CHAMBERS
ENCYCLOPEDIC
ENGLISH
DICTIONARY

CHAMBERS
ENCYCLOPEDIC
ENGLISH
DICTIONARY

EDITOR-IN-CHIEF
ROBERT ALLEN

Chambers

CHAMBERS
An imprint of Larousse plc
43–45 Annandale Street Edinburgh, EH7 4AZ

First published by Chambers 1994
10 9 8 7 6 5 4 3 2 1

A CIP catalogue record for this book is available from the British Library

We have made every effort to mark as such all words
which we believe to be trademarks.
We should also like to make it clear that the presence of a
word in the dictionary, whether marked or unmarked, in
no way affects its legal status as a trademark.

ISBN 0 550 11000 3 Standard
ISBN 0 550 11001 1 Thumb-Indexed

Population data supplied by Bartholomew

Colour maps in the appendix supplied by Bartholomew,
a division of HarperCollins Publishers Ltd
Copyright © Bartholomew 1994

Typeset in Great Britain at the University Press, Cambridge
Printed in France

CONTENTS

PREFACE

Chambers Encyclopedic English Dictionary is a completely new type of English language dictionary. This will be immediately apparent on comparing it with any other dictionary, even one called *encyclopedic*. Drawn from the unique Chambers database of language and reference materials, this new dictionary provides in one volume an exceptional range of information about words and concepts that could normally only be obtained from a whole shelf of reference books.

In the 17th and 18th centuries, and especially before the appearance of Dr Johnson's famous *Dictionary* in 1755, there were far fewer constraints than now on the kinds of material that dictionaries could include. More recently, a convention has developed that divides the domain of the dictionary (which defines terms) from that of the encyclopedia (which explains concepts). A dictionary will not normally provide detailed information about the concepts behind the words it defines, or give proper names (with the occasional exception of relatively few biographies and place-names); an encyclopedia will not provide information about terminology or linguistic patterns, or about word origins; and neither will provide information on items such as first names, institutional names, literary characters, and historical events, which are normally found only in specialist works if at all, but are as much a part of the language as the accepted 'dictionary words' are.

Words and names in all these categories will be found in this book, which is far more than simply a dictionary with added proper names in the manner of other dictionaries that are called *encyclopedic*. The wordlist has been built up from first principles, and with the usual constraints removed, to produce an integrated text of terms, names, and concepts that look behind the language labels to the things they represent. 'Language as culture' is the watchword here.

Much thought has been given to the illustrations, and each has had to earn its place as a set of information that supports and clarifies the text. Aesthetic considerations have not been ignored, but they have not been allowed to be the sole or even the primary consideration. Practicality rather than prettiness predominates. The same applies to the tables and maps, which are designed to draw together strands of information normally scattered through the alphabetical text: for example, French words and phrases, names of language families, and divisions of the natural world. These enable whole areas of information to be identified and explored, a facility normally denied to the user of dictionaries and encyclopedias.

A major challenge to any English dictionary lies in the need to explain how words are used in conjunction with other words; after all, we speak and write in phrases and sentences, and meaning emerges from the interaction of words rather than from the individual words themselves. In this dictionary, we have paid a great deal of attention to the phrasal and idiomatic aspects of language, by explaining words in their typical surroundings (or *collocation*). This will be especially noticeable in highly functional and productive words such as *get* and *turn*, which often have little meaning in themselves and derive their meaning from the words that accompany them. No other dictionary for native speakers of English has attempted this.

We have made every effort to include as much information as possible that will be immediately useful to users from a wide range of ages to answer the needs of everyday enquiry, and we have paid particular attention to the vocabulary of modern life and culture. However, I must stress to the user that any reference book of whatever size can only be a selection from a vast number of names and terms available for consideration. There are thought to be over 500 000 words and word-groups on record in English; the number of place-names runs into many thousands; and the scope for inclusion of famous people and institutional names is virtually infinite. The compiler's art lies in making a judicious selection, but it can only be a selection, and no two compilers will make the same choices. The publishers will therefore be pleased to receive suggestions for inclusion in future editions.

I would like to express my personal thanks to editorial colleagues who have worked with great dedication on this original and stimulating project, and in particular Min Lee, who oversaw the editing of the reference material and co-ordinated the logistical basis of the exercise; also Ann MacDougall, for organizational work (especially in the early stages) and work on the place-names; Jim Miles and his team, for provision of the artwork; Ilona Bellos-Morison, our Computer Officer, for her help and support; and Simon Mills and his colleagues at Compulexis Ltd for provision of database programs and other systems support in the development of the text.

We believe that the text presented here will find a permanent place as a standard one-stop source of information for family and general reference.

Robert Allen
April 1994

CONTRIBUTORS

Editor-in-Chief
Robert Allen

Reference Editor
Min Lee

Senior Editor
Ann MacDougall

EDITORIAL TEAM

Science Editor
Jo Hargreaves

Science Contributor
Hazel Muir

Text Editors
Angela Cran
Judyth Lightbody
Melanie Parry
Ingalo Thomson

Usage
George Davidson

New Words and Reading Programme
Susan Rennie

Administrative and Editorial Assistants
Helen Bleck
Siri Hansen
Alison Jones
Louise McGinnity
Marion Shepherd

External Editors and Readers
Andrew Burnet
Kay Cullen
Nick McDowell
Ruth Martin
Catherine Schwarz
Steven Scott

COMPUTING

Computer Officer
Ilona Bellos-Morison

Computer Software
Compulexis Ltd
Charlton-on-Otmoor
Oxford

ARTWORK

Publishing Director
Jim Miles

Design Director
Paul Wilkinson

Artwork Co-ordinators
Angela Holroyd
Janice McNaughton

Artwork Researchers
Rebecca Lister
Rob Perry

CARTOGRAPHY

Colour maps and population data
Bartholomew

Black-and-white maps
Thames Cartographic

GUIDE TO
USING THE DICTIONARY

1 In this dictionary, we have tried to make the information as easy to find as possible by combining the best features of dictionary and encyclopedia practice. Items are arranged as far as possible in separate articles, and apart from phrasal idioms (such as **make up** and **on the make**), no defined items are buried or 'nested' in others; the user should therefore normally look for an item as a headword in its own right. This applies to derivative words such as **bitterness** and **occasionally** (which are often left undefined as attachments to other words in normal dictionaries), and to complex names such as **elder statesman** and **Parliamentary Commissioner for Administration**.

2.1 Headwords appear in bold type, or in bold italics if they normally appear in italics in print (eg words and phrases that are not naturalized in English) or by convention (eg the names of literary works):

spoonbill *noun* any bird of a family similar to the ibises, with a long flat broad bill that is spoon-shaped at the tip.

Spooner, William Archibald (1844–1930) English Anglican clergyman and educationalist, Dean (1876–89) and Warden (1903–24) of New College, Oxford. As an albino he suffered all his life from weak eyesight but he surmounted his disabilities and earned a reputation for kindness. His nervous tendency to transpose initial letters or half-syllables in speech (metathesis) became known as the spoonerism.

Stagecoach a US film directed by John Ford (1939). ...

sub judice under consideration by a court. ...

2.2 When more than one word exists with the same spelling (*homographs*, eg **bank**), they are distinguished by raised numerals following the headwords (**bank**[1], **bank**[2]).

3 When a particular form or variant of the headword applies in some but not all of its uses this is noted in brackets at the relevant definition:

macrocosm *noun* **1** (**the macrocosm**) the universe as a whole. **2** any large or complex system or structure made up of similar smaller systems or structures. [from MACRO- + Greek *kosmos*, world]

packet *noun* **1** a paper, cardboard, or plastic bag, wrapper, or container, with its contents. **2** a small pack or package. **3** (*also* **packet boat**) a mail boat also carrying cargo and passengers, plying a fixed route. **4** *colloq.* a large sum of money: *cost a packet.* [from Old French *pacquet*]

4 Some English words and names have more than one correct spelling (eg **dispatch** and **despatch**; **Hercules** and **Heracles**). If an item is spelled in more than one way, a preferred spelling is given as the headword with variants following:

dispatch *or* **despatch** — *verb* **1** to send to a place for a particular reason. **2** to finish off or deal with quickly: *dispatch a meal.* **3** *euphemistic* to kill. — *noun* **1** (*often* **dispatches**) an official (especially military or diplomatic) report. **2** a journalist's report sent to a newspaper. **3** the act of dispatching; the fact of being dispatched. **4** *old use* speed or haste. [from Old French *despeechier*, to set free]

Hercules, Greek **Heracles** in Greek mythology, a hero famous for his strength, the son of Zeus and Alcmene. ...

5 The parts of speech (or wordclasses) are the standard ones used for English: noun, verb, adjective (adj.), adverb (adv.), pronoun (pron.), preposition (prep.), conjunction (conj.), interjection (interj.). Further information on these terms can be found at their entries in the dictionary.

6 Irregular or noteworthy inflections (plurals of nouns, parts of verbs, etc) are given in brackets after the headword and part of speech:

gadfly *noun* (PL. **gadflies**) **1** a fly that bites horses and cattle. **2** *old derog.* use a person who deliberately and persistently annoys others. [from Anglo-Saxon *gad*, goad]

nab *verb trans.* (**nabbed, nabbing**) *colloq.* **1** to catch in the act of doing wrong. **2** to arrest. **3** to grab or take.

7.1 In English, verbs commonly take a subject and an object and are called *transitive* (as in *people watch television*, in which *people* is the subject, *watch* is the verb, and *television* is the object of the verb). Transitivity is regarded as the normal function of verbs, and is only indicated (*trans.*) when it is noteworthy in particular cases. The typical object of transitive verbs is identified by being put in round brackets:

watch — *verb* **1** *trans., intrans.* to look at or focus one's attention on (someone or something moving, doing something, etc). **2** *trans., intrans.* to pass time looking at (television, a programme, entertainment, sports event, etc). ...

7.2 Some verbs describe an action in which no object is involved, such as verbs of motion including **go** and **arrive**, and verbs of state including **be** and **exist**. These are called *intransitive* and are labelled *intrans.* in the dictionary:

> **arrive** *verb* *intrans.* **1** to reach a place or destination. **2** (**arrive at something**) to come to a conclusion, decision, etc. **3** *colloq.* to be successful. **4** *said of a child* to be born. **5** *said of a thing* to be brought. **6** *said of a time* to occur. [from Old French *ariver*, from Latin *ad*, to + *ripa*, shore]

7.3 Other verbs are both transitive and intransitive in different uses (eg **move** is transitive in *we moved the car* and intransitive in *the car has moved*). In these cases the less usual uses are noted, normally intransitive (as at **break**) but sometimes transitive:

> **break** — *verb* (PAST TENSE **broke**; PAST PARTICIPLE **broken**) **1** *trans., intrans.* to divide or become divided into two or more parts as a result of stress or a blow. **2** *trans., intrans.* *said of a machine or tool, etc* to damage or become damaged, so as to stop working and be in need of repair: *the scissors have broken / try not to break the radio.* **3** to fracture a bone in (a limb, etc): *break one's leg.* **4** to burst or cut (the skin) or the skin of (the head). **5** to do something not allowed by (a law, agreement, promise, etc). **6** to interrupt (a journey). **7** *intrans.* to stop work, etc for a short period of time: *break for tea.* **8** to achieve better than (a sporting record, etc). **9** *trans., intrans.* *said of news, etc* to make or become known. **10** *intrans.* *said of the weather* to change suddenly, especially after a fine spell. **11** *trans., intrans.* to make or become weaker: *tried to break his spirit.*

> **go**[1] — *verb* *usually intrans.* (**goes**; PAST TENSE **went**; PAST PARTICIPLE **gone**) **1** (*often* **go about**, **by**, **down**, *etc*) to walk, move, or travel in the direction specified. **2** to lead or extend: *a path going across the field / the road goes all the way to the farm.* **3** (**go to somewhere**) to visit or attend it, once or regularly: *go to the cinema / go to school.* **4** to leave or move away. **5** to be destroyed or taken away; to disappear: *the old door had to go / the peaceful atmosphere has gone.* **6** to proceed or fare: *the scheme is going well.* **7** to be used up: *money going on drink.* **8** to be given or sold for a stated amount: *went for £20.* **9** to leave or set out for a stated purpose: *go for a ride / go on holiday / gone fishing.* **10** *intrans., trans.* to perform (an action) or produce (a sound): *go like this / go bang.* **11** to break, break down, or fail: *the old TV finally went / his eyes have gone.* **12** to work or be in working order: *get it going.* **13** to become; to pass into a certain condition: *go mad.* **14** to belong; to be placed correctly: *where does this go?* **15** to fit, or be contained: *my foot won't go into the shoe / four into three won't go.* **16** to continue in a certain state: *go hungry.* **17** *said of time* to pass. **18** to run in words or notes: *as the story goes.* **19** (*often* **go for someone** *or* **something**) to apply to them; to be valid or accepted for them: *the same goes for you / in this office, anything goes.* **20** *colloq.* to carry authority: *what she says goes.* **21** (*often* **go with something**) *said of colours, etc* to match or blend. **22** (**go with something**) to co-exist with it: *goodness doesn't always go with beauty.* **23** (**go by something**) to be guided by it: *don't go by what he says.* **24** to subject oneself: *go to much trouble.* **25** to adopt a system: *go metric.* **26** *trans.* to bet, especially at cards: *went five pounds.* **27** *colloq.* to be in general, for the purpose of comparison: *as girls go, she's quite naughty.* **28** to exist or be on offer: *the best offer going at the moment.* **29** *trans.* *colloq.* to welcome or enjoy: *I could go a cup of tea.* **30** *trans.* *colloq.*, *usually with quoted speech* to say.

7.4 The typical subject of a verb is given in the form '*said of ...*' before the definition proper:

> **reflect** *verb* **1** *trans., intrans.* *said of a surface* to send back (light, heat, sound, etc). **2** *trans., intrans.* *said of a mirror, etc* to give an image of. **3** *intrans.* *said of a sound, image, etc* to be reflected back. **4** to have as a cause or be a consequence of: *price increases reflect greater demand for the goods.* **5** to show or give an idea of: *a poem which reflects one's mood.* **6** (**reflect on** *or* **upon something**) to consider it carefully. **7** (**reflect on** *or* **upon someone**) *said of an action, etc* to bring praise, or blame, to them: *her behaviour reflects on (= reflects badly on) her mother / your behaviour reflects well on you.* [from Latin *reflectere*, to bend back]

7.5 Similar information is given for adjectives and other parts of speech.

8.1 The ways in which words fit into their immediate context are noted in bold type:

> **engaged** *adj.* **1** (**engaged to someone**) bound by a promise to marry them. **2** (**engaged in something**) busy or occupied with it. **3** *said of a room, etc* not free or vacant; occupied; being used.

8.2 Similarly, phrasal idioms are given in a contextualized form:

> **bring something in 1** to introduce it, make it effective, etc. **2** to produce income or profit.
> **bring something off** *colloq.* to succeed in doing something difficult.
> **bring something on 1** to cause it to happen or appear. **2** to help it to develop or progress.
> **bring something out 1** to emphasize or clarify it. **2** to publish it.
> **bring someone out in spots, a rash,** *etc* to cause them to be affected with spots or a rash: *cats bring me out in spots.*

9 Usage Labels

Items are labelled in various ways to indicate the type and level of typical use. There are three principal types of label:

register: indicates the degree of formality of an item (slang, colloq., formal, technical, etc)

subject: indicates the domain or sphere of reference in which an item is used (botany, music, etc)

geographical: indicates the area of the English-speaking world where the item is principally (but not always exclusively) found (North America, Australia, etc)

10 Usage Examples

Examples of words and phrases in use are given in italics after the definition; if there are more than one example, these are separated by an oblique:

> **occur** *verb* *intrans.* (**occurred**, **occurring**) **1** to happen or take place. **2** (**occur to someone**) to come into the mind, especially unexpectedly or by chance: *it occurred to her that the train might be late / an idea has occurred to me.* **3** to be found or exist. [from Latin *occurrere*, to run towards]

11 Word Origins

11.1 Word origins or etymologies, ie the sources from which words have come into English, are given in square brackets at the end of entries (before a usage note or text extension if any). These are largely self-explanatory, since no special symbols or abbreviations are used. Word origins are not given when these are unknown (as is often the case even with quite common words such as **boy** and **girl**), when they are self-evident (as with many compounds, eg **bathroom**, **newspaper**), or when they share the same source as a related word already given (eg the group **celebrant**, **celebrate**, **celebrated**, **celebration**, etc).

11.2 The core vocabulary of English is mainly derived by two principal routes: from Anglo-Saxon (also called Old English), ie the form of English in use from c.500 to the Norman Conquest (late 11c), and from a late form of Latin called Vulgar Latin, sometimes directly and sometimes via Old French. This second strand was a major influence on the language after the Norman Conquest.

12 Usage Notes

12.1 Notes introduced by the symbol ◆ are given to clarify particular points of usage (for example, whether **none** takes a singular or plural verb) and to distinguish between words that are often confused (such as **militate** and **mitigate**):

> **none**[1] *pron.* **1** not any. **2** no one…
>
> ◆ When referring to a plural noun, *none* may be followed by either a singular or a plural verb, whichever is logically appropriate. If the emphasis is on the individuals in a group (and *none* is equivalent to *no one* or *not one*), the verb should be singular, eg *none of us has the answer*, but if the emphasis is on the group as a whole, the verb should be plural, eg *none of us speak French*.
>
> **militate** *verb intrans.* (**militate for** or **against something**) to act, or have a strong influence in favour of or against something. [from Latin *militare*, to serve as a soldier]
>
> ◆ Often confused with *mitigate*.

12.2 Rulings are based on the norms of Standard English, ie the form of English generally regarded as correct and socially acceptable, which apply in particular to written and more formal uses of English.

13 Text Extensions

Over 1000 entries have special text extensions, introduced by the symbol ◇, which continue the explanations with encyclopedic information on the concept that lies behind the linguistic explanation given:

> **orchestra** *noun* **1** a usually large group of musicians who play a variety of different instruments as an ensemble, led by a conductor. **2** (*also* **orchestra pit**) that part of a theatre or opera-house where the orchestra sits, usually in front of or under the stage. **3** in the ancient Greek theatre, a semicircular area in front of the stage where the chorus danced. [from Greek, from *orcheisthai*, to dance]
>
> ◇ The orchestra as it is known today developed from the groups of instruments used in 17c opera houses and at the courts of London, Paris, and Vienna. Division into the four standard groups of strings, woodwind, brass, and percussion took place in the classical period and the symphony orchestra was further expanded in the 19c. A modern symphony orchestra is normally made up of around 100 players including sixty or more stringed instruments, triple or quadruple woodwind, brass including tuba, and at least three trombones, harp, and a wide array

14 Biographies

14.1 The biographical entries follow the normal conventions, with the nomenclature in bold followed by the date of birth (and death when appropriate). Subjects who are still alive at the time of editing are shown in the form (1921–). A question mark (⸮) indicates that a date is uncertain or approximate.

14.2 Kings and queens are ordered by dynastic numbers; when more than one of the same title is included, the ordering is by date, with the earliest first. For example, **Henry III** (1207–72) King of England precedes **Henry III** (1551–89) King of France.

14.3 Related biographical and institutional entries are normally put together, so that **Henry V** King of England is followed by *Henry V* (the Shakespeare play and the films based on it).

15 Place-names

15.1 Population figures and other statistics are based on the most up-to-date census information available; the date of this information varies from country to country and is specified in each entry. The letter 'e' indicates that the figure is estimated and not based on exact information.

15.2 At the time of going to press, the most up-to-date census figures for the United Kingdom are from 1981. However, for some districts, provisional estimates from 1987 and 1992 are available and these are given. Population figures over 1m are rounded to the nearest 100 000 (eg 1 654 200 is given as 1.7m); those below 1m are rounded to the nearest thousand or hundred as appropriate.

15.3 Anglicized forms of names are normally used, and the local forms are also noted.

15.4 The term 'chief town' is used to indicate the largest or most important towns or cities in a country or region.

15.5 The history sections of these entries pick out the most significant events, and do not attempt to be comprehensive.

16 Cross-references

Explicit references to other parts of the text are indicated by 'see' or 'see also' followed in small capitals by the item referred to, where related or additional information will be found:

bought see BUY.

Users should bear in mind that other terms used in the explanations will have entries of their own, even though they are not explicitly referred to.

17 Tables

The tables have been designed to bring together and sometimes supplement the information given at different places in the text. By this means, a collected list of related items, such as French words and phrases used in English, or animal families, can be found, enabling sets of information to be identified and further explored.

ABBREVIATIONS
USED IN THE DICTIONARY

In the interests of clarity, editorial abbreviations have been kept to a minimum. When they are used, this is normally for one of two reasons: to avoid distracting the user at a prominent place in the text (which is why *adjective* is shortened to *adj.*, for example), or to give a special status to the information which would not be conveyed by ordinary prose (which is why 11c is used to represent 'eleventh century', for example).

abbrev. = abbreviation
adj. = adjective
adv. = adverb
Aeron. = Aeronautics
Afr. = Africa, African
Agric. = Agriculture
Amer. = America, American
Anat. = Anatomy
Anthropol. = Anthropology
Antiq. = Antiquity
Archaeol. = Archaeology
Archit. = Architecture
Astrol. = Astrology
Astron. = Astronomy
Austral. = Australian
aux. = auxiliary

Biochem. = Biochemistry
Biol. = Biology
Bot. = Botany
Brit. = British

c = century (5c, 11c, etc)
c. = circa (about, around, especially before a date)
Chem. = Chemistry
Church of E. = Church of England
colloq. = colloquial
Comput. = Computing
conj. = conjunction
contr. = contraction

derog. = derogatory

e (following a population figure) = estimated figure
Econ. = Economics
Electr. = Electricity
Electron. = Electronics
Environ. = Environment
esp. = especially (only in labels; see above)

fig. = figurative

Geog. = Geography
Geol. = Geology
Geom. = Geometry

Hist. = History

I(s) = island(s)
interj. = interjection
intrans. = intransitive

m = metre(s), million
Maths. = Mathematics
Mech. = Mechanics
Metall. = Metallurgy
Meteorol. = Meteorology
mi = miles
Microbiol. = Microbiology
Mil. = Military
Mt(s) = Mountains

Mus. = Music
Mythol. = Mythology

Naut. = Nautical

Pathol. = Pathology
Philos. = Philosophy
Photog. = Photography
Physiol. = Physiology
pl. = plural
POP (as a heading) = population
prep. = preposition
pron. = pronoun
Psychol. = Psychology

R = River
RC = Roman Catholic
rel. = relative
Relig. = Religion

Scot. = Scottish
sing. = singular
Sociol. = Sociology

Telecomm. = Telecommunications
Theatr. = Theatre
trans. = transitive

Zool. = Zoology

The following symbols are also used:

◆ for a usage note (see section 12 above)
◇ for a text extension (see section 13 above)
ʠ indicates an uncertain or approximate date (see section 14.1 above)
ə indicates the indeterminate vowel sound as used in the second syllables of *farmer* and *garden.*

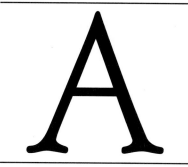

A¹ *or* **a** *noun* (PL. **As, A's, a's**) **1** the first letter of the English alphabet. **2** (*usually* **A**) the highest grade or quality, or a mark indicating this. **3** (**A**) *Mus.* **a** the sixth note in the scale of C major. **b** a musical key with the note A as its base.
— **from A to B** from one unspecified place to another.
from A to Z from beginning to end; completely.

A² *abbrev.* **1** advanced. **2** alto. **3** America. **4** ampere. **5** answer. **6** Associate (of a society, etc). **7** atomic: *A-bomb.* **8** Australia. **9** *as an international vehicle mark* Austria.

Å *abbrev.* angstrom.

a¹ *or* **an** *indefinite article* **a** is used before words beginning with a consonant or consonant sound (eg *one, united, historical*), and *an* before words beginning with a vowel or vowel sound (eg *apple, only, heir, honour*) **1** one: *here is a book.* **2** used before a word describing quantity: *a dozen eggs / a lot of trouble.* **3** any; every: *a fire is hot.* **4** each or every; per: *once a day / 60p a pound.* **5** one of a stated type: *a real Romeo.* [from Anglo-Saxon *an*, one]

a² *abbrev.* **1** *ante* (Latin), before. **2** acre.

a³ *prefix* **1** to or towards: *ashore.* **2** in the process of: *abuzz.* **3** on: *afire.* **4** in: *nowadays.* [from Anglo-Saxon *an*, on]

a-¹ *prefix* (*also* **an-** before a vowel) not; without; opposite to: *amoral / asymmetrical / agnostic.* [from Greek]

a-² *prefix* of: *akin / afresh.* [from Anglo-Saxon *of*]

AA *abbrev.* **1** Automobile Association, a UK organization which helps drivers with breakdowns or technical problems, gives travel information, etc. **2** Alcoholics Anonymous, an association for alcoholics who are trying to give up alcohol completely.

AAA *abbrev.* **1** *Brit.* Amateur Athletic Association. **2** *North Amer.* American Automobile Association.

AAC *abbrev.* Amateur Athletics Club.

Aachen, French **Aix-la-Chapelle** POP (1991e) 242 000, a manufacturing city in North Rhine-Westphalia, western Germany. It is 64km/40mi SW of Cologne, near the Dutch and Belgian borders. HISTORY the N capital of Charlemagne's empire; 32 German emperors were crowned here; annexed by France in 1801; given to Prussia in 1815; badly bombed in World War II. NOTABLE FEATURES cathedral; town hall (1350); Bad Aachen hot springs.

Aachen Cathedral a cathedral in Aachen, Germany, founded in c.790–805, and extended in the 14c. It contains the chair and tomb of Charlemagne. It is a World Heritage site.

Aalto, Alvar (1898–1976) Finnish architect, born in Kuortane. In 1940 he went to the USA and taught architecture at Yale University and the Massachusetts Institute of Technology. He

designed modern public and industrial buildings in Finland, and also contemporary furniture.

AAM *abbrev.* air-to-air missile.

aardvark *noun* a nocturnal African burrowing mammal with a stumpy thick-set body, large snout, donkey-like ears, and a tough grey skin sparsely covered with coarse hair. It feeds on termites, using its powerful claws to rip through the walls of their nests. [from Dutch *aarde*, earth + *vark*, pig]

aardvark

Aare, River, French **Aar** the largest river that is entirely in Switzerland, length 295km/183mi. It emerges from L Grimsel in the Bernese Alps and flows N, then W through the Lake of Brienz, the Lake of Thun, and L Biel to enter the Rhine. It is navigable from the Rhine to Thun.

Aarhus see ÅRHUS.

Aaron (15c–13c BC) **1** biblical patriarch, elder brother of Moses, and the first high priest of the Israelites. He was spokesman for Moses to the Egyptian Pharaoh in his attempts to lead the Israelites out of Egypt, but gave in to their rebelliousness and organized idolatrous worship in Moses' absence. Aaron and his sons were ordained as priests after the construction of the Ark of the Covenant and the Tabernacle. **2** a male first name.

Aaron, Hank (Henry Louis) (1934–   ) US baseball player, born in Mobile, Alabama. He started his career with the Milwaukee Braves in 1954, and also played for the Atlanta Braves and Milwaukee Brewers. In 1974 he surpassed Babe Ruth's 39-year-old record of career home runs, and retired in 1976 with a total of 755 home runs.

AB *abbrev.* **1** *Brit.* able seaman. **2** *North Amer., esp. US artium baccalaureus* (Latin), Bachelor of Arts.

aback
— **taken aback** surprised or shocked, especially by something unpleasant or unexpected. [from Anglo-Saxon *on bæc*, on back]

abacus *noun* **1** a frame holding a number of wires along which small balls can be moved, used for counting. **2** *Archit.* the flat upper part of a column or capital. [from Latin *abacus*, from Greek *abax*, drawing-board]

Abadan POP (1991e) 85 000, an oil port in Khuzestan province, W central Iran. It is situated close to the border with Iraq, on Abadan I, in the Shatt al-Arab delta, at the head of the Arabian Gulf. It is the terminus of Iran's major oil pipelines and was severely damaged in the Iran–Iraq War.

abaft — *adv.* in or towards the stern of a ship.
— *prep.* behind. [from A³ + Anglo-Saxon *beæftan*, after]

abalone *noun* a kind of edible shellfish with a shell lined with mother-of-pearl. [from Spanish *abulón*]

abandon — *verb* (**abandoned, abandoning**) **1** to give up completely: *abandon hope.* **2** to leave (a person, post of responsibility, etc) usually intending not to return. **3** to leave (a place of danger or difficulty, etc) intending either not to return at all or not until the danger or difficulty is past. **4** to give up to another person's control. **5** (**abandon oneself to something**) to let oneself be overcome by strong emotion, passion, etc.
— *noun* uncontrolled, uninhibited, reckless feelings.
— **abandon ship** *said of the crew and passengers* to leave a ship at sea when it is in danger of sinking. [from Old French *abandoner*, to put under someone's control]

abandoned *adj.* **1** having been abandoned. **2** having, or behaving as if one has, no sense of shame or morality.

abandonment *noun* **1** the act of abandoning or the condition of being abandoned. **2** *Legal* the act of relinquishing a legal right; eg a tenant may abandon a tenanted property. However, it is often difficult to establish in law that abandonment has taken place, and it cannot be used by people to extricate themselves from a continuing liability.

abase *verb* to humiliate or degrade (a person or oneself). [from Old French *abaissier*, from Latin *bassus*, low]

abasement *noun* **1** being humbled or degraded. **2** humiliation.

abashed *adj.* embarrassed and ashamed, especially because of shyness. [from Old French *esbahir*, to astound]

abate *verb intrans., trans.* to become or make less strong or severe. [from Old French *abatre*, to bring down]

abatement *noun* **1** the act of abating. **2** the sum or quantity abated.

abattoir *noun* a slaughterhouse. [from Old French *abatre*, to bring down]

abbacy *noun* (PL. **abbacies**) the office or authority of an abbot or abbess. [from Latin *abbatia*, abbey]

Abbado, Claudio (1933–) Italian conductor, born in Milan. He made his début in 1967 at La Scala (where he was musical director, 1968–86), and in 1968 at Covent Garden. Acclaimed for his performances of late 19c, early 20c, and some contemporary composers, he was principal conductor of the London Symphony Orchestra (1979–88), musical director of the Vienna State Opera (1986–91), and has been chief conductor of the Berlin Philharmonic since 1989.

Abbasids (8c–13c) a dynasty of caliphs that replaced the Ummayyad dynasty in 749, reached the peak of its power under Harun al-Rashid (786–809), and remained in Baghdad until its sack by the Mongols (1258). The Abbasids traced their descent from al-Abbas, the uncle of the prophet Muhammad, and so were legitimate in the eyes of the pious.

Abbas the Great (1557–1628) Shah of Persia (1588–1629), who won back lost territory from the Uzbeks, Turks, and the Great Mughal. His reign marked a peak of Persian artistic achievement, especially in the fields of painting, weaving, and manuscript illumination (elaborate decoration).

Abbe, Ernst (1840–1905) German physicist, born in Eisenach. He became professor at the University of Jena and a partner in the optical works of Carl Zeiss, on whose death he became owner in 1888. Famous for his researches in optics, he applied scientific theory to the design of improved microscope lenses.

Abbé, Lake a lake on the Ethiopia–Djibouti frontier, 145km/90mi SW of Djibouti. It is noted for its population of pink flamingoes, ibises, and pelicans; other interesting features include limestone spires and sulphur-laden vapour streams.

abbess *noun* a woman in charge of a group of nuns living in an abbey. [from Old French *abbesse*]

abbey *noun* (PL. **abbeys**) **1** a group of nuns or monks living as a community under an abbot or abbess. **2** the buildings occupied by such a community. **3** a church associated with such a community. [from Old French *abeie*]

Abbey Theatre a theatre in Abbey Street, Dublin. At the centre of the Irish dramatic movement initiated by Lady Gregory and W B Yeats, it championed J M Synge and the early plays of Sean O'Casey, and was a major early-20c venue.

abbot *noun* the man in charge of a group of monks living in an abbey. [from Latin *abbas*, from Aramaic *abba*, father]

abbrev. *or* **abbr.** *abbrev.* **1** abbreviated. **2** abbreviation.

abbreviate *verb* to shorten, especially to represent (a long word) by a shortened form. [from Latin *abbreviare*, to shorten]

abbreviation *noun* **1** the act of shortening. **2** a part of a word used to stand for the whole.
◆ Abbreviations which end with the final letter of the abbreviated word are often not followed by a full stop in British English: *Mr, Rd, St*, etc. A full stop is not incorrect, and is still generally preferred in American English. Abbreviated names of countries and organizations are usually written with capital letters and without full stops, eg *EC, OAU*; but in Amercian English *U.S.A.* is preferred. Acronyms such as *NATO* are usually written without full stops, and often as ordinary words, eg *Nato*.

ABC¹ *noun* (PL. **ABCs, ABC's**) **1** the alphabet. **2** the basic facts about a subject, especially when arranged alphabetically in a book. **3** an alphabetical guide.

ABC² *abbrev.* **1** American Broadcasting Company. **2** Australian Broadcasting Corporation.

ABC Islands an abbreviated name often applied to the three main islands of Aruba, Bonaire, and Curaçao in the Caribbean Sea, off the N coast of S America.

Abd-Al-Rahman the name of five amirs of Córdoba, Muslim Spain – most notably, Abd-Al-Rahman III (891–961), who ruled from 912. Under him the caliphate reached the peak of its power, extending its boundaries in successful campaigns against the Fatimids and the kings of Leon and Navarre. He was a patron of the arts and made Córdoba a cultural centre.

abdicate *verb* **1** *intrans., trans.* to give up one's right to (the throne). **2** to refuse or fail to carry out (one's responsibilities). [from Latin *ab-*, away, from + *dicare*, to proclaim]

abdication *noun* the act of giving up an office, especially the throne.

abdomen *noun* **1** in vertebrates, the lower part of the main body cavity, containing the digestive, excretory, and reproductive organs, and in mammals separated from the thorax (chest) by the diaphragm. **2** *Zool.* in arthropods (eg insects), the rear part of the body, behind the head and thorax. [from Latin *abdomen*]

abdominal *adj.* relating to or concerning the abdomen.

abduct *verb* to take (someone) away illegally by force or deception. [from Latin *abducere*, to lead away]

abduction *noun* kidnapping.

Some Common Abbreviations	
AD	*anno Domini*, in the year of our Lord
AH	*anno Hegirae*, in the year of the hegira, the Muslim era
am	*ante meridiem*, before noon
BC	before Christ
c	*circa*, about
cf	*confer*, compare
do	*ditto*, the same thing
eg	*exempli gratia*, for example
et al	*et alibi*, and elsewhere
et alli, aliae or alia	*and other* (people or things)
et cetera	*et cetera*, and so on
et seq, seqq.	*et sequens, sequentes*, or *sequentia*, and that, or those, following
ff	following (pages, lines, etc)
fl	*floruit*, flourished
ibid	*ibidem*, in the same place of a book, chapter, etc already mentioned
ie	*id est*, that is, that is to say
l, ll	line, lines
loc cit	*loco citato*, in the passage or place just quoted
ms, mss	manuscript, manuscripts
NB, nb	*nota bene*, note well
nem con	*nemine contradicente*, without opposition
op cit	*opere citato*, in the work or book just quoted
p, pp	page, pages
pm	*post meridiem*, in the afternoon
PS	postscript, an addition to a letter, etc
pto	please turn over
qed	*quod erat demonstrandum*, which was to be demonstrated (ie proved)
qv, qqv	*quod vide*, see this item, these items
sc	*scilicet*, namely
sv	*sub verbo* or *sub voce*, under the word or heading specified
v	*versus*, against; *vide*, see
viz	*videlicet*, namely
vs	*versus*, against

abductor *noun* a person who abducts.

Abdul-Jabbar, Kareem, originally **Lewis Ferdinand Alcindor Jr** (1947–) US basketball player, born in New York City. His change of name came with his conversion to Islam in 1969. He turned professional with Milwaukee in 1970, and during his career played more National Basketball League games (1 560) than any other player, and scored more points, 38 387. He retired in 1989.

abeam *adv.* in a line at right angles to the length of a ship or aircraft. [from A³ + BEAM]

Abegg, Richard Wilhelm Heinrich (1869–1910) German chemist, born in Danzig (now Gdańsk, Poland). Professor at Breslau from 1899, he was one of the first scientists to perceive the chemical significance of the electron, helping to develop the theory of valence which is fundamental to modern chemistry. He realized that the manner in which an element combines chemically with other elements is determined by the number of electrons in the outer shell of its atom, and observed that the inert properties of the rare gases are due to the stable configuration of eight outer electrons.

Abel a biblical character, the brother of Cain and second son of Adam and Eve. He was a shepherd, whose gift was accepted by God, and he was murdered by his brother, Cain, whose gift God did not accept (Genesis 4. 2–16).

Abel, John Jacob (1857–1938) US biochemist, born in Cleveland, Ohio. He studied at Johns Hopkins University and in Europe before returning to Johns Hopkins as its first Professor of Pharmacology (1893–1932). In 1897 he isolated from the adrenal gland the hormone adrenaline, and in pioneering work on dialysis he showed that blood contains amino acids. He also crystallized insulin (1927) and showed it to be a protein.

Abel, Niels Henrik (1802–29) Norwegian mathematician, born in Finnøy. He showed mathematical genius by the age of 15, and entered Oslo University in 1821. He developed concepts of functions which became a central theme of later 19c analysis, although his work was not fully understood, or even published, in his lifetime.

Abelard *or* **Abailard, Peter** (1079–1142) French philosopher and theologian, born near Nantes. He secretly married his pupil Héloïse, the 17-year-old niece of the canon Fulbert, but her relatives exacted revenge by castrating him. He then entered the abbey of St Denis as a monk, and Héloïse entered the convent of Argenteuil. After his teaching on the Trinity was condemned as heretical, he retired to a hermitage, which later became a monastic school known as Paraclete. Paraclete was given to a sisterhood and to Héloïse, with whom he compiled a collection of their correspondence. Later, at Cluny, he lived a model life of asceticism and theological labour, but again his adversaries, headed by Bernard of Clairvaux, accused him of heresies. He died on his way to Rome to defend himself.

Abercromby, Sir Ralph (1734–1801) Scottish soldier, born in Menstrie, Clackmannanshire. He studied law, then joined the Dragoons in 1756 and fought in the Seven Years' War. He became an MP in 1774, served in Holland and the West Indies, and captured Trinidad (1797). In 1801 he commanded the expedition to the Mediterranean, and effected a successful landing at Aboukir Bay, but was fatally wounded in the ensuing battle.

Aberdeen, George Hamilton Gordon, 4th Earl of (1784–1860) Scottish statesman, born in Edinburgh. He succeeded to his earldom in 1801, and became a Scottish representative peer (1806), Ambassador to Vienna (1813–14), and Foreign Secretary (1828–30, 1841–6). As Prime Minister of Great Britain (1852–5) he headed a coalition ministry, which for some time was very popular, but ill-defined policy during the Crimean War forced his resignation.

Aberdeen, ancient **Devana** POP (1992e) 217 000, the seaport capital of Grampian region, NE Scotland. It is on the North Sea, between the rivers Dee in the S and Don in the N, 92km/57mi NE of Dundee. It has been a royal burgh since 1179. Local silver granite is used as the fabric for many of the buildings and Aberdeen is known as 'the Granite City'. Its economy relies heavily on port trade and fishing, and it received a major boost as a result of the discovery of oil in the North Sea in the 1960s and 1970s; the rigs are supplied from the Aberdeen heliport. NOTABLE FEATURES art gallery; Gordon Highlanders Regimental Museum; Maritime Museum; St Machar's Cathedral (1131); Bridge of Dee (1500), Brig o' Balgownie (c.1320, repaired in 1607); university (1494).

Aberdeen Angus a Scottish breed of cattle with a black coat and no horns. [from *Aberdeen* and *Angus*, in Scotland]

Aberfan a village in a coal-mining region of Mid Glamorgan, S Wales. It was the scene of a major disaster in 1966, when a landslip of mining waste engulfed several houses and the school, killing 144 people, including 116 children.

aberrance *or* **aberrancy** *noun* (PL. **aberrancies**) a departure from what is normal.

aberrant *adj.* changing or departing from what is normal or accepted as standard. [from Latin *aberrare*, to wander away]

aberration *noun* **1** a temporary, usually brief and often surprising change from what is normal or accepted as standard. **2** a sudden and usually temporary drop in standards of behaviour, thought, etc. **3** *Optics* the failure of a lens in an optical system to form a perfect image, eg chromatic aberration (production of an image with coloured fringes), spherical aberration (production of a blurred image), both of which are due to the properties of the lens material.

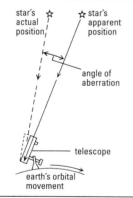

aberration of starlight

aberration of starlight *Astron.* an optical illusion in which a star appears to be displaced from its true position, caused by the effects of the finite speed of light rays travelling from the star, and the movement of the observer relative to the star as the Earth orbits around the Sun.

Aberystwyth POP (1981) 11 000, a university town and resort in Ceredigion district, Dyfed, SW Wales. It stands at the mouth of the R Ystwyth and the R Rheidol on Cardigan Bay and was built in 1227 around a castle of Edward I. NOTABLE FEATURES College of University of Wales (1872); National Library of Wales (1955).

abet *verb* (**abetted, abetting**) *especially Legal* to help or encourage (someone) to commit an offence. [from Old French *abeter*, to entice]

abetter *Legal* **abettor** *noun* a person who abets.

abeyance *noun* **1** *said of laws, customs, etc* the condition, usually temporary, of not being used or followed: *fall into abeyance*. **2** *said of a position, eg a peerage* the state, usually temporary, of not being filled or occupied. [from Old French *abeance*, from *a*, to + *baer*, to gape]

abhor *verb* (**abhorred, abhorring**) to hate or dislike very much (usually something one considers morally wrong). [from Latin *ab-* from, away+ *horrere*, to shudder]

abhorrence *noun* **1** disgust; hatred. **2** something that is abhorred.

abhorrent *adj.* (**abhorrent to someone**) hated or disliked by them.

abhorrently *adv.* so as to cause disgust, hatred, or loathing.

abide *verb* (PAST TENSE AND PAST PARTICIPLE **abode, abided**) **1** (*usually* **cannot** *or* **could not abide** or as a question) to put up with or tolerate: *we cannot abide dishonesty / how could you abide him?* **2** *intrans.* (**abide by something**) to follow, stay faithful to or obey (a decision, rule, etc). **3** *intrans. old use* to live. [from Anglo-Saxon *abidan*]

abiding *adj.* permanent; lasting or continuing for a long time.

Abidjan POP (1990e) 2.2m, an industrial seaport in the Ivory Coast, on the N shore of Ebrié Lagoon. It was the nation's capital from 1935 until 1983. NOTABLE FEATURE Ifan Museum.

Abigail 1 a female first name. **2** (**abigail**) a lady's maid. [from Hebrew, = father of exaltation]

ability *noun* (PL. **abilities**) **1** the power, skill, or knowledge to do something. **2** great skill or intelligence. [from Old French *ablete*, from Latin *habilitas*, suitability]

-ability *suffix* forming nouns corresponding to adjectives in -able: *capability*.

ab initio from the beginning; afresh. [Latin, = from the beginning]

abject *adj.* **1** *said of conditions, etc* extremely sad, miserable or poor; wretched. **2** *said of people* showing lack of courage or pride, etc; shameful. [from Latin *abjicere*, to throw away]

abjection *noun* a state of degradation or misery.

abjectly *adv.* in a defeated, humiliated manner.

abjectness *noun* misery.

abjuration *noun* the act of abjuring.

abjure *verb* to promise solemnly, especially under oath, to stop believing, doing, etc (something). [from Latin *ab*, away, from + *jurare*, to swear]

ablative — *noun* *Grammar* the case which, especially in Latin, expresses the place, means, manner or instrument of an action. — *adj.* of or in the ablative case. [from Latin *ablativus*, from *ablatus*, carried off, removed]

ablaut *noun* *Grammar* a variation of a root vowel in the forms of a word, as in *sing, sang, song*, and *sung*. [from German *ab*, off + *Laut*, sound]

ablaze *adj.* **1** burning, especially strongly. **2** brightly lit. **3** (**ablaze with something**) feeling an emotion with great passion.

able *adj.* **1** having the necessary knowledge, power, time, opportunity, etc to do something. **2** clever, skilful. [from Latin *habilis*, handy]

-able *suffix* forming adjectives meaning. **1** that may or must be: *eatable / payable*. **2** that may be the subject of: *objectionable*. **3** that is suitable for: *seasonable / fashionable*. See also -IBLE. [from Latin *-abilis*]

able-bodied — *adj.* fit and healthy. — *pl. noun* fit and healthy people.

able seaman *or* **able-bodied seaman** a sailor able to perform all duties, with more training and a higher rating than an ordinary seaman.

ablution *noun* (*usually in pl.*) **1** the washing of parts of the body as part of a religious ceremony. **2** *colloq.* the ordinary washing of oneself. **3** a place for washing oneself in a camp, on board ship, etc. [from Latin *abluere*, to wash away]

ably *adv.* **1** capably. **2** cleverly, skilfully.

-ably *suffix* forming adverbs corresponding to adjectives in -able: *capably / understandably*.

ABM *abbrev.* anti-ballistic missile, a type of rocket which can destroy an enemy's ballistic missile in the air.

abnegation *noun* **1** the act of giving up something one has or would like to have. **2** the act of renouncing a doctrine, etc. [from Latin *abnegare*, to deny]

abnormal *adj.* not normal; different from what is expected or usual. [from French *anormal*, from Greek *anomalos*]

abnormality *noun* (PL. **abnormalities**) **1** something which is abnormal. **2** the condition of being abnormal.

abnormally *adv.* unusually; unnaturally.

Abo *or* **abo** — *noun* (PL. **Abos**) *offensive slang* an Australian aborigine. — *adj.* aboriginal.

Åbo see TURKU.

aboard *adv., prep.* **1** on, on to, in or into (a ship, train, aircraft, etc). **2** *Naut.* alongside. [from Middle English *aborde*]

ABO blood group system *Medicine* a classification of human blood into four types (A, B, AB, and O), based on the presence or absence of antigens A and B.
◇ The red blood cells of the A, B, AB, and O groups carry, respectively, the A antigen, B antigen, both antigens, and neither. The blood contains natural antibodies against the blood group antigen which is absent from the red cells. Before a transfusion, the blood of the recipient and donor is cross-matched to ensure that red cells from the donor are not given to a person possessing antibodies against them, with possible fatal consequences.

ABO Blood Group			
Blood group	Antigens on red cells	Antibodies in plasma	Can receive blood type
A	A	B	A and O
B	B	A	B and O
AB[1]	A and B	none	A, B, AB, O
O[2]	none	A and B	O

[1] Universal recipient   [2] Universal donor

abode[1] *noun formal* the house or place where one lives; a dwelling.
— **of no fixed abode** *Brit. Legal* having no regular home or address.
[from ABIDE]

abode[2] see ABIDE.

abolish *verb* to stop or put an end to (customs, laws, etc). [from French *abolir*]

abolition *noun* **1** the act of abolishing something; the state of being abolished. **2** *Hist.* the abolishing of slavery.

abolitionism *noun* a 19c movement to end slavery in the southern states of the USA. It was actively promoted by the American Anti-slavery Society, founded in 1833.

abolitionist *noun* a person who seeks to abolish a custom or practice, especially capital punishment or (formerly) slavery.

A-bomb see ATOM BOMB.

Abomey a town in Zou province, S Benin, W Africa. The capital of the old Yoruba kingdom of

Dahomey, it was burned by the Portuguese and abandoned to the French in 1892. The Royal Palace of Djema, which includes the tomb of King Gbehanzin (still guarded by women), is a World Heritage site.

abominable *adj.* **1** greatly disliked, usually because morally bad. **2** *colloq.* very bad. [from Latin *abominari*, to hate]

abominable snowman a yeti. [a loose translation of Tibetan *metohkangmi*, literally 'snowfield man-bear']

abominably *adv.* **1** with an abominable manner. **2** very badly.

abominate *verb* to dislike or hate greatly. [from Latin *abominari*]

abomination *noun* **1** anything one hates or dislikes greatly. **2** great dislike or hatred.

aboriginal *or* **Aboriginal** — *noun* **1** a member of a people forming the original inhabitants of a place. **2** an Australian Aboriginal language. — *adj.* earliest, primitive, or indigenous.
◆ See note at *aborigine*.

aborigine *noun* **1** (*also* **Aborigine**) a member of a people forming the original inhabitants of Australia. **2** a member of any people who were the first to live in a country or region, especially as compared to later arrivals. [from Latin *aborigines*, pre-Roman inhabitants of Italy, from *ab origine*, from the beginning]
◇ *Aboriginal* is now the preferred form when referring to the original inhabitants of Australia; *Aborigine* may be considered offensive by people living in Australia.
Aboriginals numbered about 300 000 when white settlers first reached Australia. Now only a few thousand carry on a traditional way of life based on the tribal culture of their ancestors and many more live in poverty on the fringes of society.

abort *verb* **1** *intrans.* to lose a baby because it is born before it has developed enough to survive outside the womb; to miscarry. **2** *intrans. said of a baby* to be lost in this way. **3** to remove (a baby) from the womb of (a woman) before it has developed enough to be able to survive on its own. **4** *trans., intrans.* to stop (a plan, space flight, etc), or to be stopped, earlier than expected and before reaching a successful conclusion, usually because of technical problems or danger. [from Latin *abortus*, miscarried]

abortion *noun* **1** the removal of an embryo or fetus from the uterus (womb) before it is sufficiently developed to survive independently, deliberately induced by the use of drugs such as prostaglandins, or by surgical procedures, for medical or social reasons. — Also called *termination*. **2** the spontaneous expulsion of an embryo or fetus from the uterus (womb) before it is sufficiently developed to survive independently. — Also called *miscarriage*. **3** the failure of a plan, project, etc. **4** anything which has failed to grow properly or enough.
◇ Spontaneous abortion (miscarriage) occurs in about 20 per cent of apparently normal pregnancies, most commonly during the first 12 weeks of pregnancy, and it may not even be recognized. Certain factors, such as fetal abnormalities, smoking by the mother, and a large number of previous pregnancies, have been associated with spontaneous abortion.
Unless carried out within the terms of the Abortion Act (1967), induced abortion is a criminal offence. Two doctors must agree that continuation of the pregnancy would have a seriously detrimental effect on the physical and mental health of the mother or any existing children, and the termination must be performed at an approved hospital or clinic within the first 24 weeks of pregnancy (in the UK). There is an increased risk of complications if it is carried out after the 13th week.

abortionist *noun* **1** a person who performs abortions, especially illegally. **2** a person who is in favour of abortion.

abortion pill *Medicine* a pill containing prostaglandins or other drugs that is taken by mouth in order to induce labour and bring about termination of pregnancy.

abortive *adj.* unsuccessful.

abortively *adv.* **1** unsuccessfully. **2** incompletely.

Aboukir Bay, Battle of **1** also called **Battle of the Nile** a naval battle (Aug 1798) during the War of the Second Coalition, in which Nelson destroyed the French fleet off the coast of Egypt, a victory that forced Napoleon to abandon his Egyptian campaign of threatening British territory in India. **2** the last French victory (Jul 1799) of the Egyptian campaign, in which Napoleon's Army of Egypt captured Aboukir citadel, NE of Alexandria, defeating a huge Ottoman Turkish force.

abound *verb intrans.* **1** to exist in large numbers. **2** (**abound in** *or* **with something**) to be rich in it or filled with it. [from Latin *abundare*, to overflow]

abounding *adj.* plentifully supplied.

about — *prep.* **1** concerning; relating to; on the subject of. **2** near to. **3** around; centring on. **4** here and there in; at points throughout. **5** all around; surrounding. **6** occupied or busy with: *What are you about?* **7** on the person of. — *adv.* **1** nearly or just over; approximately. **2** nearby; close: *is there anyone about?* **3** scattered here and there. **4** all around; in all directions. **5** in or to the opposite direction: *turn about.* **6** on the move; in action: *be up and about again after an illness.*
— **about to do something** on the point of doing it.
not about to do something determined not to do it.
that's about it *or* **about all** *colloq.* almost everything that needs to be said or done has been. [from Anglo-Saxon *onbutan*]

A Bout De Souffle (Breathless) a French film directed by Jean-Luc Godard (1959). It is a drama starring Jean Seberg and Jean-Paul Belmondo about a criminal on the run who visits his US student lover in Paris, and it signalled the arrival of the Nouvelle Vague genre.

about turn *or* **about face** **1** a turn made so that one is facing in the opposite direction. **2** a complete change of direction.

about-turn *or* **about-face** *verb intrans.* to turn round so as to be facing in the opposite direction.

above — *prep.* **1** higher than; over. **2** more or greater than in quantity or degree. **3** higher or superior to in rank, importance, ability, etc. **4** too good or great for: *above petty quarrels.* **5** too good, respected, etc to be affected by or subject to. **6** too difficult to be understood by; beyond the abilities of. — *adv.* **1** at, in or to a higher position, place, rank, etc. **2** in addition: *over and above.* **3** in an earlier passage of written or printed text. **4** *literary* in heaven. — *adj.* appearing or mentioned in an earlier or preceding passage of written or printed text. — *noun* something already mentioned.
— **above all** most of all; more than anything else.
above and beyond more than is required by.
above oneself having an inflated opinion of one's importance; conceited, arrogant. [from Anglo-Saxon *abufan*]

above-board *adj.* honest; open; not secret.

abracadabra *interj.* a word which supposedly has magic power, often used by people when doing magic tricks.

abrade *verb* to scrape or wear away, especially by rubbing. [from Latin *abradere*, to scrape away]

Abraham a male first name. [from Hebrew, of uncertain origin]

Abraham *or* **Abram** (c.2000–1650 BC) a biblical character regarded as the ancestor of Israel and of several other nations; he is also an important figure in Islam. God called him to travel with his wife Sarah and nephew Lot from the Chaldaean town of Ur to Haran in NW Mesopotamia and finally to Canaan, and promised him a land and descendants which would become a great nation (Genesis 12, 15). Abraham had a son Ishmael by his wife's maid Hagar, and at 100 years of age, he and his previously barren wife Sarah had Isaac, the son whom he nearly had to sacrifice as a test of faith (Genesis 21, 22).

abrasion *noun* **1** a damaged area of skin, rock, etc, which has been worn away by scraping or rubbing. **2** the act of scraping or rubbing away.

abrasive — *adj.* **1** able to damage skin, rock, etc by rubbing and scraping. **2** able to polish or make smooth by rubbing. **3** *said of people or their actions* likely to offend others by being harsh and rude. — *noun* an abrasive substance.

abrasively *adv.* with an abrasive manner.

abrasiveness *noun* an abrasive quality, especially of manner.

abreast — *adv.* side by side and facing in the same direction. — *adj.* (**abreast of something**) up to date concerning it; having the most recent information: *keep abreast of events.* [from A³ + BREAST]

abridge *verb* to make (a book, etc) shorter. [from Old French *abregier*, from Latin *abbreviare*, to abbreviate]

abridged *adj.* shortened.

abridgement *or* **abridgment** *noun* **1** a shortening or curtailment. **2** a shorter form of a work, especially a book.

abroad *adv.* **1** in or to a foreign country or countries. **2** in circulation; at large. **3** over a wide area; in different directions. **4** *old use* out of or away from one's home. [from Middle English *abrod*]

abrogate *verb* to cancel (a law, agreement, etc) formally or officially. [from Latin *abrogare*]

abrogation *noun* the act of abrogating.

abrupt *adj.* **1** sudden and unexpected; very quick. **2** *said especially of speech, etc* rather sharp and rude. **3** steep. [from Latin *abrumpere*, to break off]

abruptly *adv.* in an abrupt way.

abruptness *noun* **1** suddenness, unexpectedness. **2** curtness.

Abruzzi *or* **Abruzzo** **1** POP (1991) 1.3m, a mountainous region in E central Italy, comprising four provinces. AREA 10 795sq km/4 167sq mi. The region rises to 2 914m at Gran Sasso d'Italia, the highest point in the Apennines. ECONOMY arable farming is possible only in valleys running from the Apennines to the Adriatic Sea; tourism, small businesses (in the 'Val Vibrata'). **2** a national park in the S of Abruzzi region, E central Italy. Established in 1922, it lies between the Apennines and the Adriatic Sea, in the valley of the upper Sangro. The park is noted for its beech forests. The resort village of Pescasseroli lies within the park. AREA 400sq km/154sq mi.

ABS *abbrev.* anti-lock braking system, a system which prevents the locking of road wheels when braking, giving improved control in difficult conditions. A sensor detects over-rapid deceleration of the wheels and signals for a reduction in braking effort.

abscess *noun* a painful and inflamed swelling in a part of the body, containing pus. [from Latin *abscessus*, going away]

abscisic acid *Bot.* a plant growth substance that plays an important role in plant develop-

...by inhibiting growth, and promoting leaf ...eing and the shedding of leaves, fruit, etc from ...he plant.

abscissa *noun* (PL. **abscissas, abscissae**) *Maths.* in coordinate geometry, the first of a pair of numbers (x, y), known as the x coordinate. It specifies the distance of a point from the vertical or y-axis. See also ORDINATE. [from Latin *abscissus*, cut off]

abscission *noun* 1 an act of cutting off, or the state of being cut off. 2 *Bot.* the shedding of leaves, fruit, and other parts from a plant by the formation of a layer of thin-walled cells, which subsequently breaks down, at the base of the part which is to be shed. [from Latin *abscindere abscissum*, to cut off]

abscond *verb intrans.* to depart or leave quickly and usually secretly, especially because one has done something wrong and wants to avoid punishment or arrest. [from Latin *abscondere*, to hide]

absconder *noun* a person who has absconded.

abseil — *verb intrans.* to make a descent down a rock face, etc using a double rope wound round the body and fixed to a point higher up. — *noun* an act of abseiling. [from German *abseilen*, from *ab*, down + *Seil*, rope]

abseiling *noun* the sport of making a descent of a rock face etc by means of a doubled rope fixed to a point higher up.

absence *noun* 1 the state of being away from work, etc. 2 the time when a person is away from work, etc. 3 the state of not existing or being lacking. — **absence of mind** a lack of attention or concentration. [from Latin *absentia*, from *abesse*, to be away]

absent — *adj.* 1 not in its or one's expected place; not present. 2 not existing, especially where normally to be expected. 3 showing that one is not paying attention or concentrating. — *verb* (**absent onself**) to stay away from a meeting, gathering, etc.

absentee *noun* a person who is not present at a particular or required time.

absenteeism *noun* frequent and continued absence from work, school, etc.

absentee landlord a landlord who does not live in the property he lets out.

absentia see IN ABSENTIA.

absently *adv.* in a way which shows one is not paying attention or concentrating.

absent-minded *adj.* not noticing what one is doing or what is going on around one, especially because one is thinking about something else; preoccupied.

absent-mindedly *adv.* in an absent-minded way.

absent-mindedness *noun* 1 forgetfulness. 2 preoccupation.

absinthe *or* **absinth** *noun* a strong green alcoholic drink flavoured with substances from certain plants, such as aniseed and wormwood. [from French *absinthe*, from Latin *absinthium*, wormwood]

Absinthe Drinker an early painting by Edouard Manet (1859, Copenhagen).

Absolute, Capt the son of Sir Anthony Absolute in Sheridan's *The Rivals*, who disguises himself as Ensign Beverley in order to woo his beloved, Lydia Languish.

absolute — *adj.* 1 complete; total; perfect. 2 without limits; not controlled by anything or anyone else. 3 certain; undoubted. 4 not measured in comparison with other things; not relative: *an absolute standard.* 5 pure; not mixed with anything else. 6 *Grammar, said of a part of a sentence, etc* not dependent on the rest of the sentence, but able to stand alone. See also RELATIVE 6. — *noun* 1 a rule, standard, etc which is thought to be true or right in all situations. 2 (**the absolute**) *Philos.* that which can exist without being related to anything else.

absolute alcohol *Chem.* ethanol containing not more than one per cent water.

absolutely *adv.* 1 completely. 2 independently of anything else. 3 *colloq.* in actual fact; really; very much. 4 (*with negatives*) at all: *absolutely nothing / absolutely no use.* 5 yes; certainly.

absolute majority *noun* a number of votes for a candidate in an election which is greater than the number of votes received by all the other candidates put together.

absolute music music which does not attempt to illustrate or describe but is for simple appreciation; the opposite to programme music.

absoluteness *noun* the quality or state of being absolute.

absolute pitch see PERFECT PITCH.

absolute zero the lowest temperature theoretically possible, 0 K (-273.15°C, or -459.67°F).

absolution *noun* the formal forgiving of a person's sins, especially by a priest. [from Latin *absolutio*, acquittal]

absolutism *noun* the theory or practice of government by a person who has total power.
◇ The theory of kingship in which the ruler had unrestricted power was elaborated and practised in early modern Europe, most notably by Louis XIV of France. Absolute power was justified by the belief that monarchs were God's representatives on Earth, and that by this Divine Right kings were owed unquestioning allegiance by their subjects.

absolutist — *noun* a person who supports absolute government. — *adj.* practising or supporting absolute government; despotic.

absolve *verb* 1 (**absolve someone from** *or* **of something**) to release them or pronounce them free from a promise, duty, blame, etc. 2 *said of a priest* to forgive (someone) formally for the sins they have committed. [from Latin *absolvere*, to loosen]

absorb *verb* 1 to take in, suck up (heat, liquid, knowledge, etc). 2 to receive or take in as part of oneself or itself. 3 to have all of the attention or interest of. 4 to reduce or lessen (the shock, force, impact, etc of something). [from Latin *ab*, away, from + *sorbere*, to suck in]

absorbed *adj.* 1 soaked up, swallowed up; taken in, incorporated. 2 engrossed.

absorbedly *adv.* with an absorbed manner.

absorbency *noun* (PL. **absorbencies**) 1 the ability to absorb liquids, etc. 2 the degree to which something is able to absorb liquids, etc.

absorbent — *noun* an absorbent material. — *adj.* able to absorb liquid, etc.

absorbing *adj.* 1 soaking up; incorporating. 2 occupying or engrossing the mind.

absorptance *noun Physics* (SYMBOL **α**) a measure of the ability of a body to absorb radiation, measured as the ratio of energy absorbed by that body to the energy that is incident (falling) on it, and formerly known as *absorptivity.*

absorption *noun* 1 the act of taking in, sucking up or absorbing, or the process of being taken in, absorbed, etc. 2 the state of having all one's interest or attention occupied by something. [from Latin *absorptio*]

absorptive *adj.* 1 capable of absorbing. 2 engrossing.

abstain *verb intrans.* (**abstain from something** *or* **from doing something**) 1 to choose not to take or have it, or to do or undertake it: *abstain from alcohol / abstain from having fun.* 2 to formally record one's intention not to vote in an election. See also ABSTENTION, ABSTINENCE. [from Latin *ab*, away, from + *tenere*, to hold]

abstainer *noun* a person who abstains, especially from alcohol.

abstemious *adj., said of people, habits, etc* taking food, alcohol, etc in very limited amounts; moderate or restrained in what one eats or drinks. [from Latin *abstemius*, from *abs*, away, from + *temetum*, strong drink]

abstemiously *adv.* with an abstemious manner.

abstemiousness *noun* being abstemious.

abstention *noun* 1 the act of choosing not to do or take something, especially not to take food or alcohol. 2 a refusal to vote; a person who has abstained from voting. [from Latin *abstinere*, to abstain]

abstinence *noun* the practice or state of choosing not to do or take something, especially alcohol. [from Latin *abstinere*, to abstain]

abstinent *adj.* keeping oneself from indulgence, especially in alcohol.

abstract — *adj.* 1 referring to something which exists only as an idea or quality. 2 concerned with ideas and theory rather than with things which really exist or could exist. 3 *said of art forms, especially painting* representing the subject by shapes and patterns, etc rather than in the shape or form it actually has. — *noun* 1 a brief statement of the main points (of a book, speech, etc). 2 an abstract idea, theory, etc. 3 an example of abstract painting, etc. — *verb* 1 to take out or remove. 2 to summarize (a book, speech, etc). — **in the abstract** in theory rather than in reality. [from Latin *abs*, away, from + *trahere*, to draw]

abstract art a general term for the many forms of non-figurative art which have developed since the beginning of the 20c. Abstract art is defined by its rejection of any attempt to represent the exterior world, and instead makes use of arrangements of lines, shapes, and colours to establish an independent 'reality' and aesthetic appeal. Since its emergence (c.1910) in Russia and Germany, with the experiments of such artists as Kandinsky, Miró, Pevsner, and Brancusi, many styles and movements have evolved in both painting and sculpture. Among the most significant were: the experimental work of Mondrian and the De Styl movement (Neo Plasticism); Constructivism, and American Abstract Expressionism (which aimed to arouse and express emotion through pure abstraction).

abstracted *adj.* thinking about something so much that one does not notice what is happening around one.

abstractedly *adv.* with an absent-minded manner.

abstraction *noun* 1 the act, or an example of, abstracting. 2 something which exists as a general idea rather than as an actual example. 3 the state of thinking about something so much that one does not notice what is happening around one.

abstruse *adj.* hard to understand. [from Latin *abstrusus*, pushed away]

abstrusely *adv.* with an abstruse manner.

absurd *adj.* not at all suitable; ridiculous. [from Latin *absurdus*, out of tune]

Absurd, Theatre of the see THEATRE OF THE ABSURD.

absurdism *noun* the expression in art of a vision of mankind as being essentially absurd and without purpose. Camus described the absurdity of the human condition in his collection of essays *Le Mythe de Sisyphe* (1942), and other writings. See also THEATRE OF THE ABSURD.

absurdity *noun* (PL. **absurdities**) 1 being absurd. 2 something that is absurd.

absurdly *adv.* with an absurd manner.

absurdness *noun* the quality of being absurd.

ABTA *abbrev.* Association of British Travel Agents.

Abu Dhabi *or* **Abu Zabi** POP (1985) 670 000, the largest of the seven member states and the capital of the United Arab Emirates. AREA c.67 600sq km/26 100sq mi. It is bounded NW by Qatar, S and W by Saudi Arabia, and N by the Arabian Gulf; the coastline is 400km/250mi long. Abu Dhabi is a major oil region, with vast areas of desert and salt flats. CAPITAL Abu Dhabi. The main oasis settlement is at Al Ayn.

Abuja POP (1991) 379 000, the capital of Nigeria, in Federal Capital Territory. The building of Abuja as the new capital was planned in 1976, to relieve pressure on the infrastructure of Lagos.

abulia *or* **aboulia** *noun Psychol.* a reduction in or absence of willpower, a common symptom of schizophrenia. [from A-¹ + Greek *boule*, will]

Abu Mena a site in NW Egypt sacred to the 3c BC martyr Abu Mena (St Menas). Many miracles were associated with his burial place, which was a centre of pilgrimage for 400 years. The ruins of the early 5c basilica erected here by Emperor Arcadius are a World Heritage site.

abundance *noun* **1** a large amount, sometimes more than is needed. **2** wealth. [from Old French *abundance*, from Latin *abundare*, to overflow]

abundant *adj.* **1** existing in large amounts. **2** (**abundant in something**) having or providing a large amount or variety of something.

abundantly *adv.* **1** very; completely. **2** in large amounts.

abuse — *verb* (pronounced *-yuze*) **1** to use (one's position, power, etc) wrongly. **2** to treat (someone or something) cruelly or wrongly. **3** to speak rudely or insultingly to or about (someone). — *noun* (pronounced *-yuse*) **1** wrong use of one's position, power, etc. **2** bad or cruel treatment of someone or something. **3** rude or insulting words said to or about someone. [from Latin *abusus*, using up, wasting]

Abu Simbel the site of two huge sandstone temples carved by Pharaoh Rameses II (c.1304–1273 BC) out of the Nile bank near Aswan. They were dismantled and relocated in the 1960s when the rising waters of the newly-constructed Aswan High Dam threatened their safety. It is a World Heritage site.

abusive *adj.* insulting or rude; using insulting or rude language.

abusively *adv.* with an abusive manner.

abusiveness *noun* being abusive.

abut *verb* (**abutted**, **abutting**) **1** *intrans.* (**abut against** *or* **on something**) *said of countries, areas of land, buildings, etc* to join, touch, or lean against another. **2** to lean on or touch (something): *a wall abutting the house.* [from Old French *abouter*, to touch with an end]

abutment *noun* the support at the end of an arch, eg in a bridge or similar structure.

abuzz *adj.* in a state of noisy activity or excitement.

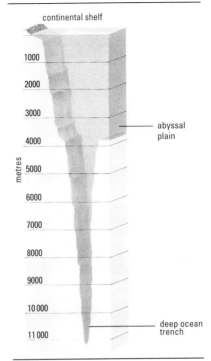

continental shelf

abyssal plain

deep ocean trench

abyss

abysmal *adj.* **1** *colloq.* extremely bad. **2** very deep; very great: *abysmal ignorance.* [from Old French *abisme*, abyss]

abysmally *adv.* **1** with an abysmal manner. **2** badly; dreadfully.

abyss *noun* **1** a very large and deep hole. **2** hell. [from Latin *abyssus*, from Greek *abyssos*, bottomless]

abyssal *adj. Biol.* deep or bottomless, especially of ocean depths. [from Greek *abyssos* bottomless]

abyssal hills *Geol.* low hills which occur on the deep sea floor, often as a series of parallel ridges 1 to 10km across. Large areas of the Atlantic and Indian Ocean floors and more than 75 per cent of the Pacific floor are covered by these hills.

abyssal plains *Geol.* extremely flat areas of the deep ocean floor which may extend for more than 1 000km. They are common in the Atlantic and Indian Oceans, but rare in the Pacific.

Abyssinia see ETHIOPIA.

AC *abbrev.* alternating current.

Ac *symbol Chem.* actinium.

a/c *abbrev.* account.

acacia *noun* a shrub or small tree with small yellow or white flowers. [from Greek *akakia*]

academe *noun formal* the world of scholars or academic life. [see ACADEMY]

academic — *adj.* **1** to do with learning, st education or teaching. **2** to do with a universi college or academy. **3** theoretical rather tha practical. **4** of no practical importance, eg because impossible or unreal: *what we would do with a car is quite academic, since we can't afford one.* **5** *said of a person* fond of intellectual pursuits. — *noun* a member of the teaching or research staff at a university or college.

academically *adv.* as regards academic matters.

academician *noun* a member of an academy (sense 2), especially the Royal Academy of Arts, the French Académie Française, or the Russian Academy of Sciences.

academy *noun* (PL. **academies**) **1** a school or college giving training in a particular subject or skill. **2** a society which encourages the study of science, literature, art, or music. **3** (*usually* **Academy**) a society of distinguished scholars, scientists, painters, etc. **4** in Scotland, a school for children between the ages of 11 and 18. [from Greek *Akademeia*, the garden outside Athens where the philosopher Plato taught, named after the hero *Akademos*]

Academy Award *or* **Oscar** *noun* any of the various prizes given each year by the American Academy of Motion Picture Arts and Sciences to the best film, actor, actress, etc.

Academy of St Martin-in-the Fields, The an English chamber orchestra formed (1959) from a string ensemble by Sir Neville Marriner. Named after its original venue (St Martin's Church in Trafalgar Square, London), its wide range of recordings has resulted in international acclaim.

acanthus *noun* **1** a plant or shrub with prickly leaves. **2** *Archit.* a stone carving of an acanthus leaf used for decorations on columns. [from Greek *akanthos*]

Acapulco *or* **Acapulco de Juarez** POP (1990) 592 000, a port and resort town in Guerrero state, S Mexico. It is situated in the Yucatán Peninsula, on the Pacific Ocean, 310km/193mi SW of Mexico City. The city is a leading Mexican tourist resort ('the Mexican Riviera'). NOTABLE FEATURE Fort San Diego.

ACAS *abbrev.* in the UK, the Advisory, Conciliation, and Arbitration Service, a body set up under the Employment Protection Act (1975). Its function is to provide facilities for conciliation, arbitration, and mediation in industrial disputes.

acc. *abbrev.* **1** (*also* **acc**) account. **2** accusative.

Accademia, in full **Accademia di Belli Arti** the municipal picture-gallery in Venice, founded by Napoleon in 1807. It houses one of the major collections in Italy.

accede *verb intrans.* (*often* **accede to something**) **1** to take office, especially to become king or queen. **2** to agree: *accede to the proposal.* **3** to join with others in a formal agreement. [from Latin *accedere*, to go near]

accelerate *verb* **1** *intrans., trans.* to increase or cause to increase speed. **2** *intrans.* to be completed more quickly. **3** to make (something) happen sooner. [from Latin *accelare*]

acceleration *noun* **1** *Physics* (SYMBOL *a*) the rate of change of velocity with time, equal to force divided by mass. It is a vector quantity, and is expressed in metres per second per second (m s⁻²). **2** any increase of speed, eg of a vehicle.

acceleration due to gravity *Physics* (SYMBOL *g*) the downward acceleration of an object falling freely due to the Earth's gravitational attraction alone. Close to the Earth's surface, it has an international standard value of 9.81m s⁻², which is the same for all objects regardless of their mass. It decreases with increasing height above sea level.

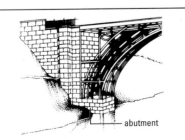

abutment

abutment

acacia

accelerator *noun* **1** *Engineering* a pedal or lever designed to control the speed of an electric motor or engine by varying the amount of electric current or fuel supplied. **2** a piece of apparatus designed to increase the velocity of charged atomic particles, eg a cyclotron, used to accelerate protons, etc. **3** any substance that increases the rate at which a process occurs, eg a catalyst.

accent — *noun* **1** the particular way in which words are pronounced by speakers who live in a particular place, belong to a particular social group, etc. **2** emphasis or stress put on a particular syllable in speaking. **3** a mark put over or under a letter or syllable to show how it is pronounced. **4** a feature, mark, or characteristic which makes something distinct or special. **5** emphasis or stress placed on certain notes or chords in a piece of music. — *verb* **1** to pronounce with an accent. **2** to write accents on. **3** to emphasize or stress. [from Latin *accentus*]
◇ In spoken language, differences in accent result from a combination of loudness, pitch, and duration. Variations in pronunciation between speakers from different countries and regions, or those belonging to a particular social class or caste, have to be distinguished from *dialect*, which also involves differences in vocabulary and grammar. For example, English may be spoken with a Scottish accent, but this is not the same as Scots dialect.

Oscar

accentor *noun* a sparrow-like bird native to N Africa, Europe, and Asia, brownish-grey to chestnut above, often streaked, and grey beneath. It feeds on insects in the summer and seeds in winter. [from Latin *accentor*, one who sings with another, from *cantor*, singer]

accentuate *verb* to emphasize or make more evident or prominent. [from Latin *accentuare*]

accentuation *noun* emphasis; stress.

accept *verb* **1** to agree to take or receive (something offered). **2** *trans., intrans.* to agree to (a suggestion, proposal, etc). **3** to agree to do (a job, etc) or take on (a responsibility, etc). **4** to believe to be true or correct. **5** to be willing to listen to and follow (advice, etc). **6** to be willing to suffer or take (blame, etc). **7** to take as suitable or appropriate: *won't accept cheques.* **8** to allow into a group, treat as a colleague, etc. **9** to tolerate calmly. [from Latin *acceptare*, to receive]

acceptability *noun* being acceptable.

acceptable *adj.* **1** worth accepting. **2** welcome or pleasing; suitable. **3** good enough, but usually only just; tolerable.

acceptably *adv.* in an acceptable way.

acceptance *noun* **1** the act or state of accepting something. **2** favourable or positive reception of something.

accepting house *Commerce* a merchant bank which 'accepts', ie buys three-month bills of exchange issued by companies. The top accepting houses in London form the Accepting Houses Committee.

acceptor *noun* **1** someone who accepts something, especially a bill of exchange. **2** a substance which is added as an impurity to a semiconductor material in order to increase the conductivity of the material by attracting electrons.

access — *noun* **1** a means of approaching or entering a place. **2** the right, opportunity, or ability to use, approach, meet with, or enter. **3** a sudden and usually brief period of strong emotion. — *verb* to get and be able to use (information, files, etc) on a computer. [from Latin *accessus*, from *ad*, to + *cedere*, to go]

accessary see ACCESSORY.

accessibility *noun* being accessible.

accessible *adj.* **1** able to be reached easily. **2** willing to talk to or have friendly discussions with other people. **3** easy to understand and enjoy or get some benefit from.

accessibly *adv.* with an accessible manner.

accession *noun* **1** the act or process of taking up a new office or responsibility, or becoming a king or queen. **2** a person or thing added, eg a new book to a library. **3** the formal act of agreeing to, and coming under the rules of, an international agreement or treaty. [from Latin *accedere*, to accede]

accessory — *noun* (PL. **accessories**) **1** something additional to, but less important than, something else. **2** an item of dress, such as a bag, hat, etc which goes with a dress, coat, etc. **3** (*also* **accessary**) *Legal* a person who helps a criminal do something wrong. — *adj.* adding to something but only in a minor way.
— **accessory before** *or* **after the fact** *Legal* a person who helps a criminal before or after the crime.
[from Latin *accessorius*]

access road a minor road built specially to give access to a house, etc.

access time the length of time it takes to get information out of the computer it is stored in.

accident *noun* **1** an unexpected event which causes damage or harm. **2** something which happens without planning or intention; chance: *managed it by accident.* [from Latin *accidere*, to happen]

accidental — *adj.* happening or done by accident; not planned. — *noun* **1** a sign, such as a sharp or flat, put in front of a note in written music to show that it is to be played higher or lower. **2** something which is not a necessary feature of something.

Accidental Death of an Anarchist (Morte accidentale di un anarchico) a play by Dario Fo (1970). It is a farce that dramatizes political issues related to oppressive capitalist governments.

accidentally *adv.* by chance.

accident-prone *adj., said of a person* frequently causing or involved in accidents, usually minor ones.

acclaim — *verb* **1** to declare (someone) to be (something) with noisy enthusiasm. **2** to receive or welcome with noisy enthusiasm. — *noun* a shout of applause or welcome. [from Latin *acclamare*]

acclamation *noun* a loud showing of approval, agreement, applause, etc.

acclimatization *or* **acclimatisation** *noun* becoming accustomed to a new climate or environment.

acclimatize *or* **acclimatise** *verb trans., intrans.* to make or become accustomed to a new place, situation, climate, etc. [from French *acclimater*, from *climat*, climate]

acclivity *noun* (PL. **acclivities**) *formal* an upward slope. See also DECLIVITY. [from Latin *acclivitas*]

accolade *noun* **1** a sign or expression of great praise or approval. **2** a touch on the shoulder with a sword when giving a person a knighthood. [from Old French *accoler*, to embrace]

accommodate *verb* **1** to provide (someone) with a place in which to stay. **2** to be large enough for; to be able to hold. **3** to do what (someone) wants; to do (someone) a favour. **4** (**accommodate oneself to something**) to adapt one's habits or plans in order to be more like, more acceptable to, or more helpful to someone or something. [from Latin *accommodare*, to adapt]

accommodating *adj.* helpful; willing to do what another person wants.

accommodatingly *adv.* with an obliging manner.

accommodation *noun* **1** (*also North Amer.* **accommodations**) a room or rooms in a house or hotel in which to live. **2** willingness to accept other people's wishes, etc. **3** (**accommodations**) *North Amer.* a reserved place on a bus, train, ship, or aircraft. **4** in vertebrates, adjustment of the shape of the lens of the eye by ciliary muscles, which contract to make the lens thinner in order to focus on distant objects, or relax to make it thicker in order to focus on nearby objects.

accommodation address an address used on letters to a person who cannot give, or does not want to give, his or her permanent address.

accommodation ladder a small ladder on the side of a large ship by means of which one can get to or from a smaller boat.

accompaniment *noun* **1** something that happens or exists at the same time as something else, or which comes with something else. **2** music played to accompany or support a singer or another instrument.

accompanist *noun* a person who plays a musical instrument to accompany or support a singer or another player.

accompany *verb* (**accompanies, accompanied**) **1** to come or go with. **2** to be done or found with. **3** to play a musical instrument to support (someone who is playing another instrument or singing). [from Old French *accompagnier*, from *a*, to + *compaignon*, companion]

accomplice *noun* a person who helps another commit a crime. [from Middle English *complice*, from Latin *complex*, joined]

accomplish *verb* **1** to manage to do. **2** to complete. [from Old French *acomplir*]

accomplishable *adj.* capable of being achieved or done.

accomplished *adj.* **1** clever or skilled. **2** completed or finished.

accomplishment *noun* **1** a social or other skill developed through practice. **2** something special or remarkable which has been done; an achievement. **3** the finishing or completing of something.

accord — *verb* **1** *intrans.* (**accord with someone** *or* **something**) to agree or be in harmony with them. **2** to give (a welcome, etc) or grant (permission, a request, etc). — *noun* agreement or consent; harmony.
— **of one's own accord** willingly; without being told to or forced to.
with one accord with everyone in agreement and acting at the same time.
[from Old French *acorder*, from Latin *ad*, to + *cor*, heart]

accordance *noun* agreement or harmony: *in accordance with the law.*

according *adv.* **1** (**according to someone**) as said or told by: *according to my doctor.* **2** (**according to something**) in agreement with: *live according to one's principles.* **3** (**according as ...**) *formal* in proportion as ... ; depending on whether: *pay according as one is able.*

accordingly *adv.* **1** in an appropriate way: *act accordingly.* **2** therefore; for that reason.

accordion *noun* a musical instrument consisting of two box-like parts joined by a folding middle section, played by pushing the box-like parts together and pulling them apart again to create a sound which is changed into different notes by pressing a series of buttons and piano-like keys with the fingers. [from German *Akkordion,* from French *accorder* or Italian *accordare,* to harmonize]

accordionist *noun* a person who plays the accordion.

accost *verb* **1** to approach and speak to (someone), especially boldly or in a threatening way. **2** *said of a prostitute* to offer to have sexual intercourse with (a person) in return for money. [from Latin *accostare*]

account — *noun* **1** a description or report. **2** an explanation, especially of one's behaviour. **3** an arrangement by which a bank or building society allows a person to have banking or credit facilities; a deposit of money in a bank or building society. **4** a statement of the money owed to someone for goods or services. **5** (*usually* **accounts**) a record of money received and spent. **6** an arrangement by which a shop allows a person to buy goods on credit and pay for them later. **7** importance or value. **8** behalf or sake. — *verb formal* to consider (someone or something) to be as specified: *accounted them all fools.*
— **account for something** to give a reason or explanation for it. **2** to make or give a reckoning of money spent, etc.
account for something or someone to succeed in destroying or disposing of them.
bring someone to account to punish them for something wrong that has been done.
by all accounts according to general opinion.
call someone to account to demand an explanation from them for their action or behaviour.
give a good *or* **poor account of oneself** to give a good or bad performance; to make a good or bad impression.
hold someone to account to consider them responsible.
leave something out of account not to consider (a problem, factor, etc) when making a decision, calculation, etc.
on account 1 to be paid for at a later date. **2** as partial payment.
on account of something because of it.
on no account not for any reason.
on one's own account 1 on one's own responsibility. **2** for one's own benefit.
put something to good account to use a situation, ability, etc to one's advantage.
take something into account *or* **take account of something** to consider (a problem, opinion, or other factor) when making a decision or assessment.
turn something to good account to use it to one's advantage.
[from Old French *aconter*]

accountability *noun* responsibility.

accountable *adj.* **1** responsible; having to explain or defend one's actions or conduct. **2** explicable.

accountancy *noun* the profession of preparing and keeping the financial records of a business or organization.
◇ The profession is also concerned in a wide range of activities including financial planning, management accounting, taxation, treasury management, and specialist areas, such as liquidation. The presentation of published accounts is governed by company law and the Stock Exchange.

accountant *noun* a person who is trained to keep accounts.

accounting *noun* the skill or practice of preparing or keeping the financial records of a company, etc.

accoutrements *pl. noun* **1** equipment. **2** a soldier's equipment apart from clothing and weapons. [from Old French *acoustrer,* to equip]

Accra POP (1988e) 949 000, the seaport capital of Ghana. It is situated on the Gulf of Guinea coast, 415km/258mi SW of Lagos. HISTORY founded as three forts and trading posts in the 17c; capital of the Gold Coast in 1877; became capital of Ghana in 1957.

accredit *verb* (**accredited, accrediting**) **1** (**accredit something to someone** *or* **someone with something**) to attribute a saying, action, etc to someone: *accredited the idea to us / should accredit them with devising the scheme.* **2** (**accredit someone to** *or* **at a place**) to send an ambassador or diplomat to a foreign country with official authority. **3** to state officially that (something) is of a satisfactory standard. [from Old French *acrediter*]

accreditation *noun* the action of accrediting or being accredited.

accredited *adj.* **1** officially recognized. **2** *said of a belief, etc* generally accepted.

accretion *noun* **1** *Geol.* a gradual increase in land area resulting from offshore deposition of sediment carried by river or stream currents, tides, or wave action. **2** the process of separate things growing into one. **3** an increase in size of a particle, eg a hailstone, as a result of the formation of additional outer layers. [from Latin *accretio,* growing together]

accrual *noun* **1** the act of accruing. **2** something which has been accrued.

accrue *verb* **1** *intrans.* (*usually* **accrue to someone or something**) to come in addition, as a product, result, or development. **2** *intrans.* to fall to naturally. **3** to collect: *accrued a collection of antique vases.* [from Old French *acrue,* from Latin *accrescere,* to grow together]

acct. *abbrev.* (*also* **acct**) account.

acculturation *noun* the process of one group of people becoming more like another group of people in behaviour, customs, etc, usually because of living near them for a long time. [from Latin *ad,* to + CULTURE]

accumulate *verb* **1** to collect or gather (something) in an increasing quantity. **2** *intrans.* to grow greater in number or quantity. [from Latin *accumulare,* from *cumulus,* heap]

accumulation *noun* **1** the act of piling up. **2** a mass or pile.

accumulative *adj.* **1** becoming greater over a period of time. **2** tending to gather, buy, etc many things.

accumulatively *adv.* in an accumulative manner.

accumulator *noun* **1** *Electr.* a storage battery that can be recharged by passing a current through it from an external DC (direct current) supply. **2** *Brit.* (*also* **accumulator bet**) a bet on four or more races, where the original money bet and any money won are bet on the next race, so that the better either wins a lot of money or loses it all. **3** *Comput.* a part of the memory of a computer that is used as a temporary store for the results of an arithmetical calculation or logic operation.

accuracy *noun* exactness; the state of being absolutely correct and making no mistakes, especially through careful effort.

accurate *adj.* **1** exact; absolutely correct; making no mistakes. **2** agreeing exactly with the truth or a standard. [from Latin *accuratus,* performed with care]

accurately *adv.* **1** without mistakes or faults. **2** exactly.

accursed *adj.* **1** *colloq.* disliked or hated. **2** having been cursed. [from Anglo-Saxon *acursod*]

accursedly *adv.* in an accursed state or manner.

accusation *noun* **1** the act of accusing someone of having done something wrong. **2** *Legal* a statement charging a person with having committed a crime.

accusative *Grammar* — *noun* in certain languages, eg Latin, Greek and German, the grammatical case of a noun, etc when it is the object of an action or the point towards which something is moving. — *adj.* of or in the accusative. [from Latin *accusativus*]

accuse *verb* (**accuse someone of something**) to charge them with an offence.
— **the accused** the person or people accused of an offence.
stand accused *Legal* to appear in court charged with an offence.
[from Latin *accusare*]

accuser *noun* a person who accuses or blames.

accusing *adj.* blaming, condemning; reproachful.

accusingly *adv.* in an accusing way.

accustom *verb* (**accustomed, accustoming**) (**accustom someone** *or* **oneself to something**) to make them become familiar with it. [from Old French *acostumer*]

accustomed *adj.* **1** (**accustomed to someone** *or* **something**) familiar with them; experienced in something. **2** usual; customary: *the accustomed practice.*

AC/DC *or* **ac/dc** — *abbrev.* alternating current/direct current. — *adj. slang* sexually attracted to both men and women.

ACE *abbrev.* Advisory Centre for Education.

ace — *noun* **1** *Cards* the card in each of the four suits with a single symbol on it, having either the highest value or the value one. **2** a person who is extremely good at something. **3** a fighter pilot who has shot down many enemy aircraft. **4** *Tennis* a serve that is so fast and cleverly placed that the opposing player cannot hit the ball. — *adj. colloq.* excellent.
— **an ace up one's sleeve** a hidden or secret advantage, argument, etc that will help one to beat an opponent.
hold all the aces to be in a powerful or winning position.
play one's ace to put into action a plan for the final defeat of one's opponent.
within an ace of something *or* **of doing something** very close to it: *came within an ace of winning.*
[from Old French *as,* from Latin *as,* unit]

acellular *adj. Biol.* not containing cells; not made up of cells.

acerbic *adj.* **1** bitter and sour in taste. **2** bitter and harsh in manner, speech, etc. [from Latin *acerbus,* sour]

acerbity *noun* **1** bitterness, sourness. **2** harshness.

acesulfame K *Chem.* an artificial sweetener, 130 times sweeter than sugar. [from *K* for *potassium,* + *sulfamic acid*]

acetal *noun Chem.* a substance formed by the reaction of an alcohol with an aldehyde. [from Latin *acetum,* vinegar]

acetaldehyde *noun Chem.* (FORMULA CH_3CHO) a colourless volatile pungent-smelling liquid used as a solvent and reducing agent, and in the manufacture of acetic acid and polymers such as paraldehyde (a sleep-inducing drug) and metaldehyde (a slug poison and fuel for portable stoves).

acetate *noun* **1** a salt of acetic acid. **2** a smooth shiny man-made material.

acetic *adj.* of or like vinegar. [from Latin *acetum,* vinegar]

acetic acid the clear, liquid acid that gives vinegar its sour taste.

acetone *noun Chem.* a strong-smelling, colourless liquid used as a solvent. [from ACETIC]

acetylcholine *noun Biochem.* a neurotransmitter found in the brain, spinal cord, and ganglia of the autonomic nervous system in mammals.

acetylene *noun Chem.* (FORMULA C_2H_2) a colourless highly flammable gas with a characteristic sweet odour, used for lighting, oxyacetylene welding, and in the manufacture of organic compounds. It is the simplest member of the alkyne series of hydrocarbons. – Also called *ethyne.* [from ACETIC]

acetyl group *Chem.* in organic chemical compounds, the CH_3CO- group.

Achaeans 1 the archaic name for the Greeks, found frequently in Homer. **2** in Classical Greece, the inhabitants of Achaea, the territory to the south of the Corinthian Gulf.

Achaemenids the first royal house of Persia, founded by the early 7c ruler, Achaemenes. Its capitals included Pasargadae and Persepolis.

ache — *verb intrans.* **1** to feel or be the source of a dull continuous pain. **2** (**ache for something**) to want it very much. — *noun* a dull continuous pain. [from Anglo-Saxon *acan*, to ache; *æce*, an ache]

Achebe, Chinua (1930–) Nigerian novelist, born in Ogidi. His novel *Things Fall Apart* (1958) was the first of four describing inter-tribal and inter-racial tensions in pre- and post-colonial Nigerian society. After *A Man of the People* (1966), he devoted most of his time to politics and education, producing no more fiction until *Anthills of the Savannah* (1987).

Achelous, River, Greek **Akhelóös** the second longest river in Greece, length 220km/137mi. It rises in the Pindus Mts, N central Greece, flowing S through mountain gorges to the fertile Agrinion Plain. It enters the Ionian Sea opposite Cephalonia I.

achene *noun Bot.* a dry one-seeded fruit that is indehiscent (ie it does not split to release its seed), formed from a single carpel, as in the buttercup. [from A-¹ + Greek *chainein*, to gape]

Acheron in Greek mythology, the chasm or abyss of the Underworld, and the name of one of the rivers there. It is also the name of a river in Epirus, which disappeared underground and was thought to be an entrance to Hades.

Acheson, Dean (Gooderham) (1893–1971) US lawyer and politician, born in Middletown, Connecticut. As under-secretary (1945–7) and then Secretary of State (1949–53) in the Truman administration, he helped to establish the Marshall Plan (1947) and also the North Atlantic Treaty Organization (1949).

Acheulian in Europe, Africa, and Asia, a broad term for early prehistoric cultures which used symmetrically-flaked stone handaxes. The name derives from finds made (c.1850) at Saint-Acheul, a suburb of Amiens in the Somme Valley, N France.

achievable *adj.* capable of being achieved.

achieve *verb* **1** to reach, realize, or attain (a goal, ambition, etc), especially through hard work. **2** to earn or gain (a reputation, etc). **3** *intrans.* to be successful. [from Old French *achever*]

achievement *noun* **1** the gaining of something, usually after working hard for it. **2** something that has been done or gained by effort.

achiever *noun* a person who achieves success.

Achilles in Greek mythology, the son of Peleus and Thetis. Thetis dipped Achilles in the R Styx so that his body was invulnerable to injury, except for the heel where she had held him. He killed Hector and was himself killed by Paris, who shot him in the heel with a poisoned arrow. Homer's *Iliad* describes Achilles' exploits in Troy.

Achilles' heel a person's weak or vulnerable point.

Achilles' tendon the tendon that connects the muscles in the calf of the leg to the heel.

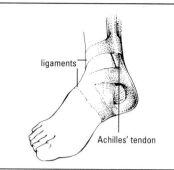

ligaments

Achilles' tendon

Achilles' tendon

achondroplasia *Medicine* an inherited form of dwarfism, in which the arms and legs are abnormally short, but the head and body are of normal size. [from A-¹ + Greek *chondros*, cartilage + *plassein*, to make]

achromatic *adj.* **1** having no colour. **2** transmitting light without separating it into the colours which go to form it. [from A-¹ + Greek *khroma*, colour]

achromatically *adv.* in an achromatic way; without colour.

achromatic lens *Astron.* a composite lens, consisting of two or more lenses each made of a different type of glass, that has the same focal length for two or more wavelengths of light, and greatly reduces the effects of chromatic aberration in optical systems.

achy *adj.* (**achier**, **achiest**) full of or troubled by pain.

acid — *noun* **1** any of a group of chemical compounds that have a sour or sharp taste, turn blue litmus paper red, and react with bases to form salts. Acids dissociate (break down) in water to form positively charged hydrogen ions and negatively charged anions. *Strong acids*, eg sulphuric acid, dissociate almost completely, whereas *weak acids*, eg acetic acid (ethanoic acid) only partially dissociate. **2** any sour substance. **3** *slang* LSD. — *adj.* **1** containing acid; sour to taste. **2** *said of remarks, etc* expressing bitterness or anger. [from Latin *acidus*, sour]

acid house a type of electronically produced disco music with a repetitive hypnotic beat, often associated with the use of certain drugs, and usually played at large parties.

acidic *adj.* like, or containing, acid.

acidification *noun* the act or process of acidifying.

acidify *verb trans., intrans.* (**acidifies**, **acidified**) to make or become acid.

acidity *noun* (PL. **acidities**) an acid quality, especially an over-acid condition of the stomach.

acidly *adv.* bitterly, sourly.

acidosis *noun Medicine* a condition in which the blood and other body fluids are abnormally acidic, eg as a result of kidney failure or diabetes.

acid rain rain or other forms of precipitation (eg snow) containing dissolved sulphur dioxide and nitrogen oxides that have been released into the atmosphere as a result of the burning of fossil fuels, eg coal or oil.
◇ Acid rain is produced when water in the atmosphere reacts with sulphur dioxide and nitrogen oxides from waste gases produced by various industrial processes, power stations, and vehicle exhaust fumes, and also by natural sources such as volcanoes and forest fires. The acid gases then fall with the rain as weak sulphuric acid and nitric acid. Waste gases originating in one country can fall as acid rain in another, causing irreparable damage to vegetation and aquatic life, polluting soil, streams, and lakes, eroding buildings, and contaminating drinking water supplies.
Many forests have been severely affected by acid rain. The Black Forest in Germany is losing many of its trees, and 80 per cent of the lakes in S Norway no longer contain fish life. A number of countries are attempting to reduce acid rain, eg by burning fuels with a low sulphur content, running cars on lead-free petrol, and fitting the smokestacks of power stations with special equipment to remove pollutants from smoke before it is released into the air.

acid test a decisive test to determine that something is genuine or valid. [originally a test using acid to determine whether a substance contained gold]

ack-ack *adj. old colloq. use* anti-aircraft. [formerly, British signaller's code for the letters *AA*, standing for *anti-aircraft*]

acknowledge *verb* **1** to admit or accept the truth of (a fact or situation). **2** to accept as valid or legal; to recognize. **3** to report that one has received (what has been sent). **4** to express thanks for. **5** to show that one has noticed or recognized (someone), by greeting them, nodding one's head, etc. **6** to accept someone (as something); to accept a person's claim to be (something). [from obsolete *acknow*, to acknowledge]

acknowledgement *or* **acknowledgment** *noun* **1** the act of acknowledging someone or something. **2** something done, given, or said to acknowledge something.

acme *noun* the highest point of achievement, success, excellence, etc. [from Greek *akme*]

acne *noun Medicine* a skin disorder, common in adolescence, caused by overactivity of the sebaceous glands, especially on the face, chest, and back. The pores become blocked by *sebum*, an oily secretion of the sebaceous glands, forming a plug which develops into a pimple or blackhead. [from Latin *acne*]

acolyte *noun* **1** a person who assists a priest in certain religious ceremonies. **2** an assistant or attendant. [from Latin *acolytus*, from Greek *akolouthos*, follower]

Aconcagua, Cerro the highest peak in the W hemisphere, situated in Mendoza province, W Argentina. HEIGHT 6 960m. It lies in the Andes, E of the Chilean border, 112km/70mi NW of Mendoza, with the Uspallata Pass at its S foot.

aconite *noun* **1** a poisonous wild plant with hood-like blue or yellow flowers, especially monkshood and wolfsbane. **2** a drug obtained from the roots of this plant. [from Latin *aconitum*]

acorn *noun* the nut-like fruit of the oak tree, which has a cup-shaped outer case. [from Anglo-Saxon *æcern*]

acorn

acoustic *adj.* **1** of sound, the sense of hearing, or acoustics. **2** *said of a musical instrument, eg a guitar* amplifying the sound by means of its body, not using an electrical amplifier. **3** *said of building materials, etc* absorbing sound. [from Greek *akoustikos*, from *akouein*, to hear]

acoustically *adv.* **1** relating to the hearing of sound. **2** without electronic amplification.

acoustic coupler an instrument that makes it possible for computers to pass information by means of an ordinary telephone.

acoustics *noun* **1** (*sing.*) the scientific study of the production and properties of sound waves. **2** (*pl.*) the characteristics of a room, concert hall, theatre, etc, that determine the nature and quality of sounds such as music and speech heard within it.

acquaint *verb* (**acquaint someone with something**) to make them aware of or familiar with it. [from Old French *acointer*]

acquaintance *noun* **1** slight knowledge of something or someone. **2** someone whom one knows slightly.
— **make someone's acquaintance** to get to know them.

acquaintanceship *noun* slight knowledge, especially of a person.

acquainted *adj.* **1** (**acquainted with someone**) knowing them personally but only slightly. **2** (**acquainted with something**) familiar with it: *acquainted with her books.*

acquiesce *verb intrans.* (**acquiesce in** *or* **to something**) to accept it or agree to it without objection. [from Latin *acquiescere*]

acquiescence *noun* quiet or tacit agreement or acceptance.

acquiescent *adj.* quietly accepting or agreeing.

acquiescently *adv.* in an acquiescent manner.

acquire *verb* **1** to get, gain or develop, especially through skill or effort. **2** to achieve or reach (a reputation). [from Latin *acquirere*]

acquired immune deficiency syndrome see AIDS.

acquired taste 1 a liking for something that develops as one has more experience of it. **2** the thing liked.

acquirement *noun* something learned or developed through hard work and not a natural gift.

acquisition *noun* **1** a thing obtained or acquired, especially through hard work or effort. **2** the act of obtaining, developing, or acquiring a skill, etc. [from Latin *acquisitio*]

acquisitive *adj.* very eager to obtain and possess things. [from Latin *acquisitivus*]

acquisitiveness *noun* a desire or tendency to collect possessions.

acquit *verb* (**acquitted, acquitting**) **1** (**acquit someone of something**) *said of a court or jury, etc* to declare a person accused of a crime to be innocent. **2** (**acquit oneself**) to behave or perform in a particular way: *acquitted themselves with distinction.* [from Old French *aquiter*]

acquittal *noun* **1** a declaration in a court of law that someone is not guilty of the crime, etc of which they have been accused. **2** performance of a duty.

Acrasia the wife of Cymochles in Edmund Spenser's *The Faerie Queene*, who dwells in the Bower of Bliss and represents Intemperance.

Acre, Hebrew **Akko**, ancient **Ptolemais** POP (1988e) 37 000, an ancient town in Northern district, NW Israel. Situated on the Mediterranean Sea, it is now a resort centre. The town became the capital of the Crusader Kingdom after Jerusalem was captured by Saladin in 1187. NOTABLE FEATURES ancient and modern harbour; Crypt of the Knights Hospitaller of St John; city walls (18c); mosque (18c).

acre *noun* **1** a unit of measurement for land, equal to 4 840sq yd or 4 047sq m. **2** (**acres**) a large area of land. [from Anglo-Saxon *æcer*, field]

acreage *noun* the number of acres in a piece of land.

acrid *adj.* **1** having a very strong, bitter taste, or smell. **2** *said of speech, manner, etc* sharp or bitter. [from Latin *acer*, sharp, keen]

acridity *noun* being acrid, bitterness.

acridly *adv.* in an acrid manner.

acrimonious *adj., said of speech, etc* bitter; accusing.

acrimoniously *adv.* bitterly; accusingly.

acrimony *noun* bitterness in feeling, temper, or speech. [from Latin *acrimonia*]

acrobat *noun* an entertainer, eg in a circus, who performs skilful balancing acts and other athletic tricks. [from French *acrobate*, from Greek *akrobatos*, walking on tiptoe]

acrobatic *adj.* **1** able to perform gymnastic feats; agile. **2** liable to change one's opinion or allegiance frequently.

acrobatically *adv.* in an acrobatic way.

acrobatics *noun* **1** (*sing.*) the art or skill of an acrobat. **2** (*pl.*) acrobatic movements.

acromegaly *noun Medicine* a disorder characterized by abnormal enlargement of the face, hands, and feet. It is caused by overproduction of growth hormone. [from Greek *akron* point, *megas, megalos* great]

acronym *noun* a word made from the first letters or syllables of other words, eg NATO is an acronym of North Atlantic Treaty Organization. An acronym is usually pronounced as a word in its own right, as distinct from *initialisms*, which are pronounced as separate letters, eg BBC. [from Greek *akron*, point, end + *onyma*, name]
◆ See note at *abbreviation.*

acrophobia *noun* fear of heights. [from Greek *akron*, point, summit + *phobos*, fear]

acropolis *noun* **1** the upper fortified part or citadel of an ancient Greek city. **2** (**Acropolis**) the citadel of ancient Athens. [from Greek *akron*, point, summit + *polis*, city]
◇ The Athenian Acropolis contained the national treasury and many sacred sites and shrines, most of which (eg the Parthenon and the Erechtheum) were associated with the worship of Athene, the patron goddess of Athens. The present ruins date mainly from the second half of the 5c BC.

across — *prep.* **1** to, at, or on the other side of. **2** from one side of to the other. **3** so as to cross: *arms folded across the chest.* — *adv.* **1** to, at, or on the other side. **2** from one side to the other.
— **across the board** general or generally; applying in all cases.
[from A³ + CROSS]

acrostic *noun* a poem in which the first letters in each line form a word or proverb. [from Greek *akron*, end + *stichos*, line]

acrylic — *noun* **1** a man-made material made from acrylic acid. **2** same as ACRYLIC RESIN. — *adj.* of the material acrylic. [from Latin *acer*, sharp + *olere*, to smell]

acrylic acid a type of naturally occurring acid used in the manufacture of paints, resins, materials, etc.

acrylic painting in art, the use of plastic paints, ie pigments mixed with an acrylic resin binder such as polymethyl methacrylate in mineral spirits. Developed from the 1930s onwards, acrylic paints have enabled many modern artists to explore and develop new painting techniques which exploit the quick-drying, chemically stable, strongly adhesive, and durable qualities of the medium.

acrylic resin *Chem.* any of a large number of synthetic resins, eg Acrilan, Perspex, formed by the polymerization of derivatives of acrylic acid. Acrylic resins are used to make artificial fibres, lenses for optical instruments, protective coatings, waxes, paints, and adhesives.

ACT *abbrev.* Australian Capital Territory.

act — *noun* **1** a thing done; a deed. **2** the process of doing something: *caught in the act.* **3** behaviour that is intended to make an impression on people and is not a sincere expression of feeling. **4** a short piece of entertainment, usually one of a series in a show; the person or people performing this. **5** a major division of a play, opera, etc. See also SCENE. **6** a formal decision reached or a law passed by a law-making body. — *verb* **1** *intrans.* to behave. **2** *intrans.* to do something: *need to act fast.* **3** *intrans.* (**act as, act for**) to perform the actions or functions (of). **4** *intrans.* to perform in a play or film. **5** to perform (a part) in a play or film; to perform (a play). **6** to show (feelings one does not really have). **7** *intrans.* (**act on**) to have an effect or influence on.
— **act of God** an event beyond human control, especially a natural disaster such as an earthquake.
act on *or* **upon something** to follow advice, etc; to obey instructions, etc.
act something out to express one's feelings, fears, etc in one's behaviour, usually unconsciously.
act up *intrans. colloq.* **1** *said of a machine, etc* to fail or function erratically. **2** to behave badly.
get in on the act *colloq.* to start taking part in some profitable activity, plan, etc in order to share in the benefits.
get one's act together *colloq.* to become organized and able to act, especially in relation to a specific undertaking.
[from Latin *actum*, thing done]

Actaeon in Greek mythology, a hunter who came upon Artemis, the goddess of chastity, while she was bathing naked. She threw water at him, changing him into a stag, and he was pursued and killed by his own hounds.

acting — *noun* the profession or art of performing in a play or film. — *adj.* temporarily doing someone else's job or duties.

actinic radiation *Physics* electromagnetic radiation, especially ultraviolet light, that is capable of initiating chemical reactions, especially changes in a light-sensitive emulsion.

actinide *or* **actinoid** *noun Chem.* any chemical element with an atomic number between 89 and 104, the best-known being uranium (92) and plutonium (94). All actinides are radioactive. [from Greek *aktis aktinos*, ray]

actinium *noun Chem.* (SYMBOL **Ac**, ATOMIC NUMBER **89**) a silvery-white radioactive metal,

Acropolis

found in uranium ores, and formed by the decay of uranium-235, or by bombarding radium with neutrons. It is used as a source of alpha particles. [from Greek *aktis*, ray (from its being radioactive)]

actinotherapy *noun Medicine* the treatment of diseases and disorders by exposure to infrared or ultraviolet radiation.

action *noun* **1** the process of doing something: *put ideas into action*. **2** something done. **3** activity, force, or energy: *a woman of action*. **4** a movement or gesture. **5** the working part of a machine, instrument, etc; a mechanism. **6** a battle; fighting. **7** (**the action**) the events of a play, film, etc. **8** *colloq.* exciting activity or events going on around one: *get a piece of the action*. **9** a legal case. — **out of action** not working. [from Latin *actio*, from *agere*, to do, drive]

actionable *adj.* giving reasonable cause for legal action.

action-packed *adj. colloq.* filled with exciting activity.

action painting a style of painting in which paint is dripped, splashed, or spilled on to the canvas; it drew attention to the significance of the act of painting in itself. The term was first used by the US art critic, Harold Rosenberg, in 1952. The style became well known through the drip paintings of Jackson Pollock.

action potential *Physiol.* a brief electrical signal consisting of a change in electrical potential, produced across the membrane of a nerve or muscle fibre in response to stimulation. It is an easily measurable indication of the passage of a nerve impulse.

action replay the repeating, often in slow-motion, of a piece of film on television, especially of some important act such as scoring a goal.

action stations positions taken by soldiers, etc who are ready for battle, etc.

Actium, Battle of a naval battle (31 BC) off the NW coast of Greece. Octavian (later the emperor Augustus) defeated the forces of Antony and Cleopatra. It has traditionally been seen as the end of the Roman Republic and the beginning of the Roman Empire.

activate *verb* **1** to make (something) start working or go into operation. **2** to make (something) radioactive. **3** to make (a chemical reaction) happen faster.

activated charcoal *or* **activated carbon** *Chem.* a form of charcoal that is a very efficient absorber of gases. It is prepared by heating wood in a limited supply of air, and is used in gas masks and cooker hoods, and also for removing the colouring matter from solutions.

activation *noun* the act or process of activating.

activation energy *Chem.* the amount of energy that is needed to start a chemical reaction by breaking and reforming chemical bonds.

active — *adj.* **1** moving, working, and doing things; full of energy. **2** operating; working. **3** having an effect: *the active ingredients*. **4** radioactive. **5** *said of verbs* in the form used when the subject of the sentence performs the action of the verb. See also PASSIVE. — *noun* **1** (*also* **active voice**) the form a verb takes when its subject performs the action or has the state that the verb denotes, eg the verbs in *the man fell, smoking kills you*, and *God exists* (see also PASSIVE). **2** a verb in the active. [from Latin *activus*]

actively *adv.* in an active way; effectively, positively.

active service *Mil.* service by a member of the armed forces, or by a military unit, in a battle area. The term is also applied, especially in the USA, to service in the fighting forces at any time, whether in peacetime or in war.

active transport *Biochem.* the transport of a solute across a cell membrane against a concentration gradient or electrochemical potential gradient (ions), and therefore requiring the input of energy.

activist *noun* a person who is very active, especially as a member of a political group.

activity *noun* (PL. **activities**) **1** the state of being active or busy. **2** (*often* **activities**) something that a person does or people do, especially for pleasure, interest, exercise, etc. **3** *Physics* the rate at which the atoms of a radioactive substance disintegrate per unit time. [from Latin *activitas*]

Act of Congress a bill sanctioned by the US legislature (ie the two houses of Congress: the House of Representatives and the Senate) and then signed by the president to become law.

act of God *Legal* an extraordinary event, beyond human control, which could not be foreseen and guarded against. Natural disasters, such as earthquakes or hurricanes may be regarded as acts of God. Damage or an accident which is a direct consequence of such events is usually not covered by insurance.

Act of Parliament a bill which has passed five stages (first reading, second reading, committee stage, report stage, third reading) in both houses of the UK parliament (the House of Commons and the House of Lords), and received the royal assent. The same kind of procedure applies in other parliamentary systems, although the specific stages through which a bill passes may vary.

actor *noun* a man or woman who performs in plays or films, especially professionally. [from Latin *actor*, doer]

Actors Studio a workshop for professional actors founded (1947) in New York City by Elia Kazan, Cheryl Crawford, and Robert Lewis. Under Lee Strasberg, it was the major centre for US acting where trained actors could work free from the pressures of a production.

actress *noun* a woman whose job is performing in plays or films.

Acts of the Apostles a New Testament book, the second part of a narrative begun in Luke's Gospel. Focusing on the early progress of Jesus' followers as they spread the Christian faith, it begins with the resurrection and ascension of Jesus, but concentrates largely upon the growth of the Jerusalem Church, its spread to Samaria and Antioch, and the missionary journeys of Paul to Asia Minor, the Aegean lands, and Rome.

actual *adj.* **1** existing as fact; real. **2** not imagined, estimated, or guessed. [from Latin *actualis*]

actuality *noun* (PL. **actualities**) **1** fact; reality. **2** (*usually* **actualities**) an existing condition.

actually *adv.* **1** really; in fact. **2** *usually said in surprise or disagreement* as a matter of fact: *actually, I think she's right*.

actuarial *adj.* relating to actuaries or their work.

actuary *noun* (PL. **actuaries**) a person who calculates insurance risks, and gives advice to insurance companies, etc on what premiums to set. [from Latin *actuarius*, clerk]

actuate *verb* **1** to cause (a mechanism, etc) to go into action. **2** to cause (someone) to act the way he or she does. [from Latin *actuare*, from *actus*, act]

actuation *noun* putting in motion, movement.

acuity *noun* **1** sharpness or acuteness, eg of the mind or senses. **2** (*also* **visual acuity**) sharpness of vision. [from Latin *acuitas*, from *acus*, needle]

acumen *noun* the ability to judge quickly and well; keen insight. [from Latin *acumen*, point, from *acus*, needle]

acupressure *noun Medicine* **1** the arrest of a haemorrhage by a needle pressing across the artery. **2** in acupuncture or related treatments, pressure (as opposed to a needle) applied to specified points (acupoints). [from Latin *acus*, needle + PRESSURE]

acupuncture *noun* a traditional Chinese method of healing in which symptoms are relieved by the insertion of thin needles at specific points beneath the skin. Despite the lack of an acceptable scientific explanation, its effectiveness is widely recognized by orthodox medical practitioners.

◇ Acupuncture has been practised for over 4 000 years in China, where it is often used as an anaesthetic during surgery. However, it has only recently attracted attention in the West. Hot or cold needles, usually made of steel, are inserted beneath the skin and stimulated, either by rotation or by an electric current, at specific sites that correspond to the tissue or organ that requires treatment. About 800 'acupuncture points' have been identified on body maps. The effects produced depend on the site of the needles, and include loss of pain sensation (usually in one particular part of the body), anaesthesia, and feelings of well-being and relaxation. Acupuncture has been used to treat chronic headache, migraine, backache, and neuralgia, and also to relieve stress and overcome habits such as smoking. Acupuncture treatment is based on the belief that there is a network of energy pathways or 'meridians' in the body, and that disease results from a disturbance of the balance of Yin and Yang energy. It is thought that by inserting needles at certain acupuncture points, the energy balance can be restored by altering the flow of energy in the various meridians. Western doctors have suggested that the effectiveness of acupuncture may be due to the fact that it stimulates deep sensory nerves, resulting in the production of endorphins, which are the body's natural painkillers. [from Latin *acus*, needle + PUNCTURE]

acupuncturist *noun* a practitioner of acupuncture.

acute — *adj.* **1** extremely severe; very bad. **2** *said of the senses* keen, sharp, penetrating. **3** *said of mental powers, etc* quick and accurate. **4** *said of a disease or symptoms* arising suddenly and often severe, but of short duration: *acute bronchitis / acute pain*. **5** *said of a sound* high, sharp, and shrill. **6** *Geom., said of an angle* of less than 90°. — *noun* (*also* **acute accent**) a mark placed over a vowel (eg *á, é*) in some languages, showing pronunciation. [from Latin *acuere*, to sharpen]

acutely *adv.* in an acute manner; severely.

acuteness *noun* the quality of being acute, especially mental perception.

-acy *suffix* forming nouns denoting **1** a quality: *accuracy*. **2** a state, condition, office, etc: *supremacy / piracy*. [from Latin *-acia*]

acyl group *Chem.* in an organic chemical compound, the general name for the functional group RCO-, where R is either hydrogen or a hydrocarbon group (eg CH_3).

AD *or* **A.D.** *abbrev.* Anno Domini: used in dates of the modern era. See also BC.

◆ Strictly, AD should precede the date, since it means 'in the year of the Lord'. However, it is commonly used following the date, and in uses such as *the tenth century* AD. CE (= common era), which is culturally neutral, is sometimes used instead.

ad *noun colloq.* short form of ADVERTISEMENT.

ADA *or* **Ada** *noun Comput.* a programming language originally devised for military use, one of its applications being simultaneous control of diverse operations. [named after Ada Lovelace (1816–52), daughter of Byron and assistant to the computer pioneer, Charles Babbage]

Adad the Mesopotamian god of storms; the Syrians called him Hadad, and in the Bible he is

Rimmon, the god of thunder. His symbol was the lightning held in his hand.

adage *noun* a proverb or maxim. [from French *adage*, from Latin *adagium*]

adagio *Mus.* — *adv.* slowly. — *noun* (PL. **adagios**) a slow movement or piece of music. [from Italian *adagio*]

Adam 1 the first man, according to the Biblical account in the Book of Genesis. 2 a male first name.
— **not know someone from Adam** to be unable to distinguish or recognize someone. [from Hebrew *adam*, man]

Adam, Adolphe (Charles) (1803–56) French composer, born in Paris. He wrote several successful operas, such as *Le Postillon de Lonjumeau* (1836), but is chiefly remembered for the ballet *Giselle* (1841).

Adam, Robert (1728–92) Scottish architect, born in Kirkcaldy. He was architect of the king's works (1761–9). In 1758 he established a London practice and during the next 40 years he and his brother James (1730–94) succeeded in transforming the prevailing Palladian fashion in architecture by a series of romantically elegant variations on diverse Classical originals, as in Home House, Portland Square, London. They also designed furniture and fittings to suit the houses they planned and decorated.

Adam and Eve biblical characters, the first man and woman created by God. Adam was formed from the dust of the ground and God's breath or spirit (Genesis 2.7); Eve was made from Adam's rib. Tempted by the serpent (the Devil), they fell into sin by disobeying God's command not to eat the fruit of the tree of the knowledge of good and evil (Genesis 3), and were expelled from the Garden of Eden. As a result, sin entered the world and the human condition was marked by toil and pain. Their sons were Cain, Abel, and Seth.

adamant *adj.* completely determined; not likely to change one's mind or opinion. [from Old French *adamaunt*, from Latin *adamas*, hard steel]

adamantly *adv.* in an adamant way; resolutely.

Adam Bede a novel by George Eliot (1859). Her first, it charts the unrequited love of carpenter Adam Bede for the tragic heroine Hetty Sorrel.

Adamnan, St (c.625–704) Irish monk, born in Donegal. He joined the Columban brotherhood of Iona at 28, and became abbot in 679. He came to support the Roman views on the dating of Easter and the shape of the tonsure. His works include the *Vita Sancti Columbae* (Life of St Columba), which reveals much about the Iona community. His feast day is 23 Sep.

Adams, Gerry (Gerald) (1948–) Northern Irish politician, born in Belfast. At an early age he joined the Irish Nationalist party Sinn Fein, the political wing of the IRA, and became its leader in 1984. From 1983 to 1992 he was MP for Belfast West, but declined to take up his seat at Westminster. He has been frequently criticized for his association with the IRA, and the UK government protested when he was granted a visa to visit the USA in 1994.

Adams, John (1735–1826) US statesman, the second President, born in Braintree (now Quincy), Massachusetts. He was a leader of American resistance to Britain, and was described as the 'colossus' of the debate on the Declaration of Independence (1776). He retired from Congress in 1777, then served as a diplomat in France and Holland. After a period as Minister to England (1785–8), he became the first US Vice-President under Washington (1789), and in 1796 was chosen by the Federalists as President (1796–1800).

Adams, John Couch (1819–92) English astronomer, born in Lidcot, Cornwall. In 1843 he graduated from Cambridge, where he was later appointed Professor of Astronomy (1858). He deduced mathematically the existence and location of the planet Neptune (1845), first observed in 1846.

Adams, John Quincy (1767–1848) US statesman, the sixth President, son of John Adams, born in Quincy, Massachusetts. Successively Minister to the Hague, London, Lisbon, and Berlin, he was elected to the US Senate in 1803. In 1809 he became Minister to St Petersburg, and was Minister at the Court of St James (1815–17). As Secretary of State under Monroe, he negotiated with Spain the treaty for the acquisition of Florida, and was alleged to be the real author of the Monroe Doctrine. He became sixth President (1825–9) and in 1830 was elected to the lower house of Congress, where he became a strong promoter of anti-slavery views.

Adams, Richard (1920–) English novelist, born in Berkshire. He worked in the Civil Service from 1948, and came to prominence with his first novel, *Watership Down* (1972), a fable about a warren of rabbits fleeing from land threatened by builders. Later novels include *Shardik* (1974) and *The Plague Dogs* (1977).

Adams, Samuel (1722–1803) US statesman, born in Boston (second cousin of John Adams). He was Lt-Governor (1789–94) and Governor (1794–7) of Massachusetts, and as a strong supporter of revolution against Britain he helped to plan the Boston Tea Party, and was one of the signatories of the Declaration of Independence (1776).

Adams, Walter Sydney (1876–1956) US astronomer, born in Antioch, Syria. In 1904 he helped to establish the Mount Wilson Observatory, where he later became director. His pioneering work on stellar spectra led to the discovery of a spectroscopic method of measuring the velocities and distances of stars.

Adams, Will(iam) (1564–1620) English sailor, born in Gillingham, Kent. He was pilot of a Dutch ship stranded off Japan in 1600, and was kept by Ieyasu Tokugawa, first Shogun, as an advisor on such areas as shipbuilding, navigation, gunnery, foreign relations, and trade. He built the first European type of ocean-going vessel in Japan. The first Englishman to enter the service of a Japanese ruler, he lived at Edo (now Tokyo), where he was given an estate by Ieyasu.

adam's apple the slight lump, part of the thyroid gland, that projects from the front of a man's neck.

Adamson, Joy (Friedericke Victoria), née **Gessner** (1910–80) Austrian-born naturalist and writer. Living in Kenya with her third husband, British game warden George Adamson (1906–89), she studied and painted wildlife, and made her name with a series of books about the lioness Elsa: *Born Free* (1960), *Elsa* (1961), *Forever Free* (1962), and *Elsa and Her Cubs* (1965). She was murdered in her home by tribesmen.

Adana 1 POP (1990) 1.4m, the commercial capital of Adana province, S Turkey and the fourth largest city in the country. It lies on the R Seyhan and is the centre of a fertile agricultural region. 2 a province of S Turkey with Adana as its capital.

adapt *verb* 1 *trans., intrans.* to change (something, oneself, etc) so as to fit new circumstances, etc; to make suitable for a new purpose. 2 to alter or modify. [from Latin *ad*, to + *aptare*, to fit]

adaptability *noun* the capability of adapting; versatility.

adaptable *adj.* 1 *said of a person* good at fitting into new circumstances, situations, etc. 2 *said of a machine, device, etc* that can be adapted.

adaptation *noun* 1 a thing which is adapted. 2 the process of adapting. 3 *Biol.* a particular change in the structure, function, or behaviour of a living organism that improves its chances of survival in its environment.

adaptive radiation *Biol.* a burst of evolution in which a single ancestral type gives rise to a number of different forms, each of which occupies a different ecological niche. It usually takes place over a relatively short period of time, and may occur after the colonization of a new habitat.

adaptor *or* **adapter** *noun* 1 a type of electrical plug used for connecting a plug of one type to a socket of another type, or for connecting several plugs to the same socket. 2 a person who adapts.

ADAS *abbrev.* Agricultural Development and Advisory Service.

ADC *abbrev.* aide-de-camp.

add *verb* 1 (**add something to something else**) to put something together with something else, so that they are counted or regarded together: *we'll add our money to yours.* 2 (**add things** *or* **add things together**) to put together or combine (two or more things). 3 (*also* **add up**) to put (two or more numbers or values) together to get their total: *when we added our money, it was more than we thought.* 4 to say or write (something) further: *they added a remark about the bad weather.*
— **add something in** to include it, especially as an extra.
add something on to attach (something) to something else. See also ADD-ON.
add up *colloq.* to make sense; to be coherent.
add up to something to be the equivalent of it or amount to it: *it all adds up to a great success.* [from Latin *addere*, from *ad*, to + *dare*, to put]

added *adj.* 1 attached. 2 extra, additional.

addendum *noun* (PL. **addenda**) 1 an addition. 2 (*usually* **addenda**) an extra piece of text added to the end of a book. [from Latin *addere*, to add]

adder *noun* a brown, olive, grey, or cream-coloured snake with a dark zigzag line running down its back, belonging to the viper family and found in most of Europe and across Asia. Adder bites are poisonous to the small animals on which they feed, eg lizards, mice, voles, and shrews, but are seldom fatal to humans. [from Anglo-Saxon *nædre*; in Middle English *a nadder* became understood to be *an adder*]

adder

addict *noun* 1 a person who is physically or psychologically dependent on the habitual intake of a drug such as alcohol, nicotine, caffeine, barbiturates, heroin, etc. 2 *colloq.* a person who is extremely fond of a hobby, etc: *a chess addict.* [from Latin *addicere*, to surrender]

addicted *adj.* (**addicted to something**) unable to do without it, especially a habit or drug.

addiction *noun* 1 the state of being addicted. 2 a habit that has become impossible to break.

addictive *adj.* causing users, etc to become addicts: *addictive drugs.*

Addis Ababa *or* **Adis Abeba** POP (1990e) 1.9m, the capital of Ethiopia, situated in the centre of the country, at a height of 2 400m. HISTORY founded by Menelik II in 1887; became capital in 1889; occupied by Italy from 1936 until 1941 when it was declared the capital of Italian

East Africa. NOTABLE FEATURES National Museum; National Library; St George Cathedral; Menelik II's Tomb. It is the headquarters of the UN Economic Commission for Africa and also of the Organization of African Unity (OAU).

Addison, Joseph (1672–1719) English essayist and poet, born in Milston, Wiltshire. An MP from 1708, he was appointed Secretary of State in 1717 but resigned because of illness a year later. He contributed to the *Tatler*, and in 1711 co-founded the *Spectator* with Sir Richard Steele. He was satirized by Pope as 'Atticus', often the correspondent of Cicero.

Addison, Thomas (1793–1860) English physician, born near Newcastle. He held positions at several hospitals and dispensaries, including Guy's Hospital, where for many years he was the leading medical teacher and diagnostician. He left outstanding descriptions of many diseases and their pathological signs, including pneumonia, tuberculosis, 'Addison's disease', and 'Addison's anaemia' (now known as pernicious anaemia).

addition *noun* **1** the act or operation of adding. **2** a person or thing that is added. **3** the combining of two or more numbers in such a way as to obtain their sum. **4** *Chem.* a chemical reaction in which one molecule combines with another to form a third more complex molecule, without the formation of a by-product such as water. Addition reactions most commonly occur between a hydrocarbon compound containing double or triple bonds, and a reagent such as hydrogen or a halogen. — **in addition to** ... as well as ...; besides ... [from Latin *additio*, from *addere*, to add]

additional *adj.* extra; more than usual.

additionally *adv.* also, besides.

additive — *noun* any chemical substance that is deliberately added to another substance, usually in small quantities, for a specific purpose, eg food flavouring or colouring, or antiknock compounds added to petrol to improve engine performance. — *adj. Maths.* relating to addition. [from Latin *additivus*]
◇ A food additive is any naturally occurring or artificially manufactured chemical compound that is added in small quantities to a food product, eg to improve its flavour, nutritional value, or visual appeal, or to prolong its shelf-life. Additives include preservatives, flavour enhancers (eg monosodium glutamate), colourings, emulsifiers, thickeners, stabilizers, bleaching agents, artificial sweeteners, vitamins, etc. See panel pp. 478–9.

addle *verb* **1** to confuse or muddle. **2** *intrans.* said of an egg to go bad. [from Anglo-Saxon *adela*, mud]

addle-brained *adj.* confused; crazy.

addled *adj.* **1** rotten. **2** confused.

add-on *noun* **1** anything added to supplement something else. **2** *Comput.* any device that can be added to a basic computer system in order to increase its capabilities, eg an extra program, circuit, or piece of hardware: *add-on memory*. **3** an extra charge added to the basic charge of something.

address — *noun* **1** the number or name of the house or building, and the name of the street and town, where a person lives or works. **2** a speech or lecture. **3** a number giving the place in a computer memory where a particular piece of information is stored. — *verb* **1** to put the name and address on (an envelope, etc). **2** to make a speech, give a lecture, etc to. **3** to speak to. **4** to give one's attention to (a problem, etc). — **address oneself to someone** *or* **something** **1** to speak or write to them. **2** to deal with a problem, matter, etc. [from Old French *adresser*]

address bus *Comput.* a set of wires connecting the processor to the memory, used to inform the memory of the address which the processor wishes to read or write to.

addressee *noun* the person to whom a letter, etc is addressed.

adduce *verb* to mention (a fact) as a supporting reason, piece of evidence, etc. [from Latin *ad*, to + *ducere*, to lead]

adducible *adj.* capable of being adduced.

Adelaide a female first name. [a French variant of *Adelheid*, derived from German *adal*, noble + *heid*, kind, sort]

Adelaide POP (1990e) 1m, the port capital of South Australia. It is situated on the Torrens R where it meets the St Vincent Gulf. The city was founded in 1837; in 1840 it became the first municipal government to be incorporated in Australia. NOTABLE FEATURES fine beaches to the W, including Maslin Beach (first nude bathing beach in Australia); many parks; two cathedrals; Adelaide Festival Centre; South Australian Museum (large collection of aboriginal art); Art Gallery of South Australia; Constitutional Museum; Ayers House (1846), headquarters of the South Australian National Trust; Maritime Museum in Port Adelaide. There are major wine-growing areas to the S (McLaren Vale) and to the N (Barossa Valley).

Adélie Land *or* **Adélie Coast**, French **Terre Adélie** à territory in Antarctica. AREA c.432 000sq km/166 800sq mi. HISTORY first seen by the French navy in 1840; explored in 1911–14 and 1929–31; became a French territory in 1938. There is a French research station at Base Dumont d'Urville.

Aden *or* **Adan** POP (1987e) 417 000, the commercial centre of Yemen. It is situated on the Gulf of Aden, at the entrance to the Red Sea. HISTORY taken by the British in 1839; capital of the former Aden protectorate; after the opening of the Suez Canal in 1869 it became an important coaling station and transshipment point; it became a British Crown Colony in 1937; scene of fighting between nationalist groups in the 1960s; capital of the new republic in 1968 until 1990 when the People's Democratic Republic of Yemen and the Yemen Arab Republic unified with San'a as its capital.

Aden, Gulf of the western arm of the Red Sea, lying between Yemen in the N and Somalia in the S, length 885km/550mi. It is connected to the Red Sea by the Strait of Bāb al Mandab.

Adenauer, Konrad (1876–1967) German statesman, born in Cologne. He practised law in Cologne, where he became Lord Mayor (1917), then President of the Prussian State Council (1920–33). In 1933 the Nazis dismissed him from all his offices, and imprisoned him twice (1934, 1944). In 1945, under Allied occupation, he founded the Christian Democratic Union. As the first Chancellor of the Federal Republic of Germany (1949–63), he established closer links with the Russians and the French, and aimed to rebuild West Germany on a basis of partnership with other European nations through NATO and the EEC.

adenine *noun Biochem.* a base derived from purine, and one of the four bases found in nucleic acids (RNA and DNA). [from Greek *aden*, gland]

adenoidal *adj.* **1** relating to the adenoids. **2** having the sound made by someone with swollen adenoids.

adenoids *pl. noun Anat.* a pair of lymph glands found in the upper part of the throat, at the back of the nasal cavity, in children. Infected adenoids may become swollen and require removal by surgery. [from Greek *adenoiedes*, from *aden*, gland]

adenosine triphosphate (ABBREV. **ATP**) *Biochem.* an organic compound, composed of adenine, ribose, and three phosphate groups, the main form in which energy is stored in the cells of living organisms. Energy is released, and so made available for muscle contraction, synthesis of complex molecules, etc, when ATP loses one or two of its phosphate groups.

adept — *adj.* (often **adept at something**) skilful at doing it; proficient. — *noun* an expert at something. [from Latin *adeptus*, having attained an art]

adeptly *adv.* expertly, skilfully.

adequacy *noun* being adequate; sufficiency.

adequate *adj.* **1** enough; sufficient. **2** (**adequate to something**) competent to do a particular job, task, etc. **3** only just satisfactory. [from Latin *ad*, to + *aequus*, equal]

adequately *adv.* in an adequate way or to an adequate extent.

à deux for two people; involving two people. [French, = for two]

adhere *verb intrans.* (often **adhere to something**) **1** to stick or remain fixed to it. **2** to remain loyal to a religion, etc. **3** to follow a plan, rule, etc exactly. [from Latin *ad*, to + *haerere*, to stick]

adherence *noun* **1** the act of adhering. **2** steady loyalty.

adherent — *noun* a follower; a supporter. — *adj.* sticking or adhering to.

adhesion *noun* **1** the process of sticking or adhering. **2** the sticking together of two surfaces, especially by means of an adhesive. **3** *Physics* the attraction between atoms or molecules of different substances, eg water and glass, that produces surface tension effects such as the formation of a meniscus. See also COHESION. **4** (often **adhesions**) *Medicine* a mass or band of fibrous connective tissue that develops between membranes or other structures which are normally separate, such as the stomach and intestines. It is caused by inflammation, especially following surgery or injury. [from Latin *adhaesio*]

adhesive — *adj.* sticky; able to make things stick together. — *noun* a substance that is used to bond two surfaces together. Adhesives can be made from natural materials, eg gelatine or vegetable gums, or manufactured synthetically, eg epoxy resins which set when mixed with a separate hardener. [from French *adhésif*, from Latin *adhaerere*, to adhere]

ad hoc *adj., adv.* for one particular purpose, situation, etc only. [from Latin *ad hoc*, to this]

ad hominem relating to a individual person. [Latin, = to the man]

adiabatic process *Physics* any process that occurs without the exchange of heat between a system and its surroundings. [from A-1 + Greek *dia*, through + *batos*, passable]

Adie, Kate (Kathryn) (1945–) English television reporter, born in Sunderland, Tyne and Wear. She joined BBC radio in 1969 as a technician, then became a producer, entering television in 1977. She progressed to become chief news correspondent in 1989 and is known for her authoritative broadcasts from trouble spots around the world.

adieu — *noun* (PL. **adieus, adieux**) a goodbye. — *interj.* goodbye. [from French *adieu*, from *à*, to + *dieu*, God]

Adige, River, German **Etsch**, ancient **Athesis** a river in N Italy, length 408km/253mi. It rises in three small alpine lakes and flows E, S, then E into the Adriatic Sea, SE of Chioggia. After the Po, it is the chief river in Italy.

Adi Granth the principal Sikh scripture, originally called the *Granth Sahib* ('Revered Book'). The word *Adi* means 'first' or 'original', which distinguishes it from the *Dasam Granth*, a later, secondary scripture. The text used today is an expanded version of an original compilation of 1604, and is revered by all Sikhs. [Punjabi, = first book]

ad infinitum *adv.* for ever; without limit. [from Latin *ad infinitum*, to infinity]

adipose *adj.* containing, or consisting of, fat; fatty. [from Latin *adiposus*, from *adeps*, soft fat]

adiposity *noun* **1** fatness. **2** tendency to fatness.

Adirondack Mountains a mountain range largely in NE New York state, USA, rising to 1 629m at Mt Marcy. The range, named after a Native American tribe, is the source of the Hudson and Ausable rivers. It is the largest state park in the USA; locations such as Lake Placid are noted winter resorts.

Adis Abeba see ADDIS ABABA.

Aditi in Hindu mythology, the mother of the Adityas, a group of supreme deities. She is celebrated as the goddess of all existence. Her name means 'the unbounded'.

adj. *abbrev.* adjective.

adjacent *adj.* (*often* **adjacent to something**) lying beside or next to it: *adjacent houses / a house adjacent to the church.* [from Latin *adjacere*, to lie by the side of]

adjectival *adj. Grammar* **1** having the role of an adjective. **2** using many adjectives.

adjectivally *adv.* as an adjective.

adjective *noun* a word that describes or modifies a noun or pronoun, as *dark* describes *hair* in *she has dark hair*, and *sad* describes *him* in *the story made him sad.* [from Latin *adjicere*, to throw to, to apply]
◇ Most adjectives in English may be placed before the noun to which they refer, ie they may be used *attributively*, as in *the blue sky*; they may also be placed after the noun and a linking verb (eg *be* or *become*), ie they may be used *predicatively*, as in *the sky became blue*. Some adjectives are normally used only predicatively, eg *afraid* as in *the boy is afraid* (and some adjectives of this type must have a following phrase, eg *devoid* as in *they were devoid of compassion*); and others are only used attributively, eg *undue* as in *avoid undue delay.*

adjoin *verb* to be next to and joined to (something). [from Old French *ajoindre*, from Latin *ad*, to + *jungere*, to join]

adjoining *adj.* **1** lying next to; neighbouring. **2** in contact, connected.

adjourn *verb* **1** to put off (a meeting, etc) to another time. **2** to finish (a meeting, etc), intending to continue it at another time or place. **3** *intrans.* to move to another place, usually for refreshment or rest. **4** *intrans.* to finish a meeting and separate. [from Old French *ajorner*]

adjournment *noun* an act of adjourning; postponement.

adjudge *verb* to declare or judge officially. [from Old French *ajuger*, from Latin *adjudicare*, to adjudicate]

adjudgement *or* **adjudgment** *noun* an official judgement or declaration.

adjudicate *verb* **1** *intrans.* to act as judge in a court, competition, etc. **2** to give a decision on (a disagreement between two parties, etc). [from Latin *adjudicare*, from *judex*, judge]

adjudication *noun* **1** the act or process of adjudicating. **2** a judgement. **3** a decision.

adjudicator *noun* a person who adjudicates.

adjunct *noun* **1** something attached or added to something else but not an essential part of it. **2** a person who is below someone else in rank. **3** *Grammar* a word or clause that adds information about the subject, etc of a sentence. [from Latin *adjungere*, to join to]

adjuration *noun* the act of adjuring.

adjure *verb formal* to request, beg, or command formally or solemnly. [from Latin *adjurare*, to swear to]

adjust *verb* **1** to change slightly so as to be more suitable for a situation, etc. **2** to change or alter, especially only slightly, to make more correct or accurate. **3** to calculate or assess (the amount of money payable in an insurance claim, etc). **4** (**adjust to something**) to change so that one fits in with it or becomes suited to it. [from Old French *ajuster*, to make conform to]

adjustable *adj.* capable of adjustment.

adjustment *noun* the act or process of adjusting; the state of being adjusted.

adjutant *noun* an army officer who does administrative work. [from Latin *adjutare*, to assist]

Adler, Alfred (1870–1937) Austrian psychiatrist, born in Vienna. He graduated as a doctor in 1895, and became a member of the psychoanalytical group that formed around Sigmund Freud. His best-known work was *Studie über Minderwertigkeit von Organen* (Study of Organ Inferiority and its Psychical Compensation, 1907), which aroused great controversy, and led to one of the early schisms in psychoanalysis.

ad-lib — *verb intrans., trans.* (**ad-libbed, ad-libbing**) to say (something) without preparation, especially as a departure from a prepared text or to fill time; to improvise (music, etc). — *adj., said of speeches, etc* made up as the speaker speaks; improvised. — *adv.* (**ad lib**) **1** without preparation. **2** *colloq.* without limit; freely. [short for Latin *ad libitum*, at pleasure]

ad litem *said of a guardian* appointed to act in court. [Latin, = for the lawsuit]

Adm. *abbrev.* Admiral.

adman *noun colloq.* a person whose job is to produce or write advertisements for commercial organizations, etc.

admin *noun colloq.* short form of ADMINISTRATION.

administer *verb* (**administered, administering**) **1** to manage, govern, or direct (one's affairs, an organization, etc). **2** to give out formally: *administer justice.* **3** to supervise a person taking (an oath). **4** to apply or provide (medicine). **5** to give: *administer a rebuke.* **6** *intrans.* to act as an administrator. [from Latin *administrare*]

administrate *verb* **1** to administer (a company, organization, etc). **2** *intrans.* to act as an administrator.

administration *noun* **1** the directing, managing or governing of a company's affairs, etc. **2** a period of government by a particular party, etc. **3** *North Amer., esp. US* a period of government by a particular president. **4** the group of people who manage a company's affairs or run the business of government.

administrative *adj.* of or concerned with administration.

administrative law the body of law relating to powers exercised by central and local government. The exercise of these administrative powers may be subject to scrutiny by the courts on legal, but not policy, grounds.

administratively *adv.* as regards administration.

administrator *noun* a person who manages, governs, directs, etc the affairs of an organization, estate, etc.

admirable *adj.* **1** worthy of being admired. **2** very good; excellent.

admirably *adv.* in an admirable way; excellently.

admiral *noun* **1** a high-ranking naval officer commanding a fleet of ships. **2** a name applied to several species of butterfly. [from Old French *amiral*, from Arabic *amir-al-bahr*, lord of the sea]

admiral of the fleet *noun* the highest-ranking admiral in the Royal Navy.

Admiral's Cup a biennial series of yacht races in the English Channel around Fastnet rock and at Cowes, first held in 1957. Competing national teams can enter up to three boats per team.

Admiralty *noun* (**the Admiralty**) *Brit. Hist.* the government department that managed the Royal Navy until the responsibility passed to the Ministry of Defence in 1964.

Admiralty Court an English court which is part of the Queen's Bench Division of the High Court. Its work deals with maritime claims in civil law, such as salvage.

Admiralty Islands POP (1980) 26 000, an island group in N Papua New Guinea, part of the Bismarck Archipelago. AREA 2 000sq km/800sq mi. There are c.40 islands. MAIN ISLAND Manus. CHIEF TOWN Lorengau. HISTORY became a German protectorate in 1884 and an Australian mandate in 1920. ECONOMY fishing; copra; pearls.

Admiralty Submarine Detection Investigation Committee (ABBREV. ASDIC) an early form (1917) of submarine detection device used on warships of the Royal Navy. ASDIC used echo-sounding and sonar as its operating principles.

admiration *noun* **1** an act of admiring. **2** wonder, approval. **3** an object of wonder or approval.

admire *verb* to regard with respect or approval. [from Latin *admirari*]

admirer *noun* **1** someone who admires a particular person or thing. **2** a man who is attracted to a particular woman.

admiring *adj.* full of admiration.

admiringly *adv.* with admiration.

admissibility *noun* fitness or ability to be admitted.

admissible *adj.* that can be allowed or accepted, especially as proof in a court of law. [from Latin *admissibilis*, from *admittere*, to admit]

admission *noun* **1** the act of allowing in or being allowed in. **2** the cost of entry. **3** an act of admitting the truth of something. [from Latin *admissio*]

admit *verb* (**admitted, admitting**) **1** *trans., intrans.* to agree to the truth of (something), especially unwillingly. **2** *trans., intrans.* (**admit something** *or* **admit to something**) to agree that one is responsible for a deed or action, especially an offence or wrongdoing. **3** to allow to enter. **4** to allow to take part in; to accept as a member or patient. **5** *formal* to have the capacity for: *a room admitting forty people.*
— **admit of something** to agree that it is possible or valid.
[from Latin *admittere*]

admittance *noun* **1** the right to enter; permission to enter. **2** the act of entering; entry.

admittedly *adv.* as is known to be true; as one must admit.

admixture *noun* **1** a thing added to the main ingredient of something. **2** the mixing in of something extra. [from Latin *ad*, to + *miscere*, to mix]

admonish *verb* **1** to warn. **2** to scold or tell off firmly but mildly. **3** to advise or urge. [from Old French *amonester*]

admonishingly *adv.* so as to admonish.

admonition *noun* a scolding or warning. [from Latin *admonitio*, from *admonere*, to admonish]

admonitory *adj.* containing a scolding or warning.

ADN *abbrev., as an international vehicle mark* Republic of Yemen (capital Aden).

ad nauseam to the point of producing disgust; excessively. [Latin, = to sickness]

ado *noun* (PL. **ados**) difficulty or trouble; fuss or bustle.
— **without more** *or* **further ado** without any more delay; immediately; promptly.
[from Middle English *at do*, to do]

adobe *noun* (pronounced as three syllables) **1** a kind of building material made of clay and straw, which is dried in the sun. **2** a sun-dried brick made from such material. **3** a building made from such bricks. [from Spanish *adobe*, from Arabic *at tub*, the brick]

adolescence *noun* the period of human development between the onset of puberty and adulthood, during which physical and emotional changes take place as a result of hormonal activity.

adolescent — *adj.* **1** *said of young people* at the stage of development between child and adult, usually between the ages of 13 and 16. **2** *colloq.*, *said of behaviour* silly; immature. — *noun* a young person between childhood and adulthood. [from Latin *adolescere*, to grow up]

Adonis 1 in Greek mythology, a beautiful young man who was loved by Aphrodite. Persephone, the goddess of the underworld, also fell in love with him and Zeus decided that Adonis should spend one third of the year with Aphrodite, one third with Persephone, and the remaining third with whomsoever he wished; he chose to spend it with Aphrodite. He was killed by a wild boar, an event which was celebrated annually in either funereal or joyous festivals. He is sometimes represented as a god of vegetation. **2** a beautiful young man.

adopt *verb* **1** *trans., intrans.* to take (a child of other parents) into one's own family, becoming its legal parent. **2** to take up (a habit, position, policy, etc). **3** to take (an idea, etc) over from someone else. **4** to choose formally (especially a candidate for an election). [from Old French *adopter*, from Latin *ad*, to + *optare*, to choose]

adopted *adj.* **1** taken as one's own. **2** taken up. **3** chosen. **4** approved.
◆ Do not confuse with *adoptive*: *adopted* children are adopted by their *adoptive* parents.

adoption *noun* the act of adopting; the state of being adopted.

adoptive *adj.* that adopts or is adopted.
◆ See note at *adopted*.

adorable *adj.* **1** worthy of being adored. **2** *colloq.* very charming and attractive. [from Latin *adorare*, from *ad*, to + *orare*, to pray]

adorably *adv.* **1** so as to inspire adoration. **2** charmingly.

adoration *noun* **1** great love. **2** worship.

Adoration of the Golden Calf, The 1 a painting by Tintoretto (c.1560). **2** a painting by Nicholas Poussin (c.1635, National Gallery, London).

Adoration of the Magi 1 the worship of the baby Jesus in Bethlehem by (traditionally) three 'Wise Men' or pagan kings. **2** a painting of this scene by various artists including Leonardo da Vinci (unfinished, 1481–c.1482, Uffizi, Florence), Jan Gossaert (National Gallery, London), Paolo Veronese (1573, National Gallery, London), and Diego Velázquez (1619, Prado, Madrid).

adore *verb* **1** to love deeply. **2** *colloq.* to like very much. **3** to worship (a god).

adorer *noun* a worshipper, a lover.

adoring *adj.* **1** loving, doting. **2** worshipful.

adoringly *adv.* in an adoring manner.

adorn *verb* **1** to decorate. **2** to add beauty to. [from Latin *adornare*]

adornment *noun* decoration, ornament.

Adorno, Theodor (1903–69) German social philosopher and musicologist, born in Frankfurt. A leading member (with Max Horkheimer and

Herbert Marcuse) of the Frankfurt School, he joined it in exile in New York City in 1934, and returned to Frankfurt in 1960. His philosophy is most fully presented in *Negative Dialectics* (1966). He argues that the task of 'critical theory' is to dissove all conceptual distinctions so that they cannot deform the true nature of reality. His sociological writings on music include *Philosophie der neuen Musik* (1949).

ADP *abbrev.* automatic data processing, the processing of large quantities of data by computer as part of a company's daily routine, to provide the information the company needs every day.

adrenal *adj.* **1** on or near the kidneys. **2** relating to the adrenal glands. [from Latin *ad*, to + RENAL]

adrenal gland *Anat.* in mammals, either of a pair of flattened endocrine glands situated one above each kidney, and consisting of a central region or *medulla* that secretes the hormones adrenaline and noradrenaline, and an outer region or *cortex* that secretes small amounts of sex hormones (androgens and oestrogens) and various corticosteroids, such as as cortisol and cortisone.

adrenaline *or* **adrenalin** *noun* **1** *Biochem.* a hormone secreted by the *medulla* (inner part) of the adrenal glands in response to fear, excitement, or anger. It causes an increase in heartbeat, blood pressure, blood sugar levels, muscle power, and the rate and depth of breathing, and it constricts certain blood vessels, diverting blood away from the intestines and towards the muscles. **2** this hormone produced synthetically, used to reduce blood loss during surgery (by constricting blood vessels), and to treat asthma.

adrenocorticotrophic hormone (ABBREV. **ACTH**) *Physiol.* a hormone that is produced by the front lobe of the pituitary gland. It controls the release of corticosteroid hormones from the adrenal glands, and is released in response to physical or emotional stress. It is also used to treat rheumatic diseases and asthma.

Adrian, Edgar Douglas, 1st Baron (1889–1977) English physiologist, born in London. Professor of Physiology at Cambridge (1937–51), he was one of the founders of modern neurophysiology. He designed equipment to study the minute electrical impulses of nerves, and showed that there is only one kind of nervous impulse, neural information being conveyed by variations in the frequency at which those impulses are transmitted, the 'frequency code'. He also developed electroencephalography (EEG), used clinically for the study of epilepsy and other brain disorders. For his work on the function of neurones he shared the 1932 Nobel Prize for Physiology or Medicine with Charles Sherrington.

Adrian a male first name. [an English form of Latin *Hadrianus*, man from Hadria]

Adrian IV, also called **Hadrian**, originally **Nicholas Breakspear** (c.1100–59) the first and only English pope (1154–9), born in Abbots Langley, Hertfordshire. He joined the monastery of St Rufus, near Avignon, and in 1137 was elected its abbot. Complaints about his strict discipline meant that he had to appear before Eugenius III at Rome, who recognized his good qualities and appointed him Cardinal Bishop of Albano (1146). As papal legate in Scandinavia (1152), he earned the title 'Apostle of the North', and as pope, he is said to have granted Ireland to Henry II.

Adriana the hot-headed wife of Antipholus of Ephesus in Shakespeare's *The Comedy of Errors*, who pursues her husband and jealously mistakes his brother for him.

Adrianople, Battle of a battle (AD 379) at present-day Edirne in European Turkey in which the Visigoths under Fritigern defeated the Roman army, two thirds of whom were killed, including

Emperor Valens. One of the crucial battles of the ancient world, it opened up Roman territory to Germanic invasion.

Adrianople, Treaty of the treaty in 1829 that ended the 1828–9 Russo-Turkish war, by which Russia gained territory from Turkey at the mouth of the Danube and along the eastern shore of the Black Sea. It recognized Russia's growing influence in the Near East and marked an important stage in the advance of both Serbia and Greece towards independent statehood.

Adriatic Sea an arm of the Mediterranean Sea, between the E coast of Italy and the Balkan Peninsula. It is separated from the Ionian Sea in the S by the Strait of Otranto; the Gulf of Venice lies to the NW. It measures 800km/500mi in length and 93–225km/58–140mi in width; maximum depth 1 250m. The Italian coast of the highly saline sea is flat and sandy, while the Balkan coast is rugged and irregular. The chief ports are Venice, Rijeka, Ancona, Bari, and Brindisi.

adrift *adj., adv.* **1** *said of a boat* not tied up; floating about without being steered. **2** without help or guidance. **3** *colloq.* off course.

adroit *adj.* quick and clever in action or thought. [from French *à droit*, according to the right, rightly]

adroitly *adj.* in an adroit way; skilfully.

adroitness *noun* dexterity, skill.

adsorb *verb Chem., said of a solid or liquid* to hold a thin layer of atoms or molecules of a solid, liquid, or gas on its surface. [from Latin *ad*, to + *sorbere*, to suck in]

adsorbent *adj.* capable of adsorption.

adsorption *noun Chem.* the accumulation of a thin layer of atoms or molecules of a solid, liquid, or gas on the surface of a solid (eg charcoal, silica) or, more rarely, a liquid. This process is utilized in certain types of chromatography.

adulate *verb* to praise or flatter far too much. [from Latin *adulari*, to fawn upon]

adulation *noun* excessive praise; flattery.

adulatory *adj.* flattering, fawning.

adult — *adj.* **1** fully grown; mature. **2** typical of, or suitable for, a fully grown person. **3** *said especially of films* containing sexually explicit or indecent scenes, and therefore regarded as unsuitable for children. — *noun* a fully grown person, animal, bird, or plant. [from Latin *adultus*, grown-up]

adult education the provision of further or continuing educational opportunities for people over the minimum school-leaving age. This may take place in institutions specially set up to cater for mature learners, or in schools, colleges, and other centres of learning. There are also numerous informal sources of adult education, such as broadcast programmes on radio and television, as well as correspondence and distance-learning courses, for people who wish to or must learn from home, or as part of their job.

adulterate *verb* to add a substance to (something) so that it is no longer pure. [from Latin *adulterare*]

adulteration *noun* **1** the act of adulterating or making less pure. **2** the state of being adulterated.

adulterer *noun* a man or woman who commits adultery.

adulteress *noun* a woman who commits adultery.

adulterous *adj.* **1** relating to or in the nature of adultery. **2** *said of a person* who has committed adultery.

adulterously *adv.* so as to involve adultery: *behave adulterously.*

adultery *noun* sexual relations willingly undertaken between a married person and a person who is not his or her spouse. [from Latin *adulterare*, to defile]

adulthood *noun* maturity.

adumbrate *verb* **1** to indicate or describe in a general way. **2** to suggest or indicate (something likely to happen in the future); to foreshadow. **3** to throw a shadow over. [from Latin *adumbrare*, to shade in, sketch]

adumbration *noun* act or process of adumbrating.

adv. *abbrev.* adverb.

Advaita Vedanta an influential school of Vedanta Hinduism, revived in a modern form during the 20c. Associated primarily with the thought of Shankara, it holds that there is only one absolute reality, Brahman, and that all selves are in effect identical, since in essence they are one with Brahman. [Sanskrit, = non-dual]

advance — *verb* **1** *trans., intrans.* to put, move, or go forward, sometimes in a threatening way. **2** *intrans.* to make progress. **3** to help the progress of; to improve or promote. **4** to propose or suggest (an idea, etc). **5** to put at an earlier time or date than that previously planned. **6** (**advance someone something**) to lend them money, or pay them money before payment is due. **7** *trans., intrans.* to increase (a price) or be increased. — *noun* **1** progress; a move forward. **2** a payment made before it is due. **3** money lent to someone. **4** an increase, especially in price. **5** (**advances**) friendly or sexual approaches to a person. — *adj.* done, made or given beforehand.
— **in advance** ahead in time, place, or development.
[from Old French *avancer*, from Latin *abante*, in front]

advanced *adj.* **1** having progressed or developed well or far. **2** modern; new; revolutionary.

Advanced-level see A-LEVEL.

advancement *noun* **1** progress and development. **2** promotion in rank or improvement in status. **3** payment in advance.

advantage *noun* **1** a favourable circumstance; benefit or usefulness. **2** a circumstance that may help one to succeed, win, etc. **3** superiority over another. **4** *Tennis* the point scored after deuce.
— **have the advantage of someone** to know something that is not known to them; to be in a better position than them.
take advantage of someone *or* **something 1** to make use of a situation, a person's good nature, etc in such a way as to benefit oneself. **2** *old use* to seduce someone.
to advantage in such a way as to emphasize the good qualities.
to one's advantage of benefit or importance to one.
turn something to advantage to use a circumstance, situation, etc in such a way as to get some benefit from it.
[from Old French *avantage*, from *avant*, before; see also ADVANCE]

advantaged *adj.* having a good social or financial situation.

advantageous *adj.* giving help or benefit in some way.

advantageously *adv.* **1** in an advantageous manner. **2** so as to produce an advantage.

advantageousness *noun* a state or condition of advantage.

advent *noun* **1** coming or arrival; first appearance. **2** (**Advent**) the period including the four Sundays before Christmas. **3** (**Advent**) the first or second coming of Christ. [from Latin *adventus*, arrival]

Adventist *noun* a member of a Christian group which believes the second coming of Christ will happen very soon.

adventitious *adj.* **1** happening by chance; accidental. **2** denoting tissues or organs that grow in an unusual position, eg a root arising from a stem. [from Latin *adventicius*, coming from the outside]

adventitiously *adv.* in an adventitious manner.

adventure *noun* **1** an exciting and often dangerous experience. **2** the excitement of risk or danger: *a sense of adventure*. [from Latin *adventurus*, about to happen]

adventure playground a playground with things for children to climb on and equipment for them to build with.

adventurer *noun* **1** a person who is eager for personal adventure. **2** a person who enjoys taking risks in business.

adventuress *noun* a woman who is eager for personal adventure.

adventurous *adj.* **1** ready to act boldly and take risks; enjoying adventure; daring. **2** full of excitement, danger, daring activities, etc.

adventurously *adv.* in an adventurous way.

adverb *noun* a word or group of words which describes or adds to the meaning of a verb, adjective, or another adverb, such as *very* and *quietly* in *they were talking very quietly*. [from Latin *adverbium*, a word added after]

adverbial *adj.* having the role of an adverb.

adverbially *adv.* like an adverb.

adversarial *adj.* **1** involving opposition. **2** hostile.

adversary *noun* (PL. **adversaries**) **1** an opponent in a competition, etc. **2** an enemy. [from Latin *adversarius*]

adverse *adj.* **1** unfavourable to one's interests. **2** disapproving. **3** hurtful. **4** *said of a wind* coming from in front of one and not from behind. [from Latin *adversus*, hostile]

adversely *adv.* in an adverse way.

adversity *noun* (PL. **adversities**) **1** circumstances that cause trouble or sorrow. **2** an event or circumstance that causes trouble or sorrow; a misfortune.

advert[1] *noun* (with stress on *ad-*) *colloq.* short form of ADVERTISEMENT.

advert[2] *verb intrans.* (with stress on *-vert*) *formal* (**advert to something**) to refer to it or mention it in speaking or writing. [from Old French *avertir*, from Latin *advertere*, to direct one's attention to]

advertise *verb* **1** to draw attention to or describe (goods for sale, services offered, etc) in newspapers, on the television, etc, to encourage people to buy or use them. **2** to make known publically or generally. **3** *intrans.* to ask for or seek (something or someone) by putting a notice in a newspaper, shop window, etc. [from Old French *avertir*, from Latin *advertere*, to direct one's attention to]

advertisement *noun* a public notice, announcement, picture, etc in a newspaper, on a wall in the street, etc, which advertises something; a short television film advertising something.

advertiser *noun* a person who advertises.

advertising *noun* the business of producing advertisements for goods.
◇ From humble origins advertising has developed in parallel with the modern industrial society and the mass media, especially from the late 19c with the advent of mass production of consumer goods. Governments, political parties, service industries (such as banking), pressure groups, and charities, as well as manufacturers and retailers, are all aware of the value of communicating with the public through advertising, and employ it to promote ideas and causes, as well as to sell products and services. Most modern advertising agencies offer a complete service to their customers, including market research, creative expertise, media planning, and media buying. Regulations on who may advertise and on the quantity and nature of ads, especially commercials, vary from country to country.

advice *noun* **1** suggestions or opinions given to someone about what he or she should do in a particular situation. **2** in business, etc, an official note about a transaction, etc.
— **take advice 1** to ask someone for an opinion about what one should do. **2** to act on advice given.
[from Old French *avis*]

advisability *noun* being recommended, sensible, or wise.

advisable *adj.* **1** said of action to be taken, etc, to be recommended; wise. **2** sensible.

advise *verb* **1** to give advice to. **2** to recommend. **3** (**advise someone of something**) to inform them about it. **4** *trans., intrans.* to act as an adviser to someone. [from Old French *aviser*]

advised *adj.* (especially in compounds) considered; judged: *well-advised / ill-advised*.

advisedly *adv.* after careful thought; on purpose.

adviser *or* **advisor** *noun* a person who advises, especially professionally.

advisory *adj.* giving advice.

advocaat *noun* a liqueur made from raw eggs, sugar, and brandy. [from Dutch *advocaatenborrel*, a lawyer's drink, originally to clear the throat]

advocacy *noun* **1** recommendation or active support of an idea, etc. **2** the function or job of an advocate, eg in a particular trial. [from Latin *advocatia*, from *advocatus*, legal counsellor]

advocate — *noun* (pronounced *-kət*) **1** especially in Scotland, a lawyer who speaks for the defence or prosecution in a trial. See also BARRISTER, SOLICITOR. **2** a person who supports or recommends an idea, proposal, etc. — *verb* (pronounced *-kate*) to recommend or support (an idea, proposal, etc), especially in public. [from Old French *avocat*, from Latin *advocatus*, legal adviser]

adze *noun* a heavy tool with a blade at right angles to its handle, used for cutting and shaping wood. [from Anglo-Saxon *adesa*]

adze

AEA *abbrev.* Atomic Energy Authority (UK).

AEB *abbrev.* Associated Examining Board.

Aegean civilization the Bronze Age cultures which flourished in the third and second millennia BC on the islands of the Aegean Sea and around its coasts.

Aegean Islands POP (1991) 456 000, an island group and region of Greece. AREA 9 122sq km/3 521sq mi. The name is generally applied to the islands of the Aegean Sea, between Greece and Turkey, which include Lesbos, Chios, Samos, Limnos, and Thasos. It is a major tourist area.

Aegean Sea an arm of the Mediterranean Sea, bounded W and N by Greece, NE and E by Turkey, and S by the islands of Crete and Rhodes. It measures (N–S) 645km/400mi in length and 320km/200mi in width; its greatest depth is 2 013m. It is dotted with islands on which the Aegean civilization of 3000–1000 BC flourished. The area is a popular tourist destination. There is natural gas off the NE coast of Greece.

Aegina, Greek **Aiyna** POP (1981) 11 000, a large island of the Saronic Is, Greece. AREA 83sq km/ 32sq mi. Its chief town is Aiyna. The island is a popular resort; a principal attraction is the Temple of Aphaia.

Aegir in Norse mythology, the god of the sea. He was a giant who collected dead sailors in his hall on the island of Hlesey.

aegis
— **under the aegis of someone** *or* **something** under the supervision and with the support of an official organization, etc.
[from Greek *aigis*, the shield of Zeus in Greek mythology]

Aegisthus in Greek legend, the son of Thyestes. While Agamemnon was absent at Troy he became the lover of Clytemnestra. Together they killed Agamemnon on his return to Argos. Aegisthus was later killed by Orestes.

Aelfric, Grammaticus (c.955–c.1020) English writer, known for his use of the Anglo-Saxon vernacular. He taught at the monastery of Cerne Abbas, later becoming abbot of Eynsham. His writings include a collection of homilies, *Lives of the Saints*, and a Latin/English grammar, glossary, and dialogue (*Colloquium*).

Aemilian Way a continuation of the Flaminian Way, Rome's major trunk road to the north. It ran from Rimini on the Adriatic coast to the R Po.

Aeneas in Roman legend, the ancestor of the Romans. He was a Trojan hero, the son of Anchises and Aphrodite, who escaped after the fall of Troy, bearing his father on his shoulders. He was shipwrecked near Carthage, where Queen Dido fell in love with him. In Cumae he visited the Underworld, then he married the daughter of the King of Latium and allied himself to the Latins in local wars. His son Ascanius founded Alba Longa, and Romulus, one of his descendants, founded the city of Rome.

Aeneid, The a Latin epic poem by Virgil (c.29–19 BC). It is based on the wanderings of the Trojan hero Aeneas, the legendary founder of Rome.

aeolian harp a box-like musical instrument which has strings stretched across a hole, and which makes musical sounds when the wind passes through it. [from Latin *Aeolus*, god of the winds]

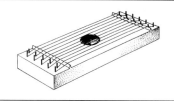

aeolian harp

Aeolians a sub-group of Hellenic peoples who colonized the NW coast of Asia Minor and the islands of the N Aegean (eg Lesbos) towards the end of the second millennium BC.

Aeolus in Greek mythology, the god of the winds. In Homer's *Odyssey*, Aeolus lived on an island and gave Odysseus the winds tied in a bag so that his ship would not be blown off course. Odysseus's men opened the bag, thinking it contained treasure, and the ship was blown far away.

aeon *noun* same as EON.

aerate *verb* **1** to force gas, especially carbon dioxide, into (a liquid), eg when making fizzy drinks. **2** to put oxygen into (the blood) by breathing. **3** to expose to the air, especially in order to introduce oxygen. [from Latin *aer*, air]

aeration *noun* **1** mixing or saturating with air or other gas. **2** oxygenation of the blood by breathing. **3** exposure to the air.

aerenchyma *noun Bot.* a type of tissue most commonly found in aquatic plants, in which there are large air spaces between the cells. [from Greek *aer*, air + *en*, in + *chyma*, that which is poured]

aerial — *noun* a wire or rod on a radio or television set, able to send or receive signals. — *adj.* **1** in or belonging to the air. **2** like air; ethereal. **3** in or from aircraft. [from Latin *aerius*, from *aer*, air]

aerially *adv.* in or through the air.

aerial photography photography of the Earth's surface from an aerial viewpoint such as a balloon, aircraft, spacecraft, or satellite. It has important applications in archaeology, ecology, geology, and military reconnaissance. In *aerial survey mapping*, an aircraft flies at a constant height along specified paths, taking pictures at regular intervals.

aerie *noun* same as EYRIE.

aero- *combining form* **1** relating to air: *aerodynamics*. **2** relating to aircraft: *aerodrome*. [from Greek *aer*, air]

aerobatic *adj.* relating to aerobatics.

aerobatics *noun* **1** (*pl.*) dangerous and difficult movements of an aeroplane, such as flying upside down, etc. **2** (*sing.*) the art of making an aeroplane perform such movements. [from AERO-+ ACROBATICS]

aerobe *Biol.* any organism that requires oxygen in order to obtain energy from the breakdown of carbohydrates or other foodstuffs by the process of respiration. With the exception of certain bacteria and yeasts, most living organisms are aerobes. [from AERO- + Greek *bios*, life]

aerobic *adj.* **1** *Biol.* denoting an organism that requires oxygen in order to obtain energy from the breakdown of carbohydrates or other foodstuffs by the process of respiration. **2** relating to any form of physical exercise that produces an increase in the use of oxygen by the body, eg walking, jogging, swimming, cycling. **3** *Biochem.* denoting a form of respiration in living organisms in which oxygen is required for the complete oxidation (breakdown) of foodstuffs, especially carbohydrates, to carbon dioxide and water. [from AERO- + Greek *bios*, life]

aerobics *noun* **1** (*sing.*) a system of physical exercise consisting of rapidly repeated, energetic movements, which increases the supply of oxygen in the blood and strengthens the heart and lungs. **2** (*sing., pl.*) energetic exercises.

aerodrome *noun Brit.* an airfield for private or military aircraft. [from AERO- + Greek *dromos*, course]

aerodynamic *adj.* **1** relating to aerodynamics. **2** making effective use of aerodynamics so as to move fast through the air.

aerodynamically *adv.* so as to be aerodynamic; as regards aerodynamics.

aerodynamics *noun* **1** (*sing.*) *Aeron.* the scientific study of the movement of air or other gases relative to solid bodies immersed in them. **2** (*pl.*) the qualities required for fast and efficient movement through the air.
◇ Aerodynamics is concerned with the flow of air around both stationary objects (eg bridges, buildings) and moving objects (eg aircraft, cars). An important aspect of aerodynamics is streamlining, which involves the shaping of an object in such a way that air flows around it with a minimum of turbulence. New models of aircraft, cars, trains, etc are tested in wind tunnels (which use fans to generate air speeds of up to 30 000kph) to assess their air resistance or *drag*. Vehicles with a streamlined shape, which minimizes drag, can reach higher speeds and consume less fuel.

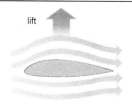

wing shape: low drag

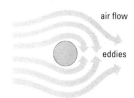

air flow

eddies

round shape: medium drag

square shape: high drag

aerodynamics

aerofoil *noun* a structure, eg a wing, tailplane, etc with a curved surface, designed to give lift when flying. [from AERO- + FOIL[2]]

aerogramme *or* **aerogram** *noun* a thin piece of paper on which to write letters for sending by air, designed so that it can be folded and sealed without being put into an envelope. [from AERO- + GRAM]

aerometry *noun Phonetics* the measurement of airflow through the nose and mouth during speech. In the pronunciation of most sounds, air passes through the mouth; but, for nasal consonants, eg [m] and [n], and vowels, eg [ō] as in French *bon*, air passes wholly or partly through the nose. Variations in oral and nasal airflow are plotted on instruments such as an *aerometer*.

aeronautic *or* **aeronautical** *adj.* relating to aeronautics.

aeronautics *sing. noun* the scientific study of travel through the Earth's atmosphere.

aerophone *noun* any musical instrument in which sound is produced using air as the main vibrating agent. These include the so-called 'free' aerophones, eg the mouth organ and harmonium, in which a reed is vibrated by air passing across it; and wind instruments of all types. Wind instruments are generally classified according to the type of material from which they are made (eg brass and woodwind), or how they are played (eg via a mouthpiece, a reed, or neither). [from Greek *aer*, air + *phone*, sound]

aeroplane *noun* a powered machine used for travelling in the air that is heavier than air and supported in its flight by fixed wings. [from AERO- + PLANE[1]]
◇ An aeroplane flies as a result of the *lift* generated by the movement of the wings through the air. The wing of an aircraft has a curved upper surface and a relatively flat lower surface, this shape being known as an *aerofoil*. When air passes over the upper surface it has to travel more rapidly than the air beneath the wing,

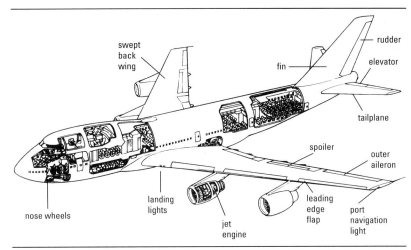

swept back wing · rudder · fin · elevator · tailplane · spoiler · outer aileron · landing lights · nose wheels · jet engine · leading edge flap · port navigation light

structural features of a 747 aeroplane

because it has a greater distance to cover. Air pressure decreases when the flow of air becomes more rapid, so the air pressure above the wing is lower than the pressure beneath it, and the suction produced lifts the wing. The higher the speed of the aeroplane, the greater the lift, and when the lift produced exceeds the weight of the aircraft, it takes off the ground.

To produce lift, the wings of an aircraft must move through the air at high speed, and a second force, known as *thrust*, provided by a propeller or jet engine, pushes the aeroplane forward. With increasing speed of flight, air resistance or *drag* increases. The forward thrust of the engines balances the air resistance, which is reduced by streamlining all parts of the aircraft that are in contact with the air. The horizontal tail surfaces of an aeroplane help to reduce *pitch* (up-and-down movement of the nose and tail), and the vertical fin of the tail helps to reduce *yaw* (slewing from side to side). The upward slant of the wings helps to counteract *roll* (dipping of the wings to one side or the other).

The most important navigation instruments on an aeroplane are the *altimeter* (which indicates altitude or height), the *air-speed indicator* (which indicates the speed of flight through the air), the *compass*, the *vertical-speed indicator* (which indicates how rapidly the plane is climbing or dropping), and the *altitude director* (which indicates whether the aircraft is flying straight and level).

aerosol *noun* **1** a cloud of fine particles of a solid or liquid suspended in a gas. **2** a can containing a product that can be sprayed to produce such a suspension, eg paint, polish, insecticide. ◇ The product to be sprayed is mixed with an inert *propellant* (a gas that is liquefied under pressure). When a button on the top of the can is pressed, a valve is opened and the pressure of the liquefied propellant forces the product up through a tube and out of the nozzle as a spray. Common propellants such as chlorofluorocarbons accumulate in the atmosphere, depleting the ozone layer. For this reason their use is being phased out, and they are being replaced by 'ozone-friendly' aerosols that contain less environmentally damaging chemicals. [from AERO- + SOL²]

aerospace *noun* **1** the Earth's atmosphere and outer space beyond it. **2** the branch of technology or of industry concerned with the flight of aircraft and space vehicles.

Aeschines (c.390 –c.322 BC) Athenian orator. He was prominent in Athenian politics between 348 and 330 BC and his advocacy of peace with Macedon brought him into frequent conflict with Demosthenes, his chief opponent. He was defeated in his attempt to undermine

Demosthenes in 330 BC and went into voluntary exile in Rhodes, where he taught rhetoric.

Aeschylus (c.525–c.456 BC) Greek tragic dramatist, born in Eleusis, near Athens. He fought for Athens at the battle of Marathon in 490 BC, and had his first victory as a poet in 485 BC at the annual dramatic festival. Only seven out of some 60 plays ascribed to him have survived, including the trilogy of the *Oresteia*: *Agamemnon*, *Choephori* (The Libation Bearers), and *Eumenides* (The Furies).

Aesculapius see ASCLEPIUS.

Aesop (?6c BC) the traditional name of a Greek writer of fables. He is supposed to have been a native of Phrygia and a slave who, after being set free, travelled to Greece. The fables are moral anecdotes with animal characters, some of which are known from the folklore of earlier periods. None of his actual writings have survived, but versions bearing the name of Aesop have remained popular throughout history.

aesthete *noun* a person who has or claims to have a special appreciation of art and beauty. [from Greek *aisthetes*, one who perceives]

aesthetic *adj.* **1** able to appreciate beauty. **2** artistic; tasteful. [from Greek *aisthetikos*, from *aisthanesthai*, to perceive]

aesthetically *adv.* in an aesthetic way.

Aesthetic or **Esthetic Movement** a view of art which flourished in the 19c. It was based on the theory that art is autonomous and

should not be judged by non-aesthetic criteria, whether moral, religious, or political. The phrase *l'art pour l'art* ('art for art's sake') was first used by French writer Victor Cousin in 1836, but the doctrine occurs in various forms in the writings of (among others) Kant, Coleridge, and Emerson. Aestheticism was attacked for its exaggerated detachment from everyday life by Ruskin and later by Tolstoy.

aesthetics *sing. noun* **1** the branch of philosophy concerned with the study of the principles of beauty, especially in art. **2** the principles of good taste and the appreciation of beauty.

aestivation *noun Bot.* **1** in certain animals, eg tropical amphibians, a state of inactivity that enables them to survive prolonged periods of heat or drought. **2** the arrangement of the petals and sepals in a flower bud. [from Latin *aestivus*, relating to summer]

aether same as ETHER 2, 3.

aetiological *adj.* **1** relating to aetiology. **2** giving a cause or reason.

aetiologically *adv.* in an aetiological way; so as to give a reason or cause.

aetiology *noun* **1** the science or philosophy of causes. **2** the study of the origins or causes of disease. [from Latin *aetiologia*, from Greek *aitia*, cause + *logos*, discourse]

AEU *abbrev.* Amalgamated Engineering Union.

AF *abbrev.* audio frequency.

AFA *abbrev.* Amateur Football Association.

Afar a Cushitic-speaking people of the Horn of Africa, also known as Danakil. One of the dominant groups in NE Ethiopia and Djibouti, they are pastoral nomads, organized into small kinship groups, which combine only in warfare and are much feared by their neighbours.

afar *adv.* at a distance; far away.
— **from afar** from a great distance.

AFC *abbrev.* **1** Air Force Cross. **2** Association Football Club.

affability *noun* being affable.

affable *adj.* pleasant and friendly in manner; easy to talk to. [from Latin *affabilis*, from *affari*, to speak to]

affably *adv.* in an affable manner.

affair *noun* **1** a concern, matter, or thing to be done. **2** an event or connected series of events. **3** a sexual relationship between two people, usually when at least one of them is married to someone else. **4** (**affairs**) matters of importance and public interest: *current affairs*. **5** (**affairs**) private or public business matters. [from Old French *afaire*, from *a*, to + *faire*, to do]

affaire *noun* **1** a liaison or intrigue. **2** an incident arousing speculation and scandal. [French, = affair]

affect¹ *verb* **1** to have an effect on. **2** to cause (someone) to feel strong emotions, especially sadness or pity. **3** *said of diseases* to attack or infect. [from Latin *afficere*]
◆ Often confused with *effect*.

affect² *verb* **1** to pretend to feel or have. **2** to use, wear, etc (something) in a way that is intended to attract attention. **3** to have an obvious liking for: *affect fast cars*. [from Old French *affecter*, from Latin *afficere*, to affect = have an effect on]

affectation *noun* **1** unnatural behaviour or pretence which is intended to impress people. **2** the act of pretending.

affected *adj.* **1** not genuine; false; pretended. **2** *said of a manner of speaking or behaving* put on to impress people.

affectedly *adv.* in an affected way.

affecting *adj.* causing people to feel strong emotion, especially sadness, pity, sympathy, joy, etc.

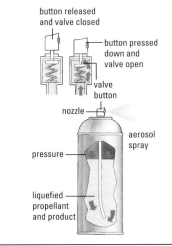

button released and valve closed · button pressed down and valve open · valve button · nozzle · aerosol spray · pressure · liquefied propellant and product

aerosol

affection *noun* **1** a feeling of love or strong liking. **2** (**affections**) feelings: *play on his affections*. **3** a disease. [from Latin *affectio*, from *afficere*, to affect = have an effect on]

affectionate *adj.* showing love or fondness.

affectionately *adv.* with affection.

affective disorder *Psychol.* any of various disorders whose primary characteristic is a disturbance of mood or emotion, eg depression, mania.

afferent *adj. Medicine, said of a nerve* carrying impulses to the brain. See also EFFERENT. [from Latin *afferre*, from *ad*, to + *ferre*, to carry]

affianced *adj. old use* engaged to be married. [from Old French *afiancer*, to pledge in marriage]

affidavit *noun* a written statement, sworn to be true by the person who makes it, for use as evidence in a court of law. [from Latin *affidavit*, he or she swears on oath]

affiliate — *verb trans., intrans.* (pronounced -*ət*) (usually **be affiliated with** *or* **to something**) to connect or associate a person or organization to a group or a larger organization. — *noun* (pronounced -*ate*) a person or organization, etc having an association with a group or larger body. [from Latin *affiliatus*, adopted]

affiliation *noun* the act or process of affiliating; the state of being affiliated.

affiliation order *Legal* a court order instructing a man to pay money towards the support of his illegitimate child.

affinity *noun* (PL. **affinities**) **1** a strong natural liking for or feeling of attraction or closeness towards someone or something. **2** (**affinity with someone**) relationship to them, especially by marriage. **3** similarity in appearance, structure, etc, especially one suggesting relatedness. **4** (**affinity for something**) chemical attraction between substances; readiness to combine chemically with another substance and remain in combination. [from Latin *affinitas*, from *affinis*, neighbouring]

affirm *verb* **1** to state positively and firmly; to state as a fact. **2** to uphold or confirm (an idea, belief, etc). **3** *intrans.* in a court of law, to promise solemnly to tell the truth, without swearing a religious oath. [from Old French *afermer*, from Latin *ad*, to + *firmare*, to make firm]

affirmation *noun* **1** assertion. **2** something which is affirmed. **3** a positive judgement or proposition. **4** a solemn declaration.

affirmative — *adj.* expressing agreement; giving the answer 'yes'. — *noun* an affirmative word or phrase.

affirmatively *adv.* in an affirmative way.

affix — *verb* to attach or fasten. — *noun* a word or syllable added to the beginning or end of a word to form another, related, word, eg *un-* to *happy* to make *unhappy*, and *-ness* to *sad* to make *sadness* ; a prefix or suffix. [from Latin *affixus*, fastened to]

afflict *verb* to cause (someone) physical or mental suffering. [from Latin *affligere*, to cast down]

affliction *noun* distress or suffering, or a cause of this.

affluence *noun* wealth, abundance.

affluent *adj.* having more than enough money; rich. [from Latin *affluere*, to flow freely]

affluent society a society in which ordinary people benefit materially from general prosperity, especially in being able to afford things that were once regarded as luxuries.

afford *verb* **1** (*used with can, could, be able to*) **a** to have enough money, time, etc to spend on (something). **b** to be able to do (something), or allow (something) to happen, without risk: *cannot afford to take chances*. **2** to give; to provide: *a room affording a view of the sea*. [from Anglo-Saxon *geforthian*, to further, promote]

affordable *adj.* that can be afforded.

afforest *verb* to plant trees on. [from Latin *afforestare*]

afforestation *noun* systematic planting with trees. See also FORESTATION.

affray *noun* a fight in a public place; a breach of the peace by fighting. [from Old French *esfrei*]

affront — *noun* an insult, especially one delivered in public. — *verb* **1** to insult, especially in public. **2** to offend the pride of; to embarrass. [from Old French *afronter*, to slap in the face]

AFG *abbrev., as an international vehicle mark* Afghanistan.

Afghan — *adj.* of Afghanistan or its inhabitants. — *noun* **1** (*also* **Afghani**) a citizen of, or person born in, Afghanistan. **2** the official language of Afghanistan. **3** (*also* **Afghan hound**) a type of tall thin dog with long silky hair, originally used for hunting. [from Pashto]

Afghanistan, official name (**Democratic**) **Republic of Afghanistan**, **De Afghanistan Democrateek Jamhuriat** POP (1992e) 19m (plus an estimated 2.5m nomadic tribesmen and c.5m living in Pakistan and Iran as refugees), a republic in S Asia, divided into 29 provinces. AREA 647 497sq km/249 934sq mi. It is bounded N by Turkmenistan, Uzbekistan, and Tajikistan, E and S by Pakistan, W by Iran, and in the extreme NE by China and India. CAPITAL Kabul. CHIEF TOWNS Herat, Kandahar. TIME ZONE GMT +4.5. OFFICIAL LANGUAGES Pushtu, Dari. Islam (mostly Sunni) is the chief religion. CURRENCY the Afghani. PHYSICAL DESCRIPTION a mountainous country centred on the Hindu Kush system which reaches over 7 000m in the centre and NE, making it the second highest range in the world; many secondary ranges; NW of the Hindu Kush, heights decrease towards the Turkmenistan border; also NW is the fertile valley of Herat; arid uplands lie to the S of the Hindu Kush descending into desert in the SW; Afghanistan is landlocked and is over 500km/300mi from the sea. CLIMATE continental climate with winter severity increased by altitude; summers are warm everywhere except on the highest peaks; protected from summer monsoons by the S mountains; rain mostly occurs during spring and autumn; annual rainfall averages 338mm; lower levels have a desert or semi-arid climate. HISTORY the nation first formed in 1747 under Ahmed Shah Durrani; Britain saw Afghanistan as a bridge between India and the Middle East but failed to gain control during a series of Afghan Wars (the last in 1919); the feudal monarchy survived until after World War II, when the constitution became more liberal under several Soviet-influenced five-year economic plans; the king was deposed in 1973, and a republic was formed; a new constitution was adopted in 1977, but a coup in 1978 installed a new government under the communist leader, Nur Mohammad Taraki; a further coup in 1979 brought to power Hafizullah Amin, which led to invasion by Soviet forces; the troops effected their final withdrawal in 1989 but faction fighting continued. GOVERNMENT new constitution (1987) provides for an Executive President, bicameral National Assembly, and Council of Ministers; the regime has met heavy guerrilla resistance from the Mujahadeen (Islamic fighters), and its influence extends effectively over only 20% of the population. ECONOMY traditionally based on agriculture, especially wheat, fruit and vegetables, maize, barley, cotton, sugar-beet, sugar cane; sheep, cattle, goats; forest wood for fuel; food processing, textiles (especially carpets), leather goods, plastics, furniture, footwear, mechanical spares; natural gas production in the N, largely for export; most sectors have been affected by Civil War, especially sugar and textiles.

Afghan Wars a series of wars (1838–42, 1878–80, 1919) between Britain and Afghanistan. They were instigated by an unsuccessful British attempt to control the region in order to prevent the advance of Russian influence towards India; and they resulted, after the third Afghan War, in the country's independence.

aficionado *noun* (PL. **aficionados**) a person who takes an enthusiastic interest in a particular sport or pastime. [Spanish, = amateur]

afield *adv.* to or at a distance; away from home: *far afield*. [from Anglo-Saxon, from A³ + FIELD]

afire *adj., adv.* on fire; burning.

aflame *adj.* **1** in flames; burning. **2** very excited.

aflatoxin *noun Biol.* a toxic substance produced by the fungus *Aspergillus flavus*, which contaminates stored corn, soya beans, peanuts, etc, in warm humid regions. Aflatoxins cause cancer in some animals, and it is thought that they may cause liver cancer in humans. [from *Aspergillus flavus*, from Latin *aspergere*, to sprinkle + *flavus*, yellow]

AFL/CIO *abbrev.* American Federation of Labor–Congress of Industrial Organizations.

afloat *adj., adv.* **1** floating. **2** at sea; aboard ship. **3** out of debt; financially secure. [from Anglo-Saxon, from A³ + FLOAT]

AFM *abbrev.* **1** Air Force medal. **2** audio frequency modulation.

afoot *adj., adv.* being prepared or already in progress.

afore *adv., prep. old use, dialect* before. [from Anglo-Saxon *onforan*]

afore- *combining form* before; previously: *aforementioned*.

aforementioned — *adj.* already mentioned. — *sing. or pl. noun* a person or group of people already mentioned.

aforesaid *adj.* said or mentioned already.

aforethought
— **with malice aforethought** *Legal, said of a criminal act* done deliberately; planned beforehand.

a fortiori for an even better or stronger reason. [from Latin *a fortiori*, from the stronger]

AFP *abbrev.* Agence France Press.

afraid *adj.* **1** (*often* **afraid of someone** *or* **something**) feeling fear; frightened. **2** (**afraid to do something**) reluctant to do something out of fear or concern for the consequences: *they are afraid to go out at night*. **3** as a formula of regret, politely sorry: *I'm afraid we're going to be late*. [past tense of the obsolete verb *affray*, to disturb or frighten]

AFRC *abbrev.* Agricultural and Food Research Council.

afresh *adv.* again, especially from the beginning; with a fresh start.

Africa the second-largest continent. AREA c.29.8m sq km/11.5m sq mi. It extends S from the Mediterranean Sea and is bounded W by the

Afghanistan

Atlantic Ocean, E by the Indian Ocean and the Red Sea, and is bisected by the Equator. Mt Kilimanjaro at 5 895m is Africa's highest point. Major rivers include the Congo, Niger, Nile, and Zambezi.

Africa, Partition of the division of the continent of Africa into colonial territories, which occurred in the last three decades of the 19c and involved Britain, France, Germany, Portugal, Italy, the Boers in the south, and (in his private capacity) King Leopold of the Belgians. The Partition of N Africa was completed by the French and the Italians in the years before World War I, after which only Liberia and Ethiopia remained independent. A repartitioning occurred at the end of the two World Wars, when German and Italian territories were confiscated. Most of the countries created by the Partition achieved independence from the 1960s, and the Organization of African Unity pledged to maintain the existing boundaries.

African — *adj.* belonging to the continent of Africa, its inhabitants or languages. — *noun* a person, especially a dark-skinned person, who is native to Africa or of African descent. [from Latin *Africanus*]

African elephant the larger of the two living species of elephant (*Loxodonta africana*), also differing from the other species in that it has larger ears, and a triangular lip on the top and bottom of the trunk (not just on the top as in the other species).

African lily see AGAPANTHUS.

African National Congress (ABBREV. **ANC**) the most important of the black South African organizations opposed to the Pretoria regime. It began life in 1912 as the South African Native National Congress, and under the influence of M K Gandhi organized passive resistance to white power. After World War II, Oliver Tambo and Nelson Mandela organized its youth wing. Its central policy document, the social democratic *Freedom Charter* (1956), advocates non-racialism rather than the racial exclusivity of its rival Pan-Africanist Congress. During the 1950s it led opposition to the Afrikaner Nationalist government, but the government banned it (1961), and Mandela was imprisoned (1964). The ANC then began a campaign of industrial and economic sabotage through its military wing, but had little success, so began attacking persons as well as property. Political progress in the 1980s led to it being unbanned and Mandela released in Feb 1990. It suspended its armed struggle in Aug 1990 and its leaders, notably Nelson Mandela, Walter Sisulu and Cyril Ramaphosa, were involved in talks about a transition to a democratic South Africa. In Dec 1993 Parliament approved a new interim constitution to enable the establishment of mult-racial democracy in the Apr 1994 elections.

African Queen, The a US film directed by John Huston (1951). Set on the treacherous rivers of Africa during World War I, it is an adventure story starring Humphrey Bogart and Katharine Hepburn.

African violet *noun* a tropical plant from E Africa, with purple, white, or pink flowers and hairy leaves, usually grown indoors in Britain.

Afrikaans *noun* one of the official languages of South Africa, developed from Dutch. [from Dutch *Afrikaans*, African]

Afrika Corps a German expeditionary force of two divisions under the command of Erwin Rommel, sent to reinforce Italian troops in N Africa (Mar 1941). Its special desert training received in Germany proved highly effective in desert warfare between 1941 and 1944.

Afrikaner *noun* a white inhabitant of S Africa whose native language is Afrikaans and who is usually of Dutch descent. [from Dutch *Afrikaans*, African]

Afro *noun* (PL. **Afros**) a hairstyle consisting of thick bushy curls standing out from the head.

Afro- *combining form* forming words meaning 'African, African and ...': *Afro-Caribbean*. [from Latin *Afer*, African]

Afro-American — *noun* an American whose ancestors came from Africa. — *adj.* of Afro-Americans, their music, culture, etc.

Afro-Asiatic — *adj.* denoting a major family of African languages used in Africa and SW Asia. It contains over 200 languages and is usually divided into six groups (thought to be derived from a common language of the 7th millennium BC), Semitic, Berber, Chadic, Cushitic, Egyptian (now extinct), and Omotic. — *noun* the languages forming this family.

Afro-Caribbean — *noun* a person living in the Caribbean whose ancestors came originally from Africa. — *adj.* of Afro-Caribbeans, their music, culture, etc.

Afsluitdijk Sea Dam a sea dam (32km/20mi long) built in 1927–32 across the Zuider Zee in the Netherlands to facilitate land reclamation.

aft *adv., adj.* at or towards the stern, rear, or tail. [from Anglo-Saxon *æftan*, behind]

after — *prep.* **1** coming later in time than. **2** following in position; behind. **3** next to and following in importance, order, arrangement, etc. **4** because of; considering: *you can't expect to be promoted after that mistake.* **5** in spite of: *he's still no better after all that medicine.* **6** about: *ask after her.* **7** in pursuit of: *run after him.* **8** said of a painting or other work of art in the style or manner of (someone else). **9** given the same name as; in imitation of: *called her Mary after her aunt.* **10** North Amer., esp. US past (an hour): *it's twenty after six.* — *adv.* later in time, behind in place. — *conj.* after the time when. — *adj.* **1** later; following: *in after years.* **2** further towards the stern of a ship: *after cabins.* See also AFT.

— **after all 1** in spite of all that has happened or has been said. **2** contrary to what is or was expected: *the shop was closed after all.*

after one's own heart of exactly the kind one likes.

after you please go before me.

be after someone *or* **something** to be pursuing or chasing a person or animal.

[from Anglo-Saxon *æfter*]

afterbirth *noun* Medicine the placenta, blood, and ruptured membranes expelled from the uterus after the birth of a mammal.

afterburning *noun* Aeron. a system whereby the thrust of a jet engine is increased by injecting fuel into the hot exhaust gases leaving the engine. The fuel is ignited by the hot gases, providing additional thrust.

aftercare *noun* care and support given to someone after a period of treatment, a surgical operation, a prison sentence, etc.

after-effect *noun* a circumstance or event, usually an unpleasant one, that follows as the result of something.

afterglow *noun* **1** a glow remaining in the sky after the sun has set. **2** an impression or feeling, usually a pleasant one, that remains when the experience, etc that caused it is over.

afterlife *noun* the continued existence of one's spirit or soul after one's death.

aftermath *noun* circumstances that follow and are a result of something, especially a great and terrible event. [from Anglo-Saxon *mæth*, mowing]

afternoon *noun* the period of the day between noon and the evening.

afters *pl. noun* Brit. colloq. dessert; pudding.

aftershave *noun* a scented lotion for putting on the face after shaving.

aftertaste *noun* the taste that remains in the mouth after one has eaten or drunk something.

afterthought *noun* an idea thought of after the main plan, etc has been formed.

afterwards *or* **afterward** *adv.* later; following (an earlier event of time).

Ag *symbol Chem.* silver. [from Latin *argentum*, silver]

Agadez 1 POP (1988) 50 000, the capital of Agadez department, central Niger. It is an ancient caravan trading city and the former capital of a Tuareg Kingdom. Agadez is renowned for its traditional silversmiths and leather workers. NOTABLE FEATURES mosque (16c); Sudanic mud architecture. **2** a department in central Niger with Agadez as its capital.

Agadir POP (1982) 110 000, a seaport in Sud province, W Morocco, on the Atlantic coast, 8km/5mi N of the mouth of the R Sous. HISTORY named Santa Cruz by the Portuguese in 1505–41; taken by the French in 1913; extensive rebuilding after an earthquake in 1960. NOTABLE FEATURE Kasbah Fortress (16c).

again *adv.* **1** once more; another time. **2** back to a previous condition, situation, etc: *get well again.* **3** in addition: *twice as much again.* **4** however; on the other hand: *He might come, but then again he might not.* **5** further; besides.

— **again and again** very often; repeatedly. [from Anglo-Saxon *ongean*]

against *prep.* **1** close to or leaning on; in contact with. **2** into collision with. **3** in opposition to: *against the law.* **4** in contrast to: *against a dark background.* **5** with a bad or unfavourable effect on: *His youth is against him.* **6** as a protection from; in anticipation of or preparation for. **7** in return for: *exchange rate against the franc.*

— **as against something** in comparison with it. **have something against someone** *or* **something** to have a reason for disliking or disapproving of them.

[from Middle English *ageynes*]

Aga Khan III, in full **Aga Sultan Sir Mohammed Shah** (1877–1957) imam (leader) of the Ismaili sect of Muslims, born in Karachi. He succeeded to the title of Aga Khan in 1885, worked for the British cause in both World Wars, and in 1937 was President of the League of Nations. A horse-racing enthusiast, he owned several Derby winners. He was succeeded as 49th imam by his grandson Karim (1936–), the son of Aly Khan, as Aga Khan IV.

Agamemnon the King of Argos and commander of the Greek army in the Trojan War. He captured Troy and returned with Cassandra, the daughter of King Priam. He was then murdered by his wife Clytemnestra and her lover Aegisthus.

agamid *noun* a lizard native to Africa (except Madagascar), S and SE Asia, and Australia. Its body is usually broad, and it has a large head, scales with ridges and spines, and a thick fleshy tongue. Its tail cannot be shed, and some species are able to change colour. [from a Carib name]

Agaña POP (1990) 1 000, the port capital of Guam, Mariana Is, W Pacific Ocean. HISTORY taken by Japan in 1941; destroyed during its recapture by the USA in 1944. NOTABLE FEATURE cathedral (1669).

agapanthus *noun* an evergreen perennial plant (*Agapanthus africanus*), native to S Africa, up to 1m tall, with strap-shaped leathery leaves, and bell-shaped blue (or rarely white) flowers borne in large heads on long leafless stalks. — Also called *African lily*. [from Greek *agape*, love + *anthos*, flower]

agape¹ *adj.* **1** said of the mouth gaping; open wide. **2** said of a person very surprised.

agape² *noun* (pronounced as three syllables) Christian brotherly love, as distinct from erotic love. [from Greek *agape*, love]

agar *noun* a type of jelly obtained from seaweed, used especially in medicine and cookery. [from Malay]

agaric *noun* any fungus with a cap and stalk, such as the edible mushroom. [from Latin *agaricum*]

Agassi, Andre (1970–) US tennis player, born in Las Vegas. He defeated Stefan Edberg to win the inaugural ATP world championship in 1991, and went on to win the men's singles at Wimbledon in 1992. In 1990 he was a member of the victorious US Davis Cup team.

Agassiz, Jean Louis Rodolphe (1807–73) Swiss-born US naturalist, born in Môtier-en-Vuly. Professor of Natural History at Neuchâtel from 1832, he wrote widely on zoology and glaciology. Following studies of the glacial phenomena of the Alps, he demonstrated in *Études sur les glaciers* (Studies on Glaciers, 1840) and *Système glaciaire* (1847) that glaciers are not static but move, indicating the existence of an Ice Age. He later became professor at Harvard University, where he founded the Museum of Comparative Zoology (1859).

Agate, James Evershed (1877–1947) English critic and essayist, born in Manchester. As drama critic of the *Sunday Times* from 1923 he established a formidable reputation. He published several works of criticism, and nine volumes of selections from his diary, *Ego* (1932–47).

agate *noun* *Geol.* a fine-grained variety of chalcedony (a form of quartz), which usually forms within rock cavities, and consists of concentrically arranged bands of two or more colours, eg black and white, as in onyx. It is used as a semiprecious stone in jewellery and ornaments. [from Old French *agathes*]

Agatha a female first name. [a Latin form of Greek *agathos*, good, honourable]

agave *noun* an American plant with thorny leaves from which fibres such as sisal are produced. [from Latin, from the Greek name *Agave*]

age — *noun* **1** the length of time a person or thing has existed. **2** a particular stage in life. **3** the fact of being old. **4** a period in the geological development or history of the world marked by some particular feature. **5** (*usually* **ages**) *colloq.* a very long time. — *verb* (**ageing, aging**) **1** *intrans.* to show signs of growing old. **2** *intrans.* to grow old. **3** *intrans.* to mature. **4** to cause to seem older or look old.
— **act** *or* **be one's age** to behave sensibly.
come of age to become legally old enough to have an adult's rights and duties.
of an age of the same, or a similar, age.
over age too old.
under age too young to be legally allowed to do something, eg buy alcoholic drink.
[from Old French *aage*, from Latin *aetas*]

-age *suffix* forming nouns meaning: **1** a collection or set: *baggage*. **2** an action: *breakage*. **3** the result of an action or event: *wreckage*. **4** a condition: *bondage*. **5** the home, house, or place of: *orphanage* / *anchorage*. **6** cost: *postage*. [from Old French]

aged — *adj.* **1** having a particular age. **2** very old. — *noun* old people as a group.

Age d'Or, L' (The Golden Age) a French film directed by Luis Buñuel (1930). A surrealist fantasy, co-written by Buñuel and Salvador Dali, it focuses on two lovers (played by Gaston Modot and Lya Lys) who are kept apart by the constraints of the Church and the hypocrisy of bourgeois morality.

Agee, James (1909–55) US novelist, born in Knoxville, Tennessee. A journalist and film critic, he is best known for *Let Us Now Praise Famous Men* (1941), a documentary account of sharecroppers in the deep South during the Depression. Other works include *A Death in the Family* (1955), a semi-autobiographical novel about his father's death, and *Agee on Film* (1958).

age group *or* **age bracket** the people between two particular ages, considered as a group.

ageing *or* **aging** *noun* the period during which the physical condition of a living organism deteriorates, leading to death; in biological terms this corresponds to the entire life process.
◇ Human ageing involves obvious physical changes, including loss of hair and hair pigment, and a reduction in skin elasticity, resulting in wrinkles. The bones become more brittle and shrink slightly, resulting in curvature of the spine and a stooped posture. Joint movements become restricted, arthritis and rheumatism may develop, and there is a decline in muscular strength and activity. The blood vessel walls thicken and become more brittle, increasing the risk of coronary artery disease and brain haemorrhage. Loss of elasticity in the lens of the eye eventually necessitates the use of spectacles for reading, or an opaque area (cataract) may form in the lens, so interfering with sight that the lens requires surgical removal. The senses of hearing and taste may also deteriorate, and there is normally a gradual decline in sexual activity, but little change in intellectual capacity.
The causes of ageing are the subject of intensive research. One theory is that the process is genetically determined, to remove individuals no longer capable of reproduction. An alternative view is that ageing is caused by the accumulation of mistakes during the duplication of genetic material (DNA) at cell division. It has also been suggested that DNA fragments or cancer-causing viruses proliferate in old cells, programming them to produce unwanted proteins that interfere with normal cell functioning.

ageism *or* **agism** *noun* the practice of treating people differently, usually unfairly, on the grounds of age only, especially because they are too old.

ageist *or* **agist** — *noun* a person who discriminates against people on the grounds of age. — *adj.* discriminating on the grounds of age.

ageless *adj.* never growing old or fading; never looking older.

age limit the age under or over which one may not do something.

Agence France Press (ABBREV. **AFP**) an international news agency, with headquarters in Paris. It is the direct successor to Havas (established 1832), and is the oldest surviving world agency.

agency *noun* (PL. **agencies**) **1** an office or business providing a particular service. **2** an active part played by someone in bringing something about. **3** *North Amer., esp. US* a government department providing a particular service. **4** the business of an agent. [from Latin *agere*, to do]

agenda *noun* a list of things to be done or discussed; a written list of subjects to be dealt with at a meeting, etc. [from Latin *agenda*, things to be done]

agent *noun* **1** a person who represents an organization and acts on its behalf; a person who deals with someone else's business matters, etc. **2** (*also* **secret agent**) a spy. **3** a substance that is used for producing a particular result. **4** a person who is the cause of something. [from Latin *agens*, from *agere*, to do]

Agent Orange *Environ.* a highly poisonous herbicide, used as a defoliant to remove the leaves from plants, including crops, during the Vietnam War.

agent provocateur *noun* (PL. **agents provocateurs**) a person employed to incite others by pretended sympathy to perform illegal acts. [French, = provocative agent]

Age of Bronze, The a sculpture by Auguste Rodin (1877). It was so realistic that Rodin was accused of having taken the cast from the living man.

age of consent the age at which consent to sexual intercourse is permitted by law.

age-old *adj.* done, known, etc for a very long time.

aggiornamento *noun* **1** political or religious reform. **2** *Christianity* the process of modernizing the belief, structure, and discipline of the Roman Catholic Church and making it more effective in the modern world. It was one of the aims of the Second Vatican Council (1962–5) called by Pope John XXIII. [from Italian *aggiornamento*, modernization]

agglomerate — *verb* *trans., intrans.* (pronounced *-rate*) to make into or become an untidy mass. — *noun* (pronounced *-rat*) **1** an untidy mass or collection of things. **2** a type of stone formed from small pieces of volcanic rock melted into a mass. — *adj.* (pronounced *-rat*) formed into a mass. [from Latin *agglomerare*, to wind on to a ball]

agglomeration *noun* **1** the act of collecting in a mass; heaping together. **2** a mass or cluster.

agglutinate *verb* **1** to stick or glue together. **2** *trans., intrans. Grammar, said of a language* to create (words) by joining together simpler words or word elements, each of which corresponds to a particular element of meaning. **3** *Biol., said of red blood cells, bacteria, etc* to clump together forming a visible precipitate as a result of mixing blood cells from two incompatible blood groups, or of the reaction of an antigen (foreign particle) to its specific antibody. [from Latin *agglutinare*, to glue together]

agglutinating language *or* **agglutinative language** *Linguistics* a language type in which words are typically made up of elements, with each element expressing a particular grammatical meaning, as in the English word *de-human-ize*. Japanese, Turkish, and Finnish are good examples of agglutinating languages. See also ANALYTIC LANGUAGE, FUSIONAL LANGUAGE.

agglutination *noun* **1** act of agglutinating. **2** an agglutinated mass. **3** a process of word-formation in which words are inflected by the addition of one or more meaningful elements to the stem. **4** *Biol.* the process of agglutinating. Agglutination tests are used to determine blood groups, and to establish the identity of bacteria.

agglutinative *adj.* tending to or able to agglutinate.

aggrandize *or* **aggrandise** *verb* **1** to increase the power, wealth, etc of (a person, country, etc). **2** to make (someone or something) seem greater than they really are. [from Old French *aggrandir*]

aggrandizement *or* **aggrandisement** *noun* making someone or something seem greater than they really are.

aggravate *verb* **1** to make (a bad situation, an illness, etc) worse. **2** to make (someone) angry; to annoy. [from Latin *aggravare*, to make heavier or worse]

aggravating *adj.* **1** worsening. **2** annoying.

aggravatingly *adv.* so as to aggravate or annoy.

aggravation *noun* **1** something that increases the gravity of an illness or crime etc. **2** irritation, annoyance.

aggregate — *noun* (pronounced *-gat*) **1** a collection of separate units brought together; a total. **2** the sand and broken stone that are mixed with water and cement to make concrete. **3** rock, eg granite, formed from a mixture of different minerals. — *adj.* (pronounced *-gat*) *said of separate units* combined together. — *verb* (pronounced *-gate*) **1** *trans., intrans.* to combine or be combined into a single unit or whole. **2** *colloq.* to amount to. **3** *formal* to add as a member to a society, group, etc.
— **in the aggregate** taken all together.
on aggregate in total.
[from Latin *aggregare*, to herd or bring together]

aggregation *noun* the act or process of aggregating.

aggression *noun* **1** the act of attacking another person or country without being provoked; an instance of hostile behaviour towards someone. **2** the tendency to make unprovoked attacks. **3** hostile feelings or behaviour. [from Latin *aggredi*, to attack]

aggressive *adj.* **1** *said of a person* always ready to attack; hostile. **2** *said of a person* strong and determined; self-assertive. **3** *said of an action* hostile.

aggressively *adv.* in an aggressive way.

aggressiveness *noun* being aggressive.

aggressor *noun* in a fight, war, etc, the person, group or country that attacks first, especially if the attack is unprovoked.

aggrieved *adj.* **1** angry, hurt, or upset because one feels that one has been badly or unfairly treated. **2** *Legal* having suffered because of someone else's illegal behaviour. [from Old French *agrever*, to press heavily upon]

aggro *noun Brit. slang* **1** fighting; violent or threatening behaviour. **2** problems or difficulties. [abbreviation of AGGRAVATION or AGGRESSION]

aghast *adj.* filled with fear or horror. [from Anglo-Saxon *gæstan*, to frighten]

agile *adj.* able to move, change direction, etc quickly and easily; nimble; active. [from Latin *agilis*, from *agere*, to do]

agilely *adv.* in an agile way.

agility *noun* being agile; the ability to move quickly and easily.

agin *prep. Scot. colloq.* against. [from Anglo-Saxon *ongean*, opposite to]

Agincourt, Battle of a battle (1415) between France and England near Hesdin (Pas-de-Calais) during the Hundred Years War, in which the French cavalry were defeated by a smaller English force of dismounted men-at-arms and archers under Henry V, who returned in 1417 to begin the systematic conquest of Normandy.

agitate *verb* **1** to excite or trouble (a person, their feelings, nerves, etc). **2** *intrans.* to stir up public opinion for or against an issue. **3** to shake or stir (a liquid). [from Latin *agitare*]

agitated *adj.* distressed, excited, and worried.

agitatedly *adv.* in an agitated way.

agitation *noun* **1** public discussion for or against something. **2** a disturbed or nervous state of mind; anxiety.

agitator *noun* **1** a person who tries continually to stir up public feeling, especially over serious political or social issues. **2** a tool or machine for stirring or shaking a liquid.

agitprop *noun* the spreading of political propaganda, especially by communists. [from Russian *agitatsiya*, agitation + *propaganda*, propaganda]

aglow *adj., adv.* shining with colour or warmth; glowing.

AGM *abbrev.* annual general meeting.

Agnes a female first name. [a Latin form of Greek *hagnos*, pure, holy]

Agnew, Spiro T(heodore) (1918–) US Republican politician, born in Baltimore, son of a Greek immigrant. In 1966 he was elected Governor of Maryland on a liberal platform. He introduced anti-racial-discrimination legislation, but by 1968 his attitude to such problems as race rioting and civil disorders had become much more conservative. He was Nixon's running mate in the 1968 election, and was Vice-President (1969–73).

Agni the Hindu god of fire. He is the personification of fire, and his ritualistic descriptions of swift tongues and sharp teeth emphasise this. He

is a guide and protector of men and has two faces, one calm and one malevolent. He acts as an intermediary between mortals and the gods.

Agnon, Shmuel Yosef, originally **Shmuel Czaczkes** (1888–1970) Israeli writer, born in Buczacz, Galicia (now Poland). He went to Palestine in 1907, studied in Berlin (1913–24), then settled in Jerusalem and changed his surname to Agnon. He wrote several volumes of short stories, and an epic trilogy of novels on Eastern European Jewry in the early 20c, culminating in *Tmol Shilshom* (The Day Before Yesterday, 1945). He was awarded the Nobel Prize for Literature in 1966.

agnosia *noun Medicine* a brain disorder characterized by inability to interpret information from the sense organs correctly, eg an affected person may have unimpaired hearing, but be unable to interpret sounds. [from A-¹ + Greek *gnosis*, knowledge, recognition]

agnostic — *noun* a person who believes that one can know only about material things and so believes that nothing can be known about the existence of God. — *adj.* relating to this view. [from Greek *agnostos*, not known]

agnosticism *noun* the belief that nothing can be known about the existence of God.

ago *adv.* in the past; earlier. [from Anglo-Saxon *agan*, to pass by]

agog — *adj.* very interested and excited; eager to know more. — *adv.* eagerly; expectantly. [from Old French *en gogues*, in fun]

agonist *noun* **1** someone engaged in a struggle, whether physical or spiritual. **2** *Biol.* a muscle whose contraction results in movement of a body part. **3** a drug whose action is complementary to that of another drug.

agonize *or* **agonise** *verb* **1** *intrans.* (**agonize about** *or* **over something**) to worry intensely or suffer great anxiety about it. **2** *trans.* to cause great anxiety or worry to. [from Greek *agonizesthai*, to struggle]

agonized *or* **agonised** *adj.* suffering or showing great anxiety, worry or agony.

agonizing *or* **agonising** *adj.* causing great bodily or mental suffering.

agonizingly *or* **agonisingly** *adv.* **1** so as to cause agony; painfully. **2** acutely, severely: *an agonizingly difficult decision.*

agony *noun* (PL. **agonies**) severe bodily or mental pain. [from Latin *agonia*, from Greek *agon*, struggle]

agony aunt *colloq.* a person who answers letters sent in to an agony column.

agony column part of a newspaper or magazine where advice is offered to readers who write in with their problems.

Agony in the Garden 1 a painting by Andrea Mantegna (c.1450, National Gallery, London). **2** a painting by Giovanni Bellini (c.1465, National Gallery, London).

agoraphobia *noun* an illogical fear of open and public places. [from Greek *agora*, marketplace + *phobos*, fear]

agoraphobic — *noun* a person who is suffering from agoraphobia. — *adj.* suffering from agoraphobia.

Agostini, Giacomo (1943–) Italian motorcyclist, born in Lovere, Bergamo. He won a record 15 world titles between 1966 and 1975, including the 500cc title a record eight times (1966–72, 1975); 13 of the titles were on an MV Agusta, the others on a Yamaha. He won 10 Isle of Man TT Races (1966–75), including the Senior TT five times (1968–72). After retirement in 1975 he became manager of the Yamaha racing team.

agouti *noun* a rodent like a cavy, native to Central and S America and the Caribbean Islands, about 500mm in length, resembling a rat

in appearance, and having long legs and a minute black tail. [from Guarani *acuti*]

AGR *abbrev.* advanced gas or gas-cooled (nuclear) reactor. A reactor in which fission reactions are produced in uranium oxide fuel. Carbon dioxide gas is circulated around the core to extract the heat released; this is then transferred to water to produce steam, which drives turbines to generate electricity. This type of reactor is used at many locations in the UK.

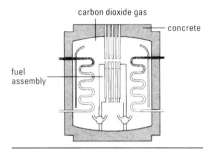

advanced gas-cooled reactor (AGR)

Agra POP (1991) 899 000, a city in Uttar Pradesh, NE India. It lies 190km/118mi SE of Delhi. HISTORY founded in 1566; Mughal capital until 1659; taken by the British in 1803; seat of the government of the North West Provinces from 1835 until 1862. NOTABLE FEATURES World Heritage sites, the Taj Mahal (1630–48) and Mirror Palace (Shish Mahal), fort (16c) with the Pearl Mosque of Shah Jahan; Great Mosque; tomb of Akbar to the N at Sikandra.

Agra Fort a 16c fort in Agra, India. It contains the Pearl Mosque (Moti Masjid) of Shah Jahan. It is a World Heritage site.

agranulocytosis *noun Medicine* a disorder in which there is a marked decrease in the number of granulocytes (a particular type of white blood cell) in the blood as a result of damage to the bone marrow, eg by toxic drugs. It results in greatly increased vulnerability to infection. [from A-¹ + GRANULE]

agraphia *noun Psychol.* loss of the ability to write, although hand co-ordination remains unaffected, caused by brain disorder. [from A-¹ + Greek *graphein*, to write]

agrarian *adj.* of or concerning land and its uses, especially farming. [from Latin *agrarius*, from *ager*, field]

agree *verb usually intrans.* **1** (**agree with something**) to be of the same opinion as someone else about something. **2** (**agree to something**) to say yes to a suggestion, request, or instruction. **3** (**agree on** *or* **upon something**) to reach a joint decision about something after discussion. **4** *trans.* to reach agreement about (something). **5** (**agree with someone**) *usually said of food* to be suitable or good for them: *milk doesn't agree with me.* **6** (**agree with something**) to be consistent with it. **7** *Grammar* to have the same number, person, gender, or case.

— **agree to differ** *said of two or more people* to agree to accept each other's different opinions.

be agreed to have reached the same conclusion. [from Old French *agreer*]

agreeable *adj.* **1** *said of things* pleasant. **2** *said of people* friendly. **3** (**agreeable to something**) *said of people* willing to accept a suggestion, etc.

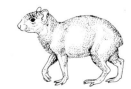

agouti

agreeably *adv.* in an agreeable way; pleasantly.

agreement *noun* **1** a contract or promise. **2** a joint decision made after discussion. **3** the state of holding the same opinion. **4** *Grammar* the state of having the same number, person, gender, or case.

Agricola, Gnaeus Julius, (AD 40–93) Roman general and the longest-serving governor in Britain (78–84). He pacified the country and advanced northward into Scotland, a gradual conquest which culminated in his victory at the battle of Mons Graupius in 84. In southern Britain, he pursued a policy of benevolent Romanization, actively encouraging the development of Roman-style towns. After his victory in Scotland, his fleet circumnavigated the mainland of Britain. He was recalled to Rome by the emperor Domitian in 85, and was not given another command. He was the father-in-law of the historian Tacitus, who wrote a short account of his life.

Agricola, Johann, originally **Schneider**, or **Schnitter**, also called **Magister Islebius** (1492–1566) German reformer, born in Eisleben. One of the most zealous founders of Protestantism, he was sent by Luther to Frankfurt (1525) to institute Protestant worship there. In 1536 he was appointed to a chair at Wittenberg, but he resigned in 1540 because of his doctrinal opposition to Luther. He wrote many theological books, and made a collection of German proverbs.

agricultural *adj.* relating to agriculture.

agricultural controls a term most commonly applied to UK government controls over agricultural production and pricing during World War II, continuing up to 1953. Agricultural controls are mainly concerned with the restriction of surplus production, and with disease prevention and limitation.

agriculturalist *or* **agriculturist** *noun* an expert on agriculture.

Agricultural Revolution a series of changes in farming practice that started in England and then spread throughout W Europe between 1700 and 1850. The main changes included greater intensity of productive land use, a reduction in the area of fallow land and wasteland, the introduction of crop rotation, the development of artificially bred grasses, and scientific animal breeding.

agriculture *noun* the cultivation of the land in order to grow crops or raise animal livestock as a source of food or other useful products, eg wool, cotton. [from Latin *ager*, field + *cultura*, cultivation]
◇ The earliest centres of agriculture are thought to be Egypt (the fertile strip fed by the Nile) and Mesopotamia (the fertile belt between the rivers Tigris and Euphrates), and the planting of crops and rearing of animals for food probably began during the Neolithic period (9 000–7 000 BC). Today agriculture is the world's largest and most important industry, producing over 95 per cent of the world's food. Sheep and goats were the first animals to be domesticated, but cattle have now assumed primary importance, with over 12 billion cattle worldwide providing milk, meat, and leather.
About one third of the world's total land area is used for farming, and about a third of this land is used to grow crops. Agriculture has been forced to become more productive in order to feed the expanding world population, and during the last century there have been significant advances in plant and animal breeding, which together with the use of fertilizers and pesticides have led to the development of hardier and more productive strains of crops, and animals that produce more meat. The availability of sophisticated machinery has also radically improved the efficiency of farming. For example, a combine harvester can cut and thresh one acre of wheat in just seven minutes.

Agriculture, Fisheries, and Food, Ministry of (ABBREV. **MAFF**) in the UK, the government department that deals with policy on agriculture, horticulture, and fisheries in England, and works in association with the Agriculture Departments of the Scottish, Welsh, and Northern Ireland Offices to ensure the administration of related EC policies. Its responsibilities also include policies relating to food quality safety in the UK, the eradication of disease (in animals, plants, and fish), assistance to businesses, and the protection of the environment.

agrimony *noun* an erect perennial plant (*Agrimonia eupatoria*), native to Europe, W Asia, and N Africa. It has hairy leaves with pairs of small leaflets alternating with large ones, and small yellow flowers borne in long terminal spikes. [from Greek *argemone*, a long prickly-headed poppy]

Agrippa, Marcus Vipsanius (c.63–12 BC) Roman general, administrator and right-hand man of Octavian (Augustus). He played an important role in various of Octavian's military campaigns, including his victory over Mark Antony at Actium in 31 BC. He was also responsible for the administration of several parts of the new Roman Empire, including the improvement of the public amenities of Rome. The Emperors Gaius (Caligula) and Nero were descendants of his marriage with Augustus's daughter, Julia.

Agrippina the Elder (c.14 BC–AD 33) the daughter of Agrippa, granddaughter of the Roman emperor Augustus, and mother of the emperor Caligula. She became the focal point of opposition to the emperor Tiberius, and hence the chief target of his henchman, Sejanus, after the suspicious death of her husband, Germanicus in 19. She was banished to the barren island of Pandateria in 29, where she died of voluntary starvation.

Agrippina the Younger (AD 15–59) the eldest daughter of Agrippina (the Elder) and Germanicus, and mother of the emperor Nero by her first husband Cnaeus Domitius Ahenobarbus. It seems likely that she engineered Nero's succession to the throne in 54 by supplanting the true heir Britannicus, and poisoning his father, the reigning emperor Claudius, her husband at the time. Initially she ruled as virtual co-regent with Nero, but he later had her murdered.

agro- *combining form* agricultural: *agrochemical*. [from Latin *ager*, field]

agrochemical *or* **agrichemical** — *noun* *Agric.* any chemical compound that is used to improve the quality of farm products, eg inorganic fertilizers, insecticides, and herbicides. — *adj.* relating to the use of such chemical compounds.

agro-industry *noun* an industry embracing all the aspects of agricultural production and distribution, including the supply of equipment and chemicals, finance, marketing, processing, and transportation of commodities.

agronomy *noun* *Agric.* the scientific study of the cultivation of field crops and soil management. It includes plant breeding and other methods of improving crop production, and soil conservation. [from AGRO- + Greek *nomos*, law]

aground *adj. adv., said of ships* stuck on the bottom of the sea or rocks, usually in shallow water.

ague *noun* **1** *old use* malaria. **2** a fit of shivering. [from Old French *fièvre ague*, acute fever]

Aguecheek, Sir Andrew the thin and foolish knight in Shakespeare's *Twelfth Night*, who is brought in by Sir Toby Belch to woo his niece, Olivia.

Agulhas, Cape the most southerly point of the African continent, 160km/100mi SE of the

Cape of Good Hope, South Africa. Running past it, round the whole S coast, is a reef called the Agulhas Bank, which is an important fishing ground. In 1852 the troopship *Birkenhead* was wrecked off the cape with the loss of 400 crew.

AH *abbrev.* anno Hegirae (Latin), in the year of the Hegira.

ah *interj.* used to express surprise, sympathy, admiration, pleasure, etc, according to the intonation of the speaker's voice.

aha *interj.* used to express pleasure, satisfaction, triumph or surprise, according to the intonation of the speaker's voice.

Ahab, Capt the monomaniac one-legged captain of the *Pequod*, obsessed with exacting revenge on the great white whale in Herman Melville's *Moby Dick*.

Ahaggar Mountains see HOGGAR MOUNTAINS.

ahead *adv.* **1** at or in the front; forwards. **2** earlier in time; before. **3** in the lead; further advanced: *ahead on points*.
— **ahead of someone** *or* **something** in advance of them.
get ahead to make progress, especially socially.

ahem *interj.* a sound made in the back of the throat, used to gain people's attention or express doubt or disapproval.

Ahimsa the principle of respect for all life and the practice of non-injury to living things, found in certain Hindu sects, Buddhism, and especially Jainism, and practised by Mahatma Gandhi. It is based on the belief that violence has harmful effects on those who commit it, including an unfavourable future rebirth. [Sanskrit, = non-injury]

Ahmadabad *or* **Ahmedabad** POP (1991) 3.3m, a commercial centre and industrial city in Gujarat, W India. It lies on the R Sabarmati, 440km/273mi N of Bombay and is a centre of the cotton industry. HISTORY founded in 1411; fell to the Mughals in 1572; British trading post in 1619; centre of Gandhi's activities during the 1920s and 1930s. NOTABLE FEATURES several temples, mosques, forts; Gandhi's Sabarmati Ashram retreat.

Ahmadiyya *or* **Ahmadis** an Islamic religious movement founded in India by Mirza Ghulam Ahmad (c.1839–1908), who was believed to be the Messiah Mahdi prophesied in the Koran. Rejected by orthodox Islam (which holds Muhammad to be the last manifestation of God), the sect, marked by its missionary zeal, is active in Asia, Africa, and Europe.

-aholic *or* **-oholic** *colloq.* an element forming words meaning 'addicted to': *workaholic*. [modelled on ALCOHOLIC]

ahoy *interj. Naut.* a shout to greet or attract the attention of another ship. [from AH + HOY]

Ahriman *or* **Angra Mainyu** in Zoroastrianism, the supreme evil spirit, the Lord of darkness and death. Ahriman is engaged in a continuing struggle with Ahura Mazda (Zoroaster's name for God).

Ahura Mazda in Zoroastrianism, the name for God. He created the world and was opposed to Ahriman, the supreme evil spirit. [Persian, = Wise Lord]

Ahvenanmaa, Swedish **Åland** POP (1992e) 25 000, an island group forming a district of Finland, in the Gulf of Bothnia between Sweden and Finland. AREA 1 552sq km/599sq mi. There are 6 554 islands, of which 80 are inhabited. CAPITAL Maarianhamina. The first language of the island group is Swedish.

AI *abbrev.* **1** artificial insemination. **2** artificial intelligence.

AID *abbrev.* artificial insemination by donor.

aid — *noun* **1** help. **2** help or support in the form of money, supplies or services given to people who need it. **3** a person or thing that helps do something: *a hearing-aid.* — *verb* **1** to help or support (someone). **2** to help (something) happen; to promote.

— **aid and abet** *Legal* to help and encourage (someone) to do something wrong, especially disobey the law.

in aid of someone *or* **something** in support of them.

what's this in aid of *colloq.* what is the reason for, or purpose of, this?

[from Old French *aidier*]

Aida *or* **Aïda** an opera by Giuseppe Verdi (1871), commissioned for the opening of the new opera house in Cairo. Set in Egypt, it concerns an Ethiopian slave Aida, who is torn between love for her father King Amonasro, whose army has attacked Egypt, and love for her secret lover Radames, the leader of the Egyptian forces. He is also loved by Aida's mistress, the Egyptian princess Amneris.

Aidan a male first name, borne by various early Irish saints. [from Gaelic *Aodh*, fire, name of the Celtic sun god]

Aidan, St (d.651), known as **the Apostle of Northumbria** Irish monk who became Bishop of Northumbria. In 635 he was summoned from Iona by King Oswald of Northumbria to evangelize the north. He established the monastery at Lindisfarne, and made many missionary journeys to the mainland. His feast day is 31 Aug.

aide *noun* an assistant or adviser, especially to the head of a government. [from French *aide*]

aide-de-camp *noun* (PL. **aides-de-camp**) an officer in the armed forces who acts as assistant to a senior officer.

aide-mémoire *noun* (PL. **aides-mémoire**) something that helps one to remember something, especially a note listing the main points mentioned in a paper, speech, etc. [from French *aide-mémoire*, help-memory]

AIDS *or* **Aids** *noun* acquired immunodeficiency syndrome: caused by infection with the human immunodeficiency virus (HIV).

◇ First identified in 1983, and now known to be a retrovirus, HIV is transmitted in blood, semen, and vaginal fluids. The virus destroys the immune system, in particular T-helper cells (which manufacture antibodies) and macrophages (which engulf invading bacteria), leaving the body susceptible to potentially fatal infections, including pneumonia and an otherwise rare skin tumour. Other symptoms may include fatigue, fever, sweating, enlarged lymph nodes, dermatitis, weight loss, herpes virus infections, meningitis, progressive blindness, and dementia.

Groups at high risk of acquiring the disease include homosexual and bisexual men, prostitutes, individuals with a history of intravenous drug abuse, haemophiliacs treated with contaminated blood products prior to 1986, and heterosexual men and women who have had casual sexual relationships. There is as yet no cure for the disease, and by 1991 the World Health Organization (WHO) had estimated that at least 10 million individuals worldwide were infected with the virus. Of these, one million had reached the stage known as AIDS. They have also predicted that 40 million people will be infected worldwide by the year 2000.

A large-scale research effort is being made to find an effective AIDS vaccine. Drugs such as zidovudine (formerly known as AZT) can slow down deterioration of the immune system, thus delaying death, but have serious side-effects. Health education initiatives, by encouraging the general population to modify their sexual behaviour and/or drug-injecting practices, have a central role in preventing further spread of the disease.

AIF *abbrev.* Australian Imperial Force.

Aiken, Howard Hathaway (1900–73) US mathematician and computer engineer, born in Hoboken, New Jersey. He spent a period working in industry, then joined the staff at Harvard (1939–61), where he built with colleagues the Automatic Sequence-Controlled Calculator (ASCC), or Harvard Mark I. Completed in 1943 and weighing 35 tons, this was the world's first program-controlled calculator. He was later professor at Miami (1961–73).

aikido *noun* a Japanese form of self-defence, based on a system of locks and holds and the movements of the attacker or opponent. [from Japanese *ai*, to harmonise + *ki*, breath + *do*, way]

ail *verb* **1** *intrans.* to be ill and weak. **2** *trans. old use* to cause pain or trouble to. [from Anglo-Saxon *eglan*, to trouble]

aileron *noun* a flap on the back of an aircraft wing which helps it balance. [a French diminutive of *aile*, wing]

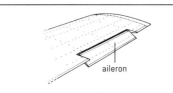

aileron

ailing *adj.* unwell; in poor health.

ailment *noun* an illness, especially a minor one.

Ailsa a female first name, after the islet *Ailsa Craig* on the Ayrshire coast of Scotland. [from 'island of Alfsigr', Old Norse *alf*, elf, supernatural + *sigi*, victory]

aim — *verb* **1** *trans., intrans.* (**aim at** *or* **for something**) to point or direct a weapon, attack, remark, etc at someone or something. **2** *intrans.* to plan, intend, or try. — *noun* **1** what a person, etc intends to do; the achievement aimed at. **2** the ability to hit what is aimed at: *good aim.*

— **take aim** to point a weapon at a target so as to be ready to fire.

[from Old French *esmer*, from Latin *aestimare*, to estimate]

aimless *adj.* without any purpose.

aimlessly *adv.* in an aimless way.

ain't *contr. colloq.* **1** am not; is not; are not. **2** has not; have not.

Aintree a racecourse in Aintree, Liverpool, since 1839 the location of the Grand National.

Ainu a people living on Hokkaido, Sakhalin, and other Japanese islands, historically physically distinct, but now intermarried with other Japanese and culturally assimilated; their own language and religion has largely disappeared. Traditionally hunters and fishermen, today many are factory workers and labourers.

air — *noun* **1** the mixture of gases, consisting mainly of oxygen, nitrogen, and carbon dioxide, which people and animals breathe and which forms the earth's atmosphere. **2** the space above and around the earth, where birds and aircraft fly. **3** an appearance, look, or manner. **4** (**airs**) behaviour intended to impress others, to show off, etc: *put on airs / airs and graces.* **5** a tune. **6** a breeze. — *verb* **1** *trans., intrans.* to hang (laundry) in a warm dry place to make it completely dry or to remove unpleasant smells. **b** *said of laundry* to be hung in a warm dry place for this purpose. **2** *trans., intrans.* to let fresh air into (a room, etc); (of a room, etc) to become cooler or fresher in this way. **3** to make warm (the sheets and blankets of a bed, especially one that has not been used recently). **4** to make (one's thoughts, opinions, etc) known publicly. **5** *old use* to make a show of or parade. **6** *trans., intrans. North Amer., esp. US* to broadcast or be broadcast on radio or television.

— **by air** in an aircraft.

a change of air a beneficial change from one's usual routine.

clear the air to remove or reduce misunderstanding or disagreement by speaking openly and honestly.

in the air 1 *said of projects, etc* uncertain or undecided. **2** *said of opinions, news, etc* being generally considered, thought, or talked about.

into thin air mysteriously and leaving no trace.

off the air no longer or not yet broadcasting on radio or television.

on the air broadcasting on radio or television.

take the air *old use* to go for a walk.

take to the air to start to fly.

walk on air to be elated.

[from Old French, from Greek *aer*]

airbag *noun* a safety device installed in some motor vehicles, consisting of a bag which inflates automatically if the vehicle is involved in a collision, preventing the driver and front-seat passenger from coming into immediate contact with the steering-wheel and dashboard.

air base a centre from which military aircraft operate.

air bed an inflated mattress.

airborne *adj.* **1** *said of aircraft* flying in the air, having just taken off. **2** transported by air.

Airborne Warning and Control System (ABBREV. **AWACS**) a radar system mounted on an aircraft and able to detect and track hostile intruders at long range, and direct friendly fighters to intercept them.

air brake a brake on large vehicles operated by compressed air.

air brick a brick with small holes, put into the side of a building to allow ventilation.

airbrush — *noun* an instrument for painting which uses compressed air to form a spray. — *verb* to paint using an air brush.

◇ The airbrush is mainly used by commercial artists and illustrators to create tonal gradations of almost photographic quality, and to produce large areas of flat colour, as well as fine line.

Airbus *trademark* **1** an aeroplane first flown in 1987. It was the first form of commercial transport other than Concorde to use fly by wire control (controlled by computer and operated electronically, not mechanically) for normal operations. Standard accommodation is for a flight crew of two, four cabin attendants, and a maximum of 179 passengers in a high-density layout. **2** any aircraft which can carry a large number of passengers, especially on short flights.

air chief marshal *Brit.* an air force officer equal in rank to a general or admiral.

air commodore *Brit.* a senior officer in the air force.

air-conditioned *adj., said of a building, etc* equipped with air-conditioning.

air-conditioner *noun* an apparatus for providing air-conditioning.

air-conditioning *noun* **1** the apparatus used to control the temperature, dryness or dampness, and sometimes the cleanness, of the air in a building, room, etc. **2** the controlling of room temperature, etc using such apparatus.

air cover the use of aircraft to protect against enemy attack.

aircraft *noun* (PL. **aircraft**) any of various types of machine which can fly in the air.

aircraft carrier a large naval warship with a flat deck, serving as a base for military aircraft.

◇ The first aircraft carrier, HMS *Furious* (1918), was a battle cruiser fitted with forward and after flight decks. In 1925 it was refitted with an island bridge on the starboard side of a continuous flight deck, and this became the standard carrier layout. By World War II, the USA and Japan had developed carriers to hold many more aircraft, and after the war technical innovations such as the steam catapult, the angled flight deck, and the mirror landing sight were introduced. Today, the largest carriers belong to the US navy, eg USS *Nimitz* (323m long, with a crew of 5 684, and carrying 90 aircraft). The first nuclear-powered carrier, the USS *Enterprise*, was completed in 1961.

aircraftman *or* **aircraftwoman**. *noun Brit.* a man or woman of the lowest rank in the air force.

aircrew *noun* the people in an aircraft who are responsible for flying it and looking after the passengers.

air cushion 1 a cushion that can be filled with air. **2** a pocket of air used for supporting a hovercraft, etc.

Airdrie POP (1981) 46 000, a town in Monklands district, Strathclyde, W central Scotland. It is 17km/11mi E of Glasgow, falling within the Clydeside urban area.

air-drop — *noun* a delivery of military equipment, troops, supplies, etc by air. — *verb* to deliver by aircraft.

airfield *noun* a small airport, usually with few buildings, where private or military aircraft are kept, and can take off and land.

air force that part of a country's defence forces which uses aircraft for fighting.

airgun *noun* a gun that uses air under pressure to fire small pellets.

airhead *noun slang* a stupid or dull person.

air hostess *Brit.* a woman member of an airliner's crew, responsible for the comfort of passengers.

airily *adv.* in an airy manner; jauntily.

airiness *noun* an airy or jaunty manner or state.

airing *noun* **1** the act of airing (laundry, a room, the sheets, etc on a bed, etc) or fact of being aired. **2** the stating and discussing of opinions, etc publicly. **3** a short walk, etc taken in order to get some fresh air.

airing-cupboard *noun* a heated cupboard in which laundry is put to become completely dry and warm.

air lane a route through the air regularly used by aircraft.

airless *adj.* **1** *said of the weather* unpleasantly warm, with no wind. **2** *said of a room* lacking fresh air; stuffy.

air letter same as AEROGRAMME.

airlift — *noun* the transporting of large numbers of people or large amounts of goods in aircraft when other routes are blocked. — *verb* to transport in this way.

rolling— ailerons roll aircraft from side to side

pitching— elevators move nose up and down

yawing— rudder moves nose left or right

aircraft movements

airline *noun* a company or organization which provides a regular transport service for passengers or cargo by aircraft.

airliner *noun* a large passenger aeroplane.

airlock *noun* **1** a bubble of air in a pipe which prevents air from flowing along the pipe. **2** a small room with controllable air pressure and two entrances, which allows a person to pass between places with different air pressures (eg between outer space and a spaceship) without air escaping or between air and water (eg between the sea and a submarine) without water getting in.

airmail *noun* **1** the system of carrying mail by air. **2** mail carried by air.

airman *or* **airwoman** *noun* a pilot or member of the crew of an aeroplane, especially in an air force.

air miss a situation in which two aircraft on different routes come dangerously close together.

airplane *noun North Amer.* an aeroplane.

air plant *Bot.* a plant that grows on another plant and uses it for support, but is not a parasite. — Also called *epiphyte*.

air pocket an area of reduced pressure in the air or a downward current which can cause an aircraft to suddenly lose height.

air pollution *Environ.* the presence of gases, smoke, dust, fumes, and other contaminants in the atmosphere at levels considered to be detrimental to living organisms. Air pollution is often a result of human activity, eg the burning of fossil fuels in industrial processes, emissions from car exhausts. Acid rain is a form of air pollution.

airport *noun* a place where civil aircraft arrive and depart, with facilities for passengers and cargo, etc.

air pressure the pressure exerted by the air as a result of the movements of air molecules.

air pump an instrument for pumping air out or in.

air raid an attack by aircraft.

air resistance *Aeron.* the drag experienced by a body passing through air.

air-rifle *noun* a rifle that is fired by air under pressure.

air sac *Zool.* **1** in birds, any of nine thin-walled extensions of the lung, which increase the efficiency of breathing. **2** in insects, an extension of the trachea (one of various tubes through which air moves into the body tissues).

air-sea rescue the use of both aircraft and boats to rescue people from the sea.

airship *noun* a type of aircraft that consists of a long gas-filled balloon-like structure with an engine to make it move and a room-like structure under it for passengers or cargo.

airsick *adj.* sick due to the motion of an aircraft.

airsickness *noun* nausea affecting travellers by air.

airspace *noun* the part of the sky directly above a country, considered as part of the country.

airstrip *noun* a strip of ground where aircraft can land and take off but which has no facilities.

air terminal an office or other place in a town from where passengers are taken, usually by bus, to an airport nearby.

airtight *adj.* **1** *said of a container, etc* which air cannot get into, out of, or through. **2** *said of an opinion, argument, etc* having no weak points.

airtime *noun* the length of time given to a particular item or programme on television or radio.

air-to-air *adj., said of a weapon* fired from one aircraft to another in flight.

air-traffic control a system or organization which manages the passage of aircraft and sends instructions to aircraft by radio communication.

air vice-marshal a senior rank in the air force.

airwaves *pl. noun* the radio waves used by radio and television stations for their broadcasts.

airway *noun* **1** a route regularly followed by aircraft. **2** (**airways**) an airline.

airwoman see AIRMAN.

airworthiness *noun* the condition of being airworthy.

airworthy *adj., said of aircraft* in a condition to fly safely.

Airy, Sir George Biddell (1801–92) English astronomer, born in Alnwick, Lincolnshire. He graduated from Cambridge (1823), where he later became professor. From 1835 to 1881 he was Astronomer Royal and Director of the Greenwich Observatory. In wide-ranging research he applied the wave theory of light to analysis of the structure of images of point sources formed by lenses, investigated planetary theory, pioneered the transmission of telegraphic time signals for the railways, achieved worldwide acceptance of the Greenwich zero meridian, and determined the mean density of the Earth through pendulum experiments.

airy *adj.* (**airier**, **airiest**) **1** with plenty of fresh, cool air. **2** not thinking about or dealing with something as seriously as one should; flippant. **3** lively; light-hearted.

airy-fairy *adj. colloq.* showing or suggesting a lack of sense or good planning; not based on facts or on awareness of real situations.

aisle *noun* **1** a passage between rows of seats, eg in a church or theatre. **2** the side part of the inside of a church. [from Latin *ala*, wing; spelling influenced by ISLE]

Ait-Ben-Haddou, Ksar of a walled village in S central Morocco. It is an example of a pre-Saharan ksar, or fortified village, with red earth houses and decorated kasbahs clinging to the steep side of an escarpment. It is a World Heritage site.

aitch *noun* the letter H or h.
— **drop one's aitches** to fail to pronounce the sound of the letter *h* when it comes at the beginning of words. [from Old French *ache*]

aitchbone *noun* **1** the rump bone in cattle. **2** a cut of beef from this. [from Old French *nache*, from Latin *natis*, buttocks]

Aix-en-Provence POP (1990) 131 000, an ancient city in Bouches-du-Rhône department, Provence-Alpes-Côte d'Azur region, SW France. Situated 30km/19mi N of Marseilles, it lies in a fertile plain surrounded by mountains. The town was founded by Romans as Aquae Sextiae in 123 BC. Since the 15c it has been an important centre for Provençal literature. The artist Paul Cézanne (1839–1906) was born and died here. NOTABLE FEATURES St Saver Cathedral (11c–16c); Baroque town hall (1658); art galleries; thermal springs; fountains; casino.

Ajaccio POP (1990) 59 000, the seaport capital of the Island of Corsica, France. It lies on the W coast, at the head of the Golfe de Ajaccio. Founded by the Genoese in 1492, it was made capital by Napoleon in 1811. It is Corsica's second largest port. NOTABLE FEATURES Maison Bonaparte (the birthplace of Napoleon); casino.

Ajanta Caves a group of 29 Buddhist cave-temples and monasteries cut into cliffs over R Wagurna, near Ajanta, Maharashtra, India. The caves, which were built from the 2c BC to the 7c AD, are noted for their wall paintings. It is a World Heritage site.

ajar *adj., adv.* partly open. [from Anglo-Saxon *on*, on + *cierr*, turn]

Ajax, Greek **Aias** the name of two Greek heroes during the Trojan war. **1** the son of Telamon, King of Salamis, known as Telamonian Ajax. He was proverbial for his size and strength, and when he was defeated by Odysseus in the contest for the armour of the dead Achilles, he went mad and killed himself. **2** the son of Oileus, King of Locris. When he returned from Troy, he provoked the anger of the gods and was killed by Poseidon as he reached the shore of Greece.

Ajman POP (1985) 64 000, the smallest of the seven member states in the United Arab Emirates. AREA c.250sq km/100sq mi. It is entirely surrounded by the territory of Shariqah, except on the coast. CAPITAL Ajman. Relatively undeveloped, it has no significant oil or gas reserves yet discovered.

AK *abbrev.* Alaska.

AKA *or* **aka** *abbrev.* also known as.

Akahito, Yamabe no (8c) Japanese poet, one of the 'twin stars' (with Hitomaro) of the great anthology of classical Japanese poetry known as the *Manyoshu* (Collection of a Myriad Leaves).

Akashi–Kaikyo Bridge a major steel suspension bridge across the Akashi Straits between Honshu and Shikoku, Japan, begun in 1978 and due for completion in 1998. It will carry a road and railway on two decks and have a main span of 1 990m.

Akbar the Great, originally **Jalal ud-Din Muhammad Akbar** (1542–1605) Mughal Emperor of India, born in Umarkot, Sind. He succeeded his father, Humayun, in 1556, and took over from his regent in 1560. He soon gained control of the whole of India north of the Vindhya Mts. Roads were constructed, a uniform system of weights and measures established, and taxation adjusted. He was unusually tolerant towards non-Muslims, and greatly encouraged literature and the arts.

Akela the old wolf pack-leader in Rudyard Kipling's *The Jungle Book*.

Akhenaton *or* **Akh(e)naten**, also called **Amenhotep** (**Amenophis**) **IV** (14c BC) King of Egypt, of the 18th dynasty, who renounced the old gods (especially Amun) and introduced a monotheistic cult worshipping the sun god Aten. One of his wives was Nefertiti.

Akihito (1933–) Emperor of Japan (1989–), the eldest son of Emperor Hirohito, born in Tokyo. Invested as Crown Prince in 1952, in 1959 he became the first Crown Prince to marry a commoner (Michiko Shoda, 1934–). He has three children: Crown Prince Naruhito (1960–), Prince Fumihito (1963–), and Princess Sayako (1969–). He is a regular contributor to the Japanese Icthyological Society's journal, and is especially interested in conservation.

akimbo *adj., adv.* with hand on hip and elbow bent outward. [from Middle English *in kenebowe*, in a sharp bend]

akin *adj.* **1** similar; of the same kind. **2** related by blood. [from A-² + KIN]

Akkadian — *noun* an ancient Semitic language of the Afro-Asiatic family. It was used in Babylonia and Assyria and had a substantial literature written in cuneiform script. It takes its name from the ancient kingdom of Akkad. — *adj.* relating to or spoken or written in Akkadian.

Akosombo Dam a major rock-fill dam (141m high) on the Volta River in Ghana, completed in 1965. It impounds L Volta and has the capacity to generate 786 megawatts of hydroelectricity.

Akrotiri a bay on the S coast of Cyprus. Its main port town is Limassol. There is a British base on the peninsula separating Akrotiri Bay on the E from Episkopi Bay on the W.

Aksakov, Sergei (Timofeyevitch) (1791–1859) Russian novelist, born in Ufa, Orenburg. He held government posts at St Petersburg and Moscow before he turned to literature in 1832 after meeting the writer Gogol. His works, which include *The Blizzard* (1834) and *Chronicles of a Russian Family* (1846–56), show his love of country sports and nature.

Aksum an ancient city in N Ethiopia. It was the capital of a powerful kingdom (1c–7c AD), and dominated trade — particularly in ivory and skins — between the Sudanese Nile Valley and the Roman Mediterranean. It is a World Heritage site.

Akureyri POP (1983) 14 000, the capital of Nordurland, N Iceland, 436km/271mi NE of Reykjavík. It is Iceland's second largest town, and the centre of trade, industry, and education in N Iceland. It attained municipal status in 1862. NOTABLE FEATURES three memorial museums to poets; Lystigardurinn Park (over 400 species of Icelandic plants).

AL *abbrev.* **1** Alabama. **2** *as an international vehicle mark* Albania.

Al *symbol Chem.* aluminium.

-al *suffix* **1** forming adjectives from nouns: *parental*. **2** forming nouns denoting an action or occurrence: *arrival*.

Ala. *abbrev.* Alabama.

Alabama POP (1990) 4.1m, a state in SE USA, divided into 67 counties, bounded S by Florida and the Gulf of Mexico. It is known as the 'Heart of Dixie', the 'Camellia State', or the 'Cotton State'. AREA 133 911sq km/51 705sq mi. PHYSICAL DESCRIPTION rivers include the Alabama (formed by the confluence of the Tallapoosa and Coosa rivers), Tombigbee, Mobile, Tennessee, and Chattahoochee; the highest point is Mt Cheaha (734m); the NE is mountainous, separated from the S coastal plain by the rolling plain of the Appalachian Piedmont. HISTORY first permanently settled by the French at Mobile in 1711; N Alabama became part of the USA in 1783, the remainder being acquired by the Louisiana Purchase in 1803; in 1819 it was the 22nd state to be admitted to the Union, but seceded in 1861; slavery was abolished in 1865; refused to ratify the 14th Amendment to the US Constitution and was placed under military rule in 1867; readmitted to the Union in 1868, but Federal troops remained until 1876; in the 1950s and 1960s many civil rights protests occurred in the area. CAPITAL Montgomery. CHIEF TOWNS Birmingham, Mobile, Huntsville. ECONOMY following the boll-weevil blight of 1915, agriculture has diversified; cattle, poultry; cotton, soya beans, peanuts; chemicals; textiles; paper products; processed food; the iron and steel industry is centred on Birmingham; coal, oil; stone; lumbering; fishing.

alabaster — *noun* a type of white stone used for ornaments, etc. — *adj.* of or like alabaster. [from Old French *alabastre*]

à la carte *said of a meal in a restaurant* with each dish priced and ordered separately. [French, = from the menu]

alacrity *noun* quick and cheerful enthusiasm. [from Latin *alacritas*]

Alain-Fournier, Henri (1886–1914) French writer, born in Sologne. He left a few short stories, and one completed novel, the nostalgic *Le Grand Meaulnes* (The Lost Domain, 1913). He was killed at St Rémy in World War I.

Alamo a battle fought during the 1836 Texan War of Independence against Mexico, when 180 Texans and US citizens held the fortified mission of Alamo against a large number of Mexican troops. They held out for 12 days until the last survivors were overwhelmed.

à la mode in fashion; according to current fashion. [French, = in fashion]

Alan a male first name. [of Celtic origin, possibly derived from a word meaning 'rock']

Alanbrooke (of Brookeborough), Alan Francis Brooke, 1st Viscount (1883–1963) British soldier, born in Bagnères-de-Bigorre, France. He joined the Royal Field Artillery in 1902, and fought in World War I. A leading strategist in World War II, he commanded the 2nd corps of the British Expeditionary Force in France (1940), and was Commander-in-Chief Home Forces, Chief of the Imperial General Staff (1941–6), and Churchill's principal strategic adviser at the conferences with Roosevelt and Stalin.

Åland see AHVENANMAA.

alanine *noun Biochem.* an amino acid that is found in proteins. [from German *Alanin*]

A la recherche du temps perdu (Remembrance of Things Past) a novel in seven sections by Marcel Proust (1913–27). It is a reflective circular narrative which explores the power of the memory and the unconscious. Its main thrust is the final realization by the narrator Marcel of his vocation as a writer.

Alaric I (c.370–410 AD) King of the Visigoths from 395, and the leader of the troops which sacked Rome in 410. It was the first time in 800 years that the city had been captured by foreigners, and it signified the beginning of the end of the Western Roman Empire.

alarm — *noun* **1** sudden fear produced by awareness of danger. **2** a noise warning of danger. **3** a bell, etc which sounds to warn of danger or, eg on a clock, to waken a person from sleep. **4** an alarm clock. — *verb* **1** to frighten. **2** to warn of danger. **3** to fit an alarm on (a house, car, etc). — **give** *or* **raise** *or* **sound the alarm** to give warning of danger by shouting, ringing a bell, etc. [from Old French *alarme*, from Italian *all'arme*, to arms]

alarm clock a clock that can be set to make a noise at a particular time to wake someone up.

alarming *adj.* disturbing or frightening.

alarmingly *adv.* so as to alarm or cause anxiety.

alarmism *noun* the spreading of unnecessary alarm.

alarmist — *noun* a person who feels or spreads unnecessary alarm. — *adj.* causing unnecessary alarm.

Alas. *abbrev.* Alaska.

alas *interj. old use, literary* used to express grief or misfortune. [from Old French *ha*, ah + *las*, wretched, from Latin *lassus* weary]

Alasdair a male first name, generally given to Scots. [a Gaelic form of ALEXANDER]

Alaska POP (1990) 587 000, a US state in the extreme NW corner of the continent, separated from the rest of the nation by Canada. It has 23 boroughs and is known as 'The Last Frontier'. AREA 1 518 748sq km/586 412sq mi. Alaska is bounded by the Beaufort Sea and the Arctic Ocean in the N, the Chukchi Sea, Bering Strait, and Bering Sea in the W, the Gulf of Alaska and the Pacific Ocean in the S, and Canada (Yukon Territory and British Columbia) in the E. It is the largest state, but the least populated. PHYSICAL DESCRIPTION one third of the area lies within the Arctic Circle; rivers include the Yukon (with tributaries the Porcupine, Tanana, and Koyukuk), Colville, Kuskokwim, Susitna and Copper; the low North Slope in the N rises to the Brooks Range, a part of the Rocky Mts; in the SW are the Kuskokwim Mts, the Aleutian Is and the Aleutian Range; the Chugach Mts lie along the S coast, and the Wrangell Mts are in the SE; the highest point is Mt McKinley (6 194m). HISTORY Russians made the first permanent settlement in 1792 on Kodiak I; the area was managed by the Russian-American Fur Company from 1799 to

1861, and there was a period of decline when the Russians withdrew from the area; bought by the USA in 1867 (known as Seward's Folly, after the chief US negotiator); gold was discovered in 1889 (at Nome) and 1902 (at Fairbanks); territorial status was achieved in 1912; the Aleutian islands of Attu and Kiska were occupied by the Japanese in 1942–3; Alaska became the 49th state of the Union in 1959; large oil reserves were discovered in 1968 (the Alaska Pipeline from Prudhoe Bay to Valdez was completed in 1977). CAPITAL Juneau. CHIEF TOWN Anchorage. ECONOMY oil, natural gas; wide range of minerals; food processing; paper; lumber; seafood; tourism. The balance between industrial development and landscape preservation is an ongoing controversy. NOTABLE FEATURES eight national parks.

Alaska, Gulf of the N part of the Pacific Ocean, between the Alaskan Peninsula in the W and the mainland Alaskan Panhandle in the E. The warm Alaskan Current keeps ports ice-free. Valdez is the main port.

Alaska Highway an all-weather road which runs from Dawson Creek in British Columbia, Canada, to Fairbanks in Alaska, linking the state to the N American highway system. It was built in 1942 to supply military forces stationed in Alaska during World War II.

al-Assad, Hafez see ASSAD, HAFEZ AL-.

Alastor in Greek mythology, an avenging demon or power. The name was used by Shelley as the title of a poem outlining a myth of his own making, in which a young poet is led through various symbolic states and ultimately to destruction.

alb *noun* a long white garment reaching to the feet, worn by some Christian priests. [from Latin *albus*, white]

alb

Albacete 1 POP (1991) 129 000, the capital of Albacete province, Castilla-La Mancha, SE Spain, 251km/156mi SE of Madrid. It is the centre of the fertile La Mancha wine-producing region. NOTABLE FEATURE cathedral (16c). **2** a hilly province in SE Spain with Albacete as its capital.

Alba Iulia, German **Karlsburg**, Latin **Apulum** POP (1990e) 73 000, the capital of Alba county, W central Romania, on the R Mureş Founded by the Romans in the 2c, it was formerly the seat of the princes of Transylvania. NOTABLE FEATURES Romanesque church (12c); Bathyaneum Building.

Albania, Albanian **Shqipni**, **Shqipri**, **Shqipëri**, official name (1991) **Republic of Albania**, Albanian **Republica e Shqipërisë** POP (1992e) 3.4m, a republic in the W part of the Balkan Peninsula, divided into 26 districts (*rrethet*). AREA 28 748sq km/11 097sq mi. It is bounded on the W by the Adriatic Sea, N by Yugoslavia, NE by Macedonia, and SE by Greece. CAPITAL Tirana. CHIEF TOWNS Shkodër, Durrës, Vlorë, Korçë, Elbasan. TIME ZONE GMT +1. Constitutionally an atheist state, the population is mainly Muslim with some Orthodox and Catholic Christians. OFFICIAL LANGUAGE Albanian.

Albania

CURRENCY the lek. PHYSICAL DESCRIPTION a mountainous country, relatively inaccessible and untravelled; the N Albanian Alps rise to 2 692m; rivers include the Drin, Shkumbin, Seman, Vijosë; there are many lakes throughout the country; half the population is concentrated in the W low-lying area, which occupies only one quarter of the country's territory. CLIMATE a Mediterranean-type climate: hot and dry on the plains in summer (average Jul temperature 24°–25°C), with frequent thunderstorms; winters are mild, damp, and cyclonic (average Jan temperature 8°–9°C); winters in the mountains are often severe, with snow cover lasting for several months; annual mountain precipitation exceeds 1 000mm. HISTORY independence followed the end of Turkish rule in 1912, but Italian forces occupied the country from 1914 until 1920; it became a republic in 1925, and a monarchy in 1928, under King Zog I; occupied by Germany and Italy in World War II, it became a new republic in 1946; it was involved in a dispute with the Soviet Union in 1961, and withdrew from the Warsaw Pact in 1968; close links with China were maintained; the Socialist People's Republic was instituted in 1976. GOVERNMENT the first free elections were held in 1991 as the country began to move towards democratic reform and westernization. ECONOMY oil, mining, chemicals, and natural gas; hydroelectric power plants on several rivers; agricultural product processing; textiles; oil products; cement; main crops are wheat, sugar-beet, maize, potatoes, fruit, and oats; in the early 1990s the economy declined and severe food shortages led to violent rioting. All industry is nationalized; the economy is also committed to eliminating private farming through the progressive transformation of farm co-operatives into state farms; forest land occupies 47% of Albanian territory.

Albanian — *noun* **1** a person born in, or a citizen of, Albania. **2** the language spoken in Albania. — *adj.* of Albania, its inhabitants, or its language.

◇ Albanian constitutes a single branch of the Indo-European family. Spoken by some three million people in Albania and neighbouring areas of Greece, Italy, and former Yugoslavia, it has two main dialects, Tosk and Gheg. The history of the language is obscure; it has no written records before the 15c and in the modern form there are a large number of words borrowed from other languages.

al-Banna, Hassan see BANNA, HASSAN AL-.

Albany POP (1991) 19 000, a resort and seaport in Western Australia, situated in Lower Great Southern statistical division. Founded in 1826, it is one of the oldest towns in Australia. The city was once used as a stopover point for vessels on their way to India.

Albany POP (1990) 101 000, the capital of New York State, USA, in Albany County, in the E of the state. It stands on the Hudson R, 232km/144mi N of New York City. It is the second oldest continuously inhabited settlement in the 13 original colonies. Settled by the Dutch in 1614, it became state capital in 1797. NOTABLE FEATURES State Capitol; Schuyler Mansion.

Albany Congress a meeting (1754) in Albany, New York, of representatives from seven British colonies, at which Benjamin Franklin proposed his 'plan of union' to unite the separate American British colonies. Although the plan was rejected by both the colonial governments and the Crown, it served as a model for the joint action of the mainland colonies in the American Revolution.

albatross *noun* a large, long-winged gull-like sea bird of the southern oceans. [from Portuguese *alcatraz*, pelican]

albatross

Albee, Edward (1928–) US dramatist, born near Washington, DC. His major works are *The Zoo Story* (1958), a one-act duologue on the lack of communication in modern society, *The American Dream* (1960), and *Who's Afraid of Virginia Woolf?* (1962, filmed 1966), a searing analysis of a failing marriage.

albeit *conj.* even if; although. [from Middle English *al be it*, although it be]

Albéniz, Isaac (Manuel Francisco) (1860–1909) Spanish composer and pianist, born in Camprodón, Catalonia. He studied under Liszt and became known especially for his picturesque piano works based on Spanish folk music. He also wrote several operas.

Albert, Prince (1819–61) prince-consort of Queen Victoria of Great Britain and Ireland, born in the Schloss Rosenau, near Coburg, Germany, the youngest son of the Duke of Saxe-Coburg-Gotha. He married his cousin Queen Victoria in 1840, and became her chief adviser, first as Consort (1842), then as Prince Consort (1857). He was kept out of politics by the public's and the government's distrust of a foreigner, but he encouraged the arts and social and industrial reforms, and it was largely on his initiative that the Great Exhibition of 1851 took place.

Albert a male first name. [from German *adal*, noble + *behrt*, bright]

Albert, Lake see MOBUTO SÉSÉ SEKO.

Albert I (1875–1934) King of the Belgians (1909–34), born in Brussels. He succeeded his uncle, Leopold II, and gained respect for his conduct while his kingdom was in German hands (1914–18) and during the subsequent restoration. He was killed by a fall while rock-climbing in the Ardennes and was succeeded by his son, Leopold III.

Alberta POP (1991) 2.5m, a province in W Canada, bordered in the S by the USA. AREA 661 190sq km/255 219sq mi. PHYSICAL DESCRIPTION it is mainly a rolling plain, with the edge of the Rocky Mts in the W; rivers, lakes, and forests are in the N, with much open prairie; treeless prairie lies in the S; drained in the N by the Peace, Slave, and Athabasca rivers, and in the S by the North Saskatchewan, Red Deer, and Bow rivers; largest lakes are L Athabasca, L Claire, and Lesser Slave L; it has several national parks. HISTORY the province was originally part of Rupert's Land, the territory granted to the Hudson's Bay Company in 1670; sovereignty was acquired by the Dominion in 1870; it achieved province status in 1905. GOVERNMENT it is governed by a Lieutenant-Governor and an elected 79-member Legislative Assembly. CAPITAL Edmonton. CHIEF TOWNS Calgary, Medicine Hat. ECONOMY oil, natural gas, coal; grain; cattle; timber products; food processing; chemicals; fabricated metals; tourism.

Alberti, Leon Battista (1404–72) Italian architect, born in Genoa. A major Renaissance figure, he was also skilled as a musician, painter, poet, and philosopher. His designs include the Churches of San Francesco in Rimini and San Maria Novella in Florence.

Albertina an art gallery founded in 1768 by Duke Albert of Saxony-Tescha. Since 1795 it has been housed in the former Taroucca Palace in Vienna. Its holdings include a major collection of graphic material.

Albert Medal in the UK, a civilian decoration, instituted (1866) in memory of Prince Albert to reward gallantry in saving life. In October 1971 all surviving holders of the medal exchanged it for the George Cross.

Albert Nile the upper reach of the R Nile in NW Uganda. It flows out from the NE corner of L Albert, close to the Victoria Nile Delta, and continues NE into the Sudan. The river is known in Sudan as the Bahr el Jebel until its meeting point with the Bahr el Ghazal to form the White Nile.

Albertus Magnus, St, Count of Bollstädt, known as the **Doctor Universalis** (c.1200–80) German philosopher, bishop, and Doctor of the Church, born in Lauingen. He joined the Dominican order and became a teacher of theology, whose pupils included Thomas Aquinas. In 1254 he became provincial of the Dominicans in Germany, and in 1260 was named Bishop of Ratisbon. In 1262 he retired to his convent in Cologne to devote himself to literary pursuits. He excelled all his contemporaries in the breadth of his learning, and helped to bring together theology and Aristotelianism. He was canonized in 1932 and his feast day is 15 Nov.

Albigenses or **Albigensians** the followers of a form of Christianity especially strong in the 11c and 12c in the town of Albi, SW France. It was derived from 3c followers of the Persian religious teacher Mani (the founder of Manichaeism), whose ideas gradually spread along trade routes to Europe. Formerly known as Cathars, and called Bogomiles in Bulgaria, they believed life on earth to be a struggle between good (spirit) and evil (matter), and they believed in the transmigration of souls; some were rigidly ascetic. Condemned by Rome and the Inquisition, they were devastated in the early 13c crusade against them, which also broke down the distinctive civilization of Provence, France.

albinism *noun* the condition of being an albino.

albino *noun* (PL. **albinos**) in an animal or human being, an abnormal lack of pigmentation in the hair, skin, and eyes; in a plant, a total or partial lack of chlorophyll or other pigments. [from Portuguese, from Latin *albus*, white]

Albion a poetic name of Celtic origin referring originally to Great Britain, and later to England specifically. In 1793, at the start of the wars with Revolutionary France, the Marquis of Ximénèz declared: 'Let us attack in her own waters perfidious Albion'.

Alboin (d.574) King of the Lombards (561–72), who fought against the Ostrogoths. In 568 he invaded Italy, and established Pavia as the

Lombard capital. He was generally considered to be a just ruler, but at a feast in Verona he made his queen drink from her father's skull, and she incited her lover to murder him.

Albufeira POP (1991) 26 000, a fishing village and resort in Faro district, S Portugal. It lies in a bay on the S coast, 43km/27mi W of Faro and is Portugal's busiest seaside resort. NOTABLE FEATURE some Moorish-style architecture.

album *noun* **1** a book with blank pages for holding photographs, stamps, etc. **2** a long-playing record. [from Latin *album*, blank tablet, from *albus*, white]

albumen *noun* the white part of an egg. [from Latin *albumen*, white of egg, from *albus*, white]

albumin *noun* a protein found in egg white and blood.

albuminuria *noun* *Medicine* the presence of albumin (a soluble protein) in the urine, sometimes but not always associated with kidney or heart disease. [from Latin *albumen*, from *albus* white]

Albuquerque, Affonso d', known as **the Great** (1453–1515) Portuguese Viceroy of the Indies, born near Lisbon. He landed on the Malabar coast of India in 1502, and conquered Goa, Ceylon, the Sundra Is, Malacca, and (in 1515) the island of Hormuz in the Persian Gulf. He gained a reputation for wisdom and justice, but had enemies at court who effected his fall from office, shortly before his death.

Albuquerque POP (1990) 481 000, the seat of Bernalillo County, central New Mexico, USA, on the Rio Grande. The largest city in the state, it was settled in 1706. It was a military post during the Mexican War (1846–70) and achieved city status in 1890. It is a health resort, an industrial centre, and the base for many federal agencies (eg Atomic Energy Commission). NOTABLE FEATURES Church of San Felipe de Neri (1706); the Old Town Plaza; National Atomic Museum.

Alcalá de Henares, ancient **Complutim**, Arabic **Alkal'a** POP (1991) 159 000, a town in Madrid province, central Spain. It stands on the R Henares, 25km/15mi NE of Madrid. Its famous university, founded in 1498, moved to Madrid in 1836. The town was rebuilt after the Civil War (1936–9). The author Miguel de Cervantes was born here in 1547. NOTABLE FEATURES 16c College of San Ildefonso (former university); Church of St Mary.

Alcazar the name of several palaces built by the Moors in cities of S Spain. In 1936 the Alcazar of Toledo was the scene of a protracted siege during the Spanish Civil War.

Alcestis in Greek mythology, the wife of Admetus. He was doomed to die, and she saved him by offering to die in his place. The action so impressed Heracles that he wrestled with the messenger of death and brought her back to life.

Alchemist, The a play by Ben Jonson (1610). Considered one of his masterpieces, it is a comedy about a fake alchemist (Subtle) who hoodwinks a variety of people by promising them their desires.

alchemist *noun* a person who practises or studies alchemy.

alchemy *noun* the forerunner of modern chemistry, which centred around attempts to convert ordinary metals such as lead into gold, and to discover a universal remedy for illness, known as the *elixir of life*. Alchemy originated in Alexandria, and was practised from about 300 BC until about 1600 AD. It was popular in Europe during the Middle Ages. [from Latin *alchymia*, from Arabic *al*, the + *kimiya*, from Greek *kemeia*, transmutation]

Alcibiades (c.450–404 BC) Athenian statesman and general from the aristocratic Alcmaeonid family. A ward of Pericles and a pupil of Socrates, he was a leader against Sparta

in the Peloponnesian War, and a commander of the Sicilian expedition (415 BC). He was then accused of sacrilege in Athens and fled to Sparta, where he was influential in the defeat of Athens in Sicily (413 BC). He fell out with the Spartans (412 BC), returned his allegiance to the Athenians, and won several notable victories in the E Aegean. In 406 BC he was blamed for the Athenian defeat off Notium, and went into voluntary exile. He was assassinated in Phrygia.

Alcmaeon in Greek mythology, the son of Amphiaraos. He was commanded by Apollo to lead the expedition of the Epigoni (the sons of the original Seven who marched on Thebes) against Thebes. He killed his mother to avenge his father's death, and was pursued by the Furies until he came to a land which had not seen the Sun at the time of his mother's death; he found this recently-emerged land at the mouth of the R Achelous. He was killed by Phegeus and his sons.

Alcmaeon (fl. 520 BC) Greek philosopher, born in Crotona, Italy, the first recorded anatomist in history. He was a pioneer of dissection, and advanced the Pythagorean doctrine that health depends on the equal balance of opposites (such as dry and wet, hot and cold). He also founded original medical theories based on empirical surgical practice.

Alcmaeonids an aristocratic Athenian family to which many prominent Athenian politicians belonged. It was particularly influential in the period 632–415 BC.

Alcobaça, Monastery of a Cistercian monastery, founded in 1152 in the town of Alcobaça, W central Portugal. It is a World Heritage site.

Alcock, Sir John William (1892–1919) English aviator, born in Manchester, who with Arthur Whitten Brown was the first to fly the Atlantic Ocean (14 Jun 1919). The trip, from Newfoundland to Ireland, was made in a Vickers-Vimy machine, and took 16 hours 27 minutes. Soon after, he died of injuries received in an aeroplane accident.

alcohol *noun* **1** any of a large group of organic chemical compounds that contain one or more hydroxyl (-OH) groups and react with acids to form esters, eg ethanol (C_2H_5OH), methanol (CH_3OH). Alcohols are used as solvents for dyes, resins, varnishes, perfume oils, etc, and as fuels and antiseptic medical products, eg surgical spirit. **2** ethanol (C_2H_5OH), a colourless volatile flammable liquid that is produced by fermentation of the sugar in fruit or cereals, and is used as an intoxicant in alcoholic beverages. **3** any beverage containing this substance, eg wine, beer, spirits. [from Arabic *al*, the + *kohl*, kohl]

alcohol: ethanol

alcohol abuse excessive drinking of alcoholic liquor, to the point where it becomes harmful.

alcoholic — *adj.* of, containing, or caused by alcohol. — *noun* a person who is addicted to alcohol liquor.

alcoholically *adv.* in terms of alcohol or alcoholic content.

Alcoholics Anonymous a self-help group for alcoholics trying to stop drinking. Founded (1935) in the USA by 'Bill W' (William Griffith Wilson, 1895–1971) and 'Dr Bob S' (Robert Holbrook Smith, 1879–1950), it now consists of local groups worldwide where members (identified by first names only) meet to give each other support.

alcoholism *noun* **1** a severe and potentially fatal condition caused by physical dependence on alcohol, habitual consumption of which occurs to such an extent that it interferes with normal everyday activities and impairs physical and mental health. **2** used loosely to refer to heavy drinking habits.
◇ Alcoholism occurs in all social classes, although there is evidence that those suffering from anxiety or depression are most susceptible, with a recent notable increase in the disorder among young mothers, and the young and long-term unemployed. Excessive alcohol consumption causes impaired memory and judgement, loss of physical co-ordination, nutritional and emotional disorders, and may eventually cause brain damage, cirrhosis of the liver, or heart disease. There are various methods of treatment, including use of the drug disulfiram (Antabuse), which causes nausea and vomiting if alcohol is consumed, psychotherapy, and support from organizations such as Alcoholics Anonymous.

Alcott, Louisa M(ay) (1832–88) US children's writer, born in Germantown, Philadelphia. She was a nurse during the Civil War before achieving success as a writer with the children's novel, *Little Women* (1868–9). Other works include *Old-fashioned Girl* (1870), *Little Men* (1871), and *Jo's Boys* (1886).

alcove *noun* a recess in the wall of a room or garden. [from Spanish *alcoba*, from Arabic *al*, the + *qubbah*, vault]

Alcuin, originally **Ealhwine**, or **Albinus** (c.735–804) writer, theologian, and adviser to the emperor Charlemagne. He was born in York, where he became master of the cloister school (778), then was invited to Charlemagne's court (781). His dedication to the education of the royal family led to the court becoming a school of culture for the almost barbarous Frankish Empire. In 796 he settled as abbot at Tours, and the school there became one of the most important in the Empire. His works comprise poems; works on grammar, rhetoric, and dialectics; theological and ethical treatises; lives of several saints; and over 200 letters.

Alcyone see HALCYONE.

Aldabra Islands a coral atoll nature reserve in the SW Indian Ocean, NW of Madagascar. AREA 154sq km/59sq mi. It lies 1 200km/750mi SW of Mahé. The atoll is an outlying dependency of the Seychelles and is occupied by scientific staff. It is the habitat of the giant land tortoise. The nature reserve, established in 1976, is a World Heritage site.

Aldeburgh Festival a June festival of music and the arts, founded (1948) in Suffolk, England, by Benjamim Britten and Peter Pears. Many of Britten's works have been premièred there, and a purpose-built concert hall was opened in the Maltings at nearby Snape in 1970.

aldehyde *noun Chem.* any member of a class of organic chemical compounds that are formed by the oxidation of alcohols and contain the -CHO group, eg formaldehyde (methanal), acetaldehyde (ethanal). Aromatic aldehydes, eg benzaldehyde, are used as flavourings and perfumes. See also ACETALDEHYDE, FORMALDEHYDE. [a shortening of Latin *alcohol dehydrogenatum*, alcohol derived from hydrogen]

aldehyde: ethanal (acetaldehyde)

al dente *adj.*, *said of pasta and vegetables* cooked so as to remain firm when bitten. [from Italian *al dente*, to the tooth]

alder *noun* a tree with catkins and toothed leaves, which grows in damp areas. [from Anglo-Saxon *alor*]

alderman *noun* **1** *in England and Wales until 1974* a member of a town, county or borough council elected by fellow councillors, below the rank of mayor. **2** *in the US and Canada* a member of the governing body of a city. [from Anglo-Saxon *ealdormann*, nobleman of the highest rank]

Alderney, French **Aurigny**, ancient **Riduna** POP (1991) 2 000, the third largest of the Channel Is, situated off the coast of French Normandy. It lies W of Cherbourg and is separated from France by the Race of Alderney. AREA 8sq km/3sq mi. It is in the Bailiwick of Guernsey and has its own legislative assembly. CHIEF TOWNS Saint Anne. ECONOMY dairy farming; tourism.

Aldershot POP (1981) 54 000, a town in Rushmoor district, Hampshire, S England. It lies 13km/8mi W of Guildford and an important military depot is located in the town.

Aldiss, Brian (Wilson) (1925–) English novelist and short-story writer, born in Dereham, Norfolk. He is best known for his science-fiction writing, and his works include *The Brightfount Diaries* (1955), *Hothouse* (1962), and *The Saliva Tree* (1966). He has also produced a history of science fiction, *Billion Year Spree* (1973).

aldosterone *noun Physiol.* a steroid hormone that is secreted into the bloodstream by the adrenal cortex of the adrenal glands. It stimulates the reabsorption of sodium ions and the excretion of potassium ions by the kidneys, in order to help maintain the balance of salts and water in the body.

Aldrin, Edwin Eugene, also known as **Buzz** (1930–) US astronaut, born in Montclair, New Jersey, the second man to set foot on the Moon (1969). Educated at West Point and the Massachusetts Institute of Technology, he was an air force pilot in the Korean War, becoming an astronaut in 1963. He set up a space-walking record in 1966 during the flight of Gemini 12.

Aldus Manutius or **Aldo Manucci/Manuzio** (c.1450–1515) Venetian printer, born in Bassiano, after whom are named the Aldine editions of the Greek and Roman classics and of the great Italian writers. The first to print Greek books, he had beautiful founts of Greek and Latin type made, and was also the first to use italics on a large scale.

Aldwych Theatre a theatre founded 1905 in London's West End by Seymour Hicks and Charles Frohman. For a time it was noted for its farces (1925–33), and was home to the RSC (1960–82).

ale *noun* **1** a light-coloured beer, higher in alcohol content than lager and with a fuller body, flavoured with hops. **2** beer. [from Anglo-Saxon *ealu*]

aleatory *adj.* depending on chance. [from Latin *aleator*, dice-player]

aleatory music music in which the choice of notes in the composition or performance is determined to a greater or lesser extent by chance or whim. Random elements have been included in certain musical compositions since c.1945, most notably by Stockhausen and John Cage (1912–). These elements may be decided on using systems of divination or by dice-throwing; the composer may provide the notes, but not the order in which they are to be played; there may be no notes written down with only an abstract representation of the general pattern for performers to interpret intuitively. The performance of aleatory music often depends on the presence of the composer to direct the musicians. [from Latin *aleatorius*, from *aleator*, a dicer, from *alea*, a die]

alehouse *noun old use* an inn or public house.

Aleixandre, Vicente (1898–1984) Spanish poet, born in Seville. He achieved recognition as a writer in 1937, but his loyalty to the Republic impeded the publication of his work for several years, his *Antología Total* (Complete Works) not appearing until 1976. He was awarded the Nobel Prize for Literature in 1977.

Alembert, Jean le Rond d' (1717–83) French philosopher and mathematician, born in Paris. He wrote an influential treatise on dynamics (1743), and several other major mathematical works. He collaborated with Diderot in the editing of the *Encyclopédie*, in which he also wrote several articles and the *Discours préliminaire* introducing the first volume (1751).

Alentejo a former region of SE central Portugal, situated SE of the R Tagus. In 1936 it was divided into the two provinces of Alto Alentejo and Baixo Alentejo. The land of this sparsely populated agricultural area forms a low-lying plain with cork tree forests, heaths, and maquis. CHIEF TOWNS Évora, Beja. ECONOMY corn; cattle, pigs; the area is also noted for the Alter Real breed of horse. NOTABLE FEATURES prehistoric standing stones and chambered cairns. [from Arabic *alem Tejo*, beyond the Tagus]

Aleppo, Arabic **Halab** POP (1990e) 2.5m, the capital city of Halab governorate, NW Syria, 350km/217mi N of Damascus. It is the chief commercial and industrial centre of N Syria. The old city is a World Heritage site.

alert — *adj.* **1** thinking and acting quickly. **2** (**alert to something**) watchful and aware of a danger, etc. — *noun* **1** a warning of danger. **2** the period of time covered by such a warning. — *verb* (**alert someone to something**) to warn them of a danger; to make them aware of a fact or circumstance.

— **on the alert** watchful.

[from French *alerte*, from Italian *all'erta*, to the watch-tower]

alertly *adv.* in an alert way.

alertness *noun* an alert state.

Alessandri (Palma), Arturo (1868–1950) Chilean politician, born in Longaví, Linares province. He was a member of the Chamber of Deputies (1897–1915), Senator (1915–18, 1944–50), and Minister of the Interior (1918–20). Elected President on a reform platform in 1920, he was ousted, but soon recalled by the armed forces (1924–5). His second term was more conservative (1932–8).

Aletsch a glacier in S central Switzerland, W and S of the Aletschhorn. It is the largest glacier in Europe. AREA 118sq km/46sq mi; length 24km/15mi.

Aleut — *noun* (PL. **Aleut**, **Aleuts**) **1** a member of a people, related to the Inuit, inhabiting the Aleutian Islands and part of Alaska. **2** the language of this people. — *adj.* (also **Aleutian**) relating to this people or their language. [from Russian]

Aleutian Islands or **Aleutians**, formerly **Catherine Archipelago** POP (1990) 12 000, a group of c.150 islands stretching c.1 600km/1 000mi from the Alaskan Peninsula, USA. AREA 17 666sq km/6 821sq mi. There are many volcanic peaks over 1 000m. MAIN ISLANDS Attu, Andreanof, Rat, Umnak, Unimak, Unalaska. CHIEF TOWN Dutch Harbor. HISTORY the group was discovered by Russian explorers in the 18c, and purchased by the USA in 1867. Several military bases and a wildlife refuge are situated on the islands.

A-level or **Advanced-level** in England, Wales, and Northern Ireland, an examination taken by school and college students which qualifies them for entrance to higher education and the professions. It is a single-subject examination at a level representing two further years of study beyond the GCSE. One A-level is deemed equivalent to two passes in the Advanced Supplementary (A/S level) examination.

Alexander I (1777–1825) Emperor of Russia (1801–25), born in St Petersburg, the grandson of Catherine the Great. He early instituted a wide range of reforms, and in 1805 Russia joined the coalition against Napoleon, but after a series of military defeats was forced to conclude the Treaty of Tilsit (1807) with France. When Napoleon broke the Treaty by invading Russia in 1812, Alexander pursued the French back to Paris. He claimed and received Poland at the Congress of Vienna (1814–15). During the last years of his reign his increased religious mysticism contributed to his founding of the Holy Alliance (1815), a document delineating Christian principles, and intended to exclude the House of Bonaparte from power in France, which was signed by Emperor Francis I, Frederick William III, and other European leaders.

Alexander I (of Scotland) (c.1077–1124) King of Scots (1107–24), son of Malcolm Canmore and Queen (later St) Margaret. He succeeded his brother Edgar and ruled north of the Forth–Clyde line while his younger brother David (later David I) controlled S Scotland in his name. He founded an Augustinian monastery at Scone, and maintained friendly relations with England by marrying Sybilla, an illegitimate daughter of Henry I, and fighting alongside Henry in Wales (1114).

Alexander II (1198–1249) King of Scots (1214–49), born in Haddington, E Lothian. He succeeded his father, William the Lion, supported the English barons against John, and later concluded a peace treaty with Henry III (1217). He renounced his hereditary claims to Northumberland, Cumberland, and Westmorland by the Treaty of York (1237), and asserted royal authority in the north and west of Scotland. His reign was a landmark in the establishment of the kingdom of Scotland.

Alexander II (of Russia), known as **the Liberator** (1818–81) Emperor of Russia (1855–81), born in St Petersburg, the son of Nicholas I. His achievements included the emancipation of the serfs (1861); local government, judicial, and military reforms; the extension of the Russian Empire into central Asia and the Far East; and the defeat of Turkey in the war of 1877–8. His struggle with populist terrorists during the latter part of his reign culminated in his assassination.

Alexander III, also called **Alexander the Great** (356–323 BC) King of Macedonia (336–323 BC), born in Pella, the son of Philip II. He was tutored by Aristotle before ascending the throne when he was 20 years old. He crushed all opposition at home, then conquered Greece's hereditary enemy, Achaemenid Persia, in a series of battles: Granicus (334 BC), Issus (333 BC), and Gaugamela (331 BC). He conquered Egypt and founded the city of Alexandria, consulting the oracle of Ammon at Siwah Oasis (which apparently fostered his belief in his divine descent). By 330 BC, Darius III had fled, and the capitals of Babylon, Susa, Persepolis, and Ecbatana had been taken. In the next three years, he conquered the eastern half of the empire then set out to invade India (327 BC). He conquered the Punjab, but was forced to return when his troops mutinied. He died shortly after in Babylon.

Alexander III, originally **Orlando Bandinelli** (c.1105–81) pope from 1159 to 1181, born in Siena, Italy. He taught law at Bologna, and became adviser to Pope Adrian IV. As pope he struggled with the emperor Frederick Barbarossa who refused to recognize him and set up antipopes. The Emperor was finally defeated and compelled to sign the Treaty of Venice (1177). Alexander was also involved in the quarrel between Henry II of England and Thomas à Becket.

Alexander VI, originally **Rodrigo Borgia** (1431–1503) pope from 1492 to 1503, born in Játiva, Spain. He was made a cardinal (1455) by his uncle, Calixtus III, and by flagrant bribery acquired the papal chair on the death of Innocent VIII. Father to Cesare, Lucretia, and two other illegitimate children, he endeavoured to break the power of the Italian princes, and to gain their possessions for his own family. He apportioned the New World between Spain and Portugal and introduced the censorship of books.

Alexander 1 a male first name, made famous by Alexander the Great of Macedonia. 2 see PARIS. [a Latin form of Greek *alexein*, to defend + *aner*, man, warrior]

Alexander of Hales, known as **the Irrefragable Doctor** (c.1170–1245) English scholastic philosopher, born in Hales, Gloucestershire. He became Professor of Philosophy and Theology in Paris, and later entered the Franciscan order. His chief work was the *Summa Universae Theologiae*, a system of instruction for the schools of Christendom.

Alexander (of Tunis), Harold Rupert Leofric George Alexander, 1st Earl (1891–1969) British soldier, born in London. He commanded a brigade on the Western Front in World War I, and in World War II was the last officer out of Dunkirk (1940). He served in Burma, and in 1942–3 was Commander-in-Chief Middle East, when his N African campaign was noted for its complete success. Appointed field marshal on the capture of Rome in Jun 1944, he became Supreme Allied Commander, Mediterranean Theatre, for the rest of the war. He later became Governor-General of Canada (1946–52), Minister of Defence (1952–4), and earl (1952).

Alexander, Franz Gabriel (1891–1964) US psychoanalyst, born in Budapest. A medical officer during World War I, he later studied and worked in Berlin. In 1932 he settled in the USA, where he founded the Chicago Institute for Psychoanalysis. Although he wrote widely on psychoanalytic and cultural issues, his work on diseases with a psychological origin, among which he included peptic ulcers and rheumatic arthritis, was especially influential.

Alexander Archipelago a group of 1 100 mountainous islands of Alaska, USA, lying off the SE coast. MAIN ISLANDS Chichagof, Baranof, Admiralty, Kupreanof, Kuiu, Prince of Wales. The naval base of Sitka and a national monument are on Baranof I.

Alexander Nevsky (c.1220–63) Russian hero and saint, born in Vladimir, who received his surname from his victory over the Swedes on the R Neva (1240). He later defeated the Teutonic Knights (1242) and the Lithuanians (1245), and also helped maintain the city of Novgorod's independence from the Mongol Empire. He was canonized (feast day 30 Aug or 23 Nov) by the Russian Church in 1547, and is the subject of a film by Sergei Eisenstein.

Alexander technique *Medicine* a system of exercises, etc, designed to improve posture and breathing habits, and by reducing muscular tension and promoting relaxation to bring about a general improvement in health. [named after the Australian therapist F M Alexander]

Alexandra Feodorovna (1872–1918) Empress of Russia upon her marriage with Nicholas II (1894), Princess of Hesse-Darmstadt, and granddaughter of Queen Victoria, born in Darmstadt, Germany. She came under the influence of Rasputin, meddled disastrously in politics, and was eventually imprisoned and shot by Bolshevik revolutionaries.

Alexandra (Helen Elizabeth Olga Christabel), Princess, the Hon Lady Ogilvy (1936–) British princess, the daughter of George, Duke of Kent, and Princess Marina of Greece. In 1963 she married the Hon Angus James Bruce Ogilvy (1928–); they have a son, James Robert Bruce (1964–) and a daughter, Marina Victoria Alexandra (1966–).

Alexandria, Arabic **El Iskandariya** POP (1990e) 3.7m, the seaport capital of Alexandria governorate, N Egypt, on the Mediterranean coast, 180km/112mi NW of Cairo. It is the second largest city in Egypt and the country's main port. HISTORY founded in 332 BC by Alexander the Great; capital of the Ptolemies from 330 BC until 304 BC and a former centre of Hellenistic and Jewish culture. NOTABLE FEATURES Royal Libraries; Catacombs of Kom El Shugafa (1c–2c); Graeco-Roman Museum; Pompey's Pillar (AD 297); Serapium temple ruins; Abu'l Abbas Mosque.

Alexandria, Library of a library founded by Ptolemy I and greatly extended by Ptolemy II. It was considered the greatest library in the Ancient World and the most important centre for literary studies. At one time it was reputed to have contained 700 000 volumes.

alexandrine — *noun* a verse of six iambic feet (in English) or twelve syllables (in French). — *adj.*, *said of verse* written in alexandrines. [from French *Alexandre*; Alexander the Great was the subject of an Old French romance written in this metre]

Alexeyev, Vasiliy (1942–) Russian weightlifter, born in Pokrovo-Shishkino. He set 80 world records (Jan 1970–Nov 1977), more than any other athlete in any sport. He was Olympic super-heavyweight champion in 1972 and 1976, and won eight world titles and nine European titles.

alexia *noun Psychol.* loss of the ability to read, caused by brain disease. [from A-¹ + Greek *legein*, to speak, confused with Latin *legere*, to read]

Alexis a male first name, also given to females outside of Eastern Europe. [from Greek *alexein*, to defend]

ALF *abbrev.* Animal Liberation Front.

alfalfa *noun* **1** a perennial plant (*Medicago sativa*) of the pea family (Leguminosae) with purple flowers, small divided leaves, and spirally twisted pods. It is one of the most important forage crops, especially in the USA. — Also called *lucerne*. **2** the young leaves of this plant used as a salad vegetable. [from Spanish, from Arabic *al-fasfasah*]

Alföld the Great Plain region of S Hungary, E of the R Danube and extending into Yugoslavia and W Romania. It is a flat area covering about half of Hungary, crossed by a system of canals which provides irrigation for grain and fruit. The arid grasslands (*pusztas*) support livestock. There are national parks at Hortobágy, Bükk, and Kiskunság.

Alfonso I *or* **Affonso Henriques** (c.1110–1185) the earliest King of Portugal (1139–85), born in Guimarães. Only two years old at the death of his father, Henry of Burgundy, he later wrested power from his mother (1128), fought the Moors, defeating them at Ourique (1139), and proclaimed himself king. He took Lisbon (1147), and later all Galicia, Estremadura, and Elvas.

Alfred, known as **the Great** (849–99) King of Wessex, born in Wantage, Berkshire, the fifth son of King Ethelwulf. When he came to the throne in 871, the Danes had already conquered Northumbria, E Mercia, and East Anglia, and were threatening Wessex itself. He defeated them at the battle of Edington, Wiltshire (878), and began to win back Danish-occupied territory by capturing the former Mercian town of London (886), and by organizing his forces into a standing army, building a navy, and establishing a network of burgs (fortified centres). He forged ties with other English peoples not under Danish rule, and enabled his successors to reconquer the Danelaw and secure the unity of England. He also revived religion and learning, aiming to win God's support for victory over the pagan Danes, and loyalty to himself as a Christian king, and he translated several Latin works into English. The story of his being scolded by a peasant woman for letting her cakes burn was first recorded in the 11c.

Alfred a male first name. [from Anglo-Saxon *aelf*, elf, supernatural being + *raed*, counsel]

alfresco *adj., adv.* in the open air. [from Italian *al fresco* in the fresh air]

Alfvén, Hannes Olof Gösta (1908–) Swedish theoretical physicist, born in Norrköping. He became professor at the Royal Institute of Technology in Stockholm in 1945. In pioneering research on ionized gases, or plasmas, and their behaviour in electric and magnetic fields, he predicted the existence of 'Alfvén waves' in plasmas (1942), which were later observed. His theories have led to important advances in analysis of stellar structure, and in the attempts to develop nuclear fusion reactors. He shared the 1970 Nobel Prize for Physics with Louis Néel.

alga *noun* (PL. **algae**) (*usually* **algae**) *Bot.* any of a large and very diverse group of mainly aquatic organisms, ranging from single-celled members of the plant plankton, eg diatoms, to large multicellular algae, including nearly all brown, green, and red seaweeds. [from Latin *alga*, seaweed]
◇ Algae contain chlorophyll and can therefore carry out photosynthesis, but they lack true leaves, stems, or roots. The majority are marine or freshwater species, but some are found in damp terrestrial habitats. Although traditionally classified as simple plants, the algae are now often included in a separate kingdom, Protista.

Algarve a province in S Portugal, co-extensive with Faro district. The name also refers to a former region, which is bounded W and S by the Atlantic Ocean, and E by the R Guadiana. HISTORY it became a Moorish kingdom in 1140; Now the most popular tourist area in Portugal, it has resorts at Luz de Lagos, Praia da Rocha, Praia do Carvoeiro, Albufeira, and Vilamoura. Costo do Algarve comprises the S Atlantic coast of Portugal, from Cape St Vincent in the W to the R Guadiana on the Spanish border. CAPITAL Faro. ECONOMY figs, olives, maize, almonds, fishing; tourism. [from Arab *al gharb*, the west]

algebra *noun* the branch of mathematics that uses letters and symbols to represent variable quantities and numbers, and to express generalizations about them. Most algebraic relationships are expressed in the form of equations that can be manipulated into suitable forms and then solved. [from Italian and Spanish, from Arabic *al-jebr*, from *al*, the + *jebr*, reunion of broken parts]

algebraic *adj.* relating to or occurring in algebra.

algebraically *adv.* by the use of algebra.

Algeciras POP (1991) 101 000, a seaport and resort in Cádiz province, Andalusia, SW Spain. It lies on the W side of Algeciras Bay, opposite Gibraltar. HISTORY founded by the Moors in 713, it was largely destroyed in the 14c and rebuilt in the 18c; the Algeciras Conference over the future of Morocco was held here in 1906. NOTABLE FEATURE the remains of Old Algeciras (dating from the 8c).

Algeria, French **L'Algérie**, official name **The Democratic and Popular Republic of Algeria**, Arabic **Al-Jumhuriya Al-Jazairiya** POP (1992e) 26m, a N African republic, divided into 31 departments (*wilaya*). AREA 2 460 500sq km/ 949 753sq mi. The republic is bounded W by Morocco, SW by Western Sahara, Mauritania, and Mali, SE by Mali, E by Libya, NE by Tunisia, and N by the Mediterranean Sea. CAPITAL Algiers (Alger). CHIEF TOWNS Constantine, Oran, Skikda, Annaba, Mostaganem, Blida, Tlemcen. TIME ZONE GMT +1. Most of the population is Arab-Berber (99%); Islam (Sunni Muslim) is the chief religion. OFFICIAL LANGUAGE Arabic; French is also spoken.

Algeria

CURRENCY the dinar. PHYSICAL DESCRIPTION from the Mediterranean coast, the mountains rise in a series of ridges and plateaux to the Atlas Saharien; 91% of the population is located on the narrow coastal plain; part of the Sahara Desert lies to the S of the Atlas Saharien; in the NE of this region is a major depression, the Chott Melrhir, which extends E into Tunisia; the Hoggar Mts in the far S rise to 2 918m at Mt Tahat. CLIMATE typical Mediterranean climate on the N coast; annual average rainfall of 400–800mm (mostly Nov–Mar); snow on the higher ground; Algiers, representative of the coastal region, has an annual rainfall of 760mm with average maximum daily temperatures of 15–29°C; the rest of the country has an essentially rainless Saharan climate. HISTORY the indigenous peoples (Berbers) have been driven back from the coast by many invaders, including the Phoenicians, Romans, Vandals, Arabs, Turks, and French; became a province of the Roman Empire; Islam and Arabic were introduced by the Arabs (8c–11c); Turkish invasion in the 16c; French colonial campaign in the 19c led to control by 1902; the National Liberation Front (FLN) engaged in guerrilla war with French forces in 1954–62; gained independence in 1962; the first president of the republic, Ahmed Ben Bella, was replaced after a coup in 1965; governed by decree until elections and a new constitution in 1976; a state of emergency was declared in 1992 as a result of clashes between government forces and the Islamic Salvation Front. GOVERNMENT a President is elected as head of state every five years by universal suffrage and he appoints a Cabinet; the President and a 430-member National Assembly share legislative power. ECONOMY large-scale nationalization after 1963; agriculture, mainly on the N coast (wheat, barley, oats, grapes, citrus fruits, vegetables); food processing, textiles, clothing; petroleum products account for c.30% of the national income; natural gas reserves are estimated to be the world's fourth largest; pioneer in the development of liquid natural gas; constructed with Italy the first trans-Mediterranean gas pipeline.

-algia *combining form* pain in the part of the body stated: *neuralgia*. [from Greek *algos*, pain]

Algiers, French **Alger** POP (1990e) 3m, the seaport capital of Algeria. HISTORY founded in the 10c by Berbers on the site of Roman Icosium; Turkish rule was established in 1518 by Barbarossa; taken by the French in 1830; Allied headquarters and seat of de Gaulle's provisional government in World War II. NOTABLE FEATURES Sidi Abderrahman Mosque, Sidi Muhammad Sherif Mosque, Djama Djehid Mosque (16c); cathedral; National Library; Bardo Museum, Museum of Antiquities, National Museum of Fine Arts.

alginate *noun Biochem.* a salt of alginic acid, found in seaweeds and forming viscous solutions

which hold large amounts of water. Alginates are used in food manufacturing as thickening agents. [from Latin *alga*, seaweed]

ALGOL *noun Comput.* an acronym for the first high-level computer programming language to be used as much for scientific problem solving as for manipulating mathematical data. It is no longer widely used, but many subsequent computer languages have been influenced by it. [from *algorithmic language*]

Algonkian *or* **Algonquian** — *adj.* denoting a family of over 30 Amerindian languages used in central and E Canada and parts of the USA. — *noun* the languages forming this family.

Algonkin *or* **Algonquin** any of the scattered small groups of Native Americans speaking Algonkian languages, living in forest regions around the Ottawa River in Canada. Most were slaughtered by the Iroquois or died from European diseases: only c.2 000 survive.

algorithm *noun* a process or set of rules used for solving problems, calculations, etc, especially by computer. [from Latin *algorismus*, from *Al-Khwarizmi*, 9c Arab mathematician]

algorithmic *adj.* relating to algorithms; involving the use of an algorithm.

Alhambra the palace-fortress of the Moorish kings built in Granada, Spain (13c–14c). It displays the ornate horseshoe arches and tinkling pools and fountains that are the essence of Moorish architecture. It is a World Heritage site.

Alhambra

Alhazen, properly **Ibn al-Haytham** (c.965–c.1040) Arab mathematician, born in Basra. He wrote a work on optics (known in Europe in Latin translation from the 13c) giving the first account of atmospheric refraction and reflection from curved surfaces, and the structure of the eye. He also constructed spherical and parabolic mirrors, and in later life turned to mathematics, developing some of the themes which had occupied the ancient Greeks.

Ali, (Chaudri) Muhammad (1905–80) Pakistani politician, born in Jullundur, E Punjab. On the partition of India, he became the first Secretary-General of the Pakistani government (1947), Finance Minister (1951), and then Prime Minister (1955–6). He resigned after a year due to lack of support from members of his own party, the Muslim League.

Ali, Muhammad, originally **Cassius Marcellus Clay, Jr** (1942–) US boxer, born in Louisville, Kentucky. He became the Olympic light-heavyweight champion in 1960, and in 1964 won the professional world heavyweight title, defeating Sonny Liston. He then joined the Black Muslims and changed his name to Muhammad Ali, and in 1967 was stripped of his title and barred from the ring for refusing to be drafted into the US army. His title was restored in 1970. In 1971 he was defeated by Joe Frazier, but beat him in 1974, and in the same year went on to regain his world heavyweight title, defeating George Foreman. He was beaten by Leon

Spinks in a split decision in Feb 1978, but regained the title later that year — the first man to win the world heavyweight title three times. He was famed for his extrovert style and his catchphrase 'I am the greatest'.

Aliákmon, River, ancient **Haliacmon** the longest river in Greece, length 297km/185mi. Rising near the Albanian border in N Greece, it flows SE then NE, discharging into the Gulf of Salonika.

alias — *noun* a false or assumed name. — *adv.* also known as: *John Smith, alias Mr X.* [from Latin *alias*, at another time, otherwise]

Ali Bey (1728–73) Caucasian slave who in 1763 rose to be chief of the Mamluks in Egypt. After being proclaimed Sultan (1768), he made himself independent of Turkey, and conquered Syria and part of Arabia. He died soon after being defeated by an army raised by one of his sons-in-law.

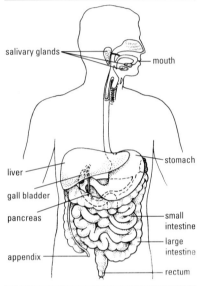

human alimentary canal

alibi *noun* **1** a plea of being somewhere else when a crime was committed. **2** *colloq.* an excuse. [from Latin *alibi*, elsewhere]

Alicante, Latin **Lucentum** POP (1991) 261 000, the seaport capital of Alicante province, SE Spain, situated 422km/262mi SE of Madrid. It is a popular winter resort. NOTABLE FEATURES palm-lined promenade; Castle of St Barbara; Church of St Mary (14c).

Alice a female first name, popularized by the heroine of Lewis Carroll's *Alice's Adventures in Wonderland* (1865). [a Norman French variant of ADELAIDE]

Alice's Adventures in Wonderland a children's novel by Lewis Carroll (1865). It tells of the bizarre experiences Alice has in the 'Wonderland' of her dreams.

Alice Springs, formerly **Stuart** (to 1933) POP (1991) 20 000, an urban centre in Northern Territory, central Australia. Established in 1890 it has become the administrative and supply centre for the settlements and cattle stations of the Outback. It is also the regional headquarters of the Flying Doctor Service. NOTABLE FEATURES Aviation Museum; Chateau Hornsby Winery nearby; tourist centre for the region.

alien — *noun* **1** a foreign-born resident of a country who has not adopted that country's nationality. **2** an inhabitant of another planet, especially in science fiction stories. **3** a plant introduced to an area by people rather than by nature. — *adj.* **1** foreign. **2** (**alien to someone** *or* **something**) not in keeping with them; unfamiliar to them. [from Latin *alienus*, foreign]

alienable *adj. Legal, said of property* able to be transferred to another owner.

Alien and Sedition Acts US laws (1798–1800) passed by a Federalist-controlled Congress to restrain political opposition. The Alien Acts delayed citizenship and gave President Adams great power over foreigners, and the Sedition Act authorized fining and imprisonment for public criticism of the government.

alienate *verb* **1** to make (someone) feel unfriendly or strange. **2** to make (someone) feel unwelcome or isolated. **3** *Legal* to transfer ownership of (property) to another person.

alienation *noun* **1** estrangement. **2** mental or emotional detachment; the state of not being involved. **3** *Legal* the transfer of ownership of property to another person.

alienation effect *Theatr.* a device or series of devices used to create a sense of detachment from the subject-matter of a play and intended to remind the audience of the strangeness of familiar things which hitherto they had taken for granted. These include interruption of the action, deliberate lowering of dramatic tension, and the introduction of placards, strip cartoons, and film. [a translation of German *Verfremdungseffekt*]

alight[1] *adj.* **1** on fire. **2** lighted up; excited: *a face alight with wonder.*

alight[2] *verb intrans.* **1** *old use* to get down from or out of a vehicle. **2** (**alight on something**) to settle or land on it. [from Anglo-Saxon *alihtan*]

align *verb* **1** to put in a straight line or bring into line. **2** *trans., intrans.* to bring (someone, a country, etc) into agreement with others, or with a political belief, cause, etc. [from French *à ligne*, into line]

alignment *noun* **1** setting in a line or lines. **2** a row arranged in this way. **3** the taking of a side, or the side taken with others in a debate, dispute, etc.

alike — *adj.* like one another; similar. — *adv.* in a similar manner. [from Anglo-Saxon *gelic*]

alimentary *adj.* relating to food and nutrition. [from Latin *alimentarius*, from *alere*, to nourish]

alimentary canal *Anat.* in vertebrate animals, a tubular organ along which food passes, and in which it is digested. It extends from the mouth, where food is ingested (taken in) to the anus, where waste material is eliminated. In humans the alimentary canal consists of the mouth cavity, pharynx, oesophagus, stomach, duodenum, small intestine, large intestine, and rectum. Specialized regions such as the duodenum and small intestine secrete different digestive enzymes and absorb the products of digestion.

alimony *noun Legal* money for support paid by a man to his wife or by a woman to her husband, when they are legally separated or divorced. See also MAINTENANCE. [from Latin *alimonia*, nourishment]

aliphatic *adj. Chem., said of organic compounds* with carbon atoms in chains rather than rings. See also AROMATIC. [from Greek *aleiphar*, oil]

aliquot *noun* **1** *Maths.* a number or quantity into which a given number or quantity can be exactly divided without any remainder. **2** *Chem.* a sample of a material or chemical substance that is analysed in order to determine its properties. [Latin, = some, several]

Alison a female first name. [a Norman French diminutive of ALICE]

alive *adj.* **1** living; having life; in existence. **2** lively; active. **3** (**alive to something**) aware of it; responsive to it. **4** (**alive with something**) full of it; abounding in it.

— **alive and kicking** *colloq.* living and active. [from Anglo-Saxon *on life*, in life]

Aliyah Jewish migrations from Europe to Palestine, which began in 1882 and were the

basis of the modern state of Israel. The second Aliyah (1904–14) focused on the redemption of the soil and personal labour as a means of salvation, and pioneered the co-operative settlement (now the *kibbutz*). The third Aliyah was a search for a National Home, the fourth (1925) a result of Jewish persecution in E Europe (mainly Poland), and the fifth (1932) represented flight from early Nazi persecution.

alkali *noun* a hydroxide of any of the alkali metals, eg sodium hydroxide, that dissolves in water to produce a solution with a pH greater than 7, known as a *basic solution.* Alkalis turn red litmus paper blue, and neutralize acids to form salts and water. [from Arabic *al-qaly*, calcinated ashes]

alkali metal *Chem.* any of the metals belonging to group IA of the periodic table of chemical elements, namely lithium, sodium, potassium, rubidium, caesium, and francium.

alkaline *adj.* containing an alkali; acting like an alkali.

alkaline earth *Chem.* any of the metals belonging to group IIA of the periodic table of chemical elements, namely beryllium, magnesium, calcium, strontium, barium, and radium.

alkalinity *noun* **1** the quality of being alkaline. **2** the extent to which a substance is alkaline.

alkaloid *noun Biochem.* any of a group of nitrogen-containing organic compounds occurring naturally in certain plants, with toxic or medicinal properties, eg caffeine, morphine, nicotine, codeine. More than 1 000 alkaloids have been identified to date.

alkalosis *noun Medicine* a condition in which the blood and other body fluids are abnormally alkaline, eg as a result of excessive vomiting, or overconsumption of antacids.

alkane *noun Chem.* the general name for any of a series of hydrocarbons having the general formula C_nH_{2n+2}, eg methane (CH_4), ethane (C_2H_6). Alkanes are saturated, ie they contain only single bonds. — Also called *paraffin.*

alkane: methane, ethane

alkene *noun Chem.* the general name for any of a series of hydrocarbons having the general formula C_nH_{2n}, eg ethene (ethylene) (C_2H_4). Alkenes contain one or more double bonds, and are therefore said to be unsaturated. — Also called *olefin.*

alkene: ethene (ethylene)

al-Khwarizmi, Abu Ja'far Muhammad ibn Musa see KHWARIZMI, ABU JA'FAR MUHAMMAD IBN MUSA AL-.

alkyl group *Chem.* in an organic chemical compound, the general name for the hydrocarbon group that is formed by the removal of one hydrogen atom from an alkane, eg the methyl group (CH_3), which is derived from methane (CH_4), and the ethyl group (C_2H_5), which is derived from ethane (C_2H_6).

alkyne *noun Chem.* the general name for any of a series of hydrocarbons having the general

alkyne: ethyne (acetylene)

formula C_nH_{2n+2}, eg ethyne (acetylene) (C_2H_2). Alkynes contain one or more triple bonds, and are therefore said to be unsaturated. — Also called *acetylene*. [*alkyd* and *ethyne*]

all — *adj.* **1** the whole amount, number, or extent of; every. **2** the greatest possible: *run with all speed*. **3** any whatever: *beyond all doubt*. — *noun* **1** every one of the people or things concerned; the whole of (something). **2** one's whole strength, resources, etc: *give one's all*. **3** *in scores in games* on each side. — *adv.* **1** entirely, quite. **2** *colloq.* very: *go all shy*.
— **after all** in spite of what has been said, been done or happened.
all along the whole time.
all and sundry everyone.
all but ... very nearly...: *he all but drowned*.
all in 1 *colloq.* exhausted. **2** with all expenses included.
all in all considering everything.
all over 1 finished. **2** everywhere in or on: *all over the world*. **3** *colloq.* exactly what one would expect from someone: *that's her all over*.
all right see as separate entry.
all there *colloq.* completely sane; mentally alert.
all told including everyone or everything.
be all for something be enthusiastic about it.
for all that in spite of it.
in all all together.
[from Anglo-Saxon *eall*]

alla breve *adj., adv. Mus.* played quickly with two beats to the bar instead of four. [from Italian *alla breve*, at the breve, there originally being one breve to the bar]

Allahabad POP (1991) 807 000, a city in Uttar Pradesh, NE India. It is situated on the N bank of the R Yamuna where it joins the R Ganges, 560km/348mi SE of New Delhi. The city was founded in 1583 and was ceded to the British in 1801. It is the centre of Hindi literature. NOTABLE FEATURES Great Mosque; Sultan Khossor's Caravanserai; fort containing the Asoka pillar (240 BC).

all-American *adj.* typically American in quality, appearance, etc.

allantois *noun Anat.* a membranous sac-like appendage for effecting oxygenation in the embryos of mammals, birds, and reptiles. [from Greek *allas -antos*, sausage + *eidos*, form]

allay *verb* to make (pain, fear, suspicion, etc) less intense. [from Anglo-Saxon *alecgan*]

all clear a signal or statement that the threat of danger is over.

allegation *noun* an unsupported claim, statement, or assertion, especially when unfavourable or depreciatory. [from Latin *allegatio*, from *allegare*, to allege]

allege *verb* to claim or declare to be the case, usually without proof. [from Old French *aleguer*, from Latin *allegare*, to allege, mixed with Old French *alegier*, from Latin *alleviare*, to justify, lighten]

alleged *adj.* presumed or claimed to be so, but not proved.

allegedly *adv.* seemingly, supposedly.

Allegheny Mountains a mountain range in E USA, forming the W part of the Appalachian Mts. From N Pennsylvania it extends over 805km/500mi SW through Maryland, West Virginia, and Virginia, forming the watershed between the Atlantic Ocean and the Mississippi R. The highest point is Spruce Knob (1 481m). The area is rich in timber, coal, iron, and limestone.

allegiance *noun* commitment and duty to obey and be loyal to a government, sovereign, etc. [from Middle English *aliegiaunce*, from Old French *liege*, liege]

allegorical *adj.* **1** relating to or in the nature of an allegory. **2** being or containing an allegory.

allegorically *adv.* in an allegorical way; in terms of allegory.

allegorize *or* **allegorise** *verb* to put in the form of an allegory.

allegory *noun* (PL. **allegories**) a story, play, poem, picture, etc in which the characters represent moral or spiritual ideas or messages. [from Old French *allegorie*, from Greek *allos*, other + *agoreuein*, to speak]

allegro *Mus.* — *adj., adv.* in a quick, lively manner. — *noun* (PL. **allegros**) a piece of music to be played like this. [from Italian *allegro*]

allele *Genetics* one of the alternative forms of a gene which can occur at a given point on a chromosome. There is usually a pair of alleles for any one gene, one having been received from each parent. [from German *Allel*, a shortening of *allelomorph*, from Greek *allelos*, one another]

alleluia *or* **hallelujah** *interj.* praise the Lord. [from Greek *allelouia*, from Hebrew *halleluyah*, praise Jehovah]

allemande *noun* **1** a dance originating in Germany in the 16c and adopted by the French and English; also, the music for it. In the 17c and 18c it became a standard movement following the prelude. It is in 4:4 time and moderate tempo, usually beginning with a semiquaver before the first main beat. **2** a quick dance in triple time, popular in Swabia and Switzerland in the late 18c and early 19c. [from French *allemande*, (feminine) German]

all-embracing *adj.* including everything; missing nothing out.

Allen, Ethan (1738–89) US soldier, revolutionary leader, and writer, born in Litchfield, Connecticut. Having distinguished himself early in the revolutionary war by the surprise and capture of Fort Ticonderoga (1775), he served on Montgomery's expedition to Canada, but was taken prisoner. He was instrumental in the separation of Vermont from New York state in 1777, and in his old age published the deist tract known as *Ethan Allen's Bible*.

Allen, Woody, originally **Allen Stewart Konigsberg** (1935–) US screenwriter, actor, and director, born in New York City. He wrote and acted in *What's New, Pussycat* (1965). *Take the Money and Run* (1969) was the first of his own films, which are mainly comedies centred on psychological problems in modern US city life. He won Academy Awards for *Annie Hall* (1977) (Best Director) and *Hannah and Her Sisters* (1986) (Best Original Screen Play).

Allen, James Alfred Van see VAN ALLEN, JAMES ALFRED.

Allenby, Edmund Henry Hynman Allenby, 1st Viscount (1861–1936) English soldier, born in Brackenhurst, Nottinghamshire. He was Commander of the 3rd Army during the battle of Arras (1917), when he almost breached the German line. Then he commanded the Egyptian Expeditionary Force and conducted a successful campaign against the Turks in Palestine and Syria, during which he captured Jerusalem (1917), Damascus and Aleppo (1918), and secured an armistice. Promoted field marshal in 1919, he was High Commissioner for Egypt (1919–25).

Allende (Gossens), Salvador (1908–73) Chilean politician, born in Valparaíso. A medical doctor who helped found the Chilean Socialist Party (1933), he became a member of the Chamber of Deputies (1937–9), Minister of Health (1939–41), and Senator (1945–70). He stood unsuccessfully for the presidency in 1952, 1958, and 1964, but was finally elected in 1970 as Leader of the left-wing Unidad Popular coalition, which promised a 'transition to socialism'. He was killed in 1973, when his government was overthrown by the armed forces.

allergen *noun Medicine* any foreign substance, usually a protein, that induces an allergic reaction in the body of a person who is hypersensitive to it, eg pollen. See also ALLERGY.

allergic *adj.* (**allergic to something**) having an allergy caused by it: *allergic to shellfish*.

allergy *noun* (PL. **allergies**) **1** a hypersensitive reaction of the body to certain foreign substances, called allergens. These react with antibodies produced within the body by the immune system, resulting in the release of histamine and other substances that cause cell damage, inflammation, and the symptoms of the particular allergy. **2** *colloq.* a dislike. [from Greek *allos*, other + *ergia*, activity]
◇ Symptoms of allergies in the medical sense include asthma, hay fever, headache, dyspepsia, nettle-rash, eczema, dermatitis, gastroenteritis and, in severe cases, extreme shock. Food substances that may produce allergies include eggs, milk, coffee, potatoes, strawberries, tomatoes, walnuts and shellfish, as well as food colouring agents and preservatives. Allergies may also be caused by inhalation of dust or pollen (particularly from grasses), contact with the hair of dogs, cats, or horses, and certain drugs.
Skin testing is often used to determine which allergen is responsible for an allergy in a particular individual. If practicable, the allergen can then be avoided. In cases where the allergen cannot be identified, antihistamine drugs are frequently used to prevent the production of histamines.

alleviate *verb* to make (pain, a problem, suffering, etc) less severe. [from Latin *alleviare*, to lighten]

alleviation *noun* making (pain, a problem, suffering, etc) less severe; relief.

alley *noun* (PL. **alleys**) **1** (**alleyway**) a narrow passage behind or between buildings. **2** a long narrow channel used for bowling or skittles. **3** a path through a garden or park. [from Old French *alee*, passage, from *aler*, to go]

Alleyn, Edward (1566–1626) English actor, a contemporary of Shakespeare, who acted in many of Christopher Marlowe's plays. He founded Dulwich College (1619) and deposited in its library documents relating to his career (including the *Diary* of Philip Henslowe, whose stepdaughter he married), which give a unique insight into the financial aspects of Elizabethan theatre.

All for Love, or The World Well Lost a play by John Dryden (1678). Written in blank verse, it is a tragedy based on William Shakespeare's *Antony and Cleopatra*, delineating the last years of the protagonists' lives.

Allgäu Alps, German **Allgäuer Alpen** a mountain range extending E from L Constance along the Austria–Germany border to the Lech R Valley. The highest peak is the Mädelegabel (2 645m). The area is noted for its intensive cattle-rearing (of the Allgäu breed). There are many spas and medicinal springs in the range.

alliance *noun* **1** the state of being allied. **2** an agreement or treaty by which people, countries, etc ally themselves with one another.

Alliance for Progress a largely fruitless 10-year programme of modernization and reform for 22 countries in Latin America, sponsored by the US government in 1961 on the initiative of President Kennedy.

allied *adj.* **1** joined by political agreement or treaty. **2** (**Allied**) of Britain and her allies in World Wars I and II. **3** similar; related.

Allies the term generally applied to the nations that fought the 'Axis' powers during World War

II. By 1942 the combatant countries comprising the Allies included Great Britain and the British Commonwealth, the USA, the Soviet Union, France, and China, while Costa Rica, Cuba, Brazil, and Mexico had also declared war on Germany and Japan. By Mar 1945 they had been joined by Bulgaria, Finland, Hungary, Italy (which nations had been previously allied to Nazi Germany), and Turkey.

alligator *noun* a large reptile similar to a crocodile but with a broader head and blunter snout. The fourth tooth from the front on each side of the lower jaw is hidden when the mouth is closed, whereas in the crocodile it is visible. There are two species, the American alligator, found in the SE USA, and the rare Chinese alligator, found only in the Yangtze River Basin. Both species live on the banks of rivers and in the water, and feed on fish, small mammals, and birds. [from Spanish *el lagarto*, the lizard]

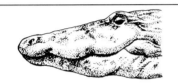

alligator

Allingham, Margery (1904–66) English detective-story writer born in London. Her books featuring the character Albert Campion include *Flowers for the Judge* (1936), *The Tiger in the Smoke* (1952), and *Cargo of Eagles* (1968).

all-in wrestling a style of wrestling with few rules or restrictions.

alliterate *verb intrans.* to use or show alliteration.

alliteration *noun* the repetition of the same sound at the beginning of each word or each stressed word in a phrase, as in *sing a song of sixpence*. [from Latin *alliteratio*, from *ad*, to + *littera*, letter]

alliterative *adj.* in the nature of or using alliteration.

alliteratively *adv.* with alliteration.

allocate *verb* to give, set apart, or assign (something) to someone or for some particular purpose. [from Latin *ad*, to + *locus*, place]

allocation *noun* 1 allocating. 2 a share or part allocated.

allophone *noun Linguistics* a phonetic variant of a phoneme. A phoneme may be produced using two (or more) different 'shapes', without altering the basic sound: for example, the English phoneme /t/ is pronounced with the lips spread in the word *tan*, but with the lips rounded in the word *too*. [from Greek *allos*, other + *phone*, sound, voice]

allot *verb* (**allotted**, **allotting**) to give to (each of a group) a share of or place in (something). [from Old French *aloter*]

allotment *noun* 1 a small part of a larger piece of public ground rented to a person to grow vegetables, etc. 2 the act of allotting.

allotrope *noun Chem.* one of the forms of a chemical element that shows allotropy.

allotropic *adj.* 1 relating to allotropy. 2 having the property of allotropy.

allotropy *noun Chem.* the existence of an element in two or more structural forms (allotropes), often due to differences in crystal structure, eg graphite and diamond (allotropes of carbon), red and white phosphorus. [from Greek *allos*, other + *tropos*, manner]

all-out *adj.* using all one's strength, powers, etc.

allow *verb* 1 to permit (someone to do something, something to happen, etc). 2 *intrans.*

(**allow for something**) to take it into consideration when judging or deciding something. 3 to give or provide: *allow £10 for food*. 4 to admit or agree to (a point, claim, etc). 5 to permit (oneself to do something). [from Old French *aloer*]

allowable *adj.* able to be admitted or accepted.

allowably *adv.* so as to be allowable.

allowance *noun* 1 a fixed sum of money, amount of something, etc given regularly. 2 something allowed.
— **make allowances for something** to take it into consideration in one's plans.
make allowances for someone to judge them less severely, or expect less of them, because of particular circumstances applying to them.

allowedly *adv.* as is generally admitted or believed.

alloy — *noun* a material consisting of a mixture of two or more metals, or a metal and a non-metal, eg bronze, brass, steel. Alloys often have superior properties to any of their individual constituents, eg increased hardness, high tensile strength, resistance to high temperature or to acids and other forms of corrosion. — *verb* to add one metal or alloy to another. [from Old French *alei*, from Latin *alligare*, to bind]

all-purpose *adj.* useful for many different purposes.

All Quiet on The Western Front 1 an anti-war novel by Erich Remarque (1929), which depicts the horror and heroism of life in the trenches during World War I. 2 a US film based on the novel, directed by Lewis Milestone (1930), and starring Lew Ayres. It includes the famous image of a hand stretching out to catch a butterfly.

all right 1 unhurt; safe: *are you all right?* 2 adequate; satisfactory. 3 satisfactorily; properly: *it worked out all right*. 4 *colloq.* used as an intensive, with little real meaning: *it's broken all right*. 5 used to express agreement or approval: *all right, you can go*.
◆ This spelling is generally more acceptable than *alright*, although the one-word form is increasingly common, on the analogy of *almighty*, *altogether*, and other words.

all-round *adj.* 1 having many different skills. 2 including everyone or everything: *an all-round education*.

all-rounder *noun* a person with a lot of different skills.

All Saints' Day a Christian festival commemorating all Church saints collectively. Formerly known as All Hallows' Day, it is held on 1 Nov in the Catholic and Anglican churches (the preceding evening being Hallowe'en), and on the first Sunday after Pentecost in the Eastern Churches.

all-singing all-dancing *colloq.* 1 performing superlatively. 2 having many special features.

All Souls' Day the day (2 Nov) set apart in the Roman Catholic Church as a day of prayer for souls in purgatory; also celebrated by some Anglicans. In the Eastern Orthodox Church, it is celebrated about two months before Easter.

allspice *noun* the berry of the pimento, used as a spice.

All's Well That End's Well a play by William Shakespeare (1602–3). It is a 'dark comedy' or 'problem play' focusing on the virtuous Helena who manages to trick the arrogant young count Bertram, her unwilling husband, into recognizing her as his wife.

All The President's Men a US film directed by Alan J Pakula (1976). It is a political documentary-style political thriller about the Watergate investigation, starring Dustin Hoffman and Robert Redford.

all-time *adj. colloq.* 1 said *eg* of a sporting record best to date; unsurpassed. 2 of great and permanent importance: *one of the all-time greats of jazz*.

allude *verb intrans.* (**allude to something**) to speak of it indirectly or mention it in passing. [from Latin *alludere*]

allure — *noun* attractiveness, appeal or charm. — *verb* to attract, charm or fascinate. [from Old French *alurer*, from *a*, to + *lurer*, to lure]

allurement *noun* 1 the act of alluring. 2 fascination, attraction. 3 someone or something that allures.

alluring *adj.* enticing, seductive, attractive.

alluringly *adv.* in an alluring way.

allusion *noun* an indirect reference. [from Latin *allusio*, from *alure*, to allure]
◆ Often confused with *illusion*.

allusive *adj.* referring indirectly.

allusively *adv.* in an allusive way.

alluvial *adj.* relating to or consisting of alluvium.

alluvium *noun* (PL. **alluvia**) fertile soil and sand, etc deposited by rivers or floods, especially in river valleys. [from Latin *alluvius*, washed up]

ally — *noun* (PL. **allies**) a country or person, etc that has formally agreed to help and support another. — *verb* (*usually* **ally oneself** *or* **be allied with** *or* **to someone**) to align oneself politically or militarily with another person or country, especially by a formal agreement. [from Old French *aleier*, from Latin *alligare*, to bind]

Alma a female first name, popular in the mid-19c. [probably from Latin *almus*, nourishing, kind]

Alma-Ata, formerly **Vernyi** (to 1921) POP (1990e) 1.2m, the capital city of Kazakhstan, in the N foothills of the Zailiyskiy Alatau Range, c.300km/185mi from the Chinese frontier. Established in 1854 as a military fortress and trading centre, it was destroyed by an earthquake in 1887. NOTABLE FEATURE Ascension Cathedral (1904, the world's second highest wooden building).

Almagro, Diego de (c.1475–1538) Spanish conquistador. He collaborated with Francisco Pizarro in two expeditions against the Incas and a brief invasion of Chile (1536), but bitter rivalry then developed between the two and Pizarro defeated him in a dispute near Cuzco, which was soon followed by Almagro's execution.

alma mater the school, college, or university that one attended, and from which one graduated. [from Latin *alma mater*, bountiful mother]

almanac *noun* a book, published yearly, with a calendar, information about the moon and stars, religious festivals, public holidays, etc. [from Latin *almanach*, from Arabic *al*, the + *manakh*, calendar]

Alma-Tadema, Sir Lawrence (1836–1912) Dutch-born British painter, born in Dronryp, Friesland. He specialized in subjects from Greek, Roman, and Egyptian antiquity. In 1873 he settled permanently in England.

almighty — *adj.* 1 having complete power. 2 *colloq.* very great. 3 (**the Almighty**) God. — *adv. colloq.* extremely. [from Anglo-Saxon *ælmihtig*]

almond *noun* 1 a kind of small tree related to the peach. 2 the nut-like seed from the fruit of this tree. [from Old French *almende*]

almond

almond-eyed *adj.* with long, almond-shaped eyes.

almoner *noun old use* a medical social worker. [from Old French *aumonier*]

almost *adv.* nearly but not quite. [from Anglo-Saxon *ælmæst*]

alms *pl. noun Hist.* donations of money, food, etc to the poor. [from Anglo-Saxon *ælmesse*, from Greek *eleemosyne*]

alms-house *noun Hist.* a house for the poor, paid for by charity.

al-Nasser, Gamal Abd see NASSER, GAMAL ABD AL-.

Alnico *noun trademark* a high-energy permanent magnet material, an alloy of aluminium, nickel, cobalt, iron, and copper.

Alnwick POP (1981) 7 500, a market town in Alnwick district, Northumberland, NE England. It stands on the R Aln, 48km/30mi N of Newcastle upon Tyne. NOTABLE FEATURE castle, seat of the Dukes of Northumberland.

aloe *noun* **1** a type of plant or tree with fleshy leaves. **2** (*usually* **aloes**) a bitter drug made from aloe leaves. [from Anglo-Saxon *alewe*]

aloe vera *noun* a type of aloe, of which the juice from the leaves is supposed to have healing powers and is used in cosmetics.

aloft *adv.* **1** in the air; overhead. **2** *Naut.* in a ship's rigging. [from Norse *a lopti*, in the sky]

alone *adj., adv.* without anyone else; by oneself; apart from other people.
— **go it alone** *colloq.* to act on one's own and without help.
leave someone *or* **something alone** to avoid bothering or interfering with them. [from Middle English *al one*, all one]

along — *adv.* **1** in some direction: *saw him walking along.* **2** in company with others: *go along for the ride.* **3** into a more advanced state: *coming along nicely.* — *prep.* beside or over all or part of the length of.
— **along with something** *or* **someone** in addition to them; as well as them. [from Anglo-Saxon *andlang*]

alongside — *prep.* close to the side of. — *adv.* to or at the side.

Alonso the king of Naples and father of Ferdinand, in Shakespeare's *The Tempest*, who repents of the part he has played in the overthrow of Prospero.

aloof — *adj.* unfriendly and distant. — *adv.* away; apart; distant: *stand aloof from the group.* [from A³ + Middle English *loof* = LUFF]

aloofly *adv.* with an aloof manner.

aloofness *noun* being aloof.

alopecia *noun Medicine* hair loss resulting from failure of the hair follicles to form hairs. It may be hereditary (eg the usual gradual loss of head hair in men), or it may be a result of disease or old age. [from Greek *alopekia*, fox-mange]

aloud *adv.* **1** loud enough to be able to be heard; not silently. **2** loudly.

Alouette, L' (**The Lark**) a play by Jean Anouilh (1953). Set in the Middle Ages, it is based on the story of St Joan.

ALP *abbrev.* Australian Labor Party.

alp *noun* **1** a high mountain. **2** in Switzerland, pasture land on a mountainside. [from Latin *Alpes*, the Alps, a mountain range running through Switzerland, France and Italy]

alpaca *noun* **1** a S American animal, related to the llama, with long silky hair. **2** the wool or cloth made from this animal's hair. [from Spanish *alpaca*, from Aymara (a S American Indian language) *allpaqa*]

Alp-Arslan (1029–72) Persian Sultan from 1059. He conquered Armenia and Georgia, and in

1071 defeated the Greek emperor at Manzikert. On the march to conquer Turkestan, he was stabbed to death by a captive enemy.

alpha *noun* **1** the first letter of the Greek alphabet (A, α). **2** a mark indicating the best or top grade.
— **alpha and omega 1** the beginning and the end. **2** the most important part.
[from Greek *alpha*]

alphabet *noun* the set of letters, usually in a fixed order, used in writing and printing a language. [from Greek *alphabetos*, from *alpha* + *beta*, the first two letters of the Greek alphabet]
◇ Most alphabets contain fewer than 30 symbols, and all western alphabets are based on the Latin and Etruscan, which were in turn derived from the Greek alphabet. This had added vowels to the Semitic consonant system, in which vowels were marked by accents called *diacritics* (as also used in the Arabic and Hebrew systems). Some special alphabets have been created for specific forms of communication, or for use by a particular group of people, eg the NATO alphabet for radio communication, Braille for the blind, and the Initial Teaching Alphabet for teaching and learning English.

alphabetical *or* **alphabetic** *adj.* in the form of an alphabet; in the order of the letters of an alphabet.

alphabetically *adv.* in terms of or in relation to the alphabet or alphabetical order: *listed alphabetically.*

alphabetize *or* **alphabetise** *verb* to arrange or list alphabetically.

Alpha Boötis see ARCTURUS.

Alpha Centauri *Astron.* the brightest star in the constellation Centaurus, and the third brightest star in the sky. It in fact consists of a group of three stars, the faintest of which, Proxima Centauri, is the closest star to the Sun.

alpha decay *Physics* a form of radioactive decay in which a radioactive nucleus spontaneously emits an alpha particle that is identical to a helium nucleus.

alphanumeric *or* **alphanumerical** *adj.* **1** containing both letters and numbers. **2** *said of a machine* using instructions which consist of letters and numbers; able to display information in the form of letters and numbers. [from ALPHABET + NUMERICAL]

alphanumerically *adv.* in an alphanumeric way; so as to be alphanumeric.

alpha particle a positively charged particle produced by radioactive decay and consisting of two protons and two neutrons bound together, identical to the nucleus of a helium atom. Alpha particles have a low energy content and are stopped by a sheet of paper or a few centimetres of air.

alpha ray a stream of alpha particles.

alpha test *Comput.* an initial test of new software by the manufacturer.

Alpher, Ralph Asher (1921–) US physicist, born in Washington, DC. With George Gamow and Hans Bethe, he proposed in 1948 the 'alpha, beta, gamma' theory which suggests the possibility of explaining the abundances of chemical elements as the result of thermonuclear processes in the early stages of a hot, evolving universe. These ideas were developed to become part of the 'Big Bang' model of the universe. He also predicted that a hot Big Bang must have produced intense electromagnetic radiation which would have 'cooled' (or 'redshifted'); this background radiation was first observed in 1964.

alphorn *or* **alpenhorn** *noun* a long straight or slightly curved horn with an upturned bell, used by Alpine cowherds. Constructed of wood and bark, alphorns are usually about 180cm (6ft) long and can sound the first five or six notes of the harmonic series.

alpine — *adj.* **1** of alps or high mountains. **2** (**Alpine**) of the Alps. — *noun* a plant growing in high mountain areas.

Alps the principal mountain range of Europe, which covers 259 000sq km/100 000sq mi in Switzerland, France, Germany, Austria, Liechtenstein, Italy, Slovenia, and Croatia. A series of parallel chains extending over 1 000km/600mi SW–NE, the Alps were originally formed by a collision of the African and European tectonic plates. The range is the source of many great European rivers, notably the Rhine, Po, and Rhône. The Western Alps consist of the Alpes-Maritimes, Cottian Alps, Alpes Dauphine, and the Graian Alps; the highest peak is Barre des Ecrins (4 101m). The Middle Alps consist of the Alpi Pennine, Alpi Lepontine, Rhaetian Alps, Bernese Alps, Alpi Orobie, Ötztaler Alpen, Dolomites, and the Lechtaler Alpen; the highest peak is Mont Blanc (4 807m); other peaks include the Matterhorn (4 477m), the Jungfrau (4 148m), and the Eiger (3 970m). The Eastern Alps consist of the Zillertaler Alpen or Alpi Aurine, Kitzbühler Alpen, Carnic Alps, Julian Alps, Hohe Tauern or Noric Alps, and the Niedere Tauern; the highest peak is Grossglockner (3 797m). In 1911 Karl Blodig was the first person to climb all peaks over 4 000m. It is a major tourist region, with highly developed facilities for skiing and mountaineering.

already *adv.* **1** before the present time or the time in question: *we've already paid.* **2** so soon or so early: *was already reading at the age of four.* [from Middle English *al redy*, completely ready]

alright a less acceptable spelling of *all right.*
◆ See note at *all right.*

Alsace, German **Elsass**, Latin **Alsatia** POP (1991) 1.6m, a region of NE France, comprising the departments of Bas-Rhin and Haut-Rhin. AREA 8 280sq km/3 196sq mi. Part of the Upper Rhine Plain on the frontier with Germany, the region is crossed S–N by the Rhine and Ill rivers. HISTORY a traditional scene of French–German conflict; formerly part of Lorraine, before becoming part of the German Empire; the 1648 Treaty of Westphalia returned most of Alsace to France; ceded to Germany in 1871, the region was returned to France in 1919; it was occupied by Germany in World War II. CHIEF TOWNS Strasbourg, Mulhouse, Colmar. ECONOMY a fertile and industrially productive region; wine, beer; pottery; chemicals; paper; printed fabrics; textile dyeing and spinning; machinery; car manufacture. There are several spas, wine towns, and vineyards.

Alsatian *noun* **1** a large wolf-like dog, often used as a guard dog or by the police. **2** a person born or living in Alsace, a region in NE France. [from Latin *Alsatia*, Alsace]

also *adv.* in addition; too; besides. [from Anglo-Saxon *ealswa*, all so, wholly]

also-ran *noun* **1** a horse, dog, person, etc not finishing in one of the top three places in a race. **2** an unimportant, undistinguished person.

Altaic — *adj.* denoting a family of languages covering the area from the Balkan Peninsula to the NE of Asia. It includes about 40 languages classified into three main groups: (1) Turkic, with written remains dating from the 8c, includes Turkish, Azerbaijani, Uzbek, Uighur, Tatar, and Kazakh; (2) Mongolian, with no written records before the 13c, includes Mongol, Buryat, Oyrat, and Kalmuk; and (3) Manchu-Tungus, which includes the now largely disused Manchu language which served as an important lingua franca between China and the outside world for nearly 200 years, and Tungus (now known as Evenki). — *noun* the languages forming this family.

Altai Mountains, Chinese **Altai Shan** a major mountain system in central Asia. It extends SE from Russia in the NW along the border between NW China and Mongolia and then into Mongolia itself. It is the source of the Irtysh and Ob rivers. Mt Belukha at 4 506m is the highest point. There are major mineral reserves in the mountains.

Altamira a Palaeolithic limestone cave of c.13 500 BC on the N Spanish coast near Santander. It is celebrated for its ceiling paintings of game animals (principally bison, bulls, horses, hinds, and boars). It was discovered in 1879 by local landowner Marcellino de Sautuola; doubts about its authenticity were dispelled by 1902. It is a World Heritage site.

altar *noun* **1** a special table at the front of a Christian church, near which the priest stands. **2** a table on which sacrifices are made to a god.
— **lead a woman to the altar** to marry her. [from Anglo-Saxon *alter*, from Latin *altaria*]

altar boy a young man or boy who assists a priest during a service.

altarpiece *noun* a religious picture or carving placed above and behind an altar, usually a carved or painted screen made up of a single panel, or a series of panels, often elaborately decorated.
◇ In Christian churches, the earliest examples date from the 10c, and were numerous by the late Middle Ages and Renaissance, notably in Venice. At the Reformation many were destroyed in Protestant countries (including almost all English examples), but in Catholic countries they continued to be produced in large numbers, especially in the Baroque period. The modern preference for plain altars set forward leaves no place for the altarpiece.
An altarpiece is called a *diptych* when it has two panels, and a *triptych* when it has three.

alter *verb trans., intrans.* (**altered**, **altering**) to make or become different. [from Old French *alterer*, from Latin *alter*, other]

alterable *adj.* capable of being altered.

alteration *noun* **1** altering or being altered. **2** a change made.

altercation *noun* a heated argument. [from Latin *altercari*, to quarrel]

alter ego *noun* (PL. **alter egos**) **1** a person's second or alternative character. **2** a close and trusted friend. [from Latin *alter ego*, other self]

alternate — *adj.* (pronounced *-nət*) **1** arranged or coming one after the other by turns: *alternate periods of misery and joy.* **2** (*with plural nouns*) every other; one out of two: *alternate Mondays.* — *verb* (pronounced *-nate*) **1** *intrans., trans. said of two things* to succeed, or cause them to succeed, each other by turns. **2** *intrans.* (**alternate between two things**) to change from one thing to another by turns. [from Latin *alternare*, to do things by turns]
♦ Often confused with *alternative*.

alternate angles *pl. noun* two equal angles which lie at opposite ends and on opposite sides of a line which intersects two parallel lines.

alternately *adv.* in an alternating position or sequence: *houses that were alternately grey and black.*

alternating current (ABBREV. **AC**) an electric current that reverses its direction at regular periods. See also DIRECT CURRENT.

alternation *noun* a pattern or sequence of repeated change from one action, state, etc, to another and back again.

alternation of generations *Biol.* the occurrence within the life cycle of certain living organisms (such as ferns, mosses, and coelenterates, eg corals) of a sexually reproducing generation that alternates with an asexually reproducing generation.
◇ In plants, alternation of generations involves a *gametophyte generation*, which bears gametes and reproduces sexually to produce a *sporophyte generation*, which bears spores and reproduces asexually. In ferns the dominant generation is the

sporophyte (the visible plant), which has the diploid number of chromosomes (a double set of chromosomes). It undergoes meiosis to produce spores that germinate and develop into a very small free-living gametophyte (known as a *prothallus*), which has the haploid number of chromosomes (a single set of chromosomes) and bears gametes. The diploid *zygote* formed by fusion of male and female gametes then develops into a new sporophyte. In mosses, by contrast, the gametophyte is the dominant generation.

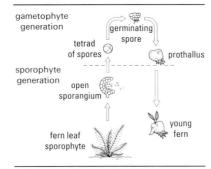

alternation of generations

alternative — *adj.* **1** available as a choice between two or more possibilities. **2** *said of a lifestyle, culture, etc* different from what is usually done, especially in being less conventional or materialistic, and more natural. — *noun* **1** the possibility of choice between two or more things. **2** any one of two or more choices or possibilities. [from Latin *alternare*, to do things by turns]
♦ Often confused with *alternate*.

alternative energy *Environ.* energy derived from sources other than nuclear power or the burning of fossil fuels such as coal, oil, and natural gas. The main sources of alternative energy are tidal power, wind power, wave power, hydroelectricity, solar radiation, and geothermal energy.

alternatively *adv.* as an alternative.

alternative medicine the treatment of disease using procedures other than those practised in orthodox medicine.
◇ Alternative medicine has become increasingly popular in recent years, especially for treatment of complaints that have not been relieved by orthodox methods. There are over 50 different approaches, including acupuncture, aromatherapy, autosuggestion, bioenergetics, chiropractic, herbalism, homeopathy and herbal medicine, hydrotherapy, massage, naturopathy, and osteopathy. Some of these treatments, eg acupuncture, have now been incorporated into orthodox medical practice.

alternative technology intermediate technology.

alternator *noun* a machine which produces an alternating current.

although *conj.* in spite of the fact that; apart from the fact that; though. [from Middle English *al thogh*, all though]

Althusser, Louis (1918–) French political philosopher, born in Birmandreis, Algeria. A member of the Communist Party from 1948, he wrote influential works on the interpretation of Marxist theory, including *Pour Marx* (For Marx, 1965) and *Lénin et la Philosophie* (Lenin and Philosophy, 1969). In 1980 he murdered his wife, and has since been confined in an asylum.

altimeter *noun Aeron.* an instrument used in aircraft for measuring height (altitude) above sea or ground level, and usually based on the change in air pressure with height, or the time taken for radio waves to be reflected back to a recording

device on the aircraft. [from Latin *altus*, high + -METER]

Altiplano an arid plateau in W Bolivia and S Peru, lying between the W and E Cordilleras at a height of 3 000–5 000m. It is covered by widespread alluvial and glacial deposits. The rivers and streams on the plateau drain into L Titicaca (Bolivia/Peru) and L Poopo (Bolivia). Both are closed lake basins, which means that they do not drain to the sea.

altitude *noun* **1** height, especially above sea level. **2** *Astron.* the angular distance between a celestial body and the horizon. See also AZIMUTH. **3** *Geom.* in a plane or solid figure, eg a triangle or pyramid, the perpendicular distance from an angle or *vertex* to the side opposite the angle (the *base*). [from Latin *altitudo*, from *altus*, high]

alto — *noun* (PL. **altos**) **1** the lowest female singing voice. **2** the highest adult male singing voice. **3** a singer with an alto voice. **4** a part or piece of music written for a voice or instrument at this pitch. — *adj., said of a musical instrument, etc* having this pitch. [from Italian *alto*, from Latin *altus*, high]

altocumulus *adj. Meteorol.* denoting middle-level clouds of the cumulus family that occur at altitudes of about 2 000m to 7 000m. They are white and/or grey in colour, and usually indicate fine weather. [from Latin *altus*, high + CUMULUS]

altogether *adv.* **1** completely. **2** on the whole. **3** taking everything into consideration.
— **in the altogether** *colloq.* naked.
[from Middle English *altogeder*, all together]

Alto Paraná, River see PARANA, RIVER.

altostratus *adj. Meteorol.* denoting middle-level clouds of the stratus family, similar to stratus clouds but less dense and occurring at higher altitudes, typically about 2 000m to 7 000m. They are greyish in colour with a sheet-like appearance, and give a warning of warm rainy weather associated with the passage of a warm front. [from Latin *altus*, high + STRATUS]

altruism *noun* an unselfish concern for the welfare of others. [from French *altruisme*, from Italian *altrui*, someone else]

altruist *noun* an altruistic person.

altruistic *adj.* having or involving an unselfish concern for the welfare of others.

altruistically *adv.* in an altruistic way.

alum *noun* **1** *Chem.* aluminium potassium sulphate, a white crystalline compound that occurs naturally as the mineral kalinite, used in dyeing and tanning, and as a medical astringent to stop bleeding. **2** any of various double-sulphate salts with a similar composition to this compound. [from Latin *alumen*]

alumina *Chem.* (FORMULA Al_2O_3) aluminium(III) oxide, a white crystalline compound that is the main ingredient of bauxite (the chief ore of aluminium), and also occurs in the form of the mineral corundum, which is used as an abrasive.

aluminium *noun* (SYMBOL **Al**, ATOMIC NUMBER **13**) a silvery-white metal that is strong when alloyed, light, a good electrical conductor, and protected against corrosion by the formation of a thin surface layer of its oxide. It is the third most abundant element in the Earth's crust, where it is a constituent of many rocks and clays, and of *bauxite*, the ore from which it is extracted. Aluminium alloys are used in the construction of aircraft and vehicles, and in door and window frames, household utensils, drink cans, etc. [from ALUM]

aluminosilicate *Chem.* a chemical compound, consisting mainly of alumina and silica, that is found in many rocks and minerals (eg clays and mica) and is also a constituent of glass and some ceramics.

alumnus *noun* (PL. **alumni**) a former pupil or student of a school, college or university. [from Latin *alumnus*, pupil]

Alva *or* **Alba Fernando Álvarez de Toledo, Duke of** (1507–82) Spanish soldier and statesman, born in Piedratita. He was sent to quell the Revolt of the Netherlands (1567), and his Council of Blood promoted a ruthless campaign of repression. He defeated Prince Louis of Nassau, compelled William of Orange to retire to Germany, then triumphantly entered Brussels (1568).

Alvarado, Pedro de (c.1495–1541) Spanish conquistador, born in Badajoz, who took part in the conquest of Mexico and later became Governor of Guatemala.

Alvarez, Luis Walter (1911–88) US experimental physicist, born in San Francisco. At the University of Chicago he built one of the first Geiger counters in the USA and used it to study cosmic rays. He later discovered electron capture by nuclei, tritium radioactivity, and the magnetic moment of the neutron, and invented a radar guidance system for landing aircraft in conditions of poor visibility. At Berkeley, where he became Professor of Physics in 1945, he developed larger bubble chamber detectors and used these to discover many new elementary particles. He was awarded the 1968 Nobel Prize for Physics.

alveolar *adj., said of a speech sound* produced by putting the tip of the tongue against the ridge behind the upper front teeth, eg *t* and *n*. [from Latin *alveolus*, small cavity]

alveolitis *noun Medicine* inflammation of the alveoli in the lungs.

alveolus *noun* (PL. **alveoli**) **1** *Anat.* each of the millions of thin-walled air sacs in the lungs, in which oxygen from inhaled air is exchanged for carbon dioxide in the blood. **2** a tooth socket in the jaw bone. **3** *Zool.* any small depression in the surface of an organ. [from Latin *alveolus*, a diminutive of *alveus*, a hollow]

always *adv.* **1** at all times. **2** continually. **3** in any case; if necessary: *you can always stay if you want to*. [from Middle English *alweys*]

alyssum *noun* a garden plant with clusters of white, yellow, or mauve flowers. [from Greek *alysson*]

Alzheimer, Alois (1864–1915) German psychiatrist and neuropathologist, born in Markbreit. After working in psychiatric hospitals, he became head of the anatomical laboratories of a psychiatric clinic in Munich and professor at Breslau University. He is best remembered for his full clinical and pathological description, in 1907, of dementia (see ALZHEIMER'S DISEASE).

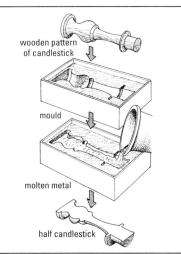

wooden pattern of candlestick

mould

molten metal

half candlestick

casting process for aluminium

Alzheimer's disease a disease in which degeneration of the brain cells results in gradual loss of memory, confusion, and impairment of other mental functions, eventually leading to total disintegration of the personality.
◇ Alzheimer's disease usually occurs in middle age or later, and there is no known cure. Current theories regarding its cause include a slow viral infection, environmental toxins (eg aluminium), and the involvement of a hereditary factor in certain forms.

AM *abbrev.* amplitude modulation.

Am *symbol Chem.* americium.

am see BE.

a.m. *or* **am** *abbrev. ante meridiem* (Latin), before midday; in the morning.

Amadeus a play by Peter Shaffer (1979). It is based on the bitter rivalry felt by the composer Antonio Salieri for Amadeus Mozart and the strange circumstances surrounding the latter's death.

Amadeus Quartet an English quartet founded in 1947. Highly acclaimed in the concert hall and recording studio (playing predominantly Mozart and Schubert), it comprised Norbert Brainin (violin), Siegmund Nissel (violin), Peter Schidlof (viola), and Martin Lovett (cello), and lasted until the death of Schidlof in 1987.

Amal a Lebanese Shiite movement established by the Imam Musa Sadr in the early 1970s. After Sadr's disappearance in 1978 during a trip to Libya, Nabih Berri took over the leadership. During the 1980s the Amal carried out several kidnappings in Lebanon, and the militia (a fighting force of over 4 000) fought with the Hizbollah (1988). It has come to be regarded as a mainstream component of Lebanese politics.

Amalekites an ancient nomadic people, notorious for their treachery, who lived S of Canaan. According to Genesis 36.12, they were descended from Esau.

amalgam *noun* **1** a mixture or blend. **2** *Chem.* an alloy of mercury with one or more other metals, eg silver or tin, which forms a soft paste on mixing, and later hardens, used in dentistry to fill holes in drilled teeth. [from Latin *amalgama*]

amalgamate *verb* **1** *trans., intrans.* to join together or unite to form a single unit, organization, etc. **2** *intrans. said of metals* to form an alloy with mercury. [from AMALGAM]

amalgamation *noun* blending; merging; joining together.

Amalthea *noun Astron.* one of Jupiter's moons, until 1979 thought to be the innermost moon. It is about 240km in diameter and has an elongated shape as a result of the gravitational pull of Jupiter.

Amanda a female first name, popular since the 1940s. [from Latin *amare*, to love]

amanuensis *noun* (PL. **amanuenses**) a literary assistant or secretary, especially one who writes from dictation or copies from manuscripts. [from Latin *amanuensis*, from *manu*, by hand]

amaranth *noun* **1** a plant with small green, red, or purple flowers. **2** *poetic* an imaginary flower that never fades. [from Greek *amarantos*, everlasting]

Amarillo POP (1990) 188 000, the seat of Potter County, NW Texas, USA. It is the commercial, banking, and industrial centre of the Texas panhandle.

amaryllis *noun* a lily-like plant native to S Africa, with large trumpet-like white, pink, or red flowers. [from the name of a shepherdess in Virgil's *Eclogues*]

amass *verb* to gather or collect (money, possessions, knowledge, etc) in great quantity. [from French *amasser*]

Amaterasu in Japanese mythology, the goddess of the sun and light, considered to be the

divine origin of the imperial family. She shut herself in a cave after a conflict with her brother, and the whole world was plunged into darkness. Light returned to the world when the other gods managed to tempt her back out by placing a mirror so that she could see what was happening outside, and grew curious.

amateur — *noun* **1** a person who takes part in a sport, pastime, etc as a hobby and without being paid for it. **2** a person who is not very skilled in an activity, etc. — *adj.* of amateurs; not professional. [from French *amateur*, from Latin *amator*, lover]

Amateur Athletic Association (ABBREV. **AAA**) the governing body for men's athletics in England and Wales. It was founded in Oxford in 1880, and the first championships were held in Lillie Bridge, London. The Women's Amateur Athletic Association was founded in 1922.

amateurish *adj., said of a person or a person's work, etc* characteristic of an amateur; not particularly skilful; inexperienced.

amateurishly *adv.* in an amateurish way.

amateurism *noun* attitudes or behaviour associated with amateurs.

amatory *adj.* of or showing sexual love. [from Latin *amatorius*, loving]

amaze *verb* to surprise greatly; to astonish. [from Anglo-Saxon *amasian*]

amazed *adj.* astonished.

amazedly *adv.* so as to astonish.

amazement *noun* astonishment; incredulity.

amazing *adj.* astonishing; wonderful.

amazingly *adv.* so as to cause amazement or surprise: *an amazingly quiet child / amazingly, he said nothing*.

Amazon *noun* **1** *Greek Mythol.* a member of a nation of women warriors from Scythia. **2** (**amazon**) an immensely strong woman, usually one who is good at sport. [from Greek; the Greeks understood it to mean 'lacking a breast', from *mazos*, breast (see below), but it was more probably a foreign word]
◇ The Amazons are described by the Greek historian Herodotus (5c BC), and were a common subject in Greek art. According to legend, there were no men in the Amazon nation; any male offspring were either killed or banished at birth. The women were said to cut off their right breasts in order to use the bow. None of these stories has any verifiable basis in fact.

Amazon, River, Portuguese **Río Amazônas** a river in the N of S America, the largest in the world by volume, and the second longest. There are two major headstreams, the Marañón and the Ucayali, rising in the Andes of Peru and joining S of Iquitos. The length from L Lauricocha (situated at the headwaters of the Marañón) is 6 280km/3 902mi; from L Vilafro, following the Ucayali and Apurímac headwaters to the mouth of the Amazon via the Canal do Norte, it measures 6 449km/4 007mi. Flowing generally W–E across Brazil, it enters the Atlantic Ocean in a wide delta, where there is a large island called Ilha de Marajó. It drains a basin of area c.7 000 000sq km/2 700 000sq mi and has more than 1 100 tributaries; the rivers of the Amazon basin carry one fifth of the world's running water. Despite difficulty in navigation, ocean steamers are able to sail as far as Iquitos, 3 680km/2 287mi from the Atlantic Ocean. The deepest point is 37m at the influx of the Trombetas R. River levels at Manaus fluctuate by more than 15m and the N channels of the delta are made dangerous by a frequent tidal bore (*Pororoca*) moving up river at up to 65kph/40mph, with waves sometimes 5m high. Cargo launches use the Amazon to reach the interior, carrying fish, cedarwood, flour, rubber, and jute. HISTORY discovered in 1500; first descended in 1541, ascended 1637; opened to world shipping in

1866; free navigation was guaranteed by treaty between Colombia and Brazil in 1929.

Amazonian *adj.* **1** relating to or like an Amazon. **2** relating to or in the region of the River Amazon.

ambassador *noun* **1** a diplomat of the highest rank appointed by a government to act for or represent it abroad. **2** a representative, messenger, or agent. [from Old French *ambassateur*, from Latin *ambactus*, servant]

ambassadorial *adj.* relating to or having the status of an ambassador.

ambassadorship *noun* the office or function of an ambassador.

Ambassadors, The 1 a group portrait by Hans Holbein the Younger (1533, National Gallery, London). **2** a novel by Henry James (1903). It explores the effect on various characters of the cultural differences between Paris and Woollett, Massachusetts.

ambassadress *noun* **1** a woman ambassador. **2** the wife of an ambassador.

Ambedkar, Bhimrao Ranji (1893–1956) Indian politician and champion of the depressed classes, born in a Ratnagiri village, Bombay. After practising as a barrister in London, he joined the Bombay Legislative Assembly and became leader of 60 000 000 untouchables (members of the lowest caste). As Minister of Law from 1947, he had a leading part in forming the Indian Constitution. Together with thousands of his followers, he publicly embraced the Buddhist faith not long before his death.

amber — *noun Geol.* a transparent yellow or reddish fossilized resin that was exuded by coniferous trees, and is found in rock strata worldwide. It can be carved and polished, and is used to make jewellery and ornaments. Extinct insects and plants are sometimes found trapped in amber. — *adj.* relating to this substance or to its colour. [from Old French *ambre*, from Arabic *anbar*, ambergris]

amber with fossilized insect

ambergris *noun* a pale grey waxy substance with a strong smell produced in the intestines of sperm whales, found in lumps floating on the water or washed ashore. Until the recent decline in whaling it was widely used in the perfume industry. [from Old French *ambre gris*, grey amber]

ambidextrous *adj.* able to use both hands equally well. [from Latin *ambi-*, both + *dexter*, right]

ambidextrously *adv.* in an ambidextrous way.

ambience *or* **ambiance** *noun* the surroundings or atmosphere of a place. [from Latin *ambiens*, surrounding, from *ambi-*, about + *ire*, to go]

ambient *adj.*, *said of air, temperature, etc* surrounding.

ambiguity *noun* (PL. **ambiguities**) **1** uncertainty of meaning. **2** an ambiguous word or statement.

ambiguous *adj.* having more than one possible meaning; not clear. [from Latin *ambiguus*, from *ambi-*, both ways + *agere*, to drive]

ambiguously *adv.* in an ambiguous way.

ambit *noun* range, extent, or bounds. [from Latin *ambitus*, from *ambi-*, about + *ire*, to go]

ambition *noun* **1** a strong desire for success, fame, or power. **2** a thing one desires to do or achieve. [from Latin *ambitio*, going round, canvassing, from *ambi-*, about + *ire*, to go]

ambitious *adj.* **1** having a strong desire for success, etc. **2** requiring hard work and skill.

ambitiously *adv.* in an ambitious way; to an ambitious extent.

ambitiousness *noun* being ambitious.

ambivalence *noun* the state of holding two opposite views or feelings about a person or subject at the same time. [from Latin *ambi-*, both + *valere*, to be worth]

ambivalent *adj.* relating to or involving ambivalence.

ambivalently *adv.* in an ambivalent way.

amble — *verb intrans.* to walk without hurrying; to stroll. — *noun* a leisurely walk. [from Old French *ambler*, from Latin *ambulare*, to walk about]

Ambler, Eric (1909–) English novelist, born in London. After an apprenticeship in engineering (1927–8), he served in Italy (1943) during World War II and at the War Office (1944–6). He specializes in the writing of spy thrillers, and his works include *Epitaph for a Spy* (1938) and *The Mask of Dimitrios* (1939).

Ambleside POP (1981) 3 200, a town in South Lakeland district, Cumbria, NW England. It lies N of L Windermere and is a popular tourism centre for the Lake District. NOTABLE FEATURES Church of St Mary (19c); tollhouse on the R Rothay Bridge (18c).

amblygonite *noun Geol.* a mineral that occurs as white or greenish masses in pegmatites in Europe and the USA. It is an important ore of lithium. [from Greek *amblus*, dull + *gonia* angle]

Ambo *or* **Ovambo** a Bantu-speaking agricultural and cattle-rearing people of N Namibia and S Angola. They are called Ovambo in Namibia, and Ambo in Angola, and are divided into several small kingdoms and chiefdoms.

Ambrose, St (c.339–97 AD) Italian bishop and writer, born in Trier. He practised law and became consular prefect of Upper Italy (369). Though he was an unbaptized layman, his fairness in dealing with the Arian/Catholic controversy led to his appointment as Bishop of Milan in 374. One of the four Latin Doctors of the Church (with St Augustine, St Jerome, and Gregory the Great), he is remembered for his preaching (which greatly influenced St Augustine), his literary works and hymns, and for his improvements of the church service, the Ambrosian ritual and chant. His feast day is 7 Dec.

ambrosia *noun* **1** *Greek Mythol.* the food of the gods, which gave them eternal youth and beauty. **2** something with a delicious taste or smell. [from Greek *ambrosia*, from *ambrotos*, immortal]

Ambrosian Library a library founded in 1609 in Milan, Italy, by Cardinal Frederico Borromeo (1564–1631). It was one of the first libraries to be opened to the general public, and has holdings of over 850 000 volumes and 2 100 incunabula.

ambulance *noun* a specially equipped vehicle for carrying sick or injured people to hospital. [from Latin *ambulare*, to walk about]

ambush — *noun* **1** the act of lying in wait to attack someone by surprise. **2** an attack made in this way. **3** the person or people making such an attack. **4** a place of concealment from which the attack is made. — *verb* to lie in wait for or attack (someone) in this way. [from Old French *embuschier*, to place men in the woods]

Amelia a female first name, first used as the central character of Henry Fielding's *Amelia*.

[probably a mixture of Latin *Emilia* + Germanic *Amalia*]

ameliorate *verb trans., intrans.* to make or become better. [from Old French *ameillorer*, from Latin *melior*, better]

amelioration *noun* making better; improvement.

Amen see AMUN.

amen *interj.*, *usually said at the end of a prayer* so be it. [from Hebrew *amen*, certainly]

amenable *adj.* **1** ready to accept advice or guidance. **2** legally responsible. [from Old French *amener*, to lead to]

amend *verb* to correct, improve, or make minor changes to (a book, document, etc).
— **make amends for something** to make up for or compensate for some injury, insult, etc. See also EMEND.
[from Old French *amender*, from Latin *emendare*]

amendment *noun* correction, improvement, alteration.

Amenhotep III (c.1411–1375 BC) King of Egypt of the 18th dynasty. His reign was marked by peaceful progress and cultural and artistic achievements at home, and the consolidation of Egyptian supremacy in Babylonia and Assyria. He had the ancient capital of Thebes rebuilt, and its monuments included the Colossi of Memnon, the Luxor temple, and the pylon at Karnak.

amenity *noun* (PL. **amenities**) **1** anything that makes life more comfortable and pleasant. **2** pleasantness of situation. **3** a public facility. [from Latin *amoenus*, pleasant]

amenorrhoea *or* **amenorrhea** *noun Medicine* the absence or stopping of normal menstruation. [from A-[1] without + Greek *men*, mouth + *rhoia*, a flowing]

American — *adj.* of the United States of America or the American continent, the people who live or were born there, and the languages they speak. — *noun* a person born or living in the United States of America, or the American continent. [from *America*, named after *Amerigo Vespucci* (1454–1512), Italian navigator]

American Academy of Motion Picture Arts and Sciences, The in the USA, an organization known since 1927 for its annual awards ('Oscars') for creative merit and craftsmanship in film production. It has been influential in establishing technical standards.

American Civil Liberties Union a US pressure group concerned to promote civil rights, especially of blacks and ethnic minorities.

American Civil War, also called **Second American Revolution** a conflict in the USA (1861–5) which resolved both the issue of the nature of the Federal Union and the relative power of the states and the central government, and the issue of black slavery. The war began soon after Lincoln won the presidential election, proof that the South could no longer expect to control the high offices of state. Although Lincoln disagreed with slavery, he did not want to interfere where it existed, but to Southerners, he and the Republican Party were intolerable; consequently, 11 Southern states seceded from the Union to establish the Confederate States of America. War broke out (12 Apr 1861) when Southern batteries fired on a Union emplacement in the harbour of Charleston, South Carolina. At first Lincoln defined the war aim as the preservation of the Union, without reference to slavery, but he broadened it (1 Jan 1863) and proclaimed the emancipation without compensation of all slaves in areas then under arms against the government. The Union had greater manpower and far greater industrial resources. The battles of Vicksburg and Gettysburg in 1863 saw the tide turn, and the Confederate general Robert E Lee surrendered to Ulysses S Grant at Appomattox Court House on 9 Apr 1865.

American Colonization Society a US pre-abolitionist anti-slavery group founded in 1816 whose goal was to resettle freed slaves in Africa. It was supported by some slaveholders anxious to keep freed blacks separate from slaves, and was dissolved in 1912.

American Federation of Labor–Congress of Industrial Organizations (ABBREV. **AFL/CIO**) in the US, a federation of trade unions, formed in 1955 from the merger of the AFL (mainly craft unions, founded in 1866) with the CIO (mainly industrial workers' unions, founded in 1935). Its aims include educational campaigns on behalf of the labour movement, the settlement of disputes among affiliates, and political support for beneficial legislation.

American football a form of football resembling rugby, but forward passing of the ball is permitted. It is the national winter sport in the USA, played on a rectangular field 300ft (91m) by 160ft (49m), known as the gridiron because it is divided into 5yd (4.6m) segments. The object is to score touchdowns (similar to tries in rugby) but progress has to be made upfield by a series of 'plays'. Six points are awarded for a touchdown and one point for a 'point after', for kicking the ball between the posts and over the crossbar. A goal kicked from anywhere on the field (a 'field goal') is worth three points. Teams consist of more than 40 squad members, but only 11 are allowed on to the field at any one time. The game was first played in US colleges in the mid-19c, and the first rules were drawn up at Princeton College in 1867. The professional game in the USA comes under the auspices of the National Football League (NFL), which is divided into two 'leagues': the American Football Conference (AFC) and National Football Conference (NFC). The winners of the two conferences play-off each January for the Super Bowl tournament.

American Indian a member of any of the original peoples of N America.

American in Paris, An an orchestral work by George Gershwin (1928) which includes taxi horns in the score.

Americanism *noun* a word, phrase, custom, etc that is characteristic of Americans.

American Revolution the war (1775–83) that established the 13 American colonies as independent from Britain, often called the American War of Independence. Relations between the N American colonies and Britain became increasingly strained (1763–75). Colonial resistance was especially high over the issue of whether the British parliament had the right to tax the colonies without their representation. The tension during this period was reflected in the Stamp Act crisis (1765–6), resistance to the Townshend Acts (1767–70), the Boston Massacre (1770), the burning of the customs cruiser Gaspée (1772), and the Boston Tea Party (1773). The British parliament's passage of the Intolerable Acts (1774) to punish Massachusetts for the Tea Party led to the calling of the First Continental Congress (1774). In Apr 1775 fighting broke out between British troops and the colonial militia known as the Minutemen at the battles of Lexington and Concord in Massachusetts. Other military engagements followed, including the colonial capture of Fort Ticonderoga (May 1775), the battle of Bunker Hill, and the unsuccessful colonial expedition in Quebec, Canada. In June 1775 the Second Continental Congress elected George Washington to command the Continental Army and in July adopted the Declaration of Independence. Following the British evacuation of Boston in May 1776, the main theatre shifted to New York, New Jersey, and Pennsylvania. Washington's troops suffered a number of defeats in the New York area, and lost the battle of Brandywine (Sep 1777) in Pennsylvania. In Jun 1777 British troops had begun to move down from Canada but shrewd American manoeuvring resulted in defeat of the

British and the surrender of Burgoyne following the battle of Saratoga in upstate New York. The French entered the war officially, bringing to the colonists badly needed material support, troops, monetary credit, and a fleet. During the winter of 1778 Washington's troops suffered great hardship while wintering in Valley Forge. By the spring the colonial forces had regathered their strength. Later that year fighting shifted southward, when Sir Henry Clinton commanded an invasion of South Carolina. Clinton's successor, Lord Cornwallis, led the army gradually north until Washington and the French Admiral de Grasse trapped him on the Yorktown Peninsula in Virginia, where he surrendered in 1781. The defeat resulted in the fall of the British Prime Minister, Lord North, who had prosecuted the war, and ended British will for further fighting. After almost two years of negotiating, the Treaty of Paris was signed in Sep 1783, recognizing the independence of the USA.

American Samoa, formerly **Loanda**, Portuguese **São Paulo de Loanda** POP (1990) 47 000, a Territory of the USA, in the central S Pacific Ocean, some 3 500km/2 175mi NE of New Zealand. AREA 197sq km/76sq mi. It comprises five principal volcanic islands and two coral atolls, and is divided into five counties. CAPITAL Pago Pago. TIME ZONE GMT −11. Its people are largely of Polynesian origin; the main religion is Christianity. LANGUAGES English; Samoan. CURRENCY US dollar. PHYSICAL DESCRIPTION the main island is Tutuila; to the E and N are Aunu'u, the Manu'a Group (Ta'u, Olosega, Ofu), the atolls of Swain's I, and the uninhabited Rose I; the main islands are hilly, with large areas covered by thick bush and forest; Tutuila rises to 653m on Ta'u to 970m. CLIMATE a tropical maritime climate, with small annual range of temperature, eg Pago Pago average in Jan is 28°C, and in Jul is 27°C; rainfall is plentiful with an annual average of 5 000mm. HISTORY the USA acquired rights to American Samoa in 1899, and the islands were ceded by their chiefs in 1900–25; it is now an unincorporated and unorganized Territory of the USA, administered by the Department of the Interior. GOVERNMENT a bicameral legislature was established in 1948; the governor is the administrative head of the executive branch; legislature (the *Fono*) comprises the Senate (18 members, chosen every four years by county councils according to Samoan custom) and the House of Representatives (20 members, plus one non-voting member, chosen every two years by popular vote). ECONOMY principal crops are taro, breadfruit, yams, bananas, coconuts; fish canning, tuna fishing, local inshore fishing; handicrafts.

American War of Independence see AMERICAN REVOLUTION.

America's Cup, originally the **Hundred Guinea Cup** one of the best-known races in yachting, now held in a different location approximately every four years, when challengers compete in a series of races to find which of them races against the holder. The trophy was won by the USA from 1870 until 1983, when it was won by Australia. The USA won it back in 1987, and then successfully held off a challenge from New Zealand in 1988, which resulted in a lengthy legal battle. In 1992, the USA retained the trophy.

americium *noun* (SYMBOL **Am**, ATOMIC NUMBER **95**) a radioactive white metallic element produced artificially from plutonium and uranium. [from *America*, where it was first produced]

Amerigo, Prince the penniless Italian aristocrat in Henry James's *The Golden Bowl*, who has an affair with Charlotte Stant and marries Maggie Verver.

Amerindian — *adj.* **1** Native American. **2** denoting a family of over 1 000 languages used by Native Americans in N, Central, and S America. It is divided into North American (including the group Eskimo-Aleut, Na-Dené,

Algonkian, and Macro-Siouan), Mesoamerican, and South American. — *noun* **1** a Native American. **2** the languages forming the Amerindian family.

amethyst — *noun* a type of purple or violet quartz used as a gemstone. — *adj.* purple or violet in colour. [from Greek *amethystos*, not drunken; the stone was supposed to prevent drunkenness]

Amhara a Semitic-speaking people of the Ethiopian central highlands who, with the Tigray, dominate the country. They are descended from the original Semitic conquerors from S Arabia. The Christian empire of Ethiopia was ruled by Amhara dynasties (1260–1974) which, by intermarriage and cultural assimilation, incorporated people from almost every ethnic group of the empire.

Amharic — *noun* the official language of Ethiopia, related to Hebrew and Arabic. — *adj.* of or in this language.

amiability *noun* being amiable.

amiable *adj.* likeable; friendly, pleasant and good-tempered. [from Latin *amicabilis*, amicable, confused with Old French *amable*, lovable]

amiably *adv.* in an amiable way.

amicability *noun* **1** being amicable. **2** friendly feelings; a friendly relationship.

amicable *adj.* friendly. [from Latin *amicabilis*, from *amicus*, friend]

amicably *adv.* in an amicable or friendly way.

amid *or* **amidst** *prep.* in the middle of; among. [from Anglo-Saxon *onmiddan*, in the centre]

Amidah the principal component of the daily prayers of Talmudic Judaism, recited while standing, and said silently except when in a congregational service. Its 19 benedictions comprise sections of praise, petition, and thanksgiving to God. An altered form of the prayer is also recited on sabbaths and festivals. [Hebrew, = standing]

amide *noun* a compound formed from ammonia, in which an acid or metal radical takes the place of one or more of the hydrogen atoms. [from AMMONIA]

amidships *or* **midships** *adv.* in, into, or near the middle of a ship.

Amiens, ancient **Samarobriva** POP (1990) 156 000, the capital of Picardy region and of Somme department, N France. Situated 130km/80mi N of Paris, on the left bank of the R Somme, it is an agricultural market town. NOTABLE FEATURES war-time cemeteries at Arras to the E; 13c Gothic Cathedral of Notre-Dame, a World Heritage site.

Amiens, Treaty of A treaty (1802) between Britain and France that marked the end of the first stage of the wars with Revolutionary France. Both powers agreed to return most of their conquests made since 1793, but peace was short-lived — war soon broke out afresh (1803–15).

Amin (Dada), Idi (c.1925–) Ugandan soldier and politician, born in Koboko of a peasant family. After a rudimentary education, he rose rapidly to become commander of the army and air force (1966). He staged a coup to depose Milton Obote in 1971, dissolved parliament, and was proclaimed President of Uganda (1971–9) by the army. Throughout his presidency there were continual reports of widespread atrocities, including the massacre of thousands of hostile tribesmen by government forces. He expelled 500 Israeli citizens (all Ugandan Asians with British passports) and the British High Commissioner, and organized the seizure of foreign-owned businesses and estates, and mass arrests. Deposed by exiled Ugandans with the help of the Tanzanian army in 1979, he fled to Libya and lived in Jeddah, Saudi Arabia (1980–8).

amine *noun* a compound formed from ammonia, in which one or more hydrocarbon radicals take the place of one or more of the hydrogen atoms. [from AMMONIA]

amino acid any of a group of water-soluble organic compounds that contain an amino (-NH₂) group and a carboxyl (-COOH) group, and form the individual subunits of proteins.
◇ Twenty amino acids are commonly found in living organisms, and the order in which they occur in a particular protein determines its properties and three-dimensional structure, and therefore its function. *Essential amino acids* are required for growth and metabolism but are not manufactured by humans and animals, so must be obtained from the diet, eg phenylalanine, tryptophan. *Non-essential amino acids* are manufactured by the body, eg alanine, glutamine.

amino acid: glycine

amino group *Chem.* the -NH₂ group in amino acids and other nitrogen-containing organic compounds.

amir same as EMIR.

Amis, Kingsley (1922–) English novelist and poet, born in London. He established his reputation with his comic second novel, *Lucky Jim* (1954), followed by *That Uncertain Feeling* (1955) and *I Like It Here* (1958). *The Old Devils* won the Booker Prize in 1986. Other works include *Collected Poems 1944–79* (1979), *The James Bond Dossier* (1965), and a James Bond novel, *Colonel Sun* (1968), written under the pseudonym of Robert Markham after the death of Ian Fleming.

Amis, Martin (Louis) (1949–) English novelist and journalist, born in Oxford, the son of Kingsley Amis. He acted in the film *A High Wind in Jamaica* (1965) and worked for the *Times Literary Supplement* before becoming a full-time writer in 1979. His first novel *The Rachel Papers* (1973) was followed by two more socio-cultural satires: *Dead Babies* (1975) and *Success* (1978). Other novels include *Money* (1984), *London Fields* (1989), and *Time's Arrow* (1991), which plays with the concepts of time and history.

Amish a US pietistic sect, founded (c.1693) in Berne, Switzerland, by Jacob Amman, a conservative Mennonite preacher. They began to emigrate to America in 1727. Now about 80 000 in number, the Amish live in rural communities, speak in a German dialect, forbid the use of modern technological developments, and are mostly dependent on non-mechanized farming for their livelihood. Resistant to institutionalization, they refuse to establish churches or colleges, and educate their own children, a practice supported by a 1972 Supreme Court decision. Together with the Mennonites they represent the last vestiges of Reformation anabaptism in the modern world.

amiss — *adj.* wrong; out of order. — *adv.* wrongly.
— **take something amiss** to be upset or offended by it.
[from MISS¹]

amity *noun formal* friendship. [from Old French *amitie*, from Latin *amicus*, friend]

Amman 1 POP (1989e) 1.3m, the capital of Jordan. An industrial and commercial city, it is situated in Amman governorate, East Bank, on the R Zarqa. Amman was the capital of the Ammonite Kingdom in biblical times and became the capital of Transjordan in 1923. Many refugees arrived after the Arab–Israeli Wars. The city is famous for its locally-quarried coloured marble. NOTABLE FEATURES Roman amphitheatre (1c BC), Archaeological Museum. **2** a governorate in Jordan with Amman as its capital.

ammeter *noun* an instrument used to measure an electric current, usually in amperes. [from AMPERE + METER]

ammo *noun colloq.* short form of AMMUNITION.

Ammon see AMUN.

ammonia *noun* **1** (FORMULA NH₃) a colourless pungent gas that is very soluble in water, formed naturally by the bacterial decomposition of proteins, urea, etc, and manufactured industrially from nitrogen and hydrogen in the Haber process. Its compounds are used as fertilizers and explosives, and liquefied ammonia is used as a refrigerant. **2** an alkaline solution of ammonia in water (ammonium hydroxide), used as a bleach and household cleaning agent. [from Latin *sal ammoniacus*, salt of Ammon, ammonia in salt form first found near a temple to the god Ammon in Libya]

ammonite *noun Geol.* an extinct marine cephalopod mollusc, with a flat tightly coiled shell, widespread during the Mesozoic era; the fossilized remains, especially the shell, of this animal. [from Latin *ammonites*, horn of Ammon]

ammonite

Ammonites an ancient Semitic people who in Old Testament times lived in S Transjordan. According to tradition, they were descended from Lot.

ammonium *Chem.* (FORMULA NH₄⁺) a cation (a positively charged ion) formed by the reaction of ammonia with acid. It behaves like a metal ion, and is found in many salts, particularly ammonium chloride (sal ammoniac) and ammonium carbonate (sal volatile). Ammonium hydroxide is an aqueous solution of ammonia.

ammunition *noun* **1** bullets, shells, bombs, etc made to be fired from a weapon. **2** facts, etc which can be used against someone in an argument. [from French *amunitions*, military supplies]

amnesia *noun* loss of memory. [from Greek *amnesia*, forgetfulness]

amnesiac *noun* a person who suffers from amnesia.

amnesic *adj.* **1** relating to amnesia. **2** suffering loss of memory.

amnesty *noun* (PL. **amnesties**) **1** a general pardon, especially for people convicted or accused of political crimes. **2** a period of time during which criminals may admit to crimes, hand in weapons, etc, with the promise of a pardon. [from Greek *amnestia*, oblivion]

Amnesty International a British-based pressure group, founded (1961) in London by Peter Benenson (1921–), a Catholic lawyer. It campaigns for the release of any person detained for their political or religious beliefs or who has been unjustly imprisoned for any other reason.

amniocentesis *noun Medicine* the insertion of a hollow needle through the abdominal wall into the uterus (womb) of a pregnant woman in order to withdraw a sample of the amniotic fluid surrounding the embryo. The sample is analysed in order to detect fetal abnormalities such as Down's syndrome or spina bifida. [from *amnion*, the membrane enclosing the foetus + *centesis*, puncture]

amnion *noun* (PL. **amnia**) *Anat.* the innermost membrane that surrounds the embryo of mammals, birds, and reptiles.

amniotic fluid *Zool.* the clear fluid that surrounds and protects the embryo in the amniotic cavity of mammals, birds, and reptiles. [from *amnion*, the membrane enclosing the foetus]

amoeba *noun* (PL. **amoebae**, **amoebas**) a microscopic animal belonging to the phylum Protozoa, which has no fixed shape and moves by continually pushing out 'arms' or *pseudopodia* in different directions. Most species live in water, but a few are found in damp soil. Some of the parasitic species are capable of causing disease, eg amoebic dysentery. [from Greek *amoibe*, change]

amoebic *adj.* relating to or characteristic of amoebae.

amok *or* **amuck**
— **run amok** *or* **amuck** to rush about violently and out of control.
[from Malay *amoq*, frenzied]

Amon see AMUN.

among *or* **amongst** *prep., used of more than two things, people, etc* **1** in the middle of: *among friends*. **2** between: *divide it among them*. **3** in the group or number of: *among his best plays*. **4** with one another: *decide among yourselves*. [from Anglo-Saxon *ongemang*]

Amontons, Guillaume (1663–1705) French instrument-maker and experimental physicist, born in Paris. He designed many instruments including a hygrometer (1687), a 'folded' barometer (1688), a conical nautical barometer (1695), and various air thermometers. In early work on gas laws he derived basic relationships between pressure, volume, and temperature, and hinted at the existence of a physically unattainable zero of temperature.

amoral *adj.* having no moral standards or principles.

amorality *noun* being amoral.

Amoret the angelic daughter of the wood nymph Chrysogone and twin sister to Belphoebe in Spenser's *The Faerie Queene*, who is imprisoned by Busirane after being snatched from her husband Sir Scudamour on their wedding-day.

Amorites the name of various Semitic peoples who lived in Mesopotamia, Syria, and Palestine in Old Testament times.

amorous *adj.* showing, feeling, or relating to love, especially sexual love. [from Latin *amorosus*, from *amor*, love]

amorously *adv.* in an amorous way.

amorphous *adj.* with no definite shape or structure. [from Greek *amorphos*, shapeless]

amortization *or* **amortisation** *noun* **1** the process of amortizing a debt. **2** the money used for this.

amortize *or* **amortise** *verb* **1** to gradually pay off (a debt) by regular payments of money. **2** to gradually write off the initial cost of (an asset) over a period. [from Old French *amortir*, to kill]

Amory, Derick Heathcoat, 1st Viscount (1899–1981) English Conservative politician, born in Tiverton, Devon. He entered parliament in 1945 and held a number of ministerial posts before serving as Chancellor of the Exchequer for two years from 1958.

Amos 1 a prophet of the 8c BC whose writings form one book of the Old Testament. **2** a male first name, now rare. [possibly from Hebrew *amos*, to carry]

Amos, Book of one of the 12 so-called 'minor' prophetic writings in the Hebrew Bible and Old Testament. Attributed to the prophet Amos, who was active in the N kingdom of Israel in the mid-8c BC, it proclaims judgement on Israel's neighbours for idolatry, and on Israel itself for social injustices and immorality.

amount — *noun* a quantity; a total or extent: *a large amount of money.* — *verb intrans.* (**amount to something**) to be equal to it or add up to it in size, number, etc: *their assets amounted to several millions.* [from Old French *amonter*, to climb up]

amour *noun old use* a love affair, especially one that is kept secret. [from French *amour*, love]

amour-propre *noun* self-esteem. [from French *amour-propre*]

Amoy see XIAMEN.

amp *noun* **1** an ampere. **2** *colloq.* an amplifier.

Ampato, Nevado de an Andean massif in the Cordillera Occidental, S Peru, rising to 6 310m. Nearby is the Cañon del Colca, a gorge cut by the R Colca. The gorge is 60km/37mi long and 3 000m deep, and is thought to be the deepest canyon in the world.

amperage *noun* the strength of an electrical current, measured in amperes.

Ampère, André Marie (1775–1836) French mathematician, chemist, and physicist, born in Lyons. He taught at the École Polytechnique in Paris, the University of Paris, and the Collège de France, and became best known for laying the foundations of of the study of electricity and electromagnetism. His name is given to the basic SI unit of electric current (ampere, amp).

ampere *noun* (SYMBOL **A**) the SI unit of electric current, equivalent to one coulomb per second. One ampere is the current that would produce a force of $2 \times 10^{-7} Nm^{-1}$ between two parallel conductors of infinite length placed 1m apart in a vacuum. [named after the French physicist André Marie Ampère]

ampersand *noun* the sign &, meaning 'and'. [short form of *and per se and*, ie 'and' by itself means 'and']

amphetamine *noun Medicine* any of a group of potentially addictive drugs that stimulate the central nervous system and produce a sense of well-being and mental alertness. Amphetamines were formerly used as appetite suppressants to treat obesity, and as antidepressants, but are now seldom prescribed because of the risk that prolonged use may lead to addiction. [from the chemical name *alphamethylphenethylamine*]

Amphibia *noun Zool.* in the classification of the animal kingdom, a class of cold-blooded semi-aquatic vertebrates that includes frogs, toads, newts, and salamanders.

amphibian *noun* **1** *Zool.* any cold-blooded vertebrate animal belonging to the class Amphibia, which includes frogs, toads, newts, and salamanders. Amphibians have a moist, thin skin without scales, and the adults live partly or entirely on land, but can usually only survive in damp habitats. They return to water to lay their eggs, which hatch to form fish-like larvae or tadpoles that breathe by means of gills, but gradually develop lungs as they approach adulthood. **2** a vehicle that can operate both on land and in water, eg an aircraft that can land and take off on either land or water. [from Greek *amphi*, both + *bios*, life]

amphibious *adj.* **1** living or operating both on land and in water. **2** *said of a military attack, etc* using troops landed from the sea.

amphibole *noun Geol.* any of a group of complex silicate minerals that are widely distributed in igneous and metamorphic rocks. Common varieties include hornblende, and fibrous forms belong to the asbestos group of minerals. [from

Greek *amphibolos*, ambiguous, on account of the resemblance between hornblende and tourmaline]

amphipod *noun* any of more than 4 600 species of crustacean belonging to the order Amphipoda, eg sandhoppers, freshwater shrimps, with different pairs of legs specialized for swimming, walking, and jumping. [from Greek *amphi*, both + *pous podos*, foot]

amphitheatre *noun Hist.* a round building without a roof, with tiers of seats round a central open area, used as a theatre. [from Greek *amphi*, around + *theatron*, theatre]

amphitheatre

Amphitrite in Greek mythology, a goddess of the sea, married to Poseidon. She is the mother of Triton and other minor deities.

Amphitryon in Greek mythology, the husband of Alcmene. In his absence, Zeus took his shape and so became the father of Heracles.

amphora *noun* (PL. **amphoras**, **amphorae**) *Hist.* a Greek or Roman narrow-necked jar with a handle on each side and a pointed bottom, used to hold wine. [from Latin and Greek *amphora*, from Greek *amphi*, on both sides + *phoreus*, bearer]

amphoteric *adj. Chem., said of a chemical compound* having two different properties, usually that of being an acid and a base, eg aluminium hydroxide is amphoteric, because it forms salts both with acids (by behaving as a base) and with alkalis (by behaving as an acid). [from Greek *amphoteros*, both]

ample *adj.* **1** more than enough; plenty. **2** extensive, abundant. **3** *said especially of people* very large. [from Latin *amplus*]

amplification *noun* **1** the act, process, or result of amplifying. **2** material added to a report, story, etc to expand or explain it. **3** a story or account with details added.

amplifier *noun* an electronic device that increases the strength of an electrical or radio signal without appreciably altering its characteristics, by transferring power from an external source to the signal. The increase in power produced, ie the ratio of the strength of the output signal to that of the input signal, is known as the *gain*. Amplifiers are used in audio equipment, radio and television sets, etc.

amplify *verb* (**amplifies**, **amplified**) **1** to make (a sound or electrical signal) stronger. **2** *trans., intrans.* (**amplify on** *or* **upon something**) to add details or further explanation to an account, story, etc. [from Latin *amplificare*, from *amplus*, ample]

amplitude *noun* **1** spaciousness, wide range or extent. **2** *Physics* for any quantity that varies in periodic cycles, eg a wave or vibration, the maximum displacement from its mean position, eg the angle between the vertical and the peak position during the swing of a pendulum. [from Latin *amplitudo*, from *amplus*, ample]

amplitude modulation *Radio* (ABBREV. **AM**) in radio transmission, the process whereby the amplitude of the carrier wave (signal-carrying wave) is made to increase or decrease instantaneously in response to variations in the characteristics of the signal being transmitted.

amply *adv.* well; more than is necessary.

ampoule *noun Medicine* a small sealed container, usually of glass or plastic, containing one sterile dose of a drug for injecting. [from French, from Latin *ampulla*, bottle]

ampulla *noun* (PL. **ampullae**) **1** *Hist.* a small round glass bottle with two handles, used by ancient Romans for holding oil, perfume, or wine. **2** a container for oil, water, or wine used in religious ceremonies. [from Latin *ampulla*]

amputate *verb Medicine* to remove surgically all or part of (a limb), usually in cases of severe injury or following death and decay of the tissue caused by gangrene or frostbite. [from Latin *amputare*, to cut off]

amputation *noun* the surgical removal of a part of the body.

amputee *noun* someone who has had a limb amputated.

Amritsar POP (1991) 710 000, a city in Punjab, NW India, and the centre of the Sikh religion. HISTORY founded in 1577 by Ram Das around a sacred tank, known as the pool of immortality; centre of the Sikh Empire in the 19c, and of modern Sikh nationalism; massacre of Indian nationalists in 1919; a battle between the Indian Army and Sikh militants inside the Golden Temple led to c.1000 deaths, including that of a Sikh leader in 1984. The Golden Temple, found at the centre of the tank, is particularly sacred to Sikhs.

Amritsar Massacre a massacre at Amritsar (13 Apr 1919), where local agitation for Indian self-rule had broken out. During a public meeting staged in a walled garden (the Jallianwalabagh), the British army commander General Dyer, believing a mutiny was imminent, ordered his troops to open fire on an unarmed crowd that had no chance of escape, killing 380 and injuring 1 200. Dyer was censured and resigned, but a public fund was opened for him in Britain. The massacre drove many Indians to support the Indian National Congress, convinced Gandhi of the impossibility of just rule under the British, and also spurred the opening of his Non-Co-operation Movement.

Amru *or* **Amr** (d.664) Arab soldier, who joined the prophet Mohammed c.629, and took part in the conquest of Palestine (638). In 642 he took Alexandria after a 14-month siege, and was the first Muslim governor of Egypt (642–4, 661–3).

Amsterdam POP (1991e) 1.1m, the capital city of the Netherlands and a major European port, situated in North Holland province. It lies at the junction of the R Amstel and an arm of the Ijsselmeer and is a major transshipping point and an important commercial and cultural centre. HISTORY chartered in 1300, Amsterdam became a member of the Hanseatic League in 1369; diamond cutting was introduced after the sacking of Antwerp in 1576 and developed into a specialized industry; became capital in 1808; the whole of the centre was destroyed by bombing in 1940, then rebuilt; harbour industry developed after

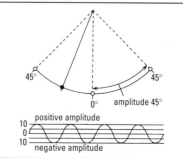

amplitude

World War II. NOTABLE FEATURES Rijksmuseum, Stedelijk Museum, Van Gogh Museum; House of Anne Frank, Rembrandt House (1606); Oude Kerk (consecrated in 1306), Nieuwe Kerk (15c); Royal Palace (17c); Concertgebouw Orchestra.

amt. *abbrev.* amount.

amuck see AMOK.

Amudarya, River, ancient **Oxus** a river in central Asia. It is 1 415km/879mi long. Its source is at the junction of the Vakhsh and Pyandzh rivers on the Turkmenistan–Afghanistan frontier, and it forms part of the border. The river flows W and NW through Turkmenistan and Uzbekistan to enter the Aral Sea in a wide delta. It is an important source of irrigation.

amulet *noun* a small object or jewel worn to protect the wearer from evil or disease. [from Latin *amuletum*]

Amun or **Amen** or **Ammon** or **Amon** in Egyptian religion, the supreme deity from the time of the Middle Kingdom onwards. He was later given the qualities of the sun-god Re and became known as Amun-Re. He was renounced by the heretic pharoah Akhenaton, but reinstated by his successors. The Great Temple of Amun is in Karnak.

Amundsen, Roald (Engelbregt Gravning) (1872–1928) Norwegian explorer, born in Borge, the first man to reach the South Pole. He abandoned medical studies in favour of a life at sea, served on the Belgian Antarctic expedition (1897), and sailed the Northwest passage (1903). His Antarctic expedition of 1910 reached the Pole in Dec 1911, one month ahead of R F Scott. In 1926 with Umberto Nobile (1885–1978) and Lincoln Ellsworth (1880–1951) he flew a dirigible over the North Pole. In 1928 he flew to assist in a search for Nobile (whose dirigible had crashed in the Arctic Ocean) and was lost at sea.

Amur River, Chinese **Heilong Jiang** a river in NE China and Russia, forming part of the international border. It is 4 350km/2 700mi long. From its main source in the Da Hinggan Ling Range, Inner Mongolia, the river flows generally E, then NE to enter the Sea of Okhotsk. It has been the scene of several border incidents.

amuse *verb* **1** to make (someone) laugh. **2** to keep (someone) entertained and interested. [from Old French *amuser*, to cause to muse]

amused *adj.* **1** made to laugh. **2** entertained; happily occupied.

amusedly *adv.* in an amused way.

amusement *noun* **1** the state of being amused. **2** something that amuses. **3** a machine for riding on or playing games of chance.

amusement arcade a public building with machines for gambling, video games, etc.

amusement park *North Amer.* a funfair.

amusing *adj.* mildly funny, diverting, entertaining.

amusingly *adv.* in an amusing way; so as to amuse: *spoke amusingly about their holidays.*

Amy a female first name. [an Anglicized form of Old French *Amee*, beloved, from *amare*, to love]

amylase *noun Biochem.* any of various enzymes present in digestive juices, which play a part in the breakdown of starch and glycogen. [from Greek *amylon*, starch]

an see A¹.

an- see A-¹.

Anabaptism *noun* belief in adult baptism. [from Greek *ana*, again + *baptizein*, to dip]

Anabaptist *noun* a member of various groups of believers who adopted the more radical elements of the 16c Reformation and advocated the baptism of believing adults only, refusing to recognize infant baptism. — Also called *Rebaptizers*.
◇ Emphasizing adherence to the word of scripture, strict Church discipline, and the separation

of Church and State, which led to severe persecution, the Anabaptists were associated with Thomas Müntzer and the Zwinglian prophets in Wittenberg (1521); the Swiss brethren in Zürich (1525); and Jan Mattys (d.1534) in Münster (1533–4), where they achieved supremacy; and spread to Moravia, N and W Germany, the Low Countries (especially the Mennonites in Holland), and later the USA.
The Baptists are in many respects their spiritual heirs.

anabatic *adj. Geol.* denoting a local upward-moving wind, which most commonly develops in a valley, and reaches speeds of 10 to 15 metres per second. [from Greek *anabasis* going up]

anabolic steroid *Biochem.* a synthetic male sex hormone (androgen) that promotes tissue growth by increasing protein synthesis. Anabolic steroids are sometimes prescribed to aid weight gain in the elderly and seriously ill, but they can produce masculine characteristics in women, and their use by athletes to increase muscle bulk and strength has been banned by most sports authorities. [from ANABOLISM]

anabolism *noun* chemical reactions in plants and animals by which complex substances are built up from simpler ones. [from Greek *ana*, up + *bole*, throw]

anachronism *noun* **1** the attribution of something to a historical period in which it did not exist. **2** a person, thing, or attitude that is out of date and old-fashioned. [from Greek *ana*, backwards + *chronos*, time]

anachronistic *adj.* involving an anachronism.

anachronistically *adv.* in an anachronistic way.

anaconda *noun* a large S American snake. [from Sinhalese *henakandaya*, the name of a Sri Lankan snake]

Anacreon (c.6c BC) Greek lyric poet, born in Teos, Asia Minor. He moved to Abdera in Thrace when Teos came under Persian rule, and later lived in Samos at the court of Polycrates. Of the five books of his poems, only a few genuine fragments of love-songs and drinking-songs have been preserved.

anaemia or **anemia** *noun Medicine* a condition characterized by a reduction in the amount of the oxygen-carrying pigment haemoglobin in the red blood cells. [from Greek *an-*, without + *haima*, blood]
◇ The main symptoms of anaemia are skin pallor, fatigue, and breathlessness, and the condition, which is often a symptom of other disorders, has many possible causes, including blood loss (eg as a result of injury or surgery), lack of iron (which is needed for the production of haemoglobin), destruction of red blood cells (eg by the malaria parasite), impaired production of red blood cells in the bone marrow (eg in leukaemia), or the production of abnormal forms of haemoglobin (eg in sickle-cell anaemia).

anaemic *adj.* **1** suffering from anaemia. **2** pale or weak; lacking in energy.

anaemically *adv.* in an anaemic way; without energy.

anaerobe *Biol.* any organism that does not require oxygen in order to obtain energy from the breakdown of carbohydrates or other foodstuffs by the process of respiration, or that cannot survive in the presence of oxygen, eg certain bacteria and yeasts.

anaerobic *Biol.* **1** denoting an organism, especially a bacterium, that does not require oxygen in order to obtain energy from the breakdown of carbohydrates or other foodstuffs, or that cannot survive in the presence of oxygen. **2** *Biochem.* denoting a form of respiration in which oxygen is not required for the oxidation (breakdown) of foodstuffs, especially of carbohydrates. This process releases much less energy than aerobic

respiration. It occurs in certain bacteria and yeasts, and in muscle tissue when all the available oxygen has been used up. Alcoholic fermentation is a form of anaerobic respiration.

anaesthesia *noun* **1** a reversible loss of sensation in all or part of the body, usually induced by drugs which may be inhaled or injected intravenously, although in suitable cases it is sometimes induced by acupuncture or hypnosis. **2** loss of sensation that may be a symptom of disease. [from Greek *an-*, without + *aisthesis*, feeling]
◇ *Local anaesthesia* is used to produce loss of sensation in a specific part of the body, the anaesthetic being injected close to the nerves that would transmit pain. It is widely used in dentistry. *Epidural anaesthetics* are injected into the space surrounding the spinal cord, and produce loss of sensation in the abdomen and lower limbs. They are often used to reduce pain during childbirth. *General anaesthesia* produces complete loss of consciousness by depressing the conduction of nerve impulses in the central nervous system (the brain and spinal cord), and it enables surgical operations to be performed without causing the patient pain or distress. In most cases general anaesthesia is first induced by injecting a drug, and then maintained by administering a mixture of gases that are inhaled (usually a mixture of nitrous oxide and oxygen, containing a volatile anaesthetic agent such as halothane). Chloroform and ether are no longer used. General anaesthesia is reversed by allowing the patient to breathe oxygen-enriched air, and the volatile anaesthetic agent is exhaled from the lungs.

anaesthetic *noun* a drug or gas that causes either total unconsciousness (*general anaesthetic*) or lack of feeling in part of the body (*local anaesthetic*), so that surgery can be performed without causing pain.

anaesthetist *noun* a doctor who gives anaesthetics to patients.

anaesthetize or **anaesthetise** *verb* to give an anaesthetic to (someone).

anaglyph *noun* **1** an ornament in low relief. **2** a picture made up of two prints in complementary colours, seen stereoscopically through spectacles of these colours. [from Greek *anaplyphos*, in low relief]

anaglypta *noun* plain white wallpaper with a raised pattern on it, usually for painting over. [from Greek *anaglyptos*, in low relief]

anagram *noun* a word, phrase, or sentence formed from a changed arrangement of the letters of another. [from Greek *ana*, back + *gramma*, letter]
◇ Historically, anagrams were commonly regarded as having mystical or religious significance, especially when formed from the letters of a person's name or title. Nowadays, they are especially familiar to crossword and word-game enthusiasts, as in the example 'painter out in *sea mist*' = Matisse.

anal *adj.* relating to or in the region of the anus.

analgesia *noun Physiol.* a reduction in or loss of the ability to feel pain, without loss of consciousness or deadening of sensation. It may be deliberately induced by pain-killing drugs such as aspirin or paracetamol, or it may be a symptom of diseased or damaged nerves. [from Greek *an*, not + *algein*, to feel pain]

analgesic — *noun* any drug or other agent that relieves pain. — *adj.* having the effect of relieving pain.
◇ *Narcotic analgesics* (eg morphine, codeine) are used to relieve severe and persistent pain, eg in terminal cancer. *Non-narcotic analgesics* (eg aspirin, paracetamol, ibuprofen) are used to treat headaches and other minor pains, and they act by preventing the formation of prostaglandins (substances formed at the site of injury or inflammation and involved in the production of pain

responses). Unlike narcotic analgesics, they are non-addictive and usually have no serious side-effects.

analogical *adj.* relating to or expressing an analogy.

analogically *adv.* by way of analogy.

analogous *adj.* **1** similar or alike in some way. **2** *Biol.* denoting plant or animal structures that are similar in function, but that have evolved completely independently of each other in different plant or animal groups, eg the wings of insects and birds. See also HOMOLOGOUS. [from Greek *analogos*, proportionate]

analogously *adv.* in an analogous way.

analogue *noun* **1** a thing regarded in terms of its similarity or parallelism to something else. **2** a physical quantity which varies according to variations in some other physical quantity and which is used to measure or record them. See also DIGITAL. [from Greek *analogos*, analogous]

analogue computer *or* **analog computer** *Comput.* a computer in which data is stored and processed in the form of continuously varying signals representing the changing size of a physical quantity such as voltage or current, rather than in the form of individual numerical values as in a digital computer. See also DIGITAL COMPUTER.

analogy *noun* (PL. **analogies**) **1** a likeness or similarity in some ways. **2** a way of reasoning which makes it possible to explain one thing or event by comparing it with something else. [from Greek *analogia*, from *analogos*, analogous]

analysable *adj.* capable of being analysed.

analyse *verb* **1** to examine the structure or content of (something) in detail. **2** to work out the ingredients or component parts of (especially a chemical compound). **3** to psychoanalyse (someone). [from Greek *analyein*, to undo, set free]

analysis *noun* (PL. **analyses**) **1** a detailed examination of the structure and content of something. **2** a statement of the results of such an examination. **3** *North Amer.* psychoanalysis. — **in the final analysis** after everything has been considered.

analysis of variance *Maths.* a procedure that is widely used in statistics to separate the different factors which cause *variance* (which for a set of numerical values is the mean of the squares of the deviations of each value from the mean of the set).

analyst *noun* **1** someone who is skilled in analysis, especially chemical, political, or economic. **2** *North Amer.* a psychoanalyst.

analytic *or* **analytical** *adj.* **1** concerning or involving analysis. **2** examining or able to examine things in detail to learn or make judgements about them.

analytically *adv.* in an analytic way.

analytic language *Linguistics* a language type in which words do not vary in their internal structure, and their grammatical function is determined solely by their position in the sentence. Examples of analytic languages include Chinese and Samoan, although many languages, including English, display features of the type. — Also called *isolating or root language*. See also AGGLUTINATING LANGUAGE, FUSIONAL LANGUAGE.

analytic philosophy a movement, associated particularly with Bertrand Russell and the early work of Ludwig Wittenstein, which sees the primary task of philosophy as one of analysing language (usually by means of formal logic) in order to resolve philosophical issues. The analytic approach has been the dominant tradition in Anglo-American academic philosophy for most of the 20c.

anamorphosis *noun* (PL. **anamorphoses**) in drawing and painting, an image executed in trick perspective so that it is distorted when seen from

a normal viewpoint but appears in normal proportion when seen from a particular angle, or reflected in a curved mirror. The skull in Holbein's *Ambassadors* (National Gallery, London) is a well-known example. [from Greek *anamorphsis*, transformation]

anapaest *noun Prosody* a foot consisting of two short or unstressed beats followed by one long or stressed beat, as in *with a leap* and *and a bound*. [from Greek *anapaistos*, reversed, because it is the reverse of a dactyl]

anapaestic *adj.*, said of verse composed using anapaests.

anaphase *noun Genetics* the stage of mitosis during which the chromosomes move to opposite poles (ends) of the cell by means of a structure composed of protein fibres, known as the *spindle*, that is formed in the cytoplasm. [from Greek *ana* up, back + PHASE]

anaphylaxis *or* **anaphylaxy** *noun Medicine* a sudden severe hypersensitive reaction to the injection of a particular foreign substance or antigen (eg certain drugs) into the body of a person who has already been exposed to that substance and is abnormally sensitive to it. [from Greek *ana* back, *phylaxis* protection]

anarchic *adj.* involving anarchy; lawless.

anarchically *adv.* in an anarchic way; lawlessly.

anarchism *noun* a political belief that governments and laws are unnecessary and should be abolished.

anarchist *noun* **1** a person who believes in anarchism. **2** a person who tries to overthrow the government by violence. **3** a person who tries to cause disorder of any kind.

anarchistic *adj.* characterized by anarchism; believing in anarchy.

anarchistically *adv.* in an anarchistic way.

anarchy *noun* **1** confusion and lack of order, especially political; the failure of law and government. **2** the absence of law and government. [from Greek *an*, without + *arche*, government]

Anasazi the prehistoric Native American inhabitants (c.200 BC–AD 1500) of the arid 'Four Corners' region of the US South-West, where Arizona, New Mexico, Colorado, and Utah meet. The modern descendants are the Hopi of Arizona, and the Rio Grande Pueblo groups of New Mexico.

Anastasia, properly **Grand Duchess Anastasia Nikolaievna Romanova** (1901–1918?) daughter of the Tsar Nicholas II, born near St Petersburg, thought to have died when the Romanov family were executed by the Bolsheviks in Yekaterinburg (19 Jul 1918). Several women have claimed to be Anastasia (eg Anna Anderson, from the Black Forest, d.1984), but conflicting opinions of members of the Romanov family and others have failed to establish the truth. The mystery has been the theme of books, plays, and films. In 1993 documentary evidence appeared of a meeting between Pius XII and two of the Tsar's daughters, suggesting that the Empress and her four daughters (including Anastasia) did survive.

anathema *noun* **1** a person or thing one detests. **2** *Christianity* a person or doctrine that has been cursed or denounced. [from Greek *anathema*, thing devoted to evil]

anathematize *or* **anathematise** *verb trans., intrans.* to curse or denounce.

Anatolia, Turkish **Anadolu** an Asiatic region of Turkey, usually synonymous with Asia Minor. It forms a mountainous peninsula between the Black Sea in the N, the Aegean Sea in the W, and the Mediterranean Sea in the S.

Anatolian — *noun* a group of extinct languages, mainly of the Indo-European family, and spoken c.2 000 BC in Anatolia, in the area of

present-day Turkey and Syria. The main Anatolian language is Hittite, recorded on cuneiform tablets dating from the 17c BC (the oldest known Indo-European texts). — *adj.* relating to this group of languages.

anatomical *adj.* relating to anatomy; concerning the body.

anatomically *adv.* as regards anatomy or the body.

anatomist *noun* a person skilled in anatomy.

anatomy *noun* (PL. **anatomies**) **1** the science of the structure of the human or animal body, or plants, especially studied through dissection. **2** the structure of an animal or plant. **3** *colloq.* a person's body. [from Greek *anatome*, dissection]

Anatomy Lesson of Dr Tulp a group portrait by Rembrandt (1632, Mauritshuis, The Hague).

Anatomy of Melancholy, The a satirical 'medical' work by Robert Burton (1621). It is a witty compendium of knowledge about the causes and cures of the 'disease' of melancholy.

Anaxagoras (500–428 BC) Ionian philosopher, born in Clazomenae. He taught in Athens, where his pupils included Pericles. His explanations of physical phenomena by natural causes brought accusations of impiety, and he withdrew to Lampsacus. He held that matter is infinitely divisible (ie that any piece of matter, regardless of how small it is, contains portions of all kinds of matter), and that order is produced from chaos by an intelligent principle.

Anaximander (611–547 BC) Ionian philosopher and successor of Thales, born in Miletus. He was the first thinker to develop a systematic philosophical view of the universe and Earth's place in it, and is sometimes called the father of astronomy. He held that the origin of the cosmos was the 'Boundless' (*apeiron*), which he conceived of in both physical and theological terms.

Anaximenes (d.c.500 BC) Greek philosopher, born in Miletus. He proposed that the first principle and basic form of matter was air, which could be transformed into other substances by a process of condensation and expansion. He also believed that the Earth and the heavenly bodies were flat and floated on the air like leaves.

ANC *abbrev.* African National Congress.

-ance *suffix* forming nouns denoting a state, quality, or action: *abundance / performance*. [from French *-ance*, from Latin *-antia*]

ancestor *noun* **1** a person who was a member of one's family a long time ago, and from whom one is descended. **2** a forerunner. [from Latin *antecessor*, from *ante*, before + *cedere*, to go]

ancestor worship deification or veneration of dead members of a family, group, or society, found in many primitive societies and religious cults. It is usually believed that the souls of the dead are able to influence the world of the living in some way, or may be invoked by ritual, etc, to assist in some endeavour. Ancestor worship is particularly associated with the Confucian tradition in China, and despite a move away from tradition in Marxist China, the dead are still venerated and family graves assiduously tended.

ancestral *adj.* of or inherited from one's ancestors.

ancestry *noun* (PL. **ancestries**) one's family descent.

Anchises in Roman mythology, the Trojan father of Aeneas. The *Aeneid* gives an account of how Aeneas carried Anchises on his shoulders out of the blazing city of Troy.

anchor — *noun* **1** a heavy piece of metal with hooks which dig into the seabed, attached by a cable to a ship and used to restrict its movement. **2** a weight used to hold a balloon to the ground. **3** anything that gives security or stability. See also ANCHORMAN. — *verb* **1** to fasten (a ship or

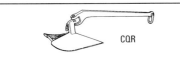

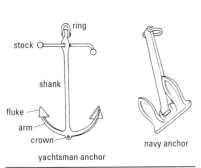

types of anchors

balloon) using an anchor. **2** to fasten securely. **3** *intrans.* to drop an anchor and become moored by it; to be moored by an anchor. [from Anglo-Saxon *ancor*]

Anchorage POP (1990) 226 000, a city and seaport in S central Alaska, USA, at the head of the Cook Inlet. It is the largest city in the state and the administrative and commercial centre. In 1918 it was founded as a railway construction camp. It is an important transportation hub and a vital defence centre, with the Fort Richardson military base and the Elmendorf air force base nearby. The city was severely damaged by an earthquake in 1964. NOTABLE FEATURES Earthquake Park; National Bank Heritage Library.

anchorage *noun* **1** a place where a ship may anchor. **2** a safe place in which to rest. **3** the act of anchoring.

anchorite *noun* a man or woman who, for religious reasons, lives alone and separate from other people. [from Greek *anachoretes*, from *ana*, apart + *choreein*, to withdraw]

anchorman *or* **anchorwoman** *noun* **1** a man or woman who presents a television programme and is responsible for keeping the discussion running smoothly, linking up with reporters outside, etc. **2** (*also* **anchor**) a man or woman running last in a relay team.

anchovy *noun* (PL. **anchovies**) a small fish of the herring family, with a strong, salty taste, usually preserved in oil. [from Spanish and Portuguese *anchova*]

ancien régime **1** the social and political system of France existing from the late 16c to the outbreak of the French Revolution in 1789. The term denotes a hierarchical, corporative society, bound closely to the dynastic state, and is associated particularly with mechanisms upholding traditional orders and privileges. **2** any superseded or outdated system or ruling class. [French, = old order]

ancient — *adj.* **1** dating from very long ago. **2** very old. **3** dating from before the end of the Western Roman Empire in AD 476. — *noun* (*usually* **ancients**) people who lived in ancient times, especially the Greeks and Romans. [from Old French *ancien*, from Latin *antianus*, former, old]

ancient history **1** the history of the countries surrounding the Mediterranean Sea, especially Greece, Asia Minor, Italy, and Egypt, before the end of the Western Roman Empire in AD 476. **2** *colloq.* information, news, etc one has known for a long time.

Ancient Mariner, The the old sailor in Coleridge's poem 'The Rime of the Ancient Mariner', who is doomed to wander the earth constantly recounting his disturbing tale.

ancillary *adj.* **1** helping or giving support to eg medical services. **2** being used as an extra. [from Latin *ancillaris*, from *ancilla*, maid-servant]

-ancy *suffix* forming nouns denoting a state or quality, or something which shows this: *expectancy / vacancy.* [from Latin *-antia*]

AND *abbrev., as an international vehicle mark* Andorra.

and *conj., used to join two or more statements, words, or clauses* **1** used to show addition: *two and two.* **2** used to show a result or reason: *fall and bang one's head.* **3** used to show repetition or duration: *It rained and rained.* **4** used to show progression: *bigger and bigger.* **5** used to show variety or contrast: *There are good cars and bad cars.* **6** *colloq.* used instead of *to* after some verbs: *come and try.* — **and/or** either or both of two possibilities stated: *cakes and/or biscuits.* [from Anglo-Saxon *and*]

Andalusia, Spanish **Andalucía** POP (1991) 6.9m, a large and fertile autonomous region of S Spain. AREA 87 268sq km/33 685sq mi. PHYSICAL DESCRIPTION dominated by the great basin of the R Guadalquivir and in the S by the Baetic Cordillera, rising to 3 478m at Cerro de Mulhacén, Spain's highest peak. CHIEF TOWNS Málaga, Cádiz, Granada, Córdoba. economy sugar cane, fruit, bananas, wine, cotton; tourism. The S coastal strip is known for its tourist resorts on the Costa del Sol and the Costa de la Luz. NOTABLE FEATURES there are many remains of Moorish rule (8–15c).

andalusite *noun Geol.* one of the three varieties of mineral aluminium silicate found in metamorphic rocks. It is an important indicator of the pressure and temperature of metamorphism in rocks. [from *Andalusia* in Spain, where it was first found]

Andaman and Nicobar Islands POP (1991) 281 000, a union territory of India, comprising two island groups in the Bay of Bengal. It is separated from Burma (Mynama), Thailand, and Sumatra by the Andaman Sea. AREA 8 293sq km/3 201sq mi. There are over 300 islands, stretching 725km/450mi N to S. Occupied by Japan in World War II, they became part of India in 1950. The Andaman Is were used as a British penal colony from 1858 to 1942 and the Cellular Jail in the penal town of Port Blair is now a national shrine. A mountainous group of 19 islands form the Nicobar Is, 120km/75mi S. Denmark occupied the Nicobar Is from 1756 until 1848 and Britain annexed them in 1869. Tropical forest covers both island groups. Monsoons occur frequently between May and Oct.

Andaman Sea the NE arm of the Indian Ocean. AREA 564 900sq km/218 000sq mi. It is bounded E by Burma (Myanma) and Thailand, N by the Gulf of Martaban, S by Sumatra, and W by the Andaman and Nicobar Is.

andante — *adj., adv. Mus.* played at a slow steady tempo. — *noun* a piece of music to be played like this. [from Italian *andante*, from *andare*, to go]

Anders, Władysław (1892–1970) Polish soldier, born in Błonie. He was Commander-in-Chief of the Polish forces in the Middle East and Italy in World War II, after which he was deprived of his nationality by the Polish Communist government (1946), became Inspector-General of the Polish forces in exile, and was a leading figure in the 140 000-strong Free Polish community in Britain.

Andersen, Hans Christian (1805–75) Danish writer, born in Odense. He worked in a factory before being educated at Copenhagen. He travelled widely in Europe writing poetry, travel books, novels, and plays. He is mainly remembered for his fairytales for children, including 'The Tin Soldier', 'The Emperor's New Clothes', 'The Tinderbox', 'The Snow Queen', and 'The Ugly Duckling'.

Anderson, Pastor Anthony the shrewd Presbyterian pastor in George Bernard Shaw's *The Devil's Disciple*, who is transformed into a man of action at the end of the play. His much younger wife, Judith, becomes infatuated with Richard Dudgeon.

Anderson, Carl David (1905–) US physicist, born in New York. In 1932 he discovered the positron, the positively charged electron-type particle, giving confirmation of the existence of antimatter. He also did notable work on gamma and cosmic rays, and was awarded the 1936 Nobel Prize for Physics jointly with Victor Hess. Later he confirmed the existence of intermediate-mass particles known as '*m*-mesons' or muons.

Anderson, Elizabeth Garrett (1836–1917) British physician, who was born in London. She pioneered the admission of women into medicine, receiving an MD degree from the University of Paris in 1870. She later practised as a physician in London, and was elected Mayor of Aldeburgh in 1908 — the first woman mayor in England.

Anderson, Philip Warren (1923–) US physicist, born in Indianapolis. He joined Bell Telephone Laboratories in 1949 to carry out theoretical work on the electrical properties of disordered systems, and demonstrated that it is possible for an electron in these materials to be trapped in a small region (1958). The discovery of this process, later known as *Anderson localization*, was an important contribution to the development of amorphous silicon solar cells, thin film transistors, and xerography. He also revealed the microscopic origin of magnets in bulk materials, and shared the 1977 Nobel Prize for Physics with Nevill Mott and John van Vleck.

Andes a major mountain range in S America. It runs parallel to the Pacific coast from the Tierra del Fuego in the S to the Caribbean Sea in the N, passing through Argentina, Chile, Bolivia, Peru, Ecuador, Colombia, and Venezuela. It extends over 6 400km/4 000mi and rises to 6 960m in the Cerro Aconcagua (Argentina), the highest point in S America. In N Argentina, Bolivia, Peru, and Colombia, there are several parallel ranges (*cordilleras*) and high plateaux. The highest peaks are in the Cordillera Agostini on the Chile–Argentina border and there are many lakes and tourist resorts in the area. Puna de Atacama to the N, a desolate plateau, has an average height of 3 350–3 900m. The central part of the Andes Range in Bolivia covers two fifths of the country in an elevated plateau (*altiplano*) of 3 000–3 600m, enclosing L Poopó and L Titicaca. The Bolivian section of the Andes Range splits into Eastern and Western ranges (Cordillera Oriental/Occidental). In Peru, the system divides into many separate ranges. It narrows in Ecuador, and includes some active volcanoes such as Chimborazo (6 310m) and Cotopaxi (5 896m). There are three main ranges in Colombia (Cordillera Occidental/Central/Oriental). The system continues NE into Venezuela as the Sierra Nevada de Mérida and connects via E Panama to the Central American ranges.

andesite *noun Geol.* a dark-coloured igneous rock, containing large amounts of feldspar minerals, produced during the eruption of volcanoes.

Andhra Pradesh POP (1991) 66.5m, a state in S India, bounded E by the Bay of Bengal. AREA 276 814sq km/106 850sq mi. CAPITAL Hyderabad. It was made a separate state based on the Telugu-speaking area of Madras in 1953. GOVERNMENT a unicameral Legislative Assembly with 295 seats. ECONOMY sugar cane, groundnuts, cotton, rice, tobacco; textiles; sugar milling; chemicals; cement; fertilizer; paper; carpets; natural gas; oil refining; shipbuilding; forestry.

andiron *noun* an iron bar, usually one of a pair, supporting logs and coal in a fireplace. [from Old French *andier*]

Andorra *or* **the Valleys of Andorra**, Catalan **Valls d'Andorra**, French **Vallée**

d'Andorre, official name **Principality of Andorra**, **Principat d'Andorra** POP (1992e) 47 000, a small, semi-independent, neutral state on the S slopes of the central Pyrenees between France and Spain, divided into seven parishes. AREA 468sq km/181sq mi. TIME ZONE GMT +1. CAPITAL Andorra la Vella. OFFICIAL LANGUAGE Catalan; French and Spanish are also spoken. CURRENCY French franc, Spanish peseta. PHYSICAL DESCRIPTION a mountainous country, reaching 2 946m at Coma Pedrosa, occupying two valleys (del Norte and del Orient) of the R Valira. CLIMATE winters are cold but dry and sunny; the lowest average monthly rainfall is 34mm in Jan; the midsummer months are slightly drier than spring and autumn. HISTORY one of the oldest states in Europe, under the joint protection of France and Spain since 1278. GOVERNMENT the Co-Princes of the Principality are the President of France and the Bishop of Urgel; the General Council of the Valleys appoints the Head of Government, who appoints four Councillors elected from the parishes. ECONOMY hydroelectric power on the R Valira; no restriction on currency exchange, and no direct or value-added taxes; commerce; tobacco; potatoes; construction; forestry; in recent years, textiles, publishing, leather, mineral water, furniture; tourism; skiing at five mountain resorts.

Andorra

Andorra-la-Vella, Spanish **Andorra la Vieja**, French **Andorre la Vielle** POP (1990e) 20 000, the capital of Andorra and one of the seven parishes of the principality. It is situated on the E side of the Pic d'Enclar (2 317m), 613km/381mi NE of Madrid and stands at an altitude of 1 029m.

Andrássy, Julius, Gróf (Count) (1823–90) Hungarian statesman, born in Kassa, Austrian Empire. A supporter of Kossuth, he was prominent in the struggle for independence (1848–9), after which he remained in exile until 1858. When the Dual Monarchy came into being, he was made Prime Minister of Hungary (1867–71).

Andrea a female first name and feminine form of *Andrew*, in use since the 17c.

Andrea del Sarto see SARTO, ANDREA DEL.

Andrew, St (1c AD) one of the 12 Apostles of Jesus Christ, brother of Simon Peter. A fisherman who previously followed John the Baptist, according to tradition he preached the Gospel in Asia Minor and Scythia, and was crucified in Achaia (Greece) by order of the Roman governor. The belief that his cross was X-shaped dates only from the 14c. He is the patron saint of Scotland and of Greece and Russia, and his feast day is 30 Nov.

Andrew a male first name, given by Christ to his first disciple, later the patron saint of Scotland, Greece, and Russia. [an Anglicized form of Greek *Andreas*, from *andr-*, man, warrior]

Andrew (Albert Christian Edward), Prince, Duke of York (1960–) British prince, second son of Elizabeth II and Prince Philip, Duke of Edinburgh. He was commissioned in the Royal Navy, qualified as a helicopter pilot and served in the Falklands War (1982). In 1986 he was made Duke of York and married Sarah Margaret Ferguson; they separated in 1992. Their children are Princess Beatrice Elizabeth Mary (1988–) and Princess Eugenie Victoria Helena (1990–).

Andrewes, Lancelot (1555–1626) English prelate, born in Barking, Essex. He was ordained in 1580, and made a prebendary of St Paul's in 1589. Elizabeth I appointed him a prebendary (1597) and Dean (1601) of Westminster. He continued to rise in favour with James VI and I, who appreciated his great learning and oratory. He took part in the translation of the Authorized Version of the Bible (1607), and became Bishop of Chichester (1605), Ely (1609), and Winchester (1618).

Andrews, Julie, originally **Julia Elizabeth Wells** (1935–) English actress, born in Walton-on-Thames, Surrey. She worked as a child star on the variety stage and later on Broadway, then played the lead in two very successful film musicals, *Mary Poppins* (1964), for which she won an Oscar, and *The Sound of Music* (1965).

Andrews, Pamela see PAMELA.

Andrews, Roy Chapman (1884–1960) US naturalist and explorer, born in Beloit, Wisconsin. He worked at the American Museum of Natural History, New York, and is best known as the discoverer of fossil dinosaur eggs and fossil mammals in Mongolia. He explored Alaska before World War I, and took part in several expeditions to central Asia.

Andrianov, Nikolai, also called **Old One-Leg** (1952–) Russian gymnast, born in Vladimir. He won 15 Olympic medals (seven gold) between 1972 and 1980. In addition, he won 12 world championship medals, including the overall individual title in 1978.

Androcles Roman slave in a story by Aulus Gellus. He escaped from his master, met a lion, and extracted a thorn from its paw. When recaptured, he was made to confront a lion in the arena and found it was the same animal. The lion did not attack him, and both were set free.

androecium *noun* *Bot.* the male reproductive parts of a flower, consisting of the stamens. [from Greek *oikion*, house]

androgen *noun* **1** *Physiol.* any of a group of steroid hormones, produced mainly by the testes, that control the growth and functioning of the male sex organs and the appearance of male secondary sexual characteristics, eg beard growth, deepening of the voice. **2** a synthetic form of any of these hormones that has a similar effect. [from Greek *aner andros*, man, male]

androgynous *adj.* **1** *Biol.* denoting an animal or plant that shows both male and female characteristics, especially one that possesses both male and female sex organs; hermaphrodite. **2** *Psychol.* showing both male and female traits, eg a woman who resembles a man in outward appearance. [from Greek *androgynos*, from *aner*, man + *gyne*, woman]

android *noun* a robot that looks, moves, and behaves like a human. [from Greek *aner*, man]

Andromache in Greek mythology, the wife of Hector, the hero of Troy. After the fall of the city she became the slave of the Greek Neoptolemus, son of Achilles, to whom she bore three sons.

Andromaque a play by Jean Racine (1667). It is a tragedy based on the story of Hector's widow, Andromaque, whose marriage to Pyrrhus leads to his murder by the jealous and suicidal Hermione.

Andromeda in Greek mythology, the daughter of Cepheus, King of the Ethiopians, and Cassiopeia. To appease Poseidon for her mother's boasting, she was fastened to a rock by the sea-shore as an offering to a sea-monster. She was rescued by Perseus, who fell in love with and married her.

Andromeda galaxy *or* **Andromeda nebula** *Astron.* a bright spiral galaxy in the constellation Andromeda, about 2.2m light years away from Earth. It is the largest of the nearby galaxies, and the most distant object visible to the naked eye.

Andropov, Yuri (1914–84) Soviet politician, born in Nagutskoye, the son of a railwayman. He became head of the KGB (1967–72), and in 1973 was made a member of the Politburo. On Brezhnev's death he became General Secretary of the Soviet Communist Party (1982–4) and consolidated his power when he became President of the USSR (1983–4), but he died soon after.

Andros POP (1988) 11 000, the northernmost island of the Cyclades, Greece, situated in the Aegean Sea between Euboea and Tinos. AREA 380sq km/150sq mi; length 40km/25mi. The island rises to 994m. CHIEF TOWN Andros. There are bathing beaches at Batsi and Gavrion.

Andros POP (1990) 8 000, an island in the W Bahamas, W of New Providence I, on the Great Bahama Bank. AREA 5 955sq km/2 299sq mi. It is the largest island in the Bahamas. The chief towns lie on the E coast. The W shore is a long, low, barren bank.

anecdotal *adj.* **1** consisting of or in the nature of anecdotes. **2** *said of information, etc* based on chance accounts of incidents rather than systematic explanation; unsystematic.

anecdote *noun* a short and entertaining account of an incident. [from Greek *anekdota*, unpublished things, from *an*, not + *ekdotos*, published]

anechoic *adj.* **1** *Physics* denoting a room, chamber, etc, in which there is little or no reflection of sound, and hence no echoes. **2** denoting wall tiles that absorb sound and so prevent reflection of sound waves by the wall.

anemia *North Amer., esp. US* same as ANAEMIA.

anemometer *noun* *Meteorol.* an instrument for measuring and recording wind speed. [from Greek *anemos*, wind + -METER]

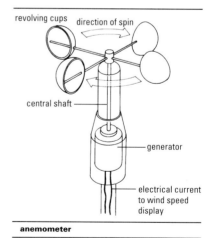

anemometer

anemone *noun* any plant of the genus *Anemone* of the buttercup family (Ranunculaceae), including the cultivated anemone, which bears red, purple, blue, or white cup-shaped flowers on a tall slender stem, and wild species such as the wood anemone. [from Greek, = flower of the wind]

aneroid *noun* (*also* **aneroid barometer**) *Meteorol.* a type of barometer used to measure atmospheric pressure and to estimate altitude. It consists of a sealed metal box from which most of the air has been removed, that expands or contracts like a bellows as the atmospheric pressure rises or falls, respectively. [from Greek *a*, without + *neros*, water]

anesthesia, anesthetic *North Amer., esp. US* same as ANAESTHESIA, ANAESTHETIC.

Aneto, Pico de the highest peak of the Pyrenees Mts, in Huesca province, NE Spain. HEIGHT 3 404m.

Aneurin *or* **Aneirin** (6c) Welsh poet, whose principal work, the *Gododdin*, celebrates the British heroes who fell in conflict with the Saxons in the bloody battle of Cattraeth.

aneurysm *or* **aneurism** *noun Medicine* a balloon-like swelling in the wall of an artery, caused by a congenital defect in the muscular wall, or a disorder such as arteriosclerosis (formation of fatty deposits on the inner walls of arteries). Aneurysms most commonly occur in the aorta. [from Greek *aneurysma*, from *ana*, up + *eurys*, wide]

anew *adv.* **1** again. **2** in a different way. [from NEW]

Anfinsen, Christian Boehmer (1916–) US biochemist, born in Monessen, Pennsylvania. He worked at the National Institutes of Health in Bethesda, Maryland, and shared the 1972 Nobel Prize for Chemistry with Stanford Moore and William Stein for work which improved the understanding of the shape and structure of the enzyme ribonuclease.

angel *noun* **1** a messenger or attendant of God. **2** a representation of this in human form, with a halo and wings. **3** *colloq.* a good, helpful, pure, or beautiful person. **4** *colloq.* a person who puts money into an enterprise, in particular in the theatre.
— **angels on horseback** oysters wrapped in slices of bacon, grilled until crisp.
[from Greek *angelos*, messenger]
◇ Angels are acknowledged in most religions, and are usually represented as benevolent. In Christian art they are normally depicted with a human body and wings. They are commonly grouped into hierarchies, such as the nine orders of Christian belief. In Christianity, Judaism, and Islam, certain angels are given special significance (for example, Michael and Gabriel are common to all three religions), and are sometimes objects of devotion. As created beings, they are held to be inferior to Christ and the prophets, although they are closer to God than the human race is.

Angela a female first name. [from Greek *angelos*, messenger, via late Latin *angelus*, angel]

angel cake a light sponge cake.

angel dust *Medicine* the street name of the drug phencyclidine piperidine (PCP), a hallucinogen, abuse of which can lead to serious psychological disturbances. [from Greek *angelos* a messenger]

Angel Falls the highest waterfall in the world, on a tributary of the R Caroní in SE Venezuela. The total drop, from a plateau in the Guiana Highlands, is 979m. The falls are named after the US aviator, Jimmy Angel, who crashed nearby in 1937.

angelfish *noun* a small tropical fish with very large fins.

angelic *adj.* of or like an angel, especially in being pure and innocent.

angelica *noun* **1** a pleasant-smelling plant, used in medicine and cooking. **2** the stalks of this plant, coated in sugar and used as a decoration for food. [from Latin *herba angelica*, angelic herb]

angelically *adv.* in an angelic way.

Angell, Sir (Ralph) Norman, originally **Ralph Norman Angell Lane** (1872–1967) English writer and pacifist, born in Holbeach, Lincolnshire. He wrote *The Great Illusion* (1910)

and *The Great Illusion 1933* (1933) to prove the economic futility of war, even for the victors. He won the Nobel Prize for Peace in 1933.

Angelo the apparently puritanical deputy to Duke Vincentio in Shakespeare's *Measure for Measure*, who abuses the power he is given, trying to blackmail Isabella into becoming his mistress.

angel shark monkfish.

angelus *noun* **1** a Roman Catholic prayer said in the morning, at noon, and at sunset, in honour of the Incarnation. **2** a bell rung to announce these prayers. [from Latin *Angelus domini*, angel of the Lord, the opening words of the prayer]

Angelus, The a painting by Jean François Millet (1859, Musée d'Orsay, Paris).

anger — *noun* a feeling of great or violent displeasure. — *verb* (**angered, angering**) to make angry; to displease. [from Norse *angr*, grief]

Angevins three ruling families of the medieval county (and later duchy) of Anjou in W France. (1) Henry II, who was descended from the earliest counts of Anjou, founded the Angevin or Plantagenet Dynasty in England, and established the 'Angevin Empire' when he took control of Normandy, Anjou, and Maine (1150–1), acquired Aquitaine (1152), and succeeded Stephen in England (1154). (2) The French Crown had annexed Anjou by 1205, and in 1246 Louis IX's brother Charles, future King of Naples and Sicily, became count. (3) The third line was descended from Charles of Valois, brother of Philip IV, who married Charles of Anjou's granddaughter in 1290. This family died out in 1481.

angina *noun* (*in full* **angina pectoris**) *Medicine* severe pain behind the chest-bone, which often spreads to the left shoulder and arm, and is induced by exertion, eg physical exercise, and usually relieved within a few minutes by rest. [from Latin *angina*, a throat disease + *pectus*, breast]
◇ Angina occurs when the coronary arteries are no longer able to supply the heart muscle with sufficient blood during exertion, usually because of a disorder of the arteries, such as thickening of their walls by the accumulation of fatty deposits and scar tissue. It may also be caused by hypertension (high blood pressure) or anaemia. It is relieved or prevented by restriction of physical activity and diet, and in severe cases by drug treatment or coronary artery bypass surgery.

angiosperm *Bot.* any plant belonging to the subdivision Angiospermae (often referred to as flowering plants), which characteristically produce flowers, and bear ovules that subsequently develop into seeds, enclosed within an ovary, the wall of which subsequently develops into a fruit. [from Greek *angeion*, vessel + *sperma*, seed]
◇ Angiosperms are the most structurally advanced members of the plant kingdom, with an estimated 250 000 species, including flowers, herbs, grasses, and many trees, found in a very diverse range of habitats. They are divided into *monocotyledons* (with one cotyledon or seed leaf), eg lily, daffodil, cereals and other grasses, palms, and *dicotyledons* (with two cotyledons), eg potato, rose, oak. The male gametes (pollen) are produced within stamens, and the female gametes (ovules) are produced within ovaries. Together with the gymnosperms (cone-bearing plants) the angiosperms belong to the division called Spermatophyta (seed-bearing plants) of the plant kingdom.

Angkor Thom the ancient capital of the Khmer Empire, 240km/150mi NW of Phnom Penh, Cambodia. The moated and walled city was built on a square plan and completed in the 12c. It was abandoned in the 15c, and rediscovered in 1861. It is surrounded by various richly-sculptured temples, including Angkor Wat, the largest of these.

Angle, *noun* (*usually* **Angles**) a member of a N German tribe who settled in N and E England and southern Scotland in the 5c. [from Anglo-Saxon *Angel*]

angle[1] — *noun* **1** *Maths.* a measure of the rotation of a line about a point, usually measured in degrees, radians, or revolutions. A complete revolution or circle corresponds to $360°$ or 2π radians. Angles are formed at the point where two lines or planes intersect. An acute angle is less than $90°$, a right angle is exactly $90°$, an obtuse angle is greater than $90°$ but less than $180°$, and a reflex angle is greater than $180°$ but less than $360°$. **2** the amount by which one line slopes away from another. **3** a corner. **4** a point of view; an aspect; a way of considering or being involved in something. — *verb* **1** *trans., intrans.* to move in or place at an angle. **2** *trans.* to present (a news story, information, etc) from a particular point of view. [Latin *angulus*]

angle[2] *verb intrans.* **1** to use a rod and line for catching fish. **2** (**angle for something**) to try to get it in a devious or indirect way. [from Anglo-Saxon *angul*, hook]

angle of incidence *Physics* the angle between a ray (eg a light ray) that strikes a surface (eg glass) and the normal (a line drawn perpendicular to that surface) at the point where the ray strikes the surface.

angle of reflection *Physics* the angle between a ray (eg a light ray) leaving a reflecting surface (eg glass) and the normal (a line drawn perpendicular to that surface) at the point where the ray leaves the surface. It is equal to the angle of incidence.

angle of refraction *Physics* the angle between a ray (eg a light ray) that is refracted (bent) at an interface between two different media (eg water and glass) and the normal (a line drawn perpendicular to that interface) at the point where the ray is refracted.

angler *noun* a person who fishes with a rod and line.

anglerfish *noun* any of about 13 families of bizarre shallow to deep-sea fishes which have a dorsal fin spine modified to form a lure to attract prey. — Also called *goosefish*.

Angles Germanic people from the S Danish Peninsula and neighbourhood. With the Saxons, they formed the bulk of the invaders who, in the two centuries following the Roman withdrawal from Britain (409), conquered and colonized most of what became England. Anglian rulers were apparently dominant by the 8c, and the Angles ultimately gave their name to England, its language, and people.

Anglesey, Henry William Paget, 1st Marquis of (1768–1854) English soldier, born in London. He sat in parliament at various times between 1790 and 1810, and served in the army with distinction in Flanders (1794), Holland (1799), and the Peninsular War (1808). He was made Marquis of Anglesey for commanding the British cavalry at the battle of Waterloo (1815), where he lost a leg. He was Lord-Lieutenant of Ireland (1828–9, 1830–3), where he supported Catholic emancipation, field marshal (1946), and Master-General of the Ordnance (1846–52).

Anglesey, Welsh **Ynys Môn** an island district of the county of Gwynedd, NW Wales. AREA 715sq km/276sq mi. The island is separated from Arfon by the Menai Strait, spanned by two bridges. CHIEF TOWNS Holyhead, Beaumaris, Amlwch, Llangefni, Menai Bridge. It is linked to Holy I by an embankment. ECONOMY agriculture; aluminium; sheep rearing; marine engineering; tourism.

Anglican — *adj.* relating to the Church of England or another Church in communion with it. — *noun* a member of an Anglican Church. [from Latin *Anglicanus*, from *Anglus*, Angle]

Anglican Communion a religious fellowship of independent, provincial or national Churches spread throughout the world, which all share a close ecclesiastical and doctrinal relationship with the Church of England, and recognize the Archbishop of Canterbury as their titular leader. Most of these Churches are in the British Commonwealth, and owe their origins to 19c missionary activities of the Church of England; a major exception is the Episcopal Church in the USA, which was fostered by the Scottish Episcopal Church. Every 10 years the Archbishop of Canterbury invites bishops throughout the Anglican Communion to take part in the Lambeth Conference.

Anglicanism *noun* the principles of the Church of England and other Anglican churches.

Anglican–Roman Catholic International Commission (ABBREV. **ARCIC**) a religious body instituted (1966) by Pope Paul VI and Archbishop Michael Ramsey (1904–88), which meets regularly and produces statements on areas of substantial agreement between the two Churches on important points of doctrine.

anglicism *noun* a word or custom that is peculiar to the English.

anglicization *or* **anglicisation** *noun* making or becoming English.

anglicize *or* **anglicise** *verb* to make English in form or character. [from Latin *Anglus*, Angle]

angling *noun* the sport of catching fish with rod, line, and hook; one of the world's most popular pastimes. There are many forms, including freshwater fishing, fly fishing, game fishing, coarse fishing, and deep sea fishing.

Anglo- *combining form* forming words meaning 'English, British' or 'English or British and ...': *Anglo-American*. [from Latin *Anglus*, English]

Anglo-Burmese Wars two wars fought largely to advance British trade and the East India Company. In 1885 Mandalay was occupied, and in 1886 all Burma was proclaimed a province of British India.

Anglo-Catholic — *noun* a member of an Anglican Church which emphasizes the Church's Catholic traditions. — *adj.* relating to Anglo-Catholics.

Anglo-Catholicism *noun* the beliefs and practices of Anglo-Catholics.

Anglo-Indian — *noun* 1 a person of British descent who has lived in India for a long time. 2 a person of mixed English and Indian descent. — *adj.* of Anglo-Indians.

Anglo-Irish Agreement a joint agreement allowing the Irish Republic to contribute to policy in Northern Ireland for the first time since 1922, signed (15 Nov 1985) by Margaret Thatcher and Garrett Fitzgerald. In Feb 1992 John Major and Albert Reynolds resolved to try and bring peace to Northern Ireland during their time of office. On 15 Dec 1993 they signed the 12-point Downing Street Declaration setting out the principles for peace talks. It included the statement that 'the British government agree that it is for the people of the island of Ireland alone, by agreement between the two parts respectively, to exercise their right of self-determination on the basis of consent, freely and concurrently given, North and South, to bring about a united Ireland, if that is their wish'.

Anglo-Norman — *noun* 1 the Old French dialect introduced into England by the Norman invaders in 1066, and spoken in England by the aristocracy for about 200 years. 2 a Norman inhabitant of England after 1066. — *adj.* of the Anglo-Norman language or people.

anglophile *noun* a person who admires England and the English. [from ANGLO- + Greek *philos*, friend]

anglophobe *noun* a person who hates or fears England and the English. [from ANGLO- + Greek *phobos*, fear]

anglophone *noun* an English-speaking person, especially in states where other languages are also spoken. [from ANGLO- + Greek *phone*, voice]

Anglo-Saxon — *noun* 1 a member of any of the Germanic tribes which settled in England and parts of Scotland in the 5c. 2 Old English, the English language before about 1150. — *adj.* of the Anglo-Saxons or the Old English language.

◇ Anglo-Saxon, or Old English, originated in the group of dialects spoken by the Angles, Jutes, and Saxons who settled in England and S Scotland from the 5c AD. From the 9c to the 11c it developed, under Danish influence, from an inflecting language to a more analytic form. It has written records dating from the 8c, including an 11c manuscript version of the epic poem *Beowulf*. Anglo-Saxon was written in the form of letters called *runes*.

Anglo-Saxon Attitudes a novel by Sir Angus Wilson (1956). It tells of the attempt by a historian to make sense of the past.

Anglo-Saxon Chronicle a series of historical records in English prose and verse from the 9c. King Alfred inspired and may have written some of the earlier material.

Angola, official name **Republic of Angola**, formerly (until 1992) **People's Republic of Angola**, Portuguese **República de Angola** POP (1992e) 10.6m, a republic in SW Africa, which consists of 18 different provinces. AREA 1 245 790sq km/480 875sq mi. It is bounded S by Namibia, E by Zambia, and N by Zaire, with the separate province of Cabinda enclosed by the Congo. CAPITAL Luanda. CHIEF TOWNS Huambo, Benguela, Lobito, Namibe (Moçâmedes), Cabinda, Malanje, Lubango. TIME ZONE GMT +1. The population consists largely of the following groups: the Bakongo, Mbundu, Ovimbundu, Lunda-Tchokwe, Nganguela, Nyaneka-Humbe, Herero, and Ambo; there are c.30 000 Europeans (mainly Portuguese); Roman Catholicism is the main religion. OFFICIAL LANGUAGE Portuguese; many Bantu languages are also spoken. CURRENCY the kwanza. PHYSICAL DESCRIPTION a narrow coastal plain, widening in the N towards the Congo Delta; high plateau inland with an average elevation of 1 200m; the highest point is Serro Môco (2 619m); numerous rivers rise in the plateau but few are navigable for any length. CLIMATE mostly a tropical plateau climate, with a single wet season in Oct–Mar and a long dry season; more temperate above 1 500m; Huambo is representative of the upland region with an average annual rainfall of 1 450mm and average daily temperatures of 24°C–29°C; temperature and rainfall are much reduced on the coast, which is semi-desert as far N as Luanda (eg Namibe in the S has an average annual rainfall of 55mm; in the far N it is 600mm). HISTORY the area became a Portuguese colony after exploration in 1483; an estimated three million slaves were sent to Brazil during the next 300 years; boundaries were formally defined during the Berlin West Africa Congress in 1884–5; became an Overseas Province of Portugal in 1951; Civil War followed independence in 1975, with three internal factions: the Marxist MPLA (Popular Movement for the Liberation of Angola), the UNITA (the National Union for the Total Independence of Angola), and the FNLA (National Front for the Liberation of Angola); the USA supplied arms to the FNLA and UNITA in 1975–6; Cuban combat troops arrived from 1976 at the request of MPLA; South African forces occupied an area along the Angola–Namibia frontier in 1975–6, and were active again in support of UNITA in 1981–4; Angola gave refuge to the Namibian independence movement SWAPO (South West Africa Peoples' Organization), who launched attacks on Namibia from Angolan territory; at the end of 1988, the Geneva agreement linked arrangements for the independence of Namibia with the withdrawal of Cuban troops, the cessation of South African attacks, and support for UNITA; a peace agreement between UNITA and the government in 1991 was followed by multiparty elections but the first results were not accepted by UNITA and fighting resumed. GOVERNMENT officially a democratic state, governed by a President (also head of state) who exercises power via a Council of Ministers (c.20) and a National Assembly. ECONOMY agriculture (cassava, corn, vegetables, plantains, bananas, coffee, cotton, sisal, timber, tobacco, palm oil, maize); reserves of diamonds, manganese, iron ore, gypsum, asphalt, limestone, salt, phosphates; extraction and refining of oil (mainly off the coast of Cabinda province), provides over 75% of recent export earnings; food processing; textiles; cement; paper; pulp.

Angola

angora — *noun* 1 a kind of goat, cat, or rabbit with long silky hair. 2 the wool or cloth made from the hair of an angora rabbit or goat. — *adj.* made from such wool or cloth. [from *Angora*, old name for Ankara, capital of Turkey]

angostura *noun* the bitter bark of a tree, used originally to reduce fever, and now used to flavour drinks. [from *Angostura*, now called Ciudad Bolivar, a town in Venezuela]

Angostura bitters *trademark* a bitter liquid for flavouring drinks, made from angostura bark.

Angra do Heroísmo POP (1991) 36 000, a fortified town and seaport in the Azores, Portugal, lying on the S coast of Terceira I. Founded in 1464, it was capital of the Azores until 1832. The centre of the town is a World Heritage site.

angrily *adv.* with an angry manner.

angry *adj.* (**angrier, angriest**) 1 feeling or showing anger. 2 *said of a wound* red and sore. 3 dark and stormy: *an angry sky*.

Angry Brigade a left-wing group with anarchist sympathies, active in Britain in the 1960s and early 1970s, which took sporadic violent action against representatives of the establishment in the name of the working class. Its leaders were tried and imprisoned for a bomb attack on the Secretary of State for Employment in 1971.

angst *noun* a feeling of anxiety or foreboding. [from German *Angst*, fear]

Ångström, Anders Jonas (1814–74) Swedish physicist, born in Lödgö. He became Professor of Physics at the University of Uppsala in 1858. A pioneering spectroscopist, he reported the finding that an incandescent gas emits the wavelengths which the same gas will absorb when cold, and studied the spectrum of the Sun, which he implied contained hydrogen. He wrote on heat, magnetism, and especially optics; the angstrom unit, for measuring wavelengths of light, is named after him.

angstrom *or* **ångstrom** *noun* (SYMBOL **Å**) a unit of length equal to 10^{-10}m, sometimes used to measure wavelengths of electromagnetic radiation (eg visible light, X-rays) and the sizes of molecules and atoms. In the SI system it has been replaced by the nanometre (10^{-9}m). [named after the Swedish physicist Anders Ångström]

Anguilla POP (1992e) 9 000, the most northerly of the Leeward Is, E Caribbean Sea. AREA 155sq km/60sq mi. It lies 112km/70mi NW of St Christopher and is a British Overseas Territory. CAPITAL The Valley. TIME ZONE GMT –4. The chief religion is Christianity. OFFICIAL LANGUAGE English. CURRENCY the E Caribbean dollar. PHYSICAL DESCRIPTION the territory of Anguilla also includes Sombrero I and several other offshore islets and cays; Anguilla I is a low-lying coral island covered in scrub. CLIMATE tropical; it has a low and erratic annual rainfall ranging from 550–1 250mm; the hurricane season is Jul–Oct. HISTORY colonized by English settlers from St Christopher in 1650; ultimately incorporated in the Colony of St Kitts-Nevis-Anguilla; separated in 1980. GOVERNMENT a governor is appointed by the British sovereign; 11-member Legislative Assembly. ECONOMY peas, corn, sweet potatoes, salt; boatbuilding; fishing; tourism.

anguish *noun* great pain or suffering, especially mental. [from Latin *angustia*, tightness]

anguished *adj.* feeling, showing, or suggesting great pain.

angular *adj.* **1** *said of a person, etc* thin and bony; sharp or awkward in manner. **2** having an angle or angles. **3** measured by an angle: *angular distance*. [from Latin *angularis*, from *angulus*, angle]

angularity *noun* **1** being angular. **2** an angular shape or form.

angular momentum *Physics* for a particle moving about an axis, the product of its angular velocity and its moment of inertia about the axis of rotation.

Angus 1 a region of Scotland etc. **2** a male first name. [from Gaelic *Aonghus*, from Celtic elements meaning 'one' + 'choice']

anhydride *noun Chem.* any chemical compound formed by the removal of water from another compound, especially an acid. [from A-¹ + Greek *hydor hydr-*, water]

anhydrous *adj., said of a chemical compound* containing no water. [from Greek *an*, without + *hydor*, water]

aniline *noun* a poisonous oily liquid obtained from coal tar, and used for making dyes, drugs, plastics, and explosives. [from Arabic *an-nil*, indigo, from which it was first obtained]

animadversion *noun* criticism or censure. [from Latin *animus*, mind + *ad*, to + *vertere*, to turn]

animal — *noun* **1** any member of the kingdom of organisms that are capable of voluntary movement, possess specialized sense organs that enable them to respond rapidly to stimuli, can only grow to a limited size, lack the pigment chlorophyll, and are unable to manufacture complex organic compounds from simple molecules obtained from the environment. Animal cells differ from plant cells in that they are surrounded by a cell membrane instead of a cell wall. **2** a person who behaves in a rough, uncivilized way. **3** *colloq.* a person or thing. — *adj.* **1** of, from, or like an animal. **2** of the physical desires of animals; brutal; sensual. [from Latin *animalis*, having breath]

animalcule *noun* a microscopic animal. [from Latin *animalculum*]

animal experimentation any type of experiment performed on living animals, especially in order to test the effects of chemical compounds, such as new drugs, cosmetics, food additives, and pesticides, on the body functions and behaviour of animals (eg guinea pigs, rabbits, hamsters, rats, mice, dogs, cats, monkeys), as an alternative to using human subjects.

The Main Groups of the Animal Kingdom

Some of the smaller groups have been omitted

Division	Representative classes	Examples
Protozoa	Sarcodina	Amoeba
	Sporozoa	Plasmodium (malaria parasite)
Porifera		sponges
Coelenterata	Anthozoa	corals, sea anemones
	Hydrozoa	Portuguese man-of-war
	Scyphozoa	jellyfish
Platyhelminthes	Cestoda	tapeworms
	Trematoda	liver flukes
	Turbellaria	flatworms
Nematoda		roundworms
Rotifera		rotifers
Bryozoa		moss animals
Brachiopoda		lampshells
Annelida	Hirudinea	leeches
	Oligochaeta	earthworms
	Polychaeta	lugworms, bristleworms
Mollusca	Bivalvia	cockles, mussels, oysters
	Cephalopoda	octopuses, nautilus, squid
	Gastropoda	snails, slugs
Arthropoda	Arachnida	spiders, scorpions
	Crustacea	crabs, shrimps, woodlice
	Insecta	flies, bees, butterflies
	Myriapoda	centipedes, millipedes
Echinodermata	Crinoidea	sea lily
	Asteroidea	starfish
	Echinoidea	sea urchins
	Holothuroidea	sea cucumbers
	Ophiuroidea	brittlestars
Hemichordata	Enteropneusta	acorn worms
Chordata	Agnatha	jawless fish, eg hagfish, lampreys
	Elasmobranchii (also called Chondrichthyes)	cartilaginous fish, eg skates, rays sharks
	Osteichthyes	bony fish, eg goldfish, eels, cod, salmon
	Amphibia	frogs, toads, newts, salamanders
	Reptilia	lizards, snakes, tortoises, crocodiles, dinosaurs
	Aves	birds
	Mammalia	humans, dogs, bats, whales

◇ Animal experimentation is illegal in most Western countries unless it is carried out under an official government licence by qualified research workers, using animals obtained from licensed breeders. The majority of such research is concerned with the development of medical products, or the study of body function, but its use for testing non-medical products, such as cosmetics and toiletries, has provoked considerable public opposition, and the general principle of using animals for experimentation is being increasingly criticized, sometimes involving the use of violence against research establishments by animal rights extremists.

Animal Farm a novel by George Orwell (1945). It is a satire on communist ideology, set in a farmyard with animals as the protagonists.

animal husbandry the breeding, rearing, and management of domesticated animals for the use of man, eg for food, fibres, skins, or the pulling of loads. Domestication of animals is thought to have started in the Middle East c.9 000 BC with sheep; pigs were domesticated c.6 000 BC, and cattle c.5 500 BC. Modern animal husbandry ranges from the keeping of small numbers of animals for domestic use, to ranching, commercial farming, and factory farming.

animalism *noun* **1** the state of having the physical desires of an animal. **2** the belief that man is no better than other animals.

animality *noun* **1** animal nature or behaviour. **2** the state of being an animal, especially a lower animal.

animalize *or* **animalise** *verb* to make (a person) brutal or sensual.

animal rights the rights of animals to exist without being exploited by humans. Animal rights campaigners oppose blood sports, the fur, ivory, and whaling trades, factory farming, and the use of animals in experiments.

animate — *verb* (pronounced *-mate*) **1** to give life to. **2** to make lively. **3** to record (still drawings telling a story) on film in such a way as to make the images seem to move: *animated cartoon.* — *adj.* (pronounced *-mət*) alive. [from Latin *animare*, from *anima*, breath, life or soul]

animated *adj.* **1** lively, spirited. **2** living. **3** moving as if alive.

animatedly *adv.* in an animated way.

animation *noun* **1** liveliness, vivacity. **2** the techniques used to record still drawings on film in such a way as to make the images seem to move.

animator *noun* a person who makes the drawings used to develop animated films and cartoons.

animatronics *noun* the use of computer-operated lifelike puppets, especially to simulate live animals in film-making. [from ANIMAL + ELECTRONICS]

animism *noun* the belief that plants and natural phenomena (eg rivers, mountains, etc) have souls. [from Latin *anima*, soul]

animist *noun* a believer in animism.

animistic *adj.* relating to or characterized by animism.

animosity *noun* (PL. **animosities**) a strong dislike or hatred. [from Latin *animositas*]

animus *noun* a feeling of strong dislike or hatred. [from Latin *animus*, spirit, soul]

anion *noun Physics* any negatively charged ion, which moves towards the anode during electrolysis. See also CATION. [from Greek *ana*, up + *ienai*, to go]

anise *noun* a Mediterranean plant with liquorice-flavoured seeds. [from Greek *anison*]

aniseed *noun* the liquorice-flavoured seeds of the anise plant, used in making sweets, drinks, and some medicines.

Anjou a former province in the Paris Basin of NW France, now occupying the department of Maine-et-Loire and small parts of Indre-et-Loire, Mayenne, and Sarthe departments. It lost provincial status in 1790. The capital of the province was Angers. Henry II of England, first of the Plantagenets (or Angevins), was son of Geoffrey Plantagenet, Count of Anjou. Anjou also gave a line of kings to Sicily and Naples.

Anjouan *or* **Johanna** *or* **Nzwani** POP (1990e) 193 000, an island of the Comoros group in the Mozambique Channel, situated between Grand Comore and Mayotte. AREA 424sq km/164sq mi.

Ankara, ancient **Ancyra**, or **Angora 1** POP (1990) 3m, the capital city of Turkey and of Ankara province. It stands on a tributary of the R Ova, in W central Turkey, and is the country's second largest city. HISTORY formerly an important location on the caravan route from Istanbul to the E; conquered by Alexander the Great in the 4c BC; part of the Roman and Byzantine Empires; under Turkish rule in the 11c; the Turkish government transferred here from Istanbul in 1923. **2** a province of W central Turkey with Ankara as its capital.

ankh *noun* a T-shaped cross with a loop above the horizontal bar. It was a symbol of life in ancient Egypt. [from Egyptian *ankh*, life]

ankle *noun* **1** the joint connecting the leg and the foot. **2** the part of the leg just above the foot. [from Anglo-Saxon *ancleow*]

anklet *noun* a chain or ring worn around the ankle.

ankylosaur *noun* a small plant-eating dinosaur, known from the Cretaceous period, with a small head, a flattened body covered with rectangular bony plates, and short legs. [from Greek *ankylos*, crooked + *sauros*, lizard]

ankylosis *noun* an abnormal stiffening of a joint, caused by bone disease, injury, or surgery. [from Greek *ankylosis*]

Ann *or* **Anne** a female first name. Many of its variants and diminutives (eg *Anna, Annette, Anita*) are now independent names. [from the Hebrew name *Chana* meaning 'He (God) has favoured me (with a child)']

Annaba 1 formerly **Bône** POP (1987) 306 000, a Mediterranean seaport in Annaba department, N Algeria. NOTABLE FEATURE the remains of Hippo Regius, an ancient Phoenician and Roman port, are nearby. **2** a department in N Algeria.

Annabel a female first name. [probably a variant of Old French *Amabel*, from Latin *amabilis*, lovable]

Anna Comnena (1083–1148) Byzantine princess, the daughter of Emperor Alexius Comnenus. She tried in vain to secure the imperial Crown, and failed in her attempt to overthrow or poison her brother (1118). Disappointed and ashamed, she withdrew from the court and sought solace in literature. On the death of her husband (1137), she retired to a convent and wrote the *Alexiad* on her father's life, which contains an account of the early Crusades.

Anna Karenina a novel by Leo Tolstoy (1873–7). It describes the tragic events surrounding a bored married woman's obsession with a young officer.

annalist *noun* a person who compiles annals.

annals *pl. noun* **1** a yearly historical record of events. **2** regular reports of the work of an organization. [from Latin *annales libri*, yearly books]

Anna of the Five Towns a novel by Arnold Bennett (1902). It focuses on the life of a young woman bound by the forces of class and religion.

Annapolis POP (1990) 33 000, the capital of Maryland state, USA, in Anne Arundel County. A port on the S bank of the Severn R, it was the US capital in 1783–4. It is now a business, shipping, and tourist centre, and is the base of the US Naval Academy (1845). In 1784 the ratification of the treaty ending the American War of Independence took place in a former statehouse of the town. [named after Princess (later Queen) Anne in 1695.]

Annapolis Convention a gathering (1786) during the American Revolution at Annapolis, Maryland, where delegates from five states met to discuss commercial problems. Consequently a meeting was called for the following year to consider changes in the Articles of Confederation, which resulted in the writing of the present federal constitution.

Annapurna, Mount a mountain massif extending c.56km/35mi in the central Himalayas, Nepal. It includes Annapurna I (8 091m), Annapurna II (7 937m), Annapurna III (7 556m), Annapurna IV (7 525m), and several other peaks over 6 000m.

Anne, Queen (1665–1714) Queen of Great Britain and Ireland (1702–14), daughter of James II, and sister of Mary II (wife of William of Orange). In 1683 she married Prince George of Denmark (1653–1708) and bore him 17 children, but only William, Duke of Gloucester (1689–1700), survived infancy. During her father's reign, Anne lived in retirement, taking no part in politics, but later was drawn into intrigues for the restoration of her father, or to secure the succession for his son. When Sarah Jennings (1660–1744), the wife of Lord Churchill (afterwards Duke of Marlborough), was appointed a lady of the bedchamber, she quickly became a close confidante. The influence of the Marlboroughs was powerfully felt in all public affairs during the greater part of Anne's reign, which was marked by the union of England and Scotland (1707), and the long struggle against Louis XIV of France known as the War of the Spanish Succession. The Marlboroughs (with Godolphin) headed the Whig Party, but Anne quarrelled with them and then found a new favourite in Abigail Masham, under whose influence she appointed a Tory government (1710). She was the last Stuart monarch; on her death the throne passed to George I of Hanover.

Anne (Elizabeth Alice Louise), Princess, Mrs Timothy Laurence (1950–) British princess, the daughter of Elizabeth II and Prince Philip, Duke of Edinburgh, born in London (at Clarence House). She married Mark Anthony Peter Phillips (1948–) in 1973 (separated 1989); they have a son, Peter Mark Andrew (1977–), and a daughter, Zara Anne Elizabeth (1981–). She married Commander Timothy Laurence in 1992. A noted horsewoman, she has ridden in the British Equestrian Team. She was created Princess Royal in 1987.

Anne, Lady the widow of Edward, Prince of Wales, who meets an unfortunate end after marrying Richard of Gloucester (Richard III) in Shakespeare's *Richard III*.

Anne of Austria (1601–66) eldest daughter of Philip III of Spain, born in Valladolid, the wife of Louis XIII of France, and the mother of Louis XIV. The marriage was not a happy one, the royal couple living for the first 22 years in a state of virtual separation (due chiefly to the influence of Cardinal Richelieu). Anne was Queen Regent for the baby Louis XIV (1643–51). After the death of her prime minister and lover Jules Mazarin in 1661, she retired to the convent of Val de Grâce.

Anne of Cleves (1515–57) Lutheran princess, who became the fourth queen-consort of Henry VIII (Jan 1540) as part of Thomas Cromwell's strategy of developing an alliance with German Protestant rulers. The marriage was declared null and void six months afterwards, and on agreeing to the divorce, Anne was given a large income.

Anne of Denmark (1574–1619) wife (from 1589) of James VI of Scotland, later James I of England. Much of her time was spent in planning extravagant court entertainments, and she became a patron of the masque and other art forms.

anneal *verb Engineering* to heat a material such as metal or glass and then slowly cool it in order to make it softer, less brittle, and easier to work. [from Anglo-Saxon *onælan*, to burn]

annealing *noun Chem.* the relief of internal stresses in metals after heat treatment, hammering, or forging, or in glass after moulding or blowing, by maintaining it at a moderate temperature. This improves its properties, or restores its original properties when it has eventually cooled.

Annecy POP (1990) 123 000, the industrial capital of Haute-Savoie department, Rhône-Alpes region, E France. It lies in the foothills of the French Alps, on the N shore of Lac d'Annecy. A popular tourist resort, it is situated on the route to the alpine passes of Little St Bernard and Mont Cenis.

annelid *noun Zool.* any invertebrate animal belonging to the phylum Annelida, consisting of segmented or true worms, which characteristically have long, soft, cylindrical bodies consisting of many similar ring-shaped body segments. [from Latin *annellus*, little ring]
◊ Annelids have a proper blood system and a simple brain, and the muscular body wall is separated from the long tubular gut by a fluid-filled body cavity or *coelom* that acts as a hydrostatic skeleton. The annelids are divided into three main classes: the Polychaeta (marine worms), the Oligochaeta (which includes the common earthworm), and the Hirudinea (leeches).

Annelida *noun Zool.* in the classification of the animal kingdom, a phylum of invertebrate animals that includes worms with segmented bodies (true worms), such as marine worms, the common earthworm, and leeches. [from Latin *annellus*, a diminutive of *anulus*, ring]

annex *verb* **1** to take possession of (land, territory), especially by conquest or occupation. **2** to add or attach (something) to something larger. **3** *colloq.* to take without permission. [from Latin *annectere*, to tie to]

annexation *noun* **1** annexing or being annexed. **2** something annexed.

annexe *or* **annex** *noun* a building added on to, or used as an addition to, another.

Annigoni, Pietro (1910–88) Italian painter, born in Milan. He held his first one-man show in Florence in 1932 and worked in England during the 1950s. His most usual medium was tempera (a mixture of powdered pigment and an emulsion of (usually) egg yolks and water), although there are also frescoes by him in the Convent of St Mark at Florence (1937). His Renaissance manner is most apparent in his portraits (eg of Queen Elizabeth II, 1955, 1970).

annihilate *verb* **1** to destroy completely. **2** to defeat or crush, especially in an argument. [from Latin *annihilare*, from *ad*, to + *nihil*, nothing]

annihilation *noun* **1** destruction; reduction to nothing. **2** an act of annihilating.

Anning, Mary (1799–1847) English fossil collector, born in Lyme Regis. She discovered in a local cliff the fossil skeleton of an ichthyosaur (1811); later she found the first pleisiosaur (1821) and the first pterodactyl, *Dimorphodon* (1828).

anniversary *noun* (PL. **anniversaries**) **1** the date on which some event took place in a previous year. **2** the celebration of this event on the same date each year. [from Latin *anniversarius*, from *annus*, year + *vertere*, to turn] See also p. 50.

Wedding Anniversaries

In many Western countries, different wedding anniversaries have become associated with gifts of different materials. There is some variation between countries.

1st	Cotton	14th	Ivory
2nd	Paper	15th	Crystal
3rd	Leather	20th	China
4th	Fruit, Flowers	25th	Silver
5th	Wood	30th	Pearl
6th	Sugar	35th	Coral
7th	Copper, Wool	40th	Ruby
8th	Bronze, Pottery	45th	Sapphire
9th	Pottery, Willow	50th	Gold
10th	Tin	55th	Emerald
11th	Steel	60th	Diamond
12th	Silk, Linen	70th	Platinum
13th	Lace		

Anno Domini 1 'in the year of our Lord', used in giving dates since the birth of Christ. **2** *colloq.* old age.

annotate *verb* to add notes and explanations to (a book, etc). [from Latin *annotare*]

annotation *noun* **1** the making of notes. **2** an explanatory note or comment.

annotator *noun* a person who annotates a book.

announce *verb* **1** to make known publicly. **2** to make known (someone's) arrival. **3** to be a sign of: *dark clouds announcing a storm.* [from Latin *annuntiare*]

announcement *noun* **1** a public or official statement, notice, or advertisement. **2** the act of announcing.

announcer *noun* a person who introduces programmes on radio or television.

annoy *verb* **1** to anger or distress. **2** to harass or pester, especially sexually. [from Latin *inodiare*, to cause aversion]

annoyance *noun* **1** something that annoys. **2** the act of annoying. **3** the state of being annoyed.

annoyed *adj.* displeased, irritated.

annoying *adj.* irritating, troublesome.

annoyingly *adv.* in an annoying or troublesome way.

annual — *adj.* **1** happening every year. **2** lasting for a year. — *noun* **1** *Bot.* a plant that germinates, flowers, produces seed, and dies within a period of one year, eg marigold. See also BIENNIAL, PERENNIAL. **2** a book published every year, especially an illustrated gift-book for children. [from Latin *annualis*, from *annus*, year]

annual general meeting (ABBREV. **AGM**) a yearly meeting of a public company, society, etc to report on the year's activity and to hold elections, etc.

annualize *or* **annualise** *verb* to calculate (rates of interest, inflation, etc) for a year based on the figures for only part of it.

annually *adv.* yearly.

annual ring *Bot.* each of the concentric rings visible in a cross-section of the stem of a woody plant, eg certain trees. It generally represents the amount of new wood produced in one year, and can thus be used to estimate the age of the plant.

annuity *noun* (PL. **annuities**) **1** a yearly grant or allowance. **2** money invested providing a fixed amount of interest every year. [from Latin *annuitas*, from *annus*, year]

annul *verb* (**annulled, annulling**) to declare publicly that (a marriage, legal contract, etc) is no longer valid. [from Latin *annullare*, from *ad*, to + *nullus*, none]

annular *adj.* ring-shaped. [from Latin *annularis*, from *anulus*, ring]

annular eclipse *Astron.* an eclipse in which a thin ring of light can be seen around the edge of the obscuring body, eg a solar eclipse during which a ring of sunlight remains visible around the Moon's shadow.

annulate *adj.* formed from or marked with rings.

annulment *noun* **1** the act of annulling. **2** the formal ending of a marriage, legal contract, etc. ◇ Annulment occurs when court proceedings, or their outcome, are declared no longer effective. There are various circumstances where annulment of a marriage may be granted. For example, where the marriage is void (ie when it was not valid in the first place), because the couple are too closely related or under age, or the marriage is bigamous; or, where the marriage is voidable (ie if it is defective in some way), such as when there has been no consummation of the marriage, or when there was lack of consent by one partner at the time of marriage.

annulus *noun* **1** *Geom.* the figure formed by two concentric circles on a plane surface, ie a disc with a central hole. **2** *Biol.* any ring-shaped structure, eg the ring of cells that surrounds the spore-bearing structure in ferns, and by constriction causes the structure to rupture, releasing its spores. [from Latin *annularis*, little ring]

Annunciation, The a painting of the Annunciation by various artists including Simone Martini (1333, Uffizi, Florence) and Antonio Pisanello (1423–4, Saint Fermo, Verona).

Annunciation *noun* **1** (**the Annunciation**) *Christianity* the announcement by the Angel Gabriel to Mary that she would be the mother of Christ. **2** the festival celebrating this, on 25 March; Lady Day. [from Latin *annuntiare*]

annus mirabilis a remarkably successful or auspicious year. [Latin, = year of wonders]

anode *noun* **1** the positive electrode in an electrolytic cell, towards which negatively charged ions, usually in solution, are attracted. **2** the negative terminal in a battery. See also CATHODE. [from Greek *anodos*, way up, from *ana*, up + *hodos*, way]

anodize *or* **anodise** *verb* to coat (a metal) with a protective oxide covering, by electrolysis. [from ANODE]

anodyne — *adj.* **1** able to relieve physical pain or mental distress. **2** able to prevent argument or criticism. — *noun* an anodyne medicine or drug. [from Greek *an*, without + *odyne*, pain]

anoint *verb* to put oil or ointment on (especially a person's head) as part of a religious ceremony, eg baptism. [from Latin *inungere*, from *in*, on + *ungere*, to smear with oil]

anointment *noun* **1** the action of anointing. **2** ointment, material to use in anointing.

anomalous *adj.* different from the usual; irregular.

anomalously *adv.* in an anomalous way.

anomaly *noun* (PL. **anomalies**) something which is unusual or different from what is normal. [from Greek *an*, without + *homalos*, even]

anomia *noun Psychol.* a disorder characterized by an inability to name familiar objects, although their uses are understood, and the affected person's speech is not impaired in any other way. [from Greek *anomia*, lawlessness]

anomie *or* **anomy** *noun* a lack of moral standards in a person or social group. [from Greek *an*, without + *nomos*, law]

anon *adv.* old use soon. [from Anglo-Saxon *on an*, into one]

anon. *abbrev.* anonymous.

anonymity *noun* the state of being anonymous.

anonymous *adj.* **1** having no name. **2** *said of an act, piece of writing, etc* by a person whose name is not known or not given. **3** without character. [from Greek *an*, without + *onoma*, name]

anonymously *adv.* without giving a name or revealing one's identity: *an obituary written anonymously.*

anorak *noun* a hooded waterproof jacket. [from Inuit]

anorexia *noun* **1** loss of appetite. **2** a common name for anorexia nervosa. [from Greek *an*, without + *orexis*, longing]

anorexia nervosa a psychological illness, mainly affecting adolescent girls and young women, and characterized by a significant decrease in body weight, deliberately induced by refusal to eat because of an obsessive desire to lose weight, usually associated with a distorted perception of actual body shape. ◇ The symptoms of anorexia nervosa include faddish eating habits, hyperactivity, and often the stopping of normal menstrual periods. In severe cases it can result in death from starvation. The disorder is often associated with problems within the sufferer's family, eg difficulties in communication, and it is treated mainly by psychotherapy, together with encouragement and incentives to eat sufficient food to regain and then maintain a normal body weight.

anorexic — *noun* a person suffering from anorexia or anorexia nervosa. — *adj.* **1** relating to or suffering from anorexia or anorexia nervosa. **2** relating to anorexics.

another *adj., pron.* **1** one more. **2** a person comparable to one already known: *another Mozart.* **3** one of a different kind: *another country.* [Middle English, from *an other*]

Anouilh, Jean (Marie Lucien Pierre) (1910–87) French dramatist, born in Bordeaux. A leading dramatist of contemporary theatre, he was influenced by the neoclassical fashion inspired by Giraudoux. Among his many successful plays are *Antigone* (1944), *Medée* (1946), *L'Alouette* (The Lark, 1953), *Becket* (1959), and *La Culotte* (The Trousers, 1978).

Anquetil, Jacques (1934–87) French cyclist, born in Mont-St Aigan, the first man to win the Tour de France five times (1957, 1961–64). In 1960 and 1964 he won the Tour of Italy, and in 1963 the Tour of Spain. He won the Grand Prix des Nations a record nine times between 1953 and 1965. He retired in 1969.

Anschluss the concept of union between Austria and Germany, expressly forbidden by the Treaties of Versailles and St Germain (1919) but supported in both countries after the collapse of the Habsburg Empire. Hitler pursued the idea once in power, and in 1938, after the resignation of Austrian Chancellor Schuschnigg, Germany occupied Austria; the union was formally proclaimed on 13 Mar 1938. [German, = joining together]

Anselm, St (1033–1109) Italian theologian and philosopher, born into a noble family near Aosta, Piedmont. In 1078 he became abbot of the Abbey of Bec, in Normandy, then was appointed Archbishop of Canterbury (1093). Frequently in conflict over Church rights, first with William II (William Rufus), then with Henry I, his resoluteness led to his being exiled by both kings, but in 1107 he threatened excommunication, and a compromise was reached. A follower of Augustine, Anselm was a major figure in early scholastic philosophy, remembered especially for his theory of atonement and his ontological proof for the existence of God. He defined God as 'something than which nothing greater can be conceived'. Since anything that exists in reality is by nature greater than anything that exists only in the mind, God must exist in reality, for otherwise he would not be 'the greatest conceivable being'. He was possibly canonized in 1163 and his feast day is 21 Apr.

anserine *adj. formal* of or like a goose. [from Latin *anser*, goose]

Anshan or **An-shan** POP (1990) 1.4m, a city in Liaoning province, NE China. Organized mining and smelting began here in c.100 BC and, today, it is the site of China's largest iron and steel complex. NOTABLE FEATURES Qianlian Shan (Thousand Lotuses Hill); Buddhist Hermitage (10c); Eryijiu (19 Feb) Park; Tanggangzi Hot Springs Park, located c.10km/6mi SE.

answer — noun **1** something said or done in reply or response to a question, request, letter, etc. **2** the solution to a mathematical problem. — verb (**answered**, **answering**) **1** trans., intrans. to make a reply or answer to someone. **2** to react or respond to (a doorbell, the telephone, etc). **3** intrans. (**answer to someone for something**) to have to account to them for it. **4** trans., intrans. to be suitable (for something). **5** to match or be the same as, especially a description. **6** intrans. (**answer for something**) to be punished for it. — **answer back** to reply rudely. [from Anglo-Saxon andswaru]

answerability noun the state or obligation of being answerable.

answerable adj. (**answerable to someone for something**) accountable for it to them.

answering machine a machine which records telephone messages when one is absent.

answering service an organization which takes messages and answers telephone calls for its customers.

ant noun any of a vast family of insects belonging to the same order (Hymenoptera) as the bees and wasps, and characteristically having elbowed antennae and narrow waists. [from Anglo-Saxon æmette]
◇ Ants are found in all parts of the world except for very cold regions, and most form perennial colonies in nests excavated in wood, soil, or plant cavities. The nest contains one or more fertile females (queens), a number of winged males, and many wingless sterile females (workers). The workers hunt for food, build the nest, and care for the developing young. The larvae that hatch from the eggs spin silken cocoons around themselves, from which the adults eventually emerge. In many species the workers defend themselves with stings, or squirt acid at their predators. Some species feed on small insects, while others feed on fungi, seeds, or honeydew, the sticky liquid produced by greenfly and other aphids.

leaf-cutter ant

-ant suffix used to form words denoting: **1** a quality or function: pleasant / expectant. **2** a person who performs an action: assistant. [from Latin -ant-, the stem of verb participles]

antacid — noun Medicine an alkaline substance that neutralizes excess acidity in the digestive juices of the stomach, and is used to relieve pain and discomfort in disorders of the digestive system. Overuse of antacids may lead to alkalosis. — adj. denoting a substance, especially a medicine, that neutralizes the acidity of the stomach.

antagonism noun openly expressed dislike or opposition.

antagonist noun **1** an opponent or enemy. **2** a muscle whose contraction opposes the action of another muscle. **3** Physiol. a drug, hormone, or other chemical substance which has the opposite effect to that of another drug, hormone, or chemical substance in the body, and therefore inhibits it. [from Greek anti, against+ agon, contest]

antagonistic adj. hostile; actively opposing.

antagonistically adv. in an antagonistic or hostile way.

antagonize or **antagonise** verb to make (someone) feel anger or hostility.

Antananarivo, formerly **Tananarive**, or **Tananarivo** (to 1975) POP (1990e) 802 000, the capital of Madagascar, situated on a ridge in the E central part of the island. The city is divided into upper and lower towns. NOTABLE FEATURES two cathedrals; Queen's Palace, Ambohitsorahitra Palace; Museum of Art and Archaeology; Zoma Market; casinos; Mohamasina Sports Stadium and racecourses.

Antarctic — noun (**the Antarctic**) the area round the South Pole. — adj. relating to this area. [from Greek anti, against+ arktikos, the Arctic]

Antarctica the S Polar continent, surrounded by an ice-filled ring of ocean waters containing scattered island groups. AREA c.15.5m sq km/6m sq mi. Mainly S of 65°S, the region is almost entirely within the Antarctic Circle. There is no permanent population. PHYSICAL DESCRIPTION it has a c.22 400km/14 000mi coastline, mainly of high ice cliffs, indented by the Ross and the Weddell seas; the divisions of Greater and Lesser Antarctica are separated by the Transantarctic Mts, with the highest point of 5 140m at Vinson Massif; animals include fishes, penguin and other seabirds, seals, and whales; plants include sea plankton, algae, mosses, and lichens, but virtually no higher plants; the average depth of the surface ice sheet is 1 500m; inland ice moves slowly towards the periphery, pushing long tongues into the sea and creating shelf ice over large areas; drift ice develops along the whole coastline; there are many icebergs in the adjacent waters, the largest of the tabular types are 10–60m high; movement of pack ice varies widely in different longitudes. CLIMATE outward blowing winds prevail, often of hurricane force; blizzards are common, especially in autumn and winter; the lowest temperature on Earth, –88.3°C, was recorded at Vostok Station. There have been major scientific explorations in this area since the first winter base was established in 1899. During International Geophysical Year (1957–8) 12 countries maintained 65 bases in Antarctica. They signed the Antarctic Treaty in 1959, providing for international co-operation in scientific research, and prohibiting military operations, nuclear explosions, and disposal of radioactive waste; in 1991 further agreement to maintain its unspoilt status was signed. Territorial claims have been made by the UK (British Antarctic Territory), Norway (Dronning Maud Land), France (Terre Adélie), Australia (Enderby Land, Wilkes Land, George V Coast, part of Oates Coast), New Zealand (160°E to 150°W), Chile (90°W to 53°W), and Argentina (74°W to 25°W). The South Pole was first reached by Amundsen in 1911.

Antarctic Circle an imaginary line on the surface of the Earth at 66°30S. It marks the southernmost point at which the sun can be seen during the summer solstice, and the northernmost point at which the midnight sun can be seen in S polar regions.

Antarctic Ocean see SOUTHERN OCEAN.

antbird noun Zool. a forest-dwelling bird, native to the New World tropics, that feeds on insects, spiders, lizards, and frogs, so called because it follows army ants, feeding on the animals they disturb.

ante — noun **1** a stake put up by a player in poker before receiving any cards. **2** an advance payment. — verb **1** to put up as a stake. **2** (**ante up**) to pay. [from Latin ante, before]

ante- combining form before in place or time: anteroom / antenatal. [from Latin ante, before]

anteater noun any of various mammals found in swamps, grasslands, and open forests of Central and S America and belonging to the same order (Edentata) as armadillos and sloths. The giant anteater has a long cylindrical snout balanced by an untidily bushy tail, and may reach a length of 2m. It feeds on ants and termites.

anteater

antecedence noun the act or state of going before.

antecedent — noun **1** an event or circumstance which precedes another. **2** Grammar a word or phrase to which another word, especially a relative pronoun, refers. **3** (usually **antecedents**) a person's past history. — adj. going before in time. [from Latin ante, before + cedere, to go]

antechamber noun an anteroom.

antedate verb **1** to belong to an earlier period than. **2** to put a date (on a document, letter, etc) that is earlier than the actual date.

antediluvian adj. **1** belonging to the time before the Flood. **2** facetious very old or old-fashioned. [from ANTE- + Latin dilivium, flood]

antelope noun (PL. **antelope**, **antelopes**) any of various species of hoofed mammal with a smooth brown or grey coat, belonging to the same family (Bovidae) as cattle, goats, and sheep, and found mainly in Africa, although a few species live in Asia. [from Greek antholops]
◇ The majority of antelopes have horns, which may be short and straight or long and elaborately curved, the horns of the females generally being shorter than those of the males. The most well-known species include the gazelles and gnus (the pronghorn antelope of N America is not a true antelope). Antelopes are generally capable of running at great speed when threated by predators, and they feed on a very wide range of plants.

ante meridiem see A.M.

antenatal adj. before birth; during pregnancy. [from ANTE- + Latin natalis, of one's birth]

antenna noun **1** (PL. **antennae**) one of a pair of feelers on the head of some insects, crabs, etc used for touching. **2** (PL. **antennas**) an aerial. [from Latin antenna, yard of a mast]

antepenultimate noun, adj. third from last.

anterior adj. **1** earlier in time. **2** at or nearer the front. [from Latin anterior, from ante, before]

anteroom noun a small room which opens into another, more important, room.

Anthea a female first name, first used in the Classical period and reinvented by 17c English pastoral poets. [from Greek antheios, flowery]

anthem noun **1** a usually complicated piece of music sung by a church choir, usually with words from the Bible. **2** a song of praise or celebration, especially of a nation: national anthem. [from Anglo-Saxon antefn, from Latin antiphona, antiphon]

anther noun that part of a flower's stamen containing the pollen. [from Greek anthos, flower]

anthesis noun Bot. **1** the opening of a flower-bud. **2** the period of time during which a flower is in full bloom. [from Greek anthesis, flowering]

ant hill a heap of earth built by ants over their nest.

anthocyanin *noun Bot.* any of a group of pigments that are found in certain cells in plants, and are responsible for many of the red, purple, and blue colours of flowers, fruits, and leaves. [from Greek *anthos*, flower + *kyanos*, blue]

anthologist *noun* a person who compiles an anthology.

anthology *noun* (PL. **anthologies**) a collection of pieces of poetry or other writing. [from Greek *anthos*, flower + *logia*, gathering]

Anthony *or* **Antony** a male first name. [from the Roman family name *Antonius*]

Anthony see also ANTONY.

Anthony, Susan B(rownell) (1820–1906) US women's suffrage leader, born in Adams, Massachusetts. Her interest in labour problems stemmed from observing the mill her father managed. After teaching and temperance work, she became a champion of women's rights; she was a leader of the National Woman Suffrage Association (from 1869), then President of the US branch (1892).

Anthony Island a provincial park in the Queen Charlotte Is, off the coast of British Columbia, Canada. The island was inhabited by Native Americans of the NW Pacific for 2 000 years. Although the Native Americans abandoned the area in the late 19c, their village with its longhouses and totem poles has been preserved. The park is a World Heritage site.

anthracite *noun Geol.* a hard shiny black coal with a very high carbon content, that burns with a short blue flame and generates much heat but little or no smoke. It is the highest grade of coal, and is widely used for domestic heating. [from Greek *anthrax*, coal]

anthrax *noun Medicine* an acute infectious disease, now rare in the UK, that is most common in sheep and cattle, but can be transmitted to humans by contact with infected meat, hides, excrement, etc. It causes fever and either pneumonia or severe ulceration of the skin, and may be fatal. It is prevented by vaccination. [from Greek *anthrax*, = coal, carbuncle]

anthropo- *combining form* of or like human beings. [from Greek *anthropos*, man]

anthropocentric *adj.* believing that mankind is the central element of existence.

anthropocentrically *adv.* in an anthropocentric way.

anthropoid — *adj.* like a human being in form. — *noun* an ape that is like a human being in form, eg the gorilla. [from Greek *anthropoeides*, man-like]

anthropoidal *adj.* like an anthropoid.

anthropological *adj.* relating to anthropology; relating to the nature and natural history of human beings.

anthropologically *adv.* as regards anthropology.

anthropologist *noun* a person who studies anthropology.

anthropology *noun* the study of human beings, especially their society, customs, and beliefs.
◇ Anthropology is traditionally identified as a 'four-field' discipline, encompassing archaeology, social and cultural anthropology, physical anthropology, and even linguistics.

anthropomorphic *adj.* **1** characterized by anthropomorphism. **2** human in form.

anthropomorphism *noun* the attribution of human behaviour, feelings, and beliefs to animals, gods, objects, etc. [from ANTHROPO- *Greek morphe*, form]

anthropomorphous *adj.* human in form.

anti — *adj.* opposed to something. — *noun* a person who is opposed to something. [from Greek *anti*, against]

anti- *combining form* **1** opposed to; against: *anti-aircraft*. **2** opposite to: *anticlockwise / anticlimax*. [from Greek *anti*, against]

anti-aircraft *adj.*, *said of a gun or missile* used to attack enemy aircraft.

Antibes, ancient **Antipolis** POP (1990) 71 000, a fishing port and fashionable resort in Alpes-Maritimes department, Provence-Alpes-Côte d'Azur region, SE France. It is on the French Riviera, facing Nice across a long bay, and is best known for its luxurious villas and hotels sheltered by the pines of Cap d'Antibes. In 1815, Napoleon and 1 000 men landed 3km/2mi to the W of Antibes on his return from Elba. NOTABLE FEATURES Roman remains; several museums, including the Musée Picasso.

antibiotic — *noun* a substance, produced by or derived from a micro-organism, that can selectively destroy or inhibit other bacteria and fungi without damaging the host. — *adj.* of or relating to antibiotics. [from ANTI- + Greek *bios*, life]
◇ The first safe and effective antibiotics, the penicillins, were extracted from the fungus *Penicillium* by Alexander Fleming. Antibiotics discovered subsequently include streptomycin, chloramphenicol, cephalosporin, erythromycin and tetracycline. These are often chemically modified to increase their stability and specificity. Most antibiotics are only effective against a few types of micro-organism, but a range of 'broad-spectrum' antibiotics, active against either a wide range of micro-organisms or a specific type of infectious agent, was developed in 1989.
Antibiotics are extremely effective in the treatment of bacterial infections, but have virtually no effect on viruses. They may also occasionally be harmful to the host, and some patients are allergic to penicillin. Furthermore, following repeated or insufficient doses of antibiotics, resistant strains of bacteria can develop, which may result in epidemics that cannot be treated by the usual antibiotics. Many infective bacteria are now resistant to early forms of penicillin. Even so, antibiotics have revolutionized human and veterinary medicine in developed countries, and have made a major contribution to the dramatic decline in deaths from communicable diseases over the last 50 years.

antibody *noun* (PL. **antibodies**) a protein that is produced by certain white blood cells in response to the presence in the body of an *antigen* (a foreign substance, usually a protein). The antibody combines with the antigen that caused its production, and renders it harmless. The production of antibodies is an important part of the body's immune response.

Antichrist *noun* **1** an enemy of Christ. **2** *Christianity* the great enemy of Christ who is expected to appear before the end of the world. [from Greek *anti*, against + *Christos*, Christ]

anticipate *verb* **1** to see what will be needed or wanted in the future and do what is necessary in advance. **2** to expect. **3** to look forward to. **4** to mention (part of a story, what a person thinks, etc) before the proper time. **5** to spend (eg one's salary) before receiving it. [from Latin *anticipare*, from *ante*, before + *capere*, to take]

anticipation *noun* anticipating, expectation.

anticipatory *adj.* anticipating.

anticlerical *adj.* opposed to public and political power being held by members of the clergy.

anticlericalism *noun* opposition to the clergy, especially to their having power in politics.

anticlimactic *adj.* relating to or in the nature of an anticlimax.

anticlimax *noun* a dull or disappointing end to a series of events which seemed to be leading to a climax.

anticline *noun Geol.* a geological fold in the form of an arch, formed as a result of compressional forces acting in a horizontal plane on rock strata. [from ANTI- + Greek *klinein*, to lean]

anticlockwise *adv., adj.* in the opposite direction to that in which the hands of a clock move.

anticoagulant *noun Medicine* a drug or other substance that prevents or slows the clotting of blood. Some anticoagulants, eg heparin and warfarin, are used to prevent the formation of blood clots, or to break up existing clots, eg in the treatment of thrombosis or embolism.

Anti-Comintern Pact an agreement (concluded 1936) between Germany and Japan, which outlined both countries' hostility to international communism. The Pact was also signed by Italy (1937). It was specifically aimed against the Soviet Union, but also recognized Japanese rule in Manchuria.

anticonvulsant *noun Medicine* a drug that is used to prevent or reduce convulsions, especially in epilepsy.

Anti-Corn-Law League an association formed (Sep 1838) in Manchester mainly by businessmen and industrialists to repeal the British Corn Laws, which imposed protective tariffs on the import of foreign corn. League propaganda aided the growing movement for free trade in early 19c Britain, and the League itself was an important political pressure group. The Corn Laws were repealed by Robert Peel in 1846.

antics *pl. noun* odd or foolish behaviour. [from Italian *antico*, grotesque]

anticyclone *noun Meteorol.* an area of relatively high atmospheric pressure from which light winds spiral outward in the opposite direction to that of the Earth's rotation. Anticyclones are generally associated with calm settled weather, and are shown on weather charts as a series of widely spaced concentric isobars.

antidepressant — *adj.* used or able to treat depression. — *noun* an antidepressant drug.

antidote *noun* **1** a medicine given to stop the harmful effects of a poison. **2** anything that prevents or counteracts something bad. [from Greek *anti*, against + *didonai*, to give]

antifreeze *noun* a substance which is added to a liquid to stop it from freezing, especially to the water in a car radiator.

antigen *noun Biol.* any foreign substance, usually a protein, that stimulates the body's immune system to produce antibodies. Common antigens include bacteria, viruses, allergens, and the proteins of incompatible blood groups or tissues. [from ANTI- + Greek *genes*, born, produced]

Antigone in Greek mythology, the daughter of Oedipus, King of Thebes, and Jocasta. She buried the body of her brother Polynices (who had attacked Thebes in opposition to his brother Eteocles and King Creon) in defiance of Creon's order that such a traitor should remain unburied. She was then, on the orders of Creon, buried alive in the family tomb where she hanged herself.

Antigone **1** a play by Sophocles (c.442 BC). Set against a background of war, it is a tragedy about a clash between Antigone's sisterly compassion for a dead traitor brother (Polynices) and the stately proprieties of King Creon, who causes her death but later suffers guilt. **2** a play by Jean Anouilh (1944), based on the one by Sophocles. Antigone is depicted as a martyr to virtue and Creon avoids the guilt suffered by the Sophocles' character.

Antigonus one of the Sicilian lords in Shakespeare's *The Winter's Tale*, who is killed by a bear after abandoning Hermione's new-born baby on a shore in Bohemia.

Antigonus Gonatas (c.320–239 BC) King of Macedonia, son of Demetrius Poliorcetes (the

Besieger). It took him seven years to regain the throne of his father in 276 BC. His defeat of the invading Gauls in the winter of 279–8 greatly enhanced his authority. He had to defend his kingdom against several rivals, including Pyrrhus of Epirus. He also fought a war against an Egyptian-backed alliance of Athens and Sparta, and defeated Ptolemy II in a naval battle off Cos. The dynasty he founded lasted until the Roman conquest in 167 BC.

Antigonus Monophthalmos ('One-Eyed') (c.382–301 BC) Macedonian soldier, one of the generals of Alexander III 'the Great'. After Alexander's death he was confirmed in control of Phrygia Major, Lycia, and Pamphylia. He was the only one of Alexander's generals who aspired to reunite the empire after Alexander's death. He waged war against the other generals, making himself master of all Asia Minor and Syria. In 306 BC he assumed the title of king together with his son Demetrius Poliorcetes, but was defeated and killed in a battle with his rivals at Ipsus in Phrygia.

Antigua and Barbuda POP (1991) 66 000, an independent group of three islands in the Leeward group of the Lesser Antilles, E Caribbean Sea: Antigua, Barbuda, which lie 40km/25mi to the N, and Redonda, uninhabited, which is 40km/25mi to the SW. AREA 442sq km/171sq mi. CAPITAL St John's (on Antigua). CHIEF TOWN Codrington (on Barbuda). TIME ZONE GMT –4. Christianity is the dominant religion. OFFICIAL LANGUAGE English. CURRENCY the E Caribbean dollar. PHYSICAL DESCRIPTION the W part of Antigua rises to 470m at Boggy Peak; Barbuda is a flat, coral island reaching only 44m at its highest point, with a large lagoon on its W side. CLIMATE tropical, with temperatures ranging from 24°C in Jan, to 27°C in Aug/Sep, and an average annual rainfall of 1 000mm. HISTORY Antigua was discovered by Columbus in 1493; colonized by the English in 1632 and ceded to Britain in 1667; Barbuda was colonized from Antigua in 1661; administered as part of the Leeward Is Federation from 1871 until 1956; became an associated state of the UK in 1967; independence was achieved in 1981. GOVERNMENT The Queen is head of state, represented by a Governor-General; there is a bicameral Legislature consisting of a 17-member Senate and a 17-member House of Representatives elected for five year periods. ECONOMY rum; sugar (marked decline in 1960s, now recovering); cotton; tourism (40% of the national income).

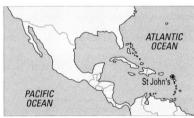

Antigua and Barbuda

antihero *noun* (PL. **antiheroes**) a principal character in a book, play, film, etc who has no noble qualities but is just like an ordinary person.

antihistamine *noun Medicine* any of a group of drugs that counteract the effects of histamines in allergic reactions, such as hay fever. Antihistamines are also used to treat disorders that cause nausea and vomiting, such as travel sickness.

anti-inflammatory *adj. Medicine* denoting a drug that reduces inflammation.

antiknock *noun* a substance added to motor fuel to slow down the rate of combustion and so prevent a knocking sound in the engine.

Antilles the whole of the West Indies except the Bahamas. The Greater Antilles include Cuba,

Jamaica, Hispaniola (Haiti and the Dominican Republic), and Puerto Rico. The Lesser Antilles include the Windward Is in the S, the Leeward Is in the N, and the Netherlands Antilles off the coast of Venezuela.

anti-lock *adj., said of a braking system* designed to prevent the wheels of a vehicle locking when the brakes are applied.

antilog *abbrev.* antilogarithm.

antilogarithm *noun Maths.* the number of which a given number is the logarithm.

antimacassar *noun* a covering for the back of a chair to stop it getting dirty. [from ANTI- + *macassar*, an oil once used on hair]

Anti-Masonic Party a US political group (1830–6). Dedicated to driving Freemasons out of public life, it arose from the highly publicized disappearance (1826) of the author of a book revealing Masonic secrets. It was the first 'third party' in the USA, and nominated a presidential candidate at the first national party convention (1832).

antimatter *noun* hypothetical particles of matter with the opposite electrical charge to those forming the Earth.

antimony *noun Chem.* (SYMBOL **Sb**, ATOMIC NUMBER **51**) a brittle bluish-white metal that is a poor conductor of heat and electricity, and is added to lead alloys to increase their hardness. It is used in storage batteries, semiconductors, flameproofing, paints, ceramics, and enamels, and its compounds are used in paint pigments. [from Latin *antimonium*]

antinode *noun Physics* a point that is halfway between the nodes in a stationary wave (a standing wave, produced when a travelling wave is reflected back along its own path). It indicates a position of maximum displacement or intensity.

antinomian — *adj.* denoting the view that Christians do not have to observe moral law. — *noun* a person holding this view. [from Latin *Antinomi*, the name of a sect believing this, from ANTI- + Greek *nomos*, law]

antinomy *noun* (PL. **antinomies**) a contradiction between two laws or beliefs that are reasonable in themselves. [from Greek *anti*, against + *nomos*, law]

antinovel *noun* a novel in which the accepted elements of novel-writing are ignored or avoided.

antinuclear *adj.* opposed to the use of nuclear power or nuclear weapons.

Antioch, Turkish **Antakya**, ancient **Hatay Antiochia** POP (1990) 284 000, the capital of Hatay province, S Turkey. It is near the Mediterranean Sea, 90km/56mi W of Aleppo in Syria. HISTORY founded in 300BC; a centre of early Christianity; destroyed by an earthquake in 526. NOTABLE FEATURE Archaeological Museum.

Antiochus III, also called **the Great** (c.242–187 BC) King of Syria (223–187 BC), of the Seleucid dynasty. He restored Seleucid prestige in the East (209–204 BC), and by his successes against the Ptolemies gained possession of Palestine and Coele Syria (198 BC). He invaded Greece but was defeated by the Romans at Thermopylae (191 BC), Magnesia (190 BC), and at sea. As a result, he was forced to evacuate all Asia Minor west of the Taurus Mts and pay Rome a crippling war indemnity.

antioxidant *noun Chem.* a substance that slows down the oxidation of other substances, often by being oxidized itself. The term is usually applied to additives in foods and plastics.

antiparticle *noun Physics* an elementary particle that has the same mass and spin as another elementary particle, but opposite electrical and magnetic properties, eg the positron is the antiparticle of the electron, because it has a positive charge of the same magnitude as the negative charge of an electron. When an elementary

particle is brought together with its antiparticle, mutual destruction results.

antipasto *noun* (PL. **antipasti**, **antipastos**) food served at the beginning of a meal to sharpen the appetite. [from Italian *antipasto*]

antipathetic *adj.* arousing or having an antipathy.

antipathetically *adv.* in an antipathetic way.

antipathy *noun* (PL. **antipathies**) strong dislike or hostility.

anti-personnel *adj., said of weapons and bombs* designed to attack and kill people rather than destroy buildings and other weapons.

antiperspirant *noun* a substance applied to the skin to help stop perspiration.

Antipholus of Ephesus one of the twin brothers in Shakespeare's *The Comedy of Errors*, who is married to Adriana.

Antipholus of Syracuse one of the twin brothers in Shakespeare's *The Comedy of Errors*, who sets out in search of his brother.

antiphon *noun* a hymn or psalm sung alternately by two groups of singers. [from Latin *antiphona*, from Greek *anti*, in return + *phone*, voice]

antipodean *adj.* relating to the antipodes.

antipodes *pl. noun* (also **Antipodes**) places on the Earth's surface exactly opposite each other, especially Australia and New Zealand as being opposite Europe. [from Greek *antipodes*, from *antipous*, having the feet opposite]

antipope *noun* a pope elected in opposition to one already elected.

antipyretic — *adj.* reducing fever. — *noun* an antipyretic drug. [from ANTI- + Greek *pyretos*, fever]

antiquarian — *adj.* of or dealing in antiques and rare books. — *noun* an antiquary.

antiquary *noun* (PL. **antiquaries**) a person who collects, studies, or deals in antiques and antiquities. [from Latin *antiquarius*, from *antiquus*, ancient]

antiquated *adj.* old and out of date; old-fashioned. [from Latin *antiquare*, to make old]

antique — *noun* **1** a piece of furniture, china, etc which is old and often valuable, and is sought after by collectors. **2** (**the Antique**) art from the time of Classical antiquity, especially sculpture. It is regarded by artists since the Renaissance both as a source of motifs, and as a model for style. — *adj.* **1** old and often valuable. **2** *colloq.* old-fashioned. [from Latin *antiquus*, ancient]

antiquity *noun* (PL. **antiquities**) **1** ancient times, especially before the end of the Roman Empire in AD 476. **2** great age. **3** (**antiquities**) works of art or buildings surviving from ancient times. [from Latin *antiquitas*, from *antiquus*, ancient]

antiracism *noun* support for policies that promote equality among, and tolerance between, groups of different racial origins, and opposition to prejudice or persecution on grounds of race.

antiracist *adj.* supporting or characterized by antiracism.

antirrhinum *noun* a plant with white, red, or yellow two-lipped flowers; a snapdragon. [from Greek *antirrinon*, from *anti*, mimicking + *rhis*, nose]

Anti-Saloon League a US organization (established 1895) aimed at forbidding alcoholic drink by the amendment of the US Constitution and by state and local anti-alcohol laws. It remained in being through the Prohibition period (1920–33), and became part of the National Temperance League in 1950.

antiscorbutic — *adj.* preventing or curing scurvy. — *noun* an antiscorbutic drug.

anti-semite *noun* a person who is hostile to or prejudiced against Jews.

anti-semitic *adj.* disliking or prejudiced against Jews.

anti-semitism *noun* hostility to or prejudice against Jews.

antiseptic — *adj.* describing a substance or drug that kills germs and so prevents infection or disease. — *noun* an antiseptic substance or drug.

antiserum *noun* (PL. **antisera**) a blood serum containing particular antibodies, used to treat or prevent a particular disease. [from ANTIBODY + SERUM]

antisocial *adj.* **1** unwilling to mix socially with other people. **2** *said of behaviour* harmful or annoying.

antisocially *adv.* in an antisocial way.

antistatic *adj.* reducing the effects of static electricity.

antitank *adj.*, *said of weapons* designed to destroy military tanks.

antithesis *noun* (PL. **antitheses**) **1** a direct opposite. **2** the placing together of contrasting ideas, words, or themes in any oral or written argument, especially to produce an effect. [from Greek *antitithenai*, to set against]

antithetic *or* **antithetical** *adj.* **1** of the nature of antithesis. **2** directly opposite; contrasted.

antithetically *adv.* in direct opposition.

antitoxin *noun Medicine* a type of antibody produced by the body in order to neutralize a toxin released by invading bacteria, viruses, etc. Some antitoxins are deliberately introduced into the body by vaccination.

antitrades *pl. noun* winds blowing above, and in the opposite direction to, trade winds.

anti-trust *adj. North Amer., esp. US, said of a law* protecting small companies and trade from domination by monopolies.

Anti-Trust Acts US legislation passed to control the development of monopoly capitalism. The Sherman Act (1890) forbade all combinations 'in restraint of trade', but ambiguities in wording led to its use against labour unions instead of the monopolistic corporations, or *trusts*. The Clayton Act (1914) was intended to clear up the ambiguities and facilitate enforcement.

antiviral *adj. Medicine* denoting a drug that destroys viruses or prevents their multiplication.

anti-vivisection *noun* opposition to scientific experiments on living animals.

anti-vivisectionist *noun* a person who opposes scientific experiments being made on living animals.

antler *noun* either of the two branched horns on the head of a stag. [from French *antoillier*]

Antofagasta 1 POP (1991e) 221 000, the port capital of Antofagasta region, Chile. The largest

antler formation

city in N Chile, it was developed as a result of the mineral and agricultural trade in the 19c. NOTABLE FEATURES geographical and archaeological museums; public gardens and beaches; sports stadium. **2** A region in Chile with Antofagasta as its capital.

Antonescu, Ion (1882–1946) Romanian soldier and dictator, born in Pitesti. He was military attaché in Rome and London, and became Chief-of-Staff in 1937. Suspended from the army (1938) and imprisoned as one of the leaders of an unsuccessful revolt, he was soon released and made Minister of War. In 1940 he became premier, forced the abdication of King Carol, and was dictator until 1944. He was executed as a war criminal.

Antonia a female first name. [a feminine version of ANTHONY, a more accurate representation of the Classical form]

Antonine Wall a defensive barrier built by the Roman emperor, Antoninus Pius, in AD 142, at the northern end of the British province. It was constructed of turf upon a foundation of cobbles, and ran from the Forth estuary to the Clyde.

Antoninus Pius (AD 86–161) Roman emperor (138–61), whose title *Pius* ('dutiful') was probably conferred because of his exemplary behaviour towards his adoptive father, Hadrian. His reign saw unrest in Germany, Africa, Palestine and Dacia. In Britain, the Antonine Wall was built (142) as a defensive measure.

Antonio 1 the rich merchant of the title in Shakespeare's *The Merchant of Venice* who, as guarantor to his friend Bassanio, wagers a pound of his flesh with Shylock. **2** The usurping brother of Prospero in Shakespeare's *The Tempest*, who is irredeemably evil. **3** The sea-captain in Shakespeare's *Twelfth Night*, who rescues Sebastian from drowning and lends him his money.

Antonioni, Michelangelo (1912–) Italian film director, born in Ferrara. After making documentaries (1945–50), he turned to feature films, which are notable for their preoccupation with character study rather than plot. He gained an international reputation with *L'Avventura* (The Adventure, 1959). Later films include *La Notte* (The Night, 1961), *Blow-up* (1967), *Zabriskie Point* (1970), and *The Oberwald Mystery* (1980).

Antonius, Marcus *or* **Mark Antony** (c.83–30 BC) Roman statesman and soldier. He was related to Julius Caesar and assisted him in Gaul (54–50 BC) and in his war against Pompey, which saw victory for the Romans at Pharsalus in 48 BC. In 44 BC, as consul, he tried in vain to have Caesar made emperor. After Caesar's assassination, his speeches caused conspirators (Brutus and Cassius) to flee from Rome and he was left with almost absolute power. He was defeated at Mutina (43 BC) by Octavian, but returned to form a triumvirate (the 'Second Triumvirate') with Octavian and Lepidus. The 'triumvirs' secured Italy, then defeated Brutus and Cassius at Philippi (42 BC). He first met Cleopatra in 41 BC, but returned from Alexandria to Italy in 40 BC. A new division of the Roman world was made at Brundisium, with Antony taking the East and Octavian the West. Antony's desertion of his wife Octavia (Octavian's sister) in favour of his renewed liaison with Cleopatra (c.37 BC), and his donation to his children by her of large parts of the Roman Empire, provided Octavian with reasons to arouse the Roman people against him. War on Egypt was declared and after defeat at Actium (31 BC), Antony and Cleopatra both committed suicide (30 BC).

Antony *or* **Anthony, St**, also called **Antony of Egypt**, or **Antony the Great** (c.251–356AD) Egyptian ascetic, the father of Christian monasticism, born in Koman, Upper Egypt. At 20 he sold his possessions for the poor, then spent 20 years in the desert, where he withstood a famous series of temptations, often rep-

resented in later art. In 305 he left his retreat and founded a monastery near Memphis and Arsinoë. Aged over 100, he made a journey to Alexandria in c.355 to dispute with the Arians, but soon retired to his desert home. His feast day is 17 Jan.

Antony see ANTHONY.

Antony of Padua, St (1195–1231) Portuguese friar, born in Lisbon. At first an Augustinian monk, in 1220 he joined the Franciscan order, and, noted for his preaching, became one of its most active propagators. Canonized in 1232, he is the patron saint of Portugal, the lower animals (legend has it that he preached to fishes when men refused to listen), and lost property; his feast day is 13 Jun.

Antony and Cleopatra a play by William Shakespeare (1606–7). It is a tragedy about the doomed love of the Roman aristocrat and soldier Mark Antony for the Egyptian queen Cleopatra.

antonym *noun* a word opposite in meaning to another word. [from Greek *anti*, opposite + *onyma* or *onoma*, name]
◇ There are several kinds of antonym, depending on the type of word involved: (1) *gradable*, eg *big/small* and *hard/soft*, which may be expressed in degrees, ie, *bigger/smaller* and *harder/softer*; (2) *non-gradable* or *complementary* terms, eg *single/married* and *male/female*; and (3) *converse*, eg *buy/sell* and *peace/war*, in which one word presupposes the existence of the other.

antonymous *adj.*, *said of a word* opposite in meaning to another word.

antonymy *noun* oppositeness of meaning.

Antrim, Gaelic **Aontroim** POP (1981) 378 000, a county in NE Northern Ireland. AREA 2 831sq km/1 093sq mi. It is bounded SW by Lough Neagh, N by the Atlantic Ocean, E by the Irish Sea, and S by Co Down. Antrim includes the islands of Rathlin, the Skerries, and the Maidens. It rises in the N and E to the Antrim Mts. CHIEF TOWNS Belfast (county town), Lisburn, Ballymena, Carrickfergus. ECONOMY Irish linen, textiles, cattle, sheep, potatoes, flax, oats, shipbuilding. NOTABLE FEATURE the Giant's Causeway, a basalt rock formation, is on the N coast.

antrum *noun* (PL. **antra**) *Anat.* a natural cavity in the body, especially in a bone. [from Greek *antron*, cave]

Antwerp, Flemish **Antwerpen**, French **Anvers 1** POP (1992e) 466 000, the chief port in Belgium and the fourth largest in the world. Situated on the R Scheldt, 88km/55mi from the North Sea, it is the capital of Antwerp district. It is a major international diamond centre. HISTORY chartered in 1291; centre of the mediaeval cloth trade with England; the city was the home of Rubens, van Dyck, and Plantin. NOTABLE FEATURES town hall (16c); Cathedral of Our Lady (1352), Church of St Jacob (15–16c); Royal Museum of Fine Arts; Antwerp Zoo, one of the world's most famous. **2** a district in Belgium with the city of Antwerp as its capital.

ANU *abbrev.* Australian National University.

Anubis in Egyptian religion, the god associated with death. He was often represented as a jackal-headed man, and was responsible for the protection of tombs, the embalming of bodies, and the guiding of souls to the world beyond.

Anuradhapura 1 POP (1981) 36 000, the capital of Anuradhapura district in Sri Lanka, 205km/127mi N of Colombo. It was the country's first capital, founded in the 4c BC. NOTABLE FEATURES the Sri Mahabodhi Tree, allegedly the oldest tree in the world (2 200 years), is all that remains of the Bo Tree, beneath which Buddha found Enlightenment; the Thuparama Dagaba, built to enshrine the collarbone of Buddha. The city is a World Heritage site. **2** a district in N central Sri Lanka.

anus *noun* the opening at the end of the alimentary canal between the buttocks, through which faeces leave the bowels. [from Latin *anus*, ring]

Anvers see ANTWERP.

anvil *noun* a heavy iron block on which metal objects can be hammered into shape. [from Anglo-Saxon *anfilt*]

anxiety (PL. **anxieties**) *noun* a strong feeling of fear or distress either as a normal response to a dangerous or stressful situation, or as a form of neurosis in which there is excessive and lasting fear, often for no apparent reason. Symptoms of anxiety may include trembling, sweating, breathlessness, rapid pulse rate, dry mouth, and nausea.

anxious *adj.* **1** worried, nervous, or fearful about what will or may happen. **2** causing worry, fear, or uncertainty. **3** very eager: *anxious to do well.* [from Latin *anxius*, from *angere*, to press tightly]

anxiously *adv.* in an anxious state; nervously.

anxiousness *noun* a state of anxiety.

any — *adj.* **1** one, no matter which: *can't find any answer.* **2** some, no matter which: *have you any apples?* **3** a very small amount of: *won't tolerate any nonsense.* **4** large or indefinite: *have any number of dresses.* **5** whichever or whatever: *any child could tell you.* — *pron.* any one or any amount. — *adv.* (*in questions and negative sentences*) in any way whatever: *it isn't any better.* [from Anglo-Saxon *ænig*]

anybody *pron.* **1** any person, no matter which. **2** *in questions and negative sentences* an important person.

anyhow *adv.* **1** in spite of what has been said, done, etc; anyway. **2** carelessly; in an untidy state.

anyone same as ANYBODY.

anyplace *North Amer., esp. US* same as ANYWHERE.

anything — *pron.* a thing of any kind; a thing, no matter which. — *adv.* in any way; to any extent: *she isn't anything like her sister.* — **anything but** ... not ... at all: *was anything but straightforward.* **like anything** *colloq.* with great speed or enthusiasm.

anyway *adv.* **1** nevertheless; in spite of what has been said, done, etc. **2** in any way or manner.

anywhere — *adv.* in, at, or to any place. — *pron.* any place.

Anzac *noun* **1** (also **ANZAC**) the Australia and New Zealand Army Corps, a unit in which troops from both countries fought during World War I in the Middle East and on the Western Front. **2** a soldier serving in this unit.

Anzac Day 25 Apr, a public holiday in Australia and New Zealand in memory of the Anzac landing in Gallipoli in 1915.

Anzio Landing the landing (22–3 Jan 1944) by 50 000 US and British troops during World War II at a small port 97km/60mi behind the German defences of the so-called Gustav line. Although the Germans were taken by surprise, they were able to confine the Allied troops and prevent them from using Anzio as a bridgehead.

AOB *or* **AOCB** *abbrev.* any other business or competent business: the last item on the agenda for a meeting, when any matter not already dealt with may be raised.

AOC *abbrev.* appellation d'origine contrôlée.

A1 *or* **A-1** *adj. colloq.* first-class; of the highest quality.

aorist *noun Grammar* a tense of a verb in some inflecting languages, especially Greek, expressing action in simple past time with no implications of completion, duration, or repetition. [from Greek *aoristos*, indefinite]

aorta *noun Anat.* in mammals, the main artery in the body, that carries oxygenated blood from the heart to the smaller arteries that in turn supply the rest of the body. [from Greek *aorte*]

Aosta, French **Aoste** POP (1990e) 36 000, the capital of Valle d'Aosta autonomous region and of Aosta province, NW Italy. It lies in the fertile valley of the R Dora Baltea, ringed by mountains. The town is an important traffic junction for routes across the Alps. Its population is largely French-speaking. NOTABLE FEATURES cathedral; old town surrounded by well-preserved Roman walls.

Aouita, Said (1960–   ) Moroccan track athlete, born in Rabat. He set world records at 1 500m and 5 000m in 1985, becoming the first man for 30 years to hold both records. He has since broken world records at 2mi, 2 000m, and 3 000m. He was the 1984 Olympic champion, 1986 overall Grand Prix winner, and 1987 world 5 000m champion.

Aozou Strip a 100km/60mi-wide strip of mountainous desert in N Chad, N central Africa. It is a disputed territory on the frontier with Libya, which occupied the area in 1973. Libya's claim is based on an unratified 1935 agreement between France and Italy. The area is rich in uranium and mineral deposits.

AP *abbrev.* Associated Press.

apace *adv. literary* quickly. [from A³ + PACE¹]

Apache a Native American people who dominated much of the SW during the 19c. They were divided into many smaller groups, which lacked any centralized organization. They subsisted on hunting, farming, and raiding Pueblo and Spanish settlements. From 1861 they fought against Federal troops in the Apache and Navajo wars, the last of which ended in 1886 with the surrender of the Apache chief Geronimo. The surviving Apache population (c.11 000) live on reservations (eg in Arizona and New Mexico).

apart *adv.* **1** in or into pieces: *come apart.* **2** separated by a certain distance or time. **3** to or on one side. **4** (*after a noun*) leaving aside: *joking apart.* — **apart from something** *or* **someone** except for them; leaving them out of consideration. [from Old French *a part*, to one side]

apartheid *noun* an official policy of separate development for different races in a state, especially in South Africa. [from Afrikaans *apart*, apart + *-heid*, *-hood*]
◇ In South Africa, this policy is being dismantled. Under this policy, different races have been given different rights, and in practice the system has been one of white supremacy, with the black majority having no representation in the central state parliament. The policy has traditionally been supported by the Nationalist Party, although many of its provisions regarding labour, social and educational segregation, and a virtually exclusive white franchise were in place before the Nationalist victory in 1948. It was, however, erected into a complete political, social, and economic system after that date; its principal architect was Hendrik Verwoerd, who was assassinated in 1966. The commitment of the de Klerk government to universal suffrage and the dismantling of apartheid culminated in all-race elections in 1994, although the process of change was vehemently opposed by certain extremist whites and also by some blacks.

apartment *noun* **1** a large room. **2** *North Amer.* a set of rooms for living in on one floor; a flat. **3** (**apartments**) a set of rooms used for accommodation, usually in a large building. [from French *appartement*, from Italian *appartare*, to separate]

apathetic *adj.* feeling or showing little or no emotion; indifferent.

apathetically *adv.* with an apathetic manner; without caring.

apathy *noun* lack of interest or enthusiasm. [from Greek *a*, without + *pathos*, feeling]

apatite *noun Geol.* a common phosphate mineral widely distributed in small amounts in many igneous and metamorphic rocks. [from Greek *apate* deceit, from its having been confused with other minerals]

apatosaurus *noun* (*formerly called* **brontosaurus**) a huge semi-aquatic dinosaur of the Jurassic period, up to 20m in length and weighing about 30 tonnes, with massive limbs, a small head and tiny teeth, a long neck, and a whip-like tail. It is thought to have fed on plant material and to have lived in swamps. [from Greek *apate*, deceit + *sauros*, lizard]

ape — *noun* **1** any of 11 species of primate that differ from most monkeys, and resemble humans, in having no tail and in walking upright some of the time. Their brains are much more highly developed than those of other primates. **2** an ugly, stupid, or clumsy person. — *verb* to imitate (someone's behaviour, speech, etc). — **go ape** *North Amer. slang* to go crazy. [from Anglo-Saxon *apa*]
◇ There are two main groups of apes: the *lesser apes* (gibbons) and the *great apes* (orang-utans, gorillas, and chimpanzees). The orang-utan (now an endangered species) and gibbon are native to Asia, and the chimpanzee and gorilla are native to Africa. Of all the animals, apes are most similar to humans in structure and development, and are said to be *anthropoid*, although they have shorter legs and longer arms than humans, and their big toes are more thumb-like. It was once thought that humans were descended from the apes, but it now seems much more likely that apes and humans had a common ancestor.

apeman *noun* any of several extinct apes thought to be the forerunners of humans.

Apennines, Italian **Appennino** a mountain range extending down the whole length of the Italian Peninsula into Sicily. Length 1 400km/870mi; width 30–150km/20–90mi. The highest points include Gran Sasso d'Italia (2 914m) in the central division, Monte Cimone (2 165m) in the N division, and Monte Pollino (2 248m) in the S division, an area which has suffered a number of earthquakes. The range is the source of many Italian rivers. In the foothills there are numerous mineral springs where the typically Mediterranean vegetation includes olive groves, vineyards, nut trees, and orchards. Above is open forest, but at c.1 800m, the slopes are covered with stones and scree; here there is stock-farming, some arable farming, and forestry.

aperient — *adj.* having a mild laxative effect. — *noun* an aperient substance or drug. [from Latin *aperire*, to open]

aperitif *noun* an alcoholic drink taken before a meal to stimulate the appetite. [from French *apéritif*, from Latin *aperire*, to open]

aperture *noun* **1** a small hole or opening. **2** the opening through which light enters an optical instrument such as a camera or telescope. **3** the effective diameter of the lens in such an instrument. [from Latin *apertura*, from *aperire*, to open]

APEX *abbrev.* advance purchase excursion: a reduced fare for journeys booked a certain period in advance.

apex *noun* (PL. **apexes**, **apices**) the highest point or tip. [from Latin *apex*, peak]

aphasia *noun Psychol.* loss or impairment of the ability to speak or write, or to understand the meaning of written or spoken language. In right-handed people it is caused by damage to the left side of the brain. It is treated by similar methods to those used for teaching deaf people. [from A-¹ not + Greek *phanai*, to speak]

aphelion *noun* (PL. **aphelia**) the point in a planet's orbit when it is furthest from the sun. See also PERIHELION. [from Greek *apo*, from + *helios*, sun]

aphid *or* **aphis** *noun* (PL. **aphids**, **aphides**) a small insect which feeds by sucking the juices from plants, eg a greenfly.

aphonia *noun Psychol.* inability to speak, which may be caused by hysteria, laryngitis or some other disorder of the larynx or brain damage. [from A-¹ + Greek *phone*, voice]

aphorism *noun* a short, often clever or humorous saying expressing some well-known truth. [from Greek *aphorizein*, to define]

aphoristic *adj.* characteristic of an aphorism; short and pithy.

aphrodisiac — *noun* a food, drink, or drug that is said to stimulate sexual desire, eg oysters, ginseng. — *adj.* sexually exciting. [from Greek *aphrodisiakos*, from *Aphrodite*, the goddess of love]

Aphrodite in Greek mythology, the goddess of sexual love and beauty, said to have been born from the sea-foam at Paphos in Cyprus. She bribed Paris with the most beautiful mortal, Helen of Troy, an offer which caused the Trojan War. The Romans identified her with Venus.

Apia POP (1991) 33 000, the capital town of Western Samoa. It is situated on the N coast of Upolu I, in the SW Pacific Ocean. The town is a rapidly expanding cluster of villages.

apiarist *noun* a bee-keeper.

apiary *noun* (PL. **apiaries**) a place where bees are kept. [from Latin *apiarum*, from *apis*, bee]

apical *adj.* of, at, or forming an apex.

apiculture *noun* bee-keeping. [from Latin *apis*, bee]

apiece *adv.* to, for, by, or from each one.

Apis in Egyptian religion, the bull-god (originally of fertility) who became associated with the Ptah of Memphis, and later with Osiris, when he became known as Serapis. A black bull with a triangular white patch on the forehead was selected from the herd and kept at Memphis; after death it was mummified and placed in a special necropolis, the Serapeum.

apish *adj.* **1** like an ape. **2** imitative. **3** affected; silly.

aplomb *noun* calm self-assurance and poise. [from French *à plomb*, straight up and down]

apnoea *or* **apnea** *noun Medicine* a temporary cessation of breathing, as occurs in some adults during sleep (*sleep apnoea*) and in some newborn babies. [from Greek *apnoia*]

Apo, Mount an active volcano and the highest mountain in the Philippines. The mountain is located near the SE coast of Mindanao I and forms part of a national park. It rises to 2 954m.

apocalypse *noun* **1** (**Apocalypse**) the last book of the New Testament, also called the Revelation of St John, which describes the end of the world. **2** any revelation of the future, especially future destruction or violence. [from Greek *apocalypsis*, uncovering]

Apocalypse Now a US film directed by Francis Ford Coppola (1979). Based on Joseph Conrad's *Heart of Darkness* (1902) and starring Marlon Brando and Robert Duvall, it combines a statement on America's involvement in Vietnam with an examination of human evil.

apocalyptic *adj.* **1** like an apocalypse. **2** *said of an event* signalling or foretelling an upheaval, disaster, etc.

Apocrypha *pl. noun* those books of the Bible included in the ancient Greek and Latin versions of the Old Testament, but not in the Hebrew version. They are excluded from modern Protestant Bibles but included in Roman Catholic and Orthodox Bibles. [from Greek *apocryphos*, hidden]

◇ Most of these writings, composed in the last two centuries BC, were approved at the Council of Trent, and so Roman Catholics tend to consider them as inspired and authoritative, while Protestants and most others attribute less authority to them, referring to them as *Apocrypha*.

In non-Catholic Bibles the Apocrypha appears as a separate collection before or after the New Testament; in Catholic Bibles they are placed among the Old Testament works themselves.

Modern studies prefer to limit the Apocrypha to 13 writings found in most Septuagint manuscripts, and to assign additional works found only in the Vulgate to a much larger body of writings called the Old Testament *Pseudepigrapha*.

apocryphal *adj.*, *said of a story, etc* unlikely to be true.

apogee *noun* **1** *Astron.* the point in the orbit of the Moon or an artifical satellite around the Earth when it is at its greatest distance from the Earth. See also PERIGEE. **2** *Physics* the greatest height reached by a missile whose velocity is not high enough for it to escape from a gravitational field. [from Greek *apo*, away + *gaia*, Earth]

apolitical *adj.* not interested or active in politics.

apolitically *adv.* without concern for politics.

Apollinaire, Guillaume, pseudonym of **Wilhelm Apollinaris de Kostrowitzky** (1880–1918) French poet, born in Rome of Italian-Polish parents. A leader of the Parisian movement which was akin to the Cubist school in painting, his work, which includes *Alcools* (1913) and *Calligrammes* (1918), rejects conventional poetic traditions.

Apollo, also called **Phoebus** in Greek mythology, the son of Zeus, twin brother of Artemis, and the god of poetic and musical inspiration. He was said to be the most powerful of the gods, and is often depicted as an ideal of male beauty, or as an archer. He established his oracle at Delphi, and spoke through a priestess called the Pythia. He later came to be associated with the Sun.

Apollo asteroid *Astron.* any of a group of small faint asteroids whose paths cross the Earth's orbit. In Jan 1991 an Apollo asteroid passed within 170 000km of Earth, closer than any other observed asteroid.

Apollonius of Perga (fl. 250–220 BC) Greek mathematician, known as 'the Great Geometer'. He was the author of the *Conica*, the definitive ancient work on conic sections which laid the foundations of later teaching on the subject. He also wrote on various geometrical problems, including that of finding a circle touching three given circles, and put forward two descriptions of planetary motion, one in terms of epicycles and the other in terms of eccentric motion.

Apollonius Rhodius (3c BC) Greek scholar and epic poet, born in Alexandria, Egypt, and long resident in Rhodes. He wrote many works on grammar, and a long poem about the quest for the Golden Fleece, the *Argonautica*, which was greatly admired by the Romans.

Apollo-Soyuz project *Astron.* a joint space mission conducted by the USA and the former Soviet Union in 1975, intended primarily as a political gesture during a period of US-Soviet détente. It involved the docking of a US Apollo spacecraft with a Soviet Soyuz spacecraft while in orbit around the Earth.

Apollo space programme *Astron.* the most ambitious space achievement to date, that involved landing men on the Moon and then returning them safely to Earth.

◇ The programme was undertaken by NASA at the direction of President Kennedy in response to the space leadership position established by the former Soviet Union. Six crewed lunar landings were made between 1969 and 1972, at a cost of over $24 billion. The first landing was made on 20 July 1969 by Neil Armstrong and Edwin Aldrin in the spacecraft *Eagle*. A *Saturn V* rocket was used to launch a command module containing a three-man crew which, on reaching the Moon, remained in lunar orbit, while a lunar module containing two of the crew members descended to the Moon's surface.

Apollyon a Biblical character, who appears as the evil dragon in John Bunyan's *The Pilgrim's Progress*.

apologetic *adj.* showing or expressing regret for a mistake or offence.

apologetically *adv.* in an apologetic way.

apologia *noun* a formal statement in defence of a belief or cause.

apologist *noun* a person who formally defends a belief or cause.

apologize *or* **apologise** *verb intrans.* to acknowledge or express regret for a mistake or offence.

apology *noun* (PL. **apologies**) **1** an expression of regret for a mistake or offence. **2** a formal defence of a belief or cause.

— **apology for something** a poor example of it: *what's that apology for a pudding?* [from Greek *apologia*, from *apologeisthai*, to speak in defence]

apophthegm *noun* a short saying expressing some general truth. [from Greek *apophthegma*, from *apo*, forth + *phthengesthai*, to speak]

apoplectic *adj.* **1** of or relating to apoplexy. **2** *colloq.* red-faced and very angry.

apoplectically *adv.* with, or as if with, symptoms of apoplexy.

apoplexy *noun* a former name for a stroke caused by a cerebral haemorrhage. [from Greek *apoplexia*, being struck down]

apostasy *noun* (PL. **apostasies**) the giving up of one's religion, principles, or political party. [from Greek *apo*, away + *stasis*, standing]

apostate — *noun* a person who renounces a former religion or belief. — *adj.* relating to or involved in this renunciation.

a posteriori *said of an argument or reasoning* working from effect to cause or from particular cases to general principles; based on observation or experience. See also A PRIORI. [from Latin *a posteriori*, from what comes after]

apostle *noun* **1** (*often* **Apostle**) a person sent out to preach about Christ in the early Christian church, especially one of his twelve original disciples. **2** an enthusiastic champion or supporter of a cause, belief, etc. [from Greek *apostolos*, from *apo*, away + *stellein*, to send]

◇ The apostles are generally taken to include the twelve original followers of Christ (excluding Judas Iscariot in some versions), who witnessed the resurrected Jesus and were charged with proclaiming his gospel. They were Peter, Andrew, James and his brother John, Philip, Bartholomew, Thomas, Matthew, James (the Less), Jude, and Simon. Matthias and Paul were subsequent additions, as were other early Christian missionaries and itinerant preachers.

Apostles' Creed *Christianity* the most ancient creed of the Christian faith, widely used in Roman Catholic and Protestant churches, and recognized by Orthodox Churches. It is a statement which stresses the threefold nature of God (as Father, Son, and Holy Spirit) and the work of Christ as God's representative on Earth. In its present form, it dates back to the 8c, though its origins go back at least as far as the 3c.

apostolic *adj.* **1** relating to the apostles in the early Christian Church, or to their teaching. **2** relating to the Pope: *the Apostolic See*.

apostolically *adv.* as regards the apostles or the Pope.

Apostolic Constitution one of the most solemn documents issued in the name of a pope, concerned with major matters of doctrine or discipline for the Roman Catholic Church.

Apollo Launches

Mission	Launch	Duration (h:min)	Crew	Comment
Apollo I	Jan 67		Grissom White Chaffee	Astronauts killed in command module in fire at launch site
Apollo IV	9 Nov 67			First launch by Saturn V rocket; successful launch of unmanned module
Apollo V	22 Jan 68– 24 Jan 68			Flight test of lunar module in earth orbit
Apollo VII	11 Oct 68– 22 Oct 68	260:90	Schirra Eisele Cunningham	First manned Apollo flight in earth orbit
Apollo VIII	21 Dec 68– 27 Dec 68	147:01	Borman Lovell Anders	First manned orbit of moon (10 orbits)
Apollo IX	3 Mar 69– 13 Mar 69	241:01	McDivitt Scott Schweickart	First manned lunar module flight in earth orbit
Apollo X	18 May 69– 26 May 69	192:03	Stafford Young Cernan	First lunar module orbit of moon
Apollo XI	16 Jul 69– 24 Jul 69	195:18	Armstrong[1] Aldrin[1] Collins	First men on moon, 20 Jul, Sea of Tranquillity
Apollo 12	14 Nov 69– 24 Nov 69	244:36	Conrad[1] Bean[1] Gordon	Moon landing, 19 Nov, Ocean of Storms
Apollo 13	11 Apr 70– 17 Apr 70	142:54	Lovell Swigert Haise	Mission aborted, ruptured oxygen tank
Apollo 14	31 Jan 71– 9 Feb 71	216:02	Shepard[1] Mitchell[1] Roosa	Moon landing, 5 Feb, Fra Mauro area
Apollo 15	26 Jul 71– 7 Aug 71	295:12	Scott[1] Irwin[1] Worden	Moon landing, 30 Jul, Hadley Rille; Lunar Roving Vehicle used
Apollo 16	16 Apr 72– 27 Apr 72	265:51	Young[1] Duke[1] Mattingly	Moon landing, 20 Apr, Descartes
Apollo 17	7 Dec 72– 19 Dec 72	301:52	Cernan[1] Schmitt[1] Evans	Longest Apollo mission, 11 Dec, Taurus-Littrow
Apollo-Soyuz Test project	15 Jul 75– 24 Jul 75	217:28	Stafford Brand Slayton	Rendezvous/docking with Soyuzia

[1]Astronauts who landed on the moon; the remaining astronaut was the pilot of the command module.

apostolic succession *Christianity* the theory in the Christian Church (notably the Roman Catholic Church), that certain spiritual powers conferred on the first Apostles by Christ have been handed down from one generation of bishops to the next in an unbroken chain of transmission. It is disputed by many New Testament scholars, and rejected by many Churches.

apostrophe *noun* **1** a punctuation mark ('), used to show the omission of a letter or letters, eg *I'm* for *I am*, and possession, eg *Ann's book*. **2** a passage in a speech, poem, etc which turns away from its course to address a person (especially dead or absent) or thing. [from Greek *apostrephein*, to turn away]

apostrophize or **apostrophise** *verb* to speak an apostrophe to.

apothecary *noun* (PL. **apothecaries**) *old use* a chemist licensed to dispense drugs. [from Greek *apotheke*, storehouse]

apotheosis *noun* (PL. **apotheoses**) **1** a raising to the rank of god. **2** a perfect example. [from Greek *apo*, completely + *theos*, god]

appal *verb* (**appalled**, **appalling**) to shock or horrify. [from French *appallir*, to grow pale]

Appalachian Mountains a mountain system in E North America extending SW from the Gulf of St Lawrence to central Alabama, length 2 570km/1 600mi. The system is a series of parallel ranges separated by wide valleys. The Appalachian Plateau lies to the W, the Folded or

Newer Appalachians are in the central area and the Older Appalachians lie to the E. The highest peak is in the Blue Ridge Mts in the E at Mt Mitchell (2 037m) in North Carolina. There are glaciers in the Canadian and New England areas. The range was a major barrier to westward exploration in early US history. It is an area rich in minerals, especially coal. NOTABLE FEATURES Great Smoky Mountains National Park (Tennessee), Shenandoah National Park (Virginia); the Appalachian Trail.

appalling *adj.* **1** causing feelings of shock or horror. **2** *colloq.* extremely bad.

appallingly *adv.* in an appalling way.

apparatchik *noun* **1** a member of a communist bureaucracy or party machine. **2** a bureaucratic hack. [from Russian *apparat*, apparatus, machine]

apparatus *noun* (PL. **apparatuses**, **apparatus**) **1** the equipment needed for a particular purpose. **2** an organization or system made up of many different parts. [from Latin *apparatus*, from *apparare*, to prepare for]

apparel *noun old use*, *formal* clothing. [from French *apareillier*, to make fit]

apparent *adj.* **1** easy to see or understand. **2** seeming to be real but perhaps not actually so. See also HEIR. [from Latin *apparere*, to appear]

apparently *adv.* as it seems; evidently, clearly.

apparition *noun* **1** a sudden, unexpected appearance, especially of a ghost. **2** a ghost. [from Latin *apparitio*]

Appassionata Sonata a piano sonata by Ludwig van Beethoven (Op 57 in F Minor, 1804–5). His publisher coined the term to describe the mood of the work. [from Italian, = impassioned]

appeal — *verb intrans.* **1** to make an urgent or formal request. **2** (**appeal to someone**) to be pleasing, interesting, or attractive. **3** *Legal* to request a higher authority or law court to review or change a decision given by a lower one. **4** (**appeal to someone**) to call on them for support: *tried to appeal to her better nature.* **5** *Cricket* to ask the umpire whether a batsman is out or not. — *noun* **1** an urgent or formal request for help, money, etc. **2** *Legal* a request to a higher authority or law court for a review or change of a decision taken by a lower one. **3** the quality of attracting, interesting, or pleasing. [from Latin *appellare*, to address by name]

appealing *adj.* **1** pleasing, attractive, or interesting. **2** arousing sympathy.

appealingly *adv.* with an appealing manner.

appear *verb intrans.* **1** to become visible or come into sight. **2** to seem. **3** to present oneself formally or in public, eg on stage. **4** to be present in a law court as either accused or counsel. **5** to be published. [from Latin *apparere*]

appearance *noun* **1** an act or instance of appearing. **2** how a person or thing looks, whether or not this reflects reality.
— **keep up appearances** to keep up an outward show of happiness, wealth, etc when this is really lacking.
put in an appearance to attend a meeting, party, etc only briefly.
to all appearances so far as it can be seen.

appease *verb* **1** to calm or pacify, especially by agreeing to demands made on one. **2** to satisfy (an appetite or doubt). [from French *apeser*, from *a*, to + *pes*, peace]

appeasement *noun* **1** the act or process of appeasing; conciliation. **2** the state of being appeased or conciliated.

appellant — *noun* a person who makes an appeal to a higher court to review or change the decision of a lower one. — *adj.* of an appeal or appellant. [from Latin *appellare*, to address by name]

appellate *adj. Legal, said especially of a court* concerned with appeals. [from Latin *appellare*, to address by name]

appellation *noun formal* a name or title. [from Latin *appellare*, to address by name]

appellation d'origine contrôlée (ABBREV. **AOC**) a term used in the labelling of French wines. It guarantees that the wine conforms to certain specified conditions of origin, strength, etc. [French, = certified name]

append *verb* to add or attach, especially as a supplement to a document. [from Latin *appendere*, to hang]

appendage *noun* anything added or attached to a larger or more important part.

appendectomy or **appendicectomy** *noun* (PL. **appendectomies**, **appendicectomies**) *Medicine* an operation for the surgical removal of the appendix. It is the commonest surgical emergency. [from APPENDIX + Greek *ektome*, a cutting out]

appendicitis *noun Medicine* inflammation of the appendix, causing abdominal pain and vomiting. Usually the appendix is surgically removed to prevent it bursting and leading to the development of peritonitis.

appendix *noun* (PL. **appendixes**, **appendices**) **1** a section containing extra information, notes, etc at the end of a book or document. **2** *Anat.* a short tube-like sac attached to the lower end of the caecum at the junction of the small and large intestines. [from Latin *appendere*, to hang]

appertain *verb intrans.* to belong or relate. [from Latin *ad*, to + *pertinere*, to belong]

appetite *noun* 1 a natural physical desire, especially for food. 2 (**have an appetite for something**) to favour or enjoy it. [from Latin *appetitus*, from *appetere*, to seek after]

appetizer *or* **appetiser** *noun* a small amount of food or drink eaten before a meal to increase the appetite.

appetizing *or* **appetising** *adj.* increasing the appetite, especially by looking or smelling delicious.

appetizingly *adv.* so as to stimulate the appetite.

Appian Way the first of Rome's major trunk roads, constructed in 312 BC by Appius Claudius Caecus. It ran initially from Rome SE to Capua, and was later extended across the peninsula to Brundisium on the Adriatic coast.

applaud *verb* 1 *trans., intrans.* to praise or show approval by clapping. 2 to express approval of. [from Latin *applaudere*, to clap]

applause *noun* praise or approval shown by clapping.

apple *noun* 1 any small deciduous tree of the genus *Malus* of the rose family (Rosaceae), with pink or white flowers and edible fruit. There are thousands of varieties of cooking, dessert, and cider apples. 2 the firm round edible fruit of this tree, with a green, red, or yellow skin and white flesh. It is consumed fresh or cooked, or used to make fruit juice, cider, etc.
— **the apple of one's eye** a person or thing one is proud or fond of.
in apple-pie order neat and tidy.
upset the apple cart to disrupt carefully made plans.
[from Anglo-Saxon *æppel*]

Apple Cart, The a play by George Bernard Shaw (1929). It is a political comedy on the relationship between democracy and the monarchy, and on political morality, in a story set in the late 20c.

apple-pie bed a bed made with the sheets doubled up so that one cannot stretch out one's legs, usually as a joke.

Appleton, Sir Edward Victor (1892–1965) English physicist, born in Bradford. He was appointed professor at London University (1924) and later at Cambridge (1936). His research revealed the existence of a layer of electrically charged particles in the Earth's upper atmosphere (the *Appleton layer*). For this work he was awarded the 1947 Nobel Prize for Physics.

Appleton layer *Physics* an ionized region of the Earth's atmosphere that reflects radio waves at frequencies of up to 50 MHz, and is widely used for radio transmission around the curved surface of the Earth.

appliance *noun* a machine, instrument, or tool used for a particular job. [from APPLY]

applicable *adj.* that may be applied; suitable; appropriate. [from Latin *applicare*, to apply]

applicant *noun* a person applying for a job, a university place, a grant, etc. [from Latin *applicare*, to apply]

application *noun* 1 a formal request, eg for a job. 2 the act of putting something on to a surface; the thing put on to a surface. 3 the act of using something for a particular purpose. 4 hard work and effort. 5 relevance. 6 *Comput.* a program designed to perform a particular function as a complement to other software. [from Latin *applicare*, to apply]

applications package *Comput.* a set of programs forming a single package designed to per-

form a particular function or set of functions, such as the creation of graphics.

applicator *noun* a device for putting something on to a surface, especially the skin. [from Latin *applicare*, to apply]

applied *adj., said of a skill, theory, etc* put to practical use: *applied science.*

applied linguistics the application of linguistic theory, methods, and practice to situations which present language-related problems and tasks. In foreign language teaching and learning, the applied linguist may provide significant background information, such as analysis of the structure of the learner's native language contrasted with that of the language being learned, in order to help predict potential sources of difficulty and error. Other areas of interest include interpretaion, translation, dictionary-making, clinical linguistics, and educational linguistics.

applied mathematics *Maths.* the branch of mathematics concerned with the formation and solution of equations whose variables relate to real physical systems, such as experimental data. ◇ Applied mathematics is widely used in all branches of engineering, many scientific subjects, and in the formation of mathematical models for use in computer simulations. At the atomic level it is used in quantum mechanics to describe subatomic particles.

appliqué *noun* decoration for clothes, fabric, etc, in which material is cut into shapes which are sewn on to the clothes, etc to make patterns and designs. [from French *appliqué*, applied]

apply *verb* (**applies, applied**) 1 *intrans.* (**apply for something**) to make a formal request, eg for a job. 2 to put or spread on a surface: *applied three coats of paint to each wall.* 3 *intrans.* to be relevant or suitable. 4 to put (a skill, rule, theory, etc) to practical use.
— **apply oneself to something** to give one's full attention or energy to a task, etc.
[from Latin *applicare*, to attach]

appoint *verb* 1 to give (a person) a job or position: *appointed him to the chairmanship / was appointed chairman.* 2 to fix or agree on (a date, time, or place). 3 to equip or furnish: *well-appointed rooms.* [from French *apointer*, from *à*, to + *point*, point]

appointee *noun* a person appointed.

appointment *noun* 1 an arrangement to meet someone. 2 the act of giving someone a job or position. 3 the job or position a person is given. 4 the person given a job or position: *you were a surprise appointment.* 5 (**appointments**) *formal* equipment and furnishings.

Appomattox Court House the site in Virginia, USA, of the surrender (9 Apr 1865) of the Confederate army under Robert E Lee to Union forces under Ulysses S Grant, which, although a few Confederates remained under arms, marked the effective end of the American Civil War.

apportion *verb* to share out fairly. [from Latin *apportionare*]

apposite *adj.* suitable; well chosen. [from Latin *appositus*, from *apponere*, to put to]

appositely *adv.* in an apposite way.

appositeness *noun* relevance, applicability.

apposition *noun* a grammatical construction in which two or more nouns or noun phrases are put together without being linked by *and, but, or,* etc, eg *his wife the doctor.* [from Latin *appositio*, from *apponere*, to put to]

appraisal *noun* evaluation; estimation of quality.

appraise *verb* 1 to decide the value or quality of (a person's skills, ability, etc). 2 to put a price on, especially officially. [from Old French *aprisier*, from *a*, to + *prisier*, to price or prize]

appraiser *noun* 1 a person who values property. 2 a person who estimates quality.

appreciable *adj.* noticeable; significant. [from Latin *appretiare*, to appreciate]

appreciably *adv.* so as to be appreciable; significantly.

appreciate *verb* 1 to be grateful or thankful for. 2 to be aware of the value, quality, etc of. 3 to understand or be aware of. 4 *intrans., trans.* to increase in value. [from Latin *appretiare*, from *ad*, to + *pretium*, price]

appreciation *noun* 1 gratitude or thanks. 2 sensitive understanding and enjoyment of the value or quality of something: *an appreciation of good music.* 3 the state of knowing or being aware of. 4 an increase in value.

appreciative *adj.* feeling or expressing appreciation.

appreciatively *adv.* in an appreciative way.

apprehend *verb* 1 to arrest. 2 to understand. [from Latin *apprehendere*, to seize]

apprehension *noun* 1 uneasy concern about the imminent future; fear or anxiety. 2 the act of arresting. 3 understanding. [from Latin *apprehendere*, to seize]

apprehensive *adj.* anxious or worried; uneasily concerned about the imminent future.

apprehensively *adv.* anxiously, nervously.

apprentice — *noun* a young person who works for an agreed period of time in order to learn a craft or trade. — *verb* to assign as an apprentice. [from French *apprentiz*, from Latin *apprehendere*, to lay hold of]

apprenticeship *noun* 1 the status of an apprentice. 2 a time of training for a trade, etc.

apprize *or* **apprise** *verb* (**apprize someone of something**) to give them information about it. [from French *appris*, learnt]

appro *noun*
— **on appro** *colloq.* on approval.

approach — *verb* 1 *trans., intrans.* to come near or nearer in space or time. 2 to suggest or propose something to. 3 to begin to deal with (a problem, subject, etc). 4 to be like or similar to: *nothing approaches this for quality.* — *noun* 1 the act of coming near. 2 a way to, or means of reaching, a place. 3 a request for help, support, etc; a suggestion or proposal. 4 a way of considering or dealing with, eg a problem: *a new approach.* 5 the course that an aircraft follows as it comes in to land. 6 an approximation. [from Latin *appropriare*, from *ad*, to + *prope*, near]

approachable *adj.* 1 friendly and ready to listen and help. 2 that can be reached.

approbation *noun* approval; consent. [from Latin *approbatio*, from *approbare*, to approve of]

appropriate — *adj.* (pronounced -*ət*) suitable or proper. — *verb* (pronounced -*ate*) 1 to take (something) as one's own, especially without permission. 2 to put (money) aside for a particular purpose. [from Latin *appropriare*, from *ad*, to + *proprius*, one's own]

appropriately *adv.* in an appropriate way; suitably.

appropriateness *noun* correctness, suitability.

appropriation *noun* the act of appropriating.

approval *noun* 1 a favourable opinion. 2 official permission.
— **on approval** *said of goods for sale* that may be returned if not satisfactory.

approve *verb* 1 to agree to or permit. 2 *intrans.* (**approve of someone** *or* **something**) to be pleased with or think well of them. [from Latin *approbare*, to approve of]

approving *adj.* favourable.

approvingly *adv.* with approval.

approx. *abbrev.* approximate.

approximate — *adj.* (pronounced *-mət*) almost exact or accurate. — *verb trans., intrans.* (pronounced *-mate*) (**approximate to something**) to come close to it in value, quality, accuracy, etc. [from Latin *approximare*, from *ad*, to + *proximus*, nearest]

approximately *adv., said of a number, estimate, etc* nearly; roughly.

approximation *noun* **1** a figure, answer, etc which is almost exact. **2** the process of estimating a figure, etc.

appurtenance *noun* (*usually* **appurtenances**) an accessory to, or minor detail of, something larger, such as duties or rights connected with owning property. [from French *apertenance*, from Latin *appertinere*, to belong]

APR *abbrev.* annual percentage rate.

Apr *or* **Apr.** *abbrev.* April.

apraxia *noun Psychol.* an inability to make deliberate movements with accuracy, usually as a result of brain disease. [from Greek *apraxia*, inaction]

après-ski — *noun* evening social activities after a day's skiing. — *adj., said of clothes, etc* suitable for such activities. [French, = after-skiing]

apricot — *noun* a small, round, pale-orange fruit with a soft furry skin, related to the peach and plum. — *adj.* apricot-coloured or apricot-flavoured. [from Portuguese *albricoque*, from Latin *praecox*, early-ripening]

April *noun* **1** the fourth month of the year, following March. **2** a female first name, taken from the month and associated with growth and new birth. [probably from Latin *aperire*, to open]

April fool a person tricked or made a fool of on 1 Apr (All Fools' Day or April Fools' Day); also, the trick made.
◇ Originally, this may have been the final day of the festivities celebrating the spring equinox, which began on Old New Year's Day (25 Mar until 1564).
The tradition, found throughout Europe, may have originated in France; outside Europe, there is an example of similar fooling during the Huli Festival in India (ending 31 Mar).

April Theses a programme of revolutionary action announced by Lenin (Apr 1917) shortly after the February Revolution and his return to Russia. In it he advocated the transformation of the Russian 'bourgeois-democratic' revolution into a 'proletarian-socialist' revolution under the slogan: 'All power to the Soviets'.

a priori *said of an argument or reasoning* working from cause to effect or from general principles to particular cases. See also A POSTERIORI. [from Latin *a priori*, from what is before]

apron *noun* **1** a piece of cloth, plastic, etc worn over the front of clothes to protect them. **2** a hard-surface area at an airport where aircraft are loaded. **3** the part of a theatre stage in front of the curtain.
— **tied to his mother's** *or* **wife's apron strings** *said of a boy or man* completely dominated by and dependent on his mother or wife.
[from Middle English *napron*, from Old French *naperon*; *a napron* came to be understood as *an apron*]

apropos — *adj., said of remarks* suitable or to the point. — *prep.* (**apropos of something**) with reference to it. — *adv.* by the way; appropriately. [from French *à propos*, to the purpose]

apse *noun* the arched, domed east end of a church. [from Greek *hapsis*, arch]

apsis *noun* (PL. **apsides**) either of the points in the orbit of a planet or satellite furthest from and nearest to the body it is orbiting. [from Greek *hapsis*, arch]

APT *abbrev.* Advanced Passenger Train.

apt *adj.* **1** suitable. **2** (**apt to do something**) inclined or likely to do it. **3** (**apt at something**) clever or quick to learn it. [from Latin *aptus*, fit]

apteryx *noun* a kiwi. [from Greek *a*, without + *pteryx*, wing]

aptitude *noun* **1** (**aptitude for something**) a natural skill or talent. **2** ability or fitness. [from Latin *aptitudo*]

aptly *adv.* in an apt way; suitably.

aptness *noun* suitability, being apt.

Apuleius, Lucius (2c) Roman satirist and rhetorician, born in Madaura, Numidia, Africa. He travelled widely, obtaining knowledge of many priestly fraternities, which he employed in his romance *Metamorphoses* or *The Golden Ass*. It is generally regarded as the only Latin novel to have survived in its entirety.

Aqaba, ancient **Aelana** POP (1986e) 37 000, a seaport in Maan governorate, East Bank, SW Jordan, at the N end of the Gulf of Aqaba, on the border with Israel. It is Jordan's only outlet to the sea and was an ancient trade route through the Red Sea–Jordan Rift Valley. It is a popular winter seaside resort.

aqua- *combining form denoting water*: *aqualung*.

aquaculture *or* **aquiculture** *noun Agric.* the practice of using the sea, lakes, and rivers for cultivating aquatic animals (eg fish, shellfish) and plants (eg seaweed), mainly for consumption as food. [from Latin *aqua* water + CULTURE]

aquafit *noun* a system of aerobic exercises performed in chest-high water.

aqua fortis *old use* nitric acid. [from Latin *aqua fortis*, strong water]

aqualung *noun* an apparatus consisting of air cylinders worn by divers on their backs, with tubes leading to the mouth, allowing them to breathe under water.

aquamarine — *noun* **1** *Geol.* a transparent bluish-green gemstone that is a variety of the mineral beryl. **2** the colour of this gemstone. — *adj.* relating to this stone or its colour. [from Latin *aqua marina*, sea water]

aquaplane — *noun* a thin board which a person stands on to be towed very fast by a motor boat. — *verb intrans.* **1** to ride on an aquaplane. **2** *said of a vehicle* to slide along out of control on a thin film of water.

aqua regia a mixture of acids used to dissolve gold and platinum. [from Latin *aqua regia*, royal water]

Aquarian — *noun* a person born under the sign of Aquarius. — *adj.* born under or characteristic of the sign of Aquarius.

aquarium *noun* (PL. **aquariums, aquaria**) a glass tank, or a building containing several such tanks (eg in a zoo), for keeping fish and other water animals. [from Latin *aquarius*, of water]

Aquarius *noun* **1** *Astron.* the Water Bearer, a large but dim southern constellation of the

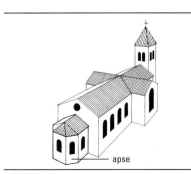

apse

zodiac, lying between Pisces and Capricornus. **2** a person born between 21 January and 19 February, under this sign. [from Latin *aquarius*, water-carrier]

aquatic — *adj.* **1** living or growing in water. **2** *said of sports* taking place in water. — *noun* **1** an aquatic animal or plant. **2** (**aquatics**) water sports. [from Latin *aquaticus*, from *aqua*, water]

aquatint *noun* a picture produced by printing with a copper plate that has been etched using acid and wax. [from Italian *aqua tinta*, dyed water]

aquatube *noun* an extended water chute with twists and bends, down which users slide on a stream of water into a swimming pool.

aqua vitae a strong alcoholic drink, especially brandy. [from Latin *aqua vitae*, water of life]

aqueduct *noun* a channel or canal carrying water, especially in the form of a tall bridge across a valley. [from Latin *aqua*, water + *ducere*, to lead]

aqueous *adj.* consisting of, like, or produced by water; watery. [from Latin *aqua*, water]

aqueous humour *Anat.* the clear liquid between the lens and the cornea of the eye.

aqueous solution *Chem.* any solution in which the solvent is water.

aquifer *noun Geol.* water-bearing rock strata, commonly sandstones or chalk, that are highly porous and permeable to water. They provide much of the world's water supply, which may be tapped directly by sinking wells or pumping the water into a reservoir. [from Latin *aqua*, water, + *ferre*, to carry]

aquilegia *noun* any of various garden hybrids of a perennial plant (*Aquilegia vulgaris*, or columbine), native to Europe, N Africa, and Asia, and having pink, crimson, violet, yellow, orange, or white flowers in which each of the five petals has a long straight backward-pointing spur containing nectar. [probably from Latin *aquila*, eagle]

aquiline *adj.* **1** of or like an eagle. **2** *said of a nose* curved like an eagle's beak. [from Latin *aquila*, eagle]

Aquinas, St Thomas known as **Doctor Angelicus** (1225–74) Italian scholastic philosopher and theologian, born in the family castle near Aquino. Against the will of his family, he entered the Dominican order (1243), but his brothers abducted him and kept him prisoner for two years. He escaped to Cologne and became a pupil of Albertus Magnus, then began to teach (1248). He published commentaries on Aristotle, and obtained great distinction as a philosophic theologian in Paris (1252), until in 1258 he was summoned by the pope to teach successively in Anagni, Orvieto, and Rome. He was canonized in 1323; his feast day is 28 Jan. The first 13c metaphysician to stress the importance of sense perception and the experimental foundation of human knowledge, he wrote *Summa Theologiae*, the first attempt at a complete theological system, which remains the general teaching of the Roman Catholic Church. His only scholastic rival was Duns Scotus (Doctor Subtilis). The Franciscans followed Scotus, and the Dominicans followed Thomas, so medieval theologians were thereafter divided into two schools (Scotists and Thomists) whose differences permeated almost every branch of doctrine.

Aquitaine, ancient **Aquitania** POP (1991e) 2.8m, a region in SW France comprising the departments of Dordogne, Gironde, Landes, Lot-et-Garonne, and Pyrénées-Atlantiques. AREA 41 308sq km/15 945sq mi. It is drained by the rivers Garonne, Dordogne, and Gironde. HISTORY the region roughly corresponds to the W part of the Roman province of *Aquitania* (c.1c BC–5c AD); united with Gascony under the French crown in the 11c; acquired by England on the marriage of Henry II to Eleanor of Aquitaine in 1152; it remained in English hands until 1453. CAPITAL Bordeaux. ECONOMY wine (Bergerac and Bordeaux are two important wine-producing areas); fruit; resin; tobacco; shipbuilding; chemicals; oil refining. NOTABLE FEATURES Parc des Landes de Gascogne Regional Nature Park; caves with ancient rock paintings; several spas.

AR *abbrev.* Arkansas.

Ar *symbol Chem.* argon.

Arab — *noun* **1** a member of a Semitic people living in the Middle East and N Africa. **2** a breed of horse famous for its grace and speed. — *adj.* relating to Arabs or Arabia. [from Greek *Araps*]
◇ Arabs are mostly Caucasoid, but Negroid and Mongoloid admixtures exist in some regions. Although they are a diverse group, the unifying force is Islam, the religion of 95% of Arabs. The majority live in the cities and towns; 5% are pastoral nomads living in deserts.

Arabella a female first name. [of Scottish origin and unclear derivation; either a variant of ANNABEL or of *Arabel*, from Latin *orabilis*, able to be called on]

arabesque *noun* **1** *Ballet* a position in which the dancer stands with one leg stretched out backwards and the body bent forwards from the hips. **2** a complex design of leaves, flowers, etc woven together. **3** a short ornate piece of music. [from Italian *arabesco*, in the Arabian style]

Arabia a peninsula in SW Asia, bounded N by the Syrian Desert, E by the Arabian Gulf, W by the Red Sea, and S by the Arabian Sea. AREA c.2 600 000sq km/1 000 000sq mi. It is divided politically into the states of Saudi Arabia, Yemen, Oman, United Arab Emirates, Bahrain, Qatar, and Kuwait. The area is an important world source of petroleum.

Arabian — *adj.* of Arabia or the Arabs. — *noun old use* an Arab.

Arabian Gulf *or* **The Gulf,** *or* **Persian Gulf,** ancient **Sinus Persicus** an arm of the Arabian Sea bounded N by Iran, NW by Iraq and Kuwait, W by Saudi Arabia and Qatar, and S by the United Arab Emirates. AREA 238 800sq km/92 200sq mi; average depth 100m. The Gulf of Oman and the Strait of Hormuz link it to the Arabian Sea. MAIN ISLANDS Bahrain, Qeshm (Iran). The Arabian Gulf is an important source of oil and a pipeline in the N links offshore oilfields with Iran and Saudi Arabia via a terminal on Khârg I. There was great tension in the Gulf during the Iran–Iraq War in the 1980s and again in the early 1990s during the Gulf War between Iraq and UN coalition forces following Iraq's invasion of Kuwait.

Arabian Nights, also called **The Thousand and One Nights** a series of fantastic tales from the East, written in Arabic and widely translated. The 'frame' story tells how Scheherazade saves herself from the daily threat of execution by enthralling her husband the Caliph with tales of Ali Baba, Sinbad the Sailor, and many others.

Arabian Sea the NW part of the Indian Ocean. It is bounded N by Pakistan and Iran, E by India, and W by Oman and South Yemen. Depths vary from 2 895m in the N to 4 392m in the SW. Principal arms include the Gulf of Oman in the NW and the Gulf of Aden in the W. The sea is a trade route between the Indian subcontinent, Arabian Gulf states, and the Mediterranean Sea.

Arabic — *noun* the Semitic language of the Arabs. — *adj.* of the Arabs, their language or culture.
◇ Arabic is spoken by c.150 million people as a first language. It spread, with Islam in the 7c and 8c, from the Arabian Peninsula to North Africa and throughout the Middle East. Classical Arabic is the literary form of the Koran, and the standard form of communication between Arab states, and in writing; colloquial Arabic has developed into many dialect forms spoken in the various

Arab states. The language has a consonantal alphabet and is written from right to left.

The Arabic Alphabet					
Letter	Name	Usual trans- literation	Letter	Name	Usual trans- literation
ا	'alif	'	ص	dad	d
ب	ba	b	ط	ta	t
ت	ta	t	ظ	za	z
ث	tha	th	ع	'ain	'
ج	jim	j	غ	ghain	gh
ح	ha	h	ف	fa	f
خ	kha	kh	ق	qaf	q
د	dal	d	ك	kaf	k
ذ	dha	th	ل	lam	l
ر	ra	r	م	mim	m
ز	za	z	ن	nun	n
س	sin	s	ه	ha	h
ش	shin	sh	و	waw	w
ص	sad	s	ي	ya	y

Arabic numeral any of the numbers 0, 1, 2, 3, 4, 5, 6, 7, 8, and 9, based on Arabic characters.

Arab–Israeli Wars four wars (1948, 1956, 1967, 1973) fought between Israel and the Arab states over the existence of the state of Israel and the rights of the Palestinians. The June 1967 war is known by supporters of Israel as the 'Six Day War' and by others as the 'June War'. The 1973 war is called the 'Yom Kippur War' by Israelis, the 'Ramadan War' by Arabs, and the 'October War' by others.

Arabist *noun* an expert in or student of Arabic culture, history, and language.

arable *adj. Agric.* **1** *said of land* suitable or used for ploughing and growing crops. **2** *said of a crop* that has to be sown on ploughed land, eg cereals, potatoes, root crops. [from Latin *arare*, to plough]

Arab League a League of Arab states, founded (Mar 1945) with the aim of encouraging Arab unity. The League's headquarters was established in Egypt, but moved to Tunis after the signing of Egypt's peace treaty with Israel in 1979. Today the Arab League has 22 member states including Palestine (represented by the Palestine Liberation Organization).

Arachne in Greek mythology, a weaver from Lydia, who challenged Athena to a contest. When Arachne's work was seen to be superior, Athena destroyed the web and Arachne hanged herself. Athena saved her, but changed her into a spider.

arachnid *noun* any of a class of eight-legged insect-like creatures, such as spiders and scorpions. [from Greek *arachne*, spider]

arachnoid — *adj.* like a cobweb. — *noun Anat.* (*also* **arachnoid membrane**) the membrane between the dura mater and the pia mater.

Arafat, Yasser, *or* **Yasir,** originally **Mohammed Abed Ar'ouf Arafat** (1929–) Palestinian resistance leader, born in Cairo of Palestinian parents. He led the Palestinian Students' Union at Cairo University, and co-founded the Fatah resistance group in 1956, which later gained control of the Palestinian Liberation Organization (PLO) in 1964. Acknowledged (though not universally popular) as the PLO leader, he skilfully managed the uneasy juxtaposition of militancy and diplomacy, and gradually gained world acceptance of the PLO. In 1983 however, his policies lost majority PLO support, and he was forced to leave Lebanon with his remaining followers. Since then he has been based at the PLO headquarters in Tunis, though he spends much of his time in Baghdad. The *intifada* (uprising) in the West Bank in 1988 paved the way for his dramatic recogni-

tion of Israel and renunciation of terrorism in Dec 1988. In 1993 he and the Prime Minister of Israel, Yitzhak Rabin, negotiated a peace agreement at the White House (signed in Cairo in 1994), by which Israel agreed to withdraw from Jericho and the Gaza Strip.

Arafura Sea a section of the Pacific Ocean, bounded in the N and NE by Indonesia and New Guinea, and in the S by Australia. Shallow depths of 27–55m are caused by the underlying continental shelf.

Aragon, Louis (1897–1983) French novelist, poet and journalist, born in Paris. A Surrealist, his first novel was *Le Paysan de Paris* (1926, The Night-Walker). He became a communist in 1930, and edited the communist weekly *Les Lettres Françaises* (1953–72). Later works include several collections of poems and the novel *La semaine sainte* (1958, Holy Week).

Aragon POP (1991) 1.2m, an autonomous sparsely-populated region of NE Spain. AREA 47 770sq km/18 400sq mi. CAPITAL Saragossa. It is a featureless upland region, largely occupying the basin of the R Ebro, with the Pyrenees in the N. HISTORY a Roman province until it was taken by the Visigoths in AD 476; captured by the Moors in the 8c; from 1035 to 1479 it was a kingdom which controlled much of N Spain and conquered parts of S Italy. ECONOMY almonds, figs, vines, and olives, grown by irrigation near rivers.

Aragon, House of the ruling house of one of Spain's component kingdoms, founded (1035) by Ramiro I, the illegitimate son of Sancho the Great of Navarre. It was united by marriage with the ruling house of Barcelona in 1131. Fernando II of Aragon married Isabel of Castile in 1469, and the crowns of Aragon and Castile were finally united in 1479.

aragonite *noun Geol.* a mineral form of calcium carbonate that occurs in some alpine metamorphic rocks, sedimentary rocks, and the shells of certain molluscs, of which it forms the lining (mother-of-pearl). [from *Aragon*, in Spain]

Araguaia, River the main tributary of the Tocantins R, NE Brazil. It rises in central Brazil, and flows NE for an estimated length of 1 770–2 410km/1 100–1 500mi. In its mid course it separates into two branches and encloses Bananal I, on which there is a national park.

arak same as ARRACK.

Arakan Yoma a mountain range in SW Burma (Myanma), between the Arakan coast on the Bay of Bengal and the Irrawaddy R valley. It rises to over 3 000m and forms a climatic barrier, cutting off central Burma (Myanma) from the effects of the SW monsoon.

Aral Sea, Russian **Aral'skoye More** an inland sea in Kazakhstan and Uzbekistan, E of the Caspian Sea. There are several small islands in the Aral Sea, which is generally shallow. It is one of the world's largest lakes but is rapidly decreasing in size; the sea level has dropped by 12m since 1960, and its area has reduced by one third. Water from rivers supplying the sea has been diverted for cotton irrigation projects and this has seriously upset the ecological balance. The water is heavily polluted, and almost all native fish life has been destroyed. Salt and dust storms following gradual exposure of the bottom of the lake have ruined nearby vegetation and more than doubled the salinity of the water. Sodium and magnesium sulphate are mined along its shores.

Aramaic — *noun* any of a group of Semitic languages, including the language spoken by Christ and modern forms spoken in parts of Syria. — *adj.* of or in Aramaic. [from Greek *Aramaios*]
◇ The group includes Old Aramaic, dating from c.2 000 BC, the language spoken by Christ; and modern forms, eg Syriac (or Assyrian), spoken in parts of the Middle East.

Aramis the third Musketeer, set on entering the Church, in Alexandre Dumas's *The Three Musketeers*.

Aran Islands POP (1991) 1 000, a group of three islands off the SW coast of Galway county, Connacht province, W Irish Republic. The islands (Inishmore, Inishmaan, and Inisheer) are located at the mouth of Galway Bay. NOTABLE FEATURES several monastic ruins and the Dun Aengus fort.

Arany, János (1817–82) Hungarian epic poet, born in Nagy-Szalonta. With Petöfi he was a leader of the popular national school, and was chief secretary of the Hungarian Academy (1870–9). His works include the satire *The Lost Constitution* (1945) and the *Toldi* trilogy (1847–54). He also published a successful translation of Shakespeare.

Ararat, (Great) Mount, Turkish (**Büyük**) **Ağri Daği** the highest peak in Turkey, situated in the E part of the country, close to the frontier with Iran and Armenia. HEIGHT 5 165m. It is said to be the landing place of Noah's Ark. Little Ararat (Küçük Ağri Daği) lies to the SE, rising to 3 907m.

Araucanians a S American Indian group of central Chile. Two divisions, the Picunche and the Huilliche, were assimilated into Spanish society in the 17c; the Mapuche resisted for over three centuries, but were finally defeated by the Chilean army in the 1880s, and were settled on reservations, which were abolished in the 1980s. They presently number c.200 000, on private former reservations and in towns and cities in Chile and Argentina.

Arawak an American Indian people of the Greater Antilles and S America. In the Antilles, they settled in villages and cultivated cassava and maize; they were frequently attacked by the Caribs, and many were later killed by the Spanish. In S America, they lived in isolated small settlements in tropical Amazonian forests, and practised hunting, fishing, and farming. A few survivors live along the coastal strip of Guyana and Surinam.

Arber, Werner (1929–) Swiss microbiologist, born in Gränichen. He became Professor of Molecular Biology at Basle in 1970. In 1962 he proposed the existence of 'restriction enzymes', which kill the viruses which invade bacteria (*bacteriophages*) by cutting phage DNA at specific points in the chain. Such enzymes allowed the development of new techniques to cut and rejoin lengths of DNA, heralding the birth of genetic engineering. He shared the 1978 Nobel Prize for Physiology or Medicine with Hamilton Smith and Daniel Nathans.

arbiter *noun* **1** a person with the authority or influence to settle arguments between other people. **2** a person with great influence in matters of style, taste, etc. [from Latin *arbiter*]

arbitrarily *adv.* in an arbitrary or random way; capriciously, despotically.

arbitrariness *noun* **1** being arbitrary; capriciousness. **2** tyranny.

arbitrary *adj.* **1** based on subjective factors or random choice, and not on objective principles. **2** *said of a person* unpredictably dictatorial or authoritarian. [from Latin *arbitrarius*]

arbitrate *verb trans., intrans.* to act as a judge in a quarrel or disagreement. [from Latin *arbitrari*, to judge]

arbitration *noun* the settling of a quarrel or disagreement between two or more groups by a neutral person.

arbitrator *noun* a person who arbitrates; an arbiter.

arbor *noun* a shaft or axle on which a piece of machinery revolves. [from Latin *arbor*, tree]

Arbor Day in the USA, New Zealand, and parts of Canada and Australia, a day (which varies from place to place) set apart each year for planting trees and increasing public awareness of the value of trees. It was first observed in the

state of Nebraska, USA in 1872 and became an official holiday there in 1885.

arboreal *adj.* of or living in trees. [from Latin *arboreus*, from *arbor*, tree]

arboretum *noun* (PL. **arboreta**) *Bot.* a botanical garden used for the display of trees and shrubs for scientific, educational, and recreational purposes. [from Latin *arbor*, tree]

arboriculture *noun* the cultivation of trees and shrubs. [from Latin *arbor*, tree]

arbour *noun* a shady area in a garden formed by trees or climbing plants, usually with a seat. [from Latin *herba*, grass, influenced by Latin *arbor*, tree]

Arbroath, ancient **Aberbrothock** POP (1981) 24 000, a port in Angus district, Tayside, E Scotland. It lies on the North Sea coast, 27km/17mi NE of Dundee. In 1320 the Declaration of Arbroath, which asserted Scotland's independence from England, was signed here by King Robert Bruce. NOTABLE FEATURE the remains of Arbroath Abbey (1178).

Arbuthnot, John (1667–1735) Scottish physician and wit, born in Inverbervie, Kincardineshire. He qualified as a doctor from St Andrews University (1696), and was appointed physician to Queen Anne (1705). Although he wrote on many scientific subjects, he is best known for his literary accomplishments, including *The History of John Bull* (1712). With Swift, Pope, and Gay, he was a founder member of the satirical Scriblerus Club, and he was the chief contributor to *Memoirs of Martinus Scriblerus*, first published in Pope's works (1741).

ARC *abbrev.* AIDS-related complex.

arc — *noun* **1** a part of the line which forms a circle or other curve. **2** a curve of bright light formed by a strong electric current passing across a space between two electrodes. — *verb intrans.* (**arced, arcing**) to form an arc. [from Latin *arcus*, bow]

arcade *noun* **1** a covered walk or passage, usually lined with shops. **2** a row of arches supporting a roof, wall, etc. [from Italian *arcata*]

Arcadia **1** a mountainous area in the centre of the Peloponnese in Greece. In antiquity, its inhabitants claimed to be pre-Dorian, and the oldest settlers of Hellenic stock in Greece. **2** (also **Arcady**) in mythology, and in the literature of Greece, Rome, and the Renaissance, a paradise of ideal pastoral existence.

Arcadian *adj.* relating to or like Arcadia; characterized by simple rural pleasures.

arcane *adj.* mysterious, secret; understood only by a few. [from Latin *arcanus*, shut]

Arc de Triomphe a triumphal arch commemorating Napoleon's victories, designed by Jean Chalgrin (1739–1811) and erected at the end of the Champs Elysées, Paris. The body of an unknown soldier was buried under the arch after World War I, and an eternal flame burns on the tomb.

Arc-et-Senans a royal saltworks situated N of Arbois, France. The idea was to incorporate a saline extraction plant with an ideal town, but building came to a halt in 1779. The works were abandoned by the end of the 19c. It is a World Heritage site.

arch¹ — *noun* **1** a curved structure forming an opening, supporting a roof, bridge, etc, or as an ornament. **2** anything shaped like an arch, especially a monument. **3** the raised part of the sole of the foot, between the heel and the toes. — *verb* **1** *intrans.* to form an arch. **2** *trans.* to span as an arch or like an arch. [from Latin *arcus*, bow]

arch² *adj.* self-consciously playful or coy. [from ARCH-, originally in *arch rogue*, etc]

arch- *or* **archi-** *combining form* chief; most important: *archangel / archduke*. [from Anglo-Saxon *arce-*, from Greek *archos*, chief]

Archaean *or* **Archean** *adj. Geol.* the earlier of the two geological eons into which the Precambrian period is divided, corresponding to the period of time from the formation of the Earth (about 4 600 million years ago) to about 2 500 million years ago. [from Greek *archaios*, ancient]

Archaebacteria *Biol.* a recently established kingdom of anaerobic bacteria that are thought to be living representatives of the oldest known life forms, which existed about four billion years ago when the Earth's atmosphere contained little oxygen. They are typically found in extreme environments such as salt lakes and hot springs, and their DNA differs markedly from that of other bacteria.

archaeological *adj.* relating to archaeology; discovered or known from archaeology.

archaeologist *noun* a person who studies or practises archaeology.

archaeology *noun* the excavation and study of the physical remains of earlier civilizations, especially buildings and artefacts. [from Greek *archaiologia*, ancient history]
◇ Modern archaeology is generally regarded as having begun with the publication of J J Winckelmann's *Geschichte der Kunst des Altertums* (History of Ancient Art), in 1764. It is mainly concerned with the rediscovery and analysis of physical remains, primarily buildings, records, and artefacts. The excavation of major sites such as Ephesus in Asia Minor and Delphi in Greece have led to the discovery of many new records and texts, which greatly increase our knowledge of past civilizations. In recent years, computer analysis of finds has enhanced the value of many finds.

archaeopteryx *noun* the oldest fossil bird, known from the Jurassic period in Europe, and having feathers and a wishbone, but distinguished from modern birds by reptilian features such as a long bony tail supported by vertebrae, three clawed fingers on the wings, and sharp teeth on both jaws. [from Greek *archaios*, ancient + *pteryx*, wing]

archaic *adj.* **1** ancient; of or from a much earlier period. **2** out of date; old-fashioned. **3** *said of a word, phrase, etc* no longer in general use, but sometimes used for special effect. [from Greek *archaikos*, from *archaios*, ancient]

archaically *adv.* in an archaic way.

archaism *noun* **1** an archaic word or expression. **2** the deliberate use of archaic words or expressions.

Archangel, Russian **Arkhangel'sk** **1** POP (1991e) 428 000, the river-port capital of Archangel oblast, NW Russia. It lies on the Northern Dvina R, on an inlet of the White Sea. Founded in 1584, it is one of the country's largest sea and river ports. The harbour is often ice-bound in winter. NOTABLE FEATURE monastery dedicated to the Archangel Michael. **2** an oblast in NW Russia with the city of Archangel as its capital.

archangel *noun* an angel of the highest order. [from Greek *archos*, chief + *angelos*, messenger]

archbishop *noun* a chief bishop, in charge of all the other bishops, clergy, and churches in a particular area. [from Anglo-Saxon *arcebiscop*]

archbishopric *noun* the office or diocese of an archbishop.

archdeacon *noun* in the Church of England, a member of the clergy ranking just below a bishop. See also ARCHIDIACONAL. [from Anglo-Saxon *arcediacon*]

archdeaconry *noun* (PL. **archdeaconries**) the office or residence of an archdeacon.

archdiocese *noun* in the Church of England, an area under the control of an archbishop.

archduchess *noun* **1** *Hist.* a princess in the Austrian royal family. **2** the wife of an archduke.

archduchy *noun* (PL. **archduchies**) the area ruled by an archduke.

archduke *noun* the title of some princes, especially formerly the son of the Emperor of Austria.

arched *adj.* **1** having an arch or arches. **2** shaped like an arch.

archenemy *noun* (PL. **archenemies**) **1** a chief enemy. **2** the Devil.

archeology *North Amer., esp. US* same as ARCHAEOLOGY.

Archer, Fred(erick) (1857–86) English jockey, born in Cheltenham. The first great jockey, he rode 2748 winners in his brief career (1870–86), and was the first man to ride 200 winners in a season. He rode 21 Classic winners, including the Derby five times (1877, 1880–1, 1885–6). His 246 wins in 1885 was a record that stood until 1933, and he was champion jockey 13 times. He committed suicide in Newmarket.

Archer, Isabel the beautiful, unhappy heroine of Henry James's *Portrait of a Lady*.

archer *noun* **1** a person who shoots with a bow and arrows. **2** (**the Archer**) the constellation and sign of the zodiac Sagittarius. [from Latin *arcus*, bow]

archery *noun* the art or sport of shooting with a bow.

archetypal *adj.* serving as an archetype or an original or typical model of something.

archetypally *adv.* in an archetypal or fundamentally typical way.

archetype *noun* **1** an original model; a prototype. **2** a perfect example. [from Greek *arche*, beginning + *typos*, model]

archfiend *noun* the Devil.

Archibald a male first name, mainly associated with Scotland. [Norman French, from the Germanic elements *ercan*, genuine + *bald*, bold, brave]

archidiaconal *adj.* of an archdeacon or archdeaconry. [from Greek *archidiakonos*]

archiepiscopal *adj.* of an archbishop or an archbishopric. [from Greek *archiepiskopos*]

Archimago *or* **Archimage** the wicked, hypocritical enchanter in Spenser's *The Faerie Queene*, who takes on many disguises to deceive people.

archimandrite *noun* *Christianity* in the Greek Church, a priest in charge of a group of monks. [from Greek *archos*, chief + *mandra*, monastery]

Archimedes (c.287–c.212 BC) Greek mathematician, born in Syracuse. The most celebrated of the ancient mathematicians, he is said to have constructed siege-engines against the Romans and the Archimedean screw still used for raising water. He discovered many formulae for the areas and volumes of various plane and solid figures, anticipating integration theories to be developed 1800 years later. In legend he discovered 'Archimedes principle' while in the bath and ran into the street with a cry of 'Eureka!' ('I have found it'). He was killed at the siege of Syracuse by a Roman soldier whose challenge he supposedly ignored while immersed in a mathematical problem.

Archimedes' principle *Physics* the principle that, when a body is wholly or partly immersed in a liquid, the weight of the fluid displaced by the body is equal to the weight of the body.

Archimedes screw an ancient device for raising water; named after the Greek mathematician who is said to have invented it. It consists of a broad threaded screw inside an inclined cylinder; as the screw is turned, the water is raised gradually between the threads and is run off at the top.

archipelago *noun* (PL. **archipelagos**) **1** *Geog.* a group or chain of islands separated from each other by narrow bodies of water. **2** formerly used to refer to an area of sea containing many small islands, eg the Aegean. [from Italian *arcipelago*, from Greek *archi-*, chief + *pelagos*, sea]

architect *noun* **1** a person qualified to design buildings and other large structures. **2** a person responsible for creating something: *the architect of the European Community*. [from Greek *archi-*, chief + *tekton*, builder]

architectural *adj.* relating to or belonging to the realm of architecture.

architecturally *adv.* as regards architecture.

architecture *noun* **1** the art of designing and constructing buildings. **2** a particular historical, regional, etc style of building design: *Victorian architecture*. **3** the buildings built in any particular style.
◇ Architecture in its broadest sense covers the design of any structure for the use of man, and the practice of architecture, especially from the 19c, and particularly in the 20c, has included a wide range of technical, functional, environmental, and aesthetic considerations. However, the study of architecture has traditionally concentrated on aspects of higher culture and art, looking at the ennobling qualities of buildings down the ages, such as the Parthenon and Pantheon from the classical period, great churches from the Middle Ages onwards, and the work of individual artist-architects such as Christopher Wren.

architrave *noun* **1** a beam that rests on top of a row of columns. **2** a moulded frame around a door or window. [from French, from Greek *archi*, chief + *trabs*, beam]

archive *noun* (*usually* **archives**) **1** a collection of old public documents, records, etc. **2** a place where such documents are kept. [from Greek *archeion*, public office]

archivist *noun* a person in charge of archives.

archly *adv.* with an arch or self-consciously playful manner.

arch stone see VOUSSOIR.

archway *noun* a passage or entrance under an arch or arches.

ARCIC *abbrev.* Anglican–Roman Catholic International Commission.

arc lamp *Engineering* a type of electric lamp, no longer in general use, in which the source of light is an arc produced when an electric current flows through ionized gas between two electrodes.

Arctic the area in the N hemisphere which lies N of the tree-line or, more loosely, to the N of the Arctic Circle. Arctic conditions of climate, vegetation, and life-forms prevail in Greenland, Svalbard, and the N parts of Canada, Russia, Alaska, and Iceland.

Arctic — *noun* (**the Arctic**) the area round the North Pole. — *adj.* **1** relating to this area. **2** (**arctic**) *colloq.* extremely cold. [from Greek *arktikos*, from *arktos*, (the constellation of the) bear]

Arctic Circle *or* **Polar Circle** an arbitrary boundary marking the southernmost extremity of the northernmost area of the Earth. It is the area to the N of the tree-line, placed at 66°17'N, but often defined as the area N of 70°N.

Arctic fox a fox (*Alopex lagopus*) widespread on Arctic land masses, having hairy feet and small ears. There are two forms, one of which is white in winter and brown in the summer, and the other is pale blue-grey in winter and darker blue-grey in the summer. The Arctic fox feeds on lemmings, birds, hares, fish, and carrion.

Arctic Ocean a body of water which is situated within the Arctic Circle. AREA 9 485 000sq km/3 661 000sq mi. It is the world's smallest ocean and is frozen all year except in marginal areas. The deepest point is the Eurasia Basin at 5122m. The cold East Greenland Current and the Labrador Current are formed by the ocean's outflow. In winter, hummocky ice-fields form; pack-ice forms during summer, carried S by surface currents and generally melts to the N of the major shipping lanes. The area was unexplored until Amundsen's flight in 1926. Research suggests the ocean is experiencing a period of warming.

Arctic tern a small tern, found worldwide, that migrates further than any other bird (approximately 36 000km per year), spending the northern summer in the Arctic, and the northern winter in the Antarctic.

Arcturus *noun* *Astron.* the brightest star in the constellation Boötes, and the fourth brightest star in the sky. It is a red giant. — Also called *Alpha Boötis*. [from Greek *Arktouros*, from *arktos* bear, *ouros* guard]

arc welding *Engineering* a form of welding in which two pieces of metal are joined by raising the temperature at the joint by means of a continuous electric arc. The high temperature melts the material on either side of the join, forming a welded joint.

Arden, John (1930–) English playwright, born in Barnsley, Yorkshire. His first play was a romantic comedy entitled *All Fall Down* (1955). Other well-known plays include *The Workhouse Donkey* (1963), a caricature of local politics in N England, and *Sergeant Musgrave's Dance* (1959), which follows Brechtian tradition in its staging.

Ardennes POP (1991e) 296 000, a department in the Champagne-Ardenne region of NE France situated on the Belgian border. AREA 5 229sq km/ 2 018sq mi. The department comprises 4 arrondissements, 37 cantons and 460 communes. CAPITAL Charleville-Mézières. ECONOMY the fertile valley of the Aisne and the centre of the department produce cereals and wine, while in the N cider and beer are made.

ardent *adj.* **1** enthusiastic; eager. **2** burning; passionate. [from Latin *ardere*, to burn]

ardently *adv.* with great enthusiasm; passionately.

Ardnamurchan Point a cape in SW Highland region, W Scotland, to the N of Mull I. It is the westernmost point on the British mainland. Its lighthouse (1849) has a fixed light visible for 29km/18mi.

ardour *noun* a great enthusiasm or passion. [from Latin *ardor*, from *ardere*, to burn]

arduous *adj.* **1** difficult; needing much work or energy. **2** steep. [from Latin *arduus*, steep]

arduously *adv.* with difficulty; laboriously.

arduousness *noun* lasting difficulty.

are¹ see BE.

are² *noun* (pronounced as in *bar*) a unit of land measure equal to 100 m². [from French *are*, from Latin *area*, open space]

area *noun* **1** a measure of the size of a flat surface, measured in square units, eg m². **2** a region or part. **3** any space set aside for a particular purpose. **4** the range of a subject, activity, or topic. **5** *North Amer., esp. US* a sunken space in front of a building's basement. [from Latin *area*, open space]

Area of Outstanding Natural Beauty (ABBREV. **AONB**) an area in England and Wales which does not merit national park status, but where special measures are needed to preserve its natural interest and beauty. They are generally smaller than national parks, and are the responsibility of local authorities and the Countryside Commission in England and, since 1991, the Countryside Council in Wales.

arena *noun* **1** an area surrounded by seats, for public shows, sports contests, etc. **2** a place of great activity, especially conflict: *the political arena*. **3** the open area in the middle of an amphitheatre. [from Latin *arena*, sanded area for combats]

Arena Chapel frescoes a cycle of frescoes by Giotto di Bondone depicting *The Lives of the Virgin and Christ* (Arena Chapel, Padua, 1305–8).

arena stage *North Amer.* same as THEATRE-IN-THE-ROUND.

aren't *contr.* **1** are not: *they aren't coming.* **2** (*in questions*) am not: *aren't I lucky?*

areola *noun* (PL. **areolae**) a faintly coloured circular area, especially that around a nipple. [a Latin diminutive of *area*, open space]

Areopagus in ancient Greece, the name for the hill in Athens which was the seat of the oldest council of state, and also for the council whose meetings took place there. The name literally means 'the hill of Ares' (the god of war).

Arequipa POP (1990e) 622 000, **1** the capital of Arequipa department, S Peru. It is situated in a valley at the foot of El Misti Volcano; altitude 2 380m. Built on the site of an ancient Inca city, it is the main commercial centre for S Peru. NOTABLE FEATURES Puente Bolívar; Plaza de Armas; cathedral (1612, rebuilt in the 19c); La Compañía Church; Santa Catalina Convent. **2** a department in S Peru with the city of Arequipa as its capital.

Ares in Greek mythology, the god of war, identified with the Roman god Mars. The son of Zeus and Hera, he was often perceived as hostile and represented the violent aspects of warfare. He had three offspring by Aphrodite.

Arethusa in Greek mythology, a nymph who was pursued by the river-god Alpheus from Arcadia in Greece to Ortygia in Sicily, where she was turned into a spring. The myth attempts to account for the fresh-water fountain which appears in the harbour of Syracuse and is believed to have flowed under the Ionian Sea.

Aretino, Pietro (1492–1557) Italian poet and satirist, born in Arezzo, Tuscany. He became well-known in Rome and secured the papal patronage, but lost it when he published his *Sonetti Lussuriosi* (1524, Lewd Sonnets). His poetical works include five comedies and a tragedy, and he also wrote several volumes of letters.

Arezzo POP (1990e) 92 000, the capital of Arezzo province, Tuscany region, NW central Italy. It lies 80km/50mi SE of Florence on the site of an Etruscan settlement near the confluence of the Chiana and Arno rivers. The poet Petrarch was born here in 1304. NOTABLE FEATURES Church of Santa Maria della Pieve (11c–13c); Gothic cathedral (begun in 1277).

Argentina, official name **Argentine Republic**, Spanish **República Argentina** POP (1992e) 33.1m, a republic in SE South America, divided into a Federal District (Buenos Aires), 22 provinces, and a Territory (Tierra del Fuego). AREA 3 761 274sq km/1 451 852sq mi (total area claimed); on the mainland of the American continent: 2 780 092sq km/1 073 115sq mi (excluding the Falkland Islands); on the Antarctic continent: 964 250sq km/372 200sq mi (excluding S Georgia, Orkney Is, and S Sandwich Is). It is bounded E by the S Atlantic Ocean, W by Chile, N by Bolivia and Paraguay, and NE by Brazil and Uruguay. The Atlantic coastline is 4 725km/2 936mi long. CAPITAL Buenos Aires. CHIEF TOWNS Córdoba, Rosario, Mendoza, La Plata, San Miguel de Tucumán. TIME ZONE GMT −3. The majority of the population is of European origin and the remainder is of mestizo or S American Indian origin; Roman Catholicism is the main religion. OFFICIAL LANGUAGE Spanish. CURRENCY the austral. PHYSICAL DESCRIPTION the Andes stretch the entire length of Argentina (N–S), forming the boundary with Chile; the mountains extend far to the E in N Argentina, but their width decreases towards the S; high ranges, plateaux, and rocky spurs are found in the NW; the highest peak is Aconcagua (6 960m); a grassy, treeless plain (the *pampa*) is to the E; uneven, arid steppes lie to the S; the island of Tierra del Fuego is situated off the S tip; N Argentina is drained by the Paraguay, Paraná, and Uruguay rivers, which

join in the R Plate estuary; several rivers flow to the Atlantic Ocean in the S; there are many lakes in the *pampa* and Patagonia regions, the largest being Lago Argentino (1 415sq km/546sq mi). CLIMATE most of Argentina lies in the rainshadow of the Andes; dry steppe or elevated desert in the NW corner; moderately humid sub-tropical climate in the NE, with average annual temperature 16°C and rainfall 500–1 000mm at Buenos Aires; the central *pampa* region and a strip along the foot of the mountains are semi-arid with temperatures ranging from tropical to moderately cool; between these two semi-arid areas lies the rainshadow; desert plateau extends to the coast; some rainfall prevents absolute barrenness; the S part is directly influenced by strong prevailing westerlies. HISTORY settled in the 16c by the Spanish; independence declared in 1816, and the United Provinces of the Río de la Plata were established; federal constitution in 1853; acquisition of the Gran Chaco after war with Paraguay (1865–70); an attempt to gain control of the Falkland Is in 1982 failed following war with the UK; following years of military rule, civilian rule was re-established in 1983. GOVERNMENT a bicameral National Congress, with a 254-member Chamber of Deputies is elected for four years and a 46-member Senate is elected for nine years; a President is elected for a six-year term. ECONOMY considerable European settlement since the opening up of the pampas in the 19c; agricultural produce, chiefly cereals and meat; also potatoes, cotton, sugar cane, sugar beet, tobacco, linseed oil, rice, soya, grapes, olives, peanuts; meat processing; cement; fertilizer; steel; plastics; paper; pulp; textiles; motor vehicles; oil and gas, chiefly off the coast of Patagonia; coal, gold, silver, copper, iron ore, beryllium, mica, tungsten, manganese, limestone, uranium.

Argentine–Brazilian War a war fought (1825-8) to decide the possession of the Banda Oriental, territory to the east of the R Uruguay occupied by Brazil in 1817. The British mediated, and the province became the independent buffer republic of Uruguay (1828).

arginine *noun Biochem.* one of the essential amino acids, and a constituent of many proteins.

Argolid the fertile plain between the mountains and the sea in the E Peloponnese near the town of Argos. It flourished particularly in Mycenaean times, when as well as Argos, the towns of Mycenae and Tiryns were located there.

argon *noun Chem.* (SYMBOL **Ar**, ATOMIC NUMBER **18**) a colourless odourless inert gas, representing 0.93% of the air by volume. It is one of the rare or noble gases, does not form any compounds, and is used to provide inert atmospheres in light bulbs, discharge tubes, and in arc welding. [from Greek, = inactive, from *a*, without + *ergon*, work]

Argonauts in Greek mythology, the 50 heroes who sailed with Jason in the ship the *Argo* to find the Golden Fleece. On the way they had to overcome various trials including the Harpies and the Symplegades.

Argos POP (1991) 22 000, an ancient town in Peleponnese region, S Greece, lying in a fertile plain near the Gulf of Argolikos. It was involved in wars with Sparta from the 7c–4c BC. It is a commercial and agricultural centre and has many archaeological remains.

argot *noun* slang used and understood only by a particular group of people. [from French *argot*]

arguable *adj.* **1** capable of being argued or disputed. **2** *said of a proposition, statement, etc* capable of being maintained.

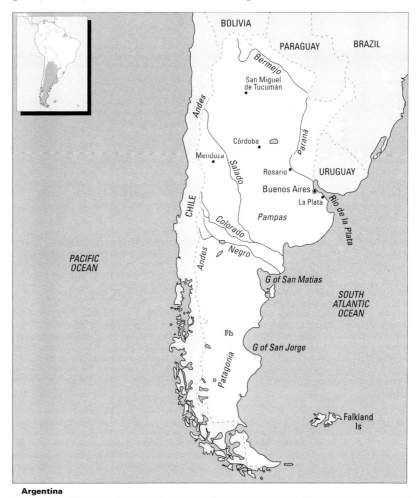

Argentina

arguably *adv.* as can be defended by argument; possibly: *arguably the finest singer in Italy.*

argue *verb* **1** *intrans.* (**argue with someone**) to exchange views with them, especially heatedly or angrily. **2** *trans., intrans.* to suggest reasons for or against (something), especially clearly and in a proper order: *declined to argue the point / argued against capital punishment.* **3** (**argue someone into** *or* **out of something**) to persuade them to do or not to do something: *persuaded us to stay.* **4** to show or be evidence for: *it argues a degree of enthusiasm on their part.* [from Latin *arguere*, to show, accuse]

argument *noun* **1** a quarrel or unfriendly discussion. **2** a reason for or against an idea, etc. **3** the use of reason in making decisions. **4** a summary of the theme or subject of a book, etc. [from Latin *argumentum*, from *arguere*, to show, accuse]

argumentation *noun* sensible and methodical reasoning.

argumentative *adj.* fond of arguing; always ready to quarrel.

argumentatively *adv.* in an argumentative way; with an argumentative manner.

Argus in Greek mythology, a watchman with a hundred eyes, appointed by Hera to guard her rival Io. After Argus was killed by Hermes, the eyes were placed in the tail of the peacock.

Århus *or* **Aarhus 1** POP (1992e) 268 000, the capital of Århus county, E Jutland, Denmark. It lies in a wide bay of the Kattegat, S of Ålborg, and is the cultural and educational hub of central Jutland. NOTABLE FEATURE Cathedral of St Clement (1201). **2** a county in E Jutland, Denmark, with Århus as its capital.

aria *noun Mus.* a long accompanied song for one voice, especially in an opera or oratorio. [from Italian *aria*]

Ariadne in Greek mythology, the daughter of Minos, the King of Crete. She enabled Theseus to escape from the labyrinth by giving him a ball of thread. He fled with her, but deserted her on the island of Naxos, where she eventually became the wife of Dionysus.

Ariadne auf Naxos (Ariadne on Naxos) an opera by Richard Strauss (1912). Set in 18c Vienna, it combines the opera seria and commedia dell'arte traditions and tells of the staging of an opera combined with a farce. The main story focuses on Ariadne, who, abandoned by Theseus, is comforted by the young god Bacchus.

Arian[1] — *noun* a person born under the sign of Aries. — *adj.* born under or characteristic of the sign of Aries.

Arian[2] — *noun* a person who believes in the doctrine of Arianism. — *adj.* relating to or following Arius or Arianism.

Arianism *noun* the doctrine of Arius of Alexandria, who denied that Christ was God.

Arica POP (1991e) 195 000, the port capital of Arica province, Tarapacá, Chile. The city is situated on the Pacific coast, SW of La Paz in Bolivia. It is the most northerly city in Chile, acquired from Peru in 1929. Arica is a major trading outlet for Bolivia. NOTABLE FEATURES Pacific War Museum; San Martín Cathedral, Customs House (both designed by Eiffel).

arid *adj.* **1** dry and barren; having very little water. **2** lacking interest; dull. [from Latin *aridus*]

aridity *noun* an arid or dry state.

Ariel 1 a magical spirit of the air in Shakespeare's *The Tempest*, who is beholden to Prospero after being freed by him from the witch Sycorax. **2** one of the larger moons of the planet Uranus. **3** each of a series of six artificial satellites launched by the USA between 1962 and 1979. The first four satellites were used to study the ionosphere, and *Ariel V* made an extensive study of X-ray sources in the sky.

Aries *noun* **1** *Astron.* the Ram, a small zodiacal constellation, most clearly seen in the autumn, situated between Pisces and Taurus. Its brightest star is *Hamal.* **2** the first sign of the zodiac, falling between 21 Mar and 20 Apr, represented by the Ram. **3** a person born under this sign. [from Latin *aries*, ram]

aright *adv.* old use correctly. [from Anglo-Saxon *ariht*]

Ariosto, Ludovico (1474–1533) Italian poet, born in Reggio nell'Emilia. Initially a student of law, he wrote his Roland epic *Orlando Furioso* (1516, enlarged 3rd edition, 1532) over a ten-year period while serving in the court of the Cardinal d'Este. He also wrote comedies, satires, sonnets, and a number of Latin poems.

arise *verb intrans.* (PAST TENSE **arose**; PAST PARTICIPLE **arisen**) **1** to come into being. **2** (**arise from** *or* **out of something**) to result from it or be caused by it. **3** to get up or stand up. **4** to come to one's notice. [from Anglo-Saxon *arisan*]

Aristaeus in Greek mythology, a minor deity of the countryside, who introduced bee-keeping, vines, and olives. His pursuit of Eurydice, the wife of Orpheus, is said to have caused her death.

Aristarchos of Samos (fl. c.270 BC) Greek astronomer. He lived in Alexandria, and is famous for maintaining not only that the Earth revolves on its axis but that it travels in a circle around the Sun, contrary to traditional beliefs. He also devised a method for determining the relative distances of the Sun and Moon.

Aristarchus of Samothrace (c.215–145 BC) Greek grammarian and critic, known for his revision of Homer's epics. He was in charge of the Library of Alexandria for over 30 years.

Aristippus (410–350 BC) Greek philosopher, born in Cyrene, a pupil of Socrates. He was founder of the Cyrenaic school of hedonism, which argued that pleasure was the highest good. He taught philosophy both in Athens and Aegina, but lived much of his life in Syracuse, at the court of Dionysius the tyrant.

aristocracy *noun* (PL. **aristocracies**) **1** the highest social class, usually owning land and having titles. **2** government by this class. **3** people considered to be the best representatives of something. [from Greek *aristos*, best + *kratos*, power]

aristocrat *noun* a member of the aristocracy.

aristocratic *adj.* **1** of the aristocracy. **2** proud and noble-looking.

aristocratically *adv.* with an aristocratic manner.

Aristophanes (c.448–388 BC) Greek comic dramatist, said to have written 54 plays, of which only 11 survive. His most sharply satirical works belong to his early period (up to c.425 BC): the *Clouds, Wasps, Acharnians, Knights,* and *Peace*. In later years he wrote the *Lysistrata, Frogs, Birds, Thesmophoriazusae, Ecclesiazusae,* and *Plutus*.

Aristotelian — *adj.* relating to Aristotle or his ideas. — *noun* a student or follower of Aristotle.

Aristotle (384–322 BC) Greek philosopher, scientist, and physician, born in Stagira, Macedonia. He was associated with Plato's Academy in Athens for 20 years, which he left after Plato's death (347 BC). In 342 BC he was appointed tutor of Philip of Macedon's son Alexander. On his return to Athens (335 BC), he opened a school (the Lyceum); his followers were called 'Peripatetics'. After Alexander's death, anti-Macedonian sentiment in Athens forced him to flee to Calchis (322 BC), where he died. He wrote the first systematic treatises on logic, made major contributions to the study of natural change, psychology, and biology, and wrote some of the most influential philosophical works in the history of thought (eg *Metaphysics, Nicomachean*

Ethics, Politics, Rhetoric, Poetics). Major Aristotelian themes include the theses that the Earth is the centre of the eternal universe; everything beneath the orbit of the Moon is composed of earth, air, fire, and water, and is subject to generation, destruction, qualitative change, and rectilinear motion; everything above the orbit of the Moon is composed of ether, and is subject to no change but circular motion. His influence was such that in the Middle Ages he was referred to simply as 'the Philosopher'.

arithmetic — *noun* (with stress on -*rith*-) **1** the branch of mathematics that uses numbers to solve theoretical or practical problems, mainly by the processes of addition, subtraction, multiplication, and division. **2** ability or skill at this: *my arithmetic is poor.* — *adj.* (with stress on -*met*-) (*also* **arithmetical**) relating to arithmetic. [from Greek *arithmetike*, of numbers, from *arithmos*, number]

arithmetically *adv.* in terms of or by means of arithmetic.

arithmetician *noun* a person skilled in arithmetic.

arithmetic mean *Maths.* see MEAN[3] 2a.

arithmetic progression a sequence of numbers in which each differs from the preceding and following ones by a constant amount, eg 2, 4, 6, 8, 10.

Arius, Greek **Areios** (c.250–336AD) Libyan theologian, the founder of the heresy called *Arianism*. In c.319 he claimed that, in the doctrine of the Trinity, the Son was not co-equal or co-eternal with the Father, but only the first and highest of all finite beings, created out of nothing by an act of God's free will. He won some support, but was excommunicated in 321 by a synod of bishops at Alexandria, which instigated fierce controversy. To resolve it the Council of Nicaea (Nice) was called (325), which defined the absolute unity of the divine essence, and the equality of the three persons of the Trinity. Arius was banished, but recalled in 334. After his death the strife spread more widely abroad: the West was mainly orthodox, the East largely Arian or semi-Arian, but by the end of the 4c the doctrine was largely suppressed.

Ariz. *abbrev.* Arizona.

Arizona POP (1990) 3.8m, a state in SW USA, bounded in the S by Mexico, and divided into 14 counties. AREA 295 249sq km/113 966sq mi. PHYSICAL DESCRIPTION rivers include the Colorado (which forms most of the W border), Gila, and Salt; the Hoover Dam causes the Colorado R to swell into L Mead; there are several mountain ranges (highest is the San Francisco Mts); the highest point is Humphreys Peak (3 862m); the Colorado Plateaux in the N are high, dry plains incised by deep canyons, notably the Grand Canyon on the Colorado R (Arizona is known as the 'Grand Canyon State'); to the S are desert basins interspersed with bare mountain peaks, then relatively low desert plains; there is a huge area of national and state forest in the centre. HISTORY the state was explored by the Spanish in 1539 and was part of New Spain from 1598 to 1821; it was then included in the newly-independent Mexico; acquired by the USA in the Treaty of Guadalupe Hidalgo (1848) and the Gadsden Purchase (1853); became a separate territory in 1863; until 1886 it was frequently attacked by the Apache (led by Cochise, and later Geronimo); Arizona joined the Union as the 48th state in 1912. The state has the largest Native American population in the USA and there are Navajo, Hopi, Apache, Papago, and other reservations. CAPITAL Phoenix. CHIEF TOWNS Tucson, Mesa, Tempe. ECONOMY tourism is the most important industry; the state also produces two thirds of the nation's copper supply; cattle are grazed on irrigated land; chief crops are dairy products, cotton, lettuce, and hay; manufacturing industries produce computer equipment, aerospace components, timber products, and machinery. NOTABLE

FEATURES Grand Canyon; Kitt Peak National Observatory; Organ Pipe Cactus National Monument Park; Painted and Sonoran deserts; Petrified Forest; meteor craters.

Arjuna in Hinduism, one of the heroes of the *Mahabharata*. In the *Bhagavadgita*, a poem which forms part of this epic, he hesitates before entering the battle, and is given the courage to go on with his duty by his charioteer Krishna.

ark *noun* **1** *Biblical* the vessel built by Noah in which his family and animals survived the Flood. **2** (**Ark**) *Judaism* a chest or cupboard in a synagogue in which the law scrolls are kept. [from Anglo-Saxon *arc*, from Latin *arca*, chest]

ark. *abbrev.* Arkansas.

Arkansas POP (1990) 2.4m, a state in S central USA, which is divided into 75 counties. AREA 137 749sq km/53 171sq mi. PHYSICAL DESCRIPTION rivers include the Mississippi (forms the E border), Red (part of the SW border), and Arkansas; the Boston Mts, part of the Ozark Plateau, rise in the NW, and the Ouachita Mts rise in the W; the highest point is Mt Magazine (860m); the mountainous region is bisected by the Arkansas R Valley; in the S and E are extensive plains; over half the state is covered by commercial forest; there are many lakes. HISTORY known as the 'Land of Opportunity', Arkansas was the first white settlement established by the French as part of French Louisiana in 1686; it was ceded to the USA as part of the Louisiana Purchase in 1803; in 1812 it was included in the Territory of Missouri, becoming a separate territory in 1819; it joined the Union as the 25th state in 1836, seceded in 1861, and was readmitted in 1868; in 1957 resistance to school desegregation made Little Rock a focus of world attention. CAPITAL Little Rock. CHIEF TOWNS Fort Smith, North Little Rock, Pine Bluff. ECONOMY a major tourist area; chief agricultural products are poultry, soya beans, rice (the nation's leading producer), cattle, dairy, and cotton; manufacturing industries produce processed foods, electrical equipment, paper, timber products, and chemicals; there is also petroleum and natural gas; Arkansas is the nation's leading producer of bauxite. NOTABLE FEATURE Hot Springs National Park.

Arkansas River a river in S central USA, length 2 330km/1 450mi. Rising in the Rocky Mts, Colorado, it flows SE through Kansas, Oklahoma, and Arkansas, joining the R Mississippi S of Memphis. Major tributaries are the Cimmaron, Canadian, Neosho, and Verdigris. The river is navigable for its length in Arkansas.

Ark of the Covenant a portable wooden chest described in the Hebrew Bible and Old Testament. It was overlaid with gold and had a cherub with extended wings mounted at each end of the golden lid (the 'mercy seat'). It contained two tablets of the Decalogue and served as a symbol of the divine presence guiding Israel. Constructed under Moses, in David's time it was taken into battle, and under Solomon was housed in the Temple, but is now lost. Torah scrolls are still kept in containers called 'arks' in Jewish synagogues.

Arles *or* **Arles-sur-Rhône** POP (1990) 53 000, an old town in Bouches-du-Rhône department, Provence-Alpes-Côte d'Azur region, SE France. It lies 72km/45mi NE of Marseilles, at the head of the delta of the Rhône. The 4c capital of Gaul, it was an important crossroads and has also been capital of Provence. The town has associations with van Gogh and Gauguin. NOTABLE FEATURES Roman remains, including a huge arena and theatre (a World Heritage site); cathedral (11c); several art museums.

Arlington, Henry Bennet, 1st Earl of (1618–85) English statesman, born in Arlington, Middlesex. A member of the cabal ministry under Charles II, he was Secretary of State (1662–74), negotiated the Triple Alliance against France (1668), and helped to develop the English party system. In 1674 he was cleared of an embezzlement charge, but resigned and became Lord Chamberlain.

Arlington POP (1990) 171 000, a county of Virginia, E USA, and a suburb of Washington DC. AREA 68sq km/26sq mi. NOTABLE FEATURES Arlington National Cemetery (1920), with a memorial amphitheatre and the Tomb of the Unknown Soldier; the Pentagon Building (US Dept of Defense headquarters).

Arlott, (Leslie Thomas) John (1914–91) English broadcaster and writer, born in Basingstoke, Hampshire. He was a clerk in a mental hospital and a detective before joining the BBC in 1945, where he made his name as a top cricket commentator.

arm¹ *noun* **1** either of the two upper limbs of the body, from the shoulders to the hands. **2** anything shaped like or similar to this: *an arm of the sea.* **3** the sleeve of a garment. **4** the part of a chair, etc that supports an arm. **5** a section or division of a larger group, eg of the army, etc. **6** power and influence: *the long arm of the law.*
— **arm in arm** with arms linked together.
at arm's length at a distance, especially to avoid becoming too friendly.
with open arms with a very friendly welcome. [from Anglo-Saxon *earm*]

arm² — *noun* **1** (*usually* **arms** or in compounds such as *firearm, sidearm*) a weapon. **2** a branch of a military force. **3** (**arms**) fighting; soldiering. **4** (**arms**) the heraldic design which is the symbol of a family, school, country, etc. — *verb* **1** to equip with weapons. **2** *intrans.* to equip oneself with weapons. **3** (**arm someone with something**) to supply them with whatever is needed. **4** to prepare (a bomb) for use.
— **bear arms** to serve as a soldier.
lay down one's arms to stop fighting.
take up arms to begin fighting.
under arms armed and ready to fight.
up in arms openly angry and protesting. [from Latin *arma*]

armada *noun* **1** a fleet of ships. **2** (**Armada**) *Hist.* the fleet of Spanish ships sent to attack England in 1588. [from Spanish *armada*, from Latin *armata*, armed forces]

armadillo *noun* (PL. **armadillos**) a small nocturnal burrowing mammal of N and S America, belonging to the same order (Edentata) as anteaters and sloths. Its head and body are covered with horny plates, and it uses its large sickle-like claws to forage for ants, termites, small reptiles, leaves, and shoots. [from Spanish, from *armado*, armed]

Armado, Don Adriano de the 'fantastical Spaniard', expert in the hyperbolic statement, in Shakespeare's *Love's Labour's Lost*.

Armageddon *noun* a large-scale and bloody battle, especially the final battle between good and evil before the Day of Judgement, as described in the New Testament (Revelation 16.16). [from Hebrew *Megiddo*, a place in northern Palestine]

Armagh, Gaelic **Ard Mhacha** POP (1981) 119 000, a county in SE Northern Ireland. AREA 1 254sq km/484sq mi. It is bounded E by Co Down, N by Lough Neagh, NW by Co Tyrone, and S and SW by the Republic of Ireland. CHIEF TOWNS Armagh (county town), Lurgan, Portadown. ECONOMY potatoes, flax, apples; linen.

Armagh POP (1991) 14 000, the county town of Co Armagh, SE Northern Ireland, in Armagh district. It was the seat of the kings of Ulster (400 BC– AD 333) and the religious centre of Ireland in the 5c. St Patrick was made archbishop here in AD 445. NOTABLE FEATURES St Patrick's Cathedral (Protestant, 1834; Roman Catholic, 1840–73); observatory (1791); Royal School (1627); Navan Fort; the palace of the kings of Ulster, is nearby.

armament *noun* **1** (*usually* **armaments**) arms, weapons, and military equipment. **2** preparation for war. [from Latin *armamenta*]

Armani, Giorgio (1935–) Italian fashion designer, born in Piacenza. He worked in a department store then became a designer for Nino Cerruti (1964–70). He set up his own company (Giorgio Armani) with Sergio Galecti in 1975, designing first for men, then also for women. He has received numerous awards for his designs.

armature *noun* **1** *Engineering* the moving part of an electromagnetic device in which an electromotive force (voltage) is induced by a magnetic field, eg the rotating wire-wound coil of an electric motor or generator. **2** a piece of soft iron placed across the two poles of a permanent magnet that is not in use, in order to preserve its magnetic properties. — *Also called* keeper. **3** a wire framework around which a sculpture is modelled. [from Latin *armatura*, armour]

armband *noun* **1** a strip of cloth worn round the arm, usually to indicate an official position or as a sign of mourning. **2** an inflatable plastic band worn round the arm by beginners in swimming.

armchair — *noun* a comfortable chair with arms at each side. — *adj.* taking no active part.

armed *adj.* **1** supplied with arms. **2** provided with means of defence. **3** *said of a weapon or bomb* ready for use.

armed forces *or* **armed services** the military forces of a country, such as the army and navy.

Armenia, ancient **Minni** an ancient kingdom largely occupying the present-day Van region of E Turkey and parts of NW Iran. It is situated SE of the Black Sea and SW of the Caspian Sea. HISTORY ruled by the Ottoman Turks from 1514; E territory ceded to Persia in 1620; further districts lost to Russia in 1828–9. Today Turkish Armenia comprises the NE provinces of Turkey. CHIEF TOWNS Kars, Erzurum, Erzincan. The Armenian nationalist movement developed in the 19c, with terrorist activities beginning in the 1970s.

Armenia

Armenia, Republic of *or* **Armeniya**, Russian **Armyanskaya** POP (1992e) 3.7m, a republic in S Transcaucasia. AREA 29 800sq km/11 500sq mi. It is bounded N by Georgia, E and SW by Azerbaijan, SE by Iran, and NW by Turkey. CAPITAL Yerevan. CHIEF TOWNS Karaklis, Kumayri. TIME ZONE GMT +4. The population is largely

armadillo

Armenian with Azerbaijani, Kurd, and Russian minorities. OFFICIAL LANGUAGE Armenian. CURRENCY the dram. PHYSICAL DESCRIPTION mountainous, rising to 4 090m at Mt Aragats in the W; the largest lake is the Sevan in the E; the chief river is the Araks. HISTORY proclaimed a Soviet Socialist Republic in 1920; became a constituent republic of the Soviet Union in 1936; Soviet Armenia laid claim to Turkish Armenia; there was a severe earthquake in 1988; dispute with neighbouring Azerbaijan over Nagorno Karabakh region; declaration of independence as the Republic of Armenia in 1991; a state of emergency was declared in 1992 as a result of the worsening economic situation; the dispute with Azerbaijan over Nagorno Karabakh escalated into full-scale war in 1992. ECONOMY seriously affected by the 1988 earthquake and conflict with Azerbaijan; building materials, chemicals, carpets, electrical engineering, foodstuffs, machine tools, textiles; hydroelectric power on the R Razdan; grains, cotton, tropical fruits, grapes, olives, livestock.

Armenian — *noun* **1** a member of the people of Armenia. **2** an Indo-European language spoken by some 5–6 million people in the Republic of Armenia, parts of Turkey, and the Middle East. — *adj.* relating to Armenia, or its people or language.
◇ The Armenians are Christians of Indo-European origin, whose highly developed ancient culture reached its zenith in the 14c. They were dominated by Russian and Turkish rulers during the 19c–20c. During World War I, the Turks deported two thirds of Armenians (1.75m) to Syria and Palestine; 600 000 were either killed or died of starvation during the journey; later, many settled in Europe, the USA, and the former Soviet Union, from which they achieved their independence in 1990.
There are two standard varieties of the modern Armenian language: Eastern Armenian, the official language of the Republic; and Western Armenian, spoken elsewhere. The language had no written form until the introduction of Christianity, with the oldest surviving texts using the 38-letter alphabet of classical Armenian dating from the 5c.

armful *noun* (PL. **armfuls**) an amount that can be held in one's arms.

armhole *noun* the opening at the shoulder of a garment through which the arm is put.

Arminius (c.18 BC–AD 19) the chief of the German Cherusci, who ambushed three Roman legions in the Teutoberg Forest, probably near Detmold, in the 9c. It was called the 'Varian' disaster, after the defeated Roman commander, P Quinctilius Varus.

Arminius, Jacobus, properly **Jakob Hermandszoon** (1560–1609) Dutch Protestant theologian, born in Oudewater. He was ordained in 1588, and became Professor of Theology at Leyden in 1603. He opposed the Calvinistic doctrine of predestination, arguing that God forgives all who repent and believe in Christ. His teaching was formalized in the 'Remonstrance' of 1610, and refuted at the Synod of Dort (1618–19). The 'Remonstrants' persisted in their belief, however, and Arminianism influenced the development of religious thought all over Europe.

armistice *noun* a stopping of hostilities; a truce. [from Latin *armistitium*, from *arma*, arms + *sistere*, to stop]

Armistice Day the anniversary of the day (11 Nov 1918) when fighting ended in World War I; replaced after World War II by Remembrance Day.

armlet *noun* a band or bracelet worn round the arm.

armorial *adj.* relating to heraldry or coats of arms. [from Latin *arma*, arms]

Armoricain, Massif a range of low lying hills in Brittany and Normandy, W France. They rise to 417m at Monts des Avaloirs in the Alpes Mancelles.

Armory show an art exhibition, officially entitled 'The International Exhibition of Modern Art', held at the 69th Regiment Armory in New York, 1913. It introduced modern art to the USA.

armour *noun* **1** *Hist.* a metal suit or covering worn by men or horses as a protection against injury in battle. **2** metal covering to protect ships, tanks, etc against damage from weapons. **3** armoured fighting vehicles as a group. **4** a protective covering on some animals and plants. **5** heraldic designs and symbols. [from French *armure*, from Latin *armatura*, armour]

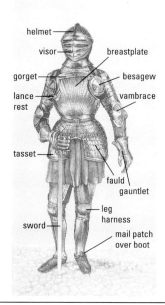

armour

armoured *adj.* **1** protected by armour. **2** *Mil.* made up of armoured vehicles.

armoured car a light-armoured fighting vehicle, usually with four-wheel drive and armed with a machine gun or small calibre cannon on a rotating turret. First developed just before 1914, their roles today on the battlefield are largely unchanged, ie reconnaissance and rear area protection.

armoured fighting vehicle (**AFV**) any military vehicle, whether on tracks or on wheels, that is protected by metal armour. Armoured vehicles have been developed for many purposes and include the tank, armoured car, armoured personnel carrier, and armoured reconnaissance vehicle.

armourer *noun* **1** a person who makes or repairs arms and armour. **2** a person in charge of a regiment's arms.

armour-plate *noun* strong metal or steel for protecting ships, tanks, etc.

armour-plated *adj.* fitted with armour-plate.

armoury *noun* (PL. **armouries**) **1** a place where arms are kept. **2** a collection of arms and weapons.

armpit *noun* the hollow under the arm at the shoulder.

arms race a contest between countries for superiority in weapons.

Armstrong, Edwin Howard (1890–1954) US electrical engineer and inventor, born in New York City. He discovered the principle of the feedback circuit, an important advance in the design of early radio receivers, and devised the circuit which became the basis for amplitude-modulation radio receivers. Professor of Electrical Engineering at Columbia University from 1935 to 1954, he also perfected the frequency-modulation system of radio transmission which virtually eliminated the problem of interference from static.

Armstrong, Henry, originally **Henry Jackson** (1912–88) US boxer, born in Columbus, Mississippi, the only man to hold world titles at three weights simultaneously. In Aug 1938 he held the featherweight, lightweight, and welterweight titles. In 1940 he fought a draw with Cerefino Garcia for the middleweight title. He had the last of his 175 fights in 1945.

Armstrong, (Daniel) Louis, also called **Satchmo** (1900–71) US jazz trumpeter and singer, born in New Orleans. He learned to play the cornet in a waifs' home, then joined Joe (King) Oliver's band in Chicago. His melodic inventiveness established his reputation as the leading improvising soloist, especially in the 'Hot Fives' and 'Hot Sevens' recordings (1925–8), after which many jazz musicians emulated his style. He toured the world with his New Orleans-style sextet, and was also a singer (songs include 'When It's Sleepy Time Down South', 'Mack the Knife', and 'Hello Dolly!') and entertainer (films include *Pennies from Heaven*, 1936, and *High Society*, 1956).

Armstrong, Neil Alden (1930–) US astronaut, born in Wapakoneta, Ohio. A fighter pilot in Korea and later a civilian test pilot, in 1962 he was chosen as an astronaut. In 1966 he commanded Gemini 8, and as commander of Apollo 11 in 1969 he became the first man to set foot on the Moon.

army *noun* (PL. **armies**) **1** a large number of people armed and organized for fighting on land. **2** the military profession. **3** a large number. **4** a group of people organized for a particular cause: *Salvation Army*. [from French *armee*, from Latin *armare*, to arm]

Arnauld, Antoine (1612–94) French theologian and philosopher. He became famous for his controversial writings against the Jesuits and in defence of the Jansenists, which led to persecution, expulsion from the Sorbonne, and finally refuge in Brussels. As religious director of the nuns of Port Royal des Champs, he and other 'Port Royalists' produced many works on grammar, geometry, and logic (eg the *Port Royal Logic*).

Arne, Thomas (Augustine) (1710–78) English composer, born in London. He began his musical career as a violinist, and produced his first opera, *Rosamond*, in 1733. He wrote over 50 operas and other works, including (as composer to Drury Lane Theatre) settings of several Shakespearean songs. His best-known work is *Rule, Britannia*, from *The Masque of Alfred*.

Arnhem (1992e) 133 000. the capital of Gelderland province, E Netherlands. It stands on the right bank of the lower Rhine, 53km/33mi SE of Utrecht. HISTORY founded on the site of a Roman settlement; received its charter in 1233; heavily damaged during World War II; the scene of an airborne landing of British troops in 1944. Arnhem is the seat of the law courts, several government agencies, and the provincial government. NOTABLE FEATURES Grote Kerk (15c); town hall (1540); St Walburgisbasiliek (1422); Dutch Open-air Museum; safari park; Burgers Zoo.

Arnhem, Battle of a major conflict (Sep 1944) in occupied Dutch territory towards the end of World War II, in which the German forces thwarted Allied attempts to break through. Operation 'Market Garden' was designed by Field Marshal Montgomery, and involved the largest airlift operation of the War, parachuting 10 000 troops on 17 Sep 1944 into the Dutch rivers area, to take key bridges over the Rhine, Maas, and Waal.

Arnhem Land the peninsular plateau in N Australia, E of Darwin. CHIEF TOWN Nhulunbuy.

NOTABLE FEATURES Kakadu National Park. A reserve for Aborigines is located in the area. ECONOMY bauxite and uranium mining. [named after the Dutch ship which arrived here in 1618]

Arno, River a river in Tuscany region, Italy. It rises in the Apennines and flows through Florence and Pisa.

Arnold, Benedict (1741–1801) US soldier and traitor, born in Norwich, Connecticut. In the War of Independence he joined the colonial forces, and for his gallantry at the siege of Quebec (1775) was made a brigadier-general. He fought at Ridgefield and Saratoga, and in 1778 was placed in command of Philadelphia. Resentment at being passed over for promotion, followed by marriage to a woman of loyalist sympathies, led him to conspire with John André to betray West Point, but André was captured and Arnold then fled to the British lines. From 1781 he lived in obscurity in London, UK.

Arnold, Matthew (1822–88) English poet and critic, born in Laleham, Middlesex. He was an inspector of schools (1851–86), and was also appointed Professor of Poetry at Oxford (1857–67). As well as his many poems, he wrote works of criticism (eg *Culture and Anarchy*, 1869), and of religious belief (eg *God and the Bible*, 1875).

Arnold, Thomas (1795–1842) English scholar and educationalist, born in East Cowes, Isle of Wight, the headmaster of Rugby School, and father of Matthew Arnold. He became headmaster of Rugby in 1828, and reformed the school system, especially by introducing sports and ending bullying. His life inspired Thomas Hughes's novel, *Tom Brown's Schooldays*. He wrote sermons and works on classical and modern history, and in 1841, shortly before his death, he became Regius Professor of Modern History at Oxford.

Arnold a male first name. [Norman French, from the Germanic elements *arn*, eagle + *warn*, rule]

Arnold of Brescia (c.1100–55) Italian churchman and politician, born in Brescia, Venice. He adopted the monastic life, but his preaching against the wealth and power of the Church led to his banishment from Italy (1139). He returned to Rome in 1145 and became involved in an insurrection against the papal government. After some 10 years it failed and he fled, but he was captured by the forces of Emperor Frederick Barbarossa and hanged for heresy.

A-road *noun Brit.* a main or principal road.

aroma *noun* 1 a distinctive, usually pleasant smell that a substance has or gives off. 2 a subtle quality or charm. [from Greek *aroma*, spice]

aromatherapist *noun* a person skilled in aromatherapy.

aromatherapy *noun* a form of therapy involving the use of essential plant oils (which are usually diluted in a 'carrier' oil), generally in combination with massage. It is used to treat physical ailments, and many of the oils are also reputed to have calming or mood-elevating properties.

aromatic *adj.* 1 having a strong, but sweet or pleasant smell. 2 *Chem.*, said of organic compounds with carbon atoms in one or more rings rather than open chains. See also ALIPHATIC.

aromatically *adv.* in an aromatic way; fragrantly.

aromatic compound any of a major class of organic chemical compounds that contain one or more *benzene rings* (five or six carbon atoms joined in a very stable ring structure), or that resemble benzene in their chemical properties. Aromatic compounds are unsaturated hydrocarbons, and usually have a strong odour, eg benzene, naphthalene.

Aroostook War a dispute (1838) over the boundary between the state of Maine and the province of New Brunswick, which led to near-hostilities between Britain and the USA but was eventually settled by the Webster–Ashburton Treaty (1842).

arose see ARISE.

around — *adv.* 1 on every side. 2 here and there; in different directions or to different places. 3 in existence. 4 near at hand. — *prep.* 1 on all sides of. 2 at or to different points in. 3 somewhere in or near. 4 approximately in or at; about. 5 *North Amer., esp. US* round.
— **have been around** *colloq.* to have a great deal of experience of life.

Around the World in Eighty Days a novel by Jules Verne (1873). It tells of the globetrotting adventures of Phileas Fogg.

arousal *noun* being aroused; an aroused state.

arouse *verb* 1 to cause or produce (an emotion, reaction, sexual desire, etc). 2 to cause to become awake or active.

Arp, Jean, also called **Hans Arp** (1887–1966) French (Alsatian) sculptor, born in Strasbourg. He was one of the founders of the Dada movement in Zürich in 1916. During the 1920s he produced many abstract reliefs in wood, but after 1928 worked increasingly in three dimensions. He was influential in the development of organic abstract sculpture, based on natural forms.

arpeggio *noun* (PL. **arpeggios**) a chord whose notes are played one at a time in rapid succession. [from Italian *arpeggiare*, to play the harp]

arquebus *noun Hist.* an early type of portable gun. [from Dutch *hakebusse*, from *hake*, hook + *busse*, gun]

arr. *abbrev.* 1 *Mus.* arranged by. 2 arrival; arrives.

Arrabal, Fernando (1932–) Spanish dramatist and novelist, born in Melilla, Spanish Morocco. His first play, *Pique-nique en campagne* (Picnic on the Battlefield, 1958), established him in the tradition of the Theatre of the Absurd. He coined the term 'panic theatre', intended to disorder the senses by shock, and has employed sadism and blasphemy to accomplish its aims. Much of his writing is inspired by the repression of Franco's Spain, which he left for Paris in 1954.

arrack *noun* an alcoholic drink made from grain or rice. [from Arabic *'araq*, sweat]

arraign *verb* 1 to bring into a court of law, usually to face serious charges. 2 to find fault with. [from French *aresnier*]

arraignment *noun* arraigning or being arraigned.

Arran an island in Strathclyde region, W Scotland, separated from the W coast mainland by the Firth of Clyde. AREA 430sq km/166sq mi. It rises to 874m at Goat Fell. CHIEF TOWN Brodick. The island is a major tourist area. NOTABLE FEATURES Brodick Castle and Country Park, ancient seat of the Dukes of Hamilton; Bronze Age Moss Farm Road Stone Circle; Lochranza Castle (13–14c).

arrange *verb* 1 to put into the proper order. 2 *trans., intrans.* (**arrange something** *or* **for something**) to plan it in advance. 3 *intrans.* (**arrange with someone**) to come to an agreement about something: *arrange with him to take time off.* 4 to make (a piece of music) suitable for particular voices or instruments. [from Old French *arangier*, from *a*, to + *rangier*, to put in a row]

arrangement *noun* 1 (*usually* **arrangements**) a plan or preparation for some future event. 2 the act of putting things into a proper order or pattern. 3 the order, pattern, etc which results from things being arranged. 4 an agreement. 5 a piece of music which has been made suitable for particular voices or instruments.

arrant *adj.* out-and-out; notorious: *an arrant liar.* [a Middle English variant of *errant*]

Arras POP (1990) 80 000, the capital of Pas-de-Calais department, Nord-Pas-de-Calais region, N France, between Lille and Amiens. It is an old frontier town, formerly famous for its tapestries. The revolutionary leader Robespierre was born here in 1758. NOTABLE FEATURES town hall (16c); cathedral (18c); there are many war cemeteries nearby; the Vimy Ridge Memorial is 10km/6mi to the N.

arras *noun* a tapestry for hanging on a wall or concealing an alcove. [from ARRAS]

array — *noun* 1 a large and impressive number or collection. 2 a well-ordered arrangement: *troops in battle array.* 3 an arrangement of numbers, figures and symbols in rows and columns. 4 *Comput.* an arrangement of individual elements of data, each of which has a reference number allowing it to be found. 5 *poetic* fine clothes. — *verb* 1 to put in order, eg for battle. 2 to dress (someone or oneself) in fine clothes. [from Old French *areer*, to arrange]

arrears *pl. noun* an amount or quantity which still needs to be done or paid back.
— **in arrears** late in paying money owed or doing the required work.
[from Old French *arere*, from Latin *ad*, to + *retro*, back, behind]

arrest — *verb* 1 to take (a person) into custody, especially by legal authority. 2 to stop or slow the development of (a disease, etc). 3 to catch or attract (a person's attention). — *noun* 1 the act of taking, or being taken, into custody, especially by the police. 2 a stopping: *cardiac arrest.*
— **under arrest** having been arrested by the police.
[from Old French *arester*, from Latin *ad*, to + *restare*, to stand still]

arresting *adj.* strikingly individual or attractive.

Arrhenius, Svante August (1859–1927) Swedish physical chemist, born in Wijk, near Uppsala. He became professor in Stockholm (1895), and later Director of the Nobel Institute of Physical Chemistry there (1905). His theory of electrolytic dissociation explained electrolytic conductivity and elucidated many other properties of electrolyte solutions. He was awarded the 1903 Nobel Prize for Chemistry.

Arrian, Latin **Flavius Arrianus** (c.95–180 AD) Greek historian, a native of Nicomedia in Bithynia, who served in the Roman army, and was appointed by Hadrian Governor of Cappadocia. His chief work is the *Anabasis Alexandrou*, a history of the campaigns of Alexander the Great.

arris *noun Archit.* a sharp edge on stone, metal, or wood where two surfaces meet. An arris rail is a wood or metal rail of triangular section; and an arris tile is an angular roofing tile used where hips and ridges intersect. [from French *arête*, a sharp ridge]

arrival *noun* 1 the act of arriving. 2 a person or thing that has arrived, especially a newborn baby.

arrive *verb intrans.* 1 to reach a place or destination. 2 (**arrive at something**) to come to a conclusion, decision, etc. 3 *colloq.* to be successful. 4 *said of a child* to be born. 5 *said of a thing* to be brought. 6 *said of a time* to occur. [from Old French *ariver*, from Latin *ad*, to + *ripa*, shore]

arrogance *noun* arrogant behaviour; an arrogant manner.

arrogant *adj.*, *said of a person or behaviour* aggressively and offensively self-assertive; having or showing too high an opinion of one's own abilities or importance. [from Latin *arrogare*, to arrogate]

arrogantly *adv.* with an arrogant manner; with offensive self-assertion.

arrogate *verb* (**arrogate something to one-self**) to claim a responsibility, power, etc without having any legal right to it. [from Latin *ad*, to + *rogare*, to ask]

arrogation *noun* an act of arrogating; an undue claim or attribution.

arrow *noun* **1** a thin, straight stick with a point at one end and feathers at the other, fired from a bow. **2** an arrow-shaped sign, eg one showing the way to go or the position of something. [from Anglo-Saxon *arwe*]

arrowhead *noun* the pointed tip of an arrow.

arrow-poison frog, a slender frog, native to Central and S America, and often brightly coloured. It inhabits woodland, its eggs are laid on the ground, and the adults carry the tadpoles to water. Its skin is highly poisonous, and local American Indians rub arrow-heads on live frogs to poison the tips for hunting. — Also called *poison-arrow frog*.

arrowroot *noun* a starch, obtained from a W Indian plant, used in foods and medicines and, formerly, to treat wounds made by poisoned arrows.

Ars Amatoria a poem in three books by Ovid (c.1 BC). It is a tongue-in-cheek exposition of love and sex.

arse *noun coarse slang* the buttocks. [from Anglo-Saxon *ears*]

arsehole *noun coarse slang* **1** the anus. **2** a term of contempt for a person.

arsenal *noun* **1** a factory or store for weapons, explosives, etc. **2** the weapons, etc available to a country or group. [from Arabic *dar sina'ah*, workshop]

arsenic — *noun* **1** (SYMBOL **As**, ATOMIC NUMBER **33**) a metalloid chemical element that occurs in three different forms, the commonest and most stable of which is a highly toxic grey shiny solid. **2** a powerful poison, an oxide of arsenic, usually found in the form of a white powder, used in insecticides. — *adj.* of, containing or using arsenic. [from Greek *arsenikon*, yellow arsenic] ◇ Arsenic occurs naturally in many ores and sometimes as the free element. It is present in minute quantities in the soil, the sea, and the human body. In larger doses is is extremely toxic, causing nausea, vomiting, diarrhoea, convulsions, and coma, and it finds frequent mention in detective novels. Arsenic was formerly used in medical drugs such as Salvarsan to treat syphilis, and is now used in insecticides, rodent poisons, weedkillers, wood preservatives, semiconductor devices, yellow and green paints, and for toughening alloys such as lead shot.

arson *noun* the crime of deliberately setting fire to a building, etc. [from Latin *arsio*, from *ardere*, to burn] ◇ In English law, there is a further criminal offence of unlawful damage, however caused. Nonetheless, the relevant statute retains the separate crime of arson. In Scots law, arson is known as *fire-raising*.

arsonist *noun* a person who commits arson.

art¹ *noun* **1** the creation of works of beauty. **2** (**arts**) the different branches of creative activity, eg music, painting, and literature, as a group. **3** one of these branches. **4** (**arts**) the branches of learning linked to creative skills, eg languages, literature and history: *Faculty of Arts*. **5** human skill and work as opposed to nature. **6** a skill, especially gained through practice. **7** (**arts**) *colloq.* cunning schemes. [from Latin *ars*]

art² *verb old use* the form of the present tense of the verb *be* used with *thou*.

Artaud, Antoni (1896–1948) French poet, actor, theatre director, and theorist of the Surrealist movement, born in Marseilles. He worked in Paris as an actor and became an active member of the Surrealists (1924–6). He wrote the

influential *Le Théâtre et son double* (The Theatre and its Double, 1938), in which he describes his Theatre of Cruelty, but spent the rest of his life in psychiatric institutions.

Artaxerxes I *or* **Ardashir** (c.211–42 AD) King of Persia (224–42), destroyer of the Arsacid dynasty of Parthia, and founder of the new Persian dynasty of the Sassanids. His expansionist policies brought him twice into conflict with Rome (230–2, 238).

Artaxerxes I, Longimanus, also called **the Long-handed** (5c BC) King of Persia (fl.464–425 BC). The second son of Xerxes I, in a long and peaceful reign he sanctioned Jewish religion in Jerusalem, and appointed Nehemiah Governor of Judea (445 BC).

Artaxerxes II, Mnemon, also called **the Mindful** (4c BC) King of Persia (404–358 BC). He lost control of Egypt, but rebuilt the royal palace at Susa.

Artaxerxes III, Ochus King of Persia (358–338 BC). The son of Artaxerxes II Mnemon, he found the empire disintegrating on his accession, but did much to build it up again. He was poisoned in 338 BC by his favourite eunuch, Bagoas.

Art Brut a term coined by French painter Jean Dubuffet (1901–85) to refer to works of art by untrained people, especially mental patients, prisoners, and socially dispossessed persons generally. Dubuffet built up a collection of c.5 000 such items, which was presented to the city of Lausanne in 1972.

Art Deco a style of art and decoration popular in Europe and the USA in the 1920s and 1930s, based on geometric shapes and strong colours. The term is abbreviated from the Paris Exposition Internationale des Arts Décoratifs et Industriels Modernes (1925).

artefact *noun* an object made by human effort, eg a tool, especially one having historical or archaeological interest. [from Latin *arte*, by art + *factum*, made]

Artegall the temperate Knight of Justice in Spenser's *The Faerie Queene*, who is eventually married to Britomart, and whose quest it is to rescue Irena from Grantorto.

Artemis in Greek mythology, the daughter of Zeus and Leto, twin sister of Apollo, and goddess of the Moon. She was originally a mother-goddess of Asia, with her most famous places of worship in Ephesus; in Greece she was a virgin-goddess, the protector of children, women in labour, and animals. She was a hunter, and is

depicted with bow and arrows. The Romans identified her with Diana.

artemisia *noun Bot.* any plant of the genus *Artemisia* of composites, including wormwood, southernwood, etc. [from Greek *artemisia*]

arterial *adj.* **1** of or like an artery. **2** *said of a road, etc* connecting large towns or cities; main.

arteriole *noun Anat.* a small artery.

arteriosclerosis *noun* (PL. **arterioscleroses**) *Medicine* a general term for any of various disorders of the arteries, especially atherosclerosis (atheroma or hardening of the arteries), in which fatty deposits and scar tissue develop on the inner walls of arteries, making them narrower and eventually obstructing the flow of blood. [from ARTERY + SCLEROSIS]

artery *noun* (PL. **arteries**) **1** *Anat.* a blood vessel that carries oxygenated blood from the heart to the body tissues, the only exception being the pulmonary artery, which conveys deoxygenated blood from the heart to the lungs. Artery walls are thicker than those of veins, and contain a layer of muscle. **2** a main road, railway or shipping lane. [from Greek *arteria*, windpipe]

artesian basin *Geol.* a shallow basin-shaped aquifer surrounded above and below by rocks that are impermeable to water, so that the groundwater in the aquifer is confined under pressure. Consequently, if a well is sunk into the aquifer, water will rise to the surface without the need for pumping. [from *Artesian*, of Artois (Latin *Artesium*) in N France]

artesian well *Geol.* a deep well that is drilled into an aquifer in an artesian basin, so that water trapped under pressure in the aquifer is forced to flow upward in the well. Artesian wells are often used as a source of drinking water. [from *Artesian*, of Artois (Latin *Artesium*) in N France, where such wells were common]

art form a recognized form for music or literature, eg the novel or the sonnet.

artful *adj.* **1** cunning; able to achieve what one wants, often by illicit or underhand means. **2** skilful.

Artful Dodger, The the name applied to Jack Dawkins, a swaggering member of Fagin's gang of child pickpockets, in Charles Dickens's *Oliver Twist*.

artfully *adv.* in an artful way; craftily.

artfulness *noun* being artful; craftiness.

arthritic — *noun* a person suffering from arthritis. — *adj.* relating to or typical of arthritis.

arthritis *noun* inflammation of one or more joints, associated with swelling, pain, redness,

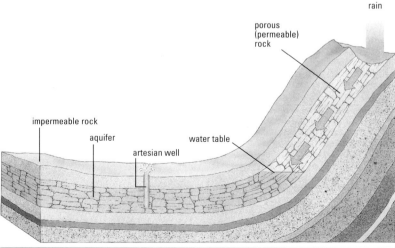

artesian well

local heat, and often restricted movement of the affected part. [from Greek *arthron*, joint + -ITIS]

◇ There are two main types of arthritis. *Osteoarthritis* is caused by degeneration of the cartilage. *Rheumatoid arthritis*, in which there is inflammation of the joints, is more common in women than in men, and may occur from the age of about 30 years onwards. In the initial stages it mainly affects the joints of the fingers, wrists, feet, and ankles. Arthritis may also be associated with gout, tuberculosis, and many other infections. Most forms of the disorder are treated with analgesics (painkillers) and anti-inflammatory drugs.

arthropod *noun Zool.* any invertebrate animal belonging to the phylum Arthropoda, the largest phylum in the animal kingdom, which contains over a million species, including insects, crustaceans (eg crabs, shrimps), arachnids (eg spiders, scorpions), and myriapods (eg centipedes, millipedes).

◇ Arthropods typically have segmented bodies, jointed appendages variously modified to form legs, antennae, mouthparts, wings, or reproductive organs, and a hard protective outer layer or *exoskeleton* made of chitin, which is moulted periodically to allow growth to occur. Arthropods have representatives in marine, freshwater, and terrestrial habitats worldwide.
[from Greek *arthron*, joint + *pous*, foot]

Arthropoda *noun Zool.* a major phylum of the animal kingdom, which includes the insects, arachnids (spiders and scorpions), crustaceans, millipedes, centipedes, and several minor groups. [from Greek *arthron*, joint + *pous podos*, foot]

Arthur (?6c) **1** in Celtic mythology, a half-legendary British king. In the version made familiar by Malory, he was brought up by Merlin and, armed with his magical sword Excalibur, he united the British tribes against pagan invaders and conquered the continent, emerging as the champion of Christianity. His story is told in many medieval romances, and various legends became interwoven with it, including those of the Round Table and the Holy Grail (both from the 12c–13c). His origins are variously claimed to have been in Brittany, Cornwall, and Wales, but it is possible that the historical Arthur was a Romanized Britain who led a force against Saxon invaders. **2** a male first name, popular in the Victorian period.

Arthur, Prince (1187–1203) posthumous son of Geoffrey (Henry II's fourth son) and Constance, Duchess of Brittany. On the death of Richard I (1199), Arthur claimed the English Crown. He was supported for a while by the French king, Philip II, but King John eventually had him murdered.

Arthur's Pass a mountain pass through the Southern Alps, N central South I, New Zealand. It lies at an altitude of 924m. The pass is set in a national park which was established in 1929.

Arthur's Tomb a painting by Dante Gabriel Rossetti (Tate Gallery, London).

artichoke *noun* (*also* **globe artichoke**) a plant with large thistle-like flower-heads, parts of which can be eaten when cooked. [from Arabic *al-kharshuf*]

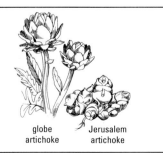

globe   Jerusalem
artichoke   artichoke

artichokes

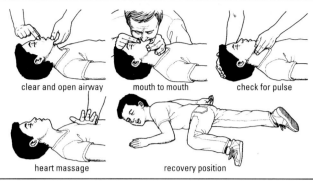

clear and open airway   mouth to mouth   check for pulse

heart massage   recovery position

artificial respiration

article *noun* **1** a thing or object. **2** a usually short written composition in a newspaper or magazine. **3** a clause or paragraph in a document, legal agreement, etc. **4** *Grammar* the definite article *the* or the indefinite article *a* or *an*, or an equivalent word in another language. [from Latin *articulus*, little joint]

articled *adj.*, *said of a lawyer, accountant, etc* bound by a legal contract while working in an office to learn the job.

Articles of Confederation the constitution of the USA from 1781 to 1788. Prepared by the Continental Congress, it established a single-house Congress, with one vote for each state and with no executive, courts, or independent revenue. Its weaknesses quickly became obvious, and it was replaced by the present constitution in 1788.

articular *adj.* relating to or associated with the joints in the body. [from Latin *articularis*, from *articulus*, little joint]

articulate — *verb* (pronounced *-late*) **1** *trans.*, *intrans.* to pronounce (words) or speak clearly and distinctly. **2** to express (one's thoughts, feelings, ideas, etc) clearly. — *adj.* (pronounced *-lət*) **1** able to express one's thoughts clearly. **2** *said of speech* pronounced clearly and distinctly so that each sound can be heard. **3** having joints. [from Latin *articulare*, to divide into distinct parts]

articulated *adj.* having joints.

articulated lorry a lorry constructed in two main sections, of which the front section can turn at an angle to the rear section, making it easier to deviate from a straight course.

articulately *adv.* in an articulate way; clearly.

articulation *noun* **1** the act of speaking or expressing an idea in words. **2** the word, idea, etc expressed. **3** the state of being jointed together. **4** a joint.

artifact same as ARTEFACT.

artifice *noun* **1** a clever trick. **2** clever skill and tricks; cunning. [from Latin *artificium*, from *ars*, *arts* + *facere*, to make]

artificer *noun* a skilled craftsman, especially a mechanic in the army or navy.

artificial *adj.* **1** made by human effort; not occurring naturally. **2** made in imitation of a natural product. **3** *said of a person, behaviour, etc* not genuine or sincere. [from Latin *artificialis*, from *ars*, art + *facere*, to make]

artificial insemination (ABBREV. **AI**) the introduction of semen into the vagina using some form of instrument in order to facilitate conception. The semen may be that of the husband or partner, in which case the procedure is known as AIH (artificial insemination by husband), or in cases where the partner is infertile it may be that of an anonymous donor, in which case the procedure is known as AID (artificial insemination by donor).

artificial intelligence *noun Comput.* (ABBREV. **AI**) the development and use of computer systems that can perform some of the functions normally associated with human intelligence, such as learning, problem-solving, decision-making, and pattern recognition.

◇ Artificial intelligence (AI) encompasses many branches of computer science, including cybernetics, knowledge-based systems, and natural language processing, that are closely allied to research in fields such as linguistics, mathematics, neurology, and psychology.
As a result of AI research, important developments have been made in robotics, natural language recognition and use, human speech recognition, and the development of *neural networks*. In *optical character recognition*, a computer recognizes and reads printed words by scanning the pattern of each character with a laser and comparing the result with patterns that have already been programmed into the machine. *Expert systems*, which can be used to make important decisions by analysing large amounts of information rapidly and accurately, were among the first applications of AI techniques. Research on *computer vision* is now in progress, involving the linking of cameras with computers so that they can identify shapes.

artificiality *noun* being artificial.

artificial language **1** an invented language, created to overcome difficulties of understanding caused by the diversity of the world's languages. Artificial languages usually seek to express the most common range of meanings using simple and regular grammar, word-formation, and pronunciation. They may be composed of an invented set of elements or symbols, or may be based on elements drawn from natural languages. Many such languages have been devised over the centuries, with Esperanto achieving the widest international success. See also AUXILIARY LANGUAGE. **2** an invented language used in computer programming. See also COMPUTER LANGUAGE.

artificially *adv.* in an artificial way.

artificial radioactivity *Physics* a form of radioactivity that results from the absorption of ionizing radiation, eg alpha particles, neutrons, by a stable substance that is not normally radioactive.

artificial respiration the process of forcing air into and out of the lungs of a person who has stopped breathing, to try to make him or her start breathing naturally again.

artificial satellite *Astron.* a man-made spacecraft that is placed in orbit around the Earth or a celestial object such as a planet.

◇ Several thousand artificial satellites are in orbit around the Earth at any one time (not all of them still functional). Communications satellites are used to relay radio, television, and telephone signals around the curved surface of the Earth, and other artificial satellites are used to gather and transmit scientific information about space and the Earth's surface, and for mapmaking, weather forecasting, navigation, scientific and technological experiments, and military purposes, eg 'spy' satellites for overlooking another nation's territory.

Artigas, José Gervasio (1764–1850) the national hero of Uruguay, born in Montevideo. The most important local patriot leader in the wars of independence against Spain, he also resisted the centralizing pretensions of Buenos Aires. The last 30 years of his life were spent in exile in Paraguay.

artillery *noun* (PL. **artilleries**) **1** large guns for use on land. **2** the part of an army equipped with such guns. [from French *artillier*, to arm]

artiness *noun* affected or ostentatious artistry.

artisan *noun* a person who does skilled work with his or her hands. [from French *artisan*, from Latin *artitus*, trained in arts and crafts]

artist *noun* **1** a person who produces works of art, especially paintings. **2** a person who is skilled at some particular thing. **3** an artiste. [from Latin *ars*, art]

artiste *noun* a professional performer, especially a singer or dancer, in a theatre, circus, etc. [from French *artiste*]

artistic *adj.* **1** liking or skilled in painting, music, etc. **2** made or done with skill and good taste.

artistically *adv.* in an artistic way.

artistry *noun* artistic skill and imagination.

Artist's Mother, The, also called ***Arrangement in Grey and Black: the Artist's Mother*** a portrait of his mother by James Abbott McNeill Whistler (1871–2, Louvre, Paris).

artless *adj.* **1** simple and natural in manner. **2** honest, not deceitful.

artlessly *adv.* in an artless way.

artlessness *noun* being artless.

Art Nouveau a style of art and decoration popular in Europe and the USA at the end of the 19c, characterized by naturalistic plant and flower motifs, and patterns of sinuous, curling lines. Examples include the drawings of Beardsley, the furniture of Mackintosh, the architecture of Gaudí, and the jewellery of Lalique.

Art of Fugue, The (Die Kunst der Fuge) a collection of fugues and canons composed in 1745–51 by J S Bach, first performed in 1927. Thought originally to have been a series of teaching pieces, the c.20 contrapuntal variations are elaborated from a principal subject in D minor, and employ the full range of contrapuntal devices (eg inversion, stretto, augmentation, and diminution).

Artois, Latin **Artesium** a former province of NE France, now occupying the department of Pas-de-Calais. Its capital was Arras. The province belonged to Flanders until 1180, was part of the Austrian and Spanish Netherlands in the Middle Ages, and was ceded to France in 1659.

Arts and Crafts Movement a predominantly English architecture, art, and applied arts movement of the second half of the 19c. The movement centred on William Morris, whose *Red House* (1859) by the architect Philip Webb is an early example of the style. Its origins lie in the writings of Pugin and Ruskin, and its intention was to change both the appearance and the way in which art and architecture were produced. It had a lasting effect on British, German, and American architecture, particularly the Garden City town-planning movement.

arts centre a building or buildings set aside for exhibitions, dramatic productions, music, poetry readings, etc.

art therapy *Psychol.* art used as a means of communication, or as a creative activity, to gain insight into psychological and emotional disorders, and to aid recovery.

artwork *noun* any original material in the form of illustrations, drawings, design, etc, produced by an artist, illustrator, or designer for reproduction in a book, magazine, or other printed medium.

arty *adj.* (**artier**, **artiest**) *colloq.* affectedly or ostentatiously artistic.

Aruba POP (1991) 67 000, a Self-Governing Dependency of the Netherlands in the E Caribbean Sea. AREA 193sq km/75sq mi. It lies 30km/19mi N of the Paraguana Peninsula, Venezuela. PHYSICAL DESCRIPTION composed of coralline limestone; rises to 189m at Jamanota in the hilly SE. HISTORY claimed by the Spanish in 1499; taken by the Dutch in 1634; formed part of the Netherlands Antilles Federation from 1845 until it was formally separated in 1986. CAPITAL Oranjestad. ECONOMY oil refining; rum distilling; cigarettes; beverages; tourism.

arum *noun* a plant with arrow-shaped leaves and flowers enclosed in bracts. [from Greek *aron*]

arum lily a plant with spikes of yellow flowers enclosed in white, yellow, or pink bracts.

Arundel, Thomas (1353–1414) English prelate and statesman, third son of Robert Fitzalan, 4th Earl of Arundel. He became Archdeacon of Taunton and Bishop of Ely (1373), then Archbishop of York (1388), and finally of Canterbury (1396). He supported the nobles who were in opposition to Richard II, who banished him (1397), but he returned to help seat Henry of Lancaster on the throne (1399). He was a vigorous opponent of the Lollards.

Arusha **1** POP (1984e) 69 000, the capital of Arusha region, NE Tanzania. It is located at the S foot of Mt Meru, 322km/200mi W of Tanga. In 1929 the railway reached the town, used as a base for trips to Mount Kilimanjaro, the Ngorongoro Crater, and the national parks of N Tanzania. **2** a region of NE Tanzania with Arusha as its capital.

Arusha Declaration an important policy statement (1967) by President Nyerere of Tanzania. It proclaimed village socialism, self-reliance, nationalization, and anti-corruption measures against politicians, and was a significant (but fruitless) attempt to create a socialist route to African development.

-ary *suffix* forming adjectives or nouns meaning 'of or connected with': *budgetary / dignitary*. [from Latin *-arius*]

Aryan — *noun* **1** a member of the peoples speaking any of the Indo-European languages, now especially the Indo-Iranian languages. **2** *Hist., in Nazi Germany* a Caucasian, especially of northern European type. — *adj.* of the Aryans or Aryan languages. [from Sanskrit *arya*, noble]

As *symbol Chem.* arsenic.

as¹ — *conj.* **1** when; while; during. **2** because; since. **3** in the manner which: *behave as one likes.* **4** that which; what: *do as one's told.* **5** although: *Try as he might, he still couldn't reach.* **6** for instance: *large books, as this one for example.* — *prep.* in the role of: *speaking as her friend.* — *adv.* to whatever extent or amount. — *pron.* **1** that, who, or which also: *She is a singer, as is her husband.* **2** (after **so**) for the reason that: *Come early so as to avoid the rush.* **3** a fact that: *he'll be late, as you know.*
— **as for** *or* **to** ... with regard to ...; concerning ...
as from *or* **as of** ... starting at (a particular time).
as if *or* **as though** ... as it would be if ...
as it were in a way; to some extent.
as well also.
as yet until now.
[from Anglo-Saxon *eallswa*, just as]

as² *noun* (PL. **asses**) an ancient Roman copper coin. [from Latin *as*, unit]

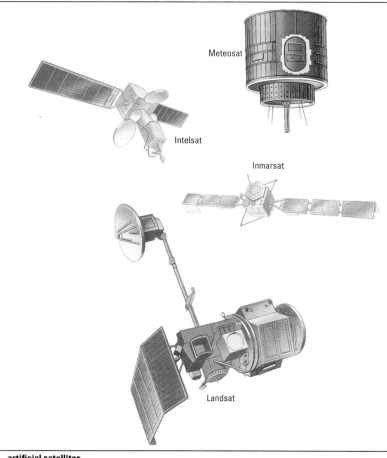

Meteosat

Intelsat

Inmarsat

Landsat

artificial satellites

ASA *abbrev.* American Standards Association, used eg in labelling photographic film speeds.

asafoetida *noun* a plant resin with an unpleasant smell, used in medicine and Indian cooking. [from Persian *aza*, gum + Latin *foetida*, fetid]

ASAP *or* **asap** *abbrev.* as soon as possible.

asbestos *noun Geol.* any of a group of fibrous silicate minerals that are resistant to heat and chemically inert.
◇ Asbestos fibres were formerly woven into fireproof cloth to make fireproof curtains, protective clothing, etc, and asbestos was used in the building industry as a thermal and electrical insulator, and in felt, plaster, pipe coverings, and roofing materials. It is also a component of brake linings. If inhaled, asbestos fibres can cause lung cancer and the respiratory disease asbestosis, and there is now strict legislation regarding the use of this material.
[from A-1, not + Greek *sbestos*, extinguished]

asbestosis *noun* a lung disease caused by breathing in asbestos dust.

ascend *verb trans., intrans.* to climb, go, or rise up.
— **ascend the throne** to become king or queen. [from Latin *ascendere*]

ascendancy *or* **ascendency** *noun* controlling or dominating power.

ascendant *or* **ascendent** — *adj.* **1** having more influence or power. **2** *Astrol.* rising over the eastern horizon. — *noun* **1** increasing influence or power. **2** *Astrol.* the sign of the zodiac rising over the eastern horizon at the time of an event, especially birth.

ascending *adj.* from the lowest to the highest, the least to the greatest, or the worst to the best.

ascension *noun* **1** an ascent. **2** (**Ascension**) *Christianity* Christ's ascent to heaven on the fortieth day after the Resurrection. [from Latin *ascensio*, from *ascendere*, to ascend]

Ascension Day *Christianity* the Thursday ten days before Whit Sunday, on which Christ's Ascension is commemorated.

Ascension Island POP (1988) 1 000, a British volcanic island in the S Atlantic. It is situated 1 125km/700mi NW of St Helena. AREA 88sq km/34sq mi. The highest point on this small and arid island is Green Mountain (859m). Its chief settlement is Georgetown. HISTORY discovered by the Portuguese on Ascension Day in 1501; British territory since 1815, administered under the Admiralty; made a dependency of St Helena in 1922; British forces were sent to the island in 1982 in support of the Falkland Islands Task Force. There are British and US air bases and a NASA tracking station on the island. It serves as an Atlantic relay station for the BBC and a cable station.

ascent *noun* **1** the act of climbing, ascending, or rising. **2** an upward slope.

ascertain *verb* to find out; to discover (the truth, etc). [from Old French *acertener*]

ascertainable *adj.* capable of being ascertained; verifiable.

ascetic — *noun* a person who avoids all physical comfort and pleasure, especially as a way of achieving holiness. — *adj.* avoiding physical pleasure and comfort; self-denying. [from Greek *asketikos*, from *askein*, to practise, train]

ascetically *adv.* in an ascetic way.

asceticism *noun* the philosophy or practice of an ascetic.

Ascham, Roger (1515–68) English humanist, born in Kirby Wiske, Yorkshire. He was tutor to the Princess Elizabeth (1548–50), and later became Latin secretary to Queen Mary and Queen Elizabeth I. His main works were *Toxophilus* (1545), a treatise in defence of archery, and *The Scholemaster* (1578), a treatise on classical education.

ASCII *abbrev. Comput.* acronym for American Standard Code for Information Interchange, the most common way of representing text characters by binary code in digital computing systems.
◇ Numbers between 0 and 127 are assigned to all the alphanumeric characters as well as a number of control functions, such as backspace and carriage return. An ASCII file consists only of text or data, without special characters for controlling output and input devices, and in general it can be read by other types of computer. It is therefore widely used for transmission of data between computers, as well as for storage of text.

Asclepius *or* **Aesculapius** in Greek and Roman mythology, the son of Apollo and a god of healing, educated by Chiron the centaur. He overreached himself by restoring Hippolytus to life, and was killed by the thunderbolt of Zeus.

Asclepius

Ascomycetes *noun Biol.* one of the main subdivisions of the fungi, characterized by the formation of asci (elongated reproductive structures that usually contain eight spores known as ascospores). The Ascomycetes include truffles, morels, most yeasts, and many parasitic fungi. [from Greek *askos*, bag]

ascorbic acid *noun* vitamin C. [from A-1 + SCORBUTIC]

Ascot a racecourse, founded in 1711 at the request of Queen Anne, on Ascot Heath in the village of Ascot, Berkshire. It is the location of Royal Ascot, a four-day social and sporting event usually attended by the British monarch. Its main event is the Ascot Gold Cup (founded in 1807), a 4km/2.5mi flat race for horses over three years old.

ascribable *adj.* capable of being ascribed; attributable.

ascribe *verb* to think of (something) as done, made, or caused by someone or something: *ascribe their success to hard work.* [from Latin *ascribere*]

ascus *noun Bot.* in fungi belonging to the subdivision Ascomycetes, a small elongated reproductive structure that usually contains eight spores known as *ascospores*. [from Greek *askos*, bag]

asdic *noun* the name for the system of submarine detection using ultrasonic waves which was used on warships of the Royal Navy up to 1963, and which afterwards was known as sonar (see also SONAR). [an acronym for *Allied Submarine Detection Investigation Committee*, the body set up in 1917 to develop the system]

ASE *abbrev.* Association for Science Education.

aseptic *adj.* free from harmful bacteria; sterile. [from A-1 + Greek *sepein*, to cause to decay]

asexual *adj.* **1** denoting reproduction that does not involve sexual processes, and in which genetically identical offspring are produced from a single parent, eg budding of yeasts, asexual spore formation in fungi, vegetative propagation in plants. **2** without functional sexual organs. **3** not sexually attracted to others.

asexuality *noun* being asexual.

asexually *adv.* in an asexual way.

asexual reproduction *Biol.* a form of reproduction in which new individuals are produced from a single parent without the involvement of gametes (specialized male and female reproductive cells) and fertilization. All the offspring are genetically identical to the parent and to each other, and are often referred to as *clones*.
◇ Asexual reproduction occurs mainly in plants (usually in addition to sexual reproduction), lower animals, and micro-organisms, eg bacteria. In plants, it may take place by *vegetative propagation* (the formation of new individuals from bulbs, corms, tubers, runners, etc), or by the production of *asexual spores* (as in ferns and mosses). In lower animals it usually occurs by *budding*, in which one or more outgrowths from the body of the parent become detached and develop into new individuals (as in yeast), or *fission*, where the parent organism split into two parts (a form of reproduction that is also very common in bacteria). The disadvantage of asexual reproduction is that no new combinations of genes are produced, so the offspring may be unable to adapt to a change in the environment.

Asgard in Norse mythology, the home of the gods and heroes slain in battle. It was created by Odin in the upper branches of the World-Tree, and included the realm of Valhalla. It was reached from earth by the bridge Bifrost (the rainbow).

ASH *abbrev.* Action on Smoking and Health.

ash¹ *noun* **1** the dust that remains after something is burnt. **2** (**ashes**) the remains of a human body after cremation. [from Anglo-Saxon *asce*]

ash² *noun* **1** any deciduous tree or shrub of the genus *Fraxinus* of the olive family, with compound leaves, small clusters of greenish flowers, and winged fruits. **2** the strong pale timber obtained from this tree, used to make hockey sticks, tool handles, furniture, etc. [from Anglo-Saxon *æsc*]

ashamed *adj.* **1** (*often* **ashamed of someone** *or* **something**) feeling shame or embarrassment about them. **2** (**ashamed to do something**) hesitant or reluctant to do it through shame or a fear of disapproval. [from Anglo-Saxon *ascamian*, to feel shame]

ashamedly *adv.* in an ashamed or shameful way.

Ashanti *or* **Asante** a Kwa-speaking Akan people of S Ghana and adjacent areas of Togo and the Ivory Coast. They are primarily an agricultural people, who form a confederacy of chiefdoms, founded by the ruler Osei Tutu in the late 17c. The independent Ashanti state was at the height of its powers in the early 19c until it was defeated (1873) and annexed (1902) by the British.

Ashbery, John (1927–) US poet, born in New York City. He has worked as an art critic in France, and since 1980 in the USA, where he has also been a professor of English. His volumes of verse, characterized by their abstract obscurity, include *The Tennis Court Oath* (1962), *Rivers and Mountains* (1966), *Self-Portrait in a Convex Mirror* (1975, Pulitzer Prize), and *A Wave* (1984). Other works include *Selected Poems* (1985), *Flow Chart* (1991), and *Hotel Lautréamont* (1992).

ashcan *noun North Amer., esp. US* a dustbin.

Ashcan School, also called **The Eight** a derisive name given to a group of US Realist painters and illustrators, formed in 1907. The group included Robert Henri (1865–1929), John Sloan (1871– 1951), and later George Bellows (1882–1925). They painted everyday, non-academic subjects in an attempt to bring art back into direct contact with ordinary life, especially street life in New York City.

Ashcroft, Dame Peggy, properly **Edith Margaret Emily** (1907–91) English actress, born in Croydon, Greater London. Her first major success in the West End was in *Jew Süss* (1929). Her great roles included Juliet in John Gielgud's production of *Romeo and Juliet* (1935), Cleopatra (1935), and Hedda Gabler (1954). She won a Best Supporting Actress Oscar for her role in the film *A Passage to India* (1984).

Ashdod POP (1988e) 75 000, a seaport in Southern district, W Israel, on the Mediterranean Sea. Formerly an ancient Philistine city, the modern city was founded in 1956 as the major port of S Israel.

Ashdown, Paddy (Jeremy John Durham) (1941–) British politician, born in India. He joined the Royal Marines (1959–71), worked for the diplomatic service (1971–6), spent some time in industry, and was elected to parliament (1983). In 1988 he became Leader of the new Social and Liberal Democratic Party.

Ashe, Arthur Robert Jr (1943–93) US tennis player, born in Richmond. He won the US national singles championship in 1968 and the first US Open championship later the same year. He was a professional tennis player from 1969 to 1979, and won the men's singles at the Australian Open (1970) and at Wimbledon (1975). After his retiral from playing he was in charge of the US Davis Cup squad, and later became a sports consultant.

ashen *adj.*, *said of a face* grey or very pale, usually from shock.

Asher, Tribe of one of the 12 tribes of ancient Israel, said to be descended from Jacob's eighth son Asher (Genesis 30.13; Numbers 1.41). Its territory included the narrow coastal plain from Carmel to the outskirts of Sidon, bordered on the E by the Galilean hills.

Ashes *pl. noun* (**the Ashes**) a trophy which goes to the team winning the regular series of cricket matches played by England and Australia. [thought to be so called from a newspaper announcement after Australia's defeat of England in 1882, that the ashes of English cricket were to be taken to Australia]

Ashkenazim Jews of central and E European descent, as distinguished from Sephardim Jews, who are of Spanish or Portuguese descent. In the Middle Ages, Europe and W Asia became divided between Christian and Islamic countries, resulting in the Ashkenazim being cut off. They developed their own customs, interpretation of the Talmud, music, and language (Yiddish).

Ashkenazy, Vladimir (1937–) Russianborn Icelandic pianist and conductor, born in Gorky. He was joint winner (with John Ogdon) of the Tchaikovsky Piano Competition in Moscow in 1962 and earned an international reputation as a concert pianist before concentrating more on conducting. He took Icelandic nationality in 1972, and became director of the Royal Philharmonic Orchestra in 1987.

Ashkhabad, formerly **Poltoratsk** POP (1991e) 412 000, the capital city of Turkmenistan. It is situated close to the Iranian border and stands at the centre of an oasis. The city was established in 1881 as a military fortification.

ashlar *or* **ashler** *noun* **1** a large stone cut square, used for building or facing walls. **2** masonry made of ashlars. [from Old French *aiseler*, from Latin *axilla*, small plank]

Ashley, Laura, née **Mountney** (1925–85) Welsh fashion designer, born in Merthyr, Wales. She married Bernard Ashley in 1949, and started up a business designing and producing furnishing materials. She then experimented with designing and making clothes, and it was this aspect which transformed their business from one small shop to an international chain of boutiques selling clothes, furnishing fabrics, and wallpapers. Her work was characterized by a romantic style and the use of natural fabrics, especially cotton.

Ashmolean Museum a museum in Oxford University, England, opened in 1683. The core of the collection was donated to the University in 1675 by Elias Ashmole (1617–92). Its holdings include a collection of archaeological relics, paintings, prints, and silverware.

Ashmore and Cartier Islands an uninhabited Australian external territory in the Indian Ocean 320km/200mi off the NW coast of Australia. AREA c.3sq km/1sq mi. The group consists of the Ashmore Is (Middle, East and West) and Cartier I. Formerly administered by the Northern Territory, it became a separate Commonwealth Territory in 1978. Ashmore Reef is a national nature reserve.

ashore *adv.* on or on to the shore or land (from water).

ashram *noun Relig.* especially in India, a hermitage for a holy man, or a place of retreat for a religious community where members lead lives of austere self-discipline and dedicated service according to the teachings and practice of their particular school. The ashram of Mahatma Gandhi is a well known example. [from Sanskrit]

Ashton, Sir Frederick (William Mallandaine) (1904–88) British dancer and choreographer, born in Guayaquil, Ecuador. He trained under Massine and Marie Rambert, choreographed his first public performance in 1926, and in 1935 became choreographer at Sadler's Wells Ballet (later the Royal Ballet), where he later became director (1963–70). He also worked with the New York City Ballet, the Royal Danish Ballet Company, and produced such works as *Façade* (1931), *Ondine* (1958), and *The Dream* (1964).

ashtray *noun* a dish or other container for the ash from cigarettes.

Ashura *noun* a Muslim fast day observed on the 10th of Muharram, the first month of the Muslim calendar. It is of special significance to Shiite Muslims, being a day of mourning for Husain, grandson of Muhammed, who was killed in 680 by soldiers of Caliph Yazid. It is an official holiday in predominantly Shiite Muslim countries such as Iran. [from Arabic *'Ashūrā*]

Ash Wednesday the first day of Lent.

ashy *adj.* (**ashier**, **ashiest**) **1** covered in ash. **2** grey; ashen.

Asia the largest continent, bounded N by the Arctic Ocean, E by the Pacific Ocean, S by the Indian Ocean, and W by Europe. AREA c.44.5m sq km/17.2m sq mi. The chief mountain system is the Himalayas, rising to 8 848m at Mt Everest. Major rivers include the Yangtze, Yellow, Brahmaputra, Irrawaddy, Indus, and Ganges.

Asia Minor see ANATOLIA.

Asian — *noun* **1** a person born and living in Asia. **2** a person of Asian descent. — *adj.* of Asia, its people, languages, and culture. [from Greek *Asianos*]

Asian Games a multi-sport competition first held in New Delhi, India in 1951, and since 1954 held quadrennially. The Far Eastern Games, the predecessors of the Asian Games, were first held in Manila in 1913.

Asiatic *adj.* Asian. [from Greek *Asiatikos*]
◆ Often considered offensive when used to refer to people.

A-side *noun* the side of a two-sided gramophone record that is more actively promoted. See also B-SIDE.

aside — *adv.* **1** on or to one side. **2** (**aside from something**) apart from it. — *noun* **1** words said by a character in a play which the audience hears, but the other characters do not. **2** a remark unrelated to the main subject of a conversation.

Asimov, Isaac (1920–92) US biochemist and science-fiction writer, born in Petrovichi, Russia. His family emigrated to the USA in 1923 and he was naturalized in 1928. From 1949 he worked at Boston University, where he eventually became Professor of Biochemistry (1979–92). He began contributing stories to science-fiction magazines in 1939, and his first book, *Pebble in the Sky*, was published in 1950. His many novels and story collections include *I, Robot* (1950), *The Caves of Steel* (1954), and *The Foundation Trilogy* (1963). From 1958 he worked mainly on textbooks and works of popular science.

asinine *adj.* of or like an ass, especially in being stupid and stubborn. [from Latin *asininus*, from *asinus*, ass]

ask *verb* **1** *trans.*, *intrans.* to put a question to (someone) or call for an answer to (a question). **2** to inquire about: *ask the way*. **3** *trans.*, *intrans.* (*often* **ask for something**) to make a request for it; to seek it. **4** to invite. **5** *intrans.* (**ask something of someone**) to expect it of them: *don't ask too much of him*.
— **ask after someone** to ask for news of them.
ask for it *or* **ask for trouble** *colloq.* to behave in a way that is likely to bring trouble on oneself. [from Anglo-Saxon *ascian*]

askance *adv.* sideways.
— **look askance at something** *or* **someone** to consider them with suspicion or disapproval.

askew *adv.*, *adj.* not properly straight or level; awry. [from A³ + SKEW]

asking price the price of an object proposed by the seller.

ASL *abbrev.* American Sign Language.

asleep *adj.*, *adv.* **1** in or into a sleeping state: *fall asleep*. **2** *colloq.* not paying attention. **3** *said of limbs* numb. [from Anglo-Saxon *on slæpe*]

ASLEF *abbrev.* Associated Society of Locomotive Engineers and Firemen.

ASM *abbrev.* air-to-surface missile.

Asmara *or* **Asmera** POP (1989e) 343 000, the capital of Eritrea, situated 2 350m above sea level. HISTORY occupied by the Italians in 1889; became regional capital in 1897; occupied by British forces in 1941. NOTABLE FEATURES cathedral (1922); mosque (1937); Archaeological Museum.

asocial *adj.* **1** not social, antisocial; not gregarious. **2** hostile to, or against the interests of, society.

asp *noun* a small poisonous snake of various kinds, found in S Europe, N Africa and Arabia. [from Greek *aspis*]

asparagine *noun Biochem.* an amino acid, first discovered in asparagus, derived from aspartic acid. It is an important nitrogen reserve in many plants, and a requirement of the human diet.

asparagus *noun* **1** any plant of the genus *Asparagus* of the lily family (Liliaceae), such as *A. officinalis*, which is cultivated as a garden vegetable and has cylindrical green shoots or 'spears' that function as leaves. The true leaves are reduced to scales. **2** the harvested shoots of this plant, which can be cooked and eaten. [from Greek *asparagos*]

aspartame *noun Food Science* an artificial sweetener, 200 times sweeter than sugar, but without the bitter aftertaste of saccharin. It is widely used in the food industry, and by diabetics and dieters. [from *asparagine*]

aspartic acid *Biochem.* an amino acid formed by the hydrolysis of asparagine. [from ASPARAGINE + ACID]

aspect *noun* **1** a particular or distinct part or element of a problem, subject, etc. **2** a particular way of considering a matter. **3** look or appearance. **4** the direction in which a building faces. **5** *Astron.* the position of a planet in relation to the Sun as viewed from the Earth. [from Latin *aspectus*, from *ad*, to + *specere*, to look]

Aspen POP (1990) 4 000, a resort town in Pitkin County, W central Colorado, USA. It is an old silver-mining town which was converted into a year-round resort and a cultural centre. There are popular ski slopes nearby.

aspen *noun* a poplar tree with flat leaves that make a tremulous rustling noise in the wind. [from Anglo-Saxon *æspe*]

aspergillosis *noun Medicine* a rare disease in which spores of the fungus *Aspergillus*, normally harmless when inhaled, settle and multiply in parts of the lung that have previously been damaged, eg by tuberculosis. [from Latin *aspergere*, from *ad* to, *spargere* to sprinkle]

asperity *noun* (PL. **asperities**) roughness, bitterness, or harshness, especially of temper. [from Latin *asper*, rough]

aspersion
— **cast aspersions on someone** *or* **something** to make damaging or spiteful remarks about them.
[from Latin *aspersio*, sprinkling, slander]

asphalt — *noun* a black tar-like substance used as a surface for roads, roofs, etc. — *verb* to cover with asphalt. [from Greek *asphaltos*]

asphyxia *noun* 1 the absence of pulse. 2 suffocation caused by any factor that interferes with respiration and prevents oxygen from reaching the body tissues, such as choking, drowning, inhaling poisonous gases, and some diseases, eg diphtheria. Unless emergency treatment is given asphyxia causes death within minutes. [from A-[1], without + Greek *sphyxis*, pulse]

asphyxiate *verb trans., intrans.* to stop or cause to stop breathing.

asphyxiation *noun* 1 producing asphyxia. 2 being asphyxiated; suffocation.

aspic *noun* a savoury jelly, made from meat or fish, used as a glaze, or to make a mould for fish, eggs, etc. [from French *aspic*, possibly connected with ASP]

aspidistra *noun* a house plant with long broad leaves. [from Greek *aspis*, shield]

aspirant *noun* a person who aspires to something.

aspirate — *noun* (pronounced -*rət*) the sound represented in English and several other languages by the letter *h*. — *verb* (pronounced -*rate*) 1 *trans., intrans.* to pronounce (a word, etc) with a breath at the beginning. 2 to remove (liquid or gas) out of a hole by sucking. [from Latin *aspirare*, from *ad*, to + *spirare*, to breathe]

aspiration *noun* 1 eager desire, ambition. 2 *Medicine* the removal of fluid from a cavity in the body such as a cyst or an inflamed joint, or from the mouth during dental treatment, by suction using an instrument known as an aspirator.

aspirator *noun* an apparatus for sucking gas, liquid, etc out of a hole, especially in the body.

aspire *verb intrans.* (**aspire to** *or* **after something**) to have a strong desire to achieve or reach an objective or ambition. [from Latin *aspirare*, from *ad*, to + *spirare*, to breathe]

aspirin *noun* acetylsalicylic acid, an analgesic drug that is widely used to relieve mild to moderate pain, eg headache, toothache, rheumatic pain, or neuralgia, and to reduce inflammation and fever caused by influenza and the common cold. It may irritate the stomach lining, causing bleeding. Daily doses are used to prevent coronary thrombosis (heart attack) and stroke in susceptible individuals. [from German (originally a trademark), from *acetyl* + *spiraeic* (= salicylic) acid]

aspiring *adj.* ambitious, hopeful.

Asquith, H(erbert) H(enry) Asquith, 1st Earl of Oxford and (1852–1928) English Liberal politician and Prime Minister, born in Morley, Yorkshire. He was called to the Bar (1876), became a QC (1890), MP for E Fife (1886–1918), Home Secretary (1892–5), Chancellor of the Exchequer (1905–8), and Prime Minister (1908–16). His administration was notable for the upholding of free trade, the introduction of old age pensions, payment for MPs, the Parliament Act of 1911, Welsh disestablishment, suffragette troubles, the declaration of war (1914), the coalition ministry (1915), and the Sinn Féin rebellion (1916). After World War I, he led the Independent Liberals who rejected Lloyd George's coalition policies.

ass[1] *noun* 1 an animal like a horse but smaller and with longer ears. 2 *colloq.* a stupid person. [from Anglo-Saxon *assa*]

ass[2] *North Amer., esp. US* same as ARSE.

Assad, Hafez al- (1928–) Syrian soldier and politician, born in Qardaha. He was Minister of Defence and Commander of the Air Force (1966–70), instigated a coup in 1970, became Prime Minister and then President (1971–). He belongs to the minority Alawi sect of Islam. After the 1973 Arab-Israeli War, he negotiated a partial withdrawal of Israeli troops from Syria. In 1976 and early 1987 he sent Syrian troops into Lebanon, and by 1989 had imposed Syrian control over the greater part of Lebanon. He enjoyed Soviet support, and was one of the few Arab leaders to support Iran in its war with Iraq. In Dec 1991 he entered his fourth seven-year term as President. In 1993 he objected to the Israeli–Palestinian agreement signed by Yitzhak Rabin and Yasser Arafat mainly because it had been concluded in secret rather than within the framework of a comprehensive settlement involving all the Arab countries.

assagai same as ASSEGAI.

assail *verb* 1 to make a strong physical or verbal attack on. 2 to make a determined start on (a task). [from Latin *ad*, to + *salire*, to leap]

assailant *noun* an attacker.

Assam POP (1991) 22.4m, a state in E India. AREA 78 523sq km/30 310sq mi. It is bounded NW by Bhutan and SE by Bangladesh. The state is almost completely separated from India by Bangladesh and played an important strategic role in World War II during the Allied advance into Burma (Myanma). It is crossed by the R Brahmaputra, in which lies Majuli I, a pilgrimage centre. GOVERNMENT a unicameral legislature of 126 members. CHIEF TOWNS Dispur, Shillong, Gauhati. ECONOMY produces almost half of India's crude oil; oil refining; timber; tea; rice; jute; cotton; oilseed.

Assamese — *noun* a language spoken in the eastern parts of N and Central India. — *adj.* relating to or spoken or written in Assamese.

assassin *noun* a killer, especially for political or religious reasons. [from Arabic *hashshashin*, hashish-eaters: originally applied to Muslim fanatics sent on murder missions at the time of the Crusades]

assassinate *verb* 1 to murder, especially for political or religious reasons. 2 to destroy the good reputation of (someone).

assassination *noun* 1 murder by an assassin. 2 the malicious ruining of a person's reputation.

assassin bug a small bug that feeds mainly on the body fluids of small arthropods. Some species suck the blood of vertebrates and are carriers of disease.

assault — *noun* 1 a violent physical or verbal attack. 2 *euphemistic* rape. — *verb* to make an assault on. [from French *asaut*, from Latin *ad*, to + *saltus*, leap]

assault and battery *Legal* the crime of threatening to attack a person, followed by an actual attack.
◇ In law, a mere attempt to strike another person constitutes an assault. When contact is made, whether it results in lasting damage or not, this is battery. Therefore, in practice, assault is always taken to include battery.

assault course an obstacle course with walls, pools, nets, etc, used for training soldiers.

assay — *noun Metall.* the analysis and assessment of the composition and purity of a metal in an ore or mineral, or of a chemical compound in a mixture of compounds. — *verb* to perform such an analysis, or to determine the commercial value of an ore or mineral on the basis of such an analysis. [from Old French *assaier*]

assegai *noun* a thin light iron-tipped wooden spear used in southern Africa. [from Arabic *azzagayah*, the spear]

assemblage *noun* 1 a collection of people or things. 2 a gathering together.
◇ The technique of assembling and fixing together various materials to create a three-dimensional whole. Any material may be used: paper, wood, metal, sacks, rubbish, or even crushed motor cars. Examples are Jean Dubuffet's works of the 1950s combining collage with natural materials, such as grasses, and Robert Rauschenberg's so-called 'combine paintings'.

assemble *verb* 1 *trans., intrans.* to gather or collect together. 2 *trans.* to put together the parts of (a machine, etc). [from Old French *asembler*, from Latin *ad*, to + *simul*, together]

assembler *noun* a computer program which converts a program in an assembly language to a code that the computer can process.

Assemblies of God a Christian pentecostalist denomination formed in the USA and Canada in the early 20c, which promotes mission work all over the world. They accept the doctrines of the Trinity, grace, and free will, practice Baptism (by total immersion) and Holy Communion, and hold that personal sanctification is gradual rather than immediate on conversion. They were also pre-millennial (believing that Christ would return within 1 000 years of the start of his reign).

assembly *noun* (PL. **assemblies**) 1 a group of people gathered together, especially for a meeting. 2 the act of assembling.

assembly language a language used for writing computer programs, which are then translated by an assembler into a code the computer can understand.

assembly line a continuous series of machines and workers along which an article, product, etc passes in the stages of its manufacture.

assent — *noun* consent or approval, especially official. See also ROYAL ASSENT. — *verb intrans.* (**assent to something**) to agree to it. [from Latin *assentari*]

assert *verb* 1 to state firmly. 2 to insist on or defend (one's rights, opinions, etc).
— **assert oneself** to state one's wishes, defend one's opinions, etc confidently and vigorously. [from Latin *asserere*]

assertion *noun* a positive or strong statement or claim.

assertive *adj.* expressing one's wishes and opinions in a firm and confident manner.

assertively *adv.* with an assertive manner.

assertiveness *noun* being assertive.

assertiveness training *Psychol.* a system whereby more positive behaviour patterns are learned, mainly by adopting a more self-confident non-aggressive approach to dealing with difficult people or situations.

assess *verb* 1 to judge the quality or importance of. 2 to estimate the cost, value, etc of. 3 to fine or tax by an amount stated: *were assessed at £500.* [from Latin *assidere*, to sit as a judge]

assessment *noun* 1 the act of assessing. 2 evaluation, estimation. 3 a valuation or estimate. 4 an amount to be paid.

assessor noun **1** a person who assesses the value of property, etc for taxation. **2** a person who advises a judge, etc on technical matters. **3** a person who assesses the importance or quality of eg a job.

asset noun **1** a valuable skill, quality, or person. **2** (**assets**) the total value of the property and possessions of a person or company, especially as able to cover debts. [from Old French *asez*, enough]

asset-stripping noun the practice of buying an unsuccessful company at a low price and selling off its assets separately for a profit.

asseverate verb to state solemnly. [from Latin *asseverare*]

assiduity noun (PL. **assiduities**) constant care and attention to a person, or to what one is doing.

assiduous adj. **1** hard-working. **2** done carefully and exactly. [from Latin *assiduus*, persistent]

assiduously adv. in an assiduous way; diligently.

assiduousness noun being assiduous; diligence.

assign verb **1** to give (a task, etc) to someone or appoint (someone) to a position or task. **2** to fix (a time, place, etc) for a purpose. **3** Legal (**assign something to someone**) to give one's title, property, interest, etc to someone else by contract. [from Latin *assignare*, to mark out]

assignation noun a secret appointment to meet, especially between lovers.

Assignats originally, paper bonds issued by the Constituent Assembly in France (1789). They were later (1790) accepted as currency notes, in view of the shortage of coin, until the abolition of paper currency in 1797.

assignee noun Legal a person to whom property, interest, etc is given by contract.

assignment noun **1** a task or duty assigned to someone. **2** the act of assigning. **3** Legal a transfer of property, interest, etc to someone else.

assignor noun Legal a person who gives property, interest, etc by contract.

assimilable adj. capable of being assimilated.

assimilate — noun Biol. any of the complex organic compounds initially produced by green plants and certain bacteria that manufacture complex molecules from simple molecules obtained from the environment, such as carbon dioxide, nitrogen, or water. — verb **1** to become familiar with and understand (facts, information, etc) completely. **2** trans., intrans. to become part of, or make (people) part of, a larger group, especially of a different race or culture. **3** Biol., said of a plant or animal to manufacture complex organic compounds. **4** to cause to resemble, especially to make (a sound) like another. [from Latin *ad*, to + *similis*, like]

assimilation noun Biol. in autotrophic organisms (green plants and certain bacteria), the manufacture of complex organic compounds from simple molecules obtained from the environment, such as carbon dioxide, nitrogen, or water; in animals, the manufacture of complex organic compounds, such as proteins and fats, from simple molecules derived from digested food material.

assist verb **1** trans., intrans. (often **assist in** or **with something**) to help with it. **2** intrans. to take part in a ceremony, etc. [from Latin *assistere*, to take a stand beside]

assistance noun help.

assistant noun **1** a person employed to help someone of higher rank, position, etc. **2** a person who serves customers in a shop.

Assize Court a legal system in England and Wales, dating from the time of Henry II, which was abolished by the Courts Act in 1971. Assize courts were presided over by High Court judges, who travelled on circuit to hear criminal and civil cases. The functions of Assize courts continue to be exercised by High Court judges sitting in Crown Courts throughout England and Wales.

assizes pl. noun Hist. a court sitting at regular intervals in each county in England and Wales. [from Latin *assidere*, to sit as a judge]

assoc. abbrev. **1** associated. **2** association.

associate — verb (pronounced -ate) **1** to connect in the mind: *associate lambs with spring*. **2** intrans. to mix socially: *don't associate with him*. **3** to involve (oneself) in a group because of shared views or aims. **4** intrans. to join with people for a common purpose. — noun (pronounced -ət) **1** a business partner. **2** a colleague or friend. **3** a person admitted to a society without full membership. — adj. **1** joined with another, especially in a business: *an associate director*. **2** not having full membership of a society. [from Latin *associare*, from *ad*, to + *socius*, companion]

associated adj. (usually **Associated**) used in the name of a company to show that it has been formed from several smaller companies.

Associated Press (ABBREV. **AP**) an international news agency, with headquarters in New York City. Founded in 1848, it is the world's largest news-gathering co-operative, and also provides a specialized economic and financial news service.

association noun **1** an organization or club. **2** a friendship or partnership. **3** a connection in the mind. **4** the act of associating.

Association football an 11-a-side team game played on a grass or synthetic pitch. At each end of the pitch is a goal net. The object is to move the ball around the field, with the feet or head, until a player is in a position to put the ball into the net and score a goal. The goalkeeper is the only person allowed to touch the ball with his hands while it is in play, provided he touches it within his specifically defined area. The ancient Greeks, Chinese, Egyptians, and Romans all played a form of football. In the early 19c it became an organized game in Britain. The Football Association was formed in 1863 and the first FA Cup final was played in 1872. The Football League was formed in 1888. The world governing body, the Fédération Internationale de Football Association (FIFA), was formed in Paris in 1904. The first World Cup was organized in Uruguay in 1930 The European governing body, the Union of European Football Associations (UEFA), was formed in 1954, and they control the major European club competitions. — Also called *soccer*.

Association of South-East Asian Nations (ABBREV. **ASEAN**) an association formed in 1967 to promote economic and cultural co-operation between Indonesia, Malaysia, the Philippines, Singapore, and Thailand. Brunei joined in 1984.

associative adj. Maths., said of calculations involving multiplication and addition giving the same answer irrespective of the position of the brackets, eg $(1 + 2) + 3 = 6$ and $1 + (2 + 3) = 6$.

assonance noun Poetry **1** the rhyming of vowel sounds but not consonants, as in *load* and *cold*. **2** the use of a consonant or consonants with different vowel sounds, as in *milled* and *mulled*. [from Latin *assonare*, to sound]

assorted adj. **1** mixed; of or containing various different kinds. **2** arranged in sorts; classified. [from Latin *ad*, to + *sors*, lot]

assortment noun a mixed collection.

assuage verb to make (a pain, sorrow, hunger, etc) less severe. [from Latin *ad*, to + *suavis*, mild, sweet]

assume verb **1** to accept (something), though without proof; to take for granted. **2** to take upon oneself (a responsibility, duty, etc). **3** to take on or adopt (an appearance, quality, etc): *an issue assuming immense importance*. **4** to pretend to have or feel. [from Latin *assumere*, to take to oneself]

assumed adj. **1** false; not genuine. **2** accepted as true before proof is available.

assuming adj., said of a person arrogant; presumptuous.

Assumption Christianity the belief in Roman Catholic and Eastern Christian theology that when the Virgin Mary died, she was 'assumed' (taken up, body and soul) to heaven. It was defined by Pope Pius XII as an article of faith in 1950.

Assumption a painting of the Assumption by Titian (1516–18, Santa Maria dei Frari, Venice).

assumption noun **1** something accepted as true without proof. **2** the act of accepting something as true without proof. **3** the act of assuming. **4** (**Assumption**) Christianity see separate entry. [from Latin *assumptio*, from *assumere*, to take to oneself]

Assumption of the Virgin a painting of the Assumption by El Greco (1577, Chicago). It was originally painted in the Santa Domingo el Antiquo, Toledo, Spain.

assurance noun **1** a promise, guarantee, or statement that a thing is true. **2** confidence. **3** Brit. insurance, especially of one's life.

Assurbanipal or **Ashurbanipal** (7c BC) King of Assyria (668–627 BC), the son of Esarhaddon and grandson of Sennacherib. The last of the Assyrian kings, he founded in Nineveh the first systematically gathered and organized library in the ancient Middle East.

assure verb **1** to state positively and confidently. **2** (**assure someone of something**) to convince them or make them sure about it: *can assure you of my innocence*. **3** to make (an event, etc) certain: *assure her success*. **4** Brit. to insure, especially one's life. [from Latin *ad*, to + *securus*, safe]

assured adj. **1** said of a person confident. **2** certain to happen.

assuredly adv. certainly.

Assyria the name given first to the area around the town of Assur on the Tigris in Upper Mesopotamia, and then much later to the empire that the rulers of Assur acquired through conquering their neighbours on all sides. At its height in the 9c and 8c BC, the Assyrian Empire stretched from the E Mediterranean to Iran, and from the Persian Gulf as far north as the mountains of E Turkey. The Empire was destroyed in an uprising of Medes and Babylonians in 612 BC.

Assyrian Hist. — noun **1** an inhabitant of Assyria. **2** the Semitic language of Assyria. — adj. of Assyria, its people, language and culture. [from Greek *Assyrios*]
◇ The Assyrian kingdom lasted from c.1530–612 BC. By the 7c BC, it was the most powerful state in the Near East, and its empire, reaching its greatest extent in the reign of Ashurbanipal (668–c.627 BC), extended from the E Mediterranean to Iran, and from the Persian Gulf to the mountains of E Turkey. The Assyrians were renowned for their brutality, both to their own lower orders and to conquered peoples, and the kings maintained their power by ruthless oppression, by extensive transportation of peoples, and by a process of self-deification. Assyrian art was similar in style to Babylonian art; the best known surviving examples are sculptures and wall decorations in bas-relief, and colossal stone winged lions or bulls that guarded the entrances to palaces and other buildings.

Astaire, Fred, originally **Frederick Austerlitz** (1899–1987) US actor and dancer, born in Omaha, Nebraska. He and his elder sister Adele began as a vaudeville team (1916) and rose to stardom in *Lady be Good* and other stage shows. When Adele married, Fred continued with various partners, notably Ginger Rogers. His many films include *Top Hat* (1935), *Follow the Fleet* (1936), and *Easter Parade* (1948). He revolutionized the film musical with his original tap-dance routines.

Astarte see ISHTAR.

astatine *noun Chem.* (SYMBOL **At**, ATOMIC NUMBER **85**) a radioactive element, the heaviest of the halogens, that has several isotopes, all of which are radioactive but have very short half-lives, ranging from fractions of a second to eight hours. Astatine is prepared by bombarding bismuth with alpha particles. [from Greek *astatos*, unstable]

aster *noun* a garden plant with small pink, white, blue, or purple daisy-like flowers. [from Greek *aster*, star]

asterisk — *noun* a star-shaped mark (*) used in printing and writing to mark especially a reference to a note or an omission. — *verb* to mark with an asterisk. [from Greek *asteriskos*, small star]

astern *adv., adj.* **1** in or towards the stern. **2** backwards. **3** behind. [from A³ + STERN]

asteroid *noun* any of thousands of small rocky objects, 1km to 1 000km in diameter, that revolve around the Sun, mainly between the orbits of Mars and Jupiter. Asteroids are thought to be fragments of the material from which the Solar System was formed. — Also called *minor planet.* [from Greek *asteroeides*, star-like]

asthenosphere *noun Geol.* the upper layer of the mantle that lies immediately below the Earth's crust. [from Greek *astheneia*, weakness]

asthma *noun* a respiratory disorder in which breathlessness and wheezing occur as a result of narrowing and obstruction of the bronchi and bronchioles (the air passages). [from Greek *asthma*, from *aazein*, to breathe hard]
◇ Asthma attacks, which are caused when muscles in the walls of the air passages go into spasm (contract excessively), are most commonly associated with allergic reactions (eg to pollen, house dust, some drugs), but they may also be precipitated by infections, physical exertion, stress, or emotional upset. The disorder is treated with *bronchodilators* (drugs that relax the muscles of the bronchi) and steroids (which reduce inflammation), usually administered in the form of an aerosol spray which is inhaled.

asthmatic — *adj.* relating to or suffering from asthma. — *noun* a person who suffers from asthma.

asthmatically *adv.* with symptoms of asthma.

astigmatic *adj.* relating to or characteristic of astigmatism; suffering from astigmatism.

astigmatism *noun Physics* a defect in a lens, especially abnormal curvature of the lens or cornea of the eye. Astigmatism causes distortion of the image of an object because not all light rays from it are brought to the same focus on the retina. It is corrected by wearing spectacles or contact lenses that produce exactly the opposite degree of distortion. [from A-¹ without + Greek *stigma*, point]

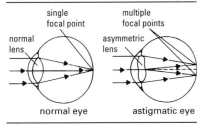

normal and astigmatic eye

astir *adj., adv.* **1** awake and out of bed. **2** in a state of motion or excitement. [from A³ + STIR]

Aston, Francis William (1877–1945) English physicist, born in Birmingham. In 1919 he developed the mass spectrograph, with which he identified 212 naturally occurring isotopes. He also stated the 'whole number rule' which observes that all isotopes have very nearly whole number masses relative to the defined mass of the one of the isotopes of oxygen (O¹⁶). He was awarded the 1922 Nobel Prize for Physics.

astonish *verb* to surprise greatly. [from Old French *estoner*, from Latin *ex*, out + *tonare*, to thunder]

astonished *adj.* extremely surprised.

astonishing *adj.* wonderful or surprising; extraordinary.

astonishingly *adv.* in an astonishing way; to an astonishing extent: *they were astonishingly brave.*

astonishment *noun* wonder; complete surprise.

Astor (of Hever), John Jacob Astor, 1st Baron (1886–1971) British newspaper proprietor, born in New York City, USA. He became an MP in 1922, and Chairman of the Times Publishing Company (1922–59) after the death of Lord Northcliffe.

Astor (of Hever Castle), Nancy Witcher Astor, Viscountess *née* **Langhorne** (1879–1964) US-born British politician, born in Danville, Virginia. In 1919, on succeeding her husband as Conservative MP for Plymouth, she became the first woman MP to sit in the House of Commons. She was known for her interest in social problems, especially women's rights and temperance. Her husband, William Waldorf, 2nd Viscount Astor (1879–1952), was proprieter of the *Observer* (1919–45).

astound *verb* to amaze or shock. [from obsolete *astone*, to astonish]

astounded *adj.* amazed, shocked, bewildered.

astounding *adj.* amazing, shocking.

astoundingly *adv.* in a surprising and shocking way.

Astrakhan, formerly **Khadzhi-Tarkhan 1** POP (1991e) 512 000, the capital of Astrakhan oblast, SE Russia, standing on a huge island in the delta of the Volga. It lies at an altitude of 22m below sea level and is protected from floods by 75km/47mi of dykes. Founded in the 13c, it is the most important port in the Volga–Caspian basin and a major transshipment centre for oil, fish, grain, and wood. The city is also known for its Astrakhan fur. NOTABLE FEATURE Kremlin fortress (16c). **2** an oblast in SE Russia with Astrakhan as its capital.

astrakhan *noun* dark tightly curled wool from lambs, used to make cloth. [from ASTRAKHAN]

astral *adj.* of or like the stars. [from Latin *astralis*, from *astrum*, star]

astray *adj., adv.* out of the right or expected way.
— **go astray** to become lost.

Astrid a female first name. [from Norse elements *ans*, god + *fridr*, fair, beautiful]

astride — *adv.* **1** with a leg on each side. **2** with legs apart. — *prep.* **1** with a leg on each side of. **2** stretching across.

astringency *noun* being astringent; severity, harshness.

astringent — *adj.* **1** severe and harsh. **2** *said of a substance* causing cells to shrink. — *noun* a substance that causes cells to shrink, used in medical preparations to stop bleeding from minor cuts, etc, and in cosmetic lotions to harden and protect the skin. Astringents are also used in throat lozenges and antiperspirants. [from Latin *astringere*, to draw tight]

astringently *adv.* with an astringent or harsh manner.

astro- *combining form* relating to stars or space. [from Greek *astron*, star]

astrodome *noun* an open space or building covered by a large translucent plastic dome, usually a sports centre or arena. The first and most famous example is the one built at Houston, Texas, in 1964.

astrolabe *noun Astron.* a former navigational instrument used to observe the positions of the Sun and bright stars, and to estimate the local time by estimating the altitude of the Sun or specific stars above the horizon. [from ASTRO- + *lab-*, root of Greek *lambanein* to take]

astrologer *noun* a person who studies or practises astrology.

astrological *adj.* relating to astrology.

astrologically *adv.* as regards or in terms of astrology.

astrology *noun* the study of the movements of the stars and planets and their influence on people's lives. [from Greek *astron*, star + *logos*, discourse]

astrometry *noun Astron.* the branch of astronomy concerned with the precise measurement of the positions of stars, planets, and other celestial bodies on the celestial sphere.

astronaut *noun* a person trained for space-travel. [from ASTRO- + Latin *nautes*, sailor]

astronautics *sing. noun* the science of space travel.

astronomer *noun* a person who studies or practises astronomy.

Astronomer Royal formerly the title of the Director of the Royal Greenwich Observatory, but since 1972 an honorary title awarded to a distinguished British astronomer.

astronomical *or* **astronomic** *adj.* **1** *said of numbers, amounts, etc* large; extreme. **2** relating to astronomy.

astronomically *adv.* **1** *colloq.* extremely; enormously: *an astronomically large bill.* **2** as regards or in terms of astronomy.

astronomical unit (ABBREV. **AU**) *Astron.* the mean distance between the Earth and the Sun, about 149.6m km (93m mi), used to measure distances within the Solar System. There are 63 240 astronomical units in a light year.

astronomy *noun* the scientific study of celestial bodies, including the planets, stars, and galaxies, as well as interstellar and intergalactic space, and the universe as a whole. [from Greek *astron*, star + *nomos*, law]

astrophysical *adj.* relating to astrophysics.

astrophysicist *noun* a person who studies astrophysics.

astrophysics *sing. noun Astron.* the application of physical laws and theories to astronomical objects and phenomena, especially stars and galaxies, with the aim of deriving theoretical models to explain their behaviour.

Asturias, Miguel Angel (1899–1974) Guatemalan novelist, born in Guatemala City. He is best known for his first novel, *El señor presidente* (Mr President, 1946), about the fall and trial of the hated dictator of an unnamed Latin-American country. Later novels include *Hombres de maíz* (Men of Maize, 1949) and *Mulatta de tal* (The Mulatta and Mr Fly, 1963). He was awarded the Nobel Prize for Literature in 1967.

Asturias POP (1991) 1.1m, an autonomous region and former principality of N Spain, co-extensive with the modern province of Oviedo. AREA 10 565sq km/4 078sq mi. PHYSICAL DESCRIPTION it is a mountainous region extending along the Bay of Biscay; largely occupied by the Cordillera Cantabrica, which rise to 2 646m in the Picos de Europa. HISTORY the centre of Christian resistance to Muslim invasion in the 8c–9c; part of the Kingdom of Leon in 911; the scene of an unsuccessful left-wing revolution in 1934. ECONOMY the region supplies nearly half of Spain's coal requirements; the mines also provide fluorspar, zinc, and iron ore; agriculture is based on maize, fruit, and livestock.

astute *adj.* able to judge and act intelligently and decisively; mentally perceptive. [from Latin *astutus*, from *astus*, craft]

astutely *adv.* in an astute way.

astuteness *noun* being astute; keen mental perception.

Asunción POP (1990e) 608 000, the federal capital of Paraguay. A port on the E bank of the R Paraguay, it is an important transport and commercial centre. It was founded in 1537 and was the capital of La Plata region until 1580. NOTABLE FEATURES La Encarnación Church; Pantheon of Heroes.

asunder *adv.* apart or into pieces. [from Anglo-Saxon *onsundran*]

Aswan, ancient **Syene 1** POP (1986) 192 000, the capital of Aswan governorate, S Egypt. It is situated on the E bank of the R Nile, 900km/560mi S of Cairo. The Aswan Dam, built between 1898 and 1902, lies to the S at the limit of navigation. The Aswan High Dam, completed in 1971, is further S at the head of L Nasser. NOTABLE FEATURES Aswan Museum; Roman Nilometer; Temples of Ptolemy VII, Seti I, and Rameses II; Tombs of the Ancient Nobles; Aga Khan Mausoleum; Coptic Monastery of St Simeon (6c); Temples of Philae; Temple of Kalabsha (transported 55km/34mi from its original site and re-erected near the Aswan High Dam). **2** a governorate in S Egypt with the town of Aswan as its capital.

Aswan High Dam a major gravity dam (height 111m, length 3 600m) on the R Nile in Egypt, completed in 1970. Situated 6.4km/4mi upstream from the lesser Aswan Dam, it impounds L Nasser and has the capacity to generate 2 100 megawatts of hydroelectricity.

asylum *noun* (PL. **asylums**) **1** a place of safety or protection. **2** the granting of protection. See also POLITICAL ASYLUM. **3** *Hist.* a mental hospital. [from Greek *asylon*, from A-¹, not + Greek *sylon*, right of seizure]

asymmetric *or* **asymmetrical** *adj.* lacking symmetry.

asymmetrically *adv.* without symmetry; in an asymmetrical way.

asymmetry *noun* a lack of symmetry. [from A-¹ not + Greek *symmetria*, symmetry]

asymptote *noun* *Geom.* a line (usually straight) which is continually approached by a curve that never actually meets the line. [from Greek *asymptotos*, apt to fall together]

As You Like It a play by William Shakespeare (1599). It is a comedy that revolves around four key couples, contrasting the world of the court with that of the pastoral Arden, and also uses songs and the reflections of Jacques and Touchstone to provide entertainment.

At *symbol Chem.* astatine.

at *prep.* expressing **1** position or location. **2** direction: *look at the book.* **3** position in time. **4** state or occupation: *children at play.* **5** time during which: *work at night.* **6** rate or level: *work at speed.* **7** cost: *sell at £5 each.* **8** cause: *shocked at his behaviour.*
— **at that 1** at that point. **2** as well.
[from Anglo-Saxon *æt*]

Atacama Desert, Spanish **Desierto de Atacama** an arid desert region in N Chile, claimed to be the world's driest area. It is made up of a series of dry salt basins, extending 960km/597mi S from the Peru border to the R

Copiapó. The desert, which supports almost no vegetation, is bounded W by the Pacific coastal range and E by the Cordillera de Domeyko. Water is piped to the towns and nitrate fields from the Cordillera. A 400-year drought up to 1971 was recorded at the town of Calama. The desert was ceded to Chile by Peru and Bolivia in 1883–4. ECONOMY copper, nitrates, iodine, borax deposits.

Atahualpa (d.1533) the last king of the Incas. On his father's death (1525) he received the kingdom of Quito, and in 1532 overwhelmed his elder brother Huascar and seized Peru. He was captured by the Spaniards, and despite agreeing to a large ransom, was accused of plotting against Pizarro and executed.

Atalanta in Greek mythology, a fleet-footed huntress who was nurtured by a she-bear. She promised to marry any man who could run faster than her in a race: those who lost were killed. Eventually Hippomenes (or Milanion) threw three golden apples of the Hesperides at her feet, so that her attention was diverted and she lost.

Atalante, L' a French film directed by Jean Vigo (1934). It is a story of romance between the captain of a barge and his wife (played by Michel Simon and Dita Parlo) who are separated and reunited.

Atatürk, Mustapha Kemal (1881–1938) Turkish soldier and statesman, born in Salonika. He raised a nationalist rebellion in Anatolia in protest against the postwar division of Turkey, and in 1921 established a provisional government in Ankara. In 1922 the Ottoman Sultanate was formally abolished, and in 1923 Turkey was declared a secular republic, with Kemal as President (1923–38). He became virtual dictator, and launched a social and political revolution introducing Western fashions, the emancipation of women, educational reform, the replacement of Arabic script with the Latin alphabet, and the discouragement of traditional Islamic loyalties in favour of a strictly Turkish nationalism. In 1935 he assumed the surname Atatürk ('Father of the Turks').

atavism *noun* **1** a resemblance to ancestors rather than immediate parents. **2** reversion to an earlier, especially more primitive, type. [from Latin *atavus*, great-great-great-grandfather]

atavistic *adj.* **1** relating to or resembling ancestors. **2** involving reversion to an earlier type.

ataxia *noun Medicine* inability of the brain to coordinate voluntary movements of the limbs, resulting in jerky movements and a staggering gait. It is caused by a disorder of the sensory nerves or by disease of the cerebellum. [from Greek *ataxia*, disorder]

Atbara POP (1983) 73 000, a town in Northern region, Sudan. It lies on the R Atbara at its junction with the R Nile, 16km/10mi N of Ed Damer. Lord Kitchener's army defeated the Khalifa's troops here in 1898.

ATC *abbrev.* Air Training Corps.

ate see EAT.

-ate *suffix* **1** forming verbs meaning 'cause to be': *hyphenate.* **2** forming nouns denoting rank, profession, or group: *doctorate / magistrate / electorate.* **3** forming nouns denoting a salt: *carbonate.* See also -IDE, -ITE. **4** forming adjectives meaning 'having, showing features of, like or related to': *passionate / fortunate.* [from the Latin ending *-atus*, sometimes via Old French]

atelier *noun* **1** a workshop or artist's studio. **2** an abbreviated form of *atelier libre*, free studio (free in the sense that anyone may attend, on payment of a fee). Found throughout Europe, these studios provide a nude model for artists to work from, but offer no instruction. [from French *atelier*]

Aten *or* **Aton** in Egypt, originally the name of the Sun's disc, and then that of the sun-god who

was the creator of all things. He had no connection with any of the other gods, and in the reign of the Pharaoh Akhenaton the cult of Aten temporarily replaced that of Amun-Re.

Athabasca 1 a lake in NE Alberta and NW Saskatchewan, central Canada. AREA 8 080sq km/3 120sq mi. It is 335km/208mi long. Large deposits of oil sand are mined in the area. **2** a river in W central Canada. It is the southernmost tributary of the Mackenzie R. The river rises in the Rocky Mts on the border between Alberta and British Columbia, to the N of Mt Columbia, and is 1 231km/765mi long.

Athabascan *or* **Athapascan** various Athabascan-speaking Native American groups living in Alaska and NW Canada, W of Hudson Bay. They lived mainly in small independent hunting-and-gathering bands and later, after Europeans reached N America, they engaged in the fur trade. Today some supply trapped animals for the fur trade and are hunters' guides, and a few are assimilated into US culture.

Athanasian Creed a statement of Christian faith, written in Latin probably in the 5c AD. Called *quicunque vult* after the opening words, it is a historic statement of Trinitarian doctrine, still sometimes used liturgically. The Greek text is known in Eastern Churches, but omits the *Filioque* clause.

Athanasius, St (c.296–373 AD) Greek Christian theologian and prelate, born in Alexandria. He distinguished himself at the Council of Nicaea (325), and was chosen Patriarch of Alexandria and Primate of Egypt. As a result of his stand against the heretic Arius, he was dismissed from his see on several occasions by emperors sympathetic to the Arian cause. His writings include works on the Trinity, the Incarnation, and the divinity of the Holy Spirit. His feast day is 2 May.

atheism *noun* the belief that there is no God. [from A-¹ without + Greek *theos*, god]

atheist *noun* a person who believes that there is no God.

atheistic *or* **atheistical** *adj.* **1** characteristic or typical of an atheist. **2** relating to or involving atheism.

atheistically *adv.* in an atheistic way.

Athelstan *or* **Aethelstan** (c.895–939) son of Edward the Elder, and grandson of Alfred the Great. Acknowledged as King of Wessex and Mercia (924), he built upon his predecessors' achievements by invading Northumbria, thus establishing himself as the first King of all England (927).

Athena *or* **Athene** in Greek mythology, the goddess of war and wisdom. She was not born, but sprang fully armed from the head of Zeus. The protectress of Athens, she was honoured by the citizens with three temples on the Acropolis, and many festivals, the chief of which was the Panathenaea. She was a warrior goddess and protected heroes; she helped the Greeks in the Trojan war. The Romans identified her with the goddess Minerva.

Athens, Greek **Athínai**, ancient **Athenae** POP (1991) 862 133; Greater Athens 3.1m, the capital of Greece, lying in a wide coastal plain between the Ilissus and Cephissus rivers, surrounded by hills. The city is badly affected by air and noise pollution. HISTORY an ancient Greek city-state which had extended over Attica by the 7c BC; it reached its height of economic and cultural prosperity under Pericles (5c BC); became part of the Roman protectorate (later province) in 146 BC; became part of the Ottoman Empire in 1456; from 1835 it has been the capital of modern Greece; it was occupied by the Germans during World War II. The city is an important tourist centre. NOTABLE FEATURES the hill of the Acropolis (156m), with the Parthenon (5c BC), the Propylaea (437–432 BC), the Temple of Athena

Niki (432–421 BC), the Ionic Erechtheion (421–406 BC), and the Acropolis Museum; S of the Acropolis are the Odeon of Herod Atticus (2c BC), the Portico of Eumenes, remains of the Asklepieion (4c BC), the rock-cut theatre of Dionysus (4c BC), and the site of the Odeum of Pericles; to the N of the Acropolis lies the excavated area of the Ancient Agora (market-place); other monuments include the Olympieion, the Arch of Hadrian (AD 131–2), and the Stadion; Parliament Building, National Garden, National Archaeological Museum.

atherosclerosis *noun* (PL. **atheroscleroses**) *Medicine* a form of arteriosclerosis (thickening and hardening of the arteries) in which cholesterol and other fatty substances are deposited on the inner walls of arteries, making·them narrow and eventually obstructing the flow of blood. [from Greek *athere*, gruel + SCLEROSIS]
◇ Arteriosclerosis can often be prevented from developing at a relatively early age by a low-cholesterol diet and regular exercise, but in old age thickening and hardening of the arteries is a natural change. Blood flow in the affected artery may eventually cease altogether, causing a heart attack or stroke.

atherosclerotic *adj.* relating to or typical of atherosclerosis.

athlete *noun* 1 a person who is good at sport, especially track and field events such as running. 2 a healthy person with athletic ability. [from Greek *athlos*, contest]

athlete's foot a disease which damages the skin between the toes, caused by a fungus.

athletic *adj.* 1 *said of people* physically fit and strong. 2 relating to athletics.

athletics *sing. noun* competitive track and field sports for athletes, including running, jumping, throwing, and walking.
◇ Modern track events include sprint races, relay races, middle and long distance races, hurdle races, and steeplechase. Field events include high jump, long jump, triple jump, pole vault, discus, javelin, and hammer throwing. Athletics competitions have a long history dating back to ancient Egypt and the ancient Greek Olympics; they dominate the modern Olympics and other international games, with most athletes at the highest

level training and competing full-time. The governing body is the International Amateur Athletics Federation, founded in 1912.

Athos the first of Alexandre Dumas's *The Three Musketeers*, unwittingly married to the evil Milady.

athwart *adv., prep.* across, from side to side (of). [from A³ + THWART]

-ation *suffix* forming nouns meaning 'the process or result of'; sometimes corresponding to verbs in *-ize*: *expectation / mechanization / representation*.

-ative *suffix* forming adjectives denoting a particular attribute or tendency: *authoritative / talkative*.

Atlanta POP (1990) 2.8m, the capital of the state of Georgia, USA, in Fulton County. It lies in the W of the state, near the Appalachian foothills. HISTORY the region was ceded by Creek Native Americans to Georgia in 1821; founded in 1837 at the end of the railway, it was named Terminus; in 1845 it was renamed Atlanta; a Confederate supply depot during the Civil War, it was partially burned in 1864 by General Sharman; became state capital in 1887. The largest city in the state, it is an industrial, transportation, and cultural centre. NOTABLE FEATURES High Museum of Art; Alliance Theatre; Oakland Cemetery; Martin Luther King Jr historic site; Grant Park.

Atlantic — *noun* (**the Atlantic**) see ATLANTIC OCEAN. — *adj.* in or relating to the area of the Atlantic. [from Greek *Atlantikos*, from *Atlas*. It was so called because it lay beyond the Atlas mountains]

Atlantic, Battle of the the conflict (1940–3) that arose out of German submarine attacks on shipping in the Atlantic during World War II, which were aimed at cutting off Britain's supplies of food and munitions, and were only brought under control in 1943.

Atlantic Charter a declaration of principles to govern national policies issued by Roosevelt and Churchill after a secret meeting off Newfoundland (Aug 1941). Echoing Woodrow Wilson's Fourteen Points of 1918 and the Four Freedoms of Roosevelt's State of the Union Address (Jan 1941), it called for such rights as

self-government and free speech for all peoples, and promised a more equitable international economic system. The Charter was endorsed by the USSR and 14 other states at war with the Axis Powers, and served as an ideological basis for Allied co-operation during World War II.

Atlantic City POP (1990) 319 000, a town in Atlantic County, SE New Jersey, USA. It is on the Atlantic coast, 96km/60mi SE of Philadelphia. A popular seaside resort, it has a famed boardwalk (over 9km/5.5mi long), piers, many casinos, and a convention centre.

Atlantic Ocean a body of water extending from the Arctic to the Antarctic. On its W side are N and S America and on the ocean's E side are the European and African continents. AREA c.86 557 000sq km/33 411 000sq mi. The average depth is 3 700m and the maximum depth is 8 648m at the Puerto Rico Trench. Principal arms are the Labrador Sea, Gulf of Mexico, and the Caribbean Sea in the W; the North Sea, Baltic Sea, Mediterranean Sea, Black Sea, Bay of Biscay, Gulf of Guinea in the E; the Weddell Sea in the S. The continental shelf is narrow off the coast of Africa and Spain and broader in NW Europe and off the Americas. Between Iceland and the Antarctic Circle, the S-shaped, underwater Mid-Atlantic Ridge is the centre of earthquake and volcanic activity. The seafloor is spreading, so that N and S America are moving away from Africa and Europe at a rate of 2cm N and 4.1cm S per year. There is major surface circulation, clockwise in the N, and counter-clockwise in the S. Main currents include the Gulf Stream (North Atlantic Drift), and the N Equatorial, Canary, S Equatorial, Brazil, Benguela, and Equatorial Counter Currents. The Sargasso Sea is a sluggish region at the centre of movement in the N Atlantic Ocean. MAIN ISLANDS Greenland, Iceland, Faroes, British Is, Newfoundland, Azores, Bermuda, Madeira, Canary Is, Cape Verde Is, Trinidad and Tobago, Ascension, St Helena, Tristan da Cunha, Falkland Is, S Georgia. Mineral resources include manganese nodules, offshore oil and gas, and metal-rich sediments; there are several major fishing areas. The Atlantic Ocean is an important international communications highway, particularly from the Americas to Europe.

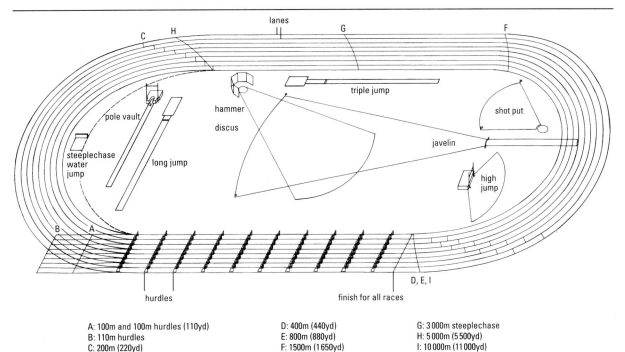

A: 100m and 100m hurdles (110yd)
B: 110m hurdles
C: 200m (220yd)
D: 400m (440yd)
E: 800m (880yd)
F: 1500m (1650yd)
G: 3000m steeplechase
H: 5000m (5500yd)
I: 10 000m (11 000yd)

athletic events

Atlantis in Greek mythology, an island identified by Plato in the Atlantic Ocean west of the Straits of Gibraltar, whose armies once threatened Europe and Africa, and which disappeared into the sea.

Atlas 1 in Greek mythology, a Titan who was made to hold up the heavens with his hands, as a punishment for taking part in the revolt against the Olympians. In early atlases, he was often portrayed as a frontispiece, hence the name. **2** *Astron.* the innermost moon of Saturn, irregular in shape and having an average diameter of 30km.

atlas *noun* (PL. **atlases**) **1** a book of maps and geographical charts. **2** *Anat.* the topmost vertebra of the spine. [from Greek *Atlas:* see ATLAS]

Atlas Mountains a system of folded mountain chains in Morocco, Algeria, and Tunisia, NW Africa. There are six main ranges. The volcanic Anti-Atlas Range in SW Morocco which runs SW–NE for 250km/155mi rises to heights of over 2 500m. The Haut Atlas Range, the largest in the group, running SW–NE for 650km/400mi from Morocco's Atlantic coast, rises to 4 165m at Mt Toubkal. To the N, the Moyen Atlas rises to 3 343m at Caberral. Situated on Morocco's Mediterranean coast, running E–W, the Er Rif Mts rise to over 2 000m. The Atlas Saharien extends NE of the Haut Atlas across N Algeria and the Tell Atlas, a smaller coastal range, runs along Algeria's Mediterranean seaboard.

atlas vertebra *Anat.* the topmost bone of the spine, which joins the skull to the spine and pivots on the axis vertebra, enabling nodding movements of the head to be made.

ATM *abbrev.* automatic teller machine.

atman *noun Hinduism* the human soul or essential self. In the teachings of the Upanishads (Sanskrit texts that form the basis of much Hindu philosophy), it is seen as being one with the Absolute, and is identified with Brahman. [from Sanskrit *atman*, self, soul]

atmosphere *noun* **1** the layer of gas surrounding a planet, and held to it by gravity. **2** the air in a particular place. **3** the mood of a place, book, etc or the general impression one has of it. **4** a unit of atmospheric pressure, equal to normal air pressure at sea level. [from Greek *atmos*, vapour + *sphaira*, ball]
◇ The Earth's atmosphere is composed of air, generally containing 78% nitrogen, 21% oxygen, and 1% argon, together with carbon dioxide, hydrogen, ozone, and methane, and traces of the other rare gases. The amount of water vapour present depends on the temperature and humidity. The atmosphere is divided into several layers, the lowest being the *troposphere*, which contains almost all of the clouds. Above it is the *stratosphere*, which extends up to 48km above the Earth, and contains very few clouds. Aircraft usually fly in this layer above the weather disturbances in the troposphere. The ozone layer is between the stratosphere and the *mesosphere*. The latter extends to 80km above the Earth, and above it lies the *thermosphere* where the air is very thin. The lower part of the thermosphere, the *ionosphere*, reflects radio waves back to Earth, enabling signals to be transmitted around the curved surface of the Earth. The outermost layer of the atmosphere, from which light gases can escape, is known as the *exosphere*.

atmospheric *adj.* **1** of a planet's atmosphere. **2** *said of a place* strongly suggestive of a particular mood or feeling.

atmospherically *adv.* as regards the atmosphere.

atmospheric pollution *Environ.* air pollution.

atmospheric pressure *Physics* the pressure exerted by the atmosphere at any point on the Earth's surface, due to the weight of the air above it. Atmospheric pressure decreases with increasing altitude.

atmospherics *pl. noun* noises caused by electrical disturbances in the air, especially when interfering with radio broadcasts.

atoll *noun* a ring-shaped coral reef surrounding a lagoon. [from *Atolu*, a name in the Maldive Islands]

atom *noun* **1** the smallest unit of a chemical element that can display the properties of that element. Atoms are composed of subatomic particles, and combine to form molecules. **2** formerly used to refer to the smallest particle of matter that can exist. [from Greek *atomos*, undivided]
◇ An atom consists of a tiny central core or *nucleus* surrounded by moving *electrons*. The nucleus, which is extremely dense, accounts for almost the entire mass of the atom, and contains *protons* (positively charged particles) and, except in the case of hydrogen, *neutrons* (uncharged particles). The electrons, which are negatively charged, orbit around the nucleus, the number of electrons being equal to the number of protons in the nucleus, so the atom carries no net charge. The chemical and electrical properties of an atom are determined by the number of electrons in the outermost orbits, and by the type of chemical bonds that are formed by the transfer or sharing of these electrons between atoms. The number of protons (or electrons) is known as the *atomic number*, which is the same for all atoms of a particular element. The total number of protons and neutrons in the nucleus is known as the *mass number*.

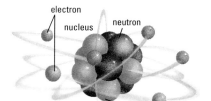

atom

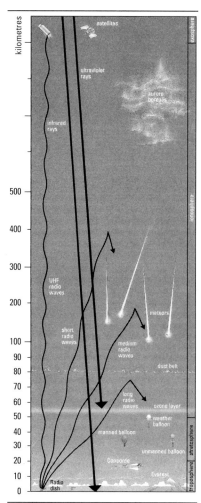

atmosphere

atom bomb *or* **atomic bomb** *Mil.* a powerful explosive device that derives its force from the sudden release of enormous amounts of nuclear (atomic) energy during nuclear fission. — Also called *nuclear bomb.*

atomic *adj.* **1** using atomic energy or atom bombs. **2** of atoms.

atomically *adv.* as regards atoms or atomic energy.

atomic clock *Physics* a precise clock that measures time by using the regular oscillations of individual atoms or molecules to regulate its movement.

atomic energy nuclear energy.

atomicity *noun Chem.* the number of atoms in a molecule of a chemical element.

atomic mass unit *Chem.* an arbitrary unit that is used to denote the masses of individual atoms or molecules. It is equal to one twelfth of the mass of an atom of the carbon-12 isotope of carbon. – Also called *dalton.*

atomic number *Chem.* (SYMBOL *Z*) the number of protons in the nucleus of an atom of a particular element. In the periodic table, the chemical elements are arranged in order of increasing atomic number.

atomic orbital *Chem.* a wave function that represents the region in space occupied by an electron that is orbiting round the nucleus of an atom.

atomic weight relative atomic mass.

atomism *noun* (*also* **atomic theory**) a philosophical tradition dating back to the 5c BC and particularly associated with the Greek philosophers Leucippus, Democritus, and Epicurus. It maintains that all that exists is made up of minute indivisible particles, and that all phenomena must be explained in terms of these 'fundamental particles' and their interactions in space (the *void*). The early philosophy was associated with atheism, and it was not until the 17c that it was adopted as scientific theory in Europe. Since that time it has led to many of the successes of modern physical sciences.

atomize *or* **atomise** *verb* **1** to reduce to atoms or small particles. **2** to reduce (a liquid or solid) to small particles or a fine spray.

atomizer *or* **atomiser** *noun* a container from which liquid can be released as a fine spray.

atonal *adj. Mus.* lacking tonality; not written in a particular key. [from Greek *atonos*, toneless]

atonality *noun* being atonal; lack of tonality.

atone *verb intrans.* (**atone for something**) to make amends for a wrongdoing. [from Middle English; originally to 'make at one', to reconcile]

atonement *noun* **1** an act of atoning. **2** (**Atonement**) *Christianity* the reconciliation of God and man through the death of Christ.

ATP *abbrev. Biochem.* adenosine triphosphate.

Atreus in Greek mythology, the king of Mycenae, the son of Pelops and father of Agamemnon and Menelaus. He quarrelled with his brother Thyestes, and placed the flesh of Thyestes' children before him at a banquet.

atrial *adj.* relating to or in the style of an atrium.

atrium *noun* (PL. **atria**, **atriums**) **1** a central court or entrance hall in an ancient Roman house. **2** either of the two upper parts of the heart that receive blood from the veins. [from Latin *atrium*]

atrocious *adj.* **1** *colloq.* very bad. **2** extremely cruel or wicked. [from Latin *atrox*, cruel]

atrociousness *noun* being atrocious; extreme wickedness.

atrocity *noun* (PL. **atrocities**) **1** wicked or cruel behaviour. **2** (*usually* **atrocities**) an act of wickedness or cruelty.

atrophy — *verb trans., intrans.* (**atrophies**, **atrophied**) to make or become weak and thin through lack of use or nourishment. — *noun* the process of atrophying. [from Greek *a*, not + *trophe*, nourishment]

atropine *or* **atropin** *noun Medicine* a poisonous alkaloid drug, obtained from deadly nightshade, that relaxes smooth muscle and reduces secretions of the salivary glands, stomach, and intestines. It is used as a premedication before general anaesthesia, as a treatment for peptic ulcers, and for dilating the pupil during examination of the eye. – Also called *belladonna*. [from Greek *Atropos*, the Fate that cut the thread of life]

Atropos see MOERAE.

attach *verb* **1** to fasten or join. **2** to associate (oneself) with or join. **3** to attribute or assign: *attach great importance to detail.* **4** *intrans.* (**attach to something**) to be connected with or form part of it: *certain conditions attach to the offer.* **5** *Legal* to arrest (a person) or seize (property) by legal authority.
— **be attached to someone** *or* **something** be fond of them.
[from French *atachier*]

attaché *noun* a junior official in an embassy. [from French *attaché*, attached]

attaché-case *noun* a small rigid leather case for documents, etc.

attached *adj.* joined, connected.

attachment *noun* **1** an act or means of fastening. **2** liking or affection. **3** an extra part that can be fitted to a machine to change its function slightly. **4** a legal seizure of a person or property. **5** a temporary period of working with a different group.

attack — *verb* **1** to make a sudden, violent attempt to hurt, damage, or capture. **2** to criticize strongly in speech or writing. **3** *intrans.* to make an attack. **4** to begin to do (something) with enthusiasm or determination. **5** to begin to damage. **6** *intrans.* to take the initiative in a game, contest, etc to attempt to score points. — *noun* **1** an act or the action of attacking. **2** a sudden spell of illness. [from Italian *attaccare*]

attacker *noun* a person who makes an attack.

attack helicopter a military helicopter designed or adapted for attacking or engaging an enemy, whether on land or at sea. In the Vietnam War, the US made extensive use of attack helicopters, mounted with guns, which proved useful in supporting troops on the ground. Modern attack helicopters are faster and more heavily armed with both guns and rocket launchers.

attain *verb* **1** to complete successfully; to accomplish. **2** to reach. [from Latin *ad*, to + *tangere*, to touch]

attainable *adj.* capable of being attained; achievable.

attainment *noun* **1** attaining; achieving by effort. **2** something that is attained.

Attalids a Hellenistic dynasty that ruled over large parts of W Asia Minor from the 3c to the 1c BC. They were keen patrons of the arts and made their capital, Pergamum, one of the main cultural centres of the Greco-Roman world.

attar *noun* a fragrant oil made from rose petals. [from Persian]

attempt — *verb* **1** to try. **2** to try to climb or master (a mountain, problem, etc). — *noun* (**attempt at something**) an endeavour to achieve something.
— **an attempt on someone's life** an attempt to kill them.
[from Latin *attemptare*, to test]

Attenborough, Sir David Frederick (1926–) English naturalist and broadcaster, born in London, brother of Richard Attenborough. He joined the BBC in 1952 as a trainee producer, and undertook expeditions for the series *Zoo Quest* (1954–64). He became Controller of BBC2 and subsequently Director of Programmes before returning to documentary-making, with such ambitious series as *Life on Earth* (1979), *The Living Planet* (1984), and *The Trials of Life* (1990).

Attenborough, Richard Attenborough, Baron (1923–) English film actor, producer, and director, born in Cambridge, brother of David Attenborough. His early film appearances included a seaman in Noël Coward's *In Which We Serve* (1942) and the young hooligan in *Brighton Rock* (1947). He was actor–producer of several feature films in the 1960s, and became a director in 1969 with *O What a Lovely War!*, followed by *A Bridge Too Far* (1977), *Gandhi* (1982), which won eight Oscars, *A Chorus Line* (1985), *Cry Freedom* (1987), and *Chaplin* (1992).

attend *verb* **1** *trans., intrans.* to be present (at). **2** to go regularly to (eg a school). **3** *intrans.* (**attend to something** *or* **someone**) to devote oneself to them or take action about them. **4** *formal* to accompany or escort. **5** *trans. formal* (**attend on** *or* **upon something**) to follow as a result of it. **6** *trans.* to serve or wait on. [from Latin *attendere*, to direct one's attention to]

attendance *noun* **1** the act of attending. **2** the number of people attending. **3** regularity of attending.

attendance allowance *Brit.* money paid by the government to severely disabled people to pay for a nurse, etc to help them.

attendant — *noun* a person employed to help, especially the public. — *adj.* **1** giving attendance. **2** accompanying.

attention *noun* **1** the act of concentrating or directing the mind. **2** special care and consideration. **3** (**attentions**) an act of politeness or courtship. **4** *Mil.* a position in which one stands rigidly erect with heels together and hands by one's sides. [from Latin *attentio*]

attentive *adj.* **1** concentrating. **2** polite and courteous.

attentively *adv.* in an attentive way; with concentration.

attentiveness *noun* being attentive; concentration.

attenuate *verb* **1** *trans., intrans.* to make or become thin and weak. **2** to reduce the strength or value of. **3** *Physics, said of sound, radiation, electric current, etc* to decrease in intensity as a result of absorption or scattering on passing through a medium. **4** *Medicine* to treat bacteria or viruses in such a way as to diminish greatly their capacity to cause disease, while retaining their ability to evoke an immune response. This procedure is used to produce certain vaccines. [from Latin *attenuare*]

attenuated *adj.* **1** thin. **2** thinned, diluted. **3** tapering.

attenuation *noun* **1** the process of making slender. **2** reduction in strength, virulence, etc. **3** *Physics* a reduction in amplitude or intensity of sound, electromagnetic radiation, etc, caused by absorption, scattering, or friction as it passes through a medium.

Attersee *or* **Kammersee**, English **Lake Atter**, or **Lake Kammer** the largest Alpine lake in Austria. It is situated in Oberösterreich state, N Austria, lying E of Salzburg. AREA 46sq km/ 18sq mi; length 20km/12mi; width 2–3km/ 1–2mi; maximum depth 171m. There are lakeside summer resorts at Seewalchen, Kammer, Weyregg, Steinbach, and Weissenbach.

attest *verb* **1** to affirm or be proof of the truth or validity of. **2** *trans., intrans.* (**attest to something**) to certify that it is so. [from Latin *attestari*, from *ad*, to + *testare*, to witness]

attestation *noun* **1** an act of attesting. **2** the administration of an oath.

attested *adj.* **1** *said of a fact, statement, etc* supported by evidence or proof. **2** *Brit., said of cattle* officially certified free from disease, especially tuberculosis.

Attic — *adj.* **1** relating to ancient Athens or Attica, or the form of Greek spoken there. **2** elegant. — *noun* the form of Greek spoken in ancient Athens. [from Greek *attikos*]

attic *noun* a space or room at the top of a house under the roof. [from ATTIC; such a structure is supposedly in the Athenian style]

Attica the SE promontory of central Greece, and the most easterly part of the Greek mainland. In Classical Greece, it was the territory which made up the city-state of Athens.

Attila (c.406–453 AD) Hunnish king (434–53), called the 'Scourge of God', whose empire extended from the Rhine to the frontiers of China but decayed after his death. In 447 he devastated all the countries between the Black Sea and the Mediterranean, and defeated the emperor Theodosius. He invaded Gaul in 451, and though defeated there he invaded Italy in 452, where Rome itself was saved only by the personal intervention of Pope Leo I, who bribed Attila with large sums of money.

attire *noun* clothing, especially formal or elegant. [from French *atirier*, to put in order]

attired *adj.* dressed, especially formally or elegantly.

Attis *or* **Atys** in Greek mythology, the young male vegetation god connected with the Asiatic cult of Cybele; he died after castrating himself, and was resurrected. The story was later associated with the spring festival.

attitude *noun* **1** a way of thinking or behaving. **2** a position of the body. **3** a pose, especially adopted for dramatic effect: *strike an attitude.* **4** the angle of an aircraft relative to the direction of the air flowing round it or to the horizontal plane, or of a spacecraft relative to its direction of movement. [from French *attitude*, from Latin *aptitudo*, suitability]

attitudinize *or* **attitudinise** *verb intrans.* to adopt an opinion or position for effect.

Attlee (of Walthamstow), Clement (Richard) Attlee, 1st Earl (1883–1967) English Labour politician and Prime Minister, born in Putney, near London. Called to the Bar in 1905, he quickly converted to socialism and became the first Labour Mayor of Stepney (1919–20), MP (1922), Deputy Leader (1931–5), and then Leader of the Opposition (1935). He was Dominions Secretary (1942–3) and Deputy Prime Minister (1942–5) in Churchill's War Cabinet. As Prime Minister (1945–51), he carried through a vigorous programme of nationalization, the National Health Service was introduced, and independence was granted to India (1947) and Burma (1948). He was Leader of the Opposition again in 1951–5.

atto- *combining form* a million million millionth, 10⁻¹⁸. [from Danish or Norwegian *atten*, eighteen]

attorney *noun* (PL. **attorneys**) **1** a person able to act for another in legal or business matters. **2** *North Amer., esp. US* a lawyer.

— power of attorney the right to act for another person in legal and business matters. [from French *atourner*, to turn over to]

Attorney General *noun* (PL. **Attorneys General**, **Attorney Generals**) the principal law officer in England, the USA, and several other countries. In England and Wales, he is a member of the House of Commons and of the government.

attract *verb* **1** to cause to come close or stay close. **2** to arouse or draw to oneself. **3** to arouse liking or admiration; to be attractive to. [from Latin *ad*, to + *trahere*, to draw]

attraction *noun* **1** the act or power of attracting. **2** a person or thing that attracts. **3** *Physics* a force that tends to pull two objects closer together, such as that between opposite electric charges or opposite magnetic poles. See also REPULSION.

attractive *adj.* **1** capable of attracting attention; appealing. **2** good-looking.

attractively *adv.* in an attractive way; pleasingly.

attractiveness *noun* the quality of being attractive.

attributable *adj.* capable of being attributed.

attribute — *verb* (with stress on *-trib-*) (**attribute something to someone** *or* **something**) to think of it as being written, made, said, or caused by them. — *noun* (with stress on *at-*) a quality, characteristic, or feature. [from Latin *attribuere*, to assign to]

attribution *noun* **1** the act of attributing. **2** something that is attributed.

attributive *adj. Grammar, said of an adjective or noun* placed before the noun which it modifies, eg in *young girl* and *buffet car*. See also PREDICATIVE.

attributively *adv. Grammar* with an attributive function.

attrition *noun* **1** a rubbing together; friction. **2** a wearing away or making weaker, especially by continual friction or attacks: *a war of attrition*. [from Latin *attritio*, from *atterere*, to rub]

attune *verb* **1** to adjust to or prepare for (a situation, etc). **2** to put (a musical instrument, an orchestra, etc) into tune.

Attwell, Mabel Lucie (1879–1964) English artist and writer, born in London. She was noted for her studies of children with which she illustrated her own and others' stories for children. From 1911 onwards she drew humorous postcards for Valentines, usually featuring chubby children.

Atwell, Winifred (1914–83) Trinidadian pianist and entertainer, born in Trinidad. A piano-player from early childhood, she turned from a career in pharmacy to become a pop cabaret performer. She had a string of 'ragtime' hits, featuring a jangly, public-bar piano sound, including 'Black and White Rag', 'Coronation Rag', and 'Let's Have a Party'. She enjoyed success later with concerts and records, but faded from view in the 1960s and emigrated to Australia.

Atwood, Margaret (1939–) Canadian poet, novelist, and critic, born in Ottawa. Her major collections include *The Circle Game* (1966), *Procedure for Underground* (1970), *You are Happy* (1974), and *Poems Selected and New, 1976–86* (1986). Among her novels are *The Edible Woman* (1970), *Lady Oracle* (1976), *The Handmaid's Tale* (1985) and *Cat's Eye* (1988). Other works include *Survival* (1972), a celebrated guide to Canadian literature.

atypical *adj.* not typical.

Au *symbol Chem.* gold. [from Latin *aurum*]

aubergine *noun* a tropical plant which produces a dark purple fruit which can be cooked and eaten as a vegetable. [from Sanskrit *vatinganah*]

aubrietia *noun* a small trailing rock plant with pink or purple flowers. [named after Claude Aubriet (1665–1742), French botanist]

auburn *adj., said especially of hair* reddish-brown. [from Latin *alburnus*, whitish, from *albus*, white]

Aubusson, Pierre d' (1423–1503) French grandmaster of the Knights Hospitallers of St John of Jerusalem, born into a noble family in Monteil-au-Vicomte. After fighting against the Turks, and later the Swiss, he joined the Knights (c.1453), and became grandmaster in 1476. Mohammed II's career of conquest, which threatened to spread over W Europe, was halted by d'Aubusson and his small colony of Christian soldiers in Rhodes (1480). He was made a cardinal in 1489.

Auchinleck, Sir Claude (John Eyre) (1884–1981) British soldier. He joined the 62nd Punjabis in 1904, and served in Egypt and Mesopotamia. In World War II, he commanded in N Norway and India, and then moved to the Middle East (1941). He made a successful advance into Cyrenaica, but was later thrown back by Rommel. His regrouping of the 8th Army on El Alamein is now recognized as a successful defensive operation, but at the time he was made a scapegoat for the retreat, and replaced (1942). In 1943 he returned to India, and then served as Supreme Commander India and Pakistan (1947).

Auckland POP (1991) 886 000 (urban area), a seaport city in North I, New Zealand. Founded in 1840, it was the capital between 1840 and 1865 and is now the principal port of New Zealand. NOTABLE FEATURES Waitemata Harbour spanned by Auckland Harbour Bridge (1959); two cathedrals; New Zealand Heritage Park; Howick Colonial Village; Auckland War Memorial Museum; and the Museum of Transport and Technology.

auction — *noun* a public sale in which each item is sold to the person who offers the most money. — *verb* (also **auction something off**) to sell it by auction. [from Latin *auctio*, an increase]

auctioneer *noun* a person who conducts an auction, especially professionally.

audacious *adj.* **1** bold and daring. **2** disrespectful; impudent. [from Latin *audax*, bold]

audaciously *adv.* in an audacious way; daringly.

audacity *noun* boldness.

Auden, W(ystan) H(ugh) (1907–73) English-born US poet, born in York. His early lyric poems reflect his deep concern with the social problems of the 1930s. He wrote *Spain* (1937) in support of the Spanish Republic's cause and (with Isherwood) published *Journey to a War* (1939), a report on Japanese aggression in China. In 1939 he emigrated to New York, but he returned to live in England while he was Professor of Poetry at Oxford (1956–61). His conversion to Anglicanism is evident in the more serious, contemplative nature of his later work. He also collaborated with Isherwood in three plays and, with Chester Kallman, wrote several opera libretti, including *The Rake's Progress* (1951) for Stravinsky.

Audenarde see OUDENAARDE.

audibility *noun* capacity to be heard.

audible *adj.* loud enough to be heard. [from Latin *audire*, to hear]

audibly *adv.* so as to audible.

audience *noun* **1** a group of people watching a performance. **2** the people reached by a film, radio broadcast, book, magazine, etc. **3** a formal interview with an important person. [from Latin *audientia*, from *audire*, to hear]

audio *adj., combining form* relating to hearing, sound, or the recording and broadcasting of sound. [from Latin *audire*, to hear]

audio frequency any frequency that can be detected by the human ear, in the range 20 to 20 000Hz for normal hearing.

audiogram *noun Medicine* a record of a person's hearing ability, in the form of a graph, as measured by an audiometer. It usually indicates hearing ability for a range of sounds of different frequency.

audiometer *noun* **1** *Medicine* an instrument used to measure a person's hearing ability at different sound frequencies. It is used in the diagnosis of deafness. **2** an instrument that is used to measure the intensity of sounds.

audio-typing *noun* the typing of material recorded on a dictating machine.

audio-typist *noun* a person who types letters, etc which have been recorded on a dictation machine.

audiovisual *adj., said of teaching aids, etc* using both sound and vision.

audit — *noun* an official inspection of an organization's accounts by an accountant. — *verb* (**audited**, **auditing**) to examine accounts officially. [from Latin *audire*, to hear]

audition — *noun* a short performance as a test of the suitability of an actor, singer, musician, etc for a particular part or role. — *verb trans., intrans.* (**auditioned**, **auditioning**) to test or be tested by means of an audition. [from Latin *auditio*, from *audire*, to hear]

auditor *noun* a person who audits accounts, especially professionally.

auditorium *noun* (PL. **auditoriums**, **auditoria**) the part of a theatre, hall, etc where the audience sits. [from Latin *auditorium*, a lecture-room, court, etc.]

auditory *adj.* relating to hearing. [from Latin *audire*, to hear]

auditory nerve *Anat.* the eighth cranial nerve, which carries nerve impulses concerned with hearing and balance from the inner ear to the brain.

Audrey 1 a female first name. **2** the simple country goatherd in Shakespeare's *As You Like It*, who is wooed by the nonsensical attentions of Touchstone. [a reduced form of the Anglo-Saxon name *Aedelpryd*, composed of *aedel*, noble + *pryd*, strength]

Audubon, John James (1785–1851) US ornithologist, born in Les Cayes, Santo Domingo. His early life was spent in France, where he studied painting and developed an interest in natural history. Returning to the USA (1804), he travelled and built up his vast collection of bird illustrations, later published in Europe as *The Birds of America* (1827–38), a work which contains coloured figures of 1 065 birds.

AUEW *abbrev.* Amalgamated Union of Engineering Workers.

au fait well informed or familiar. [French, = to the point]

Aug *or* **Aug.** *abbrev.* August.

Augean *adj. literary* filthy. [from the name *Augeas*, a king in Greek mythology whose stables were cleaned by Heracles]

Auger, Pierre Victor (1899–) French physicist, born in Paris. Professor at the University of Paris, he discovered that an atom can de-excite from a state of high energy to a lower energy state non-radiatively, by losing one of its own electrons rather than emitting a photon. He also discovered extended air showers, also known as Auger showers, in which the interaction of cosmic rays with Earth's upper atmosphere produces cascades of large numbers of secondary particles.

auger *noun* a hand-tool with a corkscrew-like point for boring holes in wood. [from Anglo-Saxon *nafogar*; in Middle English, *a nauger* was understood as *an auger*]

aught *pron. old use* anything. [from Anglo-Saxon *awiht*]

augment *verb trans., intrans.* to make or become greater in size, number, strength, amount, etc. [from Latin *augere*, to increase]

augmentation *noun* increase, addition.

augmentative *adj.* tending to augment or increase.

augmented *adj.* **1** having become or been made greater in size, etc. **2** *Mus.* increased by a semitone.

au gratin *adj., said of food* covered and cooked with breadcrumbs and often with grated cheese. [from French *au gratin*]

Augsburg, ancient **Augusta Vindelicorum** POP (1991e) 257 000, an industrial and commercial city in Bavaria, S Germany. It lies at the confluence of the Lech and Wertach rivers, 48km/30mi NW of Munich. HISTORY founded by the Romans in 15 BC; an influential commercial centre in the 15c, the seat of the famous Diets of 1530 and 1555. It is the birthplace of the artist Hans Holbein (1497) and the playwright Bertolt Brecht (1898). NOTABLE FEATURES Renaissance town hall (1615–20); St Ulrich's Minster (1500); Rococo Schaezler Palais.

Augsburg, League of an alliance (1686) against French territorial expansionism formed by Emperor Leopold I, Bavaria, Spain, Sweden, and several German states and circles of the empire. It aimed to defend the Treaties of Nijmegen (1678–9) and Ratisbon (1684), and to challenge Louis XIV's *réunion* policy (legalistic pursuit of territory, especially in disputed border areas). However, continuing mutual provocation between France and the League resulted in the War of the League of Augsburg (1689–97). The war concluded with the restored independence of Lorraine but France retained Alsace.

Augsburg Confession a statement of faith composed by Luther, Melanchthon, and others for the Diet of Augsburg (1530), the official text of which was written by Melanchthon (1531). The earliest of Protestant Confessions, it became authoritative for the Lutheran Church and influenced the Thirty-Nine Articles.

augur *verb intrans.* (*usually* **augur well** *or* **ill**) to be a good or bad sign for the future. [from Latin *augur*, soothsayer]

augury *noun* (PL. **auguries**) **1** a sign or omen. **2** the practice of predicting the future.

August *noun* the eighth month of the year. [from Latin *Augustus*, the first Roman emperor]

august *adj.* (with stress on *-gust*) noble; imposing. [from Latin *augustus*, grand]

Augusta POP (1990) 397 000, the seat of Richmond County, E Georgia, USA, lying on the Savannah R. It is an industrial centre and a popular resort with a notable golf club. HISTORY founded as a river trading post c.1717, it changed hands many times during the War of Independence, and was state capital from 1786 to 1795; during the Civil War the town housed the Confederate powder works.

Augusta POP (1990) 22 000, the capital of the state of Maine, USA, situated in Kennebec County, S Maine. It lies on the Kennebec R, 72km/45mi from the river mouth. Established as a trading post in 1628, it achieved city status in 1849.

Augustan age the age of the emperor Augustus in Rome (27 BC–AD 14) graced by the poets Horace, Ovid, and Virgil. It also lends its name to the classical period of any national literature (eg the age of Dryden, Pope, and Swift in England).

Augustine (of Canterbury), St (d.604) Italian prelate, the first Archbishop of Canterbury. He was prior of a Benedictine monastery in Rome, when in 596 Pope Gregory I sent him with 40 other monks to convert the Anglo-Saxons to Christianity. He was kindly received by Ethelbert, King of Kent, whose wife was a Christian, and whose conversion and baptism enhanced Augustine's influence. As Bishop of the English from 597, he established his church at Canterbury, but did not succeed in extending his authority over the native British Church. After his death his body was transferred to the abbey of Saints Peter and Paul in 612, now the site of St Augustine's Missionary College (1848). His feast day is 26 May.

Augustine (of Hippo), St, originally **Aurelius Augustinus** (AD 354–430) an early Christian and one of the four Latin Doctors of the Church, born in Tagaste, Numidia (modern Tunisia). Brought up a Christian by his devout mother (who became St Monica), he left to study in Carthage, where he took a mistress and fathered a son, Adeonatus (372). He read Cicero and became interested in philosophy, particularly Plato and then the Manichaeans. An enthusiastic student also of the Bible, he and Adeonatus finally became Christians (387). Ordained priest in 391, he proved a formidable antagonist to the heretical schools in the Donatist and Pelagian controversies, and became Bishop of Hippo in 396. He wrote his autobiography *Confessions* (397), *De Civitate Dei*, a vindication of the Christian Church (413–26), and *De Trinitate*, a massive exposition of the doctrine of the Trinity. The central tenets of his creed were the corruption of human nature through the fall of man, the consequent slavery of the human will, predestination, and the perseverance of the saints. His feast day is 28 Aug.

Augustinians, also known as the **Augustinian**, or **Austin Friars**, in full the **Order of the Hermit Friars of St Augustine** (ABBREV. **OSA**) a religious order united in 1255 which follows the monastic teaching and 'rule' of St Augustine (of Hippo). It established missions, monasteries, and hospitals throughout the world. There are also Augustinian nuns of second or third orders ('tertiaries').

augustly *adv.* with an august or imposing manner.

Augustus, also called **Octavian**, adopted name **Gaius Julius Caesar Octavianus** (63 BC–AD 14) the founder of the Roman Empire, son of Gaius Octavius and great-nephew and adopted son of Julius Caesar. After Caesar's assassination (44 BC), he raised an army and defeated Antony (43 BC), but later in the same year formed a triumvirate (the 'Second Triumvirate') with him and Lepidus. They defeated Brutus and Cassius (Caesar's assassins) at Philippi (42 BC), and the Empire was re-divided up between Octavian and Antony, with Octavian receiving the western half of the Empire and Antony the eastern. While Antony was distracted there by his military schemes against Parthia and his liaison with Cleopatra, Octavian aroused opposition to him at home. He defeated Antony in the battle of Actium in 31 BC, emerging as the sole ruler of the Roman world. He ruled as 'princeps' ('first citizen'), until 27 BC, when the name Augustus ('sacred') was conferred on him. During his largely peaceful reign (27 BC–AD 14) he reorganised the administration of the Empire and added several territories to its domain. He was awarded the title Pater Patriae ('Father of his Country') in 2 BC, and was deified on his death.

Augustusburg the 18c Baroque residence of the former electors of Cologne in Brühl, NW Germany. It was designed by Konrad Schlaun, and later Francois Cuvillié for Elector Clemens August (1700–61). It is a World Heritage site.

auk *noun* a seabird with a heavy body, short wings and black and white feathers. [from Norse *alka*]

Auld Lang Syne a Scottish song evoking the days of long ago or old friendship, sung communally with hands linked at moments of leave-taking or at the end of a year. The words were adapted by Robert Burns in 1791 from an earlier lyric.

auld lang syne *Scot.* days of long ago.

aunt *noun* **1** the sister of one's father or mother, or the wife of one's uncle. **2** a close female friend of a child's parents. [from Latin *amita*, father's sister]

auntie *or* **aunty** *noun* (PL. **aunties**) *colloq.* an aunt.

Aunt Sally *noun* (PL. **Aunt Sallies**) **1** a game in which sticks or balls are thrown at a dummy. **2** any target of abuse.

au pair *noun* a young person from abroad, usually a woman, who lives with a family and helps with housework, looking after children, etc in return for board and lodging. [from French *au pair*]

aura *noun* (PL. **auras**, **aurae**) **1** a distinctive character or quality around a person or in a place. **2** a fine substance coming out of something, especially that supposedly coming out of and surrounding the body, which many mystics claim is visible as a faint light. [from Greek *aura*, breeze]

aural *adj.* relating to the sense of hearing or the ears. [from Latin *auris*, ear]
◆ Often confused with *oral*, which refers to the mouth and speaking.

aurally *adv.* by hearing; by ear.

aureate *adj.* **1** golden. **2** elaborately ornamental. [from Latin *aurum*, gold]

Aurelian, originally **Lucius Aurelius Aurelianus** (AD 215–75) Roman emperor (270–5) who reunified the Empire after 40 years of disintegration. He restored army discipline and domestic order, and took successful action against the Goths and Carpi on the Danube, Zenobia of Palmyra in the East, and the breakaway Gallic Empire in the West. For his efforts, he was awarded the title 'Restorer of the Roman World'.

Aurelius, originally **Marcus Aurelius Antoninus** (AD 121–80) Roman emperor (161–80). The adopted son of Antoninus Pius, he ruled as his consul from 146. On his succession to the throne, he voluntarily divided the government with his adopted brother, Lucius Aurelius Verus, until 169. His reign saw constant warfare in Britain, the East, and Germany, and he himself directed operations for almost a decade on the Danube frontier, where he died. One of the most respected of Roman emperors in his lifetime, he was idealized after his death as the model of the perfect emperor. His *Meditations* survive to reveal his innermost thoughts and provide a unique document.

aureole *or* **aureola** *noun* **1** *said in painting* a bright light surrounding the head or body of a holy figure. **2** a circle of light round the sun or moon. [from Latin *aureolus*, golden]

au revoir *interj.* goodbye; until we meet again. [from French *au revoir*]

Auric, Georges (1899–1983) French composer, born in Lodève, Hérault. He studied under D'Indy and became one of the group of young French composers known as 'Les Six'. Inspired by Satie and Stravinsky, his music exemplifies the modern return to counterpoint, and his compositions range from orchestral pieces to ballets, songs and film scores. He was director of the Paris Opéra and Opéra Comique (1962–8), then resigned to compose.

auricle *noun Anat.* **1** the outer part of the ear. **2** the ear-shaped tip of the atrium of the heart. **3** any ear-shaped appendage. [from Latin *auricula*, little ear]

auricular *adj.* **1** belonging or relating to the ear or sense of hearing. **2** known by hearing or report. **3** shaped like an ear. **4** relating to an auricle.

auriferous *adj.* containing gold. [from Latin *aurum*, gold]

Aurignacian in European prehistory, a division of Upper Palaeolithic culture, named after the cave site at Aurignac, Haute Garonne, SW France, excavated in 1852–60 by French archaeologist Eduard Lartet (1801–71). It is characterised by stone scrapers, blades, and bone points (c.33 000–23 000 BC) which occur throughout France/Germany, and less frequently in Hungary/Austria.

aurochs *noun* (PL. **aurochsen**) an extinct wild ox. [from German *urohso*]

Aurora in Roman mythology, the name of the goddess of the dawn, equivalent to the Greek goddess Eos.

aurora *noun* (PL. **auroras**, **aurorae**) 1 *Astron.* the appearance of diffuse bands or curtains of red, green or yellow coloured lights in the night sky, most often observed from the Arctic and Antarctic regions. It is known as the *aurora borealis* (northern lights) in the northern hemisphere, and the *aurora australis* (southern lights) in the southern hemisphere. The phenomenon is caused by a burst of charged particles from the Sun that are deflected by the Earth's magnetic field around the two poles, and collide with oxygen and nitrogen atoms in the upper atmosphere to produce electrical discharges. 2 *poetic* the dawn. [from Latin *aurora*, dawn]

Aurungzebe *or* **Aurangzib (Ornament of the Throne),** kingly title **Alamgir** (1618–1707) the last and most magnificent of the Mughal Emperors of India (1658–1707), born in Dhod, Malwa. The youngest son of Shah Jahan, his struggle for power with his brothers ended when he put them to death. He was a fervent Muslim, which alienated the Hindus and led to war with the Marathas. Though his long reign was distinguished by prosperity, most of his enterprises failed and the empire began to decline.

AUS *abbrev., as an international vehicle mark* Australia.

Auschwitz the largest Nazi concentration camp, on the outskirts of Oświeim, SW Poland, where 3–4 million people, mainly Jews and Poles, were murdered (1940–5). It is a World Heritage Site, and gas chambers, watchtowers, and prison huts are preserved at the camp, part of which is now a museum.

auscultation *noun Medicine* the practice of listening, usually with a stethoscope, to the sounds made by the organs of the body, as a way of diagnosing illness. [from Latin *ascultare*, to listen]

Ausonius, Decimus Magnus (c.309–92 AD) Latin poet, born in Burdigala (Bordeaux). He was tutor to Valentinian's son Gratian, and afterwards held several offices in Gaul. His works include epigrams, poems, epistles in verse and prose, and idylls.

auspices *pl. noun* protection; patronage.
— **under the auspices of someone** *or* **something** *said of an activity or undertaking* arranged or supported by a person, society, etc.
[from Latin *auspicium*, foretelling the future by watching birds]

auspicious *adj.* promising future success; favourable. [see AUSPICES]

auspiciously *adv.* so as to be auspicious; favourably.

auspiciousness *noun* being auspicious or favourable.

Aussie *noun, adj. colloq.* Australian.

Austen, Jane (1775–1817) English novelist, born in Steventon, Hampshire. Of her six major novels, four were published anonymously during her lifetime and two posthumously: *Sense and Sensibility* (1811), *Pride and Prejudice* (1813), *Mansfield Park* (1814), *Emma* (1815), *Persuasion* (1818), and *Northanger Abbey* (1818). The novels are characterized by the psychological insight and muted irony with which she deals with her unextraordinary, usually well-to-do characters.

austere *adj.* 1 severely simple and plain. 2 serious; severe; stern. 3 severe in self-discipline. [from Greek *austeros*, strict, rigorous]

austerely *adv.* with an austere or severe manner.

austerity *noun* (PL. **austerities**) 1 the state of being austere; strictness or harshness. 2 severity and extreme simplicity of dress, etc. 3 a period of economic depression.

Austerlitz, Battle of the victory (2 Dec 1805) of Napoleon I over a combined Austrian–Russian army in Moravia. The Treaty of Pressburg (Bratislava) followed on 26 Dec, by which Austria renounced all interests in Italy, lost most of her western Alpine lands, and saw French hegemony established in western Germany.

Austin (of Longbridge), Herbert Austin, 1st Baron (1866–1941) English car manufacturer, the founder of the Austin Motor Company, born in Little Missenden, Buckinghamshire. After managing several engineering works in Australia, he returned to England and in 1895 produced his first car, the Wolseley – a three-wheeler. In 1905 he opened his own works near Birmingham. Output included the popular 'Baby' Austin 7 (1921). Austin Motor Company merged with Morris Motors in 1952 to form the British Motor Corporation Ltd.

Austin POP (1990) 782 000, the capital of the state of Texas, USA, situated in Travis County, S central Texas. It stands on the Colorado R, 236km/147mi NW of Houston and is the commercial centre for an extensive agricultural region. Electronic and scientific research is also carried out there. HISTORY settled in 1835, it became capital of the independent Republic of Texas in 1839; the Texas government moved to Houston in 1842 for fear of marauding Mexicans and Native Americans; the government returned to Austin in 1845 when Texas joined the Union.

austral *adj.* southern. [from Latin *Auster*, the south wind]

Australasia a term used loosely to include Australia and the islands of New Zealand, New Guinea (including New Britain), New Caledonia, and Vanuatu. It is often described as equivalent to all of Oceania below the Equator and N of 47°S. The name is not used commonly in these areas.

Australasian *adj.* of or relating to Australia, New Zealand, and the nearby Pacific islands.

Australia, official name **Commonwealth of Australia** POP (1992e) 17.6m, an independent country and the smallest continent in the world, situated entirely in the S hemisphere. AREA 7 692 300sq km/2 969 228sq mi. The country is divided into six states and two territories. It is bounded N by the Timor and Arafura seas, NE by the Coral Sea, E by the S Pacific Ocean, and S and W by the Indian Ocean. CAPITAL Canberra. CHIEF TOWNS Melbourne, Brisbane, Perth, Adelaide, Sydney. TIME ZONES GMT +8 (Western Australia), GMT +9.5 (Northern Territory and South Australia), GMT +10 (New South Wales, Queensland, Tasmania, Victoria, Australian Capital Territory). The population is made up of 1% Aborigine and Asian, and 99% Caucasian; Anglicanism and Roman Catholicism are the main religions. OFFICIAL LANGUAGE English. CURRENCY the Australian dollar. PHYSICAL DESCRIPTION almost 40% of its land mass is N of the Tropic of Capricorn; the Australian continent consists largely of plains and plateaus, most of which average 600m above sea level; the West Australian Plateau occupies nearly half the whole area; in the centre are the MacDonnell Ranges: the highest points being Mt Liebig (1 524m) and Mt Zeil (1 510m); in the NW the Kimberley Plateau rises to 936m at Mt Ord and in the W the Hamersley Ranges rise to 1 226m at Mt Bruce; most of the plateau is dry and barren desert, notably the Gibson Desert in the W, the Great Sandy Desert in the NW, the Great Victoria Desert in the S, and the Simpson Desert in the central area; in the S is the Nullarbor Plain; the Eastern Highlands or Great Dividing Range lie parallel to the E seaboard, rising to 2 228m at Mt Kosciusko, in the Australian Alps; between the Western Plateau and the Eastern Highlands lies a broad lowland belt extending S into the Murray-Darling plains; off the NE coast, stretching for over 1 900km/1 200mi, is the Great Barrier Reef; the island of Tasmania, a S extension of the E Highlands, rises to 1 617m at Mt Ossa, and is separated from the mainland by the Bass Strait; Australia's longest river is the Murray, its chief tributaries being the Darling, Murrumbidgee, and Lachlan. Fertile land with a temperate climate and reliable rainfall is limited to the lowlands and valleys near the coast in the E and SE, and to a small part of the SW corner. The population is concentrated in these two regions. CLIMATE more than one third of Australia receives under 260mm average annual rainfall; less than one third receives over 500mm; half the country has a rainfall variability of more than 30%, with many areas experiencing prolonged drought; Darwin's average daily temperature is 26°–34°C in Nov and 19°–31°C in Jul; rainfall varies from 386mm in Jan to zero in Jul; Melbourne's average daily temperature is 6°–13°C in Jul and 14°–26°C in Jan–Feb, with a monthly rainfall averaging 48–66mm; in Tasmania, climatic conditions vary greatly between mountain and coast; there is much heavier rainfall in the W (over 2 500mm per annum in places) than in the E (500–700mm per annum). HISTORY the Aborigines are thought to have arrived in Australia from SE Asia c.40 000 years ago; the first European visitors were the Dutch, who explored the Gulf of Carpentaria in 1606 and landed in 1642; Captain James Cook arrived in Botany Bay in 1770, and claimed the E coast for Britain; New South Wales was established as a penal colony in 1788; in 1829, all the territory now known as Australia was constituted a dependency of Britain; increasing numbers of settlers were attracted to Australia, especially after the introduction of Spanish Merino sheep; gold was discovered in New South Wales and Victoria in 1851 and in Western Australia in

Prime Ministers of Australia	
1901–3	Edmund Barton
1903–4	Alfred Deakin
1904	John Christian Watson
1904–5	George Houston Reid
1905–8	Alfred Deakin
1908–9	Andrew Fisher
1909–10	Alfred Deakin
1910–13	Andrew Fisher
1913–14	Joseph Cook
1914–15	Andrew Fisher
1915–23	William Morris Hughes
1923–9	Stanley Melbourne Bruce
1929–32	James Henry Scullin
1932–9	Joseph Aloysius Lyons
1939	Earle Christmas Page
1939–41	Robert Gordon Menzies
1941	Arthur William Fadden
1941–5	John Joseph Curtin
1945	Francis Michael Forde
1945–9	Joseph Benedict Chifley
1949–66	Robert Gordon Menzies
1966–7	Harold Edward Holt
1967–8	John McEwen
1968–71	John Grey Gorton
1971–2	William McMahon
1972–5	Edward Gough Whitlam
1975–83	John Malcolm Fraser
1983–91	Robert James Lee Hawke
1991–	Paul Keating

1892; transportation of convicts to E Australia ended in 1840, but continued until 1853 in Tasmania and 1868 in Western Australia; during this period, the colonies drafted their own constitutions and set up governments: New South Wales in 1855, Tasmania and Victoria in 1856, South Australia in 1857, Queensland in 1860, and Western Australia in 1890; in 1901 the Commonwealth of Australia was established with Canberra chosen as the site for its capital; a policy of preventing immigration by non-Whites stayed in force from the end of the 19c until 1974. GOVERNMENT the legislature (as of 1980) comprises a bicameral Federal Parliament with a 64-member Senate elected for six years, and a 125-member House of Representatives elected every three years; the Prime Minister and the Cabinet of Ministers are responsible to the House; a Governor-General, representing the Queen (as Queen of Australia), presides over an Executive Council. Northern Territory has been self-governing since 1978. ECONOMY about 26% of total land area is unused (mainly desert); c.67% is used for agricultural purposes, including arid grazing (44%) and non-arid grazing (17%), the country is the world's largest wool producer, and a top exporter of veal and beef; its most important crop is wheat; other major cereals are barley, oats, maize, and sorghum; discoveries of petroleum reserves, bauxite, nickel, lead, zinc, copper, tin, uranium, iron ore, and other minerals in the early 1960s have turned Australia into a major mineral producer; commercial oil production began in 1964; the Gippsland basin produces two-thirds of Australia's oil and most of its natural gas, but major discoveries have been made off the NW coast; manufacturing has expanded rapidly since 1945, especially in engineering, shipbuilding, car manufacture, metals, textiles, clothing, chemicals, food processing, and wine.

Australia, Order of an order established (1975) by Queen Elizabeth II for according recognition to Australian citizens (and others). The order comprises the sovereign, the Governor-General of Australia, the Prince of Wales, and Knights, Dames, Companions, Officers, Members, and Holders. The ribbon is royal blue silk with a central band of golden mimosa blossoms.

Australia Day a public holiday in Australia, 26 January or the first Monday after that, celebrating the landing of the British in 1788.

Australian — *adj.* relating to Australia. — *noun* a person born or living in Australia. [from Latin *australis*, southern]

Australian Alps a chain of mountains in SE Australia forming the S part of the Great Dividing Range. It extends c.300km/185mi SW from Australian Capital Territory to the Goulburn R, Victoria. The range includes the Snowy Mts, Bowen Mts, and Barry Mts. HEIGHT rises to 2 228m at Mt Kosciusko, the highest peak in Australia. This is a popular area for winter sports.

Australian Antarctic Territory an Antarctic territory claimed by Australia in 1936.

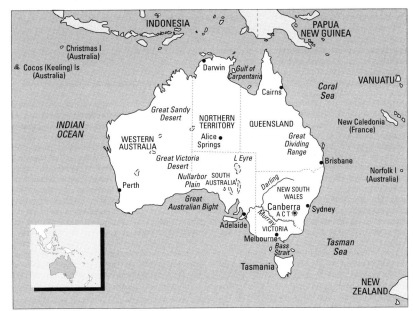

Australia

AREA 6 043 852sq km/2 332 927sq mi of land and 84 798 sq km/32 732sq mi of ice shelf. Scientific stations were established here at Mawson in 1954 and at Vestfold Hills (Davis Base) in 1957. Australia assumed custody of the US Wilkes Station on the Budd Coast in 1959, replacing it with the Casey Station in 1961.

Australian Capital Territory POP (1992e) 295 000, a territory in SE Australia. AREA 2 400sq km/925sq mi. It is bordered on all sides by New South Wales. The territory was created in 1911 to provide a location for the national capital, Canberra. PHYSICAL DESCRIPTION mountainous in the S and drops N through low hills to the urbanized floodplains of the Murrumbidgee and Molonglo rivers. ECONOMY c.60% of the workforce is employed by the government, with electronics and computing being the main manufacturing industries.

Australian East Coast Temperate and Sub-Tropical Rainforest Parks a series of national parks, and nature and flora reserves, extending along the length of the New South Wales coast. The region provides a representative sample of the whole animal and plant life of E Australia, as well as striking examples of landscape diversity, including the Mt Warning Volcano and segments of the Great Escarpment. The parks form a World Heritage area.

Australian gold rush the first significant discovery of gold in Australia, made in 1851 by Edward Hargraves, who publicized his find and attracted 2 000 to the site at Ophir in New South Wales. In the same year, large gold finds were made in Victoria, which accounted for 35% of world gold production (1851–60). Gold was also found in Queensland (1867) and Western Australia (1893). The discovery drew thousands of immigrants into Australia, created a mass movement for democracy, and gave a tremendous boost to the economy. Gold also attracted thousands of Chinese miners, who were greatly resented by the Europeans; this led to anti-Chinese laws and the beginning of the 'White Australia' Policy.

Australian Imperial Force (ABBREV. **AIF**) the volunteer military forces raised in Australia in both World Wars. In World War I, 330 770 men served overseas in the first AIF, of whom 54 000 were killed and 155 000 were wounded. In World War II, 690 000 men and 35 000 women served in the second AIF.

Australian Labor Party (ABBREV. **ALP**) the oldest political party of Australia, founded in 1891 in New South Wales following the defeat of the trade unions in the 1890 strike. The Party spread to all States by the mid-1900s and formed the world's first Labour government in Queensland in 1899 for one week. Its most important national figures have been Prime Ministers W M ('Billy') Hughes (1915–16), James Scullin (1929–32), John Curtin (1941–5), Ben Chifley (1945–9), Gough Whitlam (1972–4), and R J L ('Bob') Hawke (1983–).

Australian Rules football an Australian version of football, developed in Melbourne, Victoria, c.1858. It is a handling and kicking game which is a cross between association football, rugby, and Gaelic football. A match comprises four 25-minute quarters, and is played by two teams of 18 players per side on an oval pitch measuring c.165m long by c.137m wide. The object is to score goals, worth six points, by kicking the oval ball between the opponent's main goal posts. Smaller posts are positioned either side of the main goals, and any kick that goes through that area scores a 'behind', worth one point.

Austral Islands see TUBUAI ISLANDS.

Australopithecus an extinct human-like ape known from fossil remains found particularly in Ethiopia and Kenya, which lived from 5m to 1.5m years ago. It probably walked on two legs, and skeletal and facial characters link australopithecines closely to chimpanzees and gorillas as well as to humans. Four species have been named: *Australopithecus afarensis, Australopithecus africanus, Australopithecus robustus*, and *Australo-*

Australian States and Territories				
	Area		Population	
State or territory	sq km	sq mi	(1992e)	Capital
Australian Capital Territory	2 400	925	295 000	Canberra
New South Wales	801 428	309 351	6 000 000	Sydney
Northern Territory	1 346 200	520 000	168 000 (1991e)	Darwin
Queensland	1 727 200	666 700	3 000 000	Brisbane
South Australia	984 000	380 000	1 500 000	Adelaide
Tasmania	67 800	26 200	470 000	Hobart
Victoria	227 600	87 900	4 500 000	Melbourne
Western Australia	2 525 500	975 000	1 700 000	Perth

pithecus boisei (possibly an E African variant of *A. robustus*), formerly known as *Zinjanthropus*. The superfamily is called *Hominoidea*.

Austria, German **Österreich**, official name **Republic of Austria**, German **Republik Österreich** POP (1992e) 7.9m, a republic in central Europe, divided into nine federal states (*Länder*). AREA 83 854sq km/32 368sq mi. It is bordered to the N by Germany and the Czech and Slovak Republics, to the S by Italy and Slovenia, to the W by Switzerland and Liechtenstein, and to the E by Hungary. CAPITAL Vienna. CHIEF TOWNS Graz, Linz, Salzburg, Innsbruck, Klagenfurt. TIME ZONE GMT + 1. The population is mostly of German origin, with Croatian and Slovene minorities; Roman Catholicism is the main religion. OFFICIAL LANGUAGE German. CURRENCY the Schilling. PHYSICAL DESCRIPTION situated at the E end of the Alps, the country is almost entirely mountainous; the ranges of the Ötztal, Zillertal, Hohe Tauern, and Niedere Tauern stretch eastwards from the main Alpine massif; the highest point is Grossglockner, at 3 797m; chief passes into Italy are the Brenner and Plöcken; most of the country is in the drainage basin of the R Danube; the Neusiedler See on the Hungarian border is the largest lake in Austria. CLIMATE there are three climatic regions: the Alps (often sunny in winter but cloudy in summer); the Danube valley and the Vienna basin (the driest region); and the SE, a region of heavy thunderstorms, with often severe winters but warmer summers than N of the Alps. In general, most rain falls in the summer months; winters are cold; there is a warm, dry wind (the Föhn) in some N–S valleys, especially in autumn and spring, which can be responsible for fires and snow-melt leading to avalanches. HISTORY it was part of the Roman Empire until the 5c, then occupied by Germanic tribes; a frontier area of Charlemagne's empire; became a duchy and passed to the Habsburg family (1282), who made it the foundation of their Empire; the head of the Habsburg house was almost continually the Holy Roman Emperor, making Austria the leading German state; Habsburg defeats in the 19c (notably the Austro-Prussian War) and Hungarian nationalism led to the Dual Monarchy of Austria–Hungary; the assassination of Archduke Franz Ferdinand by Serbian nationalists triggered World War I; a republic was established in 1918 but was annexed by the German Reich in 1938 (Anschluss), under the name *Ostmark*; from 1945 Austria was occupied by British, American, French, and Russian troops; in 1955 it was recognized as an independent democratic state; its neutrality was also declared, since when Austria has been a haven for many refugees. GOVERNMENT the Assembly includes a National Council elected for four years, (183 deputies) and a Council (63 members); a president holds office for six years, and appoints a chancellor; each *Land* is administered by its own government headed by a governor elected by the provincial parliament. ECONOMY the principal agricultural areas along the R Danube and to the N of the Alps produce crops, cattle, orchards, and vineyards; there is forestry on the lower mountain slopes; iron and steel are the main metal and mineral resources, which also include lignite, lead and zinc ores, graphite, talc, kaolin, clay, and salt; other natural resources include oil (and petrochemicals), natural gas, and hydroelectric power; diverse manufacturing industry; tourism.

Austria-Hungary, Dual Monarchy of a constitutional arrangement created by the *Ausgleich* ('compromise') reached in 1867. In Austria–Hungary the Habsburg emperors Francis Joseph (until 1916), and Charles (1916–18), ruled over the twin kingdoms of Austria (the German-, Czech-, Polish-, Slovenian-, and Ruthenian-speaking regions of their empire) as well as Dalmatia and Hungary (the Magyar, Romanian, Slovak, and most Croat and Serb regions). Although the separate kingdoms had consider-

able autonomy over internal policy, foreign and financial policy remained in the hands of the Imperial government. The Dual Monarchy provided a temporary solution to the internal problems of the Habsburg Empire, but was ultimately destroyed by defeat in World War I.

Austrian Succession, War of the a European conflict over the succession to the hereditary Habsburg lands of Maria Theresa, which developed after 1744 into a colonial conflict between Britain and the Franco-Spanish bloc. On the death of Emperor Charles VI, Bavaria, Saxony, and Spain, backed by France, refused to recognize the Pragmatic Sanction and invaded Bohemia and Upper Austria. The wars began when Frederick II of Prussia seized and eventually conquered Silesia in two campaigns (1740–5). In 1745 Bavaria withdrew from the struggle, when the son and successor of Charles Albert, holder of the Bohemian and imperial crowns, renounced all claims to them. The subsequent intervention of Russia on Austria's side led to peace negotiations and to the Treaty of Aix-la-Chapelle (1748), under the terms of which the Habsburg monarchy retained almost all its dominions with the exception of Silesia.

Austro-Asiatic — *adj.* denoting a family of over 100 languages used in SE Asia. It includes three main branches, Mon-Khmer, Munda, and Nicobarese. — *noun* the languages forming this family.

Austronesian — *adj.* denoting the most numerous and (after Indo-European) the most widely dispersed of the world's great language families. It includes some 700 languages in two main groups: the western group of c.400 languages spoken in Madagascar, Malaysia, Indonesia, the Philippines, Taiwan, and W New Guinea; and the smaller eastern group, also known as Oceanic, spoken in Melanesia, Micronesia, and Polynesia. — *noun* the languages forming this group.

Austro-Prussian War a war (1866) fought between Austria and Prussia over the duchies of Schleswig and Holstein. It was declared on 14 June, decided by the Prussian victory at Königgrätz (sometimes known as Sadowa) on 3 July, and ended by the Treaty of Prague on 23 August. The defeat of Austria hastened German unification, allowed Italy (Prussia's ally) to acquire Venetia, and precipitated the creation of Austria–Hungary.

AUT *abbrev.* Association of University Teachers.

autarchy *noun* (PL. **autarchies**) government of a country by a ruler who has absolute power. [from Greek *autos*, self + *archein*, to rule]

autarky *noun* (PL. **autarkies**) economic self-sufficiency: the condition of a country that is a closed economy conducting no international trade. This is sometimes the aim of national economic policy, with tariffs and other trade barriers being erected as in Germany and Italy in the 1930s. [from Greek *autarkeia*, from *autos*, self + *arkeein*, to suffice]

Austria

authentic *adj.* **1** genuine. **2** reliable; trustworthy. [from Greek *authentikos*]

authentically *adv.* in an authentic way; so as to be authentic.

authenticate *verb* to prove to be true or genuine.

authentication *noun* **1** proof of being genuine or valid. **2** the state of having validity.

authenticity *noun* **1** the quality of being authentic; genuineness. **2** being true.

author *noun* **1** the writer of a book, article, play, etc. **2** the creator or originator of an idea, event, etc. [from Latin *auctor*]

authoritarian — *adj.* in favour of, or insisting on, strict authority. — *noun* an authoritarian person.

authoritarianism *noun* being authoritarian; authoritarian behaviour.

authoritative *adj.* **1** accepted as a reliable source of knowledge. **2** having authority; official.

authoritatively *adv.* with authority; in an authoritative way.

authority *noun* (PL. **authorities**) **1** the power or right to control or judge others. **2** (*often* **authorities**) the person or people who have power, especially political or administrative. **3** a position which has such a power or right: *be in authority*. **4** the ability to influence others, usually as a result of knowledge or expertise. **5** an expert: *an authority on birds*. **6** a passage in a book used to support a statement. [from Latin *auctoritas*, from *auctor*, author]

authorization *or* **authorisation** *noun* **1** the act of authorizing; permission. **2** legality, right.

authorize *or* **authorise** *verb* **1** to give (someone) the power or right to do something. **2** to give permission for. [from Latin *auctorizare*, from *auctor*, author]

Authorized Version, also known as the **King James Bible** an English translation of the Bible, commissioned by James VI and I. Accomplished by a panel of leading scholars of the day who used Greek and Hebrew texts and earlier English translations, it was noted for its literary excellence and became very popular after its first publication (1611). It was never formally 'authorized' by king or Parliament.

authorship *noun* **1** the origin, or attribution to an author, of a particular piece of writing. **2** the profession of writing.

autism *noun Psychol.* a rare and severe mental disorder that develops in early childhood, characterized by learning difficulties, extreme self-absorption, inability to relate to other people and the outside world, repetitive body movements, and strong resistance to changes in familiar surroundings. [from Greek *autos*, self]

autistic *adj.* characteristic of or suffering from autism.

autistically *adv.* in a way suggestive of or characterized by autism.

auto *noun* (PL. **autos**) *North Amer. colloq.* a motor car. [abbreviation of AUTOMOBILE]

auto- *combining form* of or by oneself or itself: *autograph / automatic*. [from Greek *autos*, self]

autobahn *noun* a motorway in Austria, Switzerland, or Germany. [from German *Auto*, car + *Bahn*, road]

autobiographer *noun* a person who writes an autobiography.

autobiographical *adj.* relating to or in the nature of autobiography.

autobiography *noun* (PL. **autobiographies**) **1** the story of a person's life written by that person. **2** this as a literary form.

autocatalysis *noun Chem.* a catalytic reaction initiated by the products of another catalytic reaction.

autoclave *noun* an apparatus for sterilizing objects using steam under high pressure. [from Greek *autos*, self + Latin *clavis*, key or *clavus*, nail]

autocracy *noun* (PL. **autocracies**) absolute government by one person; dictatorship. [from Greek *autos*, self + *kratos*, power]

autocrat *noun* 1 a ruler with absolute power. 2 an authoritarian person.

autocratic *adj.* typical of an autocrat; authoritarian.

autocratically *adv.* with an autocratic manner.

autocross *noun* motor-racing on a rough grass track.

Autocue *noun trademark* a screen, unseen by an audience, which displays a speaker's script, so that he or she may speak without being seen to be reading.

auto-da-fé *noun* (PL. **autos-da-fé**) 1 *Hist.* the ceremonial passing of sentence on heretics by the Spanish Inquisition. 2 the public burning of a heretic. [from Portuguese *auto da fé*, act of the faith]

autogenics *sing. noun Medicine* a system of relaxation, also used in the treatment of psychosomatic disorders, designed to facilitate voluntary control of bodily tension. [from Greek *autogenes*, self-generated]

autogiro *or* **autogyro** *noun* (PL. **autogiros**, **autogyros**) an aircraft like a helicopter with large horizontal rotating blades turned by the forward motion of the aircraft and so keeping the machine in the air. It was designed by the Spaniard Juan de la Cierva (1895–1936) in 1923. [from Greek *autos*, self + *gyros*, circle.]

autograph — *noun* 1 a person's signature, especially a famous person's, kept as a souvenir. 2 a manuscript in the author's handwriting. — *verb* to sign (a photograph, etc). [from Greek *autos*, self + *graphein*, to write]

autoimmunity *noun* the production by the body of antibodies that attack constituents of its own tissues, treating them as foreign material.

Autolycus 1 in Greek mythology, a well-known thief who was the maternal grandfather of Odysseus. He was said to be a son of Hermes. 2 the endearing rogue in Shakespeare's *The Winter's Tale*, who scrapes a living by stealing and selling sheets.

autolysis *noun Biol.* the breaking down of dead tissue by enzymes produced in the organism's own cells. [from Greek *autos*, self + *lysis*, loosening]

automat *noun North Amer., esp. US* an automatic vending machine.

automate *verb* to convert (a factory, etc) to automation.

automated *adj.* mechanized and automatic.

automatic — *adj.* 1 *said of a machine or instrument* capable of operating on its own by means of a self-regulating mechanism, and requiring little human control once it has been activated, eg a vehicle assembly plant. 2 *said of an action* done without thinking; unconscious; spontaneous. 3 happening as a necessary and inevitable result. 4 *said of a firearm* able to reload itself and so able to fire continuously. 5 *said of a motor vehicle* having automatic transmission. — *noun* 1 an automatic firearm. 2 a vehicle with automatic transmission. [from Greek *automatos*, self-moving]

automatically *adv.* 1 with automatic action; in an automatic way. 2 as a necessary consequence: *unattended bags are automatically impounded.*

automatic pilot a device that keeps an aircraft on a preset course.

automatic teller machine (ABBREV. **ATM**) an electronic panel set into the exterior wall of a bank, etc from which (on insertion of one's cash card and the keying of one's personal identification or 'PIN' number) cash or account information can be obtained.

automatic transmission in a motor vehicle, a system that allows the gears to be selected and engaged automatically in response to variations in speed, gradient, etc, as opposed to a manually controlled gearbox.

automation *noun* the use of automatic machinery in manufacturing and data-processing, so that entire procedures can be automatically controlled with minimal or no human intervention.
◇ Automated systems are used to perform repetitive tasks, such as the assembly of components of motor vehicles, welding, machining, and stock control, using automatically controlled robots, machine tools, etc. Such systems can also be used for decision-making processes, eg to pilot aircraft or to control the flow of vehicles through sets of traffic lights.

automaton *noun* (PL. **automatons**, **automata**) 1 a machine with a usually hidden electronic or clockwork control which makes it move. 2 a person who acts like a machine, according to routine and without thinking.

automobile *noun North Amer., esp. US* a motor car. [from French *automobile*, from Greek *autos*, self + Latin *mobilis*, mobile]

automotive *adj.* relating to motor vehicles. [from Greek *autos*, self + Latin *motivus*, causing to move]

autonomic nervous system *Physiol.* (ABBREV. **ANS**) that part of the nervous system which supplies the glands (eg the salivary and sweat glands), heart muscle, and smooth muscle (eg the walls of blood vessels and the bladder). It consists of the sympathetic nervous system and the parasympathetic nervous system. See also SYMPATHETIC NERVOUS SYSTEM, PARASYMPATHETIC NERVOUS SYSTEM.

autonomous *adj.* 1 self-governing. 2 independent of others.

autonomously *adv.* with autonomy; independently of others.

autonomy *noun* (PL. **autonomies**) 1 the power or right of self-government. 2 personal freedom. [from Greek *autos*, self + *nomos*, law]

auto-oxidation *noun Chem.* oxidation brought about by oxygen in the atmosphere.

autopilot same as AUTOMATIC PILOT.

autopsy *noun* (PL. **autopsies**) an examination of a dead body to find out the cause of death. [from Greek *autos*, self + *opsis*, sight]

autoradiography *noun Physics, Biol.* a technique for showing the positions of radioactively labelled molecules within the cells or tissues of a specimen, by placing the specimen over a photographic emulsion. The emulsion is then devel-

oped, and the image formed represents the distribution of the radioactive content of the specimen.

auto-reverse *noun* a feature on a cassette recorder, etc causing automatic playing of the reverse side after completion of the first.

autoroute *noun* a motorway in France. [French, from *auto*, car + *route*, road]

autosome *noun Genetics* a chromosome other than a sex-chromosome. [from Greek *autos*, self + *soma*, body]

autostrada *noun* a motorway in Italy. [Italian, from *auto*, car + *strada*, road]

auto-suggestion *noun Psychol.* a form of psychotherapy that involves repeating ideas to oneself in order to change attitudes or habits, eg to reduce anxiety.

auto-suggestive *adj.* relating to or typical of auto-suggestion.

autotrophism *Biol.* the capability of building up food materials from inorganic matter. [from Greek *autos*, self + *trophe*, food]

autumn *noun* 1 the season of the year, between summer and winter, when leaves change colour and fall. 2 a period of maturity before decay. [from Latin *autumnus*]

autumnal *adj.* 1 associated with or typical of autumn. 2 characteristic of the later part of a person's life.

autumnal equinox *Astron.* the equinox that occurs annually around 23 Sep, when the Sun's path crosses the celestial equator from north to south, so that day and night are of equal length.

autumnally *adv.* in an autumnal way; so as to suggest autumn.

autumn crocus, a plant (*Colchicum autumnale*) that produces corms and has lance-shaped glossy leaves, so called because the lilac goblet-shaped flowers appear during the autumn. Each flower consists of six petals fused below to form a long tube. — Also called *meadow saffron*.

Auvergne POP (1991e) 1.3m, a region and former province of central France, comprising the departments of Allier, Cantal, Haute-Loire, and Puy-de-Dôme. AREA 26 013sq km/10 041sq mi. PHYSICAL DESCRIPTION Haute-Auvergne is a mountainous area in the W, Basse-Auvergne is in the R Allier Valley; the highest peaks are in the Monts Dore, with Puy de Sancy at 1 886m; the sources of the rivers Loire, Cher, Allier, Dordogne, and Lot lie in the region. HISTORY formerly a Roman province, it later became a duchy and in the 10c a principality which was united to France in 1527. CAPITAL Clermont-Ferrand. ECONOMY agriculture, mineral springs, cattle, wheat, wine, cheese. [named after the Arverni, whose chieftain was Caesar's most famous opponent in the Gallic Wars.]

Auxerre, Latin **Autissiodorum** POP (1990) 41 000, a market town and the capital of Yonne department, Burgundy, central France. It stands on the R Yonne, surrounded by orchards and

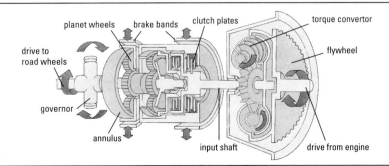

automatic transmission

vineyards, and is one of the oldest towns in France. NOTABLE FEATURES St Etienne Gothic cathedral; abbey church of St Germain with 9c frescoes.

auxiliary — *adj.* **1** helping or supporting. **2** additional or extra. — *noun* (PL. **auxiliaries**) **1** a helper. **2** (**auxiliaries**) foreign troops helping another nation at war. **3** *Grammar* an auxiliary verb. [from Latin *auxiliarius*, from *auxilium*, help]

auxiliary language a natural language adopted by people of different speech communities to aid communication. English and French are often used in this way, for example, in many parts of Africa, and particularly in the spheres of trade and education. The term is also used for certain artificial languages, especially Esperanto.

auxiliary verb *noun* a verb which shows the tense, voice, or mood of the main verb in a phrase, eg *should, will, can.*

auxin *noun Bot.* any of a large group of plant hormones that promote growth of plant tissues by an increase in the size of existing cells, rather than an increase in cell number. Low levels of auxin promote growth and high levels inhibit it. Auxins are used commercially as 'rooting powders' and weedkillers. [from Greek *auxein*, to increase]

AV *abbrev.* Authorized Version (of the Bible).

Ava a female first name, popularized by the film star Ava Gardner. [probably of Germanic origin, or a modern invention]

avail — *verb trans., intrans.* to help or be of use. — *noun* use; advantage: *of no avail.* — **avail oneself of something** to make use of it or take advantage of it. [from Latin *valere*, to be worth]

availability *noun* the state or degree of being available: *special offers are subject to availability.*

available *adj.* able or ready to be obtained or used.

availably *adv.* so as to be available.

avalanche *noun* **1** the rapid movement of a large mass of snow or ice down a mountain slope under the force of gravity. **2** a sudden appearance of a large number of people or things. [from French *avalanche*]

Avalon in Celtic mythology, the land of the dead, the place to which King Arthur was taken after his death. The name possibly means 'land of apples'.

avant-garde — *noun* those writers, painters, musicians, etc whose ideas and techniques are the most modern or advanced. — *adj., said of a work of art, idea, etc* using or supporting the most modern and advanced ideas in literature, art, music, etc. [from French *avant-garde*, vanguard]

avarice *noun* a great desire for money, possessions, etc. [from Latin *avaritia*, from *avere*, to crave]

avaricious *adj.* greedy for money, possessions, etc.

avariciously *adv.* in an avaricious way; greedily.

Avarua the port capital of the Cook Is, S Pacific Ocean. It is situated on the island of Rarotonga.

avatar *noun* the appearance of a Hindu god in human or animal form. [from Sanskrit *ava*, down + *tar-*, pass over]

Ave or **Ave Maria**, a prayer to the Virgin Mary. See also HAIL MARY. [from Latin *ave*, from *avere*, to be well; the opening words of the angel's greeting to Mary in Luke 1.28]

Ave. *abbrev.* avenue.

Avebury a village in North Wiltshire district, Wiltshire, England, on the R Kennet. It is the site of the largest megalithic monument in England, which was in use c.2600–1600 BC. The site consists of a 427m diameter earthwork, with a 9m-

deep ditch and a 5m-high outer bank. The enclosure, which comprises three stone circles, is approached by a 2.4km/1.5mi avenue of 100 paired stones. It is a World Heritage site.

avenge *verb* to punish (someone) in return for (harm they have done to someone). [from Old French *avengier*, from Latin *vindicare*, to claim]

avenger *noun* a person who takes avenging action.

avenging *adj.* wanting to be avenged; in or for revenge.

avenue *noun* **1** a broad road or street, often with trees along the sides. **2** a tree-lined approach to a house. **3** a means or way: *explored several avenues before deciding on a plan.* [from Latin *advenire*, to come to]

Avenue at Middelharnis, The a painting by Meindert Hobbema (1689, National Gallery, London).

aver *verb* (**averred, averring**) to state firmly. [from Latin *ad*, to + *verus*, true]

average — *noun* **1** the usual or typical amount or number. **2** the result obtained by adding together a group of numbers and dividing the total by the number of numbers in the group; eg the average of 4 and 8 is (4+8)÷2, ie 6. — *adj.* **1** usual or ordinary. **2** estimated by taking an average. **3** mediocre. — *verb* **1** to obtain the numerical average of. **2** to amount to on average. — **average out** to result in an average or balance: *it averaged out at 3 each.* **on average** usually; normally. [from Arabic *awariya*, damaged goods]

Averroës or **Averrhoës**, properly **Ibn Rushd** (1126–98) Islamic philosopher, born in Córdoba. He served as a judge and physician in Córdoba, Seville, and Morocco. He wrote extensive commentaries on many of Aristotle's works, which were both influential and controversial in the development of scholastic philosophy in the Middle Ages.

averse *adj.* (**averse to something**) reluctant about it or opposed to it: *not averse to helping.* [from Latin *aversus*]

aversion *noun* **1** a strong dislike. **2** an object of strong dislike. [from Latin *aversio*, from *aversus*, averse]

aversion therapy treatment which changes part of a person's behaviour by associating it with an unpleasant feeling.

avert *verb* **1** to turn away: *avert one's eyes.* **2** to prevent (especially danger). [from Latin *ab*, from + *vertere*, to turn]

Avery, Oswald Theodore (1877–1955) Canadian-born US bacteriologist, born in Halifax, Nova Scotia. During his career at the Rockefeller Institute Hospital, New York (1913–48), he confirmed that a non-virulent, rough-coated strain of the bacteria which causes pneumonia could be transformed into the virulent smooth strain in mouse serum, by the mere presence of some of the dead (heat-killed) smooth bacteria. He went on to show that the transformation is actually caused by deoxyribonucleic acid (DNA) present in the dead bacteria. This work was a prelude to the realization that the informational molecules which carry the whole reproductive pattern of any living species (the genes) are simply DNA, an idea which emerged around 1950.

Aves *pl. noun Zool.* in the animal kingdom, the class of vertebrates that comprises the birds. [from Latin *avis*, bird]

Avesta the scriptures of Zoroastrianism, written in Avestan (a language of the eastern branch of the Indo-European family) and assembled in the 3c–7c AD . Traditionally believed to have been revealed to Zoroaster, only the *Gathas*, a set of 17 hymns, may be attributed to him, and only a few parts of the original survive.

aviary *noun* (PL. **aviaries**) a large enclosed area in which birds are kept. [from Latin *aviarium*, from *avis*, bird]

aviation *noun* **1** the science or practice of flying in aircraft. **2** the aircraft industry. [from Latin *avis*, bird]

aviator *noun old use* an aircraft pilot.

Avicebrón, properly **Solomon ben Yehuda ibn Gabirol** (1020–c.1070) Jewish poet and philosopher, born in Malaga, Spain. His major work, *Fons Vitae* (Fountain of Life), translated from the Arabic, is largely Neoplatonist and inspired the Kaballists.

Avicenna, Arabic **Ibn Sina** (980–1037) Islamic philosopher and physician, born near Bokhara. He was physician to several sultans, and for some time vizier in Hamadan, in Persia. His philosophy was Aristotelianism modified by Neoplatonism; his medical system, set out in *The Canon of Medicine*, was a standard text in Europe and the Middle East.

avid *adj.* **1** enthusiastic. **2** (**avid for something**) eagerly wanting it. [from Latin *avidus*, from *avere*, to crave]

avidity *noun* greediness, eagerness.

avidly *adv.* greedily, eagerly.

Aviemore POP (1981) 2 500, a town in Badenoch and Strathspey district, Highland region, N central Scotland. It is situated on the R Spey between the Cairngorms to the E and the Monadhliath Mts to the W. The town is an all-year tourist resort and a skiing and winter sports centre.

Avignon, Latin **Avenio** POP (1990) 181 000, the walled capital of Vaucluse department, Provence-Alpes-Côte d'Azur region, SE France, situated on the left bank of the R Rhône. It was the papal residence from 1309 to 1376, and the centre of an important school of painting. Today it is a popular tourist destination. NOTABLE FEATURES ruins of the 12c Pont St Benezet, subject of the folk-song 'Sur le Pont d'Avignon'; Gothic Palais des Papes; many churches and museums. The British philosopher John Stuart Mill died here in 1873.

Avignon School a group of artists, mostly Italian, who worked for the papal court in exile in Avignon (1309–77), especially Simone Martini. The *Pietà* by an unknown artist (c.1460, Louvre) is generally considered to be the major work of the school.

Ávila or **Ávila de los Caballeros**, ancient **Avela, Abula,** or **Abyla** POP (1987e) 44 000, an ancient walled city, and the capital of Ávila province, Castilla-León, central Spain. It lies 115km/71mi W of Madrid at an altitude of 1 130m. Ávila was the birthplace of Queen Isabella and St Teresa. NOTABLE FEATURES cathedral (11c); Monastery of St Thomas; Churches of St Peter and St Vincent; town walls. The old town and churches are a World Heritage site.

avionics *Aeron.* the scientific study of the development and use of electronic and electrical devices for aircraft and spacecraft. [from AVIATION + ELECTRONICS]

avocado *noun* (PL. **avocados**) **1** a tropical evergreen tree of the genus *Persea* of the laurel family (Lauraceae), with large oval leaves, small yellowish flowers, and a pear-shaped fruit. **2** (*also* **avocado pear**) the edible pear-shaped fruit of this tree, which has a large hard seed enclosed by creamy flesh and a rough thick greenish-brown skin. It is eaten fresh, eg as a starter or in salads. [from Aztec *ahuacatl*]

avocado oil an edible oil used in salad dressings, hair and skin conditioners, and as a base for cosmetics.

avocation *noun old use* **1** a diversion or distraction from one's main occupation; a hobby. **2** *colloq.* a vocation. [from Latin *avocatio*, from *ab*, from + *vocare*, to call]

avocet *noun* a wading bird with long legs, black and white feathers, and a long thin beak curving up at the end. [from French *avocette*]

Avogadro, (Lorenzo Romano) Amedeo (Carlo) (1776–1856) Italian (Piedmontese) physicist and chemist, born in Turin, where he was later appointed professor. He succeeded his father as Count of Quaregna in 1787, and later abandoned official law and public positions to concentrate on science. In 1811 he formulated the famous hypothesis that equal volumes of all gases contain equal numbers of molecules when at the same temperature and pressure (Avogadro's law), an idea which was ignored during his own lifetime. He also introduced the idea of a polyatomic molecule.

Avogadro's constant *or* **Avogadro's number** *Chem.* the number of atoms, molecules, or ions that are present in a mole of any substance. It has a value of 6.02×10^{23}.

Avogadro's law *or* **Avogadro's rule** *Chem.* the law which states that under the same conditions of temperature and pressure equal volumes of gases contain the same number of molecules.

avoid *verb* **1** to keep away from (a place, person, action, etc). **2** to stop, prevent, manage not to, or escape. [from French *avoidier*]

avoidable *adj.* capable of being avoided; unnecessary.

avoidably *adv.* so as to be avoidable; unnecessarily.

avoidance *noun* the act of avoiding or shunning, especially a duty or responsibility.
◆ Note that *tax avoidance* involves legal ways of reducing the amount of tax one pays, whereas *tax evasion* involves illegal ways.

avoirdupois *noun* a system of weights based on a pound weighing 16 ounces. [from Old French *aveir de pes*, to have weight]

Avon POP (1992e) 968 000, a county in SW England, divided into six districts. AREA 1 347sq km/520sq mi. It is bounded N by Gloucestershire, E by Wiltshire, S by Somerset, and W by the estuary of the R Severn. Avon includes parts of the Cotswolds and Mendip Hills. CHIEF TOWNS Bristol (county town), Bath, Weston-super-Mare. ECONOMY food processing, high technology, tourism.

Avon, River **1** a river in S England, length 112km/70mi. It rises in NW Wiltshire, and flows S, W, and NE through Bath and Bristol to meet the Bristol Channel at Avonmouth. **2** a river in central England, length 75km/47mi. It rises at Naseby in Northamptonshire, and flows SW through Warwickshire, then Hereford and Worcester to meet the R Severn at Tewkesbury in N Gloucestershire. [from Celtic *avon*, river, stream]

avow *verb* to state openly; to declare; to admit. [from Latin *advocare*]

avowal *noun* a declaration, acknowledgement, or confession.

avowed *adj.* declared; admitted: *their avowed intention.*

avowedly *adv.* as is avowed; admittedly.

Avril a female first name. [from Anglo-Saxon *eofor*, boar + *hild*, battle; possibly a French variant of APRIL]

avuncular *adj.* of or like an uncle, especially in being kind and caring. [from Latin *avunculus*, maternal uncle]

AWACS *abbrev.* Airborne Warning and Control System, an aircraft-mounted radar system able to detect and track hostile intruders at long range and direct friendly fighters to intercept them. The US air force operates the Boeing E-3 Sentry AWACS. The Sentry is also flown by a joint European NATO unit, has been supplied to Saudi Arabia, and is on order for the British and French air forces.

await *verb* **1** to wait for. **2** to be certain to happen (to someone) in the future. [from French *awaitier*]

awake — *verb intrans., trans.* (PAST TENSE **awoke**; PAST PARTICIPLE **awoken**) **1** to stop sleeping or cause to stop sleeping. **2** to become active or cause to become active. — *adj.* **1** not sleeping. **2** alert or aware. [from Anglo-Saxon *awæcnian* & *awacian*]

awaken *verb trans., intrans.* (**awakened, awakening**) **1** to awake. **2** to start feeling or be aware of.

awakening *noun* **1** becoming awake. **2** wakening. **3** reanimating.

award — *verb* to give (someone something) especially as a payment or prize. — *noun* **1** a payment, prize, etc awarded. **2** a legal judgement. [from French *awarder*]

aware *adj.* **1** (*often* **aware of something** *or* **someone**) knowing about them or conscious of them. **2** well informed. [from Anglo-Saxon *gewær*]

awareness *noun* being aware, consciousness.

Awash a valley in E Ethiopia, which contains the Awash National Park. The lower valley is a World Heritage site.

awash *adj.* **1** covered or flooded by water. **2** (**awash with something**) covered by a large amount of it.

away — *adv.* **1** (*often* **away from something**) showing distance or movement from a particular place, position, person, or time. **2** in or to another, usual, or proper place: *put the books away.* **3** gradually into nothing: *fade away.* **4** continuously: *work away.* **5** as one wishes: *ask away.* **6** *said of a sporting event* on the opponent's ground. — *adj.* **1** not present. **2** distant: *not far away.* **3** *said of a sporting event* played on the opponent's ground. — *noun* a match won by a team playing on their opponent's ground. [from Anglo-Saxon *aweg, onweg*]

awe — *noun* admiration, fear, and wonder. — *verb* to fill with awe. [from Norse *agi*]

aweigh *adv., said of an anchor* in the process of being raised from the bottom of the sea. [from A³ + WEIGH]

awe-inspiring *adj.* causing awe.

awesome *adj.* causing awe; dreaded.

awestricken *or* **awestruck** *adj.* filled with awe.

awful — *adj.* **1** *colloq.* very bad. **2** *colloq.* very great: *an awful shame.* **3** awe-inspiring, terrible or shocking. — *adv. colloq.* very.

awfully *adv.* **1** very badly. **2** *colloq.* very; extremely: *awfully expensive.*

awfulness *noun* being bad or awful; horror.

awhile *adv.* for a short time. [from Anglo-Saxon *æne hwil*, a while]

awkward *adj.* **1** clumsy and ungraceful. **2** embarrassed or embarrassing. **3** difficult, dangerous or inconvenient to deal with: *an awkward customer / make things awkward for him.* [from Norse *ofugr*, turned the wrong way + -WARD]

awkwardly *adv.* with an awkward or clumsy manner; so as to cause embarrassment.

awkwardness *noun* **1** being awkward. **2** clumsiness. **3** an embarrassing situation or circumstance.

awl *noun* a pointed tool for making small holes, especially in leather. [from Anglo-Saxon *æl*]

awn *noun Bot.* in some grasses, eg barley, a small stiff bristle projecting from the lemma (one of the bracts enclosing a floret) or glumes (bracts at the base of the spikelet); a similar structure projecting from a fruit or leaf tip. [from Norse *ogn*]

awning *noun* a soft plastic or canvas covering above the entrance to a shop, hotel, etc which can be extended to give shelter from the sun or rain.

awoke, awoken *see* AWAKE.

AWOL *abbrev.* absent without leave: absent from one's place of duty without official permission.

awry *adj., adv.* **1** twisted to one side; crooked(ly). **2** wrong; amiss. [from A³ + WRY]

AWU *abbrev.* Australian Workers' Union, the largest Australian trade union from the early 1900s to 1970, and still one of the largest, with 120 000 members in 1985. It was formed in 1894 by the amalgamation of the shearers' union (formed 1886) and the rural labourers' union (formed 1890).

axe — *noun* **1** a tool with a long handle and a heavy metal blade, for cutting down trees, chopping wood, etc. **2** a severe cut in spending or staff. — *verb* **1** to get rid of or dismiss. **2** to reduce (costs, services, etc).
— **have an axe to grind** to have a personal, often selfish, reason for being involved in something.
[from Anglo-Saxon *æcs*]

Axelrod, Julius (1912–) US pharmacologist, born in New York City. Working at the Clinical Sciences Laboratory at the National Institutes for Mental Health (1955–84), he discovered the substance which inhibits nerve impulses, laying the basis for significant advances in the treatment of mental illnesses such as schizophrenia. He shared the 1970 Nobel Prize for Physiology or Medicine with Ulf von Euler and Bernard Katz.

axial *adj.* of, forming, or placed along an axis.

axiality *noun* an axial state or quality.

axil *noun Bot.* the upper angle between a leaf and the stem from which it grows. [from Latin *axilla*, armpit]

axillary *adj. Bot.* relating to the axil. [from Latin *axilla*, armpit]

axiom *noun* **1** a fact or principle which is generally accepted as true. **2** a self-evident statement. [from Greek *axios*, worthy]

axiomatic *adj.* **1** obvious; self-evident. **2** containing or based on axioms.

axiomatically *adv.* so as to be axiomatic; self-evidently.

Axis the name coined by Mussolini for the co-operation of Nazi Germany and Fascist Italy (1936–45). In May 1939 the two countries signed a formal treaty, the *Pact of Steel*. In September 1940, Germany, Italy, and Japan signed a tripartite agreement, after which all three were referred to as Axis Powers.

axis *noun* (PL. **axes**) **1** an imaginary straight line around which an object, eg a planet, rotates. **2** an imaginary straight line about which a body is symmetrical. **3** *Geom.* one of the lines of reference used to specify the position of points on a graph, eg the horizontal x-axis and vertical y-axis in Cartesian co-ordinates. **4** *Anat.* in vertebrates, the second cervical vertebra, which articulates with the atlas vertebra and enables the head to be moved from side to side. **5** (**Axis**) see as separate entry. [from Latin *axis*, axle, pivot]

axle *noun* a rod on which a wheel or pair of wheels turns. [from Norse *öxull*]

axolotl *noun* a newt-like salamander which lives in Mexican lakes. [an Aztec word, from *atl*, water + *xolotl*, servant]

axonometric *noun* an architectural drawing showing a building in three dimensions. It is produced by placing the plan at an angle and projecting the verticals upwards; all lines are drawn to scale, with parallel lines remaining parallel, so that the drawing appears distorted due to lack of perspective. [from Greek *axon*, axis + *metron*, measure]

Axum *or* **Aksum** an ancient town on the Eritrean coast in N Ethiopia. A Greek-influenced Semitic trading state, it was founded about the beginning of the Christian era. From its port at Adulis it dominated the trade of the Red Sea, and in the 3c extended its power to Yemen. At the height of its influence under King Ezana (c.320–50), who accepted Christianity, it later became the basis of the Christian kingdom of Ethiopia.

Ayacucho, Battle of the last major battle (1824) of the Spanish–American wars of independence, fought in the Peruvian Andes, and a notable victory for the Venezuelan General de Sucre.

ayah *noun* a native maid, especially formerly in India and some other parts of the British Empire. [from Hindi *aya*, from Latin *avia*, grandmother]

ayatollah *noun* a Shi'ite religious leader in Iran. [from Arabic *ayatollah*, sign of God]

Ayckbourn, Alan (1939–) English playwright, born in London, who since 1964 has worked as a producer in Scarborough. The first of many West End successes was *Relatively Speaking* (1967). Soon established as a master of farce and later a savage social commentator, among his most successful farces are *Absurd Person Singular* (1973) and *Joking Apart* (1979). He has also written two musicals, and plays for children.

aye¹ *or* **ay** — *interj. dialect* yes. — *noun* a vote in favour. [equivalent to *I*, expressing agreement]

aye² *adv. old use, poetic* always. [from Norse *ei*, ever]

aye-aye *noun* a nocturnal primitive primate from Madagascar, having a shaggy coat, a long bushy tail, large ears, and extremely long slender fingers, especially the third finger, which is used to probe for wood-boring insects. It lives in trees. [from Malagasy *aiay*]

aye-aye

Ayer, Sir A(lfred) J(ules) (1910–89) British philosopher who became Grote Professor at University College London in 1947, and was Wykeham Professor of Logic at Oxford (1959–78). His antimetaphysical *Language, Truth, and Logic* (1936) rendered in English the doctrines of the 'Vienna Circle' of logical positivist philosophers, whom he visited in 1932. He also wrote *The Problem of Knowledge* (1956) and several collections of essays.

Ayers Rock, aboriginal name **Uluru** a huge, red rock in SW Northern Territory, Australia, 450km/280mi SW of Alice Springs. It is the largest monolith in the world and lies within the Uluru National Park. HEIGHT rises from the desert to 348m; it is 3.6km/2.2mi long, 2.4km/1.5mi wide, and 8.8km/5.5mi in circumference. The resort town of Yulara is situated 20km/12mi NW.

Ayeshah *or* **Aïsha** (c.610–77) the third and favourite of Muhammad's nine wives. She bore him no children, and on his death, when she was about 22, she resisted Ali, the Prophet's son-in-law, and secured the caliphate for her father, Abu-Bekr.

Ayia Napa POP (1987e) 1 000, an old fishing village in Famagusta district, SE Cyprus. Ayia

Napa and nearby Paralimni have become the second most important tourist areas on the island. NOTABLE FEATURE Monastery of Ayia Napa (16c).

Aylesbury POP (1981) 53 000, the county town in Aylesbury Vale district, Buckinghamshire, S central England. It lies N of the Chiltern Hills, 60km/37mi NW of London. NOTABLE FEATURE St Mary's Church (13c).

Aylward, Gladys (1902–70) English missionary in China, born in London. She arrived in China in 1930, and with a Scottish missionary, Mrs Jeannie Lawson, founded the Inn of the Sixth Happiness in Yangcheng. From there in 1938 she made a great trek across the mountains leading over 100 children to safety during the war with Japan. After nine years with the Nationalists caring for the wounded, she returned to England in 1948, preached for five years, then in 1953 settled in Taiwan as head of an orphanage. The 1958 film *The Inn of the Sixth Happiness*, starring Ingrid Bergman, was based on her life.

Ayn, Al POP (1989e) 176 000, a rapidly developing new city in the emirate of Abu Dhabi, United Arab Emirates. It lies 150km/93mi E of the city of Abu Dhabi and has developed on the site of an oasis village. NOTABLE FEATURES fort; archaeological sites nearby; Al Ayn National Park, 16km/10mi S.

Ayr POP (1981) 50 000, the capital of Kyle and Carrick district, Strathclyde, SW Scotland. It stands on the Firth of Clyde, at the mouth of the R Ayr, 48km/30mi SW of Glasgow. NOTABLE FEATURES Loudoun Hall (15c–16c); Tam o' Shanter Museum; the town of Alloway, birthplace of poet Robert Burns, is 3km/2mi S; Culzean Castle (1777) is 19km/12mi SW.

ayurveda *noun* a traditional Indian system of medicine, based on correcting disharmonies in the body which are considered the causes of disease. [Sanskrit, from *ayur*, life, and *veda*, knowledge]

Ayutthaya a city in central Thailand, the former capital of the country. The remains of the old city are a World Heritage site.

AZ *abbrev.* Arizona.

azalea *noun* a garden shrub related to the rhododendron, with pink or purple flowers. [from Greek *azaleos*, dry]

Azaña (y Díaz), Manuel (1880–1940) Spanish politician, born in Alcalá de Henares. A qualified lawyer, he founded a political party, *Acción Republicana* in 1925. In the nascent Second Republic (1931), he was Minister of War and then Prime Minister (1931–3) of a reforming government, where he became identified with army reform and anticlericalism. After a period of opposition, he resumed the premiership (Feb 1936) and was elevated to the presidency (May 1936), where he remained throughout most of the Spanish Civil War, before Franco forced him into exile in France (1939).

Azariah, Prayer of one of three Additions to the Book of Daniel in the Old Testament Apocrypha or Catholic Bible, usually linked with the Song of the Three Young Men. Known also as the *Benedictus es* in Catholic forms of worship, it consists of a lamentation for the sins of Israel by Azariah (Abednego in Daniel 1.6ff), who with Shadrach and Meshach was cast into a furnace for his adherence to Israel's religion (Daniel 3).

Azerbaijan *or* **Azarbaijchan Respublikasky** *or* **Azerbaydzhan** *or* **Azerbaydzhanskaya** POP (1993e) 7.4m, a republic in E Transcaucasia. AREA 86 600sq km/33 428sq mi. It is bounded E by the Caspian Sea and S by Iran; Armenia splits the country in the SW and forms the W boundary; Georgia and the Russian Federation lie to the N. PHYSICAL DESCRIPTION crossed by the Greater Caucasus in the N and the Lesser Caucasus in the SW; they are separated by the plain of R Kura; the highest peak is Mt Bazar-

Dyuzi (4 480m) in the NE; forests cover 10.5% of the country's total area. HISTORY proclaimed a Soviet Socialist Republic in 1920; became a constituent republic of the Soviet Union in 1936; dispute from 1988 with neighbouring Armenia over the Nagorno Karabakh region; riots promoted by the nationalist Azerbaijan Popular Front (Dec 1988–Jan 1990) culminated in an anti-Armenian pogrom in the capital; Soviet troops mounted a violent assault on the city to restore order; independence was declared in 1991; full-scale war with Armenia erupted in 1992; internal unrest continued. CAPITAL Baku. CHIEF TOWNS Kirovabad, Sumgait. ECONOMY oil extraction and refining; iron; steel; aluminium; copper; chemicals; cement; foodstuffs; textiles; carpets; fishing; timber; salt extraction; grain; cotton; rice; grapes; fruit; vegetables; tobacco; silk.

Azerbaijan

Azhar, al- a Muslim university and mosque founded in 970 in Cairo, Egypt. Allegedly the oldest university in the world, it was once the centre of Islamic learning, and is now chiefly a school of Koranic teaching. [Arabic, = the resplendent]

Azikiwe, Nnamdi (1904–) Nigerian journalist and politician, born in Zungeri. He studied and taught in the USA before returning to Africa to edit the *African Morning Post* (1934–7) in Accra and the *West African Pilot* (1937) in Nigeria. He took a leading part in the Nigerian nationalist movement and helped found the National Council of Nigeria and the Cameroons (NCNC) of which he was President (1946–60). He became Prime Minister of the Eastern region (1954–9), Governor-General of Nigeria (1960–3), and first President of the Nigerian republic (1963–6). He was in Britain during the military uprising of 1966, when his office was suspended, but he returned to Nigeria and became Leader of the Nigeria People's Party in 1979 and a member of the Council of State (1979–83).

azimuth *noun Astron.* in astronomy and surveying, the bearing (direction) of an object, eg a planet or star, measured in degrees as the angle around the observer's horizon clockwise from north, which is the zero point. See also ALTITUDE. [from Arabic *al*, the + *sumut*, directions]

Azores, Portuguese **Ilhas dos Açôres** POP (1991) 242 000, an island archipelago of volcanic origin in the N Atlantic Ocean. It constitutes an autonomous region of Portugal and lies 1 400–1 800km/870–1 100mi to the W of the Cabo da Roca on mainland Portugal. AREA 2 300sq km/900sq mi. There are three widely separated groups of islands: Flores and Corvo in the NW; Terceira, Graciosa, São Jorge, Faial, and Pico in the centre; and Santa Maria with the Formigas Islands and São Miguel, the principal island, in the E. The highest point is Pico, at 2 351m. HISTORY the Azores were settled by the Portuguese in 1439; in 1466 the islands were made over to Isabella of Burgundy; thereafter there was a considerable influx of Flemish settlers. CHIEF TOWN Ponta Delgada (on São Miguel). ECONOMY grain, fruit, tea, tobacco, wine. [from Portuguese *ilhas dos açôres*, islands of the hawks]

Azov, Sea of, Russian **Azovskoye More** the NE gulf of the Black Sea, bordering Russia and Ukraine. The Kerch Strait connects it to the Black Sea. The gulf's main arms are the Gulf of Taganrog in the NE and the Sivash or Putrid Sea in the W. The latter is mostly swamp, almost completely cut off from the Sea of Azov by a sandspit. The water of the Black Sea is shallow and almost fresh, tending to freeze in the winter months (Nov–Mar). River deposits cause further shallowing and silting of the harbours. The gulf is an important source of freshwater fish for Russia.

Aztec — *noun* **1** a member of a Mexican Indian people whose great empire was overthrown by the Spanish in the 16c. **2** the language spoken by this people, also called *Nahuatl*. — *adj.* of the Aztec people, their language and culture. [from Aztec *aztecatl*, men of the north]
◇ The Aztecs built up a powerful despotic state with a strong military force, and subjugated neighbouring peoples, who paid tribute in raw materials and produce. Their largest city was Tenochtitlan (present-day Mexico City), and their best known ruler Montezuma II. They had a highly developed system of agriculture, introducing irrigation, draining swamps, and creating artificial islands in the lakes. They developed a form of hieroglyphic writing and a complex calendar, and built monumental pyramids and temples.

Azuero a peninsula in W central Panama, on the Pacific Ocean coast. It forms the W side of the Gulf of Panama and is 80km/50mi long. The peninsula rises to 829m at Cerro Canajagua.

azure — *adj.* of a deep sky-blue colour. — *noun* a deep sky-blue colour. [from Persian *lajward*, lapis lazuli]

B

B¹ *or* **b** *noun* (PL. **Bs**, **B's**, **b's**) **1** the second letter of the English alphabet. **2** (*usually* **B**) the second highest grade or quality, or a mark indicating this. **3** (**B**) *Mus.* **a** the seventh note in the scale of C major. **b** a musical key with the note B as its base.

B² *abbrev.* **1** Bachelor. **2** bass. **3** *as an international vehicle mark* Belgium. **4** *Chess* bishop. **5** *on pencils* black.

B³ *symbol Chem.* boron.

b. *abbrev.* **1** born. **2** *Cricket* bowled.

BA *abbrev.* **1** Bachelor of Arts. **2** British Airways.

BAA *abbrev.* British Airports Authority.

baa — *noun* the cry of a sheep or lamb. — *verb intrans.* (**baaed**, **baaing**) to make this cry.

Baade, (Wilhelm Heinrich) Walter (1893–1960) German-born US astronomer, born in Schröttinghausen. Working at Mount Wilson Observatory in California from 1931, he discovered the existence of two discrete stellar types or 'populations', characterized by blue stars in spiral galaxies and fainter red stars in elliptical galaxies. His telescope observations also succeeded in resolving the centre of the Andromeda galaxy and two of its companions into stars.

Baader–Meinhof Group the popular name for *Rote Armee Fraktion* (RAF), after its leaders, Andreas Baade (1943–77) and Ulrike Meinhof (1934–76). It was a left-wing German revolutionary terrorist group, and carried out political bombings in Germany in the early 1970s. Baader, Meinhoff, and 18 other members were arrested in 1972.

Baal the Phoenician god of clouds and tempest, and fertility. He is named in the Hebrew Bible, where his Canaanite fertility cult is condemned. In the Ras Shamra texts, he fights various enemies (including Yam, the god of the sea, and Mot, the god of death and sterility) to achieve supremacy over the gods. [Hebrew, = lord]

Baal

Baalbek, ancient **Heliopolis** POP (1982e) 14 000, a town in E Lebanon. The Phoenicians built a temple at Baalbek to Baal. NOTABLE FEATURES Temple of Jupiter, Temple of Bacchus. The town is a World Heritage site.

Ba'ath Socialist Party the political manifestation of Ba'athism, an Islamic ideology of the 1930s. Founded in 1943 by Michel Aflaq (1910–) and Salah al-Din Bitar, the party's ideology faced problems in combining a Marxist social analysis with an Islamic religious basis, but eventually became the ruling party in both Syria and Iraq. However the term became divorced from its ideological bases and failed to improve relations between the two countries. [from Arabic, = resurgence]

baba *or* **rum baba** *noun* a type of small sponge cake soaked in a rum-flavoured syrup. [from French *baba*, from Polish]

Babbage, Charles (1792–1871) English mathematician, born in London. Lucasian Professor of Mathematics at Cambridge (1828–39), he spent most of his life attempting to build two calculating machines. His 'difference engine' was designed for the calculation of tables of logarithms and similar functions by repeated addition performed by trains of gear wheels, but was never completed. His 'analytical engine' was designed to be programmed by punched cards and perform many different computations, but was too ambitious to be constructed with the mechanical devices of the time.

Babbitt, Irving (1865–1933) US scholar and critic, born in Dayton, Ohio. He was Professor of French at Harvard (1894–1933). Primarily a moralist and teacher, he was a leader of the 'new humanism' which flourished in the USA in the 1920s.

Babbitt a novel by Sinclair Lewis (1922). It tells of the estate agent George Babbitt's uneasy co-existence with the middle-class society of the city of Zenith.

babble *verb* **1** *trans.*, *intrans.* to talk or say quickly, especially in a way that is hard to understand. **2** *intrans. colloq.* to talk foolishly. **3** *intrans. formal literary, used of water, especially a stream* to make a low murmuring sound. **4** *trans.* to give away (a secret) carelessly. [probably imitative]

babbler *noun* a songbird native to warmer regions of the Old World, and having soft, usually brown, fluffy plumage and short wings. It feeds on insects, seeds, fruit, and nectar, and usually lives in small groups.

babbling *adj.* **1** making a murmuring sound, as of gently flowing water. **2** *said of a person* making incomprehensible sounds.

Babcock, Harold Delos (1882–1968) US physicist and astronomer, born in Edgerton, Wisconsin. He joined the staff of the Mount Wilson Observatory in 1909. With his son, he invented the solar magnetograph (1951), which made possible detailed observations of the Sun's magnetic field and resulted in the discovery of magnetically variable stars. He also discovered that the Sun reverses its magnetic polarity periodically (1959).

babe *noun* **1** *colloq. North Amer., esp. US, often used as a term of affection* a girl or young woman. **2** *old use, literary* a baby. [probably imitative of the sound made by a baby]

Babel, Tower of a structure described in the Old Testament (Genesis 11.1–9), which was probably an important temple shrine in the ancient city of Babylon. Its construction led to the confusion of languages, and the consequent dispersion of peoples, as a punishment by God for human pride.

babel *noun* **1** a confused sound of voices. **2** a scene of noise and confusion. [from Hebrew *Babel*]

Babeuf, François-Noël (1760–97) French communist, born in St Quentin, who during the Revolution (as 'Gracchus Babeuf') advocated a rigorous system of communism (Babouvism). His conspiracy to destroy the Directory (1796) and establish an extreme democratic and communistic system (a 'Republic of Equals') was discovered, and he was guillotined.

Babe Zaharias, pseudonym of **Mildred Zaharias**, *née* **Didrikson** (1914–56) US sportswoman, born in Port Arthur, Texas. At the age of 16 she set a world javelin record of 40.61m, and at the age of 18, in the 1932 Olympics, she won gold medals in the 80m hurdles (in world record time) and javelin, and a silver medal in the high jump. In golf she won the US Amateur championship in 1946, and the British Amateur title in 1947 — the first American to win both titles. As a professional she won the US Women's Open in 1948, 1950, and 1954. She also excelled at diving, billiards, and lacrosse.

Babington, Antony (1561–86) English Roman Catholic conspirator, born in Dethick, Derbyshire. He served as a page to Queen Mary of Scotland when she was a prisoner in Sheffield, and in 1586 John Ballard and others persuaded him to lead a conspiracy to effect Elizabeth's murder and Mary's release (the Babington Plot). Coded messages intercepted by Francis Walsingham led to the execution of the conspirators and were also used against Mary.

Babinski reflex *or* **Babinski effect** *Psychol.* a reflex curling upwards of the big toe when the outer side of the foot is stroked, normal in children up to two years of age. [named after the French neurologist Joseph Babinski (1857–1932)]

Babi Yar a ravine near Kiev in the Ukraine into which over 30 000 Jews were herded and massacred by Nazi German troops in 1941. It is also the title of a poem by Yevegeny Yevtushenko (1961) and a novel by Anatoly Kuznetsov (1966) dedicated to the victims.

baboon *noun* **1** any of various large ground-dwelling monkeys, most of which are native to Africa, although the hamadryas or sacred baboon also occurs in Arabia. They are smaller than chimpanzees, and have long dog-like muzzles with large teeth, and long tails. **2** *derog.* a clumsy or stupid person. [from Old French *babuin*]
◇ Baboons live in close family groups called troops, feed mainly on fruit, insects, and roots, and can be serious pests when raiding crops. Old males can be fierce fighters, and have been known to force a lion or other predator to retreat. Baboons are fast runners because their front and hind legs are of about the same length, and although they spend most of their life on the ground, they sleep in trees at night.

Babur, Zahiruddin Muhammad (1493–1530) the first Mughal Emperor of India, born in Fergana, central Asia. A descendant of Ghengis Khan and founder of the Mughal dynasty, he occupied Delhi and Agra in 1526. As well as a distinguished soldier, he was a poet and diarist.

baby — *noun* (PL. **babies**) **1** a newborn or very young child or animal. **2** an unborn child. **3** the youngest member of a group. **4** *derog.* a childish person. **5** *colloq.* a person's own particular project, responsibility, etc. **6** *colloq. North Amer., esp. US* a term of affection. — *verb* (**babies, babied**) to treat as a baby.
— **be left holding the baby** *colloq.* to be left with the responsibility for something.
throw out the baby with the bathwater *colloq.* to give up or throw away the important part of something when getting rid of an unwanted part.
[probably imitative of the sound a baby makes]

babyhood *noun* the time of life when one is a baby.

babyish *adj. derog.* childish; immature.

Babylon the capital of the Babylonian Empire from the 18c BC, situated on the R Euphrates S of Baghdad, modern Iraq. Its city walls and 'hanging gardens', attributed by classical tradition to Semiramis, who was wife of Shamshi-Adad V (823–811 BC), regent (811–806 BC), were one of the wonders of the ancient world. It was destroyed by Sennacherib in 689 BC, then rebuilt, particularly during the reign of Nebuchadnezzar II (605–562 BC). Archaeologists began to visit the site in the 18c, but the most important work was done in the early 20c by Robert Koldewey who excavated the Processional Street and the Ishtar Gate as well as palaces and temples and the site of the Tower of Babel.

Babylonia the region in Lower Mesopotamia around the ancient city of Babylon, which in antiquity twice formed the core of extensive but short-lived empires. The first, covering the whole of Mesopotamia, was created by the Amorite king Hammurabi (c.1795–1750 BC) but destroyed by the Hittites (c.1595 BC). The second arose from the Babylonian overthrow of Assyria in 612 BC; under Nebuchadnezzar II (605–562 BC) it stretched as far east as the Mediterranean. It was finally conquered by the Persians in 539–538 BC.

Babylonian exile the mass deportation of the Jews from Palestine to Babylonia in 587–586 BC, after the failure of their revolt against Nebuchadnezzar.

baby-sit *verb trans., intrans.* to look after a child (usually in its own home) while the parents are out.

baby-sitter *noun* a person who looks after a child while the parents are out.

baby-sitting *noun* looking after a child while the parents are out.

baby talk, the way in which adults talk to very young children, mimicking the immature speech forms perceived as the main features of infant language. These include simplified sentences, such as *apple all gone*, or word pronunciation, such as *doggie*. Most parents naturally adopt this form of speech, and while it is disapproved of by some people, there is no evidence that its use harms the process of language acquisition. See also CARETAKER SPEECH, MOTHERESE.

baby-walker *noun* a frame with a seat and wheels in which a baby can sit while learning to walk.

BAC *abbrev.* British Aircraft Corporation.

Bacall, Lauren, originally **Betty Perske** (1924–) US film actress, born in New York City. She first appeared in *To Have and Have Not* (1944), opposite Humphrey Bogart, whom she later married, appearing again with him in *The Big Sleep* (1946), *Dark Passage* (1947), and *Key Largo* (1948). After his death in 1957, she continued in tough sophisticated parts on screen and stage. Later films include *The Shootist* (1976), *The Fan* (1981), and *Misery* (1990).

baccalaureate *noun* **1** *formal* a Bachelor's degree. **2** a diploma of a lower status than a degree. [from French *baccalauréat*, from Latin *baccalaureus*, bachelor]

baccarat *noun* a card game in which players bet money against the banker. [from French *baccarat*]
◇ The object of the game is to assemble, in no more than two or three cards, a total points value of 9: picture cards and the 10 count as 0, the ace as 1, and other cards according to their face value. If the total points value is a double figure, the first figure is ignored, eg 18 becomes 8. Variations, which differ only in the banking arrangements, include *baccarat banque*, *chemin de fer*, and *punto banco*.

Bacchae, The a play by Euripides (c.406 BC). It is a tragedy about Dionysus, the god of wild and uncontrolled ecstasy, and his prudish enemy Pentheus.

Bacchanal a painting by Titian (c.1518, Prado, Madrid).

bacchanal *noun* **1** *literary* a noisy and drunken party. **2** a follower of Bacchus (Dionysus), the god of wine and pleasure in ancient Greece and Rome. [from Latin *bacchanalis*]

Bacchanalia the ancient orgiastic rites of Bacchus (Dionysus), the god of nature, fertility, and wine. They were banned from Rome in 186 BC on the grounds that they were a threat to morality and public order.

bacchanalian *adj. literary* characteristic of a bacchanal; riotous.

Bacchus see DIONYSUS.

Bacchus a statue by Michelangelo (1496–7).

Bacchus and Ariadne a painting by Titian (c.1523, National Gallery, London).

baccy *noun* (PL. **baccies**) *colloq.* tobacco.

Bach, C(arl) P(hilipp) E(manuel) (1714–88) German composer, born in Weimar, the second surviving son of Johann Sebastian Bach. In 1740 he became cembalist (a cembalo is an instrument like a harpsichord or dulcimer) to the young Frederick (later 'the Great') and in 1768 director of music at the main churches in Hamburg. He wrote the first methodical treatment of clavier playing, and composed numerous concertos, keyboard sonatas, church, and chamber music.

Bach, Johann Christian, known as **the London Bach** (1735–82) German composer, the eleventh and youngest son of Johann Sebastian, born in Leipzig. After becoming a Catholic, in 1760 he was appointed organist in Milan, where he composed ecclesiastical music, including a 'Requiem' and two settings of the 'Te Deum', as well as operas. In 1762 he settled in London, became composer to the London Italian Opera and musician to Queen Charlotte, and later collaborated with K F Abel (1723–87) and developed symphonic form.

Bach, Johann Sebastian (1685–1750) German composer, one of the world's greatest musicians, born in Eisenach. Orphaned by the age of 10, he was brought up by his older brother, Johann Christoph (1671–1721), organist at Ohrdruf, who taught him the organ and clavier. In 1703 he became organist at Arnstadt, but found his duties as choirmaster irksome, and he left to become organist at Mühlhausen. In 1711 he became kapellmeister to Prince Leopold of Anhalt-Cöthen, where he wrote mainly instrumental music, including the *Brandenburg Concertos* (1721) and *The Well-tempered Clavier* (1722). Widowed and left with four children, in 1721 he married Anna Magdalena Wilcke (1701–60); only six of his 13 children survived. In 1723 he was appointed cantor of the St Thomas School in Leipzig, and produced such works as c.300 church cantatas, the *St Matthew Passion* (1727), the *Mass in B Minor*, and *The Art of Fugue*. He was almost totally blind when he died. One of his main achievements was his remarkable development of polyphony. Known to his contemporaries mainly as an organist, his genius as a composer was not fully recognized until the following century.

bachelor *noun* **1** an unmarried man. **2** (**Bachelor**) a first university degree, or a person who has taken a degree: *Bachelor of Arts*. See also MASTER. [from Old French *bacheler*]

bachelorhood *noun* the time of life when one is a bachelor.

Bach flower healing *Medicine* a form of homeopathic therapy in which the healing properties of flowers are used to treat disease by relieving mental and emotional symptoms which are thought to be its cause. [named after the UK physician Edward Bach]

bacillus *noun* (PL. **bacilli**) **1** *Biol.* any of a large group of rod-shaped Gram-positive bacteria of the genus *Bacillus* that are widely distributed in soil and air, mainly as spores. Most bacilli are harmless to humans, but many species cause food spoilage, and some are responsible for serious diseases, eg anthrax, tuberculosis, diphtheria, and tetanus. **2** any rod-shaped bacterium. [from Latin *bacillus*, little stick]

back — *noun* **1** the rear part of the human body from the neck to the base of the spine. **2** the upper part of an animal's body. **3** the part of an object that is opposite to or furthest from the front. **4** the side of an object that is not normally seen or used. **5** the upright part of a chair. **6** *Football, Hockey* a player whose role is to defend. — *adj.* **1** located or situated behind or at the back. **2** of or from an earlier date: *back pay*. **3** away from or behind (especially something more important): *back roads*. — *adv.* **1** to or towards the rear; away from the front. **2** in or into an original position or condition. **3** in return or in response: *hit back*. **4** in or into the past: *look back to happier days*. — *verb* **1** to help or support, usually with money. **2** *trans., intrans.* (*usually* **back away** *or* **out** *or* **out of**) to move or cause to move backwards. **3** to bet on the success of (a horse, etc). **4** to provide a back or support for. **5** to accompany (a singer) with music. **6** to lie at the back of. **7** *intrans. Naut., said of the wind* to change direction anticlockwise.
— **back down** to concede an argument or claim, especially under pressure or opposition.
back off 1 to move backwards or retreat. **2** to back down.
back on to something *said of a building, etc* to have its back next to or facing something.
back out of something to withdraw from a promise or agreement, etc.
back to front 1 with the back where the front should be. **2** in the wrong order.
back someone up to support or assist them.
back something up to copy computer data on to a disk or tape.
get off someone's back *colloq.* to stop annoying or troubling them.

have one's back to the wall *colloq.* to be in a very difficult or desperate situation.

put one's back into something *colloq.* to do a task with all one's energy.

put someone's back up *colloq.* to make them annoyed or resentful.

see the back of someone or **something** *colloq.* to be rid of or finished with someone or something unpleasant or tiresome.
[from Anglo-Saxon *bæc*]

backache *noun* a pain in the back.

backbench *adj.* relating to the back benches in parliament.

backbencher *noun* in the UK, Australia, etc, a Member of Parliament who sits on the back benches, ie does not hold an official position in either the government or the opposition. See also FRONTBENCHER.

Backbite, Sir Benjamin one of the frivolous gossip-mongers in Sheridan's *The School for Scandal.*

backbite *verb intrans. colloq.* to speak unkindly about someone who is absent.

backbiting *noun* unkind remarks about someone who is absent.

backbone *noun* **1** the spine. **2** the main support of something (in physical and abstract senses): *the chairman is often the backbone of a company.* **3** firmness and strength of character.

backbreaking *adj., said of a task, etc* extremely hard or tiring.

backchat *noun Brit.* impertinent or rude replies, especially to a superior.

backcloth or **backdrop** *noun* the painted cloth at the back of a stage, forming part of the scenery.

backcomb *verb* to comb (the hair) towards the roots to make it look thicker.

back-cross *Genetics* a cross between a hybrid and a parent.

backdate *verb* **1** to put a date on (a document, etc) that is earlier than the actual date. **2** to make effective from a date in the past.

back door **1** the rear door to a building. **2** a clandestine or illicit means of achieving an objective: *by the back door.* **3** (*attributive*) (*often* **back-door**) denoting an activity done secretly, and often dishonestly.

backdrop see BACKCLOTH.

backer *noun* a person who gives financial support to a project, etc.

backfire *verb intrans.* **1** *said of an engine or vehicle* to produce a loud bang caused by the explosion of accumulated unburned or partially burned gases in the exhaust or inlet system. **2** *said of a plan, etc* to go wrong and have a bad effect on the originator.

back-formation *noun Grammar* **1** the making of a new word as if it were the root or simpler form of an existing word. **2** a word made in this way, eg *laze* from *lazy.*

backgammon *noun* a board game for two people, with pieces moved according to the throws of a dice. [from BACK + Middle English *gamen*, game]

background *noun* **1** the space behind the main figures of a picture. **2** a less noticeable or less public position: *stay in the background.* **3** the events or circumstances that precede and help to explain an event, etc. **4** a person's social origins, education, etc.

background radiation *Physics* naturally occurring radiation which can be detected at any place on Earth, and results from cosmic rays reaching the Earth from outer space, and from natural radioactive sources on Earth, eg certain rocks.

backhand *noun* **1** *Tennis* a stroke made with the back of the hand turned towards the ball (see also FOREHAND). **2** handwriting with the letters sloping backwards.

backhanded *adj.* **1** made with or as a backhand. **2** *said of a compliment* ambiguous or doubtful in effect.

backhander *noun* **1** a backhand stroke of a ball. **2** *colloq.* a bribe.

Back I–IV, The a series of sculptures in bronze by Henri Matisse (1909–30).

backing *noun* **1** support, especially financial. **2** material, etc that supports the back of something. **3** music accompanying a singer.

backing store *Comput.* a large-capacity computer data store supplementary to a computer's main memory.

backlash *noun* **1** a sudden violent reaction to an action, situation, etc. **2** a jarring or recoil between parts of a machine that do not fit together properly.

backless *adj.* lacking or not requiring a back.

backlog *noun* a pile or amount of uncompleted work.

backmarker *noun* a competitor at the back of the field in a race.

back number **1** a copy or issue of a newspaper or magazine that is earlier than the current one. **2** *colloq.* a person or thing that is out of date or no longer useful.

backpack — *noun North Amer., esp. US* a rucksack. — *verb intrans.* to go hiking with a pack on the back.

backpacker *noun* a person who travels with a backpack.

backpacking *noun* the activity of travelling with a backpack.

back passage *colloq.* the rectum.

back-pedal *verb intrans.* **1** to turn the pedals on a bicycle backwards. **2** to withdraw rapidly or suddenly from one's previous opinion or course of action.

back projection **1** the technique of projecting an image from film, transparency, or video, on to a translucent screen, to be viewed from the opposite side. It is particularly useful when the audience area cannot be darkened, as in museums, exhibitions, etc. **2** *Cinema* this technique used in cinematography, so that a static or moving scene is projected on to a screen which forms a background to action taking place in front of it, both being photographed together to create a single image.

backroom *attributive noun* denoting important work done secretly behind the scenes.

back seat an inferior or unimportant position: *take a back seat.*

back-seat driver *noun* a person, especially a passenger in a car, who gives unwanted advice.

back shift **1** a group of workers whose working period comes between the night shift and day shift. **2** this period.

backside *noun colloq.* the buttocks.

back slang a type of language in which words are spelt backwards and pronounced according to the new spelling, as in English *neetrith*, 'thirteen', and '*yob*', 'boy'. In the UK, back slang is most often used among children, especially public schoolboys, and certain groups of adults, such as market traders and shopkeepers.

backslide *verb intrans.* to relapse into former bad behaviour, habits, etc.

backslider *noun* a person who declines into bad habits.

backsliding *noun* a decline into former bad habits.

backspace — *verb intrans.* to move the carriage of a typewriter or a computer cursor back one or more spaces. — *noun* the key on a typewriter or computer keyboard used for backspacing.

backspin *noun Sport* the spinning of a ball in the opposite direction to the way it is travelling, reducing its speed on hitting a surface. See also SIDESPIN, TOPSPIN.

backstage *adj., adv.* **1** behind a theatre stage. **2** not seen by the public.

backstreet *noun* **1** a street away from a town's main streets. **2** (*attributive*) secret or illicit: *a backstreet abortion.*

backstroke *noun* a swimming stroke performed on the back, with the arms raised alternately in a backward circular motion, and the legs kicked in a paddling action.

backtrack *verb intrans.* **1** to return the way one came. **2** to reverse one's previous opinion or course of action.

back translation the retranslation of a translated text into the original language. The result is compared with the original translation, as a test of the quality of the original translation. The closer the correspondence between the two versions, the better the translation.

backup *noun* **1** support, assistance. **2** *Comput.* a procedure for backing up (ie copying) data for security purposes, or the copy made.

Backus, John (1924–) US computer programmer. He joined IBM in 1950 as a computer programmer, and was responsible for the development of the programming language called FORTRAN (FORmula TRANslation), completed in 1957.

backward — *adj.* **1** directed behind or towards the back. **2** less advanced than normal in mental, physical, or intellectual development. **3** reluctant or shy. — *adv.* same as BACKWARDS.

backwardness *noun* **1** being backward, especially mentally or intellectually. **2** sluggishness; slowness.

backwards *adv.* **1** towards the back or rear. **2** with one's back facing the direction of movement. **3** in reverse order. **4** in or into a worse state.

— **backwards and forwards** first in one direction, and then in the opposite direction.

bend or **fall** or **lean over backwards** *colloq.* to try extremely hard to please or accommodate someone.

know something backwards *colloq.* to know it thoroughly.

backwash *noun* **1** waves washed backwards by the movement of a ship, oars, etc through the water. **2** a repercussion.

backwater *noun* **1** a pool of stagnant water connected to a river. **2** *derog.* an isolated place, not affected by what is happening elsewhere.

backwoods *pl. noun* **1** remote uncleared forest. **2** a remote region.

backwoodsman *noun* **1** an inhabitant of backwoods. **2** a coarse person.

Bacon, Francis, Viscount St Albans (1561–1626) English philosopher and statesman, born in London. He was called to the Bar in 1582 and became an MP in 1584. He became in turn Solicitor-General (1607), Attorney-General (1613), Privy Councillor (1616), Lord Keeper (1617), and Lord Chancellor (1618). He became Lord Verulam in 1618, and was made Viscount in 1621. However, he was publicly accused before his fellow peers of bribery and corruption, fined, imprisoned, and banished from parliament and the court. Although he was later pardoned, he never returned to public office. His philosophical works include *The Advancement of Learning* (1605) and *Novum Organum* (1620), which stresses the scientific method of induction.

Bacon, Francis (1909–92) Irish artist, born in Dublin. He had no formal art education, and began painting at the age of 19. He used repellent images and repulsive human forms, and treated religious subjects in a very individual manner. His works include the controversial *Three Studies for Figures at the base of a Crucifixion* (1944) and *Painting, 1946*.

Bacon, Roger (c.1214–92) English Franciscan philosopher, known as 'Doctor Mirabilis', probably born in Ilchester, Somerset. He went to Paris and wrote commentaries on Aristotle's physics and metaphysics. In 1247 he began to devote himself to experimental science, and returned to Oxford in 1250. Again in Paris, he compiled (1266–7), at the request of Pope Clement IV, his *Opus Majus* (Great Work) along with two other works, a summary of all his learning. In 1277 his writings were condemned by the Franciscans for 'suspected novelties', and he was imprisoned until shortly before his death.

bacon *noun* meat from the back and sides of a pig, usually salted or smoked. [from Old French *bacon*]

bacteraemia *or* **bacteremia** *noun Medicine* the presence of bacteria in the blood.

bacteria see BACTERIUM.

bacterial *adj.* relating to or caused by bacteria.

bactericide *noun Chem.* a substance that destroys bacteria.

bacteriological *adj.* relating to bacteriology.

bacteriologist *noun* a person who studies bacteriology, especially professionally.

bacteriology *noun* the scientific study of bacteria and their effects.

bacteriolysis *noun Biol.* the breakdown of bacterial cells.

bacteriolytic *adj. Biol.* relating to or involving bacteriolysis.

bacteriophage *noun Biol.* a virus that infects bacteria. Bacteriophages are widely used in genetic research. [from BACTERIUM + Greek *phagein*, to eat]

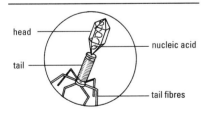

bacteriophage

bacteriostatic *adj. Chem.* denoting a substance that inhibits the growth of bacteria but does not kill them.

bacterium *noun* (PL. **bacteria**) *Biol.* any of an extremely diverse group of microscopic and usually single-celled organisms that are prokaryotes, ie their genetic material consists of a large loop of DNA in the cytoplasm, and there is no distinct nucleus containing chromosomes. [from Greek *bakterion*, little stick]
◊ Bacteria occur in soil, water, and air, and many species live as saprophytes or parasites on other living organisms, the parasitic forms being responsible for such infectious diseases of humans as anthrax, cholera, plague, pneumonia, syphilis, tetanus, and tuberculosis. A few bacteria

are autotrophic, ie they can carry out photosynthesis.
Bacteria range in size from less than one micrometre to about 500 micrometres in diameter. They are often classified according to their shape, which may be rod-shaped (*bacillus*), spherical (*coccus*), a spiral (*spirillum*), corkscrew-shaped (*spirochaete*), or filamentous, and they may occur singly, or in pairs, chains, or colonies. Most bacteria have a rigid cell wall, and many are enclosed within a slimy outer capsule. They reproduce very rapidly, usually by binary fission (division into two equal parts), although some bacteria produce asexual spores, and certain types undergo a form of sexual reproduction.
Bacteria play an important role in the decomposition and decay of organic matter, and the recycling of important chemical elements such as nitrogen, carbon, and sulphur, and they are also used in the production of butter, cheese, and yoghurt, and the breakdown of sewage and other waste products. They frequently contain small circular loops of DNA known as *plasmids* that move from one bacterium to another, transferring genetic information, and often endowing their 'hosts' with useful characteristics, eg resistance to antibiotics. Such plasmids have proved to be a very useful tool for genetic engineering.

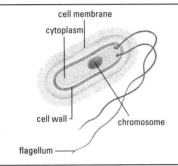

bacterium

Bactria the name given in antiquity to the area roughly corresponding to N Afghanistan and the adjacent parts of S Russia. It was ruled for centuries by foreign conquerors, notably the Achaemenids and the Seleucids. In the second half of the 3c BC, Bactria finally became an independent state, and under a series of Indo-Greek rulers went on to establish an empire that at its height covered all of Afghanistan and large parts of Soviet central Asia and Pakistan.

bad — *adj.* (**worse**, **worst**) **1** not good. **2** wicked; immoral. **3** naughty. **4** (**bad at something**) not skilled or clever at some activity. **5** (**bad for someone**) harmful to them. **6** unpleasant; unwelcome. **7** rotten; decayed. **8** serious; severe. **9** unhealthy; injured; painful. **10** sorry, upset, or ashamed. **11** not valid; worthless. **12** *slang* very good. — *noun* **1** unpleasant events. **2** evil; badness: *take the good with the bad.*
— **go to the bad** to become morally bad.
in a bad way very ill or in serious trouble.
not bad *colloq.* quite good.
too bad *colloq.* unfortunate.
[from Middle English *badde*]

Badajoz, ancient **Pax Augusta** POP (1991) 122 000, the capital of Badajoz province, Extremadura, SW Spain. It lies on the R Guadiana near the Portuguese border, 401km/249mi SW of Madrid. A former Moorish capital, it was the scene of a battle in the Peninsular War (1812). NOTABLE FEATURE cathedral (13c).

bad blood *or* **bad feeling** angry or bitter feelings.

bad debt a debt which will never be repaid.

baddy *noun* (PL. **baddies**) *colloq.* a criminal or villain, especially in films, etc.

bade see BID.

Baden, ancient **Thermae Pannonicae** POP (1991) 24 000, the capital of Baden district, Niederösterreich, NE Austria. It stands on the R Schwechat, 30km/19mi S of Vienna. The sulphurous waters of Baden, Austria's principal spa, have been appreciated since Roman times.

Baden-Powell (of Gilwell), Robert (Stephenson Smyth) Baden-Powell, 1st Baron (1857–1941) English soldier, born in London, who founded the Boy Scout movement in 1908 (now called the Scout Association) and, with his sister Agnes (1858–1945), founded the Girl Guides in 1910 (now called the Guide Association). He served with the army in India and Afghanistan, was on the staff in Ashanti and Matabeleland, and won fame as the defender of Mafeking (1899–1900).

Bader, Sir Douglas (Robert Stuart) (1910–82) English airman, born in London. After losing both legs in a flying accident in 1931, he was invalided out of the RAF, but overcame his disability and returned in 1939. He commanded the first RAF Canadian Fighter Squadron, and developed tactics that contributed to victory in the Battle of Britain, but was captured in Aug 1941 after a collision with an enemy aircraft over Béthune. His many honours included a knighthood for his work for the disabled.

bad faith dishonesty; treachery.

bad feeling see BAD BLOOD.

badge *noun* **1** a small emblem or mark worn to show rank, membership of a society, etc. **2** any distinguishing feature or mark. [from Middle English *bage*]

Badger a gruff but kind character in Kenneth Grahame's *The Wind in the Willows*.

badger — *noun* a small burrowing mammal belonging to the same family (Mustelidae) as stoats and weasels, and having a stocky body about 1m long, a short tail, and short powerful legs, with strong claws on the front feet. Like other members of the family, they have musk glands at the base of the tail. — *verb* (**badgered**, **badgering**) to pester or worry. [probably from BADGE, from the white mark on its forehead]
◊ The European badger is found throughout Europe and Asia, but is rarely seen because it is nocturnal. Its coat consists of black and white hairs which give it a grey appearance from a distance, and the fur on its head is white, with two broad black stripes running from behind the ears to near the tip of the muzzle. Badgers live in holes or *sets* excavated in the ground, and they emerge at night to feed mainly on earthworms, but also on small rodents, insects, snails, grass, nuts, and berries.

Badlands an arid region of SW South Dakota and NW Nebraska, USA. Lying E of the Black Hills, it is an area of barren, eroded landscapes and fossil deposits.

bad language coarse words and swearing.

badly *adv.* (**worse**, **worst**) **1** poorly; inefficiently. **2** unfavourably. **3** extremely; severely: *they are badly in arrears with the rent.*
— **badly off** poor.

Badminton annual three-day horse trials, held in the park of Badminton House (built 1862) in the village of Badminton, Avon. Badminton House is the seat of the Duke of Beaufort.

badminton *noun* a game for two or four players played with rackets and a shuttlecock which is hit across a high net. [from BADMINTON]
◊ Points are won by the server who aims to force errors from the opposing player(s). Developed from the children's game battledore and shuttlecock, it takes its name from Badminton House, seat of the Duke of Beaufort,

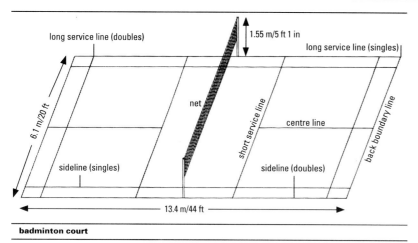

long service line (doubles)

1.55 m/5 ft 1 in

long service line (singles)

6.1 m/20 ft

net

short service line

centre line

back boundary line

sideline (singles)

sideline (doubles)

13.4 m/44 ft

badminton court

where the game was played by house-guests in the 19c.

badmouth *verb colloq.* to criticize or malign.

badness *noun* being bad; poor or evil quality.

Badoglio, Pietro (1871–1956) Italian soldier and politician, born in Grazzano Monferrato, Piedmont. On Italy's entry into World War II (Jun 1940) he was made Commander-in-Chief, but resigned after the Italian army was humiliated by the Greeks in Epirus and Albania. As Prime Minister (1943–4) after Mussolini's downfall, he formed a non-fascist government, negotiated an armistice with the Allies, and declared war on Germany, but was forced to resign.

bad-tempered *adj.* easily annoyed or made angry.

Baedeker, Karl (1801–59) German publisher, born in Essen. He started his own publishing business in 1827 in Koblenz, and is best known for the guidebooks which bear his name, published since 1872 in Leipzig.

Baekeland, Leo Hendrik (1863–1944) Belgian-born US chemist, born in Ghent. He emigrated to the USA in 1889 and founded a chemical company to manufacture one of his inventions, photographic printing paper which could be used with artificial light. A founder of the plastics industry, he made the first synthetic phenolic resin (Bakelite), which replaced hard rubber and amber as an insulator.

Baer, Karl Ernst Ritter von (1792–1876) Estonian-born German naturalist and pioneer in embryology. He was appointed professor at Königsberg (1817–34) and from 1834 taught at St Petersburg. He discovered the mammalian egg (ovum) in the ovary, and the notochord (embryonic backbone); he also formulated the 'biogenetic law', that in embryonic development general characters appear before specialized ones.

Baerlein, (Edgar) Maximillian (1879–1971) English amateur rackets and real tennis player, born in Manchester. He won the British amateur rackets title nine times between 1903 and 1923, sharing the doubles title six times (between 1902 and 1920). He won 13 British Amateur real tennis singles titles and 11 doubles titles.

Baeyer, (Johann Friedrich Wilhelm) Adolf von (1835–1917) German chemist, born in Berlin. He taught in Berlin and Strassburg, and from 1875 was professor at Munich. Best known for synthesizing the blue dye indigo and revealing details about its structure, his work also resulted in a theory which explained the instability and non-planar shape of certain molecules. He was awarded the 1905 Nobel Prize for Chemistry.

Baez, Joan (1941–) US folk singer, born in Staten Island, New York. Her crystalline soprano voice was first acclaimed at the Newport Folk Festival of 1960, and her subsequent recordings created a mass folk-music audience. She now also sings country and western songs and soft rock. A Quaker, she actively opposes racial discrimination, wars, and political imprisonment.

BAF *abbrev.* British Athletics Federation.

Baffin, William (c.1584–1622) English navigator, born probably in London. He was pilot in several expeditions in search of the Northwest Passage (1612–16), during which he examined Hudson Strait (1615), discovered Baffin Bay (1616), and named Lancaster, Smith, and Jones Sounds (1616). He sailed as far north as latitude 77°45'N, and was possibly the first person to determine a degree of longitude at sea by lunar observation. His later voyages (1616–21) were to the East, and he was killed at the siege of Ormuz.

Baffin Bay an ice-blocked Arctic gulf between Greenland to the E and Baffin, Bylot, Devon, and Ellesmere I to the W. It is c.1 125km/700mi long; 110–650km/70–400mi wide; over 2 400m deep. As there are numerous icebergs in winter, navigation is limited to the summer months. HISTORY first entered by John Davis in 1587; explored by William Baffin in 1616. Seafowl and fur-bearing animals are found along the coast.

Baffin Island the largest island of the Canadian Arctic Archipelago, in the Arctic Ocean. It is separated from Labrador by the Hudson Strait, and from Greenland to the E by the Davis Strait and Baffin Bay. AREA 318 186sq km/122 820sq mi; length c.1 600km/994mi; maximum width 725km/450mi. PHYSICAL DESCRIPTION most of the island is a plateau rising to c.915m; it has an irregular coastline, with several peninsulas and deep bays. Chief settlements are at Frobisher Bay, Lake Harbour, and Pond Inlet. The population is mainly Inuit. [named after William Baffin who studied the island in 1616]

baffle — *verb* 1 to confuse or puzzle. 2 to hinder. — *noun* a device for controlling the flow of gas, liquid, or sound through an opening. [perhaps related to Old French *befe*, mockery]

bafflement *noun* mental confusion; bewilderment.

baffling *adj.* causing mental confusion; mystifying.

bafflingly *adv.* so as to confuse or mystify: *a bafflingly strange story*.

BAFTA *abbrev.* in the UK, the British Academy of Film and Television Arts, an organization formed in 1959 from the union of the British Film Academy and the Guild of Television Producers and Directors. Each year it presents a series of awards.

bag — *noun* 1 a container made of a soft material with an opening at the top, for carrying things. 2 (**bags of something**) *colloq.* a large amount of it. 3 the amount a bag will hold. 4 an amount of fish or game caught. 5 *offensive colloq.* a woman, especially an unpleasant or ugly one. 6 (**bags**) loose wide-legged trousers. — *verb* (**bagged**, **bagging**) 1 *trans., intrans.* (also **bag up**) to put (something) into a bag. 2 to kill (game). 3 *colloq.* to obtain or reserve (a seat, etc). 4 *intrans.* said especially of clothes to hang loosely or bulge.
— **bag and baggage** completely: *clear out bag and baggage.*
in the bag *colloq.* as good as secured or done. [from Middle English *bagge*]

bagatelle *noun* 1 a game played on a board with holes into which balls are rolled. 2 an unimportant thing. 3 a short piece of music. [from French *bagatelle*, from Italian *bagatella*, trick, trifle]

Bagehot, Walter (1826–77) English economist, journalist, and political theorist, born in Langport, Somerset. Called to the Bar in 1852, he worked as a banker, then became editor of the *Economist* (1860). His *English Constitution* (1867) is still considered a standard work, and *Physics and Politics* (1872), which applied the theory of evolution to politics, influenced 19c political and economic thinking. Among the many constitutional reforms he advocated was the introduction of life peers.

bagel *or* **beigel** *noun* a hard ring-shaped bread roll. [from Yiddish *beygel*]

Bagerat the former city of Khalifatabad, founded in the 15c by General Ulugh Khan Jahan in the S Ganges delta, present-day Bangladesh. Its mosques and palaces spring from a unique marriage of local architectural styles with that of imperial Delhi. It is a World Heritage site.

baggage *noun* 1 a traveller's luggage. 2 the portable equipment of an army. [from Old French *bagage*]

baggily *adv.* in a loose or baggy manner.

bagginess *noun* a loose or baggy state or quality.

Baggins, Bilbo the hero of J R R Tolkien's *The Hobbit*, and a minor but significant character in *The Lord of the Rings*, he is a comfort-loving furry-footed hobbit who finds himself unwittingly embroiled in a series of heart-stopping adventures. His young cousin and heir, Frodo Baggins, is the hero of *The Lord of the Rings*.

baggy *adj.* (**baggier, baggiest**) hanging loose or bulging.

Baghdad POP (1990e) 4m, the capital of Iraq, on the R Tigris. The city, founded in 762, is enclosed on three sides by ancient walls. It suffered bombing in air raids during the Gulf War in 1991. NOTABLE FEATURES Abbasid Palace; Mustansiriyah Law College (13c).

Bagheera the black panther who undertakes Mowgli's physical training in Rudyard Kipling's *The Jungle Book*.

Baghlan POP (1984e) 537 000, a province in NE Afghanistan, N of Kabul. AREA 17 109sq km/6 604sq mi. The Salang Pass and Tunnel, which lay on the main Soviet supply route from the border of the former USSR to Kabul, was the focus of resistance by Mujahadeen guerrillas during the Russian occupation of Afghanistan in 1979–89. CAPITAL Baghlan Jadid.

bag lady a homeless woman who carries her belongings around with her in bags.

Bagot, Bushy and Green the king's sycophantic favourites in Shakespeare's *Richard II*, who advise him badly and, in the case of Bushy and Green, desert him at the first real sign of danger.

bagpiper *noun* a person who plays the bagpipes; a piper.

bagpipes *pl. noun* a musical instrument consisting of a bag into which air is blown through a pipe and from which air flows through other pipes to form notes. Drone pipes make single sustained notes, and a 'chanter' or fingered pipe makes the melody.

baguette *noun* a long narrow French loaf. [from French *baguette*]

Baguio POP (1990) 183 000, the summer capital of the Philippines, in Benguet province, NW Luzon I. The town is a mountain resort and the official summer residence of the president. A military academy is based at this site.

bah *interj.* expressing displeasure or disgust.

Baha'i *or* **Bahai** *noun Relig.* **1** same as BAHA'ISM. **2** an adherent of Baha'ism. [from Persian *baha*, splendour]

Baha'ism a religious movement that arose out of the Persian Islamic sect Babi in the 1860s, when Mirza Husayn Ali (1817–92), known as Baha Allah ('Glory of God'), declared himself the prophet foretold by the founder of the Babi movement, Mirza Ali Muhammad (1819–50). Baha'ism teaches the oneness of God, the unity of all faiths, the inevitable unification of humankind, the harmony of all people, universal education, and obedience to government. It has no priesthood, and its adherents are expected to teach the faith. Local assemblies meet for informal devotions in homes or rented halls, and there are ceremonies only for marriage, funerals, and the naming of babies.

Bahamas, official name **Commonwealth of the Bahamas** POP (1992e) 262 000, an independent archipelago of c.700 low-lying islands and over 2 000 cays, forming a chain extending c.800km/500mi SE from the coast of Florida. AREA 13 934sq km/5 379sq mi. CAPITAL Nassau. CHIEF TOWN Freeport. TIME ZONE GMT –5. Over 75% of the population live on Providence or Grand Bahama Is; 85% are black and 15% are white; Christianity is the dominant religion. OFFICIAL LANGUAGE English. CURRENCY Bahamian dollar. PHYSICAL DESCRIPTION the coralline limestone islands of the Bahamas comprise the two oceanic banks of Little Bahama and Great Bahama; the highest point is only 120m above sea level. CLIMATE subtropical, with average temperatures of 21°C in winter and 27°C in summer; the average annual rainfall is 750–1 500mm; hurricanes are frequent in Jun–Nov. HISTORY discovered by Columbus in 1492, but the first permanent European settlement was not until 1647, by English and Bermudan religious refugees; became a British Crown Colony in 1717; notorious rendezvous of buccaneers and pirates; gained independence in 1973. GOVERNMENT a bicameral assembly, consisting of a House of Assembly with 49 elected members and a Senate with 16 nominated members; the head of state, the British monarch, is represented by a Governor-General. ECONOMY tourism is the mainstay of the economy, especially at New Providence (Nassau and Paradise I) and Grand Bahama; important financial centre (status as a tax haven); oil refining; fishing; rum and liqueur distilling; cement; pharmaceuticals; steel pipes; fruit, vegetables.

Bahamas

Bahasa Indonesian the Malay dialect of the S Malay Peninsula, given official status as the standard language of Malaysia by the Japanese occupiers during World War II, and the official language of Indonesia since 1949. It is now also known simply as Indonesian. [from Malay *bahasa*, language]

Bahia POP (1991) 11.8m, a state in Nordeste region, NE Brazil, bounded E by the Atlantic Ocean. AREA 561 026sq km/216 556sq mi. Brazil was first claimed for Portugal by Pedro Cabral in 1500, when he stepped ashore at Pôrto Seguro, in SE Bahia. CAPITAL Salvador. ECONOMY agriculture; chemical and petrochemical industries; oil.

Bahía Blanca POP (1991) 272 000, a city in Buenos Aires province, E Argentina, founded in 1828. It is situated at the head of Bahía Blanca Bay, SW of Buenos Aires. The city has five ports on the R Naposta, including the naval base of Puerto Belgrano.

Bahrain, official name **State of Bahrain** POP (1992e) 533 000, a group of 35 islands comprising an independent state in the Arabian Gulf, midway between the Qatar Peninsula and mainland Saudi Arabia. A long causeway (25km/16mi) connects Bahrain to Saudi Arabia. AREA 678sq km/262sq mi. CAPITAL Manama. CHIEF TOWN Al Muharraq. TIME ZONE GMT +3. The population is 73% Arabic and 9% Iranian, with Pakistani and Indian minorities; Islam is the main religion. OFFICIAL LANGUAGE Arabic. CURRENCY Bahrain dinar. PHYSICAL DESCRIPTION the island of Bahrain is c.48km/30mi long and 13–16km/8–10mi wide, comprising a total area of 562sq km/217sq mi; the highest point is Jabal Dukhan (135m); largely bare and infertile, though helped by many major drainage schemes since 1973. CLIMATE cool N/NE winds with a little rain in Dec–Mar (the average temperature in Jan is 19°C); the rest of the year is dominated by either a moist NE wind (the *Shamal*) or the hot, sand-bearing *Qaws* from the S; in summer the average temperature is 36°C. HISTORY a flourishing trade centre in 2 000–1 800 BC; since the late 18c, governed by the Khalifa family; treaty of protection with the UK in 1861; gained independence in 1971; experimental parliamentary system established in 1973–5. GOVERNMENT a constitutional monarchy governed by the Amir, who appoints a Council of Ministers headed by a Prime Minister. ECONOMY oil (on land and offshore), natural gas, lime, gypsum; oil refining, aluminium smelting, ship repairing; a major centre for oil trading, banking, and commerce.

Baignade Asnières, Une a painting by Georges Seurat (1883–4, Tate Gallery, London). It was rejected by the Salon in 1884 but exhibited instead at the Salon des Indépendants.

Baikal, Lake, Russian **Baykal** a crescent-shaped lake in S Siberia, Russia. It is the largest freshwater lake in Eurasia, and also the deepest in the world (maximum depth 1 620m). AREA 31 500sq km/12 159sq mi; length (SW–NE) 636km/395mi; width 24–80km/15–50mi. It lies in a deep tectonic basin, fed by over 300 rivers and streams, but its only outlet is the R Angara. The lake, which freezes over from Jan to Apr, contains 22 islands, the largest being Ostrov Ol'khon (length 51km/32mi). There are many hot springs on the shores and earthquakes are frequent. The Trans-Siberian railway passes round the rocky S shore.

bail[1] *noun* money required as security for a person's temporary release while awaiting trial. — *verb (also* **bail out**) to provide bail for.
— **forfeit** *or* **jump bail** to fail to return for trial after being released on bail.
on bail released once bail money has been given to the court.
put up *or* **stand** *or* **go bail** to provide bail for a prisoner.
[from Old French *bail*, custody]

bail[2] *or* **bale** *verb trans., intrans. (usually* **bail** *or* **bale out**) **1** to remove (water) from a boat with a bucket. **2** to escape from an aeroplane by jumping out. [from French *baille*, bucket]

bail[3] *noun (usually* **bails**) one of the cross-pieces laid on top of the stumps in cricket.

bailey *noun* (PL. **baileys**) the outer wall of a

Bahrain

castle, or a courtyard within the wall. [from Old French *baille*, enclosure]

Bailey bridge a temporary lattice bridge that can be assembled rapidly from prefabricated pieces of welded steel, widely used as a military bridge during World War II. [named after the UK engineer Sir Donald Bailey (1901–85)]

bailiff *noun* **1** an officer of a lawcourt, especially one with the power to seize the property of a person who has not paid money owed to the court. **2** a person who looks after property for its owner. [from Old French *baillier*, to control, hand over]

Baillie, Dame Isobel (1895–1983) Scottish soprano, born in Hawick, Roxburghshire. She studied music in Manchester and Milan, and won immediate success in her opening London season in 1923. Regarded as one of this century's greatest oratorio singers, she regularly sang with Sir Thomas Beecham and gave over 1 000 performances of Handel's *Messiah*.

Bailly, Harry the handsome, diplomatic Host of the Tabard Inn where the pilgrims assemble in Chaucer's *The Canterbury Tales*.

Baily, Francis (1774–1844) English astronomer, born in Newbury, Berkshire. When he retired from a business career in 1825 fitted his house in London with an observatory. He produced an accurate catalogue of nearly 3 000 star positions, and during a total eclipse of the Sun in 1836, he observed the brilliant cluster of spots of sunlight (*Baily's beads*) which appear between the mountains of the Moon just before the Sun disappears behind it. His description of the solar corona after the 1842 eclipse was the first realistic description of this region of the solar outer atmosphere.

Baily's beads *Astron.* a broken ring of bright spots of sunlight, seen around the edge of the Moon immediately before and after a total eclipse of the Sun. It is caused by sunlight shining between mountains and valleys on the extreme rim of the Moon. [named after the UK astronomer Francis Baily]

bain-marie *noun* a pan filled with hot water in which a container of food can be cooked gently or kept warm. [from French *bain-marie*, bath of Mary, from medieval Latin *balneum Mariae*, 'Maria' being the name of an alleged alchemist]

Baird, John Logie (1888–1946) Scottish electrical engineer and television pioneer, born in Helensburgh. After poor health compelled him to give up engineering posts, he settled in Hastings (1922) and began research into the possibilities of television. In 1926 gave the first demonstration in London of a television image, and the following year he transmitted primitive television pictures over the telephone lines from London to Glasgow; in 1928 his signals were picked up in the USA. His system was adopted by the BBC from 1929 to 1937.

Bairiki POP (1990) 25 000, the capital town of Kiribati, on Tarawa atoll in the Gilbert Is, central Pacific Ocean.

bairn *noun dialect* a child. [from Anglo-Saxon *bearn*, to bear]

Bairnsfather, (Charles) Bruce (1888–1959) British soldier and cartoonist, born in Murree, India. He served in France during World War I, and became famous for his war cartoons featuring the character 'Old Bill'. During World War II, he was an official war cartoonist attached to the US Army.

Baisaki *noun* a Sikh festival (generally celebrated on 13 Apr) commemorating the founding of the Khalsa order of baptized Sikhs by the tenth guru, Gobind Singh, in 1699. [from Hindi *Baisakh*, the month of April, from Sanskrit *Vaisākha*]

bait — *noun* **1** food put on a hook or in a trap to attract fish or animals. **2** anything intended to attract or tempt. — *verb* **1** to put food on or in (a hook or trap). **2** to harass or tease wilfully. **3** to set dogs on (another animal). [from Norse *beita*, to cause to bite]

baize *noun* a woollen cloth, usually green and used as a covering on snooker and card tables. [from Old French *baies*, chestnut-coloured]

Bajazet *or* **Bayazid I** (1354–1403) Sultan in the Ottoman Empire (1389–1402). After coming to power, he quickly conquered Bulgaria, parts of Serbia, Macedonia and Thessaly, and most of Asia Minor, earning the name of 'Yildirim' (Thunderbolt). He blockaded Constantinople, and defeated Sigismund of Hungary (1396) in his attempt to rescue the city. In 1402 he was himself defeated near Ankara by Timur (Tamerlane).

bake *verb* **1** *trans., intrans.* to cook (cakes, bread, vegetables, etc) using dry heat in an oven. **2** *trans., intrans.* to dry or harden by heat from the sun or a fire. **3** *intrans. colloq.* to be extremely hot. [from Anglo-Saxon *bacan*]

baked beans *pl. noun* haricot beans baked in tomato sauce and usually tinned.

bakehouse *noun old use* a bakery.

Bakelite *noun trademark* a type of hard plastic formerly used to make dishes, buttons, etc. [named after L H Baekeland (1863–1944), its inventor]

Baker, Sir Benjamin (1840–1907) British engineer, born in Frome, Somerset. In 1861 he began a long association with the consulting engineer John Fowler, and together they constructed the London Metropolitan railway, Victoria station, and several bridges. Their greatest achievement was the Forth Rail Bridge (opened 1890).

Baker, James A(ddison) (1930–) US Republican politician, born in Houston, Texas. He served President Ford as Under-Secretary of Commerce, President Reagan as White House Chief of Staff (1981–5) and Secretary of the Treasury (1985–8), and then resigned to manage the successful presidential campaign for George Bush (1988), under whom he was Secretary of State (1989–92).

Baker, Dame Janet (Abbott) (1933–) English mezzo-soprano, born in Hatfield, Yorkshire. She made her début in the chorus at Glyndebourne (1956), worked as a soloist for Sir John Barbirolli, and enjoyed an extensive operatic career, especially in early Italian opera and the works of Benjamin Britten, until she retired from the operatic stage in 1982. Also a concert performer, she is a noted interpreter of Mahler and Elgar.

Baker, Kenneth (Wilfred) (1934–) English Conservative politician. He became an MP in 1968, and under Margaret Thatcher held various posts in the departments of Trade and Industry (1981–4) and the Environment (1984–5) before he rose to become Secretary of State for

the Environment (1985–6), then Education Secretary (1986–9), when he introduced a controversial education reform bill, and Chairman of the Conservative Party (1989–90). He was Home Secretary (1990–2) under John Major, then turned his attention to writing.

baker *noun* a person who bakes and sells bread, cakes, etc.

baker's dozen thirteen.

bakery *noun* (PL. **bakeries**) a place where bread, cakes, etc are made or sold.

Bakewell, Robert (1725–95) English stock breeder, born in Dishley, Leicestershire. By selection and inbreeding he improved the standard and management of sheep, cattle, and draught horses, thus widening interest in breeding methods. He also established the Leicester breed of sheep.

baking *adj. very* hot, especially from the sun.

baking powder a powder containing sodium bicarbonate, used to make cakes, etc rise.

baking soda sodium bicarbonate, used to make baking powder.

baklava *or* **baclava** *noun* a rich cake of Middle Eastern origin made of layers of flaky pastry with a filling of honey, nuts, and spices. [from Turkish]

baksheesh *noun* in some eastern countries, money given as a tip or present. [from Persian *bakhshish*]

Bakst, Léon, originally **Lev Samoilovich Rosenberg** (1866–1924) Russian painter, born in St Petersburg. He was associated with Sergei Diaghilev from the beginnings of the Russian ballet, designing the decor and costumes for numerous productions (1909–21). His rich, exuberant colours produced a powerful theatrical effect, which revolutionized fashion and decoration.

Baku POP (1990e) 1.8m, the seaport capital of Azerbaijan. It is situated on the Apsheron Peninsula, on the W coast of the Caspian Sea and is an industrial, scientific, and cultural centre. NOTABLE FEATURES Kiz Kalasyi (Virgin's Tower, 12c); Shirvan Shah's Palace.

Bakunin, Mikhail Alekseyevich (1814–76) Russian anarchist, born near Moscow. He took part in the German revolutionary movement (1848–9) and was condemned to death. Sent to Siberia in 1855, he escaped to Japan, and arrived in England in 1861. As the leader of anarchism, in the First Communist International (1868) he was the opponent of Karl Marx, but at the Hague Congress (1872) he was outvoted and expelled.

Balaclava, Battle of a battle (1854) fought between British and Russian forces during the early stages of the Crimean War. The Russian attack on the British base at Balaclava was unsuccessful, but the British sustained heavier losses.

balaclava *noun* a knitted hat that covers the head and neck, with an opening for the face. [from *Balaclava* in the Crimea]

balalaika *noun* a Russian stringed musical instrument with a triangular body, a neck like a guitar and normally three strings. [from Russian *balalaika*]

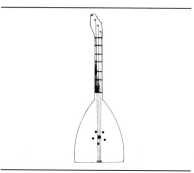

balalaika

balance — *noun* **1** an instrument for weighing, usually with two dishes hanging from a bar supported in the middle. **2** a state of physical stability in which the weight of a body is evenly distributed. **3** a state of mental or emotional stability. **4** a state existing when two opposite forces are equal. **5** something that is needed to create such equality. **6** the amount by which the two sides of an account (money spent and money received) differ. **7** an amount left over. **8** a device which regulates the speed of a clock or watch. — *verb* **1** *trans., intrans.* to be or put into a state of physical balance. **2** to compare two or more things in one's mind. **3** to find the difference between money put into an account and money taken out of it, and to make them equal: *balance the books.* **4** *intrans.* (also **balance out**) to be or become equal in amount.

— **in the balance** not yet decided.

on balance having taken all the advantages and disadvantages into consideration.

[from Latin *bilanx*, having two scales]

balanced *adj.* **1** in a state of balance. **2** fair; considering all sides of an argument, etc. **3** *said of a person* calm and sensible.

balance of payments the difference in value between the amount of money coming into a country and the amount going out of it, over a period of time.

balance of power the equal distribution of political or military power, with no one nation or group having supremacy.

— **hold the balance of power** to be in a position where either of two equal and opposed groups, etc can be made more powerful than the other through one's support.

balance of trade the difference in value of a country's imports and exports.

balance sheet a summary and balance of financial accounts.

Balanchine, George, originally **Georgi Melitonovich Balanchivadze** (1904–83) US ballet-dancer and choreographer, born in St Petersburg, Russia. The innovations of his own company were badly received by the theatre authorities, but during a foreign tour in 1924, he and some other dancers remained in Berlin, then performed in Europe as the Soviet State Dancers, and were adopted by Sergei Diaghilev into the Ballets Russes in Paris. In 1934 Balanchine opened the School of American Ballet in New York and he was director of the New York City Ballet from 1948. He also choreographed many Broadway shows and Hollywood musicals.

Balaton, Lake a lake in W central Hungary, the largest and shallowest in central Europe. AREA 598sq km/231sq mi; length 77km/48mi; width 8–14km/5–9mi. It is Hungary's largest recreation area, with resorts at Siófok, Keszthely, and Balatonfüred (a spa with carbonic waters).

Balboa, Vasco Núñez de (1475–1517) Spanish explorer, born in Jerez de los Caballeros. He settled in Santo Domingo in 1501, and in 1511 joined the expedition to Darién, S Panama, as a stowaway. Following an insurrection, he took command, and founded a colony. He was the first European to see the Pacific Ocean (1513). In 1514, the governorship of Darién was granted to Pedrarias Davila, for whom he undertook many expeditions, but on their first disagreement, Balboa was executed.

balcony *noun* (PL. **balconies**) **1** a platform surrounded by a wall or railing, projecting from the wall of a building. **2** an upper tier in a theatre or cinema. [from Italian *balcone*]

bald *adj.* **1** *said of a person* having little or no hair on the head. **2** *said of birds or animals* not having any feathers or fur. **3** bare or plain. [perhaps from Middle English *balled*, rounded]

baldacchino *or* **baldachin** *or* **baldaquin** *noun* **1** a canopy, especially the canopy supported at each corner by a pole and carried over a sacred object in a religious procession, or placed over a throne, altar, or pulpit. **2** *Archit.* a fixed structure with a canopy supported at each corner by a column, found over the high altar in many Baroque churches. A famous example is the huge bronze baldacchino in St Peter's, Rome, designed by Bernini. [from Italian *Baldacco*, Baghdad, originally the source of the silk used for the canopy]

bald eagle a kind of eagle with a white head, the national emblem of the USA.

Balder *or* **Baldur** *or* **Baldr** in Norse mythology, a god of sovereignty and power, the beautiful and kind son of Odin and Frigg. He was invulnerable to harm, but was mistakenly killed by the blind god Hodur, who had been deceived by the evil god Loki into throwing a dart of mistletoe (the only plant which could harm him) at Balder.

balderdash *noun old use* nonsense.

balding *adj.* becoming bald.

baldly *adv.* in a plain and often hurtful way: *told them baldly they were not wanted.*

baldness *noun* the partial or total loss of hair from parts of the body where it normally grows, especially the head. The gradual loss of head hair in men is hereditary, and influenced by the level of male sex hormones. Baldness may also be caused by disease, head injury, hormonal factors (in women), exposure to radiation, or old age. See also ALOPECIA.

baldric *or* **baldrick** *noun Hist.* a broad leather belt or silk sash (often highly ornate), worn around the waist or over the right shoulder to support a sword. [from Old French *baudrei*; related to Middle High German *balderick*, girdle]

Baldwin I (1172–1205) Count of Flanders (from 1194) and Hainault (from 1195), the youngest brother of Godfrey of Bouillon. He was a leader of the Fourth Crusade, and in 1204 he was crowned as the first Latin Emperor of Constantinople, but was defeated and captured at Adrianople (1205).

Baldwin, James (Arthur) (1924–88) US writer, born and brought up in Harlem, New York City. He lived in Europe (mainly in Paris) for some years, returning to the USA in 1957, where he became an active member of the civil rights movement. His novels include *Go Tell it on the Mountain* (1954), *Tell Me How Long The Train's Been Gone* (1968), and *Just Above My Head* (1979).

Baldwin (of Bewdley), Stanley Baldwin, 1st Earl (1867–1947) English Conservative politician and Prime Minister (three times). He became an MP in 1908, was President of the Board of Trade (1921–2), Chancellor of the Exchequer (1922–3), and then unexpectedly succeeded Bonar Law as Prime Minister. His period of office (1923–4, 1924–9, 1935–7) included the General Strike (1926) and was interrupted by the two minority Labour governments and also the MacDonald Coalition (1931–5), in which he served as Lord President of the Council. He arranged the abdication of Edward VIII in 1937, the year he resigned from politics.

bale¹ — *noun* a large tied bundle of a commodity such as cloth or hay. — *verb* to make into bales. [from Old French *bale*]

bale² see BAIL².

Balearic Islands, Spanish **Islas Baleares** POP (1991) 703 000, a Spanish archipelago of 5 major islands and 11 islets in the W Mediterranean Sea, situated near the E coast of Spain. AREA 5 014sq km/1 935sq mi. MAIN ISLANDS the E group chiefly comprises Majorca, Minorca, and Cabrera; the W group chiefly comprises Ibiza and Formentera. They are highly popular tourist resorts. CAPITAL Palma de Mallorca. The islands were conquered by Aragon in the 14c.

baleen *noun* whalebone. [from Latin *balaena*, whale]

baleful *adj.* **1** evil; harmful. **2** threatening; gloomy. [from Anglo-Saxon *bealu*, evil]

balefully *adv.* with menace; threateningly.

balefulness *noun* a harmful or threatening state.

Balenciaga, Cristobal (1895–1972) Spanish couturier, born in Guetaria, which is in the Basque country. He trained as a tailor, and eventually opened dressmaking and tailoring shops of his own. He left Spain for Paris as a result of the Spanish Civil War, and became a couturier. His clothes were noted for dramatic simplicity and elegant design.

Balewa, Sir Abubakar Tafawa (1912–66) Nigerian politician, born in Bauchi. He was a founder-member of the Northern People's Congress, then entered the Federal Assembly (1947), became Minister of Works (1952) and Transport (1953), then was first Federal Prime Minister (1957). He was knighted when Nigeria became independent in 1960, and was assassinated in the military uprising of 1966.

Balfour, Arthur James Balfour, 1st Earl (1848–1930) Scottish Conservative politician and Prime Minister, born in Whittinghame, East Lothian. After succeeding to the family estate (1856), he entered parliament (1874), and became Chief Secretary for Ireland (1887–91), where his policy of suppression earned him the name of 'Bloody Balfour'. His premiership (1902–5) saw the end of the South African War (1905), the Education Act (1905), and the establishment of the Committee of Imperial Defence. As Foreign Secretary (1916–19) he was responsible for the Balfour Declaration (1917) which promised Zionists a national home in Palestine, and as Lord President of the Council (1921) he was responsible for the controversial note cancelling Allied war debts to the USA.

Balfour, David the young narrator and hero of Robert Louis Stevenson's *Kidnapped* and *Catriona*, who has a series of adventures after falling in with Alan Breck. His miserly uncle, Ebenezer Balfour, is responsible for having David kidnapped.

Balfour, Francis Maitland (1851–82) Scottish embryologist, born in Edinburgh. Distinguished by his painstaking microscopic accounts of the development process, he became the first Professor of Animal Morphology at Cambridge in 1882, after publishing his *Treatise on Comparative Embryology* (1880). He lost his life in a climbing accident on Mont Blanc.

Balfour of Burley, John the religious extremist Cameronian Covenanter in Sir Walter Scott's *Old Mortality.*

Bali POP (1990) 2.8m, an island province of Indonesia, between Java in the W and Lombok in the E. AREA 5 561sq km/2 146sq mi. It is mountainous, with peaks rising to 3 142m at Gunung Agung in the E. Most of the population is Hindu. The Dutch gained full control of the island by 1908. CAPITAL Denpasar. ECONOMY rice, coffee, salt, onions, copra; cattle; handicrafts; a major tourist area.

Balinese — *noun* **1** (PL. **Balinese**) a native of Bali. **2** the Austronesian language of Bali, spoken by c.2–3 million people. — *adj.* relating to Bali or its language or Hindu culture, especially its distinctive dance, music, and drama.

◇ Balinese culture is influenced by Javanese, and the religion, which is essentially Hindu, incorporates elements of Buddhism, ancestor worship, and spiritualism, with some caste practices preserved.

balk *or* **baulk** *verb* **1** *intrans.* (*usually* **balk at something**) to hesitate or refuse to go on because of some obstacle. **2** *trans.* to check or block. [from Anglo-Saxon *balca*, ridge]

Balkan — *adj.* **1** of the peninsula in SE Europe surrounded by the Adriatic, Aegean, and Black seas. **2** of its peoples or countries. — *noun* (**Balkans**) the Balkan countries.

Balkan Wars a series of military campaigns fought (1912–13) in the Balkans. In 1912, Bulgaria, Serbia, Greece, and Montenegro successfully attacked Turkey. A preliminary peace was drawn up by the Great Powers in May 1913, in which Turkey surrendered most of its European territories, including Macedonia and Albania. Disputes between the Balkan allies led to a second war, in which Bulgaria attacked its former allies, and was defeated. The wars resulted in the reduction of Ottoman Empire territory in Europe to an area around Adrianople and Constantinople, the establishment of the state of Albania, the doubling in size of Serbia and Montenegro, and a considerable increase in the tension among the Great Powers in Europe.

Balkhash, Lake, Russian **Balkhash Ozero** a crescent-shaped lake in SE Kazakhstan, 160km/100mi W of the Chinese border. AREA 18 300sq km/7 064sq mi; length 605km/376mi; maximum width 74km/46mi; maximum depth 26m; the lake has no outlet. Salt extraction and fishing are important activities and copper deposits are found on the N shore. Chief harbours are Burylbaytal and Burlyu-Tobe. The lake is shrinking gradually.

ball¹ — *noun* **1** a round or roundish object used in some sports. **2** anything round or nearly round in shape: *a snowball.* **3** the act of throwing a ball, or the way a ball is thrown. **4** a rounded fleshy part of the body: *the ball of the foot.* **5** (*usually* **balls**) *coarse slang* a testicle (see also BALLS). — *verb trans., intrans.* to form or gather into a ball.

— **have the ball at one's feet** to have the opportunity to do something.
on the ball *colloq.* well-informed; alert.
play ball *colloq.* to co-operate.
start *or* **set** *or* **keep the ball rolling** to begin, or continue, an activity, conversation, etc.
[from Middle English *bal*]

ball² *noun* **1** a formal social meeting for dancing. **2** *colloq.* an enjoyable time: *have a ball.* [from French *bal*]

ballad *noun* **1** a slow, usually romantic song. **2** a poem or song with short verses, which tells a popular story. [from Provençal *balada*, dance]

ballade *noun* **1** a poem consisting of verses grouped in threes, with a repeated refrain, and a final short concluding verse (an envoy). **2** *Mus.* a short lyrical piece for piano. [an earlier form of BALLAD]

ball-and-socket joint a joint, especially in the body, in which the ball-shaped end of one part fits into the cup-shaped end of the other part.

Ballarat *or* **Ballaarat** POP (1991) 65 000, a city in SW central Victoria, Australia, NW of Melbourne. The largest gold reserves in the country were discovered here in 1851. In 1854, the famous Eureka Stockade, the gold-diggers' rebellion against state authority, took place at Ballarat. It is the centre of a wool-producing district. NOTABLE FEATURES Eureka Stockade reconstruction; Sovereign Hill Historic Park; Gold Museum; vintage trams.

Ballard, J(ames) G(raham) (1930–) British novelist and short-story writer, born in Shanghai, China. Initially a science-fiction writer, his novels in that genre include his first, *The Drowned World* (1962). Other novels include the semi-autobiographical *Empire of the Sun* (1984), *The Day of Creation* (1987), and *The Kindness of Women* (1991). His short-story collections include *The Terminal Beach* (1964) and *Vermilion Sands* (1973).

ballast *noun* **1** heavy material used to keep a balloon or a ship without cargo steady. **2** broken rocks or stones used as a base for roads and railway lines. [probably from Old Swedish *bar*, bare + *last*, load]

ball-bearing *noun* **1** an arrangement of small steel balls between the moving parts of some machines, to help reduce friction. **2** one of these balls.

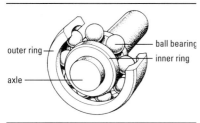

ball-bearing

ballcock *noun* a floating ball attached to a hinged rod, by which the level of water in a tank or cistern operates a valve and controls the inflow of water.

ballerina *noun* a female ballet-dancer, especially one taking leading roles. [from Italian *ballerina*, feminine of *ballerino* dancing-master]

Ballesteros, Seve(riano) (1957–) Spanish golfer, born in Pedrena. He had his first win in the 1976 Dutch Open, and his first win on the US professional circuit in 1978 (Greater Greensboro' Open). He has won three British Opens (1979, 1984, 1988), the US Masters twice (1980, 1983), and was the leading money winner in Europe in the years 1976–8, 1986, and 1988. He is the first to have won 50 European golf tournaments.

ballet *noun* a classical style of dancing and mime, using set steps and body movements; a performance of this. [from French *ballet*, diminutive of *bal*, dance]
◇ Ballet, as an independent theatre form, developed from the elaborate entertainments with music, singing, dialogue, and dance, performed at the Italian and French courts in the Renaissance. In the 18c, French ballet was adopted by other countries, most notably Russia, and a formalized technique was gradually developed which produced, in the 19c, the great Romantic ballets (eg *Les Sylphides* and *Giselle*) and Russian classics (eg *Swan Lake*, *The Sleeping Beauty*, and *The Nutcracker*). In the early 20c, the Russian impresario Sergei Diaghilev revitalized ballet in Western Europe by encouraging collaborative efforts between some great composers, choreographers, artists, and dancers. Important 20c choreographers include in the USA, George Balanchine, and in the UK, Frederick Ashton and Kenneth Macmillan.

ballet-dancer *noun* a dancer of ballet.

balletic *adj.* of or like ballet or a ballet; dance-like.

balletically *adv.* with dance-like movement; gracefully.

Ballet Rambert a touring ballet company founded (1926) in London by Marie Rambert. Its first performance *A Tragedy of Fashion* was to Frederick Ashton's choreography and Eugene Goossens's music.

Ballets Russes a ballet company created by the Russian impresario Sergei Diaghilev in 1909. Active in Europe until Diaghilev's death in 1929, it was famous for nurturing new talents and for collaborations between great painters (Bakst, Benois, Picasso), composers (Rimsky Korsakov, Satie, Stravinsky), and choreographers (Fokine, Nijinsky, Massine, Balanchine). Its repertoire of 20c classics included *Les Sylphides*, *Petrushka*, and *Le Sacre du printemps* (The Rite of Spring). In 1987 a reconstruction of Nijinsky's long-lost 1913 version of the last-named was performed by the Joffrey Ballet in the USA and Europe.

ball game *noun* **1** *North Amer.* a baseball game. **2** *colloq.* a situation: *a whole new ball game*.

ballistic *adj.* **1** relating to projectiles. **2** operating under the force of gravity.

ballistic missile a type of missile which is initially guided but drops on its target under gravity.

ballistics *sing. noun* the scientific study of the movement, behaviour and effects of projectiles, such as bullets, rockets, and guided missiles. [from Latin *ballista*, a military machine for throwing large rocks at buildings, etc]

balloon — *noun* **1** a small rubber pouch with a neck, filled with air or other gas and used as a toy or decoration. **2** a large bag, made of light material and filled with a light gas or hot air, designed to float in the air carrying people in a basket underneath. **3** an outline containing the words or thoughts of characters in a cartoon. — *verb intrans.* **1** to swell out like a balloon. **2** to increase dramatically: *the costs started ballooning alarmingly*. **3** to travel by balloon.
— **go down like a lead balloon** *colloq.*, *said of an action or statement* to be received with hostility or disapproval.
when the balloon goes up when the trouble starts.
[from Italian *ballone*]
◇ The envelope of a modern hot-air balloon is usually made of nylon or Dacron®, coated with polyurethane applied under pressure to make it more airtight. The first manned flight in a balloon was by Pilatre de Rozier and Marquis d'Arlandes at Paris in 1783, in a balloon designed by the Montgolfier brothers.

ballooning *noun* the activity of travelling in a balloon, especially for recreation.

balloonist *noun* a person who travels in a balloon, especially for recreation.

ballot — *noun* **1** a method or act of voting, usually in secret, by putting a marked paper into a box or other container. **2** the total number of votes recorded in an election. **3** a piece of paper, etc used in voting. — *verb* (**balloted, balloting**) **1** *intrans.* to vote by ballot. **2** *trans.* to take a ballot of. [from Italian *ballotta*, little ball]

ballot-box *noun* **1** the box into which voters put marked ballot-papers. **2** the system of voting in secret by ballot, especially as a sign of political freedom.

ballot-paper *noun* a piece of paper used for voting in a ballot.

ballpark *North Amer.*, *esp. US* — *noun* a baseball field. — *adj.* approximate, rough: *a ballpark figure*.
— **in the right ballpark** approximately correct or relevant.

ballpoint *or* **ballpoint pen** *noun* a pen having a tiny ball as the writing point.

ballroom *noun* a large hall where balls are held.

ballroom dancing *noun* a formal kind of dancing, in which couples dance to music with a strict rhythm.

balls *sing. noun coarse slang* **1** *North Amer.*, *esp. US* courage or bravery. **2** *also interj.* rubbish or nonsense.
— **balls something up** *Brit. coarse slang* to make a complete mess of it; to bungle it. See also BALL[1] 5.

bally *adj. Brit. old colloq. use* a mild form of BLOODY.

ballyhoo *noun colloq.* **1** a noisy confused situation. **2** noisy or sensational publicity or advertising.

balm *noun* **1** an oil obtained from certain types of trees, having a pleasant smell, and used in healing or reducing pain. **2** something comforting to either the body or the spirit. [from Old French *basme*]

Balmain, Pierre (Alexandre) (1914–82) French fashion designer, born in St Jean-de-Maurienne. He studied architecture in Paris, then turned to dress design, working for Molyneux and other designers. He opened his own fashion house in 1945. His designs were famous for elegant simplicity and included evening dresses, sportswear, and stoles. He also designed for the theatre and cinema.

Balmer, Johann Jakob (1825–98) Swiss physicist, born in Lausanne. Self-educated, he became interested in spectra late in life and produced a simple formula for the frequencies of lines in the visible part of the spectrum of hydrogen. This was deduced empirically, but a full explanation of the form of the relation later became clear through Niels Bohr's theory of atomic structure.

balmily *adv.*, *said of the air* warmly and softly.

balminess *noun*, *said of the air* being warm and soft.

Balmoral Castle a castle and estate of 9 700ha located on upper Deeside, Grampian, Scotland. It has been in the possession of the British royal family since 1852, and is used by them as a holiday home. The 19c castle was rebuilt under the direction of Prince Albert.

balmy[1] *adj.* (**balmier, balmiest**) *said of the air* warm and soft. [from Old French *basme*, balm]

balmy[2] same as BARMY.

baloney *or* **boloney** *noun slang* nonsense. [perhaps from *Bologna*, a type of sausage]

Baloo the bear who teaches Mowgli 'the Law of the Jungle' in Rudyard Kipling's *The Jungle Book*.

balsa *noun* **1** a tropical American tree. **2** (*also* **balsa-wood**) the very light wood of this tree. [from Spanish *balsa*, raft]

balsam *noun* **1** a pleasant-smelling thick sticky substance obtained from some trees and plants, used to make medicines and perfumes. **2** a tree or plant from which this substance is obtained. [from Latin *balsamum*]

Balt an Indo-European-speaking people living on the SE shores of the Baltic Sea, including Lithuanians, Latvians, and several extinct groups, such as Selonians and Prussians. They migrated to the area in the 3rd millennium BC and converted to Christianity in the 13c. Apart from the period 1917–40, they were under Russian rule from 1795 until 1991.

balti *noun* **1** a style of Indian cooking originating in Britain, in which food is both cooked and served in a pan resembling a wok. **2** the pan in which this is cooked. [from Hindi, = bucket]

Baltic Exchange the Baltic Mercantile and Shipping Exchange, a major world market for cargo space on sea and air freight, which originated in the London coffee houses, and is still found in the City of London. The Exchange also handles the market in some commodities (eg grain). It was blown up by terrorists in Apr 1992.

Baltic languages, a group of Indo-European languages, of which the main surviving examples are Latvian and Lithuanian. Both of these have written records dating from the 14c, and each has a standard form (with official status in its country), and many dialects too. Strong similarities between the Baltic and Slavic languages suggest the two groups may have a common origin, rather than being, as some people believe, the consequence of prolonged mutual influence. The Old Prussian language which is a member of the Baltic group is now extinct. See also SLAVIC LANGUAGES.

Baltic Sea, German **Ostsee**, ancient **Mare Suevicum** an arm of the Atlantic Ocean enclosed by Denmark, Sweden, Germany, Poland, Lithuania, Latvia, Estonia, Russia, Finland, and Sweden. It is connected to the North Sea by the Kattegat, Skagerrak, and Danish Straits, and the Kiel Canal. AREA 414 000sq km/160 000sq mi. Its deepest point is at Gotland Deep (c.463m). Chief arms are the gulfs of Bothnia, Finland, and Riga. The sea is generally shallow (average depth c.55m) with low salt levels and large areas frozen in winter. Navigation is impossible for three to five months each year. MAIN ISLANDS Hiiumma, Saaremaa, Aland, Gotland, Öland, Bornholm, Rüdgen, Fehmarn. Main ports include Kiel, Gdańsk, St Petersburg, Riga, Copenhagen, Stockholm, and Helsinki.

Baltic states the countries of Estonia, Latvia, and Lithuania on the E shore of the Baltic Sea. They were formed in 1918 from the Russian Baltic provinces or governments of Estonia, Livonia, and Courland, and parts of the governments of Pskov, Vitebsk, Kovno, Vilna, and Suvalki. The states were independent until 1940, when they were annexed by the USSR. They reclaimed their independence in 1991.

Baltimore, David (1938–) US molecular biologist, born in New York City. He discovered the enzyme 'reverse transcriptase' (1970) which could make DNA from RNA and allow scientists to manipulate the genetic code. He became a professor at the Massachusetts Institute of Technology in 1972. For his research into the connection between viruses and cancer, he shared the 1975 Nobel Prize for Physiology or Medicine with Howard Temin and Renato Dulbecco.

Baltimore POP (1990) 2.4m, a port in N Maryland, USA, on the Patapsco R, at the upper end of Chesapeake Bay. It is the largest city in the state and is a principal centre for culture and the arts. Its railway was the first in the USA. Established in 1729, it developed as a seaport and shipbuilding centre (famous for the Baltimore clippers) and achieved city status in 1797; rebuilt after a fire in 1904. Building of the first Roman Catholic cathedral in the USA began in the city in 1806. NOTABLE FEATURES the Inner Harbour; Edgar Allen Poe House.

Baltimore Incident a brief but serious dispute (1891) between the USA and Chile that stemmed from the death of two American sailors from the cruiser *Baltimore* in a brawl in Valparaiso. War between the two countries was averted by a Chilean apology.

Baluchistan POP (1985e) 4.9m, a province in W and SW Pakistan. AREA 347 190sq km/ 134 015sq mi. It is bounded W by Iran, N by Afghanistan, and S by the Arabian Sea. The province has a mountainous terrain, with large areas of desert. HISTORY ancient trading centre between India and the Middle East; the treaties of 1879 and 1891 brought the N section under direct British control; incorporated into Pakistan in 1947–8. CAPITAL Quetta. ECONOMY cotton; natural gas; fishing; salt; mineral reserves.

baluster *noun* each of a series of posts or pillars supporting a rail. [from French *balustre*]

balustrade *noun* a row of posts or pillars, joined by a rail, on the edge of a balcony, staircase, bridge, etc. [from French *balustrade*, from *balustre*, baluster]

Balzac, Honoré de (1799–1850) French novelist, born in Tours. He left Tours in 1819 to seek his fortune as an author in Paris and his first success was *Les Chouans* (1829), a novel about Breton peasants. After writing some other novels, he formed the design of presenting in the *Comédie humaine* (Human Comedy) a complete picture of modern civilization. The cycle of almost 90 novels contains his best-known works, including *Eugénie Grandet* (1833) and *Le Père Goriot* (Father Goriot, 1834). Despite producing 85 novels in 20 years, he never became wealthy.

Balzac a statue in bronze of Honoré de Balzac created by Auguste Rodin (1898, erected 1939, Montmartre, Paris).

Bamako POP (1992e) 746 000, the river-port capital of Mali, on the R Niger. It is a medieval centre of Islamic learning. The city became the capital of French Sudan in 1905.

bamboo *noun* 1 a tall grass that very rarely flowers, found mainly in tropical regions, with jointed hollow woody stems and deciduous leaves. Bamboo shoots are a popular food. 2 the stem of this grass, used in furniture making, basketry, building, etc, and as a garden cane. [probably from Malay *bambu*]

bamboo curtain *Politics* a term used in the West for the political and military barrier to communications around the People's Republic of China, especially in the 1950s and 1960s.

bamboozle *verb colloq.* 1 to trick or cheat. 2 to confuse.

bamboozlement *noun* cheating, trickery.

Bamian, Buddhas of two enormous images of Buddha cut into the cliffs of the Bamian Valley, Afghanistan, in the 6c. The figures, which are 53m and 35m high, were defaced by Nadir Shah's troops in the 18c.

ban — *noun* an official order that something may not be done: *a ban on advertising.* — *verb* (**banned, banning**) to forbid or prevent, especially officially or formally. [from Anglo-Saxon *bannan*, to summon]

banal *adj.* not original or interesting; tedious. [earlier meanings 'compulsory, common to all': from French *banal*]

banality *noun* (PL. **banalities**) something tedious or commonplace.

banana *noun* 1 a large perennial plant of the genus *Musa*, superficially resembling a tree, native to SE Asia, but cultivated throughout the tropics as a staple food crop. It has an underground stem, which at intervals bears buds that produce large oar-shaped leaves, the closely sheathing bases of which form a false 'stem' that rises to a height of several metres. The flower stalk grows up the hollow centre of the stem, emerging from the crown of leaves to droop towards the ground, and the bunches of fruit that develop after fertilization of the female flowers bend backwards to point away from the ground. 2 the long curved fruit of this plant, which despite its appearance is in fact a berry. It is often sold as an unblemished yellow fruit, but is not fully ripe until it is flecked with brown spots. The seeds within the fruit are sterile. [from a native name in Guinea]

banana republic *noun derog.* a poor country whose economy is dependent on foreign capital.

Banares see BENARES.

Banbury POP (1981) 38 000, a town in Cherwell district, Oxfordshire, S central England. It stands on the R Cherwell and the Oxford Canal, 35km/22mi N of Oxford. The cross famous in the nursery rhyme *Ride a Cock Horse* was destroyed by the Puritans in the 17c, but was replaced in 1858.

bancassurance *noun* the selling of insurance policies by a bank or building society through a wholly-owned subsidiary company.

Ban Chiang an archaeological site in NE Thailand, occupied c.4500–350 BC. It is a World Heritage site.

band[1] — *noun* 1 a flat narrow strip of cloth, metal, paper, etc used to hold things together or as a decoration. 2 a stripe of colour or strip of material differing from its background or surroundings. 3 a belt for driving machinery. 4 a group or range of radio frequencies between two limits: *waveband.* 5 a range of values between two limits. — *verb* to fasten or mark with a band. [from Old French *bande*]

band[2] — *noun* 1 a group of people with a common purpose or interest. 2 a group of musicians who play music other than classical music: *a rock band.* — *verb intrans., trans.* (**band together**) to unite to work for a common purpose. [from Old French *bande*]

Banda, Hastings Kamuzu (1906–) Malawi statesman, born near Kasungu. Trained as a physician in the USA and Britain, his opposition to the Central African Federation caused him to give up his successful London practice (1955) and return to Nyasaland (1958). As leader of the Malawi African Congress, he was gaoled in 1959, then became Minister of National Resources (1961), Prime Minister (1963), President of the Malawi (formerly Nyasaland) Republic (1966–), and was made Life President in 1971.

bandage — *noun* a strip of cloth for winding round a wound or a broken limb. — *verb* to wrap (a wound or a broken limb) in a bandage. [from French *bandage*]

Band Aid a pop charity established (1984) by Irish rock musician Bob Geldof (1954–) in response to Ethiopian famine appeals. The record 'Do They Know It's Christmas?' raised around £8 million.

bandana *or* **bandanna** *noun* a large brightly coloured cotton or silk square, folded and worn around the neck or head. [from Hindi *ba(n)dhnu*, a type of dyeing]

Bandaranaike, S(olomon) W(est) R(idgeway) D(ias) (1899–1959) Ceylonese (Sri Lankan) statesman, born in Colombo. He became the President of the Ceylon National Congress, and helped to found the United National Party. In Ceylon's first parliament, he was Leader of the House and Minister of Health. After resigning from government (1951) he organized the Sri Lanka Freedom Party, which returned him to parliament as Opposition Leader and as Prime Minister (1956–9) to pursue a policy of nationalization and neutralism. When he was assassinated by a Buddhist monk, he was succeeded by his wife Sirimavo Ratwatte Dias Bandaranaike (1916–), the world's first female Prime Minister (1960–5, 1970–7).

Bandar Seri Begawan, formerly **Brunei Town** POP (1991) 46 000, the capital of Brunei. It lies on the NW coast of Borneo, 20km/12mi from the mouth of the Brunei R. The town wharf has been used mainly for local vessels since the opening of the deep-water port at Muara in 1972. NOTABLE FEATURES Mesjid Sultan Omar Ali Saifuddin Mosque (1958); Churchill Museum; Sultan Hassanal Bolkiah Aquarium.

B and B *or* **B & B** *or* **b & b** *abbrev.* bed and breakfast.

bandbox *noun* a light round box for holding hats.

bandeau *noun* (PL. **bandeaux**) a narrow band of soft material worn around the head. [from French *bandeau*]

banded *adj.* marked with a stripe or stripes of a different colour.

banderole *noun* 1 a long narrow flag, usually with a forked end. 2 a flat, ribbon-like band carved into a stone wall, etc with writing on it. [from French *banderole*]

Bandiagara, Cliff of a cliff at the edge of the Dogon Plateau, at whose foot is located Bandiagara, a Dogon settlement. It is a World Heritage site.

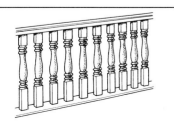

balustrade

bandicoot *noun* a large marsupial, native to Australia, Tasmania and Papua New Guinea. Its pouch opens towards the tail. There are 19 species, all of which have a rat-like appearance. They are nocturnal and dig for food (roots, insects, and worms) with their sharp claws.

bandicoot rat a giant rat found in India and Sri Lanka, where it is an agricultural pest. It is unrelated to the marsupial bandicoot.

bandit *noun* an armed robber, especially a member of a gang which attacks travellers. [from Italian *bandito*, outlaw]

bandmaster *noun* the conductor of a musical, especially brass, band.

bandog *noun* **1** an aggressive dog kept chained or tied up. **2** a dog that is a cross between an American pit bull terrier and a mastiff, rottweiler, or Rhodesian ridgeback, bred for exceptional ferocity. [from Middle English *band-dogge*, from *bande*, a tie or bond + DOG]

bandoleer *or* **bandolier** *noun* a leather shoulder belt, especially for carrying bullets. [from Old French *bandouillere*]

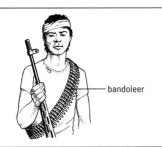

—— bandoleer

bandoleer

band-saw *noun* a saw consisting of a blade with teeth attached to a metal band which moves very fast around two wheels.

bandsman *noun* a member of a musical, especially brass, band.

bandstand *noun* a platform with a roof, often in a park, where bands play music.

Bandung POP (1990e) 2.5m, the capital of Java Barat province, W Java, Indonesia. It is situated 180km/112mi SE of Jakarta. The city was founded in 1810 and was the former administrative centre of the Dutch East Indies. At the Bandung Conference in 1955, 29 non-aligned countries met to facilitate joint diplomatic action. NOTABLE FEATURES Sundanese Cultural Centre.

bandwagon
— **jump** *or* **climb on the bandwagon** to join or show interest in an activity that is fashionable and likely to succeed.

bandwidth *noun Telecomm.* **1** the width or spread of the range of frequencies used for the transmission of radio or television signals. For television, it is determined by the field frequency, the number of scanning lines, and the colour-coding system. **2** the space in the frequency-domain occupied by signals a specified nature, eg television, radar, telephone-quality speech, etc.

bandy¹ *verb* (**bandies**, **bandied**) (**bandy something about** *or* **around**) **1** to pass (a story, information, etc) from one person to another. **2** to mention (someone's name) in rumour: *her name is being bandied about.*
— **bandy words with someone** to exchange (cross words, etc) with someone: *don't bandy words with me!*
[origin unknown]

bandy² *adj.* (**bandier**, **bandiest**) *said of a person's or animal's legs* curved or bending wide apart at the knee.

bandy-legged *adj.* having bandy legs.

bane *noun* the cause of trouble or evil: *the bane of my life.* [from Anglo-Saxon *bana*, murderer]

baneful *adj.* evil; causing harm.

Banff POP (1981) 3 900, the capital of Banff and Buchan district, Grampian region, NE Scotland. Situated on the N coast, on the left bank of the R Deveron, it is joined to the town of Macduff on the right bank. NOTABLE FEATURES museum, Duff House.

bang¹ — *noun* **1** a sudden loud explosive noise. **2** a heavy blow. **3** *coarse slang* an act of sexual intercourse. **4** *slang* an injection of an illegal drug. — *verb trans., intrans.* **1** to make a loud noise by hitting, dropping, closing violently, etc. **2** to hit sharply, especially by accident: *banged her elbow on the table.* **3** to make or cause to make the sound of an explosion. **4** *coarse slang* to have sexual intercourse with (someone). — *adv. colloq.* **1** exactly: *bang on time.* **2** suddenly.
— **bang away** *colloq.* to make a continuous noise.
go off with a bang to be a great success.
[from Norse *banga*, to hammer]

bang² *noun North Amer., esp. US (usually* **bangs***)* hair cut in a straight line across the forehead.

Bangalore POP (1991) 4.1m, the capital of Karnataka state, S central India. It lies 290km/ 180mi W of Madras. The city was founded in 1537 and served as the military headquarters of the British-administered district of Mysore from 1831 to 1947.

banger *noun* **1** *colloq.* a sausage. **2** *colloq.* an old car, usually noisy and in poor condition. **3** a loud firework.

Banghazi see BENGHAZI.

Bangkok POP (1990) 5.9m, the capital of Thailand. It lies on the Chao Praya R, 25km/15mi from its mouth on the Bight of Thailand. The city became capital of Thailand in 1782. There are many canals in the old city and these are accessible to small, ocean-going vessels. It has been the headquarters of the SE Asia Treaty Organization since 1955. NOTABLE FEATURES Grand Palace; temples of the Golden Buddha and Reclining Buddha; the Phra Pathom Chedi, the world's tallest Buddhist monument, is located 60km/ 37mi W of the city.

Bangladesh, formerly **East Pakistan**, official name **People's Republic of Bangladesh**, **Gana Prajatantri Bangladesh** POP (1992e) 119.3m, an Asian republic lying between the foothills of the Himalayas and the Indian Ocean, and divided into 24 regions. AREA 143 998sq km/55 583sq mi. It is bounded W, NW and E by India, SE by Burma (Myanma), and S by the Bay of Bengal. CAPITAL Dhaka. CHIEF TOWNS Chittagong, Khulna, Narayanganj. TIME ZONE GMT +6. It is one of the world's most densely populated areas. Most of the population is Bengali (98%), with Biharis and tribal minorities; Islam is the chief religion with some Hinduism, Buddhism, and Christianity. OFFICIAL LANGUAGE Bengali (Bangla); English is the second language. CURRENCY the taka. PHYSICAL DESCRIPTION mainly a vast, low-lying alluvial plain, cut by a network of rivers, canals, swamps, and marshes; main rivers are the Ganges (Padma), Brahmaputra (Jamuna), and Meghna, joining in the S to form the largest delta in the world; subject to frequent flooding; in the E, fertile valleys and peaks of Chittagong Hill Tracts rise to c.1 000m; lush vegetation, with bamboo and palm forests in the E, mixed monsoon forest in the Madhuper Jungle, vast areas of the S delta are covered in mangroves and hardwood forest. CLIMATE tropical monsoon climate; a hot season in Mar–Jun with heavy thunderstorms; very humid, with higher temperatures inland; the main rainy season is Jun–Sep; cyclones in the Bay of Bengal cause sea surges and widespread inundation of coastal areas. HISTORY part of the State of Bengal until Muslim East Bengal was created

in 1905, separate from Hindu West Bengal; reunited in 1911; again partitioned in 1947, with West Bengal remaining in India and East Bengal forming East Pakistan; disparity in investment and development between East and West Pakistan (separated by over 1 600km/1 000mi), coupled with language differences, caused East Pakistan to seek autonomy; rebellion in 1971 led to independence, helped by India; political unrest led to the suspension of the constitution in 1975, and the assassination of the first president, Sheikh Mujib; further coups in 1975, 1977, and 1982; constitution restored in 1986; the nation came to a stand during strikes in 1992 and there were many deaths and injuries. GOVERNMENT parliament has one 300-member chamber, with 30 seats reserved for women; members are elected every five years. ECONOMY 85% of the working population is employed in agriculture, especially rice; tea, tobacco, sugar; supplies 80% of the world's jute; jute mills, paper, aluminium, textiles, glass; shipbuilding; fishing; natural gas; coal; peat; limestone.

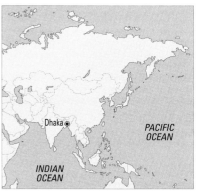

Bangladesh

bangle *noun* a piece of jewellery in the form of a solid band, worn round the arm or leg. [from Hindi *bangri*, glass ring]

Bangor POP (1981) 47 000 a city in Afon district, Gwynedd NW Wales. It is situated opposite the island of Anglesey. NOTABLE FEATURES university (1884); cathedral founded in the 6c.

Bangui POP (1988) 452 000, the capital of the Central African Republic. It lies on the R Ubangi, 1 030km/640mi NE of Brazzaville. Bangui was founded in 1889. NOTABLE FEATURE Boganda Museum.

banian see BANYAN.

Bani-Sadr, Abolhassan (1933–) Iranian politician. He studied in Paris, having fled there in 1963 after being imprisoned in Iran for involvement in riots against Shah Mohammed Reza Pahlvavi's regime. An important figure in the Iranian Revolution of 1978–9, he joined the Revolutionary Council and was elected the first President of the Islamic Republic of Iran (1980–1). Threatened throughout by a deepening conflict with the fundamentalist Muslim clergy, he was eventually criticised by the Ayatollah Khomeini, and dismissed (mid-1981). He fled to France, where he was granted political asylum.

banish *verb* **1** to send (someone) away from a place, usually the country of origin. **2** to put (thoughts, etc) out of one's mind. [from Old French *bannir*]

banishment *noun* the act or an instance of banishing.

banister *or* **bannister** *noun* (*usually* **banisters**) a row of posts and the hand-rail they support, running up the side of a staircase. [from BALUSTER]

banjo *noun* (PL. **banjos**, **banjoes**) a stringed musical instrument with a long neck and a round body, played like a guitar. [probably of African origin]

banjoist *noun* a person who plays a banjo.

Banjul, formerly **Bathurst** (to 1973) POP (1986e) 44 000, the seaport capital of The Gambia. It is situated on the Island of St Mary in the estuary of the R Gambia, 195km/121mi SE of Dakar. In 1816 it was established as a settlement for freed slaves. NOTABLE FEATURE Fort Bullen (1826).

bank[1] — *noun* **1** a long raised pile of earth, snow, etc. **2** the side or slope of a hill. **3** the ground at the edge of a river, lake, etc. **4** a raised area of sand under the sea. **5** a mass of cloud, mist, or fog. — *verb* **1** *trans., intrans.* (**bank up**) to form into a bank or banks. **2** (**bank something up**) to cover a fire with a large amount of coal to keep it burning. **3** *intrans., trans. said of an aircraft* to change direction, with one wing higher than the other. [from Middle English *banke*]

bank[2] — *noun* **1** a financial organization which keeps money in accounts for its clients, lends money, exchanges currency, etc. **2** a box in which money can be saved, especially by children. **3** a place where something is stored or collected for later use: *blood bank*. **4** in some games, a stock of money controlled by one of the players (the banker). — *verb* **1** to put (money) into a bank. **2** *intrans.* to have a bank account: *they bank with Lloyds*.
— **bank on something** to rely on or expect (something).
[from French *banque*]

bank[3] *noun* a collection of similar things arranged in rows: *a bank of switches*. [from Old French *banc*, bench]

bank account an arrangement by which a person or company keeps money in a bank and makes withdrawals when necessary.

bank base-rate a base lending rate for UK clearing banks, used as the primary measure for interest rates since 1981. It is influenced by government economic policy through the Bank of England, and is the basis on which banks calculate their interest rates to borrowers and depositors.

bank book a book recording the amounts of money put into and taken out of a bank account.

bank card *or* **banker's card** (same as cheque card)

bank draft a written order sent from a one bank to another for paying money to a customer.

banker *noun* **1** a person who owns or manages a bank. **2** a person in charge of the bank in some games.

banker's order see STANDING ORDER.

bank holiday *noun Brit.* any of several days in the year on which banks are closed, observed as a public holiday in England and Wales.

banking *noun* the business done by a bank.

banknote *noun* a piece of paper money issued by a bank.

Bank of England the official government bank of Britain, founded in London in 1694 by William Paterson, and in state ownership since 1946. It controls the supply of money, prints notes and mints coins, acts as a banker to the government and to other banks, and manages the gold and currency reserves.

bankroll — *noun* money or cash resources. — *verb colloq.* to finance.

bankrupt — *noun* a person who is legally recognized as not being able to pay debts. — *adj.* **1** not having money to pay one's debts. **2** (**bankrupt of something**) exhausted of or lacking some quality, etc: *bankrupt of ideas*. — *verb* to make bankrupt. [from French *banqueroute*, altered

under the influence of Latin *banca rupta*, bank broken]

bankruptcy *noun* (PL. **bankruptcies**) a state of being bankrupt.
◇ A person who cannot pay his or her debts is *insolvent*, and only becomes bankrupt when a court has made an adjudication order. When this order is made, ownership and control of all the bankrupt's assets and property passes to a trustee in bankruptcy, appointed by the court to administer the debtor's affairs. Bankrupt individuals may not obtain credit above a certain limit, or be a company director, MP, JP, or local councillor, and may only be discharged from bankruptcy by order of the court (this is granted automatically after a certain period in the majority of cases). Bankruptcy is not the same as *liquidation*.

Banks, Sir Joseph (1744–1820) English botanist, born in London. Between 1768 and 1771 he accompanied James Cook's expedition round the world in the *Endeavour*, and in 1778 he was elected President of the Royal Society, an office which he held for 41 years. Significant for his far-reaching influence, he was responsible for the introduction of the mango from Bengal, and many fruits of Ceylon and Australia; the colony of New South Wales owed its origin mainly to him. His name is commemorated in the genus *Banksia*.

banksia *noun* a low shrub or small tree of the genus *Banksia*, native to Australia, and having small sharply-toothed leathery leaves, and cream, orange, red, or purplish flowers with four petals and a protruding style. Up to 1 000 flowers are borne in spectacular spherical or cylindrical flower heads which develop into cone-like fruits with woody capsules. [named after the UK botanist Sir Joseph Banks]

bank switching *Comput.* a method of accessing more memory than can normally be addressed at one time, by switching between one bank of memory and another.

Banna, Hassan al- (1906–49) Islamic fundamentalist, born in Mahmudiya, near Cairo. In 1928 he founded the Society of Muslim Brothers (better known as the Muslim Brotherhood or Brethren) in Egypt. It preached a return to the purity of early Islam, and began a movement that has had considerable influence on contemporary Islamic fundamentalism. In 1948 the Egyptian Prime Minister, Nuqrashi Pasha, was killed by a Brotherhood member, and in 1949 al-Banna too was murdered, though he had condemned the assassination.

banner *noun* **1** a large piece of cloth or cardboard, with a design, slogan, etc carried at public meetings and parades. **2** a military flag. [from Old French *baniere*]

banner headline a newspaper headline written in large letters across the width of the page.

Bannister, Sir Roger (Gilbert) (1929–) English track athlete, born in Harrow, the first man to run the mile in under four minutes. He won a silver medal in the 800m in the 1950 European championship, ran in the 1952 Olympics, and in 1954 won the European 1500m title. His record-breaking mile (3 min 59.4 sec) was run in Oxford on 6 May 1954. He also ran a mile in under three minutes to win the Commonwealth Games title in 1954.

bannock *noun dialect* a small flat round cake, usually made from oatmeal. [from Anglo-Saxon *bannuc*]

Bannockburn, Battle of a battle (1314) fought near Stirling between English forces under Edward II and the Scots under Robert Bruce. The Scots were victorious, having largely destroyed the English army and killed or captured many English nobles. The battle made Bruce a national hero, and instigated Scottish counter-attacks against N England.

Bann, River a major river in Northern Ireland, length 93km/58mi. Rising in the Mourne Mts, it flows 40km/25mi NW to enter the S end of Lough Neagh, then flows N for 53km/33mi through Lough Beg to enter the Atlantic Ocean.

banns *pl. noun* a public announcement in church of two people's intention to marry. [from Anglo-Saxon *bannan*, to summon]

banquet — *noun* **1** a sumptuous formal dinner. **2** *loosely* an elaborate meal. — *verb trans., intrans.* (**banqueted, banqueting**) to entertain with or take part in a banquet. [from French *banquet*]

Banquet of the Officers of the St George Militia Company, The a group portrait by Frans Hals (Haarlem, 1616).

Banquo the fellow general of Macbeth in Shakespeare's *Macbeth* who, after being told by the Witches that his descendants will be kings, is murdered by Macbeth.

banshee *noun, especially in Irish and Scottish folklore* a female spirit whose sad cries outside a house warn that a member of the family will die. [from Irish Gaelic *bean sídhe*, woman of the fairies]

Banská Bystrica POP (1990) 87 000, the capital of Středoslovenský region, Slovakia. It is situated in the foothills of the low Tatra Mts, at the junction of the Hron and Bystrica rivers. The town, founded in the 13c, was formerly important for gold-mining.

bantam *noun* **1** a small breed of farm chicken. **2** a small but forceful person. [probably from *Bantam* in Java, from where such chickens may have been first imported]

bantamweight *noun* **1** a class for boxers, wrestlers, and weightlifters of not more than a specified weight (54kg in professional boxing, slightly more in the other sports). **2** a boxer, etc of this weight.

banter — *noun* light-hearted friendly talk. — *verb intrans.* (**bantered, bantering**) to tease or joke.

bantering *adj., noun* light-heartedly teasing.

Banting, Sir Frederick Grant (1891–1941) Canadian physiologist, born in Alliston, Ontario. While working at the laboratory of John Macleod in Toronto, he isolated pancreatic extracts (the hormone insulin) for the treatment of diabetes in 1921 (with Charles Best and James Collip). He was appointed Professor of Medical Research at Toronto in 1923, and shared the 1923 Nobel Prize for Physiology or Medicine with Macleod. A pioneer in aviation medicine, he was killed in a wartime air crash.

Bantu — *noun* **1** a group of languages spoken in southern and central Africa. **2** (*pl.*) the group of peoples who speak these languages. **3** *offensive* a black speaker of one of these languages. — *adj.* of the Bantu languages or Bantu-speaking people. [from Bantu people]
◇ The Bantu-speaking peoples are ethnically diverse, and comprise altogether some 60 million people in the S part of Africa. They may have originated in the region of modern Cameroon, and from there dispersed S, E, and NE. They have mingled with Khoisan peoples and with coastal Arab traders in the E. Their dispersal occurred in the early years of the Christian era.

Bantustan *noun, often offensive* any of the partially self-governing regions reserved for black South Africans. [from BANTU + -*stan* as in Hindustan]

Banville, (Etienne Claude Jean Baptiste) Théodore (Faullain) de (1823–91) French poet and dramatist, born in Moulins. Known as the 'roi des rimes' for his ingenuity in handling medieval ballades and rondels, his comedy *Gringoire* (1866) holds an established place in French repertory.

banyan *or* **banian** *noun* an Indian fruit tree with branches from which shoots grow down into the ground and take root. [from Portuguese *banian*, from Gujarati *vaniyo*, man of the trading caste]

baobab *noun* a large deciduous African tree of the genus *Adansonia*, with a massive soft trunk which serves as a water store, and a relatively small crown. It produces an edible fruit (monkey-bread) resembling a gourd, and the trunk is sometimes hollowed out for use as a human dwelling. [probably from an African language]

baobab tree

BAOR *abbrev.* British Army of the Rhine.

baptism *noun* the religious ceremony of baptizing a person.
◇ The Christian ritual is usually traced to the New Testament, where new converts were immersed in water (Acts 8.38–9) and where the rite is linked with the imparting of the Spirit and with repentance (Acts 2.38, 10.47). Nowadays, practices vary in different Churches: some denominations favour infant baptism, others adult baptism; some practise total immersion, others the sprinkling of water on the head.

baptismal *adj.* relating to or for baptism.

baptist *noun* **1** a person who baptizes, especially John the Baptist. **2** (**Baptist**) a member of a Christian group which believes that only people who are able to profess their religious beliefs should be baptized, and that they should be completely immersed in water.
◇ Baptists originated in early 17c England and Wales, and, in the USA, Baptist churches spread rapidly in the late 19c. There is now a worldwide communion; the Baptist World Alliance was formed in 1905. The emphasis in worship is on scripture and preaching, and each congregation is self-governing.

baptistery *or* **baptistry** *noun* (PL. **baptisteries**) **1** the part of a church where baptisms are carried out. **2** a tank of water for baptisms in a Baptist church.

Baptistery Doors 1 the earliest bronze doors made for the Baptistery (Battistero S Giovanni) in Florence by Andrea Pisano (1336). **2** three sculptured bronze doors carved by Lorenzo Ghiberti (1403–c.1453).

baptize *or* **baptise** *verb* **1** to sprinkle with or dip in water as a sign of having become a member of the Christian Church. In the case of babies, this is usually accompanied by name-giving. **2** to give a name to. [from Greek *baptizein*, to immerse]

Barbados

bar¹ — *noun* **1** a block of some solid substance: *bar of soap.* **2** a rod or long piece of a strong rigid material used as a fastening, weapon, obstruction, etc. **3** anything that prevents or hinders: *a bar to progress.* **4** a line or band of colour, light, etc, especially a stripe on a shield. **5** a room or counter in a restaurant, hotel, etc, or a separate establishment, where alcoholic drinks are sold and drunk. **6** a small café where drinks and snacks are served: *a coffee bar.* **7** a counter where some special service is available: *a heel bar.* **8** a vertical line marked on music, dividing it into sections of equal value; one of these sections. **9** the rail in a law court where the accused person stands. **10** (**the Bar**) the profession of barristers and advocates. **11** a raised area of sand, mud, stones, etc at the mouth of a river or harbour. **12** an addition to a medal, usually to show that it has been won more than once: *DSO and bar.* — *verb* (**barred**, **barring**) **1** to fasten with a bar. **2** (**bar someone from a place**) to forbid them to enter it. **3** to prevent (progress). **4** to mark with a stripe or bar. — *prep.* except.
— **be called to the Bar** to be made a barrister.
behind bars in prison.
[from Old French *barre*]

bar² *noun* a unit of (especially atmospheric) pressure, 10_5 newtons per square metre. See also MILLIBAR. [from Greek *baros*, weight]

Barabbas (1c AD) a political rebel and murderer (as described in Mark 15, Luke 23) who was released from captivity by popular acclaim in preference to Pilate's offer to release Jesus of Nazareth. He was possibly also called 'Jesus Barabbas' (in some manuscripts of Matthew 27. 16–17).

Bar aux Folies-Bergère, Un a painting by Edouard Manet (1881–2, Courtauld Institute, London). It was his last major work.

barb — *noun* **1** a point on a hook facing in the opposite direction to the main point, which makes it difficult to pull the hook out. **2** a humorous but hurtful remark. — *verb* to fit with barbs. [from Latin *barba*, beard]

Barba, Eugenio (1936–) Italian theatre director and founder of Odin Teatret, an experimental theatre company and centre for collective research in performance. In 1979 he established the International School of Theatre Anthropology. His theoretical writings include *The Floating Islands* (1984) and *Beyond the Floating Islands* (1986).

Barbados POP (1992e) 259 000, an independent state and the most easterly of the Caribbean Is, divided into 11 districts. AREA 430sq km/166sq mi. It is situated in the Atlantic Ocean, 320km/199mi NW of Trinidad. CAPITAL Bridgetown. CHIEF TOWN Speightstown. TIME ZONE GMT –4. The population is 80% of African descent, 16% mixed race, and 4% European; Protestantism is the main religion. OFFICIAL LANGUAGE English. CURRENCY Barbados dollar. PHYSICAL DESCRIPTION a small, triangular island, 32km/20mi long (NW–SE); it rises to 340m at Mt Hillaby and is ringed by a coral reef. CLIMATE tropical, with an average annual temperature of 27°C and an average annual rainfall of 1 420mm. HISTORY colonized by the British in 1627; self-government attained in 1961; it became an independent sovereign state within the Commonwealth in 1966. GOVERNMENT executive power rests with the Prime Minister, appointed by a Governor-General; there is a 21-member Senate, and a House of Assembly with 27 elected members. ECONOMY sugar cane; rum; molasses; cotton; bananas; vegetables; natural gas; garments, electronic and electrical equipment; medical supplies; tourism.

Barbara a female first name, borne by the patron saint of architects. [from Latin *barbarus*, foreign]

barbarian — *noun* **1** a person who is cruel and wild in behaviour. **2** a person who is uncivilized

and uncultured. [from Greek *barbaros*, foreign] — *adj.* cruel and wild; uncivilized.

barbaric *adj.* **1** cruel and brutal. **2** coarse and rude.

barbarically *adv.* in a barbaric or cruel manner; brutally.

barbarism *noun* **1** the state of being uncivilized, coarse, etc. **2** a coarse or ignorant act. **3** an utterance which is considered coarse or ungrammatical.

barbarity *noun* (PL. **barbarities**) **1** the state of being cruel, coarse, uncivilized, etc. **2** a cruel, coarse, or uncivilized act.

Barbarossa *or* **Redbeard** (16c) European name for two Turkish pirates, whose activities brought Algeria and Tunisia into the Ottoman Empire. Aruj was killed fighting the Spaniards in 1518. Khayr al-Din, his brother, entered the service of the Ottoman Sultan, and drove the Spaniards from Algiers, which became the main base of piracy in the S Mediterranean.

barbarous *adj.* **1** uncultured and uncivilized. **2** extremely cruel or brutal. **3** coarse or rude.

barbarously *adv.* in an uncivilized or brutal manner.

Barbary Coast the coast of N Africa from Morocco to Tripolitania (Libya), famous for piracy between the 16c and 18c. This coast and the Barbary States of Morocco, Algeria, Tunisia, and Tripolitania have taken their names from Barbarossa, who led the Turkish conquest of the region in the 1530s, preventing Spanish invasion.

barbecue — *noun* **1** a frame on which food is grilled over an open fire. **2** food cooked in this way. **3** a party held out of doors at which food is cooked on a barbecue. — *verb* to cook on a barbecue. [from S American Arawak *barbacòa*, framework of sticks]

barbed *adj.* having a barb or barbs. *said of a remark* spiteful, vindictive.

barbed wire wire with short sharp points twisted on at intervals, used for making fences, etc.

barbel *noun* **1** a long beard-like growth at the mouth of some fishes. **2** a type of fish with such growths. [from Latin *barba*, beard]

barbel

barbell *noun* a bar with heavy metal weights at each end, used for weightlifting exercises.

Barber, Chris (Donald Christopher) (1930–) English jazz trombonist and band-leader, born in Welwyn Garden City, Hertfordshire. A leading figure in the trad movement, he took over the Ken Colyer band in 1953, and replaced its former purism with a flexible repertoire. His successes include 'Rock Island Line' (1956) and 'Petite Fleur' (1959), which feature skiffle pioneer Lonnie Donegan (1931–) and clarinettist Monty Sunshine (1928–) respectively, rather than his own characteristic trombone sound. He is also a skilled musicologist.

barber *noun* a person who cuts and styles men's hair, and shaves their beards. [from Old French *barbeor*, from Latin *barba*, beard]

Barber of Seville, The (Il barbiere de Siviglia) an opera buffa by Gioacchino Rossini (1816), based on a play by Beaumarchais. One of the most popular comic operas ever, it centres around the attempts of the roguish barber Figaro to arrange the marriage of Count Almaviva to Rosina, the ward of Dr Bartolo, who also wants to marry her.

barberry *noun* (PL. **barberries**) a bushy plant or shrub with thorns, yellow flowers, and red berries. [from Latin *berberis*]

barbershop *noun* a type of singing in which four men sing in close harmony without musical accompaniment.

barbet *noun* a plump brightly coloured bird that inhabits the tropics worldwide, especially Africa, and is usually a forest-dweller, named after its 'beard' of feathers at the base of its large bill. It feeds on fruit, flowers, and insects. [from Latin *barba*, beard]

barbican *noun* a tower over the outer gate of a castle or town, allowing the gate to be defended. [from Old French *barbacane*]

Barbican Centre, in full **Barbican Arts and Conference Centre** a cultural complex in central London, opened in 1982. It includes the Barbican Theatre (the London home of the Royal Shakespeare Company), the Barbican Hall (the home of the London Symphony Orchestra), and cinemas, art galleries, and restaurants.

Barbirolli, Sir John (1899–1970) British conductor and cellist, born in London of Franco-Italian parents. After service in World War I, he played in several leading string quartets (1920–4), succeeded Toscanini as conductor of the New York Philharmonic (1937), and returned to England as permanent conductor (1943–58) of the Hallé Orchestra, which under him was reinstated as one of the world's finest. He married the oboist Evelyn Rothwell (1911–) in 1939 and became principal conductor of the Hallé in 1958.

barbiturate *noun Medicine* a salt or ester of barbituric acid, used as a source of sedative and hypnotic drugs, eg sleeping pills, and anaesthetics. Barbiturates have toxic side-effects and are potentially addictive when used over long periods, so are increasingly being replaced by safer drugs.

Barbizon School a group of French landscape painters working (c.1830–80) in Barbizon, a village in the Forest of Fontainebleau. They were pioneers of *plein air* (open air) painting, and sketched out-of-doors, directly from nature, in a way that foreshadowed the Pre-Raphaelites in England and also the Impressionists in France. Leading members included Théodore Rousseau (1812–67), Charles François Daubigny (1817–78), Narciso-Virgilio Díaz (1807–76), and Constant Troyon (1810–65).

Barbour, John (c.1316–96) Scottish poet and historian. His national epic, *The Brus* (first printing 1571), is a narrative poem on the deeds of King Robert the Bruce. He was Archdeacon of Aberdeen from c.1357 until his death.

Barbusse, Henri (1873–1935) French novelist, born in Asnières. He fought in World War I, an experience which inspired *Le Feu* (Under Fire, 1916), a realistic portrayal of life in the trenches.

barcarole *or* **barcarolle** *noun* a gondolier's song, or a piece of music with a similar rhythm. [from Italian *barcarola*, boat-song]

Barcelona, ancient **Barcino Barcinona** POP (1991) 1.7m, a major seaport and the capital of Barcelona province, Catalonia, NE Spain. It is 621km/386mi NE of Madrid, and Spain's second largest city. It is the centre of Catalan art and literature, and the base of a separatist political movement. NOTABLE FEATURES Gothic Quarter, including cathedral (13c), Ramblas Palace, Church of the Holy Family, Museum of Catalan Art, Maritime Museum, Bishop's Palace, Palace of la Virreina Art Gallery; Casa Mila (1906–10), Casa Güell (1900–14), and Parque Güell (1900–14) are World Heritage monuments by Gaudí.

Barcelona, Battle of the final event (1713–14) in the War of the Spanish Succession, when the Catalans were abandoned by their allies (the Germans and the English) and forced to defend themselves or accept unconditional surrender. After a bloody siege, the Duke of Berwick at the head of the Franco-Spanish army entered the city. The date of the surrender (11 Sep) is now commemorated as the national day of Catalonia.

bar chart *or* **bar graph**, a graph which shows values or amounts by means of vertical bars. See also PIE CHART.

bar code a machine-readable code consisting of a sequence of parallel stripes of varying thickness. The code is put on the cover or wrapping of retail products, and contains information for sales checkouts and stock control.

bar code

bard *noun* **1** *literary* a poet. **2** a poet who has won a prize at the Eisteddfod in Wales. [from Scots Gaelic *bàrd* and Irish Gaelic *bard*, poet]

Bardeen, John (1908–) US physicist, born in Madison, Wisconsin. He joined a new solid-state physics group at Bell Telephone Laboratories in 1945, and together with Walter Brattain and William Shockley he developed the point-contact transistor (1947), for which they shared the 1956 Nobel Prize for Physics. Professor at Illinois University (1951–75), he was awarded the Nobel Prize for Physics again in 1972 jointly with Leon Cooper and John Schrieffer for developing 'BCS' theory, the first satisfactory theory of how superconductivity arises.

bardic *adj.* relating to bards or to heroic poetry.

Bardolph the cowardly thief endowed with a bulbous red nose, in Shakespeare's *Henry IV Part I, Henry IV Part II, Henry V*, and *The Merry Wives of Windsor*.

Bardot, Brigitte (1934–) French film actress, born in Paris. She was 'discovered' while working as a photographic model by the director Roger Vadim, who later married her, and from 1952 made her an international sex-symbol. Their greatest success was in *Et Dieu Créa La Femme* (And God Created Woman, 1956) and she played many 'sex-kitten' parts throughout the 1960s. Her last major film was *Si Don Juan Etait Une Femme* (If Don Juan were a Woman, 1973), and in later years she has become closely concerned with animal welfare and the cause of endangered animal species.

bare — *adj.* **1** not covered by clothes; naked. **2** without the usual or natural covering: *bare trees.* **3** empty: *the cupboard was bare.* **4** simple; plain: *the bare facts.* **5** basic; essential: *the bare necessities.* — *verb* to uncover.
— **bare one's heart** *or* **soul** to make known one's private thoughts and feelings.
lay something bare to make known a secret, etc.
with one's bare hands without weapons or tools.
[from Anglo-Saxon *bær*]

bareback *adv., adj.* riding on a horse without a saddle.

bare bones the essential facts.

Barebones Parliament the British 'Parliament of Saints' (4 Jul–12 Dec 1653), named after radical member Praise-God Barebone, and nominated by the Council of Officers of the Army to succeed the Rump Parliament. It instituted civil marriage and sought legal reforms, but collapsed after disagreements over the abolition of tithes and lay patronage in Church.

barefaced *adj.* having no shame or regret.

barefacedly *adv.* without shame; openly.

barefoot *or* **barefooted** *adj., adv.* not wearing shoes or socks.

bareheaded *adj., adv.* not wearing a hat.

barelegged *adj., adv.* with the legs uncovered.

barely *adv.* **1** scarcely or only just: *barely enough.* **2** plainly, simply: *barely furnished.*

Barenboim, Daniel (1942–) Israeli pianist and conductor, born in Buenos Aires, where he made his début at the age of seven. He studied with Igor Markevich and Nadia Boulanger, and has performed regularly in Europe since 1954. A noted exponent of Mozart and Beethoven, he gained his reputation as pianist/conductor with the English Chamber Orchestra, then became musical director of the Orchestre de Paris (1975–89) and of the Chicago Symphony Orchestra (1991–), and musical and artistic director of the Deutsche Staatsoper, Berlin (1991–). He was married to the cellist Jacqueline du Pré from 1967.

bareness *noun* being bare or naked.

Barents Sea, Russian **Barentsovo More**, Norwegian **Barents Havet** a shallow arm of the Arctic Ocean, lying N of Norway and Russia. The warm North Cape Current, a continuation of the North Atlantic Drift, disperses pack ice in the S. The ports of Murmansk and Vardö are ice-free throughout the year. The Barents Sea is a rich fishing area.

Barentz *or* **Barents, William** (c.1550–1597) Dutch navigator, who was pilot to three Dutch expeditions (1594–6) in search of the Northeast Passage. He died off Novaya Zemlya, and in 1871, his winter quarters were found undisturbed after 274 years by another expedition.

bargain — *noun* **1** an agreement made between people buying and selling things, offering and accepting services, etc: *strike a bargain.* **2** something offered for sale, or bought, at a low price. — *verb intrans.* to discuss the terms for buying or selling, etc.
— **not bargain for something** to be unprepared for it.
bargain on something to rely on it or expect it to happen.
drive a hard bargain to enter into an agreement only after bargaining hard for the best terms.
into the bargain in addition; besides.
[from Old French *bargaine*]

bargainer *noun* a person who bargains, especially of a specified kind: *a hard bargainer.*

barge — *noun* **1** a long flat-bottomed boat used on rivers and canals. **2** a large boat, often decorated, used in ceremonies, celebrations, etc. — *verb* **1** (**barge about** *or* **around**) to move in a clumsy ungraceful way. **2** (**barge in** *or* **into something**) to hit or knock it clumsily. **3** (**barge past** *or* **through**) to make one's way rudely or roughly. **4** (**barge in**) to interrupt a conversation, especially rudely or abruptly. [from Old French *barge*, from Latin *barga*]

bargee *noun* a person in charge of a barge.

bargepole *noun* a long pole used to move or guide a barge.
— **not touch someone or something with a bargepole** *colloq.* to refuse to have anything to do with them.

Bari POP (1991e) 353 000, the seaport capital of Puglia region, SE Italy, situated in Bari province. It lies on a peninsula in the Adriatic Sea, NW of Brindisi. An important industrial and commercial centre, it is the site of Italy's first atomic power station. NOTABLE FEATURE Cathedral of San Nicola (begun in 1087).

barite *noun Geol.* barytes.

baritone *noun* **1** the second lowest male singing voice, between bass and tenor. **2** a singer with such a voice. **3** in music, a part that is written for such a voice. [from Greek *barytonos*, deep-sounding]

barium *noun Chem.* (SYMBOL **Ba**, ATOMIC NUMBER **56**) a soft silvery-white metal mainly obtained from the mineral barytes. Barium compounds, the soluble forms of which are highly poisonous, burn with a green flame and are used in fireworks and flares, and as paint pigments. Barium sulphate is used as a contrast medium in medicine to show the outline of the digestive system when it is being X-rayed. [from Greek *barys*, heavy]

barium meal *Medicine* a preparation of barium sulphate and water drunk by a patient prior to X-ray of the digestive system. It cannot be penetrated by X-rays, and so forms an opaque shadow which shows the outline of the stomach and intestines.

bark¹ — *noun* the short sharp cry of a dog, fox, etc. — *verb* **1** *intrans.* to make this sound. **2** (**bark out** *or* **bark something out**) to speak loudly and sharply: *barked out a series of commands.*
— **bark up the wrong tree** *colloq.* to have the wrong idea.
[from Anglo-Saxon *beorcan*]

bark² — *noun Bot.* the tough protective outer layer, consisting mainly of dead cells, that covers the stems and roots of woody plants, eg trees. It includes all the tissue lying external to the cambium. — *verb* **1** to scrape or rub off the skin from (one's leg). **2** to strip or remove the bark from (a tree, etc). [from Norse *börkr*]

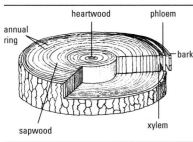

cross section through a tree

bark³ see BARQUE.

barker *noun* a person outside a circus, show, etc who shouts to attract customers.

Barkhausen, Heinrich Georg (1881–1956) German physicist, born in Bremen. As professor in Dresden from 1911, he carried out fundamental research on electron tubes and electrical oscillations, and he also developed the *Barkhausen–Kurz oscillator*, an electron tube capable of continuous-wave oscillations at ultra-high frequencies which was the forerunner of modern microwave tubes. In 1919 he discovered the 'Barkhausen effect', that the magnetization of iron proceeds in discrete steps, and he devised a loudspeaker system to render this discontinuity audible.

Barkis the taciturn carrier in Charles Dickens's *David Copperfield*, who doggedly woos Clara Peggotty.

Bar Kokhba *or* **Bar Kosiba, Simon** (d.AD 135) the leader of the Jews in their great but fruitless insurrection against the emperor Hadrian (132–4). In 1960 some of his letters were found in caves near the Dead Sea.

barley *noun* **1** a cereal (*Hordeum vulgare*) of the grass family (Gramineae), which bears a dense head of grains with long slender bristles (awns). It is more tolerant of low temperatures, drought, and poor soil than wheat, and is an important crop in north temperate regions, especially the former Soviet Union and N Europe. **2** the grain of this plant, which when partially germinated is used in the brewing of beer and the production of whisky. It is also used as feed for animal livestock. [from Anglo-Saxon *bærlic*, of barley]

barleycorn *noun* same as BARLEY 2.

barley sugar a kind of hard orange-coloured sweet, made by melting and cooling sugar.

barley water a drink made from water in which barley has been boiled, usually with orange or lemon juice added.

barmaid *noun* a woman who serves drinks in a bar.

barman *noun* (PL. **barmen**) a man who serves drinks in a bar.

bar mitzvah **1** a Jewish ceremony in which a boy usually aged 13 formally accepts full religious responsibilities. **2** a boy for whom this ceremony is conducted. [from Hebrew *bar mitzvah*, son of the law]

barmy *adj.* (**barmier**, **barmiest**) *colloq.* crazy. [originally 'bubbling or fermenting', from Anglo-Saxon *beorma*, froth on fermenting liquor]

barn *noun* **1** a building in which grain, hay, etc is stored, or for cattle, etc. **2** a large, bare building. [from Anglo-Saxon *bere*, barley + *ærn*, house]

Barna, Viktor, originally **Gyözö Braun** (1911–72) Hungarian-British table-tennis player, born in Budapest. He won a record 20 English titles between 1931 and 1953, including five singles titles (1933–5, 1937–8), and also won 15 world titles, including five singles (1930, 1932–5). After retirement, he played exhibitions and formed the Swaythling Club, a social club for ex-table-tennis internationals.

Barnaby a male first name. [an English form of *Barnabas*, a name in Aramaic meaning 'son of consolation']

Barnaby Rudge a novel by Charles Dickens (1841). It is set against the background of the 'No-Popery' Gordon riots of 1780.

barnacle *noun* a marine crustacean that cements itself firmly by means of its head to rocks, hulls of boats, and other underwater objects. Its shell consists of several plates which open when the animal is submerged, enabling it to feed, and close when it is exposed to air at low tide. [from Old French *bernaque*]

barnacle

barnacle goose a goose with a white face and black neck and breast, native to the N Atlantic Ocean, so called because in the Middle Ages it was thought that these geese hatched from goose-necked barnacles.

Barnard, Christian Neethling (1922–) South African surgeon, born in Beaufort West. He studied in Cape Town, and after a period of research in the USA, he returned to Cape Town in 1958 to work on open-heart surgery and organ transplantation. In Dec 1967, at Groote Schuur Hospital, he performed the first successful human heart transplant. The recipient died 18 days later; a second patient, operated on in Jan 1968, survived for 594 days.

Barnard, Edward Emerson (1857–1923) US astronomer, born in Nashville, Tennessee. Originally an amateur astronomer, he worked at the observatory of Vanderbilt University and Lick Observatory before being appointed professor at Yerkes Observatory in 1895. Following a systematic photographic survey of the sky, he correctly concluded that the 'black nebulae' of the Milky Way, which appear to be devoid of stars, are in fact clouds of obscuring matter. He also discovered the fifth satellite of Jupiter (1892), later named Amalthea, and identified the star with the greatest known apparent motion across the sky, now known as Barnard's star (1916).

Barnardo, Thomas John (1845–1905) Anglo-Irish founder of homes for destitute children, born in Dublin, Ireland. He preached in the Dublin slums, then went to London (1866) to study medicine. There he founded (1867) the East End Mission for destitute children, and several homes later known as the 'Barnardo Homes'.

Barnardo's a charity that originally provided homes for destitute children. It developed from the East End Mission founded in 1867 by Thomas John Barnardo. The first 'Dr Barnardo's Home' for boys opened in 1870; the first for girls in 1876. The present-day organization is responsible for over 140 schools, hostels, and youth centres, and has branches worldwide.

Barnard's star *Astron.* a faint red dwarf star in the constellation Ophiuchus. It is the third-closest star to the Sun. [named after the US astronomer Edward Emerson Barnard]

Barnave, Antoine (Pierre Joseph Marie) (1761–93) French revolutionary, born in Grenoble. He was a member of the new National Assembly (1799), where he established a reputation as an orator, and helped to carry through the Civil Constitution of the Clergy. He brought back the royal family from their flight to Varennes (1791), but developed Royalist sympathies and was guillotined.

barn dance **1** a kind of party at which there is music and country dancing, originally held in a barn. **2** a particular kind of country dance.

Barnes, William (1800–86) English pastoral poet, born in Rushay, Dorset. Formerly a teacher, he became a clergyman in 1847 and was widely known for his idyllic poetry in the Dorset dialect. His three books of poetry were collected as *Poems of Rural Life in the Dorset Dialect* (1879), and he also wrote several philological works.

barney *noun* (PL. **barneys**) *colloq.* a rough noisy quarrel.

barn owl an owl of worldwide distribution, which inhabits forests and open country, has a pale heart-shaped face, feathered legs, and feeds on small vertebrates, especially mammals and insects. It nests in crevices high above the ground, eg in trees, or in buildings.

barn owl

Barnsley POP (1981) 78 000; urban area (1981) 128 000, an industrial town in South Yorkshire, N England. It is situated on the R Dearne, 18km/11mi N of Sheffield. NOTABLE FEATURES Church of St Mary (15c); Monk Bretton Priory (3km/2mi NE).

barnstorm *verb intrans.* **1** to tour a country, stopping briefly in each town to give theatrical performances, formerly often in barns. **2** *North Amer.* to travel about the country making political speeches just before an election.

barnstormer *noun* a person who barnstorms, especially a politician.

Barnum, P(hineas) T(aylor) (1810–91) American showman, born in Bethel, Connecticut. He ran a museum in New York and with flamboyant publicity introduced freak shows, at which he sponsored the famous dwarf, General Tom Thumb (1842). In 1881 he joined with his rival James Anthony Bailey (1847–1906) to found the Barnum and Bailey circus, the 'greatest show on earth'.

barnyard *noun* the area around a barn.

barograph *noun Meteorol.* a type of barometer that produces a continous printed chart recording fluctuations in atmospheric pressure over a period of time. [from Greek *baros*, weight + *graphein*, to write]

barometer *noun* **1** *Meteorol.* an instrument for measuring atmospheric pressure, especially in order to predict changes in the weather, or to estimate height above sea level. In its simplest form it consists of a glass tube sealed at one end, filled with mercury, and inverted in a container of mercury. The height of the column of mercury that can be supported by atmospheric pressure is then measured. See also ANEROID BAROMETER. **2** anything that indicates a change: *a barometer of public opinion*. [from Greek *baros*, weight + *metron*, measure]

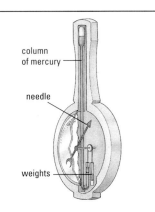

column of mercury

needle

weights

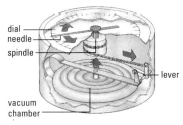

dial
needle
spindle
lever
vacuum chamber

barometer

barometric *adj.* relating to the barometer or to atmospheric pressure.

barometrically *adv.* as shown by a barometer.

baron *noun* **1** a man holding the lowest rank of nobility. **2** a powerful businessman: *an oil baron*. [from Latin *baro*, man]

baroness *noun* **1** a baron's wife. **2** a woman holding the title of baron in her own right.

baronet *noun* (ABBREV. **Bart**) in the UK, a title below that of baron. [diminutive of BARON]
◇ It is a hereditary title, not part of the peerage, and not a knighthood. It was created for England by James I in 1611 to raise money to pay the army in Ireland (the holder being required to purchase the title), and was later extended to Scotland and Ireland. Since 1801 new baronets have been of the United Kingdom as a whole.

baronetcy *noun* (PL. **baronetcies**) the rank or title of a baronet.

baronial *adj.* relating to or suitable for barons.

Barons' Wars two wars in England during the reigns of John and Henry III. The first (1215–17) took place after the sealing of Magna Carta, when many barons defied John and offered the Crown to Prince Louis of France. After John's death, the French and baronial army was routed at Lincoln (May 1217), and the war was ended by the Treaty of Kingston-on-Thames (Sep 1217). The second war (1263–7) occurred after the Provisions of Oxford failed to achieve a settlement. Simon de Montfort led some barons to capture Henry III at Lewes (1264), but he was killed at Evesham (1265), and the King was restored to power by the Dictum of Kenilworth (1266).

barony *noun* (PL. **baronies**) **1** the rank of baron. **2** land belonging to a baron.

baroque — *noun* **1** (*also* **Baroque**) a bold complex decorative style of architecture, art, decoration, and music, popular in Europe from the late 16c to the early 18c. **2** (*also* **the Baroque**) this period in European cultural history. — *adj.* (*also* **Baroque**) written or executed in such a style. [from French *baroque*, from Portuguese *barroco*, irregularly shaped pearl]
◇ Baroque art and architecture was developed in Italy c.1600, and subsequently spread across central Europe, and into Latin America. It appeared in modified form in Britain. The hallmarks of Baroque architecture were flamboyant decoration (in stone, coloured marble, gilt, and bronze), a bold and ingenious handling of classical forms (massive columns, intricately-detailed arches, and overlapping pilasters), and an overall sense of movement and vigour (undulating façades, spires, and towers). Pre-eminent architects included: in Italy, Francesco Borromini and Guarino Guarini (1624–83); in Germany, Balthasar Neumann (1687–1753); and in Britain, Christopher Wren, Nicholas Hawksmoor (1661–1736), and John Vanbrugh.
Baroque music was characterized by a gradual replacement of modality by tonality, melodic ornamentation, and the enrichment of harmony by more essential chromaticism. Instrumental music gained in prominence, the orchestra was formed, and the genres of opera, oratorio, cantata, sonata, and concerto began.

Barossa a NE suburb of Outer Adelaide, South Australia. The Barossa Valley is a noted wine-producing area and a wine festival is held every two years to celebrate the grape harvest.

barperson *noun* a person who serves drinks in a bar.

barque *or* **bark** *noun* **1** a small sailing ship with three masts. **2** *literary* any boat or small ship. [from French *barque*, from Latin *barca*, small boat]

barrack¹ — *noun* (**barracks**) a building or group of buildings for housing soldiers. — *verb* to house (soldiers) in barracks. [from French *baraque*]

barrack² *verb trans., intrans.* to shout and laugh rudely at (a speaker, sports team, etc).

barracking *noun* shouting and jeering at a public meeting, sports event, etc.

Barrack-Room Ballads a collection of poems by Rudyard Kipling (1892). It includes the poems 'Gunga Din', 'Danny Deever', and 'Mandalay'.

barracuda *noun* (PL. **barracuda, barracudas**) a large tropical sea fish which feeds on other fish and sometimes attacks people. [from Spanish *barracuda*]

barrage *noun* **1** a long burst of gunfire which keeps an enemy back while soldiers move forward. **2** a large number of questions, criticisms, etc coming in quickly one after the other. **3** a man-made barrier across a river. [from French *barrage*, from *barrer*, to block]

barrage balloon a large balloon attached to the ground by a cable and often with a net hanging from it, used to prevent attack by low-flying aircraft.

barracuda

Barranquilla POP (1992e) 1m, the modern industrial capital of Atlántico department, N Colombia. It is situated on the R Magdalena, 18km/11mi from its mouth. Founded in 1721, it is Colombia's principal Caribbean port.

Barras, Paul François Jean Nicolas, Comte de (1755–1829) French revolutionary, born in Fos-Emphoux, Var. An original member of the Jacobin Club, and a regicide, he was instrumental in the overthrow of Robespierre, and was granted dictatorial powers by the National Convention. In 1795 he acted against a Royalist uprising with his friend Bonaparte, who fired on the rebels (the 'whiff of grape-shot'). Barras became one of the five members of the Directory (1795), and was dictator again in 1797, but his hedonism and corruption made him so unpopular that he was easily overthrown by Bonaparte (1799).

Barrault, Jean-Louis (1910–94) French actor and producer, born in le Vesinet. He was a member of the Comédie-Française (1940–6), then with his wife, Madeleine Renaud, founded his own company, le Troupe Marigny. He was director of various French theatre companies. His films include *Les Enfants du Paradis* (The Children of Paradise, 1945) and *The Longest Day* (1962). His theories of dramatic art are expressed in his autobiographical *Réflexions sur le théâtre* (Reflections on the Theatre, 1949).

Barre, Raymond (1924–) French conservative politician, born in Réunion. He made his reputation as an influential neo-liberal economist at the Sorbonne, and as vice-president of the European commission (1967–72). As prime minister (1976–81) he became deeply unpopular as he cut budgets and unemployment mounted, but was regarded more favourably after his successor's failed attempts at reflation. He stood for president in 1988 but was eliminated in the first ballot.

barre *noun* a rail fixed to a wall at waist level, which ballet dancers use to balance themselves while exercising. [from French *barre*]

barred *adj.* **1** having bars. **2** closed off; blocked.

barrel — *noun* **1** a large round container with a flat bottom and curving out in the middle, usually made of planks of wood held together with metal bands. **2** the amount a barrel will hold. **3** a measure of capacity, especially of industrial oil. **4** the long hollow tube-shaped part of a gun, pen, etc. — *verb* (**barrelled, barrelling**) to put in barrels.
— **have someone over a barrel** to be in a position to get whatever one wants from them. [from Old French *baril*]

barrel-chested *adj., said of a person* having a large round chest.

barrel organ a large instrument which plays music when a handle is turned.

barrel vault *Archit.* a vault which has a semi-cylindrical roof.
◇ Barrel or tunnel vaults were much used by the Romans who developed the groined vault (formed at the intersection of two barrel vaults), and the massive domes found in many classical Roman buildings, from the basic barrel-shaped vault. Continuous barrel vaults were used, espe-

cially in the choirs, and occasionally in the naves, of medieval churches, although barrel-vaulting based on Roman architectural principles was not reintroduced until the Renaissance.

barren *adj.* **1** *said of a woman* not able to bear children. **2** not able to produce crops, fruit, etc: *barren land.* **3** not producing results. **4** dull. [from Old French *brahaigne*]

barrenness *noun* **1** a barren or unproductive state. **2** inability to produce children.

barricade — *noun* a barrier made of anything which can be piled up quickly, eg to block a street. — *verb* **1** to block or defend with a barricade. **2** (**barricade someone or oneself in**) to shut them away behind a barrier. [from French *barricade*, from *barrique*, barrel: barricades were often made from barrels]

Barrie, Sir J(ames) M(atthew) (1860–1937) Scottish novelist and dramatist, born in Kirriemuir, Angus. He became a journalist in London, and wrote a series of autobiographical prose works, including *The Little Minister* (1891). From 1890 he wrote for the theatre, his plays including *The Admirable Crichton* (1902), *Dear Brutus* (1917), and *Peter Pan* (1904), the work for which he is chiefly remembered.

barrier *noun* **1** a fence, gate, bar, etc put up to defend, block, protect, separate, etc. **2** any thing, circumstance, etc that separates things, people, etc: *a language barrier.* [from Old French *barriere*]

barrier cream cream used to protect the skin, especially on the hands, from damage or infection.

barrier island *Geol.* a long straight narrow island or peninsula which generally lies parallel to the coast and is separated from the mainland by a lagoon or salt marsh.

barrier reef a long narrow actively growing coral reef that lies parallel to the coast of a continent or encircles a volcanic island, but is separated from the land by a wide deep lagoon.

barring *prep.* except for; leaving out of consideration: *barring accidents.*

barrister *noun* in England and Wales, a lawyer qualified to act for someone in the higher law courts. [from Latin *barra*, bar]

barrow[1] *noun* **1** a small one-wheeled cart used to carry tools, earth, etc. **2** a larger cart, with two or four wheels, from which goods are often sold in the street. [from Anglo-Saxon *bearwe*, bier]

barrow[2] *noun Archaeol.* a large pile of earth over an ancient grave. [from Anglo-Saxon *beorg*, hill]

barrow boy a boy or man who sells goods from a barrow.

Barrow-in-Furness POP (1992e) 74 000, a port and industrial town in Barrow-in-Furness district, Cumbria, NW England. It lies on Furness Peninsula, 19km/12mi NW of Lancaster.

Barry a male first name, taken from the surname, and especially popular in Ireland. [it represents both the Norman word *barri* meaning 'rampart' + a Gaelic name meaning 'spear']

Barrymore, Lionel (1878–1954) US actor, born in Philadelphia. He began on stage, then became known as a film actor. His early appearances include *A Free Soul* (1931) and *Grand Hotel* (1932). Though later confined to a wheelchair, he successfully played Dr Gillespie in the original *Dr Kildare* film series. He also had etchings exhibited, and was a talented composer.

Barsetshire novels, The a series of novels by Anthony Trollope. It includes *The Warden* (1855), *Barchester Towers* (1857), *Doctor Thorne* (1858), *Framley Parsonage* (1861), *The Small House at Allington* (1864), and *The Last Chronicle of Barset* (1867).

Bart or **Barth, Jean** (1650–1702) French privateer, born in Dunkirk. He served first in the Dutch navy, turning to French service on the outbreak of the war with Holland (1672). In 1691 he commanded a small squadron in the North Sea, destroying many English vessels. During the War of the Grand Alliance (1689–97), he was taken prisoner, but escaped from Plymouth to France, where Louis XIV rewarded him with the command of a squadron (1697) and noble status.

Bart, Lionel (1930–) English composer, born in London. He first attracted attention for the songs he wrote for the British popular singer Tommy Steele in the 1950s, and went on to compose scores for a number of successful musicals, including *Lock up your Daughters!* and *Oliver!* (both 1960).

Bart *abbrev.* (also **Bart.**) Baronet.

bartender *noun North Amer.* a person who serves drinks in a bar.

barter — *verb trans., intrans.* to trade or exchange (goods or services) without using money. — *noun* trade by exchanging goods rather than selling them for money. [from Old French *barater*, to trick or cheat]

Bartered Bride, The (Prodaná nevěsta) an opera by Bedřich Smetana (1866). Set in 19c rural Bohemia, it is a story of two lovers, Jenik and Mařenka, whose betrothal is interrupted by a marriage-broker's success in persuading the latter's parents that she should marry someone wealthy instead.

barterer *noun* a person who barters or exchanges goods.

Barth, Heinrich (1821–65) German geographer, historian, and explorer, born in Hamburg. A member of a British expedition to central Africa (1850), he crossed the Great Desert, and despite the death of his companions, completed a journey of over 19 000km/12 000mi, reaching Timbuktu in 1853. His journey was described in *Travels and Discoveries in North and Central Africa* (1857–8).

Barth, Karl (1886–1968) Swiss Protestant theologian, born in Basle. Whilst pastor at Safenwil, he wrote a commentary on St Paul's Epistle to the Romans (1919) which established his theological reputation. He became a professor at Göttingen (1921), Münster (1925), and Bonn (1930), refused to take an unconditional oath to Hitler, was dismissed, and so became professor at Basle (1935–62). He played a leading role in the German Confessing Church and Barmen Declaration (1934). The major exponent of Reformed theology, his many works include *Church Dogmatics* (1932–67).

Bartholin, Erasmus (1625–98) Danish physician, physicist and mathematician, born in Roskilde. Son of Caspar Bartholin the Elder and brother of Thomas Bartholin the Elder, he was appointed the Professor of Medicine and Mathematics at Copenhagen in 1656. He discovered that when an object is viewed through Iceland feldspar (calcite), a double image is produced (1669), although he did not find an explanation of the phenomenon of double refraction.

Bartholomew 1 an apostle mentioned in the Acts of the Apostles and the synoptic gospels of the New Testament. **2** a male first name. [from Aramaic, = son of Talmai]

Bartók, Béla (1881–1945) Hungarian composer, born in Nagyszentmiklós (now Sînnocolau Mare, Romania). He became a virtuoso pianist and toured widely, during which a growing interest in folk-song led him to study Hungarian and Balkan folk music — traditions that greatly influenced his own compositions. He was Professor of Pianoforte in the Budapest Conservatory (1907–34) and later became known throughout Europe as a composer, but was driven into exile by World War II and settled in the USA. His many works include the opera *Duke Bluebeard's Castle*, the ballet *The Miraculous Mandarin*, and the *Concerto for Orchestra*.

Barton, Sir Derek Harold Richard (1918–) English chemist, born in Gravesend. He was professor at Imperial College, London, for over 20 years before moving in 1985 to Texas A & M University. He introduced conformational analysis (the study of the spatial arrangement of atoms in molecules) as a method for studying the shape of organic molecules and the effect of shape on reactivity. He shared the 1969 Nobel Prize for Chemistry with Odd Hassell (1897–1981).

Bartram, John (1699–1777) US botanist, born in Marple, Pennsylvania. Considered the 'father of American botany', he became a successful small farmer and also built up an unrivalled collection of N American plants, which he began selling to European botanists and horticulturists. This successful business allowed Bartram to travel to Virginia, the Allegheny Mts, the Carolinas, and elsewhere in search of plants.

Bary, Heinrich Anton de (1831–88) German botanist, born in Frankfurt, the founder of modern mycology. Successively professor at Freiburg, Halle, and Strassburg, he was the first rector of its recognized university. He studied the morphology and physiology of the fungi, discovering many of the complexities of their life cycles, and the Myxomycetae (slime moulds).

baryon *noun Physics* a heavy subatomic particle involved in strong interactions with other atomic particles and composed of three quarks bound together by gluons. Baryons represent a subdivision of the hadrons, and are themselves divided into nucleons (protons and neutrons) and hyperons. [from Greek *barys*, heavy]

Baryshnikov, Mikhail (Nikolaievich) (1948–) Russian-born US dancer and choreographer, born in Rīga, Latvia. He joined the Kirov Ballet, but while on tour in 1974 he defected to Canada, and then went to the USA. He appeared most often with the American Ballet Theatre, where he was artistic director (1980–90), and has also taken part in films.

barytes *noun Geol.* the mineral form of barium sulphate, the chief ore of barium. — Also called *barite*.

baryton *or* **barytone** *noun* an obsolete stringed musical instrument of the violin family, popular during the 17c and 18c, especially in Germany. It had six bowed strings like a bass viol, with the addition of a course of 10 to 15 strings which vibrated in sympathy. These sympathetic strings could also be plucked from behind the open neck of the instrument. [from Greek *barytonos*, deep-sounded, not accented]

BAS *abbrev.* **1** Bachelor of Agricultural Science. **2** British Antarctic Survey.

basal *adj.* at or forming a base.

basalt *noun Geol.* a fine-grained dark igneous (volcanic) rock formed by the solidification of thin layers of molten lava that spread out following a volcanic eruption. It is the commonest volcanic rock in the Earth's crust, and is quarried for use in the construction of buildings and roads. [from Greek *basanites*]

basaltic *adj.* consisting of basalt.

base[1] — *noun* **1** the lowest part or bottom; the part which supports something or on which something stands. **2** the origin, root, or foundation of something. **3** a headquarters; a centre of activity or operations. **4** a starting point. **5** the main part of a mixture: *rice is the base of this dish.* **6** *Chem.* any of a group of chemical compounds, eg metal oxides and hydroxides, that can neutralize an acid to form a salt and water. An aqueous solution of a base contains OH⁻ ions and will turn litmus blue. **7** *Baseball* one of several fixed points which players run between. **8** *Maths.* in a numerical system, the number of different symbols used, eg in the binary number system the base is two, because only the symbols 0 and 1 are used. In the decimal system the base is 10. **9** *Maths.* in

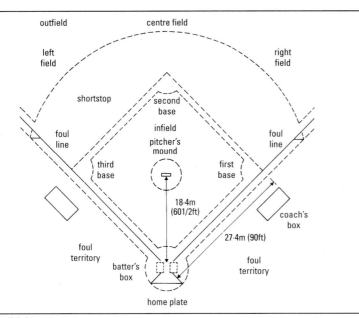

baseball field

logarithms, the number that when raised to a certain power has a logarithm equal in value to that power. In common logarithms the base is 10; in natural logarithms the base is *e*. **10** *Geom.* the usually horizontal line or surface on which a geometric figure rests. — *verb* **1** to found or establish (an argument, etc): *reasoning based on self-interest*. **2** to give as a headquarters or centre of operations: *troops based in France*. [from Latin *basis*, pedestal]

base² *adj.* **1** lacking morals; wicked. **2** not pure. **3** low in value. [from Latin *bassus*, low, short]

baseball *noun* **1** a team game played with a bat and ball on a diamond-shaped pitch by two teams each with nine players. **2** the ball used in this game.
◇ The team at bat tries to score the most runs by having their players circle the bases before they are put out by the other team. An out is made when the fielding team catches a batted ball before it touches the ground, tags a member of the offensive team between bases, or touches a base before an offensive player reaches that base. The defensive team fields batted balls with an oversized leather glove or mitt. Each game is made up of nine innings unless the score is tied, in which case the game is extended into extra innings. Each team at bat is allowed three outs in its half inning. The pitcher hurls the ball at upwards of 145kph/90mph from the mound towards the batter. If the batter swings at the ball and fails to hit it, or if the pitcher throws the ball into a designated strike zone, between the batter's knees and his chest, without the batter swinging at the ball, a strike is called. Three strikes cause a batter to be declared out. If the pitcher fails to throw the ball into the strike zone and the batter does not swing, a ball is called. Four balls allow the batter to take first base. The home plate umpire, who stands behind the catcher, determines if the ball is within the strike zone. If the batter strikes the ball and circles all the bases before being put out, he has hit a home run. Professional teams in N America are divided into the American and National Leagues. The American League consists of 14 teams and the National of 12 based in the USA and Canada. The culmination of the season, which runs from April through October, is a best-of-seven game World Series between the champions of each league.

baseless *adj.* having no cause or foundation: *baseless fears*.

baseline *noun* **1** one of the two lines which mark the ends of a tennis court. **2** an amount or value taken as a basis for comparison.

basely *adv.* impurely, immorally.

basement *noun* the lowest floor of a building, usually below ground level.

base metal *noun* any metal other than the precious metals, eg iron, tin, copper.

baseness *noun* immorality; wickedness.

base rate the rate used by a bank to fix its charges for lending money to customers.

bases pl. of BASE¹, BASE², BASIS.

BASF *abbrev.* Badische Anilin und Soda-Fabrik (a German chemical company).

bash — *verb colloq.* **1** to strike or smash bluntly. **2 (bash someone up)** to attack someone violently. **3 (bash something down** *or* **in)** to damage or break by striking very hard. **4 (bash into something)** to collide violently with it. — *noun* **1** a heavy blow or knock. **2** a mark caused by a heavy blow. **3** *slang* a noisy party.
— **have a bash at something** *colloq.* attempt it.

bashful *adj.* lacking confidence; shy. [from Old French *abaissier*, to bring low]

bashfully *adv.* with a shy or bashful manner.

bashfulness *noun* being shy or bashful.

-bashing *combining form colloq.* forming words meaning: **1** making strong and often unjustified physical or verbal attacks on a person or group of people that one dislikes or is opposed to: *union-bashing*. **2** any of various other activities associated with the word *bash*: *Bible-bashing* (enthusiastic evangelical Christian preaching).

Basho, Matsuo (1644–94) Japanese poet, born in Ueno (Iga). Becoming master of the miniature *haiku*, he started his own school, but later retired to a hermitage. Influenced by Zen Buddhism, he then travelled widely, and composed his book of travels *The Narrow Road to the Deep North* (1689) in a mixture of poetic prose and *haiku*.

BASIC *noun* a computer programming language which uses normal English vocabulary. [from *Beginner's All-purpose Symbolic Instruction Code*]

basic — *adj.* **1** of or forming the base or basis. **2** of or at a very simple or low level. **3** without additions: *basic pay*. — *noun* (*usually* **basics**) the essential parts or facts; the simplest principles. [from Latin *basis*, pedestal]

basically *adv.* mostly, essentially; described in simple or general terms: *the argument is basically sound*.

Basic English a simplified version of English, devised in 1930 by Charles Kay Ogden (1889–1957) as a means of facilitating international communication. It consists of a basic vocabulary of 850 words supplemented by international words (eg names of countries), and scientific words.

basic-oxygen process *or* **basic process** *Engineering* the most widely used method of producing steel, in which oxygen is blown at high pressure through molten pig iron.

Basidiomycetes *pl. noun Biol.* one of the main subdivisions of the fungi, characterized by the production of a terminal club-shaped reproductive structure known as a basidium, which contains spores known as basidiospores. The Basidiomycetes include mushrooms and toadstools, as well as parasitic fungi such as the rusts and smuts. [from Greek *basis*, basis]

Basie, Count (William Allen) (1904–84) US bandleader and pianist, born in Red Bank, New Jersey. He began as an itinerant piano player in vaudeville and saloons, then became leader of a successful 16-piece Kansas City band, which he took to New York. When the Swing Era waned, Basie maintained his stature with the reorganization of his band (1951) by emphasizing precision ensemble playing in more complex orchestrations.

Basil I, known as **the Macedonian** (c.812–886) Byzantine emperor (867–86), born in Thrace. He was founder of the Macedonian dynasty, and began ruling jointly with Michael III, but assassinated him in 868. He formulated the Greek legal code, in a text known as the Basilica.

Basil (the Great), St (c.329–79 AD) an early Greek Father of the Church, born in Caesarea, Cappadocia. He lived for a time as a hermit, then in 370 succeeded Eusebius as Bishop of Caesarea. Along with his brother St Gregory of Nyssa, and St Gregory of Nazianzus, he defended Christian philosophy against Arianism. His feast day is 2 Jan (W) or 1 Jan (E).

Basil a male first name. [from Greek *basileus*, king]

basil *noun* a small sweet-smelling herb used in cooking. [from Old French *basile*, from Greek *basilikon*, royal]

basilica *noun* **1** an ancient Roman public hall, with a rounded wall at one end and a row of stone pillars along each side, used as a lawcourt. **2** a church shaped like this. [from Greek *basilike*, hall]

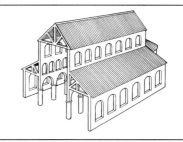

basilica

Basiliensis, Regio POP (1984e) 2.1m, a transnational 'natural region' in the Upper Rhine Valley, between the Jura Mts and the Black Forest, which encompasses the frontier districts of France, Switzerland, and Germany. AREA 234sq km/90sq mi. Its administrative centre is Basle, with regional centres at Mulhouse and Freiburg. International co-operation between the region's local governments, industries, and universities has been promoted since 1963.

basilisk *noun* **1** in legends, a snake which can kill people by breathing on them or looking at them. **2** a type of lizard found in S America. [from Greek *basiliskos*, prince]

basilisk

basin *noun* **1** a wide open dish, especially for holding water. **2** a bowl or sink in a bathroom, etc for washing oneself in. **3** the amount a basin will hold. **4** a valley or area of land drained by a river, or streams running into a river. **5** the deep part of a harbour. [from Latin *bacinum*, water vessel]

Basingstoke POP (1981) 74 000, an industrial town in Basingstoke and Deane district in Hampshire, S England. It lies 27km/17mi NE of Winchester. NOTABLE FEATURES Willis Museum; Silchester Roman site (17km/10mi N).

basis *noun* (PL. **bases**) **1** a principle on which an idea, theory, etc is based. **2** a starting point: *a basis for discussion*. **3** the main part of a mixture. [from Latin *basis*, pedestal]

bask *verb intrans.* **1** to lie in comfort, especially in warmth or sunshine. **2** to enjoy and take great pleasure: *basking in her approval*. [from Norse *bathask*, to bathe]

Baskerville, John (1706–75) English printer, born in Sion Hill, Worcestershire. He became a writing master in Birmingham, and from 1740 carried on a successful japanning business there. Following experiments in letter founding, he produced several types, one of which bears his name. His works include editions of Virgil, Milton, and the Bible. In 1758 he became printer to Cambridge University.

basket *noun* **1** a container made of strips of wood or cane, woven together. **2** the amount a basket will hold. **3** one of two nets into which the ball is thrown in basketball. **4** a goal scored in basketball.

basketball *noun* **1** a game in which two teams of five players score by throwing a ball into a net on a high post at each end of the court. **2** the ball used in this game.
◇ The game was invented by James Naismith in 1891 in Springfield, Massachusetts, USA; a similar game was played by the Olmecs in Mexico in the 10c BC. It is played on a court and the object is to throw the ball through your opponents' (bottomless) basket, situated at the end of the court, and 3.05m above the ground. Players may throw or bounce the ball, but not run with it. It is also a major sport in US colleges.

basket chair a chair made from strips of wood or cane woven together.

basketful *noun* (PL. **basketfuls**) the amount a basket will hold.

basketry *noun* the art or business of making baskets.

basketwork *noun* **1** articles made of strips of wood or cane woven together. **2** the art of making these.

basking shark a large but harmless shark, the second-largest living fish, up to 10m in length, and weighing about 6 000kg. It lives in oceanic surface waters and feeds entirely on plankton filtered by stiff bristles on its long gill arches.

Basle, German **Basel**, French **Bâle** POP (1991e) 360 000, the capital of Basel-Stadt demicanton and of Basel canton, NE Switzerland. It stands on the R Rhine, 69km/43mi N of Bern. The second largest city in Switzerland, it is also the centre of the Regio Basiliensis 'natural region' and a river port at the terminus of Rhine navigation. HISTORY built on the site of a Roman fort, the town was a medieval centre for silk, dyeing, and printing; joined the Swiss Confederation in 1501; an influential centre during the Reformation; it was the scene of the first Zionist conference in 1897. A major European communications crossroads, Basle is Switzerland's leading centre for transshipment and international commerce. NOTABLE FEATURES Gothic minster (11c, largely rebuilt in the 14c); town hall (1504–14); Spalentor (1400); European World Trade and Convention Centre; zoological and botanical gardens; many museums and theatres; space-age pylon (symbolizing the city's location at the junction of France, Germany, and Switzerland); the university (1460) is the oldest in Switzerland.

Basle, Council of a controversial Council of the Church (1431–49). It was intended to continue the work (against heresy and initiating reform) of the Council of Constance, but fell into dispute with Pope Eugenius IV for asserting the authority of the Council over that of the pope. When he attempted to dissolve the Council, it appointed Felix V, the last of the antipopes.

Basque — *noun* **1** a member of a people living in the western Pyrenees, in Spain and France. **2** the language spoken by these people. — *adj.* relating to the Basque people or their language. [from French *Basque*, from Latin *Vasco*]
◇ The Basque language is unrelated to any other European language, and is thought to be a remnant of the languages spoken in W Europe before the advent of the Indo-European family. The Basque people retain strong ethnic identity and their main city, Bilbao, is a centre of Basque nationalism. Despite being granted some local autonomy by the liberal Spanish monarchy in 1978–9, the more militant continue to agitate for a separate Basque state.

basque *noun* a tight-fitting garment for women, covering the body between the shoulders and the hips.

Basque Provinces, Spanish **País Vasco Provincias Vascongadas**, Basque **Euskadi** POP (1991) 2.1m, an autonomous region of N Spain, comprising the provinces of Àlava, Guipúzcoa, and Biscay. AREA 7 261sq km/2 803sq mi. CAPITAL Vitoria. CHIEF TOWN Bilbao. Coastal hills are separated from the main ridge of the Cordillera Cantabrica to the S by valleys growing wheat. Dammed rivers provide hydroelectric power. Industries centred around Bilbao and San Sebastian include metallurgy, paper, and furniture. The Basque Country also extends to S France and comprises Labourd, Basse-Navarre, and Soule.

Basra, Arabic **Al Basrah** **1** POP (1985e) 617 000, the port capital of Basra governorate in SE Iraq, at the head of the Shatt al-Arab, c.120km/75mi from the Arabian Gulf. The city is an administrative and commercial centre. It was a major centre of literature, theology, and scholarship in the 8c–9c. The port was badly affected in the 1980s by the Iran–Iraq war and in 1991 by bombing during the Gulf War. **2** a governorate in SE Iraq with the city of Basra as its capital.

bas-relief *noun* a technique of cutting and shaping stone or wood so that the figures on it are only slightly raised from the background. [a French word, from Italian *basso rilievo*, low relief]

bass[1] *noun* (pronounced like *base*) **1** the lowest male singing voice. **2** a singer with such a voice. **3** in music, a part written for such a voice or for an instrument of the lowest range. **4** *colloq.* a bass guitar or double bass. [from Latin *bassus*, low]

bass[2] *noun* (pronounced like *mass*) (PL. **bass**, **basses**) a type of fish found in rivers and seas, often used as food. [from Anglo-Saxon *bærs*, perch]

Bassae a temple dedicated to Apollo Epicurius on the slopes of Mt Lykaion, SW Arcadia, Greece. It was built in the 5c BC by Ictinus for the people of Phigalia after their city escaped a plague epidemic. Rediscovered in 1763, it has since been largely re-erected. It is a World Heritage site.

Bassanio the poor friend of Antonio in Shakespeare's *The Merchant of Venice*, who successfully wins the hand of Portia.

bass clef a sign at the beginning of a piece of written music which places the note F below middle C on the fourth line of the staff.

bass drum a large drum that produces a very low sound.

Bassenthwaite a lake in the Lake District of Cumbria, NW England, situated 5km/3mi NW of Keswick. Skiddaw Forest lies to the E and Thornthwaite Forest lies to the W.

basset or **basset hound** *noun* a type of dog with a long body, smooth hair, short legs, and long ears. [from French *bas*, low]

Basse-Terre POP (1990) 150 000, an island of the French Overseas Department of Guadeloupe, Lesser Antilles, in the E Caribbean Sea. AREA 848sq km/327sq mi. PHYSICAL DESCRIPTION one of Guadeloupe's two main islands, it is separated from Grande-Terre I by the narrow Rivière Salée; mountainous, with the active volcano Grande Soufrière rising to 1 484m. There is a national park at the centre of the island. CAPITAL Basse-Terre. ECONOMY agriculture, especially sugar cane.

Basseterre POP (1985e) 19 000, the capital and chief port of St Christopher-Nevis. It lies on the

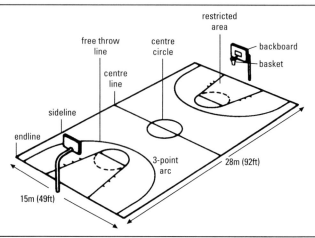

basketball court

SW coast of St Christopher I. NOTABLE FEATURE cathedral.

basset horn a musical instrument of the clarinet family, with a lower range of pitch than that of a standard clarinet. It is usually built in the key of F with notes written a fifth higher than they sound. It originated in the 18c and was used by Mozart, eg in the *Requiem* and *The Magic Flute*. [a partial translation of French *cor de bassette* and Italian *corno di bassetto*]

bass guitar *or* **bass** in popular music, an electric guitar which plays the bass part.

bassinet *noun* a baby's basket-like bed or pram, usually covered at one end. [diminutive of French *bassin*, basin]

bassist *noun* a person who plays a bass guitar or double bass.

bassoon *noun* a woodwind instrument with a double reed, producing a deep plangent sound. It consists of a jointed wooden tube doubled back on itself, fitted with metal keys and a curved crook with a double reed. It dates from the 16c. [from Italian *basso*, low]

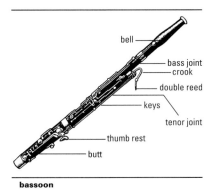

bassoon

bassoonist *noun* a person who plays a bassoon.

Bass Strait the channel separating Tasmania from Victoria, Australia. It has a maximum width of 240km/150mi and a depth of 50–70m. The strait is a source of oil and natural gas. [named in 1798 after the British explorer, George Bass (d.1812)]

bast *noun* threads of the soft inner bark of some trees, woven together and used to make ropes, mats, etc. [from Anglo-Saxon *bæst*]

bastard — *noun* **1** often *offensive* a child born of parents not married to each other. **2** *coarse slang* a term of abuse or sympathy for a man: *rotten bastard / poor bastard*. **3** *coarse slang* something annoying or difficult. — *adj.* **1** born to parents not married to each other. **2** not genuine, standard, original or pure. [from Latin *bastardus*]

bastardization *or* **bastardisation** *noun* making something less genuine or pure.

bastardize *or* **bastardise** *verb* to make less genuine or pure.

bastardized *or* **bastardised** *adj.* impure; no longer genuine.

bastardy *noun* the state of being a bastard.

baste[1] *verb* to pour hot fat or butter over (especially roasting meat).

baste[2] *verb* to sew with temporary loose stitches. [from German *basten*, to sew]

baste[3] *verb* to beat or thrash. [probably from Norse *beysta*]

Bastia POP (1990) 39 000, the port capital of Haute-Corse department, NW Corsica, France. Lying in the NE corner of the narrow Cap Corse between mountains and sea, it is the island's chief town and its largest port. The Genoese founded Bastia in 1380. It was capital of Corsica until 1811. [from Italian *bastiglia*, fortress]

Bastille a medieval fortress and prison in E Paris. The symbol of Bourbon despotism, it was stormed and destroyed by a Parisian mob on 14 Jul 1789, an event that was seen in French Revolutionary ideology to mark the end of the *ancien régime*. The anniversary of the day is a French national holiday.

bastinado — *noun* (PL. **bastinadoes**) beating of the soles of the feet with a stick as torture or punishment. — *verb* (**bastinadoes**, **bastinadoed**) to beat on the soles of the feet with a stick. [from Spanish *bastonada*, from *bastón*, stick]

bastion *noun* **1** a kind of tower which sticks out at an angle from a castle wall. **2** a person, place, or thing regarded as a defender of a principle, etc. [from Italian *bastire*, to build]

BASW *abbrev.* British Association of Social Workers.

BAT *abbrev.* British-American Tobacco Company.

bat[1] — *noun* **1** a shaped piece of wood, with a flat or curved surface, for hitting the ball in cricket, baseball, table tennis, etc. See also RACKET. **2** a batsman, especially in cricket. — *verb* (**batted**, **batting**) **1** *intrans.* to take a turn at hitting a ball with a bat in cricket, baseball, etc. **2** to hit with, or as if with, a bat.
— **off one's own bat 1** without help. **2** without being prompted by anyone else.
[from Anglo-Saxon *batt*]

bat[2] *noun* any of more than 1000 species of nocturnal mammal, the only mammal capable of sustained flight, found mainly in the tropics, but also widely distributed in warm and temperate regions.
— **have bats in the belfry** *colloq.* to be crazy or slightly mad. See also BATS, BATTY.
like a bat out of hell *colloq.* very fast.
[from Middle English *bakke*]
◊ The body of a bat is covered in fur, and the skin of the belly and back is extended to form wings that are stretched between the 'fingers' of the forelimbs, the sides of the body, and the hind limbs. The bat operates its wings by moving its limbs in a manner similar to a swimmer doing breast stroke. Contrary to popular belief, bats can see quite well, but most species hunt for food at night, relying partly on their sense of smell, but mainly on echo-location. They produce high-pitched sounds between 100 and 200 times a second, and these sound waves strike obstacles in the bat's flight path and are echoed back, enabling the animal to navigate even in total darkness. Bats eat a wide variety of foods, including insects, fish, blood, fruit, and nectar.

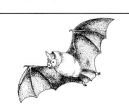

bat

bat[3] *verb* (**batted**, **batting**) to open and close (one's eyelids) very quickly, usually to attract sympathy or admiration.
— **not bat an eye** *or* **eyelid** *colloq.* to show no surprise or emotion.
[from Middle English *baten*, to flap]

Batalha, Monastery of a Dominican abbey, in Batalha, W Portugal. An example of Christian Gothic architecture, it was founded in 1388 by King João I (reigned 1385–1433) in fulfilment of a vow made at the battle of Aljubarrota, where Portuguese independence was established. It is a World Heritage site.

Batavian Republic the name given to Holland (1795–1806), after that country had been conquered by Revolutionary French forces in 1794–5. The Kingdom of Holland was ruled (1806–10) by Louis Bonaparte, Napoleon's brother, but then Holland was incorporated into France (between 1810 and the collapse of French rule in 1813).

batch — *noun* a number of things or people prepared, delivered, dealt with, etc at the same time. — *verb* to arrange in batches. [from Middle English *bache*, from Anglo-Saxon *bacan*, to bake]

batch file *Comput.* a text file containing a series of commands which are executed in order when the name of the file is called.

batch processing the processing of several batches of similar data by a single computer at the same time.

bated
— **with bated breath** feeling anxiety, excitement, or fear.
[from ABATE]

Bates, Henry Walter (1825–92) English naturalist, born in Leicester. With Alfred Wallace he explored the Amazon (1848–59), returning with 14 700 specimens, including almost 8 000 species of insect new to science. His *Contributions to an Insect Fauna of the Amazon Valley* (1861) described the phenomenon now known as *Batesian mimicry* by which harmless, edible species of animal are found resembling others, which may be distantly related and are distasteful or poisonous, for protection from predators. This discovery came amidst the controversy surrounding Charles Darwin's theory of evolution, and provided strong evidence in favour of natural selection.

Bates, H(erbert) E(rnest) (1905–74) English novelist, playwright, and short-story writer, born in Rushden, Northamptonshire. His first play, *The Last Bread*, and his first novel, *The Two Sisters*, were published in 1926. Other works include the novels *Fair Stood the Wind for France* (1944) and *The Darling Buds of May* (1958), an essay on literary criticism, *The Modern Short Story*, and several volumes of short stories. Many of his works have been televised.

Bates, Miss the very talkative aunt of Jane Fairfax in Jane Austen's *Emma*.

Bateson, William (1861–1926) English geneticist, born in Whitby, N Yorkshire. He introduced the term 'genetics' in 1909, and became the UK's first Professor of Genetics at Cambridge (1908–10). He left to become Director of the new John Innes Horticultural Institution (1910–26). A dominant proponent of Gregor Mendel's theories of heredity, he produced the first English translation of Mendel's work. Although an ardent evolutionist, he was opposed to Charles Darwin's theory of natural selection, believing the small changes demanded by the theory to be insufficient to account for the evolutionary process.

Bath, Latin **Aquae Calidae**, Anglo-Saxon **Akermanceaster** POP (1992e) 84 000, a spa town in Bath district, Avon, SW England. It lies on the R Avon, 19km/12mi SE of Bristol. HISTORY noted since Roman times for its hot springs; chartered in 1189; a fashionable spa centre in the 18c. NOTABLE FEATURES the City of Bath is a World Heritage site; Roman Baths, 15c Roman Bath Museum; abbey church; notable Georgian crescents.

Bath, Order of the (ABBREV. **OB**) a British order of chivalry, formally created (1725) by George I, but traditionally founded by Henry IV in 1399 at the Tower of London, when he conferred the honour on the 46 esquires who had attended him at his bath the night before his coronation. The order comprises the sovereign and three classes: Knights and Dames Grand Cross, Knights and Dames Commander, and Companions. The ribbon is crimson, and the Latin motto is *Tria juncta in uno* ('three joined in one').

bath — *noun* **1** a large open container for water, in which to wash the whole body. **2** an act of washing the body in a bath. **3** the water filling a bath: *run a bath*. **4** (**baths**) a public swimming pool. **5** a liquid, or its container, in which something is washed, etc, usually as part of a technical process such as developing photographs. — *verb trans., intrans.* to wash in a bath. [from Anglo-Saxon *bæth*]

Bath bun a small sweet cake.

Bath chair *formerly* a kind of chair with three wheels in which an invalid can be pushed.

bathcube *noun* a small block of bath salts.

bathe — *verb* **1** *intrans.* to swim in the sea, etc for pleasure. **2** *intrans. chiefly North Amer.* to have a bath. **3** to wash or treat (part of the body) with water, a liquid, etc to clean it or to lessen pain. **4** to cover and surround (eg in light). — *noun* an act of swimming in the sea, etc. [from Anglo-Saxon *bathian*, to wash]

bather *noun* a person who bathes or is bathing.

bathetic *adj.* characterized by bathos.

bathing cap a tight rubber cap worn to keep the hair dry when swimming.

bathing costume a swimming costume or swimsuit.

batholith *noun Geol.* a large igneous rock mass, typically granite, that has intruded while molten into the surrounding rock. [from Greek *bathos*, depth, or *bathys* deep + *lithos*, stone]

bathos *noun literary* in speech or writing, a sudden change from very important, serious, or beautiful ones to very ordinary or trivial ones. [from Greek *bathos*, depth]

bathrobe *noun* a loose towelling coat used before and after taking a bath.

bathroom *noun* **1** a room containing a bath and often other washing facilities. **2** a room with a lavatory.

bath salts a sweet-smelling substance in the form of large grains, which perfumes and softens the water in a bath.

bathtub *noun* a movable or fixed receptacle for a bath.

Bathurst see BANJUL.

Bathurst and Melville Islands POP (1981) 1 600, the two islands lying off the NW coast of Northern Territory, Australia, situated c.80km/ 50mi N of Darwin. AREA 7 487sq km/ 2 890sq mi. Aboriginal communities live on these islands. The town of Nguiu on Bathurst I was founded as a Catholic mission in 1911. ECONOMY wood-carving, pottery.

bathymetry *noun Geol.* the measurement of the depths of sea bottom features in large bodies of water, especially by echo-sounding. [from Greek *bathys*, deep]

bathyscaphe *noun* a vessel for deep-sea diving. [from Greek *bathys*, deep + *skaphos*, ship]

bathysphere *noun* a large, round, steel container, lowered deep into the sea to allow a person to observe sea animals, plants, etc. [from Greek *bathys*, deep + SPHERE]

batik *noun* **1** a technique of printing coloured patterns on cloth, in which those parts not to be coloured or dyed are covered with wax. **2** cloth coloured in this way. [from Malay]

Batista (y Zaldívar), Fulgencio (1901–73) Cuban dictator, born in Oriente province. He organized a military coup (the 'sergeants' revolt') in 1933, consolidated his power, and became President (1940–4). In 1952 he overthrew President Prío Socorras and ruled as dictator until overthrown by Fidel Castro (Jan 1959), when he found refuge in the Dominican Republic.

Batman a US film directed by Tim Burton (1989). A comic-strip story of revenge and romance, starring Michael Keaton as the wealthy crimefighter and Jack Nicholson as The Joker, it is one of the most commercially successful films ever made.

batman *noun* (PL. **batmen**) an officer's personal servant in the armed forces. [from French *bat*, pack-saddle]

baton *noun* **1** a light thin stick used by the conductor of an orchestra. **2** a short heavy stick carried by a policeman as a weapon. **3** a short stick passed from one runner to another in a relay race. **4** a stick carried by a person at the head of a marching band. [from French *bâton*, stick]

Baton Rouge POP (1990) 528 000, the capital of the state of Louisiana, USA, in East Baton Rouge parish. It is a deep-water port on the Mississippi R. HISTORY founded in 1719, it was governed successively by France, Britain, and Spain; ceded to the USA as part of the 1803 Louisiana Purchase; declared its independence under the name Feliciana in 1810; incorporated as a town within Louisiana in 1817; state capital from 1849 to 1861 and since 1882. NOTABLE FEATURES State Museum, Riverside Museum; the old capitol; Huey Long Grave and Memorial.

bats *adj. colloq.* crazy. [from the phrase *have bats in the belfry*]

batsman *or* **batswoman** *noun* a person who bats or is batting in cricket.

battalion *noun* an army unit made up of several smaller units (companies), and forming part of a larger unit (a brigade). [from French *bataillon*, from Italian *battaglione*, squadron of soldiers]

battels *pl. noun Brit.* accounts for provisions received from college kitchens and butteries, especially at Oxford University. [perhaps connected with dialect *battle*, to feed]

batten — *noun* **1** a long flat piece of wood used for keeping other pieces in place. **2** a strip of wood used to fasten the covers over the hatches in a ship's deck, etc. — *verb* to fasten or shut with battens.

— **batten down the hatches** to prepare for a danger or crisis.

[from Old French *batre*, to beat]

batter¹ *verb* (**battered, battering**) **1** *trans., intrans.* to strike or hit hard and often, or continuously. **2** (**batter something down** *or* **in**) to break down or to destroy by battering. **3** to damage or wear through continual use. [from Old French *batre*, to beat]

batter² *noun* a mixture of eggs, flour, and either milk or water, beaten together and used in cooking. [from Old French *bateure*, beating]

batter³ *noun* a person who bats or is batting, especially in baseball. See also BATSMAN.

battered *adj.* coated and cooked in batter.

battering *noun* a beating.

battering-ram *noun* a large wooden beam with a metal head, formerly used in war for breaking down walls or gates.

battery *noun* (PL. **batteries**) **1** a device that converts chemical energy into electrical energy in the form of direct current, eg a car battery. Dry batteries, in which the electrolyte is in the form of a paste instead of a liquid, are used as portable energy sources in torches, etc. See also ELECTROLYTIC CELL. **2** a number of similar things: *a battery of questions*. **3** a long line of small cages in which eg hens are kept. **4** *Legal* a physical attack on a person. See also ASSAULT AND BATTERY. **5** a group of heavy guns and the place where they are mounted. [from French *batterie*, from *battre*, to strike]

battle — *noun* **1** a fight between opposing armies or people. **2** a competition between opposing groups or people: *a battle of wits*. **3** a long or difficult struggle: *a battle for equality*. — *verb intrans.* **1** to fight. **2** to struggle; to campaign vigorously or defiantly.

— **do battle** to fight.

fight a losing battle to try to do something which is sure to fail.

half the battle something that takes one well on the way to success.

join battle to begin to fight. [from French *bataille*]

battle-axe *noun* **1** a type of axe formerly used in warfare. **2** *colloq.* a fierce and domineering older woman.

battle-cruiser *noun* a large warship, the same size as a battleship but faster and with fewer guns.

battle-cry *noun* **1** a shout given by soldiers charging into battle. **2** a slogan.

battledress *noun* a soldier's ordinary uniform.

battle fatigue *or* **combat fatigue** a usually temporary mental disorder caused by the anxiety of fighting for a long time.

battlement *noun* a low wall around the top of a castle, etc with gaps for shooting through. [from Old French *bataillier*, to provide with ramparts]

Battle of Britain see BRITAIN, BATTLE OF.

Battle of the Lapiths and Centaurs, The a painting by Piero de Cosimo (1486, National Gallery, London).

battleship *noun* the largest type of warship.

Battleship Potemkin a Russian film directed by Sergei Eisenstein (1925). It tells the story of a sailors' revolt that continues on land, and includes the famous scene of slaughter on the Odessa steps.

batty *adj.* (**battier, battiest**) *colloq.* crazy; eccentric. [from BAT²]

bauble *noun* a small cheap ornament or piece of jewellery. [from Old French *babel*, a child's toy]

Baudelaire, Charles (Pierre) (1821–67) French Symbolist poet, born in Paris. After abandoning a voyage to India, he returned to Paris in 1843 where he began to make his living by writing. One of his inspirations was his mistress, Jeanne Duval, who is the *Venus noire* of his poems. Also the author of several works of art criticism, his best-known work is the poetry collection *Les Fleurs du mal* (1857), for which author, printer, and publisher were prosecuted for impropriety in 1864. He later took to drink and opium, was struck down with paralysis, and died in poverty.

Baudouin I (1930–93) King of the Belgians, born in Stuyvenberg Castle, near Brussels, the elder son of Leopold III and his first wife, Queen Astrid. He acceded to the throne on the abdication of his father (Jul 1951), and in 1960 married the Spanish Doña Fabiola de Mora y Aragón. Considered a moral tower of strength, he was succeeded by his brother, Albert II.

baud rate *Comput.* the speed at which information is passed between computers, eg along a telephone line, given in bits per second. [named after the French inventor Emil Baudot]

Bauhaus a school of arts and crafts founded in the Weimar Republic by Walter Gropius (1919).

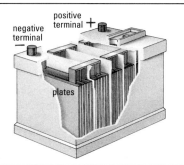

battery

Its aim was for artists and architects to work together to create a new unity in the arts. It was at first expressionist, then functionalist in style. Students and teachers included Feininger, van Doesburg, Moholy-Nagy, Kandinsky, Klee, and Mies van der Rohe. It moved to Dessau in 1925, but was closed by Hitler in 1933.

baulk see BALK.

Baur, Ferdinand Christian (1792–1860) German Protestant theologian and New Testament critic, born in Schmiden, near Stuttgart. He held the Tübingen chair of theology from 1826, and founded the Tübingen School, the first to use strict historical research methods in the study of early Christianity.

bauxite *noun Geol.* the main ore of aluminium, consisting of a white, yellow, red, or brown clay-like substance that is formed by the weathering of igneous rocks in tropical regions. [from the name *Les Baux* in S France, where it was first found]

Bavaria, German **Bayern** POP (1991e) 11.5m, a state in SE Germany, bounded by the Czech Republic in the E and by Austria in the S. AREA 70 553sq km/27 233sq mi. It is Europe's oldest existing political entity and is the largest state in Germany. PHYSICAL DESCRIPTION surrounded by the Bavarian Forest in the E, the Fichtelgebirge in the NE, and the Bavarian Alps in the S; one third of the area is forested; chief rivers are the Danube, Isar, Lech, and Main. CAPITAL Munich. CHIEF TOWNS Augsburg, Passau, Nuremberg, Würzburg, Regensburg. ECONOMY agriculture; electrical and mechanical engineering; clothing; timber; tourism; there are many spas and climatic health resorts.

Bavarian Alps see TIROL ALPS.

Bavarian Forest, German **Bayerische Wald** a mountain range bounded NW by the R Chamb and the R Regen, and SW by the Danube Valley. It forms the largest continuous forest in Europe. The highest peak is the Einodriegel (1 126m). Germany's first national park falls within the Bavarian Forest.

Bavarian Succession, War of the a brief campaign (1778–9) waged by Frederick II of Prussia against Austria. On the dying out of the Bavarian branch of the Wittelsbach family Joseph II wanted to strengthen the Habsburg position in Germany by gaining parts of Bavaria, but military manoeuvring reached stalemate, and the Treaty of Teschen eventually affirmed the status quo. Austria was forced to recognize the succession of the Palatinate line of the Wittelsbachs to the Bavarian throne, but succeeded in winning the Innviertel. Its inconclusiveness earned it the name the 'Potato War'.

bawdily *adv.* with bawdy or coarse humour.

bawdiness *noun* being bawdy; coarse humour.

bawdy *adj.* (**bawdier, bawdiest**) *said of language, writing, etc* containing coarsely humorous references to sex. [from Old French *baude*, dissolute]

bawl *verb intrans., trans.* (*also* **bawl out**) to cry or shout loudly.
— **bawl someone out** *colloq.* to scold them angrily.
[from Latin *baulare*, to bark]

Bax, Sir Arnold (Edward Trevor) (1883–1953) English composer, born in London. A visit to Russia (1910) directly inspired some pieces (eg *Gopak*, 1911), but it was the Celtic revival that had the most influence on Bax. He wrote several Irish short stories (under the name of Dermot O'Byrne), and composed orchestral pieces and songs set to the words of revival poets. He wrote seven symphonies (1921–39), tone poems (such as *Tintagel*, 1917), choral works, chamber music, piano solos and concertos. In 1942 he became Master of the King's (from 1952 Queen's) Musick.

Baxter, Richard (1615–91) English Nonconformist churchman, born in Rowton, Shropshire. He acquired immense knowledge by private study, and in 1638 he was made a deacon. He adopted Nonconformist views, and during the English Civil War was army chaplain for the Puritans. At the Restoration he was appointed a royal chaplain, but the Act of Uniformity (1662) drove him out of the English Church. He returned to London in 1672, where he preached and wrote, arguing for the toleration of dissent within the Church. His controversial opinions led him in 1685 to be brought before Judge Jeffreys for alleged sedition, and he was imprisoned for 18 months.

bay[1] *noun* a body of water that forms a wide-mouthed indentation in the coastline. It is larger than a cove, and differs from a gulf in that it is usually broader at its seaward end than it is long. [from Old French *baie*]

bay[2] *noun* 1 a small area of a room set back into a wall. 2 an area for parking vehicles, or for loading and unloading them. 3 a compartment for storing or carrying. 4 an enclosed or partly enclosed area within a building for storage or some other purpose. [from Old French *baer*, to gape]

bay[3] — *adj., said of a horse* reddish-brown in colour. — *noun* a bay-coloured horse. [from Old French *bai*, chestnut-coloured]

bay[4] *noun* 1 a type of laurel tree, with dark green shiny leaves. 2 (*usually* **bays**) a wreath of bay leaves, usually worn on the head by champions in some competitions, etc. [from Old French *baie*]

bay[5] *verb intrans., said of a dog* to make a deep howling bark or cry, especially when hunting. — *noun* the baying sound of a dog.
— **at bay 1** not able to escape, forced to face an attacker. **2** at a distance: *keep poverty at bay*.
bring to bay to trap.
[from Old French *abai*, barking]

Bayamón POP (1990) 220 000, a city in Puerto Rico, E Caribbean Sea. It is situated on the R Bayamón, SW of San Juan.

Bayeux Tapestry an embroidered wall-hanging in coloured wool on linen, which narrates events leading up to the invasion of England by William of Normandy, and the battle of Hastings in 1066. It was probably commissioned by William's half-brother Odo, Bishop of Bayeux in N France, and embroidered in S England (c.1067–77); it measures 68m long and 46–54cm high.

Bayle, Pierre (1647–1706) French Protestant philosopher and critic, born in Carlat, in Languedoc. He became Professor of Philosophy at Sedan in 1675, and at Rotterdam in 1681. There he wrote a strong defence of toleration, but was attacked by the theologian Jurieu as an agent of France and the enemy of Protestantism, and was dismissed in 1693. He then concentrated on his major work, the encyclopedic *Dictionnaire* (1697) though he was continually persecuted on account of his philosophical scepticism.

Baylis, Lilian Mary (1874–1937) English theatrical manager, born in London. She was manager of the first Old Vic company from 1912, establishing its reputation for Shakespearean theatre. In 1931 she reopened Sadler's Wells Theatre for the exclusive presentation of opera and ballet, founding the companies that were to become the English National Opera and the Royal Ballet.

Bay of Pigs the failed invasion of Cuba (Apr 1961) by Cuban exiles supported by the USA. The invasion force of 1 300 men landed at Bahía de Cochinos (Bay of Pigs) on the south coast, but was rapidly defeated by Cuban troops under Fidel Castro. The episode was an embarrassment to John F Kennedy's administration.

bayonet — *noun* a steel knife fixed to the end of a soldier's rifle. — *verb* (**bayoneted, bayonet-**ing) to stab with a bayonet. [from French *baïonnette*, from *Bayonne* in SW France, where bayonets were first made]

bayou *noun* in the US, a marshy offshoot of a lake or river. [from Louisiana French]

Bayreuth POP (1991e) 72 000, an industrial and marketing town in Bavaria, E central Germany. It lies on a tributary of R Main, and is world famous as a festival city committed to the operas of Wagner. NOTABLE FEATURES old palace (16c), new palace (1753); the Wagner Theatre (1872–6). EVENT Wagner Festival (Jul–Aug).

Bayreuth Festival a summer music festival of Wagner's operas held in Bayreuth, Germany, established by Wagner in a purpose-built theatre in 1876, when the entire *Ring* cycle was performed. The Richard Wagner Foundation Bayreuth took over the administration from Wagner's descendants in 1973.

bay window a three-sided or rounded window that juts out from the wall of a building.

bazaar *noun* 1 *in Eastern countries* a market place. 2 a sale of goods, etc, usually in order to raise money for a particular organization or purpose. [from Persian *bazar*, market]

Bazaine, Achille (François) (1811–88) French soldier, born in Versailles. He joined the army in 1831, and served notably in the French expedition to Mexico (1862–7). In 1864 he was promoted Marshal of France. For his surrender at Metz (1870), during the Franco-Prussian War, he was court-martialled and imprisoned, but he later escaped and fled to Spain.

Bazalgette, Sir Joseph William (1819–91) English engineer. He constructed London's drainage system and the Thames embankment, and was a notable pioneer of public health engineering.

bazooka *noun* a gun which fires small rockets, especially at tanks. [from the name of a toy wind-instrument]

bazouki same as BOUZOUKI.

BB *abbrev.* **1** Boys' Brigade. **2** *on pencils* very black.

BBB *abbrev., on pencils* blacker than BB.

BBBC *abbrev.* British Boxing Board of Control.

BBC *abbrev.* in the UK, the British Broadcasting Corporation, an organization operating under Royal Charter, responsible for making and transmitting its own programmes. It began its radio service in 1927 and its television service in 1936 and is financed almost wholly by licence fees.

BBC Symphony Orchestra in London, UK, the chief orchestra owned by the British Broadcasting Corporation, founded in 1930 with 114 players under Adrian Boult (from 1931 to 1950). Its guest conductors have included Bruno Walter and Arturo Toscanini. Malcolm Sargent succeeded Boult (until 1957); later conductors have included Colin Davis (1967–71), Rudolf Kempe (1975–6), and Andrew Davis since 1989. Other BBC symphony orchestras are the Scottish, Welsh, and Philharmonic.

BBFC *abbrev.* **1** British Board of Film Censors. **2** British Board of Film Classification.

BBSRC *abbrev.* Biotechnology and Biological Sciences Research Council.

BC or **B.C.** *abbrev.* **1** before (the birth of) Christ: used in dates. See also AD. **2** British Columbia.
◆ BCE (= before the common era), which is culturally neutral, is sometimes used instead.

BCC *abbrev.* British Council of Churches.

BCE or **B.C.E.** *abbrev.* before the common era: used instead of BC in dates.
◆ See note at AD.

BCG or **bcg** *abbrev.* bacillus Calmette-Guérin, a vaccine given to a person to prevent tuberculosis.

BCL *abbrev.* Bachelor of Civil Law.

BCom. *or* **BComm**. *abbrev.* Bachelor of Commerce.

BD *abbrev.* **1** Bachelor of Divinity. **2** *as an international vehicle mark* Bangladesh.

BDA *abbrev.* British Dental Association.

BDI *abbrev. Bundesverband der Deutschen Industrie* (German) Federation of German Industry.

BDS *abbrev., as an international vehicle mark* Barbados.

BE *abbrev.* Bachelor of Engineering.

Be *symbol Chem.* beryllium.

be *verb* (PRESENT TENSE **am, are, is, are**; PAST TENSE **was, were**; PAST PARTICIPLE **been**) *intrans.* **1** to exist or live: *I think, therefore I am.* **2** to occur or take place: *lunch is in an hour.* **3** to occupy a position in space: *she is at home.* **4** (*in past tense*) to go: *he's never been to Italy.* **5** to remain or continue without change: *let it be.* **6** used to link a subject and what is said about it: *she is a doctor / he is ill.* **7** *intrans.* used with the infinitive form of a verb to express a possibility, command, intention, outcome, etc: *if it were to rain / we are to come tomorrow / it was not to be.* — *verb, aux.* **1** used with the past participle of a verb to form a passive: *the film was shown last night.* **2** used with a present participle to form the continuous tenses: *he was running.* — **the be-all and end-all** the only thing of importance.

be that as it may although that may be true.
[present tense from Anglo-Saxon *beon*, to live or exist; past tense from Anglo-Saxon *weran*, to be]

be- an element forming words meaning: **1** all over or all around; thoroughly or completely: *beset / bedazzle.* **2** considering as or causing to be: *befriend / benumb.* **3** having or covered with; affected by: *bejewelled.* **4** affecting someone or something by an action: *bereave.* [from Anglo-Saxon]

BEAB *abbrev.* British Electrical Approvals Board.

beach — *noun* the sandy or stony shore of a sea or lake. — *verb* to push or pull (a boat) on to a beach.

beachcomber *noun* a person who searches beaches for things of interest or value.

beachcombing *noun* the activity of searching beaches for things of interest or value.

beachhead *noun* an area of shore captured from the enemy, on which an army can land men and equipment.

beacon *noun* **1** a fire on a hill or mountain, lit as a signal. **2** *Brit.* (chiefly in place names) a hill on which a beacon could be lit. **3** a warning or guiding device for aircraft or ships, eg a lighthouse. **4** (*in full* **radio beacon**) a radio transmitter that broadcasts signals. [from Anglo-Saxon *beacen*]

bead — *noun* **1** a small and usually round ball of glass, stone, etc strung with others, eg in a necklace. **2** (**beads**) a string of beads worn as jewellery, or one used when praying; a rosary. **3** a small drop of liquid: *beads of sweat.* — *verb* to decorate with beads. — **draw a bead on something** *colloq.* to aim a gun at it.
[from Anglo-Saxon *biddan*, to pray]

beaded *adj.* consisting of or in the form of beads.

beading *noun* thin strips of patterned wood used to decorate the edges of furniture, walls, etc.

Beadle, George Wells (1903–89) US molecular geneticist, born in Wahoo, Nebraska. He was professor at the California Institute of Technology (1946–61) and President of Chicago University (1961–8). He studied the genetics of maize, the fruit fly (*Drosophila*), and the bread mould *Neurospora*, and with colleagues developed the idea that specific genes control the pro-

duction of specific enzymes. For this work he shared the 1958 Nobel Prize for Physiology or Medicine with Edward Tatum and Joshua Lederberg.

beadle *noun* **1** a person who leads formal processions in church or some old British universities. **2** in Scotland, a church officer. **3** formerly in England, a minor parish official who had the power to punish minor offences. [from Anglo-Saxon *bydel*, from *beodan*, to proclaim]

beady *adj.* (**beadier, beadiest**) usually *derog.*, *said of a person's eyes* small, round, and bright.

beagle — *noun* a type of small hunting-dog with a short coat. — *verb intrans.* to hunt with beagles. [from Old French *baer*, to gape + *goule*, throat, mouth]

beagling *noun* hunting with beagles.

beak *noun* **1** the hard pointed or hooked part of a bird's mouth. **2** *colloq.* a nose, especially if big and pointed. **3** *Brit. old slang use* a headmaster, judge, or magistrate. [from Old French *bec*]

beaked *adj.* having a beak.

beaker *noun* **1** a large drinking-glass, or a large (often plastic) cup without a handle. **2** a deep glass container with a lip, used in chemistry. **3** the amount a beaker will hold. [from Norse *bikarr*]

Beaker culture a prehistoric culture defined archaeologically by finely-made, pottery drinking vessels for mead or beer, often burnished and geometrically decorated. They have been found in graves of the third millennium BC from Spain, Czechoslovakia, and Hungary to Italy and Britain, and have often been taken as evidence of trans-European migrations perhaps originating in Spain.

beakerful *noun* (PL. **beakerfuls**) the amount a beaker will hold.

Beale, Dorothea (1831–1906) English pioneer of women's education, born in London. From 1858 she was principal of Cheltenham Ladies' College. An advocate of higher education for women, she sponsored St Hilda's Hall, Oxford (1894), and later became a suffragette.

beam — *noun* **1** a long straight thick piece of wood, used eg in a building. **2** the widest part of a ship or boat. **3** a ray of light. **4** the part of a set of scales from which the weighing-pans hang. **5** a narrow wooden bar on which gymnasts perform balancing exercises. — *verb* **1** *intrans.* to smile broadly with pleasure. **2** *intrans.* to shine. **3** *trans.* to send out (rays of light, radio waves, etc). — **broad in the beam** *colloq.* having wide hips. **off beam** *colloq.* wrong; misguided. **on the beam** *colloq.* on the right track. **on one's beam ends** *Brit. colloq.* with only a very small amount of money left. **on the port** *or* **starboard beam** *Naut.* on the left, or right, side of a ship. [from Anglo-Saxon, = tree]

bean *noun* **1** a general name applied to the edible kidney-shaped seeds of plants belonging to the pea family (Leguminosae), especially those of the genus *Phaseolus*, eg runner bean. Beans have a high protein content and are cultivated worldwide as a food crop, many of them being used as a substitute for meat, eg soya bean. **2** any plant belonging to the pea family that bears such seeds. **3** any other seed that superficially resembles those of the pea family, eg coffee bean. — **full of beans** *colloq.* full of energy; lively and cheerful.
[from Anglo-Saxon]

bean bag 1 a small cloth bag filled with dried beans, or something similar, thrown like a ball in children's games. **2** a very large floor cushion.

beanfeast *noun Brit. colloq.* a party or celebration.

beansprout *or* **beanshoot** *noun* a young shoot of a bean plant, especially of the mung bean, used as food.

beanstalk *noun* the stem of a bean plant.

bear¹ *verb* (PAST TENSE **bore**; PAST PARTICIPLE **borne**, in sense 4 also **born**) **1** to carry, bring, or take: *bear gifts.* **2** to support (a weight). **3** to produce: *bear fruit.* **4** (PAST PARTICIPLE in the passive is **born**, *or* **borne** when followed by *by* and a name) to give birth to: *has she borne children? / a child borne by Mary / he was born in 1960.* **5** to take or accept: *bear the blame.* **6** to put up with or like. **7** to show or be marked by: *bear the traces of tears.* **8** to carry in thought or memory: *bear a grudge.* **9** *intrans.* to turn slightly in a given direction: *bear left.* **10** to have: *bear no resemblance to.* **11** to behave: *bear oneself well.*
— **bear down on someone** to move towards them threateningly.
bear on something to affect or concern it.
bear something or someone out to support or confirm them: *the evidence bears him out.*
bear up *said of a person* to remain strong, brave, etc under strain.
bear with someone to be patient with them.
bring something to bear to apply pressure or influence.
[from Anglo-Saxon *beran*]

bear² *noun* **1** any of various large carnivorous animals belonging to the family Ursidae, and having heavily built bodies covered with thick fur, short powerful limbs, small eyes and ears, strong claws, and short tails. **2** a rough ill-mannered person. **3** *Stock Exchange* a person who sells shares, hoping to buy them back later at a much lower price. [from Anglo-Saxon *bera*]
◇ Bears, like badgers, differ from many other carnivores in that they eat plant material as well as flesh. They are mainly slow-moving ground-dwellers, but they are capable of walking on their hind legs and climbing trees. The most common species is the brown bear, found in N America, E Europe, and the Himalayas. The polar bear is adapted to life in the Arctic, having hair on the soles of its feet to provide insulation and a grip on the ice, and partially webbed front paws to enable it to swim. The various black bears found in N America and Asia are smaller species, and often good tree climbers. The only bear in S America is the spectacled bear, so called because it has white rings around its eyes.

bearable *adj.* able to be suffered or tolerated.

bearably *adv.* in a bearable or tolerable way; to a tolerable degree: *bearably cold.*

bearbaiting a popular sport in Britain in the 16c, forbidden by law in 1835. The bear was chained to a stake or put into a pit, and then attacked by dogs. Bets were placed on the performance of individual dogs The Master of Bears was a Crown office with a daily stipend. See also BLOOD SPORTS.

beard — *noun* **1** the hair that grows on a man's chin and neck. **2** a beard-like growth on some animals, eg goats. **3** a hair-like growth on an ear of corn, grass, etc. — *verb* to face or oppose openly or boldly. [from Anglo-Saxon]

bearded *adj.* having a beard, or a growth resembling a beard.

beardless *adj.* lacking a beard.

Beardsley, Aubrey (1872–98) English illustrator, born in Brighton. He became well known through his posters and his black and white illustrations for *Morte d'Arthur* (1893) and other books, as well as for the *Yellow Book* magazine (1894–5) and his own *Book of Fifty Drawings*. He was one of the leaders of the 'Decadents' in the 1890s.

bearer *noun* **1** a person or thing that bears or carries. **2** a person who helps carry equipment on an expedition. **3** a person who holds a banknote, cheque, or other money order which can be exchanged for money.

bear hug *colloq.* a rough tight squeeze with the arms.

bearing *noun* **1** the way a person stands, walks, etc. **2** a relation or effect: *that has no bearing on the situation*. **3** angular direction or position relative to a known point, or a calculation of this. **4** (*usually* **bearings**) position, or a calculation of position: *a ship's bearings*. **5** (**bearings**) *colloq*. a sense or awareness of one's own position or surroundings: *lose one's bearings*. **6** a part of a machine which supports another moving part.

bearish *adj*. **1** *said of a person* bad-tempered. **2** *Stock Exchange* causing or linked with a fall in prices.

bearskin *noun* **1** the skin of a bear. **2** a tall fur cap worn as part of some military uniforms.

beast *noun* **1** any large wild animal, especially a four-footed one. **2** *colloq*. a cruel brutal person. **3** *colloq*. a difficult or unpleasant person or thing. [from Old French *beste*]

beastliness *noun* fierceness; unpleasantness.

beastly — *adj*. (**beastlier, beastliest**) **1** like a beast in actions or behaviour; fierce, brutal. **2** *colloq*. unpleasant; horrid. — *adv*. extremely and unpleasantly: *beastly hot. bestial*

beat — *verb* (PAST TENSE **beat**; PAST PARTICIPLE **beaten**) **1** to hit violently and repeatedly, especially to harm or punish. **2** to strike repeatedly, eg to remove dust or make a sound. **3** *intrans*. to knock or strike repeatedly: *rain beating against the door*. **4** to defeat; to do something better, sooner, or quicker than (someone else). **5** to be too difficult to be solved or understood by: *the last puzzle had me beaten*. **6** to mix or stir thoroughly: *beat eggs*. **7** (**beat something** or **beat something out**) to make or shape it by striking the raw material. **8** *intrans*. to move in a regular pattern of strokes, etc: *a beating heart*. **9** (**beat out time**) to mark or show musical time. **10** *trans., intrans*. to move rhythmically up and down. **11** (**beat someone** or **something back** or **down** or **off**) to push, drive, or force them away. **12** *trans., intrans*. to strike (bushes, trees, etc) to force birds or animals into the open for shooting. — *noun* **1** a regular stroke, or its sound: *the beat of a heart*. **2** the main accent in music. **3** a regular or usual course or journey, especially one made by a policeman or policewoman.
— **beat about the bush** to talk tediously about a subject without coming to the main point.
beat down *said of the sun* to give out great heat.
beat someone down to force (a person) to reduce (the price of something) by bargaining.
beat a hasty retreat to go away in a hurry.
beat it *slang* to go away immediately and quickly.
beat someone off to check them, or succeed in overcoming them.
beat someone up to punch, kick, or hit them severely and repeatedly.
dead beat *colloq*. very tired.
off the beaten track away from main roads and towns; isolated.
[from Anglo-Saxon *beatan*]

Beata Beatrix a painting by Dante Gabriel Rossetti (1863, Tate Gallery, London). It is one of several paintings featuring his wife, Elizabeth Siddal.

beater *noun* **1** a person who forces animals into the open for shooting. **2** an instrument used for beating: *an egg-beater*.

beat generation a group of US writers and poets whose work was popular in the 1950s. They sought truth through individual experience, advocating religious meditation, sexual freedom, drug use, and jazz as means to that end, and rejected the conventional values of modern Western society, with its commercialism and militarism. The writers developed their own slang and an often provocative and idiosyncratic style: they included the poets Allen Ginsberg, Gregory Corso, and Laurence Ferlinghetti; the novelist Jack Kerouac's semi-autobiographical *On the Road* achieved cult status.

beatific *adj*. **1** showing great happiness: *a beatific smile*. **2** making blessed. [from Latin *beatus*, blessed + *facere*, to make]

beatification *noun RC Church* the act of declaring a dead person 'blessed', as a step towards full canonization.

beatify *verb* (**beatifies, beatified**) **1** *RC Church* to declare the blessed status of (someone who has died), usually as the first step towards canonization. **2** to make extremely happy. [from Latin *beatus*, blessed + *facere*, to make]

beating *noun* physical assault or punishment.

beating the bounds in England, a traditional ceremonial walk at Rogationtide around parish lands, tracing the boundaries and beating stones and other boundary marks with peeled willow wands as a method of fixing their position in the collective memory.

beatitude *noun* a state of extreme happiness and peace. [from Latin *beatitudo*, from *beatus*, blessed]

Beatitudes the common name for the opening pronouncements of blessing on certain classes of people, recorded in Matthew 5.3–11 in Christ's Sermon on the Mount, and in Luke 6.20–2 in his Sermon on the Plain.

Beatles English pop group, established in Liverpool in 1960, which consisted of John Lennon (rhythm guitar, keyboards, vocals); Paul McCartney (bass guitar, vocals); George Harrison (1943–) (lead guitar, sitar, vocals); and Pete Best (1941–) (drums), replaced in 1962 by Ringo Starr (1940–), originally Richard Starkey. 'Love Me Do' was their first UK hit, and their club appearances soon created many idolizing fans. International hits (eg 'She Loves You' and 'I Wanna Hold Your Hand') and a US concert tour led to the worldwide spread of 'Beatlemania' (1964). The Beatles' image (a carefree, somewhat cynical approach to life, long hair and 'granny' glasses) influenced both the attitudes and appearance of their fans and was reinforced by the films *A Hard Day's Night* (1964) and *Help* (1965). Many of their early hits (eg 'Yesterday' and 'Eleanor Rigby') were written by Lennon and McCartney. In 1966 the Beatles stopped performing in public and turned to studio production (eg *Sergeant Pepper's Lonely Hearts Club Band*, 1967), but the group dissolved acrimoniously in 1970. Lennon lived in New York with his wife Yoko Ono (1933–); he was murdered by a deranged fan in 1980. McCartney has formed bands and toured and recorded frequently. Harrison records occasionally, and Starr has acted in several films and recorded some albums on his own.

beatnik *noun* a young person, especially in the 1950s, who rejected conventional social and political ideas and wore unusual clothes, long hair, etc.

Beaton, Sir Cecil (Walter Hardy) (1904–80) English photographer and designer, born in London. In the 1920s, as a staff photographer for *Vanity Fair* and *Vogue*, he became famous for his society portraits. He produced several photographic books, eg *The Book of Beauty* (1930). After World War II, he designed scenery and costumes for many ballet, operatic, theatrical, and film productions, including *My Fair Lady* and *Gigi*.

Beaton *or* **Bethune, David** (1494–1546) Scottish statesman and Roman Catholic prelate, born in Balfour, Fife. After studying at St Andrews, Glasgow, and Paris, he resided at the French court (1519) and was appointed Bishop of Mirepoix by Francis I (1537). In 1525 he entered the Scots parliament as Abbot of Arbroath and became Privy Seal (1528), and was later elevated to cardinal (1538) and Archbishop of St Andrews (1539). He was a vigorous supporter of French interests and a persecutor of the Scottish Protestants, but after he had the reformer George

Wishart burnt at St Andrews (1546), he was murdered in revenge three months later.

Beatrice 1 a female first name, known largely as the name of Dante's beloved. **2** the nimble, quick-witted heroine of Shakespeare's *Much Ado About Nothing*, who wickedly teases Benedick before eventually marrying him. [a French variant of *Beatrix*, from Latin *viator*, voyager through life + *beatus*, blessed]

Beatrix (Wilhelmina Armgard) (1938–) Queen of the Netherlands, born in Soestdijk, the eldest daughter of Juliana and Prince Bernhard zur Lippe-Biesterfeld. In 1966 she married the German diplomat Claus-Georg Wilhelm Otto Friedrich Gerd von Amsberg (1926–) and in 1980 acceded to the throne on the abdication of her mother. Their son, Prince Willem-Alexander Claus George Ferdinand (1967–) is the first male heir to the Dutch throne in over a century. There are two other sons: Johan Friso Bernhard Christiaan David (1968–) and Constantijn Christof Frederik Aschwin (1969–).

Beatty, David Beatty, 1st Earl (1871–1936) English admiral, born in Nantwich, Cheshire. He served in the Sudan (1896–8), and as battleship commander took part in the China War (1900). At the outbreak of World War I he steamed into Heligoland Bight, and destroyed three German cruisers. He later sank the *Blücher* (Jan 1915), and took part in the battle of Jutland (May 1916). He became Commander-in-Chief of the Grand Fleet in 1916 and First Sea Lord in 1919.

Beatty, (Henry) Warren (1937–) US film actor and producer, born in Richmond, Virginia. His first film was *Splendor in the Grass* (1961) which was followed by various roles exploiting his boyish good looks and air of sullen rebelliousness. Among his other successful films are *Bonnie and Clyde* (1967), *McCabe and Mrs Miller* (1971), *The Parallax View* (1974), *Heaven Can Wait* (1978), *Reds* (1981), for which he won a Best Director Oscar, and *Bugsy* (1991).

beat-up *adj. colloq*. old and worn; in very bad condition.

beau *noun* (PL. **beaux**) *old use* **1** a boyfriend or male lover. **2** a man who thinks a lot about his clothes and appearance. [from French *beau*, beautiful]

Beaufort, Sir Francis (1774–1857) British naval officer and hydrographer, born in Navan, Co Meath. From 1829 to 1855 he was hydrographer to the navy, devising the Beaufort scale of wind force and a tabulated system of weather registration.

Beaufort, Henry (1377–1447) English cardinal, a major figure in English politics in the early 15c. He was consecrated Bishop of Lincoln (1398) and Winchester (1405), became cardinal in 1426, and was Lord Chancellor (1403–5, 1413–17, 1424–6). In 1427 the pope sent him as legate into Germany, to organize a crusade against the Hussites, but the undertaking failed. During the 1430s he controlled the government of the young King Henry VI.

Beaufort, Lady Margaret, Countess of Richmond (1443–1509) great-granddaughter of John of Gaunt, Duke of Lancaster, she married Edmund Tudor, Earl of Richmond (1455), and was mother of Henry VII, to whom she conveyed the Lancastrian claim to the English Crown. Her third husband, Thomas, Lord Stanley, was instrumental in helping Henry VII assume the Crown. She was a benefactress of William Caxton, and of Oxford and Cambridge Universities.

Beaufort scale *Geol*. a system for estimating wind speeds without using instruments, based on a scale ranging from 0 (calm) to 12 (hurricane), as assessed by the effect of wind on observable indicators such as smoke, trees, and the surface of the sea. It is commonly used in weather fore-

Beaufort scale

In 1805 Admiral Sir Francis Beaufort worked out a scale for measuring wind speed. The scale is numbered from 1 to 12 and represents wind force out in the open.

No.	Wind force	km/h	mph	Observable effects
0	calm	<1.6	<1	smoke rises vertically
1	light air	1.6–4.8	1–3	direction shown by smoke
2	slight breeze	6.4–11.3	4–7	felt on face; wind vanes move
3	gentle breeze	12.9–19.3	8–12	leaves, twigs move; flags extended
4	moderate breeze	20.9–29.0	13–18	dust, paper, small branches move
5	fresh breeze	30.6–38.6	19–24	small trees sway; flags ripple
6	strong breeze	40.2–50.0	25–31	large branches move; flags beat
7	moderate gale	51.5–61.2	32–38	whole trees sway; walking difficult
8	fresh gale	62.8–74.0	39–46	twigs break off; walking hindered
9	strong gale	75.6–86.9	47–54	slight damage – chimney-pots, slates
10	whole gale	88.5–101.4	55–63	severe damage; trees uprooted
11	storm	103.0–115.9	64–72	widespread damage
12	hurricane	>117.5	>73	devastation

casting for shipping. [named after the British admiral Sir Francis Beaufort]

Beaufort Sea a region of the Arctic Ocean, N of Alaska and W of the Canadian Arctic Archipelago. It is covered with pack ice. A major oil deposit discovered in Prudhoe Bay in 1968 is linked by pipeline to Valdez.

Beaujolais a subdivision of the old province of Lyonnais in E central France, now forming part of the Rhône and the Loire departments. It is a granite upland on the edge of the Massif Central. The slopes above the river valleys yield the good Burgundy wine named Beaujolais. Villefranche is the trade centre of this major wine-growing region. The N part is known as Beaujolais Villages.

Beaumarchais, Pierre-Augustin Caron de (1732–99) French comic dramatist, born in Paris. His most successful comedies were *Le Barbier de Séville* (The Barber of Seville, 1775) and *Le Mariage de Figaro* (The Marriage of Figaro, 1784).

Beaumont, Francis (c.1584–1616) English dramatist, born in Gracedieu, Leicestershire. He formed a close association with John Fletcher, apparently writing at least 87 plays, but modern research finds Beaumont's hand in only about 10 of them. *The Woman Hater* (1607) is attributed solely to him, and he had the major share in *The Knight of the Burning Pestle* (1609).

Beaumont, William (1785–1853) US army surgeon, born in Lebanon, Connecticut. Through experiments on a willing patient he confirmed the chemical nature of digestion, established that the presence of food stimulated the secretion of gastric juice and directly observed the role of alcohol in the causation of gastric inflammation (gastritis). His *Experiments and Observations on the Gastric Juice and the Physiology of Digestion* (1833) was the first major US contribution to physiology.

Beauregard, P(ierre) G(ustave) T(outant) (1818–93) US soldier, born near New Orleans. He graduated at West Point (1838), served with distinction in the Mexican War, and was appointed by the Confederate government to the command at Charleston, where he commenced the American Civil War by the bombardment of Fort Sumter (12 Apr 1861). He fought at Bull Run (1861), took command at Shiloh (1862), and later defended Charleston and Richmond.

beauteous *adj. poetic* beautiful.

beauteously *adv. poetic* beautifully.

beautician *noun* a person who styles women's hair, treats their skin, applies their make-up, etc, especially in a beauty parlour.

beautification *noun* making beautiful, especially by decoration.

beautiful *adj.* **1** having an appearance or qualities which please the senses. **2** pleasing or enjoyable.

beautifully *adv.* in a manner that pleases the senses: *the stories are beautifully written.*

beautify *verb* (**beautifies**, **beautified**) to make beautiful, often by decorating.

beauty *noun* (PL. **beauties**) **1** a quality pleasing to the senses, especially the eye or ear. **2** a beautiful woman or girl. **3** *colloq.* an excellent example of something. **4** a benefit: *the beauty of the plan.* [from Old French *biaute*]

beauty contest a competition in which young women are judged by the beauty of their faces and bodies.

beauty parlour *or* **beauty salon** a place which offers hairdressing, make-up, massage, etc to women.

beauty queen the winner in a beauty contest.

beauty spot **1** a place of great natural beauty. **2** a small dark natural or artificial mark on the face, considered to enhance beauty.

Beauvais POP (1990) 56 000, the capital of Oise department, Picardy region, N France. It lies on the R Thérain, 76km/47mi N of Paris. It was formerly a tapestry-making centre and is today a market town. NOTABLE FEATURES tallest cathedral in France (68m).

Beauvoir, Simone de (1908–86) French existentialist writer and novelist, born in Paris. She studied philosophy with Sartre at the Sorbonne, where she became professor (1941–3), and (with Sartre) co-founded the avant-garde monthly, *Les Temps modernes* (1945). Closely associated with Sartre until his death (1980), her own works provide existentialism with an essentially feminine sensibility, notably the pioneering *Le Deuxième sexe* (The Second Sex, 1949) and *Les Mandarins* (1954, Prix Goncourt).

Beaux-Arts a decorative Classical architectural style of the late 19c, particularly popular in France. The name derives from the Ecole des Beaux-Arts in Paris.

Beaux-Arts, Ecole des the principal official art school in Paris. It dates from 1648, when the first class was taught by Charles Le Brun. It was abolished during the Revolution, refounded in 1796, and installed in its present quarters on the Left Bank of the Seine by 1830.

beaver *noun* **1** either of two species of a large semi-aquatic squirrel-like rodent. The European beaver is now found only in Scandinavia, E Europe, and the Elbe and Rhone valleys. The N American beaver has been reduced in numbers by hunting (for its fur and its musk) and destruction of its habitat, and it survives only in Canada and the northern USA. **2** its fur. **3** a hat made of beaver fur.

— **beaver away at something** *colloq.* to work very hard at it.
[from Anglo-Saxon *befer*]
◇ Beavers are about 1m in length, with stout bodies, soft dark brown fur, a blunt muzzle, webbed hind feet, and a broad flat scaly tail that is used as a rudder when the beaver is swimming, and as a support when it is standing on dry land. Beavers feed on bark and sapwood, and may dig a burrow in a river bank, or build a 'lodge' from twigs and mud in a pond that has been formed for this purpose by damming a stream with logs or large branches. The animal fells trees by using its large cutting incisor teeth as chisels to chew chips out of the trunks. The upper half of the lodge projects above water, and contains a dry central chamber with one or more escape tunnels leading to underwater exits.

Beaverbrook, Sir Max (William Maxwell) Aitken, 1st Baron (1879–1964) British newspaper magnate and politician, born in Maple, Ontario. A successful stockbroker, he went to Britain (1910) and entered Parliament, becoming private secretary to Bonar Law. He was made Minister of Information under David Lloyd George and in 1916 entered journalism, taking over the *Daily Express*, which became the world's most widely-read daily newspaper. A dynamic character, he also founded the *Sunday Express* (1921) and bought the London *Evening Standard* (1929), and campaigned for Empire Free Trade. During World War II he was Minister of Supply (1941–2), Minister of Production (1942), Lord Privy Seal (1943–5), and lend-lease administrator in the USA.

bebop *noun* a revolutionary jazz style which evolved in the decade after World War II, also called *bop* or *rebop*. It was so named in imitation of the two quavers used in the rhythm, and was characterized by fast tempos, complex agitated rhythms, and a continuous, improvised melodic line. Its major exponents included Charlie 'Bird' Parker, Dizzy Gillespie, and Thelonius Monk.

becalmed *adj., said of a sailing ship* unable to move because of lack of wind.

became see BECOME.

because *conj.* for the reason that.
— **because of something** *or* **someone** on account of them; by reason of them.
[from *by cause of*]

Beche, Sir Henry Thomas De La (1796–1855) English geologist, born near London. He studied the geology of England, the Alps, and Jamaica, and became the first Director of the newly established Geological Survey of Great Britain in 1835.

Bechet, Sidney (1897–1959) US soprano saxophonist, born in New Orleans. He began on the clarinet, but switched to soprano saxophone reportedly to dominate the brass in ensembles. His boldly lyrical solos made him second only to Louis Armstrong in the first jazz generation. Lionized in France on the first of many tours (1919), he later became a permanent resident there (1949).

Beck, Aaron T(emkin) (1921–) US psychiatrist, born in Rhode Island. Professor at the University of Pennsylvania, he introduced cognitive therapy as a treatment approach for neurotic disorders, particularly depression. His books include *Depression: Causes and Treatment* (1972) and *Love is Never Enough* (1988).

beck[1]
— **at someone's beck and call** having to be always ready to carry out their orders or wishes.
[from Anglo-Saxon *biecnan*, to beckon]

beck[2] *noun* a stream. [from Norse *bekkr*]

Beckenbauer, Franz (1945–) German footballer, born in Munich. He made his first-team début for Bayern Munich at the age of 18, and after only 27 matches made his international début. He played in the West German side beaten by England in the 1966 World Cup, led his country to World Cup success in 1974, and won three successive European Cup winner's medals with Bayern Munich (1974–6). After a period playing in the USA, he returned to West Germany and won a fifth League title with Hamburg in 1982. He retired in 1983, and in 1984 was appointed coach to the West German national team, a post he held until their victory in the 1990 World Cup.

Becker, Boris (1967–) German lawn tennis player, born in Leiman, the inaugural winner of the World Young Masters title, and the youngest winner of the men's singles at Wimbledon (17 yrs 227 days), both in 1985. He also won at Wimbledon in 1986 and 1989, and was a beaten finalist in 1988, 1990, and 1991. He was named World Championship Tennis champion in 1988 and world champion in 1991, Masters champion in 1988, and was a member of the West German Davis Cup-winning team in 1988 and 1989. He also won the US Open in 1989, and the Australian Open in 1991.

Becket, St Thomas (à) (1118–70) English saint and martyr, born in London. He studied canon law at Bologna and Auxerre and in 1155 became Chancellor and a brilliant figure at court, the first Englishman since the Norman Conquest to hold high office. On becoming Archbishop of Canterbury (1162) he changed dramatically: he resigned the Chancellorship and became a zealous ascetic, serving the Church as vigorously as he had the king. However, Henry II wanted to keep the clergy in subordination to the State, and although Becket consented to the Constitutions of Clarendon (1164), which defined the powers of Church and State, he remained in disfavour. His goods and the revenues of his sees were confiscated and he fled the country and spent two years in France. In 1170 he was reconciled with Henry, and returned to Canterbury, to public delight. New quarrels soon broke out however, and Henry's wish to be rid of the 'turbulent priest' led to Becket's murder in Canterbury cathedral (29 Dec 1170). He was canonized in 1173 and his feast day is 29 Dec. In 1220 his bones were transferred to the Trinity Chapel, which for many years attracted pilgrims, as described by Chaucer in the prologue to the *Canterbury Tales*.

Becket, ou l'honneur de Dieu (Becket, or The Honour of God) a play by Jean Anouilh (1959), based on the story of the quarrel between Thomas Becket and Henry II.

Beckett, Samuel (Barclay) (1906–89) Irish novelist, poet, and playwright, born in Dublin. He settled in France in 1937 and later wrote in French, notably the trilogy of novels: *Molloy* (1951), *Malone Meurt* (Malone Dies, 1951) and *L'Innommable* (The Unnamable, 1953). His play *Waiting for Godot* (En attendant Godot, 1954) was so original that it made a big impact in both Paris and London. His work shows a preoccupation with the failure of humans to communicate successfully, and mirrors the pointlessness of life which they strive to make purposeful. He was awarded the 1969 Nobel Prize for Literature.

Beckford, William Thomas (1760–1844) English writer and collector, born in Fonthill, Wiltshire. He inherited a fortune in 1770 and spent several years travelling in Europe. In 1784 he entered parliament but became involved in a scandal and was excluded from society. His main work was the Gothic novel, *Vathek* (1786), which first appeared in French. He returned to England in 1796 and commissioned the building of the Gothic Fonthill Abbey and Lansdown Tower.

Beckmann, Ernst Otto (1853–1923) German chemist, born in Solingen. Professor at Erlangen and Leipzig, he became Director of the newly founded Kaiser Wilhelm Institute in 1912. He is best known for his discovery of an important reaction by which amides are produced, and for the accurate thermometer (used to determine

molecular weights by freezing point depression or boiling point elevation) which bears his name.

beckon *verb trans., intrans.* (**beckoned, beckoning**) to call (someone) towards oneself, especially by making a sign with the hand. [from Anglo-Saxon *biecnan*]

become *verb usually intrans.* (PAST TENSE **became**; PAST PARTICIPLE **become**) **1** to come or grow to be. **2** (**become of someone** *or* **something**) to happen to: *whatever became of Donald?* **3** *trans. formal, said especially of dress* to suit, or look good on: *that hat becomes you.* [from Anglo-Saxon *becuman*, to come, approach]

becoming *adj.* **1** attractive. **2** *said of behaviour, etc* suitable or proper.

becomingly *adv.* in a proper or attractive way: *he is becomingly modest.*

Becquerel, Antoine Henri (1852–1908) French physicist, born in Paris. He succeeded his father Alexandre-Edmond Becquerel as professor at the Natural History Museum there, and in research on a fluorescent uranium salt, he discovered by chance that it emitted a penetrating radiation which he concluded to be an atomic property. This discovery of radioactivity prompted the beginning of the nuclear age. He shared the 1903 Nobel Prize for Physics with Marie and Pierre Curie.

becquerel *noun* (SYMBOL **Bq**) the SI unit of radioactivity, equivalent to one disintegration of a radioactive source per second. It has now largely replaced the curie (one becquerel is equal to 2.7×10^{-11} curies).

BEd. *abbrev.* Bachelor of Education.

bed — *noun* **1** a piece of furniture for sleeping on. **2** the bottom of a river, lake, or sea. **3** an area of ground in a garden, for growing plants: *flowerbed.* **4** a support or foundation. **5** a layer, especially of rock. — *verb* (**bedded, bedding**) **1** (**bed down** *or* **bed someone down**) to go to bed, or put him in bed or a place to sleep: *bedded down on the sofa.* **2** *colloq.* to have sexual intercourse with. **3** (**bed something out**) to plant it in a garden. **4** to place or fix firmly. **5** *trans., intrans.* to arrange in, or form, layers.

— **bed and board** lodgings and food.

a bed of roses an easy or comfortable place or situation.

go to bed with someone *colloq.* to have sexual intercourse with someone.

make the bed to make the bedclothes tidy after the bed has been slept in.

[from Anglo-Saxon *bedd*]

bedazzle *verb* **1** to impress greatly. **2** to confuse.

bedazzled *adj.* impressed; confused.

bedazzlement *noun* a state of dazzlement or confusion.

bedbath *noun* a complete wash of the body of a person who is unable get out of bed.

bedbug *noun* the common name for any of various species of household pest that infest bedding, and feed on human blood.

Bedchamber Crisis a British political crisis (May 1839). Lord Melbourne, the Whig Prime Minister, offered to resign and advised the young Queen Victoria to appoint Peel and the Tories. However, the Queen exercised her royal prerogative and refused to dismiss certain ladies of the Bedchamber with Whig sympathies, whereupon Peel refused office and the Whig government continued.

bedclothes *pl. noun* the sheets, blankets, etc used to cover a bed.

bedcover *noun* a top cover for a bed.

bedding *noun* **1** mattresses, blankets, etc. **2** straw, etc for animals to sleep on.

Beddoes, Thomas Lovell (1803–49) English poet and physiologist, born in Clifton,

Somerset. In 1822 he published *The Bride's Tragedy,* a sombre murder drama. He studied medicine at Göttingen in 1825, and then travelled in Germany and Switzerland. He is best known for his dramatic poem *Death's Jest-Book*, published in 1850, a year after his suicide.

Bede *or* **Baeda, St**, also called **the Venerable Bede** (c.673–735) Anglo-Saxon historian and theologian, born near Monkwearmouth, Durham. After studying at the Benedictine monastery there, he was later transferred to Jarrow, where he wrote homilies, lives of the saints, hymns, epigrams, works on chronology and grammar, and commentaries on the Old and New Testaments. His most valuable work is the *Historia Ecclesiastica Gentis Anglorum* (Ecclesiastical History of the English People), virtually the only source of English history before 731. He was buried in Jarrow, but in the 11c his bones were removed to Durham. His feast day is 27 May.

Bede, Adam see ADAM BEDE.

bedeck *verb* to cover with decorations; to adorn.

bedevil *verb* (**bedevilled, bedevilling**) **1** to cause continual difficulties or trouble to. **2** to confuse.

bedevilment *noun* continual difficulty or trouble, bedevil.

bedfellow *noun* **1** a person with whom one shares a bed. **2** a partner or associate.

Bedford, John of Lancaster, Duke of (1389–1435) English soldier and statesman, the third son of Henry IV. In 1414 his brother (Henry V) created him Duke of Bedford and after Henry's death (1422), he became Guardian of England and Regent of France. When his uncle (Charles VI) died, he was proclaimed King of France as Henry VI. During the Hundred Years War, he defeated the French in several battles, notably at Verneuil (1424), but an army under Joan of Arc forced him onto the defensive (1429).

Bedford POP (1981) 77 000, the county town of Bedfordshire, S central England, situated in N Bedfordshire district. It is a residential town situated 32km/20mi SE of Northampton and 75km/47mi N of London. John Bunyan (1628–88) was imprisoned here.

Bedfordshire POP (1992e) 537 000, a county in S central England, divided into four districts. AREA 1 235sq km/477sq mi. It is bounded W by Buckinghamshire, NW by Northamptonshire, NE by Cambridgeshire, and SE by Hertfordshire. The R Ouse flows W–E through the county. CHIEF TOWNS Bedford (county town), Luton, Dunstable. ECONOMY distribution centre; motor vehicles; bricks; wheat, barley.

Bedivere, Sir the only surviving knight of King Arthur's Round Table in Alfred Lord Tennyson's 'Morte d'Arthur'. He throws the sword Excalibur into the lake.

Bedlam the popular name for Bethlehem Royal Hospital, founded (1247) as a priory in London. In 1547 Henry VIII gave it to the city as a public lunatic asylum and for centuries it remained notorious for the cruel treatment suffered by its inmates.

bedlam *noun colloq.* a noisy confused place or situation. [from BEDLAM]

bed linen the sheets and pillowcases used on a bed.

Bedlington terrier a UK breed of dog with a tapering muzzle and no obvious forehead in side view. Its curly coat is usually pale, but may be grey or brown. The original short-legged breed was crossed with the whippet to produce the longer-legged modern form. [from Bedlington in NE England, where it was first bred]

Bedouin *noun* (PL. **Bedouin, Bedouins**) a member of a wandering Arab tribe that lives in the deserts of the Middle East. [from Arabic *badawi*, desert-dweller]

bedpan *noun* a wide shallow pan used as a toilet by people who are unable to get out of bed.

bedraggled *adj., said of a person or animal* very wet and untidy.

bedridden *adj.* not able to get out of bed, especially because of old age or sickness.

bedrock *noun* **1** the solid rock forming the lowest layer under soil and rock fragments. **2** the basic principle, idea, etc on which something rests.

bedroom *noun* **1** a room for sleeping in. **2** (*attributive*) denoting sexual relations: *bedroom comedy.*

Beds. *abbrev.* Bedfordshire.

bedside *noun* the place or position next to a bed, especially of a sick person.

bedsit *or* **bedsitter** *noun Brit. colloq.* a bedsitting room.

bedsitting room *noun Brit.* a single room for both eating and sleeping in.

bedsore *noun* an ulcer on a person's skin, caused by lying in bed for long periods.

bedspread *noun* a top cover for a bed.

bedstead *noun* the frame of a bed.

bedstraw *noun* a small annual or perennial plant of the genus *Gallium*, found almost everywhere, and having a fragile stem, narrow leaves arranged in whorls, and tiny white, yellow, or greenish flowers borne in open clusters.

bed-wetting *noun* accidental urination in bed at night.

bee *noun* **1** any of a large number of insects that have four membranous wings, belong to the family Apidae, and are members of the same order (Hymenoptera) as ants and wasps. They are found worldwide except in very cold regions, and the female almost always bears a sting, which is used for defence. **2** *North Amer., esp. US* a meeting of friends or neighbours to work for or enjoyment. **3** *old use* a friendly competition. — **a bee in one's bonnet** *colloq.* a notion or wish with which one is preoccupied. **the bee's knees** *Brit. colloq.* a person or thing that is extremely good. [from Anglo-Saxon *beo*] ◇ Bees have sucking and biting mouthparts, and they feed on nectar and pollen which they collect from flowers. They play an important role in the pollination of many plants, including numerous important food crops. Nectar is collected with the tongue, while pollen is picked up on the body hairs, and much of the food is taken back to the nest to be stored or fed to the grubs, although nectar is converted to honey before it is stored. Most bees are solitary, but a few, including the honey bee and bumble bee, are social insects, living in colonies of a few dozen to several thousand individuals.

Beebe, Charles William (1877–1962) US naturalist and explorer, born in New York City. He was curator of ornithology for the New York Zoological Society from 1899, wrote many widely read books, including *Galapagos* (1923) and *The Arcturus Adventure* (1925), and explored ocean depths down to almost 1000m in a bathysphere (1934).

beech — *noun* **1** a deciduous tree or shrub of the genus *Fagus* which has smooth grey bark, pale green glossy leaves, and produces triangular edible nuts. **2** the hard straight-grained wood of this tree, widely used for furniture making. — *adj.* made from the wood of the beech tree. [from Anglo-Saxon *bece*]

Beecham, Sir Thomas (1879–1961) English conductor, born in St Helens, Lancashire. He began his career with the New Symphony Orchestra in 1906 and introduced 60 works unknown to British audiences, in addition to Diaghilev's Russian ballet. He conducted opera at Covent Garden, was made artistic director there (1933), and founded the Royal Philharmonic Orchestra (1946). A champion of the works of Delius, Sibelius, and Richard Strauss, as a foremost conductor he was also known for his candid pronouncements on musical matters, his 'lollipop' encores (of popular works of classical music), and his after-concert speeches.

beech mast *pl. noun* the nuts of the beech tree.

bee dancing the movements of honey-bees in patterns, used to commmunicate the direction and distance of pollen and nectar sources to other members of the colony. The phenomenon was first documented by the Austrian biologist Karl von Frisch (1886–1982), who plotted the way in which worker bees perform circling or tail-wagging dances depending on the distance of the food from the hive.

bee-eater a brilliantly coloured bird, usually bright green with red, blue, or yellow patches, native to the Old World, especially Africa and S Asia, and having a slender pointed bill. It feeds on ants, bees, and wasps caught in flight.

beef — *noun* **1** the flesh of a bull, cow, or ox, used as food. **2** *colloq.* muscle, strength. **3** *colloq.* a complaint. — *verb intrans. colloq.* to complain. — **beef something up** *colloq.* **1** to make something stronger or heavier. **2** to make something more interesting or exciting. [from Old French *boef*, ox]

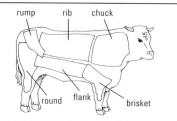

beef cuts

beefburger *noun* a piece of finely chopped beef, made into a flat round shape, grilled or fried.

beefcake *noun colloq., derog.* very muscular men displayed in photographs. See also CHEESECAKE.

Beefeater *noun* a guard at the Tower of London.

beefiness *noun* a beefy or fat condition.

beefsteak *noun* a thick slice of beef for grilling or frying.

beef tea the juice of chopped beef, sometimes taken by people who are ill.

beefy *adj.* (**beefier, beefiest**) **1** of or like beef. **2** *colloq.* having a lot of fat or muscle.

beehive *noun* **1** a box or hut in which bees are kept, and where they store their honey. **2** a place where a lot of people are working hard. **3** shaped like a traditional round-topped beehive: *a beehive hairstyle.*

beekeeper *noun* a person who keeps bees for their honey.

beekeeping *noun* the keeping of bees for their honey.

beeline *noun* a straight line between two places. — **make a beeline for something** to go to it directly or purposefully: *made a beeline for the cake-stall.*

Beelzebub, Greek *Beelzebul* a being referred to in the New Testament Gospels as the 'prince of devils' (eg Matthew 12.24), the equivalent of Satan. He is possibly linked with the Old Testament figure *Baal-zebub* ('lord of flies'), the god of Ekron (2 Kings 1.2), or with the Canaanite *Baal-zebul* ('lord of the high place'). The name is also afforded to Satan's second-in-command in Milton's *Paradise Lost.*

been see BE.

beep — *noun* a short high-pitched sound, eg made by a car horn. — *verb intrans., trans.* to produce a beep (on or for something): *do stop beeping the horn.* [imitative of the sound]

beeper *noun* an instrument that makes a beep, eg to attract someone's attention.

Beer, Sir Gavin Rylands de (1899–1972) English zoologist, born in London. He taught at Oxford (1923–38) and was later Professor of Embryology in London and Director of the British Museum (Natural History). His work refuted some early theories in embryology; he went on to contribute to theories of animal evolution, and to historical problems such as the origin of the Etruscans.

beer *noun* **1** an alcoholic beverage prepared by the slow fermentation of malted cereal grains, usually barley, flavoured with hops, eg ale, lager, stout. **2** a glass, can, or bottle of this beverage. **3** any other fermented liquor, eg ginger beer. — **beer and skittles** *Brit.* fun; pleasure. [from Anglo-Saxon *beor*]

Beerbohm, Sir (Henry) Max(imilian) (1872–1956) English writer and caricaturist, born in London. His first book of essays and drawings appeared in 1896, and he was drama critic of *The Saturday Review* until 1910 when he moved to Rapallo in Italy. He produced many volumes of caricatures and parodying essays, but is best known for his only novel *Zuleika Dobson* (1912).

beer garden a garden, usually attached to a pub, where beer and other refreshments can be drunk.

Beersheba POP (1990e) 114 000, an industrial town in Southern district, S Israel, on the N edge of the Negev Desert. Ruins of the ancient town lie to the E.

beery *adj.* (**beerier, beeriest**) **1** of or like beer. **2** *colloq.* affected by drinking beer.

Beeston POP (1981) 65 000, a town linked with Stapleford in Broxtowe district, Nottinghamshire, central England. It is 5km/3mi SW of Nottingham.

beeswax *noun* a solid yellowish substance produced by bees for making the cells in which they live, used as a polish.

beet *noun* any of several types of plant with large round or carrot-shaped roots, used as food or for making sugar. [from Anglo-Saxon *bete*]

table beet   sugar beet

beet

two pairs of wings
head   thorax   abdomen
antenna   compound eye

bee

Beethoven, Ludwig van (1770–1827) German composer, born in Bonn. Miserably raised by a father who had plans for him to become a profitable infant prodigy, he joined the Elector of Cologne's orchestra at Bonn. In 1787 he had lessons from Mozart in Vienna, where he spent most of his life. He first joined Prince Lichnowsky's household and studied under Haydn, Albrechtsberger, and possibly Salieri. His music is usually divided into three periods. The first (1792–1802), which includes the first two symphonies, the first six quartets, and the 'Pathétique' and 'Moonlight' sonatas, his style gradually develops its own individuality. The second (1803–12) begins with the 'Eroica' Symphony (1803), and includes his next five symphonies, the difficult 'Kreutzer' sonata (1803), the Violin Concerto, the 'Razumovsky' quartets (1805–6), and the 'Archduke' trio (1811). His third great period begins in 1813, and includes the mass, the Choral Symphony (1823), and the last five quartets. Though physically unattractive and arrogant, Beethoven was tolerated by Vienna society, but just as he was developing a reputation as a composer, he began to go deaf, and from 1812 he was increasingly assailed by health, business, and family worries, including prolonged litigation to obtain custody of his dead brother's son, Karl.

beetle¹ — noun any of over 350 000 species of winged insect belonging to the order Coleoptera, distributed worldwide. They characteristically have thickened forewings that are not used for flight but modified to form rigid horny cases (known as elytra) which cover and protect the delicate membranous hindwings, and in most beetles cover the whole of the abdomen. — verb intrans. (**beetle about, around**, etc) Brit. to move quickly or as if in a hurry. [from Anglo-Saxon bitela]
◇ Some beetles, such as the female glow-worm, have no wings, but all members of the order have three pairs of legs, a pair of antennae, and strong biting jaws. Beetles include both terrestrial and aquatic species, and most of them feed on plant material, including hard dry seeds and the wood of tree trunks, although a large number are scavengers, feeding on dung and carrion. Many species are serious pests, causing huge losses of cereal grain in the fields and also eating stored foodstuffs. Wood-boring beetles, such as the Death Watch beetle, destroy the timber of old buildings. Other species, such as ladybirds, are regarded as useful because they feed on aphids and other plant pests.

beetle² noun a tool with a heavy head for crushing, beating, etc. [from Anglo-Saxon bietle]

beetle³ verb intrans. to project; to overhang.

beetle-browed adj. having bushy eyebrows.

beetling adj. projecting; overhanging.

Beeton, Mrs, née **Isabella Mary Mayson** (1836–65) British writer on cookery. She was educated at Heidelberg, and became an accomplished pianist. Her book Household Management (1859–60), which covers cookery and other fields of domestic science, made her a household name.

beetroot noun a type of plant with a round red root which is cooked and used as a vegetable. [from Anglo-Saxon bete, beet]

BEF abbrev. British Expeditionary Force.

befall verb intrans., trans. (PAST TENSE **befell**; PAST PARTICIPLE **befallen**) old use, literary to happen; to happen to (someone). [from Anglo-Saxon befeallan]

befit verb (**befitted, befitting**) formal to be suitable or right for.

befitting adj. formal suitable for.

befittingly adv. formal in a way that is suitable.

before — prep. **1** earlier than: before noon. **2** ahead of; in front of: stand before the table. **3** in the presence of; for the attention of: the question before us. **4** formal, literary in the face of: draw back before the blast. **5** rather than; in preference to: put money before friendship. — conj. **1** earlier than the time when: do it before you forget. **2** rather than; in preference to: I'd die before I'd surrender. — adv. **1** formal in front of; ahead of: go before. **2** previously; in the past: haven't we met before? [from Anglo-Saxon beforan]

beforehand adv. in advance; in preparation.

befriend verb to become the friend of.

befuddle verb to confuse, especially with the effects of alcohol.

befuddled adj. confused, especially by the effects of alcohol.

beg verb intrans., trans. (**begged, begging**) (usually **beg for something**) **1** to ask for (money, food, etc). **2** to ask earnestly or humbly.
— **beg the question** to assume in an argument the truth of something which is part of what is to be proved.
beg to differ to disagree.
go begging to be unused or unwanted.
[from Anglo-Saxon bedecian]

began see BEGIN.

beget verb (**begetting**; PAST TENSE **begot**, **begat**; PAST PARTICIPLE **begotten**) **1** old use to be the father of. **2** to cause. [from Anglo-Saxon begietan]

beggar noun **1** a person who lives by begging. **2** colloq. an affectionate term for a person: cheeky beggar.
— **beggar description** or **belief** to be impossible to describe or believe.

beggarly adj. extremely small or poor.

Beggar's Opera, The a ballad opera by John Gay (1728), set to music by Johann Pepusch. It tells of the efforts of Peachum, a receiver of stolen goods, to avert the love of his daughter Polly for her highwayman husband Macheath, who is also jealously loved by his fellow-prisoner Lucy.

Begin, Menachem (1913–92) Israeli politician, born in Brest-Litovsk, Poland (now Russia). He was an active Zionist and became head of the Polish Zionist movement (1931). He fled to Russia (1939), enlisted in the Free Polish Army (1941), and was then sent to British-mandated Palestine. In 1943 he commanded the Irgun Zvai Leumi resistance group in Israel, and in 1948 founded the Herut Freedom Movement and later became Chairman of the Herut Party. In 1973 three parties combined to form the nationalist Likud Front with Begin as its leader, and in the 1977 elections he formed a coalition government. During his period as Prime Minister (1977 to 1983, when he resigned) he attended peace conferences in Jerusalem (Dec 1977) and at the invitation of US President Carter at Camp David (Sep 1978). In 1978 he and President Sadat of Egypt were jointly awarded the Nobel Peace Prize.

begin verb (**beginning**, PAST TENSE **began**; PAST PARTICIPLE **begun**) **1** trans., intrans. to start. **2** trans., intrans. to bring or come into being. **3** intrans. to start speaking. **4** intrans. to be the first, or take the first step. **5** (**begin with someone** or **something**) to deal with them first. **6** intrans. colloq. to have the ability or possibility: I can't even begin to understand.
— **to begin with** at first; firstly.
[from Anglo-Saxon beginnan]

beginner noun someone who is still learning how to do something.

beginning noun the point or occasion at which something begins.

begone interj. old use, poetic go away.

begonia noun a kind of tropical plant with brightly coloured waxy flowers and unevenly shaped leaves. [named after Michel Bégon (1638–1710), French patron of botany]

begot see BEGET.

begrudge verb **1** to do, give, or allow unwillingly or with regret. **2** (**begrudge someone something**) to envy or resent them for it.

beguile verb **1** to charm. **2** to cheat, trick, or deceive. [from BE- + guile, to deceive]

beguilement noun charm; deception.

beguiling adj. deceptively charming or amusing.

beguilingly adv. with deceptive charm: a beguilingly friendly person.

begun see BEGIN.

behalf
— **on behalf of 1** of, for, or in the interests of. **2** as a representative of.
[from Anglo-Saxon be, by + healfe, side]

Behan, Brendan (Francis) (1923–64) Irish writer, born in Dublin. Between 1939 and 1946 he was twice imprisoned for IRA activities, but was released by a general amnesty (1946). He was later imprisoned again in Manchester (1947) and deported (1952). His plays include The Quare Fellow (1956) and the The Hostage (1958). Other works include an autobiographical novel, Borstal Boy (1958).

Behar see BIHAR.

behave verb **1** intrans. to act in a specified way: behave well. **2** intrans., trans. to act or conduct (oneself) in a suitable, polite or orderly way: mind you behave yourself at the party. [from BE- + HAVE]

behaviour noun **1** way of behaving; manners: good behaviour. **2** Psychol. a response to a stimulus.
— **be on one's best behaviour** to behave as well as one can.

behavioural adj. relating or concerned with to behaviour.

behaviourally adv. in terms of behaviour.

behaviourism noun Psychol. an approach to psychology that interprets behaviour solely in terms of events that can be physically observed or measured, such as the activity of nerves and glands, and that does not take account of mental experiences such as thoughts and emotions.

behaviourist noun, adj. a person who studies or advocates behaviourism.

behaviour therapy Psychol. a form of psychotherapy which aims to modify undesirable behaviour patterns. It is often used in the treatment of neuroses, such as phobias, on the presumption that these are 'learned' forms of behaviour which can be 'unlearned'.

behead verb to cut off the head of (someone), usually as a form of capital punishment. [from Anglo-Saxon beheafdian]

beheading noun the cutting off of someone's head, usually as a form of capital punishment.

beheld see BEHOLD.

behest noun old use, formal a command or request: at his behest. [from Anglo-Saxon behæs, vow]

behind — prep. **1** at or towards the back of or the far side of. **2** later or slower than; after in time: behind schedule. **3** supporting: we're all behind you. **4** in the past with respect to: those problems are all behind me now. **5** not as far advanced as. **6** being the cause of: reasons behind the decision. — adv. **1** in or to the back or far side of. **2** remaining: leave something behind. **3** following: run behind. — adj. (**behind with**) **1** not up to date; late: behind with the payments. **2** not having progressed enough: get behind with one's work. — noun the part of the body a person sits on.
— **behind someone's back** without their knowledge or permission.
put something behind one to try to forget something unpleasant.
[from Anglo-Saxon behindan]

behindhand *adj.* **1** late. **2** (**behindhand with something**) not up to date with regard to it; in arrears.

Behn, Aphra (1640–89) English writer, born in Wye, Kent. She was brought up in Surinam, where she met the slave who was later to be the subject of her best-known work, the anti-slavery novel *Oroonoko* (1688). She returned to England in 1663, and later became a professional spy at Antwerp. Generally considered to be the first professional English woman writer, her other works include poetry and Restoration plays.

behold *old use, literary* — *verb* (PAST TENSE AND PAST PARTICIPLE **beheld**) to see; to look at. — *interj.* look. [from Anglo-Saxon *behealdan*, to hold, observe]

beholden *adj.* (**beholden to someone**) *formal* owing them a debt or favour; grateful to them. [from Anglo-Saxon *behealdan*, to hold, observe]

beholder *noun literary* an observer or onlooker.

behove *verb old use* to be necessary or fitting on the part of: *it behoves me to tell you the truth.* [from Anglo-Saxon *behofian*, to have need of]

Behrens, Peter (1868–1940) German architect and designer, born in Hamburg. He began as a painter, but in 1909 was responsible for the 'first modern building', the AEG turbine factory in Berlin. His appointment as the designer of AEG electrical products was a landmark in the history of industrial design, the first time that an artistic influence had been widely applied. He trained several leading modern architects, including Gropius and Le Corbusier.

Behring, Emil von (1854–1917) German bacteriologist and pioneer in immunology, born in Hansdorf, W Prussia. Professor of Hygiene at Halle (1894–5) and Marburg (from 1895), he discovered antitoxins for diphtheria and tetanus. He was awarded the first Nobel Prize for Physiology or Medicine in 1901.

beige *noun* a pale pinkish-yellow colour. — *adj.* of this colour. [from French *beige*]

beigel see BAGEL.

Beijing *or* **Peking** *or* **Peiping** POP municipality (1990) 10.8m, the capital city and a municipality of NE China. AREA 17 800sq km/ 6 871sq mi (municipality). HISTORY secondary capital of the Liao dynasty in the 10c and then the capital of succeeding dynasties; occupied by the Japanese in 1937–45; became the capital of China in 1949. NOTABLE FEATURES Imperial Palace, formerly known as the 'Forbidden City'; Tiananmen (Gate of Heavenly Peace, built in 1417, restored in 1651); Tiananmen Square (People's Republic proclaimed here in 1949, also the scene in 1989 of mass protests against the Chinese government, crushed by troops of the Chinese army with many civilians killed); Mao Zedong Memorial Hall (1977); Niu Jie (oldest Muslim temple, 996); Fayuan Si Temple (696); Tiantan (Temple of Heaven, 15c); Yiheyuan (Summer Palace, rebuilt in 1888); Lugouqiao Bridge (or Marco Polo Bridge); to the N, tombs of 13 Ming emperors; part of the Great Wall of China lies 75km/47mi to the NW.

Beijing Spring the period of political and cultural liberalization in China in the late 1970s and 1980s, following the death of Mao Zedong and the return to power of Deng Xiaoping. [by analogy with PRAGUE SPRING]

being *noun* **1** existence; life. **2** any living person or thing.

Beira POP (1991e) 299 000, the chief port in Mozambique and the capital of Sofala province. It lies at the mouth of the Buzi and Pungué rivers, 725km/450mi NE of Maputo. It was occupied by the Portuguese in 1506.

Beirut, Arabic **Bayrut**, French **Beyrouth**, ancient **Berytus** POP (1991e) 1.5m, the seaport capital of Lebanon. It is situated on a promontory which juts into the Mediterranean Sea. The

'Green Line' refers to the division of the city during the 1975–6 civil war into sectors, Muslim in the W and Christian in the E. An Israeli attack on Palestinian and Syrian forces in 1982 led to the evacuation of Palestinians to camps such as Sabra, Chatila, and Bourj Barajneh. The city was severely damaged by continuous fighting between rival political and religious factions in the 1980s. NOTABLE FEATURES Grand Seraglio; Cathedrals of St Elie and St George; national museum.

Béjart, Maurice (Jean), originally **Maurice Berger** (1928–) French dancer and choreographer, born in Marseilles. He toured as a dancer, then started his own company (1954) and a school called Mudra. His company became the Brussels-based Ballet of the Twentieth Century in 1959, which he directed, gradually developing a popular expressionistic form of modern ballet. In 1988 the company moved to Lausanne, Switzerland.

bejewelled *adj.* wearing or decorated with jewels.

Bekka, the, Arabic **el Beqaa** a governorate in E Lebanon, bounded NE and E by Syria. El Beqaa Valley is of strategic importance to both Israel and Syria, and is a centre of Muslim Shiite activity. CAPITAL Zahle. ECONOMY poultry, sheep; wheat; vineyards.

bel *noun* (SYMBOL **B**) a quantity used to represent the ratio of two different power levels, eg of sound, equal to 10 decibels. [named after the US inventor Alexander Graham Bell]

belabour *verb old use* **1** to beat thoroughly. **2** to argue about or discuss at excessive length.

Bel and the Dragon part of the Old Testament Apocrypha, one of the Additions to the Book of Daniel, or Daniel 14 in Catholic versions of the Bible. It contains two popular tales, probably from the 2c BC: one of how Daniel discredited Bel (patron god of Babylon) and its priests, and the other of Daniel in the lion's den.

belated *adj.* happening or coming late or too late.

belatedly *adv.* tardily; too late.

belay — *verb* **1** *Mountaineering* to make (a climber) safe by tying his or her rope to a rock or pin. **2** *Naut.* to make (a rope) secure by winding it round a hook, peg, etc. — *noun* **1** an act of belaying. **2** a piece of rock used for belaying. [from Anglo-Saxon *belecgan*]

bel canto *Mus.* a term applied to operatic singing in the Italian manner with the emphasis on beauty of tone and phrasing, agility, fluidity, and effortless transition to and sustaining of the highest notes in the range. [Italian, = beautiful singing]

Belch, Sir Toby the uproarious uncle of Olivia in Shakespeare's *Twelfth Night*, who is uncommonly fond of practical jokes, and eventually marries Maria.

belch — *verb* **1** *intrans.* to give out air noisily from the stomach through the mouth. **2** *trans.* (*also* **belch something out**) *said of a chimney, volcano, etc* to send out smoke, etc. — *noun* an act of belching. [from Anglo-Saxon *bealcan*]

beleaguer *verb* (**beleaguered, beleaguering**) **1** to surround with an army and lay siege to. **2** to cause (someone) bother or worry. [from Dutch *belegeren*, to besiege]

beleaguered *adj.* besieged, overwhelmed with criticism, difficulty, etc.

Belém, also called **Pará** POP (1991) 1.3m, the port capital of Pará state, in Norte region, N Brazil. It is situated at the mouth of the Tocantins R and was founded in 1616. NOTABLE FEATURES cathedral (1748); Paz Theatre; Santo Aleixandre Museum of Religious Art, Goeldi Museum; Mercês Church (17c), Basilica of Nossa Senhora de Nazaré (1909).

Belém, Tower of a white tower built (1515–21) on the mouth of the R Tagus in Lisbon, Portugal. It is a World Heritage site.

Tower of Belém

Belém Monastery a monastery of the Hieronymite hermit order founded by Emmanuel I (1499) in Belém, a present-day suburb of Lisbon, Portugal. It commemorates Vasco da Gama's discovery of a sea-passage to India. It is a World Heritage site.

belemnite *noun Geol.* an extinct mollusc, resembling a squid, found extensively as fossil shells from the Carboniferous period to the Eocene epoch. Its shell was internal (ie located within the body), and was typically bullet-shaped. [from Greek *belemnon*, dart]

Belfast, Gaelic **Beal Feirste** POP (1992e) 289 000, the capital of Northern Ireland, in Belfast district, Co Antrim, NE Northern Ireland. It lies at the mouth of the Lagan R, on Belfast Lough. HISTORY the original settlement and castle were destroyed in 1177; settled in the 17c by English, Scots, and Huguenots, it became a centre of Irish Protestanism; it has been capital since 1920; it has well-defined Nationalist (Catholic) and Unionist (Protestant) areas and civil unrest has disrupted the city since 1968. NOTABLE FEATURES city hall (1900); St Anne's Cathedral (begun in 1898); Ulster Museum; Parliament House at Stormont.

belfry *noun* (PL. **belfries**) **1** a tower for bells, usually attached to a church. **2** the upper part of it, containing the bells.
— **have bats in the belfry** see BAT[2].
[from French *berfroi*, watch tower]

Belgium, official name **Kingdom of Belgium**, French **Royaume de Belgique**, Flemish **Koninkrijk België** POP (1992e) 10m, a kingdom in NW Europe, divided into nine provinces. AREA 30 540sq km/11 788sq mi. It is bounded N by the Netherlands, S by France, E by Germany and Luxembourg, and W by the North Sea. CAPITAL Brussels. CHIEF TOWNS Antwerp, Ghent, Charleroi, Liège, Bruges, Namur, Mons. TIME ZONE GMT +1. A line drawn E–W just to the S of Brussels divides the population by race and language into two approximately equal parts; N of the line the inhabitants are Flemings of Teutonic stock who speak Flemish, while S of the line they are French-speaking Latins known as Walloons. The population is 55% Fleming, 33% Walloon, and 12% are of mixed or other ethnic origin. OFFICIAL LANGUAGES 56% Flemish (Dutch), 32% French, 1% German (mainly on the E border); Brussels is officially a bilingual city. Roman Catholicism is the chief religion (75%). CURRENCY the Belgian franc. PHYSICAL DESCRIPTION mostly low-lying, with some hills in the SE region (Ardennes); there are large areas of fertile soil which have been intensively cultivated for many centuries; the main river systems, the Sambre-Meuse and the Scheldt, drain across the Dutch border and are linked by a complex network of canals; Belgium has a low-lying dune-fringed coastline of 64km/40mi along the North Sea. CLIMATE cool and temperate with strong maritime influences. HISTORY part of the Roman Empire until the 2c AD; after invasion by Germanic tribes it became part of the Frankish Empire; in the early Middle Ages, some semi-independent provinces and cities grew up and from 1385 were absorbed by the House of Burgundy; known as the Spanish Netherlands, they were ruled by the Habsburgs from 1477 until the Peace of Utrecht (1713); the Spanish provinces were then transferred to Austria as the Austrian Netherlands; the country was conquered by the French in 1794 and formed part of the French Republic and Empire until uniting in 1815 with the Netherlands; in 1830 the Belgian rebellion against this union led to its recognition as an independent kingdom under Leopold of Saxe-Coburg; occupied by Germany in both World Wars; in recent decades, political tension between Walloons and Flemings has caused the collapse of several governments; in 1980 Wallonia and Flanders were given regional 'subgovernments'; a new federal constitution of 1989 divided Belgium into the autonomous regions of Flanders, Wallonia, and Brussels; constitutional amendments in 1993 were designed to continue the trend of devolving power to the regions. GOVERNMENT a hereditary and constitutional monarchy, with legislative power vested in a monarch, a Senate, and a Chamber of Representatives. ECONOMY one of the earliest countries in Europe to industrialize, using the rich coalfields of the Ardennes; Flanders has had a famous textile industry since the Middle Ages; Belgium is a long-standing centre for European trade; its important iron and steel industry, dependent on raw materials from Luxembourg and Germany, has led to many related industries, including metallurgical and engineering products, processed food and beverages, chemicals, textiles, glass, and petroleum; there is trade in gemstones (especially diamonds); agriculture is mainly livestock, also wheat, potatoes, sugar-beet, and flax; in 1948 there was full economic union between Belgium, Netherlands, and Luxembourg (Benelux Economic Union); a founder-member of the EC; Brussels is the headquarters of several major international organizations.

Belgium

Belgrade, Serbo-Croatian **Beograd**, ancient **Singidunum** POP (1991) 1.6m, the capital of the Federal Republic of Yugoslavia, situated at the junction of the Danube and Sava rivers. NOTABLE FEATURES Kalemegdan Fortress; Prince Eugene's Gate (1719); Palace of Princess Ljubica; St Mark's Church; Tomb of Sheikh Mustapha; cathedral; several museums.

Belgrano, General an Argentinian cruiser, formerly owned by the US Navy in World War II, sunk by HM submarine *Conqueror* during the Falklands conflict in 1982 with great loss of life. Its sinking proved to be one of the most controversial incidents of the war.

Belial the Biblical name given to one of the fallen angels in John Milton's *Paradise Lost*.

belie *verb* (**belied**, **belying**) **1** to show to be untrue or false. **2** to give a false idea or impression of. **3** to fail to fulfil or justify (a hope, etc). [from Anglo-Saxon *beleogan*, to deceive by lying]

belief *noun* **1** a principle, idea, etc accepted as true, especially without proof: *belief in the afterlife.*

2 trust or confidence: *has no belief in people.* **3** a person's religious faith. **4** a firm opinion.
— **beyond belief** difficult to believe; incredible.
to the best of one's belief as far as one knows. [from Anglo-Saxon *geleafa*]

believable *adj.* capable of being believed; credible.

believe *verb* **1** to accept (something said or proposed) as true. **2** to accept what is said by (a person) as true. **3** to think, assume, or suppose. **4** (**believe in something**) **a** to have religious faith or other forms of conviction about it. **b** to consider it right or good: *believe in telling the truth.* **5** (**believe in someone or something**) to be convinced of the existence of a God or another supreme being. **6** (**believe in someone**) to have trust or confidence in them.
— **not be able to believe one's ears** *or* **eyes** *colloq.* to find it hard to believe in what one is hearing or seeing. [from Anglo-Saxon *belyfan*]

believer *noun* a person who believes, especially in God.

Belinda a female first name, first used in the 17c. [only in English, but of uncertain origin]

Belisarius (505–65) Byzantine soldier under the emperor Justinian, born in Germania, Illyria. He defeated the Persians (530), suppressed an insurrection in Constantinople (532), defeated the Vandals in Africa (533–4) and the Ostrogoths in Italy (535–40), and later repelled an assault of the Huns on Constantinople (559). Falsely accused of conspiracy against the emperor, he was imprisoned (562), but was restored to favour soon after.

Belisha beacon in the UK, a tall black and white post with a flashing orange light on top, marking a pedestrian crossing on a road. [named after L Hore-Belisha, the Minister of Transport who introduced them in 1934]

belittle *verb* to treat as unimportant, especially disparagingly.

belittlement *noun* treating as unimportant; disparagement.

belittling *adj.* treating as unimportant; disparaging.

Belize, formerly **British Honduras** (to 1973) POP (1992e) 198 000, an independent state in Central America, divided into six districts. AREA 22 963sq km/8 864sq mi. It is bounded N by Mexico, W and S by Guatemala, and E by the Caribbean Sea. CAPITAL Belmopan. CHIEF TOWNS Belize City, Dangriga, Punta Gorda, San Ignacio. TIME ZONE GMT –6. The population largely consists of Creoles, Spanish-Maya Mestizos, Caribs, and several minorities; Roman Catholicism is the main religion. OFFICIAL LANGUAGE English; Spanish and local Maya languages are also spoken. CURRENCY the Belize dollar. PHYSICAL DESCRIPTION the country has an extensive coastal plain, swampy in the N, more fertile in the S; the Maya Mts extend almost to the E coast, rising to 1 120m at Victoria Peak; they are flanked by pine ridges, tropical forests, savannahs, and farm land; the Belize R flows W–E; inner coastal waters are protected by the world's second longest barrier reef. CLIMATE generally subtropical but tempered by trade winds; coastal temperatures vary between 10°C and 36°C, with a greater range in the mountains; there is variable rainfall with an average of 1 295mm in the N and 4 445mm in the S; dry season in Feb–May; hurricanes have caused severe damage. HISTORY there is evidence of early Maya settlement; colonized in the 17c by shipwrecked British sailors and disbanded soldiers from Jamaica, who defended the territory against the Spanish; it was created a British colony in 1862, administered from Jamaica; the tie with Jamaica was severed in 1884; a ministerial system of government was introduced in 1961; in 1964 internal self-government was achieved; it changed its name from British Honduras to Belize in 1973

and later gained full independence in 1981; Guatemalan claims over Belize territory led to a British military presence; in the early 1990s Guatemala established diplomatic relations with Belize and almost all of the British presence has now been withdrawn. GOVERNMENT a Governor-General represents the British Monarchy, and appoints a Prime Minister; a bicameral National Assembly, with an eight-member Senate and a 28-member House of Representatives. ECONOMY traditionally based on timber and forest products, more recently on agriculture, especially sugar, citrus fruit, cocoa, rice, tobacco, bananas, beef; fishing; boatbuilding; food processing; textiles; furniture; batteries; cigarettes.

Belize

Belize City POP (1990) 44 000, the seaport capital of Belize district, Belize. It is situated at the mouth of the Belize R where it meets the Caribbean Sea. The city is vulnerable to hurricanes and suffered severe damage in 1961, resulting in the decision in 1970 to replace it as capital with the inland city of Belmopan.

Bell, Alexander Graham (1847–1922) Scots-born US inventor, born in Edinburgh. He worked as assistant to his father in teaching elocution, and in 1871 moved to the USA and became Professor of Vocal Physiology at Boston (1873), devoting himself to the teaching of deaf-mutes and to spreading his father's system of 'visible speech'. After experimenting with various acoustic devices he produced the first intelligible telephonic transmission with the famous words to his assistant 'Mr Watson, come here — I want you', on 5 Jun 1875. He was granted three patents relating to his invention between 1875 and 1877, and formed the Bell Telephone Company in 1877.

Bell, Sir Charles (1774–1842) Scottish anatomist, surgeon and neurophysiological pioneer, born in Edinburgh. He lectured in anatomy and surgery in London, and in 1812 he was appointed surgeon to the Middlesex Hospital. After Waterloo, Bell organized a hospital in Brussels, and in 1836 he was appointed Professor of Surgery at Edinburgh. He demonstrated that, far from being single units, nerves consist of separate fibres sheathed together, and that fibres convey either sensory or motor stimuli but never both — fibres transmit impulses only in one direction. His experimental work led to the discovery of the long thoracic nerve (Bell's nerve); we speak of 'Bell's palsy' as a result of his demonstration that lesions of the seventh cranial nerve could create facial paralysis.

bell *noun* **1** a deep hollow object, usually of metal, rounded at one end and wide and open at the other, with a small hammer or clapper inside, which gives a ringing sound when struck. **2** the sound made by such an object. **3** any other device which makes a ringing sound. **4** anything shaped like a bell. **5** the ringing of a bell on board ship to tell the time. **6** *Brit. colloq.* a telephone call: *give me a bell.*
— **bell the cat** to do something daring and dangerous.
ring a bell *Brit. colloq.* to sound familiar; to remind one of something.
sound as a bell *Brit. colloq.* in very good condition or health.
[from Anglo-Saxon *belle*]

belladonna *noun* **1** a poisonous plant, deadly nightshade. **2** a drug obtained from this plant, used in medicine. [from Italian *bella donna*, beautiful lady, so called because the drug was formerly used as a cosmetic]

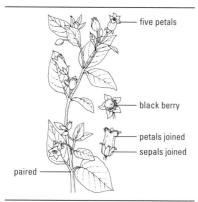

five petals

black berry

petals joined

sepals joined

paired

belladonna

Bellarmine, St Robert (Francis Romulus) (1542–1621) Italian Jesuit theologian, born in Montepulciano. He joined the Jesuits in 1560, and became Professor of Theology at Louvain (1570), then lecturer (1576) and Rector (1592) at the Roman College. In 1599 he was made a cardinal, against his own inclination, then Archbishop of Capua (1602), and he worked in the Vatican from 1605. The chief defender of the Church in the 16c, he was canonized in 1931. His feast day is 17 May.

Bellay, Joachim du (1522–60) French poet and prose writer, born in Liré, Anjou. His *Défence et Illustration de la langue françoise* (1549) was the manifesto of the Pléiade, advocating a return to classical and Italian models. It was exemplified by a set of Petrarchian sonnets, *L'Olive*.

bell-bottomed *adj.* having bell-bottoms.

bell-bottoms *pl. noun* trousers with legs which are much wider at the bottom than at the top.

bell-boy *or North Amer.* **bell-hop** a man or boy who works in a hotel, carrying guests' bags, delivering messages, etc.

belle *noun old use* a beautiful woman, especially the most beautiful woman at a dance: *belle of the ball*. [from French *belle*, beautiful, fine]

Bellenden, Lady Margaret the Royalist owner of Tillietudlem Castle who comes into conflict with Henry Morton in Sir Walter Scott's *Old Mortality*. Her brother-in-law is Major Miles Bellenden, and her granddaughter, Edith, eventually marries Morton.

Bellerophon in Greek mythology, a hero who was sent to the King of Lycia with a letter telling the King to put him to death. The King set him impossible adventures, notably the killing of the Chimera. In later accounts it is said that Athena helped him to tame the winged horse Pegasus, and that he used him to attack the Chimera.

belles-lettres *pl. noun* works of literature, especially poetry and essays, valued for their style rather than their content. [from French *belles-lettres*, beautiful letters]

bell-hop *noun North Amer.* same as BELL-BOY.

bellicose *adj. literary* likely or wanting to cause an argument or war. [from Latin *bellicosus*]

belligerence *or* **belligerency** *noun* aggressiveness; hostility.

belligerent — *adj.* **1** aggressive and unfriendly. **2** fighting a war. — *noun* a person or country fighting a war. [from Latin *belligerare*, to wage war]

belligerently *adv.* in a belligerent or warlike way.

Bellingshausen, Fabian Gottlieb von (1778–1852) Russian explorer, born in Oesel. In 1819–21 he led an Antarctic expedition as far south as 70°, and he gave his name to the Bellingshausen Sea.

Bellini, Giovanni (c.1430–1516) Italian painter who worked in Venice. He was instrumental in making Venice an artistic centre to rival Florence, and his innovations of light and colour became the hallmark of Venetian art. His work is mainly religious in theme and includes the *Agony in the Garden* (c.1465) and a series of *Madonna* pictures. Other works include the pagan allegory *The Feast of the Gods* (1514). His father Jacopo Bellini (c.1400–70) and brother Gentile Bellini (c.1429–1507) were also painters.

Bellini, Vincenzo (1801–35) Italian operatic composer, born in Catania, Sicily. An organist's son, he studied at the Conservatorio of Naples and wrote many operas, notably *Il Pirata* (1827), *La Sonnambula* (1831), and *Norma* (1831), which are noted for their elaborate vocal melodies.

bell jar a bell-shaped glass cover put over instruments, experiments, etc in a laboratory, to stop gases escaping.

Bello, Andrés (1781–1865) Venezuelan writer and polymath, born in Caracas. Educated in Caracas, he lived in London (1810–29) before settling in Chile, where he became a senior public servant, senator, and first Rector of the university (1843). Considered the most remarkable Latin American intellectual of the 19c, his writings embrace language, law, education, history, philosophy, poetry, drama, and science.

Belloc, (Joseph) Hilaire (Pierre) (1870–1953) Anglo-French writer and poet, born in St Cloud, near Paris. Educated in England, he served in the French army and then became a Liberal MP (1906–10). The author of *The Servile State* (1912), he is best known for his nonsensical verse for children, *The Bad Child's Book of Beasts* (1896) and the *Cautionary Tales* (1907). He also wrote numerous travel books, historical studies, and religious books, and was a devoted Roman Catholic.

Bellow, Saul (1915–) US novelist, born in Lachine, Quebec. He has taught at various universities and was appointed Professor of English at Chicago University (1963–). Bellow's works include the novels *Dangling Man* (1944), *The Adventures of Augie March* (1953), *Herzog* (1964), *Humboldt's Gift* (1975, Pulitzer Prize), and *Something to Remember Me By: Three Tales* (1991). He was awarded the Nobel Prize for Literature in 1976.

bellow — *verb* **1** *intrans.* to make a loud deep cry like that of a bull. **2** *trans.* to shout loudly or angrily. — *noun* **1** the loud roar of a bull. **2** a deep loud sound or cry. [from Anglo-Saxon *bylgan*]

bellows *sing. or pl. noun* **1** a device consisting of or containing a bag-like or box-like part with folds in it which is squeezed to create a current of air. **2** on some cameras, a sleeve with bellows-like folds connecting the body of the camera to the lens. [from Anglo-Saxon *belg*, bag]

bell-pull *noun* a handle or cord which operates a bell.

bell-push *noun* a button which, when pressed, operates an electric bell.

bell-ringer *noun* a person who rings a bell in a church, or who plays tunes with hand-held bells.

bell-ringing *noun* the art or practice of ringing bells.

bells and whistles *colloq.* additional, largely decorative rather than functional features.

Bell's palsy *Medicine* a sudden paralysis of the muscles of one side of the face, caused by damage to the facial nerve (a nerve that arises directly from the brain and supplies the muscles of the face). It results in distortion of the features and may also affect hearing and the sense of taste. [named after the UK surgeon Sir Charles Bell]

Bell, The a novel by Iris Murdoch (1958). It presents the philosophic standpoint of the various members of a lay community in the events leading up to the installation of a new bell in the nearby Abbey convent.

bellwether *noun* the leading sheep in a flock, with a bell on its neck.

belly — *noun* (PL. **bellies**) **1** the part of the body below the chest containing the organs used for digesting food. **2** the stomach. **3** the lower or under part of an animal's body, which contains the stomach and other organs. **4** a part of a structure shaped like a belly. — *verb intrans.* (**bellies**, **bellied**) (*usually* **belly out**) to swell out. [from Anglo-Saxon *belg*, bag]

bellyache — *noun* a pain in the belly. — *verb intrans. slang* to complain noisily or repeatedly.

belly button *colloq.* the navel.

belly-dance — *noun* an erotic eastern dance performed by women, in which the belly and hips are moved around, often very fast. — *verb intrans.* to perform a belly-dance.

belly-dancer *noun* a woman who performs belly-dances.

belly-flop *noun* a dive into water in which the body hits the surface flat, instead of at an angle.

bellyful *noun* (PL. **bellyfuls**) enough to eat. — **have had a bellyful of something** *colloq.* to have had more of it than one can bear.

belly-landing *noun* the landing of an aeroplane without using its wheels, usually because of a fault.

belly laugh a loud deep laugh.

Belmopan POP (1990e) 5 000, the capital of Belize, Central America. It is situated between the Belize and Sibun rivers, 80km/50mi W of Belize City. In was made the capital in 1970, following major hurricane damage to Belize City in 1961. A new settlement at the Valley of Peace, for refugees from El Salvador and Guatemala, was made permanent in 1985.

Belo Horizonte POP (1991) 3.5m, the commercial and industrial capital of Minas Gerais state, in Sudeste region, SE Brazil. It was Brazil's first planned modern city, built in the 1890s. The industrial area, situated c.10km/6mi from the city centre is the third largest industrial centre in Brazil. NOTABLE FEATURES Minascentro Convention Centre (1984); Mineirão Sports Stadium; Museum of Modern Art; monument in the Parque de Mangabeiras commemorating the pope's visit in 1982; modern architecture in the suburb of Pampulha.

belong *verb intrans.* **1** (**belong to**) to be the property or right of. **2** (**belong to**) to be a native of, member of a group, etc. **3** (**belong with** *or* **in something**) to have a proper place; to go together; to have the right qualities to fit in. [from Middle English *belongen*]

belongings *pl. noun* personal possessions.

Belorussia *or* **Belarus, Belorusskaya, Byelarus,** *or* **White Russia** POP (1991e) 10.3m, a republic in E Europe. AREA 207 600sq km/ 80 134sq mi. It is bounded W by Poland, NW by Lithuania, N by Latvia, E by Russia, and S by the Ukraine. CAPITAL Minsk. CHIEF TOWNS Gomel', Vitebsk, Mogilev, Bobruysk, Grodno, Brest. TIME ZONE GMT +2. OFFICIAL LANGUAGE Belorussian. CURRENCY rouble. PHYSICAL DESCRIPTION is largely flat, with low hills in the NW rising to 345m; chief rivers are the Dnieper, Zapadnaya Dvina, and Neman; there are c.11 000 lakes; a third of the country is covered by forests. CLIMATE mild winters and cool summers. HISTORY proclaimed a Soviet Socialist Republic in 1919, it became independent in 1991. ECONOMY machine tools, vehicles, agricultural machinery, glass, foodstuffs, fertilizers, textiles, electronics, artificial silk, and leather; oil extraction and refining, salt extraction; farm land covers 46% of the land area; it is an important flax-growing area, and other agricultural activities include meat and dairy production.

Belorussia

beloved — *adj.* much loved. — *noun* a much loved person. [from an obsolete verb *belove*, to love]

below — *prep.* **1** lower in position, rank, amount, etc than. **2** not worthy of. — *adv.* **1** at, to, or in a lower place, point, or level. **2** further on in a book, etc: *see page 23 below*. [from Middle English *bilooghe*]

Belphoebe the noble daughter of the wood nymph Chrysogone, and the twin sister to Amoret in Spenser's *The Faerie Queene*. She mixes herbal remedies in the forests of Fairyland to heal Timias.

Belshazzar, Greek **Balthasar**, or **Baltasar** (d.539 BC) King of Babylon from 556 BC to 539 BC, when Babylon was captured and the Neo-Babylonian Empire fell. According to the Book of Daniel, mysterious writing appeared on the wall of his palace which Daniel interpreted as predicting the fall of the Empire to the Persians and Medes.

Belshazzar's Feast a cantata for baritone, chorus, and orchestra by William Walton (1931). Its text was written from biblical sources by Osbert Sitwell.

belt — *noun* **1** a long narrow piece of leather or cloth worn around the waist to keep clothing in place or for decoration. **2** a strap passed across the body, to secure a person in a seat: *a seat-belt*. **3** an area, usually relatively long and narrow: *a belt of rain*. **4** a band of rubber, etc moving the wheels, or round the wheels, of a machine: *a conveyor belt*. **5** *slang* a hard blow. — *verb* **1** to put a belt round. **2** (**belt something on**) to fasten it with a belt. **3** to beat with a belt. **4** *trans., intrans. colloq.* (**belt into someone**) to hit them repeatedly. **5** *intrans. colloq.* (**belt along** or **home**, *etc*) to move very fast in the direction stated.
— **below the belt** *colloq.* unfair; unfairly.
belt something out *colloq.* to sing or say it very loudly.
belt up 1 to attach a seat-belt. **2** *colloq.* to stop talking.
tighten one's belt *colloq.* to reduce one's spending, and live more economically.
under one's belt *colloq.* as part of one's experience: *have a good education under one's belt*. [from Anglo-Saxon, **from Latin** *balteus*]

Beltane *noun* an ancient Celtic festival held at the beginning of May, and also in late June, when bonfires (*bel-fires*) were lighted on the hills. The custom continued into the last century in many parts of Scotland (especially in the North), and still persists in Peebles. Beltane was also one of the old quarter-days in Scotland (the others being Lammas, Hallowmas, and Candlemas). [from Gaelic *bealtainn*, apparently 'bright fire']

belted *adj.* **1** having or wearing a belt. **2** *said especially of an animal* marked with a band of different colour.

beluga *noun* **1** a kind of large sturgeon. **2** caviar from this type of sturgeon. **3** a white whale. [a Russian word, from *beliy*, white]

Belukha, Mount the highest peak in the Altai Range. It is situated at the border between Russia and Kazakhstan. HEIGHT 4 506m.

belvedere *noun Archit.* a pavilion, or a raised turret or lantern on the top of a house, built to provide a view (or admit light and air). The term is also applied to a summer-house built on high ground. [from Italian, from *bel*, beautiful + *vedere*, to see]

BEM *abbrev.* British Empire Medal.

bemoan *verb* to express great sadness or regret about (something).

bemuse *verb* to puzzle or confuse.

bemused *adj.* bewildered, confused.

ben *noun Scot., in place names* a mountain. [from Gaelic *beann*]

Benares or **Banares** or **Varanasi**, ancient *Kasi* POP (1991) 1m, a city in Uttar Pradesh state, N India. It is situated on the N bank of the R Ganges, 120km/75mi E of Allahabad and is one of the seven most sacred Hindu cities. It is also a holy city of Buddhists, Sikhs, and Jains. HISTORY Hindu city since the 6c; invaded by Afghans in 1033; ceded to Britain in 1775. NOTABLE FEATURES over 1 400 Hindu temples and shrines including the Golden Temple (1777) and Durga Temple; steps (ghats) along c.7km/4mi of the high bank of the Ganges, used by pilgrims to bathe in the sacred waters; mosque dedicated to the Muslim emperor, Aurangzeb.

Ben Bella, Ahmed (1918–) Algerian politician, born in Maghnia, a key figure in the Algerian War of Independence against France. He fought with the Free French in World War II, and became head of the Organisation Spéciale (1949), the paramilitary wing of the Algerian nationalist Parti du Peuple Algérien. In 1952 he escaped from a French-Algerian prison to Cairo, where he became a key member of the Front de Libération Nationale (FLN). Captured by the French in 1956, he spent the remainder of the war in a French prison. Following independence he was Algeria's first Prime Minister (1962–3) and then President (1963–5). Deposed in 1965 in a coup led by Houari Boumedienne, he was imprisoned until 1980.

Benbow, John (1653–1702) English admiral, born in Shrewsbury, Shropshire. He served in the Nine Years' War (1690, 1693, 1694) and the War of the Spanish Succession.

bench *noun* **1** a long wooden or stone seat. **2** a work-table for a carpenter, scientist, etc. **3** (**the bench**) a judge's seat in court. **4** (**the bench**) judges and magistrates as a group. See also QUEEN'S BENCH. **5** a seat in the House of Commons. See also BACKBENCH, FRONTBENCH.
— **raise someone to the bench** to make someone a judge or a bishop.
[from Anglo-Saxon *benc*]

benchmark *noun* **1** a mark on a post, etc giving the height above sea level of the land at that exact spot, used when measuring land and making maps. **2** anything used as a standard or point of reference.

bend — *verb* (PAST TENSE AND PAST PARTICIPLE **bent**) **1** *trans., intrans.* to make or become angled or curved. **2** *intrans.* to move or stretch in a curve: *a road bending to the left.* **3** *intrans.* (**bend down** or **over**) to move the top part of the body forward and down to reach the ground. **4** *trans., intrans.* to submit or force to submit: *bent them to his will.* — *noun* **1** a curve or bent part. **2** the act of curving or bending.
— **bend over backwards** *Brit.* to try very hard to be helpful.

bend the rules interpret the rules in one's favour, without actually breaking them.
round the bend *colloq.* mad; crazy.
[from Anglo-Saxon *bendan*]

Bendigo POP (1986e) 54 000, a city in N central Victoria, Australia, situated NW of Melbourne. It is the centre of a wine-producing area. Gold was mined here until the 1950s. NOTABLE FEATURES Central Deborah Gold Mine; Wax Museum; reconstructed Sandhurst Town; Bendigo Pottery founded in 1858 (Australia's oldest pottery); the only surviving Chinese Joss House of the 1860s.

bends *sing. or pl. noun* (**the bends**) decompression sickness: severe pains affecting divers who come to the surface too quickly from deep in the sea.

bendy *adj.* (**bendier, bendiest**) **1** having many bends or curves. **2** able to bend easily.

beneath — *prep.* **1** under; below. **2** not worthy of. — *adv.* below, underneath. [from Anglo-Saxon *beneothan*]

Beneden, Edouard Joseph Louis-Marie van (1846–1910) Belgian cytologist and embryologist, born in Liège. In 1887 he demonstrated the constancy of the number of chromosomes in the cells of an organism, which decrease during maturation and are restored at fertilization.

Benedick the confirmed bachelor in Shakespeare's *Much Ado About Nothing*, who nevertheless participates in the 'merry war' with Beatrice; he falls in love with, and eventually marries, her.

Benedict a male first name, usually given to Roman Catholics. [from Church Latin *benedictus*, blessed]

Benedict (of Nursia), St (c.480–c.547 AD) Italian saint, the founder of Western monasticism, born in Nursia. As a teenager he withdrew from society to live as a hermit. His piety led to his appointment as abbot of a monastery at Vicovaro, but he disliked the slack morals of the monks there and retreated to Subiaco, where he founded 12 small monastic communities which followed the rule he devised (c.515). He established a monastery on Monte Cassino, later one of Italy's most famous, and his Benedictine rule, fusing prayer and labour with community life, eventually became the common rule of all Western monasticism. He is the patron saint of all Europe, and his feast day is 11 Jul (formerly 21 Mar).

Benedictine — *noun* **1** a member of the Christian community that follows the teachings of St Benedict (see BENEDICTINES). **2** a strong greenish-yellow alcoholic drink first made by Benedictine monks in France in the 16c. — *adj.* relating to the Benedictines or to St Benedict.

Benedictines, properly the **Order of St Benedict (OSB)** a religious order following the rule of St Benedict of Nursia. The order consists of autonomous congregations, and has a long tradition of scholarship and promotion of learning.

benediction *noun* **1** a prayer giving blessing, especially at the end of a religious service. **2** in the Roman Catholic church, a short service in which the congregation is blessed. [from Latin *benedictio*]

benedictory *adj.* in the nature of or serving as a blessing.

benefaction *noun* a gift or donation from a benefactor.

benefactor *noun* a person who gives financial help to an institution or cause. [from Latin *bene*, good + *facere*, to do]

benefactory *adj.* serving as a gift or donation.

benefice *noun* a position as priest or a church office, and the income (from land, buildings, etc) which is attached to it. [from Latin *beneficium*, favour]

beneficed *adj., said of a person* holding a benefice or church office.

beneficence *noun formal* generosity.

beneficent *adj.* actively kind and generous. [from Latin *beneficium*, favour]

beneficently *adv.* with kindness and generosity.

beneficial *adj.* having good results or benefits. [from Latin *beneficialis*, generous]

beneficially *adv.* with good results or benefits.

beneficiary *noun* (PL. **beneficiaries**) **1** a person who benefits from something. **2** *Legal* a person who receives land, money, etc, in a will. [from Latin *beneficiarius*]

benefit — *noun* **1** something good gained or received. **2** advantage or sake: *for your benefit*. **3** (*often* **benefits**) a payment made by a government or company insurance scheme, usually to someone who is ill or out of work: *social security benefit*. **4** a game, performance at a theatre, etc from which the profits are given to a person or people in need. — *verb* (**benefited, benefiting**) **1** (**benefit from** *or* **by something**) to gain an advantage or receive something good. **2** to do good to. — **give someone the benefit of the doubt** to believe them although there may be doubts. [from Old French *benfet*, from Latin *benefactum*, good deed]

benefit society *noun* a society to which people pay money, as an investment against illness or old age.

Benelux an economic union between Belgium, the Netherlands, and Luxembourg. It began as a customs union in 1948, the result of a convention concluded in London in 1944. Despite the difficulties of achieving economic integration and the exclusion of agriculture from the union, mutual trade between the three countries expanded. A treaty established a more ambitious economic union between the three in 1958.

Benét, Stephen Vincent (1898–1943) US poet and novelist, born in Bethlehem, Pennsylvania. He is best known for his poem on the Civil War, *John Brown's Body* (1929, Pulitzer Prize).

benevolence *noun* **1** the desire to do good; kindness; generosity. **2** an act of kindness or generosity. [from French *benivolence*, from Latin *bene*, good + *volens*, wishing]

benevolent *adj.* showing or involving kindness and generosity.

benevolently *adv.* with kindness and generosity.

Bengal, Bay of an arm of the Indian Ocean, on the S coast of Asia. It is bounded by India and Sri Lanka in the W, Bangladesh in the N, and Burma (Myanma) and the Andaman and Nicobar Is in the E. Length c.2 000km/1 200mi; width c.1 600km/1 000mi; maximum depth 4 150m in the S. It receives many large rivers, including the Krishna, Ganges, Brahmaputra, and Irrawaddy. Madras, Calcutta, and Chittagong are the main ports. The Bay of Bengal is subject to heavy monsoon rains and cyclones.

Bengali — *noun* **1** a member of a people living in Bangladesh and the state of West Bengal in India. **2** the language of this people. — *adj.* relating to this people or language.

Benghazi *or* **Banghazi** **1** POP (1988e) 446 000, the second largest city in Libya and a seaport in Benghazi province. It is situated in the N of the country, on the Gulf of Sirte, 645km/400mi E of Tripoli. HISTORY first settled by the Greeks; controlled by the Turks from the 16c to 1911; under Italian rule from 1911 to 1942; used as a military and naval supply base during World War II. The modern town is partly situated on the Hellenistic and Roman towns of Berenice. **2** a province in Libya.

Benguela **1** POP (1983e) 155 000, the capital of Benguela province, W Angola. It is located 31km/19mi S of Lobito. The town was founded in 1617. **2** a province in W Angola with Benguela as its capital.

Ben-Gurion, David, originally **David Gruen** (1886–1973) Israeli politician, born in Plonsk, Poland. Attracted to the Zionist Socialist movement, he emigrated to Palestine (1906), where he formed the first Jewish trade union (1915). Expelled by the Turks, he helped to raise the Jewish Legion in America. In 1930 he became Leader of the Mapai (Labour) Party, which was the ruling party when the state of Israel was announced (May 1948). He was Prime Minister (1948–53, 1955–63).

Ben-Hur a US film directed by William Wyler (1959). It is an epic Biblical story set in Jerusalem at the time of Christ. It features Charlton Heston as a man who lives to avenge himself on the childhood friend who, as a Roman magistrate, condemned him to slavery.

Benidorm POP (1987e) 35 000, a resort town in Alicante province, Valencia, E Spain. Situated on the Mediterranean Costa Blanca, it consists of two beaches on either side of a rocky promontory. It is a popular package-holiday destination.

benighted *adj.* lacking intelligence or a sense of morality. [from obsolete *benight*, to overcome with darkness]

benign *adj.* **1** kind; gentle. **2** favourable. **3** *Medicine, said of a disorder* not having harmful effects, especially a non-cancerous tumour, ie one that does not invade and destroy the surrounding tissue or spread to more distant parts of the body. See also MALIGNANT. [from Latin *benignus*, gentle]

benignant *adj.* **1** kind. **2** favourable. **3** *said of a disease, growth, etc* not fatal.

benignity *noun* (PL. **benignities**) kindness, or an act of kindness.

benignly *adv.* in a benign or gentle way.

Benin a powerful kingdom in the S Nigerian rainforest, founded in the 13c. Benin was a source of cloth, beads, and slaves for the Portuguese in the 15c–16c, and was later involved in the slave trade. The culture is renowned for the life-size brass heads and human/animal plaques cast from the 15c onwards for its ruler, the Oba. Benin survived until conquered by the British in 1897, when many of its treasures were taken to London. The name was adopted by the former French colony of Dahomey in 1975.

Benin, formerly **Dahomey** (to 1975), official name **Republic of Benin**, French **République du Benin**, formerly (to 1990) **The People's Republic of Benin** POP (1992e) 4.9m, a Republic in W Africa, divided into six provinces. AREA 112 622sq km/43 472sq mi. It is bounded N by Niger, E by Nigeria, S by the Bight of Benin, W by Togo, and NW by Burkina. CAPITAL Porto Novo (nominal), Cotonou (political and economic). CHIEF TOWNS Ouidah, Abomey, Kandi, Parakou, Natitingou. TIME ZONE GMT +1. The main ethnic groups are the Fon, Adja, Yoruba, and Bariba; there is also a small European community. The majority of the population follows local beliefs, the remainder being either Christian or Muslim. OFFICIAL LANGUAGE French; several local languages are also spoken. CURRENCY CFA franc. PHYSICAL DESCRIPTION rises from a 100km/62mi-long sandy coast with lagoons, to low-lying plains, then to a savannah plateau at c.400m; the Atakora Mts rise to over 500m in the NW; the Alibori R valley lies in the NE and joins the R Niger valley; several rivers flow S to the Gulf of Guinea. CLIMATE tropical climate, divided into three zones; in the S, there is rain throughout the year, especially during the 'Guinea Monsoon' (May–Oct); in the central area there are two rainy seasons (peaks in

Benin

May–Jun and Oct); in the N, there is one (Jul–Sep); the N dry season (Oct–Apr) is hot, has low humidity, and is subject to the dry *harmattan* wind from the NE.

Benjamin **1** in the Old Testament, the youngest of Jacob's 12 sons and the founder of one of the 12 tribes of Israel. **2** a male first name. [from Hebrew, = son of the right hand]

Benjamin, Tribe of one of the 12 tribes of ancient Israel, said to be descended from Jacob's youngest son by Rachel (Genesis 35.16–18, 24). Its territories included the land between the hill country of Ephraim and the hills of Judah. Saul, first King of Israel, and the prophet Jeremiah were of this tribe.

Ben Macdhui, Gaelic **Ben Muich-Dhui** the second highest mountain in the United Kingdom. It is situated in the Cairngorm Mts, SW Grampian region, N central Scotland. HEIGHT 1 309m. Braemar is 29km/18mi NW.

Benn, Gottfried (1886–1956) German poet, born in Mansfeld, West Prussia. He embraced the philosophy of nihilism as a young man, and became one of the few intellectuals to favour Nazi doctrines. Trained in medicine, he wrote Expressionist verse about his profession (eg *Morgue*, 1912). His later poetry was more diverse, though still pessimistic, as in *Statische Gedichte* (Static Poems, 1948).

Benn, Tony (Anthony Neil Wedgwood) (1925–) English Labour politician, son of Viscount Stansgate, born in London. He became a Labour MP (1950–60), but was debarred from the House of Commons on succeeding to his father's title. He renounced it in 1963, then was re-elected. His various government posts include Postmaster-General (1964–6), Minister of Technology (1966–70), Secretary for Industry (1974–5), and Secretary for Energy (1975–9). Representing the left wing of the Labour Party, in 1988 he unsuccessfully challenged Neil Kinnock for the leadership.

Bennett, (Enoch) Arnold (1867–1931) English novelist, born near Hanley, Staffordshire. He worked as a solicitor's clerk and journalist and lived in Paris for some years before becoming a full-time writer. Among his 30 novels are *Anna of the Five Towns* (1902), *The Old Wives' Tale* (1908), and the *Clayhanger* (1910–16) series, all of which reflect life in the Potteries. He also wrote several plays.

Bennett, Elizabeth the spirited heroine of Jane Austen's *Pride and Prejudice*, who marries Fitzwilliam Darcy. Other members of the Bennett family are her mother and father, Mr and Mrs Bennett, and her sisters Jane, Mary, Kitty, and Lydia.

Bennett, James Gordon (1795–1872) American newspaper editor, born in Keith, Banffshire, Scotland. Trained as a journalist, in

1819 he emigrated to America, where he founded the *New York Herald* (1835).

Ben Nevis the highest mountain in the UK. It is situated in the Grampian Mts, Highland region, NW Scotland. HEIGHT 1 344m. Fort William is 7km/4mi E.

Benoît (de Sainte-Maure) (12c) French poet, born in either Sainte-Maure, near Poiters, or Sainte-More, near Tours. His romance *Roman de Troie* was a source for many later writers, notably Boccaccio.

bent — *adj.* **1** not straight. **2 (bent on something)** with one's attention or energy directed on it: *bent on revenge.* **3** *Brit. slang* dishonest. **4** *Brit. derog. slang* homosexual. — *noun* a natural liking or aptitude.

Bentham, George (1800–84) English botanist, born in Stoke, Plymouth, nephew of Jeremy Bentham. He was secretary to his uncle from 1826 to 1832. He abandoned law for botany, became Secretary of the Horticultural Society of London (1829–40), and compiled, with Joseph Hooker, the great *Genera Plantarum* (3 vols, 1862–83), among many other important botanical works.

Bentham, Jeremy (1748–1832) English philosopher, writer on jurisprudence, and pioneer of utilitarianism, born in London. He was called to the Bar in 1767, but was more interested in the theory of the law. His publications include *A Fragment on Government* (1776), and *Introduction to the Principles of Morals and Legislation* (1789), which present his theory of hedonistic utilitarianism. He held that laws should be socially useful and not merely reflect the *status quo*, and that all actions are right when they promote 'the happiness of the greatest number' — a phrase which he popularized.

benthic *adj. Biol.* denoting or relating to benthos.

benthos *noun Biol.* the living organisms that are found at the bottom of a sea or lake. [from Greek *benthos*, depth]

Bentinck, William Henry Cavendish Bentinck, 3rd Duke of Portland (1738–1809) English statesman, born in Bulstrode, Buckinghamshire. He entered Lord Rockingham's Cabinet in 1765, and succeeded him as Leader of the Whig Party. Although twice Prime Minister, (1783, 1807–9), he is best remembered as Home Secretary under Pitt the Younger, with charge of Irish affairs (1794–1801).

Bentinck, Lord William (Henry Cavendish) (1774–1839) English soldier, born in Bulstrode, Buckinghamshire, the second son of the 3rd Duke of Portland. He became an army officer (1791) and was appointed Governor of Madras (1803), but was recalled from India following a mutiny of native troops. During the Napoleonic Wars he fought in Spain and Sicily, then entered parliament. As Governor-General of India (1828–35) he introduced important administrative reforms.

Bentine, Michael (1922–) Anglo-Peruvian comedian and author, born in Watford. He made his stage début in *Sweet Lavender* (1941) and was one of the early members of *The Goons* (1951–2), but he left the popular radio series to pursue a solo career as comic and raconteur. He also appeared on television in *After Hours* (1959–60) and *It's A Square World* (1960–4) which allowed him to indulge his zany humour. Later television series, often for children, include *The Golden Silents* (1965), *Potty Time* (1973–80), and *Mad About It* (1981). He has also written numerous novels and autobiographies.

Benton, Thomas Hart (1782–1858) US statesman, born near Hillsborough, North Carolina. He was a Missouri Senator for over 30 years, and a Leader of the Democratic Party. Known as 'Old Bullion' because of his opposition to paper currency, in his later years he adopted

an anti-slavery position which finally lost him his seat in the Senate.

bentonite *noun Geol.* a type of clay formed by the decomposition of volcanic ash, used in papermaking. [from Fort Benton, Montana, USA, where it was found]

Benue, River, French **Beboué** a major tributary of the R Niger, in Nigeria. It is 1 295km/805mi long. The river rises in Cameroon and flows generally SW across E and S central Nigeria. It is navigable below Garoua, in Cameroon, and joins the R Niger at Lokoja, Nigeria.

benumb *verb* to make numb.

Benz, Karl (Friedrich) (1844–1929) German engineer, born in Karlsruhe. In 1879 he constructed a two-stroke engine model and founded a factory for its manufacture; in 1883 he founded a second company at Mannheim. His first car — one of the earliest petrol-driven vehicles — was completed in 1885. In 1926 his firm was merged with the Daimler-Motoren-Gesellschaft.

benzene *noun* a colourless flammable liquid hydrocarbon that has an aromatic odour. [see BENZOIN]
◇ Benzene is the simplest aromatic compound, and is mainly obtained from petroleum. It consists of six carbon atoms arranged in a stable ring structure, often represented in chemical formulae by a circle surrounded by a hexagon. Benzene and its derivatives are widely used as solvents, and in the manufacture of plastics, dyes, drugs, and other organic chemicals.

benzene

benzene ring *Chem.* a ring consisting of six linked carbon atoms, as in a molecule of benzene.

benzine *noun* a motor fuel obtained from petroleum.

benzodiazepine *noun Psychol.* any of various minor tranquillizers and hypnotic drugs, eg diazepam (Valium). There is increasing evidence that long-term use of such drugs can lead to addiction, and they are now generally only used to treat severe anxiety and insomnia for periods of not more than a few weeks.

benzoic acid *Chem.* (FORMULA C_6H_5COOH) a white crystalline compound obtained by the oxidation of toluene. Its sodium salt, sodium benzoate, is used as a preservative.

benzoin *noun* a thick liquid obtained from a tree native to Java and Sumatra, used to make perfumes. [from Arabic *luban jawa*, incense of Java]

Beowulf an Anglo-Saxon epic poem in 3 000 lines (c.8c), surviving in the single late-10c Cotton manuscript. It describes the heroic life of Beowulf the dragon slayer.

Beqaa, el see BEKKA, THE.

bequeath *verb* to leave (personal belongings) in a will. [from Anglo-Saxon *becwethan*]

bequest *noun* **1** an act of leaving (personal belongings) in a will. **2** anything left or bequeathed in someone's will. [from Anglo-Saxon *becwethan*, to bequeath]

berate *verb* to scold severely. [from *rate*, to scold]

Berber — *noun* **1** a person belonging to a Muslim race of North Africa. **2** the language spoken by these people. — *adj.* of the Berber people or language. [from Arabic *barbar*]

Berbera POP (1981) 65 000, a port in Woqooyi Galbeed province, Somalia. It is situated on the Gulf of Aden coast, 225km/140mi SE of Djibouti. The port was the winter capital of British Somaliland until 1941 when Hargeysa became capital.

Berbérati POP (1988) 92 000, the chief town in Haute-Sangha prefecture, SW Central African Republic. It lies 314km/195mi W of Bangui.

bereaved *adj.* having recently suffered the death of a close friend or relative. [from Anglo-Saxon *bereafian*]

bereavement *noun* the death of a close friend or relative.

bereft *adj.* **(bereft of something)** deprived of it; having had it taken away. [from the past tense of *bereave*: see BEREAVED]

Berenice a female first name. [from Greek *Pherenike*, bringer of victory]

Beresford, Jack (1899–1977) British oarsman. He competed for Great Britain at five Olympics (1920–36) as sculler and oarsman, winning three gold and two silver medals, and in 1949 received the Olympic Diploma of Merit. He won the Diamond Sculls at Henley four times, and was elected President of the Thames Rowing Club in 1971.

beret *noun* a round flat cap made of soft material. [from French *béret*, cap]

Berg, Alban (1885–1935) Austrian composer, born in Vienna. He studied under Schönberg, and welded the 12-tone system to a deeply traditional style. He is best known for his opera *Wozzeck* (first performed 1925), his Violin Concerto (1935), and the *Lyric Suite* for string quartet (1926). His unfinished opera *Lulu* was posthumously produced.

Berg, Paul (1926–) US molecular biologist, born in Brooklyn, New York City. He later became professor at Stanford (1959) and Washington (1970), and since 1985 has been director of a research centre at Stanford. In the 1960s, Berg purified several transfer RNA molecules, which carry specific amino acids through the cell to the ribosomes for assembly into proteins. In the following decade, he developed techniques to cut and splice genes from one organism into another; he has also been much concerned with the introduction of guidelines for genetic engineering. He shared the 1980 Nobel Prize for Chemistry with Frederick Sanger and Walter Gilbert.

Bergama, ancient **Pergamon** or **Pergamum** POP (1990) 101 000, a town in Izmir province, W Turkey, situated N of Izmir. It was the capital of the ancient kingdom of Pergamum, and of the Roman province of Asia. Parchment is supposed to have been invented here. NOTABLE FEATURES Acropolis; remains of temples of Trajan and Dionysus; Sanctuary of Athena; Altar of Zeus.

Bergamo POP (1991e) 118 000, the capital town of Bergamo province, Lombardy, N Italy. It lies between the Brembo and Serio rivers, NE of Milan. Bergamo was the first seat of the Republican fascist government set up in N Italy by Mussolini after his fall from power in 1943. NOTABLE FEATURES Romanesque basilica (1137–1355); cathedral (15c).

bergamot *noun* a fruit related to the orange and lemon, from which an oil is obtained which is used in perfumes and for flavouring food. [from Bergamo in N Italy]

Bergen POP (1992e) 216 000, a seaport and the administrative capital of Hordaland county, SW Norway. Lying on a promontory at the head of a deep bay, it is Norway's second largest city. It is an old shipping and trading town and an important tourist and cultural centre. HISTORY founded in 1070; capital of Norway in the 12c–13c; occupied by Germans during World War II. The composer Edvard Grieg was born here in 1843.

NOTABLE FEATURES restored cathedral (13c); Hanseatic Museum; Håkonshall (13c palace); Mariakirke (12c); art gallery; museums.

Bergen see MONS.

Berger, Hans (1873–1941) German psychiatrist, born in Neuses bei Coburg. He studied medicine at Jena University, where he remained for the rest of his career, becoming Professor of Psychiatry in 1919. In the course of psychological and physiological research, he invented electroencephalography (EEG) to measure the electrical activity of the brain; this has become a useful tool of research and diagnosis in the study of brain functions and diseases.

Bergius, Friedrich (1884–1949) German chemist, born in Goldschmieden, near Breslau. Working in Hanover from 1909, he studied the effects of high pressures and temperatures on wood, conditions necessary for its conversion into coal. He also developed a process for the conversion of coal into oil. He continued this work when he became head of the research laboratory of the Goldschmidt company in Essen in 1914, and later studied the hydrolysis of wood to sugar. He shared the 1931 Nobel Prize for Chemistry with Carl Bosch.

Bergman, (Ernst) Ingmar (1918–) Swedish film director and writer, born at Uppsala. He worked in the theatre in the late 1930s, and on screen from 1950. His films became something of a cult with art-cinema audiences, with the elegaic *Smiles of a Summer Night* (1955) and the sombre *The Seventh Seal* (1956) and *Wild Strawberries* (1957). Later films include *Herbstsonate* (Autumn Sonata, 1978) and *Fanny och Alexander* (1983).

Bergman, Ingrid (1915–82) Swedish film actress, born in Stockholm. Her first starring role at Hollywood (in *Intermezzo*, 1939) led to the successful *Casablanca* (1942), *For Whom the Bell Tolls* (1943), and *Gaslight* (1944), for which she won her first Oscar. *Anastasia* (1956) brought her another Oscar. Later appearances in film and television include *Herbstsonate* (Autumn Sonata, 1978) and *A Woman Called Golda* (1982).

Bergström, Sune Karl (1916–) Swedish biochemist, born in Stockholm. Professor at the Karolinska Institute in Stockholm (1958–81), he isolated and purified prostaglandins, for which he shared the 1982 Nobel Prize for Physiology or Medicine with John Vane and his former student Bengt Samuelsson.

Beria, Lavrenti (Pavlovich) (1899–1953) Soviet secret police chief, born in Mercheuli, Georgia. He became Soviet Commissar for Internal Affairs in 1938 and during World War II was Vice-President of the State Committee for Defence, when he was active in purging Stalin's opponents. After the death of Stalin (1953), he belonged briefly with Malenkov and Molotov to the collective leadership, but was accused by his colleagues of conspiracy and shot after a brief 'treason' trial.

beribboned *adj.* decorated with ribbons.

beriberi *noun Medicine* a deficiency disease caused by lack of vitamin B$_1$ (thiamine), which results in inflammation of the nerves, paralysis of the limbs, oedema, and heart failure. It is most widespread in parts of the tropics where the diet consists mainly of polished rice. [from Sinhalese *beri*, weakness]

Bering *or* **Behring, Vitus (Jonassen)** (1681–1741) Danish-Russian navigator, born in Horsens, Denmark. He joined the navy of Tsar Peter the Great, and fought in the Swedish wars. He was then appointed to explore the Sea of Kamchatka (1724), to determine whether Russia and America were connected by land. In 1728 and again in 1741 he sailed towards the American continent, and finally sighted Alaska. However, he was forced to return because of sickness and storms, and was wrecked on the island of Avatcha (now Bering Island), where he

died. Bering Sea and Bering Strait are named after him.

Bering Sea the part of the Pacific Ocean between Siberia in the W and Alaska in the E, bounded S by the Aleutian Is and the Aleutian Trench. AREA 2 261 100sq km/872 800sq mi. It is connected to the Arctic by the Bering Strait (90km/56mi wide at its narrowest point) and is often ice-bound (Nov–May). The boundary between Russia and the USA divides the Bering Sea. Depths reach 4 000m in the SW, but only 25–75m over the continental shelf in the NE. The sea was first explored in the 17c. Its seal herds were exploited for their fur and were under threat of extinction but the herds have been built up again after a 1911 agreement made by the UK, USA, Russia, and Japan to regulate sealing. [named after Russian navigator Vitus Bering]

Berio, Luciano (1925–) Italian avant-garde composer and teacher of music, born in Oneglia. After studying with Luigi Dallapiccola (1904–75) in the USA, he and Bruno Maderna (1920–73) founded an electronic studio in Milan (1954–61). He was married (1950–66) to the US soprano Cathy Berberian (1928–83), for whom he wrote several works. His compositions often combine live and prerecorded sound, or use tapes and electronic music, eg *Mutazioni* (1955), *Visage* (1961), and the *Sequenza* series (1958–75).

berk *or* **burk** *noun Brit. slang* a fool. [short for *Berkeley Hunt*, rhyming slang for CUNT]

Berkeley, Busby (1895–1976) US director and choreographer, born in Los Angeles. Known for his extravagant stagings of dance numbers in Hollywood films, in which the camera moves among the dancers, he was also one of Broadway's busiest stage directors of the 1920s. His films include *Gold Diggers of 1933* and *Lady Be Good* (1941).

Berkeley, George (1685–1753) Anglican bishop and philosopher, born near Kilkenny, Ireland. He was appointed Dean of Derry (1724), became Bishop of Cloyne (1734), and in 1752 moved to Oxford. In his *Essay towards a New Theory of Vision* (1709), he argued that spatial distance is not directly perceived, but inferred from the habitual association of visual and tactile sensations. Other works which expound his idealistic philosophy include the *Treatise Concerning the Principles of Human Knowledge* (1710) and *Three Dialogues between Hylas and Philonous* (1713). He argued that 'to be is to be perceived or a perceiver' – everything that exists is either a mind or in a mind.

Berkeley, Sir Lennox (Randall Francis) (1903–89) English composer, born in Oxford. His early compositions, including the oratorio *Jonah* (1935), show the influence of his French training in their conciseness and lucidity. Later works, notably the *Stabat Mater* (1946), the operas *Nelson* (1953) and *Ruth* (1956), and the orchestral *Windsor Variations* (1969) and *Voices of the Night* (1973), won him wide recognition for their combination of technical refinement and emotional appeal.

Berkeley a city in Alameda, W California, USA, on the NE shore of San Francisco Bay. It is the location of the main campus of the University of California.

berkelium *noun* (SYMBOL **Bk**, ATOMIC NUMBER 97) a radioactive metallic element manufactured artificially by bombarding americium-241 with alpha particles. [from Berkeley, California, where it was first made]

Berks. *abbrev.* Berkshire.

Berkshire, also known as **Royal Berkshire** POP (1992e) 758 000, a county in S England, divided into six districts. AREA 1 259sq km/486sq mi. It is bounded W by Wiltshire, N by Oxfordshire, NE by Buckinghamshire, E by Greater London and Surrey, and S by Hampshire. The Kennet and Thames rivers run through the county. CHIEF TOWNS Reading (county town),

Newbury, Windsor, Maidenhead, Bracknell. NOTABLE FEATURES Atomic Research Establishment at Aldermaston; Windsor Castle.

Berlin, Irving, originally **Israel Baline** (1888–1989) US songwriter, born in Temum, Russia. During his youth in New York City he began promoting his own songs as a singing waiter. 'Alexander's Ragtime Band' was an international success (1911), the first hit among more than 900 songs for which he wrote both the words and music. His score for *Annie Get Your Gun* (1946) is a model of theatre music. Sentimental lyrics and simple melodies are often considered Berlin's main strengths (eg 'Always', 1925, 'Easter Parade', 1933, 'God Bless America', 1939, and 'White Christmas', 1942), but he also had many hits with sly urbane lyrics and advanced harmonies (eg 'Heat Wave', 1933 and 'Cheek to Cheek', 1935).

Berlin, Sir Isaiah (1909–) British philosopher, born in Riga, Latvia. Most of his academic career has been at Oxford, where he was Chichele Professor of Social and Political theory (1957–67), and also served in the diplomatic service during World War II. His works on political philosophy include *Historical Inevitability* (1954), *The Age of Enlightenment* (1956), and *Two Concepts of Liberty* (1959).

Berlin POP (1991e) 3.4m, the capital of Germany. HISTORY founded in the 13c, it was the former residence of the Hohenzollerns and the capital of Brandenburg; later it was capital of Prussia, and became an industrial and commercial centre in the 18c; the city was divided into eastern and western sectors in 1945; in 1949 West Berlin became a province of the Federal Republic of Germany, and East Berlin became the capital and a county of the German Democratic Republic; the two halves of the city were separated by a wall built in 1961 by the East German government to prevent citizens moving from East to West; in 1989 contact between East and West Berlin was restored, following government changes in East Germany and the dismantling of the Berlin Wall; a unified Berlin became capital of the unified Germany in 1990. NOTABLE FEATURES Brandenburg Gate; Unter den Linden (tree-lined avenue); Pergamum Museum; National Gallery; Rotes Rathaus (red town hall); Kaiser Wilhelm Church (preserved ruins).

Berlin, Congress of an international congress (1878) that followed the Russian defeat of Turkey (1877–8) and resulted in: the gaining of independence from Turkey for Serbia, Romania, and Bulgaria; the occupation of Bosnia-Herzegovina by Austria-Hungary; the retention by Russia of gains in S Bessarabia and the Caucasus, though there was a reduction in the size of the satellite Bulgaria; and the occupation of Cyprus by Britain.

Berlin, East the capital of the former East Germany. West and East Berlin became one city when West Germany and East Germany unified in 1990. See BERLIN.

Berlin, West a former West German enclave (city and province) lying entirely within East Germany. West Berlin and East Berlin became one city when West Germany and East Germany unified in 1990. See BERLIN.

Berlin Airlift a massive airlift (1948–9) of essential supplies to postwar Berlin by British and US aircraft, undertaken in response to the attempt by the Soviet military authorities in Berlin to isolate the city from the West by severing all overland communication routes (Jun 1948). Stalin lifted the blockade in May 1949.

Berliner Ensemble a theatre company formed by Bertolt Brecht in the former East Berlin (1949). It had much influence on Western theatre, chiefly through Brecht's own productions of his later plays.

Berlin Philharmonic Orchestra a world-famous orchestra, founded (1882) in Berlin,

Germany. Among its conductors are von Bülow, Furtwängler, von Karajan, and Claudio Abbado (from 1989).

Berlin Wall a concrete wall built by the East German government in 1961 to seal off East Berlin from the part of the city occupied by the three main Western powers. Built largely to prevent mass illegal emigration to the West (a threat to the East German economy) the wall saw the deaths of many who tried to escape. Following revolutionary upheaval in East Germany, it was unexpectedly opened in 1989. Reunification has led to the dismantling of the wall.

Berlioz, (Louis) Hector (1803–69) French composer, born in Côte-Saint-André. After studying medicine, he produced some large-scale works, then entered the Paris Conservatoire (1826). He fell in love with the Irish Shakespearean actress Harriet Smithson (1800–54) and wrote the *Symphonie Fantastique* (1830) for her; they married in 1833. After winning the Prix de Rome (1830), he spent two years in Italy. His other works include his symphony *Harold en Italie* (1834), the *Grande Messe des morts* (1837), the dramatic symphony *Roméo et Juliette* (1839), the cantata *La Damnation de Faust* (1846), and his operas *Les Troyens* (1856–8) and *Béatrice et Bénédict* (1860–2). One of the founders of 19c programme music, Berlioz also wrote several books, including a treatise on orchestration.

Berlusconi, Silvio (1936–) Italian businessman and politician, born in Milan. He has interests in television stations, housing, financial services, a cinema chain, and Milan AC football club. He is leader of the right-wing Forza Italia Party, which won more seats (155) in the 1994 election than any other (though not an absolute majority). He formed a government which included neo-Fascist ministers.

Bermuda, formerly **Somers Is** POP (1992e) 62 000, a British Colony, divided into nine parishes. AREA 53sq km/20sq mi. It is situated in the W Atlantic Ocean c.900km/560mi E of Cape Hatteras, N Carolina. It comprises c.150 low-lying, coral islands and islets of which 20 are inhabited and seven are linked by causeways and bridges. The largest island is (Great) Bermuda. St George's I and St David's I lie to the E. The highest point is Gibb's Hill (78m). CAPITAL Hamilton. There are deepwater ports at Hamilton, St George (St George's I), and Freeport (Ireland I). TIME ZONE GMT –4. OFFICIAL LANGUAGE English. CURRENCY the Bermuda dollar. CLIMATE sub-tropical, generally humid; rain throughout year; summers warm to hot, winters mild. HISTORY discovered by Spanish mariner, Juan Bermudez, in the early 16c; colonized by English settlers in 1612; important naval station, and (until 1862) penal settlement; a new constitution providing internal self-government came into force in 1968; movement for independence caused tension in the 1970s, including the assassination of the Governor-General in 1973. GOVERNMENT the British monarch is represented by a Governor-General; governed by a Senate (11 members), a House of Assembly (40 members, elected for 5 years), and a 12-member Cabinet headed by a Prime Minister. ECONOMY mainly year-round tourism; increasingly an international company business centre; petroleum products; pharmaceuticals; aircraft supplies; boatbuilding, ship repair; vegetables; citrus and banana plantations; fish processing centre.

Bermuda shorts or **Bermudas** close-fitting shorts reaching almost to the knee. [from *Bermuda*, in the west Atlantic]

Bermuda Triangle a name for the area of sea between Florida, Bermuda, and Puerto Rico, where there is an unusually high number of unexplained disappearances of ships and aircraft.

Bern, French **Berne** 1 POP (1991e) 300 000, the federal capital of Switzerland, in Bern canton, lying 94km/58mi SW of Zürich. It joined the Swiss Confederation in 1353 and became capital in 1848. The city is the headquarters of several

international organizations. NOTABLE FEATURES the old city is a World Heritage site; Gothic cathedral (1421–1573); medieval town hall; clock tower; many museums. **2** a canton in W Switzerland with Bern as its capital.

Bernadette, St, originally **Marie Bernarde Soubirous** (1844–79) French visionary, born in Lourdes. She claimed to have received in 1858 18 apparitions of the Blessed Virgin at the Massabielle Rock, near Lourdes, which has since become a place of pilgrimage. A nun from 1866, she was beatified in 1925, canonized in 1933, and her feast day is 18 Feb or 16 Apr.

Bernard, Claude (1813–78) French physiologist, born near Villefranche, Beaujolais. Trained in medicine, in 1855 he became professor at the Collège de France. One of the founders of modern physiology, he was first to suggest that life requires a constant internal environment; cells function best within a narrow range of osmotic pressure and temperature when bathed in a fairly constant concentration of chemical constituents. His wide-ranging studies included the action of the secretions of the alimentary canal, the pancreatic juice, the connection between the liver and nervous system, the oxygen in blood, the opium alkaloids, curare, and the sympathetic nerves.

Bernard a male first name. [from the Germanic elements *ber*, bear + *hard*, hardy, brave]

Bernard of Clairvaux, St, also known as **the Mellifluous Doctor** (1090–1153) French theologian and reformer, born of a noble family near Dijon. In 1113 he entered the Cistercian monastery of Cîteaux, and in 1115 became the first abbot of Clairvaux. He led a studious, ascetic life, and founded more than 70 monasteries, and by his rousing eloquence he incited France for the second Crusade (1146). His writings include hundreds of epistles and sermons, and several theological treatises. He was canonized in 1174 and his feast day is 20 Aug. The monks of his reformed branch of the Cistercians are often called Bernardines.

Bernard of Menthon, St, also called **the Apostle of the Alps** (923–1008) Italian churchman, born in Savoy. As Archdeacon of Aosta he founded the hospices in the Alpine passes that were named after him, as were St Bernard dogs, trained by the monks to go to the aid of travellers. He was canonized in 1115 and his feast day is 28 May or 15 Jun.

Bernese Alps, German **Berner Alpen**, or **Bernese Oberland**, French **Alpes Bernoises** a mountain range in Bern and Valais cantons, W Switzerland. It is a N division of the Central Alps, extending from L Geneva to the Grimsel Pass. The highest peak of the range is the Finsteraarhorn (4 274m); other peaks include the Aletschhorn and Jungfrau. Interlaken and Grindelwald are among many tourist resorts in the area.

Bernhard Leopold Frederik Everhard Julius Coert Karel Godfried Pieter, Prince (1911–) prince of the Netherlands, born in Jena. He married Juliana (1937–80), the only daughter of Wilhelmina, Queen of the Netherlands; they had four daughters. During World War II, he commanded the Netherlands Forces of the Interior (1944–5).

Bernhardt, Sarah, originally **Henriette Rosine Bernard** (1844–1923) French actress, born in Paris, who became a legendary figure through her talent for acting and publicity. She won fame playing in François Coppée's *Le Passant* (1869) and her other most famous roles included *Phèdre* (1877) and Marguerite (1884) in *La Dame aux camélias*. She founded the Théâtre Sarah Bernhardt in 1899.

Bernini, Gian Lorenzo (1598–1680) Italian Baroque sculptor, architect and painter, born in Naples. He went to Rome at an early age, and was introduced to the papal court. In 1633 he completed the bronze baldacchino in St Peter's,

and in 1655 was commissioned to work on the fountain of the four river gods in the Piazza Navona. He decorated the apse of St Peter's with the *Cathedra Petri* (1657–66), designed the colonnade in front of the cathedral, and (in 1663) the grand staircase to the Vatican. Other works include the sculptures *Neptune and Triton* (c.1620) and *David* (1623).

Bernoulli, Daniel (1700–82) Swiss mathematician, born in Groningen. Born into a well-known family of mathematicians, he became Professor of Mathematics at St Petersburg (1725) and from 1732 held various professorships in Basle. He worked on trigonometric series, mechanics, vibrating systems and hydrodynamics (anticipating the kinetic theory of gases), and solved a differential equation proposed by Jacopo Riccati, now known as Bernoulli's equation.

Bernstein, Leonard (1918–90) US conductor, pianist, and composer, born in Lawrence, Massachusetts. He achieved fame suddenly in 1943, when he conducted the New York Philharmonic as a substitute for Bruno Walter. His compositions include three symphonies, a television opera, a mass, a ballet, and many choral works and songs, but he is best known for his two musical comedies *On the Town* (1944) and *West Side Story* (1957), and for his concerts for young people.

Bernstein, Sidney Lewis Bernstein, Baron (1899–1993) English businessman, born in Ilford. He bought a derelict music hall, the Empire Theatre, in Edmonton in 1922 and later turned it into a cinema. In 1929 he built the first new cinema in Dover, the design of which was copied across the country. During World War II he was Films Adviser to the Ministry of Information. He spent five years in Hollywood, then returned to the UK and in 1954 established Granada Television, which became renowned for its drama and current affairs programmes (eg *Brideshead Revisited*, 1981, and the long-running *World in Action* series).

Berowne or **Biron** one of the three lords accompanying King Ferdinand in Shakespeare's *Love's Labour's Lost*, who woos Rosaline enthusiastically despite having denounced the power of love.

Berry, Chuck, originally **Charles Edward Anderson Berry** (1926–) US rock singer, guitarist, and songwriter, born in St Louis, Missouri. He grew up playing and singing Baptist hymns, swing music, and the blues, and then used these elements in writing songs, starting with 'Maybelline', his first recording. Many of them belong to the standard repertoire of rock and roll, and are known as other singers' hits, eg 'Roll Over Beethoven' by the Beatles and 'Sweet Little Sixteen' by the Beach Boys.

berry noun (PL. **berries**) **1** *Bot.* a fleshy fruit containing several to many seeds which are not surrounded by a stony protective layer. It is indehiscent, the entire fruit being shed from the plant without opening to release the seeds, eg grape, cucumber, tomato, citrus fruits. Raspberries and blackberries are not true berries. **2** *Zool.* a dark structure resembling a knob on the bill of a swan. [from Anglo-Saxon *berie*]

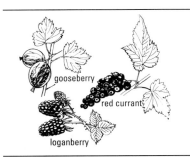

gooseberry
red currant
loganberry

types of berries

berserk *adj.* violently angry; wild and destructive. [from Norse *berserkr*, probably from *bern*, bear + *serkr*, coat]

berth — *noun* **1** a sleeping-place in a ship, train, etc. **2** a place in a port where a ship or boat can be tied up. **3** enough room for a ship to be able to turn round in. — *verb* **1** to tie up (a ship) in its berth. **2** *intrans. said of a ship* to arrive at its berth. **3** to provide a sleeping-place for.
— **give a wide berth to someone** *or* **something** to stay well away from them.

Bertha a female first name, reintroduced from Germany in the 19c. [from a Germanic short form of names beginning with *berht*, famous]

Berthelot, (Pierre Eugène) Marcellin (1827–1907) French chemist and politician, born in Paris. Appointed professor at the Collège de France (1865), he was put in charge of Paris defences in 1870, and later served as Foreign Minister (1895–6). He helped to found thermochemistry, introduced a standard method for determining the latent heat of steam, discovered many of the derivatives of coal tar, and studied the mechanism of explosion. His syntheses of many fundamental organic compounds helped to destroy the classical division between organic and inorganic compounds.

Bertolucci, Bernardo (1940–) Italian film director, born in Parma. After working on short films, his first feature as a director was *La Commare Secco* (The Grim Reaper, 1962). In the UK and the USA he is best known for *Last Tango in Paris* (1972), *The Tragedy of a Ridiculous Man* (1981), and the epic *The Last Emperor* (1987), which won him an Oscar.

Bertram, Count of Rousillon the hero, and somewhat reluctant husband of Helena, in Shakespeare's *All's Well that Ends Well*.

Bertram, Sir Thomas *and* **Lady** characters in Jane Austen's *Mansfield Park*. Their children are Tom, Edmund, Maria, and Julia.

Bertram a male first name. [Norman French, from Germanic *berht*, famous + *hramn*, raven]

Bertrand, Henri Gratien, Comte (1773–1844) French military engineer, born in Châteauroux. He fought in Italy and Egypt before becoming Napoleon's aide-de-camp (1804) and Grand Marshal (1813). He shared the Emperor's banishment to St Helena, and on his death returned to France, where in 1830 he was appointed commandant of the Polytechnic School. His shorthand diary provided a detailed account of Napoleon's life in exile.

Berwick-upon-Tweed POP (1981) 13 000, a town in Berwick-upon-Tweed district, Northumberland, NE England. It lies on the North Sea at the mouth of the R Tweed, on the Scottish-English border. HISTORY disputed by England and Scotland, it changed ownership 14 times; part of England since 1482. NOTABLE FEATURES ramparts (16c); Church of the Holy Trinity (1652); 16km/10mi SW is Flodden Field (1513); 12km/7mi SW is Norham Castle (15c).

Beryl a female first name, taken from the gemstone and first in fashion at the end of the 19c.

beryl *noun Geol.* beryllium aluminium silicate, a mineral that occurs in the form of green, blue, yellow, or white crystals, and is often used as a gemstone, the most valuable varieties being emerald and aquamarine. It is also the main source of the element beryllium. [from Greek *beryllos*]

beryllium *noun Chem.* (SYMBOL **Be**, ATOMIC NUMBER **4**) a silvery-grey metal, obtained from the mineral beryl, which is used for windows in X-ray tubes, and together with copper is used to make very strong alloys. [from BERYL]

Berzelius, Jöns Jacob (1779–1848) Swedish chemist, born near Linköping, one of the founders of modern chemistry. Professor in Stockholm (1807–32), his accurate determination of atomic weights established the laws of the way elements combine in fixed proportions and the atomic theory. He introduced modern symbols and an electrochemical theory, and discovered the elements selenium, thorium, and cerium.

Bes in Egyptian religion, a dwarf god of recreation, bandy-legged and horrific in appearance, but congenial in temperament. He was the protector in child-birth, and guardian of the family.

Besançon, ancient **Vesontio**, or **Besontium** POP (1990) 123 000, an industrial town and the capital of Doubs department, Franche-Comté region, NE France. It lies on the R Doubs at the NW edge of the Jura and has been a strategic site between the Vosges and the Jura since Gallo-Roman times. The writer Victor Hugo was born here in 1802 and it was also the birthplace of the Lumière brothers, who invented cinematography. In 1890 the first factory in the world to produce artificial fibres was established in the town. NOTABLE FEATURES cathedral (11c–13c); citadel on high rock overlooking river; Roman remains; museums; university (1485).

Besant, Annie, *née* Wood (1847–1933) English theosophist and social reformer, born in London. After her separation from the Rev Frank Besant (1873), she became Vice-President of the National Secular Society (1874). A close associate of Charles Bradlaugh, she was an ardent supporter of birth control and socialism, then met Madame Blavatsky (1889) and turned to theosophy. Later involved in politics in India, she championed nationalism and education there, and was President of the Indian National Congress (1917–23).

beseech *verb* (PAST TENSE AND PAST PARTICIPLE **beseeched**, **besought**) *formal, literary* to ask earnestly; to beg. [from obsolete *secan*, to seek]

beseeching *adj.* imploring; earnestly seeking something: *a beseeching smile.*

beseechingly *adv.* in an earnest and imploring way.

beset *verb* (**besetting**; PAST TENSE AND PAST PARTICIPLE **beset**) *literary* to attack on all sides; to worry: *beset by problems.* [from Anglo-Saxon *besettan*]

beside *prep.* **1** next to, by the side of or near. **2** compared with. **3** not relevant to: *beside the point.*
— **beside oneself** in a state of uncontrollable anger, excitement, or other emotion: *beside oneself with worry.*
[from Anglo-Saxon *be*, by + *sidan*, side]

besides — *prep.* in addition to; as well as. — *adv.* also; as well.

besiege *verb* **1** to surround (a town or stronghold) with an army in order to force it to surrender. **2** to gather round in a crowd. **3** to bother; to annoy constantly: *were besieged with questions.*

Beskids *or* **Beskidy** a mountain group in the Carpathian range on the Polish–Slovak frontier. It rises to 1 725m at Babia Gora.

besmirch *verb formal* **1** to make dirty. **2** to spoil the reputation of.

besom *noun* a large brush made from sticks tied to a long wooden handle. [from Anglo-Saxon *besma*]

besotted *adj.* **1** foolishly infatuated. **2** confused, especially through having drunk too much alcohol.

besottedly *adv.* in a foolishly infatuated way: *he was besottedly devoted to her.*

besought see BESEECH.

bespangle *verb* to decorate with objects which shine or sparkle.

bespatter *verb* (**bespattered**, **bespattering**) to cover with spots, splashes, large drops, etc.

bespeak *verb* (PAST TENSE **bespoke**; PAST PARTICIPLE **bespoken**) *formal* **1** to claim in advance. **2** to show or be evidence of.

bespoke *adj.* **1** *said of clothes* made to fit a particular person. **2** *said of a tailor* making clothes to fit individual customers.

Bessarion *or* **Basilius, John** (1403–72) Byzantine theologian, born in Trebizond (now Trabzon), one of the earliest scholars to transplant Greek literature and philosophy into the West. As Archbishop of Nicaea (now Iznik) from 1437, he accompanied the Greek emperor to the councils of Ferrara and Florence in Italy, to bring about union between the Byzantine and Latin Churches (1438). He joined the Roman Church, was made cardinal by Pope Eugenius IV (1439), served as papal governor of Bologna (1450–5), and was twice nearly elected pope.

Bessel, Friedrich Wilhelm (1784–1846) German mathematician and astronomer, born in Minden. Starting as a ship's clerk, in 1810 he was appointed director of the observatory and professor at Königsberg. He predicted the existence of a planet beyond Uranus, and was the first to identify the nearest stars and determine their distances. In the course of his astronomical work he systematized the mathematical functions which bear his name.

Bessemer, Sir Henry (1813–98) English metallurgist and inventor, born in Charlton, Hertfordshire. Self-taught, he learned metallurgy in his father's type foundry, and set up his own small iron-works in London. In 1855 he patented an economical process for manufacturing steel; although the Bessemer process was only reluctantly accepted in Britain, US entrepreneurs made a fortune from it. Bessemer established a steelworks at Sheffield in 1859, specializing at first in armaments, and later expanding to meet the worldwide demand for steel rails, locomotives, and bridges.

Bessemer process *Chem.* a process for converting pig iron (which has a high carbon content) into steel (an iron alloy with a low carbon content). Air is blown through the molten iron, and oxygen in the air converts the carbon in the iron to carbon dioxide, which escapes. This reaction produces heat which keeps the iron molten.

Best, Charles Herbert (1899–1978) Canadian physiologist, born in West Pembroke, Maine. As a research student in Toronto in 1921 he helped Frederick Banting to isolate the hormone insulin, used in the treatment of diabetes; for this work he received half of Banting's share of the 1923 Nobel Prize for Physiology or Medicine. In 1929 he became professor at Toronto University.

Best, George (1946–) Northern Irish footballer, born in Belfast. He made his début for Manchester United in 1963 at the age of 17, and won championship medals in 1965 and 1967. In 1968 he was a member of the Manchester United team which won the European Cup. He was Footballer of the Year in England and Europe in 1969, and played for Northern Ireland 37 times, but never in the World Cup. After 361 League appearances and 137 goals for Manchester United, he finished his career playing for several smaller clubs.

best — *adj.* **1** most excellent, suitable, or desirable. **2** most successful, clever, etc: *is the best at swimming.* **3** the greatest or most: *the best part of an hour.* — *adv.* **1** most successfully, etc: *who did best in the exam?* **2** more than all others: *I like her best.* — *noun* **1** the most excellent or suitable person or thing, most desirable quality, etc: *the best of the bunch / bring out the best in them.* **2** the greatest effort: *do one's best.* **3** a person's finest clothes: *Sunday best.* **4** victory or success: *get the best of an argument.* — *verb* to beat or defeat.
— **as best one can** as well as one can.
at best considered in the most favourable way; in the best circumstances.

at the best of times in the most favourable circumstances.

the best bet *colloq.* the most appropriate course of action.

for the best likely or intended to have the best results possible.

had best would find it wisest to.

make the best of something to do as well as possible in unfavourable circumstances.

put one's best foot forward to make the best attempt possible.

to the best of one's knowledge *or* **belief** *or* **ability** as far as one knows, or believes, or is able. [from Anglo-Saxon *betst*]

best-before date a date stamped on a perishable product (especially food) to indicate the day or month by which the product should be used.

best boy the charge-hand electrician in a film or television production crew, working directly under the gaffer.

bestial *adj.* **1** of or like an animal. **2** *derog.* cruel. [from Latin *bestia*, animal]

bestiality *noun* **1** disgusting or cruel behaviour. **2** sexual intercourse between a human and an animal.

bestially *adv.* with great cruelty.

bestiary *noun* (PL. **bestiaries**) a kind of book popular in Europe in the Middle Ages, containing pictures and descriptions of animals, often used for moral instruction. [from Latin *bestia*, animal]

bestir *verb* (**bestirred**, **bestirring**) (**bestir oneself**) to make an effort to become active, start moving, etc.

best man a bridegroom's main male attendant at a wedding.

bestow *verb formal* (**bestow something on** *or* **upon someone**) to give them a title, award, quality, etc. [from Anglo-Saxon *stow*, spot or position]

bestowal *noun* an act or instance of bestowing.

bestrewn *adj. formal, literary* covered loosely, usually with things which have been thrown or scattered: *a beach bestrewn with shells.* [from Anglo-Saxon *bestreowian*, to strew]

bestride *verb* (PAST TENSE **bestrode**; PAST PARTICIPLE **bestridden**) *formal, literary* to sit or stand across (something) with one leg on each side. [from Anglo-Saxon *bestridan*]

best seller **1** a book or other item which sells in large numbers. **2** the author of a best-selling book.

best-selling *adj.* that sells in large numbers.

bet — *verb* (**betting**; PAST TENSE AND PAST PARTICIPLE **betted**, **bet**) *intrans., trans.* to risk (an asset, usually money) on predicting the outcome or result of a future event, especially a race or other sporting event. The better wins money if the outcome is as predicted, and loses the money betted if it is not. **2** *trans. colloq.* to feel sure or confident: *I bet they'll be late.* — *noun* **1** an act of betting. **2** a sum of money betted. **3** *colloq.* an opinion.

— an even bet an equal chance that something will happen or not.

you bet *North Amer., esp. US slang* certainly; definitely; of course.

[origin uncertain]

beta *noun* **1** the second letter of the Greek alphabet (Β, β). **2** a mark indicating the second highest grade or quality.

beta-blocker *noun Medicine* a drug that slows the heartbeat by blocking certain receptors of the sympathetic nervous system. Beta-blockers such as propranolol are used to treat hypertension (high blood pressure), angina, and abnormal heart rhythms.

Betacam *trademark* a videotape recorder and camera system of television broadcast standard, introduced by Sony (1981). Initially for electronic news-gathering, it was adopted internationally for all forms of video production.

beta decay *Physics* a form of radioactive decay in which a neutron in an atomic nucleus spontaneously breaks up into a proton, which remains within the nucleus, and an electron, which is emitted.

betake *verb* (PAST TENSE **betook**; PAST PARTICIPLE **betaken**) *literary* (**betake oneself**) to go somewhere specified.

Betamax *trademark* a videotape cassette recorder system developed by Sony (1975) for the domestic market. Although economical, it never achieved the popularity of the VHS system.

Betancourt, Rómulo (1908–81) Venezuelan politician and reformer, born in Guatire, Miranda state. One of the founders of the Acción Democrática Party, he held power from 1945 to 1947, and when the Pérez Jiménez dictatorship (1950–8) fell, he was elected President (1959–64) of the new Venezuelan democracy.

beta particle an electron or positron produced when a neutron inside an unstable radioactive nucleus turns into a proton, or a proton turns into a neutron. Beta particles will penetrate several metres of air or a piece of paper, but are stopped by a thin sheet of aluminium.

beta test *Comput.* a second round of tests run on new software before it is marketed, designed to recreate normal working conditions.

betel *noun* an Asian climbing plant whose leaves are wrapped around the seeds of the plant and chewed. [from Malayalam (S Indian language) *vettila*]

Betelgeuse *noun Astron.* a red supergiant star (one of the largest known) of variable brightness in the constellation of Orion. It is the tenth brightest star in the sky. – Also called *Alpha Orionis.* [from French, from Arabic *bayt-al-jawzā*, Orion]

betel nut the seed of the betel plant.

bête noire *noun* (PL. **bêtes noires**) a person or thing that especially bothers, annoys or frightens one. [French, = black beast]

Bethe, Hans Albrecht (1906–) German-born US physicist, born in Strassburg (now Strasbourg, France). He taught in Germany until 1933 when he moved first to England and then to the USA, where he became professor at Cornell University (1935–75). During World War II he was Director of Theoretical Physics for the atomic bomb project. In 1939 he proposed the first detailed theory for the generation of energy by stars through a series of nuclear reactions, for which he was awarded the 1967 Nobel Prize for Physics. He also contributed with Ralph Alpher and George Gamow to the 'alpha, beta, gamma' theory of the origin of the chemical elements during the early development of the universe.

Bethlehem, Arabic **Beit Lahm 1** POP (1980) 14 000, a Biblical town in Jerusalem governorate, in the Israeli-occupied West Bank, W Jordan. It lies 8km/5mi SW of Jerusalem. The town is the birthplace of Christ and the home of David. It serves as a trade centre for the surrounding agricultural area. NOTABLE FEATURES Church of the Nativity, built by Constantine in AD 330; Monastery of Elijah (6c, later restored). **2** a subdistrict of Judea-Samaria district, Israel.

betide

— woe betide see WOE.

[from Anglo-Saxon *tidan*, to befall]

Betjeman, Sir John (1906–84) English poet, born in London. He is best known for his light verse, much of which is to be found in his *Collected Poems* (1958) and in his verse autobiography, *Summoned by Bells* (1960). He also championed Victorian and Edwardian art and architecture, and wrote numerous guide books and essays. He was made Poet Laureate in 1972.

betoken *verb* (**betokened, betokening**) *formal* to be evidence or a sign of. [from Anglo-Saxon *betacnian*]

betook see BETAKE.

betray *verb* **1** to hand over (a friend, one's country, etc) to an enemy. **2** to give away (a secret, etc). **3** to break (a promise, confidence, etc) or be unfaithful to (someone): *betray a trust.* **4** to be evidence of: *her face betrayed her unhappiness.* [from Latin *tradere*, to hand over]

betrayal *noun* an act or instance of betraying.

betrayer *noun* a person who betrays or breaks a confidence.

betrothal *noun formal* engagement to be married.

betrothed *noun, adj. formal* engaged to marry someone. [from Middle English *betrouth*, from *treuth*, truth]

better¹ — *adj.* **1** good to a greater extent; more excellent, suitable, desirable, etc. **2** (**better at something**) more successful, etc in doing it. **3** partly or fully recovered from illness. **4** greater: *the better part of a day.* — *adv.* **1** more excellently, successfully, etc. **2** in or to a greater degree. — *noun* (often **betters**) a person superior in quality, rank, etc: *one's elders and betters.* — *verb* (**bettered, bettering**) **1** to beat; to improve on. **2** *trans., intrans.* to make or become better. **3** (**better oneself**) to improve one's position or social standing.

— all the better for something very much better as a result of it.

better off more affluent or fortunate.

a change for the better an improvement.

for better or for worse no matter what happens.

get the better of someone to gain the advantage over them.

go one better than someone to do, offer, etc something better or more than them.

had better ought to: *we'd better hurry or we'll be late.*

so much the better that is, or would be, preferable.

[from Anglo-Saxon *betera*]

better² *or* **bettor** *noun* a person who bets.

Better Business Bureau one of many local organizations, mainly in the USA and Canada, formed to protect communities against unfair or misleading advertising and selling practices. They were established in the early 20c, and nowadays set standards for business practice, and investigate complaints.

betterment *noun* improvement; advancement.

betting *noun* gambling by predicting the outcome of a race etc.

betting-shop *noun Brit.* a licensed establishment where the public can place bets; a bookmaker.

between — *prep.* **1** in, to, through, or across the space dividing (two people, places, times, etc). **2** to and from: *a regular bus service between Leeds and Bradford.* **3** in combination; acting together: *they bought a car between them.* **4** shared out among: *divide the money between them.* **5** involving choice: *choose between right and wrong.* **6** including; involving: *a fight between rivals.* — *adv.* (**in between**) in, into the middle (of two points in space, time, etc): *time for a quick lunch (in) between.*

— between you and me *or* **between ourselves** as a matter of confidence.

[from Anglo-Saxon *betweonum*]

Between the Clock and the Bed a self-portrait by Edvard Munch (1940, Oslo).

betweentimes *adv.* (also **in betweentimes**) at intervals between other events.

betwixt *prep., adv. old use* between. [from Anglo-Saxon *betweox*]

betwixt and between undecided; in a middle position.

Bevan, Aneurin (1897–1960) Welsh Labour politician, born in Tredegar, Monmouthshire. One of 13 children, he began work in the pits at the age of 13, and led the Welsh miners in the 1926 General Strike. He entered parliament for the Independent Labour Party in 1929, and joined the Labour Party (1931), where he established a reputation as a brilliant, irreverent, and often tempestuous orator. As Minister of Health (1945–51), he introduced the National Health Service (1948). He became Minister of Labour in 1951, but resigned that year over the National Health charges proposed in the Budget. 'Bevanism', the left-wing movement to make the Labour Party more socialist and less 'reformist', dated from this period.

Bevan, Brian, also called **the Galloping Ghost** (1924–91) Australian rugby league player, born in Sydney. A wing-threequarter, he scored a record 796 tries in 18 seasons (1945–64). He played for Blackpool Borough and Warrington, and was one of the inaugural members of the Rugby League Hall of Fame in 1988.

bevel — *noun* **1** a sloping edge. **2** a tool which makes a sloping edge on a piece of wood or stone. — *verb* (**bevelled, bevelling**) **1** to give a bevel or slant to. **2** *intrans.* to slope at an angle. [from Old French *baif*, from *baer*, to gape]

bevelled *adj.* having a bevel or slant.

beverage *noun formal* a prepared drink, especially a hot or alcoholic drink. [from Old French *beuvrage*, from Latin *bibere*, to drink]

Beveridge, William Henry Beveridge, 1st Baron (1879–1963) British economist, administrator, and social reformer, born in Rangpur, Bengal. He entered the Board of Trade (1908) and became Director of Labour Exchanges (1909–16). He was Director of the London School of Economics (1919–37) and Master of University College, Oxford (1937–45). He is best known as the author of the *Report on Social Insurance and Allied Services* (The Beveridge Report, 1942), which helped to create the welfare state.

Beverley a female first name, sometimes given to a male, taken from the surname. [from Anglo-Saxon *beofor*, beaver + *leac*, stream]

Beverly Hills POP (1990) 32 000, a residential city in Los Angeles County, SW California, USA, surrounded by Los Angeles. It is the home of many film and television celebrities.

Bevin, Ernest (1881–1951) English Labour politician, born in Winsford, Somerset. Orphaned by the age of seven, and self-taught, he was influenced by trade unionism and became a paid official of the dockers' union. He gained a national reputation in 1920 when he won most of his union's claims against an eminent barrister, and earned himself the title of 'the dockers' KC'. He built up the National Transport and General Workers' Union, and became its General Secretary (1921–40). In 1940 he became an MP and Minister of Labour and National Service in Churchill's coalition government. In the Labour government he was Foreign Secretary (1945–51).

bevy *noun* (PL. **bevies**) **1** a group, originally of women or girls. **2** a flock of larks, quails, or swans.

bewail *verb literary* to express great sorrow or be very sad about.

beware *verb* **1** *intrans.* (**beware of something**) to be careful of it; to be on one's guard. **2** *trans. old use, literary* to be on one's guard against. [from Anglo-Saxon *bewarenian*, to be on one's guard]

Bewick, Thomas (1753–1828) English wood engraver, born in Ovingham, Northumberland, who revived the art of wood engraving as a printmaking technique. He became a partner of a Newcastle metal engraver, but began to specialize in wood. His many works include *A General History of Quadrupeds* (1790), *Chillingham Bull* (1789), and *A History of British Birds* (1797–1804).

Bewick's swan the smallest of the European swans, with a short neck, which it often holds straight, a small bill, and a concave forehead. Its faster wing-beats and musical goose-like honking help to distinguish it from other swans. [named after the English illustrator Thomas Bewick]

bewilder *verb* (**bewildered, bewildering**) to confuse or puzzle. [from obsolete *wilder*, to lose one's way]

bewildered *adj.* utterly confused.

bewildering *adj.* confusing; puzzling.

bewilderingly *adv.* so as to confuse or puzzle: *a bewilderingly large choice.*

bewilderment *noun* being confused or puzzled.

bewitch *verb* **1** to cast a spell on. **2** to charm. [from Anglo-Saxon *wiccian*, to use witchcraft]

bewitching *adj.* alluring; charming.

bewitchingly *adv.* in a bewitching way; alluringly.

Bexhill *or* **Bexhill-on-Sea** POP (1981) 35 000, a residential and resort town in Rother district, East Sussex, SE England. It lies on the English Channel, 7km/4mi W of Hastings. NOTABLE FEATURES De la Warr Pavilion (1936); 15c Herstmonceux Castle (9km/6mi NW), which has housed a royal observatory since 1949.

bey *noun Hist.* a title given to a Turkish governor in the Ottoman Empire. [from Turkish *bey*]

beyond — *prep.* **1** on the far side of: *beyond the hills.* **2** farther on than (something) in time or place. **3** out of the range, reach, power, understanding, possibility, etc of: *it's quite beyond me / beyond recognition.* **4** greater or better than in amount, size, or level. **5** other than; apart from: *unable to help beyond giving money.* — *adv.* farther away; to or on the far side of.
— **the back of beyond** a lonely isolated place.
the beyond the unknown, especially life after death.
beyond a joke more than one can reasonably tolerate.
[from Anglo-Saxon *begeondan*]

bezique *noun* a card game for two, three, or four players. It is played with two packs of cards from which all cards of a value below seven have been removed. [from French *bésigue*]
◇ Popular in the gaming-houses of France in the 19c and brought to England in the 1860s, the rules for the game were drawn up by the Portland club in 1887. The player of a winning trick is entitled to declare and score for any card combinations he may hold, including the combination of queen of spades with jack of diamonds, also called *bezique*.

b.f. *abbrev., in accounts, etc* brought forward.

B-film *or* **B-movie** *noun* a supporting film in a cinema programme, usually less ambitious than the main film.

BFPO *abbrev.* British Forces Post Office (written on mail sent to British forces abroad, with the number or name of the military unit).

BG *abbrev., as an international vehicle mark* Bulgaria.

BH *abbrev., as an international vehicle mark* Belize (formerly British Honduras).

Bhadgaon, also **Bhaktapur** POP (1981) 48 000, a city and religious centre in central Nepal, situated 14km/9mi E of Kathmandu at an altitude of 1 400m. The city, which is believed to have been founded in the 9c, is shaped like a conch-shell, with the urban area occupying c.10sq km/4sq mi. NOTABLE FEATURES Lion Gate; Golden Gate; Palace of 55 Windows; Bell of Barking Dogs; Batsala Temple; replica of Pashupatinath Temple. [from Nepali *Bhadgaon*, city of the devotees]

Bhagavadgita a poem that is part of the Hindu epic, the Mahabharata. It consists of an eve-of-battle dialogue between the warrior prince Arjuna and Lord Krishna (in the person of his charioteer), and teaches that there are many valid ways to salvation, but that not all are universally appropriate. Most Hindus regard the poem as the supreme expression of their religion. [Sanskrit, = song of the Lord]

bhaji *noun Cookery* an Indian appetizer of vegetables, chickpea flour, and spices, formed into a ball and deep-fried. [Hindi]

bhakti *noun Hinduism* loving devotion and surrender to God, recommended as the most effective path to salvation in most popular Hindu texts. [from Sanskrit *bhakti*, portion]

bhangra *noun* a style of music combining traditional Punjabi and Western pop rhythms. [Punjabi, the name of a traditional harvest dance]

Bhopal POP (1991) 1.1m, the capital of Madhya Pradesh, central India, situated 170km/106mi NE of Indore. The city was founded in 1723. It was the scene of a major industrial disaster in 1984, when poisonous isocyanate gas escaped from the Union Carbide factory, killing c.2 500 people and leaving 100 000 homeless.

BHP *abbrev.* (in Australia) the Broken Hill Proprietary Company Ltd, the largest company for much of the 20c, created in 1885 to mine silver, lead, and zinc at Broken Hill, New South Wales. After 1960 BHP expanded into oil and natural gas production, and iron, gold, and manganese mining, and in 1983 gained oil exploration rights in the China seas.

bhp *abbrev.* brake horsepower.

Bhutan, in Bhutan **Druk-yul**, official name **Kingdom of Bhutan** POP (1992e) 1.6m, a small state in the E Himalayas, divided into four regions. AREA 46 600sq km/18 000sq mi; 305km/190mi from E to W. It is bounded N by the Tibet region of China and S, E, and W by India. CAPITAL Thimphu. TIME ZONE GMT +5.5. The population includes Bhote (60%), Nepalese (25%), and indigenous or migrant tribes (15%); Lamaistic Buddhism and Buddhist-influenced Hinduism are the main religions. OFFICIAL LANGUAGE Dzongkha; Nepalese and English are also spoken. CURRENCY the ngultrum; Indian currency is also legal tender. PHYSICAL DESCRIPTION high peaks of the E Himalayas, reaching over 7 000m in the N; forested mountain ridges with fertile valleys descend to low foothills in the S; many rivers flow to meet the R Brahmaputra. CLIMATE permanent snowfields and glaciers in the mountains; subtropical forest in the S; torrential rain is common, with an average of 1 000mm in the central valleys and 5 000mm in the S. HISTORY British involvement dates from the treaty of 1774 with the East India Company; the S part of the country was annexed in 1865; Britain agreed not to interfere in internal affairs in 1910; Bhutan signed a similar treaty with India in 1949; in 1990 large numbers of ethnic Nepalese moved to Nepal and India following the introduction of strict cultural laws. GOVERNMENT governed by a Maharajah, from 1907, now addressed as King of Bhutan; an absolute monarchy was replaced by a form of democratic monarchy in 1969; the King is the head of government, advised by a nine-member Royal Advisory Council and a six-member Council of Ministers; a 151-member unicameral legislative National Assembly (*Tsongdu*) meets twice a year, comprising village elders, monastic representatives, and administrative officials, elected every three years. ECONOMY largely based on agriculture, mainly rice, wheat, maize, mountain barley, potatoes, vegetables, fruit (especially oranges); large area of plantation forest; hydroelectric power; local handicrafts; food processing; cement processing; plywood; postage stamps; tourism.

Bhutto, Benazir (1953–) Pakistani politician, daughter of Zulfikar Ali Bhutto, educated at Harvard and Oxford. She became head of the Pakistani People's Party and was exiled in London (1984–6). After her return to Pakistan (1986) she was the focus of unrest, and became Prime Minister in 1988. Removed from power by presidential decree (1990) and defeated in the general elections that year, she returned to power in the elections of 1993.

Bhutto, Zulfikar Ali (1928–79) Pakistani politician, born in Larkana, Sind. He joined the Pakistani Cabinet in 1958 as Minister of Commerce, and became Foreign Minister in 1963. Dropped from the Cabinet, he founded the Pakistan People's Party (PPP) in 1967. After the secession of E Pakistan (now Bangladesh) in 1971, he was President (1971–3) and then Prime Minister (1973–7). He introduced social and economic reforms, but opposition, especially from right-wing Islamic parties, led to the army under General Zia ul-Haq seizing control after the 1977 elections. Tried for corruption and murder, Bhutto was hanged in 1979. His elder daughter Benazir became head of the PPP.

Bi *symbol Chem.* bismuth.

bi- *prefix* forming words meaning: **1** having, involving, etc two: *bifocal.* **2** happening twice in every one, or once in every two: *bi-monthly.* **3** on or from both sides: *bilateral.* **4** *Chem.* indicating a salt which contains hydrogen: *bicarbonate.* [from Latin *bis*, twice]

Bialowieza Forest *or* **Belovezhskaya Pushcha** an area of primeval forest and nature reserves in Belorussia and E Poland, covering c.1 165sq km/450sq mi. It is a World Heritage site.

Białystok 1 POP (1992e) 272 000, the industrial capital of Białystok voivodship, NE Poland, situated on the Polasie Plain. The largest city in NE Poland, it developed as a textile centre in the 19c. It was devastated in World War II but was rebuilt after 1945. NOTABLE FEATURES Revolutionary Movement Museum; residence of the Branicki family; Church of St Roch (1924); Baroque town hall. **2** a voivodship in NE Poland with Białystok as its capital.

Bianca 1 the younger sister of Katharina in Shakespeare's *The Taming of the Shrew*, who eventually marries Lucentio. **2** The lover of Cassio in Shakespeare's *Othello.*

biannual *adj.* occurring twice a year.
◆ Often confused with *biennial*, which means 'occurring every two years'.

biannually *adv.* twice a year.

Biarritz POP (1990) 29 000, a fashionable resort town in Pyrénées-Atlantiques department, Aquitaine region, SW France. It lies on the Bay of Biscay and is noted for its mild climate and beaches.

bias — *noun* **1** a disposition to favour or disfavour one side against another in a dispute or rival claim. **2** a tendency or principal quality of a person's character. **3** a weight on or in an object, such as a bowl in the game of bowls, which makes it move in a particular direction. **4** *Statistics* a lack of balance in a result. **5** a line cut across the grain of a fabric. — *verb* (**biased, biasing** *or* **biassed, biassing**) **1** to influence or prejudice. **2** to give a bias to. [from French *biais*]

bias binding a long narrow strip of cloth sewn on or into the edges or corners of garments to make them strong.

biased *or* **biassed** *adj.* predisposed to favour one side rather than another.

biathlon *noun* an outdoor sporting event in which competitors cross a 20km course on skis, stopping at intervals to shoot at targets with rifles. [from BI- + Greek *athlon*, contest]

bib *noun* **1** a piece of cloth or plastic fastened under a child's chin to protect its clothes while eating. **2** the top part of an apron or overalls, covering the chest.

Bible *noun* **1** the sacred writings of the Christian Church, consisting of the Old and New Testaments. **2** (**bible**) a copy of these. **3** (**bible**) an authoritative and comprehensive book on a subject, regarded as definitive. [from Latin *biblia*, from Greek *biblos*, papyrus]
◊ The Christian Scriptures are divided between two *testaments*: the Old Testament (which corresponds roughly to the canon of Jewish Scriptures), and the New Testament. The Old Testament, or Hebrew Bible, is a collection of writings originally composed in Hebrew, except for parts of Daniel and Ezra, which are in Aramaic. These writings depict Israelite religion from its beginnings to about the 2c BC. The New Testament, which was written in Greek, is so-called because it constitutes a new 'testament' or 'covenant' in the history of God's dealings with his people; it focuses on the ministry of Jesus and the early development of the apostolic churches. The process of determining precisely which writings were to be accepted in the Jewish or Christian Scriptures is known as the formation of the *canon* of Scripture.
It was only in c.100 AD that the final selection of authorized Jewish Scriptures was completed, following a decision taken by the council at Jabneh. The early Christians largely accepted the Jewish Scriptures, but frequently had access to the larger collection of writings in the Septuagint and some other translations of the Hebrew Bible.
Debates about the precise limits of the Old Testament continued into the Reformation period, and at the Council of Trent (1546), the Catholics accepted as *deuterocanonical* several works which Protestants labelled as *Apocrypha* and considered of secondary value.
The first evidence for a canonical list which completely matches that widely accepted for the New Testament today was the 39th Easter letter of Athanasius (AD 367), which designates 27 books of the New Testament alongside the canon of the Old Testament.

Bible belt those areas of the Southern USA where the population is predominantly Christian fundamentalist.

Bible Society an agency for the translation and dissemination of the Bible. The first was the Van Canstein Bible Society (1710) in Germany. The modern movement proper began with the British and Foreign Bible Society, formed (1804) in London. The United Bible Society now provides a worldwide network of mainly protestant and evangelical autonomous societies, responsible for the translation of the Bible in over 1500 languages, and for its distribution at subsidized prices.

biblical *or* **Biblical** *adj.* relating to or in accordance with the Bible.

bibliographer *noun* a person who compiles a bibliography.

bibliographic *or* **bibliographical** *adj.* relating to or in the nature of bibliography.

bibliography *noun* (PL. **bibliographies**) **1** a list of books by one author or on one subject. **2** a list of books used as the sources of a book and usually given in a list at the back of it. [from Greek *biblion*, book + *graphein*, to write]

bibliophile *noun* an admirer or collector of books. [from Greek *biblion*, book + *philos*, friend]

Bibliothèque Nationale the national library of France, located in Paris. It evolved from the libraries of the French monarchs, and was designated a national depository in 1537. Its holdings include over 7 million volumes and 155 000 manuscripts.

Books of the Bible

Old Testament

Books of the Law (known as the Pentateuch)

Genesis	Numbers
Exodus	Deuteronomy
Leviticus	

Historical Books

Joshua	2 Kings
Judges	1 Chronicles
Ruth	2 Chronicles
1 Samuel	Ezra
2 Samuel	Nehemiah
1 Kings	Esther

Books of Poetry and Wisdom

Job	Ecclesiastes
Psalms	Song of Solomon
Proverbs	

Books of the Prophets

Isaiah	Jonah
Jeremiah	Micah
Lamentations	Nahum
Ezekiel	Habakkuk
Daniel	Zephaniah
Hosea	Haggai
Joel	Zechariah
Amos	Malachi
Obadiah	

New Testament

The Gospels and Acts

Matthew	John
Mark	Acts of the Apostles
Luke	

The Epistles or Letters

Romans	Titus
1 Corinthians	Philemon
2 Corinthians	Hebrews
Galatians	James
Ephesians	1 Peter
Philippians	2 Peter
Colossians	1 John
1 Thessalonians	2 John
2 Thessalonians	3 John
1 Timothy	Jude
2 Timothy	

Book of Revelation, or Apocalypse of St John

Apocrypha

1 Esdras	Prayer of Azariah
2 Esdras	Song of the Three
Tobit	Young Men
Judith	History of Susanna
Additions to Esther	Bel and the Dragon
Wisdom of Solomon	Prayer of the Manasseh
Ecclesiasticus	1 Maccabees
Baruch	2 Maccabees
Epistle of Jeremiah	

The Roman Catholic Church includes Tobit, Judith, all of Esther, Maccabees 1 and 2, Wisdom of Solomon, Ecclesiasticus and Baruch in its canon.

Bhutan

bibulous *adj. humorous* liking alcohol too much, or drinking too much of it. [from Latin *bibulus*, drinking freely]

bicameral *adj., said of a legislative body* made up of two parts, such as the House of Commons and the House of Lords in the British parliament. [from BI- + Latin *camera*, a chamber]

bicarb short form of BICARBONATE OF SODA.

bicarbonate *noun Chem.* a common name for hydrogencarbonate.

bicarbonate of soda *colloq.* sodium bicarbonate, a white powder used in baking, as a cure for indigestion, and in some types of fire extinguishers. See also BAKING SODA.

BICC *abbrev.* British Insulated Callender's Cables.

bicentenary — *noun* (PL. **bicentenaries**) a two-hundredth anniversary of an event, especially as a cause for celebration. — *adj.* of or concerning a bicentenary.

bicentennial *noun North Amer., esp. US* a bicentenary.

biceps *noun* (PL. **biceps**) a muscle with two heads or attachments, such as the muscle in the arm which bends the elbow. [from BI- + Latin *caput*, head]

Bichat, Marie François Xavier (1771–1802) French physician, born in Thoirette, Jura. From 1797 he taught medicine, from 1801 working at the Hôtel-Dieu, Paris's huge hospital for the poor. He was the first to simplify anatomy and physiology by reducing the complex structures of the organs to their simple or elementary tissues.

bicker *verb intrans.* (**bickered**, **bickering**) *colloq.* to argue or quarrel, especially about trivial matters. [from Middle English **biker**]

bickering *noun* tedious and usually trivial quarrelling.

biconcave *noun Physics* denoting a structure, especially a lens, that is concave on both surfaces.

biconvex *noun Physics* denoting a structure, especially a lens, that is convex on both surfaces.

bicuspid — *adj.* having two cusps or points. — *noun* an adult tooth having two points.

bicycle — *noun* a vehicle consisting of a metal frame with two wheels, one behind the other, and a saddle. It is driven by turning pedals with the feet and steered by handlebars attached to the front wheel. — *verb intrans.* to ride a bicycle. [from BI- + Greek *kyklos*, circle, wheel]
◇ It is generally held that the first pedal cycle was invented by a Scotsman, Kirkpatrick Macmillan, and first ridden by him in 1840. Early versions were propelled by pedals driving the front wheel through a series of cranks. The chain-driven 'safety' bicycle with pneumatic tyres appeared in 1888; it was a basic design which has changed little up to the present day.

bicycle chain a metal chain connecting the pedals to the back wheel of a bicycle, making it move when the pedals are turned.

bicycle clip a metal clip worn around the bottoms of a cyclist's trousers, keeping them close to the leg and free of the chain.

bicycle pump a long thin pump for inflating bicycle tyres.

Bicycle Thieves (Ladri Di Biciclette) an Italian film directed by Vittorio De Sica (1948). It is a story in the neorealist genre about ordinary folk, told through the actions of a man (played by Lamberto Maggiorani) following the theft of his bicycle.

bicyclist *noun formal* a rider of a bicycle; a cyclist.

bid¹ — *verb* (**bidding**; PAST TENSE AND PAST PARTICIPLE **bid**) **1** *trans., intrans.* to offer (an amount of money) when trying to buy something, especially at an auction. **2** *intrans., trans. Cards* to state in advance (the number of tricks one will try to win). **3** *intrans.* to state a price one will charge for work to be done. — *noun* **1** an offer of a price, especially at an auction. **2** *Cards* a statement of how many tricks one hopes to win. **3** an attempt to obtain something: *make a bid for freedom.*
— **bid fair** *formal* to seem likely.
[from Anglo-Saxon *beodan*, to command, summon]

bid² *verb* (**bidding**; PAST TENSE **bade**; PAST PARTICIPLE **bidden**) *formal* **1** to command. **2** to invite: *bid her to start.* **3** to express a wish, greeting, etc: *bid him welcome.* [from Anglo-Saxon *biddan*, to beg, pray]

Bidault, Georges (1899–1982) French politician, born in Paris. A professor of history, he served in both World Wars and was a member of the French resistance. He became leader of the Movement Républicaine Populaire, and apart from his periods as Prime Minister (1946, 1949–50), he was Deputy Prime Minister (1950, 1951), and Foreign Minister (1944, 1947, 1953–54). After 1958 he opposed de Gaulle over the Algerian War, was charged with plotting against the security of the state, and went into exile (1962–8).

biddable *adj.* compliant; obedient.

bidder *noun* a person who bids, especially at an auction.

bidding *noun* **1** a command, request, or invitation. **2** the offers at an auction. **3** *Cards* the act of making bids.
— **be at** *or* **do someone's bidding** to be ready to carry out someone's orders or commands.

bide *verb intrans.* (PAST TENSE **bided**, **bode**; PAST PARTICIPLE **bided**) *old use* to wait or stay.
— **bide one's time** to wait patiently for a good opportunity.
[from Anglo-Saxon *bidan*]

bidet *noun* a small low basin with taps, on which one sits to wash the genital area. [from French *bidet*, pony]

Biedermeierstil a satirical name for the simple, plain ('bourgeois philistine') style of furniture and decoration popular in Austria and Germany (1815–48). *Biedermeier* painting is often characterized by a mild sentimentalism and homely naturalism. The term is sometimes extended to architecture.

Biennale an international art exhibition held in Venice regularly since 1895, and imitated at Paris, Tokyo, and elsewhere. It was originally conservative, but since 1948 has been a major showcase for the avant garde.

biennial — *adj.* **1** occurring once in every two years. **2** lasting two years. — *noun Bot.* a plant that takes two years to complete its life cycle, eg carrot. Biennials germinate and accumulate food reserves in the first year, and flower, produce seed, and die during the second year. See also ANNUAL, PERENNIAL. [from BI- + Latin *annus*, year]
◆ Often confused with *biannual*, which means 'occurring twice a year'.

biennially *adv.* every two years.

bier *noun* a movable stand on which a coffin rests or is transported. [from Anglo-Saxon *bær*]

Bierce, Ambrose (Gwinett) (1842–?1914) US journalist and writer, born in Meigs Co, Ohio. He served in the Civil War (1861–5) before becoming a journalist in San Francisco, England, and Washington. His works include collections of sardonically humorous tales on the theme of death, such as *Tales of Soldiers and Civilians* (1891, retitled *In the Midst of Life* 1892, revised 1898). He disappeared in Mexico in 1913 during the revolution of Pancho Villa.

biff — *verb slang* to hit very hard. — *noun* a blow.

Biffen, Sir Rowland Harry (1874–1949) English botanist and geneticist, born in Cheltenham. He travelled in Brazil and the West Indies studying natural sources for rubber, and in 1908 became the first Professor of Agricultural Botany at Cambridge. Using Mendelian genetic principles, he pioneered the breeding of hybrid rust-resistant strains of wheat. He wrote *The Auricula*, published posthumously in 1951.

bifocal *adj., said of a lens* having two different parts, allowing both near and distant vision.

bifocals *pl. noun* a pair of glasses with bifocal lenses, which allow the wearer to look at distant objects through the upper part of the lens, and to read through the lower part.

bifurcate *verb intrans. formal, said of roads, etc* to divide into two parts; to fork. [from Latin *bifurcus*, two-forked]

bifurcated *adj.* divided into two parts.

bifurcation *noun* division into two parts or branches.

big — *adj.* (**bigger**, **biggest**) **1** large or largest in size, weight, or number: *the big toe.* **2** significant or important to someone: *his big day.* **3** important, powerful, successful: *the big four.* **4** older or adult: *my big sister.* **5** *often ironic* generous: *that was big of him.* **6** boastful; extravagant; ambitious: *big ideas.* **7** *old use* in an advanced stage of pregnancy: *big with child.* — *adv. colloq.* boastfully; extravagantly: *talk big / think big.*
— **big deal!** *slang* an expression of indifference.
make it big *colloq.* to become successful and famous.
too big for one's boots *colloq.* having an inflated view of one's importance; conceited.
[from Middle English, of uncertain origin]

bigamist *noun* a person who commits bigamy.

bigamous *adj.* married to two wives or husbands at the same time.

bigamously *adv.* with two wives or husbands.

bigamy *noun* (PL. **bigamies**) the crime of being married to two wives or husbands at the same time. [from BI- + Greek *gamos*, marriage]

Big Bang **1** a hypothetical model of the origin of the universe, now generally accepted, which postulates that all matter and energy were once concentrated into an unimaginably dense state, which underwent a gigantic explosion (the Big Bang) between 13 and 20 billion years ago. Physicists have calculated that in just three minutes these particles were converted into all the hydrogen atoms that now represent 90% of the universe. As the hydrogen cloud expanded, it began to break up into separate clouds, which eventually became galaxies of stars like our own Milky Way galaxy. The universe is still expanding, and may do so indefinitely, although some astronomers predict that in about 70 billion years time the galaxies will start to move closer together again. **2** *Brit. colloq.* the change, in 1986, of the rules controlling the British Stock Exchange.

Big Ben originally the nickname of the bell in the clock tower of the Houses of Parliament, London, and now by association the clock and its tower. The bell, 2.7m in diameter and weighing 13 tonnes, was cast in 1858 and named after Sir Benjamin Hall (1802–67), who was commissioner of works at the time of its installation in 1859.

Big Boy US locomotives, the biggest and most powerful to be driven by steam. Their purpose was to transport heavy freight in the USA during World War II. A typical Big Boy weighed 534 tonnes and measured 40m. Their existence (1941–59) was cut short by the emergence of diesel engine trains.

Big Brother **1** the remote and tyrannical leader of Eurasia in George Orwell's novel *Nineteen Eighty-Four* (1949). **2** any figure who is seen as attempting to exercise a repressive surveillance and authority.

big business 1 powerful commercial and industrial organizations, especially considered as a group. **2** an activity that is commercially attractive or ambitious: *modern sport is big business*.

big cat a large member of the cat family, such as the lion or tiger.

big dipper 1 a rollercoaster. **2** (**Big Dipper**) a group of seven bright stars in the Great Bear constellation; the Plough.

big end *Brit.* the larger end of the main connecting rod in an internal-combustion engine.

Bigfoot, also called **Sasquatch** in the mountaineering folklore of N America, a creature equivalent to the abominable snowman or yeti, said to be 2–3m tall. Its footprints are reported to be 43cm long.

big game large animals, such as lions, tigers, etc that are hunted for sport.

biggish *adj.* fairly big.

Biggles, in full **Major James Bigglesworth** the heroic, crime-busting British airman in *The Camels are Coming* and other books by Capt W E Johns.

Biggs, Ronald (1929–) English thief and member of the gang who perpetrated the Great Train Robbery (8 Aug 1963), when £2.5m was taken from a night mail train. Biggs was convicted and sentenced to 25 years for conspiracy and 30 years (to run concurrently) for armed robbery, but he escaped from Wandsworth Prison on 8 Jul 1965, fled to Australia, and settled in Brazil.

big guns *colloq.* the most important or powerful people in an organization.

bighead *noun colloq., derog.* a conceited or arrogant person.

big-headed *adj.* conceited; arrogant.

big-headedness *noun* conceit; arrogance.

big-hearted *adj.* thoughtful and generous.

bighorn *noun* either of two species of a wild sheep that inhabit mountains, especially cliffs: the American bighorn sheep from N America, and the Siberan bighorn or snow sheep from NE Siberia. In both species the male has large curling horns.

bight *noun* **1** a stretch of gently curving coastline. **2** a loose curve or loop in a length of rope. [from Anglo-Saxon *byht*]

big mouth *colloq.* a boastful talkative person.

bigot *noun* a person who is persistently prejudiced, especially about religion and politics, and refuses to tolerate the opinions of others. [from Old French *bigot*]

bigoted *adj.* prejudiced and intolerant.

bigotry *noun* persistent prejudice and intolerance.

Big Sleep, The a US film directed by Howard Hawks (1946). Based on a novel by Raymond Chandler, it is a complex thriller starring Humphrey Bogart as Chicago detective Philip Marlowe.

big time *colloq.* success in an activity or profession, especially in show business: *hit the big time*.

big top a large round tent in which a circus gives its performances.

bigwig *noun colloq.* an important person.

Bihar *or* **Behar** POP (1991) 86.4m, a state in E India, bounded N by Nepal and crossed by the R Ganges. AREA 173 876sq km/67 116sq mi. The Rajmahal Hills lie to the S of the river. CAPITAL Patna. GOVERNMENT governed by a 325-member Legislative Assembly. ECONOMY major mineral deposits, including coal, copper, mica; rice, jute, sugar cane, oilseed, wheat, maize; iron and steel; machine tools; fertilizers; electrical engineering; paper milling; cement.

Bijagos Islands, Portuguese **Arquipélago dos Bijagós** POP (1979) 26 000, an archipelago off the coast of Guinea-Bissau. The group includes numerous islets and 15 larger islands, including Orango, Formosa, Caravela, Roxa, and Bolama.

bijou *— noun* a small delicate jewel or object. *— adj.* small and elegant. [from French *bijou*]

bike *noun colloq.* a bicycle or motorcycle.

biker *noun colloq.* a person who rides a motorcycle.

bikeway *noun chiefly North Amer.* a lane, road, etc, specially designed or set aside for the use of pedal cycles.

biking *noun* the sport or pastime of cycling or riding a motorcycle.

Bikini an atoll in the Marshall Is, W Pacific Ocean. It lies 3 200km/2 000mi SW of Hawaii. HISTORY the site of 23 US nuclear tests from 1946 to 1958; the first H-bomb was tested here; the inhabitants were evacuated in 1946; many returned in 1972, but were evacuated again when it was discovered that they had ingested the largest dose of plutonium ever monitored in any population.

bikini *noun* a two-piece swimming costume for women. [from BIKINI, with reference to the costume's supposed 'explosive' effect]

Biko, Stephen (1946–77) South African black activist, born in King William's Town, the founder and leader of the Black Consciousness Movement. While studying medicine at Natal University he was the first President of the all-black South African Students Organization (1969), and Honorary President of the Black People's Convention (1972). In 1973 a banning order severely restricted his movements and freedom of speech and association, and he was detained four times before he died in police custody, allegedly as a result of beatings received. He was the subject of the successful film *Cry Freedom* (1987), directed by Richard Attenborough.

bilabial *— adj., said of a consonant* made with both lips touching, or almost touching, each other, as with the letter *b*. *— noun* a bilabial consonant. [from BI- + Latin *labium*, lip]

bilateral *adj.* **1** of or on two sides. **2** affecting, or signed or agreed by, two countries, groups, etc: *a bilateral agreement*. [from BI- + Latin *latus*, side]

bilateralism *noun* equality, especially in the value of trade between two countries.

bilaterally *adv.* **1** on two sides. **2** concerning two countries or parties.

bilateral symmetry *Biol.* the condition in which an organism is divisible into similar halves by one plane only.

Bilbao POP (1991) 369 000, the capital of Biscay province and a major seaport, situated in the Basque Provinces, N Spain. It lies on the R Nervión, 395km/245mi N of Madrid. Founded in 1300, it is now the commercial centre of the region. NOTABLE FEATURES cathedral (14c); Art Museum; Churches of St Anton and St Nicholas de Bari.

bilberry *noun* (PL. **bilberries**) **1** a small bushy plant or shrub with dark blue edible berries. **2** a berry from this plant.

Bildungsroman *noun* a novel which deals with the formative stages of the life of the hero or heroine. [German, = education novel]

◇ Early examples include Rousseau's *Emile* (1762). The genre was popularized in Germany by Goethe's *Wilhelm Meisters Lehrjahre* ('Wilhelm Meister's Apprenticeship', 1796). Examples in English include Dickens's *David Copperfield* (1850), Samuel Butler's *The Way of All Flesh* (1903), and James Joyce's *A Portrait of the Artist as a Young Man* (1914–15).

bile *noun* **1** a yellowish or greenish thick bitter liquid produced by the liver to help digest fats in food. **2** *literary* anger or bad temper (see also BILIOUS). [from Latin *bilis*]

bilge *noun* **1** the broadest part of a ship's bottom. **2** (*also* **bilge-water**) the dirty water that collects in a ship's bilge. **3** *colloq.* rubbish or nonsense. [probably a variant of BULGE]

bilingual *adj.* **1** written or spoken in two languages. **2** speaking two languages very well. [from BI- + Latin *lingua*, tongue]

bilingualism *noun* the ability to speak two languages fluently.

bilinguist *noun* a person who speaks two languages.

bilious *adj.* **1** sick. **2** *derog.*, *said of a colour* unpleasant, nauseous. **3** peevish; bad-tempered. See BILE [from Latin *biliosus*, from *bilis*, bile]

biliously *adv.* with a bilious or bad-tempered manner.

bilirubin *noun Biochem.* a yellowish-orange pigment that is found in the bile, and is formed from another bile pigment, biliverdin. Excess bilirubin in the blood causes jaundice (yellowing of the skin and whites of the eyes). [from Latin *bilis* bile, *ruber* red]

biliverdin *noun Biochem.* a green pigment that is found in the bile, and is formed as a result of the breakdown of the pigment haem during the disintegration of old red blood cells. Biliverdin is converted to bilirubin. [from Latin *bilis* bile, *verd* as in VERDURE]

bilk *verb* **1** to avoid paying (someone) money one owes. **2** (**bilk someone out of something**) to cheat or trick someone. [perhaps from *balk*, a term in cribbage]

bill¹ *— noun* **1** a printed or written statement of the amount of money owed for goods or services received. **2** a written plan for a proposed law. **3** *North Amer., esp. US* a banknote. **4** an advertising poster. **5** a list of items, events, performers, etc. *— verb* **1** to send a bill to (someone), requesting payment for goods, etc. **2** to advertise or announce (a person or event) in a poster, etc. *— fit or fill the bill colloq.* to be suitable, or what is required. [from Latin *bulla*, seal, document bearing a seal]

bill² *noun* **1** a bird's beak. **2** a long thin piece of land that extends into the sea. *— bill and coo colloq.* to kiss and whisper affectionately. [from Anglo-Saxon *bile*]

bill³ *noun Hist.* a weapon with a long handle and a hook-shaped blade. [from Anglo-Saxon *bil*]

billabong *noun Austral.* **1** a pool of water left when most of a river or stream has become dry. **2** a branch of a river which comes to an end without flowing into a sea, lake, or other river. [from Australian Aboriginal *billa*, river + *bung*, dead]

billboard *noun* a large board on which advertising posters are displayed.

billet¹ *— noun* **1** a formal order to provide lodgings for a soldier. **2** a house, often a private home, where soldiers are given food and lodging temporarily. *— verb* (**billeted**, **billeting**) to give lodging to (soldiers, etc). [from Old French *billette*]

billet² *noun* **1** a small log of wood. **2** a bar of metal. [from Old French *billette*]

billet-doux *noun* (PL. **billets-doux**) *old use* a love-letter. [from French *billet*, letter + *doux*, sweet]

billiards *sing. noun* an indoor table game played on a cloth-covered table with pockets at the sides and corners. Coloured balls must be struck into the pockets with the tips of long thin sticks (cues). See also SNOOKER, POOL. [from French *billard*, from *bille*, narrow stick]

◇ The earliest record of the game was in France in 1429. The most popular form is played on a standard English table c.12 ft x 6ft (3.66m x 1.83m), with one red and two white balls. Scoring is achieved by potting balls and making cannons.

billing *noun* the importance of a performer in a play or concert, especially as shown by the position of the name on the poster advertising the performance: *top billing*.

Billingsgate Market a market in London, dating from the 9c, which was situated on the bank of the River Thames at the N end of London Bridge. From the 16c, it was primarily a fish-market. It was closed in 1982, and moved to the peninsular Isle of Dogs near the Thames.

billion — *noun* (PL. **billions**, after a number **billion**) **1** a thousand million; in the UK formerly also a million million. **2** *colloq.* a billion pounds or dollars. **3** (*often* **billions**) *colloq.* a great number: *billions of books*. — *adj.* a thousand million in number. [from BI- + MILLION]

billionaire *noun* a person owning money and property worth a billion pounds, dollars, etc.

billionairess *noun* a female billionaire.

billionth *noun, adj.* a thousand millionth.

bill of exchange a written order to a person to pay a specified sum of money to some other person on a certain date or when payment is asked for.

bill of fare a menu.

bill of lading a receipt for goods transported by ship.

Bill of Rights a written declaration of the rights of the citizens of a country.

bill of sale in English law, a formal legal paper stating that something has been sold by one person to another.

billow — *noun* **1** a large wave. **2** an upward-moving mass of smoke, mist, etc. — *verb intrans.* **1** to move in large waves or clouds. **2** (**billow out**) to swell or bulge like a sail in the wind. [from Norse *bylgja*]

billowing *or* **billowy** *noun* moving in large waves; swelling.

billowy *adj.* same as BILLOWING.

billposter *or* **billsticker** *noun* a person who puts up advertising posters.

Billroth, (Christian Albert) Theodor (1821–94) Austrian surgeon, born in Bergen auf Rügen, Prussia. Professor of Surgery at Zürich (1860–7) and Vienna (1867–94), he pioneered modern abdominal surgery, performing the first successful excision of the larynx (1874) and the first removal of part of the stomach and intestine (1881). He was also the first European surgeon to adopt antisepsis.

billy *or* **billycan** *noun* (PL. **billies**) *Brit., Austral.* a metal container used for cooking in or for eating and drinking from, especially when camping.

Billy Budd **1** a novella by Herman Melville (1924). It focuses on the tragic life of a handsome, innocent sailor, who is hanged for trying to defend his name. **2** an opera by Benjamin Britten (1951) with text by E M Forster and Eric Crozier, based on Melville's story. Set on board HMS *Indomitable* and narrated as memory by the ship's guilt-ridden elderly Capt Vere, it tells the story of a sailor whose affability angered the sadistic master-at-arms Claggart, leading to a false accusation of mutiny, Claggart's accidental death, and the hanging of Billy Budd, although Vere believed he was innocent and could have saved him.

billy goat *noun* a male goat. See also NANNY GOAT. [from the name *Billy*]

billy-o *or* **billy-oh**
— **like billy-o** *or* **-oh** *Brit. old slang use* quickly, powerfully, or forcefully: *raining like billy-oh.*

Billy the Kid a ballet by Aaron Copland (1938), based on the story of the Wild West bandit William Bonney.

Biloxi POP (1990) 197 000, a town in Harrison County, SE Mississippi, USA. It lies on the Gulf of Mexico at the mouth of the Biloxi R. HISTORY first settled in 1699; the modern town was founded in 1719; it was the first permanent white settlement in the Mississippi Valley. NOTABLE FEATURE Keesler Air Force Base. [named after a Native American tribe]

BIM *abbrev.* British Institute of Management.

bimbo *noun* (PL. **bimbos**) *slang* a young woman who is physically attractive but empty-headed. [from Italian *bimbo*, baby, small child]

bimetallic *adj.* made of or using two metals.

bimetallic strip *Physics* a strip consisting of two lengths of different metals welded or riveted together face to face, which expand to different extents on heating. One can become longer than the other only if the whole takes up a curved shape, with the metal which expands most on the outer face. Bimetallic strips are used in thermostats.

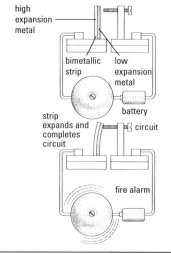

high expansion metal

bimetallic strip

low expansion metal

battery

strip expands and completes circuit

circuit

fire alarm

bimetallic strip

bimonthly — *adj.* **1** occurring once every two months. **2** occurring twice a month. — *adv.* **1** every two months. **2** twice a month.

bin *noun* **1** a large container for storing or depositing rubbish. **2** a container for storing some kinds of food: *a bread bin.* **3** a large industrial container for storing goods in large quantities. **4** a stand or case with sections in, for storing bottles of wine. [from Anglo-Saxon *binn*]

binary — *adj.* **1** consisting of two. **2** relating to the binary system. — *noun* (PL. **binaries**) a thing made up of two parts. [from Latin *binarius*]

binary code *Comput.* a code of numbers that involves only two digits, 0 and 1. See also BINARY SYSTEM.

binary fission *Biol.* the division of an organism or cell into two parts.

binary star *Astron.* a system of two stars that share and orbit around the same centre of mass, and are held together by gravitational attraction.

binary system *Maths.* a number system to the base 2 that uses only the binary digits (*bits*) 0 and 1. It forms the basis of the internal coding of information in electronics and computers, where 1 and 0 represent high and low voltages in circuits, or on and off states of switches.

binary weapon a type of chemical weapon, usually an artillery shell, packed with two chemicals which are individually harmless but which

combine on detonation to form a deadly toxic agent.

bind — *verb* (PAST TENSE AND PAST PARTICIPLE **bound**) **1** to tie or fasten tightly. **2** (**bind something up**) to tie or pass strips of cloth, bandage, etc around it. **3** to control or prevent from moving. See also BOUND¹. **4** to make (someone) promise (to do something). **5** to require or oblige (to do something): *legally bound to reply.* **6** to fasten together and put a cover on (the separate pages of a book). **7** to put a strip of cloth on the edge of (something) to strengthen it. **8** to cause dry ingredients to stick together. **9** *intrans.* to stick together. — *noun colloq.* a difficult or boring situation.
— **bind someone over** to make them legally obliged to do a particular thing, eg to keep the peace and not cause a disturbance. [from Anglo-Saxon *bindan*]

binder *noun* **1** a person who binds books. **2** a hard book-like cover in which loose pieces of paper can be kept in order. **3** a machine used for harvesting grain that binds it as it cuts it.

bindery *noun* (PL. **binderies**) a place where books are bound.

binding — *noun* **1** the part of a book cover on to which the pages are stuck. **2** cloth, etc used to bind something. — *adj.* formally or legally obliging (someone) to do (something).

bindweed *noun* a type of wild plant that attaches itself to other plants. See also CONVOLVULUS.

Binet, Alfred (1857–1911) French psychologist, born in Nice. Initially trained as a lawyer, he developed wide interests in psychology and founded the first journal French journal devoted to the subject, *L'Année Psychologique* (1894). He is principally remembered for the Binet-Simon scale (with colleague Theodore Simon) for measuring the intelligence of schoolchildren (1905) – this was the precursor of many of today's mental tests.

Binford, Lewis (Roberts) (1930–) US archaeologist, the pioneer of the anthropologically-oriented school of archaeology which has influenced the discipline since the late 1960s. He has directed attention to the systemic nature of human culture, and to the complex interaction between the technological, social, and ideological subsystems of all societies.

Bing, Sir Rudolf (1902–) British opera administrator, born in Vienna. He worked in Berlin and Darmstadt (1928–33) before managing the opera at Glyndebourne (1935–49). He took British nationality (1946), was co-founder and director (1947–9) of the Edinburgh Festival, and general manager of the Metropolitan Opera, New York.

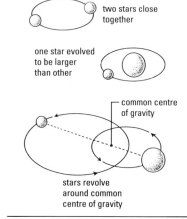

two stars close together

one star evolved to be larger than other

common centre of gravity

stars revolve around common centre of gravity

binary star

binge — *noun colloq.* a bout of extravagant eating and drinking. — *verb intrans.* to indulge in a binge. [perhaps originally a dialect word meaning 'soak']

bingo — *noun* a game of chance in which each player has a card with a set of numbers on it. Numbers are called out at random, and the winner is the first player with a card on which all the numbers have been called out. — *interj.* **1** the word shouted by the winner of a game of bingo. **2** an expression of success or sudden pleasure.
◇ The game became universally known as bingo in the 1960s; before that time it was also called *lotto* and *housey-housey*. Its increased popularity led to the establishment of bingo halls in many towns and cities in the UK, in which large numbers of players could be accommodated.

bin-liner *noun* a disposable plastic bag used as a lining in a rubbish bin.

binnacle *noun* a case for a ship's compass. [earlier *bittacle*, from Latin *habitaculum*, habitation]

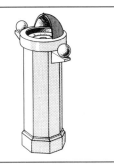

binnacle

binocular *adj.* (pronounced *by-*) with or suitable for two eyes.

binoculars *pl. noun* an optical instrument designed for viewing distant objects, and consisting of two small telescopes arranged side by side so that the observer is able to use both eyes at once. Focusing is achieved by varying the distance between the eyepiece and the object lens. [from Latin *bini*, two by two + *oculus*, eye]

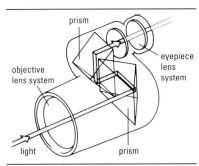

binoculars

binocular vision the ability of animals with forward-facing eyes to focus both eyes on an object at the same time. A slightly different view of the same object is presented to the retina of each eye, and the two images are co-ordinated by the brain so that the observer perceives a single three-dimensional image.

binomial — *noun Maths.* an algebraic expression that contains two variables (terms consisting of numbers or letters), eg $6x-3y$. — *adj.* containing two variables. [from BI- + Latin *nomen*, name]

binomial nomenclature *Biol.* the system (introduced by Linnaeus) of denoting a plant or animal by two Latin words, the first (with an initial capital letter) being the name of the genus, and the second (with an initial small letter) that

of the species. Both names are conventionally written in italics.

binomial theorem a formula for finding any power of a binomial without lengthy multiplication, eg $(a + b)^2 = (a' + 2ab + b')$.

Binyon, (Robert) Laurence (1869–1943) English poet and art critic, born in Lancaster, Lancashire. He worked in the British Museum (1913–33), and was Professor of Poetry at Harvard (1933–4). His poetic works include *Lyric Poems* (1894), *Odes* (1901), and *Collected Poems* (1931), and extracts from his poem 'For the Fallen' (also set to music by Elgar) adorn war memorials throughout the British commonwealth. He also wrote plays, several works of art criticism, and translated Dante's *Divine Comedy* into terza rima.

bio- *combining form* forming words denoting life or living things: *biology*. [from Greek *bios*, life]

bioassay *noun Biol.* the assessment of the concentration of a chemical substance by testing its effect on a living organism, eg its effect on plant or bacterial growth.

biochemical *adj.* relating to biochemistry.

biochemist *noun* a person who studies or practises biochemistry.

biochemistry *noun* the branch of chemistry concerned with the chemical reactions that take place in living cells.

biocontrol *noun* biological control.

biodegradable *adj.* denoting a substance that is capable of being broken down by living organisms (mainly bacteria and fungi), so that its constituents are released and can then be recycled. Many synthetic materials, eg most plastics, are non-biodegradable and do not decay naturally, presenting problems of disposal.

biodegradation *noun Biol.* the breakdown of substances by living organisms, especially bacteria and fungi.

biodiversity *noun Biol.* a measure of the number of different species of living organism that are present within a given area. It also takes account of the number of representatives of each species that are present, and the variety of habitats that exist within that area. [a shortening of *biological diversity*]
◇ The highest levels of biodiversity are found in undisturbed habitats, but in many parts of the world the Earth's biodiversity has been drastically reduced by pollution and destruction of habitats (especially rainforests), perhaps to a greater extent in this century than at any other time in the history of the planet. An international convention for the preservation of biodiversity was signed in 1992 by representatives from over 100 countries at the Earth Summit in Rio de Janeiro.

bioenergetics *sing. noun Biol.* the scientific study of the use of energy by living organisms, including its conversion from one form to another.

bioengineering *noun Medicine* the application of engineering methods and technology to biology and medicine, especially with regard to the design and manufacture of artificial limbs, hip joints, heart pacemakers, and other prostheses to replace damaged, diseased, or missing body parts.

biofeedback *noun Psychol.* the technique of learning to control certain body functions by monitoring and displaying them to the patient using electronic instruments, so that the patient becomes aware of them and can learn to control the underlying process. Subjects can learn to control heart rate, blood pressure, muscle activity, and electrical activity in the brain.

biogeography *noun. Biol.* the scientific study of the distributions of plants and animals.

biographer *noun* a writer of biography or of a particular biography: *one of Shaw's biographers.*

biographical *or* **biographic** *adj.* relating to or in the nature of biography.

biographically *adv.* in the nature of or as regards biography.

biography *noun* (PL. **biographies**) **1** an account a person's life, usually written by someone else and published or intended for publication. **2** the art of writing biographies. [from BIO- + Greek *graphein*, to write]

Bioko, formerly **Fernando Po**, or **Póo** (to 1973), **Macias Nguema Bijogo** (to 1979) a volcanic island in the Bight of Biafra, off the coast of Cameroon. AREA 2 017sq km/779sq mi. It is a province of Equatorial Guinea, rising to 3 007m at Pico de Basilé. Malabo is the chief town and capital of Equatorial Guinea. HISTORY discovered by the Portuguese in 1471; originally named after the Portuguese navigator; occupied at various times by the British, Portuguese, and Spanish. ECONOMY coffee; cocoa; copra.

biolinguistics *or* **biological linguistics** the study of biological factors which enable human beings to develop and use language. It is particularly concerned with genetic transmission of language, and neurophysical studies of the way language is produced and understood.

biological *adj.* relating to biology or living organisms.

biological clock a supposed natural mechanism inside the body which controls rhythm of the body's functions.

biological control *or* **biological pest control** *Biol.* the control of plant or animal pests by the introduction of natural predators, parasites, etc, that are only harmful to the pest, or by interfering with the reproductive behaviour of the pest.
◇ When successful, biological control represents a very cheap alternative to the use of chemical pesticides, and is much less harmful to the environment. Recently developed techniques include disruption of the pest's reproductive behaviour by the release of sterile males (so that offspring are not produced), by the strategic dispersal of pheromones that play an important role in the pest's mating behaviour, or by the use of sexual attractants to bait traps.

biological engineering See BIOENGINEERING.

biologically *adv.* as regards biology or living organisms.

biological rhythm. See BIORHYTHM.

biological warfare the use of toxins and micro-organisms as weapons in war.

biologist *noun* a person who studies or practises biology.

biology *noun* the scientific study of living organisms.

bioluminescence *noun Biol.* the emission of light by living organisms, such as certain insects, deep-sea fishes, bacteria, and fungi.

biomass *noun Biol.* the total mass of living organisms in an ecosystem, population, or designated area at a given time. It is usually expressed as dry weight per unit area.

biome *noun Biol.* a major ecological community of living organisms, usually defined by the plant habitat with which they are associated, eg grassland, rainforest.

biomechanics *noun* **1** the mechanics of movement in living things. **2** *Theatr.* a system of mechanical acrobatic exercises evolved by the Russian theatre director Vsevolod Meyerhold (1874–1940), intended to reduce actors to puppet-like figures to be manipulated at the whim of the director.

biomorphic art a type of abstract art which makes use of forms reminiscent of, but not necessarily drawn directly from, the shapes of living things. The most celebrated exponent was Jean (Hans) Arp (1887–1966), whose works influenced the Surrealists. [from Greek *bios*, life + *morphe*, form]

Biondi, Matt(hew) (1965–) US swimmer, born in Morego, California. At the 1986 world championships he won a record seven medals, including three golds, and at the 1988 Olympics won seven medals, including five golds. He set the 100m freestyle world record of 48.74 seconds in Orlando, Florida, in 1986. He won silver in the 50m freestyle at the 1992 Olympics, and announced his retirement in 1993.

bionic *adj.* **1** of or using bionics. **2** *colloq.* having extraordinary powers of speed, strength, etc.

bionics *sing. noun* **1** the study of how living organisms function and the application of the principles observed to develop computers and other machines which work in similar ways. **2** the replacement of damaged parts of the body, such as limbs and heart valves, by electronic devices. [from BIO- + ELECTRONICS]

biophysicist *noun* a person who studies or practises biophysics.

biophysics *sing. noun* the application of the ideas and methods of physics to the study of biological processes.

biopsy *noun* (PL. **biopsies**) *Pathol.* the removal of a small piece of living tissue from an organ or part of the body in order to determine the nature of any suspected disease. It is an important means of diagnosing cancer. [from BIO- + Greek *opsis*, sight or appearance]

biorhythm *noun* **1** *Biol.* a periodic change in the behaviour or physiology of many animals and plants (eg winter hibernation or migration, spring flowering), mediated by hormones which are in turn influenced by changes in daylength. **2** a circadian (24-hour) rhythm associated, for example, with sleep, and independent of daylength. **3** any of three cyclical patterns which have been suggested as influencing physical, intellectual, and emotional aspects of human behaviour. There is no scientific basis for such a phenomenon.

biosphere *noun* that part of the Earth's surface and its atmosphere in which living organisms are known to exist. – Also called *ecosphere*.

biosynthesis *noun* the manufacture by living organisms of complex organic compounds, such as proteins, fats, and other major components of cells from simpler molecules.

Biot, Jean-Baptiste (1774–1862) French physicist and astronomer, born in Paris. Professor of Mathematical Physics at the Collège de France, he made a balloon ascent with Joseph Louis Gay-Lussac to study magnetism at high altitudes in 1804. In 1806 he travelled to Spain to determine the length of a degree of longitude. He also invented a polariscope (an instrument which reveals the polarization of light), and established the fundamental laws of the rotation of the plane of polarization of light by an optically active substance.

biota *noun Biol.* the living organisms present in a particular area. [from Greek *bios*, life]

biotechnology *noun Biol.* the use of living organisms, eg bacteria, or the enzymes produced by them, in the industrial manufacture of useful products, or the development of useful processes. ◇ Some applications of biotechnology have existed since early times, eg the conversion of milk into cheese and yoghurt, and the production of alcoholic beverages and bread by fermentation using yeast. Recent applications of biotechnology centre around the modification of nuclear DNA (the genetic material) in bacterial cells using genetic engineering techniques, so that the cells are 'programmed' to produce large amounts of a desirable product, such a drug (eg antibiotics, interferon) or a hormone (eg insulin, human

growth hormone). Genetic engineering also enables commercially desirable characteristics to be conferred upon organisms, and has been used to produce crop plants resistant to certain diseases or pests, and bacteria that concentrate metals from low-grade ores. Biotechnology has been applied to such processes as the breakdown and recycling of waste in order to minimize environmental damage.

biotin *noun Biochem.* a member of the vitamin B complex that functions as a *coenzyme* for various enzymes involved in the chemical reactions in living cells. It is normally produced in adequate amounts by the bacteria that inhabit the gut of animals, but is also found in yeast, liver, egg yolk, cereals, and milk. – Also called *vitamin H*. [from Greek *bios*, life]

bipartisan *adj.* of or involving two groups or political parties. [from BI- + PARTISAN]

bipartite *adj.* **1** consisting of two parts. **2** involving, or agreed by, two parties: *a bipartite agreement.* [from BI- + Latin *partire*, to divide]

biped *noun* an animal with two feet, eg man. — *adj.* (*also* **bipedal**) having two feet. [from BI- + Latin *pes*, foot]

biplane *noun* an early type of aeroplane having two sets of wings, one above the other.

BIPM *abbrev. Bureau International des Poids et Mesures* (French) International Bureau of Weights and Measures.

bipolar *adj.* have two poles or extremes.

birch — *noun* **1** a slender deciduous tree or shrub of the genus *Betula*, found in north temperate and Arctic regions, with smooth silvery-white bark that often peels off in long papery strips. It is widely grown as an ornamental plant. **2** the strong fine-textured wood of this tree, used to make furniture, plywood, charcoal, etc. **3** a bundle of birch branches, formerly used as a punishment. — *adj.* made of birch wood. — *verb* to beat with a birch. [from Anglo-Saxon *beorc*]

bird *noun* **1** any warm-blooded vertebrate animal belonging to the class Aves, which consists of about 8 600 species, distinguished from all other animals by the possession of feathers. **2** *Brit. slang* a girl or woman. **3** *old colloq. use* a person, especially a strange or unusual one. **4** (**the bird**) harsh criticism: *gave them the bird.* — **the birds and the bees** *colloq.* sex and reproduction.

birds of a feather *Brit. colloq.* people who are like each other, share the same ideas, the same way of life, etc.

do bird *Brit. slang* to serve a prison sentence.

kill two birds with one stone *colloq.* to achieve two things with a single action.

strictly for the birds *colloq.* worthless; unimportant.

[from Anglo-Saxon *bridd*, young bird]

◇ The front limbs of birds are modified to form wings, although not all birds can fly, and the projecting jaws are modified to form a horny beak, which varies widely in shape, each type being adapted to a certain diet. The females of all bird species lay eggs with hard shells, which are usually incubated in a nest, and there is generally a prolonged period of parental care after the young birds have hatched.

Birds have exceptionally good eyesight and hearing, but very little sense of smell. Their bodies are specially adapted for flight, having a strong but very light skeleton, usually with hollow bones. Much of the wing and all of the tail is composed of long strong but very light feathers, and the body is streamlined with a smooth covering of short overlapping feathers. There is usually a pronounced vertical blade or keel on the breastbone, which serves as an attachment for the large muscles that move the wings. Birds evolved from reptiles, and present-day birds still have scaly legs.

birder *noun colloq.* a bird-watcher.

birdie — *noun* **1** a child's word for a little bird. **2** *Golf* a score of one stroke less than the fixed standard number of strokes (par) for a particular hole on a course. — *verb* (**birdying**) *Golf* to complete a hole with a birdie score.

bird-lime *noun* a sticky substance put on the branches of trees to catch small birds.

bird of paradise any of various brightly-coloured birds found in and around New Guinea.

bird-of-paradise flower an evergreen perennial plant (*Strelitzia reginae*), up to 1m high, that forms clumps of long-stalked oblong leaves, and is native to Cape province, South Africa, but widely cultivated elsewhere for its conspicuous flowers. Each 'flower' in fact represents an inflorescence of several flowers enclosed in a sheathing bract. The flowers have orange sepals and blue petals, and emerge from the bract, the whole structure resembling a bird of paradise in flight.

bird of passage 1 a bird that flies to different parts of the world as the seasons change. **2** a person who constantly moves around and never settles in one place.

bird of prey any of several types of bird, eg eagle, vulture, hawk, that hunt other birds and small mammals for food.

Birdseye, Clarence (1886–1956) US businessman and inventor, born in Brooklyn, New York. He is best known for having developed a process for freezing food in small packages suitable for retailing. He was a fur trader in Labrador, where he observed that food was often kept frozen during winter. On his return to the USA he helped found the General Seafoods Company in 1924, marketing quick frozen foods. He was President of Birdseye Frosted Foods (1930–4), and of Birdseye Electric Company (1935–8). He is also credited with the invention of the infrared heat lamp, the recoilless harpoon gun, and a method of removing water from food.

bird's-eye view 1 a general view from above. **2** a general impression.

birdsfoot trefoil a small perennial plant (*Lotus corniculatus*), native to Europe, Asia, and Africa, and having leaves composed of five oval leaflets, and stalked flat-topped clusters of two to eight yellow flowers (similar in shape to pea flowers), often tinged with red. The fruit is a long many-seeded pod.

bird's nest fern a perennial fern (*Asplenium nidus*), native to Old World tropical forests, with leaves consisting of bright green undivided fronds that form a nest-like rosette in which humus accumulates. The roots of the plant then grow into the humus, obtaining nutrients and water from it.

Birds of America a series of life-size colour plates of birds by John James Audubon (1827–38). It was accompanied by the text *Ornithological Biography* (1831–9), which he co-wrote.

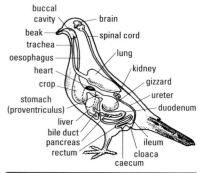

internal anatomy of a bird

Classification of Birds

Order	Common name	No. of species	Order	Common name	No. of species
Passeriformes	perching birds; passerines	5100	Gruiformes	cranes and relatives	197
Piciformes	woodpeckers and relatives	400	Galliformes	game birds	250
			Falconiformes	birds of prey	271
Coraciiformes	kingfishers and relatives	190	Anseriformes	ducks and relatives	148
Coliformes	mousebirds	6	Ciconiiformes	storks and relatives	115
Trogoniformes	trogons	36			
Apodiformes	swifts and hummingbirds	400	Pelecaniformes	pelicans and relatives	59
Caprimulgiformes	nightjars and relatives	94	Procellariiformes	albatrosses and relatives	91
Strigiformes	owls	130	Sphenisciformes	penguins	18
Cuculiformes	cuckoos and relatives	147	Gaviiformes	divers	5
			Podicipediformes	grebes	21
Psittaciformes	parrot family	315	Tinamiformes	tinamous	50
Columbiformes	pigeons and relatives	300	Casuariiformes	emu and cassowaries	4
			Rheiformes	rheas	2
Charadriiformes	gulls and relatives (mainly waders)	295	Struthioniformes	ostriches	1
			Dinornithiormes	kiwis	1

bird strike a crash between a bird or birds and the engine of an aeroplane.

bird-watcher *noun* a person who studies birds by observing them closely, especially as a hobby.

bird-watching *noun* the scientific observation of birds.

bireme *noun* a type of ancient galley, used especially in warfare by the Phoenicians, Greeks, and Romans. It was propelled by two banks of oars on either side, and a square sail. [from Latin *biremis*, from *bi-*, two + *remus*, an oar]

biretta *noun* a stiff square cap worn by Roman Catholic clergy. It has three flat upright projections on top, and may be black (worn by priests), purple (worn by bishops) or red (worn by cardinals). [from Italian *berretta*]

biriani *or* **biryani** *noun* a type of highly seasoned Indian dish consisting mainly of rice, with meat or fish. [from Urdu]

Birkbeck, George (1776–1841) English educationalist, born in Settle, Yorkshire. In 1799, as Professor of Chemistry and Natural Philosophy at Glasgow, he gave his first free lectures to the working classes. In 1804 he became a physician in London, where he took a leading part in the formation of the London Mechanics' or Birkbeck Institute (1824), now Birkbeck College, part of London University.

Birkeland, Kristian Olaf Bernhard (1867–1917) Norwegian physicist, born in Christiania (now Oslo). Professor of Physics at the university there, he demonstrated the electromagnetic nature of the northern lights, and in 1903 developed a method for obtaining nitrogen from the air.

Birkenhead, Frederick Edwin Smith, 1st Earl of (1872–1930) English Conservative politician and lawyer, born in Birkenhead, Cheshire. Called to the Bar in 1899, he entered parliament (1906) and made his name as a brilliant orator. In the Irish crisis (1914) he supported resistance to Home Rule, but later helped to negotiate the Irish settlement of 1921. He was Attorney-General (1915–19) and Lord Chancellor (1919–22), but his conduct as Secretary of State for India (1924–8) caused much criticism, and he resigned to devote himself to a commercial career.

Birkenhead POP (1981) 100 000, urban area (1981) 281 000, a town and seaport in Wirral borough, Merseyside, NW England. It stands on the Wirral Peninsula opposite Liverpool, to which it is linked by rail and road tunnels under the R Mersey.

Birkhoff, George David (1884–1944) US mathematician, born in Overisel, Michigan. Professor at Wisconsin, Princeton, and Harvard, he had many contacts with European mathematicians and was regarded as the leading US mathematician of the early part of the 20c. In 1913 he proved 'Poincaré's last theorem', which Poincaré had left unproven at his death. Later he developed 'ergodic theory', which relates to probability and has its roots in such problems as the stability of the solar system and the analysis of motion in thermodynamics.

Birmingham POP (1992e) 1m, a city and the chief town in the West Midlands, central England, 175km/109mi NW of London. It is Britain's second largest city and is part of the West Midlands urban area; motorways meet to the N at 'Spaghetti Junction'. A noted centre for metalwork since the 16c, it developed rapidly during the Industrial Revolution in an area with a large supply of iron ore and coal. The city was heavily bombed in World War II. NOTABLE FEATURES Church of St Philip (18c); Cathedral of St Chad (1839); Aston Hall (1618–35); National Exhibition Centre (1976); Aston Science Park; art gallery; Symphony Hall (CBSO); theatre; Bull Ring shopping complex.

Birmingham POP (1990) 908 000, the seat of Jefferson County, N central Alabama, USA. Settled in 1813, it is an industrial, commercial, and financial city, the largest in the state, and a leading iron and steel centre. It was the scene of civil rights protests in the 1960s. NOTABLE FEATURES Sloss Furnaces; an iron statue of Vulcan, god of the forge; Alabama Symphony Orchestra.

Biro *noun* (PL. **Biros**) *Brit. trademark* a type of pen with a writing tip consisting of a small ball. [named after L Biró (1899–1985), the inventor]

birth *noun* **1** the act or process of being born or of bearing children. **2** family history or origin: *of humble birth.* **3** beginning; origins: *the birth of socialism.*
— **give birth to someone** *said of a mother* to bear or produce a baby.
give birth to something to produce or be the cause of something: *give birth to a new idea.*
[from Norse *byrthr*]

birth certificate an official record of a person's birth, stating the time and place, the parents, etc.

birth control the prevention of pregnancy, especially by means of contraception.

birthday *noun* **1** the anniversary of the day on which a person was born. **2** (*also* **birth day**) the day on which a person was born.

birthday honours in the UK, titles or medals awarded to people on the official birthday of the king or queen.

Birthday Party, The a play by Harold Pinter (1958). It is a drama full of menace and confusion in which unemployed pianist Stanley's identity is questioned and destroyed by two sinister intruders who claim to want to celebrate his birthday.

birthday suit
— **in one's birthday suit** *humorous colloq.* naked.

birthing pool a portable pool in which a woman can sit partially immersed in water during labour and childbirth.

birthmark *noun* a blemish or mark that is present on the skin at birth and may be harmless and temporary, eg a strawberry mark, or permanent, eg a port-wine stain. Moles (raised pigment spots) are generally harmless unless they change colour or spread.

Birth of a Nation, The a US film directed by D W Griffith (1915). A silent epic set in pre-Civil War America and starring Lilian Gish, it exhibits innovative artistry and explicit racism.

Birth of Venus, The a mythological painting by Sandro Botticelli (c.1482–4, Uffizi, Florence).

birthplace *noun* **1** the place where a person was born. **2** the place where something important or well known began: *the birthplace of medicine.*

birth rate the ratio of the number of live births occurring over a period of a year in a given area per thousand inhabitants, or per thousand women of childbearing age. It is a measure of population growth.

birthright *noun* the rights a person may claim by being born into a particular family, social class, etc.

Birtwistle, Sir Harrison (1934–) English composer, born in Accrington, Lancashire. While studying in Manchester, he helped to form the New Manchester Group (with eg Peter Maxwell Davies and John Ogdon) for the performance of modern music. He also helped to form the Pierrot Players (1967); much of his work was written for them and the English Opera Group. In 1965 he wrote the instrumental *Tragoedia* and vocal/instrumental *Ring a Dumb Carillon* that established him as a leading composer. Among his later works are the operas *Punch and Judy* (1966–7), *The Mask of Orpheus* (produced 1986), and *Gawain* (1990).

Biscay, Bay of, Spanish **Golfe de Vizcaya**, French **Golfe de Gascogne**, ancient **Mar Cantabrico** an arm of the Atlantic Ocean, bounded E by France and S by Spain. A major fishing region, it has irregular coasts with many fine harbours. It is known for its strong currents and sudden storms. Major ports include St Nazaire, La Rochelle, San Sebastian, and Santander; resorts such as Biarritz lie on the straight, sandy shores of the SE French coast.

biscuit — *noun* **1** a crisp flat cake. **2** (*also* **biscuitware**) objects made from baked clay that have not been glazed. **3** a pale brown colour. — *adj.* pale brown in colour.
— **take the biscuit** *colloq.* to be worse than everything else that has happened.
[from Old French *bescoit*, from Latin *bis*, twice + *coquere*, to cook]

bisect *verb* to divide into two equal parts. [from BI- + Latin *secare*, to cut]

bisection *noun* division into two equal parts.

bisexual — *adj.* **1** sexually attracted to both males and females. **2** having the sexual organs of both male and female. — *noun* a bisexual person. See also UNISEXUAL.

bisexuality *noun* the state of being bisexual.

Bishkek, formerly **Pishpek** (to 1926), and **Frunze** (1926–91) POP (1991e) 641 000, the capital city of Kirghizia, central Asia, situated in the N of the country. The city was founded in 1825 and is a major transportation, industrial, and cultural centre.

Bishop, Sir Henry R(owley) (1786–1855) English composer, born in London. He was musical director at Covent Garden (1810–24), held professorships at Edinburgh and Oxford, and in 1842 received the first knighthood conferred upon a musician. Few of his many glees and operas have survived, but he is remembered for 'Home, Sweet Home'.

bishop noun **1** a senior Christian priest or minister in the Roman Catholic, Anglican, and Orthodox Churches, in charge of a group of churches in an area, or of a diocese. **2** Chess a piece shaped like a bishop's mitre at the top. It may only be moved diagonally across the board. [from Anglo-Saxon bisceop, from Greek episkopos, overseer]

bishopric noun **1** the post or position of bishop. **2** the area under the charge of a bishop.

Bishop's Stortford POP (1981) 23 000, a town in East Hertfordshire district, Hertfordshire, SE England. It lies on the R Stort, 13km/8mi N of Harlow. The South African politician Cecil Rhodes was born here in 1853.

Bishops' Wars two wars (1639–40) between Charles I of England and the Scottish Covenanters, caused by his unpopular policies towards the Scottish Kirk. They resulted in English defeats and bankruptcy for Charles, who was then forced to call the Short and Long Parliaments (1640), which ended his 'personal rule' (1629–40).

Bismarck, Otto Edward Leopold, Fürst von (Prince of) (1815–98) Prusso-German statesman, the first Chancellor of the German Empire (1871–90), born in Schönhausen, Brandenburg. In the new Prussian parliament (1847) he became known as an ultraroyalist, resenting Austria's predominance and demanding equal rights for Prussia. He was appointed Prime Minister in 1862 and during the Schleswig-Holstein question and the 'seven weeks' war' between Prussia and Austria, he became a national hero. Uniting German feeling, he provoked the Franco-Prussian War (1870–1) and acted as Germany's spokesman, and after the Peace of Frankfurt (1871), he developed policies aimed at consolidating and protecting the young empire. His domestic policy included universal suffrage, reformed coinage, and the codification of the law, and he also engaged in a lengthy but fruitless conflict with the Vatican (known as the Kulturkampf). In 1879, to counteract Russia and France, he formed the Austro-German Treaty of Alliance, which Italy later joined. Called the 'Iron Chancellor', he resigned the Chancellorship in 1890, out of disapproval of Emperor William II's policy, but the two were later reconciled (1894).

Bismarck POP (1990) 84 000, the capital of the state of North Dakota, USA, in Burleigh County, central North Dakota. It lies on the Missouri R. Established in 1873, it was first a territorial capital (1883) and has been state capital since 1889. Bismarck is the trade and distribution centre for the agricultural region. NOTABLE FEATURES Camp Hancock Museum; Heritage Centre. [named after the German statesman]

Bismarck Archipelago POP (1980) 314 000, an island group which is part of Papua New Guinea, lying NE of New Guinea in the SW Pacific Ocean. AREA 49 709sq km/19 188sq mi. The main islands, New Britain, New Ireland, Admiralty Is, and Lavongai, are mountainous, with several active volcanoes. HISTORY annexed by Germany in 1884; became a mandated territory of Australia in 1920; occupied by Japan in World War II; part of the UN Trust Territory of New Guinea until 1975. CHIEF TOWN Rabaul, on New Britain. ECONOMY copra; cocoa; oil palm.

Bismarck Sea the SW arm of the Pacific Ocean, NE of New Guinea. It measures c.800km/500mi E–W and contains many islands. The Battle of the Bismarck Sea, fought in 1943, saw the destruction of a Japanese naval force by the USA.

bismuth noun (SYMBOL **Bi**, ATOMIC NUMBER **83**) a hard silvery-white metal with a pinkish tinge. It is used to make lead alloys with low melting points, especially for use in fire-detection devices, automatic sprinkler systems, and electrical fuses. Its insoluble compounds are used in medicine to treat stomach upsets and skin disorders, eg eczema. [from German Wismut]

bison noun (PL. **bison**) either of two species of shaggy wild cattle with large heads, short horns, heavy front bodies and humps on their backs. [from Latin bison, probably of Germanic origin]

bisque¹ noun a thick rich soup, usually made from shellfish, cream, and wine. [from French bisque]

bisque² noun a type of baked clay or china, which has not been glazed. [see BISCUIT 2]

Bissau POP (1990e) 966 000, the seaport capital of Guinea-Bissau. It is situated on Bissau I, in the estuary of the R Geba. HISTORY established as a fortified slave-trading centre in 1687; became a free port in 1869; replaced Bolama as capital in 1941. NOTABLE FEATURES National Museum; cathedral.

bistort noun any of various plants belonging to the genus Polygonum, found mainly in north temperate regions, and including some aquatic species. It has lance-shaped or oblong leaves, with small white, pink, or red flowers borne in terminal spikes. [from Latin bis torta, twice twisted]

bistro noun (PL. **bistros**) a small bar or informal restaurant. [from French bistro]

bisulphate noun Chem. hydrogensulphate.

bit¹ noun a small piece.
— **a bit** colloq. **1** a short time or distance: wait a bit. **2** a little; slightly; rather: a bit of a fool. **3** a lot: takes a bit of doing.
a bit much or **thick** or **rich** colloq. behaviour that is unacceptable, unreasonable, or unfair.
a bit off Brit. colloq. bad manners, taste, or behaviour.
bit by bit gradually.
do one's bit to do one's fair share.
[from Anglo-Saxon bita]

bit² see BITE.

bit³ noun **1** a small metal bar which a horse holds in its mouth as part of the bridle with which it is controlled. **2** a tool with a cutting edge, which can be fitted into a drill and turned at high speed. **3** the part of a key which connects with the lever in a lock.
— **take the bit between one's teeth** to act decisively and with determination.
[from BITE]

bit⁴ noun Comput. a binary digit with a value of either 0 or 1, representing the smallest piece of information that can be dealt with by a computer. [a contraction of binary digit]

bitch — noun **1** a female of the dog family. **2** offensive slang a bad-tempered, unpleasant, spiteful woman. **3** slang a difficult or unpleasant thing. — verb intrans. **1** to speak scathingly or spitefully. **2** to complain. [from Anglo-Saxon bicce]

bitchily adv. with a bitchy or spiteful manner.

bitchiness noun being bitchy or spiteful.

bitchy adj. (**bitchier, bitchiest**) colloq. spiteful; petulantly bad-tempered.

bite — verb (**biting**; PAST TENSE **bit**; PAST PARTICIPLE **bitten**) **1** (**bite something away** or **off** or **out**) to grasp, seize, or tear it with the teeth. **2** trans., intrans. said of insects and snakes to penetrate a victim's skin and suck blood. **3** intrans. said

of fish to be caught on the hook on a fishing line. **4** intrans. to start to have an effect (usually adverse): the spending cuts are beginning to bite. **5** intrans. said of a wheel, screw, etc to grip firmly. **6** colloq. to annoy or worry: what's biting him? — noun **1** an act of biting. **2** a wound caused by biting. **3** a small amount of food: a bite to eat. **4** strength, sharpness, or bitterness of taste.
— **bite something back** colloq. to restrain oneself from saying something as if by biting the lips.
bite someone's head off colloq. to reply with unexpected fierceness or anger.
bite one's tongue to restrain oneself from saying something one wants to say.
[from Anglo-Saxon bitan]

Bithynia the name given in antiquity to the area to the SW of the Black Sea. It eluded Achaemenid and Seleucid control and became an independent kingdom under a Hellenizing dynasty of Thracian stock in c.300 BC. In 75–74 BC, under the will of its last king, Nicomedes IV, it passed to Rome. Its strategic status rose during the imperial period, and in the late 3c AD , its leading city, Nicomedia, became for a while the capital of the E half of the Empire.

biting adj. **1** bitterly and painfully cold: a biting wind. **2** said of a remark sharp and hurtful.

bit-mapping noun Comput. a method of organizing the display on a computer screen so that each pixel is assigned to one or more bits in memory, depending on the shading or number of colours required.

Bitola or **Bitolj**, Turkish **Monastir** POP (1991e) 122 000, a town in SW Macedonia. It is situated 112km/70mi S of Skopje. HISTORY under Turkish rule from 1382 until 1912; taken by the Serbs in 1913 and held by the Bulgarians during World War I; recaptured in 1918 by Franco-Serbian forces; fell to Axis powers in 1941; liberated in 1944 by Yugoslav forces. NOTABLE FEATURES excavations at Heraclea; Ajdar Kadi Mosque.

bit-part noun a small acting part in a play or film.

bits and pieces or **bits and bobs** Brit. colloq. small objects or possessions.

bitter — adj. **1** having a sharp, acid, and often unpleasant taste. **2** feeling or causing sadness or pain: bitter memories. **3** difficult to accept: a bitter disappointment. **4** showing an intense dislike, hatred, or opposition: bitter criticism. **5** said of the weather, etc extremely and painfully cold. — noun Brit. a type of beer with a slightly bitter taste, strongly flavoured with hops.
— **a bitter pill to swallow** something difficult to accept.
to the bitter end up to the very end, however unpleasant, and in spite of difficulties.
[from Anglo-Saxon biter]

bitter lemon a carbonated lemon-flavoured drink.

bitterly adv. in a bitter manner, especially with fierce resentment: he looked bitterly back at them. extremely, painfully: bitterly cold.

bittern noun a long-legged European bird that lives on or near water and makes a very loud deep sound. [from Old French butor]

bitterness noun a bitter state or quality, especially a feeling of fierce resentment: I felt no bitterness towards them.

bitters pl. noun a liquid made from bitter herbs or roots, used to help digestion or to flavour certain alcoholic drinks.

bittersweet adj. pleasant and unpleasant, or bitter and sweet, at the same time.

bittiness noun being bitty or scrappy.

bitty adj. (**bittier, bittiest**) colloq. consisting of small unrelated pieces or parts, especially awkwardly or untidily.

bitumen *noun* a brown or black sticky substance obtained from petroleum and used for surfacing roads, etc. [from Latin *bitumen*]

bituminous *adj.* containing bitumen.

bituminous coal *Geol.* a dark brown or black coal containing more than 80% carbon, which burns with a smoky yellowish flame. It is the form of coal that is most widely used for domestic and industrial purposes.

bivalent *adj.* same as DIVALENT.

bivalve — *adj.*, *said of shellfish* having a shell made up of two parts held together by a type of hinge. — *noun* any of several kinds of shellfish, including oysters.

bivariate *adj. Maths.* involving two variables.

bivouac — *noun* a temporary camp without tents, especially used by soldiers and mountaineers. — *verb intrans.* (**bivouacked, bivouacking**) to camp out temporarily at night without a tent. [from French *bivouac*, from Swiss German *Beiwacht*, an additional guard at night]

Biwa, Lake, Japanese **Biwa-ko**, also **Lake Omi** the largest lake in Japan. AREA 676sq km/261sq mi. It is situated in the Kinki region, central Honshu, 8km/5mi NE of Kyoto. The lake measures 64km/40mi long, 3–19km/2–12mi wide, and 96m deep. A canal connects the lake with Kyoto.

bizarre *adj.* weirdly odd or strange. [from Spanish *bizarro*, gallant or brave]

bizarrely *adv.* in a weird or bizarre way.

Bizerta *or* **Bizerte**, Latin **Hippo Diarrhytus 1** POP (1984) 95 000, the capital of Bizerta governorate, N Tunisia, situated 60km/37mi NW of Tunis. It is strategically important because of its prominent position on the Mediterranean coastline. HISTORY the town has been occupied by the Romans, Vandals, Arabs, Moors, Spanish, and the French; it was a German base in World War II and was heavily bombed by the allies. It later became a French naval base (until 1963). NOTABLE FEATURE kasbah in the old city. **2** a governorate in N Tunisia with Bizerta as its capital.

Bizet, Georges, originally **Alexandre César Léopold Bizet** (1838–75) French composer, born in Paris. He studied at the Paris Conservatoire and in Italy, and won the Prix de Rome (1857). His incidental music to Daudet's play *L'Arlésienne* (1872) was remarkably popular, and survived as two orchestral suites. He wrote the operas *The Pearl Fishers* (1863) and *Carmen* (1875); the latter was his masterpiece, though its realism was criticized at the time.

Bjerknes, Vilhelm Friman Koren (1862–1951) Norwegian mathematician, meteorologist, and geophysicist, born in Christiania (now Oslo). Professor in Stockholm, Oslo, and Leipzig, he later became founder Director of the Bergen Geophysical Institute. He produced his famous circulation theorem in 1898, and became a pioneer of weather forecasting.

Björnson, Björnstjerne (Martinius) (1832–1910) Norwegian novelist and playwright, born in Kvikne. He worked as a newspaper editor and theatre director, was politically active as a Home Ruler and republican, and sought to revive Norwegian as a literary language. His early works were inspired by Norway's epic past but he later turned to social themes, as in his major play, *Over Aevne* (Beyond our Power, 1883). One of his poems (1870) became Norway's national anthem. He was awarded the Nobel Prize for Literature in 1903.

Bk *symbol Chem.* berkelium.

BL *abbrev.* **1** Bachelor of Law. **2** British Library.

blab *verb* (**blabbed, blabbing**) **1** *intrans., trans.* (*usually* **blab out** *or* **blab something out**) to tell a secret, etc. **2** *intrans.* to chatter foolishly. [from Middle English *blabbe*]

blabber *verb intrans.* (**blabbered, blabbering**) to talk nonsense, especially without stopping.

blabbermouth *noun* a person who talks foolishly and indiscreetly.

Black, Sir James Whyte (1924–) Scottish pharmacologist, born in Uddingston. He taught at various universities before becoming Professor of Analytical Pharmacology at King's College, London. His research on heart disease led to the discovery of betablocker drugs (to lower heart rate and decrease blood pressure) in 1964, and his deductions in 1972 on acid secretion in the stomach resulted in the introduction of new treatments for ulcers. He shared the 1988 Nobel Prize for Physiology or Medicine with Gertrude Elion and George Hitchings.

Black, Joseph (1728–99) Scottish chemist, born in Bordeaux, France. Professor at the universities of Glasgow and Edinburgh, he was one of the most influential chemists of his generation. Around 1756 he discovered carbon dioxide, and in later studies he introduced the ideas of latent heat (the amount of heat needed to change a solid into a liquid or a liquid into a gas at the same temperature) and specific heat (the heat required to raise the temperature of a substance by a certain amount). Famed as a teacher, his chemistry classes drew students from all over Europe and America.

black — *adj.* **1** of the colour of coal, the night sky, etc. **2** without light. **3** (*also* **Black**) *used of people* dark-skinned, especially of African, West Indian, or Australian Aboriginal origin. **4** (*also* **Black**) belonging or relating to black people: *black rights.* **5** *used of drinks* without added milk: *black coffee.* **6** angry, threatening: *black looks.* **7** dirty: *they came in from the garden with their hands black.* **8** sad, gloomy, or depressed: *a black mood.* **9** promising trouble; likely to be bad in some way: *the future looks black.* **10** wicked or sinister: *black-hearted / black comedy.* **11** *said of goods, etc* not allowed by a trade union to be handled, especially during a strike. — *noun* **1** the colour of coal, the night sky, etc. **2** anything which is black in colour. **3** (*also* **Black**) a person of African, West Indian, or Australian Aboriginal origin. **4** black clothes worn when in mourning. — *verb* **1** to make black. **2** to clean with black polish. **3** to forbid work to be done on or with (certain goods).
— **black and blue** *colloq.* covered in bruises.
black and white 1 *used of photographs or television images* having no colours except black, white, and shades of grey. **2** either good or bad, right or wrong, etc, with no compromise.
black out to lose consciousness.
black something or someone out 1 to deprive them of light. **2** to prevent information from being broadcast or published.
in the black with assets on the credit side of an account.
in black and white in writing or print.
[from Anglo-Saxon *blæc*]

Black Africa the part of Africa south of the Sahara desert, where the population is mainly black.

Black Americans the US citizens descended from those brought from Africa as slaves between 1619 and the American Civil War, when emancipation took place. Nevertheless, they were still subject to institutionalized discrimination and segregation, and their struggle to achieve social and economic equality with white Americans is a major factor in US politics. African-Americans constitute around 12 per cent of the US population, and around 41 per cent of the non-white population. Since the New Deal, black Americans have voted predominantly for the Democratic Party.

blackamoor *noun old use*, usually *derog.* a dark-skinned or black person.

Black and Tans additional members of the Royal Irish Constabulary, recruited by the British government to cope with Irish national unrest in 1920. Due to the shortage of regulation uniforms, they were issued with khaki tunics and trousers and very dark green caps, hence their name.

black art same as BLACK MAGIC.

blackball *verb* **1** to vote against (a candidate for membership), originally by putting a black ball in the ballot-box. **2** to refuse to see or speak to (someone).

Black Beauty a children's novel by Anna Sewell (1877). The autobiography of a horse, it describes the varying fortunes of Beauty at the hands of numerous owners.

black belt 1 a belt indicating that the wearer has reached the highest level of skill in judo and karate. **2** a person who is entitled to wear a black belt.

blackberry *noun* **1** a thorny shrub bearing dark purple-coloured berries. **2** a berry from this shrub.

blackbird *noun* **1** a small European bird, the male of which is black with a yellow beak. **2** any of various similar N American birds.

blackboard *noun* a dark-coloured board for writing on with chalk, especially used in schools.

black body *Physics* a hypothetical body that absorbs all the radiation that falls on it, reflecting none.

black box a flight recorder in an aircraft.

Blackburn POP (1992e) 138 000, a town in Blackburn district, Lancashire, NW England. It lies 13km/8mi E of Preston, on the Leeds–Liverpool Canal. Blackburn was one of the early cotton-weaving towns.

blackcap *noun* a small songbird, the male of which has a black-topped head.

blackcock *noun* the male of the black grouse.

black comedy a kind of comedy (in narrative or dramatic form) which derives its often bitter humour from exposing and confronting the grotesque and absurd accidents and misfortunes of life. Examples include Evelyn Waugh's *Black Mischief* (1932), Nathanael West's *The Day of the Locust* (1939), Edward Albee's *Who's Afraid of Virginia Woolf* (1962), and Joe Orton's *Loot* (1965).

Black Consciousness 1 a movement formed by Steve Biko in 1969, when he led African students out of the multi-racial National Union of South African Students and founded the South African Students Organization. The Black Peoples' Convention emerged to promote co-operation in social and cultural fields among all non-white peoples, but most of its leaders were imprisoned (1977), and Biko died in police custody. The film *Cry Freedom* (1988) was based on these events. **2** a movement in the USA, which asserts the opinion that blacks possess a distinct cultural tradition, and rejects the notion that they have been totally absorbed into white society.

Black Country an industrial area of the English Midlands during and after the Industrial Revolution, centred on the counties of Staffordshire, Warwickshire, and Worcestershire.

blackcurrant *noun* **1** a garden shrub grown for its small round black fruit. **2** the fruit of this shrub.

Black Death a virulent bubonic and pneumonic plague which swept through W and central Europe from Asia (1347–51), killing approximately 25 million people, about a third of the population.

black economy unofficial business, trade, etc, undertaken clandestinely to evade payment of tax.

blacken *verb* (**blackened, blackening**) **1** *trans., intrans.* to make or become black or very dark in colour. **2** *trans.* to speak evil or badly of: *tried to blacken their name.*

Blackett, Patrick Maynard Stuart, Baron (1897–1974) English physicist, born in London. Professor at London University, Manchester University, and London's Imperial College of Science and Technology, he was awarded the 1948 Nobel Prize for Physics for developing the cloud chamber particle detector, and using it to confirm the existence of the positron (the antiparticle of the electron).

black eye an eye with darkened swollen skin around it, usually caused by a blow.

black fly *noun* a small biting fly found near running water. The females of some species are bloodsuckers and serious cattle pests.

Blackfoot three Algonkian-speaking Native American groups (Blackfoot, Blood, Piegan) originally from the east who settled in Montana, USA and Alberta, Canada. Many died of starvation after the bison were exterminated; others turned to farming and cattle rearing. Today c.10 000 live on reservations.

Black Forest, German **Schwarzwald** a coniferous forested mountain range in the Baden-Württenburg province of Germany which extends 160km/100mi from Pforzheim in the N to Waldshut on the Upper Rhine in the S. Its highest peak is the Feldberg at 1 493m. The source of the Danube and Neckar rivers, it is divided by the R Kinzig into the Lower Schwarzwald (to the N) and the Upper Schwarzwald (to the S). There are many medicinal baths and spas in the area.

Black Friar *Relig.* a monk of the Dominican Order: from their black mantles worn over white habits.

Black Friday the name given to 24 Sep 1869, the day of a US financial crisis, when the price of gold dropped severely due to an attempt by such financiers as Jay Gould (1836–92) and James Fisk (1834–72) to corner the gold market. Many speculators lost their fortunes in the ensuing panic.

blackguard *noun* (pronounced blag-) *old use* a rogue or villain.

blackguardly *adj.* (pronounced blag-) *old use* villainous; unscrupulous.

Black Hawk War a military conflict (1832) between the USA and Sauk and Fox Native Americans, which led to the completion of the policy of removing Native Americans from the 'Old Northwest' to beyond the Mississippi R.

blackhead *noun* a small black spot on the skin caused by sweat blocking one of the skin's tiny pores.

black hole *Astron.* a region in space believed to be formed when a star has collapsed in on itself in a huge implosion at the end of its life, when it has exhausted all its nuclear fuel. It is seen as a 'hole' because the force of gravity is so strong that not even light waves can escape from the star.
◇ Single stars that behave like members of a binary star system may have black holes as invisible 'companions'. It is thought that giant black holes may exist at the centre of galaxies, providing the power source for objects such as quasars. There are probably millions of black holes in the Milky Way alone.

Black Hole of Calcutta a small, badly-ventilated room in which 146 British defenders were imprisoned following Calcutta's capture (Jun 1756) by Siraj ud Daula, Nawab of Bengal, but from which allegedly only 23 emerged alive, an incident that became infamous in the history of British imperialism.

black ice a type of ice that is thin and transparent. It forms on road surfaces, where the blackness of the road makes it barely visible and therefore highly dangerous.

blacking *noun old use* black polish, especially for shining shoes.

Black Iris a painting by Georgia O'Keefe (1949, New York).

blackjack *noun* **1** pontoon or a similar card-game. **2** *North Amer.* a length of hard flexible leather, especially used for hitting people.

black lead same as GRAPHITE.

blackleg — *noun derog.* a person who refuses to take part in a strike. — *verb intrans.* (**blacklegged, blacklegging**) to refuse to take part in a strike.

blacklist — *noun* a list of people convicted or suspected of something, or not approved of. — *verb* to put (a person, etc) on such a list.

blackly *adv.* in an angry or threatening way.

black magic magic which supposedly invokes the power of the devil to perform evil.

blackmail — *verb* **1** to extort money illegally from (a person) by threatening to reveal harmful information about them. **2** to try to influence (a person) using unfair pressure. — *noun* an act of blackmailing someone.
◇ In England and Wales, blackmail, or the making of an unwarranted demand with menaces, is an offence under the Theft Act. In many states in the USA, the offence comes under the general theft statute as theft by extortion (a term also used in Scottish law).

blackmailer *noun* a person who commits blackmail.

Blackman, Frederick Frost (1866–1947) English botanist, born in Lambeth, London. From 1891 to 1936 he worked at the Cambridge Botany School, where he became renowned for his fundamental research on the respiration of plants, and on the limiting factors affecting their growth.

Black Maria *colloq.* a police van for transporting prisoners.

black mark an indication of disapproval or criticism.

black market the illegal buying and selling, at high prices, of goods which are scarce or in great demand.

black-marketeer *noun* a person who trades in a black market.

black mass a ceremony parodying the Christian mass, conducted in worship of Satan.

Blackmore, R(ichard) D(oddridge) (1825–1900) English novelist, born in Longworth, Berkshire. He was called to the Bar in 1852, but poor health made him turn to market gardening and literature in Teddington. After publishing several collections of poetry, he wrote 15 novels, mostly with a Devonshire background, of which *Lorna Doone* (1869) is the best-known.

Black Muslims in the USA, a black religious movement, also known as the Nation of Islam, founded in 1930 by Wali Farad (Wallace D Fard). It proclaimed that black Americans are descended from an ancient Muslim tribe, and its followers adopted Muslim names and believed Farad to be an incarnation of God. Farad mysteriously disappeared in 1934 and was succeeded by Elijah Muhammad (1925–75), who urged the members of the movement to avoid contact with whites, and demanded a separate state for blacks, as well as reparation for injustices. Malcolm X was one of their foremost preachers, while Muhammad Ali (Cassius Clay) was a famous member. Now led by Elijah, Muhammad's son, the movement mainly repudiates its early separatism, and has adopted orthodox Muslim beliefs. However a separatist faction has developed, led by Louis Farrakhan, which retains the original tenets of the movement.

blackness *noun* a black or very dark state or quality.

Black on Black a painting of a black square by Alexander Rodchenko (1918). It was inspired by Kazimir Malevich's *White on White* square (1915).

blackout 1 a loss of memory or consciousness. **2** a loss of sight or vision. **3** a suppression of information. **4** an enforced period during which lights are turned out over an area as a precaution during an air raid at night.

Black Panthers Party a US militant black political party, founded by Huey P Newton and Bobby Seale in 1966. It promoted the use of physical force and armed confrontation for black liberation, but was split by rival groups in the 1970s and diminished in importance.

black pepper *noun* pepper produced by grinding the dried fruits of the pepper plant without removing their dark outer covering.

Blackpool POP (1992e) 152 000, a town in Blackpool district, Lancashire, NW England. It lies on the Irish Sea coast, 25km/15mi W of Preston. It is the largest holiday resort in N England, with an estimated 8.5m visitors annually. NOTABLE FEATURES Tower (based on Eiffel Tower); Grundy Art Gallery; illuminations (autumn).

Black Power in the USA, a term used by black activists from the late 1950s that reflected their desire for increased political influence. A part of the civil rights movement, it advocated the use of force, opposed integrationist policies, and achieved results in terms of registering black voters.

black pudding a dark sausage made from pig's blood and fat.

Black Rod in the UK, an official of the House of Lords since 1522, whose chief ceremonial function is to act as the official messenger from the Lords to the House of Commons. By a tradition dating from 1643, he must knock three times with his ebony staff of office (the black rod) to gain entrance to the Commons.

Black Sea, ancient **Pontius Euxinus (Euxine Sea)**, Bulgarian **Cherno More**, Romanian **Marea Neagra**, Russian **Chernoye More**, Turkish **Karadeniz** an inland sea between Europe and Asia, connected to the Mediterranean Sea in the SW by the Bosporus, the Sea of Marmara, and the Dardanelles. AREA 507 900sq km/196 000sq mi; length 1 210km/750mi; width 120–560km/75–350mi; maximum depth 2 246m. It is bounded N by the Ukraine, E by Russia and Georgia, S by Turkey, and W by Bulgaria and Romania. The Sea of Azov is its largest arm. There are steep rocky coasts in the S and NE, but sandy shores in the N and NW. The main ports include Burgas, Varna, Odessa, Sebastopol, and Trabzon; fishing is important, especially in the N. HISTORY navigated since ancient times, its shores were first colonized by the Greeks and then the Romans; the Genoese established colonies in the 13c, and from the 15c–18c the Black Sea was part of the Turkish Empire; in 1774 Russia gained the right to trade in the Black Sea, to be followed by Austria (1784), then France, and Britain (1802); the Treaty of Paris (1856) opened the Black Sea to commerce of all nations but closed to ships of war.

black sheep a member of a family or group who is disapproved of in some way.

Blackshirt *noun* a member of the Italian Fascist Party before and during World War II.

blacksmith *noun* a person who makes and repairs by hand things made of iron, such as horseshoes.

black spot *Brit.* **1** a dangerous stretch of road where accidents often occur. **2** an area where an adverse social condition is prevalent: *an unemployment black spot.*

Black Studies educational courses centred on the history, culture, and development of black people, especially those of African origin or descent in N America, the Caribbean, and Europe.

black swan a swan native to Australia and Tasmania, and now introduced to New Zealand, so called because of its dark plumage. It nests in reed beds.

blackthorn *noun* a shrub with black twigs and white flowers, which produces sour plum-like fruit called sloes.

Black Thursday the date (24 Oct 1929) of the crash of the New York stockmarket that marked the onset of the Great Depression.

black-tie — *noun* a black bow-tie. — *adj.*, *said of a celebration or function* very formal, with guests expected to wear evening dress.

Black Watch the name of a famous Highland regiment of the British Army, first raised in 1704. The name derives from their distinctive very dark tartan. The two battalions known as the 42nd and 73rd Foot were amalgamated in 1881, and given the traditional title.

Blackwell, Sir Basil (Henry) (1889–1984) English publisher and bookseller, born in Oxford. Son of the founder of the famous Oxford bookshop (1846), he joined the family business in 1913 and later also founded the Shakespeare Head Press (1921). Succeeding to the chairmanship (1924–69), he combined the bookselling interest with that of publishing, mostly on academic subjects.

Blackwell, Elizabeth (1821–1910) US physician and feminist, born in Bristol, UK. She was the first woman to receive a degree in medicine in the USA, from Geneva College, New York state. Throughout her education and career she encountered hostility, and was responsible both for making medical education available to her sex and for founding an infirmary for the poor of New York City.

black widow *noun* a poisonous kind of spider, of which the female devours the male after mating.

Black Zionism the term applied to quasi-nationalist, messianic movements founded among black Americans and West Indians who, proud of Black history, look with reverence to Africa as the land from which their forefathers came as slaves.

bladder *noun* 1 the bag-like organ in the body in which urine collects. 2 a hollow bag made of leather, etc stretched by filling with air or liquid. 3 a small air-filled pouch in certain plants, eg seaweed. [from Anglo-Saxon *blædre*, blister, pimple]

bladder wrack a tough brown seaweed (*Fucus vesiculosus*) whose fronds can be recognized by the paired air-filled bladders which buoy them up in the water. Bladder wrack occupies large areas of the middle shore, and also grows on groynes and piers. The tips of the fronds contain the reproductive organs.

blade *noun* 1 the cutting part of a knife, sword, etc. 2 the flat, usually long and narrow part of a leaf or petal. 3 the wide flat part of an oar, bat, etc. 4 a flat bone, especially in the shoulder. [from Anglo-Saxon *blæd*]

Bladud a legendary king of Britain, who discovered the hot spring at Bath and founded the city. One story is that he was a leper who found that the mud cured him.

BLAISE *abbrev.* British Library Automated Information Service.

Blake, Robert (1599–1657) English admiral after Nelson, born in Bridgwater, Somerset. He lived in Oxford as a quiet country gentleman until 1640, when he became MP for Bridgwater in the Short Parliament, later serving in the Long Parliament (1645–53). In 1649 he blockaded Lisbon, destroyed the squadron of Prince Rupert, and in 1652–3 routed the Dutch in several battles. His greatest victory was at Santa Cruz, when he

destroyed a Spanish treasure fleet off Tenerife (1657).

Blake, William (1757–1827) English poet, painter, engraver, and mystic, born in London. Both his writing and his art reveal his mysticism and the importance he attached to imagination. His poetic works include *Poetical Sketches* (1783), *Songs of Innocence* (1789), *Songs of Experience* (1794) which include 'The Tyger', and the prophetic poem 'Jerusalem' (1804–20); his prose includes *The Marriage of Heaven and Hell* (1791). Among his paintings are *The Canterbury Pilgrims* and *Jacob's Dream*, and he also illustrated Young's *Night Thoughts* (1797), Linnell's *The Book of Job* (1826), and Dante's *Divine Comedy*, as well as doing engravings for his own works.

Blake a male first name, taken from the surname. Originally a nickname for somebody with extremely light or extremely dark hair or complexion. [from Anglo-Saxon *blaec*, black + *blac*, pale]

blame — *verb* (**blame someone for something** *or* **blame something on someone**) 1 to consider a person or thing as responsible for something bad or undesirable. 2 to find fault with a person. — *noun* responsibility for something bad or undesirable.
— **be to blame for something** to be responsible for something bad or undesirable.
[from Old French *blasmer*, from Latin *blasphemare*, to blaspheme]

blameless *adj.* free from blame; innocent.

blamelessly *adv.* without incurring or involving blame: *they were judged to have acted blamelessly.*

blamelessness *noun* lack of blame; innocence.

blameworthy *adj.* deserving blame.

Blamey, Sir Thomas Albert (1884–1951) Australian soldier, born near Wagga Wagga, New South Wales. He played an important part in the evacuation of Gallipoli, and became Chief-of-Staff of the Australian Corps in 1918. On the outbreak of World War II he commanded the Australian Imperial Forces in the Middle East, and organized the withdrawal from the Balkan area. In 1942 he became Commander-in-Chief of the Australian army, and commanded Allied Land Forces in New Guinea (1942–3).

Blanc, Mont see MONT BLANC.

blanch *verb* 1 to make white by removing the colour. 2 *intrans., trans.* to make or become white, especially through fear. 3 to prepare (vegetables or meat) for cooking or freezing by boiling in water for a few seconds. 4 to remove the skins (from almonds, etc) by soaking them in boiling water. [from Old French *blanchir*]

Blanche a female first name, originally a nickname for a blonde-haired woman, and also associated with purity. [from French *blanc*, white]

Blanchflower, Danny, properly **Robert Dennio Blanchflower** (1926–93) Northern Irish footballer, born in Belfast. He played in the Northern Ireland side which reached the World Cup quarter-finals in 1958. He played for Aston Villa, then Tottenham Hotspur, with whom he won both the League and the FA Cup in 1960–1. He was British Footballer of the Year in 1960–1, and also won a European Cup medal with Tottenham. On his retirement, he became a newspaper columnist and television commentator.

blancmange *noun* a cold sweet jelly-like pudding made with milk. [from Old French *blanc*, white + *manger*, food]

bland *adj. derog.* 1 *said of food* having a very mild taste. 2 *said of people or their actions* mild or gentle; showing no strong emotions. 3 insipid; lacking interest: *a bland appearance.* [from Latin *blandus*, soft, smooth]

Blanda, (George) Frederick (1927–) US footballer, born in Youngwood, Pennsylvania. He holds the record for the most points (2 002) in any National Football League (NFL) career. He played for the Chicago Bears, Baltimore Colts, Houston Oilers, and Oakland Raiders (1949–75).

blandish *verb* to persuade by gentle flattery; to cajole. [from Old French *blandir*]

blandishments *pl. noun* flattery intended to persuade.

blandly *adv.* in a bland or insipid manner; without interest.

blandness *noun* a bland or insipid state or quality.

blank — *adj.* 1 *said of paper* not written or printed on. 2 *said of magnetic tape, etc* with no sound or pictures yet recorded on it. 3 with spaces left for details, information, a signature, etc: *a blank form.* 4 not filled in; empty. 5 showing no expression or interest: *a blank look.* 6 having no thoughts or ideas: *my mind suddenly went blank.* 7 without a break or relieving feature: *a blank wall.* — *noun* 1 an empty space. 2 an empty space left on forms, etc to be filled in with particular information. 3 a printed form with blank spaces. 4 a state of having no thoughts or ideas: *my mind went a complete blank.* 5 a dash written in place of a word. 6 a blank cartridge. — *verb* (**blank something off** *or* **out**) to hide it or form a screen in front it: *clouds blanking out the sun.*
— **draw a blank** to get no results; to fail. [from French *blanc*, white]

blank cartridge *noun* a cartridge containing an explosive but no bullet.

blank cheque *noun* 1 a cheque which has been signed but on which the amount to be paid has been left blank. 2 complete freedom or authority.

blanket — *noun* 1 a thick covering of wool or other material, used to cover beds or for wrapping a person in for warmth. 2 a thick layer or mass which covers something: *a blanket of fog.* 3 (*attributive*) general; applying to or covering all cases, etc: *a blanket rule.* — *verb* (**blanketed, blanketing**) 1 to cover with, or as if with, a blanket. 2 to keep quiet or suppress. [from Old French *blankeete*, from *blanc*, white]

blanket bath *noun* the washing of a sick person in bed.

blankly *adv.* in a blank or inexpressive manner: *stared at us blankly.*

blankness *noun* lack of interest or expression.

blank verse *noun* poetry which does not rhyme, especially iambic pentameters.

blanquette *noun* a dish made with white meat such as chicken or veal, cooked in a white sauce. [from French *blanquette*, related to BLANKET]

Blanqui, (Louis) Auguste (1805–81) French revolutionary socialist leader, born in Puget-Théniers. He organized an abortive insurrection against the Bourbon regime in 1839, which led to his imprisonment until 1848. He founded the Central Republican Society, and was again imprisoned (1948). Remaining politically active during the Second Empire, he was arrested on the eve of the Paris Commune, of which he was nevertheless elected President (1871). A passionate extremist, whose supporters were known as Blanquists, he spent 37 years of his life in prison.

Blantyre POP (1981) 20 000, a town in Hamilton district, Strathclyde, W central Scotland. It is part of the Clydeside urban area. The missionary, David Livingstone, was born here in 1813. NOTABLE FEATURE Livingstone National Memorial.

Blantyre POP (1987) 333 000, a city in Southern region, S Malawi. It is Malawi's main commercial and industrial centre. NOTABLE FEATURES museum; two cathedrals; Kapachira Falls nearby. [named after the birthplace of the Scottish missionary, David Livingstone]

blare — *verb* **1** *intrans.* to make a sound like a trumpet. **2** *intrans., trans.* to sound or say loudly and harshly. — *noun* a loud, harsh sound. [from Middle English *blaren*]

Blarney POP (1991) 2 000, a small village in Cork county, Munster province, S Irish Republic. It is situated 8km/5mi NW of Cork. Visitors to Blarney Castle are supposed to gain the power of eloquent speech as they hang upside down to kiss the Blarney Stone. The legend dates from the 16c, when Lord Blarney, by pure loquaciousness, avoided acknowledging to Queen Elizabeth's deputy that the lands of Blarney were held as a grant from the Queen and not as a chiefship.

blarney — *noun* flattering words used to persuade or deceive. — *verb* (PAST TENSE AND PAST PARTICIPLE **blarneyed**) to persuade using flattery. [from BLARNEY]

blasé *adj.* lacking enthusiasm or interest, unconcerned, especially through over-familiarity. [from French *blasé*]

Blasis, Carlo (1797–1878) Italian dancer, choreographer, and teacher, born in Naples. He danced in France, Italy, London, and Russia, and became director of the Dance Academy in Milan in 1837. The author of noted treatises on the codification of ballet technique (1820, 1840, 1857), he is regarded as the most important ballet teacher of the 19c.

blaspheme *verb* **1** *intrans., trans.* to speak disrespectfully or rudely about God or sacred matters. **2** *intrans.* to swear or curse using the name of God. [from Latin *blasphemare*]

blasphemer *noun* a person who blasphemes.

blasphemous *adj.* involving blasphemy; using divine names profanely.

blasphemously *adv.* with blasphemy; profanely.

blasphemy *noun* (PL. **blasphemies**) speaking about God or sacred matters in a disrespectful or profane way.

◇ In many Christian countries, blasphemy is still technically a crime, and is extended to include denial or ridicule of God, Christ, or the Bible; but the law is seldom if ever invoked. Until the Enlightenment, it was punishable by death, and in some non-Christian countries (notably those adhering to Islamic fundamentalism), the crime of blasphemy is still punishable by death in some circumstances. The contemporary relevance and range of application of the law of blasphemy became a particular issue in the UK in 1989, following the publication of Salman Rushdie's book, *Satanic Verses*, considered to be blasphemous by the Muslim community at large.

blast — *noun* **1** an explosion, or the strong shock-waves spreading out from it. **2** a strong sudden stream or gust (of air, wind, etc). **3** a sudden loud sound of a trumpet, car horn, etc. **4** a sudden and violent outburst of anger or criticism. — *verb* **1** to blow up (a tunnel, rock, etc) with explosives. **2** to destroy: *blast one's hopes*. **3** to wither or cause to shrivel up. **4** to criticize severely. — *interj. colloq.* an expression of annoyance, etc.

— **at full blast** at full power, speed, etc.

blast off *said of a spacecraft* to take off from its launching pad.

blast out to make a loud noise: *music was blasting out from the radio*.

[from Anglo-Saxon *blæst*]

blasted — *adj. colloq.* annoying. — *adv. colloq.* extremely: *blasted cold*.

blast furnace *noun* a furnace for melting iron, into which blasts of hot air are blown.

blasting *noun* **1** blowing up with explosives. **2** swearing; cursing.

blastula *noun Zool.* an early embryonic stage in the development of multicellular animals. It typically consists of a hollow ball of cells. [from Greek *blastos*, bud]

blatant *adj.* **1** very obvious and without shame: *a blatant lie*. **2** very noticeable and obtrusive. [probably invented by Edmund Spenser (1596)]

Blatant Beast the babbling, malicious monster in Spenser's *The Faerie Queene*, who is the enemy to courtesy and is pursued by Sir Calidore.

blatantly *adv.* in a blatant or flagrant manner.

blather see BLETHER.

Blaue Reiter, der the name adopted by a group of avant-garde artists in Munich in 1911. It was apparently inspired by a coloured illustration of a horseman on the cover of a book. Leading members included Vasily Kandinsky (1866–1944) and Paul Klee (1879–1940). [German, = blue rider]

Blavatsky, Helena Petrovna (1831–91) Russian theosophist, born in Ekaterinoslav (now Dnepropetrovsk, Ukraine). After travelling widely, she helped to found the Theosophical Society in New York (1875), and later carried on her work in India. Her psychic powers were widely acclaimed but did not survive scientific investigation. Her writings include *Isis Unveiled* (1877).

blaze² — *noun* **1** a white mark on an animal's face. **2** a mark made on the bark of a tree, especially to show a route or path. — *verb* to mark (a tree, path, etc) with blazes.

— **blaze a trail** to be the first to do, study, discover, etc something.

[perhaps related to Norse *blesi*]

blaze³ *verb* (*usually* **blaze something abroad**) to make news or information widely known. [related to Norse *blasa*, to blow]

blaze¹ — *noun* **1** a bright strong fire or flame. **2** a sudden and sharp bursting out of feeling or emotion. **3** a brilliant display. — *verb intrans.* **1** to burn or shine brightly. **2** to show great emotion, especially anger.

— **blaze away 1** to fire a gun rapidly and without stopping. **2** *colloq.* to work very hard.

blaze up 1 to suddenly burn much more brightly. **2** to become very angry.

like blazes *colloq.* with great energy, speed, or enthusiasm.

[from Anglo-Saxon *blæse*, torch]

blazer *noun* a light jacket, often in the colours of a school or club and sometimes worn as part of a uniform. [from BLAZE¹]

blazing *adj.* **1** burning brightly. **2** *colloq.* extremely angry.

blazon — *verb* (**blazoned**, **blazoning**) **1** to make public. **2** to describe (a coat of arms) in technical terms. **3** to paint names, designs, etc on (a coat of arms). — *noun* a shield or coat of arms. [from Old French *blason*, shield]

bleach — *verb trans., intrans.* to whiten or remove colour from a substance by exposure to

sunlight or certain chemicals. — *noun* any liquid chemical, eg hydrogen peroxide, sodium hypochlorite, used to whiten or remove colour from cloth, paper, hair, etc. All bleaches are oxidizing agents. [from Anglo-Saxon *blæcan*]

bleaching powder *noun* a white powder used in bleaching, a compound of calcium, chlorine, and oxygen.

bleak *adj.* **1** exposed and desolate. **2** cold and not welcoming. **3** offering little or no hope. [from Anglo-Saxon *blac*, pale]

Bleak House a novel by Charles Dickens (1852–3). It centres around the involvements, legal and otherwise, of various members of the Jarndyce household.

bleakly *adj.* drearily; without promise.

bleakness *noun* a bleak or desolate state or quality.

blearily *adv.* dimly; indistinctly.

bleary *adj.* (**blearier**, **bleariest**) **1** *said of a person's eyes* red and dim, usually from tiredness or through crying. **2** blurred, indistinct, and unclear.

bleat *verb* **1** *intrans.* to cry like a sheep, goat or calf. **2** *intrans., trans.* (**bleat something out**) to speak or say something foolishly and in a weak, high voice. [from Anglo-Saxon *blætan*]

Bled, Lake, Serbo-Croatian **Blejsko Jezero** a lake in NW Slovenia, situated 48km/30mi NW of Ljubljana. It is an all-year tourist region, with a skiing complex nearby at Zatrnik. The spa in the village of Bled is noted for its solar treatment.

bleed *verb* (PAST TENSE AND PAST PARTICIPLE **bled**) **1** *intrans.* to lose or let out blood. **2** to remove or take blood from. **3** *intrans. said of plants, etc* to lose juice or sap. **4** to empty liquid or air from (a machine, radiator, etc). **5** *colloq.* to obtain money from (someone), usually illegally. **6** *intrans. said of dye* to come out of the material when wet.

— **one's heart bleeds** *ironic* one is sad or pitying.

[from Anglo-Saxon *bledan*]

bleeding *adj., adv. coarse slang* expressing anger or disgust: *a bleeding fool / he's bleeding lying*.

bleep — *noun* **1** a short high burst of sound, usually made by an electronic machine. **2** same as BLEEPER. — *verb* **1** *intrans.* to give out a short, high sound. **2** *trans.* to call (someone) using a bleeper. [probably imitative]

bleeper *noun* a small portable radio receiver which makes a bleeping sound when it picks up a signal, used especially to call a doctor in a hospital.

blemish — *noun* a stain, mark, or fault. — *verb* to stain or spoil the beauty of. [from Old French *blesmir*]

blench *verb intrans.* to start back or move away, especially in fear. [from Anglo-Saxon *blencan*]

blend *verb* **1** to mix (different sorts or varieties) into one. **2** *intrans.* (**blend in** *or* **with some-**

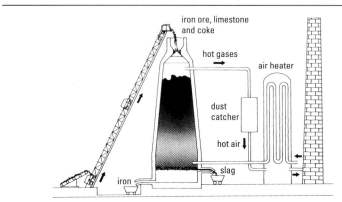

blast furnace

thing) to form a mixture or harmonious combination; to go well together. **3** to mix together. **4** *intrans. said especially of colours* to shade gradually into another: *the blue of the sea blending into the sky.* — *noun* a mixture or combination. [from Middle English *blenden*]

blende *noun* a mineral containing zinc sulphide. [from German *blenden*, to deceive]

blender *noun* a machine for mixing food or making it into a liquid.

Blenheim, Battle of the greatest military triumph (1704) of Marlborough and his Imperial ally Prince Eugene of Savoy, in the War of the Spanish Succession. Fought on the Danube to prevent a combined Franco-Bavarian assault on Vienna, it marked the first major defeat of the armies of Louis XIV of France, and the first major English victory on the European mainland since Agincourt.

Blenheim Palace a Baroque palace designed by Vanbrugh, and built (1705–24) in Woodstock, near Oxford. It is a World Heritage site.

blenny *noun* (PL. **blennies**) a type of small fish with a scaleless, slimy skin. [from Greek *blennos*, mucus]

Blériot, Louis (1872–1936) French aviator, born in Cambrai, who made the first flight across the English Channel (25 Jul 1909) from Baraques to Dover in a small 24-hp monoplane. He later became an aircraft manufacturer.

bless *verb* (PAST TENSE **blessed**; PAST PARTICIPLE **blessed**, **blest**) **1** to ask for divine favour or protection for. **2** to make or pronounce holy; to consecrate. **3** to praise; to give honour or glory to. **4** to thank or be thankful for: *I bless the day I met him.*
— **be blessed with something** to have the benefit or advantage of a natural quality or attribute: *to be blessed with good health.*
bless me *or* **bless my soul** an expression of surprise, pleasure, dismay, etc.
bless you! said to a person who has just sneezed.
[from Anglo-Saxon *bletsian*]

blessed *adj.* **1** holy. **2** *RC Church, said of a dead person* pronounced holy by the Pope, usually as the first stage of becoming a saint. **3** *euphemistic colloq.* damned.

Blessed Damozel, The a poem (1850) and painting (1871–9) by Dante Gabriel Rossetti.

blessedly *adv.* fortunately; happily.

blessing *noun* **1** a wish or prayer for happiness or success. **2** a cause of happiness; a benefit or advantage. **3** approval or good wishes. **4** a short prayer said before or after a meal.
— **a blessing in disguise** something that has proved to be fortunate after seeming unfortunate.
count one's blessings to be grateful for one's advantages.

blether *or* **blather** *verb intrans.* (**blethered**, **blethering**) *chiefly Scot.* to talk foolishly. [from Norse *blathra*]

blew see BLOW[1].

Blida POP (1987) 171 000, the chief town of El Blida department, N Algeria. It is situated 40km/25mi SW of Algiers. HISTORY dates from the 16c; occupied by the French in 1839; suffered earthquakes in 1825 and 1867.

Bligh, William (c.1753–c.1817) English sailor, born in Plymouth. He sailed under Capt Cook on Cook's second world voyage (1772–4), and in 1787 was sent as commander of the *Bounty* to Tahiti. On the return voyage, the men mutinied under his harsh treatment and in Apr 1789, Bligh and 18 men were cast adrift in an open boat without charts. In June, he arrived at Timor, near Java, having navigated his frail craft for 3 618mi/5 822km. In 1805 he was appointed Governor of New South Wales, where his conduct led to his imprisonment for two years.

blight — *noun* **1** *Agric.* a fungal disease of plants that usually attacks an entire crop, or one specific crop throughout a particular region, eg potato blight. **2** a person or thing that causes decay or destruction, or spoils things. — *verb* **1** to affect with blight. **2** to harm or destroy. **3** to disappoint or frustrate: *blighted hopes.* [origin unknown]

blighter *noun old colloq. use* **1** a person one dislikes. **2** a person one feels some sympathy for or envy of: *poor old blighter.* [from BLIGHT]

blimey *interj. Brit. slang* used to express surprise or annoyance. [from *gorblimey*, God blind me]

Blimp *or* **blimp** *noun* a very conservative, old-fashioned, reactionary person. [from the fat pompous cartoon character Colonel *Blimp*, used in anti-German and anti-government cartoons during World War II]

blimp *noun* **1** a type of large balloon or airship, used for publicity, observation, or defence. **2** a soundproof cover for a camera used to shoot films.

blimpish *adj.* characteristic of (Colonel) Blimp; reactionary.

blind — *adj.* **1** not able to see. **2** (**blind to something**) unable or unwilling to understand or appreciate something unwelcome: *blind to one's faults.* **3** without preparation or previous knowledge. **4** unthinking; without reason or purpose: *blind hatred.* **5** hidden from sight: *a blind entrance.* **6** not allowing sight of what is beyond: *a blind summit.* **7** (in flying) using instruments only, without visual contact. **8** having no openings: *a blind wall.* **9** closed at one end. **10** *said of a pastry case* cooked without a filling. **11** *said of plants* failing to produce flowers. **12** *colloq.* for the use of people who are blind: *a blind crossing.* — *adv.* blindly: *flying blind.* — *noun* **1** a screen to stop light coming through a window. **2** a person, action, or thing which hides the truth or deceives. **3** anything which prevents sight or blocks out light. **4** (**the blind**) people who cannot see. — *verb* **1** to make blind. **2** to make unreasonable, foolish, etc: *blinded by anger.* **3** (**blind someone with something**) to confuse or dazzle them: *tried to blind me with science.*
— **blind drunk** *colloq.* completely drunk.
swear blind *colloq.* to state with certainty.
turn a blind eye to something to pretend not to notice it.
[an Anglo-Saxon word]

blind alley *noun* **1** a narrow road with an opening at one end only. **2** a situation or course of action which is leading nowhere.

blind date 1 a date with a person one has not met before, often arranged by a third person. **2** the person met on such a date.

blindfold — *noun* a piece of cloth used to cover the eyes to prevent a person from seeing. — *adj., adv.* with one's eyes covered. — *verb* to cover the eyes of (someone) to prevent them from seeing.

blinding *noun* **1** making someone blind, especially violently. **2** the process of filling the cracks of a newly made road with grit. — *adj., said of a light, etc* intensely strong and bright, causing temporary lack of vision. — clear and intense: *the answer came in a blinding flash.*

Blinding of Samson, The a painting by Rembrandt (1636, Frankfurt).

blindly *adv.* in a blind manner; without vision or perception: *ran blindly ahead.*

blindman's-buff *noun* a children's game in which one child wears a blindfold and tries to catch the other children.

blindness *noun* serious or total loss of vision in one or both eyes.
◇ In developed countries the commonest causes of blindness are diabetes, degeneration of the retina of the eye, cataract and glaucoma. In developing countries many of the causes are infectious

and therefore preventible, including trachoma, gonorrhoea, river blindness, and leprosy. Blindness may also be due to hereditary or congenital factors (eg infection of the mother during pregnancy), injury, or the normal ageing process. Night blindness (inability to see in the dark) is associated with vitamin A deficiency.
Aids to the blind include guide dogs, the Braille and Moon alphabets for reading and writing, and electronic devices currently being developed that convert print to recognizable mechanical speech. When blindness is due to clouding of the lens or cornea of the eye, sight can be restored by removal of the lens or corneal grafting.

blind spot 1 *Anat.* a small area on the retina of the eye where nerve fibres from the light-sensitive rods and cones lead into the optic nerve. There are no rods and cones in this area, and so no visual images can be transmitted from it. **2** an area of poor reception within the normal range of radio transmission, caused by tall buildings or other obstructions. **3** an area of poor or no visibility, especially in the window area of a motor vehicle. **4** a subject in which a particular person lacks understanding or interest: *communication was his blind spot.*

blindworm *noun* same as SLOW-WORM.

blink — *verb usually intrans.* **1** to open and shut the eyes quickly. **2** *trans.* to open and shut (an eyelid or an eye) very quickly. **3** *said of a light* to flash on and off or shine unsteadily. **4** (**blink at something**) to refuse to recognize or accept something unwelcome. — *noun* **1** an act of blinking. **2** a brief period of sunshine, etc.
— **in the blink of an eye** quickly; suddenly.
on the blink *colloq.* not working properly.
[from Middle English *blinken*]

blinker — *noun* (*usually* **blinkers**) one of two small flat pieces of leather attached to a horse's bridle to prevent it from seeing sideways. — *verb* (**blinkered**, **blinkering**) **1** to provide (a horse) with blinkers. **2** to limit or obscure sight or awareness. [from BLINK]

blinkered *adj.* **1** *said of a horse* wearing blinkers. **2** *derog., said of a person* narrow in outlook; unwilling to consider the opinions of others.

blinking *colloq.* — *adj.* used to express mild annoyance or disapproval: *broke the blinking thing.* — *adv.* very. [from BLINK]

blip — *noun* **1** a sudden sharp sound produced by a machine. **2** a spot of light on a screen showing the position of an object. **3** a sudden and fleeting deviation from what is normal or correct. — *verb intrans.* (**blipped**, **blipping**) to make a blip. [imitative]

Bliss, Sir Arthur (Drummond) (1891–1975) English composer, born in London. He studied under Holst, Stanford, and Vaughan Williams at the Royal College of Music, and in 1921 became Professor of Composition, but resigned to compose such works as the film music for Wells's *Things to Come* (1935), the ballet *Checkmate* (1937), the opera *The Olympians* (1949), chamber music, and piano and violin works. He was music director of the BBC (1942–4), and in 1953 succeeded Bax as Master of the Queen's Musick.

bliss *noun* **1** very great happiness. **2** the special happiness of heaven. [from Anglo-Saxon *bliths*]

blissful *adj.* completely happy; utterly joyful.

blissfully *adv.* happily; joyfully.

blister — *noun* **1** a small swelling on or just beneath the surface of the skin, containing watery fluid (serum) and occasionally blood or pus, usually caused by friction or a burn, but sometimes occurring as an allergic reaction. **2** a bubble in a thin surface coating of paint, varnish, etc, or on the surface of previously molten metal or plastic that has solidified. — *verb* **1** to cause a blister on (skin, a surface, etc). **2** *intrans.* to erupt in blisters. **3** to criticize or attack sharply. [from Norse *blastr*]

blistered *adj.* having many blisters.

blistering *adj.* **1** very hot. **2** angry and aggressive: *blistering criticism.*

blister pack same as BUBBLE PACK.

blithe *adj.* **1** happy, without worries or cares. **2** *derog.* done without serious thought; casual. [an Anglo-Saxon word]

blithely *adv.* without concern; casually.

blithering *adj. colloq.* stupid. [from *blither*, a form of BLETHER]

Blithe Spirit a play by Noël Coward (1941). It is a comedy about a newly married man's encounters with his deceased wife Elvira through a medium (Madame Arcati).

BLitt *abbrev. Baccalaureus Litterarum*, Bachelor of Letters.

blitz — *noun* **1** (*also* **blitzkrieg**) a sudden strong attack, or period of such attacks, especially from the air. **2** (**the Blitz**) the German air raids on Britain in 1940. **3** a period of hard work, etc to get something finished. — *verb* **1** to attack, damage, or destroy as if by a blitz or air raid. **2** to work hard at for a short period. [from German *Blitzkrieg*, lightning war, a sudden and intensive attack to win a quick victory in war]

Blixen, Karen, Baroness, pseudonym **Isak Dinesen** (1885–1962) Danish novelist and storyteller, born in Rungsted. She travelled widely in Europe, and lived in Kenya for many years where she ran a coffee plantation. In 1931 she returned to Denmark and began to write in both Danish and English. Her works include *Seven Gothic Tales* (1934) and the autobiographical *Out of Africa* (1937, filmed in 1985 with Meryl Streep and Robert Redford).

blizzard *noun* a severe snowstorm characterized by low temperatures and strong winds that blow large drifts of dry powdery snow upward from the ground, resulting in much reduced visibility.

bloat *verb* **1** *trans., intrans.* to swell or cause to swell or puff out with air, pride, etc. **2** *trans.* to prepare (fish, especially herring) by salting and half drying in smoke. [from Norse *blautr*, wet, soft]

bloated *adj.* inflated; swollen; puffed out.

bloater *noun* a fish, especially a herring, which has been salted and half dried in smoke.

blob *noun* **1** a small soft round mass of something: *a blob of jam.* **2** a small drop of liquid. [imitative of the sound of dripping]

bloc *noun* a group of countries, people, etc who have a common interest, purpose or policy. [from French *bloc*, block, group]

Bloch, Felix (1905–83) Swiss-born US physicist, born in Zurich. Following World War II he developed the technique of nuclear magnetic resonance (NMR); this provides information about nuclei and chemical structures, and has led to a powerful imaging technique for medical diagnosis. He shared the 1952 Nobel Prize for Physics with Edward Purcell.

block — *noun* **1** a mass of solid wood, stone, ice, or other hard material, usually with flat sides. **2** a piece of wood, stone, etc used for chopping and cutting on. **3** (*usually* **blocks**) a wooden or plastic cube, used as a child's toy. **4** a large building containing offices, flats, etc. **5** a group of buildings with roads on all four sides. **6** a group of seats, tickets, etc thought of as a single unit: *a block booking.* **7** something which causes or acts as a stopping of movement, thought, etc: *a road block.* **8** a piece of wood or metal which has been cut to be used in printing. **9** *Athletics* same as STARTING-BLOCK. **10** a series of ropes and wheels for lifting things, or pulleys, mounted in a case. See also BLOCK AND TACKLE. **11** *slang* a person's head. — *verb* **1** to obstruct or impede; to put an obstacle in the way of. **2** to print (a design, title, etc) on (the cover of a book, piece of material,

etc). **3** *Cricket* to stop (a ball) with one's bat resting upright on the ground.

— **block someone** *or* **something in 1** to prevent them from moving or from getting out; to confine them. **2** to draw or sketch them roughly. **3** (**block something off**) to restrict or limit the use of an area: *the police have blocked off several streets.*

block something out 1 to shut out light, an idea, etc. **2** to draw or sketch something roughly.

block something up 1 to block it completely. **2** to fill a window, doorway, etc with bricks, etc. [from French *bloc*]

blockade — *noun* the closing off of a port, region, etc by military means in order to stop people, goods, etc from passing in and out. — *verb* to put a blockade round (a port, etc).

blockage *noun* **1** anything that causes a pipe, etc to be blocked. **2** the state of being blocked.

block and tackle *noun* a series of ropes and wheels used for lifting heavy objects. See also BLOCK 10.

blockbuster *noun colloq.* **1** a highly popular and successful film, book, etc. **2** an extremely powerful bomb.

block capital *or* **block letter** *noun* a capital letter written in imitation of printed type.

blocked *adj.* affected by an obstruction or blockage.

blockhead *noun colloq.* a stupid person.

blockhouse *noun* **1** a small shelter made from very strong concrete, used for watching battles, spacecraft take off, etc. **2** a small, temporary fort.

block letter same as BLOCK CAPITAL.

block vote *noun* a vote by a delegate, eg at a conference, that is proportional in power to the number of people the delegate represents.

Bloemfontein POP (1985e) 104 000, the capital of Orange Free State province, E central South Africa, 370km/230mi SW of Johannesburg. It is the judicial capital of South Africa and the trade centre for Orange Free State province and Lesotho. HISTORY founded as a fort in 1846; seat of government of Orange River Sovereignty and of Orange Free State Republic from 1849 until 1857; taken by Lord Roberts in 1900 during the Boer War. NOTABLE FEATURES Anglican Cathedral; National Museum (1877); War Museum (1931).

Blok, Alexander Alexandrovich (1880–1921) Russian poet, born in St Petersburg. His poetry collections include *Songs about the Lady Fair* (1904), and *Nocturnal Hours* (1911). He welcomed the 1917 Revolution and in 1918 wrote two pro-revolutionary poems, *The Twelve* and *The Scythians*.

bloke *noun Brit. colloq.* a man.

blond *adj.* **1** *said of a person* having pale yellow hair and light-coloured or pale skin. **2** *said of a person's hair* pale yellow. [from Latin *blondus*, yellow]

blonde — *noun* a woman with pale yellow hair. — *adj., said of a woman* having pale yellow hair.

Blondel (12c) French minstrel. He is said to have accompanied Richard Coeur de Lion to Palestine, and to have found him in the Austrian prison of Dürrenstein (1193) by means of a song they had jointly composed.

Blondin, Charles, pseudonym of **Jean François Gravelet** (1824–97) French tightrope walker, born in Hesdin, near Calais. In 1859 he crossed Niagara Falls on a tightrope and later repeated the feat with variations (blindfold, with a wheelbarrow, with a man on his back, on stilts, etc).

Blood, Thomas (c.1618–80) Irish criminal adventurer. Known for his activities during the English Civil War and Restoration, he attempted to steal the Crown jewels from the Tower of

London (May 1671). Disguised as a clergyman, he took the Crown, while an associate took the orb, but he was pursued, captured, and imprisoned. He was later pardoned by Charles II.

Blood, Council of, also called **Council of Troubles** a council of seven members (three of them Spaniards) established (1567–76) on Philip II's orders by the Duke of Alva, the Spanish Habsburg military commander in the Low Countries, to suppress heresy and opposition during the Revolt of the Netherlands. The Council's proceedings (1567–73) included some 12 200 trials, 9 000 convictions, and 1 000 executions, which caused widespread fear and alienation among the population.

blood — *noun* **1** a fluid tissue that circulates in the arteries, veins, and capillaries of the body as a result of muscular contractions of the heart. It conveys nutrients and oxygen to the organs and tissues, and removes carbon dioxide and other waste products. **2** the taking of life; murder. **3** relationship through belonging to the same family, race, etc.; descent: *of royal blood.* **4** near family: *my own flesh and blood.* **5** temper, passion. **6** a group of people seen as adding new strength to an existing group: *new blood in the teaching profession.* **7** a man who is interested in fashion, etc and takes a strong interest in his appearance. — *verb* **1** to give a (young hunting dog) its first taste of a freshly killed animal. **2** to give (a person, etc) the first experience of (war, battle, etc).

— **be after** *or* **out for someone's blood** to be extremely angry with a person and to want revenge, to fight him or her, etc.

in cold blood deliberately and cruelly, showing no concern or passion.

make one's blood boil to make one extremely angry.

make one's blood run cold to frighten or horrify one.

sweat blood to work very hard. [from Anglo-Saxon *blod*]

◊ The body of an average male adult contains about 5 litres of blood, 90% of which passes through the body every minute when the body is resting. As well as transporting oxygen, nutrients, hormones, waste products, etc, the blood circulates heat throughout the body. Blood volume and composition are closely regulated by the kidneys, adrenal glands, and hypothalamus. Mammalian blood consists of liquid plasma in which the blood cells are suspended. The doughnut-shaped red blood cells (*erythrocytes*), produced in the bone marrow, contain the pigment haemoglobin, which takes up oxygen in the lungs and releases it in the tissues. White blood cells (*leucocytes*), produced in the bone marrow and lymphoid tissue, protect the body against disease and infection. They engulf invading bacteria and foreign bodies, and aid the repair of injured tissues. They also produce antibodies, and are major components of the body's immune system. *Blood platelets* are the smallest components of the blood, and are involved in the process of clotting.

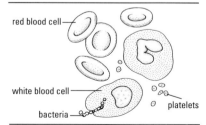

blood cells

blood-and-thunder *adj., said of a film, etc* including much violent action and excitement.

blood bank a department in a hospital or blood transfusion centre where blood collected from donors is stored, categorized according to blood group, and tested (for the presence of the HIV virus), prior to transfusion into patients.

bloodbath *noun* a massacre.

blood brother *noun* a man or boy who has promised to treat another as his brother, usually in a ceremony in which some of their blood has mixed.

blood count *noun* a medical examination to count the red or white blood cells in a person's blood.

bloodcurdling *adj.* causing great fear.

blood donor a person who donates blood under medical supervision for storage in a blood bank until it is required for transfusion into a patient with a compatible blood group.

blood group *or* **blood type** any one of the four types into which human blood may be classified, A, B, AB and O.

blood heat the normal temperature of human blood, about 37°C, 98·4°F.

bloodhound *noun* a large dog with a keen sense of smell, used for tracking.

bloodily *adv.* in a bloody or cruel manner.

bloodiness *noun* 1 being bloody or covered in blood. 2 cruelty; much killing.

bloodless *adj.* 1 without violence or anybody being killed. 2 pale and lifeless. 3 dull and tedious.

bloodlessly *adv.* without violence or killing.

bloodletting *noun* 1 killing. 2 the treating, especially formerly, of sick people by removing some of their blood.

blood-money *noun* 1 money paid for committing murder. 2 money paid in compensation to the relatives of a murdered person.

blood orange *noun* a type of orange with red flesh.

blood poisoning a serious condition caused by the presence of either bacterial toxins or large numbers of bacteria in the bloodstream.

blood pressure the pressure of the blood within the blood vessels. It usually refers to the pressure within the arteries, the pressure within capillaries and veins being much lower. In a healthy person the arterial blood pressure reaches a peak of about 120 to 130 millimetres of mercury when the heart muscle contracts, and falls to about 70 millimetres of mercury when the heart muscle relaxes.

blood relation a person related to one by birth rather than by marriage.

bloodshed *noun* the shedding of blood or killing of people.

bloodshot *adj., said of the eyes* sore and red with blood.

blood sports sports that involve the killing of animals.
◇ In Britain, blood sports are frequently referred to, especially by their supporters, as *field sports* or *country sports*. Fox-hunting, hare coursing, and other legal sports regarded by some as being unnecessarily cruel to animals have been the subject of continuous and vociferous campaigns (especially by animal-rights groups) which seek to have them banned. In the past, popular blood sports have included deer- and stag-hunting with hounds, otter hunting, cock-fighting (still practised in Asia and elsewhere but illegal in Britain since 1840), and dog-fighting (illegal but still practised clandestinely in certain parts of Britain).

bloodstained *adj.* stained with blood.

bloodstock *noun* horses that have been bred specially for racing.

bloodstone *noun Geol.* a type of chalcedony, a fine-grained variety of the mineral quartz. It is dark green with red flecks.

bloodstream *noun* the blood flowing through the body.

bloodsucker *noun* 1 an animal that sucks blood, eg the leech. 2 *colloq.* a person who extorts money from another.

bloodsucking *adj.* extortionate.

blood test a test in which a small amount of blood is analysed in order to determine its blood group, or to detect the presence of alcohol, drugs, bacteria, or viruses (eg the HIV virus). It is also used to determine whether a particular inherited or sexually transmitted disease is present, or to establish paternity where this is in dispute.

bloodthirstily *adv.* with eagerness or fondness for killing.

bloodthirstiness *noun* eagerness or fondness for killing.

bloodthirsty *adj.* 1 eager for or fond of killing or violence. 2 *said of a film, etc* including much violence and killing.

blood transfusion *noun* the process of giving a sick person blood which has been donated by another person.

blood type same as BLOOD GROUP.

blood vessel *noun* any of the tubes, arteries, veins, etc in the body, through which blood flows.

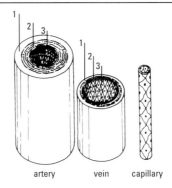

artery   vein   capillary

1: fibrous outer layer
2: muscle fibres
3: endothelium (lining)

blood vessels

Blood Wedding (Bodas de Sangre) a play by Federico García Lorca (1933). The first of a trilogy of folk tragedies (followed by *Yerma*, 1934, and *The House of Bernarda Alba*, 1936), it focuses on the conflict between love and honour in a fatal dispute involving a bride's two jealous suitors.

bloody — *adj.* (**bloodier, bloodiest**) 1 stained or covered with blood. 2 involving or including much killing. 3 cruel. 4 *slang* used to express annoyance, etc: *a bloody fool.* — *adv. slang* extremely. — *verb* (**bloodies, bloodied**) to stain or cover with blood.

Bloody Assizes the western circuit assizes in England in the summer of 1685, presided over by Lord Chief Justice George Jeffreys after the defeat of the Duke of Monmouth at the battle of Sedgemoor. About 150 of Monmouth's followers, mostly poorer farmers and clothworkers, were executed, and 800 transported to the West Indies.

bloody Mary *noun* a drink made from vodka and tomato juice.

bloody-minded *adj. derog.* deliberately uncooperative and inclined to cause difficulties for others.

bloody-mindedness *noun* being deliberately unco-operative and causing difficulties.

Bloody Sunday the name given, especially by Republicans in Northern Ireland, to events occurring during a Catholic civil rights protest march in Londonderry (30 Jan 1972). The British army opened fire, killing 14 mainly young demonstrators. Indirectly this action led to the ending of the Stormont parliament and the reimposition of direct rule by the British government over Northern Ireland.

Bloom, Leopold the endearing, commonplace Jewish man at the centre of James Joyce's *Ulysses*. Molly is his earthy, passionate wife.

bloom — *noun* 1 a flower, especially on a plant valued for its flowers. 2 the state of flowering: *in bloom.* 3 a state of perfection or great beauty: *in full bloom.* 4 a glow or flush on the skin. 5 a fine white powder on leaves, fruit, etc. — *verb intrans.* 1 to be in flower. 2 to be in or achieve a state of great beauty or perfection. 3 to be healthy; to be growing well; to flourish. [from Norse *blom*]

bloomer *noun colloq.* a silly mistake. [from BLOOMING]

bloomers *pl. noun* 1 *formerly* short loose trousers gathered at the knee, worn by women. 2 *old colloq. use* women's underpants or knickers. [named after Amelia *Bloomer* (1818–94), an American social reformer who believed women should dress in short full skirts and bloomers]

blooming — *adj.* 1 flowering. 2 bright; beautiful. 3 healthy and flourishing. 4 *slang* used as an expression of annoyance, etc: *a blooming idiot.* — *adv. slang* very.

Bloomsbury group a group of writers and artists taking their name from Bloomsbury Square in London who were active around the time of World War I. Influenced by George Moore's *Principia Ethica* (1903), they reacted against Victorian values and had a significant impact on the Modernist movement in England. They included Leonard and Virginia Woolf, Clive and Vanessa Bell, Maynard Keynes, Lytton Strachey, Roger Fry, Duncan Grant, and E M Forster.

blossom — *noun* 1 a flower or mass of flowers, especially on a fruit tree. 2 the state of flowering: *in blossom.* — *verb intrans.* (**blossomed, blossoming**) 1 to develop flowers. 2 to grow well or develop: *she has blossomed into an accomplished dancer.* [from Anglo-Saxon *blostm*]

blossoming *adj.* flowering; maturing, thriving.

blot — *noun* 1 a spot or stain, especially of ink. 2 a spot or blemish which spoils the beauty of something. 3 a stain on a person's good reputation or character. — *verb* (**blotted, blotting**) 1 to make a spot or stain on, especially with ink. 2 to dry with blotting-paper.
— **blot one's copybook** to spoil one's good reputation, etc, especially through a small mistake.
blot something out 1 to hide it from sight. 2 to refuse to think about or remember a painful memory.
[from Middle English *blotte*]

blotch — *noun* a large coloured or sore spot or mark on the skin, etc. — *verb* to cover or mark with blotches. [perhaps from **blot**]

blotchy *adj.* (**blotchier, blotchiest**) covered in blotches; discoloured in patches.

blotter *noun* a large sheet or pad of blotting-paper with a hard backing.

blotting-paper *noun* soft, thick paper used for drying wet ink when writing.

blouse — *noun* 1 a woman's shirt-like garment. 2 a loose jacket gathered in at the waist, part of a soldier's uniform. — *verb* to arrange in loose folds. [from French *blouse*]

blouson *noun* a loose jacket fitting tightly at the waist. [from French *blouson*]

blow[1] — *verb* (PAST TENSE **blew**; PAST PARTICIPLE **blown**) 1 *said of a current of air, wind, etc* to be moving, especially rapidly. **2** *intrans., trans.* (*often* **blow along** *or* **down**, *etc*) to move or be moved by a current of air, wind, etc. **3** to send (air) from the mouth. **4** to form or shape by blowing air from the mouth: *blow bubbles / blow glass*. **5** to shatter or destroy by an explosion: *the blast blew the chimney off the roof*. **6** to produce (a sound) by blowing: *blow a whistle*. **7** *intrans.* to breathe heavily. **8** to clear by blowing through: *blow one's nose*. **9 a** to cause (a fuse) to break. **b** *said of a fuse* to break, causing an interruption in the flow of current. **10** to break into (a safe, etc) using explosives. **11** *colloq.* to spoil or bungle (an opportunity, etc): *he had his chance, and he blew it*. **12** *colloq.* to spend a large amount of money: *blew £10 on a round of drinks*. **13** *intrans., trans. slang* to leave (a place) quickly and suddenly. **14** *intrans. said of a whale* to send out air and water through a hole in the top of its head. — *noun* **1** an act or example of blowing. **2** a spell of exposure to fresh air: *let's go for a blow on the cliffs*. — *interj.* an expression of annoyance.

— **blow someone away** *North Amer. slang* to murder them with a gun.

blow something away *or* **off** to remove it by blowing.

blow hot and cold *colloq.* to keep changing one's mind.

blow something out 1 to put a flame, etc out by blowing. **2** to send something forcibly outwards through an explosion. See also BLOW-OUT.

blow over *said of an incident, threat, etc* to pass by without having any harmful effect.

blow one's own trumpet *colloq.* to praise oneself and one's abilities, etc.

blow something sky-high to destroy it completely.

blow one's top *colloq.* to lose one's temper.

blow up 1 to explode. **2** to fill up or swell up with air or gas. **3** *colloq.* to lose one's temper.

blow someone up *colloq.* to lose one's temper with them.

blow something up 1 to produce a larger version of (a photograph, etc). **2** *colloq.* to make something seem more serious or important than it really is.

blow the whistle on someone *colloq.* to inform on them.

blow the whistle on something *colloq.* to bring it to an abrupt end.

[from Anglo-Saxon *blawan*]

blow[2] *noun* **1** a stroke or knock with the hand or a weapon. **2** a sudden shock or misfortune.

— **come to blows** to end up fighting.

blow-by-blow *adj., said of a description, account, etc* giving all the details in the right order.

blow-dry — *verb* to dry (hair) in a particular style with a hair-drier. — *noun* an act of blow-drying.

blower *noun* **1** a device for blowing out a current of air. **2** (**the blower**) *colloq.* the telephone.

blowfly *noun* a type of fly that lays its eggs on meat or in wounds.

blowhole *noun* **1** a nostril high on the head of a whale, which can be closed by means of valves during diving, and through which a compressed stream of water droplets and air is released, forming a 'spout', as the animal surfaces. **2** *Geol.* an aperture near a clifftop through which air or water compressed in a sea cave by breaking waves and rising tides is forcibly expelled. **3** *Geol.* a small vent on the surface of a thick lava flow.

blowlamp *or* **blowtorch** *noun* a device for producing and directing an intensely hot flame at a particular spot, used for burning off paint, etc.

blown see BLOW[1].

blow-out *noun colloq.* **1** the bursting of a car tyre. **2** a violent escape of gas, etc, especially on an oil rig. **3** a large meal.

blowpipe *noun* **1** in glass-blowing, a long narrow iron tube on which a mass of molten glass is gathered. Air is then forced down the tube, forming a bubble of air within the glass, which can then be shaped as it cools. **2** a small often curved tube that carries a stream of air into a flame in order to concentrate and direct it, eg for brazing and soldering.

blowtorch same as BLOWLAMP.

blow-up 1 an enlargement of a photograph. **2** an explosion.

blowy *adj.* (**blowier**, **blowiest**) blustery; windy.

blowzy *or* **blowsy** *adj.* (**blowzier**, **blowziest**) *derog. colloq., said of a woman* **1** fat and red-faced. **2** dirty and untidy. [from *blowze*, beggar's woman]

blubber — *noun* a thick insulating layer of fat beneath the skin of whales, seals, etc. — *verb* **1** *intrans.* to weep convulsively. **2** to try to say (words, etc) while weeping. [imitative]

Blücher, Gebbard Leberecht von, Fürst von (Prince of), known as **Marshal Forward** (1742–1819) Prussian soldier, born in Rostock, Mecklenburg. He fought against the French in 1793 and 1806, and in 1813 took chief command in Silesia, defeated Napoleon at Leipzig, and entered Paris (1814). In 1815 he assumed the general command, suffered a severe defeat at Ligny, but completed Wellington's victory at Waterloo by his timely appearance on the field.

bludgeon — *noun* a stick or club with a heavy end. — *verb* (**bludgeoned**, **bludgeoning**) **1** to hit with, or as if with, a bludgeon. **2** to force or bully into doing something.

blue — *adj.* **1** of the colour of a clear, cloudless sky. **2** sad or depressed. See also BLUES. **3** *said of a film, etc* pornographic or indecent. **4** politically conservative. **5** with a skin which is pale blue or purple because of the cold. — *noun* **1** the colour of a clear, cloudless sky. **2** blue paint or dye. **3** blue material or clothes: *dressed in blue*. **4** a person who has been chosen to represent a college or university at sport, especially at Oxford or Cambridge. **5** *Brit. colloq.* a supporter of the Conservative Party. — *verb* (**bluing**, **blueing**) **1** to make blue. **2** *colloq.* to waste.

— **do something till one is blue in the face** to do it repeatedly but without any effect.

once in a blue moon hardly ever.

out of the blue without warning; unexpectedly. [from Old French *bleu*]

Blue Angel, The (Der Blaue Engel) a German film directed by Josef Von Sternberg (1930). It tells the story of a weak and masochistic professor captivated by an alluring night-club entertainer (played by Marlene Dietrich).

blue baby *Medicine* a newborn baby suffering from congenital heart disease that results in some or all of the deoxygenated (blue) blood being pumped around the body (giving the skin and lips a bluish tinge) instead of passing through the lungs. It is treated by cardiac surgery early in life.

Bluebeard in European folklore, a wicked character who gives his new wife charge of the house-keys. She discovers the bodies of six previous wives in a forbidden room. Her brothers arrive just in time to save her from becoming Bluebeard's seventh victim, and slay him.

bluebell *noun* a small wild flower which has blue bell-shaped flowers.

blueberry *noun* a dark blue berry from a bush common in N America.

bluebird *noun* a small blue-backed N American songbird.

Blue Bird, The (L'Oiseau Bleu) a play by Maurice Maeterlinck (1909). It is a sentimental allegory about the search for happiness.

blue blood royal or noble blood or descent.

bluebottle *noun* a large fly with a blue body.

blue cheese cheese with thin lines of blue mould running through it.

blue-chip *adj.* *Stock Exchange* used to describe shares that are secure, although less secure than gilt-edged.

blue-collar *adj., said of workers* doing manual or unskilled work. See also WHITE-COLLAR.

Blue Danube, The (An der schönen, blauen Donau), properly *By the Beautiful Blue Danube* a waltz for orchestra by Johann Strauss, the Younger (Op. 34, 1867).

blue-eyed boy *noun derog. colloq.* a favourite.

bluegrass *or* **bluefunk** *noun* a simple style of country music popular in southern states of America.

blue-green alga *Biol.* common name for any of a group of single-celled photosynthetic prokaryotic organisms, often blue in colour owing to the presence of the pigment phycocyanin, which masks the green colour of chlorophyll. — Also called *cyanobacteria*.
◇ Blue-green algae were formerly classified as members of the division Cyanophyta in the plant kingdom, but are now regarded as bacteria and included in the kingdom Monera. Some species can fix atmospheric nitrogen, so increasing soil fertility, eg in rice-paddy fields, while others occur in symbiotic association with fungi to form lichens. Blue-green algae are among the oldest living organisms known.

Blue Horses a painting by Franz Marc (1911). It is one of a series of paintings which uses colour symbolically to convey the spirituality of animals.

Blue Mountain a mountain peak in Jamaica. HEIGHT 2 256m. It is the highest point on the island.

Blue Mountains a mountain range in E New South Wales, Australia, part of the Great Dividing Range, rising to 1 180m at Bird Rock. A tourist area with a national park, it is becoming a popular dormitory zone for Sydney.

blue movie *or* **blue film** a titillating or pornographic film.

blueness *noun* a blue state or quality.

Blue Nile, in Ethiopia **Abay Wenz**, in Sudan **Bahr El Azraq** the upper reach of the R Nile, NE Africa, length 1 450km/901mi. It issues from the SE corner of L Tana, in the Gojam region of Ethiopia and flows SE, then S and W, crossing into Sudan at Bumbadi. The river joins the White Nile at Khartoum, to form the R Nile. During its period of high flood, it provides almost 70% of the R Nile's flow, but during the low water, it accounts for less than 20%.

blue note *Mus.* a flattened note, usually the minor third and seventh of the scale, characteristic of the blues.

blue-pencil *verb* (**blue-pencilled**, **blue-pencilling**) to correct, edit, or cut parts out of (a piece of writing).

Blue Peter *noun* a blue flag with a white square, flown on a ship which is about to sail.

blueprint *noun* **1** a photographic print of plans, designs, etc consisting of white lines on a blue background. **2** a detailed plan of work to be done.

Blue Riband a notional honour awarded to the fastest passenger ship on the North Atlantic run. First awarded in 1838, its holders included the liner the SS *United States*. In 1986, it was awarded to Richard Branson, who broke the record for the fastest crossing in his powerboat the *Virgin Atlantic Challenger II*.

Blue Ridge Mountains a mountain range in SE USA, forming the E part of the Appalachian Mts. It extends NE–SW for c.1 050km/650mi from S Pennsylvania through Maryland, Virginia, and North Carolina to Georgia. The range includes the Black Mts and the Great Smoky Mts, and its highest point is Mt Mitchell (2 037m). Other high peaks are Brasstown Bald (1 458m), Mt Rogers (1 746m), and Sassafras Mt (1 083m). The Great Smoky Mountains National Park and the Shenandoah National Park, both established in the 1930s, are within the range. Timber is the major resource in a region famous for its wooded scenery.

blues *noun* **1** (*usually* **the blues**) a feeling of sadness or depression. **2** slow melancholy jazz music of Black American origin.

bluestocking *noun often derog.* a highly educated woman who is interested in serious academic subjects.

blue tit *noun* a small bird with blue wings and tail and blue on its head, common in Britain.

blue whale a rare baleen whale of the rorqual family, the largest living animal. It grows to a length of up to 30m, and is blue with pale spots. In the summer it feeds on shrimp-like *krill*, and in the winter it breeds near the Equator, but does not feed.

bluff¹ — *verb* **1** *intrans.* to try to deceive someone by pretending to be stronger, cleverer, etc than one really is. **2** *trans.* (**bluff someone into something**) to trick them by bluffing: *let's bluff him into doing all the work.* — *noun* an act of bluffing.
— **call someone's bluff** to challenge another person's bluff.
[from Dutch *bluffen*, to play a trick at cards]

bluff² — *noun* a steep cliff or bank of ground. — *adj.* **1** *usually said of a cliff or the bow of a ship* steep and upright. **2** rough, cheerful, and honest in manner.

bluffly *adv.* **1** steeply. **2** in a straightforwardly cheerful manner.

bluffness *noun* a bluff or rough manner; abruptness.

bluish *adj.* somewhat blue; close to blue.

Blunden, Edmund Charles (1896–1974) English poet and critic, born in Yalding, Kent. He was Professor of English Literature at Tokyo (1924–7), joined the staff of *The Times Literary Supplement* in 1943, lectured at Hong Kong University (1953–64), and became Professor of Poetry at Oxford (1966–8). Though essentially a nature poet, as is evident in *Pastorals* (1916), he is best known for the prose work *Undertones of War* (1928), which describe his own experiences in World War I.

blunder — *verb intrans.* (**blundered, blundering**) **1** to make a foolish and usually serious mistake. **2** to move awkwardly and clumsily: *her brother blundered in while we were kissing.* — *noun* a foolish and usually serious mistake. [from Middle English *blunderen*, from Norse *blunda*, to shut one's eyes]

blunderbuss *noun Hist.* a type of shotgun with a short wide barrel. [from Dutch *donderbus*, from *donder*, thunder + *bus*, gun]

blunderer *noun* a person who blunders; a clumsy person.

blundering *adj.* making or involving many clumsy mistakes.

Blunt, Anthony (Frederick) (1907–83) English art historian and Soviet spy, born in Bournemouth, Hampshire. A participant in the communist tendencies at Cambridge in the 1930s, he became a 'talent-spotter' for Guy Burgess, supplying the names of likely recruits to the Russian communist cause. While serving in British Intelligence during World War II, he could pass on information to the Soviet government, and he assisted the defection of Burgess and Donald Maclean in 1951. In 1964, after the defection of Kim Philby, Blunt confessed in return for his immunity, and he continued as Surveyor of the Queen's Pictures until 1972. His full involvement in espionage was made public only in 1979, and his knighthood (awarded 1956) was anulled.

blunt — *adj.* **1** having no point or sharp edge. **2** not sharp. **3** honest and direct in a rough way. — *verb* to make blunt or less sharp.

bluntly *adv.* in a blunt direct manner: *replied bluntly that she was staying.*

bluntness *noun* directness of manner: *the bluntness of his reply took them by surprise.*

blur — *noun* **1** a thing not clearly seen or heard. **2** a smear or smudge. — *verb* (**blurred, blurring**) **1** *trans., intrans.* to make or become less clear or distinct. **2** to rub over and smudge. **3** to make (one's memory, judgement, etc) less clear.

blurb *noun* a brief description of a book, usually printed on the jacket in order to promote it. [invented by Gelett Burgess, an American author (died 1951)]

blurred *or* **blurry** *adj.* (**blurrier, blurriest**) smudged, indistinct.

blurt *verb* (*usually* **blurt something out**) to say suddenly or without thinking of the effect or result.

blush — *noun* **1** a red or pink glow on the skin of the face, caused by shame, embarrassment, etc. **2** a pink, rosy glow. — *verb intrans.* **1** to become red or pink in the face because of shame, embarrassment, etc. **2** to feel ashamed or embarrassed: *blush when one thinks of past mistakes.* [from Anglo-Saxon *blyscan*]

blusher *noun* a pink or pale orange cream or powder used to give colour to the cheeks.

blushing *adj.* red or pink in the face from embarrassment.

bluster — *verb intrans.* (**blustered, blustering**) **1** to speak in a boasting, angry, or threatening way, often to hide fear. **2** *said of the wind, waves, etc* to blow or move roughly. — *noun* **1** speech that is ostentatiously boasting, angry, or threatening. **2** the roaring noise of the wind or sea on a rough day. [probably from German dialect *blustern*, to blow violently]

blusterer *noun* **1** a person who blusters or speaks loudly and boastfully. **2** a rough windy day.

blustery *adj., said of the weather* rough and windy.

blvd *abbrev.* boulevard.

Blyth POP (1981) 35 000, a port town in Blyth Valley district, Northumberland, NE England. It lies on the R Blyth, 18km/11mi N of Newcastle upon Tyne.

Blyton, Enid (Mary) (1897–1968) English children's writer, born in London. She trained as a Froebel teacher, then became a journalist, and published her first book *Child Whispers*, a collection of verse, in 1922. In the late 1930s she began writing her many children's stories featuring such characters as Noddy, the Famous Five, and the Secret Seven. She considered her stories highly educational and moral in tone, but has often been criticised for over-simplicity and lack of style. The author of over 600 books, she is one of the most translated British authors.

BM *abbrev.* **1** Bachelor of Medicine. **2** British Museum.

BMA *abbrev.* British Medical Association.

BMEWS *abbrev.* ballistic missile early warning system.

BMJ *abbrev.* British Medical Journal.

B-movie a feature-length entertainment film made cheaply and rapidly to provide the second part of a cinema programme.

BMus *abbrev.* Bachelor of Music.

BMW *abbrev. Bayerische Motoren Werke*, Bavarian motor works.

BMX *noun* **1** bicycle riding and racing over a rough track with obstacles. **2** a bicycle designed for this. [abbreviation of *bicycle moto-cross*]

B'nai B'rith the oldest and largest Jewish service organization, founded (1843) in the USA, to pursue educational and community activities, and focus on Jews' rights throughout the world. It includes the Hillel Foundation (for Jewish college students), the Anti-Defamation League (a civil rights group), and B'nai B'rith Women. [from Hebrew, = sons of the covenant]

BNEC *abbrev.* British National Export Council.

BNFL *abbrev.* British Nuclear Fuels Ltd.

BO *abbrev. colloq.* body odour.

Bo 1 POP (1985e) 26 000, the capital of Bo district, in Southern Province, Sierra Leone. It lies 177km/110mi SE of Freetown. **2** POP (1974) 217 711, a district in Southern Province, Sierra Leone, with Bo as its capital.

boa *noun* **1** any constricting snake belonging to the family Boidae, which also includes the pythons and anaconda. **2** (*also* **boa constrictor**) a tropical American ground-dwelling snake, 3m to 4m in length, that coils around and kills its prey by suffocation rather than crushing. Boa constrictors are found in forests, where they feed mainly on large lizards, birds, and small mammals. **3** a woman's long thin scarf, usually made of feathers or fur. [from Latin *boa*, a kind of snake]

Boadicea *or* **Boudicca** (1c AD) British warrior-queen, wife of Prasutagus, King of the Iceni, a tribe who inhabited what is now Norfolk and Suffolk. On her husband's death (60), the Romans seized her territory, and treated the inhabitants brutally. She gathered a large army, destroyed the Roman colony of Camulodunum, took Londinium and Verulamium, and put to death as many as 70 000 Romans. Defeated in battle by Suetonius Paulinus, she committed suicide.

boar *noun* **1** (**wild boar**) a wild pig. **2** a male pig kept for breeding. **3** its flesh. [from Anglo-Saxon *bar*]

board — *noun* **1** a long flat strip of wood. **2** a piece of material resembling this, made from fibres compressed together: *chipboard.* **3** a flat piece of wood, etc for a stated purpose: *notice board / chessboard.* **4** thick stiff card used eg for binding books. **5** a person's meals, provided in return for money: *bed and board.* **6** an official group of people controlling or managing an organization, etc, or examining or interviewing candidates: *a board of examiners.* **7** (**boards**) a theatre stage: *tread the boards.* **8** *Naut.* the side of a ship. — *verb* **1** to enter or get on to (a ship, aeroplane, bus, etc). **2** *intrans.* to receive accommodation and meals in someone else's house, in return for payment. **3** to provide (someone) with accommodation and meals in return for payment. **4** (*also* **board someone out**) to arrange for

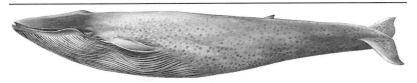
blue whale

someone to receive accommodation and meals away from home. **5** (*also* **board something up**) to cover a gap or entrance with boards.
— **across the board** see ACROSS.
go by ' the board *colloq.* to be given up or ignored.
on board on or into a ship, aeroplane, etc.
sweep the board to win everything.
take something on board to understand or accept new ideas, responsibilities, etc. [from Anglo-Saxon *bord*]

boarder *noun* **1** a person who receives accommodation and meals in someone else's house, in return for payment. **2** a pupil who lives at school during term time.

board game *noun* a game played with pieces to be moved on a board, eg chess.

boarding *noun* **1** a collection of wooden boards laid next to each other. **2** the act of boarding a ship, aeroplane, etc.

boarding-house *noun* a house where people live and take meals as paying guests.

boarding-pass *or* **boarding-card** *noun* a card or piece of paper which allows a person to board an aeroplane, etc.

boarding-school *noun* a school where pupils may live during term time.

boardroom *noun* **1** a room in which the directors of a company meet. **2** the highest level of management of a company.

boast — *verb* **1** *intrans.* to talk with excessive pride (about one's own abilities, achievements, etc.) **2** *trans.* to own or have (something it is right to be proud of): *the hotel boasts magnificent views across the valley.* — *noun* **1** an act of boasting. **2** a thing one is proud of. [from Middle English *bost*]

boastful *adj. derog.* **1** given to boasting about oneself. **2** showing or characterized by boasting.

boastfully *adv.* in a boastful manner; with excessive pride.

boastfulness *noun* tending to boast often.

boasting *noun* talking with excessive pride about oneself.

boat — *noun* **1** a small vessel for travelling over water. **2** *colloq.*, *loosely* a larger vessel; a ship. **3** a boat-shaped dish for serving sauce, etc. — *verb intrans.* to sail in a boat for pleasure.
— **in the same boat** in the same difficult circumstances.
miss the boat to lose an opportunity.
rock the boat to disturb the balance or calmness of a situation.
[from Anglo-Saxon *bat*]

boater *noun* **1** a person who sails in a boat, especially for pleasure. **2** a straw hat with a flat top and a brim.

boathook *noun* a metal hook fixed to a pole, for pulling or pushing a boat.

boathouse *noun* a building where boats are stored, especially by a lake or river.

boating *noun* the sailing of boats for pleasure.

boatman *noun* a man in charge of a small boat which carries passengers.

boat people refugees who have fled their country by boat.

Boat Race the annual rowing race between the crews of Oxford and Cambridge universities. It was first held on 10 Jun 1829 from Hambledon Lock to Henley Bridge, and is now raced over 6.78km/4mi from Putney to Mortlake. Up to (and including) 1993, the record was 70 wins for Cambridge, 68 for Oxford, and one dead heat (in 1877).

boatswain *or* **bosun** *noun* a ship's officer in charge of the lifeboats, ropes, sails, etc and crew. [from Anglo-Saxon *batswegen*, boatman]

boat train *noun* a train which takes passengers to or from a ship.

bob¹ — *verb* (**bobbed**, **bobbing**) **1** *intrans.* to move up and down quickly. **2** *intrans.* to curtsy. **3** *trans.* to move (the head) up and down, usually as a greeting. — *noun* **1** an up-and-down bouncing movement. **2** a curtsy.
— **bob up** to appear or reappear suddenly.
[from Middle English *bobben*]

bob² — *noun* **1** a short hairstyle for women and children, with the hair cut square across the face and evenly all round the head. **2** a hanging weight on a clock's pendulum. **3** a bobsleigh. — *verb* (**bobbed**, **bobbing**) **1** to cut (hair) in a bob. **2** *intrans.* to ride on a bobsleigh. [from Middle English *bobbe*, spray, cluster]

bob³ *noun* (PL. **bob**) *old colloq.* use a shilling.

bob⁴
— **bob's your uncle** *Brit. colloq.* an expression used to show that something should follow as a matter of course: *just turn the knob and bob's your uncle!*
[from *Bob*, a pet-form of the name *Robert*]

bobbin *noun* a small cylindrical object on which thread is wound, used in sewing and weaving machines. [from French *bobine*]

bobble *noun* a small ball, often made of wool, used to decorate clothes. [from BOB¹]

bobby *noun* (PL. **bobbies**) *Brit. colloq.* a policeman. [from the name *Bob*, after Sir Robert Peel, who founded the Metropolitan Police in 1828]

Bobo-Dioulasso POP (1985) 231 000, an important city of SW Burkina. It lies 322km/200mi SW of Ouagadougou.

Bobruysk POP (1991e) 223 000, a city in Belorussia, lying on the R Berezina. It was founded in the 16c and fortified by Alexander I.

bobsleigh *or* **bobsled** *noun* a sleigh with metal runners used in crossing, and sometimes racing on, snow and ice.
◊ Bobsledding is the sport of travelling or racing across snow and ice on a bobsleigh, especially the streamlined sledge developed for competitions. The first bobsleigh race was at Davros, Switzerland in 1889 on a course specially constructed for the purpose. The International Federation of Bobsleigh and Tobogganing was formed in 1923, followed by the International Bobsleigh Federation in 1957. The Olympic competitions of four-man bob and two-man bob were instituted in 1924 and 1932 respectively.

bobtail *noun* a short or cut tail, or an animal having this.

bobtailed *adj.*, *said of an animal* having a bobtail.

Boccaccio, Giovanni (1313–75) Italian writer, born (probably) in Tuscany. He started on a commercial career, but moved to Naples and took to story writing in verse and prose, his works including the *Filostrato* which tells the story of Troilus and Cressida. Until 1350, he lived alternately in Florence and Naples, and then became a diplomat and scholar, met Petrarch, and travelled widely as Florentine ambassador. His major work is the *Decameron* (completed 1358), and he influenced Chaucer, Sidney, Shakespeare, and others.

Boche *noun derog. slang* **1** a German, especially a German soldier. **2** (**the Boche**) the Germans, especially German soldiers. [from French *boche*, rascal, applied to Germans in World War I]

Bochum POP (1991e) 397 000, an industrial and commercial city in the Ruhr Valley, North Rhine-Westphalia state, W central Germany. Situated between the Emscher and Ruhr rivers, 59km/37mi SW of Münster, Bochum originally developed around the coal and steel industries.

bod *noun colloq.* a person. [FROM BODY]

bodacious *adj. slang* extraordinary; outstanding. [perhaps a mixture of BOLD and AUDACIOUS]

bode¹ *verb* to be a sign of.
— **bode ill** *or* **well** to be a bad or good sign for the future.
[from Anglo-Saxon *bodian*, to announce]

bode² see BIDE.

Bodensee see CONSTANCE, LAKE.

bodge *verb intrans., trans. colloq.* to make a mess of something; to do something badly or carelessly. [from BOTCH]

Bodhidharma (6c) Indian monk and founder of the Ch'an (or Zen) sect of Buddhism, born near Madras. In 520 he travelled to China, where he had a famous audience with the emperor. He argued that merit leading to salvation could not be accumulated through good deeds, and taught meditation as the way to return to Buddha's spiritual precepts.

Bodhisattva *noun* (*also* **bodhisattva**) *Relig.* in Mahayana Buddhism, one who has attained enlightenment but who has chosen not to pass into nirvana, voluntarily remaining in the world to help lesser beings attain enlightenment; a personal saviour. [from Sanskrit *bodhi*, enlightenment + *sattva*, existence]

bodice *noun* **1** the part of a dress covering the upper part of the body. **2** a woman's close-fitting outer garment, worn over a blouse. **3** *formerly* a similar close-fitting undergarment. [from *bodies*, plural of BODY]

-bodied a word-forming element meaning 'having a body of the type specified': *able-bodied / wide-bodied.*

bodily — *adj.* of or concerning the body. — *adv.* **1** as a whole. **2** in person.

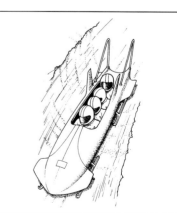

bobsleigh

---

parts of a sailing-boat

head
mast
leech
jib stay
head
battens
luft
luft
leech
battens
mainsail
boom
clew
main sheet
jib
tack
tiller
foot
foot
stern
bow
rudder
clew
hull
jib sheet
tack
centreboard

Bodin, Jean (c.1530–96) French political philosopher, born in Angers. He trained as a lawyer and served in various legal capacities for royalty. His major work, *Les Six Livres de la République* (The Six Books of the Republic, 1576), expounds the belief that property and the family form the basis of society, and that a limited monarchy is the best possible form of government. He also wrote on history, religion, and witchcraft (eg *Démonomanie des sorciers*, 1580).

bodkin *noun* a large blunt needle. [from Middle English *badeken*]

Bodleian Library the university library and national depository at Oxford, founded in 1595 by Sir Thomas Bodley (1545–1613), who restored the disused 14c library and laid the foundations of its now extensive holdings. Since 1610, it has received a free copy of every book published in England.

Bodoni, Giambattista (1740–1813) Italian printer, born in Saluzzo, who designed a modern typeface still widely used today. His press in Parma published elegant editions of the classics.

body — *noun* (PL. **bodies**) **1** the whole physical structure of a person or animal. **2** the physical structure of a person or animal excluding the head and limbs. **3** a corpse. **4** the main or central part of anything. **5** a person's physical needs and desires as opposed to spiritual concerns. **6** a substantial section or group: *a body of opinion*. **7** a group of people thought of as a single unit. **8** a quantity: *a body of water*. **9** a piece of matter: *a heavenly body*. **10** *said of wine, music, etc* a full or strong quality or tone. **11** *colloq.* a person. **12** thickness; substantial quality. — *verb* (**bodies, bodied**) to give body or form to.
— **keep body and soul together** to barely manage to survive.

over my dead body *colloq.* not if I can prevent it. [from Anglo-Saxon *bodig*]

Body Art a type of modern art popular in the 1960s which exploits the artist's (or someone else's) physical presence as a work of art in its own right; eg the artist may stand in the gallery like a living statue.

body-bag *noun* a bag made of heavy material used to transport a dead body, especially that of a war casualty or accident victim.

body-builder *noun* a person who undertakes body-building exercises.

body-building *noun* physical exercise designed to develop the muscles and strengthen the body.

bodyguard *noun* a person or group of people guarding an important person, etc.

body language *Psychol.* the communication of information by means of conscious or unconscious gestures, attitudes, facial expressions, etc.

body-piercing *noun* the practice of inserting metal studs or rings through parts of the body for decoration.

body politic all the people of a nation in their political capacity.

body-snatcher *noun Hist.* a person who robs graves of their dead bodies.

body stocking a garment worn next to the skin, covering all of the body and often the arms and legs.

bodysuit *noun* a close-fitting one-piece garment for women, worn especially during exercise and sporting activities.

bodywork *noun* **1** the outer painted structure of a motor vehicle. **2** any form of alternative therapy which concentrates on releasing tension or balancing energies in the body.

Boehm *or* **Böhm, Theobald** (1794–1881) German flautist and inventor, born in Munich. He opened a flute factory in 1828, and determined to make an acoustically perfect instrument. He devised a key mechanism to overcome the problem of requiring holes where the fingers could not reach, and in 1847 produced the model on which the modern flute is based. Some features of his system have also been used on the clarinet.

Boehme *or* **Böhme, Jakob** (1575–1624) German theosophist and mystic, born in Altseidenberg, Upper Lusatia. He was a shoemaker, but a mystical experience made him devote much time to meditation. In about 1612 he published *Aurora*, his meditations upon God, Man, and Nature, but it was condemned by the ecclesiastical authorities, and he suffered much persecution. His aim was to explain the origin of things, especially the existence of evil; he also wrote *Mysterium magnum* (The Great Mystery, 1623). His influence later spread to Holland and England, and can be found as late as the 19c.

Boeing 747 the first of the jumbo jets and the world's largest commercial airliner. Its first flight was on 9 Feb 1969 and the first passenger service was operated by Pan American from New York to London on 22 Jan 1970. It weighs 350 tonnes and is capable of carrying over 650 passengers.

Boeotia the name given in antiquity to the area in central Greece bordering on Attica. Its chief city-state was Thebes, and its inhabitants were largely of Aeolian stock.

Boer — *noun* a descendant of the early Dutch settlers in South Africa. — *adj.* of or relating to the Boers. [a Dutch word]

Boerhaave, Hermann (1668–1738) Dutch physician and botanist, born in Voorhout, near Leiden. Professor of Medicine and Botany at Leiden, he is best known for his medical works *Institutiones Medicae* (1708) and *Aphorismi de Cognoscendis et Curandis Morbis* (The Book of Aphorisms, 1709). In 1724 he also became Professor of Chemistry; his *Elementa Chemiae* (1724) is a classic.

Boer Wars two wars (1880–1, 1899–1902) fought by the British and the Boers for the mastery of southern Africa. The British had made several attempts to re-incorporate the Boers, who had left the Cape Colony in the Great Trek, within a South African confederation. The first Boer War ended with the defeat of the British at Majuba Hill, and the signing of the Pretoria and London Conventions of 1881 and 1884. In 1896 the Jameson Raid was a clumsy private effort to achieve the same objective. The second Boer War began with a series of Boer successes (Oct 1899–Jan 1900), which included the sieges of Ladysmith, Kimberley, and Mafeking, as well as victories at Stormberg, Modder River, Magersfontein, Colenso, and Modderspruit. Then Lord Roberts led counter-offensives (Feb–Aug 1900) which included the raising of the sieges, the victory at Paardeberg, and the capture of Pretoria. Finally there was a period of guerrilla warfare (Sep 1900–May 1902) when Kitchener attempted to prevent Boer commandos raiding isolated British units and lines of communication. The Boers effectively won the peace, maintained control of 'native affairs', won back representative government (1907), and federated South Africa on their terms (1910). Nevertheless, British interests in South Africa were protected, and the Union of South Africa entered both World Wars I and II on the British side.

Boethius, Anicius Manlius Severinus (c.475–524) Roman statesman and philosopher, probably born in Rome. He was appointed a court minister by the Gothic king, Theodoric. In 510, he was made consul, but was later accused of treason, imprisoned, and executed. During his imprisonment he wrote his best-known work, *De Consolatione Philosophiae* (The Consolation of Philosophy), which expresses the mutability of all earthly fortune, and the insecurity of everything except virtue.

boffin *noun Brit. colloq.* a scientist engaged in research, especially in military concerns.

bog — *noun* **1** a flat or domed area of wet spongy poorly drained ground, composed of acid peat and slowly decaying plant material, and dominated by *Sphagnum* moss, sedges, rushes, etc. **2** *Brit. slang* a lavatory. — *verb* (**bogged, bogging**) (*usually* **be bogged down**) to be prevented from progressing: *got bogged down in difficulties*. [from Gaelic *bogach*, from *bog*, soft]

Bogarde, Dirk, originally **Derek Niven Van Den Bogaerde** (1921–) English actor, born in London. He moved from the stage to films in 1946, playing mostly romantic or light comedy roles, such as *Doctor in the House* (1954). Later, more challenging parts include *The Servant* (1963), *The Damned* (1969), *Death in Venice* (1971), *The Night Porter* (1973), and *Providence* (1977). His television roles include *The Patricia Neal Story* (1981) and he is also a successful writer.

Bogart, Humphrey (De Forest) (1899–1957) US actor, born in New York City. He entered the theatre in the late 1920s and played the lead in the 1935 stage production of *The Petrified Forest*, and in the film version of 1936, which established him as a Hollywood star. Many of his performances have become classics, notably *The Maltese Falcon* (1941), *Casablanca* (1942), *The Big Sleep* (1946), *The Treasure of the Sierra Madre* (1948), and *The African Queen* (1951), for which he won an Oscar. He married Lauren Bacall in 1945.

bog asphodel a perennial plant (*Narthecium ossifragum*), native to boggy regions of NW Europe, and having yellow flowers that turn deep orange after fertilization, and woolly stamens.

bog burial *Archaeol.* a burial of prehistoric human remains found, often in a remarkable state of preservation, in peat bogs in N Europe, especially in Denmark, Germany, the Netherlands, Britain, and Ireland. Notable examples from the Iron Age are *Tollund Man* (c.200 BC) and *Grauball Man* (c.50 BC) both found in Denmark, and *Lindow Man* (c.300 BC) found in Cheshire, England: all three had died violently and it is presumed that they were either sacrificial victims or criminals of some sort.

bogey¹ *or* **bogy** *noun* (PL. **bogeys, bogies**) **1** an evil or mischievous spirit. **2** something specially feared.

bogey² *noun* (PL. **bogeys**) *Golf* a standard score for a hole or a course, formerly par but now usually a score of one stroke more than par for each hole. [perhaps from the name of an imaginary player]

bogeyman *or* **bogyman** *noun* a cruel or frightening person, existing or imaginary, used to deter or frighten children.

boggle *verb intrans. colloq.* **1** to be amazed at something, or unable to understand or imagine it: *the mind boggles*. **2** (**boggle at something**) to hesitate over it.

boggy *adj.* (**boggier, boggiest**) *said of an area of ground* wet and spongy like bog.

bogie *noun* a frame with four or six wheels which supports part of a long vehicle, such as a railway carriage.

Bognor Regis POP (1981) 53 000, a coastal resort town in Arun district, West Sussex, S England. It lies on the English Channel, 20km/12mi W of Worthing. The title 'Regis' dates from 1929, when King George V came here to recuperate.

Bogomiles see CATHARS.

Bogotá, formerly **Santa Fe de Bogotá** POP (1992e) 4.9m, the federal capital of Colombia, standing on a plateau at a height of 2 650m, in the central area of the country. HISTORY once the centre of the Chibcha culture, the city was founded by the Spanish in 1538; former capital of Greater Colombia and of New Granada. NOTABLE FEATURES cathedral; Museum of Colonial Art; Palace of San Carlos; Municipal Palace; National

Capitol; Churches of San Ignacio, Santa Clara, and San Agustín; Parque Santander, with Gold Museum; the city is linked to Monserrate National Park by a funicular railway and cable car.

bogus *adj.* false; not genuine.

bogy same as BOGEY[1].

Bohème, La (Bohemian Life) an opera by Giacomo Puccini (1896). Set in 19c Paris, the story tells of the life of four impoverished friends — poet, painter, musician, and philospher — and the love that Rodolfo (the poet) develops for a fatally ill seamstress called Mimi.

Bohemia, Czech **Čechy**, German **Böhmen** a historic province in the Czech Republic, bounded E by the historic province of Moravia, W and S by Germany and Austria, and N by Germany and Poland. PHYSICAL DESCRIPTION consists of a plateau enclosed by mountains; natural boundaries include the Erzgebirge in the N, the Bohemian Forest in the SW, and the Sudetes Mts in the NE; chief rivers include the Elbe (Labe), Vltava (Moldau), Ohre (Eger), Jihlava, and Jizera. CHIEF TOWNS Prague, České Budějovice, Plzeň, Ústí, Labem. HISTORY part of the Moravian Empire in the 9c, it was at its peak during the early Middle Ages, especially under Charles I in the 14c; in the 15c religious dissension led to the Hussite Wars; the house of Habsburg ruled from the early 16c; Bohemia became a province of Czechoslovakia in 1918; since 1990 it has formed part of the Czech Republic. ECONOMY a highly industrialized area, with reserves of coal, iron ore, and uranium; there are mineral springs.

bohemian — *noun* 1 (**Bohemian**) a person from Bohemia, formerly a kingdom, later a part of the Czech Republic. 2 a person, especially a writer or an artist, who lives in a way which ignores standard customs and rules of social behaviour. — *adj.* 1 (**Bohemian**) of or from Bohemia. 2 ignoring standard customs and rules of social behaviour. [from French *bohémien*, Bohemian, gypsy]

Bohemian Forest, German **Böhmerwald**, Czech **Český Les** a forested mountain range along the boundary between Germany and Bohemia, Czech Republic.

Böhm, Karl (1894–1981) Austrian conductor, born in Graz. His permanent posts as an opera conductor included Dresden (1934–43) and Vienna (1943–5, 1954–6), but he also appeared frequently in London, New York, and Bayreuth. Remembered chiefly for his Mozart performances, he also conducted premières of operas by Richard Strauss, a personal friend.

Bohr, Niels Henrik David (1885–1962) Danish physicist, born in Copenhagen. He developed a theory of the hydrogen atom based on two recent discoveries; evidence for the nuclear atom and the idea that energy exists in 'packets', each of which is known as a quantum. Professor at Copenhagen University from 1916, he escaped from German-occupied Denmark during World War II and assisted atom bomb research in the USA, returning to Copenhagen in 1945. He was awarded the 1922 Nobel Prize for Physics.

Boiardo, Matteo Maria, Count of Scandiano (1434–94) Italian poet, born in Scandiano. He was appointed Governor of Modena in 1841, and in 1487 of Reggio. Known as the 'Flower of Chivalry', his fame rests on the *Orlando Innamorato* (1486), a long narrative poem about the Charlemagne hero, Roland.

boil[1] — *verb* 1 *intrans.* *said of a liquid* to start to bubble and turn from liquid to gas when heated. 2 *said of a container* to have its contents at boiling point. 3 *to bring (a liquid or its container) to a heat at which the liquid boils. 4 *trans., intrans.* *said of food* to cook or be cooked by boiling. 5 (**be boiling**) *colloq.* **a** to be very hot. **b** *said of a person* to be extremely angry. 6 to treat with boiling water, especially to clean. 7 *intrans.* *said of the sea,* etc to move and bubble as if boiling. — *noun* the act or point of boiling.
— **boil away** *or* **down** *said of a liquid* to be reduced by boiling.
boil something away *or* **down** to reduce a liquid by boiling.
boil down to something *colloq.* to mean; to have as the most important part or factor: *it all boils down to a question of cost.*
boil over 1 *said of a liquid* to boil and flow over the edge of its container. 2 to speak out angrily.
boil up 1 *said of a liquid* to become heated to boiling point. 2 to come to a dangerous level.
boil something up to heat a liquid until it boils. [from Old French *boillir*, from Latin *bullire*, to bubble]

boil[2] *noun* a painful red pus-filled swelling on the skin. [from Anglo-Saxon *byl*]

Boileau (Despréaux), Nicolas (1636–1711) French critic, born in Paris. He studied law and theology at Beauvais before devoting himself to literature, and in 1677 was appointed royal historiographer. His works include satires (1660–6), epistles, critical dissertations (eg the influential *L'Art poétique*, The Art of Poetry, 1674), epigrams, and translations.

boiler *noun* 1 any closed vessel that is used to convert water into steam, especially by burning coal, oil, or other fuel, used to drive steam turbines (eg in power stations), steamships, steam locomotives, etc. 2 an apparatus for heating a building's hot water supply. 3 a metal vessel, tub, etc for boiling and washing clothes in.

boiler suit a one-piece suit worn over normal clothes to protect them while doing manual or heavy work.

boiling point 1 (ABBREV. **bp, b.p.**) the temperature at which a particular substance changes from a liquid to a vapour. The boiling point can be lowered by decreasing the air pressure, eg water boils at a lower temperature at high altitudes. 2 a point of great anger, high excitement, etc at which emotions can no longer be controlled.

Bois, W(illiam) E(dward) B(urghardt) du (1868–1963) US historian, sociologist, and equal rights campaigner, born into a small black community in Great Barrington, Massachusetts. He studied at Fisk, Harvard, and Berlin, and in his writings explored the history and lives of black Americans. In politics he campaigned for full equality, opposing the tactics of Booker T Washington. He helped found the National Organization for the Advancement of Colored People, and in his old age lived in Ghana.

Bois de Boulogne a park situated on the W outskirts of Paris. Originally a royal hunting forest, it became a popular recreation area for Parisians in the 17c, and in 1852 was relandscaped along the lines of London's Hyde Park. The Longchamps racecourse was opened here in 1857.

Boise POP (1990) 206 000, the capital of the state of Idaho, USA, situated in Ada County in the SW of the state. It lies on the Boise R. Founded after the 1862 gold rush, it is now the largest city in the state and a trade and transportation centre. NOTABLE FEATURES Old Idaho Penitentiary; Idaho State Museum.

boisterous *adj.* 1 very lively, noisy, and cheerful. 2 *said of the sea, etc* rough and stormy. [from Middle English *boistous*]

boisterously *adv.* with a lively, noisy manner.

Boito, Arrigo (1842–1918) Italian composer and poet, born in Padua. He studied at the Milan Conservatorio, and wrote his first major work, the opera *Mefistofele*, in 1868. His libretti included those for Verdi's *Otello* and *Falstaff*.

bold *adj.* 1 daring or brave. 2 not showing respect; impudent. 3 striking and clearly marked. 4 *Printing* printed in boldface. [from Anglo-Saxon *beald*]

boldface *noun Printing* thicker stronger letters, as used in the word **boldface**.

boldly *adv.* in a daring or striking manner; so as to attract the attention.

boldness *noun* daring; forwardness of manner; impertinence.

Boldwood, William the farm-owner in Thomas Hardy's *Far from the Madding Crowd*, who becomes obsessed to the point of insanity with Bathsheba Everdene.

bole *noun* the trunk of a tree. [from Norse *bolr*]

Boléro a miniature ballet by Maurice Ravel (1928), the music of which has one theme repeated throughout in the form of a prolonged crescendo.

bolero *noun* (PL. **boleros**) 1 a traditional Spanish dance, or the music for it. 2 a short open jacket reaching not quite to the waist. [from Spanish *bolero*]

Boleyn, Anne (c.1504–36) English queen, the second wife of Henry VIII (1533–6). Secretly married to Henry (Jan 1533), she was soon declared his legal wife (May). His quickly cooling passion for her was not revived by the birth (Sep 1533) of a princess (later Elizabeth I), still less by that of a stillborn son (Jan 1536). She was charged with treason and beheaded (19 May), and Henry married Jane Seymour 11 days later.

Bolingbroke, Henry St John, 1st Viscount (1678–1751) English statesman, born in London. After travelling in Europe, he entered parliament (1701), becoming Secretary for War (1704), Foreign Secretary (1710), and joint leader of the Tory Party. On the death of Queen Anne (1714), his Jacobite sympathies forced him to flee to France, where he wrote *Reflections on Exile*. His last years were spent in London, writing works such as the influential *Idea of a Patriot King* (1749).

Bolívar, Simón, known as **the Liberator** (1783–1830) the national hero of Venezuela, Colombia, Ecuador, Peru, and Bolivia, born in Caracas, who played a prominent part in the wars of independence in northern S America. In 1819 he proclaimed and became President of the vast republic of Colombia (modern Colombia, Venezuela, and Ecuador), which was finally liberated in 1822. He then led the last campaigns of independence in Peru (1824) and returned to the north in 1826 to face growing political dissension. He resigned office (1830) and died on his way into exile in Colombia.

Bolívar, Pico an Andean peak in Mérida state, W Venezuela. At 5 007m, it is the highest peak both in the Cordillera de Mérida and in Venezuela. A bust of Simón Bolívar is on its summit.

Bolivia, official name **Republic of Bolivia**, Spanish **República de Bolivia** POP (1992) 6.3m, a republic in W central S America, divided into nine departments. AREA 1 098 580sq km/ 424 052sq mi. The republic is bounded N and E by Brazil, W by Peru, SW by Chile, S by Argentina, and SE by Paraguay. CAPITAL La Paz (government), Sucre (legal and judicial). TIME ZONE GMT –4. The population is 30% Quechua, 25% Ayamará, and 25–30% mixed, the remainder being European; Roman Catholicism is the main religion (95%). OFFICIAL LANGUAGES Spanish, Quechua, Ayamará. CURRENCY the peso boliviano. PHYSICAL DESCRIPTION a landlocked country, bounded W by the Cordillera Occidental of the Andes, rising to 6 542m at Sajama; separated from the Cordillera Real to the E by the flat, 400km/250mi-long Altiplano Plateau which lies at 3 600m above sea level; major lakes in this region are Titicaca and Poopó; several rivers flow from the Andes towards the Brazilian frontier. HISTORY part of the Inca Empire, and evidence of earlier civilization; conquered by the Spanish in the 16c; independence after the war of liberation in 1825; much territory was lost after wars with neighbouring countries; there have been several changes of government and military coups in recent decades. GOVERNMENT a bicameral Congress, with a 27-member Senate and a 130-member Chamber of Deputies elected for four years; an elected President appoints a Cabinet of 18 Ministers. ECONOMY largely dependent on minerals for foreign exchange; silver largely exhausted, but replaced by tin (one fifth of world supply), tungsten, antimony, lead, gold; oil and natural gas, pipelines to Argentina and Chile; sugar cane, rice, cotton, potatoes, cereals; livestock; illegally-produced cocaine.

Bolivia

Böll, Heinrich (1917–85) German writer, born in Cologne. His many novels include *Der Zug war Pünktlich* (The Train was on Time, 1949), and a trilogy depicting life in Germany during and after the Nazi regime, *Und Sagte kein Einziges Worte* (And Never said a Solitary Word, 1953), *Haus ohne Hüter* (The Unguarded House, 1954), and *Das Brot der Frühen Jahre* (The Bread of our Early Years, 1955). He was awarded the Nobel Prize for Literature in 1972.

boll *noun* that part of a cotton plant, etc which contains the seeds. [from Anglo-Saxon *bolla*, bowl]

bollard *noun* **1** *Brit.* a small post used to mark a traffic island or to keep traffic away from a certain area. **2** a short but strong post on a ship, quay, etc round which ropes are fastened. [probably from BOLE]

bollocks *noun coarse slang* **1** (*pl.*) the testicles. **2** (*sing.*) rubbish, nonsense. [from Anglo-Saxon *beallucas*, testicles]

boll-weevil *noun* an insect which attacks cotton bolls.

Bologna POP (1991e) 412 000, the capital city of Bologna province, and of Emilia-Romagna region, N Italy. It lies at the foot of the Apennines, 83km/52mi N of Florence. An ancient Etruscan city, it is enclosed by the remains of 13c–14c walls. NOTABLE FEATURES Church of San Petronio (14c); Church of San Domenico (13c); Pinacoteca Nazionale; two leaning towers (12c), the Asinelli and the Garisenda; university (11c), one of the two prototypal universities of Europe.

Bologna, University of one of the oldest and most distinguished of European universities. It was founded as a law school in Bologna, Italy, in the 11c, and received a charter from Emperor Frederick I Barbarossa in 1158. For the next two centuries the university was pre-eminent in the study of jurisprudence.

boloney same as BALONEY.

Bolshevik — *noun* **1** *Hist.* a member of the radical faction of the Russian socialist party, which became the Communist Party in 1918. **2** a Russian communist. **3** *derog. colloq.* (often **bolshevik**) any radical socialist. — *adj.* **1** of the Bolsheviks. **2** communist. [from Russian, from *bolshe*, greater, because they were in the majority at the 1903 party congress or because they favoured more extreme measures]

Bolshevism *noun* the political principles and philosophy of the Bolsheviks.

Bolshevist *noun* an adherent of Bolshevism; a Bolshevik. — *adj.* relating to Bolshevism.

bolshie or **bolshy** *derog. slang* — *adj.* (**bolshier**, **bolshiest**) **1** bad-tempered and unco-operative. **2** left-wing. — *noun* (PL. **bolshies**) a Bolshevik.

Bolshoi Ballet a Russian ballet company (founded 1776), named when the Bolshoi Theatre took over the Petrovsky Theatre's ballet company in Moscow. Marius Petipa was among its eminent choreographers. [from Russian *bolshoy balet* = great ballet]

bolster — *noun* **1** a long narrow pillow. **2** any pad or support. — *verb* (**bolstered**, **bolstering**) (*usually* **bolster something up**) to support it, make it stronger, or hold it up. [an Anglo-Saxon word]

Bolt, Robert (1924–) English dramatist, born in Manchester. He achieved success with *A Man for All Seasons* (1960), and his later plays include *The Tiger and the Horse* (1960) and *State of Revolution* (1977). Among his screenplays are *Lawrence of Arabia* (1962), *Dr Zhivago* (1965), *Ryan's Daughter* (1970), and *The Mission* (1986).

bolt¹ — *noun* **1** a bar to fasten a door, gate, etc. **2** a small thick round bar of metal with a screw thread, used with a nut to fasten things together. **3** a flash of lightning. **4** a sudden movement or dash away, especially to escape: *make a bolt for it.* **5** a roll of cloth. **6** a short arrow fired from a crossbow. — *verb* **1** to fasten (a door, window, etc) with a bolt. **2** to eat very quickly. **3** *intrans.* to run or dash away suddenly and quickly. **4** *intrans. said of a horse* to run away out of control. **5** to fasten together with bolts. **6** *intrans. Bot.* to flower and produce seed too early, usually in response to low temperatures; (of a biennial) to behave like an annual.

— **a bolt from the blue** a sudden, unexpected, and usually unwelcome event.

bolt upright very straight and stiff.

have shot one's bolt to have failed in one's final or only available attempt. [from Anglo-Saxon]

bolt² or **boult** *verb* **1** to pass (flour, etc) through a sieve. **2** to examine or investigate. [from Old French *bulter*]

bolthole *noun* a refuge from danger; a means of escape.

Bolton, formerly **Bolton-le-Moors** POP (1981) 144 000, a town in Bolton borough, Greater Manchester, NW England. It lies 18km/11mi NW of Manchester. Until the 18c, the main industry in Bolton was wool. It then became an important cotton centre. NOTABLE FEATURES Textile Machinery Museum; Hall i' th' Wood, a local history museum.

Boltzmann, Ludwig (1844–1906) Austrian physicist, born in Vienna. From 1869 he held professorships in mathematics and physics at Graz, Vienna, Munich, and Leipzig. He did important work on the kinetic theory of gases, establishing the principle of equipartition of energy and calculating the theoretical distribution of energy between particles. He also gave a new definition of the 'entropy', or disorder of a system.

Bolzano, German **Bozen** POP (1991e) 100 000, the capital town of Bolzano province, Trentino-Alto Adige, N Italy. It lies on the R Isarco, SW of the Brenner Pass. Bolzano is the chief commer-

cial, industrial, and tourist centre of the region. Most of its inhabitants speak German.

bomb — *noun* **1** a hollow case or other device containing substances capable of causing explosions, fires, etc. **2** (**the bomb**) the atomic bomb, especially regarded as the most powerful destructive weapon. **3** (**a bomb**) *Brit. colloq.* a lot of money: *it cost a bomb.* **4** *North Amer. colloq.* a failure: *the film was a bomb.* — *verb* **1** to attack, damage, etc with a bomb or bombs. **2** *intrans. colloq.* to move or drive quickly: *bombing along the road.* **3** *intrans. colloq. North Amer.* to fail badly.

— **go like a bomb** *colloq.* **1** to move very quickly. **2** to sell extremely well; to be very successful.

[from French *bombe*, from Greek *bombos*, humming sound]

◇ Aerial bombing using free-falling bombs began in World War I. In World War II, huge tonnages were dropped in bombing raids by German and Allied air forces; and the ten-ton bomb was developed by the end of the war. Germany pioneered new methods of delivery with the V1 flying bombs and V2 rocket bombs that were targeted on Britain in 1944 and 1945. With the development of the atom bomb and hydrogen bomb, the destructive capability of a single bomb was increased to such a degree that the nuclear arsenals held by the USA and the USSR were capable of destroying all human life: the relatively small atomic bombs dropped on Hiroshima and Nagasaki were each equivalent to the explosive power of 20 000 tonnes of TNT. Modern 'smart' bombs have a guidance package in the nose which can pick up signals from targets on the ground and generate steering commands to direct the bomb to a target.

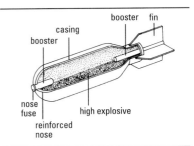

bomb

bombard *verb* **1** to attack with large heavy guns or bombs. **2** to direct questions or abuse at (someone) very quickly and without stopping. **3** *Physics* to direct a stream of high-speed particles at (a substance). [from French *bombarder*, from *bombarde*, machine for throwing stones]

bombardier *noun* **1** *Brit.* a noncommissioned officer in the Royal Artillery. **2** *North Amer., esp. US* the member of an aircraft's crew who releases the bombs. [from BOMBARD]

bombardment *noun* **1** a fierce attack with heavy weapons. **2** a fierce onslaught of questions or criticism.

bombast *noun* pretentious, boastful, or insincere words having little real force or meaning. [from Middle English *bombace*, cotton padding]

bombastic *adj., said of language* sounding impressive but insincere or meaningless.

bombastically *adv.* with an impressive but insincere manner.

Bombay POP (1991) 12.6m, the second largest city in India, and the port capital of Maharashtra state, W India. It has the only natural deep-water harbour on the W coast of the country. The city is built on a group of islands, linked by causeways. HISTORY ceded to Portugal in 1534; ceded to Britain in 1661; headquarters of the East India Company from 1685 until 1708. NOTABLE FEATURES Afghan Church (1847); Gateway of India (an archway commemorating the visit to India of

King George V and Queen Mary in 1911); Mani Bhavan (Gandhi Memorial); Raudat Tahera Mosque and Mausoleum; Victoria and Albert Museum.

Bombay duck a slender-bodied fish with large jaws and barb-like teeth, common in the tropical Indian Ocean, especially the Bay of Bengal. It is up to 40cm in length, and has soft translucent flesh. It is an important food fish, caught in fixed nets in brackish waters, and dried in the sun.

bomb calorimeter *Chem.* an apparatus that is used to determine the amount of heat energy (often expressed as the number of calories) released during the complete combustion (burning) of a fuel, food, etc.

bomb disposal the act or technique of making unexploded bombs harmless.

bomber *noun* 1 an aeroplane built for bombing. 2 a person who bombs something.

bomber jacket a short jacket gathered tightly at the waist.

bombing *noun* a period of dropping bombs; an attack with bombs.

bombshell *noun* 1 a piece of surprising and usually disappointing news. 2 *colloq.* a stunningly attractive woman.

bombsite *noun* an area where buildings have been destroyed by a bomb.

Bon the religion of Tibet before the introduction of Buddhism, apparently a form of nature worship similar to Shamanism. Many of its practices were eventually absorbed into what has become Tibetan Buddhism.

bona fide — *adj.* genuine or sincere. — *adv.* genuinely or sincerely. [from Latin *bona fide*]

bona fides 1 (*sing.*) genuineness; honesty. 2 (*sing. or pl.*) proof or evidence of trustworthiness.

Bonaire POP (1991e) 11 000, an island of the S Netherlands Antilles, E Caribbean Sea. AREA 288sq km/111sq mi. It lies 60km/37mi N of Venezuela. PHYSICAL DESCRIPTION composed of coralline limestone; rises to 241m in the hilly NW; low-lying coastal plain in the S; length 35km/22mi. CAPITAL Kralendijk. ECONOMY salt; textiles; tourism. NOTABLE FEATURES Washington-Slagbaai National Park, established in 1969; underwater park.

bonanza *noun* 1 an unexpected and sudden source of good luck or wealth. 2 a large amount, especially of gold from a mine. [from Spanish *bonanza*, good weather at sea]

Bonaparte, Jérôme (1784–1860) youngest brother of Napoleon, born in Ajaccio, Corsica. He served in the war against Prussia, became king and ruled Westphalia (1807–14), and fought at Waterloo. He lived for many years in exile in Florence, but in 1848 was appointed Governor of the Invalides, and in 1850 was made a French Marshal by Napoleon III.

Bonaparte, Joseph (1768–1844) eldest brother of Napoleon, born in Corte, Corsica. He was a diplomat for his brother, and was made ruler of the Two Sicilies (1805) and King of Naples (1806). In 1808 he became King of Spain, but after the defeat of the French at Vitoria (1813) he abdicated and returned to France. After Waterloo he escaped to the USA, and lived in New Jersey as a farmer, but in 1832 returned to Europe.

Bonapartism *noun* advocacy or support of the policies of the French emperor Napoleon Bonaparte, and his dynasty.

Bonaventure *or* **Bonaventura, St**, originally **Giovanni di Fidanza**, known as **Doctor Seraphicus** (1221–74) Italian theologian, born near Orvieto, Tuscany. He became a Franciscan in 1243, taught in Paris, was general of his order by 1257, and in 1273 was made Cardinal Bishop

of Albano. He died from ascetic exhaustion during the Council of Lyons. In 1482 he was canonized, and in 1587 Pope Sixtus V declared him the sixth of the great Doctors of the Church. His feast day is 14 Jul.

bonbon *noun* a sweet. [from French *bon-bon*]

Bond, Alan (1938–) English-born Australian businessman, born in Ealing, London. He emigrated to Australia in 1951, and established his own company at the age of 19. He was Chairman of the Bond Corporation (1969–90), which developed interests in Australian newspapers and television, brewing, oil and gas, and gold mining. His syndicate's yacht *Australia II* won the 1983 America's Cup Challenge.

Bond, James the handsome, heroic secret service agent (007) with a penchant for beautiful women and fast cars, in *Casino Royale* and other novels by Ian Fleming, many of which have been made into popular films.

bond — *noun* 1 something used for tying, binding, or holding. 2 (*usually* **bonds**) something which restrains or imprisons (a person): *break one's bonds.* 3 something that unites or joins people together: *a bond of friendship.* 4 a binding agreement or promise. 5 a certificate issued by a government or a company, which promises to pay back money borrowed at a fixed rate of interest at a stated time. 6 *Legal* a written agreement to pay money or carry out the terms of a contract. 7 *Chem.* the strong force of attraction that holds together two atoms in a molecule or a crystalline salt; a chemical bond. — *verb* 1 to join or tie together. 2 *intrans.* to hold or stick together. 3 to put (goods) into a bonded warehouse.

— **in** *or* **out of bond** *said of goods* in or out of a bonded warehouse.
[from Norse *band*]

bondage *noun* 1 slavery. 2 the state of being confined, imprisoned, etc. 3 a sado-masochistic sexual practice in which one partner is physically restrained. [from Latin *bondagium*]

bonded warehouse a building in which goods are kept until customs or other duty on them is paid.

bond energy *Chem.* the energy released or absorbed during the formation of a chemical bond.

Bondi, Sir Hermann (1919–) Austrian mathematical physicist, born in Vienna. He became Professor of Applied Mathematics at King's College, London, in 1954. He is best known for his proposal that our expanding universe is in a 'steady state', looking the same at all times and retaining the same density, matter being continuously created to fill the gaps left by the expansion. This was an important contribution to cosmological debates, although there is now more evidence for the alternative 'Big Bang' theory.

Bondi a well-known resort beach in the Sydney suburb of Waverley, New South Wales, SE Australia.

bonding *noun* 1 an act or process of making a bond. 2 *Psychol.* the forming of a close emotional attachment, especially between a mother and her newborn child.

bond paper a type of very good quality paper.

bone — *noun* 1 the hard dense tissue that forms the skeleton of vertebrates. It provides structural support for the body, and serves as an attachment for muscles, as well as being the site of red blood cell production, and a store for mineral salts. 2 any of the components of the skeleton, made of this material. 3 (**bones**) the skeleton. 4 (**bones**) the body as the place where feelings come from: *feel it in one's bones.* 5 a substance similar to human bone, such as ivory, whalebone, etc. 6 (**bones**) the basic or essential part: *the bare bones.* — *verb* 1 to take bone out of (meat, etc). 2 to make (a piece of clothing) stiff by

adding pieces of bone or some other hard substance.

— **a bone of contention** something which causes arguments or disagreement.

bone up on something *colloq.* to learn or study a subject.

have a bone to pick with someone to have a reason to argue with them about something.

make no bones about something 1 to admit or allow it without fuss or bother. **2** to be quite willing to say or do it openly.

near *or* **close to the bone** *colloq.* **1** lewd or mildly indecent. **2** *said of criticism, etc* personal; almost offensive.

to the bone 1 thoroughly and completely. **2** to the minimum.

work one's fingers to the bone to work long and hard, especially in physical work.
[from Anglo-Saxon *ban*]

◇ Bone consists of a network of soft rubbery collagen fibres reinforced by calcium salts (mainly calcium carbonate and calcium phosphate). This collagen matrix is secreted by specialized cells called *osteoblasts.* Compact bone, which is virtually solid, forms the outer shell of bones, while the interior consists of spongy bone, a honeycomb arrangement of bony bars (*trabeculae*) with many interconnecting spaces containing bone marrow. The toughest bone is comparable in strength with reinforced concrete.

There are about 206 bones in the human skeleton. Bone growth is regulated by growth hormone (somatotrophin), but bone shape and size are genetically determined, as well as being influenced by hormonal, nutritional, and mechanical factors, eg physical exercise. Calcium, phosphorus, and vitamins A, C, and D are all required for normal bone growth and development.

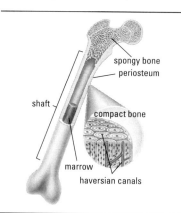

spongy bone
periosteum
shaft
compact bone
marrow
haversian canals

bone structure

bone china a type of fine china made from clay mixed with ash from burnt bones.

bone-dry *adj.* completely dry.

bonehead *noun slang* a stupid person.

bone-headed *adj.* stupid; dense.

bone idle *colloq.* utterly lazy.

boneless *adj.* lacking bones; having the bones removed.

bone meal ground bones, used as fertilizer and in animal feed.

bone of contention a point over which there is much disagreement.

boneshaker *noun colloq.* an old uncomfortable and unsteady vehicle, especially a bicycle.

bonfire *noun* a large outdoor fire, often burned as a celebration or signal. [from Middle English *bonefire*: bones were formerly used as fuel]

Bonfire Night the evening of 5 Nov, Guy Fawkes Day, when bonfires are lit, accompanied by fireworks displays.

bong *noun, verb intrans.* a long, deep sound such as is made by a large bell. — *noun* to make this sound. [imitative]

bongo *noun* (PL. **bongos**, **bongoes**) (*also* **bongo drum**) each of a pair of small drums held between the knees and played with the hands. [from Spanish *bongó*]

Bonhoeffer, Dietrich (1906–45) German Lutheran pastor and theologian, born in Breslau. He left Germany in 1933 in protest against Nazi anti-Jewish legislation, then worked in German parishes in London until 1935, when he returned to Germany to become head of a pastoral seminary until its closure by the Nazis in 1937. Deeply involved in the German resistance movement, he was arrested (1943), imprisoned, and hanged. His most influential works are *Ethik* (Ethics, 1949) and *Widerstand und Ergebung* (Letters and Papers from Prison, 1951).

bonhomie *noun* an easy, friendly nature. [from French, from *bonhomme*, good fellow]

Boniface, St, originally **Wynfrith**, known as **the Apostle of Germany** (c.680–754) Anglo-Saxon missionary, born in Wessex. A Benedictine monk from childhood, in 718 he was commissioned to preach the Gospel to all the tribes of Germany. He met with great success, and was made bishop, Primate of Germany (732), and Archbishop of Mainz (747). He resumed his missionary work among the Frisians in 754, but was killed in Dokkum by heathens. His feast day is 5 Jun.

Bonington, Chris(tian John Storey) (1934–) English mountaineer, born in London. He was a member of the British team that took part in the first successful conquest of the north face of the Eiger (1962), and of the expedition that climbed the south face of Annapurna (1970). He led the 1975 expedition, which made the first ascent of the south-west face of Everest. He reached the summit of Everest himself in 1985.

Bonin Islands, Japanese **Ogasawara-shoto** a group of 27 volcanic islands in the W Pacific Ocean, c.965km/600mi S of Tokyo, Japan. AREA 104sq km/40sq mi. The largest island in the group is Chichijima. HISTORY the islands were first colonized by Europeans and Hawaiians in 1830; annexed by Japanese in 1876; taken by USA in 1945; returned to Japan in 1968. ECONOMY sugar cane, bananas, cocoa.

bonk — *verb trans., intrans.* **1** to bang or hit. **2** *coarse slang* to have sexual intercourse with (someone). — *noun* **1** the act of banging. **2** *coarse slang* an act of sexual intercourse. [imitative]

bonkers *adj. slang* mad, crazy.

bon mot *noun* (PL. **bons mots**) a short and clever remark. [from French *bon mot*]

Bonn POP (1991e) 290 000, a city in North Rhine-Westphalia state, W central Germany. It lies on the R Rhine, 25km/15mi SE of Cologne. HISTORY one of the earliest Roman forts on the Rhine, it was later the seat of the Electors of Cologne (13–16c); the composer Ludwig van Beethoven was born in the city in 1770; Bonn became part of Prussia in 1815; badly bombed in World War II; capital of West Germany from 1949 until unification with East Germany in 1990; the seat of government is being moved in stages from Bonn to Berlin. NOTABLE FEATURES spa resort at Bad Godesberg; Minster (11–13c); Beethovenhalle.

bonne-bouche *noun* a delicious morsel. [from French *bonne bouche*, good mouth]

bonnet *noun* **1** a type of hat fastened under the chin with ribbon, formerly worn by women but now worn especially by babies. **2** *Brit.* the hinged cover over a motor vehicle's engine. **3** a soft Scottish cap. [from Old French *bonet*]

Bonney, William H, known as **Billy the Kid** (1859–81) US bandit, born in New York. After achieving legendary notoriety for his robberies

and murders in the SW states, he was captured by Sheriff Patrick F Garrett in 1880 and sentenced to hang. He escaped, but was finally tracked down and shot by Garrett.

Bonnie and Clyde 1 Bonnie Parker (1911–34) and Clyde Barrow (1909–34), born in Texas, notorious US criminals. Soon after they met in 1932, Parker helped Barrow escape from prison by smuggling a gun in to him. Their gang, which included Barrow's brother and wife, carried out robberies and murders until they were shot dead by the police at a road block in Louisiana. **2** a US film directed by Arthur Penn (1967), based on their criminal activities. Starring Warren Beatty, Faye Dunaway, and Gene Hackman, it was influenced by the French Nouvelle Vague.

bonny *adj.* (**bonnier**, **bonniest**) **1** *chiefly Scot.* attractive; pretty. **2** looking very healthy and attractive.

Bono, Edward Francis Charles Publius De see DE BONO, EDWARD FRANCIS CHARLES PUBLIUS.

bonsai *noun* (PL. **bonsai**) **1** the ancient Japanese art of cultivating artificially miniaturized trees in small containers, by restricting root growth. The roots and shoots are pruned regularly, and wires are used to bend the branches to the desired shape. **2** a miniature tree cultivated in this way, eg pine, juniper, Japanese maple, Chinese quince, cherry. [from Japanese, from *bon*, tray, bowl + *sai*, cultivation]

bonsai tree

bonus *noun* (PL. **bonuses**) **1** an extra sum of money given on top of what is due as interest or wages. **2** an unexpected extra benefit. [from Latin *bonus*, good]

bon vivant or **bon viveur** (PL. *bons vivants* or *viveurs*) a person who enjoys good food and wine. [French, = good liver]

bon voyage *interj.* an expression of good wishes said to a person about to travel. [from French *bon voyage*]

bony *adj.* (**bonier**, **boniest**) **1** of or like bone. **2** full of bones. **3** thin.

bonzer *adj. Austral. slang* good, excellent. [perhaps from French *bon*, good, influenced by BONANZA]

boo — *interj., noun* a sound expressing disapproval or made when trying to frighten or surprise someone. — *verb intrans., trans.* to shout boo to express disapproval.
— **one could not** or **would not say boo to a goose** one is very shy or easily frightened. [imitative]

boob¹ — *noun colloq.* **1** also **booboo** a stupid or foolish mistake. **2** a stupid or foolish person. — *verb intrans. colloq.* to make a stupid or foolish mistake. [from BOOBY]

boob² *noun slang* a woman's breast.

booby *noun* (PL. **boobies**) **1** *old colloq. use* a stupid or foolish person. **2** a bird related to the gannet, native to tropical and subtropical seas, and having a streamlined body and a colourful pointed bill. It catches fish by diving vertically into the water, and air sacs beneath the skin of its face absorb the shock of impact.

booby prize a prize for the lowest score, the person coming last, etc in a competition.

booby trap 1 a bomb or mine which is disguised so that it is set off by the victim. **2** something placed as a trap, eg a bucket of water put above a door so as to fall on the person who opens the door.

booby-trap *verb* to put a booby trap in or on (a place).

boodle *noun old use, slang* money, especially when gained dishonestly or as a bribe. [from Dutch *boedel*, possessions]

boogie *colloq.* — *verb intrans.* (**boogieing**, **boogying**) to dance to pop or jazz music. — *noun* a dance to pop or jazz music.

book — *noun* **1** a number of printed pages bound together along one edge and protected by covers. **2** a piece of written work intended for publication. **3** a number of sheets of blank paper bound together: *a notebook*. **4** (*usually* **books**) a record of the business done by a company, a society, etc. **5** a major division of a long literary work. **6** a number of stamps, matches, cheques, etc bound together. **7** the words of an opera or musical; a libretto. **8** a record of bets. **9** (**the book**) the current telephone directory: *they're not in the book*. — *verb* **1** *trans., intrans.* to reserve a ticket, seat, etc, or engage a person's services in advance. **2** to enter (a person's name, etc) in a book or list. **3** to record the details of (a person who is being charged with an offence).
— **be in someone's good** or **bad books** to be in, or out of, favour with them.
book in to sign one's name on the list of guests at a hotel, etc.
book someone in to reserve a place for them in a hotel, etc.
book something up to complete arrangements for (a holiday, etc).
be booked up have no more places or tickets available.
bring someone to book to punish them or make them account for their behaviour.
by the book strictly according to the rules.
in my book in my opinion.
suit one's book to be what one wants or likes.
take a leaf out of someone's book to profit or benefit from their example or experience.
throw the book at someone *colloq.* to deal with them as severely as possible. [from Anglo-Saxon *boc*]
◇ Among the earliest printed books was the Gutenberg Bible (1456), which was produced in black-letter type and closely modelled on the manuscript books produced in medieval monasteries across W Europe. From the 19c, technical innovations, such as mechanical typesetting and cheaper paper, facilitated an explosion in book production which has continued throughout the 20c.

bookable *adj.* **1** able to be booked or reserved in advance. **2** *said of an offence* that makes the offender liable to be charged.

bookbinder *noun* a person whose job is to bind books.

bookbinding *noun* the art or business of binding books.

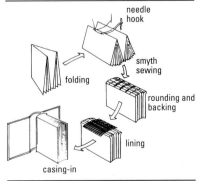

bookbinding

needle hook

smyth sewing

folding

rounding and backing

lining

casing-in

bookcase *noun* a cabinet of shelves for books.

book club a club which sells books to its members at reduced prices.

book end each of a pair of supports used to keep a row of books standing upright.

Booker Prize, in full **Booker McConnell Prize for Fiction** in the UK, a literary prize founded in 1969. It is presented annually to the best novel in English published during the preceding year.

Booker Prize	
1971	V S Naipaul *In a Free State*
1972	John Berger *G*
1973	J G Farrell *The Siege of Krishnapur*
1974	Nadine Gordimer *The Conservationist*; Stanley Middleton *Holiday*
1975	Ruth Prawer Jhabvala *Heat and Dust*
1976	David Storey *Saville*
1977	Paul Scott *Staying On*
1978	Iris Murdoch *The Sea, The Sea*
1979	Penelope Fitzgerald *Offshore*
1980	William Golding *Rites of Passage*
1981	Salman Rushdie *Midnight's Children*
1982	Thomas Keneally *Schindler's Ark*
1983	J M Coetzee *Life and Times of Michael K*
1984	Anita Brookner *Hotel du Lac*
1985	Keri Hulme *The Bone People*
1986	Kingsley Amis *The Old Devils*
1987	Penelope Lively *Moon Tiger*
1988	Peter Carey *Oscar and Lucinda*
1989	Kazuo Ishiguro *The Remains of the Day*
1990	A S Byatt *Possession*
1991	Ben Okri *The Famished Road*
1992	Barry Unsworth *Sacred Hunger*; Michael Ondaatje *The English Patient*
1993	Roddy Doyle *Paddy Clarke Ha Ha Ha*

book fair a trade fair held at regular intervals, at which publishers and booksellers present books for sale to the national and international market, and negotiate rights to publish translations, etc.

bookie *noun colloq.* a bookmaker.

booking *noun* **1** a reservation of a seat, hotel room, etc. **2** *especially in sport* the recording of an offence with details of the offender.

bookish *adj.* **1** devoted to reading. **2** often *derog.* learned and serious; with knowledge or opinions based on books rather than practical experience.

bookishness *noun* devotion to reading; learned seriousness.

bookkeeper *noun* a person who keeps official accounts.

bookkeeping *noun* the keeping of financial accounts.

booklet *noun* a small book or pamphlet with a paper cover.

bookmaker *noun* a person who takes bets on horseraces, etc and pays out winnings.

bookmark *noun* a strip of leather, card, etc put in a book to mark a particular page, especially the reader's place.

Book of Common Prayer see COMMON PRAYER, BOOK OF.

Book of Kells, The an illuminated manuscript of the Gospels (c.8c–9c). It was produced at Kells in County Meath, Eire, and is now in Trinity College, Dublin.

Book of the Dead an ancient Egyptian collection of magical and religious texts. Copies were often buried with the dead as a protection and comfort in the after-life.

bookplate *noun* a piece of decorated paper stuck into the front of a book and bearing the owner's name.

bookseller *noun* an individual or business that sells books, either direct to the public, to bookshops and book clubs, or to institutional buyers such as libraries and schools.

bookshelf *noun* (PL. **bookshelves**) a shelf for storing books in an upright position.

bookshop *noun* a shop that sells books to the public. These range from large national chains selling a wide range of new books to shops selling specialist, antiquarian, or second-hand books.

bookstall *noun* a small shop in a station, etc where books, newspapers, magazines, etc are sold.

book token a card containing a token worth a specified amount of money which can be used to buy books.

bookworm *noun* **1** *colloq.* a person devoted to reading. **2** a type of small insect which feeds on the paper and glue used in books.

Boole, George (1815–64) English mathematician and logician, born in Lincoln. Largely self-taught, he was appointed Professor of Mathematics at Cork in 1849. He is best remembered for his *Mathematical Analysis of Logic* (1847) and *Laws of Thought* (1854), in which he employed mathematical symbolism to express logical relations, greatly influencing the subsequent work of Gottlob Frege and Bertrand Russell among others.

Boolean algebra *Maths.* a form of algebra that is closely related to logic, and uses algebraic symbols and set theory, instead of arithmetical quantities, to represent logic operations. It is used to work out the logic for computer programs. [named after the UK mathematician George Boole]

boom¹ — *noun* a deep resounding sound, like that made by a large drum or gun. — *verb intrans.* to make a deep resounding sound.

— **boom something out** to say something with a booming sound.

[probably imitative]

boom² — *noun* a sudden increase or growth in business, prosperity, etc. — *verb intrans.* to prosper rapidly. [perhaps from BOOM¹]

boom³ *noun* **1** a pole to which the bottom of a ship's sail is attached, keeping the sail stretched tight. **2** a heavy pole or chain, etc across the entrance to a harbour. **3** a long pole with a microphone attached to one end, allowing the microphone to be held above the heads of people being filmed. [from Dutch *boom*, beam]

boomerang — *noun* **1** a piece of flat, curved wood used by Australian Aborigines for hunting, often so balanced that, when thrown to a distance, it returns to the thrower. **2** a malicious act or statement which harms the perpetrator rather than the intended victim. — *verb intrans., said of an act, statement, etc* to go wrong and harm the perpetrator rather than the intended victim. [from Dharuk (Australian Aboriginal language) *bumariny*]

boon¹ *noun* **1** an advantage, benefit, or blessing. **2** *old use* a gift or favour. [from Norse *bon*, prayer]

boon² *adj.* close, intimate, or favourite: *a boon companion.* [from Old French *bon*, good]

Boone, Daniel (1735–1820) US pioneer, born in Pennsylvania. He made a trail through the Cumberland Gap (1767) and became one of the first to explore Kentucky (1769–73). Twice captured by Cherokees, he repeatedly repelled (1775–8) Native American attacks on his stockade fort, now Boonesborough, and later worked as a surveyor and trapper.

boor *noun derog.* a coarse person with bad manners. [from Dutch *boer*, farmer, peasant]

boorish *adj., said of a person, or a person's manner* coarse and unfriendly.

boorishly *adv.* with a coarse and unfriendly manner.

boorishness *noun* a coarse and unfriendly manner.

boost — *verb* **1** to improve or encourage: *boost the spirits.* **2** to make greater or increase: *boost profits.* **3** to promote by advertising. — *noun* **1** a piece of help or encouragement, etc. **2** a push upwards. **3** a rise or increase.

booster *noun* **1** a person or thing that boosts. **2** *Medicine* a dose of vaccine that is given in order to renew or increase the immune response to a previous dose of the same vaccine. **3** *Engineering* an engine in a rocket that provides additional thrust at some stage of the vehicle's flight. **4** (*also* **booster rocket**) a rocket that is used to launch a space vehicle, before another engine takes over. **5** *Electron.* a radio-frequency amplifier that is used to amplify a weak television or radio signal, and to rebroadcast such a signal so that it can be received by the general public.

Boot, Sir Jesse, 1st Baron Trent (1850–1931) English drug manufacturer, born in Nottingham. He inherited his father's herbalist's shop, and in 1877 opened his first chemist's shop in Nottingham. By mass selling at reduced prices he introduced the modern chain store. By 1900 he was in control of the largest pharmaceutical retail trade in the world, with over a thousand branches in 1931.

boot¹ — *noun* **1** an outer covering, usually of leather, for the foot and lower part of the leg. **2** *Brit.* a compartment for luggage in a car, usually at the back. **3** *colloq.* a hard kick. **4** (**the boot**) *colloq.* dismissal from a job: *get the boot.* — *verb* to kick.

— **boot something** *or* **someone out** to throw them out or remove them with force.

boot someone out to dismiss them from employment, etc.

boot up *Comput.* to start (a computer) by loading the programs which control its basic functions.

the boot is on the other foot *or* **leg** *colloq.* the situation is now the reverse of what it was before, especially as regards advantage, responsibility, etc.

lick someone's boots *derog. colloq.* to try to win a person's favour by flattery, excessive obedience, etc.

[from Old French *bote*]

boot²
— **to boot** as well; in addition.
[from Anglo-Saxon *bot*, help, advantage]

bootee *noun* a soft knitted boot for a baby.

Boötes the Herdsman, a large constellation of the northern hemisphere. Its brightest star is Arcturus (Alpha Boötis).

Booth, Charles (1840–1916) English shipowner, statistician, and social reformer, born in Liverpool. An ardent radical in his youth, he settled in London (1875) and devoted 18 years to preparing *Life and Labour of the People in London* (1903), the prototype of the modern social survey. He became President of the Royal Statistical Society (1892–4) and was made a privy councillor (1904).

Booth, John Wilkes (1839–65) US assassin, born in Baltimore, brother of the actor Edwin Booth. Unsuccessful as an actor, in 1865 he entered into a conspiracy to avenge the defeat of the Confederates and shot President Lincoln at Ford's Theatre, Washington (14 Apr). He broke his leg while escaping, and fled to Virginia, but was tracked down and shot.

Booth, William (1829–1912) English religious leader, founder of the Salvation Army, born in Nottingham. He was minister of the Methodist New Connexion (1855–61), and in 1865 founded the Salvation Army (so named in 1878) to do mission work in London's East End, waging war against such evils as sweated labour and child prostitution. His wife Catherine (1829–90) was fully associated with him, and his son Bramwell (1856–1929) and daughters Kate (1859–1955) and

Evangeline (1865–1950) succeeded him in the work.

booth *noun* **1** a small temporary roofed structure, or a tent, especially at a fair. **2** a small building or structure for a stated purpose: *a polling booth*. [from Norse *buth*]

Boothroyd, Betty (1929–) English Labour politician, first female Speaker of the House of Commons, born in Dewsbury, Yorkshire. She has been MP for West Bromwich West since 1973, and became Speaker after the 1992 general election.

bootlace *noun* a piece of string, ribbon, etc used to fasten boots.

Bootle POP (1981) 71 000, a seaport in Liverpool borough, Merseyside, NW England.

bootleg — *verb* (**bootlegged, bootlegging**) to make or transport alcoholic drinks illegally, especially in a time of prohibition. — *adj., said of alcoholic drinks* illegally produced or transported.

bootlegger *noun* a person who produces or sells alcoholic drinks illegally, especially in a time of prohibition.

bootlegging *noun* the practice of producing or selling alcoholic drink illegally.
◇ The term is mainly used to refer to the smuggling of alcohol in the USA during the Prohibition era (1920–33), although it is also applied in the present day to the illegal production of goods protected by copyright or patent, such as recordings of popular music.

bootlicker *noun colloq.* a person who tries to gain the favour of someone in authority by flattery, excessive obedience, etc.

boots *noun old use* a person in a hotel who carries guests' bags and cleans their shoes.

bootstrap *Comput.* — *noun* a short program used to boot up a computer by transferring the disk-operating system program from storage on disk into a computer's working memory. — *verb trans., intrans.* to boot up (a computer) by activating the bootstrap program.

booty *noun* (PL. **booties**) valuable goods taken in wartime or by force. [from Middle English *botye*]

booze — *noun slang* **1** alcoholic drink. **2** the drinking of alcohol: *on the booze*. — *verb intrans. slang* to drink a lot of, or too much, alcohol. [from Old Dutch *busen*, to drink in excess]

boozer *noun slang* **1** a person who drinks much alcohol. **2** a public house.

booze-up *noun slang* an occasion when much alcohol is drunk.

boozy *adj.* (**boozier, booziest**) *slang* **1** given to drinking a lot of alcohol. **2** drunken.

bop¹ — *verb intrans.* (**bopped, bopping**) *colloq.* to dance to popular music. — *noun colloq.* a dance. [from *bebop*, a type of 1940s jazz music]

bop² *verb* (**bopped, bopping**) *colloq.* to hit lightly. [imitative]

Bophuthatswana, locally **Bop** POP (1985e) 1.7m, formerly an independent black homeland in South Africa. AREA 44 000sq km/17 000sq mi. It comprises seven separate units of land in Cape, Orange Free State, and Transvaal provinces. In 1971 it was granted self-governing status and became the second homeland to receive independence from South Africa (not recognized internationally) in 1977. Following violence in the lead-up to the South African elections in 1994, the President was deposed and South Africa took over the administration of the territory. The main languages spoken are English, Afrikaans, and Setswana. Around one quarter of the population are commuters or migrant workers in South Africa. ECONOMY brewing; tanning; furniture; maize; beef; platinum (one third of world production of platinum group metals), copper, nickel, gold, chromium, vanadium, asbestos, iron ore, diamonds, limestone, manganese, fluorspar.

bopper *noun colloq.* a person who dances to popular music.

boracic *adj.* **1** of or containing borax. **2** of or containing boron.

boracic acid same as BORIC ACID.

borage *noun* a plant with blue flowers, the leaves of which are used in salads or as a herb. [from Old French *bourache*]

borax *noun Chem.* (FORMULA $Na_2B_4O_7.10H_2O$) a colourless crystalline salt or white greasy powder found in saline lake deposits and used in the manufacture of enamels, ceramics, and heat-resistant glass, eg Pyrex, and as a cleaning agent, mild antiseptic, astringent, and source of boric acid. — Also called *sodium borate*. [from Latin *borax*, from Arabic *buraq*]

Bordeaux, Latin **Burdigala** POP (1990) 685 000, the capital of Aquitaine region and of Gironde department, SW France. Lying on the R Garonne, 480km/300mi SW of Paris, it is a major inland port. Bordeaux is also the cultural and commercial centre for the SW. HISTORY held by the English from 1154 until 1453; centre of the 17c Wars of the Fronde; temporary seat of government in 1870, 1914, and 1940. ECONOMY the famous Bordeaux wines are produced in the region of the town; to the N is the Médoc, to the S the Graves and Sauternes, and the Entre-deux-Mers (between the Garonne and Dordogne rivers). NOTABLE FEATURES Church of St Seurin (12c–15c); Grand Theatre (1773–80); 486m-long Pont de Pierre (1813–21); university (1441).

Border, Allan (1955–) Australian cricketer, born in Cremorne, Sydney. He has played country cricket in England for Gloucestershire and Essex. He made his Test début for Australia in 1978, and has been captain of the team since 1985. He established a world record of most Test match and one-day international appearances, and in Feb 1993 set a new world record for runs scored in Test matches when his career total reached 10 161.

border — *noun* **1** a band or margin along the edge of something. **2** the boundary of a country. **3** the land on either side of a country's border. See also BORDERS. **4** a narrow strip of ground planted with flowers, surrounding a small area of grass. **5** any decorated or ornamental edge. — *verb* **1** to provide with a border. **2** to be a border to or on the border of. **3** (**border on something**) to be nearly the same as some specified quality or condition: *actions bordering on stupidity*. [from Middle English *bordure*]

bordered *adj.* having a border.

borderer *noun* a person who lives on the border of a country.

borderland *noun* **1** land at or near the country's border. **2** a condition between two states, eg between sleeping and waking.

borderline — *noun* **1** the border between one thing, country etc and another. **2** a line dividing two opposing or extreme conditions: *the borderline between passing and failing*. — *adj.* on the border between one thing, state, etc and another.

Border Minstrelsy see MINSTRELSY OF THE SCOTTISH BORDER, THE.

Borders POP (1992e) 105 000, a Region in SE Scotland, divided into four districts. AREA 4 672sq km/1 803sq mi. It is bounded N by Lothian Region, NE by the North Sea, W by Strathclyde, SW by Dumfries and Galloway, and SE by England. PHYSICAL DESCRIPTION the region lies partly along the Cheviot Hills and is crossed E–W by the Southern Uplands; rivers include the Tweed and Teviot. CAPITAL Newtown St Boswells. CHIEF TOWNS Hawick, Peebles, Galashiels. ECONOMY livestock; forestry; textiles. NOTABLE FEATURES Melrose Abbey (12c); Abbotsford (home of Walter Scott); Dryburgh Abbey; the Muirfoot, Lammermuir, and Pentland hills.

Bordet, Jules Jean Baptiste Vincent (1870–1961) Belgian physiologist, born in Soignies. Director of the Pasteur Institute in Brussels from 1901, he discovered the immunity factors in blood serum, and the bacterium causing whooping cough. He was awarded the 1919 Nobel Prize for Physiology or Medicine.

bore¹ — *verb* **1** (*also* **bore a hole in something**) to make a hole in (something) by drilling. **2** to produce (a tunnel, mine, etc) by drilling. — *noun* **1** the hollow barrel of a gun. **2** the diameter of the hollow barrel of a gun, especially to show which size of bullets the gun requires. **3** same as BOREHOLE. [from Anglo-Saxon *borian*]

bore² — *verb* to make (someone) feel tired and uninterested, by being dull, uninteresting, unimaginative, etc. — *noun* a dull, uninteresting, tedious person or thing.

bore³ *noun* a solitary high wave of water, resembling a wall, that moves rapidly upstream and is caused by constriction of the spring tide as it enters a narrow shallow estuary. It gradually loses height as it moves upstream. [from Norse *bara*, wave]

bore⁴ see BEAR¹.

boreal forest *Bot.* the vast area of dense coniferous forest that extends from the arctic tundra to the N temperate forests in N America, Europe, and Asia.

bored *adj.* tired and without interest from being unoccupied or under-occupied.

boredom *noun* the state of being bored.

borehole *noun* a deep narrow hole made by boring, especially one made in the earth to find oil, water, etc.

Borelli, Giovanni Alfonso (1608–79) Italian mathematician and physiologist, born in Naples. He held professorships at Naples, Pisa, and Messina, and founded the 'iatrophysical' school of medicine, which sought to explain all bodily functions by physical laws.

borer *noun* a machine or tool for boring holes.

Borg, Björn (Rune) (1956–) Swedish tennis player, born in Södertälje. His first major title was the Italian Open (1974), and he went on to become Wimbledon singles champion five times (1976–80), a modern-day record. He lost to John McEnroe in the 1981 final. He also won the French singles title six times, and was the World Championship Tennis singles champion in 1976, and Masters champion in 1980 and 1981. He retired in 1981, but made comebacks in 1982, 1984, and 1991.

Borga see PORVOO.

Borghese (13c) a great 13c family of ambassadors and jurists of Siena, afterward at Rome. Their members include Camillo Borghese (1552–1621), who became pope in 1605 as Paul V, and Prince Camillo Filippo Ludovico Borghese (1775–1832), who joined the French army, married Napoleon's sister Marie Pauline (1803), and became Governor-General of Piedmont. The Borghese Palace contains one of Rome's finest art collections.

Borgia, Italian form of **Borja** an ancient family in the Spanish province of Valencia. Its members include Alfonso (1378–1458), who accompanied Alfonso of Aragon to Rome, and was elected pope as Calixtus III. Rodrigo (1431–1503), his nephew, became pope as Alexander VI (1492). Two of Rodrigo's children became especially notorious: Cesare (1476–1507) was a brilliant general and administrator; in two campaigns he became master of Romagna, Perugia, Siena, Piombino, and Urbino, and planned a Kingdom of Central Italy, and he succeeded his brother (whom he may have murdered) as Capt-General of the Church. Lucrezia (1480–1519), who has been represented both as a criminal and a patroness of learning, was married off three times by her father, for political reasons, finally becoming the wife of Alfonso, son of the Duke of Este.

boric *adj.* of or containing boron.

boric acid *Chem.* (FORMULA H_3BO_3) a white or colourless crystalline solid, obtained from borax, that is soluble in water and has antiseptic properties. It is used in pharmaceutical products, glazes, enamels, borosilicate glass, detergents, adhesives, explosives, and as a food preservative.

boring *adj.* tedious and uninteresting.

boringly *adv.* with a tedious manner or effect.

Boris a male first name, introduced from Russia in the 20c. [probably from the Tartar nickname *Bogoris*, small]

Boris Godunov an opera by Modest Mussorgsky (1874), revised by Rimsky-Korsakov. Set in Russia and Poland at the turn of the 16c, it is a complex work based on a play by Alexander Pushkin and the *History of the Russian State* by Nicolai Karamzin. When Boris Godunov becomes Tsar, he suffers guilt for having murdered Dimitri, the rightful heir to the Russian throne, and also fears a pretender, the former monk Grigory.

Borlaug, Norman Ernest (1914–) US plant pathologist and geneticist, born in Cresco, Iowa. As Director of the Wheat Programme at the International Center for Maize and Wheat Improvement, he developed 'dwarf' wheats which dramatically increased yields and made possible the 'green revolution'. He was awarded the 1970 Nobel Peace Prize.

Bormann, Martin (1900–?1945) German Nazi politician, born in Halberstadt. One of Hitler's closest advisers, he became *Reichs-minister* (1941) after Hess's flight to Scotland, and was with Hitler to the last. His own fate is uncertain, but he was possibly killed by Russian snipers in the breakout from Hitler's staff from the Chancellory (1 May 1945). In his absence the Nuremberg Court sentenced him to death (1946).

Born, Max (1882–1970) German physicist, born in Breslau (now Wrocław, Poland). He was Professor of Theoretical Physics at Göttingen (1921–33) and later Professor of Natural Philosophy at Edinburgh (1936–53). For developing the probability approach to the theory of quantum mechanics, he shared the 1954 Nobel Prize for Physics with Walther Bothe.

born *adj.* **1** brought into being by birth. **2** having a natural quality or ability: *a born leader*. **3** destined to do something stated: *born to lead men*. **4** having a stated given status by birth: *Scots-born*.
— **in all one's born days** *colloq.* in all one's lifetime or experience.
not born yesterday alert; shrewd. [from BEAR¹]

born-again *adj.* **1** converted to a fundamentalist Christian faith. **2** *colloq.* showing a new and strong enthusiasm for something: *a born-again vegetarian*.

borne see BEAR.

Borneo a large island in the W Pacific Ocean, SE Asia. It lies E of Sumatra, N of Java, and W of Sulawesi. AREA 757 050sq km/292 220sq mi. The island comprises the Malaysian states of Sarawak and Sabah, as well as Brunei in the N. The remainder is made up of the four provinces of Kalimantan, which form part of Indonesia. PHYSICAL DESCRIPTION mountainous in the N, rising to 4 094m at Mt Kinabalu in Sabah; the interior is densely forested. The island was formerly divided between the British and the Dutch. ECONOMY rice; pepper; copra; tobacco; oil; bauxite; iron.

Bornholm POP (1992e) 46 000, a Danish island and county in the Baltic Sea, situated 40km/25mi S of Sweden and 168km/104mi SE of Copenhagen. AREA 588sq km/227sq mi; length

37km/23mi. The island rises to 162m; its N and central areas are formed from granite. CAPITAL Rønne. HISTORY taken by Sweden in 1645, it was returned to Denmark in 1660. ECONOMY fishing, fish-processing; farming; pottery; tourism.

Borobudur a Buddhist sanctuary built between 750 and 850 in Java, Indonesia. The monument comprises eight stepped terraces cut into the sides of a natural mound and culminating in a central shrine (stupa).

Borodin, Alexander (Porfiryevich) (1833–87) Russian composer and scientist, born in St Petersburg. He trained in medicine and distinguished himself as a chemist, then in 1862 began to study music, under Balakirev. His works include the unfinished opera *Prince Igor* (which contains the Polovtsian Dances), three symphonies, and the symphonic sketch *In the Steppes of Central Asia*.

boron *noun Chem.* (SYMBOL **B**, ATOMIC NUMBER 5) a non-metallic element consisting of a dark brown powder or black crystals, that is found only in the form of its compounds, eg borax, boric acid. It is used in semiconductors and as a component of control rods and shields in nuclear reactors. See also BORAX, BORIC ACID.

borough *noun* **1** in Britain, a town or urban area which sends a member to Parliament. **2** *Hist.* in Britain, a town with special rights granted by royal charter. **3** a division of a large town, especially of London or New York. [from Anglo-Saxon *burg*]

Borromini, Francesco, originally Francesco Castello (1599–1667) Italian architect, born in Bissone, L Lugano. He went to Rome in 1619 and designed San Carlo alle Quattro Fontane (1637–41). Although now considered one of the great Baroque architects, he had limited influence during his lifetime. He committed suicide in Rome.

Borrow, George (Henry) (1803–81) English writer and traveller, born in East Dereham, Norfolk. He trained as a solicitor, then worked for a publisher in London. From 1825 to 1832 he wandered in England, sometimes in Romany company, as described in *Lavengro* (1851) and *The Romany Rye* (1857), examples of his numerous books in which romantic fiction and autobiography often overlap. As an agent for the Bible Society he visited St Petersburg (1833–5) and many other, mainly European, countries.

borrow *verb* **1** to take (something) temporarily, usually with permission and with the intention of returning it. **2** *intrans.* to get money in this way. **3** to take, adopt, or copy (words, ideas, etc) from another language, person, etc.
— **live on borrowed time** to live longer than expected.
[from Anglo-Saxon *borgian*, from *borg*, pledge]

borrower *noun* a person who borrows, especially from a bank or building society.

borrowing *noun* a thing borrowed, especially a word taken from one language into another.

borstal *noun Brit. Hist.* an institution which was both a prison and a school, to which young criminals were formerly sent; now replaced by *detention centre* and *youth custody centre*. [from *Borstal* in Kent, where the first of these was established]

borzoi *noun* a large dog, originally used for hunting, with a narrow head and a long, soft coat. [from Russian *borzii*, swift]

Bosch, Carl (1874–1940) German industrial chemist, born in Cologne. He became President of the I G Farbenindustrie, and shared the 1931 Nobel Prize for Chemistry with Friedrich Bergius for the development of chemical high-pressure methods, such as the 'Bosch process', in which hydrogen is obtained from water gas and superheated steam.

Bosch, Hieronymus, pseudonym of Jerome van Aken (c.1450–1516) Dutch painter,

born in Hertogenbosch. He is noted for his allegorical pictures displaying macabre devils, freaks, and monsters. Among his best-known works are *The Garden of Earthly Delights* (Prado) and the *Temptation of St Anthony* (Lisbon). He had considerable influence on the Surrealists.

Bosch process *Chem.* an industrial process whereby hydrogen is obtained by reducing (removing oxygen from) steam using carbon monoxide. [named after the German chemist Carl Bosch]

Bose, Sir Jagadis Chandra (1858–1937) Indian physicist and botanist, born in Mymensingh, Bengal (now in Pakistan). Educated at Cambridge University, he was appointed Professor of Physics at Presidency College in Calcutta. He was best known for his study of electric waves, their polarization and reflection, and for his experiments demonstrating the sensitivity and growth of plants, for which he designed an extremely sensitive automatic recorder.

bosh *noun, interj. colloq.* nonsense. [from Turkish *boş*, worthless, empty]

Bosnia-Herzegovina, Serbo-Croatian **Bosna-Hercegovina** POP (1991) 4.4m, a republic in central Europe, formerly a constituent republic of central Yugoslavia comprising two provinces. AREA 51 129sq km/19 736sq mi. CAPITAL Sarajevo. CHIEF TOWNS Banja Luka, Zenica, Tuzla, Mostar. The population consists of Muslims (46%), Serbs (34%), Croats (20%); religions are Islam, Serbian Eastern Orthodoxy, Roman Catholicism. TIME ZONE GMT +1. CURRENCY the dinar. PHYSICAL DESCRIPTION the region is mountainous and includes part of the Dinaric Alps; it is noted for its limestone gorges. HISTORY under Austrian protectorate from 1878, the two provinces were annexed by Austria in 1908; Serbian opposition to the annexation led to the murder of Archduke Francis Ferdinand, and World War I; ceded to Yugoslavia in 1918; following independence in 1992, Civil War broke out between the three ethnic groups; as a result of the fierce fighting and 'ethnic cleansing' many people have been killed, there are severe shortages of food and medical supplies and thousands have been left homeless; a large UN force was sent to the area to protect the aid effort, but fighting continued. GOVERNMENT a collective presidency and a 240-member bicameral National Assembly. ECONOMY agricultural trade; mostly dependent on UN aid.

Bosnia-Herzegovina

bosom *noun* **1** a person's, especially a woman's, chest or breast. **2** *colloq.* (also **bosoms**) a woman's breasts. **3** the part of a dress covering the breasts and chest. **4** a loving or protective centre: *the bosom of one's family*. **5** the seat of emotions and feelings. [from Anglo-Saxon *bosm*]

bosom friend a close friend.

boson *noun Physics* one of two categories of subatomic particle (the other being the fermion). The spin of a boson can only take values that are whole numbers or zero, whereas the spin of a fermion can take values that are half integers, eg 1½. Bosons are of two types, gauge bosons (eg photons and gluons) and weakons. [named after the Indian physicist Satyendra Nath Bose]

Bosporus or **Bosphorus**, Turkish **Karadeniz Boğazi** a narrow strait separating European from Asiatic Turkey, and connecting the Black Sea and the Sea of Marmara. Its length is 32km/20mi. At its narrowest point (width c.640m), there are two famous castles, Anadolu Hisar (1390) on the Asian side, and Rumeli Hisar (1452) on the European side. One of the world's longest suspension bridges (1 075m) spans the strait at Istanbul. The Bosporus, together with the Dardanelles, is an area of great strategic importance.

Bosporus Bridge a major steel suspension bridge across the Golden Horn in Istanbul, Turkey, completed in 1973, with a main span of 1 074m.

Bosques Petrificados, English **Petrified Forests** a natural monument in E Santa Cruz province, Patagonia, Argentina. AREA 100sq km/39sq mi. Established in 1954, it contains 70 000-year-old araucaria trees, averaging 3m in circumference and 15–20m in height.

Bosra an ancient Syrian city 117km/73mi S of Damascus. It was originally an Arab fortress which was conquered by the Nabataeans. It was annexed by the Romans in AD 105, and subsequently flourished as capital of the province of Arabia. It is a World Heritage site.

boss[1] — *noun colloq.* a person who employs or who is in charge of others. — *verb* (*also* **boss someone about** or **around**) *colloq.* to give them orders in a domineering way. [from Dutch *baas*, master]

boss[2] *noun* **1** a round raised knob for decoration on a shield etc. **2** a round raised decorative knob, found where the ribs meet in a vaulted ceiling. [from Old French *boce*]

Bossangoa the chief town in Ouham prefecture, N Central African Republic. It is situated on the R Ouham, 274km/170mi NW of Bangui.

bossa nova 1 a dance like the samba, which originated in Brazil. **2** music for this dance. [from Portuguese *bossa*, trend + *nova*, new]

boss-eyed *adj. Brit. colloq.* **1** having only one good eye. **2** cross-eyed. **3** crooked, squint.

bossily *adv.* in a bossy or domineering manner.

bossiness *noun* a bossy or domineering manner.

bossy *adj.* (**bossier, bossiest**) *colloq.* prone to give orders; disagreeably domineering.

bossy-boots *noun colloq.* a bossy domineering person.

Boston POP (1990) 2.9m, the capital of the state of Massachusetts, USA, and the largest city in New England. It is situated in Suffolk County, on Massachusetts Bay, at the mouth of the Charles R. HISTORY settled in 1630, it became capital of the Massachusetts Bay Colony in 1632 and achieved city status in 1822; a centre of opposition to British trade restrictions and the scene of the Boston Tea Party (1773); centre of the Unitarian Church Movement. Boston is noted for its colleges and universities. NOTABLE FEATURES Boston Tea Party Ship and Museum; Christ Church (1723); Paul Revere's House; Faneuil Hall (1742); Conservatory of Music; Museum of Fine Arts.

Bostonians, The a novel by Henry James (1886). It is set against the background of the US suffragette movement.

Boston Massacre the first bloodshed (5 Mar 1770) of the American Revolution. In an atmosphere of intense resentment against British troops and regulations, British guards at the Boston Customs House opened fire on an unruly crowd and killed five. Of the nine British soldiers tried for murder, seven (including the commander) were acquitted and two were found guilty of manslaughter.

Boston Public Library the world's first free municipal library supported by taxation. It was founded in Boston, Massachusetts, in 1852.

Boston Tea Party the climactic event of resistance to British attempts at direct taxation, which took place during the American Revolution and resulted in the destruction of 342 chests of dutied tea by working men disguised as Mohawks.

bosun same as BOATSWAIN.

Boswell, James (1740–95) Scottish man of letters and biographer of Dr Johnson, born in Edinburgh. He studied civil law in Glasgow, ran away to London in 1760, and led a colourful life in Europe before being admitted advocate on his return to Scotland (1766). He first met Samuel Johnson in 1763, was elected to his famous literary club in 1773, and took him on the memorable journey to the Hebrides. His *Journal of a Tour of the Hebrides* (1785) appeared after Johnson's death, and was followed by his major work, the *Life of Samuel Johnson* (1791).

Bosworth Field, Battle of the battle (22 Aug 1485) which resulted in Henry Tudor acceding to the English throne after Richard III was killed. Henry's forces were possibly inferior in number, but proved more loyal, and they received crucial assistance from the Stanley family, who supported both sides.

botanic or **botanical** *adj.* relating to botany or the study of plants.

botanic gardens or **botanical gardens** a public park where both native and foreign plants are grown and often studied.

botanist *noun* a person who studies or practises botany, especially professionally.

botany *noun* the branch of biology concerned with the scientific study of plants, including their structure, function, ecology, evolution, and classification. [from Greek *botane*, plant]

Botany Bay a shallow inlet 8km/5mi S of Sydney, New South Wales, SE Australia. It is ringed by residential suburbs of Sydney. Captain Cook made his first landing at Botany Bay in 1770. It was chosen as a penal settlement in 1787, but was found to be unsuitable, and a location at Sydney Cove was used instead. The name Botany Bay, however, was for many years synonymous with Australian convict settlements. [named by Captain Cook after the number of new plants discovered here]

botch *colloq.* — *verb* (*also* **botch something up**) **1** to do something badly and without skill. **2** to repair something carelessly or badly. — *noun* (*also* **botch-up**) a badly or carelessly done piece of work, repair, etc.

botched *adj.* bungled; done badly or clumsily.

botcher *noun* a person who does things carelessly or clumsily.

both — *adj., pron.* the two. — *adv.* as well: *she both works and runs a family.* [from Norse *bathir*]

Botha, Louis (1862–1919) South African statesman and soldier, born in Greytown, Natal. He was a member of the Transvaal Volksraad, and commanded the Boer forces during the second Boer War. He became Prime Minister of the Transvaal colony (1907), and then as first Prime Minister of the new Union of South Africa (1910–19), he suppressed De Wet's rebellion (1914) and conquered German SW Africa (1914–15).

Botha, P(ieter) W(illem) (1916–) South African statesman, born in Paul Roux. Elected to the South African Assembly in 1948, he held various ministries, notably that of Defence (1966–80), where he presided over a strengthening of the armed forces, as well as the controversial military intervention in Angola. As Prime Minister (1978–84) and President (1984–9), he attempted to introduce constitutional reforms

involving limited power-sharing with non-whites, but this led to a right-wing defection in 1982 from his ruling National Party.

Botham, Ian (Terence) (1955–) English cricketer, born in Heswall, Wirral, Merseyside. An all-rounder, he played for England in 102 Test matches, took 383 wickets, and scored 5 200 runs. He started his career with Somerset, made his first-class début in 1974, and his Test début in 1977 against Australia. He also played for Worcestershire (1987–91) and Durham (1992–3), before his retirement in Jul 1993. He has also played League soccer for Scunthorpe United, and is well known for his walk from John o' Groats to Lands End, and for his attempt to follow Hannibal's trek across the Alps, both ventures in aid of leukaemia research.

bother — *verb* (**bothered, bothering**) **1** to annoy, worry, or trouble. **2** *intrans.* (**bother about** or **with something**) to take the time or trouble to consider it. **3** *intrans.* (**bother about something**) to worry about it. — *noun* **1** a minor trouble or worry. **2** a person or thing that causes bother. — *interj.* an exclamation of slight annoyance or impatience. [perhaps from Irish *bodhair*, to annoy]

botheration *noun, interj. colloq.* a minor trouble or worry.

bothersome *adj.* causing bother or annoyance.

Bothnia, Gulf of the N arm of the Baltic Sea, lying between Sweden and Finland. Its length is c.650km/400mi; width 80–240km/50–150mi; maximum depth c.100m. Islets and sandbars impede navigation in the gulf. It generally freezes over in winter.

Bothwell, James Hepburn, 4th Earl of (c.1535–78) the third husband of Mary, Queen of Scots, who was held responsible for the abduction and murder of Mary's second husband, Lord Darnley (1567). After marrying Mary, he faced opposition from the nobles, and fled to Denmark after Mary's surrender to rebel forces at Carberry Hill.

Botrange the highest mountain in Belgium. It is situated in the Hohe Venn (the N section of the Ardennes) in E Liège province. HEIGHT 694m.

Botswana, official name **Republic of Botswana** POP (1992e) 1.4m, a republic in southern Africa, divided into nine districts. AREA 582 096sq km/224 689sq mi. It is bounded S by the Republic of South Africa, W and N by Namibia, and E by Zimbabwe. CAPITAL Gaborone. CHIEF TOWNS Francistown, Lobatse, Selebi-Phikwe, Orapa, Jwaneng. TIME ZONE GMT +2. The population is mainly Tswana; the majority follow local beliefs and the remaining 20% are Christian. OFFICIAL LANGUAGES English, Setswana. CURRENCY the pula. PHYSICAL DESCRIPTION land-locked, undulating, sand-filled plateau with an average elevation of c.1 000m; most people live in the fertile E, bordered by the R Limpopo; to the W the environment changes progressively through dry scrubland and savannah to the sand-covered Kalahari Desert; varied fauna and flora in the rich Okavango R delta in the NW; deciduous forest in the extreme N and NW. CLIMATE largely sub-tropical, increasingly arid in the S and W; rainfall in the N and E falls almost totally in summer (Oct–Apr) with an annual average of 450mm; average maximum daily temperatures range between 23°C and 32°C; annual rainfall is erratic in the Kalahari Desert, decreasing S and W to below 200mm. HISTORY visited by missionaries in the 19c; under British protection in 1885; the S part became a British Crown Colony, then part of Cape Colony in 1895; the N part became the Bechuanaland Protectorate; self-government was achieved in 1964; gained independence and changed name in 1966. GOVERNMENT governed by a legislative National Assembly of 34 elected, and four other members; the President appoints a Cabinet of c.15 members; there is also a House of Chiefs consisting of 15 members. ECONOMY mainly subsistence farming, especially livestock; continual problems of drought and disease; some crops, especially sorghum, as well as maize, millet, beans; cotton, groundnuts, sunflower seeds; main minerals, nickel (second largest African producer), diamonds, cobalt; also coal, brine, asbestos, talc, manganese, gypsum, gold, chromium, silver, platinum; livestock processing and products; tourism, especially wildlife observation.

Botswana

Botticelli, Sandro, originally **Alessandro Filipepi** (1444–1510) Italian painter of the early Renaissance, born in Florence. He trained under Fra Fillippo Lippi and produced many works on classical subjects, including *The Birth of Venus* (c.1482–4) and *Primavera* (Spring, c.1478), both in the Uffizi, Florence. His numerous devotional pictures include the *Coronation of the Virgin* (Florence Academy) and the large circular *Madonna and Child* (Uffizi). He also painted frescoes for the Sistine Chapel in the Vatican, and his later works were of a more deeply religious character.

bottle — *noun* **1** a hollow glass or plastic container with a narrow neck, for holding liquids. **2** the amount a bottle will hold. **3** a baby's feeding bottle, or the liquid in it. **4** *slang* courage, nerve, or confidence. **5** (*usually* **the bottle**) *slang* drinking of alcohol, especially to excess. — *verb* **1** to put into or store in bottles. **2** (*usually* **bottle something up** *or* **in**) to restrain or suppress one's feelings.
— **bottle out** *slang* to lose one's courage and decide not to do something.
[from Old French *botele*, from Latin *buttis*, cask]

bottle bank a large container, usually in the street or a public place, where people can put empty bottles so that the glass can be used again.

bottle-feed *verb* to feed (a baby) with milk from a bottle.

bottle-feeding *noun* the practice of feeding a baby from a bottle.

bottle-green *noun* a dark green colour. *adj.* of this colour.

bottleneck *noun* **1** a place or thing which impedes the movement of traffic, especially a narrow part of a road. **2** an obstacle to progress.

bottlenose whale a toothed whale with a narrow projecting beak.

Bottom, Nick the weaver who wears an ass's head in Shakespeare's *A Midsummer Night's Dream*.

bottom — *noun* **1** the lowest position or part. **2** the point farthest away from the front, top, most important or most successful part: *the bottom of the garden* / *bottom of the class*. **3** the part of the body on which a person sits. **4** the base on which something stands. **5** the seat of a chair. **6** the ground underneath a sea, river, or lake. **7** the part of a ship which is under the water. — *adj.* lowest or last. — *verb* (**bottomed, bottoming**) **1** to put a bottom on. **2** *intrans. said of a ship* to reach or touch the bottom.
— **at bottom** in reality.
be at the bottom of something to be the basic cause of it.
bet one's bottom dollar *colloq.* to be quite certain.
bottom out *said of prices, etc* to reach the lowest level and begin to rise again.
get to the bottom of something to discover the real cause of a mystery, etc.
[from Anglo-Saxon *botm*]

bottom drawer *Brit.* the sheets, cups and saucers, plates, etc that a woman traditionally collects ready for when she gets married and has her own home.

bottomless *adj.* extremely deep or plentiful.

bottom line **1** the last line of a financial statement showing profit or loss. **2** *colloq.* the essential or most important part of a situation.

botulism *noun Medicine* a severe form of food poisoning, caused by swallowing a toxin produced by the bacterium *Clostridium botulinum*, which is most commonly found in canned raw meat. The toxin, which is destroyed by cooking, damages the central nervous system and often causes death by heart and lung failure. [from Latin *botulus*, sausage, from the shape of the bacteria]

Bouar POP (1988) 106 000, the chief town in Nana-Mambéré prefecture, W Central African Republic. It is situated 113km/70mi SW of Bozoum.

Boucher (de Crèvecoeur) de Perthes, Jacques (1788–1868) French archaeologist, born in Rethel. He worked in Moulin-Quignon in the Somme Valley from 1837, where he discovered flint hand axes in association with the bones of extinct animals, from which he drew conclusions about the great antiquity of the human race. His views were at first greeted with incredulity, but were upheld 20 years later.

bouclé *noun* **1** a type of wool with curled or looped threads. **2** a material made from this. [from French *bouclé*, curled, looped]

boudoir *noun old use* a woman's private sitting-room or bedroom. [from French *boudoir*, from *bouder*, to sulk]

bouffant *adj., said of a hairstyle or dress, etc* very full and puffed out. [from French *bouffant*]

bougainvillaea *or* **bougainvillea** *noun* a tropical climbing plant whose bracts (modified leaves) are red and purple and hide the flowers. [named after Louis Bougainville]

Bougainville, Louis Antoine, Comte de (Count of) (1729–1811) French navigator, born in Paris. After army service in Canada and Germany, he joined the navy (1763), occupied the Falkland Is (1764), and led the first French circumnavigation of the world (1766–9), described in *Voyage autour du monde* (A Voyage Round the World, 1771). After the outbreak of the Revolution he devoted himself to scientific pursuits, and was made a senator and count by Napoleon. Several places, as well as the plant *Bougainvillea*, are named after him.

Bougainville POP (1990e) 160 000, a mountainous volcanic island of Papua New Guinea in the SW Pacific Ocean. AREA c.10 000sq km/ 4 000sq mi. It is 190km/118mi long, 50km/31mi wide, and rises to 2 743m at Mt Balbi. The island's chief port is Kieta. HISTORY independence movement and guerrilla fighting in 1988; peace accord signed in 1991 but fighting continues. ECONOMY copper mining; copra; cocoa; timber.

bough *noun* a branch of a tree. [from Anglo-Saxon *bog*, arm, shoulder]

bought see BUY.

bouillabaisse *noun* a thick spicy fish soup from Provence. [a French word]

bouillon *noun* a thin clear soup made by boiling meat and vegetables in water, often used as a basis for thicker soups. [from French *bouillon*, from *bouillir*, to boil]

Boulanger, Nadia (1887–1979) French composer, conductor, organist, and influential teacher of music, born in Paris. She studied at the Paris Conservatoire (1879–1904), where she won several prizes, and then wrote many vocal and instrumental works. After 1918 she turned to teaching, first at home, and later at the Conservatoire and the Ecole Normale de Musique.

Boulder POP (1990) 83 000, the seat of Boulder County, N central Colorado, USA. It lies in the Rocky Mts, c.40km/25mi NW of Denver. Founded in 1858, it is a major mountain resort with mineral springs. Boulder is also a centre for scientific research.

boulder *noun* a large piece of rock with a diameter greater than 25.6cm, that has been rounded and worn smooth by weathering and abrasion during transport. [from Middle English *bulderston*]

Boulder Dam see HOOVER DAM.

boules *sing. noun* a ball-game popular in France, played on rough ground. The players try to hit a small metal ball, the jack, with larger balls rolled along the ground. [from French *boule*, bowl₂]

boulevard *noun* a broad tree-lined street. [from French *boulevard*, from German *Bollwerk*, bulwark: originally used of roads built on a town's demolished fortifications]

Boulez, Pierre (1925–) French composer and conductor, born in Montbrison. He studied at the Paris Conservatoire under Messiaen, and in 1948 became musical director of the Barrault theatre company, where he gained renown as an interpreter of contemporary music. Such works as *Le Marteau sans maître* (1955) established his reputation worldwide. He was conductor of the BBC Symphony Orchestra (1971–5) and of the New York Philharmonic (1971–7), then became director of the Institut de Recherche et de Coordination Acoustique/Musique at the Pompidou Centre in Paris (1977–91).

Boulogne *or* **Boulogne-sur-Mer** POP (1990) 96 000, a major fishing port, situated in Pas-de-Calais department, Nord-Pas-Du-Calais region, NW France. Located on the English Channel, S of Calais, it is an important ferry and hovercraft link to England.

Boult, Sir Adrian (Cedric) (1889–1983) English conductor, born in Chester. After conducting the City of Birmingham Orchestra (1924–30), he became musical director of the BBC and conductor of the newly formed BBC Symphony Orchestra. Extensive tours in Europe and the USA won him a high reputation as a champion of English music. He retired from the BBC (1950), then conducted the London Philharmonic Orchestra until 1957, was its president from 1965, and continued conducting until 1981.

Boulton, Matthew (1728–1809) British engineer, born in Birmingham. He opened a manufacturing works at Birmingham in 1762, where he entered into partnership with James Watt. In 1774 they established a steam engine factory, which proved remunerative only after 18 years. He also applied steam power for coining machinery.

bounce — *verb* **1** *intrans. said of a ball, etc* to spring or jump back from a solid surface. **2** to make (a ball, etc) spring or jump back from a solid surface. **3** *intrans.* (**bounce about** *or* **up**) to move or spring suddenly: *bounce about the room*. **4** (**bounce in** *or* **out**) to rush noisily, angrily, with a lot of energy, etc: *bounced out in a temper*.

5 *colloq., said of a cheque* to be returned without being paid, because of lack of funds in a bank account. — *noun* **1** the act of springing back from a solid surface. **2** the ability to spring back or bounce well. **3** a jump or leap. **4** *colloq.* energy and liveliness.
— **bounce back** *intrans.* to rapidly recover one's health or good fortune after a difficult or adverse period.
[from Dutch *bonzen*, to thump]

bouncer *noun colloq.* a strong person employed by clubs and restaurants, etc to stop unwanted guests entering and to throw out people who cause trouble.

bouncily *adv.* in a bouncy or lively manner.

bounciness *noun* liveliness, energy.

bouncing *adj., said especially of a baby* strong and lively.

bouncy *adj.* (**bouncier, bounciest**) **1** able to bounce well. **2** *said of a person* noticeably lively and energetic.

bound[1] *adj.* **1** tied with, or as if with, a rope, etc. **2** (*in compounds*) restricted to or by the thing specified: *housebound / snowbound.* **3** obliged: *duty bound.* **4** *said of a book* fastened with a permanent cover.
— **bound up with something** closely linked with it. See also BIND.
bound to do something certain or obliged to do it: *it is bound to happen / we are bound to comply.* [past participle of BIND]

bound[2] *adj.* **1** (**bound for a place**) going to or towards it. **2** (*in combination*) going in a specified direction: *southbound.* [from Norse *bua*, to get ready]

bound[3] — *noun* (*often* **bounds**) **1** a limit or boundary. **2** a limitation or restriction. — *verb* **1** to form a boundary of. **2** to set limits to; to restrict.
— **out of bounds** outside the permitted area or limits.
[from Old French *bonde*]

bound[4] — *noun* **1** a jump or leap upwards. **2** a bounce back from a solid surface. — *verb intrans.* **1** to move energetically; to spring or leap: *bound down the stairs.* **2** to move with leaps. **3** *said of a ball* to bounce back from a solid surface. [from French *bondir*, to spring]

boundary *noun* (PL. **boundaries**) **1** a line marking the farthest limit of an area, etc. **2** the marked limits of a cricket field. **3** *Cricket* a stroke that hits the ball across the boundary line, scoring four or six runs. [from BOUND[3]]

bounden *adj.* old use which must be done; obligatory. [old past participle of BIND]

bounder *noun old colloq. use* a badly behaved person; a cad.

boundless *adj.* having no limit; extensive: *boundless energy.*

boundlessly *adv.* without limit.

bounteous *adj.* **1** generous. **2** freely given. [from BOUNTY]

bounteously *adv.* generously or freely; plentifully.

bountiful *adj.* **1** generous. **2** in plenty. [from BOUNTY]

bountifully *adv.* generously; plentifully.

bounty *noun* (PL. **bounties**) **1** the giving of things generously; generosity. **2** a generous gift. **3** a reward given, especially by a government, as encouragement eg to kill or capture dangerous animals, criminals, etc. [from Old French *bonte*, goodness, from Latin *bonus*, good]

bouquet *noun* **1** a bunch of flowers arranged in an artistic way, given as a gift, carried by a bride, etc. **2** the delicate smell of wine. [from French *bouquet*, from *bois*, a wood]

bouquet garni *noun* a bunch or small packet of mixed herbs used to add flavour to food, usu-

ally removed before serving. [from French *bouquet + garnir*, to garnish]

Bourbaki, Nicolas (20c) 'French mathematician', the pseudonym of a group of French mathematicians from the École Normale Supérieure. In the 1930s they conceived the plan of writing a treatise on mathematics which would set out the subject in a strictly logical development from its basic principles; publication of *Éléments de mathématiques* started in 1939, and although Bourbaki was dispersed by World War II, there followed books on a wide range of mathematical topics until around 1980. Many of the books have become the definitive treatment of their subjects, and the series also includes valuable historical essays.

Bourbon, Charles, known as **Constable de Bourbon** (1490–1527) French soldier, the son of Gilbert de Bourbon, Count of Montpensier, and the only daughter of the Duke of Bourbon. Francis I made him Constable of France for his bravery at the battle of Marignano (1515), but after losing royal favour he concluded a private alliance with Emperor Charles V and Henry VIII of England. He invaded France (1524), and was commander at the victory of Pavia (where Francis I was taken prisoner), and then Charles V made him Duke of Milan.

Bourbon, House of French royal house descended from the Capetian St Louis I (1215–70) associated with absolutist traditions at home and the extension of French influence abroad. Henry III and Henry of Navarre (Henry IV) established the dynasty, which succeeded the House of Valois. Under the latter's son (Louis XIII) and grandson (Louis XIV), the long-standing rivalry between France and the Spanish Habsburgs came to a climax, but ended when a descendant, Philip of Anjou, ascended to the Spanish throne (as Philip V) and thereby founded the Spanish House of Bourbon. Under Louis XV and Louis XVI, the French Bourbons' prestige waned, and with the latter's execution, which took place in 1793, the line was interrupted, but was briefly restored (1814–30) by Louis XVIII and Charles X).

House of Bourbon

France	
1589–1610	Henry IV
1610–43	Louis XIII
1643–1715	Louis XIV
1715–74	Louis XV
1774–93	Louis XVI
1793–1814	Interregnum
1814–24	Louis XVIII
1824–30	Charles X
Spain	
1700–24	Philip V
1724–5	Louis I
1725–46	Philip V
1746–59	Ferdinand VI
1759–88	Charles III
1788–1808	Charles IV
1814–33	Ferdinand VII

---

bourbon *noun* a type of whisky made from maize and rye, popular in the US. [from *Bourbon* county, Kentucky, where it was first made]

Bourdon gauge *Engineering* an instrument for measuring the pressure of gases, which is indicated by a pointer on a circular scale. Bourdon gauges are often attached to cylinders of compressed oxygen or other gases, used in hospitals, laboratories, and industry. [named after the French engineer Eugene Bourdon]

Bourgeois, Léon (Victor Auguste) (1851–1925) French socialist statesman, born in Paris. He studied law and served as Minister of Public Instruction (1890–2, 1898) and of Labour (1912–13, 1917), and Prime Minister (1895–6). A

delegate to the Hague Conference (1907), he was one of the founders of the League of Nations, and in 1920 was awarded the Nobel Peace Prize. His form of socialism (called *solidarism*) stressed the obligations of individuals as members of society.

bourgeois — *noun* (PL. **bourgeois**) *usually derog.* a member of the middle class, especially regarded as politically conservative and socially self-interested. — *adj.* of or like the middle class or bourgeois people. [from French *bourgeois*]

Bourgeois Gentilhomme, Le (The Prodigious Snob or The Bourgeois Gentleman) a play by Molière (1670). It is a comedy about a conflict between a master and servant.

bourgeoisie *noun* (**the bourgeoisie**) *derog.* the middle classes, especially regarded as politically conservative and socially self-interested.

Bourges POP (1990) 92 000, an ancient ducal town and the capital of Cher department, Centre region, central France. It lies at the confluence of the Auron and Yèvre rivers. NOTABLE FEATURES Cathedral of St-Etienne (13c); Palais Jacques Cœur (1443); many fine Renaissance houses.

Bourget *or* **Lac du Bourget** the largest lake in France, situated in Savoie department, Rhône-Alpes region, E France. AREA 45sq km/ 17sq mi; length 18km/11mi; width 2–3km/ 1–2mi; depth 60–100m. It is a major tourist area overlooked by Aix-les-Bains in the E. NOTABLE FEATURE Benedictine Abbey.

Bourgh, Lady Catherine de the supercilious aunt of Darcy in Jane Austen's *Pride and Prejudice*.

Bourj Barajneh a Palestinian refugee camp on the outskirts of Beirut, Lebanon. It was created following the evacuation of Palestinians from the city after Israeli attacks on Palestinians and Syrians in Jun 1982. The camp was the scene of a prolonged siege in 1987.

bourn[1] *noun* a small stream. [from BURN[2]]

bourn[2] *noun old use* a boundary or limit. [from Old French *bodne*, boundary]

Bournemouth POP (1992e) 159 000, a resort town situated in Bournemouth district, Dorset, S England. It lies on Poole Bay, 40km/25mi SW of Southampton.

Boussingault, Jean Baptiste Joseph Dieudonné (1802–87) French agricultural chemist, born in Paris. Professor of Chemistry at Lyons and Professor of Agriculture at the Conservatoire des Arts et Métiers, Paris (1839–87), he demonstrated that plants have to absorb nitrogen from the soil, contrary to what was believed at the time. He went on to suggest how nitrogen is recycled, and further showed that all green plants absorb carbon from the atmosphere in the form of carbon dioxide.

boustrophedon an ancient method of writing, particularly in early Greek, in which lines go alternately from left to right and right to left. [from Greek *boustrophe*, turning like ploughing oxen, from *bous*, ox + *strophe*, a turning]

bout *noun* **1** a period or turn of some activity: *a drinking bout.* **2** a period of illness: *a bout of flu.* **3** a boxing or wrestling match. [from obsolete *bought*, bend, turn]

boutique *noun* a small shop, especially one selling fashionable clothes. [from French *boutique*]

Boutros-Ghali, Boutros (1922–) Egyptian politician and diplomat. He travelled with President Sadat to Jerusalem on the diplomatic mission that resulted in the Camp David Accords (1978), and was appointed Minister of State for Foreign Affairs (1977–91). In 1992 he became Secretary-General of the United Nations.

bouzouki *or* **bazouki** *noun* a plucked metal-stringed musical instrument, used especially in Greece. It has a long neck, a fretted fingerboard, and three or four courses of strings played with a plectrum. [from modern Greek]

Boveri, Theodor Heinrich (1862–1915) German biologist, born in Bamberg. From 1893 he taught zoology and anatomy at the University of Würzburg. His conception of chromosomes (the threads within the nuclei of cells) as independent and organized structures responsible for particular hereditary traits provided the basis for much of later genetics.

Bovet, Daniel (1907–92) Swiss-born Italian pharmacologist, born in Neuchâtel. He studied chemistry at Geneva, and later worked at the Pasteur Institute in Paris and from 1947 in Rome. He discovered the first antihistamine drugs for the relief of allergic reactions in 1939, and later made synthetic analogues of the Indian poison curare, which have been much used as muscle relaxants in anaesthesia. He was awarded the 1957 Nobel Prize for Physiology or Medicine.

bovine *adj.* **1** of or like cattle. **2** *derog.*, *said of people* dull or stupid. [from Latin *bos*, ox]

bovine spongiform encephalopathy (ABBREV. **BSE**) a highly infectious brain disease of cattle, characterized by spongy degeneration of the brain, nervousness, a clumsy gait, and eventual collapse and death. It is a notifiable disease, and all affected animals are required to be slaughtered. — Also called *mad cow disease*.

bow¹ (pronounced like *now*) — *verb* **1** *intrans.* to bend the head or the upper part of the body forwards and downwards, usually as a sign of greeting, respect, shame, etc or to acknowledge applause. **2** to bend (the head or the upper part of the body) forwards and downwards: *bow one's head.* **3** (**bow to something**) to accept or submit to it, especially unwillingly: *must bow to the inevitable.* — *noun* an act of bowing or bending the body forwards and down.
— **bow and scrape** *derog.* to behave with excessive politeness or deference.
bow down to someone to submit to them or agree to obey them: *bow down to one's enemies.*
bow out to stop taking part; withdraw: *bow out of the contest.*
take a bow to acknowledge applause.
[from Anglo-Saxon *bugan*]

bow² (pronounced like *so*) — *noun* **1** a knot with a double loop. **2** a weapon made of a piece of curved wood, bent by a string attached to each end, for shooting arrows. **3** a long thin piece of wood with horsehair stretched along its length, for playing the violin, cello, etc. **4** anything which is curved or bent in shape. — *verb* to use a bow on (a violin, cello, etc). [from Anglo-Saxon *boga*, arch]

bow³ *noun* (pronounced like *now*) **1** (*often* **bows**) the front part of a ship or boat. **2** *Rowing* the rower nearest the bow. [from German dialect *boog* or Dutch *boeg*, a ship's bow]

Bowdler, Thomas (1754–1825) English man of letters, born in Ashley, Bath. He is immortalized as the editor of the 'Family Shakespeare' (1818), in which 'those words and expressions are omitted which cannot with propriety be read aloud in a family'.

bowdlerization *or* **bowdlerisation** *noun* expurgation of a book or text.

bowdlerize *or* **bowdlerise** *verb* to remove passages or words from (a book, play, etc), especially on moral and social rather than aesthetic grounds; to expurgate. [named after Thomas Bowdler]

bowdlerized *or* **bowdlerised** *adj.*, *said of a book or text, etc* having passages removed on grounds of taste; expurgated.

bowel *noun* **1** the organs for digesting food next after the stomach; the intestines. **2** (*usually* **bowels**) the depths or innermost part of something, especially when deep or mysterious: *the bowels of the earth.* [from Old French *buel*, from Latin *botellus*, sausage]

Bowen, Elizabeth (Dorothea Cole) (1899–1973) Irish novelist and short-story writer,

born in Dublin. Set mainly in London and Ireland, her novels include *The House in Paris* (1935), *The Death of the Heart* (1938), and *The Heart of the Day* (1949). Her *Collected Stories* appeared in 1980.

Bowen, Norman Levi (1887–1956) Canadian geochemist and petrologist, born in Kingston, Ontario. Professor at the University of Chicago (1937–46), he made important contributions to the study of igneous rocks and silicates, described in his highly influential *The Evolution of the Igneous Rocks* (1928).

bower *noun* **1** a place in a garden which is shaded from the sun by plants and trees. **2** *literary* a lady's private room. [from Anglo-Saxon *bur*, chamber]

bower-bird *noun* any of 18 species of a family of birds that are native to Australia and New Guinea, so called because the males construct bowers out of twigs, usually decorated with flowers, berries, leaves, shells, etc, in order to attract the females.

Bowie, Col James, also called **Jim** (1790–1836) US adventurer, born in Logan County, Kentucky. He is mainly remembered for his role in defending the Alamo (1836) during the Texas revolution, and for inventing the curved sheath knife named after him.

bowl¹ *noun* **1** a round deep dish for mixing or serving food, for holding liquids or flowers, etc. **2** the amount a bowl will hold; the contents of a bowl. **3** the round hollow part of an object, such as a spoon or pipe. [from Anglo-Saxon *bolla*]

bowl² — *noun* a large wooden or plastic ball designed to run in a curve, used in the game of bowls; a similar metal ball used in boules. — *verb* **1** to roll (a ball, hoop, etc) smoothly along the ground. **2** *intrans.* to play bowls. **3** *intrans., trans.* *Cricket* to throw (a ball) with a straight arm towards the person batting.
— **bowl along** to move smoothly and quickly: *a little car was bowling along the road.*
bowl someone out *Cricket* to put out the person batting by hitting the wicket with the ball.
bowl someone over 1 to knock them over. **2** *colloq.* to surprise or impress them greatly.
[from French *boule*]

Bowlby, (Edward) John (Mostyn) (1907–90) English psychiatrist. He worked at the Tavistock Clinic (1946–72), and is best known for his work on the effects of maternal deprivation upon the mental health and emotional development of children. He argued that it was essential for the mother to be present during a critical formative period in order for emotional bonds to be formed (the 'attachment theory').

bow-legged *adj.*, *said of a person* having legs which curve out at the knees.

bowler¹ *noun* **1** a person who bowls the ball in cricket, etc. **2** a person who plays bowls or goes bowling.

bowler² *noun* (*also* **bowler hat**) a man's hard round felt hat with a narrow brim. [named after *Bowler*, a 19c hatter]

bowlful *noun* (PL. **bowlfuls**) the amount a bowl will hold.

bowline *noun* **1** a rope used to keep a sail taut against the wind. **2** a knot which makes a loop that will not slip at the end of a piece of rope. [from Old German dialect *boline*]

Bowling, Lieutenant Tom the naval uncle of Roderick in Tobias Smollett's *Roderick Random*.

bowling *noun* **1** the game of bowls. **2** a game played indoors, in which a ball is rolled along an alley at a group of skittles, the object being to knock over as many as possible.
◊ Bowling is a game with an old history. It was popularized by German churchgoers in the 13c and 14c, who would roll a ball at a *kegel* (a club they used to protect themselves). If they hit it, they would be absolved from sin. The game of

nine pins was taken to the USA by Dutch and German immigrants towards the end of the 19c. When the sport was outlawed, a tenth pin was added as a way round the ban. Mechanical devices for replacing the pins on their spots were developed in the 1950s, which enhanced the game's popularity. The most popular form now is tenpin bowling.

bowling-alley *noun* **1** a long narrow channel made of wooden boards used in bowling (sense 2). **2** a building containing several of these.

bowling-green *noun* an area of smooth grass set aside for the game of bowls.

bowls *sing. noun* a game played on smooth grass with bowls, the object being to roll these as close as possible to a smaller ball called the jack.

Bowman's capsule *Anat.* the cup-shaped end of a kidney tubule, which encloses a small ball of blood capillaries (the *glomerulus*). It is responsible for draining the waste products filtered from the blood by the glomerulus. [named after the UK physician Sir William Bowman]

Bow porcelain soft-paste porcelain made at a factory in London, founded by Irish painter Thomas Frye (1710–62) and a glass merchant Edward Heylyn (1695–1765), which flourished from c.1744 until 1776. It was noted for its figures, often derived from Meissen models, and service wares.

bowshot *noun* the distance which an arrow can be shot from a bow.

bowsprit *noun* (*bow-* pronounced like *so*) a pole projecting from the front of a ship, with ropes from the sails fastened to it. [from Old German dialect *boch*, bow (of a ship) + *spret*, pole]

bowstring *noun* the string on a bow, tension in which projects the arrow.

bow tie a tie which is tied in a double loop to form a horizontal bow at the collar.

bow window a window which is curved out at the centre.

bow-wow — *noun* a child's word for a dog. — *interj.* an imitation of a dog's bark.

box¹ — *noun* **1** a usually square or rectangular container made from wood, cardboard, plastic, etc and with a lid. **2** the amount a box will hold. **3** a separate compartment for a particular purpose, eg for a group of people in a theatre, for a horse in a stable or vehicle, or a witness in a law-court. **4** a small enclosed area for a particular purpose: *a telephone box.* **5** a section on a piece of paper, field, road, etc marked out by straight lines: *a penalty box.* **6** a newspaper office or agency which collects mail and sends it on to the person it is intended for: *a post-office box / a box number.* **7** (**the box**) *Brit. colloq.* the television. **8** a raised seat for the driver on a carriage. **9** a small country house, used as a base for some sports: *a shooting-box.* **10** a gift of money given to tradesmen and, formerly, servants: *a Christmas box.* — *verb* **1** (**box something up**) to put it into or provide with a box or boxes. **2** (**box someone** *or* **something in** *or* **up**) to stop them moving; confine or enclose them.
— **box the compass** to name all the 32 points of the compass in their correct order.
[from Latin *buxis*]

box² — *verb* **1** *trans., intrans.* to fight with the fists and protected by thick leather gloves, especially as a sport. **2** *trans.* to hit (especially someone's ears) with the fist. — *noun* (*usually* **a box on the ears**) a punch with the fist, especially on the ears. [from Middle English *box*, blow]

box³ *noun* **1** (**boxtree**) a small evergreen tree or shrub, with dark shiny leaves, often used for hedges. **2** (*also* **boxwood**) its wood. [from Anglo-Saxon, from Latin *buxus*]

boxed *adj.* contained in or provided with a box.

Boxer the honourable, strong, and hardworking carthorse in George Orwell's *Animal Farm*.

Boxer *noun* a member of a 19c nationalistic secret society in China, who led an anti-foreign uprising in 1898–1900. [a translation of Chinese *yi he tuan*, = right harmonious fist]

◇ The 'Boxer Rising' originated in Shandong, where churches were destroyed and missionaries expelled. It spread across N China, reaching Beijing and Tianjin. The foreign powers sent a combined force to rescue their envoys in Beijing; they occupied the city, and the rising was suppressed.

boxer *noun* 1 a person who boxes, especially as a sport. 2 a medium-sized breed of dog with a short smooth coat.

boxer shorts loose shorts worn by men as underpants.

boxful *noun* (PL. **boxfuls**) the amount a box will hold.

box girder *Engineering* a hollow girder made of steel, timber, or concrete, and having thin walls, often used in bridge construction.

boxing *noun* the sport or practice of fighting with the fists, especially in padded gloves.

◇ The foundations of the modern sport were laid in 1867, when the Marquis of Queensberry drew up rules which still largely apply. These included fighting with gloves and the stipulation that each round in a bout should be three minutes long. Boxing was not established as a legal sport in Britain until the early 1900s, although world championship contests had begun in 1884. Today four bodies recognize world championships: The World Boxing Council (WBC); the World Boxing Association (WBA); the International Boxing Federation (IBF); and the World Boxing Organization (WBO).

Weight Divisions in Professional Boxing	
Name	Maximum weight
heavyweight	any weight
cruiserweight/junior-heavyweight	88 kg/195 lb
light-heavyweight	79 kg/175 lb
super-middleweight	77 kg/170 lb
middleweight	73 kg/160 lb
light-middleweight/ junior-middleweight	70 kg/154 lb
welterweight	67 kg/147 lb
light-welterweight/ junior-welterweight	64 kg/140 lb
lightweight	61 kg/135 lb
junior-lightweight/ super-featherweight	59 kg/130 lb
featherweight	57 kg/126 lb
super-bantamweight/ junior-featherweight	55 kg/122 lb
bantamweight	54 kg/118 lb
super-flyweight/ junior-bantamweight	52 kg/115 lb
flyweight	51 kg/112 lb
light-flyweight/ junior-flyweight	49 kg/108 lb
mini-flyweight/straw-weight/ minimum weight	under 48 kg/105 lb

Boxing Day 1 26 December, the day after Christmas Day. 2 the first weekday after Christmas, a public holiday in the UK.

boxing-glove *noun* each of a pair of thick leather gloves worn by boxers.

box junction *Brit.* an area at the intersection of a road junction, marked with a grid of yellow lines painted on the ground, which vehicles may enter only if the exit is clear.

box-kite *noun* a kite in the form of a box with open ends.

box office 1 an office which sells theatre tickets. 2 theatrical entertainment regarded in terms of its commercial value: *the new show is wonderful box office.*

box pleat on a skirt or dress, a large double pleat formed by folding the material in two pleats facing in opposite directions.

boxroom *noun Brit.* a small room used to store bags, boxes, etc or as an extra bedroom.

box set *or* **box-set** *Theatr.* a system of stage scenery used to represent the interior of a room. It consists of a three-dimensional arrangement of three walls covered by a stretched canvas cloth to form the ceiling.

boy — *noun* 1 a male child. 2 a son. 3 a young man, especially regarded as still immature. 4 (**the boys**) *colloq.* a group of men with whom a man regularly socializes: *go out with the boys.* 5 *offensive* a black male servant. — *interj.* (*also* **oh boy**) an expression of excitement, surprise, or pleasure.

Boyana Church three churches situated in the former village of Boyana, a present-day suburb of Sofia, Bulgaria. The buildings date from the 10c, 13c, and 19c, but despite their differing styles, combine to form a notable architectural unit. It is a World Heritage site.

Boyce, William (1711–79) English composer, born in London. Appointed composer (1736) and organist (1758) to the Chapel Royal, in 1757 he became Master of the King's Musick. A leading composer of church music, his works include the song 'Hearts of Oak' and the serenata *Solomon* (1743), and he compiled a valuable collection of *Cathedral Music* (1760).

Boycott, Charles Cunningham (1832–97) English soldier, born in Burgh St Peter, Norfolk. As land agent for Lord Erne in Co Mayo, he was one of the first victims in 1880 of Parnell's system of social excommunication: on his refusal to lower rents, his tenants were advised to stop communicating with him. See BOYCOTT.

Boycott, Geoffrey (1940–) English cricketer, born in Fitzwilliam, Yorkshire. He made his début for Yorkshire in 1963 and for England in the following year. In 1981 he overtook Gary Sobers' world record of 8 032 Test runs, and in 108 Tests for England scored more than 150 centuries and totalled 8 114 runs. In 1971 and 1979 he averaged 100 runs per innings. He has not played first-class cricket since 1986.

boycott — *verb* (**boycotted**, **boycotting**) 1 to refuse to have any business or social dealings with (a company, a country, etc), especially as a form of disapproval or coercion. 2 to refuse to handle or buy (goods). — *noun* an act of boycotting. [named after Charles Boycott]

Boyd Orr (of Brechin Mearns), John Boyd Orr, 1st Baron (1880–1971) Scottish nutritionist, born in Kilmaurs, Ayrshire. He was director of the Rowett Research Institute, Professor of Agriculture at Aberdeen (1942–5), and first director of the United Nations Food and Agriculture Organization (1945–8). He won the Nobel Peace Prize in 1949.

Boyer, Herbert Wayne (1936–) US biochemist, born in Pittsburgh, Pennsylvania. From 1966 he worked at the University of California at San Francisco, where he was later appointed Professor of Biochemistry. A pioneer of genetic engineering, he showed in the 1970s that such methods could be used to make insulin and other costly biochemicals commercially, and in 1976 formed the company Genentech for this purpose.

boyfriend *noun* a person's regular male companion, often with a romantic or sexual relationship.

boyhood *noun* the period of life when a person is a boy.

Boyhood of Raleigh, The a painting by Sir John Everett Millais (1870).

boyish *adj.* like a boy in appearance or behaviour: *boyish good looks.*

boyishly *adv.* with a boyish manner; like a boy.

boyishness *noun* a boyish manner or quality.

Boyle, Robert (1627–91) Anglo-Irish physicist and chemist, born at Lismore Castle, Munster. He studied at Eton, and after travelling in Europe, settled in Dorset, where he devoted himself to science. He was a founding member of the Royal Society. At Oxford (1654) he researched into air, the properties of a vacuum, combustion and respiration, and his *Sceptical Chymist* (1661) criticized the current theories of matter. In 1662 he arrived at 'Boyle's law', which states that the pressure and volume of a gas are inversely proportional.

Boyle's law *Physics* a law which states that the volume of a given mass of gas at a constant temperature is inversely proportional to its pressure.

Boyne, Battle of the a battle fought (1690) near Drogheda, Co Louth, Ireland, between Protestant forces led by William III of Great Britain and smaller Catholic forces led by James VII and II. William's decisive victory enabled him to capture Dublin, marked a critical stage in the English reconquest of Ireland, and ended James's campaign to regain the English throne. The anniversary is celebrated by Protestant marches in Northern Ireland.

Boyne, River a river in the E Irish Republic, length 110km/68mi. It rises in the Bog of Allen, Kildare county, Leinster province, and flows NE to the Irish Sea near Drogheda.

Boys' Brigade an organization for boys which encourages discipline, self-respect, etc.

Boy Scout see SCOUT.

Boy Scouts see SCOUT ASSOCIATION.

BP *abbrev.* 1 blood pressure. 2 British Petroleum. 3 British Pharmacopoeia.

Bq *symbol* becquerel.

BR *abbrev.* 1 *as an international vehicle mark* Brazil. 2 British Rail.

Br¹ *abbrev.* 1 Britain. 2 British. 3 brother.

Br² *symbol Chem.* bromine.

bra *or* **brassière** *noun* an undergarment worn by a woman to support the breasts. [from French *brassière*, baby's vest]

Brabham, Jack, properly **Sir John Arthur Brabham** (1926–) Australian racing driver, born in Sydney. Australia's first world champion (1959), he won further titles in 1960 and 1966. His first two titles were in a Cooper-Climax, the third in a car bearing his own name, which he began manufacturing in 1961. He won 14 races from 126 starts during his career (1955–70). He has remained active in the motor-racing field, but no longer owns Brabham cars.

brace — *noun* 1 a device, usually made from metal, which supports, strengthens, or holds two things together. 2 (**braces**) *Brit.* straps worn over the shoulders, for holding trousers up. 3 a wire device worn on the teeth to straighten them. 4 (PL. **brace**) a pair or couple, especially of game birds: *four brace of pheasants.* 5 *Printing* either of two symbols, { or }, used to show that lines, figures, parts of text, etc are connected. 6 a rope attached to a ship's yard, used for adjusting the sails. — *verb* 1 to make tight or stronger, usually by supporting in some way. 2 (**brace oneself**) to prepare oneself for a blow, shock, etc. [from Old French *brace*, arm, power, from Latin *bracchium*]

brace and bit a hand tool for drilling holes.

Bracegirdle, Anne (c.1663–1748) English actress, who was renowned for her beauty and virtue, and for her performances (1688–1707) in the plays of William Congreve at Drury Lane.

bracelet *noun* 1 a band or chain worn as a piece of jewellery round the arm or wrist. 2 (**bracelets**) *slang* handcuffs. [from Old French, little arm]

brachiopod *noun* a sea animal like a worm, with a shell and two arm-like growths for feeding. [from Greek *brachion*, arm + *podos*, foot]

bracing *adj.*, *said of the wind, air, etc* stimulatingly cold and fresh.

bracken *noun* the commonest species of fern in the UK (*Pteridium aquilinum*), which has tall fronds and spreads rapidly across hillsides and woodland by means of its underground rhizomes. It is a troublesome weed in hill pastures as it replaces grass and is poisonous to livestock. [from Middle English *braken*]

bracket — *noun* **1** each of a pair of symbols, [ ], ( ), < >, or { }, used to group together or enclose words, figures, etc (see also BRACE 5, PARENTHESIS). **2** a group or category falling within a certain range: *out of my price bracket*. **3** an L-shaped piece of metal or strong plastic, used for attaching shelves, etc to walls. — *verb* (**bracketed**, **bracketing**) **1** to enclose or group together (words, etc) in brackets. **2** to put (people, things, etc) into a group or category.

bracket fungus the fruiting body (spore-bearing structure) of fungi belonging to the family Polyporaceae, commonly found growing on tree trunks or stumps in north temperate regions, and so called because it resembles a hemispherical shelf or bracket in shape.

brackish *adj.*, *said of water* tasting slightly salty. [from Dutch *brak*, salty]

brackishness *noun* a slightly salty taste of water.

bract *noun* a small, scaly, and often brightly coloured leaf growing at the base of a flower. [from Latin *bractea*, thin plate of metal or gold-leaf]

brad *noun* a thin flat nail with a small head. [from Norse *broddr*, spike]

bradawl *noun* a small hand tool for making holes in wood, leather, etc.

Bradbury, Malcolm (Stanley) (1932–) English novelist and critic, born in Sheffield. He co-founded a creative writing programme at the University of East Anglia and was later appointed Professor of American studies (1970–). The author of numerous critical works which embrace Modernist and post-Modernist ideas, his own novels, many of them inspired by academia, include *Stepping Westward* (1965), *The History Man* (1975), *Rates of Exchange* (1982), and *Dr Criminale* (1992). He has written short-stories and television plays, and made several television productions, including the Emmy-award winning *Porterhouse Blue*.

Bradbury, Ray (Douglas) (1920–) US science-fiction writer, born in Waukegan, Illinois. From 1940 he was making a living by selling his short stories to pulp magazines, but began to meet a wider audience with *The Martian Chronicles* (1950) and *The Golden Apples of the Sun* (1953). He is best known for film adaptations of two of his novels, *The Illustrated Man* (1951) and *Fahrenheit 451* (1953).

Bradford POP (1981) 295 000, an industrial city in West Yorkshire, N England. Part of the West Yorkshire urban area, it lies 15km/9mi W of Leeds and 310km/193mi NW of London. Its 19c development was based on the wool textile industry. In 1985, it was the scene of a major disaster when the wooden stand of Bradford City Football Club caught fire, killing 56 people. NOTABLE FEATURES City Hall (1873); Wool Exchange (1867); art gallery (1904); cathedral (15c); National Museum of Photography, Film, and Television (1983).

Bradlaugh, Charles (1833–91) English free-thinking social reformer, born in London. An anti-religious lecturer, and a pamphleteer under the name of 'Iconoclast', he campaigned as a radical and became an MP in 1880. He claimed the right as an unbeliever to make affirmation of alle-

giance instead of taking the parliamentary oath, but the House refused to allow him to do either. Re-elected on three occasions, he was finally admitted in 1886.

Bradley, James (1693–1762) English astronomer, born in Sherbourn, Gloucestershire. Professor of Astronomy at Oxford from 1721, he was responsible for significant improvements in the precision of observations of stellar positions, and discovered the aberration of starlight. He was appointed Astronomer Royal in 1742.

Bradley, Omar N(elson) (1893–1981) US soldier, born in Clark, Missouri. He played a prominent part in Tunisia and Sicily in World War II, and in 1944 led the US invading armies through France and Germany. Chairman of the joint Chiefs-of-Staff in 1949, he was promoted general in 1950.

Bradley a male first name, from the English surname. [from Anglo-Saxon *brad*, broad + *leah*, wood, clearing]

Bradman, Sir Don(ald George) (1908–) Australian cricketer, born in Cootamundra, New South Wales. He played for Australia between 1928 and 1948, and was captain from 1936. He set up many batting records, including the highest score (452 not out), and he made the greatest number of centuries in England v. Australia test matches (19). After he retired (1948), he became a cricket administrator.

Bradstreet, Anne, *née* Dudley (1612–72) American colonial poet, born in Northampton, UK, who is acknowledged as the first poet of note in British America. Born into the English gentry, she migrated with her husband to Massachusetts in 1630 and began writing poetry, which was first published in London in 1650 without her consent.

Bradwardine, Baron of a kind but prosaic Jacobite in Sir Walter Scott's *Waverley*. His fair and gentle daughter, Rose, marries Edward Waverley.

bradycardia *noun Medicine* a condition in which the heartbeat is slower than normal (less than 50 to 60 beats per minute). [from Greek *bradys*, slow, + *kardia*, heart]

brae *noun Scot.* a slope on a hill. [from Norse *bra*, brow]

Braemar a village in SW Grampian region, NE Scotland. It is situated 10km/6mi W of Balmoral Castle, in a popular tourist area. EVENT Highland Games.

brag — *verb intrans.* (**bragged**, **bragging**) to talk boastfully or too proudly about oneself, what one has done, etc. — *noun* **1** a boastful statement or boastful talk. **2** a card game like poker. [from Middle English *brag*, arrogance]

Braga, ancient **Bracara Augusta 1** POP (1991) 91 000, the industrial capital of Braga district, NW Portugal, and the country's fourth largest city. Situated 370km/230mi N of Lisbon, it was formerly capital of the old region of Entre Minho e Douro. Braga is the seat of the Primate of Portugal. NOTABLE FEATURE cathedral (11c). **2** a district in NW Portugal with Braga as its capital.

Braganza, Portuguese **Bragança**, ancient **Juliobriga 1** POP (1991) 17 000, the capital of Braganza district, NE Portugal, situated 10km/6mi from the Spanish border. It was the original seat of the House of Braganza, rulers of Portugal from 1640 to 1910, and is now an agricultural centre. NOTABLE FEATURES castle (1187); cathedral; town hall (12c); Baçal Abbey. **2** a district in NE Portugal with Braganza as its capital.

Bragg, Sir (William) Lawrence (1890–1971) Australian-born British physicist, born in Adelaide. Son of Sir William Bragg, he studied at Trinity College, Cambridge, where he discovered the 'Bragg law' (1912), which describes the conditions for X-ray diffraction by crystals. This led to the first method to study the exact posi-

tions of atoms in crystal interiors. He became professor at Manchester (1919–37) and later head of the Cavendish Laboratory in Cambridge (1938–53), where he contributed to the discovery of the structure of DNA. He shared with his father the 1915 Nobel Prize for Physics.

Bragg, Melvyn (1939–) English novelist and television arts presenter, born in Lovell, near Carlisle. He is well known as the presenter (1978–) of the *South Bank Show* on ITV. He was Head of Arts in London Weekend Television from 1982 to 1990, when he became Controller of Arts there and Chairman of Border Television. He presented BBC Television's *Second House* (1973–7) and the books programme *Read All About It* (1976–7), and has collaborated on several film and television projects, notably with Ken Russell. His novels include *Without a City Wall* (1968), *The Nerve* (1971), *The Silken Net* (1974), and *A Time to Dance* (1990, adapted for television, 1992).

Bragg, Sir William Henry (1862–1942) English physicist, born in Westward, Cumberland. He was appointed professor at Adelaide, Leeds, and London. With his son Lawrence Bragg, he founded X-ray crystallography as a means of determining the atomic structure of crystals. This was to become one of the key techniques for deducing the structures of penicillin and DNA. They shared the 1915 Nobel Prize for Physics.

braggart *noun* a person who brags a lot. [from French *bragard*, vain, bragging]

braggingly *adv.* in a boastful or over-proud manner; as if bragging.

Brahe, Tycho (1546–1601) Danish astronomer, born in Knudstrup, S Sweden (then under the Danish Crown). Aware of serious errors in astronomical tables, he started to measure the positions of stars and planets with unprecedented accuracy, becoming the greatest astronomical observer of the pre-telescope era. He did not subscribe to Copernicus's theory of a Sun-centred planetary system, but his data allowed Johannes Kepler to prove that Copernicus was essentially correct.

Brahma the personified creator god of Hinduism. The *Trimurti* of classical Indian thought consists of the three deities Vishnu and Shiva, which represent the opposite principles of preservation and destruction, and Brahma, which both represents the balance between them and is the all-inclusive deity behind all the gods of popular Hinduism.

Brahman 1 in Hinduism, the eternal, impersonal Absolute Principle. It is the neuter form of Brahma, and is equated with cosmic unity. **2** (*also* **Brahmin**) a Hindu who belongs to the highest, priestly caste. [named after BRAHMA]

Brahmanism an early religion of India, which came to dominance during the Vedic Period (c.1200–500 BC). Regarded by Indians as the source of their religious traditions, it gave supremacy to the Brahmin class, who exercised priestly authority over all aspects of life through their responsibility for the transmission of the sacred traditions and the performance of sacrificial rituals.

Brahmaputra, River, Chinese **Yarlung Zangbo**, Bengali **Jamuna** a river in SW China and India, length c.2 900km/1 800mi. It rises in the Chinese Himalayas as the Maquan He R and flows E, then S into Assam, becoming the Brahmaputra near Sadiya. The river then flows S into Bangladesh, joining the R Ganges before entering the Bay of Bengal through a vast delta.

Brahmo Samaj *or* **Divine Society** a theistic movement within Hinduism, founded (1828) by Ram Mohan Roy. Influenced by Islam, Christianity, and modern science, it argued that reason should form the true basis of Hinduism, and sought a return to the purity of Hindu worship through an emphasis on monotheism, the rejection of idol-worship, and the reform of Hindu social practices. [Sanskrit, = society of Brahma]

Brahms, Johannes (1833–97) German composer, born in Hamburg. The son of a poor orchestral musician, he had to earn his living as a pianist until 1853, when he could turn to composition. He toured with the Hungarian violinist Reményi, and met Joachim and Liszt, and then Schumann, who helped Brahms publish his piano sonatas. His great orchestral works are comparatively late – the first, *Variations on a Theme of Haydn*, appeared when he was 40. The *German Requiem* (first performed complete in 1869) is his greatest choral work.

braid — *noun* **1** a band or tape, often made from threads of gold and silver twisted together, used as a decoration on uniforms, etc. **2** a length of hair consisting of several lengths which have been twisted together. — *verb* **1** to twist (several lengths of thread, hair) together. **2** to decorate with braid. [from Anglo-Saxon *bregdan*, to weave]

braided *adj.* decorated with braid.

braiding *noun* braid decoration.

Braille, Louis (1809–52) French teacher, born in Coupvray near Paris. He was blinded in an accident at the age of three, and became a pupil at the Institution des Jeunes Aveugles in Paris. He was Professor there from 1826, and invented a system of raised-point writing which the blind could both read and write. He later used the system for the teaching of music.

Braille *noun* a system of printing for the blind, in which raised dots are used to represent printed characters. [named after Louis Braille]

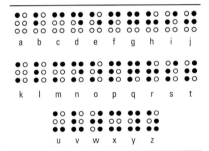

Braille alphabet

brain — *noun* **1** the highly developed mass of nervous tissue that co-ordinates and controls the activities of the central nervous system of animals. Virtually all the functions of the human body are controlled by the brain. **2** (**brains**) *colloq.* cleverness, intelligence. **3** *colloq.* a very clever person. **4** (*also* **brains**) *colloq.* the person responsible for devising a plan, undertaking, etc. — *verb colloq.* to hit hard on the head.
— **have something on the brain** *colloq.* to be preoccupied with it.
[from Anglo-Saxon *brægen*]
◊ The human brain contains more than 10 billion nerve cells, and on average weighs about 1 400g. It receives sensory information via spinal nerves from the spinal cord and cranial nerves from sense organs such as the eye and ear. When this information has been processed within the brain, appropriate instructions are sent out along motor neurones to effector organs such as muscles.
The brain is enclosed within three membranes, the *meninges*, and is protected by the rigid bones of the skull. The forebrain consists of the cerebral hemispheres, the thalamus, and the hypothalamus. The outermost layer of the cerebral hemispheres, which are deeply folded and cover most of the surface of the human brain, is known as the *cerebral cortex*. It is involved in the inte-

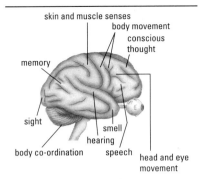

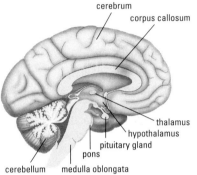

human brain

gration of all sensory input to the brain, including memory and learning, enabling behaviour to be based on past experience. The midbrain connects the forebrain to the hindbrain, which comprises the cerebellum, the medulla oblongata, and the pons. The cerebellum co-ordinates complex muscular processes such as maintaining posture, and the medulla oblongata contains centres that regulate breathing, heartbeat, and blood pressure.

brainchild *noun* a person's particular theory, idea, or plan.

brain-dead *adj.* describing a person in whom brain death has occurred or been diagnosed.

brain death the functional death of the centres in the brain stem that control breathing and other vital reflexes, so that the affected person is incapable of surviving without the aid of a ventilator. Two independent medical opinions are usually required to confirm it.

brain drain *colloq.* the loss of scientists, academics, professionals, etc to another country, usually because the prospects are better.

Braine, John (Gerard) (1922–86) English novelist, born in Bradford, Yorkshire. He served in the Royal Navy and worked as a librarian before the success of his first book, *Room at the Top* (1957), enabled him to become a full-time writer. Associated with the 'Angry Young Men' of the 1950s, his novels deal mostly with the north of England and northerners, and include *Life at the Top* (1962), *The Vodi*, and *One and Last Love* (1981).

braininess *noun* cleverness, intelligence.

brainless *adj. colloq.* stupid, silly.

brainlessly *adv.* stupidly; without intelligence.

brainstem *noun Anat.* the part of the brain that is connected to the top of the spinal cord. It consists of the midbrain, medulla oblongata, and pons.

brainstorm *noun* **1** a sudden loss of the ability to think clearly and act properly. **2** *North Amer. colloq.* same as BRAINWAVE 1.

brainstorming *noun North Amer., esp. US* the practice of trying to solve problems or develop

new ideas by rapid group discussion of spontaneous suggestions.

brainteaser *noun* a difficult exercise or puzzle.

brainwash *verb* to force (someone) to change their beliefs, ideas, etc by continually applying mental pressure.

brainwashing *noun* the process of forcing someone to change their ideas by mental pressure.

brainwave *noun* **1** *Physiol.* a wave representing the pattern of electrical activity in the brain, recorded by electrodes placed on the scalp. Alpha, beta, and delta rhythms represent, respectively, the pattern obtained when a person is awake with eyes closed, awake with eyes open, and in deep sleep. **2** *colloq.* a sudden bright or clever idea.

brainy *adj.* (**brainier, brainiest**) *colloq.* clever, intelligent.

braise *verb* to cook (meat, etc) slowly with a small amount of liquid in a closed dish. [from French *braiser*, from *braise*, live coals]

braised *adj., said of meat* cooked by braising.

brake¹ — *noun* **1** a device that is used to slow down or stop a moving vehicle or machine, usually by applying friction to the surface of a rotating part such as a wheel, brake drum, or disc. Brakes are also used to prevent the movement of parked vehicles. **2** anything which makes something stop, prevents progress, etc: *a brake on public spending.* **3** an implement for crushing flax or hemp. **4** (*also* **brake harrow**) a heavy harrow used to break up large clods of earth. — *verb* **1** *intrans.* to apply or use a brake. **2** to use a brake to make (a vehicle) slow down or stop. **3** to crush (flax or hemp) by beating.

brake² *noun* **1** an area of wild rough ground covered with low bushes, etc. **2** a thicket. [probably from an Old German dialect word meaning 'thicket']

brake drum *Engineering* a revolving cylinder, attached to a rotating piece of machinery, eg the

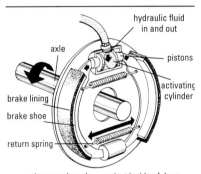

piston pushes shoe against inside of drum

drum brake

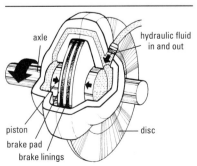

piston pushes pad against disc

disc brake

wheel of a car, against which the brake shoes press when the brake is applied.

brake horsepower (ABBREV. **bhp**) the power developed by an engine as measured either by the force that must be applied to a friction brake in order to stop it, or by a dynamometer applied to the flywheel.

brake light each of two red lights at the back of a vehicle which light up when the driver applies the brakes.

brake shoe either of two semicircular metal structures within a rotating brake drum, which press against the inner wall of the drum when the brake is applied.

braless *adj.* not wearing a bra.

Bramante, Donato, originally **Donato di Pascuccio d'Antonio** (c.1444–1514) Italian Renaissance architect and painter, born near Urbino. He lived mainly in Milan, and moved to Rome in 1499, where he built the Tempietto (c.1502). At the bequest of Pope Julius II he drew up plans for the reconstruction and renovation of the Vatican and St Peter's (1505–6).

Bramble, Matthew one of the chief letter-writers in Tobias Smollett's *Humphry Clinker*, who is later revealed to be the natural father of Humphry. Another character is his husband-hunting sister, Tabitha.

bramble *noun* **1** a common wild prickly bush which produces blackberries. **2** *Scot.* a blackberry. [from Anglo-Saxon *bremel*]

brambling *noun* a small orange-breasted bird related to the chaffinch. [from BROOM + LING]

Bran in Celtic mythology, a gigantic god who featured in the Welsh tales *The Mabinogion* as King of Britain. He died in Ireland, and his severed head provided his followers with advice and entertainment for 80 years. It was finally buried in the site of the Tower of London, from where it protected Britain from invaders until it was dug up.

bran *noun* the outer covering of cereal grain which is removed during the preparation of white flour. It is an important source of vitamin B and dietary fibre. [from Old French]

Branagh, Kenneth (Charles) (1960–) Northern Irish film and stage actor and director, born in Belfast. After three years acting with the RSC, he became co-founder and co-director of the Renaissance Theatre Company, continuing to direct and star in Shakespearean plays. His film appearances include *Henry V* (1989) and *Much Ado About Nothing* (1993), both of which he also directed, *Dead Again* (1991), and *Peter's Friends* (1992). He married the actress Emma Thompson in 1989.

branch — *noun* **1** a shoot or stem growing out like an arm from the main body of a tree. **2** a main division of a railway line, river, road, or mountain range. **3** a division in a family, subject, group of languages, etc. **4** a local office of a large company or organization. — *verb intrans.* (*also* **branch off**) **1** to send out branches. **2** to divide from the main part: *a road branching off to the left.* — **branch out** to develop different interests, projects, etc. [from Old French *branche*, from Latin *branca*, paw]

branched *adj.* having or formed into branches.

branching *adj.* forming branches.

branchless *adj.* not having branches.

brand — *noun* **1** a maker's name or trademark. **2** a variety or type: *a special brand of humour.* **3** an identifying mark on cattle, etc, usually burned on with a hot iron. **4** (*also* **branding-iron**) an iron used for burning identifying marks on cattle, etc. **5** a sign of disgrace or shame. **6** a piece of burning or smouldering wood. **7** *literary* a torch. **8** *literary* a sword. — *verb* **1** to mark (cattle, etc) with a hot iron. **2** to make a permanent impression on

(someone). **3** to give (someone) a bad name or reputation: *branded him a liar.* [from Anglo-Saxon *brand*, fire, flame]

Brandenburg a state in NE Germany. AREA 28 000sq km/10 800sq mi. CAPITAL Potsdam. CHIEF TOWNS Brandenburg, Cottbus. HISTORY came under the control of the Hohenzollern rulers from 1415 to 1918; after World War II c.12 950sq km/5 000sq mi of its territory was placed in the Soviet occupation zone and the remaining land formed a state of East Germany; the state was dissolved in 1952 but was re-established when Germany was reunited in 1990.

Brandenburg *or* **Brandenburg an der Havel** POP (1991e) 90 000, an industrial city in Brandenburg state, NE Germany. It lies on the R Havel, W of Berlin, and is the former centre of the Prussian province of Brandenburg, part of which is now in Poland. Much of the city was rebuilt after severe damage in World War II.

Brandenburg Concertos, The six pieces for different combinations of strings and wind instruments by J S Bach (1718–21).

Brandenburg Gate, a triumphal arch designed by Carl Langhans (1733–1808) and erected in Berlin (1788–91) It was badly damaged during World War II, and was restored in 1958.

brandish *verb* to wave (a weapon, etc) as a threat or display. [from Old French *brandir*]

brand-new *adj.* completely new.

Brando, Marlon (1924–) US film and stage actor, born in Omaha, Nebraska. Trained in Method acting, he achieved fame both in Tennessee Williams's stage play *A Streetcar Named Desire* (1947), and in the film version (1951). His varied film parts include Mark Antony in *Julius Caesar* (1953) and Fletcher Christian in *Mutiny on the Bounty* (1962). He won his first Oscar for *On the Waterfront* (1954), but he refused to accept a second, for *The Godfather* (1972), in protest against what he described as the persecution of the Native Americans. More recent films include *Last Tango in Paris* (1973), *Apocalypse Now* (1977), and *A Dry White Season* (1989).

Brandt, Bill (William) (1904–83) English photographer, born in London. He studied with Man Ray in Paris in 1929, and during the 1930s made striking social records contrasting the rich and the poor. He portrayed life in London during the Blitz in World War II. Later works include *Perspective of Nudes* (1961) and *Shadows of Light* (1966).

Brandt, Willy, originally **Karl Herbert Frahm** (1913–92) German politician, born in Lübeck. An anti-Nazi, he fled in 1933 to Norway, where he changed his name and worked as a journalist, until the occupation of Norway (1940) forced him to move to Sweden. In 1945 he returned to Germany, and was a member of the *Bundestag* (1949–57). A pro-Western leader, he was Mayor of West Berlin (1957–66), and as Chairman of the Social Democratic Party (1964–87) he formed a coalition government with the Christian Democrats (1966). He was elected Chancellor (1969–74) in a coalition gov-

ernment with the Free Democrats and was awarded the Nobel Peace Prize in 1971. After he resigned as Chancellor in 1974, he chaired a commission on the world economy (the Brandt Commission Report, 1980).

brandy *noun* (PL. **brandies**) a strong alcoholic drink made from wine or fermented fruit juice. [from Dutch *brandewijn*, from *branden*, to burn or distil + *wijn*, wine]

brandy-snap *noun* a thin biscuit in the form of a hollow tube, flavoured with ginger and usually served filled with cream.

Brandywine, Battle of the a battle fought (11 Sep 1777) in the US War of Independence, named after the Brandywine Creek near Philadelphia, Pennsylvania. British forces under Howe defeated Washington's troops, who were attempting to defend Pennsylvania.

Branson, Richard (Charles Nicholas) (1950–) English entrepreneur and business-man, born in London. He began the Virgin mail-order business in 1969, opened the first record shop two years later, and founded the Virgin record label in 1973. He founded Virgin Atlantic Airlines in 1984, floated the company in 1986, and bought it back two years later. Virgin Music was sold for £560 million to Thorn EMI in 1992. In 1993, with TV-am, he launched Virgin FM, the UK's second independent national radio station. He won the Blue Riband title in 1986 for the fastest sea-crossing of the Atlantic Ocean.

Brant, Joseph (1742–1807) Mohawk chief, born by the Ohio river. He fought for the British in the Indian and Revolutionary wars and helped to bring about a general peace. An earnest Christian in later years, he translated St Mark's Gospel and the Prayer Book into Mohawk, and in 1786 visited England, where he was received at court.

bran tub *Brit.* a lucky dip consisting of a tub filled with bran, paper, wood shavings, etc with prizes hidden in it.

Braque, Georges (1882–1963) French painter, born in Argenteuil. He was one of the founders of classical Cubism, and worked with Picasso (1908–1914). After World War I he developed a non-geometric semi-abstract style, and the subjects of his (mainly still life) paintings appear as a two-dimensional pattern. He was the first living artist to have his paintings exhibited in the Louvre.

brash *adj.* **1** very loud or showy. **2** rude, impudent.

brashly *adv.* in a brash or vulgar manner or style.

brashness *noun* being brash; vulgarity.

Brasília POP (1991) 1.6m, the capital of Brazil, situated in Centro-Oeste region, W central Brazil. Construction of Brasília began in 1956. It replaced Rio de Janeiro as capital in 1960. The city, designed by Oscar Niemeyer, is laid out in the shape of a bent bow and arrow. Residential areas lie along the curve of the bow. At right angles to these is the arrow, with the Congress Buildings, the President's Office, and the

Brandenburg Gate

Supreme Court at the tip. To the W lie the cathedral and the Ministry buildings. The cultural and recreational zones and the commercial and financial areas lie on either side of the intersection of the bow and arrow. The city is famous for its modern sculpture, and is a World Heritage site.

Brașov, German **Kronstadt** (to 1918), **Stalin** (1950–60) **1** POP (1992) 324 000, the industrial capital of Brașov county, central Romania. It is a summer resort and a winter sports centre. HISTORY founded in the 13c, it was an important medieval trade centre; belonged to Hungary but was handed over after World War I. **2** a county in central Romania with Brașov as its capital.

brass — noun **1** a hard yellowish metal, a mixture of copper and zinc. **2** objects, tools, etc made of brass. **3** wind instruments made of brass, such as the trumpet. **4** the people who play brass instruments in an orchestra. **5** a piece of flat brass with a figure, design, name, etc on it, usually found in a church, in memory of some dead person. **6** a small, flat, brass ornament with a design on it, for a horse's harness. **7** (**top brass**) colloq. people in authority or of high military rank. **8** (**the brass** or **the brass neck**) colloq. over-confidence or effrontery; nerve: *he had the brass to call me a wimp.* **9** colloq. money. — adj. made of brass. — **brassed off** colloq. fed up; annoyed. See also BRAZIER². [from Anglo-Saxon *bræs*]

Brassai, professional name of **Gyula Halasz** (1899–1984) French-Hungarian photographer, born in Brasso, Transylvania. He went to Paris in 1923, and recorded the nightlife of the city throughout the 1930s. During the German occupation he worked in Pablo Picasso's studio, but returned to the photographic evocation of Paris and its people during the 1950s.

brass band a band consisting mainly of brass instruments.

brasserie noun a small and usually inexpensive restaurant, especially one serving French food, and originally beer. [from French *brasserie*, brewery]

brass hat Brit. colloq. a high-ranking military officer.

brassica noun any plant belonging to the genus *Brassica* of the family Cruciferae, including several commercially important crop vegetables, eg cabbage, cauliflower, broccoli, brussels sprout, turnip, swede, kale, oilseed rape, black mustard. [from Latin *brassica*, cabbage]

brassière see BRA.

brassily adv. in a brassy or pretentious manner or style.

brassiness noun being brassy; vulgarity.

brass rubbing 1 a copy of the design on a brass (sense 5) made by putting paper on top of it and rubbing with coloured wax or charcoal. **2** the process of making such a copy.

brass tacks colloq. the essential details: *get down to brass tacks.*

brassy adj. (**brassier, brassiest**) **1** like brass in appearance, especially in colour. **2** like a brass musical instrument in sound. **3** colloq. loudly confident and rude. **4** flashy or showy.

brat noun a child, especially a rude or badly behaved one.

Bratby, John (1928–92) English artist and writer, born in London. He was one of the leading representatives of the English Realist School. With Jack Smith he represented Great Britain at the Venice Biennale in 1956. His works include *Baby in Pram* (Liverpool). He also wrote several novels, including *Breakdown* (1960).

Bratislava, German **Pressburg**, Hungarian **Pozsony**, Latin **Posonium** POP (1991) 442 000, the capital city of Slovakia, situated in the SW of the country. It is a major river port lying on the R Danube. HISTORY a stronghold of the Great

Moravian Empire in the 9c; it was capital of Hungary from 1541 to 1784; Hungarian monarchs were crowned here until 1835; it was incorporated into Czechoslovakia in 1918; Slovakia separated from the Czech Republic in 1993 with Bratislava as capital. NOTABLE FEATURES cathedral (13c); castle; Mirbach Palace; Lenin's Museum; Pharmaceutical Museum; Slovak National Theatre; Slovak National Gallery and Museum.

Bratsk Dam a major gravity earth-fill dam (125m high) on the Angara River, Russia, completed in 1961. It has the capacity to generate 4 500 megawatts of hydroelectricity.

Brattain, Walter Houser (1902–87) US physicist, born in Amoy, China. He is best known for his work on the properties of semiconductors and for helping to develop the first efficient transistor; these have been important contributions to the development of modern electronics. He shared the 1956 Nobel Prize for Physics with John Bardeen and William Shockley.

Braun, Eva (1910–45) the mistress of Adolf Hitler, born in Munich. She met Hitler in the early 1930s, when she was secretary to his staff photographer. She is said to have married Hitler before they committed suicide together in the air-raid shelter of the Chancellery during the fall of Berlin.

Braun, (Karl) Ferdinand (1850–1918) German physicist, born in Fulda. He became professor at the universities of Tübingen and Strassburg. Although his main contributions were in pure science, he is best known for the first cathode-ray (the 'Braun tube') oscilloscope introduced in 1897, providing a basic component of the television. He shared with Guglielmo Marconi the 1909 Nobel Prize for Physics for practical contributions to wireless telegraphy.

Braun, Wernher von see VON BRAUN.

bravado noun a display of confidence or daring, often boastful and insincere. [from Spanish *bravada*]

brave — adj. **1** without fear of danger, pain, etc. **2** fine, excellent. — verb (usually **brave something out**) to meet or face up to danger, pain, etc: *brave the storm.* — noun formerly a warrior from a Native American tribe. [from Old French, from Latin *barbarus*, barbarous]

bravely adv. with bravery; boldly.

Brave New World a novel by Aldous Huxley (1932). It depicts a counter-Utopia in which rulers achieve harmony in society by scientifically breeding and conditioning the population.

bravery noun a brave quality; being brave or courageous.

bravo¹ — interj. well done! excellent! — noun (PL. **bravos**) a cry of 'bravo'. [from Italian *bravo*]

bravo² noun (PL. **bravos, bravoes**) a hired killer. [from Italian *bravo*]

bravura noun **1** a display of great spirit or daring. **2** a piece of music, especially for the voice, requiring considerable technical ability. [from Italian *bravura*]

brawl — noun a noisy quarrel or fight, especially in public. — verb intrans. to quarrel or fight noisily. [from Middle English *bralle*]

brawler noun a person who brawls or is brawling, especially in public.

brawling noun noisy fighting or quarrelling.

brawn noun **1** muscle or physical strength. **2** boiled, jellied meat from the head of a pig. [from Old French *braon*, meat]

brawniness noun having strong muscles; muscularity.

brawny adj. (**brawnier, brawniest**) muscular, strong.

bray — noun the loud harsh sound made by an ass or donkey. — verb **1** intrans. said of an ass or

donkey to make a braying noise. **2** intrans. said of a person to make a loud harsh sound. **3** to say in a loud harsh voice. [from Old French *braire*]

braze verb Engineering to join (two pieces of metal) by melting an alloy with a lower melting point than either of the metals to be joined, and applying it to the joint. Brazing is similar to soldering, but requires much higher temperatures. [from French *braser*, from *braise*, live coals]

brazen — adj. **1** (**brazen-faced**) bold, impudent, shameless. **2** of or like brass, especially in sound or colour. — verb (**brazened, brazening**) (**brazen something out**) to face an embarrassing or difficult situation boldly and without shame. [from Anglo-Saxon *bræsen*, from *bræs*, brass]

brazenly adv. in a brazen or impudent manner.

brazenness noun boldness; impudence.

brazier¹ noun a metal frame or container for holding burning coal, especially used by people who have to work outside in cold weather. [from French *brasier*, from *braise*, live coals]

brazier² noun a worker in brass. [from BRASS]

Brazil, Portuguese **Brasil**, official name **The Federative Republic of Brazil**, Portuguese **República Federativa do Brasil** POP (1992e) 156.3m, a republic in E and central South America. It is divided into five geographical regions, which are subdivided into 23 states, three territories, and one federal territory (Brasília). AREA 8 511 965sq km/3 285 618sq mi. It is bounded in the N by French Guiana, Surinam, Guyana, and Venezuela; in the NW by Colombia; in the W by Peru, Bolivia, and Paraguay; in the SW by Argentina; in the S by Uruguay; in the E by the Atlantic Ocean. CAPITAL Brasília. chief towns São Paulo, Rio de Janeiro, Belo Horizonte, Recife, Salvador. TIME ZONES GMT –2 in the Atlantic islands, –3 in the E, –4 in the mid-W, and –5 in the extreme W. Most of the population are of Portuguese, Italian, German, or Japanese origin; the majority are Roman Catholic, with the remainder Protestant or Spiritualist. OFFICIAL LANGUAGE Portuguese. CURRENCY the cruzeiro. PHYSICAL DESCRIPTION the low-lying Amazon basin in the N, once an inland sea, is now drained by rivers that carry one fifth of the Earth's running water; where the forest canopy has been cleared, soils are susceptible to erosion; the Brazilian Plateau lies to the centre and S with an average height of 600–900m; vegetation changes from thorny scrub forest in the N to wooded savannah (*campo cerrado*) in the interior; the Brazilian Highlands in the N rise to 2 890m at Pico da Bandeira; the country's highest peak, Pico da Neblina (3 014m), lies in the Guiana Highlands to the S; there are eight river systems, notably the Amazon in the N, the São Francisco in the centre, and the Paraguay, Paraná, and Uruguay in the S; on the Atlantic coast a thin strip of land, c.100km/62mi wide, contains 30% of the population. CLIMATE almost entirely tropical; the Equator passes through the N region, and the Tropic of Capricorn through the SE; in the Amazon basin the annual rainfall is 1 500–2 000mm, with no dry season; the average midday temperatures are 27°–32°C; there are more distinct wet and dry seasons on the Brazilian Plateau; the dry region in the NE is susceptible to long droughts, with daily temperatures 21°–36°C, and monthly rainfall as little as 3mm in Aug, rising to 185mm in Mar; on the narrow coastal strip, the climate is hot and tropical, with rainfall varying greatly N–S; the S states lie outside the tropics, with a seasonal, temperate climate. HISTORY discovered for the Portuguese by Cabral in 1500; the first settlement was at Salvador da Bahia; there were 13 feudal principalities, which were replaced in 1572 by a Viceroyalty; the country was divided into N and S, with capitals at Salvador and Rio de Janeiro; the Portuguese court transferred to Brazil during the Napoleonic Wars; independence was declared in

1822, and a monarchy was established; a republic followed the 1889 coup; large numbers of European immigrants arrived in the early 20c; the revolution, headed by Vargas, established a dictatorship in 1930–45; a liberal republic was restored in 1946; another coup in 1964 led to a military-backed presidential regime; a military junta was established in 1969; in 1979 a process of liberalization began, allowing the return of political exiles to stand for state and federal offices; new elections ending military rule took place in 1985; elected governments face a particularly difficult economic situation. GOVERNMENT the bicameral National Congress made up of 69 senators (three from each state) is elected for eight years and 479 deputies are elected for four years by proportional representation; state governors with limited powers are elected every four years. ECONOMY one of the world's largest farming countries; the world's largest exporter of coffee, and the second largest exporter of cocoa and soya beans; beef, sugar cane, cotton, butter, maize, oranges; iron ore (reserves possibly the world's largest), manganese, bauxite, nickel, uranium, gold, gemstones; steel, chemicals, petrochemicals, machinery, motor vehicles, textiles, consumer goods, cement, lumber; shipping; fishing; tourism; offshore oil production has increased since the 1960s; large investments in hydroelectricity, cane alcohol, coal, and nuclear power; an important hydroelectric scheme at the Itaipu Dam on the R Paraná; the country is a world leader in the development of alcohol fuel; timber reserves are the third largest in the world but continuing destruction of the Amazon rainforest is causing much concern worldwide; a road network is being extended through the rainforest.

brazil *or* **Brazil** *noun* **1** a type of red wood from any of several tropical trees. **2** (*also* **Brazil nut**) a type of long, three-sided, edible white nut from a tropical American tree. [from *Brazil* in S America, the country itself being so named from the similarity of the red wood found there to that found in the East and known as *brasil*]

brazing *Engineering* the process of joining two pieces of metal by fusing a layer of brass (sometimes known as spelter) between the adjoining surfaces.

Brazos River a river in S USA, length 1 947km/1 210mi. Formed in W Texas by the Double Mountain Fork and Salt Fork rivers, it flows generally SE through Texas, past the towns of Mineral Wells and Waco, to enter the Gulf of Mexico at Freeport. Its major tributaries are the Clear Fork, Little, and Navasota rivers. Brazos River is used for irrigation, hydroelectricity, and flood-control.

Brazzaville POP (1992e) 938 000, the river-port capital of the Congo, on the right bank of the R Zaire (opposite Kinshasa, Zaire). HISTORY founded in 1880; became capital of French Equatorial Africa in 1910; served as headquarters of the Free French forces in World War II; became capital of the Congo in 1960. NOTABLE FEATURE cathedral.

BRCS *abbrev.* British Red Cross Society (see RED CROSS).

breach — *noun* **1** a breaking (of a law, promise, etc) or failure to carry out (a duty). **2** a serious disagreement. **3** a gap, break, or hole. — *verb* **1** to break (a promise, etc) or fail to carry out (a duty). **2** to make an opening or hole in.
— **in breach of something** not following or agreeing with a law, etc.
step into the breach to take responsibility, or an absent person's place, in a crisis.
[from Anglo-Saxon *bryce*]

breach of confidence a divulging of information received in confidence.

breach of contract failure to fulfil the terms of a contract.

Brazil

breach of promise the breaking of a promise, especially a promise of marriage.

breach of the peace a riot or disturbance which violates the public peace.

bread — *noun* **1** one of the oldest and most important staple foods known to man, usually prepared from wheat or rye flour that is mixed with water or milk, kneaded into a dough with yeast or some other leavening agent to make it rise, and baked. White, wheatmeal, and wholemeal loaves are usually made from flour containing more than 72%, more than 85%, and 100%, respectively, of the powdered whole grain (bran and germ). **2** food and other things one needs to live: *earn one's bread.* **3** *slang* money. — *verb* to cover (food) with breadcrumbs.
— **know which side one's bread is buttered** to know how to act for one's own best interests. [from Anglo-Saxon]

bread and butter **1** sliced and buttered bread. **2** a means of earning a living.

bread basket **1** a basket for holding bread. **2** an area which produces large amounts of grain for export. **3** *slang* the stomach.

breadboard *noun* **1** a wooden board on which bread, etc is cut. **2** a board for making a model of an electric circuit.

breadcrumbs *pl. noun* crumbs of bread, used in cooking.

breaded *adj., said of food* covered with breadcrumbs.

breadfruit *noun* the fruit of a tree found in the S Pacific islands, which looks like bread when it is roasted.

breadline
— **on the breadline** having hardly enough food and money to live on.

breadth *noun* **1** the measurement from one side to the other. **2** openness and willingness to understand and respect other people's opinions, beliefs, etc: *breadth of vision.* [from Anglo-Saxon *bræd*]

breadthways *or* **breadthwise** *adv.* as measured or regarded from one side to the other.

breadwinner *noun* the person who earns money to support a family.

break — *verb* (PAST TENSE **broke**; PAST PARTICIPLE **broken**) **1** *trans., intrans.* to divide or become

divided into two or more parts as a result of stress or a blow. **2** *trans., intrans. said of a machine or tool, etc* to damage or become damaged, so as to stop working and be in need of repair: *the scissors have broken / try not to break the radio.* **3** to fracture a bone in (a limb, etc): *break one's leg.* **4** to burst or cut (the skin) or the skin of (the head). **5** to do something not allowed by (a law, agreement, promise, etc). **6** to interrupt (a journey). **7** *intrans.* to stop work, etc for a short period of time: *break for tea.* **8** to achieve better than (a sporting record, etc). **9** *trans., intrans. said of news, etc* to make or become known. **10** *intrans. said of the weather* to change suddenly, especially after a fine spell. **11** *trans., intrans.* to make or become weaker: *tried to break his spirit.* **12** to defeat or destroy: *break a strike.* **13** to make (the force of something) less: *the trees broke her fall.* **14** to decipher: *break a code.* **15** (**break someone of something**) to make someone give up a bad habit, etc: *tried to break him of smoking.* **16** (**break with someone**) to stop associating with them: *broke with his former friends.* **17** *intrans.* to come into being: *day breaking over the hills.* **18** *intrans. said of a storm* to begin violently. **19** *intrans.* to cut or burst through: *sun breaking through the clouds.* **20** *intrans.* (**break into song or laughter**) to begin singing or laughing, especially unexpectedly. **21** *intrans. said of a boy's voice* to become lower in tone on reaching puberty. **22** to disprove (an alibi, etc). **23** to interrupt the flow of electricity in (a circuit). **24** to force open with explosives: *break a safe.* **25** *intrans. said of waves, etc* to collapse into foam. **26** to lose or disrupt the order or form of: *break ranks.* **27** *intrans. Snooker* to take the first shot at the beginning of a game. **28** *Tennis* to win (an opponent's service game). **29** *intrans. Boxing* to come out of a clinch. **30** *intrans. Cricket, said of a ball* to change direction on hitting the ground. — *noun* **1** an act of or result of breaking. **2** a brief pause in work, lessons, etc. **3** a change: *a break in the weather.* **4** a sudden rush, especially to escape: *make a break for it.* **5** *colloq.* an unexpected or sudden opportunity. **6** *colloq.* a piece of good or bad luck: *a bad break.* **7** *Snooker* a series of successful shots played one after the other. **8** *Snooker* the opening shot of a game. **9** an interruption in the electricity flowing through a circuit. **10** *Mus.* a short improvised solo passage in jazz.
— **break away** *intrans.* **1** to escape from control. **2** to put an end to one's connection with a group, etc.

break the back of something to complete the heaviest or most difficult part of a job, etc.

break camp to pack up the equipment after camping.

break cover to come out of hiding.

break down 1 *said of a person* to fail in mental health. **2** to give way to one's emotions; to burst into tears. **3** *said of a machine, etc* to stop working properly. **4** *said of human relationships* to be unsuccessful and so come to an end.

break something down 1 to use force to knock down a door, etc. **2** to divide something into parts and analyse it.

break even to make neither a profit nor a loss in a transaction.

break in to enter a building by force, especially to steal things inside, to interrupt a conversation, etc.

break in a horse to train a horse to carry a saddle and a rider.

break something in to wear new shoes, boots, etc so that they lose their stiffness.

break loose or **free 1** to escape from control. **2** to become detached: *the boat broke loose from its mooring.*

break new or **fresh ground** to do something in an original way.

break off 1 to stop talking. **2** to become detached by breaking. **3** to come to an end abruptly.

break something off 1 to detach it by breaking. **2** to end something abruptly.

break something open to open a box, door, etc by force.

break out 1 to escape from a prison, etc using force. **2** to begin suddenly and usually violently: *then war broke out.*

break out in spots, *etc* to become suddenly covered in spots, a rash, etc.

break step *said of soldiers, etc* to become irregular and out of step in marching.

break through 1 to force a way through. **2** to make a new discovery or be successful, especially after a difficult or unsuccessful period.

break up 1 to break into pieces. **2** to come to an end; to finish. **3** *said of people* to end a relationship or marriage: *his parents have broken up.* **4** *said of a relationship, marriage, etc* to come to an end: *their marriage has broken up.* **5** *said of a school or a pupil* to end term and begin the holidays.

break someone up *North Amer. colloq.* to make them laugh convulsively.

break something up 1 to divide it into pieces. **2** to make it finish or come to an end.

break wind to release gas from the bowels through the anus.

[from Anglo-Saxon *brecan*]

breakable — *adj.* able to be broken. — *noun* (*usually* **breakables**) a breakable object.

breakage *noun* **1** the act of breaking. **2** a broken object; damage caused by breaking.

breakaway *noun* **1** an act of breaking away or escaping from control. **2** (*attributive*) that has broken away; separate: *a breakaway republic.*

breakdancing *noun* an energetic style of dancing which involves complicated jumps and twists, originally developed by young black Americans.

breakdown *noun* **1** a failure in a machine or device. **2** (*attributive*) used in connection with a breakdown, especially of a road vehicle: *a breakdown van.* **3** *used of a person* a failure in mental health. **4** a failure or collapse of a process: *a breakdown in communications.*

breaker *noun* **1** a person or thing that breaks something. **2** a large wave which breaks on rocks or the beach.

breakfast — *noun* the first meal of the day. — *verb intrans.* to have breakfast. [from *break fast*, ie begin to eat after fasting]

break-in *noun* an illegal entry by force into a building, especially to steal things inside.

breaking and entering the act of breaking into a building to steal things inside.

breaking-point *noun* a point at which a person or thing can no longer stand a stress or strain.

breakneck *adj.*, *used of speed* extremely fast.

break of day *literary* dawn.

breakout *noun* an escape by force.

breakthrough *noun* **1** a decisive advance or discovery. **2** an act of breaking through something.

break-up *noun* **1** the ending of a relationship or situation. **2** a dispersal or scattering.

breakwater *noun* a wall built on a beach to break the force of the waves.

Bream, Julian (Alexander) (1933–) English guitarist and lutenist, born in London. A protégé of Andrés Segovia, he earned an international reputation in the 1950s on both guitar and lute. Several composers, including Britten, Henze, and Walton, have written works for him.

bream *noun* (PL. **bream**) **1** a type of freshwater fish. **2** (**sea bream**) a similar sea fish. [from Old French *bresme*]

breast — *noun* **1** either of the two fleshy parts on the front of a woman's body, which can produce milk. **2** the front part of the body between the neck and stomach. **3** the source or seat of emotions. **4** the part of a garment covering the breast. — *verb* **1** to face or oppose: *breast the wind.* **2** to come to the top of a hill, etc. **3** *Athletics* to touch (the tape) at the end of a race with the chest.

— **make a clean breast of something** to be frank and honest about something one has done, feels, or thinks, etc.

[from Anglo-Saxon *breost*]

breastbone *noun* the thin flat bone running down the front of the chest.

breastfed *adj.*, *said of a baby* fed with milk from the breast.

breastfeed *verb trans.*, *intrans.* to feed a baby with milk from the breast.

breastfeeding *noun* feeding a baby with milk from the breast.

breastplate *noun* a piece of armour which protects the chest.

breaststroke *noun* a style of swimming in which the arms are pushed out in front and then pulled backwards together.

breastwork *noun* a temporary wall built from earth for defence, reaching up to a person's chest.

breath *noun* **1** the air drawn into and forced out of the lungs. **2** an act of breathing air in. **3** a faint breeze. **4** a slight trace of perfume, etc. **5** a slight hint, suggestion, or rumour (especially of scandal).

— **catch one's breath** to stop breathing for a moment, from fear, amazement, pain, etc.

draw breath to breathe.

get one's breath back 1 to begin breathing normally again after strenuous exercise. **2** to recover from a shock or surprise.

hold one's breath to stop breathing, usually because of worry or to avoid being heard.

out of or **short of breath** breathless, especially after strenuous exercise.

take one's breath away to astound or amaze one (see also BREATHTAKING).

under one's breath in a whisper.

waste one's breath to speak without any effect.

[from Anglo-Saxon *bræth*]

breathalyse *verb* to test (a driver) with a Breathalyser.

Breathalyser or **Breathalyzer** *noun trademark* an instrument used to test the amount of alcohol on a driver's breath.

breathe *verb* **1** *intrans.*, *trans.* to draw air into, and force it out of, the lungs. **2** *trans.*, *intrans.* to say, speak, or sound quietly. **3** *trans.* to show or express: *breathe defiance.* **4** *intrans.* to take breath or pause. **5** *intrans.* to blow softly. **6** *intrans. said of wine* to develop flavour when exposed to the air.

— **breathe again** or **freely** to feel at ease after a period of anxiety or fear.

breathe down someone's neck to watch or supervise someone so closely that they feel uncomfortable.

breathe fire *colloq.* to speak very angrily.

breathe one's last to die.

[from BREATH]

breather *noun colloq.* a short rest or break from work.

breathily *adv.* with a sound of breathing.

breathing *noun* **1** the process of drawing air into and forcing it out of the lungs. **2** a sign in Greek indicating that the initial vowel is pronounced with an h- sound (aspirate).

breathing-space *noun* a short time allowed for rest.

breathless *adj.* **1** having difficulty in breathing normally, either from illness or from hurrying, etc. **2** very eager or excited. **3** with no wind or fresh air.

breathlessly *adv.* with difficulty in breathing normally; with a lack of breath: *replied breathlessly that she was exhausted.*

breathlessness *noun* being breathless; a lack of breath.

breathtaking *adj.* very surprising, exciting, or impressive.

breathtakingly *adv.* astoundingly; amazingly.

breath test *noun Brit.* a test given to drivers to check the amount of alcohol in their blood.

breathy *adj.* (**breathier, breathiest**) *said of the voice* producing a sound of breathing when speaking.

breccia *noun Geol.* coarse sedimentary rock composed of a mixture of angular rock cemented together by finer-grained material. It is usually formed by processes such as landslides and geological faulting, in which rocks become fractured. [from Italian *breccia*]

Brecht, (Eugene) Bertolt (Friedrich) (1898–1956) German poet, playwright, and theatre director, born in Augsburg. He established his reputation with *Die Dreigroschenoper* (The Threepenny Opera, 1928) and thereafter was concerned with encouraging audiences to think rather than identify, and with experimentation in epic theatre and alienation effects ('Verfremdungseffekt'). Hitler's rise to power forced him to leave Germany, and he lived in exile for 15 years (1933–48), during which time he wrote some of his greatest plays, including *The Life of Galileo* (Leben des Galilei, 1938), *Mother Courage and her Children* (Mutter Courage und ihre Kinder, 1939) and *The Caucasian Chalk Circle* (Der Kaukasische Kreidekreis, 1945). His directorial work on these and other plays with the Berliner Ensemble firmly established his influence as a major figure in 20c theatre.

Breck, Alan the rebellious Jacobite in Robert Louis Stevenson's *Kidnapped* and *Catriona*, who befriends David Balfour.

Breckland, The a sandy region of heathland on the border of Norfolk and Suffolk, SE England. It was an important flint mining region in Neolithic times. Today large areas are covered in conifer plantations.

Brecon Beacons a national park in SE Wales, established in 1957. AREA 1 434sq km/ 554sq mi. The park includes the three main peaks of 'The Beacons': Pen-y-Fan, Corn Du, and Cribyn, which rise to c.900m. NOTABLE FEATURES Brecon Cathedral; Llanthony Priory; Llangorse Lake.

bred see BREED.

Breda POP (1992e) 127 000, an industrial city in North Brabant province, S Netherlands, at the confluence of the Mark and Aa rivers. It is an important cultural centre and the headquarters of many research and educational institutes. HISTORY received its charter in the 13c; known for the 'Compromise of Breda' (1566), a protest against Spanish tyranny, and for Charles II's 'Declaration of Breda', made before his restoration to the throne in 1660. NOTABLE FEATURES Breda Castle (1350, now a military academy); town hall (18c); Gothic cathedral (1510).

breech *noun* **1** the back part of a gun barrel, where it is loaded. **2** *old use* the buttocks. [from Anglo-Saxon *brec*]

breech birth *or* **breech delivery** the birth of a baby buttocks first instead of the normal head-first position.

breeches *pl. noun* **1** short trousers fastened below the knee. **2** *humorous colloq.* trousers.

breeches buoy a pair of canvas breeches on a rope, used for rescuing people, especially from ships.

breed — *verb* (PAST TENSE AND PAST PARTICIPLE **bred**) **1** *intrans. said of animals and plants* to reproduce or cause them to reproduce sexually in order to transmit certain selected characteristics from parents to offspring. **2** to keep (animals or plants) for the purpose of producing offspring, or developing new types with selected characteristics. **3** to train or educate: *well-bred children*. **4** to cause or produce (usually something bad): *dirt breeds disease*. **5** *Physics* to produce more fissile fuel (atoms that can be split) than is consumed in a nuclear reaction. See also BREEDER REACTOR. — *noun* **1** an artificially maintained subdivision within an animal species, especially farm livestock or pet animals, produced by domestication and selective breeding, eg Friesian cattle, Irish wolfhound. **2** a race or lineage. **3** a kind or type. [from Anglo-Saxon *bredan*, to produce, cherish]

breeder *noun* a person who breeds animals, especially for a living.

breeder reactor a type of nuclear power station which is capable of creating more fissile material than it uses.

breeding *noun* **1** *Biol.* controlling the manner in which plants or animals reproduce in such a way that certain characteristics are selected for and passed on to the next generation. **2** the result of a good education and training: *show good breeding*.

breeding-ground *noun* **1** a place where animals, birds, etc produce their young. **2** a place, situation, etc which encourages the development of something usually regarded as bad: *a breeding-ground for crime*.

breeze¹ — *noun* **1** a gentle wind. **2** *colloq.* any job, etc which is easily done. — *verb intrans. colloq.* **1** to move briskly and confidently: *breezed into the room.* **2** (**breeze through something**) to do it easily and quickly: *breezed through the exam.* [probably from Old Spanish *briza*, north-east wind]

breeze² *noun* ashes from coal, coke or charcoal. [from French *braise*, live coals]

breezeblock *noun* a type of brick made from breeze and cement, used for building houses, etc.

breezily *adv.* in a breezy or carefree manner: *walked breezily into the room.*

breeziness *noun* a breezy or carefree manner.

breezy *adj.* (**breezier**, **breeziest**) **1** slightly windy. **2** *said of a person* lively, confident, and casual.

Bremen 1 POP (1991e) 549 000, a commercial city and the capital of Bremen state, NW Germany. Lying on both banks of the lower R Weser, 94km/58mi SW of Hamburg, Bremen is a large seaport which carries on considerable trade in grain, cotton, and tobacco. NOTABLE FEATURES

cathedral (11c); Gothic town hall (1405–10). **2** a state in NW Germany with Bremen as its capital.

Bremerhaven POP (1991e) 131 000, a seaport in Bremen state, NW Germany. It lies on the E bank of the estuary of the R Weser, 56km/35mi N of Bremen. A city from 1851, it united with Wesermunde in 1938. Bremerhaven was Europe's largest fishing port for many years before suffering a decline in deep-sea fishing in the 1980s.

Brenda a female first name, used only in Scotland until the 20c. [probably of Scandinavian origin, relating to *brand*, flaming sword]

Brendan a male first name, common in Ireland. [related to BRIAN, or possibly from Gaelic *breda + ron*, stinking hair]

Bren gun *or* **bren gun** a light, quick-firing machine-gun used during World War II. [from *Brno* in Czechoslovakia, where it was originally made + *Enfield* in England, where it was later made]

Brennan, William J(oseph) (1906–) US jurist, born in Newark, New Jersey. After practising law he rose in the New Jersey court system to the state supreme court. Named to the US Supreme Court (1956–90), he took an active role in the 'liberal' decisions it handed down under the chief justiceship of Earl Warren.

Brenner, Sydney (1927–) South African–British molecular biologist, born in Germiston, South Africa. Working at Cambridge, he made major contributions to studies of genetics and the DNA helix in the 1950s. Later he began an intensive study of the nervous system of a nematode worm, with the objective of relating the anatomy of an animal to the genetic basis of its structure.

Brenner Pass, German **Brenner Sattel**, Italian **Passo del Brennero** a mountain pass in the central Tirol Alps on the border between Italy and Austria. It lies on the main route between Bolzano and Innsbrück, at an altitude of 1 371m. Open during all seasons of the year, it is the lowest pass over the main alpine chain.

Brentano, Clemens (1778–1842) German poet, born in Ehrenbreitstein. A founder of the Heidelberg Romantic school, he wrote several poems, short stories, fairy tales, and plays, notably *Die Gründung Prags* (The Foundation of Prague, 1815). He also edited, with Achim von Arnim, *Des Knaben Wunderhorn* (1805–8), a collection of folk songs.

Brer Fox the greedy, malicious arch-enemy of Brer Rabbit in Joel Chandler Harris's *Uncle Remus*.

Brer Rabbit the cavalier rabbit who delights in helping his fellow 'creeturs' make fools of themselves in Joel Chandler Harris's *Uncle Remus*.

Brescia POP (1991e) 197 000, the capital of Brescia province, Lombardy, N Italy. It is an industrial city with firearms among its products and it serves as a market centre for local agricultural produce. NOTABLE FEATURES Tempio Capitolino (AD72), and other Roman remains; cathedrals (9c, 17c); Renaissance town hall (1492–1508).

Brest POP (1990) 201 000, a fortified port and naval station in Finistère department, Brittany, NW France. It lies on the Atlantic coast and is a natural harbour on the Penfeld Estuary. Germany used Brest as a submarine base in World War II. Heavy bombing by the Allies destroyed the town, and it was rebuilt after the War.

Brest, formerly **Brest Litovsk**, Polish **Brześć nad Bugiem** POP (1991e) 277 000, the river-port capital city of Brest region, Belorussia. It lies on the Polish border, on the R Mukhavets where it meets the R Bug, and it is a major transportation centre. HISTORY founded by Slavs in 1017; belonged to Poland until 1795 and again between 1919 and 1939; the Brest Litovsk Treaty was signed here.

Brest-Litovsk, Treaty of a bilateral treaty (1918) signed at Brest between Soviet Russia and the Central Powers, under the terms of which Russia withdrew from World War I, hostilities ceased on Germany's eastern front, and the new Soviet state ceded much territory and economic resources to Germany. Lenin decreed Russia must 'sacrifice space in order to gain time'.

brethren see BROTHER.

Brethren in Christ a Church founded in the late 18c in Pennsylvania, USA. Pietistic, evangelical, and missionary, it derived from Mennonite tradition and soon spread to Canada. Although numerically small, it now supports missionary Churches in Asia, Africa, and Central America.

Breton — *noun* **1** a person from Brittany in France. **2** the Celtic language spoken in Brittany. — *adj.* of Brittany, its people, or language. [from French *Breton*]

Bretton Woods Conference an international conference held in Bretton Woods, New Hampshire, USA, in 1944, which led to the establishment of the International Monetary System, including the International Monetary Fund (IMF) and the World Bank. The agreement, signed by the USA, UK, and 43 other nations, aimed to control exchange rates, which were fixed for members in terms of gold and the dollar. The system was used until 1973, when floating exchange rates were introduced.

Breughel *or* **Brueghel, Pieter**, also called **the Elder** (c.1520–69) Flemish painter, born (probably) in the village of Breughel, near Breda. He travelled in France and Italy then settled in Brussels, where he painted his major works. Influenced by Bosch, his genre pictures of peasant life include *The Blind Leading the Blind* (1568, Naples), the *Wedding Dance* (1566, Detroit), and the *Peasant Dance* (c.1568, Vienna). His eldest son, Pieter Breughel, the Younger (c.1564–1637) is known as 'Hell' Breughel, because of his paintings of devils, hags, and robbers. His younger son, Jan (1568–1625), known as 'Velvet' Breughel, painted still life, flowers, landscapes, and religious subjects on a small scale.

Breuil, Henri (Edouard Prosper) (1877–1961) French archaeologist, born in Mortain. He was responsible for the discovery of the caves at Combarelles and Font de Gaume in the Dordogne (1901). He was Professor at the Collège de France (1929–47), and was noted for his studies of artistic technique in cave art, and for the detailed copying of hundreds of paintings in Europe, Africa, and elsewhere.

breve *noun* **1** *Mus.* a note twice as long as a semibreve. **2** a mark ˘ sometimes put over a vowel to show that it is short or unstressed. [from Latin *brevis*, short]

breviary *noun* (PL. **breviaries**) *RC Church* a book containing the hymns, prayers, and psalms which form the daily service. [from Latin *breviarum*, summary]

brevity *noun* **1** using few words; conciseness. **2** shortness of time. [from Old French *brievete*, from Latin *brevis*, short]

brew — *verb* **1** to make beer or other alcoholic beverage by infusion, boiling, and fermentation of malted barley. **2** (*also* **brew up** *or* **brew something up**) to make (tea, coffee, etc) by mixing the leaves, grains, etc with boiling water. **3** *intrans.* to be prepared by brewing: *the tea is brewing.* **4** (*also* **brew up**) to become stronger and threatening: *there's a storm brewing.* **5** (*also* **brew something up**) to plan or prepare something (usually unwelcome): *brew up trouble.* — *noun* **1** a drink produced by brewing, especially tea or beer. **2** an amount of beer, etc produced by brewing: *last year's brew.* **3** the quality of what is brewed: *a good strong brew.* [from Anglo-Saxon *breowan*]

brewer *noun* a person or company that brews and sells beer.

brewer's yeast a type of yeast used in brewing beer, causing the sugar in the beer to change into alcohol, or as a source of the B vitamins.

brewery *noun* (PL. **breweries**) a place where beer, etc is brewed.

brewing *noun* the process by which alcoholic beverages, especially beer, are produced by the slow fermentation of malted cereal grains, usually barley, flavoured with hops.
◇ In the brewing process, barley is allowed to sprout so that it releases an enzyme (amylase) which breaks down starch to form sugars. The sprouted barley is then steeped in hot water (in a process known as *mashing*) in order to release its sugars. Hops, which give the beer a characteristic bitter taste, are added to the liquid (known as *wort*). The wort is boiled and filtered, yeast is added, and the mixture is then allowed to ferment, during which process the sugars are converted into ethanol (alcohol) and carbon dioxide.

Brewster, Sir David (1781–1868) Scottish physicist, born in Jedburgh. Educated for the church, he became editor of the *Edinburgh Encyclopaedia* in 1808. He made important discoveries concerning the polarization of reflected light, discovered stress birefringence, showing that stress on transparent materials can alter the way in which they transmit light, and invented the kaleidoscope (1816).

Brezhnev, Leoni (Ilich) (1906–82) Russian politician, born in Kamenskoye, Ukraine. Trained as a metallurgist, he became a political commissar in the Red Army in World War II, after which he was a party official in the Ukraine and Moldavia. He became a member (1952–7) and then Chairman (1960–4) of the Presidium of the Supreme Soviet. As General Secretary of the Soviet Communist Party Central Committee after Khrushchev (1964), he gradually emerged as the most powerful figure in the Soviet Union, the first to hold simultaneously the position of General Secretary and President of the Supreme Soviet (1977–82).

Brezhnev Doctrine the policies of Leonid Brezhnev, General Secretary of the Soviet Communist Party (1964–82). They combined strict political control internally with peaceful co-existence and détente abroad, and also justified intervention (including military) in the internal affairs of other socialist states (eg Czechoslovakia, 1968). The Brezhnev period was later referred to as the 'years of stagnation'.

Brian (c.926–1014) King of Ireland (1002–14), the 'Brian Boroimhe' or 'Boru' (Brian of the tribute) of the annalists. In 976 he became chief of Dál Cais, and after much fighting he made himself King of Leinster (984). Further campaigns led to his rule being acknowledged over all Ireland. He was killed after defeating the Vikings at Clontarf.

Brian a male first name. [from a Celtic element meaning 'hill' or 'eminence']

Briand, Aristide (1862–1932) French socialist politician, born in Nantes. Eleven times French Prime Minister (1909–11, 1913, 1915–17, 1921–2, 1925–6, 1929), he also acted as Foreign Minister (1925–32), and helped to conclude the Kellogg–Briand Pact (1928), which proscribed war as a means of solving disputes. He shared the 1926 Nobel Peace Prize with Gustav Stresemann, and advocated a United States of Europe.

briar¹ *or* **brier** *noun* any prickly bush, especially a wild rose bush. [from Anglo-Saxon *brer*]

briar² *or* **brier** *noun* 1 a shrub with a hard, woody root, found in southern Europe. 2 a tobacco pipe made from the root. [from French *bruyère*, heath]

bribe — *noun* a gift, usually of money, offered to someone to persuade them to do something illegal or improper. — *verb* to offer or promise a bribe, etc to (someone). [from Old French *briber*]

bribery *noun* the practice of offering bribes.

bric-à-brac *noun* small objects of little financial value kept as decorations or ornaments. [from French *à bric et à brac*, at random]

brick — *noun* 1 a rectangular block of baked clay used for building. 2 the material used for making bricks. 3 a child's plastic or wooden rectangular or cylindrical toy for building. 4 something in the shape of a brick: *a brick of ice-cream.* 5 *Brit. colloq.* (only in sing.) a trusted and helpful person. — *adj.* made of bricks, of the dull red colour of bricks. — *verb* (**brick something in** *or* **up**) to close or fill it in with bricks: *brick up the window.*
— **drop a brick** *Brit. colloq.* to do or say something embarrassing or insulting without realizing that it is.
like banging *or* **knocking one's head against a brick wall** *colloq.* having no effect despite much effort.
make bricks without straw to do a job without having the proper materials for it.
[from Old Dutch *bricke*]

brickbat *noun* 1 an insult or criticism. 2 a piece of brick, or anything hard, thrown at someone.

bricklayer *noun* a person who builds with bricks.

bricklaying *noun* the skill or practice of laying bricks in building.

brickwork that part of a building, eg the walls, that is made of brick.

brickyard *noun* a place where bricks are made.

bridal *adj.* of a wedding or a bride. [from Anglo-Saxon *brydeala*, wedding feast, from *bryd*, bride + *ealu*, ale]

Bride a female first name, common in Ireland. [from Old Irish *Brighid*, possibly meaning 'The High One']

bride *noun* a woman who has just been married, or is about to be married. [from Anglo-Saxon *bryd*]

bridegroom *noun* a man who has just been married, or is about to be married.

Brideshead Revisited a novel by Evelyn Waugh (1945). Set in war-time, it is a nostalgic evocation by the narrator, Charles Ryder, of his youth at Oxford and his involvement with the Flyte family.

bridesmaid *noun* a girl or unmarried woman attending the bride at a wedding.

bridewealth *noun* Anthropol. in some societies, property or money given by a bridegroom to the relatives of his bride, especially her parents, as a means of compensating them for her loss to the family, or to establish his rights over her.

bridge¹ — *noun* 1 a structure joining the two sides of a road, railway, river, etc to allow people, vehicles, etc to cross. 2 anything joining or connecting two separate things. 3 the narrow raised platform from which the captain of a ship directs its course. 4 the hard bony upper part of the nose. 5 a small piece of wood on a violin, guitar, etc which keeps the strings stretched tight. 6 same as BRIDGEWORK. — *verb* 1 to form or build a bridge over. 2 to make a connection, close a gap, etc.
— **cross a bridge when one comes to it** to deal with a problem when it arises and not before.
[from Anglo-Saxon *brycg*]
◇ The principal types of bridge are arch, beam, cantilever, and suspension. The greatest spans are achieved by suspension bridges (eg the Humber Bridge, England is 1 410m long). The greatest single span of the arch type is at the New River Gorge, W Virginia, USA (518m).

bridge² *noun* a card-game for four people playing in pairs, developed from whist. A player declares trumps, and also plays the hand of that player's partner, which is laid down face upwards.

◇ Bridge is thought to have originated in either Greece or Spain, and was introduced into Britain in 1880. Formerly, the most popular form was *auction bridge* in which trumps were decided by a preliminary bid or auction. This has now largely been superseded by *contract bridge* in which trumps are nominated by the highest bidder, with scoring done on a chart showing tricks contracted for and won.

bridge-builder *noun* 1 a person who builds bridges. 2 a person who tries to settle a dispute between two other people.

bridgehead *noun* a position well into enemy land from which an attack can be made.

Bridge of Sighs an enclosed 17c bridge in Venice, designed by Antonio Coritino, through which condemned prisoners would pass from the Doge's Palace to the Pozzi prison.

Bridgeport POP (1990) 142 000, a port town in Fairfield County, SW Connecticut, USA. It is situated on Long Island Sound at the mouth of the Pequonnock R. The circus manager P T Barnum lived here. The town is also the birthplace of Tom Thumb, the chief attraction of Barnum's circus. NOTABLE FEATURE Barnum Institute.

Bridges, Robert (Seymour) (1844–1930) English poet, born in Walmer, Kent. His early poetry includes three volumes of lyrics (1873, 1879, 1880), and the narrative poems *Prometheus the Firegiver* (1883) and *Eros and Psyche* (1885). His later work includes the long poem, *The Testament of Beauty* (1929). His *Collected Poems* were published in 1912 and he was made Poet Laureate in 1913. He also wrote plays and literary criticism, and was an advocate of spelling reform.

Bridget *or* **Bride, St** (453–523) Irish abbess, said to be the daughter of an Ulster prince. She founded four monasteries, the main one at Kildare. Her legendary history includes many miracles, some of which were apparently transferred to her from the Celtic goddess Ceridwen. One of the three great saints of Ireland (with Patrick and Columba), she is patron saint of Leinster, and was also revered in Scotland. Her feast day is 1 Feb.

Bridget a female first name. [an Anglicized form of Old Irish *Brighid*; see BRIDE]

Bridgetown POP (1990) 6 000, the capital of Barbados. It is a port situated on Carlisle Bay in the SW of the island. A new deep-water harbour has been built to the NW, and the resort of

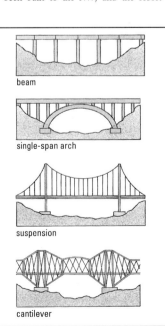

beam

single-span arch

suspension

cantilever

types of bridge

Paradise Beach is situated to the N. NOTABLE FEATURES cathedral; one of the earliest monuments commemorating Lord Nelson.

bridgework *Dentistry* a plate with false teeth, which is connected to the real teeth on either side of it (see BRIDGE[1] 6).

bridging loan a loan of money, usually from a bank, to cover the period between buying one house and selling another.

Bridgman, Percy Williams (1882–1961) US physicist, born in Cambridge, Massachusetts. Professor at Harvard, he designed equipment allowing experiments to test the strange properties of substances under unprecedentedly high pressures, demonstrating that under these conditions viscosity increases with pressure for most liquids. He also obtained a new form of phosphorus. In 1946 he was awarded the Nobel Prize for Physics.

Bridgwater POP (1981) 31 000, a town in Sedgemoor district, Somerset, SW England. It lies on the R Parret, 15km/9mi NE of Taunton. The town is the birthplace of Robert Blake (1598–1657), Oliver Cromwell's admiral. NOTABLE FEATURES Church of St Mary (14c); Admiral Blake Museum; the site of the battle of Sedgemoor (1685), where James VII defeated the Duke of Monmouth, is 6km/4mi to the E.

Bridie, James, pseudonym of **Osborne Henry Mavor** (1888–1951) Scottish dramatist, born in Glasgow. He became a successful doctor, writing a stream of plays, including *The Anatomist* (1931) and *A Sleeping Clergyman* (1933). He was also closely associated with the foundation of the Glasgow Citizen's Theatre.

bridle — *noun* **1** the leather straps on a horse's head which help the rider control the horse. **2** anything which controls or restrains. — *verb* **1** to put a bridle on (a horse). **2** to bring under control: *bridle one's anger*. **3** *intrans.* (*also* **bridle up**) to show anger or resentment by moving the head upwards proudly. [from Anglo-Saxon *bridel*]

bridle path *or* **bridle way** a path for riders and horses.

Bridlington POP (1981) 29 000, a port and resort town in E Yorkshire district, Humberside, NE England. It lies on the North Sea coast, 40km/25mi N of Hull.

Brie *noun* a French soft cheese. [from *Brie*, in NE France, where it is made]

brief — *adj.* **1** lasting only a short time. **2** short or small. **3** *said of writing or speech* using few words; concise. — *noun* **1** *Legal* **a** a summary of the facts and legal points of a case, prepared for the barrister who will be dealing with the case in court. **b** a case taken by a barrister. **c** *colloq.* a barrister: *who's your brief?* **2** instructions given for a job or task. **3** *RC Church* a letter from the Pope on a matter of discipline. — *verb* **1** to prepare a person by giving them instructions in advance: *we need to brief them in detail.* **2** *Legal* to inform a barrister about a case by brief.
— **hold no brief for someone** *or* **something** to decline to support or be in favour of them. [from Old French *brief*, from Latin *brevis*, short]

briefcase *noun* a light, usually flat case for carrying papers, etc.

Brief Encounter a British film directed by David Lean (1945). A series of chance meetings lead to an extra-marital relationship for an emotionally suppressed suburban housewife (played by Celia Johnson) and a doctor (played by Trevor Howard). It is based on Noël Coward's play *Still Life*.

briefing *noun* **1** a meeting at which instructions and information are given. **2** the instructions or information given at a meeting.

briefly *adv.* **1** using few words: *I will try to explain it briefly.* **2** for a short time: *visited her briefly at her house.*

briefness *noun* being brief, especially using few words; brevity.

brier see BRIAR[1], BRIAR[2].

Brig. *abbrev.* brigadier.

brig *noun* a type of sailing ship with two masts and square sails. [from BRIGANTINE]

brig

brigade *noun* **1** one of the divisions in the army, usually commanded by a brigadier. **2** a group of people organized for a particular purpose: *the fire brigade.* [a French word, from Old Italian *brigata*, company of soldiers]

brigadier *noun* **1** an officer commanding a brigade. **2** a staff officer of similar rank, above a colonel but below a major-general.

brigadier general in the US army, an officer ranking above a colonel.

brigand *noun* a member of a band of robbers, especially one operating in quiet mountain areas. [from French *brigand*, from Old Italian *brigante*, member of an armed band]

brigantine *noun* a type of sailing ship with two masts, with square sails on the main mast, and sails set lengthwise on the second mast. [from Old Italian *brigantino*, armed escort ship.]

Briggs, Barry (1934–) New Zealand speedway rider, born in Christchurch. He appeared in a record 17 consecutive world championship finals (1954–70), during which he scored a record 201 points and took part in 87 races, winning the title in 1957–8, 1964, and 1966. He won the British League Riders' championship six times (1965–70). His career started with Wimbledon (1952), and he also rode for New Cross, Southampton, Swindon, and Hull. He retired in 1976.

Briggs, Henry (1561–1630) English mathematician, born in Warley Wood, Halifax. Professor of Geometry at Gresham College, London, and at Oxford, he proposed the use of the base 10 for logarithms instead of the natural logarithm base used by John Napier. This was an important simplification for the practical use of logarithms in calculation.

Bright, John (1811–89) English Radical statesman and orator, born in Rochdale. He worked in his father's cotton mill, later becoming a leading member of the Anti-Corn-Law League (1839), and engaging in free trade agitation. He was MP for Durham (1843), Manchester (1847), and Birmingham (1857), and was closely associated with the Reform Act of 1867.

Bright, Richard (1789–1858) English physician, born in Bristol. In 1820 he joined the staff of Guy's Hospital, and made many important medical observations. His name is given to 'Bright's disease', in which the kidneys become inflamed.

bright — *adj.* **1** giving out or shining with much light. **2** *said of a colour* strong, light, and clear. **3** lively, cheerful. **4** (**bright at something**) clever and quick to learn it. **5** full of hope or promise: *a bright future.* — *adv.* brightly: *a fire burning bright.*
— **bright and early** very early in the morning.
look on the bright side to be cheerful and optimistic in spite of problems.
[from Anglo-Saxon *beorht*]

brighten *verb trans., intrans.* (*also* **brighten up**) **1** to make or become bright or brighter. **2** to make or become happier or more cheerful.

bright lights (**the bright lights**) a big city seen as a place of entertainment and excitement.

brightly *adv.* **1** with brightness. **2** with enthusiasm; cheerfully: *he said brightly that it would be no trouble.*

brightness *noun* being bright or shining, especially in physical senses: *the brightness of the walls took us aback.*

Brighton POP (1992e) 155 000, a resort town in Brighton district, East Sussex, SE England. It lies on the English Channel, 77km/48mi S of London. In 1782 the Prince of Wales (later George IV) took up residence here. Brighton is, today, a busy conference and tourist centre. NOTABLE FEATURES Royal Pavilion (1783), designed by John Nash; marina.

Brighton Rock a novel by Graham Greene (1938). It is set among the criminal fraternity of Brighton and tells of the tragic life of Pinkie, a 17-year old aspiring gang-leader.

bright spark *often derog.* a lively and eager young person.

Brigit *or* **Brighid** in Celtic mythology, an Irish goddess of fire, poetry, and crafts. In the Christian era a number of her attributes were taken over by St Bridget.

Brihadisvara Temple a Hindu temple at Thanjavur (formerly Tanjore), Tamil Nadu, India. It was founded by the Chola king Rajaraja I (985–1014) in the late 10c. It is renowned for its frescoes and for its 60m tower, encrusted with shrines and relief sculptures. It is a World Heritage site.

brill *noun* (PL. **brill, brills**) a European flatfish with white spots, related to the turbot.

Brillat-Savarin, Anthelme (1755–1826) French gastronome and lawyer, born in Belley. He became Mayor of Belley in 1793, but the Revolution forced him to flee to Switzerland, then to America, where he became a member of the Court of Cassation. His witty compendium of the art of dining, *La Physiologie du goût* (The Physiology of Taste, 1825), has been repeatedly republished and translated.

brilliance *or* **brilliancy** *noun* **1** being bright and sparkling. **2** outstanding intelligence or skill.

brilliant — *adj.* **1** very bright and sparkling. **2** *said of a colour* bright and vivid. **3** of outstanding intelligence or talent. **4** making a great display or show: *a brilliant display of flowers.* **5** *colloq.* excellent. — *noun* a diamond cut to have a lot of facets so that it sparkles brightly. [from French *briller*, to shine]

brilliantine *noun old use* a perfumed oil used by men to make the hair shiny. [from French *brillantine*, from *brillant*, shining]

brilliantly *adv.* with brilliance, especially with outstanding intelligence.

brim — *noun* **1** the top edge or lip of a cup, glass, bowl, etc. **2** the projecting edge of a hat. — *verb intrans.* (**brimmed, brimming**) to be full to the brim: *eyes brimming with tears.*
— **brim over** *intrans.* to become full and begin to overflow.
[from Middle English *brymme*]

brimful *or* **brim-full** *adj.* full to the brim.

brimless *adj.*, *said especially of a hat* not having a brim.

brimstone *noun old use* sulphur. [from Anglo-Saxon *bryne*, burning + STONE]

brimstone butterfly a common yellow butterfly.

Brindisi, ancient **Brundisium** POP (1990e) 93 000, the seaport capital of Brindisi province, Puglia, S Italy. It is situated on the Adriatic coast, 104km/65mi SE of Bari, and has both an inner and an outer harbour. HISTORY a centre of trade with the E Mediterranean since ancient times; used by the Crusaders as a naval base; the poet Virgil died here in 19 BC. NOTABLE FEATURES cathedral (11c, rebuilt in the 18c); Castello Svevo (1233).

brindled *adj.*, *said of animals* brown or grey, and marked with stripes of a darker colour. [from Middle English *brended*, from *brend*, burnt]

Brindley, James (1716–72) British engineer, born in Thornsett, Derbyshire. He devised a water engine for draining a coalmine and a silk mill on a new plan, and was employed (1759) to build the canal between Worsley and Manchester. In all he constructed 587km/365mi of canals. An illiterate, most of his problems were solved without writings or drawings.

brine *noun* **1** very salty water, used for preserving food. **2** *literary* the sea. [from Anglo-Saxon *bryne*]

bring *verb* (PAST TENSE AND PAST PARTICIPLE **brought**) **1** to carry or take (something or someone) to a stated or implied place or person. **2** to cause or result in: *war brings misery*. **3** to cause to be in or reach a certain state: *bring him to his senses / bring into effect*. **4** to make or force (oneself): *I can't bring myself to tell her*. **5** to be sold for; to produce as income. **6** to make (a charge) against someone: *bring a case against him*. **7** to give (evidence) to a court, etc.
— **bring something about** to cause it to happen.
bring something *or* **someone along 1** to bring or convey them with one. **2** to help something develop.
bring something back to cause a thought or memory to return.
bring something down to cause it to fall.
bring someone down to make them sad, disappointed, etc.
bring forth *formal* to give birth to or produce (an offspring).
bring something forward 1 to move an arrangement to an earlier date or time. **2** to draw attention to it.
bring something home to someone to prove or show it clearly.
bring the house down (of an actor, performer, etc) to receive ecstatic applause; to be brilliantly successful.
bring something in 1 to introduce it, make it effective, etc. **2** to produce income or profit.
bring something off *colloq.* to succeed in doing something difficult.
bring something on 1 to cause it to happen or appear. **2** to help it to develop or progress.
bring something out 1 to emphasize or clarify it. **2** to publish it.
bring someone out in spots, a rash, *etc* to cause them to be affected with spots or a rash: *cats bring me out in spots*.
bring someone over to convert them to one's own opinion, etc.
bring someone round 1 to cause them to recover consciousness. **2** to convince them that one's own opinions, etc are right.
bring someone to to cause someone who is asleep or unconscious to wake up.
bring something to mind to cause it to be remembered or thought about.
bring someone up to care for and educate them when young.
bring something up 1 to introduce a subject for discussion. **2** to vomit or regurgitate something eaten.
bring up the rear to come last or behind.
bring someone up short to cause them to stop suddenly.
[from Anglo-Saxon *bringan*]

brink *noun* **1** the edge or border of a steep, dangerous place or of a river. **2** the point immediately before the start of something dangerous, unknown, exciting, etc: *on the brink of new discoveries*. [probably from Danish *brink*, declivity]

brinkmanship *noun* *colloq.* the art of going to the very edge of a dangerous situation before moving back or withdrawing.

briny — *adj.* (**brinier, briniest**) *said of water* very salty. — *noun* (**the briny**) *colloq.* the sea.

brioche *noun* a type of bread-like cake made with a yeast dough, eggs, and butter. [from French *brioche*]

briquette *noun* a brick-shaped block made from coal dust, used for fuel. [from French *briquette*, little brick]

Brisbane POP (1990e) 1.3m, the state capital of Queensland, NE Australia. It lies on the Brisbane R. The city is the third largest in Australia and Brisbane statistical division has 10 suburbs. HISTORY founded as a penal colony in 1824; became state capital in 1859. NOTABLE FEATURES City Hall (1930); Lone Pine Koala Sanctuary; Botanical Gardens; Government House; Maritime Museum.

brisk *adj.* **1** lively, active, or quick: *a brisk walk*. **2** *said of the weather* pleasantly cold and fresh.

brisket *noun* the breast of an animal, especially of a bull or cow, when eaten as food. [from Middle English *brusket*]

briskly *adv.* with a lively or keen manner: *they responded briskly to our offer*.

briskness *noun* being brisk or lively.

brisling *noun* a small herring or sprat. [a Norwegian word]

Brissot de Warville, Jacques Pierre (1754–93) French revolutionary politician, born near Chartres. A writer on criminal law, in 1789 he was elected Representative for Paris in the National Assembly, where he influenced all the early movements of the Revolution. He established *Le Patriote français*, the organ of the earliest Republicans, and became leader of the Girondists (or Brissotins). In the Convention his moderation made him suspect to Robespierre and the Jacobins, and with other Girondists he was guillotined in Paris.

bristle — *noun* **1** a short stiff hair on an animal or plant. **2** something like this but man-made, used eg for brushes. — *verb* **1** *intrans., trans. said of hair* to stand or cause it to stand upright. **2** *intrans.* to show anger, rage, etc. **3** (**bristle with someone** *or* **something**) to be covered with or full of them. [from Anglo-Saxon *byrst*]

bristling *adj.*, *said of a beard, eyebrows, etc* thick and rough.

bristly *adj.* (**bristlier, bristliest**) **1** having bristles; rough. **2** likely to be or quickly get angry.

Bristol, ancient **Bricgstow** POP (1992e) 397 000, the county town, and administrative centre of Avon county, SW England. Situated 187km/116mi W of London, it is an important shipping centre, with ports at Avonmouth, Royal Avonmouth, Royal Portbury, and Portishead. HISTORY achieved county status in 1373; a major port in the 17c–18c, much involved in the slave trade. NOTABLE FEATURES cathedral (12c); Roman Catholic Cathedral (1973); St Mary Redcliffe (14c); Clifton Suspension Bridge (1864); the *SS Great Britain* rests restored where she was launched in 1843.

Bristol Channel an inlet of the Atlantic Ocean between Wales and England, length 128km/80mi (E–W). The channel's width varies greatly, from 5km/3mi to 80km/50mi at its mouth. It is an extension of the estuary of the R Severn, and has the greatest tidal range in England. Chief towns on the Welsh coast include Cardiff and Swansea, and on the English coast Ilfracombe and Weston-super-Mare.

Bristow, Eric, also called **the Crafty Cockney** (1957–) English darts player, born in London. He has been world professional champion a record five times (1980–81, 1984–6), and the beaten finalist five times. His other major championships include the World Masters (1977, 1979, 1981, 1983–4), the World Cup individual (1983, 1985, 1987, 1989), and the *News of the World* championship (1983–4).

Brit *noun colloq.* a British person.

Brit. *abbrev.* **1** Britain. **2** British.

Britain *or* **Great Britain** England, Scotland, and Wales. See UNITED KINGDOM.

Britain, Battle of the name given to the air war campaign of late summer 1940 in which the German Luftwaffe attempted to destroy the Royal Air Force (RAF) as a prelude to the invasion of Great Britain. The aerial offensive began in August; the German bomber aircraft and fighter escorts concentrated on wiping out the RAF both by combat in the air and by bombing their vital airfields in the south of the country. British resistance proved stubborn, with the Spitfires and Hurricanes of RAF Fighter Command being directed by radar on to the incoming bomber streams. The Luftwaffe switched their offensive from attacks on airfields to attacks on British cities (the 'Blitz'), losing their opportunity to gain true air superiority. Between 1 Jul and 31 Oct the Luftwaffe lost 2 848 aircraft to the RAF's 1 446.

Britannia *noun* a female warrior wearing a helmet and carrying a shield and a trident, used as an image or personification of Britain. [from Latin *Britannia*, Britain]

Britannia metal a silvery metal made from tin, copper, and antimony.

Britannic *adj. formal* of Britain: *His Britannic Majesty.* [from Latin *britannicus*, from *Britannia*, Britain]

British — *adj.* of Great Britain or its people. — *noun* (**the British**) people from Great Britain. [from Anglo-Saxon *Bryttisc*, from *Bryt*, Briton]

British Academy of Film and Television Arts see BAFTA.

British Actors' Equity Association see EQUITY.

British Antarctic Territory a British colonial territory which includes the South Orkney Is, the South Shetland Is, the Antarctic Graham Land Peninsula, and the land mass extending to the South Pole. AREA 5.7m sq km/2.2m sq mi. The land area is covered by ice and fringed by floating ice shelves; the peninsula is mountainous, rising to c.3 600m at Mt Jackson. The territory (which lies 20°–80°W and S of 60°S) is populated solely by scientists of the British Antarctic Survey. It is administered by a High Commissioner in the Falkland Is.

British Association for the Advancement of Science an organization founded in 1831 by a group of scientists disillusioned with the élitist and conservative attitude of the Royal Society. Its aims are to promote interest and progress in science.

British Board of Film Censors see BRITISH BOARD OF FILM CLASSIFICATION.

British Board of Film Classification (ABBREV. **BBFC**) in the UK, an organization founded as the British Board of Film Censors in 1912. Classification of films began with 'U' (suitable for a universal audience), 'A' (adults and accompanied children) and, from 1933, 'H' (horror, over 16s only). 'H' was replaced by 'X' (sex and horror) in the 1950s. In the 1960s 'X'-rated films were restricted to over-18s, 'ΛΛ' films were for over-14s only, and 'A' meant open to everyone though it carried a warning to parents. The latest ratings are: 'U' (universal); 'PG' (parental guidance required as some scenes may be unsuitable for some children); '12' (over-12s only); '18' (over-18s only); and 'R18' (distribution restricted to segregated premises where no one under 18 years is admitted). The BBFC is also responsible for the classification of television films and computer games.

British Broadcasting Corporation see BBC.

British Columbia POP (1991) 3.3m, a mountainous province in SW Canada, bordered S by the USA and W by the Pacific Ocean. AREA 947 800sq km/365 945sq mi. PHYSICAL DESCRIPTION the Rocky Mts lie to the E and the Coast Mts to the W; the largest islands are Queen Charlotte and Vancouver; the ranges are cut by the fertile valleys of the Fraser, Thompson, and Columbia rivers; there are many lakes, the largest of which are Williston, Okanagan, Kootenay, Kinbasket, and Arrow. HISTORY Captain Cook landed at Vancouver I in 1778; flourishing development of fur trade; the border with the USA was settled by the Oregon Treaty in 1846; in 1858 there was a gold rush to Fraser R; entered the Federation of Canada in 1871; the Canadian Pacific Railway was completed in 1885; the opening of the Panama Canal (1915) increased trade with Europe. GOVERNMENT governed by a Lieutenant-Governor and an elected 57-member Legislative Assembly. CAPITAL Victoria. CHIEF TOWNS Vancouver, Kamloops, Prince George, New Westminster, Burnaby. ECONOMY timber products; hydroelectric power; mining (coal, copper, silver, gold, molybdenum); oil and natural gas; fishing; dairy products; cattle; tourism.

British Council an organization founded in 1934 to spread the influence of British culture, ideas, and education. It has its headquarters in London, with 162 offices and staff based in 95 countries throughout the world.

British Empire there were several British Empires: the empire of commerce and settlement in the Caribbean and N America, founded in the 17c and partly lost when the 13 colonies declared their independence (1776); the empire in the East, founded in the 17c but developed through the extensive conquest of India (1757–1857) and the acquisition of islands, trading posts, and strategic positions from Aden to Hong Kong; the empire of white settlement in Canada, Australia, New Zealand and the Cape in South Africa, each of which had been federated as 'dominions' by 1910; and the 'dependent territories' in Africa and elsewhere acquired during the 'New Imperialism' of the last few decades of the 19c. There was also the British 'informal empire' – territories (eg parts of S America, the Middle East, the Persian Gulf, and China) which were not ruled directly, but which were influenced by the Empire's industrial and commercial power. By the late 19c the Empire was bonded together not only by industrial strength, but by its vast merchant marine and powerful navy. In 1919 the Empire reached its fullest extent through the acquisition of mandates over German and Ottoman territories in Africa and the Middle East. After World War I it was apparent that Britain could not control such an extensive empire: the dominions secured effective independence in 1931; the Middle Eastern mandates were virtually lost by World War II; India gained independence in 1947, and the other Asian colonies soon followed; while most of the rest of the Empire was decolonized in the 1960s. Many of the countries of the Empire remained in the British Commonwealth of Nations.

British Empire, Order of the in the UK, an order of knighthood, the first to be granted to both sexes equally, instituted (1917) by George V. Its five classes are: Knights and Dames Grand Cross (GBE), Knights and Dames Commanders (KBE/DBE), Commanders (CBE), Officers (OBE), and Members (MBE). The ribbon is pink, edged with grey, and recipients may come from any walk of life.

British Expeditionary Force (ABBREV. **BEF**) an army, first established in 1906, sent to France (Aug 1914 and Sep 1939) to support the French armies against German attack. In World War II, its total strength was 394 000, of whom 224 000 were safely evacuated, mainly from Dunkirk, in May–Jun 1940.

British Film Institute (ABBREV. **BFI**) in the UK, an organization founded in 1933 and aimed at promoting film both as entertainment and as a means of recording life in the UK. Partly subsidized by the government, it includes the National Film Archive, the National Film Theatre, and the Museum of the Moving Image and has an extensive library.

British Indian Ocean Territory a British territory in the Indian Ocean, 1 900km/1 180mi NE of Mauritius, consisting of the Chagos Archipelago. AREA 60sq km/23sq mi (land). The islands cover c.54 400sq km/21 000sq mi of ocean, in six main island groups, the largest of which is Diego Garcia. HISTORY acquired by France in the 18c; annexed by Britain in 1814; dependency of Mauritius until 1965. The territory was established to meet UK and US defence requirements in the Indian Ocean. There is a UK–US naval support facility on Diego Garcia.

British Legion see ROYAL BRITISH LEGION.

British Library the national depository created by the British Library Act of 1972 through the amalgamation of the British Museum Library, the National Central Library, and the National Lending Library for Science and Technology. Its reference division is based in London, housed mainly in the British Museum, though it is eventually to be moved to new premises in St Pancras, London; its lending division is based in W Yorkshire. It receives a free copy of every book published in Britain.

British Medical Association an association founded in 1832 to promote medical and related sciences, to maintain the honour of the profession, and to address matters such as education and conditions of service. Although cited as a trade union, it is not affiliated to the Trades Union Congress.

British Museum the national museum of archaeology and ethnography in Bloomsbury, London. It dates from 1753, when the collection of Sir Hans Sloane was acquired by the government. The Harleian and Cotton manuscript collections were added to the Sloane collection, forming the nucleus of the British Library, which is still partly housed in the British Museum, though it is eventually to be transferred to new premises in St Pancras, London. Since 1881 the natural history collection has been housed separately in what is now called the Natural History Museum. The ethnographical collections are housed in the Museum of Mankind, London.

British Open Golf Championship a major world golf tournament, held annually. It was first contested in Prestwick, Scotland (17 Oct 1860), and is now played over 72 holes at a different venue each year.

British Rail (ABBREV. **BR**) formerly known as **British Railways** the national railway system of Great Britain, created by the Transport Act (1947) which took the various railway companies into public ownership. The amount of track was greatly reduced (from 28 000km to 17 600km) between 1963 and 1975. Track reconstruction and electrification of lines resulted in faster journey times (eg a reduction of over an hour on the London–Edinburgh route). In 1994 the government split British Rail into 25 franchise areas for the provision of services by private companies.

British Summer Time the system of time used in Britain in the summer to give extra daylight in the evenings, one hour ahead of Greenwich Mean Time used the rest of the year.

British thermal unit Physics (ABBREV. **Btu**) the imperial unit of heat energy, equal to the amount of heat required to raise the temperature of one pound of water by one degree Fahrenheit. It is equivalent to 1054.5 joules or 252 calories.

Britomart the chaste female knight in Book III of Spenser's *The Faerie Queene*, whose quest is to seek out Artegall, the lover she has seen in a magic looking-glass.

Briton noun **1** one of the Celtic people living in S Britain before the Roman conquest. **2** a British person. [from Old French *breton*, from Latin *britto*]

Brittain, Vera (1893–1970) English writer, born in Newcastle-under-Lyme, Staffordshire. She served as a nurse in World War 1, recording her experiences in *Testament of Youth* (1933). She often lectured in the USA, wrote several novels and volumes of poetry, and two further volumes of autobiography, including *Testament of Friendship* (1940).

Brittan, Sir Leon (1939–) English Conservative politician. Called to the Bar in 1962, he was Chairman of the Conservative Bow Group (1964–5), editor of *Crossbow* magazine (1966–8), and elected an MP in 1974. He was a Minister in the Home Office (1979–81), Chief Secretary to the Treasury (1981–3), Home Secretary (1983–5), and Secretary for Trade and Industry (1985–6). In 1986 a conflict with Michael Heseltine (Secretary for Defence) over the takeover of Westland Helicopters led him to resign from the Cabinet. He became a Vice-President of the European Commission in 1989.

Brittany, French **Bretagne** POP (1991e) 2.8m, a region and former province of NW France, comprising the departments of Côtes-du-Nord, Finistère, Ille-et-Vilaine, and Morbihan. AREA 27 208sq km/10 502sq mi. PHYSICAL DESCRIPTION the prominent NW peninsula is bounded N by the English Channel and S by the Bay of Biscay; the coastline is rugged and striking; large tracts of heathland rise to 391m at Monts d'Arrée and 326m at Montagne Noire. HISTORY part of Roman Empire, following Julius Caesar's invasion in 56 BC; with the arrival of Celts from Britain in the 5c–6c came a distinctive culture and language (Breton). CAPITAL Rennes. CHIEF TOWNS Nantes, Lorient, Quimper, Brest. ECONOMY fishing; a major tourist area; the area is noted for its seafood, onions, artichokes, strawberries, and Breton Muscadet wine. NOTABLE FEATURE high concentration of megaliths.

Britten, (Edward) Benjamin Britten, Baron (1913–76) English composer, born in Lowestoft, Suffolk. During the 1930s he wrote incidental music for plays and documentary films. In the USA (1939–42), he wrote his Violin Concerto and the *Sinfonia da Requiem*. Back in the UK, his works were largely vocal and choral (eg *A Ceremony of Carols*, 1942), apart from such as *The Young Person's Guide to the Orchestra* (Variations and Fugue on a Theme of Purcell), and he helped to found the annual Aldeburgh Festival (1948). His operas include *Peter Grimes* (1945), *Billy Budd* (1951), *Gloriana* (1953), *A Midsummer Night's Dream* (1960), *Death in Venice* (1973), and several chamber operas and children's operas. A skilful pianist, he often accompanied Peter Pears.

brittle adj. **1** hard but easily broken or likely to break. **2** sharp or hard in quality: *a brittle laugh*. [from Anglo-Saxon *breotan*, to break in pieces]

brittle bone disease a disease which leaves the bones brittle and likely to break easily.

brittlely or **brittly** adv. so as to break easily.

brittleness noun being brittle or apt to break easily.

brittlestar Zool. a starfish-like member of the Echinodermata, with five slender mobile arms radiating from a disc-like body. Each arm bears a large number of suckers called *tube feet*, which aid movement over the sea bed. In some species the arms are branched.

BRN abbrev., as an international vehicle mark Bahrain.

Brno, German **Brünn** POP (1991) 388 000, the industrial capital of Jihomoravský region, Czech Republic. It lies at the junction of the Svratka and Svitava rivers. HISTORY founded in the 10c; became part of Bohemia in 1229 and a free city in 1243; formerly capital of the Austrian crownland of Moravia; the Bren gun was developed here.

NOTABLE FEATURES Spilberk Fortress; cathedral (15c); music conservatory.

broach — *verb* **1** to raise (a subject, especially one likely to cause arguments or problems) for discussion. **2** to open (a bottle or barrel, etc) to remove liquid. **3** to open and start using the contents of: *broach a new bottle*. — *noun* **1** a tool for making holes. **2** a roasting-spit. [from Middle English *broche*]

B-road *noun Brit.* a road of secondary importance.

broad — *adj.* **1** large in extent from one side to the other. **2** wide and open; spacious. **3** general, not detailed: *a broad inquiry.* **4** clear: *in broad daylight.* **5** strong; obvious: *a broad hint.* **6** main: *the broad facts.* **7** tolerant or liberal: *take a broad view.* **8** *said of an accent or speech* strongly marked by local features: *broad Scots.* **9** *usually said of a joke, anecdote, etc* rather rude and vulgar. — *noun* **1** the broad part of anything. **2** *North Amer., esp. US offensive slang* a woman. **3** (**Broads**) see BROADS, THE. [from Anglo-Saxon *brad*]

broad-based *adj.* including a wide range of opinions, people, political groups, etc.

broad bean a large flat green bean which contains large flat white seeds that can be eaten.

broadcast — *verb* (PAST TENSE AND PAST PARTICIPLE **broadcast**) **1** *trans., intrans.* to send out (a programme) by radio or television. **2** to make (something) widely known. **3** to scatter (seed) by hand. — *noun* a television or radio programme. — *adv.* **1** communicated or sent out by radio or television. **2** widely known or scattered. [from BROAD + CAST]

broadcaster *noun* a person who takes part in broadcasts, especially on a regular or professional basis.

broadcasting *noun* the transmission of radio and television programmes.
◇ From its beginnings in the 1920s, broadcasting, whether of a commercial or 'public service' variety, quickly established itself at regional, national, and international levels as a popular source of information and entertainment. It has always been subject to controls, the severity of which has varied according to the political character of the country concerned. National controls have been undermined in recent years with the advent of satellite broadcasting and increasing competition between broadcasters.

broadcloth *noun* a thick cloth of good quality made from wool, cotton, or silk.

broaden *verb trans., intrans.* (**broadened**, **broadening**) (*also* **broaden out**) to make or become broad or broader.

broad gauge a railway track wider than the standard size.

broadloom *adj., said especially of a carpet* woven on a wide loom to give broad widths.

broadly *adv.* widely; generally: *broadly speaking.*

broad-minded *adj.* tolerant of others' opinions, etc.

broad-mindedly *adv.* with tolerance; fairly, liberally.

broad-mindedness *noun* being broad-minded; tolerance.

Broadmoor a special high-security hospital for the criminally insane, established in 1863 near Camberley, Berkshire.

broadness *noun* being broad, especially extensive in scope, taste, etc.

Broads, The an area of low-lying and shallow lakes in East Anglia, E England. The lakes are flooded peat pits which were excavated during the 11c–12c. Flooding occurred during a period of climatic deterioration from the 13c. There are over 150mi/90km of navigable waterways. It is a popular holiday area with important nature reserves.

broadsheet *noun* **1** a large sheet of paper usually printed on one side only, for advertisements, etc. **2** a newspaper printed on large sheets of paper. See also TABLOID.

broadside *noun* **1** the firing of all guns on one side of a warship. **2** a strong verbal attack.
— **broadside on** sideways.

Broadstairs POP (1981) 22 186, a resort town in Thanet district, Kent, SE England. It lies SE of Margate, on the English Channel. NOTABLE FEATURE Bleak House, where Charles Dickens wrote *David Copperfield.*

broadsword *noun* a heavy sword with a broad blade, used for cutting rather than stabbing.

Broadway the name of a street in New York (25km/15.5mi long), which since the 1890s has become famous as a symbol of commercial theatre in the USA. In recent years the area has become run-down, although the theatres remain.

Broadway Boogie-Woogie a painting by Piet Mondrian (1942–3, New York). It is one of his more colourful and lively abstracts, reflecting the rhythm of city life.

Broadwood, John (1732–1812) Scottish maker of pianos and harpsichords, born in Cockburnspath, Berwickshire. He became the partner of the Swiss Burkat Shudi in London, and later took control of the firm (1782), which became a well-known family business during the next century.

Broca, Paul Pierre (1824–80) French surgeon and anthropologist, born in Sainte-Foy-le-Grande, Gironde. He first located the motor speech centre in the brain and did research on prehistoric surgical operations.

brocade *noun* a heavy silk material with a raised design on it. [from Italian or Spanish *broccato*, from *brocco*, twisted thread or spike]

brocaded *adj., said of material* woven with a brocade design on it.

Broca's area *Anat.* the region of the brain responsible for speech, located in the left frontal lobe in most right-handed people. [named after the French physician Pierre Paul Broca]

broccoli *noun* a variety of cauliflower with green or purple flower-like heads growing on thick branches. [from Italian *broccoli*, sprouts]

brochure *noun* a short book or pamphlet giving information about holidays, products, etc. [from French *brocher*, to stitch]

broderie anglaise a technique of decorating cotton and linen by making patterns with tiny holes and stitches. [French, = English embroidery]

Brodie, Miss Jean see PRIME OF MISS JEAN BRODIE, THE.

Brodsky, Joseph (1940–) Russian poet of Jewish parents, born in Leningrad (now St Petersburg). He began writing poetry in 1955, was convicted as a 'social parasite', and went into exile in the USA. He was naturalized in 1977, and

appointed Professor of Literature at Mount Holyoke College, Massachusetts (1986–). Writing in both Russian and English, his collections include *A Stop in the Desert* (1970), *A Part of Speech* (1980), *Urania* (1988), and *Watermark* (1992). He was awarded the Nobel Prize for Literature in 1987, and became US Poet Laureate in 1991.

Broglie, Louis-Victor Pierre Raymond de, 7th Duke (1892–1987) French physicist, born in Dieppe. Professor at the Sorbonne, he suggested that particles could exhibit wave-like properties and predicted some characteristics of such waves, later detected experimentally by Clinton Davisson and Lester Germer, and independently by George Thomson. He was awarded the 1929 Nobel Prize for Physics.

brogue¹ *noun* a type of strong outdoor shoe. [from Gaelic *bròg*, shoe]

brogue² *noun* a strong but gentle accent, especially of the Irish speaking English.

broil *verb chiefly North Amer.* to grill (food). [from Old French *bruiller*, to burn]

broiler *noun* **1** a small chicken suitable for broiling. **2** *North Amer.* a grill. **3** *colloq.* a very hot day.

broke *adj. colloq.* having no money.
— **go for broke** to risk all one has left in a last attempt at success. [old past participle of BREAK]

broken *adj.* **1** smashed, fractured. **2** disturbed or interrupted: *broken sleep.* **3** not working properly. **4** *said of a promise, agreement, etc* not kept. **5** *said of language, especially speech* not perfect or fluent. **6** weak or tired, especially through illness. [from BREAK]

broken chord *noun Mus.* an arpeggio.

broken-down *adj.* **1** not in working order. **2** not in good condition or good health.

broken-hearted *adj.* overwhelmed with sadness or grief.

broken-heartedly *adv.* with overwhelming sadness or grief.

Broken Hill POP (1991) 23 000, a mining town in Far West statistical division, New South Wales, SE Australia. Silver, lead, and zinc are mined in the area. The town is a centre of the trade union movement and is administered by the Barrier Industrial Council. HISTORY School of the Air founded in 1956; base for the Royal Flying Doctor Service since 1938. NOTABLE FEATURE 19c Afghan Mosque.

broken home a home that has been disrupted by the separation or divorce of parents.

broken-in *adj.* **1** *said of an animal* made tame through training. **2** *said of shoes, etc* made comfortable by being worn.

brokenly *adv., said of language* imperfectly; without fluency.

brokenness *noun* being broken; a broken state.

broken reed a weak person that can no longer be relied on.

broker *noun* **1** a person employed to buy and sell shares for others (see also STOCKBROKER). **2** a person who buys and sells secondhand goods. [from Old French *brocour*]

brokerage *noun* the profit or fee charged by a broker.

broking *noun* the trade or business of a broker.

brolly *noun* (PL. **brollies**) *Brit. colloq.* an umbrella. [a shortening of UMBRELLA]

bromeliad *noun Bot.* any plant belonging to the pineapple family (Bromeliaceae). Bromeliads are particularly common in the canopy of tropical rainforests, and most of them are epiphytes, ie they grow on other plants (but not as parasites). They typically have large strap-shaped fleshy

brittlestar

leaves that form a rosette around a central cup in which water accumulates and is then slowly absorbed by hairs on the leaves of the plant. The cup also provides an ideal habitat for certain insects, amphibians, and aquatic plants. Bromeliads are native to tropical and subtropical regions of N, Central and S America, although several species are widely grown as ornamental house plants.

bromide *noun* **1** *Chem.* any chemical compound that is a salt of hydrobromic acid (HBr). Various bromides are used as sedatives in medicine, and silver bromide is used to coat photographic film. **2** a much-used and now meaningless statement or phrase. [from BROMINE + -IDE]

bromide paper a type of paper with a surface which has been coated with silver bromide to make it sensitive to light, used for printing photographs.

bromine *noun Chem.* (SYMBOL **Br**, ATOMIC NUMBER **35**) a non-metallic element consisting of a dark red highly corrosive liquid with a pungent smell, that gives off a reddish-brown vapour. It is extracted from sea-water and salt deposits, and its compounds are used in photographic film, water purification, anti-knock petrol additives, and in the manufacture of plastics and organic chemicals. [from Greek *bromos*, stink]

bronchial *adj.* relating to the two large air tubes, the bronchi, in the lungs, or the smaller tubes they divide into.

bronchitic — *adj.* relating to or suffering from bronchitis. — *noun* a person suffering from bronchitis.

bronchitis *noun Medicine* inflammation of the mucous membrane of the bronchi (the two main airways to the lungs), which often also affects the throat, larynx, and bronchioles.

◇ The symptoms of *acute bronchitis*, which is caused by bacterial or viral infection (especially after exposure to low temperatures), are coughing, contraction and narrowing of the bronchi, and fever. Such attacks are usually severe and of short duration, whereas *chronic bronchitis*, which is associated with swelling of the bronchial mucous glands and with cigarette smoking and air pollution, causes persistent coughing up of mucus, and lasts for relatively long periods. It tends to recur, and is a common cause of death in the UK, due in part to the climate.

bronchodilator *noun Medicine* any drug or other agent that relaxes the smooth muscle of the bronchi, causing the air passages in the lungs to widen. Bronchodilators are used in the treatment of asthma and chronic bronchitis.

bronchus *noun* (PL. **bronchi**) *Anat.* either of the two main airways to the lungs that branch off the lower end of the trachea (windpipe). [from Greek *bronchus*, windpipe]

bronco *noun* (PL. **broncos**) a wild or half-tamed horse from the western USA. [from Spanish *bronco*, rough]

Brongniart, Alexandre (1770–1847) French naturalist, chemist and geologist, born in Paris. He was professor at the Sorbonne and Museum of Natural History in Paris, and also director of the porcelain factory at Sèvres. He introduced the term *Jurassic* for the limestones and clays of the Cotswolds.

Bronowski, Jacob (1908–74) Mathematician, poet, and humanist, born in Łódź, Poland. He became a lecturer at University College, Hull (1934–42), and later Director of the Coal Research Establishment of the National Coal Board, overseeing the development of smokeless fuel. He was a popular broadcaster, particularly on the BBC's *Brains Trust* and *The Ascent of Man* (1973).

Brontë, Anne, pseudonym **Acton Bell** (1820–49) English poet and novelist, born in Thornton, Yorkshire. She worked as a governess, and shared in the joint publication, under pseu-

donyms, of the three sisters' *Poems* (1846). Her two novels are *Agnes Grey* (1845) and *The Tenant of Wildfell Hall* (1848).

Brontë, Charlotte, pseudonym **Currer Bell** (1816–55) English novelist, born in Thornton, Yorkshire. She worked in England and Brussels as a teacher, and her chance discovery of Emily's poems (1845) led to the joint publication under pseudonyms of the three sisters' *Poems* (1846). Her first novel *The Professor* was published posthumously (1857). Her most famous novel *Jane Eyre* appeared in 1847, and was followed by *Shirley* (1849). She died at Haworth during pregnancy, leaving the fragment of another novel, *Emma*.

Brontë, Emily (Jane), pseudonym **Ellis Bell** (1818–48) English novelist and poet, born in Thornton, Yorkshire. She became a governess in Halifax (1837), attended the Héger Pensionat in Brussels with Charlotte (1842), and in 1845 embarked with her sisters upon a joint publication of their poetry, after Charlotte discovered her *Gondal* verse. She is best-known for her single novel *Wuthering Heights* (1847).

brontosaurus *noun* the former name for *apatosaurus*. [from Greek *bronte*, thunder + *sauros*, lizard]

Bronx *or* **the Bronx** POP (1990) 1.2m, a mainland borough of N New York City and county in New York State, NE USA. AREA 109sq km/42sq mi. [named after Jonas Bronck, an early Dutch settler]

bronze — *noun* **1** a mixture of copper and tin. **2** the dark red-brown colour of bronze. **3** a work of art made of bronze. — *adj.* **1** made of bronze. **2** of the colour of bronze. — *verb* **1** to give a bronze colour or surface to: *sun bronzing the skin.* **2** *intrans.* to become the colour of bronze. [a French word]

Bronze Age (*usually* **the Bronze Age**) the period in the history of mankind when tools, weapons, etc were made out of bronze, between about 3000 and 1000 BC.

bronzed *adj.* having a bronze colour; suntanned.

bronze medal a medal given to the person who comes third in a race, etc.

brooch *noun* a decoration or piece of jewellery, fastened to clothes by a pin. [from Middle English *broche*]

brood — *noun* **1** a number of young animals, especially birds, that are produced or hatched at the same time, or that are being cared for by adults. **2** *often humorous* all the children in a family. — *verb intrans.* **1** *said of a bird* to sit on eggs in order to hatch them. **2** (**brood about** *or* **on** *or* **over something**) to think anxiously or resentfully about it for a period of time. **3** (**brood over someone**) to be imminent or threatening. [from Anglo-Saxon *brod*]

broodily *adv.* with a broody or sullen manner.

broodiness *noun* a broody or sullen manner.

brooding *adj.* thinking anxiously or resentfully about something.

broodingly *adv.* with brooding or sullen thoughts: *sat broodingly over his coffee.*

broody *adj.* (**broodier, broodiest**) **1** *said of a bird* ready and wanting to brood. **2** deep in anxious thought. **3** *colloq., said of a woman* eager to have children.

Brook, Peter (Stephen Paul) (1925–) English theatre and film director, born in London. His work with the Royal Shakespeare Company in the 1960s was innovative, and his successes were international, notably *King Lear* (1962), *Marat/Sade* (1964), *US* (1966), and *A Midsummer Night's Dream* (1970). In 1970 he founded the International Centre of Theatre Research in Paris. Among his films are *Lord of the Flies* (1962) and *Meetings with Remarkable Men* (1979).

brook[1] *noun* a small stream. [from Anglo-Saxon *broc*]

brook[2] *verb* to tolerate or accept: *brook no criticism.* [from Anglo-Saxon *brucan*, to enjoy]

Brooke, Dorothea the saintly heroine of George Eliot's *Middlemarch.*

Brooke, Rupert (Chawner) (1887–1915) English poet, born at Rugby. His *Poems* appeared in 1911, and *1914 and Other Poems* was published posthumously in 1915. He died and was buried on Skyros, after contracting blood-poisoning on his way to serve as a commissioned officer in the Dardanelles. He was a popular poet among young people in the interwar period.

Brookeborough, Basil Stanlake Brooke, 1st Viscount (1888–1973) Irish politician and Prime Minister of Northern Ireland, born in Fermanagh. A staunch supporter of union with Great Britain, he was elected to the Northern Ireland parliament in 1929, became Minister of Agriculture (1933), Commerce (1941–5), and then Prime Minister (1943–63).

Brooklyn POP (1990) 2.3m, a borough of New York City, co-extensive with Kings County, New York State, USA. AREA 182sq km/70sq mi. This major port, situated at the SW corner of Long Island, was incorporated into New York City in 1898. It is linked to Staten I by the Verrazano Bridge, and to Manhattan by the Brooklyn Bridge. NOTABLE FEATURES Brooklyn Institute of Arts and Sciences (1823); New York Naval Shipyard (1801), now in civilian use.

Brooklyn Bridge a suspension bridge built (1869–83) across East River from Brooklyn to Manhattan I, New York City. It has a main span of 486m.

Brooks, Mel, originally **Melvin Kaminsky** (1926–) US film actor and director, born in New York City. After working as a gag-writer and comic, he made his cinema début as writer–director of *The Producers* (1967). A number of zany comic spoofs followed, among them *Blazing Saddles* (1974) and *Silent Movie* (1976). He usually writes the script, directs, and acts in his productions. Later films include *High Anxiety* (1977) and he co-produced *The Fly* (1986).

broom *noun* **1** a brush with a long handle for sweeping the floor. **2** a wild shrub of the pea family, with yellow flowers. [from Anglo-Saxon *brom*]

Broome, David (1940–) Welsh show jumper, born in Cardiff, Wales. He won the world championship on *Beethoven* in 1970, was three times European champion, on *Sunsalve* (1961) and *Mister Softee* (1967, 1969), and was the individual bronze medallist at the 1960 and 1968 Olympics. He returned to the British Olympic team in 1988 after a 20-year absence.

broomrape *noun* an annual or perennial plant, belonging to the genus *Orobanche*, that is a parasite and lacks chlorophyll. Dense spikes of brownish flowers appear above ground, and the leaves are reduced to scales. Despite its name, broom is not the only host of this plant, and it will parasitize ivy and members of the daisy family. It is found mainly in warm temperate regions of the Old World.

broomstick *noun* the long handle of a broom.

Bros. *abbrev.* Brothers, especially in the name of a company.

broth *noun* a thin, clear soup made by boiling meat, fish, or vegetables. [from Anglo-Saxon *broth*]

brothel *noun* a house where men pay money for sexual intercourse with women. [from Middle English *brothel*, worthless person, prostitute]

brother *noun* (PL. **brothers**) **1** a boy or man with the same parents as another person or people. **2** a man belonging to the same group, society, church, trade union, etc as another or others. **3** (PL. ALSO **brethren**) a man who is a member of a religious group, especially a monk. [from Anglo-Saxon *brothor*]

brotherhood *noun* **1** the state of being a brother. **2** friendliness felt towards people one has something in common with. **3** an association of men for a particular, especially religious, purpose.

brother-in-law *noun* (PL. **brothers-in-law**) **1** the brother of one's husband or wife. **2** the husband of one's sister. **3** the husband of the sister of one's own wife or husband.

brotherly *adj.* like a brother; kind, affectionate.

Brothers Karamazov, The a novel by Fyodor Dostoevsky (1880). The first part of an unfinished trilogy, it attempts to show the strength of human charity and solidarity in the face of suffering and humiliation.

brougham *noun* a type of light closed carriage pulled by four horses, with a raised open seat for the driver. [named after Lord Brougham (1778–1868)]

brought see BRING.

brouhaha *noun* noisy, excited, and confused activity. [from French *brouhaha*]

brow *noun* **1** (*usually* **brows**) an eyebrow. **2** the forehead. **3** the top (of a hill, road, pass, etc). **4** the edge (of a cliff, etc). [from Anglo-Saxon *bru*]

browbeat *verb* (PAST TENSE **browbeat**; PAST PARTICIPLE **browbeaten**) to frighten (someone) by speaking angrily or looking fierce; to bully.

browbeaten *adj.* bullied and intimidated.

Brown, Sir Arthur Whitten (1886–1948) British aviator, born in Glasgow, Scotland, of US parents. He trained as an engineer, and was the companion of John William Alcock on the first transatlantic flight (1919). He later became manager of an engineering company.

Brown, Father the unassuming priest with an instinctive talent for criminal detection in G K Chesterton's short stories, collected in *The Innocence of Father Brown* and other books.

Brown, Ford Madox (1821–93) British historical painter, born in Calais, France. He produced the dramatic *Manfred on the Jungfrau* (1841) in Paris. A visit to Italy (1845) led him to seek a greater richness of colouring, as in *Chaucer reciting his Poetry* (1851). Later works include *Work* (Manchester) and *The Last of England* (1855, Birmingham).

Brown, Jim, properly **James (Nathaniel)** (1936–) US footballer, born in St Simons, Georgia. He spent all of his career with the Cleveland Browns, was three times the National Football League's top scorer (1958–59, 1963), and led the NFL eight times in rushing (1957–65). After his retirement as a footballer, he had roles in several films.

Brown, John (1800–59) US militant abolitionist, born in Torrington, Connecticut. He had many different jobs while wandering through the country advocating antislavery. He was twice married and had 20 children. In 1859 he led a raid on the US Armory at Harper's Ferry in Virginia, intending to launch a slave insurrection. The raid failed and he was convicted of treason against Virginia and hanged. The song 'John Brown's Body' commemorates the Harper's Ferry raid, and was popular with Republican soldiers in the Civil War.

Brown, Lancelot, also known as **Capability Brown** (1716–83) British landscape gardener, born in Kirkharle, Northumberland. His gardens, such as those at Blenheim Palace, Kew, Stowe, and Warwick Castle, are characterized by an imitation of nature, and contrast with the formal continental style. His nickname arose from his habit of saying that a place had 'capabilities'.

Brown, Robert (1773–1858) Scottish botanist, born in Montrose. He was educated at Aberdeen and Edinburgh, and in 1801 travelled to Australia, bringing back nearly 4 000 species of plants. In 1831 he was the first to recognize the nucleus as the basis of a cell. He also discovered the effect later known as 'Brownian movement'.

brown — *adj.* **1** of the colour of dark soil or wood. **2** made from wholemeal flour and therefore darker in colour than white bread. **3** having a dark skin or complexion. **4** having a skin tanned from being in the sun. — *noun* **1** any of various dark colours similar to bark, tanned skin, coffee, etc. **2** brown paint, dye, material or clothes. — *verb trans., intrans.* to make or become brown by cooking, burning in the sun, etc. — **browned off** *colloq.* **1** bored; fed up. **2** discouraged. [from Anglo-Saxon *brun*]

brown alga *noun* (PL. **algae**) *Bot.* any alga belonging to the class Phaeophyceae, characterized by the presence of a brown pigment known as fucoxanthin, which masks the green pigment chlorophyll. Most brown algae are marine species, eg the kelps.

brown bear a bear widespread in the N hemisphere, and having a thick brown coat and a pronounced hump on its shoulders. In N America it prefers open habitats, and in the Old World it inhabits forest.

brown dwarf *Astron.* a hypothetical very cool 'star' with a mass that is intermediate between that of a planet and a small star. Its mass would be too low for nuclear reactions to be ignited in its core. No brown dwarfs have yet been identified with certainty, although a number of candidates have been suggested.

Browne, Robert (c.1550–1633) English Puritan separatist churchman, born in Tolethorpe, Rutland. A schoolmaster and open-air preacher, in 1580 he began to attack the established Church, and soon after formed a distinct Church on congregational principles in Norwich. In 1581 he and his followers (Brownists) were forced to flee to Holland, but in 1584 he returned and was reconciled with the Church. From the age of 80 he was in jail for assault, until his death.

Browne, Sir Thomas (1605–82) English writer, born in London. He studied medicine and travelled in Europe before settling in Norwich where he was knighted in 1671. His major work is the *Religio Medici* (c.1635), revealing a deep insight into the spiritual life. Other works include *Pseudodoxia Epidemica, or Enquiries into...Vulgar and Common Errors* (1646).

Brownian movement *or* **Brownian motion** *Physics* the ceaseless random movement of small particles suspended in a liquid or gas. It is caused by the continual bombardment of the particles by molecules of the liquid or gas, which are in a state of constant agitation. [named after Robert BROWN]

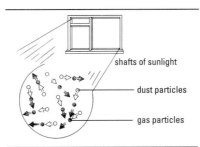

shafts of sunlight

dust particles

gas particles

Brownian movement

brownie *noun* **1** *Folklore* a friendly goblin or fairy. **2** (**Brownie** *or* **Brownie Guide**) a young member of the Girl Guides in Britain or of the Girl Scouts in the US. **3** *North Amer., esp. US* a small square chocolate cake with nuts.

Brownie Guider a woman in charge of a group of Brownie Guides.

brownie point *colloq.* a mark of approval earned by doing something good, useful, etc.

Browning, Elizabeth Barrett (1806–61) English poet, born in Durham. She seriously injured her spine as a teenager, and was an invalid for a long time. Her first poems were published at 19, and subsequent volumes appeared in 1838 and 1844. In 1845 she met Robert Browning, with whom she eloped in 1846. Her best-known work is *Sonnets from the Portuguese* (1850).

Browning, Robert (1812–89) English poet, born in London. His early work attracted little attention until the publication of *Paracelsus* (1835). *Bells and Pomegranates* (1841–6) include several of his best-known dramatic lyrics (eg 'My Last Duchess' and 'The Pied Piper of Hamelin'). In 1846 he married Elizabeth Barrett, and with her settled in Florence, where their son, Robert Barrett (1849–1912), the sculptor, was born. After the death of his wife (1861) he settled in London, where he wrote *The Ring and the Book* (1869).

browning *noun Brit.* a substance used to turn gravy brown.

Browning automatic rifle a gas-operated light machine-gun designed by US gunsmith John Moses Browning (1855–1926) in 1917, and produced in various countries until 1950. The weapon had a 20-round magazine and an effective range of 600m.

Browning Version, The a play by Terence Rattigan (1948). It is a one-act psychological study depicting a repressed classics teacher's relationships with his adulterous wife, one of her lovers, and a thoughtful schoolboy.

brownish *adj.* somewhat brown in colour.

brownness *noun* a brown state or colour.

brown owl 1 the tawny owl. **2** (**Brown Owl**) same as BROWNIE GUIDER.

brown paper very thick brown-coloured paper used eg for wrapping up parcels sent through the post.

brown rice rice which has not had its outer covering removed.

Brownshirt *noun* **1** a member of the Nazi Brownshirts. **2** a member of any fascist organization.

Brownshirts, official name *Sturmabteilungen* (**SA**) German Nazi storm troopers, formed in 1920, who by late 1931 had expanded to 500 000. They developed a radical, pseudo-socialist outlook under Ernst Röhm, and after the Nazi accession to power (1933), challenged the autonomy of the German army, but were crushed in the 'Night of the Long Knives' (30 Jun 1934), and superseded by the SS (*Schutzstaffel*, Hitler's bodyguard).

brown study 1 deep thought. **2** absent-mindedness.

brown sugar sugar which has not been completely refined and which has kept some of its original brown colour.

Brownsville POP (1990) 99 000, the seat of Cameron County, S Texas, USA. It is a port on the Rio Grande, opposite Matamoros, Mexico. HISTORY the establishment of Fort Texas here (1846) led to the Mexican War; renamed Fort Brown after Major Jacob Brown who died commanding its defence; the town, which grew up around the fort, served as an important Confederate port during the Civil War. It is the trade, processing, and distributing centre for the irrigated lower Rio Grande valley.

Brown University in the USA, a university in Providence, Rhode Island, founded in 1764 as Rhode Island College; it was renamed in 1804. It became co-educational in 1971 after merging with Pembroke College.

browse — *verb* **1** *intrans., trans.* to read a book or look around casually or haphazardly. **2** *intrans., trans. said of animals* to feed by nibbling on plants. **3** *Comput.* to read through data consecutively, as if it were a book. — *noun* **1** an act of browsing. **2** young shoots, twigs, leaves, etc used as food for cattle. [from Old French *brost*, new shoot]

BRS *abbrev.* British Road Services.

BRU *abbrev., as an international vehicle mark* Brunei.

Bruce, Sir David (1855–1931) Australian-born Scottish microbiologist and physician, born in Melbourne. As an officer in the Royal Army Medical Corps (1883–1919), he identified in Malta the bacterium that causes undulant fever in humans, named *Brucella* (1887). In 1895 in South Africa he discovered that the tsetse fly was the carrier of the parasite responsible for the cattle disease nagana and sleeping sickness in humans. The cattle disease brucellosis is named after him.

Bruce, James, known as **the Abyssinian** (1730–94) Scottish explorer, born in Larbert, Stirlingshire, Scotland. After serving as Consul-General at Algiers (1763–5), in 1768 he set out from Cairo on his journey to Abyssinia, and in 1770 reached the source of the Blue Nile. He returned to Scotland, where he published his *Travels to Discover the Sources of the Nile* (1790).

Bruce, Lenny, originally **Leonard Alfred Schneider** (1925–66) American comedian, born in New York City. His mainly improvised act often ferociously attacked hypocrisy, but his satirical, 'black' humour often transgressed the conventional rules of respectability and in 1961 he was imprisoned for obscenity.

Bruce, Robert (1274–1329) hero of the Scottish War of Independence. As Earl of Carrick, in 1296 he swore loyalty to Edward I of England, but soon joined the Scottish revolt under Wallace. In 1306, after a quarrel with his political rival, John Comyn, in which he stabbed Comyn to death, he assembled his vassals and was crowned king at Scone. He was forced to flee to Ireland, but returned in 1307 and defeated the English at Loudoun Hill. After Edward's death (1307), the English were forced from the country and all the great castles recovered except Berwick and Stirling. This led to Scottish victory at the battle of Bannockburn (1314), but sporadic war with England continued until the Treaty of Northampton (1328), which recognized the independence of Scotland, and Bruce's right to the throne.

Bruce a male first name, from the Scottish surname, common in Australia. [origin obscure]

brucellosis *noun Agric.* an infectious disease, mainly associated with cattle, in which it causes reduced milk yields, infertility, and abortion of calves. It can be transmitted to humans, as undulant fever, by contact or by consumption of unpasteurized milk. [from *Brucella*, the name of the bacterium causing the disease]

Brücke, die the name adopted by a group of avant-garde artists active in Dresden, (1905–13). Unlike the more abstract Blaue Reiter group, they painted portraits, landscapes, and figurative subjects in a crude, harsh style based on van Gogh and Gauguin. They also produced bold and expressive woodcuts and prints. Leading members included Ernst Ludwig Kirchne (1880–1938), Karl Schmitt-Rottluff (1884–1976), Erich Heckel (1883–1970), and slightly later, Emil Nolde (1867–1956) and Max Pechstein (1881–1955). [German, = the bridge]

Bruckner, Anton (1824–96) Austrian composer and organist, born in Ansfelden. He held several posts as organist, and became Professor of Composition at the Vienna Conservatory (1868–91). His fame rests chiefly on his nine symphonies (the last unfinished), but he also wrote four impressive masses, several smaller sacred

works, and many choral works. His music shows the influence of Wagner and Schubert; it received a mixed reception during his lifetime.

Brueghel, Pieter see BREUGHEL, PIETER.

Bruges, Flemish **Brugge** POP (1992e) 117 000, a port and the capital town of Brugge district and of West Flanders province, NW Belgium. It lies 12km/8mi S of Zeebrugge. Known as the 'Venice of the north', it is connected by canals to several cities and the North Sea. Bruges was the chief market town of the Hanseatic League and a major centre of the woollen and cloth trade. It remains a traditional centre for lace and is one of the best-preserved medieval cities in Europe. NOTABLE FEATURES Gothic town hall (1376–1420), Chapel of the Holy Blood, Church of Our Lady (12c–13c), market hall (13c–14c), with a belfry.

Brugge see BRUGES.

bruise — *noun* an area of skin discoloration and swelling caused by the leakage of blood from damaged blood vessels following injury. The colour of a bruise changes from red to pink to bluish and finally greenish-yellow as the blood pigment haemoglobin breaks down chemically. — *verb* **1** to mark and discolour (the surface of the skin) in this way. **2** *intrans.* to develop bruises. **3** *trans., intrans.* to hurt or be hurt emotionally or mentally. [from Anglo-Saxon *brysan*, to crush, and Old French *bruiser*, to break]

bruised *adj.* **1** affected by bruising. **2** emotionally hurt.

bruiser *noun colloq.* a big strong person, especially one who likes fighting.

bruising *noun* dark-coloured marks which show on bruised skin.

bruit *verb* (**bruit something about** *or* **around**) *old use* to spread or report news, rumours, etc. [from French *bruit*, noise]

brûlé *adj., said of food* having brown sugar on top and cooked so that the sugar melts. [French, = burnt]

Brummell, George Bryan, also called **Beau Brummell** (1778–1840) English dandy, a leader of early 19c fashion, born in London. Known at Oxford for the exquisiteness of his dress and manners, he became a leader of early 19c fashionable society, and for 20 years had the Prince Regent (later George IV) as friend and admirer. Forced to flee to France (1816) due to a quarrel and gambling debts, he had varied fortune thereafter, and died in a pauper lunatic asylum in Caen.

brunch *noun colloq.* a meal eaten late in the morning combining breakfast and lunch. [from *breakfast* + *lunch*]

Brunei, official name **State of Brunei Darussalam** (**Islamic Sultanate of Brunei**) POP (1992e) 270 000, a state on the NW coast of Borneo, SE Asia, divided into four districts. AREA 5 765sq km/2 225sq mi. It is bounded by the S China Sea in the NW, and on all other sides by Sarawak state. The Limbang R valley in Sarawak divides the state into two sections. CAPITAL Bandar Seri Begawan (formerly Brunei Town). CHIEF TOWNS Kuala Belait, Seria. TIME ZONE GMT +8. Ethnic groups include Malay (65%) and Chinese (20%); Islam is the official religion. OFFICIAL LANGUAGE Malay; English is widely spoken. CURRENCY the Brunei dollar. PHYSICAL DESCRIPTION swampy coastal plain rising through foothills to a mountainous region on the Sarawak border; equatorial rainforest covers 75% of the land area. CLIMATE tropical climate, with high temperatures and humidity, and no marked seasons; average daily temperature ranges between 24°C and 30°C; annual average rainfall is 2 540mm on the coast, doubling in the interior. HISTORY formerly a powerful Muslim sultanate, the whole island was given the name Borneo by the Europeans; under British protection in 1888; achieved internal self-government in 1971; gained independence in 1983. GOVERNMENT a constitutional

monarchy with the Sultan as head of state, advised by a Privy Council, and a Council of Ministers. ECONOMY largely dependent on oil (discovered in 1929) and gas resources; main crops are rice, bananas, peppers; some rubber and timber.

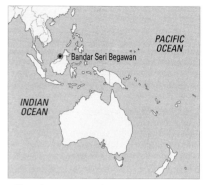

Brunei

Brunel, Isambard Kingdom (1806–59) English engineer and inventor, born in Portsmouth. He worked in his father Marc Isambard Brunel's office, and helped to plan the Thames Tunnel. He himself designed the Clifton Suspension Bridge (1829–31, completed in 1864) and the Hungerford Suspension Bridge (1841–5) over the Thames. He designed the *Great Western* (1838), the first steamship built to cross the Atlantic, the *Great Britain* (1845), the first ocean screw-steamer, and the *Great Eastern*, until 1899 the largest vessel ever built. He was also appointed engineer to the Great Western Railway, and constructed many docks and harbours.

Brunel, Sir Marc Isambard (1769–1849) French engineer and inventor, born in Hacqueville. He fled from the French Revolution in 1793, going first to the USA, where he was architect and chief engineer in New York. He settled in England in 1799, constructed many public works, and solved many of the problems of underwater tunnelling. His main achievement was the 460m Thames Tunnel from Rotherhithe to Wapping (1825–43).

Brunelleschi, Filippo (1377–1446) Italian Renaissance architect, born in Florence. He trained first as a goldsmith and sculptor before his failure in 1402 to win the competition for the second door of the Florence Baptistry led him to architecture. In Florence he designed the dome for the Cathedral (1417–34), the Ospedale degli Innocenti (1419), and the Church of San Lorenzo (1418 onwards).

brunette *noun* a woman with brown or dark hair and a fair skin. [from French *brunette*, from *brun*, brown]

Brunhild *or* **Brunhilde** *or* **Brynhild** in Norse mythology, a Valkyrie (Maiden of Odin) who has assumed human form. In the *Volsungasaga*, Odin places her behind a wall of flame where she lies in an enchanted sleep until she is woken by Sigurd. Tricked into marrying Gunnar, Sigurd's brother-in-law, she has Sigurd killed and finally kills herself on his funeral pyre. In the similar German *Nibelungenlied*, she is the wife of Gunther.

Bruno, Frank (1961–) English boxer, born in London. He won the ABA heavyweight championship when he was 18. In Oct 1985 he took the European championship, and in Jul 1986 he challenged for the WBA heavyweight world championship, but lost to the holder, Tim Witherspoon. He was also unsuccessful in his second attempt at the title, against Mike Tyson in Feb 1989. In 1993 he unsuccessfully challenged Lennox Lewis for the WBC world title. He has latterly become involved in pantomime and television.

Bruno (of Cologne), St (c.1030–1101) German churchman and founder of the Carthusian order, born in Cologne. He was Rector of the cathedral school at Reims, but withdrew in 1084 to the wild mountains of Chartreuse, near Grenoble, where with six friends he founded the austere Carthusian order. In 1091 he established a second monastery at La Torre, Calabria. His feast day is 6 Oct.

Bruno, Giordano (1548–1600) Italian hermetic thinker, born in Nola, near Naples. He was a Dominican, but his opinions forced him to flee to Geneva (1578), then to Paris (1581) and London (1583). He travelled throughout Europe until 1591, when he was arrested by the Inquisition and, after an eight-year trial, burnt in Rome. His philosophy was pantheist and sympathetic to Copernicus's theory of the universe. Among his works are *De l'infinito universo et mondi* (On the Infinite Universe and Worlds, 1584) and *Spaccio de la bestia trionfante* (The Expulsion of the Triumphant Beast, 1584).

Brunswick, German **Braunschweig** POP (1991e) 259 000, the capital of Brunswick district, Lower Saxony province, central Germany. It is a manufacturing and commercial city on the R Oker. It was capital of the duchy of Brunswick before being incorporated into Lower Saxony in 1946. NOTABLE FEATURES Romanesque cathedral (12c); castle (12c); town hall (14c–15c).

brunt *noun* the main force or shock of a blow, attack, etc: *his wife bore the brunt of his anger.* [Middle English, of unknown origin]

brush — *noun* **1** a tool with lengths of stiff nylon, wire, hair, bristles, etc, for tidying the hair, cleaning, painting, etc. **2** an act of brushing. **3** a short fight or disagreement: *a brush with the law.* **4** a fox's brush-like tail. **5** *Engineering* a metal or carbon conductor that maintains sliding contact between the stationary and moving parts of an electric motor or generator. **6** brushwood. — *verb* **1** (*also* **brush something down**) to rub it with a brush or other object to remove dirt, dust, etc. **2** (**brush something on** *or* **away, off,** *etc*) to apply or remove with a brush or brushing movement. **3** (**brush against something**) to touch it lightly in passing.
— **brush something aside** to pay no attention to it; to dismiss it as unimportant.
brush something off to refuse to listen to it; to ignore it.
brush up to make oneself clean, tidy one's appearance, etc.
brush something up *or* **brush up on something** to improve or refresh one's knowledge of a subject, language, etc.
[from Old French *brosse*, brushwood]

brushed *adj.*, *said of a material* treated by a brushing process so that it feels soft and warm: *brushed cotton.*

brush fire a fire of dead and dry bushes and trees, which usually spreads quickly.

brush-off *noun colloq.* an abrupt dismissal; a rebuff or rejection.

brush-up *noun* a tidying or cleaning up.

brushwood *noun* **1** dead and broken branches, etc from trees and bushes. **2** small trees and bushes on rough land. **3** rough land covered by such trees and bushes.

brushwork *noun* the particular way a painter has of putting paint on to canvas.

brusque *adj.* blunt and often impolite in manner. [from French *brusque*, from Italian *brusco*, sour]

brusquely *adv.* bluntly; impolitely.

brusqueness *noun* a brusque or blunt manner.

Brussels, Flemish **Brussel**, French **Bruxelles**, ancient **Broucsella** POP (1992e) 951 000 (excluding suburbs), the capital city of Belgium, and of Brabant province, central Belgium. It is divided into the Lower Town, intersected by several branches of the R Senne, and the Upper Town, set on the crest of the hills to the E. The inner city is surrounded by 18 suburbs with independent administrations. Brussels is linked to the North Sea by the Willebroek Canal. A major medieval wool centre, later the capital of the Spanish and Austrian Netherlands, it is today an important commercial, industrial, and cultural city. The headquarters of many international organizations are located in Brussels, such as the EC and NATO. The linguistic frontier between Flemings and Walloons runs just S of the city; officially Brussels is bilingual, but French predominates in the centre, and Flemish in the suburbs. NOTABLE FEATURES Royal Military School; several royal academies of fine arts and royal conservatories; town hall (15–18c); royal palace (1827–9, rebuilt in 1905); Palais de la Nation (1779–83); cathedral (13–15c); Church of Notre-Dame de la Chapelle (begun in 1210); Mannekin Pis; Mini Europe; Atomium; the largest cinema complex in the world.

Brussels, Treaty of 1 a treaty (1948) of economic, social, and cultural collaboration and collective self-defence signed by Belgium, France, Luxembourg, the Netherlands, and the UK. It was superseded by the Treaty of Paris and the Western European Union. **2** a treaty which enabled Britain, Denmark, and Ireland to join the European Economic Community. They had applied with Norway to join in 1961, but further negotiations had been vetoed by President de Gaulle (1963). Fresh negotiations followed his resignation (1969) however, and the treaty was signed, but Norway failed to ratify following a referendum.

Brussels sprout *noun* (*usually* **Brussels sprouts**) a small round cabbage-like bud, eaten as a vegetable. [first grown near *Brussels*, capital of Belgium]

brutal *adj.* **1** savagely cruel or violent. **2** ruthlessly harsh. [from Latin *brutalis*]

Brutalism *or* **New Brutalism** an architectural concept of the 1950s, in which the buildings often have large distinct blocks of exposed concrete. It is typified by the work of Le Corbusier and by his British followers James Stirling, William Gowan, and Alison and Peter Smithson.

brutality *noun* (PL. **brutalities**) **1** a brutal act. **2** brutal behaviour or treatment.

brutalization *or* **brutalisation** *noun* making brutal; brutal treatment.

brutalize *or* **brutalise** *verb* **1** to make brutal. **2** to treat brutally.

brutally *adv.* with a brutal or cruel manner.

brute — *noun* **1** an animal other than man. **2** a cruel and violent person. — *adj.* **1** not able to use reason or intelligence. **2** coarse and animal-like. [from Latin *brutus*, heavy, irrational]

brute force sheer physical strength, with no thought or skill.

brutish *adj.* of or like a brute.

brutishly *adv.* with cruelty or violence.

brutishness *noun* being brutish; cruelty.

Brutus, Marcus Junius (c.85–42 BC) Roman soldier and a leader of the group who assassinated Julius Caesar. He sided with Pompey when the civil war broke out (49 BC), but was pardoned by Caesar and appointed Governor of Cisalpine Gaul (46 BC). Cassius prevailed on him to join the conspiracy against Caesar (44 BC). He was defeated by Antony and Octavian at Philippi (42 BC), and committed suicide.

Bruxelles see BRUSSELS.

Bryggen a town in Bergen, SW Norway. It was probably founded in the 11c, and retains a large number of traditional wooden gabled buildings. It is a World Heritage site.

Bryn Mawr College a college for women opened in 1855 by the Society of Friends in Bryn Mawr village, Pennsylvania. It was one of the first women's colleges in the USA to offer graduate degrees. Since 1937 the graduate school has been open to men.

Bryony *or* **Briony** a female first name. [from the Greek plant name *bryonia*]

bryony *noun* (PL. **bryonies**) a climbing plant with green-white flowers and either red or black berries, usually found in hedges. [from Latin *bryonia*]

Bryophyta *noun Bot.* one of the main groups of the vegetable kingdom, consisting of mosses and liverworts. [from Greek *bryon*, moss, liverwort + *phyton*, plant]

bryophyte *noun Bot.* any plant belonging to the division Bryophyta of the plant kingdom, which includes mosses (Musci) and liverworts (Hepaticae).
◇ Bryophytes are generally small primitive plants without a vascular system. They are mainly terrestrial, but very vulnerable to desiccation, and so are largely restricted to damp or humid habitats. Bryophytes show *alternation of generations*, in which a visible free-living *gametophyte* (which bears gametes), capable of carrying out photosynthesis, alternates with a *sporophyte* (which bears spores) that is partly or completely dependent on the gametophyte for nutrients and water. They have rudimentary organs resembling roots, known as *rhizoids*, that anchor the plant in the ground.

Brythonic — *noun* one of two distinct branches of the early Celtic language of Britain, also known simply as British. Brythonic developed from c.4c BC with the second wave of Celtic-speaking people from Europe who settled in S England and Wales. In the 6c AD, the invading Anglo-Saxons pushed these British Celts to the west and north where the regional variations, Cornish, Welsh, and Cumbric, developed. A similar movement from S England into Brittany led to the related variation, Breton. — *adj.* relating to Brythonic.

BS *abbrev.* **1** Bachelor of Surgery. **2** *as an international vehicle mark* Bahamas. **3** British Standard(s): marked on manufactured goods that conform to an acceptable standard.

BSc. *abbrev.* Bachelor of Science.

BSE *abbrev.* bovine spongiform encephalopathy.

BSI *abbrev.* British Standards Institution, an organization which controls the quality and safety of manufactured goods, etc.

B-side *noun* the side of a two-sided gramophone record that is less actively promoted.

BSkyB *abbrev.* British Satellite Broadcasting.

BSL *abbrev.* British Sign Language.

BSM *abbrev.* British School of Motoring.

BST *abbrev.* British Summer Time.

BT *abbrev.* British Telecom.

Bt. *abbrev.* Baronet.

BTA *abbrev.* British Tourist Authority.

BTEC *abbrev.* Business and Technician Education Council.

bubble 1 a thin film of liquid forming a ball round air or gas, especially one which floats in liquid: *soap bubbles.* **2** a ball of air or gas which has formed in a solid: *an air bubble in glass.* **3** a dome made of clear plastic or glass. **4** an unrealistic or over-ambitious plan or scheme. — *verb intrans.* **1** to form or rise in bubbles. **2** (**bubble away**) to make the sound of bubbling liquid: *water bubbling away in the pan.*
— **bubble over** *intrans.* **1** to boil over. **2** to be full of happiness, excitement, enthusiasm, good ideas, etc: *they're bubbling over with excitement.* [from Middle English *bobel*]

bubble and squeak *Brit.* cold cooked cabbage and potatoes mixed together and then fried.

bubble bath a scented liquid which is put into bath water to make bubbles.

bubble chamber *Physics* a device for making visible the paths of charged particles through a liquid; devised in 1952 by Donald Glaser. Liquid hydrogen, kept heated just above its boiling point, becomes superheated if the applied pressure is suddenly released. Bubbles of vapour are formed on the ions produced by the passage of charged particles through the chamber; if the bubbles are suitably illuminated they may be photographed for later analysis.

bubble gum a type of chewing gum which can be blown into bubbles.

bubble-jet *noun* a type of ink-jet printer which heats the ink to form a bubble, which bursts and projects the ink on to the paper.

bubble memory a type of computer memory in which information is stored in magnetic bubbles which move through a layer of magnetized material.

bubble pack a clear plastic bubble, usually on cardboard, in which goods for sale are packed.

Bubbles a painting by Sir John Everett Millais (1886). It was used for a soap advertisement and became one of his best-known works.

bubbly — *adj.* (**bubblier**, **bubbliest**) **1** having or being like bubbles. **2** very lively and cheerful and full of high spirits. — *noun colloq.* champagne.

Buber, Martin (1878–1965) Jewish theologian and philosopher, born in Vienna. He was founding editor of *Der Jude* (1916–24, The Jew), Professor of Comparative Religion at Frankfurt (1923–33), then Director of the Central Office for Jewish Adult Education until 1938 when he fled to Palestine. He became Professor of the Sociology of Religion at Jerusalem, and his most influential work as a figure of religious existentialism was the early *Ich und Du* (I and Thou, 1922).

Bubka, Sergei (1963–) Ukrainian field athlete, born in Donetsk. He made his international début as a pole-vaulter at the 1983 world championship in Helsinki, where he won the gold medal. He retained this title in 1987, 1991, and 1993, and also won gold at the 1988 Olympics. In 1992, he took the world pole vault record to 6.12m.

bubo *noun* (PL. **buboes**) an inflamed swelling, especially in the armpit or groin. [from Latin *bubo*, swelling]

bubonic plague an often fatal infectious disease which causes buboes, and which is spread by fleas from rats.

Bucaramanga POP (1992e) 349 000, the capital of Santander department, N central Colombia, NE of Bogotá. It is situated in the Cordillera Oriental, 1 018m above sea level. The city, founded in 1622, is known as the 'garden city of Colombia'. NOTABLE FEATURES Parque Santander; Parque García Romero; amusement park.

buccal *adj. Anat.* relating to the mouth or the inside of the cheek. [from Latin *bucca* cheek]

buccaneer *noun* a pirate, especially one who attacked Spanish ships in the Caribbean during the 17c. [from French *boucanier*]

buccaneering *noun* pirating; unscrupulous adventuring.

Buchan, John, 1st Baron Tweedsmuir (1875–1940) Scottish writer and statesman, born in Perth. He was called to the Bar in 1901, and served on HQ staff during World War I (1916–17), before becoming Director of Information. He was MP for the Scottish Universities (1927–35), and was made a baron in 1935, when he became Governor-General of Canada (until 1940). In 1937 he became a Privy Councillor and Chancellor of Edinburgh University. The author of over 50 books, he is best known for his fast-moving adventure stories, including *Prester John* (1910), *The Thirty-nine Steps* (1915, his best-known work), and *Greenmantle* (1916).

Buchanan, George (1506–82) Scottish scholar and humanist, born near Killearn, Stirlingshire. He was imprisoned for writing a satirical poem on the Franciscans, but escaped to France (1539), and took up teaching there and in Portugal (1547), where he was arrested as a suspected heretic. Released in 1552, he returned to Scotland in 1561, and was tutor to Mary, Queen of Scots. He abandoned Mary after the death of Darnley (1567), became tutor to James VI, and keeper of the privy seal (1570–8). His works include an attack on the divine right of monarchs *De juri regni apud Scotos* (1579), and a Latin paraphrase of the Book of Psalms, which was used as a textbook until the 19c.

Buchanan, James (1791–1868) US statesman, the 15th President, born in Stony Batter, Pennsylvania. He was admitted to the Bar (1812), became a Senator (1834), Secretary of State (1845), and Democratic President (1857–61). He tried to maintain a balance between pro-salvery and anti-slavery but his attempts at compromise failed to avert the Civil War (1861–5) and he retired from politics in 1861.

Buchanan, James M (1919–) US economist, born in Murfreesboro, Tennessee. He has held numerous chairs since 1950, and is currently Professor of Economics at George Mason University (1983–), and since 1969 has been Director of the Center for Public Choice. He was awarded the Nobel Prize for Economics in 1986 for his work on the theories of public choice.

Bucharest, Romanian **Bucureşti**, ancient **Cetatea Dâmboviţei** POP (1992) 2.1m, the capital of Romania and its largest city, situated in the SE of the country on the R Dâmboviţ. HISTORY founded in the 14c; an important commercial centre on the trade route to Constantinople; it became capital of the principality of Wallachia in 1698 and capital of Romania in 1861; badly damaged by German bombing during World War II. NOTABLE FEATURES Domnita Baleasa Church (18c), St George Church (17c), Palace of the Republic, Palace of St Synod, Athenaeum arts and music centre.

Bucharest, Treaties of two treaties (1812 and 1913) concerning Balkan nationhood. The 1812 Russo-Turkish treaty concluded the Serbian revolt (begun in 1804), granted Serbia autonomy within the Ottoman Empire, and paved the way for Serbian independence (1878). The August 1913 treaty ended the second Balkan War during which Bulgaria had fought Greece, Serbia, and Romania over the division of their joint conquests in Macedonia from their defeat of Turkey in the first of the Balkan Wars (1912–13). Its terms, which involved Bulgaria's surrender of N Macedonia to Serbia, S Macedonia to Greece, and the S Dobrudja to Romania, dissolved any prospect of a 'Greater Bulgaria'.

Buchenwald a German concentration camp established near Weimar in Aug 1937. Among its 239 000 internees (of whom 56 000 died) were many Soviet and Polish prisoners of war as well as German political detainees. Liberated by the US Army in Apr 1945, Buchenwald subsequently passed under Soviet control and served as an internment camp until 1950.

Buchman, Frank (Nathan Daniel) (1878–1961) US evangelist, founder of the 'Group' and 'Moral Rearmament' movements, born in Pennsburg, Pennsylvania. He was a Lutheran minister in charge of a hospice for under-privileged boys in Philadelphia (1902–7), travelled extensively in the East, and in 1921 was led by his fear of the potential collapse of civilization to found the 'First Century Christian Fellowship' in Oxford. It was labelled the 'Oxford Group' until 1938, when it adopted the slogan 'Moral Rearmament'. After World War II the movement emerged in a more political guise as an alternative to capitalism and communism.

Buchner, Eduard (1860–1917) German chemist, born in Munich. He was awarded the 1907 Nobel Prize for Chemistry for demonstrating that alcoholic fermentation is due not to physiological processes but to chemical processes in yeast.

Büchner, Georg (1813–37) German poet and dramatist, born in Goddelau, Darmstadt. He studied medicine, but after the Paris rising of 1830 he published a pamphlet (1834) advocating economic and political revolution, and had to flee to Zürich. His best-known works are the poetical dramas *Dantons Tod* (Danton's Death, 1835) and *Woyzeck* (1837), on which Alban Berg based his opera *Wozzeck*.

Buck, Pearl S(ydenstricker) (1892–1973) US novelist, born in Hillsboro, West Virginia. She was brought up in China and was later a teacher and missionary there. Her many novels include *The Good Earth* (1931, Pulitzer Prize), the first of a trilogy about China. Other works include *The Patriot* (1939), *Dragon Seed* (1942), and five novels written under the pseudonym of John Sedges. She was awarded the Nobel Prize for Literature in 1938.

Buck, Peter Henry, also called **Te Rangi Hiroa** (1879–1951) New Zealand Maori scholar and writer. He practised medicine, was an MP (1909–14), served in World War I, then became an anthropologist. In 1927 he joined the Bishop Museum in Honolulu, Hawaii, and was Director there from 1936 until his death.

buck¹ — *noun* **1** the male of some animals, especially the rabbit, hare, or deer. **2** a lively young man. **3** an act of bucking. — *verb* **1** *intrans. said of a horse* to make a series of rapid jumps into the air, with the back arched and legs held stiff, especially in an attempt to throw a rider. **2** *said of a horse* to throw (a rider) from its back in this way. **3** *colloq.* to oppose or resist (an idea, etc.). — **buck up** *colloq.* **1** to become more cheerful. **2** to hurry. **buck someone up** to make them more cheerful. **buck something up** to improve one's ways, ideas, etc. [from Anglo-Saxon *bucca*]

buck² *noun North Amer. colloq.* a dollar. — **make a fast** *or* **quick buck** to make money quickly and often dishonestly. [perhaps from BUCKSKIN: deer-skins were used as a unit of exchange by Native Americans and frontiersmen in the 19c in the US]

buck³ *noun* **1** an item placed before the person who is to deal next in poker. **2** *colloq.* the responsibility, especially to deal with a problem: *pass the buck*. [from *buckhorn knife*, an item which used to be used as a buck in poker]

bucked *adj. Brit. colloq.* pleased and encouraged.

bucket — *noun* **1** a round open-topped container for holding or carrying liquids, sand, etc. **2** the amount a bucket will hold. **3** the scoop of a dredging machine. — *verb intrans.* (**bucketed**, **bucketing**) *colloq.* (*also* **bucket down**) *said of rain* to pour down heavily. — **kick the bucket** *slang* to die. **rain buckets** to rain hard and continuously. **weep buckets** weep long and bitterly. [from Anglo-Saxon *buc*]

bucketful *noun* (PL. **bucketfuls**) the amount a bucket will hold.

bucket seat a small seat with a round back, for one person, eg in a car.

bucket shop 1 *Brit. colloq.* a travel agent which sells cheap airline tickets. **2** an office where one may deal in shares, gamble on the money market, etc.

Buckingham, George Villiers, 1st Duke of (1592–1628) English statesman and court favourite, born in Brooksby, Leicestershire. Following several other honours, he was made Duke by James I in 1623, the year he failed to negotiate the marriage of Prince Charles (the future Charles I) to the daughter of the Spanish king, but he later succeeded in arranging the marriage to Henrietta Maria of France. The abortive expedition against Cadiz (1625) exposed him to impeachment by the Commons, and only a dissolution rescued him. An expedition against France failed (1627), and while planning a second attack, he was assassinated by a discontented subaltern.

Buckingham, George Villiers, 2nd Duke of (1628–87) English statesman, born in London. After his father's assassination, he was brought up with Charles I's children, and went into exile after the Royalist defeat in the Civil War. His estates were recovered at the Restoration, and he became a member of the cabal under Charles II. He was instrumental in Clarendon's downfall (1667), but lost power to Arlington, and was dismissed in 1674 for alleged Catholic sympathies.

Buckingham Palace the 600-room residence of the British sovereign in London, rebuilt by John Nash in 1825 for George IV, on the site of his parents' home, Buckingham House. It remained unused until Queen Victoria's accession in 1837. The front façade was redesigned in 1913 by Aston Webb.

Buckinghamshire POP (1992e) 646 000, a county in S central England, divided into five districts. AREA 1 883sq km/727sq mi. It is bounded N by Northamptonshire, E by Bedfordshire and Hertfordshire, SE by Greater London, S by Berkshire, and W by Oxfordshire. PHYSICAL DESCRIPTION drained by the Ouse and Thames rivers; crossed in the S by the Chiltern Hills; there is extensive woodland. CHIEF TOWNS Aylesbury (county town), Bletchley, Buckingham, High Wycombe, Milton Keynes. ECONOMY mainly agriculture, also furniture, bricks, printing, high technology.

buckle — *noun* a flat piece of metal attached to one end of a strap or belt, with a pin in the middle which goes through a hole in the other end of the strap or belt to fasten it. — *verb* **1** *trans.*, *intrans.* to fasten or be fastened with a buckle. **2** *trans.*, *intrans.* said of metal to bend or become bent out of shape, especially as a result of great heat or force.
— **buckle down** or **to** to begin working seriously at something.
buckle under *intrans.* to collapse under strain. [from Old French *boucle*, from Latin *buccula*, cheek-strap of a helmet]

buckled *adj.*, *said of metal* bent out of shape, especially from heat or force.

buckler *noun* a small round shield. [from Old French *bocler*, from *bocle*, boss (round knob)]

Buckley, William F(rank), Jr (1925–) US political writer and editor, born in New York City. He founded the conservative political journal *National Review* in 1955, and made it the primary voice of the intellectual US right. He ran unsuccessfully for Mayor of New York in 1963, and is a prolific author of fiction and non-fiction works, from *God and Man at Yale* (1951) to *The End of the Affair* (1992).

buckminsterfullerene *Chem.* (FORMULA **C₆₀**) an almost spherical molecule, thought to be an ingredient of soots. Each of its carbon atoms is bonded to three others, so that the surface of the molecule consists of 12 pentagons and 20 hexagons. — Also called *buckyball*. [named after Buckminster FULLER]

buckram *noun* stiffened cotton or linen, used to line clothes or cover books. [from Middle

English *bukeram*, perhaps from *Bukhara*, a town in central Asia once noted for its textiles]

Bucks *abbrev.* Buckinghamshire.

buckshee *adj.*, *adv. slang* free of charge. [from BAKSHEESH]

buckshot *noun* large lead shot used in hunting.

buckskin *noun* **1** the skin of a deer. **2** a soft leather made from deer-skin.

buckthorn *noun* a thorny shrub with berries which supply a green dye used by painters.

bucktooth *noun* a tooth which sticks out in front.

bucktoothed *adj.* having projecting front teeth.

buckwheat *noun* a type of small black grain used for feeding animals or made into flour. [from Dutch *boekweit*, beech wheat, from the shape of the seeds]

buckyball *Chem.* common name for buckminsterfullerene.

bucolic — *adj.* concerned with the countryside or people living there; pastoral. — *noun* a poem about the countryside. [from Greek *boukolos*, herdsman]

bucolically *adv.* with reference to the countryside or pastoral life.

bud — *noun* **1 a** in a plant, an immature knob-like shoot, often enclosed by protective scales, that will eventually develop into a leaf or flower. **b** a flower or leaf that is not yet fully open. **2** in yeasts and simple animals, a small outgrowth from the body of the parent that becomes detached and develops into a new individual capable of independent existence. **3** in an embryo, an outgrowth from which a limb develops. — *verb intrans.* (**budded**, **budding**) **1** to put out buds. **2** *Bot.* to reproduce asexually by the production of small outgrowths from the body of the parent, which become detached and develop into new individuals.
— **in bud** producing buds.
nip something in the bud to put a stop to an activity or plan at an early stage.
[from Middle English *budde*]

Budapest POP (1991e) 2m, the capital of Hungary and its largest city, situated in Pest county on the R Danube. It comprises old-world Buda on the W bank hills, on the site of the Roman colony of Aquinum, and modern Pest on the E bank. HISTORY a major cultural and trading centre in the 15c; Buda and Pest were unified in 1873; scene of the 1956 popular uprising, crushed by Soviet troops. NOTABLE FEATURES St Matthias Church (13c), Royal Palace, Parliament Building, museum of fine arts, national theatre, opera house; Buda Castle and the banks of the Danube are a World Heritage site.

Budd, Billy see BILLY BUDD.

Budd, Zola see PIETERSE, ZOLA.

Buddha (the enlightened one) (c.563–c.483 BC) the title of Prince Gautama Siddhartha, the founder of Buddhism, born the son of the rajah of the Sakya tribe ruling in Kapilavastu, Nepal. When about 30, he left the luxuries of the court, his beautiful wife, and all earthly ambitions for the life of an ascetic; after several years of severe austerities he saw in the contemplative life the perfect way to self-enlightenment. He taught for around 40 years, and gained many disciples and followers.

Buddh Gaya or **Bodh Gaya** a village and sacred Buddhist site in Bihar, India. Since the 3c BC, shrines have marked the spot where Gautama Buddha attained enlightenment.

Buddhism *noun* the religion founded by the Buddha, Gautama, in the 6c BC, which teaches spiritual purity and freedom from human concerns. [from Sanskrit *budh*, to awaken, notice or understand]

◇ Buddhist teaching is summarized in the Four Noble Truths, the last of which (the Eightfold Path) affirms the existence of a path leading to deliverance from the universal human experience of suffering. A central tenet is the law of *karma*, by which good and evil deeds result in appropriate reward or punishment in this life or in a succession of rebirths, a chain which can be broken by obedience to the right path.
The Buddha's path to deliverance is through morality (*sila*), meditation (*samadhi*), and wisdom (*panna*), as set out in the Eightfold Path. The goal is nirvana, which means 'the blowing out' of the fires of all desires, and the absorption of the self into the infinite.
There are two main traditions within Buddhism. Theravada Buddhism adheres to the strict and narrow teachings of the early Buddhist writings: salvation is possible for only the few who accept the severe discipline and effort necessary to achieve it. Mahayana Buddhism is more liberal, and makes concessions to popular piety: it teaches that salvation is possible for everyone, and introduced the doctrine of the Bodhisattva (or personal saviour).
The only complete canon of Buddhist scripture is the Pali canon, named after the language in which it is written.
It forms the basic teaching for traditional Theravada Buddhism, but other schools have essentially the same canon written in Sanskrit.

Buddhist *noun* a person who practises Buddhism. *adj.* relating to Buddhism.

budding *adj.* **1** developing, beginning to show talent: *a budding pianist*. **2** the formation of buds on a plant shoot, or the artificial propagation of a plant by grafting of a bud. **3** a method of asexual reproduction involving the production of one or more outgrowths or buds that develop into new individuals.

buddleia *noun* a shrub with long spikes of purple, white or yellow flowers, attractive to butterflies. [named after the English botanist Adam Buddle (d.1715)]

buddy — *noun* (PL. **buddies**) **1** North Amer. colloq. a friend or companion. **2** a volunteer who helps care for a person suffering from AIDS. — *verb* (**buddies**, **buddied**) **1** *intrans. colloq.* (usually **buddy up**) to become friendly. **2** *trans.* to help care for (someone suffering from AIDS). [perhaps from *butty*, companion]

buddy movie *colloq.* a film, usually with two central characters, exploring male or female camaraderie.

Budge, Don, properly **John Donald** (1915–) US lawn tennis player, born in Oakland, California. He was the first person to complete the Grand Slam (the four major singles championships of Australia, France, Britain, and the USA) in one year (1938). He was also triple champion (singles, men's doubles, and mixed doubles) at Wimbledon in 1937 and 1938, and between 1935 and 1938 won 25 out of 29 Davis Cup rubbers in 11 ties. He turned professional in 1939.

budge *verb intrans.*, *trans.* **1** to move or cause to move. **2** to change or cause to change one's mind or opinions: *nothing you say will make me budge*. [from Old French *bouger*]

budgerigar *noun* a type of small parrot native to Australia, often kept as a pet. [from Australian Aboriginal *gijirrigaa*]

budget — *noun* **1** a plan, especially for a particular period of time, showing how money coming in will be spent. **2** (**the Budget**) *Brit.* a periodic assessment of national revenue and expenditure proposed by the government. **3** the amount of money set aside for a particular purpose. **4** (*attributive*) low in cost: *a budget holiday*. — *verb* (**budgeted**, **budgeting**) **1** *intrans.* to calculate how much money one is earning and spending, so that one does not spend more than one has. **2** *intrans.* (**budget for something**) to allow for it in a budget: *next year we'll budget for a new car.* **3** to provide (an amount of money) in a budget: *budget £600 for a holiday.* [from Old French *bougette*, diminutive of *bouge*, pouch]

◇ In the UK, a unified Budget (dealing with both income and expenditure) was introduced for the first time by the Conservative government in November 1993. Before this time, the government's expenditure programme had been announced in November each year, with taxation measures and borrowing requirements detailed separately the following March.

budget account an account with a bank or shop into which regular payments are made to sustain a credit level.

budgetary *adj.* relating to or connected with a budget or finance.

budgeting *noun* the process or practice of drawing up budgets; financial planning.

budgie *noun colloq.* a budgerigar.

Buenaventura POP (1985) 160 000, the most important Pacific trading port in Colombia. It is situated in Cauca department in the SW of the country and was founded in 1540.

Buenos Aires **1** POP (1991e) 12.2m, the federal capital of Argentina in Gran Buenos Aires federal district, E Argentina. The city is situated on the S bank of the R Plate. HISTORY founded in 1536 as the city of the 'Puerto de Santa Maria del Buen Aire'; destroyed by S American Indians, and refounded in 1580; formerly the capital of the Spanish viceroyalty of La Plata. NOTABLE FEATURES National Gallery; Plaza de Mayo; Presidential Palace (Casa Rosada); opera house; town hall (Cabildo); cathedral; horse racing course. **2** a federal district of Argentina. **3** a province in E Argentina with the city of La Plata as its capital.

Buerk, Michael (Duncan) (1946–) English television reporter, born in Solihull. A BBC television news correspondent from 1973, he was based in Scotland and reported on energy before he went to Africa and became known for his moving reports on the famine in Ethiopia. Later he returned to the UK to front the BBC's *Nine O'Clock News.*

buff — *noun* **1** a dull yellow colour. **2** a soft undyed leather. **3** a piece of soft material used for polishing. **4** *colloq.* a person who is enthusiastic about and knows much about a subject: *an opera buff.* — *adj.* dull yellow in colour. — *verb* **1** (*also* **buff something up**) to polish with a buff or piece of soft material: *buff up one's shoes.* **2** to make (leather) soft like buff.
— **in the buff** *Brit. colloq.* naked.
[from French *buffle*, buffalo]

Buffalo POP (1990) 969 000, the seat of Erie County, W New York state, USA. It is a port on the Niagara R, at the NE end of L Erie, and is the second largest city in the state of New York. NOTABLE FEATURES Albright-Knox art gallery; science museum; the Niagara Falls are 27km/17mi to the N.

buffalo *noun* (PL. **buffalo, buffaloes**) **1** (*in full* **African buffalo**) a member of the cattle family (*Syncerus caffer*) native to S and E Africa, and having a heavy black or brown body, thick horns curving upwards at their tips, and large drooping ears. **2** (*in full* **Indian buffalo**) a SE Asian member of the cattle family (*Bubalus bubalis*), that lives in swampy areas or near rivers. Wild Indian buffaloes live in small herds, and have a black coat, but domesticated animals may be grey, black, pink, or white, and are noted for their docility. The horns of this animal are semicircular, spreading out sideways and backwards. **3** sometimes used generally to refer to the American bison. [from Portuguese *bufalo*]

buffer¹ *noun* **1** an apparatus, especially one using springs, on railway carriages, etc, or a cushion of rope on a ship, which takes the shock when the carriage or ship hits something. **2** a person or thing which protects from harm or shock. **3** *Comput.* a temporary storage area for data that is being transmitted from the central processing unit to an output device such as a printer. **4** *Chem.* a chemical solution that maintains its pH at a constant level when an acid or alkali is added to it, or when the solution is diluted. Buffers are used to prepare solutions that are required to have a specific pH, eg for dyeing, food technology, brewing, or for intravenous medical injections. [from Middle English *buffe*, blow]

buffer² *noun Brit. colloq.* a rather foolish or dull person, especially a man: *old buffer.*

buffer³ *noun* a person or thing that buffs or polishes.

buffered *adj.* **1** equipped with a buffer or buffers. **2** protected.

buffer state a neutral country situated between two larger countries which are potentially hostile towards each other, making war less likely.

buffer stock stock held in reserve to try and control prices.

buffet¹ *noun* (pronounced *boofay*) **1** a place where light meals and drinks may be bought and eaten. **2** a meal set out on tables from which people help themselves. **3** a sideboard or cupboard for holding china, glasses, etc. [from Old French *buffet*]

buffet² (pronounced like *tuffet*) — *noun* a blow with the hand. — *verb* (**buffeted, buffeting**) **1** to strike or knock with the fist. **2** to knock about: *a ship buffeted by the waves.* [from Old French *buffe*, blow]

buffet car a carriage in a train, in which light meals and drinks can be bought.

buffeting *noun* repeated knocks or blows.

Buffon, George-Louis Leclerc, Comte de (1707–88) French naturalist, born in Montbard, Burgundy. After studying law at the Jesuit college in Dijon, he devoted himself to science, and in 1739 was appointed Director of the King's Botanic Garden (Jardin du Roi) and the Royal Museum. His monumental *Histoire Naturelle* (44 vols, 1749–67) attempted to discuss all the then-known facts of natural science. He gave an early evolutionary perspective, suggesting that related species could arise from a common ancestor, and anticipated later 'uniformitarian' principles in geology, believing that the Earth's features as formed by processes currently observable rather than by catastrophic events.

buffoon *noun often derog.* a person who does amusing or foolish things. [from French *bouffon*, from Italian *buffone*]

buffoonery *noun* comic or foolish behaviour.

bug — *noun* **1** a common name for any of thousands of species of insect belonging to the order Hemiptera, eg aphids and bedbugs. True bugs have flattened oval bodies and mouthparts modified into a beak for piercing and sucking. **2** North Amer. a popular name for any kind of insect. **3** *colloq.* a popular name for a bacterium or virus that causes infection or illness: *a stomach bug.* **4** *colloq.* a small microphone hidden so as to spy on conversations. **5** *colloq.* a fault in a computer program or hardware. **6** *colloq.* an obsession or craze: *get the skiing bug.* — *verb* (**bugged, bugging**) **1** *colloq.* to hide a microphone in (a room, etc) so as to spy on conversations. **2** *slang* to annoy or worry. [from Anglo-Saxon *budda*, beetle]

bugaboo *noun* an imaginary thing which causes fear.

Bugatti, Ettore (Arco Isidoro) (1882–1947) Italian car manufacturer, born in Milan. He began designing cars in 1899 and set up his works in Strasbourg in 1907. World War I caused him to move to Italy and later to France, where his racing cars won international fame in the 1930s.

bugbear *noun* a thing which causes fear or annoyance. [originally a hobgoblin, from Middle English *bugge*, perhaps from Welsh *bwg*, hobgoblin]

bug-eyed *adj.* with eyes that stick out from the face, especially with astonishment.

bugger *coarse slang* — *noun* **1** a person or thing considered to be difficult or awkward. **2** a person one feels affection or pity for: *poor old bugger.* **3** a person who practises anal sex. — *verb* (**buggered, buggering**) **1** to practise anal sex with (someone). **2** to tire or exhaust. — *interj.* (*also* **bugger it**) an expression of annoyance.
— **bugger about** *or* **around** to waste time; to do things flippantly or without due attention.
bugger someone about to mislead them or cause them problems.
bugger all nothing at all.
bugger off to go away.
bugger something up to spoil or ruin it.
[from Old French *bougre*, from Latin *Bulgarus*, a heretic (literally, a Bulgarian), from the large number of heretical beliefs, including deviant sexual practices, thought to have come from the Balkans]

buggery *noun* anal sex.

buggy *noun* (PL. **buggies**) **1** a light open carriage pulled by one horse. **2** *North Amer., esp. US* a pram.

bugle — *noun* a brass instrument like a small trumpet, used mainly for military signals. — *verb* **1** *intrans.* to sound a bugle. **2** *trans.* to sound (a call) on a bugle. [an Old French word, from Latin *bos*, ox]

bugler *noun* a person who plays a bugle.

Buhl *or* **Boulle André Charles** (1642–1732) French cabinet-maker, born in Paris. He studied drawing, painting, and sculpture, and became a furniture designer in the service of Louis XIV.

buhl *or* **boulle** *noun* **1** a technique of furniture decoration developed by André Buhl, similar to but more elaborate than marquetry, with inlaid patterns of gold, silver, brass, pewter, ivory, and mother-of-pearl as well as coloured woods. **2** furniture decorated in this way.

build — *verb* (PAST TENSE AND PAST PARTICIPLE **built**) **1** to make or construct from parts. **2** to develop gradually. **3** to make in a particular way or for a particular purpose. — *noun* physical form, especially of the human body: *a slim build.*
— **build one thing into** *or* **on to another** to make a construction such that it is a permanent part of or addition to a larger one: *built a garage on to the side of the house.*
build on something 1 to add on by building. **2** to use (a previous success, etc) as a basis from which to develop: *build on previous experience.* **3** to base hopes, achieve success, etc on something: *success built on a popular product.* **4** to depend on something.
build up to increase gradually in size, strength, amount, etc.
build something up 1 to build it in stages. **2** to speak with great enthusiasm about it. See also BUILD-UP.
[from Anglo-Saxon *byldan*]

builder *noun* **1** a person who builds, or organizes the building of, houses, etc. **2** anything which helps to develop or build something.

building *noun* **1** the business of constructing houses, etc. **2** a structure with walls and a roof, such as a house.

building-block *noun* any of the separate parts out of which something is built.

building society *Brit.* a finance company that lends money for buying or improving houses and in which customers can invest money to earn interest.

◇ Interest paid to the society by the borrower is higher than that paid by the society to investors. In the UK, the Building Societies Act (1987) allowed societies to provide other services and to raise 20 per cent of their funds on the capital markets. The US equivalent is the *savings and loan association*.

build-up *noun* **1** a gradual increase. **2** a gradual approach to a conclusion or climax. **3** publicity or praise of something or someone given in advance of its, his, or her appearance.

built-up *adj.* **1** *said of land, etc* covered with buildings, especially houses. **2** increased in height by additions. **3** made up of separate parts.

Bujumbura, formerly **Usumbura** POP (1990e) 227 000, **1** the capital of Burundi, central Africa, at the NE end of L Tanganyika. The city, which is also a port, was founded in 1899 by German colonists. NOTABLE FEATURE Museum of African Civilization. **2** a province in NW Burundi with Bujumbura as its capital.

Bukharin, Nikolay Ivanovich (1888–1938) Russian Marxist revolutionary and political theorist, born in Moscow, and called by Lenin 'the darling of the Party'. He was active in the Bolshevik underground (1905–17), and after the February Revolution returned to Russia, and was instrumental in the organization of the October Revolution in Moscow. As a member of the Politburo (1924–9) he was a firm supporter of Lenin's New Economic Policy, and opposed Stalin's collectivization campaign. In 1937 he was arrested in Stalin's Great Purge and shot, but was posthumously readmitted to the Party in 1988.

Bulawayo POP (1982) 495 000, the second largest city in Zimbabwe and the capital of Matabeleland North province. It lies 370km/230mi SW of Harare and was founded in 1893.

bulb *noun* **1** *Bot.* in certain plants, eg tulip, onion, a swollen underground organ consisting of a modified shoot, with overlapping layers of fleshy leaf bases or scales, and roots growing from the lower surface. It functions as a food store between one growing season and the next, and is also involved in the production of new plants from daughter bulbs. **2** a flower grown from a bulb, eg a daffodil or hyacinth. **3** *Electr.* the airtight glass envelope that encloses the electric filament of an incandescent lamp, the electrodes of a vacuum tube, etc. **4** anything which is shaped like a pear. [from Latin *bulbus*, from Greek *bolbos*, onion]

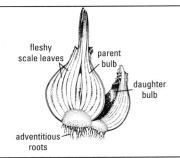

fleshy
scale leaves
parent
bulb
daughter
bulb
adventitious
roots

bulb

bulbous *adj.* **1** like a bulb in shape; fat or bulging. **2** having or growing from a bulb.

Bulganin, Nikolai Aleksandrovich (1895–1975) Soviet politician, born in Nizhniy-Novgorod. An early member of the Communist Party, he was Mayor of Moscow (1933–7), a member of the Military Council in World War II, and Minister of Defence (1946). After Stalin's death Bulganin became vice-premier in Malenkov's government, and when Malenkov

resigned (1955) he was made Prime Minister. With the real power being wielded by Khrushchev, 'B and K' travelled extensively abroad, and conducted propaganda through lengthy letters to Western statesmen, until Bulganin was dismissed in 1958.

Bulgaria, official name **People's Republic of Bulgaria**, Bulgarian **Narodna Republika Bulgariya** POP (1992e) 8.5m, a republic in the E of the Balkan Peninsula, SE Europe, divided into 28 provinces. AREA 110 912sq km/42 812sq mi. It is bounded to the N by Romania, W by Yugoslavia (Serbia) and Macedonia, SE by Turkey, S by Greece, and E by the Black Sea. CAPITAL Sofia. CHIEF TOWNS Plovdiv, Varna, Ruse, Burgas, Stara Zagora, Pleven. TIME ZONE GMT +2. The population is c.85% Bulgarian, with Turkish, Romany, and Macedonian minorities; religions are 85% Bulgarian Orthodox and 13% Muslim. OFFICIAL LANGUAGE Bulgarian. CURRENCY the lev. PHYSICAL DESCRIPTION central Bulgaria is traversed W–E by the Balkan Mts, rising to over 2 000m; the Rhodope Mts in the SW rise to nearly 3 000m just S of Sofia; the Bulgarian lowlands stretch S from the R Danube with an average width of 100km/60mi; rivers flow N to the Danube or S to the Aegean; they include the Maritsa, Iskur, Yantra, and Struma. CLIMATE largely continental, with hot summers and cold winters, but to the S the climate is increasingly Mediterranean; winters are slightly warmer on the Black Sea coast. HISTORY Bulgars crossed the Danube in the 7c and gradually merged in with the Slavonic population; Kingdom of Bulgaria was continually at war with the Byzantine Empire until it was destroyed by the Turks in the 14c; under Turkish rule until 1878 but full independence was only achieved in 1908; Bulgaria was a kingdom from 1908 to 1946, when it was proclaimed a Socialist People's Republic; it had aligned with Germany in the World Wars and in 1944 had been occupied by the USSR; in the early 1990s a multiparty government introduced political and economic reforms. GOVERNMENT a President is Head of State; a unicameral 250-member National Assembly is elected for up to five years. ECONOMY mainly agricultural produce, especially grain, fruits, vegetables, rice, tobacco, sheep, hogs, poultry, cheese, sunflower seeds, unginned cotton, attar of roses, wine; manufacturing industries include food processing, machine building, chemicals, metal products, electronics, textiles; there are natural reserves of coal, iron ore, offshore oil (Black Sea), and natural gas; tourism.

Bulgarian — *noun* **1** a native or citizen of Bulgaria. **2** the language of Bulgaria, a S Slavic language of the Indo-European family, spoken by c.8 million people in Bulgaria and neighbouring countries. — *adj.* of Bulgaria or its people or language.

Bulgars originally a Turkic-speaking people who inhabited the steppes north of the Black Sea, renowned as fierce warriors and horsemen. In the 5c they split into two groups, one of which later migrated west into the Danube region, became assimilated with the Balkan Slavs, and established the kingdom of Bulgaria.

Bulge, Battle of the the last German counter-offensive (1944) through the Ardennes in World War II (beginning 16 Dec) to prevent the Allied invasion of Germany. It achieved early success, but the Germans were eventually pushed to retreat by the Allies by the end of January 1945.

bulge — *noun* **1** a swelling, especially where one would expect to see something flat. **2** a sudden and usually temporary increase, eg in population. — *verb intrans.* to swell outwards. [from Old French *boulge*, from Latin *bulga*, knapsack]

bulghar wheat *or* **bulgur wheat** *Food Science* wheat that has been boiled, dried, lightly milled, and cracked. [from Turkish]

bulging *adj.* swelling or increasing suddenly.

Bulgaria

bulgy *adj.* having a bulge or bulges; swollen.

bulimia *noun Medicine* **1** compulsive overeating, caused either by psychological factors or by damage to the hypothalamus of the brain. **2** same as BULIMIA NERVOSA. [from Greek *boulimia*, great hunger, from *bous*, ox + *limos*, hunger]

bulimia nervosa *Medicine* a psychological disorder, most common in female adolescents and young women, in which episodes of excessive eating are followed by self-induced vomiting or laxative abuse in an attempt to avoid any weight gain.

bulk *noun* **1** size, especially when large and awkward. **2** the greater or main part of: *the bulk of the task is routine*. **3** a large body, shape, or person. **4** a large quantity: *buy in bulk / bulk buying*. **5** roughage.
— **bulk large** to be or seem important: *an issue which bulks large in his mind.*
[from Norse *bulki*, cargo]

bulk carrier a ship which carries dry goods such as grain, in bulk and unpackaged.

bulked yarn *Textiles* a yarn made of (usually synthetic) fibres modified chemically or physically to induce a high volume or loftiness to the yarn by crimping the fibres during processing.

bulkhead *noun* a wall in a ship or aircraft which separates one section from another, so that if one section is damaged, the rest is not affected. [from Middle English *bulk*, stall]

bulkily *adv.* with a large and awkward size.

bulkiness *noun* being bulky or awkward in size.

bulky *adj.* (**bulkier, bulkiest**) large in size and awkward to carry or move.

Bull, John (c.1563–1628) English organist and composer, born (possibly) in Radnorshire. He has been credited with composing 'God save the King'.

bull¹ *noun* **1** the uncastrated male of animals in the cattle family. **2** the male of the elephant, whale, and some other large animals. **3** (**the Bull**) the constellation and sign of the zodiac Taurus. **4** *Stock Exchange* a person who buys shares hoping to sell them at a higher price at a later date. **5** same as BULL'S-EYE¹.
— **a bull in a china shop** a person who acts in a rough and careless way and is likely to cause damage.
take the bull by the horns to deal boldly and positively with a challenge or difficulty.
[from Middle English *bole*]

bull² *noun* an official letter or written instruction from the Pope. [from Old French *bulle*, from Latin *bulla*, seal]

bull³ *noun* **1** an illogical, nonsensical statement, eg 'if you don't receive this card, you must write and tell me'. **2** *slang* nonsense. **3** tedious and sometimes unnecessary routine tasks.

Bullard, Sir Edward Crisp (1907–80) English geophysicist, born in Norwich. Professor at Toronto, Director of the National Physical Laboratory in London, and finally professor at

Cambridge, he made the first satisfactory measurements of heat-flow through the Earth's oceanic crust, and helped to develop the theory of continental drift. He also reintroduced the idea that the thermal convection currents in the Earth's core are responsible for the origin of the Earth's magnetism.

bull-baiting a popular sport in 16c England, forbidden by law in 1835. The bull, sometimes blinded, would be tied up and attacked by dogs Bets were placed on the performance of the dogs; the bull rarely survived. See also BLOOD SPORTS.

bulldog *noun* a small fierce heavily built dog with a large head.

bulldog clip a clip with a spring, used to hold papers together or on to a board.

bulldoze *verb* **1** to use a bulldozer to move, flatten, or demolish. **2** (**bulldoze someone into something**) to force them to do something they do not want to do: *bulldoze him into taking part.*

bulldozer *noun* a large powerful tractor with a vertical blade at the front, for pushing heavy objects, clearing the ground or making it level.

bullet *noun* a small metal cylinder with a pointed end, for firing from small guns and rifles. [from French *boulette*, little ball]

bulletin *noun* **1** a short official statement of news issued as soon as the news is known. **2** a short printed newspaper or leaflet, especially one produced regularly by a group or organization. [from French *bulletin*, from Italian *bullettino*]

bulletin-board *noun North Amer., esp. US* **1** a notice-board. **2** *Comput.* an electronic data system containing messages and programs accessible to a number of users.

bullet-proof *adj., said of a material, etc* strong enough to prevent bullets passing through.

bullet train a high-speed passenger train, especially in Japan.

bullfight *noun* a public show, especially in Spain, in which men on horseback and on foot bait and kill a bull. See BULLFIGHTING.

bullfighter *noun* a person who takes part in a bullfight.

bullfighting *noun* the sport or practice of baiting and killing bulls as a spectacle.
◇ It is the national sport of Spain, and is popular in some regions of S France, and in Latin American countries. A bull, specially bred for fighting, is released into a ring where it is goaded and weakened by the picadors (who may be mounted or on foot), before the matador enters the arena to make the final kill. Bullfighting is regarded as an art in Spain, and leading matadors are accorded the status of national heroes.

bullfinch *noun* a small European bird with a red breast, black head, and a strong beak.

bullfrog *noun* a large frog with a loud croak, found in the US.

bullhead *noun* a small bottom-dwelling fish found in clear streams and lakes of N Europe, and having a stout body up to 10cm in length, with a broad flattened head. Its eggs are laid under stones and guarded by the male, and the fish feeds on invertebrates, especially crustaceans.

bullion *noun* gold or silver in large bars. [from Old French *bouillon*, boiling]

bullish *adj.* **1** like a bull, especially in temper. **2** *Stock Exchange* tending to cause or hoping for rising prices. **3** very confident about the future.

bullishly *adv.* with a bullish or very confident manner.

bullishness *noun* being bullish or confident.

bull-mastiff *noun* a type of dog, a cross between a mastiff and a bulldog.

bull-necked *adj., said of a person* having a short thick strong neck.

bullock *noun* a castrated bull.

bullring *noun* an arena where bullfights take place.

Bull Run, Battles of, also called **Battles of Manassas** two major victories (21 Jul 1861, 29–30 Aug 1862) by Confederate forces in the American Civil War. In the first battle, the first major clash of the war, untrained Northern troops attempting to capture Richmond, Virginia (the Southern capital), were pitted against well-commanded Southerners, and in the second a large Northern force under John Pope was trapped by combined Confederate forces under 'Stonewall' Jackson and James Longstreet (1821–1904).

bull's-eye *noun* **1** the small circular centre of a target used in shooting, darts, etc. **2** a shot hitting this. **3** *colloq.* anything which hits its target or achieves its aim, etc. **4** a large, hard, round peppermint sweet. **5** a thick round disc of glass forming a window, especially on a ship. **6** a thick round boss in a sheet of glass. **7** a round lens in a lantern, or a lantern with such a lens.

bullshit *coarse slang* — *noun* nonsense. — *verb intrans.* (**bullshitted, bullshitting**) to talk bullshit.

bull terrier a terrier with a short smooth coat and strong body, originally a cross between a bulldog and a terrier.

bully[1] — *noun* (PL. **bullies**) a person who hurts or frightens weaker or smaller people. — *verb* (**bullies, bullied**) **1** to act like a bully towards. **2** (**bully someone into something**) to force them to do something they do not want to do: *they bullied us into helping.* — *adj.* excellent; very good. [from Old Dutch *boele*, lover]

bully[2] or **bully beef** corned beef. [from French *bouilli*, boiled beef]

bully[3] *verb intrans.* (**bullies, bullied**) (*usually* **bully off**) to begin a game, especially hockey, by hitting one's stick three times against an opponent's before going for the ball.

bully-boy *noun colloq.* a rough person employed to bully and threaten people.

bullying *noun* pressuring or coercing someone weaker by use of force.

Bülow, Hans (Guido), Baron von (1830–94) German pianist and conductor, born in Dresden. He joined radical social groups in Berlin, made the acquaintance of Wagner in Zurich, took piano lessons from Liszt in Wiemar, and married his daughter (1857). He became an outstanding conductor and in 1864 was appointed court pianist and director of the music school in Munich, but resigned when his wife left him for Wagner (1869), and undertook extensive conducting tours in England and the USA.

bulrush *noun* **1** a tall waterside plant of the genus *Typha* with long narrow greyish leaves and one or two thick spikes of tightly packed dark brown flowers. Bulrushes are usually found growing together in large numbers. **2** *Biblical* a papyrus plant. [perhaps from BULL[1] + RUSH[2]]

bulwark *noun* **1** a wall built as a defence, often made of earth. **2** a thing or person that defends a cause, way of life, etc. **3** (*usually* **bulwarks**) the side of a ship projecting above the deck. [from Old Dutch *bolwerc*]

bum[1] *noun Brit. colloq.* the buttocks. [from Middle English *bom*]

bum[2] *colloq. esp. North Amer.* — *noun* **1** a person who lives by begging. **2** a person who is lazy and shows no sense of responsibility. — *verb* (**bummed, bumming**) to get by begging, borrowing or cadging: *bum a lift.* — **bum around** *or* **about** to travel around or spend one's time doing nothing in particular. [perhaps from German *Bummler*, loafer]

bumbag *noun colloq.* a small bag on a belt, worn round the waist.

Bumble, Mr the cruel and officious workhouse Beadle who refuses Oliver more gruel in Charles Dickens's *Oliver Twist*.

bumble *verb intrans.* **1** to speak in a confused or confusing way. **2** to move or do something in an awkward or clumsy way.

bumble bee a large hairy black and yellow bee found in most temperate regions. Like the honey bee it is a social insect, but it forms smaller colonies, and only the queen bee survives the winter. It pollinates many plants that are important food for livestock, eg clover, but produces only small amounts of honey. [from Middle English *bomblen*, to boom or buzz]

bumbling *adj.* inept; blundering.

bumf or **bumph** *noun Brit. colloq.* miscellaneous useless leaflets, documents. [short for *bum-fodder*]

bummer *noun* **1** a lazy or idle person. **2** *colloq.* a difficult or unpleasant thing.

bump — *verb* **1** *trans., intrans.* to knock or hit something. **2** to hurt or damage by hitting. **3** *intrans.* (*usually* **bump together**) said of two moving objects to collide. **4** *intrans.* (*also* **bump along**) to move or travel with jerky or bumpy movements: *bump along the road.* — *noun* **1** a knock, jolt, or collision. **2** a dull sound caused by a knock, collision, etc. **3** a lump or swelling on the body, especially one caused by a blow. **4** a lump on a road surface.
— **bump into someone** *colloq.* to meet them by chance.
bump someone off *slang* to kill them.
bump something up *colloq.* to increase it: *bump up production.*
[imitative]

bumper — *noun* **1** *Brit.* a bar on the front or back of a motor vehicle which lessens the shock or damage if it hits anything. **2** an exceptionally good or large example. **3** a large full glass. — *adj.* exceptionally good or large: *a bumper crop.*

bumph same as BUMF.

bumpily *adv.* with a bumpy or uneven manner, ride, etc.

bumpiness *noun* being bumpy or uneven.

bumpkin *noun colloq.* an awkward, simple or stupid person, especially one from the country. [from Old Dutch *bommekijn*, little barrel]

Bumppo, Natty the rough but virtuous lone woodsman and adventurer in James Fenimore Cooper's 'Leather-Stocking Tales', also known as Deerslayer, Hawkeye, Pathfinder, and Leather-Stocking.

bumptious *adj.* offensively or irritatingly conceited. [from BUMP + FRACTIOUS]

bumptiously *adv.* with a bumptious or conceited manner.

bumptiousness *noun* being bumptious or conceited.

bumpy *adj.* (**bumpier, bumpiest**) **1** having a lot of bumps: *a bumpy road.* **2** affected by bumps: *a bumpy ride.*

bun *noun* **1** a small round sweetened roll, often containing currants, etc. **2** a mass of hair fastened in a round shape on the back of the head. [from Middle English *bunne*]

bulrush

BUNAC *abbrev.* British Universities North America Club.

bunch — *noun* **1** a number of things fastened or growing together. **2** (**bunches**) long hair divided into two pieces and tied separately at each side or the back of the head. **3** *colloq.* a group or collection. **4** *colloq.* a group of people; gang. — *verb trans., intrans.* to group together in or form a bunch. [from Middle English *bunche*]

Bunche, Ralph (Johnson) (1904–71) US diplomat, born in Detroit. He taught political science at Howard University, Washington (1928–50), played a major role in drafting the UN Charter and in planning its first General Assembly (1946), directed the UN Trusteeship department (1947–54), and became UN mediator in Palestine, where he arranged for a cease-fire. Awarded the Nobel Peace Prize in 1950, he became a UN Under-Secretary for Special Political Affairs (1954–67), and was Under-Secretary-General (1968–71).

bunching *noun* **1** gathering together in bunches. **2** a situation in which traffic on a motorway travels in groups with little distance between vehicles.

bunch of fives *noun Brit. slang* a fist; a blow with a fist.

bunchy *adj.* (**bunchier**, **bunchiest**) resembling or in the form of a bunch or bunches.

Bundesbank *noun* the state bank of Germany. [German, from *Bund*, confederacy + *Bank*, bank]

Bundestag the lower house of parliament of the Federal Republic of Germany, elections for which are held every four years in the autumn. In addition to legislating, the Bundestag selects the Chancellor and supports his government.

bundle — *noun* **1** a number of things loosely fastened or tied together. **2** a loose parcel, especially one made from cloth. **3** *Biol.* a strand of nerve or muscle fibres. **4** *slang* a large amount of money. — *verb* to make into a bundle.
— **be a bundle of nerves** to be extremely nervous.
bundle someone or **something away** or **off**, *etc* to put them somewhere quickly and roughly or untidily: *let's bundle him into a taxi / bundled the papers into the drawer.*
go a bundle on someone or **something** *slang* to like them.
[from Middle English *bundel*]

Bundy, McGeorge (1919–) US educator and politician, born in Boston, Massachusetts. He worked in public service, then taught at Harvard, where he became Dean of Arts and Sciences (1953–61). As National Security Adviser to Presidents Kennedy and Johnson he was one of the architects of the Vietnam War. He has been Professor of History at New York University since 1979.

bun fight *Brit. colloq.* a noisy tea party.

bung — *noun* a small round piece of wood, rubber, cork, etc, which closes a hole in the bottom of a barrel, a small boat, etc. — *verb* **1** to block (a hole) with a bung. **2** *slang* to throw or put in a careless way.
— *colloq.* **bung something up** to block it.
[from Old Dutch *bonge*, stopper]

bungalow *noun* a single-storey house. [from Gujarati *bangalo*, from Hindi *bangla*, in the style of Bengal]

bungee jumping the sport of jumping from a height with strong rubber ropes or cables attached to the ankles to ensure that the jumper bounces up before reaching the ground or other surface.

bunghole *noun* a hole by which a barrel, etc is emptied or filled.

bungle — *verb trans., intrans.* to do (something)

carelessly or badly. — *noun* carelessly or badly done work; a mistake.

bungled *adj.* done badly; mishandled.

bungler *noun* a person who does things badly.

bungling *noun, adj.* doing things badly or carelessly: *their bungling attempts to put things right.*

Bunin, Ivan Alexeievich (1870–1953) Russian writer, born in Voronezh. He worked as a journalist and clerk, writing lyrics and novels of the decay of the Russian nobility and of peasant life, and lived in Paris after the 1917 Revolution. His best-known work is *The Gentleman from San Francisco* (1922). He was awarded the Nobel Prize for Literature in 1933.

bunion *noun* a painful swelling on the first joint of the big toe. [perhaps from Old French *buigne*, bump on the head]

bunisexual *adj., said of an organism* possessing either male or female sex organs, but not both. See also BISEXUAL.

bunk[1] — *noun* a narrow bed attached to the wall in a cabin in a ship, caravan, etc. — *verb intrans. colloq.* (**bunk down**) to lie down and go to sleep, especially in an improvised place.

bunk[2] same as BUNKUM.

bunk[3] *Brit. slang noun* the act of running away: *do a bunk.*
— **bunk off** *intrans.* to stay away from school or work when one ought to be there.

bunk bed each of a pair of narrow beds fixed one on top of the other.

bunker *noun* **1** a large container or cupboard for storing coal. **2** an obstacle on a golf course consisting of a hollow containing sand. **3** an underground shelter. [from Scots *bonker*, box or chest]

Bunker Hill, Battle of the first pitched battle (1775) of the US War of Independence, technically a US defeat. The British garrison dislodged New England troops from their position overlooking occupied Boston, but very high British casualties demonstrated American fighting capacity and forbade attempts on other American emplacements. It was actually fought on Breed's Hill, above Charlestown, not on nearby Bunker Hill.

bunkhouse *noun* a building with many beds, usually for workers.

bunkum or **bunk** *noun colloq.* nonsense; foolish talk. [from *Buncombe*, a county in N Carolina, whose congressman is said to have excused a rambling speech in Congress on the grounds that he was only speaking for Buncombe]

bunny *noun* (PL. **bunnies**) (*also* **bunny rabbit**) a child's word for rabbit. [from *bun*, rabbit, from Scots Gaelic *bun*, bottom.]

bunny girl a club hostess or waitress whose costume includes false rabbit's ears and tail.

bunraku *noun* the classical Japanese puppet theatre which reached the peak of its popularity in the 17c–18c. Puppets are two-thirds life size, hand-held by a puppet master, generally with two 'invisible' assistants dressed in black. The action is accompanied by musicians and a singer-narrator who voices all the roles. [from Japanese]

Bunsen, Robert Wilhelm (1811–99) German chemist and physicist, born in Göttingen. Professor of Chemistry at Heidelberg (1852–99), he was one of the first to carry out spectrum analysis (1859). He also invented the grease-spot photometer, a galvanic battery, and an ice calorimeter, and worked on arsenic compounds, gas analysis and electrolysis. Although he played little part in the invention of the burner named after him, it was manufactured and sold under that name by his assistant.

bunsen burner *Chem.* a gas burner, used mainly in chemistry laboratories. Natural gas enters via a jet at the lower end of a vertical metal

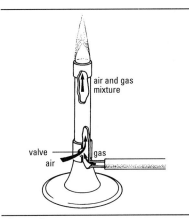

bunsen burner

tube, and air is drawn through an adjustable inlet hole. By controlling the gas-air mixture, it is possible to produce a very hot flame with no smoke. [named after Robert Bunsen]

Bunter, Billy the bespectacled, greedy, foolish 'Fat Owl of the Remove' in Frank Richards's *Billy Bunter of Greyfriars School* and other books. His sister is called Bessie.

bunting[1] *noun* **1** a row of small cloth or paper flags and other decorations. **2** thin loosely woven cotton used to make flags, especially for ships.

bunting[2] *noun* any of various small birds related to finches and sparrows.

Buñuel, Luis (1900–83) Spanish film director, born in Calanda. His first films (made with Salvador Dali) were a sensation with their surrealistic, macabre approach: *Un Chien Andalou* (An Andalusian Dog, 1928) and *L'Age d'or* (The Golden Age, 1930). He then settled in Mexico (1947) and returned to his career with *Los Olvidados* (The Young and the Damned, 1950). Later films include *Viridiana* (1961), *Le Charme Discèt de la Bourgeoisie* (The Discreet Charm of the Bourgeoisie, 1972), and *Cet Obscur Objet du Désir* (That Obscure Object of Desire, 1977). His work is characterized by a poetic, often erotic, use of imagery, a black humour, and a hatred of Catholicism.

Bunyan, John (1628–88) English writer and preacher, born in Elstow, Bedfordshire. He worked as a tinker, and fought in the parliamentary army during the Civil War (1644–5). In 1653 he joined a Christian fellowship and became a preacher, and was arrested in 1660 and spent 12 years in Bedford county gaol, where his many writings included *Grace Abounding* (1666). Briefly released after the Declaration of Indulgence (1672), he was reimprisoned for six months during which time he wrote the first part of the *Pilgrim's Progress* (1678). Returning to his career, he acted as pastor in Bedford for 16 years, where he wrote the second part of the *Pilgrim's Progress* (1684).

Bunyan, Paul in American folklore, a lumberjack of superhuman size and strength. He could not only break up log-jams with spectacular ease, but could also refashion geography, creating lakes, rivers, and even the Grand Canyon.

Bunyoro, Kingdom of one of the kingdoms of Uganda occupying territory north of Buganda. Originally known as Kitara, it was formerly the most powerful of these states, and was colonized by the Nilotic Bito. It declined in influence when Buganda rose in the 17c.

buoy — *noun* a brightly coloured floating object fastened to the bottom of the sea by an anchor, to warn ships of rocks, etc or to mark channels, etc. — *verb* to mark with a buoy or buoys.
— **buoy something up** to keep it afloat.
be buoyed up to be in good spirits, excited, etc.
[from Middle English *boye*, float]

buoyancy *noun* the upward force exerted on an object that is immersed in or floating on the surface of a fluid (a liquid or gas). It is equal to the weight of fluid displaced (Archimedes' principle).

buoyant *adj.* 1 *said of an object* able to float in a liquid. 2 *said of a liquid or gas* able to keep an object afloat. 3 *said of a person* cheerful. 4 *said of sales, profits, etc* increasing. 5 *said of a business, etc* having increasing trade, rising profits, etc. [from BUOY]

buoyantly *adv.* with a buoyant or cheerful manner.

BUPA *abbrev.* British United Provident Association, a private medical insurance scheme.

BUR *abbrev., as an international vehicle mark* Burma (Myanmar).

bur *or* **burr** *noun* 1 the rough prickly seed-case or flower of some plants, which sticks readily to things it touches. 2 any plant which produces burs. [from Middle English *burre*]

Burbage, Richard (c.1569–1619) English actor, born and died in London. He was the leading performer with Shakespeare's company from 1594 until his death, and was the first creator on stage of many of Shakespeare's greatest roles, including Hamlet, Othello, and Lear.

Burbank, Luther (1849–1926) US horticulturalist, born in Lancaster, Massachusetts. He received little formal education, but bought some land in Santa Rosa, California, and spent over 50 years in experiments breeding new vegetables, fruits, grasses, and flowers. The city of Burbank is named after him.

Burbidge, Geoffrey (1925–) English astrophysicist, born in Chipping Norton. Working in the USA with his wife Margaret Burbidge and others, he applied nuclear physics to solve the problem of the creation of the heavy elements in evolved stars. He also worked on quasars, and in 1970 showed that the light-emitting stars in elliptical galaxies only account for 25% of the total mass, highlighting the 'missing mass' mystery, which continues to this day – most of the matter in the universe cannot be detected by its radiation.

Burbidge, (Eleanor) Margaret, née **Margaret Peachey** (1923–) British astronomer, born in Davenport. She became Professor of Astronomy at the University of California in 1964. In collaboration with her husband Geoffrey Burbidge and others, she made important discoveries about the processes whereby the heavy chemical elements are built up in the cores of massive stars.

burble *verb* 1 *intrans.* to speak at length but with little meaning. 2 *intrans. said of a stream, etc* to make a bubbling, murmuring sound. 3 to say (something) in a way that is hard to understand. [probably imitative]

burbot *noun* (PL. **burbot, burbots**) an eel-like, freshwater fish. [from Old French *bourbotte*]

burden[1] — *noun* 1 something to be carried; a load. 2 a duty, obligation, etc which is difficult, time-consuming, costly, etc. 3 the carrying of loads: *a beast of burden*. 4 (*also* **burthen**) the amount a ship can carry. — *verb* (**burdened, burdening**) to load with a burden, difficulty, problem, etc.
— **the burden of proof** the responsibility for proving something, especially in a law court. [from Anglo-Saxon *byrthen*]

burden[2] *noun* 1 the main theme (of a book, speech, etc). 2 a line repeated at the end of each verse of a song; a refrain. [from Old French *bourdon*, droning sound]

burdensome *adj.* difficult to carry, support, or tolerate.

burdock *noun* a weed with prickly flowers and broad leaves. [from BUR + DOCK[3]]

bureau *noun* (PL. **bureaux, bureaus**) 1 *Brit.* a desk for writing at, with drawers and usually a front flap which opens downwards to provide the writing surface. 2 *North Amer., esp. US* a chest of drawers. 3 an office or department for business, especially for collecting and supplying information. 4 *North Amer., esp. US* a government or newspaper department. [from Old French *burel*, dark red cloth]

bureaucracy *noun* (PL. **bureaucracies**) 1 a system of government by officials who are responsible to their department heads and are not elected. 2 these officials as a group, especially when regarded as oppressive. 3 a country governed by officials. 4 any system of administration in which matters are complicated by complex procedures amd trivial rules. [from BUREAU + Greek *kratos*, power]

bureaucrat *noun* 1 a government official. 2 an official who follows rules rigidly, so creating delays and difficulties.

bureaucratic *adj.* involving a complex and inflexible administration or organization.

bureaucratically *adv.* with a bureaucratic or inflexible manner.

bureau de change a place where one can change money from one currency to another.

Bureau of Indian Affairs (ABBREV. **BIA**) a US government agency established in 1824 as part of the War Department and transferred in 1849 to the Department of the Interior. The BIA is in charge of the administration of Native American affairs, acting on behalf of the USA, which is the trustee of tribal lands and property.

burette *noun Chem.* a long vertical glass tube marked with a scale and having a tap at the bottom, used to deliver controlled volumes of liquid, eg during chemical titrations. [from French *burette*]

burgeon *verb intrans. literary* to grow or develop quickly; to flourish. [from Old French *burjon*, bud, shoot]

burgeoning *adj. literary* beginning to grow or flourish.

burger *noun* 1 a hamburger. 2 a hamburger covered or flavoured with something: *a cheeseburger.* 3 an item of food shaped like a hamburger but made of something different: *a nutburger.* [a shortening of HAMBURGER]

Burgess, Anthony (1917–93) English novelist and critic, born in Manchester. He lectured at Birmingham University (1946–48), worked for the Ministry of Education (1948–50), and taught at Banbury Grammar School (1950–4). He then became an education officer in Malaya and Brunei (1954–9), where his experiences inspired his *Malayan Trilogy* (1965). His many novels include *A Clockwork Orange* (1962), *1985* (1978), *Earthly Powers* (1980), *The Kingdom of the Wicked* (1985), *Mozart and the Wolf Gang (1991)*, and *A Dead Man in Deptford* (1993). He also wrote several critical studies and film scripts, including *Jesus of Nazareth* (1977), and published works under the names of Joseph Kell and John Burgess Wilson (his original name). His two volumes of autobiography are *Little Wilson and Big God* (1987) and *You've Had Your Time* (1990).

Burgess, Guy (Francis de Moncy) (1910–63) English spy, born in Devonport, Devon. He became a communist at Cambridge in the 1930s and was recruited as a Soviet agent. He worked with the BBC (1936–9), wrote war propaganda (1939–41), and again joined the BBC (1941–4) while working for MI5. After World War II he joined the Foreign Office, and became embassy second secretary in Washington (1950) under Kim Philby. Recalled in 1951 for 'serious misconduct', he fled Britain with Donald Maclean, and publicly resurfaced in 1956 in the USSR.

burgess *noun* 1 *Brit., in England* an inhabitant of a town or borough, especially a person who has the right to elect people to government. 2 *Brit. Hist.* a Member of Parliament for a borough, a town with a municipal corporation or a university. [from Old French *burgeis*, from Latin *burgus*, borough]

Burgh, Hubert de (d.1243) a chief justice of England under King John and Henry III (1215–32), the gaoler of Prince Arthur. He was created Earl of Kent (1227), but was imprisoned after falling from favour (1232–4), then pardoned.

burgh *noun, in Scotland until 1975* a town or borough with a certain amount of self-government under a town council. [Scots form of BOROUGH]

burgher *noun* a citizen of a town or borough, especially on the Continent. [from Old German *burger*, from *burg*, borough]

Burghers of Calais, The a group sculpture by Auguste Rodin (1886, erected 1895).

burglar *noun* a person who enters a building, etc illegally to steal. [from Old French *burgler*]

burglar alarm an alarm fitted to a building, which is activated by an intruder.

burglary *noun* (PL. **burglaries**) the crime of entering a building, etc illegally to steal.

burgle *verb* 1 *trans.* to enter (a building, etc) illegally and steal from it; to steal from (a person). 2 *intrans.* to commit burglary.

burgomaster *noun* a mayor of a town in Germany, Belgium, the Netherlands, and Austria. [from Dutch *burgemeester*, from *burg*, borough + *meester*, master]

Burgos POP (1991) 160 000, the capital of Burgos province, Castilla-León region, N Spain. It lies on the R Arlanzón, 243km/151mi N of Madrid and was the capital of the historical region of Old Castile. El Cid lived and was buried here. NOTABLE FEATURES 13–16c cathedral (burial place of El Cid), a World Heritage site; castle of the counts of Castile; Santa Maria de Gerona nuclear power station. EVENT fair and fiestas of St Peter (Jun).

Burgoyne, General, known as **Gentlemanly Johnny** the sleek, quick-witted General in George Bernard Shaw's *The Devil's Disciple.*

Burgoyne, John (1723–92) English soldier and dramatist, born in Sutton, Bedfordshire. After army service in the Seven Years' War (1756–63), he sat in parliament as a Tory. Sent to America in 1774, he led an expedition from Canada (1777), and took Ticonderoga, but was forced to surrender at Saratoga. He later joined the Whigs, and commanded in Ireland (1782–3). His best-known work is his comedy, *The Heiress* (1786).

Burgundy, French **Bourgogne** POP (1991e) 1.6m, a region and former province in E central France, comprising the departments of Côte-d'Or, Nièvre, Saône-et-Loire, and Yonne. AREA 31 582sq km/12 191sq mi. The Yonne, Cure, and Armançon rivers flow from the wooded Monts du Morvan (902m) in the region's centre, and converge en route to the R Seine near Paris. Burgundy was formerly the kingdom of Burgundia or Burgundy (5–10c). CHIEF TOWN Dijon. ECONOMY is a famous wine-producing area (eg Beaujolais, Beaune, Chablis); industry is centred on Le Creusot. NOTABLE FEATURES caves at Arcy-sur-Cure; Parc de Morvan regional nature park; there are several spas.

burial *noun* 1 the burying of a dead body in a grave. 2 *Archaeol.* a grave and the remains found in it. [from Anglo-Saxon *byrgels*, tomb]

Burial of Count Orgaz, The a painting by El Greco (1586, Church of San Tomé, Toledo).

burial rites ceremonies associated with the burial of the dead. These commonly had, and still have, some religious significance, marking the passage of the soul into the spirit world, etc, or serving to define the social status of the dead person.

Buridan, Jean (14c) French scholastic philosopher, born in Béthune. He became a teacher of a conservative nominalist philosophy, and was Rector of the University of Paris in 1328 and 1340. He wrote on logic, metaphysics, physics, and ethics. He is best-known for his contributions to the theory of choice, illustrated by 'Buridan's ass'; an ass standing equidistant between two bales of equally desirable hay has no reason to prefer one to the other, and so dies of starvation.

burin *noun* a steel tool for engraving copper, wood, etc. [from French *burin*]

burk same as BERK.

Burke, Edmund (1729–97) British statesman and political philosopher, born in Dublin, Ireland. His early writing includes his *Philosophical Inquiry into the Origin of our Ideas of the Sublime and Beautiful* (1756). He became Secretary for Ireland, and entered parliament in 1765. His main speeches and writings belong to the period when his party was opposed to Lord North's American policy (1770–82). Other works include his *Reflections on the French Revolution* (1790).

Burke, William (1792–1829) Irish murderer, born in Orrery. With William Hare (c.1790–c.1860), he carried out a series of murders in Edinburgh in the 1820s to supply dissection subjects to the anatomist Dr Robert Knox. Hare turned king's evidence, and died a beggar in London in the 1860s; Burke was hanged in front of a satisfied crowd.

Burke's Peerage a reference guide to the aristocratic and titled families of the UK, first published by John Burke (1787–1848) in 1826 as the *Genealogical and Heraldic Dictionary of the Peerage and Baronetage of the United Kingdom*.

Burkina, official name **People's Republic of Burkina Faso**, formerly **Upper Volta** (to 1984), then French **République de Haute-Volta** POP (1992e) 9.5m, a landlocked republic situated in W Africa, divided into 25 provinces. AREA 274 540sq km/105 972sq mi. It is bounded N by Mali, E by Niger, SE by Benin, S by Togo and Ghana, and SW by the Ivory Coast. CAPITAL Ouagadougou. CHIEF TOWNS Bobo-Dioulasso, Koudougou, Ouahigouya, Tenkodogo. TIME ZONE GMT. There are over 50 tribes, notably the Mossi (48%); most of the population follows local beliefs and the remainder are Muslim and Christian. OFFICIAL LANGUAGE French; many local languages are also spoken. CURRENCY the CFA franc. PHYSICAL DESCRIPTION low-lying plateau, falling away to the S; many rivers (tributaries of the Volta or Niger) are unnavigable in the dry season; wooded savannahs in the S; semi-desert in the N. CLIMATE tropical climate, with an average temperature of 27°C in the dry season (Dec–May); rainy season (Jun–Oct), with violent storms (Aug); the *harmattan* wind blows from the

NE (Dec–Mar); rainfall decreases from S to N. HISTORY Mossi empire in the 18–19c; Upper Volta was created by the French in 1919; abolished in 1932, with most land joined to the Ivory Coast; original borders reconstituted in 1947; autonomy within the French community in 1958; gained independence as Upper Volta in 1960, since when there have been several military coups; renamed Burkina Faso in 1984; military rule ended in 1991. GOVERNMENT governed by a President elected for seven years and a 107-member National Assembly elected for five years under a multiparty constitution. ECONOMY an agricultural country, largely at subsistence level and subject to drought conditions (especially in 1973–4); mainly sorghum, millet, maize, rice, cotton, groundnuts, sesame, sugar cane, livestock; reserves of titanium, limestone, iron ore, vanadium, manganese, zinc, nickel, copper, phosphate, gold; processed foods; cigarettes; shoes; bicycles.

Burkitt, Denis Parsons (1911–93) British surgeon and nutritionist, born in Enniskillen, N Ireland. Working in Uganda, he began a series of investigations of a common childhood cancer found there from 1957. It behaved as if it were infectious and subsequent research showed that the cancer – now known as 'Burkitt's lymphoma' – was caused by a virus. Burkitt's other major contribution related the low African incidence of coronary heart disease, bowel cancer and other diseases to the high unrefined fibre in the native diet.

burlesque — *noun* 1 a piece of literature, acting, etc which exaggerates and mocks a serious subject or art form. 2 *North Amer., esp. US* a type of theatrical entertainment involving humorous sketches, songs, and usually strip-tease. — *adj.* of or like a burlesque. — *verb* to make fun of (something) using burlesque. [from Italian *burlesco*, from *burla*, jest]

burliness *noun*, *said especially of a person* a strong heavy build.

burly *adj.* (**burlier, burliest**) *said of a person* strong and heavy in build. [from Middle English *borli*]

Burma (Myanma), official name **Union of Myanma** (1989), formerly **The Socialist Republic of the Union of Burma**, Burmese **Pyidaungsu Socialist Thammada Myanma Naingngandaw** POP (1992e) 43.7m, a republic in SE Asia, which is divided into 14 administrative divisions, including seven states. AREA 678 576sq km/261 930sq mi. It is bordered by China in the N and NE, Laos and Thailand in the E, India in the NW, Bangladesh in the W, and the Bay of Bengal and the Andaman Sea in the S and W. CAPITAL Rangoon (Yangon). CHIEF CITIES Mandalay, Henzada, Pegu, Myingyan. TIME ZONE GMT +6.5. Most of the population is Burman (72%); Theravada Buddhism is the main religion. OFFICIAL LANGUAGE Burmese; several minority languages are also spoken. CURRENCY the kyat. PHYSICAL DESCRIPTION rimmed in the N, E, and W by mountain ranges rising in the N to Hkakabo Razi (5 881m) and descending in a series of ridges and valleys; the principal rivers, the Irrawaddy, Salween, and Sittang all run from N–S; the Irrawaddy R delta extends over 240km/150mi of tidal forest. CLIMATE tropical monsoon climate, with a marked change between the cooler, dry season of Nov–Apr, which is dominated by the NE monsoon, and the hotter, wet season of May–Sep, dominated by the SW monsoon; coastal and higher mountains in the E and N have heavy annual rainfall (2 500–5 000mm); sheltered interior lowlands often as low as 1 000mm; lowland temperatures are high all year round (especially Mar–May); there is high humidity on the coast. HISTORY first unified in the 11c by King Anawrahta; invasion by Kubla Khan in 1287; second dynasty established in 1486, but plagued by internal disunity and wars with Siam from the 16c; new dynasty under King Alaungpaya in

1752; annexed to British India following Anglo-Burmese wars in 1824–86; separated from India in 1937; occupied by the Japanese in World War II; independence as the Union of Burma under Prime Minister U Nu in 1948; military coup under U Ne Win in 1962; became a single-party socialist republic in 1974; in 1988 there was a military coup; the National League for Democracy opposes the military government. GOVERNMENT a military council and a Cabinet head a State Law and Order Restoration Council. ECONOMY largely dependent on agriculture (especially rice, beans, maize, sugar cane, pulses, oilseed) and forestry (teak and other hardwoods); agricultural processing; textiles; footwear; pharmaceuticals; fertilizers; wood and wood products; petroleum refining; zinc, lead, tin, copper, gypsum, limestone, chromium, asbestos, oil, coal.

Burma (Myanma)

Burma Road a road linking the railhead in Lashio, Burma (Myanma) with Kunming, 1 150km/700mi distant in Yunnan province, China. It was completed by the Chinese in 1938, and was of great strategic importance to the Allies during World War II.

Burmese — *noun* 1 (PL. **Burmese**) a native or citizen of Burma (Myanma). 2 a Sino-Tibetan language spoken by c.25 million people in Burma (Myanma), the official language of the country. — *adj.* of Burma (Myanma) or its people or language.

burn¹ — *verb* (PAST TENSE AND PAST PARTICIPLE **burned, burnt**) 1 *trans., intrans.* to be on fire or set on fire. 2 *trans., intrans.* to damage or injure, or be damaged or injured, by fire or heat. 3 to use as fuel. 4 to make (a hole, etc) by or as if by fire, heat, etc: *acid can burn holes in material*. 5 *trans., intrans.* to kill or die by fire. 6 *intrans.* to be or feel hot: *my face is burning*. 7 *intrans., trans.* to feel or cause to feel a stinging pain: *vodka burns my throat*. 8 *intrans.* to feel strong emotion: *burn with shame*. 9 *intrans. colloq.* to want to do something very much: *is burning to get his revenge*. 10 *trans., intrans.* to char or scorch or become charred or scorched: *I think the potatoes are burning*. — *noun* 1 an injury or mark caused by fire, heat, acid, etc. 2 an act of burning. 3 an act of firing the engines of a space rocket.

— **burn one's boats** or **bridges** *colloq.* to destroy all chance of escape or retreat.

burn the candle at both ends to become overtired by working for excessively long periods, especially from early in the morning till late at night.

burn down *said of a large structure such as a building* to be destroyed by fire.

burn something down to destroy a building, etc by fire.

burn one's fingers or **get one's fingers burnt** *colloq.* to become involved in something foolish, dangerous, etc and suffer as a result.

burn the midnight oil to work late into the night.

burn out 1 to be completely burnt and reduced to nothing. **2** *said of a rocket engine* to stop working when the fuel is used up.

Burkina

burn out or **burn something out** to stop or cause something to stop working because of too much use or heat.

burn out or **burn oneself out** North Amer., esp. US to be exhausted from too much work or exercise.

burn up 1 to be destroyed by fire, heat, acid, etc. **2** North Amer. slang to become very angry.

burn up fuel said of an engine to use it in large quantities.

burn someone up North Amer., esp. US slang to make them very angry.
[from Anglo-Saxon biernan, to be on fire, & bær-nan, to cause to burn]

burn² noun Scot. a small stream. [from Anglo-Saxon burna, brook]

Burne-Jones, Sir Edward Coley, 1st Baronet (1833–98) English painter and designer, born in Birmingham. He trained for the Church but turned to art when he met first William Morris, then Rossetti. His later oils, inspired by the early Italian Renaissance, are characterized by a romantic and contrived Mannerism. His subjects, drawn from Arthurian romances and Greek myths, include *The Days of Creation*, *The Beguiling of Merlin*, *The Mirror of Venus* (1877), and *King Cophetua and the Beggar Maid* (1884). He also designed stained glass and tapestries.

burner noun the part of a gas lamp, stove, etc which produces the flame.
— **put something on the back burner** colloq. to put it aside for future consideration.

Burnet, Sir Alastair, originally **James William Alexander Burnet** (1928–) Scottish journalist and broadcaster, born in Edinburgh. His 40-year career since joining the *Glasgow Herald* in 1951 included posts as editor of the *Economist* (1965–74) and of the *Daily Express* (1974–6). From 1976 he was a broadcaster with Independent Television News and made his name as a distinguished newsreader on *News At Ten*. He retired in 1991.

Burnet, Sir (Frank) Macfarlane (1899–1985) Australian immunologist and virologist, born in Traralgon, Victoria. From 1928 he worked at the Walter and Eliza Hall Institute for Medical Research in Melbourne, becoming Assistant Director in 1934 and Director in 1944. His studies of immunological intolerance in relation to skin and organ grafting transformed our understanding of how the entry of foreign substances (antigens) into the body results in the production of specific antibodies which bind and neutralize the invader. He shared the 1960 Nobel Prize for Physiology or Medicine with Peter Medawar.

Burnett, Frances (Eliza), née Hodgson (1849–1924) US novelist, born in Manchester, England. In 1865 her family emigrated to Tennessee, where she had her first literary success with *That Lass o' Lowrie's* (1877). She wrote several plays and over 40 novels, notably *Little Lord Fauntleroy* (1886) and *The Secret Garden* (1909).

Burney, Fanny (Frances), later **Madame d'Arblay** (1752–1840) English novelist and diarist, born in King's Lynn, Norfolk. Her first and best-known novel, *Evelina*, was published anonymously in 1778, and influenced Jane Austen. She was given a post in the court of Queen Charlotte in 1786, but retired soon after when her health declined. Other works include *Cecilia* (1782) and *Letters and Diaries* (1846).

burning adj. **1** on fire. **2** feeling extremely hot. **3** very strong or intense: *a burning desire.* **4** very important or urgent: *a burning issue.*

burnish verb to make (metal) bright by polishing. [from Old French brunir, from brun, brown]

burnished adj. made bright by polishing.

burnishing noun making bright by polishing.

Burnley POP (1992e) 93 000, a town in Burnley district, Lancashire, NW England. It lies at the junction of the Brun and Calder rivers, 35km/22mi N of Manchester. It was one of the early cotton-weaving towns.

burnous noun a long cloak with a hood, worn by Arabs. [from Arabic burnus]

burn-out noun North Amer., esp. US **1** physical or emotional exhaustion caused by overwork or stress. **2** the point at which a rocket engine stops working when the fuel is used up.

Burns, John (Elliott) (1858–1943) English engineer and Socialist politician, born in London. He became an MP in 1892, and President of the Board of Trade in 1914. Known as a brilliant orator, he advocated the cause of the working classes of S London.

Burns, Robert (1759–96) Scottish poet, born in Alloway, near Ayr. The son of a poor farmer, he nonetheless received a literary education, and was also much influenced by popular tales and songs. On his father's death (1784) he was left to run the farm, but he did not prove a good farmer. At the same time his entanglement with Jean Armour (1767–1834) began, and as the farm went to ruin he produced a prolific output of poetry celebrating love, lust, and country life and, as in 'Holy Willie's Prayer' (1785), satirizing Calvinism. The success of the Kilmarnock edition of his poems (1786) provided him with some money, and he decided to emigrate to Jamaica. However, the praise and admiration given to his poetry persuaded him to stay in Scotland, and he began the epistolary flirtations with 'Clarinda' (Agnes Maclehose, 1759–1841). In 1788 he married Jean Armour and leased a farm near Dumfries, and was made an excise officer in 1789. He wrote 'Tam o' Shanter' in 1790, by which time his farm was failing. He is commonly regarded as the national poet of Scotland and also has a wide international reputation as both poet and songwriter.

Burnside, Ambrose Everett (1824–81) US soldier, born in Liberty, Indiana. In the Civil War he commanded a brigade at Bull Run, and captured Roanoke I. Though driven back at Fredericksburg (1862), he held Knoxville (1863), and led a corps under Grant through the battles of the Wilderness and Cold Harbor (1864). After the war he became Governor of Rhode Island, and was elected Senator (1875). A style of cheek whiskers (later known as 'sideburns') were named after him.

Burns Night the evening of 25 Jan, anniversary of the birth of Robert Burns, celebrated in Scotland and many other parts of the world with a special meal (*Burns Supper*) including haggis, potatoes, and turnips, followed by speeches, recitations of Burns's poetry, and singing of his songs.

burnt see BURN.

burnt ochre or **burnt sienna** a natural reddish-brown pigment made dark by being burnt.

burnt umber umber heated to a dark reddish-brown colour.

burp colloq. — verb **1** intrans. to let air escape noisily from one's stomach through one's mouth. **2** trans. to rub or pat (a baby) on the back to help get rid of air in its stomach. — noun a belch. [imitative]

Burr, Aaron (1756–1836) US statesman, born in Newark, New Jersey. He was called to the Bar in 1782, and became Attorney-General (1789–91), Senator (1791–7), and Republican Vice-President (1800–4). In 1804 he killed his political rival Alexander Hamilton in a duel, and fled to South Carolina. He then prepared to raise a force to conquer Texas and establish a republic, but was tried for treason (1807). Acquitted, he spent some wretched years in Europe, and in 1812 resumed his law practice in New York City.

burr¹ same as BUR.

burr² — noun **1** in some accents of English, a rough 'r' sound pronounced at the back of the throat. **2** a continual humming sound. **3** a rough edge on metal or paper. **4** a small drill used by a dentist or surgeon. — verb **1** intrans. to make a burring sound. **2** trans. to pronounce with a burr.

Burrell, Sir William (1861–1958) Scottish shipowner and art collector, born in Glasgow, the son of a shipping agent. He entered his father's business at the age of 15, and during his lifetime accumulated a collection of 8 000 works of art from all over the world, which he gave in 1944 to the city of Glasgow, with provision for a gallery. In 1949 he gifted an art gallery and a number of pictures to Berwick-on-Tweed. The Burrell Collection was finally opened to the public in 1983 in a new gallery built for it on the south side of Glasgow.

burrito noun (PL. **burritos**) a Mexican dish of a folded flour tortilla stuffed with meat, beans, chillis, etc. [from Spanish, a diminutive of burro, donkey]

Burroughs, Edgar Rice (1875–1950) US novelist, born in Chicago. He had a variety of jobs before making his name and his fortune with the series of 'Tarzan' stories, beginning with *Tarzan of the Apes* (1914), which inspired many films, radio programmes and comic strips.

Burroughs, William S(eward) (1914–) US writer, born in St Louis, Missouri. He travelled in the USA and Europe and became a heroin addict while doing odd jobs in New York. In 1953 he published *Junkie*, an account of his experiences, and his novels *Naked Lunch* (1959) and *The Soft Machine* (1961) established him as a spokesman of the late 1950s 'Beat' movement. His later work, much concerned with innovations in the novel form, includes *Nova Express* (1964), *The Wild Boys* (1971), *Cities of the Red Night* (1981), and *Ghost of Chance* (1991).

burrow — noun a hole or tunnel dug by rabbits and other small animals for shelter. — verb **1** intrans., trans. (**burrow in** or **into something**) to make a hole or tunnel in or under it. **2** intrans. to live in a burrow. **3** intrans. said of people to hide or keep warm as if in a burrow. **4** (**burrow into something**) to search or investigate it: *burrow into one's pockets.* [from Middle English berg, refuge]

Bursa, ancient **Brusa**, or **Prusa** POP (1990) 1m, the capital city of Bursa province, NW Turkey, and the fifth largest city in the country. Founded in the 3c BC, it is today a commercial and industrial centre, noted for its silk textiles. NOTABLE FEATURE Green Mosque (1421).

bursar noun **1** a treasurer in a school, college, or university. **2** a student or pupil who has a bursary. [from Latin bursa, bag, purse]

bursary noun (PL. **bursaries**) **1** an award or grant of money made to a student; a scholarship. **2** the bursar's room in a school, college, etc.

burst — verb (PAST TENSE AND PAST PARTICIPLE **burst**) **1** intrans., trans. to break open or into pieces, usually suddenly and violently. **2** intrans. to make one's way suddenly or violently: *burst into the room.* **3** intrans. to appear suddenly and be immediately important or noteworthy: *burst on to the political scene.* **4** intrans. (**be bursting**) **a** to be quite full. **b** to break open, overflow, etc. **c** to be consumed with emotion, vitality, etc: *bursting with life / bursting with anger.* — noun **1** an instance of, or the place of, bursting or breaking open. **2** a sudden brief period of some activity: *a burst of speed / a burst of gunfire.*
— **burst into song** to begin singing, especially suddenly or unexpectedly.

burst into tears to begin weeping suddenly or unexpectedly.

burst open usually said of a door to open suddenly and violently.

burst out laughing to begin laughing suddenly or unexpectedly.
[from Anglo-Saxon berstan]

bursting *adj. colloq.* **1** very eager to do something: *we're bursting to tell you the news.* **2** (**bursting with something**) having too much of it: *bursting with pride.* **3** urgently needing to urinate.

burthen see BURDEN.

Burton, Richard, originally **Richard Walter Jenkins** (1925–84) British stage and film actor, born in Pontrhydfen, South Wales. The tenth surviving child of a coalminer, he was adopted by his English teacher, Philip H Burton, who encouraged his acting. He made his stage reputation in Christopher Fry's *The Lady's Not for Burning* (1949), and had a triumphant season at Stratford (1951). His first Hollywood film was *My Cousin Rachel* (1952), followed by *The Robe* (1953), for which he received one of his six Academy Award nominations. Among his later films were *Becket* (1964), *The Spy Who Came in From the Cold* (1965), *Equus* (1977), and *1984* (released, in 1984, after his death). He was twice married to Elizabeth Taylor (1964–74 and 1975–6), his co-star in *Cleopatra* (1963) and *Who's Afraid of Virginia Woolf* (1966).

Burton, Sir Richard (Francis) (1829–90) English explorer, born in Torquay, Devon. In 1856 he set out with John Hanning Speke on the journey which led to the discovery (1858) of L Tanganyika, and afterwards travelled in N America, and held consular posts at Fernando Pó, Santos, Damascus, and Trieste. He wrote many books on his travels, and translated several Eastern works. Lady Burton (née Isabel Arundell, 1831–96), who shared in much of his travelling and writing, burned her husband's journals after his death.

Burton, Robert (1577–1640) English writer, born in Lindley, Leicestershire. He took holy orders in Oxford in 1614, and spent most of his life at Christ Church. His major work was the *Anatomy of Melancholy* (1621, 6th edition, 1651–2), a satirical miscellany on the ideas of his time.

burton
— **gone for a burton** *Brit. slang* lost, broken, dead, no longer in existence, etc.

Burton-upon-Trent *or* **Burton-on-Trent** POP (1981) 60 000, a town in East Staffordshire district, Staffordshire, central England. It lies on the R Trent, 15km/9mi SW of Derby. The town has a long tradition of brewing (Benedictines of Burton Abbey, 11c).

Burundi

Burundi, official name **Republic of Burundi** POP (1992e) 5.8m, a republic in central Africa, which is divided into eight provinces. AREA 27 834sq km/10 744sq mi. It is bounded N by Rwanda, E and S by Tanzania, SW by L Tanganyika, and W by Zaire. CAPITAL Bujumbura. CHIEF TOWNS Bubanza, Ngozi, Muyinga,

Muramvya, Gitega, Bururi, Rutana. TIME ZONE GMT +2. The population is mainly Hutu (85%), with Tutsi (14%), and other tribal minorities; Roman Catholicism and local beliefs are the chief religions. OFFICIAL LANGUAGES French and Kirundi. CURRENCY the Burundi franc. PHYSICAL DESCRIPTION lies across the Nile-Congo watershed; bounded W by a narrow plain of the R Ruizi in the NW and L Tanganyika in the W; the R Akanyaru forms the N border with Rwanda; average height of the interior plateau is c. 1 500m, sloping E towards Tanzania; the highest point is at Mt Karonje (2 685m). CLIMATE equatorial climate, varying with altitude and season; moderately wet, except during the dry season (Jun–Sept); the average annual rainfall at Bujumbura is 850mm. HISTORY from the 16c the country was ruled by the Tutsi kingdom; following the German occupation in 1890 the area was included in German East Africa; League of Nations mandated territory, administered by the Belgians in 1919; joined with Rwanda to become the UN Trust Territory of Ruanda-Urundi in 1946; gained independence in 1962 and became a full republic in 1966; civil war in 1972; military coups in 1976 and 1987; in 1993 there was a coup which resulted in the new constitution implemented with multiparty elections being abolished; over 150 000 people were reported killed in the violence; government was restored at the end of the year. ECONOMY a very poor country, relying mainly on agriculture: main subsistence crops include manioc, yams, corn, haricot beans; cash crops include coffee, cotton, tea; light consumer goods (eg shoes, soap, beverages, blankets); reserve of rare-earth metals, peat, nickel, tungsten, columbium, tantalum, phosphate.

Bury POP (1981) 62 000, a town in Bury borough, Greater Manchester, NW England. It lies 8km/5mi E of Bolton. Bury was the home town of Robert Peel, founder of the British police force, and John Kay, inventor of the 'flying shuttle' weaving loom. NOTABLE FEATURES Lancashire Fusiliers museum; city museum with the Wrigley collection of 19c English paintings.

bury *verb* (**buries, buried**) **1** to place (a dead body) in a grave, the sea, etc. **2** to hide in the ground: *a dog burying a bone.* **3** to put out of sight; to cover: *bury one's face in one's hands.* **4** to lose (a close relative) by death: *she has already buried three husbands.*
— **bury oneself in something** to occupy oneself completely with it: *bury oneself in one's work.*
bury the hatchet to stop quarrelling and become friends again.
bury one's head in the sand to refuse to think about or accept something unpleasant.
[from Anglo-Saxon *byrgan*]

Bury St Edmunds, Anglo-Saxon **Beodericsworth** POP (1981) 31 000, a market town in St Edmundsbury district, Suffolk, E England. It lies on the R Lark, 37km/23mi NW of Ipswich. NOTABLE FEATURES 5c Cathedral of St James, 14–15c Church of St Mary, Suffolk Regiment museum, Moyes Hall museum; the 7c monastery, converted to an abbey in 1032, was an important centre for the production of illustrated manuscripts, including the Bury Bible. [named after St Edmund (c.840–69), King of East Anglia, who was buried in the town and was later canonized.]

bus — *noun* **1** a usually large road vehicle which carries passengers to and from established stopping points along a fixed route for payment. **2** *colloq.* a car or aeroplane, especially one which is old and shaky. **3** a number of conductors forming a link between different parts of a computer system or network, which allow information to be passed from one part to another. — *verb* (**bused, busing** *or* **bussed, bussing**) **1** *intrans., trans.* to go or take by bus. **2** *trans. North Amer., esp. US* to transport (children) by bus to a school in a different area, as a way of promoting racial integration.

— **miss the bus** to lose an opportunity.
[from OMNIBUS]
◇ The first (horse-drawn) omnibus service was established in Paris in the 1820s. It was not until about 1910 that bus services using petrol-driven vehicles were introduced in London and other large cities.

Busan see PUSAN.

Busby, Sir Matt(hew) (1909–94) Scottish footballer and football manager, born in Bellshill, Lanarkshire. After a playing career with Manchester City (1929–36) and Liverpool (1936–9), he became manager of Manchester United in 1945. He guided the club to the first of two FA Cup wins in 1948, and under his management Manchester United also won the League championship five times. In 1958, several of his players (the 'Busby Babes') died in an air crash at Munich airport; he later rebuilt the team, which went on to win the European Cup in 1968. He retired as manager in 1969, but continued his involvement with the club, and was its President from 1980.

busby *noun* (PL. **busbies**) a tall fur hat worn as part of the uniform of some British soldiers.

busby

bus conductor a person on a bus who collects the fares from passengers and gives out tickets.

Bush, George (Herbert Walker) (1924–) US Republican politician, the 41st President, born in Milton, Massachusetts. During World War II he joined the US Navy (1942) as its youngest pilot, then he read Economics at Yale and went into business in the Texas oilfields. From 1966 he devoted himself to politics, and was elected to the House of Representatives. Unsuccessful for the Senate in 1970, he became US Permanent Representative to the United Nations. During the Watergate scandal he was Chairman of the Republican National Committee. Under President Ford he headed the US Mission to Beijing (Peking), then became Director of the CIA. In 1980 he campaigned for the Republican nomination, but lost to Reagan, and later became his Vice-President, but he was nominated in 1988 and elected President (1989–92). As President, he focused on US foreign policy, which was changed most dramatically by the dissolution of the USSR, and he presided over the US-led UN coalition to defeat Iraq in the Gulf War. He was defeated by Bill Clinton in the 1992 election, perhaps because of the perception that he had ignored US domestic issues.

bush¹ *noun* **1** a thick, woody plant with many branches, smaller than a tree. **2** a dense group of such plants. **3** a thing like a bush, especially in thickness or density: *a bush of hair.* **4** (*usually* **the bush**) wild, uncultivated country, covered with shrubs, and sometimes trees, especially in Australia, New Zealand, and Africa. [from Middle English *busshe*; some uses are from Dutch *bosch*]

bush² *noun* a sheet of thin metal lining a cylinder in which an axle revolves. — *verb* to provide with a bush. [from Old Dutch *bussche*, box]

bushbaby *noun* an agile nocturnal primate of sub-Saharan Africa with thick fur, large eyes and ears, a long tail, and long hind legs that enable it to leap easily from branch to branch. It feeds on

bushbaby

insects, especially locusts, birds' eggs, fruit, flowers, and honey.

bushed *adj. colloq.* extremely tired.

bushel *noun* a unit of measurement used for weighing grains, fruit, liquid, etc, equivalent to 8 gallons (36.4 litres).
— **hide one's light under a bushel** to keep one's good qualities or abilities hidden from other people.
[from Old French *boissiel*]

bushido *noun* a Japanese code of chivalry, the 'way of the warrior' practised by the samurai until 1868. It taught personal loyalty to a master, death rather than capture or surrender, and stoic indifference to material goods. [from Japanese *bushi*, warrior + *dō*, doctrine]

bushily *adv.* with a bushy style or appearance.

bushiness *noun* a bushy style or appearance.

bush jacket same as BUSH SHIRT.

bushman *noun* **1** a person who lives or travels in the bush in Australia or New Zealand. **2** (**Bushman**) a member of an aboriginal tribe in S Africa. **3** (**Bushman**) the language spoken by this tribe.

bushranger *noun Austral. Hist.* a robber or criminal living in the bush.

bush shirt *or* **bush jacket** a light cotton jacket with four pockets and a belt.

bush telegraph the rapid spreading of information, rumours, etc, usually by word of mouth.

bushwhack *verb intrans.* to travel through woods or bush clearing it.

bushwhacker *noun* a person who lives or travels in bush country.

bushwhacking *noun* living or travelling in bush country.

bushy *adj.* (**bushier, bushiest**) **1** covered in bushes. **2** *said of hair, etc* thick and spreading.

busily *adv.* with a busy or occupied manner.

business *noun* **1** the buying and selling of goods and services. **2** a shop, firm, commercial company, etc. **3** one's regular occupation, trade, or profession. **4** the things that are one's proper or rightful concern: *mind one's own business.* **5** serious work or activity: *get down to business.* **6** an affair, matter: *a nasty business.* **7** *colloq.* a difficult or complicated problem; a bother or nuisance: *It's a real business filling in this form.*
— **like nobody's business** *colloq.* very fast, very well, or very efficiently.
mean business *colloq.* to be very serious about something.
on business in the process of doing business or something official.
out of business no longer able to function as a business.
send someone about their business to dismiss them or send them away.
[from Anglo-Saxon *bisig*, busy + -*nes*, -ness]
◆ See note at *busyness*.

business card a card carried by businessmen and businesswomen showing their name and business address.

business class on an aeroplane, etc, seats between the standard and first classes in price and quality.

business end *colloq.* the part of something which does the work the thing is made for.

businesslike *adj.* practical and efficient.

businessman *noun* a man who works in trade or commerce, especially at a senior level.

business park an area, usually on the edge of a town, specially designed to accommodate business offices and light industry.

businesswoman *noun* a woman who works in trade or commerce, especially at a senior level.

Busirane the evil enchanter in Spenser's *The Faerie Queene*, who imprisons and tortures Amoret in his castle.

busk *verb intrans.* to sing, play music, etc in the street for money. [probably from Spanish *buscar*, to seek]

busker *noun* a person who performs in the street for money.

busking *noun* the activity of performing in the street for money.

busman's holiday leisure time spent doing what one normally does at work.

Busoni, Ferruccio (Benvenuto) (1866–1924) Italian composer and pianist, born in Empoli, Tuscany. An infant prodigy, in 1889 he became Professor of Pianoforte at Helsinki, and taught and played in Moscow, Boston, Berlin (where he lived from 1920), Weimar, and Zurich. The influence of Liszt is apparent in his great piano concerto. His opera *Doktor Faust* was completed posthumously by a pupil in 1925.

Buss, Frances Mary (1827–94) English pioneer of higher education of women. She founded the North London Collegiate School for Ladies, which became a model for the High Schools of the Girls' Public Day Schools Company. She also campaigned for women to be admitted to university.

bust[1] *noun* **1** the upper front part of a woman's body. **2** a sculpture of a person's head, shoulders, and chest. [from French *buste*]

bust[2] — *verb* (PAST TENSE AND PAST PARTICIPLE **bust, busted**) **1** *trans., intrans. colloq.* to break or burst. **2** *slang* to raid or search. — *noun slang* **1** a police raid. **2** a drinking bout; a spree. — *adj. colloq.* **1** broken or burst. **2** having no money left; bankrupt.
— **go bust** *colloq.* to go bankrupt.
[from BURST]

bustard *noun* a large bird with long legs and a long neck. [from Old French *bistarde*, from Latin *avis tarda*, slow bird (although it is not slow)]

bustard

buster *noun North Amer. slang* a form of address used for a man or boy.

bustle[1] — *verb* **1** (*usually* **bustle about**) to busy oneself noisily and energetically. **2** to make (someone) hurry, work hard, etc: *bustled her out of the room.* — *noun* hurried, noisy, and excited activity. [from Middle English *bustelen*, to hurry along aimlessly]

bustle[2] *noun Hist.* a frame or pad for holding a skirt out from the back of the waist.

bustler *noun* a person who bustles or works with ostentatious haste.

bustling *adj.* ostentatiously lively and busy.

bust-up *noun colloq.* **1** a quarrel; the ending of a relationship or partnership. **2** an explosion or collapse.

busty *adj.* (**bustier, bustiest**) *colloq., said of a woman* having large breasts.

busy — *adj.* (**busier, busiest**) **1** fully occupied; having much work to do. **2** full of activity: *a busy day / a busy street.* **3** *North Amer., esp. US, said of a telephone line* engaged. **4** constantly working or occupied. **5** fussy and tending to interfere in the affairs of others. — *verb* (**busies, busied**) (**busy someone with something**) to occupy them with a task, etc. [from Anglo-Saxon *bisig*]

busybody *noun* a person who is always interfering in other people's affairs.

busy Lizzie a popular house-plant with pink or white flowers.

busyness *noun* a busy or occupied state.
◆ Do not confuse with *business*, which has a special meaning.

but — *conj.* **1** contrary to expectation: *she fell down but didn't hurt herself.* **2** in contrast: *you've been to Spain but I haven't.* **3** other than: *you can't do anything but wait.* — *prep.* except: *they are all here but him.* — *adv.* only: *I can but try.* — *noun* an objection or doubt: *no buts about it.*
— **but for** were it not for; without: *I couldn't have managed but for your help.*
the last but one the one before the last.
[from Anglo-Saxon *butan*, outside of, without]

butane *noun Chem.* (FORMULA C_4H_{10}) a colourless highly flammable gas belonging to the alkane series of hydrocarbon compounds, and obtained from petroleum. It is used in the manufacture of synthetic rubber, and liquid butane is used as a fuel supply for portable stoves, etc. [from Latin *butyrum*, butter]

butch *adj. slang, of a person, usually a man* tough and strong-looking. [from a boy's nickname in the US]

butcher — *noun* **1** a person or shop that sells meat. **2** a person who kills animals for food. **3** a person who kills people needlessly and savagely. — *verb* **1** to kill and prepare (an animal) for sale as food. **2** to kill cruelly. **3** to ruin or spoil. [from Anglo-Saxon *bouchier*, person who kills and sells he-goats]

butcher bird *Zool.* **1** any of six species of a bird from Australia and New Guinea that impales its prey on thorns. It is similar in size to the crow, and has a large powerful hooked beak. **2** the name sometimes given to shrikes that impale their prey on thorns.

butcher's broom a stiff leathery dark green shrub (*Ruscus aculeatus*), native to Europe and the Mediterranean region, and having true leaves reduced to scales, white flowers, and red berries borne in the centre of what appear to be leaves, but are in fact flattened leaf-like branches.

butchery *noun* **1** the preparing of meat for sale as food. **2** senseless or cruel killing.

Bute, John Stuart, 3rd Earl of (1713–92) Scottish statesman, born in Edinburgh. After early court appointments, he became a favourite of George III, who made him one of the principal Secretaries of State (1761). He was an unpopular Prime Minister (1762–3), focusing his government on the supremacy of the royal prerogative, and was soon forced to resign.

Butenandt, Adolf Friedrich Johann (1903–) German biochemist, born in Bremerhaven-Lehe (now Wesermünde). Educated at Marburg and Göttingen, where he remained as a researcher, he isolated the female hormone oestrone (1929) and the male hormone androsterone (1931). He was awarded the 1939 Nobel Prize for Chemistry jointly with Leopold Ružička, but was forbidden to accept it by the Nazi regime.

Buthelezi, Chief Mangosuthu Gatsha South African politician and Zulu leader, chief of the Buthelezi tribe since 1957, and Chief Minister of the KwaZulu homeland (which ceased to exist on 1 May 1994). He founded, and remains President of, the Inkatha Freedom Party. Although opposed to apartheid, he disagreed with the imposition of international sanctions against South Africa. Since 1989 policy disagreements with the ANC have resulted in continuing violence and bloodshed. At first refusing to participate in the 1994 election, he lifted the boycott a week before polling day when agreement was reached that the Kingdom of Zululand would be recognized in the constitution.

Butler, Benjamin F(ranklin) (1818–93) US lawyer, soldier, and congressman, born in Deerfield, New Hampshire. Admitted to the Bar in 1840, he became a noted criminal lawyer, champion of the working classes, and ardent Democrat. In the Civil War, he was appointed major-general of volunteers (1861) and took possession of New Orleans (1862), where he crushed all opposition. Elected to Congress in 1866, he was prominent in the Republican efforts for the reconstruction of the southern states and the impeachment of President Johnson. He was Governor of Massachusetts in 1882, and unsuccessfully ran for president in 1884.

Butler, Joseph (1692–1752) English moral philosopher and theologian, born in Wantage, Berkshire. His first appointment was as preacher at the Rolls Chapel, London (1718), where he preached the *Fifteen Sermons* (1726). His other major work was *The Analogy of Religion* (1736), a defence of revealed religion. He became successively Bishop of Bristol (1738), Dean of St Paul's (1740), and Bishop of Durham (1750).

Butler, Samuel (1612–80) English satirist, born in Strensham, Worcestershire. He held several secretarial posts, before becoming steward of Ludlow Castle (1661) and in later years secretary to the Duke of Buckingham. His major poetic work, *Hudibras*, a burlesque satire on Puritanism, appeared in three parts (1663, 1664, 1678).

Butler, Samuel (1835–1902) English writer, painter, and musician, born in Langar Rectory, Nottinghamshire. He became a sheep farmer in New Zealand (1859–64) and on returning to England, wrote his Utopian satire, *Erewhon* (1872) and its supplement *Erewhon Revisited* (1901), which deals with the origin of religious belief. His best-known work is his autobiographical novel *The Way of All Flesh* (1903).

Butler, Rhett the devil-may-care hero of Margaret Mitchell's *Gone with the Wind*, who makes an unhappy marriage with Scarlett O'Hara.

butler *noun* the head male servant in a house, in charge of the wine cellar, dining table, etc. [from Old French *bouteillier*, from *botele*, bottle]

Butler (of Saffron Walden), R(ichard) A(usten) Butler, Baron, also called **Rab** (1902–82) British Conservative politician, born in Attock Serai, India. He became MP for Saffron Walden in 1929, and after some junior ministerial appointments, became Minister of Education (1941–5) and introduced the forward-looking Education Act of 1944. He was Chancellor of the Exchequer (1951) under Winston Churchill, Lord Privy Seal (1955), Leader of the House of Commons (1955), Home Secretary (1957), First Secretary of State, and Deputy Prime Minister (1962). In 1963 he narrowly lost the premiership to Alec Douglas-Home, and became Foreign Secretary (1963–4).

Butlin, Billy, properly **Sir William (Edmund)** (1899–1980) British holiday camp promoter, born in South Africa. He moved with his parents to Canada, served in World War I, and worked his passage to England. After a short period in a fun fair he went into business on his own, opening his first camp at Skegness (1936). In World War II he served as Director-General of hostels to the Ministry of Supply. After the war more camps and hotels were opened both at home and abroad.

Butt, Dame Clara (Ellen) (1872–1936) English contralto singer, born in Southwick,

Sussex. She made her début in 1892, and was renowned for her performances of ballads and oratorios. Elgar's *Sea Pictures* were especially composed for her.

butt¹ — *verb trans., intrans.* **1** to push or hit hard or roughly with the head like a ram or goat. **2** to join or be joined end to end. — *noun* **1** a blow with the head or horns. **2** the place where two edges join.
— **butt in** *colloq.* to interrupt or interfere. [from Old French *boter*, to push or strike]

butt² *noun* a large barrel for beer, rain, etc. [from Old French *bout*, from Latin *buttis*, cask]

butt³ *noun* **1** a person who is often a target (of jokes, ridicule, criticism, etc). **2** a mound of earth behind a target on a shooting range. [from French *but*, goal]

butt⁴ *noun* **1** the thick, heavy, or bottom end of a tool or weapon. **2** the unused end of a finished cigar, cigarette, etc. **3** *North Amer. colloq.* the buttocks. [from Middle English *bott*, from Anglo-Saxon *butt*, tree stump]

butte *noun Geol.* an isolated flat-topped residual hill with steep sides, formed by erosion of a mesa (an area of high flat land with steep escarpments), when a remnant of hard rock protects the softer rock underneath. [from French *butte*]

butter — *noun* **1** a food that is made from the fats contained in milk. The cream from milk is pasteurized and cooled, soured by adding a bacterial culture (a *starter*), and then churned to give a solid yellowish product that usually contains at least 80% fat (by weight), and is often salted. **2** any of various substances that resemble this food in appearance or texture, eg peanut butter, coconut butter. — *verb* to put butter on or in.
— **butter someone up** *colloq.* to flatter them, especially in order to gain a favour.
[from Anglo-Saxon *butere*, from Greek *boutyron*, probably meaning 'ox-cheese']

butter bean *noun* a large flat cream-coloured bean.

buttercup *noun* a wild plant with small yellow cup-shaped flowers.

buttered *adj.* coated in or made with butter.

butterfingers *noun colloq.* a person who often drops things, or who does not manage to catch things.

butterfly *noun* (PL. **butterflies**) **1** the common name for any of about 20 000 species of winged insect belonging to the same order (Lepidoptera) as moths, and having four broad wings covered with tiny overlapping scales, and a feeding tube (known as a *proboscis*) for sucking nectar from flowers. **2** a not very serious person, only interested in pleasure: *a social butterfly.* **3** (**butterflies**) a nervous feeling in the stomach. **4** same as BUTTERFLY STROKE. [from Anglo-Saxon *buter-fleoge*, butter-fly]
◇ Butterflies are found in virtually all parts of the world, but are most abundant in tropical rainforests. They differ from moths in that they have small knobs at the tips of their antennae, and hold their wings vertically above their bodies when resting. In general, butterflies are also much more brightly coloured than moths, and tend to be active during the daytime, whereas moths are nocturnal. The life cycle of the butterfly consists of four stages (egg, caterpillar, chrysalis, and adult), and the lifespan of the adult is usually very short.

butterfly fish angelfish.

butterfly nut a screw or nut with two flat projections which allow it to be turned with the fingers.

butterfly stroke a swimming stroke in which both arms are brought out of the water and over the head at the same time.

butter-knife *noun* a blunt knife for spreading butter.

buttermilk *noun* the slightly sharp-tasting liq-

uid left after all the butter has been removed from milk.

butter muslin a loosely woven cloth, originally used for wrapping butter.

butterpat *noun* **1** a small lump of butter. **2** a piece of wood used for shaping butter.

butterscotch *noun* a kind of hard sweet made from butter and sugar.

butterwort *noun* a small carnivorous perennial plant of the genus *Pinguicula*, native to the northern hemisphere and the mountains of S America. It has a rosette of oval slightly inrolled leaves, and produces solitary white, lilac, or violet flowers on leafless stems. Insects are trapped by a sticky coating on the leaves, and then washed by rain toward the leaf margins, which inroll over them, secrete digestive enzymes, and absorb the products of digestion before unrolling again.

buttery¹ *adj.* having a taste or consistency of butter.

buttery² *noun* (PL. **butteries**) a room, especially in a college or university, where food is kept and supplied to students. [from Old French *boterie*, place for storing butts]

buttock *noun* **1** (*usually* **buttocks**) each of the fleshy parts of the body between the back and the legs. **2** the similar part of some animals. [probably from BUTT⁴]

button — *noun* **1** a small round piece of metal, plastic, etc sewn on to clothes, which fastens them by being passed through a slit or hole. **2** a small disc pressed to operate a door, bell, etc. **3** a small round object worn as decoration or a badge. **4** any small round object more or less like a button: *chocolate buttons / a button nose.* — *verb* (*usually* **button something up**) to fasten it using a button or buttons.
— **button up** *slang* to stop talking.
button something up to bring it to a successful conclusion.
on the button *colloq.* exactly right or correct. [from Old French *bouton*]

button cell a small flat circular battery used to power a watch, etc.

buttonhole — *noun* **1** a small slit or hole through which a button is passed to fasten a garment. **2** a flower or flowers worn in a buttonhole or pinned to a lapel. — *verb* to stop and force conversation on (a usually reluctant person).

button mushroom a small mushroom which has not opened out.

buttress — *noun* **1** a support built on to the outside of a wall. **2** any support or prop. — *verb* **1** to support (a wall, etc) with buttresses. **2** to support or encourage (an argument, etc). [from Old French *bouterez*, thrusting]

butty *noun* (PL. **butties**) *Brit. colloq.* a sandwich. [from BUTTER]

buxom *adj., said of a woman* attractively plump and healthy-looking. [from Middle English *buhsum*, pliant]

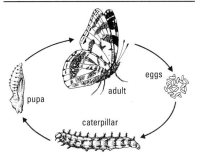
life cycle of a butterfly

Buxtehude, Diderik, German **Dietrich** (1637–1707) Danish composer and organist, born in Oldesloe or Helsingborg (now in Sweden). In 1668 he was appointed organist at the Marienkirche, Lübeck, where he began the famous *Abendmusiken* – evening concerts during Advent of his own sacred music and organ works. In 1705 Bach walked 200mi across Germany and Handel travelled from Hamburg to attend his concerts.

Buxton, Latin **Aquae Arnemetiae** POP (1981) 20 000, a spa town in Derbyshire, central England, situated 34km/21mi SE of Manchester. Its mineral waters date from Roman times. NOTABLE FEATURE Buxton Opera House (1903). EVENT well-dressing on Ascension Day.

buy — *verb* (PAST TENSE AND PAST PARTICIPLE **bought**) *usually trans.* **1** to obtain something by paying a sum of money for it. **2** to be a means of obtaining something: *there are some things money can't buy.* **3** to obtain by giving up or sacrificing something: *success bought at the expense of happiness.* **4** *colloq.* to believe or accept as true. **5** to bribe someone. — *noun* a thing bought: *a good buy.*
— **buy something in** to buy a stock or supply of it.
buy into something to buy shares in a company, etc.
buy someone off to get rid of a threatening person, etc by paying them money.
buy someone out to buy all the shares held by someone in a company.
buy oneself out to pay to be released from the armed forces.
buy time *colloq.* to gain more time before a decision, action, etc is taken.
buy something up to buy the whole stock of it.
have bought it *slang* to have been killed.
[from Anglo-Saxon *bycgan*]

buyer *noun* **1** a person who buys; a customer. **2** a person employed by a large shop or firm to buy goods on its behalf.

buyer's market a situation where there are more goods for sale than people wanting to buy them, so keeping prices low.

buyout *noun Commerce* the purchase of all the shares in a company in order to gain control of it.

buzz — *verb* **1** *intrans.* to make a continuous humming or rapidly vibrating sound. **2** *intrans.* to be filled with activity or excitement: *buzzing with activity.* **3** *colloq.* to call (someone) on the telephone. **4** *colloq.* to call (someone) using a buzzer. **5** *colloq.*, *said of an aircraft* to fly very low over or very close to (another aircraft, a building, etc. — *noun* **1** a humming or rapidly vibrating sound, eg as made by a bee. **2** a low murmuring sound eg as made by many people talking. **3** *colloq.* a telephone call. **4** *colloq.* a sense of activity, excitement, etc. **5** *colloq.* a rumour.
— **buzz about** or **around** to move quickly or excitedly.
buzz off *colloq.* to go away.
[imitative]

buzzard *noun* **1** one of a number of large hawks that resemble eagles in their effortless gliding flight, rising on warm air currents for long distances. Buzzards hunt by pouncing on rabbits, voles, mice, lizards, and other small animals. **2** *North Amer.*, *esp. US* a vulture. [from Old French *busard*]

buzzer *noun* an electrical device which makes a buzzing sound.

buzz word *colloq.* a fashionable new word or expression, often in a particular subject or social group.

BV *abbrev. Beata Virgo* (Latin) Blessed Virgin. See MARY (MOTHER OF JESUS).

BVM *abbrev. Beata Virgo Maria* (Latin) Blessed Virgin Mary. See MARY (MOTHER OF JESUS).

bwana *noun, often used as a form of address in E Africa* master; sir. [a Swahili word]

by — *prep.* **1** next to, beside, near. **2** past: *drive by the house.* **3** through, along, or across: *enter by the window.* **4** used to show the person or thing that does, causes, produces, etc something: *bitten by a dog / a play by Shakespeare.* **5** used to show method or means: *travel by air.* **6** not later than: *be home by 10 pm.* **7** during: *escape by night.* **8** used to show extent or amount: *bigger by six feet.* **9** used in stating rates of payment, etc: *paid by the hour.* **10** according to: *by my watch.* **11** used in giving measurements, compass directions, etc: *a room measuring six feet by ten / north-north-east by north.* **12** used to show the number which must perform a mathematical operation on another: *divide six by two / multiply three by four.* **13** with regard to: *do his duty by them.* — *adv.* **1** near: *live close by.* **2** past: *drive by without stopping.* **3** aside; away; in reserve: *put money by.* — *noun* (PL. **byes**) same as BYE[1].
— **by and by** after a short time.
by the by or **bye** *colloq.* while I think of it; incidentally.
by and large generally; all things considered.
by oneself 1 alone. **2** without anyone else's help.
[from Anglo-Saxon *be*]

Byblos an ancient trading city on the Lebanese coast N of Beirut. It was the chief supplier of papyrus to the Greeks, which they accordingly nicknamed 'byblos' – hence the word 'bible' (literally, the papyrus book). It is a World Heritage site.

bye[1] or **by** *noun* **1** a pass to the next round of a competition given to a competitor or team that has not been given an opponent in the current round. **2** *Cricket* a run scored from a ball which the batsman has not hit or touched.
— **by the bye** see BY.
[from BY]

bye[2] or **bye-bye** *interj. colloq.* goodbye.

bye-law same as BY-LAW.

by-election *noun* an election during the sitting of parliament to fill a seat which has become empty because the member has died or resigned.

bygone — *adj.* past, former. — *noun* (*usually* **bygones**) a past event or argument.
— **let bygones be bygones** to agree to forget past disagreements.

by-law or **bye-law** *noun* a law or rule made by a local authority. [from Norse *byjar-log*, town law]

byline *noun* a line under the title of a newspaper or magazine article which has the author's name on it.

byname *noun* another name by which a person is known; a nickname.

Byng, George, 1st Viscount Torrington (1663–1733) English sailor, born in Wrotham, Kent. He joined the navy at 15, and gained rapid promotion as a supporter of William of Orange. Made rear admiral in 1703, he captured Gibraltar, and was knighted by Queen Anne for his conduct at Málaga. He later defeated the French fleet of James Stuart, the Old Pretender (1708) and destroyed the Spanish fleet off Messina (1718).

Byng, John (1704–57) English sailor, the fourth son of George Byng, born in Southill, Bedfordshire. He joined the navy at 14, and was rapidly promoted, becoming admiral in 1756. Found guilty of neglect of duty, both for failing to relieve Minorca, blockaded by a French fleet, and for retreating to Gibraltar, he was shot at Portsmouth, presumably, in Voltaire's words, 'pour encourager les autres' (as a lesson to others).

Byng (of Vimy), Julian Hedworth George Byng, 1st Viscount (1862–1935) English soldier, born in Wrotham Park, Middlesex. He commanded the 9th Army Corps in Gallipoli (1915), the Canadian Army Corps

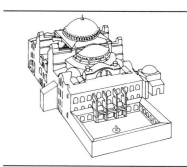

Byzantine architecture

(1916–17), and the 3rd Army (1917–18). After World War I he became Governor-General of Canada (1921–6) and Commissioner of the Metropolitan Police (1928–31), and was made a viscount (1928) and a field marshal (1932).

bypass — *noun* **1** a road which avoids a busy area or town. **2** a channel, pipe, etc which carries gas, electricity, etc when the main channel is blocked. **3** a tube inserted into a blood vessel to provide an alternative route for the blood flow, either temporarily during an operation or permanently to get round a blockage in the blood vessel. — *verb* **1** to avoid (a place) by taking a road which goes around it or avoids it. **2** to leave out (a step in a process) or ignore and not discuss something with (a person). **3** to provide with a bypass.

by-play *noun* less important action happening at the same time as the main action.

by-product *noun* **1** a secondary product that is formed at the same time as the main product during a chemical reaction or manufacturing process. By-products of industrial processes are often commercially important. **2** an unexpected, extra result; a side effect.

Byrd, Richard E(velyn) (1888–1957) US rear admiral, explorer, and aviator, born in Winchester, Virginia. He made the first aeroplane flight over the North Pole (9 May 1926), then flew over the South Pole (28–9 Nov 1929). He carried out Antarctic explorations in 1933–4 and 1939–41.

Byrd, William (1543–1623) English composer, born probably in Lincoln. Organist of Lincoln Cathedral until 1572, he then became joint organist with Tallis of the Chapel Royal. In 1575 Queen Elizabeth gave them an exclusive licence for the printing and sale of music. A great Tudor composer and a firm Catholic, Byrd wrote music of power and beauty for both the Catholic and the Anglican services, as well as madrigals, songs, keyboard pieces, and music for strings.

byre *noun Scot.* a cowshed. [from Anglo-Saxon *byre*, stall, shed]

byroad or **byway** *noun* a minor road.

Byron (of Rochdale), George (Gordon), 6th Baron (1788–1824) English poet of Scottish antecedents, born in London. He spent his first 10 years in comparative poverty in Aberdeen with his mother, before he inherited the title of his great-uncle and went eventually to Cambridge, where he followed a dissipated lifestyle. The collection of poems, *Hours of Idleness* (1807), was badly reviewed, but after his grand tour in Europe he published *Childe Harold's Pilgrimage* (1812) and several other works. These introduced the concept of the 'Byronic hero', a gloomy romantic figure like himself. He married in 1815, but was suspected of a having an incestuous relationship with his half-sister, and left for Europe, where he met Shelley. He lived in Venice for two years, and his works from this period include *Beppo* (1818) and *Don Juan* (1819–24). He gave active help to the Italian revolutionaries, and in 1823 joined the Greek rebels who had risen against the Turks, but died of marsh fever in Missolonghi.

bystander *noun* a person who watches but does not take part in what is happening.

byte *noun Comput.* a group of eight binary digits forming a unit of memory.

byway same as BYROAD.

byword *noun* a person or thing well known as an example of something: *a byword for luxury*.

Byzantine — *adj.* **1** relating to Byzantium (now Istanbul in Turkey) or the eastern part of the Roman Empire from AD 395 to 1453. **2** of the style of architecture or painting developed by the Byzantine Empire, with domes, arches, mosaics, etc. **3** secret; complex and impenetrable. — *noun* an inhabitant of Byzantium. [from Latin *byzantinus*]

Byzantine Empire the E half of the Roman Empire, with its capital at Constantinople, formerly Byzantium. Constantinople survived the collapse of the W Empire by nearly a thousand years; it finally fell to the Ottoman Turks in 1453. Its rulers included Justinian (527–65).

Byzantine music the liturgical chant of the Eastern Orthodox Churches from the rise of Constantinople (4c) to the Ottoman conquest (1453).

Byzantium an ancient Greek city on the European side of the Bosporus. It was refounded as Constantinople by Constantine, and is now Istanbul.

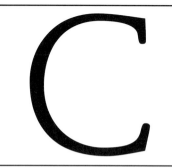

C¹ *or* **c** *noun* (PL. **Cs, C's, c's**) **1** the third letter of the English alphabet. **2** (*usually* **C**) the third highest grade or quality, or a mark indicating this. **3** (**C**) *Mus.* the note on which the Western system of music is based. **4** a musical key with the note C as its base.

C² *abbrev.* **1** Celsius. **2** centigrade. **3** century: *C19*. **4** *as an international vehicle mark* Cuba.

C³ *symbol* **1** the Roman numeral for 100. **2** *Chem.* carbon.

c *abbrev.* **1** centi-. **2** cubic. **3** *Physics* the speed of light.

c. *abbrev.* **1** *Cricket* caught. **2** cent. **3** century. **4** *circa* (Latin), approximately. **5** chapter.

© *symbol* copyright.

CA *abbrev.* **1** California. **2** Chartered Accountant.

Ca *symbol Chem.* calcium.

ca. *abbrev. circa* (Latin), approximately.

CAA *abbrev.* Civil Aviation Authority.

CAB *abbrev.* **1** Civil Aeronautics Board (USA). **2** Citizens Advice Bureaux.

cab *noun* **1** a taxi. **2** the driver's compartment in a lorry, railway engine, etc. **3** *Hist.* a carriage for hire, pulled by a horse. [short for CABRIOLET]

Cabal an acronym taken from the initials of the five leading advisers of Charles II of England between 1667 and 1673: Clifford, Arlington, Buckingham, Ashley Cooper (Shaftesbury), and Lauderdale. The name is misleading, since these five were not Charles's only advisers, nor did they agree on a common policy, and Arlington and Buckingham were bitter rivals.

cabal *noun* **1** a small group formed within a larger body, for secret, especially political, discussion, planning, etc. **2** a political plot or conspiracy. [from French *cabale*, from Hebrew *qabbalah*, tradition]

Caballé, Montserrat (1933–) Spanish soprano, born in Barcelona. In addition to her concert repertoire, she is internationally renowned for her stage roles from Rossini to Puccini, in contemporary opera, in Zarzuela, and in the German tradition (eg Wagner and Strauss).

cabaret *noun* **1** an entertainment with songs, dancing, etc at a restaurant or nightclub. **2** a restaurant or nightclub providing this. [from French *cabaret*, tavern]

cabbage *noun* **1** any of several varieties of a leafy biennial plant (*Brassica oleracea*), grown for its compact head of edible leaves, which are usually green, although in some varieties they are white or red. **2** the leaves of this plant, which can be cooked, eaten raw in salads, or pickled. **3** *derog.* a dull inactive person. **4** *offensive* a person so severely brain-damaged or mentally subnormal as to be completely dependent on other people for survival. [from French *caboche*, head]

cabbage-white butterfly a large butterfly, found in Europe and N Africa, and having wings that are mainly white with black markings, and yellow on the undersides of the hind wings. The caterpillars are pests of plants belonging to the cabbage family (Cruciferae).

cabby *or* **cabbie** *noun* (PL. **cabbies**) *colloq.* a taxi-driver. [from CAB]

caber *noun Athletics* in the contest of *tossing the caber*, a heavy wooden pole, c.3-4m in length, that must be carried upright and then tipped end over end. [from Gaelic *cabar*, pole]

cabin *noun* **1** a small house, especially made of wood. **2** a small room on a ship for living, sleeping or working in. **3** the passenger section of a plane. **4** the section at the front of a plane for pilot and crew. **5** the driving compartment of a large commercial vehicle. [from French *cabane*, cabin]

cabin boy *Hist.* a boy who serves officers and passengers on board ship.

cabin crew the members of an aircraft crew who attend to the passengers.

cabin cruiser a large, especially luxurious, power-driven boat with living and sleeping accommodation.

Cabinda 1 the seaport capital of Cabinda province, 55km/34mi N of the estuary of the R Congo. **2** a province in Angola with Cabinda as its capital. AREA 7 270sq km/2 800sq mi. Separated from the rest of Angola, it is bound W by the Atlantic Ocean and surrounded by the Congo. The province became part of Angola in 1886 by agreement with Belgium.

cabinet *noun* **1** a piece of furniture with shelves and doors, for storing or displaying things. **2** the casing round a television set, music centre, etc. **3** (*also* **Cabinet**) the group of ministers in charge of the various departments of government who meet regularly for discussion with the prime minister. [diminutive of CABIN]
◇ In Britain (where cabinet government originated), although it has no constitutional status, the cabinet forms a link between the executive and legislative branches of government, as its members must be drawn from the legislature. Members are bound by the doctrine of collective responsibility, ie ministers must publicly support decisions or resign. A cabinet may also be found in non-parliamentrary systems, such as the USA where it provides the president with an additional consultative body.

cabinet-maker *noun* a skilled maker and repairer of fine furniture.

cabinet-making *noun* the occupation or skills of a cabinet-maker.

cabinet minister *Politics* in the UK, a senior government minister with responsibility for a particular government department who is also a member of the policy- and decision-making coun-

cil chaired by the prime minister. Not all government ministers are members of the cabinet.

Cabinet of Dr Caligari, The (Das Kabinett Des Dr Caligari) a German film directed by Robert Wiene (1919). The first major German Expressionist film, it recounts a madman's imaginings and suspicions concerning Dr Caligari (played by Werner Krauss).

cabinet picture a small easel painting, carefully executed in minute detail, intended for close viewing and suitable for display in a small private room; a speciality of the 17c Dutch masters.

cable — *noun* **1** a strong wire cord or rope used for supporting loads, lifting, hauling, towing, etc, or for attaching a ship or boat to its mooring. **2** two or more electrical wires bound together but separated from each other by insulating material, and covered by a protective outer sheath, used to carry electricity, telephone messages, television signals, etc. **3** *Naut.* a measure of length or depth, about 600 ft (220 m). **4** a telegram sent by cable. **5** (*in full* **cable stitch**) a pattern in knitting that looks like twisted cable. — *verb intrans., trans.* to send a cable, or send (a message) to (a person) by cable. [from Latin *caplum*, halter]

cable car a small box-shaped vehicle suspended from a continuous moving cable, for carrying passengers up or down a steep mountain, across a valley, etc.

cablegram *noun* same as CABLE *noun* 4.

cable television *or* **cable TV** *or* **cable-vision** a television broadcasting system in which television signals are relayed directly to individual subscribers by means of underground or overhead cables, instead of being broadcast by radio waves and received by an aerial.

caboodle
— **the whole caboodle** *colloq.* the whole lot; everything.
[originally US; perhaps from *boodle*, collection]

caboose *noun* **1** *North Amer.* a guard's van on a railway train. **2** *Naut.* a ship's galley or kitchen. [from Dutch *cabuse*, ship's galley]

Cabot, John *or* **Caboto Giovanni** (1425–c.1500) Genoese pilot, who discovered the mainland of N America. Little is known about his life. About 1490 he settled in Bristol, and in 1497 set sail with two ships, accompanied by his three sons, and sighted Cape Breton Island and Nova Scotia on 24 Jun. He set out on another voyage in 1498, and died at sea.

Cabot, Sebastian (1474–1557) an explorer and navigator, the son of John Cabot, born in Venice or Bristol. He accompanied his father to the American coast, then in 1512 entered the service of Ferdinand V of Spain as a cartographer. In 1526 he explored the coast of S America for Charles V, but failed to colonize the area, and was imprisoned and banished to Africa. He returned to Spain in 1533, and later to England, where he was made inspector of the navy by Edward VI.

Cabral *or* **Cabrera Pedro Álvarez** (15c) Portuguese discoverer, born in Belmonte. In 1500 he sailed from Lisbon bound for the East Indies, but was carried to the unknown coast of Brazil, which he claimed on behalf of Portugal. He then made for India, but was forced to land at Mozambique; he was the first to provide a description of that country. He made the first commercial treaty between Portugal and India, and returned to Lisbon in 1501.

Cabrera a small Spanish island in the Balearic Is, Mediterranean Sea, lying 15km/9mi S of Majorca. ECONOMY tourism.

cabriole *noun* a furniture leg ornamentally curved to resemble an animal's leg. [from French *cabriole*, goat-like leap]

stool with cabriole legs

cabriolet *noun* **1** *Hist.* a light two-wheeled carriage drawn by one horse. **2** a car with a folding roof. [from French *cabriole*, goat-like leap]

cacao *noun* **1** a small evergreen tree (*Theobroma cacao*), native to S and Central America, but widely cultivated in other tropical regions, and of great economic importance. It has oblong leaves and pink flowers borne in clusters directly on trunks and older branches. The fruit is a yellow leathery grooved pod, enclosing up to 60 seeds embedded in soft pink pulp. The seeds (commonly referred to as 'beans' at this stage) are fermented, dried, roasted, and ground to produce cocoa powder, which is used in drinks and in the manufacture of chocolate. Pressed beans yield cocoa butter, a pale yellow fat that is used in cosmetics and as a base for chocolate manufacture. **2** the edible seed of this tree. [from Spanish, from Aztec *cacauatl*, cacao tree]

Cáceres, Arabic **Qazris 1** POP (1991) 72 000, a walled town and the capital of Cáceres province, W Spain. It lies on the R Cáceres, 297km/185mi SW of Madrid. A Roman settlement was founded here in 1c BC. The town is a World Heritage site. NOTABLE FEATURES Plaza Santa Maria; Lower Golfines Palace; Church of San Mateo; Maltravieso cave paintings. **2** a province in W Spain with Cáeres as its capital.

cache — *noun* **1** a hiding-place, eg for weapons. **2** a collection of hidden things. — *verb* to put or collect in a cache. [from French *cacher*, to hide]

cache memory *Comput.* an extremely fast part of the main store of computer memory, often used to execute instructions.

cachet **1** something that brings one respect or admiration; a distinction. **2** a distinguishing mark. **3** an official seal. **4** a special commemorative postmark. **5** *old medical use* a small edible container for a pill, etc. [from French *cachet*, something compressed]

cachexia *noun Medicine* a condition characterized by physical weakness, abnormally low body weight, and general ill health, usually associated with a chronic disease such as cancer or tuberculosis. [from Greek *kachexia*, from *kakos* bad, *hexis* condition]

cack-handed *adj. colloq.* **1** clumsy; awkward. **2** left-handed. [from dialect *cack*, excrement]

cackle — *noun* **1** the sound that a hen or goose makes. **2** *derog.* a laugh like this. **3** shrill, silly chatter. — *verb intrans.* **1** to laugh with a hen-like sound. **2** to chatter shrilly.
— **cut the cackle** *colloq.* to stop meaningless talk and come to the point.
[imitative]

CACM *abbrev.* Central American Common Market.

cacophonous *adj.* harsh, jarring.

cacophony *noun* a disagreeable combination of loud noises. [from Greek *kakos*, bad + *phone*, sound]

cactus *noun* (PL. **cacti, cactuses**) any member of a large family of mostly spiny plants (the Cactaceae), almost all of which are confined to the arid deserts of N and Central America. Cacti are succulent and store water, sometimes in the roots, but usually in swollen, often barrel-like stems, which may enable them to survive for several years without rain. The stem of a cactus often has pleat-like ribs which allow it to expand or contract as its water content changes. Cacti show various adaptations to reduce water loss. The plant surfaces are covered with a thick waxy cuticle, and in many species the leaves are absent or reduced to spines, photosynthesis being carried out by the green stem. The spines shade or insulate the cactus, protect it from animals, reflect light, and collect and absorb droplets of dew. Those cacti that flower do so very briefly, sometimes for only a few hours, and usually have conspicuous flowers, with large numbers of petals and stamens. Bird-pollinated 'day' flowers are predominantly red or yellow and unscented, whereas 'night' flowers, pollinated by moths or bats, are usually white and strongly perfumed. The fruits are berries, which are often fleshy and sometimes edible (eg the prickly pear). Many cacti are grown as house plants. [from Greek *kaktos*, prickly plant in Sicily]

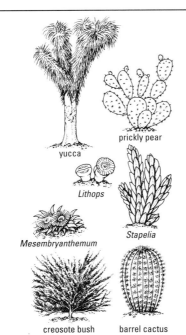

yucca
prickly pear
Lithops
Mesembryanthemum
Stapelia
creosote bush
barrel cactus

cactus types

CAD *abbrev.* computer-aided design.

cad *noun old derog. use* a man who behaves discourteously or dishonourably. [short for *caddie*, odd-job man]

cadaver *noun* a dead body, especially a human one. [from Latin *cadaver*]

cadaverous *adj.* corpse-like in appearance; pale and gaunt.

Cadbury, George (1839–1922) English businessman, born in Birmingham. In partnership with his brother Richard (1835–99), he expanded his father's cocoa and chocolate business, and established for the workers the model village of Bournville (1879), a prototype for modern methods of housing and town planning. He also became proprietor of the *Daily News* (1902).

caddie *or* **caddy** — *noun* (PL. **caddies**) a person whose job is to carry the golf clubs for a golf-player. — *verb intrans.* (**caddies, caddied, caddying**) (**caddie for someone**) to act as their caddy. [originally Scot., from French *cadet*, cadet]

caddis fly a small or medium-sized moth-like insect with brown or black wings covered with fine hairs. Caddis-fly larvae are found in ponds and streams, each larva building itself a protective cylindrical case consisting of sand grains, fragments of shell, small pieces of twig, and leaf fragments.

caddish *adj.* dishonourable, ungentlemanly.

caddy[1] *noun* (**caddies**) a small container for tea leaves. [from Malay *kati*, a unit of weight]

caddy[2] see CADDIE.

Cade, Jack (d.1450) Irish leader of the rebellion of 1450 against Henry VI. Assuming the name of Mortimer and the title of Captain of Kent, he marched on London with c.40 000 followers, demanding government reform and the return of the Duke of York to power. A promise of pardon resulted in discord among the insurgents, and they dispersed. A price was put on Cade's head, and he was killed in Sussex while trying to reach the coast.

cadence *noun* **1** a fall of pitch in the voice. **2** the rising and falling of the voice in speaking. **3** rhythm or beat. **4** a pattern of notes that closes a musical passage. [from French *cadence*, from Latin *cadere*]

cadenza *noun* an elaborate variation played by a solo musician at the end of a concerto movement, etc. [from Italian *cadenza*, from Latin *cadere*, to fall]

Cader Idris a mountain ridge in Snowdonia National Park, Gwynedd, NW Wales. It rises to 892m at Pen-y-Gader. [from Welsh *cader Idris*, chair of Idris]

cadet *noun* **1** a student at a military, naval or police training school. **2** a schoolboy or schoolgirl training in a cadet corps. [from French dialect *capdet*, chief]

cadet corps in some schools, a group of pupils organized into a unit for military training.

cadge *verb trans., intrans. derog.* (**cadge something from** *or* **off someone**) to get it by begging or scrounging.

cadger *noun* a scrounger or sponger.

cadi *or* **kadi** *noun* a judge in Muslim countries. [from Arabic *qadi*, judge]

Cadillac a make of car, first produced in 1903 by US engineer Henry Martyn Leland (1843–1932). The original model was known as the Model A Cadillac.

Cádiz, ancient **Gadier** *or* **Gades** POP (1991) 154 000, the seaport capital of Cádiz province, Andalusia, SW Spain, situated 663km/412mi SW of Madrid. It is a naval base, lying on a promontory in the Bay of Cádiz. history a base for Spanish treasure ships from the Americas in the 16–18c; in 1587 Francis Drake burned the ships of Philip II at anchor here. NOTABLE FEATURES cathedral (18c); Chapel of Santa Catalina.

cadmium *noun Chem.* (SYMBOL **Cd**, ATOMIC NUMBER **48**) a soft bluish-white metal used in alloys with low melting points, and as a corrosion-resistant plating, a component of control rods in nuclear reactors, and in nickel–cadmium batteries. Cadmium compounds, the soluble forms of which are highly toxic, are used as yellow and red pigments, and as phosphorescent coatings in television tubes. [from Greek *kadmeia*, calamine]

Cadmus in Greek mythology, the son of Agenor, King of Tyre, and sister of Europa. He followed a cow which led him to Boetia, where he founded the city of Thebes and taught its citizens to write. He later sowed dragon's teeth in the ground, from which grew a race of armed men.

cadre *noun* **1** a basic, highly trained military unit that can be expanded in emergencies. **2** an inner group of politically active people, eg within the Communist party. **3** a member of a cadre. [from French *cadre*, framework]

CAE *abbrev.* **1** College of Advanced Education. **2** *Comput.* computer-aided engineering, the use of computers to replace the manual control of machine tools by automatic control in order to increase accuracy and efficiency.

caecal *adj.* relating to or in the region of the caecum.

caecilian *noun* an amphibian found in tropical regions worldwide, up to 1.5m in length, and having a worm-like body with encircling rings and no legs. Some species have fish-like scales. It burrows into forest floors or river beds, and feeds on invertebrates. [from Latin *caecus*, blind]

caecum (PL. **caeca**) *Anat.* the blind-ended pouch, to the lower end of which the appendix is attached, at the junction of the small and large intestines. [from Latin *intestinum caecum*, blind-ended intestine]

Caedmon (7c) Anglo-Saxon poet, the first English poet known by name. According to Bede, the elderly Caedmon received a divine call in a dream to sing of the Creation. He became a monk at Whitby, and spent the rest of his life composing religious poems. The 'Hymn of Creation' is the only extant poem which can be attributed to him with any certainty.

Caen POP (1990) 189 000, the port capital of Calvados department, Basse-Normandie region, NW France. It lies on the R Orne, 15km/9mi S of the R Seine. The local limestone was used to build many of the cathedrals and churches of S England. HISTORY the principal seat of William the Conqueror; the university was founded in 1432; badly damaged during the Normandy campaign in World War II. NOTABLE FEATURES Abbey Church of St-Etienne, with the tomb of William the Conqueror; church of St-Pierre, with a famous clock tower.

Caenozoic same as CENOZOIC.

Caernarvon, Welsh **Caernarfon** POP (1981) 9 400, the administrative centre of Gwynedd, NW Wales, situated in Arfon district. It is a historic town, lying on the shore of the Menai Strait. HISTORY the castle (1284) was the birthplace of Edward II, the first Prince of Wales, and Prince Charles was invested here as Prince of Wales in 1969.

Caerphilly POP (1981) 29 000, a market town in Rhymney Valley district, Mid Glamorgan, S Wales. It is situated N of Cardiff. The town gives its name to the fine, white Caerphilly cheese. NOTABLE FEATURE castle (c.1270).

Caesar, (Gaius) Julius (c.100–44 BC) Roman general and statesman from an ancient patrician family, whose career led to the breakdown of the Republican system of government in Rome. His career progressed after service in Asia and Spain until in 60 BC he formed a triumvirate (the 'First Triumvirate') with Pompey and Crassus to protect his interests in the state. He was elected consul (59 BC) and conquered Gaul in a series of campaigns (58–50 BC), invading Britain in 55 and 54. The triumvirate came to an end in 50 BC and Caesar was asked by the Senate to surrender his command (49 BC). He refused, and instead led his army across the R Rubicon into Italy, a move which signalled the start of the Roman Civil War. Victory over the Pompeian forces at Pharsalus (48

BC), Zela (47 BC), Thapsus (46 BC), and Munda (45 BC) left him in sole control at Rome, where he received the title 'Father of his Country' and was made dictator for life. He went to Egypt where he fought on behalf of Cleopatra. His person was declared sacred and the month of Quintilis was renamed Julius in his honour. He had reformed the calendar and had many other plans for reform and improvement but he was assassinated on the Ides of March (15 Mar, 44 BC) by a group of Republican conspirators led by Brutus and Cassius. He was a talented and successful orator and general; he left well-known writings on the Gallic and Civil Wars.

caesarean *noun* (*in full* **caesarean section**) *Medicine* a surgical operation in which a baby is delivered through an incision in the lower abdomen. It is usually performed when normal delivery through the vagina would place the mother or baby at risk. [from the name of Julius Caesar, who was said to have been delivered by this method]

caesium *noun* *Chem.* (SYMBOL **Cs**, ATOMIC NUMBER **55**) a soft silvery-white metal formed by the fission of uranium, and used in photoelectric cells and certain optical instruments. The radioactive isotope caesium-137 is used in radiotherapy to treat cancer. [from Latin *caesius*, bluish-grey]

caesura *noun* a pause in a line of poetry, usually in the middle of it. [from Latin *caedere*, to cut]

café *or* **cafe** *noun* a usually small restaurant serving meals or snacks. [from French *café*, coffee, coffee house]

cafeteria *noun* a self-service restaurant. [from Spanish *cafetería*, coffee shop]

cafetière *noun* a coffee-pot with a plunger mechanism for separating the grounds from the liquid. [from French]

Caffaggiolo-maiolica maiolica made at a factory near Florence, founded in 1498 by the brothers Stefano and Pietro di Filippo. It produced brightly-coloured maiolica earthenware (1500–30), and lasted altogether for over a century.

caffeine *noun* *Biochem.* an alkaloid with a bitter taste, found in coffee beans, tea leaves, and kola nuts. It is a stimulant of the central nervous system and a diuretic. [from French *caféine*, from *café*, coffee]

caftan *or* **kaftan** *noun* **1** a long loose-fitting garment worn by men in Middle Eastern countries. **2** a similarly shaped garment worn as a dress by Western women. [from Turkish *qaftan*]

Cage, John (1912–92) US composer, born in Los Angeles. A pupil of Schoenberg and of Henry Cecil, he developed as an avant-garde composer who not only used such experimental resources as indeterminacy, chance, electronics and the 'prepared piano' (distorting the sound of the instrument with objects placed inside), but produced pieces, such as *4′ 33″* (1952, silent throughout) and *Radio Music* (1956, for one to eight radios), that challenge received ideas about what music is.

cage — *noun* **1** a container with bars, etc, in which to keep captive birds or animals. **2** a lift for taking mineworkers up and down a shaft in a mine. **3** any structure or framework something like a bird's or animal's cage: *the ribcage*. — *verb* to put in a cage.
— **cage someone in 1** to imprison or confine them. **2** to limit their freedom of action; to inhibit them.
[from French *cage*, from Latin *cavea*, hollow place]

cagebird *noun* a bird, eg a canary, suitable for keeping in a cage.

caged *adj.* kept in a cage.

cagey *adj.* (**cagier**, **cagiest**) *colloq.* not speaking frankly and openly; secretive and cautious. [possibly from CAGE]

cagily *adv.* with a cagey manner.

caginess *noun* secretiveness, wariness.

Cagliari, ancient **Carales** POP (1991e) 212 000, the seaport capital of Sardinia, Italy, and of Cagliari province. It lies on the S coast, in the Gulf of Cagliari. NOTABLE FEATURES cathedral (1312); Roman Amphitheatre; Museum of Archaeology.

Cagney, James (Francis) (1899–1986) US film actor, born in New York City. After 10 years as an actor and dancer in vaudeville, his film performance as the gangster in *The Public Enemy* (1931) brought him stardom. His ebullient energy and aggressive personality kept him in demand for the next 30 years, for such varied productions as *A Midsummer Night's Dream* (1935), *Angels with Dirty Faces* (1938), and *Yankee Doodle Dandy* (1942), for which he won an Oscar. He retired after 1961, but returned on doctor's orders for *Ragtime* (1981) and the television film *Terrible for Moran* (1984).

cagoule *noun* a light waterproof hooded outer garment, especially one that is made of thin nylon, is pulled on over the head, and reaches down to the knees. [from French *cagoule*, hood]

Cahokia a prehistoric city in East St Louis, Illinois, USA, founded in c.600, the largest such settlement in N America. At its height (c.1050–1250), the population of Middle Mississippi Native Americans reached c.10 000. The central plaza has 17 platform mounds, notably Monks Mound (c.1200), a 6 000m³ earthen pyramid, 316m by 241m at the base, standing 30m high. It is a World Heritage site.

cahoots
— **in cahoots with someone** *colloq.*, usually *derog.* working in close partnership with them, especially in the planning of something unlawful.

Caiaphas (1c AD) high priest of Israel (c.18–36), appointed by the Romans to succeed Annas. In the New Testament, he interrogated both Jesus after his arrest (Matthew 26; John 18), and Peter after his detention in Jerusalem (Acts 4).

Caicos Islands an island group in the W Atlantic Ocean, SE of the Bahamas. It forms a British Colony with the Turks Is. HISTORY settled by Loyalist planters from the S States of America after the War of Independence; following the abolition of slavery in 1838, the planters left the islands to their former slaves.

Cailletet, Louis Paul (1832–1913) French physicist, born in Châtillon-sur-Seine. While researching the liquefaction of gases in 1877, he liquefied for the first time hydrogen, nitrogen, oxygen and air by compression, cooling and sudden expansion.

caiman see CAYMAN.

Cain a biblical character, the eldest son of Adam and Eve. He was a farmer whose offering was rejected by God, although that of Cain's herdsman brother Abel was accepted (Genesis 4). He murdered Abel, and God's punishment was to make him a vagrant.
— **raise Cain** *colloq.* to cause a great disturbance, especially deliberately, eg from anger.

Caine, Michael, originally **Maurice Joseph Micklewhite** (1933–) English film actor, born in London. After years as a small-part actor, he made his name in *The Ipcress File* (1965) and *Alfie* (1966) and became an international star known both for his Cockney accent and hard work. His various successes include *Dressed to Kill* (1980), *Educating Rita* (1983), *The Honorary Consul* (1983), *Hannah and Her Sisters* (1986), for which he won an Oscar, and *Dirty Rotten Scoundrels* (1988).

Cainozoic same as CENOZOIC. [from Greek *kainos*, new + *zoe*, life]

caique *noun* **1** a light narrow boat propelled by one or two oars and used in Turkish waters, particularly on the Bosporus. **2** any small rowing boat, skiff, or lateen-rigged sailing vessel of the

Levant (including modern motorized versions), used mainly for island trade. [from French, from Turkish *kaik*, a boat]

cairn[1] *noun* a heap of stones piled up to mark eg a grave or pathway. [from Gaelic *carn*]

cairn[2] *or* **cairn terrier** *noun* a small short-legged breed of dog with a rough coat, originally from Scotland. [from Gaelic *carn*, cairn; the dogs were believed to come from rocky areas]

cairngorm *noun Geol.* a yellow or smoky brown variety of the mineral quartz, often used as a gemstone, and so called because the Cairngorms, a group of mountains in Scotland, are among the places where it occurs. [from Gaelic *carn gorm*, blue cairn]

Cairngorms *or* **Cairngorm Mountains** a granite mountain range in SE Highland and SW Grampian regions, NE central Scotland. The range forms part of the Grampian Mts, situated between the R Dee in the S and the R Spey in the N, and rises to 1 309m at Ben Macdhui. It is a winter sports area with Aviemore as an important centre.

Cairns, Hugh John Forster (1922–) English molecular biologist. He became professor at New York State University, later head of the Imperial Cancer Research Fund Laboratory in London, and since 1980 has been professor at Harvard. In important studies of the initiation and progression of cancer, he demonstrated that cancer develops from a single abnormal cell, probably initiated by mutation of the DNA sequence, but that the further progression of a cancer is dependent on multiple environmental factors such as smoking, diet, and hormones, and does not require further alteration to the cell's DNA.

Cairns POP (1991) 64 000, a resort and seaport in Far North statistical division on the NE coast of Queensland, Australia. It is the starting point for tours to the Great Barrier Reef and the Cape York Peninsula. Offshore are Green I, Fitzroy I, and Arlington Reef.

Cairo, Arabic **El Qahira 1** POP (1991e) 15m (Greater Cairo), the capital of Egypt and of Cairo governorate. It lies at the head of the delta of the R Nile, 180km/112mi SE of Alexandria, and is Africa's largest city. HISTORY originally founded as El Fustat in 642; a new capital city was founded beside El Fusat in 969; prosperity began in the 12c; occupied by the British from 1882 until 1946; headquarters of the Allied forces in N Africa during World War II; an earthquake in 1992 resulted in many deaths and destruction of property. NOTABLE FEATURES Muslim university (972) in the Mosque of El Azhar; mosques of Amur (7c), Kait Bey (15c), Ibn Touloun (878), and Sultan Hassan (14c); major archaeological sites nearby, including Heliopolis, pyramids at El Giza, and ruins of Memphis; Egyptian Museum of Antiquities, Coptic Museum, Museum of Islamic art; Royal Library. Islamic Cairo is a World Heritage site. **2** a governorate in NE Egypt with the city of Cairo as its capital.

caisson *noun* a watertight rectangular or cylindrical chamber used to protect construction workers during the building of underwater foundations, bridges, piers, etc. [from French *caisson*, large box]

caisson disease decompression sickness.

Caitanya *or* **Chaitanya** *Hinduism* a 15c sect of the Krishna *bhakti* movement, the forerunner of the Hare Krishna movement, named after the Indian mystic Caitanya (c.1486–1533) and established in northeast India, principally Bengal. Devotion to Krishna is expressed in utterance of his name (calling on his divine mercy), and in music, dance, and ecstatic trance.

cajole *verb* (**cajole someone into something**) to use flattery, promises, etc to persuade them to do something. [from French *cajoler*, to coax]

cajolery *noun* coaxing, flattery, wheedling.

cake — *noun* **1** a solid food made by baking a mixture of flour, fat, eggs, sugar, etc. **2** an individually baked portion of this food. **3** a portion of some other food pressed into a particular shape. **4** a solid block of soap, etc. — *verb* **1** *intrans.* to dry as a thick hard crust. **2** *trans.* to cover in a thick crust: *skin caked with blood.*
— **a piece of cake** *colloq.* a very easy task.
have one's cake and eat it *colloq.* enjoy the advantages of two alternatives, usually as an unattainable ideal when each excludes the other.
sell *or* **go like hot cakes** *said especially of a new product* to be bought enthusiastically in large numbers.
[from Norse *kaka*]

cakehole *noun slang* the mouth.

cakewalk *noun* **1** a prancing march with intricate improvised steps once performed by Black Americans in competition for the prize of a cake. **2** a dance developed from this. **3** *colloq.* something accomplished with extreme ease. — *verb intrans.* **1** to perform a cakewalk. **2** to accomplish something with extreme ease.

Cal. *abbrev.* California.

cal. *abbrev.* calorie.

calabash *noun* **1** a tropical American tree that bears large round gourd-like fruits. **2** the dried, hollowed-out shell of one of these fruits used as a bowl or a pipe. [from French *calebasse*]

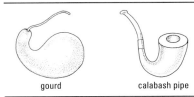

gourd   calabash pipe

calabash

calaboose *North Amer. noun slang* a small local prison. [from Spanish *calabozo*, dungeon]

calabrese *noun* a kind of broccoli. [from Italian *calabrese*, Calabrian]

Calabria POP (1991) 2m, a region in S Italy, occupying the 'toe' of the country, between the Ionian Sea and Tyrrhenian Sea. AREA 15 079sq km/5 820sq mi. PHYSICAL DESCRIPTION a mountainous region, subject to earthquakes, floods, and erosion; ranges in the N (La Sila) and S (Aspromonte) are separated by low-lying land; the coast is heavily indented with bays and coves. CAPITAL Catanzaro. CHIEF TOWNS Cosenza, Crotone, Reggio di Calabria, Locri. ECONOMY an underdeveloped area with mixed Mediterranean agriculture; wheat, olives, figs, wine, citrus fruit; mineral resources. NOTABLE FEATURE Calabria National Park.

Calais POP (1990) 102 000, a seaport in Pas-de-Calais department, Nord-Pas-de-Calais region, NW France. It lies on the Straits of Dover, at the shortest crossing to England. It is 34km/21mi SE of Dover and 238km/148mi N of Paris. HISTORY captured by England in 1346; retaken by France in 1558; a British base in World War I; there was heavy fighting here in World War II.

calamine *noun* zinc carbonate, or sometimes zinc oxide, in the form of a pink powder, used in lotions and creams for soothing stings and bites, reducing itching, etc. [from Latin *calamina*]

calamitous *adj.* disastrous, tragic, or dreadful.

calamitously *adv.* so as to be calamitous.

calamity *noun* (PL. **calamities**) a catastrophe, disaster or serious misfortune, causing great loss or damage. [from Latin *calamitas*, harm]

Calamity Jane, originally **Martha Jane Burke** (c.1852–1903) US frontierswoman, possibly born in Princeton, Missouri. Of eccentric character, usually dressed in man's clothes, she was celebrated for her bravery and her skill in

riding and shooting, particularly during the gold rush days in the Black Hills of Dakota. She is said to have threatened 'calamity' for any man who tried to court her.

calcareous *adj.* containing, or relating to, calcium carbonate; chalky. [from Latin *calcarius*, from *calx*, lime]

calceolaria *noun* any of various annual and perennial plants and shrubs belonging to the genus *Calceolaria*, native to Central and S America, and having wrinkled leaves and characteristic two-lipped yellow, orange, or red spotted flowers, the lower lip being inflated and pouchlike. [from Latin *calceus*, shoe]

Calchas in Greek mythology, a seer on the Greek side during the Trojan War. He predicted the duration of the Trojan War, recommended that Iphigeneia should be sacrificed at Aulis, and advised the construction of the wooden horse in which the Greeks finally captured Troy. He died after being defeated in a combat of 'seeing' with Mopsos.

calcicole *noun Bot.* a plant that requires soil rich in lime or chalk. [from Latin *calx calcis*, lime, limestone + *colere*, to dwell]

calciferol *noun* vitamin D₂. [from *calciferous*, calcium-carrying, as it increases the absorption of calcium, from Latin *calx*, lime]

calciferous *adj. Chem.* containing lime. [from Latin *calx calcis*, lime, limestone, + *ferre*, to bear]

calcification *noun* the process of calcifying or becoming calcified; a conversion into lime.

calcifuge *noun Bot.* a plant that requires an acid soil with a low lime or chalk content. [from Latin *calx calcis*, lime, limestone + *fugere*, to flee]

calcify *verb trans., intrans.* (**calcifies, calcified**) **1** to harden as a result of the deposit of calcium salts. **2** to change or be changed into lime. [from CALCIUM + -*ify*]

calcite *noun Geol.* crystalline calcium carbonate, a white or colourless mineral that is the main constituent of limestone and marble rocks. [from Latin *calx*, lime]

calcium *noun* (SYMBOL **Ca**, ATOMIC NUMBER **20**) a soft silvery-white metal (an alkaline earth) that is the fifth most abundant element in the Earth's crust, occurring mainly in the form of calcium carbonate minerals such as chalk, limestone, and marble. ◊ Calcium is used as a reducing agent during the extraction of metals such as uranium, and as a de-oxidizer during the production of alloys. Its compounds are used in the manufacture of plaster, cement, concrete, paper, paint, and glass. It is essential for the normal growth and development of living organisms, and it is an important constituent of bones, teeth, milk, and plant cell walls, as well as playing a major role in the clotting of blood and the control of the heartbeat. [from Latin *calx*, lime]

calcium carbide *Chem.* (FORMULA **CaC₂**) a solid grey compound, formerly used to produce acetylene in acetylene lamps.

calcium carbonate *Chem.* (FORMULA **CaCO₃**) the white solid substance of which chalk, limestone and marble are composed.

calcium chloride *Chem.* (FORMULA **CaCl₂**) a white crystalline compound that absorbs moisture from the atmosphere and is used to dry gases, and as a de-icing agent.

calcium hydroxide *Chem.* (FORMULA **Ca(OH)₂**) a white crystalline powder that dissolves sparingly in water to give an alkaline solution known as limewater. It is used as a neutralizer for acid soil, and in the manufacture of mortar, cement, bleaching powder, whitewash, and water softeners. — Also called *slaked lime*.

calcium oxide *Chem.* (FORMULA **CaO**) a white crystalline powder, formed by heating limestone, which is used in mortar and cement, and as a neutralizer for acid soils. — Also called *quicklime*.

calcium phosphate *Chem.* (FORMULA $Ca_3(PO_4)_2$) a white crystalline salt that is essential for the formation of bones and teeth in animals, and for the healthy growth of plants. It occurs in the mineral apatite.

calcium sulphate *Chem.* (FORMULA $CaSO_4$) a white crystalline solid that occurs naturally as the mineral gypsum, and is used to make plaster of Paris, paint, paper, ceramics, and blackboard chalk. It causes permanent hardness of water.

calculable *adj.* **1** capable of being calculated. **2** predictable.

calculably *adv.* in a calculable or predictable way.

calculate *verb* **1** to work out, find out, or estimate, especially by mathematical means. **2** *intrans.* (**calculate on something**) to make plans that depend on or take into consideration some probability or possibility, designed to, intended to, or likely to do something: *measures calculated to increase profits.* [from Latin *calculare*, to calculate]

calculated *adj.* intentional; deliberate: *a calculated insult.*

calculated risk a possibility of failure that has been taken into consideration before some action is taken.

calculating *adj. derog.* inclined to see other people, or situations, in terms of how one can use them to benefit oneself.

calculatingly *adv.* in a calculating way.

calculation *noun* **1** the act or process of calculating. **2** something estimated or calculated. **3** *derog.* the cold and deliberate use of people or situations to benefit oneself.

calculator *noun* a small electronic machine for doing mathematical calculations.

calculus *noun* (PL. **calculi**) **1** *Maths.* the branch of mathematics concerned with the differentiation and integration of functions. **2** *Medicine* a hard mass or 'stone' consisting of calcium salts and other compounds (eg cholesterol) that forms within hollow body structures such as the kidney, urinary bladder, gallbladder, or bile ducts. Calculi often cause pain and are usually removed by surgery. [from Latin *calculus*, pebble, as formerly used in counting]
◇ Calculus developed as a result of attempts to determine the exact gradient of a curved line. *Differential calculus* is used to calculate the rate of change of one continuously varying quantity produced by changes in another variable, by treating the quantity as if it consisted of a very large number of infinitely small changes. This form of calculus is used to determine rates of change (eg changing speed of projectiles), gradients of curves, and maximum and minimum values. *Integral calculus* involves summing the effects of continuously varying quantities by treating each quantity as if it consists of a large number of infinitely small quantities. It can be used to solve differential equations, and to calculate the area enclosed by a curve, or the volume enclosed by an irregular surface.

Calcutta POP (1991) 10.9m, the largest city in India and the port capital of West Bengal. It is situated on the R Hugli, in the delta of the R Ganges, 128km/80mi from the Bay of Bengal. HISTORY founded by the British East India Company in 1690; capital of British India from 1773 until 1912. NOTABLE FEATURES Ochterlony Monument; Raj Bhaven; St John's Cathedral (1787); Nakhoda Mosque (1926); Marble Palace (1835); Jain Temple (1867), Hindu Bengali Temple of Kali (1809).

Calcutta Cup an annual rugby union match (and the trophy awarded to the winner) between Scotland and England during the Five Nations' Championship.

caldera *noun Geol.* a large crater formed when the remains of a volcano subside down into a magma chamber that has been emptied during a violent eruption. The caldera may subsequently fill with water and become a *crater lake.* [from Spanish CALDERA, cauldron]

Calderón de la Barca, Pedro (1600–81) Spanish dramatist, born in Madrid. He was chaplain of honour to Philip IV and wrote plays, masques, and operas for the court, the Church, and the public theatres. He wrote over 100 plays on secular themes, such as *El príncipe constante* (The Constant Prince, 1629) and *El alcalde de Zalamea* (The Mayor of Zalamea, 1640), as well as many religious plays, including over 70 for the festival of Corpus Christi.

Caldwell, Erskine (1903–87) US writer, born in White Oak, Georgia. His best-known novels are *Tobacco Road* (1932) and *God's Little Acre* (1933). Much of his work, both fiction and non-fiction, addresses issues of social injustice in the US South.

Caledonian — *adj.* concerning or belonging to Scotland. — *noun facetious* a Scot. [from Latin *Caledonia,* Scotland]

Caledonian Canal a line of inland navigable waterway in Highland region, Scotland, length 96km/60mi. Following the Great Glen (Glen Mor), it extends from Inverness in the NE to Loch Eil near Fort William in the SW, linking the North Sea and the Irish Sea. Built by Thomas Telford between 1803 and 1823, it passes through Lochs Ness, Oich, and Lochy, and 35km/22mi of man-made channels (excavated between 1803 and 1847). The canal has 29 locks.

calendar *noun* **1** a booklet or chart, or an adjustable device, that shows the months and days of the year. **2** any system by which the beginning, length, and divisions of the year are fixed: *the Julian calendar.* **3** a timetable or list of important dates, events, appointments, etc. [from Latin *calendrium,* account book]

calender — *noun* a machine with heated rollers for pressing, smoothing and giving a shiny surface to cloth or paper. — *verb* (**calendered**, **calendering**) to press (cloth or paper) in a calender. [from French *calandre,* from Greek *kylindros,* cylinder, roller]

calends *pl. noun* in the Roman calendar, the first day of the month. [from Latin *calendae*]

calf¹ *noun* (PL. **calves**) **1** the young of a cow, and of several other animals, eg the elephant, the whale, and the larger deer. **2** same as CALFSKIN.
— **in calf** pregnant with a calf.
[from Anglo-Saxon *cælf*]

calf² *noun* (PL. **calves**) the thick fleshy back part of the leg below the knee. [from Norse *kálfi*]

calf love romantic love between adolescents, or the love of an adolescent for an older person.

calfskin *noun* leather made from the skin of a calf.

Calgary POP (1991) 711 000, a city in S Alberta, SW Canada. It is situated on the Bow R where it meets the Elbow R, near the foothills of the Rocky Mts. Oil is the most important industry; Calgary is also the centre of a rich grain and livestock area. HISTORY a fort was first built in 1875; growth followed the arrival of the Canadian Pacific Railway in 1883; a large part of Calgary was destroyed by fire in 1886; oil was found to the S in 1914. NOTABLE FEATURES Glenbow Alberta Art Gallery and Museum; Heritage Park Open-Air Museum; Dinosaur Park; Calgary Zoo; Calgary Tower (1967, 190m high); Centennial Planetarium.

Cali POP (1992e) 1.6m, the third largest city in Colombia and the capital of Valle de Cauca department in the W of the country. The city, which is situated at the centre of a rich sugar-producing region, was founded in 1536. NOTABLE FEATURES colonial ranch-house of Cañas Gordas; Church and 18c Monastery of San Francisco; church and convent of La Merced; cathedral; National Palace; Modern Art Museum.

Caliban the semi-human, immoral offspring of the witch Sycorax in Shakespeare's *The Tempest,* who is the sole inhabitant of the island on which Prospero ends up.

calibrate *verb* **1** to mark the scale on (a measuring instrument). **2** to correct or adjust (the scale or instrument). [see CALIBRE]

calibrated airspeed *Aeron.* an airspeed value obtained from an airspeed indicator and corrected for instrument error but not for altitude. See also TRUE AIRSPEED.

calibration *noun* **1** the act of calibrating a measuring instrument by checking it against fixed standards and then marking a scale on it. **2** one of the individual marks on the scale of a measuring instrument. **3** any measurement that is made against a fixed standard.

calibre *noun* **1** the inner diameter of the barrel of a gun or of any tube. **2** the diameter of a bullet or shell. **3** quality; standard; ability. [from French *calibre,* from Arabic *qalib,* mould]

calico *noun* (PL. **calicoes**) a kind of cotton cloth, usually plain white or in its natural, unbleached state. [from *Calicut* in India, from where the cloth was first brought]

Calicut see KOZHIKODE.

Calidore, Sir the gentle Knight of Courtesy in Spenser's *The Faerie Queene,* who pursues the Blatant Beast in an attempt to overcome the vulgarities in the world.

Calif. *abbrev.* California.

California POP (1990) 30.9m, a state in SW USA, divided into 58 counties. AREA 411 033sq km/158 706sq mi. It is bounded S by Mexico and W by the Pacific Ocean. California is known as the 'Golden State'. CAPITAL Sacramento. CHIEF TOWNS San Francisco, Los Angeles, Oakland, San Diego. PHYSICAL DESCRIPTION mountainous in the N, W, and E, with dry, arid depressions in the S (Mojave and Colorado deserts) and SE (Death Valley); the Klamath Mts lie in the N; Coast Ranges in the W run parallel to the Pacific; the Sierra Nevada in the E rises to 4 418m at Mt Whitney (the state's highest point); the foothills of the Sierra Nevada contain the Mother Lode, a belt of gold-bearing quartz; the Sierra Nevada and Coast Ranges are separated by the Central Valley which is drained by the San Joaquin and Sacramento rivers; a zone of faults (the San Andreas Fault) extends S from N California along the coast; earth tremors are commonplace; there have been major earthquakes during the 20c. HISTORY originally populated by several Native American tribes; discovered by the Spanish in 1542; colonized in the mid-18c; developed after gold was discovered in the Mother Lode in 1848; ceded to the USA by the treaty of Guadalupe Hidalgo in 1848; joined the Union as the 31st state in 1850; a major US growth area in the 20c and now the most populous US state. ECONOMY fruit, vegetables, grain; livestock; oil, natural gas, and a wide range of minerals; food processing; machinery; defence industries (but these suffered major cuts in the 1980s and 1990s); transportation equipment; fabricated metals; cotton; wine (vineyards in over 40 Californian counties); tourism; Silicon Valley is the centre of the US microelectronics industry. NOTABLE FEATURES several national monuments and parks (Yosemite, Kings Canyon, Sequoia, Redwood); the film industry; Disneyland.

California, Gulf of an arm of the Pacific Ocean between the Mexican mainland in the E and Baja California in the W. The Colorado R delta lies to the N. The gulf broadens and deepens towards the S, where it reaches a maximum depth of 2 595m. It is 1 130km/700mi long by 80–130km/50–80mi wide. Tourism, fishing, and the harvesting of sponge, pearl, and oyster are important.

California Institute of Technology a university and major centre for scientific and engineering research founded in 1891 at Pasadena, California. Originally known as the Throop Polytechnic, it was renamed in 1920, and is commonly known as 'CalTech'. The university has been co-educational since 1970.

Californian Indians once a very large concentration of many distinct Native American groups, including the Yurok, Maidu, Cahuilla, Miwok, Pomo, Mojave, Hupa, and Chumash. Before the Spanish conquest of California in the 18c there were an estimated 105 tribes, speaking many different dialects. With the Spanish conquest, their population was reduced from an estimated 350 000 to 100 000, and during the 19c many groups became extinct. The present population is c.40 000, living both on and off reservations.

californium *noun Chem.* (SYMBOL **Cf**, ATOMIC NUMBER **98**) a synthetic radioactive metal produced by bombarding curium-242 with alpha particles. One of its isotopes, californium-252, is produced in nuclear reactors, and is a strong neutron source. [from the name *California*, where the element was first made]

Caligula, properly **Gaius Julius Caesar Germanicus** (AD 12–41) Roman emperor (37–41), the youngest son of Germanicus and Agrippina, born in Antium. He was brought up in an army camp and nicknamed Caligula from his little soldier's boots (*caligae*), though his official name on accession to the throne was Gaius. His extravagant, autocratic, vicious, and mentally unstable behaviour eventually resulted in his assassination.

caliph *or* **khalif** *noun* a Muslim civil and religious leader. [from Arabic *khalifah*, successor (of Mohammed)]

caliphate *noun* the rank of, or area ruled by, a caliph.

call — *verb* **1** *trans., intrans.* (also **call out**) to shout or speak loudly in order to attract attention or in announcing something. **2** to ask (someone) to come, especially with a shout. **3** to ask for a professional visit from. **4** to summon or invite. **5** *trans., intrans.* to telephone. **6** to waken. **7** *intrans.* to make a visit: *call at the grocer's.* **8** *intrans.* to stop at a place during a journey: *does the train call at York?* **9** to give a name to: *called her Mary.* **10** to regard or consider (something) as: *I call that strange.* **11** to say or imply that (someone) is (something unpleasant): *are you calling me a liar?* **12** to summon or assemble people for (a meeting). **13** to announce or declare: *call an election.* **14** *intrans.* (**call for something**) to make a demand or appeal for it. **15** *trans., intrans.* to make a bid, or choose (a suit for trumps), in a card game. **16** *said of an umpire, etc* to judge (a ball) to be in or out of play. **17** *intrans. said of a bird, etc* to make its typical or characteristic sound. — *noun* **1** a shout or cry. **2** the cry of a bird or animal. **3** an invitation; a summons. **4** a demand, request, or appeal. **5** (**call on something**) a claim or demand for it: *too many calls on my time.* **6** a brief visit. **7** an act of contacting someone by telephone; a telephone conversation. **8** a need or reason: *not much call for Latin teachers.* **9** an act of waking someone, usually by arrangement. **10** a signal blown on a bugle, etc. **11** a feeling that one has been chosen to do a particular job; a vocation. **12** a player's turn to bid or choose trumps in a card game. **13** the decision of a referee, etc on whether a ball is in or out of play. **14** an instrument that imitates a bird's call.
— **call back** to visit or telephone again.
call someone back to contact them again or in return by telephone.
call collect *North Amer., esp. US* to have the telephone call one is making charged to the receiver of the call; to reverse the charges.
call something down on someone to try to inflict on them as if from heaven.
call for something or someone 1 to require them. **2** to collect or fetch them.
call something forth to elicit or evoke it.

call someone in to invite or request their help.
call something in to request the return of (eg library books, a batch of faulty products, etc).
call in on *or* **in at someone** to visit them, usually briefly.
call something into question to suggest reasons for doubting it.
call it a day to decide to finish work, etc.
call something off 1 to cancel a meeting, arrangement, etc. **2** to order (a dog) to stop attacking (someone). **3** to give orders for (something) to be stopped: *call off the search.*
call on *or* **upon someone 1** to visit them. **2** to appeal to them. **3** to request or invite them: *call on the secretary to read the minutes.*
call on something to gather or summon up one's strength, etc.
call people out 1 to instruct (workers) to strike. **2** to summon (eg the fire brigade, the army, etc) to help with an emergency, etc.
call round to make an informal visit.
call something *or* **someone to mind 1** to remember them. **2** to remind one of something.
call someone up 1 to conscript them into the armed forces. **2** *colloq.* to telephone them.
call something up to cause (memories, images, etc) to come into the mind.
have first call on something to have the right to (someone's help, attention, etc) before anyone else.
on call *said eg of a doctor* available if needed, eg to deal with an emergency.
within call close enough to hear if called.
[from Anglo-Saxon *ceallian*]

Callaghan (of Cardiff), (Leonard) James Callaghan, Baron, also called **Jim** (1912–) English Labour politician and Prime Minister, born in Portsmouth. He was elected MP for S Cardiff from 1945, and as Chancellor of the Exchequer under Harold Wilson (1964–7), he introduced the controversial corporation and selective employment taxes. He was Home Secretary (1967–70) and Foreign Secretary (1974–6), and on Wilson's resignation became Prime Minister (1976–9). He resigned as Leader of the Opposition in 1980.

Callao 1 POP (1990e) 589 000, the port capital of Callao department, W Peru. It handles 75% of Peru's imports and c.25% of its exports. The city was under Chilean occupation from 1879 to 1884. The rail link to Lima, built in 1851, was the first railway in S America. NOTABLE FEATURE Real Felipe fortress (1774). **2** a department in W Peru with Callao as its capital.

Callas, Maria (Meneghini) (1923–77) US operatic soprano, born in New York City of Greek parents. She studied at Athens Conservatory, and in 1947 appeared in *La Gioconda* in Verona, where she won immediate recognition. She sang with great authority in all the most exacting soprano roles, and excelled in the intricate *bel canto* style of pre-Verdian Italian opera.

call box a public telephone box.

Callendar, Hugh Longbourne (1863–1930) English physicist, born in Hatherop, Gloucestershire. Professor at McGill University in Montreal, University College London and Imperial College of Science, he devised a constant-pressure air thermometer which could measure up to 450°C, and also an accurate platinum resistance thermometer.

caller *noun* a person visiting or making a telephone call.

Calles, Plutarco Elías (1877–1945) Mexican politician, born in Guaymas, Sonora. He began as a teacher, and then became Governor of Sonora (1917) and President of Mexico (1924–8). Known for his anticlericalism and for his efforts to restrict foreign influence in the oil industry, he was defeated by Cárdenas and exiled to the USA (1936), but was allowed to return in 1941.

call girl a prostitute with whom appointments are made by telephone.

calligrapher *or* **calligraphist** *noun* a person skilled in calligraphy.

calligraphy *noun* **1** handwriting as an art. **2** beautiful, decorative handwriting. [from Greek *kallos*, beauty + *graphein*, to write]
◇ Calligraphy is a major art form in many countries of E Asia (most particularly in China and Japan), and in Arabic-speaking countries (where much of the art is based on or drawn from the sacred writings of Islam). In the West, there has been a revival of interest in calligraphy, both as a general means of improving or standardizing handwriting, and as an art form in its own right. Edward Johnston's teachings pubished in *Writing and Illumination and Lettering* (1906) were particularly influential in the UK and Europe.

calling *noun* **1** a trade or profession. **2** an urge to follow a particular profession, especially the ministry or one involving the care of other people.

calling-card *noun* **1** *North Amer.* a card bearing one's name, etc that one leaves when calling at someone's house; a visiting-card. **2** an unmistakable and usually disagreeable sign, especially deliberately left, that a particular person has been present.

Calliope in Greek mythology, the muse of epic poetry, and the most important of the nine muses. She was loved by Apollo, and is usually said to be the mother of Orpheus.

calliper *noun* **1** (**callipers**) a measuring instrument with two prongs, resembling a large pair of geometrical dividers attached to a scale which is used to measure the linear distance between them, eg to determine the diameters of pipes. **2** a splint for supporting an injured or paralysed leg by keeping it rigid and taking most of the weight of the body. It consists of metal rods that extend from a metal plate under the foot to a padded ring surrounding the upper thigh. [another form of CALIBRE]

callisthenic *adj.* relating to or typical of callisthenics.

callisthenics *noun* a system of physical exercises for increasing the body's strength and grace. [from Greek *kallos*, beauty + *sthenos*, strength]

Callisto 1 in Greek mythology, an Arcadian nymph attendant upon Artemis. She was seduced by Zeus, became pregnant, and was changed into a she-bear by either Artemis or Hera. Later, her son Arcas tried to spear her, and Zeus took pity on them and changed her into the constellation Ursa Major (Great Bear) and her son likewise into Arctophylax. **2** *Astron.* the second largest moon of Jupiter, 4 800km in diameter. Its dark surface, which is thought to consist of a mixture of ice and rocky material, is covered with large craters.

callosity *noun* (PL. **callosities**) an area of skin that has become hardened and thickened as a result of pressure or friction. [from Latin *callositas*]

callous[1] *adj.* lacking any concern for others; unfeeling; coldly and deliberately cruel. [from Latin *callosus*, thick-skinned]

callous[2] see CALLUS.

callously *adv.* in a callous way.

callousness *noun* lack of feeling, brutality.

callow *adj. derog.* young and inexperienced. [from Anglo-Saxon *calu*, bald]

call sign *or* **call signal** a word, letter, or number that identifies a ship, plane, etc when communicating with another by radio.

call-up *noun* an order to join the armed forces as a conscript.

callus *or* **callous** *noun* **1** a thickened hardened pad of skin which develops on parts of the body that are subjected to constant friction or pressure, such as the palms of the hands and soles of the feet. **2** a mass of tissue, consisting of large thin-walled parenchyma cells, that forms around a wound on the surface of a plant. **3** a mass of blood and connective tissue that forms around the exposed ends of a fractured bone, and represents an important part of the healing process. [from Latin *callus*, hardened skin or tissue]

calm — *adj.* **1** relaxed and in control; not anxious, upset, angry, etc. **2** *said of the weather, etc* still, quiet, peaceful; not rough or stormy. — *noun* **1** peace, quiet, tranquillity. **2** stillness of weather. **3** a lack of sufficient wind for sailing. — *verb trans., intrans.* **1** (**calm down**) to become calmer. **2** (**calm someone** *or* **something down**) to make them calmer. [from French *calme*, from Greek *kauma*, (a rest during) the heat of noon]

Calmar see KALMAR.

Calmette, (Léon Charles) Albert (1863–1933) French bacteriologist, born in Nice. Founder of the Pasteur institutes at Saigon and Lille, he discovered an anti-snakebite serum and described a diagnostic test for tuberculosis known as 'Calmette's reaction'. He is best known for the vaccine BCG (Bacillus Calmette–Guérin), for inoculation against tuberculosis, which he jointly discovered with Camille Guérin in 1908.

calmly *adv.* with a calm manner.

calmness *noun* the quality or state of being calm.

Calor gas *trademark* a mixture of liquefied butane and propane gases, stored under pressure in metal cylinders, and used as a fuel supply for portable stoves, etc. [from Latin *calor*, heat]

calorie *noun* the amount of heat required to raise the temperature of one gram of water by 1°C (1K) at one atmospheric pressure. — Also called *small calorie*. See also KILOCALORIE. [from French, from Latin *calor*, heat]

Calorific Values

Food (raw)	Approx. calorie value
apple	60
orange	60
tomato	15
onion	40
potato (per 100g)	75
egg	80
pasteurized whole milk (1 pint)	380
butter (per 100g)	750
Cheddar cheese (per 100g)	420
wholemeal bread (per 100g)	220
brown rice (per 100g)	360
minced beef (per 100g)	230
cod fillet (per 100g)	80
white or brown sugar (per 100g)	400
milk chocolate (per 100g)	525
instant coffee (per 100g)	0
white or red wine (1 glass)	100
beer or lager ($\frac{1}{2}$ pint)	90

calorific *adj.* relating to, or producing, heat. [from Latin *calorificus*, warming]

calorific value *Physics* the amount of heat liberated during the complete combustion of unit mass of a fuel or food.

calorimeter *noun Chem.* an instrument for measuring the thermal properties of a substance, especially its calorific value. [from Latin *calor*, heat + -METER]

Calotype a very early method of photography patented by Fox Talbot in 1841, using paper sensitized with silver iodide to produce a negative image.

calque *noun* a loan translation, ie a compound word or phrase that is a literal translation of the parts of a foreign expression, as in the German word for 'telephone', *Fernsprecher* (= *Fern*, distant,

+ *sprecher*, speaker). In English, *superman* is a calque of German *Übermensch*. [from Latin *calcare*, to tread]

Calum a male first name. [from Gaelic *columba*, dove]

calumniate *verb* to utter a calumny against (someone).

calumniator *noun* a person who utters calumny.

calumnious *adj.* of the nature of calumny; slanderous.

calumny *noun* (PL. **calumnies**) an untrue and malicious spoken statement about a person, or the act of uttering this. [from Latin *calumnia*, false accusation]

Calvary, Semitic **Golgotha** the site where Jesus Christ was crucified, presumed to be a place of execution just outside of Jerusalem (Luke 23.33). [from Latin *calvaria*, skull]

calve *verb intrans.* to give birth to a calf.

calves pl. of CALF[1], CALF[2].

Calvin, John (1509–64) French Protestant reformer, born in Noyon, Picardy. He began to preach the Reformed doctrines around France, but was forced to flee the country to escape persecution. He issued his influential *Christianae Religionis Institutio* (Institutes of the Christian Religion, 1536) in Basle, and in Geneva was persuaded by Guillaume Farel to take part in the reformation but they were both expelled from the city (1538). Calvin withdrew to Strasbourg, but in 1541 he was recalled to Geneva. He founded a theocracy which controlled most of the city's affairs, and by 1555 his authority was supreme. The father of Reformed Theology, he left a double legacy to Protestantism by systematizing its doctrine and organizing its ecclesiastical discipline. His commentaries on most of the Old and New Testaments were collected and published in 1617.

Calvin, Melvin (1911–) US chemist, born in Minnesota. Professor at the University of California (1947–71) and head of its Lawrence Radiation Laboratory (1963–80), he is best known for his researches into the role of chlorophyll in photosynthesis, for which he was awarded the 1961 Nobel Prize for Chemistry.

Calvinism *noun* the teachings of John Calvin, laying emphasis on mankind's inability to repent and believe in Christ without God's help, and on predestination (God's deciding in advance who will go to heaven and who will not).

Calvinist *noun* a follower of Calvinism.

Calvinistic *adj.* **1** relating to or typical of Calvinism. **2** following the doctrines of Calvinism.

calx *noun* (PL. **calces**, **calxes**) the powdery remains of a metal or mineral after strong heating. [from Latin *calx*, lime]

Calydonian hunt in Greek mythology, the hunting of a giant boar, sent by Artemis to ravage the kingdom of Calydon, after she had been provoked by King Oineus. The boar was killed by Meleager and he gave the spoils to Atalanta, which brought about a quarrel leading to Meleager's death.

Calypso *Astron.* the fourteenth moon of Saturn, 30km in diameter, discovered in 1980.

calypso *noun* (PL. **calypsos**) a type of popular song invented in the West Indies, usually dealing with current happenings in an amusing way, and often made up by the singer as he or she goes along.

calyx *noun* (PL. **calyces**, **calyxes**) *Bot.* the outermost whorl (circle) of a flower, consisting of the sepals, which are often green and leaf-like. The calyx encloses the petals, stamens, and carpels, and protects the developing flower bud. [from Greek *calyx*, covering, husk]

calzone *noun* a folded round of pizza dough stuffed with a savoury filling. [from Italian *calzone*, trouser leg]

CAM *Comput.* computer-aided manufacture, the use of computers to control any part of a manufacturing process.

cam *noun Engineering* an irregular projection on a wheel or rotating shaft, shaped so as to transmit regular movement to another part, eg to operate the cylinder valves of a car engine. [from Dutch *kam*, comb]

camaraderie *noun* a feeling of friendship and cheerful support for one another within a group or team of people. [from French *camaraderie*]

Camargue a district in the R Rhône delta, SE France, situated S of Arles. It is an alluvial island, mainly consisting of saltmarsh and lagoon. CHIEF TOWN Saintes-Maries-de-la-Mer. ECONOMY rice and vines (on reclaimed land in the N); tourism. NOTABLE FEATURES Etang de Vaccares nature reserve for migratory birds; the Camargue is famous for its breeding of black bulls and white horses.

Cambell the courageous brother of Canacee in Spenser's *The Faerie Queene*, who, protected by a magic ring which stops wounds from bleeding, fights Triamond and his two brothers to determine who will win his sister's hand, becoming in the process firm friends with Triamond.

camber *noun* a slight curve across the surface of a road, etc that makes water run off it, down to the sides. [from French *cambre*]

cambium *noun Bot.* in the roots and stems of woody plants, a layer of actively dividing cells between the xylem and the phloem, which produces an increase in lateral growth or girth. [from Latin *camire*, to exchange]

Cambodia, formerly **Kampuchea** (1975–89), and **Khmer Republic** (1970–5) POP (1992e) 9.1m, a republic in S Indo-China, SE Asia, divided into 18 provinces. AREA 181 035sq km/69 880sq mi. It is bounded NW by Thailand, N by Laos, E by Vietnam, and S and SW by the Gulf of Thailand. CAPITAL Phnom Penh. CHIEF TOWNS Battambang, Kompong, Som, Kompong Cham. The population is mainly Khmer (93%); Theravada Buddhism is the chief religion. TIME ZONE GMT +9. OFFICIAL LANGUAGE Khmer; French is also widely spoken. CURRENCY the riel. PHYSICAL DESCRIPTION occupies an area surrounding the Tonlé Sap (lake), a freshwater depression on the Cambodian Plain, which is crossed by the floodplain of the Mekong R in the E; the highest land lies in the SW, where the Cardamom Mts run for 160km/100mi across the Thailand border, rising to 1 813m at Phnom Aural. CLIMATE tropical monsoon climate, with a wet season in May–Sep; heavy rainfall in the SW mountains; high temperatures in the lowland region throughout the year; the average monthly rainfall at Phnom Penh is 257mm in Oct, 7mm in Jan. HISTORY originally part of the Kingdom of Fou-Nan, taken over by

Cambodia

the Khmers in the 6c; in dispute with the Vietnamese and the Thais from the 15c; established as a French Protectorate in 1863; became part of Indo-China in 1887; gained independence from France in 1953, with Prince Sihanouk as Prime Minister; Sihanouk was deposed in 1970 and a right-wing government was formed; the country was renamed the Khmer Republic; fighting throughout the country involved troops from N and S Vietnam and the USA; surrender in 1975 of Phnom Penh to the Khmer Rouge, a Communist guerrilla force which opposed the government; the country became known as Kampuchea; an attempt to reform the economy on co-operative lines by Pol Pot in 1975-8 caused the deaths of an estimated three million people; further fighting in 1977-8; Phnom Penh was captured by the Vietnamese in 1979, causing the Khmer Rouge to flee; in 1981 a constitution established a seven-member Council of State and a 16-member Council of Ministers; the Paris conference in 1988-9 between the Phnom Penh regime, the opposition coalition led by Prince Sihanouk, and the Khmer Rouge ended with no agreement; the name of Cambodia was restored in 1989; Vietnamese troops completed their withdrawal from Cambodia in 1989; a UN peace plan was agreed in 1991; in 1992 a UN Transitional Authority in Cambodia was planned but the Khmer Rouge refused to comply and UN trade sanctions were imposed in 1993; a new constitution was adopted in 1993. GOVERNMENT a pluralistic political system and a limited monarchy. ECONOMY most of the population are employed in subsistence agriculture, especially rice and corn; rubber; pepper; forestry; rice milling; fish processing; phosphates; gemstones; motor-assembly; cigarettes; industrial development disrupted by Civil War.

Cambrian *adj.* **1** *Geol.* relating to the earliest geological period of the Palaeozoic era, lasting from about 580 million to 505 million years ago. During this period there were widespread seas, and Cambrian rocks contain a large variety of marine invertebrate fossils, including trilobites, and primitive shellfish, corals, and crustaceans. **2** relating to rocks formed during this period. [from Latin *Cambria*, from Welsh *Cymru*, Wales]

cambric *noun* a fine white cotton or linen cloth. [from *Cambrai*, in N France, where the cloth was first made]

Cambridge, Latin **Cantabrigia** POP (1992e) 111 000, a university city and the county town of Cambridgeshire, E central England, situated in Cambridge district. It lies on the R Cam (Granta), 82km/51mi N of London. HISTORY a Roman settlement in AD 70; the famous university was established in the 13c. NOTABLE FEATURES churches of St Benedict and the Holy Sepulchre, King's College Chapel; university colleges.

Cambridge, formerly **New Towne** (to 1638) POP (1990) 96 000, the seat of Middlesex County, E Massachusetts, USA, situated on one side of the Charles R, with Boston on the other. HISTORY

Cambridge Colleges	
College	Founded
Peterhouse	1284
Clare	1326
Pembroke	1347
Gonville	1348
(*refounded as* Gonville and Caius *1558*)	
Trinity Hall	1350
Corpus Christi	1352
King's	1441
Queens'	1448
St Catharine's	1473
Jesus	1496
Christ's	1505
St John's	1511
Magdalene	1542
Trinity	1546
Emmanuel	1584
Sidney Sussex	1596
Downing	1800
Homerton	1824
Girton	1869
Newnham[1]	1871
Selwyn	1882
Hughes Hall	1885
St Edmund's	1896
New Hall[1]	1954
Churchill	1960
Lucy Cavendish[1]	1964
Darwin	1964
Wolfson	1965
Clare Hall	1966
Fitzwilliam	1966
Robinson	1977

[1]Women's colleges

founded in 1630; achieved city status in 1846; the first printing press in the USA was set up here in 1640; Harvard University (1636) is the oldest college in the USA; Massachusetts Institute of Technology (1859) moved from Boston in 1915.

Cambridgeshire POP (1992e) 678 000, a county in E central England, divided into six districts. AREA 3 409sq km/1 316sq mi. It is drained by the Nene, Ouse, and Cam rivers. There is flat fenland to the N. CHIEF TOWNS Cambridge (county town), Peterborough, Ely, Huntingdon. ECONOMY grain; vegetables; food processing; electronics; engineering.

Cambridge University the second oldest university in England, after Oxford. The first college, Peterhouse, was founded in 1284 and further colleges were founded after the pope formally recognized Cambridge as a *universitas* (1318). The university institutions include the Fitzwilliam Museum, the Cavendish Laboratory of experimental physics, the Cambridge University Press (founded 1534), and the University Library, a national depository. Girton College, the first for women, was founded in 1869.

Cambs. *abbrev.* Cambridgeshire.

camcorder *noun* a portable video camera that is used to record images and sound as electronic signals on a small cassette of video tape. The tape can then be played back through a standard television receiver using a videocassette recorder that is incorporated within the camera. [a shortening of *camera video recorder*]

Camden POP (1987e) 185 000, a borough in N Greater London, England. It includes the suburbs of Hampstead, St Pancras, and Holborn. There are railway stations at Euston (1849), King's Cross (1852), and St Pancras (1874). NOTABLE FEATURES British Museum; John Keats House; Gray's Inn; Lincoln's Inn; Telecom Tower (1964). [named after an 18c Lord Chancellor.]

Camden POP (1990) 87 000, the seat of Camden County, W New Jersey, USA. It is a port

on the E bank of the Delaware R, opposite Philadelphia. HISTORY became a city in 1828; the home of the poet Walt Whitman (1873-92).

Camden Town Group a group of artists who flourished (1905-13) in London. Leading members included Walter Sickert (1860-1942), Harold Gilman (1878-1919) and Spencer Gore (1878-1914). They shared an enthusiasm for recent French painting.

came see COME.

camel *noun* **1** a herbivorous (plant-eating) mammal belonging to the family Camelidae, standing up to 1.8m high at the shoulder, and having a long neck and legs, coarse hair, a tufted tail, and one or two humps on its back, which contain fat and serve as a food reserve. **2** the pale brown colour of this animal. [from Greek *kamelos*, from a Semitic source]
◇ There are two species of camel. The Arabian camel (or dromedary) has one hump, and is found mainly in Africa. The Bactrian camel, which is confined to Asia, has two humps and a heavier body and shorter legs than the Arabian camel. Both species are well adapted to life in the desert, having long eyelashes that protect the eyes from windblown sand, and easily closed slit-like nostrils. Their broad feet enable them to walk over soft sand, and they are able to survive for several weeks without water. Camels provide the main means of transportation for the desert people of Asia and Africa, and are also kept for their milk and meat, and their hairy coats, which are used to make clothing, etc.

camelhair *noun* **1** a soft usually pale brown cloth made from camels' hair. **2** hair from a squirrel's tail used to make paintbrushes.

camellia *noun* **1** an evergreen shrub of the genus *Camellia*, native to SE Asia, but widely cultivated for its conspicuous white, pink, or crimson flowers and glossy dark green leaves. **2** the flower of this plant. [named after the 17c plant collector Josef Kamel]

Camelot in Arthurian legend, the capital of King Arthur's Britain, variously located at Cadbury in the West Country, Colchester (Camulodunum), and Winchester.

Camembert *noun* a kind of soft white French cheese with a strong flavour and smell. [from *Camembert* in N France, where originally made]

cameo *noun* (PL. **cameos**) **1** a smooth rounded gemstone with a raised design, especially a head in profile, carved on it. See also INTAGLIO. **2** a piece of jewellery containing such a gemstone. **3** the design itself. **4** (*also* **cameo role**) a small part in a play or film performed by a well-known actor. **5** a short descriptive piece of writing. [from Italian *cammeo* or *cameo*]

camera[1] *noun* **1** an optical device that focuses light from an object on to light-sensitive film, in order to record the image as a photograph. **2** a device in a television broadcasting system that

camcorder

viewfinder
video circuit boards
microphone
video cassette
video tape
lens
zoom lens control

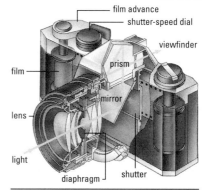

single lens reflex camera

film advance
shutter-speed dial
viewfinder
film
prism
lens
mirror
light
diaphragm
shutter

converts visual images into electrical signals for transmission.

— **on camera** in front of the camera; being filmed.

[from Latin *camera*, vaulted chamber]

◇ Light enters a camera through an opening or aperture at the front, and is then focused by a lens to form a sharp image on the light-sensitive film at the back of the camera. In the single lens reflex (SLR) camera, light entering the lens is reflected by a mirror up to the viewfinder, enabling the photographer to see the exact image that will be formed on the film. When a photograph is being taken, the mirror lifts up, the shutter opens to expose the film and then closes again. An inverted image of the object being photographed is formed on the film, which is then wound on by one frame so that another picture can be taken. When a complete roll of film has been used, it is developed and made into negatives from which prints or slides are prepared.

camera² see IN CAMERA.

camera lucida a mechanical aid used in drawing and painting, whereby an image is projected through a prism onto the paper, thus providing the artist with an accurate guide from which to work. It makes use of light reflected from a scene in the same way as the camera obscura, but has no 'chamber', and is operated in full daylight. [from Latin, = light chamber]

cameraman *noun* a person who operates a camera in television or film-making.

camera obscura a darkened room with a small hole in one wall through which light reflected from an exterior scene may be projected to form an inverted image on the opposite wall. [from Latin *camera obscura*, dark chamber]

◇ It was first mentioned in the 10c, and described by the Arabian scholar Alhazen, who used the device to make observations of solar eclipses. It was used by artists from the 16c to make quick accurate sketches of exterior scenes, and portable versions developed in the 17c and 18c became popular with landscape artists seeking to achieve a high degree of topographical accuracy in their pictures.

Camerarius, Rudolph Jacob (1665–1721) German physician and botanist, born in Tübingen. Director of the botanic garden at Tübingen and Professor of Botany, he was renowned for his experimental proof of sexuality in plants, described in *De Sexu Plantarum* (On the Sex of Plants, 1694).

camera-shy *adj.* having a dislike of being photographed.

Cameron, James (1911–85) English journalist, author and broadcaster, born in London. He worked on newspapers in Dundee and Glasgow before moving to Fleet St in 1940, where he was with the *Daily Express*, *Picture Post*, and the *News Chronicle*. His reports from all over the world, in print and broadcast form, were marked by their acute observation. His radio play, *The Pump*, won the Prix Italia in 1973.

Cameron, Julia Margaret, *née* **Pattle** (1815–79) British photographer, born in Calcutta. In 1838 she married the Indian jurist, Charles Hay Cameron (1795–1880). In England, she took highly acclaimed portrait photographs of Tennyson, Darwin, Carlyle, Newman, and others.

Cameron a male first name, transferred from the surname of the Highland clan. [from Gaelic *cam shron*, crooked nose]

Cameroon, official name **Republic of Cameroon**, French **République du Cameroun** POP (1992e) 12.2m, a republic in W Africa, divided into ten provinces. AREA 475 439sq km/183 519sq mi. It is bounded SW by Equatorial Guinea, S by Gabon, SE by the Congo, E by the Central African Republic, NE by Chad, and NW by Nigeria. CAPITAL Yaoundé. CHIEF TOWN Douala.

TIME ZONE GMT + 1. The population includes Highlanders (31%), Equatorial Bantu (19%), Kirdi (11%), and Fulani (10%); the majority follow local beliefs, and the remainder are Christian or Muslim. OFFICIAL LANGUAGES French and English; many local languages are also spoken. CURRENCY the franc CFA. PHYSICAL DESCRIPTION equatorial forest on the low coastal plain rising to a central plateau of over 1 300m; the W region is forested and mountainous, rising to 4 070m at Mt Cameroon, an active volcano and the highest peak in W Africa; the N central land rises towards the Massif d'Adamaoua; low savannah and semi-desert towards L Chad, with several national parks; rivers flowing from the central plateau to the Gulf of Guinea include the R Sanaga. CLIMATE the N has a wet season in Apr–Sep, with the remainder of the year being dry; annual rainfall in the N is 1 000–1 750mm; the N plains are semi-arid; the equatorial S experiences rain throughout the year, with two wet seasons and two dry seasons; Yaoundé, representative of the S, has an average annual rainfall of 4 030mm and maximum daily temperatures ranging between 27°C and 30°C; a small part of Mt Cameroon receives over 10 000mm of rain per annum. HISTORY first explored by the Portuguese navigator Fernando Po, later by traders from Spain, the Netherlands, and Britain; German protectorate of Kamerun in 1884; divided into French and British Cameroon in 1919; confirmed by the League of Nations mandate in 1922; UN turned mandates into trusteeships in 1946; French Cameroon acquired independence as the Republic of Cameroon in 1960; the N sector of British Cameroon voted to become part of Nigeria, and the S sector part of Cameroon; the Federal Republic of Cameroon was established, with separate parliaments in 1961; the federal system was abolished in 1972, and its name changed to the United Republic of Cameroon; the word 'United' was dropped from the name after a constitutional amendment in 1984. GOVERNMENT governed by an executive President, Cabinet, and a 180-member National Assembly elected for five years. ECONOMY agriculture employs c.80% of the workforce; the world's fifth largest cocoa producer; coffee, cotton, rubber, bananas, timber; light manufacturing; assembly; domestic processing; aluminium; crude oil; fertilizers; cement; gold; bauxite; natural gas; tin; tourism, especially to national parks and reserves.

Cameroon

Cameroon, Mount *or* **Mongo-Ma-Loba** a volcanic massif in S Cameroon. It runs inland for 37km/23mi from the Gulf of Guinea. With its main peak at 4 070m, the massif is the highest mountain group in W Africa. The last eruption was in 1959.

camiknickers *pl. noun* **1** loose-legged knickers for women, usually of a silky material. **2** a woman's undergarment consisting of a camisole and knickers combined.

Camilla a female first name. [from the Latin family name *Camillus*]

Camisards the last major Protestant rebellion in early modern Europe, centred on the Cévennes Mts in N Languedoc (1700–4). It was provoked by the Revocation of the Edict of Nantes (1685), which had guaranteed limited toleration, and the failure of the Treaty of Ryswick (1697) to safeguard French Protestants. The uprising was put down with difficulty by royal troops under Marshal Villars.

camisole *noun* a woman's loose undergarment for the top half of the body with narrow shoulder straps. [from French *camisole*]

Camões *or* **Camoens, Luís de** (1524–80) Portuguese poet, born in Lisbon. He studied for the Church at Coimbra, but declined to take orders. He went to India (1553) and Macao (1556), and was shipwrecked while returning to Goa (1558), losing everything except his major poem, *Os Lusíados* (The Lusiads, or Lusitanians). After returning to Portugal in 1570, he lived in poverty and obscurity. *Lusiads* was published to acclaim in 1572, and though it did little for his fortunes, it has since come to be regarded as the Portuguese national epic.

camomile *noun* **1** a plant with white or yellow sweet-smelling flowers. **2** the crushed flowers and leaves of this plant, used in drinks, etc, eg for medicinal purposes. [from Greek *chamaimelon*, literally 'earth apple' (from its smell)]

Camorra a secret society formed c.1820 in Naples and S Italy, which developed into a complex network of patronage, protection, and ultimately crime. As with the similar Sicilian Mafia, no unified organization has ever existed.

camouflage — *noun* **1** colouring used on military equipment, vehicles or buildings, or for soldiers' uniforms, that imitates the colours of nature and so makes them difficult for an enemy to see. **2** covering, consisting eg of tree branches or undergrowth, used to disguise military equipment, etc. **3** colouring on an animal or bird that blends with the animal's or bird's natural surroundings and makes it difficult to see. **4** devices of any kind used to disguise identity or make someone or something less distinguishable in particular surroundings. — *verb* to disguise or conceal with some kind of camouflage. [from French *camouflage*, from *camoufler*, to disguise]

camp¹ — *noun* **1** a piece of ground on which tents have been erected. **2** a collection of buildings, huts, tents, etc used as temporary accommodation or for short stays for a particular purpose. **3** a permanent site where troops are housed or trained. **4** *Archaeol.* an ancient fortified site. **5** a party or side in a dispute, etc.; a group having a particular set of opinions, beliefs, etc. — *verb intrans.* to stay in a tent or tents, cooking meals in the open, etc.

— **break camp** to take down tents, etc when leaving a campsite.

camp out 1 to live and sleep in the open, with or without a tent. **2** to stay in temporary accommodation with a minimum of furniture, equipment, etc.

[from Latin *campus*, field]

camp² *derog. colloq.* — *adj.* **1** *said of a man or his behaviour* using mannerisms that are typically associated with women, especially in a deliberate, exaggerated, or theatrical way. **2** *said of a man* homosexual. **3** theatrical and exaggerated, especially amusingly so. — *noun* camp behaviour or style. — *verb* **1** *intrans.* to behave in a camp way. **2** (**camp something up**) to make it camp.

— **camp it up** to behave in an exaggerated, theatrical way; to overact.

campaign — *noun* **1** an organized series of actions to gain support for or build up opposition to a particular practice, group, etc. **2** the operations of an army while fighting in a particular area or to achieve a particular goal or objective. — *verb intrans.* (**campaign for** *or* **against some-**

thing) to organize, or take part in, a campaign in support of or against something. [from French *campagne*, countryside, campaign]

campaigner *noun* **1** a person actively involved in a campaign. **2** an army veteran; someone who has served in several campaigns.

Campaign for Nuclear Disarmament
see CND.

campanile *noun* a bell tower standing by itself, ie not attached to a church, etc, found especially in Italy. [from Italian *campanile*, from Latin *campana*, bell]

campanologist *noun* a bell-ringer.

campanology *noun* **1** the art of bell-ringing. **2** the study of bells. [from Latin *campana*, bell + -LOGY]

campanula *noun* a tall plant with bell-shaped white or blue flowers. [diminutive of Latin *campana*, bell]

camp bed a light folding bed consisting of a metal or wooden frame with canvas stretched across it.

Campbell, Colin, also called the **Red Fox of Glenure** the factor of Ardshiel estate who is murdered in Robert Louis Stevenson's *Kidnapped*.

Campbell, Sir Colin, Baron Clyde (1792–1863) Scottish soldier, born in Glasgow. He fought in the Peninsular War against Napoleon, where he was twice badly wounded, and after 30 years of duty in various garrisons, fought in China (1842) and in the second Sikh war (1848–9). In the Crimean War he commanded the Highland Brigade in a campaign which included victory at the battle of Alma and the repulse of the Russians by the 'thin red line' at the battle of Balaclava. During the Indian Mutiny he commanded the forces in India, and effected the final relief of Lucknow (1857), and he was made field marshal in 1862.

Campbell, Donald (1921–67) English car and speedboat racer, the son of Sir Malcolm Campbell. He broke the water speed record on Ullswater, Cumbria in 1955, and breaking his own record yearly, reached 276.3mph/444.7kph on L Dumbleyung, Australia, in 1964. Like his father, he named all his vehicles 'Bluebird'. He also set a land vehicle record of 403.1mph/648.58kph in 1964 at L Eyre, Australia. He died in an accident on Coniston Water, Cumbria while trying to break his own water speed record (achieving 328mph/527.9kph). His daughter, Gina (1948–) broke the women's water speed record in 1984.

Campbell, Sir Malcolm (1885–1948) English racing motorist, born in Chislehurst, Kent. From 1927 onwards he established successive world speed records in motor and speedboat racing, and was the first motorist to exceed 300mph/483kph (at Bonneville Salt Flats, Utah, 1935).

Campbell, Mrs Patrick, *née* **Beatrice Stella Tanner** (1865–1940) English actress, born in London. She went on the stage in 1888, achieving fame with *The Second Mrs Tanqueray* (1893). Her mercurial temperament made her the terror of managers. She played Eliza in George Bernard Shaw's *Pygmalion* (1914) and formed a long friendship with the author.

Campbell, (Ignatius) Roy (Dunnachie) (1901–57) South African poet and journalist, born in Durban. He became an ardent admirer of things Spanish and fought with Franco's armies during the Civil War. His books include *The Flaming Terrapin* (1924), an allegory on the flood, *Flowering Rifle* (1939), and the autobiographical *Light on a Dark Horse* (1951), as well as many translations.

Campbell a male first name, transferred from the surname of the Highland clan. [from Gaelic *cam beul*, crooked mouth]

Campbell-Bannerman, Sir Henry (1836–1908) Scottish Liberal politician and Prime Minister, born in Glasgow. He became an MP in 1868, was Chief Secretary for Ireland (1884), War Secretary (1886, 1892–5), Liberal leader (1899), and Prime Minister (1905–8). During his administration, when his popularity united the Liberal Party, he generously granted self-government to the Boer ex-republics (out of which grew the Union of South Africa), and began the process of dismantling the obstructive power of the Upper House which eventually led to the Parliament Act of 1911.

Camp David the US presidential retreat established as 'Shangri La' (1942) by President Roosevelt in Catoctin Mountain Park, Maryland. Renamed in 1953, the retreat covers 81ha and includes a main residence (Aspen Lodge), conference hall, and office.

Camp David Accords the documents signed (Sep 1978) by the President of Egypt (Anwar Sadat) and the Prime Minister of Israel (Menachem Begin) and witnessed by US President Jimmy Carter at Camp David, Maryland, USA. Regarded by many as a triumph of US diplomacy, they were a preliminary to the signing of the formal peace treaty (1979) between the two countries, which gave Egypt back the Sinai Desert, captured by Israel in the 1967 War.

camper *noun* **1** a person who camps. **2** a motor vehicle equipped for sleeping in, with cooking and washing facilities, etc.

Camperdown, Battle of a naval battle (1797) fought between British and Dutch fleets off Texel I, Holland. Admiral Adam Duncan (1731–1804) virtually destroyed the Dutch fleet and thereby frustrated its attempt to disable the British North Sea squadron and facilitate the invasion of Britain.

camp-follower *noun* **1** *derog.* a person who supports a particular group, party, etc only because it is fashionable. **2** a person who travels about with an army or other moving group in order to earn money eg as a prostitute or by doing odd jobs for them.

camphor *noun* a strong-smelling oil in solid form obtained from a type of laurel tree or made artificially, used in ointments, etc and in industry, eg in manufacturing celluloid. [from Latin *camphora*]

camphorated *adj.* containing camphor.

Campinas POP (1991) 846 000, a town in São Paulo state, Sudeste region, SE Brazil. It lies NW of São Paulo. NOTABLE FEATURES cathedral; old market; colonial buildings.

camping *noun* living in a tent or makeshift accommodation, especially for recreation.

Campion, St Edmund (1540–81) the first of the English Jesuit martyrs, born in London. He became a deacon in the Church of England (1569), but his Roman Catholic sympathies were noticed, so he escaped to Douai in France, and in 1573 joined the Society of Jesus in Bohemia. He became Professor of Rhetoric at Prague, but in 1580 was recalled for a Jesuit mission to England. He circulated his *Decem Rationes* (Ten Reasons) against Anglicanism in 1581, was arrested, tortured, tried on a charge of conspiracy, and hanged in London. He was beatified in 1886 and canonized as one of the Forty Martyrs of England and Wales in 1970; his feast day is 25 Oct.

Campion, Albert the upper-class amateur detective in the crime novels of Margery Allingham, which include *The Crime at Black Dudley*, *Look to the Lady*, and *The Case of the Late Pig*.

Campion, Thomas (1567–1620) English physician, poet, and composer, born in Witham, Essex. He studied at Cambridge and abroad and set his own lyrics to music. As well as poetry in Latin and English he left several books of 'ayres' for voice and lute.

campion *noun* a wild plant with small red, pink, or white flowers with notched petals. [old form of CHAMPION, translating *stephanomatikos*, part of the Greek name meaning 'for making champions' wreaths']

campsite *noun* a piece of land for camping on.

campus *noun* **1** the grounds of a college or university. **2** a university, or the university as an institution. **3** the academic world.
— **on campus** within university premises or grounds.
[from Latin *campus*, field]

Campylobacter *noun Biol.* a spiral-shaped Gram-negative bacterium of the genus *Campylobacter*, that occurs in the reproductive and digestive tracts of humans and animals, and can cause diarrhoea and gastritis (inflammation of the stomach lining) in humans, and genital diseases in cattle and sheep. [from Greek *kampylos* bent, *bacterion* a little rod (from its shape)]

CAMRA *abbrev.* Campaign for Real Ale.

camshaft *noun Engineering* a rod in an engine bearing one or more cams.

Camulodunum the name for ancient Colchester, the capital first of the Belgic kingdom of Cunobelinus and then of the Roman province of Britain. It was destroyed in the revolt of Boadicea in AD 60. Though it later recovered, it yielded its capital status to Londinium (London).

Camus, Albert (1913–1960) French Existentialist writer, born in Mondovi, Algeria. He studied philosophy at Algiers, and worked as actor, teacher, playwright, and journalist there and in Paris. Active in the French resistance during World War II, he became co-editor with Sartre of the left-wing newspaper *Combat* until 1948. He earned an international reputation with his nihilistic novel, *L'Etranger* (The Outsider, 1942). Later novels include *La Peste* (The Plague, 1947) and *La Chute* (The Fall, 1956), and he also wrote plays and several political works. He was awarded the Nobel Prize for Literature in 1957.

Can. *abbrev.* **1** Canada. **2** Canadian.

can¹ *verb, aux.* **1** to be able to: *Can you lift that?* **2** to know how to: *Can he swim yet?* **3** to feel able to; to feel it right to: *How can you believe that?* **4** used to express surprise: *Can it really be that late?* **5** used to express a possibility: *The weather can change so quickly in the mountains.* **6** to have permission to: *Can I take an apple?* **7** used when asking for help, etc: *Can you give me the time?* See also CANNOT, CAN'T, COULD, COULDN'T. [from Anglo-Saxon *cunnan*, to know]

can² *noun* **1** a sealed container, usually of tin plate or aluminium, for preventing bacterial contamination of preserved food, or for retaining the carbon dioxide in fizzy drinks. **2** a large container made of metal or another material, for holding liquids, eg oil, paint. **3** the amount a can will hold. **4** *slang* prison. **5** *North Amer. slang* a lavatory. — *verb* (**canned**, **canning**) to seal (food or drink) in metal containers in order to preserve it.
— **carry the can** *colloq.* to take the blame.
in the can *colloq.* completed; finished.
[from Anglo-Saxon *canne*, pot, can]

Canaan the land of the ancient Semitic-speaking peoples, in the Bible the 'Promised Land' of the Israelites, named after one of the sons of Ham (Genesis 10). It comprised the coastal areas of modern Israel and Syria, and perhaps also the inland areas up to the R Jordan and the Dead Sea. Divided into various city-states during the early 2nd millennium BC, it mostly fell under the control of Israelites and other powers from the late 13c BC.

Canacee the daughter of King Cambuscan who receives a magical ring in 'The Squire's Tale', in Chaucer's *The Canterbury Tales*. She also appears as the wise, chaste sister of Cambell in Spenser's *The Faerie Queene*, who has many suitors and is eventually married to Triamond.

Canada, formerly **British North America** (to 1867) POP (1992e) 27.6m, an independent country in N America, divided into 10 provinces and two territories. The country is bordered S by the USA, W by the Pacific Ocean, NW by Alaska, N by the Arctic Ocean and Baffin Bay, NE by the Davis Strait, and E by the Labrador Sea and the Atlantic Ocean. AREA 9 971 500sq km/3 849 000sq mi. CAPITAL Ottawa. CHIEF TOWNS Calgary, Edmonton, Montreal, Quebec, Toronto, Vancouver, Victoria, Winnipeg. TIME ZONES W Yukon GMT −9, Yukon and Pacific −8, Mountain −7, Central −6, East −4, and Newfoundland −3. Of the population, 45% are of British origin, 29% French, and 23% other European; there are also Native American and Inuit minorities. Religion is predominantly Roman Catholic (49%), with 18% United Church and 12% Anglican. OFFICIAL LANGUAGES English, French. CURRENCY the Canadian dollar. PHYSICAL DESCRIPTION dominated in the NE by the pre-Cambrian Canadian Shield; the mountains of Nova Scotia and New Brunswick rise in the E; the fertile St Lawrence lowlands are in S Quebec and Ontario; there is flat prairie country S and W of the Shield, stretching to the Western Cordillera, which includes the Rocky, Cassiar, and Mackenzie Mts; the Coast Mts flank a rugged, heavily indented coastline, rising to 5 950m at Mt Logan, the highest peak in Canada; major rivers include the Yukon and Mackenzie in the W, North Saskatchewan, South Saskatchewan, Saskatchewan, and Athabasca in the centre, and Ottawa and St Lawrence in the E; the Great Lakes occupy the SE of the country. CLIMATE the N coast is permanently ice-bound or obstructed by ice floes, except for Hudson Bay (frozen for c.9 months each year); cold air from the Arctic sweeps S and E in winter and spring; mild winters and warm summers on the W coast and some inland valleys of British Columbia; winter temperatures on the Atlantic shores are warmer than those of the interior, but summer temperatures are lower; much of the S interior has warm summers and long, cold winters. HISTORY evidence of Viking settlement in c.1000; visited by Cabot in 1497; in 1504 St John's, Newfoundland, was established as the shore base for the English fisheries; St Lawrence was explored for France by Cartier in 1534; Newfoundland was claimed for England in 1583, making it England's first overseas colony; Champlain founded the city of Quebec in 1608; Hudson's Bay Company was founded in 1670; there was conflict between the British and the colonists of New France in the late 17c; Britain gained large areas from the 1713 Treaty of Utrecht; after the Seven Years' War, during which Wolfe captured Quebec (1759), the Treaty of Paris gave Britain almost all of France's possessions in N America; the province of Quebec was created in 1774; migration of loyalists from the USA after the War of Independence led to the division of Quebec into Upper and Lower Canada; reunited as Canada in 1841; the Dominion of Canada was created in 1867 by a confederation of Quebec, Ontario, Nova Scotia, and New Brunswick; Rupert's Land and Northwest Territories were bought from Hudson's Bay Company in 1869–70; joined by Manitoba (1870), British Columbia (1871, after promise of a transcontinental railroad), Prince Edward I (1873), Yukon (1898, following the Klondike gold rush), Alberta and Saskatchewan (1905), and Newfoundland (1949); the Canada Act (1982) gave Canada full responsibility for its constitution; there has been recurring political tension in recent decades arising from the

French–Canadian separatist movement in Quebec, and from the desire for autonomy of the Native American and Inuit populations; a 1992 referendum approved the creation of the vast autonomous territory of Nunavut for the Inuit people. GOVERNMENT a bicameral federal parliament includes a Senate of 104 nominated members and a House of Commons of 295 elected members; provinces administer and legislate on education, property laws, health, and local affairs; the British monarch is head of state, represented by a Governor-General, usually appointed for a 5-year term. ECONOMY traditionally based on natural resources and agriculture; the world's second largest exporter of wheat; forest covers 44% of the land area; widespread minerals (world's largest producer of asbestos, zinc, silver, and nickel; second largest producer of potash, gypsum, molybdenum, and sulphur); hydroelectricity, oil (especially Alberta), natural gas; major industrial development in recent decades involves food processing, vehicles and parts, chemicals, and machinery; petroleum, metal, and metal products; fishing; tourism (especially from the USA).

Canada, Order of a decoration established (1967) in Canada, with three categories: Companion, Medal of Courage, and Medal of Service. The Medal of Courage was converted to three decorations in 1972: the Cross of Valour, the Star of Courage, and the Medal of Bravery. Three levels of membership were created: Companions, Officers, and Members, with the

Governor-General of Canada as the Chancellor and principal Companion of the Order.

Canada Day a public holiday in Canada (1 Jul), commemorating the anniversary of the union of the provinces in 1867 which created the Dominion of Canada.

Canada goose a goose native to N America, and introduced to Europe and New Zealand. It has a black head and neck and a white chin, and feeds on grass and water plants. It migrates, the females often returning to their birthplace to breed.

Canadian — *noun* a native or citizen of Canada. — *adj.* relating or belonging to Canada.

Canadian River a river in S central USA, length 1 458km/906mi. Rising in the Sangre de Cristo Mts, New Mexico, it flows through Texas and Oklahoma to join the R Arkansas SE of Muskogee. Its major tributary is the North Canadian R. The river is dammed by the Conchas Dam in New Mexico; the dam is used for flood-control and irrigation.

Canadian Rocky Mountain Parks a group of five national parks (Banff, Jasper, Waterton Lakes, Kootenay, and Yoho) in Alberta and British Columbia, Canada. Together with the Burgess Shale site (an important geological fossil site in the Selkirk Mts of British Columbia) these constitute a World Heritage area.

Canadian Shield *or* **Laurentian Shield** a vast area of ancient pre-Cambrian rocks, form-

Canada

Provinces and Territories of Canada

Province or territory	Area sq km	Area sq mi	Population 1991	Capital
Alberta	661 190	255 219	2 500 000	Edmonton
British Columbia	947 800	365 945	3 300 000	Victoria
Manitoba	649 950	250 945	1 100 000	Winnipeg
New Brunswick	73 440	28 350	724 000	Fredericton
Newfoundland	405 720	156 648	568 000	St John's
Northwest Territories	3 426 320	1 322 902	58 000	Yellowknife
Nova Scotia	55 490	21 424	900 000	Halifax
Ontario	1 068 580	412 578	10 100 000	Toronto
Prince Edward Island	5 660	2 185	130 000	Charlottetown
Quebec	1 540 680	594 703	6 900 000	Quebec
Saskatchewan	652 380	251 819	989 000	Regina
Yukon	483 450	186 600	28 000	Whitehorse

Prime Ministers of Canada	
1867–73	John A MacDonald
1873–8	Alexander Mackenzie
1878–91	John A MacDonald
1891–2	John J C Abbot
1892–4	John S D Thompson
1894–6	Mackenzie Bowell
1896	Charles Tupper
1896–1911	Wilfrid Laurier
1911–20	Robert Borden
1920–1	Arthur Meighen
1921–6	William Lyon Mackenzie King
1926	Arthur Meighen
1926–30	William Lyon Mackenzie King
1930–5	Richard Bedford Bennett
1935–48	William Lyon Mackenzie King
1948–57	Louis St Laurent
1957–63	John George Diefenbaker
1963–8	Lester Bowles Pearson
1968–79	Pierre Elliott Trudeau
1979–80	Joseph Clark
1980–4	Pierre Elliott Trudeau
1984	John Turner
1984–	Brian Mulroney

ing a low plateau covering over half of Canada, extending into parts of N USA. Its S boundary runs from the Labrador coast around Hudson Bay, through Quebec and Ontario to the Arctic near the mouth of the Mackenzie R. The many lakes and swamps are remnants of Pleistocene glaciation. The land is generally infertile, but is a rich source of minerals, forest products, and hydroelectricity.

canal *noun* **1** an artificial channel or waterway for ships, barges, etc, or for bringing water into a particular area, irrigating land, etc. **2** *Anat.* a tube-shaped passage in the body. [from Latin *canalis*, water pipe, channel]

canal boat a barge.

Canaletto, originally **Canal**, **Giovanni Antonio** (1697–1768) Italian painter, born in Venice. A topographical painter, he became known for his series of views of Venice. He spent most of the years 1746–56 in England, where his views of London and elsewhere proved popular. His nephew and pupil, Bernardo Bellotto (1720–80), known as Canaletto the Younger, was also born in Venice, where he worked as a painter and engraver.

canalization *or* **canalisation** *noun* **1** the act or process of canalizing. **2** direction into a fixed channel.

canalize *or* **canalise** *verb* **1** to deepen, widen, or straighten (a river) to stop it flooding or to allow shipping along it. **2** to guide or direct into a useful, practical, or profitable course.

canapé *noun* a type of food served at parties, etc consisting of a small piece of bread or toast spread or topped with something savoury. [from French *canapé*]

canard *noun* an untrue report or piece of news; a rumour, hoax, etc. [from French *canard*, duck]

canary *noun* (PL. **canaries**) a small bird belonging to the finch family, and native to the Canary Islands, the Azores, and Madeira, which has been bred to produce varieties with bright yellow plumage, although in the wild form it is usually green or grey. It is best known for its melodic song, and is very popular as a caged bird. [named after the *Canary* Islands]

Canary Islands, Spanish **Islas Canarias** POP (1991) 1.5m, an island archipelago in the Atlantic Ocean, lying 100km/62mi off the NW coast of Africa, W of Morocco and S of Madeira. It forms the Spanish autonomous region of Canarias. AREA 7 273sq km/2 807sq mi. It comprises Tenerife, Gomera, La Palma, Hierro, Lanzarote, Fuerteventura, Grand Canary (Gran Canaria),

and several uninhabited islands. CHIEF TOWN Las Palmas. PHYSICAL DESCRIPTION a volcanic and mountainous archipelago; the Pico de Teide rises to 3 718m at the centre of a national park on Tenerife. ECONOMY a major tourist area; agriculture (fruit and vegetables grown under irrigation); fishing; canning; textiles; leatherwork, footwear; cork, timber; chemical and metal products. [the name is explained by the elder Pliny as referring to the many dogs found on Gran Canaria (from Latin *canis*, dog).]

canasta *noun* a card game played with two packs of cards, in which the aim is to collect sets of cards of the same value. [from Spanish *canasta*, basket, into which rejected cards were thrown]
◇ Technically an extension of rummy, canasta originated in Uruguay, reached the USA in the late 1940s, and by the 1950s was fashionable throughout Europe and the Americas. Basic canasta is played by four players with two standard packs of cards plus four jokers; cards are picked up and discarded, and all cards have a points value (the jokers and twos are 'wild', ie can take any value). There are many variants of the game, including Bolivian, Chilean, Italian, and wild-card canasta.

Canaveral, Cape, formerly **Cape Kennedy** (1963–73) a Cape in Brevard County, E Florida, USA, on the E coast of the Canaveral peninsula. It has been the launching site of NASA crewed space flights since 1961.

Canberra POP (1990e) 310 000, the capital of Australia and of Australian Capital Territory in the SE of the country. It lies on the Molonglo R. HISTORY the city was planned by US architect Walter Burley Griffin after a competition in 1911; building started in 1913; the Commonwealth Parliament moved here from Melbourne in 1927. NOTABLE FEATURES Australian War Memorial; National Library; National Gallery; High Court; Parliament House (1927, new building opened in 1988 by the Queen).

cancan *noun* a lively dance originally from Paris, usually performed in the theatre by dancing girls, who execute high kicks, raising their skirts to reveal their petticoats, etc. [from French *cancan*]

cancel *verb* (**cancelled**, **cancelling**) **1** to stop (something already arranged) from taking place, by an official announcement, etc. **2** to stop (something in progress) from continuing. **3** *intrans.* to withdraw from an engagement, etc. **4** to tell a supplier that one no longer wants (something). **5** to put an end to (an existing arrangement, rule, law, etc). **6** to cross out, delete. **7** to put an official stamp on (eg a cheque or postage stamp) so that it cannot be re-used. **8** *Maths.* to strike out (factors common to both numbers) from the numbers above the line (numerator) and below the line (denominator) of a fraction, or take out (equal quantities) from either side of an equation.
— **cancel something out** to remove the effect of it, by having an exactly opposite effect. [from Latin *cancellare*, to cross out]

cancellation *noun* **1** cancelling. **2** something which has been cancelled, especially a theatre ticket which can then be transferred to another person.

Cancer *noun* **1** *Astron.* the Crab, a faint uniform constellation lying on the zodiac between Gemini and Leo. At its centre is a star cluster, Praesepe, which can be seen with the naked eye. **2** the Crab, the fourth sign of the zodiac. **3** a person born between 22 June and 22 July, under the sign of Cancer. [from Latin *cancer*, crab]

cancer *noun* **1** any form of malignant tumour that develops when the cells of a tissue or organ multiply in an uncontrolled manner. In contrast to benign tumours, malignant tumours invade and destroy the surrounding tissues, and may then spread to other parts of the body via the bloodstream or the lymphatic system, lodging in

organs distant from the first tumour, and forming secondary tumours known as *metastases*. If left untreated, cancer is generally fatal. **2** one of these diseased areas. **3** an evil within an organization, community, etc that is gradually destroying it. [from Latin *cancer*, crab, cancerous growth]
◇ The precise cause of cancer is unknown, but a number of contributory factors have been identified. For example, lung cancer is associated with smoking, leukaemia is associated with exposure to radiation, and skin cancer is linked with exposure to strong sunlight. Agents that are capable of inducing cancer, eg certain chemicals and drugs, and ionizing radiation, are known as *carcinogens*. They damage the DNA of cells, and if the damage is not repaired before the cells divide, cancer may develop. Other factors that have been implicated in the development of cancer are diet, hereditary factors, and hormonal imbalance (sometimes induced by drugs). It is now known that certain genes in viruses and mammalian cells, known as *oncogenes*, can cause normal cells to develop into cancerous cells.
Cancer is usually treated by surgery, chemotherapy (the use of drugs), or radiotherapy (the use of X-rays or the radiation produced by various radioactive isotopes to destroy tumours), or some combination of these. See also ONCOGENE.

Cancerian — *noun* a person born under the sign Cancer. — *adj.* relating to this sign.

cancerous *adj.* like or affected with cancer.

Cancún POP (1980) 27 500, a city and resort island in Quintana Roo on the Yucatán Peninsula, S Mexico. It was developed during the late 1970s as a major beach resort.

candela *noun* a unit of measurement of the strength or intensity of a source of light. [from Latin *candela*, candle]

candelabrum *noun* (PL. **candelabra** sometimes used as a singular, **candelabrums**) a decorative candle-holder with branches for several candles. [from Latin *candela*, candle]

Candice a female first name. [a respelling of *Candace*, the name of a succession of Ethiopian queens, probably influenced by Latin *canditia*, whiteness]

candid *adj.* **1** saying honestly and openly what one thinks; outspoken. **2** *colloq., said of a photograph* taken of someone without their knowledge so as to catch them unawares in an informal situation. [from Latin *candidus*, shining white, pure, honest]

Candida a play by George Bernard Shaw (1897). The conflict between practicality and poetry is examined through the relationship between Candida and the poet Marchbanks, whom she later rejects in favour of her conventional Christian Socialist husband.

candidacy *or* **candidature** *noun* (PL. **candidacies**) the position or status of being a candidate.

candidate *noun* **1** a person who is competing with others for a job, prize, parliamentary seat, etc. **2** a person taking an examination. **3** a person or thing considered suitable for a particular purpose or likely to suffer a particular fate: *is a candidate for promotion.* [from Latin *candidatus*; Roman candidates always wore white (Latin *candidus*)]

Candide a philosophical tale by Voltaire (1759). It chronicles the disastrous fortunes of Candide, an idealistic young man, and in doing so satirizes the optimistic theology of Leibniz and Rousseau.

candidly *adv.* in a candid way.

candidness *noun* being candid; honesty, frankness.

candied *adj.* preserved or encrusted with sugar; crystallized.

candle *noun* a stick or block of wax or (especially formerly) tallow, usually long and cylindrical in shape but sometimes more ornamental, containing a wick that is burnt to provide light. — **burn the candle at both ends** to exhaust oneself with work or activity from early morning till late in the night; to try to do too many things. **not fit** *or* **able to hold a candle to something** *or* **someone** to be noticeably inferior to them. **not worth the candle** *said of a task, etc* not worth the trouble and effort it would take. [from Latin *candela*]

candlelight *noun* the light given by a candle or candles.

candlelit *adj.* lit by candles.

Candlemas *noun* a festival of the Christian church on 2 February celebrating the purification of the Virgin Mary after childbirth, at which candles are carried in procession. [from Anglo-Saxon *Cændelmæsse*, candle mass]

candlestick *noun* a holder for a candle.

candlewick *noun* a cotton fabric with a tufted surface formed by cut loops of thread, used for bedcovers, etc. [from the similarity of the thread used to a candle's wick]

Candolle, Augustin Pyrame de (1778–1841) Swiss botanist, born in Geneva. Professor at Montpellier and Geneva, he defined the natural method of plant classification in *Théorie élémentaire de la botanique* (Elementary Theory of Botany, 1813), devising a method which dominated for 50 years. On his extensive expeditions he did much to establish plant geography.

candour *noun* the quality of being candid; frankness and honesty. [from Latin *candor*, purity, sincerity]

candy — *noun* (PL. **candies**) *North Amer.* **1** a sweet. **2** sweets or confectionery. — *verb* **1** to reduce (sugar) to a crystalline form by boiling and evaporating slowly. **2** to preserve (fruit, peel, etc) by boiling in sugar or syrup. **3** to coat or encrust with sugar or candied sugar. [from Old French *sucre candi*, candied sugar, from Persian *qandi*, sugar]

candyfloss *noun* a fluffy mass of spun sugar usually coloured and served on a stick.

candy-striped *adj.* having a pattern of stripes, usually pink or red on a white background.

candytuft *noun* an evergreen plant with narrow leaves and white, pink or purple flowers. [from *Candia*, in Crete, from where the plant was brought + TUFT]

cane — *noun* **1** the hollow stem of any of several large plants of the grass or reed families, eg bamboo, or of one of the small palms. **2** same as SUGAR CANE. **3** the stem of a raspberry plant. **4** thin stems or strips cut from stems, eg of rattan, for weaving into baskets, etc. **5** a walking-stick. **6** a long slim stick for beating people as a punishment, or for supporting plants. — *verb* **1** to beat with a cane, as a punishment. **2** to construct or mend with cane. [from Greek *kanna*, reed]

Canea see CHANIA.

cane-sugar *Biochem.* sucrose, especially that obtained from sugar-cane.

Canetti, Elias (1905–) British writer of Spanish–Jewish origin, born in Russe, Bulgaria. He has lived in England from 1939, continuing to write in German. His interest in crowd psychology produced the novel *Die Blendung* (1935, trans. as both Auto da Fe and The Tower of Babel) and the study *Masse und Macht* (Crowds and Power, 1960). His volumes of autobiography include *Das Augenspiel* (The Play of the Eyes, 1985). He was awarded the Nobel Prize for Literature in 1981.

canful *noun* (PL. **canfuls**) the amount a can will hold.

canine — *adj.* **1** relating to, belonging to, or like, a dog. **2** relating to the dog family in general, including wolves and foxes. — *noun* **1** an animal of the dog family. **2** a canine tooth. [from Latin *canis*, dog]

canine tooth any of the four sharp-pointed teeth situated one on each side of the front four top and bottom teeth in the human mouth.

caning *noun* **1** a beating with a cane. **2** *colloq.* a severe defeat or humiliation.

Canis Major *Astron.* the Greater Dog, a small but very bright constellation in the southern hemisphere, lying partly in the Milky Way, and easily visible with the naked eye. It contains Sirius (the Dog Star), the brightest star in the sky. [from Latin *canis major*, greater dog]

Canis Minor *Astron.* the Lesser Dog, a small constellation in the northern hemisphere, lying partly in the Milky Way. Its brightest star is Procyon, the eighth brightest star in the sky. [from Latin *canis minor*, lesser dog]

canister *noun* **1** a metal or plastic container for tea or other dry foods. **2** *Mil.* a metal cylinder filled with gas or metal shot, which explodes when thrown or fired. [from Latin *canistrum*, basket]

canker *noun* **1** a fungal, bacterial, or viral disease of trees and woody shrubs, eg fruit trees, in which hardened tissue forms over sunken or cracked dead areas on the bark or near a wound. The affected stem eventually dies. **2** ulceration of the lips, mouth, or tongue. **3** an ulcerous disease of animals that causes several conditions, eg inflammation and decay of the hooves of horses, inflammation of the ears of cats and dogs. **4** an evil, destructive influence, etc. [from Anglo-Saxon, from Latin *cancer*, crab, ulcer]

cankerous *adj.* corroding like a canker.

cannabis *noun* **1** a narcotic drug, prepared from the leaves and flowers of the hemp plant (*Cannabis sativa*), that produces euphoria or hallucinations when smoked or swallowed. It produces psychological rather than physical dependence, but its use is prohibited in many countries because it may lead to addiction to hard drugs such as heroin. — Also called *marijuana, hashish, pot.* **2** a common name for the hemp plant from which this drug is obtained. [from Greek *kannabis*, hemp]

cannabis resin the drug cannabis prepared for sale in solid form.

Cannae, Battle of a battle (216 BC) fought at Cannae in S Italy during the Second Punic War. The Carthaginians under Hannibal conquered the Romans in what is their worst recorded defeat.

canned *adj.* **1** contained or preserved in cans. **2** *slang* drunk. **3** *colloq.* previously recorded.

cannelloni *noun* a kind of pasta in the form of large tubes, served with a filling of meat, cheese, etc. [from Italian *cannelloni*, from *cannello*, tube]

cannery *noun* (PL. **canneries**) a factory where goods are canned.

Cannes POP (1990) 336 000, a fashionable resort town in Alpes-Maritimes department, Provence-Alpes-Côte d'Azur region, SE France. Part of the French Riviera, it lies on the Golfe de la Napoule (a bay of the Mediterranean Sea). It is a major tourist destination, with a mild winter and temperate summer climate. There are many beaches, yachting harbours, and casinos. EVENT International Film Festival (Apr–May).

Cannes Film Festival a two-week spring festival established at Cannes in 1947. It consists of showings of many new films, and provides an international marketplace for the exchange of ideas and contracts.

cannibal *noun* **1** a person who eats human flesh. **2** an animal that eats others of its own kind. [from Spanish *caníbal*, from *Caribes*, the Caribs of the W Indies, once believed to be cannibals]

cannibalism *noun* the practice of eating human flesh.

cannibalistic *adj.* relating to or practising cannibalism.

cannibalize *or* **cannibalise** *verb colloq.* to take parts from (a machine, vehicle, etc) for use in repairing another.

cannily *adv.* in a canny way.

canniness *noun* being canny.

Canning, George (1770–1827) English statesman, born in London. He entered parliament in 1794 as a supporter of William Pitt, and his posts included Under-Secretary of State (1796), Treasurer of the Navy (1804–6), Minister for Foreign Affairs (1807), Ambassador to Lisbon (1814), and President of the Board of Control (1816). He unexpectedly became Foreign Secretary in 1822 after the suicide of Castlereagh (with whom Canning had once had a duel over the failed Walcheren expedition), and he gave a new impetus to commerce by advocating tariff reductions. He was the first to recognize the free states of Spanish America; promoted the union of Britain, France, and Russia in the cause of Greece (1827); protected Portugal from Spanish invasion; campaigned for Catholic emancipation; and prepared the way for a repeal of the Corn Laws. In 1827 he formed an administration with the aid of the Whigs, but he died that year.

Cannizzaro, Stanislao (1826–1910) Italian organic chemist and legislator, born in Palermo. Condemned to death for his part in the Sicilian Revolution in 1848, he fled to Paris and later taught in Alessandria, Piedmont, before returning to Italy as Professor of Chemistry at Genoa in 1855; in 1860 he supported Garibaldi's Sicilian revolt. He later became professor at Palermo and Rome. Realizing the significance of Amedeo Avogadro's work, his greatest achievement was to recognize the difference between atomic weight and molecular weight. He did much to co-ordinate organic and inorganic chemistry, and discovered the reaction named after him.

Cannon, Walter Bradford (1871–1945) US physiologist, born in Prairie du Chien, Wisconsin. Working throughout his career at Harvard University, he studied digestion and the functions of the nervous system. His results indicated how the nervous system prepares an animal for 'fight or flight', through stimulation of the adrenal glands and by increasing heart rate and blood pressure, and how it maintains a large number of physiological functions, including body temperature and the composition of the body's fluids.

cannon — *noun* (PL. **cannon, cannons**) **1** *Hist.* a large gun mounted on wheels. **2** a rapid-firing gun fitted to an aircraft or ship. **3** a stroke in billiards in which the cue ball strikes the other balls one after the other; a similar stroke in other related games. — *verb* **1** (**cannon into something**) to hit or collide with it while moving at speed. **2** (**cannon off something**) to hit with force and bounce off it. [from Old French *canon*, from Italian *cannone*, from *canna*, tube]

cannonade *noun* a continuous bombardment by heavy guns. [from French *canonnade*, from Italian *cannonata*, cannon shot]

cannonball *noun Hist.* a ball, usually of iron, for shooting from a cannon.

cannon fodder *colloq.* soldiers regarded merely as material to be sacrificed in war.

cannot *verb, aux.* can not. See also CAN'T. — **cannot but** see CAN'T.

cannula *or* **canula** *noun Medicine* a thin hollow tube that is used to remove fluid from body cavities. [from Latin, a diminutive of *canna*, reed]

canny *adj.* (**cannier, canniest**) **1** wise, clever, and alert, especially in business matters; shrewd. **2** careful; cautious. **3** *dialect, said of a person* nice; good. [from CAN[1], in the sense of 'to know how']

Cano, Juan Sebastian del (d.1526) Spanish navigator, born in Guetaria, the first to journey around the world. In 1519 he sailed with Ferdinand Magellan, after whose death he safely navigated the *Victoria* home to Spain. He died during a second expedition.

canoe — *noun* a light narrow boat propelled by one or more single- or double-bladed paddles by an occupant or occupants facing the direction of travel. — *verb intrans.* (**canoes, canoed, canoeing**) to travel by canoe.
— **paddle one's own canoe** *colloq.* **1** to manage without other people's help. **2** to look after one's own affairs; to mind one's own business. [from Spanish *canoa*]
◇ Historically, the canoe has consisted of a light wooden framework covered with birch bark or, later, thin wooden planks. Oceangoing Pacific dugout canoes are often fitted with an outrigger; Maori war canoes were up to 20m long, fashioned from a single pine tree, fitted with a single sail, and propelled by as many as 60 paddlers. The two types of canoe used in competitive water sports are the *kayak* and the *Canadian canoe*.

canoeing *noun* the sport or activity of paddling a canoe.

canoeist *noun* a person who canoes.

canon *noun* **1** a basic law, rule, or principle. **2** a member of the clergy attached to a cathedral or, in the Church of England, a member of the clergy having special rights with regard to the election of bishops. **3** an officially accepted collection of eg religious writings, or of works considered to be by a particular writer. **4** in the Christian church, a list of saints. **5** a section of the Roman Catholic mass. **6** a piece of music similar to a round, in which a particular sequence is repeated, with a regular overlapping pattern, by different voices or instruments. [from Greek *kanon*, rod, rule; sense 2 via Anglo-Saxon *canonic*, from Latin *canonicus*, person under a monastic rule]

canonical *adj.* **1** of the nature of, according to, or included in a canon. **2** regular. **3** orthodox or accepted. **4** ecclesiastical.

canonical hours *RC Church* set hours for prayer. See also COMPLINE, LAUDS, MATINS, NONE[2], SEXT, TERCE, VESPERS.

canonization *or* **canonisation** *noun* **1** the action of canonizing a saint. **2** being canonized.

canonize *or* **canonise** *verb* to declare (someone) officially to be a saint.

canon law the law of the Christian church.

canoodle *verb intrans. colloq.* to hug and kiss; to cuddle.

can-opener *noun* a small tool for opening cans.

canopied *adj.* covered by or provided with a canopy.

canopy *noun* (PL. **canopies**) **1** a covering hung or held up over something or someone for shelter or ornament, or ceremonially. **2** a wide overhead covering. **3** *Archit.* a roof-like structure over an altar, recess, etc. **4** a transparent cover over the cockpit of an aeroplane. **5** *Bot.* the top layer of a wood or forest, consisting of the uppermost leaves and branches of trees. **6** the fabric part of a parachute, that opens like an umbrella. [from Latin *conopeum*, mosquito net]

Canova, Antonio (1757–1822) Italian sculptor, born in Possagno. He studied in Venice and Rome, and came to be regarded as the founder of a new Neoclassical school. His best-known works include the tombs of Popes Clement XIII (1787–92) and XIV (1783–7), statues of Napoleon, and one of his sister Princess Borghese reclining as Venus Victrix (1805–7), and the sculpture *The Three Graces* (begun 1814).

canst *old use* the form of the verb **can** used in the 2nd person singular with **thou**.

cant[1] — *noun* **1** *derog.* insincere talk, especially with a false display of moral or religious principles. **2** the special slang or jargon of a particular group of people, eg thieves. — *verb intrans.* to talk in a preaching way. [from Latin *cantare*, to chant]

cant[2] — *noun* **1** a slope. **2** a jerk or toss that makes something tilt. **3** a sloping or tilting position or plane. — *verb trans., intrans.* to tilt, slope or tip up. [from Middle English *cant*, border, side]

can't *contr.* cannot.
— **one can't but** ... one has to ... or is obliged to: *you can't but admire her perseverance.*

Cantab. *abbrev. Cantabrigiensis* (Latin), belonging to Cambridge.

cantabile *adj. Mus.* in an easy, flowing, melodious style. [from Italian *cantabile*, suitable for singing]

Cantabria POP (1991) 524 000, an autonomous region in N Spain, co-extensive with the modern province of Santander. AREA 5 289sq km/ 2 041sq mi. PHYSICAL DESCRIPTION stretches across the Cantabrian Mts to the headwaters of the R Ebro. CAPITAL Santander.

Cantabrian Mountains, Spanish **Cordillera Cantabrica** a mountain range in N Spain, extending 500km/310mi W–E from Galicia along the Bay of Biscay to the Pyrenees. It forms a barrier between the sea and the central plateau (Meseta) of Spain. The highest point is in the Picos de Europa Massif (2 648m). The range is rich in minerals, as well as being a source of hydroelectric power.

cantaloup *or* **cantaloupe** *noun* a large melon with a thick, ridged skin and orange-coloured flesh. [from French *cantaloup*, probably from *Cantaluppi* in Italy, where first cultivated in Europe]

cantankerous *adj.* bad-tempered; irritable.

cantankerously *adv.* in a cantankerous way.

cantankerousness *noun* a bad-tempered or quarrelsome nature or state.

Cantar de Mio Cid (Song of my Cid), also called ***Poema de Mio Cid*** an epic Spanish poem (12c). It describes the fall and rise of the 11c Castilian nobleman and military hero, Rodrigo Díaz de Vivar, commonly known as El Cid.

cantata *noun* a sung musical work (as opposed to a *sonata* which is played). The early 17c Italian cantata for one or more voices was an extended musical setting of secular verses, with alternating recitative and aria. It was imitated elsewhere in the 17c and 18c, and extended to include religious texts. In Germany, the Lutheran chorale was incorporated in the cantata with parts written for soloists, chorus, and orchestra: this was the model adopted by J S Bach. Since the late 18c, cantatas have usually been choral works accompanied by orchestra. [from Italian *cantare*, to sing]

cantata *noun* a sung musical work, especially on a religious theme, with parts for chorus and soloists. [from Italian *cantata aria*, sung air]
◇ The early 17c Italian cantata for one or more voices was an extended musical setting of secular verses, with alternating recitative and aria. It was imitated elsewhere in the 17c and 18c, and extended to include religious texts. In Germany, the Lutheran chorale was incorporated in the cantata with parts written for soloists, chorus, and orchestra; this was the model adopted by J S Bach. Since the late 18c, cantatas have usually been choral works accompanied by orchestra.

canteen *noun* **1** a restaurant, especially a cafeteria, attached to a factory, office, etc for the use of employees. **2** a shop selling food and drink in an army camp, etc. **3** a case containing cutlery; a full set of knives, forks, spoons, etc. **4** a flask for water, etc carried by soldiers or campers. [from French *cantine*, a shop in a barracks, etc.]

canter — *noun* a horse-riding pace between trotting and galloping. — *verb intrans., trans.* (**can-**

tered, cantering) to move or cause to move at this pace. [originally *Canterbury gallop*, the pace used by the pilgrims riding to Canterbury in the Middle Ages]

Canterbury, Latin **Durovernum**, Anglo-Saxon **Cantwaraburh** POP (1981) 40 000, a market town linked with Blean in Canterbury district, Kent, SE England. It is the seat of the Primate of the Anglican Church. HISTORY St Augustine began the conversion of England to Christianity here in 597; Thomas Becket was murdered in Canterbury Cathedral in 1170; the town has important literary associations with Chaucer, Marlowe, Defoe, Dickens, and Maugham. NOTABLE FEATURES cathedral (11–15c); Churches of St Dunstan, St George, St Martin, St Mildred, and St Peter; St Augustine's College; the Weavers, half-timbered Tudor houses; city walls.

Canterbury Tales a series of linked narrative poems and prose pieces by Geoffrey Chaucer (late 14c). It is modelled on Boccaccio's *Decameron* and consists of numerous tales told by a group of pilgrims (who are introduced in the Prologue) on the road to Canterbury.

canticle *noun* a hymn or chant with a text taken from the Bible. [from Latin *canticulum*, diminutive of *canticum*, song]

cantilever *noun* **1** a beam or other support projecting from a wall to support a balcony, staircase, etc. **2** *Engineering* a beam that is securely fixed at one end and hangs freely at the other, although it may be supported at some point along its length. Cantilevers are widely used in structural engineering. [perhaps from CANT[2] + LEVER]

cantilever bridge a fixed bridge consisting of two outer spans that project towards one another and support a suspended central span, eg the Forth Road Bridge in Scotland.

canting *adj.* pretending to be religious; whining.

cantingly *adv.* with a canting manner.

canto *noun* (PL. **cantos**) a section of a long poem. [from Italian *canto*, song]

Canton see GUANGZHOU.

Canton POP (1990) 394 000, the seat of Stark County, E Ohio, USA. It was the home and burial place of President McKinley, 25th President of the USA.

canton *noun* a division of a country, especially one of the separately governed regions of Switzerland. [from Old French *canton*]

Cantonese — *noun* **1** the dialect of Chinese used in the Canton area of China. **2** (*sing., pl.*) a person, or the people, belonging to Canton. — *adj.* belonging to Canton.

cantonment *noun Hist.* a permanent military station in India.

cantor *noun* **1** a man who chants the liturgy and leads the congregation in prayer in a synagogue. **2** a person who leads the choir in a Christian church service. [from Latin *cantor*, singer]

Can't Pay, Won't Pay (Non si paga! non si paga!) a play by Dario Fo (1974), in which traditional farce is used to illustrate political criticisms of bourgeois capitalist governments.

Canute *or* **Cnut,** also called **the Great** (c.995–1035) King of England (from 1016), Denmark (from 1019), and Norway (from 1028), the younger son of Sweyn Forkbeard, after whose death (1014) he successively challenged Ethelred the Unready and Edmund Ironside for the English throne. He defeated Edmund in 1016 at the battle of Assandun, secured Mercia and Northumbria, and became King of all England after Edmund's death. The story of his failure to stop the tide coming in was invented by the 12c historian, Henry of Huntingdon, to demonstrate the frailty of humanity compared to the might of God.

canvas *noun* **1** a thick heavy coarse cloth used for sails, tents, etc and for painting pictures on. **2** a painting done on canvas, or a piece of canvas prepared for painting. **3** the sails of a ship. — **under canvas 1** in tents. **2** *Naut.* with sails spread. [from Anglo-Saxon *canevas*, from Latin *cannabis*, hemp]

canvass *verb* **1** *trans., intrans.* to ask for votes or support from (someone) for a person or proposal. **2** to find out the opinions of, on a particular matter. **3** to discuss or examine (a question) in detail. [from CANVAS in an old sense, to toss in a sheet, or to criticize severely]

canvasser *noun* a person who canvasses opinions, etc.

canyon a deep gorge or ravine with steep sides, usually cut into the bedrock of arid and semi-arid regions by the action of a stream or river. [from Spanish *cañón*, tube, hollow]

Canyon de Chelly a national monument in NE Arizona, USA, established in 1931 to protect notable Native American cliff dwellings, dating from c.350 AD. AREA 339sq km/131sq mi.

CAP *abbrev.* Common Agricultural Policy.

cap — *noun* **1** a hat with a flat or rounded crown and a peak, of any of various types, some worn as part of a uniform or issued to members of a team. **2** a small hat of any of various shapes, many worn as an indication of occupation, rank, etc. **3** (*usually in compounds*) a close-fitting hat of various sorts. **4** a lid, cover, or top, eg for a bottle or pen. **5** (*also* **percussion cap**) a little metal or paper case containing a small amount of gunpowder, that explodes when struck, used eg to make a noise in toy guns. **6** a protective or cosmetic covering fitted over a damaged or decayed tooth. **7** a covering or top layer: *icecap.* **8** the top or top part. **9** a person chosen for a team representing a country, etc, or the fact of being chosen for such a team. **10** (*also* **Dutch cap**) a contraceptive device consisting of a rubber cover that fits tightly over the woman's cervix (opening into the womb) and prevents the male sperm entering; a diaphragm. — *verb* (**capped, capping**) **1** to put a cap on, or cover the top or end of, with a cap. **2** to be or form the top of. **3** to choose for a team by awarding a cap to. **4** to do better than, improve on or outdo: *cap someone's achievement.* **5** to set an upper limit to (a tax), or to the tax-gathering powers of (a local authority). — **cap in hand** humbly. **if the cap fits, wear it** *colloq.* you can take the general criticism, etc personally if you think it applies to you. **set one's cap at someone** *old colloq. use, said of a woman* to make obvious efforts to attract a particular man. **to cap it all** *colloq.* as a final blow; to make matters worse. [from Anglo-Saxon *cæppe*, from Latin *cappa*, hooded cloak]

cap. *abbrev.* capital (letter).

Capa, Robert, originally **Andrei Friedmann** (1913–54) Hungarian–US photojournalist, born in Budapest. He recorded the Spanish Civil War (1935–7), covered China under the Japanese attacks of 1938, and reported World War II in Europe from the Normandy invasion onwards. He was killed by a landmine in the Indo-China fighting which preceded the war in Vietnam.

capability *noun* (PL. **capabilities**) **1** ability or efficiency. **2** a power or ability, often one that has not yet been made full use of.

capable *adj.* **1** (**capable of something**) having the ability or the personality for a task, objective, etc. **2** clever; able; efficient. [from French *capable*, from Latin *capabilis*]

capably *adv.* in a capable way; ably.

capacious *adj. formal* having plenty of room for holding things; large; roomy. [from Latin *capax*]

capaciously *adv.* in a capacious way; with plenty of room.

capaciousness *noun* plenty of space; roominess.

capacitance *noun Electr.* the ability of the conductors in a capacitor to store electric charge. It is equal to the ratio of the stored charge on one of the conductors to the potential difference between them. The SI unit of capacitance is the farad.

capacitor *noun Electr.* a device consisting of two conducting surfaces separated by a dielectric material (insulator), eg waxed paper, that can store energy in the form of electric charge. Capacitors can smooth the flow of an electric current and are used in electrical oscillators, eg in radio.

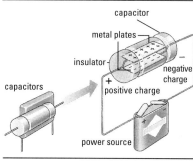

capacitor

capacity *noun* (PL. **capacities**) **1** the amount that something can hold. **2** the amount that a factory, etc can produce. **3** (**capacity for something**) the ability or power to achieve it. **4** function; role. [from Latin *capacitas*, from *capax*, capable, roomy]

caparison — *noun* **1** *Hist.* a decorative covering, harness, etc for a horse. **2** *formal* a fine set of clothes. — *verb* (**caparisoned, caparisoning**) **1** to put a caparison on. **2** *formal* FACETIOUS to dress up. [from Spanish *caparazón*, saddle cloth]

cape¹ *noun* **1** a short cloak. **2** an extra layer of cloth attached to the shoulders of a coat, etc. [from Latin *cappa*, hooded cloak]

cape² *noun* **1** a part of the coast that projects into the sea. **2** (**the Cape**) **a** the Cape of Good Hope, the most southerly part of Africa. **b** Cape Province in South Africa. [from Middle English *cap*, from Latin *caput*, head]

Cape Breton Island POP (1991) 162 000, an island in Nova Scotia province, E Canada, separated from the mainland by the Strait of Canso. Many of the people on the island are of Scottish descent, and Gaelic is still spoken. AREA 10 295sq km/3 974sq mi. PHYSICAL DESCRIPTION almost bisected by the Bras d'Or Lake (an arm of the sea); the Cape Breton Highlands National Park lies in the NW. HISTORY originally French (known as Ile Royale); taken by the British in 1758; joined to Nova Scotia in 1820. CHIEF TOWNS Sydney, Glace Bay, Louisburg. ECONOMY dairy farming; fishing; timber; coal mining, gypsum; tourism.

Cape Canaveral see CANAVERAL, CAPE.

Cape Cod a sandy peninsula in SE Massachusetts, USA, bounded E by the Atlantic Ocean and W by Cape Cod Bay. It is 105km/65mi long and up to 32km/20mi wide, and is crossed by the 13km/8mi Cape Cod Canal. The peninsula is a popular resort area. Pilgrims from the *Mayflower* landed near Provincetown in 1620.

Cape Coloured relating to the Coloured population of Cape Province in South Africa.

Cape of Good Hope a headland situated at the S tip of Cape Peninsula, SW Cape province, South Africa.

Cape Province, Afrikaans **Kaapprovinsie** POP (1991) 5m, the largest province in South Africa. AREA 641 379sq km/247 572sq mi. It is bounded W by the Atlantic Ocean and S by the Indian Ocean. The NW frontier with Namibia is formed by the Orange R. There are several mountain ranges along the Great Escarpment. The Cape of Good Hope lies S of Cape Town. Cape Agulhas is the most S point of the African continent. The province is noted for its variety of flora, best observed at the Cape Floral Kingdom Reserve on Table Mountain. HISTORY founded in 1652; formally ceded to Britain (Cape Colony) in 1814; separate parliament established in 1850; joined Union of South Africa in 1910. CAPITAL Cape Town. CHIEF TOWNS Port Elizabeth, East London. ECONOMY wine; grain; fruit; distilling; livestock; diamonds; copper; vehicles; pottery; timber; engineering; textiles; furniture.

caper¹ — *verb intrans.* (**capered, capering**) to jump or dance about playfully. — *noun* **1** a playful jump. **2** *old use* a playful trick or joke. **3** *derog.* a scheme, activity, etc, especially something dishonest or illegal. [from Latin *caper*, goat]

caper² *noun* **1** a prickly shrub of southern Europe. **2** one of its flower buds pickled for use as flavouring. [from the earlier form *capers* (mistaken as a plural), from Greek *kapparis*]

capercailzie *or* **capercaillie** *noun* a large European grouse. [from Gaelic *capull coille*, horse of the wood]

Cape St Vincent, Battle of a naval battle (1797) fought between British and Spanish fleets. Admiral Sir John Jervis (1735–1823) defeated a numerically superior Spanish force and thus prevented French plans to assemble a combined invasion fleet to conquer Britain.

Capet, Hugo, *or* **Hugh** (c.938–96) King of France, founder of the third Frankish royal dynasty (the Capetians), which ruled France until 1328. The son of Hugh the Great, whom he succeeded as Duke of the Franks in 956, he was elected king and crowned at Noyon (987). His 40 years in power were marked by constant political intrigue and struggle, both among the feudal aristocracy and with his Carolingian rivals, but his position was invariably saved by the disunity of his enemies.

Capetian Dynasty French ruling dynasty for over 300 years (987–1328) founded by Hugh Capet in succession to the Carolingians. Two dynamic royal descendants were Philip II of France and St Louis IX. By increasing territorial control, enforcing the right of an eldest son to inherit, and devoting themselves to administration and justice, the Capetians laid the foundations of the French nation-state.

Cape Town, Afrikaans **Kaapstad** POP (1990e) 2.3m, the legislative capital of South Africa and capital of Cape province, situated on Table Bay at the foot of Table Mt. It is a seaport. HISTORY founded as a victualling station for the Dutch East India Company in 1652; occupied by the British in 1795. NOTABLE FEATURES Castle of Good Hope (1666), the oldest colonial building in South Africa; Koopmans de Wet House (1777); Groote Kerk; Union Houses of Parliament; National Gallery.

Cape Verde, official name **Republic of Cape Verde**, Portuguese **Republica de Cabo Verde** POP (1992e) 384 000, an island group in the Atlantic Ocean. It lies off the W coast of Africa, c.500km/310mi W of Dakar, Senegal. AREA 4 033sq km/1 557sq mi. The two main groups define their position with reference to the prevailing NE wind: the Barlavento (windward) group in the N and the Sotavento (leeward) group in the S. CAPITAL Praia (on São Tiago I). CHIEF TOWN Mindelo. TIME ZONE GMT –1. About 50% of the population live on São Tiago I. The majority are of mixed black African and European descent (60%); Roman Catholicism is the main religion. OFFICIAL LANGUAGE Portuguese; Creole is widely spoken. CURRENCY escudo. PHYSICAL DESCRIPTION the islands are of volcanic origin, mostly mountainous; the highest peak is Cano at 2 829m, an active volcano on Fogo I; the coastal plains are semi-desert; savannah or thin forest lies on the mountains; there are fine, sandy beaches on most islands. CLIMATE located at the N limit of the tropical rain belt; low and unreliable rainfall mainly in Aug and Sep; cooler and damper in the uplands; severe drought can occur; the tropical heat is subject to only a small temperature range throughout the year. HISTORY colonized by the Portuguese in the 15c, also used as a penal colony; administered with Portuguese Guinea until 1879; became an overseas province of Portugal in 1951; gained independence in 1975. GOVERNMENT governed by a President, Council of Ministers, and unicameral People's National Assembly of 79 members, elected for five years. ECONOMY formerly an important victualling point for transatlantic shipping; the economy has suffered because of drought; substantial emigration in the early 1970s, with 80% unemployment by 1976; c.70% of the workforce are farmers occupying irrigated inland valleys; maize, beans, potatoes, cane sugar, bananas, yams, coffee; livestock; increase in fishing since 1975; mining of salt, limestone, volcanic silica ash (pozzolana).

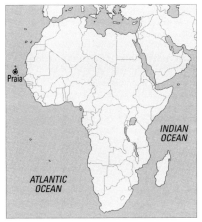

Cape Verde

Cape Verde, French **Cap Vert** the most westerly point of the African continent, in Dakar region, W Senegal.

capillarity *noun* the phenomenon whereby a liquid such as water rises up a narrow tube placed in the liquid. It is caused by surface tension effects in which water molecules at the surface of the liquid are attracted to the solid molecules of the glass tube, and the liquid rises until its weight balances the surface tension. Capillarity is largely responsible for the upward movement of water in plants, eg tall trees. — Also called *capillary action*. [from Latin *capillus*, hair]

capillary — *noun* (PL. **capillaries**) **1** a tube with a very small diameter. **2** one of the very small blood vessels in the body that connect arteries with veins. — *adj.* **1** *said of a tube* having a very small diameter. **2** relating to capillarity. **3** hair-like.

capita see PER CAPITA.

capital[1] — *noun* **1** the chief city of a country, usually where the government is based. **2** a capital letter. **3** the total amount of money or wealth possessed by a person or business, etc, especially when used to produce more wealth. — *adj.* **1** principal; chief. **2** *said of a letter of the alphabet* in its large form, as used eg at the beginnings of names and sentences. **3** *said of a crime* punished by death. **4** *Brit. old colloq. use* excellent.

— **make capital out of something** to use a situation or circumstance to one's advantage.
with a capital A *or* **B** *or* **C** *etc* in a very real or genuine sense: *poverty with a capital P*.
[from Latin *capitalis*, from *caput*, head]

capital[2] *noun Archit.* the slab of stone, etc, usually ornamentally carved, that forms the top section of a column or pillar. [from Latin *capitellum*, diminutive of *caput*, head]
◇ The capital of a column is usually designed and identified according to one of the five main orders of architecture: Doric, Ionic, Corinthian, Tuscan, and Composite. Other forms include basket, bell, crocket, cushion, lotus, palm, protomai (with animal figures), scalloped, and water-leaf.

capital assets the things a person or company owns that could be sold to raise capital.

capital expenditure the money that a company, etc uses to buy equipment, buildings, etc.

capital gains money obtained from selling possessions.

capital gains tax (ABBREV. **CGT**) *Commerce* a UK tax on the profit or gain obtained by selling or exchanging an asset.
◇ Machinery, land, shares, certain categories of commercial and private dwelling, and works of art are subject to this tax, but private cars and household goods are exempt. Individuals and trusts have exemption up to a given amount of profit from disposals in any one year; there is also a special exemption for disposals made on retirement.

capital-intensive *adj., said of an industry, etc* needing a lot of capital to keep it going. See also LABOUR-INTENSIVE.

capitalism *noun* an economic system based on private rather than state ownership of businesses, factories, transport services, etc, with free competition and profit-making.
◇ Capitalism developed in 19c Western societies after the Industrial Revolution. According to Marx, capitalism depends on exploitation of the workers (or proletariat) who own nothing but their labour, which they must sell in the market controlled and owned by the capitalist class (or bourgeoisie). Non-Marxist economists define capitalism as a system in which property is privately owned and goods are sold freely in a competitive market, but without reference to exploitation. Capitalism is a highly productive economic system, although it can give rise to environmental and social (eg unemployment) problems.

capitalist — *noun* **1** a person who believes in capitalism. **2** *derog.* a wealthy person, especially one who is obviously making a great deal of personal profit from business, etc. — *adj.* believing in capitalism.

capitalistic *adj.* relating to or typical of capitalism or capitalists.

capitalization *or* **capitalisation** *noun* the action or process of capitalizing.

capitalize *or* **capitalise** *verb* **1** to write with a capital letter or in capital letters. **2** to sell (property, etc) in order to raise money. **3** to supply (a business, etc) with needed capital. **4** (**capitalize on something**) to exploit an asset, achievement, etc to one's advantage.

capitally *adv. Brit. old colloq. use* in a capital or excellent way.

capital punishment punishment of a crime by death.
◇ Capital punishment for murder has been abolished in the UK, though it remains the penalty for high treason and piracy with violence. It is still available in several states of the USA, and in many other countries. A variety of methods are used to carry out executions, such as electrocution, hanging, gassing, shooting, and lethal injection.

capital sum a sum of money paid all at once, eg to someone insured.

capital transfer tax in the UK, a tax payable on gifts of money or property over a certain value.

capitation *noun* a tax of so much paid per person. [from Latin *capitatio*, poll tax, from *caput*, head]

Capitol the Assembly of the US Congress on Capitol Hill, Washington, DC. The building was designed in 1792 by William Thornton (1759–1828). In 1814 the British set fire to the unfinished structure, and it was not until 1827 that it .was finally completed by Benjamin Latrobe (1764–1820) and Charles Bulfinch (1763–1844). The dome was added by Thomas Walter (1804–87).

Capitoline Hill the highest of the seven hills upon which Rome was built. Once the political and religious centre of Ancient Rome, it is now the site of the Piazza del Campidoglio, designed by Michelangelo, and of the city's administrative offices.

capitulate *verb intrans.* **1** to surrender formally, usually on agreed conditions. **2** to give in to argument or persuasion. [from Latin *capitulare*, to set out (conditions) under headings]

capitulation *noun* surrender.

Capodimonte porcelain soft-paste porcelain of the royal house of Naples, started in 1743 and removed to Buen Retiro in Spain in 1759. It was notable for its delicate figures, particularly the chinoiseries, which were much copied by later factories in Italy and elsewhere.

capon *noun* a male chicken that has had its sex organs removed and been fattened for eating. [from Latin *capo*]

Capone, Al (Alphonse) (1899–1947) US gangster, born in New York City. Notorious worldwide as a racketeer during the prohibition era in Chicago, it was not until 1931 that evidence sufficient to charge him was found, and he was sentenced to 10 years' imprisonment for tax evasion. Released on health grounds in 1939, he retired to his Florida estate.

Capote, Truman, originally **Truman Streckfus Persons** (1924–84) US writer, born in New Orleans. His first novel, *Other Voices, Other Rooms*, was published in 1948. Other works include the novels *The Grass Harp* (1951), *Breakfast at Tiffany's* (1958, filmed 1961), and *In Cold Blood* (1966), a 'nonfiction novel' about a murder in Kansas.

Cappadocia, Turkish **Kapadokya** a mountainous region in central Turkey between the Black Sea and the Taurus Mts. The largest town is Neşehir. HISTORY a poor area without good natural defences, it tended to be ruled by whatever power was dominant in Asia Minor; a province of the Roman Empire from AD 17. NOTABLE FEATURES eroded landscape features and cave dwellings in the Göreme Valley.

cappuccino *noun* (PL. **cappuccinos**) coffee with frothy hot milk and usually chocolate powder on top. [from Italian *cappuccino*]

Capra, Frank (1897–1991) US film director, born at Palermo, Italy. His family emigrated to California when he was six. He began in film work in 1921, and had several box-office hits. Among his best-known films are *It Happened One Night* (1934), *Mr Deeds Goes to Town* (1936) and *You Can't Take It with You* (1938), which won Academy Awards, *Lost Horizon* (1937), *Arsenic and Old Lace* (1942), *State of the Union* (1948), and his last, *A Pocketful of Miracles* (1961).

Capri, ancient **Capreae** a rocky island in Campania, Italy, lying off the tip of the Sorrento Peninsula in the Tyrrhenian Sea. AREA 10.5sq km/4sq mi; length 6km/4mi; maximum width 2.5km/1.5mi. CAPITAL Capri. The island, which is noted for its flowers and striking scenery, is a popular tourist area; a principal attraction is the Grotta Azzurra (Blue Grotto) off the N coast.

capriccio *noun* (PL. **capricci**, **capriccios**) *Art* a picture or print depicting a scene or incident that is a product of the artist's imagination. In the 18c the term was applied to the townscapes and landscapes of such artists as Canaletto and Giovanni Pannini (1691–1765), in which buildings from different locations were combined in one picture, or anachronistic figures and scenes included. Goya's series of etchings entitled *Los Caprichos* depict bizarre and grotesque fantasies of extraordinary invention.

caprice *noun* **1** a sudden change of mind for no good or obvious reason. **2** a sudden strange wish or desire. **3** the tendency to have caprices. **4** *Mus.* a lively composition in an original style. [from Italian *capriccio*, fancy]

Caprichos, Los a series of over 80 etchings by Goya (1799). They offer a satirical depiction of the corruption of the Church and Court.

capricious *adj.* often changing one's mind for no good reason; changeable in behaviour, mood or opinion. [from Italian *capriccioso*, wayward, fanciful]

capriciously *adv.* in a capricious way.

capriciousness *noun* being capricious.

Capricorn *noun* **1** (*also* **Capricornus**) *Astron.* the Sea Goat, a large but dim zodiacal constellation lying between Sagittarius and Aquarius. **2** the Goat, the tenth sign of the zodiac. **3** a person born between 23 December and 19 January, under the sign of Capricorn. [from Latin *caper*, goat + *cornu*, horn]

Capricornian — *noun* a person born under the sign Capricorn. — *adj.* relating to this sign.

caps. *abbrev.* capital letters.

capsicum *noun* **1** a plant of tropical America bearing hollow seedy fruits. **2** the hot-tasting red, green, or yellow fruit of this plant, called a pepper, used as a vegetable or flavouring. [probably from Latin *capsa*, box, case]

capsizable *adj.* capable of being capsized.

capsize *verb* **1** *intrans. usually said of a boat* to tip over completely; to overturn. **2** *trans.* to cause (a boat) to capsize.

capstan *noun* **1** a cylinder-shaped apparatus that is turned to wind a heavy rope or cable, eg that of a ship's anchor. **2** one of a pair of shafts or spindles in a tape-recorder, round which the tape winds. [from Provençal *cabestan*]

capsular *adj.* in the form of or resembling a capsule.

capsule *noun* **1** a hard or soft soluble case, usually made of gelatine, containing a single dose of a powdered drug that is to be taken by mouth. **2** (*in full* **space capsule**) a small spacecraft or a compartment within a spacecraft that houses the instruments and crew for the duration of a space flight. **3** *Anat.* a membranous sheath, sac, or other structure that surrounds an organ or tissue, eg the capsule that surrounds the lens of the eye or the moving parts of a joint. **4** *Bot.* in some flowering plants, eg poppy, a dry dehiscent fruit, formed by the fusion of two or more carpels, that splits open to release its many seeds. **5** *Biol.* the gelatinous envelope of protein or polysaccharide that surrounds and protects certain bacteria. [from Latin *capsula*, diminutive of *capsa*, box]

capsulize *or* **capsulise** *verb* to present (information) in a concise form.

Capt. *abbrev.* Captain.

captain — *noun* **1** a leader, chief. **2** the commander of a ship. **3** the commander of a company of troops. **4** a naval officer below a commodore and above a commander in rank. **5** an army officer of the rank below major and above lieutenant. **6** the chief pilot of a civil aircraft.

7 the leader of a team or side, or chief member of a club. — *verb* to be captain of. [from Old French *capitain*, from Latin *capitaneus*, chief]

captaincy *noun* (PL. **captaincies**) the rank or office of a captain.

caption — *noun* **1** the words that accompany a photograph, cartoon, etc to explain it. **2** a heading given to a chapter, article, etc. **3** wording appearing on a television or cinema screen as part of a film or broadcast. — *verb* (**captioned**, **captioning**) to provide with a caption or heading. [from Latin *captio*, act of seizing]

captious *adj.* inclined to criticize and find fault. [from Latin *captiosus*, arguing falsely]

captiously *adv.* with a captious manner.

captiousness *noun* being captious.

captivate *verb* to delight, charm, or fascinate. [from Latin *captivare*, to take captive]

captivating *adj.* enchanting, fascinating.

captivatingly *adv.* in a captivating way.

captivation *noun* being captivated or enchanted.

captive — *noun* a person or animal that has been caught or taken prisoner. — *adj.* **1** kept prisoner. **2** held so as to be unable to get away. **3** forced into a certain state or role. [from Latin *captivus*, prisoner]

captivity *noun* the condition or period of being captive or imprisoned.

captor *noun* the capturer of a person or animal. [from Latin *captor*]

capture — *verb* **1** to catch; to take prisoner. **2** to gain possession or control of. **3** to succeed in recording (a subtle quality, etc): *the camera captured her smile*. — *noun* **1** the capturing of someone or something. **2** the person or thing captured. [from Latin *captura*]

capturer *noun* a captor.

Capuchin *noun* a member of an order of friars (see CAPUCHINS). — *adj.* relating to the Capuchins.

capuchin a New World monkey, the most numerous captive monkey in the USA and Europe. It has a prehensile tail (adapted for grasping), often carried curled at the tip, and is acrobatic and intelligent. It was formerly a popular pet for street musicians. [so called because its thick hair resembles a monk's cowl]

Capuchins, in full the **Order of Friars Minor of St Francis Capuccinorum** (ABBREV. **OM Cap** *or* **OSFC**) a monastic order which originated as a branch of the Franciscan order. Formed in 1529 by Matteo di Bassi (c.1495–1552), it observes a strict rule that stresses poverty and austerity. [from Italian *cappuccio*, a kind of cowl worn by them, from Latin *cappa*]

Capulet the father of Juliet in Shakespeare's *Romeo and Juliet*, who maintains a feud with Montague and tries to make his daughter marry for money.

Cap Vert see CAPE VERDE.

capybara *noun* a cavy-like rodent, native to Central and S America, and the largest living rodent, growing to a length of over 1m. It is dog-like in appearance, with a deep square snout, partially webbed toes, and no tail. It lives in or near water, and feeds on plant material. [from Portuguese, from a S American name]

car *noun* **1** a motor vehicle, usually four-wheeled, for carrying a small number of people. **2** *North Amer. combining form* a railway carriage or van. **3** a passenger compartment in eg a balloon, airship, lift, or cable railway. [from Middle English *carre*, from Latin *carrum*, cart]

Carabobo, Battle of a decisive victory (24 Jun 1821) by Simón Bolívar in the Spanish–American wars of independence, fought

near Valencia, Venezuela. It resulted in the liberation of Venezuela from Spanish rule.

Caracas POP (1990e) 4.1m, the federal capital of Venezuela. It is a commercial, cultural, and industrial centre. HISTORY founded in 1567; national hero, Simón Bolívar, was born here in 1783; although often damaged by earthquakes, the city has undergone greater growth since the 1940s than any other Latin American capital. A low mountain pass gives access to Caracas' port at La Guaira. NOTABLE FEATURES Plaza Bolívar; Panteón Nacional (with Bolívar's tomb); Casa Natal del Libertador; Capitolio Nacional; cathedral.

Caractacus *or* **Caratacus** *or* **Caradoc** (1c AD) Chief of the Catuvellauni tribe, the son of Cunobelinus. He mounted a resistance against the Romans in the years following the Claudian conquest of Britain in 43, but was finally defeated in Wales. He was betrayed by the Brigantian queen, Cartimandua, and taken to Rome (51), where he was exhibited in triumph, then pardoned by Claudius.

carafe *noun* a wide-necked bottle or flask for wine, etc, for use on the table. [from French *carafe*, from Spanish *garrafa*]

carambola *noun* a SE Asian tree, the fruit of which is known as star fruit. [from Spanish *carambola*, word]

caramel *noun* **1** a brown substance with a characteristic flavour produced by heating sugar solution until it darkens. It is used as a food colouring, eg in beer, and as a flavouring. **2** a toffee-like sweet made from sugar, animal fat, and milk or cream. **3** a pale yellowish brown colour. [from French, from Spanish *caramelo*]

caramelization *or* **caramelisation** *noun* the process of turning sugar into syrup.

caramelize *or* **caramelise** *verb* **1** *trans.* to change (sugar) into caramel. **2** *intrans.* to turn into caramel.

carapace *noun* **1** *Zool.* the hard thick shell, resembling a shield, that covers the upper part of the body of some reptiles of the order Chelonia (tortoises and turtles) and crustaceans, eg crabs. **2** a layer of heat-resistant tiles covering a spacecraft. [from Spanish *carapacho*, shell]

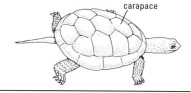

carapace

carat *noun* **1** a unit of weight used for precious stones, equal to 0·2g. **2** a measure of the purity of gold, pure gold being 24 carats. [from Arabic *qirat*, 4-grain weight, from Greek *keration*, carob bean, 3.3-grain weight]

Carausius, Marcus Aurelius Mausaeus (c.245–293 AD) Roman commander of the English Channel fleet, under Diocletian and Maximian. He rebelled and established an independent empire in Britain and NE Gaul (c.287), which he ruled until his assassination.

Caravaggio, originally **Michelangelo Merisi** (1573–1610) Italian Baroque painter, born in Caravaggio. He went to Rome in the 1590s, where Cardinal del Monte became his chief patron. His realistic works include several altarpieces and religious paintings which use dramatic contrasts of light and shade. These include several paintings of St Matthew (1599–1603) and *Christ at Emmaus* (c.1602–3, National Gallery, London).

caravan — *noun* **1** a large vehicle fitted for living in, designed for towing by a motor vehicle or,

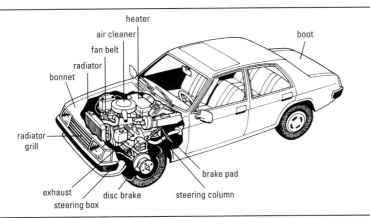

heater
air cleaner
fan belt
radiator
bonnet
radiator grill
exhaust
steering box
disc brake
steering column
brake pad
boot

mechanic and electrical components of a car

especially formerly, a horse. **2** *Hist.* a group of travellers, merchants, etc usually with camels, crossing the desert in company for safety. — *verb intrans.* (**caravanned**, **caravanning**) to go travelling with, or stay in, a caravan. [from Persian *karwan*, company of travellers]

caravanette *noun* a motor vehicle with a compartment equipped for living in while touring.

caravanning *noun* holidaying in or travelling with a caravan.

caravanserai *noun* in some Eastern countries, an inn with a central courtyard, for receiving caravans crossing the desert, etc. [from Persian *karwansarai*, caravan inn]

caravan site a place where caravans may be parked, permanently or temporarily, usually with showers and toilets, a shop, etc.

caravel *noun* a light sailing vessel used for trade in the Mediterranean in the 14c–17c. Originally lateen-rigged, they were developed in the 15c by the Spanish and Portuguese for voyages of exploration as well as trade. These larger ocean-going vessels usually had three masts with squarerigged forward masts and lateen-rigged mizzen mast. [from French *caravelle*, from Italian *caravella*; compare late Latin *cārabus*, Greek *karabos*, a light ship]

caraway *noun* a plant of Europe and Asia with small white flowers. [from Arabic *karawiya*]

caravel

caraway seed the small, strong-flavoured fruit of this plant, used in baking.

carbide *noun Chem.* any chemical compound consisting of carbon and another element (except for hydrogen), usually a metal. Carbides are extremely hard, and are widely used as abrasives.

carbine *noun* a short light rifle. [from French *carabine*]

carbohydrate *noun Biochem.* any of a group of organic compounds that are present in the cells of all living organisms, and consist of carbon, hydrogen, and oxygen. Carbohydrates are formed in green plants during photosynthesis, and are an important source of energy for both plants and animals. [from CARBON + HYDRATE]
◇ The simplest carbohydrates are the sugars, which include both *monosaccharides* (simple sugars), eg glucose, and their derivatives, and *disaccharides* (two monosaccharides linked together), eg sucrose. *Polysaccharides* such as starch, cellulose, and glycogen have much larger and more complex molecules. Starch and glycogen serve as major energy stores in plants and animals, respectively, and cellulose is responsible for the rigidity of plant cell walls. Starch is an important source of dietary carbohydrate, and is found in foods such as potatoes, bread, pasta, and rice.

carbolic acid phenol, an acid obtained from coal, used as a disinfectant. [see CARBON]

carbolic soap soap containing carbolic acid.

carbon *noun* **1** (SYMBOL **C**, ATOMIC NUMBER **6**) a non-metallic element that occurs in various pure amorphous forms, such as coal, coke, and charcoal, and as two crystalline allotropes, namely diamond and graphite. **2** a sheet of carbon paper. **3** a carbon copy. [from French *carbone*, from Latin *carbo*, charcoal]
◇ Carbon is present in all living organisms, and is ultimately derived from carbon dioxide in the atmosphere which is trapped by plants during the process of photosynthesis. It forms more compounds than any other element, mainly *organic compounds* consisting of chains or rings of carbon atoms bonded to atoms of other elements, especially hydrogen and oxygen. It also forms many important inorganic compounds, including carbon dioxide, carbon monoxide, carbonates, and carbides.
Carbon is used in the manufacture of steel, carbon fibres, electrodes, and brushes for electric motors. The isotope carbon-12 is used as a basis for determining the atomic weights of other elements, and the radioactive isotope carbon-14 is used for dating geological and archaeological specimens (carbon dating), and as a radioactive tracer.

carbonaceous *adj.* containing, or like, carbon.

carbonate — *noun Chem.* a salt of carbonic acid containing the carbonate (CO_3^{2-}) ion.

Carbonates commonly occur as rock-forming minerals, eg chalk, limestone, dolomite, and they all react with acids to produce carbon dioxide. — *adj.* relating to such a compound.

carbonated *adj.*, *said of a drink* made fizzy by being filled with carbon dioxide.

carbonation *noun Chem.* the addition of carbon dioxide gas to a liquid under pressure, eg to make fizzy drinks.

carbon black *Chem.* a form of finely divided carbon, produced by partial combustion of natural gas or petroleum oil, used in pigments and printer's ink.

carbon copy **1** a copy of typewritten matter, etc made using carbon paper. **2** *colloq.* a person or thing that looks exactly like someone or something else.

carbon cycle a series of reactions in which carbon, either as the free element or in the form of one of its many compounds, is exchanged between living organisms and their non-living environment, including the atmosphere, oceans, and soil.
◇ Carbon in the form of carbon dioxide in the atmosphere is fixed by plants during the process of *photosynthesis* and incorporated into carbohydrates. Animals feed on the plants, and also feed on herbivorous (plant-eating) animals, and the carbohydrates they obtain from their food are broken down within the animals' bodies by the process of *respiration*, which releases energy and carbon dioxide. As a result, animals obtain the energy they require for normal body functions, and carbon dioxide is returned to the atmosphere. Carbon dioxide is also released during the decay of dead animals and plants, the burning of coal and other fossil fuels, the chemical decomposition of rocks containing carbonates, eg chalk and limestone, and the activity of volcanoes. It is feared that human activities which result in the oxidation of carbon, eg the burning of fossil fuels, may disturb the cycle.

carbon dating *Archaeol.* a scientific method of estimating the age of archaeological specimens, based on measurements of the radioactive isotope carbon-14, which is present in all living organisms, but on their death gradually decays and is not replaced. As its half-life is known, the ratio of carbon-14 to stable carbon (carbon-12) in a specimen can be used to calculate the age of the latter.

carbon dioxide (FORMULA CO_2) a colourless odourless tasteless gas that is chemically unreactive and does not burn or support the combustion of other materials. It is denser than air, and represents about 0.03% of the atmosphere by volume.
◇ Carbon dioxide is produced by the combustion (burning) of carbon or its organic compounds, eg coal, coke, oil, natural gas. It is also formed by the action of dilute acids on metal carbonates, and is a product of fermentation (eg during baking or brewing), respiration of living organisms, and the decay of organic matter. It is consumed by plants during the process of photosynthesis.
Solid carbon dioxide (dry ice) is used as a refrigerant, and the gas can be liquefied under pressure or used to provide the fizzy sparkle in carbonated drinks. It is also used in fire extinguishers, as a coolant in nuclear reactors, and as an aerosol propellant. The accumulation of carbon dioxide in the atmosphere as a result of the widespread burning of fossil fuels and destruction of rainforest is thought to be a major factor contributing to the greenhouse effect.

carbon fibre a high-strength material prepared by heating textile fibres in the absence of air. Carbon fibres are more than twice as stiff as steel, and are used in fibre-reinforced plastics to make extremely strong lightweight materials which are used in components of aeroplanes and rockets, and in sports equipment such as fishing rods, racquets, and skis.

carbonic *adj.* relating to carbon.

carbonic acid a weak acid formed from carbon dioxide and water.

carboniferous *adj.* **1** producing carbon or coal. **2** (**Carboniferous**) *Geol.* relating to the fifth period of the Palaeozoic era, lasting from about 360 million to 290 million years ago, and characterized by extensive swampy forests containing clubmosses, ferns, and horsetails, which subsequently formed coal deposits. Amphibians became more numerous, and the first reptiles appeared. **3** relating to rocks formed during this period. [from CARBON + -FEROUS]

carbonization *or* **carbonisation** *noun* the action or process of carbonizing.

carbonize *or* **carbonise** *verb* **1** *trans., intrans.* to turn into or reduce to carbon, by heating. **2** to coat with carbon.

carbon monoxide *Chem.* (FORMULA **CO**) a poisonous colourless odourless gas formed by the incomplete combustion of carbon, eg in car-exhaust gases, and manufactured industrially by the oxidation of methane for use as a reducing agent, eg to extract metals from ores. It binds to iron in the blood pigment haemoglobin, preventing the uptake of oxygen, and levels as low as 0.1% in the air can be fatal.

carbon paper paper coated on one side with an ink-like substance containing carbon, placed between two or more sheets of paper eg on a typewriter so that a copy is made on the lower sheets of what is typed on the top sheet.

carbon steel *Engineering* steel containing carbon, with different properties according to the quantity of carbon used.

carbonyl group *Chem.* in certain organic chemical compounds (aldehydes, ketones, and carboxylic acids), the C=O group, consisting of a carbon atom joined to an oxygen atom by a double bond.

carborundum *noun Chem.* an extremely hard black crystalline substance, consisting of silicon carbide, that is used as an abrasive and semiconductor. [from CARBON + CORUNDUM]

carboxyl group *Chem.* in certain organic chemical compounds, the -COOH group, characteristic of carboxylic acids.

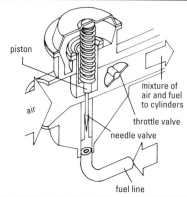

carboxylic acid: ethanoic acid (acetic acid)

carboxylic acid *Chem.* an organic acid containing a carboxyl (-COOH) group bonded to hydrogen or a hydrocarbon, eg methanoic acid (formic acid), which has the formula HCOOH, ethanoic acid (acetic acid), which has the formula CH_3COOH.

carboy *noun* a large round glass or plastic bottle used for storing dangerous acids, usually with an outer case made of basketwork, etc. [from Persian *qaraba*, glass flagon]

carbuncle *noun* **1** a very large kind of pimple or boil on the skin. **2** a round red gem, a garnet in uncut form. [from Latin *carbunculus*, diminutive of *carbo*, coal]

carburettor *noun* the part of an internal combustion engine in which the liquid fuel (eg petrol) and air are mixed in the correct proportions and vaporized before being sucked into the cylinders. [from obsolete *carburet*, carbide]

carcase *or* **carcass** *noun* **1** the dead body of an animal. **2** *colloq.* a living person's body. **3** the rotting remains of something, eg a ship. [from Old French *carcasse*]

Carcassonne, ancient **Carcaso** POP (1990) 45 000, the capital of Aude department, Languedoc-Roussillon region, S France. It lies on the R Aude and the Canal du Midi, in the foothills of the Pyrenees. NOTABLE FEATURES the Cité is the best preserved example of a French medieval fortified town, with a double circuit of walls and towers; Basilica of St-Nazaire (5c, rebuilt in the 11c–13c); Cathedral of St Michel (late 13c, restored in 1840); Gothic Church of St Vincent (late 13c).

Carchemish an ancient trading city in N Syria which controlled one of the main crossing points of the Euphrates. It was ruled by the Hittites in the second millennium BC, survived the destruction of the Hittite empire (c.1200 BC), and remained an important centre of Hittite culture until its conquest by Assyria in 716 BC.

carcinogen *noun Medicine* any substance capable of causing cancer in a living tissue that is exposed to it, eg X-rays and other ionizing radiation, many chemical compounds (eg constituents of cigarette smoke), and some viruses. Carcinogens damage the DNA of a cell, which may then become cancerous if the cell divides before the damage has been repaired. [from Greek *karkinos*, crab, cancer + -GEN]

carcinogenic *adj.* tending to cause cancer.

carcinoma *noun Medicine* any cancer that occurs in epithelial tissue, ie the skin, or the tissue that lines the internal organs of the body, such as the digestive tract and lungs. It may then spread to other parts of the body via the bloodstream. [from Greek *karkinos*, crab, cancer]

card¹ *noun* **1** a thick stiff kind of paper or thin cardboard. **2** (*also* **playing card**) a rectangular piece of card bearing a design, usually one of a set of 52, for playing games with. **3** a small rectangular piece of card or plastic, showing eg one's identity, job, membership of an organization, etc. **4** a small rectangular piece of stiff plastic issued by a bank, etc to a customer, used instead of cash or a cheque when making payments, as a guarantee for a cheque, for operating a cash machine, etc. **5** *Comput.* a piece of card on which information is stored in the form of punched holes or magnetic codes. **6** a piece of card, usually folded double, bearing a design and message, sent to someone on a special occasion. **7** a postcard. **8** *old colloq. use* an amusing person. **9** *Racing* same as RACECARD. **10** (**cards**) games played with playing cards. **11** (**cards**) an employee's personal documents held by his or her employer.
— the cards are stacked against someone *or* **something** *colloq.* circumstances do not favour them.
get one's cards *colloq.* to be dismissed from one's job.
have a card up one's sleeve in an argument or contest, to have something to one's advantage that one's opponent is not aware of and that one can still make use of.

hold all the cards *colloq.* to have the stronger or strongest position of opposing parties; to have all the advantages.
lay *or* **put one's cards on the table** *colloq.* to announce one's intentions, reveal one's thoughts, etc openly.
on the cards *colloq.* likely to happen.
play one's best *or* **strongest** *or* **trump card** *colloq.* to make use of one's strongest advantage.
play one's cards close to one's chest to be secretive about one's intentions.
play one's cards right *colloq.* to make good use of one's opportunities and advantages.
[from French *carte*]

card² *noun* a comb-like device with sharp teeth for removing knots and tangles from sheep's wool, etc before spinning, or for pulling across the surface of cloth to make it fluffy. — *verb* to treat with a card. [from Middle English *carde*, teasel head]

cardamom *or* **cardamum** *or* **cardamon** *noun* the seeds of a tropical SE Asian plant, used as a spice. [from Greek *kardamomum*]

Cardano, Girolamo (1501–76) Italian mathematician, physician, and philosopher, born in Pavia. He became famous as a physician and teacher of mathematics in Milan, and was appointed Professor of Medicine at Pavia (1543) and Bologna (1562). In 1570 he was imprisoned by the Inquisition for heresy; he soon recanted and went to Rome in 1571. He wrote over 200 treatises, including his famous work on algebra, the *Ars Magna* (The Great Skill), in which methods for solving various types of equation algebraically were published for the first time.

cardboard — *noun* a stiff material manufactured from pulped waste paper, used for making boxes, card, etc. — *adj.* **1** made of cardboard. **2** *derog., said eg of characters in a play, etc* not realistic or life-like.

cardboard city an area in which homeless people live or sleep, using cardboard boxes, etc, as shelter. These camp sites have become a feature of many large cities in Europe and the USA in the late 1980s and 1990s.

card-carrying *adj.* **1** officially registered as a member of a political party, etc and openly supporting it. **2** *colloq.* strongly supporting.

cardiac *adj.* relating to the heart. [from Greek *kardia*, heart]

cardiac arrest *Medicine* the stopping of the heartbeat and therefore the pumping action of the heart, usually as a result of myocardial infarction (death of part of the heart muscle). There is an immediate loss of consciousness, breathing stops, and brain damage and death may occur within minutes unless emergency treatment is given.

cardiac massage manual pressure applied over the heart with the rhythm of a heartbeat, to start the heart again after cardiac arrest.

cardiac muscle *Anat.* specialized muscle, found only in the walls of the heart, consisting of long fibres with unique physiological properties that enable them to expand and contract indefinitely.

Cardiff, Welsh **Caerdydd** POP (1992e) 295 000, the capital of Wales, in South Glamorgan, and the administrative centre of South and Mid Glamorgan. It lies on the Bristol Channel at the mouth of the Taff, Rhymney, and Ely rivers. HISTORY a Roman fort was founded here in the 1c AD; a Norman castle was built in c.1090; received its city charter in 1147; expanded in the 19c as trade in coal grew; loss of the coal and steel industries in recent decades; became official capital of Wales in 1955; Tiger Bay quayside area is the subject of a redevelopment programme. NOTABLE FEATURES Llandaff Cathedral; Church of St John; Cardiff Castle; Cathays Park public buildings (including the National Museum of Wales and University College); Cardiff Arms

piston

air

mixture of air and fuel to cylinders

throttle valve

needle valve

fuel line

carburettor

Park (rugby); home to the Welsh National Opera; Welsh National Folk Museum nearby.

Cardiff Arms Park, Welsh **Parc yr Arfau**, also called the **National Stadium** a rugby ground in Cardiff, Wales, the home of the Welsh national team since 1964.

Cardigan, James Thomas Brudenell, 7th Earl of (1797–1868) English soldier, born in Hambleden, Buckinghamshire. He entered the army in 1824, and purchased his promotion. After commanding the 15th Hussars (until 1833), then the 11th Hussars (1836–47), he commanded a cavalry brigade against the Russians in the Crimea, and led the fatal charge of the Six Hundred at Balaclava (the Charge of the Light Brigade, 25 Oct 1854). He then became Inspector-General of Cavalry (1855–60). The woollen jacket known as a cardigan is named after him.

cardigan noun a long-sleeved knitted jacket that fastens down the front. [named after the 7th Earl of Cardigan]

cardinal — noun **1** one of a group of leading clergy in the Roman Catholic Church, who elect the pope and advise him, their official dress being bright red. **2** a cardinal number. **3** a N American songbird of which the male is bright red. **4** (also **cardinal red**) a bright red colour. — adj. of the highest importance; principal or fundamental. [from Latin *cardinalis*, principal]

cardinalate noun **1** the rank or office of a cardinal. **2** the cardinals as a body.

cardinal number, a number expressing quantity, such as one, two, or three, as distinct from a number expressing order, such as first, second, or third. See also ORDINAL NUMBER.

cardinal point noun any of the four main points of the compass: north, south, east, and west.

Cardinals, College of an institution made up of all the cardinals of the Roman Catholic Church, originating from the reforms of Pope Urban II (reigned 1088–99). Technically of three-fold structure (bishops, priests, and deacons), in 1586 its number was restricted to 70, but this limit was removed by Pope John XXIII in 1958. It is responsible for the government of the Church during a vacancy in the papacy, and (since 1179) for the election of a pope.

cardinal virtue any of the most important virtues, usually listed as justice, prudence, temperance, fortitude, faith, hope, and charity.

cardinal vowels Phonetics a set of reference points devised by the British phonetician Daniel Jones (1881–1967), for identifying the vowel sounds of a language based on the movements of the tongue and jaws, and separated by roughly regular acoustic intervals from each other. Eighteen main tongue positions are distinguished on a grid representing vertical and horizontal tongue movements.

carding noun Weaving the process of blending and disentangling fibres in preparation for spinning. In mechanized carding systems, fibres are passed between a series of rollers covered with projecting steel wires and rotating at different speeds, and emerge in the form of a light fluffy web or sliver.

cardio- combining form belonging or relating to the heart. [from Greek *kardia*, heart]

cardiogram noun Medicine an electrocardiogram.

cardiograph noun Medicine an electrocardiograph.

cardiographer noun a person who operates an electrocardiograph.

cardiography noun the science and skill of using a cardiograph.

cardiologist noun a medical specialist concerned with cardiology.

cardiology noun the study of the structure, function, and diseases of the heart. [from CARDIO- + -LOGY]

cardiopulmonary adj. Anat. relating to the heart and lungs.

cardiovascular adj. relating to both the heart and the blood vessels. [from CARDIO- + VASCULAR]

cardphone noun a payphone operated with a phonecard. See also CASHPHONE.

Card Players, The a painting by Paul Cézanne (1890–2, Musée d'Orsay, Paris).

card-sharp or **card-sharper** noun derog. a person who makes a business of cheating at card games played for money.

card table a small folding table, usually covered with green cloth, for playing card games on.

Carducci, Giosuè (1835–1907) Italian poet, born in Valdicastello. In 1860 he became Professor of Italian Literature at Bologna, and in 1876 he was returned to the Italian parliament as a Republican, and became a senator in 1890. His poems, which include the collection *Rime nuove* (New Poems, 1861–87), are classical in form and style but emotionally far-reaching. Regarded as the national poet of Italy, he was awarded the Nobel Prize for Literature in 1906.

card vote Brit. a vote by representatives of bodies, each vote counting in proportion to the number of members represented.

care — noun **1** attention and thoroughness. **2** caution; gentleness; regard for safety. **3** the activity of looking after someone or something, or the state of being looked after. **4** worry or anxiety. **5** a cause for worry; a responsibility. — verb intrans. **1** to mind or be upset by something, or the possibility of something. **2** (**care about** or **for someone** or **something**) to concern oneself about them or be interested in them. **3** (**care for something** or **someone**) to have a wish or desire for: *would you care for a drink?* **4** to wish or be willing: *would you care to come?*
— **as if I** etc **care** or **cared** colloq. it doesn't matter to me, etc.
care for someone 1 to look after them. **2** to be fond of or love them. **3** to like or approve of them: *I don't care for mushrooms.*
care of ... (usually **c/o** ...) written on letters, etc addressed to a person at someone else's address.
for all I etc **care** colloq. without upsetting me, etc in the least.
have a care! old use be more careful, considerate, etc.
I etc **couldn't care less** colloq. it doesn't matter to me, etc in the least.
in care being looked after by a local authority, etc, or in a hospital, etc, instead of at home.
take care to be cautious, watchful, or thorough.
take care of someone or **something 1** to look after them. **2** to attend to or organize them. [from Anglo-Saxon *caru*, anxiety, sorrow]

careen verb **1** to turn (a boat) over on its side for cleaning, etc. **2** intrans. said of a ship to lean over to one side; to heel over. **3** intrans. North Amer., esp. US, said of a vehicle, etc to swerve or lurch violently from side to side. [from Latin *carina*, keel]

career — noun **1** one's professional life; one's progress in one's job. **2** a job, occupation, or profession. **3** one's progress through life generally. **4** a swift or headlong course. — verb intrans. colloq. to rush in an uncontrolled or headlong way. [from French *carrière*, racecourse, career]

careerism noun concern with the advancement of one's career.

careerist noun derog. a person who is chiefly interested in his or her own advancement or promotion.

careers adviser or **careers officer** in schools, etc, a person whose job is to help young people choose a suitable career.

carefree adj. having few worries; cheerful.

careful adj. **1** giving or showing care and attention; thorough. **2** gentle; watchful or mindful; cautious. **3** taking care to avoid harm or damage. **4** (**careful of something**) protective of it.

carefully adv. with care; in a careful way.

carefulness noun being careful.

careless adj. **1** not careful or thorough enough; inattentive. **2** lacking, or showing a lack of, a sense of responsibility. **3** effortless: *careless charm.*

carelessly adv. without care; in a careless way.

carelessness noun **1** being careless. **2** a careless action.

carer noun the person who has the responsibility for looking after an ill, disabled, or otherwise helpless person.

caress — verb to touch or stroke gently and lovingly. — noun a gentle, loving touch; a gentle embrace. [from Italian *carezza*]

caret noun a mark ⋀ made on written or printed material to show where a missing word, letter, etc should be inserted. [from Latin *caret*, there is missing]

Caretaker, The a play by Harold Pinter (1960). It is the enigmatic story of a malevolent tramp, Davies, who is given sanctuary by Aston in a cluttered room (owned by Mick) and offered the vague position of caretaker. Their power-struggle and inability to communicate effectively are revealed in inconsequential and obsessional dialogue.

caretaker — noun a person employed to look after a public building, eg a school, or a house, eg if the owner is away. — adj. taking temporary responsibility.

caretaker speech, the speech used by adults when talking to young children. It has shorter sentences, is grammatically simple, and has clear pronunciation, often with exaggerated intonation and repetition. This is the form of speech typically adopted by a child's mother (motherese) and, with certain variations, by the father, grandparents, older siblings, and others who have charge of young children. See also BABY TALK.

careworn adj. worn out with, or marked by, worry and anxiety.

cargo noun (PL. **cargoes**) the goods carried by a ship, aircraft, or other vehicle. [from Spanish *cargo*, burden]

Carib — noun **1** an aboriginal inhabitant of the southern West Indies or of parts of Central and S America. **2** their language. — adj. relating to the Caribs or their language. [from Spanish *Caribe*, from the Arawak language of the West Indies]
◇ The early Caribs were American Indian groups of the Lesser Antilles and neighbouring S America (the Guianas and Venezuela). The island Caribs were maritime people and warriors, who drove the Arawak from the area, and were themselves slaughtered by the Spanish in the 15c. The mainland Caribs led a more peaceful existence in small autonomous settlements in the tropical forests.

Caribbean adj. the part of the Atlantic between the West Indies and Central and S America. — noun relating to this region.

Caribbean Community (ABBREV. **CARICOM**) an association of former British colonies in the Caribbean, some of which (Barbados, Jamaica, and the Leeward Islands) existed as the Caribbean Federation, with the aim of full self-government, until the establishment of the Federation of the West Indies (1958–63). When Jamaica became independent (1962), the Federation was dissolved. In 1968 many of the islands agreed to the establishment of the Caribbean Free Trade Area (CARIFTA).

Caribbean Sea an arm of the Atlantic Ocean between the West Indies and Central and S

America. AREA 2 515 900sq km/971 100sq mi. It is linked to the Pacific Ocean by the Panama Canal. Depths range from 6m on the continental shelf off Nicaragua to 5 058m on the floor of the Venezuelan Basin; the deepest point is at the Cayman Trench, where it measures 6 950m. It was visited by Columbus in 1493. The sea is a major trade route and tourist area. MAIN ISLANDS Greater and Lesser Antilles.

caribou noun (PL. **caribous**, **caribou**) a type of reindeer found in N America. [from Canadian French caribou, from a Native American language]

caricature — noun **1** a representation, especially a drawing, of someone, with his or her most noticeable and distinctive features exaggerated for comic effect. **2** a ridiculously poor attempt at something. — verb to make or give a caricature of something. [from Italian caricatura, from caricare, to distort]

caricaturist noun a person who makes a caricature.

CARICOM abbrev. Caribbean Community.

caries noun the gradual decay or rotting of teeth or bones. [from Latin caries, decay]

carillon noun **1** a set of bells hung usually in a tower and played by means of a keyboard or mechanically. **2** a tune played on such bells. [from French carillon, from Latin quaternio, probably a set of four bells]

caring adj. showing concern for others; sympathetic and helpful.

caring profession a job that involves looking after people socially or medically.

carjacking noun the practice of hijacking a car with its driver and passengers.

Carl a male first name. [a respelling of German Karl, a form of CHARLES]

Carl XVI Gustaf (1946–) King of Sweden, born in Stockholm, the grandson of King Gustavus VI (1882–1973). Since his father had died in an air accident (1947), he became Crown Prince when his grandfather came to the throne (1950). A new constitution restricting monarchical powers was approved by the Swedish parliament just before his accession (1973). In 1976 he married Silvia Sommerlath (1943–). They have three children: Victoria (1977–), who is heir to the Swedish throne, Carl Philip (1979–), and Madeleine (1982–). A keen sportsman, he is proficient in yachting, skiing, and shooting.

Carlisle, Latin **Luguvallum** POP (1992e) 103 000, the county town of Cumbria, NW England, situated in Carlisle district. It lies at the West end of Hadrian's Wall, at the confluence of the Eden and Caldew rivers. HISTORY became an important fortress in Scots–English border wars; developed as a railway centre in the 19c. NOTABLE FEATURES cathedral (11c–12c); castle (11c); Church of St Cuthbert (18c).

Carlow, Gaelic **Cheatharlach** POP (1991) 41 000, a county in Leinster province, SE Irish Republic. AREA 896sq km/346sq mi. PHYSICAL DESCRIPTION lies between the Slieve Ardagh Hills in the W and the Wicklow Mts in the E where the Barrow and Slaney rivers water rich farm land; the Blackstairs Mts rise in the S. CAPITAL Carlow. ECONOMY wheat, barley, sugar beet.

Carlow POP (1991) 14 000, the capital of Carlow county, Leinster, SE Irish Republic. NOTABLE FEATURES Carlow Castle (12c); cathedral (19c); Browne's Hill Tumuli (3km/2mi E).

Carlson, Chester Floyd (1906–68) US inventor, born in Seattle. After studying physics, he took a law degree and worked as a patent lawyer in an electronics firm. By 1938, following experiments on copying processes, he had discovered the basic principles of electrostatic 'xerography'. Patented in 1940, his photocopier was later developed and marketed by the Xerox Corporation, and made him a multi-millionaire.

Carlyle, Thomas (1795–1881) Scottish man of letters, born in Ecclefechan, Dumfriesshire. He taught for several years, wrote articles for the Edinburgh Encyclopaedia, and became absorbed in German literature, notably Goethe. His best-known work Sartor Resartus, on social philosophy, appeared in 1833–4. In 1834 he moved to London where his major works included The French Revolution (3 vols, 1837) and Frederick the Great (6 vols, 1858–65).

Carmarthen POP (1981) 15 000, the administrative centre of Dyfed, SW Wales, situated in Carmarthen district. It lies on the R Towy, 13km/8mi N of the Bristol Channel, and was chartered in 1227.

Carmel a female first name, taken from a mountain in an area of the Holy Land settled by early Christian monks, later the Carmelite order. [from Hebrew carmel, garden, orchard]

Carmelite — noun a member of a monastic order (see CARMELITES). — adj. relating to the Carmelites.

Carmelites, properly the **Order of the Brothers of the Blessed Virgin Mary of Mt Carmel**, or **White Friars** (ABBREV. **OCarm**) a Roman Catholic monastic order that originated in the 12c from the Hermits of Mt Carmel (Israel) to seek the way of life of the prophet Elijah. They flourished as mendicant friars in Europe. Carmelite nuns were officially recognized in 1452, and were reformed by Teresa of Avila in Spain (1562) as strictly cloistered Discalced Carmelites (ODC, named from the practice of wearing sandals instead of shoes and stockings). The male order was reformed by St John of the Cross and recognized as a separate order in 1593. The original order specialized in teaching and preaching, but the Discalced turned to mainly parochial and foreign mission work.

Carmen an opéra comique by Georges Bizet (1875), based on a novel by Prosper Mérimée. Initially a failure, it is now a highly popular work that tells of the bewitching, impetuous gipsy-girl Carmen and her life and loves in 19c Seville.

Carmina Burana a scenic cantata by Carl Orff (1937) to (sometimes erotic) medieval poetry from a Beuren monastery; it is the first part of the Trionfi trilogy. [from Latin, = songs of Beuren]

carmine noun **1** a deep red colour; crimson. **2** a red colouring substance obtained from the cochineal insect. [from French carmine]

Carnac a peninsula on the S coast of Brittany, N France, renowned for its megalithic alignments (avenues), stone circles, and chambered tombs of Neolithic date. The main groups of alignments of standing stones are at Kermario, Kerlescan, and Ménec. In all, c.3 000 stones survive, extending over some 5km/3mi.

carnage noun great slaughter. [from French carnage, from Latin carnaticum, payment in meat]

carnal adj. **1** belonging to the body or the flesh, as opposed to the spirit or intellect. **2** sexual. [from Latin caro, flesh]

carnality noun a carnal or bodily state.

carnally adv. in a carnal way.

Carnap, Rudolf (1891–1970) German-born US philosopher, born in Wuppertal. He was a lecturer at Vienna (1926–31), and Professor of Philosophy at Prague (1931–5), Chicago (1936–52), and California (1954–70). He was one of the leaders of the 'Vienna Circle' of logical positivists. His writings include Der logische Aufbau der Welt (The Logical Construction of the World, 1928), Logische Syntax der Sprache (Logical Syntax of Language, 1934), and Meaning and Necessity (1947).

carnassial tooth Anat. in carnivorous animals, a molar or premolar tooth that is adapted for tearing flesh. [from French carnassier, flesh-eating, from Latin caro carnis, flesh]

Carnatic music the classical music of S India, similar in musical style and methods of performance to the music of the north (Hindustani). A melody is sung, or played on a plucked string or reed instrument; a second melody instrument accompanies; and drums contribute complex rhythmic patterns against a more metrical background of other percussion or hand-clapping. The two traditions differ in language (that of Carnatic music is Telugu) and in details of voice production, ornamentation, and the formation and nomenclature of ragas. Tanjore was the chief centre from which it began to spread in the 17c.

carnation noun **1** a plant with sweet-smelling flowers, originally red, white, or pink. **2** a deep pink colour. [from Latin carnatio, flesh colour, from caro, flesh]

Carné, Marcel (1906–) French film director, born in Paris. He trained as a film technician and from 1931 collaborated as director with the poet and scriptwriter Jacques Prévert. This resulted in a series of outstanding productions, including Quai des Brumes (Port of Shadows, 1938), Le Jour se lève (Daybreak, 1939) and Les Enfants du Paradis (Children of Paradise, 1944).

Carnegie, Andrew (1835–1918) Scottish-born US steel industrialist, born in Dunfermline. His family emigrated to Pittsburgh in 1848, and after several jobs he invested in the business which grew into the largest iron and steel works in the USA. He retired in 1901, a multimillionaire, to Skibo Castle in Sutherland, Scotland. He donated millions of dollars to public institutions in the UK and USA, and several buildings are named after him.

Carnegie Hall a US concert hall in New York City. Named after its first owner, the industrialist Andrew Carnegie, it was opened in 1891 and restored in 1986. Tchaikovsky was the first guest conductor there, and it was the home of the New York Philharmonic orchestra until the 1960s.

carnelian see CORNELIAN.

Carnic Alps, German **Karnische Alpen**, Italian **Alpi Carniche** a S Alpine mountain range on the border between Italy and Austria. Its highest peak is Hohe Warte (2 780m). The range is crossed by the Plöcken Pass.

carnival noun **1** a period of public festivity with eg street processions, colourful costumes, and singing and dancing. **2** a circus or fair. [from Latin carnelevarium, probably from caro, flesh + levare, to remove, the original carnival being Shrove Tuesday, the day before the start of the Lent fast]

Carnival of the Animals, The (Carnaval des animaux, Le) a 'grand zoological fantasy' by Camille Saint-Saëns (1886), for two pianos and orchestra or ensemble. Each movement, eg No.13 Le cygne (The Swan), represents an animal.

carnivore noun **1** commonly used to refer to an animal that feeds mainly on the flesh of other vertebrate animals; a meat-eating animal. **2** any of a group of mammals belonging to the order Carnivora, whose teeth are specialized for biting and tearing flesh, eg dogs, cats, seals, although some are omnivores, eg bears, or even herbivores, eg panda. See also HERBIVORE. [from Latin carnivorus, flesh-eating]

carnivorous adj. **1** denoting an animal, especially a mammal, that feeds mainly on the flesh of other vertebrate animals. **2** denoting a plant which traps animals, usually insects and small invertebrates, and secretes enzymes which digest the prey, allowing the products of digestion to be absorbed by the plant.

◇ Carnivorous plants grow in nutrient-poor habitats, and nitrogen and other nutrients obtained from the digested animal protein supplement those derived from the soil. Such plants include several unrelated groups, eg sundews, pitcher plants, Venus flytrap.

Carnot, Lazare (Nicolas Marguerite) (1753–1823) French statesman, born in Nolay, Burgundy. He entered the army as an engineer, and in 1791 became a member of the Legislative Assembly. He survived the Reign of Terror, and became one of the Directors (1795), but in 1797 was suspected of Royalist sympathies and escaped to Germany. Back in Paris, he became Minister of War (1800), and helped to organize the Italian and Rhenish campaigns, for which he became known as the 'organizer of victory' during the Revolutionary Wars. He also commanded at Antwerp (1814), and during the Hundred Days was Minister of the Interior.

Carnot, (Nicolas Léonard) Sadi (1796–1832) French engineer and physicist, born in Paris. Son of Lazare Carnot, he became an engineer, and from 1819 concentrated on scientific research. He was the first to apply scientific principles to the analysis of the working cycle and efficiency of the steam engine, arriving at an early form of the second law of thermodynamics and the concept of reversibility in the form of the ideal 'Carnot cycle'.

Carnoustie POP (1981) 9 200, a resort town in Angus district, Tayside, E Scotland. It lies on the E coast of Scotland, 17km/11mi NE of Dundee. The town's golf courses include one of championship status.

carob *noun* **1** an evergreen tree (*Ceratonia siliqua*), native to the Mediterranean region, which produces large reddish-brown seedpods rich in sugars and gums. — Also called *locust tree.* **2** the edible seedpod of this tree, ground and used as a substitute for chocolate and as a food stabilizer, or as a feed for animal livestock. [from French *carobe*]

Carol I (1839–1914) first King of Romania (1881–1914), born in Hohenzollern-Sigmaringen. He was made Prince of Romania in 1866, and became king when his country received independence from the Ottoman Empire. He carried out many reforms, but was unable to forestall the peasant revolt of 1907, when many thousands were killed.

Carol a first name, originally male, now female. [an Anglicized version of Latin *Carolus* (see CHARLES); as a female name it is probably a short form of CAROLINE]

carol — *noun* a religious song, especially one sung at Christmas in honour of Christ's birth. — *verb intrans.* (**carolled, carolling**) **1** to sing carols. **2** to sing joyfully. [from Old French *carole*]
◇ In medieval English, a carol was any song with a refrain, whether religious or secular. Some of the melodies for carols popular today are borrowed from 16c hymns, and the practice of arranging carols for two or more voices goes back to the 15c.

Caroline *or* **Carolyn** a female first name. [from a French derivative of *Carolus* (see CHARLES)]

Caroline in the UK, a 1960s pirate pop music radio station, financed by advertising, that operated illegally from a ship off the Essex coast and prompted the creation of Radio 1.

Caroline of Ansbach (1683–1737) queen-consort of George II of Great Britain, born in Ansbach, the daughter of a German prince. She exercised a strong influence over her husband, and was a leading supporter of his chief minister, Robert Walpole.

Caroline of Brunswick, Amelia Elizabeth (1768–1821) wife of King George IV of the UK, born in Brunswick, Germany, the daughter of George III's sister, Augusta. She married George, Prince of Wales in 1795, but although she bore him a daughter (Princess Charlotte), at his request they lived apart. When George became king (1820), she refused the offer of an annuity to renounce the title of queen, but although his divorce bill failed, she was not allowed into Westminster Abbey at the coronation (Jul 1821).

Carolingian — *noun* a member of a Frankish dynasty (see CAROLINGIANS). — *adj.* relating to the Carolingians.

Carolingians a Frankish ruling dynasty which rose to power as mayors of the palace, and ultimately replaced the Merovingians when Pepin III, 'the Short' became King of the Franks in 751. The Carolingian Empire created by Charlemagne embraced most of the former territory of the Roman Empire in the West, but the Frankish custom of dividing land among all male heirs meant its rapid decline after his death. In 843 it was divided at the Treaty of Verdun into E Francia, W Francia, and the 'Middle Kingdom' stretching from the North Sea to Italy, and these soon dissolved into smaller states.

carom *noun* a form of billiards popular in Europe, played on a table without pockets with the object of making cannons. [short form of *carambole*, a cannon in billiards, from French *carombole*, from Spanish *carambola*, the red ball in billiards]

carotene *or* **carotin** *noun Biochem.* any of a number of reddish-yellow pigments, widely distributed in plants, that are converted to vitamin A in the body. [from Latin *carota*, carrot]

carotenoid *or* **carotinoid** *noun Biochem.* any of a group of plant pigments that absorb light during photosynthesis.

Carothers, Wallace Hume (1896–1937) US organic and industrial chemist, born in Burlington, Iowa. At the Du Pont Company in Wilmington, he developed the synthetic rubber neoprene (first produced commercially in 1931) and later nylon, first marketed two years after his suicide in Philadelphia.

carotid *or* **carotid artery** *noun* one of two large blood vessels in the neck that carry blood to the head. [from Greek *karotides*, from *karos*, stupor, pressure on these arteries causing unconsciousness]

carousal *noun* a drinking bout or party; a noisy revel.

carouse *verb intrans.* to take part in a noisy drinking party. [from German *gar aus*, all out, ie completely emptying the glass]

carousel *noun* **1** a revolving belt in an airport, etc on to which luggage is unloaded so that passengers can collect it as it passes by. **2** a revolving case for holding photographic transparencies, for use in a projector. **3** *North Amer.* a merry-go-round. [from Italian *carusello*, kind of ball game]

carp[1] *noun* (PL. **carp, carps**) a large edible fish of lakes and rivers. [from Middle English *carpe*]

carp[2] *verb intrans.* to complain, find fault, or criticize, especially unnecessarily. [from Norse *karpa*, to boast, dispute]

carpal *Anat.* — *adj.* relating to the wrist. — *noun* any of the group of bones in the wrist. [from Greek *karpos*, wrist]

car park a building or piece of land where cars can be parked.

Carpathian Mountains a mountain system in E central Europe, forming the E wing of the great Alpine uplift. It extends 1 400km/870mi in a semi-circle from Slovakia through Poland and the Ukraine to Romania; it forms, in the middle, the boundary between Slovakia and Poland. Its main divisions (W–E) are the Little Carpathians, White Carpathians, Beskids, Low Tatra, High Tatra, E or Romanian Carpathians, and the Transylvanian Alps. Mt Gerlachovsky (2 663m) is the highest point. The range is rich in minerals and coal deposits, and is generally forested to 1 200m.

carpel *noun Bot.* the female reproductive part of a flowering plant, consisting of a stigma, style, and ovary. There may be one or many carpels in a flower, either fused together or free. [from Greek *karpos*, fruit]

Carpentaria, Gulf of a major inlet on the N coast of Australia between Cape Arnhem and Cape York. It is bounded N by the Arafura Sea. The inlet is 595km/370mi long by 491km/305mi wide with shallow depths of 25–55m. There are several islands and the area is a source of bauxite and manganese. [named in 1644 by Abel Janssoon Tasman in honour of Pieter Carpenter, Governor-General of Dutch East Indies]

carpenter *noun* a skilled workman in wood, eg in building houses, etc or in making and repairing fine furniture. [from Latin *carpentarius*, person who builds wagons]

carpentry *noun* the work or skill of a carpenter.

carper *noun* a person who carps.

carpet — *noun* **1** a covering for floors and stairs, made of heavy, usually woven and tufted, fabric. **2** something that covers a surface like a carpet does. — *verb* **1** to cover with, or as if with, a carpet. **2** *colloq.* to reprimand or scold. — **on the carpet** *colloq.* being scolded or reprimanded. [from Middle English *carpete*, from Italian *carpita*, woollen bed-covering]

carpet-bag *noun* an old-fashioned travelling-bag made of carpeting.

carpetbagger *noun derog.* a politician seeking election in a place where he or she is a stranger.
◇ Originally a derogatory term for US Northerners who went to the defeated South after the American Civil War to aid freed blacks and take advantage of the economic opportunities offered by Reconstruction. The Southerners characterized them as opportunistic transients who carried all their belongings in bags made of carpet fabric. Although many were well-intentioned, others were corrupt and gained political power by exploiting the black vote.

carpeting *noun* **1** fabric for making carpets. **2** carpets generally.

carpet slippers slippers, especially men's, with the upper part made of carpeting or a fabric resembling it.

carpet-sweeper *noun* a long-handled device fitted with a revolving brush, that picks up dust, etc from carpets as it is pushed along.

car phone, a portable telephone for use in a car, operating by cellular radio. See CELLULAR RADIO.

carping *adj.* critical, over-critical.

carpingly *adv.* with a carping manner.

carport *noun* a roofed shelter for a car, attached to the side of a house.

carpus *noun* (PL. **carpi**) *Anat.* the set of bones forming the wrist. See also CARPAL. [from Greek *karpos*, wrist]

Carrantuohill the highest peak in the Irish Republic, in the Macgillycuddy's Reeks Range, SW Irish Republic. HEIGHT 1 041m.

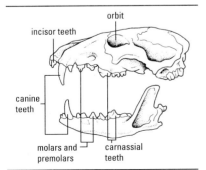

orbit
incisor teeth
canine teeth
molars and premolars
carnassial teeth

typical carnivore skull

Carrel, Alexis (1873–1944) US experimental surgeon, born in Lyons, France. He worked at the Rockefeller Institute for Medical Research from 1906, and discovered a method of suturing blood vessels which made it possible to replace arteries. In 1912 he was awarded the Nobel Prize for Physiology or Medicine. During World War I, he served the French army and helped Henry Dakin to develop 'Dakin's solution' for sterilizing deep wounds; he also did much research on prolonging the life of tissues.

carrel *or* **carrell** *noun* a small compartment or desk in a library, for private study. [from Middle English *carole*, enclosure for study in a cloister]

carriage *noun* 1 a four-wheeled horse-drawn passenger vehicle. 2 a railway coach for carrying passengers. 3 the process or cost of transporting goods. 4 a moving section of a machine, eg a typewriter, that carries some part into the required position. 5 the way one holds oneself in standing or walking. [from Middle English *cariage*, from Old French *carier*, to carry]

carriage clock a small ornamental clock with a handle on top, originally used by travellers.

carriageway *noun* the part of a road used by vehicles, or a part used by vehicles travelling in one direction.

carrier *noun* 1 a person or thing that carries. 2 a person or firm that transports goods. 3 a person or animal infected by a disease in such a way as to be able to pass it on to others without actually suffering from it. 4 a carrier bag.

carrier bag a plastic or paper bag with handles, supplied to shop customers for carrying purchased goods.

carrier pigeon a pigeon that carries messages.

carrier wave *Physics* in radio transmission, a continuously transmitted radio wave whose amplitude or frequency is made to increase or decrease instantaneously in response to variations in the characteristics of the signal being transmitted.

Carrington, Peter (Alexander Rupert) Carrington, 6th Baron (1919–) British Conservative politician. He served with distinction in World War II and his appointments in every subsequent Conservative government included High Commissioner to Australia (1956–9), First Lord of the Admiralty (1959–63), and Secretary of State for Defence (1970–4). Upon the Conservative return to office he was Foreign Secretary (1979–82), when he established independence for Zimbabwe (1980), but he resigned over the Argentinian invasion of the Falkland Islands. He later became Secretary-General of NATO (1984–8).

Carrington, Richard Christopher (1826–75) English astronomer, born in Chelsea, London. He set up his own private observatory at Redhill, Surrey, where he produced star catalogues and observed the Sun's rotation systematically over a period of seven years, noting the apparent motions of sunspots across its disc. His formula for the solar rotation's dependence on solar latitude was universally adopted.

carrion *noun* dead and rotting animal flesh. [from Old French *charogne*, from Latin *caro*, flesh]

carrion crow a crow native to Europe and Asia, usually having black plumage, that inhabits forest, grassland, and cultivated land, and eats virtually anything.

Carroll, Lewis, pseudonym of **Charles Lutwidge Dodgson** (1832–98) English writer, born in Daresbury, Cheshire. He took holy orders in 1861, and lectured in mathematics (1855–81). He is best known for his children's novel *Alice's Adventures in Wonderland* (1865) and its sequel, *Through the Looking-glass* (1872). Other works include the nonsense verse *The Hunting of the Snark* (1876).

carrot *noun* 1 a usually long and pointed orange-coloured root vegetable. 2 *colloq.* something offered as an incentive. [from Old French *carrotte*]

carroty *adj. dérog.*, *said of hair* having a strong reddish colour.

carry *verb* (**carries**, **carried**) 1 to hold in one's hands, have in a pocket, bag etc, or support the weight of on one's body, while moving from one place to another. 2 to bring, take, or convey. 3 to have on one's person. 4 to be the means of spreading (a disease, etc). 5 to support: *the walls carry the roof.* 6 to be pregnant with. 7 to hold (oneself or a part of one's body) in a certain way: *carry oneself well.* 8 to bear (responsibilities, etc). 9 to bear the burden or expense of: *we can't carry unprofitable enterprises.* 10 to do the work of (someone who is not doing enough) in addition to one's own. 11 to print or broadcast. 12 to stock or sell. 13 to have, involve, etc: *a crime carrying the death penalty.* 14 *intrans. said of a sound or the source of a sound* to be able to be heard a distance away. 15 to pass or agree to by majority vote. 16 to win the support of (voters, an audience, etc). 17 to bear the effects of: *he carries his age well.* 18 to take to a certain point: *carry politeness too far.* 19 *Maths.* to transfer (a figure) in a calculation from one column to the next. 20 *intrans. said of a golf ball, etc* to travel (a certain distance). 21 *Mil.* to capture (a town, etc).
— **be** *or* **get carried away** *colloq.* to become over-excited or over-enthusiastic.

carry something forward to transfer a number, amount, etc to the next column, page, or financial period.

carry something off 1 to manage an awkward situation, etc well. **2** to win a prize, etc. **3** to take something away by force.

carry on 1 to continue; to keep going. **2** *colloq.* to make a noisy or unnecessary fuss.

carry something on to conduct or engage in business, etc.

carry on with someone to have a love affair with someone.

carry something out to accomplish it successfully.

carry something over 1 to continue it on the following page, etc; to carry forward. **2** to postpone it.

carry someone through to help them to survive a difficult period, etc.

carry something through to complete or accomplish it.
[from Old French *carier*, from Latin *carricare*, to cart]

carrycot *noun* a light, box-like cot for a baby, with handles for carrying it.

carrying *adj., said of a voice* easily heard at a distance.

carry-on 1 an excitement or fuss. **2** a romance or love-affair.

carry-out *noun colloq.* 1 *North Amer., esp. US, Scot.* cooked food bought at a restaurant, etc for eating elsewhere. 2 *North Amer., esp. US, Scot.* a shop or restaurant supplying such food. 3 *Scot.* an alcoholic drink bought in a shop or pub for drinking elsewhere.

car-sick *adj.* feeling sick as a result of travelling in a car.

car-sickness *noun* the tendency to be car-sick; a bout of being car-sick.

Carson, Kit (Christopher) (1809–68) US frontiersman, born in Kentucky. A Missouri trapper and hunter, his knowledge of Native American habits and languages led to his being guide in John Frémont's explorations (1842). He was Indian agent in New Mexico (1853), and fought for the Union in the Civil War.

Carson, Rachel Louise (1907–64) US naturalist and publicist, born in Springdale, Pennsylvania. She worked in marine biology in the US Fish and Wildlife Service (1936–49), and during the 1940s her books on marine ecology became influential. Her *Silent Spring* (1962) directed much public attention to the problems caused by agricultural pesticides, and she became a pioneer in the conservationist movement of the 1960s.

Carson City POP (1990) 40 000, the capital of the state of Nevada, USA, founded in 1859. It is an independent city situated near L Tahoe, W Nevada, and serves as the trade centre for a mining and agricultural area. It is also a gambling centre. NOTABLE FEATURE Nevada State Museum. [named after the frontiersman Kit Carson]

cart — *noun* 1 a two- or four-wheeled, horse-drawn vehicle for carrying goods or passengers. 2 a light vehicle pushed or pulled by hand. — *verb* 1 to carry in a cart. 2 (**cart something around** *or* **off, etc**) *colloq.* to carry or convey it.
— **in the cart** *colloq.* in difficulties.
put the cart before the horse to reverse the normal or logical order of doing things.
[related to Norse *cartr*]

Cartagena, Latin **Carthago Nova** POP (1991) 167 000, a fortified seaport and naval base in Murcia province, SE Spain. It lies 48km/30mi S of Murcia and is Spain's leading commercial port and naval base. It was formerly the largest naval arsenal in Europe. The city was founded by the Carthaginians in 221 BC. NOTABLE FEATURES Castle of la Concepción; Church of Santa Maria la Vieja (13c).

Cartagena (de los Indes) POP (1992e) 688 000, the port capital of Bolivar department, NW Colombia. It lies on the Caribbean coast, SW of Barranquilla. The city was founded in 1533 and sacked by Francis Drake in 1586. The old colonial quarter is a World Heritage site.

Carte, Richard D'Oyly (1844–1901) English impresario and manager, born in London. He built the Savoy Theatre (1881) and the Royal Opera House (1887), and is best known as the first producer of the Gilbert and Sullivan operas.

carte blanche complete freedom of action or discretion. [from French *carte blanche*, blank paper]

cartel *noun* a group of firms that agree, especially illegally, on similar fixed prices for their products, so as to reduce competition and keep profits high. [from French *cartel*, from Italian *cartello*, letter of defiance]

Carter, Angela (1940–92) English novelist and short-story writer, born in London. Her fiction, characterized by feminist themes and fantasy narratives, includes the novels *The Magic Toyshop* (1967), *The Infernal Desire Machines of Dr Hoffman* (1972), *Nights at the Circus* (1984), and *Wise Children* (1991), and the short-story collections *Black Venus* (1985) and *American Ghosts and Old World Wonders* (1993). She also wrote poetry, children's stories, and radio plays and, with Neil Jordan, wrote the screenplay for *The Company of Wolves* (1984).

Carter, Howard (1874–1939) English archaeologist, born in Swaffham, Norfolk. He joined Flinders Petrie's archaeological survey of Egypt as an artist in 1891, and from 1907 conducted his own research under the patronage of George Herbert, 5th Earl of Carnarvon (1866–1923). His discoveries included the tombs of Hatshepsut, Tuthmosis IV and, most notably, that of Tutankhamen (1922).

Carter, Jimmy (James Earl) (1924–) US politician, the 39th President, born in Plains, Georgia. He served in the US Navy until 1953, when he took over the family peanut business and other enterprises. As Governor of Georgia (1970–4) he expressed an enlightened policy towards the rights of blacks and women. In 1976 he won the Democratic presidential nomination, and went on to win a narrow victory over Gerald

Ford. During his administration (1977–81) he arranged the peace treaty between Egypt and Israel (1979), and was concerned with human rights at home and abroad, but it ended in difficulties over the taking of US hostages in Iran, and the Soviet invasion of Afghanistan. Carter was defeated by Ronald Reagan in the 1980 election.

Cartesian philosophy various attempts made by Descartes' contemporaries and successors to work out the salient features of his philosophy: eg his mind–body dualism, which influenced Leibniz's doctrine of pre-established harmony.

Carthage an ancient town in Tunisia, N Africa, now a suburb of Tunis. Reputedly founded by the Phoenicians in 814 BC, it was destroyed by Rome in 146 BC following the Punic Wars. The site was colonized by Caesar and Augustus in the 1c BC, and became the capital of the Roman province of Africa. It fell to the Vandals (AD 439–533), and was destroyed again by the Arabs in 698. The few remains include the Roman baths of Antonius, the old harbour, and an aqueduct of Hadrian. It is a World Heritage site.

carthorse *noun* a large strong horse bred for heavy work on farms, etc.

Carthusian — *noun* a member of a monastic order (see CARTHUSIANS). — *adj.* relating to the Carthusians.

Carthusians, properly the **Order of Carthusians** (ABBREV. **OCart**) a Roman Catholic monastic order founded (1084) by Bruno of Cologne in Chartreuse, near Grenoble, France. The monks practise strict abstinence and live as solitaries; lay brothers live in a community. Membership is small, but there are houses in many parts of Europe. The liqueur 'La Grande Chartreuse' is distilled at the mother house, the profits from which are distributed to local charities.

Cartier-Bresson, Henri (1908–) French photographer, born in Paris. He studied painting and literature before taking up photography after a trip to Africa in 1930. His first pictures were published in 1933. In the later 1930s he worked as assistant to the film director Jean Renoir, and after World War II was a co-founder of the independent photographic agency, Magnum Photos. He works only in black-and-white, concerned exclusively with the capturing of visual moments illustrating contemporary life. His books include *The World of Henri Cartier-Bresson* (1968). In the mid-1970s he gave up photography, and returned to his earlier interests of painting and drawing.

cartilage *noun* a tough flexible semi-opaque material that forms the skeleton of cartilaginous fish, eg sharks, dogfish. In other vertebrates, including man, it forms the skeleton of the embryo, but is converted into bone before adulthood. In the adult, cartilage persists in structures such as the larynx, trachea, nose, and discs between the vertebrae, and also surrounds the ends of bones at joints. [from French *cartilage*, from Latin *cartilago*]

cartilaginous *adj.* of the nature of or like cartilage.

Cartland, Barbara (Hamilton) (1901–) English popular romantic novelist, born in Birmingham. Since her first novel, *Jigsaw* (1923), she has written over 200 books, mostly romantic novels but also biographies of 'romantic' figures, and books on food, health, and beauty. She has been active in charitable causes, and is an advocate of health foods and fitness for the elderly.

cartographer *noun* a person who makes charts or maps.

cartographic *adj.* relating to cartography.

cartography *noun* the art or science of making maps. [from French *carte*, chart + -GRAPHY]

Carton, Sydney the dissolute but goodhearted barrister whose selfless generosity makes

him a hero in Charles Dickens's *A Tale of Two Cities.*

carton *noun* **1** a plastic or cardboard container in which food of various types is packaged for sale. **2** a cardboard box. [from French *carton*, pasteboard, from Italian *cartone*, strong paper]

cartoon *noun* **1** a humorous drawing in a newspaper, etc, often ridiculing someone or something. **2** (*also* **animated cartoon**) a film made by photographing a series of drawings, each showing the subjects in a slightly altered position, giving the impression of movement when the film is run at normal speed. **3** (*also* **strip cartoon**) a strip of drawings in a newspaper, etc showing a sequence of often humorous events. **4** a preparatory drawing of a subject done by an artist before attempting a large painting of it. [from Italian *cartone*, strong paper, or a drawing on it]

cartoonist *noun* an artist who draws cartoons for newspapers, etc.

cartouche *noun Hist.* **1** a paper case containing the explosive charge for a gun, etc; a cartridge. **2** *Archit.* a scroll-like ornament or decorative border with rolled ends. **3** in Egyptian hieroglyphics, an oval figure enclosing a royal or divine name. [from French *cartouche*, from Italian *cartoccio*, from Latin *carta, charta,* paper]

cartridge *noun* **1** a small case containing the explosive charge and bullet for a gun. **2** the part of the pick-up arm of a record-player that contains the needle or stylus. **3** a tube containing ink for loading into a fountain pen. **4** a plastic case containing sound-recording tape, larger and more efficient than a cassette. **5** a plastic case containing photographic film, for loading directly into the camera. [from the earlier form *cartage*, a variant of French *cartouche*, cartridge]

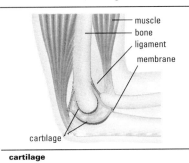

cartilage

cartridge belt a wide belt with a row of loops or pockets for gun cartridges.

cartridge paper thick rough-surfaced paper for drawing on.

cartwheel — *noun* **1** the wheel of a cart. **2** an acrobatic movement in which one throws one's body sideways with the turning action of a wheel, putting one's weight on each hand and foot in turn. — *verb intrans.* to perform a cartwheel.

Caruso, Enrico (1873–1921) Italian operatic tenor, born in Naples. Born into a poor family, the eighteenth of 20 children, he received little formal education. His first appearance was in *Faust* (1895), then he went to London (1902) and New York (1903). The extraordinary power of his voice, combined with his acting ability, won him recognition as one of the greatest tenors of all time.

carve *verb* **1** to cut (wood, stone, etc) into a shape. **2** to make (something) from wood or stone by cutting into it. **3** to produce (a design, inscription, etc) in wood or stone. **4** to cut (meat) into slices; to cut (a slice) of meat. **5** *intrans.* to cut meat into slices. **6** (**carve something out**) to establish or create an opportunity, etc for oneself through personal effort: *carve out a career.*

— **carve something up 1** to cut it up. **2** *colloq.* to divide territory, spoils, etc, especially in a crude or wholesale manner.

carve someone up *slang* to attack and cut someone with a knife.
[from Anglo-Saxon *ceorfan*, to cut]

carvel-built *adj., said of a boat* built with planks laid flush, not overlapping. See also CLINKER-BUILT. [from *carvel*, a type of ship]

Carver, George Washington (c.1864–1943) US scientist, born into a black slave family near Diamond Grove, Missouri. Despite receiving little early education, he graduated from Iowa State Agricultural College (1894), and became renowned for his research into agricultural problems and synthetic products, especially from peanuts and sweet potatoes. He also helped make Tuskegee Institute in Alabama a focus of education for the disadvantaged black farmers of the South, and was a noted teacher and humanitarian.

carver *noun* **1** a person who carves. **2** a carving-knife.

carvery *noun* (PL. **carveries**) a restaurant where meat is carved from a joint for customers on request.

carve-up *noun* a wholesale division of territory or spoils.

carving *noun* a figure or pattern etc produced by carving.

carving-fork *noun* a large fork with two long prongs, for holding meat steady during carving.

carving-knife *noun* a long sharp knife for carving meat.

car wash a place at a petrol station, etc fitted with automatic equipment for washing cars.

Cary, John (c.1754–1835) English cartographer, who began as an engraver in London and in c.1783 became a publisher and land surveyor. His *New and Correct English Atlas* appeared in 1787, followed by county atlases, and the *New Universal Atlas* of 1808. In 1794 he undertook a road survey of England and Wales, published as *Cary's New Itinerary* (1798).

Cary, (Arthur) Joyce (Lunel) (1888–1957) British novelist, born in Londonderry, Northern Ireland. He fought in W Africa in World War I, and war injuries and ill health forced his early retirement to Oxford, where he took up writing. His novels based on his African experience include *African Witch* (1936) and *Mister Johnson* (1939). He is best known for the trilogy *Herself Surprised* (1940), *To be a Pilgrim* (1942), and *The Horse's Mouth* (1944).

caryatid *noun* (PL. **caryatids, caryatides**) *Archit.* a carved female figure used as a support for a roof, etc, instead of a column or pillar. [from Greek *Karyatides*, priestesses of the goddess Artemis at Caryae in S Greece, or columns in the form of women]

Casablanca, Arabic **Dar el Beida** POP (1990e) 3.2m, a seaport in Centre province, W Morocco, on the Atlantic coast 290km/180mi SW of Tangier. The city handles over 75% of Morocco's trade. HISTORY founded by the Portuguese as Casa Branca in 1515; seriously damaged by an earthquake in 1755 and rebuilt; French occupation in 1907; meeting place of Churchill and Roosevelt in 1943.

Casablanca a US film directed by Michael Curtiz (1942). It is a wartime romance, starring Humphrey Bogart and Ingrid Bergman, that focuses on a Casablanca bar owner who helps a fugitive couple escape to America.

Casals, Pablo (Pau) (1876–1973) Spanish cellist, conductor, and composer, born in Vendrell, Tarragona. He became Professor of Cello at Barcelona (1896) and soon after began to appear as a soloist. In 1919 he founded the Barcelona Orchestra, which he conducted until he left Spain at the outbreak of the Spanish Civil War (1936). In 1950 he founded an annual festival of classical chamber music in Prades, France. His own compositions consist of choral and chamber works.

Casanova (de Seingalt), Giacomo (Girolamo) (1725–98) Italian adventurer, born in Venice, whose many occupations included clergyman, secretary, soldier, violinist, and spy. In 1755 he was imprisoned in Venice for being a magician, but he escaped in 1756, and for nearly 20 years travelled through Europe indulging in romantic escapades. He established the state lottery in Paris, mingled with the aristocracy everywhere, and usually had to 'vanish' after a brief period of felicity. His main work is his autobiography, first published in its complete form in 1960.

Casanova *noun derog.* a man with a reputation for having many love affairs. [named after Giacomo Casanova]

Casaubon, Mr the middle-aged, pedantic, and mean-spirited husband of Dorothea in George Eliot's *Middlemarch*.

cascade — *noun* **1** a waterfall or series of waterfalls. **2** something resembling a waterfall in appearance or manner of falling. **3** a large number of things arriving or to be dealt with suddenly: *cascades of letters.* — *verb intrans.* to fall like a waterfall. [from French *cascade*, from Italian *cascare*, to fall]

Cascade Range a volcanic mountain range in W North America, which extends over 1 120km/700mi from N California through Oregon and Washington in the USA to British Columbia in Canada. The highest point is Mt Rainier (4 392m), Washington. Other high peaks include Mts Adams (3 742m), Baker (3 285m), Hood (3 424m), Jefferson (3 200m), and Shasta (4 317m). Many of the peaks are snow-covered volcanic cones, notably Mt St Helens (2 549m) which erupted in 1980. There are glaciers on the higher peaks (notably Mt Rainier) and many glacial lakes (the largest is L Chelan). Crater Lake National Park is in the S. The Klamath and Columbia rivers cut through from E to W, and a 13km-8mi-long railway tunnel goes through the range E of Seattle. The range is heavily forested and is a source of hydroelectricity. [named after the cascades of the Columbia R where it passes through the range in a canyon c.1 200m deep]

case¹ — *noun* **1** a box, container, or cover, for storage, protection, carrying, etc. **2** a suitcase or briefcase. **3** *Printing* a tray with compartments for type, the terms *lower case* for small letters and *upper case* for capital letters resulting from the traditional positioning of the trays containing those letters. — *verb* **1** to put in a case. **2** *slang* to have a good look at (a house, etc) with the intention of breaking into it and stealing (see also JOINT). [from Latin *capsa*, case for holding a scroll]

case² *noun* **1** a particular occasion, situation, or set of circumstances. **2** an example, instance, or occurrence. **3** a person receiving some sort of treatment or care. **4** a matter requiring investigation: *the police are looking into the case.* **5** a matter to be decided in a law court. **6** (**case for** *or* **against something**) the argument for or against something, with the relevant facts fully presented. **7** *Grammar* the relationship of a noun, pronoun or adjective to other words in a sentence, or the form the noun, etc takes which shows this relationship. **8** an odd character.
— **as the case may be** according to how things turn out.
be the case to be true.
a case in point a good example, relevant to the present discussion.
in any case whatever happens; no matter what happens.
in case so as to be prepared or safe (if a certain thing should happen).
in case of something if a certain occurrence happens.

in that case if that happens, since that has happened, etc.
[from French *cas*, from Latin *casus*, fall]

casebook *noun* a written record of cases dealt with by a doctor, etc.

case-harden 1 *Metall.* to harden the surface layer of steel by diffusing carbon into it at high temperatures so that the outer surface is tough and resistant to wear, while the inner core remains resistant to fracture. **2** *Geol., said of a mineral* to form a coating on the surface of porous rock as a result of the evaporation of a solution containing that mineral. **3** to make (someone) insensitive or callous.

case history a record of relevant details from a person's past kept by a doctor, social worker, etc.

casein *noun Biochem.* a milk protein that is the main constituent of cheese. [from Latin *caseus*, cheese]

case law law based on decisions made about similar cases in the past, as distinct from statute law established by the government.

case load the number of cases a doctor, etc has to deal with at any particular time.

Casement, Sir Roger (David) (1864–1916) Irish patriot and British consular official, born in Kingstown (now Dun Laoghaire), Co Dublin. He acted as Consul in Africa (1895–1904) and Brazil (1906–11), and exposed the exploitation of rubber workers in the Congo and Peru. An ardent Irish nationalist, he tried to obtain German support for Irish independence, but in 1916 was arrested on landing in Ireland from a German submarine to head the Sinn Féin rebellion, and hanged for high treason in London. His controversial 'Black Diaries' were long suppressed by the government but ultimately published in 1959.

casement *or* **casement window** *noun* a window that opens outwards like a door. [from Middle English, from CASE¹]

casework *noun* social work with individuals, in which family background and environment are closely studied.

cash — *noun* **1** coins or paper money, as distinct from cheques, credit cards, etc. **2** *colloq.* money in any form. — *verb* to obtain or give cash in return for (a cheque, traveller's cheque, postal order, etc).
— **cash down** *colloq.* with payment immediately on purchase.
cash something in to exchange tokens, vouchers, etc for money.
cash in on something *colloq.* to make money, or profit in some other way, by taking advantage of a situation, etc.
cash on delivery (ABBREV. **c.o.d.**) with payment for goods immediately on delivery.
cash up *Brit. colloq., said of a shopkeeper, etc* to count up the money taken, usually at the end of a day.
[from Old French *casse*, box]

cash-and-carry — *noun* a large often wholesale shop where accredited customers pay for goods in cash and take them away immediately. — *adj., said of a business, etc* using this system.

cash book a written record of all money paid out and received by a business, etc.

cash box a box, usually metal and with a lock, for keeping cash in.

cash card a card, issued by a bank, etc, with which one can obtain money from a cash machine.

cash crop a crop that is grown for sale rather than for consumption by the farmer's household or by animal livestock.

cash desk a desk in a shop, etc at which one pays for goods.

cashew *noun* **1** a small kidney-shaped nut. **2** the evergreen tropical American tree on which it grows. [from Portuguese *cajú*, from Tupí (S American Indian language)]

cash flow the amount of money coming into, and going out of, a business, etc.

cashier¹ *noun* the person in a business firm, etc who receives, pays out, and generally deals with, the cash. [from Old French *caissier*, from *caisse*, cash box]

cashier² *verb* (**cashiered, cashiering**) to dismiss (an officer) from the armed forces in disgrace. [from Old Dutch *kasseren*]

cashless *adj.* using payment by credit card or electronic transfer of money, rather than by cash or cheque.

cash machine *or* **cash dispenser**, an electronic machine, eg fitted into the outside wall of a bank, from which one can obtain cash using one's personal cash card. See also ATM.

cashmere *noun* **1** very fine soft wool from a long-haired Asian goat. **2** a fabric made from this. [from *Kashmir*, in N India, where shawls were woven from this wool]

cashphone *noun* a coin-operated payphone, as distinct from a cardphone.

cash point 1 the place in a supermarket, etc where money is taken for goods purchased. **2** a cash machine.

cash register a machine in a shop, etc that calculates and records the amount of each sale and from which change and a receipt are usually given.

casing *noun* a protective covering, eg of plastic for electric cables.

casino *noun* (PL. **casinos**) a public building or room for gambling. [Italian diminutive of *casa*, house]

cask *noun* **1** a barrel for holding liquids, especially alcoholic liquids. **2** the amount contained by a cask. [back-formation from CASKET, the ending *-et* having been understood as a diminutive suffix]

casket *noun* **1** a small case for holding jewels, etc. **2** *North Amer.* a coffin. [from Middle English]

Casper POP (1990) 61 000, the seat of Natrona County, E central Wyoming, USA, and the largest city in the state. Situated on the North Platte R, 228km/142mi NW of Cheyenne, it is the centre of a farming and ranching area, rich in minerals. The town expanded rapidly after oil was discovered in the 1890s. Oil and oil-related industries remain important to the local economy. NOTABLE FEATURE Old Fort Casper Museum.

Caspian Sea, ancient **Mare Caspium**, or **Mare Hyrcanium** the largest inland body of water on earth, bounded W by Azerbaijan, W and N by Russia, N and E by Kazakhstan, E by Turkmenistan, and in the S by Iran. AREA 371 000sq km/143 200sq mi. It lies c.28m below sea level; maximum depth 980m in the S; the shallow N area has an average depth of only 5.2m; the sea is subject to fluctuations as a result of evaporation, river input, and dams on the R Volga. Chief ports for freight trade (especially oil and Beluga caviar) are Astrakhan in Russia and Baku in Azerbaijan. There is no outlet, salt levels are low, and there are no tides. The sea is frozen in the N for several months during severe winters. [possibly named after the Caspii tribe which once occupied the S shores]

Cass, Dunstan a spiteful, villainous character in George Eliot's *Silas Marner*. His good-natured brother Godfrey is the husband of Nancy Lammeter and natural father of Eppie.

Cassandra 1 in Greek mythology, the daughter of Priam, King of Troy. She was loved by Apollo, who gave her the gift of prophecy, but because she did not return his love he decreed that while she would always tell the truth, she would never be believed. At the fall of Troy she was taken as a concubine by Agamemnon, and was murdered with him on his return to Mycenae. **2** a female first name.

cassava *noun* **1** a perennial shrubby plant of the genus *Manihot*, belonging to the spurge family (Euphorbiaceae) and native to Brazil, but cultivated throughout the tropics for its fleshy tuberous edible roots. Cassava is a staple food crop in Africa. The roots are used to make cassava flour, bread, tapioca, and laundry starch, and the juice from the roots can be fermented to make an alcoholic drink. The leaves are eaten as a vegetable. Bitter cassava must be boiled and pressed in order to remove prussic acid, a poisonous compound that is present in its sap. — Also called *manioc*. **2** a starchy substance that is obtained from the root of this plant, and is stored and exported in the form of tapioca. [from Spanish *cazabe*, from Taino (W Indian language)]

casserole — *noun* **1** a dish with a lid, in which meat, vegetables, etc can be cooked and served. **2** the food produced in a casserole. — *verb* to cook in a casserole. [from French *casserole*]

cassette *noun* **1** a small usually plastic case, containing a long narrow ribbon of magnetic tape, that can be inserted into a suitable audio or video tape recorder for recording or playback, during which the tape passes from one reel of the cassette to the other. **2** a small lightproof plastic cartridge containing photographic film for loading into a camera. [from French *cassette*, from Italian *cassetta*, diminutive of *cassa*, box]

cassette recorder *or* **cassette-player** a machine that records or plays material on cassette.

Cassini, Giovanni Domenico (1625–1712) Italian–French astronomer, born in Perinaldo, near Nice (then in Italy). Professor at the University of Bologna and Director of the Paris Observatory, he made many important discoveries about the planets, including determinations of their rotation periods, and the distances of Mars and the Sun. He also discovered four of Saturn's moons, and the division of its rings which bears his name (1675).

Cassini *noun* a space probe scheduled by NASA and the European Space Agency to be launched in 1997, and to go into orbit around Saturn in 2004.

Cassini's division *Astron.* a dark ring, consisting of a gap about 2 600km wide, concentric with the ring of Saturn and dividing it into two parts (ring A and ring B). [named after the Italian–French astronomer Giovanni Domenico Cassini]

Cassio the young lieutenant of Othello in Shakespeare's *Othello*, who becomes a victim of Iago's treachery.

Cassirer, Ernst (1874–1945) German–Jewish neo-Kantian philosopher, born in Wrocław. He became Professor of Philosophy at Hamburg in 1919, and Rector in 1930, but he resigned when Hitler came to power, and taught at Oxford (1933–5), Göteborg (1935–41), Yale (1941–4), and Columbia (from 1944 until his death). His best-known work, *Die Philosophie der symbolischen Formen* (The Philosophy of Symbolic Forms, 1923–9), analyses the symbolic functions underlying all human thought, language, and culture.

cassiterite *noun Geol.* a hard black mineral, consisting mainly of tin oxide (SnO_2), that is the chief ore of tin. [from Greek *kassiteros*, tin]

Cassius, in full **Gaius Cassius Longinus** (d.42 BC) Roman soldier, politician, and a leader of the group who assassinated Julius Caesar. He opposed Caesar during the civil war with Pompey, but was pardoned by him after Pompey's defeat at Pharsalus (48 BC). He later turned against Caesar again, and with Brutus played a leading part in the conspiracy to murder him (44 BC). After being defeated by Caesar's

avengers (Antony and Octavian) at Philippi (42 BC), he committed suicide.

cassock *noun* a long black or red garment worn in church by clergymen and male members of a church choir. [from Old French *casaque*, type of coat]

cassowary *noun* (PL. **cassowaries**) a large flightless bird of NE Australia and New Guinea. [from Malay *kasuari*]

cassowary

cast — *verb* (PAST TENSE AND PAST PARTICIPLE **cast**) **1** *usually old use* to throw. **2** to turn, direct, shed, or cause to fall or arise: *cast doubt on / cast a shadow / cast one's eye over / cast a spell*. **3** *trans., intrans.* to throw (a fishing-line) out into the water. **4** to let down (an anchor). **5** to release from a secured state: *cast adrift*. **6** *said of animals* to get rid of or shed (a skin, horns, etc). **7** (**cast something off** *or* **aside** *or* **out**) to throw it off or away; to get rid of it. **8** to give (an actor) a part in a play or film; to distribute the parts in (a film, play, etc). **9** to shape (metal, plastic, plaster, etc) by pouring it in a molten or liquid state into a mould; to create (an object) by this means. **10** to give or record (one's vote). **11** to work out (a horoscope). **12** to present (work, facts, etc) in a certain way. — *noun* **1** a throw; an act of throwing (dice, a fishing-line, etc). **2** an object shaped by pouring metal, plastic, plaster, etc in molten or liquid form into a mould. **3** (*also* **plaster cast**) a covering of plaster moulded, when wet, round a broken limb, etc to support it while it heals. **4** the set of actors or performers in a play, opera, etc. **5** *formal* type, form, shape, or appearance: *an analytical cast of mind*. **6** a slight tinge; a faint colour. **7** the slight turning inwards of an eye; a squint. **8** a coiled heap of earth or sand thrown up by a burrowing worm, etc.
— **cast about** *or* **around for something 1** to look about for it. **2** to try to think of it: *cast about for ideas.*
cast someone away to cause them to be abandoned on a remote piece of land after shipwreck, etc.
cast someone down to depress or discourage them.
cast one's mind back to think about something in the past.
cast off *or* **cast something off 1** to untie a boat ready to sail away. **2** to finish off and remove knitting from the needles.
cast on *trans., intrans.* to form (stitches or knitting) by looping and securing the wool, etc over the needles.
cast something up 1 to mention (a person's past faults, etc) to them, as a reproach. **2** to throw (a body, etc) up on to a beach.
cast up figures to find their total.
[from Norse *kasta*, to throw]

castanets *pl. noun* a musical instrument consisting of two small hollow pieces of wood or plastic attached to each other by string, held in the palm and struck together rhythmically, used especially by Spanish dancers to accompany their movements. [from Spanish *castañeta*, from *castaña*, chestnut, the wood used]

castaway *noun* a person who has been shipwrecked.

caste *noun* **1** any of the four hereditary social classes into which Hindus are divided. **2** this system of division into classes, or any system of social division based on inherited rank or wealth. — **lose caste** to drop to a lower social class. [from Portuguese *casta*, breed, race]
◊ The Hindu caste system reflects the cultural divide between the ancient Dravidian peoples and the Aryans who conquered them. Although the caste system is not officially recognized by the state, it remains entrenched in many areas of Indian society.

castellated *adj., said of a building* having turrets and battlements like those of a castle. [from Latin *castellare*, to fortify]

castellation *noun* **1** building castles. **2** providing a house with battlements. **3** a castellated structure; a battlement.

caster[1] see CASTOR[2].

caster[2] *or* **castor** *noun* a closed container with holes in its lid, through which to sprinkle the contents, eg sugar or flour, over food. [see CAST]

caster sugar finely crushed white sugar used in baking, etc.

castigate *verb* to criticize or punish severely. [from Latin *castigare*, to whip]

castigation *noun* severe punishment or criticism.

Castiglione, Count Baldassare (1478–1529) Italian writer and diplomat, born near Mantua. In 1505 he was sent by the Duke of Urbino as envoy to Henry VII of England, who made him a knight. His chief work, *Il Cortegiano* (The Courtier, 1528), was a manual for courtiers.

casting *noun* **1** *Engineering* the process of forming a solid object with a fixed shape by pouring molten material, eg metal, alloy, glass, or plastic, into a mould and allowing it to cool and solidify. **2** an object formed in this way.

casting vote the deciding vote of a chairperson when the votes taken at a meeting, etc are equally divided.

cast iron any of a group of hard heavy alloys of iron, containing more carbon than steels, and cast into a specific shape when molten because it is too brittle to work when solid. It is used to make machine and engine parts, stoves, pipes, radiators, cooking utensils, etc.

cast-iron *adj.* **1** made of cast iron. **2** very strong. **3** *said of a rule or decision* firm; not to be altered. **4** *said of an argument, etc* with no flaws, loopholes, etc.

Castle (of Blackburn), Barbara Anne Castle, Baroness, *née* **Betts** (1911–) English Labour politician, born in Bradford. She became MP for Blackburn in 1945 and during the 1950s was a convinced 'Bevanite' in her espousal of radical causes. She was Chairman of the Labour Party (1958–9), Minister of Overseas Development (1964–5), and a controversial Minister of Transport (1965–8), responsible for a 70mph speed limit and the 'breathalyzer' test for drunken drivers. She was Secretary of State for Employment and Productivity (1968–70) and Minister of Health and Social Security (1974–6) before returning to the backbenches under Harold Wilson, but was then appointed Vice-Chairman of the Socialist Group in the European Parliament (1979–84).

castle — *noun* **1** a large fortified, especially medieval, building with battlements and towers. **2** *Chess* a piece that can be moved any number of squares forwards, backwards, or sideways (also called ROOK). — *verb intrans. Chess* to make a move allowed once to each player in a game, in which the king is moved two squares along its

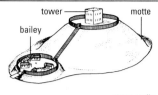

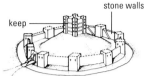

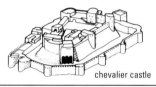

castle layouts

rank towards either castle, and the castle is placed on the square the king has passed over. [from Latin *castellum*]

Castlebar, Gaelic **Caisleán an Bharraigh** POP (1991) 8 000, the capital of Mayo county, Connacht province, W Irish Republic. It lies on the R Castlebar and is a residential and agricultural market town. The Irish Land League was founded here in 1879.

Castlereagh, Robert Stewart, Viscount (1769–1822) British statesman, born in Dublin, Ireland. He became Whig MP for Co Down in 1790, turning Tory in 1795. Created Viscount Castlereagh in 1796, he became Irish Secretary (1797), President of the Board of Control (1802), and Minister of War (1805–6, 1807–9). As Foreign Secretary under Lord Liverpool from 1812, he was at the heart of the coalition against Napoleon (1813–14). He represented England at Chaumont and Vienna (1814–15), Paris (1815), and Aix-la-Chapelle (1818). He advocated 'Congress diplomacy' among the great powers, to avoid further warfare. Believing that he was being blackmailed for homosexuality, he committed suicide at Foots Cray, his Kentish seat.

castles in the air *or* **castles in Spain** grand but impossible schemes; daydreams.

cast-off — *noun* something, especially a garment, discarded or no longer wanted. — *adj.* no longer needed; discarded.

castor¹ see CASTER².

castor² *or* **caster** *noun* a small swivelling wheel fitted to the legs or underside of a piece of furniture so that it can be moved easily. [see CAST]

Castor and Pollux, also called the **Dioscuri**, Greek **Kastor and Polydeuces** in Classical mythology, twin sons of Leda, usually pictured on horseback. Pollux was fathered by Zeus and was immortal, Castor was fathered by Tyndareus and was mortal. When Castor was killed, Zeus granted Pollux's pleas for Castor to share his immortality so that they would not be separated, and turned them into the constellation Gemini. They appear in the form of St Elmo's Fire to help mariners.

castor oil oil from the seeds of a tropical plant, used as a lubricant and medicinally as a laxative.

castrate *verb* **1** to remove the testicles of. **2** to deprive of masculinity or strength. [from Latin *castrare*]

castrated *adj.* **1** gelded. **2** made ineffective.

castration *noun* the action of castrating.

castrato *noun* (PL. **castrati**, **castratos**) a male singer castrated before puberty in order to preserve his soprano or contralto voice. The practice probably originated in the 16c at the Vatican to compensate for the lack of female voices in the choirs. In the 17c and 18c many leading parts in *opera seria* were written specifically for castrati who were renowned for their virtuosity and the beauty of their voices: roles included Idamante in Mozart's *Idomeneo*, and the title role in Monteverdi's *Orfeo* (Orpheus). They were no longer used in opera after c.1825, but continued to be used in church music until the late 19c.

Castries POP (1991e) 53 000, the port capital of St Lucia, situated on the NW coast of the island. The town was founded in 1650 and was rebuilt after a fire in 1948.

Castro (Ruz), Fidel (1927–) Cuban revolutionary, born near Birán. A practising lawyer in Havana, in 1953 he was imprisoned after an unsuccessful rising against Fulgencio Batista, but released under an amnesty. He fled to the USA and Mexico, then in 1956 landed in Cuba with a small band of insurgents. In 1958 his full-scale attack forced Batista to flee and Castro became Prime Minister (1959–76), proclaimed a 'Marxist-Leninist programme', began far-reaching reforms, and became President (1976–). He overthrew US economic dominance and routed the US-connived emigré invasion at the Bay of Pigs (1961), but remained dependent on Soviet aid. Cuba continued to suffer three decades of economic crisis, exacerbated by the US embargo and the collapse of the Soviet Union, which brought much trade to an end.

casual *adj.* **1** happening by chance. **2** careless; showing no particular interest or concern. **3** without serious purpose or intention. **4** (of clothes) informal. **5** *said of work, etc* occasional; not permanent or regular. [from Latin *casualis*, accidental]

casually *adv.* in a casual way.

casualness *noun* being casual.

casualty *noun* (PL. **casualties**) **1** a person who is killed or hurt in an accident or war. **2** the casualty department of a hospital. **3** something that is lost, destroyed, sacrificed, etc as a result of some event. [see CASUAL]

casualty department *or* **casualty ward** the part of a hospital where casualties from an accident, etc are attended to.

casuist *noun* a person who uses cleverly misleading arguments, especially to make things that are really morally wrong seem acceptable. [from French *casuiste*, from Latin *casus*, case]

casuistic *adj.* involving clever and misleading argument or casuistry.

casuistry *noun* the use of clever and misleading argument.

casus belli a circumstance or situation that causes a war. [Latin, = occasion of war]

CAT *abbrev.* College of Advanced Technology.

cat¹ *noun* **1** any of a wide range of carnivorous mammals belonging to the family Felidae, including such large cats as the lion, tiger, jaguar, leopard, cheetah, and lynx, as well as the common domestic cat. **2** a popular name for the domestic cat, *Felis catus*, which belongs to this family. **3** *derog. colloq.* a person, especially a woman, with a spiteful tongue. **4** *slang* a person. **5** same as CAT-O'-NINE-TAILS.
— **the cat's whiskers** *or* **pyjamas** *colloq.* the best or greatest thing.
fight like cat and dog *colloq.* to quarrel ferociously.
let the cat out of the bag *colloq.* to give away a secret unintentionally.
like a cat on a hot tin roof *or* **on hot bricks** *colloq.* very nervous or uneasy.

like something the cat brought in *colloq.* messy, dirty, untidy, or bedraggled in appearance.
no room to swing a cat having very little space; cramped.
not have a cat in hell's chance *colloq.* to have absolutely no chance.
play cat and mouse with someone to keep chasing and almost catching them; to tease them cruelly.
put *or* **set the cat among the pigeons** to do or say something that is generally upsetting or disturbing.
rain cats and dogs *colloq.* to rain long and hard.
see which way the cat jumps *colloq.* to wait on events before acting.
[from Latin *cattus*]
◇ All cats have lithe agile bodies, strong cutting teeth, and sharp claws that can often be retracted (drawn in), and are used for climbing. They are generally nocturnal creatures, and their eyes are adapted to see in dim light, while the long whiskers on the muzzle are probably used for feeling their way in the dark. When hunting at night they also rely on their very acute sense of hearing. Cats were probably first domesticated from wild African and European species by the ancient Egyptians. Unlike wild cats, domesticated cats normally hold their tails horizontally when walking. Most domestic cats are short-haired, and many of them are tabby, ie brownish or grey with dark markings (often striped), while other domestic breeds are ginger, tortoiseshell, or black, often with white markings. Two of the best-known breeds are the long-haired white Persian, and the Siamese, which has a fawn coat and blue eyes, and is descended from the sacred temple cat of Thailand.

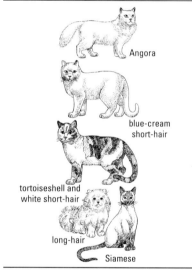

Angora

blue-cream short-hair

tortoiseshell and white short-hair

long-hair

Siamese

cat types

cat² *noun colloq.* short for CATALYTIC CONVERTER.

catabolism *noun Biochem.* the metabolic processes whereby complex organic compounds in living organisms are broken down into simple molecules. [from Greek *katabole*, throwing down]

catachumen *noun* a person who is being taught about the main beliefs of Christianity.

cataclysm *noun* **1** an event causing tremendous change or upheaval. **2** a terrible flood or other disaster. [from Greek *kataklysmos*, flood]

cataclysmic *adj.* disastrous; involving great change or upheaval.

catacomb *noun* (*usually* **catacombs**) a system of underground tunnels containing burial places. [from Latin *catacumbas*]

catafalque *noun* a platform on which the coffin of a king or other important person is placed for the lying-in-state or funeral. [from French *catafalque*, from Italian *catafalco*]

Catalan — *noun* a Romance language of the Indo-European family, spoken by c.5–7 million people in NE Spain and Andorra, and in neighbouring areas of France. — *adj.* relating to or spoken or written in Catalan.

Catalaunian Plains, Battle of the a battle (AD 451) in E France in which the Huns under Attila were defeated by the Romans and Visigoths.

catalepsy *noun* a state of unconsciousness with complete rigidity of the body, as in a hypnotic trance or severe mental illness. [from Greek *katalepsis*, seizing]

cataleptic *adj.* relating to or affected by catalepsy.

catalogue — *noun* 1 a list of items arranged in a systematic order, especially alphabetically. 2 a brochure, booklet, etc containing a list of goods for sale. 3 a list or index of all the books in a library. 4 a series of things mentioned one by one as though in a list: *the catalogue of his faults.* — *verb* 1 to make a catalogue of (a library, books, etc). 2 to enter (an item) in a catalogue. 3 to list or mention one by one: *He catalogued her virtues.* [from Greek *katalegein*, to reckon up]

cataloguer *noun* a person who compiles a catalogue.

Catalonia, Spanish **Cataluña**, Catalan **Catalunya** POP (1991) 6m, an autonomous region in NE Spain, comprising the provinces of Barcelona, Gerona, Lérida, and Tarragona, and formerly including Roussillon and Cerdana. AREA 31 932sq km/12 326sq mi. It is an area with its own distinctive culture; its Romance language, Catalan, is related to Provençal. PHYSICAL DESCRIPTION the Catalan Mts run parallel to the coast linking the Pyrenees with the central plateau (Meseta); drained by many rivers, primarily the R Ebro. HISTORY united with Aragon in 1137; a medieval trading empire in the 13c–14c; became part of Spain following the union of the Castilian and Aragonese crowns (1469–79); there has been a strong separatist movement since the 17c; the Catalan republic (established in 1932) was abolished by Franco during the Civil War; full autonomy was granted once more in 1980, and Catalan was recognized as an official language. CAPITAL Barcelona. ECONOMY cereals, olives, almonds, hazelnuts, grapes; industry is centred around Barcelona; hydroelectricity; major tourist resorts on the Costa Brava.

catalysis *noun* the speeding up of a chemical reaction by use of a catalyst. [from Greek *catalysis*, breaking up]

catalyst *noun* 1 *Chem.* any substance that changes the rate of a chemical reaction, especially by increasing it, without itself undergoing any permanent chemical change, eg finely divided metals, metal oxides, enzymes in living cells. 2 something or someone that causes, or speeds up the pace of, change.

catalytic *adj.* of the nature of or involving catalysis.

catalytic converter a device, fitted to the exhaust system of a motor vehicle with a petrol or diesel engine, that is designed to reduce toxic emissions from the engine, and thereby reduce environmental pollution.
◇ A catalytic converter consists of a metal casing enclosing a metal or ceramic honeycomb coated with metal catalysts, usually platinum, palladium, or rhodium. The honeycomb structure enables a very high surface area to be packed into a small volume, and as exhaust gases from the engine flow through this structure, the catalyst chemically converts carbon monoxide, oxides of nitrogen, and unburned hydrocarbon fuel, all of which cause atmospheric pollution, into water vapour, carbon dioxide, and nitrogen. All new

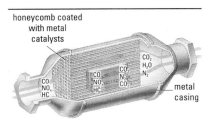

honeycomb coated with metal catalysts

CO carbon monoxide   HC hydrocarbons
CO_2 carbon dioxide N_2 nitrogen
NO_x nitrogen oxides H_2O water

catalytic converter

cars will eventually be required by law to be fitted with such a device.

catalytic cracking in the petrochemical industry, the process whereby long-chain hydrocarbons produced during petroleum refining, eg heavy oils, are broken down into lighter more useful short-chain products, eg petrol or kerosene, using a catalyst such as silica or alumina.

catalyze or **catalyse** *verb* to speed up (a chemical reaction) by catalysis; to act on by catalysis.

catamaran *noun* 1 a sailing-boat with two hulls lying parallel to each other, joined across the top by the deck. 2 a raft made of logs or boats lashed together. [from Tamil *kattumaram*, tied wood]

Catania POP (1991e) 364 000, the port capital of Catania province, Sicily, S Italy. It lies on the E coast at the foot of Mt Etna, 160km/100mi SE of Palermo.

cataplectic *adj.* relating to or affected by cataplexy.

cataplexis *noun Zool.* a physical state resembling death, adopted by some animals to discourage predators. [from Greek *kataplexis*, astonishment]

cataplexy *noun Medicine* a sudden attack of muscular weakness that affects the whole body and causes collapse without loss of consciousness. It is triggered by strong emotion such as laughter, anger, or excitement.

catapult — *noun* 1 a Y-shaped stick with an elastic or rubber band fitted between its prongs, used especially by children for firing stones, etc. 2 *Hist.* a weapon of war designed to fire boulders. 3 an apparatus on an aircraft-carrier for launching aircraft. — *verb* 1 to fire or send flying with, or as if with, a catapult. 2 *intrans.* to be sent flying as if from a catapult. [from Greek *kata*, against + *pallein*, to throw]

cataract *noun* 1 *Medicine* an opaque area within the lens of the eye that produces blurring of vision, and may be caused by ageing, injury, diabetes, prolonged exposure to ionizing radiation, or various hereditary disorders. It is treated by surgical replacement of the affected lens, or by its removal and the use of corrective spectacles. 2 a succession of steep waterfalls within a river. 3 an immense rush of water, eg from a large waterfall that consists of a single vertical drop. [from Greek *katarraktes*, waterfall]

catarrh *noun* inflammation of the lining of the nose and throat, causing a discharge of thick mucus. [from Greek *kata*, down + *rheein*, to flow]

catarrhal *adj.* of the nature of or relating to catarrh.

catastrophe *noun* 1 a terrible blow or calamity. 2 a great disaster, causing destruction, loss of life, etc. 3 a disastrous ending or conclusion. 4 a violent event in the geological history of the earth. [from Greek *catastrophe*, overturning, conclusion]

catastrophic *adj.* of the nature of a catastrophe; disastrous.

catastrophically *adv.* so as to cause a catastrophe; disastrously.

catatonia *noun Medicine* an abnormal mental state characterized either by stupor, mutism, and immobility, or by excessive excitement and violent or unco-ordinated activity. It may be a symptom of a form of schizophrenia, or of hysteria or encephalitis. [from Greek *kata*, down + *tonos*, tension]

catatonic *adj.* relating to or of the nature of catatonia.

cat burglar a burglar who breaks into buildings by climbing walls, water pipes, etc.

catcall *noun* a long shrill whistle expressing disagreement or disapproval.

catch — *verb* (PAST TENSE AND PAST PARTICIPLE **caught**) 1 to stop (a moving object) and hold it. 2 to manage to get hold of or trap, especially after a hunt or chase. 3 to be in time to get, reach, see, etc: *catch the last post.* 4 to overtake or draw level with. 5 to discover so as to prevent, or to encourage, the development of: *the disease can be cured if caught early / catch children young for athletic training.* 6 to surprise (someone) doing something wrong or embarrassing. 7 to trick or trap. 8 to become infected with. 9 *trans., intrans.* to become or cause to become accidentally attached or held: *my dress caught on a nail.* 10 to hit. 11 to manage to hear, see or understand. 12 to attract (attention, etc): *catch her eye.* 13 *intrans.* to start burning. 14 to succeed in recording (a subtle quality, etc): *the artist perfectly caught her expression.* 15 *Cricket* to put (a batsman) out by catching the ball he has struck before it touches the ground. — *noun* 1 an act of catching. 2 a small device for keeping a lid, door, etc closed. 3 something caught. 4 the total amount of eg fish caught. 5 a hidden problem or disadvantage; a snag; some unsuspected trick in a question. 6 something or someone that it would be advantageous to get hold of, eg a certain person as a husband or wife. 7 a slight breaking sound in one's voice, caused by emotion. 8 a children's game of throwing and catching a ball. 9 *Mus.* a humorous round sung by two or three people.
— **be caught short** see SHORT.
be or **get caught up in something** to be or get involved in it, especially unintentionally.
catch at something to try to catch or hold it; to hold on to it briefly.
catch fire to start burning.
catch hold of something to grasp or grab it.
catch it *colloq.* be scolded, punished, etc.
catch on *colloq.* to become popular. (**catch on to something**) to understand it.
catch someone out 1 to trick them into making a mistake. 2 to discover them or take them unawares in embarrassing circumstances.
catch sight of or **catch a glimpse of someone** or **something** to see them only for a brief moment.
catch up or **catch up with someone** to draw level with someone ahead. (**catch up on something**) to bring oneself up to date with one's work, the latest news, etc.
catch something up to pick it up or grab it hastily.
[from Old French *cachier*, from Latin *captiare*, to try to catch]

Catch-22 a novel by Joseph Heller (1961). It describes how US airmen seek leave from active service in World War II on grounds of mental derangement and are judged ineligible to apply, since such a request proves their sanity.

catch-22 *noun* a set of circumstances by which one is permanently frustrated and from which one cannot escape, all possible courses of action either having undesirable consequences or leading inevitably to further frustration of one's aims. [from the name of the novel]

catch-all *adj.*, *said of a phrase in an agreement, etc* covering all possibilities.

catch crop *Agric.* a fast-growing crop that is either planted between the rows of a main crop, or grown in the time interval between two main crops.

catcher *noun* *Baseball* the fielder who stands behind the batter.

Catcher in the Rye, The a novel by J D Salinger (1951). It tells of the experiences of 16-year old Holden Caulfield when he runs away to New York for two days.

catchiness *noun* being catchy.

catching *adj.* infectious.

catchment 1 the area of land that is drained by a particular river system or lake. 2 the population within the catchment area of a school, hospital, etc.

catchment area 1 the area served by a particular school, hospital, etc, to which people within the area are expected to go. 2 the area of land whose rainfall feeds a particular river, lake or reservoir.

catchpenny *adj. derog.* poor in quality but designed to appeal to the eye and sell quickly.

catchphrase *noun* a frequently used popular and fashionable phrase or slogan.

catchword *noun* 1 a much-repeated, well-known word or phrase. 2 each of the two words printed in the top corners of each page of a dictionary or encyclopedia, indicating the first and last entry to be found on that page. 3 the first word of a page, printed at the bottom of the previous page.

catchy *adj.* (**catchier**, **catchiest**) *said of a song, etc* tuneful and easily remembered.

catechism *noun* 1 a series of questions and answers about the Christian religion, or a book containing this, used for instruction. 2 any long series of difficult questions, eg in an interview.

catechize *or* **catechise** *verb* 1 to teach by means of a catechism, or using a question-and-answer method. 2 to question (a person) very thoroughly. [from Greek *katechizein*, to instruct orally]

categorical *or* **categoric** *adj.*, *said of a statement, refusal, denial, etc* absolute or definite; making no exceptions and giving no room for doubt or argument. [from Greek *kategorikos*; see CATEGORY]

Categorical Imperative the supreme moral principle of Kant's ethics. It states the unconditional command of the moral law, irrespective of ulterior end or aim, urging people to act responsibly.

categorically *adv.* so as to be categorical; definitely.

categorization *or* **categorisation** *noun* classification.

categorize *or* **categorise** *verb* to put into a category or categories; to classify.

category *noun* (PL. **categories**) a group of things, people, or concepts classed together because of some quality or qualities that they all have. [from Greek *kategoria*, statement, affirmation]

catenary *noun* 1 *Maths.* the curve formed by a flexible chain or cable supported at both ends and hanging freely, acted on by no force other than gravity. 2 *Engineering* a similar structure, consisting of an overhead cable, that is used to deliver electric current to an electric railway locomotive or tram. [from Latin *catena*, chain]

cater *verb intrans.* (**catered**, **catering**) 1 (**cater for someone**) to supply food, accommodation, or entertainment for. 2 (**cater for someone** *or* **something**) to make provision for them; to take them into account. 3 (**cater to something**) to

indulge or pander to unworthy desires, etc. [from Middle English *acatour*, buyer, from Old French]

caterer *noun* a person whose job is to provide food, etc for social occasions.

catering *noun* the job of a caterer.

caterpillar *noun* 1 the larva of a butterfly, moth, or sawfly, which has a segmented worm-like body, often hairy or conspicuously patterned, several pairs of legs, and strong jaws. It eats continually, moulting its skin at regular intervals as it grows, and eventually develops into a pupa. 2 (*usually* **Caterpillar**) *trademark* **a** a continuous band or track made up of metal plates driven by cogs, used instead of wheels on heavy vehicles for travelling over rough surfaces. **b** a vehicle fitted with such tracks. [probably from Old French *chatepelose*, hairy cat]

caterwaul — *verb intrans.* 1 *said of a cat* to make a loud high wailing noise. 2 to wail or shriek in this way. — *noun* a loud high wail. [formed from CAT¹]

caterwauling *noun* howling, wailing.

Catesby, Robert (1573–1605) English conspirator, born in Lapworth, Warwickshire. A Roman Catholic of good fortune, he suffered fines and imprisonment under Elizabeth I and James I. He organized the group of men who carried out the Gunpowder Plot (1605), but when it failed he fled to Holbeach House, Staffordshire, where he was killed.

catfish *noun* a large fish with whisker-like growths round its mouth.

catgut *noun* a string-like material produced from the dried intestines of sheep, etc, used in surgery for stitching, and for stringing violins and (now rarely) tennis racquets.

Cath. *abbrev.* Catholic.

Cathars *or* **Cathari** originally, puritan and ascetic 3c separatists from the Church who were celibate, rejected sacraments, and professed a neo-Manichaean dualism, ie they held good and evil to be separate spheres, and that everything non-spiritual was evil. By the Middle Ages, they had become a heretical sect known in Bulgaria as Bogomiles and in France as Albigenses. [from Greek *kathari*, pure ones]

catharsis *noun* (PL. **catharses**) 1 the emotional relief that results either from allowing repressed feelings to surface, as in psychoanalysis, or from an intensely dramatic experience, originally a stage tragedy that inspires acute fear and pity in the onlooker. 2 *Medicine* the clearing out or purging of the bowels. [from Greek *kathairein*, to purify]

cathartic *adj.* 1 resulting in catharsis. 2 cleansing; purgative.

cathedral *noun* the principal church of a diocese (the area presided over by a bishop), in which the bishop has his throne. [from Greek *kathedra*, seat]
◇ Among the most famous cathedrals are the W European Gothic examples built in the Middle Ages, such as Rheims and Chartres in France, and Westminster Abbey in London. In many towns and cities, the cathedral forms the centre around which social and cultural, as well as religious, life developed.

Cather, Willa (Sibert) (1873–1947) US novelist, born in Winchester, Virginia. She worked as a journalist in Pittsburgh and New York before becoming a full-time writer. Her best-known novels include *O Pioneers!* (1913) and *My Antonia* (1918), both set in the frontier country of Nebraska, and *Death Comes for the Archbishop* (1927).

Catherine II, known as **the Great** (1729–96) Empress of Russia (1762–96), born in Stettin. Originally Princess Sophia Augusta of Anhalt-Zerbst, she was baptized into the Russian Orthodox Church under the name of Catherine.

In 1745 she began an unhappy marriage to the heir to the Russian throne (later Peter III, reigned 1761–2). She spent much of her time in political intriguing, reading, and extra-marital affairs (her most notable lover was Potemkin), until a palace coup overthrew her husband, and she was proclaimed empress. Her energetic foreign policy included the extension of the Russian Empire south to the Black Sea as a result of the Russo-Turkish Wars (1774, 1792), and in the west she brought about the three partitions of Poland. In 1774 she suppressed the popular rebellion led by Pugachev, and later actively persecuted members of the progressive-minded nobility.

Catherine see KATHERINE.

Catherine de' Medici (1519–89) Queen of France, wife of Henry II, and Regent (1560–74), born in Florence, the daughter of Lorenzo de' Medici, Duke of Urbino. She was married at 14, and during the minority of her sons, Francis II (1559–60) and Charles IX (1560–3), she assumed political influence as Queen Mother. She tried to pursue moderation, to give unity to a state increasingly torn by religious division and aristocratic faction (eg among the Bourbon princes), but she nursed dynastic ambitions, was drawn into political and religious intrigues, and connived in the infamous St Bartholomew's Day Massacre (1572).

Catherine of Aragon (1485–1536) queen-consort of Henry VIII as his first wife (1509–33), and fourth daughter of Ferdinand and Isabella of Spain, born in Alcalá de Henares. She was first married in 1501 to Arthur (1486–1502), the eldest son of Henry VII, and after his early death married his young brother Henry (1509). Of their five children, only the Princess Mary (later Mary I) survived. In 1527 Henry began a procedure for divorce and obtained it in 1533, thereby breaking with the pope and starting the English Reformation. Catherine then retired to lead an austere religious life.

Catherine of Braganza (1638–1705) wife of Charles II of England, the daughter of John IV of Portugal, born in Vila Viçosa, Portugal. She was married to Charles in 1662 as part of an alliance between England and Portugal, but she was unable to produce an heir. She helped to convert Charles to Catholicism just before his death, after which she returned to Portugal (1692).

Catherine, Mount, Arabic **Katherina** a mountain in S Sinai governorate, NE Egypt. HEIGHT 2 637m. It is the highest point in Egypt. NOTABLE FEATURE St Catherine's monastery (6c), at an altitude of 1 500m.

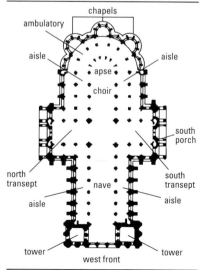

cathedral plan

Catherine wheel a wheel-like firework which is fixed to a post, etc and which whirls round when set off. [named after St Catherine, who escaped being martyred on a spiked wheel]

catheter *noun Medicine* a long narrow flexible tube inserted into a part of the body, especially the bladder, to drain off fluids. [from Greek *kathienai*, to send down]

cathode *noun* **1** the negative electrode in an electrolytic cell, towards which positively charged ions, usually in solution, are attracted. **2** the positive terminal of a battery. See also ANODE. [from Greek *kathodos*, descent]

cathode rays streams of negatively charged electrons issuing from the cathode of a vacuum tube.

cathode-ray tube an evacuated glass tube (vacuum tube) in which streams of electrons, known as cathode rays, are produced. Cathode-ray tubes are used to display images in television sets, the visual display units of computers, cathode-ray oscilloscopes, and radar equipment.
◇ A very narrow beam of electrons is emitted from a heated metal plate, known as the *cathode*, which is maintained at a negative voltage that repels the electrons. The electron beam is accelerated to a high speed by a series of positively charged grids, and finally strikes a screen coated with phosphors at the other end of the tube. The phosphors glow when struck by an electron, and the beam is deflected by magnetic or electric deflecting plates, and traces out an image on the screen. In a television set, three separate beams of electrons, corresponding to red, blue, and green light, are controlled by a microcomputer and guided to the correct positions on the screen.

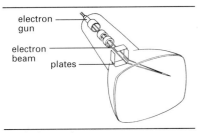

electron gun
electron beam
plates

cathode-ray tube

catholic — *adj.* **1** (**Catholic**) relating or belonging to the Roman Catholic Church. **2** (**Catholic**) relating to the whole Christian Church, or to the Church before the East–West split of 1054, or to the Western Church before the split caused by the Reformation. **3** *said especially of a person's interests and tastes* broad; wide-ranging. — *noun* (**Catholic**) a member of the Roman Catholic Church. [from Greek *katholikos*, universal]

Catholic Church 1 as in the Apostles' Creed, the universal Church which confesses Jesus Christ as Lord. **2** Christian Churches with episcopal order and confessing ancient creeds. **3** specifically, the Roman Catholic church and other Churches recognizing the primacy of the pope, as distinct from Protestant and Orthodox Churches. [from Greek *katholikos*, general, universal]

Catholic Emancipation a religious concession reluctantly granted (1829) by the British Tory government under the Duke of Wellington, following mounting agitation in Ireland led by Daniel O'Connell and the Catholic Association. Roman Catholics were permitted to become MPs, and all offices of state in Ireland, except Viceroy and Chancellor, were also opened to Catholics.

catholicity *noun* **1** universality. **2** liberality or breadth of view. **3** Catholicism.

Catiline, in full **Lucius Sergius Catalina** (d.62 BC) Roman politician who tried to exploit the economic unrest of Rome and Italy in the 60s BC for his own political ends. His conspiracy to assassinate Cicero and other senators was foiled by Cicero who denounced him in the senate late in 63 BC. He escaped from Rome but fell in battle at Pistoria early in 62 BC.

cation *noun Physics* any positively charged ion, which moves towards the cathode during electrolysis. See also ANION. [from Greek *kateinai*, to go down]

catkin *noun Bot.* in certain tree species, eg birch, hazel, a flowering shoot that bears many small unisexual flowers, adapted for wind pollination. Male catkins usually hang down from the stem and shed vast amounts of pollen, which is intercepted by the feathery stigmas of the much smaller and often erect female catkins. [from Old Dutch *kateken*, kitten]

catmint *or* **catnip** *noun Bot.* a square-stemmed perennial plant (*Nepeta cataria*), native to Europe and Asia, and having oval toothed leaves and spikes of white two-lipped flowers spotted with purple, so called because its strong scent is attractive to cats.

catnap — *noun* a short sleep. — *verb intrans.* (**catnapped**, **catnapping**) to doze; to sleep briefly, especially without lying down.

Cato, Marcus Porcius, also called **the Elder**, or **the Censor** (234–149 BC) Roman statesman, orator, and man of letters. He was noted for his conservative, anti-Greek policies, and when made censor (184 BC), he introduced rigorous legislative reforms (including the taxing of luxury goods) which led to him being known as 'the Censor'. His mission to Carthage (153 BC) fuelled his fear of the Carthaginians, and afterwards he ended every speech in the Senate with the words 'Carthage must be destroyed' until war was finally declared on Carthage in 149 BC. His treatise on agriculture is the oldest extant literary prose work in Latin; he also wrote the first Latin history of Rome, of which only fragments survive.

Cat on a Hot Tin Roof a play by Tennessee Williams (1955, Pulitzer Prize). It is a Freudian tale about the dismay felt by Maggie, who wants to save her marriage and have a child with Brick, her impotent, alcoholic husband, and the annoyance felt by Brick's wealthy father who wants a grandson.

cat-o'-nine-tails *noun Hist.* a whip with nine knotted rope lashes, used as an instrument of punishment in the navy.

Cato Street Conspiracy a plot (Feb 1820) formulated by Arthur Thistlewood (1770–1820) and fellow radical conspirators, to blow up the British Tory Cabinet during a dinner at the Earl of Harrowby's house. The plot was infiltrated by a government agent, and the leaders were arrested and hanged.

Catriona a female first name, popularized outside Scotland by Robert Louis Stevenson's novel *Catriona* (1893). [a form of KATHERINE]

Cats a musical by Andrew Lloyd Webber (1981), based on poetry by T S Eliot. Set in and around a rubbish tip, it depicts various cats' lives through song and the cat-like costumes and movements of the actors.

CAT scanner *abbrev. Medicine* computer-assisted or computed axial tomography scanner, a machine that produces X-ray images of cross-sectional 'slices' through the brain or other soft body tissues.
◇ The images produced are integrated by means of a computer to give a three-dimensional picture which can be viewed at specific depths and from specific angles on a video screen, and used to aid diagnosis of tumours, abscesses, etc, without the need for exploratory surgery.

cat's cradle a game with a long piece of string, which is looped over the fingers and passed from person to person in a series of changing patterns.

cat's eye 1 (**Cat's eye** *trademark*) a small glass reflecting device, one of a series set into the surface along the centre of a road to guide drivers. **2** a type of precious stone.

Catskill Mountains a mountain group in SE New York State, USA, part of the Appalachian system. Slide Mt (1 282m) is the highest point.

cat's paw a person used by someone else to perform an unpleasant job.

catsuit *noun* a woman's close-fitting garment, combining trousers and top.

Cattell, Raymond Bernard (1905–) English psychologist, born in Staffordshire. He was professor at Illinois University and later moved to the University of Hawaii. He applied the statistical techniques of factor analysis to the study of personality differences, with the aim of being able to establish psychological dimensions along which people could be measured and compared.

cattery *noun* (PL. **catteries**) a place where cats are bred or looked after. [see CAT¹]

cattily *adv.* in a catty way.

cattiness *noun* being catty.

cattle *pl. noun* **1** any of various large heavily built grass-eating mammals, including wild species, which are all horned (eg the bison, buffalo, and yak), and domestic cattle, which are descended from the auroch, a wild species that once lived in Europe but is now extinct. **2** often used to refer to domesticated forms of this animal which are farmed for their milk, meat, and hides. [from Old French *catel*, property]
◇ Cattle were first domesticated about 6 000 years ago, and since then they have become indispensable to humans, and are kept worldwide for their milk and meat, and other products, including leather. They are ruminants, ie they have complex stomachs divided into four chambers. Grass is swallowed whole and temporarily stored in the first chamber or *rumen*, and it is then passed into the second chamber to be softened and formed into balls called *cuds*. These are returned to the mouth for chewing, and are then passed to the third chamber of the stomach, and finally digested in the fourth chamber.

cattle cake blocks of concentrated food for cattle.

cattle grid a trench covered by a grid, taking up the width of a road, that can be crossed by wheeled vehicles, but not by cattle and sheep.

cattleya *noun* one of the most popular cultivated orchids, an epiphyte, native to SE Asia and S America. It has swollen green bulb-like stems for storing water, and produces spikes of up to 47 large showy flowers. [named after the English botanist William Cattley]

catty *adj.* (**cattier**, **cattiest**) inclined to talk spitefully about other people. [see CAT¹]

Catullus, Gaius Valerius (c.84–c.54 BC) Latin lyric poet, born in Verona. He settled in Rome (c.62 BC), where he met the 'Lesbia' whom he addresses in his verses (although her identity is uncertain). His extant works comprise 116 pieces, several of which attack Caesar and his other political enemies. It is, however, for his love poetry that he is mainly remembered.

catwalk *noun* **1** a narrow walkway, usually at a high level, eg alongside a bridge. **2** the narrow raised stage along which models walk at a fashion show.

Cauca, River a river in Colombia. It rises in the Cordillera Central, 51km/32mi S of Popayán, and is the main tributary of the R Magdalena. The river flows 970km/603mi N through the fertile Cauca Valley between the Cordilleras Occidental and Central, and through rainforests and swamps in its lower course near its junction with the R Magdalena. Its lower and mid courses are partly navigable by small craft.

Caucasian — *adj.* **1** relating to the Caucasus, a mountain range between the Black Sea and the Caspian Sea, representing the boundary between Europe and Asia. **2** belonging to one of the light-skinned or white races of mankind. **3** denoting a family of 38 languages spoken in the area of the Caucasus mountains, between the Black Sea and the Caspian Sea. — *noun* **1** an inhabitant or native of the Caucasus. **2** a white-skinned person. **3** the languages forming the Caucasian family.

Caucasoid *adj.* belonging to the Caucasian race.

Caucasus Mountains, Russian **Kavkaz** a major mountain system, extending c.1 250km/780mi between the Black Sea and the Caspian Sea SE across Russia, Georgia, Armenia, and Azerbaijan. It is bounded S by Turkey and Iran and comprises the Greater Caucasus and the Lesser Caucasus. Mt Elbrus in the W (5 642m) is the highest point in the range. The mountains widen in the E to over 160km/100mi.

Cauchy, Augustin Louis Cauchy, Baron (1789–1857) French mathematician, born in Paris. He did important work on ordinary and partial differential equations, being one of the first to argue the need to establish conditions that ensure that such equations have solutions. A proponent of the wave theory of light, he was also the founder of the theory of functions of a complex variable, which was to play a leading role in the development of mathematics during the rest of the 19c.

caucus *noun* (PL. **caucuses**) **1** *derog.* a small dominant group of people taking independent decisions within a larger organization. **2** *North Amer., esp. US* a group of members of a political party, or a meeting of such a group for some purpose.

caudal *adj.* **1** *Anat.* relating to the area of the buttocks. **2** *Zool.* relating to, or like, a tail. [from Latin *cauda*, tail]

caudate *adj. Zool.* having a tail. [from Latin *caudatus*, from *cauda*, tail]

caught see CATCH.

caul *noun* **1** the membrane in which the foetus is enclosed. **2** part of this sometimes found over a baby's head at birth. [from Old French *cale*, little cap]

cauldron *noun* a very large bowl-shaped metal pot for boiling or heating liquids. [from Old French *cauderon*]

Caulfield, Holden the lonely, adolescent hero, who runs away to New York, in J D Salinger's *The Catcher in the Rye.*

cauliflower *noun* a variety of cabbage with an edible white flower, used as a vegetable. [from the earlier *colieflorie*, with spelling influenced by Latin *caulis*, cabbage, and FLOWER]

cauliflower ear an ear permanently swollen and misshapen by injury, especially from repeated blows.

caulk *verb* to fill up (the seams or joints of a boat) with tarred rope, called oakum; to make (a boat) watertight by this means. [from Latin *calcare*, to trample]

causal *adj.* **1** relating to, or being, a cause. **2** relating to cause and effect. [from Latin *causalis*]

causality *noun* **1** the relationship between cause and effect. **2** the principle that everything has a cause. **3** the process at work in the causing of something.

causally *adv.* in a causal way.

causation *noun* **1** the relationship of cause and effect; causality. **2** the process of causing. [from Latin *causatio*]

causative — *adj.* **1** making something happen; producing an effect. **2** *Grammar* expressing

the action of causing. — *noun* a causative verb. [from Latin *causativus*]

causatively *adv.* in a causative way.

cause — *noun* **1** something which produces an effect; the person or thing through which something happens. **2** a reason or justification: *there is no cause for concern.* **3** an ideal, principle, aim, etc, that people support and work for. **4** a matter that is to be settled by a lawsuit; the lawsuit itself. — *verb* to produce as an effect; to bring about. — **make common cause with someone** to co-operate with them, so as to achieve a common aim. [from Latin *causa*]

'cause *contr. colloq.* because.

cause célèbre *noun* (PL. **causes célèbres**) a legal case, or some other matter, that attracts much attention and causes controversy. [French, = famous case]

causeway *noun* **1** a raised roadway crossing low-lying, marshy ground or shallow water. **2** a stone-paved pathway. [from Old French *caucie*, from Latin *(via) calciata*, limestone-paved (way)]

caustic — *adj.* **1** *Chem.*, said of a chemical substance strongly alkaline and corrosive to living tissue, eg sodium hydroxide (caustic soda). **2** *said of remarks, etc* sarcastic; cutting; bitter. — *noun* **1** caustic soda. **2** *Optics* the curve produced when parallel rays of light are reflected in a large concave mirror, or refracted by a convex lens. [from Greek *kaustikos*, capable of burning]

caustically *adv.* with a caustic effect or manner.

causticity *noun* being caustic.

caustic soda *noun* sodium hydroxide, used in making soap and paper.

cauterization *or* **cauterisation** *noun Medicine* the intentional destruction of living tissue by the direct application of a heated instrument (a cautery), an electric current, a laser beam, or a caustic chemical, in order to remove small warts, seal blood vessels, etc.

cauterize *or* **cauterise** *verb* to burn away (infected or damaged tissue in the body) using a caustic substance or hot iron. [from Latin *cauterizare*, from Greek *kauter*, branding-iron]

caution **1** care in avoiding danger; prudent wariness. **2** a warning. **3** a reprimand or scolding for an offence, accompanied by a warning not to repeat it. **4** *Legal* a warning from the police to someone suspected of an offence, that anything he or she says may be used as evidence. **5** *old colloq. use* an amusing person or thing. — *verb* (**cautioned, cautioning**) **1** *trans., intrans.* to warn or admonish someone. **2** to give (someone) a legal caution. [from Latin *cautio*]

cautionary *adj.* giving, or acting as, a warning: *cautionary remarks.*

cautious *adj.* having or showing caution; careful; wary. [see CAUTION]

cautiously *adv.* in a cautious way.

cautiousness *noun* being cautious.

cavalcade *noun* a ceremonial procession of cars, horseback riders, etc. [from French *cavalcade*, from Italian *cavalcata*, raid on horseback]

cavalier — *noun* **1** *old use* a horseman or knight. **2** *old use* a courtly gentleman. **3** *now facetious* a man acting as escort to a lady. **4** (**Cavalier**) *Hist.* a supporter of Charles I during the 17c English Civil War. — *adj. derog., said of a person's behaviour, attitude, etc* thoughtless, offhand, casual or disrespectful. [from Italian *cavaliere*, from Latin *caballarius*, horseman]

cavalierly *adv.* with a cavalier manner.

cavalry *noun* (PL. **cavalries**) *(sing.)* **1** *usually Hist.* the part of an army consisting of soldiers on horseback. **2** the part of an army consisting of

soldiers in armoured vehicles. [from French *cavallerie*, from Latin *caballarius*, horseman]

cavalryman *noun* a member of a cavalry troop.

Cavan POP (1991) 53 000, a county in Ulster province, N central Irish Republic. AREA 1 891sq km/730sq mi. To the N lies Northern Ireland. The county is drained by the Analee, Boyne, and Erne rivers. CAPITAL Cavan. ECONOMY oats, potatoes; dairy farming.

Cavan, Gaelic **Cabháin** POP (1991) 5 000, the capital of Cavan county, Ulster province, Irish Republic, situated NW of Dublin. It is an agricultural market town.

cave *noun* a large natural hollow chamber either underground, usually with an opening to the surface, or in the side of a mountain, hillside, or cliff. Underground caves are often associated with limestone rocks, which are slowly dissolved by underground streams, and frequently contain stalactites and stalagmites. Sea caves are formed as a result of wave action.
— **cave in 1** *said of walls, a roof, etc* to collapse inwards. **2** *colloq., said of a person* to give way to persuasion.
[from Latin *cavus*, hollow]

cave art the art of the Palaeolithic period (Old Stone Age), created c.30 000 years ago. Paintings preserved on the walls of limestone caves in France and Germany show hunting scenes, and realistic drawings of animals. Small stone carvings have also been found from the period. Cave art is not 'art' in the modern sense; it seems likely that it was done for some magical purpose.

caveat *noun* **1** a warning. **2** *Legal* an official request that a court should not take some particular action without warning the person who is making the request. [from Latin *caveat*, let him or her beware]

cave-in *noun* **1** a collapse. **2** a submission or surrender.

Cavell, Edith (1865–1915) English nurse, born in Swardeston, Norfolk. She became a nurse in 1895, and matron of the Berkendael Institute, Brussels, in 1907. During World War I she tended friend and foe alike (1914–15), yet was executed by the Germans for helping Belgian and Allied fugitives to escape capture.

caveman *noun* **1** (*also* **cave-dweller**) a person of prehistoric times, living in caves. **2** *derog.* a man of crude, brutish behaviour.

Cavendish, Henry (1731–1810) English natural philosopher and chemist, born in Nice. He studied at Cambridge, but left to devote himself to science, after being bequeathed a fortune. In 1760 he studied 'inflammable air', now known as hydrogen gas; he later ascertained that water resulted from the union of two gases. The 'Cavendish experiment' was an ingenious means of estimating the density of the Earth.

Cavendish, Spencer Compton, 8th Duke of Devonshire, known as the **Marquis of Hartington** (1833–1908) English Liberal politician, born in Lower Holker, Lancashire. He became an MP in 1857, and from 1863 to 1874 his posts included Lord of the Admiralty, War Secretary, Postmaster-General, and Chief Secretary for Ireland. In 1875 he became Leader of the Liberal Opposition during Gladstone's temporary abdication, and later became Secretary of State for India (1880–2) and War Secretary (1882–5) under him. Disapproving of Irish Home Rule, he led the breakaway from the Liberal Party, became head of the Liberal Unionists (from 1886), and served in the Unionist government as Lord President of the Council (1895–1903).

Cavendish, William, Duke of Newcastle (1592–1676) English soldier and patron of the arts. He gave strong support to Charles I in the Civil War, and was general of all forces north of the Trent. After the battle of

Marston Moor (1644) he lived on the Continent, at times in great poverty, until the Restoration. A noted patron of poets and dramatists, he was himself the author of several plays, and of two works on horsemanship.

Cavendish, House of the surname of the ducal house of Devonshire, a family directly descended from the chief justice Sir John Cavendish, who in 1381 was beheaded by Jack Straw's followers, and from Sir William Cavendish of Cavendish, Suffolk (c.1505–1557).

caver *noun* a person whose pastime is exploring caves.

cavern *noun* a large dark cave. [from Latin *caverna*, from *cavus*, hollow]

cavernous *adj.* **1** *said of a hole or space* deep and vast. **2** *said of rocks* full of caverns.

cavernously *adv.* in a cavernous way.

cavetto *noun* (PL. **cavetti**) *Archit.* a hollowed moulding with a curvature of a quarter of a circle, used chiefly in cornices, eg on ancient Egyptian buildings. [an Italian diminutive of *cavo*, from Latin *cavus*, hollow]

caviare *or* **caviar** *noun* the roe of the sturgeon, a spiny fish of the N hemisphere, used as food and considered a delicacy. [perhaps from Turkish *havyar*]

cavil — *verb intrans.* (**cavilled, cavilling**) (**cavil at** *or* **about something**) to object to it, or find fault with it, especially trivially or unnecessarily. — *noun* a trivial objection. [from Latin *cavillari*, to scoff]

caviller *noun* a person who cavils.

caving *noun* the sport of exploring caves.

cavitation *noun Physics* **1** the formation of cavities in a structure. **2** the formation of gas bubbles in a liquid. **3** the formation of a partial vacuum in a liquid moving at high speed.

cavity *noun* (PL. **cavities**) **1** a hollow or hole. **2** a hole in a tooth, caused by decay. [from Latin *cavitas*, hollowness]

cavity wall a wall of a building constructed in two separate layers or partitions with a space between them.

cavort *verb intrans.* to jump, prance, or caper about.

Cavour, Camillo Benso, Conte di (Count of) (1810–61) Piedmontese statesman who brought about the unification of Italy (1861), born in Turin. As premier (1852–9), he greatly improved economic conditions, and brought the Italian question before the Congress of Paris. He resigned over the Peace of Villafranca (which left Venetia Austrian), but returned in 1860, and secretly encouraged the expedition of Garibaldi, which gained Sicily and S Italy.

cavy *noun* (PL. **cavies**) any of various rodents native to S America, including guinea pigs and a wide range of rodents. The domestic guinea pig was bred as food by the Incas, and is still eaten in S America. [from *Cabiai*, a native name in French Guiana]

caw — *noun* the loud harsh cry of a crow or rook. — *verb intrans.* to make this cry. [imitative]

Caxton, William (c.1422–91) the first English printer, born in the Weald of Kent. He learned the art of printing probably in Cologne (1471–2), and printed the first book in English, the *Recuyell of the Historyes of Troye* (1475). He then set up his wooden press in Westminster (c.1476), and produced the *Dictes or Sayengis of the Philosophres* (1477), the first book printed in England. Of about 100 books printed by him, including the *Canterbury Tales*, over a third survive only in unique copies or fragments.

cay see KEY².

Cayenne POP (1990) 42 000, the federal and district capital of French Guiana, NE S America. It is a major port on Cayenne I, at the mouth of the

R Cayenne, on the Atlantic coast. Founded in 1643, it was used as a penal settlement from 1854 until 1938. NOTABLE FEATURES Canal Laussant (1777); Jesuit-built residence of the Prefect in the Place de Grenoble (1890). The city is known for its pepper.

cayenne *or* **cayenne pepper** *noun* a hot spice made from the seeds of certain types of capsicum, a tropical American vegetable. [formerly *čayan*, from Tupí (S American language), changed by association with Cayenne in French Guiana]

Cayley, Arthur (1821–95) English mathematician, born in Richmond, Surrey. Called to the Bar in 1849, he wrote nearly 300 mathematical papers during 14 years' practice in conveyancing. In 1863 he became Professor of Pure Mathematics at Cambridge. His principal contributions to mathematics were in algebra, his 'theory of invariants and covariants', and his work on matrices; his collected mathematical papers fill 13 volumes.

Cayley, Sir George (1773–1857) English amateur scientist and pioneer of aviation, born in Scarborough. He constructed and flew (1808) a glider with a wing area of 28m², probably the first practical heavier-than-air flying machine. In 1853 he constructed the first successful man-carrying glider, which safely flew a few hundred metres across a valley.

cayman *or* **caiman** *noun* (PL. **caymans**) a S American reptile similar to an alligator. [from Spanish *caimán*, from Carib, a West Indian language]

Cayman Islands POP (1991e) 27 000, a British colony in the W Caribbean Sea. AREA 260sq km/100sq mi. It comprises the islands of Grand Cayman, Cayman Brac, and Little Cayman, c.240km/150mi S of Cuba. CAPITAL George Town. CHIEF TOWN West Bay. TIME ZONE GMT –5. The population is mainly of mixed descent (c.60%); Christianity is the chief religion. OFFICIAL LANGUAGE English. CURRENCY the Cayman Is dollar. PHYSICAL DESCRIPTION low-lying, rising to 42m on the Cayman Brac Plateau; ringed by coral reefs. CLIMATE tropical, with an average annual rainfall of 1 420mm; the hurricane season is Jul–Nov; average temperatures are 24–32°C from May to Oct and 16–24°C from Nov to Apr. HISTORY discovered by Columbus in 1503; ceded to Britain in 1670; colonized by British settlers from Jamaica; became a British Colony in 1959. GOVERNMENT a Governor represents the British Sovereign, and presides over a 15-member Legislative Assembly. ECONOMY mainly tourism; international finance; property development; marked increase in cruise ship traffic; over 450 banks and trust companies established on the islands; oil transshipment; crafts, jewellery; cattle, poultry; vegetables; tropical fish; turtle products.

CB *abbrev.* **1** Citizens' Band. **2** Companion of the Order of the Bath.

CBC *abbrev.* Canadian Broadcasting Corporation.

CBE *abbrev.* Commander of the Order of the British Empire.

CBI *abbrev.* in the UK, the Confederation of British Industry, a federation of UK employers, founded in 1965, with a membership of c.250 000 companies. It carries out surveys and research into matters affecting business, and promotes the needs and intentions of its members to the government.

CBS *abbrev.* Columbia Broadcasting System.

CBSO *abbrev.* City of Birmingham Symphony Orchestra.

cc *abbrev.* **1** carbon copy. **2** cubic centimetre.

CCC *abbrev.* County Cricket Club.

CCD *abbrev. Electron.* charge-coupled device.

CCTV *abbrev.* closed-circuit television.

CD *abbrev.* **1** compact disc. **2** civil defence, or Civil Defence (Corps), a voluntary organization of civilians, active especially in World War II, trained to cope with the effects of enemy attack. **3** *Corps Diplomatique* (French), Diplomatic Corps, the body of diplomats in the service of any country.

Cd *symbol Chem.* cadmium.

cd *abbrev.* candela.

CD-i *or* **CDI** *abbrev.* compact disc interactive, a multimedia compact disc which stores sound, text, graphics, animation, and video in a single format.

CDN *abbrev., as an international vehicle mark* Canada.

Cdr *abbrev.* Commander.

CD-ROM *abbrev. Comput.* compact disc read-only memory, a facility allowing examination, but not alteration, of a text on compact disc.

CDT *abbrev.* craft, design, technology.

CE *or* **C.E.** *abbrev.* Common Era: used instead of AD in dates.
◆ See note at AD.

Ce *symbol Chem.* cerium.

cease *verb trans., intrans.* to bring or come to an end.
— **without cease** *formal* continuously.
[from Old French *cesser*]

cease-fire *noun* **1** a break in the fighting during a war, agreed to by both sides. **2** the order to stop firing.

ceaseless *adj.* continuous; going on without a pause or break.

ceaselessly *adv.* without ceasing; endlessly.

Ceauşescu, Nicolae (1918–89) Romanian politician, born in Scorniceşti. He joined the Communist Party at 15, and held several junior political posts before becoming President of the State Council (1967) and General Secretary of the Romanian Communist Party (1969). Under his leadership, Romania became increasingly independent of the USSR, and for many years Romania was the only Warsaw Pact country to have cordial relations with China. He became the first President of the Republic in 1974, and his personalized way of ruling included giving senior posts to family members. His policy of replacing traditional villages by collectives of concrete apartments caused much controversy in the late 1980s. In 1989 he was deposed when the army joined a popular revolt against his repressive government, and after a trial by military tribunal, he and his wife Elena were shot.

Cebu *or* **Cebu City** POP (1990) 610 000, a seaport in Cebu province, on the E coast of Cebu I, Philippines. Founded in 1565, it was the first Spanish settlement in the Philippines. NOTABLE FEATURES Spanish Fort; Santo Niño Church.

Cecil, Robert (Arthur Talbot Gascoyne), 3rd Marquis of Salisbury (1830–1903) English Conservative statesman, born in Hatfield, Hertfordshire. He became an MP in 1853, and was appointed Indian Secretary (1866 and 1874), Foreign Secretary (1878), Leader of the Opposition (on Disraeli's death, 1881), and Prime Minister three times (1885–6, 1886–92, 1895–1902), when he often served as his own Foreign Secretary, a post from which he resigned in 1900. He remained as head of government during the Boer War (1899–1902), then retired.

Cecil, William, 1st Baron Burghley, or **Burghleigh** (1520–98) English statesman, born in Bourn, Lincolnshire. He was MP for Somerset and Northumberland, and became Secretary of State (1550). During Mary I's reign (1553–8) he conformed to Catholicism. In 1558 Elizabeth I appointed him chief Secretary of State, and throughout her reign he was the main architect of Elizabethan greatness, which included influencing her pro-Protestant foreign policy, securing the execution of Mary, Queen of Scots, and preparing for the Spanish Armada. From 1572 until his death he was Lord High Treasurer.

Cecil the surname of an English family of statesmen, descended from David Cecil, sheriff of Northamptonshire (1532–3) and an MP. The earldoms of Exeter and Salisbury are two branches of the family founded by two sons of William Cecil, 1st Baron Burghley; these became marquisates in 1789 (Salisbury) and 1801 (Exeter).

Cecil a male first name. [from the Welsh surname, itself derived from the Old Welsh form of Latin *sextus* sixth; used in the Middle Ages as an English form of Latin *Caecilius*, from Latin *caecus*, blind]

Cecilia, St (c.2c–3c AD) Christian martyr and patron saint of music. Tradition relates that she was a Roman maiden whose vow of celibacy was respected even by her pagan husband Valerian, who later became a Christian. They were both put to death for their faith. Her feast day is 22 Nov.

Cecilia a female first name, associated with St Cecilia, 2c–3c martyr and patron saint of music. [the feminine form of Latin *Caecilius* (see CECIL)]

Cecrops or **Kekrops** in Greek mythology, the ancestor and first king of the Athenians. He was born from the earth, and formed with snake-like appendages instead of legs. During his reign Athena and Poseidon fought for the possession of Attica.

cedar *noun* **1** any of various tall coniferous trees of the genus *Cedrus* of the pine family, noted for its flat crown with widely spreading branches, its needle-like foliage and reddish-brown bark. **2** the hard yellow sweet-smelling wood of this tree, used as building timber and for making furniture. [from Greek *kedros*]

cedarwood same as CEDAR 2.

cede *verb* **1** to hand over or give up formally. **2** *intrans.* to yield or give way: *cede to a higher authority.* [from Latin *cedere*, to yield]

cedilla *noun* **1** in French and Portuguese, a mark put under *c* in some words (eg *façade*) to show that it is to be pronounced like *s*, not like *k*. **2** the same mark used under other letters in other languages to indicate various sounds. [from Spanish, a variant of *zedilla*, diminutive of *zeda*, z]

Cedric a male first name, unknown before the character Cedric of Rotherwood in Sir Walter Scott's *Ivanhoe* (1819). [an altered form of the Anglo-Saxon name *Cerdic*]

Ceefax *noun trademark* a television information service provided by the BBC. [from the phrase *see facts*]

CEGB *abbrev.* Central Electricity Generating Board.

ceilidh *noun* originally in Scotland and Ireland, an informal gathering, especially with entertainment in the form of songs, story-telling, instrumental music and dancing. [from Gaelic *ceilidh*, visit]

ceiling *noun* **1** the inner roof of a room, etc. **2** an upper limit. **3** the maximum height that a particular aircraft can reach. **4** the height above the ground of the base of the cloud-layer. [from Middle English *celen*, to panel]

celandine *noun* a small wild plant with glossy yellow flowers, similar to a buttercup. [from Greek *chelidonion*, from *chelidon*, swallow, the flowering of the plant coinciding with the arrival of the swallows in spring]

Celebes see SULAWESI.

Celebes Sea, Indonesian **Laut Sulawesi** a sea in SE Asia. AREA 280 000sq km/110 000sq mi; maximum depth 5 090m. It is bounded by Indonesian islands in the W and S, Malaysia in the NW, and the Philippines in the NE.

celebrant *noun* a person who performs a religious ceremony.

celebrate *verb* **1** to mark (eg a success or other happy occasion, a birthday or other anniversary) with festivities. **2** *intrans.* to do something enjoyable to mark a happy occasion, anniversary, etc. **3** to give public praise or recognition to, eg in the form of a poem. **4** to conduct (a religious ceremony, eg a marriage or mass). [from Latin *celebrare*, to honour]

celebrated *adj.* famous.

celebration *noun* the action or state of celebrating.

celebrator *noun* a person who celebrates.

celebratory *adj.* of the nature of a celebration.

celebrity *noun* (PL. **celebrities**) **1** a famous person. **2** fame. [from Latin *celebritas*, fame]

celeriac *noun* a variety of celery with a turnip-like root that is eaten as a vegetable.

celerity *noun formal* quickness. [from Latin *celeritas*]

celery *noun* a plant with crisp juicy stalks eaten as a vegetable. [from French *céleri*, from Greek *selinon*, parsley]

celesta *noun* a keyboard instrument, resembling a small upright piano, from which soft bell-like sounds are produced by hammers striking steel plates suspended over wooden resonators. It was invented in 1886 by the French instrument-maker Auguste Mustel (1842–1919). [from French *céleste*, heavenly]

celestial *adj.* **1** belonging to, or relating to, the sky: *celestial bodies.* **2** belonging to heaven; heavenly; divine: *celestial voices.* [from Latin *celestialis*, from *caelum*, the heavens]

celestial equator *Astron.* the great circle in which the plane of the Earth's equator meets the celestial sphere and divides it into northern and southern hemispheres. The angular distance of a star or planet north or south of the celestial equator is known as *declination*.

celestial mechanics *Astron.* the branch of astronomy concerned with the movement of celestial bodies in gravitational fields, especially the motion of planets, binary stars, artificial satellites, and other objects that are in orbit. It is based on Newton's laws of motion and gravity.

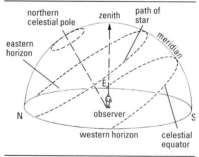

celestial sphere

celestial sphere *Astron.* an infinitely large imaginary sphere on which the stars and other celestial bodies appear to lie when viewed by an observer at the centre of the sphere, represented by the Earth. It is used to specify the position of stars and other celestial bodies in relation to the Earth.

Celia 1 the daughter of Duke Frederick in Shakespeare's *As You Like It*, who accompanies her cousin Rosalind into the Forest of Arden disguised as Aliena. **2** a female first name, associated with Shakespeare's character. [from a Roman family name derived from *caelum*, heaven]

celiac *adj., noun North Amer., esp. US* same as COELIAC.

celibacy *noun* the state or habit of being celibate.

celibate — *adj.* **1** unmarried, especially in obedience to a religious vow. **2** having no sexual relations with anyone. — *noun* a person who is unmarried, especially because of a religious vow. [from Latin *caelebs*, unmarried]

cell *noun* **1** a small room for an inmate in a prison or monastery. **2** *Biol.* the basic structural unit of all living organisms (except viruses), consisting of a mass of protein material (the protoplasm), which is composed of the cytoplasm (a watery jelly-like material) and usually a nucleus. **3** *Electr.* an electrolytic cell, consisting of two electrodes (an anode and a cathode) immersed in an electrolyte. When an electric current is passed through the electrolyte from an external source, electrolysis occurs. **4** a voltaic cell, which produces a current as a result of the conversion of chemical energy to electrical energy at the surface of two electrodes (an anode and a cathode) immersed in an electrolyte. **5** one of the cavities or compartments in a honeycomb or in a structure similarly divided. **6** *Radio* a radio transmitter serving one of the geographical areas into which a country is divided for coverage by cellular radio. **7** one of these geographical areas. **8** *Comput.* a unit or area of storage in computing, eg the smallest unit capable of storing a single bit. **9** a small group of people (especially spies or terrorists) conducting their own operation within a larger organization. **10** *Hist.* a tiny one-roomed dwelling used by a hermit. [from Latin *cella*, room, small apartment]

◇ The average diameter of most cells is of the order of 0.01 to 0.1mm. The number of cells within an organism ranges from one (as in bacteria, protozoans, and certain fungi, eg yeasts) to billions (in higher animals and plants). The cells of all living organisms except bacteria contain a distinct nucleus which encloses the genetic material. The nucleus and cytoplasm are enclosed within a very thin cell membrane, which regulates the movement of substances into and out of the cell. In plants, fungi, and bacteria there is also a rigid outer cell wall, which in plants consists mainly of cellulose. All the biochemical reactions necessary for the maintenance of life are associated with the cytoplasm, nucleus, or cell membrane.

According to the internal structure of their cells, all organisms can be classified as *prokaryotes* or *eukaryotes*. Prokaryotic cells, which are found only in bacteria and blue-green algae (cyanobacteria) contain a single loop of DNA instead of a distinct nucleus. There is a rigid cell wall, and the cytoplasm does not contain organelles (specialized structures with a specific function). Eukaryotic cells, which are found in all other living organisms, do have a distinct nucleus (with the exception of red blood cells). The nucleus contains DNA organized into chromosomes, and it is separated from the cytoplasm by a nuclear membrane. The cytoplasm contains many organelles, including mitochondria (which produce energy by breaking down carbohydrate molecules), ribosomes (which manufacture proteins), and (in green plants only) chloroplasts, which contain the pigment chlorophyll and are the site of photosynthesis. Unlike prokaryotic cells, eukaryotic cells divide by mitosis or meiosis.

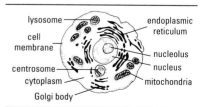

animal cell

cellar — *noun* **1** a room, usually underground, for storage, eg of wine. **2** a stock of wines. — *verb* (**cellared**, **cellaring**) to store in a cellar. [from Latin *cellarium*, storeroom, pantry]

cellarage *noun* **1** the volume of cellar space in a building. **2** the cost of storing goods in a cellar.

cell body *Anat.* the enlarged part of a neurone (nerve cell) that contains the nucleus and cytoplasm, and from which the long thread-like axon extends.

Cellini, Benvenuto (1500–71) Italian goldsmith, sculptor, and engraver, born in Florence, and particularly known for his autobiography (1558–62). His best work includes the gold saltcellar of *Neptune and Triton* made for Francis I of France, and his bronze *Perseus with the Head of Medusa*. He was imprisoned several times for murdering or maiming his rivals.

cellist *noun* a person who plays the cello.

cell membrane *Biol.* the surface membrane surrounding a cell.

cello *noun* (PL. **cellos**) a stringed musical instrument similar to a violin but much larger, played sitting, with the neck of the instrument against the player's shoulder. It has four strings tuned an octave below the viola; 17c and early 18c versions had five strings. [short for VIOLONCELLO]

cello

Cellophane *noun trademark* a material consisting of thin transparent sheeting manufactured from regenerated cellulose, used as a wrapping material for food and other products, and in dialysis tubes. [from CELLULOSE + Greek *phainein*, to shine or appear]

cellphone *noun Radio* a portable telephone for use in a cellular radio system.

cellular *adj.* **1** composed of cells, or divided into cell-like compartments. **2** containing many cavities or holes; porous. **3** knitted with an open pattern. [from Latin *cellula*, tiny cell or room]

cellular radio *noun* a system of radio communication used especially for car phones, based on a network of small geographical areas or 'cells', each served by a transmitter.

cellule *noun Biol.* a small cell. [from Latin *cellula*, tiny cell or room]

cellulite *noun* deposits of fat cells that do not respond to a change in diet or exercise regime,

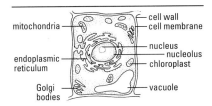

plant cell

and which give the skin a dimpled pitted appearance. [from French, from Latin *cellula*, little cell]

celluloid *noun trademark* **1** a transparent highly flammable plastic material made from cellulose nitrate and camphor, formerly widely used in photographic film, but now largely superseded by cellulose acetate, which is non-flammable. **2** cinema film.

cellulose *noun* the substance of which the cell walls of plants chiefly consist, an important ingredient of paper and used in the manufacture of synthetic fibres. [from French *cellule*, tiny cell]

cellulose acetate *Chem.* a tough flexible non-flammable thermoplastic resin formed by treating cellulose with acetic acid, and used to make photographic film, magnetic tape, lacquers, varnishes, and acetate fibres, eg rayon.

cellulose nitrate *Chem.* a highly flammable pulpy solid prepared by treating cellulose with concentrated nitric acid. It is used as an explosive and propellant, and was formerly used in photographic film, plastics, and lacquers.

cell wall *Bot.* in plant cells, the relatively rigid outer wall that surrounds the membrane of the cell, and consists mainly of cellulose. Animal cells do not have cell walls.

Celsius, Anders (1701–44) Swedish astronomer, born in Uppsala. Professor of Astronomy at the University of Uppsala from 1730, he devised the centigrade thermometer and the temperature scale named after him in 1742.

Celsius *or* **Celsius scale** (ABBREV. **C**) a scale of temperature, formerly known as the centigrade scale, in which the freezing point of water is 0°C and its boiling point is 100°C, the temperature range between these fixed points being divided into 100 degrees. [named after Anders Celsius]

Celsus, Aulus Cornelius (1c AD) Roman writer and physician who compiled an encyclopedia on medicine, rhetoric, history, philosophy, war and agriculture. The only extant portion of the work is the *De Medicina*, in which he gives accounts of symptoms and treatments of diseases, surgical methods, and medical history.

Celt *noun* a member of one of the ancient peoples that inhabited most parts of Europe in pre-Roman and Roman times, or of the peoples descended from them, eg in Scotland, Wales and Ireland. [from Greek *Keltoi*, Celts]

Celtiberia a territory in N central Spain which was inhabited by the Celtiberians, a warlike people of mixed Celtic and Iberian ancestry. They were pacified by the Romans in 133 BC after decades of intermittent but fierce resistance to Roman occupation.

Celtic — *adj.* relating to the Celts or their languages. — *noun* the group of languages spoken by the Celts, including Gaelic, Irish, Manx, Welsh, Cornish, and Breton.
◊ The Celtic language of Europe, known as Continental Celtic, included the regional dialects, Gaulish, Galatian, and Celtiberian; examples of these dialects survive only in place-names and inscriptions. The Celtic language of Britain, known as Insular Celtic and including the branches Brythonic and Goidelic, survives in the regional variants of Cornish, Welsh, Breton (in France), Irish Gaelic, Scottish Gaelic, and Manx.

Celtic Church the original Church in the British Isles, which retained its independence from the Anglo-Roman Church until the Synod of Whitby (663–4). Contacts with European Christianity were developed as early as the 4c AD. The organization was largely monastic, led by an abbot rather than a bishop, and emphasized the ascetic life, scholarship, and art as well as mission. The Church was active in Ireland, Scotland, Wales, and England (eg Saints Patrick, Ninian, Columba), and in the 6c in continental Europe.

Celtic Sea a part of the Atlantic Ocean, situated S of Ireland. It is separated from the Irish Sea by the St George's Channel. Its main inlet is the Bristol Channel. The sea has average depths of 100–200m.

cement — *noun* **1** a fine powder that hardens when mixed with water, and is formed by grinding a heated mixture of clay and limestone. It is used in building as an ingredient of mortar and concrete. **2** any of various substances used as adhesives for bonding to a hard material. **3** the thin layer of hard bony tissue that anchors the roots of the teeth to the jaws. **4** *Geol.* any material, especially precipitated mineral salts, that binds loose particles of sediment together to form solid rock. — *verb* **1** to stick together with cement. **2** to apply cement. **3** to bind or make firm (eg a friendship). [from Old French *ciment*, from Latin *caementum*, quarried stone]

cementation *noun* any process in which the surface of a metal, etc, is impregnated at high temperature by another substance, as in steelmaking, case-hardening, turning glass into porcelain, etc.

cemetery *noun* (PL. **cemeteries**) a burial ground for the dead, especially one that is not attached to a church. [from Greek *koimeterion*, sleeping-room, burial place]

cenotaph *noun* a tomb-like monument in honour of a person or people buried elsewhere, especially soldiers killed in war. [from Greek *kenos*, empty + *taphos*, tomb]

Cenozoic *or* **Cainozoic** *adj. Geol.* denoting the most recent era of the Phanerozoic eon, lasting from about 65 million years ago to the present day, and subdivided into the Tertiary and Quaternary periods. [from Greek *kainos*, new + *zoe*, life]

censer *noun* a container in which incense is burnt, used eg in some churches. [from Latin *incensarium*]

censor — *noun* an official who examines books, films, newspaper articles, etc and has the power to cut out any parts thought undesirable (eg because containing information a government wants kept secret) or offensive (eg because over-violent or sexually too explicit), and to forbid publication or showing altogether. — *verb* to alter or cut out parts of, or forbid publication, showing or delivery of. [from Latin *censor*, a Roman official empowered to punish moral and political offences]

censorial *adj.* relating to a censor or the activity of a censor.

censorious *adj.* inclined to find fault; severely critical. [from Latin *censorius*, relating to a censor, hence severe]

censoriously *adv.* in a censorious way.

censoriousness *noun* being censorious.

censorship *noun* **1** the practice of censoring. **2** the job of a censor.
◊ Censorship involving the wholesale banning of information, including works of fiction, enforced by the imposition of penalties against offenders, is regarded as a characteristic of authoritarian states. However, censorship plays a part in even the most enlightened and progressive of societies, usually deriving its legitimacy from an assumed consensus on what is not acceptable at a particular time. It is also routinely practised in time of war. Since 1972 the monthly periodical Index on Censorship has campaigned against abuses of the fundamental right of free expression throughout the world.

censurable *adj.* **1** deserving censure. **2** capable of being censured.

censure — *noun* severe criticism or disapproval. — *verb* to criticize severely or express strong disapproval of. [from French *censure*, from Latin *censura*, the job of a censor, hence judgement, especially severe]

census *noun* **1** an official count, carried out at intervals, of a population, covering information such as sex, age, job, etc. **2** an official count made of something else, eg vehicles using a particular road. [from Latin *census*, from *censere*, to assess]

cent *noun* a currency unit of several countries, worth one-hundredth of the standard unit, eg of the US dollar. [from Latin *centum*, a hundred]

cent. *abbrev.* **1** centigrade. **2** central. **3** century.

centaur *noun Greek Mythol.* a creature with a man's head, arms, and trunk joined to the four-legged body of a horse. [from Greek *kentauros*]

Centaurs in Greek mythology, a race of creatures, each with a man's upper body joined to the four-legged body of a horse. They were generally savage, riotous creatures who lived away from the towns and cities. They were defeated in a battle with the Lapiths.

Centaurus *Astron.* the Centaur, a large constellation in the S hemisphere. Its brightest star, Alpha Centauri, in fact consists of three stars, the faintest of which, Proxima Centauri, is the closest star to the Sun.

centenarian — *noun* a person who is 100 years old or more. — *adj.* **1** 100 years old or more. **2** relating to a centenarian. [from Latin *centenarius*, composed of 100]

centenary — *noun* (PL. **centenaries**) the 100th anniversary of some event, or the celebration of it. — *adj.* **1** occurring every 100 years. **2** relating to a period of 100 years. [from Latin *centenarius*, composed of 100]

centennial — *noun North Amer.* a centenary. — *adj.* **1** relating to a period of 100 years. **2** occurring every 100 years. **3** lasting 100 years. [from Latin *centum*, 100 + *-ennial* as in BIENNIAL]

centi- *combining form* denoting a hundred. [from Latin *centum*, hundred]

centigrade *or* **centigrade scale** (ABBREV. **C**) the former name for the Celsius scale of temperature. [from Latin *centum*, 100 + *gradus*, step]

centime *noun* a currency unit of several countries, worth one-hundredth of the standard unit, eg of the French franc. [from Old French *centiesme*, from Latin *centesimum*, one-hundredth]

centimetre *noun* the 100th part of a metre.

centipede *noun* a small insect-like creature with a long, many-sectioned body, each section having a pair of legs. [from CENTI- + Latin *pes*, foot]

central *adj.* **1** at, or forming, the centre of something. **2** near the centre of a city, etc; easy to reach. **3** principal or most important. [from Latin *centralis*, from *centrum*, centre]

Central African Republic, French **République Centrafricaine** POP (1992e) 3.2m, a republic in central Africa, divided into 15 prefectures. AREA 626 780sq km/241 937sq mi. It is bounded N by Chad, NE by Sudan, S by Zaire and Congo, and W by Cameroon. CAPITAL Bangui. CHIEF TOWNS Berbérati, Bouar, Bossangoa. TIME ZONE GMT +1. There are c.80 ethnic groups, including Baya (34%), Banda (28%), and Sara (10%); Christianity is the main religion (Roman Catholicism 25%, Protestantism 25%). The remainder of the population holds local or Muslim beliefs. OFFICIAL LANGUAGE French; Sangho is also widely spoken. CURRENCY the franc CFA. PHYSICAL DESCRIPTION on a plateau forming the watershed between the Chad and Congo river basins; most N rivers drain towards L Chad, and southbound rivers flow towards the R Ubangi; the highest ground is found in the NE (Massif des Bongos) and NW. CLIMATE single rainy season in the N between May and Sep with an average annual rainfall between 875mm and 1 000mm; more equatorial climate in the S, between 1 500mm and 2 000mm. HISTORY part of French Equatorial Africa (known as Ubangi Shari); became an autonomous republic within

the French community in 1958; gained independence in 1960; a monarchy known as the Central African Empire was established, under Bokassa I in 1976; Bokassa was forced to flee in 1979 (he returned in 1986 for trial and was found guilty in 1987); the constitution was amended in 1992 to allow for opposition parties and to reduce the powers of the President. ECONOMY c.85% of the working population is engaged in subsistence agriculture, growing cassava, groundnuts, cotton, maize, coffee, millet, sorghum, tobacco, rice, sesame seed, plantain, bananas, yams; timber, diamonds, uranium; sawmilling, brewing, diamond splitting, leather and tobacco processing.

Central African Republic

Central America a geographical region that encompasses the independent states S of Mexico and N of S America. The area, which includes Guatemala, El Salvador, Belize, Honduras, Nicaragua, Costa Rica, and Panama, gained independence from Spain in 1821.

Central American Common Market (ABBREV. **CACM**) an economic association initiated in 1960 between Guatemala, Honduras, El Salvador, Nicaragua, and (from 1963) Costa Rica. Its early apparent success was offset by growing political crisis in the late 1970s.

Central American Federation a federation formed (1823) by Costa Rica, Nicaragua, Honduras, El Salvador, and Guatemala, following independence from Spain. Despite vigorous leadership by Francisco Morazán (1792–1842) of Honduras, internal tensions brought about the collapse of the federation by 1838.

central bank a national bank acting as banker to the government, issuing currency and having control over interest rates.

Central Committee of the Communist Party of the Soviet Union in the former USSR, the highest decision-making authority apart from Congress, which elected it. Except in rare circumstances (twice in Nikita Khrushchev's time), it exercised little influence, partly because of its unwieldy size and partly because of the concentration of power in the Politburo.

Central Criminal Court the official title of the OLD BAILEY.

central government the government that has power over a whole country, as distinct from local government.

central heating a system for heating a whole building, by means of pipes, radiators, etc connected to a central source of heat.

Central Intelligence Agency (ABBREV. **CIA**) in the USA, the official intelligence analysis organization responsible for external security, established under the National Security Act (1947) and reporting directly to the president. As a result of abuses of power in both the domestic

(eg in the Watergate affair) and foreign arenas, the CIA must now co-ordinate domestic activities with the FBI and report on covert activities to Congress. See also FBI.

centralism *noun* the policy of bringing the administration of a country under central control, with a decrease in local administrative power.

centralist — *noun* a person who supports centralism. — *adj.* characterized by centralism.

centrality *noun* the condition or state of being central.

centralization *or* **centralisation** *noun* the action or process of centralizing; centralism.

centralize *or* **centralise** *verb trans., intrans.* to bring under central control.

central locking in a motor vehicle, a system whereby all the doors (including the boot or trunk) are locked or unlocked automatically when the key is turned in any one of the locks.

centrally *adv.* in a central way or position; in or with regard to the centre.

centrally-heated *adj.* provided with or warmed by central heating.

central nervous system the brain and the spinal cord.

Central Powers initially, the members of the Triple Alliance (Germany, Austria-Hungary, Italy) created by Bismarck (1882). Since Italy remained neutral in 1914, the term was later used to describe Germany, Austria-Hungary, their ally Turkey, and later Bulgaria in World War I.

central processing unit the part of a computer that performs arithmetical and logical operations on data, and controls the other units contained in the system.

Central Region POP (1992e) 273 000, a region in central Scotland, divided into three districts. AREA 2 631sq km/1 016sq mi. It is bounded N and

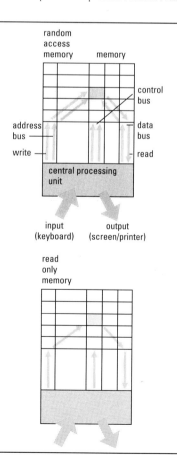

central processing unit (CPU)

NE by Tayside, E by Fife, SE by Lothian, and S and W by Strathclyde. PHYSICAL DESCRIPTION the N part of the Region is in the Highlands, and includes the Trossachs in the W; the S part encloses the Forth River Valley; drained by the Forth, Carron, and Devon rivers; contains several lochs, including Katrine, Venachar, and part of Earn. CAPITAL Stirling. CHIEF TOWNS Falkirk, Alloa, Grangemouth (all in the SE, the region's industrial area). ECONOMY brewing and distilling; engineering; agriculture. NOTABLE FEATURES Stirling Castle; Loch Lomond; Bannockburn battle site.

central reservation *Brit.* a narrow strip of grass, concrete, etc dividing the two sides of a dual carriageway, especially a motorway.

Central Treaty Organization (ABBREV. **CENTO**) a politico-military alliance signed in 1955 between Iran (which withdrew after the fall of the Shah), Turkey, Pakistan, Iraq (which withdrew in 1958), and the UK, as a defence against the USSR.

Central Valley *or* **Great Central Valley** a valley in California, USA, between the Sierra Nevada in the E and the Coast Range in the W. The Sacramento and San Joaquin rivers feed the Central Valley Project, a series of dams and reservoirs constructed for flood-control, irrigation, and hydroelectricity.

centre — *noun* **1** a part at the middle of something: *chocolates with soft centres.* **2** a point inside a circle or sphere that is an equal distance from all points on the circumference or surface, or a point on a line at an equal distance from either end. **3** a point or axis round which a body revolves or rotates. **4** a central area. **5** a place where a particular activity is concentrated or particular facilities, information, etc are available: *a sports centre.* **6** something that acts as a focus: *the centre of attraction.* **7** a point from which activities radiate and are controlled: *the centre of operations.* **8** a position that is at neither extreme, especially in politics. **9** in some playing-field sports, a position in the middle of the field, or a player in this position. — *adj.* at or in the centre; central. — *verb* **1** to place in or at the centre; to position centrally or symmetrically. **2** to adjust or focus (eg one's thoughts). **3** *intrans., trans.* (**centre on** *or* **upon something**) to concentrate on it. [from Latin *centrum*, from Greek *kentron*, sharp point, the point round which a circle is drawn]

Centre Beaubourg, also called the **Pompidou Centre** the Centre National d'Art et de Culture, situated on the Plateau Beaubourg in Paris. Designed by Renzo Piano and Richard Rogers (opened in 1977), it is a six-storey building which wears its plumbing and service structures on the outside. It houses a modern art gallery and a centre for industrial design.

centreboard *noun* a movable plate in a sailing boat or dinghy, which can be let down through the keel to prevent sideways drift.

centrefold *noun* the sheet that forms the two central facing pages of a magazine, etc, or a picture, etc occupying it.

Centre 42 a plan for a performing arts centre supported by trade-union money, as agreed at the 1960 Trades Union Congress. The Round House, London, was acquired with this aim, but the original plan for free performances never materialized.

centre-forward *noun* *Sport* in some field games, the position in the centre of the front line, or the player in this position.

centre-half *noun* *Sport* in some field games, the position in the centre of the half-back line, or the player in this position.

centre of gravity *noun* *Physics* the point at which the entire mass of an object may be considered to be concentrated.

centre of mass *or* **centre of inertia** *Physics* centre of gravity.

centrepiece *noun* **1** a central or most important item. **2** an ornament or decoration for the centre of a table.

centre spread same as CENTREFOLD.

centri- *combining form* denoting a centre or middle. [from Latin *centrum*, centre]

-centric *combining form* having a stated centre, focus, basis, etc.

centrifugal *adj.* acting or moving away from the centre of a circle along which an object is moving, or away from the axis of rotation. [from CENTRI- + Latin *fugere*, to flee]

centrifugal force an apparent force that seems to exert an outward pull on an object that is moving in a circular path. In fact such a force does not exist. See also CENTRIPETAL FORCE.

centrifuge — *verb* to separate substances by spinning them at high speed in a rotating device. — *noun* an instrument containing a rotating device that is used to separate solid or liquid particles of different densities, by spinning them at high speed in a tube in a horizontal circle. The heaviest particles become sedimented in the form of a pellet at the end of the tube.

centriole *noun* *Biol.* a cylindrical structure that plays a role in cell division in animal cells. [a diminutive of Latin *centrum*, centre]

centripetal *adj.* acting or moving towards the centre of a circle along which an object is moving, or towards the axis of rotation. [from CENTRI- + Latin *petere*, to seek]

centripetal force, the force that is required to keep an object moving in a circular path. It is directed inwards towards the centre of the circle, and for an object of mass m moving with a constant speed v in a circle of radius r, the centripetal force is mv^2/r. See also CENTRIFUGAL FORCE.

centrism *noun* the practice of sticking to the middle ground in politics; the holding of moderate political opinions.

centrist — *adj.* having moderate, non-extreme political opinions. — *noun* a person holding such opinions. [from CENTRE + -IST]

centromere *noun* *Genetics* the part of a chromosome that attaches it to the spindle during cell division. [from Latin *centrum*, from Greek *kentron*, a sharp point + *meros*, part]

centurion *noun* *Hist.* in the army of ancient Rome, an officer in charge of a century. [from Latin *centurio*, from *centum*, a hundred]

century *noun* (PL. **centuries**) **1** any of the 100-year periods counted forwards or backwards from an important event, especially the birth of Christ. **2** a period of 100 years. **3** in the game of cricket, 100 runs made by a batsman in a single innings. **4** *Hist.* in the army of ancient Rome, a company of (originally) 100 foot soldiers. [from Latin *centuria*, unit of 100 parts]

◆ Since there was no year 0, the first century AD (or CE) began with year 1 and ended with year 100, and the second century began with year 101. Strictly, therefore, the 20th century began on 1 Jan 1901 (not 1900) and will end on 31 Dec 2000 (not 1999); and the 21st century will begin on 1 Jan 2001. However, in general use, a new century is regarded as beginning on the 1 Jan of the year ending in -00.

CEO *abbrev.* Chief Executive Officer.

cephalic *adj.* relating to the head. [from Greek *kephale*, head]

cephalic index *Anthropol.* a skull's breadth as a percentage of its length. Skulls of different relative breadths are termed *brachycephalic* (broad), *mesaticephalic* (intermediate), and *dolichocephalic* (long).

Cephalonia, Greek **Kefallinía** POP (1991) 32 000, the largest of the Ionian Is, Greece, lying off the W coast in the Ionian Sea. AREA 781sq km/301sq mi; length 48km/30mi. PHYSICAL

DESCRIPTION an island of hills (rising to 1 628m), fertile plains, sandy beaches, and long stretches of rocky coast. The island was devastated by earthquakes in 1953. CAPITAL Argostolion. ECONOMY olives, grapes.

cephalopod *noun* any of a group of sea creatures, including the octopus, squid and cuttlefish, consisting of a head and a ring of tentacles equipped with suckers. [from Greek *kephale*, head + *pous podos*, foot]

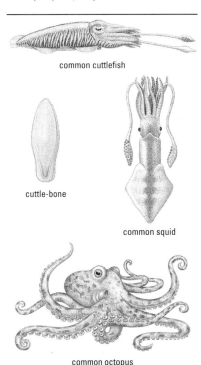

common cuttlefish

cuttle-bone

common squid

common octopus

cephalopods

Cephalopoda *noun* *Zool.* in the animal kingdom, a class of highly developed and almost exclusively marine molluscs, including cuttlefish, octopus, and squid. [from Greek *kephale*, head + *pous podos*, foot]

Cepheid variable *Astron.* any of a group of variable stars that pulsate on a very regular basis, every 1 to 100 days, such that the longer the period of pulsation, the brighter the star. The observed period of a Cepheid variable indicates its distance from Earth, and is used to measure distances in our own and nearby galaxies. [named after the prototype Cepheid star, Delta Cephei]

Cepheus *noun* *Astron.* a northern constellation, lying partly in the Milky Way, that includes the star Delta Cephei, the prototype of Cepheid variables that are used to calculate distances in our own and nearby galaxies. Its brightest star is Alderamin. [from Greek *kepheus*, named after King Cepheus, father of Andromeda]

ceramic *adj.* **1** any of a number of hard brittle materials, eg enamels, all kinds of pottery, porcelain, tiles, and brick, produced by moulding or shaping and then baking or firing non-metallic mineral substances (clays) at high temperatures. **2** relating to or made of such a material. [from Greek *keramos*, potter's clay]

◇ Ceramics are resistant to the action of water and most chemicals, and are good electrical and thermal insulators. They are used to make articles that must be highly resistant to wear over long periods, eg artificial teeth and hip joints. Heavy clay ceramics such as bricks, roofing tiles, and underground drainpipes are used in construction, and ceramics with high melting points are used as refractories to line furnaces, and in the fuel elements of nuclear reactors. Ceramic casings and parts for car and aircraft engines are being developed because they wear out more slowly than metal, and are also lighter than their cast-iron equivalents.

ceramics *noun* **1** (*sing.*) the art of making pottery. **2** (*pl.*) articles made of pottery.

Cerberus in Greek mythology, the dog with three heads which guards the entrance to the Underworld. Heracles carried him off as one of his labours.

cereal — *noun* **1** an edible member of the grass family (Gramineae) that is cultivated as a food crop for its nutritious seeds (grains). **2** the grain produced. **3** a breakfast food prepared from grain. — *adj.* relating to edible grains. [from Latin *Cerealis*, relating to *Ceres*, goddess of agriculture] ◇ Cereals form the staple food of most of the world's population, and they are also used to feed animal livestock such as cattle, sheep, and pigs. The main cereals are wheat, barley, rye, and oats, grown in temperate regions, and rice, maize, sorghum, and millet, grown in tropical and subtropical regions. The grain of cereals contains large amounts of starch (an important energy source) as well as protein, vitamins, and dietary fibre. Wheat, rice, and maize together cover over 50 per cent of the world's cultivated land, and yield about 1 000 million tonnes of grain every year. Rice is the staple diet of over 50 per cent of the world population.

barley   wheat

barley and wheat

cerebellar *adj.* relating to or in the region of the cerebellum.

cerebellum *noun* (PL. **cerebella**) *Anat.* the main part of the hindbrain in vertebrates, concerned primarily with the co-ordination of movement. [from Latin, diminutive of *cerebrum*, brain]

cerebral *adj.* **1** relating to the brain. **2** *facetious* using or requiring the use of the brain, especially too much: *a cerebral piece of music.* [from CEREBRUM]

cerebral cortex *Anat.* the outer layer of the cerebral hemispheres of the brain. In humans it consists of highly convoluted folds of *grey matter*, about 2mm deep, and contains over 12 000 million nerve cells. It is responsible for consciousness (including perception, memory, and learning) and the initiation of voluntary movement.

cerebral haemorrhage *Medicine* haemorrhage (bleeding) from a ruptured blood vessel, usually an artery, within the brain, most often caused by hypertension (high blood pressure) or degenerative disease of the blood vessel concerned, eg arteriosclerosis. Symptoms range from temporary numbness or weakness to total paralysis (stroke), coma, or death.

cerebral hemisphere *Anat.* in higher vertebrates, either of the two halves of the brain. The cerebral hemispheres form the major part of the human brain, each having a much folded outer layer of grey matter (the *cerebral cortex*) and controlling the opposite side of the body.

cerebral palsy *Medicine* a failure of the brain to develop normally in young children due to brain damage before or around the time of birth. ◇ Cerebral palsy may be caused by injury during birth, infection of the mother during pregnancy, lack of oxygen before birth, haemorrhage (bleeding), meningitis, or hereditary factors. It results in weakness, lack of co-ordination of the limbs, and in many cases *spastic paralysis*, in which the limbs may slowly become permanently deformed. Intelligence and speech may also be severely impaired.

cerebrate *verb intrans. facetious* to think; to use one's brain. [from CEREBRUM]

cerebration *noun* action of the brain, especially unconscious.

cerebrospinal *adj.* relating to the brain and spinal cord together.

cerebrum *noun* (PL. **cerebra**) *Anat.* in higher vertebrates, the part of the brain that consists of two cerebral hemispheres linked by a band of nerve fibres (the *corpus callosum*). It initiates and co-ordinates all voluntary activity. [from Latin *cerebrum*]

ceremonial *adj.* relating to, used for, or involving a ceremony. [from Latin *caerimonia*, rite]
♦ Often confused with *ceremonious*.

ceremonially *adv.* in a ceremonial way.

ceremonious *adj.* elaborately formal. [from Latin *caeremoniosus*, full of religious rites]
♦ Often confused with *ceremonial*.

ceremoniously *adv.* in a ceremonious way.

ceremony *noun* (PL. **ceremonies**) **1** a ritual performed to mark a particular, especially public or religious, occasion. **2** formal politeness.
— **stand on ceremony** to insist on behaving formally.
without ceremony in a hasty, informal way. [from Latin *caerimonia*, rite]

Ceremony of Carols, A carols set in 11 movements for treble voices and harp by Benjamin Britten (Op 28, 1942).

Ceres 1 in Roman mythology, the name for the ancient corn-goddess, Demeter, whose cult was known in Attica, Arcadia, Asia Minor, and Sicily. **2** *Astron.* the largest asteroid (minor planet), and the first to be discovered. It is about 100km in diameter.

cerise — *noun* cherry-red. — *adj.* of this colour. [from French *cerise*, cherry]

cerium *noun Chem.* (SYMBOL **Ce**, ATOMIC NUMBER **58**) a soft silvery-grey metal belonging to the lanthanide series, used in catalytic converters for car exhausts, alloys for cigarette-lighter flints, cores for carbon arc lamps, and as an agent for removing fission products from spent nuclear fuel. [named after the asteroid *Ceres*]

cermet *noun Engineering* **1** a hard strong composite material, resistant to corrosion and wear, made from a ceramic and a metal, and used to make cutting tools and brake linings. **2** a type of electronic resistor made of such material. [from CERAMIC + METAL]

CERN *abbrev.* Conseil Europeén pour la Recherche Nucléaire (French), European Organization for Nuclear Research, now known as the European Laboratory for Particle Physics.

ceroc *noun* a contemporary style of jive dancing to rock-and-roll music. [from French *Le Roc* dancing, on which it is based]

cert *noun colloq.* a certainty.

cert. *abbrev.* **1** certificate. **2** certified.

certain — *adj.* **1** proved or known beyond doubt. **2** (**certain about** *or* **of something**) having no doubt about it; absolutely sure. **3** *used with reference to the future* definitely going to happen, etc; able to rely on or be relied on. **4** particular, and, though known, not named or specified: *a*

certain friend of yours. **5** used before a person's name to indicate either their obscurity or one's own unfamiliarity with them: *a certain Mrs Smith.* **6** *said of a quality* undeniably present without being clearly definable: *the beard gave his face a certain authority.* **7** some, though not much: *that's true to a certain extent.* — *pron.* some.
— **for certain** definitely; without doubt.
make certain of something to take action so as to ensure it or be sure about it. [from Old French, from Latin *certus*, sure]

certainly *adv.* **1** without any doubt. **2** definitely. **3** *in giving permission* of course.

certainty *noun* (PL. **certainties**) **1** something that cannot be doubted or is bound to happen. **2** freedom from doubt; the state of being sure. **3** the state of being bound to happen: *the certainty of death.*

certifiable *adj.* **1** capable of or suitable for being certified. **2** *colloq.* mad, crazy.

certificate — *noun* (pronounced -*cət*) an official document that formally acknowledges or witnesses a fact (eg *a marriage certificate*), an achievement or qualification (eg *a First-Aid certificate*), or one's condition (eg *a doctor's certificate*). — *verb* (pronounced -*cate*) to provide with a certificate. See also CERTIFY. [from Latin *certificare*, to certify]

certificated *adj.* qualified by a particular course of training.

certificate of deposit a certificate representing a fixed-term interest-bearing deposit in large denominations, which may be bought and sold. First introduced by Citibank in New York in 1961, Sterling certificates were introduced in 1968.

certification *noun* **1** certifying or being certified. **2** a document that certifies something.

certified *adj.* **1** possessing a certificate. **2** endorsed or guaranteed. **3** *said of a person* insane.

certify *verb* (**certifies, certified**) **1** to declare or confirm officially. **2** to declare (someone) insane. **3** to declare to have reached a required standard, passed certain tests, etc. See also CERTIFICATE. [from Latin *certificare*]

certitude *noun* a feeling of certainty. [from Latin *certitudo*, from *certus*, sure]

Cervantes (Saavedra), Miguel de (1547–1616) Spanish writer, born in Alcalá de Henares. He is best known for his novel *Don Quixote* (2 parts 1605, 1615), the first part of which is thought to have been written while he was in prison in La Mancha. Other works include *La Galatea*, a pastoral romance (1585), and many plays, of which only two have survived.

statue of Cervantes, Madrid

cervical *adj.* relating to or in the region of the cervix.

cervical smear *Pathol.* the collection of a sample of cells from the cervix (neck) of the uterus for staining and examination under a microscope, in order to detect any abnormal changes indicative of cancer. Such tests, performed at regular intervals, help to reduce the incidence of cervical cancer by detecting precancerous or early cancerous stages of the disease. — Also called *smear test*.

cervix *noun* **1** *Anat.* the neck of the uterus (womb), consisting of a narrow passage leading to the inner end of the vagina. **2** *Anat.* the neck. [from Latin *cervix*, neck]

cesium same as CAESIUM.

cessation *noun* stopping or ceasing; a pause. [from Latin *cessare*, to cease]

cession *noun* the giving up or yielding of territories, rights, etc to someone else. [from Latin *cessio*, from *cedere*, to yield]

cesspit *or* **cesspool** *noun* a pool, pit or tank for the collection and storage of sewage and waste water. [from Italian *cesso*, latrine]

cetacean — *noun* any of a group of animals that includes the whale, dolphin and porpoise. — *adj.* relating to this group. [from Greek *ketos*, whale]

cetane *noun* a hydrocarbon present in diesel fuel, in amounts indicated by a *cetane number*, used for grading the fuel. [from Greek *ketos*, whale, cetane also being obtainable from *cetyl* compounds found in spermaceti]

Cetewayo *or* **Cetshwayo** *or* **Cetshwayo** (c.1826–1884) ruler of Zululand (1873–83), born near Eshowe, Zululand. In 1879 he defeated the invading British at Isandhlwana, but was himself defeated and taken prisoner at Ulundi. He was restored to part of his kingdom in 1883, but was soon driven out by his subjects.

Cetus *noun* *Astron.* the Whale, the fourth largest constellation, lying above the celestial equator, but inconspicuous because it has few bright stars. It contains the variable star Mira, which is a red giant.

Ceuta POP (1991) 68 000, a freeport and military station, at the E end of the Strait of Gibraltar, on the N African coast of Morocco. It became Spanish in 1580 and today is administered by Cádiz province, Spain. NOTABLE FEATURES old fortress at Monte Hacho; cathedral (15c); Church of Our Lady of Africa (18c).

Cévennes, ancient **Cebenna** the chief mountain range in the S of France, on the SE edge of the Massif Central. It extends generally NE–SW, forming a watershed between the river systems of the Loire, Rhône, and Garonne. The highest peak is Mt Mézenc (1 754m). The varied landscape includes forest, barren grassland, and deep gorges, such as the Gorges du Tarn near Les Vignes.

Cézanne, Paul (1839–1906) French Post-Impressionist painter, born in Aix-en-Provence. He studied law before he was persuaded by his friend Emile Zola to go to Paris in 1862, where he began to paint. He later worked with and was influenced by Pissarro, and began to use the glowing colours which characterize his work. In his later period (after 1886), he emphasized the underlying forms of nature by constructing his pictures from a rhythmic series of coloured planes. His paintings foreshadow Cubism and include *The Mills of Gardanne* (1885–6), *L'Estaque* (c.1888, Louvre, Paris), *The Card Players* (1890–2, Musée d'Orsay, Paris), and *The Gardener* (1906, Tate Gallery, London).

Cf *symbol Chem.* californium.

cf. *abbrev. confer* (Latin), compare.

CFC *abbrev.* chlorofluorocarbon.

CGI *or* **CLGLI** *abbrev.* City and Guilds (of London) Institute.

cgs unit *Physics* centimetre-gram-second unit, a system of measurement based on the use of the centimetre, gram, and second as the fundamental units of length, mass, and time, respectively, for most purposes now superseded by SI units.

CH *abbrev.* **1** Companion of Honour, a British title awarded to people who have given particu-

lar service to the nation. **2** *as an international vehicle mark Confederatio Helvetica* (Latin), Switzerland.

ch. *abbrev.* **1** chapter. **2** *Chess* check. **3** church.

Chac in Mayan mythology, the god of rain, characterized by two wide eyes, a long turned-up nose and two curved fangs. He was also worshipped as four gods, each associated with a different colour and one of the four points of the compass. He is the equivalent of the Aztec god, Tlaloc.

cha-cha *or* **cha-cha-cha** *noun* a Latin American dance, or music for it. [from American Spanish *cha-cha*]

Chaco Culture National Historical Park, formerly **Chaco Canyon National Monument** a remote desert canyon in New Mexico, 160km/100mi NW of Albuquerque. It was the hub in c.950–1300 AD of the Anasazi Native American culture. Established as a National Monument in 1907, it was renamed in 1980. Its 650km/400mi road network links c.125 D-shaped pueblos or planned villages. The best-known is Pueblo Bonito, a compact five-storey settlement with c.600 rooms. It is a World Heritage site.

chaconne *noun* an old Spanish dance, probably originating in Mexico; also, a piece of music for it. It is written in the form of variations on a ground bass or a stereotyped harmonic progression in triple time with slow stately tempo, and was widely used in 17c opera, ballet, and instrumental music. See also PASSACAGLIA. [from French *chaconne*, from Spanish *chacona*, from Basque *chucun*, pretty]

Chaco War a territorial struggle (1932–5) between Bolivia and Paraguay in the disputed N Chaco area. Owing to the brilliant tactics of Col José Félix Estigarribia (1888–1940), Paraguay won most of the area, and a peace treaty was signed in 1938. Around 50 000 Bolivians and 35 000 Paraguayans died in the war. The outcome of the war had a decisive effect on the future of both countries.

Chad, French **Tchad**, official name **Republic of Chad**, French **République du Tchad** POP (1992e) 6m, a republic in N central Africa, divided into 14 prefectures. AREA 1 284 640sq km/ 495 871sq mi. The republic is bounded N by Libya, E by Sudan, S by Central African Republic, and W by Cameroon, Nigeria, and Niger. CAPITAL Ndjamena. CHIEF TOWNS Moundou, Sarh, Abéché. TIME ZONE GMT +1. There are c.200 ethnic groups; Islam is the chief religion, with local religions and Christianity in the minority. OFFICIAL LANGUAGE French; many local languages are also spoken. CURRENCY the franc CFA. PHYSICAL DESCRIPTION occupies a landlocked and mostly arid, semi-desert plateau at the edge of the Sahara Desert with an average altitude of 200–500m; the Logone and Chari rivers drain into L Chad in the SW; isolated massifs along the Sudan frontier rise to 1 500m; the Tibesti Mts in the N rise to 3 415m at Emi Koussi; vegetation is generally desert scrub or steppe; most people live in the tropical S. CLIMATE moderately wet in the S between May and Oct, but dry for the rest of the year; the hot and arid N is almost rainless; the central plain is hot and dry, with a brief rainy season during Jun–Sep. HISTORY part of French Equatorial Africa in the 19c; colonial status in 1920; gained independence in 1960; rebel forces took the capital, forming a new government in 1982; fighting continued between Libyan-supported rebels and the French-supported government until a cease-fire was agreed in 1987; following a coup in 1991 a multiparty system was adopted. GOVERNMENT a President, with legislative and executive power, is assisted by a Cabinet. ECONOMY severely damaged in recent years by drought, locusts, and civil war; export of cotton, kaolin, animal products; agriculture mainly cassava, groundnuts, millet, sorghum,

Chad

rice, yams, sweet potatoes, dates; livestock, fishing; oil exploration, with refining facilities; uranium, gold, bauxite; salt is mined around L Chad.

Chad, Lake, French **Tchad** a shallow freshwater lake in N central Africa, at the meeting point of Chad, Nigeria, Cameroon, and Niger. The lake is a remnant of a former inland sea. AREA 10 400sq km/4 000sq mi (low water), 20 700sq km/8 000sq mi (high water). The lake has no visible outlets. There is a chain of inhabited islands along the E coast. Fishing and mineral extraction (natron) are important. The Douguia Wildlife Reserve is located close to the lake. Oil was discovered nearby in Niger.

Chadic — *noun* a group of more than 100 languages spoken by c.25 million people in parts of Ghana and the Central African Republic. The group is assigned to the Afro-Asiatic family of languages, although its status within the family is unclear. The most important language of the group is Hausa. — *adj.* relating to this group of languages.

chador *or* **chadar** *or* **chuddar** *noun* a thick veil worn by Muslim women covering the head and body. [from Persian *chador*]

chador

Chadwick, Sir James (1891–1974) English physicist, born near Macclesfield. In work on radioactivity he discovered the neutron (1932), for which he was awarded the 1935 Nobel Prize for Physics. He led the UK's work on the atomic bomb during World War II.

Chaeronea, Battle of a battle (338 BC) in N Boeotia in which Philip of Macedon and his troops defeated the Greeks. It effectively ended the political independence of the Greek city-states.

chafe *verb* **1** *trans., intrans.* to make or become sore or worn by rubbing. **2** to make warm by rubbing. **3** (**chafe at** *or* **under something**) to become angry or impatient at: *chafe at the rules.* [from Old French *chaufer*, to heat]

chafer *noun* any of several large, slow-moving beetles. [from Anglo-Saxon *ceafor*]

chaff¹ *noun* **1** the husks or shells separated from grain during threshing. **2** chopped hay and straw used to feed cattle. **3** worthless material. **4** strips of metal foil dropped by aircraft to confuse enemy radar. [from Anglo-Saxon *ceaf*]

chaff² — *noun* light-hearted joking or teasing. — *verb* to tease or make fun of.

Chaffanbrass the tireless barrister in Anthony Trollope's 'Palliser' novels, whose unkempt appearance belies his great talent in the courtroom.

chaffinch *noun* a songbird of the finch family, the male having a pinkish body and grey head. [from Anglo-Saxon *ceaffinc*, chaff finch]

chaffinch

Chagall, Marc (1889–1985) Russian-born French artist, born in Vitebsk. He left Russia in 1922, and settled near Paris. During World War II he moved to the USA, where he began to design ballet sets and costumes. He illustrated several books, but is best known for his fanciful painting of animals, objects, and people, both real and imaginary. The word 'Surrealist' is said to have been coined by Apollinaire to describe the work of Chagall.

chagrin *noun* acute annoyance or disappointment. [from French *chagrin*]

Chaikin, Joseph (1935–) US actor and theatre director, born in New York City. His early acting work was with The Living Theater, notably in *The Connection* (1960) and *Man is Man* (1962). In 1963 he founded The Open Theater, which for a decade produced some of the most original work in the US, such as *America Hurrah* (1965), *Terminal* (1969), and *Nightwalk* (1973).

Chain, Sir Ernst Boris (1906–79) British biochemist, born in Berlin. In 1933 he fled to Britain, where he worked at Cambridge and Oxford, and later held posts in Rome and London. He shared the 1945 Nobel Prize for Physiology or Medicine for the purification and development of penicillin, and also worked on snake venoms and insulin.

chain — *noun* **1** a series of connected links or rings, especially of metal, used for fastening, binding, holding, supporting, transmitting motion or, eg in jewellery, for ornament. **2** a series or progression: *a chain of events.* **3** a number of shops, hotels, etc under common ownership or management. **4** (**chains**) something that restricts or frustrates. **5** *Chem.* a number of atoms linked in a series to form a molecule, etc. **6** an old measure of length equal to 22 yards (about 20m). — *verb* to fasten, bind, or restrict with, or as if with, chains. — **in chains** bound by chains, as a prisoner or slave. [from Old French *chaeine*, from Latin *catena*]

chain gang a group of prisoners chained together for working outside the prison.

chain letter a letter copied to a large number of people, especially with a request for and promise of something (eg money), each recipient being asked to copy the letter to a stated number of acquaintances.

chainmail same as MAIL².

chain of office a heavy ornamental chain worn round the neck as a symbol of office, eg by a mayor.

chain reaction 1 *Physics* a nuclear reaction that is self-sustaining, eg nuclear fission, in which the splitting of atomic nuclei is accompanied by the release of neutrons, which themselves cause the splitting of more nuclei. Such chain reactions may be controlled, as in a nuclear reactor, or uncontrolled, as in a nuclear explosion. **2** *Chem.* a chemical reaction that is self-sustaining because a change in one molecule causes many other molecules to undergo change, eg during combustion. **3** a series of events, each causing the next.

chainsaw *noun* a power-driven saw, the blade of which is a fast-revolving chain composed of metal teeth.

chain-smoke *verb trans., intrans.* to smoke (cigarettes) continuously.

chain-smoker *noun* a person who smokes cigarettes continuously.

chain store one of a series of shops, especially department stores, owned by the same company and selling the same goods.

chair — *noun* **1** a seat for one person, with a back-support and usually four legs. **2** the office of chairman or chairwoman at a meeting, etc, or the person holding this office. **3** a professorship. **4** *Hist.* a sedan chair. — *verb* **1** to control or conduct (a meeting) as chairman or chairwoman. **2** to lift up and carry (a victor, etc) in triumph. **3** to place (someone) in a seat of authority. — **the chair** *colloq. North Amer., esp. US* the electric chair as a means of capital punishment. **in the chair** acting as chairman. **take the chair** to be chairman or chairwoman. [from Old French *chaiere*, from Greek *kathedra*, seat]

chairlift *noun* a series of seats suspended from a moving cable, for carrying skiers, etc up a mountain.

chairman *or* **chairwoman** *or* **chairperson** *noun* (PL. **chairmen, chairwomen, chairpersons**) **1** a person who conducts or controls a meeting or debate. **2** a person who presides over a committee, a board of directors, etc.

Chairs, The (Les Chaises) a play by Eugène Ionesco (1952). An example of the Theatre of the Absurd and described by the author as 'tragic farce', it shows a set of chairs preparing to seat the invisible guests of a suicidal couple.

chaise *noun Hist.* a light open two-wheeled horse-drawn carriage. [from French *chaise*, chair]

chaise longue (PL. **chaises longues**) a long seat with a back and one arm-rest, on which one can recline at full length. [from French *chaise longue*, long chair]

Chakri *or* **Chakkri dynasty**, also called **Bangkok dynasty** a Siamese dynasty founded in 1782 by General P'raya Chakri, who as Rama I (reigned 1782–1809), established his capital in present-day Bangkok, and instituted a period of stability and prosperity in Siam. His successors, especially Rama III (reigned 1824–51), Rama IV (reigned 1851–68), and Rama V (reigned 1868–1910), opened the country to foreign trade and championed modernization. The dynasty still rules Thailand (Siam's modern name) under the constitutional monarchy established after the bloodless revolution of 1932.

chalaza *noun* **1** *Zool.* in a bird's egg, one of two spiral strands of albumen that hold the yolk sac in position. **2** *Bot.* in a plant ovule, the region at the base of the nucellus (a mass of thin-walled cells in the centre of the ovule). [from Greek *chalaza*, hail, lump]

Chalcedon, Council of a Council of the Church (AD 451–5) which agreed that Jesus Christ is truly God and truly man, two natures in one person (the 'Chalcedonian definition'). The definition is generally accepted by the Churches, though there has been uneasiness about its interpretation.

chalcedony *noun Geol.* a fine-grained variety of the mineral quartz, which occurs in various forms, including several semiprecious gemstones, eg agate, jasper, onyx. [from Greek *chalkedon*]

Chalcis, Greek **Khalkis**, ancient **Evripos** POP (1991) 52 000, the capital of the island of Euboea, Greece. It is an administrative and economic centre. Aristotle died here.

Chalcolithic *adj.* belonging to the Copper or earliest Bronze Age: the period of transition between the Neolithic and Bronze Ages when copper was already in use. [from Greek *chalkos*, copper + *lithos*, stone]

chalcopyrite *noun Geol.* a copper iron sulphide mineral ($CuFeS_2$), found in veins associated with igneous rocks. It is golden-yellow in colour, and is the main ore of copper. — Also called *copper pyrites.* [from Greek *chalkos*, copper + PYRITE]

Chaldaeans *or* **Chaldeans 1** originally the name of a Semitic people (Kaldu) from Arabia who settled in the region of Ur in Lower Mesopotamia. **2** a generic term for Babylonians in the 7c–6c BC. **3** the practitioners in Roman times of the Babylonian science of astrology.

chalet *noun* **1** a style of house typical of snowy Alpine regions, built of wood, with windowshutters and a heavy, sloping, wide-eaved roof. **2** a small cabin for holiday accommodation, especially one of a number at a holiday camp, etc. **3** a wooden villa. [from Swiss French *chalet*]

Chaliapin, Fyodor (Ivanovich) (1873–1938) Russian bass singer of great power, born in Kazan. Also talented as an actor, he sang in opera at Tiflis (1892), Moscow (1896), and London (1913). He left Russia after the Revolution.

chalice *noun* **1** *poetic* a wine cup; a goblet. **2** in the Christian Church, the cup used for serving the wine at Communion or Mass. [from Old French *chalice*, from Latin *calix*, cup]

chalk — *noun* **1** a soft fine-grained porous rock, composed of calcium carbonate, often pure white or very light in colour, and formed from the shell fragments of countless millions of minute marine organisms that were deposited on the ocean bed during the Cretaceous period. It is used in writing materials, paints, putty, cement, and fertilizers. **2** a material similar to this, usually calcium sulphate, or a stick of it, often coloured, used for writing and drawing, especially on a blackboard. — *verb* to write or mark in chalk. — **by a long chalk** *colloq.* by a considerable amount.

chalk and cheese *colloq.* completely different things.

chalk something up to add an item to one's list of successes or experiences.

chalk something up to someone to add it to the account of money owed by or to them.

not by a long chalk *colloq.* not at all. [from Anglo-Saxon *cealc*, from Latin *calx*, limestone]

chalkboard *noun North Amer., esp. US* a blackboard.

chalkiness *noun* the quality of being chalky.

chalky *adj.* (**chalkier, chalkiest**) **1** like, or consisting of, chalk. **2** *said eg of a face* very pale.

challenge — *verb* **1** to call on (someone) to settle a matter by any sort of contest: *challenge him to a duel.* **2** to cast doubt on or call in question: *challenge her right to dismiss staff.* **3** to test, especially in a stimulating way: *a task that challenges you.* **4** (of a guard or sentry) to order (someone) to stop and show official proof of identity, etc. **5** *Legal* to object to the inclusion of (a person) on a jury. — *noun* **1** an invitation to a contest. **2** the questioning or doubting of something. **3** a problem or task that stimulates effort and interest. **4** an order from a guard or sentry to stop and prove identity. **5** *Legal* an objection to the inclusion of (someone) on a jury. [from Old French *chalenge*]

challenged *adj.* a supposedly neutral term in political correctness, meaning handicapped, impaired, or deficient in some specified way. It was first used in the USA when discussing physical or mental handicap, but is now applied in a wide variety of contexts: *physically challenged* (= disabled) / *financially challenged* (= poor).

Challenger *noun Astron.* the second Space Shuttle vehicle, which was launched for the first time in 1983, and was destroyed by an explosion during its tenth launch in 1986.

challenger *noun* a person who issues a challenge.

challenging *adj.* demanding; difficult but rewarding.

challengingly *adv.* in a challenging way.

Chalmers, Thomas (1780–1847) Scottish theologian and reformer, born in Anstruther. Ordained in 1803, he became a minister in Glasgow (1815), where his magnificent oratory took the city by storm. He became Professor of Moral Philosophy at St Andrews (1823), and of Theology at Edinburgh (1827). In 1843 he led the Disruption, when 470 ministers seceded from the Established Church of Scotland to found the Free Church of Scotland.

chalumeau *noun* **1** an early reed-pipe which evolved into the clarinet at the beginning of the 18c. **2** a term still used today for the lowest register of the clarinet. [from French *chalumeau*, from Late Latin *calamellus*, diminutive of *calamus*, a pipe, reed]

Chamaeleon *Astron.* a small faint constellation in the S hemisphere.

chamber *noun* **1** *old use* a room, especially a bedroom. **2** a hall for the meeting of an assembly, especially a legislative or judicial body. **3** one of the houses of which a parliament consists. **4** (**chambers**) a suite of rooms used by eg a judge or lawyer. **5** an enclosed space or hollow; a cavity. **6** the compartment in a gun into which the bullet or cartridge is loaded. **7** a room or compartment with a particular function: *a decompression chamber*. [from Old French *chambre*, from Latin *camera*, room]

chambered tomb *Archaeol.* a megalithic monumental tomb from the Neolithic period used, originally in the E Mediterranean and later around the coasts of W Europe, for collective burial. They were probably associated with a cult of the dead, and were constructed of massive stone uprights and roofed with corbelled blocks, often surmounted with a large mound or cairn. Notable examples dating from c.3 000 BC are to be found on Malta, at Maes Howe on Orkney, and at West Kennet in Wiltshire.

Chamberlain, Sir (Joseph) Austen (1863–1937) English Conservative politician, eldest son of Joseph Chamberlain, born in Birmingham. He was elected a Liberal Unionist MP in 1892, and sat as a Conservative MP until his death. He was Chancellor of the Exchequer (1903–6, 1919–21), Secretary for India (1915–17), Unionist leader (1921–2), Foreign Secretary (1924–9), and First Lord of the Admiralty (1931). He received the 1925 Nobel Peace Prize for negotiating the Locarno Pact.

Chamberlain, Joseph (1836–1914) English politician, born in London. A successful businessman, he became Mayor of Birmingham (1873–5) and a Liberal MP (1876). He became President of the Board of Trade (1880), but in 1886 resigned over Gladstone's Home Rule bill, which split the Liberal Party. From 1889 he was Leader of the Liberal Unionists, and in the coalition government of 1895 took office in Robert Cecil's Conservative Cabinet as Secretary of State for the Colonies. In 1903 he resigned to be free to advocate his ideas on tariff reform, until he retired after a paralysing stroke in 1906.

Chamberlain, (Arthur) Neville (1869–1940) English politician and Prime Minister, son of Joseph Chamberlain by his second marriage. A Conservative MP from 1918, he was Chancellor of the Exchequer (1923–4 and 1931–7), and three times Minister for Health (1923, 1924–9 and 1931), where he effected notable social reforms. He played a leading part in the formation of the National Government (1931). As Prime Minister (1937–40), he advocated 'appeasement' of Italy and Germany, returning from Munich with his claim to have found 'peace in our time' (1938). He resigned as a result of criticism of his war leadership and initial military reverses.

Chamberlain, Owen (1920–) US physicist, born in San Francisco. Professor at the University of California, he shared the 1959 Nobel Prize for Physics with Emilio Segrè for the discovery of the antiproton (the negatively charged particle with the same mass as the proton).

Chamberlain, Wilt(on Norman), also called **Wilt the Stilt** (1936–) US basketball player, born in Philadelphia. He played for the Philadelphia 76ers against the New York Knickerbockers in Mar 1962, and scored 100 points in a game, the only man to do so in a major league game in the USA. He scored a record 4 029 points that season, and was seven times the National Basketball Association leading scorer (1960–6). During his career (1960–73) he scored 31 419 points at an average of 30.1 per game. His nickname derives from his height (1.85m).

chamberlain *noun* **1** a person who manages a royal or noble household. See also LORD CHAMBERLAIN. **2** the treasurer of a corporation, etc. [from Old French *chambrelenc*, from Latin *camera*, room]

chambermaid *noun* a woman in a hotel, etc who cleans bedrooms.

chamber music music composed for a small group of players, suitable for performing in a room rather than a concert hall, with only one player to a part.
◇ The term is conventionally applied only to instrumental music and typical forms include the trio sonata for two violins and bass (17c and early 18c), the string quartet for two violins, viola, and cello (18c to the present day), and other combinations including a piano or wind instruments, such as the piano quartet and quintet and the clarinet trio and quintet.

chamber of commerce an association of business people formed to promote local trade.

chamber orchestra a small orchestra that plays classical music.

chamberpot *noun* a receptacle for urine, etc for use in a bedroom.

Chambers, Ephraim (c.1680–1740) English encyclopedist, born in Kendal, Westmoreland. While apprenticed to a globemaker in London, he conceived the idea of a cyclopedia (2 folio vols, 1728). A French translation gave rise to the French *Encyclopédie*.

Chambers, Robert (1802–71) Scottish publisher and author, born in Peebles, Borders. He began as a bookseller in Edinburgh (1818), and wrote many books on Scottish history, people, and institutions, also contributing regularly to his brother's *Chambers's Edinburgh Journal*.

Chambers, William (1800–83) Scottish publisher and author, born in Peebles, Borders. In 1814 he was apprenticed to a bookseller in Edinburgh, and in 1819 began his own business. In 1832 he started *Chambers's Edinburgh Journal*, and soon after united with his brother Robert in founding the printing and publishing firm of W & R Chambers.

Chambord a village 18km/11mi E of Blois, France, noted for its chateau and estate. The chateau was once a hunting lodge of the counts of Blois, and was reconstructed (1519–33) by Francis I and Henry II as a royal residence. It is a World Heritage site.

chambré *adj., said of wine* at room temperature. [French, = put into a room]

chameleon *noun* **1** a slow-moving lizard, found mainly in Africa, with a sticky tongue that can be extended further than its own body length in order to trap prey. Its eyes can be swivelled independently of each other, and its granular skin changes colour rapidly in response to changes in its environment, acting as camouflage and as a means of communication with rivals. **2** someone who readily adapts to any new environment. **3** *derog.* a changeable, unreliable person. [from Greek *chamai*, on the ground + *leon*, lion]

chameleon

chamfer — *verb* (**chamfered**, **chamfering**) to give a smooth rounded shape to (an edge or corner). — *noun* a rounded or bevelled edge. [from Old French *chamfrein*, from *chant*, edge + *fraindre*, to break]

chamois *noun* (PL. **chamois**) **1** a small goat-like antelope of mountainous regions of Europe and SW Asia. **2** soft suede leather made from its skin or from that of sheep and goats. **3 shammy leather** a piece of this used as a polishing cloth for glass, etc. [from French *chamois*]

champ¹ — *verb trans., intrans.* to munch noisily. — *noun* the sound of munching.
— **champ at the bit** to be impatient to act. [imitative]

champ² *noun colloq.* a champion.

champagne *noun* **1** a sparkling white French wine traditionally drunk at celebrations. **2** a pale pinkish-yellow colour. [from *Champagne*, the French district where the wine was originally made]

Champagne-Ardenne POP (1991e) 1.3m, a region in NE France comprising the departments of Ardennes, Aube, Marne, and Haute-Marne. AREA 25 606sq km/9 884sq mi. HISTORY there was heavy fighting in Champagne during the last three wars between France and Germany. CAPITAL Châlons-sur-Marne. The region is noted for the production of champagne wine; the 120km-75mi-long 'Route du Champagne' runs through the vine-growing areas, starting at Rheims.

champers *noun colloq.* champagne.

champion — *noun* **1** in games, competitions, etc, a competitor that has defeated all others. **2** the supporter or defender of a person or cause. — *adj., adv. dialect* fine. — *verb* to strongly support or defend (a person or cause). [from Old French, from Latin *campio*, from *campus*, battlefield, place for exercise]

championship *noun* **1** a contest held to find the champion. **2** the title or position of champion. **3** the strong defending or supporting of a cause or person.

champlevé *noun* a technique of enamelling on metal. The surface of the metal is first engraved with the pattern or image, the engraved channels are filled with vitreous pastes or powders of different colours, and then the metal is fired. The technique was applied on an almost industrial scale at Limoges in France in the 18c. [French, = raised field]

Champollion, Jean François (1790–1832) French founder of Egyptology, born in Figeac. He was Professor of History at Grenoble (1809–16), and was best known for his use of the Rosetta Stone to decipher Egyptian hieroglyphics (1822–4). In 1831 a Chair of Egyptology was founded for him in the Collège de France.

Ch'an a general term for meditation in Chinese Buddhism, referring to a school which dates perhaps from the 6c. Combining Mahayana Buddhist teachings with those of Taoism, it emphasizes meditative experience rather than an intellectual approach.

Chance, Britton (1913–) US biochemist, born in Wilkes-Barre, Pennsylvania. Professor at the University of Pennsylvania, he demonstrated the existence of a complex between an enzyme and the substance it acts on (1943). Such complexes had long been theoretically presumed to exist as an essential stage in enzyme action but had not been detected.

chance — *noun* **1** the way that things happen unplanned and unforeseen; fate or luck as causing this to happen, or something that happens in this way. **2** an unforeseen, unexpected occurrence. **3** a possibility or probability. **4** a possible or probable success: *not stand a chance.* **5** an opportunity: *your big chance.* **6** risk, or a risk: *take a chance.* — *verb* **1** to risk. **2** *intrans.* to do or happen by chance: *I chanced to meet her.*
— **be in with a chance** to have some hope of success.
a chance in a million 1 the faintest possibility. **2** (*also* **chance of a lifetime**) an opportunity not to be missed.
chance it *or* **chance one's luck** *or* **chance one's arm** to take a risk.
chance on *or* **upon someone or something** to meet or find them by accident.
the chances are ... it is likely that ...
an eye to the main chance a tendency to act from motives of personal advantage rather than consideration for others.
on the off chance in hope rather than expectation.
an outside chance a very faint possibility.
take a chance on something to act in the hope of it being the case.
take one's chance *or* **chances** to make the most of whatever opportunities arise.
[from Old French *cheance*, from Latin *cadere*, to fall]

chancel *noun* the eastern part of a church, where the altar is, formerly separated from the nave by a screen. [from Latin *cancelli*, lattice, grating]

chancellery *noun* (PL. **chancelleries**) **1** the rank of a chancellor. **2** a chancellor's department or staff. **3** — Also called *chancery.* **a** the offices or residence of a chancellor. **b** the office of an embassy or consulate.

chancellor *noun* **1** the head of the government in certain European countries. **2** a state or legal official of various kinds. See also LORD CHANCELLOR. **3** in the UK, the honorary head of a university. **4** in the US, the president of a university or college. [from Latin *cancellarius*, court usher]

Chancellor of the Exchequer *noun* the chief minister of finance in the British government.

chancellorship *noun* the position or office of chancellor.

chancer *noun colloq., derog.* a person inclined to take any opportunity to profit, whether honestly or dishonestly.

chancery *noun* (PL. **chanceries**) **1** (*usually* **Chancery**) a division of the High Court of Justice. **2** a record office containing public archives. **3** — Also called *chancellery.* **a** the offices or residence of a chancellor. **b** the office of an embassy or consulate.

— **in chancery 1** *said of a legal case* being heard in a court of chancery. **2** in the charge of a lord chancellor. **3** in an awkward or difficult situation. [a contracted form of CHANCELLERY]

Chancery Division a division of the High Court of England and Wales created by the Judicature Acts (1873–5). Its functions include dealing with trusts, bankruptcy, and probate matters (eg the validity of wills). Historically, the Court of Chancery was the court of equity presided over by the Lord Chancellor.

Chan Chan an ancient Chimu capital in the Moche Valley, Peru, occupied from c.1000 to the Inca conquest in c.1470. Its residential area had a population of c.30 000. The centre is notable for its 10 rectangular enclosures, which were the administrative centres of the kingdom. It is a World Heritage site.

chanciness *noun* being chancy; uncertainty.

chancre *noun Medicine* a small hard sore, a sign of syphilis. [from Old French]

chancrous *adj.* relating to or of the nature of a chancre.

chancy *adj.* (**chancier, chanciest**) risky; uncertain.

chandelier *noun* an ornamental light-fitting hanging from the ceiling, with branching holders for candles or light-bulbs. [from Old French *chandelier*, candle-holder]

Chandigarh POP (1991) 503 000, a city and union territory in NW India. AREA 114sq km/44sq mi. It serves as the joint state capital of the Punjab and Haryana. The city, designed by architect Le Corbusier, includes an 8km/5mi green belt. NOTABLE FEATURE the largest rose garden in Asia.

Chandler, Raymond (Thornton) (1888–1959) US detective-story writer, born in Chicago. He worked as a freelance writer in London and served in the Canadian army and RAF during World War I. His novels featuring the private-eye Philip Marlowe include *The Big Sleep* (1939), *Farewell, My Lovely* (1940), and *The Long Goodbye* (1953). Many of his novels have been made into films.

Chandler, Seth Carlo (1846–1913) US astronomer, born in Boston. After work at the US Coast Survey and at Harvard, he devoted himself to private research from 1885. He is best known for his discovery of the 'Chandler wobble', the periodic variations in latitude of points on the Earth's surface due to movement of the geographic poles with a period of 430 days (14 months).

chandler *noun* **1** a dealer in ship's supplies and equipment. **2** a dealer in certain other goods: *corn chandler.* **3** *old use* a grocer. **4** *old use* a dealer in candles, oil, etc. [from Old French *chandelier*, dealer in candles]

chandlery *noun* (PL. **chandleries**) **1** a place where candles are kept. **2** goods sold by a chandler.

Chandos an English family, descended from a follower of William the Conqueror. Its greatest member was Sir John Chandos, Edward the Black Prince's follower, who fell in battle (1370). A descendant, Sir John Brydges, was created Baron Chandos in 1554. James Brydges (1673–1744) was created Duke of Chandos in 1719. In 1796 the title passed by marriage to the family of Grenville, until 1889 Dukes of Buckingham and Chandos.

Chandrasekhar, Subrahmanyan (1910–) Indian-born US astrophysicist, born in Lahore (now in Pakistan). Educated at Cambridge, in 1936 he moved to the USA to work at the University of Chicago and Yerkes Observatory. He showed that at the end of their lives, stars of less than a certain critical mass will collapse to form white dwarfs, small hot stars in

which material is compressed to densities of millions of times that of ordinary matter. He shared the 1983 Nobel Prize for Physics with William Fowler.

Chanel, Coco, originally **Gabrielle Chanel** (c.1883–1971) French couturier, born in Saumur. She worked as a milliner until 1912, and after World War I opened a couture house in Paris. She revolutionized women's fashions during the 1920s with her designs which included the 'chemise' dress and the collarless cardigan jacket. Many of the features she introduced, such as the vogue for costume jewellery and the 'Chanel suit', still retain their popularity. She retired in 1938, but made a successful comeback in 1954.

Chaney, Lon, originally **Alonso** (1883–1930) US film actor, born in Colorado Springs. He was famous for spine-chilling deformed villains and other horrific parts, as in *The Hunchback of Notre Dame* (1923) and *The Phantom of the Opera* (1925), and was called the 'man of a thousand faces'.

Changan see XI'AN.

Changchun *or* **Ch'angch'un** POP (1990) 2.2m, the capital of Jilin province, NE China. It lies on the Yitong R in the centre of China's NE plain. HISTORY developed during Japanese military occupation between 1933 and 1945 as the capital of Manchukuo. NOTABLE FEATURE Changchun film studio.

change — *verb* **1** *trans., intrans.* to make or become different. **2** (**change one thing for another**) to give, leave, or substitute one thing for another. **3** to exchange (usually one's position or function) with another person, etc: *change places.* **4** *trans., intrans.* (**change into** *or* **out of something**) to remove (clothes, etc) and replace them with clean or different ones. **5** to put a fresh nappy or clothes on (a baby), or clean sheets on (a bed). **6** *trans., intrans.* (**change into something**) to make into or become something different. **7** to obtain or supply another kind of money for: *change pounds into francs.* **8** *intrans., trans.* to go from one vehicle, usually a train or bus, to another to continue a journey: *change trains at Didcot / we need to change at the depot.* **9** *intrans., trans.* to put a vehicle engine into (another gear): *change into third.* — *noun* **1** the process of changing or an instance of it. **2** the replacement of one thing with another; the leaving of one thing for another. **3** a variation, especially a welcome one, from one's regular habit, etc: *eat out for a change.* **4** the leaving of (one vehicle) for another during a journey. **5** a fresh set (of clothes) for changing into. **6** (**small** *or* **loose change**) coins as distinct from notes. **7** coins or notes given in exchange for ones of higher value. **8** money left over or returned from the amount given in payment. **9** (*usually* **changes**) any of the various orders in which a set of church bells can be rung. **10** (**change of life**) *colloq.* the menopause.
— **change down** to change to a lower gear.
change hands to pass into different ownership.
change one's mind to adopt a different intention or opinion.
change over 1 to change from one preference or situation to another. **2** to exchange (jobs, roles, etc): *I drove for two hours, then we changed over.*
change up to change to a higher gear.
get no change out of someone *colloq.* to get no help from them.
[from French *changer*]

changeability *or* **changeableness** *noun* **1** a tendency to be changeable; fickleness. **2** the power of being changed.

changeable *adj.* **1** inclined or liable to change often. **2** able to be changed.

changeably *adv.* in a changeable or changing way.

changeless *adj.* never-changing.

changelessly *adv.* without change.

changeling *noun* in folklore, a child substituted by the fairies for an unbaptized human baby. [see CHANGE]

change-over *noun* a change from one preference or situation to another.

change-ringing *noun* a British form of bell-ringing devised by the 17c Cambridge printer Fabian Stedman. A set of differently tuned bells is rung in various permutations so that no sequence (or 'change') is sounded more than once. With a full diatonic scale of eight bells 40 320 changes are possible: a peal of 5 000 changes takes as much as three hours to ring.

changing-room *noun* a room in a sports centre, etc where one can change one's clothes.

Changsha *or* **Ch'angsha** POP (1990) 1.4m, a river port and the capital of Hunan province, SE China. It lies on the lower Xiang R, in intensively cultivated lowlands. The town was founded before 1000 BC and was an early craft, industrial, and educational centre. Changsha was established as a foreign trade port in 1904. NOTABLE FEATURES Hunan Provincial Museum; Yuelushan Park, containing the Lushan Temple (founded in AD 268), Kaifu Temple (896).

Chania *or* **Canea** POP (1991) 66 000, the capital town of Chania department, Crete, on the N shore of the island. It was founded in the 13c. The town was capital of Crete until 1971.

channel — *noun* **1** any natural or artificially constructed water course, eg the bed of a stream, or an irrigation channel. **2** the part of a river, waterway, etc, that is deep enough for navigation by ships. **3** a wide stretch of water, especially between an island and a continent, eg the English Channel. **4** *Electron.* the frequency band that is assigned for sending or receiving a clear radio or television signal. **5** a groove, furrow or any long narrow cut, especially one along which something moves. **6** *Comput.* the path along which electrical signals or data flow. **7** (**channels**) a means by which information, etc is communicated, obtained or received. **8** a course, project, etc into which some resource may be directed: *a channel for one's energies.* **9** (**the Channel**) the English Channel, the stretch of sea between England and France. — *verb* (**channelled, channelling**) **1** to make a channel or channels in. **2** to convey (a liquid, information, etc) through a channel. **3** to direct (a resource, eg talent, energy, money) into a course, project, etc. [from Old French *chanel*]

Channel Islands, French **Iles Normandes** an island group of the British Isles in the English Channel, W of the Cotentin Peninsula of Normandy. A dependent territory of the British Crown, it has individual legislative assemblies and legal system and is divided into the Bailiwicks of Jersey and of Guernsey. Both English and Norman-French are spoken. AREA 194sq km/75sq mi. MAIN ISLANDS Guernsey, Jersey, Alderney, Sark; other islands include Herm, Jethou, Brechou, the Caskets, the Minquiers, and the Chauseys. The islands were granted to the Dukes of Normandy in the 10c; the only part of Normandy remaining with England after 1204; occupied by Germany in World War II. GOVERNMENT a Bailiff presides over the Royal Court and the Representative Assembly (the States). ECONOMY fruit, vegetables; flowers; dairy produce, Jersey and Guernsey cattle; tourism; used as a tax haven.

channel swimming swimming the English Channel from shore to shore. The first to achieve the crossing without the aid of a life jacket was Capt Matthew Webb (1848–83), who swam from Dover to Calais on 24–5 August, 1875. The record for the fastest crossing stands at 7h 40min, held by US swimmer Penny Dean.

Channel Tunnel a tunnel from Cheriton near Folkestone in England to Sangatte near Calais, begun in 1987, and completed in 1994. It consists of twin rail tunnels 50km/31mi long (38km/23mi of which are under the sea).

chansons de geste Old French epic poems popular in the 12c–14c, which celebrated the exploits of noblemen and feudal lords. Different cycles centre on Charlemagne (including the *Chanson de Roland*), and the Crusades. [French, = 'songs of deeds']

chant — *verb trans., intrans.* **1** to recite in a singing voice. **2** to keep repeating, especially loudly and rhythmically. — *noun* **1** a type of singing used in religious services for passages in prose, with a simple melody and several words sung on one note. **2** a phrase or slogan constantly repeated, especially loudly and rhythmically. [from Old French *chant*, song, and *chanter*, to sing]

chanter *noun* **1** the pipe on which the melody is played on a set of bagpipes. **2** this pipe adapted for separate use as a practice instrument. **3** someone who chants. [from Old French *chanteor*, singer]

chanterelle *noun* an edible yellow fungus with a trumpet-shaped cap. [from French *chanterelle*, from Latin *cantharellus*, diminutive of *cantharus*, tankard]

chanting *noun* **1** performing a chant. **2** the sound of a chant or chants.

chantry *noun* (PL. **chantries**) a chapel, or a sum of money, provided for the chanting of masses. [from Old French *chanter*, sing]

chanty see SHANTY[2].

Chanukkah same as HANUKKAH.

Chaos in Greek mythology, the primeval state of emptiness (according to Hesiod), but in later Greek philosophy (according to Ovid) a mass of muddled forms and elements which separated out into the universe.

chaos *noun* **1** complete confusion; utter disorder. **2** *Physics* a state of disorder and irregularity that is an intermediate stage between highly ordered motion and entirely random motion. Chaos is present in most real systems, such as weather patterns and the motion of planets around the Sun, and the long-term behaviour of chaotic systems cannot be predicted. [from Greek *khaos*]

chaotic *adj.* lacking any order; utterly confused.

chaotically *adv.* in a chaotic way.

chap[1] *noun colloq.* a man or boy; a fellow. [formerly, a customer; a shortened from CHAPMAN]

chap[2] — *verb trans., intrans.* (**chapped, chapping**) *said of skin* to make or become roughened, sore, and red from rubbing or exposure to cold. — *noun* a sore and inflamed or roughened patch on the skin. [from Middle English *chappen*]

chap[3] *noun* **1** a chop or jaw. **2** a cheek. [ultimately from Norse *kjaptr*, jaw]

chap. *abbrev.* chapter.

Chapala, Lake the largest lake in Mexico. It is situated on the central plateau, 48km/30mi S of Guadalajara, in the SW part of the country. AREA 3 366sq km/1 299sq mi. It is 77km/48mi long E–W and is c.16km/10mi wide. The resort town of Chapala lies on the N shore.

chaparral *noun* an area of dense undergrowth, shrubs and small trees. [from Spanish *chaparral*, from *chaparro*, evergreen oak]

chapati *or* **chapatti** *noun* in Indian cooking, a thin flat portion of unleavened bread. [from Hindi *capati*]

chapel *noun* **1** a recess within a church or cathedral, with its own altar. **2** a place of worship attached to a house, school, etc. **3** *especially in England and Wales* a place of Nonconformist worship, or the services held there. **4** an association of workers in a newspaper office, or a printing- or publishing-house. [from Latin *cappella*,

cloak, ie the cloak of St Martin, which was kept in a shrine, to which the word became attached]

Chapelcross a nuclear power station in Dumfries and Galloway region, Scotland, 4km/2.3mi NE of Annan. Scotland's first gas-cooled reactors came into commercial operation here in 1959–60.

chaperone *or* **chaperon** — *noun* **1** *formerly* an older woman accompanying a younger unmarried one on social occasions, for respectability's sake. **2** an older person accompanying and supervising a group of young people. — *verb* to act as chaperone to. [from Old French *chaperone*, hood]

chaplain *noun* a clergyman or -woman attached to a chapel, to a school, hospital or other institution, or to the armed forces. [from Latin *cappellanus*, custodian of St Martin's cloak; see etymology for CHAPEL]

chaplaincy *noun* (PL. **chaplaincies**) the position or office of chaplain.

chaplet *noun* **1** a wreath of flowers or a band of gold, etc for the head. **2** a string of beads, especially one used by Roman Catholics as a short version of the rosary. [from Old French *chapel*, wreath, hat]

Chaplin, Charlie, in full **Sir Charles Spencer Chaplin** (1889–1977) English film actor and director, born in London. In his numerous early comedies he adopted the bowler hat, out-turned feet, moustache, and walking cane which became his hallmark, as in *The Kid* (1914) and *The Gold Rush* (1924). His art was essentially suited to the silent film, and when sound arrived he experimented with new forms, as in *City Lights* (1931), with music only, and *Modern Times* (1936), part speech and part mime. *Limelight* (1952) won him a Best Original Score Oscar, the year his left-wing sympathies caused him to leave the USA for Switzerland.

Chapman, George (c.1559–1634) English poet and dramatist, born near Hitchin, Hertfordshire. He is best known for his translations of Homer's *Iliad* (1598–1611) and *Odyssey* (1616). With Ben Jonson and John Marston he composed *Eastward Ho* (1605), and his numerous dramas include the tragedy *Bussy d'Ambois* (1607).

Chapman, Sydney (1888–1979) English physicist and geophysicist, born in Eccles, Lancashire. Professor at Manchester, Imperial College in London, and Oxford, he worked in the USA from 1954. He made important contributions to the kinetic theory of gases, and developed the theory of thermal diffusion. He also produced the first satisfactory theory of geomagnetic storms, and studied atmospheric tides.

chapman *noun* (PL. **chapmen**) *Hist.* a travelling dealer; a pedlar. [from Anglo-Saxon *ceapman*, from *ceap*, trading]

Chappaquiddick an island to the E of Martha's Vineyard Island, USA, in the Nantucket Sound, off the SE coast of Massachusetts. [Algonkian, = separated-island-at]

chapped *adj., said of the skin* dry and cracked.

chappie *noun colloq.* diminutive of **chap**[1].

chaps *pl. noun* a cowboy's protective leather riding leggings, worn over the trousers. [from Spanish *chaparejos*]

chapter *noun* **1** one of the numbered or titled sections into which a book is divided. **2** a period associated with certain happenings: *an unfortunate chapter in my life.* **3** a sequence or series: *a chapter of accidents.* **4** *North Amer., esp. US* a branch of a society, or its meeting. **5** the body, or a meeting, of canons of a cathedral, or of the members of a religious order.

— **chapter and verse** an exact reference, description of circumstances, etc quoted in justification of a statement, etc.

[from Old French *chapitre*, from Latin *caput*, head]

chapter house the building used for the meetings of a cathedral chapter.

char[1] *verb trans., intrans.* (**charred, charring**) **1** to blacken by burning. **2** *said of wood* to turn into charcoal by partial burning. [shortened from CHARCOAL]

char[2] — *verb intrans.* (**charred, charring**) to do paid cleaning work in someone's house, an office, etc. — *noun colloq.* a charwoman. [from Anglo-Saxon *cierran*, to turn; later, as *chare*, to accomplish (a task)]

char[3] *noun old colloq. use* tea. [from Hindi *ca* and Chinese *ch'a*]

char[4] *or* **charr** *noun* (PL. **char, charr, chars, charrs**) a small fish of the salmon family found in cold northern lakes, rivers or seas.

charabanc *noun old use* a single-decker bus for tours, sightseeing, etc; a coach. [from French *char à bancs*, carriage with seats]

character *noun* **1** the combination of qualities that makes up a person's nature or personality. **2** the combination of qualities that typifies anything. **3** type or kind. **4** strong, admirable qualities such as determination, courage, and honesty. **5** interesting qualities that make for individuality: *a house with character.* **6** a person in a story or play. **7** an odd or amusing person. **8** *colloq.* a person. **9** reputation: *blacken someone's character.* **10** a letter, number, or other written or printed symbol. — **in** *or* **out of character** typical or untypical of a person's nature. [from Greek *charakter*, engraving tool, branding-iron, hence a distinctive mark impressed on something]

character actor an actor who specializes in character parts.

character assassination the destruction of a person's good name, reputation, etc, by slander, rumour, etc.

character code *Comput.* the particular binary code used to represent a character in a computer, eg ASCII.

characteristic *adj.* **1** typical. **2** distinctive.

characteristically *adv.* in a characteristic way; typically.

characterization *or* **characterisation** *noun* **1** characterizing. **2** the process by which a writer builds up the characters in a story or play so that their individual personalities emerge. **3** the art of an actor in giving a convincing performance as a particular character.

characterize *or* **characterise** *verb* **1** to describe or give the chief qualities of. **2** to be a distinctive and typical feature of.

characterless *adj. derog.* dull; uninteresting; lacking individuality.

character part a colourful part in a play or film, giving good opportunities for characterization.

character sketch a quick description of someone, mentioning his or her chief qualities.

charade *noun derog.* a ridiculous pretence; a farce. [from French *charade*, from Provençal *charrado*, entertainment]

charades *noun* a party game in which players act out each syllable of a word, or each word of a book title, etc in successive scenes, while the watching players try to guess the complete word or title.

charcoal *noun* **1** a black material, a form of carbon, produced by partially burning wood, used for drawing and as a fuel. **2** a drawing done in charcoal. **3** (*also* **charcoal grey**) a dark grey colour. [from Middle English *charcole*]

Charcot, Jean Martin (1825–93) French pathologist and neurologist, born and educated in Paris. Working at the Salpêtrière hospital from 1862, he contributed much to knowledge of chronic and nervous diseases, and made important studies of hypnotism. His pupils included Sigmund Freud.

Chardonnay *noun* **1** a grape variety, originally from the Burgundy region of France, now grown also in California, Australia, New Zealand, etc. **2** a dry white wine made from this grape. [from French *Chardon*]

Chargaff, Erwin (1905–) Czech-born US biochemist, born in Czernowitz (now in the Ukraine). Professor at Columbia University, New York, his work showed that the base composition of DNA is characteristic of a species and identical in different tissues of the same animal, and that the DNA bases occur in pairs. This was important evidence in favour of the double helix structure of DNA, proposed in 1953.

charge *verb* **1** to ask for (an amount) as the price of something: *charged us £20 for mending the window.* **2** to ask (someone) to pay an amount for something: *I'll have to charge you.* **3** (**charge something to someone**) to record it as a debt against them: *charge the breakages to me.* **4** to accuse (someone) officially of a crime: *was charged with manslaughter.* **5** *trans., intrans.* to rush at in attack. **6** *intrans.* to rush. **7** *formal* to order officially: *she was charged to appear in court.* **8** (**charge someone with something**) *formal* to give them a task or responsibility: *he was charged with looking after the books.* **9** to load (a gun, etc). **10** *old use, formal* to fill up: *charge your glasses.* **11** *said of a battery, etc* to store up, or cause to store up, electricity. **12** to load or saturate: *the liquid is made fizzy by charging it with carbon dioxide.* **13** to fill: *the moment was charged with emotion.* — *noun* **1** an amount charged; a price, fee, or cost. **2** control, care, responsibility; supervision or guardianship: *in charge of repairs / the police arrived and took charge.* **3** something or someone, eg a child, that is in one's care. **4** something of which one is accused: *a charge of murder / they face several charges.* **5** a rushing attack. **6** an amount of electricity carried by something, or stored in a device such as a battery. **7** a quantity of material appropriate for filling something. **8** an amount of explosive for loading into a gun, etc; a cartridge or shell. **9** an order. **10** a task, duty, or burden: *undertake a difficult charge.* **11** a debt or financial liability. — **press** *or* **prefer charges** to charge someone officially with a crime, etc. [from Old French *chargier* or *charger*, from Latin *carricare*, to load a vehicle]

chargeable *adj.* **1** *said of costs, etc* that may or should be charged to someone. **2** permitted or liable to be charged: *a fee is chargeable for missed appointments.* **3** incurring tax or duty: *chargeable assets.* **4** *said of an offence* serious enough to justify a legal charge by the police.

charge card a small card entitling one to make purchases on credit, supplied to one by a shop with which one has a credit account.

charge-coupled device (ABBREV. **CCD**) **1** *Comput.* a memory unit in which information is stored using electrically charged particles that circulate continuously through cells printed on a semiconductor. The memory storage capacity of a single computer chip can be greatly enhanced in this way. **2** *Electron.* a sensor in a video camera, made up of a mosaic of minute photo-conductive diodes corresponding to the pixels and lines of a television system. Charges produced in each element by incident light are stored until read off in the required scanning sequence.

charged *adj.* filled with excitement or other strong emotion: *the charged atmosphere in the room.*

chargé d'affaires (PL. **chargés d'affaires**) a deputy to, or substitute for, an ambassador. [French, = person in charge of affairs]

charge hand the deputy to a foreman in a factory, etc.

charge nurse a nurse in charge of a hospital ward, especially if a male; the equivalent of a sister.

Charge of the Light Brigade an incident during the battle of Balaclava (1854), in which the Light Brigade under Lord Cardigan misunderstood an order given by the commanding officer Lord Raglan, charged the main Russian artillery, and suffered massive loss of life.

Charge of the Light Brigade, The a poem by Alfred Lord Tennyson (1854). The poem contains the controversial line: 'Someone had blundered'.

charger *noun Hist.* a strong horse used by a knight in battle, etc.

Chari, River a river in SW Chad. It flows 800km/500mi NW to join the R Logone at Ndjamena, where it forms the border between Chad and Cameroon before entering L Chad. The length, including the main headstream (R Bamingui), is 1 060km/660mi.

charily *adv.* with a chary or guarded manner.

chariness *noun* being chary.

Charing Cross an area in central London, UK, traditionally regarded as being the heart of the city. It takes its name from a cross erected to mark the site of the resting-place of Queen Eleanor, who died in 1290.

chariot *noun Hist.* a two-wheeled vehicle pulled by horses, used in ancient times for warfare or racing. [diminutive of Old French *char*, carriage]

charioteer *noun* a chariot-driver.

Chariots of Fire a British film directed by Hugh Hudson (1981). Based on the story of Scottish Olympic champion runner Eric Liddell (played by Ian Charleson) who refused to race on the Sabbath, it won four Academy Awards, including Best Original Score for its theme music.

charisma *noun* (PL. **charismata**) **1** a strong ability to attract people, and inspire loyalty and admiration. **2** *Relig.* a divinely bestowed talent or power. [from Greek *charis*, grace]

charismatic *adj.* relating to or having charisma; attracting loyalty and admiration.

charismatic movement a movement within Christianity that emphasizes the power of the Holy Spirit at work within individuals, manifesting itself as an ability to heal, a talent for prophecy, etc.

charitable *adj.* **1** kind and understanding in one's attitude to others. **2** generous in assisting people in need. **3** relating to, belonging to, or in the nature of, a charity: *charitable institutions.* [from Old French, from *charite*, charity]

charitably *adv.* in a charitable way; with generosity.

charity *noun* (PL. **charities**) **1** assistance given to those in need. **2** an organization established to provide such assistance. **3** kindness and understanding in one's attitude towards, or judgement of, other people. **4** *Biblical* compassionate love for others. [from Old French *charite*, from Latin *caritas*, love]

charlady see CHAR[2].

charlatan *noun derog.* a person posing as an expert in some profession, eg medicine. [from Old French, from Italian *ciarlare*, to chatter]

charlatanism *noun* the practices of a charlatan.

Charlemagne *or* **Charles the Great** (742–814) King of the Franks (771–814) and Emperor of the West (800–14), the eldest son of Pepin the Short. He defeated the Saxons (772–804), as well as the Lombards (773–4), fought the Arabs in Spain, and took control of most of Christian W Europe. In 800 he was crowned emperor by Pope Leo III. In his later years, a period that has become known as the

'Carolingian Renaissance', he consolidated his vast empire, building palaces and churches, and promoting Christianity, education, agriculture, the arts, manufacture, and commerce.

Charleroi POP (1992e) 207 000, a town in Hainaut province, SW Belgium, on the R Sambre. HISTORY formerly a fortress; in World War I Charleroi was the location of a German attack against the French (1914).

Charles I (of England) (1600–49) King of Scotland and England (1625–49), born in Dunfermline, Scotland. He failed in his bid to marry the Infanta Maria of Spain (1623), marrying instead the French princess Henrietta Maria (1609–69). This was the first event to disturb the nation, for the marriage Articles permitted her the free exercise of the Catholic religion. Three parliaments were summoned and dissolved in the first four years of his reign, then for 11 years Charles ruled without one, using instead judges and Prerogative Courts (those that had jurisdiction over testamentary matters). He warred with France (1627–9), and in 1630 made peace with Spain, but his continuing need for money led to unpopular economic policies, and he further alienated the realm in his attempt to anglicize the Scottish Church (1639). In 1642 Charles entered into the Civil War, but his cause was devastated at Naseby (14 Jun 1645), and he surrendered to the Scots at Newark (1646). After many negotiations, during which his attempts at duplicity exasperated opponents, and a second Civil War (1646–8), he came to trial at Westminster, where his refusal to plead was interpreted as a confession of guilt, so he was beheaded (30 Jan 1649).

Charles I (of Austria-Hungary) (1887–1922) Emperor of Austria (Karl I) and King of Hungary (Károly IV), born in Persenbeug Castle, Austria. He became heir presumptive to both thrones on the assassination (1914) of his uncle, Archduke Franz Ferdinand, and then succeeded his great-uncle, Francis Joseph (1916), but was compelled to abdicate in 1918. Two attempts at restoration in Hungary (1921) failed, and he died in exile in Madeira.

Charles II (of England) (1630–85) King of Scotland and England (1660–85), born in London. The son of Charles I, as Prince of Wales he sided with his father in the Civil War, and was then forced into exile. On his father's execution (1649), he was crowned king at Scone (1651) and marched on England, but his forces met defeat at Worcester (1651). He remained in exile until summoned back as king (1660) by an impoverished England that was tired of military despotism. In 1662 he married the Portuguese Princess Catherine of Braganza, who bore him no heir, though Charles was the father of many illegitimate children. His war with Holland (1665–7) was unpopular, and led to the dismissal of his adviser, Lord Clarendon (1667), who was replaced by a court cabal. He negotiated skilfully between conflicting political and religious pressures, including the trumped-up 'Popish Plot', and was succeeded by his brother James.

Charles II (of Spain) (1661–1700) King of Spain (1665–1700), born in Madrid, the son of Philip IV. He went to war against France in the Grand Alliance, and precipitated the War of the Spanish Succession by naming in his will Philip of Anjou as his successor. He was the last ruler of the Spanish Habsburg dynasty, and his reign marked the end of Spanish power in Europe.

Charles IV (of Spain) (1788–1819) King of Spain (1738–1808), born in Portici, Naples, the son of Charles III. His government was largely controlled by his wife Maria Louisa (1751–1819) and her favourite, Manuel de Godoy. Nelson destroyed his fleet at Trafalgar, and in 1808 he abdicated under pressure from Napoleon, in favour of Napoleon's brother Joseph. He spent the rest of his life in exile.

Charles V (of France), known as **the Wise** (1337–80) King of France, born in Vincennes. He ascended the throne in 1364, and in a series of victories regained most of the territory lost to the English in the Hundred Years War.

Charles V (Emperor) (1500–58) Holy Roman Emperor (1519–56), born in Ghent. The son of Philip of Burgundy and Joanna of Spain, in 1517 he was made joint ruler of Spain with his mother, and in 1519 was elected to the Holy Roman Empire. His warfare against Francis I of France dominated W European affairs, leading on the defeat of Francis in 1525 to the formation of the Holy League against Charles by Pope Clement VII, Henry VIII, Francis, and the Venetians. In 1527 Rome was sacked and the Pope imprisoned, and although Charles disclaimed any part of it, the Peace of Cambrai (1529) left him master of Italy. At the Diet of Augsburg (1530) he confirmed the 1521 Edict of Worms, which had condemned Martin Luther, and the Protestants formed the League of Schmalkald. After further battles, in 1538 the Pope, Francis, and Charles agreed at Nice to a 10-year truce, but Charles's league with the Pope drove the Protestants to rebellion. They were crushed at Mühlberg (1547), but in 1552 Charles was defeated by Maurice of Saxony, and Protestantism received legal recognition. In 1555 he divided the Empire between his son (Philip II of Spain) and his brother (Ferdinand I), and retired to the monastery of Yuste in Spain.

Charles VI (of France), known as **the Foolish** (1368–1422) King of France, born in Paris. He came to the throne as a young boy in 1380. From 1392 he suffered from fits of madness, and Henry V defeated him at the battle of Agincourt (1415).

Charles VII (of France), known as **the Victorious** (1403–61) King of France (1422–61), born in Paris. When he came to the throne, the north of the country was in English hands, with Henry VI proclaimed King of France. However Joan of Arc incited the nobles and the people, leading to the end of the siege of Orléans (1429). Under his rule the English gradually lost nearly all they had gained in France.

Charles IX (of France) (1550–74) King of France (1560–74), born in St Germain-en-Laye. The second son of Henry II and Catherine de' Medici, he was successor to his brother, Francis II. His reign coincided with the Wars of Religion, and he was largely controlled by his mother, whose counsels drove him to authorize the slaughter of the Parisian Huguenots in the St Bartholomew's Day Massacre (1572).

Charles X (of France) (1757–1836) the last Bourbon King of France (1824–30), born in Versailles, the grandson of Louis XV. He married Maria Theresa of Savoy in 1773 and lived in England during the French Revolution. In 1814 he returned to France as Lt-General of the kingdom and then succeeded his brother Louis XVIII, but his repressive rule led to revolution, and his eventual abdication and exile.

Charles XII (of Sweden) (1682–1718) King of Sweden (1697–1718), born in Stockholm, the son of Charles XI. An alliance against him was made by Denmark, Poland and Russia, but he attacked Denmark (1699), compelling the Danes to sue for peace, then defeated the Russians at Narva (1700), and dethroned Augustus II of Poland (1704). He invaded Russia again in 1707, and was eventually defeated at Poltava (1709). He escaped to Turkey but in 1714 returned and formed another army to attack Norway, but was killed at the siege of Halden. By then Sweden was exhausted by war and ceased to be numbered among the great powers.

Charles XIV (of Sweden), originally **Jean Baptiste Jules Bernadotte** (1763–1844) King of Sweden (1818–44), born in Pau, France. He joined the French army in 1780, and rose to become Marshal in 1804. In 1799 he was Minister of War, and for his conduct at Austerlitz was named Prince of Pontecorvo (1805). After fighting in several Napoleonic campaigns (1805–9), in 1810 he was elected heir to the throne of Sweden, when he turned Protestant and changed his name to Charles John. He joined in fighting against Napoleon at Leipzig (1813), then in 1814 was rewarded with the Kingdom of Norway, recreating the union of the two countries.

Charles (Philip Arthur George), Prince of Wales (1948–) British prince and heir-apparent to the throne, eldest son of Elizabeth II and Prince Philip, Duke of Edinburgh, born in London (at Buckingham Palace). He was given the title of Prince of Wales in 1958, and invested at Caernarvon in 1969. He served in the RAF and Royal Navy (1971–6), and in 1981 married Lady Diana Frances, youngest daughter of the 8th Earl Spencer; they separated in 1992. They have two children: William Arthur Philip Louis (1982–) and Henry Charles Albert David (1984–). Often outspoken about his views on modern architecture, education and the environment, he has published several books, including some children's stories and his own water colours.

Charles Martel, also called **the Hammer** (c.688–741) the illegitimate son of Pepin II of Héristal, who in 1719 became mayor of the palace of Austrasia and effective ruler of the Franks. He conducted many campaigns against the Frisians and Saxons, and in Aquitaine, Bavaria, and Burgundy, and halted Muslim expansion in W Europe at the battle of Poitiers (732). By 723 he was the undisputed head of the Carolingian family, and though he ruled much of Gaul, he was never crowned king, but left the Frankish kingdom to his sons, Carolman and Pepin.

Charles a male first name, popular among European leaders since Charlemagne (Charles the Great), Holy Roman Emperor in the 9c. [from French *Charles*, from a Germanic word meaning 'man', a variant of Anglo-Saxon *ceorl*]

Charles, Jacques-Alexandre-César (1746–1823) French experimental physicist, born in Beaugency. He discovered 'Charles's law', relating the temperature of a gas to its volume, and was the first to make a hydrogen balloon ascent (1783). Professor in Paris, he also invented several ingenious scientific instruments.

Charles, Ray, originally **Ray Charles Robinson** (1930–) US singer and pianist, born in Albany, Georgia. Blind from the age of five, and orphaned at 15, he went to Seattle and, after writing arrangements for several pop groups, was contracted to Atlantic Records in 1952. With *I've got a Woman* (1955) he established an influential new style of rhythm and blues which introduced elements of gospel music.

Charles's law *Physics* a law which states that, if the pressure remains constant, the volume of a given mass of gas is directly proportional to its absolute temperature. [named after the French physicist Jacques Charles]

Charleston POP (1990) 250 000, the capital of the state of West Virginia, USA, and the state's largest city. It lies at the confluence of the Elk and Kanawha rivers, in Kanawha County. It is an important transportation and trading centre. HISTORY developed around Fort Lee in the 1780s; achieved city status in 1870; capital of West Virginia from 1870 until 1875 and from 1885.

Charleston POP (1990) 507 000, the seat of Charleston County, SE South Carolina, USA. It is a port on the Atlantic Ocean, at the mouths of the Ashley and Cooper rivers. HISTORY founded in 1670 (oldest city in the state); survived attacks by a British fleet in 1776 and 1779; finally captured and held by the British in 1780–2; the Confederate attack on nearby Fort Sumter (1861) began the Civil War; evacuated by Confederate forces in 1865 after a two-year siege; devastated by an earthquake in 1886; badly damaged by Hurricane Hugo in 1989. NOTABLE FEATURES

Charleston Museum; Old Slave Mart Museum and Gallery; Gibbes Art Gallery; several old colonial buildings.

Charleston, Battles of the victorious British siege of Charleston, South Carolina (11 Feb–12 May 1780), which marked the beginning of the Southern phase of British strategy in the US War of Independence.

Charleston *noun* a vigorous dance popular in the 1920s, its characteristic step being a pivot on one leg with a side-kick of the other from the knee. [from *Charleston*, a town in South Carolina, USA]

Charlestown POP (1985) 2 000, the capital and port of Nevis I, St Christopher-Nevis.

charlie *noun Brit. colloq.* a fool.

charlock *noun* a rough hairy annual plant (*Sinapis arvensis*) with toothed and lobed leaves and yellow cross-shaped flowers. It is related to mustard, and was formerly grown as a leaf vegetable, but is now a pernicious weed of arable land. [from Anglo-Saxon *cerlic*]

Charlotte POP (1990) 396 000, the seat of Mecklenburg County, S North Carolina, USA, and the largest city in the state. HISTORY settled in c.1750; the Mecklenburg Declaration of Independence was signed here in 1775; James K Polk, 11th President of the USA, was born here in 1795.

Charlotte a female first name, especially popular in the 18c–19c. [a French feminine diminutive of CHARLES]

Charlotte Amalie, formerly **St Thomas** (1921–36) POP (1990) 12 000, the port capital of the US Virgin Is, Lesser Antilles, Caribbean Sea. Situated on the S coast of St Thomas I, it was founded by the Danes in 1672. It is an important cruise ship port.

Charlottenburg Palace a palace in Berlin, built 1695–1796 by Elector Frederick I for his wife, Sophie Charlotte. The building houses a museum.

Charlottesville POP (1990) 131 000, the seat of Albemarle County, central Virginia, USA. It is an independent city situated on the R Rivanna, 112km/70mi NW of Richmond. It was settled in the 1730s. NOTABLE FEATURES Ash Lawn (home of President James Monroe); Monticello (home of President Thomas Jefferson) and the University of Virginia are World Heritage sites. [named after the wife of King George III]

Charlottetown POP (1991) 15 000, the provincial capital of Prince Edward I, NE Canada, situated on Hillsborough Bay, in Queen's county. HISTORY founded by the French in the 1720s; capital since 1765.

Charlton, Bobby (Robert) (1937–) English footballer, born in Ashington, Northumberland. He was a professional footballer with Manchester United (1954–73) and made his full-team début in 1956. He survived the Munich air disaster (1958) which killed eight team-mates, won three League championship medals (1956–7, 1964–5, 1966–7), a Football Association Cup winners' medal (1963), and captained Manchester United to victory in the 1968 European Cup. He played 106 games for England, scored a record 49 goals, and was a member of the England World Cup winning team in 1966. He joined Preston North End as manager in 1973, and played 38 games for them before retiring in 1975. He is now a director of Manchester United.

Charlton, Jack (John) (1935–) English footballer, born in Ashington, Northumberland, the elder brother of Bobby Charlton. He played for Leeds United (1952–73), and won 35 caps for England, including one in the 1966 World Cup Final. He was manager of Middlesbrough (1973–7), Sheffield Wednesday (1977–83), and Newcastle United (1984–5). In 1986 he was appointed manager of the Republic of Ireland,

and he led the team to the semifinals of the European Nations Cup in 1988.

charm — *noun* **1** the power of delighting, attracting or fascinating. **2** (**charms**) delightful qualities possessed by a person, place, thing, etc. **3** an object believed to have magical powers. **4** a magical saying or spell. **5** a small ornament, especially of silver, worn on a bracelet. — *verb* **1** to delight, attract, or fascinate. **2** (**charm someone into** *or* **out of something**) to influence or persuade by charm. **3** to control as if by magic: *charm snakes*.

— **work like a charm** to produce the desired result as if by magic.
[from Old French *charme*, from Latin *carmen*, song, spell]

charmed *adj.* seeming to be protected by magic: *lead a charmed life*.

charmer *noun* **1** *colloq.* a person with an attractive, winning manner. **2** *combining form* a person who can charm animals: *a snake-charmer*.

Charmian Cleopatra's loyal lady-in-waiting in Shakespeare's *Antony and Cleopatra*, and Dryden's *All for Love*.

Charminar a city landmark at Hyderabad, Andhra Pradesh, India. The archway, surmounted by four minarets 56m high, was built during the reign of Mohammed Quli Qutab Shah in 1591.

charming *adj.* delightful; pleasing; attractive; enchanting.

charmingly *adv.* in a charming way.

charmless *adj.* lacking charm; unattractive.

charmlessly *adv.* in a charmless way.

charnel house *Hist.* a building where dead bodies or bones are stored. [from Old French *charnel*, burial place]

Charnel House, The a painting by Pablo Picasso (1945).

Charnley, Sir John (1911–82) British orthopaedic surgeon, born in Bury, Lancashire. He served as an orthopaedic specialist during World War II, then returned to the Manchester Royal Infirmary, where he developed the technology and surgical techniques in the 1950s and 1960s for the replacement of arthritic hip joints.

Charon 1 in Greek mythology, the ferryman of the Underworld, who carried the souls of the dead across the rivers Styx and Acheron. **2** *Astron.* the only known moon of Pluto, 1 000km in diameter, discovered photographically in 1978. It is unusually large relative to its planet, its diameter being about 40% of that of Pluto.

chart — *noun* **1** a map, especially one designed as an aid to navigation by sea or air, or one on which weather developments are shown. **2** a sheet of information presented as a table, graph or diagram. **3** (**charts**) *colloq.* weekly lists of top-selling pop records. — *verb* **1** to make a chart of (eg part of the sea). **2** to plot the course or progress of. **3** *intrans. colloq.* to appear in the record charts. [from Old French *charte*, from Latin *charta*, leaf of paper]

charter — *noun* **1** a document guaranteeing the rights and privileges of subjects, issued by a sovereign or government. **2** a document in which the constitution and principles of an organization are presented. **3** a document creating a borough. **4** the hire of aircraft or ships for private use, or a contract for this. — *verb* (**chartered**, **chartering**) **1** to hire (an aircraft, etc) for private use. **2** to grant a charter to. [from Old French *chartre*, from Latin *charta*, paper]

chartered *adj.* **1** qualified according to the rules of a professional body that has a royal charter: *chartered accountant.* **2** having been granted a charter.

charterer *noun* **1** the holder of a charter; a freeholder. **2** a person who charters transport.

charter flight a flight in a chartered aircraft.

Charteris, Leslie, originally **Leslie Charles Bowyer Yin** (1907–93) US crime-story writer, born in Singapore of British parents. He settled in the USA in 1932 and worked as a Hollywood screenwriter. He is best known for the many novels featuring Simon Templar, 'the Saint'.

Chartism *noun* a largely working-class radical movement for political reform active in Britain from the late 1830s to the early 1850s.
◇ Its objective was democratic rights for all men, and it took its name from the 'People's Charter' (1838). Its six points were universal manhood suffrage, the abolition of property qualifications for MPs, parliamentary constituencies of equal size, a secret ballot, payment for MPs, and annual general elections. Both the Chartist petitions presented to parliament (1839 and 1842) were rejected by large majorities, but despite its immediate failure Chartism influenced the direction of working-class political and economic organizations.

Chartist — *noun* an advocate or supporter of Chartism. — *adj.* relating to or supporting Chartism.

Chartres, ancient **Autricum**, or **Civitas Carnutum** POP (1990) 42 000, the capital of Eure-et-Loire department, Centre region, N central France. Situated on the left bank of the R Eure, 100km/62mi SW of Paris, Chartres is an important agricultural centre lying in the fertile Plaine de la Beauce. NOTABLE FEATURES Gothic Cathedral of Notre-Dame (1195–1220), a World Heritage site; Abbey Church of St Pierre-en-Vallée (11c–13c).

Chartres Cathedral the cathedral of Notre Dame, built (13c) at Chartres, France and widely recognized as a masterpiece of Gothic architecture. It is a World Heritage site.

Chartreuse, La Grande the principal monastery of the Carthusian order, founded in 1084 by St Bruno in the Dauphin Alps of SE France. The monastery has been destroyed and rebuilt several times, and the present structure (which is now a museum) dates from the 17c. Chartreuse liqueur was first distilled here in 1607.

chartreuse *noun* a green or yellow liqueur made from brandy and herbs. [named after the monastery of Chartreuse]

charwoman *or* **charlady** *noun* a woman employed to clean a house, office, etc.

chary *adj.* (**charier**, **chariest**, **of**) **1** cautious; wary: *chary of lending money*. **2** sparing; rather mean: *chary of praise*. [from Anglo-Saxon *cearig*, sorrowful, anxious]

Charybdis see SCYLLA.

Chase, James Hadley, pseudonym of **René Raymond** (1906–85) English novelist, born in London. He served in the RAF during World War II and started the vogue for tough realism in gangster stories with *No Orchids for Miss Blandish* (1939) and other works.

chase¹ — *verb* **1** (**chase someone** *or* **chase after someone**) to follow or go after them in an attempt to catch them. **2** (**chase someone away** *or* **off**, *etc*) to drive or force them away, off, etc. **3** *intrans.* to rush; to hurry. **4** *colloq.* to try to achieve, especially with difficulty: *too many applicants chasing too few jobs*. **5** to pursue a particular matter urgently with (someone): *chase the post office about the missing parcel*. — *noun* **1** a pursuit. **2** (**the chase**) the hunting of animals, eg foxes. **3** a large area of open land, originally where wild animals were kept for hunting.

— **chase something up** to inquire about (a matter) or seek out (information).

chase someone up to speak to (the person responsible) in order to get something done.

give chase to rush off in pursuit.
[from Old French *chasser*, from Latin *captare*, to try to catch]

chase² *verb* to decorate (metal) with engraved or embossed work. [short for *enchase*, to engrave or emboss]

chase³ *noun Printing* a metal frame that holds assembled type in position for printing. [from Old French *chas*, from a variant of Latin *capsa*, case]

chaser *noun* **1** *colloq.* a drink taken after one of a different kind, eg beer after spirits. **2** a person, animal, etc that chases. **3** a horse for steeplechasing.

chasing *noun* the art or technique of engraving or embossing metal; also, the patterns produced.

chasm *noun* **1** a deep crack in the ground, found eg close to a cliff edge. **2** a very wide difference in opinion, feeling, etc. [from Greek *chasma*]

chassé — *noun* a gliding step used in ballroom dancing, etc. — *verb intrans.* (PAST TENSE AND PAST PARTICIPLE **chasséd**) to perform this step. [from French *chassé*]

chassis *noun* (PL. **chassis**) **1** the central structure of a vehicle, on which wheels, bodywork, etc are mounted. **2** any rigid basic structure, eg that of a radio or television, on which electronic parts, etc are mounted. **3** an aeroplane's landing-gear. [from French *châssis*, frame]

chaste *adj.* **1** sexually virtuous or pure; refraining from sexual relations either outside marriage or altogether. **2** *said of behaviour, etc* modest; decent. **3** *said of clothes, jewellery, style, etc* simple; plain; unadorned. See also CHASTITY. [from Old French *chaste*]

chastely *adv.* in a chaste way.

chasten *verb* to produce in (someone) a feeling of guilt and a resolve to improve. [from Old French *chastier*, to punish]

chasteness *noun* being chaste; chastity.

chastise *verb* **1** to punish severely, especially by beating. **2** to scold. [from Latin *castigare*, to punish]

chastisement *noun* **1** physical punishment. **2** a scolding.

chastity *noun* **1** the state of refraining entirely from sexual intercourse or from sex outside marriage; chasteness. **2** simplicity or plainness of style. [from Old French *chastete*]

chastity belt *Hist.* a leather garment covering the genitals in such a way as to prevent sexual intercourse, into which eg crusaders were said to lock their wives to ensure chastity in their absence.

chasuble

chasuble *noun* a long sleeveless garment, usually elaborately embroidered, worn by a priest when celebrating Mass or Communion. [from French *chasuble*, from Latin *casubla*, variant of *casula*, hooded cloak]

chat¹ — *verb intrans.* (**chatted, chatting**) to talk or converse in a friendly, informal way. — *noun* informal familiar talk; a friendly conversation.

— **chat someone up** *colloq.* to speak to them flirtatiously, or in the hope of gaining a favour. [shortened from CHATTER]

chat² *noun* any of several small birds of the thrush family. [imitative]

château *noun* (PL. **châteaux**) **1** a large French castle or country seat. **2** a vineyard estate around a castle or house. [from French *château*]

Chateaubriand, François Auguste René, Viscount of (1768–1848) French writer and politician, born in St Malo. He established his literary reputation with *Atala* (1801), an unfinished Romantic epic of Native American life, and *Le Génie du christianisme* (The Genius of Christianity, 1802) made him prominent among men of letters. He held various political and diplomatic posts after the Restoration, and wrote his autobiography *Mémoires d'outre-tombe* (Memoirs from Beyond the Tomb, 6 vols 1902).

Château Gaillard a castle in Les Andelys, Normandy, France, sited on a promontory overlooking the R Seine. It was built in 1196–8 by Richard I (1157–99), King of England, and Duke of Normandy. It was captured by the French king, Philip Augustus, after a long siege in 1203–4.

châtelaine *noun Hist.* **1** the mistress of a large house. **2** a chain or set of chains for attaching keys to, worn hanging from the belt by women. [from French *châtelaine*]

Chatelier, Henri Louis Le see LE CHATELIER.

Chatham Islands POP (1991) 760, a set of islands in the SW Pacific Ocean belonging to New Zealand. AREA 963sq km/372sq mi. They lie 850km/528mi E of South I and comprise Chatham I (Whairikauri), Pitt I (Rangihaute), and some rocky islets. The chief settlement on the islands is Waitangi. ECONOMY sheep-rearing; sealing; fishing.

Chatila a Palestinian refugee camp on the outskirts of Beirut, Lebanon. It was created following the evacuation of Palestinians from the city after Israeli attacks on Palestinians and Syrians in Jun 1982. It was the scene of a massacre by Christian Phalangists in Sep 1983.

chat show a television or radio programme in which well-known people are interviewed informally.

Chatsworth an English country house, built (1687–1707) for the 1st Duke of Derbyshire near Edensor village, Derbyshire. The original design by William Talman (1650–1719) was altered and extended by successive architects.

Chattanooga POP (1990) 433 000, the seat of Hamilton County, S Tennessee, USA. It is a port on the Tennessee R, just N of the Georgian border, and is almost entirely surrounded by scenic mountains (including Lookout Mt, Signal Mt, and Missionary Ridge). HISTORY settled in c.1835, after which it developed as a salt-trading centre; achieved city status in 1851; scene of battles during the Civil War (1863).

chattel *noun* a moveable possession, especially in the expression *goods and chattels*. [from Old French *chatel*, from Latin *capitale*, wealth]

chatter — *verb intrans.* (**chattered, chattering**) **1** to talk rapidly, noisily, unceasingly and heedlessly, usually about trivial matters. **2** *said of the teeth* to keep knocking together as a result of cold or fear. **3** *said of eg monkeys and birds* to make high-pitched noises similar to chattering. — *noun* chattering talk or a sound similar to it. [imitative]

chatterbox *noun derog.* a person who is inclined to chatter.

chatterer *noun* a person or thing that chatters.

Chatterji, Bankim Chandra (1838–94) Indian novelist, born in Katalpura, Bengal. One of the first Indian writers to write prose fiction, his works include *Durges Nandini* (1864) and *Ananda Math* (1882), from which the Hindu Nationalist song *Bande Mataram* ('Hail to thee, Mother'), was taken.

Chatterton, Thomas (1752–70) English poet, born in Bristol. His poems purported to be by Thomas Rowley, an imaginary 15c monk, but were eventually denounced as forgeries. He then went to London in 1770, where he wrote many successful stories, essays, and other works, but, left penniless when his patron died, he poisoned himself with arsenic.

chattily *adv.* in a chatty and amiable way.

chattiness *noun* a tendency to chat amiably.

chatty *adj.* (**chattier, chattiest**) *colloq.* **1** given to amiable chatting. **2** *said of writing* friendly and informal in style.

Chau *noun* a traditional theatre of E india, with three regional styles: *Mayurbhanj*, dance-drama without masks; *Seraikala*, dance with masks; and *Purulia*, dance-drama with masks.

Chaucer, Geoffrey (c.1345–1400) English poet, born (probably) in London. In 1357 and 1358 he was a page to the wife of Lionel, Duke of Clarence, and then transferred to the king's household. He wrote his *Book of the Duchess* in 1369, on the death of John of Gaunt's wife. He travelled extensively abroad on the king's service, and also held royal posts at home, including that of Comptroller of the Petty Customs (1382). In 1386 he was elected a knight of the shire for Kent and, influenced by Boccaccio, went on to write *Troilus and Criseyde*, and several other major works. He lost his offices in 1386 and fell upon hard times, though in 1399 he was awarded a pension. It was during this last period that he wrote his most famous work, the unfinished *Canterbury Tales*.

chauffeur — *noun* a person employed to drive a car for someone else. — *verb* to act as a driver for (someone). [from French *chauffeur*, stoker]

chauffeuse *noun* a female chauffeur.

Chaunticleer the vain, quick-witted cockerel in 'The Nun's Priest's Tale', in Chaucer's *The Canterbury Tales*, whose favourite wife is Pertelote. Also in *Reynard the Fox* (Le Roman de Renart).

chauvinism *noun derog.* an unreasonable belief, especially if aggressively expressed, in the superiority of one's own nation, sex, etc. [named after Nicolas *Chauvin* (fl.1815), a fanatically patriotic soldier under Napoleon]

chauvinist — *noun* a person whose beliefs and actions are characterized by chauvinism. — *adj.* relating to or characteristic of chauvinism.

chauvinistic *adj.* relating to or typical of chauvinism or a chauvinist.

chauvinistically *adv.* in a chauvinistic way.

Chavín de Huantar a prehistoric ceremonial centre at 3 200m in the Mosna Valley of the E Andes, the focus (c.400–200 BC) of a religious cult which embraced all of central and N Peru. Its buildings cover 50ha, and the 6ha civic centre is notable for its carved stone deities and the New Temple, which is internally a maze of galleries, ramps, and stairways. It is a World Heritage site.

ChB *abbrev. Chirurgiae Baccalaureus* (Latin), Bachelor of Surgery.

Cheadle POP (1981) 60 000, a town linked with Gatley in Stockport borough, Greater Manchester, NW England. It is situated S of Manchester and 4km/2.5mi W of Stockport.

cheap — *adj.* **1** low in price; being, or charging, less than the usual price; being, or offering, good value for money. **2** low in price but of poor quality: *cheap plastic jewellery.* **3** of little worth; valueless: *war makes human life seem cheap.* **4** mean; unfair; unpleasant; nasty. — *adv. colloq.* cheaply: *good houses don't come cheap.*

— **on the cheap** *derog.* cheaply; with minimal expense.
[from Anglo-Saxon *ceap*, trade, price, bargain]

cheapen *verb* (**cheapened, cheapening**) **1** to cause to appear cheap or not very respectable. **2** *trans., intrans.* to make or become cheaper.

cheapjack — *noun derog.* a seller of cheap, poor-quality goods. — *adj.* of poor quality.

cheaply *adv.* at a low price; economically.

cheapness *noun* being cheap.

Cheapside a road in the City of London, running from St Paul's Cathedral to the Bank of England. It was a major market area during the medieval period, with many guildhalls nearby.

cheapskate *noun colloq., derog.* a mean, miserly person.

cheat — *verb* **1** to trick, deceive, swindle. **2** (**cheat someone of** *or* **out of something**) to deprive them of it by deceit or trickery. **3** *intrans.* to act dishonestly so as to gain an advantage: *cheat at cards.* **4** (**cheat on someone**) *colloq.* to be unfaithful to (a husband, wife, or partner), especially sexually. **5** to escape (something unpleasant) by luck or skill. — *noun* **1** a person who cheats. **2** a dishonest trick. [shortened from ESCHEAT]

check — *verb* **1** *trans., intrans.* to establish that (something) is correct or satisfactory, especially by investigation or enquiry: *I need someone to check my work / will you check that I locked the front door?* **2** to hold back, prevent, stop: *he was about to complain, but checked himself.* **3** *North Amer.* to mark (something correct, etc) with a tick. **4** *North Amer.* to hand over or deposit for safekeeping. **5** *intrans. said of information, etc* to be consistent; to agree with other information: *that checks with the other boy's story.* **6** *Chess* to put (the opposing king) into check. — *noun* **1** (**check on**) an inspection or investigation made to find out about something or to ensure that something is as it should be. **2** a standard or test by means of which to check something. **3** a stoppage in, or control on, progress or development. **4** a pattern of squares: *cotton with a purple check.* **5** *North Amer., esp. US* a tick marked against something. **6** *North Amer., esp. US* a cheque. **7** *North Amer.* a restaurant bill. **8** *North Amer.* a ticket or token for claiming something left in safekeeping. **9** *Chess* the position of the king when directly threatened by an opposing piece.
— **check in** to report one's arrival at an air terminal or hotel.
check something *or* **someone in 1** to register or record the arrival of (especially guests at a hotel or passengers at an air terminal). **2** to hand in (luggage for weighing and loading) at an air terminal. See also CHECK-IN.
check something off to mark an item on a list as dealt with.
check out 1 to register one's departure, especially from a hotel on paying the bill. **2** *chiefly North Amer., said of information, etc* to be satisfactory or consistent. See also CHECKOUT.
check something *or* **someone out** to investigate them thoroughly.
[from Old French *eschec*, check in chess, from Persian *shah*, king]

checkable *adj.* capable of being checked.

checked *adj.* having a squared pattern: *purple-checked cotton.*

checker[1] *noun* **1** a person who checks. **2** *North Amer.* a person who operates a checkout at a supermarket.

checker[2] see CHEQUER, CHEQUERS.

check-in *noun* at an air terminal, the desk at which passengers' tickets are checked and luggage weighed and accepted for loading.

checklist *noun* a list of things to be done or systematically checked.

checkmate — *noun* **1** *Chess* a winning position, putting one's opponent's king under

inescapable attack. **2** frustration or defeat. — *verb* **1** *Chess* to put (the opposing king) into checkmate. **2** to foil or outwit. [from Persian *shah mata*, the king is dead]

checkout *noun* the pay desk in a supermarket.

checkpoint *noun* a place, eg at a frontier, where vehicles are stopped and travel documents checked.

check-up *noun* a thorough examination, especially a medical one.

Cheddar 1 POP (1981) 3 900, a market town in Sedgemoor district, Somerset, SW England, situated 16km/10mi SE of Weston-super-Mare. It is famous for the limestone features of the Cheddar Gorge and for the cheese originally made here. **2** any of various types of hard yellow, orange, or white cheese.

cheek *noun* **1** either side of the face below the eye. **2** impudent speech or behaviour. **3** (*usually* **cheeks**) *colloq.* either of the buttocks.
— **cheek by jowl** very close together.
turn the other cheek to refuse to retaliate.
[from Anglo-Saxon *ceace* or *cece*]

cheekbone *noun* the bone that projects below the eye.

cheekily *adv.* in a cheeky way.

cheekiness *noun* a cheeky action, remark, or behaviour.

cheeky *adj.* (**cheekier, cheekiest**) impudent; disrespectful.

cheep — *verb intrans., said especially of young birds* to make high-pitched noises. — *noun* a sound of this sort. [imitative]

cheer — *noun* **1** a shout of approval or encouragement. **2** *old use* mood; spirits: *be of good cheer.* **3** *old use* merriment. **4** *old use* food and drink: *Christmas cheer.* — *verb trans., intrans.* to give approval or encouragement by shouting.
— **cheer someone on** to encourage them by shouting.
cheer up to become more cheerful.
cheer someone up to make them more cheerful.
[from Old French *chere*, face]

cheerful *adj.* **1** happy; optimistic. **2** in a good mood. **3** bright and cheering. **4** willing; glad; ungrudging.

cheerfully *adv.* with a cheerful manner.

cheerfulness *noun* being cheerful.

cheerily *adv.* with a cheery manner.

cheeriness *noun* a cheery state.

cheering *adj.* bringing comfort; making one feel glad or happier.

cheerio *interj. Brit. colloq.* **1** goodbye. **2** cheers (sense 1). [from CHEER]

cheerleader *noun* in the USA a person who leads organized cheering, especially at sports events.

cheerless *adj.* dismal, depressing, dreary or dull.

cheerlessly *adv.* in a cheerless way; miserably.

cheerlessness *noun* being cheerless.

cheers *interj. Brit. colloq.* **1** used as a toast before drinking. **2** thank you. **3** goodbye. [from CHEER]

cheery *adj.* (**cheerier, cheeriest**) cheerful; lively; jovial.

Cheeryble, Charles and **Edwin** the benevolent, good-humoured old twin brothers in Charles Dickens's *Nicholas Nickleby*. They have a nephew called Frank Cheeryble.

cheese[1] *noun* **1** a solid or soft creamy food that is prepared from the curds of milk. **2** a wheel-

shaped solid mass of this substance. **3** a flavoured food with the consistency of soft cheese, eg lemon cheese.
— **cheesed off** *Brit. slang* fed up or annoyed.
hard cheese *Brit. old slang* use bad luck.
[from Anglo-Saxon *cyse*, from Latin *caseus*]
◊ During cheese preparation, milk (usually from cows or goats) is curdled by adding a small amount of rennin or lactic acid, which separates the milk into *curd*, a thick creamy substance containing most of the protein and fat in the milk, and *whey*, a thin watery liquid. The whey is drained off and the curd is salted, compressed into blocks, and allowed to harden and ripen. Some soft cheeses, eg cottage cheese and cream cheese, are eaten fresh. Hard cheeses may be ripened by bacteria, eg Cheddar, or by bacteria and surface fungi, eg Gouda, Port-Salut. 'Blue' cheeses, eg Blue Stilton, Wensleydale, are injected with penicillin moulds. In general, a long curing period will produce a cheese with a crumbly texture and a sharp 'bite', whereas a short curing period will produce cheese with a smooth texture and mild flavour.

Some Types of Cheese		
Cheese	**Type and characteristics**	
England		
Cheddar	hard; cow's milk; white to yellow	
Cheshire	hard; cow's milk; white to palest yellow	
Lancashire	hard; cow's milk; white; crumbly	
Leicester	hard; cow's milk; orange; crumbly	
Stilton	semihard; cow's milk; mould-ripened; blue-veined	
France		
Brie	soft; cow's milk; downy rind	
Camembert	soft; cow's milk; downy rind	
Pont l'Évêque	soft; cow's milk; washed rind	
Port Salut	semisoft; cow's milk; yellow	
Reblochon	soft; cow's milk; pressed	
Roquefort	semihard; ewe's milk; blue-veined	
Saint Paulin	semisoft; cow's milk; yellow	
Vacherin	soft; cow's milk; soft interior with hard rind	
Germany		
Münster	semisoft; cow's milk; bacteria-ripened	
Tilsit	semihard; cow's milk; bacteria-ripened	
Greece		
Feta	soft; ewe's or goat's milk; salty	
Italy		
Dolcelatte	semisoft; cow's milk; mould-ripened; blue/green-veined	
Gorgonzola	semihard; cow's milk; mould-ripened; blue/green-veined	
Parmesan	very hard; cow's milk; bacteria-ripened; long cure	
Romano	very hard; cow's, ewe's or goat's milk; bacteria-ripened	
Netherlands		
Edam	semihard; skimmed cow's milk; mild; red wax rind	
Gouda	semihard; cow's milk; mild; yellow wax rind	
Spain		
Manchego	semisoft–hard; ewe's milk; mild or sharp depending on length of cure	
Switzerland		
Emmenthal	hard; cow's milk; creamy; large holes	
Gruyère	hard; cow's milk; small holes	
Sapsago	very hard; soured cow's milk; light green (clover mixed with the curd)	

cheese² *noun slang* (**big cheese**) an important person. [perhaps from Urdu *chiz*, thing]

cheese board 1 a board on which to serve cheese. 2 the selection of cheeses served.

cheeseburger *noun* a hamburger served with a slice of cheese, usually in a bread roll.

cheesecake *noun* 1 a sweet food made with soft cheese. 2 *old colloq.* use photographs of partially clothed women, especially used to add sex appeal in advertising. See also BEEFCAKE.

cheesecloth *noun* 1 a type of thin cloth used for pressing cheese. 2 a loosely woven cloth used for shirts, etc.

cheeseparing *adj. derog.* mean with money.

cheese straw a long thin light cheese-flavoured biscuit.

cheesy *adj.* (**cheesier, cheesiest**) 1 of the nature of cheese; like cheese. 2 *colloq.* cheap, inferior.

cheetah *noun* a large member of the cat family, found in Africa and SW Asia, and having a tawny or grey body covered with black spots, a small head, and very long legs. It is the fastest land animal, reaching speeds of over 95kph over short distances, as when running down its prey, eg antelopes, ostriches, hares. The cheetah is the only cat to hunt in this way. [from Hindi *cita*]

cheetah

chef *noun* the chief cook, usually male, in a restaurant, etc. [from French *chef*, chief]

chef d'oeuvre *noun* (PL. **chefs d'oeuvre**) an artist's or writer's masterpiece. [French, = chief work]

cheiromancy see CHIROMANCY.

Cheka an acronym for the All-Russian Extraordinary Commission for Combating Counter-Revolution and Sabotage, established 1917, effectively a political police force with duties to investigate and punish anti-Bolshevik activities. During the Civil War it was responsible for executing thousands of political opponents in what came to be called the 'Red Terror'. [from Russian letters *che+ka*]

Chekhov, Anton (Pavlovich) (1860–1904) Russian dramatist and short-story writer, born in Taganrog. He began to write while a medical student and his first book of stories (1886) was a success. When *The Seagull* (Chayka, 1896) was revived in 1898 by Stanislavsky at the Moscow Art Theatre, it too was successful. His other works include *Uncle Vanya* (Dyadya Vanya, 1900), *The Three Sisters* (Tri sestry, 1901), *The Cherry Orchard* (Vishnyovy sad, 1904), and many short stories.

chelate *noun Chem.* an organic chemical compound (eg haemoglobin) in which a central metal ion is attached to one or more rings of atoms. [from Greek *chele*, claw]

Chelmsford POP (1992e) 93 000, the county town of Essex, SE England, situated in Chelmsford district. It lies on the R Chelmer, 48km/30mi NE of London. NOTABLE FEATURE cathedral (15c).

Chelsea see KENSINGTON AND CHELSEA.

Chelsea pensioners the occupants of the Royal Hospital for old and disabled soldiers in Chelsea, London, which was founded by Charles I (1682), and takes in about 420 men, usually aged over 65. Their distinctive uniforms are navy blue in winter and scarlet in summer.

Chelsea porcelain a pioneer soft-paste porcelain made at a factory in Chelsea, London, which flourished from 1743 until 1785. It was founded by a silversmith from Liège, Nicholas Sprimont (1716–71), and a jeweller, Charles Gouyn (d.1781). Like Bow, it produced both figures and finely-painted service wares. In 1770 the factory was bought by William Duesbury (1725–86) of Derby.

Cheltenham POP (1992e) 107 000, a residential town in Cheltenham district, Gloucestershire, SW central England. It lies on the western edge of the Cotswold Hills, 12km/7mi NE of Gloucester. The town was a famous spa in the 18c. The headquarters of the Government's operations in electronic surveillance (GCHQ) are located at Cheltenham.

Chelyabinsk or Tchelyabinsk 1 POP (1990e) 1.1m, the industrial capital of Chelyabinsk oblast, W Siberian Russia. It lies on the E slopes of the S Ural Mts and was founded in 1736 as a frontier outpost. 2 an oblast in W Siberian Russia with Chelyabinsk as its capital.

chemical — *adj.* relating to, or made using, chemistry or chemicals. — *noun* a substance produced by or used in chemistry. [from the earlier *chemic*, relating to alchemy or chemistry]

chemical element a substance that cannot be broken down into simpler substances by chemical means, and which is composed of similar atoms that all have the same atomic number (number of protons in the nucleus), which defines that substance and its position in the periodic table.
◇ There are more than 90 naturally occurring elements, and a number of others (all of which are radioactive) have been produced artificially. Each element is assigned a chemical symbol of one or two letters, eg H (hydrogen), Na (sodium), which is used to denote that element in chemical formulae and equations. The atoms of a particular element may differ in the number of neutrons present in the nucleus, such different varieties of a single element being known as *isotopes*. In certain nuclear reactions one element can be changed into another. Chemical elements combine with each other to form *compounds*. See panel p. 238.

chemical engineering the branch of engineering concerned with the design, manufacture, operation, and maintenance of machinery and other equipment used for chemical processing on an industrial scale.

chemical equation a way of expressing a chemical reaction symbolically, by indicating on the left-hand side of the equation the chemical formulae and relative amounts of the reactants (reacting substances), and on the right-hand side the formulae and relative amounts of the products formed. The two halves of the equation are linked either by a single arrow, indicating that the reaction is irreversible, or by double arrows, indicating that it is reversible, eg the equation $2H_2 + O_2 \rightarrow 2H_2O$.

chemical formula *Chem.* the representation of the chemical composition of a compound by means of symbols that represent atoms of an element, eg the chemical formula for water is H_2O, indicating that a molecule of water contains two hydrogen atoms and one oxygen atom.

chemically *adv.* as regards chemistry or chemicals.

chemical reaction *Chem.* the process whereby one or more substances, known as *reactants*, react to form one or more different substances, known as *products*.

chemical symbol *Chem.* a single capital letter, or a combination of a capital letter and a small one, which is used to represent an atom of a particular chemical element in a chemical formula, eg the chemical symbol for copper is Cu.

chemical toilet a toilet in which human waste is treated with chemicals, used where running water is not available.

chemical warfare warfare involving the use of toxic chemical substances, eg mustard gas and tear gas, to kill or injure human beings (or to incapacitate them temporarily by causing confusion, stupor, etc) and to damage or render useless animals, plants, and non-living materials.

chemin de fer a variation of the card game baccarat. [from French *chemin de fer*, railway]

chemise *noun* a woman's shirt or loose-fitting dress. [from Old French, from Latin *camisa*, shirt]

chemist *noun* 1 a scientist specializing in chemistry. 2 a person qualified to dispense medicines; a pharmacist. 3 a shop dealing in medicines, toiletries, cosmetics, etc. [formerly *chymist*, from Latin *alchimista*, alchemist]

chemistry *noun* 1 the science of elements and compounds and the ways in they which act on, or combine with, each other. 2 *colloq.* emotional and psychological interaction experienced in a relationship.

chemoreceptor *noun Biol.* any sense organ that responds to stimulation by chemical substances.

chemotaxis *noun Biol.* the movement of a whole organism in response to chemical stimulus.

chemotherapeutic *adj.* relating to or involving chemotherapy.

chemotherapy *noun Medicine* the treatment of a disease or disorder by means of drugs or other compounds that are designed to destroy invading micro-organisms or specific areas of tissue, especially the treatment of cancer with cytotoxic drugs (as opposed to radiotherapy). [from CHEMICAL + THERAPY]

Chenab, River a river in Kashmir, India, and Pakistan. It is one of the five rivers of the Punjab, Pakistan; length 1 087km/675mi. The river rises in the Himalayas and flows NW into Kashmir, then S into Pakistan. It is joined by the R Sutlej, E of Bahawalpur, to form the R Panjnad, which then joins the R Indus to the NE of Chachran.

Chengchow see ZHENGZHOU.

Chengde or Ch'eng-te, English **Jehol** POP (1990) 247 000, a town in NE Hebei province, N China. It is a distribution centre for forestry and agricultural products. NOTABLE FEATURES summer palace and gardens of Qing Emperor Kang Xi, now a public park; several temples, including the Temple of General Peace (1775).

Chengdu or Cheng-tu POP (1990) 3m, the capital of Sichuan province, SW central China. It was founded in 200 BC as the Zhou dynastic capital. The city has been the regional industrial base since 1949. NOTABLE FEATURES home of the Tang poet, Du Fu (712–70); the Dujiang Yan Dam (250 BC) is located 40km/25mi to the NW; Ching Yang Gong Temple; Sichuan Opera.

Cheng-hsien see ZHENGZHOU.

Cheng-tu see CHENGDU.

chenille *noun* a soft shiny velvety fabric. [from French *chenille*, caterpillar]

Chepstow, Welsh **Casgwent** POP (1981) 13 000, a town in Monmouth district, Gwent, SE Wales. It lies on the R Wye, 22km/14mi NE of Newport. NOTABLE FEATURES 11c–13c castle; 11c St Mary's Church; remains of 13c town wall and 14c town gate; ruins of Tintern Abbey (1131), 5km/3mi N.

cheque *noun* a printed form on which to fill in instructions to one's bank to pay a specified sum

Chemical Elements

Symbol	Element	Derived from	Atomic no.	Symbol	Element	Derived from	Atomic no.
Ac	actinium	Greek *aktis* = ray	89	Nd	neodymium	Greek *neos* = new and *didymos* = twin	60
Ag	silver	Anglo-Saxon *seolfor*	47				
Al	aluminium	Latin *alumen* = alum	13	Ne	neon	Greek *neos* = new	10
Am	americium	America	95	Ni	nickel	German, abbreviation of *Kupfernickel*	28
Ar	argon	Greek *argos* = inactive	18				
As	arsenic	Latin *arsenicum*	33	No	nobelium	Nobel	102
At	astatine	Greek *astatos* = unstable	85	Np	neptunium	planet Neptune	93
Au	gold	Anglo-Saxon *gold*	79	O	oxygen	Greek *oxys* = acid + *gen*	8
B	boron	Persian *burah*	5	Os	osmium	Greek *osme* = odour	76
Ba	barium	Greek *barys* = heavy	56	P	phosphorus	Latin, from Greek 'light-bearing'	15
Be	beryllium	Greek *beryllion* = beryl	4				
Bi	bismuth	German (origin unknown)	83	Pa	protactinium	Greek *protos* = first + actinium	91
Bk	berkelium	Berkeley, California	97				
Br	bromine	Greek *bromos* = stench	35	Pb	lead	Anglo-Saxon *lead*	82
C	carbon	Latin *carbo* = charcoal	6	Pd	palladium	planet Pallas	46
Ca	calcium	Latin *calx* = lime	20	Pm	promethium	Prometheus, stealer of fire from heaven (Greek myth)	61
Cd	cadmium	Greek *kadmeia* = calamine	48				
Ce	cerium	planet Ceres	58	Po	polonium	Poland	84
Cf	californium	California	98	Pr	praseodymium	Greek *prasios* = green + *dydymos* = twin	59
Cl	chlorine	Greek *chloros* = green	17				
Cm	curium	Pierre and Marie Curie	96	Pt	platinum	Spanish *platina* = silver	78
Co	cobalt	German *Kobold* = goblin	27	Pu	plutonium	planet Pluto	94
Cr	chromium	Greek *chroma* = colour	24	Ra	radium	Latin *radius* = ray	88
Cs	caesium	Latin *caesium* = bluish-grey	55	Rb	rubidium	Latin *rubidus* = red	37
Cu	copper	Cyprus	29	Re	rhenium	German *Rhein*	75
Dy	dysprosium	Greek *dysprositos*	66	Rh	rhodium	Greek *rhodon* = rose	45
Er	erbium	Ytterby, a Swedish town	68	Rn	radon	radium emanation	86
Es	einsteinium	Einstein	99	Ru	ruthenium	Ruthenia	44
Eu	europium	Europe	63	S	sulphur	Latin *sulfur*	16
F	fluorine	Latin *fluo* = flow	9	Sb	antimony	Latin *antimonium*	51
Fe	iron	Anglo-Saxon *iren*	26	Sc	scandium	Scandinavia	21
Fm	fermium	Fermi	100	Se	selenium	Greek *selene* = moon	34
Fr	francium	France	87	Si	silicon	Latin *silex* = flint	14
Ga	gallium	Latin *gallia* = France	31	Sm	samarium	Samarski, a Russian savant	62
Gd	gadolinium	Gadolin, a Finnish chemist	64	Sn	tin	Anglo-Saxon *tin*	50
Ge	germanium	Latin *Germania*	32	Sr	strontium	Strontian, a Scottish village	38
H	hydrogen	Greek *hydro* = water + *gen*	1	Ta	tantalum	Tantalus (Greek myth)	73
He	helium	Greek *helos* = sun	2	Tb	terbium	Ytterby, a Swedish town	65
Hf	hafnium	Hafnia = Copenhagen	72	Tc	technetium	Greek *technetos* = artificial	43
Hg	mercury	Mercury (Roman myth)	80	Te	tellurium	Latin *tellus* = earth	52
Ho	holmium	*Holmia* = Stockholm	67	Th	thorium	Norse god Thor	90
I	iodine	Greek *iodes* = violet	53	Ti	titanium	Latin *Titanes* = sons of the earth	22
In	indium	its indigo spectrum	49				
Ir	iridium	Latin *iris* = a rainbow	77	Tl	thallium	Greek *thallos* = budding twig	81
K	potassium	English potash	19	Tm	thulium	Greek and Roman *Thule* = Northland	69
Kr	krypton	Greek *kryptos* = hidden	36				
La	lanthanum	Greek *lanthan* = conceal	57	U	uranium	planet Uranus	92
Li	lithium	Greek *lithos* = stone	3	Une	unnilennium		109
Lu	lutetium	Lutetia, ancient name of Paris	71	Unh	unnilhexium		106
				Unp	unnilpentium		105
Lw	lawrencium	Lawrence, US physicist	103	Unq	unnilquadium		104
Md	mendelevium	Mendeléev, Russian chemist	101	Uns	unnilseptium		107
				V	vanadium	Norse goddess Vanadis (Freya)	23
Mg	magnesium	Magnesia, district in Thessaly	12				
				W	tungsten	Swedish, heavy stone	74
Mn	manganese	Latin *magnes* = magnet	25	Xe	xenon	Greek *xenos* = stranger	54
Mo	molybdenum	Greek *molybdos* = lead	42	Y	yttrium	Ytterby, a Swedish town	39
N	nitrogen	Greek *nitron* = saltpetre	7	Yb	ytterbium	Ytterby, a Swedish town	70
Na	sodium	English *soda*	11	Zn	zinc	German *zink*	30
Nb	niobium	Niobe (Greek myth)	41	Zr	zirconium	Persian *zargun* = gold-coloured	40

of money from one's account to another account. [from CHECK]

chequebook *noun* a book of cheques ready for use, printed with one's own name and that of the bank issuing it.

chequebook journalism *derog.* the practice of paying enormous prices for exclusive rights to especially sensational material for newspaper stories.

cheque card a card issued to customers by a bank, guaranteeing payment of their cheques up to a stated amount.

chequer or, in N America, **checker**. *noun* **1** a pattern of squares alternating in colour as on a chessboard. **2** one of the pieces used in the game of Chinese chequers. **3** *North Amer.* one of the

round pieces used in the game of draughts. [Old French *escheker*, chessboard, from *eschec*, check in chess; see etymology for CHECK]

chequered *adj.* **1** patterned with squares or patches of alternating colour. **2** *said of a person's life, career, etc* eventful, with alternations of good and bad fortune.

chequered flag a black-and-white-checked flag waved in front of the winner and subsequent finishers in a motor race.

Chequers the official country residence of British prime ministers, located in the Chiltern Hills, Buckinghamshire, which was donated to the nation by Viscount Lee of Fareham in 1921.

chequers or, in N America, **checkers**. *sing. noun* the game of draughts.

Cherbourg, ancient **Carusbur** POP (1990) 92 000, a fortified seaport, ferryport, and naval base in Manche department, Basse-Normandie region, NW France. It is France's third largest naval base, situated at the head of the Cotentin Peninsula.

Cherenkov, Pavel Alekseyevich (1904–) Soviet physicist, born in Voronezh. In 1934 he observed blue light emission from water bombarded by gamma rays; the 'Cherenkov effect' was later explained as being produced by particles travelling through a medium at velocities greater than the speed of light in that medium. This effect has become important for particle identification in high-energy physics; he shared the 1958 Nobel Prize for Physics with Igor Tamm and Ilya Frank.

cherish *verb* **1** to care for lovingly. **2** to take great care to keep (a tradition, etc) alive. **3** to cling fondly to (a hope, belief, or memory). [from Old French *cherir*, from *cher*, dear]

Chernenko, Konstantin Ustinovich (1911–85) Soviet politician, born in Bolshaya Tes, Siberia. He joined the Communist Party in 1931, and held several local posts. A long-time associate of Brezhnev, he became a member of the Politburo in 1978, and the Party's chief ideologist after the death of Suslov. Regarded as a conservative, in the Party leadership contest of 1982 Chernenko was a rival of Andropov, after whose death he became Party General Secretary and President (1984–5), but he fell ill and died, and was succeeded by Gorbachev.

Chernobyl a city in central Ukraine, situated N of Kiev, near the junction of the Pripyat and Ushk rivers. In 1986 one of the reactors at the Chernobyl Nuclear Power Station emitted unprecedentedly large amounts of radioactivity into the atmosphere. Traces of radiation were reported in W Europe including Scandinavia and the United Kingdom and in areas of N America. More than 30 people died in the incident and c.300 people were treated in hospital; residents in the surrounding contaminated areas were evacuated.

chernozem *noun Geol.* a dark highly fertile soil, rich in humus and soluble calcium salts, found in cool regions with low humidity, especially semi-arid grasslands. [from Russian *chernozëm* from chernyl, black + zemlya, earth]

Cherokee a Native American people, originally from the Great Lakes, who migrated to the SE after their defeat by the Iroquois and the Delaware. They were evicted from their land when gold was discovered on it, and c.15 000 were force-marched west by c.7 000 US troops (the 'trail of tears', 1838–9). The survivors were settled in Oklahoma with Creeks and other SE groups moved there by the US government in the 1830s. An estimated 66 000 still live in E Oklahoma.

cheroot *noun* a cigar that is cut square at both ends. [French *cheroute*, from Tamil *curuttu*, roll]

Cherry a female first name. [an Anglicized form of French *chérie*, and a short form of the female name *Charity*]

cherry *noun* (PL. **cherries**) **1** a small round red, purplish, or yellow fruit containing a small smooth stone surrounded by pulpy flesh, which may be sweet or sour, and a thin outer skin. It can be eaten raw, or used in jams, pies, liqueurs, etc. **2** any of various small deciduous trees of the genus *Prunus* that are cultivated for this fruit, for their wood, or in the case of ornamental varieties for their attractive white or pink, single or double flowers. **3** the fine-grained reddish wood of this tree, which darkens on exposure to light, and is highly prized for cabinetwork, panelling, and fine furniture. **4** (*also* **cherry-red**) a bright red colour. — **two bites** *or* **another bite at the cherry** *colloq.* an unexpected further opportunity. [from Anglo-Saxon *ciris* (mistaken for a plural), from Greek *kerasion*]

cherry brandy a liqueur made with brandy in which cherries have been steeped.

Cherry Orchard, The (Vishnyovy sad) a play by Anton Chekhov (1904). Set in pre-revolutionary Russia, the future of an orchard provides the background to a family discussion which becomes an analysis of their disillusionment and society's declining values.

cherry-picking *noun colloq.* the business practice of rejecting insurance applications from those considered to be bad risks.

'Cherry Ripe' a poem by Robert Herrick, published in *Hesperides* (1648).

chert *noun Geol.* flint.

cherub *noun* **1** (PL. **cherubs, cherubim**) an angel, represented in painting and sculpture as a winged child. **2** a sweet, innocent and beautiful child. [from Hebrew *k'rubh*, plural *k'rubhim*]

cherubic *adj.* of the nature of a cherub.

cherubically *adv.* like a cherub.

chervil *noun* a herb whose aniseed-flavoured leaves are used in salads, etc. [from Anglo-Saxon *cherfelle*, from Greek *chairephyllon*]

Cheryl a female first name. [formed from BERYL and CHERRY]

Ches. *abbrev.* Cheshire.

Chesapeake Bay an inlet of the Atlantic Ocean in the S of the state of Virginia and N Maryland, USA. It is over 300km/185mi long and lies at the mouth of the Susquehanna, Patuxent, Potomac, Chester, Choptank, Nanticoke, Rappahannock, and James rivers. The inlet forms part of the Intracoastal Waterway. It was an early area of US settlement (explored in 1607). The bay yields a wide range of seafood. Increasing pollution is a problem.

Cheshire POP (1992e) 967 000, a county in NW central England, divided into eight districts. AREA 2 328sq km/899sq mi. It is bounded W by Wales, N by Merseyside and Greater Manchester, E by Derbyshire, and S by Staffordshire and Shropshire. PHYSICAL DESCRIPTION drained by the Mersey, Weaver, Dee, Gowy, and Wheelock rivers; Delamere Forest lies between Chester and Northwich. CHIEF TOWNS Chester (county town), Crewe, Warrington, Widnes, Runcorn, Macclesfield. ECONOMY dairy farming; petrochemicals; motor vehicles.

Cheshire Cat the grinning cat in Lewis Carroll's *Alice's Adventures in Wonderland*.
— **grin like a Cheshire cat** to smile broadly and knowingly.

chess *noun* a board game for two people each with 16 playing-pieces, the most important pieces being the kings, and the object of the game to trap one's opponent's king. [from Old French *esches*, plural of *eschec*, check in chess, from Persian *shah*, king]

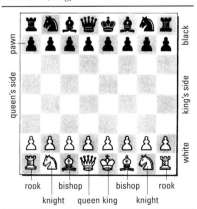

chess notation

chessboard *noun* the board, divided into alternating black (or brown) and white squares, on which chess is played.

chessman *noun* one of the 32 figures used as playing-pieces in chess.

chest[1] *noun* **1** the part of the body between the neck and the waist that contains the heart and lungs, or the front part of this. **2** a large strong box used for storage or transport. **3** a small cabinet, eg for medicines.
— **get something off one's chest** *colloq.* to relieve one's anxiety about a problem, wrongdoing, etc by talking about it.
[from Anglo-Saxon *cist, cest, cyst*, box, from Latin *cista*]

Chester, Latin **Deva Devana Castra**, Welsh **Caerleon**, Anglo-Saxon **Legaceaster** POP (1992e) 120 000, the county town of Cheshire, NW central England, situated in Chester district. It lies on the R Dee, 305km/189mi NW of London. In Roman times it was an important port and military centre. NOTABLE FEATURES cathedral (13c–15c); city walls; two-tiered shopping arcades; St John's Church (11c); town hall (1869).

Chesterfield, Philip Dormer Stanhope, 4th Earl of (1694–1773) English statesman, orator, and man of letters, born in London. After making the Grand Tour in Europe, he became an MP (1715). A bitter antagonist of Robert Walpole, he joined the Pelham ministry (1744), became Irish Lord-Lieutenant (1745), and one of the principal Secretaries of State (1746–8). Intimate with Jonathan Swift, Alexander Pope, and other contemporary authors, he wrote *Letters to his Son* (1774), a guide to manners and success.

Chesterfield POP (1992e) 101 000, a town in Chesterfield district, Derbyshire, central England. It lies on the R Rother, 16km/10mi S of Sheffield. NOTABLE FEATURES 14c Church of St Mary and All Saints (with a famous crooked spire); Chatsworth House (11km/7mi W).

chesterfield *noun* a heavily padded leather-covered sofa with arms and back of the same height. [named after a 19c Earl of Chesterfield]

Chester-le-Street POP (1992e) 53 000, a town in Chester-le-Street district, Durham, NE England, situated 9km/6mi N of Durham. It lies on the R Wear and was built on the site of the Roman station of Concangium. NOTABLE FEATURES 14c Lumley Castle; Church of St Mary and St Cuthbert.

Chesterton, G(ilbert) K(eith) (1874–1936) English critic, novelist and poet, born in London. Much of his work is in the form of essays and articles for periodicals, including those for his own *G.K.'s Weekly* (founded 1925). He also wrote poetry, literary studies (eg *Dickens*, 1906), religious works (including lives of Francis of Assisi and Thomas Aquinas), and works of social criticism. It is however for his short stories featuring the detective-priest Father Brown that he is mainly remembered (eg *The Innocence of Father Brown*, 1911).

chestily *adv.* in a chesty way.

chestiness *noun* being chesty.

chestnut *noun* **1** either of two shiny reddish-brown nuts, the edible *sweet chestnut* and the *horse chestnut*. **2** either of the two trees bearing the nuts, or their wood. **3** a reddish-brown colour, especially of hair. **4** a reddish-brown horse. **5** an often-repeated joke or anecdote.
— **pull someone's chestnuts out of the fire** *colloq.* to rescue them from difficulties.
[from the earlier *chesten nut*, from Latin *castanea*, chestnut tree]

chest of drawers a piece of furniture fitted with drawers, especially for holding clothes.

chesty *adj.* (**chestier, chestiest**) *colloq.* **1** *Brit.* liable to, suffering from, or caused by, illness affecting the lungs. **2** *said of a woman* having large breasts.

Chetniks, Serbo-Croatian *Četnici* bands of royalist Serbian guerrilla fighters active in Yugoslavia during World War II. Organized by Col Drazha Mihailovic, they fought Tito's communist Partisans rather than the Axis occupiers and so forfeited Allied support in 1944. The Partisans

defeated them, and Mihailovic was executed in 1945.

cheval glass a full-length mirror mounted on a stand with swivelling hinges that allow it to be positioned at any angle. [from French *cheval*, horse, support]

Chevalier, Maurice (1888–1972) French film and vaudeville actor, born in Paris. He began as a child singer and dancer in small cafés, and then danced at the Folies Bergères (1909–13). His first Hollywood film was *The Innocents of Paris* (1929), and 30 years later his straw-hatted, *bon-viveur* personality, with his distinctive French accent, was still much acclaimed, as in the musical *Gigi* (1958). He received a Special Academy Award in 1958.

chevalier *noun* **1** in France, a member of a modern order such as the Legion of Honour, or of one of the historical knighthood orders. **2** *old use* a knight; a chivalrous man. [from French *chevalier*, from Latin *caballarius*, horseman]

Cheviot Hills a hill range on the border between Scotland and England. It extends 56km/35mi SW along the frontier between Borders region and Northumberland and rises to 816m at The Cheviot. Many border battles between the Scots and the English have taken place in the hills over the centuries. The range gives its name to a famous breed of sheep.

Chevreul, Michel Eugène (1786–1889) French chemist and gerontologist, born in Angers. He worked at the Museum of Natural History in Paris, where he was appointed professor and later director, and was also director of the dyeworks at the Gobelins Tapestry. He decomposed soaps made of animal fats, isolating and naming many members of the fatty acid series, and showed that soaps are combinations of a fatty acid with an inorganic base, a discovery which opened up vast industries. He also investigated the physics and psychology of colour.

Chevrolet, in full **Chevrolet Motor Company** an automobile company (now a division of General Motors) founded in the USA in 1911 by Swiss-born racing driver, Louis Chevrolet (1878–1941), and William Crapo Durant (1861–1947). Chevrolet sold his interest to Durant in 1915, and the company was incorporated with General Motors in 1916.

chevron *noun* a V-shaped mark or symbol, eg one worn on a military uniform to indicate rank. [from Old French *chevron*, rafter]

chevrotain *noun* a ruminant mammal, native to tropical forests of Africa, India, Sri Lanka, and SE Asia, and having a small stocky body, short slender legs, and no horns or antlers. The male has long protruding canine teeth. – Also called *mouse deer*.

chew — *verb* **1** *trans., intrans.* to use the teeth to break up (food) inside the mouth before swallowing. **2** *trans., intrans.* (**chew at** *or* **on something**) to keep biting or nibbling at it. **3** (**chew something up**) to crush, damage, or destroy it by chewing, or as if by chewing. — *noun* **1** an act of chewing. **2** something for chewing, eg a chewy sweet.
— **chew over** *or* **on something** *colloq.* to consider or discuss it at length.
[from Anglo-Saxon *ceowan*]

chewiness *noun* being chewy.

chewing-gum *noun* a sticky sweet-flavoured substance for chewing without swallowing.

chewy *adj.* (**chewier, chewiest**) *colloq.* needing a lot of chewing.

Cheyenne POP (1990) 73 000, the capital of the state of Wyoming, USA, situated in Laramie County, SE Wyoming. It is near to the Colorado border, 157km/98mi N of Denver. HISTORY the city was founded at a railway junction in 1867; became the territorial capital in 1869; prospered in the 1870s from gold mining in the Black Hills. NOTABLE FEATURE Frontier Days Museum.

Cheyenne a Native American Plains people, divided since the 1830s into N and S groups. They were pushed west by various groups (such as the Ojibwa and Sioux), and their population was reduced by fighting and disease. They were involved in conflict with European prospectors and settlers (1857–9), and in the 1870s participated in the uprisings of other Plains tribes against the whites. Today they live mainly in Montana and Oklahoma.

Chiang Kai-shek see JIANG JIESHI.

Chiang Mai POP (1989e) 164 000, a city in NW Thailand 700km/435mi N of Bangkok. It has been the principal city of N Thailand since 1296, when it was founded as the capital of Lan Na Thai Kingdom.

Chianti *noun* a dry, usually red, Italian wine. [from *Chianti* in Italy, where the wine was first produced]

chiaroscuro *noun Art* an originally Italian painting style in which strong highlighting and deep shadow are used to give figures their shape. [from Italian *chiaroscuro*, light-dark]

chiasma *or* **chiasm** *noun* (PL. **chiasmata**) **1** *Genetics* during meiosis, any region where homologous chromosomes remain in contact after they have begun to separate from each other, and where mutual exchange of genetic material occurs as a result of crossing over. See also CROSSING OVER. **2** *Anat.* the point where the optic nerves cross each other in the brain. [from Greek *chiasma*, a cross-shaped mark]

Chiba POP (1991e) 835 000, the capital of Chiba prefecture, Kanto region, E Honshu, Japan. It is a commuter town 40km/25mi E of Tokyo, on Tokyo Bay. NOTABLE FEATURE Buddhist temple (8c).

Chibcha *or* **Miusca** an Indian people of S America who lived in the central highlands of Colombia from c.1200. They developed the largest and most highly centralized political system in the area, made up of smaller units under hereditary leaders. They were defeated by the Spanish in the 16c, and were later assimilated.

chic — *adj.* appealingly elegant or fashionable. — *noun* stylishness; elegance. [from French *chic*]

Chicago POP (1990) 6.1m, the seat of Cook County, NE Illinois, on L Michigan. It is the third largest city in the USA and the major industrial, financial, and cultural centre for the US interior. 'The Loop' area is the centre of commerce and finance; the steel industry is particularly important – one quarter of the nation's steel is produced in and around the city. Chicago is a major inland port and has one of the busiest airports in the world. HISTORY built on the site of Fort Dearborn, it was settled in the 1830s; achieved city status in 1837; developed as a result of its strategic position linking the Great Lakes with the Mississippi R after the Illinois and Michigan Canal was completed in 1848, and after the railway to the E was opened in 1853; much of the city was destroyed by fire in 1871; there was notorious gangster activity here in the Prohibition years (1920s), notably by Al Capone. NOTABLE FEATURES Sears Tower (1974), the world's tallest building (443m); Lyric Opera; Art Institute; Museum of Science and Industry; Shedd Aquarium; Planetarium; Chicago Symphony Orchestra.

Chicago School the name given to a group of Chicago architects and office buildings in the late 19c. The buildings are the forerunners of 20c skyscrapers (eg the Reliance Building, 1894–5).

chicane — *noun* **1** an obstacle, eg a series of sharp bends, on a motor-racing circuit. **2** trickery; chicanery. — *verb* **1** (**chicane someone into** *or* **out of something**) *old use* to cheat them. **2** *intrans.* to use trickery or chicanery. [from French *chicane*, quibble]

chicanery *noun* (PL. **chicaneries**) **1** clever talk intended to mislead. **2** a dishonest argument. **3** trickery; deception. [from French *chicanerie*, from *chicane*, quibble]

Chichén Itzá a Toltec/Maya city, capital of the Yucatan peninsula, Mexico (c.1000–1200), reputedly established by the Toltec ruler Topíltzin after his expulsion from Tula c.987. Its centre contains temple pyramids, the largest known Meso-American ballcourt, and a *tzompantli* (skull platform). Other features include the Cenote (Well) of Sacrifice, a water-filled pit sacred to the Rain God, into which votive offerings and human sacrifices were cast.

Chichester, Sir Francis (Charles) (1901–72) English yachtsman, born in Barnstaple, Devonshire. He emigrated to New Zealand in 1919, where he made a fortune as a land agent. He became interested in flying, and made several pioneer flights, but was badly injured by a crash in Japan (1931). In 1953 he took up yacht racing, and won the first solo transatlantic yacht race (1960) in *Gipsy Moth III*, sailing from Plymouth to New York in 40 days; he repeated the success in 1962 in 33 days. He made a successful solo circumnavigation of the world (1966–7) in *Gipsy Moth IV*, sailing from Plymouth to Sydney in 107 days and from there back to Plymouth, via Cape Horn, in 119 days.

Chichester POP (1981) 27 000, the county town of West Sussex, S England, situated 26km/16mi E of Portsmouth, in Chichester district. HISTORY founded by the Romans; later taken by the Saxons and named after their leader, Cissa. NOTABLE FEATURES cathedral (11c–12c); Bishop's Palace (12c); St Mary's Hospital (13c); market cross (15c); Chichester Festival Theatre (1962); remains of a Roman villa at Fishbourne (3km/2mi W).

chick *noun* **1** a baby bird. **2** *old slang use* a young woman. [from Middle English *chike*, variant of *chiken*, chicken]

chicken — *noun* **1** the domestic fowl, bred virtually worldwide for its meat and eggs, and thought to be derived from the red jungle fowl of India and SE Asia. There are many commercial breeds as well as ornamental ones. Chickens have short wings and can only fly for very small distances. **2** the flesh of this animal used as food. **3** *derog. colloq.* a cowardly person. **4** *slang* a youthful person: *he's no chicken.* — *adj. derog. colloq.* cowardly. — *verb* (**chicken out of something**) to avoid or withdraw from an activity or commitment from lack of nerve or confidence. [from Middle English *chiken*]

chicken-and-egg situation a situation where one cannot tell which of two happenings is cause and which effect.

chickenfeed *noun* **1** food for poultry. **2** something small and insignificant, especially a paltry sum of money.

chicken-hearted *or* **chicken-livered** *adj. derog. colloq.* cowardly.

chickenpox *noun* an infectious viral disease that is transmitted by airborne droplets and mainly affects children; an attack during childhood usually confers immunity for life. Its symptoms are fever and an itchy rash of dark red spots that develop into blisters and then scabs, which drop off after about two weeks.

chicken run a small strip of ground usually enclosed with wire netting, for keeping chickens.

Chicken Soup with Barley see ROOTS.

chicken wire wire netting.

chickpea *noun* **1** a leafy branching annual plant (*Cicer arietinum*) with white or bluish flowers, native to Asia, but cultivated since antiquity for its wrinkled yellow pea-like edible seeds, which are borne in short swollen pods, generally containing two seeds each. **2** the edible seed of this plant, usually eaten boiled or roasted. [from earlier *chich pea*, from French *chiche*]

chickweed *noun* a common weed with small white flowers. [from CHICK + WEED, the leaves and seeds being enjoyed by birds]

chicly *adv.* with a chic or stylish manner.

chicory *noun* **1** a blue-flowered plant of the daisy family. **2** its carrot-like root, ground down as a flavouring, or substitute, for coffee. **3** its leaves, especially used raw in salads. [from Greek *kichorion*]

chide *verb* (PAST TENSE **chided**, *old use* **chid**; PAST PARTICIPLE **chided**, *old use* **chidden**) to scold, rebuke. [from Anglo-Saxon *cidan*]

chiding *noun* a scolding or rebuke.

chief — *noun* **1** the head of a tribe, clan, etc. **2** a leader. **3** the person in charge of any group, organization, department, etc. — *adj.* **1** *used in titles, etc* first in rank; leading. **2** main; most important; principal.
— **in chief** mainly; especially; most of all.
[from Old French *chef*, from Latin *caput*, head]

chief constable in the UK, the officer in charge of the police force of a county or region.

chief executive the director of a business, organization, etc.

chiefly *adv.* **1** mainly. **2** especially; above all.

chief of staff (PL. **chiefs of staff**) the senior officer of each of the armed forces.

chief petty officer a senior non-commissioned officer in the Royal Navy and the navies of some other countries.

chieftain *noun* **1** the head of a tribe or clan. **2** a leader or commander. [from Old French *chevetaine*, from Latin *capitaneus*, captain]

chieftaincy *or* **chieftainship** *noun* (PL. **chieftaincies**) the position of chieftain.

chiffchaff *noun* a bird belonging to a group of Old World warblers, native to Europe, N Africa, and Asia, and inhabiting forest margins with thick undergrowth. It feeds on insects. [imitative of its call]

chiffon *noun* **1** a very fine transparent silk or nylon fabric. **2** *Cookery* a light silkily frothy mixture, made with beaten whites of eggs. [from French *chiffon*, rag]

chiffonier *or* **chiffonnier** *noun* **1** a tall elegant chest of drawers. **2** a low wide cabinet with an open or grille front. [from French *chiffonnier*, a container for *chiffons*, scraps of fabric]

chigger *or* **chigoe** *noun* a tropical flea of Africa, India and America that burrows into the skin, especially beneath the toenail. [from Carib (a W Indian language) *chigo*]

chignon *noun* a soft bun or coil of hair worn at the back of the neck. [from French *chignon*, from Old French *chaignon*, nape of the neck]

chigoe see CHIGGER.

Chihuahua 1 POP (1990) 531 000, the capital of Chihuahua state, N Mexico, lying 1 428m above sea level. The city was the centre of Pancho Villa's revolutionary activities. NOTABLE FEATURE cathedral (18c). It is famous for its breed of small dog. **2** a state in N Mexico with Chihuahua as its capital.

chihuahua *noun* a type of miniature dog, with a smooth or long-haired coat.

chilblain *noun* a painful red itchy swelling of the skin, especially on the fingers, toes, or ears, caused by abnormal constriction of the blood vessels of the skin on exposure to cold. [from CHILL + *blain*, blister]

child *noun* (PL. **children**) **1** a boy or girl between birth and physical maturity. **2** one's son or daughter. **3** someone lacking experience or understanding in something: *an absolute child in financial matters.* **4** *derog.* an innocent or naive person. **5** a person seen as a typical product of a particular historical period, movement, etc: *he was a child of his time.*
— **child's play** *colloq.* a basic or simple task.
with child *old use* pregnant.
[from Anglo-Saxon *cild*]

child abuse any form of physical, mental, or emotional maltreatment of a child, eg neglect or sexual abuse, by either of its parents or another adult.

childbearing *noun* the process of giving birth to a child.

child benefit a regular state allowance to parents for the upbringing of children below a certain age.

childbirth *noun* the process whereby a mother gives birth to a child at the end of pregnancy.

Childe, (Vere) Gordon (1892–1957) Australian archaeologist, born in Sydney. His early books, notably *The Dawn of European Civilisation* (1925), and *The Most Ancient Near East* (1928), established him as an influential archaeological theorist. He was Professor of Archaeology at Edinburgh (1927–46) and Director of the University of London Institute of Archaeology (1946–56).

Childe Harold's Pilgrimage a poem by Byron (1812–18). It describes the travelling experiences of Harold, a melancholy outsider, who is the first real example of the 'Byronic hero'.

Childers, (Robert) Erskine (1870–1922) Anglo-Irish writer and nationalist, born in London. He fought in the second Boer War and World War I, and wrote a popular spy story, *The Riddle of the Sands* (1903), and several non-fiction works. In 1921 he joined the Irish parliament as a Sinn Féin MP, denounced the treaty that created the Irish Free State, and joined the Irish Republican Army, but was captured and executed in Dublin.

Child Holding a Dove an early painting by Pablo Picasso (Courtauld College, London), from his 'blue period' (1902–4).

childhood *noun* the state or time of being a child.

childish *adj.* **1** *derog.* silly; immature. **2** relating to children or childhood; like a child.

childishly *adv.* with a childish manner.

childishness *noun* being childish.

childless *adj.* having no children.

childlike *adj.* like a child; innocent.

child-lock *noun* a feature on a video recorder, etc which prevents settings on the equipment being altered by a child playing with it.

childminder *noun* a person, usually officially registered, who looks after children for payment, eg for working parents.

childproof *or* **child-resistant** *adj.* designed so as not to be able to be opened, operated, damaged, etc by a child.

Children's Crusade a movement in 1212 of thousands of children (some as young as six) from Germany and France, who aimed to reach the Holy Land and recapture Jerusalem from the Turks. Some reached Genoa, Italy, but did not embark; others reached Marseilles, France, and were shipped to N Africa and sold into slavery.

Child Support Agency (ABBREV. **CSA**) a UK government body established in 1993 to administer the provisions of the Child Support Act by contacting and enforcing absent parents to pay child maintenance costs.

child welfare care of children's health and living conditions, as a branch of social work.

Chile, official name (**Republic of Chile** Spanish **República de Chile**) POP (1992e) 13.6m, a republic in SW South America, divided into 12 regions. AREA 756 626sq km/292 058sq mi (excluding territory claimed in Antarctica). It is bounded W by the Pacific Ocean, E by Argentina, NE by Bolivia, and NW by Peru. CAPITAL Santiago. CHIEF TOWNS Valparaíso, Concepción, Talcahuano, Antofagasta, Viña del Mar. time zone GMT −4. OFFICIAL LANGUAGE Spanish. The population is mainly of mixed Spanish and S American Indian descent; Roman Catholicism is the chief religion. CURRENCY the peso. PHYSICAL DESCRIPTION a narrow coastal belt, backed by the Andean mountain ridges rising in the N to 6 723m at Llullaillaco; the mountains are lower in

the centre and S; they are ice-capped and separated by sea channels in the far S; a fertile, central, Andean valley, 40–60 km/25–40 mi wide at 1 200m, separates the coastal range from the main inland cordilleras; the Atacama Desert lies in the far NW. CLIMATE highly varied (spans 37° of latitude, with altitudes from the Andean peaks to the coastal plain); extreme aridity in the N Atacama Desert; cold, wet, and windy in the far S at Tierra del Fuego; Mediterranean climate in central Chile, with warm, wet winters and dry summers; the average temperature at Valparaíso on the coast varies from below 12°C (Jul) to nearly 18°C (Jan), with an average annual rainfall of 505mm; at Santiago (high altitude), rainfall is below 375mm; at Antofagasta in the N, it is just over 12mm. HISTORY originally occupied by S American Indians; the arrival of the Spanish in the 16c made Chile part of the Vice-royalty of Peru; independence from Spain was declared in 1810, resulting in war until the Spanish were defeated in 1818; the first president was General Bernardo O'Higgins; border disputes with Bolivia, Peru, and Argentina brought a Chilean victory in the War of the Pacific (1879–84); economic unrest in the late 1920s led to a military dictatorship until 1931; the Marxist coalition government was ousted in 1973, and replaced by a military junta, banning all political activity, and resulting in considerable political opposition, both at home and abroad; a constitution providing for an eventual return to democracy came into effect in 1981; after 1988 there were limited political reforms, with a schedule for further elections; a National Congress was restored in 1990. GOVERNMENT executive power is exercised by a President, elected for four years; legislative power is exercised by a bicameral National Congress. ECONOMY based on agriculture and mining; wheat, corn, potatoes, sugar beet, fruit, livestock; fishing in the N, timber in the S; copper, iron ore, nitrates, silver, gold, coal, molybdenum; oil and gas were discovered in the far S (1945); steel, wood pulp, cellulose, mineral processing.

Chile

chili same as CHILLI.

chill — *noun* **1** a feeling of coldness: *a wintry chill in the air.* **2** a feverish cold. **3** a feeling, especially sudden, of depression or fear. **4** a coldness of manner; hostility. — *verb* **1** *trans., intrans.* to make or become cold. **2** to cause to feel cold. **3** to scare, depress, or discourage. **4** to harden (molten metal) quickly by putting it into a water-cooled mould.

— **chill out** *slang* to relax, especially after a period of hard work or exercise.

take the chill off something to warm it slightly.

[from Anglo-Saxon *ciele*, cold]

chilled *adj.* **1** made cold. **2** hardened by chilling. **3** preserved by chilling.

chill factor the degree by which weather conditions, eg wind, increase the effect of cold temperatures.

chilli *or* **chili** *noun* (PL. **chillis, chillies**) **1** the hot-tasting seed-case of a type of pepper or capsicum, often used in dried, powdered form as a flavouring. **2** (*in full* **chilli con carne**) a hot Mexican dish of minced meat and beans flavoured with chilli powder. [from Aztec *chilli*]

chilliness *noun* being chilly.

chilling *adj.* frightening.

chillingly *adv.* with a chilling manner.

chilly *adj.* (**chillier, chilliest**) **1** rather cold. **2** *colloq.* unfriendly; hostile.

Chiltern Hills a low, chalk hill range in SE England. It extends 88km/55mi NE from S Oxfordshire, through Buckinghamshire, Hertfordshire, and Bedfordshire, and is continued SW as the Berkshire Downs and NE as the East Anglian Ridge. The range rises to 260m at Coombe Hill.

Chiltern Hundreds in the UK, a legally fictitious office of profit under the Crown: Steward or Bailiff of Her Majesty's Chiltern Hundreds of Stoke, Desborough, and Burnham. To accept this office disqualifies an MP from the House of Commons. As an MP cannot resign, application to the Chiltern Hundreds is the conventional manner of leaving the Commons.

Chi-lung see JILONG.

Chimaera see CHIMERA.

Chimborazo an inactive Andean volcano in central Ecuador. HEIGHT 6 310m. It is the highest peak in the Ecuadorean Andes. The cone of the volcano is partly covered by glaciers.

Chimbote POP (1990e) 297 000, a port in Ancash department, N Peru. It has one of the few natural harbours on the W coast and is Peru's largest fishing port. A new port has been built to serve the national steel industry.

chime — *noun* **1** a set of tuned bells; the sound made by them. **2** (**chimes**) a percussion instrument consisting of hanging metal tubes that are struck with a hammer. — *verb* **1** *intrans. said of bells* to ring. **2** *intrans., trans. said of a clock* to indicate (the time) by chiming. **3** *intrans.* to agree or harmonize: *that chimes with what others say.*

— **chime in 1** to add a remark to a conversation, especially repeating or agreeing with something. **2** to agree with someone, or fit in with them. [formerly *chymbe belle*, probably from Anglo-Saxon *cimbal*, cymbal]

Chimera *or* **Chimaera 1** in Greek mythology, a fire-breathing monster with the head of a lion, the body of a goat, and the tail of a serpent. It was eventually slain by Bellerophon. **2** (**chimera**) a wild, impossible idea. [from Greek *chimaira*, she-goat]

chimerical *adj.* **1** of the nature of a chimera. **2** wild, fanciful.

Chimkent POP (1991e) 439 000, an industrial city in South Kazakhstan, founded in the 12c.

chimney *noun* (PL. **chimneys**) **1** a narrow vertical shaft for the escape of smoke from a fire or furnace; the top part of this, rising from a roof. **2** an outlet for steam from an engine. **3** the outlet of a volcano. **4** a glass funnel protecting the flame of a lamp. **5** a narrow vertical cleft in a rock face. [from Old French *cheminee*, from Latin *camera caminata*, room with a fireplace]

chimney breast a projecting part of a wall built round the base of a chimney.

chimneypot *noun* a short hollow rounded fitting, usually made of pottery, that sits in the opening at the top of a chimney.

chimney stack 1 a stone or brick structure rising from a roof, usually carrying several chimneys. **2** a very tall factory chimney.

chimney-sweep *noun* a person who cleans soot out of chimneys, especially for a living.

chimp *noun colloq.* a chimpanzee.

chimpanzee *noun* the most intelligent of the great apes (*Pan troglodytes*), found in tropical rainforests of Africa, up to 1.5m in height, and having long coarse black hair, except for a white patch near the rump. The face, ears, hands, and feet are hairless. [from a W African language]
◇ Chimpanzees live in groups of up to 40 individuals, and within a group the males are arranged in a social order, the socially inferior animals respecting their superiors. They feed mainly on fruit, leaves, and roots, although some chimpanzees eat meat. They often search for food on the ground, usually walking on all fours, but they can also walk upright. They use tools such as sticks to extract honey, ants, and termites from nests, and stones to crack nuts, or for hurling at predators. Chimpanzees have also been observed to chew leaves to form a pulpy sponge, which is then used to extract water from a hollow in a tree, and recent studies suggest that the adults teach their offspring how to use tools.

chimpanzee

chimpanzee language the sounds, gestures, and facial expressions used by chimpanzees to communicate with each other. Because of its complex nature and certain characteristics in common with human communication, several experiments have been conducted in the USA which have attempted to establish whether it is possible to teach young animals to communicate directly with man through sign language and other methods which exploit the chimpanzee's relatively well-developed mental abilities.

Chimu a S American Indian people of Peru, the most important political and cultural group before the Incas in the 14c. They built cities and pyramid temples, and developed sophisticated irrigation systems. They were conquered by the Incas (1465–70), who absorbed many aspects of their culture.

chin *noun* the front central part of the lower jaw.
— **keep one's chin up** *colloq.* to stay cheerful in spite of misfortune or difficulty.
take it on the chin *colloq.* to accept a difficulty or misfortune bravely.
[from Anglo-Saxon *cinn*]

China, official name **The People's Republic of China**, Chinese **Zhonghua Renmin Gonghe Guo** POP (1990) 1.2 billion, a socialist state in central and E Asia, comprising 21 provinces, three municipalities (Shanghai, Beijing, Tianjin) and five autonomous regions (Ningxia, Xinjiang, Guangxi, Xizang, Inner Mongolia). AREA 9 597 000sq km/3 704 000sq mi. It also claims the island of Taiwan. The country is bordered NW by Kirghizia and Kazakhstan, N by Mongolia, NE by Russia, E by North Korea, the Bo Hai Gulf, the Yellow Sea, and the E China Sea (Hong Kong and Macao as SE enclaves), S by the S China Sea, the Gulf of Tongking, Vietnam, Laos, Burma (Myanma), India, Bhutan, and Nepal, and W by India, Pakistan, Afghanistan, and Tajiskistan. CAPITAL Beijing. CHIEF TOWNS Shanghai, Tianjin, Shenjang, Wuhan, Guangzhou. TIME ZONE GMT + 8. Most of the population is of Han Chinese origin (93%), with over 50 minorities; the chief religions are Confucianism, Taoism, Buddhism, and ancestor-worship, but China is officially atheist. OFFICIAL LANGUAGES standard Chinese (Putonghua) or Mandarin, also Yue (Cantonese), Wu, Minbei, Minnan, Xiang, Gan, Hakka; minority languages. CURRENCY (*renminbi*) the yuan or kuai; overseas visitors use foreign exchange certificates. PHYSICAL DESCRIPTION over two thirds of the country is upland hill, mountain, and plateau; the highest mountains are in the W, where the Tibetan Plateau rises to an average altitude of 4 000m ('the roof of the world'); the land descends to the desert or semi-desert of Sinkiang and Inner Mongolia N and E of the Tibetan Plateau; the broad and fertile plains of Manchuria lie in the NE, separated from North Korea by the densely forested Changpai Shan uplands; further E and S, the prosperous Sichuan Basin is drained by the Yangtze R; the S plains and E coast, with rich, fertile soils, are heavily populated. CLIMATE varied, with seven zones: (1) NE China has cold winters, with strong N winds and warm, humid summers, but unreliable rainfall; in Manchuria, the rivers are frozen for four to six months each year, and snow lies for 100–150 days; (2) central China has warm and humid summers, sometimes typhoons or tropical cyclones on the coast; (3) S China, partly within the tropics, is the wettest area in summer; frequent typhoons (especially during Jul–Oct); (4) SW China has summer temperatures moderated by altitude, winters are mild with little rain; summers are wet on the mountains; (5) Tibet autonomous region, a high plateau surrounded by mountains, has severe winters with frequent light snow and hard frost, summers are warm, but nights are cold; (6) Xinjiang and the W interior has an arid desert climate, cold winters, and well distributed rainfall throughout the year; (7) Inner Mongolia has an extreme continental-type climate, with cold winters and warm summers and strong winds in winter and spring. HISTORY Chinese civilization is believed to date from the Xia Dynasty of 2 200–1 700 BC; the W Zhou Dynasty ruled over a prosperous feudal agricultural society in c.1066–771 BC; the E Zhou Dynasty from 770 BC until 256 BC was the era of Confucius and Lao Zi (Lao-tzu); the Qin Dynasty from 221 BC until 206 BC unified the warring states and provided a system of centralized control; there was expansion W during the W and E Han dynasties between 206 BC and AD 220, and Buddhism was introduced from India; China was split into Three Kingdoms (the Wei, Shu, and Wu) between AD 220 and AD 265; from the 4c, a series of N dynasties was set up by invaders, with several dynasties in the S; gradually reunited during the Sui (581–618) and Tang (618–907) dynasties; after a period of partition into Five Dynasties (907–60) there emerged the Song Dynasty of 960–1279, remembered for literature, philosophy, and inventions (eg movable type and gunpowder); Genghis Khan established the Mongol Yuan Dynasty between 1279 and 1368; visits by Europeans, such as Marco Polo in the 13c–14c; the Ming Dynasty from 1368 until 1644 increased contacts with the West; overthrown by Manchus, who ruled until 1911, and enlarged the empire to include Manchuria, Mongolia, Tibet, Taiwan, and parts of Turkestan; opposition to foreign imports led to the Opium Wars of 1839–42 and 1858–60, which opened ports to foreign trade; the Sino-Japanese War in 1895 gave control of Taiwan and Korea to Japan; the Boxer Rising in 1900 was the last attempt to oppose foreign influence; the Republic of China was founded by Sun Yatsen in 1912; unification under Jiang Jieshi (Chiang Kai-shek), who made Nanjing the capital in 1928; conflict between Nationalists and Communists led to the Long March in 1934–5, with Communists moving to NW China under Mao Zedong (Mao Tse-tung); Nationalist defeat and withdrawal to Taiwan in 1950; the People's Republic of China was proclaimed in 1949, with its capital at Beijing (Peking); the first Five-Year Plan (1953–7) was a period of nationalization and collectivization; the Great Leap Forward (1958–9) emphasized local authority and the establishment of rural communes; the Cultural Revolution was initiated by Mao Zedong in 1966; many policies were reversed after Mao's death in 1976, and there was a drive towards rapid industrialization and wider trade relations with the West; the killing of student-led pro-democracy protesters in Tiananmen Square, Beijing, in 1989 provoked international outrage and the introduction of economic sanctions, relaxed after 1990; tough economic controls were imposed in 1993. GOVERNMENT governed by an elected National People's Congress of 2 978 deputies; State Council of over 45 ministers, led by a Prime Minister. ECONOMY since 1949, largely based on heavy industry, producing iron and steel, coal, machinery, armaments, textiles, petroleum; more recently, light industries (eg household goods, consumables); special economic zones set up to attract foreign investment; rich mineral deposits, especially coal, tungsten, iron, tin, phosphate, aluminium, copper, lead, zinc, antimony, manganese, sulphur, bauxite, salt, asbestos; the largest oil-producing country in the Far East; major subsistence crops include rice, grain, beans, potatoes, tea, sugar, cotton, oil-seed.

china — *noun* **1** articles made from a fine translucent earthenware, originally from China. **2** articles made from similar materials. — *adj.* made of china. [from Persian *chini*, Chinese]

china clay kaolin, a fine white clay used for making porcelain.

Chinaman *noun* (PL. **Chinamen**) **1** *old derog. use* a Chinese man. **2** *Cricket* a ball, spinning from the off to the leg side, bowled by a left-handed bowler to a right-handed batsman.

Chi-nan see JINAN.

China tea a kind of smoke-cured tea grown in China.

Chinatown *noun* in any city outside China, a district where most of the inhabitants are Chinese.

chinchilla *noun* **1** a small rodent of S America, much valued for its soft grey fur. **2** the fur itself. **3** a breed of cats or of rabbits with grey fur. [from Spanish *chinchilla*]

Chindits members of the 3rd Indian Division, raised in 1942 by Brigadier Orde Wingate for long-range guerrilla operations (supported by air-supplied bases) in Japanese-occupied Burma. High casualties were sustained on the two deep penetrations of the Burmese jungle in 1943 and 1944, and their military value has been questioned.

chine¹ — *noun* **1** the backbone. **2** a cut, especially of pork, consisting of part of the backbone and adjoining parts. **3** a steep-sided ridge. — *verb* to cut (the carcass of an animal) along the backbone. [from Old French *eschine*]

chine² *noun* a deep ravine, especially in S England. [from Anglo-Saxon *cinu*, crevice]

Chinese — *noun* (PL. **Chinese**) **1** a native or citizen of China, or a member of the main ethnic group of China. **2** the language of the main ethnic group of China. — *adj.* of China or its people or language.
◇ Chinese has the largest number of mother-tongue speakers (c.1 000 million) of all the world's languages, and has eight main varieties or 'dialects'. The best known of these varieties are Cantonese, spoken in the S, and Mandarin, spoken in the N, central region, and W. The modern standard codified language (known in China as *putōnghuà*, 'common language') uses the northern form of Mandarin from the Beijing (Peking) region as the basis for standard pronunciation. After several attempts were made to write Chinese using the Roman alphabet, the *pinyin* 'phonetic spelling' system, using 58 characters, was introduced in 1958.

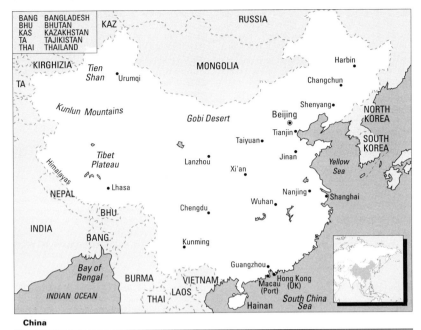

China

Chinese cabbage or **Chinese leaves** a green lettuce-like vegetable used raw in salads.

Chinese chequers a game played by moving pegs or marbles on a star-shaped board.

Chinese gooseberry the kiwi fruit.

Chinese lantern 1 a collapsible paper lantern that folds concertina-fashion. 2 a plant with bright orange papery calyxes resembling lanterns.

Chinese puzzle 1 a very difficult wooden puzzle, especially consisting of a series of boxes that fit one inside the next. 2 any highly complicated puzzle or problem.

Chingachgook the occasional companion of Natty Bumppo, and the last surviving Mohican chieftain in James Fenimore Cooper's 'Leather-Stocking Tales'.

Ching-tao see QINGDAO.

Chink or **Chinkie** or **Chinky** offensive slang — noun (PL. **Chinkies**) a Chinese person. — adj. Chinese.

chink[1] noun 1 a small slit or crack. 2 a narrow beam of light shining through such a crack. [related to CHINE[2]]

chink[2] — noun a faint, short ringing noise; a clink. — verb intrans., trans. to make or cause to make this noise. [imitative]

chinless adj. derog. 1 having a small, weak, backwards-sloping chin. 2 having a weak, indecisive character.

chinoiserie noun a European style of design and decoration which imitates or uses Chinese motifs and methods. [from French chinois, Chinese]
◇ From the time when Chinese silks, porcelain, and lacquerware were first imported into Europe in the late Middle Ages, Oriental designs and techniques were borrowed or adapted in every area of the decorative arts: in porcelain (both in materials and decoration), furniture, book illustration, fabric design, and even garden design.

Chinook a Native American people of Washington and Oregon, one of the NW groups with an artistic tradition. They were salmon fishers who traded dried fish, slaves, canoes, and shells. White contact, dating back to 1805, eventually eroded their culture, and most Chinook were moved to reservations (present-day population c.600).

Chinook a helicopter produced by Boeing which, in Mar 1959, won a US Army design competition for 'battlefield mobility'. It has extreme damage potential by being capable of carrying an internal bomb load of two tonnes or an external sling load of up to eight tonnes.

chinstrap noun a helmet strap, worn under the chin.

chintz noun a shiny cotton material originally imported from India, usually printed in bright colours on a light background, used especially for soft furnishings. [from chints, plural of chint, from Gujarati (an Indian language) chi(n)t]

chintzy adj. (**chintzier**, **chintziest**) derog. sentimentally or quaintly showy.

chinwag noun colloq. a chat.

Chios, Greek **Khíos**, Italian **Scio** POP (1991) 53 000, a Greek island in the Aegean Sea, off the W coast of Turkey. AREA 842sq km/325sq mi; length 48km/30mi. It has been noted since Classical times for its wine and figs and is one of four places claiming to be the birthplace of Homer. PHYSICAL DESCRIPTION the fifth largest of the Greek islands; crossed N–S by hills rising to 1 298m; fertile plain in the SE. CHIEF TOWN Chios.

chip — verb (**chipped**, **chipping**) 1 (**chip something** or **chip at something**) to knock or strike small pieces off a hard object or material. 2 intrans. to be broken off in small pieces; to have small pieces broken off. 3 to shape by chipping: chip a design into the stone. 4 to cut (potatoes) into strips for frying. 5 trans., intrans. Golf, Football to strike with, or play, a chip shot. — noun 1 a small piece chipped off. 2 a place from which a piece has been chipped off: a big chip in the lid. 3 Brit. (usually **chips**) a strip of potato, fried or for frying. 4 North Amer. (also **potato chip**) a potato crisp. 5 a plastic counter used as a money token in gambling. 6 Comput. a small piece of silicon, on which a large amount of information can be stored electronically (also called MICROCHIP, SILICON CHIP). 7 a small piece of stone.
— **chip in** colloq. 1 to interrupt: chip in with a suggestion. 2 to contribute.

a chip off the old block colloq. a person very like one or other parent in personality or appearance.

have a chip on one's shoulder colloq. to feel resentful about something, especially unreasonably.

have had one's chips colloq. to have lost one's chance; to have failed or been killed.

when the chips are down colloq. at the moment of crisis; when it comes to the point. [from Anglo-Saxon cipp, log, ploughshare, beam]

chipboard noun solid board made from compressed wood chips.

chipmunk noun any of several small ground squirrels found in N America and N Asia, with reddish-brown fur and a less bushy tail than that of tree squirrels. Chipmunks live in underground burrows, and feed on berries, fruits, nuts, seeds, small insects, slugs, and snails. [from earlier chitmunk, from Ojibwa, a N American Indian language]

chipolata noun a small sausage. [from French chipolata, from Italian cipollata, onion dish]

chipped adj. 1 shaped or damaged by chipping. 2 shaped into chips.

Chippendale, Thomas (1718–79) English cabinet-maker, born in Otley, Yorkshire. He set up a workshop in St Martin's Lane in 1753, and soon became famous for his elegant neoclassical furniture, especially chairs, which he made mostly from mahogany. His illustrated Gentleman and Cabinet-maker's Director (1754) was the first comprehensive trade catalogue of its kind. His son Thomas (c.1749–1822) carried on the business.

Chippendale adj. Furniture denoting furniture made by, or imitating the style of, Thomas Chippendale, with graceful and elegant lines and detailed carving.

chipper adj. North Amer. colloq., said of a person cheerful and lively. [perhaps from N English dialect]

Chippewa see OJIBWA.

chippy noun (PL. **chippies**) Brit. colloq. 1 a chip shop. 2 a carpenter or joiner.

Chips, Mr, properly **Arthur Chipping** the kind, retired old schoolmaster in James Hilton's Goodbye, Mr Chips and To You, Mr Chips.

chip shop a shop selling chips, fish, and other fried foods, for taking away to eat.

chip shot Golf, Football a short, high shot or kick.

Chirac, Jacques (René) (1932–) French Gaullist politician. First elected to the National Assembly in 1967, he gained extensive governmental experience before being appointed Prime Minister (1974–6) by Giscard d'Estaing, but resigned over differences with him and became Leader of the Gaullist Party. Mayor of Paris since 1977, he was an unsuccessful candidate in the 1981 and 1988 presidential elections but was Prime Minister again (1984–6) during François Mitterand's presidency.

chirography or **cheirography** noun the study of the forms and styles of handwriting, which differ between the writing systems of the major language families. Styles and forms in the western writing tradition include: majuscule or capital letters, used by the early Greeks and Romans from c.300 BC; minuscule or small letters, gradually developed by the Greeks from the 8c AD; with large rounded letters, found in Latin and Greek manuscripts from the 4c–8c AD; cursive, using rounded strokes to join letters; and italic, developed in Italy in the 14c. [from Greek cheir, and + graphe, writing]

chiromancy or **cheiromancy** noun palmistry. [from Greek cheir, hand + manteia, divination]

Chiron in Greek mythology, a good centaur renowned for his wisdom and knowledge of medicine, the son of Kronos and Philyra the Oceanid. He educated many Greek heroes including Asclepius, Jason the Argonaut, Heracles, and Achilles. After being accidentally wounded by a poisoned arrow of Heracles, he gave up his immortality to Prometheus, and was changed into the constellation Sagittarius.

chiropodist *noun* a person who treats minor disorders of the feet, eg corns. [from Greek *cheir*, hand + *pous*, foot; the original practitioners treated hands as well as feet]

chiropody *noun* the diagnosis, treatment, and prevention of disorders and diseases of the foot, especially in the elderly or disabled.

chiropractic *noun* a method of treating pain by manual adjustment of the spinal column, etc so as to release pressure on the nerves. [from Greek *cheir*, hand + *prattein*, to do]

chirp — *verb* **1** *intrans.* said of birds, grasshoppers, etc to produce a short high unmusical sound. **2** *trans., intrans.* to chatter, or say (something), merrily. — *noun* a chirping sound. [imitative]

chirpily *adv.* with a chirpy manner.

chirpiness *noun* being chirpy; cheeriness.

chirpy *adj.* (**chirpier, chirpiest**) *colloq.* cheerful and lively.

Chirripó Grande the highest peak in Costa Rica and S Central America. HEIGHT 3 819m. It lies in the Cordillera de Talamanca. NOTABLE FEATURE Chirripó National Park.

chirrup — *verb intrans.* (**chirruped, chirruping**) to chirp, especially in little bursts. — *noun* a burst of chirping. [imitative]

chirrupy *adj.* cheerful.

chisel — *noun* a tool with a strong metal blade with a cutting edge at the tip, used for cutting and shaping wood or stone. — *verb* (**chiselled, chiselling**) **1** to cut or shape (wood or stone) with a chisel. **2** *slang* to cheat. [from Old French *cisel*]

Chisholm Trail a cattle trail from Texas, across Oklahoma, to the railheads at Abilene, Kansas. It is named after Jesse Chisholm, who pioneered the route in 1866. The trail fell into disuse with the spread of enclosure and the growth of a rail network.

chit[1] *noun* a short note, especially an officially signed one, recording money owed or paid, an order for goods, etc. [from Hindi *citthi*]

chit[2] *noun derog.* a cheeky young girl; a mere child. [related to KITTEN]

chitarrone *noun* (PL. **chitarroni**) a large lute or theorbo popular in the 16c and 17c, both as a solo instrument and in accompanying singing. It had six pairs of stopped strings extending over a fretted fingerboard to a lower pegbox, with a further eight unstopped bass strings extending over the entire length of the long double neck to an upper pegbox. [from Italian; related to GUITAR KITHARA]

chitchat *derog.* — *noun* chatter; gossip. — *verb intrans.* (**chitchatted, chitchatting**) to gossip idly. [reduplicated form of CHAT]

chitin *noun Zool.* a complex carbohydrate substance that serves to strengthen the tough outer covering or cuticle of insects and crustaceans, and the cell walls of many fungi. As a strong lightweight supporting material it has a similar function to bone in vertebrates. [from French *chitine*, from Greek *chiton*, tunic]

chitinous *adj.* consisting of or like chitin.

Chittagong 1 POP (1990e) 2.3m, the seaport capital of Chittagong district, SE Bangladesh. It is the country's principal port, on the R Karnafuli, which flows into the Bay of Bengal. HISTORY conquered by the Nawab of Bengal in 1666; ceded to the British East India Company in 1760; damaged during the Indo-Pakistani War in 1971. NOTABLE FEATURES Hindu and Buddhist temples. **2** a district in SE Bangladesh with Chittagong as its capital.

Chittagong Hill Tracts POP (1981) 580 000, a region in SE Bangladesh, bounded E by Burma (Myanma). AREA 8 680sq km/3 350sq mi. It is a hilly area enclosed by the Feni, Karnafuli, Sangu, and Matamuhuri rivers, reaching heights of 500–1 000m in the SE. The region is divided

into four fertile valleys, covered with thick, planted forest dominated by tall teak trees. CAPITAL Rangamati. L Kaptia was formed when the Karnafuli hydroelectric dam was built at Kaptia.

chitterlings *pl. noun* a pig's or other animal's intestines, prepared as a food. [from Middle English *cheterling*]

chitty same as CHIT[1].

Chitwin or **Royal Chitwin** a national park in S central Nepal, established in 1973. AREA 932sq km/360sq mi. It is situated between the Sumesar Range in the E and the R Gandak in the W. The park is a World Heritage site.

chivalrous *adj.* **1** showing chivalry; courteous towards, and concerned for, those weaker than oneself. **2** relating to medieval chivalry.

chivalrously *adv.* with a chivalrous manner.

chivalrousness *noun* being chivalrous.

chivalry *noun* **1** courtesy and protectiveness shown to the weak, or to women by men. **2** *Hist.* a code of moral and religious behaviour followed by medieval knights; the medieval system of knighthood. [from Old French *chevalerie*, from *chevalier*, knight]

chive *noun* a plant of the onion family with purple flowers and long thin hollow leaves used as a flavouring or garnish. [from Old French *cive*]

chivvy or **chivy** *verb* (**chivvies, chivvied**) to keep urging on or nagging (someone), especially to hurry or to get some task done. [perhaps from the ballad *Chevy Chase*]

Čáslavsk, Věra (1942–) Czech gymnast, born in Prague. She switched from ice-skating to gymnastics as a 15 year-old, and went on to win 22 Olympic, World, and European titles (1959–68), and eight silver and three bronze medals. She won three Olympic gold medals in 1964, and four in 1968. She donated her medals (one each) to the four Czech leaders (Dubcek, Svoboda, Cernik, Smrkorsky) deposed following the Soviet invasion.

Chloe a female first name, adopted from the New Testament by 17c Puritans. [from Greek *khloe*, green shoot, verdure]

chlor- or **chloro-** *combining form* **1** green. **2** chlorine. [from Greek *chloros*, green]

chloral or **chloral hydrate** *noun Medicine* a colourless crystalline compound used as a sedative. [from CHLORINE + ALCOHOL]

chlorate *noun Chem.* a salt of chloric acid (HClO$_3$). [from CHLORINE + -ATE]

chloric *adj. Chem.* relating to, containing, or obtained from, chlorine: *chloric acid*. [from CHLORINE + -IC]

chloride *noun* **1** *Chem.* a compound of chlorine with another element or radical (group of atoms); a salt of hydrochloric acid (HCl). **2** chloride of lime, a bleaching agent. [from CHLORINE + -IDE]

chlorinate *verb* to treat (eg water) with, or cause (a substance) to combine with, chlorine. [from Greek *chloros*, green]

chlorinated *adj.* treated or combined with chlorine.

chlorination *noun* treatment or combination with chlorine.

chlorination *noun* **1** *Chem.* the formation of a chlorinated compound (an organic compound containing chlorine) as a result of a chemical reaction between chlorine and an organic compound. **2** the bleaching or disinfecting of a substance by treating it with chlorine.

chlorine *noun Chem.* (SYMBOL **Cl**, ATOMIC NUMBER **17**) a greenish-yellow poisonous gas with a pungent smell, that is obtained from deposits of sodium chloride (common salt) or potassium chloride, and from sea water, by electrolysis. It is widely used as a disinfectant (eg in swimming pools) and a bleach, and in the manufacture of

chlorine-containing organic chemicals such as propellants (eg chlorofluorocarbons), cleaning fluids, and monomers for the production of synthetic rubber and polyvinyl chloride (PVC).

chloro- see CHLOR-.

chlorofluorocarbon *noun Chem.* (ABBREV. **CFC**) a chemical compound composed of chlorine, fluorine, and carbon, used as an aerosol propellant, and in refrigeration systems to aid the circulation of cooling agents. It is also produced during the manufacture of plastic foam for containers.
◊ Chlorofluorocarbons are very stable over long periods, but eventually release their chlorine atoms into the atmosphere. Chlorine reacts with the ozone layer to form chlorine oxide, and this process is beginning to damage the ozone layer. Conservationists fear that CFCs may destroy the ozone layer altogether, and many countries have signed international agreements to ban the use of CFCs. By the end of the 1990s, refrigerators will not contain CFCs, and many aerosol products already contain alternative 'ozone-friendly' propellants, such as carbon dioxide and nitrous oxide.

chloroform — *noun Chem.* (FORMULA **CHCl$_3$**) a colourless volatile sweet-smelling liquid, formerly used as an anaesthetic, but now known to cause liver damage. It is used as a solvent, and in the manufacture of organic chemicals. — Also called *trichloromethane*. — *verb* to anaesthetize with chloroform. [from CHLORINE + *formic* as in FORMIC ACID]

chlorophyll *noun Bot.* the green pigment, found in the chloroplasts of all green plants, that absorbs light energy from the sun during photosynthesis, and converts it to chemical energy required for the manufacture of carbohydrates by the plant. [from CHLOR- + Greek *phyllon*, leaf]

chloroplast *noun Bot.* any of many specialized membrane-bound structures containing the green pigment chlorophyll, found within the cytoplasm of photosynthetic cells of all green plants that are regularly exposed to light. Photosynthesis takes place within these structures. [from CHLOR- + Greek *plastos*, moulded]
◊ Chloroplasts are typically biconvex in shape, and contain stacks of sheet-like membranes (*lamellae* or *thylakoids*) bearing photosynthetic pigments, including chlorophyll. The stacks of lamellae, known as *grana*, are surrounded by a watery matrix or *stroma*, which also contains DNA. The light reactions of photosynthesis, in which light energy from sunlight is converted to chemical energy in the presence of chlorophyll, take place on the thylakoid membranes. The dark reactions, in which the chemical energy produced in the light reactions is used to manufacture carbohydrates, take place in the stroma.

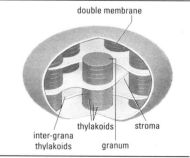

double membrane
thylakoids
stroma
inter-grana thylakoids
granum

chloroplast

choc *noun colloq.* chocolate.

chocaholic or **chocoholic** *noun* someone who is addicted to chocolate. [from CHOCOLATE by analogy with ALCOHOLIC]

chock — *noun* a heavy block or wedge used to prevent movement of a wheel, etc. — *verb* to wedge or immobilise with chocks.

chock-a-block *adj.* tightly jammed; crammed full: *a room chock-a-block with people.* [originally a nautical term, referring to a tackle with two blocks close together]

chock-full *adj.* absolutely full.

chocolate — *noun* **1** a food product, made from cacao (cocoa) beans, that is usually sold in bars or blocks, and may be eaten on its own or used to flavour biscuits, cakes, ice cream, milk drinks, etc. **2** a sweet made from or coated with this substance. **3** a beverage made by dissolving a powder prepared from this substance in hot water or milk. **4** a dark-brown colour. — *adj.* **1** made from, or coated with, chocolate. **2** dark brown. [from Aztec *chocolatl*]
◇ Chocolate is prepared by roasting and grinding the edible portion (nib) of cacao beans from the tree *Theobroma cacao* to form a thick paste consisting of cocoa solids and cocoa butter (fats). Plain chocolate, which is dark and slightly bitter, is made by removing some of the cocoa butter, whereas milk chocolate is prepared by adding milk solids (or vegetable fats) and sugar to the paste to produce a much sweeter product. White chocolate, which is flavoured with vanilla and sweetened with sugar, contains cocoa butter but no cocoa solids.

chocolate-box *adj. derog.* over-pretty or sentimental, like the designs on boxes of chocolates.

chocolaty *adj.* **1** made with or as if with chocolate. **2** tasting of or like chocolate. **3** coloured like chocolate.

choice — *noun* **1** the act or process of choosing. **2** the right, power, or opportunity to choose: *have no choice.* **3** something or someone chosen: *a good choice.* **4** a variety of things available for choosing between: *a wide choice.* — *adj.* of specially good quality.
— **from choice 1** willingly. **2** if given a choice.
of one's choice selected according to one's own preference.
take one's choice to choose whatever one wants.
[from Old French *chois*]

choiceness *noun* being choice.

choir *noun* **1** an organized group of trained singers, especially one that performs in church. **2** especially in a cathedral or large church, the area occupied by the choir; the chancel. [from Old French *cuer*, from Latin *chorus*]

choirboy *or* **choirgirl** *noun* a young boy or girl who sings in a church choir.

choirmaster *or* **choirmistress** *noun* the trainer of a choir.

choir stalls fixed wooden seats for the choir in the chancel of a church.

Choiseul-Amboise, Etienne François, Duc de (Duke of) (1719–85) French statesman, minister of Louis XV, born in Lorraine. He served in the Austrian Wars of Succession, and became Duc de Choiseul and Foreign Minister in 1758. He arranged in 1756 the alliance between France and Austria against Frederick the Great, and obtained good terms for France at the end of the Seven Years' War (1763). He also improved the army and navy, and developed trade and industry.

choke — *verb* **1** *trans., intrans.* to prevent or be prevented from breathing by an obstruction in the throat, fumes, emotion, etc. **2** to stop or interfere with breathing in this way. **3** *trans., intrans.* to make or become speechless from emotion: *choking with rage.* **4** to fill up, block, or restrict. **5** to restrict the growth or development of: *plants choked by weeds.* — *noun* **1** *Engineering* a valve in the carburettor of a petrol engine that reduces the air supply and so gives a richer fuel/air mixture while the engine is still cold. **2** (*in full choke coil*) *Electron.* a coil of wire that is included in a radio circuit in order to present a high impedance to the passage of audio-frequency or radio-frequency currents.

— **choke something back** to suppress something indicative of feelings, especially tears, laughter, or anger.
choke someone off to prevent them from continuing to speak.
choke something off to put a stop to it; to prevent it.
[from Anglo-Saxon *aceocian*, to suffocate]

choker *noun* a close-fitting necklace or broad band of velvet, etc worn round the neck.

cholecalciferol *noun* vitamin D₃. [from Greek *chole*, bile + CALCIFEROL]

choler *noun old use* anger; irritability. [earlier meaning, bile; from Greek *chole*, bile]

cholera *noun Medicine* an acute and potentially fatal bacterial infection of the small intestine, acquired by ingesting food or water contaminated with the bacterium, and often causing epidemics in areas with poor sanitation. The symptoms are severe vomiting and diarrhoea, which cause extreme dehydration, followed by shock, kidney failure, and death, if untreated. [from Greek *chole*, bile]

choleric *adj.* irritable; bad-tempered.

cholesterol *noun Biochem.* a sterol found mainly in animal tissues, especially in fat, blood, nervous tissue, bile, and the liver. [from Greek *chole*, bile + *stereos*, solid]
◇ Cholesterol is an important component of all cell membranes in animals, and is a precursor for many steroid hormones, including the sex hormones. It is manufactured in the liver, and also provided by certain dietary items, especially meat, butter, and eggs. High levels of cholesterol in the diet and in the blood are often associated with atherosclerosis (hardening of the arteries).

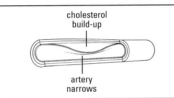

cholesterol build-up

artery narrows

cholesterol deposit

choline *noun Biochem.* an organic compound that is a component of the neurotransmitter acetylcholine, and is also involved in the transport of fats in the body. [from Greek *chole*, bile]

Choluteca 1 POP (1989e) 57 000, the capital of Choluteca department, S Honduras. It is situated in the plain of Choluteca, 34km/21mi SE of San Lorenzo. **2** a department in S Honduras with Choluteca as its capital.

chomp — *verb trans., intrans.* to munch noisily. — *noun* an act of chomping. [variant of CHAMP]

Chomsky, (Avram) Noam (1928–) US linguist and political activist, born in Philadelphia, Pennsylvania. He became Professor of Linguistics at the Massachusetts Institute of Technology, where he wrote *Syntactic Structures* (1957), introducing a new theory of language called transformational generative grammar. His opposition to the Vietnam War involved him in the radical movement, and in 1969 he published *American Power and the New Mandarins*, attacking politically liberal intellectuals who force their ideology on other nations. He has since continued to publish major works in both linguistics and politics (eg *Deterring Democracy*, 1991).

Chongqing *or* **Chungking** *or* **Pahsien** POP (1990) 3.2m, a town in Sichuan province, W central China. It lies at the confluence of the Jialing Jiang and Yangtze rivers and is the most important industrial city in the SW. HISTORY founded in the 12c; became a treaty port in 1891; capital of China in 1937–46. NOTABLE FEATURES hot springs are located nearby; US–Chiang Kai-

shek Criminal Acts Exhibition Hall; Sichuan Fine Arts Academy; Chongqing Museum.

choose *verb* (PAST TENSE **chose**; PAST PARTICIPLE **chosen**) **1** *trans., intrans.* to take or select (one or more things or persons) from a larger number, according to one's own preference or judgement. **2** to decide; to think fit.
— **nothing** *or* **not much to choose between people** *or* **things** with little difference in quality, value, etc between them.
[from Anglo-Saxon *ceosan*]

choosy *adj.* (**choosier, choosiest**) *colloq.* difficult to please; fussy.

chop¹ — *verb* (**chopped, chopping**) **1** (**chop something** *or* **chop at something**) to cut it with a vigorous downward or sideways slicing action, with an axe, knife, etc. **2** to hit (a ball) with a sharp downwards stroke. **3** *colloq.* to reduce or completely withdraw (funding, etc). — *noun* **1** a slice of pork, lamb, or mutton containing a bone, especially a rib. **2** a chopping action or stroke. **3** a sharp downward stroke given to a ball. **4** a short sharp blow. **5** (**the chop**) *colloq.* **a** a dismissal from a job: *get the chop.* **b** the sudden stopping or closing down of something: *our project got the chop.*
— **chop something off** to remove it by chopping.
[variant of CHAP²]

chop²
— **chop and change** to keep changing one's mind, plans, etc.
chop logic to use over-subtle or complicated and confusing arguments.
[from Anglo-Saxon *ceapian*, to bargain or trade]

chophouse *noun colloq.* a restaurant specialising in steak and chops.

Chopin, Frédéric (François) (1810–49) Polish composer and pianist, born in Zelazowa Wola, near Warsaw, where his French father had settled. He played in public at the age of eight, and published his first work at 15. He studied at the Warsaw Conservatory under Elsner (1826–9), then visited Vienna and Paris and became the idol of the salons. He lived with the novelist George Sand (Madame Dudevant) from 1838 to 1847, when they became estranged. Chopin wrote mainly for the piano, including 50 mazurkas, 27 études, 25 préludes, 19 nocturnes, 13 waltzes, 12 polonaises, 4 ballades, 3 impromptus, 3 sonatas, 2 piano concertos, and a funeral march.

Chopin, Kate, *née* Katherine O'Flaherty (1851–1904) US novelist and short-story writer, born in St Louis, Missouri. She lived in New Orleans, but after the death of her husband in 1882 she returned to St Louis and began to write. Her early works *Bayou Folk* (1894) and *A Night in Acadie* (1897) contain stories of Creole and Cajun life but she is mainly remembered for her last novel *The Awakening* (1899), a realistic account of a woman's struggle for sexual fulfilment and independence of social and family ties.

chopper *noun* **1** *colloq.* a helicopter. **2** *colloq.* a motorcycle with high handlebars. **3** a short-handled axe-like tool. **4** (**choppers**) *colloq.* the teeth.

choppily *adv., said of water* roughly.

choppiness *noun, said of water* being rather rough.

chopping-board *noun* a board for chopping up vegetables, etc on.

choppy *adj.* (**choppier, choppiest**) *said of the sea, etc* rather rough, with small irregular waves.

chops *pl. noun* the jaws or mouth, especially an animal's.
— **lick one's chops** *colloq.* to look forward to some pleasure with relish.
[from chap, the lower half of the cheek]

chopsticks *pl. noun* a pair of slender wooden, plastic or ivory sticks, operated in one hand like pincers, used for eating with in several Oriental countries. [from Pidgin English *chop*, quick + STICK[1]]

chop suey a Chinese dish of chopped meat and vegetables fried in a sauce, usually served with rice. [from Chinese dialect *jaahp seui*, mixed bits]

choral *adj.* relating to, or to be sung by, a choir or chorus: *choral music*. [from Latin *choralis*, from *chorus*, choir]

chorale *noun* **1** a hymn tune with a slow, dignified rhythm and strong harmonisation. **2** *North Amer., esp. US* a choir or choral society. [from German *Choral*, short for *Choralgesang*, choral singing]

chorally *adv.* **1** in the manner of a chorus. **2** for a choir.

choral society a group that meets regularly to practise and perform choral music.

Choral Symphony Ludwig van Beethoven's Symphony No.9 in D minor (Op 125, 1823). The last movement, a setting of Schiller's *Ode to Joy*, has been adopted as the European Community anthem.

chord[1] *noun Mus.* a combination of musical notes played together. [formerly *cord*, shortened from ACCORD]

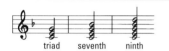

triad   seventh   ninth

music chord

chord[2] *noun* **1** *poetic* a string of a musical instrument. **2** *Anat.* same as CORD. **3** *Maths.* a straight line joining two points on a curve or curved surface.
— **strike a chord** to prompt a feeling of recognition or familiarity.

touch the right chord to get the desired emotional or sympathetic response from someone. [from Greek *chorde*, string, gut]

Chordata *noun Zool.* a phylum of the animal kingdom that includes all animals which at some stage of their development possess a *notochord* (a flexible rod-like structure which strengthens and supports the body in the embryos and adults of more primitive members of the group, but in vertebrates is replaced before birth by a spinal column). [from Greek *chorde*, a string, intestine]

chordate *noun Zool.* any animal belonging to the phylum Chordata.

chore *noun* a piece of housework or other boring and laborious task. [see CHAR[2]]

chorea *noun Medicine* either of two disorders of the nervous system that cause rapid involuntary movements of the limbs and sometimes of the face. *Sydenham's chorea* occurs mainly in children and is an allergic response to bacterial infection. *Huntingdon's chorea* is an inherited disorder in which degeneration of the nerve cells in the brain leads to progressive dementia. [from Greek *choreia*, dance]

choreograph *verb* to plan the choreography for (a dance, ballet, etc).

choreographer *noun* a person who choreographs dance.

choreographic *adj.* relating to or involving dancing.

choreography *noun* the arrangement of the sequence and pattern of movements in dancing. [from Greek *choreia*, dance + -GRAPHY]

chorionic gonadotrophin *Physiol.* in mammals, a hormone produced during pregnancy. Its presence in the urine forms the basis of many types of pregnancy test.

chorister *noun* a singer in a choir, especially a choirboy in a church or cathedral choir. [from Middle English *queristre*, from *quer*, choir, influenced by Latin *chorista*, singer in a choir]

choroid *adj. Anat.* the layer of cells, lying between the retina and the sclerotic, that lines the back of the eyeball in terrestrial vertebrates. It is rich in blood vessels, and contains a pigment that absorbs excess light, so preventing blurring of vision. [from Greek *chorion*, membrane]

chortle *verb intrans.* to give a half-suppressed, amused or triumphant laugh. [word invented by Lewis Carroll in *Through the Looking-glass*, combining SNORT and CHUCKLE]

chorus — *noun* **1** a set of lines in a song, sung after each verse. **2** a large choir. **3** a piece of music for such a choir. **4** the group of singers and dancers supporting the soloists in an opera or musical show: *a chorus girl*. **5** something uttered by a number of people at the same time: *a chorus of 'Nos'*. **6** *Theatr.* an actor who delivers an introductory or concluding passage to a play. **7** *Greek Theatr.* a group of actors, always on stage, who comment on the developments in the plot. — *verb* (**chorused**, **chorusing**) to say, sing or utter together.
— **in chorus** all together; in unison. [from Latin *chorus*, choir]

chose, chosen. See CHOOSE.

chosen few a select, privileged group of people.

Chou En-Lai see ZHOU ENLAI.

chough *noun* a red-legged black bird of the crow family.

choux pastry a very light pastry made with eggs. [from French *pâte choux*, cabbage pastry]

chow[1] *noun* a breed of dog, originally Chinese, with thick fur, a curled tail, and a blue tongue. [probably from a Chinese dialect]

chow[2] *noun North Amer., esp. US* slang food. [from Pidgin English *chow-chow*, mixed fruit preserve]

chowder *noun North Amer.* a thick soup containing clams or fish and vegetables, often made with milk. [from French *chaudière*, kettle]

chow mein a Chinese dish of chopped meat and vegetables served with fried noodles. [from Chinese *chow mein*, fried noodles]

Chrétien de Troyes (?–c.1183) French medieval poet, born in Troyes. He enjoyed the patronage of Marie de Champagne, daughter of Louis VII. His best-known works are the metrical Arthurian romances, including *Lancelot* and *Perceval*. His *Erec et Enide* (c.1160) is the earliest known Arthurian romance.

chrism *noun* **1** holy oil used in the Roman Catholic and Orthodox Churches for anointing. **2** *Relig.* confirmation. [from Greek *chrisma*, anointing]

Christ — *noun* **1** the Messiah or 'anointed one' whose coming is prophesied in the Old Testament. **2** Jesus of Nazareth, or Jesus Christ, believed by Christians to be the Messiah. **3** a figure or picture of Jesus. — *interj. offensive* (to many) expressing surprise, anger, etc. [from Greek *christos*, anointed]

Christadelphian *noun Christianity* a member of the Brothers of Christ, a Christian sect founded in the USA in 1848 by John Thomas (1805–71). Teaching a return to primitive Christianity and believing in the complete accuracy of the Bible, they claim that Christ will return to establish a theocracy, based in Jerusalem, and enduring for a millennium. They are congregational in organization, have no ordained ministers, and practise adult (but not infant) baptism. [from Greek *Christos*, Christ + *adelphos*, brother]

Christchurch POP (1991) 307 000, a city in Canterbury on the E coast of South I, New Zealand, lying on the R Avon. It was founded in 1850 by English Anglican colonists. NOTABLE FEATURES Canterbury Museum; Ferrymead Historic Park; McDougall Art Gallery.

christen *verb* (**christened, christening**) **1** to give (a person, especially a baby) a name, as part of the religious ceremony of receiving him or her into the Christian Church. **2** to give a name or nickname to. **3** *humorous* to use for the first time: *shall we christen the new wine glasses?* [from Anglo-Saxon *cristnian*, from *cristen*, Christian]

Christendom *noun* **1** all Christians. **2** the parts of the world in which Christianity is the recognized religion. [from Anglo-Saxon, from *cristen*, Christian + -DOM]

christening *noun* the ceremony of baptism.

Christian X (1870–1947) King of Denmark (1912–47), born in Charlottenlund. During his reign, Denmark's link with Iceland was severed (1918, 1944), but N Schleswig was recovered from Germany (1920). During the German occupation (1940–5), he remained in Denmark and sought with some success to save Denmark from the harshest effects of occupation without undue collaboration.

Christian 1 a male first name, occasionally female. **2** the hero in John Bunyan's *The Pilgrim's Progress*. [from Latin *Christianus*, follower of Christ]

Christian, Fletcher (18c) English seaman, the leader of the mutiny (against Capt Bligh) on the *Bounty*, during its homeward voyage from Tahiti (1789). In 1808 his descendants were found on Pitcairn I.

Christian — *noun* **1** a person who believes in, and follows the teachings and example of, Jesus Christ. **2** *colloq.* a person of Christian qualities. — *adj.* **1** relating to Jesus Christ, the Christian religion, or Christians. **2** *colloq.* showing virtues associated with Christians, such as kindness, patience, tolerance and generosity. [from Latin *Christianus*]

Christian Aid a British charity, founded in 1949, supported by most churches in Britain. It pays for development projects in the poorest countries of the world, particularly in agriculture, water supply, and health, using its own experts as advisors.

Christian Democrats members of Christian Democratic political parties, most of which were formed in W Europe (except the UK) after 1945, and which have since become a major political force. The Christian Democratic philosophy has strong links with the Catholic Church and its notions of social and economic justice. Electorally, the most successful example is the Christian Democratic Union (CDU) of Germany.

Christian era the period of time from the birth of Jesus Christ to the present.

Christianity *noun* **1** the religious faith based on the teachings of Jesus Christ. **2** the spirit, beliefs, principles, and practices of this faith. **3** Christendom.
◇ The earliest Christians were Jews who believed that Christ was the Messiah promised in the Old Testament, and that he was the Son or 'Word' (Logos) of God. His twelve chosen followers or disciples formed the nucleus of the Church as a society or communion of believers. The faith spread quickly through the Greek and Roman world; it was adopted by the emperor Constantine in AD 315, although it was not declared the official religion of the Roman Empire until the reign of Theodosius in AD 391. In the Dark Ages, Christianity survived through the life and witness of groups of monks in monasteries, and formed the basis of civilization in Europe in the Middle Ages. The Christian Church has evolved into major divisions: the Eastern or Orthodox Churches; the Roman Catholic Church, with the Pope at its head; and the Protestant Churches, which stemmed from

Immovable Christian Feasts

Jan 1	Solemnity of Mary, Mother of God		Aug 22	Queenship of Mary
Jan 6	Epiphany		Sep 8	Birthday of the Virgin Mary
Jan 7	Christmas Day (*Eastern Orthodox*)[1]		Sep 14	Exaltation of the Holy Cross
Jan 11	Baptism of Jesus		Oct 2	Guardian Angels
Jan 25	Conversion of Apostle Paul		Nov 1	All Saints
Feb 2	Presentation of Jesus (*Candlemas Day*)		Nov 2	All Souls
Feb 22	The Chair of Peter, Apostle		Nov 9	Dedication of the Lateran Basilica
Mar 25	Annunciation of the Virgin Mary		Nov 21	Presentation of the Virgin Mary
Jun 24	Birth of John the Baptist		Dec 8	Immaculate Conception
Aug 6	Transfiguration		Dec 25	Christmas Day
Aug 15	Assumption of the Virgin Mary		Dec 28	Holy Innocents

[1] Fixed feasts in the Julian Calendar fall 13 days later than the Gregorian Calendar date.

Movable Christian Feasts

Year	Ash Wednesday	Easter	Ascension	Whit Sunday	Sundays after Trinity	Advent	Trinity Sunday	Corpus Christi
1994	16 Feb	3 Apr	12 May	22 May	25	27 Nov	29 May	2 Jun
1995	1 Mar	16 Apr	25 May	4 Jun	24	3 Dec	11 Jun	15 Jun
1996	21 Feb	7 Apr	16 May	26 May	25	1 Dec	2 Jun	6 Jun
1997	12 Feb	30 Mar	8 May	18 May	26	30 Nov	25 May	29 May
1998	25 Feb	12 Apr	21 May	31 May	24	29 Nov	7 Jun	11 Jun
1999	17 Feb	4 Apr	13 May	23 May	25	28 Nov	30 May	3 Jun
2000	8 Mar	23 Apr	1 Jun	11 Jun	23	3 Dec	18 Jun	22 Jun

Ash Wednesday, the first day of Lent, can fall at the earliest on 4 February and at the latest on 10 March.

Palm (Passion) Sunday is the Sunday before Easter; Good Friday is the Friday before Easter; Holy Saturday (often referred to as Easter Saturday) is the Saturday before Easter; Easter Saturday, in traditional usage, is the Saturday following Easter.

Easter Day can fall at the earliest on 22 March and at the latest on 25 April. Ascension Day can fall at the earliest on 30 April and at the latest on 3 June. Whit Sunday can fall at the earliest on 10 May and at the latest on 13 June. There are not less than 22 and not more than 27 Sundays after Trinity. The first Sunday of Advent is the Sunday nearest to 30 November.

the split with the Church of Rome in the Reformation. Christianity has been spread round the world through the process of colonization, and by the work of missionaries.

christian name 1 the personal name given to a Christian at baptism. 2 anyone's first or given name; a forename.

Christian Science a movement, founded by Mary Baker Eddy, which seeks to reinstate the original Christian message of salvation from all evil, including sickness and disease as well as sin. The first Church of Christ, Scientist, was established in 1879 in Boston, USA. Eddy's *Science and Health with Key to the Scriptures* (1875) and the Bible are the principal texts of the movement. Christian Scientists decline conventional medical treatment in the belief that health is restored by living in a way that is in keeping with the principle of divine harmony. The society publishes the newspaper, *The Christian Science Monitor*.

Christian Scientist a follower of Christian Science.

Christian Socialism a range of movements aimed at combining Christian and socialist, or collectivist, ethical principles, and which attempt to promote socialism by enlisting Christ's help. They originated in 19c Britain and have since spread to Scandinavia, Switzerland, France, Germany, and the USA.

Christians of St Thomas a group of Indian Christians living on the Malabar coast. Named after Jesus' Apostle Thomas, who allegedly brought Christianity to India, they were founded by Nestorians in the 5c. They are now part of the Syrian Church, and have their own patriarch.

Christie, Dame Agatha (Mary Clarissa), *née* **Miller** (1891–1976) English writer, born in Torquay, Devon. She wrote more than 70 detec-

tive novels featuring the Belgian detective, Hercule Poirot, or the inquiring village lady, Miss Marple. Her play *The Mousetrap* opened in 1952 and holds the record for the longest unbroken run in a London theatre. Several of her novels have been filmed, including *Murder on the Orient Express* (1974) and *Death on the Nile* (1978).

Christie, John Reginald Halliday (1898–1953) English murderer, born in Yorkshire. In 1953 he was hanged in London for the murder of his wife, but he also confessed to strangling five other women and killing the wife of Timothy John Evans. In 1950 Evans had been been hanged for the murder of his infant daughter, and also charged with his wife's murder. A special inquiry resulted in the opinion that Christie had committed both murders, and Evans was granted a free pardon (1966). The trial of Christie played an important part in the alteration of British legislation affecting the death penalty.

Christie, Linford (1960–) English track athlete, born in St Andrews, Jamaica. He made his international début for the UK in 1980. He won the European 100m title in 1986, and established himself as the fastest man outside the USA. He retained that title in 1990, and also won a gold medal at the Commonwealth Games. In 1992, he was the Olympic 100m gold medallist, displacing Allan Wells (1952–) as the oldest man to take the title. In 1993, he won the 100m gold medal in the world championships in Stuttgart.

Christina a female first name. [a variant of *Christiana*, feminine of *Christianus* (see CHRISTIAN), or a Latinized form of Middle English *christin*, christian]

Christine a female first name, originally associated with Scotland. [a French form of CHRISTINA]

Christ in Glory a tapestry by Graham Sutherland (1962, Coventry Cathedral). It is his largest religious work.

Christ in Majesty a sculpture in aluminium by Sir Jacob Epstein (1957).

Christ in the House of his Parents a Pre-Raphaelite painting by Sir John Everett Millais (1850, Tate Gallery, London). Its realistic depiction of Christ aroused great controversy on its exhibition.

Christ in the House of Martha a painting by Diego Velázquez (c.1618, National Gallery, London).

Christmas *noun* 1 the annual Christian festival commemorating the birth of Christ, held on 25 December. 2 the period of celebration surrounding this date. [from Anglo-Saxon *Cristesmæsse*, Christ's Mass]

Christmas box a small gift of money given at Christmas to a postman or tradesman providing regular services.

Christmas cactus a hybrid cactus (*Schlumbergera × buckleyi*) that has spineless arching green stems consisting of flattened jointed segments, and magenta flowers, so called because it flowers in winter. It is a popular house plant.

Christmas cake a large rich iced fruitcake, eaten at Christmas.

Christmas Carol, A a novella by Charles Dickens (1843). The first and best-known of his *Christmas Books* (1852), it tells of the ghostly experiences of the miser Scrooge.

Christmas Day 25 December.

Christmas Eve 24 December, or the evening of this day.

Christmas Island *or* **Kiritimati** POP (1990) 3 000, the largest atoll in the world, one of the Line Is, in Kiribati. AREA 390sq km/150sq mi. It lies 2 000km/1 250mi S of Honolulu. HISTORY discovered by Captain Cook in 1777; annexed by the British in 1888; used as a nuclear testing site in the late 1950s. ECONOMY coconut plantations.

Christmas pudding a rich steamed pudding containing dried fruit, spices, etc, eaten especially at Christmas.

Christmas rose an evergreen plant with white or pink flowers that bloom in the winter.

Christmas stocking a long sock, traditionally hung up by children on Christmas Eve to be filled with presents.

Christmassy *adj.* of or suitable for Christmas.

Christmas tree a small fir tree, sometimes artificial, on which decorations, lights and presents are hung at Christmas.

Christ of St John of the Cross a painting by Salvador Dali (1951, Glasgow). It is a representation of the Crucifixion.

Christology *noun Christianity* the branch of theology which is concerned with the significance of Jesus Christ for the Christian faith. Traditionally, the term was restricted to the study of the person of Christ, particularly the way in which he was both human and divine. With the later emphasis on the inseparability of Christ's person and his work, it now encompasses enquiry into Christ as saviour.

Christopher, St (3c AD) Syrian saint, said to have been 3.6m tall, and to have suffered martyrdom under the emperor Decius (249–51). According to tradition, he carried the Christ-child (and all the weight of the world's sin) across a river. The patron saint of travellers, his feast day is 25 Jul. [from Greek elements *khristos*, Christ + *pherein*, to bear.]

Christopher a male first name.

Christopher Robin the child (based on his son) in A A Milne's *Winnie-the-Pooh* and other works.

Christ Reproved by his Parents a painting by Simone Martini (1342, Walker Art Gallery, Liverpool).

Christ's Hospital a boy's public school, founded in London (1552) but since 1906 at Horsham, Sussex. It was known as the 'blue coat' school, because of the blue cloak which was part of the pupils' uniform.

chromakey *noun Television* a special effect in which an area of strong colour (usually a blue background) can be removed from an image and replaced by a picture or background from another source.

chromatic *adj.* **1** relating to colours; coloured. **2** *Mus.* relating to, or using notes from, the 12-note form of scale (*chromatic scale*) that includes semitones. See also DIATONIC. [from Greek *chromatikos*, from *chroma*, colour]

chromatically *adv.* in a chromatic way.

chromaticism *noun* an attribute in music which uses notes, intervals, and chords foreign to the prevailing mode or key. A *chromatic note* is one which does not belong to the diatonic scale; a *chromatic chord* is one which includes one or more chromatic notes; a *chromatic harmony* makes use of chromatic chords; a *chromatic scale* is one which proceeds by semitones; and a *chromatic instrument* is one whose compass includes all the notes of the chromatic scale. See also DIATONICISM. [from Greek *chrōmatikos*, coloured, embellished]

chromatid *noun Genetics* one of the two thread-like structures formed by the longitudinal division of a chromosome.

chromatin *noun Biol.* in a cell nucleus, the material that appears as a loose network of threads until the time of cell division, when it becomes organized into visible chromosomes. It consists of DNA and histone protein, and can be easily stained to allow study of cell division under the microscope. [from Greek *chroma*, colour]

chromato- see CHROMO-.

chromatography *noun* a technique for separating the components of a mixture of liquids or gases. It is widely used in biochemical and pharmaceutical research to detect minute quantities of a substance (eg a drug in blood), to separate and measure the quantities of several substances in a mixture, and to remove impurities. [from Greek *chroma*, colour + -GRAPHY]
◇ A *mobile phase* (liquid or gas) containing a mixture of substances that are to be analysed is allowed to pass through a *stationary phase* (liquid or solid). The latter may be in a tubular column, on paper, or in a thin layer on a glass or plastic support. The various components of the mixture are absorbed to different extents by the stationary phase, and each becomes separated into a distinct layer. A simple example of paper chromatography is the separation of the constituent dyes of an ink spilled on paper tissue.

chromatophore *noun Zool.* a pigment-bearing cell or structure within a cell. In many animals, chromatophores are cells containing granules of pigment, and by dispersing or contracting the granules, the animal is able to change colour. [from Greek *chroma*, colour + PHORE]

chrome *noun* a non-technical word for chromium, especially when used as a silvery plating for other metals. [from Greek *chroma*, colour]

chrome yellow a yellow colouring matter obtained from a lead compound of chromium.

chrominance *noun* **1** the quality of light that produces colour, or a colour, measured by comparison with a reference colour source (usually a white) of equal brightness and specified chromaticity. **2** in television and video signals, the component that defines the colour as distinct

from its brightness or *luminance*. [from CHROMO- + *luminance*]

chromite *noun Geol.* a mineral composed of chromium and iron oxides, that occurs as compact masses of black crystals with a metallic lustre. It is the main source of chromium.

chromium *noun Chem.* (SYMBOL **Cr**, ATOMIC NUMBER **24**) a hard silvery metal that is resistant to corrosion, and is used in alloys with iron and nickel to make stainless steel. It is also used as an electroplated coating on other metals, especially steel, to give a shiny decorative finish and prevent rust. Several of its compounds are used in dyes and pigments. [a Latinized form of CHROME]

chromo- or **chromato-** *combining form* colour. [from Greek *chroma*, colour]

chromophore *noun Chem.* that part of a molecule of a chemical compound that gives rise to the colour of the compound. Most chromophores in dyestuffs involve double bonds, which lower the energy of radiation absorbed by the molecule, so that visible light as well as ultraviolet radiation is absorbed by the compound.

chromosomal *adj.* relating to chromosomes.

chromosome *noun* in the nucleus of a cell, any of a number of microscopic threadlike structures that become visible as small deeply staining rod-shaped bodies at the time of cell division, and which contain in the form of DNA all the genetic information that is needed for the development of the cell and the whole organism. [from Greek *chroma*, colour + *soma*, body]
◇ Each chromosome contains a single molecule of DNA that carries the genes, which are arranged in a specific order. There may be hundreds of genes on a chromosome, and the position of a particular gene on a chromosome is known as its *locus*. The number of chromosomes in the nucleus differs from one species to another, and is usually characteristic of a particular species, eg the cells of the human body contain 22 pairs of ordinary chromosomes, plus a pair of sex chromosomes (a matching pair of X-chromosomes in females, or an X-chromosome and a Y-chromosome in males). In diploid cells (cells containing a double set of chromosomes), the chromosomes occur in *homologous pairs* containing identical genetic loci, each member of a pair having originated from a different parent.

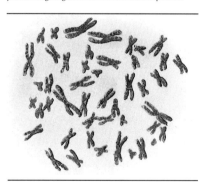
human chromosomes about to divide

chromosome map *Genetics* a diagram showing the positions (*loci*) of genes along an individual chromosome.

chromosphere or **chromatosphere** *noun Astron.* a layer of gas (mainly hydrogen) about 10 000km deep that lies above the Sun's visible surface (the photosphere). It can be seen as a thin crescent of pinkish-red light during a total eclipse of the Sun, when light from the photosphere is blocked by the Moon. [from Greek *chroma*, colour + SPHERE]

Chron. *abbrev. Biblical* Chronicles.

chron- or **chrono-** *combining form* time. [from Greek *chronos*, time]

chronic *adj.* **1** *said of a disease or symptom* of long duration, usually of gradual onset and often difficult to treat, eg chronic pain. It may or may not be severe. See also ACUTE. **2** *Brit. colloq.* very bad; severe; grave. **3** habitual. [from Greek *chronikos*, relating to time]

chronically *adv.* **1** in a chronic way. **2** *Brit., colloq* badly; extremely.

chronicity *noun* a chronic condition or quality of a disease.

chronicle — *noun* (often **chronicles**) a record of historical events year by year in the order in which they occurred. — *verb* to record (an event) in a chronicle. [diminutive of Old French *chronique*, from Greek *chronika*, annals]

chronicle play a play based on recorded history, rather than myth or legend.
◇ Marlowe and Shakespeare used Raphael Holinshed's *The Chronicles of England, Scotland, and Ireland* as a source for their plays on the English monarchy. In the 20c, Thomas Hardy wrote *The Dynasts* (1904–8) after extensive research on the Napoleonic Wars, and other modern examples include Robert Bolt's *A Man for all Seasons* (1960), on the life of Sir Thomas More.

chronicler *noun* a person who compiles a chronicle.

Chronicles, Books of, also called **Paralipomenon I and II** two books of the Hebrew Bible or Old Testament. Originally a single work, which perhaps included the books of Ezra and Nehemiah, it presents a history of Judah from its beginnings to its restoration under Ezra and Nehemiah. It has many parallels with the Books of Samuel and Kings, but the Chronicler's interests are mainly in the Temple and its cult.

chrono- see CHRON-.

chronogram *noun* a date made up of the letters of Roman numerals (C, D, I, L, M, V, and X) hidden within the letters of a phrase or sentence. Chronograms may be found in inscriptions on tombstones and foundation stones, where the letters making up the date to be commemorated are usually written in capitals. [from Greek *chronos*, time + *gramma*, letter]

chronological *adj.* **1** according to order of occurrence: *in chronological order*. **2** relating to chronology.

chronologically *adv.* in a chronological way or order.

chronologist *noun* a person who studies chronology.

chronology *noun* (PL. **chronologies**) **1** the study or science of determining the correct order of historical events. **2** the arrangement of events in order of occurrence. **3** a table or list showing events in order of occurrence.

chronometer *noun* a very accurate type of watch or clock designed to keep accurate time in all conditions, used especially at sea.

chrysalis *noun* **1** the pupa of insects that undergo metamorphosis (transformation of a lava into a mature adult), eg butterflies, moths. **2** the protective case that surrounds the pupa. [from Greek *chrysallis*, from *chrysos*, gold]

chrysanthemum *noun* a garden plant of the daisy family, with large bushy flowers, pale yellow to deep gold. [from Greek *chrysos*, gold + *anthemon*, flower]

Chrysler, in full **Chrsyler Corporation** an automobile company founded in the USA in 1925 by Walter Percy Chrsyler (1875–1940). It was formed from an amalgamation of the Maxwell Motor Company and Willys-Overland Company. Chrysler designed the first high compression engine, and introduced the Plymouth motor car.

Chrysler Building an office block in Manhattan, New York City, designed by William Van Alen (1926–30). Its spire and various decorative features on other parts of the building are made from stainless steel. It was the tallest building in the world (319.4m) until the opening of the Empire State Building in 1931.

chrysoberyl *noun Geol.* a green, yellow, or brown mineral, some varieties of which are used as gemstones. [from Greek *chrysos*, gold + *beryllos*, beryl]

chrysolite *noun Geol.* a light yellowish-green gemstone that is a variety of the mineral olivine. [from Greek *chrysos*, gold + *lithos*, stone]

chrysoprase *noun Geol.* a translucent bright green gemstone that is a variety of chalcedony. [from Greek *chrysos*, gold + *prason*, leek]

Chrysostom, St John (c.347–407AD) Syrian churchman, and one of the Doctors of the Church, born in Antioch, and named from the Greek meaning 'golden-mouthed', due to his eloquence. He spent six years as a monk in the mountains, but returned in 381 to Antioch, where he was ordained, and gained a reputation as a great religious orator. In 398 he was made Archbishop of Constantinople, where he carried out many reforms, but his reproof of vices moved the empress Eudoxia to have him deposed and banished (403), following which he moved from one place of exile to another. His feast day is 27 Jan.

chub *noun* a small fat river-fish of the carp family.

Chubb Crater or Ungava-Quebec Crater a meteorite crater in N Quebec, Canada. It is 3km/2mi in diameter, with a depth of c.410m and it is occupied by Crater Lake (260m deep). [named after the prospector F W Chubb, who discovered the crater in 1949]

chubbily *adv.* with a chubby appearance.

chubbiness *noun* being chubby.

chubby *adj.* (**chubbier, chubbiest**) plump, especially in a childishly attractive way. [perhaps from CHUB]

chuck[1] — *verb* **1** *colloq.* to throw or fling. **2** to give (a child, etc) an affectionate tap under the chin. **3** *slang* (**chuck something up**) to abandon or reject it. — *noun* **1** *colloq.* a toss, fling, or throw. **2** (**the chuck**) *slang* dismissal; rejection: *gave her boyfriend the chuck.* **3** an affectionate tap under the chin.
— **chuck something out** *colloq.* to get rid of it; to reject it.
chuck someone out *colloq.* to order them to leave.

chuck[2] **or chuck steak** *noun* beef cut from the area between the neck and shoulder. [variant of CHOCK]

chuck[3] *noun* a device for holding a piece of work in a lathe, or for holding the blade or bit in a drill. [variant of CHOCK]

chuckle — *verb* **1** *intrans.* to laugh quietly, especially in a half-suppressed private way. **2** *trans.* to utter with a little laugh. — *noun* an amused little laugh. [from an old word *chuck*, to cluck like a hen]

chuff *verb intrans., said of a steam train* to progress with regular puffing noises. [imitative]

chuffed *adj. Brit. colloq.* very pleased. [from dialect *chuff*, plump, swollen with pride]

chug — *verb intrans.* (**chugged, chugging**) *said of a motor boat, motor car, etc* to progress while making the typical quiet thudding noise of an unsophisticated engine. — *noun* this noise. [imitative]

Chukchi Peninsula, Russian **Chukotskiy Poluostrov** the NE extremity of the Eurasian landmass, in Magadan oblast, Siberian Russia. It is bounded N by the Chukchi Sea, E by the Bering Strait, and S by the Anadyr Gulf of the Bering Sea. It lies at the E end of the Chukchi Range and rises to heights above 1 000m. Cape Dezhnev forms the E point of the peninsula.

Chu-kiang see ZHU JIANG.

chukka boot a leather ankle boot.

chukker or chukka *noun* one of the six seven-and-a-half-minute periods of play in the game of polo. [from Hindi *cakkar*, round]

chum — *noun colloq.* a close friend. — *verb* (**chummed, chumming**) (**chum up with someone**) to make friends with them. [perhaps from *chamber fellow*, a fellow student, etc sharing one's room]

chummy *adj.* (**chummier, chummiest**) *colloq.* friendly.

chump *noun* **1** *colloq.* an idiot; a fool. **2** the thick end of a loin cut of lamb or mutton: *a chump chop.* **3** a short thick heavy block of wood.
— **off one's chump** *Brit. colloq.* crazy; extremely foolish.
[perhaps a combination of CHUNK and LUMP]

chunder *Austral. slang* — *verb intrans.* to vomit; to be sick. — *noun* vomit. [origin unknown]

Chungking see CHONGQING.

chunk *noun* **1** a thick, especially irregularly shaped, piece. **2** *colloq.* a large or considerable amount. [variant of CHUCK[3]]

chunky *adj.* (**chunkier, chunkiest**) **1** thickset; stockily or strongly built. **2** *said of clothes, fabrics, etc* thick; bulky. **3** solid and strong. **4** containing chunks: *chunky marmalade.*

church *noun* **1** a building for public Christian worship. **2** the religious services held in a church: *go to church.* **3** (**Church**) the profession of a clergyman: *enter the Church.* **4** (**Church**) the clergy considered as an especially political group: *quarrels between Church and State.* **5** (**Church**) any of many branches of Christians with their own doctrines, style of worship, etc: *the Methodist Church.* **6** the whole Christian establishment: *studying church history.* [from Anglo-Saxon *cirice*, from Greek *kyriakon* (*doma*), the house of the Lord, from *kyrios*, lord]

Church Army an Anglican organization of volunteer lay workers, founded in 1882. Its aims are evangelical, but it concentrates on social welfare and rehabilitation work, mainly in cities.

churchgoer *noun* a person who attends church services, especially regularly.

Churchill, Frank a careless flirtatious character, engaged to Jane Fairfax, in Jane Austen's *Emma.*

Churchill, Lord Randolph (Henry Spencer) (1849–95) English Conservative politician, born in Blenheim Palace, Oxfordshire, the third son of the 7th Duke of Marlborough, and the father of Winston Churchill. He entered parliament in 1874, and was leader in 1880 of a guerrilla band of Conservatives known as the 'Fourth Party'. He was Secretary for India (1885–6), and for a short while in 1886 Chancellor of the Exchequer and Leader of the House of Commons, but he resigned after his first budget proved unacceptable.

Churchill, Sir Winston (Leonard Spencer) (1874–1965) English politician, Prime Minister (1940–5, 1951–5), and writer, born in Blenheim Palace, Oxfordshire, the eldest son of Randolph Churchill. He fought at Omdurman during the 1898 Nile Expeditionary Force, was a newspaper correspondent during the second Boer War, and became a Conservative MP in 1900. After differences with the Party, he joined the Liberals in 1904, and was Colonial Under-Secretary (1905), President of the Board of Trade (1908), Home Secretary (1910), and First Lord of the Admiralty (1911). In 1915 he was made the scapegoat for the Dardanelles disaster, but in 1917 became Minister of Munitions. After World War I he was Secretary of State for War and Air (1919–21), and — as a 'Constitutionalist' supporter of the Conservatives — Chancellor of the Exchequer (1924–9). In 1929 he returned to the

Conservative fold, but remained out of step with the leadership until World War II, when he returned to the Admiralty. On Chamberlain's defeat (May 1940) he formed a coalition government and, holding both the premiership and the defence portfolio, led Britain through the War against Germany and Italy with steely resolution. Defeated in the Jul 1945 election, he became a pugnacious Leader of the Opposition. In 1951 he became Prime Minister again, and retired in 1955. He remained a venerated backbencher, having achieved a world reputation not only as a great strategist and inspiring war leader, but as a classic orator with a supreme command of English. He was also a talented painter and a broad-minded writer with an Augustan style and a profound sense of history. He won the 1953 Nobel Prize for Literature.

churchman or churchwoman *noun* a member of the clergy or of a church.

Church of England the official state Church of England, a national Church that has both Protestant and Catholic features, is based on episcopal authority, and has the sovereign as its head.
◊ It originated when Henry VIII broke ties with the Roman Catholic Church (c.1532–4) and was declared by Parliament to be the 'supreme head on earth of the English Church'. However, the Church remained largely Catholic in character until reforms of doctrine and liturgy under Edward VI, when the new Book of Common Prayer appeared (1549, 1552). Under Elizabeth I the moderately Protestant set of doctrinal statements (the 'Thirty-Nine Articles') emerged. She and James I resisted efforts towards both a Catholic revival and Puritan attempts to take a more Calvinist stance, but under Charles I a presbyterian form of government was temporarily established until the episcopacy and Prayer Book were restored under Charles II.
The Church of England today consists of some 44 dioceses in the two provinces of Canterbury and York, with over 16 000 churches and other places of worship. Local parishes are arranged into rural deaneries and dioceses, with each diocese led by a bishop and sometimes assisted by a suffragan or assistant bishop.
In 1970 the General Synod was established for the purpose of reaching decisions and expressing views on issues of interest to the Church. It meets three times a year and is presided over by the Archbishops of Canterbury and York. In Nov 1992, amid much contoversy, it voted to permit the ordination of women as priests.

church officer in some churches, a person acting as church caretaker, with certain other duties.

Church of Scotland the national Church in Scotland, founded at the Reformation of 1560 under the leadership of John Knox.
◊ Presbyterian in its governing organization and discipline, elders (ordained laymen) play a leading part with ministers in church courts at local, congregational level (in Kirk Session), district level (presbyteries, overseeing congregations in a given area), provincial synods, and the General Assembly.
Ministers (women and men), who are ordained by presbytery, are alone authorized to administer the sacraments of Baptism (of infants as well as adults) and the Lord's Supper (communion).
It has a strong missionary tradition, especially in Africa and India, and supports many Churches in developing countries.

churchwarden *noun* **1** in the Church of England, one of two lay members of a congregation elected to look after the church's property, money, etc. **2** an old-fashioned long clay pipe.

churchyard *noun* the burial ground round a church.

churlish *adj.* bad-tempered; rude; ill-mannered. [from *churl*, surly person, peasant]

churlishly *adv.* with a churlish manner.

churlishness *noun* being churlish.

churn — *noun* **1** a machine in which milk is shaken about to make butter. **2** a large milk can. — *verb* **1** to make (butter) in a churn, or to turn (milk) into butter in a churn. **2** (**churn something up**) to shake or agitate it violently.
— **churn something out** to keep producing things of tedious similarity in large quantities. [from Anglo-Saxon *cirin* or *cyrn*]

chute[1] *noun* **1** a sloping channel down which to send water, rubbish, etc. **2** a slide in a children's playground or swimming-pool. [from French *chute*, fall]

chute[2] *noun colloq.* a parachute.

Chu Teh see ZHU DE.

chutney *noun* an Indian type of pickle made with fruit, vinegar, spices, sugar, etc. [from Hindi *catni*]

chutzpah *noun chiefly North Amer. colloq.* self-assurance bordering on impudence; audacity; effrontery; nerve. [from Yiddish *chutzpah*]

Chuzzlewit, Martin, also called **Old Martin** the rich and suspicious head of the family in Charles Dickens's *Martin Chuzzlewit*. Other members of the family include his brother Anthony, nephew Jonas, and grandson Martin.

chyle *noun Physiol.* a milky fluid, consisting of lymph containing fats that have been absorbed from the small intestine during digestion. [from Greek *chylos*, juice]

chyme *noun Physiol.* the partially digested food that passes into the duodenum and small intestine from the stomach. [from Greek *chymos*, juice]

CI *abbrev.* **1** Channel Islands. **2** *as an international vehicle mark* Côte d'Ivoire (French), Ivory Coast.

Ci *symbol* curie.

CIA *abbrev.* Central Intelligence Agency (USA).

ciabatta *noun* Italian bread with a sponge-like texture, made with olive oil. [Italian, = slipper]

CIB *abbrev.* Chartered Institute of Bankers.

cicada *noun* a large hemipteran insect of mainly tropical regions that spends most of its life in trees, sucking sap from beneath the bark, against which it is well camouflaged. The males attract females with a high-pitched warbling whistle produced by vibrating tambourine-like membranes on either side of the body. [from Latin *cicada*]

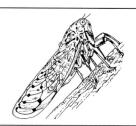

cicada

cicatrice *or* **cicatrix** *noun* (PL. **cicatrices**) a scar left by a wound after healing. [from Latin *cicatrix*]

CICB *abbrev. Brit.* Criminal Injuries Compensation Board.

cicely *noun* a plant with a strong smell of aniseed, used as a flavouring, especially sweet cicely. [from Greek *seselis*, with spelling influenced by the name *Cicely*]

Cicero, Marcus Tullius (106–43 BC) Roman orator, statesman, and man of letters, born in Arpinum, Latium. He embarked upon a political career and was elected consul in 63 BC. He foiled Cataline's revolutionary plot but broke the law by executing some of the conspirators

(Roman citizens) without a trial and when charges were pressed, he went into exile in Thessalonica (58 BC). In 57 BC he was recalled by the people, but lost the esteem of both Caesar's and Pompey's factions by vacillating between the two. He lived in retirement in Rome (46–44 BC), where he wrote most of his major works on rhetoric and philosophy. Following the assassination of Caesar, he delivered his speeches (the 'Philippics') against Antony (43 BC), which resulted in his assassination by Antony's soldiers.

CID *abbrev.* Criminal Investigation Department, the detective branch of the British police force.

Cid, El, real name **Rodrigo**, or **Ruy Díaz de Vivar** (c.1043–99) Spanish hero, born in Burgos, who soon became known as the 'Cid' (from the Moorish Sidi, 'lord'); 'Campeador' (warrior) is often added. A soldier of fortune and a great patriot, he was constantly fighting. His great achievement was the capture of Valencia from the Moors (1094).

-cide *combining form* forming nouns denoting: **1** the act of killing; murder: *homicide*. **2** a person, substance, or thing that kills. [from Latin *-cida*, -killer, and *-cidium*, -killing]

cider *noun* an alcoholic drink made from apples. [from French *cidre*]

Cid, Le a play by Pierre Corneille (1636). A tragedy, its plot revolves around the conflicts of loyalty, love and honour. Though highly successful, it provoked much rivalry and a bitter exchange of pamphlets known as the 'Querelle du Cid'.

Cienfuegos 1 POP (1989e) 119 000, the port capital of Cienfuegos province, W central Cuba. It lies on the S coast, 337km/209mi SE of Havana. The city was founded in 1819 and is an important industrial centre. NOTABLE FEATURES botanical garden; Castillo de Jagua (1738–45); museum. **2** a province in W central Cuba with Cienfuegos as its capital.

cigar *noun* a long slender roll of tobacco leaves for smoking. [from Spanish *cigarro*]

cigarette *noun* a tube of finely cut tobacco rolled in thin paper, for smoking. [from French *cigarette*, diminutive of *cigare*, cigar]

cigarette end *or* **cigarette butt** the unsmoked stub of a cigarette.

cigarette-holder *noun* a long slim mouthpiece into which a cigarette can be fitted for smoking.

cigarette-lighter *noun* a petrol- or gas-fuelled device with a flint, for lighting cigarettes.

cigar-shaped *adj.* having an elongated oval shape with pointed ends.

CII *abbrev.* Chartered Insurance Institute.

ciliary muscle *Anat.* a muscle that controls the curvature of the lens of the eye, by contracting to make it thin (for viewing distant objects), or relaxing to make it thicker (for viewing nearby objects). [from Latin *cilium*, eyelash]

ciliate *noun Zool.* a microscopic single-celled organism that typically possesses short hair-like appendages, known as *cilia*, on its surface, which are used to aid locomotion. Ciliates are found free-living in all kinds of aquatic and terrestrial habitats, and as parasites. [from Latin *cilium*, eyelash]

Cilicia the ancient name for the S coastal part of Turkey around the Taurus Mts. It was famous for its timber and its pirates.

cilium *noun* (PL. **cilia**) *Biol.* any of the short hair-like appendages that project from the surface of certain cells, and move rhythmically, usually to aid locomotion, or to cause movement of the water surrounding some single-celled aquatic organisms. [from Latin *cilium*, eyelash]

cimbalom *noun* a form of dulcimer used in Hungary and other E European countries. It con-

sists of a wooden box with a series of metal strings strung on pegs, and is played by striking the strings with sticks. Smaller types are portable, carried on a strap round the player's shoulders. Though mainly used in folk music, it has been used as a concert instrument, notably by Stravinsky, Kodály, Liszt, and Bartók. [Hungarian, from Italian *cembala*, cymbal]

Cimmerians a nomadic people of S Russia who were driven out by the Scythians in the 8c BC. They migrated through the Caucasus Mts to Assyria and Asia Minor, where they caused widespread havoc and destruction.

Cimon (c.507–c.450 BC) Athenian soldier and politician, the son of Miltiades, the conqueror at Marathon. He fought at the battle of Salamis (480 BC) and from 476 BC was the most notable commander of the forces of the Delian League in the patriotic struggle against the Persians. His greatest exploit was his destruction of a Persian fleet and army at the River Eurymedon (c.476 BC). He led an unsuccessful expedition to support the Spartans during the helot uprising in 462 BC, and was dismissed and ostracized in 461 BC. He was recalled in 454 BC, and may have been instrumental in obtaining a five-years armistice with Sparta. He died at the siege of a town in Cyprus.

C-in-C *abbrev.* Commander-in-Chief.

cinch *noun colloq.* **1** an easily accomplished task. **2** a certainty. [from Spanish *cincha*, saddle girth]

cinchona *noun* **1** any tree of the Cinchona genus, yielding bark from which quinine and related by-products are obtained. **2** the dried bark of these trees.

Cincinnati POP (1990) 1.5m, the seat of Hamilton County, SW Ohio, USA, situated on the Ohio R. HISTORY Fort Washington was built here in 1789; large numbers of German immigrants arrived in the 1840s; William Howard Taft, 27th US President, was born here in 1909. NOTABLE FEATURES Taft Museum; Contemporary Arts Centre; Kings Island Park; several centres for culture, music, and the arts.

Cincinnatus, Lucius Quinctius (5c BC) Roman statesman, farmer and folk hero. He was called from the plough and given absolute power to rescue the Roman army of the consul Minucius, which had been trapped by the Aequi (458 BC). After his victory, he voluntarily gave up this power and returned to his farm.

cincture *noun literary* a belt or girdle. [from Latin *cinctura*]

cinder *noun* **1** a piece of burnt coal or wood. **2** (**cinders**) ashes. [from Anglo-Saxon *sinder*, slag]

Cinderella *noun* someone or something whose charms or merits go unnoticed; a neglected member of a set or group. [from the fairy-tale character Cinderella]

cindery *adj.* of the nature of or composed of cinders.

cine *adj.*, *combining form* relating to moving pictures: *a cinecamera* / *a cine projector*. [shortened from CINEMA]

cinema *noun* **1** a theatre in which motion pictures are shown. **2** cinemas in general: *don't go to the cinema much.* **3** (*usually* **the cinema**) motion pictures or films generally. **4** the art or business of making films. [from CINEMATOGRAPH]
◇ The first cinema audiences in 1895 were shown single-reel films, usually depicting scenes of real life in movement. These were soon followed by stories in continuous action, fantastic trick films, and music hall turns. By 1912, productions of more than a single reel had been developed, and by the 1920s the silent cinema had become an established international medium for entertainment, instruction, and propaganda. Sound was added in 1927, and colour was available from the 1930s (though it did not become

universal until the 1950s). Various forms of wide-screen presentation were introduced from the 1950s. Feature films made for the cinema are still a major source of popular entertainment, despite competition from television and video.

CinemaScope *trademark* a system of wide-screen cinematography, based on Henri Chrétien's invention of 1927 and adopted by 20th Century-Fox in 1953.

cinematic *adj.* relating to or characteristic of the cinema.

cinematograph *noun* an apparatus for taking and projecting moving pictures, ie a series of still photographs each representing an instant of time, in rapid succession.

cinematographer *noun* a person skilled in cinematography.

cinematographic *adj.* relating to or characteristic of cinematography.

cinematography *noun* the art of making motion pictures. [from Greek *kinema*, motion + -GRAPHY]

cinema vérité *Cinema* a style of film production characterized by documentary treatment, giving the appearance of real life even for fictional drama. The approach usually favours non-professional actors and minimal script and rehearsal, and often makes use of the mobile viewpoint of a hand-held camera and natural sound. [French, = cinema truth]

Cinerama *trademark* one of the first systems of wide-screen cinema presentation (1952), using three synchronized projectors to cover a large curved screen in three blended panels. It was available only in specially-adapted cinemas, and was discontinued after 1962 because of its cost and complexity. [from CINEMA + PANORAMA]

cineraria *noun* a plant with brightly coloured daisy-like flowers and leaves with a thick white down. [from Latin *cinerarius*, relating to ashes]

cinerary *adj.* relating to ashes; for holding ashes: *a cinerary urn.* [from Latin *cinerarius*, relating to ashes]

cinnabar *noun* 1 *Geol.* a bright red transparent to translucent mineral form of mercury sulphide, that is the principal source of mercury, and is also used to make the orange-red pigment vermilion. 2 vermilion, an orange-red colour. 3 a moth with red and black wings. [from Greek *kinnabari*, from Persian]

cinnamon *noun* 1 a spice obtained from the inner bark of a SE Asian tree. 2 a brownish-orange colour. [from Greek *kinnamon*]

cinquecento *noun* Italian art and literature of the 16c Renaissance. [from Italian, = 500, referring to the century 1500–99]

cinquefoil *noun* 1 a plant of the rose family with five-petalled flowers and leaves divided into five sections. 2 *Heraldry* a five-petalled flower. 3 *Archit.* a design composed of five petal-like arcs, found at the top of an arch, in a circular window, etc. [from Old French *cincfoille*, from Latin *quinquefolium*, five-leaved plant]

Cinque Ports originally, the five S English coast ports of Dover, Hastings, Hythe, Romney, and Sandwich (and later Rye and Winchelsea), associated by royal authority (under Edward the Confessor) to provide ships for naval defence. They received royal privileges, including (from 1265) the right to send barons to parliament, and charters (from 1278), and were governed by a Lord Warden who was also Constable of Dover Castle. Their role declined with the growth of the navy under the Tudors and Stuarts, and the status was abolished in 1835.

CIOB *abbrev.* Chartered Institute of Building.

CIPA *abbrev.* Chartered Institute of Patent Agents.

CIPFA *abbrev.* Chartered Institute of Public Finance and Accountancy.

cipher — *noun* 1 a secret code. 2 something written in code. 3 the key to a code. 4 an interlaced set of initials; a monogram. 5 *Maths. old use* the symbol 0, used to fill blanks in writing numbers, but of no value itself. 6 a person or thing of little importance. 7 any Arabic numeral. — *verb* (**ciphered, ciphering**) to write (a message, etc) in code. [from Latin *ciphra*, from Arabic *sifr*, empty, zero]

circa *prep., used especially with dates* about; approximately: *circa 1250.* [from Latin *circa*]

circadian *adj. Biol.* denoting a biological rhythm that is more or less synchronized to a 24-hour cycle, eg the pattern of sleeping and waking in adult humans. [from CIRCA + Latin *dies*, day]

Circassians a people from the Caucasus, speaking a NW Caucasian language, who are divided into Adyghians (Lower Circassians) and Kabardians (Upper Circassians). Most live in Russia, but there are also Circassian communities in Syria and Turkey, and small groups in Iraq, Jordan, and Israel.

Circe in Greek mythology, an enchantress who detained Odysseus and his followers on the island of Aeaea. She transformed Odysseus's men into swine with a magic drink, but he was able to defeat her charms through the protection of the herb moly.

Circinus *Astron.* the Compasses, a small obscure constellation in the southern hemisphere, lying in the Milky Way.

circle — *noun* 1 a perfectly round plane (two-dimensional) figure that is bordered by a line, known as the *circumference*, which consists of all points that are an equal distance (the *radius*) from a fixed point within the figure (the *centre*). 2 anything in the form of a circle. 3 a circular route, eg the orbit of a planet, etc. 4 a curved upper floor of seats in a theatre, etc. 5 a series of events, steps or developments, ending at the point where it began. See also VICIOUS CIRCLE. 6 a group of people associated in some way: *his circle of acquaintances.* — *verb* 1 *trans., intrans.* to move in a circle; to move in a circle round. 2 to draw a circle round.
— **come full circle** 1 to complete a full cycle. 2 to reach or arrive back at the starting-point.
go round in circles to be trapped in an endless and frustrating cycle of repetitive discussion or activity.
run round in circles to rush around frantically, making little progress.
[from Anglo-Saxon *circul*, from Latin *circulus*]
◇ The *diameter* of a circle is equal to twice the radius, and consists of a straight line that crosses the circle from one side to the other and passes through the centre. A *chord* is a line joining any two points on the circumference. For a circle of radius *r*, the circumference is equal to $2\pi r$, and the area is equal to πr^2, where π is a constant with a value of approximately 3.142.

circlet *noun* 1 a simple band or hoop of gold, silver, etc worn on the head. 2 a small circle. [from Old French *cerclet*, diminutive of *cercle*, circle]

circotherm oven an oven with a fan to circulate internal hot air. It is designed to achieve uniformity of heating and to economize in heating and cooking time. Also popularly known as a *fan oven.*

circuit *noun* 1 a complete course, journey, or route round something. 2 a race track, running-track, etc. 3 (*in full* **electric circuit**) a path consisting of various electrical devices joined together by wires so that an electric current can flow continuously through it. 4 the places or venues visited in turn and regularly by entertainers, etc. 5 a round of places made by a travelling judge. 6 a group of cinemas, theatres, etc under common control, with shows moving on from one to the next. [from French *circuit*, from Latin *circuitus*, round trip, revolution]

circuit-breaker *noun* a device that automatically interrupts an electric current when a fault occurs.

circuitous *adj.* taking a long complicated route; indirect; roundabout.

circuitously *adv.* in a circuitous way.

circuitousness *noun* being circuitous.

circuitry *noun* (PL. **circuitries**) *Electr.* 1 a plan or system of circuits. 2 the equipment or components making up such a system.

circuit training athletic training in the form of a repeated series of exercises.

circular — *adj.* 1 having the form of a circle. 2 moving or going round in a circle, leading back to the starting-point. 3 *said of reasoning, etc* containing a fallacy, the truth of the conclusion depending on a point that depends on the conclusion being true. 4 *said of a letter, etc* addressed and copied to a number of people. — *noun* a circular letter or notice. [from Latin *circularis*]

circularity *noun* (PL. **circularities**) a circular form, position, or quality.

circularize *or* **circularise** *verb* to send circulars to.

circularly *adv.* in a circular way.

circular saw a power-driven saw with a rotating disc-shaped toothed blade.

circulate *verb* 1 *trans., intrans.* to move or cause to move round freely, especially in a fixed route: *traffic circulating through the town centre.* 2 *trans., intrans.* to spread; to pass round: *circulate the report.* 3 *intrans.* to move around talking to different people, eg at a party. [from Latin *circulare*, to encircle]

circulation *noun* 1 the act or process of circulating. 2 *Anat.* in all except very simple animals, the system of vessels that transports blood and other tissue fluids, eg lymph, to and from all the parts of the body via a regular circuitous course; specifically, the system of blood vessels that supplies oxygenated blood pumped by the heart to all parts of the body, and that transports deoxygenated blood to the lungs. 3 the distribution of a newspaper or magazine, or the number of copies of it that are sold.

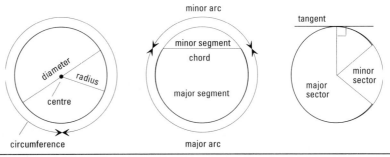

circle

— in or **out of circulation 1** said of money being, or not being, used by the public. **2** taking part, or not taking part, in one's usual social activities.

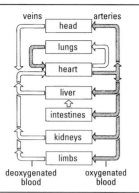

human circulation

circulatory adj. relating to circulation, especially of the blood.

circum- combining form round about. [from Latin circum, about]

circumcise verb **1** to cut away the foreskin of (a male), as a religious rite or medical necessity. **2** to cut away the clitoris of (a woman), or the skin covering it, for the same reasons. [from Latin circum, around + caedere, to cut round]

Circumcision noun Christianity a festival (1 Jan) in honour of the circumcision of Christ, eight days after his birth.

circumcision noun **1** in males, the surgical removal of all or part of the foreskin of the penis, usually performed during early childhood for religious or ethnic reasons, or on medical grounds. **2** in females, the surgical removal of the clitoris (and sometimes the labia).

circumference noun **1** Geom. the length of the boundary of a circle or other closed curve, eg an ellipse, or the length of a path around a sphere at its widest point. For a circle, the circumference is equal to $2\pi r$, where r is the radius of the circle, and π has a value of approximately 3.14. **2** the boundary of an area of any shape. **3** the distance represented by any of these. [from Latin circum, around + ferre, to carry]

circumferential adj. relating to or of the nature of a circumference.

circumflex noun a mark placed over a vowel (eg ô, û) in some languages as an indication of pronunciation, length, or the omission of a letter. [from Latin circumflexus, arch]

circumlocution noun an unnecessarily long or indirect way of saying something. [from Latin circum, around + loqui, to speak]

circumlocutory adj. given to or marked by circumlocution.

circumnavigate verb to sail or fly round (the world). [from Latin circum, around + navigare, to sail]

circumnavigation noun the act of circumnavigating.

circumnavigator noun a person who circumnavigates.

circumscribe verb **1** to put a line or boundary round. **2** to limit or restrict. **3** Geom. to draw a figure round (another figure) so that they touch without intersecting. See also INSCRIBE. [from Latin circum, around + scribere, to write]

circumscription noun the act of circumscribing.

circumspect adj. cautious; prudent; wary. [from Latin circum, around + specere, to look]

circumspection noun caution; vigilance.

circumspectly adv. in a circumspect way.

circumstance noun **1** (often **circumstances**) a fact, occurrence, or condition, especially when relating to an act or event: died in mysterious circumstances. **2** (**circumstances**) one's financial situation. **3** events that one cannot control; fate: a victim of circumstance. **4** ceremony: pomp and circumstance.
— in or **under no circumstances** never, not for any reason at all.
in or **under the circumstances** the situation being what it is or was.
reduced cirumstances poverty.
[from Latin circum, around + stare, to stand]

circumstantial adj., said of an account of an event full of detailed description, etc.

circumstantial evidence Legal details or facts that give a statement, etc the appearance of truth, but do not prove it.

circumstantially adv. in a circumstantial way.

circumvent verb **1** to find a way of getting round or evading (a rule, law, etc). **2** to outwit or frustrate (someone). [from Latin circum, around + venire, to come]

circumvention noun the act of circumventing; avoidance.

circus noun **1** a travelling company of performers including acrobats, clowns, and often trained animals, etc; a performance by such a company, traditionally in a circular tent. **2** colloq. a scene of noisy confusion. **3** a travelling group of professional sportspeople, etc who put on displays. **4** often in place names an open space, especially one roughly circular, at the junction of a number of streets; a circular terrace of houses. **5** in ancient Rome, an oval or circular open-air stadium for chariot-racing and other competitive sports. [from Latin circus, circle, ring, stadium]
◊ The ring associated with the modern-day circus was introduced in 1768 by the trick horseback rider Philip Astley (1742–1814). Charles Hughes built his Royal Circus in 1782 — the first modern-day use of the word. Famous 19c circuses included Barnum and Bailey's, Astley's and Spengler's, and in more recent times, Betram Mills, Billy Smart, David Chipperfield, and the Moscow State Circus.

Cirencester, ancient **Corinium Dobunorum** POP (1981) 14 000, a market town in Cotswold district, Gloucestershire, SW central England. It lies in the Cotswolds on the R Churn, 22km/14mi NW of Swindon. During the 2c, it was the second largest town in Roman Britain. NOTABLE FEATURES Royal Agricultural College; Church of St John the Baptist (14c); Corinium Museum.

cirque noun Geog. a deep semicircular hollow resembling an amphitheatre, with steep side and back walls, located high on a mountain slope and often containing a small lake. Cirques are formed as a result of the erosion of bedrock by a small glacier. — Also called corrie, cwm. [from French cirque, circus]

cirrhosis noun Medicine a progressive disease of the liver, caused especially by persistent excessive drinking of alcohol, with a wasting away of normal tissue, and an overgrowth of abnormal lumpy tissue. [from Greek kirrhos, tawny, from the colour of the diseased liver + -OSIS]

cirriped or **cirripede** noun Zool. any of the class of sea creatures that includes barnacles. [from Latin cirrus, curl + pes, foot]

cirrocumulus noun (PL. **cirrocumuli**) Meteorol. a type of high cloud, often referred to as a 'mackerel sky' because it consists of small masses of white clouds that form a rippled pattern. It is associated with warm fronts. [from CIRRUS + CUMULUS]

cirrostratus noun (PL. **cirrostrati**) Meteorol. a type of high cloud that forms a thin whitish layer with a fibrous appearance, and which may cover most or all of the sky. It is associated with the approach of a depression. [from CIRRUS + STRATUS]

cirrus noun (PL. **cirri**) Meteorol. a common type of high cloud with a wispy fibrous or feathery appearance. It is composed of ice crystals, and is associated with fair weather. [from Latin cirrus, curl]

CIS abbrev. **1** Chartered Institute of Secretaries. **2** Commonwealth of Independent States.

Cisalpine Republic N Italian state created by Napoleon I at the Peace of Campoformio (1797). It comprised Milan and Lombardy, the Valtellina, the Romagna, the Venetian territories of Brescia and Bergamo, and the Duchy of Massa Carrara, and by the Treaty of Lunéville (1802), it became the Italian Republic, with Bonaparte as President.

Ciscaucasia the N Caucasus territory of Kuban, Stavropol, Terek, and the Black Sea, formed in 1924. It existed until 1934, when it was split into the Asov Black Sea, Ordzhonikidze, and Stavropol Territories.

Ciskei POP (1991e) 847 000, an independent black homeland in NE Cape province, South Africa. AREA 7 700sq km/2 972sq mi. Ciskei is bounded SW by the Indian Ocean. It was the fourth homeland to gain independence from South Africa (1981), although its independent status is not recognized internationally. CAPITAL Bisho. The majority of the population are Xhosa and are dependent on subsistence agriculture; many people are commuters or migrant workers in South Africa.

cissy see SISSY.

cist noun Archaeol. a grave lined and covered with slabs of stone. [from Welsh cist, chest, from Latin cista]

Cistercian — noun a member of a religious order formed in 1098 (see CISTERCIANS). — adj. relating to the Cistercians. [from Latin Cistercium, Citeaux]

Cistercians a religious order formed (1098) in Citeaux, France, by Benedictine monks led by St Robert of Molesme. They followed a strict rule, with an emphasis on solitude, poverty, and simplicity. The order was prominent in the Middle Ages, and Bernard of Clairvaux was among its leaders. By the 13c it had over 500 houses in Europe, but thereafter declined. In the 17c it was divided into communities of Common Observance (now abbreviated SOCist) and of Strict Observance (in full, the Order of the Reformed Cistercians of the Strict Observance, abbreviated OCSO). The latter were revived in France after the Revolution by Trappists (former members of the monastery of La Trappe). Common Observance is now prominent in the USA and in parts of W Europe, with an abbot-general in Rome; Strict Observance, with a mother-house in Citeaux and an abbot in Rome, is active in France, Switzerland, England, and Poland.

cistern noun **1** a tank storing water, usually in the roof-space of a house, or serving a flushing toilet. **2** Archaeol. an underground reservoir. [from Latin cisterna, reservoir]

cistron noun Genetics that part of a chain of DNA that is functionally equivalent to a gene. [from cis-trans test, a test defining the unit of genetic function]

citadel noun a stronghold or fortress close to, or dominating the centre of, a city, built for its protection and as a place of refuge. [from Italian cittadella, diminutive of città, city]

citation noun **1** the quoting or citing of something as example or proof. **2** a passage quoted from a book, etc. **3** Legal an order to appear in court. **4** a special official commendation or award for merit, bravery, etc, or a list of the reasons for such an award.

citation analysis the quantitative analysis of the use of bibliographical citations in academic publications. The number of times a research study or a journal is cited by others can be interpreted as a valid indicator of its importance.

cite *verb* **1** to quote (a book, its author, or a passage from it) as an example or proof. **2** to mention as an example or illustration. **3** *Legal* to summon (a person) to appear in court; to name (a person) as being involved in a case. **4** to mention (someone) in an official report by way of commendation: *cited for bravery*. [from Old French *citer*, to summon]

CITES *abbrev.* Convention on International Trade in Endangered Species (of Wild Fauna and Flora).

citizen *noun* **1** an inhabitant of a city or town. **2** a native of a country or state, or a naturalized member of it. [from Middle English *citesein*, from Old French *citeain*, from *cite*, city]

Citizen Kane a US film directed by Orson Welles (1941). Considered a milestone in cinema history, the story develops from a journalist's attempts to uncover the significance of the last word, 'Rosebud', uttered by a dying millionaire (played by Orson Welles).

citizenry *noun* the citizens of a town, country, etc.

Citizens Advice Bureaux, National Association of (ABBREV. **CAB**) in the UK, a national network of information offices, set up in 1939 to inform the public about the emergency regulations in World War II. It now provides free and confidential information, particularly concerning the social services, housing, legal aid, consumer services, and family matters. It is funded mainly by the government and the majority of its staff are trained volunteers.

citizen's arrest an arrest, allowable in some countries, made by a member of the public.

Citizens' Band a set of radio frequencies that members of the public may use for sending messages to each other.

citizens' charter a set of proposals drawn up by the government, or other body such as a local authority, outlining eg the minimum acceptable standards of service in health care, education, etc, people's rights with regard to public bodies, compensation for unacceptably poor service, etc.

citizenship *noun* **1** the status or position of a citizen. **2** the rights and duties of a citizen.

Citlaltépetl or **Pico de Orizaba** the highest peak in Mexico, situated in the E of the country. HEIGHT 5 699m. A dormant volcano, it has been inactive since 1687. It is situated in the Pico de Orizaba National Park, established in 1936.

citrate *noun Chem.* a salt of citric acid.

citric *adj.* relating to, or obtained from, citrus fruits or citric acid. [see CITRUS]

citric acid *Chem.* (FORMULA $C_6H_8O_7$) an organic acid, present in the juice of citrus fruit, that plays an important role in the energy-generating biochemical reactions of the Krebs cycle in plant and animal cells. It is used as a food flavouring and antioxidant.

citrin *noun* vitamin P. [from CITRUS]

Citroën, André Gustave (1878–1935) French engineer and motor manufacturer, born in Paris. He was responsible for the mass production of armaments during World War I. After the war he applied these techniques to the manufacture of low-priced small cars; the first of these Citroën models appeared in 1919. He became bankrupt in 1934 and lost control of his company.

citron *noun* **1** a fruit like a large lemon, with a thick sweet-smelling yellow rind. **2** the candied rind of this fruit, used for flavouring or decorating cakes, etc. **3** the Asian tree bearing the fruit.

[from Italian *citrone*, from Latin *citrus*, the citron tree]

citrus *noun* (*also* **citrus fruit**) any of a group of edible fruits with a tough outer peel enclosing membranous segments filled with juicy flesh rich in vitamin C, citric acid, and water, obtained from trees or shrubs of the orange family (genus *Citrus*), eg orange, lemon, grapefruit, lime, tangerine, and kumquat. They may be eaten fresh, squeezed for their juice, or used to produce flavourings, essential oils, etc. [from Latin *citrus*, the citron tree]

cittern or **cithern** or **cither** *noun* a plucked stringed instrument popular in the 16c and 17c, and known in England in the 18c as the *English guitar*. It resembled a lute, but had a smaller pear-shaped body, a flat back, and wire strings played with a plectrum or the fingers. The zither is a different instrument. [from Greek *kithara*]

city *noun* (PL. **cities**) **1** any large town; in the UK, a town with a royal charter, and usually a cathedral. **2** the body of inhabitants of a city. **3** (**the City**) the business centre of a city, especially London. [from Old French *cite*, from Latin *civitas*, state]
◇ In classical Greece, cities were self-governing and (usually) economically self-sufficient states; in early medieval times, they were usually those towns which were the seats of bishops. In the UK, the term is used of cathedral towns (eg Ely) and certain other towns on which the title has been conferred by royal authority (eg Birmingham in 1889); in the USA, cities are those urban centres that have a particular local government structure.

city desk in a newspaper office, the department of the **city editor**, dealing with financial news.

city fathers the magistrates of a city, or members of its council.

city hall (*often* **City Hall**) the local government of a city, or the building in which it is housed.

City Lights a US film directed by Charles Chaplin (1931). A silent comedy, it tells the moving story of a tramp (Chaplin) who enables a blind flower-seller to have her sight restored.

City of Birmingham Symphony Orchestra (ABBREV. **CBSO**) an English orchestra, founded as the City of Birmingham Orchestra in 1920 (renamed 1948), with a first performance of works composed and conducted by Elgar. Simon Rattle has conducted there since 1980.

city-state *noun Hist.* a city that possesses its own territory and forms an independent state.
◇ The city-state, or *polis*, was the principal political and economic unit of ancient Greece. Some were democracies, others more oligarchic in character; all, however, had the same basic organs of government, ie assemblies composed of male citizens, an advisory council, and executive officers who were either elected or (in some democracies) chosen by lot. The city-state declined in the 4c BC, especially after the emergence of Macedon as the dominant power in Greece. In the empire of Alexander, and in the Hellenistic kingdoms, city-states existed as part of the constitutional structure; their relations with the kings is one of the main historical interests of this period. Rome is the most famous example of a city-state that grew to rule an empire.

Ciudad Guayana or **San Félix de Guayana** POP (1990e) 537 000, a new city in Bolívar state, E Venezuela, on the Orinoco and Caroní rivers. It was founded in 1961 to link the towns of San Félix, Puerto Ordaz, Palúa, and Matanzas.

Ciudad Juárez POP (1990) 798 000, a town in Chihuahua state, N Mexico. It is situated on the US border, opposite El Paso, Texas, on the R

Grande. The town was the headquarters of the Mexican president Benito Juárez in 1865.

civet *noun* **1** (*also* **civet cat**) a small spotted cat-like animal, found in Asia and Africa. **2** a strong-smelling fluid produced by the animal's glands, used in perfumes to make their scent last. **3** the fur of the animal. [from French *civette*]

civet

civic *adj.* relating to a city, citizen, or citizenship. [from Latin *civicus*, from *civis*, citizen]

civically *adv.* in a civic way.

civic centre a place, sometimes a specially designed complex, where the administrative offices and chief public buildings of a city are grouped.

civics *sing. noun* the study of local government and of the rights and duties of citizenship.

Civic Trust a charitable organization which exists to promote conservation and improvement of the environment in town and country, through encouraging high standards in architecture, town planning, and the preservation of buildings of historic and architectural interest. There are separate Civic Trusts for England, Scotland, and Wales.

civil *adj.* **1** relating to the community: *civil affairs*. **2** relating to or occurring between citizens: *civil disturbances*. **3** relating to ordinary citizens; not military, legal, or religious. **4** *Legal* relating to cases about individual rights, etc, not criminal cases. **5** polite; not discourteous. [from Latin *civilis*, relating to citizens, from *civis*, citizen]

civil defence **1** the organization and training of ordinary citizens to assist the armed forces in wartime, especially during enemy attack. **2** the body of people involved in this.
◇ Civil defence became a vital part of a nation's defences during the bombing campaigns in World War II. In the age of nuclear weapons, however, faced with the prospect of massive casualties, Britain has largely disbanded its Civil Defence operation. Countries which maintain active organizations include Switzerland and Sweden; in the USA, Civil Defense is chiefly concerned with the effects of natural disasters.

civil disobedience the refusal to obey regulations, pay taxes, etc, as a form of non-violent protest.

civil engineer an engineer who designs and builds roads, bridges, tunnels, etc.

civil engineering the branch of engineering concerned with the design, construction, and maintenance of roads, bridges, railways, canals, tunnels, docks, and other large non-mechanical structures, as well as land drainage, water supply, and sewage treatment.

civilian — *noun* anyone who is not a member of the armed forces or the police force. — *adj.* relating to civilians. [from Old French *civilien*, relating to civil law]

civility *noun* (PL. **civilities**) **1** politeness. **2** an act of politeness; a polite remark or gesture. [from Old French *civilite*]

civilization or **civilisation** *noun* **1** the state of being, or process of becoming, civilized; the act of civilizing. **2** a stage of development in human society that is socially, politically, culturally, and technologically advanced. **3** the parts of the world that have reached such a stage. **4** *usually Hist.* a people and their society and culture: *the Minoan civilization.* **5** built-up areas as opposed to wild, uncultivated, or sparsely populated parts. **6** intellectual or spiritual enlightenment, as opposed to brutishness or coarseness.

civilize *or* **civilise** *verb* **1** to lead out of a state of barbarity to a more advanced stage of social development. **2** to educate and enlighten morally, intellectually, and spiritually. [from French *civiliser*, from Latin *civilis*, relating to political life]

civilized *or* **civilised** *adj.* **1** socially, politically, and technologically advanced. **2** agreeably refined, sophisticated, or comfortable. **3** *facetious* trained to behave and speak politely.

civil law the part of a country's law that deals with its citizens' rights, etc, not with crimes.

civil liberty (*often in pl.*) personal freedom of thought, word, action, etc.

civil list in the UK, the annual Parliamentary allowance to the sovereign and the Royal family for household expenses.

civilly *adv.* with a civil manner.

civil rights the personal rights of any citizen of a country, especially to freedom and equality regardless of race, religion, sex, or sexuality.

civil servant a person employed in the civil service.

civil service the body of officials employed by a government to administer the affairs of a country.

civil war a war between citizens of the same state.
◇ Notable examples include: the American Civil War (1861–5) between the southern states and the northern or Federal States; the English Civil War (1642–6 and 1648) between the king, supported by the Royalists (Cavaliers), and the Parliamentarians (Roundheads); and in the 20c, the Spanish Civil War (1936–9) between the (fascist) Nationalists and the Republicans.

civvies *pl. noun colloq.* ordinary civilian clothes as opposed to a military uniform.

civvy street *colloq.* ordinary civilian life outside the armed forces.

Ci Xi *or* **Tz'u Hsi**, personal name **Yehenala** (1835–1908) Chinese consort of the Xiangfeng Emperor (1851–62). She bore his only son, who succeeded at the age of five as the T'ung Chih Emperor. After his death (1875), she flouted the succession laws of the Imperial clan to ensure the succession of another minor, aged three, as the Guang Xu (Kuang Hsu) Emperor. In 1900 she took China into war against the combined treaty powers in support of the Boxer movement.

CL *abbrev.,* as an international vehicle mark Sri Lanka (formerly Ceylon).

Cl *symbol Chem.* chlorine.

clack — *noun* a sharp noise made by one hard object striking another. — *verb* **1** *trans., intrans.* to make or cause to make this kind of noise. **2** *intrans.* to talk noisily. [imitative]

clad — *adj. literary* **1** clothed: *clad in velvet.* **2** covered. — *verb* (**cladding**; PAST TENSE AND PAST PARTICIPLE **clad**) to cover (one material) with another, as protection, etc. [a past tense and past participle of CLOTHE]

cladding *noun Engineering* **1** a thin covering applied to the external surface of a building in order to improve its appearance or to increase its weather or fire resistance. **2** a thin layer of an expensive metal that is used to coat a cheaper metal. **3** in nuclear reactors, a thin layer of metal, eg zirconium or stainless steel, that covers the fuel elements and protects them from corrosion. It also prevents the release of fission products into the coolant. **4** the process whereby one material is covered with another, and the two are

then bonded together under conditions of high temperature and pressure.

cladistics *sing. noun Biol.* a system of animal and plant classification in which organisms are grouped together on the basis of similarities due to recent origin from a common ancestor. [from Greek *klados*, branch]

claim — *verb* **1** to state (something) firmly, insisting on its truth. **2** to declare oneself (to be, to have done, etc). **3** to assert that one has. **4** *trans., intrans.* to demand or assert as a right. **5** to take, use up. **6** to need; to deserve; to have a right to. **7** to declare that one is the owner of. **8** to identify oneself as having (responsibility). — *noun* **1** a statement one insists on the truth of. **2** a demand, especially for something that one has, or believes one has, a right to: *lay claim to the throne / stake one's claim / make claims on someone's time.* **3** (**claim to**) a right to or reason for: *a claim to fame.* **4** something one has claimed, eg a piece of land or a sum of money.
— **jump a claim** to claim land containing gold, oil, etc which already belongs to someone else. [from Latin *clamare*, to cry out]

claimant *noun* a person who makes a claim.

Clairvaux a Cistercian abbey founded in 1115 by St Bernard near Ville-sous-la-Ferté, Champagne, France. The site was changed into a prison during the 19c.

clairvoyance *noun* the ability, claimed by some, to see into the future, or know things that cannot be discovered through the normal range of senses. [from French *clairvoyance*, from *clair*, clear + *voir*, to see].

clairvoyant — *adj.* involving or claiming the power of clairvoyance. — *noun* a person who claims to have the power of clairvoyance.

clam — *noun* **1** any of various edible bivalve molluscs. **2** *colloq.* an uncommunicative person. — *verb* (**clammed, clamming**) (**clam up**) *colloq.* to stop talking suddenly; to refuse to speak, answer questions, etc. [a shortening of *clamshell*, from *clam*, an old word related to CLAMP]

clamber — *verb intrans.* to climb, especially using hands as well as feet. — *noun* an act of clambering. [related to CLIMB]

clammily *adv.* in a clammy way.

clamminess *noun* the state or condition of being clammy.

clammy *adj.* (**clammier, clammiest**) moist or damp, especially unpleasantly so. [from Anglo-Saxon *clæman*, to smear]

clamorous *adj.* noisy, boisterous.

clamorously *adv.* in a clamorous or noisy way.

clamorousness *noun* being clamorous or noisy.

clamour — *noun* **1** a noise of shouting or loud talking. **2** an outcry; loud protesting or loud demands. **3** any loud noise. — *verb intrans.* (**clamour for something**) to demand it noisily. [from Latin *clamor*, shout]

clamp¹ — *noun* **1** a tool with adjustable jaws for gripping things firmly or pressing parts together. **2** a reinforcing or fastening device, used in woodwork, etc. **3** (*also* **wheel clamp**) a heavy metal device that can be fitted to the wheels of a car to prevent it being moved. — *verb* **1** to fasten together or hold with a clamp. **2** to fit a clamp to a wheel of (a parked car) to stop it being moved. **3** to hold, grip, shut, or press tightly.
— **clamp down on something** *or* **someone** to put a stop to it/them or control it/them strictly. [from Old Dutch *clampe*]

clamp² *noun* a mound of dug potatoes or other root crop, covered with earth and straw as protection against cold. [from Old Dutch *clamp*, heap]

clampdown *noun* a restriction; a suppression of activity.

clan *noun* **1** a group of families, in Scotland or of Scots origin, generally with the same surname, and (especially formerly) led by a chief. **2** *humorous* one's family or relations. **3** a group of people who have similar interests, concerns, etc. **4** a division of a tribe. [from Gaelic *clann*, children]

clandestine *adj.* **1** concealed; kept secret. **2** furtive; sly; surreptitious. [from Latin *clandestinus*, from *clam*, secretly]

clandestinely *adv.* in a clandestine way.

clang — *verb intrans., trans.* to make or cause to make a loud deep ringing sound. — *noun* this sound. [from Latin *clangere*, to clang, resound]

clanger *noun colloq.* a tactless, embarrassing and all too obvious blunder: *drop a clanger.*

clangour *noun poetic* a continuous, loud, confused, and intrusive noise. [from Latin *clangor*, noise]

clank — *verb intrans., trans.* to make or cause to make a sharp sound of metal striking metal or some other hard surface. — *noun* this sound. [imitative]

clannish *adj. derog.*, *said of a group of people* closely united, with little interest or trust in people not belonging to the group.

clannishly *adv.* in a clannish way.

clannishness *noun* being clannish.

clansman *or* **clanswoman** *noun* (PL. **clansmen, clanswomen**) a member of a clan.

clap¹ — *verb* (**clapped, clapping**) **1** *intrans., trans.* to strike (especially the palms of one's hands) together with a loud noise, to applaud (someone), mark (a rhythm), gain attention, etc. **2** to strike (someone) with the palm of the hand, usually as a friendly gesture. **3** to place forcefully: *clapped the book on the table.* **4** *colloq.* to put suddenly (into prison, chains, etc). — *noun* **1** an act of clapping. **2** the sudden loud explosion of noise that thunder makes.
— **clap eyes on** *colloq.* to see.

clapped out *colloq.* **1** *said of a machine, etc* old, worn out, and no longer working properly. **2** *said of a person* exhausted.
[from Anglo-Saxon *clæppan*]

clap² *noun coarse slang* (**the clap**) a venereal disease, especially gonorrhoea. [related to Old French *clapier*, brothel]

Clapeyron, (Bénoit-Paul-) Emile (1799–1864) French civil engineer, born in Paris. He worked in Russia and on the construction of railways and bridges in France; he also designed locomotives, becoming the first to make deliberate use of the expansive action of steam in the cylinder. In 1834 he publicized Sadi Carnot's classic but previously neglected work on the power and efficiency of various types of heat engine.

Clapham Sect, also called the **Saints** a movement for evangelical reform of the Church of England. Active in the 1780s and 1790s, its members were all Anglicans. It was named after the estate at Battersea Rise, Clapham, owned by English economist Henry Thornton (1760–1815), where he and his cousin William Wilberforce lived. John Venn (1759–1813), vicar of Clapham, was also a prominent member.

clapper *noun* **1** the dangling piece of metal inside a bell that strikes against the side to make it ring. **2** a device that produces a loud clattering noise, for scaring birds from crops, etc.
— **like the clappers** *colloq.* very quickly.

clapperboard *noun* a pair of hinged boards clapped together in front of the camera before and after shooting a piece of film, so as to help synchronize sound and vision.

Clapton, Eric (1945–) English guitarist, born in London. One of the most significant white exponents of Black music, particularly the blues, he began his recording career with the Yardbirds and John Mayall's Bluesbreakers, before he joined the rock–jazz–blues group Cream and attracted many worshipful fans. He then played with Blind Faith and formed his own band Derek and the Dominos, whose song 'Layla' (1972) was a hit. After overcoming a drug problem, he developed a middle-of-the-road blues style, and continued his stardom into the 1990s.

claptrap *noun* meaningless, insincere or pompous talk. [from CLAP[1] + TRAP]

claque *noun* **1** a group of people paid to applaud a speaker at a meeting or performer in a theatre, etc. **2** a circle of flatterers or admirers. [from French *claquer*, to clap]

Clara a female first name. [a late Latin name, from *clarus*, famous]

Clare, St (1194–1253) Italian abbess, born of a noble family in Assisi. In 1212, she gave up her possessions and joined a Benedictine convent, and in 1215 founded with St Francis the order of Franciscan nuns, known as the Poor Clares. Canonized in 1255, in 1958 she was designated patron saint of television, for at Christmas 1252, while in her cell in the Convent of San Damiano, she both saw and heard the Mass in the Church of St Francis at Assisi. Her feast day is 11 (formerly 12) Aug.

Clare *or* **Claire** a female first name. [an English form of CLARA, sometimes taking the French spelling *Claire*]

Clare, Angel a minister's son in Thomas Hardy's *Tess of the D'Urbervilles*, who marries Tess only to immediately abandon her on learning of her past.

Clare, John (1793–1864) English poet, born in Helpston, Cambridgeshire. Though almost without schooling, he began to write verse and his *Poems Descriptive of Rural Life* (1820) were well-received. Despite some patronage, he was forced to live in poverty, and spent the last 23 years of his life in an asylum at Northampton, where he wrote some of his best poetry.

Clare, Gaelic **An Chláir** POP (1991) 91 000, a county in Munster province, W Irish Republic. AREA 3 188sq km/1 231sq mi. It is bounded W by the Atlantic Ocean and E by the Slieve Aughty Mts. PHYSICAL DESCRIPTION the Cliffs of Moher are on the Atlantic coast; there are limestone outcrops at Burren. CAPITAL Ennis. ECONOMY cattle, dairy farming; fishing.

Clarence a male first name, now rare, from the royal title 'Duke of Clarence'. [of Celtic origin]

Clarendon, Edward Hyde, 1st Earl of (1609–74) English statesman and historian, born near Salisbury, Wiltshire. He became a member of the Short Parliament (1640), where he at first supported the popular party, but in 1641 became a close adviser of Charles, and headed the Royalist opposition in the Commons until 1642. He became Chancellor of the Exchequer (1643) and High Chancellor (1658). In 1660 his daughter Anne (1638–71) secretly married the King's brother, James (later James II). Unpopular as a statesman, Clarendon apparently irritated Cavaliers and Puritans alike, and in 1667, after the disastrous war with Holland, he was usurped by a court cabal. Impeached for high treason, he left the country for France. His major work is the *History of the Rebellion in England* (3 vols, 1704–7).

Clarendon, Constitutions of a written declaration of rights (1164) claimed by Henry II of England in ecclesiastical affairs, with the purpose of restoring royal control over the English Church. Promulgated at Clarendon, near Salisbury, the Constitutions (especially Clause 3, which threatened clerical criminals with secular penalties) brought Thomas Becket and Henry II into open conflict.

Clarendon Code a series of British Acts passed by the Cavalier Parliament between 1661 and 1665 which reasserted the supremacy of the Church of England over Protestant nonconfor-

mity after the collapse of the 'Puritan Revolution' in 1660. The most important were the Corporation Act (1661) and the Act of Uniformity (1662). Nonconformity was recognized as lawful, but many restrictions were placed on nonconformists' activities.

claret *noun* **1** a French red wine, especially from the Bordeaux district. **2** the deep reddish-purple colour of this wine. [from Old French *clare*, spiced wine]

clarification *noun* the process of making clear.

clarify *verb trans., intrans.* (**clarifies**, **clarified**) **1** to make or become clearer or easier to understand. **2** *said of butter, fat, etc* to make or become clear by heating. [from Latin *clarus*, clear + *facere*, to make]

clarinet *noun* a woodwind instrument, with a cylindrical tube and a single reed. [from French *clarinette*, diminutive of Old French *clarin*, clarion] ◇ The clarinet was in regular use as a solo and orchestral instrument by the end of the 18c; the later addition of a key mechanism facilitated accurate intonation and the playing of passages in keys that had previously been difficult. The clarinet is a transposing instrument with the most common models pitched in A or B♭.

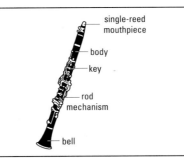

single-reed mouthpiece
body
key
rod mechanism
bell

clarinet

clarinettist *noun* a person who plays the clarinet.

clarion *noun* an old kind of trumpet with a shrill sound, used to call men to arms, etc: *a clarion call*. [from Latin *clario*, from *clarus*, clear]

Clarissa a novel by Samuel Richardson (1747–8). It tells, in epistolary form, of the violent, tragic relationship between genteel Clarissa Harlowe and the manipulative libertine, Robert Lovelace.

clarity *noun* **1** the quality of being clear and pure. **2** the quality of being easy to see, hear, or understand. **3** clearness and accuracy of thought, reasoning, and expression. [from Latin *claritas*]

Clark, Jim (James) (1936–68) Scottish motor racing driver, born in Kilmany, Fife. He won his first race in 1956, and was Scottish National Speed champion in 1958 and 1959. After joining the Lotus Team in 1960, he went on to become world champion racing driver in 1963 and 1965. In all, he won 25 Grand Prix events. He was killed during a Formula Two race in Hockenheim, Germany.

Clark, William (1770–1838) US explorer, born in Caroline Co, Virginia. He joined the army in 1789, and was appointed joint leader with Meriwether Lewis of the successful transcontinental expedition to the Pacific coast and back (1804–6). He later became superintendent of Indian affairs in Louisiana Territory, and then Governor of Missouri Territory.

Clark (of Saltwood), Kenneth (Mackenzie) Clark, Baron (1903–83) English art historian, born in London. He was Keeper of the Department of Fine Art in the Ashmolean Museum (1931–3), Director of the National Gallery (1934–45), and Slade Professor of Fine Art at Oxford (1946–50). He wrote many

popular books on his subject and became widely known through his television series *Civilisation* (1969).

Clarke, Jeremiah (c.1674–1707) English composer, born probably in London. He studied under Blow at the Chapel Royal, became organist of Winchester College (1692), vicar-choral of St Paul's, London (1695), and followed his master at the Chapel Royal (1704). He committed suicide after an unhappy love affair. The real composer of the *Trumpet Voluntary* long attributed to Purcell, Clarke wrote theatre music, religious and secular choral works, and music for the harpsichord.

Clarke, Kenneth (1940–) English politician. Called to the Bar in 1963, he entered parliament in 1970. After junior posts in the Heath administration (1971–4), he entered Margaret Thatcher's government in 1979 and gained a reputation as an affable and capable politician. He became Secretary of State for Health (1988), with the task of overseeing a major reform of the National Health Service, Secretary of State for Education and Science (1990), Home Secretary (1992), and Chancellor (1993–).

Clarke, Michael (1962–) Scottish dancer and choreographer, born near Aberdeen. He attended the Royal Ballet School at 13, danced with Ballet Rambert, and started his own company in 1984. Known for his innovative technique and inventive choreography, his original style incorporates such things as punk, 1960s fantasy, nudity, video, and platform shoes. In 1991 he appeared as Caliban in Peter Greenaway's film *Prospero's Books*. His major productions include *Mmm . . . Modern Masterpiece* (1992), which combines punk music with Stravinsky's *Rite of Spring*.

Clarkson, Thomas (1760–1846) English philanthropist, born in Wisbech, Cambridgeshire. He crusaded against African slavery, and after the passing of the anti-slavery laws (1807), wrote a two-volume *History of the Abolition of the African Slave-trade* (1808). He was also a leading member of the Anti-Slavery Society, which was formed in 1823 for the abolition of slavery in the West Indies, and achieved its aim in 1833.

clarsach *noun* a small harp strung with wire, played in Scotland and Ireland. [from Gaelic *clarsach*]

clash — *noun* **1** a loud noise, like that of metal objects striking each other. **2** a serious disagreement; a quarrel or argument. **3** a fight, battle, or match. **4** the coinciding in one's timetable of two or more events, both or all of which one ought to or would like to attend. — *verb* **1** *intrans., trans. said of metal objects, etc* to strike against each other noisily. **2** *intrans.* to fight; to have a battle. **3** *intrans.* (**clash with someone**) to disagree violently. **4** *intrans. said of commitments, etc* to coincide, usually fortuitously. **5** *intrans. said of colours, styles, etc* to be unpleasing or unharmonious together. [imitative]

clasp *noun* **1** a fastening on jewellery, a bag, etc made of two parts that link together. **2** a firm grip, or act of gripping. — *verb* **1** to hold, or take hold of, firmly. **2** to fasten or secure with a clasp.

clasp knife a folding pocket knife, originally one held open by a catch.

class — *noun* **1** a lesson or lecture. **2** a number of pupils taught together. **3** the body of students that begin or finish university or school in the same year. **4** a category, kind, or type. **5** a grade or standard. **6** any of the social groupings into which people fall according to their job, wealth, etc. **7** the system by which society is divided into these groups. **8** *colloq.* stylishness in dress, behaviour, etc; good quality. — *verb* to regard as belonging to a certain class; to put into a category.

— **in a class of its own** outstanding; with no equal.

[from Latin *classis*, rank, class, division]

class-conscious *adj. derog.* aware of one's own and other people's social class.

class-consciousness *noun* awareness of social classification.

classic — *adj.* **1** of the highest quality; established as the best. **2** entirely typical. **3** simple, neat, and elegant, especially in a traditional style: *a classic black suit.* — *noun* **1** an established work of literature. **2** an outstanding example of its type. **3** something, eg an item of clothing, always approved of and essential to have: *the little black dress, a classic of the 50s.* **4** (*also* **Classic**) a celebrated annual sporting event, especially a horse race (see also CLASSICS). [from Latin *classicus*, relating to classes, especially the best]

classical — *adj.* **1** *said of literature, art, etc* of ancient Greece and Rome. **2** *said of architecture or the other arts* showing the influence of ancient Greece and Rome: *a classical façade.* **3** *said of music and arts related to it* having an established, traditional, and somewhat formal style and form: *classical music.* **4** *said of procedures, etc* following the well-known traditional pattern: *the classical method.* **5** *said of a shape, design, etc* simple; pure; without complicated decoration. **6** *said of a language* being the older, literary form. — *noun colloq.* classical music.

classically *adv.* **1** in a classic or classical way. **2** so as to be classic.

classical music music which is relatively formal or 'serious', which is part of a long written tradition, which lends itself to sophisticated study and analysis, and which is (most often) performed in concert halls, opera houses, and churches. In this sense 'classical' is usually used to distinguish such music from jazz, folk music, light music, and pop. However, the term is used more specifically to describe the music of the 18c and early 19c (roughly the period from Bach to Beethoven) in which there were certain accepted conventions of form and structure used as a framework for the expression of ideas.

classical revival a form of Western art characterized by a return to the classical orders in architecture, and interest in themes from classical literature, and on emphasis on the human form (with proportions based on Roman sculpture), as in central motif. Major revivals occurred in the Carolingian period (8c), 13c France, 15c Italy, 17c France, and in 18c Rome (from where it spread throughout Europe and N America in the 18c and early 19c and became known as the Neoclassical movement).

Classical Symphony Sergei Prokofiev's Symphony No.1 in D (Op 25, 1916–17), written in parody of Haydn's style.

classicism *noun* in art, architecture, prose, and poetry, a simple, elegant style typical in 18c and early 19c Europe.
◇ The term is applied to an adherence in any period to the standards of Greek and Roman art, as exemplified in correct proportion and power of expression in representations of the human figure. In literature, classicism is associated especially with the Latin poets such as Horace and Virgil.

classicist *noun* someone who has studied classics, especially as a university subject.

Classics the name given to the principal horse races in several countries. There are five Classics in England: the *One Thousand Guineas*, run over 1.6km/1mi at Newmarket, first run in 1814; the *Two Thousand Guineas*, run over 1.6km/1mi at Newmarket, first run in 1809; the *Derby* or *Derby Stakes* (named after the 12th Earl of Derby), run over 2.4km/1.5mi at Epsom Downs, first run in 1780; the *Oaks* (named after the Epsom home of the 12th Earl of Derby), run over 2.4km/1.5mi at Epsom, first run in 1779 ; the *St Leger*, run over c.2.9km/1mi 6 furlongs at Doncaster, first run in 1776. The *Oaks* and the *One Thousand Guineas* are open to fillies only.

classics *sing. noun* (*often* **Classics**) the study of Latin and Greek and the literature and history of ancient Greece and Rome.

classifiable *adj.* capable of being classified.

classification *noun* **1** the arrangement and division of things and people into classes. **2** a group or class into which a thing or person is put.

classified *adj.* **1** arranged in groups or classes. **2** *said of information* kept secret by the government. **3** *said of a road* classed as a motorway or major route.

classified ad a small advertisement in a newspaper offering something for sale, advertising a job, etc.

classify *verb* (**classifies**, **classified**) **1** to put into a particular class or group. **2** to declare (information) secret, and not for publication. [Latin *classis*, class, division + *facere*, to make]

classless *adj.* **1** *said of a community* not divided into social classes. **2** not belonging to any particular social class.

classlessness *noun* **1** being without social classification. **2** not belonging to any class.

classmate *noun* a fellow pupil or student in one's class at school or college.

classroom *noun* a room in a school or college where classes are taught.

classy *adj.* (**classier**, **classiest**) *colloq.* stylish; fashionable; superior.

clatter — *noun* a loud noise made by hard objects striking each other, or falling on to a hard surface. — *verb intrans., trans.* (**clattered**, **clattering**) to make or cause to make this noise. [imitative]

Claude, Georges (1870–1960) French technologist, born in Paris. Noted for important work on gases, he devised a process for the liquefaction of air (1902) and is credited with the invention of neon lighting for signs.

Claude a male first name, also given to females in France. [from French, from the Roman family name *Claudius*, derived from *claudius*, lame]

Claudia a female first name. [from the Roman family name; see CLAUDE]

Claudian, properly **Claudius Claudianus** (AD 340–410) Roman poet, born in Alexandria, Egypt, the last of the great Latin poets. Several of his works have survived, notably his epic poem *The Rape of Proserpine*.

Claudio 1 the well-meaning brother of Isabella in Shakespeare's *Measure for Measure*, who is condemned to death for seducing his intended wife, Juliette. **2** The lover of Hero in Shakespeare's *Much Ado About Nothing*.

Claudius, in full **Tiberius Claudius Nero Germanicus** (10 BC–AD 54) Roman emperor (41–54), grandson of the empress Livia, brother of Germanicus, and nephew of the emperor Tiberius. He was considered unattractive in his youth and rumoured to be an imbecile, so he was not involved in politics and spent much of his time in historical studies under the historian Livy. He became emperor largely by accident in the chaos following his nephew Caligula's murder, and proved to be an able and progressive ruler, although a hostile tradition portrays him as unduly influenced by his wives and freedmen. He introduced many administrative reforms, and extended the empire through the annexation of Britain (43), Mauretania (41–2), and Thrace (46). He is believed to have been poisoned by his fourth wife Agrippina who wished to secure the succession of her son, Nero.

Claudius the fratricidal king in Shakespeare's *Hamlet*, who has married his former sister-in-law, Gertrude, and plots the murder of Hamlet.

clause *noun* **1** *Grammar* part of a sentence that has its own subject, verb, object, etc. **2** *Legal* a

paragraph or section in a contract, will, or act of parliament. [from Latin *clausa*]

Clausewitz, Karl (Philip Gottlieb) von (1780–1831) Prussian soldier, born in Burg. He served in the Prussian and Russian armies, and as major general became director of the Prussian army school, and Gneisenau's chief of staff. His posthumously published *Vom Kriege* (On War, 1833), which advocated a policy of total war, revolutionized military theory and was very influential in Germany and beyond.

Clausius, Rudolf Julius Emmanuel (1822–88) German physicist, born in Köslin, Prussia. He studied at Berlin, and in 1869 became professor at Bonn. He worked on optics and electricity, formulated the second law of thermodynamics, and was influential in establishing thermodynamics as a science.

claustrophobia *noun* **1** fear felt in, or fear of being in, confined spaces. **2** an uncomfortable feeling of being shut in or confined. [from Latin *claustrum*, bolt, barrier + -PHOBIA]

claustrophobic *adj.* relating to or of the nature of claustrophobia.

Claverhouse, Graham of see DUNDEE, JOHN GRAHAM OF CLAVERHOUSE, 1ST VISCOUNT OF.

clavichord *noun* an early keyboard instrument with a soft tone. [from Latin *clavis*, key + *chorda*, string]
◇ Clavichords are usually oblong, with the strings running parallel to the keyboard. When a key is depressed a small brass blade (or tangent) strikes the string, causing it to vibrate along part of its length and to be damped (by a small piece of cloth or felt) on the remainder. In early 'fretted' clavichords, each string could produce several notes depending on where the tangent struck; later versions had a single string for each note. They were popular from the 15c to the late 18c but fell into disuse with the advent of the piano. They are now mainly used in the performance of early music.

clavicle *noun Anat.* in vertebrates, either of two short slender bones linking the shoulder-blades with the top of the breastbone. It is the most frequently broken bone in the human body. [from Latin *clavicula*, diminutive of *clavis*, key]

claw — *noun* **1** one of the sharply pointed hooked nails of an animal or bird. **2** the foot of an animal or bird with claws. **3** either of the feet of a crab or lobster which ends in pincers. **4** something with the shape or action of a claw, eg part of a mechanical device. — *verb trans., intrans.* (**claw at something**) to tear or scratch it with claws, nails, or fingers.
— **claw something back 1** *said of a government* to recover money given in the form of benefits and allowances by imposing a new tax. **2** to regain a commercial advantage, etc with difficulty.
[from Anglo-Saxon *clawu*]

clawback the process of clawing back; recovery of expenditure by taxation.

clawed frog *or* **clawed toad** an African or S American frog, so called because it has claws on three hind toes. It is aquatic, has no tongue, and catches its prey with its hands.

claw hammer a hammer with two points on one side of its head, that can be used for pulling out nails.

Clay, Cassius see ALI, MUHAMMAD.

Clay, Henry (1777–1852) US statesman and orator, born in Hanover Co, Virginia, the son of a Baptist preacher. He became a lawyer (1797), entered the lower house of Congress in 1811, and was chosen its speaker, a post he held for many years. Active in bringing on the war of 1812–15 with Britain, he was also one of the commissioners who arranged the Treaty of Ghent which ended it. He made several attempts to hold the Union together during the slavery question, for which he earned the title of 'the great pacificator'. In 1824, 1831, and 1844 he was an unsuccessful candidate for the presidency.

clay *noun* **1** *Geol.* a poorly draining soil with a very fine texture, consisting mainly of aluminium silicates. It is hard when dry, but can absorb large quantities of water, swelling to become soft, pliable, and sticky. It is used to make pottery, bricks, ceramics, etc. **2** earth or soil generally. **3** *Tennis* the hard surface of clay courts. **4** *poetic* the substance of which the human body is formed. — **have feet of clay** to lack moral courage. [from Anglo-Saxon *clæg*]

clay court a tennis court with a hard surface of clay or a similar substance.

clayey *adj.* **1** like or made of clay. **2** covered with clay.

Clayhanger a novel by Arnold Bennett (1910). The first of the Clayhanger trilogy, it describes the life of Edwin Clayhanger and his relationship with his overbearing father, Darius.

claymation *noun* animation using clay or plasticine figures.

clay mineral *Geol.* any of various silicates of aluminium that are the chief constituents of clay, and form fine flaky crystals which can absorb water, giving clay its characteristic plasticity when wet. They are formed as a result of the weathering of rocks, and are often deposited by rivers. Clay minerals are used to make bricks and pottery, and as a filler for paper, rubber, and paint.

claymore *noun Hist.* a two-edged broadsword used by Scottish highlanders. [from Gaelic *claidheamh mór*, large sword]

clay pigeon a clay disc that is thrown up mechanically as a target in the sport of **clay-pigeon shooting**.

clay pipe a tobacco pipe made of baked clay.

Clayton-Bulwer Treaty a US/British agreement formed (1850) by US Secretary of State John M Clayton and the British Minister to Washington, Sir Henry Lytton Bulwer, on the terms for building a canal across Central America. In effect until 1901, its major provision was to forbid either party to exercise exclusive control or to build fortifications.

clean — *adj.* **1** free from dirt. **2** not containing anything harmful to health; pure. **3** pleasantly fresh: *a clean taste.* **4** hygienic in habits: *a clean animal.* **5** unused; unmarked: *a clean sheet of paper.* **6** neat and even: *a clean cut.* **7** simple and elegant: *a ship with good clean lines.* **8** clear of legal offences: *a clean driving licence.* **9** morally pure; innocent. **10** *said of humour, etc* not offensive or obscene. **11** fair: *a clean fight.* **12** *slang* not carrying drugs or offensive weapons. **13** *said of nuclear installations, etc* not producing a harmful level of radioactivity. **14** *Relig., said of certain animals* allowed for people to eat. **15** *said of musical sounds* pure and accurate. **16** absolute; complete: *make a clean break.* — *adv.* **1** *colloq.* completely: *get clean away / I clean forgot.* **2** straight; directly; encountering no obstruction: *sailed clean through the window.* — *verb* **1** *trans., intrans.* to make or become free from dirt. **2** *trans., intrans.* to dry-clean or be dry-cleaned. **3** *intrans.* to dust, polish floors and furniture, etc in a house or office, especially as a job. **4** to prepare (vegetables, etc) for cooking or eating by cutting away the inedible parts. — *noun* **1** an act of cleaning. **2** *Weight-lifting* a lift of the weight as far as the shoulders cleanly. — **clean bill of health** a medical certificate or report confirming that one is in good health, especially after being ill.

clean something out to clean a room or cupboard, etc thoroughly.

clean someone out *slang* to deprive or cheat them of money.

clean up 1 to clean a place thoroughly. **2** *slang* to make a large profit.

clean something up to make a dirty place or person clean; to get rid of a mess.

clean up after someone to clean up a mess, etc left by them.

come clean *colloq.* to admit or tell the truth about something that one has previously concealed or lied about.

have clean hands *colloq.* to have no connection with the crime, etc in question.

make a clean sweep 1 to make sweeping changes. **2** to win all the prizes at a sporting event, etc.

with a clean slate *or* **sheet** with a fresh start, as though beginning from the beginning again, especially after an error or misdeed. [from Anglo-Saxon *clæne*]

clean bill of health a declaration that a person is healthy, or that a machine or organization is working satisfactorily.

clean-cut *adj.* **1** pleasingly regular in outline or shape: *clean-cut features.* **2** neat; respectable.

cleaner *noun* **1** a person employed to clean inside buildings, offices, etc. **2** a machine or substance used for cleaning. **3** (*also* **cleaners**) a shop where clothes, etc can be taken for cleaning. — **take someone to the cleaners** *colloq.* to extort all or most of their money from them.

cleaning lady *or* **cleaning woman** a woman whose job is to clean inside a house, factory, office, etc.

clean-limbed *adj.* having a tall, slim, shapely body.

cleanliness *noun* (pronounced *clen-*) habitual cleanness or purity.

clean-living *adj.* leading a decent, healthy existence.

cleanly[1] *adv.* **1** in a clean way. **2** tidily; efficiently; easily.

cleanly[2] *adj.* (pronounced *clen-*) *old use* hygienic in one's personal habits.

cleanness *noun* being clean.

clean-out *noun* **1** a thorough cleaning. **2** *colloq.* a swindle.

clean room an area in a factory kept free of dust, etc for the manufacturing of computer or other precision components.

cleanse *verb* **1** to clean or get rid of dirt from. **2** to purify; to remove sin or guilt from. [from Anglo-Saxon *clænsian*]

cleanser *noun* a substance that cleans, eg a cream or liquid for cleaning the face.

clean-shaven *adj.* without a beard or moustache.

cleansing department the local-government department responsible for cleaning the streets and collecting rubbish.

clean-up *noun* a thorough cleaning.

clear — *adj.* **1** transparent; easy to see through. **2** *said of weather, etc* not misty or cloudy. **3** *said of the skin* healthy; unblemished by spots, etc. **4** easy to see, hear or understand. **5** bright; sharp; well-defined; *a clear picture.* **6** *said of vision* able to see well. **7** *said of musical sounds* pure and accurate. **8** certain; convinced; having no doubts or confusion: *are you clear about that point?* **9** definite; free of doubt, ambiguity, or confusion. **10** capable of, or resulting from, accurate observation, logical thinking, etc. **11** evident; obvious. **12** (**clear of something**) free of obstruction. **13** (**clear of something**) well away from it; out of range of or contact with it: *well clear of the rocks.* **14** (**clear of something**) free of it; no longer affected by it. **15** remaining after all charges, taxes, expenses, etc have been paid. **16** *said of the conscience, etc* free from guilt, etc. **17** entire; without interruption: *need a clear week to finish.* **18** free of appointments, etc. — *adv.* **1** in a clear manner. **2** completely: *get clear away.* **3** *North Amer.* all the way: *see clear to the hills.* **4** (**clear of something**)

well away from it; out of the way of it: *keep/steer clear of trouble / stand clear.* — *verb* **1** *trans., intrans.* to make or become clear, free of obstruction, etc. **2** to remove or move out of the way. **3** to prove or declare to be innocent. **4** to get over or past without touching: *clear the fence.* **5** to make as profit over expenses. **6** to pass inspection by (customs). **7** to give or get official permission for (a plan, etc). **8** to approve (someone) for a special assignment, access to secret information, etc. **9** *trans., intrans.* to pass (a cheque), or (of a cheque) to pass from one bank to another through a clearing-house. **10** to decode. **11** to pay (a debt). — **clear the air** *colloq.* to get rid of bad feeling, suspicion or tension, especially by frank discussion.

clear the decks see DECK.

clear off *colloq.* to go away.

clear something off to finish paying debts, etc.

clear out *colloq.* to go away.

clear something out to rid it of rubbish, etc.

clear up *said of the weather* to brighten after rain, a storm, etc.

clear something up 1 to tidy up a mess, room, etc. **2** to solve a mystery, etc. **3** to make something better.

in the clear no longer under suspicion, in difficulties, or in danger. [from Old French *cler*]

clearance *noun* **1** the act of clearing. **2** the distance between one object and another passing beside or under it. **3** permission, or a certificate granting this. **4** (*also* **security clearance**) official acknowledgement that one can be trusted not to pass secrets to an enemy.

clear-cut *adj.* clear; sharp.

clear-headed *adj.* capable of, or showing, clear, logical thought.

clear-headedly *adv.* in a clear-headed way.

clearing *noun* an area in a forest, etc that has been cleared of trees, etc.

clearing bank a bank using the services of a central clearing-house.

clearing-house *noun* **1** an establishment that deals with transactions between its member banks. **2** a central agency that collects, organizes and distributes information.

clearly *adv.* **1** in a clear manner. **2** obviously: *clearly, he's wrong.*

clearness *noun* the quality of being clear.

clear-out *noun* a clearing out of rubbish, etc.

clear-sighted *adj.* capable of, or showing, accurate observation and good judgement.

clear-sightedly *adv.* in a clear-sighted way.

clear-sightedness *noun* the quality of being clear-sighted.

clearway *noun* a stretch of road on which cars may not stop except in an emergency.

cleavage *noun* **1** a series of cell divisions of an ovum immediately after it has been fertilized, which transform it into a group of small cells called a blastula. **2** *Biochem.* the breakdown of a complex molecule, such as a protein, into simpler molecules by the splitting of chemical bonds within its structure. **3** *Geol.* the splitting of rocks into thin parallel sheets, or the splitting of a crystal in one or more specific directions to give smooth surfaces. **4** *colloq.* the hollow between a woman's breasts, especially as revealed by a dress with a low neck. [from CLEAVE[1]]

cleave[1] *verb* (PAST **clove, cleft, cleaved**; PAST PARTICIPLE **cloven, cleft, cleaved**) *trans., intrans. formal, literary* **1** to split or divide. **2** to cut or slice: *cleave a way through the undergrowth.* See also CLOVEN. [from Anglo-Saxon *cleofan*]

cleave[2] *verb intrans.* (PAST TENSE AND PAST PARTICIPLE **cleaved**) to cling or stick. [from Anglo-Saxon *cleofian*]

cleaver *noun* a knife with a large square blade, used by butchers for chopping meat. [from CLEAVE[1]]

Cleethorpes POP (1992e) 70 000, a resort town in Cleethorpes district, Humberside, NE England. It is situated on the R Humber estuary, SE of Grimsby.

clef *noun* Mus. each of three symbols placed on a stave to indicate the pitch of the notes written on it: the *treble clef* or *G clef* on the second line up, the *bass clef* or *F clef* on the second line down, and the *alto clef* or *C clef* on the middle line. [from French *clef*, key]

cleft[1] *noun* a split, fissure, wide crack, or deep indentation. [related to CLEAVE[1]]

cleft[2] *adj.* split; divided.
— **in a cleft stick** in a difficult or awkward situation.
[past participle of CLEAVE[1]]

cleft palate *Medicine* a deformity of the palate caused by failure of the two sides of the roof of the mouth to meet and fuse together in the developing fetus, resulting in an abnormal opening between the mouth cavity and nasal cavities at birth. It can be corrected by a series of surgical operations during childhood.

Cleland, John (1709–89) English novelist born in London. After working and travelling abroad, he published *Fanny Hill, or the Memoirs of a Woman of Pleasure* (1750). A best-seller in its time, it achieved a second *succès de scandale* on its revival and prosecution under the Obscene Publications Act in 1963.

clematis *noun* a garden climbing plant of the buttercup family, with purple, yellow, or white flowers. [from Greek *clematis*, periwinkle, convolvulus, or traveller's joy]

Clemenceau, Georges (1841–1929) French statesman, born in Mouilleron-en-Pareds. He trained as a doctor, worked as a teacher in the USA (1865–9), then returned to France, where he became a member of the National Assembly, and (1876) a leader of the extreme left in the Chamber of Deputies. Twice Prime Minister (1906–9, 1917–20), he became known as 'the tiger' for his autocratic manner, and as Chairman of the Peace Conference in 1919 he displayed an intransigent hatred of Germany. A brilliant journalist, he founded *L'Aurore* (1897), and other papers.

clemency *noun* 1 the quality of being clement. 2 mercy.

Clement I, St, known as **Clemens Romanus** (d.c.101 AD) pope from 88 to 89 or 92 to 101, the first of the Apostolic Fathers, and either the second or third successor of St Peter in the see of Rome. He may have been a freedman of Jewish parentage belonging to the imperial household. He wrote the *Epistle to the Corinthian Church* (c.95), which discusses social dissensions and the Resurrection. A tradition suggests that he was martyred. His feast day is 23 Nov.

Clement VII, originally **Giulio de' Medici** (1478–1534) Italian pope (1523–34), born in Florence, who was a patron of artists and scholars. He allied himself with Francis I of France against the Holy Roman Emperor Charles V, was besieged by the Constable Bourbon, and became his prisoner. His indecisiveness, along with his refusal to sanction Henry VIII's divorce from Catherine of Aragon, hastened the Reformation.

clement *adj.* 1 *said of the weather* mild; not harsh or severe. 2 merciful. [from Latin *clemens*, mild, calm, merciful]

clementine *noun* a citrus fruit like a small tangerine. [from French *clementine*]

clemently *adv.* 1 mildly. 2 mercifully.

clench — *verb* 1 to close (one's teeth or one's fists) tightly, especially in anger. 2 to hold or grip firmly. — *noun* 1 the action of clenching. 2 a very

tight grasp. [from Anglo-Saxon *beclencan*, to hold fast]

Cleon (d.422 BC) Athenian soldier and politician. When Mytilene fell to Athens in 427 BC, he suggested that its citizens be executed, but this was never carried out. He defeated the Spartans on the island of Sphacteria (425 BC), but was later killed in battle with the Spartans at Amphipolis.

Cleopatra VII (69–30 BC) Queen of Egypt (51–48 BC, 47–30 BC), the daughter of Ptolemy Auletes, and well known as the lover of Julius Caesar and Mark Antony. With the help of Caesar, to whom she bore a son Caesarion, she regained the throne from her brother (47 BC). She first met Antony, by whom she had three children, in 41 BC, and he restored to her several portions of the old Ptolemaic Empire, and gave to their joint offspring substantial areas of the Roman East (34 BC). After the battle of Actium (31 BC) in which she and Antony were defeated by Octavian, she committed suicide. The asp which, according to tradition, she used to cause her death, was an Egyptian symbol of royalty.

clerestory *or* **clearstory** *noun* (PL. **clerestories**) *Archit.* in a church, an upper row of windows in the nave wall, above the roof of the aisle. [from CLEAR (referring to the windows) + STOREY]

clergy *noun pl., or, sometimes, sing.* (PL. **clergies**) the ordained ministers of the Christian church, or the priests of any religion. [from French *clergé*]

clergyman *or* **clergywoman** *noun* a member of the clergy.

cleric *noun* a clergyman. [from Latin *clericus*, priest]

clerical *adj.* 1 relating to the clergy. 2 relating to clerks, office workers or office work.

clerical collar the stiff white collar, fastening at the back, worn by clergymen.

clerihew *noun* a humorous poem four lines long, especially about a famous person. [named after the inventor, E Clerihew Bentley.]

Clerk, the a soberly-dressed ponderous clerical student in Chaucer's *The Canterbury Tales*, who tells the tale of Patient Griselda.

clerk *noun* 1 a person in an office or bank who deals with letters, accounts, records, files, etc. 2 in a law court, a person who keeps records or accounts. 3 a public official in charge of the records and business affairs of the town council. 4 an unordained or lay minister of the church. 5 *North Amer.* a shop assistant or hotel receptionist. 6 *old use* a scholar or clergyman. [from Anglo-Saxon *clerc*, variant of CLERIC]

clerkess *noun* a female clerk.

clerk of works the person in charge of the construction and care of a building.

Clermont-Ferrand POP (1990) 254 000, the chief town of Auvergne region and capital of Puy-de-Dôme department, central France. It is the geographical and economic centre of the Massif Central. Clermont-Ferrand is a major source of mineral water, with over 20 mineral springs. It is also the centre of car tyre manufacture in France. HISTORY capital of Auvergne in the 16c; Clermont merged with Montferrand in 1630; Blaise Pascal was born here in 1632. NOTABLE FEATURES Gothic Cathedral of Notre-Dame (begun in 1248); Basilica of Notre-Dame-du-Port (11c–12c).

Clevedon POP (1981) 18 000, a summer resort town in Woodspring district, Avon, SW England. It lies on the R Severn estuary, SW of Bristol. The town has associations with the writers Thackeray and Coleridge.

Cleveland, (Stephen) Grover (1837–1908) US statesman, the 22nd and 24th President, born in Caldwell, New Jersey, the son of a Presbyterian minister. As a lawyer, he became Mayor of Buffalo, and in 1882 Governor of New York. In

his first term as President (1885–9), he strongly advised a readjustment of the tariff on various imports. During his second term (1893–7), in 1895 he evoked intense excitement throughout the world by applying the Monroe Doctrine to Britain's dispute with Venezuela over the frontier question.

Cleveland POP (1992e) 560 000, a county in NE England, divided into four districts. AREA 583sq km/225sq mi. It is bounded E by the North Sea, S by North Yorkshire, and W by Durham. It includes Teesside urban area with port facilities on the R Tees estuary. CHIEF TOWNS Middlesbrough (county town), Stockton-on-Tees, Hartlepool. ECONOMY oil; fertilizers; iron; steel; chemicals; petrochemicals. NOTABLE FEATURE North York Moors National Park.

Cleveland POP (1990) 1.8m, the seat of Cuyahoga County, NE Ohio, USA, and the largest city in the state. It is a port on L Erie at the mouth of the Cuyahoga R. HISTORY developed with the opening of the Ohio and Erie Canal in 1827; achieved city status in 1836. NOTABLE FEATURES Play House; Holden Arboretum; Museum of Art.

Cleveland Way a long-distance footpath in North Yorkshire, N England, which stretches c.150km/90mi from Helmsley to near Filey.

clever *adj.* 1 good or quick at learning and understanding. 2 skilful, dexterous, nimble, or adroit. 3 well thought out; ingenious. [from Middle English *cliver*, related to Anglo-Saxon *clifer*, claw]

clever dick *derog. colloq.* a person who is over-sure of his or her cleverness.

cleverly *adv.* in a clever way.

cleverness *noun* the quality of being clever.

clew — *noun* 1 *Naut.* the corner of a ship's sail. 2 *old use* a ball of thread. 3 the arrangement of cords by which a hammock is suspended. — *verb* (**clew a sail up** *or* **down**) to haul it up or let it down. [from Anglo-Saxon *cliewen*, ball of thread]

cliché *noun derog.* 1 a phrase or combination of words that was striking and effective when first used, but has become stale and feeble through repetition. 2 a too-frequently used idea or image; a stereotype. [from French *cliché*, a stereotype plate or stencil]

clichéd *adj.* of the nature of a cliché.

click — *noun* 1 a short sharp sound like that made by two parts of a mechanism locking into place. 2 *Mech.* a catch in a piece of machinery. 3 in some African languages, a click-like speech sound produced by a sucking action with the tongue. 4 *Comput.* to press and release one of the buttons on a mouse input device in order to send an instruction to the computer to which it is attached, eg to select a particular item from a menu displayed on the screen. — *verb* 1 *trans., intrans.* to make or cause to make a click. 2 *intrans. colloq.* to meet with approval. 3 *intrans. colloq.* to become clear or understood.
— **click with someone** *colloq.* to become friendly with them.
[imitative]

client *noun* 1 a person using the professional services of eg a lawyer, bank manager, architect, etc. 2 a customer. [from Latin *cliens*, dependant]

clientèle *noun* the clients of a professional person, customers of a shopkeeper, etc, or people habitually attending a theatre. [from French *clientèle*]

cliff *noun* a high steep rock face, especially on the coast. [from Anglo-Saxon *clif*]

cliff dwellings the houses of the Pueblo Indians in SW USA from the Pueblo III cultural period, c.1100–1300 AD. They were built in arched recesses of cliff walls, stone blocks, and adobe mortar, often several storeys high. They were deserted by 1300, when the people moved further S and established pueblo villages, where they still live. Some cliff dwellings are preserved, such as the Cliff Palace at Mesa Verde, Colorado.

cliffhanger *noun* **1** a story that keeps one in suspense up to the end. **2** the ending of an episode of a serial story which leaves the audience in suspense, as if with the hero clinging to a cliff edge. **3** an exciting situation, especially a contest, of which the conclusion is in doubt until the very last minute.

cliffhanging *adj.* of the nature of a cliffhanger; full of suspense.

Clifford a male first name, after the surname, commonly shortened to *Cliff*. [from Anglo-Saxon *clif*, cliff, slope + *ford*, ford]

climacteric *noun* **1** *Biol.* in living organisms, a period of changes, especially those associated with the menopause in women, and with a reduction in sexual desire in men. **2** *Bot.* in plants, an increase in respiration rate associated with the ripening of fruit. It can be artificially delayed so as to prevent the deterioration of fruit during transport and storage. [from Greek *klimakter*, rung of a ladder]

climactic *adj.* of the nature of a climax.

climactically *adv.* in a climactic way.

climate *noun* **1** the average weather conditions of a particular region of the world over a long period of time, usually at least 50 years. These conditions include the average temperature, rainfall, air pressure, humidity, hours of sunshine, and wind speed and direction. **2** a part of the world considered from the point of view of its weather conditions: *move to a warmer climate.* **3** a current trend in general feeling, opinion, policies, etc. [from Greek *klima*, latitude, region]

◇ Climate is determined mainly by temperature and rainfall, but is also affected by the distribution of land and sea, because continental areas heat up and cool down more quickly than the sea, which tends to have a moderating effect on the weather pattern of an area.

Warm air holds far more water than cold air. Close to the equator, air is warmed by the Sun and holds large amounts of water vapour that has evaporated from the oceans. As it rises, the air cools and the water vapour condenses to form water droplets that develop into clouds, and then fall as rain, so this part of the world tends to have a hot wet climate. Further north and south, at the tropics of Cancer and Capricorn, the air which has risen and circulated from the equatorial region falls again, warming up as it does so, so that it is able to hold more water. As a result there is very little rainfall in these areas, which contain the world's hot dry deserts.

In the polar regions, the Sun's rays have to travel much further through the atmosphere before reaching the Earth's surface (at the equator the Sun shines directly overhead), and much of their heat energy is dissipated before they reach the ground. As a result, the air at the poles is so cold that the small amount of water vapour that is present falls as snow. The climate of areas between the equator, tropics, and poles tends to be more variable, and can also be affected by the presence of mountains, forests, or large cities.

climatic *adj.* relating to climate.

climatically *adv.* as regards climate.

climatological *adj.* relating to climatology.

climatologist *noun* a person who studies climatology.

climatology *noun* the scientific study of climate.

climax — *noun* **1** the high point or culmination of a series of events or of an experience. **2** a sexual orgasm. — *verb intrans., trans.* to come or bring to a climax. [from Greek *climax*, ladder, climax]

climax community *Biol.* a stable plant com-

munity representing the final stage in the colonization of a habitat, eg oak woodland in the UK.

climb — *verb* **1** *trans., intrans.* (*also* **climb up**) to go towards the top of (a hill, ladder, etc). **2** *intrans.* (**climb down** *or* **in** *or* **out**, etc) to reach somewhere with difficulty, especially by using hands and feet. **3** *intrans.* to rise or go up. **4** *intrans.* to increase. — *noun* **1** an act of climbing. **2** a slope to be climbed.
— **climb down** to concede one's position on some issue, etc, especially publicly or humiliatingly.
[from Anglo-Saxon *climban*]

climbable *adj.* capable of being climbed.

climb-down *noun* a dramatic or humiliating change of mind or concession.

climber *noun* **1** a climbing plant. **2** a mountaineer. **3** *derog.* a person who is too obviously trying to rise through the social ranks.

climbing *noun* the sport of climbing rock faces, especially with the help of ropes and other devices.

climbing-frame *noun* a strong framework of metal or wooden bars for children to climb around on.

climbing perch an Asiatic freshwater fish common in rivers, lakes, and canals, up to 25cm in length and having a special respiratory organ above the gills for breathing air. It is able to move overland by jerky thrusts of its tail fin, and is a popular food fish.

climbing plant *Bot.* a plant which reaches toward the light by clinging to neighbouring plants, walls, or other supports. — Also called VINE.

clime *noun poetic, humorous* a part of the world: *foreign climes.* [from Greek *klima*, region, latitude]

clinch — *verb* **1** to settle (an argument or bargain) finally and decisively. **2** *intrans. Boxing, Wrestling, said of contestants* to hold each other in a firm grip. **3** *intrans. colloq.* to embrace. **4** *Joinery* to bend over and hammer down the projecting point of (a nail or rivet that has been driven through a piece of wood, etc). — *noun* **1** an act of clinching. **2** *Boxing, Wrestling* an act of clinging to each other to prevent further blows, create a breathing space, etc. **3** *colloq.* an embrace. [variant of CLENCH]

clincher *noun* a point, argument or circumstance that finally settles or decides a matter.

cline *noun Biol.* a gradual change in the form of an animal or plant species across different parts of its geographical or environmental range, so that the populations at either end of the cline may be very different from each other. [from Greek *klinein*, to lean]

cling — *verb intrans.* (PAST TENSE AND PAST PARTICIPLE **clung**) **1** to hold firmly or tightly; to stick. **2** to be emotionally over-dependent: *still clinging to his mother.* **3** to refuse to drop or let go. — *adj.* same as CLINGSTONE. [from Anglo-Saxon *clingan*]

clinger *noun* someone or something that clings.

clingfilm *noun* a thin, clear plastic material that adheres to itself, used for wrapping food, covering containers, etc.

clinginess *noun* being clingy.

clingstone *adj., said of a fruit, eg a peach* having a stone that sticks to the flesh.

clingy *adj.* (**clingier, clingiest**) inclined to cling.

clinic *noun* **1** a private hospital or nursing home that specializes in the treatment and care of patients with particular diseases or disorders. **2** a department of a hospital or a health centre that specializes in the diagnosis, treatment, and medical care of one type of patient, or in one form of treatment, eg a family planning clinic. **3** a session during which patients are given medical treatment or advice in such a specialized department. **4** the instruction in examination and treatment of patients that is given to medical students, usu-

ally at the patient's bedside in a hospital ward. **5** a session in which an expert is available for consultation. [from Greek *klinikos*, relating to the sickbed]

clinical *adj.* **1** relating to, or like, a clinic or hospital. **2** *said of medical studies* based on, or relating to, direct observation and treatment of the patient, as distinct from theoretical or experimental work. **3** *said of manner, behaviour, etc* cold; impersonal; unemotional; detached. **4** *said of surroundings, etc* severely plain and simple, with no personal touches.

clinical death the state of the body in which the brain has ceased to function, though artificial means can be used to maintain the action of the heart, lungs, etc.

clinical linguistics the application of linguistics to analysis of disorders of spoken, written, or signed language, including those language handicaps with a clear physical cause (deafness, aphasia, etc), and those which have no apparent physical cause (stuttering, stammering, dyslexia, etc). Clinical linguistics emerged in the 1970s as an ancillary subject to speech pathology and has since developed into a separate academic field.

clinically *adv.* in a clinical way; in terms of medical observation rather than theory.

clinical psychology the practical application of psychological research findings to the diagnosis, treatment, and prevention of a wide range of mental disorders, including anxiety, depression, sexual and marital problems, childhood behavioural problems, eating disorders, drug and alcohol dependence, phobias, obsessions, schizophrenia, mental handicap, and dementia.

clinical thermometer a thermometer used for finding the temperature of the body.

clinician *noun* a doctor who works directly with patients, in a clinic, etc.

clink¹ — *noun* a short sharp ringing sound. — *verb intrans., trans.* to make or cause to make a clink. [perhaps from Old Dutch *klinken*, to ring]

clink² *noun slang* prison. [originally the name of a prison in Southwark]

Clinker, Humphry see HUMPHRY CLINKER, THE EXPEDITION OF.

clinker *noun* **1** a mass of fused ash or slag left unburnt in a furnace. **2** the cindery crust on a lava flow. [from Dutch *klinker*, hard brick]

clinker-built *adj., said of a boat* with a hull each of whose planks overlaps the one below it on the outside. See also CARVEL-BUILT. [from *clink*, a form of CLINCH, from the use of clinched nails]

clinometer *noun* a hand-held surveying instrument used to measure the angles of a slope by bringing a level-bubble on a graduated circle into alignment with a wire in a sighting tube.

clint *noun Geol.* **1** one of a series of limestone blocks or ridges divided by fissures. **2** any exposed outcrop of hard flinty rock that forms a projection or ledge. [from Middle English, = cliff]

Clinton, Bill (William) (1946–) US Democratic politician and 42nd President. He taught law at the University of Arkansas (1973–6) before he was elected state attorney general (1976). Elected Governor of Arkansas in 1978, he was the youngest person ever to hold that office, and served for five terms (1979–81 and 1983–92). In 1992, on a platform of hope and change in a climate of economic recession and voter disillusionment, he was elected President, thus ending a 12-year Republican hold on the office. Since his inauguration (20 Jan 1993) he has been faced with problems at home, such as the need to break his election promise and raise taxes to reduce budget deficit, and problems abroad involving decisions on the intervention of US troops in the Somalian and Yugoslav civil wars.

Clio in Greek mythology, the Muse of history and of lyre-playing.

clip¹ — *verb* (**clipped**, **clipping**) **1** to cut (hair, wool, etc). **2** to trim or cut off the hair, wool or fur of. **3** to punch out a piece from (a ticket) to show that it has been used. **4** to cut (an article, etc) from a newspaper, etc. **5** *colloq.* to hit or strike sharply. **6** to cut (a small amount) from something. — *noun* **1** an act of clipping. **2** a short sequence extracted from a film. **3** *colloq.* a sharp blow. **4** *colloq.* speed; rapid speed: *going at a fair clip.* **5** *Austral., New Zealand* the total amount of wool shorn from sheep, at one time, place, etc.
— **clip someone's wings** to reduce their power or scope for activity.
[from Norse *klippa*, to cut]

clip² — *noun* **1** (*often in compounds*) any of various usually small devices for holding things together or in position. **2** (*also* **cartridge clip**) a container for bullets attached to a gun, that feeds bullets directly into it. **3** a piece of jewellery in the form of a clip, for attaching to clothing. — *verb trans., intrans.* (**clipped**, **clipping**) to fasten with a clip. [from Anglo-Saxon *clyppan*, to embrace, clasp]

clipboard *noun* a board serving as a portable writing surface, with a clip at the top for holding paper, forms, etc.

clip joint *slang* a bar, restaurant or nightclub charging excessively high prices.

clip-on *adj.*, *said eg of earrings* fastening with a clip.

clipped *adj.* **1** *said of the form of a word* shortened, eg *sec* from *second*. **2** *said of speaking style* tending to shorten vowels, omit syllables, etc.

clipper *noun Hist.* a fast sailing ship with large sails. [from CLIP¹]

clippers *pl. noun* (*often in compounds*) a clipping instrument.

clipping *noun* **1** a piece clipped off: *hair clippings.* **2** a cutting from a newspaper, etc.

clique *noun derog.* a group of friends, professional colleagues, etc who stick together and are hostile towards outsiders. [from French *clique*]

cliquey *or* **cliquish** *adj.* (**cliquier**, **cliquiest**) characteristic of a clique; socially exclusive.

cliquiness *or* **cliquishness** *noun* being cliquey.

clitoral *adj.* relating to or in the region of the clitoris.

clitoridectomy *noun Medicine* the surgical removal of the clitoris. See also CIRCUMCISION.

clitoris *noun Anat.* in female mammals, a small highly sensitive organ located in front of the opening of the vagina, which like the penis in males becomes erect when sexually stimulated. [from Greek *kleitoris*]

Clive a male first name, after the surname. [from Anglo-Saxon *clif*, cliff, slope]

Clive (of Plassey), Robert Clive, Baron (1725–74) English soldier and administrator in India, born in Styche, Shropshire. He joined the East India Company (1743), and took part in the campaigns against the French. In 1755 he was called to avenge the so-called Black Hole of Calcutta, and at the battle of Plassey (1757) he defeated a large Indian-French force. For three years he was sole ruler of Bengal, in all but name. He returned to England (1760) and entered parliament, but in 1765 went back to Calcutta, effectively reformed the civil service, and also re-established military discipline. His measures were seen as drastic, and he was subjected to a select committee enquiry upon his return to England in 1767. Though vindicated, he committed suicide in London.

Cllr *abbrev.* Councillor.

cloaca *noun Zool.* in most vertebrates apart from mammals, the terminal region of the gut, into which the alimentary canal, urinary system, and reproductive system all open and discharge their contents, which are then expelled from the body via a single common aperture. [from Latin *cloaca*, from *cluere*, to purge]

cloak — *noun* **1** a loose outdoor garment, usually sleeveless, fastened at the neck so as to hang from the shoulders. **2** a covering: *a cloak of mist.* **3** a concealment or disguise: *use one's job as a cloak for spying activities.* — *verb* to cover up or conceal: *cloaked in mystery.* [from Old French *cloke*, from Latin *clocca*, bell, bell-shaped cape]

cloak-and-dagger *adj.*, *said of stories, situations, etc* full of adventure, mystery, plots, spying, etc.

cloakroom *noun* **1** a room in a theatre, restaurant, etc where coats, hats, etc may be left. **2** a toilet, especially in a public building.

clobber¹ *verb* (**clobbered**, **clobbering**) *colloq.* **1** to hit. **2** to defeat completely. **3** to criticize severely.

clobber² *noun slang* **1** clothing. **2** personal belongings, equipment, etc.

cloche *noun* **1** a covering of glass or transparent plastic for protecting young plants. **2** a woman's close-fitting dome-shaped hat. [from French *cloche*, bell, bell jar, from Latin *clocca*, bell]

clock¹ — *noun* **1** an instrument for measuring and indicating time, usually by means of a digital display or pointers on a dial. **2** a device that controls the speed of the central processing unit in a computer. **3** a device that synchronizes the timing in switching circuits, transmission systems, etc. **4** a device in a vehicle for showing distance travelled or speed of travel. **5** (*in full* **time clock**) an instrument for recording employees' times of arrival and departure. **6** the downy seedhead of a dandelion. **7** *slang* the face. — *verb* **1** to measure or record time using such an instrument. **2** to record with a stopwatch the time taken by (a racer, etc) to complete a distance, etc. **3** *colloq.* to travel at (a speed as shown on a speedometer). **4** *slang* to hit (someone).
— **against the clock** with a time deadline.

beat the clock to finish before the set time limit or deadline.

clock in *or* **on** to record one's time of arrival at a place of work.

clock out *or* **off** to record one's time of departure from a place of work.

clock something up to reach a particular speed, cover a particular distance, or achieve a particular score, etc.

put back the clock to seek to return to the conditions of an earlier period.

round the clock throughout the day and night.

watch the clock to pay close attention to the time of day, especially in order not to exceed minimum working hours.
[from Old Dutch *clocke*, bell, clock]
◊ The operation of a clock depends on the generation of a series of pulses or vibrations that occur at finely controlled and regular intervals. Mechanical clocks depend on the regular swing of a pendulum, or the oscillation of a mass connected to a coiled spring, while electric clocks depend on the frequency of alternating current to drive a synchronized motor. Quartz clocks are driven by the vibrations of a piezoelectric quartz crystal.

clock² *noun* a decoration on the side of a sock.

Clock Symphony Joseph Haydn's Symphony No.101 in D (1794). It is named after the clock-like accompaniment in the second movement.

clock tower a four-walled tower with a clock face on each wall.

clockwatcher *noun* a person who pays close attention to the time of day, especially in order not to exceed minimum working hours.

clockwise *adj.*, *adv.* moving, etc in the same direction as that in which the hands of a clock move.

clockwork — *noun* a mechanism like that of a clock, working by means of gears and a spring that must be wound periodically. — *adj.* operated by clockwork.
— **like clockwork** smoothly and with regularity; without difficulties.

clod *noun* **1** a lump of earth, clay, etc. **2** *colloq.* a stupid person. [from Middle English *clodde*]

cloddish *adj.* **1** like a clod or clods. **2** stupid.

cloddishly *adv.* in a cloddish way.

cloddishness *noun* being cloddish.

clodhopper *noun colloq.* **1** a clumsy person. **2** a large, heavy boot or shoe. [from CLOD + HOP¹]

clodhopping *adj.* like a clodhopper.

clog — *noun* a shoe carved entirely from wood, or having a thick wooden sole. — *verb trans., intrans.* (**clogged**, **clogging**) (*also* **clog up**) to obstruct or become obstructed so that movement is difficult or impossible. [from Middle English]

cloisonné *noun* a form of decoration for vases, etc, the pattern being formed in wire and filled in with coloured enamel. [from French = compartmented]

cloister

cloister — *noun* **1** a covered walk built against the wall of a church, college, etc with arches along its other side that open on to a garden, quadrangle, etc. **2** a place of religious retreat, eg a monastery or convent; the quiet secluded life of such a place. — *verb* (**cloistered**, **cloistering**) to keep (someone) away from the problems of normal life in the world. [from Old French *cloistre*]

Cloisters, the a complex in Fort Tryon Park, New York City, incorporating several medieval structures. The Cloisters were opened as a branch of the Metropolitan Museum of Art in 1938, and house George Grey Barnard's notable collection of medieval art.

cloistral *adj.* **1** relating to or like a cloister. **2** living in a cloister.

clonal *adj.* relating to or like a clone.

clone — *noun* **1** *Biol.* any of a group of genetically identical cells or organisms derived from a single parent cell or organism by asexual re-

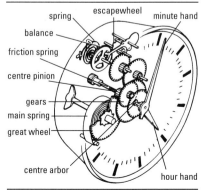

clock mechanisms

production, eg vegetatively propagated plants. **2** *Biol.* any of a large number of identical copies of a gene produced by genetic engineering. **3** *Comput.* a usually cheaper imitation of an existing computer or software product, produced by a different manufacturer. **4** *colloq.* a person or thing that looks like a replica of someone or something else. — *verb trans., intrans.* to produce a set of identical cells or organisms from a single parent cell or organism, or to produce many identical copies of a gene by genetic engineering. [from Greek *klon*, twig]

clonk — *noun* a noise of a heavy, especially metal, object striking something. — *verb intrans., trans.* to make or cause to make this noise. [imitative]

Clonmel, Gaelic **Cluain Meala** POP (1991) 16 000, the capital of Tipperary county (South Riding), Munster province, S Irish Republic. It lies on the R Suir and is the centre of Irish greyhound racing and salmon fishing.

clop — *noun* the hollow sound of a horse's hooves on hard ground. — *verb intrans.* (**clopped, clopping**) *said of a horse* to walk along making this noise. [imitative]

Close, Glenn (1947–) US film and stage actress, born in Greenwich, Connecticut. A well-established career on television and Broadway led to her acclaimed feature-film début in *The World According to Garp* (1982). Among her subsequent successes are *Jagged Edge* (1985), *Fatal Attraction* (1987), *Dangerous Liaisons* (1988), and *Hamlet* (1990).

close¹ — *adj.* **1** near in space or time; at a short distance: *at close range.* **2** near in relationship, friendship, or connection. **3** touching or almost touching. **4** tight, not loose; dense or compact; with little space between. **5** near to the surface: *a close haircut.* **6** thorough; searching. **7** *said of a contest, etc* with little difference between entrants, etc. **8** (**close to something**) about to happen, do something, etc: *close to tears.* **9** similar to the original, or to something else: *a close translation / a close resemblance.* **10** uncomfortably warm; stuffy. **11** secretive. **12** mean: *close with money.* **13** heavily guarded: *under close arrest.* **14** *old use* shut; closed; confined. **15** *said of an organization, etc* restricted in membership. — *adv.* **1** (*often in compounds*) in a close manner; closely: *close-fitting / follow close behind.* **2** at close range. **3** (**close on** or **to** ...) nearly: *close on a thousand.*
— **at close quarters 1** at close range; near to. **2** *said of fighting* hand-to-hand, one individual fighting another.
close at or **to hand** close by; easily available.
a close call or **shave** a narrow or lucky escape.
a close thing 1 a narrow escape. **2** something only just managed or achieved.
close to home uncomfortably close to the truth, or to a sensitive matter.
[from Old French *clos*, closed, from Latin *claudere*, to close]

close² — *verb* **1** *trans., intrans.* to shut. **2** to block (a road, etc) so as to prevent use. **3** *trans., intrans. said of shops, etc* to stop or cause to stop being open to the public for a period of time. **4** *trans., intrans. said of a factory, business, etc* to stop or cause to stop operating permanently. **5** *trans., intrans.* to finish; to come or bring to an end; to stop discussion, etc of. **6** *trans., intrans.* to join up or come together; to cause edges etc, of something to come together. **7** to settle or agree on: *close a deal.* **8** *intrans. Econ., said of currency, shares, etc* to be worth at the end of a period of trading. **9** (**close on someone**) to catch them up: *the police were closing on him.* — *noun* an end or conclusion.
— **close down 1** *said of a business* to close permanently. **2** *said of a television or radio station, etc* to stop broadcasting at the end of the day.
close something down to close it permanently.
close one's eyes to something to pretend not to notice it.

close in *said of days* to become shorter in winter, while nights get longer.
close in on someone to approach and surround them: *the police were closing in on them.*
close up to move closer together.
close something up to bring closer together: *close up the gaps.*
close with someone 1 to strike a bargain with; to agree to (an offer, etc). **2** *old use* to begin fighting them.
[from Latin *claudere*, to close]

close³ *noun* **1** in Scotland, a narrow passage leading from the street to the stair of a tenement building. **2** (**Close**) used as the name of a street, usually one closed to traffic at one end. **3** the land and buildings surrounding and belonging to a cathedral; a quadrangle. [from Middle English *clos*, enclosure, from Latin *claudere*, to close]

closed *adj.* **1** shut; blocked. **2** *said of a community or society* with membership restricted to a chosen few.
— **behind closed doors** privately, the public being excluded.

closed book a person or subject that one cannot understand.

closed circuit a complete electrical circuit.

closed-circuit television a television system serving a limited number of receivers, eg within a building, the signal being transmitted by wires.

closed-loop *Comput. adj.* denoting a computer system in which performance is controlled by comparing an amount of output with an expected standard in order to identify and reduce deviations.

close-down *noun* **1** the permanent closing of a business. **2** *Brit.* the closing of broadcasting at the end of the day.

closed shop, a factory, etc in which only members of a trade union are employed. See also OPEN SHOP.

closed syllable a syllable ending in a consonant.

close-fisted *adj. colloq.* mean; miserly.

close harmony a style of singing in harmony with the voice parts nearly coinciding.

close-hauled *adj. Naut.* with sails set for sailing as nearly into the wind as possible.

close-knit *adj., said of a group, community, etc* closely bound together.

closely *adv.* in a close way; with close attention: *shall watch them closely.*

closeness *noun* a close quality or state.

close season the time of year when it is illegal to kill certain birds, animals or fish for sport.

closet — *noun* **1** a cupboard. **2** *old use* a small private room. **3** *old use* same as WATER CLOSET. — *adj.* secret, not openly declared. — *verb* (**closeted, closeting**) (**closet someone** or **oneself away**) to shut them or oneself away in private, eg for confidential discussion. [from Old French diminutive of *clos*, enclosed place]

close-up *noun* **1** a photograph, television shot, etc taken at close range. **2** a detailed look at, or examination of, something.

closing date the last possible date on which something can be done, sent in, etc.

closing-time *noun* the time when pubs must stop serving drinks and close.

clostridium *noun* (PL. **clostridia**) *Biol.* a rod-shaped Gram-negative bacterium of the genus *Clostridium* that occurs in soil and in the digestive tract of humans and animals. Species of *Clostridium* cause botulism (a severe form of food poisoning) and tetanus. [from Greek *kloster*, spindle]

closure — *noun* **1** the act of closing something, eg a business or a transport route. **2** a device for closing or sealing something. **3** a parliamentary procedure for cutting short a debate and taking an immediate vote. — *verb* to use this procedure for ending (a debate). [from Latin *clausura*, from *claudere*, to close]

clot — *noun* **1** a soft mass, especially of solidified liquid matter such as blood. **2** *colloq.* a fool. — *verb intrans., trans.* (**clotted, clotting**) to form into clots. [from Anglo-Saxon *clott*, lump, mass]

Cloten the posturing, ridiculous son of the Queen in Shakespeare's *Cymbeline*, whose malicious plans for Imogen and Posthumus come to nothing.

cloth *noun* **1** woven, knitted, or felted material. **2** (*often in compounds*) a piece of fabric for a special use: *tablecloth.* **3** (**the cloth**) the clergy. [from Anglo-Saxon *clath*]

cloth cap a flat cap, especially made of tweed, with a stiff brim.

clothe *verb* (PAST TENSE AND PAST PARTICIPLE **clothed**, *old use* **clad**) **1** to cover or provide with clothes. **2** to dress. **3** to cover, conceal, or disguise: *hills clothed in mist.* See also CLAD. [from Anglo-Saxon *clathian*]

clothes *pl. noun* **1** articles of dress for covering the body, for warmth, decoration, etc. **2** same as BEDCLOTHES. [from Anglo-Saxon *clathas*, plural of *clath*, cloth]

clothes horse a hinged frame on which to dry or air clothes indoors.

clothesline *noun* a rope suspended usually outdoors, on which to hang clothes to dry.

clothes moth a small drab moth, whose larvae feed on dried organic matter, including woollen materials and fur. It can be a serious household pest.

clothes peg a small clip-like or forked device for securing clothes to a clothesline.

clothes pole a fixed vertical pole for tying a clothesline to.

clothier *noun old use* a person who makes, sells, or deals in cloth or especially men's clothing. [from Middle English *clothier*, altered from *clother*, from CLOTH]

clothing *noun* **1** clothes. **2** something forming a covering: *a clothing of snow.* [from CLOTHE]

Clotho see MOERAE.

cloth of gold a silk or woollen fabric interwoven with gold thread.

clotted cream thick cream made by slowly heating milk and taking the cream from the top.

cloud — *noun* **1** *Meteorol.* a visible floating mass of small water droplets or ice crystals suspended in the atmosphere above the Earth's surface. **2** a visible mass of particles of dust or smoke in the atmosphere. **3** a dark or dull spot. **4** a circumstance that causes anxiety. **5** a state of gloom, depression, or suspicion: *he left the firm under a cloud.* — *verb* **1** (*usually* **cloud over**) to become overcast with clouds. **2** *trans., intrans.* (*usually* **cloud over** or **cloud something over**) to make or become misty or cloudy. **3** (*also* **cloud over**) *said of the face* to develop a troubled expression. **4** to make dull or confused. **5** to spoil or mar.
— **on cloud nine** *colloq.* extremely happy.
up in the clouds *colloq.* out of touch with reality.
with one's head in the clouds *colloq.* preoccupied with one's own thoughts.
[from Anglo-Saxon *clud*, hill, mass of rock]
◊ Cloud is formed by the condensation or freezing of water vapour on minute particles in the atmosphere when air masses move upward as a result of convection currents, unstable conditions, etc, and in so doing cool rapidly. Clouds are usually classified according to their height and shape. See illustration p. 262.

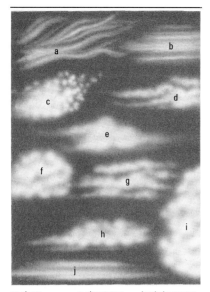

a: cirrus   e: altostratus   h: nimbostratus
b: cirrostratus   f: cumulus   i: cumulonimbus
c: cirrocumulus   g: stratocumulus   j: stratus
d: altocumulus

cloud types

cloud base *Meteorol.* the height above sea level of the lowest part of a cloud.

cloudburst *noun* a sudden downpour of rain.

cloud chamber a device for detecting subatomic particles. As charged particles pass through a chamber containing vapour, the size of the chamber is suddenly increased so that the temperature falls. Droplets of vapour then condense on the particles so that their tracks become visible as trails of mist.

cloud chamber *Physics* a device for detecting subatomic particles, consisting of a chamber containing vapour prone to condensing to form a liquid. The movement of particles forms ions, which act as centres for the condensation of liquid, and the paths of the particles then become visible as trails of mist. The cloud chamber has now been superseded by other particle detectors.

cloud-cuckoo-land *noun* a place where everything goes well, the apparent dwelling-place of over-optimistic people who refuse to see the problems of the real world.

cloudily *adv.* in a cloudy way.

cloudiness *noun* being cloudy.

cloudless *adj., said especially of the sky* having no clouds; clear and bright.

Clouds, The a Greek play by Aristophanes (c.423 BC). It is a political satire ridiculing the philosopher Socrates.

cloudy *adj.* (**cloudier, cloudiest**) **1** full of clouds; overcast. **2** *said eg of a liquid* not clear; milky. **3** confused; muddled.

clout — *noun* **1** *colloq.* a blow. **2** *colloq.* influence or power. **3** *dialect* a piece of clothing. — *verb colloq.* to hit. [from Anglo-Saxon *clut*, piece of cloth]

clove¹ *noun* the strong-smelling dried flower-bud of a tropical Asian tree, used as a spice. [from French *clou*, nail, from its shape]

clove² *noun* one of the sections into which a bulb, especially of garlic, naturally splits. [from Anglo-Saxon *clufu*, bulb]

clove³ see CLEAVE¹.

cloven *adj. old use, poetic* split; divided. [past participle of CLEAVE¹]

cloven hoof the partly split hoof of cattle, sheep or goats, and, in folklore, etc, of the Devil.

clover *noun* a small herbaceous plant of the genus *Trifolium* that grows wild in temperate regions. It has leaves divided into three leaflets (a four-leafed clover is sometimes considered lucky), and small dense red or white flowers. It is widely cultivated as a fodder crop for animal livestock, and is a good source of nectar for honey. — **in clover** *colloq.* in great comfort and luxury. [from Anglo-Saxon *clæfre*]

cloverleaf *noun* an arrangement of curving roads at the junction of two motorways, etc, having, from the air, the shape of a four-leaved clover.

Clovis the earliest identifiable Native American culture of N America (c.10000–9000 BC). It was part of the tradition of mammoth hunting, and is characterized archaeologically by fluted spear points found across the USA, notably near Clovis, New Mexico, in 1963.

Clovis I (c.465–511 AD) Merovingian king. In 481 he succeeded his father, Childeric, as King of the Franks, then overthrew the Gallo-Romans, and had taken possession of the whole country between the Somme and the Loire by 496. In 493 he married (St) Clotilda, and after routing the Alemanni was converted to Christianity along with several thousand warriors. In 507, he defeated the Visigoth, Alaric II, then captured Bordeaux and Toulouse, but was checked at Arles by the Ostrogoth, Theodoric.

clown — *noun* **1** a comic performer in a circus or pantomime, usually wearing ridiculous clothes and make-up. **2** someone who behaves comically. **3** *derog.* a fool. — *verb intrans.* (*usually* **clown about** *or* **around**) to behave ridiculously.

clownish *adj.* like a clown; foolish or playful.

clownishly *adv.* in a clownish way.

clownishness *noun* being like a clown.

cloy *verb intrans.* to become distasteful through excess, especially of sweetness. [variant of earlier *acloy*, originally meaning to nail, from Latin *clavus*, nail]

cloying *adj.* sickly sweet.

cloze testing a procedure used to establish a student's level of comprehension of a reading passage. The passage is presented with words omitted at regular intervals and the student must supply the missing words, or plausible substitutes. Cloze testing is mainly used in foreign language teaching. [formed from CLOSURE]

club — *noun* **1** a stick, usually thicker at one end, used as a weapon. **2** a stick with a specially shaped head, for playing golf or putting with. **3** (*also* **Indian club**) a bottle-shaped wooden object for swinging and throwing, for exercise. **4** a society or association. **5** the place where such a group meets. **6** a building with dining, reading, and sleeping facilities for members. **7** same as NIGHTCLUB. **8** (**clubs**) one of the four suits of playing-cards with black cloverleaf-shaped symbols. **9** one of the playing-cards of this suit. — *verb* (**clubbed, clubbing**) **1** to beat or strike with a club. **2** (**club together**) to contribute money jointly for a special purpose. — **in the club** *or* **pudding club** *colloq.* pregnant. [from Norse *klubba*, cudgel]

clubbable *adj.* friendly; able to mix well socially.

clubbed *adj., said of the fingers* thickened at the tips.

club foot a deformity in which the foot is turned inwards.

clubhouse *noun* a building where a club meets, especially the premises of a sports club.

clubmoss *Bot.* a spore-bearing vascular plant of the genus *Lycopodium*, related to ferns and horsetails. It has a long regularly branched stem with numerous small leaves, and sporangia (spore-bearing structures) in the leaf axils, often arranged in a terminal cone-like *strobilus*.

Clubmosses are found mainly in moist tropical or subtropical regions, and they are the only living representatives of a very primitive class, the Lycopsida, which flourished during the Carboniferous period, and included giant forms resembling trees.

clubmoss

clubroot *noun Bot.* a disease of plants of the cabbage family (Cruciferae), characterized by gall-like swellings of the roots and discoloration of the leaves, caused by the parasitic slime mould *Plasmodiophora brassicae*.

cluck — *noun* the sound that a hen makes. — *verb intrans.* **1** *said of a hen* to make clucks. **2** to express disapproval by making a similar sound with the tongue. [imitative]

clue — *noun* **1** a fact or circumstance the discovery of which helps one to solve a mystery or to make progress in investigating something, eg a crime. **2** a word or words representing, in a more or less disguised form, something to be entered in a crossword. — **not have a clue** *colloq.* to be completely ignorant about something. — *verb trans., intrans.* (**cluing**) (**clue someone in** *or* **up**) *colloq.* to inform them. [variant of *clew*, ball of thread, from its use in finding the way out of a maze]

clueless *adj. derog.* stupid, incompetent or ignorant.

Cluj-Napoca *or* **Cluj**, German **Klausenberg** POP (1989e) 329 000, the capital of Cluj county, NE central Romania. It lies on the R Someş in the foothills of the Apuseni Mts. HISTORY founded in the 12c on the site of a former Roman colony; a former capital of Transylvania; ceded from Hungary in 1920; the chief cultural and religious centre of Transylvania since the 16c. NOTABLE FEATURES St Michael Church; Austrian Fort; Franciscan Monastery; Botanical Gardens; winter sports facilities nearby.

clump — *noun* **1** a group of eg trees, plants or people standing close together. **2** a dull heavy sound, eg of treading feet. — *verb* **1** *intrans.* to walk with a heavy tread. **2** *trans., intrans.* to form into clumps. [related to Dutch *klompe*, lump, mass]

clumpiness *noun* being clumpy.

clumpy *adj.* (**clumpier, clumpiest**) **1** large and heavy: *clumpy shoes*. **2** clumping.

clumsily *adv.* in a clumsy way.

clumsiness *noun* being clumsy.

clumsy *adj.* (**clumsier, clumsiest**) **1** unskilful with the hands or awkward and ungainly in movement. **2** badly or awkwardly made. [from Middle English *clumse*, to be numb with cold]

clung see CLING.

clunk — *noun* the sound of a heavy, especially metal, object striking something. — *verb intrans., trans.* to make or cause to make this sound. [imitative]

Clurman, Harold (1901–80) US theatre director and critic, born in New York City. He was co-founder of the Group Theater (1931–40), and one of its directors, and he later worked as a director in Hollywood and on Broadway. An influential drama critic, his writings include *Lies Like Truths* (1958) and *The Divine Pastime* (1974).

cluster — *noun* **1** a small group or gathering. **2** a number of flowers growing together on one stem. — *verb trans., intrans.* (**clustered**, **clustering**) to form into a cluster or clusters. [from Anglo-Saxon *clyster*, bunch]

clutch[1] — *verb* **1** to grasp tightly. **2** *intrans.* (**clutch at something**) to try to grasp it. — *noun* **1** (**usually clutches**) control or power. **2** a device in a motor vehicle that connects or disconnects two revolving shafts, thereby passing, or preventing the passing of, the driving force from engine to gearbox. **3** the pedal operating this device.
— **clutch at straws** to try anything, however unlikely, in one's desperation.
[from Anglo-Saxon *clyccan*]

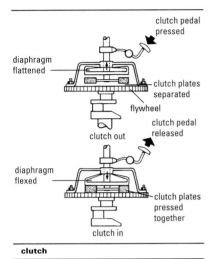

diaphragm flattened

clutch pedal pressed

clutch plates separated

flywheel

clutch out

clutch pedal released

diaphragm flexed

clutch plates pressed together

clutch in

clutch

clutch[2] *noun* **1** a number of eggs laid at the same time. **2** a brood of chickens. [from Norse *klekja*, to hatch]

clutch bag a small handbag without handles, held in the hand or under the arm.

Clutha, River the longest river on South I, New Zealand. From its source, the Makarora R, it is c.320km/200mi long. It rises in L Wanaka, W South I, and flows SE to enter the Pacific Ocean near Kaitangata. There are major hydroelectric schemes on the river near Alexandra.

clutter — *noun* an untidy accumulation of objects, or the confused, overcrowded state caused by it. — *verb* (**cluttered**, **cluttering**) (**clutter something up**) to overcrowd or make it untidy with accumulated objects. [variant of earlier *clotter*, from CLOT]

Clwyd POP (1992e) 415 000, a county in NE Wales, which is divided into six districts. AREA 2 426sq km/936sq mi. It is bounded W by Gwynedd, N by the Irish Sea, E by Cheshire and Shropshire, and S by Powys. CHIEF TOWN Mold; other main towns are Wrexham, Prestatyn, Rhyl, Flint, Colwyn Bay. ECONOMY coal; steel; engineering; chemicals; plastics; clothing; paper; microprocessors; the N Wales coast is a major tourist area. NOTABLE FEATURES castle remains at Chirk, Flint, Rhuddlan, and Denbigh; Ffestiniog Railway (steam); Llechwedd slate caverns.

Clyde, River a river in S Scotland, length 170km/106mi. Its main headstream, the Daer Water, rises in S Strathclyde, near the Dumfries and Galloway border, and flows generally N and NW. It then passes through Scotland's most important industrial area, S of Glasgow and through the city itself. At Dumbarton it expands into the estuary of the Firth of Clyde (2–30km/ 1–19mi wide, increasing to c.60km/37mi at its mouth), leading to the Atlantic Ocean. Glasgow is the head of navigation for ocean-going vessels. The Clyde, which is used for hydroelectricity, is linked to the R Forth by canal. Waterfalls near

Lanark are known as the Falls of Clyde. The Clyde Valley is noted for the breeding of Clydesdale horses.

Clydeside POP (1981) 1.7m, an urban area in W Strathclyde, W central Scotland. It comprises the 11 districts of Bearsden and Milngavie, Clydebank, Cumbernauld and Kilsyth, East Kilbride, Eastwood, Glasgow City, Hamilton, Monklands, Motherwell, Renfrew, and Strathkelvin. It is a major industrial area.

Clytemnestra *or* **Clytemestra** in Greek mythology, the twin sister of Helen and the wife of Agamemnon. She murdered him on his return from Troy, assisted by her lover Aegisthus. She was killed in revenge by her son Orestes.

Cm *symbol Chem.* curium.

cm *abbrev.* centimetre.

CMG *abbrev.* Companion of the Order of St Michael and St George.

CNAA *abbrev.* Council for National Academic Awards.

CND *abbrev.* in the UK, the Campaign for Nuclear Disarmament, an organization formed in 1958 to oppose Britain's development of a nuclear-weapons programme. It was an effective pressure group in the 1960s, but its popularity and influence had already begun to decline before the signing of nuclear non-proliferation pacts in the 1980s.

CNN *abbrev.* Cable News Network (USA).

CNR *abbrev.* Canadian National Railway.

C N Tower *or* **Canadian National Tower** the world's tallest self-supporting tower. It was erected in Toronto, Ontario in 1973–5, and is 555.3m high.

CO *abbrev.* **1** *as an international vehicle mark* Colombia. **2** Colorado. **3** Commanding Officer.

Co[1] *abbrev.* **1** Company. **2** County.

Co[2] *symbol Chem.* cobalt.

co- *prefix* forming words meaning 'with, together, jointly': *co-star / co-exist / co-operate.*

c/o *abbrev.* care of.

coach — *noun* **1** a railway carriage. **2** a bus designed for long-distance travel. **3** *Hist.* a closed horse-drawn carriage. **4** a trainer or instructor in a sport, etc, or a private tutor, especially one who prepares pupils for examinations. — *verb trans., intrans.* to train in a sport, etc, or teach privately.
— **drive a coach and horses through something** *colloq.* to ignore and therefore make nonsense of laws, regulations, existing arrangements, etc.
[from Old French *coche*, from Hungarian *kocsi*, from *Kocs* in Hungary]

coachbuilder *noun* a person who builds the bodies of motor vehicles.

coaching *noun* **1** tutoring, instruction. **2** *Hist.* travelling by coach.

coachman *noun Hist.* the driver of a horse-drawn coach.

coachwork *noun* the painted outer bodywork of a motor or rail vehicle.

coagulant *noun* a substance that causes coagulation.

coagulate *verb intrans., trans.* to pass or cause to pass from a liquid state to a semi-solid one; to curdle or clot. [from Latin *coagulare*]

coagulation *noun* **1** the action or process of coagulating. **2** the forming or uniting into a mass.

coal *noun* **1** a hard brittle generally brown or black combustible rock consisting mainly of carbon, and formed by the compaction of partially decomposed plant material. It is widely burned as a fuel, and is also used to make coke. **2** a piece of this.
— **coals to Newcastle** something brought to a place where it is already plentiful.

haul someone over the coals *colloq.* to scold them severely.

heap coals of fire on someone's head to make them feel guilty by repaying evil with good.
[from Anglo-Saxon *col*]
◊ Coal is one of the main fossil fuels, formed during the Carboniferous period from the rotting vegetation of tropical forests, which became overlaid by other rocks, subjected to great pressure, and over thousands of years turned into coal, most of which is now found in bands or seams at varying depths under the ground. Coal was the most important fuel of the Industrial Revolution, and was formerly the main type of domestic fuel, but has now been largely replaced by other fossil fuels. Many by-products of coal are used in detergents, antiseptics, dyes, pesticides, and medical drugs. Coal-burning power plants still produce almost two-thirds of the world's electricity.

coalesce *verb intrans.* to come together so as to form a single mass. [from Latin *co-*, together + *alescere*, to grow]

coalescence *noun* growing into each other; fusion.

coalescent *adj.* **1** that coalesces. **2** coalescing. **3** growing together.

coalface *noun* **1** the exposed face in a coalmine from which coal is being cut. **2** the area where the essential practical work is carried on in any particular field of activity.

coalfield *noun* an area where there is coal underground.

coal-fired *adj.* fuelled by coal.

coal gas a flammable gas, consisting mainly of hydrogen and methane, obtained by the destructive distillation of coal, or by heating coal in the absence of air. Formerly used as a domestic fuel, it has now been superseded by natural gas.

coalition *noun Politics* **1** a combination or temporary alliance, especially between political parties. **2** (*in full* **coalition government**) government by, or a government made up of, representatives of two or more political parties. Coalition governments are more common in electoral systems using proportional representation. [from Latin *coalitio*]

coalmine *noun* a place where coal is mined.

coal tar a thick black liquid obtained as a by-product during the manufacture of coke. It was formerly a major source of organic compounds, eg benzene and phenol, for the manufacture of drugs, dyes, etc, but most of these compounds are now obtained from petroleum or natural gas.

coal tit a small grey bird with a black head.

coaming *noun Naut.* the raised edging round the hatches on a ship, to keep out water.

coarse *adj.* **1** rough or open in texture. **2** rough or crude; not refined. **3** *said of behaviour, speech, etc* rude or offensive.

coarse fish freshwater fish, other than trout and salmon.

coarse fishing the sport of fishing for coarse fish.

coarsely *adv.* with a coarse manner.

coarsen *verb trans., intrans.* (**coarsened**, **coarsening**) to make or become coarse.

coarseness *noun* being coarse.

coast — *noun* the zone of land that borders the sea; the seashore. — *verb intrans.* **1** to travel downhill, eg on a bicycle or in a motor vehicle, using no kind of propelling power, relying on gravity or momentum. **2** to progress smoothly and satisfactorily without much effort.
— **the coast is clear** *colloq.* there is no danger of being spotted or caught.
[from Old French *coste*]

coastal *adj.* **1** relating to the coast. **2** situated near a coast.

Coastal Command a separate functional Command within the British Royal Air Force (1936–69). Moves to transfer it to the Royal Navy caused a political storm in 1958–9. During World War II, the Command destroyed 184 German U-boats and 470 000 tonnes of enemy shipping, and played a major role in winning the battle of the Atlantic.

coaster *noun* **1** a vessel that sails along the coast taking goods to coastal ports. **2** a small mat or tray for slipping under a glass, bottle, decanter, etc to protect the table surface. [from COAST]

coastguard *noun* a person stationed on the coast to watch for ships or swimmers in difficulties, and to give help.

coastline *noun* the shape of the coast, especially as seen on a map, or from the sea.

Coast Mountains a mountain range lying in the W of the Canadian province of British Columbia and in Alaska, USA. It extends c.1 600km/1 000mi NW–SE and runs parallel to the Pacific Ocean, forming the NW border between British Columbia and Alaska. The range rises to 4 042m at Mt Waddington, in British Columbia. It has a rugged terrain with several glaciers.

Coast Range a mountain belt in W North America. It extends along the coast of the Pacific Ocean from Alaska through British Columbia (Canada), Washington, Oregon, California (all USA), and Baja California (Mexico). It includes the Kenai, Chugach, St Elias, Olympic, and Klamath Mts. The highest point is Mt Logan (5 950m) in the St Elias Mts, Canada. In British Columbia the range continues on the Alexander Archipelago, Queen Charlotte I, and Vancouver I; here it is separated from the Coast Mts to the E by several straits along the British Columbia coast. The Central Valley lies to the E in California.

coat — *noun* **1** an outer garment with long sleeves, typically reaching to the knees. **2** a jacket. **3** the hair, fur, or wool of an animal. **4** a covering or application (of something, eg paint, dust, sugar, etc). — *verb* to cover with a layer of something. [from Old French *cote*]

Coatbridge POP (1981) 51 000, the industrial capital of Monklands district, Strathclyde, W central Scotland. It lies 14km/9mi E of Glasgow and is part of the Clydeside urban area.

Coates, Eric (1886–1957) English composer, born in Hucknall, Nottinghamshire. He worked as a violinist in small chamber groups until in 1912 he became leading violist in the Queen's Hall Orchestra under Sir Henry Wood, who produced several of his early works at Promenade Concerts. Success as a composer of attractive light music enabled him to devote himself to composition after 1918. Among his best-known compositions are the *London Suite* (1933), *The Three Elizabeths* (1944), and a number of popular waltzes and marches.

coat-hanger *noun* a shaped piece of wood, plastic, or metal, with a hook, on which to hang garments.

coati *noun* a raccoon-like N and S American mammal, having reddish-brown fur, a long narrow muzzle with an overhanging tip, and a long banded tail. It lives in woodland and feeds on fruit and small animals. Solitary males are called *coatimundis* (or *koatimundis*). [from a S American name]

coating *noun* **1** a covering or outer layer. **2** material for making a coat or coating.

coat of arms a heraldic design consisting of a shield bearing the special symbols of a particular person, family, organization, or town.

coat of mail *Hist.* a protective garment made of interlinked metal rings, worn by soldiers.

coat-tails *pl. noun* two long pieces that hang down at the back of a man's tailcoat.

— **on someone's coat-tails** enjoying undeserved success as a result of someone else's achievement.

co-author — *noun* one's fellow author. — *verb* to write (a book, etc) with one or more others.

coax *verb* **1** (**coax someone into** *or* **out of something**) to persuade them, using flattery, promises, kind words, etc. **2** to get by coaxing. [from earlier *cokes*, fool]

coaxial *adj.* **1** having a common axis. **2** *Electr.*, said of a cable consisting of two conductors arranged concentrically and insulated from each other. [from CO- + AXIS]

coaxingly *adv.* in a coaxing way.

cob *noun* **1** a strong horse with short legs. **2** a male swan. **3** a hazelnut or hazel tree. **4** a corncob. **5** a loaf with a rounded top.

cobalt *noun* **1** *Chem.* (SYMBOL **Co**, ATOMIC NUMBER **27**) a silvery-white metal that is commonly used in the form of an alloy, eg stainless steel, high-strength alloys for cutting tools, and magnetic alloys. The radioactive isotope cobalt-60 is used in radiotherapy to treat cancer. **2** (*also* **cobalt blue**) a mixture of cobalt oxide and alumina that is used as a bright blue pigment in paints, ceramics, etc. **3** the colour of this compound. [from German *Kobold*, goblin, the name given to the material by frustrated miners looking for silver]

cobaltic *adj.* relating to or of the nature of cobalt.

Cobb, Ty (Tyrus Raymond), also called the **Georgia Peach** (1886–1961) US baseball player, born in Narrows, Georgia. In a 23-year career with Detroit and Philadelphia he hit over 4 000 base hits, a record which survived 57 years until broken in 1985. His career batting average was an all-time record at 0.367, and he led the American League 12 times in batting.

cobber *noun* Austral., New Zealand colloq. often used as a form of address) a pal.

Cobbett, William (1763–1835) English journalist and reformer, born in Farnham, Surrey. After spending a year reading widely, he did army service in New Brunswick (1785–91), then went to the USA, where he wrote fierce pieces against the native Democrats under the name 'Peter Porcupine'. His return to England in 1800 was welcomed by the Tories, and he started his *Weekly Political Register* (1802), which changed in 1804 from its original Toryism to an uncompromising Radicalism. His other works include a *History of the Protestant Reformation* (1824–7) and *Rural Rides* (1830).

cobble[1] *noun* (*also* **cobblestone**) a rounded stone used especially formerly to surface streets. [from COB]

cobble[2] *verb* **1** *trans., intrans.* to mend (shoes). **2** (**cobble something together**) to construct or concoct it roughly or hastily. [back-formation from COBBLER]

cobbled *adj.* having a cobbled surface.

cobbler *noun* a person who mends shoes.

cobblers *noun slang* nonsense. [rhyming slang: *cobblers' awls*, ie *balls*]

Cobden, Richard, known as the **Apostle of Free Trade** (1804–65) English economist and politician, born in Heyshott, Sussex. He settled in a Manchester calico business and in 1835 visited the USA, and in 1836–7 the Levant, after which he published two pamphlets preaching free trade, non-intervention, and speaking against 'Russophobia'. In 1838 he helped to found the Anti-Corn-Law League, becoming its most prominent member, and as an MP from 1841, he focused his speeches on this cause, which resulted in the repeal of the Corn Laws in 1846.

Coblenz, German **Koblenz**, ancient **Confluentes** POP (1991e) 109 000, a city situated in Rhineland-Palatinate state, W central Germany.

It lies at the confluence of the Mosel and Rhine rivers, 80km/50mi SE of Cologne. It is one of the leading centres of the Rhine wine trade. HISTORY the seat of the Frankish kings in the 6c; badly bombed in World War II. The Austrian statesman Metternich was born here in 1773. NOTABLE FEATURES St Castor's Church (836); Fortress of Ehrenbreitstein.

COBOL *noun* short for *Common Business-Oriented Language*, a computer programming language used in commerce, based on English.

cobra *noun* any of various species of venomous snake, usually about 2m long, found in Africa and Asia. When threatened, it rears up and movable ribs spread the skin behind the head to form a flattened hood. It feeds mainly on rodents, frogs, toads, and birds, and its venom is highly poisonous. The Indian cobra is believed to be one of the most dangerous snakes, killing thousands of people every year. [from Portuguese, from Latin *colubra*, snake]

cobweb *noun* **1** a web formed of fine sticky threads spun by a spider. **2** a single thread from this. [from Middle English *coppeweb*, from Anglo-Saxon *atorcoppe*, spider]

cobwebby *adj.* **1** full of cobwebs. **2** like a cobweb.

coca *noun* a S American shrub, or its leaves, which contain cocaine and are chewed as a stimulant. [from Spanish *coca*, from Quechua *kuka*]

cocaine *noun* *Medicine* an alkaloid drug obtained from the leaves of the coca plant, sometimes used medicinally as a local anaesthetic. It is toxic, potentially hallucinogenic, and its habitual use causes addiction, leading to mental and physical deterioration. Its use as a stimulant is illegal in many countries, and addiction to the derivative *crack* can cause social problems.

coccus *noun* (PL.; **cocci**) *Biol.* a spherical bacterium. [from Greek *kokkos*, berry]

coccyx *noun* (PL. **coccyxes**, **coccyges**) *Anat.* a small triangular tail-like bone at the base of the human spine. [from Greek *coccyx*, cuckoo, from its triangular beak]

Cochabamba **1** POP (1989e) 404 000, the third largest city in Bolivia and capital of Cochabamba department. It is situated in the central part of the country at an altitude of 2 500m. The city was founded in 1542 and is an important agricultural centre. NOTABLE FEATURES Palacio de Cultura; Los Portales Museum; Monument to War of Independence; thermal baths nearby. **2** a department in central Bolivia with the city of Cochabamba as its capital.

Cochin POP (1991) 1.1m, a naval base and seaport in Kerala state, SW India. It is situated on the Malabar coast of the Arabian Sea, 1 080km/671mi SE of Bombay. A Portuguese trading station was established here by Vasco da Gama in 1502. Fort Cochin was the first European settlement in India. NOTABLE FEATURE Tomb of Vasco da Gama.

cochineal *noun* **1** a bright red pigment widely used as a food colouring, eg in alcoholic drinks. **2** an insect found in Mexico and the West Indies, the dried body of which yields this dye. [from Spanish *cochinilla*]

cochlea *noun* (PL. **cochleae**) *Anat.* in the inner ear of mammals, crocodiles and birds, a hollow spirally coiled structure that converts the vibrations of sound waves into nerve impulses, which can then be interpreted by the brain as sound. [from Greek *cochlias*, snail with spiral shell]

cochlear *adj.* relating to or in the region of the cochlea.

cock[1] — *noun* **1** a male bird, especially an adult male chicken. **2** a stopcock for controlling the flow of liquid, gas, etc. **3** the hammer of a gun, raised and let go by the trigger. **4** *coarse slang* the penis. **5** *coarse slang* nonsense. **6** *slang* a pal, usually used as a form of address. — *verb* **1** *trans.*,

intrans. to lift; to stick up. **2** to turn in a particular direction: *cock an ear towards the door.* **3** to draw back the hammer of (a gun). **4** to set (one's hat) at an angle.
— **go off at half cock** to begin too soon, without being fully prepared.
[from Anglo-Saxon *cocc*]

cock² *noun* a small pile of hay, etc. [related to Norse *kökkr*, lump]

cockade *noun Hist.* a feather or a rosette of ribbon worn on the hat as a badge. [from COCK¹]

cock-a-hoop *adj. colloq.* jubilant; exultant.

cock-a-leekie *noun* soup made from chicken boiled with leeks. [from COCK¹ + LEEK]

cock-and-bull story *noun colloq.* an unlikely story, especially one used as an excuse or explanation.

cockatoo

cockatoo *noun* any of 16 species of the parrot family, usually found in woodland areas in Australasia, and resembling a parrot but with a large brightly coloured crest on its head that can be erected at will. Most species are white, or tinged with pink or yellow, and they feed on seeds, fruit, and nuts. Cockatoos can mimic human speech and other sounds, and are popular cage birds. [from Malay *kakatua*]

cockatrice *noun* **1** *Mythol.* a monster with the head, wings, and legs of a cock and the body and tail of a serpent. **2** *Biblical* a poisonous snake. [from Old French *cocatris*]

cockchafer *noun* a large grey-brown beetle. [from COCK 1 + *chafer*, beetle]

Cockcroft, Sir John Douglas (1897–1967) English nuclear physicist, born in Yorkshire. Professor at Cambridge (1939–46), he induced the first artificial disintegration of a nucleus by bombarding a lithium nucleus with protons (1932), pioneering the use of particle accelerators. For this work he shared the 1951 Nobel Prize for Physics with Ernest Walton.

cock-crow *noun* dawn; early morning.

cocked hat *Hist.* a three-cornered hat with upturned brim.
— **knock into a cocked hat** *colloq.* to surpass spectacularly or defeat utterly.
[from COCK¹]

cocker *noun* (*also* **cocker spaniel**) a small, especially copper-coloured, spaniel. [from WOODCOCK, which it was bred to hunt]

cockerel *noun* a young cock. [diminutive of COCK¹]

Cockerell, Sir Christopher Sydney (1910–) English radio-engineer and inventor, born in Cambridge. He first worked on radio and radar, and in the early 1950s invented the hovercraft.

Cockermouth POP (1981) 7 000, a town in Allerdale district, Cumbria, NW England. It lies at the junction of the Cocker and Derwent rivers, 40km/25mi SW of Carlisle. It was the home-town of the poet William Wordsworth.

cock-eyed *adj.* **1** crooked; lopsided. **2** senseless; crazy; impractical. [from COCK¹]

cockfight *noun* a fight between cocks armed with sharp metal spurs.

cockfighting *noun* contests in which cocks are set to fight each other.

cockily *adv.* with a cocky manner.

cockiness *noun* being cocky.

cockle *noun* an edible shellfish with a rounded, ribbed, hinged shell in two equal halves.
— **warm the cockles of one's heart** *colloq.* to delight and gladden one.
[from French *coquille*, shell]

cockleshell *noun* **1** the shell of the cockle. **2** any tiny insubstantial boat.

cockney — *noun* (PL. **cockneys**) **1** (*often* **Cockney**) a native of London, especially of the East End. **2** the dialect used by Cockneys. — *adj.* relating to Cockneys or their dialect. [from Middle English *cokeney*, a cock's egg (ie a misshapen egg), contemptuous name for a town-dweller]

cockpit *noun* **1** the compartment for the pilot and crew aboard an aircraft. **2** the driver's seat in a racing-car. **3** the part of a small yacht, etc containing the wheel and tiller. **4** *Hist.* a pit into which cocks were put to fight each other. **5** any scene of prolonged conflict, especially in war. [from COCK¹ + PIT¹]

cockroach *noun* a large insect with a flattened body, long slender antennae, and biting mouthparts, found mainly in the tropics, where it feeds nocturnally on decaying animal and vegetable matter. Several species are serious pests in human dwellings, and may spread disease, eg outbreaks of food poisoning. [from Spanish *cucaracha*]

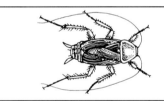

cockroach

cockscomb *noun* **1** the fleshy red crest on a cock's head. **2** (*also* **coxcomb**) *old derog. use* a conceited fellow. [from *cock's comb*]

Cockscomb Basin a region in the Maya mountains, Belize. AREA 15sq km/6sq mi. It is a forest reserve, part of which was designated the world's first jaguar reserve in 1986.

cocksure *adj.* foolishly over-confident. [from COCK¹]

cocktail *noun* **1** a mixed drink of spirits and other liquors. **2** a mixed dish especially of seafood and mayonnaise. **3** a mixture of different things.

cocktail stick a short thin pointed wooden stick on which to impale small items of food for serving at parties, etc.

cock-up *noun slang* a mess or muddle resulting from incompetence. [from COCK 1]

cocky *adj.* (**cockier, cockiest**) *derog.* cheekily self-confident. [from COCK¹]

coco see COCONUT.

cocoa *noun* **1** the seed of the cacao tree (*Theobroma cacao*). **2** a powder prepared from the seeds of the cacao tree after they have been fermented, dried, and roasted. **3** a drink prepared by mixing this powder with hot milk or water. [a variant of CACAO]

cocoa bean one of the seeds from the cacao tree (cocoa plant) after it has been fermented,

removed from the pod, and roasted. Cocoa beans form the raw material for chocolate manufacture.

cocoa butter a pale yellow fat obtained from cocoa beans, used as a base in the manufacture of chocolate and in cosmetics.

coconut *noun* **1** (*in full* **coconut palm**) a tropical palm tree (*Cocos nucifera*) with a characteristic curved trunk, up to 30m in height, with a crown of feathery leaves up to 6m long, probably native to Polynesia, and a characteristic tree of oceanic islands. It is cultivated throughout the tropics for its edible fruit. The trunk of the tree provides timber, and the leaves are woven into mats and baskets, and used for thatching. **2** the large single-seeded fruit of this tree, with a thick fibrous outer husk and a hard woody inner shell enclosing a layer of white edible flesh and a central cavity. The cavity contains a clear sweet-tasting liquid known as coconut milk, which is gradually absorbed as the fruit ripens. The white flesh is eaten raw or cooked, sold as desiccated coconut, or dried to form *copra*. Coconut milk is a nutritious drink. The oil obtained from pressed copra is used in margarine, soap, and other products, and the residue is used as feed for animals. [from Portuguese *coco*, grimace or ugly face, from the face-like markings on a coconut]

coconut shy a stall at a fair where contestants throw balls to knock coconuts off stands.

cocoon — *noun* the protective silky covering that many animals, eg spiders, earthworms, spin around their eggs; a similar covering that a lava spins around itself before it develops into a pupa. — *verb* **1** to wrap up as if in a cocoon. **2** to protect from the problems of everyday life. [from Provençal *coucoun*, eggshell]

cocooning *noun* the practice of choosing to spend one's spare time with a partner or one's family, rather than taking part in more social activities.

Cocos Islands *or* **Keeling Islands** POP (1991) 647, an Australian external territory comprising two separate groups of atolls in the Indian Ocean, 3 685km/2 290mi W of Darwin. AREA 14.2sq km/5.5sq mi (total land). There are 27 small, flat, palm-covered coral islands in the territory. The main islands are West I, 10km/6mi long, mostly occupied by Europeans, and Home I, occupied by the Cocos Malay community. HISTORY discovered in 1609 by Captain William Keeling of the East India Company; first settled in 1826, and developed by the Clunies-Ross family; annexed to the British Crown in 1857; granted by Queen Victoria to George Clunies-Ross in 1886; incorporated with the Settlement of Singapore in 1903; placed under Australian administration in 1955 as the Territory of Cocos (Keeling) Islands; Australia purchased the Clunies-Ross interests in the islands in 1978, and the inhabitants voted to become part of Northern Territory in 1984. GOVERNMENT an islands council, established by the Malay community, advises the administrator on all issues. ECONOMY copra plantation. NOTABLE FEATURE meteorological station.

cocotte *noun* a small lidded pot for oven and table use, especially intended for an individual portion. [from French *cocotte*]

co-counselling *noun* a form of self-help therapy in which two or more people take turns at being client and counsellor.

Cocteau, Jean (1889–1963) French poet, playwright, and film director, born in Maisons-Lafitte, near Paris. He had early success with his poems and figured as the sponsor of Picasso, Stravinsky, Giorgio di Chirico, and the musical group known as Les Six. His best-known works include the novel *Les Enfants terribles* (Children of the Game, 1929), the play *Orphée* (Orpheus, 1926), and the films *Le Sang du poète* (The Blood of the Poet, 1932) and *La Belle et la bête* (Beauty and the Beast, 1945).

cod¹ *noun* (PL. **cod**) a large soft-finned fish, found mainly in the N Atlantic Ocean, with a plump olive-green or brown body, covered with spots, and a silvery underside. It is second only in importance to the herring as a food fish in western countries. However cod populations are now becoming depleted by overfishing.

cod² *slang* — *noun* **1** a hoax. **2** a parody. — *verb* (**codded, codding**) **1** *intrans., trans.* to hoax (someone). **2** to parody.

cod³ *noun slang* nonsense. [from CODSWALLOP]

coda *noun Mus.* a passage added at the end of a movement or piece, to bring it to a satisfying conclusion. [from Italian *coda*, tail]

coddle *verb* **1** to cook (eggs) gently in hot, rather than boiling, water. **2** to pamper, mollycoddle, or over-protect. [variant of *caudle*, spiced egg drink for an invalid, from Latin *calidus*, warm]

code — *noun* **1** a system of words, letters, or symbols, used in place of those really intended, for secrecy's or brevity's sake. **2** a set of signals for sending messages, etc. **3** *Comput.* a set of symbols that represent numbers, letters, etc in binary form so that information can be stored or exchanged between different computer systems, eg the ASCII code. **4** *Comput.* the set of written instructions or statements that make up a computer program. **5** a group of numbers and letters used as means of identification. **6** a set of principles of behaviour. **7** a systematically organized set of laws. — *verb* **1** to put (a message, etc) into a code. **2** to generate a set of written instructions or statements that make up a computer program. [from Old French, from Latin *codex*, book]

codeine *noun Medicine* a morphine derivative that relieves mild to moderate pain, has a sedative effect, and suppresses the coughing reflex. It causes constipation, and is sometimes used to treat diarrhoea. [from Greek *kodeia*, poppy head]

Code Napoléon the French Civil Code, introduced (though not devised) by Napoleon Bonaparte as First Consul (1804) to fill the void left by the abolition of the legal and social customs of pre-revolutionary France. It established the principles of equality between people, liberty of person and contract, and the inviolability of private property, and was introduced into those areas of Europe under direct French control. The Civil Code of the newly-united Italian state (1865) bore close affinity to it, and it was widely emulated in S America. It remains extant in France, Belgium, Luxembourg, and Monaco.

co-dependency *noun* the condition of seeking to fulfil one's emotional needs by caring for or controlling a dependant.

code switching *Linguistics* a phenomenon commonly found in bilingual speakers, in which a speaker changes from one language to another in the course of a conversation with another bilingual speaker of the same language background. Code switching may be used to exclude other listeners from the conversation; or, if speakers cannot adequately express themselves in one language, they may switch to another language for short spells.

code word a word or phrase of special and secret significance, agreed on by its users for a purpose.

codex *noun* (PL. **codices**) an ancient manuscript bound in book form. [from Latin *codex*, set of tablets, book]

codfish *noun* a cod.

codger *noun colloq.* a man, especially an old and strange man. [perhaps a variant of CADGER]

codicil *noun Legal* a short addition to a will, added after the will has been written. [from Latin *codicillus*, diminutive of *codex*, book]

codification *noun* **1** the process of codifying. **2** the state of being codified.

codify *verb* (**codifies, codified**) to arrange (laws, etc) into a systematic code.

codling¹ *noun* a kind of cooking-apple. [from Middle English *querdling*]

codling² *noun* the young of the cod.

cod-liver oil a medicinal oil obtained from cods' livers, rich in vitamins A and D.

codon *noun Genetics* in a molecule of messenger RNA, a set of three bases that is specific for one particular amino acid. The order of codons determines the order in which amino acids are added to form a chain during the manufacture of a protein molecule.

codpiece *noun Hist.* a flap of material attached to a man's breeches, covering his genitals. [from earlier *cod*, scrotum]

codswallop *noun slang* nonsense.

Cody, William F(rederick), known as **Buffalo Bill** (1846–1917) US showman, born in Scott Co, Iowa. He gained his nickname after killing nearly 5 000 buffalo in eight months for a contract to supply meat to the workers on the Kansas Pacific Railway. He served as a scout in the Sioux wars, but from 1883 toured with his own Wild West Show. The town of Cody in Wyoming is situated on part of his ranch.

Coe, Sebastian (1956–) English track athlete, born in London. In the 800m at the European championships he successively won the bronze (1978), silver (1982), and gold (1986) medals. He broke his first world records (800m and 1mi) in 1979 and in total broke eight world records including the 800m, the 1 000m, and the mile (three times, most recently in 1981). He won the gold medal in the 1 500m and the silver in the 800m at both the 1980 and 1984 Olympics. Fitness problems followed, and he was omitted from the British team that went to the 1988 Olympics. He retired from running after the 1990 Commonwealth Games, to pursue a career in politics. In 1992 he became Conservative MP for Falmouth and Cambourne.

co-ed — *abbrev. colloq.* co-education or co-educational. — *noun North Amer., esp. US* a female student in a co-educational school or college.

co-education *noun* education of pupils of both sexes in the same school or college.
◇ In some countries, for religious and cultural reasons, schools are predominantly for children of the same sex. In most European countries, the 20c trend has been away from single-sex education, though there is a continuing debate about whether girls in particular are disadvantaged by co-education.

co-educational *adj.* teaching both sexes together.

coefficient *noun* **1** *Maths.* in an algebraic expression, a number or other constant factor, which may be represented by a letter, placed before a variable to signify that the variable is to be multiplied by that factor, eg in the expression $3x^2$, the coefficient of x^2 is 3, and in the equation $ax^2 + bx + c = 0$, a is the coefficient of x^2 and b is the coefficient of x. **2** *Physics* a number or parameter that is a measure of a specified property of a particular substance under certain conditions, eg the coefficient of viscosity.

coelacanth *noun* a primitive bony fish believed extinct till a live specimen was found in 1938. [from Greek *koilos*, hollow + *akantha*, spine]

Coelenterata *noun Zool.* in the animal kingdom, a phylum of invertebrate animals that have a single body cavity and usually show radial symmetry, eg jellyfish, sea anemones, and corals. [from Greek *koilos*, hollow + *enteron*, intestine]

coelenterate *noun Zool.* any invertebrate animal of the phylum Coelenterata. They are mainly marine organisms, many of which possess stinging cells that are used for capturing prey, and for defence, eg jellyfish, sea anemones, corals. [from Greek *koilos*, hollow + *enteron*, intestine]

coeliac — *adj.* **1** relating to the abdomen. **2** relating to coeliac disease. — *noun* a person suffering from coeliac disease. [from Greek *koilia*, belly]

coeliac disease *Medicine* a condition in which the lining of the small intestine is abnormally sensitive to the protein gluten, found in wheat, rye, and barley. Food is not digested and absorbed properly, giving rise to symptoms of malnutrition, including deficiency disorders, as well as fatigue and breathlessness. The disorder is treated with a strict gluten-free diet.

coelom *noun Zool.* the main body cavity in multicellular animals, which typically forms the cavity around the gut in annelids (eg earthworms), echinoderms (eg starfish), and vertebrates. [from Greek *koiloma*, cavity]

coenobite *noun* a member of a monastic community. [from Greek *koinos*, common + *bios*, life]

coenobitic *adj.* relating to, or characterized by, a coenobite or the monastic way of life.

co-enzyme *noun Biochem.* an organic molecule (such as a vitamin) that bonds with a specific enzyme only while a biochemical reaction is being catalysed. It is essential to, but remains unaffected by, the reaction.

coerce *verb* (**coerce someone into something**) to force or compel them, using threats, etc. [from Latin *coercere*, to restrain]

coercible *adj.* capable of being coerced.

coercion *noun* **1** the action of coercing. **2** constraint, restraint, force.

coercive *adj.* **1** coercing. **2** of the nature of coercion.

coeval *formal* — *adj.* of the same age or period of time. — *noun* someone of the same age or period of time. [from Latin *co-*, with + *aevum*, age]

co-exist *verb intrans.* **1** to exist together, or simultaneously. **2** to live peacefully side by side in spite of differences, etc.

co-existence *noun* a state of co-existing.

co-existent *adj.* existing together.

co-extensive *adj.* covering the same distance or time.

C of E *abbrev.* Church of England.

coffee *noun* **1** an evergreen tree or shrub of the genus *Coffea*. It belongs to the madder family (Rubiaceae), and has oval leaves, white fragrant flowers, and red fleshy fruits which typically contain two seeds (the coffee beans) rich in caffeine. Arabian coffee (*Coffea arabica*), which represents most of the world's coffee crop, is native to Ethiopia, and was first introduced to Arabia, and subsequently to the E Indies, W Indies, and S America. It requires a hot humid climate and a fertile soil, and is now mainly cultivated in Central and S America, especially Brazil. **2** the seeds of this plant, roasted whole or ground to a powder. **3** a popular beverage that contains the stimulant caffeine and is prepared from the roasted and ground 'beans' (the seeds) of the coffee plant, especially *Coffea arabica*. Decaffeinated coffee is produced by extracting the caffeine from powdered coffee beans using a suitable solvent. **4** the brown colour of the drink when mixed with milk. [from Turkish *kahveh*, from Arabic *qahwah*, coffee or wine]

coffee bar a place where coffee and snacks are sold at a counter.

coffee bean the seed of the coffee plant.

coffee break a pause for a cup of coffee during working hours.

coffee house *Hist.* an establishment serving coffee, used by fashionable people especially in the 18c.

coffee mill a machine for grinding coffee beans.

coffee table a small low table.

coffee-table book *often derog.* a large expensive highly illustrated book, suitable for visitors to browse through.

coffer *noun* 1 a large chest for holding valuables. 2 (**coffers**) a treasury or supply of funds. 3 *Archit.* a hollow or sunken section in the elaborate panelling or plasterwork of a ceiling. [from Old French *cofre*, from Greek *kophinos*, basket]

cofferdam *noun* a caisson.

coffin *noun* a box in which to bury or cremate a corpse. [from Old French *cofin*, from Greek *kophinos*, basket]

cog *noun* 1 one of a series of teeth on the edge of a wheel or bar which engage with another series of teeth to bring about motion. 2 a person unimportant to, or a process or organization. [from Middle English *cogge*]

cogency *noun* convincing or persuasive force.

cogent *adj.*, *said of arguments, reasons, etc* strong; persuasive; convincing. [from Latin *cogere*, to drive]

cogently *adv.* in a cogent way.

Coggan, (Frederick) Donald Coggan, Baron (1909–) English prelate, born in London. He lectured in Semitic languages at Manchester (1931–4), then became Professor of the New Testament at Wycliffe College, Toronto (1937–44), Principal of London College of Divinity (1944–56), Bishop of Bradford (1956–61), Archbishop of York (1961–74), and finally Archbishop of Canterbury (1974–80). Among his theological works are *On Preaching* (1978), *Mission to the World* (1982), and *God of Hope* (1991).

cogitate *verb intrans.* to think deeply; to ponder. [from Latin *cogitare*, to think]

cogitation *noun* deep thought; meditation.

cogitative *adj.* having the power of thinking; given to cogitating.

cognac *noun* a high-quality French brandy from *Cognac* in SW France.

cognate *adj.* (**cognate with someone** *or* **something**) 1 descended from or related to a common ancestor. 2 *said of words or languages* derived from the same original form. 3 related; akin. [from Latin *co-*, with + *gnasci*, to be born]

cognition *noun Psychol.* the combination of mental activities, which include perception, memory, reasoning, judgement, problem-solving, language, symbolism, and conceptual thought, that enable a person to experience and learn about his or her environment. [from Latin *cognitio*, study, knowledge]

cognitive *adj.* relating to or capable of cognition.

cognitively *adv.* in a cognitive way.

cognitive therapy *Psychol.* a form of psychotherapy based on the view that the manner in which people perceive themselves and the world about them strongly influences their feelings and emotions. In cognitive therapy, the therapist helps the patient to identify false or distorted perceptions and modify them accordingly, in an attempt to alleviate disorders such as depression, addictive behaviour, etc.

cognizance *or* **cognisance** *noun* 1 knowledge; understanding; perception; awareness. 2 the range or scope of one's awareness or knowledge. 3 *Legal* the right of a court to deal with a particular matter. 4 *Heraldry* a distinctive mark or sign.
— **take cognizance of something** to take it into consideration.
[from Old French *conoisance*, from Latin *cognoscere*, to know; *g* added later under the influence of Latin]

cognizant *or* **cognisant** *adj.* (**cognizant of something**) aware of it.

cognomen *noun* 1 *Roman Hist.* a Roman's third name, often in origin an epithet or nickname. 2 a nickname or surname. [from Latin, *co-*, with + *nomen*, name]

cognoscenti *pl. noun* knowledgeable or refined people; connoisseurs. [Italian, from Latin *cognoscere*, to know]

cogwheel *noun* a wheel with cogs.

cohabit *verb intrans.* (**cohabited, cohabiting**) to live together as, or as if, husband and wife. [from Latin *cohabitare*, to live together]

cohabitation *noun* living together.

cohabiter *or* **cohabitee** *noun* a person who lives with another or others.

Cohan, Robert (Paul) (1925–) US-born British dancer, choreographer, and director. Born in Brooklyn, New York, he took British citizenship in 1989. He trained with the Martha Graham Company in New York, and from 1946 to 1957 was Martha Graham's partner. He founded a company in 1957, but returned to Graham's group, where he became co-director (1966). From 1967 to 1983 he was the founding artistic director of London Contemporary Dance Theatre, which was to play a key role in the development of modern dance performance and education in the UK. His many works include *Cell* (1969), *Stages* (1971), *Class* (1975), *Forest* (1977), and *Video-Life* (1987).

cohere *verb intrans.* 1 to stick together. 2 to be consistent; to have a clear logical connection or development. [from Latin *cohaerere*, to be connected]

coherence *noun* 1 a tendency to cohere. 2 a sticking together. 3 consistency.

coherence theory *Philos.* a theory of truth which maintains either that a proposition is true if it fits into a network of propositions, or that a necessary condition for justifying a belief is that it should fit with the believer's other beliefs.

coherent *adj.* 1 *said of a description or argument* logically and clearly developed; consistent. 2 speaking intelligibly. 3 sticking together; cohering. 4 *Physics, said of radiating waves* having the same frequency and a constant phase difference. [from Latin *cohaerere*, to be connected]

coherently *adv.* in a coherent way.

cohesion *noun* 1 the process or state of sticking together. 2 the tendency to stick together. 3 *Physics* the attraction between atoms or molecules of the same substance, eg water molecules, that produces surface tension effects such as the formation of droplets and thin films. See also ADHESION. [from Latin *cohaerere*, to stick together]

cohesive *adj.* 1 having the power of cohering. 2 tending to unite into a mass.

Cohn, Ferdinand Julius (1828–98) German botanist and bacteriologist, born in Breslau (now Wrocław, Poland). Professor of Botany at Breslau from 1859 and founder of the world's first institute specializing in plant physiology, he is regarded as the father of bacteriology in that he was the first to account it a separate science. He did important research in plant pathology, and worked with Robert Koch on anthrax.

Cohnheim, Julius Friedrich (1839–84) German pathologist, born in Demmin, Pomerania (now in Poland). Professor at Kiel, Breslau, and Leipzig, his brilliant experimental work included important studies of infection and cancer. He first elucidated completely the microscopic events of inflammation, and provided the first proof that tuberculosis was an infectious disease.

cohort *noun* 1 *Hist.* in the ancient Roman army, one of the ten divisions of a legion. 2 a band of warriors. 3 a group of people sharing a common quality or belief. 4 *colloq.* a follower, supporter, or companion. [from Latin *cohors*]

COHSE *abbrev.* Confederation of Health Service Employees.

coif¹ *noun* a close-fitting cap worn especially by women in medieval times or by nuns under a veil. [from Old French *coiffe*]

coif² — *noun* a hairstyle. — *verb* (**coiffed, coiffing**) to dress (hair); to dress the hair of. [probably from COIFFURE]

coiffeur *noun* a male hairdresser. [from French *coiffeur*]

coiffeuse *noun* a female hairdresser.

coiffure — *noun* a hairstyle. — *verb* to dress (hair); to dress the hair of. [from French *coiffure*]

coil¹ — *verb trans., intrans.* (*also* **coil up**) to wind round and round in loops to forms rings or a spiral. — *noun* 1 something looped into rings or a spiral. 2 a single loop in such an arrangement. 3 a wound length of wire for conducting electricity. 4 a piece of plastic-covered wire inserted into the womb to prevent pregnancy. [from Old French *cuillir*, to gather together]

coil² *noun old use* trouble and tumult.
— **this mortal coil** the troubles of the world.

Coimbatore POP (1991) 1.1m, a city in Tamil Nadu state, S India. It lies 425km/264mi SW of Madras. HISTORY a stronghold of successive Tamil kingdoms from the 9c until the 17c; ceded to Britain in 1799.

Coimbra, ancient **Conimbriga** 1 POP (1991) 97 000, the capital of Coimbra district, central Portugal. It lies on the R Mondego, 173km/108mi NE of Lisbon. In the 12c–13c it was the capital of Portugal. NOTABLE FEATURES the country's oldest university was founded in Lisbon in 1290 and transferred here in 1537; two cathedrals; São Sebastião Aqueduct; Monastery of the Holy Cross; National Museum; Conimbriga Roman Site and Children's Portugal Village nearby. 2 a district in central Portugal with Coimbra as its capital.

coin — *noun* 1 a small metal disc stamped for use as money. 2 coins generally. — *verb* 1 to manufacture (coins) from metal; to make (metal) into coins. 2 to invent (a new word or phrase).
— **be coining it** *colloq.* to be making a lot of money.
the other side of the coin the opposite way of looking at the issue under consideration.
pay someone back in their own coin to respond to their discourteous or unfair treatment with similar behaviour.
to coin a phrase *ironic* used to introduce an over-used expression.
[from Old French *coin*, wedge, die]

coinage *noun* 1 the process of coining. 2 coins. 3 a newly invented word or phrase. 4 the official currency of a country.

coincide *verb intrans.* 1 to happen at the same time. 2 to be the same; to agree. 3 to occupy the same position. [from Latin *co-*, together + *incidere*, to happen]

coincidence *noun* 1 the occurrence of events together or in sequence in a startling way, without any causal connection. 2 the fact of being the same.

coincident *adj.* 1 coinciding in space or time. 2 in agreement.

coincidental *adj.* happening by coincidence.

coincidentally *adv.* by coincidence; at the same time.

coin-operated *adj.*, *said of a machine* operating on the insertion of a coin.

coir *noun* fibre from coconut shells, used for making ropes, matting, etc. [from Malayalam (a SW Indian language) *kayaru*, cord]

coital *adj.* involving or relating to sexual intercourse.

coition *or* **coitus** *noun* sexual intercourse. [from Latin *coire*, to unite]

Coke, Sir Edward (1552–1634) English jurist, born in Mileham, Norfolk. He was called to the Bar in 1578, and rose to become Speaker of the House of Commons in 1593, Attorney-General (1594), Chief Justice of the Common Pleas (1606), Chief Justice of the King's Bench (1613), and Privy Councillor. He prosecuted Essex, Raleigh, and the Gunpowder conspirators, but after 1606 he vindicated national liberties against the royal prerogative. He was dismissed in 1617, and from 1620 led the popular party in parliament, and was largely responsible for the Petition of Right (1628).

Coke (of Holkham), Thomas William, Earl of Leicester (1754–1842) English agriculturalist, the 'father of experimental farms', born in London. People visited his estate from all over the world, and special meetings were held at sheep-clipping time ('Coke's Clippings'), the last of which took place over three days in 1821 and attracted 7 000 visitors. As MP for Norfolk from age 21, he held the seat for 57 years and was responsible for bringing forward the motion to recognize the independence of the American Colonies.

coke¹ — noun a brittle greyish-black porous solid consisting of the residue of carbon and ash that remains after heating bituminous coal in the absence of air. It is used as a carbon source in the smelting of metal ores, and as a smokeless fuel for domestic heating. — verb trans., intrans. to convert coal into this material. [from dialect colk, core]

coke² noun colloq. cocaine.

Col. abbrev. 1 Colonel. 2 Colorado (US state). 3 (also **Col**) Biblical Colossians.

col noun 1 Geol. in a mountain range, a pass between two adjacent peaks, or the lowest point in a ridge, often used for lines of communication, eg roads. 2 Meteorol. in a weather chart, a zone of low pressure and light winds between two anticyclones. [from French col, neck]

col. abbrev. 1 colour. 2 column.

col- see CON-.

cola or **kola** 1 noun an evergreen tree (Cola acuminata), native to Africa but cultivated in other tropical regions for its seeds (cola nuts), which are borne in pods and contain caffeine. They are exported for use in soft-drink flavourings and certain medicines. 2 a soft-drink flavoured with the extract obtained from the seeds of this tree. [from W African kolo, nut]

colander noun a perforated metal or plastic bowl in which to drain the water from cooked vegetables, etc. [from Latin colare, to strain]

Colbert, Claudette, originally **Lily Claudette Chauchoin** (1903–) US film and stage actress, born in Paris. She started in films with spirited comedy roles, and won an Oscar for It Happened One Night (1934). Ten years of romantic comedy successes followed, including Tovarich (1937) and The Palm Beach Story (1942). She had varied character parts up to the 1960s, such as in Parrish (1960), and then turned to the theatre.

Colbert, Jean Baptiste (1619–83) French statesman, born in Rheims. In 1651 he entered the service of Mazarin, and in 1661 became the chief financial minister of Louis XIV. His series of successful financial reforms doubled the revenue in 10 years, and he also reorganized the colonies, provided a strong fleet, improved the civil code, and introduced a marine code. The Academies of Inscriptions, Science, and Architecture were founded by him, and he became a patron of industry, commerce, art, science, and literature.

Colchester, Latin **Camulodunum**, Anglo-Saxon **Colneceaster** POP (1992e) 149 000, a town in Colchester district, Essex, SE England. It lies S of the R Colne, 82km/51mi NE of London. HISTORY claims to be the oldest town in England, founded by Cymbeline in c.10 AD; burnt by Boadicea in c.60 AD. NOTABLE FEATURES city walls; castle (12c); St Botolph's Priory.

cold — adj. 1 low in temperature; not hot or warm. 2 lower in temperature than is normal, comfortable, or pleasant. 3 said of food cooked, but not eaten hot: cold meat. 4 unfriendly. 5 comfortless; depressing. 6 colloq. unenthusiastic: the suggestion left me cold. 7 without warmth or emotion: a cold, calculating person. 8 sexually unresponsive. 9 said of colours producing a feeling of coldness rather than warmth. 10 colloq. unconscious, usually after a blow, fall, etc: out cold. 11 dead. 12 in trying to guess or find something, far from the answer or the hidden object. 13 said of a trail or scent not fresh; too old to follow. — adv. without preparation or rehearsal. — noun 1 lack of heat or warmth; cold weather. 2 a contagious viral infection, common in colder climates, that causes inflammation of the mucous membranes of the nose, throat, and bronchial tubes. Its symptoms are a sore throat, coughing and sneezing, a congested nose, headache, and sometimes fever, as well as a general feeling of fatigue.
— **catch cold** to become ill with a cold.
get cold feet colloq. to lose courage; to become reluctant to carry something out.
give someone the cold shoulder colloq. to respond aloofly to them; to rebuff or snub them.
in cold blood deliberately and unemotionally.
make someone's blood run cold to terrify or horrify them.
out in the cold colloq. ignored, disregarded, and neglected by others.
pour or **throw cold water on something** colloq. to be discouraging or unenthusiastic about a plan, idea, etc.
[from Anglo-Saxon cald]

cold-blooded adj. 1 said of an animal having a body temperature that varies with the temperature of the surrounding environment, eg reptiles, amphibians, fish. — Also called poikilothermic. 2 lacking emotion; callous; cruel.

cold-bloodedly adv. in a cold-blooded way.

cold-bloodedness noun being cold-blooded.

cold boot Comput. a reboot activated by completely switching off and restarting a computer from the power source.

cold calling a marketing technique in which a sales representative contacts potential customers by telephone, without advance warning.

cold chisel a chisel for cutting cold metal, stone, etc.

cold comfort no comfort at all.

Cold Comfort Farm a novel by Stella Gibbons (1933). It is a parody on the melodramatic rural novels which were popular at the time.

cold cream face cream for cleaning the skin and keeping it soft.

cold frame a glass-covered frame for protecting young plants growing outdoors.

cold front Meteorol. the edge of a mass of cold air pushing against a mass of warm air.

Cold Harbor, Battles of a battle in the American Civil War, fought in Virginia (1–3 Jun 1864), with General Grant's forces suffering heavy losses (12 000 men in one day's fighting) in an ill-advised attack on General Lee's secure Confederate position. Nevertheless, the battle did further Grant's strategy of unrelenting pressure on the South.

cold-hearted adj. unkind.

cold-heartedly adv. in a cold-hearted way.

cold-heartedness noun being cold-hearted.

coldly adv. with a cold or unfriendly manner; without warmth: replied coldly that he did not know.

coldness noun being cold.

cold-shoulder verb to give (someone) the cold shoulder.

cold sore a patch of small blister-like spots around or near the mouth, caused by a virus.

cold storage 1 the storage of food, etc under refrigeration. 2 the state of being put aside or saved till another time; postponement; abeyance.

cold sweat sweating from fear or nervousness.

cold turkey slang the acute discomfort felt by someone withdrawing from an addictive drug.

cold war a state of hostility and antagonism between nations, without actual warfare.
◇ The term is most commonly used to describe relations between the former Soviet Union and the major Western non-communist powers (in particular the USA) between 1945 and the late 1960s when the nuclear arms race intensified. The process of detente, begun in the late 1960s, led to a 'thaw' in relations between the major powers, with treaties limiting the increase in nuclear weapons. The Cold War has been generally perceived as ending with the break-up of the Soviet Union, the demolition of the Berlin Wall, and the reunification of Germany in 1990.

cole noun any of various vegetables of the cabbage type. [from Anglo-Saxon cawl, from Latin caulis]

colectomy noun Medicine the surgical removal of the colon.

Colenso, Battle of a reverse suffered (1899) by the British in the Boer War. General Sir Redvers Buller (1838–1908), fearing that his forces might be cut off in his efforts to relieve Ladysmith, changed his plans and attempted to take Colenso, an important crossing-point on the Tugela River, but he was defeated by Boer forces under Louis Botha.

Coleridge, Samuel Taylor (1772–1834) English poet, born in Ottery St Mary, Devon. He married Sara Fricker (Robert Southey's sister-in-law) in 1795 and moved to Nether Stowey in 1797, where they became close friends with William and Dorothy Wordsworth. From this connection a new poetry emerged, in reaction against neoclassical artificiality. The influential Lyrical Ballads (1798) opened with his 'Ancient Mariner'. He suffered a moral collapse due partly to his use of opium, and his relations with Wordsworth deteriorated. His unhappiness was made evident in 'Ode to Dejection' (1802). He began a weekly paper, The Friend (1809), and settled in London, writing and lecturing. In 1816 he published 'Christabel' and the fragment, 'Kubla Khan', both written in his earlier period of inspiration. He is also remembered for his critical writing (eg Biographia Literaria, 1817, and Aids to Reflection, 1825).

coleslaw noun a salad made with finely-cut raw cabbage and carrots. [from Dutch koolsla, cabbage salad]

Colet, John (c.1467–1519) English scholar and theologian, born in London. After travelling in Italy, he became a priest in England, and worked with Thomas More and Erasmus while lecturing at Oxford. In 1505 he became Dean of St Paul's, where he continued to deliver controversial lectures on the interpretation of Scripture, and he founded St Paul's School (1509–12).

Colette, (Sidonie Gabrielle) (1873–1954) French novelist, born in Saint-Sauveur-en-Puisaye. Her early books were written in collaboration with her first husband, Henri Gauthier-Villars (pen name Willy). Her novels, for which she won many awards, are characterized by a preoccupation with sensual experiences. They include the Claudine series (1900–3), Chéri (1920), and Gigi (1945).

Colette a female first name. [a French feminine diminutive of Col, Colle (see COLIN)]

coleus noun a perennial plant (Coleus blumei), native to Java. It has square stems, oval toothed leaves borne in opposite pairs, and slender spikes of small pale blue or white flowers. It is widely grown as a house plant for its ornamental foliage, which is variegated in a range of colours, including deep crimson, scarlet, pink, and yellow. [from Greek *koleos*, sheath]

coley *noun* (PL. **coleys**) a large edible fish of the cod family, found in the N Atlantic, with white or grey flesh.

colic *noun Medicine* severe abdominal pain that usually occurs in short waves minutes or seconds apart. It is common in babies, and is due to wind in the intestines caused by swallowing air or overfeeding. In adults it is usually caused by constipation, or partial or complete obstruction of the intestine. [from Greek *kolon*, colon SEE COLON²]

colicky *adj.* suffering from colic.

Coligny, Gaspard II de, Seigneur de (Lord of) Châtillon (1519–72) French Huguenot leader, born in Châtillon-sur-Loing. He fought in the wars of Francis I and Henry II, and in 1552 was made Admiral of France. In 1557 he became a Protestant, and commanded the Huguenots during the second and third Wars of Religion. He was one of the first victims in the St Bartholomew's Day massacre in Paris (1572).

Colin a male first name. [originally short for NICHOLAS; now an independent name]

coliseum *noun Hist.* a large stadium or amphitheatre for sports and other entertainment. [a Latin variant of *Colosseum*, the largest Roman amphitheatre]

colitis *noun Medicine* inflammation of the lining of the large intestine. [from COLON² + -ITIS]

Coll a flat, rocky island in Strathclyde region, W Scotland. It lies 30km/19mi NW of Tobermory, Mull. It measures 20km/12mi in length and rises to 103m at Ben Hogh; its chief village is Arinagour. The island is associated with the history of the Clan Maclean.

collaborate *verb intrans.* **1** to work together with another or others on something. **2** *derog.* to co-operate with or help (an enemy occupying one's country). [from Latin *com-*, together + *laborare*, to work]

collaboration *noun* the act of collaborating.

collaborationism *noun* a policy of collaboration.

collaborationist *noun derog.* a supporter of collaboration.

collaborative *adj.* collaborating; involving or given to collaborating.

collaboratively *adv.* in a collaborative way.

collaborator *noun* a person who collaborates.

collage *noun* **1** a design or picture made up of pieces of paper or cloth, or parts of photographs, etc fixed to a background surface. **2** the art of producing such works. [from French *collage*, pasting, gluing]
◇ Collage was invented c.1912 by Picasso and Braque. It was widely used by other Cubists and the Surrealists, and was an innovation that had a major effect on the subsequent course of 20c art.

collagen *noun Biol.* a tough fibrous protein that is the main constituent of connective tissue found in skin, bones, teeth, cartilage, ligaments, etc. [from Greek *kolla*, glue + -GEN]

collapse — *verb usually intrans.* **1** to fall, give way, or cave in. **2** to drop unconscious; to faint; to drop exhausted or helpless. **3** to break down emotionally. **4** to fail suddenly: *several firms collapsed*. **5** *intrans., trans.* to fold up compactly for storage or space-saving. **6** *intrans., trans. said of the lungs or blood vessels, etc* to become or cause to become flattened. **7** *Stock Exchange* to suffer a sudden steep drop in value. — *noun* the process of collapsing. [from Latin *collabi*, to slide, fall]

collapsibility *noun* the quality of being collapsible.

collapsible *adj.* capable of collapsing or being collapsed.

collar — *noun* **1** a band or flap of any of various shapes, folded over or standing up round the neck of a garment; the neck of a garment generally. **2** something worn round the neck. **3** a band of leather, etc worn round the neck by a dog, etc. **4** a padded leather object, shaped to fit round a horse's neck, to ease the strain of pulling a vehicle. **5** a distinctively coloured ring of fur or feathers round an animal's or bird's neck. **6** a cut of meat from the neck of an animal. **7** a ring-shaped fitting for joining two pipes, etc together. **8** any collar-like part. — *verb* (**collared, collaring**) **1** to seize by the collar. **2** *colloq.* to catch or capture. **3** *colloq.* to grab for oneself.
— **hot under the collar** *colloq.* angry or flustered.
[from Old French *colier*, from Latin *collum*, neck]

collarbone *noun* either of two bones, the clavicles, linking the shoulder-blades with the top of the breastbone.

collarless *adj.* lacking a collar.

collate *verb* **1** to examine and compare (texts, evidence, etc). **2** to check and arrange in order (sheets of paper, pages of a book, etc) ready for fastening together. [from Latin *collatus*, past participle of *conferre*, to put together, compare]

collateral — *adj.* **1** descended from a common ancestor, but through a different branch of the family. **2** additional; secondary in importance; subsidiary. — *noun* (also **collateral security**) assets offered to a creditor as security for a loan. [from Latin *collateralis*, from Latin *com-*, with + *latus*, side]

collaterally *adv.* **1** side by side. **2** additionally. **3** with descent from a different family branch.

Collatinus *or* **Collatine** the husband of Lucretia in Shakespeare's *The Rape of Lucrece*.

collation *noun* **1** the act of collating. **2** a light meal.

collator *noun* a person or device which collates.

colleague *noun* a fellow-worker, especially in a profession. [from Latin *collega*, partner, colleague]

collect — *verb* (with stress on -*lect*) **1** *trans., intrans.* to bring or come together; to gather; to accumulate. **2** to build up an assortment of (things of a particular type) out of enthusiasm for them: *collect stamps.* **3** to call for; to fetch; to pick up. **4** *trans., intrans.* to get (eg money owed or voluntary contributions) from people: *offered to collect for Oxfam.* **5** to calm or control (oneself); to get (one's thoughts, etc) under control. — *adj.* (with stress on -*lect*) *North Amer., esp. US, said of a telephone call* paid for by the person receiving it. — *adv.* (with stress on -*lect*) *North Amer., esp. US* reversing the charges. — *noun* (with stress on *coll*-) *Christianity* a short form of prayer used in the Anglican and Roman Catholic Churches. [from Latin *colligere*, to gather]

collectable *adj.* **1** capable of being collected. **2** desirable.

collected *adj.* **1** *said of a writer's works* all published together in a single volume or a uniform set of volumes. **2** cool; calm; self-possessed.

collectedly *adv.* in a collected way.

collectedness *noun* self-possession; coolness.

collection *noun* **1** the act of collecting. **2** an accumulated assortment of things of a particular type. **3** an amount of money collected. **4** the removal of mail from a postbox at scheduled times.

collective *adj.* of, belonging to, or involving all the members of a group.

collective bargaining talks between a trade union and a company's management to settle questions of pay and working conditions.

collective farm *Agric.* a large state-owned farm run on co-operative principles, and formed by the merging of several smaller farms that were previously owned by individuals. Collective farming originated in the former Soviet Union, and is also practised in China and Israel.

collectively *adv.* in a collective way; as a whole, together.

collective *noun* a noun standing for a group of people, animals, etc, usually taking a singular verb, eg *swarm/herd/gang/committee*.

collective security *Politics* the concept of maintaining security and territorial integrity by the collective actions of nation states, especially through international organizations such as NATO, the League of Nations, and the United Nations (where the principle is embodied in its Charter). Individual member states must be prepared to accept collective decisions and implement them, if necessary, through military action.

collectivism *noun* **1** the economic theory that industry should be carried on with a collective capital. **2** a system embodying this.

collectivization *or* **collectivisation** *noun* organization according to collectivism.

collectivize *or* **collectivise** *verb* to group (farms, factories, etc) into larger units and bring under state control and ownership.

collector *noun* (often in compounds) a person who collects, as a job or hobby: *stamp-collector.*

collector's item something that is a good specimen of its type and would interest a collector.

Colleen a female first name. [from COLLEEN]

colleen *noun Irish* a girl. [from Irish *cailín*, girl]

college *noun* **1** an institution, either self-contained or part of a university, providing higher education, further education, or professional training. **2** one of a number of self-governing establishments that make up certain universities. **3** the staff and students of a college. **4** (*often* **College**) a name used by some larger secondary schools. **5** a body of people with particular duties and rights: *College of Cardinals.* **6** an official body of members of a profession, concerned with maintaining standards, etc. [from Latin *collegium*, group of associates, fellowship]

College of Arms in England, the organization that authorizes the use of heraldry (the granting and designing of pictorial devices or arms originally used on the shields of knights in armour to identify them in battle), and the official archive of the pedigrees and arms of English, Northern Irish, and Commonwealth families.

college of education *Brit.* a college specializing in the initial and in-service training of teachers, usually offering BA as well as BEd degrees. Since the 1970s, many colleges of education have merged with polytechnics and universities, as the numbers of pupils in British schools fell, and the demand for teachers decreased accordingly.

collegiate *adj.* **1** of, relating to, or belonging to a college. **2** having the form of a college. **3** *said of a university* consisting of individual colleges. [from Latin *collegiatus*, from *collegium*, fellowship]

collegiate church **1** in Scotland, a church served by two clergymen of equal rank. **2** a church having a chapter of canons attached to it.

collide *verb intrans.* **1** to crash together, or crash into someone or something. **2** *said of people* to disagree or clash. [from Latin *collidere*, from *com-*, with + *laedere*, to strike]

collie *noun* a usually long-haired black- or tan-and-white dog used for herding sheep, etc. [perhaps from Scot. *colle*, coal, the breed having once been black]

collier *noun* **1** a coal-miner. **2** a ship that transport's coal. [from Middle English *coliere*, from Anglo-Saxon *col*, coal]

colliery *noun* (PL. **collieries**) a coalmine with its buildings.

collimator *noun* **1** a device for obtaining a beam of parallel rays of light or other radiation, or one for obtaining a beam of particles moving in parallel paths. **2** a small telescope fixed to a large one, to assist in preliminary alignment. [from Latin *collineare*, to bring into line with]

collinear *adj. Maths.* lying on the same straight line.

Collingwood, Cuthbert Collingwood, Baron (1750–1810) English admiral, born in Newcastle upon Tyne. He joined the navy at 11, and from 1778 his career was closely connected with that of Nelson. He fought at Brest (1794), Cape St Vincent (1797), and at Trafalgar (1805), where he succeeded Nelson as commander.

Collins, Michael (1890–1922) Irish politician and Sinn Féin leader, born near Clonakilty, Co Cork. He became an MP in 1918, directed the guerilla campaign during the Anglo-Irish War (1919–21), and with Arthur Griffith was largely responsible for the negotiation of the treaty with Great Britain in 1921. He was killed in an ambush between Bandon and Macroom.

Collins, Phil(ip) (1951–) English singer, drummer and songwriter, born in Hounslow, West London. He began with the band Flaming Youth, joined Genesis as drummer in 1970, and took over as lead vocalist when Peter Gabriel left the group (1985). Under his leadership the band gained international success, which was maintained with *We Can't Dance* (1991), but as a solo artist his success was greater, with the albums *Face Value* (1981), *No Jacket Required* (1985), and *But Seriously . . .* (1989). He has also acted on film and television.

Collins, (William) Wilkie (1824–89) English novelist, born in London. He spent four years in business and was then called to the Bar but turned instead to literature, specializing in the genre of suspense and mystery. His best-known novels are *The Woman in White* (1860) and *The Moonstone* (1868).

Collins, William the foolish, bumptious clergyman in Jane Austen's *Pride and Prejudice*.

collision *noun* **1** the violent meeting of objects; a crash. **2** a disagreement or conflict. [from Latin *collisio*]

collision course a direction taken, or course of action begun, that is bound to result in collision with something or someone.

collocate *verb intrans. Grammar, said of a word* to occur frequently alongside another word, often as part of the construction that relates to its context: *'different' collocates with 'from' and 'to', and sometimes with 'than'.* [from Latin *collocare*, to place together]

collocation *noun* **1** grouping together in a certain order. **2** *Grammar* the occurring of certain words together; grammatical interdependence: *the frequent collocation of 'different' and 'to'.*

colloid *noun Chem.* a state that is intermediate between a suspension and a true solution, in which fine particles of one substance are spread evenly throughout another substance. *Aerosols* are colloids in which a liquid or a solid is dispersed in a gas, eg smoke, fog. *Emulsions* are colloids in which a liquid is dispersed in a liquid, eg milk. Emulsion paint is a *sol* (a solid dispersed in a liquid). [from Greek *kolla*, glue]

colloquial *adj., said of language or vocabulary* informal; used in conversation rather than in formal speech or writing. [from Latin *colloquium*, conversation]

colloquialism *noun* a colloquial expression.

colloquially *adv.* in a colloquial or informal way.

colloquium *noun* (PL. **colloquia**) an academic conference; a seminar. [from Latin *colloquium*, conversation]

colloquy *noun* (PL. **colloquies**) a conversation; talk. [from Latin *colloquium*, conversation]

collusion *noun* secret and illegal co-operation for the purpose of fraud or other criminal activity, etc. [from Latin *collusio*]

collusive *adj.* **1** involving collusion. **2** conspiratorial.

collywobbles *pl. noun colloq.* **1** pain or discomfort in the abdomen. **2** nervousness; apprehensiveness. [probably from COLIC + WOBBLE]

Colman, George, known as **the Elder** (1732–94) British dramatist and theatre manager, born in Florence, Italy. A lawyer by profession, he began his theatrical career by taking part in the management of Drury Lane (1764), where his *Polly Honeycombe* had been successfully produced (1760). His best-known play, *The Clandestine Marriage* (1766), was written in collaboration with David Garrick. In 1767 he purchased a share in Covent Garden Theatre, and in 1776 bought the Haymarket Theatre.

Colo. *abbrev.* Colorado.

Cologne, German **Köln** POP (1990e) 950 000, a manufacturing and commercial river-port in North Rhine-Westphalia state in W central Germany. It lies on the W bank of the R Rhine and is a major traffic junction and commercial centre, noted for its trade fairs. HISTORY capital of the N Roman Empire in the 3c; an influential centre during the Middle Ages; badly bombed in World War II. NOTABLE FEATURE cathedral (begun in 1248).

Cologne cathedral

cologne *noun* eau-de-Cologne. [from Cologne, the place of manufacture]

Colombia, official name **Republic of Colombia**, Spanish **República de Colombia** POP (1992e) 33.4m, a republic in the NW of S America. AREA 1 140 105sq km/440 080sq mi. It is bounded N by Panama and the Caribbean Sea, W by the Pacific Ocean, E by Venezuela, SE by Brazil, and S by Ecuador and Peru. CAPITAL Bogotá. chief towns Medellín, Cali, Barranquilla. TIME ZONE GMT –5. The majority of the people live in temperate Andean valleys (90%). The population includes many people of mixed Spanish and S American Indian descent; Roman Catholicism is the main religion. OFFICIAL LANGUAGE Spanish. CURRENCY the peso. PHYSICAL DESCRIPTION Caribbean and Pacific coastlines, with several island possessions; on the mainland, the Andes run N–S, branching into three ranges dividing narrow, coastal plains from the forested lowlands of the Amazon basin; the Cordillera Central, separated from the Cordillera Occidental in the W by the R Cauca, rises up to 5 750m at Huila, the highest peak; the Cordillera Oriental in the E surrounds large areas of plateau;

Colombia

rivers flow to the Pacific Ocean, Caribbean Sea, and Amazon. CLIMATE hot and humid coastal plains in the NW and W, annual rainfall is over 2 500mm; drier period on the Caribbean coast (Dec–Apr); the annual rainfall of the Andes is 1 000–2 500mm, falling evenly throughout the year; hot and humid tropical lowlands in the E, with annual rainfall of 2 000–2 500mm. HISTORY Spanish occupation from the early 16c, displacing Amerindian peoples; governed by Spain within the Vice-royalty of Peru, later the Vice-royalty of New Granada; gained independence in 1819, after the campaigns of Simón Bolívar and formed a union with Ecuador, Venezuela, and Panama as Gran Colombia; the union ended with the secession of Venezuela in 1829, Ecuador in 1830, and Panama in 1903; Civil War in the 1950s; considerable political unrest in the 1980s continued into the 1990s, when a State of Emergency was declared in 1992. GOVERNMENT a new constitution in 1991; governed by a bicameral Congress (a 100-member Senate and a Chamber of Representatives with 160 members elected for four years); a President, elected for a four-year term, appoints a Cabinet and is advised by a Council of State. ECONOMY virtually self-sufficient in food; major crops include coffee, bananas, cotton, sugar, maize, rice, beans, wheat, potatoes, cut flowers; textiles, leather, chemicals, consumer goods; gold, silver, platinum, emeralds, nickel, coal, oil, natural gas; development of the interior is hampered by a lack of good communications. There is widespread illegal cocaine trafficking, which the government has been attempting to eradicate with help from the USA since mid-1989.

Colombo, originally **Kalan-Totta** POP (1990e) 615 000, the seaport capital of Sri Lanka, on the W coast, S of the R Kelani. The city's outer suburb of Sri-Jayawardenapura has been the administrative capital since 1983. HISTORY settled by the Portuguese in 1517 and by the Dutch in 1656; under British control in 1796; British defence base from 1942 until 1945; location of the 1950 Commonwealth Conference which established the Colombo Plan. NOTABLE FEATURES National Museum; Independence Hall; Hindu shrines; Moorish mosques; large artificial harbour.

Colombo Plan, in full the **Colombo Plan for Cooperative Economic and Social Development in Asia and the Pacific** a plan drawn up in 1951 and renamed in 1977. The founding countries were the UK, India, Pakistan, Australia, and New Zealand, which were later joined by the USA, Japan, and some other Pacific and S and SE Asian countries.

Colón, formerly **Aspinwall** **1** POP (1990) 141 000, the second largest city in Panama and the port capital of Colón province in the N of the country. It is situated at the Caribbean end of the Panama Canal. Founded in 1850, it was originally named after William Aspinwall, the railway builder, and renamed in honour of Christopher Columbus. **2** a province in N Panama.

colon¹ *noun* a punctuation mark (:), properly used to introduce a list, an example, or an explanation. [from Greek *colon*, clause]

colon² *noun* in vertebrates, the large intestine except for the rectum. Its main function is to reabsorb water from the indigestible remains of food, which are converted to solid faeces. [from Greek *kolon*, large intestine]

colonel *noun* a senior army officer, in charge of a regiment, below a brigadier in rank. [from Italian *colonello*, leader of a column]

Colonel Blimp see BLIMP, COLONEL.

colonelcy *noun* (PL. **colonelcies**) the rank or office of colonel.

colonel-in-chief *noun* in the British army, an honorary rank and title often held by a member of the Royal family.

colonial — *adj.* **1** relating to, belonging to, or living in a colony or colonies. **2** possessing colonies: *colonial powers.* — *noun* an inhabitant of a colony. [from COLONY]

Colonial and Imperial Conferences a series of conferences held in 1887, 1894, 1897, 1902 and 1907, usually in London, at which representatives of the British colonies and dominions discussed matters of common imperial concern, especially defence, trade, and communications. The first Imperial Conference (the change of name implied a new status for the colonies) was held in 1911, and was followed by others in 1921, 1923, 1926, 1930, and 1937, concerned mainly with constitutional changes and economic matters. After World War II they were replaced by the Conferences of Commonwealth Prime Ministers.

colonialism *noun often derog.* the policy of acquiring colonies, especially as a source of profit.

colonialist *noun* a supporter of colonialism.

colonially *adv.* as regards colonies or colonialism.

colonic *adj.* relating to or in the region of the colon (see COLON²).

colonization *or* **colonisation** *noun* **1** the act of colonizing or the process of being colonized. **2** setting up a colony or colonies.

colonize *or* **colonise** *verb* **1** to establish a colony in (an area or country). **2** to settle (people) in a colony.

colonnade *noun* a row of columns, usually supporting a roof. [from French *colonnade*, from Latin *columna*, column]

colonnaded *adj.* having a colonnade.

Colonsay *or* **St Columba's Isle** an island in Strathclyde region, W Scotland. It lies N of Islay and W of Jura, and is separated from Oronsay by a low channel which is dry at low water. The island rises to 134m at Carn Mor. NOTABLE FEATURES the islet of Eilean nan Ron (SW) is a nature reserve with a breeding colony of grey seals; Augustinian Priory.

colony *noun* (PL. **colonies**) **1** a settlement abroad founded and controlled by the founding country; the settlers living there; the territory they occupy. **2** a group of the same nationality or occupation forming a distinctive community within a city, etc. **3** a group of animals or plants of the same species living together in close proximity, sometimes with physical connections between individual members, eg sponges, corals, or a large number of animals living together in a highly organized social group, eg bees, ants, termites. **4** an isolated group of bacteria or fungi growing on a solid medium, and forming a visible mass. [from Latin *colonia*, farm, colony]

colophon *noun* **1** an inscription at the end of a printed book or manuscript giving the name of

the writer, printer, etc and place and date of production. **2** a publisher's ornamental mark or device. [from Greek *colophon*, summit, finishing touch]

Colorado POP (1990) 3.5m, a state in W central USA, divided into 63 counties. It is known as the 'Centennial State'. AREA 269 585sq km/104 060sq mi. PHYSICAL DESCRIPTION its rivers include the Colorado, Arkansas, Grande, and South Platte; the Rocky Mts run N–S through the centre, divided into several ranges (Front Range, Sangre de Cristo Mts, Park Range, Sawatch Mts, and San Juan Mts); over 50 peaks rise above 4 000m; the highest point is Mt Elbert (4 399m); E Colorado, part of the High Plains, is the centre of cattle and sheep ranching in the state; the Colorado Plateau in the W has many canyons cut by the Colorado and Gunnison rivers; there are several notable national parks and monuments (Rocky Mountain National Park, Dinosaur National Monument, and Great Sand Dunes National Monument); the Ute Native American reservation lies in the SW. HISTORY the E part was included in the 1803 Louisiana Purchase; the W part was gained from Mexico by the Treaty of Guadalupe Hidalgo in 1848; the settlement expanded after the gold strike of 1858; became a territory in 1861; joined the Union as the 38th state in 1876. CAPITAL Denver. CHIEF TOWNS Colorado Springs, Aurora, Lakewood, Pueblo. ECONOMY wheat, hay, corn, sugar-beet; livestock; major industries include food processing, printing and publishing, and the manufacture of electrical and transportation equipment, fabricated metals, chemicals, and lumber, stone, clay, and glass products; mineral reserves include oil, coal, and uranium; Colorado has the world's largest deposits of molybdenum; there is a flourishing tourist industry especially catering for fishing, hunting, and skiing.

Colorado beetle a small beetle that has a yellow back with 10 longitudinal black stripes on its wing cases. The females lay eggs on potato plants, and the larvae are reddish-yellow with black side spots. The Colorado beetle is a serious pest of potato crops.

Colorado Desert a depressed arid region in SE California, USA and N Baja California, Mexico. AREA c.5 000–8 000sq km/2 000–3 000sq mi. Part of the Great Basin, it contains the Salton Sea, a shallow saline lake lying 71m below sea level.

Colorado River a river in SW USA, length c.2 350km/1 460mi. Rising in the Continental Divide, N Colorado, it flows through Utah and Arizona (via Marble Canyon and the Grand Canyon) and forms part of the Nevada–Arizona, California–Arizona, and Arizona–Mexico borders. It empties into the Gulf of California. Major tributaries are the Gunnison, Green, San Juan, Little Colorado, Gila, and Virgin rivers. It is used extensively for irrigation, flood-control, and for hydroelectric power (via the Hoover, Davis, Parker, and Imperial dams).

Colorado Springs POP (1990) 397 000, the seat of El Paso County, central Colorado, USA. It

lies at the foot of Pikes Peak, 102km/63mi S of Denver. Mineral springs nearby make it a popular health resort. It was established in 1872 and achieved city status in 1886. NOTABLE FEATURE US Air Force Academy.

colorant *noun* a substance used for colouring. [from Latin *color*, colour]

coloration *noun* arrangement or combination of colours; colouring. [from Latin *colorare*, to colour]

coloratura *noun* **1** an elaborate and intricate passage or style in singing. **2** a soprano specializing in such singing. [from Italian *coloratura*, colouring]

colorimeter *noun Chem.* an instrument for measuring the colour intensity of a solution, in order to determine the concentration of the coloured constituent. This is done by comparing the result with the colour intensities of standard solutions of known concentrations of the constituent.

colossal *adj.* **1** huge; vast. **2** *colloq.* splendid; marvellous. [from COLOSSUS]

colossally *adv.* immensely, hugely.

Colosseum an amphitheatre in Rome, Italy, begun by the emperor Vespasian in c.70 AD, dedicated by his son Titus in AD 80, and completed by Domitian in AD 82. It could seat 50 000 spectators who watched gladiators battle, fights between men and wild animals (including the sacrifice of Christians to lions), and feigned sea battles, for which the amphitheatre could be flooded.

Colossians, Letter of Paul to the a New Testament writing attributed to Paul while he was in prison, although his authorship is disputed. It was apparently written to counter the false teaching in Colossae by some people who claimed a higher spiritual knowledge associated with an ascetic and ritualistic way of life and with the worship of angels (Colossians 2.8–23).

colossus *noun* (PL. **colossi**, **colossuses**) **1** a gigantic statue. **2** an overwhelmingly powerful person or organization. [from Greek *kolossos*]

Colossus of Rhodes a colossal bronze statue (thought to be c.31m high) of the sun-god Helios, which stood at the entrance to the harbour of Rhodes. It was built in c.280 BC, and was one of the seven wonders of the ancient world. It collapsed in an earthquake in 224 BC.

colostomy *noun* (PL. **colostomies**) *Surgery* an operation to construct an opening in the colon through which it can be emptied, when emptying through the anus is not possible. [from COLON² + Greek *stoma*, mouth]

colostrum *noun Zool.* in mammals, the yellowish milky fluid secreted by the mammary glands immediately before and after giving birth. It contains more white blood cells and antibodies, and less fat and carbohydrate, than the true milk which is secreted later. [from Latin *colostrum*]

colour — *noun* **1** the visual sensation produced in the brain as a result of nerve impulses relayed from the cones of the retina when they absorb

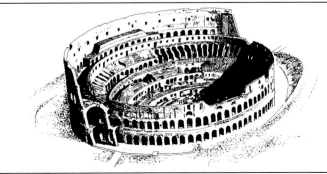

Colosseum

light energy of a particular wavelength. Thus the colour of an object depends on the wavelength of the light it reflects. **2** any of these variations or colours, often with the addition of black and white. **3** *Photog., Art* the use of some or all colours, as distinct from black and white only: *in full colour*. **4** a colouring substance, especially paint. **5** the shade of a person's skin, as related to race; the darker skin shades. **6** pinkness of the face or cheeeks. **7** lively or convincing detail: *add local colour to the story*. **8** richness of quality in music, or its mood and quality generally. See also COLOURS. — *verb* **1** to put colour on; to paint or dye. **2** (*also* **colour something in**) to fill in an outlined area or a black and white picture with colour. **3** to influence: *feelings can colour one's judgement*. **4** *intrans.* to blush. — **off colour** *colloq.* unwell. [from Old French *color*]

colour bar *noun* discrimination against coloured people.

colour-blindness *noun* any of various conditions characterized by an inability to distinguish between certain colours, due to a congenital defect (present from birth) in the light-sensitive cone cells of the retina that are responsible for colour perception. The commonest type is inability to distinguish between reds and greens.

colour-coded *adj.* marked by a system of colours for the purposes of identification or classification.

colour coding *noun* the systematic use of colour as a means of identification or classification, as in electrical wiring.

coloured — *adj.* **1** (**also in compounds**) having colour, or a specified colour: *lemon-coloured*. **2** belonging to a dark-skinned race; non-white. **3** (**Coloured**) *South Afr.* of mixed white and non-white descent. — *noun* **1** a person of dark-skinned race. **2** (**Coloured**) *South Afr.* a person of mixed white and non-white descent.

colour-fast *adj., said of fabrics* dyed with colours that will not run when washed.

colour filter *Photog.* a transparent material which transmits light for only a selected portion of the visible spectrum, partially or completely absorbing the remainder. In colour photography, filters may be used to provide light of a required spectral composition, or to give an overall colour balance to a photograph. In black-and-white photography, their use can alter the tonal values of coloured subjects, eg the depth of a blue sky may be emphasized.

colourful *adj.* **1** full of especially bright colour. **2** lively; vivid; full of interest or character.

colourfully *adv.* in a colourful way.

colouring *noun* **1** a substance used to give colour, eg to food. **2** the applying of colour. **3** arrangement or combination of colour. **4** facial complexion, or this in combination with eye and hair colour.

colourist *noun* someone skilled in the use of colour; an artist.

colourization *or* **colourisation** *noun Cinema* the process of adding colour to a motion picture previously shot in black-and-white. It is now normally carried out by electronic means on a videotape transfer intended for television broadcasting.

colourize *or* **colourise** *verb trans.* to add colour to (a cinema film made in black and white) with the aid of a computer.

colourless *adj.* **1** without, or lacking, colour. **2** uninteresting; dull; lifeless. **3** pale.

colourlessly *adv.* in a colourless way.

colours *pl. noun* **1** the flag of a nation, regiment, or ship. **2** the coloured uniform or other distinguishing badge awarded to team-members in certain games. **3** a badge of ribbons in colours representing a particular party, etc, worn to show support for it. **4** the coloured dress of a jockey and horse, identifying the horse's owner.

— **in one's true colours** as one really is.
nail one's colours to the mast to announce openly one's support for something or someone.
with flying colours with great success.

colour scheme *noun* a choice or combination of colours in house decoration, etc.

colour sergeant *noun* a sergeant who carries the company's colours.

colour supplement *noun* an illustrated magazine accompanying a newspaper.

colour television a television system in which separate signals corresponding to the three primary colours of light (red, blue, and green) are used to form a full-colour image on the screen of a specially designed television receiver.

colour therapy a form of therapy that involves the selection and use of appropriate colours that are said to promote healing and well-being.

colourway *noun* a combination of colours in patterned material, etc.

Colt *noun* trademark a type of small pistol. [named after Samuel Colt, the inventor]

colt *noun* **1** a young male horse. **2** an inexperienced young team-player or member of a junior team. [from Anglo-Saxon]

coltish *adj.* youthfully awkward in movement or behaviour.

coltishly *adv.* in a coltish or awkward way.

Coltrane, John (William) (1926–67) US tenor and soprano saxophonist, composer, and bandleader, born in Hamlet, North Carolina. He developed his unique style after joining Miles Davis's band (1955) and although his impassioned aggressive tenor solos led to disputes among critics, younger saxophonists emulated him. He formed his own quartet in 1960, and attained a creative peak in such recordings as 'Giant Steps' (1960), 'Africa/Brass' (1961), 'Impressions' (1961), 'Live at Birdland' (1963), and 'A Love Supreme' (1964).

coltsfoot *noun* a wild plant with bright yellow flowers.

colugo *noun* a nocturnal mammal, native to SE Asia, that has a lemur-like face, and a large membrane along each side of the body, extending to the tips of the fingers, toes, and long tail. It lives in trees, and glides through the air by extending the membrane. It feeds on plant material. — Also called *flying lemur*. [probably from a Malaysian word]

Columba, St, also called **Colmcille**, or **Colm** (521–97) Irish missionary in Scotland, born in Gartan, Donegal. He was the founder of many monasteries in Ireland (eg in 546 at Derry, and later at Durrow), and then on the Hebridean island of Iona, where he founded a monastery that later became the mother Church of Celtic Christianity in Scotland. He is said to have transcribed 300 books with his own hand.

Columba *Astron.* the Dove, a small constellation in the southern hemisphere, lying near Canis Major.

Columbia POP (1990) 453 000, the capital of the state of South Carolina, USA, situated in Richland County, central South Carolina. It lies at the confluence of the Broad and Saluda rivers, which join to form the Congaree R. HISTORY settled in the early 1700s; became state capital in 1786; achieved city status in 1854; burned by General Sherman in 1865.

Columbia Broadcasting System, properly **CBS Inc** a major US broadcasting company, based in New York City. It was founded (1927) as United Independent Broadcasts, Inc, and was called Columbia Broadcasting System, Inc from 1928 to 1974, when it assumed its present name. It grew from being a small radio station to

become the controller of the CBS national television and radio networks.

Columbia River a river in SW Canada and NW USA, length 1 953km/1 214mi. The river rises in the Rocky Mts in E British Columbia, flows into Washington state, USA, and enters the Pacific at Cape Disappointment, SW of Tacoma, Oregon. It has many rapids and falls and has cut a major gorge through the Cascade Range. The river is a source of irrigation and hydroelectric power.

Columbia University in the USA, a university in New York City, founded in 1754 as King's College. It was closed during the American Revolution, and was renamed Columbia College when it reopened in 1784; it was given its current name in 1896. The affiliated college for women is called Barnard College (founded in 1889).

columbine *noun* a wild flower related to the buttercup, with spurred petals that look like a group of pigeons. [from Latin *columba*, dove, pigeon]

columbium *noun Chem.* former name for niobium.

Columbus, Christopher, Italian **Cristoforo Colombo**, Spanish **Cristóbal Coln** (1451–1506) Genoese discoverer of the New World, born in Genoa. He went to sea at 14, and after being shipwrecked off Portugal, settled there in about 1470. Supported by Ferdinand and Isabella of Spain, he set sail in the *Santa Maria* with the aim of reaching India by sailing W from Saltes (3 Aug 1492). He reached the Bahamas (12 Oct), and then visited Cuba and Hispaniola (Haiti), where he left a small colony. He returned (15 Mar 1493) to be received with the highest honours by the court. On his second voyage (1493–6) he discovered several of the Caribbean islands, and on his third (1498–1500) he discovered the S American mainland, but after a revolt against his command, was sent home in irons by a newly appointed royal governor. Restored to favour in Spain, he went on his last great voyage (1502–4) along the south side of the Gulf of Mexico.

Columbus POP (1990) 1.4m, the capital of the state of Ohio, USA. It lies at the confluence of the Olentangy and Scioto rivers, in Franklin County, central Ohio. HISTORY laid out opposite the earlier settlement of Franklinton in 1812; became state capital in 1824; achieved city status in 1834. NOTABLE FEATURES Centre of Science and Industry; Ohio Historical Centre; Ohio Railway Museum; Ballet Metropolitan.

Columbus Day a national holiday in the USA, held in most states on the second Monday in October in commemoration of Christopher Columbus's discovery of America in 1492; also celebrated in several countries of Central and S America.

column *noun* **1** *Archit.* a usually cylindrical pillar with a base and capital. **2** something similarly shaped; a long, more or less cylindrical mass. **3** a vertical row of numbers. **4** a vertical strip of print on a newspaper page, etc. **5** a regular section in a newspaper concerned with a particular topic, or by a regular writer. **6** a troop of soldiers or of vehicles standing or moving a few abreast. [from Latin *columna*, pillar]

columnar *adj.* **1** relating to columns. **2** like a column. **3** arranged or formed in columns.

columnist *noun* a person writing a regular section of a newspaper.

Colwyn Bay, Welsh **Bae Colwyn** POP (1981) 28 000, a seaside resort town in Colwyn district, Clwyd, N Wales. NOTABLE FEATURES Eirias Park; Welsh Mountain Zoo; Pier Pavilion.

com- see CON-.

coma *noun* a prolonged state of deep unconsciousness from which a person cannot be awakened. It is usually caused by brain damage or infection, brain tumour, severe hypoglycaemia (low blood-sugar levels) due to diabetes, or poisoning, eg by alcohol. In deep coma there may be no response to painful or reflex stimuli. [from Greek *koma*, deep sleep]

Coma Berenices *Astron.* Berenice's Hair, a small faint constellation of the northern hemisphere, noted for the large number of galaxies it contains, including the Coma Cluster, a huge cluster of faint galaxies.

Comanche a Shoshonean-speaking Native American Plains group who migrated S from Wyoming. One of the first groups to acquire horses from the Spanish, they hunted buffalo, raided and displaced others (eg the Apache), and attacked white settlers. The S Comanche were settled on reservations in the mid-19c, and the N Comanche finally agreed to settle on a reservation in Oklahoma in 1867 (present-day population c.4 250).

Comaneci, Nadia (1961–   ) Romanian gymnast, born in Onesti, Moldavia. In the 1976 Olympic Games, at the age of 14, she won gold medals in the parallel bars and beam disciplines, and bronze in the floor, becoming the first gymnast to obtain a perfect score of 10.00 for her performance on the bars and beam. She also won a gold medal in the beam at the 1978 World Championships. She won both the beam and floor exercise gold medals in the 1980 Olympics. Later she became an international judge, and coach to the Romanian national team. In 1989 she defected to the USA via Hungary.

comatose *adj.* **1** in a coma. **2** *facetious* sleepy; asleep. [from Greek *koma*, deep sleep]

comb — *noun* **1** a rigid toothed device for tidying and arranging the hair, sometimes worn in the hair to keep it in place. **2** a toothed tool for disentangling and cleaning strands of wool or cotton. **3** an act of combing. **4** a honeycomb. **5** the fleshy crest on the head of the male chicken or other cock bird. — *verb* **1** to arrange, smooth or clean with a comb. **2** to search (a place) thoroughly.
— **comb something out 1** to remove (dirt, etc) by combing. **2** to find and get rid of (unwanted elements).
[from Anglo-Saxon *camb*]

combat — *noun* fighting; a struggle or contest: *single combat.* — *verb* (**combated, combating**) to fight against; to oppose. [from French *combat*]

combatant — *adj.* involved in a fight. — *noun* a combatant person.

combative *adj.* inclined to fight or argue.

combination *noun* **1** the process of combining or state of being combined. **2** two or more things, people, etc combined; the resulting mixture or union. **3** a set of numbers or letters for opening a combination lock. **4** a motorcycle with sidecar. **5** *Maths.* a set of numbers or objects selected from a given set of numbers or objects, regardless of their order. **6** (**combinations**) an old-fashioned one-piece undergarment combining long-sleeved vest and long underpants.

Combination Acts British legislation passed in 1799 and 1800 to prohibit the coming together ('combination') of workers in trade unions. The Acts were part of the anti-reformist legislation passed by the Pitt government during the French wars. When they were repealed in 1824–5, trade unions were legalized, though under severe restrictions.

combination lock a lock with a numbered dial or rotating sections, that must be turned so as to register or line up a particular combination of numbers before it will open.

combinatory *adj.* able to be or tending to be combined.

combine — *verb* **1** *trans., intrans.* to join together; to unite. **2** to possess (two contrasting qualities, etc); to manage or achieve (two different things) at the same time. — *noun* **1** a group of people or businesses associated for a common purpose. **2** *colloq.* a combine harvester. [from Latin *combinare*, from *com*-, with + *bini*, two each]

Combined Operations Command a British force established (1940) when Churchill appointed Admiral of the Fleet Lord Keyes to co-ordinate British commando raids against German-occupied Europe. Keyes' successor Lord Mountbatten (1941–3) directed larger operations involving the army, navy, and air force, and prepared for the eventual Allied invasion of France, in which Combined Operations techniques were to play a crucial role.

combine harvester *Agric.* a machine used to harvest cereals and other arable crops, so called because it is equipped both to reap (cut) the crop, and to thresh it by separating the grain or seed, which is lifted to a hopper, from the straw, which is left in a swathe on the ground.

combining form *noun Grammar* a word-form that occurs in combinations or compounds, eg *Anglo-* as in *Anglo-American* and *-lysis* in *electrolysis*.

combo *noun* (PL. **combos**) *colloq.* a small jazz dance band. [from COMBINATION]

combustibility *noun* a combustible quality.

combustible — *adj.* **1** easily catching fire; burning readily; capable of being burnt as fuel. **2** easily exploding into violent passion. — *noun* a combustible material. [from Latin *combustibilis*]

combustion *noun* **1** the process of catching fire and burning. **2** *Chem.* a chemical reaction in which a gas, liquid, or solid is rapidly oxidized, usually by oxygen, with the production of heat and often light. [from Latin *combustio*]

come — *verb usually intrans.* (PAST TENSE **came**; PAST PARTICIPLE **come**) **1** to move in the direction of speaker or hearer. **2** to reach a place; to arrive. **3** (**come to an opinion, conclusion**, *etc*) to reach it after consideration. **4** (**come to** *or* **into something**) to reach a certain stage; to pass into a certain state: *come to power.* **5** (**come to harm**, *etc*) to suffer it. **6** (**come up to something**) to extend to or reach a level, standard, etc. **7** (**come to an amount**) to reach it in total: *that comes to £20 exactly.* **8** to travel or traverse (a distance, etc). **9** (**come from a place**) to have as a source or place of origin: *do you come from Australia?* **10** (**come to do** *or* **be something**) to happen: *how did you come to hurt yourself?* **11** to enter one's consciousness or perception: *come into view.* **12** to occupy a specific place in order, etc: *in 'ceiling', 'e' comes before 'i'.* **13** to be available; to exist or be found: *come in several sizes.* **14** to become: *come undone.* **15** to turn out: *come true.* **16** (**come to something**) to be a case of it: *when it comes to hard work, Jim's your man.* **17** to descend or result from: *come from healthy stock / this is what comes of being indulgent.* **18** (*with complement*) to act like; to pretend to be: *don't come the innocent.* **19** *colloq.* to have a sexual orgasm. **20** on the arrival of (a particular point in time): *come next Tuesday I'll be free.* — *interj.* used to reassure or admonish: *oh, come now, don't exaggerate.*
— **come about 1** to happen. **2** *Naut.* to change direction.
come across (*with complement*) to make a certain impression: *her speech came across well.*
come across something *or* **someone** to discover them; to encounter them.
come across with something *slang* to provide what is required.
come again? *colloq.* could you repeat that?
come along 1 to progress; to improve. **2** to arrive. **3** to hurry up.
come and go to reappear from time to time.
come apart to fall to pieces.
come at something *or* **someone 1** to attack them. **2** to approach them.
come away to become detached.
come back 1 to be recalled to mind: *it's all coming back to me now.* **2** (*also* **come in**) to become fashionable again.
come back at someone to answer them rudely.
come between people to interfere or cause trouble between them.
come by something to obtain it: *how did you come by that cut?*
come down 1 to lose one's social position: *come down in the world.* **2** *said of an heirloom, etc* to be inherited. **3** to leave university. **4** to decide.
come down on someone *or* **something** to deal with them severely; to be very disapproving: *come down heavily on bullying.* **1** (**come down to something**) to be equivalent to it, in simple terms: *it comes down to this.* **2** (**come down with something**) to develop an illness.
come for someone *or* **something 1** to attack them. **2** to call to receive something: *came for our subscription.*
come forward to offer oneself: *several witnesses came forward.*
come in 1 to arrive; to be received. **2** to have a particular role, function, or use: *this is where you come in / come in useful.* **3** *said of the tide* to rise. **4** to become fashionable.
come in for something to deserve or incur it: *came in for some criticism.*
come into something to inherit money, etc.
come into one's own to have the opportunity to display one's talents.
come it over *slang* to put on an act: *don't come it over me.*
come off 1 to become detached. **2** to succeed. **3** to take place.
come off it! *colloq.* stop talking nonsense!
come on 1 to start. **2** to hurry up, cheer up, not talk nonsense.
come one's way to become available.
come out 1 *said of the sun or stars* to appear. **2** to become known. **3** to fade in the wash: *the mark won't come out.* **4** to strike: *come out in sympathy.* **5** to declare one's opinion openly: *come out in favour of the plan.* **6** to work out: *can't get the sum to come out.* **7** to emerge in a certain position or state: *come out well from the affair.* **8** *said of a photograph* to be developed: *come out nice and clear.* **9** *colloq.* to declare openly that one is a homosexual. **10** *old use, said of a girl* to be launched in society.
come out in something to develop a rash, etc: *come out in spots.*
come out with something to make a remark, etc: *what will she come out with next?*
come over 1 to change one's opinion or side: *come over to our side.* **2** to make a certain impression: *comes over well on television.* **3** (*with complement*) *colloq.* to feel or become: *come over a bit faint.*
come over someone to affect them: *what came over them?*
come round 1 to regain consciousness. **2** to regain one's temper; to calm down. **3** to change one's opinion. **4** to recur in order or routine.
come through to survive.
come through something to survive it.
come to to regain consciousness.
come to nothing to fail.

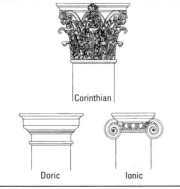

Corinthian

Doric   Ionic

columns

come to oneself 1 to regain consciousness. **2** to calm down; to regain one's self-control.

come under something *or* **someone 1** to belong to a category. **2** to be a specified responsibility: *swimming-pools come under the local authority.*

come up 1 to occur; to happen: *I'll contact you if anything comes up.* **2** to be considered or discussed: *the question didn't come up.* **3** to rise socially: *come up in the world.*

come up against someone *or* **something** to be faced with them as an opponent, challenge, etc.

come up to someone to approach them.

come up with something to offer it; to put it forward: *come up with an idea.*

come upon something *or* **someone** to discover it by chance.

have it coming to one *colloq.* to deserve whatever unpleasant fate befalls one.

not know whether one is coming or going to be in a dazed or bewildered state.

when it comes to ... when it is a question of...: *when it comes to hard work, he's your man.* [from Anglo-Saxon *cuman*]

comeback 1 *noun* a return to former success, or to the stage, etc after a period of retirement or obscurity: *stage a comeback.* **2** a retort. **3** an opportunity for redress or retaliation.

COMECON *or* **Comecon** *abbrev.* Council for Mutual Economic Assistance.

comedian *noun* **1** an entertainer who tells jokes, performs comic sketches, etc. **2** an actor in comedy. [from COMEDY]

Comédie-Française the oldest surviving theatre company in France. Dating (officially) from 1680, seven years after the death of Molière, it was formed by a combination of troupes that included his former company, and was soon known as *La Maison de Molière.* Still the guardian of the French classical tradition, it is organized as a co-operative society, with the longest-serving actor as its head and all full members as share-holders.

Comédie Humaine, La the collective name given to approximately 92 fictional works by Honoré de Balzac. The novels included under this title are intended to give an overall, realistic portrayal of French life in the late 18c and early 19c.

comedienne *noun* a female comedian.

comedo *noun* (PL. **comedos**) *Medicine* a blackhead in the skin. [from Latin *comedo*, glutton]

comedown *noun* **1** a decline in social status. **2** an anticlimax.

comedy *noun* (PL. **comedies**) **1** a light, amusing play or film. **2** drama of this type generally. **3** in earlier literature, a play with a fortunate outcome. **4** funny incidents or situations. [from Greek *komoidia*, from *komos*, comic chorus + *aoidos*, singer]

come-hither *adj. colloq.* flirtatious: *a come-hither look.*

comeliness *noun* a comely or attractive quality.

comely *adj.* (**comelier**, **comeliest**) *said of a woman* wholesomely attractive. [from Anglo-Saxon *cymlic*, beautiful]

Comenius, John Amos, Czech **Komenský Jan Ámos** (1592–1670) Czech educational reformer, born in Moravia. He was Rector of the Moravian school of Prerau (1614–16) and minister at Fulnek, but fled to Poland at the beginning of the Thirty Years War. He settled at Lissa in 1628, where he worked out his new theory of education, and was chosen Bishop of the Moravian Brethren in 1632. In 1650 he went to Hungary, where he composed his *Orbis Sensualium Pictus* (The Visible World in Pictures, 1658), the first picture book for children.

come-on *noun colloq.* sexual encouragement: *give someone the come-on.*

comer *noun* (*often in compounds*) a person who comes: *latecomers / a newcomer / challenge all comers.*

comestible *noun* (*usually in pl.*) something to eat. [from French *comestible*, from Latin *comedere*, to eat up]

comet *noun Astron.* in the solar system, a small body composed mainly of frozen gases, ice, and dust, that follows an elliptical orbit around the Sun, and has a characteristic bright head (*coma*) and a streaming tail when its orbit takes it close to the Sun. [from Greek *kometes*, literally 'long-haired', from *kome*, hair]

◇ The solid part of a comet, the *nucleus*, is very small (usually only a few kilometres in diameter), irregularly shaped, and has been likened to a 'dirty snowball' consisting mainly of ice and solid rock particles. When the comet's orbit takes it close to the Sun, a cloud of gas, dust, and water vapour boils away from the nucleus, forming the tail of the comet, which can extend for millions of kilometres, and always points away from the Sun. When its orbit takes it away from the Sun, the comet's tail gradually fades until it is invisible, and the comet in its frozen state resembles an asteroid, and is not normally visible from Earth until it swings round and approaches the Sun once more.

come-uppance *noun colloq.* a well-deserved punishment or retribution: *get one's come-uppance.*

comfit *noun Hist.* an old type of sweet, usually a sugar-coated nut, etc. [from French *confit*]

comfort — *noun* **1** a state of physical and mental contentedness or wellbeing. **2** relief from suffering, or consolation in grief. **3** a person or thing that provides such relief or consolation. **4** (*usually* **comforts**) something that makes for ease and physical wellbeing. — *verb* to relieve from suffering; to console or soothe. [from French *conforter*]

comfortable *adj.* **1** in a state of especially physical wellbeing; at ease. **2** providing comfort. **3** *colloq.* financially secure. **4** *said of a hospital patient, etc* in a stable, more or less pain-free condition. **5** quite large: *win by a comfortable margin.* [from French *confortable*]

comfortably *adv.* **1** so as to be comfortable. **2** in a comfortable way.

— **comfortably off** *colloq.* financially secure; able to live in comfort.

comforter *noun* **1** a person who comforts. **2** *old use* a warm scarf. **3** *old use* a baby's dummy. **4** *North Amer., esp. US* a quilt.

comfrey *noun* a bristly plant of the borage family, with bell-shaped blue flowers, formerly used medicinally. [from Latin *conferva*, healing water plant]

comfy *adj.* (**comfier**, **comfiest**) *colloq.* comfortable.

comic — *adj.* **1** characterized by or relating to comedy; intended to amuse. **2** funny. — *noun* **1** a comedian. **2** (*also* **comic book**) a paper or magazine, especially one aimed at children or teenagers, which includes strip cartoons, illustrated stories, etc. The term is now applied to the format rather than the content, which may be serious (and even horrific) as well as comic. [from Greek *komikos*, from *komos*, comic chorus]

comical *adj.* funny; amusing; humorous; ludicrous.

comicality *noun* a comical quality.

comically *adv.* in a comical way.

comic opera a lighthearted opera with spoken dialogue as well as singing.

◇ Various forms of comic opera in Europe include: in Italy, *opera buffa*; in France, *opéra-comique*; and in Germany, *Singspiel*. They all share the characteristic of spoken dialogue interspersed with song; although the subject matter is generally more light-hearted than serious opera, it may

not necessarily be wholly comic. In Britain, the term is used to refer to a form of musical drama which was influenced by Restoration parodies of plays with music and song. These 'comic' operas (also known as *ballad operas*) were usually satirical dramas which included songs set to popular tunes of the day: one of the earliest examples was John Gay's *The Beggar's Opera*, first produced in 1728.

comic strip a brief story or episode told through a short series of pictures, in a newspaper, etc.

Comines *or* **Commynes, Philippe de** (c.1445–1511) French statesman and historian, born in Comines, Flanders. In 1463 he entered the court of Burgundy, but from 1472 served Louis XI of France, after whose death he was imprisoned. Restored to favour in 1493, he accompanied Charles VIII on his Italian expedition (1494). His *Mémoires* provide an important record of the era.

Cominform *abbrev.* in the USSR, Communist Information Bureau.

coming — *noun* an arrival; an approach: *await their coming.* — *adj.* **1** *colloq.* looking like a winner: *the coming man.* **2** approaching: *in the coming months.*

— **comings and goings** *colloq.* bustle; activity; movement.

Comino the smallest of the three main islands of the Maltese group. It lies midway between the islands of Malta and Gozo. AREA 2.7sq km/ 1sq mi. It is a 20-minute boat trip from the main island across the South Comino Channel. The highest point on the island is 247m; the Blue Lagoon is its chief attraction. Comino was a harbour for pirates until the 1700s.

Comintern *abbrev.* in the USSR, Communist International.

comity *noun* civility; politeness; courtesy. [from Latin *comitas*, from *comis*, friendly]

comity of nations mutual respect between nations for one another's laws and customs.

comma *noun* a punctuation mark (,) indicating a slight pause or break made for the sake of clarity, etc. [from Greek *comma*, clause]

command — *verb* **1** to order formally. **2** to have authority over or be in control of. **3** to have at one's disposal. **4** to deserve or be entitled to. **5** to look down over: *the window commands a view of the bay.* — *noun* **1** an order. **2** control; charge; *second in command.* **3** knowledge of and ability to use. **4** a military unit, or a district, under one's command. **5** a specialized section of an army, air force, etc: *Bomber Command.* **6** a group of high-ranking army officers, etc: *the British High Command.* **7** an instruction to a computer to carry out some operation. [from French *commander*]

commandant *noun* a commanding officer, especially of a prisoner-of-war camp or a military training establishment. [from French *commandant*, present participle of *commander*, to command]

command economy a centrally controlled economy in which the state takes all economic decisions. Most countries of the former communist bloc were command economies (see also MARKET ECONOMY).

commandeer *verb* **1** to seize (property) for military use in wartime, official use in an emergency, etc. **2** to seize without justification. [from Afrikaans *commandeer*, from French *commander*, to command]

commander *noun* **1** a person who commands. **2** in the British navy, an officer just below captain in rank. **3** a high-ranking police officer. **4** (*also* **knight commander**) a senior member in some orders of knighthood.

commander-in-chief *noun* (PL. **commanders-in-chief**) the officer in supreme command of a nation's forces.

commanding *adj.* **1** powerful; leading; controlling. **2** in charge. **3** inspiring respect or awe. **4** giving good views all round: *a house with a commanding position.*

commandment *noun* a divine command, especially (*usually* **Commandment**) one of 10 given to Moses, listed in the Bible in Exodus 20.

command module the section of a spacecraft from which operations are directed, serving also as living quarters.

commando *noun* (PL. **commandos**) a member of a unit of soldiers specially trained to carry out dangerous and difficult attacks or raids. [from Afrikaans *commando*, originally from Portuguese *commandar*, to command]

command paper, a government document presenting a report on some matter or outlining government policy. See also GREEN PAPER, WHITE PAPER.

command performance a special performance of a play, etc given at the request, and in the presence, of the head of state.

command post a temporary military headquarters.

commedia dell'arte a 16c Italian form of comedy with stock characters and plots full of intrigue. [Italian, = comedy of the arts]

commemorate *verb* **1** to honour the memory of (a person or event) with a ceremony, etc. **2** to be a memorial to. [from Latin *commemorare*, to keep in mind]

commemoration *noun* an act or ceremony of preserving the memory of some person or thing.

commemorative *adj.* tending or serving to commemorate.

commence *verb trans., intrans.* to begin. [from Old French *commencier*, from Latin *initiare*, to begin]

commencement *noun* **1** a beginning. **2** *North Amer.* a graduation ceremony.

commend *verb* **1** to praise. **2** to entrust (someone or something) to someone. **3** to recommend or make acceptable: *if the idea commends itself to you.* [from Latin *commendare*]

commendable *adj.* praiseworthy; creditable.

commendably *adv.* in a commendable way.

commendation *noun* **1** praise; approval. **2** an award or honour.

commendatory *adj.* commending; involving commendation.

commensalism *noun Biol.* the partnership or association of two organisms of different species which does not affect or benefit either of them. [from COM- + Latin *mensa*, table]

commensurable *adj.* (*often* **commensurable with** *or* **to something**) **1** *Maths.* having a common factor; divisible by a common unit with an integer or whole number as a result. **2** measurable by a common standard. [from Latin *com-*, with+ *mensurare*, to measure]

commensurate *adj.* (**commensurate with something**) **1** in proportion to it; appropriate to it. **2** equal to it in extent, quantity, etc. [from Latin *com-*, with+ *mensurare*, to measure]

commensurately *adv.* so as to be commensurate.

comment — *noun* **1** a remark or observation, especially a critical one. **2** talk, discussion, or gossip. **3** an explanatory or analytical note on a passage of text. — *verb trans., intrans.* (**comment on something**) to make observations about it. — **no comment** I decline to comment. [from Latin *commentum*, commentary]

commentary *noun* (PL. **commentaries**) **1** a continuous, especially broadcast, report on an event, match, etc as it actually takes place. **2** an explanation accompanying a film, etc. **3** a set of

notes explaining or interpreting points in a text, etc. [from Latin *commentarium*, notebook]

commentate *verb intrans.* to give a running commentary.

commentator *noun* **1** a broadcaster giving a commentary on a match, event, etc. **2** the writer of a textual commentary. [from Latin *commentator*, interpreter]

commerce *noun* **1** the buying and selling of commodities and services; trade, including banking, insurance, etc. **2** *old use* social dealings or communication. [from French *commerce*, from Latin *commercium*, trade]

commercial — *adj.* **1** relating to, engaged in or used for commerce. **2** profitable; having profit as chief aim; exploited or exploitable for profit. **3** paid for by advertising. — *noun* a radio or television advertisement. [from Latin *commercium*, trade]

Commercial Court a court within the Queen's Bench Division which hears major commercial cases in England and Wales. Cases often involve litigants from overseas, and are usually heard in private, with the judge in the role of arbitrator.

commercialism *noun* **1** commercial attitudes and aims. **2** undue emphasis on profit-making.

commerciality *noun* a commercial quality or nature.

commercialization *or* **commercialisation** *noun* **1** exploitation for profit. **2** making commercial.

commercialize *or* **commercialise** *verb* **1** to exploit for profit, especially by sacrificing quality. **2** to make commercial.

commercially *adv.* in a commercial way; as regards commerce.

commercial traveller *noun* a person who travels around the country representing a business firm and selling their goods.

commie *colloq., derog.* — *noun* a communist. — *adj.* communist: *commie talk.*

comminute *verb technical* **1** to crush (eg minerals) into tiny pieces. **2** to reduce to small portions. [from Latin *comminuere*]

comminution *noun* act of comminuting.

commis *or* **commis chef** *noun* (PL. **commis**, **commis chefs**) an assistant or trainee waiter or chef. [from French *commis*]

commiserate *verb intrans.* (**commiserate with someone**) to express sympathy for them. [from Latin *com-*, with + *miserari*, to lament]

commiseration *noun* pity, sympathy.

commissar *noun* in the former Soviet Union, the head of a government department, or a Communist Party official responsible for the political education of military units. [from Russian *komisar*, from Latin *commissarius*, officer in charge]

commissarial *adj.* relating to or associated with a commissary.

commissariat *noun* **1** a department in the army responsible for food supplies. **2** *formerly* a government department in the Soviet Union. [from French and Russian, from Latin *commissarius*, officer in charge]

commissary *noun* (PL. **commissaries**) **1** an officer responsible for supplies and provisions in the army. **2** *North Amer.* a store supplying provisions and equipment to a military force. **3** *orig. North Amer., esp. US* a canteen serving a film studio, etc. [from Latin *commissarius*, officer in charge]

commission — *noun* **1** a formal or official request to someone to perform a task or duty; the authority to perform it; the task or duty. **2** a military rank above a certain level, or the document conferring this. **3** an order for a piece of work,

especially a work of art. **4** a board or committee entrusted with a particular task. **5** a fee or percentage given to the agent arranging a sale. **6** the act of committing, eg a crime. — *verb* **1** to give a commission or authority to. **2** to grant military rank above a certain level to. **3** to request (someone to do something). **4** to place an order for (a work of art, etc). **5** to prepare (a ship) for active service.
— **in** *or* **out of commission** in use, or not in use or working condition.
[from Latin *commissio*, entrusting]

commissionaire *noun* a uniformed attendant at the door of a cinema, theatre, office, or hotel. [from French *commissionaire*]

commissioned officer, a military officer who is holding a commission. See also NON-COMMISSIONED OFFICER.

commissioner *noun* **1** a representative of the government in a district, department, etc. **2** a member of a commission.

commissionership *noun* the position or office of a commissioner.

commit *verb* (**committed**, **committing**) **1** to carry out or perpetrate (a crime, offence, error, etc). **2** to have (someone) put in prison or a mental institution. **3** to promise or engage (especially oneself) for some undertaking, etc. **4** to dedicate (oneself) to a cause, etc from a sense of conviction: *a committed Christian.* **5** to entrust or give, eg facts to memory (ie memorize them), or thoughts to paper (ie write them down). **6** to send (a person) for trial in a higher court.
— **commit oneself** to make a definite decision. [from Latin *committere*, to give, entrust, perpetrate]

commitment *noun* **1** the act of committing someone or oneself; the state of being committed. **2** dedication or devotion; strong conviction. **3** an undertaking or responsibility: *taking on too many commitments.*

committal *noun* the action of committing someone to a prison or mental institution.

committee *sing. or pl. noun* **1** a group of people selected by, and from, a larger body, eg a club, to undertake especially administrative work on its behalf. **2** a body specially appointed to undertake an investigation, enquiry, etc. [from earlier *committen*, to entrust + -EE]

Committee of the Regions a committee of the European Union, made up of 189 members, delegates from the regional government of each member country. It has the right of consultation on all matters which would effect the regions, eg public health, education, European transport.

committee stage *Politics* the stage between the second and third readings of a parliamentary bill, when it is examined in detail by members sitting in committee.

commode *noun* **1** a chair with a hinged seat covering a chamber pot. **2** a chest of drawers. [from French *commode*, from Latin *commodus*, convenient]

commodious *adj.* comfortably spacious. [from Latin *commodus*, convenient]

commodiously *adv.* in a commodious way.

commodiousness *noun* the quality of being commodious.

commodity *noun* (PL. **commodities**) **1** something that is bought and sold, especially a manufactured product or raw material. **2** something, eg a quality, from the point of view of its value in society: *courtesy is a scarce commodity.* [from Latin *commoditas*, benefit]

commodity market *or* **commodity exchange** a market where buyers and sellers of commodities (eg wool, sugar, coffee, wheat, metals) trade. Often prices are fixed on a bargain-by-bargain basis. The London Commodity

Exchange is one of the most important in the world and deals in many different commodities; some markets deal with only one commodity.

commodore *noun* **1** in the British navy, an officer just below a rear admiral in rank. **2** the president of a yacht club. **3** the senior captain in charge of a fleet of merchant ships. [perhaps through Dutch from French *commandeur*, commander]

Commodore Keppel a portrait painting by Sir Joshua Reynolds (1753, National Maritime Museum, London). The subject's pose derives from that of a Classical statue, *The Apollo Belvedere.*

common — *adj.* **1** often met with; frequent; familiar. **2** shared by two or more people, things, etc: *characteristics common to both animals.* **3** publicly owned. **4** of a standard one has a right to expect: *common decency.* **5** widespread: *common knowledge.* **6** *derog.* lacking taste or refinement; vulgar. **7** of the ordinary type: *the common cold.* **8** not of high rank or class: *the common people.* **9** *Maths.* shared by two or more numbers: *highest common factor.* — *noun* **1** a piece of land that is publicly owned or available for public use. **2** *Legal* a right to something, or to do something, on someone else's land. **3** *slang* common sense. See also COMMONS.
— **the common touch** an ability, in someone distinguished by accomplishment or rank, to relate sociably to ordinary people.
in common 1 *said of interests, etc* shared: *they have little in common.* **2** in joint use or ownership: *a garden owned in common by the residents.*
make common cause to co-operate to achieve a common aim.
[from Latin *communis*]

Common Agricultural Policy (ABBREV. **CAP**) the most important of the common policies of the European Community, which accounts for about 65 per cent of EC expenditure. Its basic principles are free trade for agricultural commodities within the Community, Community preference for domestic production, control of imports from the rest of the world, and common prices and subsidization. The main objectives are increased agricultural productivity, a fair standard of living for farmers, reasonable market prices for the consumer, stability of markets, and secure food supplies. Most of these objectives have been met through the use of subsidies on certain types of farming or certain crops, which in turn have generated surpluses of most major commodities, such as the 'butter mountain' and 'wine lake'. An important additional objective for the CAP is to contain these surpluses and limit the huge cost associated with their disposal. Radical reforms involving the reduction of target prices for cereals, beef, and dairy produce were introduced in May 1992.

common denominator 1 *Maths.* a whole number that is a multiple of each of the denominators of two or more fractions, eg 15 (3 × 5) is a common denominator of ⅓ and ⅗. See also LOWEST COMMON DENOMINATOR. **2** something that enables comparison, agreement, etc between people or things.

commoner *noun* a person who is not a member of the nobility.

common era a culturally neutral term for the present era, reckoned since the birth of Christ. See also BCE, CE.

common gender *Grammar* the gender of such nouns as *doctor, scientist, baby,* that can refer to either sex.

common ground an area of agreement between people, as a starting-point for discussion.

common law in England, law based on custom and decisions by judges, as distinct from written law.

common-law *adj.* denoting a relationship of two people living together as husband and wife but not legally married: *common-law marriage.*

commonly *adv.* **1** usually, often; generally, ordinarily. **2** in a common way. **3** vulgarly.

Common Market the European Community.

commonness *noun* being common.

common noun *Grammar* a noun that is not a proper name and which can refer to any member of a class of things, eg *car table girl* as opposed to *Paris John.* See also PROPER NOUN.

common-or-garden *adj.* of the ordinary, everyday kind.

commonplace — *adj.* **1** ordinary; everyday. **2** *derog.* unoriginal; lacking individuality; trite. — *noun* **1** *derog.* a trite comment; a cliché. **2** an everyday occurrence. [translation of Latin *locus communis,* an argument widely used]

Common Prayer, Book of the official directory of worship or service-book of the Church of England, widely followed in Churches of the Anglican Communion. Largely composed by Archbishop Cranmer, it was first introduced in 1549, and revised in 1552, 1604, and 1662.

common-riding *noun* in the Scottish Borders, a ceremonial progress by riders on horseback around the boundaries of common land, by tradition intended to deter encroachment by neighbouring landowners, and to guard against invasion by the English. In some border towns, notably Hawick and Selkirk, the common-riding is led by a young unmarried man (the cornet) chosen each year as the representative of the townspeople. During the ride, various ceremonies peculiar to the particular area (analogous to *beating the bounds*) are performed.

common room in a college, school, etc a sitting-room for general use by students or staff.

common rorqual see RORQUAL.

commons *noun* **1** *Hist.* (**the commons**) (*pl.*) the ordinary people. **2** (**the Commons**) the House of Commons. **3** *old use, facetious* shared food rations.
— **on short commons** having reduced rations.

common seal a true seal native to the N Pacific and N Atlantic oceans, usually grey with dark blotches. It dives to depths of more than 90m, and feeds on fish, squid, and crabs.

common sense practical good sense.

common-sense *or* **commonsensical** *adj.* having or noted for common sense.

common time *Mus.* a rhythm with two or four beats to the bar.

Commonwealth an English republican regime created by Oliver Cromwell, based on the Rump Parliament established in 1649, which lasted until the *Instrument of Government* created a Protectorate in 1653. It failed to achieve political settlement at home, but its armies pacified Scotland and Ireland. The Navigation Acts (1650, 1651) and the Anglo-Dutch Wars (1652–4) fostered overseas trade and colonies.

commonwealth *noun* **1** a country or state. **2** an association of states that have joined together for their common good. **3** (**the Commonwealth**) **a** see as separate entry. **b** same as COMMONWEALTH OF NATIONS. **4** a title used by certain US states. [from COMMON + WEALTH]

Commonwealth Conference an annual meeting of prime ministers of the independent nations that evolved from the former British Empire and now belong to the Commonwealth of Nations.

Commonwealth Day the second Monday in March, celebrated throughout the Commonwealth of nations. Until 1960 it was celebrated, as *Empire Day,* on 24 May (Queen Victoria's

birthday); from 1967 it was celebrated on the Queen's official birthday in June; and it was changed to its present day in 1977.

Commonwealth Development Corporation an organization established as the Colonial Development Corporation by the British government under the Overseas Resources Development Act (1948, renamed 1963). Its functions were to develop trade and defence in former British colonial territories and countries through a loans programme, which lasted until the early 1970s.

Commonwealth Games a multi-sport gathering held every four years by representatives of the nations of the Commonwealth. The first Games were held as the British Empire Games in Hamilton, Canada, in 1930. They were renamed the British Empire and Commonwealth Games in 1954; the current title was adopted in 1970.

Commonwealth Institute an organization founded in 1959 to replace the Imperial Institute, itself founded in 1886 to promote commerce and industry between the countries of the British Empire. Its main activity is the promotion of the heritage and culture of its member nations. It is made up of the centre in Kensington, London, a regional branch in Bradford, and the separately run Scottish Institute in Edinburgh. In Sep 1993, it was announced that government funding for it (c.80 per cent of its costs) would be withdrawn after Mar 1996.

Commonwealth of Independent States (ABBREV. **CIS**) a grouping (1991) of 11 independent states out of the 15 republics which formerly made up the Soviet Union. They are: Armenia, Azerbaijan, Belorussia, Kazakhstan, Kirghizia, Moldavia, Russia, Tajikistan, Turkmenistan, Ukraine, and Uzbekistan.

Commonwealth of Nations, former name **British Commonwealth** a voluntary organization of autonomous states which had been imperial possessions of Britain. Its head is the reigning British monarch. It was formally established by the Statute of Westminster (1931)

Commonwealth Membership

The Commonwealth is an informal association of sovereign states.

Member countries are grouped by year of entry.

1931	Australia, Canada, New Zealand, United Kingdom
1947	India, Pakistan (left 1972, rejoined 1989)
1948	Sri Lanka
1957	Ghana, Malaysia
1960	Nigeria
1961	Cyprus, Sierra Leone, Tanzania
1962	Jamaica, Trinidad and Tobago, Uganda
1963	Kenya
1964	Malawi, Malta, Zambia
1965	the Gambia, Singapore
1966	Barbados, Botswana, Guyana, Lesotho
1968	Mauritius, Nauru, Swaziland
1970	Tonga, Western Samoa
1972	Bangladesh
1973	Bahamas
1974	Grenada
1975	Papua New Guinea
1976	Seychelles
1978	Dominica, Solomon Islands, Tuvalu
1979	Kiribati, St Lucia, St Vincent and the Grenadines
1980	Vanuatu, Zimbabwe
1981	Antigua and Barbuda, Belize
1982	Maldives
1983	St Christopher and Nevis
1984	Brunei

Three countries have left the Commonwealth:
Fiji (1987), Ireland (1949), South Africa (1961)

Commonwealth Games

Venues

1930	Hamilton, Canada
1934	London, England
1938	Sydney, Australia
1950	Auckland, New Zealand
1954	Vancouver, Canada
1958	Cardiff, Wales
1962	Perth, Australia
1966	Kingston, Jamaica
1970	Edinburgh, Scotland
1974	Christchurch, New Zealand
1978	Edmonton, Canada
1982	Brisbane, Australia
1986	Edinburgh, Scotland
1990	Auckland, New Zealand
1994	Victoria, Canada

Leading Medal Winners

	Nation	Gold	Silver	Bronze	Total
1	England	420	368	368	1156
2	Australia	397	374	382	1153
3	Canada	287	301	299	887
4	New Zealand	94	121	161	376
5	Scotland	56	74	109	239
6	South Africa	60	44	47	151
7	Wales	32	39	60	131
8	Kenya	35	24	33	92
9	India	37	36	31	104
10	Northern Ireland	15	20	34	69

and meets frequently to discuss matters of mutual interest and concern. While most states, on independence, chose to become members of the Commonwealth, four have left: Irish Republic, 1949; South Africa, 1961; Pakistan, 1972; Fiji, 1987.

commotion *noun* **1** a disturbance; an upheaval; tumult. **2** noisy confusion; uproar; din. [from Latin *commotio*, from *movere*, to move]

communal *adj.* **1** relating to, or belonging to, a community. **2** shared; owned in common. **3** relating to a commune or communes. [from Latin *communalis*, from *communis*, common]

communally *adv.* as regards a community; collectively rather than individually.

commune¹ *noun* (with stress on *com-*) **1** a number of unrelated families and individuals living as a mutually supportive community, with shared accommodation, supplies, responsibilities, etc. **2** in some European countries, the smallest local administrative unit. [from Latin *communa*, from *communis*, common]

commune² *verb intrans.* (with stress on *-mune*) **1** to communicate intimately or confidentially. **2** to get close to or relate spiritually to (eg nature). [from French *communer*, to share]

communicable *adj.* **1** capable of being communicated. **2** *Medicine* denoting an infectious or contagious disease, such as the common cold, that can be transmitted from one organism to another by direct physical contact, infected airborne droplets, etc. The most serious communicable diseases are known as *notifiable diseases*, eg diphtheria, meningitis, rabies. [from Latin *communicabilis*, from *communicare*, to share or impart]

communicant *noun* **1** a person who receives Communion. **2** an informant. [from Latin *communicare*, to partake, impart]

communicate *verb* **1** *trans., intrans.* to impart (information, ideas, etc); to make (something) known or understood; to get in touch. **2** to pass on or transmit (a disease, feeling, etc). **3** *intrans.* to understand someone; to have a comfortable social relationship. **4** *intrans. said of rooms, etc* to be connected: *a communicating door.* **5** *intrans.* in

the Christian Church, to receive Communion. [from Latin *communicare*, to share]

communication *noun* **1** the process or act of communicating; the exchanging or imparting of ideas and information, etc. **2** a piece of information, a letter, or a message. **3** social contact. **4** (**communications**) the systems involved in transmission of information, etc especially by electronic means or radio waves. **5** (**communications**) means or routes used for moving troops or supplies. **6** (**communications**) the science and activity of transmitting information, etc.

communication cord *Brit.* a chain or cord fitted in a railway carriage, to be pulled in an emergency to stop the train.

communications satellite *Astron.* an unmanned artificial satellite sent by rocket into orbit around the Earth, and used to relay radio, television, and telephone signals.

◊ Communications satellites relay signals around the Earth's curved surface, either by reflecting them or by amplifying and retransmitting them. Most such satellites are placed in geostationary orbit, remaining fixed over one point on the Earth's surface. The entire world is linked by a series of communications satellites known as *Intelsat*.

communication theory the application of information theory to human communication in general. Communication is seen as involving an information source which encodes a message to be transmitted through a channel to a receiver, where it is decoded and has an effect. Efficient, error-free transmission is assumed to be the primary goal, especially in engineering contexts. However, more general applications of the model have been criticized for neglecting the importance of factors such as feedback, social context, and the active role of human receivers in the production of meaning.

communicative *adj.* **1** sociable; talkative. **2** relating to communication: *communicative skills.*

communicatively *adv.* in a communicative way.

communion *noun* **1** the sharing of thoughts, beliefs, or feelings. **2** a group of people sharing the same religious beliefs. **3** (*also* **Holy Communion**) in the Christian Church, a service at which bread and wine are taken as symbols of Christ's body and blood; the consecrated bread and wine. [from Latin *communio*, mutual participation]

communiqué *noun* an official bulletin, communication, or announcement. [from French *communiqué*, something communicated]

communism *noun* **1** a political theory advocating that society should be classless, private property should be abolished, and land, factories, and other sources of wealth should be collectively owned and controlled by the people. **2** (**Communism**) a political movement founded on the principles of communism set out by Karl Marx. **3** the political and social system established on these principles in the former Soviet Union and other countries of E Europe. [from French *communisme*, from *commun*, common]

◊ Modern communism is particularly associated with the theories of Karl Marx, who saw the emergence of a communist society as being the final stage in a historical process that was rooted in human material needs, preceded by feudalism, capitalism, and (a transitional stage) socialism. The working class, or proletariat, would be the instrument of a revolution that would overthrow the capitalist system, abolishing class distinctions, and ending exploitation of the masses. Marx's writings have provided a powerful ideological basis for communist and socialist parties and governments round the world. His ideology formed the political basis of the Communist Party of the Soviet Union, under Lenin and Stalin. Communism declined rapidly in the countries of eastern Europe in the 1980s. The other major

form of revolutionary communism is Maoism (in China). Most socialist and social democratic parties reject the revolutionary path to socialism, and advocate a gradual reformist strategy which operates within a constitutional framework.

Communism Peak, Russian **Pik Kommunizma**, formerly **Mt Garmo** (to 1933), or **Mt Stalin** (1933–62) the highest peak in Tajikistan. It is part of the Pamir Range, situated in the N of the country. HEIGHT 7 495m. It was first climbed in 1933.

communist — *noun* **1** a supporter of or believer in communism. **2** (*often* **Communist**) a member of a Communist party. — *adj.* **1** relating to communism. **2** believing in or favouring communism.

communistic *adj.* **1** believing in or favouring communism. **2** involving or favouring communal living and ownership.

Communist Information Bureau (ABBREV. **Cominform**) an organization formed (1947–56) by Stalin to succeed the Comintern. Its purpose was the co-ordination of the propaganda and politics of the communist parties of Bulgaria, Czechoslovakia, France, Hungary, Italy, Poland, Romania, the USSR, and Yugoslavia.

Communist International (ABBREV. **Comintern**) an organization formed (1919–43) in Moscow at the behest of the Soviet Communist Party. Adopting Leninist principles in its policies, it rallied left-wing socialists and communists, and rejected reformism in favour of revolutionary action, which it encouraged against capitalist governments.

communitarian *noun* **1** a member of a community. **2** an advocate of community life.

community *noun* (PL. **communities**) **1** the group of people living in a particular locality. **2** a group of people bonded together by a common religion, nationality or occupation. **3** a religious or spiritual fellowship of people living together. **4** the quality or fact of being shared or common: *community of interests.* **5** a group of states with common interests. **6** the public; society in general. **7** *Biol.* a collection of different plant or animal species that occupy the same habitat and interact with each other. [from Latin *communitas*, fellowship]

community centre a place where members of a community may meet for social, sporting or educational activities.

community charge, a tax levied on individuals to pay for local services; the poll tax. See also RATE¹ NOUN 6, COUNCIL TAX.

community home an institution in which young offenders are accommodated.

community school *or* **college** a school or college which is open to the whole community, not just to those of school age. Its facilities may be made available at evenings and at weekends, and in some cases children and adults may study in the same class or take part in the same recreational activities.

community service work of benefit to the local community, sometimes prescribed for offenders in place of a prison sentence.

◊ A convicted defendant may be required by the court to undertake constructive unpaid work in the community (under a community service order) for a stated number of hours within the following 12 months. If the terms of the order are not adhered to the court may impose a further sentence.

community singing organized singing at a large gathering, with everyone taking part.

community work work that serves the social and economic needs of members of a community.

community worker a person who works to meet the needs of a community, eg a social worker.

commutable *adj.* capable of being commuted or exchanged.

commutation *noun* the act of being commuted or exchanged.

commutative *adj. Maths., said of an arithmetical process* performed on two quantities, the order of which does not affect the result, eg addition and multiplication, because $a + b$ is equal to $b + a$, and $a \times b$ is equal to $b \times a$. Subtraction and division are not commutative operations.

commutator *noun* an apparatus for reversing an electric current.

commute *verb* **1** *intrans.* to travel regularly between two places, especially between home and work in a city, etc. **2** to alter (a criminal sentence) to one less severe. **3** to substitute; to convert. **4** to exchange (a pension, etc) for another form of payment, especially a lump sum. [from Latin *commutare*, to alter or exchange]

commuter *noun* a person who travels regularly between home and work.

Como POP (1990e) 89 000, the capital of Como province, Lombardy, NW Italy. A popular tourist destination, it is situated at the SW end of L Como, surrounded by rocky heights. NOTABLE FEATURES marble cathedral (1396); twin-towered Church of Sant'Abbondio (11c); old town largely encircled by its medieval wall; some Roman remains.

Como *or* **Lario, Lake,** ancient **Larius Lacus** a narrow lake in Como province, Lombardy, NW Italy, situated at the foot of the Bernese Alps, 50km/31mi N of Milan. AREA 146sq km/56sq mi; length 50km/31mi; 4km/2.5mi wide at its halfway point. With a maximum depth of 410m, it is the deepest of the N Italian lakes. The promontory of Bellagio divides it into two branches, with the town of Como at the S end of the SW branch. Lake resorts include Tremezzo and Menaggio.

Comodoro Rivadavia POP (1991) 124 000, a seaport and the largest city in Chubut province, Patagonia, S Argentina. It is situated on the Golfo San Jorge, on the Atlantic coast.

Comoé a national park, largely in Bouna department, NE Ivory Coast. AREA 11 500sq km/4 450sq mi. The park, established in 1968, is a World Heritage site.

Comoros, official name **Federal and Islamic Republic of the Comoros**, French **République Fédérale Islamique des Comores** POP (1992e) 585 000, a group of three volcanic islands (Grand Comore, Anjouan, and Mohéli), at the N end of the Mozambique Channel, between Mozambique and Madagascar. AREA 1 862sq km/719sq mi. CAPITAL Moroni. TIME ZONE GMT +3. The chief religion is Islam. OFFICIAL LANGUAGE Kiswahili. CURRENCY the franc CFA. CLIMATE tropical; May–Oct is the dry season and Nov–Apr is the hot, humid season; average temperatures are 20°C in Jul and 28°C in Nov. HISTORY under French control from 1843 to 1912; French Overseas Territory in 1947; internal political autonomy was achieved in 1961; unilateral independence was declared in 1975; Mayotte decided to remain under French administration; established as a Federal Islamic Republic in 1978; political instability continued through the 1980s and in the early 1990s. GOVERNMENT governed by a President (elected for a six-year term) who is head of Government as well as head of state, a Council of Ministers, and a 42-member unicameral Federal Assembly, elected every five years. ECONOMY largely agricultural; vanilla, copra, cacao, sisal, coffee, cloves, vegetable oils, perfume.

compact¹ — *adj.* (with stress on *-pact*) **1** firm and dense in form or texture. **2** small, but with all essentials neatly contained. **3** neatly concise. — *verb* (with stress on *-pact*) to compress. — *noun* (with stress on *com-*) a small case for women's face powder, usually including a mirror. [from Latin *compactus*, put together]

compact² *noun* (with stress on *com-*) a contract or agreement. [from Latin *com-*, with + *pacisci*, to, agree]

compact disc (ABBREV. **CD**) an aluminium disc that is used to store digital data, mainly recorded music, but also large collections of computer data, eg the text of catalogues and encyclopedias, especially using the CD-ROM (compact disc with read-only memory) format.
◇ Unlike a vinyl record, a compact disc has no grooves. Recorded sound, eg music, is converted into digital signals which are represented by microscopic pits etched into the aluminium by a laser beam. The aluminium surface is then protected by sealing it inside a transparent plastic coating. The recorded sound is played back by directing a beam of laser light on to the disc, and the beam is reflected back to a light-sensitive detector by the smooth aluminium, but not by the rough surface of the pits. As the disc spins at high speed and the laser beam scans across its surface, the detector produces a series of light pulses representing the pattern of pits etched into the disc. These pulses are converted to electrical signals by a photocell, and are then passed via an amplifier to loudspeakers which convert them to an almost exact replica of the original sound.

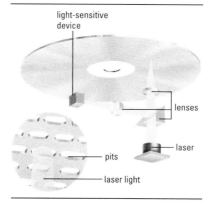

compact disc player

compaction *noun* the act of compacting or state of being compacted.

compactly *adv.* in a compact way; so as to be compact.

compactness *noun* the quality of being compact.

companion¹ *noun* **1** a friend, comrade, or frequent associate. **2** someone who accompanies one on a journey. **3** *Hist.* a woman paid to live or travel with, and be company for, another. **4** *especially as a title* a book of advice; a handbook or guide. **5** one of a pair of matching objects.

Comoros

6 (**Companion**) an honourable title denoting a low-ranking member of any of various orders of knighthood. [from French *compagnon*, from Latin *companio*, literally food-sharer, from *panis*, bread]

companion² *noun Naut.* a hatch admitting light to a cabin or lower deck. [from Dutch *kompanje*, quarterdeck]

companionable *adj.* friendly; sociable; comfortable as a companion.

companionably *adv.* in a companionable way.

companionship *noun* **1** fellowship, company. **2** a body of companions.

Companions of Honour, Order of the (ABBREV. **CH**) in the UK, an award instituted (1917) for outstanding service to the nation. It now consists of the sovereign and a maximum of 65 members (of either sex). The ribbon is carmine edged in gold.

companionway *noun* a staircase between decks.

company *noun* (PL. **companies**) **1** the presence of another person or other people; companionship. **2** the presence of guests or visitors, or the people involved: *expecting company*. **3** one's friends, companions, or associates: *get into bad company*. **4** a business organization. **5** a troop of actors or entertainers. **6** a military unit of about 120 men. **7** a ship's crew. **8** a gathering of people, at a social function, etc.
— **be good** *or* **bad company** to be an entertaining, or dreary, companion.
be in good company to be not the only one in a situation.
in company with ... together with ...; along with: *in company with other reasons*.
keep someone company to act as their companion to.
part company with someone 1 to separate from them. **2** to disagree with them.
[from Old French *compaignie*, from the same root as COMPANION]

company secretary *noun* a senior member of a business organization, in charge of financial and legal matters.

comparability *noun* the fact or extent of being comparable.

comparable *adj.* **1** of the same or equivalent kind. **2** able to be compared; similar enough to allow comparison.

comparably *adv.* in a comparable way; so as to be comparable.

comparative — *adj.* **1** judged by comparison; as compared with others. **2** relating to, or using the method of, comparison. **3** as observed by comparing one another: *their comparative strengths*. **4** *Grammar, said of adjectives and adverbs* in the form denoting a greater degree of the quality in question, either using the suffix *-er* as in *larger, faster* or the word *more*, as in *more usual, more usually*. — *noun Grammar* **1** a comparative adjective or adverb. **2** the comparative form of a word. [from Latin *comparare*, to match]

comparative history a form of historical inquiry that studies the relative development of different societies within the same period of history, or similar phenomena across different periods, rather than concentrating on the development of a particular nation. An example is the analysis of why Britain underwent industrialization in the late 18c and early 19c while its European neighbours did not.

comparative linguistics the study of the similarities and differences between languages and dialects; also, the comparison of features found in the various forms in the historical development of a single language. In the 19c, linguists were primarily concerned with exploring these similarities and differences with a view to setting up language typologies. In the field of comparative philology, correspondences in sounds were used to classify languages; for example, Greek, Latin, and the Germanic languages were shown to belong to the Indo-European family, and, using the process known as *internal reconstruction*, the characteristics of antecedent or parent languages were deduced.

comparative literature the study of the literatures of different languages and nations, and the relationships and similarities which may exist between them.

comparatively *adv.* **1** relatively; rather, somewhat: *the weather is comparatively mild.* **2** by way of comparison.

compare *verb* **1** (**compare one thing with another**) to examine (things of the same kind) to see what differences there are between them. **2** (**compare one person or thing to another**) to liken them: *compare her to an angel.* **3** (**compare with something** *or* **someone**) to stand comparison with them; to be comparable with them: *he can't compare with his predecessor in ability.* — **beyond compare** *or* **without compare** *formal* without equal; incomparable. **compare notes** to exchange ideas and opinions. [from Latin *comparare*, to match]

comparison *noun* **1** the process of, an act of, or a reasonable basis for, comparing: *it doesn't bear comparison with them / there can be no comparison between them.* **2** *Grammar* the positive, comparative, and superlative forms of adjective and adverbs: *the degrees of comparison.* [from French *comparaison*]

compartment *noun* **1** a separated-off or enclosed section. **2** any of several enclosed sections into which a railway carriage is divided. [from French *compartiment*]

compartmental *adj.* involving or consisting of compartments.

compartmentalization *or* **compartmentalisation** *noun* the process or state of being compartmentalized.

compartmentalize *or* **compartmentalise** *verb* to divide, distribute or force into categories.

compass *noun* **1** a direction-finding instrument containing a dial (**compass card**) marked with 32 points, with a magnetized needle that always points to magnetic north. **2** (*usually* **compasses** *or* **pair of compasses**) an instrument consisting of two hinged arms, for drawing circles, measuring distances on maps, etc. **3** range or scope. **4** *Mus.* the range, from highest to lowest possible note, of a voice or instrument. [from French *compas*, from *compasser*, to measure] ◇ The magnetic compass, first introduced into Europe in the 12c, consists of a freely suspended or pivoted magnetic needle which turns to align itself with the magnetic north or south poles. It is subject to the irregularity of the short- and long-period variation of the Earth, and has been largely replaced in modern navigation with the gyrocompass.

compassion *noun* a feeling of sorrow and pity for someone in trouble, usually inclining one to help, show mercy, etc. [from Latin *compassio*]

compassionate *adj.* **1** inclined to pity or mercy. **2** merciful.

compassionate leave special leave granted in cases of bereavement.

compassionately *adv.* in a compassionate way.

compassion fatigue progressive disinclination to show compassion because of continued or excessive exposure to deserving cases.

compatibility *noun* the quality of being compatible.

compatible *adj.* (*often* **compatible with something** *or* **someone**) **1** able to associate or co-exist agreeably. **2** *Comput.*, *said of a program or device* capable of being used with a particular

computer system, especially one produced by another manufacturer. **3** *Engineering, said of a device or piece of machinery* capable of being used in conjunction with another, especially a newer version, without the need for special modification. [from Latin *compatibilis*]

compatibly *adv.* in a way that is compatible; so as to be compatible.

compatriot *noun* someone from one's own country; a fellow-citizen. [from Latin *compatriota*, from *com-* with + *patria*, one's country]

compeer *noun* an equal; a companion or comrade. [from French *comper*, from Latin *com-* with + *par*, equal]

compel *verb* (**compelled, compelling**) **1** to force; to drive. **2** to arouse; to draw forth: *their plight compels sympathy.* [from Latin *compellere*, to force]

compelling *adj.* **1** powerful; forcing one to agree, etc. **2** irresistibly fascinating.

compellingly *adv.* in a compelling or convincing way.

compendious *adj.* concise but comprehensive. [from Latin *compendiosus*, from *compendium*, summary]

compendiously *adv.* in a compendious way.

compendium *noun* (PL. **compendiums, compendia**) **1** a concise summary; an abridgement. **2** a collection of boardgames, puzzles, etc in a single container. [from Latin *compendium*, from *com-*, together + *pendere*, to weigh]

compensate *verb* **1** (**compensate someone for something**) to make amends to them for loss, injury, or wrong, especially by a suitable payment. **2** (**compensate for something**) to make up for a disadvantage, loss, etc. [from Latin *compensare*]

compensation *noun* **1** the process of compensating. **2** something that compensates. **3** a sum of money given to make up for loss, injury, etc.

compensatory *adj.* involving or giving compensation.

compère — *noun* a person who presents a radio or television show, introduces performers, etc. — *verb* to act as compère for (a show). [from French *compère*, godfather]

compete *verb intrans.* (*often* **compete with** *or* **against someone** *or* **something**) **1** to take part in a contest. **2** to strive or struggle: *compete with other firms.* **3** *said of a product, firm, etc* to give good value, be reasonably cheap, etc when compared to market rivals. [from Latin *competere*, to coincide, ask for, seek]

competence *noun* (*also occasionally* **competency**) **1** capability; efficiency. **2** legal authority or capability. **3** *old use* sufficient income to live comfortably.

competent *adj.* **1** efficient. **2** having sufficient skill or training to do something. **3** legally capable. [from Latin *competere*, to meet, be sufficient]

competently *adv.* in a competent way; ably.

competition *noun* **1** an event in which people compete. **2** the process or fact of competing. **3** one's rivals, eg in business, or their products. **4** *Biol.* in a community of plants and animals, the simultaneous demand for the same limited resource, eg light, water, by two or more organisms or species, which leads to a struggle for continued survival. [from Latin *competitio*, meeting together]

competitive *adj.* **1** involving rivalry. **2** enjoying rivalry; aggressive; ambitious. **3** *said of a price or product* reasonably cheap; comparing well with those of market rivals. [from Latin *competere*, to meet together]

competitively *adv.* in a competitive way.

competitiveness *noun* the quality of being competitive.

competitor *noun* a person, team, firm, or product that competes; a rival. [from Latin *competitor*, from *competere*, to meet]

compilation *noun* **1** the process of compiling. **2** the book, etc compiled.

compile *verb* **1** to collect and organize (information, etc); to produce (a list, reference book, etc) from information collected. **2** *Comput.* to devise (a set of instructions) from a programming language by means of a compiler. [from Latin *compilare*, to plunder]

compiler *noun* **1** a person who compiles information, etc. **2** *Comput.* a program for converting a programming language into a language usable with a particular computer.

complacence *or* **complacency** *noun* being complacent.

complacent *adj.* **1** self-satisfied; smug. **2** too easily satisfied; disinclined to worry. [from Latin *complacere*, to be pleasing]

complacently *adv.* with a complacent manner.

complain *verb intrans.* **1** to express one's dissatisfaction or displeasure. **2** (**complain of something**) to say that one is suffering from a pain, disease, etc. [from Old French *complaindre*, to pity]

complainant *noun Legal* a plaintiff.

complainer *noun* a person who complains.

complaint *noun* **1** the act of complaining. **2** an expression of dissatisfaction; a cause for this. **3** a disorder, illness, etc.

complaisance *noun* **1** a desire to please, especially in excess. **2** an obliging manner or attitude. ◆ Often confused with *complacence*.

complaisant *adj.* wanting to please; obliging; amenable. [from French *complaisant*, from *complaire*, to please] ◆ Often confused with *complacent*.

complaisantly *adv.* in a complaisant way.

Compleat Angler, The a work on fishing by Izaak Walton (1653). It is a manual which is interspersed with reflective passages, songs, verse, and glimpses of country life.

complement — *noun* **1** something that completes or perfects; something that provides a needed balance or contrast. **2** the number or quantity required to fill something, eg the crew of a ship. **3** *Grammar* a word or phrase added to a verb to complete the predicate of a sentence, eg *dark* in *it grew dark.* **4** *Maths.* in set theory, all the members of a universal set that do not belong to a specified set S. For example, if the universal set represents all positive whole numbers, and set S represents all odd numbers, the complement of set S will represent all even numbers. **5** *Geom.* that amount by which an angle or arc falls short of a right angle or quadrant. **6** *Biol.* in blood serum, a group of proteins that combine with antibodies and participate in the destruction of foreign particles following an immune response. — *verb* to be a complement to. [from Latin *complementum*, from *complere*, to fill] ◆ Often confused with *compliment*.

complementarily *adv.* in a complementary way; so as to complement.

complementary *adj.* **1** serving as a complement to something. **2** complementing each other. **3** *Physics, said of two colours* producing white when combined.

complementary medicine *Medicine* alternative medicine.

complete — *adj.* **1** whole; finished; with nothing missing. **2** thorough; utter; absolute; total. — *verb* **1** to finish; to make complete or perfect. **2** to fill in (a form). — **complete with** ... having the additional feature of ... [from Latin *complere*, to fill up]

completely *adv.* **1** so as to be complete: *completely full.* **2** to a full or extreme extent; without reserve: *was completely satisfied.*

completeness *noun* a complete state or quality.

completion *noun* **1** the fact or process of completing. **2** the state of being complete. **3** fulfilment.

complex — *adj.* **1** composed of many interrelated parts. **2** complicated; involved; tangled. **3** *Grammar, said of a sentence* having a main clause and one or more subordinate clauses. — *noun* **1** something made of interrelating parts, eg a multi-purpose building: *a leisure complex.* **2** *Psychol.* in psychoanalysis, a set of repressed thoughts and emotions that strongly influence an individual's behaviour and attitudes. **3** *colloq.* an obsession or phobia. [from Latin *complex*, closely connected]

complexion *noun* **1** the colour or appearance of the skin, especially of the face. **2** character or appearance: *that puts a different complexion on the matter.* [from Latin *complexio*, combination]

complexity *noun* (PL. **complexities**) **1** the quality of being complex. **2** a complication; an intricacy.

complex number *Maths.* the sum of a real and an imaginary number.

complex sentence, a sentence comprising a main clause word and one or more subordinate clauses. See also COMPOUND SENTENCE, SIMPLE SENTENCE.

compliance *noun* **1** yielding. **2** agreement, assent. **3** submission.

compliant *adj.* inclined to comply with or yield to the wishes of others; obedient; submissive.

compliantly *adv.* in a compliant way.

complicate *verb* to add difficulties or intricacies to; to make complex or involved. [from Latin *com-*, together + *plicare*, to fold]

complicated *adj.* **1** difficult to understand or deal with. **2** intricate; complex. **3** *said of a fracture in a bone* accompanied by damage to blood vessels, nerves, or organs.

complication *noun* **1** the process of becoming complicated. **2** a circumstance that causes difficulties. **3** *Medicine* a second and possibly worse disease or disorder that arises during the course of (and often as a result of) an existing disease or disorder.

complicity *noun* participation in a crime or wrongdoing. [from Latin *complex*, closely connected]

compliment — *noun* **1** an expression of praise, admiration, or approval. **2** a gesture implying approval: *paid her the compliment of dancing with her.* **3** (**compliments**) formal regards accompanying a gift, etc. — *verb* (**compliment someone on something**) to congratulate them for it. [from French *compliment*, from Italian *complimento*]

◆ Often confused with *complement.*

complimentary *adj.* **1** paying a compliment; admiring or approving. **2** given free.

compline *noun* in Roman Catholic liturgy, the seventh and last service of the day, at 9pm, completing the set hours for prayer. See also LAUDS, MATINS, NONE[2], SEXT, TERCE, VESPERS. [from French *complie*, from Latin *completa hora*, complete hour]

comply *verb intrans.* (**complies, complied**) (*often* **comply with something**) to act in obedience to an order, command, request, etc: *we had to comply / complied with their wishes.* [from Italian *complire*, to fulfil]

component — *noun* any of the parts that make up a machine, engine, instrument, etc. — *adj.* being one of the parts of something. [from Latin *componere*, to assemble into a whole]

componential analysis *Linguistics* the analysis of vocabulary into a series of basic identifying features or 'components' of meaning. For example, *woman* could be analysed using the components 'female', 'adult', and 'human', and *boy* using the components 'male', 'young' (or 'non-adult'), and 'human'.

comport *verb* **1** (**comport oneself**) to behave in a specified way. **2** *intrans.* (**comport with something**) to suit or be appropriate to it. [from Latin *com-*, together + *portare*, to carry]

comportment *noun* behaviour, bearing.

compose *verb* **1** *trans., intrans.* to create (music). **2** to write (a poem, letter, article, etc). **3** to make up or constitute. **4** to arrange as a balanced, artistic whole: *compose a painting.* **5** to calm (oneself); to get (one's thoughts, etc) under control. **6** to settle (differences between people in dispute). **7** *Printing* to arrange (type) or set (a page, etc) in type ready for printing. [from Latin *com-*, together + *ponere*, to put]

composed *adj., said of a person* calm; controlled.

composedly *adv.* with a composed manner.

composer *noun* someone who composes, especially music.

composite — *adj.* **1** made up of different parts, materials, or styles. **2** *Bot.* of or relating to the Compositae (a family of flowering plants). — *noun* **1** *Bot.* a member of a large family of flowering plants (Compositae) in which the flower head consists of many tiny florets crowded together and often surrounded by a circle of bracts, eg daisy, sunflower. **2** *Chem.* a combination of two or more materials which has superior properties to any of its individual components, eg carbon-fibre reinforced plastics, combinations of metal alloys. **3** *Archit.* (*often* **Composite**) the most decorative of the five main orders of architecture. It was introduced by the Romans and was characterized by the combination of the Corinthian acanthus with the Ionic volute, carved mouldings, and decorated entablature.

composite cinematography *Cinema* motion picture photography involving the combination and blending of images from two or more different sources, eg live actors and miniature or painted settings.

composition *noun* **1** something composed, especially a musical or literary work. **2** the process of composing. **3** *Art* arrangement, especially with regard to balance and visual effect: *photographic composition.* **4** *old use* a school essay. **5** what something consists of. **6** a synthetic material of any of various kinds. **7** *Printing* the arrangement of pages of type ready for printing.

compositor *noun Printing* a person who sets or arranges pages of type ready for printing.

compos mentis *adj. Legal* being of sound mind; perfectly rational. [Latin, = in control of the mind]

compost *noun* rotting vegetable matter, etc kept for mixing into soil to enrich it and to nourish plants. [from Latin *com-*, together + *ponere*, to put]

composure *noun* mental and emotional calmness; self-control. [from COMPOSE]

compound[1] — *noun* (with stress on *com-*) **1** (*in full* **chemical compound**) *Chem.* a substance that is composed of two or more chemical elements combined in fixed proportions. It differs from a mixture in that its constituents cannot be separated from each other by physical means. **2** something composed of two or more ingredients or parts. **3** a word made up of two or more words, eg *tablecloth.* See also DERIVATIVE. — *adj.* (with stress on *com-*) **1** composed of a number of parts or ingredients. **2** *Grammar, said of a sentence* made up of two or more main clauses. — *verb* (with stress on *-pound*) **1** to make (especially something bad) much worse; to complicate or

add to (a difficulty, error, etc). **2** to mix or combine (ingredients); to make up (a mixture, etc) by doing this. **3** *Legal* to agree to overlook (an offence, etc) in return for payment. **4** *intrans.* (**compound with someone**) to come to an agreement (especially a financial agreement) with them. [from French *compoundre*, from Latin *componere*, to put together]

compound[2] *noun* (with stress on *com-*) **1** in China, India, etc, an area enclosed by a wall or fence and containing a house or factory. **2** an enclosed area in a prison, used for a particular purpose. **3** in S Africa, an enclosure in which labourers are housed. [from Malay *kampong*]

compound fracture *Medicine* a type of bone fracture in which one or both broken ends of the bone pierce the overlying skin. — Also called *open fracture.*

compound interest, interest on the original sum and on any interest already accumulated. See also SIMPLE INTEREST.

compound sentence, a sentence comprising more than one main clause. See also COMPLEX SENTENCE, SIMPLE SENTENCE.

compound time *Mus.* with three, or a multiple of three, beats to a bar.

comprehend *verb* **1** to understand; to envisage. **2** to include. [from Latin *comprehendere*, to seize, understand]

comprehensibility *noun* the quality of being comprehensible.

comprehensible *adj.* capable of being understood. [from Latin *comprehensibilis*]

comprehensibly *adv.* in a comprehensible way.

comprehension *noun* **1** the process or power of understanding; the scope or range of one's knowledge or understanding. **2** a school exercise for testing students' understanding of a passage of text. [from Latin *comprehensio*]

comprehensive — *adj.* **1** covering or including everything or a great deal. **2** *said of a school or education* providing teaching for children of all abilities between the ages of 11 and 18. — *noun* a comprehensive school. [from Latin *comprehendere*, to comprise, include]

comprehensively *adv.* so as to include everything; completely.

comprehensiveness *noun* the quality of being comprehensive.

compress — *verb* **1** to press together, squeeze or squash. **2** to reduce in bulk; to condense. — *noun* a pad pressed against a part of the body to reduce swelling, stop bleeding, etc. [from Latin *compressare*, to squeeze together]

compressibility *noun* the property of being reduced in volume by pressure.

compressible *adj.* able to be compressed.

compression *noun* **1** the process of compressing or the state of being compressed. **2** the process whereby the volume of a substance, especially a gas, is reduced as a result of an increase in pressure. **3** the stroke that compresses the gases in an internal combustion engine.

compressor *noun Engineering* a device that compresses a gas, especially air, by raising its pressure and decreasing its volume. Compressors are used as power sources for pneumatic tools, eg road drills, sprayers, tyre pumps.

comprise *verb* **1** to contain, include or consist of. **2** to go together to make up. [from French *compris*, included]

compromise — *noun* something agreed on after concessions have been made on each side. — *verb* **1** *intrans.* to make concessions; to reach a compromise. **2** to endanger, or expose to scandal, by acting indiscreetly. **3** to settle (a dispute) by making concessions; to relax (one's principles, etc). [from Latin *compromittere*, to promise reciprocally]

Compromise of 1850 a major but ultimately unsuccessful attempt by the US Congress to resolve by legislation the conflict between the North and South over slavery, in particular its expansion into new territories (eg California and the South-West). Its major terms were the admission of California as a free state, and the passage of a strong fugitive slave law to placate the South.

Compton, Arthur Holly (1892–1962) US physicist, born in Wooster, Ohio. He held posts at Washington University in St Louis, and at Chicago. His theory of how X-rays are scattered by matter provided important evidence that light may be considered to behave as particles as well as waves. For this work he shared the 1927 Nobel Prize for Physics with Charles Wilson. He played a major part in developing the atomic bomb and in building the first nuclear reactor (1942).

Compton, Denis (Charles Scott) (1918–) English cricketer, born in London. He played cricket for England 78 times, and scored 5 807 runs. His county team was Middlesex. In the 1947 season he scored a record 3 816 runs, including a record 18 centuries. During his career (1936–57) he made 38 942 runs and took 622 wickets. He was also a football player, and won a cap for England in 1943. His career was spent with Arsenal, and along with his brother, Leslie, he won a Football Association Cup winner's medal in 1950. More recently, he has been a cricket journalist and broadcaster.

Compton, Fay (1894–1978) English actress, born in London, daughter of the actor Edward Compton, and sister of Sir Compton Mackenzie. She first appeared on the stage in 1911, and won acclaim in London in *Peter Pan* (1918). She later played many famous parts, especially in other plays by J M Barrie.

Compton-Burnett, Dame Ivy (1892–1969) English novelist, born in Pinner, Middlesex. Her stylized novels, usually set in upper-class Victorian or Edwardian households and focusing on several generations of large families, include *Pastors and Masters* (1925), *Manservant and Maidservant* (1947), and *Mother and Son* (1955).

compulsion *noun* **1** the act of compelling or condition of being compelled. **2** an irresistible urge to perform a certain action, especially an irrational one. **3** *Psychol.* a specific action or ritual that is repeated many times and usually represents a form of obsession, eg repetitive washing based on fear of contamination. [from Latin *compulsio*]

compulsive *adj.* **1** *said of an action* resulting from a compulsion. **2** *said of a person* acting on compulsion. **3** *said of a book, film, etc* holding one's attention. [from Latin *compulsivus*]

compulsively *adv.* in a compulsive way.

compulsorily *adv.* so as to be compulsory.

compulsory *adj.* required by the rules, law, etc; obligatory. [from Latin *compulsorius*]

compulsory purchase the purchase, against the will of the owner, of property or land needed for some public project, etc by a local authority.

compunction *noun* a feeling of guilt, remorse or regret; scruples or misgivings. [from Latin *compungere*, to puncture]

computable *adj.* able to be computed or calculated.

computation *noun* the process or art, or a system, of calculating or computing; a result calculated or computed.

computational *adj.* **1** involving calculation. **2** involving computer processes.

computational linguistics the application and development of techniques and concepts, used in statistics and computer science, to the analysis of language. Fields of interest include the development of computer models of language structure and interaction as part of research into artificial intelligence, the use of computers in speech analysis and synthesis, automatic ('machine') translation, and information retrieval.

computationally *adv.* by means of computer processes; with computers.

compute *verb trans., intrans.* to calculate, estimate or reckon, with or without the help of a computer. [from Latin *computare*, to reckon]

computer *noun* an electronic device that is capable of accepting data, processing it at great speed according to a set of instructions (a program) stored within the device, and presenting the results.
◊ The term computer usually refers to a *digital computer*, which manipulates data coded in the form of binary numbers. *Analogue computers*, in which data is stored and processed in the form of continually varying signals, are used for scientific research, quality control in manufacturing, etc.
A typical digital computer has a central processing unit (CPU) which performs operations on the data according to the instructions specified by a program. Data is supplied to the computer via an *input device*, usually a keyboard, mouse, disk drive, or tape drive, or a joystick (often used for computer games). The processed data is displayed to the user via an *output device*, usually either a visual-display unit (VDU), or a printer which provides information on paper (known as *hard copy*). Data and programs are stored in *computer memory*.
Computers range in size from hand-held electronic organizers, laptop computers, and microcomputers designed for use by one person in homes, schools, small businesses, etc, to large mainframe computers which may be used by several hundred people simultaneously, eg in universities, national companies, and governmental departments. The largest computers, known as *supercomputers*, are used for weather forecasting and other complex scientific tasks.
All computer systems consist of *hardware* (electronic, electrical, magnetic, and mechanical components) and *software* (the programs used by the computer, including the *operating system* that controls all the main activities of the computer, as well as the running of other programs). Computers have a wide range of uses, such as data processing, word processing, information storage and retrieval, computer graphics, computer-aided design (CAD), computer-aided manufacture (CAM), robotics, scientific research, weather forecasting, aircraft simulators for training pilots, and computer games. They are also used as an educational tool in schools, and for training.

computer-aided design (ABBREV. **CAD**) the use of a computer system to create and edit design drawings, using an electronic 'drawing board' in the form of a computer screen, and incorporating many of the techniques of computer graphics. It is widely used in architecture, manufacturing, engineering (eg car design), and electronics.
◊ Computer-aided design enables the user to view designs from different angles, to test the effect of changes on an existing design, to incorporate components of diagrams that are stored in memory, and to test alternative designs by simulating them. Rough sketches made with a light pen or mouse can be converted into precise technical drawings, and the results can be plotted or printed out in the form of technical drawings or design specifications. Diagrams can also be saved in electronic form for incorporation in future designs.

computer art a type of art which began after 1945 when wartime analogue computers were adapted to make abstract drawings; for example, the work of the English artist and philosopher Desmond Paul Henry (1921–). Since the mid-1960s, modern digital computers have been used to produce paintings, drawing, and even sculpture. An artist may design programs, incorporating some randomizing element, with the results printed out by machine. Light and sound may be incorporated in the program, and frequently the artist intervenes during production of the image.

computer game *Comput.* a game on cassette or disk for playing on a home computer, the player manipulating moving images on the screen by pressing certain keys, or using a control pad or joystick.

computer generation any of five broad groups used to denote the different eras of technological development of digital computers.
◊ *First-generation* computers were the early devices, developed in the 1940s and 1950s, consisting of thermionic valves. From the early 1960s they were replaced by *second-generation* computers, built using transistors and printed circuits. In *third-generation* computers transistors were replaced by integrated circuits. *Fourth-generation* computers, still in use today, are built with very large integrated circuits, and are being used to design *fifth-generation* computers specifically for use in artificial intelligence. It is hoped that computers of this category will be capable of *parallel processing*, ie performing several actions simultaneously rather than in a sequence of steps, so that their speed of operation is greatly increased and they can be used with very powerful programming languages.

computer graphics the use of computers to display and manipulate information in graphical or pictorial form, either on a visual-display unit (VDU), or via a printer or plotter.
◊ In computer graphics, input is achieved by drawing with a mouse on a graphics tablet, by drawing directly on the screen with a light pen, or by using a scanner. Anything that can be drawn on paper can be drawn on the VDU screen, from a simple histogram to a three-dimensional engineering drawing, and from a complex colour map to an animated film sequence. The main advantage of computer graphics is that pictorial information can be manipulated almost instantly in ways that are impossible on paper, eg lines can be straightened, details expanded, and whole areas deleted.
Applications of computer graphics include desktop publishing (DTP), computer-aided design (CAD), image processing, flight simulators, engineering, meteorology, medicine, molecular modelling, and computer games.

computerization *or* **computerisation** *noun* the use or equipment of computer processes.

computerize *or* **computerise** *verb* to transfer (a procedure, operation, system, etc) to control by computer; to organize (information) by computer; to equip with computers.

computer language a defined set of numbers, symbols, or words that is used to write a computer program. It translates the user's instructions into the machine code that is used by the computer, and converts the coded responses of the computer back into a form that can be understood by the user.
◊ There are two main types of computer language. In *low-level languages* each instruction represents a single machine code operation, whereas in *high-level languages* each instruction is equivalent to several or many machine code instructions. High-level languages are written using notations that are relatively easily understood by the user, and programs written in such languages can be run on computers with different types of processor. Examples of high-level languages include BASIC, one of the most widely used computer languages in the world, FORTRAN, which is used for scientific work, and COBOL, which is used to write financial programs.

computer literacy the condition of being competent or fully versed in the use of computers.

computer memory the part of a computer system that stores programs and data, either temporarily or permanently, and is connected to the central processing unit (CPU) of the computer. Memory capacity is measured in bytes, kilobytes, or megabytes.
◇ Two basic types of *internal memory* (also known as *immediate access memory*) are used in digital computers. *Read-only memory (ROM)* stores the programs that control the operation of the computer, and cannot be altered. The information contained in ROM is not lost when the computer is switched off. *Random-access memory (RAM)* is used for storing (writing) data temporarily, and for obtaining (reading) data. Programs and data stored in RAM are lost when the computer is switched off, and for this reason when not in use they are held in *external memory* (also known as *backing storage*), which usually consists of a hard or floppy disk, a magnetic tape, or an optical disc (eg CD-ROM).

computer science the study of the development, operations, and applications of computers.

computer scientist a person who studies or is an expert in computer science.

comrade *noun* **1** a friend or companion; an associate, fellow worker, etc. **2** a fellow communist or socialist. [from Spanish *camarada*, the soldiers sharing a billet, a room-mate, from Latin *camera*, room]

comrade-in-arms *noun* a fellow soldier or campaigner.

comradely *adj.* like a comrade.

comradeship *noun* **1** friendship, camaraderie. **2** the state or position of a comrade.

COMSAT *or* **comsat** *abbrev. North Amer.* Communications Satellite.

Comte, Auguste (1798–1857) French philosopher and sociologist, and pioneer of Positivism, born in Montpellier. His lectures on positivist philosophy (*Cours de Philosophie positive*) were published in six volumes (1830–42). In his philosophy, he argues that there are three stages of intellectual and scientific development: theological, metaphysical, and positive or experiential. Sociology (a term he coined) is seen as the most important of the theoretical sciences.

con¹ *colloq.* — *noun* a confidence trick; a deception, trick, or bluff. — *verb* (**conned, conning**) to swindle or trick (someone), especially after winning their trust.

con² *verb trans., intrans.* (**conned, conning**) *old use* to read over and learn by heart. [from CAN¹]

con³ *verb* (**conned, conning**) *Naut.* to direct the steering of (a ship). [earlier *cond*, from French *conduire*, to conduct]

con- *or* **col-** *or* **com-** *or* **cor-** *prefix, found usually in words derived from Latin* with or together; sometimes used with emphatic or intensifying effect. [from Latin *com-*, form of *cum*, with]

Conakry POP (1983) 705 000, the seaport capital of Guinea, on Tumbo I, 710km/441mi SE of Dakar (Senegal). It is linked to the mainland by a causeway. The city was established in 1889.

conc. *abbrev.* concentrated.

concatenate *verb* to link up into a connected series. [from Latin *con-*, with + *catena*, chain]

concatenation *noun* a series of things, eg events, each linked to the one before in chain-like fashion.

concave *adj., said of a surface or shape* inward-curving, like the inside of a bowl. See also CONVEX. [from Latin *concavus*, vaulted, from *cavus*, hollow]

concavity *noun* (PL. **concavities**) **1** the quality of being concave. **2** a hollow.

conceal *verb* **1** to hide; to place out of sight. **2** to keep secret. [from Latin *concelare*]

concealment *noun* **1** keeping secret or hidden; secrecy. **2** a hiding place.

concede *verb* **1** to admit to be true or correct. **2** to give or grant. **3** to yield or give up. **4** to admit defeat in (a contest) before, or without continuing to, the end.
— **concede defeat** to admit that one is beaten. [from Latin *concedere*, from, to yield]

conceit *noun* **1** too good an opinion of oneself; vanity. **2** *old use* a witty, fanciful, or ingenious thought or idea. [from CONCEIVE]

conceited *adj.* having too good an opinion of oneself.

conceitedly *adv.* with a conceited manner.

conceivability *noun* a conceivable quality or state.

conceivable *adj.* imaginable; possible: *try every conceivable method.*

conceivably *adv.* possibly; perhaps.

conceive *verb* **1** *trans., intrans.* to become pregnant; to begin to form (a baby). **2** to form (an idea, etc). **3** *trans., intrans.* (**conceive of something**) to think of or imagine an idea, etc. [from French *concever*, from Latin *concipere*, to conceive or perceive]

concentrate — *verb* **1** (**concentrate on something** *or* **someone**) to give all one's attention and energy to them. **2** to focus: *concentrate our efforts.* **3** *trans., intrans.* to bring or come together in one place. **4** *Chem.* to increase the amount of a dissolved substance in a solution, either by adding more of it, or by evaporating the solvent in which it is dissolved. **5** *Chem.* to make a chemical substance denser or purer. — *noun* a concentrated liquid. [from Latin *con-*, together + *centrum*, centre]

concentrated *adj.* **1** attentive, focussed. **2** contracted. **3** condensed, compressed.

concentration *noun* **1** intensive mental effort. **2** the act of concentration, or state of being concentrated. **3** the proportion in which a substance is present in a solution, etc. **4** a concentrate.

concentration camp a prison camp for civilians who are not tolerated by the authorities.

concentric *adj. Geom.* denoting two or more circles of different sizes but with a common centre, or two or more cylinders with a common axis. [from Latin *con-*, same + *centrum*, centre]

concentrically *adv.* in a concentric way.

concentricity *noun* the quality of being concentric.

Concepción POP (1991e) 312 000, the industrial capital of Concepción province, central Chile. It lies 15km/9mi up the R Bío-Bo and is the third largest city in the country. Concepción was founded in 1550. It is often damaged by earthquakes. NOTABLE FEATURE Cerro Caracol to the SE, with major views at Mirador Chileno and Mirador Alemán.

concept *noun* a notion; an abstract or general idea. [from Latin *conceptum*]

conception *noun* **1** an idea or notion. **2** the origin or start of something, especially something intricate. **3** the act of conceiving. **4** *Biol.* the fertilization of an ovum (egg cell) by a sperm, representing the start of pregnancy. [from Latin, from *concipere*, to conceive]

conceptual *adj.* relating to or existing as concepts or conceptions.

Conceptual Art a movement dating from the 1960s, in which the artist, instead of producing a physical object (eg a painted canvas) presents ideas, often in the form of eg a written text, a map, or a sound cassette.

conceptualism *noun Philos.* any theory of universals (ie general terms and abstract objects, such as qualities, relations, and numbers) that maintains that these are formed and constructed in the mind, and therefore exist only in the mind. For example, there are many things in nature that are red, but redness is a concept that has no independent existence outside the mind.

conceptualization *or* **conceptualisation** *noun* **1** the process of conceptualizing. **2** something that is conceptualized.

conceptualize *or* **conceptualise** *verb* to form a concept of.

conceptually *adv.* in a conceptual way; as a concept.

concern — *verb* **1** to have to do with; to be about: *it concerns your son.* **2** (*often* **be concerned about something** *or* **someone**) to worry, bother, or interest. **3** to affect; to involve: *a perfectionist where food is concerned.* — *noun* **1** a worry, or a cause of worry. **b** interest, or a subject of interest. **2** one's business or responsibility: *no concern of yours.* **3** an organization; a company or business. [from Latin *concernere*, to distinguish or relate to]

concerned *adj.* worried.
— **concerned with something** *or* **someone** having to do with them; involving them.

concernedly *adv.* with a concerned manner.

concernedness *noun* the quality of being concerned.

concerning *prep.* about; regarding.

concernment *noun* concern.

concert — *noun* (with stress on *con-*) a musical performance given before an audience by singers or players. — *verb* (with stress on *-cert*) to endeavour or plan by arrangement.
— **in concert 1** jointly; in co-operation. **2** *said of singers, etc* in a live performance.
[from French *concert*, from Italian *concerto*, from *concertare*, to organize]

concerted *adj.* (with stress on *-cert-*) planned and carried out jointly.

Concertgebouw Orchestra a Dutch orchestra, founded (1888) in Amsterdam at the opening of the concert hall of that name. Its first conductor, Willem Kes (1856–1934), was succeeded by Willem Mengelburg (1871–1951), under whom the orchestra saw international fame (1895–1945). The present conductor (since 1988) is the Italian Riccardo Chailly (1953–   ).

concertina — *noun* a musical instrument like a small accordion. — *verb intrans., trans.* (**concertinaed, concertinaing**) to fold or collapse like a concertina. [made up by inventor]

concertino *noun* (PL. **concertinos**) **1** a musical work for solo instrument(s) and orchestra, shorter than a concerto and usually with lighter accompaniment. **2** the passages in a concerto grosso for solo instrument(s), typically for two violins and a cello.

concerto *noun* (PL. **concertos, concerti**) a musical composition for one or more solo instruments and orchestra. [from Italian *concerto*, from *concertare*, to organize]

concerto grosso (PL. **concerti grossi**) **1** an orchestral work, usually in four or more movements, with passages for solo instruments (*concertino*) alternating with the full body of the orchestra (*ripieno*). The Baroque model of the concerto grosso employed by composers such as Bach, Corelli, and Handel has been revived in the 20c, eg by Ernest Bloch (1880–1959). **2** the main body of instruments in an orchestral work of this kind. [Italian, = large concerto]

concert pitch *noun Mus.* the standard pitch that instruments are tuned to for concert performances.

concession *noun* **1** the act of conceding. **2** something conceded or allowed. **3** the right, granted under government licence, to extract minerals, etc in an area; the right to conduct a business from within a larger concern. **4** a reduction in price, fare, etc for categories such as students, the elderly, the disabled, the unemployed. [from Latin *concessio*, yielding]

concessionaire *noun* the holder of a mining or trading concession.

concessionary *adj.* involving or obtained by a concession, especially a reduction in price: *concessionary fares for students.*

concessive *adj. Grammar* expressing concession, especially by means of words such as *although, though,* and *even if.* [from Latin *concessivus*]

conch *noun* **1** a large spiral shell of any of several similar shellfish. **2** a shellfish having such a shell. [from Greek *konche*]

conchologist *noun* a person who collects or studies shells.

conchology *noun* the study of shells and shellfish.

conciliate *verb* **1** to win over; to overcome the hostility of; to placate. **2** to reconcile (people in dispute, etc). [from Latin *conciliare*, to unite in friendship]

conciliation *noun* the act or process of conciliating.

conciliator *noun* a person who tries to bring about conciliation.

conciliatory *adj.* intended to conciliate: *conciliatory remarks.*

concise *adj.* brief, but covering essential points. [from Latin *concisus*, cut short]

concisely *adv.* in a concise way; briefly.

concision or **conciseness** *noun, said especially of writing* the quality of being concise or brief.

conclave *noun* **1** a private or secret meeting. **2** in the RC Church, the body of cardinals gathered to elect a new pope; their meeting-place. [from Latin *conclave*, a room that can be locked, from *clavis*, key]

conclude *verb* **1** *trans., intrans.* to come or bring to an end. **2** to reach an opinion based on reasoning. **3** to settle or arrange: *conclude a treaty with a neighbour state.* [from Latin *concludere*, from *claudere*, to close]

conclusion *noun* **1** an end. **2** a reasoned judgement; an opinion based on reasoning: *come to / draw a conclusion.* **3** settling of terms, an agreement, etc.
— **in conclusion** finally; lastly.
jump to conclusions to presume something with inadequate evidence.
[from Latin *conclusio*, from *concludere*, to end]

conclusive *adj., said of evidence, proof, etc* decisive, convincing; leaving no room for doubt. [from Latin *conclusivus*]

conclusively *adv.* decisively, convincingly.

conclusiveness *noun* being conclusive or decisive.

concoct *verb* **1** to make, especially ingeniously from a variety of ingredients. **2** to invent (a story, excuse, etc). [from Latin *concoctus*, cooked together]

concoction *noun* **1** the act of concocting. **2** something that is concocted.

concomitant — *adj.* accompanying: *fever with concomitant headache, sore throat, etc.* — *noun* something that is concomitant. [from Latin *concomitare*, to accompany]

concomitantly *adv.* in a concomitant way.

Concord POP (1990) 36 000, the capital of the state of New Hampshire, USA, situated in Merrimack County, S New Hampshire. It lies on the Merrimack R, 24km/15mi N of Manchester.

HISTORY established in 1727; became a city in 1853 and state capital in 1808. Mary Baker Eddy, founder of the Christian Scientists, lived here.

Concord POP (1984e) 17 000, a town in Middlesex County, E Massachusetts, USA. It lies on the R Concord, 30km/19mi NW of Boston. HISTORY settled in 1635; in April 1775 British soldiers attempted to seize military stores in Concord but were resisted by minutemen; the resulting battles at Concord and Lexington marked the start of the American War of Independence. Concord was the home of the writers Alcott, Emerson, Hawthorne, and Thoreau.

concord *noun* **1** agreement; peace or harmony. **2** *Grammar* agreement between words, especially in number and gender, eg between verb and subject. **3** *Mus.* a chord with a harmonious sound, the opposite of a *discord.* **4** a treaty; a pact. [from Latin *concordia*, agreement]

concordance *noun* **1** a state of harmony. **2** an alphabetical index of words used by an author or in a book, giving the reference and usually meaning. [from Latin *concordantia*, from Latin *concordare*, to agree]

concordant *adj.* harmonious, united.

concordat *noun* an agreement, especially between church and state. [from French *concordat*, from Latin *concordare*, to agree]

Concorde the world's first (and only remaining) supersonic airliner, built jointly by the British Aircraft Corporation and the French company, Aérospatiale. It entered full-time operational service in Jan 1976. Its maximum speed is 2.2 times the speed of sound, though normal cruising speed is reduced to twice the speed of sound (Mach 2, 1 920kph/1 200mph).

concourse *noun* **1** a large open area for people, in a railway station, airport, etc. **2** a throng; a gathering. [from French *concours*, from Latin *concursus*, assembly]

concrete — *noun* a building material consisting of cement, sand, and gravel mixed with water, which forms a hard rock-like mass when allowed to dry. — *adj.* **1** relating to such a material. **2** able to be felt, touched, seen, etc, as opposed to abstract: *concrete objects.* **3** definite or positive, as opposed to vague or general: *concrete evidence.* **4** *Grammar, said of a noun* denoting a physical thing rather than a quality, condition, or action. **5** *said of music* produced from sounds and music already recorded. **6** *said of poetry* relying partly for its effect on the physical arrangement of words on the page. — *verb* **1** to cover with or embed in concrete. **2** *trans., intrans.* to solidify. [from Latin *concretus*, from *con-*, together + *crescere*, to grow]

concrete art a term applied from c.1930 to various styles of non-figurative art in which the picture is constructed from geometrical forms and simple planes. Theo van Doesburg (1883–1931), and Max Bill (1908–) suggested the term as an alternative to abstract art, and it is synonymous with Constructivism in its broadest sense.

concretely *adv.* in a concrete way.

concreteness *noun* being concrete; material existence.

concretion *noun* **1** *Medicine* a hard stony mass occurring in a body tissue or natural cavity. **2** *Geol.* a hard rounded nodule of mineral matter formed within the pores of a sedimentary or igneous rock as a result of precipitation of dissolved mineral salts. [from Latin *concretio*, from *con-*, together + *crescere*, to grow]

concubinage *noun* **1** the state of a man and a woman living together but not married to each other. **2** the status of a concubine.

concubine — *noun usually Hist.* a woman who lives with a man and has sexual intercourse with him, without being married to him. [from Latin *concubina*, from *con-*, together + *cumbere*, to lie]

concupiscence *noun* strong sexual desire. [from Latin *concupiscere*, to long for]

concupiscent *adj.* lustful.

concur *verb intrans.* (**concurred, concurring**) **1** to agree. **2** to happen at the same time; to coincide. [from Latin *con-*, together + *currere*, to run]

concurrence *noun* **1** agreement; consent. **2** the coinciding of events, etc.

concurrent *adj.* **1** running in parallel; happening or taking place simultaneously. **2** *said of lines* meeting or intersecting. **3** in agreement. [from Latin *con-*, together + *currere*, to run]

concurrently *adv.* so as to be concurrent; at the same time.

concuss *verb* to cause concussion in. [from Latin *concutere*, to shake together]

concussion *noun* **1** temporary injury to the brain caused by a blow or fall, usually producing unconsciousness. **2** violent shaking or jarring.

Condé, Louis I de Bourbon, Prince de (Prince of) (1530–69) leader of the Huguenots during the French Wars of Religion, born in Vendôme, the younger brother of Antony of Bourbon, King of Navarre. He fought in the wars between Henry II and Spain (1551–7), and joined the Huguenots on the accession of Francis II (1559). He was defeated at Dreux during the first civil war (1562), and in the second war (1567–9) was defeated at Jarnac.

Condé, Louis II de Bourbon, Prince de (Prince of), known as **the Great Condé** (1621–86) French military leader, born in Paris. During the Thirty Years War he defeated the Spaniards (1643, 1648) and Bavarians (1645–6). He was instrumental in helping the court party come to terms with the disturbances of The Fronde, but his arrogance led to his imprisonment, and on his release he joined the rebels. Defeated at the battle of the Dunes, near Dunkirk (1658), he was then pardoned. He became one of Louis XIV's greatest generals, and defeated the Spanish in Franche-Comté (1668) and William of Orange at Seneffe (1674).

Condé, House of the junior branch of the French royal line the House of Bourbon, which played a prominent role in French dynastic politics, particularly in the 16–17c. Ten generations bore the title of *Prince de Condé*, of whom the most eminent was Louis II de Bourbon, the *Great Condé.*

condemn *verb* **1** to declare to be wrong or evil. **2** to find guilty; to convict. **3** (**condemn someone to something**) **a** to sentence them to a punishment, especially death. **b** to be the cause of someone's disagreeable fate: *was condemned to a friendless existence by his own ill-temper.* **4** to betray the guilt of; to give away: *his obvious nervousness condemned him.* **5** to declare (a building) unfit to be used or lived in. **6** [from Latin *condemnare*, to condemn]

condemnation *noun* **1** the act of condemning. **2** the state of being condemned.

condemnatory *adj.* expressing or implying condemnation.

condensation *noun* **1** *Physics* the process whereby a gas or vapour turns into a liquid as a result of cooling. **2** *Chem.* a chemical reaction in which two or more small molecules combine to form a larger molecule, usually with the elimination of a molecule of water. **3** *Optics* in an optical instrument, the process of focusing a beam of light.

condensation reaction *Chem.* a reaction in which two or more relatively small molecules combine to form a larger one, with the elimination of a relatively simple byproduct, usually a molecule of water.

condense *verb* **1** to concentrate or compress; to make denser. **2** *trans., intrans.* to turn from gas or vapour to liquid or solid. **3** to express more briefly; to summarize. [from Latin *condensare*, to compress]

condensed milk milk thickened by evaporation and sweetened.

condenser *noun* **1** *Electr.* a capacitor. **2** *Chem.* an apparatus for changing a vapour into a liquid by cooling it and allowing it to condense. Condensers are standard equipment in chemistry laboratories, and are also built into steam engines, steam turbines, etc. **3** *Optics* in an optical instrument such as a microscope, a lens or series of lenses that is used to concentrate a light source.

condescend *verb intrans.* **1** to act in a gracious manner to those one considers one's inferior. **2** to be gracious enough to do something, especially as though it were a favour: *they condescended to meet us.* [from Latin *condescendere*, from *descendere*, to descend]

condescending *adj.* **1** gracious. **2** offensively patronizing.

condescendingly *adv.* with a condescending manner.

condescension *noun* **1** the action of being condescending. **2** condescending behaviour.

condign *adj., said of praise, reward, punishment, etc* well-deserved. [from Latin *condignus*, from *dignus*, worthy]

condiment *noun* a seasoning, eg salt, pepper, mustard, etc, used at table to give flavour to food. [from Latin *condimentum*]

condition — *noun* **1** a particular state. **2** a state of health, fitness, or suitability for use: *out of condition.* **3** an ailment or disorder: *a heart condition.* **4** (**conditions**) circumstances: *poor working conditions.* **5** a requirement or qualification: *a necessary condition for membership.* — *verb* (**conditioned**, **conditioning**) **1** to accustom or train to behave or react in a particular way; to influence. **2** to affect or control; to determine. **3** to get (an animal, one's hair, skin, etc) into good condition.
— **on condition that** ... only if: *will go on condition that you come too.*
on no condition absolutely not.
[from Latin *conditio*, from *condicere*, to agree]

conditional *adj.* (**conditional on something**) dependent on a particular condition, etc.

conditionally *adv.* in a conditional way; with conditions.

conditioned reflex *Physiol.* a type of reflex action in which the response occurs not to a *sensory stimulus*, such as hunger, but to a *neutral stimulus* that has become firmly associated by learning with the sensory stimulus, eg the sound of a bell which is linked to the imminent presence of food.

conditioner *noun* (*often in compounds*) a substance for improving the condition of something.

conditioning *noun* **1** the process of making or becoming conditioned. **2** *Psychol.* a reflex response to a stimulus which depends upon the former experience of the individual, and can be modified, eg by rewarding or punishing a particular response so that it comes to occur more or less frequently.

condole *verb intrans.* (**condole with someone**) to express one's sympathy to them. [from Latin *con-*, with + *dolere*, to grieve]

condolence *noun* (*often* **condolences**) sympathy, or an expression of sympathy: *offer one's condolences.*

condom *noun* a contraceptive device consisting of a thin rubber sheath worn on the penis during sexual intercourse, to prevent the release of sperm into the vagina and so avoid pregnancy, and to prevent the spread of disease.

condominium *noun* **1** *North Amer.* a block of individually owned apartments. **2** joint control

of a state by two or more other states. [from Latin *con-*, with + *dominium*, dominion, rule]

condonable *adj.* capable of being condoned.

condone *verb* to pardon or overlook (an offence or wrong). [from Latin *condonare*, to present, overlook]

condor *noun* either of two species of large American vulture, with the largest wingspan of any living bird (up to 3m). The Andean condor is still relatively common, but the Californian condor, which only lays one egg every other year, has been hunted almost to extinction. [from Spanish *cóndor*, from Quechua *kuntur*]

condor

Condorcet, Marie Jean Antoine Nicolas de Caritat, Marquis de (1743–94) French statesman, philosopher, and mathematician, born in Ribemont. At the Revolution he made eloquent speeches and wrote famous pamphlets on the popular side. He was sent to the Legislative Assembly (1791), and became its President, siding usually with the Girondists, but, condemned by the extreme party, he went into hiding. Later he was placed in jail and died on his first night of captivity. His work in mathematics had become highly regarded in the 1760s, and his philosophy embraced the ideal of progress and the indefinite perfectibility of the human race.

conduce *verb intrans.* (**conduce to something**) to help or tend towards a result, especially a desirable one. [from Latin *con-*, together + *ducere*, to lead]

conducive *adj.* (**conducive to something**) likely to achieve a desirable result.

conduct — *verb* (with stress on *-duct*) **1** to lead or guide. **2** to manage; to control: *conduct the firm's business.* **3** *trans., intrans.* to direct the performance of an orchestra or choir by movements of the hands or a baton. **4** to transmit (heat or electricity) by conduction: *metal conducts heat.* **5** to direct, channel, or convey: *hot air conducted through pipes.* **6** (**conduct oneself**) to behave in a specified way: *one should always conduct oneself with dignity.* — *noun* (with stress on *con-*) **1** behaviour. **2** the managing or organizing of something: *the conduct of the war.* [from Latin *conductus*, guide]

conductance *noun* the ability of a material to conduct heat or electricity. In a direct current circuit it is the reciprocal of resistance. The SI unit of conductance is the siemens. See also CONDUCTIVITY.

conduction *noun* the process by which heat or electricity is transmitted through a material, body, etc.

conductivity *noun* **1** (*in full* **electrical conductivity**) a measure of the ability of a material to conduct electricity. It is the reciprocal of resistivity. **2** (*in full* **thermal conductivity**) the ability of a material to conduct heat.

conductor *noun* **1** the director of a choir's or orchestra's performance. **2** a material, etc that conducts heat or electricity. **3** a person who collects the fares from passengers on a bus, etc.

conductress *noun* a woman who collects fares on a bus, etc.

conduit *noun* a channel, trough or pipe carrying water or electric cables. [from French *conduit*, from Latin *conductus*, channel]

cone — *noun* **1** *Geom.* a solid (three-dimensional) figure with a flat base in the shape of a circle or ellipse, and a curved upper surface that tapers to a fixed point (the *vertex*). A *right circular cone* has a circular base and its vertex is directly above the centre of the circle. The volume of such a cone is equal to $\frac{1}{3}\pi r^2 h$, where r is the radius of the base, h is the perpendicular height of the vertex above the base, and π is a constant with a value of approximately 3.142. **2** something similar to this in shape, eg a pointed holder for ice cream, made of wafer biscuit, or a plastic object used to mark off temporary lanes for traffic, etc. **3** *Anat.* one of the two types of light-sensitive receptor cell in the retina of the eye of vertebrates. Cones are specialized for the detection of colour, and function best in bright light. **4** *Bot.* the reproductive structure of gymnosperms, eg conifers and cycads, consisting of a central axis bearing many overlapping sporophylls (modified leaves resembling scales) that in turn bear the reproductive organs. Most gymnosperms produce separate male and female cones. — Also called *strobilus*. — *verb* (*usually* **cone something off**) to close off an area or part of a road with a line of traffic cones. [from Greek *konos*]

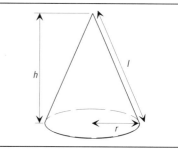

cone

Coney Island a resort on the S coast of Long Island in Brooklyn borough, New York State, USA, near the mouth of the Hudson R. It has been a pleasure resort since the 1840s. NOTABLE FEATURE New York Aquarium. [from Dutch *konijn*, rabbit]

confab *colloq.* — *noun* a confabulation. — *verb intrans.* (**confabbed**, **confabbing**) to confabulate.

confabulate *verb intrans. formal* to talk, discuss or confer. [from Latin *confabulari*, to converse]

confabulation *noun* a discussion.

confection *noun* **1** any sweet food, eg a cake, sweet, biscuit, pudding. **2** *old use, facetious* a fancy or elaborate garment, eg a hat. [from Latin *confectio*, making]

confectioner *noun* a person who makes or sells sweets or cakes.

confectionery *noun* **1** sweets, biscuits, and cakes. **2** the art or business of a confectioner.

confederacy *noun* (PL. **confederacies**) **1** a league or alliance of states. **2** (**the Confederacy**) *Hist.* the union of 11 southern states that seceded from the USA in 1860–1, so causing the American Civil War. They were Virginia, North Carolina, South Carolina, Georgia, Florida, Tennessee, Alabama, Mississippi, Louisiana, Texas, and Arkansas. **3** a conspiracy; an association formed for illegal purposes. [from Latin *confoederatio*, league]

confederate — *noun* (pronounced *-rət*) **1** a member of a confederacy. **2** a friend or an ally; an accomplice or a fellow conspirator. **3** (**Confederate**) *Hist.* a supporter of the Confederacy of American states that seceded in 1860–1. — *adj.* (pronounced *-rət*) **1** allied; united. **2** (**Confederate**) *Hist.* belonging to the Confederacy. — *verb* (pronounced *-rate*) to unite into a confederacy. [from Latin *confoederatus*, united in a league]

Confederate States of America the official name of the states that seceded in 1860–1, precipitating the American Civil War: Virginia, North Carolina, South Carolina, Georgia, Florida, Tennessee, Alabama, Mississippi, Louisiana, Texas, and Arkansas. The Confederacy's constitution was modelled on the US Constitution. Its only president was Jefferson Davis of Mississippi. It never won foreign recognition, and collapsed after military defeat by the North in 1865. The other four slave states (Delaware, Maryland, Kentucky, and Missouri) and the NW counties of Virginia (later West Virginia) did not secede.

confederation *noun* **1** the uniting of states into a league. **2** the league so formed.

Confédération Générale du Travail (ABBREV. **CGT**) English **General Confederation of Labour** the largest labour trade union federation in France, formed in 1895, with over 2m members, mainly representing production and blue-collar workers. The other French federations are the *Confédération Française Démocratique du Travail*, established in 1919, historically associated with the Church, and drawing most of its members from the private sector of the economy; the *Confédération Générale des Cadres* (CGC), set up in 1944, renamed in 1979, consisting mainly of white-collar workers; and the *CGT-Force Ouvrière* (CGT-FO) ('Workers' Force), consisting mainly of civil servants and clerical workers, which was formed in 1948 when it broke away from CGT.

Confederation of British Industry see CBI.

confer *verb* (**conferred, conferring**) **1** *intrans.* to consult. **2** (**confer something on someone**) to grant them an honour or distinction. [from Latin *con-*, together + *ferre*, to bring]

conference *noun* **1** a formally organized gathering for the discussion of matters of common interest or concern. **2** consultation; the formal exchanging of views: *in conference with the Prime Minister.* **3** an assembly of representatives of an association, church denomination, etc. [from Latin *conferentia*, from *con-*, together + *ferre*, to bring]

conferencing *noun* the practice of holding a business conference in which the participants are linked by telephone, video equipment, and/or computer.

conferment *noun* the bestowing of honours.

confess *verb* **1** *trans., intrans.* to own up to (a fault, wrongdoing, etc); to admit (a disagreeable fact, etc) reluctantly. **2** *trans., intrans.* to recount (one's sins) to a priest, in order to gain absolution. **3** *said of a priest* to hear the confession of (someone). [from Latin *confiteri*, to admit]

confessed *adj.* having openly admitted a weakness: *a confessed alcoholic.*

confessedly *adv.* admittedly, avowedly.

Confessing Church a Church formed in Germany by evangelical Christians opposed to Nazism and the Nazi-supported 'German Christian Church Movement'. Its Synod of Barmen published the *Barmen Declaration* (1934), which became influential in Germany and beyond as a basis for resistance to oppressive civil authorities. In 1948 it was succeeded by the Evangelical Church in Germany.

confession *noun* **1** the admission of a sin, fault, crime, distasteful or shocking fact, etc.

2 the formal act of confessing one's sins to a priest. **3** a declaration of one's religious faith or principles: *a confession of faith.* **4** a religious body with its own creed or set of beliefs.

confessional *noun* the small enclosed stall in a church where a priest sits when hearing confessions.

confessor *noun* **1** a priest, especially one to whom members of the church go regularly, who hears confessions and gives spiritual advice. **2** *Hist.* a person whose holy life serves as a demonstration of his or her religious faith: *Edward the Confessor.* [from Latin *confessor*, martyr, witness]

confetti *noun* tiny pieces of coloured paper traditionally thrown at the bride and groom by wedding guests. [from Italian, plural of *confetto*, sweetmeat]

confidant *or* **confidante** *noun* respectively a male or female friend with whom one discusses personal matters. [from French *confident(e)*, from Latin *confidere*, to trust]

confide *verb intrans., trans.* **1** (**confide in someone**) to speak freely with them about personal matters. **2** to tell (a secret, etc) to someone. **3** to entrust to someone's care. [from Latin *confidere*, to trust]

confidence *noun* **1** trust in, or reliance on, a person or thing. **2** faith in one's own ability; self-assurance. **3** a secret, etc confided to someone. **4** a relationship of mutual trust: *took her into his confidence.*
— **in confidence** in secret; confidentially. [from Latin *confidentia*]

confidence interval *Maths.* in statistical analyses, an interval that can with reasonable confidence be expected to contain the true value of an unknown parameter.

confidence trick *noun* a form of swindle in which the swindler first wins the trust of the victim.

confidence trickster a swindler.

confident *adj.* **1** certain; sure: *confident of success.* **2** self-assured.

confidential *adj.* **1** secret; not to be divulged: *confidential information.* **2** trusted with private matters: *a confidential secretary.* **3** used for privacy's sake: *a confidential whisper.* [from Latin *confidentia*, confidence]

confidentiality *noun* a confidential quality or requirement.

confidentially *adv.* in a confidential way; in confidence.

confiding *adj.* trustful; not suspicious.

confidingly *adv.* with a confiding manner.

configuration *noun* **1** the positioning or distribution of the parts of something relative to each other. **2** an outline or external shape. **3** *Physics* the arrangement of atoms in a molecule, or the arrangement of electrons in orbitals around the nucleus of an atom. [from Latin *configurare*, to form, fashion]

confine *verb* (with stress on *-fine*) **1** to restrict; to limit: *shall confine my remarks to the main points.* **2** to prevent the spread of (eg a fire). **3** to keep prisoner or keep from moving. **4** *old use* to keep (a woman about to give birth) indoors or in bed. [from Latin *confinis*, border]

confined *adj.* narrow; restricted.

confinement *noun* **1** the state of being shut up or kept in an enclosed space. **2** the period surrounding childbirth: *her fourth confinement.*

confines *pl. noun* (with stress on *con-*) limits; boundaries; restrictions.

confirm *verb* **1** to provide support for the truth or validity of (something): *refused to confirm or deny the rumour.* **2** to finalize or make definite (a booking, arrangement etc). **3** (**confirm someone in**

an opinion, etc) to make them more convinced about it: *I was confirmed in my suspicion that he was cheating us.* **4** to give formal approval to; to establish officially: *confirm someone in his appointment.* **5** to accept (someone) formally into full membership of the Christian Church. [from Latin *confirmare*]

confirmation *noun* **1** the act of confirming. **2** proof or support. **3** finalization. **4** the religious ceremony in which a person is admitted to full membership of the church.

confirmatory *adj.* **1** giving additional support to an argument, etc. **2** confirming.

confirmed *adj.* so settled into the state or condition mentioned as to be unlikely to change.

confiscate *verb* to take away (something) from someone, as a penalty. [from Latin *confiscare*, to transfer to the state treasury]

confiscation *noun* the act of confiscating.

conflagration *noun* a fierce and destructive blaze. [from Latin *conflagrare*]

conflate *verb* to blend or combine (eg two different versions of a text, story, etc) into a single whole. [from Latin *conflare*, to smelt or fuse]

conflation *noun* **1** the act of conflating. **2** a fusion or combination.

conflict — *noun* (with stress on *con-*) **1** disagreement; fierce argument; a quarrel. **2** a clash between different aims, interests, ideas, etc. **3** a struggle, fight, battle, or war. — *verb intrans.* (with stress on *-flict*) to be incompatible or in opposition: *the demands of a career often conflict with those of family life.* [from Latin *confligere*, to dash together, clash]

conflict theory *Sociol.* the theory that conflict and social division are inevitable in all social structures because the mechanisms by which society integrates and exercises control over its members are never wholly successful.

confluence *noun* the place where one river flows into another *con-*. [from Latin *con-*, together + *fluere*, to flow]

confluent *adj.* **1** flowing together. **2** running into one. **3** uniting.

conform *verb intrans.* **1** to behave, dress, etc in obedience to some standard considered normal by the majority. **2** (**conform to something**) to obey rules, etc; to meet or comply with standards, etc. **3** (**conform to or with something**) to be in agreement with it; to match or correspond to it. [from Latin *conformare*, to shape]

conformable *adj.* **1** corresponding or matching. **2** compliant; agreeable. **3** *Geol.*, *said of rock layers* still lying as originally laid down.

conformation *noun* a shape, structure or arrangement.

conformist *noun* a person who conforms to the norm, obeys rules, does the expected thing, etc.

conformity *noun* **1** obedience to rules, normal standards, etc. **2** accordance; compliance: *in conformity with safety standards.*

confound *verb* **1** to puzzle; to baffle. **2** to defeat or thwart (one's enemies or their schemes). **3** to mix up or confuse (one thing with another). **4** as an exclamation of annoyance: *confound it!* [from Latin *confundere*, to pour together, throw into disorder, overthrow]

confounded *adj.* used to indicate annoyance: *a confounded nuisance.*

confoundedly *adv.* **1** *colloq.* hatefully, shamefully. **2** cursedly.

confrère *noun* a fellow member of one's profession, etc; a colleague. [from Old French *confrère*, from Latin *con-*, with + *frater*, brother]

confront *verb* **1** to face, especially defiantly or accusingly: *he confronted his accusers.* **2** to prepare to deal firmly with: *confront the problem.* **3** (**con-**

front someone with something) to bring them face to face with a damning or revealing circumstance: *decided to confront him with his error.* **4** *said of an unpleasant prospect* to present itself to (someone): *certain death confronted them.* [from Latin *confrontari*, from *frons*, forehead, brow]

confrontation *noun* an act of confronting; a hostile meeting or exchange of words.

Confucian — *noun* a follower or supporter of Confucianism. — *adj.* of or belonging to Confucianism.

Confucianism the teachings of the Chinese philosopher Confucius (551–479 BC), with emphasis on morality, consideration for others, obedience, and good education.
◇ It has two ethical strands: one, associated with Confucius and Hsün Tzu (c.298–238 BC), is based on convention; we ought to follow traditional codes of behaviour for their own sake. The other, associated with Mencius and the medieval Neo-Confucians, is based on intuition; we ought to do as our moral natures dictate.

Confucianist *noun* a follower of Confucius.

Confucius, Latin for **K'ung Fu-tse, 'the Master K'ung'** (551–479 BC) Chinese philosopher, born in the state of Lu (modern Shantung). He became a teacher in 531 BC, and in 501 BC was appointed Governor of Chung-tu, then Minister of Works, and later Minister of Justice. His ideas for social reform were popular with the people, but his enemies caused him to leave Lu, and he travelled widely. The *Confucian Analects*, memorabilia compiled soon after his death, are a collection of his sayings and doings.

confuse *verb* **1** to put into a muddle or mess. **2** (**confuse one thing with another, or several things**) to fail to distinguish; to mix up: *confuse 'ascetic' with 'aesthetic' / tended to confuse the different brands.* **3** to puzzle, bewilder, or muddle. **4** to complicate. **5** to embarrass. [from Latin *confundere*, to mix]

confused *adj.* **1** perplexed, muddled. **2** disordered. **3** embarrassed.

confusedly *adv.* in a confused way.

confusing *adj.* causing confusion.

confusingly *adv.* in a confusing way.

confusion *noun* **1** the act of confusing or state of being confused. **2** disorder; muddle. **3** mental bewilderment. [from Latin *confusio*, from *confundere*, to mix]

confutation *noun* **1** the action of confuting. **2** something that confutes a person or theory etc.

confute *verb* to prove (a person) wrong, or (a theory, etc) false. [from Latin *confutare*, to pour cold water on]

conga — *noun* **1** an originally Cuban dance performed in single file, with three steps followed by a kick. **2** a large drum beaten with the fingers. — *verb intrans.* (**congaed, congaing**) to dance the conga. [from Spanish *conga*]

congé *noun* **1** permission to depart. **2** abrupt dismissal. [from French *congé*]

congeal *verb trans., intrans., said of liquid* to thicken, coagulate or solidify, especially through cooling. [from Latin *congelare*, to freeze completely]

congealment or **congelation** *noun* **1** the act or process of congealing. **2** anything congealed.

congener *noun* a plant or animal that is a member of the same genus as another plant or animal. [from Latin *con-*, same + *genus*, kind]

congenial *adj.* **1** companionable; having a personality and interests that fit well with one's own. **2** pleasant or agreeable. [from Latin *con-*, same + *genius*, spirit]

congeniality *noun* being congenial.

congenially *adv.* with a congenial manner.

congenital *adj.* **1** *said of bodily and mental disorders* present since birth. **2** affected since birth by a particular condition: *a congenital idiot.* [from Latin *con-*, with + *gignere*, to give birth to]

congenitally *adv.* from birth.

conger *noun* (*also* **conger eel**) a large sea eel. [from Latin *conger*, from Greek *gongros*]

congeries *noun* (PL. **congeries**) a miscellaneous accumulation; a confused heap. [from Latin *congeries*, heap]

congested *adj.* **1** crowded; too full; obstructed. **2** *Pathol., said of a part of the body* over-full of blood. **3** *said of the nose or air passages* obstructed with mucus. [from Latin *congerere*, to heap together]

congestion *noun* **1** an overcrowded condition. **2** an accumulation of blood, lymph, or mucus in a part of the body. **3** fullness.

conglomerate — *noun* (pronounced *-rət*) **1** a mass formed from things of different kinds. **2** *Geol.* a sedimentary rock consisting of small rounded pebbles embedded in a matrix of sand, silt, or some other fine-textured material. **3** a business group composed of a large number of firms merged together. — *adj.* (pronounced *-rət*) composed of things of different kinds formed into a mass. — *verb intrans.* (pronounced *-rate*) to accumulate to form a mass. [from Latin *con-*, together + *glomus*, ball of yarn]

conglomeration *noun* **1** the state of being conglomerated. **2** a collection or jumble of things.

Congo, official name **The Republic of the Congo**, formerly **People's Republic of the Congo** POP (1992e) 2.4m, a W central African republic, divided into nine provinces. AREA 341 945sq km/131 990sq mi. It is bounded W by Gabon, NW by Cameroon, N by the Central African Republic, E and S by Zaire, and SW by the Atlantic Ocean. It encloses the Angolan province of Cabinda, apart from its coast. CAPITAL Brazzaville. CHIEF TOWNS Pointe-Noire (port), Loubomo, Nkayi. TIME ZONE GMT +1. There are c.15 main ethnic groups, notably the Kongo (48%), Sangha (20%), M'Bochi (12%), and Téké (17%); Christianity and local beliefs are the main religions. OFFICIAL LANGUAGE French. CURRENCY the franc CFA. PHYSICAL DESCRIPTION a short Atlantic coastline fringing a broad mangrove plain that rises inland to a ridge of mountains reaching 900m; the inland mountain ridge is deeply cut by the R Congo flowing SW to the coast; beyond this ridge, the Niari Valley rises up through terraced hills to reach 1 040m at Mont de la Lékéti on the Gabon frontier; mainly covered by dense grassland, mangrove, and forest; several rivers flow E and S to meet the Oubangui and Congo rivers, which form the E and S borders. CLIMATE hot, humid, equatorial climate; annual rainfall is 1 250–1 750mm, decreasing near the Atlantic coast and in the S; temperatures vary little, with average daily maximum temperatures at Brazzaville 28–33°C; the dry season is Jun–Sep. HISTORY discovered by the Portuguese in the 14c; the French established a colonial presence in the 19c; became part of French Equatorial Africa, known as the 'Middle Congo', in 1908 until 1958; gained independence as the Republic of Congo in 1960; a military coup created the first Marxist state in Africa, renaming the country the People's Republic of the Congo in 1968; Marxism was renounced in 1990 and opposition parties were permitted; fighting between ethnic and political groups followed the disputed election results of 1993. GOVERNMENT a President appoints a Prime Minister and Cabinet; legislative power is held by a bicameral Parliament consisting of a National Assembly of 125 members and a Senate of 60 members. ECONOMY based on agriculture and forestry; the main cash crops are sugar cane, coffee, cocoa, palm oil, tobacco, groundnuts; the main subsistence crops are manioc, rice, yams, potatoes, maize, bananas; oil; timber; diamonds;

Congo

lead; zinc; gold; potash; cement; oil refining; timber processing; brewing; sugar refining; soap.

Congo, River see ZAIRE, RIVER.

Congonhas a town in the Brazilian highlands, noted for its 18c sanctuary of Bom ('good') Jesus, a church with chapels and gardens. The sanctuary, which contains Antonio Francisco Lisboa's (1738–1814) sculptures of the 12 Apostles, is a major centre of pilgrimage. It is a World Heritage site.

congrats *pl. noun* (*often as an exclamation*) *colloq.* congratulations.

congratulate *verb* (**congratulate someone on something**) **1** to express one's pleasure to someone at their success, good fortune, happiness, etc. **2** to consider (oneself) lucky or clever to have managed something: *congratulated herself on her narrow escape.* [from Latin *congratulari*, to wish one another joy]

congratulation *noun* **1** the action or an expression of congratulating. **2** (*also* **congratulations**) (*often as an exclamation*) an expression used to congratulate someone.

congratulatory *adj.* expressing congratulations.

congregate *verb trans., intrans.* to gather together into a crowd. [from Latin *congregare*, from *grex*, herd]

congregation *noun* **1** a gathering or assembly of people, especially for worship in church. **2** the people regularly attending a particular church.

congregational *adj.* **1** relating to or administered by a congregation or separate congregations. **2** (**Congregational**) belonging to a Protestant denomination in which the affairs of each individual church are run by its own congregation.

Congregationalism a movement which sees the Christian Church as essentially a gathered community of believers, covenanting with God, keeping God's law, and living under the Lordship of Christ. It derived from the Separatists of the 16c Reformation in England, of whom Robert Browne was an early leader, but persecution drove its followers to Holland and the USA (the Pilgrim Fathers, 1620). Church affairs, including calling a minister and appointing deacons, are regulated by members at a 'church meeting'. As a world denomination, it has a strong missionary tradition. One denomination formed (1949) the International Congregational Council, which merged with Presbyterians as the World Alliance of Reformed Churches (1970). It has a strong tradition of tolerance and freedom of belief, and has contributed to ecumenism by insisting on the importance of the local church in the event of union with other denominations.

Congregationalist *noun* a member of a Congregational Church.

congress 1 a large, especially international assembly of delegates, gathered for discussion. **2** a name used for the law-making body in some countries, especially (**Congress**) that of the US. [from Latin *congredi*, to meet]

congressional *adj.* relating or belonging to a congress.

Congress Kingdom of Poland the name of that part of Poland given to Russia at the Congress of Vienna (1815). Tsar Alexander I granted it a constitution which established it theoretically as a constitutional monarchy united to the Russian Empire. After the Polish uprising of 1830 the constitution was suspended, and after that of 1863 the kingdom was fully absorbed and subjected to a campaign of Russianization (the imposition of Russian culture and ways of life).

congressman *and* **congresswoman**. *noun* respectively a male and female member of a congress.

Congress of Racial Equality (ABBREV. **CORE**) a US civil rights organization, founded in 1942, which includes community issues and the registration of black voters in the South in its projects. In the 1960s CORE sponsored the freedom riders' challenge to segregation in interstate public transport.

Congreve, William (1670–1729) English dramatist and poet, born in Bardsey, Yorkshire. His first comedy, *The Old Bachelor*, was produced under John Dryden's auspices in 1693, and was highly successful, as were *Love for Love* (1695), *The Way of the World* (1700), and his one tragedy, *The Mourning Bride* (1697).

congruence *or* **congruency** *noun* **1** suitability or appropriateness. **2** agreement. **3** *Geom.* the quality of being congruent.

congruent *adj.* **1** *Geom.*, said of two or more figures identical in size and shape. **2** (**congruent with something**) suitable or appropriate to it. [from Latin *congruere*, to meet together]

congruently *adv.* in a congruent way.

congruity *noun* **1** agreement between things. **2** consistency. **3** suitability.

congruous *adj.* (**congruous with something**) fitting; suitable; proper. [from Latin *congruus*, from *congruere*, to meet together]

congruously *adv.* in a congruous way.

conic *adj.* *Geom.* relating to a cone. [from Greek *konikos*, from *konos*, cone]

conical *adj.* cone-shaped. [from Greek *konikos*, cone-shaped]

conic section *Geom.* the curved figure produced when a plane (flat surface) intersects a cone. Depending on the angle at which it cuts through the cone, it may be a circle, ellipse, hyperbola, or parabola.

conifer *noun* any of various mostly evergreen trees and shrubs that have narrow needle-like leaves and produce their pollen and seeds in cones, eg pine, spruce (Christmas tree), cedar, and yew. Conifers represent the majority of living gymnosperms (cone-bearing plants), and are found mainly in regions with cool climates. They grow relatively fast, and are widely planted as a source of softwood timber. [from Latin, *conus*, cone + *ferre*, to carry]

coniferous *adj.*, *said of trees* bearing cones.

Conisbrough POP (1981) 16 000, a coal-mining town in Doncaster borough, South Yorkshire, N England. It is situated 8km/5mi SW of Doncaster. NOTABLE FEATURE 12c Norman castle, the site of Sir Walter Scott's novel *Ivanhoe*.

Coniston Water a lake in the Lake District of Cumbria, NW England. It lies W of L Windermere and Grizedale Forest and is 9km/6mi long. The village of Coniston lies on the NW shore; on the E shore is Brantwood, former home of John Ruskin. The Old Man of Coniston rises to 802m in the W. Malcom Campbell broke the world water speed record on Consiton Water in 1939 and his son Donald Campbell was killed here in 1967 while attempting to break his own record.

conj. *abbrev. Grammar* conjunction.

conjectural *adj.*, *said of an argument, conclusion, etc* based on conjecture.

conjecturally *adv.* with conjecture.

conjecture — *noun* **1** an opinion based on incomplete evidence. **2** the process of forming such an opinion. — *verb intrans.* to make a conjecture. [from Latin *conjectura*, conclusion]

conjoin *verb trans., intrans.* to join together, combine, or unite. [from French *conjoindre*, to join together]

conjoint *adj.* joint; associated; united.

conjointly *adv.* in a united fashion.

conjugal *adj.* relating to marriage, or to the relationship between husband and wife. [from Latin *conjugalis*, from *con-*, together + *jugum*, yoke]

conjugal family the family of one's husband or wife.

conjugality *noun* the state or condition of being married.

conjugally *adv.* in a conjugal way.

conjugate — *verb trans., intrans.* (pronounced -*gate*) **1** *Grammar* **a** to give the inflected parts of (a verb), indicating number, person, tense, voice, and mood. **b** *intrans.* *said of a verb* to have inflected parts. **2** *Biol.* to reproduce by fusion of two cells, eg in protozoa, or by formation of a tube between two cells, eg in certain algae. — *adj.* (pronounced -*gət*) **1** joined, connected, or coupled. **2** *Chem.*, *said of an acid and base* related to each other such that the acid is converted into the base by losing a proton, and the base is converted into the acid by gaining a proton. **3** *Geom.* denoting a pair of angles whose sum is 360°. **4** *said of words* having a common origin. — *noun* (pronounced -*gət*) a conjugate word or thing. [from Latin *con-*, with + *jugum*, yoke]

conjugation *noun* **1** *Grammar* the inflection of a verb to indicate number, person, tense, voice and mood, or a particular class of verbs having the same set of inflections. See also DECLENSION. **2** a uniting, joining or fusing.

conjunction *noun* **1** *Grammar* a word used to link sentences, clauses, or words, eg *and*, *but*, *if*, *or*, *because*. **2** a joining together; combination. **3** the coinciding of two or more events. **4** *Astrol.* the apparent meeting or passing of two or more heavenly bodies.

— **in conjunction with something** together with it.

[from Latin *con-*, with + *jungere*, to join]

◇ Where two main clauses are connected, the linking word is known as a *coordinating conjunction*: these include *and*, *but*, *either*, *or*, *neither*, *nor*, and *yet*. Where a main clause is connected to one or more subordinate clauses, the linking word is known as a *subordinating conjunction*: these include *which*, *what*, *why*, *when*, *where*, *who*, *since*, *if*, *because*, and *that*. Some conjunctions may also be used as pronouns (*who*, *what*) or adverbs (*either*, *yet*).

conjunctiva *noun* (PL. **conjunctivas**, **conjunctivae**) *Anat.* the membrane that covers the eyeball and the inside of the eyelid. [from Latin *membrana conjunctiva*, conjunctive membrane]

conjunctival *adj.* relating to or in the region of the conjunctiva.

conjunctive — *adj.* **1** connecting; linking. **2** *Grammar* used as a conjunction. — *noun* *Grammar* a word or phrase used as a conjunction. [from Latin *conjunctivus*, connecting]

conjunctively *adv.* as or like a conjunction.

conjunctivitis *noun* inflammation of the conjunctiva.

conjuncture *noun* a combination of circumstances, especially one leading to a crisis. [from Latin *conjungere*, to join]

conjure *verb* **1** *intrans.* to practise conjuring. **2** to summon (a spirit, demon, etc) to appear. **3** *old use* to beg (someone) earnestly to do something.

— **conjure something up 1** to produce it as though from nothing. **2** to call up, evoke, or stir (images, memories, etc).

a name to conjure with a name of great importance or significance.

[from Latin *conjurare*, to swear together]

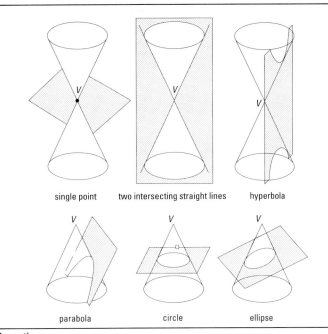

single point   two intersecting straight lines   hyperbola

parabola   circle   ellipse

conic sections

conjurer or **conjuror** *noun* an entertainer who performs conjuring tricks.

conjuring *noun* the performing of tricks that deceive the eye or seem to defy nature, especially by adroit use of the hands.

conk[1] *noun slang* the nose.

conk[2] *verb slang* to hit (someone) on the head.

conk[3] *verb intrans. slang* (usually **conk out**) **1** *said of a machine, etc* to break down. **2** *said of a person* to collapse with fatigue, etc.

conker *noun colloq.* the nut of the horse chestnut tree. [either dialect *conker*, snail shell, originally used in the game, or a form of CONQUER]

conkers *sing. noun* a children's game played with conkers on strings, in which players try to shatter each other's conkers by hitting them with their own.

con man *noun colloq.* a swindler using confidence tricks.

Conn. *abbrev.* Connecticut.

Connacht or **Connaught** POP (1991) 423 000, a province situated in the W Irish Republic, comprising the counties of Sligo, Leitrim, Mayo, Roscommon, and Galway. AREA 17 121sq km/6 609sq mi. CHIEF TOWNS Sligo, Galway, Castlebar. ECONOMY agriculture; livestock.

Connaught see CONNACHT.

connect *verb* (usually **connect to** or **with something** or **someone**) **1** *trans., intrans.* to join; to link. **2** to associate or involve: *is connected with advertising.* **3** to associate or relate mentally. **4** to join by telephone. **5** to relate by marriage or birth. **6** *intrans. said of aeroplanes, trains, buses, etc* to be timed so as to allow transfer from one to another. **7** *intrans. humorous, said of the fist, etc* to strike. **8** *intrans. colloq.* to make sense. — **well connected** with important or aristocratic relatives. [from Latin *con-*, together + *nectere*, to fasten]

cnnectable or **connectible** *adj.* capable of being connected.

Connecticut POP (1990) 3.3m, a densely populated New England state in NE USA, divided into eight counties. It is known as the 'Constitution State' or 'Nutmeg State'. AREA 12 996sq km/5 017sq mi. PHYSICAL DESCRIPTION the Thames, Connecticut, and Housatonic rivers flow S through the state to empty into Long Island Sound; the highest point is Mt Frissell (725m). HISTORY explored by Adriaen Block in 1614; first colonized by Puritans in the 1630s; one of the original states of the Union, and the fifth to ratify the Federal Constitution. CAPITAL Hartford. CHIEF TOWNS Bridgeport, New Haven, Waterbury, Stamford. ECONOMY the coast is largely urbanized and highly industrial; the interior is mainly woodland and forest, with some cropland producing dairy produce, poultry, and tobacco; manufactures include defence industries, machinery, transport equipment, electrical goods, firearms, and metal products.

connecting-rod *noun* the metal rod connecting the piston to the crankshaft in a motor vehicle.

connection or **connexion** *noun* **1** the act of connecting or state of being connected. **2** something that connects; a link. **3** a relationship through marriage or birth. **4** an especially influential person whom one meets through one's job, etc; a contact. **5** a train, bus, etc timed so as allow transfer to it from another passenger service; the transfer from one vehicle to another. — **in connection with something** to do with it; concerning it.
in this connection with reference to the matter being considered.

connective — *adj.* **1** serving to connect. **2** *Grammar* linking two sentences, clauses, etc. — *noun Grammar* a connective word.

connective tissue *Anat.* any of several widely differing tissues, usually containing collagen, that provide the animal body and its internal organs with structural support, eg bone, cartilage, tendons, ligaments.

connector *noun* that which joins or links one thing to another.

Connemara a mountainous region in W Galway county, Connacht province, Irish Republic. PHYSICAL DESCRIPTION L Corrib lies to the E; the rocky coastline has mountains rising to 765m at Croagh Patrick in the Twelve Bens; there are peat bogs and numerous lakes.

Connery, Sean, originally **Thomas Connery** (1930–) Scottish film actor, born in Edinburgh. He achieved celebrity with his part as James Bond in *Dr No* (1962), a role that he played on seven occasions, including *From Russia With Love* (1963) and *Diamonds are Forever* (1971). He won a Best Actor Oscar for his role in *The Name of the Rose* (1986) and a Best Supporting Actor Oscar for *The Untouchables* (1987).

conning-tower *noun* **1** the raised part of a submarine containing the periscope. **2** the wheelhouse of a warship. [from CON[3]]

connivance *noun* the act or practice of conniving.

connive *verb intrans.* **1** (**connive at something**) to pretend not to notice a wrongdoing, and thereby share responsibility for it. **2** (**connive with someone**) to conspire. [from Latin *connivere*, to blink]

conniver *noun* a person who connives.

connoisseur *noun* a person who is knowledgeable about, and a good judge of, eg the arts, wine, food, etc. [from French *connoisseur*, from *connaître*, to know]

Connolly, Maureen (Catherine), also called **Little Mo** (1934–69) US lawn tennis player, born in San Diego, California, the first woman to win all four major titles in one year (1953). She won the US championship in 1951 at the age of 16, and thereafter lost only four matches in her career. She won the Wimbledon singles in 1952–4, the US title in 1951–3, the French Open in 1953–4, and the Australian title in 1953. She was forced to retire in 1954 after breaking her leg in a riding accident.

Connor a male first name. [from Old Irish elements *con(n)*, high + *cobar*, desire]

Connors, Jimmy, properly **James Scott** (1952–) US lawn tennis player, born in East St Louis, Illinois. He was Wimbledon men's singles champion in 1974 and 1982. He won the Australian Open in 1974, and the US Open in 1974, 1976, 1978, 1982, and 1983. With Ilie Nastase, he won the Wimbledon men's doubles in 1973, and the US Open men's doubles in 1975. He was World Championship Tennis champion in 1977 and 1980, Masters champion in 1978, and was a member of the US Davis Cup team in 1976 and 1981. A left-handed player, he was one of the first to use the double-fisted backhand.

connotation *noun* **1** the act of connoting. **2** an idea, association, or implication additional to the main idea or object expressed.

connotative *adj.* connoting; relating to connotation.

connote *verb formal* **1** *said of a word* to suggest, in addition to its literal meaning: *'portly' somehow connotes pomposity.* **2** to mean; to imply. [from Latin *connotare*, to mark in addition]

connubial *adj.* of or relating to marriage or to relations between a husband and wife. [from Latin *connubium*, marriage]

connubially *adv.* in a connubial way.

conquer *verb* (**conquered**, **conquering**) **1** to gain possession or dominion over (territory) by force. **2** to defeat. **3** to overcome or put an end to (a failing, difficulty, evil, etc). **4** to succeed in climbing, reaching, traversing, etc. **5** to become a celebrity in: *the singer who conquered America.* **6** *intrans.* to win; to succeed. [from Latin *conquirere*, to go in search of]

conquering *adj.* victorious.

conqueror *noun* a person who conquers.

conquest *noun* **1** the act of conquering. **2** a conquered territory. **3** something won by effort or force. **4** a person whose affection or admiration one has won. [from French *conqueste*, from Latin *conquirere*, to seek out]

conquistador *noun* (PL. **conquistadores**, **conquistadors**) any of the 16th-century Spanish conquerors of Peru and Mexico. [from Spanish *conquistador*, conqueror]

Conrad, Joseph, originally **Józef Teodor Konrad Korzeniowski** (1857–1924) British novelist, born of Polish parents in Berdichev, Ukraine. He joined the British merchant navy, and his experiences at sea inspired much of his writing. His best-known novels include *The Nigger of the Narcissus* (1897), *Lord Jim* (1900), *Nostromo* (1904), *The Secret Agent* (1907), *Under Western Eyes* (1911), and *Chance* (1914). Other notable works include the short story *The Heart of Darkness* (1902). This formed the basis for the film *Apocalypse Now*.

Conrad a male first name. [an Anglicized form of German *Konrad*, from the elements *kuoni*, bold + *rad*, counsel]

Conran, Sir Terence (Orby) (1931–) English designer and businessman, born in Esher, Surrey. He founded and ran the Habitat Company (1971), based on his own success as a furniture designer and the virtues of good design and marketing. He has since been involved in the management of several related businesses and has won many design awards.

consanguineous *adj.* descended from a common ancestor. [from Latin *con-*, same + *sanguis*, blood]

consanguinity *noun* descent from a common ancestor.

conscience *noun* the sense of moral right and wrong that affects a person and affects behaviour. — **in all conscience** by any normal standard of fairness.
on one's conscience making one feel guilty. [from Latin *conscientia*]

conscience-stricken *adj.* feeling guilty over something one has done.

conscientious *adj.* **1** careful; thorough; painstaking. **2** guided by conscience. [from Latin *conscientiosus*]

conscientiously *adv.* in a conscientious way.

conscientiousness *noun* the quality of being conscientious.

conscientious objector a person who refuses on moral grounds to serve in the armed forces.

conscious *adj.* **1** awake and aware of one's surroundings: *half-conscious.* **2** aware, knowing. **3** deliberate: *a conscious effort to be polite.* **4** (*often in compounds*) concerned, especially too concerned, with: *class-conscious.* — *noun* the conscious part of the mind. [from Latin *conscius*, from *scire*, to know]

consciously *adv.* in a conscious way; knowingly.

consciousness *noun* **1** the state of being conscious. **2** awareness. **3** *Psychol.* the physical and mental state of being awake and fully aware of one's environment, thoughts, and feelings.

conscript — *verb trans.* (with stress on second syllable) to enrol for compulsory military service. — *noun* (with stress on first syllable) a person who has been conscripted. [from Latin *conscribere*, to enlist]

conscription *noun* the compulsory enrolment of recruits for military service.

consecrate *verb* **1** to set apart for a holy use; to make sacred; to dedicate to God. **2** to devote to a special use. [from Latin *consecrare*, from *sacer*, sacred]

consecration *noun* the act or process of making holy.

consecutive *adj.* **1** following one after the other: *consecutive numbers.* **2** *Grammar* expressing result or consequence. [from Latin *consequi*, to follow]

consecutively *adv.* in a consecutive way; successively.

consensus *noun* general feeling or opinion; agreement; a majority view. [from Latin *consensus*, agreement, from *con-*, same + *sensus*, feeling]

consent — *verb* **1** *intrans.* (**consent to something**) to give one's permission for it; to agree to it. **2** to agree to do something. — *noun* agreement; assent; permission: *give one's consent.* — **by common consent** as is generally agreed. [from Latin *consentire*, to agree]

Consentes Dii *or* **Consentes Di** the Roman name for the twelve major gods, whose statues, grouped in male/female pairs, stood in the Forum. They were Jupiter/Juno, Neptune/Minerva, Mars/Venus, Apollo/Diana, Volcanus/Vesta, and Mercury/Ceres.

consequence *noun* **1** something that follows from, or is caused by, an action or set of circumstances. **2** a conclusion reached from reasoning. **3** importance: *of no consequence.* — **in consequence of something** as a result of it. **take the consequences** to accept whatever results from one's decision or action. [from Latin *consequi*, to follow]

consequent *adj.* (**consequent on** *or* **upon something**) resulting from it.

consequential *adj.* **1** important. **2** *said of a person* self-important; pompous. **3** following as a result. [from Latin *consequentia*, consequence]

consequently *adv.* as a result; therefore.

conservable *adj.* capable of being conserved.

conservancy *noun* **1** a body controlling a port or river. **2** an area under special environmental protection. **3** a body concerned with environmental conservation. **4** conservation. [from Latin *conservare*, to preserve]

conservation *noun* **1** the act of conserving; the state of being conserved. **2** the management of the environment in such a way that that its wildlife, natural resources, and quality are preserved and protected. **3** the preservation of historical artefacts, eg books, paintings, monuments, for future generations. **4** *Physics* (*also* **conservation law**) a law which states that the energy, mass, electrical charge, or some other physical property of a closed system will remain constant, eg energy cannot be created or destroyed, although it can be converted from one form to another. [from Latin *conservare*, to save] ◇ The aim of environmental conservation is to mimimize environmental damage caused by human activity. The underlying principles of conservation are the preservation of a wide variety of animals and plants, a reduction in environmental pollution, and the sparing use of nonrenewable resources, eg by recycling paper and glass products. The World Conservation Strategy (1980) concluded that conservation was necessary in order to maintain viable stocks of all plant and animal species, unpolluted air and water, and fertile soil, so that both present and future generations are able to make maximum use of available resources. Other motives for conservation include the enjoyment of wildlife and unspoiled landscapes, the continued use of the land for recreation, and the moral responsibility to conserve the Earth and its resources.

conservation area an area, especially in a village, town, or city, designated as being of special architectural or historic interest, and therefore protected from any alterations that may threaten its character.

conservationist *noun* a supporter of environmental conservation.

conservation of energy *Physics* the law which states that the total energy of a closed (isolated) system remains constant, ie energy can be converted from one form to another, but it cannot be created or destroyed.

conservation of mass *Physics* the law which states that the total mass of the substances that take part in a chemical reaction (the reactants) is equal to the total mass of the products formed, ie mass cannot be created or destroyed.

conservatism *noun* **1** the inclination to preserve the existing state of affairs and to avoid especially sudden or radical change. **2** (**Conservatism**) the policies and principles of a Conservative Party.

conservative — *adj.* **1** favouring the keeping of what is established or traditional; disliking change. **2** *said of an estimate or calculation* deliberately low, for the sake of caution. **3** *said of tastes, clothing, etc* restrained; not flamboyant. **4** (**Conservative**) relating to the Conservative Party, a UK political party supporting free enterprise and private ownership of industry, or any other Conservative Party. — *noun* **1** a traditionalist. **2** (**Conservative**) a member or supporter of a Conservative Party. [from Latin *conservare*, to preserve]

conservatively *adv.* in a conservative way.

Conservative Party in the UK, Canada, and Australia, a political party on the right of the political spectrum, advocating support of established customs and institutions, opposition to socialism, and usually favouring free enterprise. The British Conservative Party (full name *Conservative and Unionist Party*; also known by its historic name *Tory*) has been the most successful party electorally this century. Between 1914 and 1945, it was almost continuously in power, benefiting from the split in the opposition vote that resulted from the decline of the Liberal Party and the rise of the Labour Party. Under Margaret Thatcher's leadership, the party moved towards a more right-wing position, and from 1979 has had a continuous period in office in which radical reforms, such as privatization of nationalized industries and utilities, have been instituted.

conservatoire *noun* a school specialising in music or any of the fine arts. [from French *conservatoire*, from Italian *conservatorio*, originally an orphanage]

conservatory *noun* (PL. **conservatories**) **1** a greenhouse for plants, or a similar room used as a lounge, attached to, and entered from, the house. **2** a conservatoire. [from Latin *conservare*, to conserve]

conserve — *verb* (with stress on *-serve*) to keep safe from damage, deterioration, loss or undesirable change. — *noun* (with stress on *con-*) a jam made especially from fresh fruit. [from Latin *conservare*, to save]

consider *verb* (**considered, considering**) **1** to go over in one's mind. **2** to look at thoughtfully. **3** to call to mind for comparison, etc. **4** to assess with regard to employing, using, etc: *consider someone for a job.* **5** to contemplate doing something. **6** to regard as. **7** to think; to have as one's opinion. **8** to take into account; to make allowances for. **9** *intrans.* to think carefully. — **all things considered** taking all the circumstances into account. [from Latin *considerare*, to examine]

considerable *adj.* **1** large; great. **2** having many admirable qualities: *a considerable person.* [from Latin *considerabilis*]

considerably *adv.* largely; to a large extent.

considerate *adj.* careful not to hurt or inconvenience others. [from Latin *consideratus*, careful]

considerately *adv.* with a considerate manner.

considerateness *noun* the quality of being considerate.

consideration *noun* **1** thoughtfulness on behalf of others. **2** careful thought. **3** a fact, circumstance, etc to be taken into account. **4** a payment, reward, or recompense. — **in consideration of something** in return for it: *a small fee in consideration of your efforts.* **take something into consideration** to allow for it. **under consideration** being considered. [from Latin *considerare*, to consider]

considered *adj.* **1** carefully thought about: *my considered opinion.* **2** (*with an adverb*) thought of or valued in some way: *highly considered.*

considering — *conj.* taking into account: *still very active, considering her age.* — *adv.* taking the circumstances into account: *pretty good, considering.*

consign *verb* **1** to hand over; to entrust. **2** to send, commit, or deliver. **3** to send (goods). [from Latin *consignare*, to put one's seal to]

consignee *noun* the addressee or recipient of goods, etc.

consignment *noun* **1** a load of goods, etc sent or delivered. **2** the act of consigning. — **on consignment** *said of retail goods* to be paid for only if sold, and returned if unsold.

consignor *noun* the sender or deliverer of goods.

consist *verb intrans.* **1** (**consist of something**) to be composed or made up of several elements or ingredients: *the mixture consists of flour, eggs, and water.* **2** (**consist in** *or* **of something**) to have it as an essential feature: *their character consists in their heroism.* [from Latin *consistere*, to stand firm]

consistency *noun* (PL. **consistencies**) **1** the texture or composition of something, with regard to density, thickness, firmness, solidity, etc. **2** the quality of being consistent. **3** agreement; harmony. [from Latin *consistere*, to stand together]

consistent *adj.* **1** (**consistent with something**) in agreement with it; in keeping with it: *injuries consistent with a heavy blow.* **2** unchanging, reliable, regular, steady. [from Latin *consistere*, to stand firm]

consistently *adv.* in a consistent way.

consistory *noun* (PL. **consistories**) an ecclesiastical council, especially one composed of the pope and cardinals. [from Latin *consistorium*, meeting-place]

consolable *adj.* capable of being consoled.

consolation *noun* **1** a circumstance or person that brings one comfort. **2** the act of consoling.

consolation prize *noun* a prize given to someone who just fails to win a major prize.

consolatory *adj.* comforting.

console[1] *verb* (with stress on *-sole*) to comfort in distress, grief, or disappointment. [from Latin *consolari*, to comfort]

console[2] *noun* (with stress on *con-*) **1** *Mus.* the part of an organ with the keys, pedals and panels of stops. **2** a panel of dials, switches, etc for operating an electronic machine. **3** a freestanding cabinet for audio or video equipment. **4** an ornamental bracket for a shelf, etc. [from French *console*, from *consolateur*, comforter, supporter]

consolidate *verb trans., intrans.* **1** to make or become solid or strong. **2** *said of businesses, etc* to combine or merge. [from Latin *consolidare*]

consolidation *noun* 1 making solid or strong. 2 the merging of businesses, etc.

consolidator *noun* a person or thing that consolidates.

consols *pl. noun Brit.* government securities. [from consolidated annuities]

consommé *noun* thin clear soup made from meat stock. [from French *consommé*, finished]

consonance *noun* 1 the state of agreement. 2 *Mus.* a pleasant-sounding combination of musical notes.

consonant[1] *noun* 1 any speech-sound produced by obstructing the passage of the breath in any of several ways. 2 a letter, used alone or in combination (as in *ch*, *ll*, *st*, etc), representing such a sound. [from Latin *consonans litera*, letter having the same sound]

consonant[2] *adj.* (**consonant with something**) in harmony or agreement with it. [from Latin *consonare*, to sound together]

consonantal *adj.* 1 characteristic of a consonant. 2 *said of an alphabet, etc* using only consonants, and usually marking vowels by means of accents.

consort[1] — *noun* (with stress on *con-*) 1 a wife or husband, especially of a reigning sovereign. 2 *Naut.* an accompanying ship. — *verb intrans.* (with stress on *-sort*) (**consort with someone**) to associate or keep company with them (usually with unfavourable implications). [from Latin *consors*, sharer]

consort[2] *noun* (with stress on *con-*) a group of players, singers or instruments, especially specialising in early music. [variant of CONCERT]

consortium *noun* (PL. **consortia**, **consortiums**) an association or combination of several banks, businesses, etc. [from Latin *consortium*, partnership]

conspectus *noun* a survey or report; a summary. [from Latin *conspectus*, view, survey]

conspicuous *adj.* 1 very noticeable or obvious. 2 notable; striking; glaring. [from Latin *conspicuus*, visible]

conspicuously *adv.* in a conspicuous or obvious way.

conspicuousness *noun* the quality of being conspicuous.

conspiracy *noun* (PL. **conspiracies**) 1 the activity of conspiring. 2 a plot. 3 a group of conspirators. [from Latin *conspiratio*, plot] ◇ In law, conspiracy is an agreement by two or more people to commit an unlawful act. In civil law, a conspiracy to cause damage to a third party may be actionable as a tort.

conspiracy of silence an agreement to keep quiet about something.

conspirator *noun* someone who plots, or joins a conspiracy. [from Latin *conspirator*, from *conspirare*, to plot]

conspiratorial *adj.* relating to or involving conspiracy.

conspiratorially *adv.* in a conspiratorial way.

conspire *verb intrans.* 1 to plot secretly together especially for an unlawful purpose. 2 *said of events* to seem to be working together to thwart one: *everything conspired to make me miss my train.* [from Latin *conspirare*]

Constable, John (1776–1837) English landscape painter, born in East Bergholt, Suffolk. He trained at the Royal Academy and in 1828 received an inheritance which enabled him to continue as a painter. His best-received works include *View on the Stour* (1819), *The Haywain* (1821, National Gallery, London) and *White Horse* (1825, New York), all of which won gold medals. Other works include *Salisbury Cathedral* (1823, Victoria and Albert Museum, London).

constable *noun* 1 a policeman or policewoman of the most junior rank. 2 *Hist.* the chief officer of a royal household. 3 the governor of a royal castle. [from French *conestable*, from Latin *comes stabuli*, count of the stable]

constabulary — *noun* (PL. **constabularies**) the police force of a district or county. — *adj.* of or relating to constables or the police. [from Latin *constabularius*, from Middle English *constablerie*, from French *conestable*, constable]

Constance 1 the virtuous Roman heroine of 'The Man of Law's Tale', in Chaucer's *The Canterbury Tales*. 2 a female first name, now relatively rare. [from Latin *Constantia*, either a derivative of *constans*, steadfast, or an abstract noun meaning 'constancy']

Constance, German **Konstanz**, ancient **Constantia** POP (1990e) 75 000, a lake port in Baden-Würtemmberg state, SW Germany, situated on L Constance, close to the Swiss border. It was once an episcopal see and later an imperial city. NOTABLE FEATURES cathedral (15c); council hall (1388).

Constance, Lake, German **Bodensee**, ancient **Lacus Brigantinus** a lake on the N side of the Swiss Alps, forming a meeting point of Switzerland, Austria, and Germany. AREA 541sq km/209sq mi; length 64km/40mi. It forms part of the course of the R Rhine and contains the islands of Mainau and Reichenau. Its NW arm is known as the Überlingersee. The chief towns on the shore are Constance, Friedrichshafen, Lindau, and Bregenz.

constancy *noun* being constant.

Constant (de Rebeque), (Henri) Benjamin (1767–1830) French novelist and politician, born in Lausanne, Switzerland. After studying at Oxford, Erlangen, and Edinburgh, he settled as a publicist in Paris (1795), where he supported the Revolution. Banished in 1802 for opposing Napoleon, on his return in 1814 he became leader of the liberal opposition. His best-known work is the novel *Adolphe* (1816), based on his relationship with Mme de Staël.

constant *adj.* 1 never stopping. 2 frequently recurring. 3 unchanging. 4 faithful; loyal. 5 *Maths.* a symbol (usually a numeral) that remains unchanged, unlike a *variable*, for which one or more values may be substituted. For example, in the expression $3y^2 - 4$, *y* is a variable and the numbers 3 and 4 are constants. [from Latin *constare*, to be unchanging or steadfast]

Constanţa, ancient **Tomis**, or **Constantiniana** 1 POP (1989e) 355 000, the capital of Constanţa county, SE Romania, situated on the W shores of the Black Sea. It is the third largest city in Romania and a major port connected to the Romanian oilfields. HISTORY established as a Greek colony in the 7c BC; under Roman rule from 72 BC; Ovid lived in exile here; ceded to Romania in 1878. 2 a county in SE Romania with Constanţa as its capital. [named after Constantine I (4c)]

Constantine I, also called **the Great**, in full **Flavius Valerius Constantinus** (c.274–337) Roman emperor, the eldest son of Constantius Chlorus. He became emperor of the West on his defeat of Maxentius at the Milvian Bridge in Rome (312) and sole emperor (324) on his defeat of Licinius, the emperor of the East. He believed that his victory in 312 was the work of the Christian God, and became the first emperor to promote Christianity, whence his title 'Great'. His edict of Milan (313), issued jointly with Licinius, brought toleration to Christians throughout the empire, and his new capital at Constantinople, founded on the strategically important site of Byzantium (324), was from the outset a Christian city. Christianity became a state religion in 324 and the great Church Council of Nicaea was held. On his death the empire was partitioned between his three sons, Constantine II, Constans, and Constantius II.

Constantine I (of Greece) (1841–1929) King of Greece (1913–17, 1920–22), born in Athens. After playing a leading part in Greece's victories in the Balkan Wars (1912–13), he succeeded his father George I as king. During World War I, his policy of neutrality led to bitter conflict with interventionist forces led by liberal politician Venizelos, culminating (1916–17) in virtual civil war, Anglo-French intervention, and his abdication. Restored after the war, he abdicated once again (1922) following Greece's defeat by Turkey and an internal military revolt.

Constantine II (1940–) King of Greece (1964–73), born near Athens. In 1964 he succeeded his father Paul I and married Princess Anne-Marie of Denmark (1946–). He fled to Rome (Dec 1967) after an abortive attempt against the military government which had seized power in a coup, and was officially deposed in 1973. The monarchy was abolished by a national referendum in 1974.

Constantine, ancient **Ciria**, **Qacentina** 1 POP (1987) 441 000, the oldest city in Algeria and the chief town in Constantine department, N Africa. It lies 320km/200mi SE of Algiers. HISTORY important since the 3c–4c BC; Roman provincial capital of Numidia; destroyed in AD 311 during a Civil War, rebuilt by Constantine I; seat of successive Muslim dynasties in the Middle Ages; prospered under the Turks in the 18c; French occupation in 1837. 2 a department in NE Algeria with Constantine as its chief town.

Constantinople, Latin Empire of a 13c empire based at Constantinople (ancient Byzantium, modern Istanbul), the capital of the medieval (Eastern) Roman or Byzantine Empire. The army of the Fourth Crusade took Constantinople (1204) and created a Latin Empire, with Baldwin I, Count of Flanders as the first emperor. It finally succumbed to the army of Michael VIII Palaeologus in 1261.

constantly *adv.* in a constant way; steadily, regularly.

constellation *noun* 1 any of 88 regions into which the sky is conceptually divided, each consisting of a group of stars that often form a distinctive shape in the sky, although their distances from the Earth may differ greatly, eg Ursa Major (great bear), Centaurus (centaur). 2 a group of associated people or things. [from Latin *constellatio*, from *stella*, star]

consternation *noun* dismay, alarm, agitation or anxiety. [from Latin *consternatio*]

constipate *verb* to cause constipation in. [from Latin *con-*, together + *stipare*, to press]

constipated *adj.* suffering from constipation.

constipation *noun* a condition in which the faeces become hard and difficult to pass from the bowels.

constituency *noun* (PL. **constituencies**) 1 the district represented by a member of parliament or other representative in a legislative body. 2 the voters in that district. [from CONSTITUENT]

constituent — *adj.* 1 forming part of a whole. 2 having the power to create or alter a constitution: *a constituent assembly*. 3 having the power to elect. — *noun* 1 a necessary part; a component. 2 a resident in a constituency. [from Latin *constituere*, to establish]

constituent analysis *Linguistics* the process of analysing linguistic constructions into the components or constituents from which they are made. For example, the sentence *John helped the girl* may be divided into the major constituents 'John' and 'helped the girl'. Further divisions may be made of the remaining constituents, including division of words into stems and affixes. The order of division is usually represented using a series of lines or brackets, or by a tree diagram.

constitute *verb* 1 to be; to go together to make. 2 to establish; to appoint: *the recently consti-*

Constellations

Latin name	English name	Latin name	English name
Andromeda	Andromeda	Leo (Z)	Lion
Antlia	Air Pump	Leo Minor	Little Lion
Apus	Bird of Paradise	Lepus	Hare
Aquarius (Z)	Water Bearer	Libra (Z)	Scales
Aquila	Eagle	Lupus	Wolf
Ara	Altar	Lynx	Lynx
Aries (Z)	Ram	Lyra	Harp
Auriga	Charioteer	Mensa	Table
Boötes	Herdsman	Microscopium	Microscope
Caelum	Chisel	Monoceros	Unicorn
Camelopardalis	Giraffe	Musca	Fly
Cancer (Z)	Crab	Norma	Level
Canes Venatici	Hunting Dogs	Octans	Octant
Canis Major	Great Dog	Ophiuchus	Serpent Bearer
Canis Minor	Little Dog	Orion	Orion
Capricornus (Z)	Sea Goat	Pavo	Peacock
Carina	Keel	Pegasus	Winged Horse
Cassiopeia	Cassiopeia	Perseus	Perseus
Centaurus	Centaur	Phoenix	Phoenix
Cepheus	Cepheus	Pictor	Easel
Cetus	Whale	Pisces (Z)	Fishes
Chamaeleon	Chameleon	Piscis Austrinus	Southern Fish
Circinus	Compasses	Puppis	Ship's Stern
Columba	Dove	Pyxis	Mariner's Compass
Coma Berenices	Berenice's Hair	Reticulum	Net
Corona Australis	Southern Crown	Sagitta	Arrow
Corona Borealis	Northern Crown	Sagittarius (Z)	Archer
Corvus	Crow	Scorpius (Z)	Scorpion
Crater	Cup	Sculptor	Sculptor
Crux	Southern Cross	Scutum	Shield
Cygnus	Swan	Serpens	Serpent
Delphinus	Dolphin	Sextans	Sextant
Dorado	Swordfish	Taurus (Z)	Bull
Draco	Dragon	Telescopium	Telescope
Equuleus	Little Horse	Triangulum	Triangle
Eridanus	River Eridanus	Triangulum	
Fornax	Furnace	Australe	Southern Triangle
Gemini (Z)	Twins	Tucana	Toucan
Grus	Crane	Ursa Major	Great Bear
Hercules	Hercules	Ursa Minor	Little Bear
Horologium	Clock	Vela	Sails
Hydra	Sea Serpent	Virgo (Z)	Virgin
Hydrus	Water Snake	Volans	Flying Fish
Indus	Indian	Vulpecula	Fox
Lacerta	Lizard		

Z: Found on the Zodiac

tuted board of enquiry. [from Latin constituere, to establish]

constitution noun **1** a set of rules governing an organization; the supreme laws and rights of a country's people, etc. **2** the way in which something is formed or made up. **3** one's physical make-up, health, etc. **4** the act of forming or constituting. [from Latin constitutio, arrangement, physical make-up]
◇ Usually a written document determining the way that a country may be governed in terms of the sources, purpose, use, and limits upon the exercise of political power. Written constitutions normally include a description of government institutions and their powers, processes for amending the constitution, and a bill of rights. The UK is one of the few exceptions in not having a written constitution.

constitutional — adj. **1** legal according to a given constitution. **2** relating to, or controlled by, the law of the land. **3** relating to one's physical make-up, health, etc. — noun old use a regular walk taken for the sake of one's health.

Constitutional Convention a gathering (1787) in Philadelphia that drafted the US Constitution; 12 of the original 13 states were represented (Rhode I did not send a delegate). The term is also used for any political meeting which is empowered to write a state or national constitution.

constitutionally adv. in a constitutional way; in terms of a constitution.

Constitution of the United States the US constitution embodies the concepts on which the US system of government is based. The law of the land since 1789, it establishes a federal republic, balancing the power of the states and that of the federal government. In the federal government, power is divided among three independent branches: legislative, executive and judicial. The constitutional document comprises a short preamble and seven Articles which are followed by 26 amendments, the first 10 of which are known as the Bill of Rights (although later amendments also deal with civil rights issues). The others cover such matters as the election, death or removal of the President, and eligibility to stand for election to Congress. Drafted at the Constitutional Convention of 1787 held in Philadelphia, the Constitution was adopted after it had been ratified by nine of the states.

constrain verb **1** (usually **be constrained**) to force; to compel: feel constrained to tell the truth. **2** to limit the freedom, scope, or range of. [from French constraindre]

constrained adj. awkward; embarrassed; forced.

constraint noun **1** a limit or restriction. **2** force; compulsion. **3** awkwardness, unnaturalness, embarrassment or inhibition.

constrict verb **1** to squeeze or compress; to enclose tightly, especially too tightly; to cause to tighten. **2** to inhibit. [from Latin constringere, to bind]

constriction noun **1** the process of constricting. **2** something that is constricted. **3** contraction, tightness.

constrictive adj. causing a constriction.

constrictor noun **1** a snake that kills by coiling around its prey, then squeezing and suffocating it. **2** Anat. any muscle that compresses an organ or narrows an opening.

construct — verb (with stress on -struct) **1** to build. **2** to form, compose, or put together. **3** Geom. to draw (a figure). — noun (with stress on con-) **1** something constructed, especially in the mind. **2** a mental image constructed from a number of sense-impressions. [from Latin construere, to build, pile together]

construction noun **1** the process of building or constructing. **2** something built or constructed; a building. **3** Grammar the arrangement of words in a particular grammatical relationship, to form a sentence, clause, etc. **4** interpretation: put a wrong construction on someone's words.

constructional adj. **1** involving construction. **2** used for structures. **3** using structures.

constructive adj. **1** helping towards progress or development; useful. **2** Legal, said of facts realized from what has been stated, rather than actually stated themselves. **3** relating to construction.

constructively adv. in a constructive way.

Constructivism a term usually applied to a form of abstract art that began in Russia in 1917, using machine-age materials such as steel, glass, and plastic. Leading practitioners included Vladimir Tatlin (1885–1953), and the brothers Antoine Pevsner and Naum Gabo. In Russia this impetus was channelled into industrial design (Soviet Constructivism). Pevsner and Gabo left Russia in the early 1920s, and their ideas subsequently influenced abstract artists in the West (International Constructivism).

constructor noun a person who constructs.

construe verb **1** to interpret or explain. **2** Grammar to analyse the grammatical structure of (a sentence, etc). **3** Grammar (**construe one word with another**) to combine them grammatically. **4** Grammar to translate word for word. **5** to deduce; to infer. [from Latin construere, to construct]

consubstantiation noun Christianity a doctrine attributed to Luther, describing the presence of Christ in the Eucharist 'under and with the elements of bread and wine'. It is to be contrasted with the Roman Catholic doctrine of transubstantiation.

consul noun **1** an official repesentative of a state, stationed in a foreign country to look after eg the interests of fellow citizens living there. **2** Hist. either of the two joint chief magistrates in ancient Rome. [from Latin consul]

consular adj. relating to a consul.

consulate noun the post or official residence of a consul (see CONSUL 1).

consulship noun the office or position of a consul.

consult verb **1** to ask the advice of: consult a lawyer. **2** to refer to (a map, book, etc). **3** to consider (wishes, feelings, etc). **4** (**consult with someone**) to have discussions with them. **5** intrans. to give advice as a consultant: the doctor's consulting hours. [from Latin consultare]

consultancy noun **1** the post of consultant. **2** an agency offering professional advice.

consultant noun **1** a person who gives professional advice. **2** the most senior grade of doctor in a given speciality in a hospital or clinic, who accepts ultimate responsiblity for the treatment and care of patients.

consultation *noun* **1** the act or process of consulting. **2** a meeting for the obtaining of advice or for discussion.

consultative *adj.* available for consultation; advisory: *a consultative committee.*

consulting *adj.* acting as an adviser: *a consulting architect.*

consulting room the room in which a doctor sees patients.

consumable *adj.* capable of being consumed.

consume *verb* **1** to eat or drink. **2** to use up. **3** to destroy. **4** (**be consumed with something**) to be obsessed or overcome by a feeling, etc: *they are consumed with jealousy.* [from Latin *consumere*]

consumer *noun* **1** the person who uses a product; any member of the public buying and using goods and services. **2** someone or something that consumes.

consumer durables goods that do not need frequent replacement, eg furniture, television sets, etc.

consumer goods goods bought to satisfy personal needs, as distinct from eg machinery and other equipment used in the production of goods.

consumerism *noun* **1** the protection of the interests of consumers. **2** *Econ.* the theory that steady growth in the consumption of goods is necessary for a sound economy.

consumer protection activities devised to protect buyers of goods and services against inferior or dangerous products and misleading advertising. This protection may be statutory or may operate through a voluntary code within an industry. They may also be introduced through the representations of consumer organizations.

consumer research the study of the needs and preferences of consumers.

Consumers' Association in the UK, an organization, founded in 1957, which undertakes the comparative analysis of products and services, and reports to its members on such matters as quality, safety, value for money, price, and design features of available models or brands. The reports are published in the magazine *Which.*

consumer society the advanced stage of industrial society, in which there is a high availability and consumption of consumer goods and services. The term is associated with the notion of consumer sovereignty, in that goods are produced to meet consumer needs and demands, and consumption is increased through production of convenience or disposable goods.

consumer terrorism the deliberate contamination by harmful substances of certain food products, usually in order to blackmail the producers or retailers of the products.

consuming *adj., said of an enthusiasm, etc* obsessive; overwhelming.

consummate — *verb* (pronounced *-mate*, with stress on *con-*) **1** to finish, perfect, or complete. **2** to make (a marriage) into a marriage in its full legal sense through the act of sexual intercourse. — *adj.* (with stress on *-summ-*) **1** supreme; very great; very skilled. **2** complete; utter: *a consummate idiot.* [from Latin *consummare*, to complete, perfect]

consummately *adv.* perfectly; with great skill.

consummation *noun* **1** the act of consummating. **2** perfection.

consumption *noun* **1** the act or process of consuming. **2** the amount consumed. **3** the buying and using of goods. **4** *old use* tuberculosis of the lungs. [from Latin *consumptio*]

consumptive — *adj.* **1** relating to consumption; wasteful or destructive. **2** suffering from tuberculosis of the lungs. — *noun* a person suffering from tuberculosis of the lungs.

cont. *abbrev.* continued.

contact — *noun* (with stress on *con-*) **1** the condition of touching physically. **2** communication, or a means of communication. **3** an acquaintance whose influence or knowledge may prove useful to one, especially in business. **4** an electrical connection, allowing passage of a current. **5** a person who has been exposed to an infectious disease through being near a person who has it. — *verb* (with stress on *-tact*) to get in touch with; to communicate with. [from Latin *contactus*, touching]

contactable *adv.* able to be contacted.

contact lens a small lens, consisting of hard, soft, or gas-permeable plastic material, that is worn in direct contact with the front of the eyeball as an alternative to spectacles for the correction of visual defects.

contact process *Chem.* the process whereby sulphuric acid is manufactured on an industrial scale by the oxidation of sulphur dioxide to sulphur trioxide in the presence of a catalyst.

Contadora, Isla an island of Panama, in the Pearl Is, Gulf of Panama. It was the meeting place of the foreign ministers of Colombia, Mexico, Panama, and Venezuela (the Contadora Group) in 1983 to discuss the problems of Central America. Their proposed solutions became known as the Contadora Process.

contagion *noun* **1** the transmission of a disease by direct physical contact with the body of an infected person. **2** *old use* a disease that is transmitted in this way and not by physical contact or by the inhalation of infected airborne droplets, etc. **3** a spreading social evil; a corrupting influence. [from Latin *contagio*, touching, contact]

contagious *adj.* **1** *said of a disease* spread by bodily contact. **2** *said of a person* in an infectious condition; likely to infect others. **3** *said of a mood, laughter, etc* spreading from person to person; affecting everyone in the vicinity.

contain *verb* **1** to hold or have; to have in or inside; to consist of. **2** to control, limit, check, or prevent the spread of. **3** to control (oneself or one's feelings). **4** to enclose or surround. **5** *Maths.* to be divisible by (a number) without a remainder. [from Latin *continere*, to contain, restrain]

containable *adj.* able to be contained; controllable.

container *noun* **1** an object designed for holding or storing, such as a box, tin, carton, etc. **2** a huge sealed metal box of standard size and design for carrying goods by lorry or ship.

containerization *or* **containerisation** *noun* the process of containerizing goods.

containerize *or* **containerise** *verb* to put (cargo) into containers.

container ship a cargo ship designed to carry 6m or 12m containers in pre-determined positions, largely dispensing with the loading and stowage problems associated with traditional cargo. The first purpose-built ships were commissioned in 1966 by a British company.

containment *noun* the action of preventing the expansion of a hostile power, etc.

containment building a steel or concrete structure enclosing a nuclear reactor, designed to withstand high pressure and high temperature and, in emergency, to contain the escape of radiation.

contaminant *noun* something which contaminates.

contaminate *verb* **1** to make impure; to pollute or infect. **2** to make radioactive. [from Latin *contaminare*]

contamination *noun* **1** pollution. **2** adulteration, corruption. **3** infection.

contd *or* **contd.** *abbrev.* continued.

contemn *verb literary* to despise, disdain or scorn. [from Latin *contemnere*]

contemplate *verb* **1** *trans., intrans.* to think about; to go over (something) mentally; to meditate. **2** to look thoughtfully at. **3** to consider as a possibility. [from Latin *contemplari*, to survey, look at carefully]

contemplation *noun* thought, meditation.

contemplative — *adj.* **1** thoughtful; meditative. **2** relating to religious contemplation. — *noun* a person whose life is spent in religious contemplation.

contemplatively *adv.* in a contemplative way.

contemporaneity *noun* being contemporaneous.

contemporaneous *adj.* (**contemporaneous with something**) existing or happening at the same time or period as something. [from Latin *contemporaneus*, from *con-*, same + *tempus*, time]

contemporaneously *adv.* at the same time or period.

contemporary — *adj.* **1** (**contemporary with something**) belonging to the same period or time as something. **2** (**contemporary with someone**) of the same age as them. **3** modern. — *noun* (PL. **contemporaries**) **1** a person who lives or lived, or thing that exists or existed, at the same time as another. **2** a person of about the same age as another. [from Latin *con-*, same + *tempus*, time]

contempt *noun* **1** scorn. **2** *Legal* disregard of, disrespect for, or disobedience to the rules of a court of law. — **hold someone in contempt** to despise them. [from Latin *contemnere*, to scorn]

contemptible *adj.* **1** despicable; disgusting; vile. **2** worthless; paltry.

contemptibly *adv.* in a contemptible way.

contemptuous *adj.* (**contemptuous of someone** *or* **something**) showing contempt for them; scornful of them. [from Latin *contemnere*, to scorn]

contemptuously *adv.* with a contemptuous manner.

contend *verb* **1** *intrans.* to struggle, strive, fight, or compete. **2** *intrans.* to argue earnestly. **3** to say, maintain, or assert. [from Latin *contendere*, to strive]

contender *noun* a contestant or competitor.

content¹ (with stress on *-tent*) — *adj.* (**content with something**) satisfied about it; happy; uncomplaining. — *verb* **1** to satisfy. **2** (**content oneself with something**) to limit oneself to a particular choice, or course of action: *contented themselves with a cream tea.* — *noun* peaceful satisfaction; peace of mind. [from Latin *contentus*]

content² *noun* (with stress on *con-*) **1** the subject-matter of a book, speech, etc. **2** the proportion in which a particular ingredient is present in something: *a diet with a high starch content.* **3** (**contents**) the things contained in something. **4** (**contents**) the text of a book; a summary of the text by chapters, etc given at the beginning of a book. [from Latin *continere*, to contain]

content analysis *Linguistics* the process of analysing linguistic constructions into units of independent meaning. For example, in the sentence *Dog eats man*, there are three clear units of meaning; however, in the sentence *The car has* *broken down*, there are only two clear units of meaning, ie 'car' and 'broken down'.

contented *adj.* peacefully happy or satisfied.

contentedly *adv.* in a contented way.

contentedness *noun* being contented.

contention *noun* **1** a point that one asserts or maintains in an argument. **2** argument or debate. [from Latin *contentio*, strife, controversy]

contentious *adj.* **1** likely to cause argument or quarrelling. **2** quarrelsome or argumentative. [from Latin *contendere*, to strive]

contentiously *adv.* in a contentious way.

contentment *noun* the quality of being content.

contest — *noun* (with stress on *con*-) **1** a competition. **2** a struggle. — *verb* (with stress on *-test*) **1** to enter the competition or struggle for. **2** to dispute (a claim, someone's will, etc). [from Latin *contestari*, to call to witness]

contestable *adj.* able to be contested.

contestant *noun* a person who takes part in a contest; a competitor.

context *noun* **1** the passage in a text or speech within which a particular word, statement, etc occurs. **2** circumstances, background, or setting. — **out of context** without reference to context. [from Latin *contextus*, connection]

contextual *adj.* relating to or depending on a context.

contiguity *noun* being contiguous.

contiguous *adj.* (**contiguous with** *or* **to something**) **1** touching it; neighbouring or adjacent to it. **2** near or next in order or time. [from Latin *contiguus*, touching]

contiguously *adv.* in a contiguous way.

continence *noun* **1** the ability to control one's bowels and bladder. **2** self-control; control over one's appetites and passions. [from Latin *continentia*, self-control]

continent[1] *noun* **1** any of the seven main land masses of the world, namely Europe, Asia, N America, S America, Africa, Australia, and Antarctica. **2** the mainland portion of one of these land masses. **3** (**the Continent**) the mainland of Europe, regarded from the British Isles. [from Latin *continere*, to contain]
◊ The Earth's crust beneath the continents is thicker and more complex than that beneath the oceans. Continental crust is, on average, about 35km/22mi thick, although where major mountains chains occur, eg the Himalayas, the crust may be up to 50km/31mi thick. Whereas oceanic crust consists mainly of basalt-like rocks, the continents consist mainly of granite overlain by various sedimentary and metamorphic rocks. Most scientists now believe that the continents are still growing, with new continental crust being formed by remelting oceanic crust.

continent[2] *adj.* **1** able to control one's bowels and bladder. **2** self-controlled.

continental — *adj.* **1** belonging or relating to the mainland of the continent of Europe. **2** relating to any of the continents of the world. — *noun old use* an inhabitant of the mainland of Europe.

continental breakfast a light breakfast, eg of rolls and coffee.

Continental Congress the federal legislature (1774–8) that declared the struggle for American independence. It was made up of delegates from each of the 13 colonies (states after 1776). The First Congress met (5 Sep–26 Oct 1774) in response to Britain passing the Intolerable Acts, and its delegates (unsuccessfully) petitioned King George III. The Second convened in May 1775, shortly after the battles of Lexington and Concord, and created an army, but later adopted the Declaration of Independence (Jul 1776) and remained the voice

of the young country under the Articles of Conferation until the US Constitution took effect in 1789.

Continental Divide *or* **Great Divide** a line of mountain peaks in N America extending SE from NW Canada down the western USA into Mexico, central America, and S America where it meets the N end of the Andes. A major watershed, it includes the Rocky Mts in Canada and the USA and the Sierra Madre Ranges in Mexico.

continental drift *Geol.* the theory that the continents were formed as a result of the breaking up of a single land mass into several smaller land masses which slowly drifted apart across the Earth's surface.

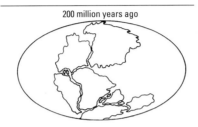
200 million years ago

135 million years ago

today

← direction of drift

continental drift

continental quilt a duvet.

continental shelf *Geol.* the gently sloping seabed, underlying an area of relatively shallow sea, that surrounds the continents.

contingency *noun* (PL. **contingencies**) **1** something liable, but not certain, to occur; a chance happening. **2** something dependent on a chance future happening.

contingency plans plans made in case a certain situation should arise.

contingent — *noun* **1** a body of troops. **2** any identifiable body of people: *there were boos from the Welsh contingent.* — *adj.* **1** (**contingent on** or **upon something**) dependent on some uncertain circumstance. **2** liable, but not certain, to occur; accidental. [from Latin *contingere*, to touch, happen]

continual *adj.* **1** constantly happening or done; frequent. **2** constant; never ceasing. [from Latin *continualis*, from *continuus*, uninterrupted]
◆ Often confused with *continuous*.

continually *adv.* repeatedly, persistently.

continuance *noun* **1** the act or state of continuing. **2** duration. [from Latin *continuare*, to make continuous]

continuation *noun* **1** the act or process of continuing, often after a break or pause. **2** that

which adds to something or carries it on, eg a further episode of or sequel to a story.

continue *verb* **1** *trans., intrans.* to go on; not to stop. **2** *trans., intrans.* to last or cause to last. **3** *trans., intrans.* to carry on or start again after a break. **4** *intrans.* (**continue with something**) to persist in it; to keep on with it. **5** *intrans.* to keep moving in the same direction: *continue up the hill.* [from Latin *continuare*]

continuity *noun* **1** the state of being continuous, unbroken or consistent. **2** *Television, Cinema* the arrangement of scenes so that one progresses smoothly from another. [from Latin *continuitas*, from *continuus*, unbroken]

continuo *noun* (PL. **continuos**) *Mus.* a bass part for a keyboard or stringed instrument; the instrument or instruments playing this. [from Italian *continuo*, continuous]

continuous *adj.* **1** never ceasing. **2** unbroken; uninterrupted. **3** *Grammar, said of tense* formed with the verb *be* and the present participle, and representing continuing action or a continuing state, as in *I am waiting, they were dancing,* and *you will be needing this.* [from Latin *continuus*, unbroken]
◆ Often confused with *continual*.

continuous assessment *Education* the judging of pupils' progress by means of frequent tests throughout the year, as an alternative to occasional examinations.

continuously *adv.* so as to be continuous; without stopping.

continuous representation *Art* the practice of illustrating several consecutive stages of a story in one picture. For example, in paintings of the Nativity, the shepherds may be shown in the foreground adoring the new-born Jesus and again in the background watching their flocks.

continuum *noun* (PL. **continua**, **continuums**) a continuous sequence; an unbroken progression. [from Latin *continuus*, unbroken]

contort *verb trans., intrans.* to twist violently out of shape. [from Latin *contorquere*, to twist]

contortion *noun* **1** a violent twisting. **2** a deformed shape.

contortionist *noun* an entertainer who is able to twist his body into spectacularly unnatural positions.

contour — *noun* **1** (*usually* **contours**) the distinctive outline of something. **2** (*also* **contour line**) a line on a map joining points of the same height or depth. — *verb* **1** to shape the contour of, or shape so as to fit a contour. **2** to mark the contour lines on (a map). [from French *contour*, from Italian *contornare*, to outline]

contra- *prefix* **1** against: *contraception.* **2** opposite: *contraflow.* **3** contrasting: *contradistinction.* **4** *Mus.* lower in pitch: *contrabass.* [from Latin *contra*]

contraband — *noun* **1** the smuggling of goods prohibited from being imported or exported. **2** smuggled goods: *police found crates of contraband in the warehouse.* — *adj.* prohibited from being imported or exported; smuggled. [from Spanish *contrabanda*, from Latin *contra-* + *bandum*, ban]

contrabass *noun* another name for the double bass.

contra bassoon a double bassoon which sounds an octave lower than the standard instrument. It is made of either wood or metal. [from Italian prefix *contra-* indicating an octave lower]

contraception *noun* the prevention of pregnancy; birth control. [from CONTRA- + CONCEPTION]

contraceptive — *noun* a drug or device that prevents pregnancy following sexual intercourse; used to plan the timing and number of children in individual families, and so control population growth. Some contraceptives are also used to provide protection against sexually transmitted diseases. — *adj.* having the effect of preventing pregnancy.

◊ Methods of contraception vary widely in safety and reliability. *Barrier methods* prevent sperm from reaching the cervix (the neck of the womb), and also provide protection against AIDS and other sexually transmitted diseases. They include the condom or sheath, and the diaphragm or cap (which fits over the cervix). In 1992 the female condom, a thin polyurethane pouch that fits inside the vagina, became available. *Intra-uterine devices* such as the coil are thought to prevent implantation of the fertilized egg in the wall of the uterus. '*Natural*' methods of contraception, eg abstention from intercourse during the fertile period, or withdrawal of the penis from the vagina before ejaculation, are very unreliable, and normally only used on religious grounds. *Oral contraceptives*, which contain synthetic steroids similar to oestrogen and progesterone, prevent the normal release of an egg from the ovaries, and combined oestrogen and progesterone pills are one of the most reliable methods of contraception, although they may increase the risk of strokes and heart attacks, particularly in smokers over 35 years of age. *Post-coital contraceptives* (the 'morning-after pill'), which contain the synthetic oestrogen stilboestrol, can be taken up to 72 hours after unprotected intercourse, but are generally only used in emergencies. Other hormonal methods include long-acting injections, and capsules implanted under the skin. Research is currently in progress to develop an effective male contraceptive pill. Sterilization, by vasectomy in men, or by cutting and tying of the Fallopian tubes in women, is the only form of permanent contraception.

contract — *noun* (with stress on *con-*) **1** an agreement, especially a legally binding one. **2** a document setting out the terms of such an agreement. — *verb* (with stress on -*tract*) **1** *intrans., trans.* to make or become smaller. **2** *intrans., trans. said of muscles* to make or become shorter, so as to bend a joint, etc. **3** *intrans., trans. said of the brows* to draw together into a frown. **4** to catch (a disease). **5** to enter into (an alliance or marriage). **6** to incur or accumulate (a debt). **7** *trans., intrans. said of a word, phrase, etc* to reduce to a short form: '*are not*' *is contracted to* '*aren't*'. **8** *intrans., trans.* (**contract with someone**) to enter a legal contract concerning them.
— **contract in** *or* **out** to arrange to participate, or not to participate, eg in a pension scheme.
contract something out *or* **put something out to contract** *said of a business company, etc* to arrange for part of a job to be done by another company. [from Latin *contractus*, contraction, agreement]

contractable *adj., said eg of a disease or habit* liable to be contracted.

contract bridge the usual form of the card game bridge, in which only tricks bid and won count in one's score.

contractible *adj., said eg of muscles* capable of being contracted.

contractile vacuole *Zool.* in single-celled animals, eg amoeba, a cavity that fills with water and periodically contracts, expelling its contents into the surrounding medium. It controls the water content of the animal, and also provides a means whereby waste products can be excreted.

contraction *noun* **1** the process of contracting or state of being contracted. **2** a tightening of a muscle or set of muscles, especially those of the abdomen in childbirth. **3** a shortened form of a word or phrase: '*aren't*' *is a contraction of* '*are not*'.

contractor *noun* a person or firm that undertakes work on contract, especially connected with building, installation of equipment, or the transportation of goods.

contractual *adj.* relating to a contract or binding agreement.

contractually *adv.* on a contractual basis.

contradict *verb* **1** to assert the opposite of or deny (a statement, etc) made by (a person). **2** *said of a statement, etc* to disagree or be inconsistent with (another): *the two accounts contradict each other.* [from Latin *contra-*, opposite + *dicere*, to say]

contradiction *noun* **1** the act of contradicting. **2** one statement contradicting another, etc. **3** denial. **4** inconsistency.

contradictory *adj.* **1** inconsistent. **2** denying. **3** contrary.

contradistinction *noun* a distinction made in terms of a contrast between qualities, properties, etc.

contraflow *noun* a form of traffic diversion used on dual carriageways, with vehicles moving in opposite directions sharing the same carriageway.

contraindicate *verb Medicine* to be a reason for not using (a treatment, operation, etc).

contraindication *noun Medicine* a contraindicating factor.

contralto *noun* (PL. **contraltos**) **1** the female singing voice that is lowest in pitch. **2** a singer with this voice. **3** a part to be sung by this voice. [from Italian *contralto*, lower than alto]

contraption *noun humorous, colloq.* a machine or apparatus.

contrapuntal *adj. Mus.* relating to, or arranged as, counterpoint. [from Italian *contrappunto*, counterpoint]

contrapuntally *adv.* in a contrapuntal way.

contrariety *or* **contrariness** *noun* **1** opposition. **2** inconsistency, discrepancy.

contrarily *adv.* in a contrary way.

contrariwise *adv.* reversing the situation; the opposite way round.

contrary — *adj.* **1** (**contrary to something**) opposite; quite different; opposed. **2** *said of a wind* blowing against one; unfavourable. **3** obstinate, perverse, self-willed, or wayward. — *noun* (PL. **contraries**) **1** an extreme opposite. **2** either of a pair of opposites. **3** *Logic* either of two propositions that cannot both be true of the same thing.
— **contrary to something** in opposition or contrast to it.
on the contrary in opposition or contrast to what has just been said.
to the contrary to the opposite effect; giving the contrasting position.
[from Latin *contrarius*, from *contra*, opposite]

contrast — *noun* (with stress on *con-*) **1** difference or dissimilarity between things or people that are being compared. **2** a person or thing that is strikingly different from another. **3** the degree of difference in tone between the colours, or the light and dark parts, of a photograph or television picture. — *verb* (with stress on -*trast*) **1** to compare so as to reveal contrasts. **2** (**contrast with something**) to be distinct from it; to show a contrast.
— **in contrast to** *or* **with something** *or* **someone** as an opposite to them or something distinct from them.
[from CONTRA-[1] + Latin *stare*, to stand]

contravene *verb* to break or disobey (a law or rule). [from CONTRA-[1] + Latin *venire*, to come]

contravention *noun* (*usually* **in contravention**) infringement of a law, etc.

Contreras, Battle of an engagement (1847) in the Mexican War in which the Mexican army under Santa Anna was badly defeated by a smaller US force under Winfield Scott (1786–1866). It opened the way to Mexico City and led to the collapse of Mexican resistance.

contretemps *noun* **1** an awkward or embarrassing moment, happening, etc. **2** a slight disagreement. [from French *contretemps*, from *contre*, against + *temps*, time]

contribute *verb* (*usually* **contribute to something**) **1** *trans., intrans.* to give for some joint purpose. **2** *intrans.* to be one of the causes of something. **3** to supply (an article, etc) for publication in a magazine, etc. [from Latin *contribuere*, to bring together]

contribution *noun* **1** the act of contributing. **2** something contributed, eg money, or an article for a magazine.

contributor *noun* a person or organization that contributes.

contributory *adj.* **1** giving or given to a common purpose or fund. **2** having partial responsibility. **3** *said of a pension scheme* involving contribution from the employee as well as the employer.

con trick *colloq.* a confidence trick.

contrite *adj.* sorry for something one has done. [from Latin *contritus*, crushed]

contritely *adv.* with a contrite manner.

contrition *noun* **1** remorse. **2** *Christianity* deep sorrow for past sin and resolve to avoid future sin.

contrivance *noun* **1** the act or power of contriving. **2** a device or apparatus. **3** a scheme; a piece of cunning.

contrive *verb* **1** to manage or succeed. **2** to bring about: *contrive one's escape*. **3** to make or construct, especially with difficulty. [from Old French *controver*, to find]

contrived *adj.* forced or artificial: *a contrived ending to a play*.

control — *noun* **1** authority or charge; power to influence or guide: *in control / take control / under control / out of control*. **2** a means of limitation: *impose strict controls on spending*. **3** (**controls**) the levers, switches, etc by which a machine, etc is operated. **4** the people in control of some operation: *mission control*. **5** the place where something is checked: *go through passport control*. **6** something used as a standard against which to check the results of an experiment. **7** *Spiritualism* a dead person guiding a medium. — *verb* (**controlled, controlling**) **1** to have or exercise control over. **2** to regulate. **3** to limit. **4** to check or verify against a standard: *a controlled experiment*. [from Old French *contrerolle*, duplicate account or register]

control engineering the branch of engineering concerned with the control and adjustment of systems. Control is achieved by using closed loop systems; when an error is detected, the information is returned to the input and used to correct the error.

controllability *noun* the quality of being controllable.

controllable *adj.* capable of being controlled.

controller *noun* **1** a person or thing that controls. **2** an official in charge of public finance. **3** a person in charge of the finances of an enterprise, etc.

control tower a tall building at an airport from which take-off and landing instructions are given.

controversial *adj.* involving or causing controversy.

controversially *adv.* in a controversial way.

controversy *noun* (PL. **controversies**) a usually long-standing disagreement or dispute. [from CONTRA-[1] + Latin *vertere*, to turn]

contumacious *adj.* **1** obstinately disobedient. **2** opposing lawful authority with contempt.

contumaciously *adv.* in a contumacious way.

contumacy *noun formal* obstinate refusal to obey; resistance to authority. [from Latin *contumacia*, stubbornness]

contumelious *adj.* haughtily insolent.

contumely *noun* (PL. **contumelies**) *formal* scornful or insulting treatment or words. [from Latin *contumelia*, outrage, insult]

contuse *verb Medicine* to bruise. [from Latin *contundere*, to beat, bruise]

contusion *noun technical* a bruise.

conundrum *noun* 1 a confusing problem. 2 a riddle, especially involving a pun.

conurbation *noun* an extensive built-up area, consisting of several towns whose outskirts have merged. [from CON- + Latin *urbs*, city]

convalesce *verb intrans.* to recover one's strength after an illness, operation or injury, especially by resting. [from Latin *convalescere*, to recover]

convalescence *noun* a period of recovery after illness or injury.

convalescent — *adj.* recovering from an illness. — *noun* a convalescent person.

convection *noun* the transmission of heat through liquids or gases by means of currents that begin to circulate as heated particles rise from the cooler and denser areas to the warmer, less dense areas. [from Latin *con-*, together + *vehere*, to carry]

convector *noun* a heating apparatus that circulates warm air by convection. [from Latin *con-*, together + *vehere*, to carry]

convene *verb trans., intrans.* to assemble or summon to assemble: *convene a meeting*. [from Latin *con-*, together + *venire*, to come]

convener *or* **convenor** *noun* a person who convenes or chairs a meeting.

convenience *noun* 1 the quality of being convenient. 2 something useful or advantageous. 3 *Brit.* a lavatory, especially a public one. — **at one's convenience** when and where it suits one.

convenience food any food which has been partially or entirely prepared by the manufacturer, and requires only to be cooked, eg cook-chill meals, and frozen, canned, or dried foods.

convenient *adj.* 1 fitting in with one's plans, etc; not causing trouble or difficulty. 2 useful; handy; saving time and trouble. 3 available; at hand. [from Latin *convenire*, to fit, be suitable]

conveniently *adv.* in a convenient way.

convent *noun* 1 a community of nuns, or the building they occupy. 2 a school where the teaching is done by nuns. [from Latin *conventus*, assembly]

conventicle *noun Hist.* a secret, especially unlawful, religious meeting. [from Latin *conventiculum*, assembly]

Convention, National the assembly which ruled France (1792–5). It originated with the insurrection of 10 Aug 1792, which overthrew the Legislative Assembly and called for new elections on a completely democratic franchise. In practice, however, very few dared to vote. The Convention proclaimed the First Republic, tried and executed King Louis XVI, and was forced to authorize the extreme measures of the French Revolution (1793–4), under Robespierre and the Committee of Public Safety. With the downfall of Robespierre at Thermidor (July 1794), the Convention recovered its own authority, recalled the surviving Girondins, established a new constitution, the Directory (1795), and dissolved itself.

convention *noun* 1 a large and formal conference or assembly. 2 a formal treaty or agreement. 3 a custom or generally accepted practice, especially in social behaviour. [from Latin *conventio*, meeting, agreement]

conventional *adj.* 1 traditional; normal; customary. 2 conservative or unoriginal: *conventional attitudes*. 3 *said of weapons or warfare* non-nuclear.

conventionality *noun* (PL. **conventionalities**) 1 being conventional. 2 something which is established by use or custom.

conventionalize *or* **conventionalise** *verb* to make conventional.

conventionally *adv.* in a conventional way; by way of convention.

Convention on International Trade in Endangered Species (ABBREV. **CITES**) *Environ.* an international convention founded in 1973 with the aim of controlling the trade in endangered plant and animal species.

converge *verb intrans.* 1 (**converge on** *or* **upon something** *or* **someone**) to move towards or meet at one point. 2 *said eg of opinions* to tend towards one another; to coincide.

convergence *noun* the act or point of converging.

convergent *adj.* 1 converging; coming together. 2 agreeing.

convergent evolution *Biol.* the tendency of unrelated species that inhabit a similar environment to develop superficially similar structures, eg the wings of birds and insects.

converging lens *Physics* a lens that causes light rays to converge to a focus, eg a convex lens.

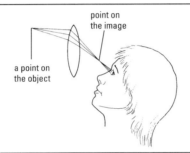

point on the image

a point on the object

converging lens

conversant *adj.* (**conversant with something**) having a thorough knowledge of it. [from Latin *conversari*, to associate with]

conversation *noun* informal talk between people. [from Latin *conversatio*]

conversational *adj.* 1 relating to conversation. 2 used in conversation rather than formal language. 3 communicative; talkative.

conversationalist *noun* a person fond of, or skilled in, conversation.

conversation analysis *Linguistics* the study of real-life conversations and analysis of their sequential structure with the aim of understanding the strategies used to link different strands and themes, and the ways in which people interact. See also DISCOURSE ANALYSIS.

conversation piece 1 a striking object that stimulates conversation. 2 a group portrait, eg showing members of a family engaged in characteristic activities in their usual setting.

converse[1] *verb intrans.* (with stress on -*verse*) (**converse with someone**) *formal* to hold a conversation with them; to talk to them. [from Latin *conversari*, to associate with]

converse[2] (with stress on *con-*) — *adj.* reverse; opposite. — *noun* opposite. [from Latin *conversus*, opposite]

conversely *adv.* in a converse way; on the contrary.

conversion *noun* 1 the act of converting. 2 something converted to another use. 3 *Rugby* the scoring of one or two further points after a try by kicking the ball over the goal.

convert — *verb* (with stress on -*vert*) 1 *trans., intrans.* (**convert something into something else**) to change it in form or function. 2 *trans., intrans.* to win over, or be won over, to another religion, opinion, etc: *many were converted to Christianity / decided to convert to Judaism*. 3 to change into another measuring system or currency. 4 *Rugby* to achieve a conversion after (a try). — *noun* (with stress on *con-*) a person who has been converted to a new religion, practice, etc. [from Latin *convertere*, to change]

converter *or* **convertor** *noun* a person or thing that converts, especially an electrical or electronic device for converting a current or signal.

convertible *adj.* capable of being converted.

convex *adj., said of a surface or shape* outward-curving, like the surface of the eye. See also CONCAVE. [from Latin *convexus*, arched]

convexity *noun* (PL. **convexities**) 1 roundness of form on the outside. 2 a round form or figure.

convey *verb* 1 to carry; to transport. 2 to communicate: *difficult to convey exactly what I mean*. 3 *Legal* to transfer the ownership of (property). [from Old French *conveier*, from Latin *via*, way]

conveyable *adj.* capable of being conveyed.

conveyance *noun* the process of conveying. 1 a vehicle of any kind. 2 *Legal* the transfer of the ownership of property.

conveyancer *noun* a person who prepares deeds for the transfer of property.

conveyancing *noun* the act or process of transferring the ownership of property.

conveyer *or* **conveyor** *noun* a person or thing that conveys.

conveyor belt an endless moving rubber or metal belt for conveying articles, eg in a factory.

convict — *verb* (with stress on -*vict*) (**convict someone of something**) to prove or declare them guilty of a crime. — *noun* (with stress on *con-*) a person serving a prison sentence. [from Latin *convincere*]

conviction *noun* 1 the act of convicting; an instance of being convicted. 2 the state of being convinced; a strong belief. — **carry conviction** to be convincing. [from Latin *convincere*, to overcome, convict]

convince *verb* (**convince someone of something**) to persuade them of it; to cause them to believe it. [from Latin *convincere*, to overcome]

convinced *adj.* firm in one's belief: *a convinced atheist*.

convincing *adj.* 1 believable. 2 certain, positive. 3 *said of a victory* achieved by a significant margin.

convincingly *adv.* in a convincing way; so as to convince.

convivial *adj.* 1 lively, jovial, sociable and cheerful. 2 festive. [from Latin *convivialis*, from *convivium*, feast]

conviviality *noun* 1 cheerful sociability. 2 festivity.

convivially *adv.* in a convivial way.

Convocation a gathering of Church of England clergy, originally in the provinces of Canterbury and York, to regulate affairs of the Church. The *Upper House* consists of the archbishop and bishops; the *Lower House* of representatives of the lower clergy. Since the early 20c the two convocations have met together as the Church Assembly, which meets two or three times a year, with powers regulated by Parliament.

convocation *noun* 1 the act of summoning together. 2 an assembly. 3 (**Convocation**) *Church of E.* see as separate entry. 4 a formal assembly of graduates of a college or university. [from Latin *convocatio*, summoning together]

convoke *verb* to call together; to assemble: *convoke the committee*. [from Latin *convocare*]

convoluted *adj.* **1** coiled and twisted. **2** complicated: *convoluted reasoning*. [from Latin *convolvere*, to roll together]

convolution *noun* a twist or coil.

convolvulus *noun* the bindweed, or other twining plant of the same family. [from Latin *convolvere*, to roll up]

convoy — *noun* a group of vehicles or merchant ships travelling together, or under escort. — *verb* to accompany for protection. [from Old French *convoier*, from Latin *con-*, with + *via*, way]

convulse *verb trans., intrans.* to jerk or distort violently by or as if by a powerful spasm. [from Latin *convellere*, to pull violently]

convulsion *noun* **1** the state of being convulsed. **2** (*often* **convulsions**) a violent involuntary contraction of the muscles of the body, or a series of such contractions, resulting in contortion of the limbs and face, and sometimes accompanied by loss of consciousness. Convulsions may be caused by grand mal epilepsy, high fever, poisoning, meningitis, brain damage, etc. **3** (**convulsions**) *colloq.* spasms of laughter. [from Latin *convulsio*]

convulsive *adj.* **1** causing or affected by convulsions. **2** spasmodic.

convulsively *adv.* in a convulsive way.

Conwy, English **Conway** POP (1981) 13 000, a historic market town and resort in Aberconwy district, Gwynedd, NW Wales. It lies at the head of the R Conwy. A road tunnel runs beneath the river. NOTABLE FEATURES castle (13c); walls around the town.

cony *noun* (PL. **conies**) **1** a rabbit. **2** its fur used for clothing, etc. [from Old French *conil*]

coo¹ — *noun* the soft murmuring call of a dove. — *verb* (**cooed, cooing**) **1** *intrans.* to make this sound. **2** *intrans., trans.* to murmur affectionately. [imitative]

coo² *interj. colloq.* used to express amazement.

cooee — *interj.* used to attract attention. — *verb intrans.* (**cooed, cooeeing**) to call 'cooee'. [from an Australian Aboriginal language]

Cook, James (1728–79) English navigator, born in Marton, Yorkshire. He joined the navy in 1755 and became master in 1759. He surveyed the area around the St Lawrence R, Quebec, then in the *Endeavour* carried the Royal Society expedition to Tahiti to observe the transit of Venus across the Sun (1768–71). On the return, he circumnavigated New Zealand and charted parts of Australia. In his second voyage he sailed round Antarctica (1772–5), and discovered several Pacific island groups. His third voyage (1776–9) aimed to discover a passage round the north coast of America from the Pacific, but he was forced to turn back, and on his return journey was killed by natives on Hawaii.

Cook, Thomas (1808–92) British railway excursion and tourist pioneer, born in Melbourne, Derbyshire. He worked at several jobs before becoming a Baptist missionary in 1828. He organized his first railway excursion in 1841, from Leicester to Loughborough. His travel agency is now a worldwide organization.

Cook, Mount a mountain in W South I, New Zealand, in the Southern Alps. It is the highest peak in New Zealand at a height of 3 764m. The Tasman Glacier is 29km/18mi long and 2km/1.2mi wide.

cook — *verb* **1** *trans., intrans.* to prepare or be prepared by heating. **2** *colloq.* to alter (accounts, etc) dishonestly. — *noun* a person who cooks or prepares food.

— **cook something up** *colloq.* to concoct or invent it: *tried to cook up an excuse*.

what's cooking? *colloq.* what's up?; what's the plan?

[from Anglo-Saxon *coc*, from Latin *coquus*]

cook-chill *adj. Food Science* denoting foods, especially individual meals, that are cooked, packaged, and stored in a refrigerated state, and require reheating before serving.

Cooke, (Alfred) Alistair (1908–) British journalist and broadcaster. He joined the BBC as a film critic in 1934 but then became a foreign correspondent and specialized in American affairs. He wrote and narrated *America: a personal history of the United States* (1971–2) and has broadcast the weekly radio programme *Letter From America* since 1946.

cooker *noun* **1** an apparatus, or special pot, for cooking food. **2** *colloq.* (*also* **cooking-apple**) an apple for cooking rather than eating raw.

cookery *noun* the art or practice of cooking food.

cookery book *or* **cookbook** a book of recipes.

cookie *noun* **1** *North Amer.* a biscuit. **2** *Scot.* a bun. **3** *colloq.* a person: *a smart cookie*.

— **that's the way the cookie crumbles** *North Amer. colloq.* that's how things usually turn out. [from Dutch *koekje*, little cake]

Cook Islands POP (1992e) 17 000, a widely scattered group of 15 volcanic and coral islands, c.3 200km/2 000mi NE of New Zealand, S Pacific Ocean. AREA 238sq km/92sq mi. It is a Self-Governing Territory in free association with New Zealand. CAPITAL Avarua (on Rarotonga I). TIME ZONE GMT +10. The population is largely Polynesian; Christianity is the main religion. OFFICIAL LANGUAGE English with local languages spoken widely. CURRENCY the New Zealand dollar. PHYSICAL DESCRIPTION the islands comprise the Northern Group and the Southern Group; the Northern Group, except Nassau, are low-lying coral atolls with central lagoons; in the Southern Group, Palmerston and Manuae are typical atolls, while Takutea, like Nassau, is a low coral island without a central lagoon; others are mainly volcanic with fringing coral reefs; the highest island, Rarotonga, rises to 650m. CLIMATE damp and tropical, with rainfall heavy on forested volcanic slopes of S islands; the hurricane season lasts from Nov to Apr. HISTORY placed under British protection between 1888 and 1901; became a New Zealand dependency in 1901; internally self-governing since 1965. GOVERNMENT governed by an elected 24-member Legislative Assembly, with a Premier as head of state; a high commissioner represents British sovereign and New Zealand interests. ECONOMY mainly fishing and agriculture, especially copra, citrus fruits, pineapples, tomatoes, bananas; fruit processing; tourism (especially in Rarotonga and Aitutaki).

Cookson, Catherine (Ann) (1906–) English novelist, born in East Jarrow, Tyneside. She did not begin to write until in her 40s, publishing her first novel, *Kate Hannigan*, in 1950. Most of her novels are set in NE England and are full of tragedy and romance. They include the Mallen trilogy (1973–4), *Tilly Trotter* (1981), *The Moth* (1986), and *The House of Women* (1992).

Cook Strait the channel of the Pacific Ocean separating North I from South I, New Zealand. It is 23–130km/14–80mi wide. Captain Cook visited the strait in 1770.

cool — *adj.* **1** between cold and warm; fairly cold. **2** pleasantly fresh; free of heat: *a cool breeze*. **3** calm: *keep a cool head*. **4** lacking enthusiasm; unfriendly: *a cool response*. **5** impudent; audacious; brazen. **6** *said of a large sum* at least: *made a cool million*. **7** *colloq.* admirable; excellent. **8** *said of colours* suggestive of coolness, typically pale and containing blue. — *noun* **1** a cool part or period; coolness: *in the cool of the evening*. **2** *colloq.* self-control; composure: *lose/keep one's cool*. — *verb trans., intrans.* (**cool down** *or* **off**) **1** to become cool. **2** to become less interested or enthusiastic. (**to cool something down** *or* **off**) to make it cool.

— **cool it** *colloq.* to calm down.

cool one's heels to be kept waiting.

play it cool to deal with a situation calmly but warily.

[from Anglo-Saxon *col*]

coolant *noun* a liquid or gas used as a cooling agent, especially a fluid used to remove heat from a working engine.

cooler *noun* **1** a container or device for cooling things. **2** *slang* prison.

Coolidge, (John) Calvin (1872–1933) US Republican politician, the 30th President, born in Plymouth, Vermont. He became a lawyer, was Governor of Massachusetts (1919–20), Vice-President 1921–3, then President (1923–9) on Harding's death. A strong supporter of US business interests, he was triumphantly re-elected by the Republicans in 1924, but refused renomination in 1928.

coolie *noun offensive* **1** an unskilled native labourer in Eastern countries. **2** *South Afr.* an Indian. [from Tamil *kuli*, hired person]

cooling-off period an interval for reflection and negotiation before taking action.

cooling tower a tall structure resembling a tower, in which water heated in an industrial process is cooled for re-use.

coolly *adv.* **1** with a cool manner. **2** calmly, indifferently. **3** impudently.

coolness *noun* **1** being cool. **2** moderate cold. **3** loss of friendship. **4** lack of enthusiasm. **5** calmness.

coomb *noun* a hollow in a hillside, or a short valley. [from Anglo-Saxon *cumb*, valley]

coon *noun* **1** *offensive slang* a black person. **2** *North Amer. colloq.* a raccoon.

coop *noun* a cage for hens.

— **coop someone** *or* **something up** to confine them in a small space.

[related to Anglo-Saxon *cypa*, basket]

co-op *noun colloq.* a co-operative society, or a shop run by one.

Cooper, Sir Astley (1768–1841) English surgeon, born at Brooke Hall, Norfolk. In 1800 he became surgeon to Guy's Hospital, and in 1813 professor at the College of Surgeons. Famous for raising surgery from its primitive state to a science, he removed a tumour from the head of King George IV (1820) and in 1828 was appointed Sergeant-Surgeon to the King. His major work was *Anatomy and Surgical Treatment of Hernia* (1804–7).

Cooper, Gary (Frank James) (1901–61) US film actor, born in Helena, Montana. A newspaper cartoonist in Los Angeles before working as an extra in silent films, his first leading role came in *The Winning of Barbara Worth* (1926). He then starred as the archetypal hero of many westerns, including the Hemingway epics *A Farewell to Arms* (1932) and *For Whom the Bell Tolls* (1943), as well as *High Noon* (1952), for which he won an Oscar. His roles also represented the best of US small-town virtues in, for example, *Mr Deeds Goes to Town* (1936), his first Oscar-winner. He received a Special Academy Award in 1960.

Cooper, Henry (1934–) English boxer, born in Bellingham, Kent, the only man to win the Lonsdale Belt outright on three occasions (1961, 1965, and 1970). He beat Brian London to win his first British heavyweight title in 1959. He floored Muhammad Ali (then known as Cassius Clay) in 1963, though he did not win the fight, and in 1966 he fought him for the World heavyweight title but was forced to retire in the 6th round on account of a bad cut. In 1971 he lost his British heavyweight title in a disputed contest against Joe Bugner, and announced his retirement. In 1993 he sold his Lonsdale Belts, following losses incurred as a Lloyds' 'name'.

Cooper, James Fenimore (1789–1851) US novelist, born in Burlington, New Jersey. He joined the navy in 1806, but resigned in 1811 and began to write novels. He is best known for his five 'Leather-Stocking Tales', American frontier adventure novels including *The Last of the Mohicans* (1826) and *The Pathfinder* (1840).

Cooper, Leon Neil (1930–) US physicist, born in New York City. Working at the University of Illinois, he developed 'BCS' theory, the first satisfactory theory of how superconductivity arises, jointly with John Bardeen and John Schrieffer. For this work they shared the 1972 Nobel Prize for Physics.

cooper *noun* a person who makes or repairs barrels. [from Latin *cuparius*, from *cupa*, cask]

co-operate *verb intrans.* **1** (**co-operate with someone**) to work together with them. **2** to be helpful, or willing to fit in with others' plans. [from CO- + OPERATE]

co-operation *noun* **1** the act of co-operating. **2** willingness to help. **3** assistance.

co-operative — *adj.* **1** relating to, or giving, co-operation. **2** helpful; willing to fit in with others' plans, etc. **3** *said of a business or farm* jointly owned by workers, with profits shared equally. — *noun* a co-operative business or farm.

co-operatively *adv.* in a co-operative way.

Co-operative Party a British political party (established 1917), which grew out of the ideas of voluntary mutual economic assistance developed in the 19c by Robert Owen. It soon became closely integrated with the Labour Party.

co-operative society a profit-sharing association for the cheaper purchase of goods.

Co-operative Wholesale Society (ABBREV. **CWS**) an organization, founded in 1863, to which most co-operative retail stores were affiliated by the 1900s. The co-operative movement was inspired by the work of Robert Owen in the early 19c, and the early co-operative stores followed the principles of the first one, which was established in Rochdale in 1844. The CWS acted as manufacturer, wholesaler, and banker, and profits were distributed to consumers in the form of a dividend (later stamps) which could be redeemed for cash or against later purchases.

co-operator *noun* a person who co-operates.

co-opt *verb*, *said of the members of a body, etc* to choose as an additional member. [from Latin *cooptare*, to appoint, admit as member]

co-option *noun* the act or process of co-opting.

co-optive *adj.* that is co-opted.

co-ordinate — *verb* (pronounced *-nate*) **1** to combine, integrate, and adjust (a number of different parts or processes) so as to relate smoothly one to another. **2** to bring (one's limbs or bodily movements) into a smoothly functioning relationship. — *adj.* (pronounced *-nət*) **1** relating to, or involving, co-ordination or co-ordinates. **2** *Grammar, said of clauses* equal in status, as when joined by *and* or *but*. — *noun* (pronounced *-nət*) **1** (*usually* **coordinate**) *Maths., Geog.* either of a pair of numbers taken from a vertical and horizontal axis which together establish the position of a fixed point, eg on a map. **2** (**co-ordinates**) garments designed to be worn together.

coordinate geometry *Geom.* a system of geometry in which points, lines, and surfaces are located in two-dimensional or three-dimensional space by means of coordinates. For example, a point on a two-dimensional plane can be represented by a pair of coordinates that define its position in relation to a horizontal x-axis and a vertical y-axis that are set at right angles to each other, meeting at a point called the *origin*. A line or curve (such as a parabola) consisting of a series of points can be represented as an algebraic equation, so that the geometry of such a figure can be analysed by manipulating algebraic expressions without the need to plot a graph. – Also called *analytical geometry*.

co-ordination *noun* **1** ordered action together. **2** balanced or skilful movement.

co-ordinator *noun* a person who co-ordinates an activity, etc.

coot *noun* **1** a water bird with a white patch above the beak. **2** *old colloq. use* a fool. [from Middle English *cote*]

cop[1] *noun slang* a policeman. [from COPPER[2]]

cop[2] *verb* (**copped, copping**) *slang* **1** to catch. **2** to grab; to seize. **3** to suffer (a punishment, etc). — **cop it** *slang* to be punished.
cop out *colloq.* to escape or withdraw; to avoid a responsibility.
not much cop *colloq.* of little use or interest. [from Old French *caper*, to seize]

Copán an ancient Mayan city which flourished in the 8c in the Motagua Basin of W Honduras, noted for its three-dimensional stone carving. In 1839 the US explorer John Lloyd Stephens (1805–52) and artist Frederick Catherwood (1799–1856) bought the site for $50 from the local inhabitants so they could uncover and record the monuments uninterrupted. It is a World Heritage site.

cope[1] *verb intrans.* **1** (**cope with something**) to deal with a difficulty or problem, etc successfully. **2** to manage; to get by. [from Old French *couper*, to hit]

cope[2] *noun* a long sleeveless cape worn by clergy on ceremonial occasions. [from Latin *capa*]

Copeau, Jacques (1879–1949) French theatre manager, director, actor, teacher, and drama critic, born in Paris. He was co-founder of the *Nouvelle Revue Française* (1908) for which he wrote until 1913, when he established the Théâtre du Vieux-Colombier company. This initiated a major renovation in French theatre, and his theatre school's methods influenced drama training throughout the West. In 1924 he formed an acting troupe, Les Copiaus (1924–9).

Copenhagen, Danish **København**, ancient **Hafnia** POP (1992e) 1.3m, the capital of Denmark, situated on the E coast of Zealand and the N part of Amager I. It is an important shipping and commercial centre. HISTORY developed around 12c fortifications; received its charter in 1254; became capital in 1443. NOTABLE FEATURES old citadel of Frederikshavn; Tivoli Amusement Park (May–Sep); Amalienborg Palace (residence of the Danish monarch since 1794); Christiansborg Palace; town hall (1894–1905); National (Thorwaldsen) Museum; cathedral; Little Mermaid Sculpture; Trinitatiskirke (17c); Rosenborg Castle (1610–24), now a museum.

Copenhagen, Battles of British naval operations (1801, 1807) aimed at preventing Danish neutrality from benefiting France during the Napoleonic Wars. The first (Apr 1801), led by Admirals Hyde Parker (1739–1807) and Nelson, resulted in Denmark's withdrawal from the Armed Neutrality. After the bombardment of Copenhagen (Sep 1807) by Admiral James Gambier (1756–1833) and Arthur Wellesley (later Duke of Wellington), the Danes surrendered their fleet and stores.

Copernican system *Astron.* a model of the Solar System, proposed by Copernicus in 1543, in which the Sun is regarded as the centre, with the Earth and other planets moving in perfectly circular orbits around it (a *heliocentric* system). Kepler later showed that the paths of the planets are ellipses, and Newton explained the orbits in terms of gravitational theory.

Copernicus, Nicolas (1473–1543) Polish astronomer, born in Toruń, Prussia (now in Poland). He studied mathematics and optics at Kraków, then canon law at Bologna, before becoming canon of Frombork. His *De Revolutionibus Orbium Coelestium* (On the Revolution of the Celestial Spheres, 1543) received a hostile reception as it challenged ancient teaching, but finally led to acceptance

that the Sun, rather than the Earth, lies at the centre of our solar system.

copier *noun* a machine for making copies, especially photocopies.

co-pilot *noun* the assistant pilot of an aircraft.

coping *noun* the top row of stones in a wall. [related to COPE[2]]

coping-stone *noun* one of the stones forming the top row in a wall, etc.

copious *adj.* plentiful. [from Latin *copiosus*]

copiously *adv.* in abundance, plentifully.

Copland, Aaron (1900–90) US composer, born in New York City. He studied under Rubin Goldmark, and in France under Nadia Boulanger. After his return to the USA (1924), he produced a series of early works influenced by Stravinsky, neoclassical in outlook and employing jazz idioms, which was followed by compositions that drew on US tradition and folk music, as in the ballets *Billy the Kid* (1938) and *Appalachian Spring* (1944). He also composed film scores, two operas, and three symphonies.

cop-out *noun colloq.* an avoidance of a responsibility; an escape or withdrawal.

Coppélia, in full ***Coppélia, ou La fille aux yeux d'émail (Coppelia, or The Girl with Enamel Eyes)*** a ballet by Léo Delibes (1870), based on E T A Hoffman's story 'The Sandman', and later used by the composer as the basis for a suite.

copper[1] — *noun* **1** *Chem.* (SYMBOL **Cu**, ATOMIC NUMBER **29**) a soft reddish-brown metal that occurs both as the free metal and in various ores, especially copper pyrites (chalcopyrite). It is an excellent conductor of heat and electricity, and is used to make electric cables, wire, pipes, and coins. Its main alloys are brass (copper and zinc) and bronze (copper and tin), and it is an important trace element in many plants and animals. **2** any coin of low value made of copper or bronze. **3** a large metal vessel for boiling water in. — *adj.* of the brownish-red colour of copper. [from Latin *cuprum*, from *cyprium aes*, brass of Cyprus]

copper[2] *noun slang* a policeman. [from COP[2]]

Copperbelt POP (1990) 1.6m, a province in central Zambia. AREA 31 328sq km/12 093sq mi. The province is the economic centre of the country because of its vast copper and cobalt reserves. The world's largest known deposits are situated here, with chief mines at Mufulira, Nkana, and Chibuluma. The mining area extends into the N of the country and into S Zaire. CAPITAL Ndola. CHIEF TOWNS Chilonga, Kitwe, Luanshya.

copper-bottomed *adj.* **1** *said eg of ships or pans* having the bottom protected by a layer of copper. **2** *colloq.* reliable, especially financially.

Copperfield, David see DAVID COPPERFIELD.

copperhead *noun* a poisonous Australian or American snake with a copper-coloured head.

copper (II) sulphate *Chem.* (FORMULA $CuSO_4$) a white compound that tends to absorb

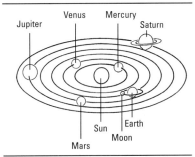

Copernican system

moisture from the atmosphere, forming a blue crystalline hydrate ($CuSO_4.5H_2O$). It is used in electroplating, and as an antiseptic, pesticide, and wood preservative.

copperplate *noun* **1** *Printing* a copper plate used for engraving or etching, or a print made from it. **2** fine regular handwriting of the style formerly taught in schools and used on copperplates.

copper pyrites *Geol.* chalcopyrite.

coppery *adj.* like copper.

coppice — *noun Bot.* an area of woodland in which trees are regularly cut back to ground level to encourage the growth of side shoots, which are then periodically harvested for firewood, fencing, etc. — *verb* to manage woodland in this way. [from Old French *copeiz*]

Coppola, Francis Ford (1939–) US film director and screenwriter, born in Detroit, Michigan. His first feature film as director was *Dementia 13* (1963), and this was followed by the musical, *Finian's Rainbow* (1967). Among his outstanding productions are *The Godfather* (1972; *Part II*, 1974; *Part III*, 1990) and his controversial study of the Vietnam War, *Apocalypse Now* (1979). Later films include *The Cotton Club* (1984), *Peggy Sue Got Married* (1987), and *Bram Stoker's Dracula* (1992).

copra *noun* the dried kernel of the coconut, yielding coconut oil. [from Portuguese *copra*, from Malayalam (Indian language) *koppara*]

coprolalia *noun Psychol.* the repetitive use of indecent language, which may be involuntary, eg as a symptom of Tourette's syndrome, a disorder characterized by severe nervous tics. [from Greek *kopros*, dung]

copse *noun* a coppice.

Copt *noun* **1** a member of the Coptic Church. **2** an Egyptian descended from the ancient Egyptians.

Coptic — *noun* the language of the Copts, now used only in the Coptic Church. — *adj.* relating to the Copts or their language. [from Greek *Aigyptios*, Egyptian]

Coptic Church the Christian Church in Egypt, of ancient origin and claiming St Mark as its Founder and scholars and bishops of Alexandria in the early centuries of Christianity as its Fathers (eg Clement and Athanasius). With the condemnation of Patriarch Dioscuros and the Monophysite doctrine (ie that Jesus Christ was divine in nature only, rather than both human and divine) by the Council of Chalcedon (451), the Copts split from the Orthodox Church. The Copts have links with other Monophysite Churches in Armenia, Ethiopia, and Syria, and have preserved the ancient liturgy in the Coptic language, and they observe the sacraments of the ancient Alexandrian rite. It maintains a monastic tradition and structure, and its head (called a 'pope') is elected by a religious tribunal and confirmed by the Egyptian government. [from Greek *aigyptos*, Egyptian]

copula *noun Grammar* a verb that links subject and complement, eg *is* in *She is a doctor*. [from Latin *copula*, bond]

copulate *verb intrans.* to have sexual intercourse. [from Latin *copulare*, to bind, couple]

copulation *noun* sexual intercourse.

copy — *noun* (PL. **copies**) **1** an imitation or reproduction. **2** one of the many specimens of a book, or of a particular issue of a magazine, newspaper, etc. **3** written material for printing, especially as distinct from illustrations, etc. **4** the wording of an advertisement. **5** material suitable for a newspaper article. — *verb* (**copies, copied**) **1** to imitate. **2** to make a copy of. **3** *trans., intrans.* to reproduce; to photocopy. **4** *trans., intrans.* to make a copy of another's work, pretending that it is one's own. **5** to give a copy to. [from Latin *copia*, transcript]

copybook — *noun* a book of handwriting examples for copying. — *adj.* **1** *derog.* unoriginal. **2** faultless; perfect.
— **blot one's copybook** to spoil one's good record by misbehaviour or error.

copycat *noun derog.* a mere imitator.

copyist *noun* **1** a person who makes copies in writing. **2** an imitator.

copyright *noun* the sole right to print, publish, translate, perform, film, or record a literary, dramatic, musical, or artistic work.
◇ Most countries (with the major exception of China) have their own copyright laws. International protection is given by means of two major conventions, the Berne Convention and the Universal Copyright Convention, which lay down minimum standards for member states. In Britain, copyright law was revised in the Copyright, Designs, and Patents Act of 1988, and is chiefly aimed at protecting works of British citizens, or works first published in Britain.

copywriter *noun* a person who writes advertising copy.

Coquelin, Benoît Constant (1841–1909) French actor, born in Boulogne. He made his début with the Comédie-Française in 1860. Unrivalled as a comic actor, his greatest successes included Figaro, Tartuffe, and Cyrano de Bergerac, a role he performed over 400 times. His *L'art et le comedien* (Art and the Actor, 1880) is an important contribution to the study of acting.

coquetry *noun* flirtation.

coquette *noun* a flirtatious woman. [from French *coquet*, diminutive of *coq*, cock]

coquettish *adj.* flirting; like a flirt.

coquettishly *adv.* with a coquettish manner.

coquettishness *noun* coquettish behaviour.

Cor. *abbrev. Biblical* Corinthians.

cor- see CON-.

Cora a female first name. [origin unclear; possibly a Latinized form of Greek *kore*, maiden]

coracle *noun* a small, oval rowing-boat made of wickerwork covered with hides or other waterproof material. [from Welsh *corwgl*]

coral — *noun* **1** a tiny invertebrate marine animal, found mainly in tropical seas, belonging to the same class (Anthozoa) as sea anemones, and consisting of a hollow tube with a mouth, surrounded by tentacles, at the top. The tentacles trap small crustaceans and pass them to the mouth. **2** a hard chalky substance of various colours, formed from the skeletons of this animal. **3** a pinkish-orange colour. — *adj.* pinkish-orange in colour. [from Greek *korallion*]
◇ Corals are surrounded and supported by a hard chalky cup-shaped skeleton made of calcium carbonate. Some corals are solitary, but the majority live in colonies built by budding, during which process branches sprout from above the skeleton and develop their own mouths and tentacles. The skeleton then grows up around the new branches, and eventually a colony consisting of millions of corals is formed, the individual members of the colony forming a continuous sheet of living tissue that covers the chalky skeleton. Such colonies can be beautifully coloured and form a variety of shapes. Reef-building corals form huge reefs thousands of kilometres long in clear water along tropical and subtropical shores, especially in the Indian Ocean.

Coral Island, The a children's novel by R M Ballantyne (1858). It describes the adventures of three boys (Ralph, Jack, and Peterkin) who are shipwrecked on a desert island.

coral island *or* **reef** a coral reef containing a central lagoon that has become raised above sea level, and has then drained to form a hollow, eventually becoming colonized by plants, insects, birds, etc. Coral islands are found mainly in the Pacific and Indian Oceans.

coralline *adj.* like or containing coral.

Coral Sea *or* **Solomon Sea** an arm of the Pacific Ocean, bounded W by NE Australia, N by Papua New Guinea and the Solomon Is, and E by Vanuatu and New Caledonia. AREA 4 791 000sq km/ 1 849 000sq mi; the maximum depth in the New Hebrides Trench is 9 175m. There are many coral islands in its waters and the Great Barrier Reef lies along the sea's western edge. It was the scene of a US naval victory over the Japanese in 1942.

Coral Sea Islands, Territory of the an uninhabited territory in the Coral Sea off the NE coast of Australia. Since 1969, it has beeen administered by the Australian government. It comprises scattered reefs and islands (including the Great Barrier Reef) over a sea area of about 1msq km/386 000sq mi. There is a manned meteorological station on Willis I.

coral snake a venomous snake native to the New World and E Asia, usually with bold alternating bands of black, yellow, and red. It produces strong venom, but is not aggressive. Its short fangs do not inject venom easily, and the snake either grips its prey in its mouth after striking it, or bites it several times.

cor anglais (PL. **cors anglais**) a woodwind musical instrument similar to, but lower in pitch than, the oboe. [from French *cor anglais*, English horn]

Corbaccio the deaf and foolish old miser in Ben Jonson's *Volpone*.

corbel *noun Archit.* a stone or timber projecting from a wall, taking the weight of eg a parapet, arch, or bracket. [from Old French *corbel*, crow]

corbelled *adj.* provided with corbels.

corbelling *noun* stone or brickwork made into corbels.

Corbières a sparsely populated upland district in Aude department, Languedoc Roussillon region, S France. It lies between the Massif Central and the Pyrenees with its highest point at Pic de Bugarach (1 231m). The lower-lying area is known for its red wine. CHIEF TOWN Quillan.

Corbusier, Le, pseudonym of **Charles Edouard Jeanneret** (1887–1965) Swiss architect and city planner, born in La Chaux-de-Fonds. He worked in Paris with Auguste Perret, and then with Peter Behrens in Germany (1910–11). In 1919 he published, with Amédée Ozenfant, the Purist manifesto, and developed a theory of the interrelation between modern machine forms and architectural techniques. His first building, based on the technique of the Modulor (a system using units whose proportions were those of the human figure), was the *Unité d'habitation*, Marseilles (1945–50). Some of his buildings are raised on stilts or *piloti* (eg the Swiss Pavilion, Cité Universitaire, Paris). His city planning designs include those used in Algiers (1938–42), Buenos Aires (1938), and Chandigarh (1951). His books, *Vers une architecture* (1923), *Le Modular* (1948), and *Le Modular 2* (1955) have had worldwide influence on town planning and building design.

cord *noun* **1** thin rope or thick string, or a piece of it. **2** *Anat.* a string-like bodily organ. **3** the cable of an electrical appliance. **4** a ribbed fabric, especially corduroy. **5** (**cords**) corduroy trousers. **6** a unit of measurement for cut wood equal to 128 cubic ft. (3.63 m³). [from Greek *chorde*, string]

Corday (d'Armont), (Marie) Charlotte (1768–93) French noblewoman, born in St Saturnin, who was guillotined for murdering the revolutionary leader Jean Paul Marat. She sympathized with the aims of the Revolution, but was horrified by the acts of the Jacobins. She obtained an audience with Marat, while he was in his bath, and stabbed him.

corded *adj., said of fabric* ribbed.

Cordelia the youngest of Lear's three daughters in Shakespeare's *King Lear*, who refuses to pander to her father but remains loyal and loving to him even after being banished from his kingdom.

cordial — *adj.* **1** warm and affectionate. **2** heartfelt; profound: *a cordial dislike.* — *noun* a fruit-flavoured drink. [from Latin *cordialis*, from *cor*, heart]

cordiality *noun* warmth and friendliness; sincerity.

cordially *adv.* warmly, heartily.

cordite *noun* a smokeless explosive, stringy in appearance, used in guns and bombs. [from CORD]

cordless *adj., said of an electrical appliance* operating without a flex; battery-powered.

Córdoba POP (1991) 300 000, the capital of Córdoba province, Andalusia, S Spain. It lies on the R Guadalquivir, 400km/250mi SW of Madrid. The city was the capital of Moorish Spain in the 8c and, today, is a bishopric. NOTABLE FEATURES cathedral; old Jewish quarter; Moorish Alcazar; the Great Mosque is a World Heritage site.

The Mosque at Córdoba, Spain

Córdoba 1 POP (1990e) 1.2m, the capital of Córdoba province, central Argentina, on the R Primero, near the foothills of the Sierra de Córdoba. It was founded by Cabrera in 1573; renowned as a Jesuit mission centre. NOTABLE FEATURES Argentina's first university (1613); cathedral (1758). **2** a province in central Argentina with Córdoba as its capital.

cordon — *noun* **1** a line of police or soldiers, or a system of road blocks, encircling an area so as to prevent or control passage into or out of it. **2** a ribbon bestowed as a mark of honour. **3** a fruit tree trained to grow as a single stem. — *verb* (**cordon something off**) to close off an area with a cordon. [from French *cordon*, diminutive of *corde*, cord]

cordon bleu — *adj., said of a cook or cookery* of the highest standard. — *noun* (PL. **cordons bleus**) a cook of the highest standard. [from French *cordon bleu*, blue ribbon]

corduroy *noun* **1** a thick ribbed cotton fabric. **2** (**corduroys**) trousers made of corduroy. **3** (*also* **corduroy road**) *North Amer.* a road made of logs lying side by side.

core — *noun* **1** the fibrous case at the centre of some fruits, eg apples and pears, containing the seeds. **2** the innermost, central, essential, or unchanging part. **3** the central region of a star or planet, especially the Earth. **4** *Archaeol.* the lump of stone left after flakes have been struck off it for shaping into tools. **5** the central part of a nuclear reactor, containing the fuel, where the nuclear reaction takes place. **6** *Electr.* a piece of magnetic material that, when placed in the centre of a wire coil through which an electric current is being passed, increases the intensity of the magnetic field and the inductance of the coil. Cores are

used in transformers, electromagnets, electric engines, etc. **7** (*in full* **core memory**) the main memory of a computer, where instructions and data are stored in such a way that they are available for immediate use. **8** the inner part of an electric cable. **9** a cylindrical sample of rock, soil, etc, removed with a hollow tubular drill. — *verb* to remove the core of (an apple, etc).

core curriculum *Education* a basic central provision for all pupils, as opposed to a set of options taken only by some. The core curriculum usually includes mathematics, science, and the child's native language.

Corelli, Arcangelo (1653–1713) Italian composer, surnamed 'Il Divino', born in Fusignano. His Concerti grossi and his solo and trio sonatas for violin mark an epoch in chamber music, and had great influence on J S Bach and on contemporary string technique.

corer *noun* a knife with a hollow cylindrical blade for coring fruit.

co-respondent *noun Legal* in divorce cases, a person said to have committed adultery with the partner (called the *respondent*) against whom the case is being brought.

Corfu, Greek **Kérkira** POP (1991) 105 000, the northernmost and second largest of the Ionian Is, Greece. It is situated off the NW coast of Greece, in the Ionian Sea, and is the seventh largest Greek island. AREA 592sq km/229sq mi; length 64km/40mi. PHYSICAL DESCRIPTION the terrain is densely vegetated and semi-mountainous, rising to 907m. CHIEF TOWN Corfu. HISTORY a Corinthian colony was established in the 8c; under Venetian control from 1386 to 1797; a British protectorate from 1815 to 1864, before being ceded to Greece. ECONOMY textiles; fishing; olive oil, fruit; tourism is important. NOTABLE FEATURES Church of St Spyridon; old fortress (1386).

CORGI *abbrev.* Confederation for Registration of Gas Installers (UK).

corgi *noun* a short-legged dog with a thick coat and fox-like head. [from Welsh *cor*, dwarf + *ci*, dog]

Cori, Carl Ferdinand (1896–1984) Czech-born US biochemist, born in Prague. Professor at Washington University in St Louis from 1931, he conducted research into carbohydrate metabolism and the enzymes of animal tissue. He shared the 1947 Nobel Prize for Physiology or Medicine with his wife Gerty Cori and Bernardo Houssay.

coriander *noun* a European plant whose strong-smelling leaves and seeds are used as a flavouring. [from Greek *koriannon*]

Corinne a female first name. [a French form of Greek *Corinna*, from *kore*, maiden]

Corinth, Greek **Kórinthos** POP (1991) 29 000, the capital of Corinth department, Peloponnese region, S Greece. It lies on an isthmus separating the Adriatic Sea from the Aegean Sea. HISTORY founded before 3000 BC; an influential Greek city-state of Dorian origins, often at odds with Ionian Athens; famous in antiquity for its commercial and colonizing activities; transferred to its new site in 1858, after a severe earthquake; construction of the Corinth Canal, bisecting the isthmus, was completed in 1893; the city was rebuilt after a further earthquake in 1928 and a great fire in 1933. NOTABLE FEATURES the site of ancient Corinth, excavated since 1896, lies 7km/4mi SW; there are extensive remains, including the Archaic Temple of Apollo and several basilicas.

Corinth Canal an artificial waterway bisecting the Isthmus of Corinth in Greece. It is 6.5km/4mi long and was built between 1881 and 1893, although excavation of a canal through the isthmus was begun as early as AD 67.

Corinthian *adj.* **1** relating to ancient Corinth in Greece. **2** *Archit.* denoting an order of classical architecture characterized by a style of column

with a fluted shaft and a heavily carved capital having a distinctive acanthus-leaf design. See also DORIC, IONIC.

Corinthians, Letters of Paul to the two New Testament writings written from the apostle Paul to the Church that he founded in Corinth. The first is his response to various ethical and doctrinal problems dividing the Church at Corinth; the second is his response to later developments in this Church, to the efforts to collect funds for the Jerusalem Church, and to charges against him by opponents.

Corinto, formerly **Punta Icacos** POP (1985e) 24 000, the chief Pacific port of Nicaragua, located in Chinandega department.

Coriolanus, Gaius *or* **Gnaeus Marcius** (5c BC) Roman folk hero, named after his capture of the Volscian town of Corioli, and the subject of Shakespeare's play *Coriolanus*. He was banished by the Romans for tyrranical behaviour during a famine (491 BC), took refuge with the Volscians, and proceeded to lead them against Rome. After entreaties from his mother and wife, he spared Rome, and was executed by the Volscians.

Coriolis effect *or* **Coriolis force** *Physics* a hypothetical force that appears to act on objects moving across the Earth's surface, and results from the Earth's rotation. In the northern hemisphere, the path of an object appears to be deflected to the right, and in the southern hemisphere it appears to be deflected to the left. The Coriolis effect is invoked to explain the patterns of trade winds in equatorial regions, and water currents in the oceans. [named after the French physicist Gaspard Gustave de Coriolis]

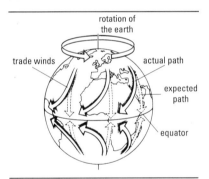

Coriolis effect

Cork, Gaelic **Chorcaigh** POP (1991) 283 000, a county in Munster province, S Irish Republic, bounded S by the Atlantic Ocean. It is a prosperous agricultural and industrial county, and the largest in the Republic. AREA 7 459sq km/2 879sq mi. PHYSICAL DESCRIPTION watered by the Lee, Bandon, and Blackwater rivers; the Boggeragh and Nagles Mts rise in the NW and N. CAPITAL Cork. ECONOMY fishing, agriculture; natural gas and oil off Kinsale Head, with terminal facilities at Whiddy I. NOTABLE FEATURE Blarney Castle.

Cork, Gaelic **Chorcaigh** POP (1991) 174 000, the capital of Cork county, Munster province, S Irish Republic. It is Ireland's third largest city and is a commercial seaport lying on the R Lee, near its mouth on Lough Mahon. NOTABLE FEATURES St Finbarr's Cathedral; St Mary's Cathedral; Shandon Church.

cork — *noun* **1** *Bot.* a layer of tissue that forms below the epidermis in the stems and roots of woody plants, eg trees. It consists of dead cells coated with suberin, a waxy substance that renders them impermeable to air and water, and so protects the underlying cells from water loss and physical injury. Cork is particularly abundant in the bark layer of certain tree species, and is stripped from the cork oak for commercial use.

2 a piece of this used as a stopper for a bottle, etc. — *verb* (*usually* **cork up** *or* **cork something up**) **1** to stop (a bottle, etc) with a cork. **2** to suppress (one's feelings, etc). **3** *intrans.* to be quiet. [from Arabic *qurq*, from Latin *quercus*, oak]

corkage *noun* the fee charged by a restaurant for serving to customers wine that they have bought elsewhere.

corked *adj., said of wine* spoilt as a result of having a faulty cork.

corker *noun old slang use* something or someone marvellous.

cork oak an evergreen tree (*Quercus suber*), native to the Mediterranean region, that grows to a height of up to 20m, and has glossy leaves with spiny margins. Its bark produces a thick cork layer which can be removed in cylindrical sheets from the tree. It is cultivated as a commercial source of cork.

corkscrew — *noun* a tool with a spiral spike for screwing into bottle corks to remove them. — *adj.* shaped like a corkscrew. — *verb intrans.* to move spirally.

corm *Bot. noun* in certain plants, eg crocus, a swollen underground stem, rounded in shape and bearing roots on its lower surface. It functions primarily as a food store between one growing season and the next, and is also involved in the production of new plants from daughter corms which develop and then separate from the parent corm. [from Greek *kormos*, lopped tree trunk]

corm

Cormack, Allan MacLeod (1924–) South African-born US physicist, born in Johannesburg. He worked at Groote Shuur Hospital in Johannesburg before moving to the USA, where he became professor at Tufts University, Massachusetts. For pioneering computerized axial X-ray tomography scanning (CAT), which enables detailed X-ray pictures of 'slices' of the human body to be produced, he shared the 1979 Nobel Prize for Physiology or Medicine with Godfrey Hounsfield.

cormorant *noun* any of over 30 species of seabird with an upright stance, dark brown or black plumage, webbed feet, a long neck, and a slender bill, found along coasts or on inland waters almost worldwide. Cormorants are expert divers and swimmers, and feed mainly on fish. They breed in large colonies. [from French, from Latin *corvus marinus*, sea raven]

Corn. *abbrev.* Cornwall.

corn¹ *noun* **1** cereal plants, in the UK especially wheat, oats, or barley, and in N America maize. **2** the seeds of these plants; grain. **3** *slang* something stale or old-fashioned. [from Anglo-Saxon]

corn² *noun* a small patch of hardened skin, especially on a toe.

— **tread on someone's corns** *colloq.* to hurt their feelings. [from Latin *cornu*, horn]

corn belt the major agricultural region of the US Midwest. It is centred on the states of Iowa and Illinois, and includes parts of South Dakota, Minnesota, Nebraska, Kansas, Missouri, Ohio, and Indiana. Its main products are corn (maize) and other feed-grain; livestock is also raised.

corncob *noun* the core part of an ear of maize, to which the grains are attached.

— **corn on the cob** a corncob cooked and served as a vegetable.

corncrake *noun* a bird with a harsh grating cry, that inhabits cornfields. [from CORN¹ + *crake*, from Norse *krakr*, crow]

corn dolly a figure made of plaited straw.

cornea *noun* the transparent covering of the eyeball. [from Latin *cornea tela*, horny tissue]

corneal *adj.* relating to or in the region of the cornea.

corned beef *adj.* beef that has been salted, cooked, and canned. [from CORN¹]

Corneille, Pierre (1606–84) French dramatist, born in Rouen. His first successful comedy was *Mélite*, and then *Le Cid* (1636), a classical tragedy, took Paris by storm. Other major tragedies were *Horace* (1639), *Cinna* (1639), and *Polyeucte* (1640). *Le Menteur* (The Liar, 1642) entitles him to be called the father of French comedy as well as of French tragedy. A master of the Alexandrine verse form, he wrote many other plays, and in 1671 joined Molière and Philippe Quinault in writing the opera *Psyché*.

cornelian *or* **carnelian** *noun Geol.* a red and white form of agate, used as a semi-precious stone and for making seals. [from Old French *corneline*]

Cornell University in the USA, a university in Ithaca, New York, named after its founder, Ezra Cornell (1807–74) in 1865. Its specialized areas of study include agriculture. Oberlin College for women was opened in 1872.

corner — *noun* **1** a point or place where lines or surface-edges meet; the inside or outside of the angle so formed. **2** an intersection between roads. **3** a quiet or remote place. **4** an awkward situation: *in a tight corner*. **5** *Econ.* control of a particular market gained by buying up the total stocks of a commodity, to re-sell at one's own price. **6** *Boxing* either of the angles of the ring used as a base between bouts by contestants. **7** *Football* a free kick from a corner of the field. — *verb* (**cornered, cornering**) **1** to force into a place or position from which escape is difficult. **2** to gain control of (a market) by buying up total stocks of a commodity. **3** *intrans. said of a driver or vehicle* to turn a corner.

— **cut corners** to spend less money, effort, time, etc on something than one should, especially to save time.

take a corner to negotiate a corner in a motor vehicle: *took the corner too fast*.

turn the corner 1 to go round a corner. **2** to get past the most dangerous stage, eg of an illness.

cormorant

[from Old French *corne*, corner, horn]

cornerstone *noun* **1** a stone built into the corner of the foundation of a building. **2** a crucial or indispensable part; a basis: *the cornerstone of his argument*.

cornet *noun* **1** a brass musical instrument similar to the trumpet. **2** a cone-shaped edible holder for ice cream; an ice-cream cone. [from Old French *cornet*, diminutive of Latin *cornu*, horn]

cornetist *or* **cornettist** *noun* a person who plays the cornet.

cornflakes *pl. noun* toasted maize flakes, eaten as a breakfast cereal.

cornflour *noun* finely ground flour, usually made from maize.

cornflower *noun* a plant with deep blue flowers that grows in cornfields.

cornice *noun* **1** a decorative border of moulded plaster round a ceiling. **2** *Archit.* the lower section of the horizontal layer of masonry surmounting a row of columns. **3** *Archit.* a projecting moulding at the top of an external wall. **4** *Art* the projecting top part of a pedestal. **5** *Mountaineering* an overhang formed of snow or ice. [from Italian *cornice*, crow]

cornily *adv.* in a corny way.

corniness *noun* being corny.

Cornish — *adj.* belonging to Cornwall, its people, or language. — *noun* the Celtic language once spoken in Cornwall, related to Welsh.

Cornish pasty a semicircular folded pastry case containing meat and vegetables.

Corn Islands, Spanish **Islas del Maíz** a pair of small islands, the Grande and Pequeña Is, in Nicaragua, off the Caribbean coast. The larger island is a popular Nicaraguan holiday resort.

Corn Laws British legislation regulating the trade in corn. The most famous Corn Law was that enacted by Lord Liverpool's government in 1815, which imposed prohibitively high duties on the import of foreign corn when the domestic price was lower than 80 shillings (£4) a quarter (eight bushels). Widely criticized by radical politicians as legislation designed to protect the landed interest at the expense of the ordinary consumer, the Corn Law was amended in 1828, with the introduction of a sliding scale. Duties were further reduced by Peel in 1842, and the Laws repealed in 1846.

cornucopia *noun Art* a horn full to overflowing with fruit and other produce, used as a symbol of abundance. [from Latin *cornu*, horn + *copia*, abundance]

cornucopian *adj.* **1** relating to a cornucopia. **2** abundant.

Cornwall, Celtic **Kernow** POP (1992e) 475 000, a county in SW England, divided into eight districts and the Isles of Scilly. It is bounded S by the English Channel, N by Devon, and W by the Atlantic Ocean. AREA 3 564sq km/1 376sq mi. The Cornish nationalist movement revived the Stannary (Tinners' Parliament) in 1974, and there is renewed interest in the Cornish language. CHIEF TOWN Truro (county town). ECONOMY dairy farming; market gardening; fishing; tourism.

Cornwallis, Charles Cornwallis, 1st Marquis (1738–1805) English soldier and statesman, born in London. After serving in part of the Seven Years' War, he accepted a command in the American War of Independence (1775–83), though he was personally opposed to taxing the American colonists. He defeated Horatio Gates at Camden (1780), but was forced to surrender at Yorktown (1781). Appointed Governor-General of India (1786–93, 1804–5), he defeated Tippoo Sahib, and introduced the series of reforms known as the Cornwallis Code. He was also Lord-Lieutenant of Ireland (1798–1801), and negotiated the Peace of Amiens (1802).

corny *adj.* (**cornier, corniest**) *colloq.* **1** *said of a joke* old and stale. **2** embarrassingly old-fashioned or sentimental. [from CORN[1]]

corolla *noun Bot.* a flower's circle of petals. [from Latin *corolla*, garland]

corollary *noun* (PL. **corollaries**) **1** something that follows from another thing that has been proved. **2** a natural or obvious consequence. [from Latin *corollarium*, gift of money, originally for a garland, from *corolla*, garland]

Coromandel Coast the E coast of India, extending more than 650km/400mi from Point Calimere in the S to the mouth of the Krishna R in the N.

coromandel screen a screen made of wood, incised with designs filled with colour or with gold, and lacquered. Such screens were imported in large numbers from the Far East in the late 17c for the European luxury trade. [from the name *Coromandel Coast* in SE India]

corona *noun* (PL. **coronae, coronas**) **1** *Astron.* the outer atmosphere of the Sun, consisting of a halo of hot luminous gases that boil from its surface, visible during a total solar eclipse. **2** *Bot.* in certain plants, eg daffodil, a trumpet-like outgrowth from the corolla of petals. **3** *Physics* the glowing region produced by ionization of the air surrounding a high-voltage conductor. [from Latin *corona*, crown]

corona

coronary — *adj. Physiol.* denoting the arteries supplying blood to the heart muscle. — *noun* (PL. **coronaries**) a coronary thrombosis. [from Latin *coronarius*, encircling (the heart) like a wreath, from *corona*, wreath]

coronary thrombosis *Medicine* the formation of a blood clot (thrombus) in one of the two coronary arteries that supply blood to the heart muscle. It blocks the flow of blood to the heart, resulting in the death of part of the heart muscle (*myocardial infarction*), which gives rise to a heart attack. It is usually caused by the accumulation of fatty deposits and scar tissue on the inner walls of the arteries.

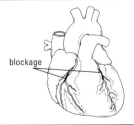

blockage

coronary thrombosis

coronation *noun* the ceremony of crowning a king, queen, or consort. [from Latin *coronatio*, from *corona*, crown]

◇ In Britain, monarchs are crowned in Westminster Abbey, where the English kings have been crowned since 1066. The coronation ceremony is made up of various elements including administration of the oath, presentation of the Bible, the anointing (a solemn and private part of the ceremony carried out under a canopy), the presentation of the various emblems of knighthood and royalty, including the robe, orb, sceptre, ring, and rod, the actual crowning (with St Edward's Crown), the benediction, the enthroning, and the homage of the princes of the blood and the peerage.

coroner *noun* **1** an official who inquires into sudden or accidental deaths, and investigates cases of treasure trove. **2** the principal officer of one of the six ancient divisions of the Isle of Man. [from Old French *corouner*, supervisor of the Crown's pleas]

coronet *noun* **1** a small crown. **2** a circlet of jewels for the head. [from Old French *coronet*, diminutive of *corone*, crown]

coronograph *or* **coronagraph** *noun Astron.* an optical instrument that is used to observe the Sun's corona (outermost layer), which, because of the overwhelming brilliance of the Sun's disc, can normally only be seen during the brief duration of a total solar eclipse. The coronograph consists of a telescope, inside which is a rounded object that produces an artificial eclipse. [from Latin *corona*, crown]

Corot, (Jean Baptiste) Camille (1796–1875) French landscape painter, born in Paris. He took up art in 1822, and after visiting Italy settled in Paris (1827). His main sketching ground was at Barbizon, in the Forest of Fontainebleau. Several of his works, including *La Danse des nymphes* (1850), are in the Louvre, Paris.

corp. *abbrev.* **1** (*also* **Corp.**) corporal. **2** corporation.

corpora see CORPUS.

corporal[1] *noun* an officer in the army or air force just below a sergeant in rank. [from Italian *caporale*, from *capo*, head]

corporal[2] *adj.* relating to the human body. [from Latin *corporalis*, from *corpus*, body]

corporal punishment physical punishment such as beating or caning.

corporate *adj.* **1** shared by members of a group; joint. **2** belonging, or relating, to a corporation: *corporate finance*. **3** formed into a corporation: *a corporate body*. [from Latin *corporare*, to form into a body]

corporately *adv.* in a corporate way.

corporate raider a company or individual who seeks to gain control of a business by acquiring a large proportion of its stock.

corporate state *Politics* a capitalist state which operates corporatism; applied to those authoritarian states in which producers' organizations theoretically have decision-making powers regarding economic policy but are merely acting as agents of the state, as in Fascist Italy from the 1920s to the 1940s where employers' and workers' organizations were represented in the Council of Corporations.

corporate strategy the broad aims and strategies that a company wishes to follow over a period of time, especially five years.

corporation *noun* **1** a body of people acting jointly eg for administration or business purposes. **2** the council of a town or city. **3** *facetious* a paunch. [from Latin *corporatio*, trade guild]

Corporation Act a British Act passed (1661) by the Cavalier Parliament soon after the Restoration of Charles II to restrict office in municipal corporations to those who took the sacrament according to Church of England usage. Part of the reassertion of Anglican supremacy represented by the Clarendon Code, the Act remained on the statute book until 1828.

corporation tax a tax paid by companies on the profits they make.

corporatism *or* **corporativism** *noun Politics* the belief that the state should intervene in a capitalist economy in order to guarantee social harmony. Corporatism operates in many modern capitalist democracies.

corporeal *adj.* relating to the body as distinct from the soul; bodily; physical; material. [from Latin *corpus*, body]

corporeality *noun* being corporeal.

corporeally *adv.* in a corporeal way.

corps *noun* (PL. **corps**) **1** a military body or division: *the intelligence corps*. **2** a body of people engaged in particular work: *the diplomatic corps*. [from French *corps*, body]

corps de ballet a company of ballet dancers, eg at a theatre. [from French *corps de ballet*]

corpse *noun* the dead body of a human being. [from Latin *corpus*, body]

corpulence *noun* extreme fatness.

corpulent *adj.* fat; fleshy; obese. [from Latin *corpulentus*]

corpus *noun* (PL. **corpora**) **1** a body of writings, eg by a particular author. **2** a body of written and/or spoken material for language research. **3** *Anat.* the name of any of various structures within the body. [from Latin *corpus*, body]

◇ A language corpus may comprise a large collection of texts and other written and spoken language covering the language as a whole and drawn from a wide variety of sources. As a representative sample of the language it may be used for many different types of linguistic research, such as dictionary-making, and studies of usage and language development. The value of text corpora has been greatly enhanced by the development of computational programs and techniques for analysing them.

corpus callosum (PL. **corpora callosa**) *Anat.* a thick bundle of about 300m nerve fibres in the centre of the brain, that serves to connect the left and right cerebral hemispheres. [from Latin *corpus*, body + *callosus* callous]

Corpus Christi a Roman Catholic festival in honour of the Blessed Sacrament, held on the Thursday after Trinity Sunday. It was instituted in 1264 by Pope Urban IV, and in pre-Reformation England was the time when trade guilds traditionally performed religious dramas.

corpuscle *noun Anat.* any small particle or cell within a tissue or organ, especially a red or white blood cell. [from Latin *corpusculum*, diminutive of *corpus*, body]

corpuscular *adj.* of or relating to corpuscles.

Corpus Juris Canonici the chief collection of Church or canon law of the Roman Catholic Church and, to an extent, of the Anglican Churches. It includes the decrees of popes and canons, and rules formulated by the Councils (eg the Decretals of Gregory IX). Canon law exercised considerable influence on the development of civil and international law. The 'Corpus' was succeeded in the Roman Catholic Church by the *Codex Juris Canonici* (1918). [Latin, = body of canon law]

corpus luteum (PL. **corpora lutea**) *Anat.* in the ovary of female mammals, the mass of yellowish tissue that develops from a ruptured Graafian follicle after ovulation. It secretes the hormone progesterone, which prepares the womb for possible implantation of a fertilized egg. If fertilization does not occur, the corpus luteum degenerates. [from Latin *corpus*, body + *luteus*, yellow]

corral *North Amer.* — *noun* an enclosure for driving horses or cattle into. — *verb* (**corralled, corralling**) to herd or pen into a corral. [from Spanish *corral*]

correct — *verb* 1 to set or put right; to remove errors from. 2 to mark the errors in. 3 to adjust or make better. 4 *old use* to rebuke or punish. — *adj.* 1 free from error; accurate; not mistaken. 2 right; proper; appropriate. 3 conforming to accepted standards: *very correct in his behaviour*.
— **stand corrected** acknowledge one's mistake. [from Latin *corrigere*]

correcting fluid a thick, usually white, liquid for covering up errors in writing or typing.

correction *noun* 1 the act of correcting. 2 an alteration that corrects something. 3 *old use* punishment.

corrective — *adj.* having the effect of correcting or adjusting. — *noun* something that has this effect.

correctly *adv.* in a correct way; so as to be correct.

correctness *noun* being correct.

corrector *noun* someone or something that corrects.

Correggio, originally **Antonio Allegri** (c.1494–1534) Italian Renaissance painter, born in Correggio. In 1518 he began his series of mythological frescoes for the convent of San Paolo at Parma, and from 1521 to 1524 was engaged upon *The Ascension* in the cupola of San Giovanni. He was commissioned for the decoration of the cathedral of Parma in 1522. He also painted many easel pictures on religious themes, including *The Nativity* known as *The Night* (Dresden).

correlate *verb* 1 *intrans., trans. said of two or more things, or of one thing in relation to another* to have a connection or correspondence; to relate one to another: *smoking in pregnancy correlates with lower birth weight.* 2 to combine, compare, show relationships between (information, reports, etc). [from Latin *cor-*, with + *relatio*, carrying back]

correlation *noun Statistics* the strength of the relationship between two random variables. A positive correlation occurs when one variable shows a tendency to increase or decrease in the same way as the other. A negative correlation occurs if one variable tends to increase as the other decreases.

correlative *adj.* 1 mutually linked. 2 *Grammar, said of words* used as an inter-related pair, like *either* and *or*.

correspond *verb intrans.* 1 (**correspond to something**) to be similar or equivalent to it: *an increase in wages followed by a corresponding increase in prices.* 2 (**correspond with *or* to something *or* someone**) to be in agreement; to match. 3 (**correspond with someone**) to write and receive letters from them. [from Latin *cor-*, with + *respondere*, to answer]

correspondence *noun* 1 similarity; equivalence. 2 agreement. 3 communication by letters; letters received or sent.

correspondence course a course of study conducted by post.

correspondent *noun* 1 a person with whom one exchanges letters. 2 a person employed by a newspaper, radio station, etc to send reports from a particular part of the world, or on a particular topic.

corridor *noun* 1 a passageway, esp one off which rooms open or, on a train, one giving access to compartments. 2 a strip of land through foreign territory, giving access eg to a port. 3 a restricted route through the air that air traffic must follow. [from Italian *corridore*, corridor, place for running]

corridors of power places where the people who make the important decisions are to be found.

corrie *noun* in the Highlands of Scotland, a hollow in the side of a hill. [from Gaelic *coire*, pot]

Corrigan-Maguire, Mairead (1944–) Northern Irish peace activist, born in Belfast, the Roman Catholic founder with Betty Williams (1943–) of the Northern Ireland Peace Movement, which consisted of both Roman Catholic and Protestant women and was known as the Community for Peace People (1976). She and Williams shared the 1976 Nobel Peace Prize.

corrigendum *noun* (PL. **corrigenda**) an error for correction, eg in a book. [from Latin *corrigendum*, something to be corrected]

corroborate *verb* to confirm (eg someone's statement): *corroborating evidence.* [from Latin *corroborare*, to strengthen]

corroboration *noun* confirmation.

corroborative *adj.* tending to confirm.

corroborator *noun* a person who corroborates.

corroboree *noun Austral.* 1 a ceremonial or warlike dance. 2 a noisy gathering. [from an Australian Aboriginal language]

corrode *verb* 1 *said eg of rust or chemicals* to eat away (a material or object) little by little. 2 *said of a material or object* to be gradually eaten away. 3 to destroy gradually: *a relationship corroded by mutual ill feeling.* [from Latin *corrodere*, to gnaw to pieces]

corrosion *noun* 1 the wearing away and eventual destruction of a metal or alloy as a result of its oxidation by air, water, or chemicals, eg the rusting of iron and steel, or the tarnishing of silver. 2 a corroded part or patch. [from Latin *corrodere*, to gnaw to pieces]

corrosive *adj.* 1 capable of eating away. 2 *said of language* hurtful, sarcastic.

corrugate *verb* to fold into parallel ridges, so as to make stronger: *corrugated iron.* [from Latin *corrugare*, to wrinkle]

corrugation *noun* 1 the act of wrinkling, or the state of being wrinkled. 2 a wrinkle.

corrupt — *verb* 1 *trans., intrans.* to change for the worse, especially morally. 2 to spoil, deform or make impure. 3 to bribe. 4 *intrans.* to decay or deteriorate. — *adj.* 1 morally evil. 2 accepting bribes. 3 dishonest. 4 *said of a text* so full of errors and alterations as to be unreliable. 5 *Comput., said of a program or data* containing errors arising eg from a fault in the hardware or software. [from Latin *corrumpere*, to spoil]

corruptibility *noun* a tendency to be corrupted.

corruptible *adj.* capable of being or liable to be corrupted.

corruption *noun* 1 the process of corrupting or condition of being corrupt. 2 a deformed form of a word or phrase: *'Santa Claus' is a corruption of 'Saint Nicholas'.*

corruptive *adj.* tending to corrupt.

corruptly *adv.* in a corrupt way.

corsage *noun* a small spray of flowers for pinning to the bodice of a dress. [from Old French *corsage*, bodily shape, later bodice, from Latin *corpus*]

corsair *noun old use* 1 a pirate or pirate ship. 2 a privately owned warship. [from Old French *corsaire*]

corselet *noun* 1 (*also* **corslet**) *Hist.* a protective garment or piece of armour for the upper part of the body. 2 (*also* **corselette**) a woman's undergarment combining girdle and brassière. [from Old French diminutive of *cors*, body, bodice]

corset — *noun* 1 a tightly fitting undergarment stiffened by strips of bone or plastic, for shaping, controlling, or supporting the figure. 2 *Commerce* government restrictions on the lending power of banks. — *verb* (**corseted, corseting**) 1 to put a

corset on. 2 to restrict. [from Old French diminutive of *cors*, body, bodice]

corsetry *noun* the making and selling of corsets.

Corsica, French **Corse** POP (1990) 250 000, a mountainous island and territorial collectivity of France in the Mediterranean Sea, comprising the departments of Corse-du-Sud and Haute-Corse. It is France's largest island, separated from Sardinia to the S by the Strait of Bonifacio. AREA 8 680sq km/3 350sq mi; length 183km/114mi; width up to 84km/52mi. It has been part of France since 1768; Napoleon was born on the island in 1769. PHYSICAL DESCRIPTION mountainous interior, rising to 2 710m at Mont Cinto; fertile alluvial plains in the E are edged with lagoons and swamps; it has c.1 000km/620mi of superb coastal scenery; there is luxuriant growth of vegetation and Corsica is known as 'the scented isle'. CAPITAL Ajaccio. CHIEF TOWNS Bastia, Calvi, Corte, Bonifacio. ECONOMY corks, asbestos, vines, olives, fruit, sheep, goats; major scenic area, with a wide range of tourist activities. NOTABLE FEATURES the 'Calanches' (above the Gulf of Porto) are granite pinnacles worn into bizarre forms resembling fabulous animals; Cape Girolata, Cape Porto, and Scandola Nature Reserve are World Heritage sites.

cortège *noun* a procession, especially at a funeral. [from French *cortège*, from Italian *corteggio*, retinue]

Cortés *or* **Cortéz, Hernán** (1485–1547) Spanish conquistador of Mexico, born in Medellín. He accompanied Velázquez on his expedition to Cuba (1511), and in 1519 commanded an expedition against Mexico, which led to his first battle at Tabasco. After founding Veracruz, he marched to Tlascala and made allies of the natives, then marched on the Aztec capital and captured the king, Montezuma. The Mexicans rose however, and Cortés was forced to flee, but he launched a successful siege of the capital and it fell in 1521. Appointed Governor and Capt-General of New Spain in 1522 (Mexico was held by the Spanish as the Vice-royalty of New Spain for 300 years), his authority was later superseded, and he returned to Spain in 1540.

Cortes the Spanish parliament. The Cortes of Leon in the late 12c is thought by many to have been the earliest of all medieval parliaments. The Cortes exercised full democratic rights for the first time under the Second Republic of 1931–6. In 1977 it was established as the lower chamber of a two-chamber parliament based on universal suffrage.

cortex (PL. **cortices**) *noun Anat.* the outer layer of an organ or tissue, when this differs in structure or function from the inner region, eg the cerebral cortex (outer layer of grey matter) of the brain. [from Latin *cortex*, tree bark]

cortical *adj.* 1 relating to or in the region of the cortex. 2 external.

corticosteroid *or* **corticoid** *noun Biochem.* any steroid hormone, eg cortisone, manufactured by the adrenal cortex.

cortisone *noun Biochem.* a naturally occurring steroid hormone that is isolated from the cortex (outer part) of the adrenal glands, and is used as an anti-inflammatory agent to treat rheumatoid arthritis, certain eye and skin disorders, and Addison's disease (in which there is a deficiency of corticosteroid hormones). [from *corticosterone*, a hormone secreted by the cortex of the adrenal gland]

corundum *noun Geol.* an extremely hard aluminium oxide mineral, used as an abrasive powder and as a constituent of emery. Its coloured crystalline forms include the gemstones ruby and sapphire. [from Tamil *kuruntam*]

Corunna, Spanish **La Coruña**, ancient **Caronium** POP (1991) 245 000, the seaport capital of La Coruña province, Galicia region, NW

Spain. It lies on the Atlantic coast, 609km/378mi NW of Madrid. HISTORY the base of the Spanish Armada in 1588; the city was sacked by Drake in 1589; scene of a British victory during the Peninsular War (1808–14) and the death of Sir John Moore (1809). NOTABLE FEATURES Hercules Tower; Church of Santiago.

coruscate *verb intrans.* to sparkle. [from Latin *coruscare*, to sparkle]

coruscation *noun* a glittering; a flash.

Corvette one of the first plastic-bodied cars to go into mass production. General Motors described it as 'America's only authentic Sports car'. Ed N Cole and Harley Earl developed it in the early 1950s for the rich young American who felt the need for speed, and it quickly became successful.

corvette *noun* **1** a small warship for escorting larger vessels. **2** *Hist.* a sailing warship with one tier of guns. [from Dutch *corver*, pursuit vessel]

Corvino one of the greedy characters trying to inherit Volpone's money in Ben Jonson's *Volpone*.

Corybantes the attendants and eunuch priests of the Phrygian nature goddess, the Cybele. Her orgiastic cult was officially introduced into Rome towards the end of the Punic Wars.

Cos, Greek **Kós**, Italian **Coo** POP (1982) 21 000, an island in the Dodecanese, E Greece, lying in the Aegean Sea off the SW coast of Turkey. AREA 290sq km/112sq mi; length 43km/27mi; width 2–11km/1–7mi. PHYSICAL DESCRIPTION hilly in the E region, rising to 846m at Mt Dikaios. HISTORY famous in antiquity for its wine, amphorae, and 'Coan garments', and for the cult of Asclepius and its doctors, notably Hippocrates; severely damaged by earthquakes in 1933. CAPITAL Cos. ECONOMY cereals, olive oil, wine, fruit; tourism. NOTABLE FEATURES sanctuary of Asclepios; Castle of the Knights of St John (15c); Plane Tree of Hippocrates.

cos¹ *noun* (*also* **cos lettuce**) a lettuce with slim crisp leaves. [from *Cos*, a Greek island where it originated]

cos² *abbrev.* cosine.

cosecant *noun Maths.* (ABBREV. **cosec**) for a given angle in a right-angled triangle, the ratio of the length of the hypotenuse to the length of the side opposite the angle under consideration; the reciprocal of the sine of an angle.

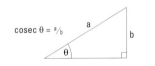

cosec $\theta = {}^a\!/_b$

cosecant

Cosgrave, William Thomas (1880–1965) Irish politician and first President of the Irish Free State, born in Dublin. He joined the Sinn Féin movement at an early age, and took part in the Easter Rising (1916). He became a Sinn Féin MP (1918–22), and after his years as President (1922–32), was Leader of the Opposition (Fine Gael, 1932–44). His son Liam (1920–) was leader of the Fine Gael Party (1965–7) and Prime Minister (1973–7).

cosh — *noun* a club, especially a rubber one filled with metal, used as a weapon. — *verb colloq.* to hit with a cosh or something heavy. [perhaps from Romany *koshter*, stick]

Così fan tutte (Women are Like That), subtitle ***La Scuola degli Amanti (The School for Lovers)*** an opera by Wolfgang Amadeus Mozart (1790). Set in late 18c Naples, it tells of two lovesick officers who accept a bet from Don Alfonso that in one day he can prove their

fiancées will not be faithful in their absence. The resultant comedy is also a cynical comment on love relationships. [from Italian, literally = they all do it]

cosily *adv.* in a cosy way.

cosine *noun Maths.* (ABBREV. **cos**) in trigonometry, a function of an angle in a right-angled triangle, defined as the length of the side adjacent to the angle divided by the length of the hypotenuse (the longest side).

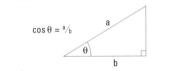

$\cos \theta = {}^a\!/_b$

cosine

cosiness *noun* being cosy.

COSLA *abbrev.* Convention of Scottish Local Authorities.

cosmetic — *adj.* **1** used to beautify the face, body, or hair. **2** improving superficially, for the sake of appearance only. — *noun* a cosmetic application, especially for the face. [from Greek *kosmetikos*, of adornment]

cosmetically *adv.* **1** by using cosmetics. **2** superficially.

cosmic *adj.* **1** relating to the Universe; universal. **2** coming from outer space: *cosmic rays.* **3** *colloq.* large or significant. [from Greek *kosmikos*, from *kosmos*, universe]

cosmically *adv.* **1** in a cosmic way. **2** *said of a star rising* with the sun.

cosmic background radiation *Astron.* short-wavelength electromagnetic radiation from outer space, consisting of heat remaining from the Big Bang. It is thought to permeate the entire Universe, which consequently is not completely cold, but has a temperature of 2.73° above absolute zero (2.73K).

cosmic rays *or* **cosmic radiation** *Astron.* radiation consisting of streams of high-energy particles from outer space, travelling at about the speed of light, most of which are thought to originate from supernovae. When *primary cosmic rays* (consisting mainly of protons) enter the Earth's atmosphere they collide with atomic nuclei in the atmosphere and generate *secondary cosmic rays* (consisting mainly of mesons, such as pions and muons) that shower the Earth.

cosmic string *Astron.* hypothetical massive filaments of matter, predicted to be an important component of the very early Universe according to supersymmetry theory (the theory that elementary particles of two classes, *fermions* and *bosons*, are paired with each other). Cosmic strings, in the form of infinite lines or closed loops, may have played an important role in the formation of galaxy clusters.

cosmogony *noun* (PL. **cosmogonies**) the study of the origin and development of the Universe as a whole, or of specific celestial objects or systems, especially the Solar System. [from Greek *kosmos*, universe + *-gonia*, giving birth to]

cosmological *adj.* relating to cosmology.

cosmological argument *Theology* an argument proposed by Aquinas and others, which attempted to prove that God exists by asserting that since the universe exists and its existence cannot be explained by things in the Universe, it may therefore be supposed that there also exists an (uncaused) *first cause*, ie God.

cosmological principle *Astron.* the principle that, at a given time, the universe would appear the same to observers in other galaxies as

it does to us, ie that all places in the Universe are alike.

cosmologist *noun* a person who studies or is an expert in cosmology.

cosmology *noun* **1** the scientific study of the origin, nature, structure, and evolution of the Universe. The most well-known theory in modern cosmology is the Big Bang theory of the origin of the Universe, according to which the Universe began with a huge explosion 13 to 20 billion years ago. **2** a theory or model of the origin and structure of the Universe. [from Greek *kosmos*, universe + -LOGY]

cosmonaut *noun* a Russian astronaut. [from Greek *kosmos*, universe + *nautes*, sailor]

cosmopolitan — *adj.* **1** belonging to, or representative of, all parts of the world. **2** free of national prejudices; international in experience and outlook. — *noun* a person of this type; a citizen of the world. [from Greek *kosmos*, universe + *polites*, citizen]

cosmopolitanism *noun* belief in a cosmopolitan outlook.

cosmos *noun* the Universe seen as an ordered system. [from Greek *kosmos*, world order, universe]

Cossack — *noun* a member of the Cossacks. — *adj.* belonging or relating to this people. [from Ukrainian *kozak*, originally freebooter]

Cossacks originally, members of semi-independent communities of fugitive peasants and military adventurers who inhabited the steppelands of S Russia and Ukraine. Attempts to limit Cossack freedom led to several large-scale rebellions against the Russian government in the 17c–18c. In the 18c–19c Cossack horsemen were formed into military organizations (*hosts*) and earned a reputation for ferocious fighting.

cosset *verb* (**cosseted, cosseting**) to treat too kindly; to pamper. [perhaps from Anglo-Saxon *kossetung*, kissing]

cost — *verb* (PAST TENSE AND PAST PARTICIPLE **cost**) **1** to be obtainable at a certain price. **2** to involve the loss or sacrifice of. **3** (**costed**) to estimate or decide the cost of. **4** *trans., intrans. colloq.* to put (someone) to some expense. — *noun* **1** what something costs. **2** loss or sacrifice. **3** (**costs**) *Legal* the expenses of a case.
— **at all costs** no matter what the risk or effort may be.
cost someone dear to prove costly to them.
count the cost 1 to consider all the risks before taking action. **2** to realize the bad effects of something done.
to one's cost with some loss or disadvantage. [from Latin *constare*, to cost]

Costa Blanca a resort region along the Spanish Mediterranean coast, situated in Murcia, Alicante, and part of Almería provinces. The area extends S from Cabo San Antonio to the Punto Almerimar and attracts tourists in both summer and winter. [from Spanish *costa blanca*, white coast]

Costa Brava a resort region along the Spanish Mediterranean coast, situated in Catalonia province and lying between Barcelona and the French border. [from Spanish *costa brava*, wild coast]

cost-accounting *noun* a branch of accountancy concerned with the analysis of costs for a product or operation. It may be carried out on a historical or projected basis, often with the aim of establishing a current standard or norm against which actual cost may be compared, so that it may be determined whether costs are getting out of line with expectations.

Costa de la Luz a resort region on the Atlantic coastline of Huelva and Cádiz provinces, S Spain. It extends from the Portuguese border to the southernmost tip of Spain at Tarifa on the

Strait of Gibraltar. [from Spanish *costa de la luz*, coast of light]

Costa del Azahar a resort region along the Spanish Mediterranean coast, situated in Castellón de la Plana and Valencia provinces. It lies between the Costa Dorada in the N and the Costa Blanca in the S, and is the longest stretch of coast in Spain. [from Spanish *costa del azahar*, orange-blossom coast]

Costa del Sol a resort region along the Spanish Mediterranean coast, situated in Andalusia province. It extends from Punto Almerimar to the southernmost point in Spain at Tarifa. [from Spanish *costa del sol*, coast of the sun]

Costa Dorada a resort region along the Spanish Mediterranean coast, to the S of the Costa Brava. It extends c.260km/162mi in Barcelona and Tarragona provinces. [from Spanish *costa dorada*, golden coast]

Costa Dourada the Atlantic coastline of W Portugal between the Ponta da Arrifana and the mouth of the R Sado.

costal *adj. Anat.* relating to the ribs. [from Latin *costa*, rib]

co-star — *noun* a fellow star in a film, play, etc. — *verb intrans.* (**co-starred, co-starring**) 1 *said of an actor* to appear alongside another star. 2 *said of a production* to feature as fellow stars: *co-starred Gielgud and Olivier.*

Costard the clown in Shakespeare's *Love's Labour's Lost.*

Costa Rica, official name **Republic of Costa Rica**, Spanish **República de Costa Rica** POP (1992e) 3.1m, the second smallest republic in Central America, divided into seven provinces. AREA 51 022sq km/19 694sq mi. It is bounded W by the Pacific Ocean, N by Nicaragua, E by the Caribbean, and SE by Panama. CAPITAL San José. CHIEF TOWNS Cartago, Heredia, Liberia, Puntarenas, Limón. TIME ZONE GMT –6. The population is mainly of Spanish descent and the main religion is Roman Catholicism. OFFICIAL LANGUAGE Spanish. CURRENCY the colón. PHYSICAL DESCRIPTION a series of volcanic ridges form the backbone of Costa Rica (some volcanoes are active); the highest peak, Chirripó Grande (3 819m), is in the Cordillera de Talamanca; the central plateau, the Meseta Central, covers an area of 5 200sq km/2 000sq mi at an altitude of 800–1 400m; it is drained W by the R Grande into the Pacific and NE by the R Reventazón into the Caribbean; much swampy land near the coast, with tropical forest as the land rises; a lowland savannah extends from just S of the mouth of the Río Grande de Tárcoles along the NE shore of the Golfo de Nicoya towards Nicaragua. CLIMATE tropical climate, with a small temperature range and abundant rainfall; more temperate in the central uplands; dry season is Dec–May; average annual rainfall is, 3 300mm, with much local variation; the average annual temperature is 26–28°C. HISTORY visited by Columbus in 1402; named Costa Rica ('rich coast') in the belief that vast gold treasures existed; gained independence from Spain in 1821; member of the Federation of Central America in 1824–39. The 20c saw political unrest, with civil war in 1948, following which the army was disbanded. A Civil Guard was established in 1992. GOVERNMENT democratic republic governed by an Executive President and Legislative Assembly of 57 deputies (elected for four years), and a 20-member Cabinet. ECONOMY primarily agriculture, mainly coffee (especially in Meseta Central), bananas, sugar, cattle; timber, fishing, gold, silver, bauxite; oil exploration in collaboration with Mexico; food processing, textiles, fertilizers, plastics, pharmaceuticals, electrical equipment.

cost-benefit analysis a type of study which compares the cost of a particular course of action (eg building a motorway) with the resulting benefits. It takes into account the social costs and benefits (such as the preservation or destruction of a community or area of countryside) as well as the strictly financial ones.

cost-effective *adj.* giving acceptable value for money.

costermonger *noun Brit.* (*also* **coster**) a person who sells fruit and vegetables from a barrow. [from *costard*, an apple + -MONGER]

costive *adj. old use* constipated. [from Old French *costivé*]

costliness *noun* 1 being costly. 2 price.

costly *adj.* (**costlier, costliest**) 1 involving much cost; expensive. 2 lavish; sumptuous. 3 involving major losses or sacrifices.

Costner, Kevin (1955–) US film actor and director, born in Los Angeles, California. After being a Hollywood stage manager, he had increasingly significant film parts during the early 1980s until achieving fame in *Silverado* (1985) and *The Untouchables* (1987). Other films include *Dances With Wolves* (1990), which he starred in and directed and which won seven Oscars, *Robin Hood: Prince of Thieves* (1991), *JFK* (1991), and *The Bodyguard* (1992).

cost of living the cost to the individual of ordinary necessities such as food and clothing.

cost price the price paid for something by the retailer, before resale at a profit.

costume *noun* 1 a set of clothing of a special kind, especially of a particular historical period or particular country. 2 a garment or outfit for a special activity: *a swimming-costume.* 3 *old use* a woman's suit. [from Italian *costume*, habit, dress]

costume jewellery jewellery made of inexpensive or artificial materials.

costumier *noun* a person who makes or supplies costumes.

cosy — *adj.* (**cosier, cosiest**) 1 warm and comfortable. 2 friendly, intimate, and confidential. — *noun* (PL. **cosies**) a warm cover to keep something warm, especially a teapot or boiled egg.

cot[1] *noun* 1 a small bed with high sides for a child. 2 *North Amer., esp. US* a camp bed. [from Hindi *khat*, bedstead]

cot[2] *noun* 1 *poetic* a cottage. 2 a cote. [from Anglo-Saxon]

cot[3] *abbrev.* cotangent.

cotangent *noun Maths.* (ABBREV. **cot**) for a given angle in a right-angled triangle, the ratio of the length of the side adjacent to the angle under consideration to the length of the side opposite it; the reciprocal of the tangent of an angle.

cot death the sudden and unexplained death of a baby during sleep.

cote *noun* (*usually in compounds*) a small shelter for birds or animals: *dovecote.* [from Anglo-Saxon]

Côte d'Ivoire see IVORY COAST.

coterie *noun* a small exclusive group of people with interests in common. [from Old French *coterie*, group of tenant farmers]

coterminous *adj.* having the same boundaries, duration, or range. [from Latin *con-*, same + *terminus*, boundary]

cotinga *noun* a bird native to the New World tropics, that inhabits woodland. Most species feed on fruit, and some catch insects in flight. [from a S American name]

cotoneaster *noun* a garden shrub with red or orange berries. [from Latin *cotonea*, quince]

Cotopaxi the highest active volcano in the world, in N central Ecuador. HEIGHT 5 896m. It lies in the Andes, 48km/30mi S of Quito, in a national park which was established in 1975. A llama breeding station and a NASA satellite tracking station are located nearby.

Cotswold Hills *or* **Cotswolds** a hill range, mainly in Gloucestershire, SE England. It extends 80km/50mi NE from Bath to Chipping Camden, separating the lower R Severn from the source of the R Thames. It rises to 333m at Cleeve Cloud, near Cheltenham. The area gives its name to a breed of sheep and is noted for its limestone, used in many picturesque villages.

cottage *noun* a small house, especially an old stone one, in a village or the countryside. [from COT[2]]

cottage cheese a type of soft white cheese made from sour milk.

cottage industry a craft industry such as knitting or weaving, employing workers in their own homes.

cottage loaf a loaf consisting of a round piece of dough with a smaller round piece on top of it.

cottager *noun* a person who lives in a cottage.

cottar *or* **cotter** *noun Hist. Scot.* a farm labourer occupying a cottage rent-free. [from COT[2]]

Cottian Alps, French **Alpes Cottiennes** a division of the W Alps in SE France along the French–Italian frontier, extending from the Alpes Maritimes at Maddalena Pass to the Alpes Graian at Mont Cenis. The highest peak is Monte Viso (3 851m).

cotton — *noun* 1 a shrubby plant of the genus *Gossypium*, belonging to the mallow family (Malvaceae), and having broad lobed leaves, creamy-white, yellow, or reddish flowers, and egg-shaped seed pods, known as *bolls*, that burst when ripe to reveal tightly packed seeds covered with creamy-white downy fibres that contain 87–90% cellulose. Cotton is widely cultivated in tropical and subtropical regions, and is of major economic importance as a source of natural fibre that is used to make textiles. 2 the soft white fibre obtained from this plant, which is used to make textiles. The bolls are picked when ripe, either by hand or by machine after the plants have been chemically defoliated, causing all the bolls to open simultaneously. This is followed by removal of the seeds (*ginning*), cleaning and separating of the fibres (*carding*), stretching (*drawing*), and finally *spinning* into yarn. 3 the cloth that is woven from fibres that have been obtained from this plant and spun into yarn. — *verb* (**cotton on to something**) *colloq.* to begin to understand it. [from Old French *coton*, from Arabic *qutun*]

cotton gin a machine for separating the seeds from the cotton.

cottongrass *noun* a genus (*Eriophorum*) of sedges, having long silky or cotton-like hairs around the ripened ovary.

cottonwool *noun* soft fluffy wadding used in treating injuries, applying cosmetics, etc, originally made from cotton fibre.

Costa Rica

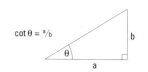

$$\cot \theta = \frac{a}{b}$$

cotangent

cottony *adj.* **1** made of or with cotton. **2** like cotton.

cotyledon *noun Bot.* in flowering plants, one of the leaves produced by the embryo, and an important feature in the classification of plants. Monocotyledons and dicotyledons have one and two cotyledons, respectively, in each seed. [from Greek, from *kotyle*, cup]

couch[1] — *noun* **1** a sofa or settee. **2** a bed-like seat with a headrest, eg for patients to lie on when being examined or treated by a doctor or psychiatrist. **3** *poetic* a bed. — *verb* to express in words of a certain kind. [from French *coucher*, to lay down]

couch[2] *noun* (pronounced *cooch*) (*also* **couch grass**) a grass of the wheat family, with creeping roots. [from Anglo-Saxon *cwice*]

couchette *noun* a sleeping-berth on a ship or train, converted from ordinary seating; a railway carriage with such berths. [from French *couchette*, diminutive of *couche*, bed]

couch potato *colloq.* someone who spends their leisure time sitting inactive in front of the television or video.

cougar *noun North Amer.* a puma. [from French *couguar*, from a S American Indian word]

cough — *verb intrans.* **1** to expel air, mucus, etc from the throat or lungs with a rough sharp noise. **2** *said of an engine, etc* to make a similar noise. — *noun* **1** an act or sound of coughing. **2** a condition of lungs or throat causing coughing. — **cough up** *slang* to provide money or information.
cough something up 1 to bring up mucus, phlegm, blood, etc by coughing. **2** *slang* to provide money or information. [imitative]

cough mixture a liquid medicine for relieving coughing.

could *verb aux.* **1** past tense of CAN: *I found I could lift it.* **2** used to express a possibility or a possible course: *you could try telephoning her.* **3** used in making requests: *could you help me?* **4** to feel like doing something or able to do something: *I could have strangled him / I could not allow that.* — **could be** *colloq.* that may be the case.

couldn't *contr.* could not.

couldst *verb old use* the form of *could* used with *thou.*

Coulomb, Charles Augustin de (1736–1806) French physicist, born in Angoulême. He experimented on friction and invented a torsion balance for measuring the force of magnetic and electrical attraction (1784–5). With 'Coulomb's law' he observed that the force between two small charged spheres is proportional to the product of the charges divided by the square of the distance between them. The SI unit of quantity of charge is named after him.

cotton plant

coulomb *noun* (SYMBOL **C**) the SI unit of electric charge. It is equal to the amount of charge transported by a current of one ampere in one second.

council *noun* **1** a body of people whose function is to advise, administer, organize, discuss, or legislate. **2** the elected body of people that directs the affairs of a town, district, region, etc. [from Old French *concile*, from Latin *concilium*]

Council for Mutual Economic Assistance (ABBREV. **COMECON**) a body founded (1949) by Stalin, dominated by the USSR. Its purpose was ostensibly the economic integration of the Eastern bloc as a means of counteracting the economic power of the West. The 10 member states were eventually the USSR, Bulgaria, Cuba, Czechoslovakia, Hungary, Poland, Romania, E Germany, Mongolia, and Vietnam. With the overthrow of communism in E Europe in 1989–90 and the weakening of the USSR, COMECON was disbanded in 1991.

Council for the Protection of Rural England a pressure group founded in 1926 as the Council for the Preservation of Rural England. It has 42 county branches and aims to promote the protection and improvement of the countryside and rural amenities. The Council for the Protection of Rural Wales is a similar organization.

council house a house owned and rented out by a local council.

councillor *noun* a member of a council, especially of a town, etc.
◆ Often confused with *counsellor.*

Council of Europe an association of European states, established in 1949. It has a Committee of Ministers, comprising the member countries' foreign ministers, a representative Parliamentary Assembly which meets in Strasbourg to discuss matters of common concern, and a European Court of Human Rights (a later addition). It had 27 members in 1992.

Council of Ministers a body that consists of ministers from the government of each EC member state, the minister involved depending on the subject under consideration. There are around 20 different types of council meetings; agriculture and foreign affairs have the most regular meetings.

Council of the Church in the Orthodox and Roman Catholic Churches, a meeting of bishops of the whole Church to regulate doctrine and discipline. The last Ecumenical Council (of the undivided Church) is generally held to be the Second Council of Nicaea (787). The Roman Catholic Church recognizes a Council if called by a pope, and its decisions as infallible (if approved by the pope). Non-Roman Catholic Churches recognize the World Council of Churches (formed in 1948), but infallibility is not claimed.

council tax a UK local government tax based on and banded according to property values, introduced in 1993 to relace the community charge or poll tax.

counsel — *noun* **1** advice. **2** consultation, discussion, or deliberation: *take counsel with one's supporters.* **3** a lawyer or group of lawyers that gives legal advice and fights cases in court. — *verb* (**counselled, counselling**) to advise.
— **keep one's own counsel** to keep one's opinions and intentions to oneself. [from Old French *conseil*, from Latin *consilium*, advice]

counsellor or *North Amer.* **counselor** *noun* **1** an adviser. **2** a lawyer.
◆ Often confused with *councillor.*

count[1] — *verb* **1** *intrans.* to say numbers in order: *count to five.* **2** to find the total amount of, by adding up item by item. **3** to include. **4** *intrans.* to be important; to matter; to have an effect or value. — *noun* **1** an act of counting. **2** the number counted. **3** a charge brought against an accused person.

— **count someone** or **something in** to include them.
count me in or **out** I am willing, or not willing, to be included.
count on someone or **something** to rely on them.
count someone out 1 to declare (a floored boxer) to have lost the match if he is unable to get up within a count of ten seconds. **2** to exclude them from consideration.
count something out to lay down or present items one at a time while counting: *counted out five pounds each.*
keep or **lose count** to keep, or fail to keep, a note of the running total.
out for the count 1 *said of a boxer* unable to rise to his feet within a count of ten. **2** unconscious. **3** *facetious* fast asleep. [from Old French *cunter*, from Latin *computare*]

count[2] *noun* a European nobleman equal in rank to a British earl. [from Latin *comes*, companion]

countable *adj.* **1** able to be counted. **2** *Grammar, said of a noun* capable of being used with *a* or *an*, or in the plural.

countdown *noun* a count backwards, with zero as the moment for action, used eg in launching a rocket.

countenance — *noun* face; expression or appearance. — *verb* to allow; to tolerate.
— **give countenance to something** to support a proposal, etc.
keep one's countenance to remained composed, manage not to laugh, etc. [from Old French *contenance*, from Latin *continentia*, self-control]

counter[1] *noun* **1** a long flat-topped fitting in a shop, cafeteria, bank, etc over which goods are sold, food is served, or business transacted. **2** a small flat disc used as a playing-piece in various board games. **3** a disc-shaped token used as a substitute coin. **4** a device for counting something.
— **over the counter** by the normal method of sale in a shop, etc.
under the counter by secret illegal sale, or by unlawful means. [from Latin *computare*, to reckon]

counter[2] — *verb trans., intrans.* (**countered, countering**) to oppose, act against, or hit back. — *adv.* (**counter to something**) in the opposite direction to it; in contradiction of it: *results ran counter to expectations.* — *noun* **1** a return blow; an opposing move. **2** an opposite or contrary. **3** something that can be used to one's advantage in negotiating or bargaining. **4** *Naut.* the curved, overhanging part of a ship's stern. [from Old French *contre*, against]

counter- *prefix* **1** against: *counter-attack.* **2** in competition or rivalry: *counter-attraction.* **3** matching or corresponding: *counterpart.* [from Old French *contre*, against]

counteract *verb* to reduce or prevent the effect of.

counteraction *noun* resistance, opposition.

counteractive *adj.* tending to counteract.

counter-attack — *noun* an attack in response to an attack. — *verb intrans.* to attack in return.

counter-attraction *noun* a rival attraction.

counterbalance — *noun* a weight, force or circumstance that balances another and cancels it out. — *verb* to act as a counterbalance to; to neutralise or cancel out.

counterblast *noun* a vigorous and indignant verbal or written response.

counter-charge *noun* an accusation made in response to one made against oneself.

counter-claim *noun* a claim or assertion made in opposition to one made by someone else.

counter-clockwise *adj., adv.* anticlockwise.

counter-culture *noun* a culture that rejects or opposes the values of the culture of the majority. Counter-cultures have arisen across the ages in many societies. Modern examples include the Beats in the USA in the 1950s, the Punks in the 1970s, and the New Age travellers in the 1980s and 90s.

counter-espionage *noun* activities undertaken to frustrate spying by an enemy or rival.

counterfeit — *adj.* **1** made in imitation of a genuine article, especially with the purpose of deceiving; forged. **2** not genuine; insincere. — *verb* **1** to copy for a dishonest purpose; to forge. **2** to pretend: *counterfeit friendship*. [from Old French *contrefait*, copied, from Latin CONTRA-, against + *facere*, to make]

counterfoil *noun* the section of a cheque, receipt, ticket, etc retained as a record by the person who issues it. [from Latin *folium*, leaf]

counter-insurgency *noun* military action taken against insurgents or rebels.

counter-intelligence *noun* counter-espionage.

countermand *verb* to cancel (an order or command). [from Old French *contremander*, from Latin CONTRA-, against + *mandare*, to order]

counter-measure *noun* an action taken to counteract a threat, dangerous development, or move.

counter-offensive *noun* an aggressive move made in response to an initial attack.

counterpane *noun* a coverlet; a bedspread. [from Old French *coitepoint*, quilt, from Latin *culcita puncta*, quilted mattress]

counterpart *noun* the matching or corresponding person or thing elsewhere.

counterpoint *noun* Mus. **1** the combining of two or more melodies sung or played simultaneously into a harmonious whole. **2** a part or melody combined with another. See also CONTRAPUNTAL.

counterpoise *noun* **1** a state of balance between two weights. **2** something that counterbalances.

counter-productive *adj.* tending to undermine productiveness and efficiency; having the opposite effect to that intended.

Counter-Reformation a general movement of reform and missionary activity in the Roman Catholic Church from the mid 16c, stimulated in part by the Protestant Reformation. It included the revival of the monastic movement (eg Capuchins, 1528; Oratorians, 1575), especially the creation of the Jesuit Order. There was a strong influence from mystics (eg John of the Cross, Teresa of Avila) and devotional teachers (eg Francis of Sales), the Council of Trent formulated doctrine, and liturgical and moral reforms were introduced throughout the Church. In a secular sense, the term also refers to the success of Roman Catholic powers in Europe in the late 16c and early 17c.

counter-revolution *noun* a revolution to overthrow a system of government established by a previous revolution.

counter-revolutionary — *adj.* opposing revolution or a revolution. — *noun* a person involved in a counter-revolution.

countersign — *verb* to sign (a document, etc) already signed by someone else) by way of confirmation. — *noun* a password or signal used in response to a sentry's challenge.

counter-signature *noun* a name countersigned on a document.

countersink *verb* (PAST TENSE **countersank**; PAST PARTICIPLE **countersunk**) **1** to widen the upper part of (a screw hole) so that the top of the screw when inserted will be level with the surrounding surface. **2** to insert (a screw) into such a hole.

counter-tenor *noun* an adult male singer who sings falsetto, using the same range as a female alto.

counterweight *noun* a counterbalancing weight.

countess *noun* **1** the wife or widow of an earl or count. **2** a woman with the rank of earl or count. [from Old French *contesse*, from Latin *comitissa*, feminine of *comes*, companion]

countless *adj.* so many as to be impossible to count.

countrified *adj.* rural; rustic in appearance or style.

country *noun* (PL. **countries**) **1** the land of any of the nations of the world. **2** the population of such land. **3** one's native land. **4** open land, with moors, woods, hills, fields, etc, as distinct from towns, etc. **5** land having a certain character or connection: *Burns country*. **6** an area of knowledge or experience: *back in the familiar country of simple arithmetic*.
— **across country** not keeping to roads.
go to the country to dissolve parliament and hold a general election.
[from Latin *contrata terra*, land lying in front of one]

country-and-western — *adj.* denoting a style of music popular among white people of the Southern USA. — *noun* folk music or songs in this style.

country club a club in a rural area with facilities for sport and recreation.

country dance a traditional British dance in which partners face each other in parallel lines.

country dancing the performance of country dances.

country house *or* **country seat** a landowner's large house in the country.

countryman *or* **countrywoman** *noun* **1** a man or woman who lives in a rural area. **2** a man or woman belonging to the same country as oneself.

countryside *noun* land outside or away from towns.

Countryside Commission for England and Wales a UK government amenity agency set up in 1968 to replace the National Parks Commission. It advises the government on matters of countryside interest, and formulates policy for National Parks. It provides grants for nature reserves, wardens, footpaths, and for public access to open countryside. The Countryside Commission for Scotland has similar functions, but there are no National Parks in Scotland.

countrywide *adj.* all over the country.

Country Wife, The a play by William Wycherley (1675). It is a bawdy satiric comedy about an elderly husband trying to keep his wife out of mischief, and the virile Horner who pretends to be a eunuch in order to expose social and sexual hypocrisy.

county — *noun* (PL. **counties**) **1** any of the geographical divisions within England, Wales, and Ireland that form the larger units of local government. **2** in the USA, the main administrative subdivision within a state. — *adj. derog. colloq.* typical of the landed gentry. [from Old French *conte*]

county court a local court for non-criminal cases.

county town the chief town of a county, acting as its seat of administration.

coup *noun* **1** a successful move. **2** a coup d'état. [from French *coup*, stroke or blow]

coup de grâce a final decisive blow. [French, = blow of mercy]

coup d'état *noun* (PL. ***coups d'état***) the sudden, usually violent, overthrow of a government. [French, = stroke of the state]

coupe *noun* a dessert made with fruit and ice cream. [from French *coupe*, glass, cup]

coupé *noun* a four-seated two-door car with a sloping rear. [from French *coupé*, from *couper*, to cut]

couple — *noun* **1** a man and wife, boyfriend and girlfriend, or other pair of people romantically attached. **2** a pair of partners, eg for dancing. **3** two, or a few. **4** *Physics* a pair of equal but opposite forces that are applied to different points on the same object, producing a turning effect or *torque*. — *verb* **1** to link; to connect. **2** *intrans.* to have sexual intercourse.

couplet *noun* a pair of consecutive lines of verse, especially rhyming. [diminutive of COUPLE]

coupling *noun* **1** a link for joining things together. **2** *derog.* the act of having sex.

coupon *noun* **1** a slip of paper entitling one to something, eg a discount. **2** a detachable order form, competition entry form, etc printed on packaging, etc. **3** a betting form for football pools. [from Old French *colpon*, piece cut off]

courage *noun* **1** bravery. **2** cheerfulness or resolution in coping with setbacks.
— **have the courage of one's convictions** to be brave enough to act in accordance with one's beliefs.
pluck up courage *or* **take one's courage in both hands** to become resolved to meet a challenge.
take courage to be resolute or cheerful in difficult circumstances.
[from Old French *corage*, from Latin *cor*, heart]

courageous *adj.* having or showing courage.

courageously *adv.* in a courageous way.

courageousness *noun* possession of courage.

courante *noun* a lively dance in triple time, originating in the 16c; also, a piece of music for it. By the 17c, two distinct forms had evolved: the French *courante* and the Italian *corante* (or *corrente*). About the same time, it became one of the four standard dances of the orchestral suite. [from French *danse courante*, running dance]

courgette *noun* a long green vegetable, a type of small marrow. [from French *courgette*]

courier *noun* **1** a guide who travels with, and looks after, parties of tourists. **2** a messenger. [from Old French *courier*, from Latin *currere*, run]

Courrèges, André (1923–) French fashion designer, born in Pau. He studied civil engineering, but later turned to fashion in Paris, where he was trained by Balenciaga, and opened his own house in 1961. Famous for stark, futuristic, 'Space Age' designs, he has featured trouser (pants) suits, white boots, and short skirts. He produces ready-to-wear as well as couture clothes.

course — *noun* **1** the path that anything moves in. **2** a direction taken or planned: *go off course*. **3** the channel of a river, etc. **4** the normal progress of something. **5** the passage of a period of time: *in the course of the next hour*. **6** a line of action: *your best course is to wait*. **7** a series of lessons, etc. **8** a prescribed treatment, eg medicine to be taken, over a period. **9** any of the successive parts of a meal. **10** (*often in compounds*) the ground over which a game is played or a race run. **11** *Archit.* a single row of bricks or stones in a wall, etc. — *verb* **1** *intrans.* to move or flow. **2** *trans.* to hunt (hares, etc) using dogs.
— **in the course of something** while doing it; during it.
in the course of time eventually.
in due course at the appropriate or expected time.
a matter of course a natural or expected action or result.

of course 1 as expected. **2** naturally; certainly; without doubt. **3** admittedly.
stay the course to endure to the end.
[from Old French *cours*, from Latin *currere*, to run]

coursebook *noun* a book to accompany a course of instruction.

courser *noun* **1** a person who courses hares, etc, or a hound used for this. **2** *poetic* a swift horse. **3** any of several swiftly running birds of Asia or Africa.

coursing *noun* hunting hares with dogs.

Court, Margaret (Jean), *née* **Smith** (1942–) Australian lawn tennis player, born in Albury, New South Wales. She was the winner of more Grand Slam events (66) than any other player: 10 Wimbledon titles (including the singles in 1963, 1965, 1970), 22 US titles, (singles in 1962, 1965, 1968–70, 1973) 13 French (singles 1962, 1964, 1969–70, 1973), and 21 Australian (singles 1960–6, 1969-71, 1973). In 1970 she became the second woman (after Maureen Connolly) to win all four major titles in one year. She retired in 1977.

court — *noun* **1** the judge, law officials, and members of the jury gathered to hear and decide on a legal case. **2** the room (*also* **courtroom**) or building (*also* **courthouse**) used for such a hearing. **3** an area marked out for a particular game, or a division of this. **4** an open space or square surrounded by houses or by sections of a building. **5** (**Court**) a name used for a group of houses so arranged, or for a block of flats or for a country mansion. **6** the palace, household, attendants, and advisers of a sovereign. — *verb* **1** *trans., intrans. old use* to try to win the love of. **2** to try to win the favour of. **3** to seek (popularity, etc). **4** to risk or invite: *court danger.*
— **the ball is in his** *or* **your,** *etc* **court** he, you, etc must make the next move.
go to court to take legal action.
hold court to be surrounded by a circle of admirers.
out of court without legal action being taken: *settle out of court.*
pay court to someone to pay them flattering attention.
put *or* **rule something out of court** to prevent it from being heard or considered.
take someone to court to bring a legal case against them.
[from Old French *cort*, from Latin *cohors* or *cors*, yard]

Courtauld Institute of Art an Institute founded in 1932 to promote the study of art history. It was established by the endowments of Viscount Lee of Fareham and Samuel Courtauld (1876–1947), and is part of London University. It is now housed with its galleries in Somerset House, London.

court card *Cards* the king, queen, or jack.

courteous *adj.* polite; considerate; respectful. [from Old French *corteis*, from *cort*, court]

courteously *adj.* with a courteous manner.

courteousness *noun* the quality of being courteous.

courtesan *noun Hist.* a prostitute with wealthy or noble clients. [from Old French *courtisane*, from Italian *cortigiana*, woman of the court]

courtesy *noun* (PL. **courtesies**) **1** courteous behaviour; politeness. **2** a courteous act.
— **by courtesy of someone 1** by their permission. **2** *colloq.* from them.
[from Old French *corteisie*, from *corteis*, courteous]

courtesy title a frequently used but legally invalid title, eg 'Lord' before the first name of a peer's younger son.

courthouse *noun* a building in which lawcourts are held.

courtier *noun* **1** a person in attendance at a royal court. **2** an elegant flatterer. [from Old French *courteiour*, attendant at court]

courtliness *noun* being courtly.

courtly *adj.* having fine manners.

court-martial — *noun* (PL. **courts-martial, court-martials**) a trial, by a group of officers, of a member of the armed forces, for a breach of military law. — *verb* to try by court-martial.

Courtney a male and female first name, after the surname. [Norman *Courtenay*, domain of Curtius; also from the nickname *court nez*, short nose]

Court of Appeal in England and Wales, a court with civil and criminal divisions, which hears appeals from other courts. The civil division hears appeals from the High Court and the county court; its head is the Master of the Rolls. The criminal division hears appeals from the Crown Court; its head is the Lord Chief Justice. Appeal on a point of law may be allowed from the Court of Appeal to the House of Lords.

Court of Justice of the European Communities the European Court which sits at Luxembourg, an institution of the European Communities, with its judges being appointed by the member states. Its functions involve the interpretation of Community treaties and legislation; it can also decide whether the conduct of any member state breaches Community law. The court also gives rulings on relevant points of law referred to it by domestic courts of member states.

Court of Session a Scottish court, sitting in Edinburgh, which deals with civil matters. It has an Outer House and a more senior Inner House, similar to the High Court and Court of Appeal respectively.

court order a direction or command of a judiciary court which, if not complied with, may lead to criminal proceedings against the offender or offenders.

courtroom *noun* a room in which a lawcourt is held.

courtship *noun* the courting or wooing of an intended spouse; the period for which this lasts.

court shoe a woman's shoe in a plain, low-cut style.

courtyard *noun* an open space surrounded by buildings or walls.

Courtyard of a House in Delft a painting by Pieter de Hooch (1658, National Gallery, London).

couscous *noun* a N African dish of crushed wheat steamed and served eg with meat. [from French *couscous*, from Arabic *kuskus*]

cousin *noun* (*also* **first cousin**) a son or daughter of one's uncle or aunt. [from Old French *cosin*, from Latin *con*-, with + *sobrinus*, cousin]

cousin once removed (*also* **first cousin once removed**) a son or daughter of one's cousin.

Cousins, Frank (1904–86) English trade union leader, born in Bulwell, Nottingham. A miner's son, he worked in the pits at 14, turned lorry driver, and by 1938 was a full-time union organizer. In 1955 he became General Secretary of the Transport and General Worker's Union, and played a controversial role in the London Transport strike (1958). He was Minister of Technology (1964–6) until he resigned over the prices and incomes policy, MP for Nuneaton (1965–6), and Chairman of the Community Relations Commission (1968–70).

Cousteau, Jacques Yves (1910–) French naval officer and underwater explorer, born in Saint André, Gironde. He invented the aqualung diving apparatus (1943), founded the French navy's undersea research group (1946), and in 1947 he made a world record free dive of 91m. As commander of the oceanographic research ship *Calypso*, he made the first underwater film. Having retired from the navy in 1956, he was appointed Director of the Oceanographic Museum of Monaco (1957–88). His famous films include *The Undersea World of Jacques Cousteau* (1968–76) and *Lilliput in Antarctica* (1990).

couture *noun* the designing, making, and selling of fashionable clothes. [from French *couture*, sewing]

couturier *noun* a fashion designer.

couturière *noun* a female fashion designer.

covalent bond *Chem.* a chemical bond in which two atoms are held together by the sharing of a pair of electrons between them.

covariance *noun* **1** the property of varying concomitantly. **2** *Maths.* a statistic that is used to measure the agreement between two sets of random variables, and differs from correlation in that it is dependent on the scale used to measure the variables.

cove¹ *noun* a small and usually sheltered bay or inlet on a rocky coast. [from Anglo-Saxon *cofa*, room]

cove² *noun old colloq. use* a fellow.

coven *noun* a gathering of witches. [from Old French *covin*, from Latin *convenire*, to meet]

covenant — *noun* **1** a formal written promise to pay a sum of money regularly, eg to a charity. **2** *Legal* a formal sealed agreement. **3** *Biblical* God's agreement with the Israelites. — *verb trans., intrans.* to agree by covenant to do something.

covenanter *noun* **1** a person who makes a covenant. **2** (**Covenanter**) *Hist.* an adherent of either of two 17c religious covenants defending Presbyterianism in Scotland. [from Old French *covenir*, to agree]

Covenanters originally, signatories (and their successors) of the National Covenant (1638) and the Solemn League and Covenant (1643) in Scotland, who resisted the theory of 'Divine Right of Kings' and the imposition of an episcopal system on the Presbyterian Church of Scotland. Until Presbyterianism was restored (1690), they were savagely persecuted, imprisoned, executed without trial, or deported (eg to Holland or the USA).

Covent Garden a square in central London, known for the fruit and vegetable market that operated there for nearly three centuries; it also gives its name to the Royal Opera House close by. The site, which was once the garden of a convent in Westminster, was developed in the 17c, and the first theatre there was opened in 1732 The market was relocated in 1974, and the buildings restored to form shops and restaurants. See also ROYAL OPERA HOUSE.

Covent Garden Theatre, properly **Theatre Royal, Covent Garden** see ROYAL OPERA HOUSE.

Coventry¹, ancient **Couentrey** POP (1992e) 305 000, a modern, industrial city in West Midlands, central England, situated 150km/93mi NW of London. HISTORY in 1043 the Earl of Mercia, husband of Lady Godiva, founded a Benedictine priory, around which the town grew; an important centre of clothing manufacture from the 17c; the poet Philip Larkin was born here in 1922. NOTABLE FEATURES old cathedral (1433), destroyed during World War II; new cathedral designed by Sir Basil Spence (consecrated in 1962); Church of Holy Trinity (15–16c); St Mary's Hall (1343), built for the merchants' guild; Museum of British Road Transport; art gallery.

Coventry²
— **send someone to Coventry** to refuse to speak to them or associate with them, especially as a punishment or protest.
[perhaps from the imprisonment of Royalists in Coventry during the Civil War]

cover — *verb* (**covered, covering**) **1** to form a layer over. **2** to protect or conceal by putting

something over. **3** to clothe. **4** to extend over.
5 to strew, sprinkle, spatter, mark all over, etc.
6 (**be covered with a feeling**, *etc*) to be overwhelmed by it: *covered with embarrassment*. **7** to
deal with (a subject). **8** *said of a reporter, etc* to
investigate or report on (a story). **9** to have as
one's area of responsibility. **10** to travel (a distance). **11** to be adequate to pay: *cover one's
expenses*. **12** to insure; to insure against. **13** to
threaten by aiming a gun at. **14** to keep (a building, its exits, etc) under armed watch. **15** to
shield with a firearm at the ready or with actual
fire. **16** *Sport* to protect (a fellow team-member)
or obstruct (an opponent). **17** *said of a stallion,
bull, etc* to mate with (a female). **18** *said of a bird*
to sit on (eggs). — *noun* **1** something that covers.
2 a lid, top, protective casing, etc. **3** the covering
of something: *plants that give good ground cover*.
4 (**covers**) the sheets and blankets on a bed.
5 the paper or board binding of a book, magazine, etc; one side of this. **6** an envelope: *a first-
day cover*. **7** shelter or protection: *take cover*.
8 insurance. **9** service: *Dr Brown will provide emergency cover*. **10** a pretence; a screen; a false identity: *his cover as a salesman was blown*. **11** armed
protection; protective fire. **12** *Cricket* cover point.
13 in restaurants, etc, a place setting at table.
— **cover for someone** to take over the duties of
an absent colleague, etc.

cover something up to conceal a dishonest act,
a mistake, etc.

under cover 1 in secret. **2** within shelter.

under cover of something using it as a protection or pretence.

under plain cover in a plain envelope without
tradename, etc.

under separate cover in a separate envelope or
parcel.
[from Old French *covrir*]

coverage *noun* an amount covered; the fullness of treatment of a news item in any of the
media, etc.

coverall — *noun* (*usually* **coveralls**) a one-
piece protective garment worn over normal
clothes. — *adj.* serving many purposes.

cover charge a service charge made per person in a restaurant, etc.

Coverdale, Miles (1488–1568) English
Protestant reformer and biblical scholar, born in
York. He was ordained priest in 1514, and joined
the Augustinian Friars in Cambridge, but was
converted to Protestantism. His own translation
of the Bible (the first complete one in English)
appeared in 1535. He then superintended the
work which led to the 'Great Bible' (1539), and
also edited 'Cranmer's Bible' (1540). Forced to
leave the country after Cromwell's fall, he
returned to England in 1548 under Cranmer's
influence and became Bishop of Exeter (1551).
On Queen Mary's accession he went abroad
again, but returned in 1559 to live in London.

cover girl a girl or woman whose photograph
is shown on a magazine cover.

covering *noun* something that covers, especially a blanket, protective casing, etc.

covering letter a letter accompanying and
explaining documents or goods.

coverlet *noun* a thin top cover for a bed; a bedspread or counterpane. [from Old French *cuver-lit*,
cover-bed]

cover note a temporary certificate of insurance.

cover point *Cricket* the fielding position forward and to the right of the batsman.

covert — *adj.* secret; secretive; stealthy.
— *noun* **1** a thicket providing cover for game.
2 *Biol.* a feather covering the base of a wing or tail
feather. [from Old French *covert*, past participle of
covrir, to cover]

covertly *adv.* in a secretive way.

cover-up *noun* an act of concealing or withholding information about something suspect or
illicit.

cover version an artist's version of a song,
etc already recorded by someone else.

covet *verb* (**coveted, coveting**) to long to possess (something belonging to someone else).
[from Old French *coveitier*, from Latin *cupiditas*,
longing, greed]

covetous *adj.* envious, greedy.

covetously *adv.* in a covetous way.

covetousness *noun* jealous desire.

covey *noun* (PL. **coveys**) **1** a small flock of
grouse or partridge. **2** a small group of people.
[from Old French *covee*, from *cover*, to hatch]

cow[1] *noun* **1** the female of any species of cattle.
2 the female of other large animals, eg the elephant, whale, seal, and moose. **3** a term of abuse
for a woman.
— **till the cows come home** *colloq.* for an
unforeseeably long time.
[from Anglo-Saxon *cu*]

cow[2] *verb* to frighten into submission. [from
Old Norse *kuga*, to subdue]

Coward, Sir Noël (Peirce) (1899–1973)
English actor, playwright, and composer, born in
Teddington, Middlesex. An actor from the age of
12, his first play, written with Esme Wynne, was
produced in 1917. Among his many successes are
Hay Fever (1925), *Private Lives* (1930), and *Blithe
Spirit* (1941). He wrote the music for most of his
works and was an accomplished singer.

coward *noun* **1** someone easily frightened, or
lacking courage to face danger or difficulty.
2 someone who acts brutally towards the weak
or undefended. [from Old French *couard*, from
Latin *cauda*, tail]

cowardice *or* **cowardliness** *noun* lack of
courage.

cowardly *adj.* like a coward.

Cowardly Lion, the one of Dorothy's companions in Frank L Baum's *The Wonderful Wizard
of Oz*.

cowbell *noun* a bell hanging from a cow's neck.

cowberry *noun* a small evergreen shrub
(*Vaccinium vitis-idaea*), native to N temperate
regions, up to 30cm tall, and having oval leaves
(often notched at the tip), drooping bell-shaped
pinkish-white flowers borne in terminal clusters,
and edible red berries.

cowboy *noun* **1** in the western USA, a man in
charge of cattle, especially as a character in films
of the Wild West. **2** *derog.* someone who undertakes building or other work without proper
training or qualifications; a dishonest businessman or entrepreneur.

cowcatcher *noun* a concave metal fender on
the front of a railway engine for clearing cattle
and other obstacles from the line.

cower *verb intrans.* (**cowered, cowering**) to
shrink away in fear. [from Middle English *couren*]

Cowes POP (1981) 16 000, a seaport in Medina
district, I of Wight, S England. It lies on the R
Medina estuary where it meets the N coast of the
island. Cowes is a well-known yachting centre.
NOTABLE FEATURES Osborne House (East Cowes),
summer residence of Queen Victoria and Prince
Albert; Cowes Castle, built by Henry VIII (1543),
is home of the Royal Yacht Squadron. EVENT
Cowes Week (Aug).

cowgirl *noun* a female worker assisting with
cattle or having charge of them.

cowhand, cowherd same as COWMAN.

cowhide *noun* a cow's hide made into leather.

cowl *noun* **1** a monk's large loose hood or
hooded habit. **2** a revolving cover for a chimneypot for improving ventilation. **3** a cowling. [from
Anglo-Saxon *cugele*, from Latin *cucullus*, hood]

cowlick *noun* a lock of hair standing up stiffly
from the forehead.

cowling *noun* a removable metal covering for
the engine of a vehicle or aircraft. [from COWL]

cowman *or* **cowhand** *or* **cowherd** *noun*
a person assisting with cattle or having charge of
them.

co-worker *noun* a fellow worker; a colleague.

cow parsley a biennial or perennial plant
(*Anthriscus sylvestris*), native to Europe, Asia, and
N Africa, and growing up to 1.5m tall. It has hollow grooved stems, leaves divided into leaflets
with toothed oval segments, and small white
flowers borne in umbels (flat-topped umbrella-
shaped clusters). — Also called *Queen Anne's lace*.

cowpat *noun* a flat circular deposit of cow
dung.

cow pea *noun Bot.* an annual plant (*Vigna sinensis*) that is a legume, cultivated in various parts of
the world for its edible seeds.

Cowpens, Battle of a conflict (1781) in
South Carolina during the US War of
Independence in which a small American army
under Daniel Morgan (1736–1802) defeated a
British force under Banastre Tarleton
(1754–1833).

Cowper, William (1731–1800) English poet,
born in Berkhamsted, Hertfordshire. He was
called to the Bar in 1754 but did not practise. He
suffered frequently from mental instability, and
attempted suicide several times. In collaboration
with the clergyman John Newton, he wrote the
Olney Hymns (1779). His other works include the
ballad 'John Gilpin' (1783), and his long poem
about rural ease, *The Task* (1785).

cowpox *noun Medicine* a viral infection of the
udders of cows that can be transmitted to
humans by direct contact, and causes mild symptoms so similar to smallpox that an attack confers
immunity. The virus is used as a smallpox vaccine.

cowrie *noun* **1** a large tropical shellfish. **2** its
brightly coloured shell, in primitive societies
used as money or prized for magic qualities.
[from Hindi *kauri*]

European cowrie shell

cowshed *or* **cowhouse** *noun* a building for
housing cattle.

cowslip *noun* a wild plant with yellow sweet-
smelling flowers. [from Anglo-Saxon *cuslyppe*,
cow dung]

cox — *noun* short for **coxswain**. — *verb trans.,
intrans.* to act as cox of (a boat).

coxcomb *noun old derog. use* a foolishly vain or
conceited man. [a contraction of *cock's comb*; originally applied to jesters from their comb-like
headgear]

coxless *adj.*, *said of a rowing boat, especially in
racing* having no cox.

◇ Coxless pairs and coxless fours are official
events in Olympic and world rowing competitions.

coxswain *noun* **1** the person who steers a
small boat. **2** a petty officer in a small ship. [from
cock, ship's boat + SWAIN]

coy *adj.* **1** shy; modest; affectedly bashful.
2 irritatingly uncommunicative about something. [from Old French *coi*, calm, from Latin *quietus*, quiet]

coyly *adv.* in a coy way.

coyness *noun* being coy.

coyote *noun* (PL. **coyote**, **coyotes**) a small N American wolf with a pointed face, tawny fur, and a black-tipped bushy tail, originally found mainly in deserts, prairies, and open woodland, but now increasingly known as an urban scavenger. Coyotes feed on small mammals, birds, fish, insects, and plants, and they pair for life. Many thousands are killed each year because they are considered dangerous to livestock. — Also called *prairie wolf*. [from Aztec *coyotl*]

coypu *noun* (PL. **coypu**, **coypus**) a S American rodent similar to a beaver, bred for its fur. [from a S American Indian language]

Cozumel, Isla a resort island in the Caribbean Sea, 19km/12mi off the coast of Quintana Roo on the Yucatán Peninsula, S Mexico. It is 47km/29mi long and 14.5km/9mi wide. CHIEF TOWN San Miguel.

CPAG *abbrev.* Child Poverty Action Group.

CPGB *abbrev.* Communist Party of Great Britain.

CPO *abbrev.* Chief Petty Officer.

CPR *abbrev.* Canadian Pacific Railway.

CPRE *abbrev.* Council for the Protection of Rural England.

CPSA *abbrev.* Civil and Public Services Association.

CPU *abbrev. Comput.* central processing unit.

CR *abbrev., as an international vehicle mark* Costa Rica.

Cr *symbol Chem.* chromium.

crab *noun* **1** any of about 4 500 species of crustacean belonging to the order Decapoda, most of which have a hard flattened shell and five pairs of jointed legs. Most crabs are marine, although there are a number of freshwater species. Many crabs are used as food. **2** (**Crab**) the sign of the zodiac and constellation Cancer. **3 a** the crab louse. **b** (**crabs**) infestation by this.
— **catch a crab** in rowing, either to sink the oar too deeply or to miss the water.
[from Anglo-Saxon *crabba*]
◇ In crabs, the front pair of legs are modified to form large pincers, which are used for picking up food, and many species use the back pair of legs as paddles for swimming. The tail is usually very small and folded forward under the rest of the body. While some crabs feed on algae, others are carnivores, and many are general scavengers. They range in size from the pea crabs, which have shells only 6mm in diameter, to the giant spider crab of Japan, whose outstretched claw tips may span 3.7m. The hermit crab does not have a shell, but makes its home in the empty shell of a sea snail or other mollusc.

crab

crab apple a small sour wild apple. [from Middle English *crabbe*]

Crabbe, George (1754–1832) English poet, born in Aldeburgh, Suffolk. He trained as a surgeon, turned to literature, and was ordained in 1782. His best-known work from this early period is *The Village* (1783), a realistic portrait of rural life, following which he wrote nothing for over 20 years. His later narrative poems include *The Parish Register* (1807), *The Borough* (1810), and other volumes of *Tales*.

crabbed *adj.* **1** bad-tempered. **2** *said of handwriting* cramped and hard to decipher. [from CRAB]

crabbedly *adv.* in a crabbed way.

crabbedness *noun* bad temper.

crabby *adj.* (**crabbier, crabbiest**) *colloq.* bad-tempered. [from CRAB]

crab louse a crab-like louse that infests the hair of the pubis.

Crab nebula *Astron.* an expanding cloud of gas in the constellation of Taurus, consisting of the remains of a star that exploded as a supernova in AD 1054 (when it was observed on Earth as a brilliant point of light).

crabwise *adj., adv.* moving sideways.

crack — *verb* **1** *trans., intrans.* to fracture partially without falling to pieces. **2** *trans., intrans.* to split. **3** *trans., intrans.* to make or cause to make a sudden sharp noise. **4** *trans., intrans.* to strike sharply. **5** *trans., intrans.* to give way or cause to give way: *crack someone's resistance*. **6** to force open (a safe). **7** to solve (a code or problem). **8** to tell (a joke). **9** *intrans. said of the voice* to change pitch or tone suddenly and unintentionally. **10** *Chem. trans., intrans.* to break down long-chain hydrocarbons produced during petroleum refining into lighter more useful short-chain products. — *noun* **1** a sudden sharp sound. **2** a fracture in a material produced by an external force or internal stress, often originating in a defective region of the material. **3** a narrow opening. **4** a resounding blow. **5** *colloq.* a joke. **6** *slang* a highly addictive derivative of cocaine, consisting of hard crystalline lumps that are heated and 'smoked' (inhaled) as a stimulant. Habitual use leads to physical and mental deterioration, and addiction to crack is a serious social problem in some countries. — *adj. colloq.* expert: *a crack shot*.
— **at the crack of dawn** *colloq.* at daybreak; very early.
crack down on someone *or* **something** *colloq.* to take firm action against them.
crack up to suffer an emotional breakdown.
crack something up *colloq.* to praise it extravagantly: *not all it's cracked up to be* = not as good as people say it is.
a fair crack of the whip a fair opportunity.
get cracking *colloq.* to make a prompt start with a journey, undertaking, etc.
have a crack at something *colloq.* to attempt it.
[from Anglo-Saxon *cracian*, to resound]

crackbrained *adj. colloq.* mad; crazy.

crackdown *noun* a firm action taken against someone or something.

cracked *adj.* **1** *colloq.* crazy; mad. **2** *said of a voice* harsh; uneven in tone.

cracker *noun* **1** a thin crisp unsweetened biscuit. **2** a small noisy firework. **3** a party toy in the form of a gaudy paper tube usually containing a paper hat, gift, and motto, that pulls apart with an explosive bang.

crackers *adj. colloq.* mad.

cracking *colloq.* — *adj.* **1** very good. **2** very fast: *a cracking pace*. — *adv.* used for emphasis: *a cracking good story*. — *noun Chem.* same as CATALYTIC CRACKING.

crackle — *verb intrans.* to make a faint continuous cracking or popping sound. — *noun* this kind of sound. [from CRACK]

crackling *noun* the crisp skin of roast pork. [from CRACK]

crackly *adj.* **1** producing a crackling sound. **2** brittle, crisp.

cracknel *noun* **1** a light brittle biscuit. **2** a hard nutty filling for chocolates. **3** (**cracknels**) *North Amer.* crisply fried pieces of fat pork. [from Middle English *krakenelle*]

crackpot *colloq.* — *adj.* crazy. — *noun* a crazy person.

Cracow see KRAKOW.

-cracy *combining form* denoting rule, government, or domination by a particular group, etc: *democracy*. [from Greek *kratos*, power]

cradle — *noun* **1** a cot for a small baby, especially one that can be rocked. **2** a place of origin; the home or source of something: *the cradle of civilization*. **3** a suspended platform or cage for workmen engaged in the construction, repair, or painting of a ship or building. **4** the support for the receiver on an old-style telephone. — *verb* to rock or hold gently: *cradle a baby in one's arms*.
— **from the cradle to the grave** throughout one's life.
[from Anglo-Saxon *kradol*]

cradle-snatcher *noun derog.* someone who chooses a much younger person as a lover or marriage partner.

craft — *noun* **1** (*also in compounds*) a skill or occupation, especially one requiring the use of the hands: *crafts such as weaving and pottery*. **2** skilled ability. **3** cunning. **4** (PL. **craft**) (*often in compounds*) a boat or ship, or an air or space vehicle. — *verb* to make skilfully. [from Anglo-Saxon *cræft*]

craftily *adv.* in a crafty way.

craftiness *noun* being crafty.

craftsman *or* **craftswoman** *noun* a man or woman skilled at a craft.

craftsmanship *noun* the skill of a craftsman or craftswoman.

crafty *adj.* (**craftier, craftiest**) clever, shrewd, cunning, or sly.

crag *noun* a rocky peak or jagged outcrop of rock. [from Celtic *crag*, related to Welsh *craig* and Gaelic *creag*]

cragginess *noun* being craggy.

craggy *adj.* (**craggier, craggiest**) **1** full of crags. **2** rough. **3** rugged.

Craig, Edward (Henry) Gordon (1872–1966) English stage designer, actor, director, and theorist, born in Stevenage, Hertfordshire. He was an actor in Henry Irving's company, but left the Lyceum in 1897 to be a director and designer. He settled in Italy (1906) and published the journal *The Mask* (1908–29) and the influential books, *On the Art of the Theatre* (1911) and *The Theatre Advancing* (1921).

Craig, Roger (1960–) US footballer, born in Preston, Mississippi. A running back with the San Francisco 49ers, in the 1985 Super Bowl he scored 18 points and three touchdowns, both records. He also became the first player in National Football League history to rush for 1 000 yards and receive passes for 1 000 yards. He then became manager of the San Francisco Giants (1985–).

Craig a male first name, after the Scottish surname. [from Gaelic *creag*, rock]

Craigie, Sir William Alexander (1867–1957) Scottish philologist and lexicographer, born in Dundee, Tayside. He was Professor of Anglo-Saxon at Oxford (1916–25), and of English at Chicago (1925–35). He was joint editor of the *New* (later *Oxford*) *English Dictionary* (1901–33), and also editor of dictionaries on Scots and on American English.

Craik, Dinah Maria (1826–87) English novelist, born in Stoke-on-Trent, Staffordshire. The author of many novels, prose essays, and poems, her best-known work is the novel *John Halifax, Gentleman* (1857), which has been translated into several languages.

Cram, Steve, properly **Stephen** (1960–) English track athlete, born in Gateshead, Durham. He was the European junior champion at 3 000m in 1979, and won senior titles at 1 500m in 1982 and 1986. He won the world championship gold medal at 1 500m in 1983, and the Commonwealth Games gold medals at 1 500m (1982, 1986) and 800m (1986). In 1985 he set three world records in 20 days at 1 500m, 1mi, and 2 000m. His time for the mile was 3 min 46.32 seconds, a record which stood until 1993 when it was surpassed by Noureddine Morceli of Algeria.

cram *verb* (**crammed, cramming**) **1** to stuff full. **2** (**cram something in or together**) to push or pack it tightly. **3** *intrans., trans.* to study intensively, or prepare (someone) rapidly for, an examination. [from Anglo-Saxon *crammian*, to stuff full]

cram-full *adj.* full to bursting.

crammer *noun* a person or school that prepares pupils for examinations by rapid study.

cramp¹ — *noun* **1** the painful involuntary contraction of a muscle. **2** (**cramps**) severe abdominal pain. — *verb* to restrict tiresomely. — **cramp someone's style** to restrict their scope for creativity or individuality. [from Old French *crampe*]

cramp² — *noun* (also **cramp-iron**) a clamp for holding stone or timbers together. — *verb* to fasten with a cramp. [from Old Dutch *crampe*, hook]

cramped *adj.* **1** *said of a space* too small; overcrowded. **2** *said of handwriting* small and closely written.

crampon *noun* a spiked iron attachment for climbing boots, to improve grip on ice or rock. [from French *crampon*]

cranberry *noun* (PL. **cranberries**) **1** an evergreen shrub bearing red acid berries. **2** one of these berries. [from German dialect *kraanbeere*, crane berry]

cranberry

Crane, (Harold) Hart (1899–1932) US poet, born in Garrettsville, Ohio. His most important work is contained in *The White Buildings* (1926), a collection on New York life, and *The Bridge* (1930), an epic using Brooklyn Bridge as its focal point. An alcoholic, he drowned himself by jumping from the ship aboard which he was returning from a visit to Mexico. His *Collected Poems* were published in 1933.

Crane, Stephen (1871–1900) US writer and war correspondent, born in Newark, New Jersey. He began as a journalist in New York, and became known as a novelist through *Maggie: a Girl of the Streets* (1893) and *The Red Badge of Courage* (1895), a realistic story of a soldier in the Civil War. He also wrote poems and short stories, and worked as a war correspondent in Greece and Cuba.

crane — *noun* **1** a machine with a long pivoted arm from which lifting gear is suspended, allowing heavy weights to be moved both horizontally and vertically. **2** a large wading bird with a long neck and long legs, found in marshlands and swamps in N America and throughout most of Europe, Asia, and Africa. It has a loud trumpeting call, and performs spectacular dances during the breeding season. — *verb trans., intrans.* to stretch (one's neck), or lean forward, in order to see better. [from Anglo-Saxon *cran*]

cranefly *noun* a long-legged two-winged insect, the daddy-long-legs.

cranesbill *noun* an annual or perennial plant of the genus *Geranium*, native to temperate regions, and having leaves with lobes radiating from a central point, and white, purple, or blue flowers with five petals. Most of the so-called geraniums of horticulture in fact belong to the genus *Pelargonium*.

Cranford a novel by Mrs Gaskell (1851–3). It is a collection of sketches depicting the lives of various middle-aged ladies in a sleepy English country village.

cranial *adj.* relating to or in the region of the skull.

cranial nerve *Anat.* in vertebrates, one of the ten to twelve pairs of nerves that arise directly from the brain.

craniosacral therapy a form of alternative therapy involving manipulation of the skull to relieve imbalances in the cranial rhythm that are believed to cause illness. [from CRANIUM + SACRUM]

cranium *noun* (PL. **crania, craniums**) **1** the dome-shaped part of the skull, consisting of several fused bones, that encloses and protects the brain. **2** the skull. [from Greek *kranion*]

crank *noun* **1** a right-angled bend in, or an arm projecting at right angles from, a shaft, for communicating motion to or from the shaft. **2** a tool bent at right angles for starting an engine by hand. **3** *derog.* an eccentric person. — **crank something up** to start an engine with a crank. [from Anglo-Saxon *crancstæf*, weaving implement]

crankshaft *noun* a shaft driving, or driven by, a crank, eg in a vehicle engine.

cranky *adj.* (**crankier, crankiest**) *colloq.* eccentric or faddy.

Cranmer, Thomas (1489–1556) English prelate and Archbishop of Canterbury (1533–53), born in Aslacton, Nottinghamshire. He said that he had sworn allegiance to the pope 'for form's sake'. He later annulled Henry's marriages to Catherine of Aragon and to Anne Boleyn (1536), and divorced him from Anne of Cleves (1540). Cranmer was largely responsible for the Book of Common Prayer (1549, 1552), and on Henry's death, he rushed Protestant changes through. He had little to do with affairs of state, but agreed to the plan to divert the succession from Mary to Lady Jane Grey (1553), for which he was later arraigned for treason. Sentenced to death, he retracted the seven recantations he had been forced to write, then was burned alive.

crannied *adj.* having crannies.

cranny *noun* (PL. **crannies**) **1** a narrow opening; a cleft or crevice. **2** an out-of-the-way corner. [from Middle English *crany*]

crap *coarse slang* — *noun* **1** faeces. **2** nonsense. — *verb intrans.* (**crapped, crapping**) to defecate. [from Middle English *crap*, chaff]

crape see CREPE.

craps *sing. noun* a gambling game in which the player rolls two dice.

crapulence *noun* sickness caused by excessive drinking. [from Latin *crapula*, drunkenness]

crapulent *or* **crapulous** *adj.* suffering from crapulence.

crash — *verb* **1** *trans., intrans.* to fall or strike with a banging or smashing noise. **2** *trans., intrans.* (*usually* **crash into something**) *said of a vehicle* to collide or cause it to collide with something. **3** *intrans.* to make a deafening noise. **4** *intrans.* to move noisily. **5** *intrans. said of a business or stock exchange* to collapse. **6** *intrans. said of a computer or program* to fail completely, because of a malfunction, etc. **7** *slang* to gatecrash. **8** (*usually* **crash out**) *slang* to fall asleep; to sleep the night. — *noun* **1** a violent impact or breakage, or the sound of it. **2** a deafening noise. **3** a traffic or air-

craft accident; a collision. **4** the collapse of a business or the stock exchange. **5** the failure of a computer or program. — *adj.* concentrated or intensive, so as to produce results in minimum time: *a crash diet.* [imitative]

crash barrier a protective metal barrier along the edge of a road or carriageway.

crash dive a rapid emergency dive by a submarine.

crash-dive *verb intrans.* to make a crash dive.

crash helmet a protective helmet worn eg by motor-cyclists.

crashing *adj. colloq.* utter; great: *a crashing bore.*

crash-land *verb trans., intrans., said of an aircraft* to land in an emergency, usually without lowering the undercarriage and with the risk of crashing.

crash-landing *noun* an emergency landing of an aircraft.

crass *adj.* **1** gross; downright. **2** colossally stupid. **3** utterly tactless or insensitive. [from Latin *crassus*, thick, stupid]

crassly *adv.* in a crass way.

crassness *noun* being crass.

Crassus, Marcus Licinius, also called **Dives** ('wealthy') (c.115–53 BC) Roman politician. As praetor, he defeated Spartacus at the battle of Lucania (71 BC), and was made consul with Pompey in 70 BC. He later formed the 'First Triumvirate' (60 BC) with Julius Caesar and Pompey to challenge the Senate. In 53 BC, as Governor of Syria, he attacked the Parthians, but was routed and killed at the battle of Carrhae.

-crat *combining form* forming nouns and adjectives corresponding to words in *-cracy*: democrat.

Cratchit, Bob the impoverished and good-natured clerk to Scrooge in Charles Dickens's *A Christmas Carol.*

crate — *noun* **1** a strong wooden, plastic, or metal case with partitions, for carrying breakable or perishable goods. **2** *derog. slang* a decrepit vehicle or aircraft. — *verb* to pack in a crate. [from Latin *cratis*, wickerwork barrier]

Crater *Astron.* the Cup, a small faint constellation in the northern sky.

crater *noun* **1** the bowl-shaped mouth of a volcano. **2** a hole left in the ground where a meteorite has landed or a bomb or mine has exploded. **3** a circular rimmed depression in the surface of the moon. [from Greek *krater*, mixing-bowl]

Crater Lake a circular crater lake in SW Oregon, USA, located in Crater Lake National Park, in the Cascade Range. AREA 52sq km/20sq mi; 9.5km/6mi across; 604m deep. It lies at an altitude of 1 879m and is situated in a large pit formed by the destruction of the summit of a prehistoric volcano (now called Mt Mazama). The lake has no inlet or outlet, but remains at a near-constant level from rainfall and melting snow. Its shore is lined by cliffs 150–600m high. Small Wizard I near the W shore rises 237m above the surface, and has a crater at the top.

Crater Lake see CHUBB CRATER.

-cratic *combining form* forming adjectives corresponding to nouns in *-cracy*: democratic.

craton *noun Geol.* a relatively rigid and immobile part of the Earth's crust that has been stable for at least 1 500m years. [from Greek *kratos*, strength]

cravat *noun* a formal style of neckerchief worn by men instead of a tie. [from French *cravate*, an imitation of the neckwear of the *Cravates* (Croatians)]

crave *verb* **1** (**crave something** *or* **crave for** *or* **after something**) to long for it; to desire it overwhelmingly. **2** *old formal use* to ask for politely; to beg. [from Anglo-Saxon *crafian*]

craven *old derog. use* — *adj.* cowardly; cringing. — *noun* a coward. [from Middle English *cravant*, defeated]

cravenly *adv.* in a cowardly or cringing way.

cravenness *noun* being craven.

craving *noun* an intense longing; an overwhelming desire.

craw *noun* **1** the crop of a bird or insect. **2** the stomach of a lower animal.
— **stick in one's craw** *colloq.* to be difficult for one to swallow or accept.
[from Middle English *crawe*]

crawfish *noun* (PL. **crawfish**) same as CRAYFISH.

Crawford, Henry and Mary the superficial brother and sister in Jane Austen's *Mansfield Park*.

Crawford, Joan, originally **Lucille Fay Le Sueur** (1904–77) US film actress, born in San Antonio, Texas. At first a nightclub dancer, she started in silent films in 1925, taking the lead in *Our Dancing Daughters* (1928). She became an established star in the 1930s and 1940s, winning an Oscar for *Mildred Pearce* (1945). Her last great role was in *Whatever Happened to Baby Jane?* (1962), in which she co-starred with her long-standing rival, Bette Davis.

crawl — *verb intrans.* **1** *said of insects, worms, etc* to move along the ground. **2** to move along on hands and knees, especially as a stage before learning to walk. **3** *said eg of traffic* to progress very slowly. **4** to be, or feel as if, covered with crawling insects. **5** (**crawl to someone**) *derog. colloq.* to behave in an over-humble way to someone whose approval one wants. — *noun* **1** a crawling motion. **2** a very slow pace. **3** a swimming-stroke with an alternate overarm action.

crawler *noun derog. colloq.* someone who behaves in an over-humble, ingratiating way to those in senior positions.

Crawley, the Rev Josiah the proud but poorly off minister in Anthony Trollope's 'Barsetshire' novels, who first appears in *Framley Parsonage* but features most prominently in *The Last Chronicle of Barset*.

Crawley, Sir Pitt a brutal character in William Makepeace Thackeray's *Vanity Fair*. Other members of his family include his rich, unpredictable sister Miss Crawley, and his sons Pitt and Rawdon.

Crawley POP (1992e) 89 000, a town in Crawley district, West Sussex, S England, situated 43km/27mi S of London. It was designated a 'new town' in 1947. London Gatwick airport lies to the N of the town.

Craxi, Bettino (1934–) Italian politician, born in Milan. He was active in the Socialist Youth Movement, and joined the Central Committee of the Italian Socialist Party in 1957. A member of the National Executive in 1965, he became Deputy Secretary (1970–6), General Secretary (1976), and Italy's first Socialist Prime Minister (1983–7).

crayfish *noun* (PL. **crayfish**) an edible shellfish similar to a lobster. [from Old French *crevice*, from Old German *krebiz*, crab]

crayfish

crayon — *noun* a coloured pencil, or stick of coloured wax or chalk. — *verb trans., intrans.* (**crayoned, crayoning**) to draw or colour with a crayon. [from French *crayon*, from *craie*, chalk]

craze — *noun* an intense but passing enthusiasm or fashion. — *verb* **1** to make crazy: *a crazed*

look. **2** *trans., intrans. said eg of a glazed or varnished surface* to develop or cause to develop a network of fine cracks. [probably from Norse]

crazily *adv.* in a crazy way.

craziness *noun* being crazy.

crazy *adj.* (**crazier, craziest**) **1** mad; insane. **2** foolish; absurd; foolhardy. **3** (**crazy about something** *or* **someone**) madly enthusiastic about them.
— **like crazy** *colloq.* keenly; fast and furious.

Crazy Horse, Sioux name **Ta-Sunko-Witko** (c.1849–77) Oglala Sioux Chief, born in South Dakota. Regarded as the foremost Sioux military leader, he defeated General Custer at the battle of Little Big Horn (1876) with a combined force of Sioux and Cheyennes. He and his followers surrendered the following year, and he died in custody in Fort Robinson, Nebraska.

crazy paving paving made up of irregularly shaped slabs of stone or concrete.

creak — *noun* the squeaking noise made typically by an unoiled hinge or loose floorboard. — *verb intrans.* **1** to make this noise. **2** *facetious* to be in an unreliable or infirm condition. [imitative]

creakily *adv.* **1** with a creaking sound. **2** stiffly.

creakiness *noun* being creaky.

creaky *adj.* (**creakier, creakiest**) **1** squeaky. **2** tending to creak. **3** badly made or performed. **4** stiff.

cream — *noun* **1** the yellowish fatty substance that rises to the surface of milk, and yields butter when churned. In the UK, single cream contains not less than 18% fat, and double cream contains 48% fat. **2** any food that resembles this substance in consistency or appearance, eg 'synthetic' cream, ice cream. **3** any cosmetic substance that resembles cream in texture or consistency, eg cold cream. **4** the best part of something; the pick. **5** a yellowish-white colour. — *verb* **1** to beat (eg butter and sugar) till creamy. **2** to remove the cream from (milk).
— *usually* **cream something off** to select or take away the best part.
[from Old French *cresme*]

creamer *noun* **1** a powdered milk substitute, used in coffee. **2** *Antiq. North Amer., esp. US* a cream jug. **3** a device for separating cream from milk.

creamery *noun* (PL. **creameries**) a place where dairy products are made or sold.

cream of tartar potassium hydrogen tartrate, a white powder used together with sodium bicarbonate in baking powder, which produces bubbles of carbon dioxide when water is added to it, lightening the texture of bakery products, eg cakes.

creamware *noun* a hard durable type of earthenware first produced in Staffordshire in the 18c, and usually having a cream-coloured glaze. Josiah Wedgwood produced a much-refined version of it around 1760.

creamy *adj.* (**creamier, creamiest**) **1** full of cream. **2** like cream in appearance or consistency.

crease — *noun* **1** a line made by folding, pressing or crushing. **2** *Cricket* a line marking the position of batsman or bowler. — *verb trans., intrans.* to make a crease or creases in; to develop creases.
— **crease up** *or* **crease someone up** *trans., intrans. colloq.* to be or make incapable with laughter, pain, or exhaustion.
[from Middle English *creeste*, connected with CREST]

create *verb* **1** to form from nothing: *create the universe.* **2** to bring into existence; to introduce: *create a system.* **3** to cause. **4** to produce or contrive. **5** *trans., intrans. said of an artist, etc* to use one's imagination to make. **6** *intrans. colloq.* to make a fuss. **7** *said of an actor* to be the first to

play (a certain role). **8** to raise to an honourable rank: *was created a peer.* [from Latin *creare*]

creatine *or* **creatin** *noun Biochem.* an organic compound, found in muscle, whose phosphate serves as an important source of energy for muscle contraction. [from Greek *kreas kreatos*, flesh]

Creation, The (Die Shöpfung) an oratorio by Joseph Haydn (1798) to a text derived indirectly from Milton's *Paradise Lost*.

creation *noun* **1** the act of creating. **2** something created. **3** the universe; all created things.

creative *adj.* having or showing the ability to create; inventive or imaginative.

creatively *adv.* in a creative way.

creativity *noun* **1** being creative. **2** the ability to create.

creator *noun* **1** a person who creates. **2** (**the Creator**) God.

creature *noun* **1** a bird, beast, or fish. **2** a person: *a wretched creature.* **3** the slavish underling or puppet of someone. [from Latin *creatura*, act of creating]

creature comforts comforts such as food, clothes, warmth, etc.

creature of habit 1 an animal with fixed, especially seasonal, behaviour patterns. **2** a person of unchanging routines.

crèche *noun* a nursery where babies can be left and cared for while their parents are at work, shopping, exercising, etc. [from French *crèche*, manger]

Crécy, Battle of a battle (1346) near Abbeville between France and England in the Hundred Years War. Using tactics perfected against the Scots, Edward III routed a larger French army, and demonstrated the superiority of a co-ordinated force of dismounted men-at-arms and longbowmen over mounted knights.

cred *noun slang* credibility: *street cred.*

credence *noun* faith or belief placed in something: *give their claims no credence.* [from Latin *credentia*]

credentials *pl. noun* personal qualifications and achievements that one can quote in evidence of one's trustworthiness; documents or other evidence of these. [from Latin *credentia*, belief]

credibility *noun* the quality of being credible.

credibility gap in politics, the discrepancy between what is claimed and what is actually, or is likely to be, the case.

credible *adj.* **1** capable of being believed. **2** reliable; trustworthy. [from Latin *credibilis*]

credibly *adv.* in a credible way.

credit — *noun* **1** faith placed in something. **2** honour, or a cause of honour: *to her credit, she didn't say anything / your loyalty does you credit.* **3** acknowledgement, recognition, or praise: *give him credit for trying / take credit for someone else's hard work.* **4** (**credits**) a list of acknowledgements to those who have helped in the preparation of a book or (*also* **credit titles**) film. **5** trust given to someone promising to pay later for goods already supplied: *buy goods on credit.* **6** one's financial reliability, especially as a basis for such trust. **7** the amount of money available to one at one's bank. **8** an entry in a bank account acknowledging a payment. **9** the side of an account on which such entries are made. See also DEBIT. **10** a certificate of completion of a course of instruction; a distinction awarded for performance on such a course. — *verb* (**credited, crediting**) **1** to believe; to place faith in. **2** (**credit something to someone** *or* **someone with something**) to enter a sum as a credit on someone's account, or allow a sum as credit. **3** (**credit someone with something**) to attribute a quality or achievement to them: *we credited you with more sense.* [from Old French *crédit*, from Latin *creditum*, loan]

creditable *adj.* praiseworthy; laudable.

creditably *adv.* in a creditable way.

credit account a financial arrangement with a shop that allows one to purchase goods on credit.

credit card a card authorizing one to purchase goods or services on credit.

credit insurance insurance taken out when a business sells on credit terms (ie asks for payment at a later date). The insurer provides a safeguard against the possibility of the customer not paying, thereby creating a 'bad debt'.

credit note a form entitling one to a certain sum as credit, eg in place of returned or faulty goods.

creditor *noun* a person to whom one owes money. See also DEBTOR.

credit rating an assessment of a person's creditworthiness.

credit squeeze restrictions on borrowing imposed by the government.

credit transfer payment made directly from one bank account to another.

credit union a co-operative and non-profit-making savings association which makes loans to its members at a low rate of interest, often for consumer items. Credit unions are becoming increasingly popular in the UK, especially in communities where people are unable to obtain other forms of credit. The system is also popular in the USA where there are some 50 000 credit unions.

creditworthiness *noun* entitlement to credit.

creditworthy *adj.* judged as deserving financial credit on the basis of earning ability and previous promptness in repaying debts.

credo *noun* (PL. **credos**) a creed. [from Latin *credo*, I believe]

credulity *noun* a tendency to believe something without proper proof.

credulous *adj.* too trusting; too ready to believe. [from Latin *credulus*, trustful]

credulously *adv.* in a credulous way.

Cree an Algonkian-speaking Native American group from the Canadian Subarctic region, originally hunters and fishermen. With guns acquired from French fur traders in the 17c, they began to expand: one group, the Plains Cree, moved west, and became bison hunters, while the Woodland Cree remained in forested areas and continued to hunt.

creed *noun* **1** (often **Creed**) a statement of the main points of Christian belief. **2** any set of beliefs or principles, personal or religious. [from Anglo-Saxon *creda*, from Latin *credo*, I believe]

Creek a Native American people, originally from Georgia and Alabama. Their territory was first invaded by the Spanish in the 16c, and in the Creek War (1813–14) against US troops, they were defeated and forced to cede much of their land. Finally they were forcibly moved to Oklahoma in 1837, where they became one of the Five Civilized Tribes. The present-day population is c.17 000, living in Oklahoma and Alabama.

creek *noun* **1** a narrow coastal inlet. **2** *North Amer., Austral., New Zealand* a small river or tributary.
— **up the creek** *colloq.* in desperate difficulties. [from Old Norse *kriki*, nook]

creel *noun* a large basket for carrying fish. [from Middle English *crele*]

creep — *verb intrans.* (PAST TENSE AND PAST PARTICIPLE **crept**) **1** to move slowly, with stealth or caution. **2** to move with the body close to the ground; to crawl. **3** *said of a plant* to grow along the ground, up a wall, etc. **4** to enter barely noticeably: *anxiety crept into her voice.* **5** to develop little by little: *creeping inflation.* **6** *said especially of the flesh* to have a strong tingling sensation as a response to fear or disgust. — *noun* **1** *derog.* an unpleasantly sly or sinister person; also as a general term of abuse. **2** the slow deformation with time of a solid material, especially a metal, under stress. It usually occurs at high temperatures, although lead, zinc, and tin show this property at ordinary temperatures. Creep is taken into account during the design of machinery, vehicles, etc. **3** the slow movement of soil, broken rock, or mining ground downward under the influence of gravity.
— **give one the creeps** *colloq.* to disgust or repel one.
[from Anglo-Saxon *creopan*]

creeper *noun* a creeping plant.

creepers *pl. noun* shoes with thick quiet soles.

creepily *adv.* in a creepy way.

creepy *adj.* (**creepier**, **creepiest**) *colloq.* slightly scary; spooky; eerie.

creepy-crawly *noun* (PL. **creepy-crawlies**) *colloq.* a small creeping insect.

cremate *verb* to burn (a corpse) to ashes, as an alternative to burial. [from Latin *cremare*, to burn]

cremation *noun* the act or process of cremating a corpse.
◊ Soldiers killed in battle in ancient Greece were cremated, and the practice was later adopted by the Romans. It is the regular method used by Hindus, and it is becoming more common in Christian countries (where it was formerly discouraged because of its non-Christian associations).

crematorium *noun* (PL. **crematoria**, **crematoriums**) a place where corpses are cremated.

crème *noun* **1** cream, or a creamy food. **2** a liqueur. [from French *crème*, cream]

crème caramel an egg custard baked in a dish lined with caramel.

crème de la crème the cream of the cream; the very best.

crème de menthe a green peppermint-flavoured liqueur.

crème fraîche cream thickened with a culture of bacteria, used in cooking. [French, = fresh cream]

crenellated *adj.*, *said of a castle, wall, etc* having battlements. [from French *crenel*, the notch or space in battlements]

crenellation

crenellation *noun* battlements along the top of a castle wall.

creole *noun* **1** a pidgin language that has become the accepted language of a region. **2** (**Creole**) the French-based creole spoken in the US states of the Caribbean Gulf. **3** (**Creole**) a native-born West Indian or Latin American of mixed European and Negro blood; a French or Spanish native of the US Gulf states. [from French *creole*, from Portuguese *crioulo*, native]

Creon *or* **Kreon** a name (meaning 'ruler') given to several legendary Greek kings, but especially to the brother of Jocasta, regent of Thebes, who awarded the throne to Oedipus. Later, after the siege of the city by the seven Champions, he commanded that Polynices should not be buried, and condemned Antigone to death for disobeying this order.

creosote *noun* **1** a dark brown oil distilled from coal tar, used for preserving wood. **2** a transparent oil distilled from wood tar, used as an antiseptic. [literally 'flesh-preserver', from Greek *kreas*, flesh + *soter*, saviour]

crêpe *or* **crepe** *noun* **1** (also **crape**) a thin finely-wrinkled silk fabric, dyed black for mourning wear; a mourning armband made of this. **2** rubber with a wrinkled surface, used for shoe soles. **3** a thin pancake. [from French *crêpe*, from Latin *crispus*, crisp]

crêpe paper paper with a wrinkled, elastic texture, used for making decorations, etc.

crept see CREEP.

crepuscular *adj.* **1** of, or relating to, twilight; dim. **2** denoting animals that are active before sunrise or at dusk, eg bats, rabbits, deer. [from Latin *crepusculum*, twilight]

crêpy *adj.* (**crêpier**, **crêpiest**) **1** like crêpe. **2** *said especially of the skin* wrinkled.

Cres. *abbrev.* Crescent.

crescendo — *noun* (PL. **crescendos**) **1** a gradual increase in loudness; a musical passage of increasing loudness. **2** a high point or climax. — *adj., adv. Mus.* played with increasing loudness. See also DIMINUENDO. [from Italian *crescendo*, from Latin *crescere*, to grow]

crescent *noun* **1** the moon in its first quarter — the new moon; loosely, the moon in its first or last quarter. **2** something similar in shape to this, eg a semicircular row of houses. [from Latin *crescere*, to grow]

cress *noun* any of several plants whose sharp-tasting leaves are used in salads, etc. [from Anglo-Saxon *cressa* or *cærse*]

Cressida in medieval accounts of the Trojan War, the daughter of Calchas, a Trojan priest. She was beloved by Troilus, a Trojan prince, but deserted him for Diomedes when transferred to the Greek camp.

crest *noun* **1** a comb, vertical tuft of feathers, or ridge-like projection on the head of certain birds or animals. **2** a plume on a helmet. **3** *Heraldry* the part of a coat of arms that appears above the shield. **4** the topmost ridge of a mountain. **5** the foaming edge of a wave. [from Latin *crista*]

crested *adj.* having a crest, or something like one.

crestfallen *adj.* dejected as a result of a blow to one's pride or ambitions. [from CREST]

Cretaceous *adj.* **1** *Geol.* relating to the last period of the Mesozoic era, lasting from about 140m to 65m years ago. During this period the first flowering plants appeared, and dinosaurs and many other reptiles became extinct at the end of the period. Ammonites also died out at this time. **2** relating to rocks formed during this period. **3** (**cretaceous**) composed of or resembling chalk. [from Latin *creta*, chalk]

Crete, Greek **Kríti**, Italian **Candia**, Latin **Creta** POP (1991) 537 000, an island region of Greece, situated in the Mediterranean Sea to the S of the Cyclades island group. It is the largest of the Greek islands and the fifth largest in the Mediterranean Sea. AREA 8 336sq km/3 218sq mi; length 256km/159mi; width 14–60km/9–37mi. PHYSICAL DESCRIPTION the White Mts in the W rise to 2 452m; the Idhi Oros in the centre rise to the highest point of the island, Psiloritis (2 456m); the N coastline is deeply indented. HISTORY evidence of settlement from c.6000 BC; important Minoan civilization in c.2000 BC; ruled at various times by Greeks, Romans, Turks, and Arabs; passed to Greece in 1913; occupied by Nazi Germany in World War II, after an airborne invasion in 1941. CAPITAL Heraklion. CHIEF TOWNS

Chania, Agios Nikolaos. ECONOMY fruit, olive oil, wine; sheep, goats; tourism. NOTABLE FEATURES ancient sites at Knossos, Gortys, Lato, and Phaistos.

cretin *noun* **1** a person who is mentally retarded and physically deformed as the result of a congenital malfunction of the thyroid gland, a disorder formerly common in alpine districts. **2** *offensive* an idiot. [from French dialect *crestin*, from Latin *christianus*, Christian, human creature]

cretinism *noun* the condition of being a cretin.

cretinous *adj.* typical of a cretin.

cretonne *noun* a strong cotton material used for curtains, chair-covers, etc. [from French *cretonne*, from *Creton* in Normandy]

Creus, Cape, Greek **Aphrodisium** the easternmost point on the Iberian Peninsula. The picturesque fishing village of Cadaques nearby is preserved by local artists.

crevasse *noun* Geol. a deep vertical crack in a glacier, formed by stresses that build up as different parts of the glacier move at different rates. [from French, from Old French *crevace*, crevice]

crevice *noun* a crack; a narrow opening; a cleft or cranny. [from Old French *crevace*, from Latin *crepare*, to crack]

crew¹ — *noun* **1** the team of people manning a ship, aircraft, train, bus, etc. **2** a ship's company excluding the officers. **3** a team engaged in some operation: *camera crew*. **4** *colloq., usually derog.* a bunch of people: *a strange crew*. — *verb intrans.* to serve as a crew member on a yacht, etc. [from Middle English *creue*, reinforcements, from Old French *creu*, increase]

crew² see CROW.

crewcut *noun* a closely cropped hairstyle for men.

Crewe POP (1981) 59 000, a town in Crewe and Nantwich district, Cheshire, NW central England. It is a major railway junction, NW of Stoke-on-Trent, and an important centre of the dairy industry.

crewel *noun* thin, loosely twisted yarn for tapestry or embroidery.

crewelwork *noun* needlework using crewels.

crew neck a firm round neckline on a sweater.

crew-necked *adj.* having a crew-neck.

crib — *noun* **1** a baby's cot or cradle. **2** a manger. **3** a model of the nativity, with the infant Christ in a manger **4** a literal translation of a text, used as an aid by students. **5** something copied or plagiarised from another's work. **6** the discarded cards in cribbage, used by the dealer in

scoring. — *verb trans., intrans.* (**cribbed, cribbing**) to copy or plagiarise. [from Anglo-Saxon *cribb*, stall, manger]

cribbage *noun* a card game for two to four players, who each try to be first to score a certain number of points. [from CRIB, the discarded cards in the game]

Crick, Francis Harry Compton (1916–) English molecular biologist, born near Northampton. Working at the Cavendish Laboratory in Cambridge from 1949, he constructed a molecular model of the complex genetic material DNA with James Watson (1953); he later made far-reaching discoveries concerning the genetic code. He shared the 1962 Nobel Prize for Physiology or Medicine with Watson and Maurice Wilkins.

crick *colloq.* — *noun* a painful spasm or stiffness, especially in the neck. — *verb* to wrench (eg one's neck or back).

cricket¹ *noun* an outdoor game played with a ball, bats, and wickets, between two sides of eleven players.

— **not cricket** *colloq.* unfair; unsporting.

◇ Each team takes it in turn to bat and bowl. The batting team defends two wickets at either end of a 22yd (20.1m) grass pitch, and tries to score as many runs as possible before being dismissed. Two batsmen are on the field at any one time. The attacking team is made up of bowler, wicket-keeper, and fielders who are placed at strategic positions around the field. The bowler delivers an *over* (usually of six balls) to one wicket, and a second bowler then repeats the process at the second wicket. When the batter has hit the ball, he may decide it is safe to make a run or runs between the two wickets, exchanging places with the other batsman. If the ball reaches the boundary four runs are automatically scored; if it reaches the boundary without first touching the ground, six runs are scored. The batsman can be got out if he is bowled, caught, stumped, run out, or leg before wicket. When all ten batsmen have been dismissed the innings ends, but a team may declare (ie stop its innings) at any time if it is judged that sufficient runs have been made to win.

cricket² *noun* any of about 2 500 species of mainly nocturnal insect found worldwide, but primarily in tropical regions. It is closely related to the grasshopper, but can be distinguished from the latter by its long slender antennae. The males produce a distinctive chirping sound by rubbing their forewings together. [imitative]

cricketer *noun* a person who plays cricket.

cri de coeur *noun* a cry from the heart; a sincere appeal. [French, = cry of the heart]

crier *noun Hist.* an official who announces news by shouting it out in public.

crikey *interj. old slang use* an expression of astonishment. [altered form of CHRIST]

crime *noun* **1** an illegal act; an act punishable by law. **2** such acts collectively. **3** an act gravely wrong morally. **4** *colloq.* a deplorable act; a shame. [from Latin *crimen*, charge, crime]

Crimea, Russian **Krym** an autonomous republic and peninsula in S Ukraine, bounded S and W by the Black Sea, and E by the Sea of Azov. It is separated from the mainland to the N by the narrow Perekop Isthmus, and from the Taman Peninsula to the E by the Kersh Strait. AREA 25 900sq km/9 997sq mi; length 320km/200mi. PHYSICAL DESCRIPTION along the S coast the Krymskiye Gory Range rises to just over 1 500m; dry steppeland extends southwards covering c.80% of the total area. HISTORY colonized by the Greeks in the 7c BC; invaded by Goths (AD 250), Huns (AD 373), Khazars (8c), Byzantine Greeks (1016), Kipchaks (1050), Tatars (13c), Ottomans (late 15c), and Russians (1736); in the Crimean War (1854–5) Britain, France, and Sardinia defeated the Russians; became an autonomous Soviet republic in 1921; was degraded to an oblast of Soviet Russia from 1946 until 1954, when it became a region of the Ukraine; Tatars were exiled from the 1940s, but regained the right to residency in 1988; in 1991 the Crimea became an autonomous republic of the Ukraine; since then, conflict between the Ukraine and Russia concerning the status of the peninsula has increased. CHIEF TOWNS Simferopol, Sebastopol, Kerch. ECONOMY rich in minerals (iron, gypsum, limestone); the subtropical Black Sea coast is a major tourist attraction, notably at Yalta.

Crime and Punishment a novel by Fyodor Dostoevsky (1866). It tells of the hero Raskolnikov's attempt to ease his conscience for his crime through his confession.

Crimean War a war fought (1854–6) on the Crimean peninsula by Britain and France against Russia. Its origins lay in Russian successes in the Black Sea area, and the British and French desire to prevent further expansion into the Ottoman Empire by the Russians, which constituted a threat to the Mediterranean and overland routes to India. Major battles were fought in 1854 at the R Alma (20 Sep), Balaclava (25 Oct), and Inkerman (5 Nov). The fall of the Russian fortress at Sebastopol (Sep 1855) led to peace negotiations, finally agreed in Paris (Mar 1856), in which Russia ceded S Bessarabia to neighbouring Moldavia and accepted the neutralization of the Black Sea; Moldavia and Wallachia were soon to unite as an independent Romania. The War was also notable for Florence Nightingale's nursing exploits in Scutari and the pioneer war reports by W H Russell in *The Times*.

criminal — *noun* a person guilty of a crime. — *adj.* **1** against the law: *criminal activities*. **2** of, or relating to, crime or criminals or their punishment. **3** *colloq.* very wrong; wicked. [from Latin *criminalis*, from *crimen*, crime]

Criminal Injuries Compensation Board a UK public body under the auspices of the Home Office, responsible for making payments to victims of violent crime. Compensation is awarded on principles applicable to civil cases.

criminality *noun* **1** the condition of being a criminal. **2** guiltiness.

criminal law a branch of law that deals with unlawful acts which are offences against the public and society generally. Breaches of criminal law are generally investigated by the police. The responsibility for prosecution varies between jurisdictions: in England and Wales it belongs to the Crown Prosecution Service; in Scotland, to the Procurator Fiscal.

cricket field positions

criminally *adv.* in a criminal way.

criminologist *noun* a person who studies or is an expert in criminals and their crimes.

criminology *noun* the study of crime and criminals. [from Latin *crimen*, crime]

crimp *verb* **1** to press into small regular ridges; to corrugate. **2** to wave or curl (hair) with curling-tongs. **3** to roll the edge of (sheet metal). **4** to seal by pinching together. [from Anglo-Saxon *crympan*, to curl]

Crimplene *noun trademark* **1** a thick polyester yarn. **2** a crease-resistant clothing material made from this.

crimson — *adj.* of a deep purplish red colour. — *noun* this colour: *dressed in crimson.* — *verb* **1** to dye crimson. **2** *intrans.* to become crimson; to blush. [from Old French *cramoisin*, from Arabic *qirmizi*, a dye made from a Mediterranean insect]

cringe *verb intrans.* **1** to cower away in fear. **2** *derog.* to behave in a submissive, over-humble way. **3** *loosely* to wince in embarrassment, etc. [from Anglo-Saxon *cringan*, to fall in battle]

cringer *noun* a person who cringes.

crinkle — *verb trans., intrans.* to wrinkle or crease. — *noun* a wrinkle or crease; a wave. [related to Anglo-Saxon *crincan*, to yield]

crinkly *adj.* (**crinklier, crinkliest**) wrinkly.

crinoline *noun Hist.* a hooped petticoat for making skirts stand out. [originally a stiff horsehair fabric, from Latin *crinis*, hair + *linum*, flax]

cripple — *verb* **1** to make lame; to disable. **2** to damage, weaken, or undermine. — *noun* **1** a person who is lame or badly disabled. **2** a person damaged psychologically: *an emotional cripple.* [from Anglo-Saxon *crypel*]

Cripps, Sir (Richard) Stafford (1889–1952) English Labour politician and economist, born in London. Called to the Bar in 1913, he made a fortune in patent and compensation cases, was appointed Solicitor-General in the second Labour government (1930), and became an MP (1931). During the 1930s he was associated with several extreme left-wing movements, and was expelled from the Labour Party (1939) for his 'popular front' opposing Chamberlain's policy of appeasement. As an independent MP during World War II, he was ambassador in Moscow (1940–2), Lord Privy Seal (1942), and later Minister of Aircraft Production. On Labour's return to power (1945), he was readmitted to the Party and appointed President of the Board of Trade. In 1947 he became Minister of Economic Affairs and then Chancellor of the Exchequer, when he introduced a successful austerity policy.

Criseyde see TROILUS AND CRISEYDE.

crisis *noun* (PL. **crises**) **1** a crucial or decisive moment. **2** a turning-point, eg in a disease. **3** a time of difficulty or distress. **4** an emergency. [from Greek *krisis*, decision, judgement]

crisis management a term first applied to international politics after the 1962 Cuban missile crisis, implying that crises have to be handled as they arise, and cannot be dealt with by long-term strategic planning. The term is now applied in a wider sense to political and business management.

crisis theology a type of Protestant theology initiated after World War I, inspired by the Swiss theologian Karl Barth (1886–1968), and highly influential in the 1920s and 1930s. The term 'crisis' essentially applied to the judgement (Greek *krisis*) of God upon all merely human, social, and religious endeavours. The approach exercised a decisive influence on the Barman Declaration (1934), drawn up in response to what was perceived as the Nazification of the German-Christian Church, which affirmed Jesus Christ as God's sole and sufficient revelation and denied any revelations in nature, history, and race apart from him.

crisp — *adj.* **1** dry and brittle: *crisp biscuits.* **2** *said of vegetables or fruit* firm and fresh. **3** *said of* weather fresh; bracing. **4** *said of a person's manner or speech* firm; decisive; brisk. **5** *said of fabric, etc* clean; starched. **6** *said of hair* springy. — *noun* (*also* **potato crisp**) a thin deep-fried slice of potato, sold in packets as a snack.

— **to a crisp** *facetious* burnt till black and brittle. [from Latin *crispus*, curly]

crispbread *noun* a brittle unsweetened rye or wheat biscuit.

crisply *adv.* in a crisp way; sharply.

crispy *adj.* (**crispier, crispiest**) **1** crisp. **2** curling, wavy.

criss-cross — *adj.* **1** *said of lines* crossing one another in different directions. **2** *said of a pattern, etc* consisting of criss-cross lines. — *adv.* running or lying across one another. — *noun* a pattern of criss-cross lines. — *verb trans., intrans.* to form, mark with, or move in, a criss-cross pattern. [from *Christ-Cross*, a decorative cross introducing the alphabet in old learning-books]

Cristóbal Coln, Pico the highest peak in Colombia, in the Sierra Nevada de Santa Marta. HEIGHT 5 800m. It lies in the N of the country, 113km/70mi E of Barranquilla.

Cristofori *or* **Cristofari Bartolommeo** (1655–1731) Italian harpsichord-maker, born in Padua. He is credited with the invention of the pianoforte.

criterion *noun* (PL. **criteria**) a standard or principle on which to base a judgement. [from Greek *kriterion*, from *krites*, judge]

◆ Note that *criteria* is a plural form; *a criteria* is incorrect, though often heard.

critic *noun* **1** a professional reviewer of literature, art, drama, or music. **2** a person who finds fault with or disapproves of something. [from Greek *kritikos*, discerning, from *krites*, judge]

critical *adj.* **1** fault-finding; disapproving. **2** relating to a critic or criticism. **3** involving analysis and assessment. **4** relating to a crisis; decisive; crucial. **5** *Physics, said eg of a measurement* marking the point of transition between one state and another. **6** *Nuclear Physics* having reached the point at which which a nuclear chain reaction will sustain itself.

critically *adv.* in a critical way.

critical mass *Physics* the smallest amount of a given fissile material (one that is able to undergo nuclear fission), formed into a given shape, that is needed to sustain a nuclear chain reaction, eg for a sphere of uranium-235, the critical mass is 52kg.

critical path analysis a procedure used to manage and produce a detailed schedule for a complex project so that it can be completed in the minimum time possible. It often involves the use of a specially written computer package.

critical temperature 1 *Physics* the temperature above which a gas cannot be liquefied by pressure alone. **2** the temperature above which a magnetic material loses its magnetic properties.

criticism *noun* **1** fault-finding. **2** reasoned analysis and assessment, especially of art, literature, music, or drama; the art of such assessment. **3** a critical comment or piece of writing.

criticize *or* **criticise** *verb trans., intrans.* **1** to find fault; to express disapproval of. **2** to analyse and assess.

critique *noun* a critical analysis; a criticism. [from French *critique*, from Greek *kritike*, the art of criticism]

Crittenden Compromise an attempt (1860) in the months preceding the American Civil War by Kentucky Senator John J Crittenden to resolve the crisis between North and South by the formal recognition of slavery in territories south of 36°30' (the repealed Missouri Compromise line). This proved unacceptable to Abraham Lincoln, whose election as President was causing secession by the slave-holding South.

croak — *noun* the harsh throaty noise typically made by a frog or crow. — *verb* **1** *intrans.* to make this sound. **2** to utter with a croak. **3** *intrans., trans. slang* to die or kill. [imitative]

Croatia, Serbo-Croatian **Hrvatska** POP (1991) 4.8m, a republic in E Europe. AREA 56 538sq km/21 824sq mi. It is bounded SW and W by the Adriatic Sea, N by Slovenia, NE by Hungary, E by Yugoslavia, and SE by Bosnia-Herzegovina. CAPITAL Zagreb. CHIEF TOWNS Rijeka, Čakovec, Split, Zadar. TIME ZONE GMT +1. Around 75% of the population are Croats, and the rest are Serbs; Roman Catholicism is the chief religion. OFFICIAL LANGUAGE Serbo-Croat. CURRENCY the dinar. PHYSICAL DESCRIPTION a mountainous republic, with islands on the Adriatic coast; the inland terrain includes fertile plains. HISTORY formed a joint crownland with Slavonia in 1888; proclaimed itself an independent state during occupation by the Axis Powers in 1941–5; part of Yugoslavia from 1945 to 1991; declaration of independence in 1991, followed by confrontation with the National Army and Civil War; an official ceasefire was declared in 1992 but fighting restarted in 1993. GOVERNMENT a directly elected President and a bicameral Assembly consisting of a Chamber of Deputies and a Chamber of Districts. ECONOMY chiefly an agricultural region; manufactures include machinery and cement; there are supplies of crude oil; the economy has been severely affected by military conflict.

Croatia

Croce, Benedetto (1866–1952) Italian philosopher, historian, and critic, born in Pescasseroli. He founded the review, *La Critica*, in 1903, and made major contributions to idealistic aesthetics in his *Estetica* (1902, Aesthetic) and *La Poesia* (1936, Poetry). In 1910 he became Senator, and was Minister of Education (1920–1) when, with the rise of Mussolini, he had to resign his professorship at Naples. He was opposed to totalitarianism, and with the fall of Mussolini (1943) helped to resurrect Liberal institutions in Italy.

crochet — *noun* decorative work consisting of intertwined loops, made with wool or thread and a hooked needle. — *verb intrans., trans.* (**crocheted, crocheting**) to work in crochet. [from French *crochet*, diminutive of *croche*, hook]

crock[1] *noun colloq.* an old decrepit person, vehicle, etc: *poor old crock.* [from Middle English *crok*, old ewe]

crock[2] *noun* an earthenware pot. [from Anglo-Saxon *crocc*, pot]

crockery *noun* earthenware or china dishes; plates, cups, etc.

crocket *noun Archit.* in Gothic architecture, a stylized leaf- or flower-shaped carved decoration. It was used in 12c French buildings as an ornamental capital on columns, and was particularly common in the English Decorated style on the sloping sides of pinnacles, spires, and canopies.

Crockett, Davy (David) (1786–1836) US backwoodsman, born in Tennessee. After distinguishing himself against the Creek Indians in Jackson's campaign of 1814, he was elected to the Tennessee state legislature (1821) and to Congress (1826). He died fighting for Texas at the battle of the Alamo, but his name has been preserved in legend through highly embellished stories of his exploits.

crocodile *noun* **1** a large aquatic reptile belonging to the genus *Crocodylus*, found in rivers and estuaries in tropical regions of Africa, Asia, Australia, and America, and having a bulky body, short legs, powerful jaws that narrow to form a long snout (which may be slender or broad), and a thick scaly skin. **2** leather made from its skin. **3** a line of schoolchildren walking in twos. [from Greek *krokodeilos*]
◇ Crocodiles may be up to 7.5m in length, and differ from alligators in that the fourth tooth from the front on each side of the lower jaw is visible when the jaws are closed. They are most often found floating just beneath the water surface, or lying on river banks, basking in the sun. Crocodiles are carnivores, and feed mainly on fish and relatively large mammals, eg antelope and zebra. Together with the alligators and gharial, they are descended from an ancient group of reptiles, the archosaurs, which included the extinct dinosaurs and pterodactyls.

crocodile

crocodile tears a show of pretended grief.

crocus *noun* (PL. **crocuses**) a small perennial flowering plant of the genus *Crocus* of the iris family, that has an underground corm and thin spiky leaves. It is widely cultivated for its single yellow, purple, or white flowers, and as a source of saffron powder, a yellow dye obtained from the stigmas of *Crocus sativus*. [from Greek *krokos*, saffron]

Croesus (d.c.546 BC) the last king of Lydia (c.560–546 BC), renowned for his wealth. He succeeded his father, Alyattes, and conquered the Greeks of Asia Minor and extended his kingdom eastward from the Aegean to the Halys. The Persian king, Cyrus II, defeated and imprisoned him (546 BC), but his death is a mystery.

croft — *noun* especially in the Scottish Highlands, a small piece of enclosed farmland attached to a house. — *verb intrans.* to farm a croft. [from Anglo-Saxon]

crofter *noun* a person who runs or farms a croft.

croissant *noun* a crescent-shaped bread roll, made with a high proportion of fat, and flaky in consistency. [from French *croissant*, crescent]

Cro-Magnon Man a prehistoric form of fully modern man named after the 1868 discovery of fossil skeletons at Cro-Magnon in SW France. Cro-Magnons were cave-dwelling big-game hunters who lived on the steppes and tundra of late Ice Age Europe.

cromlech *noun* *Archaeol.* **1** a prehistoric circle of standing stones. **2** *loosely* a dolmen. [from Welsh *crom*, curved + *llech*, stone]

Crompton, Richmal, pseudonym of **Richmal Samuel Lamburn** (1890–1969) English writer born in Bury, Lancashire. She was a Classics teacher until she contracted poliomyelitis in 1923. Primarily a children's writer, she is best known for the substantial series of 'William' books beginning with *Just William* (1922) and featuring the schoolboy hero, William Brown.

Cromwell, Oliver (1599–1658) English soldier and politician, born in Huntingdon, Cambridgeshire. A convinced Puritan, he sat in both the Short and the Long Parliaments (1640), and when war broke out (1642) fought for the parliament at Edgehill. He formed a cavalry called the Ironsides, where rigid discipline and strict morality were enforced, and with them secured victory at Marston Moor (1644). Under Fairfax he led the New Model Army to victory at Naseby (1645). After quelling an insurrection in Wales that supported Charles I, and defeating the invading army of Hamilton, he brought the King to trial, and was one of the signatories of his death warrant (1649). Having established the Commonwealth, Cromwell suppressed the Levellers, the Irish (1649–50), and the Scots (under Charles II) at Dunbar (1650) and Worcester (1651). He dissolved the Rump of the Long Parliament (1653), and after the failure of his Barebones Parliament, established a Protectorate (1653). He refused the offer of the Crown in 1657. At home he reorganized the national Church and gave Scotland and Ireland parliamentary representation. Under him the Commonwealth became the head and champion of Protestant Europe. He was succeeded by his son Richard (1626–1712), who was forced into French exile in 1659.

Cromwell, Thomas, Earl of Essex, (c.1485–1540) English statesman, born in London. He served as a soldier on the Continent (1504–12), then entered Thomas Wolsey's service in 1514, and became his agent and secretary. He arranged Henry VIII's divorce with Catherine of Aragon, and put into effect the Act of Supremacy (1534) and the dissolution of the monasteries (1536–9). His offices included Chancellor of the Exchequer (1533), Secretary of State and Master of the Rolls (1534), Lord Privy Seal (1536), and Lord Great Chamberlain (1539), in each of which he proved himself a highly efficient administrator and adviser to the king. However Henry's aversion to Anne of Cleves, the consort of Cromwell's choosing, led to his ruin, and he was beheaded.

crone *noun offensive* an old woman. [from Old Dutch *croonie*, old ewe, from Old French *caronie*, carrion]

Cronin, A(rchibald) J(oseph) (1896–1981) Scottish novelist, born in Cardross, Dunbartonshire. He studied medicine at Glasgow (1919), but took up literature in 1930 and was immediately successful with *Hatter's Castle* (1931). Subsequent works include *The Citadel* (1937) and *The Keys of the Kingdom* (1942). Several of his books were filmed, and the radio and television series *Dr Finlay's Casebook* was based on his stories.

Cronin, James Watson (1931–) US physicist, born in Chicago. Professor at Princeton from 1965 and at Chicago from 1971, he made important studies of the decay of a fundamental particle known as the 'kaon' (1964). His results, which demonstrated some unexpected properties of reactions when subatomic particles decay, have been used to explain the domination of matter over antimatter in the universe. He shared the 1980 Nobel Prize for Physics with Val Fitch.

Cronus *or* **Kronos** in Greek mythology, a Titan who became the second ruler of the universe after castrating his father Uranus. He devoured all his children apart from Zeus, who was replaced by a stone, grew up secretly in Crete, and eventually overthrew him.

crony *noun* (PL. **cronies**) a close friend. [from Greek *chronios*, long-lasting]

crook — *noun* **1** a bend or curve: *carried it in the crook of his arm*. **2** a shepherd's or bishop's hooked staff. **3** any of various hooked fittings, eg on woodwind instruments. **4** *colloq.* a thief or swindler; a professional criminal. — *adj.* Austral., New Zealand colloq. **1** ill. **2** not working properly. **3** nasty; unpleasant. — *verb* to bend or curve. [from Old Norse *kraka*, hook]

crooked *adj.* **1** bent, curved, angled, or twisted. **2** not straight; tipped at an angle. **3** colloq. dishonest.

crookedly *adv.* in a crooked way.

crookedness *noun* being crooked.

croon — *verb intrans., trans.* to sing in a subdued tone and reflective or sentimental style. — *noun* this style of singing. [from Old Dutch *cronen*, to lament]

crooner *noun* a person who croons.

crop — *noun* **1** *Agric.* a plant that is cultivated to produce food for man, fodder for animals, or raw materials, eg cereals, clover, barley. **2** *Agric.* the total yield produced by or harvested from such a plant, or from a certain area of cultivated land, such as a field. **3** a batch; a bunch: *this year's crop of graduates*. **4** a short style of haircut. **5** a whip handle; a horserider's short whip. **6** *Zool.* in the gullet of birds, the thin-walled pouch where food is stored before it is digested. — *verb* (**cropped**, **cropping**) **1** to trim; to cut short. **2** *said of animals* to feed on grass, etc. **3** to reap or harvest a cultivated crop. **4** *intrans.* *said of land* to produce a crop.
— **crop up** *intrans. colloq.* to occur or appear unexpectedly.
[from Anglo-Saxon *cropp*]

crop circle an area or pattern of flattened crops in a field of standing crops, often visible from the air.

cropper
— **come a cropper** *colloq.* **1** to fall heavily. **2** to fail disastrously.

crop rotation *Agric.* a system of farming in which two or more different crops are grown one after the other on the same piece of land. The aim of crop rotation is to maintain the fertility of the soil, because different crops take different amounts of the various nutrients from the soil. It also limits the effects of pests and diseases, and 'spreads' the risk of failure of a specific crop.

croquet *noun* a game played on a lawn, in which mallets are used to drive wooden balls through a sequence of hoops. [from French *croquet*, diminutive of *croc*, hook]
◇ The croquet lawn is laid out with six hoops and a central peg. Four balls coloured blue, red,

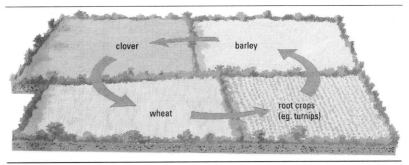

crop rotation

black, and yellow are struck through the hoops in a prescribed order. The first player to reach and hit the central peg wins.

croquette *noun* a ball or roll of eg minced meat, fish, or potato, coated in breadcrumbs and fried. [from French *croquette*, from *croquer*, to crunch]

Crosbie, Adolphus an ambitious character who marries Lady Alexandrina de Courcy in Anthony Trollope's *The Small House at Allington*, one of the 'Barsetshire' novels.

Crosby, Bing, originally **Harry Lillis Crosby** (1904–77) US singer and film actor, born in Tacoma, Washington. He began his career playing the drums while still at school, and he sang with Paul Whiteman's Rhythm Boys. His film début was in *King of Jazz* (1930) and he became a beloved and well-known name in the entertainment world. His recordings of 'White Christmas' and 'Silent Night' were very successful. He starred in many films, notably the *Road to* films with Bob Hope and Dorothy Lamour.

Crosby *or* **Great Crosby** POP (1981) 54 000, a residential town in Sefton borough, Merseyside, NW England. It lies at the mouth of the R Mersey, opposite the Crosby Channel, 10km/6mi N of Liverpool.

crosier *or* **crozier** *noun* a bishop's hooked staff, carried as a symbol of office. [from Middle English *crocer* or *croser*, staff-bearer, from Old French *croce*, hooked staff]

Crosland, Tony (Charles Anthony Raven) (1918–77) English Labour politician, born in St Leonards-on-Sea, Sussex. Elected an MP in 1950, he later became Secretary for Education and Science (1965–7), President of the Board of Trade (1967–9), Secretary for Local Government and Regional Planning (1969–70), Environment Secretary (1974–6), and Foreign Secretary (1976–7). A strong supporter of Hugh Gaitskell, he was a key member of the revisionist wing of the Labour Party, and wrote one of its seminal texts, *The Future of Socialism* (1956).

Cross, Charles Frederick (1855–1935) English industrial chemist, born in Brentford, Essex. With Edward John Bevan, he invented the modern method of producing artificial silk.

cross — *noun* **1** a mark, structure, or symbol composed of two lines, one crossing the other in the form + or ×; the mark × indicating a mistake or cancellation, as distinct from a tick. **2 a** a vertical post with a horizontal bar fixed to it, on which criminals were crucified in antiquity. **b** (**the Cross**) *Christianity* the cross on which Christ was crucified, or a representation of it; this as a symbol of Christianity. **3** a burden or affliction: *have one's own cross to bear.* **4** a monument, not necessarily in the form of a cross; (as a place name) the site of such a monument. **5** a medal in the form of a cross. **6** a plant or animal produced by crossing two different strains, breeds, or varieties of a species in order to produce an improved hybrid offspring. **7** a mixture or compromise: *a cross between a bedroom and a living room.* **8** a movement across, eg of a football from wing to centre. — *verb* **1** *trans., intrans.* (*also* **cross over**) to move, pass, or get across. **2** to place one across the other: *cross one's legs.* **3** *intrans.* to meet; to intersect. **4** *intrans. said of letters between two correspondents* to be in transit simultaneously. **5** (**cross oneself**) to make the sign of the Cross. **6** to draw a line across: *cross one's t's.* **7** to make (a cheque) payable only through a bank by drawing two parallel lines across it. **8** (*also* **cross something out, off**, *etc*) to delete or cancel it by drawing a line through. **9** to cross-breed (two different strains, breeds, or varieties of a species of animal or plant): *cross a sheep with a goat.* **10** to frustrate or thwart. **11** to cause unwanted connections between (telephone lines). — *adj.* **1** angry; in a bad temper. **2** (*in compounds*) **a** across: *cross-Channel / cross-country.* **b** intersecting or at right angles: *crossbar.* **c** contrary: *cross purposes.* **d** intermingling: *cross-breeding.*

— **be at cross purposes** *said of two or more people* to misunderstand or clash with one another.
cross one's fingers *or* **keep one's fingers crossed** to appeal for good fortune, originally by crossing one's middle finger over one's index finger.
cross one's heart to make a crossing gesture over one's heart as an indication of good faith.
cross someone's mind to occur to them.
cross someone's palm to put a coin in their hand.
cross someone's path to encounter them.
cross swords with someone to have a disagreement or argument with them. [from Anglo-Saxon *cros*, from Latin *crux*]

crossbar *noun* **1** a horizontal bar, especially between upright posts. **2** the horizontal bar on a man's bicycle.

crossbench *noun* a seat in parliament for members not belonging to the government or opposition.

crossbencher *noun* a member of parliament who sits on the crossbenches.

crossbill *noun* a finch with a beak in which the points cross instead of meeting.

crossbones *pl. noun* a pair of crossed femurs appearing beneath the skull in the skull-and-crossbones symbol eg used on pirate flags or gravestones.

crossbow *noun* a bow placed crosswise on a stock, with a crank to pull back the bow, and a trigger to release arrows.

cross-breed *Biol.* — *verb* to mate (two animals of different pure breeds) in order to produce offspring in which the best characteristics of both parents are combined. — *noun* an animal that has been bred from two different pure breeds.

cross-check — *verb* to check (information) from an independent source. — *noun* a check of this kind.

cross-country *adj.* across fields, etc rather than on roads.

cross-country running an athletic running event using a pre-determined course over natural terrain. The length of race varies, but world championships are over 12km/7.5mi for men and 5km/3.1mi for women. The first recorded international race was in May 1898, and covered a 14.5km/9mi course at Ville D'Avray near Paris.

cross cut a transverse or diagonal cut.

crosse *noun* a lacrosse stick. [from French *crosse*, hooked stick]

ankh   botoné   Celtic

papal   Latin   Lorraine

Greek   Maltese

Russian
(and other Slavs)

types of crosses

cross-examination *noun* the process of cross-examining.

cross-examine *verb* to question (especially a witness for the opposing side in a law case) so as to develop or throw doubt on his or her statement.

cross-examiner *noun* a person who makes a cross-examination.

cross-eyed *adj.* having one or both eyes turned inward; squinting.

Cross Fell the highest peak of the Pennine Chain in Cumbria, NW England, situated 32km/20mi SE of Carlisle. HEIGHT 893m.

cross-fertilization *or* **cross-fertilisation** *noun* **1** in plants and animals, the fusion of a female gamete (egg) with a male gamete (sperm or pollen) of another individual, especially one of a different species or variety. **2** the fruitful interaction of ideas from different cultures, etc.

cross-fertilize *or* **cross-fertilise** *verb trans., intrans.* to fertilize by cross-fertilization.

crossfire *noun* **1** gunfire coming from different directions. **2** a bitter or excited exchange of opinions, arguments, etc.

cross-grained *adj.* **1** *said of wood* having the grain or fibres crossing or intertwined. **2** *said of a person* perverse; awkward to deal with.

crosshatch *verb trans., intrans. Art* to shade with intersecting lines.

crossing *noun* **1** a place for crossing a river, road, etc. **2** a journey across water: *a rough crossing.*

crossing over *Genetics* in meiosis, the exchange of genetic material that occurs as a result of the exchange of segments of homologous chromosomes, giving rise to genetic variation in the offspring.

cross-legged *adj., adv.* sitting with the ankles crossed and knees wide apart.

Crossman, Richard (Howard Stafford) (1907–74) British Labour politician. He was a philosophy tutor at Oxford, and leader of the Labour group on Oxford City Council (1934–40) before he entered parliament (1945). Under Harold Wilson he was Minister of Housing and Local Government (1964–6), then Secretary of State for Social Services, and head of the Department of Health (1968–70). In 1970–2 he was editor of the *New Statesman*, where he had first worked in 1938. His best-known work is his series of political diaries, begun in 1952, which keep a detailed record of the day-to-day workings of government. They were published in four volumes (1975–81), despite attempts to suppress them.

crosspatch *noun colloq.* a bad-tempered person.

cross-ply *adj., said of a tyre* with the cords in the outer casing lying crosswise to strengthen the tread. See also RADIAL.

cross-pollination *noun Bot.* the transfer of pollen from the anther of the stamen of one flower to the stigma of another flower of the same species.

cross-question *verb* to cross-examine.

cross-refer *verb intrans., trans.* to direct (the reader) to refer from one part of a text to another.

cross-reference — *noun* a reference from one part of a text to another. — *verb* to supply with cross-references.

crossroads *sing. noun* **1** the point where two or more roads cross or meet. **2** a point at which an important choice has to be made.

cross section *noun* **1 a** the surface revealed when a solid object is sliced through, especially at right angles to its length. **b** a diagram representing this. **2** a representative sample.

cross-sectional *adj.* in the form of a cross-section.

cross-stitch *noun* an embroidery stitch made by two crossing stitches.

cross-talk *noun* **1** unwanted interference between communication channels. **2** fast and clever conversation; repartee.

cross-training *noun* a method of exercise alternating the use of gymnasium equipment with aerobic floor exercises in the same session.

crosswind *noun* a wind blowing across the path of a vehicle or aircraft.

crosswise *adj., adv.* lying or moving across, or so as to cross.

crossword *noun* a puzzle in which clues yield words that cross vertically and horizontally within a grid of squares.

crotch *noun* the place where the body or a pair of trousers forks into the two legs. [variant of CRUTCH]

crotchet *noun Mus.* a note equal to two quavers or half a minim in length. [from Old French *crochet*, hooked staff]

crotchetiness *noun* being crotchety.

crotchety *adj. colloq.* irritable; peevish. [from CROTCHET, in the sense of an odd fancy]

crouch — *verb intrans.* (*also* **crouch down**) **1** to bend low or squat with legs close to the chest and often also with one's hands on the ground. **2** *said of animals* to lie close to the ground ready to spring up. — *noun* a crouching position or action.

croup[1] *noun* (pronounced *croop*) inflammation of the trachea and larynx in children, causing difficulty in breathing and a hoarse cough. [imitative]

croup[2] *noun* (pronounced *croop*) the rump of a horse. [from Old French *crope*, related to CROP]

croupier *noun* the person who presides over a gaming-table, collecting the stakes and paying the winners. [from French *croupier*, pillion passenger on a horse]

croupy *adj.* (**croupier, croupiest**) suffering from or typical of croup.

croûton *noun* a small cube of fried or toasted bread, served in soup, etc. [from French *croûton*, diminutive of *croûte*, crust]

Crow a Native American Sioux-speaking Plains people. They separated from the Hidatsa in the 18c, and lived between the Missouri and Yellowstone Rivers, becoming nomadic buffalo hunters on horseback, and traders. They allied with whites in the Indian wars of the 1860s and 1870s, and in 1868 were settled on reservations in Montana, where most Crow still live (present-day population c.4 000).

crow — *noun* **1** any of about 100 species of large black bird, usually with a powerful black beak, including the carrion crow, rook, raven, jackdaw, and magpie. Crows are among the most intelligent of all birds, and they have a varied diet, including small animals and seeds. **2** the shrill and long-drawn-out cry of a cock. — *verb intrans.* (PAST TENSE **crowed, crew**) **1** *said of a cock* to cry shrilly. **2** *said of a baby* to make happy inarticulate sounds. **3** (**crow over someone** *or* **something**) to triumph gleefully over them; to gloat. — **as the crow flies** in a straight line. [from Anglo-Saxon *crawa*]

crowbar *noun* a heavy iron bar with a bent, flattened end, used as a lever.

crowd — *noun* **1** a large number of people gathered together. **2** the spectators or audience at an event. **3** (*usually* **crowds**) *colloq.* a large number of people. **4** a set or group of people. **5** the general mass of people: *don't just follow the crowd.* — *verb* **1** *intrans.* to gather or move in a large, usually tightly-packed, group. **2** to fill: *crowded streets.* **3** to pack; to cram. **4** to press round, or supervise (someone) too closely. — **crowd someone out** to overwhelm and force them out: *big businesses crowd out the small ones.*

crowd something out to fill it completely: *the concert hall was crowded out.* [from Anglo-Saxon *crudan*, to press]

crowded *adj.* full of people, thronged.

Crowley, Aleister, originally **Edward Alexander Crowley** (1875–1947) English writer and 'magician'. He became interested in the occult while an undergraduate at Cambridge, and later founded the order known as the Silver Star. He travelled widely, and settled for some years in Sicily with a group of disciples at the Abbey of Thelema, near Cefalù. Rumours of drugs, orgies, and magical ceremonies led to his expulsion from Italy. He liked to be known as 'the great beast' and 'the wickedest man alive'.

crown — *noun* **1** the circular, usually jewelled gold headdress of a sovereign. **2** (**Crown**) the sovereign as head of state; the authority or jurisdiction of a sovereign or of the government representing a sovereign. **3** a wreath for the head, or other honour, awarded for victory or success. **4** a highest point of achievement; a summit or climax: *the crown of one's career.* **5** the top, especially of something rounded. **6** the part of a tooth projecting from the gum; an artificial replacement for this. **7** a representation of a royal crown used as an emblem, symbol, etc. **8** a British coin worth 25 pence (formerly 5 shillings). **9** the junction of the root and stem of a plant. **10** a UK paper size, 385×505 mm. — *verb* **1** to place a crown ceremonially on the head of; to make king or queen. **2** to be on or round the top of. **3** to reward; to make complete or perfect: *efforts crowned with success.* **4** to put an artificial crown on (a tooth). **5** *colloq.* to hit on the head. **6** *Draughts* to give (a piece) the status of king. — **to crown it all** *colloq.* as the finishing touch to a series of especially unfortunate events. [from Old French *coroune*, from Latin *corona*, wreath, crown]
◇ In the UK, and in many former colonial countries, the Crown is an alternative legal definition to the state, which represents the organs of government. The powers exercised by the sovereign are now largely vested in the government of the day, although they are carried out in the name of the Crown.

Crown Agents (for Overseas Governments and Administrations) in the UK, an agency which provides professional, financial, and commercial services to governments and other public authorities in developing countries, and to international agencies. It also acts on behalf of the World Bank.

crown colony a colony under the direct control of the British government.

Crown Court a court in England and Wales, established by the Courts Act (1971) which abolished the Assizes and Quarter Sessions. Crown Courts have power to deal with indictable offences, and also hear most appeals from magistrates' courts. In addition to the criminal jurisdiction, a High Court judge may hear civil cases in this court.

Crown Estate a property belonging by heredity to the British sovereign, comprising some 109 260ha in England, Scotland, and Wales. Most of Britain's foreshore is included, together with the sea bed within territorial waters. Revenue from the Crown Estate is made over to the government at the beginning of each reign.

crowning *adj.* highest; greatest: *her crowning achievement.*

crown jewels the crown, sceptre, and other ceremonial regalia of a sovereign.

crown prince the male heir to a throne.

crown princess 1 the wife of a crown prince. **2** the female heir to a throne.

Crown Proceedings Act in the UK, an Act (1947) which permits ordinary civil actions against the Crown (ie as if it were a private individual). Before 1947, it had been possible for

someone to take certain proceedings against the Crown only by personal petition (*petition of right*), as in breach of contract cases. However, the monarch still remains personally immune from civil or criminal liability.

crow's feet the wrinkles at the outer corner of the eye.

crow's nest a platform for a lookout, fixed to the top of a ship's mast.

crozier see CROSIER.

CRT *abbrev.* cathode ray tube.

cruces see CRUX.

crucial *adj.* **1** decisive; critical. **2** very important; essential. **3** *slang* very good; great. [from Latin *crux*, cross]

crucially *adv.* in a crucial way.

Crucible, The a play by Arthur Miller (1953). Its theme of the persecution of the Salem witches is equated with the political persecution in 1950s America known as McCarthyism.

crucible *noun* an earthenware pot in which to heat metals or other substances. [from Latin *crucibulum*, lamp]

crucifix *noun* a representation, especially a model, of Christ on the cross. [from Latin *crucifixus*, man fixed to a cross]

Crucifixion a painting of the Crucifixion by various artists including Tintoretto (1565, Scuola di San Rocco), Diego Velázquez (17c, Prado, Madrid), and Graham Sutherland (1944, St Matthew's Church, Northampton).

crucifixion *noun* **1** execution by crucifying. **2** (**Crucifixion**) the crucifying of Christ, or a representation of this. [from Latin *crucifixio*, from *crux*, cross + *figere*, to fix]
◇ Crucifixion was a common form of capital punishment in the Roman world, usually inflicted only on slaves and people of low social status (*humiliores*). It was commonly preceded by flagellation.

Crucifixion of St Peter a fresco by Michelangelo (1542–50, Pauline Chapel, Vatican). It is one of his final pictorial works.

cruciform *adj.* cross-shaped. [from Latin *crux*, cross]

crucify *verb* (**crucifies, crucified**) **1** to put to death by fastening to a cross by the hands and feet. **2** to torment, torture or persecute. **3** *slang* to defeat or humiliate utterly. [from Old French *crucifier*, from Latin *crux*, cross + *figere*, to fix]

crude *adj.* **1** in its natural, unrefined state: *crude oil.* **2** rough or undeveloped: *a crude sketch.* **3** vulgar; tasteless. [from Latin *crudus*, raw]

crudely *adv.* in a crude way.

crudity *noun* **1** something crude. **2** rawness, unripeness.

cruel *adj.* **1** deliberately and pitilessly causing pain or suffering. **2** painful; distressful. [from French *cruel*]

cruelly *adv.* in a cruel way.

cruelty *noun* (PL. **cruelties**) a cruel act; cruel behaviour.

Cruelty, Theatre of a 20c theatrical genre based on Antoine Artaud's vision of a metaphysical theatre in which (eg by using shock) both actors and audience could experience existential realities, without any avoidance or illusion.

cruet *noun* **1** a small container for salt, pepper, mustard, vinegar, etc, for use at table. **2** a stand for a set of such jars. [from Old French *cruet*, diminutive of *cruye*, jar]

Cruise, Tom, in full **Tom Cruise Mapother IV** (1962–) US film actor, born in Syracuse, New Jersey. His first box-office hit was the teenage comedy *Risky Business* (1983), and subsequent successes include *Top Gun* (1986), *The Color of Money* (1986), *Cocktail* (1988), *Rain Man* (1988), *Born on the 4th of July* (1989), *A Few Good Men* (1992), and *The Firm* (1993).

The Main Crusades to the East

	Background	Leader(s)	Events
First Crusade (1096–9)	Proclaimed by Pope Urban II to safeguard pilgrim routes to the Holy. Sepulchre	Bohemond I Godfrey of Bouillon Raymond, Count of Toulouse Robert, Count of Flanders Robert Curthose, Duke of Normandy Stephen, Count of Blois	Turks vanquished at Battle of Dorylaeum (Jul 1097); capture of Antioch in Syria (Jun 1098), Jerusalem (Jul 1099). Godfrey of Bouillon became ruler of the new Latin kingdom of Jerusalem. Three other crusader states were founded: Antioch, Edessa, Tripoli.
Second Crusade (1147–8)	Proclaimed by Eugenius III to aid the crusader states after the Muslim reconquest of Edessa (1144).	Conrad III of Germany Louis VII of France	German army heavily defeated by Turks near Dorylaeum (Oct 1147), and the French defeated at Laodicea (Jan 1148). The crusaders' military reputation was destroyed.
Third Crusade (1189–92)	Proclaimed by Gregory VIII after Saladin's defeat of the Latins at the Battle of Hattin (Jul 1187) and his conquest of Jerusalem (Oct 1187).	Frederick I Barbarossa Philip II Augustus of France Richard I of England	Cyprus conquered from Greeks (May 1191), and established as new crusader kingdom (survived until 1489); capture of Acre in Palestine (Jul 1191); Saladin defeated near Arsuf (Sep 1191). Most cities and castles of the Holy Land remained in Muslim hands.
Fourth Crusade (1202–4)	Proclaimed by Innocent III to recover the Holy Places	Boniface of Montferrat	Despite papal objections, crusade diverted from Egypt or Palestine (1) to Zara, a Christian town in Dalmatia, conquered for Venetians (Nov 1202); (2) to Byzantium, (sack of Constantinople), Apr 1204, and foundation of Latin Empire of Constantinople.
Fifth Crusade (1217–21)	Proclaimed by Innocent III when a six-year truce between the kingdom of Jerusalem and Egypt expired	Andrew II of Hungary John of Brienne, King of Jerusalem Leopold, Duke of Austria	Three indecisive expeditions against Muslims in Palestine (1217); capture of Damietta in Egypt after protracted siege (May 1218–Nov 1219), but crusaders forced to relinquish Damietta (Aug 1221) and withdraw.
Sixth Crusade (1228–9)	Emperor Frederick II first took the Cross in 1215. Excommunicated by Gregory IX for delaying his departure, he finally arrived at Acre in Sep 1228.	Frederick II	Negotiations with Egyptians secured Jerusalem and other places, including Bethlehem and Nazareth (Feb 1229); Frederick crowned King of Jerusalem in church of Holy Sepulchre (Mar 1229). Jerusalem was held until recaptured by the Khorezmian Turks in 1244.
Seventh Crusade (1248–54)	Proclaimed by Innocent IV after the fall of Jerusalem and defeat of the Latin army near Gaza by the Egyptians and Khorezmians (1244).	Louis IX of France	Capture of Damietta (June 1249); defeat at Mansurah (Feb 1250); surrender of crusaders during attempted withdrawal; Damietta relinquished and large ransoms paid (May 1250).
Eighth Crusade (1270–2)	Proclaimed after the Mameluk conquest of Arsuf, Caesarea, Haifa (1265), Antioch and Joppa (1268).	Charles of Anjou, King of Naples-Sicily Edward of England (later Edward I) Louis IX of France	Attacked Tunisia in N Africa (Jul 1270); Louis died in Aug; Charles concluded treaty with Tunis and withdrew; Edward negotiated 11-years' truce with Mameluks in Palestine. By 1291 the Latins had been driven from the Holy Land.

cruise *verb intrans.* **1** to sail about for pleasure, calling at a succession of places. **2** *said eg of a vehicle or aircraft* to go at a steady comfortable speed. [from Dutch *kruisen*, to cross]

cruise missile a low-flying, long-distance, computer-controlled winged missile.

cruiser *noun* **1** a large fast warship. **2** (*also* **cabin-cruiser**) a motor boat with living quarters.

cruiserweight *noun, adj.* light heavyweight.

crumb — *noun* **1** a particle of dry food, especially bread. **2** a small amount: *a crumb of comfort*. **3** the soft interior of a loaf of bread. **4** *slang* an obnoxious person. — *verb* to coat in breadcrumbs. [from Anglo-Saxon *cruma*]

crumble — *verb* **1** *trans., intrans.* to break into crumbs or powdery fragments. **2** *intrans.* to collapse, decay or disintegrate. — *noun* a dish of cooked fruit covered with a crumbled mixture of sugar, butter, and flour. [from Middle English *kremelen*, from Anglo-Saxon *gecrymian*]

crumbly *adj.* (**crumblier, crumbliest**) easily crumbled.

crumbs *interj. colloq.* an expression of surprise, dismay, etc. [altered form of CHRIST]

crumby *adj.* (**crumbier, crumbiest**) **1** full of or in crumbs. **2** soft like the inside of a loaf.

crumminess *noun* inferiority.

Crummles, Vincent *and* Mrs touring actors in Charles Dickens's *Nicholas Nickleby*. Their daughter is Ninetta, 'The Infant Phenomenon'.

crummy *adj.* (**crummier, crummiest**) *colloq., derog.* shoddy, dingy, dirty, or generally inferior. [variant of CRUMBY]

crumpet *noun* **1** a thick round cake made of soft light dough, eaten toasted and buttered. **2** in Scotland, a type of large thin pancake. **3** *offensive slang* a girl; female company generally.

crumple *verb* **1** *trans., intrans.* to make or become creased or crushed. **2** *intrans. said of a face or features* to pucker in distress. **3** *intrans.* to collapse; to give away. [from Anglo-Saxon *crump*, crooked]

crunch — *verb* **1** *trans., intrans.* to crush or grind noisily between the teeth or under the foot. **2** *intrans.* to produce a crunching sound. **3** *intrans., trans. Comput. colloq.* to key or process at speed. — *noun* **1** a crunching action or sound. **2** *colloq.* the moment of decision or crisis: *when it comes to the crunch*. [imitative]

crunchy *adj.* (**crunchier, crunchiest**) that can be crunched.

crusade — *noun* **1** a strenuous campaign in aid of a cause. **2** *Hist.* see CRUSADES. — *verb intrans.* to engage in a crusade; to campaign. [from French *croisade* and Spanish *cruzada*, from Latin *crux*, cross]

crusader *noun* a person who goes on a crusade.

Crusades Holy Wars from 1096 onwards authorized by the pope in defence of Christendom and the Church, which were fought against the infidels in Germany, Spain, and the East, against heretics and schismatics who threatened Catholic unity, and against Christian lay powers who opposed the papacy. Crusaders committed themselves with solemn vows, and by the 13c were granted full indulgence (remission of all punishment due for sin and an assurance of direct entry into heaven). Papal authorizations of war against Islam continued to be made until the 18c.

crush — *verb* **1** to break, damage, bruise, injure, or distort by compressing violently. **2** to grind or pound into powder, crumbs, etc. **3** *trans., intrans.* to crumple or crease. **4** to defeat, subdue, or humiliate. — *noun* **1** violent compression. **2** a dense crowd. **3** a drink made from the juice of crushed fruit. **4** *colloq.* an amorous passion, usually unsuitable; an infatuation. [from Old French *cruisir*]

crush barrier a barrier for separating a crowd, eg of spectators, into sections to prevent crushing.

crusher *noun* a person or thing that crushes.

Crusoe, Robinson see ROBINSON CRUSOE.

crust — *noun* **1** the hard-baked outer surface of a loaf of bread; a piece of this; a dried-up piece of bread. **2** the pastry covering a pie, etc. **3** a crisp or brittle covering. **4** the solid outermost layer of the Earth, consisting mainly of sedimentary rocks overlying ancient igneous rocks, and varying in thickness from about 8km under the oceans to about 40km under the continents. — *verb trans., intrans.* to cover with, or form, a crust.

Crustacea *noun Zool.* in the animal kingdom, a large class of mainly aquatic arthropods, including crabs, lobsters, shrimps, woodlice, barnacles, etc. [from Latin *crusta*, shell]

crustacean — *noun Zool.* any invertebrate animal belonging to the class Crustacea (one of the classes of arthropods) and typically possessing two pairs of antennae and a segmented body covered by a calcareous (chalky) external skeleton or *carapace.* — *adj.* of or relating to these creatures. [from Latin *crusta*, shell]
◇ Most crustaceans, eg crab, lobster, prawn, shrimp, barnacle, water flea, inhabit marine or freshwater habitats, but a few live in damp terrestrial habitats, eg woodlouse. Many of the body segments bear paired appendages, which may be modified to form mouthparts or antennae, or used for walking, swimming, or catching food particles. Crustaceans breathe by means of gills which are modified limbs or outgrowths from the bases of the limbs. Small crustaceans form much of the plankton of the sea.

crustie *or* **crusty** *noun Brit. slang* a New-Age traveller. [from CRUST]

crustily *adv.* in a crusty way.

crusty *adj.* (**crustier, crustiest**) **1** having a crisp crust. **2** irritable, snappy, or cantankerous.

crutch *noun* **1** a stick, usually one of a pair, used as a support by a lame person, with a bar fitting under the armpit or a grip for the elbow. **2** a support, help, or aid. **3** same as CROTCH. [from Anglo-Saxon *crycc*]

Crux *Astron.* the Southern Cross, a constellation of the southern hemisphere, and the smallest constellation in the sky (by area), lying in the Milky Way. Its brightest stars are Alpha Crucis and Beta Crucis, and it also contains the Coalsack, a dark nebula (cloud of dust) that is silhouetted against the brilliant starry background of the Milky Way.

crux *noun* (PL. **crux, cruces**) **1** a decisive, essential, or crucial point. **2** a problem or difficulty. [from Latin *crux*, cross]

Cruyff, Johann (1947–) Dutch footballer, born in Amsterdam. He joined his first club, Ajax, at the age of 10, and at 19 made his début in the Dutch League. He won 11 Dutch League and Cup medals with Ajax, and helped them to three consecutive (1971–3) European Cup successes. In 1973 he joined Barcelona and won Spanish League and Cup medals with them. He captained Holland in the 1974 World Cup final (beaten by West Germany). He returned to Holland as a player in 1983, joined Feyenoord in 1984, then returned to Barcelona as manager in 1988.

cry — *verb usually intrans.* (**cries, cried**) **1** to shed tears; to weep. **2** (*also* **cry out**) to shout or shriek, eg in pain or fear, or to get attention or help. **3** *trans.* to exclaim. **4** *said of an animal or bird* to utter its characteristic noise. **5** *trans. old use, said of a street trader* to proclaim (one's wares). — *noun* (PL. **cries**) **1** a shout or shriek. **2** an excited utterance or exclamation. **3** an appeal or demand. **4** a rallying call or slogan. **5** a bout of weeping. **6** the characteristic utterance of an animal or bird. **7** a street trader's call: *street cries.*
— **cry something down** to be critical of it; to scorn it.
cry one's eyes *or* **heart out** to weep long and bitterly.
cry off to cancel an engagement or agreement.
cry out for something to be obviously in need of it: *an abuse crying out for justice.*
cry someone *or* **something up** to praise them.

for crying out loud *colloq.* an expression of impatience or annoyance.

in full cry in keen pursuit of something.

crybaby *noun derog. colloq.* a person who weeps at the slightest upset.

crying *adj.* demanding urgent attention: *a crying need.*

cryogenics *sing. noun* the branch of physics dealing with very low temperatures and their effects. [from Greek *kryos*, frost + -GENIC]

cryolite *noun Geol.* a pale grey mineral, composed of sodium, aluminium, and fluorine (Na_3AlF_6), used in the smelting of aluminium ores. It is found mainly in Greenland and the former Soviet Union. [from Greek *kryos*, frost + *lithos*, stone]

cryopreservation *noun Biol.* the preservation of living cells (eg blood, human eggs, and sperm) by freezing; cryonics. [from Greek *kryos*, frost]

crypt *noun* an underground chamber or vault, especially one beneath a church used for burials. [from Greek *krypte*, from *kryptein*, to hide]

cryptanalysis *noun* the deciphering of coded information or messages.
◇ It involves first intercepting a message, then analysing it to reveal its contents. Since languages can be distinguished by the different frequencies with which letters of the alphabet occur, the prime task is to search for these patterns in the code. The use of computers makes this task considerably easier, although highly sophisticated modern codes can present major problems, even for computers, because of their more arbitrary nature.

cryptic *adj.* **1** puzzling, mysterious, obscure, or enigmatic. **2** *said of a crossword puzzle* with clues in the form not of synonyms but of riddles, puns, anagrams, etc. [from Greek *kryptikos*, from *kryptein*, to hide]

cryptically *adv.* in a cryptic way.

crypto- *combining form* forming words meaning: **1** hidden or obscure: *cryptogram.* **2** secret or undeclared: *crypto-fascist.* [from Greek *kryptein*, to hide]

cryptogam *noun* **1** *Bot.* a general term for a plant such as a seaweed, moss, or fern that reproduces by means of spores. **2** *Bot.* a term often used loosely to refer to a plant that lacks flowers. [from CRYPTO- + Greek *gamos*, marriage]

cryptogram *noun* something written in a code or cipher.

cryptographer *noun* a person who writes in and deciphers codes.

cryptographic *adj.* relating to or typical of codes.

cryptography *noun* the study of, or art of writing in and deciphering, codes.

Crystal a female first name, taken from the gemstone and popular in the 19c.

crystal — *noun* **1** (*in full* **rock crystal**) a mineral, colourless transparent quartz. **2** (*also* **crystal ball**) a globe of rock crystal or glass used for crys-

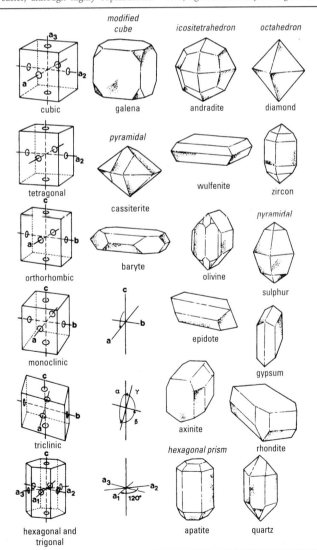

modified cube — icositetrahedron — octahedron

cubic — galena — andradite — diamond

tetragonal — pyramidal — wulfenite — zircon

cassiterite

orthorhombic — baryte — olivine — pyramidal

sulphur

monoclinic — epidote — gypsum

triclinic — axinite

hexagonal and trigonal — hexagonal prism — apatite — rhondite — quartz

types of crystals

tal-gazing. **3** a brilliant, highly transparent glass used for cut glass; cut-glass articles. **4** a small piece of a solid that has a regular three-dimensional shape, and whose plane (flat) faces are arranged in a regular order and meet each other at specific angles. **5** *Chem.* any solid substance consisting of a regularly repeating arrangement of atoms, ions, or molecules. **6** *Electr.* a crystalline element, made of piezoelectric or semiconductor material, that functions as a transducer, oscillator, etc, in an electronic device. — *adj.* like crystal in brilliance and clarity.
— **crystal clear** as clear or obvious as can be. [from Greek *krystallos*, ice]
◇ Most solids have a crystalline structure, eg rocks and minerals, metals, salt, and sugar. Crystals usually occur as a result of crystallization, which may take place when molten rocks cool down and solidify, when a solution of a crystalline solid is allowed to evaporate slowly, or when extra amounts of a crystalline solid are added to a saturated solution of the solid. Mineral crystals can be classified into various three-dimensional geometric catogories according to the size, shape, number, and angle of the faces of each crystal.

crystal-gazer *noun* a fortune-teller.

crystal-gazing *noun* **1** a fortune-teller's practice of gazing into a crystal ball long and hard enough to conjure up a vision, for interpreting as appropriate. **2** *derog.* guesswork about the future.

crystal healing the selection and use of crystals that are said to promote healing and well-being.

crystal lattice *Physics* the orderly three-dimensional arrangement of atoms or ions in a crystal.

crystalline *adj.* **1** having the clarity and brilliance of crystal. **2** *Chem.* taking the form of crystals.

crystallization *or* **crystallisation** *noun* *Chem.* the process whereby crystals are formed by cooling a molten mass, by allowing a solution of a crystalline solid to evaporate slowly, or by adding more of a crystalline solid to an already saturated solution. Crystallization occurs naturally, eg in many rocks, and is also used commercially in the manufacture of common salt, sugar crystals, synthetic gemstones, etc.

crystallize *or* **crystallise** *verb* **1** *trans., intrans.* to form crystals by the process of crystallization. **2** to coat or preserve (fruit) in sugar. **3** *trans., intrans. said of plans, ideas, etc* to make or become clear and definite.

crystallographer *noun* an expert in crystallography.

crystallography *noun* the study of the structure of crystals.

crystalloid *noun* a substance that when dissolved will pass through a membrane.

Crystal Palace an iron-framed, prefabricated glass building designed by Sir Joseph Paxton to house the Great Exhibition of 1851. The structure, dubbed the 'Crystal Palace' by *Punch* magazine, was erected in London's Hyde Park. It was re-erected in S London, but destroyed by fire in 1936.

Cry, the Beloved Country a novel by Alan Paton (1948). It focuses on the racial problems of South Africa in its realistic portrayal of an impoverished black community.

Cs *symbol Chem.* caesium.

c/s *abbrev.* cycles per second.

CSA *abbrev.* Child Support Agency.

CSE *abbrev. Brit.* Certificate of Secondary Education (replaced in 1988 by GCSE).

CSEU *abbrev.* Confederation of Shipbuilding and Engineering Unions.

CS gas *noun* a gas that irritates the air passages and eyes, used against rioters, etc. [named after the US inventors (1928), B Carson & R Staughton]

CSIRO *abbrev.* (in Australia) the Commonwealth and Scientific and Industrial Research Organization, the leading government science organization, formed in 1920; its present name dates from 1949. Its early work was in primary industry, but after 1936 its role was extended to secondary industry, and further broadened by legislation in 1978.

CSP *abbrev.* Council for Scientific Policy.

CSU *abbrev.* Civil Service Union.

CSYS *abbrev.* Certificate of Sixth Year Studies.

CT and **Ct.** *abbrev.* Connecticut.

CTOL *abbrev.* conventional take-off and landing.

Cu *symbol Chem.* copper. [from Latin *cuprum*]

cu. *abbrev.* cubic.

Cuauhtémoc (c.1495–1525) the last Aztec ruler. He succeeded Montezuma's successor, Cuitláhuac, and unsuccessfully resisted the Spaniards under Cortés at the siege of Tenochtitlán (now Mexico City) in 1521. He was executed while on an expedition with Cortés to Honduras.

cub — *noun* **1** the young of certain animals, eg the fox, bear, lion, and wolf. **2** (**Cub** *or* **Cub Scout**) a member of the junior branch of the Scout Association. **3** *old use, derog.* an impudent young man. **4** *colloq.* a beginner; a novice: *a cub reporter.* — *verb intrans.* (**cubbed**, **cubbing**) to give birth to cubs.

Cuba, official name **Republic of Cuba**, Spanish **República de Cuba** POP (1992e) 10.8m, an island republic in the Caribbean Sea, divided into 14 provinces and the city of Havana. AREA 110 860sq km/42 792sq mi. It lies W of Haiti, N of Jamaica, and S of Florida. CAPITAL Havana. CHIEF TOWNS Santiago de Cuba, Camagüey, Holguín, Santa Clara, Guantánamo. TIME ZONE GMT –5. The people are mainly of Spanish and African descent; before 1959, 85% of the population were Roman Catholic, but the Castro regime discouraged religious practices until 1992. OFFICIAL LANGUAGE Spanish. CURRENCY the peso. PHYSICAL DESCRIPTION an archipelago, comprising the island of Cuba, Isla de la Juventud, and c.1 600 islets and cays; the main island is 1 250km/777mi long, varying in width from 191km/119mi in the E to 31km/19mi in the W; heavily indented coastline; the S coast is generally low and marshy and the N coast is steep and rocky, with some fine harbours; the main ranges are the Sierra del Escambray in the centre, the Sierra de los Organos in the W, and the Sierra Maestra in the E; the highest peak is Pico Turquino (2 005m); the island is mostly flat, with wide, fertile valleys and plains. CLIMATE subtropical, warm, and humid; the average annual temperature is 25°C; the dry season is Nov–Apr; the average annual rainfall is 1 375mm; hurricanes usually occur between Jun and Nov. HISTORY visited by Columbus in 1492; it was a Spanish colony until 1898; Spain relinquished its rights over Cuba following a revolution under José Martí, with the support of the USA; gained independence in 1902, with the USA retaining naval bases, and reserving the right of intervention in domestic affairs; the struggle against the dictatorship of General Batista led by Castro, unsuccessful in 1953, was finally successful in 1959, and a Communist state was established; an invasion by Cuban exiles with US support was defeated at the Bay of Pigs in 1961; US naval blockade, after Soviet installation of missile bases in 1962; after emigration was permitted (1980) many Cubans settled in Florida; agreement was reached in 1992 for the withdrawal of Russian troops. GOVERNMENT governed by a 31-member State Council, appointed by a National Assembly of People's Power (510 deputies) following the proposal of

the head of state. ECONOMY after 1959, plantation estates were nationalized, and land plots distributed to peasants; the world's second largest sugar producer (accounting for 75% of export earnings); tobacco, rice, maize, coffee, citrus; dairy cattle; fishing; sugar milling; oil refining; food and tobacco processing; textiles; paper and wood products; metals, cement; the world's fifth largest producer of nickel; tourism; before Castro, over half of Cuba's trade was with the USA; later with the markets of the former USSR.

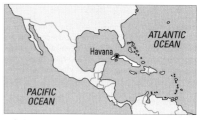

Cuba

Cuban Missile Crisis a period (Oct 1962) of acute international tension and potential military confrontation between the USA and USSR, following the USA's discovery of Soviet nuclear missile sites in Cuba. President Kennedy demanded the dismantling of the base and the return of the missiles, and set up a naval blockade around the island. The crisis ended on 28 October, when Soviet leader Khrushchev agreed to Kennedy's demands, in return for the withdrawal of US missiles from Turkey.

cubbyhole *noun colloq.* **1** a tiny room. **2** a cupboard, nook, or recess in which to accumulate miscellaneous objects. [from dialect *cub*, stall, pen]

cube — *noun* **1** a solid body having six equal square faces. **2** a block of this shape. **3** *Maths.* the product of a number multiplied by itself twice. — *verb* **1** to calculate the cube of (a number). **2** to form or cut into cubes. [from French *cube*, from Greek *kybos*, dice]

cube root the number of which a given number is the cube.

cubic *adj.* **1** shaped like a cube. **2** having three dimensions. **3** *said of a unit of measurement* indicating a volume equivalent to a cube with the unit as its edge measurement: *a cubic metre.*

cubical *adj.* **1** relating to a cube. **2** solid, three-dimensional. **3** *Maths.* equal to that contained in a cube of specified dimensions.

cubicle *noun* a small compartment for sleeping or undressing in, screened for privacy. [from Latin *cubiculum*, from *cubare*, to lie down]

Cubism an early 20c movement in painting, with objects represented as geometrical shapes. It was developed from c.1908 by Pablo Picasso and Georges Braque, who rejected Renaissance perspective and Impressionist attention to light and atmosphere. Objects, painted in sombre shades, were analysed into geometrical planes with several views depicted simultaneously (*analytic cubism*). After c.1912 a flatter, more colourful and decorative hard-edged style emerged (*synthetic cubism*), using collage and painted relief constructs.

Cubist — *adj.* relating to or characteristic of Cubism. — *noun* an artist who works in the Cubist style.

cubit *noun* an old measure, equal to the length of the forearm from the elbow to the tip of the middle finger. [from Latin *cubitum*, elbow]

Cubitt, Thomas (1788–1855) English builder, born in Buxton, Derbyshire. He revolutionized trade practices in the building industry, and with his brother Lewis (1799–1883) was responsible for many large London projects, including Belgravia, and the east front of Buckingham Palace.

Cuchulain, Irish **Cu Chulainn** the hero of many Irish legends (the Ulster cycle) and the chief warrior of Ulster, who obtained his name (meaning 'the hound of Culaan') after killing a huge dog. In his strength and exploits he is comparable to the Greek hero Achilles.

cuckold — noun old use a man whose wife is unfaithful. — verb to make a cuckold of. [from Middle English cokkewold, from Old French cocu, cuckoo]

cuckoldry noun **1** the state of being a cuckold. **2** making a cuckold.

cuckoo — noun any of about 130 species of insectivorous bird, named after the distinctive two-note call of the male common cuckoo. The common cuckoo is found in Europe, Asia, and America, and lays its eggs in the nests of other birds, which instinctively feed the young cuckoo when it hatches, even though it pushes any other eggs and chicks out of the nest. — adj. colloq. insane; crazy. [imitative]

cuckoo clock noun a clock from which a model cuckoo springs on the hour, uttering the appropriate number of cries.

cuckoo pint see LORDS-AND-LADIES.

cuckoo spit a white froth discharged by the larvae of certain insects on leaves and stems.

cucumber noun a long green vegetable with juicy white flesh, used in salads.
— **cool as a cucumber** colloq. calm and composed.
[from Latin cucumis]

Cúcuta POP (1985) 357 000, the capital of Norte de Santander department, NE Colombia. It lies 16km/10mi from the Venezuelan frontier, within a Tax Free Zone. HISTORY founded in 1733; destroyed by an earthquake in 1875, then rebuilt. Because of the town's geographical position as a gateway to Venezuela, Cúcuta was a focal point in Colombia's fight for independence.

cud noun the half-digested food that a cow or other ruminating animal brings back into the mouth from the stomach to chew again.
— **chew the cud** colloq. to meditate, ponder, or reflect.
[from Anglo-Saxon cwudu]

cuddle — verb **1** trans., intrans. to hug or embrace affectionately. **2** (**cuddle in** or **up**) to lie close and snug; to nestle. — noun an affectionate hug.

cuddlesome adj. pleasant to cuddle; cuddly.

cuddly adj. (**cuddlier**, **cuddliest**) pleasant to cuddle; attractively soft and plump.

cudgel — noun a heavy stick or club used as a weapon. — verb (**cudgelled**, **cudgelling**) to beat with a cudgel.
— **cudgel one's brains** to struggle to remember or solve something.
take up the cudgels for someone to fight for or defend them.
[from Anglo-Saxon cycgel]

Cudworth, Ralph (1617–88) English philosopher and theologian, born in Aller, Somerset. He was leader of the 'Cambridge Platonists', Professor of Hebrew (1645), Rector of North Cadbury, Somerset (1650), and Master of Christ's College, Cambridge (1654). His best-known work, The True Intellectual System of the Universe (1678), aimed to establish the reality of a supreme divine Intelligence against materialism.

cue¹ — noun **1** the final words of an actor's speech, or something else said or done by a performer, that serves as a prompt for another to say or do something. **2** anything that serves as a signal or hint to do something. — verb (**cued**, **cueing**) to give a cue to.
— **on cue** at precisely the right moment.
take one's cue from someone to follow their lead as regards behaviour, etc.
[perhaps from q for quando (Latin, when), formerly written in actors' scripts]

cue² — noun **1** a stick tapering to a point, used to strike the ball in billiards, snooker, and pool. **2** old use a tail of hair or plait at the back of the head. — verb (**cued, cueing**) to strike (a ball) with the cue. [from French queue, tail]

Cuenca POP (1990) 195 000, the third largest city in Ecuador and the capital of Azuay province. It was founded by the Spanish in 1557. NOTABLE FEATURES La Concepción Convent (1599), now a religious art museum; cathedral; Modern Art Museum; Folk Museum; sulphur baths nearby.

cuff¹ — noun **1** a band or folded-back part at the lower end of a sleeve, usually at the wrist. **2** North Amer. the turned-up part of a trouser leg. **3** (**cuffs**) slang handcuffs.
— **off the cuff** colloq. without preparation or previous thought.
[from Middle English cuffe, mitten]

cuff² — noun a blow with the open hand. — verb to hit with an open hand. [probably from Norse]

cufflink noun one of a pair of decorative fasteners for shirt cuffs.

Cugnot, Nicolas Joseph (1725–1804) French military engineer. Around 1770 he invented a three-wheeled steam-driven artillery carriage with a speed of 2–3 mph. Lack of support prevented further development.

cuirass noun Hist. a piece of armour, a breastplate with or without a back plate attached to it. [from French cuirasse]

cuisine noun **1** a style of cooking. **2** the range of food served at a restaurant, etc. [from French cuisine, kitchen]

Cukor, George D(ewey) (1899–1983) US film director, born in New York City. He worked first on Broadway, but went to Hollywood in 1929, starting a career of 50 years' solo directing with Girls About Town (1931). His films with the actresses Greta Garbo, Joan Crawford, and Katharine Hepburn were particularly successful. His range was wide, and included Gaslight (1944), A Star is Born (1954), and My Fair Lady (1964), for which he won an Oscar.

Culdees originally, monks in the Irish church in the 8c and the Scottish Church in the 9c, who later became secular clergy. In Scotland, they were respected for their high ideals and spirituality, and survived in St Andrews until the 14c.

cul-de-sac noun (PL. **culs-de-sac**) a street closed at one end. [from French cul-de-sac, sack-bottom]

Culiacán or **Culiacán Rosales** POP (1990) 602 000, the capital of Sinaloa state, NW Mexico, on the R Culiacán, 208km/129mi NW of Mazatlán. It was founded in 1599.

culinary adj. relating to cookery or the kitchen. [from Latin culina, kitchen]

Culkin, Macaulay (1980–) US film actor, born in New York City. A successful child star, his first film was Rocket Gibraltar (1988). Among his subsequent films are Jacob's Ladder (1990), Home Alone (1990), Home Alone 2 (1992) and The Good Son (1993). Despite his youth, he is one of the most highly-paid Hollywood stars.

cull — verb **1** to gather or pick up (information or ideas). **2** to select and kill (weak or surplus animals) from a group, eg seals or deer, in order to keep the population under control. — noun an act of culling. [from Old French cuillir, to gather]

Culloden a ridge forming part of Drummossie Muir in Nairn district, Highland region, Scotland, situated E of Inverness. It is famous as the site of the battle in 1746.

Culloden, Battle of a battle fought (1746) near Inverness, the last major battle on British soil. It marked the end of the 1745 Jacobite rebellion led by Charles Edward Stuart, whose force, mainly of Scottish highlanders, was crushed by a superior force of English and lowland Scots under the Duke of Cumberland.

culm noun Bot. **1** the jointed hollow stem of a grass. **2** the solid stem of a sedge. [from Latin culmus, stalk]

culminate verb intrans. (**culminate in something**) to reach the highest point or climax. [from Latin culmen, top, summit]

culmination noun the act or point of culminating; the top or climax.

culottes pl. noun flared trousers for women, looking like a skirt. [from French culottes, breeches]

culpability noun being guilty; blameworthiness.

culpable adj. deserving blame. [from Latin culpare, to blame]

culpably adv. in a way that deserves blame.

Culpeper, Nicholas (1616–54) British astrologer, born in London. He practised astrology in Spitalfields from 1660, and published an English translation of the College of Physicians' Pharmacopoeia, A Physical Directory (1649), and The English Physician Enlarged, or the Herbal (1653). Both books had enormous sales.

culprit noun **1** a person guilty of a misdeed or offence. **2** Legal a person accused of a crime. [said to be from Old French culpable, guilty + prest, ready: in legal tradition, when a prisoner pleaded not guilty, the clerk of the court replied culpable: prest daverrer notre bille, ie 'guilty, ready to prove our charge']

cult noun **1** a system of religious belief; the sect of people following such a system. **2** an especially extravagant admiration for a person, idea, etc. **3** a fashion, craze or fad. [from Latin cultus, from colere, to worship]

cultivar (ABBREV. **cv**) a variety of a plant that does not occur naturally in the wild, but has been developed and maintained by cultivation using horticultural or agricultural techniques. Many cultivars do not breed true, and are propagated vegetatively. [a shortening of cultivated variety]

cultivate verb **1** to prepare and use (land or soil) for crops. **2** to grow (a crop, plant, etc). **3** to develop or improve: cultivate one's mind / cultivate a taste for literature. **4** to try to develop a friendship with (someone), especially for personal advantage. [from Latin cultivare]

cultivated adj. **1** well bred and knowledgeable. **2** said of plants not wild; grown in a garden, etc.

cultivation noun **1** the act of cultivating. **2** education, breeding, and culture.

cultivator noun **1** a machine for breaking up ground. **2** a person who cultivates.

cultural adj. **1** relating to a culture or civilization. **2** relating to the arts.

cultural lag or **culture lag** a slower rate of cultural change found in one part of a society compared with the whole or majority, or a slower rate of change in a particular society compared to the world at large.

culturally adv. in a cultural way; as regards culture.

Cultural Revolution (1966–76) in China, a mobilization of youth in the towns, started by Mao Zedong in an attempt to move away from the Soviet style of communism. Schools were closed and students were encouraged to join Red Guard units, which persecuted teachers and 'intellectuals'. The economy was disrupted, and violence resulted in many deaths. Mao tried to draw back from the excesses of the Cultural Revolution but the Gang of Four continued to enforce the philosophy until its members were imprisoned in 1976.

culture — noun **1** the customs, ideas, art, etc of a particular civilization, society, or social group. **2** appreciation of art, music, literature, etc. **3** improvement and development through care and training: beauty culture. **4** (also in compounds) the cultivation of eg plants, trees, bees, etc, especially for commercial purposes: *silkworm culture / apiculture*. **5** a crop of bacteria grown for study. — *verb* to grow (bacteria) for study. [from Latin *cultura*, from *colere*, to cherish, practise]

cultured *adj.* **1** well-educated; having refined tastes and manners. **2** *said of a pearl* formed by an oyster round a foreign body deliberately inserted into its shell.

culture shock disorientation caused by a change from a familiar environment, culture, ideology, etc, to another that is wholly or radically different or alien.

culvert *noun* a covered drain or channel carrying water under a road or railway.

-cum- *combining form* combined with; also used as: *kitchen-cum-dining-room*. [from Latin *cum*, with]

Cumae the oldest Greek colony in Italy, founded in c.750 BC near present-day Naples. It was famous in Roman times as the home of the oracular prophetess, the Sibyl.

Cumberland, William Augustus, Duke of (1721–65) English soldier, the second son of George II, born in London. He adopted a military career, and in the War of the Austrian Succession (1740–8) was wounded at Dettingen (1743) and defeated at Fontenoy (1745). He crushed the Charles Edward Stewart's rebellion at Culloden (1746), and by his harsh policies afterwards earned the title of 'Butcher'. In the Seven Years' War (1756–63), he surrendered to the French (1757), and then retired.

Cumberland a former county of NW England which has been part of Cumbria since 1974. The area was disputed between the Scots and the English until their crowns united in 1603.

Cumbernauld POP (1992e) 64 000, the capital of Cumbernauld and Kilsyth district, Strathclyde, central Scotland. It is situated 20km/12mi NE of Glasgow and was designated a 'new town' in 1955.

cumbersome *adj.* heavy, awkward, unwieldy, clumsy, or unmanageable. [from Middle English *cummyrsum*]

Cumbria POP (1992e) 490 000, a county in NW England, divided into six districts. AREA 6 810sq km/2 629sq mi. It is bounded W by the Irish Sea, NW by the Solway Firth, N by the Scottish border, E by Northumberland, Durham, and North Yorkshire, and S by Lancashire. PHYSICAL DESCRIPTION the Pennines rise in the E, forming the border with Northumberland; 40% of the county lies within the Lake District and Yorkshire Dales national parks. CHIEF TOWNS Carlisle (county town), Penrith, Kendal, Barrow-in-Furness. ECONOMY agriculture; shipbuilding; marine engineering; chemicals; atomic energy at Sellafield and Calder Hall; tourism.

cumin

cumin *noun* a Mediterranean herb whose seeds are used as flavouring. [from Greek *kyminon*]

cummerbund *noun* a wide sash, especially one worn with a dinner jacket. [from Hindi *kamarband*, loin band]

cummings, e e, properly **E(dward)**

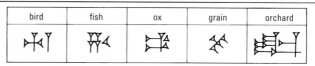

bird	fish	ox	grain	orchard

cuneiform script

E(stlin) Cummings (1894–1962) US writer and painter, born in Cambridge, Massachusetts. Better known for his writings than his paintings, his collections of poetry include *Tulips and Chimneys* (1923). His poems are striking for their unorthodox typography and linguistic style. His best-known prose work is *The Enormous Room* (1922), which describes his internment in a French concentration camp.

cumulative *adj.* increasing in amount, effect or strength with each successive addition. [from Latin *cumulare*, to pile up]

cumulatively *adv.* in a cumulative way.

cumulonimbus *adj.* *Meteorol.* denoting clouds of the cumulus family that rise to heights of up to 10km, and are often dark and threatening when seen from below. They are associated with thunderstorms and the arrival of a cold front during the passage of a depression. [from Latin *cumulus*, heap]

cumulus *noun* (PL. **cumuli**) *Meteorol.* a fluffy heaped cloud with a rounded white upper surface and a flat horizontal base. It is composed of water droplets, and usually develops over a heat source, eg a volcano or hot land surface. The height of the cloud depends on the humidity of the atmosphere. [from Latin *cumulus*, heap, mass]

cuneiform — *adj.* of, or in, any of several ancient Middle-Eastern scripts with impressed wedge-shaped characters. — *noun* cuneiform writing. [from Latin *cuneus*, wedge]

cunnilingus *noun* the stimulation of a woman's genitals by licking, etc. [from Latin *cunnus*, vulva + *lingere*, to lick]

cunning — *adj.* **1** clever, wily, sly, crafty, or artful. **2** ingenious, skilful, or subtle. — *noun* **1** slyness; wiliness. **2** skill; expertise. [from Anglo-Saxon *cunnan*, to know]

Cunningham, Merce (1919–) US dancer, choreographer, teacher, and director, born in Centralia, Washington. He danced with the Martha Graham company (1939–45), and started the Merce Cunningham Dance Company in 1953, where he furthered the concern with form and abstraction in modern dance and developed a new vocabulary for it. Among his choreographic works are *Suite for Five* (1956), *Scramble* (1967), *Duets* (1980), and *Loosestrife* (1991).

Cunning Little Vixen, The (Příhody Lišky Bystroušky) an opera by Leoš Janáček (1924). It tells of a forester who captures a young vixen and develops an attachment to her that parallels a previous human relationship. Though saddened when she escapes and is shot, the themes of death and renewal are emphasized when he sees the vixen's cubs.

cunningly *adv.* in a cunning way.

cunt *noun coarse slang* **1** the female genitals. **2** *offensive slang* used as an abusive term for a person. [from Middle English *cunte*]

cup — *noun* **1** a small round container with a handle, from which to drink especially hot liquids, eg tea or coffee. **2** the amount a cup will hold, used as a measure in cookery. **3** a container or something else shaped like a cup: *egg cups / bra cups*. **4** an ornamental, usually silver, vessel awarded as a prize in sports competitions, etc. **5** a competition in which the prize is a cup. **6** a drink based on wine, with added fruit juice, etc: *claret cup*. **7** *literary* something that one undergoes or experiences: *one's own cup of woe*. — *verb* (**cupped**, **cupping**) **1** to form (one's hands) into a cup shape. **2** to hold (something) in one's cupped hands.

— **one's cup of tea** *colloq.* one's personal preference.
[from Anglo-Saxon *cuppe*, from Latin *cupa*, cask]

cupboard *noun* a piece of furniture, or a recess, fitted with doors, shelves, etc, for storing provisions or personal effects. [from Anglo-Saxon *cup-pebord*, table for crockery]

cupboard love an insincere show of affection towards someone from whom one wants something.

cup final the final match in a football contest or other competition for a cup.

cupful *noun* (PL. **cupfuls**) the amount a cup will hold.

Cupid the Roman god of Love, son of Venus and lover of Psyche, depicted as a naked winged boy with bow and arrows. He is equivalent to the Greek god Eros.

cupid *noun* a figure of Cupid in art or sculpture. [from Latin *cupido*, desire, love]

cupidity *noun* greed for wealth and possessions. [from Latin *cupiditas*]

cupola *noun* **1** a small dome or turret on a roof; a domed roof or ceiling. **2** an armoured revolving gun turret. **3** a furnace used in iron foundries. [from Italian *cupola*, from Latin *cupula*, diminutive of *cupa*, cask]

cuppa *noun colloq.* a cup of tea. [altered form of *cup of*]

cupping *noun Medicine* the former practice of applying heated cups to the skin, which was thought to promote healing by drawing 'harmful' blood away from diseased organs to the surface of the skin.

cupric *adj. Chem.* denoting any compound of copper in which the element has a valence of two, eg cupric chloride ($CuCl_2$).

cuprite *noun Geol.* a red copper oxide mineral (Cu_2O) that is an important source of copper. [from Latin *cupreus*, from *cuprum*]

cupro-nickel *noun* an alloy of copper with nickel.

cuprous *adj. Chem.* denoting any compound of copper in which the element has a valence of one, eg cuprous chloride ($CuCl$). [from Latin *cupreus*, from *cuprum*, copper]

cup tie one of a series of knockout matches in a competition for a cup.

cur *noun old derog. use* **1** a surly mongrel dog. **2** a surly fellow; a scoundrel. [from Middle English *curdogge*, related to Norse *kurra*, to grumble]

curability *noun* the property of being curable.

curable *adj.* capable of being cured.

Curaçao POP (1991e) 144 000, the largest and most populous island of the Netherlands Antilles, E Caribbean Sea, situated 60km/37mi N of Venezuela. AREA 444sq km/171sq mi. PHYSICAL DESCRIPTION composed of coralline limestone; generally flat, but rises to 373m in the NW; length 58km/36mi; width 13km/8mi; HISTORY discovered by Europeans in 1499; became a Dutch colony in 1634. CAPITAL Willemstad. ECONOMY oil refining; phosphate mining; ship repairing; liqueur; tourism.

curacy *noun* the office or benefit of a curate.

curare *noun* a paralysing poison smeared on arrow-tips by S American Indian hunters, with medicinal uses as a muscle relaxant. [from Carib (S American Indian language) *kurari*]

curate *noun* a clergyman who acts as assistant

to a vicar or rector in the Church of England. [from Latin *curatus*, from *cura*, care]

curative — *adj.* able, or tending, to cure. — *noun* a substance that cures. [from Latin *curativus*, from *cura*, healing]

curator *noun* a person who has responsibility for a museum or other collection. [from Latin *curator*, keeper, from *cura*, care]

curb — *noun* **1** something that restrains or controls. **2** a chain or strap passing under a horse's jaw, attached at the sides to the bit; a bit with such a fitting. **3** a raised edge or border. **4** *North Amer.* a kerb. — *verb* **1** to restrain or control. **2** to put a curb on (a horse). [from Old French *courb*, curved]

curd *noun* **1** (*often* **curds**) milk thickened or coagulated by acid; the solid parts of this, as distinct from the liquid whey, used in making cheese. **2** any of several substances of similar consistency. [from Middle English *curden*, to congeal]

curdle *verb trans., intrans.* to turn into curds. — **make someone's blood curdle** to horrify or petrify them. [from CURD]

cure — *verb* **1** (**cure someone of something**) to restore them to health or normality; to heal them. **2** to get rid of (an illness, harmful habit, or other evil). **3** to preserve meat by soaking it in salt solution and then removing it in order to dehydrate it and prevent the growth of bacteria. **4** to preserve leather, tobacco, etc, by drying. **5** to vulcanize (rubber). — *noun* **1** something that cures or remedies. **2** restoration to health. **3** a course of healing or remedial treatment. **4** *Relig.* the responsibility of a minister for the souls of the parishioners. [from Latin *curare*, to care for, heal, and *cura*, healing]

cure-all *noun* a universal remedy; a panacea.

curettage *noun* the process of using a curette.

curette *or* **curet** — *noun* *Medicine* a spoon-shaped instrument that is used to scrape a tissue sample from the inner surface of an organ or body cavity for diagnostic purposes, or to remove diseased tissue from such a cavity. — *verb* (**curetted**, **curetting**) to scrape with a curette. [from French, from *curer*, to clean, clear]

curfew *noun* **1** an order forbidding people to be in the streets after a certain hour. **2** the time at which such an order applies. **3** *Hist.* the ringing of a bell as a signal to put out fires and lights. [from Old French *covrefeu*, literally 'covers the fire']

Curia Regis the king's household and a fluctuating entourage of important subjects, which conducted all the central functions of government in early medieval times, introduced in 1066. Later, in 13c England particular departments (Chancery, Exchequer, etc) were no longer part of the household, but the relationship between Curia and government nevertheless remained fundamental. [Latin, = the king's court]

Curie, Marie, originally **Marya**, née **Marya Skłodowska** (1867–1934) Polish-born French radiochemist, born in Warsaw. She emigrated to France in 1891, and studied at the Sorbonne. She worked with her husband Pierre Curie on magnetism and radioactivity, discovered radium and polonium, and shared the 1903 Nobel Prize for Physics with her husband and Antoine Henri Becquerel. Following her husband's death in 1906, she succeeded him as professor at the Sorbonne, and later won the Nobel Prize for Chemistry (1911).

Curie, Pierre (1859–1906) French physicist, born in Paris. Professor at the Sorbonne from 1904, he discovered piezoelectricity (1880), the small electric current produced when certain crystals are mechanically deformed and vice versa. He worked with his wife Marie Curie on magnetism and radioactivity; they shared the 1903 Nobel Prize for Physics with Antoine Henri Becquerel. He was killed in a traffic accident.

curie *noun* (SYMBOL **Ci**) the former unit of radioactivity, equivalent to 3.7×10^{10} disintegrations of a radioactive source per second. It has now been replaced by the becquerel in SI units. [named after the French physicists Marie and Pierre *Curie*]

curio *noun* (PL. **curios**) an article valued for its rarity or unusualness. [from CURIOSITY]

curiosity *noun* (PL. **curiosities**) **1** eagerness to know; inquisitiveness. **2** something strange, odd, rare, exotic, or unusual. [from Latin *curiositas*]

curious *adj.* **1** strange; odd. **2** eager or interested: *curious to see what happens*. **3** inquisitive. [from Latin *curiosus*, careful, inquisitive]

curiously *adv.* in a curious way.

Curitiba POP (1991) 2m, the commercial and industrial capital of Paraná state, S Brazil. It is situated SW of São Paulo at an altitude of 900m. NOTABLE FEATURES cathedral (1894); Palácio Iguaçu; Paranaense Museum; Passeio Público Park; temple in Egyptian style on L Bacacheri lies to the N.

curium *noun* *Chem.* (SYMBOL **Cm**, ATOMIC NUMBER **96**) a radioactive element formed by bombarding plutonium-239 with alpha particles. [named after Marie and Pierre Curie, the discoverers of radium]

curl — *verb* **1** *trans., intrans.* to twist, roll, or wind (hair) into coils or ringlets; to grow in coils or ringlets. **2** *intrans., trans.* to move in, or form into, a spiral, coil, or curve. **3** *intrans.* to take part in the game of curling. — *noun* **1** a small coil or ringlet of hair. **2** the tendency of hair to curl. **3** a twist, spiral, coil, or curve. — **curl up 1** to sit or lie with the legs tucked up. **2** *colloq.* to writhe in embarrassment, etc. [from Middle English *crull*, curly]

curler *noun* a device for curling the hair.

curlew *noun* a large wading bird, found on open plains, moors, and marshes across Europe and Asia, with a slender down-curved bill, long legs, and a two-syllable fluting call. It feeds on shellfish, snails, worms, and insects, using its long bill to probe for them in the sand. [from Old French *corleu*, perhaps imitative]

curlicue *noun* a fancy twist or curl; a flourish made with a pen. [from CURLY + CUE[2]]

curliness *noun* being curly.

curling *noun* a team game played on ice with smooth heavy stones with handles, that are slid towards a circular target marked on the ice. [from CURL]

◊ The sport is believed to have been introduced into Scotland by Flemings in the 15c. It is played in many countries, and is especially popular in Canada, the UK, and the Nordic countries.

curly *adj.* (**curlier**, **curliest**) having curls; full of curls.

curmudgeon *noun* a bad-tempered or mean person.

curmudgeonly *adj.* like a curmudgeon.

currant *noun* **1** a small dried seedless grape. **2** (*in compounds*) any of several small soft berries. [from Old French *raisins de Corinthe*, grapes of Corinth, the place of export]

currency *noun* (PL. **currencies**) **1** the system of money, or the coins and notes, in use in a country. **2** general acceptance or popularity, especially of an idea, theory, etc. **3** modernity; up-to-dateness. [from Latin *currere*, to run]

◊ Convertible currency is that proportion of a country's money which may be exchanged for the money of another country. When the rate of exchange between one currency and another falls, the currency depreciates; when it rises, the currency appreciates. Currency revaluation is the deliberate raising by a government of the value of its country's currency in terms of foreign currencies; currency devaluation is the reduction of the country's currency in terms of foreign currencies.

current — *adj.* **1** generally accepted: *according to the current view*. **2** of or belonging to the present:

current affairs. — *noun* **1** a continuous flow of water or air in a particular direction. **2** the flow of electricity through a circuit or wire. **3** a popular trend or tendency: *currents of opinion*.

current account a bank account from which money can be drawn without notice, and on which little or no interest is paid.

currently *adv.* at the present time.

curriculum *noun* (PL. **curricula**) a course, especially of study at school or university. [from Latin *curriculum*, course, from *currere*, to run]

curriculum vitae (PL. **curricula vitae**) a written summary of one's personal details and the main events of one's education and career, produced to accompany job applications, etc. [from Latin *vita*, life]

curry[1] *noun* (PL. **curries**) a dish, originally Indian, of meat, fish, or vegetables cooked with usually hot spices. [from Tamil *kari*, sauce]

curry[2] *verb* **1** to groom (a horse). **2** to treat (tanned leather) so as to improve its flexibility, strength and waterproof quality. — **curry favour with someone** to use flattery to gain their approval; to ingratiate oneself with them. [from Old French *correier*, to make ready]

curry powder a selection of ground spices used in making curry.

curse — *noun* **1** a blasphemous or obscene expression, usually of anger; an oath. **2** an appeal to God or other divine power to harm someone. **3** the resulting harm suffered by someone: *under a curse*. **4** an evil; a cause of harm: *the curse of drugs*. **5** *colloq.* (**the curse**) menstruation; a woman's menstrual period. — *verb* **1** to utter a curse against; to revile with curses. **2** *intrans.* to use violent language; to swear. — **be cursed with something** to be burdened or afflicted with it. [from Anglo-Saxon *curs*]

cursed *adj.* **1** under a curse. **2** *offensive* damnable; hateful.

cursive — *adj., said of writing* having letters joined up, not printed separately. — *noun* cursive writing. [from Latin *cursivus*, from *currere*, to run]

cursively *adv.* in a cursive style.

cursor *noun* **1** a flashing marker on a computer screen indicating the current position of the operator in the content. **2** the transparent movable part of a slide rule or other measuring instrument. [from Latin *cursor*, runner]

cursorily *adv.* in a cursory way.

cursory *adj.* hasty; superficial; not thorough. [from Latin *cursorius*]

cursus honorum in ancient Rome, the ordered career structure which was normal for anyone who aspired to high public office. The major offices of state, such as the quaestorship, praetorship, and consulship, had to be held in strict order, and not before a certain age. [Latin, = the course of honours]

curt *adj.* rudely brief; dismissive; abrupt. [from Latin *curtus*, short]

curtail *verb* to reduce; to cut short; to restrict. [originally *curtal*, something docked or shortened, from Latin *curtus*, short]

curtailment *noun* **1** the act of curtailing. **2** shortening.

curtain — *noun* **1** a hanging cloth over a window, round a bed, etc for privacy or to exclude light, or in front of a stage to screen it from the auditorium. **2** the rise of the curtain at the beginning, or fall of the curtain at the end, of a stage performance, act, scene, etc. **3** something resembling a curtain: *a curtain of thick dark hair*. **4** (**curtains**) *colloq.* the end; death. — *verb* **1** (*usually* **curtain something off**) to surround or enclose it with a curtain. **2** to supply (windows, etc) with curtains. [from Old French *cortine*, from Latin *cortina*]

curtain call an audience's demand for performers to appear in front of the curtain after it has fallen, to receive further applause.

curtain-raiser *noun* **1** a short play, etc before the main performance. **2** any introductory event.

curtain wall 1 *Archit.* a wall that is not load-bearing. **2** *Fortification* a wall between two towers or bastions.

curtly *adv.* with a curt manner.

curtness *noun* being curt.

curtsy — *noun* (PL. **curtsies**) a slight bend of the knees with one leg behind the other, performed as a formal gesture of respect by women. — *verb intrans.* (**curtsies**, **curtsied**) to perform a curtsy. [variant of COURTESY]

curvaceous *adj. colloq., said of a woman* having a shapely figure.

curvature *noun* the condition of being curved; the degree of curvedness. [from Latin *curvatura*]

curve — *noun* **1** a line no part of which is straight, or a surface no part of which is flat. **2** any smoothly arched line or shape, like part of a circle or sphere. **3** (**curves**) *colloq.* the roundnesses of a woman's body. **4** a graph, or a line on a graph. **5** *Maths.* a line representing an equation. — *verb intrans., trans.* to form, or form into, a curve; to move in a curve. [from Latin *curvus*, crooked]

curvilinear *adj.* consisting of, or bounded by, a curved line. [from CURVE + RECTILINEAR]

curvy *adj.* (**curvier**, **curviest**) having curves or a curved shape.

Curzon (of Kedleston), George Nathaniel Curzon, Marquis (1859–1925) English statesman, born in Kedleston Hall, Derbyshire. He became an MP in 1886, travelled widely in Eastern countries, was Under-Secretary for India (1891–2), and for Foreign Affairs (1895), and in 1898 was made Viceroy of India. He introduced many social and political reforms, established the NW Frontier Province, and partitioned Bengal. He resigned after a disagreement with Lord Kitchener (1905), but returned to politics as Lord Privy Seal (1915) and then Foreign Secretary (1919–24).

Cush the name used by the pharaohs for Nubia, the land stretching S from the First Cataract to the Sudan. Cush was secondary to Egypt in the second millennium BC, but ruled it in the first.

cushiness *noun* being cushy.

Cushing, Harvey Williams (1869–1939) US neurosurgeon, born in Cleveland, Ohio. Professor at Harvard and Yale, he developed important new techniques and procedures to control blood pressure and bleeding during surgery, and discovered a novel operative approach to the pituitary gland. His biography of the Canadian physician William Osler won a Pulitzer Prize in 1926.

Cushing's syndrome *Medicine* a condition characterized by obesity, raised blood pressure, acne, osteoporosis, and weakness, caused by the presence of excess amounts of corticosteroid hormones in the body as a result of a tumour of the pituitary gland, or a malignant tumour elsewhere in the body. [named after the US surgeon Harvey Cushing]

cushion — *noun* **1** a stuffed fabric case used for making a seat comfortable, for kneeling on, etc. **2** a thick pad, or something having a similar function. **3** something that gives protection from shock, reduces unpleasant effects, etc. **4** the resilient inner rim of a billiard table. — *verb* **1** to reduce the unpleasant or violent effect of. **2** to protect from shock, injury, or the extremes of distress. **3** to provide with cushions. [from Old French *cuissin*, from Latin *coxa*, hip]

Cushitic languages a group of about 30 Afro-Asiatic languages, spoken by c.13m people in Somalia, Kenya, Sudan, and Ethiopia. The most widely spoken are Oromo (or Gassa), and Somali. [from *Cush*, an ancient kingdom in the Nile valley]

cushy *adj.* (**cushier**, **cushiest**) *colloq.* comfortable; easy; undemanding. [from Hindi *khush*, pleasant]

cusp *noun* **1** *Geom.* a point formed by the meeting of two curves. **2** *Astron.* either point of a crescent moon. **3** *Anat.* a sharp raised point on the grinding surface of a molar tooth. **4** *Astrol.* the point of transition between one sign of the zodiac and the next. [from Latin *cuspis*, a point]

cuss *old colloq. use* — *noun* **1** a curse. **2** a person or animal, especially if stubborn. — *verb intrans., trans.* to curse. [from CURSE]

cussed *adj.* **1** obstinate, stubborn, awkward or perverse. **2** cursed.

cussedly *adv.* in a cussed way.

cussedness *noun* obstinacy, awkwardness.

custard *noun* **1** a sweet sauce made with milk and cornflour. **2** (*also* **egg custard**) a dish or sauce of baked eggs and milk. [formerly *custade*, altered from Middle English *crustade*, pie with a crust]

Custer, George Armstrong (1839–76) US soldier, born in New Rumley, Ohio. After a brilliant career as a cavalry commander in the Civil War, he served in the campaigns against the Native American tribes of the Great Plains. His actions were controversial, but his gift for self-publicity made him a symbol of the cavalry. His defeat by a combined Sioux-Cheyenne force at Little Big Horn, Montana (25 Jun 1876) shocked the nation, but did not particularly help the Native Americans' cause.

custodial *adj.* relating to custody; involving custody.

custodian *noun* a person who has care of something, eg a public building or ancient monument; a guardian or curator. [from Latin *custodia*, watch, watchman]

custodianship *noun* the office of custodian.

custody *noun* **1** protective care; the guardianship of a child, awarded to someone by a court of law. **2** the condition of being held by the police; arrest or imprisonment. — **take someone into custody** to arrest them. [from Latin *custodia*, watch, vigil]

custom *noun* **1** a traditional activity or practice. **2** a personal habit. **3** the body of established practices of a community; convention. **4** an established practice having the force of a law. **5** the trade or business that one gives to a shop, etc by regular purchases.

customarily *adv.* usually, traditionally.

customary *adj.* usual; traditional; according to custom.

custom-built *or* **custom-made** *adj.* built or made to an individual customer's requirements.

customer *noun* **1** a person who purchases goods from a shop, uses the services of a business, etc. **2** *colloq.* a person with whom one has to deal (usually with unfavourable implications): *an awkward customer.* [from CUSTOM]

customs *noun* **1** (*pl.*) taxes or duties paid on imports. **2** (*sing.*) the government department that collects these taxes. **3** (*sing.*) the place at a port, airport, frontier, etc where baggage is inspected for goods on which duty must be paid. [from CUSTOM]

customs house the office at a port, etc where customs duties are paid or collected.

customs union an economic agreement where nations adopt common excise duties, thereby eliminating the need for customs checks along their common frontiers, and creating a free trade area. The European Union is a customs union.

cut — *verb* (**cutting**; PAST TENSE AND PAST PARTICIPLE **cut**) **1** (*also* **cut something off** *or* **out**) (of a sharp-edged instrument or person using it) to slit, pierce, slice, or sever it. **2** (*also* **cut something up**) to divide it by cutting. **3** to trim (hair, nails, etc), reap (corn), mow (grass) or detach (flowers). **4** (*also* **cut something out**) to make or form it by cutting. **5** to shape the surface of (a gem) into facets, or decorate (glass), by cutting. **6** to shape the pieces of (a garment): *badly cut clothes.* **7** to bring out (a record or disc). **8** to injure or wound with a sharp edge or instrument. **9** to hurt: *cut someone to the heart.* **10** to reduce (eg prices, wages, interest rates, working hours, etc). **11** to shorten (eg a book or play). **12** to delete or omit. **13** to edit (a film). **14** *intrans.* to stop filming. **15** *intrans. Cinema, said of a film or camera* to change directly to another shot, etc. **16** *Maths.* to cross or intersect. **17** to reject or renounce: *cut one's links with one's family.* **18** to ignore or pretend not to recognize (a person). **19** to stop: *cut drinking.* **20** to absent oneself from: *cut classes.* **21** to switch off (an engine, etc). **22** *Cricket* to hit (a ball) with a slicing action, causing it to spin or swerve. **23** *said of a baby* to grow (teeth). **24** *intrans.* (**cut across** *or* **through**) to go off in a certain direction; to take a short route. **25** to dilute (eg an alcoholic drink) or adulterate (a drug). **26** to divide; to partition: *a room cut in half by a bookcase.* — *noun* **1** an act of cutting, a cutting movement or stroke. **2** a slit, incision, or injury made by cutting. **3** a reduction. **4** a deleted passage in a play, etc. **5** the stoppage of an electricity supply, etc. **6** *slang* one's share of the profits. **7** a piece of meat cut from an animal. **8** the style in which clothes or hair are cut. **9** a sarcastic remark. **10** a refusal to recognize someone; a snub. **11** a short cut. **12** a channel, passage, or canal. — **a cut above something** *colloq.* superior to it.

cut across something 1 to go against (normal procedure, etc). **2** *said of an issue, etc* to be more important than, or transcend (the barriers or divisions between parties, etc).

cut and dried decided; definite; settled beforehand.

cut and run *colloq.* to escape smartly.

cut and thrust aggressive competition; quick verbal exchange or repartee.

cut back on something to reduce spending, etc.

cut both ways to have advantages and disadvantages; to bear out both sides of an argument.

cut someone dead to ignore them completely.

cut something down to fell a tree, etc.

cut down on something to reduce one's use of it; to do less of it: *cut down on drinking.*

cut in 1 to interrupt. **2** *said of a vehicle* to overtake and squeeze in front of another vehicle.

cut it fine *colloq.* to leave barely enough time or space for something.

cut it out *slang* to stop doing something bad or undesirable.

cut something off 1 to separate or isolate it. **2** to stop the supply of gas, electricity, etc. **3** to stop it or cut it short.

cut someone off to disconnect them during a telephone call.

cut out *said of an engine, etc* to stop working.

cut something out 1 to remove or delete it. **2** to clip pictures, etc out of a magazine, etc. **3** *colloq.* to stop doing it. **4** to exclude it from consideration. **5** to block out the light or view.

cut out for *or* **to be something** having the qualities needed for it.

cut something short to reduce or shorten it.

cut someone short to silence them by interrupting.

cut up *colloq.* distressed; upset.

cut up rough *colloq.* to get angry and violent.

to cut a long story short to come straight to the point.

[from Middle English *cutten*]

cutaway *adj.* **1** *said of a diagram, etc* having outer parts omitted so as to show the interior. **2** *said of a coat* with the front part cut away below the waist.

cutback *noun* a reduction in spending, use of resources, etc.

cute *adj. colloq.* **1** attractive; pretty. **2** clever; cunning; shrewd. [from ACUTE]

cutely *adv.* in a cute way.

cuteness *noun* being cute.

cut glass glass with patterns cut into its surface.

Cuthbert, St (c.635–87) Anglo-Saxon churchman and missionary, born probably in Lauderdale (then in Northumbria). He became a monk (651), prior of Melrose (661), and of Lindisfarne (664). In 676 he left to become a hermit, but in 684 was persuaded to take the bishopric of Hexham, then of Lindisfarne. Two years later he returned to his cell, on the island of Farne, where he died. After many moves, his body was finally buried in Durham (999). His feast day is 20 Mar.

Cuthbert a male first name, borne by two English saints and now rare. [from Anglo-Saxon elements *cud*, known + *beorht*, famous]

cuticle *noun* **1** *Anat.* the epidermis or outer layer of the skin, including the outer layer of cells in a hair, and the hardened skin at the base of the fingernails and toenails. **2** *Bot.* the waxy waterproof protective layer that covers all the parts of a plant that are exposed to the air, except for the stomata. **3** *Zool.* the protective layer of horny non-cellular material that covers the surface of many invertebrates, and forms the *exoskeleton* of arthropods, eg insects and crustaceans. [from Latin *cuticula*, skin]

cutlass *noun Hist.* a short, broad, slightly curved sword with one cutting edge. [from French *coutelas*, from Latin *cultellus*, little knife]

cutler *noun* a person who manufactures cutlery. [from French *coutelier*, from Latin *culter*, knife]

cutlery *noun* knives, forks, and spoons for table use.

cutlet *noun* **1** a small piece of meat with a bone attached; a rib or neck chop. **2** a slice of veal. **3** a rissole of minced meat or flaked fish. [from Old French *costelette*, little rib, from Latin *costa*, rib]

cut-off *noun* **1** the point at which something is cut off or separated. **2** a stopping of a flow or supply.

cut-out *noun* **1** something cut out of a newspaper, etc. **2** a safety device for breaking an electrical circuit.

cutter¹ *noun* a person or thing that cuts.

cutter² *noun* **1** a small, single-masted sailing ship. **2** a ship's boat. **3** a motor launch sometimes armed. [from CUT]

cut-throat — *adj.* **1** *said of competition, etc* very keen and aggressive. **2** *said of a card game* played by three people. — *noun* **1** a murderer. **2** a long-bladed razor with a handle.

cutting — *noun* **1** an extract, article, or picture cut from a newspaper, etc. **2** a piece cut from a plant for rooting or grafting. **3** a narrow excavation made through high ground for a road or railway. — *adj.* hurtful; sarcastic.

cuttlefish *noun* (PL. **cuttlefish**, **cuttlefishes**) a 10-armed sea creature related to the squid and octopus, that squirts inky fluid. [from Anglo-Saxon *cudele*]

Cutty Sark a clipper ship built in Dumbarton in 1869 for the China tea trade. It has been preserved in dry dock at Greenwich since 1957.

cutwater *noun* **1** the sharp vertical front edge of a ship's prow. **2** a pointed projection at the base of a bridge support.

Cuvier, Georges Léopold Chrétien Frédéric Dagobert, Baron (1769–1832) French anatomist, born in Montbéliard. Professor at the Museum of Natural History in Paris and the Collège de France, he also held a number of government posts. Known as the father of comparative anatomy, he originated the natural system of animal classification, and was the first to classify fossils together with living species. A militant anti-evolutionist, he accounted for the fossil record by positing 'catastrophism': a series of extinctions due to periodic global floods after which new forms of life appeared.

Cuzco 1 POP (1990e) 275 000, the capital of Cuzco department, S Peru, lying at an altitude of 3 500m. It is the oldest continuously occupied city in the Americas and was the ancient capital of the Inca empire; it served as the ceremonial capital and was the hub of the 40 000km/ 25 000mi Inca road network. Today it is a World Heritage site. NOTABLE FEATURES colonial churches; monasteries; convents; extensive Inca ruins; cathedral (17c); Church of La Compañía de Jesús (17c); Church of Santo Domingo (17c). **2** a department in S Peru with Cuzco as its capital.

CV *abbrev.* curriculum vitae.

CVO *abbrev.* Commander of the (Royal) Victorian Order.

cwm *noun* **1** in Wales, a valley. **2** *Geog.* a cirque. [from Welsh *cwm*]

CWS *abbrev.* Co-operative Wholesale Society.

cwt *abbrev.* hundredweight. [from Latin *centum*, hundred + *wt*, weight]

CY *abbrev.*, as an international vehicle mark Cyprus.

cyan *noun* **1** a greenish blue. **2** a blue ink used as a primary colour in printing. [from Greek *kyanos*, blue]

cyanide *noun* a salt of hydrocyanic acid (HCN), especially the highly poisonous potassium salt (KCN) used to extract gold and silver. [from Greek *kyanos*, blue (hydrocyanic acid having been first obtained from Prussian blue, a blue dye)]

cyanobacteria blue-green algae. [from Greek *kyanos*, blue]

cyanocobalamin *noun* vitamin B_{12}. [from CYANIDE + COBALT + VITAMIN]

cyanogen *noun Chem.* (FORMULA **NCCN**) compound of carbon and nitrogen, consisting of a colourless inflammable poisonous gas with a smell of bitter almonds, formed by the action of acids on cyanides. [from Greek *kyanos*, blue]

cyanosed *adj.* afflicted or appearing to be afflicted with cyanosis.

cyanosis *noun Pathol.* blueness of the skin caused by lack of oxygen in the blood. [from Greek *kyanos*, blue]

Cybele in mythology, a mother-goddess, especially of wild nature, whose cult originated in Phrygia, and was taken over by the Greeks. She was depicted with a turreted mural crown, and was attended by lions.

cybernetic *adj.* relating to or involving cybernetics.

cybernetics *noun* the comparative study of communication and automatic control processes in mechanical or electronic systems (eg machines or computers) and biological systems (eg the nervous system of animals, especially humans). [from Greek *kybernetes*, steersman]

cyberpunk *noun* a genre of science fiction depicting a society rigidly controlled by computer networks and the actions of hackers who rebel against it. [from CYBERNETIC + PUNK]

cyberspace *noun* **1** the computer-generated environment of virtual reality. **2** the space in which electronic communication takes place over computer networks. [from CYBERNETIC + SPACE]

cycad *noun* a tropical or subtropical gymnosperm (cone-bearing plant), more closely resembling a palm than a conifer, and having an unbranched trunk covered with the remains of old leaf bases, and a crown of tough leathery leaves. The cycads are living representatives of a much more widespread group that flourished 100 to 150 million years ago. [from Greek *koix*, palm, from a misreading of the plural *koikas*]

Cyclades, Greek **Kikládhes** POP (1991) 95 000, a Greek island group in the Aegean Sea. The islands lie between the Peloponnese to the W and the Dodecanese to the E. AREA 2 572sq km/ 993sq mi. MAIN ISLANDS Siros, Delos, Tinos, Andros, Mikonos, Milos, Naxos, Paros, Kithnos, Serifos; the islands lie in a circle around Siros. CAPITAL Hermoupolis (on Siros). Several of the islands are popular holiday resorts.

cyclamate *noun* any of a number of sweet chemical compounds formerly used as sweetening agents. [from an invented chemical name]

cyclamen *noun* a plant with white, pink, or red flowers with turned-back petals. [from Greek *kuklaminos*]

cyclamen

cycle — *noun* **1** a constantly repeating series of events or processes. **2** *Physics* one of a regularly repeated set of similar changes, eg in the movement of a wave. The duration of one cycle is equal to the *period* of the motion, and the rate at which a cycle is repeated per unit time is equal to its *frequency*. One hertz represents a frequency of one cycle per second. **3** a series of poems, songs, plays, etc centred on a particular person or happening. **4** a bicycle or motor cycle. — *verb intrans.* **1** to ride a bicycle. **2** to happen in cycles. [from Greek *kyklos*, circle]

cyclic or **cyclical** *adj.* **1** occurring in cycles. **2** *Chem., said of a compound* having atoms forming a closed ring.

cyclically *adv.* in a cyclical way.

cycling the riding of a bicycle for fitness, pleasure, or as a sport. The first cycle race was in Paris in 1868, and won by James Moore of England. There are several popular forms of cycling as a sport. In *time trials* cyclists race against the clock. *Cyclo-cross* is a mixture of cycling and cross-country running, with the bike on the shoulder. *Track racing* takes place on purpose-built concrete or wooden velodromes. *Criteriums* are races around town or city centres. *Road races* are normally in excess of 150km/100mi in length, and take place either from one point to another, or involve several circuits around a predetermined road course. *Stage races* involve many days' racing, each consisting of 150km/100mi or more. The most famous cycle race is the Tour de France.

cyclist *noun* the rider of a bicycle or motor cycle.

cycad

cyclo- *combining form* forming words meaning: **1** circle; ring; cycle. **2** *Chem.* cyclic compound. **3** bicycle. [from Greek *kyklos*, circle]

cyclo-cross *noun* a cross-country bicycle race in the course of which bicycles have to be carried over natural obstacles.

cyclometer *noun* a device for recording the revolutions of a wheel, used on a bicycle to measure the distance travelled. [cyclo- + -meter]

cyclone *noun* **1** *Meteorol.* an area of low atmospheric pressure in which winds spiral inward towards a central low, blowing in an anticlockwise direction in the northern hemisphere and a clockwise direction in the southern hemisphere. Cyclones are often associated with stormy weather. — Also called *depression, low.* **2** a violent tropical storm caused by such an area of low atmospheric pressure, and accompanied by torrential rain and extremely strong winds, often causing widespread destruction and loss of life. [from Greek *kyklon*, a whirling round]

cyclonic *adj.* relating to or characteristic of a cyclone.

cyclopedia *or* **cyclopaedia** *noun* an encyclopedia.

Cyclops (PL. **Cyclopes**) in Greek mythology, a race of one-eyed giants who worked as smiths and were associated with volcanic activity. In the *Odyssey*, the Cyclops Polyphemus is outwitted and blinded by Odysseus, and hurls rocks into the sea at the departing ship. [from Greek *cyclops*, round-eyed]

cyclostyle — *noun* a duplicating machine that reproduces from a stencil. — *verb* to reproduce by means of a cyclostyle. [from CYCLO- + Latin *stylus*, writing tool]

cyclotron *noun* *Physics* an apparatus for accelerating charged atomic particles in a magnetic field. [from CYCLO- + -tron, denoting particle accelerator]

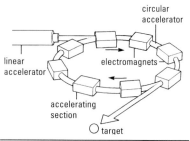

cyclotron

cygnet *noun* a young swan. [from Greek *kyknos*, swan]

Cygnus *Astron.* the Swan, a large northern constellation that contains *Cygnus A*, a double galaxy that is one of the strongest radio sources in the sky, and *Cygnus X-1*, an intense X-ray source that may be the first known example of a black hole. The constellation's brightest star is Deneb.

cylinder *noun* **1** *Geom.* a solid figure of uniform circular cross-section, in which the curved surface is at right angles to the base. The volume of a cylinder of radius r and height h is equal to $\pi r^2 h$. **2** a container, machine part, or other object of this shape, eg a storage container for compressed gas. **3** *Engineering* in an internal combustion engine, the tubular cylinder within which the chemical energy of the burning fuel is converted to the mechanical energy of a moving piston. [from Greek *kylindros*, roller]

cylindrical *adj.* having the shape of a cylinder.

cyma *or* **cymatium** *noun* an S-shaped or ogee moulding of the cornice in classical orders of architecture. When concave above and convex below it is known as a *cyma recta*; when convex above and concave below it is known as a *cyma reversa*. [from Greek *kyma*, a billow]

cymbal *noun* a plate-like brass percussion instrument, either beaten with a drumstick, or used as one of a pair that are struck together to produce a ringing clash. [from Greek *kymbalon*]

cymbalist *noun* a person who plays the cymbals.

Cymbeline *or* **Cunobelinus** (d.c.43 AD) pro-Roman king of the Catuvellauni tribe from c.10 AD, who from his capital at Camulodunum (Colchester) ruled most of SE Britain. Shakespeare's character in his play of the same name was loosely based on Holinshed's half-historical Cunobelinus.

Cymbeline a play by William Shakespeare (1609–10). A romantic comedy using elements of Roman and British history, it concerns the reconciliation of Imogen both with her father, Cymbeline, King of Britain, and with her husband Posthumus, after much mistaken identity and misunderstanding.

cymbidium *noun* an orchid of the genus *Cymbidium*, native to tropical forests from Asia to Australia. It is widely cultivated for its large showy flowers, which are much used in floristry and as cut flowers. [from Latim *cymba*, boat]

cyme *noun Bot.* an inflorescence (flowering shoot) in which the main stem and each of its branches ends in a flower, and all subsequent flowers develop from lateral buds arising below the apical flowers. [from Greek *kyma*, wave]

Cymochles the lascivious brother of Pyrochles and husband of Acrasia in Spenser's *The Faerie Queene*, who is an enemy of Christianity.

cymose *adj.* bearing cymes, or in the form of a cyme.

Cymric — *adj.* of or belonging to Wales, its people or language. — *noun* the Welsh language. [from Welsh *Cymru*, Wales]

Cynewulf (8c) Anglo-Saxon poet, from Mercia or Northumberland. The works attributed to him are restricted to the four poems, *Juliana, Christ, Elene,* and *The Fates of the Apostles*, which have his name worked into the text in runes.

cynic *noun* **1** a person who habitually doubts or questions human goodness or sincerity. **2** *Philos.* see CYNICS. [from Greek *kyon*, dog]

cynical *adj.* characterized by habitual scepticism about human goodness.

cynically *adv.* in a cynical way.

cynicism *noun* **1** the attitude, beliefs, or behaviour of a cynic. **2** a cynical act, remark, etc.

Cynics a discontinuous group of philosophers, early members of which included Antisthenes and Diogenes of Sinope, influential in Greece and Rome 4c BC–6c AD. They led and promoted an ascetic life in conformity with nature, avoiding all societal conventions and artificially-induced desires. Their thought was influential on Stoicism.

cynosure *noun* the focus of attention; the centre of attraction. [from Greek *Kynosoura*, dog's tail, ie the Little Bear constellation, used as a guide by sailors]

Cynthia a female first name, dating from the 17c classical revival. [from Greek *Kynthis*, an epithet of the goddess Artemis, who was said to be born on Mount Kynthos]

cypher same as CIPHER

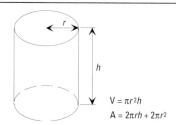

$$V = \pi r^2 h$$
$$A = 2\pi rh + 2\pi r^2$$

cylinder

cypress *noun* a slim, dark green coniferous tree, sometimes associated with death and mourning. [from Greek *kyparissos*]

Cyprian, St, originally **Thascius Caecilius Cyprianus** (c.200–258 AD) Christian bishopmartyr, born in Carthage. He became a Christian in c.245, and was Bishop of Carthage from 248, but he soon gained many enemies for trying to restore strict discipline. He fled from Roman persecution, and eventually suffered martyrdom under Valerian (reigned 253–60), but his writings remained influential. His feast day is 16 Sep.

Cypriot — *noun* **1** a native of Cyprus, an E Mediterranean island. **2** the dialect of Greek spoken in Cyprus. — *adj.* of or belonging to Cyprus, its people or language.

Cyprus, Greek **Kypros**, Turkish **Kibris**, official name **Republic of Cyprus**, Greek **Kypriaki Dimokratia**, Turkish **Kibris Cumhuriyeti** POP (1992e) 716 000, an island republic in the NE Mediterranean Sea, lying c.80km/50mi S of Turkey. It is the third largest island in the Mediterranean Sea. AREA 9 251sq km/3 571sq mi. CAPITAL Nicosia. CHIEF TOWNS Larnaca, Limassol, Kyrenia; Famagusta (the chief port prior to the 1974 Turkish invasion) is now under Turkish occupation, and declared closed by the Cyprus government. TIME ZONE GMT +3. The population consists of c.77% Greek-speaking Orthodox Christians and 18% Turkish-speaking Muslims; almost all Turks live in the N sector (37% of the island). OFFICIAL LANGUAGES Greek and Turkish, with English widely spoken. CURRENCY the Cyprus pound. PHYSICAL DESCRIPTION the Kyrenia Mts extend 150km/90mi along the N coast, rising to 1 024m at Mt Kyparissovouno; the forest-covered Troödos Mts are in the SW, rising to 1 951m at Mt Olympus; the fertile Mesaoria plain extends across the island centre; the coastline is indented, with several long, sandy beaches. CLIMATE a typical Mediterranean climate with hot, dry summers and warm, wet winters; average annual rainfall is 500mm, with great local variation; average daily temperatures (Jul–Aug) range from 22°C on the Troödos Mts to 29°C on the central plain; winters are mild, with an average temperature of 4°C in higher parts of the mountains, and 10°C on the plain; there is snow on higher land in winter. HISTORY Cyprus has a recorded history of 4 000 years, its rulers have included the Greeks, Ptolemies, Persians, Romans, Byzantines, Arabs, Franks, Venetians, Turks, and British; became a British Crown Colony in 1925; Greek Cypriot demands for union with Greece (*enosis*) led to guerrilla warfare against the British administration, under Grivas and Makarios, and a four-year state of emergency (1955–9); achieved independence in 1960, with Britain retaining sovereignty over the military bases at Akrotiri and Dhekelia; there was Greek–Turkish fighting throughout the 1960s, with a UN peacekeeping force sent in 1964; there was further terrorist activity in 1971; the 1974 Turkish invasion led to occupation of over one third of the island, with displacement of over 160 000 Greek Cypriots; the island was divided into two parts by the Attila Line, from the NW coast above Pomos to Famagusta in the E, cutting through Nicosia where it is called the Green Line; peace talks on reunification were inconclusive in both 1990 and 1992; Cyprus and Greece agreed upon a common defence policy in 1993 and Turkey affirmed its commitment to a political agreement with Cyprus. GOVERNMENT governed by a President (head of state), elected for a five-year term by the Greek community, and a House of Representatives of 80 elected members; Turkish members ceased to attend in 1983, when the Turkish community declared itself independent (as the 'Turkish Republic of Northern Cyprus', recognized only by Turkey). ECONOMY the Greek Cypriot area has now largely recovered from the 1974 invasion, with light manufacturing a main growth sector; paper, paperboard products; chemicals; food and wine; clothing;

footwear; cigarettes; petroleum refining; cement production; electricity generation; mineral exports include asbestos, clay, chrome, and umber; tourism is also recovering and now accounts for c.15% of national income; the Turkish Cypriot economy is heavily dependent on agriculture, producing potatoes, citrus fruit, grapes, cereals, carobs, vegetables, olives, and almonds; irrigation schemes aim to increase the area under cultivation.

Cyprus

Cyrankiewicz, Jozef (1911–89) Polish politician. He became Secretary of the Socialist Party in Cracow in 1935. Taken prisoner by the Germans (1939), he escaped and organized resistance, but was sent to Auschwitz in 1941. In 1945 he became Secretary-General of the Socialist Party, and after two periods as Prime Minister (1947–52, 1954–70), became Chairman of the Council of State (1970–2) and of the All-Poland Peace Committee (1973).

Cyrano de Bergerac, Savinien (1619–55) French satirist and dramatist, born in Paris. In his youth he fought more than a thousand duels, mostly on account of his extremely large nose. His works include satirical accounts of visits to the Moon and Sun, published posthumously as *Histoire comique des états et empires de la lune* and *Histoire comique des états et empires du soleil*. These stories suggested the character 'Gulliver' to Jonathan Swift.

Cyrano De Bergerac 1 a French play by Edmond Rostand (1897). **2** a French film directed by Jean-Paul Rappeneau (1990). Combining bold adventure and exquisite pathos, it is the tale of a skilled swordsman and poet (played in the film by Gérard Depardieu) who, ashamed of his oversized nose, generously woos his lady-love on behalf of another man.

Cyrenaics a school of Greek philosophers active in the 4c–3c BC, founded by Aristippus of Cyrene. They believed that the immediate sensation of pleasure is the only good, that all such sensations are equal in worth, and that past and future pleasures have no present value.

Cyrene a prosperous Greek city-state in N Africa, famous in antiquity for the export of silphium, a plant used in ancient medicine. It was ruled over by the Ptolemies and became part of the Roman province of Cyrene in 74 BC. It is now a World Heritage site, and the location of the village of Shahhat, E Libya.

Cyril, St (827–69) Greek Christian missionary, born in Thessalonica. He and his brother St Methodius (826–85) were known as the 'Apostles of the Slavs'. Cyril, traditionally the inventor of the Cyrillic alphabet, first worked among the Tartar Khazars, and Methodius among the Bulgarians of Thrace and Moesia. In Moravia they made Slav translations of the Scriptures and chief liturgical books. After Cyril's death, Methodius continued as Bishop of Moravia to evangelize the Slavs, and he gained the approval of Pope John VIII when he was called to Rome (879) to justify his celebration of the Mass in the native tongue. Their feast day is 7 Jul.

Cyril of Alexandria, St (AD 376–444) Greek theologian, a Doctor of the Church, born in Alexandria. He became Patriarch of Alexandria (412), and vigorously implemented orthodox Christian teaching. He expelled the Jews from the city (415), and relentlessly persecuted the Patriarch of Constantinople, Nestorius (d.451), who was deposed at the Council of Ephesus (431). Pope Leo XIII declared him a Doctor of the Church in 1882. His feast day is 9 Jun (E) or 27 Jun (W).

Cyril a male first name, also the name of Greek evangelists who devised the Cyrillic alphabet. [an English form of Greek *Kyrillos*, derived from *kyrios*, lord]

Cyrillic *adj.* of or in the alphabet used for Russian, Bulgarian, and related languages, said to have been invented by St Cyril.

Cyrus II, also called **the Great** (c.585–529 BC) the founder of the Achaemenid Persian Empire, and son of Cambyses I. He defeated the Medes (549 BC), became King of Persia (548 BC), and took Lydia (c.546 BC) and Babylon (539 BC). His empire eventually ran from the Mediterranean to the Hindu Kush. He had a policy of religious conciliation: the nations who had been carried into captivity in Babylon along with the Jews were restored to their native countries, and allowed to take their gods with them.

cyst *noun* **1** *Anat.* an abnormal sac or closed cavity that contains fluid, semi-solid material, or gas, eg an ovarian cyst, which forms spontaneously, or a sebaceous cyst, which forms in the skin when the duct of a sebaceous gland becomes blocked. **2** *Biol.* the dormant or resting stage in the life cycle of certain bacteria, protozoa, or other organisms which is surrounded by a tough outer layer that protects it from unfavourable environmental conditions. [from Greek *kystis*, bladder, pouch]

cysteine *noun Biochem.* an amino acid that is found in proteins.

cystic *adj.* **1** relating to or like a cyst. **2** being enclosed within or having a cyst. **3** relating to the gall bladder or urinary bladder.

cystic fibrosis *Medicine* a hereditary disease in which the exocrine glands (especially of the lungs, pancreas, mouth, and intestinal tract) produce abnormally thick mucus that blocks the bronchi, pancreas, and intestinal glands, causing recurring bronchitis and other respiratory problems, impaired absorption of food, and (in children) failure to gain weight.

cystine *noun Biochem.* an amino acid that is found in proteins, especially keratin. [from CYST]

cystitis *noun Medicine* inflammation of the urinary bladder, usually caused by bacterial infection, and more common in women than in men. The main symptoms are a desire to pass urine frequently, and pain or a burning sensation when passing urine.

-cyte *combining form* denoting a cell: *erythrocyte*. [from Greek *kytos*, vessel]

cyto- *combining form* forming words denoting a cell. [from Greek *kytos*, vessel]

cytochrome *noun Biochem.* in the cells of living organisms, any of a group of substances that play an important role in the breakdown of carbohydrates to release energy.

cytogenetics *noun Genetics* the scientific study of the relationship between inheritance and cell structure, especially the origin, structure, and function of chromosomes, and their effects on inheritance in populations.

cytokinesis *noun Genetics* during the last stages of cell division (when the nucleus has already divided), the division of the cytoplasm of the cell into two parts, resulting in the formation of two daughter cells which may or may not be equal in size.

cytokinin *noun Bot.* any of various plant hormones that control growth by stimulating the

division of plant cells. [from CYTO- + Greek *kineein*, to move]

cytological *adj.* relating to cytology.

cytologist *noun* an expert in cytology.

cytology *noun* the study of plant and animal cells.

cytoplasm *noun Biol.* that part of a living cell, excluding the nucleus, that is enclosed by the cell membrane. The cytoplasm contains a range of organelles (specialized structures with a specific function) such as mitochondria, ribosomes, and (in plants only) chloroplasts. [from CYTO- + Greek *plasma*, body]

cytosine *noun Biochem.* a base derived from pyrimidine, and one of the four bases found in nucleic acids (DNA and RNA).

cytoskeleton *noun Biol.* in the cytoplasm of a living cell, a network of protein filaments that forms the structural framework of the cell, and is also responsible for cytoplasmic streaming (the movement of cytoplasm from one part of the cell to another).

cytosol *noun Biol.* the soluble component of the cytoplasm.

cytotoxic *adj. Biol.* describing any agent, especially a drug, that destroys or prevents the division of cells, and is used in chemotherapy to treat various forms of cancer.

czar, *etc* see TSAR, etc.

Czech — *noun* **1** a native of former Czechoslovakia or the Czech Republic (since its separation from Slovakia in 1993), or formerly of Bohemia or Moravia. **2** one of the two principal languages of the Czechs (the other being Slovak). — *adj.* of or relating to the Czechs or their language. [from the Polish spelling *czech*]

Czech Legion a corps of 40 000 Czech volunteers and ex-prisoners-of-war in Russia, who rose in revolt against the Bolsheviks (May 1918) while being transported home along the Trans-Siberian railway. They seized many towns along the railway, and soon controlled much of Siberia, a revolt that sparked off the first phase of the Russian Civil War.

Czechoslovakia, Czech **Československo**, official name **Czech and Slovak Federative Republic**, Czech **Česka a Slovenska Federadivni Republika** the former federal state which consisted of the Czech Republic and the Slovak Republic. The capital was Prague. HISTORY formerly ruled by Austrian Habsburgs; the Czech lands united with Slovakia to form the separate state of Czechoslovakia in 1918; Germany occu-

The Cyrillic Alphabet					
Letter		Usual trans-literation	Letter		Usual trans-literation
А	а	a	П	п	p
Б	б	b	Р	р	r
В	в	v	С	с	s
Г	г	g	Т	т	t
Д	д	d	У	у	u
Е	е	e	Ф	ф	f
Ё	ё	ë	Х	х	h, kh, ch
Ж	ж	ž, zh	Ц	ц	c, ts
З	з	z	Ч	ч	č, ch
И	и	i	Ш	ш	š, sh
Й	й	j	Щ	щ	šč, shch
К	к	k	Ы	ы	y
Л	л	l	Ь	ь	'
М	м	m	Ъ	ъ	''
Н	н	n	Э	э	è
О	о	o	Ю	ю	ju, yu
			Я	я	ja, ya

pied the Sudetenland region in 1938, and then the whole country; the government was in exile in London during World War II; achieved independence with the loss of some territory to the USSR in 1946; communist rule followed the 1948 coup; an attempt at liberalization by Dubček was terminated in 1968 by the intervention of Warsaw Pact troops; a strong protest movement continued, culminating in the fall from power of the Communist Party in 1989; the Czech and Slovak republics were granted increasing autonomy; in 1993 separate states were created.

Czech Republic, Czech **České Zeme** POP (1991e) 10.3m, a landlocked republic in E Europe, divided into eight regions. It comprises the former provinces of Bohemia, Silesia, and Moravia, and from 1918 until 1993 it formed part of the former Czechoslovakia. AREA 78 864sq km/ 30 441sq mi. It is bounded W by Germany, N and E by Poland, SE by Slovakia, and S by Austria. CAPITAL Prague. CHIEF TOWNS Brno, Plzeň, Ostrava, Olomouc. TIME ZONE GMT +1. Most of

Czech Republic

the population are Czech, with a small Slovak minority; the chief religion is Roman Catholicism. OFFICIAL LANGUAGE Czech. CURRENCY the koruna. PHYSICAL DESCRIPTION Bohemia and W Moravia are separated from E Moravia and Slovakia by the R Morava valley; the W range of the Carpathians rise in the E; drained by the Morava, Moldau, Elbe, and Oder rivers; there are many lakes; the land is richly wooded, chiefly with mixed and coniferous forests. CLIMATE continental, with warm, humid summers and cold, dry winters; winter snow lies for 40–100 days. HISTORY became an independent republic in 1993 following the dissolution of Czechoslovakia in 1992. GOVERNMENT a Prime Minister and the Council of Ministers exercise executive power; a President is elected by the bicameral parliament which consists of a Chamber of Deputies and a Senate. ECONOMY iron, steel, chemicals, machinery, glass, vehicles, cement, armaments, wood, paper, beer; steel production around the Ostrava coalfields; agriculture produces sugar beet, potatoes, wheat, barley, and maize; there are large dams and reservoirs on rivers for energy and water conservation; large quantity of mineral springs has led to the development of many health spas.

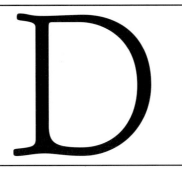

D¹ *or* d *noun* (PL. **Ds, D's, d's**) **1** the fourth letter of the English alphabet. **2** (*usually* **D**) the fourth highest grade or quality, or a mark indicating this. **3** (**D**) *Mus.* **a** the second note in the scale of C major. **b** a musical key with the note D as its base. **4** (**D**) the D-shaped mark on a billiards table.

D² *abbrev.* **1** *North Amer., esp. US* Democrat. **2** *as an international vehicle mark* Deutschland, Germany. **3** *Cards* diamonds. See also 3-D.

D³ *symbol* **1** the Roman numeral for 500. **2** *Chem.* deuterium.

d¹ *abbrev.* **1** deci-. **2** a penny or pence (in the UK before 1971). [from Latin *denarius*] see also s.

d. *abbrev.* **1** daughter. **2** died.

'd *contr.* **1** would: *I'd go.* **2** had: *he'd gone.* **3** *colloq.* did: *where'd he go?*

D1 and D2 formats videotape recording systems using digital rather than analogue techniques, developed by Sony (1987) and Ampex (1988) respectively.

DA *abbrev.* (PL. **DAs, DA's**) *North Amer., esp. US* District Attorney.

da *abbrev.* deca-.

dab¹ — *verb* (**dabbed, dabbing**) **1** *intrans., trans.* to touch lightly and usually repeatedly with a cloth, etc. **2** (**dab something on** *or* **off**) to spread it on or remove it with light touches of a cloth, etc. — *noun* **1** a small amount of something creamy or liquid. **2** a light, gentle touch. **3** a gentle blow. **4** (**dabs**) *slang* fingerprints. [from Middle English *dabben*; probably imitative]

dab² *noun* a small brown European flatfish with rough scales. [from Old French *dabbe*]

dab³
— **a dab hand** an expert.

dabble *verb* **1** *trans., intrans.* to move or shake (one's hand, foot, etc) about in water, especially playfully. **2** *intrans.* (**dabble at** *or* **in** *or* **with something**) to do it or study it without serious effort. [from DAB¹ 1 or Dutch *dabbelen*]

dabbler *noun* a person who dabbles in some activity.

dabchick *noun* a small duck-like bird, the little grebe.

da capo *Mus.* an indication to the performer to go back to the beginning of the piece. [from Italian *da capo*, from the beginning]

Dacca see DHAKA.

dace *noun* (PL. **dace, daces**) a small European river fish. [from Old French *dars*, dart]

dacha *noun* a country house or cottage in Russia, especially one provided for the use of a person of importance. [from Russian *dach*, originally meaning 'gift' (especially from a ruler)]

dachshund *noun* a breed of small dog with a long body and very short legs. [from German *Dachs*, badger + *Hund*, dog]

Dacia the name given in antiquity to the area N of the Danube roughly corresponding to modern Romania. It was conquered by the Romans in the early 2c AD .

dacoit *or* **dakoit** *noun* an armed robber or bandit, one of a gang in India or Burma, especially in the 18c and 19c. [from Hindi *dākait*, robber]

dactyl *noun Poetry* a foot consisting of one long or stressed syllable followed by two short or unstressed ones: *'Think of her / mournfully'* consists of two dactyls. [from Greek *daktylos*, finger, from the similarity between the lengths of the syllables in a dactyl and the lengths of the bones in a finger (one long and two short)]

dactylic *adj. Poetry* consisting of or written in dactyls.

dad *noun colloq.* a father. [from the sound *da da* made by a baby]

Dada *or* **Dadaism** a movement in art and literature founded in Zürich in 1916, which turned away from all traditional forms and styles. It was founded by artists and writers including the poet Tristan Tzara and the painter Hans Arp. Leading figures included Max Ernst, Francis Picabia, Man Ray, and Marcel Duchamp, whose *Fountain* (1917, a porcelain urinal) is one of the best-known Dada works. [from French *dada*, hobby-horse]

daddy *noun* (PL. **daddies**) *colloq.* **1** a father. **2** the oldest, biggest, best, worst, etc example of something: *a daddy of a thunderstorm*. [from DAD]

daddy-long-legs *noun Brit. colloq.* a cranefly.

dado *noun* (PL. **dadoes, dados**) **1** the lower part of the wall of a room when decorated differently from the upper part. **2** *Archit.* the plain square part of the base of a column or pedestal. [from Italian *dado*, dice]

Daedalus in Greek mythology, an Athenian inventor, who worked for King Minos in Crete and constructed the labyrinth. He was later imprisoned by Minos but made wings from wax and feathers for himself and his son Icarus, and escaped to Sicily.

daemon *noun* **1** a spirit occupying a position halfway between gods and men. **2** a spirit which guards a place or takes care of or helps a person. See also DEMON. [from Greek *daimon*]

daffodil — *noun* **1** a flowering plant of the genus *Narcissus* that has an underground bulb and produces a single bright yellow flower consisting of a central trumpet surrounded by six petals. It occurs wild in many parts of Europe, and there are many cultivated garden varieties that vary widely in colour and shape. **2** the flower of this plant. **3** a pale yellow. — *adj.* pale yellow. [from Middle English *affodille*; the initial *d* is unexplained]

daft *adj. Brit. colloq.* **1** silly or foolish. **2** insane or mad. **3** (**daft about** *or* **on something**) enthusias-

tic about it or keen on it. [from Anglo-Saxon *gedæfte*, meek, mild]

daftly *adv.* in a daft or silly way.

daftness *noun* being daft; silliness.

Dagda in Celtic mythology, a protective Irish deity, noted for his enormous club on wheels which both killed and restored to life, and for his cauldron which inspired and rejuvenated. Oengus and Brigit were his children.

dagger *noun* **1** *Hist.* a knife or short sword with a pointed end, used for stabbing. **2** *in books, etc* the symbol †, used as a reference mark.
— **at daggers drawn** openly showing anger or dislike and on the point of fighting.
look daggers at someone to give them a fierce or angry look.

dago *noun* (PL. **dagoes**) *offensive* a person of Spanish, Portuguese, Italian or S American origin. [probably from Spanish *Diego*, James]

Daguerre, Louis (Jacques Mandé) (1789–1851) French photographic pioneer, born in Cormeilles. He was a scene painter for the opera in Paris. From 1826 onwards, and partly in conjunction with Joseph Niepce (1765–1833), he perfected the photographic process known as the *daguerreotype*.

daguerreotype *noun* **1** an early type of photography invented by Louis Daguerre, which used mercury vapour to develop an exposure of silver iodide on a copper plate. **2** a photograph made by this method.

Dahl, Roald (1913–90) British writer, born in Llandaff, S Wales, of Norwegian parents. He worked for the Shell Oil Company in London and Africa, then served as a fighter pilot in the RAF during World War II. He specialized in writing short stories of unexpected horror and macabre surprise, such as in *Someone Like You* (1953) and *Kiss, Kiss* (1960). His children's books display a similar taste for the grotesque, eg *James and the Giant Peach* (1961) and *Charlie and the Chocolate Factory* (1964).

dahl see DAL.

dahlia *noun* a garden plant with large brightly coloured flowers, some varieties having ball-like heads with many petals. [named after the 18c Swedish botanist Anders Dahl]

Dahomey a W African kingdom based on its capital at Abomey, which in the late 17c and early 18c extended its authority from the coast to the interior, to the W of the Yoruba states. In the 1720s, the cavalry of the Oyo kingdom of the Yoruba devastated Dahomey, but when the Oyo Empire collapsed in the early 19c, Dahomey regained its power. The state was annexed by the French in 1883, and regained its independence in 1960. It was renamed Benin in 1975.

Daibutsu any Japanese statue of Buddha. Notable examples in Japan include the bronze figure cast in 1252 at Kamakura, 11.5m high.

Dáil or **Dáil Éireann** noun the lower house of the parliament of the Republic of Ireland. [from Irish Dáil, assembly of Ireland]

daily — adj. **1** happening, appearing, etc every day, or every day except Sunday, or now often every day except Saturday and Sunday. **2** relating to a single day. — adv. every day. — noun (PL. **dailies**) **1** a newspaper published every day except Sunday. **2** Brit. colloq. a person, usually a woman, who is paid to clean and tidy a house regularly, but not necessarily every day. [from DAY]

daily bread the money, food, etc one needs to live.

daily dozen old use physical exercises performed every day for the sake of one's health.

Daimler, Gottlieb (Wilhelm) (1834–1900) German engineer, born in Schorndorf. He worked from 1872 on improving the gas engine, and in 1885 designed one of the earliest roadworthy motor cars. In 1890 he founded the Daimler Automobile Company at Cannstatt.

Daimler, German **Daimler-Motoren-Gelleschaft** an automobile company founded in Germany in 1890 by Gottlieb Daimler. It produced the first Mercedes car in 1899. In 1926 it merged with Benz to form Daimler-Benz, and the diesel-powered Mercedes-Benz was produced in 1936.

daintily adv. with a dainty or neat manner.

daintiness noun being dainty or neat.

dainty — adj. (**daintier, daintiest**) **1** small and pretty, and usually delicate. **2** small and neat. **3** said of food particularly nice to eat. **4** often derog. very, or excessively, careful and sensitive about what one does or says. — noun (PL. **dainties**) something small and nice to eat, especially a small cake or sweet. [from Old French daintie, worthiness]

daiquiri noun a drink made with rum, lime juice and sugar. [from Daiquiri in Cuba]

dairy noun (PL. **dairies**) **1** the building on a farm where milk is cooled and temporarily stored before being transported by tanker to a commercial processing plant or factory. Butter and cheese are now only rarely made at farm dairies. **2** a commercial processing plant or factory that processes, bottles, and distributes milk received from farms, and manufactures other dairy products, eg cream, butter, cheese, and yoghurt. [from Middle English daierie, from daie, dairymaid]

dairy cattle Agric. cows that are kept to produce milk, and to rear calves in order to maintain a dairy herd, eg Friesian and Jersey breeds.

dairy farm a farm which specializes in producing milk, etc.

dairy farmer a farmer working in dairy products.

dairymaid noun Hist. a milkmaid.

dairyman or **dairywoman** noun a person who looks after the dairy cows on a farm.

dais noun a raised platform in a hall, eg for speakers at a meeting. [from Old French deis]

Daisy a female first name, after the name of the flower.

daisy noun (PL. **daisies**) **1** any of various common wild and cultivated flowering plants belonging to the sunflower family (Compositae), eg oxeye daisy, Michaelmas daisy. **2** the common daisy (Bellis perennis), which has a flowerhead with a yellow centre consisting of many tiny flowers (florets), surrounded by white bracts. It is a common lawn weed in Europe. [from Anglo-Saxon dæges eage, day's eye]

Daisy Miller a novel by Henry James (1878). It focuses on the experiences of an American girl in Europe who is unaware of the code of behaviour governing the societies in which she moves.

daisy-wheel noun in a typewriter, etc, a metal disc divided into separate spokes, each with a letter of the alphabet at the end, the disc rotating so that the letter printed corresponds to the letter struck on the keyboard.

Dakar POP (1992e) 1.7m, the capital of Senegal, at the S extremity of the Cape Verde peninsula. It is the second largest seaport in W Africa, serving Senegal and Mauritania. HISTORY founded in 1857; capital of French W Africa in 1902; between 1924 and 1946 it was part of a separate area known as Dakar and Dependencies; held by Vichy forces during World War II; became capital of Senegal in 1958. NOTABLE FEATURES Great Mosque; cathedral; Ethnographical Museum; markets.

dal or **dahl** or **dhal** noun **1** any of various edible dried split pea-like seeds. **2** a cooked dish made of any of these seeds. [from Hindi dal, to split]

Daladier, Edouard (1884–1970) French politician, born in Carpentras. In 1936 he was Minister of War in the Popular Front Cabinet, and as Premier again (1938–40) supported appeasement policies and signed the Munich Pact. After his resignation, he became successively War and Foreign Minister, and on the fall of France was arrested and interned until 1945, then continued in politics until 1958.

Dalai Lama the title of the hierarch of the Geluga tradition of Tibetan Buddhism, and political leader of Tibet from the 17c to 1959. It was first given by the Mongol ruler Altan Khan to Sonam Gyamtsho (1543–88); the fifth Dalai Lama, Ngawang Lopsang Gyatso (1617–82), became political leader. Each successive Dalai Lama is held to be a reincarnation of the previous one, and is also regarded as a manifestation of the Bodhisattva Avalokiteshavara. The fourteenth incarnation is Tensin Gymatsho (1935–), who ruled in Tibet from 1940 until 1959, when he went into exile in India; the Tibetans still regard him as their spiritual leader. He won the Nobel Peace Prize in 1989. [from Mongolian dalai, ocean + Tibetan lama, high priest]

Dalap-Uliga-Darrit POP (1990e) 20 000, the capital of the Marshall Is. It is situated on Majuro atoll.

Dale, Sir Henry Hallett (1875–1968) English physiologist and pharmacologist, born in London. Director of the National Institute for Medical Research in London from 1928, he discovered acetylcholine, and shared the 1936 Nobel Prize for Physiology or Medicine with Otto Loewi (1873–1961) for work on the chemical transmission of nerve impulses.

Dale, Lily the heroine of Anthony Trollope's The Small House at Allington, who is jilted by her fiancé, Adolphus Crosbie. She also features in The Last Chronicle of Barset, where she continues to be sought after by her childhood sweetheart, Johnny Eames.

Dale a male first name, after the surname. [from DALE]

dale noun a valley, especially in the N of England. [from Anglo-Saxon dæl]

d'Alembert see ALEMBERT, JEAN LE ROND D'.

Dalhousie, James Andrew Broun Ramsay, 1st Marquis of (1812–60) Scottish soldier and administrator in India, born in Dalhousie Castle, Midlothian. He became an MP (1837) and President of the Board of Trade (1845). As Governor-General of India (1847–56), he encouraged the development of railways and irrigation works, and annexed Satara (1847) and Punjab (1849). However the annexation of Oudh (1856) caused resentment which fuelled the 1857 Rebellion.

Dali, Salvador (Felipe Jacinto) (1904–89) Spanish artist, born in Figueras. He joined the Surrealists in Paris (1928), and became one of the principal figures of the movement. His study of

abnormal psychology and dream symbolism led him to represent 'paranoiac' objects in landscapes remembered from his Spanish boyhood. In 1940 he settled in the USA, became a Catholic, and devoted his art to symbolic religious paintings. He wrote The Secret Life of Salvador Dali (1942), and collaborated with Luis Buñuel in the surrealist films Un Chien Andalou (An Andalusian Dog, 1928) and L'Age d'Or (The Golden Age, 1930). His paintings include The Persistence of Memory (known as the 'Limp Watches', 1931, New York) and Christ of St John of the Cross (1951, Glasgow).

Dalian or **Luda, Lu-ta, Dairen, Dalien** POP (1990) 2.5m, a port city in Liaoning province, NE China. It has been designated a special economic zone and lies at the centre of a fruit-growing area. The city's deep, natural harbour is silt-free and ice-free. Resort beaches are located nearby. HISTORY the port was built between 1899 and 1930 by the Japanese; occupied by Soviet forces from 1945 to 1954.

Dalit noun a member of the former Untouchable class in India. [Hindi]

Dallas POP (1990) 2.6m, the seat of Dallas County, NE Texas, USA, and the seventh largest city in the country. It is situated on the Trinity R. Dallas is the commercial and financial focus of the SW, and is also a cultural, educational, and artistic centre. HISTORY founded in 1841; achieved city status in 1871; President John F Kennedy was assassinated in Dallas in 1963.

dalliance noun idle wasting of time.

Dalloway, Mrs a novel by Virginia Woolf (1925). It describes one day in the life of a wealthy London woman whose character is revealed as she prepares for her party.

dally verb intrans. (**dallies, dallied**) **1** to waste time idly or frivolously. **2** (**dally with someone**) old use to flirt with them. [from Old French dalier, to chat]

Dalmatia a name applied since early times to the strip of territory in Croatia, Bosnia-Herzegovina, and Montenegro (Yugoslavia) which borders the Adriatic Sea. There are harbours at Zadar, Split, and Dubrovnik. PHYSICAL DESCRIPTION extends from the S end of Pag I to Cavtat, S of Dubrovnik, and is largely mountainous and barren; there are few lines of communication to the interior. HISTORY formerly part of the Greek province of Illyria; settled in the 6c BC; occupied by Slavs in the 7c AD.

Dalmatian noun a large short-haired dog, white with dark spots.

Daloa POP (1975) 265 000, a department in SW central Ivory Coast. AREA 15 200sq km/5 900sq mi.

dal segno Mus. an indication that the performer must go back to the sign ꞏSꞏ. [from Italian dal segno, from the sign]

Dalton, John (1766–1844) English chemist and natural philosopher, born in Eaglesfield, Cumberland. He supported himself as a teacher, while carrying out his scientific researches. In 1794 he described colour blindness (Daltonism), but his chief physical researches were on mixed gases, the force of steam, the elasticity of vapours, and the expansion of gases by heat. His development of the atomic theory of matter elevated chemistry to a quantitative science.

dalton noun Chem. an atomic mass unit. [named after the UK chemist John Dalton]

Dalton's law of partial pressures Chem. a law which states that, in a mixture of gases, the pressure exerted by each gas is the same as that which it would exert if it were the only gas present.

DALY abbrev. disability adjusted life year, a statistical measure used to calculate the number of healthy years lost in an average life-span through premature death or disability.

dam¹ — *noun* **1** a barrier built across a river to hold back the flow of water, eg in order to form a reservoir to store water for domestic or industrial use, or to provide a head of water for a hydro-electric power station. **2** the water confined behind such a structure, often forming a lake or reservoir. — *verb* (**dammed**, **damming**) to hold back with a dam. [probably from Old German dialect *Damm*]

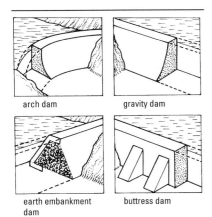

arch dam gravity dam

earth embankment dam buttress dam

types of dam

dam² *noun*, *said of horses, cattle, and sheep* a female parent. [from DAME]

damage — *noun* **1** harm or injury, or loss caused by injury. **2** (**damages**) *Legal* payment due for loss or injury caused by another person, organization, etc. — *verb* to cause harm, injury, or loss to. [from Old French *damage*, from Latin *damnum*, loss]

damaged *adj.* harmed, injured; broken.

damaging *adj.* having a bad effect on a person's reputation.

Daman and Diu POP (1991) 102 000, a Union Territory in W India. AREA 112sq km/43sq mi.

Damascus, Arabic **Dimashq** POP (1990e) 2.7m, the capital of Syria, on the R Barada. It is claimed to be the world's oldest continuously inhabited city. In ancient times it was a great trade and commercial centre. NOTABLE FEATURES medieval citadel (1219); Great Mosque (8c, burned in 1893, then restored). The ancient Via Recta, scene of the conversion of St Paul, runs E–W for 1.5km/1mi with Roman gateways at either end. The city is a World Heritage site.

damask — *noun* a type of cloth, originally silk, now usually linen, with a pattern woven into it, often used for tablecloths, curtains, etc. — *adj.* greyish-pink or greyish-red. [from *Damascus* in Syria, where such cloth was made]

damask rose a sweet-smelling pink or red variety of rose.

Damavand, Mount a volcanic cone in the Elburz Mts, N Iran. HEIGHT 5 670m. It is the highest peak in Iran, and has a permanent snowcap.

Dambulla, Golden Temple of a temple in Dambulla, Sri Lanka, built in the 1c BC into the base of a huge outcrop of wave-shaped rock. The five caverns which form the temple are gilded inside and contain 150 images of Buddha, and frescoes depicting Buddha's life. It is a World Heritage site.

dame *noun* **1** a woman who has been awarded the highest or second-highest class of distinction in any of four British orders of chivalry, or honours for service or merit awarded by the Queen or the Government. See also KNIGHT. **2** *North Amer. slang* a woman. **3** a comic female character in a pantomime, usually played by a man. [from Old French *dame*, from Latin *domina*, lady]

Damian a male first name. [probably from Greek *daman*, to tame or subdue]

Damien, Father Joseph, originally **Joseph de Veuster** (1840–89) Belgian Roman Catholic missionary, born in Tremelo. He is renowned for his work among the lepers of the Hawaiian island of Molokai, where he lived from 1873 until his death from the disease.

damn — *verb* **1** *Relig.* to sentence to never-ending punishment in hell. **2** to declare to be useless or worthless. **3** to suggest or prove the guiltiness of. — *interj.* (**damn it**) an expression of annoyance or disappointment. — *adj. often colloq.*, *for emphasis* annoying; hateful: *the damn cold.* — *adv. colloq.* used for emphasis: *it's damn cold.*
— **as near as damn it** *colloq.* as accurately, closely, etc as possible; acceptably accurate, etc; very nearly.
be damned if one will do something *colloq.* to refuse to do it.
damn all *colloq.* nothing at all.
damn someone *or* **something with faint praise** to praise them so unenthusiastically as to seem disapproving.
not give a damn *colloq.* not to care at all.
[from Latin *damnare*, to condemn]

damnable *adj.* **1** hateful; awful; deserving to be condemned. **2** annoying.

damnably *adv.* annoyingly; very.

damnation — *noun Relig.* **1** never-ending punishment in hell. **2** the act of condemning or state of being condemned to such punishment. — *interj.* an expression of annoyance or disappointment.

damned — *adj.* **1** *Relig.* sentenced to damnation. **2** *colloq.* annoying, hateful, etc. — *adv. colloq.* extremely; very: *damned cold.*
— **do one's damnedest** *colloq.* to do one's utmost.

damning *adj.* **1** very critical. **2** proving or suggesting guilt.

Damocles (4c BC) a legendary courtier of Dionysius the Elder, tyrant of Syracuse (405–367 BC). He extolled the happiness of royalty, but Dionysius showed him the precarious nature of fortune by seating him at a richly-spread table with a keen-edged sword suspended over his head by a single horsehair.

Damon and Pythias *or* **Phintias** (4c BC) two Pythagorean philosophers of Syracuse, remembered as the models of faithful friendship. Condemned to death by Dionysius the Elder, tyrant of Syracuse, Pythias begged to be allowed to go home to arrange his affairs, and Damon pledged his own life for his friend's. Pythias returned just in time to save Damon from death. Struck by so noble an example, Dionysius pardoned Pythias.

damp — *adj.* slightly wet. — *noun* slight wetness, eg in walls or the air, especially if cold and unpleasant. — *verb* **1** to make slightly wet. **2** *Mus.* to press (the strings, or a string, of an instrument) to stop or lessen vibration.
— **damp something down 1** to make (emotions, interest, etc) less strong. **2** to make (a fire) burn more slowly.
[from Middle English *damp*, harmful vapour]

damp-course *or* **damp-proof course** *noun* a horizontal layer of material in a wall of a building, usually near the ground, which stops damp rising through the bricks.

dampen *verb* (**dampened**, **dampening**) **1** to make slightly wet. **2** *trans.*, *intrans.*
— **dampen down** *said of emotions, interest, etc* to become less strong.
dampen something down 1 to make (emotions, interest, etc) less strong. **2** to make (a fire) burn more slowly.

dampener *noun* a person or thing that dampens or causes dampness.

damper *noun* **1** something which lessens enthusiasm, interest, etc. **2** a movable plate which allows the flow of air to a fire, etc to be controlled so that the amount of heat may be altered.
— **put a damper on something** to lessen enthusiasm for it, or interest in it, etc).

Dampier, William (1652–1715) English navigator and buccaneer, born near Yeovil. He journeyed to Newfoundland and the West Indies, and in 1679 joined a band of buccaneers along the Pacific coast of S America. In 1683 he sailed across the Pacific Ocean, visiting the Philippines, China, and Australia. On his return to England, he published his *New Voyage round the World* (1697). He then led a voyage of discovery to the South Seas (1699), where he explored the NW coast of Australia, and gave his name to the Dampier Archipelago and Strait. He made further journeys to the South Seas in 1703 and 1708.

damply *adv.* in a damp way.

dampness *noun* being damp; a damp state.

damp-proof *adj.*, *said of a material or substance* not allowing wetness to get through.

damp-proof course see DAMP-COURSE.

damp squib a disappointingly uninteresting or unsuccessful event.

damsel *noun old use, literary* a girl or young woman. [from Old French *dameisele*]

damselfly *noun* (PL. **damselflies**) a large insect with a long body and two pairs of slender wings, typically held together over the abdomen when at rest. Damselflies are powerful predators, both as aquatic larvae and as flying adults.

damson *noun* **1** a small purple plum. **2** the tree it grows on. [from Latin *Damascenus*, of Damascus in Syria]

Dan, Tribe of one of the 12 tribes of ancient Israel, descended from Jacob's fifth son, whose mother was Rachel's maid Bilhah (Genesis 35). Their territory was vaguely defined, but was initially a coastal plain surrounded by the territories of Ephraim, Benjamin, and Judah; later they were forced to migrate north near the sources of the R Jordan.

Dan. *abbrev.* **1** (*also* **Dan**) *Biblical* the Book of Daniel. **2** Danish.

dan *noun* any of the grades of black belt awarded for particular levels of skill in judo, karate, etc. [from Japanese]

Danaans *or* **Danaoi** in Greek legend, the collective name for the Greeks who joined together in the expedition to Troy.

Danae in Greek mythology, the daughter of King Acrisius of Argos. When an oracle prophesied that her son would kill his grandfather, Acrisius imprisoned her in a bronze tower. Zeus visited her in a shower of gold and she gave birth to a son, Perseus, who accidentally killed Acrisius with a discus.

Danakil Depression a desert area in NE Ethiopia, occupying Tigray in the E, Welo in the NE, and Harerge in the N. It also extends into parts of Eritrea. The region is low-lying, bounded by the Red Sea in the N and E and the Rift Valley in the S and W. Although mountainous in parts, the land also dips below sea level. An extremely hot area, temperatures are close to 60°C. Naturally occurring salt reserves have been the centre of the regional economy for centuries.

Da Nang, formerly **Tourane** POP (1989) 371 000, a seaport in Quang Nam-Danang province, central Vietnam, on the S China Sea. It was the site of an important US military base during the Vietnam War.

dance — *verb* **1** *intrans.* to make a usually repeated series of rhythmic steps or movements (usually in time to music). **2** to perform (a particular series of such steps or movements): *dance a waltz.* **3** (*usually* **dance about** *or* **around**) to

move or jump quickly up and down or from side to side. **4** to bounce (a baby), usually on one's knee. — *noun* **1** a series of fixed steps, usually made in time to music. **2** a social gathering at which people dance. **3** a piece of music played for dancing.
— **dance attendance on someone** *derog.* to follow them and do whatever they want.
dance to someone's tune to do what they want or expect.
lead someone a merry dance *Brit.* to involve them in unnecessary difficulties and exertions. [from Old French *danser*, to dance]

Dance of Death, The a series of 40 woodcuts depicting the Dance of Death by Hans Holbein the Younger (issued 1538).

dancer *noun* a person who dances, especially professionally.

Dancer Lacing Her Shoe a painting by Edgar Degas (c.1878, Paris).

Dances With Wolves a US film directed by Kevin Costner (1990). Starring Costner, and the winner of seven Oscars, it is a Western about a US lieutenant's friendship with a remote tribe of native Sioux people.

Dance to the Music of Time, A a series of 12 novels by Anthony Powell (1951–75). It is named after Poussin's painting, the *Dance of Time*, and chronicles 50 years of post-World War I life, narrated by the central character Nicholas Jenkins.

dancing *noun* the activity or occupation of a dancer.

D and C *abbrev.* dilatation and curettage.

dandelion *noun* a perennial plant of the genus *Taraxacum*, found in most temperate regions. It produces a rosette of deeply notched leaves and a single yellow flowerhead, which is borne on a hollow stem containing white latex sap and develops into a round white fluffy seedhead or 'dandelion clock'. Dandelion leaves are used in salads, and the common dandelion is a frequent lawn weed. [from French *dent de lion*, lion's tooth]

dander
— **get one's** *or* **someone's dander up** *colloq.* to become angry, or make someone angry.

dandle *verb* to bounce (usually a small child) on one's knee.

Dandolo, Enrico (c.1110–1205) Italian statesman, born in Venice. He was Ambassador to Constantinople (1173), and became Doge of Venice (1192). In 1202 he marched at the head of the Fourth Crusade, subduing Trieste and Zara, the coasts of Albania, the Ionian Is, and Constantinople (1205), where he established the Empire of the Latins.

dandruff *noun* a common condition in which thin whitish flakes of dead skin are deposited on the scalp as a result of an increase in the normal loss of cells from the outermost layer of the skin.

dandy — *noun* (PL. **dandies**) a man who pays a lot of attention to his appearance, dressing very fashionably or elegantly. — *adj. colloq.* (**dandier, dandiest**) good; fine.

Dane, Clemence, pseudonym of **Winifred Ashton** (c.1891–1965) English novelist and playwright, born in London. Her novels include *Regiment of Women* (1917), *Legend* (1919), and *The Flower Girls* (1954). Many of her plays have achieved long runs, notably *A Bill of Divorcement* (1921) and *Will Shakespeare* (1921).

Dane *noun* **1** a native or citizen of Denmark. **2** *Hist.* any of the Vikings from Scandinavia who invaded Britain in the 9c–11c. See also DANISH. [from Danish *Daner*, Danes]

Danegeld a royal tax levied on land in England between 991 and 1012, in order to buy peace from Danish invaders. After 1066, the term was used for a general tax, which was effectively abandoned in 1162.

Danelaw *noun* the part of England occupied by the Danes from the 9c to the 11c. [from Anglo-Saxon *Dena lagu*, Danes' law]
◇ The Danes settled an area of E England stretching from Yorkshire to E Anglia. After King Alfred's victory over the Danish commander Guthrum at Edington in 878, a treaty was made (886) confining the Danes to the region east of Watling Street. The Danes established their own system of law, social organization, and land measurement. The Danish influence can still be found, especially in the many Norse words in English (eg *egg*, *take*, and *window*), and in place-names such as those ending in *-by*, *-gate*, and *-thorp*.

danger *noun* **1** a situation or state in which someone or something may suffer harm, an injury, or a loss: *in danger of falling*. **2** something that may cause harm, injury, or loss. **3** a possibility of something unpleasant happening.
— **on the danger list** *Medicine* so ill or seriously injured that there is a high risk of death. [from Old French *dangier*, power (therefore power to harm)]

Dangerfield, Thomas (1650–85) English conspirator, born in Waltham, Essex. A thief, vagabond, and soldier, in 1679 he accused the Presbyterians of plotting to destroy the government. Imprisoned when this was shown to be a lie, he claimed he had been deceived by Catholics plotting against the life of Charles II. Convicted of libel, he was whipped and pilloried, and on returning from Tyburn was killed by a blow from a bystander.

danger money extra money paid to a person for doing a dangerous job.

dangerous *adj.* likely to or able to cause harm or injury.

dangerously *adv.* in a dangerous way; so as to cause danger.

dangle *verb* **1** *intrans., trans.* to hang loosely. **2** to offer or present (an idea, a possible reward, etc) to someone.

Daniel **1** an Israelite slave of the Old Testament who obtained favour from King Nebuchadnezzar by interpreting dreams. **2** a male first name. [from Hebrew *Daniel*, the Lord is judge]

Daniel, Glyn (Edmund) (1914–86) Welsh archaeologist, born in Barry. He lectured at Cambridge (1945–74) and was Professor of Archaeology (1974–81). He stimulated popular interest in archaeology through writing, editing, and broadcasting. He was editor of the journal *Antiquity* (1958–86) and of the book series 'Ancient Peoples and Places' published from 1955. On British television he achieved particular popularity in the 1950s as the chairman of the archaeological panel game *Animal, Vegetable, or Mineral*.

Daniel, Book of a book of the Hebrew Bible and Old Testament. The first half (chapters 1 to 6) contains narrative accounts about Daniel and his three companions, ostensibly set during the Babylonian exile in the 6c BC; the second half (chapters 7 to 12) describes apocalyptic revelations of Daniel recorded as first-person visions. Some date the work to the 6c BC; others claim it to be 3c–2c BC. The Additions to the Book of Daniel are three works found in some ancient Greek versions, in the modern Catholic Bible, and in the Apocrypha of the Protestant Bible.

Daniel Deronda a novel by George Eliot (1876). Her last, it is set against a Jewish background and focuses mainly on the lives of the adopted Daniel Deronda and the spoilt Gwendolen Harleth.

Daniell, John Frederick (1790–1845) English chemist and meteorologist, born in London. Professor of Chemistry at the newly founded King's College in London from 1831, he invented a hygrometer (1820), a pyrometer

(1830), and a constant voltage (Daniell) electric cell.

Danilova, Alexandra (Dionysievna) (1903–) Russian-born US dancer and teacher, born in Peterhof. She joined the Maryinski Theatre (now Kirov Ballet) in 1922, then in 1924 went on tour in Europe, where she joined Sergei Diaghilev. She danced as prima ballerina with the Ballets Russes de Monte Carlo (1938–52), and created leading parts in Balanchine and Massine's works. Afterwards she became a highly acclaimed teacher at the School of American Ballet.

Danish — *adj.* **1** of Denmark or its inhabitants. **2** of the language spoken in Denmark. — *noun* **1** the language spoken in Denmark. **2** (**the Danish**) the people of Denmark. See also DANE. [from Old French *daneis*]
◇ Danish is a Germanic language belonging to the continental group of Scandinavian languages. It has c.500 million speakers in Denmark, parts of Germany, and the USA.

Danish blue a type of strong-tasting cheese, white with streaks of bluish mould through it.

Danish pastry a flat cake of rich, light pastry, with any of various types of sweet filling on the top.

dank *adj., usually said of a place* unpleasantly wet and cold.

dankness *noun* being dank; a dank state.

D'Annunzio, Gabriele (1863–1938) Italian writer, born in Prescara. During the 1890s he wrote several novels, influenced by the philosophy of Nietzsche, notably *Il trionfo della morte* (The Triumph of Death, 1894). His best-known poetic work is *Laudi del cielo del mare della terra e degli eroi* (In Praise of Sky, Sea, Earth, and Heroes, 1899), and his major plays include the tragedy *La Gioconda* (1899), which he wrote for the actress Eleonor Duse. A nationalist, he served in World War I, and in 1919 occupied and became dictator of Fiume until he was removed by the Italian government (1920). He was a supporter of Mussolini.

Dante (Alighieri) (1265–1321) Italian poet, born in Florence. A lawyer's son, he was baptized Durante, later contracted into Dante. In 1274, he met 'Beatrice' (reputedly Beatrice Portinari, c.1265–90), an event which influenced the rest of his life. His platonic devotion to her continued despite her marriage, and despite his own marriage (after her death) to Gemma Donati. In 1300, he became one of the six priors of Florence. His sympathy for the moderate 'White Guelfs' led to his exile in 1302, when the 'Black faction' became dominant, and he never returned to his native city. He eventually settled in Ravenna, where he stayed until his death. The *Vita Nuova* (c.1292), which tells of his boyish passion for Beatrice, is probably the earliest of his major works. The best-known of these is the *Divina Commedia* (Divine Comedy, c.1307), a vision of hell, purgatory, and heaven. He also wrote several shorter poems, as well as treatises on government and language.

Danton, Georges (Jacques) (1759–94) French revolutionary politician, born in Arcis-sur-Aube. He was practising as a lawyer in Paris at the outbreak of the Revolution and in 1790 formed the Cordeliers' Club, a rallying point for revolutionary extremists. Appointed Minister of Justice (1792), he voted for the death of the king (1793), and was one of the original members of the Committee of Public Safety. He tried to abate the pitiless severity of his own Revolutionary Tribunal, but lost the leadership to Robespierre and was guillotined for conspiracy.

Danu in Celtic mythology, a mother-goddess who is associated with hills and the earth. Her name is linked to a race of people known as the Tuatha De Danann, who settled in Ireland in c.1500 BC.

Danube, River, German **Donau**, Bulgarian **Dunav**, Russian **Dunai**, Romanian **Dunarea** the second-longest river in Europe, length 2 850km/ 1 770mi. It rises in the Black Forest, SW Germany, and flows generally E and S through Austria, Slovakia, and Hungary, forming most of the Romania–Bulgaria border. It enters the Black Sea through a wide, swampy delta. An important commercial route, it is linked by canals to other major rivers (part of the Trans-Europe Waterway). It flows through Vienna, Budapest, and Belgrade.

Danzig see GDAŃSK.

Daphne 1 in Greek mythology, the daughter of a river-god, Ladon (or, in another story, Peneios). She was pursued by the god Apollo but was saved by being turned into a laurel, which became Apollo's sacred tree. **2** a female first name.

Daphnia noun a common type of water flea, found in bodies of freshwater.

Daphnis in Greek mythology, a Sicilian shepherd, half-brother of Pan, who was loved by a nymph. He was blinded for being unfaithful to her and, in trying to console himself by singing and playing the flute, became the inventor of pastoral poetry.

Daphnis and Chloe a Greek prose romance by Longus (c.2c–3c). It is a pastoral romance describing the sexual awakening and marriage of two young people.

Daphnis et Chloé (Daphnis and Chloe) a ballet by Maurice Ravel (1912), commissioned by Diaghilev's Ballets Russes, and later used by Ravel as the basis for two orchestral suites.

Da Ponte, Lorenzo, originally **Emanuele Conegliano** (1749–1838) Italian poet, born in Ceneda, near Venice. He was Professor of Rhetoric at Treviso until political troubles drove him to Vienna, where he wrote the libretti for Mozart's operas *Le Nozze di Figaro* (1786), *Don Giovanni* (1787), and *Così fan Tutte* (1790). After a period in London (1792–1805), he went to New York, and eventually became a lecturer in Italian at Columbia College (1825).

dapper adj., usually said of small men neat and smart in appearance and lively in movement. [from Dutch *dapper*, brave]

dappled adj. marked with spots or rounded patches of a different, usually darker, colour.

dapple-grey — adj., said of a horse of a pale grey colour with darker spots. — noun a dapple-grey horse.

Darby, Abraham (c.1678–1717) English iron-master, born near Dudley, Worcestershire. He founded the Bristol Iron Company (1708), and is generally acknowledged to be the first to use coke successfully in the smelting of iron (1709). His works at Coalbrookdale produced the finest iron yet made.

Darby and Joan an old man and old woman who have been happily married for many years. [from characters in an 18c song]

Darby and Joan club a social club for elderly men and women.

Darcy, Fitzwilliam the proud hero of Jane Austen's *Pride and Prejudice*, who marries Elizabeth Bennett.

Dardanelles or **Hellespont**, Turkish **Çanakkale Boğazi**, ancient **Hellespontus** a narrow strait in NW Turkey, connecting the Aegean Sea in the W and the Sea of Marmara in the E, and separating the Gallipoli Peninsula of European Turkey from Anatolia. The strait is 65km/40mi long and 1.6–6.4km/1–4mi wide. During World War I the Dardanelles was the scene of an unsuccessful Allied campaign.

dare — verb **1** aux. intrans. to be brave enough to do something frightening, difficult or danger-ous: *he wouldn't dare to leave / dare I tell him?* **2** to challenge (someone to do something frightening, difficult, dangerous, etc). **3** to be brave enough to risk facing: *dare his father's anger.* — noun a challenge (to do something dangerous, etc).

— **how dare you!** an expression of anger or indignation at something someone has said or done.

I dare say or **daresay** probably; I suppose: *I dare say you're right.* [from Anglo-Saxon *durran*]

dare-devil — noun a person who does dangerous or adventurous things without worrying about the risks involved. — adj., said of actions, etc daring and dangerous.

Dar es Salaam 1 POP (1990e) 1.7m, the capital of Dar es Salaam region, E Tanzania, on the Indian Ocean, 45km/28mi S of Zanzibar. HISTORY founded in 1882; occupied by the German East Africa Company in 1887; became capital of German E Africa in 1891; occupied by the British in World War I; its status as national capital is being transferred to Dodoma. Dar es Salaam is the chief seaport and industrial, commercial, and financial centre. NOTABLE FEATURES National Museum (contains the Olduvai Gorge fossils); Tanzanian State House. **2** a region in E Tanzania with Dar es Salaam as its capital. [Arabic, = haven of peace]

Dargomizhsky, Alexander (Sergei-evitch) (1813–69) Russian composer, born in Tula. Taught by Glinka and influenced by other Russian nationalist composers, he set Pushkin's *The Stone Guest* to music (completed by Rimsky-Korsakov), which anticipated the work of Mussorgsky in dramatic power and naturalist treatment of words. He also wrote the operas *Esmeralda* (completed 1840) and *Rusalka* (1856), and almost 100 songs.

Darhan or **Darkhan** POP (1990e) 90 000, a town in Selenge county, N Mongolia. It lies E of the R Haraa and NW of Ulan Bator. Darhan is a new town, constructed since 1961.

Darién POP (1990) 44 000, a province in E Panama, bounded to the SE by Colombia and W by the Gulf of Panama. AREA 16 803sq km/ 6 486sq mi. CAPITAL La Palma. CHIEF TOWNS Yaviza, El Real. The attempted settlement by the Scots in the 1690s (the Darién Scheme) is remembered in local place names such as Punta de Escores and Caledonia Bay. NOTABLE FEATURE Darién National Park, a World Heritage site.

daring — adj. **1** bold, courageous or adventurous. **2** designed or intended to shock or surprise — noun boldness, courage.

daringly adv. with a daring or bold manner.

Darius I, also called **the Great** (548–486 BC) King of Persia (521–486 BC), of the Achaemenid dynasty. He is noteworthy for his administrative reforms (he divided the empire into provinces called *satrapies*), military conquests, and religious toleration. His conquests, especially in the East and Europe (Thrace and Macedonia) consolidated the frontiers of the empire. He suppressed the Ionian revolt of 499–494 BC and then launched two expeditions against Athens and Eretria in retaliation for their support of this revolt. The first was abandoned in 492 BC after the wreck of his fleet off Mt Athos and the second (the first Persian War) was defeated by the Athenians at Marathon (490 BC).

Darjeeling or **Darjiling** POP (1991) 73 000, a hill station in W Bengal, NE India, in the Himalayan foothills near the Sikkim state frontier. The population is mainly Bhutanese and Nepalese. It is the centre of a tea-growing region and the former summer residence of the Bengal government.

dark — adj. **1** without light. **2** said of a colour not light or pale; closer to black than white. **3** said of a person or the colour of their skin or hair not light or fair. **4** sad or gloomy. **5** evil or sinister: *dark powers.* **6** mysterious and unknown: *a dark secret.* — noun **1** (usually **the dark**) the absence of light. **2** the time of day when night begins and there is no more light: *after dark.* **3** a dark colour.

— **in the dark** not knowing or aware of something.

keep it dark to keep something secret. [from Anglo-Saxon *deorc*, dark]

Dark Ages the period of European history from about the 5c to the 11c, regarded as historically obscure and culturally uneventful.

◇ The term is now considered to be misleading, and the implication that it was a period of intellectual darkness underestimates very real achievements, particularly in the areas of religion, learning, and government. Historians usually describe the whole period c.500–c.1500 as the *Middle Ages*.

darken verb trans., intrans. (**darkened, darkening**) to make or become dark or darker.

darkened adj. made dark or darker.

dark horse a person about whom little is known.

darkly adv. in a mysterious, gloomy, sinister or threatening way or tone of voice.

darkness noun being dark; a dark state.

darkroom noun a room into which no ordinary light is allowed, used for developing photographs.

darky or **darkie** noun offensive a person with black or brown skin, especially a black.

darling — noun **1** often used as a term of affection a dearly loved person. **2** a lovable person or thing. — adj. **1** well loved. **2** colloq. delightful.

Darling Range a mountain range in Western Australia, near Perth. It extends 320km/200mi S along the SW coast. HEIGHT rises to 582m at Mt Cooke.

Darling River the longest tributary of the Murray R with a length of 3 070km/1 908mi. Formed by the Dumaresq and Macintyre rivers at the New South Wales–Queensland border, it flows generally SW to join the Murray R. The waters of the Darling are used for irrigation in New South Wales.

Darlington, Cyril Dean (1903–81) English cytologist and geneticist, born in Chorley, Lancashire. Director of the John Innes Horticultural Institution, London, and Professor of Botany at Oxford, he proposed many major theories, including the idea that chromosomes themselves are the objects of evolution and selection.

Darlington POP (1992e) 100 000, an industrial town in Darlington district, Durham, NE England. It lies on the R Tees, to the W of Stockton-on-Tees. The first passenger railway ran from Stockton to Darlington, in 1825.

darn¹ verb to mend by sewing with rows of stitches which cross each other.

darn² interj. a less offensive or emphatic substitute for **damn**.

Darnay, Charles the assumed English identity of the exiled French aristocrat Charles St Evremonde, in Charles Dickens's *A Tale of Two Cities*.

darned adj. irritating; disliked.

darning noun **1** the work of darning clothes, etc. **2** clothes, etc which need to be darned or which have been darned.

Darnley, Henry Stewart, Lord (1545–67) English nobleman, the second husband of Mary, Queen of Scots and father of James I of England, born in Temple Newsom, Yorkshire. He married Mary (his cousin) in 1565, but his debauchery and arrogance made him unpopular, and his part in the murder (1566) of the Queen's secretary, David Rizzio, caused his downfall and led to his estrangement from the Queen. He was killed in

Edinburgh, when Kirk O'Field, the house in which he was sleeping, was destroyed by gunpowder — a plot probably organized by the Earl of Bothwell, perhaps with Mary's knowledge.

Darrell a male and sometimes female first name, after the surname. [from the Norman baronial name *d'Airelle*]

Darren a male first name. [of recent coinage and unclear origin]

Darrow, Clarence (Seward) (1857–1938) US lawyer, born in Kinsman, Ohio. He was admitted to the Bar in 1878, and later became counsel for Chicago and North Western Railways. He left this post when a strike of the American Railway Union occurred, and defended Eugene Debs who had called it (1894). He took on further labour cases and, after World War I, was involved in several notable defences, including the murder case against Nathan Leopold and Richard Loeb (1924), and the trial of John T Scopes (1925) for the teaching of Darwinian evolution in school.

Dart, Raymond Arthur (1893–1988) Australian-born South African anatomist, born in Toowong. Professor of Anatomy at Witwatersrand University in Johannesburg (1923–58), he described the *Taung skull*, an apelike infant part-skull (found in a mine in Taung, Bechuanaland) as belonging to an intermediate between anthropoids and man, which he named *Australopithecus africanus* (southern African ape).

dart — *noun* **1** a narrow, pointed weapon that can be thrown or fired. **2** a small sharp-pointed missile used in the game of darts. **3** a sudden quick movement. **4** a fold sewn into a piece of clothing to make it fit more neatly. — *verb* **1** *intrans.* to move suddenly and quickly. **2** *trans.* to send or give (a look or glance) quickly. [from Old French *dart*]

D'Artagnan the adventurous, fiery hero of Alexandre Dumas's *The Three Musketeers*.

dartboard *noun* a circular target used in the game of darts.

darter *noun* a slender bird native to warm regions worldwide. It spears fish underwater with its long pointed bill, and swims with only its head and long neck above the water surface.

darter

Dartford POP (1992e) 82 000, a market town in Dartford district, Kent, SE England. It stands on the R Dearent, 24km/15mi NW of Chatham, and is linked to Essex by the Dartford Tunnel. It forms part of the Greater London urban area.

darting *adj.* moving suddenly and quickly.

Dartmoor a national park in Devon, S England, established in 1951. It contains several Bronze and Iron Age settlements, and is noted for its granite tors and hanging oak woods. The area is popular for walking and riding. The highest point is High Willhays (621m). AREA 913sq km/ 352sq mi.

Dartmouth College in the USA, a liberal arts college in Hanover, New Hampshire,

founded in 1769. Primarily an undergraduate college, its specialized areas of study include courses on black studies, Native Americans, and the environment.

darts *sing. noun* a game in which darts are thrown at a circular target (*dartboard*) divided into numbered sections, points being scored according to the section each dart hits.
◇ The standard dartboard is divided into 20 segments numbered from 1 to 20, which are in turn divided into smaller segments which double or treble the score if hit. The central ring or 'bull' is worth 50 points. The throwing distance is normally 2.4m, and the height of the board at its central point is 1.7m.

Darwin, Charles Robert (1809–82) English naturalist, born in Shrewsbury. He studied medicine at Edinburgh University and biology at Cambridge, and was recommended as naturalist to HMS *Beagle*, then about to start for a scientific survey of S American waters (1831–6). By 1846 he had published several works on his zoological and geological discoveries, and become one of the leading scientists of his day. Working at Downe in Kent, he addressed himself to the great work of his life — the problem of the origin of species. His conclusions were published in *The Origin of Species by Means of Natural Selection* (1859); this controversial epoch-making work eventually succeeded in obtaining widespread recognition for the theory of natural selection, that environmental pressures act to select better adapted individuals, which survive to pass on their features to subsequent generations. His supplementary treatise *The Descent of Man* (1871) postulated the descent of the human race from the anthropoid group.

Darwin, formerly **Palmerston** (to 1911), **Port Darwin** POP (1991) 78 000, the seaport capital of Northern Territory, N Australia, on the Beagle Gulf, Clarence Strait. It is an important communications centre, serving Arnhem Land in the E and the surrounding mining districts. HISTORY the first European settlement, established in 1869, was destroyed by a hurricane in 1879; attacked by the Japanese in 1942; destroyed by cyclone Tracy in 1974. NOTABLE FEATURES Government House (1869); Overland Telegraph Memorial; Stuart Memorial (John McDouall Stuart crossed Australia from Adelaide to Darwin in 1861–2); Ross and Keith Smith Memorial (first flight from England, Dec 1919); cathedral (1902); Fannie Bay Gaol Museum; S of Darwin is Australia's first commercial crocodile farm.

Darwin a settlement on East Falkland, Falkland Is. It is situated c.70km/40mi W of Stanley at the head of Choiseul Sound, on the narrow isthmus that joins the N half of East Falkland to Lafonia in the S.

Darwinism *noun Biol.* the theory of evolution by natural selection, proposed jointly by Charles Darwin and Alfred Russel Wallace.
◇ The theory was based on Darwin's observations that within a species there is wide variation between individuals and that, on average, more offspring are produced than are needed to replace the parents, yet population size remains more or less constant. Darwin argued that this must be due to competition for survival, in which the fittest individuals, ie those best adapted to their environment, survive and reproduce, while less well-adapted individuals die out or fail to breed as successfully as their counterparts. Eventually such natural selection of favourable traits over many generations will lead to the development of a new species. The discovery of the mechanism of genetic inheritance has resulted in a modified version of the theory, known as *neo-Darwinism*.

dash¹ — *verb* **1** *intrans.* to run quickly; to rush. **2** *intrans.* to crash or smash. **3** to hit or smash violently. **4** to destroy or put an end to (hopes, etc).
— *noun* **1** a quick run or sudden rush. **2** a small amount of something added, especially a liquid.

3 a patch of colour. **4** a short line (—) used in writing to show a break in a sentence, etc. **5** in Morse code, the longer of the two lengths of signal element, written as a short line (see also DOT). **6** confidence, enthusiasm, and stylishness. **7** *North Amer. Sport* a short race for fast runners. [from Middle English *daschen* or *dassen*, to rush or strike violently]

dash² *interj.* a milder and less offensive substitute for *damn*.

dashboard *noun Brit.* a panel with dials, switches and instruments in front of the driver's seat in a motor vehicle, boat, etc. [from DASH¹; originally a board protecting the driver of a horse-drawn coach from splashes of mud]

dashing *adj.* **1** smart; stylish. **2** lively and enthusiastic.

dashingly *adv.* in a lively and enthusiastic way.

dastardly *adj. old use* cowardly, mean, and cruel. [probably connected with DAZED]

DAT *abbrev.* digital audio tape.

dat. *abbrev.* dative.

data *noun originally pl* but now treated as *sing.* See also DATUM. **1** two or more pieces of information or facts, especially those obtained by scientific observation or experiment. **2** a collection of information in the form of numbers, characters, electrical signals, etc, that can be supplied to, stored, or processed by a computer. [from Latin *data*, things given]

databank *noun Comput.* a collection of files or records containing bibliographic or textual data on a particular subject, stored in a computer so that a number of users may copy items of interest from it.

database *noun Comput.* an organized collection of computer data coded and stored in such a way that different categories of data in a wide variety of different forms can be accessed, often by many users and for a wide variety of applications. A set of programs known as a database management system (DBMS) allows data to be updated, deleted, or retrieved from one or more databases.

data capture any process of changing information from its original form into a form which can be fed into a computer.

dataglove *noun* an electronically wired glove which transmits the wearer's movements to a virtual reality monitor.

data processing the performance of operations on data by a computer system, especially the arrangement of large amounts of data into a more useful form according to specified rules and procedures.

date¹ — *noun* **1** the day of the month, and/or the year, recorded by a number or series of numbers. **2** a statement on a letter, document, etc giving usually the day, the month and the year when it was written, sent, etc. **3** a particular period of time in history: *costumes of an earlier date*. **4** *colloq.* a planned meeting or social outing, usually with a person of the opposite sex. **5** *North Amer. colloq.* a person of the opposite sex whom one is meeting or going out with. **6** *colloq.* an agreed time and place of performance. — *verb* **1** to put a date on. **2** to find, decide on, or guess the date of. **3** (**date back to** *or* **from a specified time**) to have begun or originated then. **4** to show the age of; to make (especially a person) seem old. **5** *intrans.* to become old-fashioned. **6** *trans., intrans. colloq.* to go out with (a person of the opposite sex), especially regularly.
— **to date** up to the present time.
[from Old French *date*, from Latin *datum*, given]

date² *noun* the fruit of the date-palm, brown, sticky, and sweet-tasting when dried. [from French *datte*, from Greek *daktylos*, finger, date]

dated *adj.* old-fashioned.

Date Line an imaginary line, based by international agreement on the meridian of 180° (with deviations to keep certain islands in the same zone as their respective mainlands). The date is altered to compensate for the gain or loss of time (1 hour per 15°) which occurs when circumnavigating the globe.

dateline *noun* a line, usually at the top of a newspaper article, which gives the date and place of writing.

date palm a tall tree with a crown of long spreading leaves, cultivated in N Africa and the Middle East for its yellowish to reddish-brown edible fruits, which are borne in heavy clusters and have a very high sugar content. They may be harvested before they ripen, or dried for export.

date rape rape committed by someone known to the victim while both are on a date.

date-stamp — *noun* **1** a device, usually a rubber stamp, for printing the date on something. **2** the date printed by this. — *verb* to print with a date-stamp.

dative — *noun Grammar* in some languages, a case which is mostly used to show that a noun or pronoun is the indirect object of a verb. — *adj. Grammar* of or in this case. [from Latin *dativus*, from *dare*, to give]

Datong *or* **Ta-t'ung** POP (1990) 1.1m, a city in Shanxi province, E central China. It lies W of Beijing. The city was founded in the 4c as capital of the Northern Wei dynasty. NOTABLE FEATURES Jiulong Bi (Nine Dragon Screen); Yungang Caves, 16km/10mi W (earliest Buddhist stone-carving in China, mostly carved between AD 460 and AD 494).

datum *noun* (PL. **data**) a piece of information. See also DATA. [from Latin *datum*, something given]

daub — *verb* **1** to spread roughly or unevenly on to or over a surface: *daubed paint on the walls.* **2** to cover (a surface) with a soft sticky substance or liquid. **3** *trans., intrans. derog.* to paint carelessly or without skill. — *noun* **1** soft, sticky material such as clay, often used as a covering for walls. See also WATTLE AND DAUB. **2** *derog. colloq.* an unskilful or carelessly done painting. [from Old French *dauber*, from Latin *dealbare*, to whitewash]

dauber *noun* a person or implement that daubs, especially in painting.

Daudet, Alphonse (1840–97) French writer, born in Nîmes. He moved to Paris in 1857, where he devoted himself to literature. His theatrical pieces include *L'Arlésienne* (1872), for which Bizet composed incidental music. His best-known work includes his sketches and short stories of Provençal life, notably *Lettres de mon moulin* (Letters from my Mill, 1869), and *Tartarin de Tarascon* (1872) and its two sequels.

daughter — *noun* **1** a female child considered in relation to her parents. **2** a woman closely associated with, involved with, or influenced by a person, thing, or place: *a faithful daughter of the Church.* — *adj.* derived by some process from and thought of as being like a daughter of: *French is a daughter language of Latin.* [from Anglo-Saxon *dohtor*]

daughterboard *noun* a printed circuit board which plugs into a motherboard.

daughter cell *Genetics* either of two new cells formed as a result of cell division.

daughter element *Physics* any of the elements produced as a result of the splitting of an atom by nuclear fission.

daughter-in-law *noun* (PL. **daughters-in-law**) the wife of one's son.

daughterly *adj.* like a daughter; befitting a daughter: *daughterly devotion.*

daughter nucleus *Biol.* either of the two nuclei that are produced when the nucleus of a living cell splits into two parts during cell division.

daunt *verb* to frighten, worry, or discourage.
— **nothing daunted** not at all discouraged or less enthusiastic.
[from Old French *danter*]

daunting *adj.* intimidating; discouraging.

dauntingly *adv.* so as to intimidate or discourage.

dauntless *adj.* fearless; not easily discouraged.

Dauphin *or* **dauphin** the title of the eldest son of the reigning French monarch in the period 1350–1830, acquired in 1349 when the future king Charles V purchased the lands known as *Dauphiné*.

Dauphine *or* **dauphine** the title of the wife of the Dauphin.

Dauphiné a former province in SE France, now occupying the departments of Drôme, Isère, and Hautes-Alpes. HISTORY part of the Holy Roman Empire; passed to Charles V of France in 1349; both the lands and the title became the property of the king's eldest son.

Dausset, Jean Baptiste Gabriel Joachim (1916–) French immunologist, born in Toulouse. His wartime service in the medical corps led to an interest in transfusion responses and the way in which they can lead to antibody production; his later experiments on skin grafting led to 'tissue typing', which greatly reduces rejection risks in transplant surgery. In 1978 he became Professor of Experimental Medicine at the Collège de France. He shared the 1980 Nobel Prize for Physiology or Medicine with George Snell and Baruj Benacerraf.

Davao *or* **Davao City** POP (1990) 850 000, a seaport in Davao Del Sur province, S Mindanao, Philippines. It lies at the head of the Davao Gulf. The city was founded in 1849 and was formerly held by the Japanese.

Davenant *or* **D'Avenant, Sir William** (1606–68) English poet and playwright, born in Oxford. The son of an innkeeper, he was rumoured to be the illegitimate son of Shakespeare. In 1628 he took to writing for the stage, his most successful work being *The Wits* (1636). He became Poet Laureate in 1638, and was later manager of the Drury Lane Theatre. In 1656, with *The Siege of Rhodes*, he simultaneously helped to revive drama, which had been banned under Oliver Cromwell, and brought to the stage the first public opera in England.

davenport *noun* **1** *Brit.* a type of desk. **2** *North Amer.* a large sofa.

David I (c.1085–1153) King of Scots (1124–53), the youngest son of Malcolm Canmore and Queen (later St) Margaret. During his reign he secured the foundations of the medieval kingdom of Scotland. In 1136 he supported the claims of his niece, Empress Matilda, to the English Crown, and embarked on wars against Stephen. He was defeated in 1138 at the battle of the Standard, near Northallerton, but from 1141 occupied the whole of N England to the rivers Ribble and Tees.

David II (1324–71) King of Scots (1329–71), the only surviving son of Robert Bruce, born in Dunfermline, Fife. He became king at the age of five, but in 1334, after the victory of Edward III of England at Halidon Hill (1333), he fled to France until 1341. He later invaded England, but was defeated and captured at Neville's Cross (1346), and was kept prisoner for 11 years. He was succeeded by his sister's son, Robert II.

David 1 (d.c.963 BC) the first Judean King of Israel, the youngest son of Jesse of Bethlehem, traditionally the author of several of the Psalms and the ancestor of Jesus. His success as a warrior against the Philistines (eg killing Goliath) aroused King Saul's jealousy, and he was forced to flee, but after Saul's death he became King over Judah

in Hebron, and later was chosen King of all Israel. Jerusalem became the political and religious centre of his kingdom, and he built a palace for himself on its highest hill, Zion (the 'city of David'), and placed the Ark of the Covenant there under a tent. He united the many tribes of Israel, and extended his territory from Egypt to the Euphrates. The later part of his reign was troubled by attempted revolutions by his sons Absalom and Adonijah. He may have died as early as 1018 BC, and was succeeded by his son Solomon. **2** a male first name. [of uncertain Hebrew derivation, probably meaning 'beloved']

David *or* **Dewi, St** (d.601) the patron saint of Wales, born near St Bride's Bay, Pembrokeshire. He was Bishop of Moni Judeorum, or Menevia (later St David's), presided over two Welsh synods, at Brefi and Caerleon, and founded many Welsh churches. Menevia became a shrine to him; his feast day is 1 Mar.

David, Elizabeth (1913–92) English cookery writer, born in Sussex. After time spent in France, on a Greek island, and in Cairo, she returned to a Britain beset by food rationing (1946). Her early books (eg *Mediterranean Cooking,* 1950 and *Italian Food,* 1954) are a reminder of a culinary world not restricted by the lack of butter, cream, and imported delicacies. Her best-known work is her influential *French Provincial Cooking* (1960), a work of reference as well as a collection of recipes; other works include her authoritative *English Bread and Yeast Cookery* (1977) and *An Omelette and a Glass of Wine* (1984).

David a statue of the biblical character David by various sculptors including Donatello (c.1430s, Bargello, Florence), Andrea del Verrocchio (c.1476, Bargello, Florence), Michelangelo (1504, Accademia, Florence) and Gian Lorenzo Bernini (1623, Borghese, Rome).

David Copperfield a novel by Charles Dickens (1849–50). It describes the life of a young Englishman who is orphaned as a boy.

Davies, Clement (Edward) (1884–1962) Welsh politician, born in Llanfyllin, Montgomeryshire. Called to the Bar in 1909, he was elected MP for Montgomeryshire (1929), and was Leader of the Liberal Party (1945–56). He declined a post as Education Secretary in Winston Churchill's 1951–5 government, and thus lost his only chance of holding office; however he saved the Liberal Party from being subsumed in the Conservative Party (as had the National Liberals).

Davina a female first name, originating in Scotland. [a Latin feminine form of DAVID]

da Vinci, Leonardo see LEONARDO DA VINCI.

Davis, Bette, properly **Ruth Elizabeth Davis** (1908–89) US film actress, born in Lowell, Massachusetts. After a short stage career she had her first Hollywood success in *The Man who Played God* (1932). Her numerous leading roles included *Of Human Bondage* (1934) and *Dangerous* (1935), which established her as a major star for the next three decades. She received great critical acclaim for her role in *Whatever Happened to Baby Jane?* (1962); later appearances included *Death on the Nile* (1979) and many television productions.

Davis, Sir Colin (Rex) (1927–) English conductor, born in Weybridge, Surrey. He was assistant conductor of the BBC Scottish Orchestra (1957–9), then went to Sadler's Wells, where he became musical director (1961–5). He was chief conductor of the BBC Symphony Orchestra (1967–71), and musical director at Covent Garden (1971–86), where he gained his reputation as a Wagner conductor of international standing with a new production of *The Ring.* He is also a noted interpreter of Berlioz.

Davis, Jefferson (1808–89) US statesman, born in Christian Co, Kentucky. He served in several frontier campaigns, then entered

Congress for Mississippi (1845), fought in the Mexican War (1846–7), and became Secretary of War (1853–7). In the Senate he led the extreme State Rights Party, supported slavery, and was President of the Confederate States during the Civil War (1861–5), at the close of which he was imprisoned for two years, then released on bail. Though indicted for treason, he was never brought to trial.

Davis, Joe (Joseph) (1901–78) English billiards and snooker champion, born in Whitwell, Derbyshire. He was responsible for inaugurating the world snooker championship in 1927, and won every title between then and 1946, when he retired from world championship play. He was also world billiards champion from 1928 to 1933. In 1955 at the Leicester Square Hall he became the first man to compile an officially recognized maximum snooker break of 147. His brother, Fred (1913–), followed the same career, winning the first of his 10 World Snooker titles in 1948.

Davis, Miles (Dewey III) (1926–91) US trumpeter, composer, and bandleader, born in Alton, Illinois. An influential and much admired instrumentalist of the postwar era, from 1948 he led a nonet that introduced the 'cool jazz' style. He became known for his expressive lyricism (eg 'Round About Midnight', 1955), new modal structures (eg 'Milestones', 1958), solos in elegant orchestrations (eg 'Porgy and Bess', 1958), and fusion of jazz harmonies with rock instrumentation and rhythms (eg 'In a Silent Way', 1969).

Davis, Steve (1957–) English snooker player, born in London. He dominated snooker in the 1980s, winning the world championship six times (1981, 1983–4, and 1987–9). His first major title was the Coral UK championship in 1980. In 1982, during the Lada Classic, he became the first man to compile a televised maximum 147 break. In 1985 he lost to Dennis Taylor on the final black of the 35th frame of the world championship.

Davis Cup an annual lawn tennis competition for international male teams, first held in 1900. It was held on a challenge basis up to 1972, but since then has been a knockout competition.

Davisson, Clinton Joseph (1881–1958) US physicist, born in Bloomington, Illinois. In 1927, working with Lester Germer, he accidentally observed the diffraction of electrons, confirming the theory that particles can behave as waves; this was of crucial importance in the development of the quantum theory of matter. He shared the 1937 Nobel Prize for Physics with George Paget Thomson.

Davis Strait a sea passage between Greenland and Baffin I, connecting the Atlantic Ocean and the Arctic Ocean. It is c.650km/400mi long by 290km/180mi wide at its narrowest point. The Labrador current brings icebergs along this route from the Arctic Ocean into the Atlantic Ocean. The strait was first visited in 1587 by the British navigator John Davis, after whom it is named.

davit *noun* a curved device used as a crane on a ship, especially either one of a pair of such devices from which a lifeboat is hung and by means of which it can be lowered over the side of the ship. [from a form of the name *David*]

Davitt, Michael (1846–1906) Irish founder of the Irish Land League, born in Straid, Co Mayo. He started work in a cotton mill at 10, where he lost an arm in an accident, and in 1866 joined the Fenian Movement. In 1870 he was arrested for sending guns to Ireland, and sentenced to 15 years penal servitude. Released in 1877, he began a campaign (against eg absentee landlords and unfair rents) which culminated in the Land League (1879). While in prison again, he was elected an MP (1882), but disqualified from taking his seat. A strong Home Ruler and opponent of Parnell, he was an MP again twice (1892–3, 1895–9).

Davos, Romansch **Tavau** POP (1990) 11 000, a fashionable summer and winter resort town in Graubünden canton, E Switzerland, situated SE of Chur. It lies at an altitude of 1 560m, in a high valley crossed by the R Landwasser, surrounded by forest-covered mountains. Davos is a noted health resort and winter sports centre.

Davy, Sir Humphry (1778–1829) English chemist, born in Penzance. Having taken up chemistry in 1797, he experimented with several newly discovered gases and discovered the anaesthetic effect of laughing gas (nitrous oxide). In 1801 he became a lecturer at the Royal Institution. His fame chiefly rests on his discovery that chemical compounds could be decomposed into their elements using electricity. In this way he showed that water is a compound of hydrogen and oxygen; he went on to discover potassium, sodium, barium, strontium, calcium, and magnesium. In 1815 he invented the miner's safety lamp.

Davy Jones's locker the bottom of the sea, especially as the place where the bodies of drowned sailors lie. [from *Davy Jones*, a sailors' name for the evil spirit of the sea]

Davy lamp a miner's safety-lamp, invented by Sir Humphry Davy.

dawdle *verb intrans.* **1** to walk more slowly than necessary or desirable. **2** to waste time, especially by taking longer than necessary to do something.

dawdler *noun* a person who dawdles; an idler.

Dawes, Charles G(ates) (1865–1951) US politician and financier, born in Marietta, Ohio. He was head of the Commission which drew up the Dawes Plan (1924) for German reparation payments to Europe after World War I. In 1925 he shared the Nobel Peace Prize with Sir Austen Chamberlain for negotiating the Locarno Pact, and he was Republican Vice-President under Coolidge (1925–9).

Dawkins, Jack see ARTFUL DODGER.

Dawn a female first name. [from the word for 'daybreak', perhaps a vernacular translation of Latin *Aurora*]

dawn — *noun* **1** the time of day when light first appears as the sun rises. **2** the beginning of (a new period of time, etc). — *verb, said of the day* to begin; to become light.
— **at the break of dawn** at the first light of day when the sun rises.
dawn on someone to begin to be realized by them.
[first recorded as *dawning*, probably from Old Norse, related to DAY]

dawn chorus the singing of birds at dawn.

Day, Sir Robin (1923–) English journalist and broadcaster, born in London. He trained as a lawyer, and became a freelance broadcaster in 1954. Working on radio in eg *It's Your Line* (1970–6) and *The World at One* (1979–88), and on television in eg *Question Time* (1979–89) and *The Parliament Programme* (1991–), he brought an incisive freshness to interviewing techniques and proved a formidable inquisitor of political figures. Among his books are *Grand Inquisitor — memoirs* (1989).

day *noun* **1** the period of 24 hours during which the Earth rotates once on its axis with respect to the Sun (*solar day*) or the stars (*sidereal day*). Ordinary time is expressed in terms of the solar day, which is divided into 24 hours, and is nearly four minutes longer than the sidereal day. **2** the period of time from sunrise to sunset. **3** the period of time in any 24 hours normally spent doing something, especially working: *the working day*. **4** (**day** or **days**) a particular period of time, usually in the past: *one's childhood days* / *it never happened in their day*.
— **all in a** or **the day's work** a normal or acceptable part of one's work or routine.
day by day as each day passes.

day in, **day out** continuously and tediously without change.
have had one's day to have passed the time of one's greatest success, influence, popularity, etc.
in this day and age nowadays; in modern times.
make someone's day to satisfy or delight them.
one of these days at some time in the future.
one of those days a day of difficulties or misfortunes.
that will be the day *colloq.* that is unlikely to happen.
those were the days that was a good or happy time.
win or **carry the day** to win a victory.
[from Anglo-Saxon *dæg*]

Daya Bay the site of China's largest nuclear power project, in Guangdong province, in the S part of the country. It lies 50km/30mi E of Hong Kong and was designed to supply Hong Kong and Guangdong province with power in 1993.

Dayak or **Dyak** the Malayo-Polynesian-speaking indigenous inhabitants of Borneo and Sarawak, including the Bahau, Ngaju, Land Dayak, and Iban, or Sea Dayak (present-day population c.2m). They mostly live along rivers in small longhouse communities, cultivating rice, and hunting and fishing.

Dayan, Moshe (1915–81) Israeli soldier and politician, born in Deganya, Palestine. During the 1930s he joined the illegal Jewish defence organization, Haganah, and was imprisoned by the British (1939–41), then released to fight with the Allies in World War II (when he lost his left eye and adopted his distinctive black eye-patch). He became Chief-of-Staff (1953–8), joined the Knesset as a Labour member in 1959, but left the Labour Party in 1966 to set up the Rafi Party with Ben Gurion. He won international acclaim as Defence Minister in 1967 when his heavily-outnumbered forces triumphed over Egypt, Jordan, and Syria in the 'Six-Day War', and he came to symbolize Israeli courage. As Foreign Minister, he helped to secure the historic peace treaty with Egypt (1977). He resigned from the Begin government in 1979, and launched a new centre party in 1981.

daybreak *noun* the time in the morning when light first appears in the sky; dawn.

day care supervision and care given by trained nurses or other staff to young children or elderly handicapped people during the day.

day centre or **day care centre** a place which provides supervision and care, and/or social activities, during the day for the elderly, the handicapped, people who have just left prison, etc.

daydream — *noun* pleasant thoughts which take one's attention away from what one is, or should be, doing. — *verb intrans.* to be engrossed in daydreams.

daydreamer *noun* a person who daydreams, especially habitually.

Day-Lewis, C(ecil) (1904–72) Irish poet, born in Ballintogher, Sligo. During the 1930s he became known as a leading left-wing writer, but in 1939 he broke away from communism. He was Professor of Poetry at Oxford (1951–6), and at Harvard (1964–5), and became Poet Laureate in 1968. His *Collected Poems* appeared in 1954, and his autobiography *The Buried Day* in 1960. He also published several critical works, translations and, under the pseudonym of Nicholas Blake, detective novels.

Day-Lewis, Daniel (1958–) English film and stage actor, born in London. The son of Poet Laureate Cecil Day-Lewis, he made an early film début with a non-speaking part in *Sunday, Bloody Sunday* (1971). He appeared on stage and television and then established his reputation in the films *My Beautiful Laundrette* and *A Room With a View* (both 1985). His performance as the handicapped writer Christy Brown in *My Left Foot* (1989) won him an Oscar. More recent films include *The Last of the Mohicans* (1992), *The Age of Innocence* (1994), and *In the Name of the Father* (1994).

daylight *noun* 1 the light given by the sun; natural light as opposed to electric light, etc. 2 the time in the morning when light first appears in the sky; dawn.
— **beat the living daylights out of someone** *colloq.* to beat them severely.
in broad daylight *said of a shocking or criminal act* 1 during the day. 2 openly, with no attempt to hide one's actions.
scare *or* **frighten the living daylights out of someone** *colloq.* to frighten them greatly.
see daylight 1 to begin to understand. 2 to realize that one has nearly completed a difficult or long task.

daylight robbery *colloq.* greatly overcharging for something.

Daylight Saving Time (ABBREV. **DST**) a means of making fuller use of the hours of daylight over the summer months, usually by putting the clocks forward one hour. It was adopted by Germany in 1917, by the UK (where it is known as British Summer Time) after World War I, and by the USA in 1966. Many other countries now have some form of Daylight Saving Time.

day nursery a place where young children are looked after during the day, eg while their parents are at work.

Day of Judgement *or* **Last Judgement** according to some beliefs, the time when the world will end, and God will judge all mankind.

day of reckoning a time when mistakes, failures, bad deeds, etc are punished.

day-release *noun Brit.* a system by which employees are given time off work (usually one day a week) to study at college, etc.

day return *Brit.* a reduced bus or train fare for a journey to somewhere and back again on the same day.

day shift 1 a period of working during the day. 2 the people who work during this period. See also BACK SHIFT, NIGHT SHIFT.

daytime *noun* the time when there is daylight, between sunrise and sunset.

Dayton POP (1990) 182 000, the seat of Montgomery County, W Ohio, USA, situated at the confluence of the Stillwater and Miami rivers. It has an aviation and aeronautical research centre. HISTORY established in 1796; home to the aviation pioneers, the Wright brothers.

daze — *verb* to make (someone) feel confused or unable to think clearly (eg by a blow or shock). — *noun* a confused, forgetful or inattentive state of mind. [from Norse *dasask*, to be weary]

dazed *adj.* affected by a blow or shock; mentally confused.

Dazu a town in Sichuan province, W central China. It lies 160km/100mi NW of Chongqing. NOTABLE FEATURES important Buddhist archaeological site, containing over 50 000 stone carvings (9c–13c); Bei Shan (North Hill) nearby is the site of the first Buddhist shrine in China (892), with over 10 000 figures; Baoding Shan lies 15km/9mi NE, with 10 000 figures sculpted between 1179 and 1249, including the Sleeping Buddha (over 30m) and the Yuan Jue (Total Awakening) Grotto.

dazzle *verb* 1 to cause to be unable to see properly, with or because of a strong light. 2 to impress greatly by one's beauty, charm, skill, etc. [from DAZE]

dazzling *adj.* 1 temporarily blinding. 2 highly impressive; brilliant: *a dazzling display*.

dazzlingly *adv.* with a dazzling or brilliant manner.

dB *abbrev.* decibel.

DBE *abbrev.* Dame Commander of the Order of the British Empire.

DBS *abbrev.* direct broadcasting by satellite.

DC *abbrev.* 1 *Mus.* da capo. 2 direct current. 3 District Commissioner. 4 District of Columbia.

DCC *abbrev.* digital compact cassette, a digital audio tape in standard cassette format, played via a fixed-head tape recorder.

DCL *abbrev.* Doctor of Civil Law.

DCM *abbrev.* Distinguished Conduct Medal.

DCMG *abbrev.* Dame Commander of the Order of St Michael and St George.

DCVO *abbrev.* Dame Commander of the (Royal) Victorian Order.

DD *abbrev. Divinitatis Doctor* (Latin), Doctor of Divinity.

D-Day 1 the day (6 Jun 1944) when the Allies launched the greatest amphibious operation in history (code-named 'Overlord'), and invaded German-occupied Europe. By the end of D-Day, 130 000 troops had been landed on five beach-heads along an 80km/50mi stretch of the coast of Normandy, at a cost of 10 000 casualties. 2 a day on which something important is to happen or begin. [from *D* for *day* + DAY]

DDR *abbrev. Deutsche Demokratische Republik* (German), the former German Democratic Republic (East Germany).

DDS *abbrev.* Doctor of Dental Surgery.

DDT *abbrev.* a highly toxic chemical compound formerly widely used as an insecticide. It can contaminate all the organisms within a food chain without itself degrading, resulting in extensive pollution of the environment, and its use is now restricted or banned in most countries. [from the full name *dichlorodiphenyltrichloroethane*]

DE *abbrev.* Delaware.

de- *prefix* 1 down or away. 2 reversal or removal. 3 completely. [de-1 and de-3 from Latin *de*, off, from; de-2 from Old French *des-*, from Latin *dis-* (see DIS-)]

deacon *noun* 1 a member of the lowest rank of clergy in the Roman Catholic and Anglican churches. 2 in some other churches, a member of the church with certain duties such as looking after the church's financial affairs. See also DIA-CONATE. [from Greek *diakonos*, servant]

deaconess *noun* 1 in some churches, a woman who has similar duties to those of a deacon. 2 in some churches, a woman whose duties are similar to those of a minister and who acts as an assistant to the minister.

deactivate *verb* to remove or lessen the capacity of (something such as a bomb) to function or work.

deactivation *noun* the act or process of deactivating.

dead — *adj.* 1 no longer living. 2 not alive. 3 no longer in existence; extinct. 4 with nothing living or growing on or in it. 5 not, or no longer, functioning; not connected to a source of power. 6 no longer burning. 7 no longer in use: *a dead language.* 8 no longer of interest or importance: *a dead issue.* 9 having little or no excitement or activity; boring. 10 without feeling; numb. 11 complete; absolute. 12 *said of a sound* dull. 13 *Sport*, *said of a ball* in a position where it cannot be played until brought back into the game. — *noun* 1 (**the dead**) dead people. 2 (**the dead of night**) the middle of the night, when it is most intensely dark and still. 3 (**the dead of winter**) the middle of winter, when it is most intensely cold. — *adv. slang* quite; very.
— **dead against** *or* **dead set against something** completely opposed to it.
dead from the neck up *derog. colloq.* very stupid or of little intelligence.

dead set on something determined or keen to do or acquire it.
dead to something incapable of understanding it; not affected by it.
dead to the world *colloq.* fast asleep.
one wouldn't be seen dead doing something, *etc colloq.* one would not ever do it.
stop dead to stop suddenly and abruptly.

dead-beat *noun colloq.* a useless person. See also BEAT.

dead colour *Art* in painting, the first layer of paint thinly applied to the surface of the canvas or panel. A normal technique used by the Old Masters whose paintings were built up in layers, it has been abandoned by many modern artists in favour of freer methods of applying paint.

dead duck *colloq.* someone or something with no chance of success or survival.

deaden *verb* to lessen, weaken, or make less sharp, strong, etc.

dead end 1 a road closed off at one end. 2 a situation or activity with no possibility of further progress or movement.

dead-end *adj.* allowing no progress.

dead-head *verb* to remove withered or dead flowers from (plants).

dead heat in a race, competition, etc, the result when two or more competitors produce equally good performances.

dead letter a rule or law no longer obeyed or in force.

deadline *noun* a time by which something must be done.

deadliness *noun* being deadly or fatal.

deadlock — *noun* a situation in which no further progress towards an agreement is possible. — *verb trans., intrans.* to cause or come to such a situation.

dead loss *colloq.* someone or something that is totally useless.

deadly — *adj.* 1 causing or likely to cause death. 2 *colloq.* very dull or uninteresting. 3 very great: *in deadly earnest.* — *adv.* very; absolutely.

deadly nightshade a plant with bell-shaped purple flowers and poisonous black berries from which a drug, belladonna, is obtained.

dead man's handle *or* **dead man's pedal** a device on a machine, eg a railway engine, which must be kept pressed down for the machine to operate and which stops the machine if the pressure is released.

deadness *noun* being dead; a dead state.

dead-nettle *noun* a plant like a nettle but which has no sting.

deadpan *adj., said of someone's expression, etc* showing no emotion or feeling, especially when joking but pretending to be serious.

dead reckoning the estimating of the position of a ship, aircraft, etc from the distance and direction travelled, without looking at the position of the stars, sun, or moon.

Dead Sea, ancient **Lacus Asphaltites**, Hebrew **Bahrat Lut** (**Sea of Lot**), Old Testament **Salt Sea**, **Sea of the Plain**, **East Sea** an inland lake in the Great Rift Valley on the Jordan–Israel border. It is the lowest point on earth at 394m below sea level. The lake is fed by the R Jordan to the N, but it has no outlet. It is divided by the Lashon Peninsula. One of the most salty lakes in the world, it contains magnesium, sodium, potassium, and calcium salts. Potash and magnesium bromide have been exploited since 1921. The sea level is falling because water from the R Jordan is used for irrigation and home supply. Plans for a direct link with the Mediterranean Sea to stabilize sea levels were abandoned.

Dead Sea Scrolls a collection of parchment scrolls in Hebrew and Aramaic, found accidentally in 1947 and 1952–5 concealed in pottery jars in 11 caves near Qumran on the Dead Sea. They are thought to represent the library of an ascetic Jewish sect, the Essenes, which was concealed when their settlement was overrun by the Roman army in AD 68. Many represent books of the Old Testament, and are c.1000 years older than previously known copies.

deadweight *noun* **1** a heavy load. **2** *technical* (*also* **dead weight**) the difference in the weight of a ship when unloaded and loaded.

dead wood *colloq.* someone or something that is no longer useful or needed.

deaf — *adj.* **1** unable to hear at all or to hear well. **2** (**deaf to something**) not willing to listen to advice, criticism, etc. — *pl. noun* (**the deaf**) deaf people.
— **turn a deaf ear to someone** *or* **something** to ignore or refuse to pay any attention to them. [from Anglo-Saxon *dēaf*]

deaf-aid *noun Brit.* a hearing-aid.

deafen *verb* to make deaf or temporarily unable to hear.

deafening *adj.* **1** extremely loud. **2** causing deafness.

deafeningly *adv.* extremely loudly.

deaf-mute *noun often offensive* a person who is both deaf and unable to speak.

deafness *noun* partial or total loss of hearing in one or both ears.
◇ *Conductive deafness* occurs when the normal transmission of sound waves from the external ear to the inner ear is prevented. This is usually due to infection of the middle ear or, rarely, to a degenerative condition of the inner ear. *Perceptive* or *nerve deafness* is the result of an abnormality of the cochlea in the inner ear, the auditory nerve, or the auditory centres in the brain. It may be caused by infection with German measles (rubella) before birth, or by injury, disease, lengthy exposure to high levels of noise, or the normal ageing process.
Both types of deafness can be treated with a hearing aid, most versions of which fit behind the ear, although smaller aids that fit within the ear are now becoming available. Lip reading, sign language and cued speech (in which ambiguous lip movement during speech is clarified manually) are all important aids to the deaf. In cases of profound deafness a cochlear implant with a special electronic processor may be fitted in the inner ear.

Deák, Francis (1803–76) Hungarian statesman, born in Zala. He practised as an advocate, and entered the national Diet in 1832, and played a moderate liberal role. Minister of Justice from 1848, he dissociated himself from Lajos Kossuth's more extreme Magyar nationalism, and became a leader of moderate liberalism in the restored Diet of 1861. He helped Hungary recover her constitution (1867), and established the Dual Monarchy of Austria-Hungary by negotiating the *Ausgleich* of 1867.

Deal POP (1981) 27 000, a resort town in Dover district, Kent, SE England. It is situated on the English Channel, 13km/8mi NE of Dover. NOTABLE FEATURE 16c Deal Castle, built by Henry VIII.

deal¹ — *noun* **1** a bargain, agreement, or arrangement, especially in business or politics. **2** a particular form of treatment or behaviour towards someone: *a rough deal*. **3** the act of, the way of, or a player's turn of sharing out cards among the players in a card game. — *verb* (PAST TENSE AND PAST PARTICIPLE **dealt**) **1** *intrans.* (**deal in something**) to buy and sell it. **2** *trans., intrans.* (*also* **deal out**) to divide the cards among the players in a card game. **3** *trans., intrans.* (*also* **deal out**) to give (something) out to a number of people, etc.

— **deal someone a blow** to hit or strike them.
deal with something *or* **someone** **1** to take action regarding them. **2** to be concerned with them.
a good *or* **great deal 1** a large quantity. **2** very much or often: *she sees them a great deal.* [from Anglo-Saxon *dæl*, part]

deal² *noun* a plank, or planks, of fir or pine wood, or other soft wood, used for making eg furniture. [from Old German dialect *dele*]

dealer *noun* **1** a person or firm dealing in retail goods. **2** the player who deals in a card-game.

dealership *noun* **1** a business which buys and sells things. **2** a business licensed to sell a particular product by its manufacturer.

dealings *pl. noun* business, etc contacts.

dealt see DEAL¹.

Dean, Christopher see TORVILL, JAYNE.

Dean, James (Byron) (1931–55) US film actor, born at Marion, Indiana. He started acting at university, joined the Actors Studio, and after small parts in theatre, films, and television gained overnight success in the film *East of Eden* (1955). He starred in only two more films, *Rebel Without a Cause* (1955) and *Giant* (released 1956), before he was killed in a car crash. He became a cult figure, the personification of contemporary rebellious American youth.

dean *noun* **1** a senior clergyman in an Anglican cathedral. **2** a senior official in a university or college, sometimes with responsibility for student discipline. **3** the head of a university or college faculty. [from Old French *deien*]

deanery *noun* (PL. **deaneries**) **1** the house or office of a dean. **2** a group of parishes for which a rural dean has responsibility.

Deans, Jeanie the honourable commonplace heroine of Sir Walter Scott's *The Heart of Midlothian*, who walks to London to secure a pardon for her half-sister Effie. Their father's name is Davie Deans.

dear — *adj.* **1** high in price; charging high prices. **2** lovable; attractive. **3** used in addressing someone at the start of a letter. **4** (**dear to someone**) **a** greatly loved by them. **b** very important or precious to them. — *noun* **1** a charming or lovable person. **2** *used especially as a form of address* a person one loves or likes. — *interj.* an expression of dismay, etc.
— **cost someone dear** to cause or result in a lot of trouble or suffering.
dear knows *colloq.* no one knows.
[from Anglo-Saxon *deore*]

Dearborn POP (1990) 89 000, a town in Wayne County, SE Michigan, N central USA. It lies on the R Rouge, 16km/10mi W of Detroit. Henry Ford, the car-manufacturer, was born here in 1863. NOTABLE FEATURES Greenfield Village; Henry Ford Museum.

dearly *adv.* **1** very much. **2** at a high price or cost.
— **pay dearly** to be made to suffer.

dearness *noun* being dear or expensive.

Dearne Valley POP (1981) 89 000, an urban area in S Yorkshire, N England, situated 12km/7mi SE of Barnsley. Its centre is at Bolton-upon-Dearne. The R Dearne crosses the area, and flows SE into the R Don.

dearth *noun* a scarceness or lack of something. [from DEAR + -TH²]

death *noun* **1** the time, act, or manner of dying, or the state of being dead. **2** *Biol.* the cessation of all the vital functions that are required to keep an organism alive. **3** *Medicine* the cessation of the heartbeat when this is accompanied by brain death (the functional death of the centres in the brain stem that control breathing and other vital reflexes). **4** something which causes a person to die: *be the death of someone*. **5** the end or destruc-

tion of something. **6** (**Death**) the figure of a skeleton, as a symbol of death.
— **at death's door** near death; gravely ill.
in at the death 1 present when a hunted animal, eg a fox, is killed. **2** present at the end or destruction of an enterprise, undertaking, etc.
like death warmed up *colloq.* having a sick or unhealthy appearance.
like grim death very hard or tightly.
put someone to death to kill or cause them to be killed; to execute them.
to death very much; to an extreme or excess: *bored to death.*
to the death until dead or until one's opponent is dead.
[from Anglo-Saxon *dēath*]

death-bed *noun* the bed in which a person dies or is about to die.

death blow an action, decision, etc which puts an end to or destroys (hopes, plans, etc).

death cap a mushroom (*Amanita phalloides*) that is the most poisonous of all fungi. It has a smooth shiny yellowish-green cap with darker streaks, with crowded white gills on the underside of the cap.

death cell a prison cell in which a prisoner who is condemned to death is kept before the sentence is carried out.

death certificate a certificate, signed by a doctor, stating the time and cause of someone's death.

death duty *Brit.* formerly, a tax paid on the value of property left by a person after he or she has died (now replaced by *inheritance tax*).

death-knell *noun* **1** the ringing of a bell when someone has died. **2** an action, announcement, etc that heralds the end or destruction of (hopes, plans, etc).

deathless *adj. often ironic* immortal; unforgettable: *deathless prose.*

deathly *adj., adv.* like in death.

death-mask *noun* a mask made of a person's face after he or she has died.

Death of a Salesman a play by Arthur Miller (1949, Pulitzer Prize). It is a moving study of an ageing salesman whose belief in contemporary values causes his downfall.

death penalty punishment of a crime by death.

death-rate *noun* the number of deaths as a proportion of the total population, usually calculated as a percentage or rate per thousand.

death row *North Amer., esp. US* part of a prison where people who have been sentenced to death are kept.

death's-head *noun* a human skull, or a picture, mask, etc representing one.

deathtrap *noun* a building, vehicle, etc which is unsafe and likely to cause serious or fatal accidents.

Death Valley an ancient rift-valley lake-bed in SE California, western USA, beside the Nevada border. A deep and arid desert basin, it is one of the hottest places in the world and contains the lowest point in N America (the Badwater R, altitude 86m). It is 225km/140mi long, 6–26km/4–16mi wide, and was designated a national monument in 1933 (area 8 400sq km/3 240sq mi). The highest point is at Telescope Peak (3 367m). Rainfall is less than 50mm per year and summer temperatures reach 74°C on the ground and 57°C in the air. There are numerous salt and alkali flats, colourful rock formations, desert plants, small animal life, and footprints of prehistoric animals. The valley was named in 1849 by a party of gold prospectors, some of whom died while trying to cross it; in the 1880s large deposits of borax were discovered. NOTABLE FEATURE Scott's Castle, built by the American adventurer Walter Scott (1872–1954).

death-warrant *noun* an official order that a death sentence is to be carried out.

deathwatch beetle a type of beetle which makes a ticking or tapping sound that used to be thought to mean that someone in the building was going to die.

death wish a desire to die, or that someone else should die.

deb *noun colloq.* a debutante.

debacle *or* **débâcle** *noun* total disorder, defeat, collapse of organization, etc. [from French *débâcle*]

debar *verb* (**debarred**, **debarring**) to stop (someone) from joining, taking part in, doing, etc something.

debarment *noun* exclusion from acting or taking part.

de Bary, Heinrich Anton see BARY, HEINRICH ANTON DE.

debase *verb* **1** to lower the value, quality, or status (of something). **2** to lower the value of (a coin) by adding metal of a lower value. [from DE- + ABASE]

debased *adj.* lowered in value or status; spoiled.

debasement *noun* debasing; degradation.

debatable *or* **debateable** *adj.* doubtful; which could be argued about; uncertain.

debate — *noun* **1** a formal discussion, often in front of an audience, in which two or more people put forward opposing views on a particular subject. **2** any general discussion on a subject, not necessarily in one place or at one time. — *verb trans., intrans.* **1** to hold or take part in a formal discussion on a particular topic, often in front of an audience. **2** to consider the arguments for or against (something).
— **open to debate** not certain or agreed; in doubt.
[from Old French *debatre*, to discuss]

debater *noun* a person who takes part in a debate.

debating *noun* formal discussion of a question.

debauch — *verb* to corrupt; to cause or persuade (someone) to take part in immoral (especially sexual) activities or excessive drinking. — *noun* a period of debauched behaviour. [from Old French *desbaucher*, to corrupt]

debauched *adj.* corrupted; immoral.

debauchee *noun* a person who likes sensual indulgence.

debauchery *noun* excessive sensual indulgence.

de Beauvoir, Simone see BEAUVOIR, SIMONE DE.

de Beer, Sir Gavin Rylands see BEER, SIR GAVIN RYLANDS DE.

debenture *noun* **1** a type of loan to a company or government agency which is usually made for a set period of time and carries a fixed rate of interest. **2** the document or bond acknowledging this loan. [from Latin *debentur*, there are due or owed]

debilitate *verb* to make weak or weaker. [from Latin *debilis*, weak]

debilitating *adj.* weakening; enervating.

debilitation *noun* a debilitating or weakening state or process.

debility *noun* weakness of the body or mind, especially as a result of illness or disease.

debit — *noun* **1** an entry in an account recording what is owed or has been spent. **2** a sum taken from a bank, etc account. **3** a deduction made from a bill or account. See also CREDIT. — *verb* (**debited**, **debiting**) **1** to take from (an account, etc). **2** to record in a debit entry: *debited*

£150 against them / debited them with £150. [from Latin *debitum*, what is due]

debonair *adj.*, *said especially of a man* cheerful, charming, and of elegant appearance and good manners. [from Old French *de bon aire*, of good manners]

debonairly *adv.* with a debonair or cheerful manner.

De Bono, Edward Francis Charles Publius (1933–) Maltese-born British psychologist and author. A lecturer in medicine at Cambridge (1976–83), he is involved with a number of organizations to promote the skills of thinking including the Cognitive Research Trust, Cambridge (Director since 1971). His books include *The Use of Lateral Thinking* (1967) and *Handbook for a Positive Revolution* (1990).

Deborah **1** the name of Rebecca's nurse in the Old Testament and of a female prophet. **2** a female first name, popular since the 17c. [from Hebrew *deborah*, bee]

debouch *verb intrans. technical, said of troops or a river, etc* to come out of a narrow place or opening into a wider or more open place. [from French *déboucher*, from *de*, from + *bouche*, mouth]

debouchment *noun* **1** coming out into an open place. **2** the outlet of a river, etc.

de Bourgh, Lady Catherine see BOURGH, LADY CATHERINE DE.

Debrecen POP (1991e) 214 000, the capital of Hajdú-Bihar county, E Hungary, and the third largest city in the country. It is the economic and cultural centre of the Great Plain. HISTORY in 1849 Louis Kossuth proclaimed Hungary's independence in the great church in Debrecen.

Debrett's Peerage a reference guide to the titled aristocracy of Great Britain, first published in 1802 by John Debrett (c.1752–1822). It has separate listings of peers and baronets, and also offers information on forms of address, precedence, the wearing of decorations, and etiquette.

Debreu, Gerard (1921–) French-born US economist, born in Calais. He went to the USA in 1950, was a Professor at Yale (1955–61), and became Professor of Economics (in 1962) and Maths (in 1975) at California. He was awarded the Nobel Prize for Economics in 1983 for his work on the equilibrium between prices, production, and consumer demand in a free-market economy.

debrief *verb* to gather information from (a diplomat, astronaut, soldier, etc) after a battle, event, mission, etc.

debriefing *noun* interrogation after a completed mission, etc.

debris *or* **débris** *noun* **1** what remains of something crushed, smashed, destroyed, etc. **2** rubbish. **3** small pieces of rock. [from French *debris*]

de Broglie, Louis-Victor Pierre Raymond see BROGLIE, LOUIS-VICTOR PIERRE RAYMOND DE.

Debs, Eugene V(ictor) (1855–1926) US politician, born in Terre Haute, Indiana. As a locomotive fireman he became President of the American Railroad Union (1893) and in 1894 led a successful national strike for higher wages. He helped to establish the Socialist Party of America, was imprisoned for labour agitation, and stood five times as Socialist candidate for president (1900–20). His pacifism led to his imprisonment (1918–21).

debt *noun* **1** something which is owed. **2** the state of owing something. [from Old French *dette*, from Latin *debitum*, what is owed]

debt of honour a debt one is morally but not legally obliged to pay.

debtor *noun* someone owing money. See also CREDITOR.

debug *verb* (**debugged**, **debugging**) **1** to remove secret microphones from (a room, etc). **2** to look for and remove faults in (a computer program).

debunk *verb* to show (a person's claims, good reputation, etc) to be false or unjustified. [from DE- + BUNK[2]]

Debussy, Claude (Achille) (1862–1918) French composer, born in St Germain-en-Laye. His early successes were the *Prélude à l'après-midi d'un faune* (1894), and his piano pieces *Images* and *Préludes*, in which he experimented with novel techniques and effects, producing the pictures in sound which led to his work being described as 'Musical Impressionism'. He extended this new idiom to orchestral music in *La Mer* (1905) and other pieces.

début *or* **debut** *noun* the first public appearance of a performer. [from French *début*]

débutante *noun* a young woman making her first formal appearance as an adult in upper-class society, usually at a ball. [from French *débutante*, from *débuter*, to start off]

Debye, Peter Joseph Wilhelm, originally **Petrus Josephus Wilhelmus Debije** (1884–1966) Dutch–US physicist and chemist, born in Maastricht. Professor at Zürich, Utrecht, Göttingen, and Leipzig, and Director of the Kaiser Wilhelm Institute for Physics in Berlin, he moved to the USA in 1940 as Professor of Chemistry at Cornell. Noted for his work on molecular structure and a pioneer in X-ray powder photography, he was awarded the 1936 Nobel Prize for Chemistry.

Dec *or* **Dec.** *abbrev.* December.

deca- *combining form* ten: *decahedron.* [from Greek *deka*, 10]

decade *noun* **1** a period of 10 years. **2** a group or series of 10 things, etc. [from DECA-]

decadence *noun* **1** a falling from high to low standards in morals, art, etc. **2** the state of having low or immoral standards of behaviour, etc. [from French *décadence*, from Latin *de*, from + *cadere*, to fall]

decadent *adj.* having low moral standards.

decadently *adv.* in a decadent or immoral way.

Decadents specifically, a group of French writers in the late 1880s. It included the poets Baudelaire, Verlaine, Rimbaud, and Mallarmé, and the novelist Joris Karl Huysmans. More generally, any writers exhibiting decadent tendencies (eg Edgar Allan Poe in the 1840s).

decaff *colloq.* — *adj.* decaffeinated. — *noun* decaffeinated coffee.

decaffeinate *verb* to remove all or part of the caffeine from.

decaffeinated *adj. said of coffee, etc* having all or part of the caffeine removed.

decagon *noun Geom.* a polygon with 10 sides and 10 angles. [from DECA- + Greek *gonia*, angle]

decagonal *adj.* having 10 sides and angles.

decahedral *adj., said of a solid figure* having 10 faces.

decahedron *noun* a solid figure with ten faces. [from DECA- + Greek *hedra*, seat]

Decalogue *noun* (**the Decalogue**) *Biblical* the Ten Commandments given by God to Moses. [from DECA- + Greek *logos*, word]

Decameron a series of narratives by Boccaccio (1349–51). It describes how 10 Florentines taking refuge from the plague relate one tale each for 10 days. It was influential on Chaucer's *Canterbury Tales.* [from DECA- + Greek *hemera*, day]

decamp *verb intrans.* to go away suddenly, especially secretly. [from French *décamper*]

decanal *adj. Relig.* **1** of or relating to a dean or deanery. **2** *said of part of a choir* positioned on the same side of the cathedral as the dean, ie the south side. [from late Latin *decanus*, dean]

decant *verb* **1** to pour (wine, etc) from one bottle or container to another, leaving any sediment behind. **2** to remove (people) from where they usually live to some other place. [from French *décanter*, from Latin *de*, from + *canthus*, spout]

decanter *noun* an ornamental bottle for wine, sherry, whisky, etc.

decapitate *verb* to cut off the head of. [from DE- 1 + Latin *caput*, head]

decapitation *noun* beheading.

decapod *noun Zool.* a member of the Decapoda, including crabs, lobsters, squid, and cuttlefish. [from DECA- + Greek *pous podos*, foot]

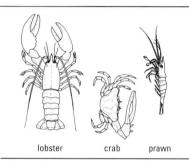

lobster   crab   prawn

decapods

Decapoda *pl. noun Zool.* in the animal kingdom, a large order of predominantly marine crustaceans that characteristically have three pairs of legs modified as pincers for feeding, and five pairs of walking legs, eg crabs, shrimps, lobsters.

decarbonization *or* **decarbonisation** *noun* removal of carbon.

decarbonize *or* **decarbonise** *verb* to remove carbon from (an internal-combustion engine).

decathlete *noun* a contestant in a decathlon.

decathlon *noun* an athletic competition (usually for men) in which competitors take part in ten different events over two days. [from DECA- + Greek *athlon*, contest]

Decatur, Stephen (1779–1820) US naval commander, born in Sinepuxent, Maryland, of French descent. He served against the French, and distinguished himself in the war with Tripoli (1801–5), when he burned the captured *Philadelphia* and escaped under the fire of 141 guns. Promoted captain in 1804 and commodore in 1810, in the war with Britain he captured the frigate *Macedonian* (1812), but surrendered in 1814, and was killed in a duel in Bladensburg, Maryland.

decay — *verb* **1** *trans., intrans.* to make or become rotten, ruined, weaker in health or power, etc. **2** *intrans. Physics, said of a radioactive substance* to break down spontaneously into one or more isotopes which may or may not be radioactive. — *noun* **1** the natural breakdown of dead organic matter. **2** *Physics* the spontaneous breakdown of an unstable nucleus of a radioactive substance into one or more isotopes which may or may not be radioactive, with the emission of alpha or beta particles, or gamma rays. **3** a gradual decrease in health, power, quality, etc. **4** rotten matter in a tooth, etc. [from Old French *decair*]

Deccan, Sanskrit **Dakshin** an eastward-sloping plateau occupying most of S central India, S of the Vindhya Mts. The average altitude is 600m. Bounded by the Eastern Ghats and the Western Ghats, it includes most of Karnataka, S Andhra Pradesh, SE Maharashtra, and the NW Tamil Nadu states. Major towns include Hyderabad and Bangalore. The area is noted for its cotton. The British struggle against the French for control of India during the 18c took place on the Carnatic Plains.

decease *noun formal Legal* death. [from Old French *deces*]

deceased *formal Legal* — *adj.* dead. — *noun* (**the deceased**) a dead person or dead people.

deceit *noun* **1** an act of deceiving or misleading. **2** dishonesty; deceitfulness; willingness to deceive. [from Old French *deceite*]

deceitful *adj.* **1** deceiving, especially as a general habit. **2** intended to deceive.

deceitfully *adv.* in a deceitful or dishonest way.

deceive *verb* **1** to mislead or lie to. **2** to convince (oneself) that something is true when it is not. See also DECEPTION. [from Old French *deceivre*]

deceiver *noun* a person who deceives, especially habitually.

decelerate *verb trans., intrans.* to slow down or cause to slow down (especially a vehicle, machine, etc). [from DE- 1 + ACCELERATE]

deceleration *noun* reduction in speed.

December *noun* the twelfth month of the year. [from Latin *December*, from *decem*, 10 (because it was at one time the tenth month of the Roman year)]

decency *noun* (PL. **decencies**) **1** decent behaviour or character. **2** (**decencies**) the generally accepted rules of respectable or moral behaviour.

decennial *adj.* **1** happening every 10 years. **2** consisting of 10 years. [from Latin *decem*, 10 + *annus*, year]

decent *adj.* **1** respectable; suitable; modest, not vulgar or immoral. **2** kind, tolerant or likeable. **3** fairly good; adequate. [from Latin *decere*, to be fitting]

decently *adv.* in a decent way; so as to be decent or reasonable: *cannot decently refuse.*

decentralization *or* **decentralisation** *noun* the process of decentralizing.

decentralize *or* **decentralise** *verb trans., intrans., said of a part of government, industry, etc* to alter or be altered by the transfer of organization, etc from one main central place to several smaller, less central positions.

deception *noun* **1** an act of deceiving or the state of being deceived. **2** something which deceives or misleads. [from Latin *decipere*, to deceive]

deceptive *adj.* deceiving; misleading.

deceptively *adv.* so as to deceive or mislead: *deceptively simple.*

deci- *combining form* one-tenth: *decilitre.* [from Latin *decimus*, tenth]

decibel *noun* (SYMBOL **dB**) a unit equal to $\frac{1}{10}$ of a bel, used for comparing levels of power, especially sound, on a logarithmic scale. One decibel corresponds to an increase in sound intensity of 26%, which is just detectable by the human ear. The sound of conversation is about 50dB, while that of a jet aircraft taking off can reach 130dB.

decide *verb* **1** (**decide on** *or* **about something**) to establish an intention or course of action regarding it. **2** (**decide to do something**) establish an intention of doing it: *decided to leave early.* **3** (**decide against something**) to reject it as an intention or course of action: *decided against making a donation.* **4** to settle (something). **5** to make the final result of (something) certain. **5** to cause (someone) to decide in a certain way: *the weather decided them to stay.* **6** to make a formal judgement about something. [from Latin *decidere*, to cut down, settle]

decided *adj.* **1** clear and definite; unmistakable. **2** determined; showing no doubt.

decidedly *adv.* undoubtedly; definitely: *decidedly ugly.*

decider *noun* **1** someone or something that decides. **2** something that decides the result of something.

deciduous *adj.* **1** *Bot.* denoting plants which shed all their leaves at a certain time of year, usually the autumn in temperate regions, eg horse chestnut. See also EVERGREEN. **2** *Biol.* denoting structures which are shed at maturity or after a period of growth, eg milk teeth. [from Latin *decidere*, to fall down]

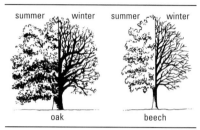

summer   winter   summer   winter

oak   beech

deciduous trees

decilitre *noun* a tenth of a litre.

decimal — *adj.* **1** based on the number 10; relating to powers of 10 or the base 10. **2** denoting a system of measurement, etc, with units that are related to each other by multiples of 10. — *noun* a decimal fraction. [from Latin *decimalis*, of tenths]

decimal currency a system of money in which each coin or note is either a tenth of or 10 times another in value.

decimal fraction a fraction in which tenths, hundredths, thousandths, etc are written in figures after a decimal point which follows the figure or figures expressing whole numbers, eg $0.5 = \frac{5}{10}$ or $\frac{1}{2}$. See also VULGAR FRACTION.

decimalization *or* **decimalisation** *noun* conversion to a decimal system of units.

decimalize *or* **decimalise** *verb* to convert (numbers, a currency, etc) from a non-decimal to a decimal form.

decimal system **1** a system of measurement with units that are related to each other by multiples of 10. **2** the number system in common use, in which the place values of the digits in a number correspond to multiples of powers of 10. **3** a system of library classification, based on the division of books into numbered classes, with further subdivision shown by numbers following a decimal point.

decimate *verb* to reduce greatly in number; to destroy a large part or number of. [from Latin *decimare*, to take a tenth person or thing, from *decem*, 10]

decimation *noun* destruction of a large number.

decipher *verb* (**deciphered**, **deciphering**) **1** to translate (a message or text in code or in an unfamiliar or strange form of writing) into ordinary, understandable language. **2** to work out the meaning of (something obscure or difficult to read).

decipherable *adj.* capable of being deciphered.

decipherment *noun* deciphering; translation from a code.

decision *noun* **1** the act of deciding. **2** something decided. **3** the ability to make decisions and act on them firmly. [from Latin *decisio*, cutting off]

decisive *adj.* **1** putting an end to doubt or dispute. **2** willing and able to make decisions quickly and with firmness.

decisively *adv.* in a decisive way; to a decisive degree; conclusively.

decisiveness *noun* the quality of being decisive, especially habitually.

deck[1] *noun* **1** a platform extending from one side of a ship to the other, and forming a floor or covering. **2** a floor in a bus, etc. **3** *North Amer., esp. US* a pack of playing-cards. **4** that part of a tape recorder or computer in which the magnetic tapes are placed, and the mechanism for running them.
— **clear the decks** to clear away obstacles or deal with preliminary jobs in preparation for further activity.
hit the deck *colloq.* to lie or fall down suddenly and quickly on the ground or floor.
[from Old Dutch *dec*, roof, covering]

deck[2] (**deck something out**) to decorate or embellish it. [from Dutch *dekken*, to cover]

deck-chair *noun Brit.* a light folding chair made of wood and canvas or other heavy fabric, usually used for sitting outside.

-decker *combining form* forming words meaning 'having a certain number of decks': *triple-decker*.

deck hand a person who does general work on the deck of a ship.

decko see DEKKO.

declaim *verb* **1** *trans., intrans.* to make (a speech) in an impressive and dramatic manner. **2** (**declaim against something**) to protest about it loudly and passionately. [from Latin *declamare*]

declamation *noun* an impressive or emotional speech, usually made in protest or condemnation. [from Latin *declamare*, to declaim]

declamatory *adj., said of speech* impassioned; rhetorical.

Declan a male first name, recently revived in Ireland and Scotland. [from Gaelic *Deaglan*, of uncertain origin]

declaration *noun* declaring; a formal statement or announcement.

Declaration of Independence a document adopted (1776) by the Continental Congress after the American Revolution to proclaim the separation of the 13 colonies from Britain. Written mainly by Thomas Jefferson, it announced the right of revolution and detailed the Americans' reasons for the break.

Declaration of Independence

We hold these Truths to be self-evident, that all Men are created equal, that they are endowed by their Creator with certain unalienable Rights, that among these are Life, Liberty, and the Pursuit of Happiness – That to secure these Rights, Governments are instituted among Men, deriving their just Powers from the Consent of the Governed, that whenever any Form of Government becomes destructive of these Ends, it is the Right of the People to alter or to abolish it, and to institute new Government, laying its Foundation on such Principles, and organizing its Powers in such Form, as to them shall seem most likely to effect their Safety and Happiness. Prudence, indeed, will dictate that Governments long established should not be changed for light and transient Causes; and accordingly all Experience hath shewn, that Mankind are more disposed to suffer, while Evils are sufferable, than to right themselves by abolishing the Forms to which they are accustomed. But when a long Train of Abuses and Usurpations, pursuing invariably the same Object, evinces a Design to reduce them under absolute Despotism, it is their Right, it is their Duty, to throw off such Government, and to provide new Guards for their future Security.

Declaration of Rights an English statute (1689) which ended the brief interregnum after James VII and II quit the throne and fled to the Continent (Dec 1688), and established William III and Mary II as joint monarchs. The bill effectively ensured that monarchs operated with the consent of parliament and did not suspend or dispense with laws passed by that body.

Declaration of the Rights of Man and Citizen a declaration made by the French National Assembly (27 Aug 1789) proclaiming liberty of conscience, of property, and of the press, and freedom from arbitrary imprisonment. It marked the end of the privileged system of the *ancien régime*.

declarative *adj. Grammar* making a statement.

Declaratory Act a British Act passed (1766) by the Rockingham government. Opposition in the American colonies to the introduction of taxes by the preceding Grenville administration had resulted in Rockingham's repeal of the Stamp Act, but the Declaratory Act reasserted the British parliament's authority to legislate for the colonies 'in all cases whatsoever'.

declare *verb* **1** to announce publicly or formally: *declare war*. **2** to say firmly or emphatically. **3** to make known (goods on which duty must be paid, income on which tax should be paid, etc). **4** *intrans. Cricket* to end an innings before 10 wickets have fallen. **5** *intrans.* (**declare for** *or* **against something**) to state one's support or opposition regarding it. **6** *trans., intrans. Cards* to state or show that one is holding (certain cards). [from Latin *declarare*, from *clarus*, clear]

declassification *noun* removal of information from an official secret list.

declassify *verb* (**declassifies, declassified**) to take (an official document, etc) off a list of secret information and allow public access to it.

declension *noun Grammar* **1** in certain languages, such as Latin, any of various sets of different forms taken by nouns, adjectives or pronouns to indicate case, number, and gender. **2** the act of stating these forms. See also CONJUGATION, DECLINE. **3** any group of nouns or adjectives showing the same pattern of forms. [from Latin *declinatio*, bending aside]

declination *noun* **1** *technical* the angle between true north (geographical north) and magnetic north (north as indicated by a magnetic compass). It varies according to time and geographical location. **2** *Astron.* the angular distance of a star or planet north or south of the celestial equator. It is measured in degrees, and is the coordinate on the celestial sphere that corresponds to latitude on the Earth. [from Latin *declinatio*, bending aside]

decline — *verb* **1** to refuse (an invitation, etc), especially politely. **2** *intrans.* to become less strong or less healthy. **3** *intrans.* to become less in quality or quantity. **4** *Grammar* to state the pattern of forms representing the various cases of (a noun, adjective, or pronoun). See also CONJUGATE, DECLENSION. — *noun* a lessening of strength, health, quality, quantity, etc. [from Latin *declinare*, to bend aside]

Decline and Fall of the Roman Empire, The a historical work by Edward Gibbon (published in 6 vols 1776, 1781, 1788). It covers more than 13 centuries of classical history up to the capture of Constantinople by the Turks in 1413.

declivity *noun* (PL. **declivities**) *formal* a downward slope. See also ACCLIVITY. [from DE- 1 + Latin *clivus*, sloping]

declutch *verb intrans.* to release the clutch of (a motor vehicle).

decoction *noun* a liquid obtained by boiling something in water, eg to extract its flavour. [from Latin *decoctio*, from *coquere*, to cook or boil]

decode *verb* to translate (a coded message) into ordinary language.

decoder *noun* a person or device that decodes.

décolletage *noun* a low-cut neckline on a woman's dress, etc.

décolleté *or* **décolletée** *adj.* **1** *said of a woman's dress, etc* having the neckline cut low at the front. **2** *said of a woman* wearing such a dress, etc. [from French *décolleter*, to bare the neck and shoulders]

decommission *verb* (**decommissioned, decommissioning**) to take (eg a warship or atomic reactor) out of use or operation.

decompose *verb* **1** *intrans. said of a dead organism* to rot, usually as a result of the activity of fungi and bacteria. **2** *said of a chemical compound* to break down into simpler compounds or its constituent elements, eg as a result of heating, exposure to light, or electrolysis. **3** *trans., intrans. technical* to separate into smaller or simpler parts or elements. [from French *décomposer*]

decomposition *noun* decaying; rotting; disintegration.

decompress *verb technical* to decrease the pressure on.

decompression *noun* reduction of air pressure.

decompression chamber a sealed room in which the air pressure can be varied, used especially to enable deep-sea divers to return gradually and safely to normal air pressure after a dive.

decompression sickness, a painful and sometimes fatal disorder that occurs when a person who has been breathing air under high pressure, eg a deep-sea diver, returns too suddenly to normal atmospheric pressure, eg by surfacing too rapidly. — Also called *the bends*.
◇ In decompression sickness, nitrogen dissolved in the bloodstream comes out of solution and forms bubbles that hinder or even block the circulation, causing pain and possible brain, heart, and lung damage. The condition is treated by returning the patient to the original high pressure, eg in a decompression chamber, and then slowly reducing the pressure to normal levels.

decongestant *noun Medicine* a drug or other agent, usually administered in the form of a nasal spray or taken by mouth, that reduces or relieves nasal congestion by clearing mucus from the nasal cavities.

deconstruction *or* **deconstructive criticism** an approach to critical analysis applied especially to literary texts which, questioning the ability of language to represent adequately any external reality, asserts that it is therefore impossible for any text to communicate a fixed and stable meaning, and that readers should eradicate or 'deconstruct' all philosophical and other concepts when approaching a text.

decontaminate *verb* to make (something) safe by removing poisons, radioactivity, etc.

decontamination *noun* removal of contaminating poisons, etc.

décor *noun* the style of decoration, furnishings, etc in a room or house. [from French *décor*, decoration]

decorate *verb* **1** to beautify with ornaments, etc. **2** to put paint or wallpaper on. **3** to give a medal or badge to as a mark of honour. [from Latin *decorare*, to beautify]

Decorated style a form of English Gothic architecture prevalent in the late 13c and 14c, characterized by a maximum of surface decoration, usually in the form of stylized leaves and the double-S curve known as an *ogee*. Examples include Wells Cathedral (1290–c.1340) and the Lady Chapel and Octagon at Ely (1321–53).

decorating *noun* painting of a building, etc.

decoration *noun* **1** something used to decorate. **2** the act of decorating. **3** a medal or badge given as a mark of honour.

decorative *adj.* ornamental or beautiful (especially if not useful).

decorative arts the applied arts, as distinct from the fine arts. The decorative arts include ceramics, metalwork, textiles, furniture, glassmaking, bookbinding, calligraphy, etc. The distinction between decorative art and fine art can become blurred in some areas, such as ceramic sculpture and hanging tapestries; in general, the decorative art object is functional as well as ornamental.

decorator *noun* a person who decorates buildings professionally.

decorous *adj.*, *said of behaviour or appearance* correct or socially acceptable; showing proper respect. [from Latin *decorus*, becoming, fitting]

decorously *adv.* with a decorous or proper manner.

decorum *noun* correct or socially acceptable behaviour. [from Latin *decorus*, becoming or fitting]

De Courcy, Lord *and* **Lady** self-seeking, aristocratical characters in Anthony Trollope's 'Barsetshire' novels.

decoy — *verb* to lead or lure into a trap. — *noun* someone or something used to lead or lure (a person or animal) into a trap. [probably from Dutch *de kooi*, the cage]

decrease — *verb trans.*, *intrans.* (with stress on *-crease*) to make or become less. — *noun* (with stress on *de-*) a lessening or loss. [from Latin *decrescere*]

decreasingly *adv.* to a lessening extent.

decree — *noun* **1** a formal order or ruling made by someone in high authority (eg a monarch) and which becomes law. **2** *Legal* a ruling made in a law court. — *verb* to order or decide (something) formally or officially. [from Latin *decretum*]

decree absolute *Legal* a decree issued by a court in divorce proceedings which officially ends a marriage.

decree nisi *Legal* a decree issued by a court in divorce proceedings which will become a decree absolute after a period of time unless some reason is shown why it should not. [from Latin *nisi*, unless]

decrepit *adj.* **1** weak or worn out because of old age. **2** in a very poor state because of age or long use. [from Latin *decrepitus*, very old]

decrepitude *noun* a decrepit or worn out state.

decretal *noun* a papal decree. [from Latin *decretalis*, of a decree]

Decroux, Etienne-Marcel (1898–) French actor responsible for the renaissance of mime in the 20c. He developed and taught a system of physical expression he termed *mime corporel*. After opening a school in Paris (1940), from 1941 he toured extensively both teaching and performing.

decry *verb* (**decries**, **decried**) to express disapproval of; to criticize as worthless or unsuitable. [from French *décrier*]

Dedalus, Stephen the scholarly central figure in James Joyce's *A Portrait of the Artist as a Young Man*, who reappears in *Ulysses*.

Dedekind, Julius Wilhelm Richard (1831–1916) German mathematician, born in Brunswick. He taught at Göttingen and Zürich before becoming professor in Brunswick in 1862. He gave one of the first precise definitions of the real number system, and did important work in number theory which led him to introduce many concepts which have become fundamental in all modern algebra, in particular that of an 'ideal'.

dedicate *verb* (*usually* **dedicate something to someone** *or* **something**) **1** to give or devote (oneself or one's time, money, etc) wholly or chiefly to some purpose. **2** to devote or address (a book, piece of music, etc) to someone as a token of affection or respect. **3** to set apart for some sacred purpose. [from Latin *dedicare*, to declare, dedicate]

dedicated *adj.* **1** working very hard at or spending a great deal of one's time and energy on something. **2** *technical*, *said especially of a computer* designed to carry out one particular function.

dedication *noun* **1** the quality of being dedicated. **2** the act of dedicating. **3** the words dedicating a book, etc to someone.

dedicator *noun* a person who makes a dedication.

dedicatory *adj.* serving as a dedication in a book, etc: *dedicatory remarks.*

deduce *verb* to think out or judge on the basis of what one knows or assumes to be fact. [from DE- 1 + Latin *ducere*, to lead]

deducible *adj.* capable of being deduced.

deduct *verb* to take away (a number, amount, etc). [from DE- 1 + Latin *ducere*, to lead]

deductible *adj.* capable of being deducted; eligible for deduction: *expenses deductible from tax.*

deduction *noun* **1** the act or process of deducting. **2** something, especially money, which has been or will be deducted. **3** the act or process of deducing, especially of deducing a particular fact from what one knows or thinks to be generally true. See also INDUCTION. **4** something that has been deduced. [from DE- 1 + Latin *ducere*, to lead]

deductive *adj.*, *said of a logical process of thought* deducing or involving deduction of particular facts from general truths. See also INDUCTIVE.

de Duve, Christian René see DUVE, CHRISTIAN RENÉ DE.

Dee, John (1527–1608) English alchemist, geographer, and mathematician, born in London. He travelled widely in Europe, brought back many astronomical instruments, and earned the reputation of a sorcerer. For most of his life he was concerned with the search for the Northwest Passage to the Far East.

deed *noun* **1** something someone has done. **2** a brave action or notable achievement. **3** *Legal* a signed statement which records the terms of an agreement, especially about a change in ownership of a house or other property. [from Anglo-Saxon *dæd* or *ded*]

deed poll *Brit. Legal* a deed made and signed by one person only, especially when changing his or her name.

dee-jay *or* **deejay** *noun colloq.* a disc jockey. [from the initials *DJ*]

deem *verb formal*, *old use* to judge, think or consider. [from Anglo-Saxon *deman*, to form a judgement]

deep — *adj.* **1** far down from the top or surface; with a relatively great distance from the top or surface to the bottom. **2** going or being far in from the outside surface or edge. **3** (*usually in a hyphened compound*) going or being far down by a specified amount: *knee-deep in mud.* **4** in a specified number of rows or layers: *lined up four deep.* **5** coming from or going far down; long and full: *a deep sigh* / *a deep breath.* **6** very great; serious: *deep trouble.* **7** *said of a colour* strong and relatively dark; not light or pale. **8** (**deep in something**) fully occupied or involved with it: *deep in thought.* **9** low in pitch. **10** *said of emotions, etc* strongly felt. **11** obscure; hard to understand: *deep thoughts.* **12** *said of a person* mysterious; keeping secret thoughts. **13** *Cricket* not close to the wickets. **14** *Football* well behind one's team's front line of players. — *adv.* **1** deeply. **2** far down or into. **3** late on in or well into (a period of time). — *noun* **1** (**the deep**) the ocean. **2** (*also* **deeps**)

old use a place far below the surface of the ground or the sea. See also DEPTH.

— **deep down** in reality, although not in appearance.

go off (**at**) **the deep end** *colloq.* to lose one's temper suddenly and violently.

in deep water *colloq.* in trouble or difficulties.

jump in *or* **dive in** *or* **be thrown in at the deep end** *colloq.* to begin or be given a difficult undertaking with little or no experience or preparation. [from Anglo-Saxon *deop*]

deepen *verb trans.*, *intrans.* (**deepened**, **deepening**) to make or become deeper, greater, more intense, etc.

deep-freeze — *noun* a specialized refrigeration unit, or a compartment in a refrigerator, that is designed for storage of perishable material, especially food, in a frozen state at a temperature below -18°C (0°F). — *verb* (PAST TENSE **deep-froze**; PAST PARTICIPLE **deep-frozen**) to preserve perishable material, especially food, by storing it in a frozen state, so as to prevent the growth and reproduction of bacteria and other micro-organisms.

deep-fry *verb* to fry (something completely submerged in hot fat or oil).

deeply *adv.* very greatly.

deep-rooted *or* **deep-seated** *adj.*, *said of ideas, habits, etc* deeply and firmly established in a person or group of people and not easily removed or changed.

deep-sea *adj.* of, for, working, etc in the deeper parts of the sea.

deep-seated see DEEP-ROOTED.

deep-set *adj.* (of the eyes) in relatively deep sockets.

Deep South (the Deep South) the SE part of the USA, roughly the states of South Carolina, Georgia, Louisiana, Mississippi, and Alabama.

deep space outer space, understood by some people as the area of space well outside the Earth's atmosphere or beyond the Moon's orbit, by others as the area outside the solar system.

deer *noun* (PL. **deer**) any of numerous ruminant mammals belonging to the family Cervidae, found throughout Europe, Asia, and N and S America, and distinguished by the presence of antlers, usually branched, in the male. [from Anglo-Saxon *deor*, animal, deer]
◇ Deer are noted for their speed, graceful movements, and agility when jumping over obstacles. Male deer, usually known as stags or bucks, are generally significantly larger than the females, which are called hinds or does. With the exception of caribou, only male deer bear antlers. These are shed each year, but new antlers develop within a few months, and are initially covered by 'velvet', a layer of soft hair-covered skin. When the antlers are fully grown, the skin peels away or is rubbed off by the deer. The tough antlers are then used to defend territory or, in the mating season, to fight rivals. Deer range in size from the giant elk of Alaska, which reaches a height of up to 2m, to the S American pudu, which is about 40cm high. They are generally found in woodland and forest, where they feed on leaves, shoots, grass, and moss. Rapidly increasing populations of deer can cause serious damage to tree plantations and crops.

deerhound *noun* a breed of dog, developed in Scotland from Mediterranean ancestors, that has a tall slim body, a shaggy grey coat, long legs, a long tail, and a small head with short soft ears.

deerskin *noun* leather made from the skin of a deer.

deerstalker *noun* a kind of hat with peaks at the front and back and flaps at the side to cover the ears.

deface *verb* to deliberately spoil the appearance of (eg by marking or cutting). [from Old French *desfacier*]

defacement *noun* defacing; spoiling the appearance of something.

de facto, actual or actually, though not necessarily legally so. See also DE JURE. [from Latin *de facto*, in fact]

defamation *noun* defaming; attacking someone's good reputation.

defamatory *adj.*, said of a remark, etc attacking someone's good reputation.

defame *verb* to attack the good reputation of (someone) by saying something unfavourable about them. [from Latin *diffamare*, to spread bad reports about]

default — *verb intrans.* (**default on something**) to fail to do what one should do, especially to fail to pay what is due. — *noun* **1** a failure to do or pay what one should. **2** *Comput.* a preset option which will always be followed unless the operator enters a command to the contrary.
— **by default** because of someone's failure to do something which would have prevented or altered the situation.
[from Old French *defaillir*, to fail]

defaulter *noun* a person who defaults, especially in paying a debt.

defeat — *verb* **1** to beat, win a victory over, eg in a war, competition, game or argument. **2** to cause (plans, etc) to fail. — *noun* the act of defeating or state of being defeated. [from Old French *desfait*, from *desfaire*, to ruin, undo]

defeatism *noun* a state of mind in which one too readily expects or accepts defeat or failure.

defeatist — *adj.* too ready to accept defeat or failure. — *noun* a person who is defeatist.

defecate *verb intrans. formal, technical* to empty the bowels of waste matter. See also FAECES. [from Latin *defaecare*]

defecation *noun* emptying of the bowels.

defect — *noun* a flaw, fault or imperfection. — *verb intrans.* to leave one's country, political party or group, especially to support or join an opposing one. [from Latin *deficere*, to fail]

defection *noun* defecting; abandoning a country, cause, etc.

defective *adj.* imperfect; having a defect or defects.

defector *noun* a person who defects, or abandons a cause.

defence *noun* **1** the act of defending against attack. **2** the method, means, or equipment used to guard or protect against attack or when attacked. **3** the armed forces of a country. **4** (**defences**) fortifications. **5** a person's answer to an accusation, justifying or denying what he or she has been accused of. **6** (**the defence**) in a law court, the person or people on trial and the lawyer or lawyers acting for them. **7** *Sport* (**the defence**) the players in a team whose main task is to prevent their opponents from scoring. [from Latin *defendere*, to defend]

defenceless *adj.* unable to defend oneself if attacked.

defence mechanism *Psychol.* a process, usually subconscious, of blocking out of one's mind a feeling or memory one finds painful.

Defence, Ministry of in the UK, a government department first established in 1940 (when it replaced the War Office), responsible for military and defence policy. The Minister (Secretary of State from 1964) is a member of the cabinet.

Defence of the Realm Act (ABBREV. **DORA**) a British Act introduced (Nov 1914) at the beginning of World War I to give the government greater controls over the activities of its citizens, most importantly concerning restrictions on press reporting and other forms of censorship. The restrictions were increased as the war progressed.

defend *verb* **1** to guard or protect against attack or when attacked. **2** to explain, justify, or argue in support of, the actions of (someone accused of doing wrong). **3** *trans., intrans.* to be the lawyer acting on behalf of (the accused) in a trial. **4** *trans., intrans. Sport* to try to prevent one's opponents from scoring. **5** *Sport* to take part in a contest against a challenger for (a title, medal, etc one holds). [from Latin *defendere*]

defendant *noun* a person against whom a charge is brought in a law-court. See also PLAINTIFF.

defender *noun* a person who defends against attack, especially in military and sporting contexts.

Defender of the Faith, Latin *fidei defensor* a title conferred (1521) on Henry VIII of England by Pope Leo X as a reward for the king's written opposition to the teachings of Martin Luther. After the Reformation, the title was confirmed by parliament, and is still used by British sovereigns.

Defenestration of Prague the dramatic gesture (1618) with which the Czech Protestants challenged the authority and religion of the Habsburg Emperors within the Czech Lands. A crowd of nobles and knights marched on Prague Castle and, after a dispute, threw two imperial councillors, the Counts Martinic and Slavata, and their secretary out of a high window. Falling on rubbish, the victims survived. But in due course the Czech estates proceeded to depose Ferdinand II from the thrones of Bohemia and Moravia and to replace him with Frederick V of the Palatinate.

defensible *adj.* able to be defended or justified. [from Latin *defensibilis*]

defensibly *adv.* so as to be defended or justified.

defensive *adj.* **1** defending or ready to defend. **2** attempting to justify one's actions when criticized or when expecting criticism.
— **on the defensive** defending oneself or prepared to defend oneself against attack or criticism.
[from Latin *defensivus*]

defensively *adv.* in a defensive way.

defensiveness *noun* being defensive.

defer[1] *verb* (**deferred, deferring**) to put off or leave until a later time. [from Latin *differre*, to delay, postpone]

defer[2] *verb intrans.* (**deferred, deferring**) (**defer to someone**) to yield to their wishes, opinions, or orders. [from French *déférer*]

deference *noun* **1** willingness to consider or respect the wishes, etc of others. **2** the act of deferring.
— **in deference to someone** *or* **something** deferring to them; showing recognition of or respect for them.

deferential *adj.* showing deference or respect.

deferentially *adv.* with a deferential or respectful manner.

deferment *or* **deferral** *noun* deferring; postponement.

deferred payment payment for goods one has received by small sums of money over a period of time.

defiance *noun* an act of defying or of open disobedience; challenging or opposition, especially in a way that shows lack of respect.

defiant *adj.* openly disobedient or challenging.

defiantly *adv.* with a defiant or openly challenging manner.

deficiency *noun* (PL. **deficiencies**) **1** a shortage or lack in quality or amount. **2** the thing or amount lacking.

deficiency disease *Medicine* any disease caused by lack of one or more specific nutrients, especially vitamins, in the diet, eg rickets, scurvy, beriberi.

deficient *adj.* not good enough; not having all that is needed. [from Latin *deficere*, to fail or be lacking]

deficit *noun* the amount by which some quantity, especially a sum of money, is less than what is required (eg the amount by which expenditure is greater than income). [from Latin *deficere*, to fail or be lacking]

deficit financing *Econ.* a government policy of stimulating the economy by deliberately planning a budget deficit, where expenditure will exceed the revenue from taxes. Money is pumped into the economy to stimulate (or maintain) demand and excess spending is financed by borrowing.

defile[1] *verb* (with stress on *-file*) **1** to make dirty or polluted. **2** to take away or spoil the goodness, purity, holiness, etc of. [from Old French *defouler*, to trample or violate; altered under the influence of the old word *befile*, from Anglo-Saxon *befylan*, to make foul]

defile[2] — *noun* (with stress on *de-*) a narrow valley or passage between mountains. — *verb intrans.* (with stress on *-file*) to march in file. [from French *défilé*, from *défiler*, to march in file]

defilement *noun* making dirty; pollution.

defiler *noun* a person or thing that defiles or pollutes.

definable *adj.* capable of being defined or described precisely.

define *verb* **1** to fix or state the exact meaning of (a word, etc). **2** to fix, describe, or explain (opinions, duties, the qualities or limits of, etc). **3** to make clear the outline or shape of: *an ill-defined splodge on the canvas*. See also DEFINITION. [from Latin *definire*, to set boundaries to]

definite *adj.* **1** fixed or firm; not liable to change. **2** sure; certain. **3** clear and precise. **4** having clear outlines. [from Latin *definire*, to set boundaries to]
◆ Often confused with *definitive*.

definite article *Grammar* a word (*the* in English) used before a noun, or before an adjective used absolutely, to denote a specific or known example, or a defined class, as in *the cat by the door, the government, the uninitiated*. See also INDEFINITE ARTICLE.

definitely *adv.* **1** as a definite fact; certainly. **2** in a definite way.

definiteness *noun* a definite state or quality.

definition *noun* **1** a statement of the meaning of a word or phrase. **2** the act of defining a word or phrase. **3** the quality of having clear, precise limits or form. **4** the degree of clearness and preciseness of limits or form.
— **by definition** because of what something or someone essentially is or does: *a carpenter is by definition a craftsman*.
[from Latin *definitio*]

definitive *adj.* **1** settling a matter once and for all. **2** most complete or authoritative. [from Latin *definitivus*]
◆ Often confused with *definite*.

definitively *adv.* in a definitive or decisive way.

deflate *verb* **1** *trans., intrans.* to collapse or grow smaller by letting out gas. **2** to reduce or take away the hopes, excitement, feelings of importance or self-confidence, etc of. **3** *trans., intrans. Econ.* to cause or undergo deflation. See also INFLATE, REFLATE. [from DE- + INFLATE]

deflated *adj.* **1** having the air or gas removed. **2** *said of a person* deprived of confidence.

deflation *noun* **1** the act of deflating or the process of being deflated. **2** the state of being or feeling deflated. **3** *Econ.* a reduction in the amount of money available in a country, resulting in lower levels of economic activity, industrial output, and employment, and a lower rate of increase in wages and prices. See also INFLATION, REFLATION.

deflationary *adj.* tending to cause deflation.

deflect *verb trans., intrans.* to turn aside from the correct or intended course or direction. [from Latin *deflectere*]

deflection *noun* deflecting; deviation.

deflower *verb literary* to deprive (a woman) of her virginity. [from Latin *deflorare*, from *de*, from + *flos*, flower]

Defoe, Daniel (1660–1731) English writer, born in London. In 1688 he joined William III's army, and supported the King's party until 1704. He was imprisoned at Newgate following the publication of his satire *The Shortest Way with the Dissenters* (1702). On his release he founded and wrote *The Review* (1704–13), and worked intermittently as a secret agent for the Tory politician Robert Harley. After the accession of George I (1714) he returned to the writing of fiction and published his best-known work, *Robinson Crusoe* (1719–20). His other major works include *A Journal of the Plague Year*, *Moll Flanders* (both 1722), and *Roxana* (1724).

defoliant *noun Chem.* a type of herbicide that causes the leaves to fall off plants.

defoliate *verb* (**defoliated, defoliating**) *technical* to cause leaves to fall off (trees, etc). [from Latin *defoliare*, from *de*, off + *folium*, leaf]

defoliation *noun* shedding or removal of leaves from trees.

De Forest, Lee (1873–1961) US physicist and inventor, born in Council Bluffs, Iowa. A pioneer of radio and wireless telegraphy, he patented more than 300 inventions and is known as the 'father of radio' in the USA. He introduced the grid into the thermionic valve (1906), invented the four-electrode valve, and did much early work on sound reproduction and television.

deforest *verb Agric.* to cut down forest trees for commercial use as timber, firewood, etc, or to clear land for agriculture, without replacing them, or without allowing the natural forest to regenerate.

deforestation *noun Environ.* the felling of all trees, usually over a large area, in a region that was previously natural forest, without planting more trees to replace those that have been lost. ◇ The main purpose of deforestation is to provide land for agricultural, industrial, or urban purposes, or to obtain timber. Deforestation in tropical regions has resulted in the clearance of large areas of land for agriculture, and for the building of towns, cities, or industrial developments. In S America and Africa trees are being cut down at the rate of 12 hectares a minute, day and night. This is equivalent to the destruction of an area of forest nearly twice the size of England every year. Deforestation has resulted in the extinction or endangering of many plant and animal species whose natural habitat is rainforest. The destruction of such forests on steep slopes causes severe soil erosion, and may lead to desertification, as the shallow exposed soils are quickly washed away by running water. Furthermore, the soil in tropical rainforests is very low in nutrients, so that the removal of trees followed by cultivation of the land rapidly results in exhaustion of the soil. An important consequence of deforestation on a large scale is the rise in atmospheric carbon dioxide levels, because fewer trees are available to absorb carbon dioxide from the atmosphere and produce oxygen by the process of photosynthesis. This factor is contributing to the greenhouse effect.

deform *verb* to change the shape of (something) without breaking it, so that it looks ugly, unpleasant, unnatural, or spoiled. [from Latin *deformis*, ugly]

deformed *adj.* put out of shape; made ugly.

deformity *noun* (PL. **deformities**) being deformed or misshapen.

defraud *verb* (**defraud someone of something**) to dishonestly prevent (someone) getting or keeping something which belongs to them or to which they have a right. [from Latin *defraudare*]

defray *verb formal* to provide the money to pay (someone's costs or expenses). [from Old French *deffroier*, to pay costs]

defrayal *or* **defrayment** *noun* provision of money to meet a cost.

defrock *verb* to remove (a priest) from office, usually because of unacceptable conduct or beliefs.

defrost *verb trans., intrans.* **1** to remove ice from or have the ice removed from; to unfreeze. **2** *said of frozen food, etc* to make or become no longer frozen.

deft *adj.* skilful, quick, and neat. [from Anglo-Saxon *gedæfte*, meek]

deftly *adv.* in a deft or skilful way.

deftness *noun* being deft or skilful.

defunct *adj. facetious, formal* no longer living, existing, active, usable, or in use. [from Latin *defungi*, to finish]

defuse *verb* **1** to remove the fuse from (a bomb, etc). **2** to make (a situation, etc) harmless or less dangerous.

defy *verb* (**defies, defied**) **1** to resist or disobey boldly and openly. **2** to dare or challenge (someone). **3** *formal* to make impossible or unsuccessful. See also DEFIANCE. [from Old French *defier*, from Latin *diffidare*, to renounce one's faith]

Degas, (Hilaire Germain) Edgar (1834–1917) French artist, born in Paris. He went to Italy, where he was influenced by the Renaissance painters. On his return to Paris he associated with the Impressionists and took part in most of their exhibitions from 1874 to 1886. He was also influenced by Japanese woodcuts and by photography. His works include *Dancer Lacing her Shoe* (c.1878, Paris) and *Jockeys in the Rain* (1879, Glasgow).

de Gaulle, Charles see GAULLE, CHARLES DE.

degaussing *noun Physics* the process by which an object's magnetic field is neutralized by encircling it with an electric field. The process is used to protect ships from magnetically activated mines.

degeneracy *noun* a degenerate or degraded state.

degenerate — *adj.* (pronounced *-rət*) **1** physically, morally, or intellectually worse than before. **2** *Biol.* having lost former structure, or changed from a complex to a simpler form. — *noun* (pronounced *-rət*) a degenerate person or animal. — *verb intrans.* (pronounced *-rate*) **1** to go from a better, more moral, etc state to a worse one. **2** *Biol.* to lose former structure, or change from a complex to a simpler form. [from Latin *degenerare*, to become unlike one's kind]

degeneration *noun* **1** the process or act of degenerating. **2** *Biol.* the breakdown, death, or decay of cells, nerve fibres, etc. **3** *Biol.* an evolutionary change from a complex structural form to an apparently simpler form, as in the wings of flightless birds such as the emu.

degenerative *adj. technical, said of a condition or disease* steadily destroying or damaging a part of the body.

degradable *adj. technical* capable of being broken down or destroyed chemically or biologically.

degradation *noun* **1** moral deterioration. **2** *Chem.* reduction of a substance to a simpler structure.

degrade *verb* **1** to disgrace or humiliate. **2** to reduce in rank, status, etc. **3** *trans., intrans. Chem.* to change or be converted into a substance with a simpler structure. [from Old French *degrader*, from Latin *de*, down + *gradus*, step]

degrading *adj.* humiliating; debasing.

degree *noun* **1** an amount or extent. **2** *Physics* (SYMBOL °) a unit of temperature used in the Celsius, Fahrenheit, and Kelvin scales. **3** *Geom.* (SYMBOL °) a unit by which angles are measured and direction is described. It is equal to the angle of one segment of a circle that has been divided into 360 equal parts. Degrees are subdivided into minutes and seconds. **4** an award or title given by a university or college, either earned by examination or research or given as a mark of honour. **5** a comparative amount of severity or seriousness (see FIRST-DEGREE, SECOND-DEGREE, THIRD-DEGREE). **6** *Grammar* any of the three categories of comparison (*positive*, *comparative*, and *superlative*) of an adjective or adverb.
— **by degrees** gradually.
to a degree to a certain or considerable extent. [from Old French *degre*, from Latin *de*, down + *gradus*, step]

De Havilland, Sir Geoffrey (1882–1965) English aircraft designer, born in Haslemere, Surrey. He built his first plane in 1908 and became director of the firm bearing his name, producing many types of aircraft during and between the two World Wars, including the Tiger Moth, the Mosquito, and the Vampire jet. He established a height record for light aircraft in 1928.

De Havilland Gypsy Moth (UK) an aircraft flown by such notables as Sir Francis Chichester, Amy Johnson, and J A Mollison. It remained in production until 1934, by which time it was in worldwide use as a civil and military aircraft and was built under licence in Australia, France, and the USA.

dehiscent *adj. Bot.* denoting a fruit, or the anther of a stamen, that bursts open spontaneously at maturity to release the seeds or pollen, eg laburnum pod. [from Latin *dehiscere*, to gape, split open]

dehumanize *or* **dehumanise** *verb* to remove the human qualities from.

dehydrate *verb* **1** to remove water from (a substance or organism). **2** *trans., intrans.* to lose or cause to lose too much water from the body. [from DE- + Greek *hydor*, water]

dehydrated *adj.* deprived of water; with water removed.

dehydration *noun* **1** the removal of water from a substance. **2** a method of preserving food by greatly reducing its moisture content, eg sundried fruit, freeze-dried coffee. **3** *Medicine* a condition in which there is insufficient water in the body, eg as a result of diarrhoea or excessive sweating.

de-ice *verb* to remove ice from; to make or keep free of ice.

de-icer *noun* **1** a mechanical device for preventing the formation of ice, eg on an aircraft wing. **2** a chemical used to remove ice, eg from a car windscreen.

deification *noun* making into a god; treating as divine.

deify *verb* (**deifies, deified**) to regard or worship (someone or something) as a god. [from Old French *deifier*, from Latin *deus*, god + *facere*, to make]

deign *verb intrans.* to do something reluctantly and in a way that shows that one considers the matter hardly important or beneath one's dignity: *didn't even deign to reply*. [from Old French *daigner*, from Latin *dignari*, to consider worthy]

Deimos *Astron.* one of the two moons of Mars, thought to be an asteroid trapped by the gravity of that planet. It is irregular in shape, and less heavily cratered than Phobos, the other moon.

deionization *noun Chem.* an ion-exchange process that is used to purify or change the composition of a solution, especially to purify water obtained from the mains water supply.

Deirdre 1 in Irish legends, a beautiful girl destined to cause deaths. She was sought after by King Conchobhar of Ulster, but eloped with Naoise, a young king, and lived with him for seven years. When Naoise was killed by treachery, she was forced to marry Conchobhar, and killed herself. **2** a female first name, popular in Ireland.

Deir el Medîna an ancient Egyptian village on the R Nile at Luxor, S of the Valley of the Kings, occupied c.1550–1080 BC by the hereditary craftsmen who built and decorated the royal tombs of Thebes. It was discovered in 1815, and excavated from 1922 to 1951.

deism *noun* belief in the existence of God without acceptance of any religion or message revealed by God to man. See also THEISM. [from Latin *deus*, god + -ISM]

deist *noun* a person who believes in God but rejects established religions.

deity *noun* (PL. **deities**) *formal* **1** a god or goddess. **2** the state of being divine. **3** (**the Deity**) God. [from Latin *deitas*, from *deus*, god]

déjà vu the feeling or illusion that one has experienced something before although one is actually experiencing it for the first time. [from French *déjà vu*, already seen]

dejected *adj.* sad; miserable. [from Latin *deicere*, to throw down, disappoint]

dejectedly *adv.* with a dejected or sad manner.

dejection *noun* being dejected or sad.

Déjeuner sur l'herbe, Le a painting by Edouard Manet (1863, Musée d'Orsay, Paris). Its depiction of naked women picnicking with fully-clothed men caused a scandal when it was first exhibited at the Salon des Refusés in 1863.

de jure *Legal* according to law; by right. See also DE FACTO. [from Latin *de jure*, by law]

Dekker, Thomas (c.1570–c.1641) English dramatist, born in London. He was a prolific writer, but only a few of his plays were printed. His best-known works are the comedy *The Shoemaker's Holiday* (1600) and *The Honest Whore* (1604; part II, 1630). He also wrote plays in collaboration with other Elizabethan dramatists, and prose pamphlets on London life.

dekko
— **have** or **take a dekko** *Brit. slang* to take a look. [from Hindi *dekhna*, to see]

De Klerk, F(rederik) W(illem) (1936–) South African politician, born in Johannesburg. He entered the South African parliament in 1972, served in the cabinets of B J Vorster and P W Botha (1978–89), and became National Party Leader for the Transvaal in 1982. He succeeded Botha as President in 1989 and began the process of gradually improving diplomatic relations and reforming the apartheid system. In 1990 he ended the ban on the African National Congress (ANC) black opposition movement and sanctioned the release from imprisonment of Nelson Mandela, with whom in 1993 he was jointly awarded the Nobel Prize for Peace. By 1994 apartheid had been abolished and South Africa experienced its first democratic elections with de Klerk appointed vice-president.

De Kooning, Willem, or **William** (1904–) Dutch-born US painter, born in Rotterdam. He emigrated to the USA in 1926. By the 1950s he had emerged as a leader of the abstract Expressionist movement (New York School), especially in the genre of action painting. A central theme in his work is the human form and his works include the controversial series *Woman I–V* (1952–3, New York).

Del. *abbrev.* Delaware.

De La Beche, Sir Henry Thomas see BECHE, SIR HENRY THOMAS DE LA.

Delacroix, (Ferdinand Victor) Eugène (1798–1863) French Romantic painter, born in Charenton. His paintings *Dante and Virgil in Hell* (1822, Paris Institute) and *The Massacre at Chios* (1823, Louvre, Paris) aroused a lot of criticism on account of their loose drawing and vivid colouring. In his later work he moved even further away from traditional classical treatment in his canvases of historical and dramatic scenes which are often violent or macabre in subject (eg *Liberty Guiding the People*, 1831, Louvre, Paris).

De La Mare, Walter (John) (1873–1956) English writer, born in Charlton, Kent. He worked for an oil company (1890–1908), before devoting himself completely to writing. His first work, *Songs of Childhood* (1902), was published under the pseudonym of Walter Ramal. Writing for both adults and children, he produced several volumes of poetry, novels, and short stories. These include the prose romance *Henry Brocken* (1904), the poetic collection *The Listeners* (1912), and the fantasy novel *Memoirs of a Midget* (1921).

De La Roche, Mazo (1885–1961) Canadian novelist, born in Newmarket, Ontario. She is best known for the series of novels about the Whiteoak family, which begins with *Jalna* (1927).

Delaunay, Robert (1885–1941) French painter, born in Paris. He began painting in 1905 and experimented with contrasting colours and the relationship between different colours and movement. He is best known for his series of vibrantly coloured pictures of Saint-Severin and the Eiffel Tower (c.1910). Later, he isolated areas of pure colour in his pictures, a method which became known as Orphism. The breaking up of the surface of his pictures into planes of colour eventually led to almost pure abstraction. He was an influence on the members of the Blaue Reiter group.

Delaware POP (1990) 689 000, a state in E USA, divided into three counties. AREA 5 296sq km/2 045sq mi. It is the second smallest state in the USA, and is bounded E by Delaware Bay and the Atlantic Ocean. PHYSICAL DESCRIPTION the Delaware R forms part of the border with New Jersey; the highest point is at Ebright Road (135m). HISTORY the original Swedish settlers were supplanted in 1655 by the Dutch, who were in turn supplanted by the British in 1664; part of Pennsylvania until 1776; one of the original states of the Union and the first to ratify the Federal Constitution in 1787; Delaware is known as the 'First State' or 'Diamond State'. CAPITAL Dover. CHIEF TOWNS Wilmington, Newark. ECONOMY poultry, soya beans, corn, dairy products; it is mainly an industrial state centred around Wilmington; industries include chemicals, transportation equipment, processed food, plastics, and metals. Several large corporations are based in Wilmington, taking advantage of the state's lenient taxation laws.

Delaware Aqueduct in the USA, a tunnel covering a total distance of 169km/105mi, built (1937–53) to carry water from Delaware River to New York City.

Delaware River a river in E USA, length 450km/280mi. Rising in the Catskill Mts, New York State, it flows SE following the state frontiers of Pennsylvania, New York, and New Jersey and empties into Delaware Bay. It is navigable to Trenton.

delay — *verb* (**delayed, delaying**) **1** to slow down or cause to be late. **2** to put off to a later time. **3** *intrans.* to be slow in doing something; to linger. — *noun* **1** the act of delaying or state of being delayed. **2** the amount of time by which someone or something is delayed. [from Old French *delaier*]

delayed action the operation of eg the switch on a camera or detonator on a bomb some

time after the setting of the operating mechanism.

Delbrück, Max (1906–81) German biophysicist, born in Berlin. He studied physics in Göttingen, worked on chemistry in Berlin, and moved to biology from 1937 at the California Institute of Technology. There he did much to create bacterial and bacteriophage (bacterial virus) genetics, and in 1946 showed that viruses can recombine genetic material. He shared the 1969 Nobel Prize for Physiology or Medicine with Salvador Luria and Alfred Hershey.

delectable *adj., said especially of food* delightful or enjoyable; delicious. [from Latin *delectare*, to delight]

delectably *adv.* delightfully; deliciously.

delectation *noun formal* delight, enjoyment, or amusement.

Deledda, Grazia (1875–1936) Italian novelist, born in Nuoro, Sardinia. She made her name with naturalistic stories of her native island, including the novel *Elias Portolu* (The Woman and the Priest, 1900). She was awarded the Nobel Prize for Literature in 1926.

delegate — *verb* (pronounced *-gate*) **1** to give (part of one's work, power, etc) to someone else. **2** to send or name (a person) as a representative, as the one to do a job, etc. — *noun* (pronounced *-gət*) someone chosen to be the representative for another person or group of people eg at a conference or meeting. [from Latin *de*, away + *legare*, to send as ambassador]

delegation *noun* **1** a group of delegates. **2** the act of delegating or the state of being delegated.

Delescluze, (Louis) Charles (1809–71) French radical Republican and journalist, born in Dreux. His revolutionary politics drove him from France to journalism in Belgium (1835), but the February Revolution (1848) brought him back to Paris. His writing made him popular but brought him imprisonment (1849–53), and he was transported until 1859. He played a prominent part in the Paris Commune (1871), and died on the last barricade.

delete *verb* to rub out, score out, or remove (especially from something written or printed). [from Latin *delere*, to blot out]

deleterious *adj. formal* harmful or destructive. [from Greek *deleterios*]

deleteriously *adv. formal* harmfully.

deletion *noun* rubbing out; something rubbed out or removed.

delf or **delph** or **delft** *noun* a kind of earthenware originally made at *Delft* in the Netherlands, typically with a blue design on a white background.

Delfont (of Stepney), Bernard, Baron, originally **Boris Winogradsky** (1909–) Russian-born theatre producer, brother of Lew Grade. Born in Tokmak, Russia, he and his family moved to Britain in 1912. He entered theatrical management in 1941, and during the next 20 years acquired many theatrical properties and gained control of more than 30 companies, embracing theatre, film, television, music, and property interests. He also presented the annual Royal Variety Performance (1958–78) and has presented a record number of West End shows.

Delft POP (1992e) 90 000, an ancient city and municipality in W South Holland province, W Netherlands. It lies on the R Schie, between Rotterdam and The Hague. HISTORY in the 14c it became famous for linen-weaving and in the 16c for pottery and porcelain (delftware porcelain is still produced); William the Silent was assassinated here in 1584; it was the birthplace of the painter Vermeer in 1632. NOTABLE FEATURES Nieuwe Kerk (1396–1496); Italian Renaissance town hall; Prisenhof.

Delftware *noun* a type of earthenware decorated with an opaque glaze containing oxide of tin, and produced in Holland (at Delft and elsewhere) and England in large quantities in the 17c. It is usually blue and white with motifs copied from Chinese porcelain.

Delhi, Hindi **Dilli**, formerly **Shahjahanabad** POP (1991) 8.4m, the capital of India and the administrative centre of Delhi union territory, N central India, 1 190km/740mi NE of Bombay. Old Delhi, enclosed within the walls, was built by Shah Jahan in 1638, on the R Yamuna. Mughal architecture and thronged bazaars contrast with the formal architecture and wide boulevards of New Delhi to the S, largely designed by Lutyens. New Delhi has been the administrative centre of India since 1912 and is the country's largest commercial centre. NOTABLE FEATURES Red Fort, containing the imperial palace of Shah Jahan (17c); Jama Masijid, the largest mosque in India (1644–58); Rajghat, where Mahatma Gandhi was cremated (1948).

Delia a female first name. [a Greek epithet of the goddess Artemis, who was said to have been born on the island of Delos]

deliberate — *adj.* (pronounced *-rət*) **1** done on purpose; not accidental. **2** slow and careful. — *verb trans.*, *intrans.* (pronounced *-rate*) to think about something carefully. [from Latin *deliberare*, to consider carefully]

deliberately *adv.* intentionally; on purpose.

deliberation *noun* **1** careful thought. **2** (**deliberations**) formal and thorough thought and discussion. **3** slowness and carefulness.

Delibes, (Clément Philibert) Léo (1836–91) French composer, born in St Germain du Val, Sarthe. He became second director at the Grand Opéra, Paris (1865) and a Conservatoire professor (1880). He wrote light operas (eg *Lakmé*), but is chiefly remembered for the ballet *Coppélia* (1870).

delicacy *noun* (PL. **delicacies**) **1** the state or quality of being delicate. **2** something considered particularly delicious to eat. [from DELICATE]

delicate *adj.* **1** easily damaged or broken. **2** not strong or healthy. **3** of fine texture or workmanship. **4** dainty; small and attractive. **5** small, neat, and careful: *delicate movements*. **6** requiring tact and careful handling: *a delicate situation*. **7** careful about what one says or does, so as not to offend others. **8** *said of colours, flavours, etc* light; not strong. [from Latin *delicatus*]

delicately *adv.* with a delicate or dainty manner.

delicatessen *noun* a shop selling foods prepared ready for the table, especially cooked meats, cheeses, and unusual or imported foods. [from German *Delikatessen*, from French *délicatesse*, delicacy]

delicious *adj.* **1** with a very pleasing taste or smell. **2** giving great pleasure. [from Old French *delicious*, from Latin *deliciae*, delight]

deliciously *adv.* in a delicious or highly pleasing way.

delight — *verb* **1** to please greatly. **2** *intrans.* (**delight in something**) to take great pleasure from it. — *noun* **1** great pleasure. **2** something or someone that gives great pleasure. [from Old French *deliter*, from Latin *delectare*; spelling influenced by LIGHT]

delighted *adj.* highly pleased; thrilled.

delightedly *adv.* with a delighted or highly pleased manner.

delightful *adj.* giving great pleasure.

delightfully *adv.* in a highly pleasing way.

Delilah a biblical character, who was persuaded by the Philistines to discover the secret of her husband Samson's great strength — his uncut hair. She contrived to cut his hair to weaken him (Judges 16).

delimit *verb* (**delimited**, **delimiting**) to mark or fix the limits or boundaries of (powers, etc). [from Latin *delimitare*]

delimitation *noun* fixing limits or boundaries.

delineate *verb* to show by drawing or by describing in words. [from Latin *delineare*, to sketch out]

delineation *noun* description in drawing or words.

delinquency *noun* minor crime, especially committed by young people.

delinquent — *noun* a person, especially a young person, guilty of a minor criminal offence. — *adj.* guilty of a minor crime or misdeed. [from Latin *delinquere*, to fail in one's duty]

deliquesce *verb intrans. Chem.*, *said especially of salts* to dissolve slowly in water absorbed from the air. [from Latin *deliquescere*, to dissolve]

deliquescence *noun* becoming liquid; deliquescing.

deliquescent *adj.* becoming liquid; dissolving in water.

delirious *adj.* **1** affected by delirium, usually as a result of fever or other illness. **2** very excited or happy. [from Latin *delirus*, from *delirare*, to rave, originally to go off a straight furrow, from *de*, from + *lira*, furrow]

deliriously *adv.* in a delirious or wildly excited way.

delirium *noun* **1** a state of madness or mental confusion and excitement, often caused by fever or other illness, drugs, etc. **2** extreme excitement or joy. [from Latin *delirare*; see etymology at DELIRIOUS]

delirium tremens *noun* (ABBREV. **DTs**) delirium caused by habitual and persistent drinking of too much alcohol, inducing hallucinations, anxiety, confusion, and trembling. [from Latin *tremere*, to tremble]

Delius, Frederick (1862–1934) British composer, of German-Scandinavian descent, born in Bradford, Yorkshire. At the age of 20 he went to Florida as an orange planter, but studied music in his spare time and entered the Leipzig Conservatory (1886) where he became a friend of Grieg. After 1890 he lived mainly in France. A prolific composer, he wrote six operas, including *A Village Romeo and Juliet* (1901), and a variety of choral and orchestral works, such as *Appalachia* (1902) and *On Hearing the First Cuckoo in Spring* (1912). By 1924 he was paralysed and blind from a syphilitic infection, but with the English musician Eric Fenby (1906–) as his amanuensis from 1928, he continued to compose.

deliver *verb* (**delivered**, **delivering**) **1** *trans.*, *intrans.* to carry (goods, letters, etc) to a person or place. **2** *formal* (**deliver something up**) to hand over. **3** to give or make (a speech, etc). **4** *formal*, *old use* (**deliver from**) to set free or rescue. **5** to help (a woman) at the birth of (a child). **6** *trans.*, *intrans. colloq.* to keep or fulfil (a promise or undertaking). **7** *formal* to aim or direct (a blow, criticism, etc) towards someone or something. — **deliver the goods** *colloq.* to fulfil a promise or undertaking.

deliverance *noun formal*, *old use* the act of rescuing, freeing, or saving from danger or harm, or the state of being rescued, freed, or saved.

deliverer *noun* a person who delivers, especially a liberator.

delivery *noun* (PL. **deliveries**) **1** the carrying of (goods, letters, etc) to a person or place. **2** the thing or things being delivered. **3** the process or manner of giving birth to a child. **4** the act of making, or one's manner of making, a speech, etc. **5** the act or manner of throwing a ball, especially in some sports.

dell *noun* a small valley or hollow, usually with trees. [from Anglo-Saxon *dell*]

Deller, Alfred (George) (1912–79) English counter-tenor, born in Margate, Kent. He made many recordings of early English songs, notably those of Dowland and Purcell, and in 1950 formed the Deller Consort, which was devoted to the authentic performance of early music. In 1963 he founded the Stour Music Festival.

de Lorris, Guillaume see LORRIS, GUILLAUME DE.

Delos one of the smallest of the Cyclades islands, Greece. It was an important religious and political centre in antiquity, until it was sacked by Mithridates (88 BC); it is now largely uninhabited. It has many archaeological remains, including a theatre and the sanctuary of Apollo. It is a World Heritage site.

De Los Angeles, Victoria, originally Victoria López Cima (1923–) Spanish soprano, born in Barcelona. She made her début in Madrid (1944) and soon achieved international recognition as both a concert and an operatic singer, noted particularly for her 19c Italian roles and for her performances of Spanish songs.

Delphi, Greek **Dhelfoí** a village and ancient site in Fokis department, Greece. It is situated on the slopes of Mt Parnassos. It was renowned throughout the ancient Greek world as the sanctuary of Apollo and the seat of his oracle. The remains of the temple and precincts were excavated in the 19c.

Delphi, Oracle of the oracular shrine of Apollo at Delphi. It was the most prestigious oracle in the Greco-Roman world. On the payment of a fee, enquirers put their questions to Apollo's medium, a priestess called the Pythia.

Delphine a female first name. [associated with *delphinium* the flower; also a French version of Latin *Delphina*, woman from Delphi]

delphinium *noun* (PL. **delphiniums**, **delphinia**) a garden plant with tall spikes of usually blue flowers. [from Greek *delphis*, dolphin (from the shape of the flowers)]

Delphinus *Astron.* the Dolphin, a small faint constellation lying just north of the celestial equator.

Delphi technique a forecasting technique used in business planning. Experts are invited to give their opinion on the likelihood of occurrence of a specific event on or by a specific date. The consensus view is taken as a forecast.

a frieze from Delphi

delta *noun* **1** at the mouth of some rivers, an often triangular area of silt, sand, gravel, or clay, formed from sediment deposited by the river as it slows down on entering the relatively still waters of a sea or lake. **2** the fourth letter of the Greek alphabet (Δ, δ). [from Greek *delta*]

Delta rocket *Astron.* any of a series of increasingly powerful versions of a US rocket with two or three stages, and up to nine solid-fuel boosters attached to the first stage, used to launch scientific and communications satellites from 1960 onward.

delude *verb* to deceive or mislead. See also DELUSION. [from Latin *deludere*, to cheat]

deluge — *noun* **1** a flood. **2** a downpour of rain. **3** a great quantity of anything coming or pouring in. — *verb* **1** (**be deluged with something**) to be overwhelmed by it. **2** *formal* to flood; to cover in water. [from Old French *deluge*, from Latin *diluvium*, flood]

delusion *noun* **1** the act of deluding or being deluded. **2** a false or mistaken belief, especially because of mental illness. [from Latin *delusio*]

delusions of grandeur a false belief in one's own importance.

delusive *or* **delusory** *adj.* deluding or likely to delude.

de luxe *or* **deluxe** *adj.* very luxurious or elegant; with special features or qualities. [from French *de luxe*, of luxury]

delve *verb intrans.* **1** (**delve into something**) to search it for information. **2** (**delve through something**) to search through it. [from Anglo-Saxon *delfan*, to dig]

Dem. *abbrev.* Democrat and Democratic.

demagnetize *or* **demagnetise** *verb* to take away the magnetic properties of.

demagogic *adj.* typical of a demagogue.

demagogue *noun derog.* a person who tries to win political power or support by appealing to people's emotions and prejudices. [from Greek *demos*, people + *agogos*, leading]

demagoguery *or* **demagogy** *noun* behaviour of a demagogue.

demand — *verb* **1** to ask or ask for firmly, forcefully or urgently. **2** to require or need. **3** to claim as a right. — *noun* **1** a forceful request or order. **2** an urgent claim for action or attention: *makes great demands on one's time.* **3** people's desire or ability to buy or obtain (goods, etc): *a slump in demand for coffee.*
— **in demand** very popular; frequently asked for.
on demand when asked for.
[from Old French *demander*, to ask]

demanding *adj.* **1** requiring a lot of effort, ability, etc: *a demanding job.* **2** needing or expecting a lot of attention: *a demanding child.*

demarcate *verb* to mark out the limits or boundaries of.

demarcation *noun* **1** the marking out of limits or boundaries. **2** the strict separation of the areas or types of work to be done by the members of the various trade unions in a factory, etc: *a demarcation dispute.* [from Spanish *demarcar*, to mark the boundaries of]

demean *verb* to lower the dignity of or lessen respect for (someone, especially oneself). [from MEAN[1]]

demeaning *adj.* humiliating; debasing.

demeanour *noun* manner of behaving; behaviour towards others. [from Old French *demener*, to treat]

demented *adj.* mad; out of one's mind. [from Latin *de*, from + *mens*, mind]

dementedly *adv.* in a demented or crazy way.

dementia *noun Psychol.* a loss or severe lessening of normal mental ability and functioning,

occurring especially in the elderly. See also SENILE DEMENTIA. [from Latin *de*, from + *mens*, mind]

demerara *or* **demerara sugar** a form of brown sugar. [from *Demerara* in Guyana, S America]

demerit *noun formal* a fault or failing. [from Latin *demereri*, to deserve]

Demeter in Greek mythology, the goddess of corn. After Hades imprisoned her daughter Persephone in the Underworld, she forced a compromise which allowed Persephone to return to the world above between spring and autumn. She was also connected with the Eleusinian Mysteries. The Romans identified her with the goddess Ceres.

Demetrius one of the two heroes in Shakespeare's *A Midsummer Night's Dream*, in love with Helena.

demi- *combining form* half or partly: *demigod.* [from French *demi*, half]

demigod *noun Mythol.* a person who is part human and part god.

demijohn *noun* a large bottle with a short narrow neck and one or two small handles, used eg for storing wine. [from French *dame-jeanne*, Dame Jane, influenced by DEMI- and the name *John*]

demilitarization *or* **demilitarisation** *noun* removal of armed forces from a region.

demilitarize *or* **demilitarise** *verb* to remove armed forces from (an area) and not allow any military activity in it.

De Mille, Cecil B(lount) (1881–1959) US film producer and director, born in Ashfield, Massachusetts. He was an actor and writer before making the first US feature film in Hollywood, *The Squaw Man* (1913). His box-office spectacles included *The Ten Commandments* (1923), *The Plainsman* (1937), and *The Greatest Show on Earth* (1952). He also organized the first commercial passenger airline service in the USA (1917).

demise *noun* **1** *formal* death. **2** a failure or end. [from Old French *demise*, from *desmettre*, to lay down]

demisemiquaver *noun Mus.* a note equal in time to half a semiquaver.

demist *verb* to free (a vehicle's windscreen) from condensation or frost by blowing warm air over it.

demister *noun* a device for clearing a windscreen of condensation.

demo *noun* (PL. **demos**) *colloq.* demonstration.

demob *Brit. colloq.* — *verb* (**demobbed**, **demobbing**) short form of DEMOBILIZE. — *noun* short form of DEMOBILIZATION.

demobilization *or* **demobilisation** *noun* release from service in the armed forces.

demobilize *or* **demobilise** *verb* to release from service in the armed forces, eg after a war.

democracy *noun* (PL. **democracies**) **1** a form of government in which the people govern themselves or elect representatives to govern them. **2** a country, state, or other body with such a form of government. [from Greek *demos*, people + *kratos*, strength]
◇ The oldest democracies are identified as those developed in some ancient Greek city-states in the 5c BC, and especially in Athens; although these were based on full assemblies of the people to vote on legislation, citizenship extended only to free adult males. In larger nation-states, democracy is representative, ie citizens elect representatives (such as MPs) to act and legislate on their behalf. It was not until the 20c, with the abolition of slavery and the extension of voting to women, that 'the people' could be taken to mean the entire adult population of a country. Further necessary conditions are the legal equality of citizens, and freedom of information to

ensure that citizens are in an equal and informed position to choose their rulers and hold them accountable. Some more radical thinkers argue that economic equality is also necessary, in order to enable all classes in society to take a full part in political life.

democrat *noun* **1** a person who believes in democracy as a principle. **2** (**Democrat**) a member or supporter of the Democratic Party in the USA, or of any political party with *Democratic* in its title. See also REPUBLICAN.

democratic *adj.* **1** concerned with or following the principles of democracy. **2** believing in or providing equal rights and privileges for all. **3** (**Democratic**) relating to or belonging to the *Democratic Party*, one of the two chief political parties of the US.

democratically *adv.* in a democratic way; on democratic principles.

Democratic Labor Party (ABBREV. **DLP**) in Australia, a political party, formed in 1957 from anti-communist groups which had formerly been part of the Australian Labor Party (ALP). The DLP was largely centred in Victoria, and at its height, in the late 1950s and through the 1960s, its importance lay in its ability to prevent the ALP from winning national government. Its policies were strongly anti-communist and pro-defence, and incorporated elements of Catholic teaching on social matters.

Democritus (c.460–370 BC) Greek philosopher, born in Abdera in Thrace. He wrote many physical, mathematical, ethical, and musical works, of which only fragments survive. His *atomic system* assumes an infinite multitude of everlasting atoms, from whose random combinations springs an infinite number of successive world-orders in which there is law but not design. His system, derived from Leucippus (about whom little is known), was developed by Epicurus and Lucretius.

demodulate *verb Radio* to perform demodulation on the carrier wave of a radio broadcast.

demodulator *noun Radio* a device that extracts information from the modulated carrier wave of a radio broadcast.

demographer *noun* a person who studies demography or the statistics of populations.

demographic *adj.* relating to demography or populations.

demography *noun technical* the scientific study of population statistics, including births, deaths, etc. [from Greek *demos*, people + *graphein*, to write]

Demoiselles d'Avignon, Les a painting by Pablo Picasso (1906–7, New York). It broke with the Impressionist tradition and, in its semi-abstract form, heralded the start of Cubism.

De Moivre, Abraham (1667–1754) French mathematician, born in Vitry, Champagne. A Protestant, he came to England around 1686, after the revocation of the Edict of Nantes, and supported himself by teaching. His principal work was *The Doctrine of Chances* (1718) on probability theory, but he is best remembered for the fundamental formula on complex numbers known as De Moivre's theorem, relating the exponential and trigonometric functions.

demolish *verb* **1** to pull or tear down (a building, etc). **2** to destroy (an argument, etc). **3** *facetious* to eat up. [from Latin *demoliri*, to throw down]

demolition *noun* the act of demolishing.

demon *noun* **1** an evil spirit. **2** a cruel or evil person. **3** a person who has great energy, enthusiasm, or skill: *a demon at football.* **4** (also **daemon**) a good or friendly spirit. [from Greek *daimon*, spirit]

demoniac *or* **demoniacal** *adj.* **1** of or like a demon or demons. **2** influenced or as if influenced by demons; frenzied or very energetic.

demonic *adj.* **1** of or like a demon or demons. **2** possessed or as if possessed by a demon or demons; evil.

demonically *adv.* like a demon; as if possessed.

demonstrable *adj.* capable of being demonstrated.

demonstrably *adv.* in a demonstrable way; as can be demonstrated.

demonstrate *verb* **1** to show or prove by reasoning or providing evidence. **2** *trans., intrans.* to show how something is done, operates, etc. **3** *intrans., trans.* to show (one's support, opposition, etc) by protesting, marching, etc in public. [from Latin *demonstrare*, to show, indicate]

demonstration *noun* **1** showing or demonstrating. **2** a public display of opinion on a political or moral issue. **3** *Maths., Philos.* establishing as true or evident by argument or proof.

demonstrative *adj.* **1** showing one's feelings openly. **2** (**demonstrative of something**) showing it or proving it to be so: *words demonstrative of anger*.

demonstratively *adv.* in a demonstrative or openly expressive way.

demonstrative pronoun *and* **adjective.** *noun Grammar* a word indicating the person or thing referred to, ie *this, that, these, those*.

demonstrator *noun* **1** a person who demonstrates equipment, etc. **2** a person who takes part in a public demonstration.

demoralization *or* **demoralisation** *noun* demoralizing; being demoralized.

demoralize *or* **demoralise** *verb* to take away the confidence, courage, or enthusiasm of; to dishearten. See also MORALE. [from French *démoraliser*]

Demosthenes (c.383–322 BC) Athenian orator and statesman. He entered politics in c.354 BC, and in 351 BC he delivered the first of a long series of speeches (the 'First Philippic') advocating all-out resistance to Philip of Macedon. The Athenians, in alliance with the Thebes, did eventually go to war against Philip (340 BC), but were defeated at Chaeronea (338 BC). Demosthenes was later put on trial by the peace party of Aeschines, and fully vindicated himself in his speech, *On the Crown* (c.330 BC). He was exiled for embezzlement (325 BC) after a large sum of money belonging to Alexander the Great, and deposited in the Athens treasury as the responsibility of Demosthenes and others, was found to be missing. He committed suicide (322 BC), after the failure of the Athenian revolt against Macedon in the aftermath of the death of Alexander.

demote *verb* to reduce to a lower rank or grade. [from DE- + PROMOTE]

demotic — *adj., said especially of a language* used in everyday affairs; popular. — *noun* **1** colloquial language. **2** (**Demotic**) a form of modern Greek based on popular usage, as distinct from formal or literary language. **3** a simplified form of ancient Egyptian writing. [from Greek *demotikos*, from *demos*, people]

demotion *noun* reduction to a lower rank.

demur — *verb intrans.* (**demurred**, **demurring**) (**demur at something**) to object mildly to it or be reluctant to do it. — *noun* (**without demur**) without objecting. [from Old French *demorer*, to wait]

demure *adj., said of a person* quiet, modest, and well-behaved. [from Old French *demorer*, to wait, influenced by *meur*, ripe]

demurely *adv.* with a demure or modest manner.

demureness *noun* being demure; modesty of manner.

demurral *noun* mild objection or reluctance.

demystification *noun* reduction of an irrational element.

demystify *verb* (**demystifies**, **demystified**) to remove the mystery from.

den *noun* **1** a wild animal's home. **2** a centre (often secret) of illegal or immoral activity. **3** a room in a house or a hut outside it, used as a place to work or play. [from Anglo-Saxon *denn*, cave, lair]

denarius *noun* (PL. **denarii**) an ancient Roman silver coin. [from Latin *denarius*, containing 10, because originally equal to 10 asses]

denationalization *or* **denationalisation** *noun* restoration of an industry to private ownership.

denationalize *or* **denationalise** *verb* to return or transfer (an industry) to private ownership from state ownership.

denature *verb* **1** *Biol.* to change the structure of a protein, eg an enzyme, by exposing it to high temperatures, certain chemicals, or extremes of pH. This usually results in a decrease in its solubility and the loss of its biological effects, eg the catalytic properties of an enzyme. **2** *Physics* to add another isotope to a material capable of nuclear fission, so that it is no longer suitable for use in a nuclear weapon. **3** to add a poisonous or unpalatable substance to alcohol, methylated spirits, etc, to render it unfit for human consumption.

dendrite *noun Zool.* any of a number of cytoplasmic projections that radiate outwards from the star-shaped cell body of a neurone (nerve cell). See also NEURONE. [from Greek *dendrites*, of a tree]

dendrochronology *noun* the analysis of the patterns of annual growth-rings found in trees and the fixing of dates by comparative study of timber from different periods. [from Greek *dendron*, tree + *chronos*, time]
◇ By working back from the present, it is possible to build up a chronological sequence by matching the patterns of early phases of growth in old, living trees, and the ring phases found in timber samples from archaeological sites.
A tree-ring sequence may thus be extended backwards over many thousands of years, and has proved to be an important check on other forms of archaeological dating.

dendrologist *noun* a person who studies dendrology.

dendrology *noun* the scientific study of trees. [from Greek *dendron*, tree + -LOGY]

dendron *noun Physiol.* a dendrite. [from Greek *dendron*, tree]

Deng Xiaoping *or* **Teng Hsiao-p'ing** (1904–) leader of the Chinese Communist Party, since 1978 the dominant figure in Chinese politics, born in Sichuan province. Educated in France, where he joined the Communist Party, and in the Soviet Union, he became associated with Mao Zedong (Mao Tse-tung) during the period of the Jiangxi Soviet (1928–34). In 1954 he became Secretary-General of the Chinese Communist Party, but reacted strongly against the excesses of the Great Leap Forward (1958–9). When Mao launched the Cultural Revolution in 1966, Deng was criticized and purged along with Liu Shaoqi, but retained the confidence of premier Zhou Enlai and was restored to power in 1974. Again dismissed in 1976, after the death of Mao he was restored once more to power.

denial *noun* **1** an act of denying or declaring something not to be true. **2** an act of refusing something to someone. **3** an act of refusing to acknowledge connections with somebody or something.

denier *noun* the unit of weight of silk, rayon, or nylon thread, usually used as a measure of the fineness of stockings or tights. [from French *denier*; originally a small coin, from DENARIUS]

denigrate *verb* to scorn or criticize; to attack or belittle the reputation, character, or worth of. [from Latin *denigrare*, to blacken]

denigration *noun* defamation; disparagement.

denigrator *noun* a person who denigrates or disparages.

denim *noun* **1** a kind of hard-wearing, usually blue, cotton cloth used for making jeans, overalls, etc. **2** (**denims**) trousers or jeans made of denim. [from French *de Nîmes*, of Nîmes in France]

De Niro, Robert (1943–) US film actor, born in New York City. Eight years after his screen début, he attracted critical attention as the baseball player in *Bang the Drum Slowly* (1973) and won a Best Supporting Actor Oscar for *The Godfather Part II* (1974). His films made with Martin Scorsese include *Taxi Driver* (1976) and *Raging Bull* (1980), for which he won a Best Actor Oscar. Others include *The Deer Hunter* (1978), *Awakenings* (1990), and *Cape Fear* (1991). He made his directorial début with *The Bronx Tale* (1994).

Denis *or* **Denys, St**, properly **Dionysius** (3c AD) Italian-born patron saint of France, who was sent from Rome in c.250 to preach the Gospel to the Gauls, and became the first Bishop of Paris. He was martyred at Paris under the Roman emperor Valerian (reigned 253–60).

denizen *noun* **1** *formal* an inhabitant (human or animal). **2** *Biol.* a species of animal or plant which has become well established in a place to which it is not native and into which it has been introduced. [from Old French *deinzein*, from *deinz*, within]

Denmark, Danish **Danmark**, official name **Kingdom of Denmark**, Danish **Kongeriget Danmark** POP (1993e) 5.2m, a kingdom of N Europe, divided into 14 counties (*amt*). It is the smallest of the Scandinavian countries and consists of most of the Jutland Peninsula, several islands in the Baltic Sea (the largest include Zealand, Fyn, Lolland, Faister, and Bornholm), and some of the N Frisian Is in the North Sea. Greenland and the Faroes are self governing regions of Denmark. AREA (excluding dependencies) 43 076sq km/16 627sq mi; coastline length is 3 400km/2 100mi. It is bounded N by the Skagerrak, E by the Kattegat, the Sound, and the Baltic Sea, S by Germany, and W by the North Sea. CAPITAL Copenhagen. CHIEF TOWNS Århus, Odense, Ålborg, Esbjerg, Randers, Kolding. TIME ZONE GMT +1. The Danes are a branch of the Scandinavian race; their chief religion is Lutheranism. OFFICIAL LANGUAGE Danish. CURRENCY the krone. PHYSICAL DESCRIPTION uniformly low-lying; the highest point (Ejer Bavnehöj in E Jylland) is less than 200m; there are no large rivers and few lakes; the shoreline is indented by many lagoons and fjords, the largest of which is Lim Fjord (which cut off the N extremity of Denmark in 1825). CLIMATE much modified by the Gulf Stream, giving cold and cloudy winters, and warm, sunny summers; annual rainfall is usually below 675mm. HISTORY part of Viking kingdoms in the 8c–10c; the centre of the Danish Empire under Canute in the 11c; joined with Sweden and Norway under one ruler in 1389; Sweden separated from the union in the 16c, as did Norway in 1814; Schleswig-Holstein was lost to Germany in 1864, but N Schleswig was returned after a plebiscite in 1920; Denmark was occupied by Germany during World War II; Iceland became independent of Danish rule in 1944; Greenland and the Faroes remain dependencies; Denmark joined the EEC in 1973. GOVERNMENT a constitutional monarchy since 1849; a unicameral system was adopted in 1953; legislative power lies jointly with the monarch and the 179-member Diet (*Folketing*). ECONOMY a lack of raw materials has resulted in development of processing industries such as foodstuffs, brewing, machinery, hardware, shipping, furniture, glass, porcelain, chemicals, and pharmaceuticals;

intensive agriculture (corn, horticulture, vegetables, pigs, cattle, and poultry); forestry; windmill production.

Denmark

Denning (of Whitchurch), Alfred Thompson, Baron (1899–) English judge, educated at Oxford. He was called to the Bar in 1923, became a KC in 1938, and a judge of the High Court of Justice in 1944. He was Master of the Rolls (1962–82), and in 1963 led the enquiry into the circumstances of Sir John Profumo's resignation as Secretary of State for War. His books include *The Road to Justice* (1955) and *What Next in the Law* (1982).

Dennis *or* **Denis** a male first name. [a form of *Theodoric*, from the Germanic elements meaning 'tribe' and 'power']

denominate *verb formal* to give a specific name or title to (something). [from Latin *denominare*, to name]

denomination *noun* **1** a religious group with its own particular beliefs, organization, and practices. **2** a particular unit of value of a postage stamp, coin, or banknote, etc.

denominational *adj.* relating to or belonging to a religious denomination.

denominator *noun Maths.* in a vulgar fraction, the number shown below the line, indicating the units into which the fraction is dividing the whole, eg '5' in the fraction ⅗. See also NUMERATOR.

denotation *noun* denoting; marking by signs or symbols.

denote *verb* **1** to mean; to be the name of or sign for. **2** to be a sign, mark, or indication of. [from Latin *denotare*, to mark out]

dénouement *noun* the final part of a story or plot, in which uncertainties are explained and previously unresolved problems and mysteries are resolved. [from French *dénouement*, from *dénouer*, to untie a knot]

denounce *verb* **1** to inform against or accuse publicly: *denounced them as traitors.* **2** to condemn (an action, proposal, idea, etc) strongly and openly. See also DENUNCIATION. [from Old French *dénoncier*, from Latin *denuntiare*, to announce]

dense *adj.* **1** closely packed or crowded together. **2** thick. **3** *colloq.* stupid; slow to understand. [from Latin *densus*]

densely *adv.* in a dense or closely packed way; to a dense degree.

denseness *noun* a dense state; stupidity.

density *noun* (PL. **densities**) **1** the state of being dense or the degree of denseness. **2** the ratio of the mass of a substance to its volume. The SI units of density measurement are kg m⁻³. **3** the number of items within a specific area or volume, eg population density. **4** *Comput.* the number of bits that can be stored on one track of a disk, or within a specific area of magnetic tape, etc.

dent — *noun* a hollow in the surface of something, especially something hard, made by pressure or a blow. — *verb* **1** to make a dent in.

2 *intrans.* to become dented. [from Anglo-Saxon *dynt*, blow]

dental *adj.* concerned with or for the teeth. [from Latin *dentalis*, from *dens*, tooth]

dental caries *Medicine* the decay of a tooth, resulting from erosion of the enamel of the tooth by acid. The acid is produced during the breakdown of sugars by bacteria present in the plaque on the tooth surface. Dental caries is the commonest cause of toothache, and if left untreated eventually destroys the tooth.

dental floss a soft thread used for cleaning between the teeth.

dental formula *Zool.* a formula that shows the number of different types of tooth present in the upper and lower jaw of a mammal in a specific order (incisors, canines, premolars, and molars). The total number of each type of tooth is given first for the upper jaw and then for the lower jaw.

dental surgeon a dentist.

dentate *adj. technical* with a tooth-like notched pattern round the edge.

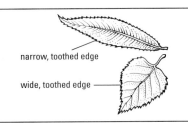

narrow, toothed edge

wide, toothed edge

dentate structure of leaves

dentifrice *noun* paste or powder for cleaning the teeth. [from French *dentifrice*, from Latin *dens*, tooth + *fricare*, to rub]

dentil *noun Archit.* each of a series of small square or rectangular blocks or projections, especially those set beneath the cornice in classical orders. Although they are principally ornamental, their use probably also mimics the ends of supporting beams used in earlier wooden structures. [from their resemblance to a row of teeth; from French *dentille*, from *dent*, tooth]

dentine *or* **dentin** *noun Anat.* in vertebrates, a hard yellowish-white material that forms the bulk of the tooth. At the crown it is covered by enamel, and at the root by cementum (a substance similar to bone). It is perforated by short nerve endings extending from the pulp, and exposed dentine is sensitive to heat, cold, and touch. [from Latin *dens*, tooth]

dentist *noun* a person who is professionally trained and qualified to practise dentistry. [from French *dentiste*, from *dent*, tooth]

dentistry *noun* the branch of medicine concerned with the diagnosis, treatment, and prevention of diseases of the mouth and teeth.

◇ General dental practitioners provide primary dental care, including the treatment of diseased, fractured, or badly worn teeth by means of fillings, inlays, crowns, and bridges, and the replacement of missing teeth by dentures. Dentists based in hospitals or dental schools are usually involved in one of several specialist areas. *Orthodontics* is concerned with improvement of the function or appearance of teeth by changing their position or angle. *Periodontics* involves the prevention and treatment of diseases of the tissues that surround and support the teeth. *Endodontics* is concerned with the treatment of disorders of the tooth pulp, a major part of which is root canal treatment. *Oral surgery* involves the repair of injury to the mouth and face as a result of accident or disease. It includes the removal of wisdom teeth, treatment of fractured bones, diagnosis and removal of tumours, and the cos-

metic restoration of disorders such as cleft palate. There has recently been an increasing emphasis on *preventive dentistry*, which includes counselling on dietary habits and oral hygiene. The use of fluoridated toothpaste and the addition of fluoride to drinking water have contributed to a significant decline in dental decay in the West since the early 1980s.

dentition *noun technical* the number, arrangement, and type of teeth in a human or animal. [from Latin *dentitio*, teething]

denture *noun* (*usually* **dentures**) a false tooth or set of false teeth. [from French *denture*, from *dent*, tooth]

denudation *noun* **1** denuding; making bare. **2** *Geol.* the process by which the surface of the land is progressively lowered as a result of weathering and erosion, so that the underlying rocks are laid bare.

denude *verb* to make completely bare; to strip. [from Latin *denudare*, to lay bare, uncover]

denunciation *noun* a public condemnation or accusation. See also DENOUNCE. [from Latin *denuntiare*, to announce]

Denver POP (1990) 1.6m, the port capital of the state of Colorado, USA, and the largest city in the state. It lies on the South Platte R, in Denver County, N central Colorado. Denver is the processing, shipping, and distribution centre for a large agricultural area. Several national parks nearby attract tourists to the city. HISTORY formed in 1860 by the union of the gold-mining settlement of Auraria with two other villages; became state capital in 1867. NOTABLE FEATURES Fornery Transport Museum; art museum; the US Mint.

deny *verb* (**denies**, **denied**) **1** to declare (something) not to be true. **2** to refuse to give or allow to (someone). **3** to refuse to acknowledge a connection with.
— **deny oneself** to do without (things that one desires or needs). See also DENIAL.
[from Old French *denier*, from Latin *denegare*]

deodorant *noun* a substance that prevents or conceals unpleasant smells, especially the smell of stale sweat on the human body. [from DE- + ODOUR]

deodorization *or* **deodorisation** *noun* removal of an unpleasant smell.

deodorize *or* **deodorise** *verb* to remove, conceal, or absorb the unpleasant smell of.

deoxyribonucleic acid *Biochem.* (ABBREV. **DNA**) the nucleic acid, containing the sugar deoxyribose, that forms the material of which the chromosomes and genes of almost all living organisms are composed. It contains coded instructions for the transmission of genetic information from one generation to the next, and for the manufacture of all the proteins that are required for growth and development of a whole new organism. [from *deoxy-*, containing less oxygen than + RIBONUCLEIC ACID] See illustration on p. 373.

◇ A DNA molecule is composed of two long twisted strands (made up of alternating sugar and phosphate groups) that are coiled around each other to form a *double helix*. Genetic information is stored on the strands in the form of a code consisting of four types of molecule, known as *bases*, which occur in pairs, forming cross-links between the two strands of the DNA molecule. There are four bases (adenine, thymine, cytosine, and guanine), and the sequence of base pairs serves as a code of instructions for the manufacture of protein from DNA. Just as a large number of words can be formed from only a few letters, so DNA can form a wide variety of different instructions from only four bases.

DNA can reproduce itself in a process known as *replication*, during which it separates into two single strands, each of which then copies its missing counterpart in order to regenerate the double helix. Very rarely, the molecule fails to copy itself correctly, and a *mutation* results. Mutations are sometimes lethal, but they can also produce advantageous changes that allow an organism to adapt to alterations in its environment. This is the basis of the theory of evolution.

depaato *noun* a large Japanese department store, often having roof gardens and restaurants, and frequently holding cultural exhibitions and other attractions.

Depardieu, Gérard (1947–) French film actor, born in Châteauroux, France. He began his career in French cinema in 1965; his first English-speaking role was in *Green Card* (1990). Noted for his imposing physique and versatility, he has had successes in many genres. His many films include *Tenue de Soirée* (1986), *Jean de Florette* (1986), *Cyrano de Bergerac* (1990), and *Tous les Matins du Monde* (1991).

depart *verb intrans.* **1** *somewhat formal* to leave. **2** (**depart from something**) to stop following or decline to follow a planned or usual course of action. [from Old French *departir*]

departed *formal — adj.* dead. *— noun* (**the departed**) a person or people recently dead.

department *noun* **1** a section of an organization (eg a government or other administration, a university, an office, or a shop), with responsibility for one particular aspect or part of the organization's work. **2** a subject or activity which is someone's special skill or particular responsibility. [from French *département*]

departmental *adj.* **1** of or concerning a department or departments. **2** divided into departments.

Department of Trade and Industry see TRADE AND INDUSTRY, DEPARTMENT OF.

department store a large shop with many different departments selling a wide variety of goods.

departure *noun* **1** an act of going away or leaving. **2** (**departure from something**) a change from a planned or usual course of action. **3** a new activity, different from what one has been doing or normally does.

depend *verb intrans.* (**depend on** *or* **upon someone** *or* **something**) **1** to rely on; to be able to trust. **2** to rely on financial or other support from. **3** to be decided by or vary according to (something else). [from Old French *dependre*, from Latin *dependere*, to hang down]

dependability *noun* being dependable or reliable.

dependable *adj.* trustworthy or reliable.

dependably *adv.* in a dependable or reliable way.

dependant *noun* a person who is kept or supported financially by another.

dependence *noun* (**dependence on** *or* **upon something** *or* **someone**) **1** the state of being dependent on them. **2** trust and reliance.

dependency *noun* (PL. **dependencies**) **1** a country governed or controlled by another. **2** addiction to drugs, etc.

dependent *adj.* (**dependent on** *or* **upon something** *or* **someone**) **1** relying on them for financial or other support. **2** *said of an issue or outcome* to be decided or influenced by them: *success is dependent on all our efforts.*

dependent clause same as SUBORDINATE CLAUSE.

depersonalization *or* **depersonalisation** *noun Psychol.* a condition in which a person feels unreal, or feels that the mind and body are becoming separated. It is a common symptom of severe stress, and of epilepsy, depression, and schizophrenia.

depersonalize *or* **depersonalise** *noun Psychol.* to take away the characteristics or personality of; to make impersonal.

depict *verb* **1** to paint or draw. **2** to describe. [from Latin *depingere*, to paint]

depiction *noun* representation in drawing or words.

depilatory *technical — noun* (PL. **depilatories**) a chemical substance used to remove unwanted hair from the body. *— adj.* able to remove hair. [from Latin *depilare*, to remove hair]

deplete *verb* to reduce greatly in number, quantity, etc; to use up (supplies, money, energy, resources, etc). [from Latin *deplere*, to empty]

depletion *noun* reduction or exhaustion in numbers or amount.

deplorable *adj.* very bad, shocking, or regrettable.

deplorably *adv.* in a deplorable way; to a deplorable extent.

deplore *verb* to feel or express great disapproval of or regret for. [from French *déplorer*, from Latin *deplorare*, to weep for]

deploy *verb* **1** to spread out and position (troops) ready for battle. **2** to organize and bring into use (resources, arguments, etc). [from French *déployer*]

deployment *noun* positioning or organization of resources, etc.

depolarization *or* **depolarisation** *noun Chem.* the removal or prevention of electrical polarization (separation into positive and negative charges).

depopulate *verb* to reduce greatly the number of people living in (an area, country, etc). [from Latin *depopulari*, to lay waste, later understood as meaning to deprive of people]

depopulated *adj., said of an area, etc* having a reduced population.

depopulation *noun* reduction of population.

deport¹ *verb* to legally remove or expel (a person) from a country. [from Latin *deportare*, to carry away]

deport² *verb* (**deport oneself**) *formal* to behave oneself in a particular way. [from Latin *deportare*, to carry away]

deportation *noun* legal expulsion of a person from a country.

deportee *noun* a person who is expelled from a country.

deportment *noun* **1** the way one holds or carries oneself; one's bearing. **2** behaviour.

depose *verb* to remove from a high office or powerful position. [from Old French *deposer*, to put down or away]

deposit *— verb* (**deposited, depositing**) **1** to put or leave. **2** to put (money, etc) in a bank, etc, for safekeeping or to earn interest. **3** to give (a sum of money) as the first part of the payment for something, so guaranteeing that one can complete the purchase later. **4** to pay (a sum of money) as a guarantee against loss or damage. *— noun* **1** a sum of money, etc deposited in a bank, etc. **2** a sum of money given as part payment for something or paid as a guarantee against loss or damage. **3** solid matter that has settled at the bottom of a liquid, or is left behind by a liquid. **4** a layer (of coal, oil, minerals, etc) occurring naturally in rock. [from Latin *depositum*, from *deponere*, to put down]

deposit account a bank account on which one is paid interest and which cannot be used for the transfer of money to other people by eg cheque or standing order.

depositary *noun* (PL. **depositaries**) *formal* a person, etc to whom something is given for safekeeping.

deposition *noun* **1** the act of deposing or process of being deposed. **2** the act of depositing or process of being deposited. **3** *Legal* a written statement made under oath and used as evidence in a court of law when the witness cannot be present. **4** *Geol.* the laying down on the Earth's surface of eroded material that has been transported by wind, rivers, glaciers, avalanches, etc. [from Latin *depositio*, putting down]

depositor *noun* a person who deposits money in a bank.

depository *noun* (PL. **depositories**) **1** a place where things such as furniture are stored. **2** a depositary.

depot *noun* **1** a storehouse or warehouse. **2** a place where buses, trains, and certain types of vehicles are kept and repaired. **3** *North Amer.* a bus or railway station. **4** a military headquarters, or military post where stores are kept and recruits trained. [from French *dépôt*, from Latin *deponere*, to put down]

deprave *verb* to make evil or morally corrupt. [from Latin *depravare*, to pervert, distort]

depraved *adj.* morally corrupted.

depravity *noun* moral wickedness, evil, or corruption.

deprecate *verb* to express disapproval of; to deplore. [from Latin *deprecari*, to try to avert]
◆ Often confused with *depreciate*.

deprecating *adj.* disapproving of something.

deprecatingly *adv.* with a disapproving manner.

deprecation *noun* expression of disapproval.

deprecatory *adj.* **1** showing or expressing disapproval. **2** apologetic; trying to avoid disapproval.

depreciate *verb* **1** *trans., intrans.* to fall or cause to fall in value. **2** to be contemptuous of the worth of; to belittle. [from Latin *depretiare*, to lower the price of]
◆ Often confused with *deprecate*.

depreciation *noun* **1** *Econ.* a fall in value of a currency against the value of other currencies. **2** the reduction in the value of fixed assets such as buildings and equipment through use or age. **3** the act of depreciating.

depreciatory *adj.* belittling; contemptuous.

depredation *noun* (*often* **depredations**) damage, destruction, or violent robbery. [from Latin *depraedatio*, from *praedari*, to plunder]

depress *verb* **1** to make sad and gloomy. **2** *formal* to make lower. **3** *formal* to press down. [from Old French *depresser*]

depressant *— adj. Medicine, said of a drug* able to reduce mental or physical activity. *— noun* a depressant drug. See also ANTIDEPRESSANT.

depressed *adj.* **1** sad and gloomy. **2** *Psychol.* suffering from a mental illness which causes feelings of sadness, inadequacy, tiredness, etc. **3** suffering from high unemployment and low standards of living: *a depressed area.*

depressing *adj.* causing low spirits.

depressingly *adv.* in a depressing way.

depression *noun* **1** *Psychol.* a mental state characterized by prolonged and disproportionate feelings of sadness, pessimism, helplessness, apathy, low self-esteem, and despair, often accompanied by an increased or decreased desire for food or sleep, and impaired concentration. **2** a period of low business and industrial activity accompanied by a rise in unemployment. **3** (**the Depression**) the period of worldwide economic depression from 1929 to 1934. **4** an area of low atmospheric pressure. **5** a hollow, especially in the ground.
◇ Depression may be caused by changes in life circumstances, especially loss of various kinds (eg bereavement, unemployment), or it may be a factor in a wide range of mental disorders and physical illnesses. It is treated with antidepressant drugs, psychotherapy, or, very rarely and only in extreme cases, by electroconvulsive therapy.

depression of freezing point *Chem.* the lowering of the freezing point of a liquid, achieved by dissolving a solid in it.

depressive *noun* a person who suffers frequently from depression.

deprivation *noun* **1** hardship, etc caused by being deprived of necessities, rights, etc. **2** the act of depriving or state of being deprived.

deprive *verb* (**deprive someone of something**) to take or keep it from them; to prevent them from using or enjoying it. [from Latin *deprivare*, to degrade]

deprived *adj.* **1** (**deprived of something**) having had it kept or taken from one. **2** *said of a person* suffering from hardship through lack of money, reasonable living conditions, etc. **3** *said of a district, etc* lacking good housing, schools, medical facilities, etc.

dept. *abbrev.* department.

depth *noun* **1** deepness; the distance from the top downwards, from the front to the back, or from the surface inwards. **2** *said of feelings or colours* intensity or strength. **3** extensiveness: *the depth of one's knowledge.* **4** (**depths, the depth**) somewhere far from the surface or edge of: *the depths of the ocean, of the country.* **5** (**depths, the depth**) an extreme feeling (of despair, sadness, etc) or great degree (of deprivation, etc). **6** (often **the depths**) the middle and severest part of (winter, etc). **7** (**depths**) serious aspects of a person's character that are not immediately obvious. **8** *said of sound* lowness of pitch.
— **in depth** deeply and thoroughly.

out of one's depth 1 in water so deep that one would be below the surface even when standing up. **2** not able to understand information or an explanation, or in a situation which is too difficult for one to deal with.
[from Anglo-Saxon *deop*, deep + -TH²]

depth charge a type of bomb dropped from a ship which explodes underwater and is used to attack submarines.

deputation *noun* a group of people appointed to represent and speak on behalf of others. [from Latin *deputare*, to select]

depute *verb formal* **1** to formally appoint (someone) to do something. **2** (**depute something to someone**) to give (one's work, etc, or part of it) to someone else to do. [from Old French *deputer*, from Latin *deputare*, to select]

deputize *or* **deputise** *verb* **1** *intrans.* (**deputize for someone**) to act as their deputy. **2** *trans.* to appoint as a deputy.

deputy — *noun* (PL. **deputies**) **1** a person appointed to act on behalf of or as an assistant to

someone else. **2** in some countries, a person elected to the lower house of parliament. — *adj.* in some organizations, next in rank to the head and having the authority to act on his or her behalf. [from Old French *deputer*, to appoint, from Latin *deputare*, to select]

de Queiros, José Mari Eca de see QUEIROS, JOSÉ MARI ECA DE.

De Quincey, Thomas (1785–1859) English writer, born in Manchester. He became an opium addict while living in Oxford, moved to Grasmere in 1809, where he stayed near Coleridge and the other Lake poets, and finally to Edinburgh in 1828. His writings consist largely of magazine articles, the most famous of which, *Confessions of an Opium-eater*, appeared as a serial in 1821.

derail *verb trans., intrans.* to leave or cause to leave the rails.

derailment *noun, said of a train* accidental separation from the rails.

derange *verb* **1** to make insane. **2** to disrupt or throw into disorder or confusion. [from French *déranger*, to disturb]

deranged *adj.* made insane; thrown into confusion.

derangement *noun* disturbance; mental disorder.

Derby, Edward Geoffrey Smith Stanley, 14th Earl of (1799–1869) English statesman and Conservative Prime Minister, born in Knowsley Hall, Lancashire. He entered parliament as a Whig in 1828, and became Chief-Secretary for Ireland (1830) and Colonial Secretary (1833), when he carried the Act for the emancipation of West Indian slaves. In 1834, he withdrew from the Whigs and joined the Conservatives. He entered the Lords as Baron Stanley of Bickerstaffe in 1844 and headed the Protectionists from 1846, the year he became Party leader. Prime Minister on three occasions (1852, 1858–9, 1866–8), he passed the Reform Bill (1867) in his third administration.

Derby POP (1992e) 227 000, an industrial city in Derbyshire, central England. It stands on the R Derwent, 56km/35mi NE of Birmingham. HISTORY founded in the 9c by the Danes as Deoraby; chartered in 1637; a porcelain centre in the 18c, producing Derby ware; first silk mill, in 1719. NOTABLE FEATURES Cathedral of All Saints (1525); old silk mill industrial museum.

derby¹ *noun* (PL. **derbies**) **1** (**the Derby**) a horse race held annually at Epsom Downs. **2** a race or a sports event or contest, especially (*local derby*) a contest between teams from the same area. [named after the Earl of *Derby*, one of the founders of the race in 1780]. See also CLASSICS.

derby² *noun* (PL. **derbies**) North Amer. a bowler hat. [from DERBY¹]

Derby china a variety of porcelain china made in Derby, England, from around the 1750s. In 1770, the factory owner William Duesbury (1725–86) bought the Chelsea Porcelain works, and transferred its moulds and patterns to Derby. The Derby factory specialized in fine neoclassical figures and wares, and should not be confused with the quite separate Crown Derby Porcelain Company, established in 1877.

Derbys. *abbrev.* Derbyshire.

Derbyshire POP (1992e) 947 000, a county in central England, divided into nine districts. AREA 2 631sq km/1 016sq mi. It is bounded NW by Greater Manchester, N by West Yorkshire, NE by South Yorkshire, E by Nottinghamshire, SE by Leicestershire, and W by Cheshire and Staffordshire. PHYSICAL DESCRIPTION rises to The Peak at 636m; drained by the Derwent, Dove, Wye, and Trent rivers. CHIEF TOWNS Matlock (county town), Derby, Chesterfield, Glossop. ECONOMY sheep and dairy farming; textiles; engineering; coal, iron smelting.

Derby, the see CLASSICS.

deregulate *verb* to remove controls and regulations from (a business or business activity).

deregulation *noun* removal of controls from a business, etc.

derelict — *adj.* abandoned and falling in ruins. — *noun* a tramp; a person with no home or money. [from Latin *derelinquere*, to abandon]

dereliction *noun* (usually **dereliction of duty**) neglect or failure.

dereliction of duty *noun formal* failure to do what one ought to do.

derestrict *verb* to remove a restriction from (something), especially a speed limit from (a road).

derestriction *noun* removal of restrictions.

Dergue *or* **Derg** the name given to the Provisional Administrative Council after the military's overthrow of Emperor Haile Selassie (1974) and chaired by Haile Mariam Mengistu in Ethiopia until its collapse in 1991. Operating like a politburo, its members increasingly also came to full governmental positions, and it established the Worker's Revolutionary Party to advance its radical socialist policies. [from Amharic, = Committee]

deride *verb* to laugh at or make fun of. See also DERISION. [from Latin *deridere*]

de rigueur required by fashion, custom or the rules of politeness. [from French *de rigueur*, of strictness]

derision *noun* the act of deriding; scornful laughter. [from Latin *derisio*]

derisive *adj.* scornful; mocking. [from DERISION]
◆ Often confused with *derisory*.

derisively *adv.* in a derisive or scornful way.

derisory *adj.* ridiculous and insulting, especially ridiculously small. [from Latin *derisorius*]
◆ Often confused with *derisive*.

derivation *noun* **1** the act of deriving or the state or process of being derived. **2** the source or origin (especially of a word). **3** *Grammar* the process of forming a word by adding one or more prefixes or suffixes to another word. [from Old French *deriver*, from Latin *de*, from + *rivus*, stream]

derivative — *adj.* not original; derived from or copying something else (especially someone else's work). — *noun* **1** something which is derived from something else. **2** *Grammar* a word formed by adding one or more prefixes or suffixes to another word, such as *happily* from *happy*, *decarbonize* from *carbon*. **3** *Chem.* a compound (usually organic) that is made from another compound. **4** *Maths.* the result of differentiation in order to calculate the changes in one variable produced by changes in another variable.

derive *verb* **1** (**derive from something**) to come or arise from it; to have it as a source. **2** (**derive one thing from another**) to obtain or produce one thing from another. **3** to trace (something) back to a source or origin.

dermatitis *noun Medicine* inflammation of the skin, which becomes red and itchy and may develop small blisters. In most cases it is associated with eczema, in which there is a change in the actual composition of the skin in response to a chemical irritant, or as part of an allergic reaction.

dermato- *or* **dermat-** *or* **-derm** *combining form* of the skin, as in. DERMATITIS and ECTODERM [from Greek *derma*, skin]

dermatologist *noun* a person who practises or studies dermatology.

dermatology *noun* the branch of medical science concerned with the study of the skin and treatment of its diseases.

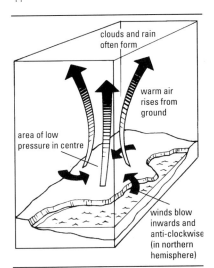

clouds and rain often form

warm air rises from ground

area of low pressure in centre

winds blow inwards and anti-clockwise (in northern hemisphere)

depression: a low pressure weather system

dermis *noun Anat.* the thick layer of skin that lies beneath the epidermis. It consists of loose connective tissue containing blood capillaries, nerve endings, hair follicles, sweat glands, lymph vessels, and some muscle fibres. [from Greek *derma*, skin]

Dermot a male first name, confined to Ireland. [from Gaelic *Diarmait*, probably from *di*, without + *hairmait*, envy]

derogate *verb intrans.* (**derogate from something**) *formal* to cause it to appear inferior; to show one's low opinion of something. [from Latin *derogare*, to detract from]

derogation *noun* **1** reduction in power or authority. **2** deterioration.

derogatorily *adv.* in a derogatory or disapproving way.

derogatory *adj.* showing, or intended to show, disapproval, dislike, scorn, or lack of respect. [from Latin *derogatorius*]

Deronda, Daniel see DANIEL DERONDA.

derrick *noun* **1** a type of crane with a movable arm. **2** a framework built over an oil-well, used for raising and lowering the drill. [named after Derrick, a 17c hangman]

Derrida, Jacques (1930–) French philosopher, born in Algeria. He taught at the Sorbonne (1960–4) and at the Ecole Normale Supérieure (1965–84) in Paris. His critique of the referentiality of language and the objectivity of structures founded the school of criticism called *deconstruction*. Among his works are *De la Grammatologie* (Of Grammatology, 1967), *L'écriture et la différence* (Writing and Difference, 1967), and *La dissémination* (Dissemination, 1972).

derring-do *noun old use, literary* daring deeds. [from a wrong understanding by Spenser, the 16c poet, of the phrase *derrynge do* (= daring to do) in the work of an earlier poet]

derris *noun* **1** a climbing plant related to peas and beans. **2** an insecticide made from its roots. [from Greek *derris*, leather jacket]

Derry see LONDONDERRY.

derv *noun Brit.* diesel oil used as a fuel for road vehicles. [from *d*iesel- *e*ngine *r*oad *v*ehicle]

dervish *noun* a member of any of various Muslim religious groups vowed to poverty, some of whom perform spinning dances as part of their religious ritual. [from Turkish *derviş*, from Persian *darvish*, poor man, dervish]

dancing dervish

Derwent Water a lake in the Lake District of Cumbria, NW England. It extends 5km/2mi S from Keswick.

DES *abbrev.* Department of Education and Science.

Desai, Morarji (Ranchhodji) (1896–) Indian politician, born in Gujarat. He entered politics in 1930 and after various ministerial posts, was a candidate for the premiership in 1964 and 1966, but was defeated by Indira Gandhi. He

became Deputy Prime Minister in 1969 to lead the Opposition Congress Party. Detained during the state of emergency (1975–7), he was then appointed leader of the newly-formed Janata Party and elected Prime Minister (1977–9). The Janata government experienced much internal strife however, and he was forced to resign.

desalinate *verb technical* to remove salt from (especially sea-water). [from DE- 2 + SALINE]

desalination *noun* the removal of salt, mainly sodium chloride, from seawater in order to produce fresh water for drinking, irrigation, etc.

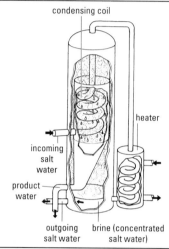

condensing coil

heater

incoming salt water

product water

outgoing salt water

brine (concentrated salt water)

desalination

descant *Mus.* — *noun* a melody played or harmony sung above the main tune. — *adj., said of a musical instrument* having a higher pitch than others of the same type. [from Old French, from DIS-, apart + *cantus*, song]

Descartes, René (1596–1650) French philosopher and mathematician, usually regarded as the father of modern philosophy, born near Tours. He studied law at Poitiers, graduating in 1616, and in 1618 he enlisted for private military service. While serving in the Bavarian army in 1619 he conceived a reconstruction of the whole of knowledge into a unified system of certain truth modelled on mathematics, based on physics and reaching via medicine to morality, all supported by a rigorous rationalism. His *Discours de la Méthode* (Discourse on Method, 1637), the *Meditationes de prima Philosophia* (Meditations of First Philosophy, 1641) and the *Principia Philosophiae* (Principles of Philosophy, 1644) set out the fundamental Cartesian doctrines: the method of systematic doubt; the first indubitably true proposition, *cogito ergo sum* (I think therefore I am); the idea of God as the absolutely perfect being; and the dualism of mind and matter. In mathematics he reformed algebraic notation and helped found coordinate geometry.

descend *verb* **1** *trans., intrans.* to go or move down from a higher to a lower place or position. **2** *intrans.* to lead or slope downwards. **3** (**descend on** *or* **upon someone** *or* **something**) to invade or attack them. **4** *intrans. said of titles, property, etc* to pass by inheritance from one generation to another.
— **be descended from someone** to have them as an ancestor.
would not descend to something *or* **to do something** would not demean oneself by resorting to unworthy or immoral behaviour. [from Old French *descendre*]

descendant *noun* a person, animal, etc that is the child, grandchild, great-grandchild, etc of another.

descending *adj.* from the highest to the lowest, the greatest to the least, or the best to the worst.

descent *noun* **1** the act or process of coming or going down. **2** a slope downwards. **3** family origins or ancestry; the fact of being descended from someone. **4** a sudden invasion or attack. [from Old French *descente*]

describe *verb* **1** to say what (someone or something) is like. **2** (**describe oneself as something**) to call oneself, or claim to be, something. **3** *technical Geom.* to draw or form. **4** *formal* to move in the shape of: *skaters describing circles on the ice*. [from Latin *describere*]

description *noun* **1** the act of describing. **2** a statement of what someone or something is like. **3** *colloq.* a sort, type, or kind: *toys of every description*. [from Latin *descriptio*]

descriptive *adj.* describing, especially describing well or vividly. [from Latin *descriptivus*]

descriptively *adv.* in a descriptive way.

descry *verb* (**descries, descried**) *formal* **1** to see or catch sight of. **2** to see or discover by looking carefully. [from Old French *descrier*, to announce and *descrire*, to describe]

Desdemona the wife, and heroine, of Shakespeare's *Othello*. The loss of her handkerchief leads to her murder at the hands of her husband.

desecrate *verb* to treat or use (a sacred object) or behave in (a holy place) in a way that shows a lack of respect or causes damage. [from DE- 2 + CONSECRATE]

desecration *noun* treating a holy place with violence or disrespect.

desecrator *noun* a person who treats a holy place with violence or disrespect.

desegregate *verb* to end (especially racial) segregation in (public places, schools, transport systems, etc).

desegregation *noun* abolition of segregation.

deselect *verb Brit.* **1** *said of a branch of a political party* to reject (the existing Member of Parliament or local councillor) as a candidate for the next election. **2** *said of a selection committee, etc* not to re-select (eg an athlete) for a place on a team, etc.

deselection *noun* failure to reselect the existing candidate in a political election.

desensitization *or* **desensitisation** *noun* making less sensitive.

desensitize *or* **desensitise** *verb* to make less sensitive to light, pain, suffering, etc.

desert[1] *verb* (with stress on *-sert*) **1** to leave or abandon (a place or person), intending not to return. **2** *intrans.* to leave, especially a branch of the armed forces, without permission. **3** to take away one's support from (a person, cause, etc). [from French *déserter*]

desert[2] *noun* (with stress on *des-*) an arid area of land where vegetation is scarce or non-existent, and which is characterized by extremely high or low temperatures, or by the evaporation of more water from the Earth's surface than is precipitated in the form of rain, snow, etc. Deserts occur in all continents except Europe, and are found mainly in inland regions where there is low rainfall and temperatures fluctuate widely. The world's largest desert is the Sahara in N Africa. Cold deserts are barren because the low temperatures restrict plant growth. [Old French, from Latin *deserere*, to abandon]

deserted *adj., said of a building, etc* empty or abandoned.

Deserted Village, The a poem by Oliver Goldsmith (1770). It is a pastoral elegy set in unspoiled 'Auburn', lamenting the decline of the English countryside in the face of industrialization.

deserter *noun* a person who deserts from military service.

desertification *noun* **1** the process by which a new desert is formed, or an existing desert spreads across an area that was formerly moist and fertile. **2**

◇ There are two main causes of desertification. A natural change in the climate may take place as a result of a major shift in the Earth's weather patterns, or bad farming practices (such as inefficient irrigation, over-cultivation, over-grazing, or forest clearance) may lead to soil erosion, drying, and eventual desertification. Frequently, both factors contribute to the formation of desert. The best-known recent example of desertification and its consequences for wildlife and the human population is in W Africa, where desert conditions have been spreading from the Sahara Desert into the neighbouring Sahel region.

desertion *noun* the act of or an instance of deserting, especially deserting one's husband or wife or deserting from military service.

Desert Rats members of the 7th British Armoured Division, which in 1940 took as its badge the jerboa or desert rat, capable of remarkable leaps. The media applied the name generally to all British servicemen in the N Africa campaign, and it was also adopted by those not entitled to wear the jerboa shoulder flash.

deserts *pl. noun* (with stress on -*serts*) what one deserves, usually something unfavourable: *get one's just deserts*. [from Old French *desert*, from *deservir*, to deserve]

deserve *verb* to have earned, be entitled to, or be worthy of (a reward or punishment, etc). [from Old French *deservir*]

deservedly *adv.* as one rightly deserves.

deserving *adj.* **1** worthy or suitable (to be given support, a reward, etc). **2** *formal* (**deserving of something**) worthy of it; meriting it.

déshabillé *adj.* the state of being only partly dressed. [from French *déshabillé*, undressed]

De Sica, Vittorio (1902–74) Italian actor and film director, born in Sera. He established himself

Largest Deserts

Name/Location	Area[1]	
	sq km	sq mi
Sahara, N Africa	7 700 000	3 000 000
Arabian, SW Asia	2 330 000	900 000
Gobi, Mongolia and NE China	1 295 000	500 000
Patagonian, Argentina	673 000	260 000
Great Basin, SW USA	492 000	190 000
Chihuahuan, Mexico	450 000	175 000
Great Sandy, NW Australia	450 000	175 000
Nubian, Sudan	400 000	155 000
Great Victoria, SW Australia	325 000	125 000
Thar, India/Pakistan	320 000	124 000
Sonoran, SW USA	310 000	120 000
Kara Kum, Turkmenistan	260 000	100 000
Kyzyl-Kum, Kazakhstan	300 000	115 000
Takla Makan, N China	270 000	105 000
Kalahari, SW Africa	260 000	100 000
Kavir, Iran	260 000	100 000
Syrian, Saudi Arabia/Jordan/Syria/Iraq	260 000	100 000
Ust'-Urt, Kazakhstan	160 000	62 000
Bet-Pak-Dala, S Kazakhstan	155 000	60 000
Simpson, C Australia	145 000	56 000
Dzungaria, China	142 000	55 000
Atacama, Chile	140 000	54 000
Namib, SE Africa	134 000	52 000
Sturt, SE Australia	130 000	50 000
Bolson de Mapimi, Mexico	130 000	50 000
Ordos, China	130 000	50 000
Alashan, China	116 000	45 000

[1] Desert areas are very approximate, because clear physical boundaries may not occur.

as a romantic star of stage and screen, and became a director in 1940, achieving international success in the neorealist style with *Sciuscià* (Shoeshine, 1946) and *Ladri di biciclette* (Bicycle Thieves, 1948).

desiccant *noun Chem.* a substance that absorbs water and so can be used as a drying agent to remove water from or prevent absorption of water by other substances. [from Latin *desiccare*, to dry up]

desiccate *verb* to dry or remove the moisture from (something, especially food, in order to preserve it). [from Latin *desiccare*, to dry up]

desiccated *adj., said of food* having the moisture removed.

desiccation *noun* removal of the moisture from food, etc.

desiccator *noun Chem.* a device, usually a closed glass vessel containing a desiccant, that is used to remove water from or prevent the absorption of water by other substances.

desideratum *noun* (PL. **desiderata**) *formal* something wanted or required. [from Latin *desiderare*, to long for]

design — *verb* **1** to develop or prepare a plan, drawing, or model of (something) before it is built or made. **2** *formal* to plan, intend, or develop for a particular purpose. — *noun* **1** a plan, drawing, or model showing how something is to be made. **2** the art or job of making such drawings, plans, etc. **3** the way in which something has been made. **4** a picture, pattern, arrangement of shapes, etc used eg as decoration. **5** one's plan, purpose, or intention: *put there by design*.
— **have designs on something** to have plans to appropriate it.
[from French *désigner*]

designate — *verb* (pronounced -*nate*) **1** to name, choose, or specify for a particular purpose or duty. **2** to mark or indicate. **3** to be a name or label for. — *adj.* (pronounced -*nət*) (*used after a noun*) having been appointed to some official position but not yet holding it: *editor-designate*. [from Latin *designare*, to plan or mark out]

designation *noun* **1** a name or title. **2** designating; the state of being designated.

Design Centre the headquarters of the Design Council, a British organization whose centre was opened in London in 1956. It is used for exhibitions of developments in design, and to promote the improvement of design in the products of British industry. There is a Scottish Design Centre in Glasgow.

designedly *adv.* intentionally; on purpose.

designer *noun* **1** a person who makes designs, plans, patterns, drawings, etc, especially professionally. **2** (*attributive*) **a** designed by and bearing the name of a famous fashion designer: *designer dresses*. **b** especially made for a particular purpose or effect: *designer drugs*. **c** *colloq.* following current fashion.

designer drug *Medicine* any of various synthetic drugs, often narcotics, which are not controlled by law in the USA, so called because they are specifically designed by chemists to be slightly different structurally from drugs that are controlled by law (ie illegal drugs), yet chemically so similar to them that they have similar biological effects. These 'legal' drugs are produced covertly and sold on the streets to drug users. The normal dangers of drug abuse are increased by the risk of chemical contamination.

designing *adj. derog.* using cunning and deceit to achieve one's purpose.

desirability *noun* being desirable or wanted.

desirable *adj.* **1** pleasing; worth having. **2** sexually attractive.

desirably *adv.* according to what is desirable or wanted.

desire — *noun* **1** a longing or wish. **2** strong sexual interest and attraction. — *verb* **1** *formal* to want. **2** to long for or feel sexual desire for. **3** *old use, formal* to ask or command. [from Old French *desirer*]

Desire Under The Elms a play by Eugene O'Neill (1924). A story of greed and incest reflecting problems in the US society of his time, it depicts a farmer's relationship with his wife and her desire for his son by a previous marriage.

desirous *adj. formal* (**desirous of something**) wanting it keenly.

desist *verb intrans. formal* (**desist from something**) to stop doing it. [from Old French *desister*]

desk *noun* **1** a sloping or flat table, often with drawers, for sitting at while writing, reading, etc. **2** a place or counter in a public building where a service is provided. **3** a section of a newspaper, etc office with responsibility for a particular subject. [from Latin *discus*, disc, table]

deskilling *noun* the process of removing the element of human skill from a job, operation, etc, through automation, computerization, etc.

desk-top *adj.* small enough to fit on the top of a desk.

desk-top publishing (ABBREV. **DTP**) the process of preparing and producing typeset output as a basis for published text, using a microcomputer with specialist software and high resolution printers. This method can produce high quality texts without the need for extensive office space.

Des Moines POP (1990) 393 000, the capital of the state of Iowa, USA. It is the state's largest city and lies at the junction of the Racoon and Des Moines rivers, in Polk County, central Iowa. Des Moines is an important industrial, commercial, and transportation centre in the heart of Iowa's Corn Belt. HISTORY developed around a fort established in 1843; became a city and state capital in 1900; damaged by flooding in 1993. NOTABLE FEATURES the Capitol; Des Moines Art Centre; Centre of Science and Industry.

Desmond, Gerald Fitzgerald, 15th Earl of (c.1538–83) Irish Catholic nobleman, who rebelled (1579–80) against Queen Elizabeth, sacked the town of Youghal by night, and was proclaimed a traitor.

Desmond a male first name. [originally an Irish local name (Gaelic *Deas Mumhan*) for someone from south Munster]

Desmoulins, (Lucie Simplice) Camille (Benoist) (1760–94) French revolutionary and journalist, born in Guise. He studied law, but owing to a stutter never practised. He was nonetheless an effective crowd orator and influential pamphleteer, and played a dramatic part in the storming of the Bastille. A member of the Cordeliers' Club from its foundation, he was elected to the National Convention, and voted for the death of the king. He actively attacked the Girondists, but by the end of 1793 argued for moderation, which incurred the hostility of Robespierre and resulted in his own execution.

desolate — *adj.* (pronounced -*lət*) **1** *said of a place* deserted, barren and lonely. **2** *said of a person* very sad; in despair. **3** lacking pleasure or comfort: *a desolate life*. **4** lonely; alone. — *verb* (pronounced -*late*) **1** to overwhelm with sadness or grief. **2** to make deserted or barren; to lay waste. [from Latin *desolare*, to forsake]

desolated *adj.* made wretched; forlorn.

desolation *noun* a state of lonely wretchedness or misery.

Despair, Giant a character in John Bunyan's *The Pilgrim's Progress*, who imprisons Christian and Faithful.

despair — *verb intrans.* (often **despair of something** *or* **despair of doing something**) to lose or lack hope. — *noun* **1** the state of having lost hope. **2** (**the despair**) someone or something that causes worry and despair: *he's the despair of his parents.* [from Old French *desperer*]

despairing *adj.* giving up hope; involving loss of hope: *he gave a despairing glance.*

despairingly *adv.* in a despairing or hopeless way.

despatch see DISPATCH.

desperado *noun* (PL. **desperados, desperadoes**) *especially in the western USA in the 19c* a bandit or outlaw. [probably a mock-Spanish word formed from DESPERATE]

desperate *adj.* **1** extremely anxious, fearful or despairing. **2** willing to take risks fearlessly because of hopelessness and despair. **3** very serious, difficult, dangerous, and almost hopeless: *a desperate situation.* **4** dangerous and likely to be violent: *a desperate criminal.* **5** extreme and carried out as a last resort because of the seriousness or hopelessness of the situation: *desperate measures.* **6** very great: *desperate need.* **7** (**desperate for something**) in great or urgent need of it: *desperate for supplies.* **8** extremely anxious or eager: *desperate to go to the concert.* [from Latin *desperare*, to despair]

desperately *adv.* **1** in a despairing or desperate manner. **2** very hard. **3** extremely.

desperation *noun* a state of despair; extreme hopelessness.

despicable *adj.* deserving one's contempt; mean. [from Latin *despicabilis*]

despicably *adv.* in a despicable or contemptible way.

despise *verb* to look down on with scorn and contempt. [from Old French *despire*, from Latin *despicere*]

despite *prep.* in spite of. [from Old French *despit*, from Latin *despicere*, to despise]

despoil *verb formal, literary* to rob or steal everything valuable from (a place). [from Old French *despoiller*, from Latin *spolium*, plunder]

despoiler *noun* a person who robs a place of its valuables.

despoliation *noun* plundering; robbing.

despondency *noun* low spirits; dejection.

despondent *adj.* sad; dejected; in low spirits. [from Latin *despondere*, to lose heart]

despondently *adv.* with a despondent or sad manner.

despot *noun* a person who has very great or total power, especially one who uses such power in a cruel or oppressive way. [from Greek *despotes*, master]

despotic *adj.* like a despot; tyrannical; overbearing.

despotically *adv.* in a despotic or overbearing way.

despotism *noun* absolute power; tyranny.

Dessalines, Jean Jacques (c.1758–1806) Emperor of Haiti, born a slave, probably in Grande Rivière du Nord, Saint Domingue (called Haiti since 1804). He was involved with Toussaint L'Ouverture in the slave revolt of 1791, and after compelling the French to leave Haiti (1803), he was created Governor and crowned Emperor as Jacques I. His supporters were alienated by his cruelty and debauchery however, and he was assassinated near Port-au-Prince.

dessert *noun* **1** a sweet food served after the main course of a meal. **2** the course at or near the end of a meal, when such food is served. [from Old French, from *desservir*, to clear the table]

dessertspoon *noun* **1** a medium-sized spoon, about half the size of a tablespoon and twice the size of a teaspoon. **2** the amount a dessertspoon will hold.

dessertspoonful *noun* (PL. **dessertspoonfuls**) the amount a dessertspoon will hold.

destabilization or **destabilisation** *noun* destabilizing; making less stable.

destabilize or **destabilise** *verb* to make (a country, economy, etc) less stable.

De Stijl a group of Dutch artists and architects formed in 1917, influenced by Cubism, Dutch Calvinism, and theosophy. The group advocated a new, wholly abstract aesthetic style composed solely of straight lines, primary colours, and black and white. Its members included Piet Mondrian, Theo van Doesburg, J J P Oud, and Gerrit Rietveld.

destination *noun* the place to which someone or something is going or being sent. [from Latin *destinatio*, purpose]

destine *verb formal* (usually **be destined for something** or **to do something**) to have it as an arranged purpose. [from Old French *destiner*]

destiny *noun* (PL. **destinies**) **1** one's purpose or future as arranged by fate or God. **2** (*also* **Destiny**) fate; the power which appears or is believed to control events. [from Old French *destinee*, from Latin *destinare*, to appoint]

destitute *adj.* **1** lacking money, food, shelter, etc; extremely poor. **2** *formal* (**destitute of something**) completely lacking in something necessary or desirable. [from Latin *destitutus*]

destitution *noun* being desititute; lack of money and food.

destroy *verb* **1** to knock down, break into pieces, completely ruin, etc. **2** to put an end to. **3** to defeat totally. **4** to ruin or seriously damage the reputation, health, financial position, etc of. **5** to kill (a dangerous, injured, or unwanted animal). [from Old French *destruire*, from Latin *de*, down + *struere*, to build]

destroyer *noun* **1** a person or thing that destroys or causes destruction. **2** a type of small, fast warship.

destruct *verb trans., intrans. chiefly North Amer., esp. US, said of equipment, especially a missile in flight* to destroy or be destroyed, especially for safety reasons.

destructibility *noun* the capacity to be or the likelihood of being destroyed.

destructible *adj.* able to be destroyed.

destruction *noun* **1** the act or process of destroying or being destroyed. **2** something that destroys. [from Latin *destruere*, to destroy, from *de*, down + *struere*, to build]

destructive *adj.* **1** causing destruction or serious damage. **2** *said of criticism, etc* pointing out faults, etc without suggesting improvements.

destructively *adv.* in a destructive or seriously damaging way.

desultorily *adv.* in a desultory or purposeless way.

desultory *adj.* jumping from one thing to another with no plan, purpose, or logical connection. [from Latin *desultorius*, from *desultor*, circus performer who jumped from horse to horse]

Det. *abbrev.* Detective.

detach *verb* **1** to unfasten or separate. **2** *Mil.* to select and separate (a group of soldiers, etc) from a larger group, especially to carry out a special task. [from Old French *destachier*, from *des-, dis-* + *atachier*, to attach]

detachable *adj.* capable of being detached; removable.

detached *adj.* **1** *said of a building* not joined to another on either side. See also SEMI-DETACHED. **2** *said of a person* feeling no personal or emotional involvement; showing no prejudice or bias.

detachedly *adv.* with a detached or uninvolved manner: *spoke detachedly about the war.*

detachment *noun* **1** the state of being emotionally detached or free from prejudice. **2** a group (eg of soldiers) detached from a larger group for a special purpose. **3** the act of detaching or state or process of being detached.

detail — *noun* **1** a small feature, fact, or item. **2** something considered unimportant. **3** all the small features and parts (of something) considered as a whole: *an artist's eye for detail.* **4** a part of a painting, map, photograph, etc considered separately, often enlarged to show small features. **5** *Mil.* a group of eg soldiers given a special task or duty. — *verb* **1** to describe or list fully. **2** to appoint (someone) to do a particular task. — **in detail** giving or looking at all the details. [from Old French *detailler*, to cut up]

detailed *adj.* having or giving many details; thorough.

detain *verb* **1** to stop, hold back, keep waiting, or delay. **2** *said of the police, etc* to keep (someone) in a cell, prison, or elsewhere, especially before trial. See also DETENTION. [from Old French *detenir*, to hold]

detainee *noun* a person held under guard eg by the police, especially for political reasons.

detect *verb* **1** to see or notice. **2** to discover, and usually indicate, the presence or existence of (something which should not be there or whose presence is not obvious). [from Latin *detegere*, to uncover]

detectable or **detectible** *adj.* capable of being detected.

detection *noun* **1** the act or process of detecting or state of being detected. **2** the work of a detective, investigating and solving crime.

detective *noun* a police officer whose job is to solve crime by observation and gathering evidence. See also PRIVATE DETECTIVE.

detective story a story whose main theme is the solving of a crime.

detector *noun* an instrument or device used for detecting the presence of something.

détente *noun* a lessening of tension, especially in the relationships between countries. [from French *détente*]

detention *noun* **1** the act of detaining or the state of being detained, especially in prison or police custody. **2** a punishment in which a pupil is kept in school after the other pupils have gone home. [from Latin *detinere*, to detain]

detention centre a place where young criminals are kept for a short time by order of a court.

deter *verb* (**deterred, deterring**) to discourage or prevent (someone) from doing (something) because of fear of unpleasant consequences. [from Latin *deterrere*, to frighten off]

detergent — *noun* a soapless and usually water-soluble substance that is added to a liquid, especially water, in order to improve its cleaning properties. It acts by reducing surface tension and so allowing fats and oils that bind dirt to skin, clothing, etc, to dissolve in water. — *adj.* having the power to clean. [from Latin *detergere*, to wipe off]

◇ Unlike soap, detergents do not form an insoluble scum in hard water. Water-soluble detergents are usually sodium salts of sulphonic (sulphur-containing) acids, produced by the petrochemical industry, and they may be liquids, as in shampoos and washing-up liquids, or powdered solids. Washing powders usually contain alkyl benzene, bleaches, and optical brighteners, and 'biological' detergents also contain enzymes. Oil-soluble detergents are used in dry-cleaning solutions and lubricating oils. Concern about the disposal of detergents, which can pollute rivers and streams with foam, phosphates, and other harmful chemicals, has led to the development of 'environmentally friendly' detergents that contain no bleaches or phosphates.

deteriorate *verb intrans.* to grow worse. [from Latin *deterior*, worse]

deterioration *noun* worsening.

determinant *noun* **1** a determining factor or circumstance. **2** *Maths.* a number obtained by multiplying and adding the elements of a square matrix according to certain rules. **3** *Biol.* in an antigen molecule, a region or regions that enable it to be recognized and bound by an antibody.

determinate *adj.* having definite, fixed limits, etc.

determination *noun* **1** firmness or strength of will, purpose or character. **2** the act of determining or process of being determined.

determinative *adj.* having the power to limit or determine.

determine *verb* **1** to fix or settle the exact limits or nature of. **2** to find out or reach a conclusion about by gathering facts, making measurements, etc. **3** *trans., intrans.* to decide or cause (someone) to decide. **4** to be the main influence on; to control. [from Old French *determiner*, from Latin *determinare*, to fix the limits of]

determined *adj.* **1** (**determined to do something**) firmly intending to do it. **2** having or showing a strong will.

determiner *noun Grammar* a word that comes before a noun or noun phrase, and limits its meaning in some way, eg *a, the, this, every, some.*

determinism *noun Philos.* the theory that every event has a cause, or that nature is uniform. *Causal determinsim* maintains that all events are determined by causes, and that each event could not have failed to have happened. Philosophers have disagreed about whether causal determinism is compatible with free will. *Logical determinism*, attributed to the Stoics, states that the laws of logic alone necessitate any event, and that it is contradictory to conceive of anything being different from what it is.

determinist *noun* a believer in determinism.

deterrence *noun* discouragement by fear of the consequences.

deterrent *noun* something which deters, especially a weapon intended to deter attack.

detest *verb* to dislike intensely; to hate. [from Old French *detester*]

detestable *adj.* hateful.

detestably *adv.* in a detestable or hateful way.

detestation *noun* great dislike; hatred.

dethrone *verb* **1** to remove (a monarch) from the throne. **2** to remove from a position of power, influence, or authority.

dethronement *noun* removal from the throne.

detonate *verb trans., intrans.* to explode or cause to explode. [from Latin *detonare*, to thunder down]

detonation *noun* detonating; explosion.

detonator *noun* an explosive substance or a device used to make a bomb, etc explode.

detour — *noun* a route away from and longer than a planned or more direct route. — *verb intrans.* to make a detour. [from French *détour*]

detoxification *noun* **1** *Physiol.* one of the functions of the liver, involving the removal of toxic substances from the blood, or the neutralization of their toxic effects. **2** *Medicine* the rehabilitation of a person who has been addicted to alcohol or other drugs, eg heroin, and the promotion of recovery from their toxic effects, usually within an institution that specializes in the treatment of addicts.

detoxify *verb* (**detoxifies, detoxified**) to remove poison, drugs, or harmful substances from (a patient). [from DE- + TOXIC]

detract *verb intrans.* (**detract from something**) to take away from it or lessen it. [from Latin *detrahere*, to pull away]

detraction *noun* detracting from a person's reputation; defamation.

detractor *noun* a person who criticizes or belittles (someone, or someone's beliefs, achievements, etc), especially unfairly.

detriment *noun* harm or loss: *to the detriment of her health.* [from Latin *detrimentum*]

detrimental *adj.* harmful; damaging.

detrimentally *adv.* in a detrimental or harmful way.

detritus *noun* **1** *Geol.* loose fragments of weathered rock, produced by disintegration or erosion, that have been transported some distance from their place of origin. **2** *Biol.* dead plants or animals, or any debris of living organisms, eg shed parts. **3** bits and pieces of rubbish left over from something. [from Latin *deterere*, to rub away]

Detroit POP (1990) 4.4m, the seat of Wayne County, SE Michigan, USA. It is a port on the Detroit R, W of L St Clair, and is the sixth largest city in the USA. Detroit is the nation's leading manufacturer of cars and trucks (one third of the country's cars are assembled in and around the city). HISTORY founded by the French as a fur-trading outpost in 1701, it became the trading and political centre for the Great Lakes region; surrendered to the British during the Seven Years War in 1760; it was handed over to the USA in 1796; much of the city was rebuilt after a fire in 1805; capital of the state from 1837 until 1847; centre of the 1960s Motown sound; in the early 1980s recession caused high unemployment and a fall in population. NOTABLE FEATURES Science Centre; Historical Museum; Institute of Arts; Motown Museum; Belle Isle.

de trop not wanted; in the way. [from French *de trop*]

Deucalion in Greek mythology, the son of Prometheus. When Zeus flooded the world, Deucalion and his wife Pyrrha built an 'ark' which grounded on the top of Parnassus. They were the only survivors but they correctly interpreted an oracle which told them how to restore the human race.

deuce[1] *noun* **1** *Tennis* a score of forty points each in a game or five games each in a match. **2** a card, dice throw, etc of the value two. [from Old French *deus*, two]

deuce[2] *noun old use* (**the deuce**) *said in exclamations* the devil. [perhaps from DEUCE[1] two being an unlucky throw in dice]

deus ex machina **1** in classical drama, a god lowered on to the stage by a mechanical device to resolve problems which have arisen in the course of the play or to decide the final outcome. **2** in any literary genre, someone or something introduced suddenly or unexpectedly to provide a contrived solution to a difficulty. [Latin, = god out of a machine]

Deut. or **Deut** *abbrev. Biblical* Deuteronomy.

deuterium *noun Chem.* (SYMBOL **D**) one of the three isotopes of hydrogen, almost identical to the latter in its chemical properties, but with slightly different physical properties, eg boiling point. Its nucleus contains one proton and one neutron. [from Greek *deuteros*, second]

deuterium oxide *Chem.* (FORMULA D_2O) A compound analogous to water, consisting of deuterium (heavy hydrogen) and oxygen. It is denser than water, has a higher freezing and boiling point, and does not support plant or animal life. It is used as a moderator to slow down neutrons in nuclear reactors. — Also called *heavy water.*

deuteron *noun Physics* the nucleus of an atom of deuterium (an isotope of hydrogen), composed of a proton and a neutron. [from Greek *deuteros*, second]

Deuteronomy, Book of the fifth and last book of the Pentateuch, in the Hebrew Bible and Old Testament. Traditionally attributed to Moses, some date it later (c.7c BC). It documents Israel's wilderness experiences, and contains an extensive code of religious laws and duties. Its title means 'a repetition of the law'. [from the Septuagint's mistaken rendering into Greek of Deuteronomy 17.18, where the Hebrew means 'a copy of the law']

Deutsches Museum the German Museum of Masterpieces in Science and Technology, founded in Munich in 1903. The museum, which includes a research institute and issues scientific publications, was established to promote the study of developments in science and industry.

Deutschmark or **Deutsche Mark** *noun* (ABBREV. **DM**) the standard unit of currency in Germany, equal to 100 pfennigs. [from German *Deutschmark*]

de Valera, Eamon see VALERA, EAMON DE.

De Valois, Dame Ninette, originally **Edris Stannus** (1898–) Irish dancer, born in Blessington, Co Wicklow. Her first stage appearance was in pantomime at the Lyceum (1914), and following a European tour with Sergei Diaghilev (1923–5), she became director of ballet at the Abbey Theatre, Dublin, and in 1931 founded the Vic–Wells Ballet (later Sadler's Wells and Royal Ballet). As artistic director there until 1963, she came to be regarded as the pioneer of British ballet, both in her own choreography, as in *The Rake's Progress* (1935) and *Checkmate* (1937), and in the development of a school and two major companies.

devaluation *noun* reduction in the value of a currency.

devalue *verb* **1** *trans., intrans.* to reduce the value of (a currency) in relation to the values of other currencies. **2** to make (a person, action, etc) seem less valuable or important.

devastate *verb* **1** to cause great destruction in or to. **2** to overwhelm with grief; to shock greatly. [from Latin *devastare*, to lay waste]

devastated *adj.* **1** *said of a person* overwhelmed with shock or grief. **2** *said of an area or country* extensively harmed or damaged.

devastating *adj.* **1** completely destructive. **2** shocking; overwhelming. **3** *colloq.* very good or impressive; extremely attractive.

devastatingly *adv.* in a devastating or destructive way.

devastation *noun* devastating; causing great harm or damage.

develop *verb* (**developed, developing**) **1** *trans., intrans.* to make or become more mature, more advanced, more complete, more organized, more detailed, etc. **2** *said of a living organism, organ, tissue, or cell* to become transformed from a simple structure to a much more complex one, usually by passing through a number of stages. **3** to begin to have; to have an increasing amount of: *develop an interest in politics.* **4** *intrans., trans.* to appear and grow, or to have or suffer from something which has appeared and grown: *be developing a cold.* **5** to use chemical agents to convert an invisible image on exposed photographic film or paper into a visible image. **6** to bring into fuller use (the natural resources, etc of a country or region). **7** to build on (land) or prepare (land) for being built on. [from French *développer*]

developer *noun* **1** a chemical used to develop photographic film. **2** a person who builds on land or improves and increases the value of buildings.

developing *adj., said of a country* relatively poor, but aiming to grow socially and economically.

developing countries *Econ.* countries with a low income per capita of population. The term is applied to most of the countries of Asia, Africa, and Latin America, predominantly agricultural economies, though including some with a well-developed industrial base (eg Brazil, India, and Pakistan) or with rich mineral wealth.

development *noun* **1** the act of developing or the process of being developed. **2** a new stage, event, or situation. **3** a result or consequence. **4** land which has been or is being developed, or the buildings built or being built on it.

development aid *Politics* financial and economic assistance given by rich industrial nations to developing countries. Official development aid is channeled through organizations such as the International Development Association (a UN agency) and the International Finance Corporation (an arm of the World Bank).

developmental *adj.* relating to or in the nature of development.

developmentally *adv.* in a developmental way.

developmental psychology *Psychol.* the branch of psychology concerned with the scientific study of human mental development and behaviour from birth to maturity.

development area *Brit.* an area of high unemployment into which the government encourages businesses and industry to move eg by offering grants.

deviance *noun* departure from normal standards or methods.

deviant — *adj.* not following the normal patterns, accepted standards, etc. — *noun* a person who does not behave in a normal or acceptable fashion, especially sexually. [from Latin *deviare*; see etymology at DEVIATE]

deviate *verb intrans.* to turn aside or move away from what is considered a correct or normal course, standard of behaviour, way of thinking, etc. [from Latin *deviare*, to turn from the road, from *de*, from + *via*, road]

deviation *noun* **1** the act of deviating. **2** *Geog.* the existence of or the amount of a difference between north as shown on a compass and true north, caused by the magnetism of objects near the compass, etc.

deviationism *noun* a tendency to dissent from some aspects of a (usually political) belief or ideology.

deviationist *noun* a person given to deviationism.

device *noun* **1** something made for a special purpose, eg a tool or instrument. **2** a plan or scheme for doing something, sometimes involving trickery or deceit. **3** a sign, pattern, or symbol used eg on a crest or shield. See also DEVISE. — **be left to one's own devices** to be left alone and without supervision or help. [from Old French *devis* and *devise*, from Latin *divisa*, mark, device]

devil — *noun* **1** (**the Devil**) *Relig.* the most powerful evil spirit; Satan. **2** any evil or wicked spirit. **3** *colloq.* a mischievous or bad person. **4** *colloq.* a person of a stated type: *lucky devil*. **5** someone or something difficult to deal with. **6** a person who excels at something. **7** (**the devil**) used for emphasis in mild oaths and exclamations: *what the devil is she doing?* — *verb* (**devilled, devilling**) to prepare or cook with a spicy seasoning. — **be a devil** *colloq.* said to encourage someone to do something they are hesitating to do. **between the devil and the deep blue sea** in a situation where the alternatives are equally undesirable. **devil take the hindmost** one should take care of one's own success, safety, etc with no thought for others. **the devil to pay** serious trouble as a consequence of an action, etc. **give the devil his due** to admit the good points of a person one dislikes.

go to the devil 1 to be ruined. **2** *usually said as a command, in anger* to go away.

like the devil *colloq.* very hard.

speak *or* **talk of the devil** said at the arrival of someone one has just been talking about. [from Anglo-Saxon *deofol*, from Greek *diabolos*, slanderer]

devilish — *adj.* **1** of or like a devil; as if from, produced by, etc a devil. **2** very wicked. **3** *colloq.* very great or very difficult. — *adv. old use* very.

devilishly *adv. old use* very; terribly.

devil-may-care *adj.* cheerfully heedless of danger, consequences, etc.

devilment *noun* mischievous fun.

devilry *noun* (PL. **devilries**) **1** mischievous fun. **2** wickedness or cruelty. **3** witchcraft; black magic.

devil's advocate a person who argues for or against something simply to encourage discussion or argument.

Devil's Disciple, The a play by George Bernard Shaw (1897). Set during the American War of Independence, it is about a romantic villain who defies his bad reputation to die in a condemned man's place.

Devil's Island see SALUT, ILES DU.

Devil's Tower the first US national monument, in NE Wyoming, USA. It is a natural tower of volcanic rock with a flat top, 263m high. It was used as the setting for Steven Spielberg's film *Close Encounters of the Third Kind* (1977).

Devine, George (Alexander Cassidy) (1910–65) English actor and theatre director, born in Hendon, Greater London. He devoted his career to reforming British theatre training. This included founding the London Theatre Studio (1936–9) with Michel Saint-Denis and others, directing the Young Vic touring company, and (at the Royal Court Theatre) developing the 'writer's theatre' at the newly formed English Stage Company, where he was artistic director from 1956.

devious *adj.* **1** not totally open or honest; deceitful. **2** cunning; able to think up clever and usually deceitful ways of achieving things, etc. **3** not direct: *came by a devious route.* [from Latin *devius*, from *de*, from + *via*, road]

deviously *adv.* in a devious or deceitful way.

deviousness *noun* being devious or deceitful.

devise *verb* **1** to invent, make up, or put together (a plan, etc) in one's mind. **2** *Legal* to leave (property such as land or buildings) to someone in a will. See also BEQUEATH. [from Old French *deviser*, from Latin *divisa*, division of goods]

Devizes POP (1981) 13 000, a market town in Kennet district, Wiltshire, S England. It lies on the Kennet and Avon Canal, 26km/16mi SE of Bath. NOTABLE FEATURES Museum of the Wiltshire Archaeological and Natural History Society; Wiltshire Regimental Museum; remains of a 12c castle destroyed during the Civil War.

Devlin, Patrick Arthur Devlin, Baron (1905–92) English lawyer and judge, the son of an Ulster-born father and Scottish mother. He was called to the Bar in 1929, built up a successful practice, and was appointed to the High Court in 1948. In 1960 he became a Lord Justice of Appeal, and was raised to the peerage in 1961. He resigned from the House of Lords in 1964. During the 1980s, he campaigned with Lord Scarman for the review of the Guildford Four conviction.

devoid *adj.* (**devoid of something**) free from it, lacking it, or empty of it. [from Old French *devoidier*, to take away]

Devolution, War of a Franco-Spanish conflict (1667–8) prompted by Louis XIV of France in pursuit of the legal claims of his wife Queen Maria Theresa (the elder daughter of Philip IV of Spain) to the Spanish Netherlands. When Louis's armies overran Flanders, the Dutch Republic, England, and Sweden were prompted to negotiate the Triple Alliance (1668). This led to France's invasion of Franche-Comté, but also, after a secret treaty of compromise between Louis and Emperor Leopold was signed in early 1668, to the signing of the peace Treaty of Aix-la-Chapelle (2 May 1668).

devolution *noun* the act of devolving, especially the giving of certain powers to a regional government by a central government. [from Latin *devolutio*, from *devolvere*, to roll down]

devolutionist *noun* an advocate of devolution.

devolve *verb* (**devolve to** *or* **on** *or* **upon someone**) **1** *trans., intrans.* said of duties, power, etc to transfer (them) or be transferred to someone else. **2** *intrans. Legal* to pass by succession: *on his death, the title will devolve on his nephew.* [from Latin *devolvere*, to roll down]

Devon POP (1992e) 1.1m, a county in SW England, divided into 10 districts. AREA 6 711sq km/2 590sq mi. It is bounded NW by the Bristol Channel and the Atlantic Ocean, E by Dorset and Somerset, S by the English Channel, and SW by Cornwall. PHYSICAL DESCRIPTION rises to Dartmoor in the SW and Exmoor in the NE; drained by the Exe, Dart, Torridge, and Tow rivers. CHIEF TOWNS Exeter (county town), Plymouth, Torbay, Torquay, Barnstaple. ECONOMY tourism, especially on the coast; livestock, dairy products (noted for clotted cream), cider.

Devonian 1 *Geol.* relating to the fourth period of the Palaeozoic era (between the Silurian and the Carboniferous), lasting from about 410 million to 360 million years ago. During this period bony and cartilaginous fishes flourished, the first amphibians appeared, and land plants became more common. **2** relating to the rocks formed during this period. [from *Devon* in SW England]

devote *verb* to use or give up (a resource such as time or money) wholly to some purpose: *devoted their time to writing letters.* [from Latin *devovere*, to consecrate]

devoted *adj.* **1** (**devoted to someone**) loving and loyal to them. **2** (**devoted to something**) given up to it; totally occupied by it.

devotedly *adv.* in a devoted way; with devotion.

devotedness *noun* being devoted.

devotee *noun* **1** a keen follower or enthusiastic supporter. **2** a keen believer in a religion or follower of a god.

devotion *noun* **1** great love or loyalty; enthusiasm for or willingness to do what is required by. **2** devoting or being devoted. **3** religious enthusiasm and piety. **4** (**devotions**) *Relig.* worship and prayers.

devotional *adj.* relating to or in the nature of devotion.

devour *verb* **1** to eat up greedily. **2** to destroy thoroughly. **3** to read eagerly. **4** to look at with obvious pleasure. **5** (*usually* **be devoured**) to be taken over totally: *was devoured by guilt.* [from Latin *devorare*, to gulp down]

devout *adj.* **1** sincerely religious in thought and behaviour. **2** deeply-felt; earnest. [from Latin *devovere*, to consecrate]

devoutly *adv.* in a devout or sincere way.

devoutness *noun* being devout or sincere.

De Vries, Hugo Marie (1848–1935) Dutch botanist and geneticist, born in Haarlem, the son of a Dutch prime minister. The first instructor in plant physiology in the Netherlands, he became Professor of Botany at Amsterdam (1878–1918). From 1890 he devoted himself to the study of heredity and variation in plants, significantly developing Mendelian genetics and evolutionary theory.

dew *noun* a form of precipitation consisting of tiny droplets of water that are deposited on objects close to the ground, eg leaves, on cool clear nights when air in contact with the ground becomes saturated. [from Anglo-Saxon *deaw*]

Dewar, Sir James (1842–1923) Scottish chemist and physicist, born in Kincardine-on-Forth. Professor at Cambridge (from 1875) and at the Royal Institution, he liquefied and froze many gases, invented the vacuum flask, and (with Frederick Abel) discovered the explosive cordite.

Dewar flask *Physics* an insulated vessel with double walls; the inner space is surrounded by a vacuum and silvered so that heat losses by convection and radiation are reduced to a minimum. Originally designed to hold gases liquefied at very low temperatures, it was later developed for domestic use for maintaining liquids, eg beverages, at constant high or low temperatures. [named after Sir James Dewar]

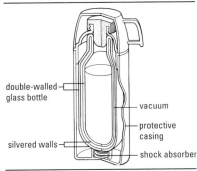

double-walled glass bottle
vacuum
protective casing
silvered walls
shock absorber

Dewar flask

dewclaw *noun* a small functionless toe or claw on the leg of some dogs and other animals.

dewdrop *noun* a drop of dew.

de Wet, Christian see WET, CHRISTIAN DE.

Dewey, John (1859–1952) US philosopher and educationalist, born in Burlington, Vermont. He taught at Michigan (1884) and Chicago (1894), and became Professor of Philosophy at Columbia (New York) in 1904. He was a leading exponent of pragmatism, and his philosophy of education, which stressed development of the person, understanding of the environment, and learning through experience, was influential. His writings include (on philosophy) *The Quest for Certainty* (1929), and (on education) *The Child and the Curriculum* (1902).

Dewey decimal system an international library classification system, devised in 1873 by US librarian Melvil Dewey (1851–1931). It is based on 10 main classes of subject-matter, each class containing 100 numbers with decimal subdivisions.

de Witt, Jan see WITT, JAN DE.

dewlap *noun* a flap of loose skin hanging down from the throat of certain cattle, dogs, and other animals. [probably from DEW + Anglo-Saxon *læppa*, loose hanging piece]

dewy *adj.* (**dewier, dewiest**) covered in dew.

dewy-eyed *adj.* naïve and too trusting.

dexterity *noun* **1** skill in using one's hands. **2** quickness of mind. [from French *dextérité*, from Latin *dexter*, right, skilful]

dexterous *or* **dextrous** *adj.* having, showing, or done with dexterity.

dexterously *or* **dextrously** *adv.* with dexterity; agilely; skilfully.

dextral *adj.* **1** associated with or located on the right side, especially of the body. **2** right-handed, or favouring the right-hand side. **3** *said of flatfish* lying right-side up. **4** *said of the shells of some gas-* tropod molluscs turning in the normal manner, ie clockwise from the top. [from medieval Latin *dextralis*, from *dextra*, right hand]

dextrin *noun Biochem.* any of a group of short-chain polysaccharides produced during the partial breakdown of starch or glycogen. [from French *dextrine*]

dextrose see GLUCOSE. [from Latin *dexter*, right]

Dezhnev, Cape the most north-easterly point of the Eurasian land mass, situated in NE Siberian Russia. It lies at the E end of the Chukchi Peninsula, projecting into the Bering Sea. [named after the Russian navigator who discovered it in 1648.]

DF *abbrev.* Defender of the Faith.

DFC *abbrev.* Distinguished Flying Cross.

DFM *abbrev.* Distinguished Flying Medal.

DG *abbrev.* **1** *Dei gratia* (Latin), by the grace of God. **2** *Deo gratias* (Latin), thanks be to God. **3** Director General.

Dhaka, former spelling **Dacca** **1** POP (1990e) 6.6m, the capital of Bangladesh, in Dhaka region, lying W of the R Meghna on a channel of the R Dhaleswari. HISTORY former French, Dutch, and English trading post; capital of the Mughal province of East Bengal (1608–1704); capital of the British province of East Bengal and Assam (1905–12); major expansion since becoming the capital of East Pakistan in 1947, with large-scale immigration and growth of industry; it became capital in 1971 of the new nation of Bangladesh. Dhaka is the centre of the world's greatest jute-growing region. NOTABLE FEATURES Suhrawardy Uddyan (city park); Central Shahid Minar Monument; known as the 'city of mosques' (over 1 000); Sadarghat Market; Langalband 12km/8mi SE, a sacred Hindu site. **2** a region in central Bangladesh with Dhaka as its capital.

dhal see DAL.

dharma *noun* **1** *Buddhism* truth. **2** *Hinduism* the universal laws, especially the moral laws to be followed by each individual. [from Sanskrit *dharma*]

dhobi *noun Hist.* in India, Malaya, etc, a man who does washing. [from Hindi *dhobī*]

dhoti *noun* a garment worn by some Hindu men, consisting of a long strip of cloth wrapped around the waist and between the legs. [from Hindi *dhotī*]

dhow *noun* a type of ship with one or more sails, used in countries around the Indian Ocean.

dhow

DHSS *abbrev.* in the UK, Department of Health and Social Security (since 1989, the Department of Social Services).

DI *Medicine abbrev.* donor insemination.

di- *prefix* **1** two or double: *dicotyledon*. **2** *Chem.* containing two atoms of the same type: *dioxide*. [from Greek *dis*, twice]

diabetes *noun* any of various disorders, especially diabetes mellitus, that are characterized by thirst and excessive production of urine. [from Greek *diabetes*, siphon]

diabetes insipidus *Medicine* a rare disorder characterized by the excretion of large amounts of dilute urine, and constant thirst. It is caused by a deficiency of antidiuretic hormone (the hormone that controls reabsorption of water by the kidneys).

diabetes mellitus *Medicine* a common metabolic disorder in which the hormone insulin, normally secreted by special cells in the pancreas called islets of Langerhans, is no longer produced in sufficient quantity or activity to control sugar (glucose) metabolism.
◇ In diabetes mellitus, the blood sugar levels rapidly become too high due to the absence of insulin, and sugar also appears in the urine. Other symptoms include excessive production of urine, dehydration, thirst, fatigue, and loss of weight. The use of fats as an alternative energy source can lead to the build-up of ketones in the bloodstream (ketoacidosis) and, eventually, to convulsions, diabetic coma, and even death. If left untreated, serious complications can occur as a result of thickening of the arteries, eg damage to the retina and lens of the eye, kidney failure, and an increased risk of heart disease.
Diabetes tends to be hereditary, but may also be triggered by factors such as alcoholism. In the form which starts in childhood, which is usually more severe than the adult-onset form, no insulin is produced, and treatment usually involves a carefully controlled diet and daily doses of insulin (normally by self-administered injection). In adult-onset diabetes the tissues fail to respond to the presence of insulin when it is produced, and this condition may respond to a simple change in diet.

diabetic — *noun* a person suffering from diabetes. — *adj.* **1** relating to or suffering from diabetes. **2** especially for people who have diabetes.

diabolic *adj.* **1** of or like a devil; devilish. **2** very wicked or cruel. [from Greek *diabolos*, slanderer, devil]

diabolical *adj. Brit. colloq.* very shocking, annoying, bad, etc.

diabolically *adv.* **1** in a diabolical way; wickedly. **2** *colloq.* exceedingly; very: *it was diabolically funny.*

diabolism *noun* the worship of the Devil or devils; witchcraft; black magic. [from Greek *diabolos*, devil + -ISM]

diachronic *or* **diachronical** *adj. Linguistics* concerned with the study of a language in terms of its origins and historical development: the opposite of *synchronic*.

diaconate *noun* **1** the position of deacon. **2** one's period of time as a deacon. **3** deacons as a group. [from Latin *diaconus*, deacon]

diacritic — *noun* a mark written or printed over, under, or through a letter to show that that letter has a particular sound, as in *é, è, ç, ñ.* — *adj.* same as DIACRITICAL. [from Greek *diakritikos*, able to distinguish]

diacritical *adj.* functioning as a diacritic; distinguishing.

diadem *noun* **1** a crown or jewelled head-band, worn by a royal person. **2** royal power or authority. [from Old French *diademe*, from Greek *dia*, around + *deein*, to bind]

diaeresis *noun* (PL. **diaereses**) a mark (¨) placed over a vowel to show that it is to be pronounced separately from the vowel before it, as in *naïve.* [from Greek *diairesis*, separation]

diagenesis *noun Geol.* the physical and chemical processes whereby unconsolidated sediment is converted to solid rock.

Diaghilev, Sergei (Pavlovich) (1872–1929) Russian ballet impresario, born in Novgorod. He ignored his law degree, became editor (1898) of *Mir Iskousstva* (World of Art), and for a few years arranged exhibitions and concerts of Russian art and music. His permanent company, the Ballets Russes (founded in 1911), triumphantly toured

Europe and remained perilously in existence for 20 years, with all the great dancers, composers, and painters of the period contributing to its success. He also encouraged such major choreographers as Fokine, Nijinsky, and Balanchine.

diagnose *verb* **1** to identify (an illness) from a consideration of its symptoms. **2** to identify (a fault).

diagnosis *noun* (PL. **diagnoses**) **1** the process whereby a disease or disorder is provisionally identified on the basis of its symptoms and the patient's medical history. It may then be confirmed or disproved by laboratory tests, X-ray examinations, etc. **2** *Biol.* in taxonomy, a formal description, eg of a plant, made on the basis of its distinguishing characteristics. **3** identification of problems in other areas, eg in mechanics and computing. [from Greek, from *diagignoskein*, to distinguish]

diagnostic *adj.* relating to or useful in diagnosis.

diagonal — *adj.* **1** *Maths.*, said of a straight line joining any two non-adjacent corners of a polygon or any two vertices not on the same face in a polyhedron. **2** sloping or slanting. — *noun* a diagonal line. [from Greek *dia*, through + *gonia*, angle]

diagonally *adv.* in a diagonal direction.

diagram *noun* a line drawing, often labelled with text, that does not show all the visible details of an object or process, but only the most important features of its structure, or the manner in which it functions. [from Greek *diagramma*, from *dia*, round + *graphein*, to write]

diagrammatic *adj.* having the form of a diagram; serving as a diagram.

diagrammatically *adv.* in the form of a diagram.

diakinesis *noun* during meiosis, the final stage of prophase, when the pairs of homologous chromosomes are almost completely separated from one another.

dial — *noun* **1** a disc or plate on a clock, radio, meter, etc with numbers or other scales or measurements marked on it and a movable pointer or indicator, used to indicate eg measurements of speed, time, etc or selected settings of time, temperature, radio frequency, etc. **2** the round numbered plate on some telephones and the movable disc fitted over it. — *verb trans., intrans.* (**dialled**, **dialling**) to use a telephone dial to call (a number). [from Latin *dialis*, daily]

dialect *noun* a form of a language spoken in a particular region or by a certain social group, differing from other forms in grammar, vocabulary, and in some cases pronunciation. [from Greek *dialektos*, manner of speech]

dialectal *adj.* relating to or belonging to dialect: *dialectal forms of words.*

dialectic *noun Philos.* **1** (*also* **dialectics**) the art or practice of establishing truth by discussion. **2** (*also* **dialectics**) a debate which aims to resolve the conflict between two opposing theories rather than to disprove either of them. **3** the art of reasoning and arguing logically. [from Greek *dialektike* (*techne*), (the art) of debating]

dialectical *adj. Philos.* of or by dialectic; depending on or proceeding by the resolving of the conflict between opposing factors, theories, etc.

dialling code the part of a telephone number that represents a town or area.

dialogue *noun* **1** a conversation, especially a formal one. **2** the words spoken by the characters in a play, book, etc. **3** a discussion or exchange of ideas and opinions, especially between two groups, with a view to resolving conflict or achieving agreement. [from Greek *dialogos*, conversation]

dialysis *noun* (PL. **dialyses**) **1** *Chem.* the separation of particles of different sizes in a solution,

based on the different rates at which the various substances diffuse through a semi-permeable membrane. It is mainly used to separate large particles such as proteins from soluble substances such as salts. **2** *Medicine* the removal of toxic substances from the blood by diffusion through a semi-permeable membrane in an artificial kidney machine, used in cases of kidney failure when a transplant is not available. — Also called *haemodialysis.* [from Greek *dialysis*, separation]

diamanté — *adj.*, said of a fabric decorated with small sparkling ornaments. — *noun* a diamanté fabric. [from French *diamanté*, decorated with diamonds]

diameter *noun Geom.* the length of a straight line drawn from one side of a circle to the other, and passing through its centre. It is equal to twice the radius of the circle. [from Greek *dia*, across + *metron*, measure]

diametric *or* **diametrical** *adj.* **1** of or along a diameter. **2** *said of opinions, etc* directly opposed; very far apart.

diametrically *adv.*, said in relation to opposition completely; utterly: *diametrically opposite opinions.*

diamond *noun* **1** a crystalline allotrope of carbon, colourless when pure, and the hardest known mineral. It is formed naturally by the crystallization of pure carbon under great pressure, and is highly prized as a gemstone for jewellery. Diamond can also be produced synthetically for use in cutting and grinding tools, and in precision instruments, eg watches. **2** a piece of this substance, used in cutting tools, etc. **3** (**diamonds**) one of the four suits of playing-cards, with red symbols of this shape. **4** one of the playing-cards of this suit. **5** a baseball pitch, or the part of it between the bases. [from Old French *diamant*, from Latin and Greek *adamas*, steel, diamond]

Diana (Frances), Princess of Wales, née **Lady Diana Spencer** (1961–) British princess, born in Sandringham, Norfolk, and wife of Charles, Prince of Wales, since 1981. They have two children: William Arthur Philip Louis (1982–) and Henry Charles Albert David (1984–). She and Charles separated in 1992, but she continued to carry out her public engagements, taking a special interest in children and the sick (notably AIDS victims) until late 1993 and in 1994 announced that she would take an advisory role with the International Red Cross.

Diana 1 Roman goddess, associated with the Moon, virginity, and hunting. She was identified with the Greek goddess Artemis. **2** a female first name, popular from the end of the 19c. [of uncertain origin, possibly connected to *Dionysos*]

Diane de Poitiers (1499–1566) mistress of Henry II of France. Married at 13, she was a widow at 32, but then won the affections of the boy dauphin (later Henry II), who was already wedded to Catharine de' Medici. On his accession (1547) Diane enjoyed great influence, and was made Duchess of Valentinois.

dianthus *noun* any plant of the genus *Dianthus* of flowers to which carnations and pinks belong. [from Latin *dianthus*, from Greek *Dios anthos*, Zeus's flower]

diapause *noun Zool.* in the life cycle of an insect, a period during which growth and development are arrested, often until environmental conditions become more favourable. [from Greek *diapausis*, pause]

diaper *noun* **1** a type of linen or cotton cloth with a pattern of small diamond or square shapes. **2** *North Amer.* a baby's nappy. [from Old French *diaspre*]

diaphanous *adj.*, said of cloth light and fine, and almost transparent. [from Greek *dia*, through + *phanein*, to show]

diaphragm *noun* **1** *Anat.* in mammals, the sheet of muscle that separates the thorax (chest)

from the abdomen. It is lowered during inhalation, when the lungs are filled with air, and raised during exhalation, when air is expelled from the lungs. **2** *Optics* an opaque disc, with a central aperture of adjustable diameter, that is used to control the amount of light entering an optical instrument such as a camera or microscope. **3** a thin vibrating disc or cone that converts sound waves to electrical signals in a microphone, or electrical signals to sound waves in a loudspeaker. **4** a contraceptive device consisting of a soft plastic or rubber cap that is fitted over the neck of the uterus before intercourse to prevent the entry of sperm. — Also called *Dutch cap*. [from Greek *diaphragma*, partition]

diarist *noun* a person who writes a diary, especially one which is published.

diarrhoea *noun* a condition in which the bowels are emptied more frequently than usual and the faeces are very soft or liquid. [from Greek *dia*, through + *rhoia*, flow]

diary *noun* (PL. **diaries**) **1** a written record of daily events in a person's life, or a book containing this. **2** *Brit.* a book with separate spaces or pages for each day of the year in which appointments, daily notes, and reminders may be written. [from Latin *diarium*, from *dies*, day]

Diary of a Nobody, The a comic novel by George and Weedon Grossmith (1892). It describes, in the form of a diary, fifteen months in the life of city clerk Charles Pooter.

Diaspora *noun* (**the Diaspora**) **1** the scattering of the Jewish people to various countries following their exile in Babylon in the 6c BC. **2** the new communities of Jews which arose in various countries as a result. **3** the Jews who do not live in the modern state of Israel. [from Greek *dia*, through + *speirein*, to scatter]

diastase *see* AMYLASE. [from Greek *diastasis*, division]

diastole *noun Medicine* the rhythmic expansion of the chambers of the heart during which they fill with blood. See also SYSTOLE. [from Greek *dia*, apart + *stellein*, to place]

diastolic *adj. Medicine* relating to diastole, when the heart fills with blood.

diatom *noun* common name for a member of the division Bacillariophyta, a group of microscopic one-celled algae found in vast numbers in plankton. Their characteristic ornately marked shells are strengthened with silica, and fit together like the two halves of a box. [from Greek *diatomos*, cut through]

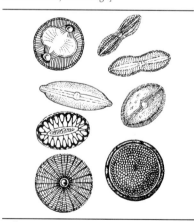

diatoms

diatomic *adj. Chem.* denoting a molecule that consists of two identical atoms, eg O_2, H_2.

diatomite *noun Geol.* kieselguhr. [from Greek *diatomos* cut through]

diatonic *adj. Mus.*, said of a scale, etc consisting of or involving only the basic notes proper to a particular key, with no additional sharps, flats or naturals. See also CHROMATIC. [from Greek *dia*, through + *tonos*, tone]

diatonicism *noun* an attribute of a piece or section of music which uses, either exclusively or predominantly, notes belonging to a major or minor scale. See also CHROMATICISM.

diatribe *noun* a bitter or abusive critical attack in speech or writing. [from Greek *diatribe*, discourse]

Diaz *or* **Dias, Bartolomeu** (c.1450–1500) Portuguese navigator and explorer. In 1487 King John II gave him two vessels to follow up the discoveries already made on the west coast of Africa. He was driven by a storm round the Cape of Good Hope (the southern extremity of Africa), and discovered Algoa Bay. He also travelled with Vasco da Gama in 1497, and with Cabrero Cabral in 1500, during whose expedition he was lost in a storm.

Díaz, (José de la Cruz) Porfirio (1830–1915) Mexican statesman, born in Oaxaca. He fought against the French occupation of Mexico (1862–7). Though defeated in the presidential election of 1875, he seized power and served as President of Mexico (1876–80, 1884–1911), exercizing strong personal control over all areas of government, until the revolution of Francisco Madero (1873–1913) forced him to resign and flee into exile. His regime encouraged foreign investment in Mexico but the wealth was concentrated into the hands of a small section of the population.

diazepam *noun Psychol.* a tranquillizing drug, sold under the trade name Valium, which relieves anxiety and also acts as a muscle relaxant, but because of increasing evidence that its long-term use causes addiction, is now generally only used to treat severe anxiety or insomnia over very short periods. [from DI- + *azo-* denoting nitrogen + *ep-* as in EPOXY]

diazo compound *Chem.* any of various organic compounds containing two adjacent nitrogen atoms, only one of which is attached to a carbon atom. Diazo compounds are used in the manufacture of many dyes and drugs.

dibasic *adj. Chem.* denoting an acid that contains two replaceable hydrogen atoms, eg sulphuric acid (H_2SO_4).

dibble *or* **dibber** *noun* a short pointed hand-tool used for making holes in the ground for seeds, young plants, etc.

dice — *noun* (PL. **dice**) **1** a small cube with a different number of spots, from 1 to 6, on each of its sides or faces, used in certain games of chance. **2** a game of chance played with one or more dice. See also DIE[2]. — *verb* **1** to cut (vegetables, etc) into small cubes. **2** *intrans.* to play or gamble with dice. — **dice with death** to take a great risk. **no dice** *colloq.* used to indicate a negative answer or unsuccessful outcome. [originally the plural of DIE[2]]

dicey *adj.* (**dicier, diciest**) *colloq.* risky.

dichotomous *adj.* divided into two parts; involving division into two parts.

dichotomy *noun* (PL. **dichotomies**) a division or separation into two groups or parts, especially when these are sharply opposed or contrasted. [from Greek *dicha*, in two + *tome*, cut]

dichroism *noun Physics* a property of some crystals, that reflect certain colours when viewed from one angle, and different colours when viewed from another angle. [from Greek *dichroos*, two-coloured]

dick *noun* **1** *coarse slang* the penis. **2** *slang* a detective. [from the name *Dick*]

Dicke, Robert Henry (1916–) US physicist, born in St Louis, Missouri. Professor at Princeton University, he independently deduced

in 1964 that a 'Big Bang' origin of the universe should have left an observable remnant of microwave radiation, detectable all around us; this background radiation was first observed in the same year. He also carried out important work on gravitation.

Dickens, Charles (John Huffam) (1812–70) English novelist, born in Landport, near Portsmouth. His family moved to London in 1814 where his father was imprisoned for debt, the whole family accompanying him to the Marshalsea Prison (apart from Charles who was sent to work in a blacking factory). He eventually took up journalism and published various papers and sketches in the *Monthly Magazine*, and the *Evening Chronicle*, many of which were later collected in *Sketches by Boz* (1836–7). His first novel *The Pickwick Papers* also appeared at this time, and other novels which first appeared in monthly instalments included *Oliver Twist* (1837–9), *Nicholas Nickleby* (1838–9), and *The Old Curiosity Shop* (1840–1). His later novels include *David Copperfield* (1849–50), *Bleak House* (1852–3), *A Tale of Two Cities* (1859), *Great Expectations* (1860–1), and the unfinished *The Mystery of Edwin Drood* (1870). He achieved great success in his lifetime and much of his later life was spent travelling and giving public readings.

dickens *noun colloq.* (**the dickens**) the devil, used especially for emphasis. [from the name *Dickon* or *Dicken*, from *Richard*]

Dickensian *adj.* resembling the 19c English social life depicted in the novels of Charles Dickens, especially the poor living and working conditions or the odd and often grotesque characters described.

dicker *verb intrans.* to argue about the price or cost of something.

Dickinson, Emily (Elizabeth) (1830–86) US poet, born in Amherst, Massachusetts. She withdrew from all social contacts at the age of 23 and lived a secluded life, writing in secret over 1000 poems. Hardly any of her work was published until after her death, when her sister brought out three highly acclaimed volumes (1890–6). Further posthumous collections include *The Single Hound* (1914), and *Bolts of Melody* (1945). Her lyrics, which show great originality in thought and in form have had considerable influence on modern poetry.

dicky[1] dickie dickey. *noun* (PL. **dickies, dickeys**) a false shirt front, especially when worn with evening dress.

dicky[2] *adj.* (**dickier, dickiest**) *colloq.* not in good condition.

dicky-bird *noun* a child's word for a small bird. [from the name *Dicky*, for *Richard*]

dicotyledon *noun Bot.* a flowering plant with an embryo that has two cotyledons (seed leaves), leaf veins arranged in a network, a ring of vascular bundles in the stem, and flower parts arranged in multiples of two or five, eg potato, rose. Dicotyledons include the hardwood trees, eg oak, beech. See also MONOCOTYLEDON.

dicta see DICTUM.

Dictaphone *noun trademark* a small tape-recorder for use especially when dictating letters.

dictate — *verb* (with stress on *-tate*) **1** *trans., intrans.* to say or read out (something) for someone else to write down. **2** to state or lay down (rules, terms, etc) forcefully or with authority. **3** *trans., intrans. derog.* to give orders to or try to impose one's wishes on (someone). — *noun* (with stress on *dict-*) (*usually* **dictates**) **1** an order or instruction. **2** a guiding principle. [from Latin *dictare*]

dictation *noun* **1** something read for another to write down. **2** the act of dictating.

dictator *noun* **1** a ruler with complete and unrestricted power. **2** a person who behaves in a dictatorial manner. **3** in ancient Rome, a person

given complete authority in the state for a period of six months at a time of crisis.

dictatorial *adj.* of, like, or suggesting a dictator; fond of using one's power and authority and imposing one's wishes on or giving orders to other people.

dictatorially *adv.* with a dictatorial or authoritarian manner.

dictatorship *noun* the status or position of a dictator.
◇ In practice, dictatorship often refers to rule by several people, who are unelected and authoritarian in character, such as a military dictatorship. Personal dictatorships are now rare.

diction *noun* **1** the way in which one speaks. **2** one's choice or use of words to express meaning. [from Latin *dicere*, to say]

dictionary *noun* (PL. **dictionaries**) **1** a book containing the words of a language arranged alphabetically with their meanings. **2** an alphabetically arranged book of information. [from Latin *dictionarium*]
◇ Dictionaries may be monolingual (explaining the words of one language), bilingual (giving equivalents of one language in another), or occasionally multilingual (giving equivalents across several languages). The first dictionaries were in fact bilingual.
Dictionaries vary widely in their coverage and treatment of language. Samuel Johnson's influential *Dictionary of the English Language* (1755), was the first English dictionary to record the language as a whole, and to include examples of usage. The *New* (later *Oxford*) *English Dictionary*, published in parts from the end of the 19c to the 1920s, was (and in later editions is) the fullest record of any living language. American English acquired its clear identity and status with the publication of Noah Webster's *American Dictionary of the English Language* (1828).
Modern dictionaries are often derived from computer databases, which allow flexible and structured storage of linguistic information, and enable the compilation, manipulation, and extraction of material for specific purposes. Many specialist dictionaries, including slang, foreign terms, and new words, are now published.

Dictionary of National Biography, The (ABBREV. **DNB**) It was founded (1882) and first published in 63 volumes (1885–1900) by George Smith, edited by Sir Leslie Stephen. It is a record of notable British people and is augmented every ten years by supplements, which are currently published by Oxford University Press.

Dictionary of the English Language, A a dictionary compiled by Samuel Johnson (1755). It was an innovative work, especially in using literary quotations to exemplify usage and clarify definitions.

dictum *noun* (PL. **dictums, dicta**) **1** a formal or authoritative statement of opinion. **2** a popular saying or maxim. [from Latin *dictum*]

did see DO[1].

didactic *adj.* **1** intended to teach or instruct. **2** *derog.* too eager or too obviously intended to instruct, in a way resented by the reader, listener, etc. [from Greek *didaskein*, to teach]

didactically *adv.* with a didactic or instructive manner.

didacticism *noun* didactic or instructive principles.

diddle *verb colloq.* to cheat or swindle. [probably from Jeremy *Diddler*, character in a 19c play]

diddler *noun colloq.* a cheat or swindler.

Diderot, Denis (1713–84) French writer and philosopher, born in Langres. In 1746 he became chief editor on the *Encyclopédie* (a major work of the Enlightenment, originally intended as a

French translation of Ephraim Chambers's *Cyclopaedia*, 1728), a post he held for 20 years. His work *Pensées philosophiques* (Philosophical Thoughts, 1746) was burned by the Parliament of Paris for its anti-Christian ideas, and he was imprisoned for his *Lettre sur les aveugles* (Essay on Blindness, 1749). He also wrote novels, plays, satires, and essays.

didgeridoo *noun* an Australian Aborigine wind instrument, consisting of a long wooden or bamboo tube which when blown into produces a low droning sound. [from an Australian Aboriginal language]

didn't *contr.* did not.

Dido in Greek mythology, the daughter of the King of Tyre, and the founder of Carthage. In Virgil's *Aeneid*, she fell in love with Aeneas, and when he deserted her she committed suicide by throwing herself upon a pyre.

Dido and Aeneas an opera by Henry Purcell (1689), based on the Fourth Book of Virgil's *Aeneid*. It focuses on Queen Dido of Carthage, and the Trojan prince Aeneas, whose marriage is destroyed by a sorceress who convinces Aeneas that Jove has ordered him to leave Carthage. The heartbroken Dido's 'When I am laid in earth' is a famously moving lament.

die[1] *verb intrans.* (**died, dying**) **1** to stop living; to cease to be alive. **2** to cease to exist, come to an end or fade away. **3** *said of an engine, etc* to stop working suddenly and unexpectedly. **4** (**die of something**) to suffer or be overcome by the effects of it: *die of boredom.*
— **be dying for something** *or* **to do something** *colloq.* to have a strong desire or need for it or to do it.
die away 1 to fade away from sight or hearing until gone. **2** to become steadily weaker and finally stop.
die back *said of a plant's soft shoots* to die or wither from the tip back to the hard wood.
die down 1 to lose strength or force. **2** *said of a plant or its soft shoots* to wither back to the root without completely dying.
die hard to be difficult to change or remove.
die off to die one after another.
die out to cease to exist anywhere; to become extinct.
never say die never give up or give in.
[from Middle English *dien*, from Norse *deyja*]

die[2] *noun* (PL. **dies** in sense 1, **dice** in sense 2) **1** a metal tool or stamp for cutting or shaping metal or making designs on coins, etc. **2** a dice.
— **the die is cast** a decision has been made or an action taken which cannot be changed or gone back on.
straight as a die 1 completely straight. **2** completely honest.
[from Old French *de*, from Latin *datum*, something given]

dieback *noun Bot.* the death of young shoots of trees and shrubs, often followed by the death of larger branches and stems. It may be due to frost damage, fungal attack, or lack of water, mineral salts, light, etc.

die casting 1 *Engineering* a form of casting in which molten metal is forced under pressure into cooled *dies* (metal moulds), usually in order to produce large numbers of small items of a particular shape. **2** an object made in this way.

diehard *noun* a person who stubbornly refuses to accept new ideas or changes.

dielectric *Physics* — *noun* a non-conducting material whose molecules align or polarize under the influence of applied electric fields. Dielectrics are an essential component of capacitors. — *adj.* denoting such a material.

Dieppe POP (1990) 37 000, a seaport in Seine-Maritime department, Haute-Normandie region, NW France. It lies below high chalk cliffs on the R Arques, where it meets the English Channel, N of Rouen. Heavy fighting took place here during World War II.

dieresis *North Amer., esp. US.* Same as DIAERESIS.

Diesel, Rudolf Christian Karl (1858–1913) German engineer, born in Paris. He demonstrated the first practical compression-ignition engine (his 'rational heat motor') in 1897; the diesel engine achieved an efficiency about twice that of comparable steam engines. At the height of his fame, he vanished from a boat and was presumed drowned.

diesel *noun* **1** diesel oil. **2** a diesel engine. **3** a train, etc driven by a diesel engine. [named after the German engineer Rudolf Diesel]

diesel engine a type of internal combustion engine in which air in the cylinder is compressed until it reaches a sufficiently high temperature to ignite the fuel. Diesel engines are heavier and more powerful than petrol engines, and are used in buses, lorries, tractors, locomotives, ships, etc. [named after the German engineer Rudolph Diesel]

diesel fuel *Engineering* a type of liquid fuel, composed mainly of hydrocarbons derived from petroleum, that is designed for use in a diesel engine.

diesel oil heavy oil used as fuel for a diesel engine.

Diet, Imperial see IMPERIAL DIET.

diet[1] — *noun* **1** the food and drink habitually consumed by a person or animal. **2** a planned or prescribed selection of food and drink, especially one designed for weight loss, maintenance of good health, or the control of a medical disorder. **3** (*attributive*) denoting a food or drink, often with a brand name, that contains less sugar than the standard version. — *verb intrans.* (**dieted, dieting**) to restrict the quantity or type of food that one eats, especially in order to lose weight. [from Old French *diete*, from Greek *diaita*, way of life]

diet[2] *noun* **1** the legislative assembly of certain countries, eg Japan. **2** *Hist.* a conference held to discuss political or church affairs. [from Latin *dieta*, public assembly, from Greek *diaita*, way of life]

dietary *adj.* of or concerning a diet.

dietary fibre, indigestible plant material, found in unrefined carbohydrate foods such as wholemeal bread and cereals, fruit and vegetables, which keeps bowel movements regular and is therefore thought to help prevent disorders such as chronic constipation and diverticular disease. – Also called *roughage*.

dieter *noun* a person who diets or is dieting.

dietetic *adj.* **1** of or concerning diet. **2** for use in a special medical diet.

dietetics *sing. noun* the scientific study of diet and its relation to health.

dietician *or* **dietitian** *noun* a person who is trained in dietetics.

Diet of Worms see WORMS, DIET OF.

Dietrich, Marlene, originally **Maria Magdalena Von Losch** (1901–92) German film actress, born in Berlin. She became famous in *Der blaue Engel* (The Blue Angel, 1930), and developed a glamorous and sensual film personality in such Hollywood films as *Morocco* (1930) and *Blond Venus* (1932). During World War II, she often appeared in cabaret shows for Allied troops, and after the war pursued her singing career. Later films include *Judgement at Nuremberg* (1961).

Diffa 1 the capital of Diffa department, SE Niger, located close to the Nigerian border. **2** a department in SE Niger. AREA 140 216sq km/ 54 123sq mi. L Chad forms the SE border and there is an extensive area of sand dunes in the N.

differ *verb intrans.* (**differed, differing**) **1** *said of two or more people or things* to be different or unlike each other in some way. **2** (**differ from something**) to be different from it or unlike it. **3** (**differ with someone**) to disagree with them. [from Old French *differer*]

Differdange POP (1991) 16 000, a town in Esch-sur-Alzette canton, Luxembourg district, S Luxembourg. It is an important industrial centre and point of departure for excursions to the French frontier.

difference *noun* **1** what makes one thing or person unlike another. **2** the state of being unlike. **3** a change from an earlier state, etc. **4** the amount by which one quantity or number is greater or less than another. **5** a quarrel or disagreement.
— **make a** *or* **no**, *etc* **difference** to have some or no, etc effect on a situation.
[from Latin *differentia*]

different *adj.* **1** (**different from** *or* **to someone**) not the same; unlike.
◆ *Different* is commonly followed by *from* and *to* in British usage. In North Amer. usage, *than*, is common; it is also used in British English when followed by a clause, as in *they are different than they used to be*. In British English, *different from* is the most widely accepted usage.
2 separate; distinct; various. **3** *colloq.* unusual.

differential — *adj.* **1** of, showing or based on a difference. **2** *Maths.* an infinitesimal change in the value of one or more variables as a result of a similarly small change in another variable or variables. — *noun* **1** (*in full* **wage differential**) a difference in the rate of pay between one category of worker and another in the same industry or company. **2** a differential gear. [from Latin *differentialis*]

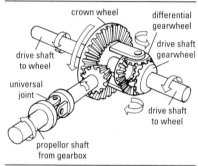

differential gear

differential calculus a procedure for calculating the rate of change of one variable quantity produced by changes in another variable. It employs *differentiation* to determine rates of change, gradients of curves, maximum and minimum values, etc.

differential coefficient *Maths.* the ratio of the rate of change of a function to that of its independent variable.

differential gear an arrangement of gears that allows the wheels on either side of a vehicle to rotate at different speeds (the outer wheels rotating more rapidly) when the vehicle is being driven round a corner.

differentiate *verb* **1** *intrans., trans.* (**differentiate between things**, *or* **one thing from another**) to establish a difference between them; to be able to distinguish one from another. **2** to constitute a difference between (things) or in (one thing as against another): *the shape of its mouth differentiates a crocodile from an alligator.* **3** (**differentiate between people**) to treat one person, etc differently from another. **4** to become different. **5** *Maths.* to use the process of differentiation to calculate the changes in one variable quantity produced by changes in a related variable, ie to find the *derivative* of a function *f.* **6** *Biol.*, *said of an unspecialized cell or tissue* to become increasingly specialized in structure and function, eg during the development of a muscle fibre or a red blood cell. [from Latin *differentiare*]

differentiation *noun* **1** the process of differentiating. **2** *Maths.* a method used in calculus to calculate the rate of change of one variable quantity produced by changes in a related variable, by finding the *derivative* of a function *f*. If $y = f(x)$, then the derivative of *y* is written as d*y*/d*x* (or *f* ′). If $y = x^n$, then the derivative d*y*/d*x* is nx^{n-1}, and is equal to the gradient of a tangent to the curve at the point *x*. **3** *Biol.* the process whereby unspecialized precursor cells or tissues develop into cells or tissues that have a highly specialized structure and function, eg the development of embryonic tissue into muscle cells, neurones (nerve cells), etc. **4** a change by which what is generalized or homogeneous becomes specialized or heterogeneous.

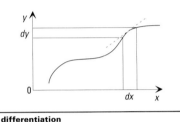

differentiation

differently *adv.* in a different way.

difficult *adj.* **1** requiring great skill, intelligence, or effort. **2** *said of a person* not easy to please; awkward, unco-operative. **3** *said of a problem, situation, etc* potentially embarrassing; hard to resolve or get out of. [from Latin *difficultas*, difficulty]

difficulty *noun* (PL. **difficulties**) **1** the state or quality of being difficult. **2** a difficult thing to do or understand. **3** a problem, obstacle, or objection. **4** (*usually* **difficulties**) trouble or embarrassment, especially financial.

diffidence *noun* being diffident or shy; lack of confidence.

diffident *adj.* lacking in confidence; too modest or shy. [from Latin *diffidere*, to distrust]

diffidently *adv.* with a diffident or shy manner.

diffract *verb Physics* to cause diffraction in. [from Latin *diffringere*, to shatter]

diffraction *noun Physics* the spreading out of waves (eg light or sound waves) as they emerge from a small opening or slit. Diffraction causes the bending of a beam of light around an obstruction.
◇ Diffraction occurs when the opening through which waves travel is of about the same size as the wavelength of the waves, which then spread out (ie are diffracted) and areas appear where there is no wave motion. This is because waves produced from different points on the opening interfere with each other. When the peaks of two waves arrive at the same point together, they combine to form a larger wave, but when a peak combines with a trough, they cancel each other out and there is no wave motion. Because of diffraction, objects smaller than the wavelength of light can never be seen. This also limits the resolving power of telescopes and microscopes, since light is diffracted as it passes through lenses. Atoms in crystals cause the diffraction of incident X-rays, producing patterns which enable the structure of the crystal to be determined.

diffraction grating *Physics* a device that contains many hundreds of slits per centimetre, and can be used to divide a light beam into its component colours, the pattern produced being known as a spectrum.

diffractive *adj.* causing diffraction.

diffuse — *verb trans., intrans.* to spread or send out in all directions. — *adj.* **1** widely spread; not concentrated. **2** *said of a style of writing or speaking* using too many words; not concise. [from Latin *diffundere*, to pour out in various directions]

diffused *adj.* widely spread; dispersed.

diffusely *adv.* in a diffuse or widely spread way.

diffuseness *noun* being diffuse or widely spread. .

diffusion *noun* **1** the act of diffusing or state of being diffused. **2** *Physics* the process whereby a fluid (a liquid or gas) gradually and spontaneously disperses from a region of high concentration to one of low concentration, as a result of the random movements of its constituent atoms, molecules, or ions. Diffusion of two substances will continue until they are completely mixed, and occurs more rapidly in gases than in liquids.

dig — *verb* (**digging**; PAST TENSE AND PAST PARTICIPLE **dug**) **1** *trans., intrans.* to turn up or move (earth, etc), especially with a spade. **2** to make (a hole, etc) by digging. **3** *trans., intrans.* to poke. **4** *old slang use* to appreciate. **5** *trans., intrans. old slang use* to understand. — *noun* **1** a remark intended to irritate, criticize, or make fun of. **2** a place where archaeologists are digging, eg to uncover ancient ruins. **3** a poke. **4** an act of digging.
— **dig in** *colloq.* to start to eat. **2** to make a protected place for oneself.
dig something in to mix it into the soil, etc by digging.
dig into something 1 *colloq.* to start eating a meal, etc. **2** to examine or search through it for information.
dig in one's heels to refuse to change one's mind.
dig one's own grave to be the cause of one's own failure or downfall.
dig something *or* **someone out 1** to get them out by digging. **2** *colloq.* to find them by extensive searching.
dig something up 1 to remove it from the ground by digging. **2** to find or reveal something buried or hidden by digging. **3** *colloq.* to search for and find information, etc.
[from Middle English *diggen*]

Digby, Sir Kenelm (1603–65) English diplomat, scientist, and writer, born in Gayhurst, Buckinghamshire. He travelled abroad and met Prince Charles in Madrid in 1623. On returning to England he was knighted and entered Charles's service. During the Civil War he was imprisoned by the parliament (1642–3), and had his estate confiscated. After the Restoration, he was Chancellor to Queen Henrietta Maria until 1664.

digest[1] *verb* (with stress on -*gest*) **1** *trans., intrans.* to break down (food), or (of food) to be

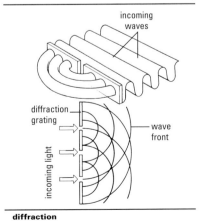

diffraction

broken down, in the stomach, intestine, etc into a form which the body can use. **2** to hear and consider the meaning and implications of (information). [from Latin *digerere*, to dissolve]

digest[2] *noun* (with stress on *di*-) **1** a usually regularly published collection of summaries or shortened versions (of news stories or current literature). **2** a summary or shortened version. **3** a systematically arranged collection of laws. [from Latin *digerere*, to arrange]

digestible *adj.* able to be digested.

digestion *noun* **1** the process whereby complex substances in food are broken down into simpler soluble compounds by enzymes, usually in the alimentary canal (stomach and intestines). Proteins are converted to amino acids, carbohydrates are converted to glucose and other simple sugars, and fats are converted to fatty acids and glycerol. These compounds are then absorbed and assimilated into the cells of the body. **2** the process of absorbing information, etc.

digestive — *adj.* of or for digestion. — *noun Brit.* (*also* **digestive biscuit**) a type of plain slightly sweetened biscuit made from wholemeal flour.

digger *noun* **1** a machine used for digging and excavating. **2** a person who digs, especially a gold-miner. **3** *colloq.* an Australian or New Zealander, especially a soldier.

Diggers a radical group in England formed during the Commonwealth. Led by Gerrard Winstanley (1609–72), it preached and practised agrarian communism on common and waste land, and established Digger communities to cultivate the land at St George's Hill, Surrey (Apr 1649) and in nine other southern and Midland counties. The movement was suppressed and its colonies dispersed by local landowners.

diggings *pl. noun* **1** a place where people dig, especially for gold or precious stones. **2** *Brit. old colloq. use* lodgings. See also DIGS.

digit *noun* **1** any of the ten figures 0 to 9. **2** *technical* a finger or toe. [from Latin *digitus*, finger, toe]

digital *adj.* **1** showing numerical information in the form of a set of digits, rather than by means of a pointer on a dial, eg digital watch. **2** denoting a process or a device that operates by processing information that is supplied and stored in the form of a series of binary digits, eg digital recording, digital computer. **3** denoting an electronic circuit that responds to and produces signals which at any given time are in one of two possible states. **4** of or involving digits in any way. See also ANALOGUE.

digital/analog converter *Comput.* a device that converts digital signals into analog (continuously varying) signals for use by an analog computer.

digital audio tape *Electron.* (ABBREV. **DAT**) **1** a magnetic audio tape on which sound has been recorded after it has been converted into a digital code. **2** this form of recorded sound, affording greater clarity and compactness, and less distortion than conventional recording.

digitalis *noun* **1** *Bot.* any plant of the genus *Digitalis*, eg the purple foxglove (*D. purpurea*). **2** *Medicine* an extract from the dried leaves of the foxglove (genus *Digitalis*) that stimulates the heart muscle by increasing contractions of the heart. It is used to treat heart failure and other cardiac disorders. [from the Latin genus name of the foxglove]

digitization *or* **digitisation** *noun* conversion into digitized form.

digitize *or* **digitise** *verb* to convert data into binary form, ie into a form that uses only the digits 0 and 1.

digitizer *or* **digitiser** *noun* a device for converting data, etc into digitized form.

dignified *adj.* stately, serious, or showing dignity.

dignify *verb* (**dignifies**, **dignified**) **1** to make (something) impressive or dignified. **2** to make (something) seem more important or impressive than it is. [from Latin *dignus*, worthy + *facere*, to make]

dignitary *noun* (PL. **dignitaries**) a person of high rank or position, especially in public life. [from DIGNITY -ARY]

dignity *noun* **1** stateliness, seriousness, and formality of manner and appearance. **2** goodness and nobility of character. **3** calmness and self-control. **4** high rank or position.
— **beneath one's dignity** not worthy of one's attention or time, etc.
— **stand on one's dignity** to demand to be treated with proper respect.
[from Latin *dignitas*, from *dignus*, worthy]

digraph *noun* a pair of letters that represent a single sound, as in the *ph* of *digraph*. [from Greek *di-*, twice + *graphe*, mark, character]

digress *verb intrans.* to wander from the point, or from the main subject in speaking or writing. [from Latin *digredi*, to move away]

digression *noun* departure from the main subject of discussion, etc.

digs *pl. noun Brit. colloq.* lodgings. See also DIGGINGS.

Digue, La POP (1985) 2 000, a granite island in the Seychelles, Indian Ocean. AREA 10sq km/4sq mi.

dihedral *adj. Geom.* formed or bounded by two planes. [from Greek *di-*, twice + *hedra*, seat]

Dijon, ancient **Dibio** POP (1990) 226 000, the industrial and commercial capital of Burgundy region, and of Côte d'Or department, E France. It stands at the confluence of the Ouche and Ruzon rivers. It is a centre of the wine trade, and is famous for Dijon mustard. NOTABLE FEATURES Palais des Ducs de Bourgogne; Gothic Church of Notre-Dame; Church of St Michel; Palais de Justice (16–17c); Cathedral of St-Benigne; the remains of the 14c Chartreuse de Champmol (now a hospital).

dike see dyke.

diktat *noun* **1** a forceful, sometimes unreasonable, order which must be obeyed. **2** a harsh settlement forced on the defeated or powerless. [from German *diktat*, something dictated]

dilapidated *adj., said of furniture, buildings, etc* falling to pieces because of neglect or age; in great need of repair. [from Latin *dilapidare*, to demolish]

dilapidation *noun* a state or process of disrepair or ruin.

dilatation *or* **dilation** *noun* dilating; becoming larger.

dilatation and curettage (ABBREV. **D and C**) *Medicine* a minor gynaecological operation, usually performed to remove small tumours or to obtain specimens of tissue in order to diagnose various disorders. The cervix (neck) of the uterus (womb) is dilated, and a special type of instrument known as a curette is passed through the dilated cervix into the uterus, the lining of which is gently scraped.

dilate *verb* **1** *trans., intrans. said especially of an opening in the body* to make or become larger, wider, or further open. **2** *intrans. formal* (**dilate on something**) to speak or write at great length about it. [from Latin *dilatare*, to spread out]

dilatorily *adv.* in a dilatory or delaying way.

dilatoriness *noun* being dilatory; delaying.

dilatory *adj.* slow in doing things; inclined to or causing delay. [from Latin *dilatorius*]

dildo *noun* (PL. **dildos**) an object shaped like an erect penis, used for sexual pleasure.

dilemma *noun* **1** a situation in which one must choose between two (or more than two) courses of action, both (or all) equally undesirable. **2** col-loq. a problem or difficult situation. [from Greek *di-*, twice + *lemma*, assumption]

dilettante *noun* (PL. **dilettantes**, **dilettanti**) *often derog.* a person who has an interest in a subject, especially art, literature, or science, but does not study it very seriously or in depth. [from Italian *dilettante*, from *dilettare*, to delight]

dilettantism *noun* superficial interest in a subject, especially in the arts.

diligence *noun* careful and hard-working effort.

diligent *adj.* **1** hard-working and careful. **2** showing or done with care and serious effort. [from Latin *diligens*, careful]

diligently *adv.* in a diligent or hard-working way.

dill *noun* a European herb, the fruit of which is used in flavouring, especially pickles. [from Anglo-Saxon *dile*]

dill

dilly-dally *verb intrans.* (**dilly-dallies**, **dilly-dallied**) *colloq.* **1** to be slow or waste time. **2** to be unable to make up one's mind. [from DALLY]

Dilthey, Wilhelm (1833–1911) German philosopher, born in Biebrich. He taught at Basle, Kiel, Breslau, and finally Berlin (1882), where he was Professor of Philosophy. He argued that human knowledge can only be understood as involving the knower's life lived in a historically conditioned culture. His ideas were influential on Heidegger.

diluent *noun Chem.* any solvent that is used to dilute a solution.

dilute — *verb* **1** to decrease the concentration of a solute (dissolved substance) in a solution by adding more solvent, especially water. **2** to reduce the strength, influence, or effect of (something). — *adj. Chem., said of a solution* containing a relatively small amount of solute (dissolved substance) compared to the amount of solvent present. [from Latin *diluere*, to wash away]

dilution *noun* making a liquid thinner or weaker.

diluvial *or* **diluvian** *adj.* **1** of or pertaining to a flood, especially the flood mentioned in the Book of Genesis in the Bible. **2** caused by a flood. [from Latin *diluvium*, flood]

Dilwara Temples a group of five Jain temples near Mt Abu, Rajasthan, India. They were built during the 11c–13c, and are renowned for the profusion and delicacy of their sculpture.

Dilys a female first name, now relatively rare. [from Welsh *dilys*, genuine]

dim — *adj.* (**dimmed**, **dimming**) **1** not bright or distinct. **2** lacking enough light to see clearly. **3** faint; not clearly remembered: *a dim memory.* **4** *colloq.* not very intelligent. **5** *said of eyes* not able to see well. **6** *colloq.* not good; not hopeful: *dim prospects.* — *verb trans., intrans.* (**dimmed**, **dimming**) to make or become dim.
— **take a dim view of something** *colloq.* to disapprove of it.
[from Anglo-Saxon *dimm*]

DiMaggio, Joe, properly **Joseph** (**Paul**), also called **the Yankee Clipper** (1914–) US baseball player, born in Martinez, California. He spent his entire career with the New York Yankees (1936–51). An outstanding fielder, he also holds the record for hitting safely in 56 consecutive games (1941). His second wife was the film star Marilyn Monroe.

Dimbleby, Richard (Frederick) (1913–65) English broadcaster, born in Richmond on Thames. He joined the BBC in 1931 and became its first foreign correspondent, first war correspondent, and was the first radio man to go into Berlin and Belsen at the end of World War II. Afterwards he presented *Panorama*, and was a commentator on major events, especially royal occasions. His sons, David (1938–) and Jonathan (1944–), followed their father into broadcasting. David has been with the BBC since 1960; Jonathan is a freelance broadcaster and author.

dime *noun* a coin of the USA and Canada worth ten cents or one tenth of a dollar. [from Old French *disme*, from Latin *decima*, tenth]

dime novel *North Amer.* a cheap popular novel.

dimension *noun* **1** a measurement of length, width, or height. **2** any directly measurable physical quantity, eg mass, length, time, charge. **3** *Geom.* the number of parameters that are needed to specify the size of a geometrical figure, and the location of particular points on it, eg a triangle has two dimensions, whereas a pyramid has three dimensions. **4** (*often* **dimensions**) size or extent. **5** a particular aspect of a problem, situation, etc. [from Old French, from Latin *dimensio*, measuring]

-dimensional *combining form* forming words meaning 'having a certain number of dimensions': *two-dimensional.*

dimer *noun Chem.* a chemical compound composed of two similar units, known as *monomers*, which may combine during either an addition reaction or a condensation reaction.

diminish *verb* **1** *trans., intrans.* to make or become less or smaller. **2** to cause to seem less important, valuable, or satisfactory. [from an obsolete word *minish* combined with Middle English *diminue*, from Latin *deminuere*, to make less]

diminished *adj.* **1** having become less, smaller, less important, etc. **2** *Mus.* reduced by a semitone.

diminishing returns (*in full* law of diminishing returns) *Econ.* a law or prediction that there is a point beyond which any additional input in the form of capital and labour, or additional taxation, results in progressively smaller output per unit of capital or labour, or smaller tax yields.

diminuendo *Mus.* — *noun* (PL. **diminuendos**) **1** a gradual lessening of sound. **2** a musical passage with gradually lessening sound. — *adj., adv.* with gradually lessening sound. See also CRESCENDO. [from Italian *diminuendo*, from Latin *deminuere*, to make less]

diminution *noun* a lessening or decrease. [from Latin *diminutio*]

diminutive — *adj.* very small. — *noun* *Grammar* **1** (*also* **diminutive suffix**) an ending added to a word to indicate smallness, eg *-let* in *booklet*. **2** a word formed in this way. [from Latin *deminuere*, to make less]

Dimitrov, Georgi (Mihailov) (1882–1949) Bulgarian politician, born near Radomir.

Imprisoned in 1917 for antimilitarist agitation, he was released, but later fled to Yugoslavia and was sentenced to death in his absence. He lived under an assumed name in Berlin, and in 1933 was one of those charged with setting fire to the Reichstag. He was acquitted, then became a Russian citizen and Executive Secretary of the Comintern (1934–43). In 1945 he returned to Bulgaria, and as premier (1946–9) ruthlessly imposed the Russian language and culture.

dimly *adv.* in a dim way; faintly: *we could dimly see the lighthouse in the distance.*

dimmer *or* **dimmer switch** a switch used to reduce the brightness of a light.

dimness *noun* being dim or faint; lack of light or brightness.

dimorphism *noun* **1** *Biol.* the occurrence of two distinct forms within a species of living organism, eg the male and female in many animals. **2** *Chem.* the crystallization of a chemical element or compound into two different crystalline forms that have the same chemical composition.

dimple *noun* a small hollow, especially in the skin of the cheeks, chin or, in babies, at the knees and elbows.

dimpled *adj.* having slight hollows on the surface.

dimwit *noun colloq.* a stupid person.

dim-witted *adj.* stupid.

DIN *abbrev.* (German) *Deutsche Industrie-Norm*, German Industry Standard, a set of standards for electrical connections, paper sizes, etc.

din — *noun* a loud, continuous, and unpleasant noise. — *verb* (**dinned**, **dinning**) (**din something into someone**) to repeat (something) forcefully to someone over and over again so that it will be remembered. [from Anglo-Saxon *dyne*]

dinar *noun* the standard unit of currency in Yugoslavia and several Arab countries. [from Arabic & Persian *dinar*]

Dinaric Alps, Serbo-Croatian **Dinara Planina**, Italian **Alpi Dinariche** a mountain range following the Adriatic coast of Croatia, Bosnia-Herzegovina, Montenegro, and NW Albania. It is linked to the main alpine system via the Julian Alps and rises to 2 522m at Durmitor. There are limestone ranges in the Karst region of Croatia.

D'Indy, (Paul Marie Théodore) Vincent (1851–1931) French composer, born in Paris. He studied law and developed his interest in musical composition under the guidance of César Franck. He helped to found the Schola Cantorum (1894), and taught there and at the Conservatoire until his death. His works include operas and orchestral pieces, notably *Symphonie sur un chant montagnard français* (Symphony on a French Mountaineer's Song, 1886).

dine *verb intrans. formal* **1** to eat dinner. **2** (**dine off** *or* **on** *or* **upon something**) to eat food for one's dinner.
— **dine out** to have dinner somewhere other than one's own house, eg in a restaurant.
[from Old French *disner*, from Latin *dis-, dis-* + *jejunare*, to fast]

diner *noun* **1** a person who dines. **2** a dining-car on a train. **3** *North Amer.* a small, cheap restaurant.

ding — *noun* a ringing sound. — *verb* to make a ding. [imitative]

ding-dong — *noun* **1** the sound of bells ringing. **2** *colloq.* a heated argument or fight. — *adj. colloq., said of a fight, argument, etc* fierce or heated. [imitative]

dinghy *noun* (PL. **dinghies**) **1** a small open boat propelled by oars, sails, or an outboard motor. **2** a small collapsible rubber boat, especially one kept for use in emergencies. [from Hindi *dingi*, small boat]

dinginess *noun* being dingy or dirty.

dingo *noun* (PL. **dingoes**) a species of wild dog found in Australia. [from Dharuk (Australian Aborigine language) *dinggu*]

dingy *adj.* (**dingier, dingiest**) **1** faded and dirty-looking: *dingy clothes.* **2** dark and rather dirty: *a dingy room.*

dining-car *noun* a carriage on a train in which meals are served.

dining-room *noun* a room in a house used mainly for eating in.

dinitrogen oxide *Chem.* nitrous oxide.

dinitrogen tetroxide *Chem.* (FORMULA N_2O_4) a colourless or pale-yellow liquid that is used as an oxidant in rocket fuel.

dinkum *adj. Austral., New Zealand colloq.* real; genuine; honest. [from dialect *dinkum*, fair share of work]

dinky *adj.* (**dinkier, dinkiest**) *colloq.* neat; dainty. [from Scot. *dink*, neat]

dinner *noun* **1** the main meal of the day, eaten in the middle of the day or in the evening. **2** a formal meal, especially in the evening, often held to honour a person or in celebration of an event. [same as DINE]

dinner-dance *noun* a social occasion consisting of a formal dinner followed by dancing.

dinner-jacket *noun* a usually black jacket worn by men at formal social gatherings, especially in the evening.

dinner-service *or* **dinner-set** *noun* a complete set of plates and dishes for serving dinner to several people.

dinosaur *noun* any member of a large group of prehistoric reptiles that dominated life on land during the Mesozoic era, from about 225 million to 65 million years ago, becoming extinct at the end of the Cretaceous period. [from Greek *deinos*, terrible + *sauros*, lizard]. See illustration on p. 364. ◇ Dinosaurs are distinguished from other reptiles by their standing posture, in which the limbs were held vertically beneath the body, rather than being directed out sideways. This allowed much more efficient movement than the sprawling gait of a typical reptile. There were over 800 species of dinosaur, all having a specialized type of hip joint to allow this upright posture, and they were divided into two groups, the reptile-hipped dinosaurs (order Saurischia) and the bird-hipped dinosaurs (order Ornithischia). The saurischian dinosaurs included the two-legged carnivores such as *Tyrannosaurus* (which stood about 6m high on its strong hind legs, and had huge dagger-like teeth) and the enormous four-legged predominantly herbivorous forms such as *Apatosaurus* (formerly known as *Brontosaurus*), *Brachiosaurus*, and *Diplodocus* (all of which had bulky bodies, long necks and tails, and small heads). The ornithischian dinosaurs included ankylosaurs, *Stegosaurus* (which had a row of large bony plates projecting from its back), and *Iguanodon*. Many dinosaurs reached an enormous size. *Diplodocus* was about 28m long, but weighed only 10 tonnes, whereas *Apatosaurus* was slightly shorter, at 25m, but weighed 30 tonnes. *Brachiosaurus* weighed about 80 tonnes, and was the heaviest of all dinosaurs. These large dinosaurs were very slow moving, and some scientists now believe that a few of them were warm-blooded. Dinosaurs suddenly became extinct at the end of the Cretaceous period, and it is thought that a combination of climatic changes and competition from mammals in the altering environment is the most likely reason for this event. The closest living relatives of the dinosaurs are crocodiles and birds.

Dinosaur Provincial Park a provincial park in Alberta, SW Canada. It is an area of severe erosion; in the early 20c the fossil remains of some 60 different species of dinosaur were discovered here. The park is a World Heritage site.

dint *noun* a hollow made by a blow; a dent.
— **by dint of something** by means of it. [from Anglo-Saxon *dynt*, blow]

diocesan *adj.* relating to or concerning a diocese.

diocese *noun* the district over which a bishop has authority. [from Greek *dioikesis*, housekeeping]

Diocletian, in full **Gaius Aurelius Valerius Diocletianus**, originally **Diocles** (AD 245–316) Roman emperor (284–305), born in Dalmatia. He rose through the ranks of the army to become emperor. He saw the answer to the Empire's problems in a division of power at the top and reorganization of the provincial structure below. In 286 the Empire was split in two, with Diocletian retaining the East, and Maximian, a loyal friend, taking the West. Further refinement followed in 293 when, under the tetrarchy, the Empire was divided into four. Britain was restored to the Empire in 296 and the Persians defected in 298. In 303 there was severe persecution of the Christians. Diocletian abdicated in 305 and built a palace (now in the centre of modern Split) on the coast of Dalmatia, and devoted himself to philosophy and gardening.

diode *noun Electron.* an electronic device containing two electrodes (an anode and a cathode) that allows current to flow in one direction only. ◇ Diodes are used as rectifiers to convert alternating current into direct current, and are of many different types, eg electron tubes, semiconductor devices, light-sensitive diodes (used in photoelectric cells), light-emitting diodes (which produce light when an electric current passes through them), and thermistors (whose resistance varies with temperature). [from Greek *di-*, twice + *hodos*, way]

dioecious *adj. Bot.* having male and female flowers on different plants. See also MONOECIOUS. [from Greek *di-*, twice + *oikos*, house]

Diogenes of Sinope (412–323 BC) Cynic philosopher, born in Sinope, Pontus. In Athens, he was influenced by the teaching of Antisthenes, and became an austere ascetic. His unconventional behaviour, which became legendary in antiquity (eg looking with a lantern in daylight for an honest man), was intended to portray the ideal of a life lived according to nature.

Diomedes *or* **Diomede** in Greek legend, a hero who fought in the Trojan War. His feats included the wounding of Aphrodite and the capture of the Trojan Palladium, the sacred image of the goddess Athena. In the medieval version of the story, he became the lover of Cressida.

Dione *Astron.* the fourth moon of Saturn, 1 120km/696 mi in diameter and heavily cratered in some areas, but also containing relatively smooth plains. Another tiny moon, Dione B, is associated with it.

Dionysia the festivals in ancient times held in honour of Dionysus, the Greek god of fertility, ecstasy, inspiration, drama, and wine.

Dionysius of Halicarnassus (1c BC) Greek critic, historian, and rhetorician, from Halicarnassus in Asia Minor, who lived and worked in Rome at the time of Augustus. Much of his writing survives, including about half of his *Early Roman History*. It traces the history of Rome from its origins to the outbreak of the First Punic War (264 BC).

Dionysius the Areopagite (1c AD) Greek or Syrian churchman, one of the few Athenians converted by the apostle Paul (Acts 17.34). Traditionally, he was the first Bishop of Athens and a martyr. The Greek writings (first mentioned in 533) that bear his name were probably

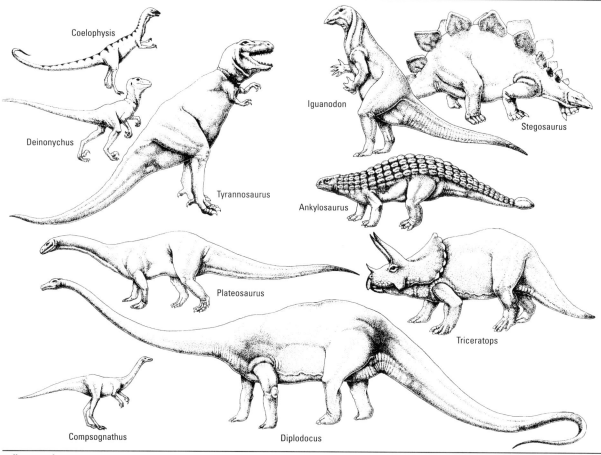

dinosaur shapes

written by an Alexandrian, and had much influence on the development of theology.

Dionysius the Elder (c.431–367 BC) tyrant of Syracuse (405–367 BC) and ruler of half of Sicily, whose influence extended over most of S Italy. His reign was dominated by intermittent warfare with the Carthaginians, his chief rivals for power in Sicily.

Dionysius the Younger (c.397 BC–?) tyrant of Syracuse (367–357/6 BC, 347/6–344 BC), the son and successor of Dionysius the Elder. He was taught by Plato as a potential philosopher-king, but turned out to be an oppressor. Twice overthrown, he ended his days in exile at Corinth.

Dionysius Thrax (1c–2c) Greek grammarian, born in Alexandria, who taught at Rhodes and at Rome. His only surviving work, *Technē Grammatikē*, is the basis of all European works on grammar.

Dionysus, also called **Bacchus** in Greek mythology, the god associated with wine, fertility, and wild ecstasy; later, specifically as Bacchus, the Roman god of wine, associated with music and dramatic festivals. He was the son of Zeus and Semele, and his foreign cult came to Greece from Thrace.

Diophantus (fl. 3c AD) Greek mathematician who lived in Alexandria. Little of his work has survived; the largest work is the *Arithmetica* which deals with the solution of problems about numbers, and in contrast to earlier Greek work, uses a rudimentary algebraic notation instead of a purely geometric one. In many problems the solution is not uniquely determined – these have become known as Diophantine problems.

dioptre *or* **diopter** *noun Optics* (ABBREV. **dpt**) a unit that is used to express the power of a lens, defined as one divided by the focal length of the

lens, when the focal length is measured in metres. It has a positive value for converging lenses and a negative value for diverging lenses. [from Greek *dioptron*, spyglass]

Dior, Christian (1905–57) French couturier, born in Granville, Normandy. He was the founder of the international Dior fashion house, and first began to design clothes in 1935. After working for Piguet and Lelong in Paris, he founded his own Paris house in 1945, and in 1947 achieved worldwide fame with his long-skirted 'New Look'. His later designs included the 'H' line and the 'A' line.

dioxide *noun Chem.* a compound formed by combining two atoms of oxygen with one atom of another element. [from Greek *di-*, twice + OXIDE]

dioxin *noun* any of various highly toxic chlorinated organic chemicals produced as a by-product of the manufacture of certain herbicides and insecticides. They are absorbed by fatty tissues, and have been associated with allergic skin reactions, cancer, birth defects, and miscarriages. The detection of low levels of dioxins in bleached paper products has resulted in the increasing use of non-chlorinated bleaches in such products.

Dip. *abbrev.* Diploma.

dip — *verb* (**dipped**, **dipping**) **1** to put into a liquid for a short time. **2** *intrans.* to go briefly under the surface of a liquid. **3** *intrans.* to drop below a surface or level. **4** *intrans., trans.* to go or push down briefly and then up again. **5** *intrans.* to slope downwards. **6** *intrans., trans.* to put (one's hand, etc) into a dish, container, etc and take out some of the contents. **7** to immerse (an animal) in a bath of disinfectant chemical that kills parasitic insects. **8** *Brit.* to lower the beam of (a vehicle's headlights). — *noun* **1** an act of dipping. **2** a

downward slope or hollow (especially in a road). **3** a short swim or bathe. **4** a chemical liquid for dipping animals. **5** a type of thick sauce into which biscuits, raw vegetables, etc are dipped.

— **dip into something 1** to take or use part of it. **2** to look briefly at a book or study a subject in a casual manner.
[from Anglo-Saxon *dyppan*]

diphtheria *noun Medicine* a highly contagious bacterial infection, now rare, in which a tough grey 'membrane' forms at the back of the throat, causing difficulty in breathing and swallowing. The bacterium also releases a toxin into the bloodstream which causes inflammation of the heart and nerves and can lead to heart failure. Immunization is highly effective in preventing this disease. [from Greek *diphthera*, leather (from the leathery covering formed in the throat)]

diphthong *noun Grammar* **1** two vowel sounds pronounced as one syllable, as the sound represented by the *ou* in *sounds*. **2** a digraph. [from Greek *di-*, twice + *phthongos*, sound]

diploid *adj. Genetics* describing an organism, cell, or nucleus in which there are two sets of chromosomes, one set being derived from each of the parents. In animals all the cells except the gametes are diploid. [from Greek *diploos*, double]

diploma *noun* a document certifying that one has passed a certain examination or completed a course of study. [from Latin *diploma*, official document, from Greek *diplōma*, letter folded over]

diplomacy *noun* **1** the art or profession of making agreements, treaties, etc between countries, or of representing and looking after the affairs and interests of one's country in a foreign country. **2** skill and tact in dealing with people.

diplomat *noun* **1** a government official or representative engaged in diplomacy. **2** a very tactful person. [from French *diplomate*, from Latin *diploma*, official document]

diplomatic *adj.* **1** concerning or involved in diplomacy. **2** tactful.

diplomatically *adv.* with a diplomatic manner; in terms of diplomacy.

diplomatic bag a bag or other container for official letters, packages, etc sent to and from an embassy, not subject to customs inspection.

diplomatic corps all the diplomats and embassy staff of all the embassies in the capital of a country.

diplomatic immunity the privilege granted to members of the diplomatic corps by which they may not be taxed, arrested, etc by the country in which they are working.

dipole *noun Physics* a separation of electric charge, in which two equal and opposite charges are separated from each other by a small distance. Certain molecules act as dipoles.

dipper *noun* **1** a type of ladle. **2** a small songbird which can swim under water and feeds on river-beds.

dipsomania *noun Medicine* an extreme form of alcoholism, in which there is an insatiable craving for alcoholic drink. [from Greek *dipsa*, thirst + *mania*, madness]

dipsomaniac *noun* a person with an abnormal craving for alcohol.

dipstick *noun* **1** a stick used to measure the level of a liquid in a container, especially the oil in a car engine. **2** *slang* a term of abuse for a person.

dipswitch *noun* a switch used to dip the headlights of a motor vehicle.

diptych *noun* a work of art, especially on a church altar, consisting of a pair of pictures painted on hinged wooden panels which can be folded together like a book. See also TRIPTYCH. [from Greek *diptychos*, folded together]

Dirac, Paul Adrien Maurice (1902–84) English mathematical physicist, born in Bristol. Professor of Mathematics at Cambridge (1932–69), he applied relativity theory to quantum mechanics, successfully accounting for electron 'spin' and predicting the existence of antimatter. He shared the 1933 Nobel Prize for Physics with Erwin Schrödinger.

dire *adj.* **1** dreadful; terrible. **2** extreme; very serious; very difficult. [from Latin *dirus*]

direct — *adj.* **1** straight; following the quickest and shortest path from beginning to end or to a destination. **2** *said of a person's manner, etc* open, straightforward and honest; going straight to the point. **3** with no other factors involved: *the direct cause of the accident.* **4** not working or communicating through other people, organizations, etc: *a direct link with the chairman.* **5** exact; complete: *a direct opposite.* **6** forming or being part of an unbroken line of descent from parent to child to grandchild, etc: *a direct descendant of Sir Walter Raleigh.* — *verb* **1** to point, aim or turn in a particular direction. **2** to show the way. **3** to order or instruct. **4** to control or manage; to be in charge of (something). **5** *trans., intrans.* to plan and supervise the production of (a play or film). **6** *formal* to put a name and address on (a letter). — *adv.* directly; by the quickest or shortest path. [from Latin *directus*]

direct action *Politics* action taken by an individual or (more usually) a group, such as a trade union, in order to obtain some demand or concession from government, an employer, etc. Strikes and civil disobedience are examples of direct action, and the term may also be applied to the activities of terrorist organizations and other extremists.

direct current electric current which flows in one direction. See also ALTERNATING CURRENT.

direct debit an order to one's bank which allows someone else to withdraw sums of money from one's account, especially in payment of bills.

directed energy weapon *Mil.* a weapon using advanced laser beam, particle beams, plasma beams, or microwave beams, all of which travel at the speed of light, and which are theoretically capable of shooting down missiles in space.

direction *noun* **1** the place or point towards which one is moving or facing. **2** the way in which someone or something is developing. **3** (*usually* **directions**) information, instructions, or advice, eg on how to construct or operate a piece of equipment. **4** (**directions**) instructions about the way to go to reach a place. **5** management or supervision. **6** the act, style, etc of directing a play or film. [from Latin *directio*]

directional *adj.* relating to direction in space.

direction-finder *noun Engineering* a radio receiver that is used in navigation to determine the direction from which an incoming radio signal is coming, and thus to establish the location of its source.

directive *noun* an official instruction issued by a higher authority, eg a government. [from Latin *directivus*]

directly *adv.* **1** in a direct manner. **2** by a direct path. **3** at once; immediately. **4** very soon. **5** exactly: *directly opposite.*

directness *noun* a direct or straightforward manner, especially of speech or thought: *they discussed the matter with a welcome directness.*

direct object *noun Grammar* the noun, noun phrase or pronoun which is directly affected by the action of a transitive verb, as *the dog* in *The boy kicked the dog.* See also INDIRECT OBJECT.

Directoire Style a French style of furniture, and women's clothes, strictly belonging to the years 1795–9, but generally used to describe furniture fashionable between the outbreak of the French Revolution and the introduction of the Empire Style (c.1804). It was a restrained neoclassical style influenced by antique Greek art.

director *noun* **1** any of the most senior managers of a business firm. **2** the person in charge of a college, organization, institution, or special activity. **3** the person directing a play, film, etc. [from DIRECT -OR]

directorate *noun* **1** the directors of a business firm. **2** the position or office of director.

directorial *adj.* relating to directors or management.

directorship *noun* the office or status of a director.

Directory the government of the First Republic of France (1795–9) established in the Thermidorian reaction to the Reign of Terror, with five executive Directors. Its limited franchise and narrow social base added to the difficulties of rampant inflation, and after political conspiracies from left and right, it was overthrown by the coup of 18 Brumaire (9–10 Nov), which brought Napoleon I to power.

directory *noun* (PL. **directories**) **1** a book with a (usually alphabetical) list of names and addresses of people or organizations. **2** *Comput.* a named grouping of files on a disk, usually with a common element, allowing a command to be applied to, or bypass, all the files it contains, etc. [from Latin *directorium*]

direct speech *noun Grammar* speech reported in the actual words of the speaker. See also INDIRECT SPEECH.

direct tax *noun* a tax paid directly to the government by a person or organization rather than one levied on goods and services (eg income tax as opposed to value-added tax). See also INDIRECT TAX.

dirge *noun* **1** a funeral song or hymn. **2** *sometimes derog.* a slow, sad song or piece of music. [from Latin *dirige*, lead, the first word in a hymn sung in the Latin Office (religious service) for the Dead]

Dirichlet, (Peter Gustav) Lejeune (1805–59) German mathematician, born in Düren. Professor at Berlin and Göttingen, his main work was in number theory, Fourier series, and boundary value problems in mathematical physics; by his teaching and example he was the dominant influence on many leading German mathematicians of the next generation.

dirigible *noun technical* an airship. [from Latin *dirigere*, to direct]

dirk *noun* a small knife or dagger. [from Scots *durk*]

dirndl *noun* **1** a traditional alpine peasantwoman's dress, tight-fitting at the top and waist, and wide and loose at the bottom. **2** a skirt that is tight at the waist and wide at the bottom. [from German dialect *dirndl*]

dirt *noun* **1** any unclean substance, eg mud or dust. **2** soil; earth. **3** a mixture of earth and cinders used to make road surfaces. **4** *euphemistic* excrement. **5** *colloq.* obscene speech or writing. **6** *colloq.* spiteful gossip; scandal: *got some dirt on him.* — **treat someone like dirt** to treat them with no consideration or respect. [from Norse *drit*, excrement]

dirt-cheap *adj., adv. colloq.* very cheap or cheaply.

dirtily *adv.* in a dirty way.

dirtiness *noun* a dirty state.

dirty — *adj.* (**dirtier, dirtiest**) **1** marked with dirt; soiled. **2** which involves one becoming soiled with dirt: *a dirty job.* **3** unfair; dishonest: *dirty tricks.* **4** obscene, lewd, or pornographic: *dirty films.* **5** for the purposes of having sex in secret: *a dirty weekend.* **6** *said of weather* rainy or stormy. **7** *said of a colour* dull. **8** showing dislike or disapproval: *a dirty look.* **9** unsportingly rough or violent: *a dirty tackle.* — *verb trans.* (**dirties, dirtied**) to make dirty. — *adv.* dirtily: *fight dirty.* — **do the dirty on someone** *colloq.* to cheat or trick them.

dirty word **1** an indecent or vulgar word. **2** *colloq.* an unpopular concept or point of view: *ambition is a dirty word.*

dirty work *noun* **1** work that makes one dirty. **2** *colloq.* unpleasant or dishonourable duties.

dis- *prefix* forming words denoting: **1** the opposite of the simple word: *disagree* / *dislike.* **2** reversal of the action of the simple word: *disassemble.* **3** removal or undoing: *dismember* / *disrobe.* [from Latin *dis-*]

disability *noun* (PL. **disabilities**) **1** the state of being disabled. **2** a condition, such as a physical handicap, that results in partial or complete loss of a person's ability to perform social, occupational, or other everyday activities.

disable *verb* **1** to deprive of a physical or mental ability. **2** to make (eg a machine) unable to work; to make useless.

disabled *adj.* **1** *said of a person* having a physical or mental handicap. **2** *said of a machine, etc* made unable to work.

disablement *noun* disabling of a person or machine.

disabuse *verb* (**disabuse someone of something**) to rid them of a mistaken idea or impression.

disaccharide *noun Biochem.* a carbohydrate that consists of two monosaccharides (simple sugars) joined together, with the elimination of a molecule of water. The most abundant disaccharides in nature are *sucrose* (table sugar), which contains a glucose molecule linked to a frucose molecule, and *lactose* (milk sugar), which contains a glucose molecule linked to a galactose molecule.

disadvantage — *noun* **1** a difficulty, drawback or weakness. **2** an unfavourable situation. — *verb* to put at a disadvantage.

disadvantaged *adj.* in an unfavourable position, especially deprived of normal social or economic benefits.

disadvantageous *adj.* having disadvantages or weaknesses.

disaffected *adj.* dissatisfied and no longer loyal or committed. [from DIS-²]

disaffection *noun* disloyalty; discontent.

disagree *verb intrans.* **1** *said of two or more people* to have conflicting opinions. **2** (**disagree with someone**) to have a different opinion from them. **3** (**disagree with something**) to be opposed to something. **4** to conflict with each other: *the two theories disagree.* **5** *euphemistic* to quarrel. **6** (**disagree with someone**) *said of food* to cause digestive problems. [from Old French *desagreer*]

disagreeable *adj.* **1** unpleasant. **2** bad-tempered; unfriendly.

disagreeably *adv.* in a disagreeable or unpleasant way; to an unpleasant degree.

disagreement *noun* **1** the state of disagreeing. **2** *euphemistic* a quarrel.

disallow *verb* to formally refuse to allow or accept; to judge to be invalid. [from Old French *desalouer*]

disallowance *noun* refusal to allow something.

disappear *verb intrans.* **1** to go out of sight; to vanish. **2** to cease to exist. **3** to go missing. [from DIS-¹]

disappearance *noun* disappearing; passing from sight.

disappoint *verb* **1** to fail to fulfil the hopes or expectations of. **2** *formal* to prevent (eg a plan) from being carried out. [from Old French *desapointer*]

disappointed *adj.* having one's hopes or expectations frustrated.

disappointing *adj.* causing disappointment; frustrating one's hopes or expectations.

disappointment *noun* **1** the state of being disappointed. **2** something that disappoints.

disapprobation *noun formal* disapproval, especially on moral grounds. [from DIS-¹]

disapproval *noun* thinking badly of someone or something.

disapprove *verb intrans.* (**disapprove of something** *or* **someone**) to have a low opinion of them; to think them bad or wrong.

disapproving *adj.* showing disapproval; thinking badly.

disarm *verb* **1** to take weapons away from. **2** *intrans.* to reduce or destroy one's own military capability. **3** to take the fuse out of (a bomb). **4** to take away the anger or suspicions of. [from Old French *desarmer*]

disarmament *noun* the reduction or destruction by a nation of its own military forces.
◇ General disarmament (applying to all countries) and comprehensive disarmament (applying to all categories of forces and weapons) were first attempted in 1927 and 1934 by the League of Nations, and by the United Nations in the 1950s, both without success. Disarmament is therefore limited to agreements between two or a few countries. The most significant arms reduction agreements in terms of world security have been those between the USA and the former Soviet Union, both in regard to their respective nuclear capabilities and in deployment of conventional forces. The principal instruments have been the rounds of talks called SALT (Strategic Arms Limitation Talks) from 1969, and START (Strategic Arms Reduction Talks) from 1982. A major concern now is preventing the extension of nuclear arms to countries that have hitherto not had them.

disarming *adj.* taking away anger or suspicion; quickly winning confidence or affection.

disarmingly *adv.* with a disarming manner.

disarrange *verb* to make untidy or disordered.

disarrangement *noun* lack of arrangement or order; putting things out of order.

disarray — *noun* a state of disorder or confusion. — *verb* throw into disorder.

disassociate same as DISSOCIATE.

disaster *noun* **1** an event causing great damage, injury or loss of life. **2** a total failure. **3** extremely bad luck: *Disaster struck.* [originally 'bad influence of the stars', from Old French *desastre*, from *des-, dis-* + *astre*, star]

disastrous *adj.* involving great damage or loss.

disavow *verb formal* to deny knowledge of, a connection with, or responsibility for. [from Old French *desavouer*]

disavowal *noun* refusal to acknowledge someone or something.

disband *verb trans., intrans.* to stop operating as a group; to break up. [from Old French *desbander*, to unbind]

disbandment *noun* breaking up of a group; formal dispersal.

disbelief *noun* inability or refusal to believe something: *they looked at us in disbelief.*

disbelieve *verb* **1** to believe to be false or lying. **2** *intrans.* to have no religious faith.

disburse *verb* to pay out, especially from a fund. [from Old French *desbourser*]

disbursement *noun* payment from a fund.

disc *noun* **1** a flat, thin circular object. **2** any disc-shaped recording medium, such as a gramophone record or compact disc. **3** *Anat.* in the spine of vertebrates, a plate of fibrous tissue between two adjacent vertebrae. **4** *Comput.* same as DISK. [from Greek *diskos*]

discard *verb* **1** to get rid of as useless or unwanted. **2** *Cards* to put down (a card of little value) especially when unable to follow suit.

disc brake a brake in which pads are pressed against a metal disc attached to the vehicle's wheel.

discern *verb* to perceive, notice, or make out; to judge. [from Latin *discernere*]

discernible *adj.* capable of being seen or perceived: *no discernible difference.*

discerning *adj.* having or showing good judgement.

discernment *noun* good judgement.

discharge — *verb* **1** to allow (someone) to leave; to send away or dismiss, especially from employment. **2** to perform or carry out (eg duties). **3** *trans., intrans.* to flow out or cause to flow out or be released. **4** *Legal* to release from custody. **5** *trans., intrans.* to fire (a gun). **6** *Legal* to pay off (a debt). **7** *trans., intrans.* to unload (a cargo). **8** *trans., intrans.* *technical* to lose or cause (a device) to lose some or all electrical charge. — *noun* **1** the act of discharging. **2** something discharged. **3** *formal Legal* release or dismissal. **4** *Physics* the flow of electric current through a gas in a discharge tube, often resulting in luminescence of the gas. **5** *Electr.* the release of stored electric charge from a capacitor, battery, or accumulator. **6** *Electr.* a high-voltage spark of electricity produced when there is a large difference in electrical potential between two points, eg lightning. [from Old French *descharger*]

disciple *noun* **1** a person who believes in, and follows the teachings of another. **2** one of the twelve close followers of Christ. [from Latin *discipulus*, from *discere*, to learn]

disciplinarian *noun* a person who enforces strict discipline on others.

disciplinary *adj.* of, relating to, or enforcing discipline; intended as punishment.

discipline — *noun* **1** strict training, or the enforcing of rules, intended to produce ordered and controlled behaviour in oneself or others; the ordered behaviour resulting from this. **2** punishment designed to create obedience. **3** an area of learning, especially a subject of academic study. — *verb* **1** to train or force (oneself or others) to behave in an ordered and controlled way. **2** to punish. [from Latin *disciplina*]

disc jockey *noun* a person who presents a programme of recorded popular music on the radio or at a disco.

disclaim *verb* **1** to deny (eg involvement with or knowledge of). **2** to give up a legal claim to. [from Old French *desclaimer*]

disclaimer *noun* **1** a written statement denying legal responsibility. **2** a denial.

disclose *verb* to make known; to show or make visible. [from Old French *desclore*]

disclosure *noun* the act of disclosing or making something known.

disco — *noun* (PL. **discos**) **1** a discotheque. **2** a party with dancing to recorded music. **3** the mobile hi-fi and lighting equipment used for such a party. — *adj.* suitable for, or designed for, discotheques.

Discobolus (Discus Thrower) a sculpture by Myron (5c BC).

discoloration *or* **discolouration** *noun* change or loss of colour.

discolour *verb trans., intrans.* to stain or dirty; to change in colour. [from Old French *descolorer*]

discomfit *verb* (**discomfited, discomfiting**) **1** to cause to feel embarrassed or uneasy; to perplex. **2** to frustrate the plans of. [from Old French *desconfire*]

discomfiture *noun* frustration; humiliating disappointment.

discomfort — *noun* a slight physical pain or mental uneasiness. — *verb* to make physically uncomfortable or mentally uneasy. [from Old French *desconfort*]

discompose *verb* to upset, worry, or agitate.

discomposure *noun* a state of upset or agitation.

disconcert *verb* to cause to feel anxious or uneasy; to fluster. [from obsolete French *disconcerter*]

disconcerting *adj.* causing anxiety or unease.

disconnect *verb* **1** to break the connection between (especially an electrical device and a power supply). **2** to stop the supply of (a public service such as the gas supply or the telephone) to (a building, etc).

disconnected *adj.* **1** no longer connected. **2** *said especially of speech* not correctly constructed, and often not making sense.

disconnection *noun* a break in a connection or link.

disconsolate *adj.* deeply sad or disappointed; not able to be consoled. [from Latin *disconsolatus*]

disconsolately *adv.* with deep sadness or disappointment.

discontent *noun* dissatisfaction; lack of contentment.

discontented *adj.* dissatisfied; unhappy.

discontinuance *or* **discontinuation** *noun* discontinuing; breaking off.

discontinue *verb* **1** *trans., intrans.* to stop or cease. **2** to stop producing: *a discontinued line*. [from Old French *discontinuer*]

discontinuity *noun* lack of continuity; interruption.

discontinuous *adj.* having breaks or interruptions.

discord *noun* **1** disagreement; conflict; failure to get on. **2** *Mus.* an unpleasant-sounding combination of notes; lack of harmony. **3** uproarious noise. [from Latin *discordia*]

discordant *adj.* lacking harmony; disagreeing.

discotheque *noun* a night-club with dancing to recorded pop music. See also DISCO. [from French *discotheque*]

discount — *noun* an amount deducted from the normal price, eg for prompt payment. — *verb* **1** to disregard as unlikely, untrue, or irrelevant. **2** to make a deduction from (a price).
— **at a discount** for less than the usual price. [from Old French *descompter*]

discount house a UK financial institution which buys short-dated government stocks (Treasury Bills) with money borrowed from commercial banks for very short periods. The difference between the borrowing rate and the lending rate provides the discount house with its profit.

discourage *verb* **1** to deprive of confidence, hope, or the will to continue. **2** to seek to prevent (a person or an action) with advice or persuasion. [from Old French *descourager*]

discouragement *noun* dissuasion; feeling discouraged.

discouraging *adj.* taking away one's courage or confidence; dissuading: *our first efforts had a discouraging response.*

discourse — *noun* **1** a formal speech or essay on a particular subject. **2** serious conversation. — *verb intrans.* to speak or write at length, formally or with authority. [from Latin *discursus*]

discourse analysis *Linguistics* the study of continuous stretches of language, both in speech and writing, to discover their structure, and the features which bind sentences in a sequence. For example, cohesion is created by the used of the pronouns *she* and *him* in the sequence *Anne met Peter yesterday. She was surprised to see him.* See also CONVERSATION ANALYSIS, TEXTLINGUISTICS

discourteous *adj.* showing a lack of courtesy; impolite. [from DIS-¹]

discourteously *adv.* with a discourteous or impolite manner.

discourtesy *noun* lack of courtesy; impoliteness.

discover *verb* (**discovered, discovering**) **1** to be the first person to find. **2** to find by chance, especially for the first time. **3** to learn of or become aware of for the first time. [from Old French *descouvrir*]

Discovery a name given to various exploration vessels. The most famous is Scott's *Discovery*, built in 1901 and moored in the Thames in 1936. It has undergone restoration by the Maritime Trust. Its name is preserved as a memorial by the admiralty in HMS *Discovery*, the flagship to the Admiral Commanding Reserves.

discovery *noun* (PL. **discoveries**) **1** the act of discovering. **2** a person or thing discovered.

discredit — *noun* loss of good reputation, or the cause of it. — *verb* (**discredited, discrediting**) **1** to cause to be disbelieved or regarded with doubt or suspicion. **2** to damage the reputation of.

discreditable *adj.* bringing discredit.

discreet *adj.* **1** careful to prevent suspicion or embarrassment, especially by keeping a secret. **2** avoiding notice; inconspicuous. See also DISCRETION. [from Latin *discretus*]

discrepancy *noun* (PL. **discrepancies**) a failure (eg of sets of information) to correspond or be the same. [from Latin *discrepare*, to differ in sound]

discrepant *adj.* showing a discrepancy or failure to correspond.

discrete *adj.* separate; distinct. [from Latin *discretus*]

discretely *adv.* in a discrete or separate manner.

discreteness *noun* being discrete; separateness.

discretion *noun* **1** the quality of behaving in a discreet way. **2** the ability to make wise judgements. **3** the freedom or right to make decisions and do as one thinks best: *allowed to change the plans at our own discretion.* [from Latin *discretio*]

discretionary *adj.* made, done, given, etc according to the wishes of a particular person or group; not compulsory or automatic.

discriminate *verb intrans.* **1** to recognize a difference between two people or things. **2** to give different treatment to different people or groups in identical circumstances, especially without justification and on political or religious grounds. [from Latin *discriminare*, to separate]

discriminating *adj.* showing good judgement; able to recognize even slight differences.

discrimination *noun* **1** unjustifiably different treatment given to different people or groups. **2** the ability to draw fine distinctions; good judgement, especially in matters of taste.

discriminatory *adj.* displaying or representing unfairly different treatment.

discursive *adj.* **1** wandering from the main point. **2** *Philos.* based on argument or reason, rather than on intuition. [from DISCOURSE]

discus *noun* **1** a heavy metal disc, thicker at the centre than the edge, thrown in athletic competitions. **2** the competition itself. [from Greek *diskos*]
◇ The athletics field event (*discus throw*) uses a circular disc of wood with metal plates, weighing 2kg for men and 1kg for women, which is thrown with one hand from within the confines of a 2.5m circle. In competition, six throws are allowed, the aim being to throw it as far as possible.

discuss *verb* to examine or consider in speech or writing. [from Latin *discutere*, to shake to pieces]

discussion *noun* a conversation or debate on a particular topic.

discus throw see DISCUS.

disdain — *noun* dislike arising out of lack of respect; contempt. — *verb* **1** to refuse or reject out of disdain. **2** to regard with disdain. [from Old French *desdaigner*, from Latin *dignus*, worthy]

disdainful *adj.* showing disdain or contempt.

disdainfully *adv.* with a disdainful or contemptuous manner.

disease *noun* **1** illness or lack of health caused by infection rather than by an accident; any one such illness with characteristic symptoms. **2** any undesirable phenomenon. [from Old French *desaise*, unease]

diseased *adj.*, *usually said of a part of the body* suffering from disease.

diseconomy *noun* (PL. **diseconomies**) an economic disadvantage, such as lower efficiency or higher costs. [from DIS-¹]

disembark *verb trans., intrans.* to take or go from a ship on to land. [from Old French *desembarquer*]

disembarkation *noun* departure or removal from a ship.

disembodied *adj.* **1** *said eg of a spirit or soul* separated from the body; having no physical existence. **2** seeming not to come from, or be connected to, a body: *a disembodied voice.*

disembowel *verb* (**disembowelled, disembowelling**) to remove the internal organs of, as a punishment, torture, etc.

disembowelment *noun* forcible or violent removal of the internal organs.

disenchant *verb* **1** to free from illusion. **2** to make dissatisfied or discontented.

disenchanted *adj.* feeling dissatisfied or disappointed, especially after high expectations.

disenchantment *noun* a feeling of disappointment, especially after high expectations.

disenfranchise see DISFRANCHISE.

disengage *verb* **1** to release or detach from a connection. **2** *trans., intrans.* to withdraw (troops) from combat. [from Old French *desengager*]

disengagement *noun* release from a connection or commitment.

disentangle *verb* **1** to free from complication, difficulty, or confusion. **2** to take the knots or tangles out of (eg hair).

disentanglement *noun* freeing from complication or entanglement.

disestablish *verb* to take away the official status or authority of.

disestablishment *noun* removal of official status or authority from an institution.

disfavour *noun* **1** a state of being disliked, unpopular, or disapproved of. **2** dislike or disapproval.

disfigure *verb* to spoil the beauty or general appearance of. [from Old French *desfigurer*]

disfigurement *noun* spoiling the appearance of something; defacement.

disfranchise *or* **disenfranchise** *verb* to deprive of the right to vote.

disfranchisement *or* **disenfranchisement** *noun* the removal of rights, especially to vote in elections.

disgorge *verb* **1** to vomit. **2** to discharge or pour out. **3** to give up or relinquish, especially under pressure. [from Old French *desgorger*, from *gorge*, throat]

disgrace — *noun* shame or loss of favour or respect, or the cause of it. — *verb* to bring shame upon. [from French *disgrâce*]

disgraceful *adj.* bringing shame; degrading.

disgruntled *adj.* annoyed and dissatisfied; in a bad mood. [from DIS-⁴ + obsolete *gruntle*, to complain]

disguise — *verb* to hide the identity of by a change of appearance, to conceal the true nature of (eg intentions). — *noun* **1** a disguised state: *in disguise.* **2** something, especially a combination of clothes and make-up, intended to disguise. [from Old French *desguiser*]

disgust — *verb* to sicken; to provoke intense dislike or disapproval in. — *noun* intense dislike; loathing. [Old French *desgouster*]

disgusted *adj.* having a feeling of intense dislike or revulsion.

disgusting *adj.* causing a feeling of intense dislike or revulsion.

dish — *noun* **1** a shallow container in which food is served or cooked. **2** its contents, or the amount it can hold. **3** anything shaped like this. **4** a particular kind of food. **5** (**dishes**) the used plates and other utensils after the end of a meal. **6** a dish aerial. **7** *colloq.* a physically attractive person. — *verb colloq.* to ruin (especially chances or hopes).
— **dish something out** *colloq.* **1** to distribute it. **2** to give it out.

dish something up *colloq.* **1** to serve (food). **2** to offer or present (eg information).

[from Anglo-Saxon *disc*, plate, bowl, table]

dishabille same as DÉSHABILLÉ.

dish aerial *noun* a large dish-shaped aerial used to receive signals in radar, radio-telescopes and satellite broadcasting.

disharmonious *adj.* lacking harmony; disagreeing.

disharmony *noun* disagreement; lack of harmony. [from DIS-¹]

dishearten *verb* (**disheartened, disheartening**) to dampen the courage, hope, or confidence of.

disheartening *adj.* dispiriting; discouraging.

disheartenment *noun* being disheartened; discouragement.

dishevelled *adj., said of clothes or hair* untidy; in a mess. [from Old French *descheveler*]

dishevelment *noun* a state of personal untidiness.

dishonest *adj.* not honest; likely to deceive or cheat; insincere. [from Old French *deshoneste*]

dishonestly *adv.* in a dishonest way.

dishonesty *noun* lack of honesty; a dishonest act.

dishonour — *noun* shame or loss of honour, or the cause of it. — *verb* **1** to bring dishonour on. **2** to treat with no respect. **3** *Commerce* to refuse to honour (a cheque). [from Old French *deshonneur*]

dishonourable *adj.* bringing dishonour or disgrace.

dishwasher *noun* **1** a machine that washes and dries dishes. **2** a person employed to wash dishes, eg in a restaurant.

dishwater *noun* water in which dirty dishes have been washed.

dishy *adj.* (**dishier, dishiest**) *colloq.* sexually attractive.

disillusion *verb* (**disillusioned, disillusioning**) to correct the mistaken beliefs or illusions of.

disillusioned *adj.* sad or disappointed at having discovered the unpleasant truth.

disillusionment *noun* being disillusioned.

disincentive *noun* something that discourages or deters.

disinclination *noun* being disinclined or unwilling.

disinclined *adj.* unwilling.

disinfect *verb* to clean with a substance that kills germs.

disinfectant *noun* a germ-killing substance.

disinformation *noun* false information intended to deceive or mislead.

disingenuous *adj.* not entirely sincere or open; creating a false impression of frankness.

disingenuously *adv.* with a disingenuous or insincere manner.

disingenuousness *noun* a disingenuous or insincere manner.

disinherit *verb* (**disinherited, disinheriting**) to legally deprive of an inheritance.

disinheritance *noun* rejection of an heir; removal from inheritance.

disintegrate *verb trans., intrans.* **1** to break into tiny pieces; to shatter or crumble. **2** to break up. **3** to undergo or cause to undergo nuclear fission.

disintegration *noun Physics* the breakdown of an atomic nucleus, either spontaneously by radioactive decay, or as a result of bombardment with high-energy particles.

disinter *verb* (**disinterred, disinterring**) **1** to dig up (especially a body from a grave). **2** to discover and make known.

disinterest or **disinterestedness** *noun* impartiality; objectivity.

disinterested *adj.* **1** not having an interest in a particular matter; impartial, objective. **2** *colloq.* showing no interest; uninterested.
◆ Use in sense 2 is often disapproved of.

disinterment *noun* removal of a body from a grave.

disjointed *adj., said of speech* not properly connected; incoherent. [from Old French *desjoindre*]

disjunctive *adj.* marked by breaks; discontinuous. [from Old French *desjoindre*]

disk *noun Comput.* a magnetic disc-shaped medium used to record and store data in a computer. See also FLOPPY DISK, HARD DISK. [a variant of DISC]

disk drive *Comput.* a device containing the mechanisms for rotating a magnetic disk at high speed. It also controls the movement of a *read-write head* which passes over the surfaces of the disk in order to read or write magnetic signals that represent the stored data.

diskette *noun Comput.* **1** an alternative name for a floppy disk. **2** formerly used to refer to a 5.25in floppy disk.

dislike — *verb* to consider unpleasant or unlikeable. — *noun* **1** mild hostility; aversion. **2** something disliked.

dislocate *verb* **1** to dislodge (a bone) from its normal position in a joint, eg by violently displacing it from the socket during a sports injury. The most common sites of dislocation include the shoulder and hip. **2** to disturb the order of; to disrupt. [from Latin *dislocare*]

dislocation *noun* dislocating, especially of a bone in the body.

dislodge *verb* **1** to force out of a fixed or established position: *dislodge a stone.* **2** to drive from a place of rest, hiding, or defence. [from Old French *desloger*]

dislodgement or **dislodgment** *noun* change from an established position.

disloyal *adj.* not loyal or faithful. [from Old French *desloyal*]

disloyalty *noun* lack of loyalty; unfaithfulness.

dismal *adj.* **1** not cheerful; causing or suggesting sadness. **2** *colloq.* third-rate; of poor quality. [from Old French, from Latin *dies mali*, unlucky days]

dismally *adv.* in a dismal way; miserably: *dismally cold weather.*

dismantle *verb* **1** to take to pieces; to demolish. **2** to abolish or close down, especially bit by bit. [from Old French *desmanteller*]

dismay — *noun* a feeling of sadness arising from deep disappointment or discouragement. — *verb* to cause this feeling in (someone). [from Old French *desmaiier*]

dismember *verb* (**dismembered, dismembering**) **1** to tear or cut the arms and legs from. **2** to divide up (especially land). [from Old French *desmembrer*]

dismemberment *noun* **1** forcible or violent removal of the arms and legs. **2** division of territory.

dismiss *verb* **1** to refuse to consider or accept. **2** to put out of one's employment. **3** to send away; to allow to leave. **4** to close (a court case). **5** *Cricket* to bowl out. [from Latin *dis-*, from, away + *mittere*, to send]

dismissal *noun* dismissing, especially of a person from employment: *an offence that warrants instant dismissal.*

dismissive *adj.* (often **dismissive of something** or **someone**) giving no consideration or respect; showing no willingness to believe.

dismount *verb* **1** *intrans.* to get off a horse, bicycle, etc. **2** to force (someone) off a horse,

bicycle, etc. **3** to remove from a stand or frame. [from Old French *desmonter*]

Disney, Walt(er Elias) (1901–66) US artist and film producer, born in Chicago. He worked as a commercial artist before setting up a small studio in which he produced animated cartoons, his most famous character being Mickey Mouse (1928). Among his early successes were the *Silly Symphonies* (from 1929) and the first full-length coloured cartoon film, *Snow White and the Seven Dwarfs* (1937). This was followed by *Pinocchio* (1940), *Dumbo* (1941), and *Fantasia* (1940), the first successful attempt to realize music in images. His other achievements include a series of coloured nature films (eg *The Living Desert*, 1953), several swashbuckling colour films for young people, such as *Treasure Island* (1959) and *Robin Hood* (1952), and family films such as *Mary Poppins* (1964). He opened the family amusement park Disneyland in California in 1955.

disobedience *noun* refusal to obey.

disobedient *adj.* refusing or failing to obey. [from DIS-¹]

disobey *verb trans., intrans.* to act contrary to the orders of; to refuse to obey. [from Old French *desobeir*]

disobliging *adj.* unwilling to help; disregarding, or tending to disregard, wishes or requests. [from DIS-¹]

disorder *noun* **1** lack of order; confusion or disturbance. **2** unruly or riotous behaviour. **3** a disease or illness. [from Old French *desordre*]

disordered *adj.* lacking order; put out of order.

disorderly *adj.* **1** not neatly arranged; disorganized. **2** causing trouble in public.

disorganization or **disorganisation** *noun* lack of organization; confusion.

disorganize or **disorganise** *verb* to disturb the order or arrangement of; to throw into confusion.

disorientate or **disorient** *verb* to cause to lose all sense of position, direction, or time.

disorientation *noun* confusion as to one's position, etc.

disown *verb* to deny having any relationship to or connection with; to refuse to recognize or acknowledge.

disownment *noun* refusal to acknowledge someone; renunciation.

disparage *verb* to speak of with contempt. [from Old French *desparager*, to marry below one's class]

disparagement *noun* speaking with contempt.

disparaging *adj.* contemptuous; showing disapproval.

disparate *adj.* completely different; too different to be compared. [from Latin *disparare*, to separate]

disparity *noun* (PL. **disparities**) great or fundamental difference; inequality.

dispassionate *adj.* **1** calm; unemotional. **2** not influenced by personal feelings; impartial. [from DIS-¹]

dispatch or **despatch** — *verb* **1** to send to a place for a particular reason. **2** to finish off or deal with quickly: *dispatch a meal.* **3** *euphemistic* to kill. — *noun* (often **dispatches**) an official (especially military or diplomatic) report. **2** a journalist's report sent to a newspaper. **3** the act of dispatching; the fact of being dispatched. **4** *old use* speed or haste. [from Old French *despeechier*, to set free]

dispatch rider *noun* a person employed to deliver messages by motorcycle or, formerly, on horseback.

dispel *verb* (**dispelled, dispelling**) to drive away or banish (thoughts or feelings). [from Latin *dispellere*]

dispensable *adj.* **1** that can be done without; expendable. **2** able to be dispensed.

dispensary *noun* (PL. **dispensaries**) a place where medicines are given out or dispensed.

dispensation *noun* **1** special exemption from a rule, obligation or (especially religious) law. **2** the act of dispensing. **3** a religious or political system regarded as the chief governing force in a nation or during a particular time. **4** *Relig.* God's management of human affairs.

dispense *verb* **1** to give out (eg advice). **2** to prepare and distribute (medicine). **3** to administer (eg the law). — **dispense with something** to do without it. [from Latin *dispendere*, to weigh out]

dispersal *or* **dispersion** *noun* dispersing; scattering.

disperse *verb trans., intrans.* **1** to spread out over a wide area. **2** to break up or cause (a crowd) to break up and leave. **3** to vanish or cause to vanish. **4** *Physics, said of light* to break up into the colours of the spectrum. **5** *Physics, said of particles* to become evenly distributed throughout a liquid or gas. [from Latin *dispergere*, to scatter widely]

dispirit *verb* (**dispirited, dispiriting**) to dishearten or discourage.

displace *verb* **1** to put or take out of the usual place. **2** to take the place of. **3** to remove from a post. [from Old French *desplacer*]

displaced person *noun* a person forced to leave his or her own country through war or persecution.

displacement *noun* **1** the act of displacing. **2** *technical* the quantity of liquid, gas, etc displaced by an immersed object, especially of water by a floating ship.

displacement activity *Psychol.* a relatively harmless activity that is substituted for a more destructive type of behaviour, eg the release of aggression during strenuous physical exercise, rather than directing it at other people.

display — *verb* **1** to put on view. **2** to show or betray (eg feelings). — *noun* **1** the act of displaying. **2** an exhibition; a show of talent; an arrangement of objects on view. **3** the visual display unit linked to a computer, or the digital characters of a liquid-crystal display unit, used in watches, calculators, etc. **4** a pattern of animal behaviour, usually involving stereotyped sounds, movements, colour patterns, etc, that produces a specific response in another individual, especially of the same species. Displays are most frequently associated with courtship or the defence of territory. [from Old French *despleier*]

displease *verb* to annoy or offend. [from Old French *desplaisir*]

displeasure *noun* a feeling of annoyance or offence.

disport *verb trans., intrans. literary* to indulge (oneself) in lively amusement. [from Old French *se desporter*, to carry oneself away]

disposable *adj.* **1** intended to be thrown away or destroyed after use. **2** *said of income or assets* remaining after tax and other commitments are paid; available for use when needed.

disposal *noun* the act of getting rid of something. — **at the disposal of someone** available for use by them.

dispose *verb* **1** (**dispose of something**) to get rid of it; to deal with or settle it. **2** to place in an arrangement or order. **3** (**be disposed**) to feel or be inclined: *am not disposed to try / ill-disposed towards us*. [from Latin *disponere*, to set out]

disposition *noun* **1** temperament; personality; a tendency. **2** arrangement; position; distribution. **3** *Legal* the act of giving over (eg property).

dispossess *verb* (**dispossess someone of something**) to take (especially property) away from them.

dispossession *noun* removal of property from a person.

disproof *noun* the act of disproving; something that disproves.

disproportion *noun* lack of balance or equality; failure to be in proportion.

disproportionate *adj.* unreasonably large or small in comparison with something else.

disproportionately *adv.* in a disproportionate way; to a disproportionate degree.

disprove *verb* to prove to be false or wrong. [from Old French *desprover*]

disputable *adj.* liable to be disputed or argued about.

disputation *noun* argument; debate; discussion.

disputatious *adj., said of a person* inclined to dispute or argue; contentious.

dispute — *verb* (with stress on *-spute*) **1** to question or deny the accuracy or validity of. **2** to quarrel over rights to or possession of: *disputed territory*. **3** *trans., intrans.* to argue about (something). — *noun* (with variable stress) an argument. [from Latin *disputare*, to discuss]

disqualification *noun* making or declaring someone ineligible, especially for infringing rules.

disqualify *verb* (**disqualifies, disqualified**) **1** to remove from a competition, especially for breaking rules. **2** to make unsuitable or ineligible.

disquiet — *noun* a feeling of anxiety or uneasiness. — *verb* to cause this feeling in (someone).

disquieting *adj.* causing a feeling of anxiety or unease.

disquietude *noun* a feeling of disquiet or unease.

disquisition *noun formal* a long and detailed discussion of a subject in speech or writing. [from Latin *disquisitio*]

Disraeli, Benjamin, 1st Earl of Beaconsfield (1804–81) English statesman, born in London, the eldest son of an Anglicized Jew. His early reputation was as a novelist, based on the political novels *Coningsby* (1844) and *Sybil* (1846), which date from his period as a Romantic Tory, critical of industrial developments. He became leader of the 'Young England' movement which espoused these values, and came to prominence as a critic of Peel's free trade policies, especially the repeal of the Corn Laws (1845–6). He became leader of the Conservatives in the Commons, after the Peelites left the Party, and was Chancellor of the Exchequer in Derby's minority governments of 1852 and 1858–9. While Chancellor in the government of 1866–8, he piloted the 1867 Reform Bill through the Commons. He became Prime Minister on Derby's resignation in 1868, but was defeated soon afterwards in the general election. His second administration (1874–80) was notable both for diplomacy and social reform, though much of the latter only consolidated legislation begun under Gladstone. During his administration, Britain became half-owner of the Suez Canal (1875), and the Queen assumed the title Empress of India (1876). His skilful diplomacy at the Congress of Berlin (1878) helped preserve European peace after conflict between the Russians and the Turks in the Balkans. He was defeated in 1880 by Gladstone and the Liberals.

disregard — *verb* to pay no attention to; to dismiss as unworthy of consideration. — *noun* dismissive lack of attention or concern.

disrepair *noun* bad condition or working order owing to a need for repair. [from DIS-¹]

disreputable *adj.* suffering from, or leading to, a bad reputation.

disreputably *adv.* in a way that causes discredit: *behave disreputably*.

disrepute *noun* the state of having a bad reputation: *bring something into disrepute*. [from DIS-¹]

disrespect *noun* lack of respect; impoliteness; rudeness. [from DIS-¹]

disrespectful *adj.* showing a lack of respect; impolite.

disrespectfully *adv.* with a disrespectful or impolite manner.

disrobe *verb trans., intrans.* **1** *literary* to undress. **2** to take ceremonial robes off. [from DIS-³]

disrupt *verb* to disturb the order or peaceful progress of. [from Latin *disrumpere*, to break into pieces]

disruption *noun* disturbance to peace or order.

disruptive *adj.* causing disturbance to peace or order.

dissatisfaction *noun* being dissatisfied; a feeling of discontent.

dissatisfied *adj.* displeased; discontented; not satisfied.

dissatisfy *verb* (**dissatisfies, dissatisfied**) to fail to satisfy; to make discontented.

dissect *verb* **1** to cut open (a plant or dead body) for scientific or medical examination. **2** to examine in minute detail, especially critically. [from Latin *dissecare*, to cut into pieces]

dissection *noun* cutting open or into pieces.

dissemble *verb trans., intrans.* to conceal or disguise (true feelings or motives); to assume a false appearance of (something). [from Latin *dissimulare*]

disseminate *verb* to cause (eg news or theories) to be widely circulated or diffused. [from Latin *disseminare*, to sow widely]

dissemination *noun* wide circulation of news, etc.

dissension *noun* disagreement leading to strife or violence.

dissent — *noun* **1** disagreement, especially open or hostile. **2** voluntary separation, especially from an established church. — *verb intrans.* (often **dissent from someone** *or* **something**) **1** to differ in opinion; to disagree. **2** to break away, especially from an established church. [from Latin *dissentire*, to disagree]

dissenter *noun* a person who dissents or disagrees, especially in religious matters.
◇ Historically, the term is associated with groups (usually Christians) who separate themselves from the established Church or general religious belief of a country. In a wider sense, the term is applied to those who dissent from the very principle of an established or national Church.

dissentient *formal* — *adj.* disagreeing with a majority or established view. — *noun* a dissentient person.

dissenting *adj.* disagreeing; differing in opinion.

dissertation *noun* **1** a long essay, especially forming part of a higher education degree course. **2** a formal lecture on a particular subject. [from Latin *disserere*, to discuss]

disservice *noun* a wrong; a bad turn. [from Old French *desservir*]

dissidence *noun* open or public disagreement.

dissident — *noun* a person who disagrees publicly, esp with a government. — *adj.* disagreeing; dissenting. [from Latin *dissidere*, to sit apart]

dissimilar *adj.* (often **dissimilar to something**) unlike; different.

dissimilarity *noun* being unlike; difference.

dissimulate *verb trans., intrans.* to hide or disguise (especially feelings). [from Latin *dissimulare*]

dissimulation *noun* hiding or disguising feelings.

dissipate *verb* 1 *trans., intrans.* to separate and scatter. 2 to use up carelessly; to squander. [from Latin *dissipare*]

dissipated *adj.* over-indulging in pleasure and enjoyment; debauched.

dissipation *noun* 1 the process of dissipating. 2 extravagant or debauched living.

dissociate *verb* 1 to regard as separate. 2 to declare (someone or oneself) to be unconnected with. 3 *Chem.*, *said of a chemical substance* to break down into its constituent molecules, atoms, or ions, eg when dissolved in water or exposed to electromagnetic radiation. [from Latin *dissociare*]

dissociation *noun* being separate; lack of connection.

dissoluble *adj.* 1 able to be disconnected. 2 soluble. [from Latin *dissolubilis*]

dissolute *adj.* indulging in pleasures considered immoral; debauched. [from Latin *dissolutus*, lax, loose]

dissoluteness *noun* indulgence in immoral pleasures.

dissolution *noun* 1 the breaking up of a meeting or assembly, eg Parliament; the ending of a formal or legal partnership, eg a marriage or business. 2 abolition, eg of the monarchy. 3 the process of breaking up into parts. [from DISSOLVE]

dissolution of the monasteries the confiscation and forced sale of Church lands by the English Crown, initiated in 1536 by Henry VIII (administered by Thomas Cromwell), and continuing up to the time of the early Stuart monarchs.

◊ Henry's move away from Rome, and the poor state of the royal finances, were the motives for the dissolution. The monastic communities owed allegiance to Rome and other institutions outside England, and were therefore perceived as a threat to the king's power. Henry also needed to buy the political allegiance of the lay nobility and gentry, and distributed some of the spoils among them. There was wholesale destruction of great Gothic buildings, religious art and artefacts, and libraries.

dissolve — *verb* 1 *trans., intrans.* to break up and merge with a liquid. 2 to bring (an assembly, eg Parliament) to a close; to end (a legal partnership, eg a business). 3 *trans., intrans.* to disappear or cause to disappear: *our support dissolved.* 4 *intrans.* (*often* **dissolve into laughter, tears,** *etc*) be overcome emotionally. 5 *intrans.* technical, *said of a film or television image* to fade out as a second image fades in. — *noun* technical a fading out of one film or television image as a second is simultaneously faded in. [from Latin *dissolvere*, to loosen]

dissonance *noun* 1 *Mus.* an unpleasant combination of sounds or notes; lack of harmony. 2 disagreement; incompatibility. [from Latin *dissonare*, to be discordant]

dissonant *adj.* lacking in harmony; harsh-sounding.

dissuade *verb* (**dissuade someone from doing something**) to deter them with advice or persuasion. [from Latin *dissuadere*]

dissuasion *noun* advice or persuasion meant to deter.

dissyllable same as DISYLLABLE.

distaff *noun* the rod on which a bunch of wool, flax, etc is held ready for spinning by hand. — **the distaff side** old use the wife's or mother's side of the family. [from Anglo-Saxon *distæf*]

distance — *noun* 1 the measured length between two points in space; the fact of being apart. 2 any faraway point or place; the furthest visible area. 3 coldness of manner. — *verb* 1 to put at a distance. 2 (*usually* **distance oneself**) to declare oneself to be unconnected or unsympathetic to something: *distanced themselves from government policy.*

— **go the distance** *colloq.* to last out until the end, usually of a sporting (especially boxing) contest.

keep one's distance to stay safely away, especially refusing involvement; to avoid friendship or familiarity.

[from Latin *distancia*]

distant *adj.* 1 far away or far apart in space or time. 2 not closely related. 3 cold and unfriendly. 4 appearing to be lost in thought.

distantly *adv.* in the distance; remotely in time or place: *they are distantly related.*

distaste *noun* dislike; aversion.

distasteful *adj.* unpleasant or offensive.

distemper[1] *noun* an infectious disease of animals, especially dogs. [from Old French *destemprer*, to derange]

distemper[2] — *noun* any water-based paint, especially when mixed with glue or size and used for poster-painting or murals. — *verb* (**distempered, distempering**) to paint with distemper. [from Latin *distemperare*, to soak]

distend *verb trans., intrans.* to make or become swollen, inflated, or stretched. [from Latin *distendere*]

distensible *adj.* capable of being distended or stretched.

distension *noun* distending; stretching.

distil *verb* (**distilled, distilling**) 1 to purify a liquid by the process of distillation. 2 to produce alcoholic spirits in this way. 3 to create a shortened version of. [from Latin *destillare*, to drip down]

distillate *noun* a concentrated extract, the product of distilling.

distillation *noun Chem.* a method of purifying a liquid by heating it to boiling point and condensing the vapour formed to a liquid (the *distillate*), which is then collected. This process is used to produce whisky and other alcoholic spirits.

distilled water *Chem.* water that has been purified by distillation.

distiller *noun* a person or company that makes alcoholic spirits.

distillery *noun* (PL. **distilleries**) a place where alcoholic spirits are distilled.

distinct *adj.* 1 easily seen, heard, or recognized; clear or obvious. 2 noticeably different or separate. [from Latin *distinctus*, from *distinguere*, to distinguish]

distinction *noun* 1 exceptional ability or achievement, or an honour awarded in recognition of it. 2 the act of differentiating. 3 the state of being noticeably different. 4 a distinguishing feature.

distinctive *adj.* easily recognized because very individual.

distinctiveness *noun* the quality of being distinctive or individual.

distinctly *adv.* clearly; unmistakably.

distinguish *verb* 1 (**distinguish one thing from another**) to mark or recognize as different. 2 *intrans.* (**distinguish between things or people**) to see the difference between them. 3 to make out; to identify. 4 (**distinguish oneself**) to be considered outstanding because of some achievement. [from Latin *distinguere*]

distinguishable *adj.* capable of being distinguished or recognized as different.

distinguished *adj.* 1 famous (and usually well respected). 2 with a noble or dignified appearance.

Distinguished Flying Cross (ABBREV. **DFC**) in the UK, a decoration instituted in 1918, awarded to officers and warrant officers in the RAF for acts of gallantry performed on active service. The ribbon is equal blue and grey diagonal stripes.

Distinguished Service Order (ABBREV. **DSO**) in the UK, a military decoration instituted in 1886, awarded in recognition of special service by officers of the army and navy. The ribbon is red edged with blue.

distinguishing *adj.* serving to identify.

distort *verb* 1 to twist out of shape. 2 to change the meaning or tone of by inaccurate retelling. 3 to alter the quality of (sound). [from Latin *distorquere*]

distorted *adj.* 1 twisted out of shape. 2 wrongly changed in meaning.

distortion *noun* distorting; impaired quality of sound, etc.

distract *verb* 1 (**distract someone from something**) to divert their attention from it. 2 to entertain or amuse. 3 to confuse, worry, or anger. [from Latin *distrahere*, to draw apart]

distracted *adj.* 1 diverted from the main topic of attention. 2 confused, troubled.

distracting *adj.* diverting one's attention from the main topic.

distraction *noun* 1 something that diverts the attention. 2 an amusement; recreation. 3 anxiety; anger. 4 madness.

distrain *verb Legal* to seize (eg property) as, or in order to force, payment of a debt. [from Old French *destraindre*]

distraint *noun Legal* seizure of property or goods in order to meet a debt or obligation.

distrait *adj. literary* thinking of other things. [from French *distrait*]

distraught *adj.* in an extremely troubled state of mind. [a form of DISTRACT]

distress — *noun* 1 mental or emotional pain. 2 financial difficulty; hardship. 3 great danger; peril: *in distress.* — *verb* to cause distress to; to upset. [from Old French *destresse*]

distressed *adj.* 1 suffering distress. 2 *said of furniture or fabric* given an antique appearance; artificially aged.

distressing *adj.* causing distress or emotional pain.

distribute *verb* 1 to give out. 2 to supply or deliver (goods). 3 to spread out widely; to disperse. [from Latin *distribuere*]

distribution *noun* 1 the process of distributing or being distributed. 2 the location or pattern of things spread out. 3 *Statistics* a set of measurements or values, together with the observed or predicted frequencies with which they occur. Such information is often presented in the form of a graph.

distributive *adj.* 1 relating to distribution. 2 *Grammar, said of a word* referring individually to all members of a group, as do the words *each, every.*

distributor *noun* 1 a person or company that distributes goods. 2 a device in the ignition system of a car or other motor vehicle that directs pulses of high-voltage electricity from the induction coil to the spark plugs in the cylinders of the engine.

district *noun* an area or region, especially one forming an administrative or geographical unit. [from Latin *districtus*, jurisdiction]

district attorney *North Amer., esp. US* a lawyer employed by a district to conduct prosecutions.

district nurse a nurse who visits patients in their homes to give them treatment.

District of Columbia POP (1990) 589 000, a federal district in E USA, co-extensive with the city of Washington. AREA 174sq km/67sq mi. It was established in 1790–1, its land taken from Maryland and Virginia.

distrust — *verb* to have no trust in; to doubt. — *noun* suspicion; lack of trust.

distrustful *adj.* having no trust in someone or something; suspicious.

disturb *verb* 1 to interrupt. 2 to inconvenience. 3 to upset the arrangement or order of. 4 to upset the peace of mind of. [from Latin *disturbare*]

disturbance *noun* 1 an outburst of noisy or violent behaviour. 2 an interruption. 3 an act of disturbing or process of being disturbed.

disturbed *adj.* *Psychol.* emotionally upset or confused.

disturbing *adj.* causing anxiety; unsettling.

disunite *verb* to drive apart; to cause disagreement or conflict between or within.

disunity *noun* lack of unity or agreement.

disuse *noun* the state of no longer being used, practised, or observed; neglect.

disused *adj.* no longer used; obsolete.

disyllabic *adj.*, *said of a word* having two syllables.

disyllable *noun* a word of two syllables. [from Greek *di-*, twice + SYLLABLE]

ditch — *noun* a narrow channel dug in the ground for drainage or irrigation, or as a boundary. — *verb* *slang* to get rid of; to abandon. [from Anglo-Saxon *dic*]

dither — *verb* *intrans.* (**dithered, dithering**) to act in a nervously uncertain manner; to waver. — *noun* a state of nervous indecision. [from Middle English *didderen*]

ditherer *noun* a person who dithers or is indecisive.

dithery *adj.*, *said of a person* dithering; indecisive.

ditsy *adj.* *North Amer. colloq.* scatterbrained; flighty. [perhaps a mixture of DOTTY and DIZZY]

ditto — *noun* (PL. **dittos**) *noun* the same thing; the above; that which has just been said. — *adv.* likewise; the same. [from Latin *dictum*, said]

ditto marks marks (”) written immediately below a word, etc in a list to mean 'same as above'.

ditty *noun* (PL. **ditties**) a short simple song or poem. [from Latin *dictare*, to dictate or compose]

diuretic — *noun* *Medicine* a drug or other substance that increases the volume of urine produced and excreted, eg coffee, beer, and many drugs that are prescribed to reduce oedema (water retention in the body tissues) or to treat hypertension (high blood pressure). — *adj.*, *said of a substance* increasing the production and excretion of urine. [from Greek *dia*, through + *ouron*, urine]

diurnal *adj.* *formal*, *technical* 1 daily. 2 during the day. 3 *said of animals* active during the day. 4 *said of flowers* open during the day. [from Latin *diurnus*]

diurnally *adv.* *formal*, *technical* during the day.

diva *noun* (PL. **divas, dive**) a great female singer, especially in opera. [from Latin *diva*, goddess]

divalent *adj.* *Chem.*, *said of an atom* able to combine with two atoms of hydrogen or the equivalent. [from DI- + VALENCY]

Divali *or* **Diwali** *noun* the Hindu festival of lights, held in October or November in honour of Lakshmi, goddess of wealth and good fortune. During the four to five days of the festival, houses are lit by oil lamps, ornate patterns are drawn on the floor near the door, and presents are given to children. [from Hindi]

divan *noun* 1 a sofa with no back or sides. 2 a bed without a headboard or footboard. [from Persian *diwan*, long seat]

dive¹ — *verb* *intrans.* 1 to leap head first into water. 2 to become submerged. 3 to fall steeply through the air. 4 to throw oneself to the side or to the ground. 5 to move quickly and suddenly out of sight. — *noun* 1 an act of diving. 2 *slang* any dirty or disreputable place, especially a bar or club. 3 *Boxing slang* a faked knockout: *take a dive*. — **dive into something** 1 to plunge one's hands (eg into a bag). 2 to involve oneself enthusiastically in an undertaking. [from Anglo-Saxon *dyfan*]

dive² see DIVA.

dive-bomb *verb* *trans.*, *intrans.* to bomb while diving in an aircraft.

dive-bomber *noun* an aeroplane that releases a bomb while diving.

dive-bombing *noun* bombing from a diving aircraft.

diver *noun* 1 a person who dives. 2 a person who swims or works underwater. 3 a large diving bird, native to northern waters of the northern hemisphere, and having plumage with fine contrasting patterns. It feeds mainly on fish, and only comes ashore to breed.

diverge *verb* *intrans.* 1 to separate and go in different directions. 2 to differ. 3 (**diverge from something**) to depart or deviate (eg from a usual course). [from Latin *di-*, apart + *vergere*, to turn]

divergence *noun* separation; deviation.

divergent *adj.* separating; going in different directions.

diverging lens *Physics* a lens that causes light rays to diverge (spread out), eg a concave lens.

divers *adj.* *old use*, *literary* various; many different. [etymology as for DIVERSE]

diverse *adj.* 1 various; assorted. 2 different; dissimilar. [from Latin *diversus*, turned different ways]

diversification *noun* engaging in different activities; branching out.

diversify *verb* (**diversifies, diversified**) 1 *trans.*, *intrans.* to make or become diverse. 2 *intrans.* to engage in new and different activities; to branch out.

diversion *noun* 1 the act of diverting; the state of being diverted. 2 a detour from a usual route. 3 something intended to draw attention away. 4 amusement. [from Latin *diversio*]

diversionary *adj.* intended to cause a diversion.

diversity *noun* variety in kind; being varied or different.

divert *verb* 1 to cause to change direction. 2 to draw away (especially attention). 3 to amuse. [from Latin *divertere*, to turn aside]

diverticular *adj.* *Medicine* relating to diverticula.

diverticulitis *noun* *Medicine* inflammation of one or more diverticula.

diverticulum *noun* (PL. **diverticula**) *Medicine* a pouch formed at a weak point in the muscular wall of the alimentary canal, especially the colon.

divertimento *noun* (PL. **divertimenti, divertimentos**) a light musical composition intended primarily for entertainment. The term originated in the 18c, and was applied to works consisting of a suite of movements for orchestra or chamber ensemble, eg by Mozart and his contemporaries. [from Italian *divertimento*, entertainment, amusement]

divest *verb* 1 to undress (oneself or another). 2 (**divest someone of something**) to take it from them. [from Latin *de-*, away from + *vestire*, to clothe]

divestment *noun* divesting; depriving of possession.

divide — *verb* 1 *trans.*, *intrans.* to split up or separate into parts. 2 (*also* **divide something up**) to share. 3 **a** to determine how many times one number is contained in (another). **b** *intrans.* *said of a number* to be a number of times greater or smaller than another: *3 divides into 9*. 4 to cause disagreement among; to set at odds. 5 to serve as a boundary between. — *noun* 1 a disagreement; a gap or split. 2 *North Amer.*, *esp. US* a ridge of high land between two rivers. [from Latin *dividere*, to force apart]

dividend *noun* 1 a portion of a company's profits paid to a shareholder. 2 a benefit: *Meeting her would pay dividends*. 3 *Maths.* a number divided by another number. [from Latin *dividendum*, what is to be divided]

dividers *pl. noun* a V-shaped device with movable arms, used in geometry, etc for measuring.

Divina Commedia see DIVINE COMEDY.

divination *noun* 1 the practice of foretelling the future (as if) by supernatural means. 2 insight. 3 a guess. [from DIVINE]

divine — *adj.* 1 of, from, or relating to God or a god. 2 *colloq.* extremely pleasant or beautiful; excellent. — *verb* 1 to foretell; to learn of by intuition; to guess. 2 *trans.*, *intrans.* to search for (underground water) with a divining-rod. — *noun* a member of the clergy expert in theology. [from Latin *divinus*, from *divus*, a god]

Divine Comedy (Divina Commedia) a poem by Dante (c.1300). It is composed in *terza rima* and consists of the *Inferno*, the *Purgatorio*, and the *Paradiso*, describing how the poet has visions of hell, purgatory, and heaven.

divinely *adv.* 1 in divine terms. 2 *colloq.* extremely finely or well: *she sang divinely*.

Divine Office *or* **Holy Office** the prayers which had to be said every day by priests and devotees of the pre-Reformation Western Church, and which are still said in the Roman Catholic Church. The practice dates from early monasticism, and derives from Jewish tradition.

Divine Right of Kings (13–17c) the concept of the divinely-ordained authority of monarchs, widely held in the medieval and early modern periods, and often associated with the absolutism of Louis XIV of France and the assertions of the Stuarts.

diving *noun* the activity or sport of plunging into water, especially from a platform or board at the side of a swimming-pool.
◇ At competitive level, the most common form is by jumping from an elevated rigid or sprung board into a swimming pool, performing a variety of twists and somersaults. Marks are gained for style, and for successfully completing the dive, based on its level of difficulty. Springboard events take place from a board 3m above the water; platform diving is from a rigid board 10m above the water.

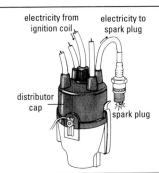

electricity from ignition coil

electricity to spark plug

distributor cap

spark plug

distributor

diving-bell *noun* a large hollow bottomless underwater container pumped full of air, to which an unequipped diver returns to take in oxygen.

diving-board *noun* a narrow platform from which swimmers can dive into a pool, etc.

diving-suit *noun* a diver's waterproof suit, especially one with a helmet and heavy boots for walking on the sea-bottom, etc.

divining-rod *noun* a stick, especially of hazel, held near the ground when divining for water, (allegedly) twitching when a discovery is made.

divinity *noun* (PL. **divinities**) 1 theology. 2 a god. 3 the state of being God or a god. [from DIVINE]

divisible *adj.* able to be divided.

division *noun* 1 the act of dividing; the state of being divided. 2 something that divides or separates; a gap or barrier. 3 one of the parts into which something is divided; a major unit of an organization, eg an army or police force. 4 *Maths.* the process of determining how many times one number (the *divisor*) is contained in another (the *dividend*). 5 a formal vote in Parliament. 6 *Bot.* in the plant kingdom, one of the major groups used for classification, corresponding to a phylum in the animal kingdom, and subdivided into classes, eg Bryophyta (mosses and liverworts).

divisional *adj.* relating to or belonging to a division or section, especially of a business or organization: *divisional headquarters*.

Divisional Court in England and Wales, a court attached to each of the three divisions of the High Court. Each Divisional Court is presided over by three judges and hears appeals from the relevant division. In addition, the Divisional Court of the Queen's Bench Division exercises supervisory jurisdiction over junior courts and tribunals.

Divisionism a technique in painting by which small patches or spots of pure colour are placed close together so that they appear to mix not on the palette or canvas, but in the eye of the viewer. It was developed systematically by some of the French Post-Impressionists, notably Georges Seurat, and labelled *Neoimpressionism* by the French critic Félix Fénéon (1861–1944). See also POINTILLISM.

division sign *noun* the symbol ÷ representing division in calculations.

divisive *adj.* tending to cause disagreement or conflict. [from DIVIDE]

divisiveness *noun* being divisive; a tendency to cause disagreement.

divisor *noun Maths.* a number by which another number is divided. [from Latin *divisor*, divider]

divorce — *noun* 1 the legal ending of a marriage. 2 a complete separation. — *verb* 1 *trans., intrans.* to legally end marriage to (someone). 2 to separate. [from Latin *divortere*, to leave one's husband]

◇ In England and Wales, divorce is granted if it is shown that there has been irretrievable breakdown of the marriage. The person applying for a divorce (the petitioner) must support the application with evidence of one of five facts: that the other party (the respondent) has committed adultery, has displayed unreasonable behaviour, is guilty of desertion, has lived apart from the petitioner for two years and consents to the divorce, or has lived apart for five years.

divorcé *noun* a divorced man.

divorced *adj., said of a partner in marriage* separated by divorce.

divorcée *noun* a divorced woman.

divot *noun* a clump of grass and earth removed, especially by the blade of a golf club. [from Scot. *divot*]

Divrigi the chief town of Divrigi district, central Turkey, near the Caltisuyu R. It has a notable 13c mosque and hospital complex which is a World Heritage site.

divulge *verb* to make known; to reveal. [from Latin *divulgare*, to publish widely]

divulgence *noun* making known; disclosing a secret, etc.

divvy *slang* — *noun* (PL. **divvies**) a dividend or share. — *verb* (**divvies**, **divvied**) (*also* **divvy up**) to divide or share.

Diwali see DIVALI.

Dix, Otto (1891–1969) German Realist painter, born in Gera-Unternhaus. He is best known for his realistic etchings and paintings of World War I casualties, and for his various portrayals of Berlin prostitutes in the post-War period. His work was disapproved of by the Nazi Party, and declared to be 'degenerate'. After World War II he painted mostly religious subjects.

Dixie 1 a popular name for the Southern Confederate states of the USA. 2 a flat marshy agricultural area in N Florida, USA.

dixie *noun* a large metal cooking-pot or kettle. [perhaps from Hindi *degci*]

Dixieland a style of jazz derived from the 'classic' New Orleans school in the early 20c, and also associated with white musicians who based their music on that of the Original Dixieland Jazz Band. Louis Armstrong, Sidney Bechet, Jelly Roll Morton, and Earl Hines were Dixieland performers.

DIY *abbrev.* do-it-yourself.

dizzily *adv.* in a dizzy or bewildered way.

dizziness *noun* a dizzy or bewildered state.

dizzy — *adj.* (**dizzier**, **dizziest**) 1 experiencing or causing a spinning sensation causing loss of balance: *feel dizzy / dizzy heights*. 2 *colloq.* silly; not reliable or responsible. 3 *colloq.* bewildered. — *verb* (**dizzies**, **dizzied**) 1 to make dizzy. 2 to bewilder. [from Anglo-Saxon *dysig*, foolish]

DJ *abbrev.* 1 *slang* dinner jacket. 2 disc jockey.

Dja Faunal Reserve a game reserve which borders on the Dja R in Cameroon, Africa. It is a World Heritage site.

Djakarta see JAKARTA.

Djem, El the world's most intact example of a Roman amphitheatre, situated in the present-day village of El Djem in W Tunisia. It is one of the few surviving relics of the ancient city of Thysdrus, and had a capacity for 35 000 people. It is a World Heritage site.

Djemila the former Roman garrison of Cuicul in N Algeria. It was founded in the late 1c, spread and flourished in the 3c–4c, and had declined by the 6c. The ruins include temples, forums, thermal baths, and Christian basilicas. It is a World Heritage site.

Djenné a town in S Mali, formerly (16c–18c) an important centre of trade and Muslim learning. It has an ancient mosque which has been restored several times. The old town is a World Heritage site.

Djibouti, official name **Republic of Djibouti**, Arabic **Jumhouriya Djibouti** POP (1992e) 467 000, a republic in NE Africa, divided into five districts. AREA 23 310sq km/8 998sq mi. It is bounded NW, W, and S by Ethiopia, SE by Somalia, and N by the Gulf of Aden. CAPITAL Djibouti. CHIEF TOWNS Tadjoura, Dikhil, Obock, Ali-Sabieh. TIME ZONE GMT + 3. The chief ethnic group is Somali (60%); Islam is the chief religion. OFFICIAL LANGUAGES Arabic, French. CURRENCY the Djibouti franc. PHYSICAL DESCRIPTION a series of plateaux dropping down from mountains to flat low-lying rocky desert; 350km/220mi of fertile coastal strip around the Gulf of Tadjoura, which juts deep into the country; highest point, Moussa Ali, rising to 2 020m in the N. CLIMATE semi-arid with a hot season (May–Sep); very high temperatures on coastal plain all year round, maximum average daily temperature dropping below 30°C for only three months (Dec–Feb); slightly lower humidity and temperatures in the interior highlands (over 600m); rainfall average 130mm annually at Djibouti. HISTORY French colonial interest in the mid 19c, setting up French Somaliland in 1896; French Overseas Territory following World War II; French Territory of the Afars and the Issas in 1967; gained independence in 1977; a new constitution introduced in 1992 permits a multiparty system. GOVERNMENT governed by a President (elected for six years), a legislative chamber of Deputies (elected for five years), an executive Prime Minister, and a Council. ECONOMY crop-based agriculture is possible only with irrigation; date palms, fruit, vegetables; raising of livestock among the nomadic population; some fishing; a small industrial sector; tourism. The economy is based on the port of Djibouti, which is well situated to handle ships using the Suez Canal and Red Sea; it was badly affected by local wars, and by the closure of the Suez Canal between 1967 and 1975.

Djibouti

Djibouti POP (1984e) 180 000, the free-port capital of Djibouti, situated in the S of the country on a coral peninsula 565km/351mi NE of Addis Ababa (Ethiopia). Built between 1886 and 1900 in Arab style, the city became the official port of Ethiopia in 1897.

Djilas, Milovan (1911–) Yugoslav politician and writer, born in Montenegro. A lifelong friend of Tito, his wartime exploits as a partisan led to his rise in government. He was discredited and imprisoned for his outspoken criticism of the communist system as practised in Yugoslavia, but was released under amnesty in late 1966. His books include *The New Class* (1957) and *Conversations with Stalin* (1962).

djinn, and **djinni**. See JINNI.

DK *abbrev., as an international vehicle mark* Denmark.

dl *abbrev.* decilitre.

DLitt or **DLit** *abbrev. Doctor litterarum litteraturae* (Latin), Doctor of Letters or Literature.

DM *abbrev.* Deutschmark.

DMs *abbrev. colloq.* Doc Martens.

DMus *abbrev.* Doctor of Music.

DMZ *abbrev.* demilitarized zone.

DNA *abbrev.* deoxyribonucleic acid.

DNB *abbrev.* Dictionary of National Biography.

Dnepropetrovsk, formerly **Ekaterinoslav** (to 1926) 1 POP (1990e) 1.2m, the industrial river-port capital of Dnepropetrovsk region, Ukraine. It lies on the R Dnieper, and was founded in 1783 on the site of a Cossack village. NOTABLE FEATURE cathedral (1830–5). 2 a region in the Ukraine with the city of Dnepropetrovsk as its capital.

Dnestr, River see DNIESTER, RIVER.

Dnieper, River, Russian **Dnepr**, ancient **Borysthenes** the third longest river in Europe, length c.2 200km/1 400mi. Rising in the S Valdayskaya Vozvyshennost Range in Russia it flows S and W past Smolensk, turns S at Orsha, and flows through Belorussia. It then makes a wide bend through the Ukraine to enter the Black Sea at Kherson. Water from the Kakhovka Reservoir irrigates large areas of the lower Dnieper Basin and the plain of N Crimea.

Dniester, River or **Dnestr**, Polish **Dniest** a river in Ukraine and Moldavia, rising in the Carpathian Mts. Flowing 1 400km/870mi generally SE, it enters the Dnestrovskiy Liman, a N inlet of the Black Sea, SW of Odessa. It formed the USSR–Romania border between 1918 and 1940. From Dec to Mar the river freezes over.

D-notice *noun* a notice sent by the government to newspapers asking them not to publish certain information for reasons of security. [from defence notice]

do¹ — *verb* (**does**, **doing**; PAST TENSE **did**; PAST PARTICIPLE **done**) **1** to carry out, perform, or commit. **2** to finish or complete. **3** *trans., intrans.* to be enough or suitable: *that will do for me / that will do me.* **4** to work at or study. **5** *intrans.* to be in a particular state: *Business is doing well.* **6** to put in order or arrange. **7** *intrans.* to act or behave. **8** to provide as a service: *do lunches.* **9** to bestow (honour, etc). **10** to cause or produce. **11** to travel (a distance); to travel at (a speed). **12** *colloq.* to be an improvement or enhancement to: *this dress doesn't do much for my figure.* **13** *colloq.* to cheat. **14** *colloq.* to copy the behaviour of; to mimic. **15** to visit as a tourist. **16** *colloq.* to ruin: *now he's done it!* **17** *colloq.* to assault or injure: *tell me, or I'll do you.* **18** *colloq.* to spend (time) in prison. **19** *colloq.* to convict. **20** *intrans. colloq.* to happen: *there was nothing doing.* **21** *slang* to take (drugs). — *verb aux.* **1** used in questions and negative statements or commands: *do you smoke? / I don't like wine / don't do that!* **2** used to avoid repetition of a verb: *she eats as much as I do.* **3** used for emphasis: *she does know you've arrived.* — *noun* (PL. **dos**, **do's**) *colloq.* **1** a party or other gathering. **2** something done as a rule or custom: *dos and don'ts.* **3** a violent scene; a fracas.

— **be done for** to face ruin or death.
be or **have done with something** or **someone** to have finished with or to have dealt with them.
could do with something or **someone** would benefit from having them.
do away with someone or **something** **1** to murder them. **2** to abolish an institution, etc.
do someone or **something down** to speak of them as if unimportant or not very good.
do for someone *colloq.* to do household cleaning for them on a regular basis.
do someone in *colloq.* **1** to kill them. **2** to exhaust them.

do something out to clear out a room, etc; to decorate it.
do someone out of something to deprive them of it, especially by trickery.
do someone over *slang* **1** to rob them. **2** to attack or injure them.
do something up *colloq.* **1** to repair, clean, or improve the decoration of a building, etc. **2** to fasten it; to tie or wrap it up.
do oneself up to dress up.
do without something to manage without it.
have or **be to do with someone** or **something** **1** *said of a thing, event, etc* to be related to or connected with something else: *that has a great deal to do with your question / it has nothing to do with me.* **2** *said of a person* to be partly or wholly responsible for something: *I had nothing to do with the arrangement.*
[from Anglo-Saxon *don*]

do² same as DOH.

do. *abbrev.* ditto.

DOA *abbrev.* dead on arrival.

doable *adj.* able to be done.

Dobbin, Col William the loyal friend of George Osborne in William Makepeace Thackeray's *Vanity Fair*, who is secretly in love with George's wife, Amelia.

Doberman pinscher or **Doberman** *noun* a large breed of dog with a smooth black-and-tan coat. [from *Dobermann*, breeder's name + German *Pinscher*, terrier]

Dobzhansky, Theodosius (1900–75) US geneticist, born in Nemirov, Ukraine. He studied in Kiev and taught genetics in Leningrad before emigrating to the USA in 1927. There he taught at the California Institute of Technology, Columbia University, Rockefeller University in New York, and the University of California. He showed that the genetic variability within a population is large, and includes many potentially lethal genes (recessives) which nevertheless confer versatility when the population is exposed to environmental change; he went on to apply his ideas to the concept of race in man.

doc *noun colloq.* a doctor.

docile *adj.* easy to manage or control; submissive. [from Latin *docilis*, easily taught]

docilely *adv.* with a docile or willing manner.

docility *noun* a docile manner.

dock¹ — *noun* **1** a harbour where ships are loaded, unloaded, and repaired. **2** (**docks**) the area surrounding this. — *verb trans., intrans.* **1** to bring or come into a dock. **2** *said of space vehicles* to link up in space.
— **in dock** being repaired.
[from Old Dutch *docke*]

dock² *verb* **1** to cut off all or part of (an animal's tail). **2** to make deductions from (especially pay); to deduct (an amount). [from Middle English *dok*]

dock³ *noun* a weed with large broad leaves and a deep root. [from Anglo-Saxon *docce*]

dock⁴ *noun* the enclosure in a court of law where the accused sits or stands. [from Flemish *dok*, cage, sty]

docker *noun* a labourer who loads and unloads ships.

docket — *noun* any label or note accompanying a parcel, eg detailing contents or recording receipt. — *verb* (**docketed**, **docketing**) to fix a label to; to record the contents or delivery of.

dockyard *noun* a shipyard.

Doc Martens *trademark* a make of lace-up leather boots with light, thick resilient soles.

doctor — *noun* **1** a person trained and qualified to practise medicine. **2** a person holding a doctorate. — *verb* (**doctored**, **doctoring**) **1** to falsify (eg information); to tamper with; to drug (food or drink). **2** *colloq.* to sterilize or castrate (an animal).

3 *often facetious* to give medical treatment to. [from Latin *doctor*, teacher]

doctoral *adj.* relating to a doctorate.

doctorate *noun* a high academic degree, awarded especially for research.

Doctor Faustus, The Tragical History of a play by Chrisopher Marlowe (c.1594). Written in blank verse, it tells of a pact made by Dr Faustus to sell his soul to the Devil in exchange for 24 hours' magical power.

Doctor Zhivago **1** a novel by Boris Pasternak (1957). It describes the life of a man in the wake of the Russian Revolution (1917). It was banned in Russia until 1987. **2** a film (1965) directed by David Lean.

doctrinaire *adj. derog.* adhering rigidly to theories or principles, often regardless of practicalities or appropriateness.

Doctrinaires (19c) in France, a group of moderate constitutional liberals who shared the views of François Guizot. They advocated constitutional monarchy and elevated their policy of the *juste milieu*, or 'middle road', to a complete political philosophy.

doctrinal *adj.* relating to or consisting of doctrine.

doctrine *noun* a thing or things taught, especially (any one of) a set of religious or political beliefs. [from Latin *doctrina*, teaching]

docudrama *noun* a play or film based on real events and characters. [a contraction of *documentary drama*]

document — *noun* **1** any piece of writing of an official nature, eg a certificate. **2** *Comput.* a file of text produced and read by a computer, especially a word processor. — *verb* **1** to record, especially in written form. **2** to provide written evidence to support or prove. [from Latin *documentum*, lesson, proof]

documentary — *noun* (PL. **documentaries**) a film or television or radio programme presenting real people in real situations. — *adj.* **1** connected with, or consisting of, documents. **2** of the nature of a documentary; undramatised.

documentation *noun* documents or documentary evidence, or the provision or collection of these.

dodder *verb intrans.* (**doddered**, **doddering**) to move in an unsteady, trembling fashion as a result of old age. [variant of old word *dadder*]

dodderer *noun* a doddering person.

doddery *adj.* tending to dodder; unsteady.

doddle *noun colloq.* something easily done or achieved.

dodecagon *noun* a flat geometric figure with 12 sides and angles. [from Greek *dodeka*, twelve + *gonia*, angle]

dodecahedron *noun* a solid geometric figure with twelve faces. [from Greek *dodeka*, twelve + *hedra*, seat]

Dodecanese, Greek **Dhodhekanisos** a group of Greek islands in the SE Aegean Sea, Greece, off the SW coast of Turkey. It consists of 12 islands and several islets. AREA 2 682sq km/1 035sq mi. MAIN ISLANDS Rhodes (largest island), Cos, Patmos. HISTORY under Turkish rule from the 16c; passed to Italy in 1912; part of Greece since 1947. ECONOMY fruit, olives, sponges; there are several major tourist centres. NOTABLE FEATURES ancient sites from the Hellenistic and Roman periods include the Asklepieion on Cos, the Acropolis of Rhodes, and the Acropolis of Lindos. [from Greek *dhodhekanisos*, twelve islands]

dodge — *verb* **1** to avoid by moving quickly away, especially sideways. **2** to escape or avoid by cleverness or deceit. — *noun* **1** a sudden movement aside. **2** a trick to escape or avoid something.

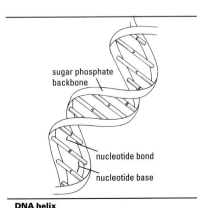

sugar phosphate backbone

nucleotide bond

nucleotide base

DNA helix

Dodgems *noun trademark* a fairground amusement consisting of a rink in which drivers of small electric cars try to bump each other.

dodger *noun* a shirker; a trickster.

dodgy *adj.* (**dodgier, dodgiest**) *colloq.* **1** difficult or risky. **2** untrustworthy; dishonest, or dishonestly obtained. **3** unstable; slightly broken.

dodo *noun* (PL. **dodos, dodoes**) **1** a large flightless bird of the pigeon family, about the size of a turkey, that once lived on the island of Mauritius, and became extinct around the middle of the 17c. **2** *colloq.* any old-fashioned person or thing. **3** *colloq.* a stupid person.
— **as dead as a dodo** *colloq.* **1** extinct. **2** out-of-date; obsolete.
[from Portuguese *doudo*, silly]

dodo

Dodoma 1 POP (1988) 204 000, the new capital of Tanzania, E Africa, situated in the central area of the country. **2** a region in central Tanzania with Dodoma as its capital.

DOE *abbrev.* Department of the Environment.

doe *noun* (PL. **does, doe**) an adult female rabbit, hare, or small deer, eg the fallow deer. [from Anglo-Saxon *da*]

doer *noun* a person who does something; an active person.

does see DO.

doesn't *contr.* does not.

doff *verb old use, literary* to take off (a piece of clothing); to lift (one's hat) in greeting. [from DO[1] + OFF]

dog — *noun* **1** any carnivorous mammal belonging to the family Canidae, which includes the wolves, jackals, and foxes. Dogs have strong jaws and sharp teeth, and they are fast runners and good hunters. **2** any of many different breeds of a domestic species of this family (*Canis familiaris*). **3** the male of any such animal. **4** any of various mammals of other families, eg prairie dog. **5** a mechanical gripping device. **6** *offensive slang* an unattractive woman. **7** *colloq.* a fellow or rogue. — *verb* (**dogged, dogging**) **1** to follow very closely; to track. **2** to trouble or plague.
— **a dog's breakfast** *or* **dinner** *colloq.* an untidy mess; a shambles.
a dog's life a life of misery.
like a dog's dinner *colloq.* dressed smartly or showily.
[from Anglo-Saxon *docga*]
◇ The dog was probably the first animal to be domesticated by humans, and it seems likely that it was used for hunting and as protection against wild animals. The origins of the domestic dog are uncertain, although it is thought that it may be descended from the wolf. Dogs have blurred eyesight, and they can only see in black and white, but this is more than compensated for by their very keen sense of smell, which is sometimes exploited for police detection work, eg drug searches, and mountain rescue operations. There are now over 100 breeds of domestic dog, usually classified as sporting, non-sporting, hounds, terriers, working, or toy breeds.

Dogberry one of the constables in Shakespeare's *Much Ado About Nothing*, whose attempted erudition results in a series of misunderstandings and malapropisms.

dogcart *noun* a two-wheeled horse-drawn passenger carriage with seats back-to-back.

dog-collar *noun* **1** a collar for a dog. **2** *colloq.* a close-fitting white collar worn by members of the clergy.

dog days the hottest period of the year, when the Dogstar rises and sets with the sun.

doge *noun* the chief magistrate in the former republics of Venice and Genoa. [from Italian dialect *doge*, duke]

dog-eared *adj.*, *said of a book* with its pages turned down at the corners; shabby; scruffy.

dog-end *noun slang* a cigarette end.

Doge's Palace the residence of the former Doges (chief magistrates) of Venice. Although parts of the structure date from the 12c, the loggias and marble façade of the present-day building are renaissance additions. It is the repository of many art treasures.

dogfight *noun* **1** a battle at close quarters between two fighter aircraft. **2** a fight between dogs. **3** any violent fight.

dogfish *noun* any of various kinds of small shark.

dogged *adj.* determined; resolute.

doggedly *adv.* in a dogged or resolute way.

doggedness *noun* being dogged or resolute.

Dogger Bank a large sandbank forming the shallowest part of the North Sea. It lies c.200km/125mi E of the Cleveland coast and c.250km/155mi N of the Norfolk coast, England. Its depth varies from 17m to 37m and it is an important breeding ground for North Sea fish.

doggerel — *noun* **1** badly written poetry. **2** poetry with an irregular rhyming pattern for

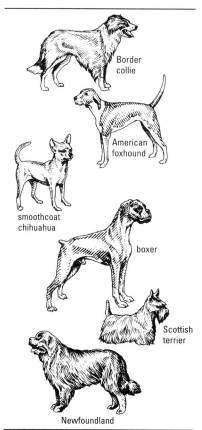

Border collie

American foxhound

smoothcoat chihuahua

boxer

Scottish terrier

Newfoundland

dog types

dogfish

comic effect. — *adj.* of poor quality. [from Middle English *dogerel*, worthless]

doggo
— **lie doggo** *old colloq. use* to hide; to lie low. [probably from DOG]

doggy — *adj.* (**doggier, doggiest**) *colloq.* **1** of, like, or relating to dogs. **2** fond of dogs. — *noun* (*also* **doggie**) (PL. **doggies**) a child's word for a dog.

doggy-bag *noun* a bag in which a customer at a restaurant can take home uneaten food.

doggy-paddle *or* **dog-paddle** — *noun* a basic swimming stroke with short paddling movements like a dog's. — *verb intrans.* to swim using this stroke.

doghouse
— **in the doghouse** *colloq.* out of favour.

dog in the manger a person who has no need of something and refuses to let others use it.

dog-in-the-manger *adj.* characteristic of a dog in the manger; possessively selfish.

dogleg *noun* a sharp bend, especially on a golf course.

dogma *noun* **1** a belief or principle laid down by an authority as unquestionably true; such beliefs or principles in general. **2** *colloq.* an opinion arrogantly stated. [from Greek *dogma*, opinion]

dogmatic *adj.* **1** *said of an opinion* forcefully and arrogantly stated as if unquestionable. **2** *said of a person* tending to make such statements of opinion.

dogmatism *noun* the quality of being, or the tendency to be, dogmatic.

dogmatist *noun* a person who is dogmatic or given to positive assertions.

dogmatize *or* **dogmatise** *verb intrans.* to state one's opinions dogmatically.

do-gooder *noun colloq.* an enthusiastically helpful person, especially one whose help is unwanted or impractical.

dog rose a European wild rose with pink or white flowers.

dogs *pl. noun* (**the dogs**) *colloq.* greyhound racing.
— **go to the dogs** *colloq.* to deteriorate greatly.

dogsbody *noun* (PL. **dogsbodies**) *colloq.* a person who does menial tasks for someone else.

Dog Star *Astron.* see SIRIUS.

dog-tired *adj. colloq.* extremely tired.

dogtrot *noun* a gentle trotting pace.

dogwood *noun* a European shrub with small white flowers and purple berries.

doh *noun* the first note of the scale in the sol-fa system of music notation. [from Italian *doh*]

Doha, Arabic **Ad Dawhah** POP (1986) 217 000, the seaport capital of Qatar, on the E coast of the Qatar Peninsula, in the Arabian Gulf. Reclamation of the West Bay has created New Doha. The city is a chief commercial and communications centre. NOTABLE FEATURE old Turkish fort (1850).

doily *or* **doyley** *noun* (PL. **doilies, doyleys**) a small decorative napkin of lace or lace-like paper laid on plates under sandwiches, cakes, etc. [named after *Doily*, London draper]

doings *sing. noun colloq.* the thing whose name cannot be remembered; a thingummy.

Doisy, Edward Adelbert (1893–) US biochemist, born in Hume, Illinois. Director of the Department of Biochemistry at St Mary's Hospital, St Louis (1924–65), he studied reproduction and isolated important hormones. In 1939 he isolated and characterized vitamin K_1 (from alfalfa) and vitamin K_2 (from fish meal); for this work he shared the 1943 Nobel Prize for Physiology or Medicine with Carl Dam.

do-it-yourself *noun* (ABBREV. DIY) the practice of doing one's own household repairs, etc without professional help.

Dolby *or* **Dolby system** a system of noise reduction in magnetic audio tape-recording, consisting of an electronic circuit that is used to reduce the background hissing sound heard during replay, and to improve the quality of stereophonic sound in cinemas. [named after the US engineer Raymond Dolby]

dolce *adj., adv. Mus.* to be sung or played gently or sweetly. [Italian, = sweet, from Latin *dulcis*]

Dolce Vita, La (The Sweet Life) an Italian–French film directed by Federico Fellini (1960). It depicts a week of caricatured, decadent, high-society life in modern Rome, through the eyes of a gossip columnist (played by Marcello Mastroianni).

Dol Common the bawdy, witty prostitute who conspires with Subtle and Face in Ben Jonson's *The Alchemist.*

doldrums *pl. noun* (**the doldrums**) **1** a depressed mood; low spirits. **2** a state of inactivity. **3** (*also* **Doldrums**) *Meteorol.* a hot humid region on either side of the Equator, lying between the trade winds of the northern and southern hemispheres, where there is generally little or no wind. [from obsolete *dold*, stupid]

Dole, Elizabeth Hanford (1936–) US public official, born in Salisbury, N Carolina. She became a lawyer in Washington and served in various offices under Presidents Johnson, Nixon, Ford, and Carter. Married to Senator Robert Dole since 1975, she was Secretary of Transportation (1983–7) in the Reagan administration and Secretary of Labor (1989–90) under President Bush, before she became President of the American Red Cross in 1991.

Dole, Robert (1923–) US politician, born in Russell, Kansas. He served in the Kansas state legislature and the House of Representatives before he won a Senate seat in 1968. Married to Elizabeth Dole, he has chaired the Republican national committee, was an unsuccessful Republican nominee for the vice-presidency (1976), and sought the Republican nomination for the presidency in 1988.

dole — *noun colloq.* (**the dole**) unemployment benefit. — *verb intrans.* (**dole something out**) to hand it out or give it out.
— **on the dole** *colloq.* unemployed; receiving unemployment benefit.
[from Anglo-Saxon *dal*, share]

doleful *adj.* sad; expressing or suggesting sadness; mournful. [from Old French *doel*, grief + -FUL]

dolefully *adv.* with a doleful or melancholy manner.

dolefulness *noun* a doleful or melancholy manner.

Dolin, Anton, originally **Patrick Healey-Kay** (1904–83) English dancer and choreographer, born in Slinfold, Sussex. He was a principal with Diaghilev's Ballet Russes from 1924 (with whom he danced in Michel Fokine's *Spectre de la Rose* and George Balanchine's *Le Bal* and *The Prodigal Son*) and with the Vic–Wells Ballet during the 1930s. With Alicia Markova he founded the Markova–Dolin Ballet Company, and from 1950 to 1961 he served as London Festival Ballet's first

artistic director, choreographing for the company. His works include *Rhapsody in Blue* (1928), *Variations for Four* (1957) and *Pas de deux for Four* (1967).

doll — *noun* **1** a toy in the form of a model of a human being, especially a baby. **2** *derog. colloq.* a showy overdressed woman. **3** *slang, often offensive* any girl or woman, especially when considered pretty. **4** *colloq.* a term of endearment, especially for a girl. — *verb* (**doll oneself up**) to dress smartly or showily. [from the name DOLLY]

dollar *noun* (SYMBOL **$**) the standard unit of currency in the US, Canada, Australia, and numerous other countries, divided into 100 cents. [from German *Thaler*, short for *Joachimsthaler*, the name of silver coins from *Joachimsthal* in Bohemia]
◇ The US dollar is the world's most important currency: much international trade is conducted in it and the prices of goods and commodities (notably oil) are often quoted in it. Over half the official reserves of countries are held in dollars, and its value (affected by US economic policy) has an important effect on the economies of other nations.

dollarization *noun* the basing of the value of a country's currency on that of the US dollar.

Dollfuss, Engelbert (1892–1934) Austrian politician, born in Texing. He became Leader of the Christian Socialist Party, and as Chancellor (1932–4) he suspended parliamentary government, drove the socialists into revolt and militarily crushed them (Feb 1934). In Jul 1934, a Nazi putsch in Vienna culminated in his assassination.

dollop *noun colloq.* a small shapeless mass of any semi-solid substance, especially food.

Doll's House, A (Et Dukkehjem) a play by Henrik Ibsen (1879). Apparently concerned with social and feminist issues, it is a realist tragedy about a woman whose wish to establish her independence means forsaking her husband.

Dolly a female first name, from which *doll* is derived. [originally a pet form of DOROTHY, now a pet form of DOLORES or an independent name]

dolly *noun* (PL. **dollies**) **1** *colloq.* a child's name for a doll. **2** *Cinema, Broadcasting* a frame with wheels on which a film or television camera is mounted for moving shots. It permits forward and sideways movement of the point of view during the action of the scene in addition to the pan and tilt of the camera itself. A *dolly shot* is a scene planned to make use of such camera movement.

dolmen *noun* a simple prehistoric monument consisting of a large flat stone supported by several vertical stones. [perhaps from Breton *dol*, table + *men*, stone]

Dolmetsch, (Eugène) Arnold (1858–1940) French-born British musician of Swiss origin, born in Le Mans, and naturalized in 1931. Known for reviving interest in early music and musical instruments, he established workshops at his home in Haslemere, Surrey, and promoted festivals on early music. In 1919 he made the first modern recorder and in 1928 the Dolmetsch Foundation was established to support his work, which was continued by his son Carl (1911–).

dolomite *noun* **1** *Geol.* a mineral composed of calcium magnesium carbonate, formed by the replacement of limestone. **2** a sedimentary carbonate rock containing more than 50 per cent dolomite. [named after the Dolomites, in which it is found]

Dolomites, Italian **Alpi Dolomitiche** an alpine mountain range in NE Italy, rising to 3 342m at Marmolada. It is a limestone formation of jagged outlines and isolated peaks. The range is a major area for walking and climbing; winter sports and health resort centres include Cortina d'Ampezzo and San Martino di Castrozza.

Dolores a female first name, mainly given to Roman Catholics. [of Spanish origin; abbreviated from *Maria de los Dolores*, Mary of Sorrows]

dolorous *adj. literary* causing, involving, or suggesting sorrow or grief. [from DOLOUR]

dolour *noun poetic* sorrow or grief. [from Latin *dolor*, pain]

dolphin *noun* **1** a small toothed whale belonging to the family Delphinidae, and found in seas virtually worldwide, both in deep water and near to coasts. **2** a freshwater (or river) dolphin. [from Greek *delphinos*]
◇ Dolphins live together in schools, and are well known for their grace and playfulness in the water – a school of dolphins will often follow a ship for days. Recent studies have revealed that the dolphin is among the most intelligent of all animals, with a communications system which some scientists believe is a form of language. They can stay submerged for up to 15 minutes, and their sense of hearing is acute, and probably the chief means by which they hunt for food. They feed mainly on fish, and also eat shrimps and cuttlefish. There are several species of dolphin, and they can be distinguished from the porpoises, to which they are related, by their beaked snouts (porpoises have blunt snouts). Like all whales, dolphins give birth to live, fully developed young.

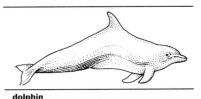

dolphin

dolphinarium *noun* a large open-air aquarium in which dolphins are kept, both for study and to display to the public. [from DOLPHIN + AQUARIUM]

dolt *noun derog.* a stupid person. [from Anglo-Saxon *dol*, stupid]

doltish *adj.* dull; stupid.

DOM *abbrev., as an international vehicle mark* Dominican Republic.

Dom the highest mountain that is entirely in Switzerland. It lies NE of Zermatt, in the Pennine Alps. HEIGHT 4 545m.

-dom *suffix* forming words denoting: **1** a state or rank: *serfdom / dukedom.* **2** an area ruled or governed: *kingdom.* **3** a group of people with a specified characteristic: *officialdom.* [from Anglo-Saxon *dom*, judgement]

Domagk, Gerhard Johannes Paul (1895–1964) German biochemist, born in Lagow (now in Poland). He taught at Greifswald and Münster before becoming Director of the I G Farbenindustrie Laboratory for Experimental Pathology and Bacteriology at Wuppertal-Elberfeld in 1927. His discovery of the chemotherapeutic properties of sulphanilamide ushered in a new age in chemotherapy. In 1939 his original acceptance of the Nobel Prize for Physiology or Medicine was cancelled upon instruction from the German government; he finally received the award, but not the remuneration, in 1947.

domain *noun* **1** the scope of any subject or area of interest. **2** a territory owned or ruled by one person or government. **3** *Maths.* the set of values specified for a given mathematical function. **4** *Physics* in a ferromagnetic substance, eg iron, nickel, a small region within which individual magnetic moments can be aligned, giving that substance permanent magnetic properties. [from French *domaine*]

dome *noun* **1** a roof in the shape of a hemisphere. **2** anything of similar shape. **3** *colloq.* a head. [from Latin *domus*, house]

domed *adj.*, *said of a building* having a dome.

Dome of the Rock a shrine completed in 691 on Mt Moriah, Jerusalem. The shrine, which is built on an octagonal plan and surmounted by a gilded wooden cupola, encloses the holy rock where, according to tradition, Muhammad ascended to heaven and Abraham prepared to sacrifice Isaac.

Dome of the Rock

Domesday Book *or* **Doomsday Book**, a survey of all lands in England, ordered by William the Conqueror in 1086, detailing their value, ownership, etc. See also DOOMSDAY. [from Anglo-Saxon *dom*, judgement]
◇ The survey covered all the lands S of the rivers Ribble and Tees (excluding London and Winchester), and was probably intended to enable the Norman conquerors to exploit their feudal rights and crown lands. The information was arranged by county, and within each county, according to the tenure of the major landowners. The Domesday Book is so called because it was considered to be as authoritative as the Last Judgement or 'doomsday'.

domestic — *adj.* **1** of or relating to the home, the family, or private life. **2** *said of animals* not wild; kept as a pet or farm animal. **3** within or relating to one's country; not foreign: *domestic sales and export sales.* **4** enjoying home life. — *noun* a household servant. [from Latin *domesticus*, from *domus*, house]

domestically *adv.* as regards the home or family.

domesticate *verb* **1** to train (an animal) for life in the company of people. **2** *often facetious* to make used to home life, especially to train in cooking, housework, etc.

domestication *noun* adaptation to home life.

domesticity *noun* home life, or a liking for it.

domestic science training in household skills, especially cooking; home economics.

domicile — *noun* **1** *formal* a house. **2** a legally recognized place of permanent residence. — *verb Legal* to establish in a fixed residence. [from Latin *domicilium*, dwelling]

domiciliary *adj.* relating to people and their homes.

dominance *noun* command or influence over others.

dominant — *adj.* **1** most important, evident, or active; foremost. **2** tending or seeking to command or influence others. **3** *said of a building, etc* overlooking others from an elevated position. **4** *Biol.* denoting a gene, or the characteristics

determined by it, whose phenotype (visible effect) is fully expressed in an individual whether there are two dominant alleles, or one dominant and one recessive allele. **5** denoting a characteristic determined by such a gene. **6** *Biol.* denoting the most prevalent plant or animal species in a particular community or during a particular period, or describing an animal that occupies a superior position within a group of its own kind. — *noun* the fifth note on a musical scale. [from DOMINATE]

dominate *verb trans., intrans.* **1** to have command or influence over (someone). **2** to be the most important, evident, or active of (a group). **3** to enjoy an elevated position over (a place). [from Latin *dominari*, to be master]

dominating *adj.* tending to dominate.

domination *noun* dominating; absolute authority.

domineer *verb intrans.* to behave in an arrogantly dominant way. [etymology as for DOMINATE]

domineering *adj.* overbearing; behaving arrogantly towards others.

Domingo, Placido (1941–) Spanish tenor, born in Madrid. He moved to Mexico with his family and studied piano and conducting there. He made his début as a baritone in 1959, took his first tenor role in 1960, and became a member of the Israeli National Opera (1962–5), then sang in New York (1966), at La Scala (1969), and at Covent Garden (1971). His vocal technique and acting ability have made him one of the world's leading lyric-dramatic tenors, notably in works by Puccini and Verdi, and he has made numerous recordings and film versions of operas.

Dominic, St (c.1170–1221) Spanish founder of the Order of Friars Preachers (1216), born in Calaruega, Old Castile. His rigorously ascetic life was focused on missionary work, notably among Muslims, 'heretics', and the Albigenses of S France, but his memory is stained by his consent to the cruel crusade instigated by Innocent I against the Albigenses, who had murdered his legate, Peter of Castelnau. By the time Dominic died, the Dominican order (based on the Augustine rule) occupied 60 houses, and had spread as far as England, where from their dress the monks were called Black Friars. He was canonized in 1234 by Gregory IX and his feast day is 4 Aug.

Dominic a male first name, mainly given to Roman Catholics. [an English form of Latin *Dominicus*, from *dominus*, lord]

Dominica, French **Dominique**, official name **Commonwealth of Dominica** POP (1991e) 109 000, an independent republic located in the Windward Is, E Caribbean Sea, divided into ten parishes. AREA 751sq km/290sq mi. It is situated between Guadeloupe in the N and Martinique in the S. CAPITAL Roseau. CHIEF TOWNS Portsmouth, Grand Bay. TIME ZONE GMT –4. The population is mainly of African or mixed African–European descent; Roman Catholicism is the main religion. OFFICIAL LANGUAGE English; French is also spoken. CURRENCY E Caribbean dollar, pound sterling, French franc. PHYSICAL DESCRIPTION roughly rectangular in shape, with a deeply-indented coastline; the island is c.50km/30mi long and 26km/16mi wide, rising to 1 447m at Morne Diablotin; volcanic origin, with many fumaroles and sulphur springs; it has a central ridge, with lateral spurs and deep valleys, with several rivers; forestry covers 67% of the land area. CLIMATE warm and humid; average monthly temperatures are 26–32°C; average annual rainfall is 1 750mm on the coast and 6 250mm in the mountains; severe hurricanes in 1979 and 1980 affected the economy. HISTORY discovered by Columbus in 1493; colonization attempts by the French and British in the 18c; became a British Crown Colony in 1805; part of the Federation of the West Indies from 1958 until 1962; gained inde-

pendence in 1978. GOVERNMENT an independent republic within the Commonwealth, governed by a House of Assembly of 30 members (21 elected for a 5-year term); a Cabinet is presided over by a Prime Minister; an elected President is head of state. ECONOMY agricultural processing; coconut-based products; cigars; citrus fruits (notably limes), bananas, coconuts, cocoa; lime juice, lime oil, bay oil, copra, rum; pumice; water bottling; tourism.

Dominican — *noun* a member of a Christian order of friars and nuns founded by St Dominic (see DOMINICANS). — *adj.* relating to this order.

Dominican Republic, Spanish **República Dominicana** POP (1992e) 7.5m, a republic of the West Indies, divided into 27 provinces. AREA 48 442sq km/18 699sq mi. It comprises the E two-thirds of the island of Hispaniola, bordering W on Haiti. CAPITAL Santo Domingo. CHIEF TOWNS Santiago, La Vega, San Juan, San Francisco de Macorís, La Romana. TIME ZONE GMT –4. The people are mainly of Spanish or mixed Spanish and Indian descent; Roman Catholicism is the state religion. OFFICIAL LANGUAGE Spanish. CURRENCY peso. PHYSICAL DESCRIPTION crossed NW–SE by the Cordillera Central, a heavily-wooded range with many peaks over 3 000m; the Pico Duarte (3 175m) is the highest peak in the Caribbean; in the SW, L Enriquillo lies in a broad valley cutting E–W; there is a wide coastal plain to the E. CLIMATE tropical maritime with a rainy season from May to Nov; the average temperature at Santo Domingo ranges between 24°C (Jan) and 27°C (Jul); average annual rainfall is 1 400mm; hurricanes may occur in Jun–Nov. HISTORY discovered by Columbus in 1492; became a Spanish colony in the 16c–17c; the E province of Santo Domingo remained Spanish after the partition of Hispaniola in 1697; taken over by Haiti on several occasions; gained independence in 1844 under its modern name; reoccupied by Spain in 1861–5. A long dictatorship at the end of the 19c was followed by revolution and bankruptcy. Dictatorships, revolutions and military coups continued through the 20c, with right wing parties holding power for most of the 1970s, 1980s and early 1990s. GOVERNMENT governed by a National Congress (30-member Senate, 120-member Chamber of Deputies); all members and the President are elected for four-year terms. ECONOMY mainly agriculture, especially sugar, cocoa; coffee, rice, cotton, tobacco, bananas, mangoes, tomatoes, oranges; sugar processing; bauxite, iron, nickel, gold; textiles; cement; tourism expanding, with resort complexes on the N coast.

Dominican Republic

Dominicans, properly **Ordo Praedicatorum (OP)**, also known as **Friars Preachers**, **Black Friars**, or **Jacobins** a religious order, founded (1216) by St Dominic in Italy to provide defenders of the Roman Catholic Faith. The order exercises individual and corporate poverty and concentrates on preaching and teaching. Known for its scholarship (eg Thomas Aquinas, Albertus Magnus) and missionary activity, it has houses in every part of the Christian world.

dominion *noun* **1** rule; power; influence. **2** a territory or country governed by a single ruler or government; formerly, a self-governing colony within the British Empire. [from Latin *dominium*, ownership]

Dominica

domino *noun* (PL. **dominoes**) **1** any of a set of small rectangular tiles marked, in two halves, with a varying number of spots. **2** a grouping of tiles with matching halves laid end to end in the game of *dominoes*. **3** a black cloak with a hood and mask attached, worn at masked balls. [perhaps from Italian *domino!*, master!, the winner's cry in dominoes]
◇ The game of dominoes has several forms, and can be played by two or more players. The object of the basic game is to lay down a line of dominoes, each player in turn being required to put down a domino which has on one of its divisions the same value as the one left at either end of the line by the previous player. Other variants require the adjoining dominoes to add up to a given total (often 7). The winner is the first player to have no dominoes left to play.

domino effect the relation of political cause and effect implied by the *domino theory*.

domino scheme a method of antenatal and postnatal care, together with hospital delivery, supervised by the mother's own midwife.

domino theory the theory that a political event can cause a series of similar events in neighbouring areas, like a falling domino causing the others in a row to fall in turn.

Domitian, in full **Titus Flavius Domitianus** (AD 51–96) Roman emperor (81–96), the younger son of Vespasian, and the last of the Flavian emperors. He was an autocratic ruler who alienated the ruling class by his tyrannical ways. After the armed revolt of Saturninus, the Governor of Upper Germany (89), he became suspicious of all opposition and unleashed a reign of terror in Rome which lasted until his own assassination.

Don *noun* the Spanish equivalent of Mr. [from Spanish *Don*, from Latin *dominus*, lord]

Don, River a river in SW Russia length 1 958km/1 217mi. Rising SE of Tula, it flows generally S and then sweeps round in a wide bend to enter the Sea of Azov. It is linked to the R Volga in the E by canal, and is accessible to sea-going vessels as far as Rostov-on-Don. There are valuable fisheries, especially in the lower course.

don¹ *noun* a university lecturer, especially at Oxford or Cambridge. [etymology as for DON]

don² *verb* (**donned, donning**) to put on (clothing). [from DO 1 *on*]

Donald a male first name, common in Scotland. [from the old Celtic name *Domhnull*, from *dubno*, world + *val*, rule]

donate *verb* to give, especially to charity. [from Latin *donare*, to give]

Donatello, properly **Donato di Betto Bardi** (c.1386–1466) Italian sculptor, born in Florence. Regarded as the forerunner of modern sculpture, he was the first sculptor since classical times to produce statues independent of an architectural setting. Among his works are the marble statues of *St Mark* and *St George* for the exterior of Or San Michele, the tomb of Pope John XXIII in the Baptistery, and the bronzes *David*, and *Judith and Holofernes*.

donation *noun* a formal gift, usually of money; an amount given as a gift.

Donatists a group of African Christian schismatics named after Donatus. The movement supported rebaptism, and declared invalid the sacraments celebrated by priests suspected of collaboration in times of persecution. It flourished in Africa in the 4c and 5c AD, and despite condemnation by Augustine (of Hippo), the Roman emperor, and the Catholic Church (AD 411), continued until the 7c–8c.

Donatus, Aelius (c.300–c.399 AD) Latin grammarian and rhetorician, who taught at Rome in c.360. His treatises on Latin grammar were the only textbooks used in schools in the Middle Ages, so that 'Donat' in W Europe came to mean a grammar book. He also wrote commentaries on Terence and Virgil.

Donau, River see DANUBE, RIVER.

Doncaster, ancient **Danum** POP (1981) 76 000; urban area 133 000, a town in Doncaster borough, South Yorkshire, N England. It stands on the R Don, 27km/17mi NE of Sheffield. HISTORY founded as a castle in the 1c AD; later an important Roman station on the road from Lincoln to York. NOTABLE FEATURES South Yorkshire Industrial Museum; ruined Conisbrough Castle nearby; racecourse. EVENT the St Leger Stakes, the oldest horse-race in England (Sep).

done — *adj.* **1** finished. **2** *said of food* fully cooked. **3** socially acceptable. **4** used up. **5** *colloq.* exhausted. — *interj.* expressing agreement or completion of a deal.
— **done for** *colloq.* facing ruin or death.

done with something or **someone** *colloq.* finished with them; having dealt with them.

Donegal, Gaelic **Dún na nGall** POP (1991) 128 000, a scenic county in Ulster province, N Irish Republic, bounded W and N by the Atlantic Ocean and E by Northern Ireland. AREA 4 830sq km/1 864sq mi. PHYSICAL DESCRIPTION watered by the Finn and Foyle rivers; the Blue Stack Mts are in the W, Derry Eagh in the NW, and Slieve Snaght in the N, rising to 752m at Errigal; Station I on Lough Derg is an important place of pilgrimage associated with St Patrick. CAPITAL Lifford. CHIEF TOWNS Ballyshannon, Letterkenny, Donegal. ECONOMY agriculture, livestock; tweed manufacture; there are uranium deposits.

doner kebab thin slices cut from a block of minced and seasoned lamb grilled on a spit and eaten on unleavened bread. [from Turkish *döner*, rotating]

Donetsk, formerly **Stalino** (to 1961), **Yuzovka** (to 1924) POP (1990e) 1.1m, the industrial capital of Donetsk oblast, E Ukraine. It lies on the R Kalmius, in the coal-mining area of the Donets Basin. HISTORY founded in 1870; during World War II it was taken by German forces, who destroyed the town; recaptured by Soviet forces in 1943; rebuilt after the War.

dong¹ — *noun* a deep ringing sound. — *verb* to make this sound. [imitative]

dong² *noun coarse slang* a penis.

Don Giovanni an opera by Wolfgang Amadeus Mozart (1787). Set in 17c Seville, the story focuses on the legendary Don Giovanni and his various attempted seductions, until one murdered father reappears as a statue and drags him away.

Dönitz, Karl (1891–1980) German naval commander, born in Grünau, near Berlin. After entering the German Navy submarine service in 1916, he strongly advocated U-boat warfare, planned Hitler's U-boat fleet, was made its commander (1936), and in 1943 became Commander-in-Chief of the German Navy. Becoming Führer on the death of Hitler, he was responsible for the final surrender to the Allies, and in 1946 was sentenced to 10 years' imprisonment for war crimes.

Donizetti, (Domenico) Gaetano (Maria) (1797–1848) Italian composer, born in Bergamo. He studied music in Italy and produced his first opera in Venice (1818). The work which carried his fame beyond Italy was *Anna Bolena* (1830), and his other successes included *Lucia di Lammermoor* (1835).

donjon *noun* a heavily fortified central tower in a medieval castle. [old variant of DUNGEON]

Don Juan a satirical epic poem by Byron (1819–24). It is written in *ottava rima* and describes the uproarious travelling adventures of young Don Juan, a character based upon the legendary Don Juan Tenorio of Seville.

Don Juan a man who is, or claims to be, a regular seducer of women.

donkey *noun* (PL. **donkeys**) **1** the domestic ass, a hoofed herbivorous mammal with a large head and long ears, related to but smaller than the horse. It is used for riding, and in many developing countries it is used to pull equipment and carry loads. **2** *colloq.* a stupid person.

donkey jacket a workman's heavy jacket made of a thick (usually black) woollen fabric.

donkey's years *colloq.* a very long time; ages.

donkey-work *noun* **1** heavy manual work. **2** preparation; groundwork.

Donleavy, J(ames) P(atrick) (1926–) Irish-US author, born in New York City, of Irish parents. He served in the US Navy during World War II, and has been an Irish citizen since 1967. Best known for his comic first novel, *The Ginger Man* (1955), his other works include *A Singular Man* (1963), *The Beastly Beatitudes of Balthazar B* (1968), *The Onion Eaters* (1971), and *Leila* (1983).

Donna a female first name. [of recent origin, from Italian *donna*, lady; further influenced by *Madonna*, title of the Virgin Mary]

Donne, John (c.1572–1631) English poet, born in London. He studied law in London, and in 1598 became secretary to Thomas Egerton, Keeper of the Great Seal, but was dismissed on account of his secret marriage to Egerton's niece. Originally a Catholic, he then joined the established Church, took Orders, and was made Dean of St Paul's (1621). His creative years fall into three main periods. The first (1590–1601) was a time of passion and cynicism, as seen in his *Elegies* and *Songs and Sonnets*. The second, from his marriage to his ordination in 1614, was a period of anguished meditation, as seen in his *Anniversaries* and funeral poems. The third period (that of his ministry) includes sonnets and hymns, (eg 'To God My God, in my Sicknesse').

donnish *adj.* of, typical of, or resembling a don; intellectual or bookish.

Donoghue, Stephen (Steve) (1884–1945) English jockey, born in Warrington. He won the Derby six times between 1915 and 1925, including a record three consecutive wins (1921–3). Champion jockey in 10 successive years (1914–23), he won a total of 14 classics.

donor *noun* **1** a person who donates something, especially money. **2** a person or animal that provides blood, semen, living tissue, or organs for medical use, eg blood for transfusion, or a kidney for transplantation. **3** *Electron.* an impurity in the form of a chemical element, such as antimony, that is deliberately added to a pure semiconductor material such as silicon, so called because it donates electrons to the semiconductor and so increases the conductivity of the latter. **4** *Chem.* an atom that donates a pair of electrons to an acceptor, resulting in the formation of a coordinate bond.

donor card a card indicating that its carrier is willing, in the event of sudden death, to have (usually specified) healthy organs removed for transplant to others.

donor insemination (ABBREV. **DI**) artificial insemination using semen from a donor.

Don Quixote a novel by Cervantes (2 parts 1605, 1615). It describes the absurd adventures of the hero, Don Quixote, who deludes himself that he is a knight after obsessively reading chivalric romances. He is accompanied on his travels by his pragmatic squire Sancho Panza.

don't — *contr.* do not. — *noun colloq.* something that must not be done: *dos and don'ts*.

don't-know *noun* a person undecided, especially as to whom to vote for.

donut same as DOUGHNUT.

doodah *noun colloq.* a thing whose name one cannot remember.

doodle — *verb intrans.* to scrawl or scribble aimlessly and meaninglessly. — *noun* a meaningless scribble.

Doolittle, Eliza the Cockney flower-seller in George Bernard Shaw's *Pygmalion*, who is taken on by Henry Higgins in an attempt to have her speech improved.

doom — *noun* inescapable death, ruin, or other unpleasant fate. — *verb* to condemn to death or some other dire fate. [from Anglo-Saxon *dom*, judgement]

doomsday *noun* the last day of the world; in Christianity, the day on which God will judge the human race.
— **till doomsday** *colloq.* for ever.

Doone, Lorna see LORNA DOONE.

door *noun* 1 a movable barrier opening and closing an entrance, eg to a room, cupboard, or vehicle. 2 an entrance. 3 a house considered in relation to others: *three doors away*. 4 a means of entry; an opportunity to gain access: *opened the door to stardom*.
— **lay something at someone's door** to blame them for it.
[from Anglo-Saxon *duru*]

doorbell *noun* a bell on or at a door, rung by visitors as a sign of arrival.

doorknocker see KNOCKER.

doorman *noun* a (usually uniformed) man employed to guard the entrance to a hotel, restaurant, theatre, etc and give assistance to guests or customers.

doormat *noun* 1 a mat for wiping shoes on before entering. 2 *colloq.* a person easily submitting to unfair treatment by others.

doorstep *noun* 1 a step positioned immediately in front of a door. 2 *slang* a thick sandwich or slice of bread.
— **on one's doorstep** situated very close, especially to one's home.

doorstop *noun* a device, especially a wedge, for holding a door open.

door-to-door *adj., adv.* 1 going from house to house. 2 *said eg of a journey time* between precise points of departure and arrival.

doorway *noun* an entrance to a building or room; the space filled by a door.

dopa *noun Biochem.* an amino acid that plays an important role in the manufacture of adrenaline and noradrenaline, and the neurotransmitter dopamine. It is used in the treatment of Parkinson's disease, in which there is a deficiency of dopamine. [from *dioxyphenylalanine*, a former name for the compound]

dopamine *noun Biochem.* an important chemical compound known as a *catecholamine*, that functions as a neurotransmitter and is also an intermediate in the manufacture of adrenaline and noradrenaline. [from DOPA + AMINE]

dope — *noun* 1 *colloq.* a drug taken for pleasure, especially cannabis. 2 *colloq.* a drug of any kind, especially one given to athletes or horses to affect performance. 3 *colloq.* a stupid person. 4 (**the dope**) *slang* information, especially when confidential. — *verb* to give or apply drugs to, especially dishonestly or furtively. [from Dutch *doop*, sauce]

dopey *or* **dopy** *adj.* (**dopier, dopiest**) *colloq.* 1 sleepy or inactive, as if drugged. 2 stupid.

dopily *adv. colloq.* in a dopey or stupid way.

dopiness *noun colloq.* a dopey or stupid manner or state.

doping *noun Physics* the addition of very small amounts of impurities (eg antimony, arsenic) to a crystal of silicon, germanium, etc, in order to convert it into a semiconductor.

doppelgänger *noun* an apparition or double of a person. [German, = double-goer]

Doppler, Christian Johann (1803–53) Austrian physicist, born in Salzburg. Professor of Physics at Vienna from 1851, he is best known for his explanation of perceived frequency variation when sources of sound or light waves move at high speed with respect to an observer (the *Doppler effect*).

Doppler effect *Physics* the change in wavelength observed when the distance between a source of waves and the observer is changing. The wavelength increases as the wave source and observer move apart, and decreases as they move closer together. The changing pitch of the siren of a passing motor vehicle is an example of the Doppler effect on sound waves. The increasing separation of the Earth and the stars is confirmed by a change in the wavelength of star light, caused by the Doppler effect. [named after the Austrian physicist Christian Doppler]

Dorado *noun Astron.* the Goldfish, a small and inconspicuous constellation of the southern hemisphere. Its brightest star is Alpha Doradus.

Dorchester, ancient **Durnovaria** POP (1981) 14 000, the county town of Dorset, S England, situated in West Dorset district. It stands on the R Frome, 12km/7mi N of Weymouth. HISTORY in the 10c King Athelstan established a mint in Dorchester; Judge Jeffreys' Bloody Assizes were held here in 1685; the town's Roman ramparts became known as 'The Walks' in the 18c; Dorchester was the model for Casterbridge in the novels of Thomas Hardy. NOTABLE FEATURES Dorset County Museum; Dorset Military Museum; Maiden Castle prehistoric fort (3km/2mi S).

Dordogne, River, ancient **Duranius** a river in SW France, length 472km/293mi. Rising in the Auvergne Hills, at the confluence of the Dor and Dogne rivers, it flows SW and W to meet the R Garonne at Bec d'Ambes, where it forms the estuary of the Gironde. The river is a source of hydroelectricity, and there are vineyards (notably those of St Emilion) along the valley slopes. The valley of the Dordogne is a popular tourist destination.

Dordrecht *or* **Dordt** *or* **Dort** POP (1992e) 112 000, a river port and industrial city in South Holland province, W Netherlands. It lies 19km/12mi SE of Rotterdam. HISTORY founded in 1008; became the wealthiest commercial town in the Netherlands, overtaken by Rotterdam in the 18c; the Synod of Dort (the greatest meeting of the Reformed churches) took place here in 1618–19. NOTABLE FEATURE Grote Kerk (14c–16c).

Doria, Andrea (c.1466–1560) Genoese mercenary and admiral, born in Oneglia. After serving under various Italian princes, he commanded the Genoese fleet, and defeated the Turks in 1519. When the imperial faction came to power (1522), he transferred his allegiance to Francis I of France, commanded the French fleet, and defeated Charles V in Italy and Provence. After a period of papal service, he rejoined the French, but in 1529, fearing Francis's power, he went over to Charles V, entered Genoa, and established an oligarchy under his domination. He continued to fight the Turks with many successes, but was defeated at Algiers (1541) and Herba (1560). His family continued to rule after his death in Genoa until the end of the 18c.

Dorian *adj.* relating or belonging to the Dorians.

Dorians a sub-group of Hellenic peoples, thought to have migrated into Greece around 1100 BC. Dorian settlements included Argos, Corinth, and Sparta, and later Halicarnassus and Syracuse.

Doric *adj. Archit.* denoting an order of classical architecture, characterized by thick fluted columns. See also CORINTHIAN, IONIC. [from Greek *Dorikos*, from *Doris*, in ancient Greece]

Dorigen the heroine of 'the Franklin's Tale' in Chaucer's *The Canterbury Tales*, who is married to Arveragus but almost forced into adultery with Aurelius, on account of a foolish bargain she makes with him.

Doris a female first name, popular at the beginning of the 20c. [an ancient Greek name, probably derived from *doron*, gift]

dorm *noun colloq.* a dormitory.

dormancy *noun* a quiet or inactive state.

dormant *adj.* temporarily quiet, inactive, or out of use. *Biol.* denoting a living organism or a reproductive body such as a seed, spore, or cyst that is in a resting state, especially in order to survive a period of unfavourable environmental conditions, eg drought, low temperature. [from Latin *dormire*, to sleep]

dormer *or* **dormer window** *noun* a window fitted vertically into an extension built out from a sloping roof. [from DORMITORY, in which they were originally fitted]

dormitory *noun* (PL. **dormitories**) 1 a large bedroom for several people, especially in a school. 2 *North Amer., esp. US* a hall of residence in a college or university. [from Latin *dormitorium*, from *dormire*, to sleep]

dormitory town *or* **dormitory suburb** a town or suburb from which most residents travel to work elsewhere.

Dormobile *noun trademark* a van equipped for living and sleeping in. [from DORMITORY + AUTOMOBILE]

dormouse *noun* (PL. **dormice**) a small nocturnal rodent with rounded ears, large eyes, velvety fur, and a bushy tail, that spends the day asleep in nests in trees or on the ground. Dormice hibernate for several months in winter, and for the rest of the year they feed on nuts, seeds, berries, young shoots, and bark. [connected with Latin *dormire*, to sleep, from its hibernating habits]

Dormouse, The a dozy character, present at The Mad Hatter's Tea-Party, in Lewis Carroll's *Alice's Adventures in Wonderland*.

Dornier, Claude (1884–1969) German aircraft engineer, born in Kempten. In 1911 he designed the first all-metal plane. He founded the Dornier works at Friedrichshafen and Altenrhein, where he made seaplanes and flying boats, including the famous 12 engined Do X (1929). The Dornier twin-engined bomber was a standard Luftwaffe type in World War II.

Dorothy 1 a female first name. 2 (*in full* **Dorothy Gale**) the orphan girl from Kansas who is transported by a cyclone to the fantastic land of Oz, in Frank L Baum's *The Wonderful Wizard of Oz*. [an Anglicization of Greek *Dorothea*, formed from *doron*, gift + *theos*, god. These also form the female name *Theodora*]

Dors. *abbrev.* Dorset.

dorsal *adj. Biol., Physiol.* of or on the back: *dorsal fin*. [from Latin *dorsum*, back]

Dorset POP (1987e) 649 000, a county in S England, divided into eight districts. AREA 2 654sq km/1 024sq mi. It is bounded S by the English Channel and from W to E by Devon, Somerset, Wiltshire, and Hampshire. Many of Thomas Hardy's novels are set in the county. PHYSICAL DESCRIPTION extensive heathlands and chalk down are drained by the Frome and Stour rivers. CHIEF TOWNS Dorchester (county town), Bournemouth, Weymouth, Poole. ECONOMY livestock; quarrying; tourism.

Dortmund POP (1991e) 599 000, an industrial and mining river port in North Rhine-Westphalia state, W central Germany. Situated 50km/31mi S of Münster in the valley of the Ruhr, the city is connected to the North Sea by the Dortmund-Ems Canal (272km/169mi long). The inland harbour is one of the largest in Germany. Dortmund is also a great sporting centre, with almost 100 sports installations.

dory *noun* (PL. **dories**) a golden-yellow fish of the mackerel family. [from French *dorée*, golden]

Doryphorus (**Spear Bearer**) a sculpture by Myron (5c BC).

DOS *abbrev. Comput.* disk operating system, a program for handling information on a disk.

dosage *noun* the prescribed amount of a dose of a medicine or drug.

dose — *noun* **1** *Medicine* the measured quantity of medicine, ionizing radiation, eg X-rays, or some other therapeutic agent that is prescribed by a doctor to be administered to a patient at any one time, or at regular intervals over a period of time. **2** the amount of ionizing radiation to which a person is exposed over a specified period of time. **3** *colloq.* a bout, especially of an illness or something unpleasant: *a dose of the flu.* **4** *slang* any sexually transmitted disease, especially gonorrhoea: *catch a dose.* — *verb* (**dose someone up with something**) to give them medicine, especially in large quantities. — **like a dose of salts** *colloq.* extremely quickly and effectively. [from Greek *dosis*, giving]

dosh *noun slang* money.

dosimeter *noun Physics* an instrument for measuring the dose of radiation received by a person, or by a laboratory or other area.

Dos Passos, John (Roderigo) (1896–1970) US novelist and war correspondent, born in Chicago, Illinois. He was an ambulance driver in the later years of World War I, an experience which inspired his antiwar novel *Three Soldiers* (1921). He then worked in Europe and elsewhere as a newspaper correspondent. His best-known work is the trilogy on US life, *U.S.A.* (1930–6).

doss *verb intrans. slang* (**doss down**) to settle down to sleep, especially on an improvised bed. [perhaps *doss*, dialect for HASSOCK]

dosser *noun slang* **1** a homeless person sleeping on the street or in a doss-house. **2** a lazy person.

doss-house *noun slang* a very cheap lodging-house for homeless people.

dossier *noun* a file of papers containing information on a person or subject. [from French *dossier*]

dost *verb old use* the form of *do* used with *thou*.

Dostoevsky *or* **Dostoyevsky, Fyodor (Mikhailovich)** (1821–81) Russian novelist, born in Moscow. He trained as a military engineer but turned to literature, publishing the short story *Poor Folk* in 1846. Condemned to death in 1849 for his participation in revolutionary circles in St Petersburg, he was reprieved at the last moment, and sent to a Siberian prison camp until 1854. In 1859 he returned to St Petersburg, where he wrote his major realistic novel, *Crime and Punishment* (1866). Other well-known novels include *The Idiot* (1868–9) and *The Brothers Karamazov* (1879–80).

dot — *noun* **1** a small round mark; a spot; a point. **2** in Morse code, the shorter of the two lengths of signal element, written as a point. See also DASH. — *verb* (**dotted, dotting**) **1** to put a dot on. **2** to scatter; to cover with a scattering. — **dot the i's and cross the t's 1** to pay close attention to detail. **2** to finish the last few details of something.
on the dot exactly on time.
the year dot *colloq.* a very long time ago.
[from Anglo-Saxon *dott*, head of a boil]

dotage *noun* a state of feeble-mindedness owing to old age; senility: *in one's dotage.* [etymology as for DOTE]

dotard *noun* a person in his or her dotage. [from DOTE]

dote *verb intrans.* (**dote on** *or* **upon someone** *or* **something**) to show a foolishly excessive fondness for them. [from Old Dutch *doten*, to be silly]

doth *old use* does.

doting *adj.* foolishly or excessively fond of someone.

dot matrix printer a computer printer using arrangements of pins from a matrix or set to form the printed characters.

dottily *adv. colloq.* in a dotty or silly way.

dottiness *noun colloq.* a dotty or silly manner or state.

dotty *adj.* (**dottier, dottiest**) *colloq.* **1** silly; crazy. **2** (**dotty about someone** *or* **something**) infatuated with them.

Douai Bible an early English translation of the Bible by Roman Catholic scholars. The New Testament was first published in Rheims in 1582; the Old Testament in 1609. It is sometimes called the Rheims–Douai translation (the English college in Douai moved to Rheims in 1578).

Douala *or* **Duala** POP (1988e) 1.2m, the seaport capital of Littoral province, Cameroon. It lies on the estuary of the R Wouri, 25km/16mi from the Gulf of Guinea coast. HISTORY capital of German Cameroon, known as Kamerunstadt from 1885 until 1901; changed to the present name in 1907; capital of French Cameroon from 1940 until 1946. NOTABLE FEATURE Pagoda of King Manga Bell.

double — *adj.* **1** made up of two similar parts; paired; in pairs. **2** of twice the (usual) weight, size, etc. **3** for two people: *a double bed.* **4** ambiguous: *double meaning.* **5** *said of a musical instrument* sounding an octave lower: *double bass.* — *adv.* **1** twice. **2** with one half over the other: *folded double.* — *noun* **1** a double quantity. **2** a duplicate or lookalike. **3** an actor's stand-in, used especially in dangerous scenes. **4** a double measure of alcoholic spirit. **5** a racing bet in which any winnings from the first stake become a stake in a subsequent race. **6** a win in two events on the same racing programme. — *verb* **1** *trans., intrans.* to make or become twice as large in size, number, etc. **2** (**double something over**) to fold one half of it over the other. **3** *intrans.* to have a second use or function: *the spare bed doubles as a couch.* **4** *intrans.* (**double for someone**) to act as their substitute. **5** *intrans.* to turn round sharply. — **at** *or* **on the double** very quickly.
double back to turn and go back, often by a different route.
double up 1 to bend sharply at the waist, especially through pain. **2** (*also* **double up with someone**) to share a bedroom.
[from Latin *duplus*]

double agent a spy working for two governments with conflicting interests.

double-barrelled *adj.* **1** *said of a gun* having two barrels. **2** *said of a surname* made up of two names (eg *Lloyd-Jones*).

double bass the contrabass, the largest and lowest in pitch of the orchestral stringed instruments. There are two basic types: the first, modelled on the double-bass viol, has sloping shoulders and a flat back; the second has squarer shoulders and a rounded (or flat) back. Modern instruments have four (or five) strings which may be bowed or plucked.

double bill *or* **triple bill** two or three films or plays presented as a single entertainment, one after the other.

double bond *Chem.* a covalent bond formed by the sharing of two pairs of electrons between two atoms.

double-breasted *adj., said of a coat or jacket* having overlapping front flaps.

double-check *verb trans., intrans.* to check twice or again.

double chin a chin with an area of loose flesh underneath.

double cream thick cream with a high fat content.

double-cross — *verb* to cheat or deceive (especially a colleague or ally, or someone one is supposed to be helping). — *noun* such a deceit.

double-crosser *noun* a person who double-crosses or cheats another.

double-dealer *noun* a cheat or deceiver.

double-dealing *noun* cheating; treachery.

double-decker *noun* **1** a bus with two decks. **2** *colloq.* anything with two levels or layers: *double-decker sandwich.*

double Dutch *colloq.* nonsense; incomprehensible jargon.

double-edged *adj.* **1** having two cutting edges. **2** having two possible meanings or purposes.

double entendre a remark having two possible meanings, one of them usually sexually suggestive; the use of such remarks. [from Old French *double entendre*, double meaning]

double exposure *Photog.* the combination of two or more images separately exposed on a single photographic record. As a photographic technique, it is widely used for artistic effects and in trick photography. Images may be superimposed so that one is seen through the other, or appear without overlapping with specific areas reserved by the use of masks and matts.

double figures the numbers between 10 and 99 inclusive, especially the lower ones.

double-glazed *adj.* having double-glazing.

double-glazing *noun* windows constructed with two panes separated by a vacuum, providing added heat insulation.

Double Indemnity a US film directed by Billy Wilder (1944). It is a film noir about an insurance salesman's fatal involvement with a murderous and deceitful femme fatale, starring Fred MacMurray and Barbara Stanwyck.

double-jointed *adj.* having extraordinarily flexible body joints.

double negative an expression containing two negative words where only one is needed, as in *He hasn't never asked me.*

double-park *verb trans., intrans.* to park at the side of another vehicle parked alongside the kerb.

double-quick *adj., adv.* very quick or quickly.

doubles *sing. noun* a competition in tennis, etc between two teams of two players each.

double standard (*also* **double standards**) a principle or rule applied firmly to one person or group and loosely or not at all to another, especially oneself.

double star *Astron.* **1** a binary star. **2** a pair of stars that appear close together when viewed through a telescope, but are in fact at very different distances from Earth, and only appear to be near each other because they lie in very nearly the same direction from Earth.

doublet *noun* **1** a close-fitting man's jacket, with or without sleeves, popular from the 14c to the 17c. **2** a pair of objects of any kind, or each of these. [from Old French *doublet*]

double take an initial inattentive reaction followed swiftly by a sudden full realisation, especially used as a comic device: *do a double take.*

double-talk *noun* ambiguous talk, or talk that seems relevant but is really meaningless, especially as offered up by politicians.

doublethink *noun* simultaneous belief in, or acceptance of, two opposing ideas or principles.

double time a rate of pay equal to double the basic rate.

doubloon *noun* a former gold coin of Spain and S America. [from Spanish *doblón*]

doubly *adv.* **1** to twice the extent; very much more. **2** in two ways.

doubt — *verb* **1** to feel uncertain about; to be suspicious, or show mistrust, of. **2** to be inclined to disbelieve. — *noun* **1** a feeling of uncertainty, suspicion, or mistrust. **2** an inclination to disbelieve; a reservation.

— **no doubt** surely; probably.

without a doubt *or* **without doubt** certainly. [from Latin *dubitare*]

doubter *noun* a person who doubts, especially habitually.

doubtful *adj.* **1** feeling doubt. **2** uncertain; able to be doubted. **3** likely not to be the case.

doubtfully *adv.* in a doubtful or uncertain way.

doubtless *adv.* probably; certainly.

douche — *noun* **1** a powerful jet of water that is used to clean a body orifice, especially the vagina. It is an unreliable method of contraception. **2** an apparatus for producing such a jet. — *verb* to apply a douche to. [from French *douche*]

Dougal a male first name, usually confined to Scots. [from Gaelic *Dubhgall*, from *dubh*, black, dark + *gall*, stranger, a reference to Danish settlers]

dough *noun* **1** a mixture of flour, liquid (water or milk), and yeast, used in the preparation of bread, pastry, etc. It usually refers to such a mixture that has been kneaded but not baked. **2** *slang* money. [from Anglo-Saxon *dah*]

doughnut *noun* a spongy ring-shaped pastry, especially filled with cream or jam, usually with a hole in the middle.

doughnutting *noun* the surrounding of a speaker in parliament by members of the same party, to give the impression on television of a packed House.

doughtily *adv. literary* bravely.

doughtiness *noun literary* bravery.

doughty *adj.* (**doughtier, doughtiest**) *literary* brave; stout-hearted. [from Anglo-Saxon *dyhtig*]

doughy *adj.* (**doughier, doughiest**) like dough, or having the consistency of dough.

Douglas, Gawain *or* **Gavin** (c.1474–1522) Scottish poet and bishop, born in Tantallon Castle, East Lothian. Educated for the priesthood, he became Dean of St Giles, Edinburgh (1501) and Bishop of Dunkeld (1515), but was forced to flee to London in 1521, after the fall of his nephew, the 6th Earl of Angus. His works include *The Palice of Honour* (c.1501) and a translation into Scots of the *Aeneid* (finished c.1513), the first translation of its kind of a Latin poet.

Douglas, Kirk, originally **Issur Danielovich** (1916–) US film actor, born in Amsterdam, New York. The son of poor Russian immigrants, he acted on Broadway and first appeared in Hollywood in *The Strange Love of Martha Ivers* (1946). Highlights from his prolific career include *Lust For Life* (1956), *Paths of Glory* (1957), *Spartacus* (1960), and the television film *Amos* (1985).

Douglas, Michael (Kirk) (1944–) US film actor and producer, born in New Brunswick, New Jersey. He gained experience of the film industry through his father (Kirk Douglas) and first appeared in *Hail Hero!* (1969). Working as a producer, he shared the Best Picture Oscar won by *One Flew Over the Cuckoo's Nest* (1975). Among the films he has starred in are *Romancing the Stone* (1984), *Jewel of the Nile* (1985), *Fatal Attraction* (1987), *Wall Street* (1987), for which he won a Best Actor Oscar, and *Basic Instinct* (1992).

Douglas, (George) Norman (1868–1952) Scottish writer, born in Deeside. Brought up in Germany, he became a diplomat, and travelled widely. He settled in Italy in 1896 and wrote several novels (eg *South Wind*, 1917), natural history memoirs, and travel books (eg *Old Calabria*, 1919).

Douglas POP (1991) 22 000, the seaport capital of the Isle of Man. It lies on the E coast of the island, 80km/50mi W of Barrow-in-Furness. NOTABLE FEATURES House of Keys; Manx National Museum; Castle Mona (1804); Tower of Refuge on Conister Rock (1832); steam railway.

Douglas a male first name, after the family of the Earls of Douglas. [originally a local name composed of Gaelic elements *dubh*, black, dark + *uis*, water]

Douglas-Home, Alec see HOME (OF THE HIRSEL), BARON.

Douglass, Andrew Ellicott (1867–1962) US astronomer, born in Windsor, Vermont. Professor of Physics and Astronomy at Arizona University (1906) and later Director of the Stewart Observatory (1918–38), he investigated the relationship between sunspots and climate by examining and measuring the annual growth-rings of long-lived Arizona pines and sequoias; he noted that variations in their width corresponded to specific climatic cycles, creating patterns which can be discerned in timbers from prehistoric archaeological sites and providing a time-sequence for dating purposes.

Douglass, Frederick (c.1817–95) US abolitionist and journalist, born into slavery in Tuckahoe, Maryland. He escaped in 1838, and in 1841 emerged as a major anti-slavery force. He also supported the cause of women's rights, and became US Minister to Haiti.

Doukhobors *or* **Dukhabors** a religious sect that originated in Russia c.1740. It teaches that God is manifested in the human soul, which is eternal, and which at death passes into another body (metempsychosis). Frequently in conflict with the authorities, especially for refusing military service, the adherents were persecuted until 1898, when they were allowed to emigrate (mainly to Canada).

Doulton an English pottery firm originally based in Lambeth, London. They began making chimney-pots and large architectural ornaments in the first half of the 19c, and by the time of their expansion to Burslem in 1854 they were renowned for tiles, figures, and decorative panels in faience.

Dounreay a nuclear research station in Caithness, Scotland, on the coast of the Pentland Firth, 13km/8mi W of Thurso. The Prototype Fast Reactor (PFR), the world's first experimental fast-breeder reactor, opened there in 1974. Its need for three cooling circuits made it an expensive plant, and it closed in 1994.

dour *adj.* stern; sullen. [from Latin *durus*, hard]

Douro, River, Spanish **Río Duero**, ancient **Durius** a river in Spain and Portugal, length 895km/556mi. It rises in N central Spain, flowing W to the Portuguese border, which it follows for 107km/66mi. It turns W across N Portugal, emptying into the Atlantic Ocean near Oporto. The river is navigable for 200km/124mi to Barca de Alva. Used extensively for irrigation and hydro-electric power, the river has five dams which are operated jointly by Spain and Portugal. Vineyards in the upper Douro Valley produce port and Mateus Rosé.

douse *or* **dowse** *verb* **1** to throw water over; to plunge into water. **2** to extinguish (a light or fire).

dove *noun* **1** any of several smaller members of the pigeon family with a small head, stout body, and pointed tail. In fact there is no real difference between a pigeon and a dove. **2** *Politics* a person favouring peace rather than hostility. See also HAWK. [from Anglo-Saxon *dufe*]

dovecote *or* **dovecot** *noun* a shed in which domestic pigeons are kept.

Dover, French **Douvres**, Latin **Dubris Portus** POP (1981) 34 000, a seaport in Dover district, Kent, SE England. The principal cross-Channel port, it provides the shortest link with France (35km/22mi). It was the largest of the Cinque Ports. NOTABLE FEATURES Dover Castle (13c–14c); 13c St Edmund's Chapel (smallest chapel in England); Roman painted house (2c).

Dover POP (1990) 28 000, the capital of the state of Delaware, USA. It is situated in Kent County, central Delaware, 65km/40mi S of Wilmington. HISTORY founded in 1683, it became state capital in 1777; achieved city status in 1929.

Dover, Treaty of a treaty (1670) between Charles II of Great Britain and Louis XIV of France. Under its terms, Charles received French subsidies and agreed to maintain amity with France and, later, declare himself a convert to Roman Catholicism. Some of the terms were kept secret for a time from the British parliament, which did much to sour relations with the King.

Dover sole, a flatfish, distributed from the Mediterranean to Norway, up to 50cm in length, and having both eyes on the right side of the body, a twisted mouth with teeth on the underside only, and dorsal and anal fins that extend to the tail. It is a very popular food fish. – Also called *European sole*.

dovetail — *noun* (*also* **dovetail joint**) a corner joint, especially in wood, made by fitting v-shaped pegs into corresponding slots. — *verb trans., intrans.* to fit or combine neatly.

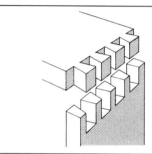

dovetail

dowager *noun* **1** a title given to a nobleman's widow, to distinguish her from the wife of her husband's heir: *dowager duchess*. **2** *colloq.* a grand-looking old lady. [from Old French *douagiere*, from Latin *dotare*, to endow]

dowdily *adv.* with a dowdy or dull manner.

dowdiness *noun* a dowdy or dull manner or appearance.

Dowding, Hugh (Caswell Tremenheere) Dowding, 1st Baron (1882–1970) Scottish airman, born in Moffat, Dumfriesshire. In World War I he served in the Royal Artillery and the Royal Flying Corps, and as air chief marshal in World War II was Commander-in-Chief of Fighter Command (1936–40) and responsible for the air defence of Britain, which resulted in the victorious Battle of Britain (1940).

dowdy *adj.* (**dowdier, dowdiest**) *said especially of a woman* dull, plain, and unfashionable. [from Middle English *dowd*, slut]

dowel *noun* a thin cylindrical (especially wooden) peg, especially used to join two pieces by fitting into corresponding holes in each. [from Old German *dovel*]

Dowell, Anthony (1943–) English dancer and director, born in London. He joined the Royal Ballet company in 1961, and became one of the premier male ballet-dancers of the period, noted for his lightness and elegance in classical roles, and for his partnership with Antoinette Sibley. He was principal dancer of the American Ballet Theatre (1978–80), but returned to the Royal Ballet as artistic director in 1986.

dower *noun* a widow's share, for life, in her deceased husband's property. [from Old French *douaire*, from Latin *dotare*, to endow]

dower house a house smaller than, and within the grounds of, a large country house, originally one forming part of a dower.

Dow Jones Index a statistic showing the state of the New York Stock Market, computed on working days by Dow Jones and Co. It enables a measurement to be made of changes in the price of shares of 30 leading US corporations, and is the primary indicator of share price movements in the USA.

Dowland, John (1563–1626) English lutenist and songwriter. He failed, as a Catholic, to become a court musician to Queen Elizabeth, but entered the service of the Duke of Brunswick (1594), and subsequently went to Italy. Following his return to England (1596) he wrote his first book of 'ayres', then became lutenist to Christian IV of Denmark (1598) and produced other collections of music. In London in 1605 he composed *Lachrymae*, which contains some of the finest instrumental consort music of the period, and he is remembered also for the songs 'Weep you no more, sad fountains' and 'Awake, sweet love'.

Down, Gaelic **An Dun** POP (1981) 341 000, a county in SE Northern Ireland. AREA 2 448sq km/ 945sq mi. It is bounded W by Co Armagh, NE by Co Antrim, N by Belfast Lough, S by Carlingford Lough, and E by the Irish Sea. PHYSICAL DESCRIPTION the coastline is indented (from N to S) by Strangford Lough, Dundrum Bay, and Carlingford Lough; the Mourne Mts are in the S; major rivers include the Newry, Lagan, and Bann; the highest point is at Slieve Donard (852m). CHIEF TOWNS Downpatrick (county town), Newry, Bangor, Newtownards. ECONOMY oats, potatoes, vegetables; stock-rearing; linen.

down[1] — *adv.* **1** towards or in a low or lower position, level, or state; on or to the ground. **2** from a greater to a lesser size, amount or level: *scaled down / calm down.* **3** towards or in a more southerly place. **4** in writing; on paper: *take down notes.* **5** as a deposit: *put down five pounds.* **6** to an end stage or finished state: *hunt someone down / grind down.* **7** from earlier to later times: *handed down through generations.* **8** not vomited up: *keep food down.* — *prep.* **1** in a lower position on. **2** along; at a further position on, by, or through: *down the road.* **3** from the top to, or towards the bottom. **4** *dialect* to or in (a particular place): *going down the town.* — *adj.* **1** sad; in low spirits. **2** going towards or reaching a lower position: *a down pipe.* **3** (**down by**) with a deficit (of): *down by three goals.* **4** made as a deposit: *a down payment.* **5** reduced in price. **6** (**down for**) noted; entered in a list, etc: *Your name is down for the hurdles.* **7** *said of a computer, etc* out of action, especially temporarily. — *verb* **1** to drink quickly, especially in one gulp. **2** to force to the ground. — *noun* **1** an unsuccessful or otherwise unpleasant period: *ups and downs.* **2** (**downs**) an area of rolling (especially treeless) hills.
— **down to the ground** *colloq.* completely; perfectly.
down tools *colloq.* to stop working, as a protest.
down under *colloq.* in or to Australia or New Zealand.
down with...! let us get rid of...!
have a down on someone *colloq.* to be ill-disposed towards them.
[from Anglo-Saxon *of dune*, from the hill]

down[2] *noun* soft fine feathers or hair. [from Norse *dunn*]

down-and-out — *adj.* homeless and penniless, with no hope of earning a living. — *noun* a down-and-out person.

down-at-heel *adj.* shabby.

downbeat — *adj.* **1** pessimistic; cheerless. **2** calm; relaxed. — *noun Mus.* the first beat of a bar.

downcast *adj.* **1** glum; dispirited. **2** *said of eyes* looking downwards.

downer *noun* **1** *colloq.* a state of depression: *be on a downer.* **2** *slang* a tranquillising or depressant drug.

downfall *noun* failure or ruin, or its cause.

downgrade *verb* to reduce to a lower grade.

downhearted *adj.* dispirited; discouraged; dismayed.

downhill — *adv.* **1** downwards. **2** to or towards a worse condition. — *adj.* **1** downwardly sloping. **2** becoming increasingly easier. **3** deteriorating.

Downing Street 1 a street off Whitehall in central London. Of the original terraced houses only numbers 10 (since 1735 the Prime Minister's official residence), 11 (used by the Chancellor of the Exchequer), and 12 (used by the Party Whip) remain. **2** used allusively for the British government or the office of Prime Minister.

down-in-the-mouth *adj.* unhappy; depressed.

download *verb* to transfer (data) from one computer to another.

down-market *adj.* cheap, poor quality, or lacking prestige.

Downpatrick, Gaelic **Dun Padraig** POP (1991) 10 000, the county town of Co Down, SE Northern Ireland, in Down district, near the S end of Strangford Lough. It is one of the chief centres of pilgrimage in Ireland. HISTORY St Patrick is said to have landed here in 432 and to have founded a church in c.440; Downpatrick is the reputed burial place of Saints Patrick, Columbus, and Bridget of Kildare. NOTABLE FEATURES St Patrick's Cathedral (1798–1812); the remains of Inch Abbey (c.1187), 3km/2mi NW; remains of the Monastery of Saul, 2km/1mi NE.

down payment a deposit.

downpour *noun* a very heavy fall of rain.

downright *adj., adv.* utter or utterly.

Downs the low-lying chalk hill ranges which rise in Dorset and Hampshire and extend into Surrey, Kent, and East and West Sussex, S England. The North Downs extend from the chalk cliffs of Dover in the E, through Kent and into Surrey; they are separated from the South Downs by the Weald. The South Downs stretch W to Beachy Head, running parallel to the S coast. The North Downs rise to 294m at Leith Hill and the South Downs rise to 264m at Butser Hill.

downside *noun* **1** the lower or under side. **2** *colloq.* a negative aspect; a disadvantage.

downsizing *noun* the practice of reducing the size of a workforce, especially by redundancies.

Down's syndrome a disorder caused by a chromosomal abnormality (the presence of three copies of chromosome 21 instead of the normal pair), which results in mental retardation, slow physical development, flattened facial features, and slight slanting of the eyes, which gave rise to the former name for the condition, mongolism. Down's syndrome is congenital (present from birth), and the incidence of the disorder rises significantly with increasing age of the mother, to one in 100 births for mothers over the age of 40 years. Down's syndrome can be diagnosed relatively early in pregnancy by amniocentesis. [named after the UK physician John Langdon Haydon Down]

downstage *adj., adv.* at or towards the front of a theatre stage.

downstairs — *adv.* to or towards a lower floor; down the stairs. — *adj.* on a lower or ground floor. — *noun* a lower or ground floor.

downstream *adj., adv.* further along a river towards the sea; with the current.

downtime *noun* time during which work ceases because a machine, especially a computer, is not working.

down-to-earth *adj.* **1** sensible and practical. **2** not at all pretentious. **3** plain-speaking.

downtown — *adj., adv.* in or towards the lower part of the city, or the city centre. — *noun* this area of a city.

downtrodden *adj.* oppressed; ruled or controlled tyrannically.

downturn *noun* a decline in economic activity.

downward — *adj.* leading or moving down; descending; declining. — *adv.* same as DOWNWARDS.

downwardly *adv.* in a downward direction.

downwards *adv.* to or towards a lower position or level.

downwind — *adv.* **1** in or towards the direction in which the wind is blowing; with the wind blowing from behind. **2** behind in terms of wind direction; with the wind carrying one's scent away from (eg an animal one is stalking). — *adj.* moving with, or sheltered from, the wind.

downy *adj.* (**downier, downiest**) covered with or made of down; soft like down.

dowry *noun* (PL. **dowries**) an amount of wealth handed over by a woman to her husband on marriage. [from DOWER]

dowse[1] *verb intrans.* to search for underground water with a divining-rod.

dowse[2] see DOUSE.

dowser *noun* a person who searches for water with a divining-rod.

doxology *noun* (PL. **doxologies**) a Christian hymn, verse, or fixed expression praising God. [from Greek *doxa*, glory + *logos*, discourse]

doyen *noun literary* the most senior and most respected member of a group or profession. [from French *doyen*]

Doyle, Sir Arthur Conan (1859–1930) Scottish writer, born in Edinburgh. He served as a physician in the Boer War (1899–1902) and wrote the pamphlet *The War in South Africa* (1902), but is best known as the creator of the detective Sherlock Holmes, who made his first appearance in *A Study in Scarlet* (1887). *The Adventures of Sherlock Holmes* were serialized in the *Strand Magazine* (1891–3) as well as being published as books, and their popularity was such that Conan Doyle was thwarted in his attempts to kill off his hero. He himself set greater stock by his historical romances, such as *The White Company* (1890).

Doyle, Roddy (1958–) Irish novelist, born in Dublin. He worked for 14 years as a teacher in a community school in Kilbarrack (N Dublin) – the 'Barrytown' of his novels *The Commitments* (1988), *The Snapper* (1990), and *The Van* (1991) spoke for communities denied a media voice, their comic style acting as a vehicle for Doyle's statement on the plight of the urban dispossessed. The Booker Prize-winning *Paddy Clarke Ha Ha Ha* (1993), narrated through the sense and senses of a 10-year-old boy, similarly exhibits the tragedy that underlines all comedy.

doyley see DOILY.

doz. *abbrev.* dozen.

doze — *verb intrans.* to sleep lightly. — *noun* a brief period of light sleep.
— **doze off** to fall into a light sleep.
[from Norse *dus*, lull]

dozen *noun* (PL. **dozen** following a number, **dozens**) **1** a set of twelve. **2** (**dozens**) *colloq.* very many: *saw dozens of them.* [from Latin *duodecim*]

dozenth *adj.* **1** twelfth. **2** denoting an indeterminately high place in a sequence: *for the dozenth time.*

dozily *adv.* in a dozy or sleepy way.

doziness *noun* a dozy or sleepy state.

dozy *adj.* (**dozier, doziest**) **1** sleepy. **2** *colloq.* stupid; slow to understand; not alert.

DPA *abbrev.* Data Protection Authority.

DPhil or **DPh** *abbrev.* Doctor of Philosophy. See also PHD.

DPP *abbrev.* Director of Public Prosecutions.

Dr *abbrev.* **1** Doctor. **2** drachma. **3** *in addresses* Drive.

drab *adj.* (**drabbier, drabbiest**) **1** dull; dreary. **2** of a dull greenish-brown colour. [perhaps from French *drap*, cloth]

Drabble, Margaret (1939–) English novelist, born in Sheffield. Her novels, which describe some of the emotional and moral problems experienced by women during the postwar years, include *The Millstone* (1965), *The Needle's Eye* (1972), and *The Radiant Way* (1987).

drably *adv.* drearily; dully.

drabness *noun* a dreary or dull state or appearance.

drachm *noun* a measure equal to ⅛ of an ounce or fluid ounce, formerly used by pharmacists. [etymology as for DRACHMA]

drachma *noun* (PL. **drachmas, drachmae**) (SYMBOL **Dr**) the standard unit of currency in Greece, divided into 100 lepta. [from Greek *drakhme*, handful]

Draco (7c BC) Athenian legislator whose harsh codification of the law in 621 BC produced the word *draconian*. The code was largely abolished by Solon (594 BC); only his law on homicide remained.

Draco *Astron.* the Dragon, a large but faint constellation of the northern hemisphere.

draconian *adj., said of a law, etc* harsh, severe. [named after Draco, 7c Athenian lawgiver]

Dracula **1** a novel by Bram Stoker (1897). It describes the experiences of Jonathan Harker in the Transylvanian castle of Count Dracula, a human vampire. The archetypal vampire story, it has inspired numerous films and parodies. **2** a British film directed by Terence Fisher (1958). This version of the Dracula legend stars Christopher Lee as a sexually alluring vampire and Peter Cushing as the expert on vampires.

draft — *noun* **1** a written plan; a preliminary sketch. **2** a written order requesting a bank to pay out money, especially to another bank. **3** a group of people drafted. **4** *North Amer., esp. US* conscription. — *verb* **1** to set out in preliminary sketchy form. **2** to select and send off (personnel) to perform a specific task. **3** *North Amer., esp. US* to conscript. [a form of DRAUGHT]

Draft Conscription in the USA, a method of compulsory enlistment into the army, first introduced (1777) when the number of volunteers failed to meet the quotas demanded by the Continental Congress. Enacted both by the South (1862) and by the North (1863) during the American Civil War, it was regarded as flouting the US tradition of voluntary service, and, in the South, as an abuse of states' rights. The Selective Service Act (1940) was invoked in various crises such as the invasion of Korea, the Berlin Airlift, and the Cuban Missile Crisis. Much of the opposition to the Vietnam War centred on the draft. Eventually offenders numbered 570 000, so that under President Nixon a fairer lottery system was introduced in 1969, and the draft was ended in 1973.

draft-dodger *noun colloq. North Amer., esp. US* a person who avoids conscription.

drag — *verb* (**dragged, dragging**) **1** to pull roughly or violently; to pull along slowly and with force. **2** *trans., intrans.* to move or cause to move along scraping the ground. **3** *colloq.* (*usually* **drag someone away**) to force or persuade them to come away. **4** to search (eg a lake) with a hook or dragnet. — *noun* **1** an act of dragging; a dragging effect. **2** a person or thing that makes progress slow. **3** *colloq.* a draw on a cigarette. **4** *colloq.* a dull or tedious person or thing. **5** *colloq.* women's clothes worn by a man. **6** the resistance to motion that is encountered by an object travelling through a fluid (a liquid or gas). Drag is counteracted by the forward thrust of the engines of aircraft, but causes a substantial increase in fuel

consumption. The effects of drag are greatly reduced in aircraft, cars, and trains with a streamlined shape.

— **drag on** *colloq.* to proceed or continue slowly and tediously.

drag one's feet *or* **heels** *colloq.* to delay; to be deliberately slow to take action.

drag something out *colloq.* to make it last as long as possible.

drag something up *colloq.* to mention an unpleasant subject long forgotten.
[from Anglo-Saxon *dragan*]

draggle *verb trans., intrans.* to make or become wet and dirty (as if) through trailing along the ground. [from DRAG]

dragnet *noun* a heavy net pulled along the bottom of a river, lake, etc in a search for something.

dragon *noun* **1** a large mythical fire-breathing reptile-like creature with wings and a long tail. **2** *colloq.* a frighteningly domineering woman. [from Greek *drakon*]

dragonfly *noun* (PL. **dragonflies**) any insect belonging to the order Odonata, with a fairly large slender brightly coloured body, often metallic in appearance, gauzy translucent wings that cannot be closed, and large eyes covering most of the head. Dragonflies are commonly found near still or slow-moving water, and they feed on small insects which they catch in mid-air.

dragoon — *noun Hist.* a heavily armed mounted soldier. — *verb* to force or bully (someone) into doing something. [from French *dragon*]

drag race a contest in acceleration between specially designed cars over a short distance. See DRAGSTER.

drag-racing *noun* the activity or sport of competing in drag races.

dragster *noun* a car designed or adapted to be used in drag races.

drain — *verb* **1** (**drain liquid off** *or* **away**) to cause or allow it to escape. **2** (**drain something of liquid**) to remove liquid from it. **3** (**drain off**) *said of liquid, etc* to escape; to flow away. **4** to drink the total contents of (a glass, etc). **5** *trans., intrans.* (**drain away** *or* **drain something away**) to disappear or cause it to disappear: *our support drained away*. **6** to use up the strength, emotion, or resources of (someone). **7** *said of a river* to carry away surface water from (land). — *noun* **1** a device, especially a pipe, for carrying away liquid. **2** (**a drain on something**) anything that exhausts or seriously depletes a supply.

— **down the drain** *colloq.* wasted; lost.
[from Anglo-Saxon *dreahnian*]

drainage *noun* the process, method, or system of draining.

draining-board *noun* a sloping (especially channelled) surface at the side of a sink allowing water from washed dishes to drain away.

drainpipe *noun* **1** a pipe carrying water from a roof into a drain below ground. **2** (**drainpipes**) *colloq.* very narrow tight-fitting trousers.

Drake, Sir Francis (c.1540–96) English Elizabethan seaman, born in Crowndale, Devon. In 1567 he commanded the *Judith* in his kinsman John Hawkins's ill-fated expedition to the West Indies, and returned there several times to recover the losses sustained from the Spaniards, his exploits gaining him great popularity in England. In 1577 he set out with five ships for the Pacific, through the Straits of Magellan, but the rest of the fleet was battered by storm and fire. He continued in the *Golden Hind* across the Pacific, reached the Pelew Is, and returned to England via the Cape of Good Hope in 1580. The following year, Queen Elizabeth I visited his ship and knighted him. In 1585 he sailed with 25 ships against the Spanish Indies, bringing home tobacco, potatoes, and the dispirited Virginian colonists. In the week-long battle against the Spanish Armada (1588) in the Channel, his sea-

manship and courage brought him further distinction.

drake *noun* a male duck.

Drakensberg Mountains, Zulu **Kwathlamba Quathlamba** a mountain range in South Africa, extending NE–SW through Transvaal, Natal, and Cape provinces. It forms the E frontier of Lesotho with Natal and the W frontier of Swaziland with Transvaal. The highest peak, at the Natal–Lesotho frontier, is Thaban Ntlenyana (3 482m).

dram *noun* **1** *colloq.* a small amount of alcoholic spirit, especially whisky. **2** a measure of weight equal to 1/16 of an ounce. [from etymology as for DRACHMA]

drama *noun* **1** a play; any work performed by actors. **2** plays in general, as an art form. **3** the art of producing, directing, and acting in plays. **4** excitement and emotion; an exciting situation. [from Greek *drama*]

dramatherapy *noun Psychol.* a form of therapy in which drama is used as a means of acting out different responses to real-life situations, in order to aid personal development and gain insight into psychological problems and difficulties in personal relationships.

dramatic *adj.* **1** of or relating to plays, the theatre, or acting in general. **2** exciting. **3** sudden and striking; drastic. **4** *said of a person or behaviour* flamboyantly emotional.

dramatically *adv.* in a dramatic or exciting way.

dramatics *sing. noun* **1** activities associated with the staging and performing of plays. **2** exaggeratedly emotional behaviour.

dramatis personae a list of the characters in a play. [from Latin *dramatis personae*, persons of the drama]

dramatist *noun* a writer of plays.

dramatization *or* **dramatisation** *noun* an adaptation of a literary work as a play or drama.

dramatize *or* **dramatise** *verb* **1** to make into a work for public performance. **2** to treat as, or cause to seem, more exciting or important.

drank see DRINK.

drape *verb* **1** to hang (cloth) loosely over (something). **2** to arrange or lay loosely. [from Old French *draper*]

Draper, John William (1811–82) British-born US author and scientist, born in St Helens, near Liverpool. Professor of Chemistry and later President of the Medical Department at the University of New York, he was an early pioneer of photography and formulated 'Draper's law', the principle that only absorbed radiation can produce chemical change. He also established that all solids become incandescent at an identical temperature, and if heated enough, afford a continuous spectrum. A prolific author, today he is best remembered for various impassioned polemical studies of the history of science.

draper *noun* a person who sells fabric.

drapery *noun* (PL. **draperies**) **1** fabric; textiles. **2** curtains and other hanging fabrics. **3** a draper's business or shop.

drapes *pl. noun North Amer., esp. US* curtains.

drastic *adj.* extreme; severe. [from Greek *drastikos*, from *draein*, to act]

drastically *adv.* extremely; severely.

drat *interj. colloq.* expressing anger or annoyance. [an alteration of *God rot*]

dratted *adj. colloq.* expressing annoyance: *the dratted handle's come off*.

draught — *noun* **1** a current of air, especially indoors. **2** a quantity of liquid swallowed in one go. **3** the amount of water required to float a ship. **4** any of the discs used in the game of draughts. **5** *colloq.* draught beer. **6** the act of pulling or drawing. **7** a dose of liquid medicine. — *adj.* **1** *said of beer* pumped direct from the cask to the glass. **2** *said of an animal* used for pulling loads. — **on draught** *said of beer* stored in casks from which it is served direct. [from Anglo-Saxon *draht*, from *dragan*, to draw]

draughts *sing. noun* a game for two people played with 24 discs on a chequered board. ◇ Each player has twelve circular pieces, either black or white, which are arranged on alternate squares on the first three rows of the 64-square board. The object is to remove one's opponent's pieces by jumping over them to a vacant diagonal square. Only forward moves are permitted until a piece reaches the back line of the opposing territory, when it becomes a king and may move backward or forward.

draughtsman *noun* **1** a person skilled in drawing. **2** a person employed to produce accurate and detailed technical drawings. **3** any of the discs used in the game of draughts.

draughtsmanship *noun* skill in drawing, especially in technical drawing.

draughty *adj.* (**draughtier, draughtiest**) prone to or suffering draughts of air.

Dravidian — *adj.* **1** denoting a dark-skinned race of S India. **2** denoting a family of over 20 languages used mainly in India, SE Asia, Africa, and the Pacific. It includes Telugu, Tamil, Kannada, and Malayalam. — *noun* the languages forming this family.

draw — *verb* (PAST TENSE **drew**; PAST PARTICIPLE **drawn**) **1** *trans., intrans.* to make a picture of (something or someone), especially with a pencil. **2** to pull out, take out, or extract: *draw water from a well / with swords drawn.* **3** *intrans.* to move or proceed steadily in a specified direction: *draw nearer.* **4** (**draw on something**) to make use of assets from a fund or source: *draw on reserves of energy.* **5** to open or close (curtains). **6** to attract (eg attention or criticism). **7** *trans., intrans.* (*also* **draw with someone**) to end a game with neither side winning; to finish on equal terms with an opponent. **8** to choose or be given as the result of random selection. **9** (**be drawn on something**) to be persuaded to talk or give information: *he refused to be drawn on his plans.* **10** to arrive at or infer (a conclusion). **11** *intrans.* to suck air (eg through a cigarette). *said of a chimney* to cause air to flow through a fire, allowing burning. **12** *technical, said of a ship* to require (a certain depth of water) to float. **13** *intrans. said of tea* to brew or infuse. **14** to disembowel: *hanged, drawn, and quartered.* — *noun* **1** a result in which neither side is the winner; a tie. **2** the making of a random selection, eg of the winners of a competition; a competition with winners chosen at random. **3** the potential to attract many people, or a person or thing having this. **4** the act of drawing a gun. — **draw back from something** to refuse to become involved in it; to avoid commitment. **draw in** *said of nights* to start earlier, making days shorter. **draw the line** to fix a limit, eg on one's actions or tolerance. **draw something out** to make it last a long time or longer than necessary. **draw someone out** to encourage to be less shy or reserved. **draw up** to come to a halt. **draw something up** to plan and write a contract or other document. **draw oneself up** to lift oneself into an upright position. [from Anglo-Saxon *dragan*]

drawback *noun* a disadvantage.

Drawbell, James Wedgwood (1899–1979) Scottish journalist, born in Falkirk. After working as a reporter in N America, he was appointed editor of the *Sunday Chronicle* at the age of 24, one of the youngest Fleet Street editors. He also pioneered the development of *Woman's Own* as a mass-circulation magazine. His autobiography, *The Sun Within Us* (1963), includes a compelling account of his boyhood in a Falkirk tenement.

drawbridge *noun* a bridge that can be lifted to prevent access across, or to allow passage beneath.

drawer *noun* **1** a sliding lidless storage box fitted as part of a desk or other piece of furniture. **2** a person who draws. **3** (**drawers**) *old use* knickers, especially when large and roomy. — **out of the top drawer** *colloq.* of the very best quality or the highest standard. [see DRAW]

drawing *noun* any picture made up of lines, especially one drawn in pencil.

drawing-board *noun* a board to which paper is fixed for drawing. — **go back to the drawing-board** to return to the planning stage, to find a more successful approach.

drawing-pin *noun* a pin with a broad flat head, used especially for fastening paper to a board or wall.

drawing-room *noun* a sitting-room or living-room.

drawl *verb trans., intrans.* to speak or say in a slow lazy manner, especially with prolonged vowel sounds. [connected with DRAW]

drawn *adj.* showing signs of mental strain or tiredness.

-drawn *combining form* forming words meaning 'pulled by': *horse-drawn.*

drawn-out *adj.* tedious; prolonged.

drawstring *noun* a cord sewn inside a hem eg on a bag or piece of clothing, closing up the hem when pulled.

dray¹ *noun* a low horse-drawn cart used for heavy loads. [from Anglo-Saxon *dræge*, from *dragan*, to draw]

dray² same as DREY.

Dr Barnardo's Homes see BARNARDO'S.

dread — *noun* great fear or apprehension. — *verb* to look ahead to (something) with dread. — *adj. literary* inspiring awe or great fear. [from Anglo-Saxon *ondrædan*]

dreaded *adj.* **1** greatly feared. **2** *loosely* much disliked.

dreadful *adj.* **1** inspiring great fear; terrible. **2** *loosely* very bad, unpleasant, or extreme.

dreadfully *adv.* **1** terribly. **2** *colloq.* extremely; very: *it's dreadfully late.*

dreadlocks *pl. noun* thin braids of hair tied tightly all over the head, especially worn by Rastafarians.

Dreadnought, HMS a British battleship armed entirely with 'big guns', launched in 1906. Its production heralded the start of the pre-World War I naval race between Britain and Germany.

dreadnought *noun* **1** a heavily armed battleship. **2** a fearless person.

dream — *noun* **1** a series of unconscious thoughts and mental images that are experienced during sleep, and may be pleasant, bizarre, or (in the case of nightmares) frightening. Most dreams are not remembered on waking. **2** a state of complete engrossment in one's own thoughts. **3** a distant ambition, especially unattainable. **4** *colloq.* an extremely pleasing person or thing. **5** *colloq.* (*attributive*) luxurious, ideal. — *verb* (PAST AND PAST PARTICIPLE **dreamed, dreamt**) **1** *trans., intrans.* to have thoughts and visions during sleep. **2** (*usually* **dream of something**) **a** to have a distant ambition or hope. **b** to imagine or conceive of something. **3** *intrans.* to have extravagant and unrealistic thoughts or plans. **4** *intrans.* to be lost in thought. — **dream something up** to devise or invent something unusual or absurd. **like a dream** *colloq.* extremely well, easily, or successfully. [from Middle English] ◇ Dreaming takes place during relatively light sleep, when brain activity is similar to that of a person who is awake and alert. During such phases of sleep the muscles are relaxed and the eyes move rapidly beneath the eyelids. This is known as REM (rapid eye movement), and a person who is woken during REM sleep (which occurs several times during the night) will remember his or her dream. Many scientists believe that dreams allow the brain to dispose of unwanted information, but some psychologists consider that the content of dreams is very important, and can indicate hidden or repressed memories that are causing psychological or emotional problems.

Dream, The a painting by Henri Rousseau (1910, New York). It is set against an exotic jungle landscape.

dreamboat *noun slang* an ideal romantic partner.

dreamer *noun* a person who dreams, especially of unrealistic schemes.

dreamily *adv.* in a dreamy or unreal way.

dreaminess *noun* a dreamy or unreal state.

dream ticket *chiefly North Amer.* an ideal or optimum list of electoral candidates.

Dreamtime *or* **The Dreaming** in the mythology of the Australian Aborigines, one of the names for the time of the Ancestors, who created the world and are still alive in the sacred places. This time continues to exist, and it may be possible to find it through dreams.

dreamy *adj.* (**dreamier, dreamiest**) **1** unreal, like a dream. **2** having or showing a wandering mind. **3** *colloq.* lovely.

drearily *adv.* in a dreary or uninteresting way.

dreariness *noun* a dreary or uninteresting state or appearance.

dreary *adj.* (**drearier, dreariest**) **1** dull and depressing. **2** uninteresting. [from Anglo-Saxon *dreorig*, bloody, mournful]

dredge¹ — *verb trans., intrans.* to clear the bottom of or deepen (the sea or a river) by bringing up mud and waste. — *noun* a machine for dredging, with a scooping or sucking action. — **dredge something up** *colloq.* to mention or bring up something long forgotten.

dredge² *verb* to sprinkle (food), eg with sugar or flour. [from Old French *dragie*, sugar-plum]

dredger *noun* a barge or ship fitted with a dredge.

dregs *pl. noun* **1** solid particles in a liquid that settle at the bottom. **2** worthless or contemptible elements. [from Norse *dregg*]

drench — *verb* **1** to make soaking wet. **2** to administer liquid medicine to (an animal). — *noun* a dose of liquid medicine for an animal. [from Anglo-Saxon *drencan*, to cause to drink]

Dresden POP (1991e) 493 000, the capital of the state of Saxony, E central Germany. It lies on the R Elbe, SE of Berlin, close to the frontier with the Czech Republic. The former capital of Saxony, it was almost totally destroyed by bombing in 1945, and has been rebuilt. Dresden china is now manufactured in Meissen.

Dresden, Battle of Napoleon's last victory (1813) in Germany, fought outside the Saxon capital Dresden, then a major French depot, against an allied force of Austrian, Prussian, and Russian troops under Prince Schwarzenberg (1771–1820). The French success did not continue however, for the Allies defeated them twice in the following 10 days.

dress — _verb_ **1** _trans., intrans._ to put clothes on; to (cause to) wear clothes (of a certain kind). **2** to treat and bandage (wounds). **3** to prepare, or add seasoning or a sauce to (food). **4** to arrange a display in (a window): _window dressing._ **5** to shape and smooth (especially stone). **6** _intrans._ to put on or have on formal evening wear. — _noun_ **1** a woman's garment with top and skirt in one piece. **2** clothing; wear: _in evening dress._ — _adj._ formal; for wear in the evenings: _dress jacket._ — **dress someone down** to scold them.

dress up 1 to put on fancy dress. **2** to dress in very smart or formal clothes.

dress something up to make it appear more pleasant or acceptable by making additions or alterations. [from Old French _dresser_, to prepare]

dressage _noun_ horses' training in, or performance of, set manoeuvres signalled by the rider. [from French _dressage_]

dress circle a balcony in a theatre, especially the first above the ground floor.

dresser _noun_ **1** a free-standing kitchen cupboard with shelves above, for storing and displaying dishes, etc. **2** a theatre assistant employed to help stage actors with their costumes. **3** a person who dresses in a particular way.

dressily _adv._ with a dressy or stylish manner.

dressing _noun_ **1** any sauce added to food, especially salad. **2** a covering for a wound. **3** _Agric._ **a** an application of fertilizer to the soil surface. **b** chemical treatment of seeds, especially those of cereal crops, before sowing in order to control fungal diseases.

dressing-down _noun_ a reprimand.

dressing-gown _noun_ a loose robe worn informally indoors, especially over nightclothes.

dressing-table _noun_ a piece of bedroom furniture typically with drawers and a large mirror.

dressmaker _noun_ a person who makes women's clothes.

dressmaking _noun_ the business of making women's clothes.

dress rehearsal 1 the last rehearsal of a play, with full costumes, lighting and other effects. **2** a practice under real conditions, or an event considered as such in relation to another more important.

dressy _adj._ (**dressier, dressiest**) **1** dressed or dressing stylishly. **2** _said of clothes_ for formal wear; elegant. **3** _colloq._ fancy; over-decorated.

drew see DRAW.

drey _noun_ a squirrel's nest.

Dreyfus, Alfred (c.1859–1935) French Jewish army officer, born in Mülhausen, Alsace. An artillery captain on the General Staff, in 1893–4 he was falsely charged with delivering defence secrets to the Germans. He was court-martialled and transported to Devil's I, French Guiana. Efforts to prove his innocence provoked a vigorous response from militarists and anti-Semites, and deeply divided the French intellectual and political world. The writer Emile Zola assailed the government in his celebrated _J'Accuse_ (1898). Proof of his innocence came when German military documents were uncovered in 1930.

dribble — _verb_ **1** _intrans._ to fall or flow in drops. **2** _intrans._ to allow saliva to run slowly down from the mouth. **3** _trans., intrans._ to move along keeping (a ball) in close control with frequent short strokes. — _noun_ **1** a small quantity of liquid, especially saliva. **2** an act of dribbling a ball. [from obsolete _drib_]

driblet _noun_ a very small amount, especially of liquid. [see DRIBBLE]

dribs and drabs very small quantities at a time. [see DRIBBLE]

drier or **dryer** _noun_ a device or substance that dries hair, paint, etc.

Driesch, Hans (Adolf Eduard) (1867–1941) German zoologist and philosopher, born in Bad Kreuznach, Prussia. He was Professor of Philosophy at Heidelberg (1912), Cologne (1919), and Leipzig (1921). He did valuable work in embryology and parapsychology, and became an exponent of vitalism (the doctrine that there is a vital life force).

drift — _noun_ **1** _Geol._ superficial deposits of rock material that have been carried from their place of origin by glaciers. **2** _Geol._ continental drift. **3** a general movement or tendency to move. **4** the movement of a stretch of sea in the direction of a prevailing wind. **5** degree of movement off course caused by wind or a current. **6** the general or essential meaning of something. — _verb intrans._ **1** to float or be blown along or into heaps. **2** to move aimlessly or passively from one place or occupation to another. **3** to move off course. [from Norse _drift_, snowdrift]

drifter _noun_ **1** a fishing-boat that uses a drift-net. **2** a person who moves from place to place, settling in none.

drift-net _noun_ a large fishing-net allowed to drift with the tide.

driftwood _noun_ wood floating near, or washed up on, a shore.

drill[1] — _noun_ **1** a tool for boring holes. **2** a training exercise, or a session of it. **3** correct procedure; routine. — _verb_ **1** _trans., intrans._ to make (a hole) with a drill; to make a hole in (something) with a drill. **2** to exercise or teach through repeated practice. [probably from Dutch _drillen_, to bore]

drill[2] _noun_ thick strong cotton cloth. [from German _Drillich_, ticking]

drill[3] — _noun_ **1** a shallow furrow in which seeds are sown; the seeds sown. **2** a machine for sowing seeds in rows. — _verb_ to sow in rows.

drill[4] _noun_ a W African baboon related to, but smaller than, the mandrill. [from a W African language]

drily see DRY.

drink — _verb_ (PAST TENSE **drank**; PAST PARTICIPLE **drunk**) **1** _trans., intrans._ to swallow (a liquid); to consume (a liquid) by swallowing. **2** _intrans._ to drink alcohol; to drink alcohol to excess. **3** to get (oneself) into a certain state by drinking alcohol: _drank himself silly / drank themselves into a stupor._ **4** _trans., intrans._ (**drink to someone** or **something**) to drink a toast to them. — _noun_ **1** an act of drinking; a liquid suitable for drinking. **2** alcohol of any kind; the habit of drinking alcohol to excess. **3** a glass or amount of drink. **4** (**the drink**) _colloq._ the sea. — **drink something in** to listen to it eagerly. [from Anglo-Saxon _drincan_]

drinkable _adj._ fit to be drunk.

drink-driver _noun_ a person who drives while under the influence of alcohol.

drink-driving _noun_ the act or practice of driving while under the influence of alcohol.

drinker _noun_ a person who drinks, especially alcohol.

drip — _verb_ (**dripped, dripping**) **1** _trans., intrans._ to release or fall in drops. **2** _intrans._ to release a liquid in drops: _a dripping tap._ **3** _trans., intrans. colloq._ to bear or contain an impressive or excessive amount of something: _a film dripping with sentimentality._ — _noun_ **1** the action or noise of dripping. **2** same as DRIP-FEED. **3** _derog. colloq._ a person lacking spirit or character. [from Anglo-Saxon _dryppan_]

drip-dry — _adj., said of a garment_ requiring little or no ironing if hung up to dry. — _verb trans., intrans._ to dry in this way.

drip-feed — _noun_ a device for passing a liquid solution slowly and continuously into a vein. — _verb_ to feed with a liquid in this way.

dripping _noun_ fat from roasted meat, especially when solidified.

drive — _verb_ (PAST TENSE **drove**; PAST PARTICIPLE **driven**) **1** _trans., intrans._ to control the movement of (a vehicle); to be legally qualified to do so. **2** _intrans._ to travel in a vehicle. **3** to take or transport in a vehicle. **4** to urge or force to move. **5** to strike or cause to strike firmly. **6** to produce motion in; to cause to function. **7** (**be driven by something**) to be motivated by it: _they were driven to steal by sheer hunger._ **8** to conduct or dictate: _drive a hard bargain._ — _noun_ **1** a trip in a vehicle; travel by road. **2** (**driveway**) a path for vehicles, leading from a private residence to the road outside. **3** energy and enthusiasm. **4** an organized campaign; a group effort: _economy drive._ **5** operating power, or a device supplying this. **6** a forceful strike of a ball in various sports. **7** a united movement forward, especially by a military force. **8** a meeting to play a game, especially cards. — **be driving at something** to intend or imply it as a meaning or conclusion: _what is he driving at?_ **drive something home** to make it clearly understood. [from Anglo-Saxon _drifan_]

drive-in _noun adj., said of a cinema, restaurant, etc_ providing a service or facility for customers remaining seated in vehicles.

drivel — _noun_ nonsense. — _verb intrans._ (**drivelled, drivelling**) **1** to talk nonsense. **2** to dribble or slaver. [from Anglo-Saxon _dreflian_, to dribble]

driver _noun_ **1** a person who drives a vehicle. **2** a large-headed golf club for hitting the ball from the tee.

driving — _noun_ the act, practice, or way of driving vehicles. — _adj._ **1** producing or transmitting operating power: _driving wheel._ **2** heavy and windblown: _driving rain._ **3** providing the motive for determined hard work.

driving licence an official licence to drive a motor vehicle.

◇ In the UK, a _provisional driving licence_ entitles a person over the age of 17 to drive certain categories of motor vehicle provided they are, at all times, accompanied by a person holding a full driving licence. A _full driving licence_ entitles a driver to drive on the public roads unaccompanied; and _heavy-goods-vehicle licence_ is a licence to drive larger vehicles, such as lorries over a certain tonnage, buses, and coaches.

driving seat
— **in the driving seat** _colloq._ in a controlling or commanding position.

driving test a test of ability to drive safely, especially an official or obligatory test. In the UK, the official driving test is administered by the Department of Transport.

drizzle — _noun_ fine light rain. — _verb intrans._ to rain lightly. [from Anglo-Saxon _dreosan_, to fall]

drizzly _adj., said of the weather_ inclined to drizzle.

Dr Jekyll and Mr Hyde, The Strange Case of a novel by Robert Louis Stevenson (1886). It describes the events following the respectable Dr Jekyll's attempts to split his nature by drinking a potion which changes him into the evil Mr Hyde.

Drogheda, Gaelic **Droichead Átha** POP (1991) 25 000, an industrial seaport in Louth county, NE Leinster province, E Irish Republic. It stands on the R Boyne, N of Dublin and was the meeting-place of the Irish parliaments until 1494. NOTABLE FEATURES Neolithic passage graves 7km/4mi W; remains of a 5c monastery at Monasterboice, 8km/5mi N; Battle of the Boyne field (1690), 6km/4mi SW.

droit de seigneur 1 _Hist._ the alleged right of a feudal lord to take the virginity of a vassal's bride on her wedding night. **2** an excessive or unreasonable demand made of a subordinate. [French, = lord's right]

droll *adj.* oddly amusing or comical. [from French *drôle*]

drollery *noun* droll or oddly amusing ideas or humour.

drolly *adv.* in a droll or oddly amusing way.

dromedary *noun* (PL. **dromedaries**) a breed of single-humped camel that is capable of moving at speed across the desert, and is much used as a means of transport in N Africa, the Middle East, and India. See also BACTRIAN. [from Greek *dromados*, running]

Dromio the name of twin brothers, Dromio of Ephesus and Dromio of Syracuse, servants of Antipholus of Ephesus and Antipholus of Syracuse respectively, in Shakespeare's *The Comedy of Errors*.

drone — *verb intrans.* **1** to make a low humming noise. **2** (**drone on**) to talk at length in a tedious monotonous voice. — *noun* **1** a deep humming sound. **2** a male social insect, eg honeybee, ant, that does not contribute to the maintenance of the colony, and whose sole function is to mate with fertile females. See also WORKER. **3** a lazy person, especially one living off others. [from Anglo-Saxon *dran*, bee]

Dronning Maud Land see QUEEN MAUD LAND.

drool *verb intrans.* **1** to dribble or slaver. **2** (**drool over something**) to show uncontrolled admiration for it or pleasure at the sight of it. [alteration of DRIVEL]

droop — *verb intrans.* **1** to hang loosely; to sag. **2** to be weak with tiredness. — *noun* drooping state. [from Norse *drupa*]

droopy *adj.* (**droopier, droopiest**) hanging loosely; drooping.

drop — *verb* (**dropped, dropping**) **1** *trans., intrans.* to fall or allow to fall. **2** *trans., intrans.* to decline or cause to decline; to lower or weaken. **3** to give up or abandon (eg a friend or a habit); to stop doing temporarily. **4** to stop discussing (a topic). **5** (*also* **drop someone** *or* **something off**) to set them down from a vehicle; to deliver or hand them in. **6** to leave or take out: *they've dropped me from the team*. **7** to mention casually: *drop a hint*. **8** to fail to pronounce: *drop one's h's*. **9** *colloq.* to write informally: *drop me a line*. **10** *intrans.* (**drop into something**) to pass idly or passively (into a habit, etc). **11** *coarse slang* to give birth to. **12** *slang* to beat to the ground. — *noun* **1** a small round or pear-shaped mass of liquid, especially falling; a small amount (of liquid). **2** a descent; a fall. **3** a vertical distance. **4** a decline or decrease. **5** any small round or pear-shaped object, eg an earring or boiled sweet. **6** (**drops**) liquid medication administered in small amounts. **7** a delivery.
— **at the drop of a hat** *colloq.* promptly; for the slightest reason.
drop back *or* **behind** to get left behind others in a group.
drop in *or* **by** to pay a brief unexpected visit.
drop off *colloq.* to fall asleep.
drop out 1 to withdraw from an activity. **2** *colloq.* to adopt an alternative lifestyle as a reaction against traditional social values.
drop out of something to withdraw eg from a pre-arranged activity.
let something drop to make it known inadvertently or as if inadvertently.
[from Anglo-Saxon *droppian*]

drop-kick — *noun Rugby* a kick in which the ball is released from the hands and struck as it hits the ground. — *verb* to kick (a ball) in this way.

droplet *noun* a tiny drop.

dropout *noun* **1** a student who quits before completing a course of study. **2** a person whose

alternative lifestyle is a reaction against traditional social values. *loosely* any unconventional person. See also DROP OUT.

drop-out *noun* **1** *Telecomm.* a brief loss of signal, especially in magnetic recording. **2** *Comput.* a patch which fails to record data on a magnetic tape.

dropper *noun* a short narrow glass tube with a rubber bulb on one end, for applying liquid in drops.

droppings *pl. noun* animal faeces.

dropsical *adj.* affected with dropsy.

dropsy *noun* the former name for oedema (the abnormal accumulation of fluid in the body tissues). [from Greek *hydrops*, from *hydor*, water]

dross *noun* **1** waste coal. **2** scum that forms on molten metal. **3** *derog. colloq.* rubbish; any worthless substance. [from Anglo-Saxon *dros*]

Droste-Hülshoff, Annette Elisabeth, Baroness von (1797–1848) German poet, born near Münster, Westphalia. She led a secluded life on her family estate and wrote poetry mainly on religious themes and on the Westphalian countryside. She also wrote a novella, *Die Judenbuche* (1842, The Jew's Beech). Her devotional verses were published posthumously as *Geistliche Jahre* (1851, Spiritual Years).

drought *noun* a prolonged lack of rainfall. [from Anglo-Saxon *drugath*, dryness]

drove¹ past tense of **drive**.

drove² *noun* **1** a moving herd of animals, especially cattle. **2** a large moving crowd. [from Anglo-Saxon *draf*, herd]

drover *noun Hist.* a person employed to drive farm animals to and from market.

drown *verb* **1** *intrans.* to die by suffocation as a result of inhaling liquid, especially water, into the lungs. **2** to kill by suffocation in this way. **3** to apply an excessive amount of liquid to; to soak or flood. **4** (**drown something out**) to suppress the effect of one sound with a louder one.
— **drown one's sorrows** *colloq.* to become drunk in order to forget one's troubles.
[from Middle English *drounen*]

drowse *verb intrans.* to sleep lightly for a short while; to be in a pleasantly sleepy state. [from Anglo-Saxon *drusian*, to be sluggish]

drowsily *adv.* in a drowsy or sleepy way.

drowsiness *noun* a drowsy or sleepy state or manner.

drowsy *adj.* (**drowsier, drowsiest**) **1** sleepy; causing sleepiness. **2** lethargic. **3** quiet and peaceful.

drub *verb* (**drubbed, drubbing**) **1** to defeat severely. **2** to beat; to thump. [from Arabic *daraba*, to beat]

drubbing *noun* a beating; a complete defeat.

drudge — *verb intrans.* to do hard, tedious, or menial work. — *noun* a servant; a labourer.

drudgery *noun* tedious or menial work.

drug — *noun* **1** any chemical substance which, when taken into the body or applied externally, has a specific effect on its functioning. Drugs may be therapeutic, when used to prevent or treat disease, or they may become progressively addictive when used for purposes of self-indulgence. **2** any narcotic drug, especially an addictive one, possession of which is illegal. **3** anything craved for. — *verb* (**drugged, drugging**) **1** to administer a drug to. **2** to poison or stupefy with drugs. **3** *said of food, etc* to mix or season with drugs.
— **a drug on the market** a commodity in plentiful supply but not in demand.
[from Old French *drogue*]
◇ The most widely used drugs are medicines, taken for the prevention, treatment, and cure of disease, and for the relief of symptoms such as pain, most drugs being active in doses of mil-

ligrams or less. Some drugs, including hormones, occur naturally in the body and are usually administered to compensate for a deficiency. A number of drugs are extracted from plants, but most are now synthesized chemically, and all new drugs are rigorously tested before being licensed for public use. Official instructions for their preparation and purity are published in a pharmacopoeia, and any dispensed drug must comply with these standards. In the UK, certain drugs are available only on prescription.

All drugs are prescribed in specific doses, as even a small overdose can lead to serious side-effects. Certain drugs in combination can also have harmful consequences, and a few can provoke an allergic reaction, or a patient may suddenly develop an allergy to a drug that was previously well tolerated. Certain drugs are addictive, so that a person gradually becomes physically or psychologically dependent on them, and withdrawal symptoms occur if the dosage is not maintained.

drug addiction the physical and psychological effects that result from taking certain drugs habitually, characterized by a compulsion to continue experiencing the mental effects of the drug, or to avoid the pain or discomfort of its absence.
◇ Long-term drug addicts often need to increase the doses of the drug they are taking in order to obtain the same effect, because they have developed *drug tolerance*, and this may lead to criminal behaviour, usually theft, in order to pay for the drug, especially if it is an illegal one. Drugs that produce *physical dependence*, in which withdrawal of a drug causes specific *withdrawal symptoms* such as vomiting, sweating, and tremors, include alcohol and 'hard' drugs such as cocaine, heroin, and morphine. Drugs that produce *psychological dependence* (in which the drug is used to induce a state of well-being, but there are no physical withdrawal symptoms on stopping the drug) include nicotine, cannabis, and amphetamines. The prolonged use of many types of minor tranquillizer has also been found to be highly addictive. Overdosing on hard drugs can be fatal, and the use of infected needles to inject such drugs is a major cause of the spread of AIDS.

drugget *noun* thick coarse woollen fabric; a protective cover for a floor or carpet made from this. [from Old French *droguet*, waste fabric]

druggist *noun North Amer., esp. US* a pharmacist.

drugstore *noun North Amer., esp. US* a chemist's shop, especially one also selling refreshments.

druid *noun* **1** a member of a Celtic order of priests in N Europe in pre-Christian times. **2** an eisteddfod official. [from Gaulish *druides*]
◇ They are known to have existed in pre-Roman Gaul and the British Isles. According to classical authors, notably Pliny, they came from a warrior aristocracy, and acted as arbitrators as well as priests, healers, seers, and divines. Their rites are said to have been conducted in oak groves, and to have included human sacrifice. At the time of the Roman conquest, they had great power among the Western Celts, although this steadily declined under Roman occupation. Various groups who have claimed to revive ancient British traditions have been influenced by romantic and unhistorical reconstructions of the Druidic cult produced by antiquaries in the 18c and 19c. There is no evidence to connect the Celtic Druids with Stonehenge.

druidic *or* **druidical** *adj.* relating to or belonging to the druids.

drum — *noun* **1** a percussion instrument consisting of a hollow frame with a skin or other membrane stretched tightly across its opening, sounding when struck. **2** any object resembling this in shape, especially a cylindrical container. **3** an eardrum. — *verb* (**drummed, drumming**) **1**

intrans. to beat a drum. **2** *trans., intrans.* to make continuous tapping or thumping sounds (with).
— **drum something in** *or* **into someone** to force something into their mind through constant repetition.
drum someone out to expel them.
drum something up *colloq.* to achieve or attract it by energetic persuasion: *managed to drum up more support.*
[from German *Trommel*, originally imitative]
◇ In the symphony orchestra, the most widely-used types are bass and tenor drums, side (or snare) drum, tabor, and timpani (which can be tuned to a definite pitch). In pop and rock music, the drum kit (played by a single member of the group) is an arrangement of snare drum, tenor drum, bass drum, and cymbals. In recent years, electronically-operated drum machines have been introduced.

drumhead *noun* the part of a drum that is struck.

drumlin *noun Geol.* a small streamlined hill produced by the pressure of moving ice over glacial deposits. Drumlins often occur in groups, producing a 'basket of eggs' topography. [from Scottish and Irish Gaelic *druim*, back]

drum machine a synthesizer for simulating the sound of drums and other percussion instruments.

drum major the leader of a marching (especially military) band.

drum majorette see MAJORETTE.

drummer *noun* a person who plays drums.

Drummond, Catriona the title character in Robert Louis Stevenson's *Catriona*, who is the daughter of James More and loved by David Balfour.

Drummond, William, of Hawthornden (1585–1649) Scottish poet, born in Hawthornden, near Edinburgh. He studied law in France, then became Laird of Hawthornden (1610) and devoted his life to poetry. His *Poems* were published in 1616, and the best-known of his prose works is *A Cypresse Grove* (1623), a meditation on death. He also wrote numerous royalist pamphlets, and a *History of Scotland 1423–1524*, published posthumously in 1655.

drumstick *noun* **1** a stick used for beating a drum. **2** the lower leg of a cooked fowl, especially a chicken.

drunk — *verb* past participle of DRINK. — *adj.* **1** lacking control in movement, speech, etc through having drunk an excess of alcohol. **2** (**drunk with something**) intoxicated or overwhelmed with it: *drunk with self-pity.* — *noun* a drunk person, especially one regularly drunk.

drunkard *noun* a person who is often drunk.

drunken *adj.* **1** drunk. **2** relating to, or brought on by, alcoholic intoxication.

drunkenly *adv.* with a drunken manner.

drunkenness *noun* being drunk; a drunken state or manner.

drupe *noun Bot.* a fleshy fruit containing one or more seeds that are surrounded by a stony protective layer or *endocarp*, eg plum, cherry, peach, holly. Raspberries and blackberries are clusters of small drupes, and not true berries. [from Greek *dryppa*, olive]

Drury Lane Theatre the oldest theatre in London, on a site originally occupied by the theatre which was built by the dramatist Thomas Killigrew and opened in 1663. It is one of the two patent theatres (the other is Covent Garden). Destroyed by fire, it was redesigned by Sir Christopher Wren (1674) and from 1711 it became well established under the management of the actors Robert Wilks, Colley Cibber, and Thomas Doggett. David Garrick made his first appearance there in Thomas Otway's *The Orphan* (1742); his years of management

(1747–76) were the greatest yet seen in the history of Drury Lane. Then Richard Brinsley Sheridan took over (1776–88) with his *School for Scandal*, and Sarah Siddons and John Kemble made their names, as did Edmund Kean in the early 1800s, and Henry Irving and Ellen Terry in the 1900s.

Druze *or* **Druz** *or* **Druse** — *sing. or pl. noun Relig.* a people, or a member of a people, inhabiting chiefly a mountainous district in the south of Syria, whose religion deviates considerably in belief and practice from the main Muslim body. The faith originated during the closing years of the Fatimid caliph al-Hakim (AD 996–1021), who some extreme Ismaelis regarded as a manifestation of Divinity. The Druze await the return from divine concealment of both al-Hakim and his disciple, Hamza ibn Ali. They assemble on Thursdays, instead of the usual Fridays, reject many of the prescriptions of the canon law of Islam, affirm monogamous marriage, and believe in the transmigration of souls. — *adj.* relating to this people or their religion. [perhaps from *Darazi*, an early exponent of the religion]

dry — *adj.* (**drier, driest**) **1** free from moisture or wetness. **2** with little or no rainfall. **3** from which all the water has evaporated or been taken: *a dry well.* **4** thirsty. **5** *said of an animal* no longer producing milk. **6** *said of wine, etc* not sweet. **7** not buttered. **8** *said of humour* expressed in a quietly sarcastic or matter-of-fact way. **9** forbidding the sale and consumption of alcohol. **10** *said of eyes* without tears. **11** dull; uninteresting. **12** lacking warmth of character. **13** *said of a cough* not producing catarrh. — *verb* (**dries, dried**) **1** *trans., intrans.* to make or become dry. **2** *trans.* to preserve (food) by removing all moisture. — *noun* (PL. **dries**) *colloq.* a staunch right-wing Conservative politician. See also WET.
— **dry out 1** to become completely dry. **2** *colloq.* to receive treatment to cure addiction to alcohol; to have one's addiction cured.
dry something out to dry it completely.
dry up 1 *colloq., said of a speaker or actor* to run out of words; to forget lines while on stage. **2** *slang* to shut up or be quiet.
dry something up to dry (dishes) after washing them.
[from Anglo-Saxon *dryge*]

dryad *noun Greek Mythol.* a woodland nymph or fairy, often with demigod status. [from Greek *dryados*]

dry battery a battery consisting of dry cells.

dry cell *Chem.* an electrolytic cell in which current is passed through an electrolyte that consists of a moist paste, eg ammonium chloride, instead of a liquid. Dry cells are used as portable energy sources in batteries for torches, radios, calculators, etc.

dry-clean *verb* to clean (especially clothes) with liquid chemicals, not with water.

dry-cleaner *noun* a business that dry-cleans clothes, etc.

dry-cleaning *noun* clothes, etc to be dry-cleaned.

Dryden, John (1631–1700) English poet, born in Aldwinkle, Northamptonshire. He went to London in 1657, where he wrote several plays and satires for the court. His first successful play was *The Indian Emperor* (1665), written in heroic couplets. After 1676, he began to write in blank verse and produced the play *All for Love* (1678). In 1668 he was made Poet Laureate and in, 1670, royal historiographer. He wrote a series of satires, notably *Absalom and Achitophel* (1681), which did much to turn opinion against the Whigs. He also wrote the didactic poem *Religio Laici* (1682), which argues the case for Anglicanism, and *The Hind and the Panther* (1687), marking his conversion to Catholicism. He lost his laureateship on the accession of William III (1688), and took to translation as a means of survival.

dry dock a dock from which the water can be pumped out to allow work on a ship's lower parts.

dryer see DRIER.

dry ice solid carbon dioxide used as a refrigerating agent.

dry land land as opposed to sea or other water.

dryness *noun* a dry state.

drypoint *noun* a technique of engraving in intaglio print-making in which the design is incised by direct pressure into the copper plate, using a strong steel or diamond-pointed tool. Dürer experimented with the technique in the 16c, executing whole prints in drypoint. It is more commonly used in combination with other engraving methods, to add tonal depth and accented line; Rembrandt used it with great mastery in many of his etchings.

dry rot 1 *Bot.* a serious type of timber decay caused by the fungus *Serpula lacrymans*, common in damp, poorly ventilated buildings. Infected wood typically shows cross-grain cracking, and eventually becomes brittle, disintegrates and crumbles into a powdery mass. **2** *Bot.* several fungal diseases of plants, eg stored potatoes, fruit.

dry run a rehearsal or practice.

dry-stone *adj., said of a wall* made of stones wedged together without mortar.

DSC *abbrev.* Distinguished Service Cross.

DSc *abbrev.* Doctor of Science.

DSM *abbrev.* Distinguished Service Medal.

DSO *abbrev.* Distinguished Service Order.

DSS *abbrev.* Department of Social Services.

DST *abbrev.* daylight saving time.

DT *or* **DTs** *abbrev.* delirium tremens.

DTh *or* **DTheol** *abbrev.* Doctor of Theology.

DTI *abbrev.* Department of Trade and Industry.

DTP *abbrev.* desktop publishing.

dual *adj.* **1** consisting of or representing two separate parts. **2** double; twofold. [from Latin *duo*, two]

Duala see DOUALA.

Dual Alliance a defensive alliance (1879) between the German and Austro-Hungarian Empires, which assured 'reciprocal protection' from direct Russian attack, and at least benevolent neutrality in case of an attack from any other power. By the inclusion of Italy it expanded to the Triple Alliance (1882), and remained the focus of German and Austro-Hungarian foreign policy until 1918.

dual carriageway a road on which traffic moving in opposite directions is separated by a central barrier or strip of land.

dualism *noun Philos.* the belief that reality is made up of two separate parts, one spiritual and one physical, or influenced by two separate forces, one good and one bad.

duality *noun* the state of being double.

Duarte, Pico formerly **Monte Trujillo** a mountain in the Cordillera Central of the Dominican Republic. HEIGHT 3 175m. It is the highest peak in the Caribbean.

dub¹ *verb* (**dubbed, dubbing**) **1** to give a name, especially a nickname, to. **2** to confer the title of knight on by touching each shoulder with a sword. **3** to smear (leather) with grease. [from Anglo-Saxon *dubbian*]

dub² — *verb* (**dubbed, dubbing**) **1** to add a new soundtrack to (eg a film), especially one in a different language. **2** to add sound effects or music to (eg a film). — *noun* a type of reggae music in which bass, drums and the artistic arrangement are given prominence over voice and other instruments. [contraction of DOUBLE]

Dubai *or* **Dubayy** POP (1985) 419 000, the second largest of the United Arab Emirates, NE of Abu Dhabi. AREA 3 900sq km/1 505sq mi. CAPITAL Dubai. CHIEF TOWN Mina Jebel Ali (a free trade zone). Oil was discovered in 1966 and the production and export of crude oil began in 1969.

Du Barry, Marie Jeanne Gomard de Vaubernier, Comtesse (Countess) (c.1743–93) the favourite mistress of Louis XV, born in Vaucouleurs. Brought up in a convent, she won the attention of Louis XV (1768), and married Comte Guillaume du Barry before she became official royal mistress. She exerted much influence until Louis died in 1774, when she was dismissed from court. She was tried before the Revolutionary Tribunal, and guillotined.

dubbin *noun* a wax-like mixture of oil and tallow for softening and waterproofing leather. [from DUB¹]

Dubček, Alexander (1921–92) Czechoslovakian statesman, born in Uhrovek, Slovakia. He joined the Communist Party in 1939, fought as a Slovak patriot against the Nazis (1944–5), and rose to become First Secretary in the Party (1968). His far-reaching economic and political reforms included the abolition of censorship and increased freedom of speech, but his liberalization policy led to the occupation of Czechoslovakia by Soviet forces (Aug 1968), and in 1969 he was replaced by Gustáv Husk. He became President of the Federal Assembly, but was then expelled from the Presidium, and deprived of Party membership in 1970. In 1989, following a popular uprising, and the resignation of the Communist government, he was elected Chairman of the Federal Assembly, but he lost his parliamentary seat in the elections of Jun 1992. He died later that year from injuries sustained in a car accident.

dubiety *noun formal* dubiousness. [from Latin *dubietas*]

dubious *adj.* 1 feeling doubt; unsure; uncertain. 2 arousing suspicion; potentially dishonest or dishonestly obtained. [from Latin *dubium*, doubt]

dubiously *adv.* in a dubious or suspicious way.

Dublin, Gaelic **Baile Átha Cliath** POP (1991) 1m, a county in Leinster province, E Irish Republic. AREA 922sq km/356sq mi. PHYSICAL DESCRIPTION bisected W–E by the R Liffey and the Grand Canal; the Wicklow Mts rise in the S; the Irish Sea to the W. CHIEF TOWNS Dublin (capital), Dunleary. ECONOMY agriculture, livestock; Dublin trade and industries.

Dublin, Gaelic **Baile Átha Cliath**, ancient **Eblana** POP (1991) 916 000, the capital of the Irish Republic and of Dublin county. It is a trading port at the mouth of the R Liffey where it meets the Irish Sea. HISTORY a Viking settlement from the 9c until the 11c; the centre of English rule from the 12c until 1919; the site of the first Sinn Féin parliament in 1919. NOTABLE FEATURES King's Inns; National Museum; National Gallery; Leinster House; Dublin Castle; Abbey Theatre; Book of Kells (in Trinity College Library). The city has literary associations with James Joyce, George Bernard Shaw, Jonathan Swift, Oscar Wilde, and W B Yeats.

Du Bois, Blanche the self-deluded Southern belle in Tennessee Williams' *A Streetcar Named Desire*, who is commited to a mental institution after being raped by her brother-in-law, Stanley Kowalski.

Dubois, Marie Eugène François Thomas (1858–1940) Dutch palaeontologist, born in Eijsden. He studied medicine in Amsterdam and taught there from 1899. In the 1890s he found the fossil hominids named *Pithecanthropus erectus* (Java Man) and which he claimed to be the 'missing link' between apes and man. When in the 1920s this idea eventually became widely accepted, he began to insist that the fossil bones were those of a giant gibbon, a view that he maintained until death.

du Bois, W E B see BOIS, W(ILLIAM) E(DWARD) B(URGHARDT) DU.

Du Bois-Reymond, Emil Heinrich (1818–96) German physiologist, born in Berlin. Professor of Physiology at Berlin from 1855, he investigated the physiology of muscles and nerves, and demonstrated electrical activity in the nervous systems of animals.

Dubrovnik, Italian **Ragusa** POP (1989e) 68 000, a port on the Dalmatia coast of Croatia, and the capital of Dalmatia. It suffered earthquake damage in 1979 and was badly damaged in 1991 during the siege by the Federal Army in the Civil War. NOTABLE FEATURES cathedral; Rector's palace; the medieval town walls surrounding the old town are a World Heritage site.

Dubuffet, Jean (1901–85) French artist, born in Le Havre. He invented the concept of Art Brut, pioneering the use of rubbish (eg discarded newspapers, broken glass) to create 'pictures'. He is regarded as a forerunner of the Pop Art and Dada-like fashions of the 1960s.

ducal *adj.* relating to a duke. [from Latin *ducalis*]

ducat *noun* a former European gold or silver coin of varying value. [from Latin *ducatus*, duchy]

Duchamp, Marcel (1887–1968) French painter, born in Blainville. He was associated with several modern movements, including Cubism and Futurism, and shocked his generation with such works as *Nude Descending a Staircase* (1912, Philadelphia). He was one of the pioneers of Dadaism. In 1915 he left Paris for New York, where he spent eight years on his best-known work, *The Large Glass: The Bride Stripped Bare by her Bachelors, Even* (1915–23, Philadelphia).

Duchenne, Guillaume Benjamin Amand (1806–75) French physician, born in Boulogne-sur-Mer. A pioneer of electrophysiology and electrical treatment of disease, he did important work on polio, locomotor ataxia and a common form of muscular (Duchenne's) dystrophy. He also developed a method of taking small pieces of muscle (biopsy) from patients for microscopical examination.

duchess *noun* 1 the wife or widow of a duke. 2 a woman of the same rank as a duke in her own right. [from Old French *duchesse*]

Duchess of Malfi, The a play by John Webster (1623). It is a tragedy in blank verse about a widowed Duchess who secretly marries her steward but is consequently cruelly hounded to her death by her scheming brothers.

duchy *noun* (PL. **duchies**) the territory owned or ruled by a duke or duchess. [from Old French *duché*]

Duchy of Cornwall the oldest of English duchies, instituted by Edward III in 1337 to provide support for his eldest son, Edward, the Black Prince. Since 1503 the eldest son of the sovereign has inherited the dukedom; it consists of lands (totalling c.52 000ha) in Cornwall, Devon, Somerset, and S London, including the Oval cricket ground. The present Prince of Wales pays income tax on the income from the Duchy of Cornwall used for personal purposes.

Duchy of Lancaster a duchy created in 1267 by Henry III of England for his son Edmund, and attached to the Crown since 1399 when the last Duke of Lancaster (John of Gaunt's son) became Henry IV. Comprising c.21 000ha of farm land and moorland, mostly in Yorkshire, the duchy produces revenue which is paid into the Privy Purse (the monarch's private allowance), thus functioning as a department of state. The monarch is taxed on the income used for personal purposes. It is controlled by the Chancellor of the Duchy of Lancaster, usually a Cabinet member.

duck¹ *noun* 1 any wild or domesticated water bird related to the swans and geese, and having short legs, webbed feet, and a large flattened beak, eg eider, teal, mallard. The females generally have a dull plumage, but the males are often brightly coloured. 2 the flesh of this animal used as food. 3 the female of such a bird, as opposed to the male drake. 4 *colloq.* a likeable person; a term of endearment or (loosely) of address. 5 *Cricket* a batsman's score of zero. — **break one's duck** *colloq.* to enjoy one's first success after several failures. **like water off a duck's back** *colloq.* having no effect at all. [from Anglo-Saxon *duce*]

duck² *verb* 1 *intrans.* to lower the head or body suddenly, to avoid notice or a blow. 2 to push briefly under water. 3 *colloq.* (**duck out of something**) to avoid something unpleasant or unwelcome. [from Middle English *douken*]

duck³ *noun* hard-wearing cotton fabric, used for tents, sails, etc. [from Dutch *doek*, linen cloth]

duck-billed platypus see PLATYPUS.

duckboard *noun* a narrow board laid across muddy ground to form a path.

ducking *noun* immersion of a person or animal in water.

ducking-stool *noun Hist.* a chair on a long wooden pole, used for ducking offenders into water as punishment.

duckling *noun* a young duck.

ducks and drakes the game of skimming stones across the surface of water. — **play ducks and drakes with something** *colloq.* to squander or waste it.

duckweed *noun* any of a family of plants whose broad flat leaves grow on the surface of water.

ducky *colloq.* — *noun* (PL. **duckies**) a term of endearment. — *adj.* (**duckier, duckiest**) excellent; attractive or pleasing.

Ducos du Hauron, Louis (1837–1920) French scientist, born in Langan. A pioneer of colour photography, he established (by 1867) the principles of additive and subtractive colour reproduction, although at that time photographic materials of the required sensitivity were not available. In 1878 he described practical methods of applying these principles. In 1891 he proposed the anaglyph method for stereoscopic images.

duct *noun* 1 *Anat.* any tube in the body, especially for carrying glandular secretions away from a gland, eg tear duct. 2 in a building, a casing or shaft that accommodates pipes or electrical cables, or a tube used for ventilation and air conditioning. [from Latin *ducere*, to lead]

ductile *adj.* 1 *Chem.* denoting certain metals, eg copper, that can be drawn out into a thin wire or thread without breaking or decreasing in strength. 2 easily influenced by others. [from Latin *ductilis*, from *ducere*, to lead]

ductility *noun* the capacity of metal to be stretched or pressed into shape.

dud *colloq.* — *noun* 1 a counterfeit article. 2 a bomb or other projectile that fails to go off. 3 any useless or ineffectual person or thing. 4 (**duds**) clothes. — *adj.* 1 useless. 2 counterfeit.

dude *noun colloq. North Amer., esp. US* 1 a man. 2 a city man, especially an Easterner holidaying in the West. 3 a man preoccupied with dressing smartly.

Dudelange *or* **Forge du Sud** POP (1991) 15 000, an industrial town in Esch-sur-Alzette canton, Luxembourg district, S Luxembourg. It is situated at the foot of Mont St Jean and is the third largest town in Luxembourg. NOTABLE FEATURES Parish Church; Lang's 'Way of the Cross'.

Dudgeon, Richard, known as **Dick** the flamboyant title character of George Bernard

Shaw's *The Devil's Disciple*, whose reputation as the family reprobate does not prevent him from taking Pastor Anthony Anderson's place on the gallows. Mrs Dudgeon is his self-righteous mother, and Essie his illegitimate young cousin.

dudgeon
— **in high dudgeon** very angry, resentful, or indignant.

Dudley POP (1981) 187 000, a town in the West Midlands, central England, situated 12km/7mi W of Birmingham. NOTABLE FEATURES Church of St Thomas the Apostle (1817–19); Dudley Castle (13c).

due — *adj.* **1** owed; payable. **2** expected according to timetable or pre-arrangement. **3** proper. — *noun* **1** what is owed; that which can be rightfully claimed or expected. **2** (**dues**) subscription fees. — *adv.* directly: *due north.*
— **due to something** or **someone 1** caused by them. **2** because of them.
give someone his or **her due** to acknowledge their qualities or achievements, especially when disapproving in other ways.
[from Old French *deü*, from *devoir*, to owe]

duel — *noun* **1** a pre-arranged fight to the death between two people, to settle a matter of honour. **2** any serious conflict between two people or groups. — *verb intrans.* (**duelled**, **duelling**) to fight a duel. [from Latin *duellum*, variation of *bellum*, war]

duellist *noun* a person who takes part in a duel.

duenna *noun* an older woman acting as a chaperone to a girl or young woman (especially formerly) in Spanish and Portuguese society. [from Spanish *dueña*]

due process *Legal* a principle, deriving from a clause of the Magna Carta (1215), which provides that no person shall be arrested, imprisoned, banished, or in any way deprived of his or her rights, except by the lawful judgement of equals and according to the law of the land. The principle is also embodied in the 5th and 14th amendments of the US Constitution.

Duessa the self-proclaimed daughter of Deceit and Shame in Spenser's *The Faerie Queene*, who is a wicked enchantress representing severally the religion of Catholicism and Mary Queen of Scots. While appearing to be beautiful she is really hideously deformed.

duet *noun* a piece of music for two singers or players; a pair of musical performers. [from Italian *duetto*, from Latin *duo*, two]

duettist *noun* a performer in a duet.

Dufay, Charles François de Cisternay (1698–1739) French chemist, born in Paris. As superintendent of gardens to the King of France, he discovered two kinds of electricity (positive and negative), and carried out research on phosphorus and double refraction.

Dufay, Guillaume (c.1400–1474) French composer, born (probably) in Cambrai, the most celebrated 15c composer. A choirboy at Cambrai, he returned there as canon in 1439 after extensive travel and residence in Italy. Almost 200 of his works are extant, including eight complete masses, many motets, and songs. His warmth of emotion, strong sense of melody and pioneering of the *cantus firmus* mass greatly influenced Renaissance composers.

duff[1] *noun* a heavy boiled or steamed pudding, especially containing fruit. [form of DOUGH]

duff[2] *adj. colloq.* useless; broken. [perhaps from DUFFER]

duff[3] *verb*
— **duff someone up** *slang* to treat them violently; to beat them up.
[perhaps from DUFFER]

duff[4] — *verb colloq.* **1** to bungle. **2** to misplay or mishit (a shot, especially in golf). — *adj.* bungled. [from DUFFER]

duffel or **duffle** *noun* a thick coarse woollen fabric. [from Dutch *duffel*, from *Duffel*, Belgian town]

duffel bag a cylindrical canvas shoulder bag with a drawstring fastening.

duffel coat a heavy (especially hooded) coat made of duffel, typically with toggle fastenings.

duffer *noun colloq.* a clumsy or incompetent person.

Dufourspitze, Italian **Punta Dufour** a mountain peak on the Swiss–Italian border. It is the highest of the Monte Rosa group of the Pennine Alps and the second highest of the entire Alpine range. HEIGHT 4 634m.

dug[1] past tense of **dig**.

dug[2] *noun* **1** an animal's udder or nipple. **2** *coarse slang* a woman's breast.

dugong *noun* a whale-like plant-eating tropical sea mammal. [from Malay *duyong*]

dugout *noun* **1** a canoe made from a hollowed-out log. **2** a soldier's rough shelter dug into a slope or bank or in a trench. **3** a covered shelter at the side of a sports field, for the trainer, substitutes, etc.

Duisburg POP (1991e) 534 000, an industrial and commercial city in North Rhine-Westphalia state, W central Germany. It is the largest inland port in Europe, situated on the western edge of the R Ruhr, at the confluence of the Ruhr and the Rhine rivers. International rowing regattas are held in the Wedau Sports Park. HISTORY a university town in the Middle Ages; the 16c Flemish map-maker Gerhardus Mercator lived here; badly bombed in World War II.

Dukas, Paul (Abraham) (1865–1935) French composer, born in Paris. Some of his music was classical in approach, but he tended mainly towards Musical Impressionism, and is noted for the symphonic poem *L'Apprenti sorcier* (The Sorcerer's Apprentice, 1897) and the opera *Ariane et Barbe-Bleu* (1907). He also wrote several orchestral and piano pieces, and was Professor of Composition at the Paris Conservatoire from 1927.

duke *noun* **1** a nobleman of the highest rank outside the royal family. **2** the ruler of a small state or principality. **3** *old slang use* a fist. [from Latin *dux*, leader]

dukedom *noun* the title or property of a duke.

Duke of Edinburgh Award Scheme a scheme launched (1956) by Prince Philip, Duke of Edinburgh, to help young people between 14 and 25 develop their social awareness and personality. There are three levels of award to attain (bronze, silver, and gold) and each has four sections: community service, expeditions and explorations, skills, and physical recreation.

Duke of York in the UK, a title often given to the second son of the sovereign, such as Albert (later George VI), the second son of George V, and Andrew, the second son of Elizabeth II.

Dukeries, The an area of NW Nottinghamshire, central England. It includes Sherwood Forest and the parks of former ducal seats at Clumber, Thoresby, Welbeck, and Worksop.

dulcet *adj. literary, said of sounds* sweet and pleasing to the ear. [from Latin *dulcis*, sweet]

dulcimer *noun* a musical instrument consisting of a flattish box with tuned strings stretched across, struck with small hammers. [from Latin *dulce melos*, sweet song]

Dull the constable in Shakespeare's *Love's Labour's Lost.*

dull — *adj.* **1** *said of colour or light* lacking brightness or clearness. **2** *said of sounds* deep and low; muffled. **3** *said of weather* cloudy; overcast. **4** *said of pain* not sharp. **5** *said of a person* slow to learn or understand. **6** uninteresting; lacking liveliness.

7 *said of a blade* blunt. — *verb trans., intrans.* to make or become dull. [from Anglo-Saxon *dol*, stupid]

dullard *noun old use* a dull person.

Dulles, John Foster (1888–1959) US Republican politician, born in Washington, DC. During World War II he advocated a world governmental organization, was an advisor at the Charter Conference of the United Nations in 1945, and then became US delegate to the General Assembly. As US Secretary of State from 1953, his vigorous diplomacy led to many personal conferences with statesmen in other countries. He resigned in 1959, and was awarded the Medal of Freedom shortly before he died.

dullness *noun* a dull or uninteresting state.

dully *adv.* in a dull or uninteresting way.

dulse *noun* an edible red seaweed. [from Gaelic *duileasg*]

Duluth POP (1990) 240 000, the seat of St Louis County, NE Minnesota, USA. It lies at the W end of L Superior, and is a major lake port, established in the 1850s. NOTABLE FEATURES Aerial Lift Bridge; Leif Erikson Park.

duly *adv.* **1** in the proper way. **2** at the proper time. [from DUE]

Dumas, Alexandre (1802–70) French novelist and playwright, born in Villers-Cotterêts, Aisne. He moved to Paris in 1823, where he obtained a clerkship, and his first literary success was the play *Henri III* (1829). After several other plays he turned to travelogues and historical novels, and his best-known works include *Le Comte de Monte Cristo* (The Count of Monte Cristo, 1844–5), *Les Trois Mousquetaires* (The Three Musketeers, 1845), and *La Tulipe noire* (The Black Tulip, 1850). His son, Alexandre (1824–95), often known as 'Dumas fils', was also a writer, whose best-known work was *La Dame aux camélias* (1848).

Dumas, Jean Baptiste André (1800–84) French chemist, born in Alais. A lecturer at the École Polytechnique, he began work on choking fumes from candles, developed a theory of substitution in organic compounds, and went on to classify these into types. He became professor at the Athenée, the École Centrale (which he founded) and the Sorbonne, and later moved into politics.

du Maurier, Dame Daphne see MAURIER, DAME DAPHNE DU.

du Maurier, George see MAURIER, GEORGE (LOUIS PALMELLA BUSSON) DU.

dumb *adj.* **1** not having the power of speech. **2** *said of animals* not having human speech. **3** temporarily deprived of the power of speech, eg by shock. **4** silent; not expressed in words. **5** *colloq. chiefly North Amer., esp. US* foolish; unintelligent. **6** performed without words: *dumb show.* [from Anglo-Saxon]

Dumbarton POP (1981) 23 000, the capital of Dumbarton district, Strathclyde, W Scotland. It lies at the confluence of the Leven and Clyde rivers, 22km/14mi NW of Glasgow. NOTABLE FEATURE Dumbarton Castle (modern barracks with a 12c gateway, a dungeon and a sundial dating from the time of Mary Queen of Scots).

dumbbell *noun* **1** a weight used in pairs in muscle-developing exercises, consisting of a short metal bar with a heavy ball or disc on each end. **2** *colloq. chiefly North Amer.* a stupid person.

dumbfound or **dumfound** *verb* to astonish or confound, originally so as to leave speechless.

dumbly *adv.* silently; without speaking.

dumbness *noun* inability to speak.

dumbo *noun* (PL. **dumbos**) *colloq.* a stupid person. [from DUMB]

dumbstruck *adj.* silent with astonishment or shock.

dumbwaiter *noun* **1** a small lift for transporting laundry, dirty dishes, etc between floors in a restaurant or hotel. **2** a movable shelved stand for food, placed near a table. **3** a revolving food tray set in the middle of a table.

dumdum *noun* a bullet that expands on impact, causing severe injury. [from *Dum-Dum*, arsenal near Calcutta, India]

dumfound see DUMBFOUND.

Dumfries POP (1981) 32 000, the capital of Dumfries and Galloway region and of Nithsdale district, SW Scotland. It is a market town on the R Nith, 97km/60mi SE of Glasgow. Robert Burns lived here from 1791 until his death in 1796. NOTABLE FEATURES Burns's House and Mausoleum; Old Bridge House (1662); Devorgilla's Bridge (originally 13c).

Dumfries and Galloway POP (1992e) 148 000, a Region in SW Scotland, divided into four districts. AREA 6 370sq km/2 459sq mi. It is bounded N by Strathclyde, E by Borders Region, SE by England (along the R Sark), S by the Solway Firth, Wigtown Bay, and Luce Bay, and W by Beaufort's Dyke. PHYSICAL DESCRIPTION drained by the Cree, Dee, Nith, and Annan rivers; the peninsula, known as the Rinns of Galloway, is in the W. CAPITAL Dumfries. CHIEF TOWNS Kirkcudbright, Stranraer. ECONOMY agriculture; livestock (cattle and sheep); forestry; tourism. NOTABLE FEATURES Ruthwell Cross; Glen Trool; Galloway Hills.

dummy — *noun* (PL. **dummies**) **1** a life-size model of the human body, eg used for displaying clothes. **2** a realistic copy, especially one misleadingly substituted for the genuine article. **3** a baby's rubber teat sucked for comfort. **4** *colloq. chiefly North Amer.* a stupid person. **5** *Sport* an act of dummying with the ball. **6** a person or company acting seemingly independently, but really the agent of another. — *adj.* false; sham; counterfeit. — *verb trans., intrans.* (**dummies, dummied**) *Sport* to make as if to move one way before sharply moving the other, in order to deceive (an opponent). [from DUMB]

dummy run a practice; a try-out.

Dumouriez, Charles François (du Périer) (1739–1823) French soldier, born in Cambrai. A leader of the Girondins, he was appointed Minister of Foreign Affairs in 1792, but resigned to command the northern army. He defeated the Prussians at Valmy and the Austrians at Jemappes, but in 1793 lost to the Austrians at Neerwinden. His leanings towards the monarchy caused him to be denounced by the revolutionaries, and to save his head he went over to the Austrians. He later settled in England.

dump — *verb* **1** to put down heavily or carelessly. **2** *trans., intrans.* to dispose of (rubbish), especially in an unauthorized place. **3** *colloq.* to break off a romantic relationship with. **4** *Econ.* to sell (goods unsaleable domestically) abroad at a much reduced price, usually to keep the domestic price high. **5** *Comput.* to transfer computer data from one program to another using a dump, or to transfer a computer program or data on to disk or tape. — *noun* **1** a place where rubbish may be dumped. **2** a military store, eg of weapons or food. **3** *Comput.* a printed copy of the contents of a computer's memory, used to transfer data from one program to another, or to find the cause of an error in a program. **4** *colloq.* a dirty or dilapidated place. [from Middle English]

dumping *noun Commerce* the sale of a commodity on a foreign market at a price below the cost of producing it. An exporting business, with or without government subsidy, may pursue the policy of dumping in order to dispose of surpluses (without causing a reduction in prices in its home market), to eliminate competition, or to break into a new market.

dumpling *noun* **1** a baked or boiled ball of dough served with meat. **2** a rich fruit pudding. **3**

colloq. a plump person. [from obsolete *dump, lump*]

dumps
— **down in the dumps** *colloq.* in low spirits; depressed.
[perhaps from German *dumpf*, gloomy]

dumpy *adj.* (**dumpier, dumpiest**) short and plump. [perhaps from DUMPLING]

dun[1] *noun* **1** a dark greyish brown colour. **2** a horse of this colour. [from Anglo-Saxon]

dun[2] — *verb* (**dunned, dunning**) to press persistently for payment. — *noun* a demand for payment.

Dunant, (Jean) Henri (1828–1910) Swiss philanthropist, born in Geneva. After seeing the plight of the wounded on the battlefield of Solferino, he inspired the foundation of the International Red Cross. His efforts eventually led to the Geneva Convention (1864). In 1901 he shared the first Nobel Peace Prize.

Dunbar, William (c.1460–c.1520) Scottish poet, born (probably) in East Lothian. Educated at St Andrews, he became a Franciscan novice and travelled widely, before leaving the order and entering the diplomatic service. He was a courtier of James IV, and his poems include *The Thrissill and the Rois* and *Lament for the Makaris*, and several satires, such as *The Twa Marriit Wemen and the Wedo*, and *The Dance of the Sevin Deadly Synnis*. His name disappears from the records after 1513.

Duncan I (c.1010–40) He was the grandson of Malcolm II and probably ruled over most of Scotland except the islands and the far north. He was killed by Macbeth at Pitgaveny, near Elgin.

Duncan, King the king of Scotland in Shakespeare's *Macbeth*, who is murdered in his sleep by Macbeth.

Duncan a male first name. [from Gaelic *Donnchadh*, formed by old Celtic elements meaning 'brown' + 'battle']

Duncan, Isadora, originally **Angela Duncan** (1877–1927) US dancer and choreographer, born in San Francisco. She travelled throughout Europe, performing her own choreography, and founded schools in Berlin, Salzburg, and Vienna. A pioneer of modern dance, she based her work on Greek-derived notions of beauty and harmony, but also used running, skipping, and walking movements. An influential and controversial figure, she held unconventional views on marriage and women's liberation. She died in a car accident when her scarf caught in the wheel.

dunce *noun* a stupid person; a slow learner. [from *Dunses*, followers of J Duns Scotus, 13th-century educationalist opposed to classical studies]

Dunciad, The a mock-heroic poem by Alexander Pope (published anonymously, 1728). It satirizes 'Dulness' and all the authors for whom he had no respect.

Dundalk, Gaelic **Dun Dealgan** POP (1991) 30 000, the capital of Louth county, Leinster province, NE Irish Republic. It lies on the R Castletown near its mouth on Dundalk Bay. NOTABLE FEATURE Dun Dealgan Mound, 3km/2mi W (birthplace of Cuchulain, the legendary Irish warrior).

Dundee, John Graham of Claverhouse, 1st Viscount of, known as **Bloody Claverse**, or **Bonnie Dundee** (c.1649–89) Scottish soldier. In 1672 he entered the horseguards of the Prince of Orange (later William III), whose life he saved at the battle of Seneff. He returned to Scotland in 1677, and defeated the Covenanters at Bothwell Brig (1679). Joined by the Jacobite clans, he raised the standard for James II against William and Mary, but died from a musket wound after his successful battle against the Loyalist forces at the Pass of

Killiecrankie. He features in Walter Scott's novel about the Covenanters, *Old Mortality* (1816).

Dundee POP (1981) 172 000, the port capital of Tayside region and of Dundee City district, E Scotland. It lies on the N side of the Firth of Tay, 29km/18mi E of Perth. The Firth of Tay is crossed here by road and rail bridges. HISTORY a royal burgh since the 12c, it developed with the jute manufacturing industry. NOTABLE FEATURES Barrack Street Natural History Museum; Caird Hall (1914–23); Broughty Castle Museum; Claypotts Castle (1569–88); Albert Institute (1867).

dunderhead *noun* a stupid person.

dunderheaded *adj.* stupid.

dune *noun* a ridge or hill formed by the accumulation of windblown sand, usually on a seashore or in a hot desert. [from Old Dutch *duna*]

Dunedin POP (1991) 110 000, a city in Otago, SE South Island, New Zealand. It lies on the E coast at the S end of the Otago Peninsula. There is a seaport at Port Chalmers, 13km/8mi to the NE. The city was founded by Scottish settlers in 1848 and their influence is evident in buildings, parks, and statues. NOTABLE FEATURES two cathedrals; Octagon; Burns Statue; Municipal Chambers (1878–80); Fortune Theatre (1869); Knox Church (1876); Early Settlers' Museum; Hocken Library.

Dunfermline POP (1981) 52 000, the industrial capital of Dunfermline district, Fife, E Scotland. It lies 27km/17mi NW of Edinburgh. HISTORY a royal burgh since 1588, it is the ancient residence of Scottish kings; several were buried here, including Robert Bruce. It was the birthplace of Charles I (1600) and also of the US industrialist Andrew Carnegie (1835). NOTABLE FEATURES Dunfermline Abbey and Palace (standing on 11c foundations).

dung *noun* animal excrement. [from Anglo-Saxon]

Dungannon, Gaelic **Dun Geanainn** POP (1991) 9 000, a market town in Dungannon district, Co Tyrone, S central Northern Ireland, situated 56km/35mi SW of Belfast. It is the former stronghold of the Earls of Tyrone. NOTABLE FEATURES 9c High Cross of Arboe nearby; prehistoric stone circles with grave mounds (c.1800 BC) at Beaghmore.

dungarees *pl. noun* loose trousers with a bib and shoulder straps attached, worn as casual wear or overalls. [from Hindi *dungri*]

dung-beetle *noun* a shiny dark coloured beetle whose larvae feed on the dung of herbivorous animals, eg cattle.

dung-beetle

Dungeness Head a headland on the S coast of Kent, S England, projecting into the English Channel SE of Lydd. Nearby is Dungeness Nuclear Power Station.

dungeon *noun* a prison cell, especially underground. [from Old French *donjon*]

Dunhuang *or* **Tunhuang** a town in Gansu province, NW China. It was founded in 200 BC. NOTABLE FEATURES the Mogao Grottoes, the oldest Buddhist shrines in China (from AD 366) lie

25km/15mi SE; the Yangguan and Hongshan mountain passes lie 62km/38mi SW: they served as China's gateway to the western world until they were blocked by the Mongols in the 14c.

dunk verb **1** to dip (eg a biscuit) into tea or a similar beverage. **2** to submerge. [from Old German dunkon]

Dunkirk, French **Dunkerque**, Flemish **Duinekerke** POP (1990) 193 000, a seaport in Nord department, Nord-Pas-de-Calais region, NW France, situated at the entrance to the Straits of Dover. It is the third largest port in France, with extensive docks and quays, and cross-Channel ferry connections. HISTORY began in the 9c as a tiny fishing harbour close to the church (kirk) on the dunes; during World War II the retreating British Expeditionary Force was rescued from the beaches near the town.

Dunleary or **Dun Laoghaire** POP (1991) 56 000, a borough and resort town in Dublin county, Leinster province, E Irish Republic. It is situated on the Irish Sea, S of Dublin, and is a fishing port, yachting centre, and suburb of Dublin. It was named Kingstown in 1821 when George IV landed here.

dunlin noun a small wading bird, native to the northern hemisphere, and having mottled brown plumage with pale underparts, and a slender probing bill. It inhabits shoreline or open areas near water, and forms large flocks. [a diminutive of DUN[1]]

Dunlop, Joey, properly **(William) Joseph** (1952–) Northern Irish motorcyclist, born in Ballymoney, Northern Ireland. Between 1977 and 1988 he won 13 Isle of Man TT races, including the Senior Tourist Trophy (TT) in 1985, and 1987–8. He won the Formula One TT for the sixth successive season in 1988, and was Formula One world champion (1982–6). In 1988, he set the TT lap record at 190.73kph/118.54mph.

Dunn, Douglas (1942–) Scottish poet, born in Inchinnan, Renfrewshire. He worked as a librarian in the USA and in Hull, and became Professor of English at St Andrews University in 1991. His collections of poetry include *Terry Street* (1969), *Barbarians* (1979), *Elegies* (1985), and *Northlight* (1988). His *New and Selected Poems 1966–88* were published in 1989. Other works include the short story collection *Secret Villages* (1985).

Dunnet Head a cape in NE Highland region, NE Scotland, and the northernmost point of the British mainland. It is situated at the W end of the Pentland Firth, 13km/8mi NE of Thurso.

Dunnett, Alastair (MacTavish) (1908–) Scottish journalist, born in Kilmacolm, Ayrshire. He gave up a job in banking to publish a magazine for Scottish boys, a venture that launched his journalistic career. He was chief press officer to the Secretary of State for Scotland (1940–6) and editor of the *Daily Record* (1946–55) before becoming editor of *The Scotsman* (1956–72).

Dunois, Jean d'Orléans, Comte (Count), known as **the Bastard of Orléans** (1403–68) French soldier in the Hundred Years War, born in Paris, the illegitimate son of Louis, Duke of Orléans. He defeated the English at Montargis (1427), defended Orléans with a small force until the defeat of the siege by Joan of Arc (1429), then inflicted further defeats on the English, forcing them out of Paris, and out of Normandy and Guienne by 1453, thereby securing the freedom of France.

Duns Scotus, John, Latin **Joannes** (c.1265–1308) Scottish Franciscan philosopher and theologian, born (probably) in Duns, Berwickshire. His works consist mainly of commentaries on the Bible, Aristotle, and the *Sentences* of Peter Lombard, and he pioneered the doctrine of the Immaculate Conception. Also presented in his philosophy was a strong criticism of Thomas Aquinas, whose followers

included the Dominicans and became known as Thomists, while those of Scotus included the Franciscans and were known as Scotists. His dialectical skill gained him the title of 'Doctor Subtilis', but his defence of the papacy against the divine right of kings resulted in ridicule by the English Reformers of the 16c (hence the word 'dunce').

Dunstable or **Dunstaple, John** (c.1390–1453) English composer, who had much influence on his continental contemporaries. An important early exponent of counterpoint, he wrote motets, masses and secular songs including the three-part *O Rosa bella*.

Dunstable POP (1981) 49 000, a town in S Bedfordshire district, Bedfordshire, S central England. It lies at the N end of the Chiltern Hills, 7km/4mi W of Luton, at the junction of the Roman Watling Street and the earlier Icknield Way. NOTABLE FEATURE Whipsnade Zoo nearby.

Dunstan, St (c.909–988) Anglo-Saxon prelate, born near Glastonbury. When he was appointed abbot of the abbey there (945), he transformed it into a centre of religious teaching. An adviser to King Edmund, he fled during Edwy's reign, but was recalled by King Edgar to become Bishop of Worcester (957) and of London (959), and, when Edgar ruled all England, Archbishop of Canterbury (959). Dunstan also introduced the Benedictine rule into England. His feast day is 19 May.

duo noun (PL. **duos**) **1** a pair of musicians or other performers. **2** any two people considered a pair. [from Latin *duo*, two]

duodecimal adj. relating to the number twelve, or multiples of it; twelfth. [from Latin *duodecim*, twelve]

duodenal adj. relating to or affecting the duodenum.

duodenal ulcer Medicine an ulcer of the duodenum, usually accompanied by inflammation, caused by the effect of increased levels of acid secretions from the stomach on the duodenum wall.

duodenum noun (PL. **duodena**, **duodenums**) Anat. the first part of the small intestine, into which food passes after leaving the stomach. Within it bile from the gall bladder and pancreatic juice from the pancreas neutralize the stomach acid and continue the digestive process. [from Latin, from *duodecim*, twelve, the portion being twelve fingers' breadth in length]

duologue noun **1** a dialogue between two actors. **2** a play for two actors. [from Latin *duo*, two + Greek *logos*, discourse]

dupe — verb to trick or deceive. — noun a person who is deceived. [from French *dupe*]

duple adj. **1** double; twofold. **2** Mus. having two beats in the bar. [from Latin *duplus*]

duple time musical time with two main beats to the bar. Simple duple time has beats divisible by two, as in 2:2, 2:4, and 2:8; compound duple time has beats divisible by three, as in 6:4, 6:8, and 6:16.

duplex — noun **1** a flat on two floors. **2** a semi-detached house. — adj. **1** double; twofold. **2** *said of a computer circuit* allowing transmission of signals in both directions simultaneously. [from Latin *duplex*]

duplicate — adj. (pronounced -kət) identical to another. — noun (pronounced -kət) **1** an exact (especially printed) copy. **2** another of the same kind; a subsidiary or spare. — verb (pronounced -kate) **1** to make or be an exact copy or copies of. **2** to repeat. — **in duplicate** in the form of two exact copies. [from Latin *duplicare*, to fold in two]

duplication noun duplicating; making an exact copy.

duplicator noun a machine for copying documents, etc.

duplicitous adj. insincere; cheating.

duplicity noun formal deception; trickery; double-dealing. [from Latin *duplicis*, double]

Du Pont, Pierre Samuel (1870–1954) US businessman and management innovator, born in Wilmington, Delaware. In 1902 he bought the family gunpowder company with his cousins, and decentralized many of its activities. As President (1915–20) he also introduced and developed many new industrial management techniques (eg a systematic approach to strategic planning, control systems, and the pioneering of modern industrial accounting methods). In 1920 he became President of General Motors after the Du Pont company had rescued it from near bankruptcy.

Du Pont Nemours, Eleuthère Irénée (1771–1834) French-born US industrialist, born in Paris, the younger son of Pierre-Samuel Du Pont de Nemours (1739–1817). He worked in his father's printing plant until it was closed down in 1797. He emigrated to the USA, and in 1802 established a gunpowder factory in Wilmington, Delaware, which developed into one of the world's largest chemical concerns.

du Pré, Jacqueline see PRÉ, JACQUELINE DU.

Dupré, Marcel (1886–1971) French organist, born in Rouen. An exceptional improviser, he became chief organist at Notre Dame Cathedral in Paris. He won the Prix de Rome for composition (1914), became professor at the Paris Conservatoire (1926), composed many chorales and an organ concerto, and was acclaimed throughout Europe for his organ recitals.

Dur. abbrev. Durham.

durability noun the capacity to last a long time.

durable — adj. **1** lasting a long time without breaking; sturdy. **2** long-lasting; enduring. — noun a durable item, especially one not frequently replaced. [from Latin *durare*, to last]

durably adv. in a durable or long-lasting way.

Dura-Europos in Roman times, a major caravan city on the middle Euphrates, and a flourishing frontier town until its sack by the Sassanids in AD 256. The wall paintings from its 3c synagogue form an important link between Hellenistic and early Christian art.

dura mater Anat. the outermost and thickest of the three membranes (*meninges*) that surround the brain and spinal cord. [from Latin *duritia*, hardness + *mater*, mother]

Durango or **Victoria de Durango 1** POP (1990) 414 000, the capital of Durango state, NW central Mexico, 903km/561mi NW of Mexico City. The city was founded in 1563. NOTABLE FEATURES cathedral (1695); famous for its iron-water spring. **2** a state in NW central Mexico with Durango as its capital.

duration noun the length of time that something lasts or continues. [from Latin *durare*, to last]

Durban or **Port Natal** POP (1990e) 1.1m, a seaport in Natal province and the third largest city in South Africa. It is situated on the Indian Ocean coast, 485km/300mi SE of Johannesburg. The population includes many Indians, descendants of those who were brought to South Africa in the 1860s to work on the sugar plantations. A mission settlement was founded here in 1834. NOTABLE FEATURES museum and art gallery; oldest Hindu temple in South Africa.

Durbar the audience-chamber or body of officials at the Indian royal court. In British India the term was applied to formal assemblies marking important state occasions to which leading Indians were invited (eg the 1911 Delhi Durbar to celebrate the visit of King George V and Queen Mary).

D'Urberville, Alec a wealthy, unscrupulous man in Thomas Hardy's *Tess of the D'Urbervilles* whose seduction of Tess has resonations throughout her life.

Durbeyfield, Tess the tragic heroine of Thomas Hardy's *Tess of the D'Urbervilles*, who is unable to escape from the torment of her past.

Dürer, Albrecht (1471–1528) German painter and engraver, born in Nuremberg. He travelled widely (1490–4), and in 1497 set up his own studio. In 1498 he published his first major series of designs on wood, the illustrations of the Apocalypse. He was employed by Emperor Maximilian I, in whose honour he drew the *Triumphal Car* and (with others) the *Triumphal Arch*, the largest known woodcut (9sq m).

duress *noun* the influence of force or threats; coercion. [from Latin *duritia*, hardness]

Durey, Louis (1888–1979) French composer, born in Paris. In 1916, under the influence of Erik Satie, he became one of the group of young French composers known as 'Les Six', but broke with them in 1921. He wrote large orchestral and choral works, but is chiefly known for his songs and chamber music.

Durga in Hindu mythology, the mother goddess in her fierce or warrior aspect, and the wife of Shiva. She was summoned by the gods to kill the buffalo-demon, Mahisha. She is depicted as a beautiful woman with eight or ten arms, riding a lion or tiger, and killing the demon with a trident.

Durham POP (1992e) 607 000, a county in NE England, divided into eight districts. AREA 2 436sq km/940sq mi. It is bounded E by the North Sea, N by Tyne and Wear and Northumberland, W by Cumbria, and S by North Yorkshire and Cleveland. PHYSICAL DESCRIPTION rises to the Pennines in the W; drained by the Tees, Derwent, and Wear rivers. CHIEF TOWNS Durham (county town), Darlington, Chester-le-Street, Bishop Auckland. ECONOMY engineering; chemicals; agriculture; coal.

Durham POP (1981) 41 000, the county town of Durham county, NE England, situated on the R Wear. It was founded in the 10c by monks who had fled from Lindisfarne. NOTABLE FEATURES Norman cathedral (1093) and castle (11c), designated a World Heritage site; Gulbenkian Museum; Durham Light Infantry Museum.

during *prep.* **1** throughout the time of. **2** in the course of. [from obsolete *dure*, to last, from Latin *durare*]

Durkheim, Emile (1858–1917) French sociologist, born in Epinal, generally regarded as one of the founders of sociology. He taught at the university of Bordeaux (1887), and at the Sorbonne. His writings include *Les Règles de la méthode sociologique* (The Rules of Sociological Method, 1894) and a definitive study of suicide (1897). His concept of 'collective representations' explains how the social power of ideas stems from their development through the interaction of many minds.

Durmitor the highest mountain in Montenegro, SW Yugoslavia, situated in the Dinaric Alps between the Piva and Tara rivers. It is part of a national park, which is a World Heritage site. HEIGHT 2 522m.

Durrell, Gerald (Malcolm) (1925–) English zoologist, writer, and traveller, born in Jamshedpur, India, the brother of Lawrence Durrell. His animal stories and reminiscences include *My Family and Other Animals* (1956), *A Zoo in My Luggage* (1960), and *Birds, Beasts and Relatives* (1969). He is the founder of a zoo and a wildlife centre in Jersey.

Durrell, Lawrence (George) (1912–90) English novelist and poet, born in Darjeeling, India, brother of Gerald Durrell. He taught English in Athens, served in the Foreign Office and settled in Cyprus in 1953. He made his name with *Prospero's Cell* (1945) and the 'Alexandria Quartet' (1957–60): *Justine, Balthazar, Mountolive* and *Clea*. Other works include a series of five

novels comprising *Monsieur* (1974), *Livia* (1978), *Constance* (1982), *Sebastian* (1983), and *Quinx* (1985). He also wrote several books of poems, short stories, and travel books.

Durrës, formerly **Durazzo**, Turkish **Draj 1** POP (1989) 83 000, the seaport capital of Durrës district, W Albania, situated on the Adriatic Sea, 30km/19mi W of Tirana. It is Albania's principal port and a health resort. HISTORY founded as Epidamnos in 627 BC and renamed Dyrrhachium in 229 BC; capital of Albania from 1912 until 1921; occupied during World War I by the Italians and Austrians. NOTABLE FEATURES a former royal villa and also the remains of Byzantine–Venetian fortifications. **2** a district in W Albania with the town of Durrës as its capital.

Duse, Eleonora, known as **the Duse** (1859–1924) Italian actress, ranked as one of the world's greatest, born near Venice. She rose to fame in Italy, then triumphed (1892–3) throughout the European capitals, mainly acting in plays by Ibsen, contemporary French dramatists, and the works of her lover, Gabriele D'Annunzio.

Dushanbe, formerly **Diushambe** (to 1929), **Stalinabad** (1929–61) POP (1991e) 582 000, the capital of Tajikistan. It is an industrial city lying on the R Dushabe and serves as an important transportation centre.

dusk *noun* twilight; the period of semi-darkness before night. [from Anglo-Saxon *dox*, dark]

duskiness *noun* partial darkness or obscurity.

dusky *adj.* (**duskier, duskiest**) **1** dark; shadowy. **2** dark-coloured; dark-skinned.

Düsseldorf POP (1991e) 575 000, the industrial capital of North Rhine-Westphalia state, W central Germany. It lies on the lower Rhine, 34km/21mi NW of Cologne. The city is the administrative centre of the province's heavy industry, and often hosts congresses and trade fairs. HISTORY became a city in 1288; it was the birthplace of the German poet Heinrich Heine (1797). NOTABLE FEATURES Schloss Benrath (18c); Rococo palace (1755–73); Art Academy (1767); opera house, theatre.

dust — *noun* **1** earth, sand, or household dirt in the form of a fine powder. **2** a cloud of this. **3** any substance in powder form. **4** *colloq.* an angry complaint; a commotion: *kick up a dust*. **5** *poetic* human remains; a dead body. — *verb* **1** *trans., intrans.* to remove dust from (furniture, etc.). **2** *trans.* to sprinkle with a substance in powder form.
— **let the dust settle** *colloq.* to wait until calm is restored before acting.
throw dust in someone's eyes *colloq.* to deceive them.
[from Anglo-Saxon]

dustbin *noun* a large (usually cylindrical) lidded container for household rubbish, especially one kept outside.

Dust Bowl the semi-arid area of the US prairie states from Kansas to Texas, which suffers from dust-storms. In the 1930s, after several years of overcultivation, strong winds and dry weather resulted in major dust storms and soil erosion.

dust bowl an area of land that has been farmed without protection against the effects of soil erosion, and from which the topsoil has been removed as a result of strong winds and drought.

dustcart *noun* a vehicle in which household rubbish is collected.

dust cover 1 a dust jacket. **2** a dust sheet.

duster *noun* **1** a cloth for removing household dust. **2** a machine for spraying crops with fertiliser or other preparations.

dustily *adv.* curtly; rudely: *replied dustily that he didn't know.*

dust jacket a loose protective paper cover on a book, carrying the title and other information.

dustman *noun* a person employed to collect household rubbish.

dustpan *noun* a handled container into which dust is swept, like a flattish open-ended box with a shovel edge.

dust sheet a cloth sheet used to protect unused furniture from dust.

dust-storm *noun* a whirling mass of dust blown up by severe winds.

dust-up *noun colloq.* an argument or fight.

dusty *adj.* (**dustier, dustiest**) **1** covered with, or containing, dust. **2** *said of a colour* dull. **3** old-fashioned; dated. **4** lacking liveliness; flat. **5** impolitely blunt.

Dutch — *noun* **1** the language of the Netherlands. See also AFRIKAANS, FLEMISH. **2** (**the Dutch**) the people of the Netherlands. — *adj.* of the Netherlands, its people or their language.
— **go Dutch** *colloq.* to each pay his or her own share of a meal, etc.
[from Old Dutch *dutsch*]
◇ Dutch (or Netherlandic) is a W Germanic language spoken by c.20 million people in the Netherlands, Belgium, and former Dutch colonies such as Surinam and the Antilles.

Dutch auction an auction at which the price is gradually lowered until someone agrees to buy.

Dutch barn an open-sided barn with a curved roof.

Dutch cap a contraceptive cap worn over a woman's cervix.

Dutch courage artificial courage gained by drinking alcohol.

Dutch elm disease *Bot.* a serious disease of elm trees, caused by the fungus *Ceratocystis ulmi*, and spread by a bark beetle. Symptoms include wilting, yellowing of leaves, and death of individual branches or whole trees.

Dutchman *or* **Dutchwoman** *noun* a native or citizen of the Netherlands.

Dutch New Guinea see IRIAN JAYA.

Dutch oven 1 an open-fronted metal box for cooking food in front of a fire. **2** a lidded earthenware or iron stewpot or casserole.

Dutch Reformed Church 1 in Holland, the largest Protestant Church. It stemmed from the Calvinist Reformation in the 16c, and its leaders and scholars have been influential in Dutch life, in former Dutch colonies, and also in Reformed theology. **2** in South Africa, the official Church of dominant white Afrikaans-speaking nationals (totally separated from the Church in Holland). It was condemned in 1982 by the other Reformed Churches for justifying both theologically and practically the policy of apartheid. However, in 1986 it denounced its support of apartheid and three years later declared it to be sinful.

Dutch Revolt see NETHERLANDS, REVOLT OF THE.

Dutch treat an amusement where each person pays for himself or herself.

Dutch uncle a person who openly criticizes or reprimands where appropriate, without sparing one's feelings.

Dutch Wars three wars (1652–4, 1664–7, 1672–4) between England and the Dutch Republic over issues of trade and the colonies. The first followed the Navigation Acts, whereby England sought increased trade; the second concerned the colonies in Africa and N America; and the third resulted from English involvement with the French in the Treaty of Dover (1670). The wars precipitated the decline of Dutch power, and signalled the growing predominance of the English.

Dutch West India Company the organization of Dutch merchants responsible for the settlement of New Netherland, now part of New York State and New Jersey. Established in 1621, the Company was dissolved in 1674 and later reorganized as a trading venture.

duteous adj. literary dutiful. [from DUTY + -OUS]

dutiable adj., said of goods on which duty is payable.

dutiful adj. having or showing a sense of duty. [from DUTY + -FUL]

dutifully adv. in a dutiful or respectful way.

Dutrochet, (René Joachim) Henri (1776–1847) French physiologist, born in Néon. He qualified in medicine in Paris, and became physician to Joseph Bonaparte of Spain. In pioneering physiological work he postulated that cellular respiration was essentially identical in animals and plants, he isolated stomata (the small openings on the surface of leaves), and recognized the role of chlorophyll. He was also the first to make wide-ranging studies of osmosis, which he identified as the cause of sap movement in plants.

duty noun (PL. **duties**) 1 something one is or feels obliged to do; a moral or legal responsibility, or the awareness of it. 2 a task to be performed, especially in connection with a job. 3 tax on goods, especially imports. 4 respect for elders or seniors. — **do duty for something** to serve in its place; to act as a substitute for it. **on** or **off duty** working, or not working; liable or not liable to be called upon to go into action. [from Old French dueté]

duty-bound adj. obliged by one's sense of duty.

duty-free — adj., said of goods, especially imports non-taxable. — noun colloq. a duty-free shop.

duty-free shop a shop, especially at an airport or on a ship, where duty-free goods are sold.

Duvalier, François, also called **Papa Doc** (1907–71) Haitian politician, born in Port-au-Prince. Trained as a doctor, he was President from 1957 until his death. He ruled in an increasingly arbitrary fashion, and his regime saw the creation of the civilian militia known as the Tonton Macoute, and the exile of many people. Made President for life in 1964, he was succeeded in this post by his son Jean-Claude (or 'Baby Doc' 1951–), who ruled until he was overthrown in a coup in 1986.

Duve, Christian René de (1917–) English-born Belgian biochemist, born in Thames Ditton, Surrey. Professor at Louvain from 1951 and at Rockefeller University in New York from 1962, he is best known for the discovery of lysosomes, small organelles within cells which contain enzymes; their malfunction may result in metabolic diseases, such as cystinosis. He shared the 1974 Nobel Prize for Physiology or Medicine with Albert Claude and George Palade.

duvet noun a thick quilt filled with feathers or man-made fibres, for use on a bed instead of a sheet and blankets. [from French duvet]

DV abbrev. Deo volente (Latin) God willing.

DVLA abbrev. Driver and Vehicle Licensing Agency (formerly Centre).

Dvořák, Antonín (Leopold) (1841–1904) Czech composer, born near Prague. He attended the organ school in Prague in 1857, and then began to earn his living from the viola. In 1877 Brahms introduced his music to Vienna, and was a great influence on him. His work, basically classical in structure, but with colourful Slavonic motifs, won increasing European recognition, especially his Stabat mater (1880). By then he had written six symphonies and much chamber and piano music. In 1891 he became director of the New York Conservatory. He wrote his ninth symphony Z nového světa (From the New World, 1893) in the USA, and then returned to Prague (1895).

dwarf — noun (PL. **dwarfs**, **dwarves**) 1 an abnormally small person, either with very short limbs and a head and body of normal size (usually due to achondroplasia, a genetic disorder) or with fairly normal but small proportions (usually due to a deficiency of growth hormone). 2 an animal or plant that is much smaller or shorter than others of its species, usually as a result of selective breeding. 3 a mythical man-like creature with magic powers. — verb 1 to cause to seem small or unimportant. 2 to stunt the growth of. [from Anglo-Saxon dweorg]

dwarfish adj. like a dwarf; very small.

dwarf star Astron. a relatively small star, of high density and low luminosity, that lies on the main sequence of the Hertzsprung–Russell diagram, eg the Sun. The source of energy in such stars is the conversion of hydrogen into helium by nuclear reactions within the core of the star.

dweeb noun North Amer., esp. US derog. slang an idiot, a nerd. [perhaps a mixture of FEEBLE and WEED]

dwell verb intrans. (PAST TENSE AND PAST PARTICIPLE **dwelt**, **dwelled**) formal, literary to reside. (**dwell on** or **upon something**) to think or speak about it obsessively. [from Anglo-Saxon dwellan, to delay or tarry]

dweller noun a person who lives in a particular place or area: a city-dweller.

dwelling noun formal, literary a place of residence; a house.

dwindle verb intrans. to shrink in size, number or intensity. [from Anglo-Saxon dwinan, to fade]

DY abbrev., as an international vehicle mark Benin, formerly Dahomey.

Dy symbol Chem. dysprosium.

dybbuk noun in Jewish folklore, an evil spirit or the soul of a dead person, which enters the body of a living person and controls their behaviour until exorcized by a religious rite. [from Hebrew dibbūq]

dye — verb trans., intrans. (**dyeing**) to colour or stain permanently. — noun a coloured substance, either natural or synthetic, that is used in solution to impart colour to another material, eg paper, textiles, leather. It differs from a pigment, which is used in suspension. [from Anglo-Saxon deagian]

dyed-in-the-wool adj. of firmly fixed opinions; out-and-out.

dyer noun a person who dyes cloth, etc, especially as a business.

Dyfed POP (1992e) 351 000, a county in SW Wales, divided into six districts. AREA 5 768sq km/2 226sq mi. It is bounded W by Cardigan Bay and St George's Channel, S by Bristol Channel, SE by West Glamorgan, and N and E by Powys. PHYSICAL DESCRIPTION drained by the Ystwyth, Towy, and Teifi rivers; the Black Mountain range is in the SE corner; the Cambrian Mts occupy much of the N and E. CHIEF TOWNS Carmarthen (the administrative centre), Aberystwyth, Cardigan, Lampeter. ECONOMY agriculture (dairy products); fishing; oil refining; coal; tinplate; tourism. NOTABLE FEATURES Brecon Beacons National Park; Laugharne (home of the poet Dylan Thomas); Pembrokeshire Coast National Park.

dying — verb present participle of DIE[1]. — adj. 1 expressed immediately before death. 2 final: dying seconds of the match.

dyke[1] or **dike** — noun 1 a wall or embankment built to prevent flooding. 2 Geol. a vertical or semi-vertical sheet of igneous rock that cuts across the layering or bedding planes in the surrounding rock. It is formed when molten magma is forced under pressure into older rocks and then solidifies below the Earth's surface. 3 Scot. a wall, eg surrounding a field. — verb to protect or drain with a dyke. [from Anglo-Saxon dic, ditch]

dyke[2] noun offensive slang a lesbian.

Dylan, Bob, originally **Robert Allen Zimmerman** (1941–) US folksinger and songwriter, born in Duluth, Minnesota. He rose to fame in the 1960s, influenced by Woody Guthrie's folk tradition. His lyrics and gravelly voice made his songs a dominant influence in the popular music and culture of the period. The themes of opposition to war, the nuclear bomb, and racial and social injustice appear in such songs as Blowin' in the Wind and The Times They are A-Changin'. In the late 1960s he changed to a more traditional country and western style of music, as in Nashville Skyline (1969). The 1970s saw him turn back to rock and roll, and turn from his Jewish faith to embrace Christianity, which led to religious albums such as Saved, but he returned to Judaism in the 1980s.

dynamic adj. 1 full of energy, enthusiasm, and new ideas. 2 relating to dynamics. [from Greek dynamis, power]

dynamically adv. 1 with energy and enthusiasm. 2 in relation to dynamics or motion.

dynamics noun 1 (sing.) Physics the branch of mechanics that deals with the motion of objects and the forces that act to produce such motion. 2 (pl.) movement or change in any sphere; also, the forces causing this: political dynamics.

dynamism noun limitless energy and enthusiasm.

dynamite — noun 1 any of a group of powerful blasting explosives, formerly consisting of nitroglycerine absorbed into a porous material such as wood pulp or charcoal, but now usually containing ammonium nitrate or sodium nitrate. 2 colloq. a thrilling or dangerous person or thing. — verb to blow up with dynamite. [from Greek dynamis, power]

dynamo noun (PL. **dynamos**) Electr. an electric generator that converts mechanical energy into electrical energy, usually in the form of direct current. It consists of conducting coils that generate an electromotive force when they are rotated in a magnetic field. colloq. a tirelessly active person. [from Greek dynamis, power]

dynamometer noun Engineering an instrument that is used to measure mechanical force, especially in order to determine the output power of a motor or engine.

dynastic adj. relating to or associated with a dynasty: a dynastic marriage.

dynasty noun (PL. **dynasties**) 1 a succession of rulers from the same family; their period of rule. 2 a succession of members of a powerful family or other connected group. [from Greek dynasteia, power, dominion]

dyne noun a unit of force, producing an acceleration of one centimetre per second per second on a mass of one gram. [from Greek dynamis, force]

dysarthria noun Psychol. an impaired ability to enunciate speech clearly, caused by a disease or disorder of the tongue or other muscles associated with speech. [from Greek dys-, amiss + Greek arthron, joint]

dysentery noun Medicine severe infection and inflammation of the intestines caused by bacteria, protozoa, or parasitic worms, characterized by violent diarrhoea containing blood and mucus, and severe abdominal pain. Amoebic dysentery, which is largely confined to areas of poor sanitation in tropical and subtropical countries, is caused by the protozoan Entamoeba histolytica. [from Greek dysenteria, bad bowels]

dyslexia noun 1 a disorder that develops in childhood, characterized by difficulty in reading and writing and in spelling correctly, although individual letters can be recognized and other intellectual abilities are unimpaired. A number of educational programmes have been developed to help sufferers. 2 a popular term for difficulties in reading and writing. [from Greek *dys-*, amiss + *lexis*, word]

dyslexic — *adj.* affected by dyslexia. — *noun* a person affected by dyslexia.

dysmenorrhoea *or* **dysmenorrhea** *noun Medicine* pain in the lower abdomen, associated with menstruation. [from Greek *dys-*, amiss + *men*, month + *rhoia*, flow]

dyspepsia *noun Medicine* indigestion. [from Greek *dys-*, amiss + *pepsis*, digestion]

dyspeptic *adj.* **1** suffering from dyspepsia. **2** *colloq.* bad-tempered; liverish.

dysplasia *noun Medicine* **1** abnormal development of a tissue, eg skin, bone. **2** an abnormal change in the size or shape of a mature cell. [from Greek *dys-*, amiss + *plasis*, moulding]

dyspnoea *or* **dyspnea** *noun Medicine* difficulty in breathing, often associated with serious disease of the heart or lungs. [from Greek *dyspnoia*, from *dys-*, amiss + *pnoe*, breathing]

dysprosium *noun* (SYMBOL **Dy**, ATOMIC NUMBER **66**) a soft silvery-white metallic element that is one of the most magnetic substances known, and a strong absorber of neutrons. [from Greek *dysprositos*, difficult to reach]

dystrophy *noun Medicine* any of various unrelated disorders of organs or tissues, especially muscle, arising from an inadequate supply of nutrients, eg muscular dystrophy (in which the muscle fibres are eventually replaced by fat). See also MUSCULAR DYSTROPHY. [from Greek *dys-*, amiss + *trophe*, nourishment]

DZ *abbrev., as an international vehicle mark* Barr al-Djaza'ir (Arabic), Algeria.

Dzerzhinsk, formerly **Chernorech** (to 1919), and **Rastiapino** (1919–29) POP (1991e) 287 000, a manufacturing city in Nizhegorod oblast, W Russia. It lies on the R Oka, 32km/20mi W of Nizhniy Novgorod. It became a city in 1930.

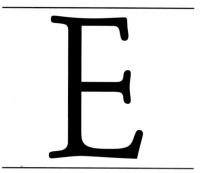

E

E¹ *or* **e** *noun* (PL. **Es**, **E's**, **e's**) **1** the fifth letter of the English alphabet. **2** the fifth highest grade or quality. **3** *Mus.* the third note in the scale of C major. **4** a musical key with the note E as its base.

E² *abbrev.* **1** East. **2** Ecstasy. **3** *Physics* electromotive force. **4** (*also* **e**) electronic: *E-mail.* **5** *Physics* energy. **6** *as an international vehicle mark España*, Spain. **7** European: *E-number.*

e¹ *abbrev.* see E² 4.

e² *symbol* used with a number to mark any of several standard sizes of pack as set out in EC law.

Ea *or* **Enki** a Mesopotamian god of water. He helped humans to survive by teaching them to plough the land, and was revered as the source of creativity and wisdom. A myth in which Enki eats the plants in a paradise garden parallels the story of Adam and Eve.

each — *adj.* every one of two or more people or items considered separately. — *pron.* every single one of two or more people, animals or things. — *adv.* to, for, or from each one: *give them one each.*
— **each other** used as the object of a verb or preposition when an action takes place between two (or more than two) people, etc: *they were talking to each other.*
each way *said of a bet* winning if the horse, dog, etc on which the bet is placed finishes first, second, or third in a race.
[from Anglo-Saxon *ælc*]

Eads, James B(uchanan) (1820–87) US civil engineer, born in Lawrenceburg, Indiana. His steel arch bridge (1867–74) across the Mississippi at St Louis, with a central span of 520ft/158m, is one of the finest in the USA. His works for improving the Mississippi mouth were completed in 1879.

eager *adj.* (often **eager for something** *or* **to do something**) feeling or showing great desire or enthusiasm; keen to do or get something. [from Old French *aigre*]

eager beaver *colloq.* a person who is exceptionally enthusiastic or willing.

eagerly *adv.* with an eager or enthusiastic manner.

eagerness *noun* being eager; enthusiasm.

eagle *noun* **1** any of various birds of prey belonging to the same family as hawks, harriers, and vultures, and found worldwide. Eagles have large bodies, powerful hooked beaks, feathered legs, and strong curved talons for grasping prey. They are noted for their soaring graceful flight and keen eyesight. **2** a figure of an eagle, used as a national emblem by various countries. **3** *Golf* a score of two under par. [from Old French *aigle*, from Latin *aquila*]

eagle eye 1 exceptionally good eyesight. **2** careful supervision, with an ability to notice small details.

eagle-eyed *adj.* having exceptionally good eyesight.

eagle owl an owl native to the Old World, including a species that is the largest of all owls. It has eyelashes, an unusual feature in owls.

eaglet *noun* a young eagle.

EAK *abbrev., as an international vehicle mark* Kenya (ie East Africa Kenya).

Eames, Johnny a character in Anthony Trollope's *The Small House at Allington* and *The Last Chronicle of Barset*, who doggedly pursues Lily Dale.

Eamonn a male first name. [Irish, the Gaelic form of EDMUND]

ear¹ *noun* **1** the sense organ, usually one of a pair situated on each side of the head (or in some animals on top of the head), that is concerned with hearing and the maintenance of balance in vertebrates. **2** the external part of the ear. **3** the sense or power of hearing, especially the ability to hear the difference between sounds. **4** anything like an ear in shape or position. **5** *formal, literary* attention; the act of listening: *lend an ear / give ear to.*
— **be all ears** *colloq.* to listen attentively or with great interest.
have someone's ear to have them willing to listen or pay attention.
have one's ear to the ground to keep oneself well informed about what is happening around one.
in one ear and out the other *colloq.* heard but quickly disregarded or forgotten.
make someone's ears burn to talk, especially unfavourably, about them in their absence.
out on one's ear *colloq.* dismissed swiftly and summarily.
play something by ear 1 to play a piece of music without the help of a score. **2** *colloq.* to do something without a fixed plan, as circumstances suggest.
up to one's ears in something *colloq.* deeply involved in or occupied with it.
[from Anglo-Saxon *eare*]
◇ In humans and other mammals the ear consists of three parts. The *outer ear* transmits sound waves from outside the ear to the *tympanic membrane* (eardrum), and consists of a *pinna* (commonly referred to as the 'ear') that projects from the head and is made of a thin layer of cartilage covered with skin. It funnels sound into a channel that leads to the tympanic membrane. In some mammals, eg dogs, the pinna can be moved independently in order to detect the direction of sounds.
The *middle ear* is an air-filled cavity containing three small bones or *ossicles*, known as the *malleus* (hammer), *incus* (anvil), and *stapes* (stirrup). The *Eustachian tube* links the middle ear to the pharynx at the back of the throat, ensuring that the air pressure remains the same on both sides of the tympanic membrane. The ossicles transmit

vibrations from the tympanic membrane to the *fenestra ovalis* (oval window), the upper of two membrane-covered openings that separate the middle ear from the fluid-filled *inner ear*. Vibrations from the fenestra ovalis are finally transmitted to the spiral-shaped *cochlea* in the inner ear. The cochlea is filled with fluid and lined with sensory cells (*hair cells*) that detect vibrations as movements of fluid and relay them as nerve impulses via the auditory nerve to the brain, where they are interpreted as the tone and pitch of the original sound.
The inner ear also contains three fluid-filled semicircular tubes, known as *semicircular canals*, which can detect movements of the head and are concerned with the maintenance of balance.

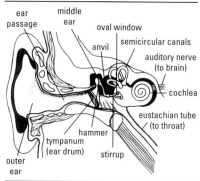

human ear

ear² *noun Bot.* the flowering head or spike of grasses, especially cereals, that contains the seeds. [from Anglo-Saxon *éar*]

earache *noun* pain in the inner part of the ear.

eardrum *noun* the small membrane that separates the outer ear from the middle ear, and transmits vibrations made by external sound waves to the tiny bones or *ossicles* of the middle ear. — Also called *tympanum.*

earful *noun colloq.* (PL. **earfuls**) (*not usually in pl.*) a long complaint or telling-off.

Earhart, Amelia (1898–1937) US aviator, born in Atchison, Kansas. She was the first woman to fly the Atlantic Ocean, as a passenger, and followed this by a solo flight in 1932. In 1935 she flew solo from Hawaii to California. In 1937 she set out to fly round the world, but her plane was lost over the Pacific.

earl *noun* a male member of the British nobility ranking below a marquess and above a viscount. See also COUNTESS. [from Anglo-Saxon *eorl*]

earldom *noun* the status or position of an earl.

earliness *noun* being early or sooner than expected.

Earl Marshal in the UK, the hereditary post held by the Howard Dukes of Norfolk. The Earl

Marshal is a great officer of state, head of the College of Arms and also responsible for organizing state ceremonies.

earlobe *noun* the soft, loosely hanging piece of flesh which forms the lower part of the ear.

early *adv., adj.* (**earlier**, **earliest**) **1** near the beginning of a period of time, period of development, etc. **2** sooner than others, sooner than usual, or sooner than expected or intended. **3** in the near future. **4** in the far-off past.
— **at the earliest** not before, and probably later than.

early on at or near the beginning of a period of time, etc.

it's early days *colloq.* it is too soon to be able to judge the outcome or expect a result.
[from Anglo-Saxon *ærlice*]

early bird *colloq.* **1** a person who gets out of bed early. **2** a person who arrives early.

Early English style a form of English Gothic architecture prevalent during the 13c, characterized by pointed arches, rib vaults, and a greater stress on the horizontals than is found in French Gothic architecture. Examples include the chancel of Lincoln Cathedral (c.1192) and Salisbury Cathedral (c.1220–70).

early warning system a radar system designed to give the earliest possible warning of attack from enemy aircraft or missiles.

earmark *verb* to set aside or intend for a particular purpose.

earmuffs *pl. noun* coverings worn over the ears to protect them from cold or noise.

earn **1** *verb trans., intrans.* to gain (money, wages, one's living) by working. **2** to gain. **3** to deserve. See also WELL-EARNED. [from Anglo-Saxon *earnian*]

Earn, Loch a loch in Perth and Kinross district, Tayside, Scotland. It is 11km/7mi long from E to W. The loch is drained by the R Earn, which flows E to meet the estuary of the R Tay, SE of Perth. It is a centre for watersports.

earner *noun* **1** a person who earns. **2** *slang* an easy and sometimes dishonest way of making money.

earnest[1] *adj.* **1** serious or over-serious. **2** showing determination, sincerity or strong feeling.
— **in earnest** serious or seriously.
[from Anglo-Saxon *eornust*]

earnest[2] *noun literary, old use* **1** a part payment made in advance, especially to confirm an agreement. **2** a sign or foretaste of what is to come. [from Middle English *ernes*, from Old French *erres*, pledges]

earnestly *adv.* with an earnest or sincere manner.

earnestness *noun* being earnest or sincere.

earnings *pl. noun* money earned.

Earnshaw, Catherine the passionate heroine of Emily Brontë's *Wuthering Heights*.

earphones same as HEADPHONES.

earpiece *noun* the part of a telephone or hearing-aid which is placed at or in the ear.

ear-piercing — *adj., said of a noise* loud and sharp. — *noun* the piercing of the earlobe for the purpose of inserting an earring.

earplug *noun* a piece of wax, rubber, etc placed in the ear as a protection against noise, cold or water.

earring *noun* a piece of jewellery worn attached to the ear, especially to the earlobe.

earshot *noun* the distance at which sound can be heard: *out of earshot / within earshot.*

ear-splitting *adj., said of a noise* extremely loud.

earth *noun* **1** (*often* **Earth**) the third planet from the Sun and the fifth-largest planet in the solar system. Its orbit lies between those of Venus and Mars. It takes 23 hours 56 minutes to rotate once on its own axis, and it revolves once around the Sun in 365.25 days. It is the only planet in the solar system known to support life. **2** the mater-

ial world, or human existence. **3** the land and sea as opposed to the sky. **4** dry land as opposed to the sea. **5** the soil, consisting of a mixture of loose fragmented rock and organic material, in which plants are rooted. **6** a burrow in which an animal, especially a fox, lives. **7** an electrical connection with the ground. **8** a wire that provides an electrical connection with the ground. **9** *Chem.* the old name for certain oxides of metals, eg alkaline earth, rare earth. **10** *Electr.* to connect to the ground electrically. **11** (*also* **earth something up**) to heap soil around the lower part of a plant, eg as a protection against frost.
— **come back** *or* **down to earth** to become aware of the realities of life.

cost the earth *colloq.* to be extremely expensive.

go to earth *said of an animal* to go into its hole or hiding-place.

on earth used for emphasis: *what on earth is that?*

run someone *or* **something to earth 1** to chase or hunt an animal to its hole or hiding-place. **2** to find them after a long search.
[from Anglo-Saxon *eorthe*]

◇ The Earth is about 150 million km from the Sun, and it has a diameter of 12 756km at the equator, and a circumference of 40 075km. It has one large natural satellite, the Moon. The Earth is not completely round, but bulges slightly at the equator and is rather flattened at the poles. It rotates on its axis, which tilts about 23° from the vertical. This tilt and the Earth's movement around the Sun are responsible for the changing seasons. About 71 per cent of the Earth's surface is covered by water and only 29 per cent by land, and there are permanent ice caps at each pole.
The Earth's interior (the *geosphere*) consists of a solid *inner core* composed of an iron–nickel alloy under pressure. Surrounding this is a liquid *outer core*, about 2 250km thick, composed mainly of nickel and iron, but with a certain amount of lighter material such as silicon and sulphur. Enclosing the outer core is another layer, the *mantle*, about 2 900km thick, consisting of solid rock within which material rises and falls as a result of heating and cooling. These movements are thought to be responsible for the processes of continental drift and plate tectonics. The rocky outer crust or *lithosphere* varies in thickness from about 8km under the oceans to about 40km under the continents, and is composed of a wide range of different rock types. The Earth is surrounded by an envelope of air, known as the *atmosphere*, which is rich in oxygen and nitrogen. The Earth is thought to have been formed about 4 550 million years ago, as a result of the condensation of a cloud of gas and dust under the attraction of gravitational forces to form a solid sphere. After millions of years the rock crust and the oceans and atmosphere formed. About 200 million years ago there was a single land mass, that subsequently divided into smaller land masses, which eventually, after millions of years of continental drift, formed the continents we know today.

earthbound *adj.* **1** attached to the earth. **2** *said of a spacecraft, etc* moving towards the earth. **3** *sometimes derog.* unable to think beyond what is known or familiar; lacking imagination.

earthen *adj.* **1** *said of a floor, etc* made of earth. **2** *said of a pot, etc* made of baked clay.

earthenware *noun* pottery made of a kind of baked clay which is rather coarse to the touch.

earthily *adv.* with an earthy or coarse manner.

earthiness *noun* being earthy or coarse; crudeness.

earthling *noun* in science fiction, a native of the Earth.

earthly *adj.* **1** *literary* of or belonging to this world; not spiritual. **2** *colloq.* used for emphasis: *have no earthly chance.*
— **not have an earthly** *colloq.* **1** not to have the slightest chance of success. **2** not to have the least idea. See also UNEARTHLY.

earthquake *noun* a series of shock waves which pass through the Earth, and may cause the

ground to shake, sometimes resulting in major destruction and loss of life. It is caused by the movement of rocks under stress deep in the Earth's crust.
◇ The source of an earthquake, known as the *focus*, may occur in rocks up to 500km below the surface of the Earth. The point on the Earth's surface directly above the focus is known as the *epicentre*. Vibrations radiate outwards from the focus, travelling through the Earth in all directions. The Earth's crust consists of a number of plates which are able to move, and major earthquakes usually occur at the edges of these plates, and may be associated with volcanic activity. Most earthquakes occur in a belt around the Pacific Ocean, and along a zone between the

Major Earthquakes

All magnitudes on the Richter scale.

Location	Year	Magnitude	Deaths
Los Angeles (USA)	1994	6.6	44
Japan	1993	7.8	2
Futuna (French Pacific)	1993	6.3	5
California (USA)	1992	7.4	2
Kirgizstan	1992	7.5	50
Nusa Tenggara	1992	6.8	2 500
Cairo (Egypt)	1992	5.9	552
Erzincum (Turkey)	1992	6.7	2 000
Uttar Pradesh (India)	1991	6.1	1 000
Costa Rica/Panama	1991	7.5	80
Georgia	1991	7.2	100
Afghanistan	1991	6.8	1 000
Pakistan	1991	6.8	300
Cabanatuan City	1990	7.7	1 653
NW Iran	1990	7.5	40 000
N Peru	1990	5.8	200
Romania	1990	6.6	70
Philippines	1990	7.7	1600
San Francisco	1989	6.9	100
Armenia	1988	7.0	25 000
SW China	1988	7.6	1 000
Nepal/India	1988	6.9	900
Mexico city	1985	8.1	7 200
N Yemen	1982	6.0	2 800
S Italy	1980	7.2	4 500
El Asnam (Algeria)	1980	7.3	5 000
NE Iran	1978	7.7	25 000
Tangshan (China)	1976	8.2	242 000
Guatemala City	1976	7.5	22 778
Kashmir	1974	6.3	5 200
Managua (Nicaragua)	1972	6.2	5 000
S Iran	1972	6.9	5 000
Chimbote (Peru)	1970	7.7	66 000
NE Iran	1968	7.4	11 600
Anchorage (USA)	1964	8.5	131
NW Iran	1962	7.1	12 000
Agadir (Morocco)	1960	5.8	12 000
Erzincan (Turkey)	1939	7.9	23 000
Chillan (Chile)	1939	7.8	30 000
Quetta (India)	1935	7.5	60 000
Gansu (China)	1932	7.6	70 000
Nan-shan (China)	1927	8.3	200 000
Kwanto (Japan)	1923	8.3	143 000
Gansu (China)	1920	8.6	180 000
Avezzano (Italy)	1915	7.5	30 000
Messina (Italy)	1908	7.5	120 000
Valparaiso (Chile)	1906	8.6	20 000
San Francisco (USA)	1906	8.3	500
Ecuador/Colombia	1868	*	70 000
Calabria (Italy)	1783	*	50 000
Lisbon (Portugal)	1755	*	70 000
Calcutta (India)	1737	*	300 000
Hokkaido (Japan)	1730	*	137 000
Catania (Italy)	1693	*	60 000
Caucasia (Caucasus)	1667	*	80 000
Shensi (China)	1556	*	830 000
Chihli (China)	1290	*	100 000
Silicia (Asia Minor)	1268	*	60 000
Corinth (Greece)	856	*	45 000
Antioch (Turkey)	526	*	250 000

*Magnitude not available

Mediterranean region and the Himalayas. The magnitude of an earthquake is usually measured on the Richter scale.

see also RICHTER SCALE.

earth science each of a group of sciences concerned with the study of the Earth and its atmosphere, especially geology, but also including geography, geomorphology, geophysics, geochemistry, oceanography, and meteorology.

earth-shattering *or* **earth-shaking** *adj. colloq.* of great importance.

earth-shatteringly *or* **earth-shakingly** *adv.* in a crucially important way; remarkably.

earthshine *or* **earthlight** *noun Astron.* a phenomenon often observable close to the time of a new moon, when sunlight reflected from the surface of the Earth on to the Moon causes the dark disc of the latter to be faintly illuminated.

earthstar *noun Biol.* a fungus, related to the puffball and found in woodland, that produces spores contained within a spherical fruit body. At maturity, the fleshy outer layer of the fruit body splits into several segments that curl backwards to form a structure resembling a star.

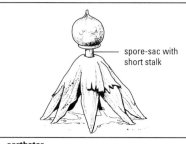

spore-sac with short stalk

earthstar

Earth Summit *Environ.* the United Nations Conference on Environment and Development, which took place in Rio de Janeiro, Brazil, in Jun 1992. An international convention for the preservation of biodiversity was signed by representatives from over 100 countries (not including the USA), and measures were drawn up to attempt to combat global warming.

earth tremor a slight earthquake.

earthwork *noun technical (often in pl.)* a man-made bank of earth, used formerly as a fortification, or as a foundation in modern road-building.

Earthworks, also called **Land Art** a modern art movement started in the late 1960s, in which holes are dug, stones arranged in patterns, etc, and the results often photographed. Examples include a work by the US artist Walter de Maria in 1968, in which he chalked two parallel white lines in the Nevada desert and exhibited photographs of them, entitled *Mile Long Drawing.*

earthworm *noun* the common name for various terrestrial worms belonging to the class Oligochaeta and having a long slender body divided into segments. They live in moist soil, feeding on decaying vegetation and continually swallowing and excreting the soil as worm casts. By mixing and aerating the soil they improve its quality.

earthy *adj.* (**earthier, earthiest**) **1** of or like earth or soil. **2** coarse or crude; lacking politeness.

ear-trumpet *noun* an old-fashioned hearing-aid consisting of a small trumpet held up to the ear.

earwig *noun* the common name for any nocturnal insect belonging to the order Dermaptera, characterized by a large pair of pincers at the hind end of the body, and named after the mistaken belief that it enters the ear of a sleeping person. [from Anglo-Saxon *eare*, ear + *wicga*, insect]

ease — *noun* **1** freedom from pain or anxiety. **2** absence of difficulty. **3** freedom from embarrass-

ment. **4** absence of restriction. — *verb* **1** to free from pain, trouble or anxiety. **2** *trans., intrans.* (**ease off** *or* **up**) to become less intense; to relax. **3** (**ease something in** *or* **out**) to move (something heavy or awkward) gently or gradually in or out of position.

— **at ease 1** relaxed; free from anxiety or embarrassment. **2** *Mil. (often as a command)* standing with legs apart and hands clasped behind the back.

ill at ease anxious or embarrassed.

take one's ease *formal* to relax; to make oneself comfortable.

[from Old French *aise*]

easel *noun* a stand for supporting a blackboard, an artist's canvas, etc. [from Dutch *ezel*, ass]

easement *noun Legal* the right of a landowner to use land which is not the landowner's own, or to prevent its owner from making an inconvenient use of it. Examples include a private right of way, and the right to light, to support of buildings, or to the taking of water.

easily *adv.* **1** without difficulty. **2** clearly; beyond doubt; by far. **3** very probably.

easiness *noun* being easy.

east — *noun* **1** (*also* **the east** *or* **the East**) the direction from which the sun rises; or any part of the earth, a country, a town, etc lying in that direction. **2** (**the East**) **a** the countries of Asia, east of Europe (see also FAR EAST, MIDDLE EAST). **b** *Politics* the former communist countries of eastern Europe. — *adj.* **1** in the east; on the side which is on or nearest the east. **2** coming from the direction of the east: *an east wind.* — *adv.* towards the east. [from Anglo-Saxon *east*]

East Anglia a region in E England. It comprises the counties of Norfolk and Suffolk, and parts of Cambridgeshire and Essex. East Anglia was a kingdom in Anglo-Saxon England and a major producer of wool in medieval times. CHIEF TOWN Norwich. ECONOMY agriculture; fishing; high technology; tourism.

East Bank a region in Jordan, E of the R Jordan. It comprises the governorates of Amman, Al Balqa, Irbid, Al Karak, and Maan, corresponding roughly to the former Amirate of Transjordan.

eastbound *adj.* going or leading towards the east.

Eastbourne POP (1992e) 86 000, a resort town in Eastbourne district, East Sussex, SE England. It lies on the English Channel, 30km/19mi SE of Brighton. HISTORY a Crown possession in Saxon times; later bought by three Sussex families; developed in the 18c into a fashionable coastal resort. NOTABLE FEATURES Lamb Inn (13c); Pilgrims Inn (14c); Towner Art Gallery; Saxon Church of St Mary.

East End the eastern part of a city, especially an area of London situated N of the R Thames and E of Shoreditch and Tower Bridge. It became a densely-populated industrial area during the 19c, and has undergone extensive reconstruction following heavy bombing during World War II.

Eastender *noun* an inhabitant of London's East End.

Easter *noun* **1** a Christian religious festival, held on the Sunday after the first full moon in spring, celebrating the resurrection of Christ. **2** the period during which the festival takes place, thought of as extending from Good Friday (the Friday before Easter Sunday) to the following Monday (Easter Monday). [from Anglo-Saxon *eastre*, perhaps from *Eostre*, a goddess associated with spring]

◇ In Western Churches, Easter Day falls between 22 Mar and 25 Apr inclusive, depending on the date of the first full moon after the spring equinox; the Eastern (Orthodox) Churches have a different method of calculating the date.

Easter Day *or* **Easter Sunday** the Sunday of Easter.

Easter egg an egg, traditionally a painted hard-boiled egg, but now more commonly a chocolate egg, given as a present at Easter.

Easter Island *or* **Rapa Nui**, Spanish **Isla de Pascua** POP (1985e) 2 000, an island of Chile, just to the S of the Tropic of Capricorn and c.3 500km/2 200mi W of the Chile coast. AREA 166sq km/64sq mi; maximum length 24km/15mi; maximum width 12km/8mi. PHYSICAL DESCRIPTION triangular, with an extinct volcano at each corner; it rises to 652m at Terevaka; undulating grassy and tree-covered hills with numerous caves and rocky outcrops; one third of the island is covered by the Rapa-Nui National Park, established in 1968. CHIEF TOWN Hanga Roa. The islanders are largely of Polynesian origin. NOTABLE FEATURES famous for its *moai* stone statues depicting local ancestors and considered by their creators to have had supernatural powers. There are nearly 1 000 carved from the slopes of Rano Raraku, where the largest (19m) still lies. Remains of the ceremonial city of Orongo are on the slopes of the Rano Kau volcano crater. [name refers to Easter Sunday, 1722 — the date on which the island was discovered by Dutch admiral Jacob Roggeveen.]

easterly — *adj.* **1** *said of a wind, etc* coming from the east. **2** looking, lying, etc towards the east. — *adv.* to or towards the east. — *noun* (PL. **easterlies**) an easterly wind.

eastern *adj.* **1** of or in the east. **2** facing or directed towards the east.

easterner *noun* a person who lives in or comes from the east, especially the eastern part of the USA.

easternmost *adj.* situated furthest east.

Eastern Woodlands Indians a Native American group living in the forested region along the Atlantic seaboard from Canada to South Carolina, and stretching west just beyond the Mississippi River. Algonkian-, Iroquoian- and Siouan-speaking, they lived by hunting, fishing, and gathering, with some farming of maize, squash, and beans in some southern areas. They were gradually pushed west and north towards the Great Plains and Canada; others were placed on reservations, some of which still exist in upstate New York and New England.

Easter Rising a rebellion (24–9 Apr 1916) of Irish nationalists in Dublin, organized by two revolutionary groups – the Irish Republican Brotherhood led by Patrick Pearse, and Sinn Féin led by James Connolly (1870–1916). Its focal point was the seizing of the General Post Office. After the rising was suppressed several leaders were executed, but the extent of the reprisals increased support for the nationalist cause in Ireland.

Easter Sunday see EASTER DAY.

East Germany, German **Deutsche Demokratische Republik** see GERMANY.

East India Company, British originally a British trading monopoly, established (1600) in India. Its first 'factory' (trading station) was in Surat (1612), with others in Madras (1639), Bombay (1688), and Calcutta (1690). During the 18c it competed with European countries, especially France. Local Indian disputes and Mughal weakness resulted in territorial benefits (eg control of Bengal, 1757) and the right to collect revenue from the Mughal emperor (1765). Financial indiscipline led to the 1773 Regulating Act and Pitt's 1784 India Act, which established a Board of Control responsible to parliament and signalled the Company's gradual loss of independence. Its monopoly was broken in 1813, its powers handed over to the British Crown in 1858, and it ceased to exist as a legal entity in 1873.

East India Company, Dutch (*Vereenigde Oostindische Compagnie*) a trading company founded in 1602 to protect trade in the Indian

Ocean and assist in the Dutch Wars of Independence against Spain. It established 'factories' (trading stations) on the Indian subcontinent, but made little political/cultural contact there. It founded long-term colonies in South Africa, Ceylon, and especially the Indonesian archipelago. The height of its prosperity was in the 17c and it was dissolved in 1799.

East India Company, French (*Compagnie des Indes Orientales*) a commercial/political organization founded in 1664 which directed French colonial activities in India. Its major trading stations were in Chandernagore, Pondicherry, and Mahé, and it competed for power with the British during the 18c. Its ambitious governer Joseph Dupleix (1697–1763) captured Madras (1746), but he was recalled to Paris in 1754, and the Company lost government support and collapsed during the French Revolution.

East Kilbride POP (1992e) 85 000, a town in Strathclyde, W central Scotland, situated in East Kilbride district. It is 11km/7mi S of Glasgow, and was designated a 'new town' in 1947. NOTABLE FEATURE Calderglen Country Park.

Eastleigh POP (1981) 59 000, a town in Eastleigh district, Hampshire, S England, situated just north of Southampton.

Eastman, George (1854–1932) US inventor and philanthropist, born in Waterville, New York. He turned from banking to photography, producing a successful roll film on paper (1884) and the 'Kodak' camera (1888). In 1889 he manufactured the transparent celluloid film used by Thomas Alva Edison and others in experiments which made possible the moving-picture industry.

East Sussex see SUSSEX, EAST.

eastward *or* **eastwards** *adv., adj.* towards the east.

Eastwood, Clint(on) (1930–) US film actor and director, born in San Francisco. He became an international star with three Italian-made 'spaghetti' westerns, beginning with *Per Un Pugno Di Dollari* (A Fistful of Dollars, 1964). In the USA his box-office status was confirmed with several violent crime thrillers (eg *Dirty Harry*, 1971). He was actor–director for the first time in *Play Misty for Me* (1971). Later films as such include *Bronco Billy* (1980), *Pale Rider* (1985), *Heartbreak Ridge* (1986), *Unforgiven* (1992), for which he won a Best Director Oscar, and *In the Line of Fire* (1993).

easy — *adj.* (**easier, easiest**) **1** not difficult. **2** free from pain, trouble, anxiety, etc. **3** not stiff or formal; friendly. **4** not tense or strained; leisurely. **5** *colloq.* having no strong preference. — *adv. colloq.* in a slow, calm or relaxed way: *take it easy.*
— **easy does it!** be careful!; (in the performing of a physical task) don't strain yourself!
easy on the eye *or* **ear** pleasant to look at or listen to.
go easy on *or* **with something** to use, take, etc not too much of: *go easy on the wine.*
go easy on *or* **with someone** to deal with them gently or calmly.
stand easy *Mil. (often as a command)* to stand less stiffly than standing at ease.
[from Old French *aisie*, from *aisier*, to ease]

easy-care *adj., said of fabrics* easy to clean and requiring little or no ironing; usually made from synthetic fibres or from specially treated natural fibres.

easy chair a soft, comfortable chair, usually with arms.

easy-going *adj.* not strict; relaxed; tolerant.

easy street *colloq.* a situation of comfort and financial well-being.

easy terms payment in instalments rather than all at once.

EAT *abbrev., as an international vehicle mark* Tanzania (ie East Africa Tanganyika).

eat *verb* (PAST TENSE **ate**; PAST PARTICIPLE **eaten**) **1** *trans., intrans.* to bite, chew and swallow (food). **2** *intrans.* to take in food. **3** to take in as food. **4** (**eat something away** *or* **eat into something**) to destroy the material, substance, form, etc of, especially by chemical action. **5** (**eat into** *or* **through something**) to use it up gradually. **6** (**eat up** *or* **eat something up**) to finish one's food. **7** (**be eaten up by** *or* **with something**) *usually of a bad feeling* to be greatly affected by it: *be eaten up with jealousy.* **8** *colloq.* to trouble or worry: *what's eating you?*
— **eat one's heart out** to suffer, especially in silence, from some longing or anxiety, or from envy.
eat humble pie to lower oneself or lose dignity, eg by admitting a mistake.
eat in to eat at home rather than in a restaurant.
eat out to eat at a restaurant rather than at home.
eat out of someone's hand *colloq.* to be very willing to follow, obey, or agree with them.
eat one's words to admit that one was wrong.
[from Anglo-Saxon *etan*]

eatable — *adj.* fit to be eaten. — *noun (usually* **eatables**) an item of food. See also EDIBLE.

eater *noun* **1** a person who eats: *a noisy eater.* **2** an eating apple, or any other fruit meant to be eaten raw.

eatery *noun* (PL. **eateries**) *colloq.* a small restaurant.

eating apple an apple for eating raw.

eats *pl. noun colloq.* food.

EAU *abbrev., as an international vehicle mark* Uganda (ie East Africa Uganda).

eau-de-cologne *or* **cologne** *noun* a mild type of perfume, originally made in Cologne in Germany. [from French *eau-de-cologne*, water of Cologne]

eaves *pl. noun* the part of a roof that sticks out beyond the wall, or the underside of it. [from Anglo-Saxon *efes*, the clipped edge of thatch]

eavesdrop *verb intrans.* (**eavesdropped, eavesdropping**) (**eavesdrop on someone**) to listen secretly to a private conversation. [from Anglo-Saxon *yfæsdrypæ*, eavesdropper, a person who stands under the eaves to listen to conversations]

eavesdropper *noun* a person who eavesdrops.

eavesdropping *noun* listening to anothers' conversation.

EAZ *abbrev., as an international vehicle mark* Tanzania (ie East Africa Zanzibar).

ebb — *verb intrans.* **1** *said of the tide* to move back from the land. **2** (**ebb away**) to grow smaller or weaker. — *noun* **1** the movement of the tide away from the land. **2** a growing smaller or weaker: *his health is on the ebb.*
— **at a low ebb** in a poor or weak state (mentally or physically).
[from Anglo-Saxon *ebba*]

Ebbw Vale POP (1981) 21 000, a town in Monmouth district, Gwent, SE Wales. It lies on the R Ebbw, 56km/35mi NW of Bristol. It was formerly a major coal-mining centre (the Big Pit is now on view to tourists). The iron and steel industries closed down in the 1970s.

Ebla a Syrian city-state of the third millennium BC, lying S of Carchemish. It traded with Anatolia, Assyria, and Sumeria.

ebony — *noun* **1** a hard heavy jet-black wood that takes a high polish and is used to make carvings, piano keys, woodwind instruments, knife handles, and jewellery, and is also used in cabinetwork. **2** the tropical hardwood tree (*Diospyros ebenum*), found in Africa and Asia, from which this wood is obtained. — *adj.* **1** made from this wood. **2** *literary* black. [from Latin *ebeninus*]

Ebro, River, ancient **Iberius** the longest river that flows entirely in Spain, length 910km/565mi. It rises in the Cantabrian Mts, NE Spain, flowing SE to enter the Mediterranean Sea at Cape Tortosa. The river, which has three major reservoirs on its course, is used for hydroelectricity and irrigation.

EBU *abbrev.* European Broadcasting Union.

ebullience *or* **ebulliency** *noun* cheerfulness; enthusiasm.

ebullient *adj. formal* very high-spirited; full of cheerfulness or enthusiasm. [from Latin *ebullire*, to boil out]

ebulliently *adv.* with cheerfulness or enthusiasm.

EC *abbrev.* **1** European Commission. **2** European Community. **3** *as an international vehicle mark* Ecuador.

eccentric — *adj.* **1** *said of a person, behaviour, etc* odd; unusual. **2** *technical, said of a wheel, etc* not having the axis at the centre. **3** *Geom.* denoting two circles that do not have a common centre, ie that are not concentric. **4** denoting a moving body that deviates from a circular path or orbit. — *noun* **1** an eccentric person. **2** *technical* a device for converting rotating motion into backward and forward motion. [from Latin *eccentricus*, from Greek *ek*, out of + *kentros*, centre]

eccentrically *adv.* in an eccentric or unusual way.

eccentricity *noun* (PL. **eccentricities**) an eccentric manner or characteristic.

Eccl. *or* **Eccl** *abbrev. Biblical* Ecclesiastes.

Ecclesiastes, Book of a book of wisdom literature in the Hebrew Bible and Old Testament, attributed to the 'Preacher, the son of David, King of Jerusalem', who is traditionally identified as Solomon, although the work is more usually now thought to belong to the period following Israel's exile (late 3c BC). [derived from the Greek rendering of the Hebrew *Koheleth*, the preacher, one who speaks or teaches in an assembly]

ecclesiastic *noun formal* a clergyman. [from Latin *ecclesiasticus*, from Greek *ekklesia*, church]

ecclesiastical *or* **ecclesiastic** *adj.* of or relating to the Church or the clergy.

ecclesiastically *adv.* as regards the Church or the clergy.

Ecclesiasticus, Book of, also called the **Wisdom of Jesus, the Son of Sirach**, or simply **Sirach**, or **Ben Sira** a book of the Apocrypha, originally attributed to a Jewish scribe (c.180 BC), and later translated into Greek by his grandson. It includes collections of proverbs and exhortations, and praises wisdom. It ends with a historical survey in praise of Israel's leaders. [from Latin *ecclesiasticus*, Church book]

ecclesiology *noun Relig.* **1** the theological study of the nature of the Christian Church. **2** the science of church construction and decoration.

Ecclus. *or* **Ecclus** *abbrev.* Ecclesiasticus (Apocrypha).

ecdysis *noun Zool.* in animals with a rigid exoskeleton, eg insects and crustaceans, the act of shedding the exoskeleton to allow growth to occur. [from Greek *ekdysis*, from *ek*, out of + *dyein*, to put on]

Ecevit, Bülent (1925–) Turkish politician, born in Istanbul. He became an MP for the centre-left Republican People's Party (1957), then Minister of Labour, then in 1966 became Secretary-General of his Party and subsequently Chairman (1972). As Prime Minister (1974, 1977, 1978–9), during his 1974 coalition government he ordered the invasion of Cyprus, and in 1978 imposed martial law on Turkey. After the military coup of 1980, he was imprisoned twice for criticizing the military regime.

ECG *abbrev.* electrocardiogram or electrocardiograph.

echelon *noun* **1** *formal* a level or rank in an organization, etc, or the people at that level. **2** *technical* a roughly V-shaped formation, used by ships, planes, birds in flight, etc in which each member is in a position slightly to the outside of the one in front. [from French *échelon*, from *échelle*, ladder]

Echidna in Greek mythology, a monster, half-woman and half-snake, who was the mother of various monsters, including the Chimera and Hydra.

echidna *noun* the spiny anteater, an egg-laying mammal of Australia and New Guinea, with a long snout and long claws. [from Greek *echidna*, viper]

echidna

echinoderm *noun Zool.* any marine invertebrate animal belonging to the phylum Echinodermata, usually characterized by the possession of five-rayed symmetry in the adult, eg starfish, brittle star, sea urchin, sea lily, sea cucumber. [from Greek *echinos*, hedgehog, sea urchin + *derma*, skin]
◇ The body of an echinoderm is typically covered with calcareous (chalky) plates embedded in the skin, often bearing protruding spines. It contains water-filled tubes, slender branches of which emerge from the body wall as *tube feet*, which are used for feeding, locomotion, and breathing.

Echinodermata *noun Zool.* in the animal kingdom, a phylum of radially symmetrical marine invertebrates, eg starfish, sea urchins, brittlestars. [from Greek *echinos*, hedgehog]

Echo in Greek mythology, a nymph of whom several stories are told. In one legend, she was beloved by Pan and torn to pieces, with only her voice surviving. In another, she was punished by Hera so that she could only repeat the last words of another speaker. In a third, she loved Narcissus, who rejected her, and she wasted away to only a voice.

echo — *noun* (PL. **echoes**) **1** the reflection of a sound wave by the surface of a nearby object so that a weaker signal is received a short time after the original signal. **2** a sound repeated in this way. **3** *often facetious* a person who imitates or repeats what others say or think. **4** an imitation or repetition (sometimes accidental). **5** (*often* **echoes**) a trace; something which brings to mind memories or thoughts of something else. **6** a reflected radio or radar beam, or the visual signal it produces on a screen. — *verb* (**echoes**, **echoed**) **1** *intrans.* to sound loudly with an echo. **2** to send back an echo of. **3** to repeat (a sound or a statement). **4** to imitate or in some way be similar to.
◇ An echo occurs when sound waves striking surfaces at different distances return to the observer at different times. The length of the delay between the two signals indicates the distance of the reflecting object. Ships and submarines use echoes in sonar equipment to measure water depth and to look for features on the sea bed. Bats use the echoes produced by high-pitched sounds made while flying to obtain information about the direction and distance of objects that they are unable to see. [from Greek *ekho*, = sound]

echocardiography *Medicine* a technique which involves the use of ultrasound waves to produce pictures of the internal structure and movements of the heart as it beats, used in the diagnosis of heart disease.

echoic *adj.* **1** *formal, said of a sound* of or like an echo. **2** *of a word* imitating the sound it represents; onomatopoeic: *'bump' is an echoic word.*

echolocation *noun Physics* the perception of objects by means of reflected sound waves, typically after high-frequency sounds have been emitted. The process is used by some animals, such as bats and whales, for navigation and for location of prey.

echo-sounder *noun* a device for testing the depth of water by echo-sounding.

echo-sounding a method used to estimate the depth of water beneath a ship or other vessel, by sending out an ultrasound signal and measuring the time taken for its echo to return to a receiver after it has been reflected from the sea bed. Echo-sounding is also used to detect shoals of fish beneath fishing boats.

Eck, Johann Mayer von (1486–1543) German Roman Catholic theologian, born in Egg, Swabia. He became Professor of Theology at Ingolstadt (1510), and was the ruling spirit of that university until his death. He disputed with Luther at Leipzig (1519), wrote on papal authority, and went to Rome in 1520, to return with the bull which declared Luther a heretic.

Eckert, John Presper (1919–) US engineer and inventor, born in Philadelphia. With John Mauchly, he developed the Electronic Numerical Integrator and Computer (ENIAC), one of the first modern computers; this led directly to their EDVAC (Electronic Discrete Variable Computer), a more advanced stored-program machine. Their next machine, UNIVAC (Universal Automatic Computer), marked the beginning of the modern US data-processing industry, becoming one of the first computers to be sold commercially.

Eckhart, Johannes, known as **Meister Eckhart** (c.1260–c.1327) German theologian and mystic, born in Hochheim, near Gotha. He was Dominican provincial in Saxony (1303–11), and from 1312 preached at Strasbourg, Frankfurt, and Cologne. His teaching is a mystic pantheism, which influenced later religious mysticism and speculative philosophy. In 1325 he was accused of heresy by the Archbishop of Cologne, and two years after his death his writings were condemned by Pope John XXII.

éclair *noun* a long cake of light pastry, with a cream filling and chocolate or coffee icing. [from French *éclair*, flash of lightning, perhaps because it is quickly eaten]

eclampsia *noun Medicine* a disorder that may occur during the last three months of pregnancy, and is characterized by convulsions, a sudden increase in blood pressure, water retention, and the presence of protein in the urine. [from Greek *eklampsis*, from *eklampein*, to flash forth, to burst forth violently]

éclat *noun literary* **1** striking effect. **2** splendid success. **3** applause; praise. [from French *éclat*]

eclectic *adj., said of a style of writing or art, or a set of beliefs* selecting material or ideas from a wide range of sources or authorities. [from Greek *ek*, from + *legein*, to choose]

eclectically *adv.* in an eclectic or widely selective manner or style.

eclecticism *noun* an eclectic manner or style.
◇ In the visual arts, especially painting and sculpture, the term is applied to the practice of borrowing formal or stylistic features from the works of other artists, and has a positive implication. For example, Tintoretto was said to have combined the colour of Titian with the drawing of Michelangelo.

eclipse — *noun* **1** a phenomenon in which light from a celestial body, eg the Sun, is partly or totally obscured by another celestial body, eg a solar eclipse occurs when the Moon passes between the Earth and the Sun, and casts a shadow on the Earth, and a *lunar eclipse* occurs when the Earth passes between the Moon and the Sun, and casts a shadow on the Moon, which therefore reflects no sunlight. **2** a loss of fame or importance. — *verb* **1** to cause an eclipse of. **2** to surpass or outshine. [from Greek *ekleipsis*, failure to appear]

eclipsing binary *Astron.* a binary star in which one star periodically passes in front of the other (as seen from Earth), eclipsing it, so that the total light received on Earth from the two stars temporarily decreases until both stars are visible again.

ecliptic — *noun* (**the ecliptic**) *Astron.* the path that the Sun appears to follow through the stars (and therefore around the celestial sphere) each year as the Earth orbits around the Sun. The ecliptic passes through the 12 constellations of the zodiac, and corresponds to the intersection of the Earth's orbit with the celestial sphere; the plane of the Earth's orbit around the Sun. — *adj.* relating to an eclipse or the ecliptic.

eclogue *noun* a short poem, or part of a longer one, in the form of a dialogue or soliloquy. Up to the 18c, the term referred specifically to pastoral poems (eg by Virgil, Dante, Petrarch, Spenser, Pope). In modern poetry it is used as a means of expressing the poet's ideas in non-pastoral poems (eg by Swift, Auden). [from Latin *ecloga*, from Greek *ekloge*, a selection]

Eclogues, The ten pastoral poems by Virgil (c.42–39 BC). They are written in imitation of the Idylls of Theocritus.

Eco, Umberto (1932–) Italian novelist and critic, born in Allesandra. He became Professor of Semiotics at the University of Bologna (1971–) and has published several important works on the subject, including *Semiotics and the Philosophy of Language* (1984). His novel *Il nome della rosa* (The Name of the Rose, 1981), an intellectual detective story in a medieval monastic setting, attracted much critical attention and was filmed in 1986. Other works include *Il pendolo di Foucault* (Foucault's Pendulum, 1989).

eco- *combining form* denoting living things in relation to their environment: *ecology / ecotourism*. [from Greek *oikos*, house]

eco-friendly *adj.* not harmful to the environment.

ecological *adj.* relating to ecology or the relation of things to their surroundings.

ecologically *adv.* as regards ecology or the relation of things to their surroundings.

ecologist *noun* a person who studies ecology.

ecology *noun* the branch of biology that is concerned with the relationship between living organisms and their natural environment, including their relationship with each other. [from Greek *oikos*, house + -LOGY]
◇ Recent ecological studies have led to concern about the adverse effects of human activity on the environment, and have highlighted the importance of conservation strategies. As a result, the word 'ecology' is sometimes used more or less interchangeably with 'environmentalism' to describe a philosophy independent of the scientific discipline.

econ. *abbrev.* economic, economics, or economy.

econometrics *sing. noun* a specialized branch of economics which uses mathematical and statistical techniques to develop and test economic theories, make economic forecasts, etc.

economic *adj.* **1** of or concerned with the economy of a nation, etc. **2** *said of a business practice, etc* likely to bring a profit. **3** of economics.

economical *adj.* not wasting money or resources.

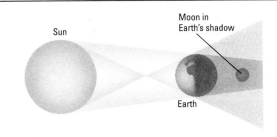

lunar eclipse

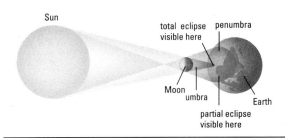

solar eclipse

---

economically *adv.* in an economical way.

Economic Community of West African States (**ECOWAS**) an organization formed (May 1975) through the Treaty of Lagos by 15 W African states : Benin, Gambia, Ghana, Guinea, Guinea-Bissau, Ivory Coast (Côte d'Ivoire), Liberia, Mali, Mauritania, Niger, Nigeria, Senegal, Sierra Leone, Togo, and Upper Volta (now Burkina). Cape Verde joined in 1977. It aims to end trade restrictions, establish a common customs tariff, harmonize economic and industrial policies, and equalize the levels of development of member states.

economic growth increase in a country's output of goods and services over a given period of time. The rate of economic growth is measured by comparing the actual output of goods and services from one year to the next, having made appropriate adjustments for changes in prices.

economics *sing. noun* **1** the study of the production, distribution, and consumption of money, goods and services. **2** financial aspects: *the economics of the situation / the economics of the situation.* See also HOME ECONOMICS.

economist *noun* an expert in economics.

economization *or* **economisation** *noun* being economical; economizing.

economize *or* **economise** *verb intrans.* to cut down on spending or waste: *we need to economize / we decided to economize on coffee.*

economy — *noun* (PL. **economies**) **1** the organization of money and resources within a nation, etc, especially in terms of the production, distribution, and consumption of goods and services. **2** a system in which these are organized in a particular way: *a socialist economy.* **3** careful management of money or other resources, avoiding waste and cutting down on spending. **4** (*usually* **economies**) an instance of economizing; a saving. **5** efficient or sparing use: *economy of movement.* — *adj.* **1** *said of a class of travel, especially air travel* of the cheapest kind. **2** (*also* **economy-size** *or* **-sized**) *said of a packet of food, etc* larger than the standard or basic size, and proportionally cheaper. [from Greek *oikos*, house + *nomos*, law]

ecosocialism *noun Politics* a branch of socialism originating in the late 1970s and early 1980s, which combines concern for environmental and ecological matters with the more established aims of socialism. In particular, it represents the view that resources should be used in a socially useful mannner.

ecosphere *noun* same as BIOSPHERE.

ecosystem *noun Biol.* a self-contained community of plants and animals and the physical environment with which it interacts and exchanges materials, eg rainforest, grassland.

◇ The relationships within an ecosystem are usually delicately balanced, and may be disrupted by the removal of a particular species, or by physical or chemical factors such as drought or pollution. The study of ecosystems is commonly based on the transfer of energy and nutrients from one organism to another along a *food*

chain. In most natural ecosystems, however, several food chains interact to form complex food webs (eg a plant may be eaten by several different herbivores, which in turn serve as food for a wide range of carnivores, that are themselves eaten by other carnivores).

ecotourism *noun* tourism in areas of unspoiled natural beauty, carefully managed so that holidaymakers have minimum impact on the environment, and where the income generated contributes to conservation.

ecotype *noun Biol.* a variety or race of a plant species that is restricted to a particular habitat.

ECSC *abbrev.* European Coal and Steel Community.

ecstasy *noun* (PL. **ecstasies**) **1** a feeling of immense joy. **2** *Psychol.* a mental state of extreme well-being and trance-like elation. **3** *slang* (*also* **Ecstasy**) methylene-dioxymethamphetamine, a 'designer drug' taken for its stimulant and hallucinogenic properties. [from French *extasie*, from Greek *ekstasis*, standing outside oneself]

ecstatic *adj.* **1** of, showing, or causing ecstasy. **2** *colloq.* very happy or pleased.

ecstatically *adv.* in an ecstatic or intensely joyful way.

ECT *abbrev.* electro-convulsive therapy.

ecto- *combining form* forming words meaning 'outside': *ectomorph.* See also ENDO-, ENTO-, EXO-. [from Greek *ektos*, outside]

ectoderm *noun Zool.* in a multicellular animal that has two or more layers of body tissue, the outermost layer of cells of the embryo, which develops into the epidermal tissues such as skin, hair, tooth enamel, and sense organs. — Also called *epiblast.* [from ECTO- + Greek *derma*, skin]

ectomorph *noun* a person of slender build with long thin limbs and a relatively low body weight, sometimes said to be associated with a sensitive inhibited personality. [from ECTO- + Greek *morphe*, form]

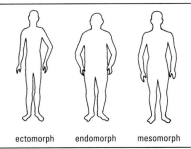

| ectomorph | endomorph | mesomorph |

ectomorph, endomorph, and mesomorph

-ectomy *combining form* (PL. **-ectomies**) *Medicine* forming words denoting removal by surgery: *hysterectomy.* [from Greek *ektome*, from *ektemnein*, to cut out]

ectopic *adj. Medicine* in an abnormal position, especially denoting the development of a fetus outside the uterus, usually in one of the Fallopian

tubes. In almost all cases the fetus is aborted within three months of conception. [from Greek *ek*, from + *topos*, place]

ectoplasm *noun* **1** *Biol.* in organisms such as the amoeba, the layer of clear non-granular and relatively rigid cytoplasm lying immediately below the cell membrane, that aids the process of *cytoplasmic streaming* necessary for movement of the animal to occur. **2** the substance thought by some people to be given off by the body of a spiritualistic medium during a trance. [from ECTO- + Greek *plasma*, something moulded]

ecu *or* **ECU** *noun* European currency unit, a trading currency whose value is based on the combined values of several European currencies.

◇ The ecu serves as a currency reserve, and is regarded as a potential single European currency. The so-called *hard ecu* is based on the narrow band of the exchange rate mechanism and is designed not to be devalued against any other European currency, thereby bringing stability and low inflation.

Ecuador, official name **Republic of Ecuador**, Spanish **República del Ecuador** POP (1992e) 10.8m, a republic in the NW of S America straddling the Equator. AREA 270 699sq km/104 490sq mi. It is bounded N by Colombia, S and E by Peru, and W by the Pacific Ocean and includes the Galápagos Is 970km/600mi to the W. CAPITAL Quito. CHIEF TOWNS Guayaquil, Cuenca, Riobamba, Esmeraldas. TIME ZONE GMT –5. The population is 25% S American Indian, 55% Mestizo, 10% Spanish, and 10% African; Roman Catholicism is the main religion. OFFICIAL LANGUAGE Spanish; Quechua is also spoken. CURRENCY the sucre. PHYSICAL DESCRIPTION coastal plain (*Costa*) in the W, descending from rolling hills in the N to a broad lowland basin averaging 100km/60mi in width before opening out into the Gulf of Guayaquil; Andean uplands (*Sierra*) in the central region, three main ranges rising to snow-capped peaks which include Cotopaxi (5 896m); forested alluvial plains of the *Oriente* in the E, dissected by rivers flowing from the Andes towards the Amazon; frequent serious earthquakes; the Galápagos Is comprise six main volcanic islands, with a land area of c.7 812sq km/3 015sq mi. CLIMATE hot and humid coast, rain throughout the year (especially Dec–Apr); varies from 2 000mm in the N to 200mm in the S; central Andes temperatures are much reduced by altitude; Quito has warm days and chilly nights, with frequent heavy rain in the afternoon; hot and wet equatorial climate in the E. HISTORY formerly part of the Inca Empire; taken by the Spanish in 1527; within the Viceroyalty of New Granada; gained independence in 1822; joined with Panama, Colombia, and Venezuela to form Gran Colombia; left the union to become an independent republic in 1830; the country's political history is highly unstable (there were 22 presidents between 1925 and 1948, none completing a term in office); following inconclusive election results and the implementation of reforms there was unrest in the early 1990s. GOVERNMENT unicameral National Congress consisting of a 71-member House of Deputies and four permanent committees of 28 members elected every four years; a president is elected for a four year term. ECONOMY agriculture employs c.50% of the workforce; beans, cereals, potatoes, livestock in the *Sierra*; bananas, coffee, cocoa, cane sugar, rice, cotton, vegetable oil in the *Costa*; fishing (especially shrimps), balsawood, food processing, textiles, petrochemicals, steel, cement, pharmaceuticals; oil piped from the *Oriente* to refineries at Esmeraldas.

Ecuador

ecumenical *adj.* **1** bringing together different branches of the Christian Church. **2** working towards the unity of the Christian Church. **3** of the whole Christian Church: *an ecumenical council*. [from Greek *oikoumenikos*, of the inhabited world]

ecumenicalism *or* **ecumenism** *noun* the principles or practice of Christian unity.

ecumenically *adv.* as regards Christian unity or the whole Christian world.

ecumenism *noun Relig.* a movement seeking the unity of divided Churches and denominations within Christianity. The 4c and 5c 'Ecumenical Councils' claimed to represent the Church in the whole world. The modern interest in ecumenism stems from the Edinburgh Missionary Conference (1910) and led to the formation in 1948 of the World Council of Churches. The movement encourages dialogue between Churches of different denominations, unions where possible, joint acts of worship, and joint service in the community. [from Greek *oikoumene*, the inhabited world]

eczema *noun Medicine* acute or chronic inflammation of the outer layer (epidermis) of the skin, usually consisting of a reddish itching rash accompanied by small blisters, followed by thickening, crusting, or discoloration of the skin. [from Greek *ekzema*, from *ek*, out of + *zeein*, to boil]

ed. *abbrev.* **1** edited. **2** edition. **3** editor. **4** educated. **5** education.

-ed *suffix* **1** used to form past tenses and past participles: *talked / waited*. **2** used to form adjectives from nouns: *bearded / bald-headed*.

Edam POP (1992e) 25 000, a town in E North Holland province, W Netherlands. It lies on reclaimed land on the Ijsselmeer, 21km/13mi NE of Amsterdam. HISTORY founded as a customs post in the 13c; developed a prosperous cheese trade in the 16c–17c. NOTABLE FEATURE Grote Kerk (15c).

Edam *noun* a type of mild yellow cheese, usually shaped into balls and covered with red wax. [from *Edam*, where it was originally made]

edaphology *noun* the study of soil as a medium for living organisms, particularly for vegetation. Any property of soil, physical or chemical, may influence which plants are capable of growing in that soil. These properties are known as *edaphic factors*, and include relative acidity or alkalinity, soil structure, soil depth, and levels of nutrient. [from Greek *edaphos*, ground, soil + -LOGY]

Edberg, Stefan (1966–) Swedish tennis player, born in Vasternik. He won the men's singles title at Wimbledon in 1988 and 1990. Other wins include the Australian Open (1985, 1987), and the US Open (1991–2).

Edda the name of two separate collections of Old Norse literature. The *Elder Edda* (9c) consist of heroic and mythological poems; the later Edda were written (mainly in prose) by the Icelandic poet Snorri Sturluson (early 13c). [Old Norse, = great-grandmother]

Eddington, Sir Arthur Stanley (1882–1944) English astronomer, born in Kendal, Westmoreland. Professor at Cambridge and director of the university observatory, he made important contributions to the study of stellar structure, and his measurements of star positions during a total solar eclipse gave the first direct confirmation of Einstein's general theory of relativity. He was also a well-known popularizer of science.

Eddy, Mary, *née* **Baker** (1821–1910) US founder of the Christian Science Church, born in Bow, New Hampshire. Brought up a Congregationalist, she suffered from ill health, and so had little formal education, but she was cured of a spinal malady by the faith healer Phineas P Quimby (1802–66). In 1866 she was severely injured in a fall, but read in the Bible about Christ healing the paralysed man, and claimed to have been similarly healed. Thereafter she developed a spiritual and metaphysical system she called Christian Science; in 1876 she founded the Christian Science Association, and in 1879 organized at Boston the Church of Christ, Scientist.

eddy — *noun* (PL. **eddies**) **1** a circular or swirling movement that develops within a current of water or air when the continuity of flow is disturbed in some way. **2** a movement of air, smoke, fog, etc similar to this. — *verb intrans., trans.* (**eddies**, **eddied**) to move or cause to move in this way.

Edelman, Gerald Maurice (1929–) US biochemist, born in New York City. Professor at Rockefeller University, he clarified the chemical structure and mode of action of the antibodies which form a major part of a vertebrate animal's defence against infection. For these discoveries he shared the 1972 Nobel Prize for Physiology or Medicine with Rodney Porter.

edelweiss *noun* (PL. **edelweiss**) a small European mountain plant with white woolly leaves around the flower-heads. [from German *edel*, noble + *weiss*, white]

Eden, Sir (Robert) Anthony, 1st Earl of Avon (1897–1977) Anglo-Irish politician and Conservative Prime Minister, born in Windlestone, Durham. He became an MP in 1923, was Foreign Under-Secretary (1931), Lord Privy Seal (1933), and Foreign Secretary (1935), but resigned in 1938 over differences with Prime Minister Neville Chamberlain. In World War II he was first Dominions Secretary, then Secretary of State for War, and Foreign Secretary (1940–5). Again Foreign Secretary (1951–5), he was involved with the negotiations in Korea and Indo-China, and the 1954 Geneva Summit Conference. He succeeded Churchill as Prime Minister (1955–7), and in 1956 ordered British forces (in collaboration with the French and Israelis) to occupy the Suez Canal Zone, a controverisal action condemned by the UN.

Eden a river in Cumbria, NW England, length 104km/65mi. It rises 16km/10mi SE of Appleby and flows NW to meet the Solway Firth NW of Carlisle.

Eden 1 (*also* **Garden of Eden**) a biblical place depicted as an earthly paradise, where Adam and Eve lived prior to their sin and expulsion (Genesis 2, 3). In the Book of Ezekiel it symbolizes the future restitution of Israel after the exile. **2** a beautiful region; a place of delight. [from Hebrew *eden*, delight, pleasure]

edentate *Biol.* — *adj.* lacking teeth. — *noun* an animal belonging to the order Edentata, a group of mammals that characteristically have few or no teeth, well-developed claws for digging and hanging from tree branches, etc, and whose bodies are often covered with an armour of bony plates, eg armadillos, anteaters, sloths. [from Latin *edentatus*, toothless]

Edgar (943–75) King of Mercia and Northumbria (957) and (from 959) King of all England, the younger son of Edmund I. He encouraged the reform of the English Church as a means of enhancing his prestige and power, though his lavish support for the monasteries caused bitterness among the nobility. In c.973 he introduced a uniform currency based on silver pennies.

Edgar the elder, more honest, but at first far too trusting, of the Earl of Gloucester's sons in Shakespeare's *King Lear*, who goes into exile from his father's house and disguises himself as a mad beggar.

Edgar a male first name. [from Anglo-Saxon *ead*, prosperity, fortune + *gar*, spear]

Edgar the Atheling (c.1050–1125) Anglo-Saxon prince, the grandson of Edmund Ironside. Though chosen as king after the battle of Hastings, he was never crowned. He submitted to William the Conqueror (by Dec 1066), but then rebelled and fled to Scotland (1068), where his sister Margaret married Malcolm Canmore, and was reconciled with King William in 1074. When fighting for Duke Robert of Normandy against Henry I of England at the battle of Tinchebrai (1106) he was taken prisoner, and after his release he retired from public life.

Edgbaston a cricket ground in Birmingham, England, one of the home grounds of Warwickshire CCC, and a regular venue for England Test matches. It was first used by Warwickshire in 1894.

edge — *noun* **1** the part farthest from the middle of something; a border or boundary. **2** the area beside a cliff or steep drop. **3** the cutting side of something sharp such as a knife. **4** *Geom.* the meeting point of two surfaces. **5** sharpness or severity: *a cold wind with an edge to it*. **6** bitterness: *there was an edge to his criticism*. — *verb* **1** to form or make a border to, edged with flowers. **2** to shape the edge or border of. **3** *trans., intrans.* (**edge forward** *or* **in** *or* **out**, *etc*) to move gradually and carefully. **4** to sharpen (a knife, etc).
— **have the edge on** *or* **over someone** *or* **something** to have an advantage over them; to be better than them.
on edge uneasy; nervous and irritable.
take the edge off something 1 to make it less unpleasant or less difficult. **2** to weaken or diminish it.
[from Anglo-Saxon *ecg*]

edgeways *or* **edgewise** *adv.* sideways.
— **not get a word in edgeways** to be unable to contribute to a conversation because the others are talking continuously.

Edgeworth, Maria (1767–1849) Anglo-Irish novelist, born in Blackbourton, Oxfordshire. She is best known for her novels of Irish life, such as *Castle Rackrent* (1800) and *The Absentee* (1812).

edgily *adv.* with a nervous or tense manner.

edginess *noun* being nervous or tense.

edging *noun* a decorative border.

edgy *adj.* (**edgier**, **edgiest**) *colloq.* easily annoyed; nervous or tense.

EDI *abbrev.* electronic data interchange, the use of computer links to exchange or provide on-line access to business data, etc.

edibility *noun* the state of being edible.

edible *adj.* fit to be eaten; suitable to eat. [from Latin *edibilis*]

edict *noun* an order issued by a monarch or government. [from Latin *edicere*, to proclaim]

edification *noun* improvement of the mind or morals.

edifice *noun formal* **1** a building, especially a large impressive one. **2** a large and complex organization. [from French *édifice*, from Latin *aedificare*, to build]

edify *verb* (**edifies**, **edified**) *formal* to improve the mind or morals of. [from French *édifier*, from Latin *aedificare*, to build]

edifying *adj.* intellectually or morally stimulating.

Edinburgh, Prince Philip, Duke of (1921–) the consort of Elizabeth II, son of Prince Andrew of Greece and Princess Alice of Battenberg, born in Corfu. He entered the Royal Navy in 1939 as Lt Philip Mountbatten. He became a naturalized British subject in 1947, and was created Duke of Edinburgh on the eve of his marriage to the Princess Elizabeth (20 Nov). In 1957 his name was styled Prince Philip. Seriously interested in science and the technology of industry, he is also a keen sportsman, yachtsman, and qualified airman. In 1956 he began the Duke of Edinburgh Award Scheme to foster the leisure activities of young people.

Edinburgh POP (1992e) 440 000, the capital of Scotland, of Lothian Region, and of Edinburgh City district. It is situated in E central Scotland, between the Pentland Hills and the S shore of the Firth of Forth. There are port facilities at Leith, which was united with Edinburgh in 1920. The city is a financial, legal, and cultural centre. Its historical significance and natural beauty make it a major tourist destination. HISTORY The castle was built by Malcolm Canmore in the 11c; in 1392 Robert Bruce granted Edinburgh its first charter; became capital of Scotland in 1482; political power diminished after the 1707 Act of Union; the original burgh was the Old Town around the castle; Edinburgh expanded first in the 1760s, with the Georgian New Town area (designed by James Craig), but the business centre remained in the Old Town; Nor' Loch, separating the Old and the New Towns, was drained and laid out to create Princes Street Gardens; an intellectual centre in the 18c. NOTABLE FEATURES Edinburgh Castle; the Royal Mile, which runs from the Castle to the Palace of Holyroodhouse, the official residence of the Queen in Scotland; Holyrood Park, in which lies Arthur's Seat, the plug of an extinct volcano; Scott Monument (1844), 61m high; Calton Hill, with an observatory and an unfinished reproduction of the Parthenon; Royal Observatory on Blackford Hill; Gladstone's Land (six-storey tenement, 1620); house of John Knox (15c); St Giles Cathedral (15c); St Mary's Cathedral (19c); National Gallery of Scotland; Scottish National Gallery of Modern Art; Scottish National Portrait Gallery; Royal Museum of Scotland; Museum of Childhood; Royal Botanic Garden; Edinburgh Zoo; Meadowbank Stadium Sports Complex; artificial ski slope (at Hillend); Edinburgh University (1583). EVENTS Royal Highland Agricultural Show (Jun); Military Tattoo (Aug); the Edinburgh Festival (Aug–Sep).

Edinburgh Festival, in full **Edinburgh International Festival** an annual festival, founded in 1947. Held over three weeks in Aug–Sep, it includes concerts, recitals, and operas. A very large 'fringe' festival, which has less formal performances, revues, and exhibitions is held at the same time, as well as a Film Festival, a Jazz Festival, and a Book Festival (in alternate years).

Edison, Thomas Alva (1847–1931) US inventor and physicist, born in Milan, Ohio. During the Civil War he worked as a telegraph operator in various cities, and invented an electric vote-recording machine. In 1871 he invented the paper ticker-tape automatic repeater for stock exchange prices, which he then sold in order to establish an industrial research laboratory. He took out more than 1 000 patents in all, including the gramophone (1877), the electric light bulb (1879), and the carbon granule microphone as an improvement for Alexander Graham Bell's telephone. In 1912 he produced the first talking motion pictures.

edit — *verb* **1** to prepare (a book, newspaper, programme, film, etc) for publication or broadcasting, especially by making corrections or alterations. **2** to be in overall charge of the process of producing (a newspaper, etc). **3** (*usually* **edit something out**) to remove (parts of a work) before printing, broadcasting, etc. **4** to prepare (a cinema film, or a television or radio programme) by putting together material previously photographed or recorded. **5** *Comput.* to add, delete, modify, or rearrange (data) in preparation for processing by a computer, or to enable it to be used by other programs. **6** *Comput.* to produce a new version of (a text or program file). — *noun* a period or instance of editing. [from French *éditer*, from Latin *edere*, to bring forth]

edited *adj.* prepared for publication or broadcasting by editing.

Edith a female first name, now relatively rare. [from Anglo-Saxon *ead*, prosperity, fortune + *gyd*, battle]

edition *noun* **1** a number of copies of a book, etc printed at one time, or at different times without alteration. **2** the form in which a book, etc is published: *paperback edition.*

editor *noun* **1** a person who edits books, etc. **2** a person who is in charge of a newspaper, magazine or programme, or one section of it. **3** a person who puts together the various sections of a cinema film, etc.

editorial — *adj.* of or relating to editors or editing. — *noun* an article written by or on behalf of the editor of a newspaper or magazine, usually one offering an opinion on a current topic.

editorialize *or* **editorialise** *verb intrans.* **1** to write an editorial. **2** *derog.* in journalism, to introduce personal opinion into what is meant to be factual reporting.

editorially *adv.* as regards editors or editing.

editorship *noun* the status or position of an editor.

Edmonton POP (1991) 617 000, the capital of Alberta province, W Canada, situated on the banks of the North Saskatchewan R. It is the most northerly large town in N America. HISTORY Fort Edmonton was built in 1795 by Hudson's Bay Company, 40km/25mi below the present site; destroyed by Native Americans in 1807, and in 1819 it was rebuilt on a new site; reached by railway from 1891; chosen to be capital in 1905; grew rapidly after the discovery of oil nearby in 1947. NOTABLE FEATURES Legislative Building; George McDougall Memorial Shrine and Museum (1871).

Edmund I (921–46) King of the English (from 939), the half-brother of Athelstan. On Edmund's accession, Scandinavian forces from Northumbria, reinforced by levies from Ireland, quickly overran the E Midlands. He re-established his control over the S Danelaw (942) and Northumbria (944), and then ruled a reunited England.

Edmund II *or* **Edmund Ironside** (c.980–1016) King of the English, the son of Ethelred the Unready. He was chosen king by the Londoners on his father's death (Apr 1016), while Canute was elected at Southampton by the Witan (Council). Edmund hastily levied an army, defeated Canute, and attempted to raise the siege of London, but was routed at Ashingdon (or possibly Ashdon), Essex (Oct 1016). He agreed to a partition of the country, but died a few weeks later, leaving Canute as sole ruler.

Edmund, St, originally **Edmund Rich** (1170–1240) English prelate and Archbishop of Canterbury, born in Abingdon, Oxfordshire. He became famous as a preacher, and was commissioned by Pope Gregory IX to preach the sixth crusade throughout England (c.1227). As archbishop (from 1234), he was the spokesman of the national party against Henry III, defending Church rights. He gave his name to St Edmund Hall, Oxford, and his feast day is 16 Nov.

Edmund 1 a male first name, borne by several early kings and saints. **2** the illegitimate son of the Earl of Gloucester in Shakespeare's *King Lear*, who ruthlessly manipulates others in an attempt to further his own ambitions. [from Anglo-Saxon *ead*, prosperity, fortune + *mund*, protection]

Edna a female first name, now rare. [probably an Anglicization of Irish *Eithne*; possibly from Hebrew *ednah*, rejuvenation, pleasure]

Edomites, Greek **Idumeans** in the Bible (Genesis 36), the descendants of Esau who settled in the mountainous area south of the Dead Sea to the Gulf of Aqabah. As Israel's enemies they were conquered by David, but they retook parts of Judah and became a kingdom in the 8c BC. They participated in the overthrow (587/6 BC) of Jerusalem by the Babylonians, but were eventually conquered by John Hyrcanus in the late 2c BC, which forced their integration with the Jewish people. Herod I (the Great) was of Edomite descent.

EDP *abbrev.* electronic data processing.

EDTA *abbrev. Chem.* ethylene diamine tetra-acetic acid.

educable *or* **educatable** *adj.* capable of being educated.

educate *verb* **1** to train and teach. **2** to provide school instruction for. **3** to train and improve (one's taste, etc). [from Latin *educare*, to bring up]

educated *adj.* **1** having received an education, especially to a level higher than average. **2** produced by or suggesting a (good) education. **3** based on experience or knowledge: *an educated guess.*

education *noun* **1** the process of teaching and training, usually from infancy. **2** the instruction received. **3** the process of training and improving (one's taste, etc).

educational *adj.* relating to education; having the function of educating: *educational television programmes.*

educational drama the use of drama and its techniques in schools and other educational institutions as a medium for creative expression, intended to develop self-awareness and self-confidence in pupils and students of all ages. Drama has been found to have an important role in the education of the mentally and physically handicapped, and is part of the curriculum in many schools.

educationalist *or* **educationist** *noun* an expert in methods of education.

educational linguistics, the application of linguistic theories and techniques to the teaching and learning of a first language in schools and other educational institutions. See also APPLIED LINGUISTICS.

educationally *adv.* as regards education or educating.

educational psychology *Psychol.* the branch of psychology concerned with the application of the findings of psychology to the understanding of the learning process.

educative *adj.* educating.

educator *noun* a person who educates; an educating experience or circumstance.

educe *verb formal* to bring out or develop. [from Latin *e*, out + *ducere*, to lead]

educible *adj.* capable of being educed or developed.

eduction *noun* the process of educing or developing.

edutainment *noun* the presentation of educational material as entertainment.

Edward I (1239–1307) King of England (1272–1307), the elder son of Henry III and Eleanor of Provence, born at Westminster. He married Eleanor of Castile (1254) and later Margaret of France, the sister of Philip IV (1299). In the Barons' War (1264–7), he at first supported Simon de Montfort, but rejoined his father, and defeated de Montfort at Evesham (1265). He then won renown as a crusader to the Holy Land, and after his return (1274), successfully campaigned (1276–7, 1282–3) to annex N and W Wales, where he built several castles to mark his conquests. He reasserted English claims to the overlordship of Scotland when the line of succession failed, and chose John Balliol as king (1292), but Edward's insistence on full rights of suzerainty provoked the Scottish magnates to force Balliol to refuse to recognize Edward and ally with France (1295). Thus began the Scottish Wars of Independence, and despite prolonged campaigning and victories such as Falkirk (1298), Edward could not subdue Scotland as he had done Wales.

Edward II (1284–1327) King of England (1307–27), the fourth son of Edward I and Eleanor of Castile, born in Caernarfon, Wales. In 1301 he was created Prince of Wales, the first English heir apparent to bear the title, and in 1308 married Isabella of France, the daughter of Philip IV. Throughout his reign, Edward mismanaged the barons, who sought to rid the country of royal favourites (such as Piers Gaveston, who was eventually captured and executed, 1312) and regain their place in government. Edward invaded Scotland in 1314 but was defeated by Robert Bruce at the battle of Bannockburn (1314). Risings followed in Wales and Ireland. Edward's wife, Queen Isabella, hated his new favourites, Hugh le Despenser and his son, and with her lover Roger Mortimer toppled them (1326) and imprisoned Edward in Kenilworth Castle. He renounced the throne in favour of his eldest son Edward (1327) and was murdered in Berkeley Castle.

Edward II a play by Christopher Marlowe (c.1592). It is a tragedy in blank verse set at the time of Edward II's accession to the throne, concerning the King's love for his favourite Piers Gaveston, which sparks off a revolt by the barons, and also the estrangement and rebellion of his Queen, Isabella.

Edward III (1312–77) King of England (1327–77), the elder son of Edward II and Isabella of France, born in Windsor, Berkshire. He married Philippa of Hainault in 1328, and their eldest child Edward, later called the Black Prince, was born in 1330. By banishing his mother from court and executing her lover Roger Mortimer, he assumed full control of the government (1330), and began to restore the monarchy's authority and prestige. He supported Edward Balliol's attempts to wrest the Scots throne from David II, who was forced by defeat at Halidon Hill (1333) to flee to France until 1341. In 1337, after Philip VI had declared Guyenne forfeit, Edward revived his hereditary claim to the French Crown through his mother Isabella (the daughter of Philip IV), thus beginning the Hundred Years War. He destroyed the French navy at the battle of Sluys (1340), and won another major victory at Crécy (1346).

Edward IV (1442–83) King of England (1461–70, 1471–83), the eldest son of Richard, Duke of York, born in Rouen, France. His father Richard claimed the throne as the lineal descendant of Edward III's third and fifth sons (Lionel, Duke of Clarence, and Edmund, Duke of York), against the Lancastrian King Henry VI (the lineal descendant of Edward III's fourth son, John of Gaunt). Richard was killed at the battle of Wakefield (1460), but Edward entered London in 1461, was recognized as king when Henry VI was deposed, and with the support of his cousin Richard Neville, Earl of Warwick, defeated the Lancastrians at Towton. He threw off his dependence on Warwick, and secretly married Elizabeth Woodville (1464), but Warwick forced him into exile in Holland (Oct 1470), and Henry VI regained the throne. Edward returned to England (Mar 1471), regained kingship (11 Apr), then defeated and killed Warwick at the battle of Barnet (14 Apr), and destroyed the remaining Lancastrian forces at Tewkesbury (4 May). Henry VI was murdered in the Tower soon afterwards, and Edward remained secure for the rest of his reign.

Edward V (1470–83) King of England (Apr–Jun 1483), born at Westminster, the son of Edward IV and Elizabeth Woodville. Shortly after his accession, he and his younger brother Richard, Duke of York, were imprisoned in the Tower by their uncle Richard, Duke of Gloucester, who usurped the throne as Richard III. The two princes were never heard of again, and were presumably murdered (Aug 1483) on their uncle's orders.

Edward VI (1537–53) King of England, born in London, the son of Henry VIII by his third queen, Jane Seymour. During his reign (1547–53), power was first in the hands of his uncle the Duke of Somerset, and then of John Dudley, Duke of Northumberland. Edward became a devout Protestant, and under the Protectors the English Reformation flourished. He died of tuberculosis, having agreed to the succession of Lady Jane Grey (who was overthrown after nine days by Mary I).

Edward VII (1841–1910) King of the United Kingdom (1901–10), born in London, the eldest son of Queen Victoria. In 1863 he married Alexandra (1844–1925), the eldest daughter of Christian IX of Denmark. They had three sons and three daughters: Albert Victor (1864–92), Duke of Clarence; George (1865–1936); Louise (1867–1931), Princess Royal; Victoria (1868–1935); Maud (1869–1938), who married Haakon VII of Norway; and Alexander (born and died 1871). As Prince of Wales, his behaviour led him into several social scandals, and the Queen excluded him from affairs of state. As king, he carried out several visits to European capitals to improve international relations.

Edward VIII (1894–1972) King of the United Kingdom (Jan–Dec 1936), born in Richmond, Surrey, the eldest son of George V. He succeeded his father in 1936, but abdicated (11 Dec) because of his proposed marriage to Mrs Ernest Simpson, a commoner well known in London society, who had been twice divorced. He was then given the title of Duke of Windsor, and the marriage took place in France in 1937. They lived in Paris, apart from a period in the Bahamas (1940–5), where Edward was Governor.

Edward (Antony Richard Louis), Prince, also called **Edward Windsor** (1964–) British prince, third son of Elizabeth II and Prince Philip, Duke of Edinburgh. He joined the Royal Marines in 1986 but left the following year and began a career in the theatre as a production assistant. In late 1993 he became joint Managing Director of a new independent television company, Ardent Productions. Among other positions, he is Chairman of the Duke of Edinburgh's Award Special Projects Group and President of the National Youth Music Theatre.

Edward a male first name, used since before the Norman Conquest. [from Anglo-Saxon *ead*, prosperity, fortune + *weard*, guard]

Edward the Black Prince (1330–76) eldest son of Edward III, born in Woodstock, Oxfordshire. He fought at Crécy at the age of 16; his popular title (first cited in a 16c work) is said to refer to his black armour. He won several victories in the Hundred Years War, including Poitiers (1356). In 1362 he was created Prince of Aquitaine, and lived there until 1371, until a revolt forced him to return to England. He had two sons: Edward (1365–70) and the future Richard II. Though considered a great soldier, he was unsuccessful as an administrator.

Edward the Confessor (c.1003–66) King of England (1042–66), the elder son of Ethelred the Unready and Emma of Normandy, and the last king of the Old English royal line. He succeeded his half-brother Hardicanute to the throne, and until 1052 maintained his position against the ambitious Godwin family by building up Norman favourites. Though in 1051 the childless Edward very probably recognized Duke William of Normandy (later William I) as his heir, the Godwins regained their ascendancy, and nominated Harold Godwin (Harold II) to succeed. The Norman Conquest followed soon after. Edward's reputation for holiness began in his lifetime, and he rebuilt Westminster Abbey in the Romanesque style. He was canonized in 1161 (feast day 13 Oct).

Edward the Elder (c.870–924) King of Wessex (899–924), the elder son of Alfred the Great. He became the strongest ruler in Britain, for in a great military campaign he conquered and annexed to Wessex the S Danelaw (910–18), and assumed control of Mercia (918). In 920, his overlordship was formally recognized by all the chief rulers beyond the Humber, including the King of Scots.

Edward the Martyr, also called **St Edward** (c.962–78) King of England (975–8), son of Edgar. During his reign there was a reaction against the policies in support of monasticism that had been espoused by his father. He was murdered at Corfe, Dorset, by supporters of his stepmother, Elfrida, and canonized in 1001 (feast day 12 Oct).

Edward, Lake, in Zaire **Lake Rutanzige** a lake in E central Africa, in the W Rift Valley, on the frontier between Zaire and Uganda. AREA 4 000sq km/1 500sq mi; length c.80km/50mi; width 50km/30mi. It receives the Rutshuru R and the Semliki R flows from its N end into L Albert. Henry Stanley discovered the lake in 1889. [named after the Prince of Wales in 1889, later Edward VII.]

Edwardian *adj.* of, or characteristic of, Britain in the years 1901–10, the reign of King *Edward* VII.

Edwards, Gareth Owen (1947–) Welsh rugby player, born in Gwaun-cae-Gurwen near Swansea. He played as half-back, full-back, and centre (excelling particularly as scrum half), and was first capped for Wales as a teenager. He was appointed captain before he was 21, and he won 63 caps, including 10 'B' internationals.

Edwards, Jonathan (1703–58) US theologian and metaphysician, born in East Windsor, Connecticut. Ordained in 1727, he ministered with success at the Congregational Church in Northampton, Massachusetts, until his hardline Calvinism led to controversy and his dismissal (1750). He then worked as a missionary with the Housatonnucks until 1758, when he became President of Princeton College. His works (eg *Freedom of the Will*, 1754) contributed to the religious revival known as the Great Awakening.

Edwin, St (584–633) King of Northumbria (616–33), brought up in N Wales. Under him, Northumbria became united, and he pushed his power west as far as the islands of Anglesey and Man, obtained the overlordship of East Anglia, and (by a victory over the West Saxons) that of all England, apart from Kent. He was converted to Christianity, and baptized with his nobles in 627. He fell in battle against Mercians and Welsh at Hatfield Chase, and was afterwards canonized (feast day 12 Oct).

Edwin a male first name. [from Anglo-Saxon *ead*, prosperity, fortune + *wine*, friend]

-ee *suffix* forming nouns denoting: **1** the person who is the object of the action of a verb: *payee / employee*. **2** a person in a stated condition: *absentee / escapee / refugee*. **3** a person with a stated association or connection: *bargee*. [from French *-é* or *-ée*]

EEC *abbrev.* European Economic Community, the former name of the European Community.

EEG *abbrev.* electroencephalogram or electroencephalograph.

eel *noun* any of several species of fish with a long slender snakelike body, small fins, and a smooth slimy skin, often without scales. Most species, eg the Moray eel and conger, are marine, but freshwater eels are common in rivers and lakes of Europe and N America. Eels are a popular food item in some parts of the world. [from Anglo-Saxon *æl*]

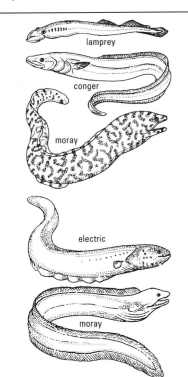

types of eel

eel grass a grass-like marine plant of the genus *Zostera*, found in shallow waters around all but tropical coasts. It is adapted to withstand saltwater, and grows completely submerged. Eel grass is a major source of food for migrating brent geese.

e'en *old use, poetic* — *adv.* even. — *noun* evening.

e'er *adv. old use, poetic* ever.

-eer *suffix* **1** forming nouns denoting a person concerned with or engaged in a stated activity: *auctioneer / mountaineer*. **2** forming verbs denoting actions or behaviour associated with a stated activity: *electioneer*. [from French *-ier*]

eerie *adj.* (**eerier**, **eeriest**) strange and disturbing or frightening. [perhaps from Anglo-Saxon *earg*, cowardly]

eerily *adv.* with a strange and disturbing manner.

eeriness *noun* being eery or strange.

Eeyore the melancholy donkey in A A Milne's *Winnie-the-Pooh* and other works.

Éfaté, French **Vaté**, English **Sandwich Island** a volcanic island of Vanuatu, lying in the SW Pacific Ocean. AREA 985sq km/380sq mi. Length 42km/26mi; width 23km/14mi. Port-Vila, the capital of Vanuatu, is situated on the island.

efface *verb* **1** to rub or wipe out. **2** to block out (a memory, etc). **3** to avoid drawing attention to (oneself). See also SELF-EFFACING. **4** to surpass or outshine. [from French *effacer*]

effacement *noun* the process of effacing or wiping out.

effect — *noun* **1** a result. **2** an impression given or produced. **3** operation; working state: *come, bring, put into effect*. **4** (*usually* **effects**) *formal* property. **5** (*usually* **effects**) devices, especially lighting and sound, used to create a particular impression in a film, on a stage, etc: *special effects*. — *verb formal* to do, cause to happen, or bring about.
— **for effect** in order to make an impression on others.
give effect to something *formal* to do it or bring it into operation.
in effect in reality; practically speaking.
take effect to begin to work; to come into force.
to the effect that *formal* with the meaning or result that.
to good, **some**, **no**, *etc* **effect** with much, some, no, etc success.
to that effect *formal* with that meaning or intended result.
with effect from ... *formal* coming into operation or becoming valid at the time stated.
with immediate effect *formal* as from now. [from Old French, from Latin *effectus*]
◆ Often confused with *affect*.

effective *adj.* **1** having the power to produce, or producing, a desired result. **2** producing a pleasing effect. **3** in, or coming into, operation; working; active. **4** actual, rather than theoretical.

effectively *adv.* **1** in an effective way. **2** in reality; for all practical purposes.

effectiveness *noun* being effective; having the intended result.

effector *noun Biol.* in an animal, any structure, usually a muscle or gland, that causes the animal, or part of it, to respond to a particular stimulus, such as a nerve impulse.

effectual *adj.* **1** producing the intended result. **2** *said of a document, etc* valid. [from Latin *effectualis*]

effectually *adv.* with the intended result.

effectuate *verb formal* to do; to carry out with success. [from Latin *effectuare*]

effectuation *noun* the process of causing something to happen.

effeminacy *noun* an effeminate state or manner.

effeminate *adj. sometimes derog., said of a man* having features of behaviour or appearance more typical of a woman. [from Latin *effeminare*, to make like a woman]

effeminately *adv.* with an effeminate manner.

efferent *adj. Medicine, said of a nerve* carrying impulses out from the brain. See also AFFERENT. [from Latin *efferre*, from *e*, from + *ferre*, to carry]

effervesce *verb intrans.* **1** to give off bubbles of gas. **2** to behave in a lively, energetic way. [from Latin *effervescere*, to boil up]

effervescence *noun* being effervescent; giving off bubbles of gas.

effervescent *adj.* effervescing; giving off bubbles of gas.

effete *adj. derog.* **1** *said of an institution, organization, etc* lacking its original power or authority.

2 *said of a person* lacking strength or energy; made weak by too much protection or refinement. [from Latin *effetus*, weakened by having given birth]

effeteness *noun* being effete or weak.

efficacious *adj. formal* producing, or certain to produce, the intended result. [from Latin *efficax*]

efficaciously *adv.* with the intended result; successfully.

efficacy *noun* effectiveness; having the intended result.

efficiency *noun Physics* **1** the state or quality of being efficient. **2** a measure of the effectiveness of the performance of a machine, engine, etc. It is equal to the ratio of the useful energy output to the energy input, and is usually expressed as a percentage.

efficient *adj.* **1** producing satisfactory results with an economy of effort and a minimum of waste. **2** *said of a person* capable of competent work within a relatively short time. [from Latin *efficere*, to accomplish]

efficiently *adv.* in an efficient way; with economical use of resources.

effigy *noun* (PL. **effigies**) **1** a crude doll or model representing a person, on which hatred of or contempt for the person can be expressed, eg by burning. **2** *formal* a portrait or sculpture of a person used as an architectural ornament. [from Latin *effigies*]

effloresce *verb intrans.* **1** *Chem., said of a crystalline salt* to undergo the process of efflorescence. **2** *Bot., said of a plant* to produce flowers. [from Latin *efflorescere*, to blossom]

efflorescence *noun* **1** *Chem.* the process whereby certain crystalline salts, known as hydrates, lose water of crystallization and become powdery on exposure to air. **2** *Bot.* the production of flowers by a plant.

efflorescent *adj.* efflorescing; producing flowers.

effluent — *noun* **1** an outflow of sewage, agricultural fertilizers, industrial waste, etc, into a river, lake, or sea. **2** *Geog.* a stream or river flowing from a larger body of water. — *adj. formal, technical* flowing out. [from Latin *effluere*, to flow out]

effluvium *noun* (PL. **effluvia**) *formal* an unpleasant smell or vapour given off by something, eg decaying matter. [from Latin *effluere*, flow out]

efflux *noun* the act of flowing out; something that flows out. [from Latin *effluere*, to flow out]

effort *noun* **1** hard mental or physical work, or something that requires it. **2** an act of trying hard. **3** the result of an attempt; an achievement. [from Old French *esfort*, from Latin *fortis*, strong]

effortless *adj.* done without effort or apparent effort.

effortlessly *adv.* without any effort or apparent effort.

effrontery *noun* (PL. **effronteries**) shameless rudeness; impudence. [from French *effronterie*, from Latin *effrons*, shameless]

effulgence *noun* an effulgent or bright quality; brilliance.

effulgent *adj. literary* shining brightly; brilliant. [from Latin *effulgere*, to shine out]

effulgently *adv.* with brilliance; brightly.

effusion *noun* **1** a pouring or flowing out. **2** *derog.* an uncontrolled flow of speech or writing. [from Latin *effusio*, pouring out]

effusive *adj. derog.* expressing feelings, especially happiness or enthusiasm, in an excessive or very showy way. [from *effuse*, to pour out]

effusively *adv.* with an effusive or enthusiastic manner.

effusiveness *noun* being effusive; enthusiasm.

EFL *abbrev.* English as a Foreign Language.

EFTA *or* **Efta** *abbrev.* European Free Trade Association.

EFTPOS *abbrev.* electronic funds transfer at point of sale.

EFTS *abbrev.* electronic funds transfer system.

eg *or* **e.g.** *abbrev. exempli gratia* (Latin), for example.

egalitarian — *adj.* relating to, promoting, or believing in the principle that all human beings are equal and should enjoy the same rights. — *noun* a person who upholds this principle. [from French *égalitaire*, from *égal*, equal]

egalitarianism *noun* egalitarian principles or beliefs.

Egas Moniz, António Caetano de Abreu Freire (1874–1955) Portuguese neurosurgeon and diplomat, born in Avanca. Professor at Coimbra and Lisbon, he developed prefrontal lobotomy for the control of schizophrenia and other mental disorders. He shared the 1949 Nobel Prize for Physiology or Medicine with Walter Hess, and also had a successful political career in the Portuguese parliament.

Egbert (d.839) King of Wessex (from 802). After his victory in 825 over the Mercians at Ellendun (now Wroughton) in Wiltshire, Essex, Kent, Surrey, and Sussex submitted to him. His conquest of Mercia itself (829) did not last long, but he extended his control over Cornwall and defeated the allied Vikings and Britons at Hingston Down (838). These successes made him master of S England from Kent to Land's End, and established Wessex as the strongest Anglo-Saxon kingdom.

egg¹ *noun* **1** *Biol.* in animals and plants, the unfertilized ovum or female gamete (reproductive cell) that is produced by the ovary. If fertilized by a sperm cell during the process of sexual reproduction, it forms a zygote, which then develops into an embryo. — Also called *ovum*. **2** *Zool.* in oviparous animals, eg birds, reptiles, amphibians, fish, and insects, a structure containing the ovum that is expelled from the body of the female either before or after fertilization. **3** the hard shell of an egg. **4** a hen's egg, used as food. **5** anything with the shape of a hen's egg. — **have** *or* **put all one's eggs in one basket** to depend entirely on a single plan, etc.

have *or* **get egg on one's face** *colloq.* to be made to look foolish.

teach one's grandmother to suck eggs *colloq.* to try to show someone more experienced than oneself how to do something. [from Norse *egg*]

◇ In viviparous animals, eg most mammals, eggs develop within the body. In oviparous animals, which lay eggs outside the body, each egg is surrounded by membranes and often a hard shell that protects it from damage and prevents water loss. Such eggs also contain nutrients that nourish the developing embryo.
Birds' eggs contain a large amount of yolk which is rich in fat, especially cholesterol, and albumen (the white of the egg), which provides the embryo with protein and water. The yolk is held in position by a twisted band of protein (the chalaza) which also serves as a shock absorber. The unfertilized eggs of domestic poultry, especially chickens, are widely used as food, although the high cholesterol content of the yolk has led some people to restrict their egg intake for health reasons.

egg² *verb* — **egg someone on** *colloq.* to urge or encourage them. [from Norse *eggja*, edge]

egg-cup *noun* a small cup-shaped container for holding a boiled egg while it is being eaten.

egg custard see CUSTARD.

egg-flip see EGG-NOG.

egghead *noun colloq., sometimes derog.* a very clever person; an intellectual.

egg-nog *or* **egg-flip** *noun* a drink made from raw eggs, milk, sugar, and an alcoholic spirit, especially rum or brandy.

eggplant *noun North Amer., esp. US* an aubergine.

eggshell — *noun* the hard, thin covering of an egg. — *adj.* **1** *said of paint or varnish* having a slightly glossy finish. **2** *said of articles of china* very thin and fragile.

egg-timer *noun* a device consisting of a sealed glass tube narrowed in the middle, containing sand or salt which, by trickling slowly from the top to the bottom of the tube through the narrow part, indicates the approximate time required to boil an egg.

egg tooth *Zool.* a hard point on the beak of an unhatched bird or reptile, which is used to break the shell of the egg.

eglantine *noun* a fragrant species of wild rose, the sweet-brier. [from French *églantine*]

Egmont *or* **Egmond Lamoral, Graaf van (Count of) Gavre** (1522–68) Flemish statesman and soldier, born in La Hamaide, Hainault. He accompanied Emperor Charles V on many campaigns, notably against the French at St Quentin (1557) and Gravelines (1558), for which he was made Governor of Flanders and Artois. He opposed Philip II of Spain's policy of encroaching on local liberties, and thereby became a hero of the people, but when he later broke with the Prince of Orange, he was executed as a traitor.

Egmont, Mount, Maori **Taranaki** a symmetrical volcanic peak, W North Island, New Zealand, situated S of New Plymouth. HEIGHT 2 518m. Mount Egmont National Park was established in 1900.

ego *noun* (PL. **egos**) **1** personal pride. **2** self-centredness or conceit. **3** *Psychol.* in psychoanalysis, the part of the mind that maintains conscious contact with the outside world, and is concerned with perception, memory, and reasoning. According to Freudian theory it reconciles the primitive desires and instincts of the *id* with the moral goals and social conscience of the *superego*. See also ID, SUPEREGO. [from Latin *ego*, I]

egocentric *adj. derog.* interested in oneself only.

egocentrically *adv.* with interest in oneself only.

egocentricity *noun* interest in oneself only.

egoism *noun* **1** *Philos.* the principle that self-interest is the basis of morality. **2** selfishness. **3** egotism.

egoist *noun* a person who believes in self-interest as a moral principle.

Egoist, The a novel by George Meredith (1879). It is a study of refined selfishness as seen in the central character Sir Willoughby Patterne.

egoistic *or* **egoistical** *adj.* relating to or characterized by self-interest.

egoistically *adv.* with self-interest.

egomania *noun Psychol.* extreme self-interest which prevents one from allowing other people to come between oneself and the achievement of one's desires.

egomaniac *noun* a person who is governed by extreme self-interest.

egotism *noun derog.* **1** the habit of speaking too much about oneself. **2** the fact of having a very high opinion of oneself.

egotist *noun* a self-centred person.

egotistic *or* **egotistical** *adj.* speaking too much about oneself.

egotistically *adv.* with too much reference to or interest in oneself.

ego trip *colloq.* an action or enterprise undertaken to enhance one's own reputation or standing.

egregious *adj. formal* outrageous; shockingly bad. [from Latin *egregius*, standing out from the herd, from *e*, out of + *grex*, herd]

egregiously *adv.* in a shockingly bad way.

egregiousness *noun* being egregious or shockingly bad.

egress *noun formal Legal* **1** the act of leaving, or the right to leave, a building or other enclosed place. **2** an exit. [from Latin *egredi*, to go out]

egret *noun* any of various white, long-legged wading birds similar to herons. [from French *aigrette*]

egret

Egypt, official name **Arab Republic of Egypt**, Arabic **Jumhuriyat Misr Al-Arabiya** POP (1992e) 55.2m, a republic in NE Africa, divided into 25 governorates. AREA 1 001 449sq km/ 386 559sq mi. It is bounded W by Libya, S by Sudan, E by the Red Sea, NE by Israel, and N by the Mediterranean Sea. CAPITAL Cairo. CHIEF

osprey

great bustard

emu

American coot

common crow

guira cuckoo

kiwi

robin

golden plover

different types of birds' eggs

TOWNS Alexandria, Port Said, Aswan, Suez, El Gîza. TIME ZONE GMT +2. The population is chiefly of E Hamitic origin (90%) and the main religion is Sunni Muslim, with a minority largely Coptic Christian. OFFICIAL LANGUAGE Arabic. CURRENCY the Egyptian pound. PHYSICAL DESCRIPTION the R Nile flows N from Sudan, dammed S of Aswan, creating L Nasser; a huge delta lies N of Cairo, 250km/160mi across and 160km/100mi N–S; the narrow Eastern Desert, sparsely inhabited, lies between the Nile and the Red Sea; the broad Western Desert covers over two thirds of the country and contains seven major depressions, the largest and lowest of which is the Qattara Depression (133m below sea level); the Sinai Peninsula in the S is a desert region with mountains rising to 2 637m at Gebel Katherîna, Egypt's highest point; 90% of the population lives on the Nile floodplain (c.3% of the country's area). CLIMATE mainly desert, except for an 80km-/50mi-wide Mediterranean coastal fringe, where annual rainfall is 100–200mm; very hot on the coast when the dust-laden *khamsin* wind blows N from the Sahara (Mar–Jun); Alexandria, representative of the coastal region, has an annual average rainfall of 180mm; elsewhere, rainfall is less than 50mm. HISTORY Neolithic cultures on the R Nile from c.6000 BC; Pharaoh dynasties from c.3100 BC; pyramids at El Gîza were constructed during the Fourth Dynasty; Egyptian power was greatest during the New Empire period from 1567 BC until 1085 BC; became a Persian province in the 6c BC; conquered by Alexander the Great in the 4c BC; Ptolemaic Pharaohs ruled Egypt until 30 BC; conquered by the Arabs in 672; occupied by France under Napoleon from 1798 until 1801; the Suez Canal was constructed in 1869; a revolt in 1879 was put down by the British in 1882; became a British protectorate in 1914; declared independent in 1922; used as a base for Allied forces during World War II; King Farouk was deposed by Nasser in 1952; Egypt was declared a republic in 1953; an attack on Israel, followed by Israeli invasion in 1967, resulted in the loss of the Sinai Peninsula and control over part of the Suez Canal (regained following negotiations in the 1970s); in 1981, Sadat was assassinated; relations with Arab nations were strained as a result of the agreement with Israel but improved throughout the 1980s; Cairo was hit by a severe earthquake in 1992; the government announced that it had uncovered an Islamic fundamentalist plot to found an Islamic State; violent attacks and clashes between Muslim and Coptic Christians in the early 1990s. GOVERNMENT governed by a People's Assembly of 454 members (including 10 presidential appointments) which elects a President every six years; the President appoints a Prime Minister and a Council; there is also a 210-member Consultative Council. ECONOMY agriculture on the floodplain of the R Nile accounts for about one third of the national income; the building of the Aswan High Dam extended irrigated cultivation; cotton, rice, fruit, vegetables; food processing, textiles, construction, light manufacturing, military equipment; oil, iron ore, aluminium, cement, gypsum, phosphates, manganese, tin, nitrates; a major tourist

Egypt

Dynasties of Ancient Egypt

Date BC	Dynasty	Period
c.3100–2890	I	Early Dynastic Period
c.2890–2686	II	First use of stone in building
c.2686–2613	III	Old Kingdom
c.2613–2494	IV	The age of the great
c.2494–2345	V	pyramid builders
c.2345–2181	VI	Longest reign in history: Pepi II, 90 years
c.2181–2173	VII	First Intermediate Period
c.2173–2160	VIII	Social order upset; few
c.2160–2130	IX	monuments built
c.2130–2040	X	
c.2133–1991	XI	
1991–1786	XII	Middle Kingdom
1786–1633	XIII	Golden age of art and craftsmanship
1786–c.1603	XIV	Second Intermediate Period
1674–1567	XV	Country divided into principalities
c.1684–1567	XVI	
c.1660–1567	XVII	
1567–1320	XVIII	New Kingdom
1320–1200	XIX	Began with colonial
1200–1085	XX	expansion, ended in divided rule
1085–945	XXI	Third Intermediate Period
945–730	XXII	Revival of prosperity
817?–730	XXIII	and restoration of cults
720–715	XXIV	
751–668	XXV	
664–525	XXVI	Late Period
525–404	XXVII	Completion of Nile –
404–399	XXVIII	Red Sea canal
399–380	XXIX	
380–343	XXX	
343–332	XXXI	Alexander the Great reached the site where he founded Alexandria in 332 BC

area (but tourism has been severely affected by terrorist activity in the 1990s).

Egyptian — *noun* 1 a native or citizen of Egypt. 2 the language of ancient Egypt. — *adj.* relating or belonging to Egypt.
◇ The Semitic language of the ancient Egyptians survives only in inscriptions and papyrus manuscripts. In the 2c AD it evolved into Coptic, which is still used by Monophysite Christians in Egypt as a language of devotion. The vernacular language of modern Egypt is a dialect of colloquial Arabic.

Egyptologist *noun* an expert in or student of Egyptology.

Egyptology *noun* the study of the language, culture, and history of ancient Egypt.
◇ The first published accounts of journeys and discoveries in ancient Egypt were produced in Europe in the 16c. The discovery of the Rosetta Stone in 1799 provided the key to the decipherment of Egyptian hieroglyphics (1822), and the first books on Egyptian architecture were published in the early 19c. Systematic excavation by European and Egyptian archaeologists followed throughout the 19c and early 20c, and continues to the present day, with an increasing emphasis on the study of the everyday lives of artisans and agrarian communities.

Ehrlich, Paul (1854–1915) German bacteriologist, born in Strehlen, Silesia (now Strzelin, Poland). After studying in Leipzig, he carried out research in Berlin and shared the 1908 Nobel Prize for Physiology or Medicine with Elie Metchnikoff for work on immunity and serum therapy. A pioneer of chemotherapy, he is most famous for his discovery in 1910 of a cure (salvarsan) for syphilis.

Eichmann, (Karl) Adolf (1906–62) Austrian Nazi war criminal, born in Solingen, Germany. A member of the SS from 1932, he organized anti-Semitic activities but was captured by US forces in 1945. He escaped from prison, having kept his identity hidden, and in 1950 reached Argentina, but was traced by Israeli agents, taken to Israel (1960), condemned, and executed.

eider *or* **eider duck** a large sea duck from northern countries. [from Icelandic *æthr*]

eiderdown *noun* 1 the down or soft feathers of the eider. 2 a quilt filled with this or some similar material.

Eiffel, (Alexandre) Gustave (1832–1923) French engineer, born in Dijon. He designed several notable bridges and viaducts, before working on his most famous project, the Eiffel Tower. He also designed the framework of the Statue of Liberty, New York, and built the first aerodynamic laboratory, near Paris. In 1893 he was imprisoned for two years for breach of trust in connection with the Panama Canal.

Eiffel Tower a tower in Paris, designed by Gustave Eiffel and erected (1887–9) in the Champs-de-Mars for the Paris Exhibition of 1889. It was the tallest building in the world (300m) until 1930, when it was exceeded by the Chrysler Building and then, in 1931, by the Empire State Building.

Eiger a mountain peak with three ridges in the Bernese Alps, S central Switzerland. HEIGHT 3 970m. Its N face is one of the most formidable climbs in the Alps.

Eigg an island in Highland region, W Scotland. It lies S of Skye, 11km/7mi from the mainland. AREA 67sq km/26sq mi. It rises to 397m at Sgurr of Eigg. The whole island is a nature reserve managed by the Scottish Wildlife Trust. Eigg is historically associated with the Clan Macdonald. ECONOMY cattle; crofting; fishing. [from Gaelic *eag*, notched]

eight — *noun* 1 the number or figure 8; any symbol for this number. 2 the age of 8. 3 something, eg a garment or a person, whose size is denoted by the number 8. 4 8 o'clock. 5 a set of 8 people or things, eg the crew of an eight-oared boat. 6 a playing-card with 8 pips. 7 a score of 8 points. — *adj.* 1 8 in number. 2 aged 8.
— **be** *or* **have had one over the eight** *colloq.* to be slightly drunk.
[from Anglo-Saxon *æhta*]

eighteen — *noun* 1 the number or figure 18; any symbol for this number. 2 the age of 18. 3 something, especially a garment, or a person, whose size is denoted by the number 18. 4 a set of 18 people or things. 5 a film classified as suitable for people aged 18 and over. — *adj.* 1 18 in number. 2 aged 18. [from Anglo-Saxon *æhtatene*]

eighteenth *noun, adj.* the position in a series corresponding to 18 in a sequence of numbers.

eightfold — *adj.* 1 equal to eight times as much or as many. 2 divided into, or consisting of, eight parts. — *adv.* by eight times as much.

Eightfold Path the fourth of Buddha's Four Noble Truths, prescribing the way to enlightenment. The Path involves right understanding, right aspiration, right speech, right conduct, right means of livelihood, right endeavour, right mindfulness, and right contemplation.

eighth *noun, adj.* **1** the position in a series corresponding to 8 in a sequence of numbers. **2** one of eight equal parts.

eighthly *adv.* as eighth in a series.

eighties *pl. noun* **1** the period of time between one's eightieth and ninetieth birthdays. **2** the range of temperatures between eighty and ninety degrees. **3** the period of time between the eightieth and ninetieth years of a century.

eightieth *noun, adj.* the position in a series corresponding to 80 in a sequence of numbers.

eightsome reel **1** a lively Scottish dance for eight people. **2** the music for this dance.

eighty — *noun* (PL. **eighties**) **1** the number or figure 80. **2** the age of 80. **3** a set of 80 people or things. — *adj.* **1** 80 in number. **2** aged 80. [from Anglo-Saxon *æhtatig*]

Eighty Years War see NETHERLANDS, REVOLT OF THE.

Eijkman, Christiaan (1858–1930) Dutch physician and pathologist, born in Nijkerk. He investigated the disease beri-beri in the Dutch East Indies (now Indonesia), and was the first to produce a dietary deficiency disease experimentally (in chickens) and to propose the concept of 'essential food factors', later called vitamins. He shared the 1929 Nobel Prize for Physiology or Medicine with Frederick Gowland Hopkins.

Eilat see ELAT.

Eileen a female first name. [from Gaelic *Eibhlin*, perhaps derived from EVELYN; -BH is also dropped in the Anglicized form *Aileen*]

Eindhoven POP (1992e) 194 000, a modern industrial city in SE North Brabant province, S Netherlands. It lies on the R Dommel, 88km/55mi SE of Rotterdam, and is an important shopping and cultural centre. HISTORY developed in the second half of the 19c around the textile and electric light industries; for a while it was the largest city in S Netherlands. NOTABLE FEATURES Philips Evoluon (museum of modern technology); Centre of Micro-Electronics.

Eine kleine Nachtmusik (A Little Night-Music) a serenade for string quartet and double bass by Wolfgang Amadeus Mozart (K525, 1787), the melodic charm of which embodies the finesse and clarity of his work.

Einstein, Albert (1879–1955) German–Swiss–US theoretical physicist, born in Ulm, Bavaria. He took Swiss nationality in 1901, was appointed examiner at the Swiss Patent Office (1902–5), and began to publish original papers on the theoretical aspects of problems in physics. His early work on the photoelectric effect (the way that electrons can be ejected from certain metals when illuminated by ultraviolet light) heralded the development of quantum theory and earned the award of the 1921 Nobel Prize for Physics. He went on to achieve world fame through his special (1905) and general (1916) theories of relativity. Professor at Zürich and Prague, and Director of the Kaiser Wilhelm Physical Institute in Berlin, he left Germany after Hitler's rise to power and from 1934 lectured at Princeton, USA, becoming a US citizen and professor at Princeton in 1940. After World War II he urged international control of atomic weapons; in 1952 he was invited to become the second President of Israel, but declined.

einsteinium *noun* (SYMBOL **Es**, ATOMIC NUMBER **99**) an artificially produced radioactive metallic element. [named after US physicist Albert Einstein]

Einthoven, Willem (1860–1927) Dutch physiologist, born in Semarang, Dutch East Indies (now Indonesia). Professor of Physiology at Leiden, he developed the string (or Einthoven) galvanometer for measuring the electrical rhythms of the heart, and introduced the term 'electrocardiogram'. He was awarded the 1924 Nobel Prize for Physiology or Medicine.

Éire see IRISH REPUBLIC.

EIS *abbrev.* Educational Institute of Scotland.

Eisenhower, Dwight D(avid), also called **Ike** (1890–1969) US soldier and politician, born of German immigrant parentage in Denison, Texas. During World War II he was chief military assistant to General MacArthur in the Philippines (by 1939), and in 1942 he commanded Allied forces for the amphibious descent on French N Africa. His smooth co-ordination of the Allied staff led to his selection as Supreme Commander for the 1944 cross-channel invasion of the continental mainland, and in 1950 he was made Supreme Commander of the Combined Land Forces in NATO. The popularity which he had gained in Europe swept him to victory as a Republican in the following presidential elections, and he became the 34th US President (1953–61). His presidency was marked by the US government's preoccupation with foreign policy, and by a campaign against communism.

Eisenstein, Sergei (Mikhailovich) (1898–1948) Russian film director, born in Rīga. Following theatrical scene painting, he began his influential career in cinema. His films often substitute the group or crowd for the traditional hero, and he uses skilful cutting to achieve mounting impressionistic effects, as in the Odessa steps sequence of *Battleship Potemkin* (1925). Later films included *Alexander Nevsky* (1938) and *Ivan the Terrible* (1944).

eisteddfod *noun* (PL. **eisteddfods, eisteddfodau**) an annual Welsh arts festival during which competitions are held to find the best poetry, drama, songs, etc. [from Welsh *eisteddfod*, session]

◇ Medieval eisteddfods were principally concerned with the testing of bards and minstrels in their art. The modern revival of the festival began in the late 18c, and the National Eisteddfod has been held annually (in August) since 1880, alternately in N and S Wales. Its central event is the award of a Chair for a poem in strict bardic verseform, and its general purpose is the promotion of Welsh literature and music.

either — *adj.* **1** any one of two. **2** each of two; both: *a garden with a fence on either side.* — *pron.* any one of two things, people, etc. — *adv.* **1** (*used in negative statements*) also; as well: *I thought him rather unpleasant, and I didn't like his wife either.* **2** (*used after a negative phrase*) what is more; besides: *he plays golf, and he's not bad, either.*
— **either... or...** introducing two choices or possibilities: *I need either a pen or a pencil / either you come or I don't go.*
either way *or* **in either case** in whichever of two cases.
[from Anglo-Saxon *ægther*]

ejaculate — *verb* (pronounced *-late*) *intrans., trans.* said of a man or male animal to discharge (semen). [from Latin *ejaculari*, to throw out]

ejaculation *noun* **1** a sudden exclamation or cry. **2** discharge of semen.

ejaculatory *adj.* relating to ejaculation or discharge of fluid.

eject *verb* **1** to throw out with force. **2** to force to leave. **3** *intrans.* to leave a moving aircraft using an ejector seat. [from Latin *ejicere*, to throw out]

ejection *noun* ejecting; the process of being ejected.

ejective *adj.* that ejects or throws out.

ejector *noun* a person or device that ejects something or someone.

ejector seat a type of seat fitted to a military aircraft, designed to eject the pilot from the cockpit in an emergency.

eke *verb* (**eke out**) **1** to make (a supply) last longer, eg by adding something else to it or by careful use. **2** to manage with difficulty to make (a living, etc). [from Anglo-Saxon *eacan*, to increase]

Ekman, Vagn Walfrid (1874–1954) Swedish oceanographer, born in Stockholm. Professor of Mathematical Physics at Lund (1910–39), he explained the variation in direction of ocean currents with depth, and showed that the general motion of near-surface water is the result of interaction between the surface wind force, the Coriolis force and the frictional effects between the various water layers.

Ekofisk an oilfield in the North Sea, linked by pipeline to Teesport, Cleveland, NE England.

elaborate — *adj.* (pronounced *-rət*) **1** complicated in design; complex. **2** carefully planned or worked out. — *verb* (pronounced *-rate*) **1** (**elaborate on** *or* **upon something**) to add detail to it. **2** to work out in great detail. **3** to make more ornate. [from Latin *elaborare*]

elaborately *adv.* in an elaborate way, or to an elaborate degree.

elaboration *noun* the process of elaborating or explaining in detail.

Elaine a female first name, first occurring in Malory's *Morte D'Arthur* (15c). [from Old French; originally a version of HELEN, now an independent name]

El Alamein *or* **Al-Alamain, Battle of** a battle fought (23 Oct–4 Nov 1943) in World War II, named after a village on Egypt's Mediterranean coast. It resulted in the defeat of Rommel's Afrika Corps by the British Eighth Army under Montgomery and proved to be a turning point in the war in Africa.

Elam the name given in antiquity to what is now SW Iran. Its main city was Susa, and at its height in the 13c BC it ruled an empire stretching from Babylonia to Persepolis.

élan *noun literary* impressive and energetic style. [from French *élan*]

eland *noun* (PL. **elands, eland**) a large African antelope with spiral horns. [from Dutch]

eland

elapse *verb intrans. formal, said of time* to pass. [from Latin *elabi*, to slide away]

elastic — *adj.* **1** *said of a material or substance* able to return to its original shape or size after being pulled or pressed out of shape. **2** *said of a force* caused by, or causing, such an ability. **3** able to be changed; flexible. **4** made of elastic. **5** *said of a person or feelings* able to recover quickly from a shock or upset. — *noun* stretchable cord or fabric woven with strips of rubber. [from Greek *elastikos*, from *elaunein*, to propel]

elastically *adv.* flexibly; so as to stretch easily.

elasticated *adj., said of a fabric* having been made elastic by being interwoven with rubber.

elastic band a thin loop of rubber for holding papers or other items together or in place. – Also called *rubber band*.

elasticity *noun Physics* the property of certain materials that allows them to return to their original shape and size after the removal of a deforming force or *stress*.

elasticize *or* **elasticise** *verb* to make elastic.

elastic limit *Physics* the maximum force that can be applied to an elastic material without it becoming permanently deformed.

elastomer *noun Physics* a material that returns to its original shape after it has been deformed by stretching or compression, eg synthetic rubber.

Elat *or* **Eilat** POP (1988e) 25 000, a seaport in Southern district, S Israel, on the N shore of the Gulf of Aqaba. The port is Israel's only outlet to the Red Sea. It was founded in 1949 on the site of the biblical town of Elath. NOTABLE FEATURE nature reserve with underwater observatory.

elate *verb* to make intensely happy; to fill with optimism. [from Latin *elatus*, elevated, exalted]

elated *adj.* highly pleased; overjoyed.

elatedly *adv.* with an elated or highly pleased manner.

elation *noun* an elated or highly pleased state.

Elba, Greek **Aithalia**, Latin **Ilva** an island in the Tyrrhenian Sea, between the N Italian coast and Corsica. AREA 223sq km/86sq mi; length 27km/17mi; width 19km/12mi. The island is separated from the Italian mainland by the 10km-/6mi-wide Strait of Piombino. CHIEF TOWN Portoferraio. ECONOMY iron working; fisheries; fruit; wine; tourism. Napoleon lived here in 1814–15 following his abdication.

Elbe, River, Czech **Labe**, ancient **Albis** a river in the Czech Republic and Germany, length 1 158km/720mi. Rising on the S slopes of the Riesengebirge, Czech Republic, it flows N and NW to enter the North Sea at Cuxhaven, Germany. It is connected by canals with the R Oder and the Baltic Sea, and is navigable beyond the Czech border.

Elbert, Mount the highest peak in the Rocky Mts, situated in Lake County, central Colorado, USA. HEIGHT 4 399m.

elbow — *noun* **1** the joint where the human arm bends. **2** the part of a coat, jacket, etc which covers this joint. **3** the corresponding joint in animals. **4** a sharp turn or bend, eg in a road or pipe. — *verb* **1** to push or strike with the elbow. **2** to make (one's way through) by pushing with the elbows.
— **at one's elbow** close to one.
give *or* **get the elbow** *slang* to dismiss or be dismissed.
out at elbow *or* **elbows 1** *said of a garment* no longer smart; worn out. **2** *said of a person* wearing worn-out clothes.
[from Anglo-Saxon *elnboga*]

elbow-grease *noun colloq.* hard work, especially hard polishing.

elbow-room *noun* **1** space enough for moving or doing something. **2** freedom; lack of constraint.

Elbrus, Mount the highest peak in Europe, in the Caucasus range, SW Russia. It is situated close to the Georgian border, 64km/40mi SW of Kislovodsk. HEIGHT 5 642m. It is formed by two extinct volcanic cones and its glaciers give rise to the Kuban, Malka, and Baksan rivers.

Elche, Latin **Illicis** POP (1991) 182 000, a town in Alicante province, Valencia region, E Spain. It stands on the R Vinalapó, 23km/14mi SW of Alicante. NOTABLE FEATURES Altimira Palace, a national monument (15c); Huerto del Cura Garden and a Palm Grove for which the town is noted – it is the largest in Europe.

elder[1] — *adj.* **1** older. **2** (**the elder**) used before or after a person's name to distinguish him or her from a younger person of the same name. — *noun* **1** a person who is older. **2** (*often* **elders**) an older person, especially when regarded as having authority. **3** in some Protestant Churches, a lay person who has some responsibility for administration. [from Anglo-Saxon *eldra*]

elder[2] *noun* a bush or small tree with white flowers and purple-black or red berries. [from Anglo-Saxon *ellærn*]

elderberry *noun* (PL. **elderberries**) the fruit of the elder.

elderliness *noun* being elderly or rather old.

elderly — *adj.* rather old. — *noun* (**the elderly**) old people.

elder statesman an old and very experienced member of a group, especially a politician, whose opinions are respected.

eldest — *adj.* oldest. — *noun* a person who is the oldest of three or more.

El Dorado an early colonial Spanish-American legend about a ruler coated in gold, believed to exist in New Granada (now Colombia). By extension, it also evoked a land of fabulous wealth, in search of which Raleigh organized two expeditions (1595, 1617). [from Spanish, = the gilded one]

Eleanor a female first name, introduced to Britain by Eleanor of Aquitaine. [from Old Provençal *Alienor*, probably formed from Germanic *ali*, other, foreign]

Eleanor of Aquitaine (c.1122–1204) queen-consort of Louis VII of France (1137–52) and, after the annulment of this marriage, of the future Henry II of England (1154–89). She was imprisoned (1174–89) for supporting the rebellion of her sons, two of whom became kings as Richard I (in 1189) and John (in 1199).

Eleanor of Castile (c.1245–1290) queen-consort of Edward I of England (1254–90), the daughter of Ferdinand III. She accompanied Edward to the Crusades, and is said to have saved his life by sucking the poison from a wound. She died at Harby, Nottinghamshire, and the 'Eleanor Crosses' at Northampton, Geddington, and Waltham Cross are survivors of the 12 erected by Edward at the halting places of her cortège. The last stopping place was Charing Cross, where a replica now stands.

Eleatics a group of Greek philosophers active in the 5c BC from Elea, Italy. Including Parmenides, Melissus, and Zeno, they argued that reality is imperishable, timeless, indivisible, motionless, and utterly changeless, and the world as it appears is a misrepresentation.

elec. *abbrev.* electric or electricity.

elect — *verb* **1** to choose by vote. **2** (**elect to do something**) to do it by choice. — *adj.* **1** (*following the noun*) elected to a position, but not yet formally occupying it. **2** specially chosen. **3** *Relig.* chosen by God for salvation. — *noun* (**the elect**) people chosen, for salvation or otherwise. [from Latin *eligere*, to choose]

electability *noun* capability of being elected.

electable *adj.* capable of being elected, especially to political office.

elected *adj.* chosen by election.

election *noun* the process or act of choosing people for (especially political) office by taking a vote. See also GENERAL ELECTION.

electioneer *verb intrans.* to take part in an (especially political) election campaign.

electioneering *noun* taking part in an election campaign.

elective *adj.* **1** *said of a position, office, etc* to which someone is appointed by election. **2** having the power to elect. **3** optional.

electively *adv.* by means of an election.

elector *noun* **1** a person who has the right to vote at an election. **2** (**Elector**) *Hist.* a German prince or archbishop in the Holy Roman Empire who had the right to elect the emperor.

electoral *adj.* of elections or electors.

electoral college in the US, the body of people who elect the President, having themselves been elected by popular vote.

electorally *adv.* as regards elections or voters.

electoral roll *or* **electoral register** the list of people in a particular area who are allowed to vote in local and general elections.

electorate *noun* (**the electorate**) all the electors of a city, country, etc.

Electra in Greek legend (but not in Homer), the daughter of Agamemnon and Clytemnestra. She assisted her brother Orestes when he came to Argos to avenge his father, and later married his friend Pylades.

Electra a play by Euripides (c.422–416 BC), about the gruesome matricide by Orestes in revenge for his father's death at the hands of his mother's lover.

electric — *adj.* **1** of, produced by, worked by, or generating electricity. **2** having or causing great excitement, tension, or expectation. — *noun* (**electrics**) **1** electrical appliances. **2** *colloq.* wiring. [from Greek *elektron*, amber, which produces electricity when rubbed]

electrical *adj.* related to or operated by electricity.

electrical engineering the branch of engineering concerned with the practical applications of electricity and magnetism in the design and construction of machinery, and in power generation, distribution, and storage.

electrically *adv.* as regards electricity; by means of electricity.

electric blanket a blanket for warming a bed, containing an electrical element controlled by a thermostat.

electric chair a chair used for executing criminals by sending a powerful electric current through them.

electric charge a quantity of electricity that is either positive or negative, such that two positive charges or two negative charges will repel each other, whereas a positive charge and a negative charge will attract each other. The SI unit of electric charge is the coulomb. A flow of moving charges in the form of electrons is known as an electric current. An electron bears a negative charge of 1.602×10^{-19} coulombs, and a proton bears a positive charge of equal magnitude, so a material that contains equal numbers of electrons and protons will be electrically neutral.

electric current the flow of electric charge, in the form of electrons, in the same direction through a conductor. The SI unit of electric current is the ampere (amp). A current of one amp corresponds to the flow of a charge of one coulomb every second.

electric eel an eel-like fish, which is able to deliver electric shocks by means of an organ in its tail.

electric eye *colloq.* a photochemical cell, a light-sensitive device which, when the beam of light completing its circuit is broken, produces an electric current, eg in order to bring an alarm system into operation.

electric fence a wire fence with an electric current passing through it.

electric field a region surrounding an electrically charged particle, within which any other particles present will experience a force.

electric guitar a guitar with an electrical amplifier.

electrician *noun* a person whose job is to install and repair electrical equipment.

electricity *noun* **1** the manifestation of a form of energy associated with separation or movement of charged particles, especially electrons and protons. **2** the scientific study of this form of energy. **3** an electric charge or current, especially when supplied as a source of power for heating, lighting, running electronic equipment, etc. **4** excitement, tension, or expectation.
◇ Electricity is concerned with the flow of positive and negative charges. The electrons in atoms

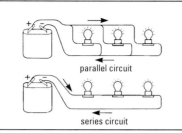

electric circuit diagram

carry negative charge, and are very much lighter than atoms, so most charges arise because electrons are moved from one place to another. An electric current is a flow of electric charge, and it is driven by an *electromotive force* (*emf*). This is often generated by a battery, in which case the force arises because it is chemically more favourable for the electrons to be at one terminal of the battery than at the other (there is said to be a *potential difference* between the two terminals). This type of current is known as *direct current* (*dc*) because it flows in one direction only.

A current can also be driven by a changing magnetic field. A dynamo changes the magnetic field through a coil of wire by spinning the coil in the field, so that the field passes through the coil first in one direction and then in the other. The field alternately increases and decreases, so an alternating emf is produced which drives the current first in one direction and then in the other. This is known as an *alternating current* (*ac*).

electricity generation the conversion of a suitable energy source (eg water power, coal, oil, nuclear energy) into electrical energy (electricity), usually by driving turbines linked to generators in a power station. Electricity so produced can then be distributed over a wide area by means of long-distance cables in order to provide a convenient source of power for heating, lighting, driving machinery and domestic appliances, etc.

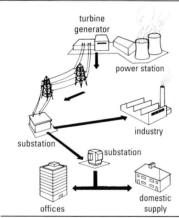

electricity supply and generation

electric motor *Physics* any device for converting electrical energy into mechanical energy.

electric ray, any of various sluggish bottom-dwelling marine fish, widespread in tropical and temperate seas, and having a rounded body, smooth skin, a robust tail, and well-developed electric organs that produce strong shocks to stun prey. — Also called *torpedo ray*.

electric shock therapy same as ELECTRO-CONVULSIVE THERAPY.

electrification *noun* the process of electrifying; installation of electricity.

electrify *verb* (**electrifies**, **electrified**) **1** to give an electric charge to. **2** to equip (eg a railway system) for the use of electricity as a power supply. **3** to cause great excitement in.

electrifying *adj.* extremely exciting.

electrifyingly *adv.* excitingly.

electro- *combining form* forming words relating to electricity.

electro-acupuncture *noun* a form of acupuncture in which manual manipulation is replaced by a low-frequency electric current passed between pairs of needles.

electrocardiogram *noun Medicine* (ABBREV. **ECG**) a recording of the electrical activity of the heart muscle, obtained by means of an electrocardiograph, and used in the diagnosis of heart disease.

electrocardiograph *noun Medicine* (ABBREV. **ECG**) a recording instrument, connected by leads to a number of electrodes taped to the chest wall and limbs, used to record the electrical activity of the heart muscle.

electrocardiography *noun Medicine* the branch of medicine concerned with the production and interpretation of electrocardiograms, whereby the electrical activity of the heart is recorded.

electrochemistry *noun Chem.* the branch of chemistry concerned with the relationships between electrical energy and chemical energy, such as the production of an electric current by a chemical reaction (eg in an electrolytic cell), and the chemical changes produced by the passage of an electric current (eg electrolysis).

electro-convulsive therapy *Medicine* (ABBREV. **ECT**) a treatment for mental disorders, especially severe depression, in which a low-voltage electric current is passed through the brain while the patient is under anaesthesia. Formerly a common treatment, it has now been largely replaced by the use of drugs.

electrocute *verb* **1** to kill accidentally by electric shock. **2** to execute by means of electricity. [from ELECTRO- + EXECUTE]

electrocution *noun* the process of electrocuting or killing by electric shock.

electrode *noun Electr.* either of the two conducting plates through which an electric current enters or leaves a battery, thermionic valve, discharge tube, semiconductor device, etc. The cathode is the negative electrode and the anode is the positive electrode. [from ELECTRIC + Greek *hodos*, way]

electroencephalogram *noun Medicine* (ABBREV. **EEG**) a diagram or tracing produced by an electroencephalograph.

electroencephalograph *noun Medicine* (ABBREV. **EEG**) an apparatus which registers, as a diagram or tracing, the electrical activity of the brain.

electrolysis *noun* **1** *Chem.* the process whereby the elements of a chemical compound are separated by passing an electric current through a solution or molten form of that compound, known as an *electrolyte*. **2** the removal of tumours, hair roots, etc, by means of an electric current.

◇ During electrolysis, direct current from a battery is passed between two solid electrodes that

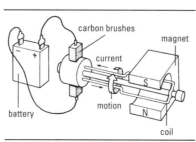

electric motor

are dipped in the electrolyte. Positively charged ions migrate to the cathode (negatively charged electrode), and negatively charged ions migrate to the anode (positively charged electrode). The applications of electrolysis include production of hydrogen and oxygen from water, extraction of pure metals from impure metal ores, and electroplating of metal objects.

electrolyte *noun Chem.* a chemical substance that can conduct electricity when in its molten state or when dissolved in water or some other solvent. [from ELECTRO- + Greek *lutos*, released]

electrolytic *adj.* relating to or involving electrolysis.

electrolytic cell *Chem.* any cell that consists of an electrolyte (a substance that when molten or in solution conducts electricity), in which electrodes (a positively charged anode and a negatively charged cathode) are immersed.

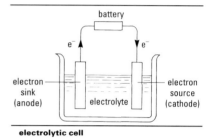

electrolytic cell

electromagnet *noun Physics* a temporary magnet consisting of a coil of insulated wire wrapped around a soft iron or steel core, which becomes strongly magnetized when an electric current flows through the wire. Electromagnets are used in switches, electric bells, loudspeakers, metal-lifting cranes, etc.

electromagnetic *adj.* having electrical and magnetic properties.

electromagnetic induction *Physics* the production of an electromotive force (a voltage) in a conductor by moving it in a magnetic field. Electromagnetic induction forms the basis of the operation of devices such as transformers, generators, and motors.

electromagnetic radiation oscillating electric and magnetic fields that are propagated together through empty space as radiated waves, eg visible light, infra-red radiation, X-rays.

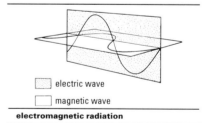

electric wave

magnetic wave

electromagnetic radiation

electromagnetic spectrum *Physics* the range of frequencies or wavelengths of the various different forms of electromagnetic radiation, ie radio waves, microwaves, infra-red, visible light, ultraviolet, X-rays, and gamma rays, in order of increasing frequency (and therefore decreasing wavelength).

electromagnetism *noun* magnetic forces produced by electricity.

electromotive *adj. Physics* producing or tending to produce an electric current.

electromotive force *Physics* the energy which forces a current to flow in an electrical circuit.

electron *noun Physics* a fundamental particle (one that cannot be subdivided further) that

Electromagnetic Spectrum

Radiation	Approximate wavelengths	Uses
Radio waves	>10cm	communications; radio and TV broadcasting
Microwaves	1mm–10cm	communications; radar; microwave ovens
Infrared	$10^{-3}–7.8 \times 10^{-7}$m	night and smoke vision systems; intruder alarms; weather forecasting; missile guidance systems
Visible	$7.8 \times 10^{-7}– 3 \times 10^{-7}$m	human eyesight
Ultraviolet	$3 \times 10^{-7}–10^{-8}$m	forensic science; medical treatment
X-rays	$10^{-8}–3 \times 10^{-11}$m	medical X-ray photographs; material structure analysis
Gamma rays	$<3 \times 10^{-11}$m	medical diagnosis

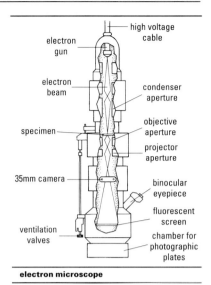

electron microscope

carries a negative electric charge. The mass of an electron is 9.110×10^{-31}kg, and it carries a charge of 1.602×10^{-19} coulombs. The flow of electrons along a conductor constitutes an electric current. ◇ Electrons are fundamental particles, ie they cannot be subdivided. In an atom, electrons orbit at great speed around a central nucleus, remaining a fixed distance from it which is determined by their energy level. The orbits of electrons can be regarded as a series of concentric 'shells' surrounding the nucleus, and the number of electrons in the outermost shell determines the properties of the atom. When atoms combine to form molecules, electrons in the outermost shell are transferred from one atom to another, or are shared between atoms.

electron capture 1 *Physics* the capture of an electron by a substance, resulting in the formation of a negatively charged ion. **2** the capture of an electron, which combines with a proton in the nucleus of an atom to form a neutron. As a result, the atomic number of the atom decreases by one.

electronegativity *noun Chem.* a measure of the ability of an atom within a molecule to attract electrons.

electron gun *Physics* a device that is used to produce a beam of electrons, eg a heated cathode. It is an essential component of television tubes, electron microscopes, and cathode-ray tubes.

electronic *adj.* **1** *said of a device* operated by the movement of electrons in very small electric circuits containing semiconductors, etc, or in a vacuum or gas. **2** produced, operated, etc using electronic apparatus: *electronic music.* **3** relating to electronics.

electronically *adv.* by means of electronics.

electronic funds transfer at point of sale *noun* (ABBREV. **EFTPOS**) a retail payment system which allows the direct transfer of money from the customer's bank account to the retailer's without the use of cash or cheques.

electronic mail *noun* (ABBREV. **E-mail**) *Comput.* the sending of messages via computer systems. Messages are usually stored centrally until they are accessed by the recipient. E-mail facilities have the advantages of speed, flexibility, and low cost, and are provided by most computer networks. They are also available on a national and international basis.

electronic photography exposure of a single picture in a special video camera, which records the image digitally on a rotating 50mm magnetic disk. Up to 25 shots may be taken and are available for immediate display on a video screen or on a paper printout within 90 seconds.

electronic point of sale (ABBREV. **EPOS**) a computerized till system at retail checkouts which links tills with bar-code readers to a stock control system.

electronic publishing *Comput.* the publishing of computer-readable texts on disk, CD-ROM, CD-I, etc.

electronics *noun* **1** (*sing.*) the scientific study of the conduction of electricity in a vacuum, in gases, and in semiconductors, and the design and applications of devices that control the movement of electrons. **2** (*pl.*) the electronic parts of a machine or system.
◇ The first electronic device was the thermionic valve, which was later replaced by the transistor. Subsequently, the development of the silicon chip and the integrated circuit, which enabled electronic components to be miniaturized, led to an enormous expansion of the electronics industry. Modern electronic devices are based on wafer-thin crystals containing tens of thousands of electronic components. The social impact of electronics is huge, and includes the development of microcomputers, word processors, television, spacecraft, pacemakers, pocket calculators, and digital watches.

electronic tagging the use of electronic tags (see TAG[1] *sense 2*).

electron microscope *Biol.* a microscope that uses a beam of electrons instead of light rays to produce a highly magnified image of an object that is too small to be seen with a light microscope. Electron microscopes are used to examine and photograph cells, viruses, and large molecules.
◇ Electron microscopes use electromagnetic coils as lenses to focus the electron beam, which has a much shorter wavelength than visible light, and so can provide a much higher *resolution* (ability to distinguish detail). There are three main types of electron microscope. In the *transmission electron microscope* (TEM), an electron beam passes through a very thinly sliced specimen and forms an image on a fluorescent screen. It can achieve magnifications of up to one million times actual size without losing definition. In the *scanning electron microscope* (SEM), the specimen is scanned by bombarding it with electrons that generate secondary electrons which are emitted from the surface of the specimen, collected, and used to construct a three-dimensional image of the object on a TV monitor. The magnification achieved (up to 200 000 times actual size), is not so high as with a transmission microscope, but the method is more suitable for thick specimens, eg tissue samples. *Scanning transmission electron microscopes* combine the features of the SEM and TEM, and can achieve even higher magnifications, and a sufficiently high resolution for individual atoms to be observed.

electron volt *or* **electronvolt** (SYMBOL **eV**) *Physics* a unit of energy equal to the energy acquired by an electron when it accelerates through a potential difference of one volt. It is equal to 1.602×10^{-19} joules.

electropalatography *noun Phonetics* the study of the way the tongue makes contact with the palate during speech. An artificial palate containing electrodes is inserted in the subject's mouth; when the tongue makes contact with the artificial palate the electrodes send impulses to a monitoring device; this displays the changing pattern of contacts made as the subject speaks as lights on a screen or dots on a computer printout.

electrophoresis *noun Chem.* the migration of charged particles in a solution under the influence of an electric field. It is used to separate individual amino acids from a mixture, by adjusting the pH of the solution so that some amino acids become positively charged and others become negatively charged. [from ELECTRO- + Greek *phoreein*, to bear]

electroplate — *verb* to plate or coat (a metal surface) with a thin layer of another metal by electrolysis, usually for decorative purposes, or to protect the underlying metal from corrosion. Metals commonly used for electroplating include silver, gold, copper, nickel, and chromium. — *noun* electroplated articles.

electroplated *adj.* coated with metal by electrolysis.

electroplating *noun* the process of coating with metal by electrolysis.

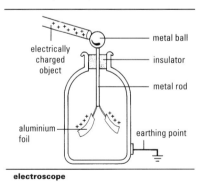

electroscope

electroscope *noun Physics* a device for detecting the presence of an electric charge and estimating its amount. The simplest form consists of two thin gold leaves which repel each other when charged, the extent to which they move apart indicating the amount of the charge.

electrostatic field *Physics* an electric field associated with stationary electric charges.

electrostatics *sing. noun Physics* the scientific study of fields and potentials caused by stationary electric charges.

elegance *noun* being elegant or graceful; refinement.

elegant *adj.* **1** having or showing good taste in dress or style, combined with dignity and gracefulness. **2** *said of a movement* graceful. **3** *said of a plan, etc* simple and ingenious. [from Latin *elegans*]

elegantly *adv.* with an elegant or graceful manner.

elegiac *adj. formal, literary* mournful or thoughtful; which is, or is like, an elegy.

elegiacally *adv.* by means of elegiacs; mournfully.

elegize *or* **elegise** *verb formal, literary* **1** *intrans., trans.* to write an elegy about someone or something. **2** *intrans.* to produce mournful or thoughtful writings or songs.

elegy *noun* a mournful or thoughtful song or poem, especially one whose subject is death or loss. [from Latin *elegia*, from Greek *elegos*, lament]

Elegy Written in a Country Churchyard a poem by Thomas Gray (1751). It is a reflective musing on mortality and country life.

element *noun* **1** a part of anything; a component or feature. **2** *Chem.* a chemical element. **3** a person or small group within a larger group. **4** a slight amount. **5** a high-resistance wire through which an electric current is passed in order to produce heat in an electric fire, kettle, or similar appliance. **6** one of a number of components in an electric circuit. **7** *Maths.* a single member of a set. **8** *Comput.* a single item in a set of computer data. **9** any one of the four basic substances (earth, air, fire, and water) from which, according to ancient philosophy, everything is formed. **10** (**elements**) weather conditions, especially when severe. **11** (**elements**) basic facts or skills. **12** (**elements**) *Relig.* bread and wine as the representation of the body and blood of Christ in the Eucharist. — **in one's element** in the surroundings that one finds most natural and enjoyable. [from Latin *elementum*]

elemental *adj.* **1** basic or primitive; of the forces of nature, especially the four elements earth, air, fire, and water. **2** immense; of the power of a force of nature.

elementary *adj.* dealing with simple or basic facts.

elementary particle *Physics* any of a number of different types of subatomic particle that do not appear to be divisible into smaller units.

elementary school *North Amer., esp. US* primary school.

elephant *noun* (PL. **elephants**, **elephant**) the largest living land mammal, belonging to the family Elephantidae, and having an almost hairless grey skin, thick pillar-like legs with broad feet, large ears that are used to radiate heat, small eyes, and upper incisor teeth modified to form tusks. Its nose and upper lip are greatly elongated and modified to form a flexible muscular trunk. See also WHITE ELEPHANT. [from Latin *elephantus*, from Greek *elephas*]
◇ The African elephant (*Loxodonta africana*), found in bush, forest, or semi-desert country south of the Sahara, and the Indian elephant (*Elephas maximus*), found in thick forests in India and SE Asia, are the two surviving representatives of the order Proboscoidea, which included many extinct forms, such as mammoths and mastodons. The African elephant is the larger of the two. A male (known as a *bull*) may stand up to 3.5m high and weigh as much as 6 tonnes. It can be distinguished from the Indian elephant by its large ears, which reach below the mouth, its sloping forehead, and the presence of two 'lips' at the tip of its trunk. The Indian elephant has smaller ears, a domed forehead, and a single lip on its trunk. In both species the trunk is used for carrying food and water to the mouth, spraying water over the body, smelling, and lifting and investigating objects. Elephants feed on grass, leaves, fruit, and young tree branches. Their ivory tusks have made them a target for hunters and poachers, and the number of elephants in the wild is now much reduced, herds surviving only in game parks.

African elephant

Indian elephant

elephant types

Elephanta Caves a group of Hindu cave-temples located on Elephanta Island off the W coast of Maharashtra, India. The temples, which were excavated in the 8c–9c, are noted for their sculptures, in particular the 'Trimurti', a three-headed bust of the gods Shiva, Vishnu, and Brahma. It is a World Heritage site.

elephantiasis *noun Medicine* a chronic disease that occurs mainly in the tropics, caused by infection with parasitic roundworms. The lymph vessels become blocked so that drainage of fluid from the surrounding tissues is prevented, resulting in massive thickening of the skin in affected areas of the body, usually the legs.

elephantine *adj.* **1** of or like an elephant. **2** huge. **3** *derog.* large and awkward; not graceful.

elephant seal any of the two largest species of seal, the males of which have large snouts.

elephant shrew an insectivorous animal that is not a true shrew, so called because it has a long flexible snout. It lives in African forests and grassland, and can move rapidly by hopping on its hind legs.

Eleusinian Mysteries in ancient Greece, secret ceremonies connected with the worship of the corn-goddess Demeter and her daughter Persephone, which were held annually at Eleusis near Athens. Initiation, preceded by ritual purification, was believed to secure happiness in the after-life for those who had led a blameless life.

elevate *verb* **1** to raise or lift. **2** to give a higher rank or status to. **3** to improve (a person's mind, etc) morally or intellectually. **4** to make more cheerful. [from Latin *elevare*]

elevated *adj.* **1** *said of a rank, position, etc* very high; important. **2** *said of thoughts, ideas, etc* intellectually advanced or very moral. **3** *said of land or buildings* raised above the level of their surroundings. **4** cheerful; elated.

elevating *adj.* improving the mind; morally uplifting.

elevation *noun* **1** the act of elevating or state of being elevated. **2** *technical* height, eg of a place above sea level. **3** *technical* a drawing or diagram of one side of a building, machine, etc. **4** *formal* a high place.

elevation of boiling point *Chem.* the raising of the boiling point of a liquid, achieved by dissolving a substance in it.

elevator *noun* **1** *North Amer.* a lift in a building. **2** a tall building in which grain is stored. **3** *Anat.* a muscle used to raise a part of the body. **4** *Aeron.* a movable flap at the tail of an aircraft, by means of which the aircraft climbs or descends.

elevatory *adj.* serving to elevate or bring to a higher position.

eleven — *noun* **1** the number or figure 11; any symbol for this number. **2** the age of 11. **3** something, eg a garment or a person, whose size is denoted by the number 11. **4** 11 o'clock. **5** a set of 11 people or things, especially a team of 11 players. **6** a score of 11 points. — *adj.* **1** 11 in number. **2** aged 11.
— **at the eleventh hour** at the last possible moment; only just in time.
[from Anglo-Saxon *endleofan*]

eleven-plus *noun* in the UK, an examination formerly taken at 11 or 12 to determine the type of secondary school a pupil will attend.

elevenses *noun colloq.* a snack, usually consisting of coffee, tea, biscuits, etc, taken at about eleven o'clock in the morning.

eleventh *noun, adj.* a position in a series corresponding to 11 in a sequence of numbers.

elf *noun* (PL. **elves**) **1** in folklore, a tiny fairy with a tendency to play tricks. **2** a mischievous child. [from Anglo-Saxon *ælf*]

elfin *adj.* **1** *said of physical features, etc* small and delicate. **2** elfish; small and mischievous, but charming.

elfish *or* **elvish** *adj.* characteristic of an elf; mischievous.

Elgar, Sir Edward (1857–1934) English composer, born in Broadheath, Worcestershire. Largely self-taught, he worked as a violinist before he became conductor of the Worcester Glee Club and the County Asylum Band, and organist of St George's Church, Worcester. The *Enigma Variations* (1899) and the oratorio *The Dream of Gerontius* (1900) made him the leading figure in English music, and after the Elgar Festival (London, 1904) he received a knighthood. From 1924 he was Master of the King's Musick. His other works include oratorios, symphonies, concertos, and incidental music.

Elgin Marbles a collection of marble sculptures of the mid-5c BC from the Parthenon of Athens. They were acquired in 1801–3 (when Greece was under Turkish rule) by Thomas Bruce, 7th Earl of Elgin (1766–1841), and shipped to England. In 1816 they were purchased by the government for the British Museum. The Greek government has campaigned (so far, unsuccessfully) for their return to Greece.

El Gîza *or* **Gîza** *or* **Gizeh** *or* **Al-Jizah** **1** POP (1990e) 2.2m, the capital of El Gîza governorate, N Egypt. The city is situated on the W bank of the R Nile, 5km/3mi SW of Cairo. NOTABLE FEATURES the Sphynx and pyramids of Cheops, Khafra, and Mankara are situated 8km/5mi SW. **2** a governorate in N Egypt with El Gîza as its capital.

El Greco see GRECO, EL.

elicit *verb* (**elicited, eliciting**) **1** (**elicit something from someone**) to succeed in getting information from them, usually with some effort or difficulty. **2** to cause or bring out. [from Latin *elicere*]

elicitation *noun* the process of eliciting or drawing out a response.

elicitor *noun* a person who elicits or draws out a response.

elide *verb* **1** *Grammar* to omit (a vowel or syllable) at the beginning or end of a word. **2** to omit (a part of anything). See also ELISION. [from Latin *elidere*, to strike out]

eligibility *noun* the status of being eligible or suitable.

eligible *adj.* (*often* **eligible for something**) **1** suitable, or deserving to be chosen (for a job, as a husband, etc). **2** having a right: *eligible for compensation*. [from Latin *eligere*, to elect]

Elijah (9c BC) Hebrew prophet, whose story is told in 1 Kings 17–19, 21, and 2 Kings 1–2. His loyalty to God inspired him to oppose the worship of Baal in Israel under King Ahab and Jezebel, and was rewarded by his direct ascent into heaven in a whirlwind.

Elijah an oratorio by Felix Mendelssohn (Op 70, 1846) to a text based on 1 Kings 17–19.

eliminable *adj.* that may be eliminated.

eliminate *verb* **1** to get rid of or exclude. **2** to exclude from a later part of a competition by defeat in an earlier part. **3** *slang* to kill. [from Latin *eliminare*, to carry outside]

elimination *noun* the process of eliminating or getting rid of.

eliminator *noun* someone or something that eliminates, eg the first round of a competition.

Elint the practice of '*electronic intelligence*' gathering, in which the performance factors of hostile weapons systems can be determined by the interpretation of their electronic emissions.

Eliot, George, pseudonym of **Mary Ann**, or **Marian Evans** (1819–80) English novelist, born near Nuneaton, Warwickshire. She took charge of the family household when her mother died (1836), and after the death of her father (1849) she travelled abroad before settling in London, where she began to write for the *Westminster Review* (1850). She became assistant editor of it (1851), and the centre of a literary circle whose members included G H Lewes, with whom she lived until his death (1878). Her first story appeared in 1857, and her major novels include *Adam Bede* (1859), *The Mill on the Floss* (1860), *Silas Marner* (1861), *Middlemarch* (1871–2), and *Daniel Deronda* (1876).

Eliot, T(homas) S(tearns) (1888–1965) US-born British poet, critic, and dramatist, born in St Louis, Missouri. He studied at Harvard and Paris and, after a year's scholarship to Oxford, was persuaded to stay in England by Ezra Pound. He worked as a teacher and in a bank before becoming a director of Faber publishers. Supported by Pound, he published his first book of poetry, *Prufrock and Other Observations* (1917), and was introduced by Bertrand Russell into the Bloomsbury Circle. He then published *The Waste Land* (1922) and *The Hollow Men* (1925), and edited the quarterly review, *The Criterion* (1922–39). In 1927 he became a British subject and was baptized and confirmed, adhering to the Anglo-Catholic movement within the Church of England. Later works include his major poetic achievement, *Four Quartets* (1944), and a series of plays, notably *Murder in the Cathedral* (1935) and *The Cocktail Party* (1950). He also wrote much literary and social criticism (eg *After Strange Gods*, 1936). He was awarded the Nobel Prize for Literature in 1948.

Elisabethville see LUBUMBASHI.

Elisha (9c BC) Hebrew prophet who succeeded Elijah and whose story is told in 1 Kings 19 and 2 Kings 2–9, 13. Active in Israel under several kings from Ahab to Jehoash, he was credited with miraculous signs, counselled kings, and attempted to guide the nation against its external enemies, especially the Syrians.

elision *noun Grammar* the omission of a vowel or syllable, as in *I'm*, *we're*. See also ELIDE. [from Latin *elidere*, to strike out]

elite *or* **élite** — *noun* **1** the best, most important, or most powerful people within society.

2 the best of a group or profession. **3** a size of letter in typewriting, twelve characters per inch. — *adj.* best, most important or most powerful. [from Old French *eslire*, to choose, from Latin *eligere*, to elect]

elitism *or* **élitism** *noun* **1** the belief in the need for a powerful social elite. **2** the belief in the natural social superiority of some people. **3** *often derog.* awareness of, or pride in, belonging to an elite group in society.

elitist *or* **élitist** *noun* a supporter of elitism. *adj.*

elixir *noun* **1** *Chem.* in alchemy, a chemical preparation that was formerly claimed to have the power to change ordinary metals into gold, or to be a universal remedy for illness (the elixir of life). **2** a panacea. **3** *Medicine* a clear sweetened liquid containing alcohol or glycerine, used to mask the taste of an unpalatable medicine that is dissolved in it. [from Arabic *al-iksir*, the philosopher's stone]

Elizabeth a female first name, dating from Queen Elizabeth I (1533–1603) and popularized by its royal associations in the 20c. [from Hebrew *Elisheba*, God is my oath + *shabbath*, rest]

Elizabeth I (1533–1603) Queen of England (1558–1603), the daughter of Henry VIII by his second wife, Anne Boleyn, born in Greenwich, near London. On the death of Edward VI (1553) she sided with her half-sister Mary (later Mary I) against Lady Jane Grey and the Duke of Northumberland, but her Protestantism made Mary suspicious, and she was imprisoned for her alleged part in the rebellion of Wyatt (1554). She ascended the throne on Mary's death, and established herself as a strong but tolerant Protestant sovereign, making peace with France and Scotland. She was guided in her government by William Cecil as Secretary of State. Later the formal establishment of the Anglican Church and the imprisonment of Mary, Queen of Scots (1568) caused endless conspiracies among English Catholics. Elizabeth eventually had Mary executed (1587), and she persecuted the Catholics and incited the Netherlands against Philip of Spain, which led him to attack England (unsuccessfully) with his 'invincible armada' (1588). She had many relationships, notably with Robert Dudley, Earl of Leicester, whom her secretary Robert Cecil advised her not to marry. Considered a strong, cruel, and capricious woman, the 'Virgin Queen' was nevertheless popular with her subjects, and she later became known as 'Good Queen Bess'. Her reign is seen as the period when England became a world power.

Elizabeth II (1926–) Queen of the United Kingdom and Head of the Commonwealth, born in London, the daughter of George VI. Formerly Princess Elizabeth Alexandra Mary, she was proclaimed queen on 6 Feb 1952, and crowned on 2 Jun 1953. Married in 1947, her husband is Prince Philip, Duke of Edinburgh. They have three sons, Charles Philip Arthur George (1948–), Andrew Albert Christian Edward (1960–), and Edward Anthony Richard Louis (1964–), and a daughter, Anne Elizabeth Alice Louise (1950–).

Elizabethan — *adj.* relating to or typical of the reign of Queen Elizabeth I of England (1558–1603). — *noun* a person who lived during this time.

Elizabethan style a form of early English Renaissance architecture of the period 1558–1603, characterized by symmetrical facades combined with Netherland decoration and over-sized windows. Plans are often E- or H-shaped (eg Longleat, c.1568 onwards).

Elizabeth Petrovna (1709–62) Empress of Russia (1741–62), the daughter of Peter the Great and Catherine I, born near Moscow. She became Empress on the deposition of Ivan VI. Features of her reign, during which she was guided by favourites, included the conclusion of a war with

Sweden and, fuelled by her animosity towards Frederick the Great, a part in the War of the Austrian Succession and in the Seven Years' War.

elk *noun* (PL. **elks**, **elk**) the largest of all deer, found in northern parts of Europe and Asia, and in N America, where it is called the moose. [probably from Anglo-Saxon *elhr*]

Ellen a female first name. [originally a variant of HELEN]

Ellesmere Island an arctic island in Northwest Territories, Canada, separated from Greenland by the Nares Strait. AREA 196 236sq km/75 747sq mi. It is barren and mountainous, with a large ice-cap in the SE and a fjord coastline. Its N point, Cape Columbia, is the northernmost point in Canada. There are several small settlements.

Ellesmere Port POP (1992e) 81 000, a port town in Ellesmere Port and Neston district, Cheshire, NW central England. It lies on the estuary of the R Mersey and the Manchester Ship Canal, 14km/9mi SE of Liverpool.

Ellice Islands see TUVALU.

Ellington, Duke, originally **Edward Kennedy** (1899–1974) US composer, arranger, bandleader, and pianist, born in Washington, DC. He was an itinerant piano player in dance bands in Washington and New York until 1924, when he became bandleader at the Kentucky Club and then (1927–32) at the Cotton Club. He developed a unique sound for his musicians by blending instruments into startling harmonies. Following early successes (eg 'Mood Indigo', 1930), he toured in Europe (1933), then worked on extended concert pieces (eg 'Reminiscing in Tempo', 1935), and began a series of annual concerts at Carnegie Hall (1943–50). His creative peak, generally said to be from 1939 to 1942, included 'Warm Valley', 'Cotton Tail', and 'Take the A Train'.

ellipse *noun Geom.* a regular oval, as formed by a diagonal cut through a cone above the base. [from Latin *ellipsis*, from Greek *elleipsis*, omission]

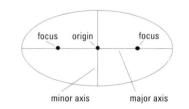

ellipse

ellipsis *noun* (PL. **ellipses**) **1** *Grammar* a figure of speech in which a word or words needed for the sense or grammar are omitted but understood. **2** a set of three dots that indicate the omission of a word or words, eg in a lengthy quotation. [see ELLIPSE]

ellipsoid *noun Geom.* a surface or solid object of which every plane section is an ellipse or a circle.

elliptical *or* **elliptic** *adj.* **1** *Maths.* of or having the shape of an ellipse. **2** *said of speech or writing* containing an ellipsis; so concise as to be unclear or ambiguous. [from Greek *elleipsis*, omission]

elliptically *adv.* in an elliptical way; over-concisely.

Ellora Caves a collection of Buddhist, Hindu, and Jaina temples carved into the rocky cliffs near Ellora, in the state of Maharashtra, India. The most notable is the Kailashanatha Temple (8c), dedicated to the Hindu god Shiva. They form a World Heritage site.

elm *noun* any of various tall deciduous trees of the genus *Ulmus*, found mainly in the northern

elm

hemisphere, that have broad serrated leaves and produce clusters of small flowers which develop into winged fruits bearing a single seed. The English elm (*U. procera*) has been severely affected by infection with the fungus that causes Dutch elm disease. [from Anglo-Saxon *elm*]

elocution *noun* the art of speaking clearly and effectively. [from Latin *eloqui*, to speak out]

elocutionary *adj.* relating to elocution or clear speech.

elocutionist *noun* a teacher of, or an expert in, elocution.

Elohim a divine name for the God of Israel. The plural form here is used as a plural of majesty. One of the most common divine names in the Hebrew Bible, where it occurs over 2 500 times, it could also refer to other gods, angels, or even to humans such as Moses. [Hebrew, = gods]

elongate *verb* to lengthen or stretch out. [from Latin *elongare*]

elongated *adj.* long and narrow.

elongation *noun* the process of elongating; making longer.

elope *verb intrans.* to run away secretly, especially to get married. [from Old French *aloper*, probably from Middle English *alopen*]

elopement *noun* an act of eloping.

eloper *noun* a person who elopes.

eloquence *noun* 1 the art or power of using speech to impress, move, or persuade. 2 fine and persuasive language. [from Latin *eloqui*, to speak out]

eloquent *adj.* having or showing eloquence.

eloquently *adv.* with eloquence.

El Paso POP (1990) 592 000, the seat of El Paso County, W Texas, USA. It is a port on the R Grande, opposite the city of Ciudad Juarez, Mexico. HISTORY founded in 1827; part of it was transferred to Mexico in 1963, after the settlement of the Chamizal border dispute.

El Salvador, official name **Republic of El Salvador**, Spanish **República de El Salvador** POP (1992) 5.1m, the smallest of the Central American republics, divided into 14 departments. AREA 21 476sq km/8 290sq mi. It is bounded N and E by Honduras, W by Guatemala, and S by the Pacific Ocean. CAPITAL San Salvador. CHIEF TOWNS Santa Ana, San Miguel, Mejicanos, Delgado. The population is chiefly Spanish–S American Indian (89%); Roman Catholicism is the main religion. OFFICIAL LANGUAGE Spanish. CURRENCY the colón. TIME ZONE GMT −6. PHYSICAL DESCRIPTION two volcanic ranges running E–W divide El Salvador into three geographical regions, ranging from a narrow coastal belt in the S through upland valleys and plateaux (average height, 600m) to mountains in the N (highest point, Santa Ana, is 2 381m); the R Lempa, dammed for hydroelectricity, flows S to the

Pacific; many volcanic lakes; earthquakes are common. CLIMATE varies greatly with altitude; hot and tropical on the coastal lowlands; single rainy season (May–Oct); temperate uplands; average annual temperature at San Salvador is 23°C; average annual rainfall is 1 775mm. HISTORY originally part of the Aztec kingdom; conquest by the Spanish in 1526; independence from Spain in 1821; member of the Central American Federation until its dissolution in 1839; became an independent republic in 1841; dictatorship followed by political unrest in the mid-20c; war with Honduras in 1965 and 1969; considerable political unrest in the 1970s, with guerrilla activity directed against the US-supported government; assassination of the Archbishop of San Salvador, Oscar Romero, in 1980; civil war followed in which 75 000 died; a peace agreement was signed in 1992; a state of emergency was declared in 1993 as a result of an outbreak of cholera. GOVERNMENT governed by a President elected for five years, and a 60-member elected National Assembly. ECONOMY largely based on agriculture; main crops coffee and cotton; sugar, maize, balsam (world's main source); food processing; textiles; shoes; furniture; chemicals, fertilizers; pharmaceuticals; cement; rubber goods; oil products.

El Salvador

else *adj., adv.* different from or in addition to something or someone known or already mentioned: *I'd like something else / where else can you buy it?*
— **or else** ... 1 or if not ...; otherwise: *hurry up, or else we'll be late.* 2 *colloq.* or I will punish or harm you: *give me the money, or else!*
[from Anglo-Saxon *elles*]

elsewhere *adv.* somewhere else.

Elsinore, Danish **Helsingor** POP (1992e) 57 000, a seaport in NE Zealand, Denmark, lying on The Sound opposite Helsingborg in Sweden. It is the site of Kronborg Castle (16c), famous as the scene of Shakespeare's *Hamlet*.

Elspeth a female first name. [a Scottish contracted form of ELIZABETH]

ELT *abbrev.* English Language Teaching.

El Tajín an ancient Meso-American city near Papantla, N Veracruz, Mexico, which flourished from c.600 to 900 but was abandoned after 1100. It has a 60ha ceremonial centre with 12 ballcourts. The 18m high Pyramid of the Niches (c.600) has 365 external niches, each reputed to have contained an idol for one day of the year.

Elton, Ben(jamin Charles) (1959–) English comedian and writer, born in Guildford, Surrey. Since the early 1980s he has been at the forefront of the alternative comedy movement, which prefers obscene and anti-establishment humour to the sexism and racism of traditional comedy. He has co-written television comedy including *The Young Ones* (1982–4) and several series of *Blackadder* (1987–9). His novels are *Stark* (1989) and *Gridlock* (1991).

Elton, Charles Sutherland (1900–91) English ecologist, born in Liverpool. Following four Arctic expeditions in the 1920s, he spent most of his career at Oxford University (1936–67) and produced classic books on animal ecology. His work on animal communities led to recognition of the ability of many animals to counter

environmental disadvantage by change of habitats, and to the use of the concepts of 'food chain' and 'niche'.

Eluard, Paul, pseudonym of **Eugène Grindal** (1895–1952) French poet, born in Saint-Denis. One of the founders of the Surrealist movement in literature, his volumes of poetry include *Le Devoir et l'Inquiétude* (1917), *Capitale de la douleur* (1926), and *Les Yeux Fertiles* (1936). He broke with the Surrealists in 1938, joined the Communist Party in 1942, and became active in the French Resistance.

elucidate *verb* to make clear or explain; to shed light on. [from Latin *elucidare*]

elucidation *noun* elucidating; clear explanation.

elucidatory *adj.* serving to elucidate or make clear.

elude *verb* 1 to escape or avoid by quickness or cleverness. 2 to fail to be understood by, discovered by, or found in the memory of. [from Latin *eludere*]

elusive *adj.* 1 difficult to find or catch. 2 difficult to remember. 3 avoiding the issue or the question. [from ELUDE]

elusively *adv.* in an elusive way; so as to be difficult to catch or understand.

elusiveness *noun* being elusive or difficult to catch or understand.

elution *noun* *Chem.* in chromatography, the removal of a substance that has been adsorbed on to the surface of another substance, usually a column of resin, by passing a solvent down the column. [from Latin *elutio -onis*, washing]

elver *noun* a young eel. [from old word *eelfare*, literally 'eel journey', a reference to the migration of young eels upstream]

elves see ELF.

Elvis a male first name, made famous by the US singer Elvis Presley (1935–78). [origin obscure]

elvish see ELFISH.

Elvström, Paul (1928–) Danish yachtsman. He is the only yachtsman to have won four individual Olympic gold medals: in the Firefly class in 1948 and the Finn class in 1952, 1956, and 1960. He was also the first to win the same event at four consecutive Olympics. He came fourth in the Tornado class at the 1984 Olympics, his seventh Games, with his daughter, Trine.

Elwyn-Jones, Frederick Elwyn-Jones, Baron (1909–89) Welsh jurist and Labour politician, born in Llanelli. He was called to the Bar in 1935, and was a member of the British War Crimes Executive in Nuremberg in 1945. An MP in England from 1945, he was involved in the founding of Amnesty International. In 1964 he was appointed Attorney-General by Prime Minister Harold Wilson, and while in this post he led the team of counsel to the investigating tribunal of the Aberfan pit disaster. He was Lord High Chancellor (1974–9) and Lord of Appeal (1979–89).

Ely POP (1981) 9 000, a small city in East Cambridgeshire district, Cambridgeshire, E central England. It lies in fertile, wheat-growing fens, on the R Ouse, 23km/14mi NE of Cambridge. NOTABLE FEATURES 12c cathedral (octagonal tower); King's School (1543); the Isle of Ely (higher ground surrounded by fens) is the location of Hereward the Wake's defence against the Normans.

Elysée, Palais de l' a palace built (1718) for the Compte d'Evreux on the Rue du Faubourg Sainte-Honoré in Paris. It later became the home of Napoleon I and Napoleon III, and since 1873 has been the official residence of the French President.

Elysian *adj.* characteristic of the happiness associated with Elysium.

Elysium *or* **Elysian fields 1** in Greek and Roman mythology, the happy fields, often located on the borders of the Underworld, where the good remain after death in perfect happiness. **2** *poetic* a state or place of perfect happiness. [from Latin *elysium*, from Greek *elysion*]

em- *prefix* a form of *en-* used before b, m, and p.

'em *contr. colloq.* them. [from Middle English *hem*, them]

emaciate *verb* to make extremely thin, especially through illness, starvation, etc. [from Latin *emaciare*]

emaciated *adj.* thin through malnutrition or starvation.

emaciation *noun* extreme leanness or wasting of the body caused by malnutrition, parasitic worms, or diseases such as cancer or tuberculosis.

emanate *verb intrans.* **1** *said of an idea, etc* to emerge or originate. **2** *said of light, gas, etc* to flow; to issue. [from Latin *emanare*, to flow out]

emanation *noun* emanating or originating.

emancipate *verb* to set free from slavery, or from some other social or political restraint. [from Latin *emancipare*, to free]

emancipated *adj.* freed, especially from a social restraint.

emancipation *noun* the process of emancipating or freeing.

Emancipation Proclamation a document issued (1 Jan 1863) during the American Civil War by President Lincoln (following a preliminary proclamation on 22 Sep 1862) that declared the freedom of all slaves in areas then in arms against the US government. It did not free slaves in areas not in rebellion.

Emanuel *or* **Manuel I**, known as **the Great**, or **the Fortunate** (1469–1521) King of Portugal (1495–1521), born in Alcochete. He consolidated royal power, and his reign marked a golden age of Portugal; he prepared the code of laws which bears his name, and made his court a centre of chivalry, art, and science, though the era was marred by his persecution of the Jews. He sponsored the voyages of Vasco da Gama, Cabral, and others, which helped to make Portugal the first naval power of Europe and a world centre of commerce.

emasculate *verb* **1** to reduce the force, strength, or effectiveness of. **2** to remove the testicles of; to take away the masculinity of. [from Latin *e*, from + *masculus*, diminutive of *mas*, male]

emasculated *adj.* reduced in force or effectiveness; made feeble.

emasculation *noun* emasculating; making feeble or ineffective.

emasculatory *adj.* serving to emasculate or make feeble.

embalm *verb* to preserve (a dead body) from decay, originally with oils and spices, but now by treatment with chemicals or drugs. [from Old French *embaumer*]

embalmer *noun* a person who embalms dead bodies, especially professionally.

embalmment *noun* the process of embalming dead bodies.

embankment *noun* **1** a bank or wall of earth made to enclose a waterway, or to carry a road or railway. **2** a slope of grass, earth, etc which rises from either side of a road or railway.

embargo — *noun* (PL. **embargoes**) **1** an official order forbidding something, especially trade with another country. **2** the resulting stoppage, especially of trade. **3** any restriction or prohibition. — *verb* (**embargoes, embargoed**) **1** to place under an embargo. **2** to take for use by the state. [from Spanish *embargar*, to impede or restrain]

embark *verb* **1** *trans., intrans.* to go or put on board ship: *embark for America.* **2** (**embark on something**) to begin a task, especially a lengthy one. [from French *embarquer*]

embarkation *noun* embarking; boarding a ship.

Embarquement pour l'île de Cythère, L' a painting by Jean-Antoine Watteau (1717, Louvre, Paris).

embarrass *verb* **1** *trans., intrans.* to cause to feel, or to become, anxious, self-conscious, or ashamed. **2** (**be embarrassed**) to be in financial difficulties. **3** to make more complicated. **4** to confuse or perplex. [from French *embarrasser*]

embarrassed *adj.* feeling awkward or self-conscious.

embarrassing *adj.*, *said of an incident, remark, etc* causing awkwardness or self-consciousness.

embarrassingly *adv.* in an embarrassing or awkward way.

embarrassment *noun* self-conscious awkwardness, or a cause of it: *he's an embarrassment to all of us.*

embassy *noun* (PL. **embassies**) **1** the official residence of an ambassador. **2** an ambassador and his or her staff. **3** a diplomatic mission to a foreign country. [from Old French *ambassee*]

embattled *adj.* **1** prepared for battle. **2** troubled by problems or difficulties. [from Old French *embataillier*, to prepare or arm for battle]

embed *verb* (**embedded, embedding**) to set or fix firmly and deeply.

embellish *verb* **1** to make (a story, etc) more interesting by adding details which may not be true. **2** to beautify with decoration. [from Old French *embellir*, to make beautiful]

embellished *adj.* beautified with decoration.

embellishment *noun* **1** beautifying with decoration. **2** elaboration of a story, etc with details.

ember *noun* (usually **embers**) **1** a piece of glowing or smouldering coal or wood in a dying fire. **2** *literary* what remains of a once strong feeling. [from Anglo-Saxon *æmyrge*]

Ember Days in the Christian Church, the Wednesday, Friday, and Saturday of the weeks (*Ember Weeks*) following the first Sunday in Lent, Whit Sunday, Holy Cross Day (14 Sep), and St Lucia's Day (13 Dec); formerly observed as special days of fasting and abstinence. [from Middle English *ymber*, from Old English *ymbren*, a period, circuit, rotation (as of the seasons)]

embezzle *verb* to take dishonestly (money with which one has been entrusted). [from Old French *embesiler*, to make away with]

embezzlement *noun* the act of embezzling.

embezzler *noun* a person who embezzles money.

embitter *verb* (**embittered, embittering**) to cause (someone) to feel bitter.

embittered *adj.* made to feel bitter and resentful.

embittering *adj.* causing feelings of bitterness and resentment.

embitterment *noun* the process of causing bitter feelings.

emblazon *verb* (**emblazoned, emblazoning**) **1** to decorate with a coat of arms or some other bright design. **2** to display in a very obvious or striking way. [from EM- + *blazon*, from French *blason*, shield]

emblazonment *noun* decoration or display, especially heraldic.

emblem *noun* an object chosen to represent an idea, a quality, a country, etc. [from Latin *emblema*]

emblematic *adj.* in the nature of an emblem; serving as an emblem.

embodiment *noun* **1** embodying; something that is embodied. **2** a typical example or representative of something: *the embodiment of evil.*

embody *verb* (**embodies, embodied**) **1** to be an expression or a representation of in words, actions, or form; to typify or personify. **2** to include or incorporate.

embolden *verb* (**emboldened, emboldening**) to make bold.

embolism *noun* *Medicine* the blockage of a blood vessel (usually in the heart, lungs, or brain) by a blood clot, air bubble, or a fragment of tissue or some other material that has travelled through the bloodstream. The commonest form is a *pulmonary embolism* (blockage of the pulmonary artery), which can result in sudden death. [from Greek *embolismos*, from *emballein*, to insert]

embolus *noun* (PL. **emboli**) *Medicine* any obstruction in a blood vessel, especially a blood clot.

emboss *verb* to carve or mould a raised design on (a surface). [from Old French *embocer*]

embossed *adj.* carved or moulded with a raised design.

embrace — *verb* **1** to hold closely in the arms, affectionately or as a greeting. **2** *intrans. said of two people* to hold each other closely in the arms, affectionately or as a greeting. **3** to take (eg an opportunity) eagerly, or accept (eg a religion) wholeheartedly. **4** to include. — *noun* **1** an act of embracing. **2** a loving hug. [from Old French *embracer*, from Latin *in*, in + *bracchium*, arm]

embrasure *noun* **1** an opening in the wall of a castle, etc for shooting through. **2** an opening in a thick wall for a door or window, with angled sides which make it narrower on the outside. **3** the sloping of these sides. [from French *embraser*, to splay]

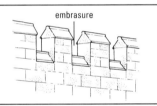

embrasure

embrasure

embrocation *noun* **1** a lotion for rubbing into the skin as a treatment for sore or pulled muscles. **2** the act of rubbing in such lotion. [from Greek *embroche*, lotion]

embroider *verb* (**embroidered, embroidering**) **1** *trans., intrans.* to decorate (cloth) with sewn designs. **2** to make (a story, etc) more interesting by adding details, usually untrue. [from Old French *embroder*]

embroiderer *noun* a person who embroiders, especially professionally.

embroidery *noun* **1** the art or practice of sewing designs on to cloth. **2** articles decorated in this way. **3** *derog.* gaudy decoration. **4** the addition of (usually false) details to a story, etc.

embroil *verb* **1** (**embroil someone in something**) to involve them in a quarrel or in a difficult situation. **2** to throw into a state of confusion. [from French *embrouiller*]

embroilment *noun* embroiling; uproar; commotion.

embryo *noun* (PL. **embryos**) **1** in animals, the developing young organism, from the first division of the zygote (fertilized ovum or egg) until hatching or birth. **2** in humans, the developing young organism during the first seven weeks after conception (fertilization of the egg cell). Thereafter it is usually referred to as a fetus. **3** in angiosperms (flowering plants), gymnosperms (cone-bearing plants), pteridophytes (eg ferns), and bryophytes (eg mosses and liverworts), the structure that develops from the zygote following fertilization, and prior to germination. It usually consists of a plumule (young shoot), radicle (young root), and either one or two cotyledons (seed leaves). In angiosperms and gymnosperms the embryo is protected within a seed. **4** anything in its earliest stages. [from Greek *embryon*, from *en*, in + *bryein*, to swell]

embryological *adj.* relating to embryology or the study of embryos.

embryologist *noun* a person who studies embryology.

embryology *noun* the scientific study of the formation and development of embryos.

embryonic *adj.* in an early stage of development.

Emelye the chaste lady who is loved by Palamon and Arcite in 'The Knight's Tale', in Chaucer's *The Canterbury Tales*.

emend *verb* to edit (a text), removing errors and making improvements. See also AMEND. [from Latin *emendare*]

emendation *noun* a change or correction, especially to a text.

emerald *noun* **1** a deep green variety of beryl, containing chromium, found mainly in metamorphic rocks in Colombia, and highly valued as a gemstone. It can also be manufactured synthetically. **2** (*also* **emerald green**) the colour of this stone. [from Old French *esmeralde*, from Greek *smaragdos*]

Emerald Isle *poetic* Ireland, so called from its greenness.

emerge *verb intrans.* **1** to come out from hiding or into view. **2** to become known or apparent. **3** to survive a difficult or dangerous situation. [from Latin *emergere*]

emergence *noun* emerging; first appearance.

emergency *noun* (PL. **emergencies**) **1** an unexpected and serious happening which calls for immediate and determined action. **2** a serious injury needing immediate medical treatment; or a patient suffering such an injury.

emergent *adj.* emerging; developing.

emeritus *adj.* retired, but retaining a former title as an honour: *emeritus professor / professor emeritus*. [from Latin *mereri*, to earn]

Emerson, Ralph Waldo (1803–82) US poet and essayist, born in Boston, Massachusetts. He became pastor of a Unitarian Church in Boston (1829), but his controversial views caused his resignation. In 1833 he came to Europe and visited Thomas Carlyle, with whom he corresponded for most of his life. In 1834 he moved to Concord, Massachusetts, where he wrote his influential prose rhapsody, *Nature* (1836), and many Transcendental poems and essays, including *The Conduct of Life* (1860).

emery *noun* *Geol.* an impure variety of corundum (aluminium oxide) containing oxides of iron and silica. It is used as an abrasive and polishing material. [from Greek *smyris*, polishing powder]

emery board a small flat strip of wood or card coated with emery powder or some other abrasive, used for filing one's nails.

emery paper *or* **emery cloth** paper or cloth coated with emery, used for cleaning or polishing metal.

emetic — *adj.* *Medicine* causing someone to vomit. *noun* an emetic medicine. [from Greek *emeein*, to vomit]

EMF *abbrev.* **1** (*also* **emf**) electromotive force. **2** European Monetary Fund.

emigrant *noun* a person who emigrates or who has emigrated. [from Latin *emigrare*, to move from a place]

emigrate *verb intrans.* to leave one's native country and settle in another. See also IMMIGRATE. [from Latin *emigrare*, to move from a place]

emigration *noun* emigrating; departure to settle in another country.

émigré *noun* a person who has emigrated, usually for political reasons. [from French *émigré*, from Latin *emigrare*, to move from a place]

Emilia 1 the wife of Iago, and honest lady-in-waiting to Desdemona, in Shakespeare's *Othello*. **2** The long-suffering beloved of Peregrine in Tobias Smollett's *Peregrine Pickle*.

Emily a female first name. [a medieval form of Latin *Aemilia*, probably from *aemulus*, rival]

eminence *noun* **1** honour, distinction, or prestige. **2** an area of high ground. **3** (**Your** *or* **His eminence**) a title of honour used in speaking to or about a cardinal. [from Latin *eminere*, to stand out]

éminence grise (PL. **éminences grises**) a person who has great influence over a ruler, government, etc, without occupying an official position of power. [French, = grey eminence, first applied to Cardinal Richelieu's private secretary, Father Joseph]

eminent *adj.* famous and admired.

eminently *adv.* **1** very. **2** obviously.

Emin Pasha, originally **Eduard Schnitzer** (1840–92) German doctor and explorer, born of Jewish parents in Neisse. He studied medicine in Germany, then adopted the Muslim faith and took the name of Emin Effendi (1876). He joined the Egyptian service and became Governor of the Equatorial Province (1878) with the title of Bey and (later) Pasha. A skilful linguist, he added to the knowledge of African languages, anthropology, geography, and natural history, and also attempted to suppress the slave trade. Although isolated and hemmed-in by enemies, he was reluctant to be 'rescued' by Stanley's expedition (1889), and soon returned to carry out further explorations, only to be murdered by Arab slave-traders.

emir *noun* a title given to various Muslim rulers, especially in the Middle East or W Africa. [from Arabic *amir*, ruler]

emirate *noun* the position or authority of, or the territory ruled by, an emir.

emissary *noun* (PL. **emissaries**) **1** a person sent on a mission, especially on behalf of a government. **2** a person sent with a message. [from Latin *emissarius*]

emission *noun* **1** the act of emitting. **2** something emitted, especially heat, light, or gas. [from Latin *emissio*, a sending out]

emissive *adj.* having the power to emit energy, eg heat, light.

emit *verb* (**emitted**, **emitting**) to give out (light, heat, a sound, a smell, etc). [from Latin *emittere*, to send out]

Emlyn a male first name. [Welsh; probably derived from Latin *Aemilius* (see EMILY)]

Emma a female first name. [originally a short form of compound names with Germanic *erm* or *irm*, entire, and now an independent name]

Emma a novel by Jane Austen (1816). It centres on the journey to maturity of the self-righteous heroine Emma Woodhouse.

Emmental *or* **Emmenthal** *noun* a mild hard Swiss cheese with holes in it. [from *Emmenthal*, a valley in Switzerland]

Emmet, Robert (1778–1803) Irish patriot, born in Dublin. He joined the United Irishmen, and during his travels for the Irish cause on the Continent, he met Napoleon. In 1803 he plotted a fruitless insurrection against the English, for which he was hanged.

emollient — *adj.* **1** *Medicine* softening or soothing the skin. **2** *formal* advocating a calmer, more peaceful attitude. — *noun* *Medicine* a substance which softens or soothes the skin. [from Latin *emollire*, to soften]

emolument *noun* *formal* (*often in pl.*) any money earned or otherwise gained through a job or position, eg salary or fees. [from Latin *emolumentum*, a corn-grinder's fee, from *molere*, to grind]

emote *verb intrans.* *derog. colloq.* to display exaggerated or insincere emotion.

emotion *noun* a strong feeling. [from Latin *emovere*, to stir up, disturb]

emotional *adj.* **1** of the emotions. **2** causing or expressing emotion. **3** *said of a person* tending to express emotions easily or excessively. **4** *often derog.* based on emotions, rather than rational thought: *an emotional response*.

emotionalism *noun* *often derog.* the tendency to be too easily affected or excited by the emotions.

emotionally *adv.* in an emotional way.

emotionless *adj.* having no emotions; without feeling.

emotive *adj.* tending, or designed, to excite emotion. [from Latin *emovere*, to stir, disturb]

emotively *adv.* so as to excite emotion: *talked emotively about her childhood*.

empanel *verb* (**empanelled**, **empanelling**) **1** to enter (the names of prospective jurors) on a list. **2** to select (a jury) from such a list.

empathetic *adj.* able to share others' feelings.

empathize *or* **empathise** *verb intrans.* (**empathize with someone**) to share their feelings.

empathy *noun* the ability to share and understand another person's feelings. [from Greek *empatheia*, passion, affection]

Empedocles (c.490–c.430 BC) Greek philosopher and poet, born in Acragas, Sicily. In *On Nature* he agreed with Parmenides that there could be no absolute coming to exist or ceasing to exist; all change in the world is the result of two contrary cosmic forces, Love and Strife, mixing and separating four everlasting elements, Earth, Water, Air, and Fire. The doctrine of four elements became central to Western thought for 2 000 years following its adoption by Aristotle.

emperor *noun* the male ruler of an empire or of a country which was once the centre of an empire. See also EMPRESS. [from Old French *emperere*, from Latin *imperator*, commander]

Emperor Concerto, The Beethoven's Piano Concerto No.5 in E flat (Op 73, 1809).

emperor moth *Zool.* a large broad-winged moth found in Europe, N America, and Asia, with a large eyespot on each of the wings, which are greyish-purple in females and brown, purple, and orange in males. The scent emitted by the females can be detected by males at a distance of over 1km.

emperor penguin the largest species of penguin, found in the Antarctic.

emphasis *noun* (PL. **emphases**) **1** (**emphasis on something**) special importance or attention given to it. **2** greater force or loudness on certain words or parts of words to show that they are important or have a special meaning. **3** force or firmness of expression. [from Greek *emphasis*, outward appearance, implied meaning]

emphasize *or* **emphasise** *verb* to put emphasis on.

emphatic *adj.* **1** expressed with or expressing emphasis. **2** *said of a person* speaking firmly and forcefully. [from Greek *emphatikos*]

emphatically *adv.* with emphasis or forceful expression: *replied emphatically that he was not going*.

emphysema *noun Medicine* the presence of air in the body tissues. In *pulmonary emphysema*, the alveoli (air sacs) of the lungs become over-inflated and damaged, resulting in a reduction in the surface area over which oxygen and carbon dioxide can be exchanged, and causing laboured breathing. This condition is associated with chronic bronchitis and smoking, particularly in elderly men. [from Greek, from *emphysaein*, to swell]

empire *noun* **1** a group of nations or states under the control of a single ruler or ruling power, especially an emperor or empress. **2** the period of time during which such control is exercised. **3** a large commercial or industrial organization controlling many separate firms, especially one headed by one person. **4** *often facetious* that part of an organization, a company, etc under the management of a particular person. **5** *formal, literary* supreme control or power. See also EMPEROR, EMPRESS, IMPERIAL. [from Old French *empire*, from Latin *imperium*, command, power]

empire-builder *noun* a person who seeks to acquire extra personal authority, responsibility, etc, within an organization.

empire-building *noun colloq., often derog.* the practice of acquiring extra personal authority within an organization, usually by expanding personnel and resources.

Empire State Building an office block in Manhattan, New York City, designed by the firm of Shreve, Lamb & Harman (1930–1). It was the tallest building in the world until 1954. It is 449m high (including a 68m high television mast added in 1951).

Empire Style a French style of decoration associated with Napoleon I's court after he became emperor in 1804. It is massive, and heavily ornamented with classicizing motifs, particularly Egyptian sphinxes, winged lions, and caryatids. The style was seen mainly in furniture, and also in costume; women wore richly embroidered floor-length 'Grecian' dresses, with high waists, while men favoured high-collared shirts, cravats, waistcoats, and tailcoats. The equivalent style in Britain was *Regency*.

empirical *or* **empiric** *adj.* **1** based on experiment, observation, or experience, rather than on theory. **2** regarding experiment and observation as more important than scientific law. [from Greek *empeiria*, experience]

empirical formula *Chem.* a chemical formula showing the simplest possible ratio of atoms in a molecule.

empirically *adv.* by means of experiment rather than theory.

empiricism *noun* **1** *Philos.* the theory or philosophy stating that knowledge can only be gained through experiment and observation. **2** the application of empirical methods, eg to science.

empiricist *noun* a person who believes in experiment as a basis of knowledge.

emplacement *noun* **1** *Mil.* a strongly defended position from which a field gun may be fired. **2** *formal* the act of putting, or the state of having been put, into place. [from French *emplacement*]

employ — *verb* **1** to give (usually paid) work to. **2** (**be employed in something**) to have one's time and attention devoted to it: *busily employed in writing letters.* **3** to use. — *noun formal* the state of being in paid work; employment. [from French *employer*]

employable *adj., said of a person* suitable to be employed.

employed *adj.* having a job; working.

employee *noun* a person who works for another in return for payment.

employer *noun* a person or company that employs workers.

employment *noun* **1** the act of employing or the state of being employed. **2** an occupation, esp regular paid work. See also UNEMPLOYMENT.

employment agency an organization which finds jobs for people, and workers for companies seeking them.

employment exchange the former name for a job centre.

emporium *noun* (PL. **emporiums, emporia**) *formal* a shop, especially a large one selling a wide variety of goods. [from Greek *emporion*, trading station]

empower *verb* (**empowered, empowering**) (**empower someone to do something**) to give them authority or official permission to do it.

empress *noun* **1** the female ruler of an empire or of a country which was once the centre of an empire. **2** the wife or widow of an emperor. [from Old French *emperesse*, from *emperere*, emperor]

Empson, Sir William (1906–84) English poet and critic, born in Howden, Yorkshire. He became Professor of English Literature at Tokyo (1931–4) and Peking (1937–9, 1947–53), working in the interim with the BBC's Far Eastern Service. In 1953 he became Professor of English Literature at Sheffield University. He wrote several major critical works, notably *Seven Types of Ambiguity* (1930); his *Collected Poems* were published in 1955.

emptily *adv.* with an empty manner; without meaning: *replied emptily that he didn't know.*

emptiness *noun* an empty state; being empty.

empty — *adj.* (**emptier, emptiest**) **1** having nothing inside. **2** not occupied, inhabited, or furnished. **3** not likely to be satisfied or carried out: *empty promises.* **4** (**empty of something**) completely without it: *a life empty of meaning.* — *verb trans., intrans.* (**empties, emptied**) **1** to make or become empty. **2** to tip, pour, or fall out of a container. — *noun* (PL. **empties**) *colloq.* an empty container, especially a bottle. [from Anglo-Saxon *æmetig*, unoccupied]

empty-handed *adj.* **1** carrying nothing. **2** having gained or achieved nothing.

empty-headed *adj.* foolish; having no capacity for serious thought.

empyreal *adj. literary* relating to the sky.

empyrean *noun poetic* (*usually* **the empyrean**) the sky. [from Latin *empyreus*, from Greek *empyros*, fiery]

EMS *abbrev.* European Monetary System.

Ems, River, Dutch **Eems**, ancient **Amisia** a river in NW Germany, length 328km/204mi. It rises N of Paderborn, and meanders W and N to the North Sea, forming a 32km-/20mi-long estuary. It is linked to the Ruhr via the Dortmund-Ems Canal.

Ems telegram a despatch (13 Jul 1870) describing the refusal of William (Wilhelm) I of Prussia to accept French conditions over the disputed candidature to the Spanish throne. Altered and published by Bismarck, it helped achieve his aim of provoking Napoleon III of France into declaring war on Prussia.

EMU *abbrev.* Economic and Monetary Union (between EC countries).

emu *noun* a large flightless but swift-running bird, almost 2m tall with coarse brown plumage, found in deserts, plains, and forests in Australia. Emus raid crops and waterholes, and are regarded as a pest by farmers. [from Portuguese *ema*, ostrich]

emulate *verb* **1** to try hard to equal or be better than. **2** to imitate. [from Latin *aemulari*, to rival]

emulation *noun* emulating; trying to equal someone else.

emulsifier *or* **emulsifying agent** a chemical substance that coats the surface of droplets of one liquid so that they can remain dispersed throughout a second liquid, forming a stable emulsion. Emulsifiers are used in the food industry to prevent the coalescence of oil droplets in oil-water emulsions such as margarine, ice cream, and salad cream.

emulsify *verb trans., intrans.* (**emulsifies, emulsified**) to make or become an emulsion.

emulsion — *noun* **1** *Chem.* a colloid consisting of a stable mixture of two immiscible liquids (such as oil and water), in which small droplets of one liquid are dispersed uniformly throughout the other, eg salad cream, low-fat spreads. **2** *Photog.* the light-sensitive material that is used to coat photographic film, paper, etc. **3** emulsion paint. — *verb colloq.* to apply emulsion paint to. [from Latin *emulgere*, to drain out]

emulsion paint water-based paint.

EN *abbrev.* Enrolled Nurse.

en- *prefix* **1** forming verbs with the meaning 'put into, on, or on to': *entrust / enthrone.* **2** forming verbs with the meaning 'cause to be': *enrich / enfeeble.* **3** forming verbs with the meaning 'in, into' or with a meaning simply stronger than that of the base verb: *entangle / enliven.*

-en *suffix* **1** forming verbs with the meaning 'make or become (more)': *deepen / sc'.en.* **2** forming verbs with the meaning 'give, endow with': *strengthen.* **3** forming adjectives with the meaning 'made or consisting of': *wooden.*

enable *verb* **1** to make able; to give the necessary means, power, or authority to. **2** to make possible.

enact *verb* **1** to act or perform, on stage or in real life. **2** to establish by law.

enactment *noun formal* **1** the act of passing, or the passing of, a parliamentary bill into law. **2** that which is enacted; a law.

enamel — *noun* **1** a hardened coloured glass-like substance applied as a decorative or protective covering to metal or glass. **2** any paint or varnish which gives a finish similar to this. **3** the hard white covering of the teeth. — *verb* (**enamelled, enamelling**) to cover or decorate with enamel. [from Old French *enameler*, from *esmail*, enamel]

enamoured *adj.* **1** (**enamoured with someone**) *formal, literary* in love with them. **2** (**enamoured of something**) very fond of it, pleased with it, or enthusiastic about it. [from Old French *enamourer*, from *amour*, love]

en bloc *adv.* all together; as one unit. [from French *en bloc*, in a block]

enc. *abbrev.* **1** enclosed. **2** enclosure.

encamp *verb trans., intrans.* to settle in a camp.

encampment *noun* settlement in a camp.

encapsulate *verb* **1** to express concisely the main points or ideas of, or capture the essence of. **2** to enclose in, or as if in, a capsule.

encapsulation *noun* encapsulating; precise expression of an idea.

emu

encase *verb* **1** to enclose in, or as if in, a case. **2** to surround or cover.

encasement *noun* enclosing in a case.

encash *verb* to convert into cash; to cash.

encaustic — *adj.*, *said of ceramics* decorated using pigments melted in wax and burnt into the clay. — *noun* **1** the technique which uses pigments in this way. **2** a piece of pottery or any other article decorated using this technique. [from Greek *enkaustikos*, from *enkaiein*, to burn in]
◇ Encaustic painting was one of the principal techniques of painting in ancient civilizations. The most famous surviving examples are the 1c BC–3c AD mummy portraits from Faiyum, Egypt.

-ence *suffix* forming nouns indicating: **1** a state or quality, or an action, etc which shows a state or quality: *confidence / diligence / impertinence*. **2** an action: *reference*. [from French *-ence*, from Latin *-entia*]

encephalin *or* **enkephalin** *noun Biochem.* either of two chemical compounds that occur naturally in the brain and spinal cord, and have pain-relieving properties similar to those of morphine and other opiates. [from Greek *en*, in + *kephale*, head]

encephalitis *noun Medicine* inflammation of the brain, usually as a result of a viral or bacterial infection, or an allergic reaction (especially to certain vaccines). Its symptoms include headache, fever, vomiting, mental confusion, and eventually coma. [from Greek *enkephalos*, brain + *-ITIS*]

encephalo- *or* **encephal-** *combining form Anat.* forming words relating to the brain. [from Greek *enkephalos*, from *en*, in + *kephale*, head]

encephalogram, encephalograph same as ELECTROENCEPHALOGRAM, ELECTROENCEPHALOGRAPH.

enchain *verb literary* **1** to put in chains. **2** to hold or fix (attention, etc). [from French *enchaîner*]

enchant *verb* **1** to charm or delight. **2** to put a magic spell on. [from French *enchanter*, from Latin *incantare*, to sing a magic spell over]

enchanted *adj.* charmed; bewitched.

enchanter *or* **enchantress** *noun* **1** a person who casts spells. **2** a charming person, especially one who sets out to be so.

enchanting *adj.* charming; delightful.

enchantingly *adv.* in an enchanting or delightful way.

enchantment *noun* **1** the act of enchanting or state of being enchanted. **2** a magic spell. **3** charm; attraction.

enchilada *noun* a Mexican dish consisting of a flour tortilla with a meat filling, served with a chilli-flavoured sauce. [from Spanish *enchilar*, to season with chilli]

encircle *verb* to surround, form a circle round.

encirclement *noun* encircling, especially of territory.

Encke's comet *Astron.* the comet with the shortest known orbital period, 3.3 years. [named after the German astronomer Johann Franz Encke]

encl. *abbrev.* **1** enclosed. **2** enclosure.

enclave *noun* **1** a small country or state entirely surrounded by foreign territory. **2** a distinct racial or cultural group isolated within a country. [from French *enclave*, from Latin *inclavare*, to lock up]

enclose *verb* **1** to put inside a letter or its envelope. **2** to shut in or surround.

enclosed *adj.* put inside something, especially an envelope.

enclosure *noun* **1** the process of enclosing or being enclosed, especially with reference to common land. **2** land surrounded by a fence or wall.

3 an enclosed space at a sporting event. **4** an additional paper or other item included with a letter.
◇ In England, the process of transferring common land to private hands had begun in the 14c, gathering pace in the 15c and 16c, as large landowners tried to increase the income from their estates. The enclosure of land caused widespread poverty and homelessness among the rural population, and there were revolts in 1536, 1569, and 1607. From c.1760 to 1820, parliamentary Enclosure Acts formalized the process, and many small landowners were reduced to agricultural labourers or forced off the land altogether. Enclosure of land was limited by statute in 1876.

encode *verb* to express in or convert into code.

encomiastic *adj. literary* serving as an encomium; flattering.

encomium *noun* (PL. **emporiums, emporia**) *formal* a formal speech or piece of writing praising someone. [from Greek *enkomion*, song of praise]

encompass *verb* **1** to include or contain, especially contain a wide range or coverage of. **2** to surround. **3** to cause or bring about.

encore — *noun* a repetition of a performance, or an additional performed item, after the end of a concert, etc. — *interj.* an enthusiastic call from the audience for such a peformance. — *verb* to call for an extra performance of or from. [from French *encore*, again]

encounter — *verb* (**encountered, encountering**) **1** to meet, especially unexpectedly. **2** to meet with (difficulties, etc). **3** to meet in battle or conflict. — *noun* **1** a chance meeting. **2** a fight or battle. [from Old French *encontrer*, from Latin *contra*, against]

encounter group *Psychol.* a group of people formed to discuss personal problems and feelings openly in order to arrive at a better understanding of themselves and others.

encourage *verb* **1** to give support, confidence, or hope to. **2** to urge someone to do something. **3** to promote or recommend. [from French *encourager*]

encouragement *noun* support; a source of increased confidence.

encouraging *adj.* giving support or courage.

encouragingly *adv.* so as to increase courage or confidence: *an encouragingly good response*.

encroach *verb intrans.* (*usually* **encroach on someone** *or* **something**) **1** to intrude or extend gradually or stealthily on someone else's land, etc. **2** to go beyond the fair limits of a right, etc. **3** to overstep proper or agreed limits. [from Old French *encrochier*, to seize]

encroachment *noun* encroaching; intrusion on another's territory or rights.

encrust *verb* to cover with a thick hard coating, eg of jewels or ice. [from Latin *incrustare*]

encrustation *noun* encrusting; a hard crust or coating.

encumber *verb* (**encumbered, encumbering**) **1** to prevent the free and easy movement of; to hamper or impede. **2** to burden with a load or debt. [from Old French *encombrer*, to block]

encumbrance *noun* an impediment, hindrance or burden.

-ency *suffix* forming nouns indicating a state or quality, or something which shows a state or quality: *efficiency / inconsistency*. [from Latin *-entia*]

encyclical — *noun Relig.* a letter sent by the pope to all Roman Catholic bishops. — *adj. formal, said of a letter* for general or wide circulation. [from Greek *enkyklios*, from *en*, in + *kyklos*, circle]

Encyclopaedia Britannica the first edition was published in Edinburgh (1768–71), edited by William Smellie. It was edited and published there until 1901, when it was bought by

two US publishers, but continued to be published in the UK. The 10th edition was sponsored by *The Times* and the 11th edition published by Cambridge University Press, with editorial work for both of these being carried out in the USA and the UK. Encyclopaedia Britannica, Inc was set up in Chicago in 1941. The 15th edition is supplied in 29 volumes.

encyclopedia *or* **encyclopaedia** *noun* a reference work containing information on every branch of knowledge, or on one particular branch, usually arranged in alphabetical order. [from Greek *enkyklios paideia*, general education]
◇ The most notable developments took place in 18c Britain and France with Ephraim Chambers' *Cyclopaedia* (1728), the 35-volume *Encyclopédie* of Diderot and his associates (1751–76), and the first edition of the *Encyclopaedia Britannica* (1768–71).

encyclopedic *or* **encyclopaedic** *adj.* **1** *said of knowledge* full and detailed. **2** of, belonging to, or like an encyclopedia.

encyclopedist *or* **encyclopaedist** *noun* a compiler of encyclopedias.

Encyclopedists a collective term for the distinguished editors (Diderot and d'Alembert) and contributors (notably Voltaire, Montesquieu, Condorcet, and Rousseau) of the *Encyclopédie*, a major work of social and political reference published in France (1751–72) and associated with the French Enlightenment.

end — *noun* **1** the point or part farthest from the beginning, or either of the points or parts farthest from the middle, where something stops. **2** a finish or conclusion: *come to an end*. **3** a piece left over: *a cigarette end*. **4** death or destruction: *meet one's end*. **5** an object or purpose: *the ends justify the means*. **6** *Sport* one of the two halves of a pitch or court defended by a team, player, etc. **7** the part of a project, etc for which one is responsible: *they've had a few problems at their end*. — *verb trans., intrans.* to finish or cause to finish; to reach a conclusion or cease to exist.
— **at the end of the day** *colloq.* when everything has been taken into account.
end it all *colloq.* to kill oneself.
the end of the road the point beyond which one cannot continue or survive.
end on *or* **end to end** with ends touching.
end up ... *colloq.* **1** to arrive or find oneself ... eventually: *we ended up in Manchester*. **2** (**end up as ...**) to become ... finally: *they ended up as circus clowns*.
in the end finally; after much discussion, work, etc.
keep *or* **hold one's end up** *colloq.* to fulfil one's promises or obligations in spite of difficulties.
make ends meet to live within one's income and avoid debts.
no end *colloq.* very much; very many.
on end 1 vertical; standing straight up. **2** continuously; without a pause.
[from Anglo-Saxon *ende*]

endanger *verb* (**endangered, endangering**) to put in danger; to expose to possible loss or injury.

endangered species any plant or animal species that is in danger of extinction in the near future. A species may become endangered because its populations have fallen to very low levels, or because it only occurs naturally in a few restricted areas.
◇ The main threat to endangered species is destruction of their natural habitats, especially as a result of deforestation or the draining of marshland to provide land for agricultural or other purposes, eg urban developments. Hunting threatens the survival of some animals, while pollution of seas and rivers is a threat to aquatic life. According to the World Wide Fund for Nature, the black rhinoceros is the most endangered of the large mammals, and has been hunted until there are only about 3 000 animals in the whole

of Africa. One of the rarest of all plants is the giant rafflesia, which grows on the rainforest floor in Malaysia, and produces the largest flowers of any known plant. Other examples of endangered animals and plants include the blue whale, monk seal, giant panda, polar bear, orangutan, whooping crane, bald eagle, and lady's slipper orchid.

Endangered Animals

Animal	Where last seen	Est. No.
Asiatic buffalo	India, Nepal	2 200
Blue whale	World oceans	7 500
Bontebok (antelope)	South Africa	800
Crested ibis (wading bird)	Japan	< 12
European bison	Poland	>1 000*
Everglades kite	Florida	100
Florida panther	Florida	< 300
Giant panda	China	200
Imperial eagle	Spain	100
Indian rhinoceros	India, Nepal	< 600
Java rhinoceros	Indonesia	< 100
Kakapo (parrot)	New Zealand	< 100
Key deer	North America	600
Mediterranean monk seal	Mediterranean Sea	500
Orang-utan	Borneo, Sumatra	5 000
Père David's deer	China	600*
Polar bear	Arctic	8 000
Przewalski's horse	Central Asia	40–60*
Siberian tiger	USSR, China, Korea	< 200
Southern bald eagle	North America	600
Whooping cranes	North America	About 50

* Saved from extinction by zoos.

endear *verb* (**endear someone to someone** *or* **something**) to cause them to be beloved or liked.

endearing *adj.* arousing feelings of affection.

endearingly *adv.* with an endearing or affectionate manner.

endearment *noun* **1** a word or phrase expressing affection. **2** affection or fondness.

endeavour — *verb* (**endeavour to do something**) to try to do it, especially seriously and with effort. — *noun* a determined attempt or effort. [from Middle English *endeveren*, to exert oneself, from French *devoir*, duty]

endemic *adj., said of a disease, etc* regularly occurring in a particular area or among a particular group of people. [from Greek *endemos*, native]

Ender, Kornelia (1958–) German swimmer, born in Bitterfeld. She won three Olympic silver medals in 1972, aged 13, and between 1973 and 1976 broke 23 world records (the most by a woman under modern conditions). At the 1973 and 1975 world championships she won 10 medals, including a record eight golds. In 1976 she became the first woman to win four gold medals at one Olympic Games: the 100m and 200m freestyle, the 100m butterfly, and the 4×100m medley relay.

Enders, John Franklin (1897–1985) US bacteriologist, born in West Hartford, Connecticut. He shared with Frederick Robbins and Thomas Weller the 1954 Nobel Prize for Physiology or Medicine for the cultivation of polio viruses in human tissue cells, thus greatly advancing virology and making possible the development of a polio vaccine. In 1962 he developed an effective vaccine against measles.

ending *noun* **1** the end, especially of a story, poem, etc. **2** *Grammar* the end part of a word, especially an inflection.

endive *noun* a plant, related to chicory, whose crisp curly or broad leaves are used in salads. [from French *endive*]

endless *adj.* having no end, or seeming to have no end.

endlessly *adv.* without end, or seemingly without end.

endlessness *noun* being endless; lasting for ever.

endmost *adj.* farthest; nearest the end.

endo- *combining form* internal; inside. See also ECTO-, ENTO-, EXO-. [from Greek *endon*, within]

endocarditis *noun Medicine* inflammation of the delicate membrane that lines the heart (the endocardium) and of the heart valves. [from Greek *endon*, within + *kardia*, heart]

endocrine *adj.* **1** *Physiol.* relating to internal secretions, or to a pathway or structure that secretes internally. **2** *said of a gland* ductless and producing and secreting one or more hormones directly into the bloodstream, eg the pituitary, thyroid, parathyroid, and adrenal glands, and the gonads (the ovary and testis). Such glands are strongly interdependent, often only secreting hormones in response to the presence of other hormones in the bloodstream. See also EXOCRINE. [from ENDO- + Greek *krinein*, to separate]

endocrinology *noun Physiol.* the scientific study of those glands, known as endocrine glands, that produce and secrete hormones, and of the hormones themselves.

endoderm *noun Zool.* in a multicellular animal that has two or more layers of body tissue, the innermost layer of cells of the embryo, which develops into the alimentary canal, liver, pancreas, and other digestive glands of the adult. It also forms the yolk sac and allantois in birds and mammals. [from ENDO- + Greek *derma*, skin]

endodontics *noun Medicine* the branch of dentistry concerned with the diagnosis, treatment, and prevention of disorders of the tooth pulp, including root canal treatment.

endogamy *noun Anthropol.* the practice or rule of marrying only within one's own group. [from ENDO- + Greek *gamos*, marriage]

endometriosis *noun Medicine* the presence of tissue similar to the membrane (the *endometrium*) that lines the uterus (womb), at other sites in the pelvic cavity, eg in the ovary or Fallopian tubes, where it continues to vary in thickness and structure at different times of the menstrual cycle.

endomorph *noun* a person of rounded or plump build, sometimes said to be associated with a calm, easy-going personality. [from ENDO- + Greek *morphe*, form]

endoplasm *noun Biol.* the central portion of the cytoplasm of a cell.

endoplasmic reticulum *Biol.* an extensive convoluted cytoplasmic membrane found in most eukaryotic cells, continuous with both the outer membrane of the nucleus and the plasma membrane of the cell. It is involved in the manufacture and transport of proteins.

endorphin *noun Biochem.* any of a group of chemical compounds that occur naturally in the brain and have similar pain-relieving properties to morphine. They are thought to be involved in the control of emotional responses. The feelings of well-being induced by physical exercise have been attributed to the release of endorphins. [from ENDO- + MORPHINE]

endorse *verb* **1** to write one's signature on the back of (a document), especially on the back of (a cheque) to specify oneself or another person as payee. **2** to make a note of an offence on (a driving licence). **3** to state one's approval of or support for. [from Old French *endosser*, to put on the back, from Latin *dorsum*, back]

endorsement *noun* **1** endorsing or confirming. **2** a signature or other mark endorsing a document. **3** a record of a conviction entered on a driving licence.

endoscope *noun Medicine* a long thin flexible instrument containing bundles of optical fibres and having a light at one end, used for viewing internal body cavities and organs.

endoscopic *adj. Medicine* involving the use of an endoscope.

endoscopy *noun Medicine* examination of the internal organs by means of an endoscope.

endoskeleton *noun Zool.* in vertebrates (animals with backbones), such as mammals, birds, and fish, an internal skeleton made of bone or cartilage.

endothelium *noun* (PL. **endothelia**) *Zool.* a single layer of cells that lines the internal surfaces of the heart, blood vessels, and lymph vessels.

endothermic reaction *Chem.* any process, especially a chemical reaction, that involves the absorption of heat.

endow *verb* **1** to provide a source of income for (a hospital, place of learning, etc). **2** (**to be endowed with something**) to have a quality, ability, etc: *endowed with common sense*. [from Old French *endouer*, from Latin *dos*, dowry]

endowment *noun* the act of endowing; a sum endowed.

endowment assurance *or* **endowment insurance** a form of insurance in which a set sum is paid at a certain date, or earlier in the event of death.

endpaper *noun* one of the two leaves at the front or back of a hardback book, fixed with paste to the inside of the cover, to give strength to the binding.

end-product *noun* the final product of a series of operations, especially industrial processes.

endue *verb* (**endue someone with something**) to provide with a certain quality. [from Old French *enduire*, from Latin *inducere*, to lead in]

endurable *adj.* capable of being endured.

endurance *noun* **1** the capacity for, or the state of, patient toleration. **2** the ability to withstand physical hardship or strain.

endure *verb* **1** to bear patiently, put up with. **2** *intrans. formal* to continue to exist; to last. [from Old French *endurer*, from Latin *indurare*, to harden]

enduring *adj.* lasting.

end-user *noun* a person, company, etc that will buy and use a product that is being sold.

endways *adv.* **1** with the end forward or upward. **2** end to end.

Endymion in Greek mythology, a handsome shepherd of Mount Latmos (or the King of Elis), who was loved by the moon goddess Selene. Zeus put him into a perpetual sleep, while Selene looked after his flocks, and visited him every night.

Endymion **1** a poem in four books by John Keats (1818). It is based on the Greek legend of the young shepherd Endymion, who falls asleep on Mount Latmos and becomes enamoured with the moon goddess. **2** a novel by Benjamin Disraeli (1880). His last, it is set against the political background of the 1830s and focuses on the rising fortunes of Endymion and his twin sister Myra.

enema *noun Medicine* **1** the injection of a liquid into the rectum. **2** the liquid injected. [from Greek *enienai*, to send in]

enemy — *noun* (PL. **enemies**) **1** a person who is actively opposed to someone else. **2** a hostile nation or force, or a member of it. **3** an opponent or adversary. **4** a person, thing, etc that opposes or acts against: *cleanliness is the enemy of disease.* — *adj.* hostile; belonging to a hostile nation or force. [from Old French *enemi*, from Latin *inimicus*]

energetic *adj.* having or displaying energy; forceful; vigorous. [from Greek *energetikos*]

energetically *adv.* with energy or vigour; forcefully.

energize *or* **energise** *verb* **1** to stimulate, invigorate, or enliven. **2** to provide energy for the operation of (a machine, etc).

energy *noun* (PL. **energies**) **1** the capacity for vigorous activity; liveliness or vitality. **2** force or forcefulness. **3** *Physics* the capacity to do work. Within a particular system, energy may be converted from one form to another, but is neither created nor destroyed, so the total energy content of the system remains constant (the law of conservation of energy). [from Greek *energeia*, from *en*, in + *ergon*, work]
◇ The many different forms of energy include electrical, chemical, mechanical, and nuclear energy, heat, light, and sound. All of these can be regarded as aspects of kinetic energy (energy of motion) or potential energy ('stored' energy of position). Most of the Earth's energy is derived from the Sun, where it is produced by nuclear fusion. The other main energy sources are fossil fuels (petroleum, coal, and natural gas), nuclear energy, and hydroelectricity. The SI unit of energy is the joule (symbol J), which is the work done when a force of one newton moves through a distance of one metre. The rate at which energy is delivered is known as power.

energy conservation *Environ.* the reduction or avoidance of energy loss or wastage by various means, including insulation, and the adoption of new or different patterns of energy use.

energy level *Physics* one of the fixed amounts of energy that an electron in an atom can possess at any given time.

enervate *verb* **1** to take energy or strength from. **2** to deprive of moral or mental vigour. [from Latin *enervare*, to weaken]

enervating *adj.* depriving of vigour.

enervation *noun* being enervated or deprived of vigour.

Enfants Du Paradis, Les (Children of Paradise) a French film directed by Marcel Carné (1944). It is a masterful romantic drama set in the theatre world of 19c Paris, starring Arletty and Jean-Louis Barrault.

enfant terrible *noun* (PL. ***enfants terribles***) a person with a reputation for rude or embarrassing behaviour in public. [French, = dreadful child]

enfeeble *verb formal* to make weak.

enfeebled *adj.* made weak.

enfeeblement *noun* making weak.

enfilade *Mil.* — *noun* a continuous burst of gunfire sweeping from end to end across a line of enemy soldiers. — *verb* to direct an enfilade at. [from French *enfiler*, to thread]

enfold *verb* **1** to wrap up, enclose. **2** to embrace.

enforce *verb* **1** to cause (a law or decision) to be carried out. **2** (**enforce something on someone**) to impose (one's will, etc) on them. **3** to strengthen (an argument). **4** to persist in (a demand). [from Old French *enforcer*]

enforceable *adj.* capable of being enforced.

enforced *adj.* not voluntary or optional.

enforcement *noun* the process of enforcing.

enfranchise *verb formal* **1** to give the right to vote in elections. **2** to set free, especially from slavery. **3** to give (a town) the right to be represented in parliament. [from Old French *enfranchir*, to set free]

enfranchisement *noun* the conferring of rights, especially to vote in elections.

engage *verb* **1** to take on as a worker. **2** to book or reserve. **3** (**engage someone in something**) to involve or occupy them in it: *she engaged me in small talk.* **4** *intrans., trans. Mil.* to come or bring into battle: *engage the enemy / engage with the enemy.* **5** *trans., intrans.* to cause

part of a machine, etc to fit into and lock with another part: *engage a gear / the gears engage.* [from French *engager*]

engagé *adj.* having or showing a political or moral commitment. [French, = engaged]

engaged *adj.* **1** (**engaged to someone**) bound by a promise to marry them. **2** (**engaged in something**) busy or occupied with it. **3** *said of a room, etc* not free or vacant; occupied; being used.

engagement *noun* **1** the act of engaging or state of being engaged. **2** a firm agreement between two people to marry. **3** an arrangement made in advance; an appointment. **4** *Mil.* a battle.

engaging *adj.* charming or attractive.

engagingly *adv.* with a charming or attractive manner.

Engels, Friedrich (1820–95) German socialist philosopher and founder of 'scientific socialism', born in Barmen. From 1842 he lived mostly in England. He first met Karl Marx in Brussels in 1844, collaborated with him on the *Communist Manifesto* (1848), and later edited and translated Marx's writings.

engender *verb* (**engendered, engendering**) to produce or cause (especially feelings or emotions). [from French *engendrer*]

engine *noun* **1** a machine that is used to convert some form of energy, especially the heat energy released by a burning fuel, into mechanical energy that can be used to perform useful work. In internal combustion engines (petrol, diesel, and gas-turbine engines) the fuel is burned inside the engine, whereas in external combustion engines (eg steam engines) it is burned outside the engine in a boiler. **2** a railway locomotive. **3** *formal* a device or instrument: *an engine of destruction.* [from Old French *engin*, from Latin *ingenium*, device]

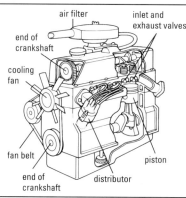

car engine

engine-driver *noun* a person who drives a railway locomotive.

engineer — *noun* **1** a person who designs, makes, or works with machinery. **2** (*also* **civil engineer**) a person who designs or constructs roads, railways, bridges, etc. **3** an officer in charge of a ship's engines. **4** a person, especially a member of the armed forces, who designs and builds military apparatus. — *verb* **1** *often derog.* to arrange or bring about by skill or deviousness. **2** to design or construct as an engineer.

engineering *noun* the application of scientific knowledge, especially that concerned with matter and energy, to the practical problems of design, construction, operation, and maintenance of devices encountered in everyday life.
◇ Such devices include machinery, engines, buildings, roads, bridges, different forms of transport (including aircraft and spacecraft), telecommunications, computers, radio, television, and other electronic devices.
The main branches of engineering are civil, mechanical, electrical, electronic, chemical, mining, metallurgical, aeronautical, agricultural and

marine, all of which have played a major role in the development of modern civilization.

England, Latin **Anglia** POP (1981) 46.2m, the largest area within the United Kingdom, forming the S part of the island of Great Britain, divided into 46 counties. AREA 130 357sq km/ 50 318sq mi. It is bounded N by Scotland, S by the English Channel, E by the North Sea, and W by Wales, the Atlantic Ocean, and the Irish Sea. The area includes the Isles of Scilly, Lundy, and the Isle of Wight. CAPITAL London. CHIEF TOWNS Birmingham, Bristol, Leeds, Liverpool, Manchester, Newcastle upon Tyne, Plymouth, Sheffield; chief ports are at Felixstowe, Grimsby, Immingham, Portsmouth, Southampton, and Tilbury. Most of the population are of Anglo-Saxon origin, with Asian, African, and many other minorities; the chief religions are Protestantism and Roman Catholicism. OFFICIAL LANGUAGE English. CURRENCY the pound sterling. HISTORY taken by Julius Caesar in 55 BC; invasion by Nordic tribes in the 5c forced many Celtic groups into Cornwall and Wales; England unified in 924–939; taken by William of Normandy in

Monarchs of England	
Saxons	
827–39	Egbert
839–58	Ethelwulf
858–60	Ethelbald
860–6	Ethelbert
866–71	Ethelred I
871–99	Alfred the Great
899–924	Edward the Elder
924–39	Athelstan
939–46	Edmund
946–55	Edred
955–9	Edwy
959–75	Edgar
975–8	Edward the Martyr
978–1016	Ethelred II the Unready
1016	Edmund Ironside
Danes	
1016–35	Canute
1035–40	Harold I Harefoot
1040–2	Hardicanute
Saxons	
1042–66	Edward the Confessor
1066	Harold II
House of Normandy	
1066–87	William I the Conqueror
1087–1100	William II
1100–35	Henry I
1135–54	Stephen
House of Plantagenet	
1154–89	Henry II
1189–99	Richard I
1199–1216	John
1216–72	Henry III
1272–1307	Edward I
1307–27	Edward II
1327–77	Edward III
1377–99	Richard II
House of Lancaster	
1399–1413	Henry IV
1413–22	Henry V
1422–61	Henry VI
House of York	
1461–83	Edward IV
1483	Edward V
1483–5	Richard III
House of Tudor	
1485–1509	Henry VII
1509–47	Henry VIII
1547–53	Edward VI
1553	Jane
1553–8	Mary I
1558–1603	Elizabeth I

see continuation at **Great Britain**

1066; the Magna Carta was signed in 1215; conquered Wales in 1284; the War of the Roses from 1455 until 1485 resulted in the Tudors becoming the ruling family; there was major colonial expansion in the 16c; Charles I was executed in 1649 after seven years of war between Royalists and Parliamentarians; the Act of Union was signed in 1707. PHYSICAL DESCRIPTION largely undulating lowland, rising in the S to the Mendips, Cotswolds, Chilterns, and North Downs, in the N to the N–S ridge of the Pennines, and in the NW to the Cumbria Mts; drained in the E by the Tyne, Tees, Humber, Ouse, and Thames rivers and in the W by the Eden, Ribble, Mersey, and Severn rivers; the Lake District in the NW includes Derwent Water, Ullswater, Windermere, and Bassenthwaite. ECONOMY minerals (coal, tin, china clay, salt, potash, lead ore, iron ore), North Sea oil and gas; vehicles, heavy engineering; petrochemicals, pharmaceuticals; textiles; food processing; electronics; telecommunications; publishing; brewing; pottery; fishing; livestock, agriculture, horticulture; tourism.

English — *adj.* **1** relating to England or the people of England. **2** *chiefly North Amer.* relating to Great Britain or its inhabitants (this use is often offensive to non-English inhabitants of Britain). **3** of or using the English language. — *noun* **1** the main language of Britain, N America, a great part of the British Commonwealth, and some other countries. **2** (**the English**) the people of England.
— **Middle English** English as spoken and written between about 1150 and 1500.
Old English English as spoken and written until about 1150.
[from Anglo-Saxon *Englisc*]
◇ English belongs to the Germanic branch of the Indo-European family of languages. It has an unbroken literary heritage going back to the inflecting language of the Anglo-Saxons (Old English). Both before and after the Norman Conquest, it has adopted a large number of loan words, particularly from Romance languages such as French and Italian. The language continues to evolve with diverse geographical and cultural influences in and from the many countries of the world in which it is spoken. It is the main international language of book and newspaper publication, science and technology, advertising and pop music, and computer information storage. See panels pp. 420 and 421.

English breakfast a cooked breakfast, usually consisting of several dishes or courses.

English Chamber Orchestra (ABBREV. **ECO**) a chamber orchestra founded (1948) as the Goldsbrough Orchestra by Arnold Goldsbrough and Lawrence Leonard. It changed its name in 1960, when it widened its repertory beyond the 18c, then became the resident orchestra at the Aldeburgh Festival (1961).

English Channel, French **La Manche**, Latin **Mare Britannicum** an arm of the Atlantic Ocean, bounded N by England and S by France. Formed with the rise in sea level after the last glacial period, it is connected to the North Sea in the E by the Straits of Dover (34km/21mi wide). The channel is 565km/351mi long and at its widest point (Lyme Bay–Gulf of St Malo) it measures 240km/149mi. MAIN ISLANDS Isle of Wight, the Channel Is. There are frequent crossings by ferry and hovercraft, linking English and French ports. It is one of the world's busiest shipping lanes. The first aeroplane crossing was made by Louis Blériot in 1909, and the first person to swim across was Matthew Webb in 1875. The Channel tunnel was opened in 1994.

English Civil Wars England's greatest internal conflict (1642–8), fought between supporters of Parliament and supporters of Charles I, following the King's attempts to rule without a parliament. Although the King left London in March

Counties of England				
County	Area sq km	sq mi	Population[1]	Admin centre
Avon[2]	1 347	520	968 000	Bristol
Bedfordshire	1 235	477	537 000	Bedford
Berkshire	1 259	486	758 000	Reading
Buckinghamshire	1 883	727	646 000	Aylesbury
Cambridgeshire	3 409	1 316	678 000	Cambridge
Cheshire	2 328	899	967 000	Chester
Cleveland[2]	583	225	560 000	Middlesbrough
Cornwall	3 564	1 376	475 000	Truro
Cumbria[2]	6 810	2 629	490 000	Carlisle
Derbyshire	2 631	1 016	947 000	Matlock
Devon	6 711	2 590	1 100 000	Exeter
Dorset	2 654	1 024	664 000	Dorchester
Durham	2 436	940	607 000	Durham
Essex	3 672	1 417	1 600 000	Chelmsford
Gloucestershire	2 643	1 022	541 000	Gloucester
Greater London[2]	1 579	609	6 900 000	–
Greater Manchester[2]	1 287	497	2 600 000	–
Hampshire	3 777	1 458	1 600 000	Winchester
Hereford and Worcester[2]	3 926	1 515	690 000	Worcester
Hertfordshire	1 634	631	994 000	Hertford
Humberside[2]	3 512	1 356	881 000	Hull
Isle of Wight	381	147	126 000	Newport
Kent	3 731	1 440	1 500 000	Maidstone
Lancashire	3 063	1 182	1 400 000	Preston
Leicestershire	2 553	985	902 000	Leicester
Lincolnshire	5 915	2 283	597 000	Lincoln
Merseyside[2]	652	252	1 500 000	Liverpool
Norfolk	5 368	2 072	763 000	Norwich
Northamptonshire	2 367	914	590 000	Northampton
Northumberland	5 032	1 942	307 000	Newcastle upon Tyne
Nottinghamshire	2 164	835	1 000 000	Nottingham
Oxfordshire	2 608	1 007	587 000	Oxford
Shropshire	3 490	1 347	413 000	Shrewsbury
Somerset	3 451	1 332	473 000	Taunton
Staffordshire	2 716	1 048	1 100 000	Stafford
Suffolk	3 797	1 466	648 000	Ipswich
Surrey	1 679	648	1 000 000	Kingston upon Thames
Sussex, East	1 795	693	721 000	Lewes
Sussex, West	1 989	768	713 000	Chichester
Tyne and Wear[2]	540	208	1 100 000	Newcastle
Warwickshire	1 981	765	492 000	Warwick
West Midlands[2]	899	559	2 600 000	Birmingham
Wiltshire	3 481	1 344	579 000	Trowbridge
Yorkshire, North	8 309	3 207	723 000	Northallerton
Yorkshire, South	1 560	602	1 300 000	Barnsley
Yorkshire, West	2 039	787	2 100 000	Wakefield

[1]1992 census
[2]New counties in 1974 were formed as follows:
Avon: parts of Somerset and Gloucestershire
Cleveland: parts of Durham and Yorkshire
Cumbria: Cumberland, Westmoreland, parts of Lancashire and Yorkshire
Greater London: London and most of Middlesex
Greater Manchester: parts of Lancashire, Cheshire, and Yorkshire
Hereford and Worcester: Hereford, most of Worcestershire
Humberside: parts of Yorkshire and Lincolnshire
Merseyside: parts of Lancashire and Cheshire
Tyne and Wear: parts of Northumberland and Durham
West Midlands: parts of Staffordshire, Warwickshire, and Worcestershire

1642, open hostilities between Royalists and Parliamentarians did not immediately break out, for both sides feared the consequences of civil strife. Charles finally raised his standard two months later in Nottingham. The first major engagement, which was inconclusive, took place at Edgehill in Oct but Royalist forces then threatened London, the key Parliamentary stronghold. By autumn 1643 the north and the west (apart from a garrison in Gloucester) were in Royalist hands, although Parliament held back the tide in the (drawn) first battle of Newbury. The crucial event of 1643 was Parliament's alliance with the Scots in the Solemn League and Covenant, which led to the major defeat inflicted by Parliament and Scottish invaders at the battle of Marston Moor (Jul 1644). However, the King's forces in the west gained victories over the Earl of Essex in the battle of Lostwithiel (1643), and in the second

battle of Newbury against the combined forces of Essex, the Earl of Manchester, and Sir William Waller. In 1645, strengthened by the creation of the New Model Army, Parliament's cause advanced in the Midlands and the west, with important victories at Naseby and Langport. The first civil war ended in 1646 when Charles surrendered to the Scots at Newark (May) and his Oxford stronghold fell in Jun. Negotiations between the King and Parliament had begun in 1645 with little success, and there was continuing disagreement over religion, in particular Parliament's disestablishment of the Church, and the King's prerogative rights, many of which had been abolished by Parliament. In 1647 the army presented the King with the Heads of Proposals, which demanded both religious toleration and Parliamentary control of the armed forces. Charles made a secret alliance with the Scots,

Speakers of English

The first column gives figures for countries where English is used as a mother-tongue or first language; for countries where no figure is given, English is not the first language of a significant number of people. (A question-mark indicates that no agreed estimates are available.) The second column gives total population figures (*mainly 1990 figures*) for countries where English has official or semi-official status as a medium of communication. These totals are likely to bear little correlation with the real use of English in the area.

Country	First language speakers of English	Country population	Country	First language speakers of English	Country population
Anguilla	8 000 –	8 000	New Zealand	3 000 000	3 389 000
Antigua and Barbuda	80 600 –	80 600	Nigeria	?	119 812 000 +
Australia	14 000 000	17 073 000	Pakistan	?	122 666 000 +
Bahamas	253 000	253 000	Papua New Guinea		3 671 000
Bangladesh	?	113 005 000 +	Philippines		61 480 000
Barbados	257 000 +	257 000 +	St Christopher and Nevis	44 100	44 100
Belize	100 000 +	189 000 +	St Lucia	?	151 000 +
Bermuda	59 300 +	59 300 +	St Vincent and the Grenadines	100 000 +	115 000 +
Bhutan	?	1 442 000 +	Senegambia		600 000
Botswana		1 295 000 –	Seychelles		68 700
Brunei		259 000 +	Sierra Leone		4 151 000
Cameroon		11 900 000 +	Singapore	?	2 718 000
Canada	17 000 000 +	26 620 000 +	Solomon Islands		319 000 +
Dominica	50 000 +	82 200 +	South Africa	2 000 000 +	30 797 000
Fiji		740 000 +	Sri Lanka	?	17 103 000 +
Ghana		15 020 000	Suriname		411 000
Gibraltar		30 689 +	Swaziland		770 000
Grenada	101 000 +	101 000 +	Tanzania		24 403 000
Guyana	700 000 +	756 000	Tonga		96 000 +
Hong Kong	?	5 841 000 –	Trinidad and Tobago	1 233 000	1 233 000
India	?	853 373 000 +	Tuvalu		9 100 +
Irish Republic	3 515 000	3 515 000	Uganda		16 928 000
Jamaica	2 300 000 +	2 391 000	UK	57 000 000 +	57 384 000
Kenya		24 872 000	USA	215 000 000	249 246 000 +
Kiribati		71 100 +	US territories in Pacific		300 000 –
Lesotho		1 760 000	Vanuatu		150 000
Liberia		2 595 000	Western Samoa		165 000 +
Malawi		8 831 000	Zambia		8 456 000
Malaysia (East)		14 300 000	Zimbabwe	200 000 +	9 369 000
Malta		353 000	Other British territories	30 000 +	30 000 +
Mauritius		1 080 000			
Montserrat	12 000	12 000			
Namibia		1 302 000			
Nauru		9 000 +			
Nepal	?	18 910 000 +	TOTALS	317 043 000 +	1 895 079 100 +

by promising to establish Presbyterianism in England (which Parliament had failed to do); they invaded England (Apr 1648), and were repulsed only after the battle of Preston (Aug). Bitterly fought, the second war earned Charles the epithet 'that man of blood' and ultimately his execution (30 Jan 1649). The two wars cost possibly 100 000 lives — one in 10 adult males.

English Heritage in the UK, a body directly responsible for over 350 buildings and monuments in England, and for protecting and preserving England's collection of 12 500 designated monuments and over 300 000 'listed' buildings. Similar functions are carried out by Historic Scotland (an agency of the Scottish Office) in Scotland and Cadw (Welsh Historic Monuments) in Wales.

English horn same as COR ANGLAIS.

Englishman *and* **Englishwoman** *noun* a native or citizen of England.

English National Ballet a dance company, called the London Festival Ballet until 1988, which emerged (1950) from Alicia Markova and Anton Dolin's groups of Ballets Russes dancers. Wide audiences are attracted by the guest stars and popular dancers, who mainly perform the classics, but also some modern works.

English National Opera an opera company based in London. Previously the Sadler's Wells Opera (renamed 1974), it developed from the Old Vic company and was based at the

Sadler's Wells Theatre (1931–68) before moving to the Coliseum.

English-Speaking Union a charity which was founded (1918) by Sir Evelyn Wrench (1882–1966) aimed at 'improving understanding about people, international issues, and culture through the bond the English language provides'. Based in London, the Union also has branches in many other countries.

English Stage Company an organization established under George Devine (1956) to encourage new playwrights. It influenced postwar British theatre by insisting on the value of contemporary drama, and made its home in the Royal Court Theatre, London.

engorged *adj.* **1** crammed full. **2** *Medicine* blocked by blood. [from EN- + GORGE]

engrave *verb* **1** to carve (letters or designs) on stone, wood, metal, etc. **2** to decorate (stone, etc) in this way. **3** to fix or impress deeply (on the mind, etc). [from EN- + obsolete *grave*, to carve]

engraver *noun* a person who engraves letters or designs, especially professionally.

engraving *noun* **1** the art of carving designs on stone, etc. **2** a piece of stone, etc decorated in this way. **3** a print taken from an engraved metal plate.

engross *verb* to take up completely the attention and interest of. [from Old French *engrosser*, from *en gros*, completely]

engrossed *adj.* having one's attention fully occupied; mentally absorbed.

engrossing *adj.* engaging one's full attention; highly interesting.

engulf *verb* **1** to swallow up completely. **2** to overwhelm. [from EN- + *gulf*, to swallow]

enhance *verb* to improve or increase the value, quality or intensity of (often something already good). [from Old French *enhauncer*]

enhanced radiation weapon (ABBREV. **ERW**) a more precise term for NEUTRON BOMB.

enhancement *noun* increase in quality; improvement.

enigma *noun* **1** a puzzle or riddle. **2** a mysterious person, thing, or situation. [from Greek *ainigma*]

enigmatic *adj.* obscure; puzzling.

enigmatically *adv.* in an obscure or puzzling way.

Enigma Variations *or* **Variations on an original theme, 'Enigma'** an orchestral work comprising 14 variations or portraits by Edward Elgar (Op 36, 1899), dedicated to his 'friends pictured within'.

enjoin *verb formal* **1** to order or command (someone) to do something. **2** (**enjoin something on someone**) to demand behaviour of a certain kind from them: *enjoin politeness on one's children.* **3** *Legal* (**enjoin someone from something**) to forbid them to do it, by means of an injunction. [from French *enjoindre*]

enjoy *verb* **1** to find pleasure in. **2** to have, experience, have the benefit of (something good): *the room enjoys sunlight all day.*
— **enjoy oneself** to experience pleasure or happiness.
[from Old French *enjoir*]

enjoyable *adj.* capable of being enjoyed; offering pleasure.

enjoyably *adv.* in an enjoyable or pleasurable way.

enjoyment *noun* enjoying; deriving pleasure.

Enki see EA.

enkindle *verb literary* **1** to set fire to. **2** to stir up (feelings), or arouse strong feelings in.

enlarge *verb* **1** *trans., intrans.* to make or become larger. **2** to reproduce (a photograph, etc) in a larger form. **3** *intrans.* (**enlarge on** *or* **upon something**) to speak or write about it at greater length or in greater detail.

enlargement *noun* **1** something enlarged, esp a photographic print larger than the standard or original print. **2** the act of enlarging or the state of being enlarged. **3** the process of admitting new member countries to the European Union.

enlighten *verb* (**enlightened, enlightening**) **1** to give more information to. **2** to free from ignorance or superstition.

enlightened *adj.* having or showing awareness and understanding and a freedom from prejudice and superstition.

enlightening *adj.* providing information; freeing from ignorance or prejudice.

Enlightenment a European philosophical movement of the 18c, rooted in the 17c Scientific Revolution and the ideas of Locke and Newton. It was founded on a belief in the superiority of reason as a guide to all knowledge and human concerns, from which issued the idea of progress and a challenging of traditional Christianity.

enlightenment *noun* the act of enlightening or the state of being enlightened; freedom from ignorance or superstition.

Enlil the Mesopotamian god of the wind, son of Anu the sky-god, and king of the gods before the creation of Marduk (the supreme god of Babylonia).

Differences Between British and American English

There are many differences of meaning, pronunciation, spelling, and syntax between British and American English. Some of the commoner differences in meaning in typical usage are listed below. The increasing influence of American usage on British English is having the effect of blurring distinctions. It should also be remembered that practice differs widely within the USA; and it is becoming increasingly difficult to establish linguistic boundaries between the language used in the USA and the language used in Canada.

There are also a number of general spelling differences between British and American English. Others are less distinct, because both varieties permit variants of form and inflections (for example, the forms **acknowledgement** and **acknowledgment** are found in both American and British English).

	British		American		British		American
-ae-	as in anaesthetic	-e-	as in anesthetic	-ogue	as in catalogue	-og	as in catalog
-oe-	as in oestrogen	-e-	as in estrogen	-ou-	as in mould	-o-	as in mold
-ence	as in defence, licence (noun)	-ense	as in defense, license (noun)	-l-	as in instil, instalment, skilful	-ll-	as in instill, installment, skillful
-re	as in centre	-er	as in center	-ll-	as in traveller	-l-	as in traveler
-our	as in flavour	-or	s in flavor				

British	American	British	American	British	American
aeroplane	airplane	estate agent	realtor	reverse charge (telephone) call	collect call
aluminium	aluminum	first floor	second floor	rise (in salary)	raise
anticlockwise	counterclockwise	flag day	tag day	roundabout (traffic)	rotary
aubergine	eggplant	flat	apartment	rowing-boat	rowboat
autumn	fall	frying pan	skillet	rubber	eraser
back garden	yard	grill	broil	rubbish	trash
banknote	bill	ground floor	first floor	scone	biscuit
bath	tub	handbag	purse, pocketbook	season ticket	commutation ticket
biscuit (savoury)	cracker	hoarding	billboard	shoelace	shoestring
biscuit (sweet)	cookie	icing	frosting	shop assistant	clerk
bonnet (of a car)	hood (of a car)	insect	bug	silencer (car)	muffler (car)
braces	suspenders	ironmonger	hardware store	spring onions	green onions
brooch	pin	kerb	curb	sweets	candy
bumper (of a car)	fender (of a car)	knickers	underpants	tap	faucet
camp-bed	cot	lavatory	washroom	tart	pie
caretaker	janitor	lawyer	attorney	terraced house	row house
chemist's shop	drugstore	lift	elevator	tights	pantihose
cheque	check	lorry	truck	timber	lumber
cinema (building)	movie theater	loud-hailer	bull-horn	traffic jam	gridlock
city centre	downtown	main road	highway	tram	streetcar
coffin	casket	murder	homicide	trolley (at supermarket, etc)	cart
cornflour	cornstarch	motorway	expressway	trousers	pants
cotton reel	spool	number plate (of a vehicle)	licence plate (of a vehicle)	turn-up (trousers)	cuff (pants)
courgette	zucchini	nappy	diaper	tyre	tire
crisps	potato chips	pavement	sidewalk	underground	subway
cupboard	closet	pedestrian crossing	crosswalk	undertaker	mortician
current account (bank)	checking account	petrol	gasoline (gas)	verandah	porch
curriculum vitae	résumé	pig	hog	vest	undershirt
curtains	drapes	plot (of ground)	lot	waistcoat	vest
draughts (game)	checkers	potato chips	french fries	wallet	billfold
drawing pin	thumb tack	pram	baby carriage	windscreen	windshield
driving licence	driver's license	queue	line	zip	zipper
dual carriageway	divided highway	railway	railroad		
dustbin	garbage can	return ticket	round-trip ticket		
engine driver	engineer				

American	British	American	British	American	British
airplane	aeroplane	drugstore	chemist's shop	pocketbook	handbag, purse
aluminum	aluminium	eggplant	aubergine	porch	verandah
apartment	flat	elevator	lift	potato chips	crisps
attorney	lawyer	engineer	engine driver	purse	handbag
baby carriage	pram	eraser	rubber	railroad	railway
bill	banknote	expressway	motorway	raise (in salary)	rise
billboard	hoarding	fall	autumn	realtor	estate agent
billfold	wallet	faucet	tap	résumé	curriculum vitae
biscuit	scone	fender (of a car)	bumper (of a car)	rotary (in traffic)	roundabout
broil	grill	first floor	ground floor	round-trip ticket	return ticket
bug	insect	french fries	potato chips	row house	terraced house
bull-horn	loud-hailer	frosting	icing	second floor	first floor
candy	sweets	garbage can	dustbin	sidewalk	pavement
cart (at supermarket, etc)	trolley	gasoline (gas)	petrol	skillet	frying pan
casket	coffin	green onions	spring onions	spool	cotton reel
check	cheque	gridlock	traffic jam	streetcar	tram
checkers	draughts	hardware store	ironmonger	string	shoelace
checking account	current account	highway	main road	subway	underground
clerk	shop assistant	hog	pig	suspenders	braces
closet	cupboard	homicide	murder	tag day	flag day
collect (telephone) call	reverse charge call	hood (of a car)	bonnet (of a car)	thumb tack	drawing pin
commutation ticket	season ticket	janitor	caretaker	tire	tyre
cookie	biscuit (sweet)	licence plate (of a vehicle)	number plate (of a vehicle)	trash	rubbish
cornstarch	cornflour	line	queue	truck	lorry
cot	camp-bed	lot	plot (of ground)	tub	bath
counterclockwise	anticlockwise	lumber	timber	underpants	knickers
cracker	biscuit (savoury)	mortician	undertaker	undershirt	vest
crosswalk	pedestrian crossing	move theater	cinema	vest	waistcoat
cuff (pants)	turn-up (trousers)	muffler (car)	silencer (car)	washroom	lavatory
curb	kerb	pantihose	tights	windshield	windscreen
diaper	nappy	pants	trousers	yard	back garden
divided highway	dual carriageway	pie	tart	zipper	zip
downtown	city centre	pin	brooch	zucchini	courgette
drapes	curtains				

enlist *verb* **1** *intrans.* to join one of the armed forces. **2** *trans.* to obtain the support and help of; to obtain (support and help).

enlisted man *or* **enlisted woman** *North Amer., esp. US* a member of the armed forces below the rank of officer.

enlistment *noun* enlisting; joining one of the armed services.

enliven *verb* (**enlivened, enlivening**) to make (more) active, lively, or cheerful.

enlivenment *noun* enlivening; making cheerful.

en masse all together; as a mass or group. [from French *en masse*]

enmesh *verb* to catch or trap in a net, or as if in a net; to entangle.

enmity *noun* **1** the state or quality of being an enemy. **2** ill-will; hostility. [from Old French *enemistie*, from Latin *inimicus*, enemy]

Enniskillen *or* **Inniskilling**, Gaelic **Inis Ceithleann** POP (1991) 11 000, the county town of Co Fermanagh, SW Northern Ireland, in Fermanagh district. It lies on an island in the R Erne. HISTORY English families were settled here after Tyrone's rebellion; in 1689 William III's forces defeated those of James II at Enniskillen and the town became an important Protestant stronghold. NOTABLE FEATURES castle ruins (15c–16c); cathedral (17c–18c).

Ennius, Quintus (c.239–169BC) Roman epic poet, born in Rudiae, Calabria. He is said to have served in the Punic Wars, and returned to Rome with Cato the Elder, where he taught Greek, and attained the rank of Roman citizen. He introduced the hexameter into Latin, but only fragments of his many writings survive, including those of the epic poem *Annales*.

ennoble *verb* **1** to make (something) noble or dignified. **2** to make (someone) a member of the nobility.

ennoblement *noun* ennobling; making someone a member of the nobility.

ennui *noun literary* boredom or discontent caused by a lack of activity or excitement. [from French *ennui*, boredom]

ENO *abbrev.* English National Opera.

Enoch a male first name, mentioned in the Old Testament as grandson of Adam. [from Hebrew, = experienced]

enormity *noun* (PL. **enormities**) **1** outrageousness or wickedness. **2** an outrageous or wicked act.
◆ The use of *enormity* to mean *enormousness* (as in *the enormity of the building*) is usually regarded as incorrect.

enormous *adj.* extremely large; huge. [from Latin *enormis*, unusual]

enormously *adv.* to a large extent; hugely: *enormously helpful.*

enormousness *noun* enormous size; hugeness.
◆ See note at *enormity.*

enough — *adj.* in the number or quantity needed: *enough food to eat.* — *adv.* **1** to the necessary degree or extent. **2** fairly: *she's pretty enough.* **3** quite: *oddly enough, I can't remember.* — *pron.* the amount needed.
— **have had enough of something** to be able to tolerate no more of it.
[from Anglo-Saxon *genoh*]

en passant in passing; by the way. [French, = in passing]

enquire, enquiry see INQUIRE, INQUIRY.

enrage *verb* to make very angry. [from Old French *enrager*]

enraged *adj.* extremely angry.

enrapture *verb* to give intense pleasure or joy to.

enraptured *or* **enrapt** *adj.* intensely pleased or delighted.

enrich *verb* **1** to make rich or richer, especially better or stronger in quality, value, flavour, etc. **2** to make wealthy or wealthier.

enriched *adj.* made rich or richer.

enrichment *noun* making rich or richer; improvement in quality, etc.

enrol *verb* (**enrolled, enrolling**) **1** to add the name of (a person) to a list or roll, eg of members; to secure the membership or participation of. **2** *intrans.* to add one's own name to such a list; to become a member. [from Old French *enroller*]

enrolment *noun* enrolling; adding a name to a list.

en route on the way to a place. [French, = on the way]

ensconce *verb trans. literary, humorous* (*usually* **be ensconced**) to settle comfortably or safely. [from EN- + *sconce*, small fort]

ensemble *noun* **1** a small group of (usually classical) musicians who regularly perform together. **2** a passage in opera, ballet, etc performed by all the singers, musicians, or dancers together. **3** a set of items of clothing worn together; an outfit. **4** all the parts of a thing considered as a whole. [from French *ensemble*, together]

enshrine *verb* **1** to enter and protect (a right, idea, etc) in the laws or constitution of a state, constitution of an organization, etc. **2** to place in a shrine.

enshroud *verb* **1** to cover completely; to hide by covering up. **2** to cover in a shroud.

ensign *noun* **1** the flag of a nation or regiment. **2** a coloured flag with a smaller union flag in one corner, especially the **White Ensign**, the flag of the Royal Navy and the Royal Yacht Squadron, or the **Red Ensign**, the flag of the Merchant Navy. **3** *Hist.* the lowest rank of officer in the infantry, or an officer of this rank. **4** *North Amer., esp. US* the lowest rank in the navy, or an officer of this rank. [from Old French *enseigne*, from Latin *insignia*, from *signum*, sign]

ensilage same as SILAGE.

enslave *verb* **1** to make into a slave. **2** to subject to a dominating influence.

enslavement *noun* making into a slave.

ensnare *verb* to catch in, or as if in, a trap; to trick or lead dishonestly (into doing something).

Ensor, Sir Robert (Charles Kirkwood) (1877–1958) English radical journalist and historian, born in Somerset. He joined the *Manchester Guardian* as a leader-writer and edited an anthology of speeches and writings, *Modern Socialism* (1904). He also worked for the liberal *Daily News* (1909–11) and the radical *Daily Chronicle* (1912–30) and was active in the Labour movement. Chosen to write the late Victorian volume of the *Oxford History of England*, he produced his masterpiece, *England 1870–1914* (1936).

ensue *verb intrans.* (**ensue from something**) **1** to follow it; to happen after it. **2** to result from it. [from Old French *ensuer*, from Latin *sequi*, to follow]

ensuing *adj.* **1** following. **2** happening as a result.

en suite forming, or attached as part of, a single unit or set: *an en suite bathroom.* [from French *en suite*, in sequence]

ensure *verb* **1** to make certain; to assure or guarantee. **2** to make safe and secure. [from Old French *enseurer*, from Latin *securus*, safe]

ENT *abbrev.* ear, nose, and throat.

-ent *suffix* forming adjectives and nouns denoting an action, activity, or function: *resident / different.* [from the Latin ending *-ens -entis*]

entablature *noun Archit.* in classical architecture, the part of a building directly supported by the columns, usually with a frieze and a cornice. [from Italian *intavolatura*]

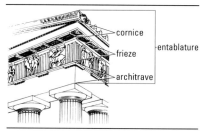

entablature

entail — *verb* **1** to have as a necessary result or requirement. **2** *Legal* (**entail something on someone**) to bequeath property to one's descendants, not allowing them the option to sell it. — *noun Legal* **1** the practice of entailing (property). **2** property which has been entailed. **3** the successive heirs to property. [from EN- + TAIL[2]]

entailment *noun* **1** the process of entailing property. **2** *Philos.* the necessity of a proposition being true as a result of another proposition.

entangle *verb* **1** to cause to get caught in some obstacle, eg a net. **2** to involve in difficulties. **3** to make complicated or confused.

entanglement *noun* the process of entangling; complication.

entasis *noun* the slightly bulging outline of a column or similar structure, intended to counteract the illusion of concavity that an absolutely straight column would create. Various formulas for correcting this illusion were devised and perfected by classical Greek architects, with most Greek columns gradually diminishing in thickness towards their tops. [from Greek *entasis*, from *en*, in + *tasis*, a stretch]

Entebbe POP (1991) 42 000, a town in S Uganda on the N shore of L Victoria, 30km/19mi SW of Kampala. Founded in 1893, it was the capital of Uganda from 1894 until 1962. It was the scene in 1976 of a dramatic rescue by Israeli forces of Israelis whose plane had been hijacked by a group of terrorists.

Entente Cordiale a term first used in the 1840s to describe a close relationship between the UK and France. It was then given to a series of agreements in 1904 between the two countries, which dealt with such issues as the establishment of the UK's predominant role in Egypt, and France's interests in Morocco. [from French *entente cordiale*, cordial understanding]

entente cordiale a friendly agreement or relationship between nations or states.

enter *verb* (**entered, entering**) **1** *intrans., trans.* to go or come in or into. **2** *trans., intrans.* to register (another person, oneself, one's work, etc) in a competition. **3** to record in a book, diary, etc. **4** to join (a profession, society, etc). **5** to submit or present: *enter a complaint.* **6** (**enter into**) to begin to take part in. **7** (**enter into**) to agree to be associated in or bound by: *enter into an agreement.* **8** (**enter on** *or* **upon something**) to begin an undertaking, especially a lengthy one: *enter upon a new stage of life.*

enteric *adj. Medicine* of the intestines. [from Greek *enteron*, intestine]

enteritis *noun Medicine* inflammation of the intestines, especially the lining of the small intestine, which usually causes vomiting, diarrhoea, and abdominal pain. It may be the result of bacterial or viral infections, poisoning, exposure to ionizing radiation, eg X-rays, or an allergic reaction.

entero- *or* **enter-** *combining form* forming words with the meaning 'intestine': *enteritis.* [from Greek *enteron*, intestine]

enterprise *noun* **1** a project, undertaking. **2** a project that requires boldness and initiative. **3** boldness and initiative. **4** a business firm. [from Old French *entreprendre*, to undertake]

enterprise zone in the UK, an area of the country designated by government as a site where industrial and commercial renewal is to be encouraged by financial and other incentives. Enterprise zones are usually located in inner cities or in areas which have lost their traditional industries (with resulting high levels of unemployment). Schemes of this kind are in operation in many W European countries and in the USA.

enterprising *adj.* showing enterprise and initiative; adventurous.

enterprisingly *adv.* in an enterprising or adventurous way.

entertain *verb* **1** to provide amusement or recreation for. **2** *intrans., trans.* to give hospitality to (a guest), especially in the form of a meal. **3** to consider or be willing to adopt (an idea, suggestion, etc). [from French *entretenir*, to maintain, to hold together]

Entertainer, The a play by John Osborne (1957). The decline of the mediocre music hall joker Archie Rice mirrors the decline of a society and illustrates the author's uncompromising hatred of outworn social and political institutions and attitudes. It was filmed in 1960 starring Laurence Olivier in the lead role.

entertainer *noun* a person who provides amusement, especially professionally.

entertaining *adj.* interesting and amusing.

entertainment *noun* **1** something that entertains, eg a theatrical show. **2** the act of entertaining. **3** amusement or recreation.

enthalpy *noun Chem.* the amount of heat energy possessed by a substance, expressed per unit mass. It is measured as the heat change that occurs during a chemical reaction that takes place at constant pressure. [from Greek *enthalpein*, to warm in]

enthral *verb* (**enthralled, enthralling**) to fascinate; to hold the attention or grip the imagination of. [from EN- + THRALL]

enthralled *adj.* having one's attention absorbed; fascinated.

enthralling *adj.* absorbing one's attention; fascinating.

enthralment *noun* being enthralled; fascination.

enthrone *verb* to place on a throne.

enthronement *noun* installing of a monarch on the throne, especially as a ceremony.

enthuse *verb intrans., trans.* to be enthusiastic, or make (someone) enthusiastic.

enthusiasm *noun* lively or passionate interest or eagerness. [from Greek *enthousiasmos*, zeal inspired by a god, from *en*, in + *theos*, god]

enthusiast *noun* a person filled with enthusiasm, especially for a particular subject; a fan or devotee.

enthusiastic *adj.* showing lively interest.

enthusiastically *adv.* with lively interest or enthusiasm.

entice *verb* to tempt or persuade, by arousing hopes or desires or by promising a reward. [from Old French *enticier*]

enticement *noun* enticing; something that allures or fascinates.

enticing *adj.* alluring; fascinating.

enticingly *adv.* in an enticing or alluring way.

entire *adj.* **1** whole, complete. **2** absolute; total. [from Old French *entier*, from Latin *integer*, whole]

entirely *adv.* **1** fully or absolutely. **2** solely.

entirety *noun* (PL. **entireties**) completeness; wholeness.

— in its entirety totally; taken as a whole.

entitle *verb* **1** (**entitle someone to something**) to give them a right to have or to do it. **2** to give a title or name to (a book, etc). [from Old French *entitler*]

entitlement *noun* having a right to something.

entity *noun* (PL. **entities**) **1** something that has a physical existence, as opposed to a quality or mood. **2** the essential nature (of something). **3** *Philos.* the fact or quality of existing. [from Latin *entitas*, from *ens*, thing that exists]

ento- *combining form* inside. See also ECTO-, ENDO-, EXO-. [from Greek *entos*, within]

entomb *verb* **1** to put in a tomb. **2** to cover, bury or hide as if in a tomb. [from Old French *entoumber*]

entombment *noun* being put in a tomb.

entomological *adj.* relating to entomology or the study of insects.

entomologist *noun* a person who studies entomology.

entomology *noun* the scientific study of insects. [from Greek *entomon*, insect, from *entomos*, cut into sections]

entourage *noun* a group of followers or assistants, especially one accompanying a famous or important person. [from French *entourage*, from *entourer*, to surround]

entr'acte *noun* **1** an interval between the acts of a play. **2** *formerly* entertainment provided during this interval. [from French *entr'acte*, from *entre*, between + *acte*, act]

entrails *pl. noun* **1** the internal organs of a person or animal. **2** *literary* the inner parts of anything. [from Old French *entrailles*, from Latin *intralia*, from *inter*, within]

entrance[1] *noun* **1** a way in, eg a door. **2** *formal* the act of entering: *gain entrance*. **3** the right to enter. [from ENTER + -ANCE]

entrance[2] *verb* (with stress on *-trance*) **1** to grip the attention and imagination of. **2** to put into a trance.

entrancement *noun* enchantment; fascination.

entrancing *adj.* gripping the imagination; fascinating.

entrant *noun* a person who enters (especially an examination, a competition, or a profession).

entrap *verb* (**entrapped, entrapping**) **1** to catch in, or as if in, a trap. **2** to trick (someone) into doing something. [from Old French *entraper*]

entrapment *noun* **1** the act of entrapping or process of being entrapped. **2** *Legal* the act or process of deliberately inducing someone to commit a crime in order to provide a reason for arresting and prosecuting him or her.

entreat *verb* to ask passionately or desperately; to beg. [from Old French *entraiter*]

entreaty *noun* (PL. **entreaties**) a passionate or desperate request.

entrecôte *noun* a boneless steak cut from between two ribs. [from French *entrecôte*, from *entre*, between + *côte*, rib]

entrée *noun* **1** a small dish served after the fish course and before the main course at a formal dinner. **2** a main course. **3** *formal* the right of admission or entry: *entrée into polite society*. [from French *entrée*, entrance]

entrench *verb* **1** to fix or establish firmly, often too firmly: *deeply entrenched ideas*. **2** to fortify with trenches dug around.

entrenchment *noun* establishing a firm position.

entrepôt *noun* a port through which goods are imported and exported, often without duty being paid on them. [from French *entrepôt*, warehouse]

entrepreneur *noun* a person who engages in business enterprises, usually with some personal financial risk. [from French *entrepreneur*, one who undertakes]

entrepreneurial *adj.* acting as an entrepreneur; undertaking business enterprises.

entropy *noun* (PL. **entropies**) *Physics* a measure of the amount of disorder in a system, or of the unavailability of energy for doing work. When a system undergoes a change, its entropy cannot decrease, but will either remain constant (during a reversible change) or increase (during an irreversible change). The entropy of the universe is increasing, because every process in which energy is released involves some energy wastage, and therefore a decrease in the amount of energy that is available for doing work. [from German *Entropie*, from Greek *en*, in + *tropos*, turn, change]

entrust *verb* (**entrust something to someone**, *or* **someone with something**) to give it to them to take care of or deal with.

entry *noun* (PL. **entries**) **1** the act of coming or going in. **2** the right to enter. **3** a place of entering such as a door or doorway. **4** a person, or the total number of people, entered for a competition, etc. **5** an item written on a list, in a book, etc, or the act of recording an item in this way. [from Old French *entree*, from *entrer*, to enter]

entryism *noun derog.* the practice of joining a political party in large enough numbers to gain power and change the party's policies.

entryist *noun derog.* a person who engages in political entryism.

Entryphone *noun trademark* an intercom system fitted at the entrance to a building, especially a block of flats, by which visitors can identify themselves to specific occupants before being admitted to the building.

entwine *verb* **1** to wind or twist two things together. **2** to make by winding or twisting something together.

E-number *noun* any of various identification codes, consisting of the letter E (for European) followed by a number, that are used to denote all food additives, except flavourings, that have been approved by the European Community (EC). Lists of ingredients on food packaging either show the full names of additives, or their E-numbers. Additives that are used in the UK but are not approved by the EC are represented by a code number without the letter E.

enumerate *verb* **1** to list one by one. **2** to count. [from Latin *enumerare*, to count up]

enumeration *noun* enumerating; counting, listing.

enumerative *adj.* serving to list or count.

enunciate *verb* **1** *trans., intrans.* to pronounce words clearly. **2** to state formally. [from Latin *enuntiare*, to announce]

enunciation *noun* clear pronunciation of words.

enuresis *noun Medicine* involuntary urination, especially during sleep. [from Greek *en*, in + *ouresis*, urination]

enuretic *adj.* involving involuntary urination.

envelop *verb* (with stress on *-vel-*) (**enveloped, enveloping**) **1** to cover or wrap completely. **2** to obscure or conceal: *an event enveloped in mystery*. [from Old French *envoloper*, from *en*, in + *voloper*, to wrap]

envelope *noun* (with stress on *en-*) **1** a thin flat sealable paper packet or cover, especially for a letter. **2** a cover or wrapper of any kind. **3** *Biol.* a plant or animal structure that contains or encloses something, eg the nuclear envelope, consisting of a double membrane that surrounds the nucleus of a cell. **4** *technical* the glass casing that surrounds an incandescent lamp. [from French *enveloppe*, from *envelopper*; related to ENVELOP]

envelopment *noun* enveloping or being enveloped; covering.

Enver Pasha (1881–1922) Turkish nationalist and politician, born in Constantinople (modern Istanbul). A leader in the revolution of Young Turks in 1908, he later became Minister of War (1914), but fled to Russia in 1918 after the Turkish surrender in World War I, and was killed in an insurrection in Turkestan.

enviable *adj.* likely to cause envy; highly desirable.

enviably *adv.* so as to cause envy or admiration: *they were enviably sure of themselves.*

envious *adj.* feeling or showing envy: *they were envious of our successes.*

enviously *adv.* with envy: *looked enviously at the winners.*

environment *noun* **1** the surroundings or conditions within which something or someone exists. **2** (*usually* **the environment**) the combination of external conditions that surround and influence a living organism, including light, temperature, availability of food and water, climatic conditions, geographical area, pollution by chemicals, radiation, noise, etc, the presence of other organisms possibly competing for the same resources, and the physical and chemical nature of the immediate surroundings, eg soil, sea water. The environment of human beings also includes social, cultural, economic, and political factors, and the room, building, town, region, or country in which a person lives. [from Old French *environnement*, from *environner*, to surround]

environmental *adj.* concerning or connected with the environment: *environmental issues.*

environmental archaeology the study of past environments and ecological interaction over time between human and contemporary animal and plant communities.
◇ It is possible, from evidence such as animal bones and teeth, preserved pollen and plants, and soils and sediments, to deduce what impact human beings made on the environment and over what period of time this happened. For example, a recent study in the Western Isles of Scotland has shown that the felling of native timber by prehistoric man resulted in the formation of peat bogs and gradually reduced the total area of cultivable land so that the original human population could not be sustained.

environmentalism *noun* concern about the natural environment and its protection from pollution and other harmful effects of human activity.

environmentalist — *noun* a person who is concerned about the harmful effects of human activity on the environment. — *adj.* used to describe a group or organization whose aims are to protect the environment and to increase public awareness of environmental issues.

environmentally *adv.* as regards the environment.

environmentally friendly not harmful to the environment, eg referring to certain detergents and non-aerosol sprays.

Environmentally Sensitive Area (ABBREV. **ESA**) an area of farmland, designated by the UK Ministry of Agriculture on the basis of its value as a wildlife habitat, which the farmer is encouraged to manage using traditional methods that minimize environmental damage. In return, a payment is made to the farmer by the Ministry of Agriculture to compensate for the financial losses incurred by farming in this way.

Environmental Protection Agency (ABBREV. **EPA**) a US government agency formed in 1970 to control air and water pollution caused by industrial waste, pesticides, and radiation, as well as excessive noise pollution.

environmental studies a relatively new scientific subject which studies the interaction between man and the environment, and which emphasizes the links between different subjects related to this issue, including ecology, geography, geology, meteorology, economics, sociology, and politics.

environs *pl. noun* surrounding areas, especially the outskirts of a town or city. [from Old French *environ*, around]

envisage *verb* **1** to picture in the mind. **2** to consider as likely in the future: *we envisage a pay-rise in the autumn.* [from French *envisager*, from *visage*, face]

envoy *noun* **1** a diplomat ranking next below an ambassador. **2** a messenger or agent, especially on a diplomatic mission. [from French *envoyer*, to send]

envy — *noun* **1** a feeling of resentment or regretful desire for another person's qualities, better fortune, or success. **2** anything that arouses envy: *a house that is the envy of his colleagues.* — *verb* (**envies**, **envied**) (**envy someone something**) to feel envy against someone on account of their fortune, success, etc: *I envy them their good luck.* [from Old French *envie*]

enzyme *noun Biochem.* a specialized protein molecule that acts as a catalyst for the biochemical reactions that occur in living cells. [from Greek *en*, in + *zume*, leaven]
◇ Most enzymes are highly specific to a particular reaction or group of reactions. A molecule of the substance on which the enzyme acts (the *substrate*) binds to an *active site* on the enzyme. After the reaction has taken place, the product separates from the enzyme molecule, which itself remains unchanged and so can be re-used, perhaps many thousands of times per second. Enzyme activity is very sensitive to temperature, pH (acidity), substrate concentration, and the presence of inhibitory compounds. The names of enzymes typically end in *-ase*, and are usually derived from the substrates on which they act, eg protease breaks down protein. Enzymes have many industrial applications, including drug manufacture, textile production, biological detergents, baking and brewing, and cheese manufacture. They are also important research tools in genetic engineering.

EOC *abbrev.* Equal Opportunities Commission.

Eocene — *noun Geol.* the second epoch of the Tertiary period, lasting from about 54 million to 38 million years ago. During this time the first horses and elephants appeared, and most plants were similar to modern types. — *adj.* **1** relating to this epoch. **2** relating to rocks formed during this epoch. [from Greek *eos*, dawn + *kainos*, recent]

Eohippus *noun Zool.* the earliest stage in the evolution of the modern horse, about the size of a small dog, with four splayed front toes and three hind toes. It was widespread in N America, Europe, and Asia during the early Eocene epoch, and became extinct about 49 million years ago. — Also called *Hyracotherium*. [from Greek *eos*, dawn + *hippos* horse]

EOKA *abbrev. Ethnike Organosis Kypriakou Agonos* (Greek) National Organization for the Cypriot Struggle.

eolian harp same as AEOLIAN HARP.

eolithic or **Eolithic** *adj.* belonging to the early part of the Stone Age, when crude stone implements were first used by man. [from Greek *eos*, dawn + *lithos*, stone]

eon or **aeon** *noun* — a long period of time. — *Geol.* the largest unit of geological time, consisting of a number of eras. — *Astron.* a period of a thousand million years.

Eos in Greek mythology, the goddess of the dawn, daughter of Helios, mother of Memnon. She abducted various mortals to be her lovers, including Tithonus. He was granted immortality by Zeus at her request, but she had forgotten to ask for perpetual youth, so he became old and decrepit and she shut him away, until the gods took pity and changed him into a cicada.

eosin *noun Biol.* a red acidic dye used to stain thin sections of plant or animal tissue before they are examined under an optical microscope. It stains cytoplasm pink and cellulose red, and is often used together with *haematoxylin*, a blue alkaline dye that stains cell nuclei blue. [from Greek *eos,* dawn]

EP *noun* an extended-play gramophone record.

EPA *abbrev.* Environmental Protection Agency (USA).

epaulette or **epaulet** *noun* a decoration on the shoulder of a coat or jacket, especially of a military uniform. [from French *épaulette*, from *épaule*, shoulder]

épée *noun* a sword with a narrow flexible blade, used formerly in duelling and, with a blunted end, in modern fencing. [from French *épée*]

Eph. or **Eph** *abbrev. Biblical* Ephesians.

ephedrine *noun Medicine* an alkaloid drug, with similar effects to adrenaline, that constricts blood vessels and widens the bronchial passages. Formerly used to treat asthma and chronic bronchitis, it is now mainly used as a nasal decongestant. [from Greek *ephedra*, horsetail (the plant)]

ephemera *pl. noun* things that are valid or useful for a short time, especially printed items. [from Greek *ephemeros*, living a day, from *epi*, for + *hemera*, day]

ephemeral — *noun Biol.* a plant or animal that completes its life cycle within weeks, days, or even hours, eg mayfly, many desert plants. — *adj.* **1** *Biol.* denoting such a plant or animal. **2** lasting a short time.

ephemeris *noun* (PL. **ephemerides**) *Astron.* **1** a table that shows the predicted future positions of celestial bodies such as the Sun, Moon, planets, certain stars, and comets. **2** a book, usually published annually, containing a collection of such tables, together with other relevant information about predictable astronomical phenomena such as eclipses.

ephemeris time (ABBREV. **ET**) *Astron.* a system of time based on the orbital movement of

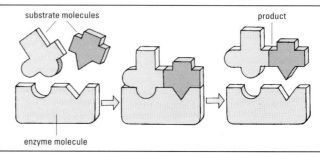

enzyme

the Earth around the Sun, as opposed to the Earth's rotation about its own axis. Ephemeris time was used to calculate the orbital movement of objects in the Solar System until 1984, when it was replaced by dynamical time.

Ephesians, Letter of Paul to the a New Testament writing attributed to Paul. It sets out God's purposes in establishing the Church, and includes advice for the Christian community in Ephesus.

Ephesus an ancient city of Lydia and important Greek city-state on the W coast of Asia Minor (now in Turkey). It was the centre of the cult of Cybele (an Anatolian fertility goddess) and the site of the Temple of Artemis, one of the Seven Wonders of the Ancient World. In Roman times, it was the principal city of the province of Asia, and the seat of the Roman governor. Its ruins were excavated during the 19c–20c.

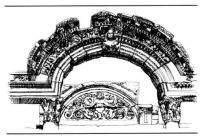

Ephesus

Ephraim, Tribe of one of the 12 tribes of ancient Israel, descended from the younger son of Jacob's son Joseph. Their territory included the central hill country of Palestine, stretching to Bethel in the south and almost to Shechem in the north.

epi- *combining form* forming words meaning 'above, over, upon': *epicentre / epidural.* [from Greek *epi,* on, over]

epiblast *noun Zool.* same as ECTODERM. [from EPI- + Greek *blastos,* shoot]

epic — *noun* **1** a long narrative poem telling of heroic acts, the birth and death of nations, etc. **2** a long adventure story, film, etc. — *adj.* of or like an epic, especially in being large-scale and imposing. [from Greek *epikos,* from *epos,* word, song]

epicene *adj.* **1** having characteristics of both sexes, or of neither sex. **2** of, or for use by, both sexes. **3** effeminate. **4** *Grammar, said of a noun* referring to people or animals of either sex, eg 'driver', as opposed to 'waiter' and 'waitress'. [from Greek *epikoinos,* common to many]

epicentre *noun* the point on the earth's surface which is directly above the focus (centre of activity) of an earthquake, or directly above or below a nuclear explosion. [from Greek *epi,* over + *kentron,* point]

epicure *noun* a person who has refined taste, especially one who enjoys good food and drink. [from *Epicurus,* the ancient Greek philosopher (see entry)]

Epicurean *noun* **1** a follower of the philosophy of Epicurus. **2** (**epicurean**) a person who likes pleasure and good living. — *adj.* (**epicurean**) **1** given to luxury or to the tastes of an epicure. **2** relating to the philosophy of Epicurus.
◇ In its general senses, the word takes on a meaning associated with pleasure and enjoyment rather than the personal happiness that Epicurus intended (see EPICUREANISM). Other words that develop new meanings in this way are *stoic, stoical,* and words with ethnic reference like *vandal.*

Epicureanism a philosophical school established by Epicurus in the 4c BC, surviving until the 3c AD. Its basic moral principle was that per-

sonal happiness is the supreme good, with freedom from fears (eg of death) and from pain. It regarded the universe as a collection of indestructible atoms moving in a void, and not guided by any divine influence.

epicurism *noun* **1** the pursuit of pleasure, especially as found in good food and drink. **2** the tendency to be critical and hard to please in matters of luxury.

Epicurus (c.341–270 BC) Greek philosopher, born in Samos. He opened a school at Mitylene (310 BC), and taught there and at Lampsacus. In 305 BC he established a successful school of philosophy in Athens, and led a life of temperance and simplicity. He held that pleasure is the chief good, by which he meant freedom from pain and anxiety, not (as the term 'epicure' has since come to mean) one who indulges sensual pleasures without stint. Only a few letters and fragments of his work survive.

epicycle *noun Maths.* a circle whose centre rolls around the circumference of another fixed circle. The curved path followed by a point on the circumference of the epicycle is known as an *epicycloid.*

Epidaurus an ancient Greek city-state situated in the E Peloponnese. It was famous for its sanctuary to Asclepius, the god of healing, and for its open theatre, which is still used today. It is a World Heritage site.

epidemic — *noun* **1** a sudden outbreak of infectious disease (such as cholera and influenza) which spreads rapidly and affects a large number of people, animals, or plants in a particular area for a limited period of time. **2** a sudden and extensive spread of anything undesirable. — *adj.* of or like an epidemic; sometimes also used to describe a non-infectious condition such as malnutrition. See also ENDEMIC. [from Greek *epi,* among + *demos,* the people]

epidemiology *noun Biol.* the study of the distribution, effects, and causes of diseases in populations, and the means by which they may be treated or prevented. It includes not only infectious diseases such as cholera and smallpox, but also conditions such as heart disease and cancer that are related to lifestyle or environmental factors, eg diet, exercise, and smoking habits.

epidermal *adj.* relating to the epidermis.

epidermis *noun Biol.* the outermost layer of a plant or animal, which serves to protect the underlying tissues from infection, injury, and water loss. In plants and many invertebrates, it is only one cell thick, and is covered by an impermeable waxy layer (*cuticle*). In vertebrates, it forms part of the skin and consists of several layers of cells which gradually become filled with keratin, a horny substance that hardens the skin. The outermost layer consists of dead cells that are continuously being worn away. [from Greek *epi,* upon + *derma,* the skin]

epididymis *noun* (PL. **epididymides**) *Anat.* a long narrow highly coiled tube in the testis of mammals, birds, and reptiles, that conveys sperm from the seminiferous tubules of the testis to the vas deferens. The sperm mature and become fertile as they pass along the epididymis, and they are stored in the lower part of the tube prior to ejaculation. [from EPI- + Greek *didymos,* twin, testicle]

epidural — *adj. Medicine* situated on, or administered into, the dura mater, the membrane enveloping the brain and the spinal cord. — *noun Medicine* an anaesthetic administered into the dura mater, used especially during childbirth to remove all sensation below the waist. [from EPI- + DURA MATER]

epiglottal *adj.* relating to the epiglottis.

epiglottis *noun Anat.* in mammals, a moveable flap of cartilage which hangs at the back of the tongue. It closes the opening of the larynx (windpipe) when food or drink is being swallowed, so

preventing obstruction of the air passages. [from Greek *epi,* over + *glottis,* glottis]

Epigoni in Greek mythology, a collective name given to the 'next generation' of heroes, the sons of the Seven against Thebes. After the failure of their fathers to take Thebes, the sons made another expedition and succeeded; this was shortly before the Trojan War.

epigram *noun* a witty or sarcastic saying, or a short poem with such an ending. [from Greek *epigramma,* from *epi,* upon + *gramma,* writing]

epigrammatic *adj.* in the nature of an epigram; short and witty.

epigraph *noun* **1** a quotation or motto at the beginning of a book or chapter. **2** an inscription on a building. [from Greek *epigraphe,* from *epi,* upon + *graphein,* to write]

epigraphy *noun* the study of inscriptions, especially those made by carving, embossing, engraving, and painting on hard surfaces such as stone, marble, clay, pottery, and wax. Inscriptions found on monuments such as the Egyptian pyramids and the Ogam stones of Celtic Britain provide important data for the historical study of ancient civilizations, as well as insights into the early development of writing systems. Our knowledge of the political and constitutional systems of the Greeks and Romans is heavily dependent on records preserved in the form of inscriptions on stone. [from Greek *epigraphe,* from *epi,* upon + *graphein,* to write]

epilepsy *noun* any of a group of disorders of the nervous system characterized by recurring attacks that involve impairment or sudden loss of consciousness. [from Greek *epilepsia,* from *epilambanein,* to seize]
◇ In the form of epilepsy known as *grand mal,* violent convulsions occur as a result of stiffening and jerking of the muscles; in the form known as *petit mal,* there may be merely a brief period of impaired consciousness. All forms of epilepsy are caused by disturbances in the electrical activity of the brain, and can be treated with anticonvulsant drugs.

epileptic — *adj.* of or suffering from epilepsy. — *noun* a person who suffers from epilepsy.

epilogue *noun* **1** the closing section of a book, programme, etc. **2** a speech addressed to the audience at the end of a play. [from Greek *epilogos,* from *epi,* upon + *logos,* speech]

epiphany *noun* (PL. **epiphanies**) **1** (*usually* **Epiphany**) a Christian festival on 6 January which, in the western churches, commemorates the showing of Christ to the three wise men, and, in the Orthodox and other eastern Churches, the baptism of Christ. **2** the sudden appearance of a god. **3** *literary* a sudden revelation or insight. [from Greek *epiphaneia,* manifestation]
◇ The eve of Epiphany is Twelfth Night. In some countries, gifts are exchanged at Epiphany rather than at Christmas.

epiphysis *noun* (PL. **epiphyses**) **1** *Anat.* the growing end of a long bone, which is initially separated from the long shaft of the bone by cartilage, and develops separately. Eventually the cartilage is converted to solid bone, and the epiphysis fuses with the shaft to form a complete bone. **2** the pineal gland. [from Greek *epiphysis,* excrescence]

epiphyte *noun Bot.* a plant that grows on another plant, using it for support, but is not a parasite, eg moss. Epiphytes are particularly common in tropical rainforests, and include many orchids and bromeliads. [from EPI- + Greek *phyton,* plant]

episcopacy *noun* (PL. **episcopacies**) **1** the government of the church by bishops. **2** bishops as a group. **3** the position or period of office of a bishop. [from Greek *episkopos,* overseer]

episcopal *adj.* relating to or governed by bishops.

Episcopal Church, Protestant the Anglican Church in the USA. It was formally established (1784) after the War of Independence when the bishops of the Episcopal Church of Scotland consecrated Samuel Seabury (1729–86) as the first Bishop of Connecticut. It is an active missionary Church, especially in the Far East and S America.

Episcopal Church in Scotland an independent Protestant Church in Scotland, founded after the presbyterian nature of the Church of Scotland was established by the Act of Settlement in 1690. Although it is in full communion with the Church of England (ie within the Anglican Communion), it is self-governing and has its own General Synod of 160 elected members, presided over by the Primus, one of the seven diocesan bishops.

episcopalian — *adj.* relating to or advocating Church government by bishops. — *noun* a member of an episcopal (especially Anglican) Church.

episcopalianism *noun* episcopalian principles.

episcopate *noun* **1** the position or period of office of a bishop. **2** bishops as a group. **3** an area under the care of a bishop; a diocese or bishopric.

episiotomy *noun* (PL. **episiotomies**) *Medicine* a surgical cut made at the opening of the vagina during childbirth, to assist the delivery of the baby. [from Greek *epision*, pubic area + -TOMY]

episode *noun* **1** one of several events or distinct periods making up a longer sequence. **2** one of the separate parts in which a radio or television serial is broadcast or a serialized novel, etc published. **3** any scene or incident forming part of a novel or narrative poem, often one providing a digression from the main story. [from Greek *epeisodion*, from *epi*, upon + *eisodos*, a coming in]

episodic *adj.* **1** consisting of several distinct periods. **2** occurring at intervals; sporadic.

episodically *adv.* at intervals; sporadically.

epistemological *adj.* relating to epistemology or the study of knowledge.

epistemology *noun* the philosophical theory of knowledge. The origins of human knowledge have long been debated by philosophers: empiricists claim that knowledge ultimately derives from sense-experience; Locke proposed that knowledge is gained only by experience and that the mind at birth is a blank sheet; rationalists claim that some, if not all, significant knowledge is *a priori*, independent of the senses or experience; and sceptics argue that we can have no knowledge at all, or at least considerably less than might be thought. Another central question is the difference between knowledge and belief. In this regard, philosophers have attempted to formulate necessary conditions for the truth and justification of beliefs. [from Greek *episteme*, knowledge]

epistle *noun* **1** *literary* a letter, especially a long one dealing with important matters. **2** a novel or poem written in the form of letters. **3** (*usually* **Epistle**) each of the letters written by Christ's Apostles which form part of the New Testament. **4** a reading from one of the Epistles as part of a religious service. [from Latin *epistola*]

epistolary *adj. formal* relating to or consisting of letters.

epistolary novel a type of novel in which the story is told entirely through an exchange of letters between the characters. The genre was made fashionable during the 18c with Samuel Richardson's *Clarissa* (1748); other notable examples are Smollett's *Expedition of Humphry Clinker* (1771), and Pierre Laclos' *Les Liaisons Dangereuses* (1782).

epitaph *noun* **1** an inscription on a gravestone. **2** a short commemorative speech or piece of writing in a similar style. [from Greek *epitaphion*, from *epi*, upon + *taphos*, tomb]

epithelial *adj.* relating to the epithelium.

epithelium *noun* (PL. **epithelia**) *Anat.* the layer of tissue covering all external surfaces of a multicellular animal, and lines all hollow structures except for blood vessels and lymph vessels. It usually provides protection, or is specialized for secreting and absorbing substances. [from Greek *epi*, upon + *thele*, nipple]

epithet *noun* an adjective or short descriptive phrase which captures the particular quality of the person or thing it describes: *King Ethelred II was given the epithet 'The Unready'.* [from Greek *epitheton*, from *epi*, on + *tithenai*, to place]

epitome *noun* **1** a miniature representation of a larger or wider idea, issue, etc. **2** a person or thing that is the embodiment of or a perfect example of (a quality, etc). **3** a summary of a written work. [from Greek *epi*, upon, + *tome*, a cut]

epitomize *or* **epitomise** *verb* to be or make an epitome of.

EPNS *abbrev.* electroplated nickel silver.

epoch *noun* **1** a major division or period of history, a person's life, etc, usually marked by some important event. **2** *Geol.* an interval of geological time representing a subdivision of a period, and during which a particular series of rocks was formed, eg the Pleistocene epoch. [from Greek *epoche*, fixed point]

epochal *adj.* relating to or lasting for an epoch.

epoch-making *adj.* highly significant or decisive.

eponym *noun* a person after whom something is named, especially the main character in a play, novel, etc whose name provides its title. [from Greek *epi*, upon + *onyma*, a name]

eponymous *adj.*, *said of a character in a story, etc* having the name from which the title is taken.

EPOS *abbrev.* electronic point of sale.

epoxy *Chem.* — *adj.* consisting of an oxygen atom bonded to two carbon atoms. — *noun* (*in full* **epoxy resin**) any of a group of synthetic thermosetting resins, so called because they contain epoxy groups, that are tough, resistant to abrasion and chemical attack, and form strong adhesive bonds. Epoxy resins are widely used as electrical insulators and adhesives. [from Greek *epi*, upon + OXYGEN]

Eppie the golden-haired natural daughter of Godfrey Cass, brought up by Silas in George Eliot's *Silas Marner*.

EPROM *abbrev. Comput.* erasable programmable read-only memory, a read-only memory in which stored data can be erased by ultraviolet light, etc, and reprogrammed.

EPS *abbrev.* earnings per share (stock exchange).

Epsom and Ewell POP (1981) 67 000, the amalgamated towns in Epsom and Ewell district, Surrey, SE England. Situated 22km/14mi SW of London, Epsom and Ewell forms part of the Greater London urban area. NOTABLE FEATURE horse-racing centre on the Epsom Downs.

Epsom salts a bitter white powder, a preparation of magnesium sulphate, used as a medicine for clearing the bowels. [from *Epsom* in Surrey, where it occurs naturally in spring water]

EPSRC *abbrev.* Engineering and Physical Sciences Research Council.

Epstein, Sir Jacob (1880–1959) British sculptor, born a Russian-Polish Jew in New York. His early commissions included 18 nude figures for the British Medical Association building in the Strand (1907–8). These, along with several of his symbolic sculptures, including *Ecce Homo* (1934), resulted in accusations of indecency and blasphemy. He was renowned for his bronze

portrait heads of celebrities and children. Works include *Christ in Majesty* (in aluminium, 1957) and *St Michael and the Devil* (in bronze, 1958–9).

equability *noun* being equable or even-tempered.

equable *adj.* **1** *said of a climate* never showing very great variations or extremes. **2** *said of a person* even-tempered. [from Latin *aequabilis*, from *aequus*, equal]

equably *adv.* with an equable manner; calmly.

equal — *adj.* **1** the same in size, amount, value, etc. **2** evenly balanced; displaying no advantage or bias. **3** having the same status; having or entitled to the same rights. **4** (**equal to something**) having the necessary ability for it. — *noun* a person or thing of the same age, rank, ability, worth, etc. — *verb* (**equalled**, **equalling**) **1** to be the same in amount, value, size, etc as. **2** to be as good as; to match. **3** to achieve something which matches (a previous achievement or achiever). [from Latin *aequus*]

equality *noun* an equal state; being equal.

equalization *or* **equalisation** *noun* making or becoming equal.

equalize *or* **equalise** *verb* **1** *trans.*, *intrans.* to make or become equal. **2** *intrans.* to reach the same score as an opponent, after being behind.

equalizer *or* **equaliser** *noun* a person or thing that equalizes, especially a goal or point scored which makes one equal to one's opponent. See also GRAPHIC EQUALIZER.

equally *adv.* in an equal way; to an equal extent.

equal opportunities the principle of equal treatment of all employees or candidates for employment, irrespective of race, religion, sex, etc.

Equal Rights Amendment a proposed amendment to the US Constitution stating that equal rights shall not be denied on account of sex. First introduced into Congress in 1923, it was not approved by Congress until 1972. Although the adoption deadline was extended from 1979 to 1982, the amendemnt fell just short of ratification by the required 38 states.

equanimity *noun* calmness of temper; composure. [from Latin *aequanimitas*, from *aequus*, equal + *animus*, mind]

equate *verb* **1** (**equate one thing to** *or* **with another**) to consider them as equivalent. **2** (**equate with something**) to be equivalent to it. [from Latin *aequare*, to make equal]

equation *noun* **1** *Maths.* a mathematical statement of the equality between two expressions involving constants and/or variables, used to find solutions to variables, or to describe a set of points, eg on a line or curve. For example, the algebraic equation $y = mx + c$ (where x and y are variables and m and c are constants) represents a straight line. **2** *Chem.* a chemical equation. **3** the act of equating.

equator *noun* **1** (**the Equator**) the imaginary great circle that passes around the Earth at latitude 0° at an equal distance from the North and South Poles, and divides the Earth's surface into the northern and southern hemispheres. It is 40 076km/24 902mi in length. **2** *Astron.* same as celestial equator. [from Latin *aequator*, equalizer (of day and night)]

equatorial *adj.* of or near the equator.

Equatorial Guinea, official name **Republic of Equatorial Guinea**, *or* **República de Guinea Ecuatorial** POP (1992e) 369 000, a republic in W central Africa, comprising a mainland area (Río Muni) and several islands (notably Bioko and Annabón) in the Gulf of Guinea. It is divided into seven provinces. AREA 26 016sq km/10 042sq mi (mainland); total area 28 051sq km/10 828sq mi. The mainland is bounded N by Cameroon, E and S by Gabon, and W by the Gulf of Guinea. CAPITAL Malabo. CHIEF TOWNS Bata and Evinayoung on the mainland, Luba and Riaba on

Bioko. TIME ZONE GMT +1. The majority of the mainland population is Fang and most are Christian. OFFICIAL LANGUAGE Spanish; pidgin English and Fang are also spoken. CURRENCY the ekuele. PHYSICAL DESCRIPTION the mainland rises sharply from a narrow coast of mangrove swamps towards the heavily-forested African plateau; deeply cut by several rivers; Bioko I, about 160km/100mi NW of the mainland, is of volcanic origin, rising to 3 007m at Pico de Basilé. CLIMATE hot and humid equatorial; average annual rainfall is c.2 000mm; average maximum daily temperature is 29–32°C. HISTORY first visited by Europeans in the 15c; the island of Fernando Póo was claimed by Portugal in 1494 and held until 1788; occupied by Britain from 1781 until 1843; rights to the area were acquired by Spain in 1844; gained independence in 1968; military coup in 1979; a new constitution was approved in 1991 and multiparty democracy was legalized in 1992. GOVERNMENT a House of Representatives elected for five years and a smaller State Council. ECONOMY largely based on agriculture; cocoa, coffee, timber, bananas, cassava, palm oil, sweet potatoes.

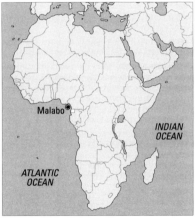

Equatorial Guinea

equerry *noun* (PL. **equerries**) an official who serves as a personal attendant to a member of a royal family. [from Old French *esquierie*, company of squires, from *esquier*, squire]

equestrian *adj.* **1** of horse-riding or horses. **2** on horseback. [from Latin *equestris*, relating to horsemen]

equi- *combining form* equal or equally: *equidistant*. [from Latin *aequus*, equal]

equiangular *adj.* having equal angles.

equidistance *noun* equality of distance.

equidistant *adj.* equally distant.

equilateral *adj.* having all sides of equal length. [from EQUI- + Latin *latus*, side]

equilibrium *noun* **1** *Physics* a state in which the various forces acting on an object or objects in a system balance each other, so that there is no tendency for any part of the system to move.

2 *Chem.* a reversible chemical reaction in which the rate of forward and backward reactions is the same, so that the concentrations of reactants and products remain unchanged. **3** a calm and composed state of mind. [from Latin *aequi librium*, from *aequus*, equal + *libra*, balance]

equilibrium constant *Chem.* at a specified temperature, the ratio of the concentrations of the products of a chemical reaction to the concentrations of the reactants (the substances that react with each other).

equine *adj. formal* of, relating to, or like a horse or horses. [from Latin *equinus*, from *equus*, horse]

equinoctial — *adj.* happening on or near an equinox. — *noun* **1** a storm or gale occurring about the time of an equinox. **2** (*also* **equinoctial line**) *Astron.* the celestial equator, the imaginary line occurring where the plane of the earth's equator cuts the celestial sphere (the imaginary sphere to which the stars appear to be fixed).

equinox *noun* either of the two occasions on which the sun crosses the equator, making night and day equal in length, the *spring equinox* occurring about 21 Mar and the *autumnal equinox* occurring about 23 Sep. [from Latin *a equi noctium*, from *aequus*, equal + *nox*, night]

equip *verb* (**equipped**, **equipping**) to fit out or provide with the necessary tools, supplies, abilities, etc. [from French *équiper*, from Old French *eschiper*, to fit out a ship, probably from Norse *skip*, ship]

equipage *noun* **1** a horse-drawn carriage with its footmen. **2** *formerly* the equipment carried by a military unit.

equipment *noun* **1** the clothes, machines, tools, instruments, etc necessary for a particular kind of work or activity. **2** *formal* the act of equipping.

equipoise *noun formal* **1** a state of balance. **2** a counterbalancing weight. [from EQUI- + POISE]

equitable *adj.* **1** fair and just. **2** *Legal* relating to, or valid according to, the concept of natural justice, or equity, as opposed to common law or statute law. [from French *équitable*: see EQUITY]

equitation *noun formal* the art of riding a horse. [from Latin *equitare*, to ride, from *equus*, horse]

Equity, in full **British Actors' Equity Association** in the UK, a trade union established in 1929 to protect the interests of professional actors (eg salaries, conditions of employment). Similar organizations exist in the USA and Canada.

equity *noun* (PL. **equities**) **1** fair or just conditions or treatment. **2** *Legal* the concept of natural justice, as opposed to common law or statute law, often invoked to support an interpretation, or the complete waiving, of a law. **3** the excess in value of a property over the mortgage and other charges held on it. **4** (*usually* **equities**) an ordinary share in a company. [from Old French *equite*, from Latin *aequitas*, equality]

equivalence *noun* the fact or state of being equivalent; having equal value.

equivalent — *adj.* equal in value, power, meaning, etc. — *noun* an equivalent thing, amount, etc. [from Latin *aequus*, equal + *valere*, to be worth]

equivalently *adv.* to a degree equal in amount or value.

equivocal *adj.* **1** ambiguous; of doubtful meaning. **2** of an uncertain nature. **3** questionable, suspicious, or mysterious. [from Latin *aequivocus*, from *aequus*, equal + *vox*, voice, word]

equivocally *adv.* in an equivocal or ambiguous manner.

equivocate *verb intrans.* to use ambiguous words in order to deceive or to avoid answering a question.

equivocation *noun* evasive ambiguity.

Equuleus *noun Astron.* the Foal, a faint constellation near the celestial equator, and the second smallest constellation in the sky.

Equus a play by Peter Shaffer (1973). It is about the relationship between an obsessed stable boy who has blinded some horses and a psychiatrist who attempts to explain his actions.

ER *abbrev.* **1** *Elizabeth Regina* (Latin), Queen Elizabeth. **2** *Edwardus Rex* (Latin), King Edward.

Er *symbol Chem.* erbium.

-er[1] *suffix* used to form the comparative of adjectives and adverbs: *happier / sooner*. [from Anglo-Saxon forms]

-er[2] *suffix* **1** used to form words meaning the person or thing performing the action of the verb: *driver / heater*. **2** used to form words meaning a person from a particular town or city: *Londoner / New Yorker*. [from Anglo-Saxon *-ere*]

ERA *abbrev.* Equal Rights Amendment.

era *noun* **1** a distinct period in history marked by or beginning at an important event. **2** *Geol.* the second largest interval of geological time, representing a subdivision of an eon, eg Mesozoic era. Each era is in turn divided into a number of periods. [from Latin *aera*, number]

eradicate *verb* to get rid of completely. [from Latin *eradicare*, to root out]

eradication *noun* getting rid of something; elimination.

erase *verb* **1** to rub out (pencil marks, etc). **2** to remove all trace of. [from Latin *eradere*, to scratch out]

eraser *noun* something that erases, especially a rubber for removing pencil or ink marks.

Erasistratus (3 BC–? AD) Greek physician, born in Ceos, who founded a school of anatomy in Alexandria. One of the founders of modern medicine, he studied the nature of the nervous system, and came near to discovering the circulation of the blood.

Erasmus, Desiderius, originally **Gerrit Gerritszoon** (1466–1536) Dutch humanist and scholar, a very influential Renaissance figure, born in Rotterdam. He joined an Augustinian monastery in 1487 and became a priest in 1492. While a professor at Cambridge, he wrote the satire *Encomium Moriae* (The Praise of Folly,

Equivalent Numbers					
%	Decimal	Fraction	%	Decimal	Fraction
1	0.01	1/100	30	0.30	3/10
2	0.02	1/50	31	0.31	31/100
3	0.03	3/100	32	0.32	8/25
4	0.04	1/25	33	0.33	33/100
5	0.05	1/20	33.3	0.333	1/3
6	0.06	3/50	34	0.34	17/50
7	0.07	7/100	35	0.35	7/20
8	0.08	2/25	36	0.36	9/25
8.3	0.089	1/12	37	0.37	37/100
9	0.09	9/100	38	0.38	19/50
10	0.10	1/10	39	0.39	39/100
11	0.11	11/100	40	0.40	2/5
12	0.12	3/25	41	0.41	41/100
12.5	0.125	1/8	42	0.42	21/50
13	0.13	13/100	43	0.43	43/100
14	0.14	7/50	44	0.44	11/25
15	0.15	3/20	45	0.45	9/20
16	0.16	4/25	46	0.46	23/50
16.7	0.167	1/6	47	0.47	47/100
17	0.17	17/100	48	0.48	12/25
18	0.18	9/50	49	0.49	49/100
19	0.19	19/100	50	0.50	1/2
20	0.20	1/5	55	0.55	11/20
21	0.21	21/100	60	0.60	3/5
22	0.22	11/50	65	0.65	13/20
23	0.23	23/100	70	0.70	7/10
24	0.24	6/25	75	0.75	3/4
25	0.25	1/4	80	0.80	4/5
26	0.26	13/50	85	0.85	17/20
27	0.27	27/100	90	0.90	9/10
28	0.28	7/25	95	0.95	19/20
29	0.29	29/100	100	1.00	1

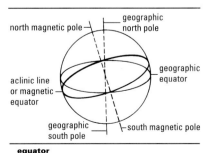

equator

Number Systems					
Arabic	Roman	Binary	Arabic	Roman	Binary
1	I	1	50	L	110010
2	II	10	60	LX	111100
3	III	11	64	LXIV	1000000
4	IV	100	90	XC	1011010
5	V	101	99	XCIX	1100011
6	VI	110	100	C	1100100
7	VII	111	128	CXXVIII	10000000
8	VIII	1000	200	CC	11001000
9	IX	1001	256	CCLVI	100000000
10	X	1010	300	CCC	100101100
11	XI	1011	400	CD	110010000
12	XII	1100	500	D	111110100
13	XIII	1101	512	DXII	1000000000
14	XIV	1110	600	DC	1001011000
15	XV	1111	900	CM	1110000100
16	XVI	10000	1 000	M	1111101000
17	XVII	10001	1 024	MXXIV	10000000000
18	XVIII	10010	1 500	MD	10111011100
19	XIX	10011	2 000	MM	11111010000
20	XX	10100	4 000	M$\bar{V}$	111110100000
21	XXI	10101	5 000	$\bar{V}$	1001110001000
30	XXX	11110	10 000	$\bar{X}$	10011100010000
32	XXXII	100000	20 000	$\bar{X}\bar{X}$	100111000100000
40	XL	101000	100 000	$\bar{C}$	11000011010100000

1509), and he later lived in Louvain and in Basle. His reaction against scholasticism, and criticism of the Catholic Church (expressed in *Colloquia familiaria* (1519), an audacious treatment of Church abuses and pedantries), as well as of the dogmatic theology of the Reformers, meant continual controversy in his life. His other works include the first translation of the Greek New Testament and editions of many other writers.

Erasmus the first of several portrait paintings of Erasmus by Hans Holbein the Younger (1523, Louvre, Paris).

erasure *noun* **1** the act of rubbing out. **2** a place where something written has been erased.

Erato in Greek mythology, the Muse responsible for lyric poetry and hymns.

Eratosthenes (c.276–194 BC) Greek mathematician, astronomer, and geographer, born in Cyrene. Head of the great library at Alexandria, he was the most versatile scholar of his time. He measured the obliquity of the ecliptic and the circumference of the Earth with considerable accuracy.

erbium *noun Chem.* (SYMBOL **Er**, ATOMIC NUMBER 68) a soft silvery metal, belonging to the lanthanide series, that absorbs neutrons and has a high electrical resistivity. It is used in alloys for nuclear reactors, and in lasers for medical applications. Erbium oxide is used as a pink pigment in ceramics. [from the name *Ytterby* in Sweden, where it was first discovered]

Erdenet POP (1990e) 56 000, a town in Bulgan county, N Mongolia, lying on a tributary of the Orhon Gol. It was founded as a new city in 1971 with Soviet help.

ere *prep., conj. poetic* before. [from Anglo-Saxon *ær*]

Erechtheum a temple on the Athenian Acropolis, named after the legendary king Erechtheus of Athens. It is a symmetrical, two-part Ionic marble temple built during the Peloponnesian War (c.420–407 BC) and dedicated to Athena and Poseidon-Erectheus. The six caryatids of the porch (one is now amongst the Elgin marbles) are particularly noteworthy.

Erechtheus in Greek mythology, an early king of Athens, born from the Earth and nurtured by Athena. He sacrificed his daughter Chthonia to secure victory over the Eleusinians, but was killed by Poseidon. The Erechtheum, a temple on the Acropolis, is probably on the site of his palace.

erect — *adj.* **1** upright; not bent or leaning. **2** *said of the penis, clitoris, or nipples* enlarged and rigid through being filled with blood, usually as a result of sexual excitement. — *verb* **1** to put up or to build. **2** to set or put (a pole, flag, etc) in a vertical position. **3** to set up or establish. [from Latin *erigere*, to set upright]

erectile *adj. Physiol., said of an organ, etc* capable of becoming erect.

erection *noun* **1** the act of erecting or the state of being erected. **2** *sometimes derog.* a building or structure. **3** *said of a sexual organ, especially the penis* the process of becoming erect or the state of being erect. **4** an erect sexual organ, especially an erect penis.

erectly *adv.* in an erect posture.

erectness *noun* an erect state or posture.

Erewhon a satirical novel by Samuel Butler (published anonymously, 1872). It is set in 'Erewhon' (an anagram of 'nowhere'), and is an attack on the hypocritical morality of English society.

erg *noun Physics* a unit of work or energy defined as the amount of work done when a force of one dyne moves through a distance of one centimetre. It is used in the centimetre-gramme-second (c.g.s.) system of measurement, and one erg is equal to 10⁻⁷ joules. [from Greek *ergon*, work]

ergo *adv. formal Logic* therefore. [from Latin *ergo*]

ergonomic *adj.* relating to ergonomics or the study of people in their work environment.

ergonomically *adv.* in terms of people and their work environment: *an ergonomically sound practice.*

ergonomics *noun Engineering* the study of the relationship between people and their working environment, including machinery, computer sytems, etc. The engineering aspects of this interaction are investigated in order to maximize work performance, minimize stress and fatigue, and improve the design of equipment. [from Greek *ergon*, work + *-nomics* as in ECONOMICS]

ergonomist *noun* a person who studies ergonomics, especially professionally.

ergot *noun* **1** a disease of rye and other cereals caused by the fungus *Claviceps purpurea*, which appears as hard purple structures (ergots) on the seedheads. Ergots contain highly toxic alkaloid substances, and in the Middle Ages consumption of infected ryebread caused convulsions and gangrene accompanied by a burning sensation

known as St Anthony's fire. **2** (**ergots**) the hard purple structures characteristic of this disease. **3** the fungus that produces this disease. It is an important source of alkaloid drugs, chemically related to LSD, that are used to treat migraine headaches and to stimulate contractions of the uterus during childbirth. [from French, from Old French *argot*, cock's spur, because of its appearance]

ergotism *noun Medicine* poisoning caused by the consumption of bread made from rye infected with the fungus *Claviceps purpurea* (ergot). The fungus contains poisonous alkaloids that constrict blood vessels, resulting in a burning sensation in the limbs, gangrene, and convulsions. Formerly known as *St Anthony's fire*.

Erhard, Ludwig (1897–1977) German economist and politician, born in Furth. Professor of Economics at Munich, in 1949 he was elected to the Federal Parliament at Bonn and became Chancellor of the Exchequer in the Adenauer administration. He pioneered West Germany's great economic recovery from wartime devastation, and succeeded Adenauer as Christian Democratic Chancellor (1963–6), but economic difficulties forced his resignation.

Eric a male first name, introduced to Britain by Scandinavian settlers. [from Old Norse *ei, ey*, forever + *rik*, power]

Erica a female first name. [a Latin feminine form of ERIC, also the Latin word for 'heather']

Ericsson, John (1803–89) Swedish inventor, born in Långbanshyttan. He was a Swedish army engineer before moving to England (1826), where he invented the first successful screw-propeller (1836). His many inventions and warship designs revolutionized their construction.

Eridu the oldest of the ancient Sumerian city-states, lying SW of Ur. Excavations of the site have revealed a series of temples which began to be built in the sixth millennium BC and ended in the third with the ziggurat (temple).

Erie, Lake the fourth largest of the Great Lakes, N America, on the frontier between Canada and the USA. AREA 25 667sq km/ 9 907sq mi; length 388km/241mi; width 48–92km/30–57mi. The Detroit R is its inlet from L Huron in the W, via L St Clair; the Niagara R in the E is its outlet to L Ontario. The Welland Ship Canal bypasses the Niagara Falls. Islands include Bass, Kelleys, and Pelee; major ports include Buffalo, Cleveland, Detroit. Ice generally closes the lake to navigation during winter months (Dec–Mar).

Erik the Red, properly **Erik Thorvaldson** (10c) Norwegian sailor who explored the Greenland coast and founded the Norse colonies there (985). His son Leif Eriksson landed in 'Vinland', often identified as America (1000). Both men are the subject of Icelandic sagas.

Erin *noun old use, poetic* Ireland. [from Old Irish *Erinn*]

Erinyes in Greek mythology, spirits of vengeance, depicted as carrying torches and covered with snakes. Their names are Alecto 'never-ceasing', Megaira 'grudger', and Tisiphone 'avenger of blood'. In Roman mythology, they were called the Furies.

Eris in Greek mythology, a goddess personifying strife, the daughter of Night and the sister of Ares. She was present at the wedding of Peleus and Thetis and threw a golden apple inscribed 'for the fairest' among the guests. This brought Hera, Athene, and Aphrodite into contention, and was the first cause of the Trojan War.

Eritrea, Amharic **Ertra** POP (1992e) 505 000, a country in NE Africa, on the Red Sea. AREA 93 679sq km/36 160sq mi. It is bounded N and NW by Sudan, W and SW by Ethiopia, S by Djibouti, and E by the Red Sea. CAPITAL Asmara. CHIEF TOWNS Assab, Massawa, Keren, Tessenai. TIME ZONE GMT +3. The main religions are Coptic Christianity and Islam. OFFICIAL LAN-

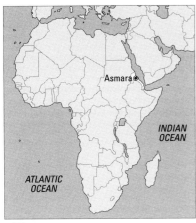

Eritrea

GUAGES Arabic, English. CURRENCY the Ethiopian birr. PHYSICAL DESCRIPTION low-lying coastline stretching 1 000km/620mi along the Red Sea, rising to an inland plateau. HISTORY taken by Italy in 1882; colony established in 1890; used as a base for the Italian invasion of Abyssinia in 1935; part of Italian East Africa in 1936; taken by the British in 1941; federated as part of Ethiopia in 1952; made a province of Ethiopia in 1962, which led to political unrest; Civil War in the 1970s, with separatists making major gains; Soviet- and Cuban-backed government forces regained most areas after a 1978 offensive; continuing conflict in the 1980s; following the collapse of the Ethiopian government in 1991, Eritrea became an autonomous region with the Eritrean People's Liberation Front (EPLF) establishing a provisional government; independence was declared in 1993. GOVERNMENT a President appoints the State Council which exercises executive power; legislative power is exercised by the National Assembly; at the end of a transition period (maximum four years) multiparty elections are planned. ECONOMY fishing; minerals, oil, gas.

Eritrea Liberation Front (ABBREV. **ELF**) a movement founded in 1958 which sought independence from Ethiopia. Eritrea, an Italian colony from 1884, was federated with Ethiopia at the request of the UN (1952) and then incorporated as a province (1962). The collapse of the Dergue in 1991 advanced its position and Eritrea became independent in 1993.

ERM abbrev. Exchange Rate Mechanism.

ermine noun **1** the winter phase of the stoat, when its fur has turned white except for the tip of the tail, which remains dark. **2** the fur of this animal, which was highly prized by the fur trade and formerly reserved for royalty. [from Old French hermine, from Latin Armenius mus, Armenian mouse]

Ernie noun the computer which applies the laws of chance to pick the prize-winning numbers of premium bonds. [from Electronic random number indicator equipment]

Ernst, Max (1891–1976) German painter, born in Brühl, near Cologne. He studied philosophy then turned to painting, and in 1919 founded the German Dada group in Cologne. He later participated in the Surrealist movement in Paris, and was one of the first to use the technique of frottage (pencil rubbings on canvas).

erode verb trans., intrans. to wear away, destroy, or be destroyed gradually. See also EROSION. [from Latin erodere, to gnaw away]

erogenous adj., said of part of the body sensitive to sexual stimulation. [from Greek eros, love + genes, born]

***Eroica Symphony**, published as **Sinfonia eroica, composta per festiggiare il sovvenire di un grand uomo** (Heroic symphony, composed to celebrate the memory of a great man) Beethoven's Symphony No.3 in E flat (Op 35, 1803), composed for Napoleon.

Eros 1 in Greek mythology, the son of Aphrodite and Ares. He is first depicted on vases as a handsome athlete, then as a boy with wings and arrows, and finally, in the Hellenistic period, as a chubby baby. He was identified with the Roman god Cupid. **2** Astron. a cigar-shaped asteroid, about 35km/22mi long and 6km/4mi wide, that orbits the Sun every 1.8 years, and in 1975 passed within 23 million km/14 million mi of Earth.

erosion noun the loosening, fragmentation, and transport from one place to another of rock material by water, wind, ice (eg glaciers), gravity, or living organisms, including human activity. Rivers are the most effective agents of erosion, forming the pattern of hills and valleys, while wave action forms the coastlines. Soil erosion is a natural geological process, but it is prevented by good land management. Certain processes (eg deforestation, overgrazing, inefficient irrigation) accelerate soil erosion and lead to loss of the fertile topsoil, often with serious economic consequences.

erosive adj. causing erosion.

erotic adj. of or arousing sexual desire, or giving sexual pleasure. [from Greek erotikos, from eros, love]

erotica pl. noun erotic literature, pictures, etc.

erotically adv. with an erotic manner or sense.

eroticism noun **1** the erotic quality of a piece of writing, a picture, etc. **2** interest in, or pursuit of, sexual sensations. **3** the use of erotic images and symbols in art, literature, etc.

err verb intrans. **1** to make a mistake, be wrong, or do wrong. **2** to sin.

— **err on the side of** ... to run the risk of a particular fault, in order to avoid an opposite and greater fault: err on the side of caution.

[from Old French errer, from Latin errare, to stray]

errand noun **1** a short journey made in order to get or do something, especially for someone else. **2** the purpose of such a journey. [from Anglo-Saxon ærende, mission]

errant adj. literary **1** doing wrong; erring. **2** wandering in search of adventure: a knight errant. [from Old French errer, in sense 1 from Latin errare, to stray, and in sense 2 from Latin itinerare, to make a journey]

errantry noun literary wandering in search of adventure.

errata see ERRATUM.

erratic adj. **1** irregular; having no fixed pattern or course. **2** unpredictable in behaviour. [from Latin errare, to stray]

erratically adv. with no fixed pattern or course; unpredictably.

erratum noun (PL. **errata**) formal an error in writing or printing. [from Latin errare, to stray]

Errol, Cedric see LITTLE LORD FAUNTLEROY.

erroneous adj., said of an impression, etc; not said of a person wrong or mistaken. [from Latin erroneus, straying]

erroneously adv. in error; by mistake.

error noun **1** a mistake, inaccuracy, or misapprehension. **2** the state of being mistaken. **3** the possible discrepancy between an estimate and an actual value or amount: a margin of error. [from Latin error, a wandering or straying, error]

ersatz derog. — noun a cheaper substitute, often used because the genuine article is unavailable. — adj. substitute; imitation. [from German ersatz]

Erse — noun the name formerly used by lowland Scots for the Gaelic language of the Scottish Highlands and Islands; now applied to the Gaelic language of Ireland. — adj. relating to or spoken or written in this language. [from Lowland Scots Erisch, Irish]

Ershad, Hossain Muhammad (1929–) Bangladeshi soldier and chief martial law administrator. Appointed army Chief-of-Staff by President Ziaur Rahman in 1978, he repeatedly demanded that the armed forces should be involved in the country's administration. In 1982 he led a bloodless military coup, and became President (1983–90) the following year, but faced continuing political opposition and demands for a full return to civilian rule until he resigned. In 1991 he was sentenced to 10 years' imprisonment for illegal arms possession, among other charges.

Erskine, Thomas, 1st Baron (1750–1823) Scottish jurist, born in Edinburgh. He was called to the Bar in 1778, became a KC and MP (1783), and acted as Lord Chancellor (1806–7). In 1781 he secured the acquittal of Lord George Gordon, following the anti-Catholic Gordon Riots of 1780. His sympathy with the French Revolution led him to join the 'Friends of the People', and to undertake the defence in many political prosecutions of 1793–4, notably of the English radical, Tom Paine.

erstwhile adj. formal, old use former; previous. [from Anglo-Saxon ærest, from ær, before]

eructation noun formal a belch or the act of belching. [from Latin eructare, to belch out]

erudite adj. showing or having a great deal of knowledge; learned. [from Latin erudire, to instruct]

eruditely adv. with an erudite or learned manner.

erudition noun scholarly learning or knowledge.

erupt verb intrans. **1** said of a volcano to throw out lava, ash, and gases. **2** to break out suddenly and violently. **3** said of a skin blemish to appear suddenly and in a severe form. [from Latin erumpere, to break out]

eruption noun **1** the process of erupting, especially of a volcano. **2** a sudden or violent breaking-out.

-ery or -ry suffix **1** indicating a place where work or an activity of the stated kind is carried out: brewery. **2** indicating a class, group, or type of the stated kind: greenery / weaponry. **3** indicating an art, skill, or practice of the stated kind: dentistry. **4** indicating behaviour of the stated kind: bravery. **5** indicating anything connected with the stated person or thing: popery. [from French -erie, from Latin -arius]

erysipelas noun an infectious disease of the skin, especially of the face, producing deep red sore patches, and accompanied by fever. [from Greek, perhaps from eruthros, red + pella, skin]

erythema noun Medicine redness of the skin, caused by dilation of the blood capillaries. [from Greek erythema, from erythros red]

erythrocyte noun Medicine a red blood corpuscle. [from Greek erythros, red + kytos, hollow vessel]

erythromycin noun Medicine an antibiotic that is used to treat a wide range of bacterial infections, especially in patients who are allergic to penicillin. [from Greek erythros red]

erythropoietin noun Physiol. a hormone, secreted mainly by the kidneys, that stimulates an increase in the rate of formation of red blood cells in bone marrow. It is produced in response to a decrease in the amount of oxygen in the tissues. [from Greek erythros, red + poiesis, making]

ES abbrev., as an international vehicle mark El Salvador.

Es symbol Chem. einsteinium.

-es suffix see -S.

ESA abbrev. **1** Environmentally Sensitive Area. **2** European Space Agency.

Esaki, Leo (1925–) Japanese physicist, born

in Osaka. In 1957, when working at the Sony Corporation in Tokyo, he developed the Esaki diode, a semiconductor device with widespread uses in computers and microwave systems. He joined IBM in the USA in 1960, and he shared the 1973 Nobel Prize for Physics with Brian Josephson and Ivar Giaever.

Esau a biblical character, the elder son of Isaac. He is depicted as his father's favourite son, but he was deprived of Isaac's blessing and his birthright by his cunning brother Jacob (Genesis 27). The story explains why Esau's descendants, the Edomites, were thereafter hostile to Jacob's descendants, the Israelites.

Esbjerg POP (1992e) 82 000, a seaport on the W coast of Ribe county, SW Jutland, Denmark. It is the most important Danish North Sea port, and a base for North Sea oil and gas exploration.

Esc. *abbrev.* escudo.

escalate *verb intrans., trans.* to increase or be increased rapidly in scale, degree, etc. [a back-formation from ESCALATOR]

escalation *noun* a rapid increase.

escalator *noun* a type of conveyor belt which forms a continuous moving staircase. [originally a trademark, probably from Spanish *escalada*, from Latin *scala*, ladder]

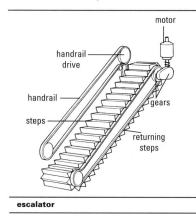

escalator

escallop *noun* same as SCALLOP.

escalope *noun* a thin slice of boneless meat, especially veal. [from French *escalope*]

escapade *noun* a daring, adventurous, or un-lawful act. [from French *escapade*]

escape — *verb* **1** *intrans.* to gain freedom. **2** to manage to avoid (punishment, disease, etc.). **3** not to be noticed or remembered by: *nothing escapes his notice*. **4** *intrans.* said of a gas, liquid, etc to leak out or get out. **5** *said of words, etc* to be uttered unintentionally by. — *noun* **1** an act of escaping. **2** a means of escape. **3** the avoidance of danger or harm: *a narrow escape*. **4** a leak or release. **5** something providing a break or distraction. [from Old French *escaper*, probably from Latin *excappare*, to remove one's cape]

escape clause a clause in a contract stating the conditions under which the contract may be broken.

escapee *noun* a person who has escaped, especially from prison.

escapement *noun* the mechanism in a clock or watch which connects the moving parts to the balance.

escape road a short side-road, eg at a bend on a hill, into which a driver can turn in order to stop if in difficulty.

escape velocity *Physics* the minimum velocity required for an object such as a space vehicle or rocket to escape from the pull of the gravitational field of the Earth, or of another planet or celestial body.

escapism *noun* the means of escaping, or the tendency to escape, from unpleasant reality into day-dreams or fantasy.

escapist — *noun* a person who indulges in escapism. — *adj.* characterized by escapism.

escapologist *noun* a person who practises escapology, especially professionally.

escapology *noun* the art or practice of freeing oneself from chains and other constraints, especially as theatrical entertainment.

Escargot, L' an abstract painting by Henri Matisse (1953, Tate Gallery, London).

escarpment *noun Geol.* a more or less continuous line of very steep slopes, formed by faulting or erosion, and found, for example, around the margins of a plateau. [from French *escarper*, to cut steeply]

Escaut, River see SCHELDE.

eschatological *adj.* relating to eschatology or the theological last things.

eschatology *noun* the branch of theology dealing with last things, eg death, divine judgement, and life after death. [from Greek *eschatos*, last]

escheat — *Legal noun* **1** *formerly* the handing over of property to the state or a feudal lord in the absence of a legal heir. **2** property handed over in this way. — *verb* **1** *intrans.* to be handed over in this way. **2** *trans.* to hand over, or confiscate (property). [from Old French *eschete*, from *escheoir*, to fall to someone]

Escherichia coli *Biol.* (ABBREV. **E. coli**) a species of bacterium that occurs naturally in the intestines of vertebrates, including humans, and sometimes causes disease. [named after the German physician T Escherich]

eschew *verb formal* to avoid, keep away from, or abstain from. [from Old French *eschever*]

eschewal *noun* avoidance; abstinence.

Escoffier, (Georges) Auguste (c.1847–1935) French chef, born in Villeneuve-Loubet. He was head chef to the general staff of the Rhine army in the Franco-Prussian War (1871) and of the Grand Hotel, Monte Carlo, before he moved to the Savoy, London, and finally to the Carlton. The inventor of *pêche melba* (peach melba) and other dishes, he wrote several books on culinary art.

Escorial, El a granite palace-monastery built (1563–84) for Philip II in New Castile, Spain by Juan Bautista de Toledo and his successor Juan de Herrera. It houses a library (founded by Philip II) and an art gallery which includes works by El Greco, Velazquez, and Titian. It is a World Heritage site.

escort — *noun* **1** one or more people, vehicles, etc accompanying another or others for protection, guidance, or as a mark of honour. **2** a person of the opposite sex asked or hired to accompany another at a social event. — *verb* to accompany as an escort. [from French *escorte*]

escritoire *noun* a writing-desk, usually ornamented and with drawers, compartments, etc. [from French *escritoire*, from Latin *scriptorium*, writing-room]

escudo *noun* (PL. **escudos**) (ABBREV. **Esc.**) the standard unit of currency in Portugal. [from Portuguese *escudo*, from Latin *scutum*, shield]

esculent *formal* — *adj.* edible. — *noun* any edible substance. [from Latin *esculentus*, from *esca*, food]

escutcheon *noun* **1** a shield decorated with a coat of arms. **2** a small metal plate around a keyhole or doorknob.
— **a blot on the escutcheon** *facetious* a stain on one's good reputation.
[from Old French *escuchon*, from Latin *scutum*, shield]

-ese *suffix* forming nouns and adjectives: **1** relating to a stated country or place: *Japanese / Vietnamese*. **2** indicating the people or language of

a stated country: *Chinese*. **3** *often derog.* the typical style or language of a particular group or profession: *journalese*. [from Old French *-eis*, from Latin *-ensis*]

esker *noun Geol.* a long narrow hill of gravel and sand which may wind for long distances along a valley floor, and is thought to be formed by water flowing in tunnels underneath glaciers. [from Irish *eiscir*, ridge]

Eskimo — *noun* (PL. **Eskimos, Eskimo**) **1** *now often offensive* a member of any of several peoples inhabiting N Canada, Greenland, Alaska, and E Siberia. **2** the family of languages spoken by these peoples. — *adj.* relating to these peoples or to their language. [from N American Indian *esquimantsic*, eaters of raw flesh]
◊ Although *Eskimo* is the established English name for the people, the people themselves find it offensive and prefer the name *Inuit*.

Eskimo dog a powerful breed of dog used by Inuit (Eskimos) to pull sledges.

ESL *abbrev.* English as a second language.

ESN *abbrev.* educationally subnormal.

esophagus same as OESOPHAGUS.

esoteric *adj.* understood only by those few people who have the necessary special knowledge; secret; mysterious. [from Greek *esoterikos*, from *eso*, within]

esoterically *adv.* in an esoteric or mysterious way.

ESP *abbrev.* **1** English for special purposes. **2** extra-sensory perception.

esp. *abbrev.* especially.

espadrille *noun* a light canvas shoe with a sole made of rope or other plaited fibre. [from French *espadrille*, from Provençal *espardillo*, from *espart*, esparto grass]

espalier *noun* **1** a trellis or arrangement of wires against which a shrub or fruit tree is trained to grow flat, eg against a wall. **2** such a shrub or tree. [from French *espalier*]

esparto *or* **esparto grass** *noun* a tough coarse grass native to Spain and N Africa, used to make rope, etc. [from Spanish *esparto*, from Latin, from Greek *sparton*, kind of rope]

especial *adj.* special. [from Old French, from Latin *specialis*, individual]

especially *adv.* principally; more than in other cases.

Esperanto *noun* a language invented for international use, published in 1887. [from the pseudonym of its inventor, Dr Zamenhof, meaning 'the one who hopes']

espionage *noun* the activity of spying, or the use of spies to gather information. [from French *espionnage*, from *espion*, spy]

esplanade *noun* a long wide pavement next to a beach. [from French *esplanade*, from Spanish *esplanar*, make level]

espousal *noun* **1** *formal* the act of espousing (a cause, etc). **2** *old use* a marriage or engagement.

espouse *verb* **1** *formal* to adopt or give one's support to (a cause, etc). **2** *old use* to marry, or to give (eg a daughter) in marriage. [from Old French *espouser*, to marry]

espresso *noun* (PL. **espressos**) **1** coffee made by forcing steam or boiling water through ground coffee beans. **2** the machine for making it. [from Italian *espresso*, pressed out]

esprit *noun formal, literary* liveliness or wit. [from French *esprit*, spirit]

esprit de corps loyalty to, or concern for the honour of, a group or body to which one belongs. [French, = spirit of the group]

espy *verb* (**espies, espied**) *literary* to catch sight of; to observe. [from Old French *espier*]

Esq. *abbrev.* esquire.

-esque *suffix* **1** in the style or fashion of: *Byronesque*. **2** like or similar to: *picturesque*. [from French]

esquire *noun* **1** *abbrev.* (**Esq.**) a title used after a man's name when no other form of address, eg Mr, is used, especially when addressing letters. **2** a squire. [from Old French *esquier*, squire]

esquisse *noun* in art, a preliminary study: for a picture or design, usually a rapid sketch or rough drawing; for a sculpture, a model, often made smaller than the final work. [from French *esquisse*, sketch]

ESRC *abbrev.* Economic and Social Research Council.

-ess *suffix* indicating a female of the type or class: *lioness / duchess*. [from French *-esse*, from Latin *-issa*]

essay — *noun* **1** a short formal piece of writing, usually dealing with a single subject. **2** *formal* an attempt. — *verb formal* to attempt. [from French *essayer*, to try]

essayist *noun* a writer of literary essays.

Essays of Elia, The the collective name for two series of miscellaneous essays by Charles Lamb (1823–33). The first series appeared in the *London Magazine* (1820–3) under the pseudonym of Elia. The essays are reflective, largely autobiographical pieces, often light-hearted or nostalgic in tone.

Essen POP (1991e) 626 000, an industrial city in North Rhine-Westphalia state, W central Germany. It lies 29km/18mi NE of Düsseldorf, between the Emscher and Ruhr rivers. Essen is the headquarters of many large industrial corporations and is an important centre of retail trade. It was badly bombed during World War II. NOTABLE FEATURES Minster (9c–14c); Werden Abbey Church.

essence *noun* **1** the basic distinctive part or quality of something, determining its nature or character. **2** a liquid obtained from a plant, drug, etc and having its properties in concentrated form.

— **in essence** basically or fundamentally.

of the essence absolutely necessary or extremely important.

[from French *essence*, from Latin *esse*, to be]

Essenes a Jewish sect renowned in antiquity for its asceticism, communistic lifestyle, and skill in predicting the future. The Dead Sea Scrolls are believed to have belonged to a local Essene community.

essential — *adj.* **1** absolutely necessary. **2** of the basic or inner nature, the essence, of something. — *noun* **1** something necessary. **2** a basic or fundamental element, principle, or piece of information.

essentialism *noun* a doctrine, articulated by Aristotle and later philosophers, which claims that everything has a nature or essence, ie a mixture of properties such that if the thing were to lose any of them, it would cease to be. For example, being a mammal is an essential property of a cow; whereas being brown is an accidental property, something a cow could lose without ceasing to be.

essentiality *noun* being essential; an essential quality or nature.

essentially *adv.* **1** basically; most importantly. **2** necessarily.

essential oil *Bot.* a mixture of volatile oils which have distinctive and characteristic odours, obtained from certain aromatic plants, eg rose, jasmine, juniper. They are widely used in perfumes, cosmetics, antiseptics, flavourings, herbal medicines, and aromatherapy.

Essequibo, River the largest river in Guyana, draining over half the country. It rises in the Guiana Highlands on the Brazilian border and flows c.970km/600mi N to meet the Atlantic Ocean at a 32km-/20mi-wide delta, NW of Georgetown. Navigable for large vessels up to Bartica (c.80km/50mi), its course is interrupted by many rapids and falls.

Essex, Robert Devereux, 2nd Earl of (1566–1601) English soldier and courtier to Elizabeth I, born in Netherwood, Herefordshire. At court, he quickly rose in the favour of Elizabeth, despite his clandestine marriage (1590) with the widow of Sir Philip Sidney. In 1591 he commanded the forces sent to help Henry IV of France, and took part in the sacking of Cadiz (1595). His quarrels with the Queen's advisers, and with Elizabeth (notably the occasion when he turned his back on her, and she boxed his ears) eventually led to his imprisonment when his six-month lord-lieutenancy of Ireland (1599) proved a failure. He plotted to destroy the City of London, but was beheaded for high treason.

Essex POP (1987e) 1.6m, a county in SE England, which is divided into 14 districts. AREA 3 672sq km/1 417sq mi. It is bounded E by the North Sea, S by the estuary of the R Thames, SW by Greater London, W by Hertfordshire, and N by Cambridgeshire and Suffolk. CHIEF TOWNS Chelmsford (county town), Harwich (ferry port), Colchester, Southend-on-Sea. ECONOMY agriculture (especially cereals); oysters; electronics, motor vehicles; tourism.

Esso *abbrev.* Standard Oil.

est. *abbrev.* **1** established. **2** estimated.

-est *suffix* forming the superlative of adjectives and some adverbs: *quickest / soonest*. [from Anglo-Saxon *-est* and *-ost*]

establish *verb* **1** to settle (someone) firmly in a position, place, job, etc. **2** to set up (eg a university or a business). **3** to find, show, or prove. **4** to cause people to accept (eg a custom or a claim). [from Old French *establir*]

established *adj.* **1** settled or accepted. **2** said of a Church, recognized as the official Church of a country.

establishment *noun* **1** the act of establishing. **2** a business, its premises, or its staff. **3** a public or government institution: *a research establishment*. **4** (**the Establishment**) the group of people in a country, society, or community who hold power and exercise authority, and are regarded as being opposed to change.

estancia *noun* a large estate or cattle ranch in Spanish America. [from Spanish *estancia*, station, dwelling]

Estaque, L' a landscape painting by Paul Cézanne (c.1888, Louvre, Paris).

estate *noun* **1** a large piece of land owned by a person or group of people. **2** an area of land on which development of a particular kind has taken place, eg houses in a **housing estate**) or factories (an **industrial trading estate**). **3** *Legal* a person's total possessions (property, money, etc), especially at death. **4** a plantation. **5** *Hist.* any of various groups or classes within the social structure of society, eg the **first estate** or lords spiritual (ie bishops and archbishops), the **second estate** or lords temporal (ie the nobility) and the **third estate** (the common people). **6** *old use* a condition or state: *the holy estate of matrimony*. [from Old French *estat*]

estate agent **1** a person whose job is the buying, selling, leasing, and valuation of houses and other property. **2** the manager of a private estate.

estate car a car with a large area behind the rear seats for luggage, etc, and a rear door.

estate duty same as DEATH DUTY.

Estates General, French *États-Généraux* an assembly representing the different provinces of the French monarchy, called by the king primarily to grant taxes. It began in 1347 but never met on a regular basis, and after the meeting of 1614 no more were called until 1789. In the intervening period the king ruled as an absolute monarch, although some provincial Estates continued to meet intermittently. Both the Estates General and the provincial Estates met and voted in three separate houses: the First Estate (the clergy), the Second Estate (the nobility) and the Third Estate (the commoners).

esteem — *verb* **1** to value, respect, or think highly of. **2** *formal* to consider to be. — *noun* high regard or respect. [from Old French *estimer*, from Latin *aestimare*, to estimate the value of]

Estella the cold-hearted beauty in Charles Dickens's *Great Expectations*, brought up by Miss Havisham, and loved by Pip.

Estelle a female first name, revived in the 19c with the Latinate form *Estella*. [an Old French form of Latin *stella*, star (see STELLA)]

ester *noun* *Chem.* an organic chemical compound formed by the reaction of an alcohol with an organic acid, with the loss of a water molecule. Some fragrant volatile esters are used as food flavourings, and many esters occur naturally in plants and animals as oils and fats. [probably a contraction of German *Essigäther*, acetic ether]

Esterházy (1600–1866) a powerful aristocratic family of Hungary, which flourished in several branches between the 16c and 19c. Among its many members were Count Pál Esterhzy of Fraknó (1635–1713), Austrian field marshal, who was made a Prince of the Empire in 1687 for his successes against the Turks. Prince Miklós IV (1765–1833) fought against Napoleon, and also gathered a splendid collection of pictures at Vienna, but by extravagance brought his vast estates into sequestration. Prince Pál Antal (1786–1866) represented Austria at London until 1842 and in 1848 became Minister of Foreign Affairs.

Esth. *abbrev. Biblical* (Book of) Esther.

Esther **1** a biblical character, slave of king Ahasuerus. **2** a female first name. [a Persian translation of Hebrew *Hadassah*, myrtle]

Esther, Book of a book of the Hebrew Bible and Old Testament. It tells how Esther, a cousin and foster daughter of the Jew, Mordecai, became the wife of the Persian king Ahasuerus (Xerxes I) and prevented the extermination of Jews by the order of Haman, a king's officer. The event is said to be the source of the Jewish feast of Purim. The Additions to the Book of Esther are not contained in the Hebrew Bible, but are found in the Septuagint, the Old Testament Apocrypha, and as Esther 11–16 in the Catholic Bible.

esthetic same as AESTHETIC.

estimable *adj.* highly respected; worthy of respect. [see ESTIMATE]

estimate — *verb* (pronounced *-mate*) **1** to judge or calculate (size, amount, value, etc) roughly or without measuring. **2** to have or form an opinion (that); to think. **3** to submit to a possible client a statement of (the likely cost) of carrying out a job. — *noun* (pronounced *-mət*) **1** a rough assessment (of size, etc). **2** a calculation of the probable cost of a job. [from Latin *aestimare*, to estimate the value of]

estimation *noun* **1** judgement; opinion. **2** the act of estimating.

estimator *noun* a person who estimates values, etc.

Estonia, Estonian **Eesti**, Russian **Estonskaya** POP (1993e) 1.5m, a republic in E Europe, bounded W by the Baltic Sea, N by the Gulf of Finland, E by Russia, and S by Latvia. AREA 45 100sq km/17 409sq mi. CAPITAL Tallinn. CHIEF

Estonia

TOWNS Tartu, Narva, Kohtla-Järve, Pärnu. TIME ZONE GMT +2. Most of the population are Estonian with Russian, Ukrainian, and Belorussian minorities; Protestantism is the chief religion. OFFICIAL LANGUAGE Estonian. CURRENCY the kroon. PHYSICAL DESCRIPTION there are over 1 500 lakes in a fairly flat terrain; there are many islands on the coast, notably Saaremaa, Hiiumaa, and Muhu; 36% of the area is forested. HISTORY ceded to Russia in 1721; achieved independence in 1918; a Soviet Socialist Republic from 1940, it was occupied by Germany during World War II; there was a resurgence of the nationalist movement in the 1980s; declared independence in 1991. GOVERNMENT parliament elects a President. ECONOMY shale oil; machines; metalworking; chemicals; food processing; cotton; fabrics; timber; dairy farming; pigs; fishing; the economy suffered as a result of the transfer to a free market system but began to stabilize in 1993.

Estonian — noun the language spoken by about one million people in Estonia; the official language of the country. It belongs to the Finno-Ugric branch of the Uralic family of languages. — adj. relating to or spoken or written in Estonian.

Estragon one of the two argumentative tramps in Samuel Beckett's *Waiting for Godot*.

estrange verb to cause (someone) to break away from a previously friendly state or relationship. [from Old French *estranger*, from Latin *extraneare*, to treat as a stranger]

estranged adj. no longer friendly or supportive: *his estranged wife*.

estrangement noun separation; loss of friendship or affection.

Estremadura a province and former region of W central Portugal. AREA 3 249sq km/1 254sq mi. It is the political and cultural centre of Portugal, and a popular tourist region. CHIEF TOWN Lisbon. ECONOMY agriculture (vines, fruit and vegetables, olives, wheat, maize, and rice); sheep, goats. NOTABLE FEATURE thermal springs. [from Latin *extrema durii*, farthest land on the Douro]

estuary noun (PL. **estuaries**) the broad mouth of a river that flows into the sea, where fresh water mixes with sea water. Estuaries are affected by the tides, and are often used as harbours because they are relatively sheltered. [from Latin *aestus*, commotion, tide]

ESU abbrev. English-Speaking Union.

Esztergom, German **Gran**, ancient **Strigonium** POP (1990) 30 000, a river-port town in Komárom county, N Hungary, situated on the R Danube, NW of Budapest. HISTORY a fortress in Roman times; capital of Hungary in the 10c; Hungary's first king, St Stephen, was born here in c.975; seat of primate in 1198. NOTABLE FEATURES 19c Basilica (the largest church in Hungary); thermal springs nearby.

ET abbrev., as an international vehicle mark Egypt.

E.T.– The Extra-Terrestrial a US film directed by Steven Spielberg (1982). It is a sentimental tale of a young boy who gives sanctuary to an abandoned alien. It was an enormous box-office success.

ETA abbrev. estimated time of arrival.

et al. abbrev. *et alia* or *et alii* (Latin), and other things or people.

etc or **etc.** abbrev. et cetera.

et cetera or **etcetera** (Latin) and the rest, and so on.

etceteras pl. noun additional things or people; extras.

etch verb 1 trans., intrans. to make designs on (metal, glass, etc) using an acid to eat out the lines. 2 to make a deep or irremovable impression. [from German *ätzen*, to etch, eat away with acid]

etcher noun a person who etches, especially professionally.

etching noun 1 the act or art of making etched designs. 2 a print made from an etched plate.

ETD abbrev. estimated time of departure.

Eteocles in Greek legend, the elder one of Oedipus's two sons; both were cursed by their father. Eteocles became king of Thebes after his father's death, and refused to share power with his brother Polynices. Seven Champions attacked the city, and Eteocles was killed by Polynices.

eternal adj. 1 without beginning or end; everlasting. 2 unchanging; valid for all time. 3 colloq. frequent, endless.
— **the Eternal** a name for God.
[from Old French *eternel*, from Latin *aeternalis*]

eternally adv. for ever; without end; constantly.

eternal triangle a relationship, involving love and jealousy, between two men and a woman, or two women and a man.

eternity noun (PL. **eternities**) 1 time regarded as having no end. 2 the state of being eternal. 3 Relig. a timeless existence after death. 4 colloq. an extremely long time. [from Old French *eternite*]

eternity ring a ring set with a circle of stones, as a symbol of lasting love.

ETH abbrev., as an international vehicle mark Ethiopia.

ethane noun Chem. (FORMULA C_2H_6) a colourless odourless flammable gas belonging to the alkane series of hydrocarbons, and found in natural gas. It is used as a fuel and refrigerant, and in the synthesis of organic compounds. [from ETHER + -*ane*]

ethanedioic acid Chem. oxalic acid.

ethanediol noun ethylene glycol.

ethanol noun Chem. (FORMULA C_2H_5OH) a colourless volatile flammable alcohol that is produced by fermentation of the sugar in fruit or cereals, and is used as an intoxicant in alcoholic beverages, and as a fuel. — Also called *ethyl alcohol*.

Ethel a female first name, now rare. [in 19c, the short form of names beginning *ethel*, noble (variant of Germanic *adal*) before becoming an independent name]

Ethelbert (c.552–616) King of Kent (560–616). During his reign Kent achieved (c.590) control over England south of the Humber, Christianity was introduced by St Augustine (597), and English laws were written down for the first time.

Ethelred or **Aethelred I** (c.830–71) King of Wessex (865–71), the elder brother of Alfred the Great. During his Reign the Danes launched their main invasion of England, and he died soon after his victory over them at Ashdown, Berkshire.

Ethelred or **Aethelred II**, also called the **Unready** (c.968–1016) King of England (from 978), the son of Edgar. He ascended the throne as a boy, after the murder of his half-brother, Edward the Martyr. In 1002 he confirmed an alliance with Normandy by marrying as his second wife Duke Richard's daughter Emma — the first dynastic link between the two countries. In 1013 the Viking Sweyn Forkbeard secured mastery over the whole of England, forcing Ethelred into exile in Normandy until Sweyn's death (1014). He returned to oppose Canute, but the unity of English resistance was broken by the rebellion of his son Edmund Ironside. 'Unready' is a mistranslation of Unraed ('ill advised'), a pun on his given name, Aethelred ('good counsel').

ethene noun Chem. same as ETHYLENE.

ether noun 1 any of a group of organic chemical compounds that are volatile and highly flammable, and contain two hydrocarbon groups linked by an oxygen atom. They are formed by the dehydration of alcohols. 2 (**diethyl ether**) (FORMULA $C_2H_5OC_2H_5$) the commonest ether, widely used as a solvent, and formerly employed as an anaesthetic. 3 (also **aether**) Physics a hypothetical medium formerly believed to be necessary for the transmission of electromagnetic radiation. This concept was abandoned when the theory of relativity was accepted. 4 (also **aether**) poetic the

clear upper air or a clear sky. [from Greek *aither*, the heavens]

ethereal adj. 1 of an unreal lightness or delicateness; fairy-like. 2 heavenly or spiritual. [see ETHER]

ethereally adv. in an ethereal way; spiritually.

ethic noun the moral system or set of principles particular to a certain person, community, group, etc. [from Greek *ethikos*, from *ethos*, custom, character]

ethical adj. 1 of or concerning morals, justice, or duty. 2 morally right. 3 said of a medicine or drug not advertised to the general public, and available only on prescription.

ethically adv. as regards ethics or moral principles: *an ethically justifiable practice*.

ethics noun 1 (sing.) the study or the science of morals. 2 (pl.) rules or principles of behaviour: *medical ethics*.

Ethiopia, formerly **Abyssinia**, official name **Socialist Ethiopia**, Amharic **Hebretesebawit Ityopia** POP (1992e) 54.6m, a state in NE Africa, which is divided into 15 regions. AREA 1 128 497sq km/435 600sq mi. It is bounded W and SW by Sudan, S by Kenya, E and NE by Somalia, and N by Djibouti and the Red Sea. CAPITAL Addis Ababa. CHIEF TOWNS Dire Dawa, Harer. TIME ZONE GMT +3. Ethnic groups include Galla (40%), Amhara and Tigray (32%). The main religions are Islam (40–45%) and Ethiopian Orthodox (35–40%). OFFICIAL LANGUAGE Amharic. CURRENCY the birr. PHYSICAL DESCRIPTION dominated by a mountainous central plateau; split diagonally by the Great Rift Valley; the highest point is Ras Dashan Mt (4 620m); the plateau is crossed E–W by the Blue Nile, which has its source in L Tana; the N and E are relatively low-lying; in the NE the Danakil Depression dips to 116m below sea level; the country is landlocked, having lost about 10% of its territory and all of its Red Sea coastline, since the former province of Eritrea separated from Ethiopia. CLIMATE tropical, moderated by higher altitudes; distinct wet season (Apr–Sep); temperatures warm, but rarely hot all year round; annual rainfall generally over 1 000mm; hot, semi-arid NE and SE lowlands receive less than 500mm annually; severe droughts in the 1980s caused widespread famine, deaths, and resettlement, with massive amounts of foreign aid. HISTORY oldest independent country in sub-Saharan Africa; first Christian country in Africa; Abyssinian independence recognized by the League of Nations in 1923; Italian invasion in 1935; annexation as Italian East Africa in 1936–41; Haile Selassie returned from exile in 1941; military coup, with the formation of the Provisional Military Administrative Council (PMAC) in 1974; opposition by left-wing civilian groups countered by mass arrests and executions in 1977–8; ongoing conflict with Somalia over Ogaden region; internal conflict with regional separatist Eritrean and Tigrean forces; government offensive successful in 1978, but received setbacks in the early 1980s; severe famine in the 1980s; PMAC dissolved in 1987, with the transfer of power to the People's Democratic Republic; attempted coup 1989; collapse of the government in 1991; famine in 1992; independence for Eritrea in 1993. GOVERNMENT a President and Prime Minister, a Council of Representatives and a Council of Ministers. ECONOMY one of the world's poorest countries; over 80% of the population is employed in agriculture, especially subsistence farming; exports mainly coffee, also sugar, cotton, pulses, oil

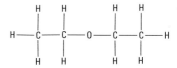

diethyl ether

Ethiopia

seeds; production severely affected by drought; small amounts of oil, gold, cement, salt; food processing, tobacco, textiles; distribution of foreign aid hindered by internal conflicts and poor local organization.

Ethiopianism a type of nationalist movement founded among US and West Indian blacks which looks towards Africa as their place of origin. It is connected with messianism and the independent black Churches that broke away from established Christianity.

ethnic *adj.* **1** relating to, or having, a common race or cultural tradition: *an ethnic group.* **2** associated with, or resembling, an exotic, especially non-European, racial or tribal group: *ethnic clothes.* **3** from the point of view of race, rather than nationality: *ethnic Asians.* **4** between or involving different racial groups: *ethnic violence.* [from Greek *ethnikos*, from *ethnos*, nation]

ethnically *adv.* as regards race; in terms of race.

ethnic cleansing genocide or forced removal inflicted by one ethnic group on all others in a particular area.

ethnicity *noun* racial status or distinctiveness.

Ethniki Organosis Kipriakou Agonos (ABBREV. **EOKA**) a Greek Cypriot underground movement that aimed to end British rule and achieve *enosis*, the union of Cyprus with Greece. Founded in 1955 by a Greek army officer Col George Grivas, with the support of Archbishop Makarios III, its campaign of anti-British violence came to a climax in 1956–7. Following Makarios' acceptance of Cypriot independence rather than *enosis*, EOKA was disbanded (1958), and in 1971–4 it was unsuccessfully resurrected as EOKA B. [from Greek, = National Organization of Cypriot Struggle]

ethnocentric *adj.* relating to, or holding, the belief that one's own cultural tradition or racial group is superior to all others. [from Greek *ethnos*, nation + -CENTRIC]

ethnocentricity *or* **ethnocentrism** *noun* the policy or practice of being ethnocentric.

ethnography *noun* a detailed description of the culture of a particular society based on fieldwork and participation in the life of the society. Ethnography was pioneered by the Polish anthropologist Bronislaw Malinowski (1884–1942), who made an intensive study of the Trobriand Islanders in the early 1920s.

ethnolinguistics *sing. noun* the study of the relationship between language and cultural behaviour. It is concerned with all aspects of language, eg its structure, usage, association with national and culture identity, etc.

ethnological *adj.* relating to ethnology or the study of race.

ethnologist *noun* a person who studies ethnology or race.

ethnology *noun* the scientific study of different races and cultural traditions, and their relations with each other. [from Greek *ethnos*, nation]

ethnomusicology *noun* the study of music in its racial, cultural, and social contexts. The term is applied particularly to the study of folk and national music outside the European tradition, eg the music of primitive cultures in S America, Asia, and Africa. Some studies based on oral tradition were made in the 18c and 19c, but it was not until sound recording became easily available that the discipline developed and established itself on a scientific basis.

ethnoscience *noun* **1** a branch of social and cultural anthropology which investigates folk beliefs or ideologies that correspond to such fields of Western Science as medicine, astronomy, and zoology. **2** ethnography.

ethology *Zool.* the study of animal behaviour, especially by direct observation and monitoring (eg by radio-tracking) of animals in their natural habitats. [from Greek *ethos*, custom + -LOGY]

ethos *noun* the typical spirit, character, or attitudes (of a group, community, etc). [from Greek *ethos*, custom, culture]

ethyl *noun Chem.* in organic chemical compounds, the (C_2H_5-) group, as for example in ethylamine $(C_2H_5NH_2)$. [from ETHER + Greek *hyle*, matter]

ethylene *noun* (FORMULA C_2H_4) a colourless flammable gas with a sweet smell, belonging to the alkene series of hydrocarbons. It is used in the manufacture of organic chemicals and polyethylene (polythene), and as an agricultural chemical to hasten the ripening of fruit. — Also called *ethene*.

ethylene diamine tetra-acetic acid *Chem.* a white crystalline compound, the sodium salt of which is used to remove small traces of metal ions from solutions, and as an antidote for poisoning by certain heavy metals.

ethylene glycol *Chem.* a thick liquid alcohol used as an antifreeze. — Also called *ethanediol*.

ethyne *noun Chem.* same as ACETYLENE.

etiolated *adj.* **1** *Bot.,* said of a plant having foliage that has become yellow through lack of sunlight. **2** *formal literary,* said of a person pale and weak in appearance. [from French *étioler*, to become pale]

etiolation *noun Bot.* the abnormal appearance of plants grown in darkness or severely reduced light, where the leaves appear yellow due to lack of chlorophyll and the stems are long and spindly.

etiology same as AETIOLOGY.

etiquette *noun* **1** conventions of correct or polite social behaviour. **2** rules, usually unwritten, regarding the behaviour of members of a particular profession, etc towards each other. [from French *étiquette*, label]

Etna, Mount, in Sicily **Mongibello** the largest active volcano in Europe, situated in Catania province, E Sicily, Italy, 29km/18mi NW of Catania. HEIGHT 3 323m. It has the form of a truncated cone with an almost circular base 40km/25mi in diameter and 145km/90mi in circumference; there are over 200 subsidiary cones on the flanks of the mountain, notably the twin-peaked Monti Rossi (948m high). Fertile lower slopes allow the cultivation of oranges, lemons, olives, and vines; higher up are forest, maquis, and a desert zone of lava and ashes. The mountain peak is snow-covered for nine months of the year. The solar power station *Eurhelios* is on the S slope, receiving an average annual sunshine of 3 000 hours. Recent major eruptions were in 1949, 1971, 1985, and 1992.

Eton see WINDSOR.

Etruria a region in ancient Italy, roughly corresponding to modern Tuscany. In antiquity, it was inhabited mainly by the Etruscans.

Etruscans a people of obscure origin who inhabited Etruria in W central Italy from the 8c BC. They succumbed to the Romans politically in the 3c BC, though culturally their influence remained strong.

-ette *suffix* **1** indicating a female of the stated type: *usherette.* **2** indicating a small thing of the type: *cigarette / kitchenette.* **3** indicating an imitation: *leatherette.* [from Old French *-ette*]

étude *noun Mus.* a short piece written for a single instrument, intended as an exercise or a means of showing talent. [from French *étude*, study]

ety. *abbrev.* etymology.

etymological *adj.* relating to etymology or the origin of words.

etymologically *adv.* as regards etymology or the origin of words.

etymologist *noun* a person who studies etymology or the origin of words.

etymology *noun* (PL. **etymologies**) **1** the study of the origin and development of words and their meanings. **2** an explanation of the history of a particular word. [from Latin *etymologia*, from Greek *etymon*, the literal sense of a word, from *etymos*, true]

E-type Jaguar a sports car first produced in 1961. One version of the E-type contained a V12 engine of 5.3l which made it capable of over 240kph/150mph. After producing some 75 000 E-Types, Jaguar discontinued the model in 1975, and it became a collector's item.

EU *abbrev.* European Union.

Eu *symbol Chem.* europium.

Euboea, Greek **Évvoia**, Italian **Negropon** POP (1991) 209 000, the second largest Greek island, situated in the Aegean Sea. Euboea is separated from the mainland by a narrow channel. AREA 3 655sq km/1 411sq mi; length 144km/89mi. CAPITAL Chalcis. CHIEF TOWNS Istiaia, Kimi, Karistos. ECONOMY olives, grapes, cereals; sheep, goats; tourism (several coastal resorts).

eucalyptus *noun* (PL. **eucalyptuses**, **eucalypti**) **1** any of various evergreen trees of the genus *Eucalyptus*, native to Australia but grown widely elsewhere. They have oval leathery leaves, and flowers modified to form woody cups with 'lids' which fall to release numerous conspicuous stamens. The different groups are identified by their bark, which may be smooth, scaly, fibrous, or black in colour. Eucalyptus trees are rapid growing, the tallest reaching a height of 97m, and they are often planted for timber. Some species produce eucalyptus oil, which is strongly antiseptic and used in various medicines, while others are grown as ornamental trees for their blue-tinted foliage. Eucalyptus trees are a major or sole source of food for various animals, eg koalas. **2** the hard durable wood of this tree,

eucalyptus

which contains strong-smelling resins, and is widely used as timber. **3** eucalyptus oil. [from Greek *eu*, well + *kalyptos*, covered]

Eucharist, also called **Mass (Roman Catholic)**, **Holy Communion**, or the **Lord's Supper (Protestant)** a sacrament, the central act of worship for most Christian denominations. Based on the example of Jesus at the Last Supper, when he identified the bread which he broke and the wine which he poured with his body and blood (1 Corinthians 11.23–5; Matthew 26.26–8; Mark 14.22–4; Luke 22.17–20), it generally consists of the consecration of bread and wine by the priest or minister and its distribution among the worshippers (*communion*). Theological interpretations vary through such interpretations as transubstantiation and consubstantiation, to symbolism representing the real presence of Christ and a simple memorial meal. [from Greek *eucharistia*, thanksgiving]

Eucharistic *adj.* relating to the Eucharist.

euchre *noun* an American card-game for two, three, or four players, played with 32 cards.

Euclid (fl.300 BC) Greek mathematician who taught in Alexandria, where he appears to have founded a mathematical school. His *Elements of Geometry*, in 13 books, is the earliest substantial Greek mathematical treatise to have survived and probably the most widely known mathematical work; with modifications and simplifications it was still being used as a school textbook in the earlier part of the 20c. The approach which obeys his axioms became known as Euclidean geometry.

Euclidean *or* **Euclidian** *adj.* of, or relating to, the geometrical system devised by *Euclid*, a Greek mathematician of the 3c BC.

Euclidean geometry *Maths.* a system of three-dimensional geometry based on the theories of the Greek mathematician Euclid.

Eudoxus of Cnidus (408–353 BC) Greek mathematician, astronomer, and geographer. Thought to have been a member of Plato's Academy, he formed his own school in Cyzicus. He made many advances in geometry, and it is possible that much of Euclid's *Elements* is largely his work. He drew maps of the stars and the known areas of the world, and correctly recalculated the length of the solar year.

Eugene POP (1990) 113 000, the capital of Lane County in W Oregon, USA. It lies on the Willamette R and was founded in 1851.

Eugene a male first name. [an Old French form of Greek *eugenes*, well-born, noble]

Eugene of Savoy, Prince, properly **François Eugène de Savoie Carignan** (1663–1736) Austrian soldier, born in Paris. After Louis XIV of France refused to commission him, he entered the service of the Emperor Leopold against the Turks, whom he defeated on several occasions to end their power in Hungary (1699–1718). He fought against France in two wars between 1689 and 1714, and while in command of the imperial army he helped Marlborough at Blenheim (1704), Oudenarde (1708), and at Malplaquet (1709). However, when Holland and England withdrew he was defeated by Villars (1712), but he later captured Belgrade (1718).

Eugene Onegin **1** a novel in verse by Alexander Pushkin (written 1823–31). It is set in St Petersburg and describes the relationship between Tatyana and Onegin. His rejection of her and flirtation with her sister results in a duel in which he kills his friend and leaves for six years, but returns to rejection by the now faithfully married Tatyana. **2** an opera by Tchaikovsky (1879), based on Pushkin's novel.

eugenic *adj.* relating to eugenics or the science of improving human populations.

eugenically *adv.* in terms of eugenics or the improvement of human populations.

eugenics *sing. noun* **1** the science concerned with the detection and elimination of human hereditary diseases and disorders by genetic counselling of parents who may be carriers of such conditions. **2** the principle or practice, now largely discredited, of improving the human race by selective breeding from individuals who are regarded as strong, healthy, intelligent, etc. [from Greek *eugenes*, well-born, of good stock]

euglena *noun* a single-celled organism of the genus *Euglena*, found in fresh water, and having a long whip-like structure or flagellum at its front end, which is used to propel it through the water. It usually contains chlorophyll in chloroplasts, and is often classified as a green alga, but sometimes lacks chlorophyll, feeds like an animal, and is classified as a member of the phylum Protozoa. [from Greek *eu*, well + *glene*, eyeball]

eukaryote *or* **eucaryote** *Biol.* an organism in which the cells have a distinct nucleus containing the genetic material and separated from the cytoplasm by a nuclear membrane. The genetic material comprises several chromosomes containing DNA associated with histone proteins. [from Greek *eu*, well + *karyon*, kernel]. See also PROKARYOTE.
◇ All living organisms apart from bacteria and cyanobacteria (blue-green algae) are eukaryotes. Eukaryotic cells divide by mitosis and meiosis, and their cytoplasm contains many organelles (specialized structures with a specific function), such as mitochondria and ribosomes. If chlorophyll is present, it is confined within organelles known as chloroplasts.

Euler, Leonhard (1707–83) Swiss mathematician, born in Basle. Professor in St Petersburg and Director of Mathematics and Physics in the Berlin Academy, he was a major figure in 18c mathematics. He published over 800 different books and papers, on every aspect of pure and applied mathematics, physics, and astronomy. In analysis he studied infinite series and differential equations, introduced or established many new functions, and created the calculus of variations; many important concepts in mathematics are named after him.

Euler, Ulf Svante von (1905–83) Swedish pharmacologist, born in Stockholm. Working at the Karolinska Institute, he isolated and named prostaglandins in 1935. Later, in the study of neurally active chemicals, he isolated and characterized the principal transmitter of the sympathetic nervous system, noradrenaline, in the early 1940s. He was appointed Professor of Physiology at the Karolinska in 1939, and shared the 1970 Nobel Prize for Physiology or Medicine with Julius Axelrod and Bernard Katz.

Euler-Chelpin, Hans Karl August Simon von (1873–1964) German-Swedish biochemist, born in Augsburg. After graduating from Berlin University in 1895, he joined the staff of the University of Stockholm, where he became Professor of Chemistry in 1906 and later director of the newly established biochemical institute (1929). Following the discovery that enzymes contain easily removable non-protein parts known as coenzymes, he determined the structure of a coenzyme involved in the fermentation of sugars. For this work he shared the 1929 Nobel Prize for Chemistry with Sir Arthur Harden. His son Ulf von Euler was awarded a Nobel prize in 1970.

eulogistic *adj.* expressing praise.

eulogistically *adv.* as an expression of praise.

eulogize *or* **eulogise** *verb* to praise highly.

eulogy *noun* (PL. **eulogies**) **1** a speech or piece of writing in praise of someone or something. **2** high praise. [from Latin *eulogium*, from Greek *eu*, well + *logos*, discourse]

Eumenides in Greek mythology, a euphemistic name given to the Furies, as in Aeschylus' play of the same name. The name means 'the kindly ones'.

eunuch *noun* **1** a man who has been castrated, especially one formerly employed as a guard of a harem in Eastern countries. **2** *derog.* a person who lacks power or effectiveness in some respect. [from Greek *eunouchos*]

Eupen POP (1991e) 17 000, a town in E Liège province, Belgium. It is the principal town in German-speaking Belgium, a popular health resort (famed for the Kneipp water-cure), and a holiday centre. NOTABLE FEATURES Belgium's largest artificial lake; St Nicholas Church (1727).

euphemism *noun* **1** a mild or inoffensive term used in place of one considered offensive or unpleasantly direct, eg *pass on* instead of *die*. **2** the use of such terms. [from Greek *eu*, well + *phanai*, to speak]

euphemistic *adj.*, *said of an expression* serving as a euphemism, or mild expression replacing a harsher one.

euphemistically *adv.* with a euphemistic manner; as a euphemism.

euphonious *adj.* pleasing to the ear.

euphoniously *adv.* in a way that sounds pleasant; harmoniously.

euphonium *noun* a brass instrument of the tuba family.
◇ The euphonium generally has four valves and is occasionally used as an orchestral instrument for parts marked 'tenor tuba' (as in Holst's *The Planets*). It is more usually found in brass and military bands.

euphony *noun* (PL. **euphonies**) **1** a pleasing sound, especially in speech. **2** pleasantness of sound, especially of pronunciation. [from Greek *eu*, well + *phone*, sound]

euphoria *noun* a feeling of wild happiness and well-being. In unjustified circumstances it may be a symptom of mania or the side-effect of certain drugs. [from Greek *euphoria*, ability to endure well]

euphoric *adj.* feeling intense happiness.

euphorically *adv.* with intense happiness.

Euphrates, River, Arabic **Al Furat**, Turkish **Firat** the longest river in W Asia, length 2 735km/ 1 700mi, formed in E central Turkey by the confluence of the Kara (W Euphrates) and Murat. It flows generally S to the Syrian border, then SE into Iraq. It unites with the Tigris NW of Basra to form the Shatt al-Arab, which flows for 192km/119mi to enter the Arabian Gulf. The upper course flows swiftly through deep canyons. It is used extensively for irrigation in Syria. Canals link with the R Tigris. There are remains of several ancient cities (eg Babylon) along present or former banks.

Euphues a romance in two parts by John Lyly (c.1578, 1580). It describes the travelling adventures of Euphues, a young Athenian. It is notable for its affected style of writing, which gave its name to the term 'euphuism'.

euphuism *noun* a pompous and affected style of writing. [from the style of John Lyly's romance *Euphues*]

euphuistic *adj.* having a pompous and affected style.

euphuistically *adv.* in a pompous and affected style.

Eur. *abbrev.* Europe.

Eurasian — *adj.* **1** of mixed European and Asian descent. **2** of, or relating to, Europe and Asia. — *noun* a person of mixed European and Asian descent.

Euratom *abbrev.* European Atomic Energy Community.

eureka *interj.* an exclamation of triumph at finding something, solving a problem, etc. [from Greek *heureka*, I have found it]

Eureka Stockade an armed clash in Australia between goldminers and a combined police and military force at the site of Ballarat,

Victoria (1854), which cost the lives of 30 miners and five soldiers, after miners objected to the expensive mining licence imposed by the government. Public opinion swung behind the miners, reforms to the goldfields were carried out, and the government was forced to back down.

eurhythmic *adj.* **1** *Archit.* in harmonious proportion. **2** relating to eurhythmics.

eurhythmics *sing. noun* the art or a system of rhythmic movement, specifically the system of musical training devised by the Swiss composer and teacher Emile Jaques-Dalcroze, which employed bodily movements to develop a quick response to changing rhythms. [from Greek *eu*, well + *rhythmos*, rhythm]

Euripides (c.480–406 BC) Greek tragic dramatist, born in Athens. He abandoned painting for literature, writing about 80 dramas, of which 19 survive, including *Medea*, *Electra*, and *Trojan Women*. Some (eg *The Bacchae*) were put on the Athenian stage only after the author's death, when his work became very popular.

Euro- *combining form* Europe or European.

Eurocheque *noun* a cheque which may be drawn on the user's own account and exchanged for cash, goods, or services in a number of European (and non-European) countries.

Eurocommunism an attempt in the 1970s and 1980s by W European communist parties to refashion Marxism–Leninism and follow a doctrine more appropriate to liberal democracies and market economies, led by the Italian Communist Party.

Eurocrat *noun sometimes derog.* an official involved in the administration of any organization in the European Community.

Eurocurrency or **Euromoney** *noun* convertible currencies, including pounds sterling, French and Swiss francs, Deutschmarks, and US dollars, held in banks in W Europe outside the country of origin. They can be borrowed by commercial undertakings for trade.

Eurodollars *pl. noun* US currency held in European banks to assist trade.

Eurofighter the name given to the standardized air-to-air and ground-attack aircraft which has been jointly developed by Britain, Germany, Italy, and Spain. It is expected to equip the air forces of these countries by the year 2000.

Euromoney see EUROCURRENCY.

Europa **1** (*also* **Europe**) in Greek mythology, the daughter of Agenor, king of Tyre. She was abducted by Zeus in the shape of a bull, who swam with her on his back to Crete. Her children were Minos, Rhadamanthus, and Sarpedon. **2** *Astron.* the fourth largest moon of Jupiter, 3 140km in diameter, discovered by Galileo.

Europa Nostra an international federation established in 1963 for the preservation of historic sites, buildings, and monuments. It represents more than 200 organizations from 20 countries. [from Italian, = our Europe]

Europe the second-smallest continent, forming an extensive peninsula of the Eurasian land-mass. It occupies c.7% of the earth's surface. It is bounded N and NE by the Arctic Ocean, NW and W by the Atlantic Ocean, S by the Mediterranean Sea, and E by Asia beyond the Ural Mts. It supports over 25% of the world's population. Major rivers include the Danube, Loire, Rhine, Rhône, and Tagus. Major mountain systems include the Alps, rising to 4 807m at Mont Blanc, and the Pyrenees, rising to 3 404m at Pico de Aneto.

European — *adj.* **1** of, or relating to, Europe. **2** showing or favouring a spirit of co-operation between the countries of Europe, especially those of the European Community. — *noun* **1** a native or inhabitant of Europe. **2** a person who favours close political and economic contact between the countries of Europe, especially those of the European Community.

European Broadcasting Union (ABBREV. **EBU**) the professional association of national broadcasting organizations of W Europe, N Africa, and the Near East, founded in 1950 to promote co-operation between its members.

European Coal and Steel Community (ABBREV. **ECSC**) the first European economic institution, set up in 1952. It has worked to remove customs duties and quota restrictions in coal, iron ore, and scrap, and aims to ensure that competition in these commodities is fair.

European Commission (ABBREV. **EC**) the administrative body of the European Community, which is collectively responsible to the European Parliament. Its functions are to uphold the European ideal, propose new policy initiatives, and ensure that existing policies are implemented. It comprises 17 commissioners from the member states — two each from the UK, France, Germany, Italy, and Spain, and one each from the others — who serve a four-year term and are each responsible for a specific area of work. In practice the Commission's intended role as the main source of direction and decision-making within the EC has fallen to the Council of Ministers.

European Community (ABBREV. **EC**) a community of 12 states in W Europe created for the purpose of achieving economic and political integration. It comprises three communities, the first of which was the *European Steel and Coal Community*, established (1952) under the Treaty of Paris by France, West Germany, Italy, Belgium, the Netherlands, and Luxembourg. Under the Treaty of Rome (1958), the six states established the *European Economic Community* and the *European Atomic Energy Community*, which provided for collaboration in the civilian sector of nuclear power. Six countries joined later: Denmark, Ireland, and the UK (1973); Greece (1981); and Portugal and Spain (1986). Turkey is seeking to become a member. To develop and oversee the policies of economic and political integration there are a number of supranational community institutions: the Commission, the

EC Membership		
Name of country	Year of joining	MEPs
Belgium	1958	24
Denmark	1973	16
France	1958	81
Germany	1958	81
Greece	1981	24
Ireland	1973	15
Italy	1958	81
Luxembourg	1958	6
Netherlands	1958	25
Portugal	1986	24
Spain	1986	60
United Kingdom	1973	81

Members of the European Parliament	
No. of seats	567
Belgium	25
Denmark	16
France	87
Germany	99
Greece	25
Ireland	15
Italy	87
Luxembourg	6
Netherlands	31
Portugal	25
Spain	64
United Kingdom	87

Council, the European Parliament, and the European Court of Justice.

European Council the body (established 1974) which twice a year brings together the heads of state and/or government of the member states of the European Community for the purpose of overall policy direction.

European Court of Justice see COURT OF JUSTICE OF THE EUROPEAN COMMUNITIES.

European Economic Community (ABBREV. **EEC**) an association within the European Community, established in 1958 after the Treaties of Rome (1957), and often referred to as the Common Market. It is essentially a customs union, with a common external tariff and a common market with the removal of barriers to trade among the members. Among its common policies is the Common Agricultural Policy, which provides for external tariffs to protect domestic agriculture and for price support mechanisms. The cost of support to agriculture takes up about 70 per cent of the European Community's budget and has shown an alarming propensity to grow. There are common policies for fisheries, regional development, industrial intervention, and economic and social affairs. In 1986 the Single European Act was passed, allowing for the completion of the process of creating a common market within the Community by 1992.

European Free Trade Association (ABBREV. **EFTA**) an association established (1960) under the Stockholm Convention by seven W European states who were not members of the European Economic Community. The members (Austria, Denmark, Norway, Portugal, Sweden, Switzerland, and the UK) agreed to eliminate over a period of time trade restrictions between them. Agriculture was excluded from the agreement, although individual arrangements were permitted. Finland, Iceland, and Liechtenstein joined later, and the UK and Denmark (1973), and Portugal (1985) left to join the EEC.

European Monetary System (ABBREV. **EMS**) a financial system set up in 1979 by members of the EEC with the aim of stabilizing and harmonizing currencies. Member-states use a special currency called the European Currency Unit (ecu). A percentage of members' foreign exchange reserves is deposited with the European Monetary Co-operation Fund, and ecus are received in exchange. Members join an exchange rate mechanism (ERM) which regulates currency exchange fluctuations.

European Monetary Union (ABBREV. **EMU**) one of the objectives of the European Union, the economic and monetary union of the 12 member states. EMU is planned to take place in three stages, which include the adoption of measures concerning the freedom of capital movement, the establishment of the European Monetary Institute in Frankfurt (the forerunner of the European Central Bank), and culminating in a common currency (or ecu) by the year 2000. Britain and Denmark have the right to opt out from the final stage.

European Parliament the representative assembly of the European Community. Despite its name, it has no legislative powers, but it does have the right to be consulted by the Council, to dismiss the Commission (a right never so far used), and to reject or amend the Community budget (exercised in 1979, 1984, 1985, and 1986). The more forceful role played by the Parliament in recent years reflects the fact that it has been directly elected since 1979. The administration of the Parliament lies in Luxembourg; its plenary sessions are held in Strasbourg; and its committees are in Brussels, where the Commission is based and the Councils meet.

European sole see DOVER SOLE.

European Union (ABBREV. **EU**) an association of 12 European countries, heralded by the Single

European Act (1986) and created by the Treaty of Maastricht (in effect from 1 Nov 1993), forming the political and economic infrastructure that enables the free movement of people, goods, and services between member countries. One of its main aims is monetary union, a project handled by the European Community (EC), which is a component part of the EU. Two other pillars of the Union that require inter-governmental co-operation are the areas of foreign and security policy (handled by the WEU) and justice and home affairs.

europium *noun Chem.* (SYMBOL **Eu**, ATOMIC NUMBER **63**) a soft silvery metal belonging to the lanthanide series, used as a neutron absorber in the control rods of nuclear reactors. Its oxide is used in the red phosphors for colour television screens. [from the name *Europe*]

Europort see ROTTERDAM.

Eurovision Song Contest an annual contest, first held (1956) in Lugano, Switzerland, to choose a winning pop song from among those entered by the participating countries.

Eurydice in Greek mythology, a dryad, the wife of Orpheus. She died of a snake bite, and Orpheus went down to the Underworld to try to get her back. She was released on the condition that she would follow him, and that he should not look at her until they reached the light. He looked back before they emerged, and she disappeared into the Underworld forever.

Eusebio, properly **Eusebio Ferreira da Silva**, also called **the Black Pearl** (1942–) Portuguese footballer, born in Lourenço Marques, Mozambique. He made his international début in 1961, and played for his country 77 times in all. At club level he played for Benfica, winning 15 Portuguese League and Cup winner's medals. He appeared in four European Cup finals, winning just once, in 1962. He retired in 1978 after a brief spell playing in the USA, and was later appointed coach to Benfica.

Eustachian tube either of the two tubes which connect the middle ear to the pharynx, serving to equalize the pressure on the two sides of the eardrum. [named after the 16c Italian anatomist B Eustachio]

eustasy *noun Geol.* worldwide change in sea-level caused by advancing or receding polar ice caps. This has caused a gradual rise in sea-level over the last century. [from Greek *eu*, well + *stasis*, standing]

Euterpe in Greek mythology, one of the Muses, usually associated with flute-playing.

euthanasia *noun* the act or practice of ending the life of a person who is suffering from an incurable and often painful or distressing illness. [from Greek, from *eu*, well + *thanatos*, death]
◇ In *positive euthanasia*, painless death is actively brought about, usually by administering a suitable drug. *Passive* (or *negative*) euthanasia involves the deliberate withholding of treatment that would keep the patient alive. In most countries positive euthanasia is illegal, and there are moral and religious objections to such a practice, but pressure groups such as *Exit* as well as some medical pracitritioners have advocated euthanasia as a dignified form of death for the elderly and chronically sick, who have lost the will or desire to live.

eutrophic *adj. Environ.* describing a body of water that has become over-enriched with nutrients, either naturally or as a result of pollution with artificial fertilizers, etc. [from Greek *eutrophiä*]

eutrophication *noun Environ.* the process whereby a body of water, eg a lake, becomes over-enriched with nutrients, mainly owing to sewage disposal and run-off of agricultural fertilizers containing nitrates and phosphates. The resulting overgrowth of algae depletes the oxygen levels in the water, and leads to the death of aquatic animals. [from Greek *eutrophiä*]

eV *abbrev.* electronvolt.

Eva, Little the delicate daughter of St Clare in Harriet Beecher Stowe's *Uncle Tom's Cabin*.

evacuate *verb* **1** to leave (a place), especially because of danger. **2** to cause (people) to leave a place, especially because of danger. **3** *Medicine* to empty (the bowels). [from Latin *evacuare*, to empty out]

evacuation *noun* the process of evacuating, especially removing people from a place because of danger.

evacuee *noun* an evacuated person.

evade *verb* **1** to escape or avoid by trickery or skill. **2** to avoid answering (a question). See also EVASION. [from Latin *evadere*, to go out]

evaluate *verb* **1** to form an idea or judgement about the worth of. **2** *Maths.* to calculate the value of. [from French *évaluation*]

evaluation *noun* an estimate of value or worth.

Evandale, Lord an officer of Claverhouse, and the rival to Henry Morton for Edith Bellenden's affections, in Sir Walter Scott's *Old Mortality*.

evanesce *verb intrans. literary* to disappear gradually; to fade from sight. [from Latin *evanescere*, to vanish]

evanescence *noun* vanishing; gradual disappearance.

evanescent *adj. literary* **1** quickly fading. **2** short-lived; transitory.

evangelical — *adj.* **1** based on the Gospels. **2** of or denoting any of various groups within the Protestant church stressing the authority of the Bible and claiming that personal acceptance of Christ as saviour is the only way to salvation. **3** enthusiastically advocating a particular cause, etc. — *noun* a member of an evangelical movement, or a supporter of evangelical beliefs. [from Greek *eu*, well + *angellein*, to bring news]

evangelicalism *noun* evangelical principles.

evangelically *adv.* according to the Gospels, or to evangelical principles.

evangelism *noun* **1** the act or practice of evangelizing. **2** evangelicalism.

Evangelist an advocate of the Gospel in John Bunyan's *The Pilgrim's Progress*.

evangelist *noun* **1** a person who preaches Christianity, especially at large public meetings. **2** (*usually* **Evangelist**) each of the writers of the four Biblical Gospels: Matthew, Mark, Luke, or John.

evangelistic *adj.* relating to evangelism.

evangelization *or* **evangelisation** *noun* evangelizing; promoting Christianity.

evangelize *or* **evangelise** *verb* **1** to attempt to persuade (someone) to adopt Christianity. **2** *intrans.* to preach Christianity, especially travelling from place to place to do so. **3** *intrans., trans. often facetious* to attempt to persuade (someone) to adopt a particular principle or cause.

Evans, Sir Arthur (John) (1851–1941) English archaeologist, born in Nash Mills, Hertfordshire. He was Curator of the Ashmolean Museum, Oxford (1884–1908), where he developed an interest in the ancient coins and seals of Crete. Between 1899 and 1935 he excavated the city of Knossos, discovering the remains of the civilization which in 1904 he named 'Minoan', after Minos, the Cretan king of Greek legend.

Evans, Dame Edith (Mary) (1888–1976) English stage and film actress, born in London. Known for her versatility, she made many notable appearances in the plays of William Shakespeare and George Bernard Shaw, but her most famous role was as Lady Bracknell in Oscar

Wilde's *The Importance of Being Earnest*. Her first film appearance was in *The Queen of Spades* (1948) and she continued to act until her eighties.

Evans, Sir Geraint (Llewellyn) (1922–92) Welsh baritone, born in Pontypridd, Wales. He made his operatic début at Covent Garden (1948) and soon earned international fame, particularly in comic roles such as Mozart's Leporello, Verdi's Falstaff, and Wagner's Beckmesser. He retired from the operatic stage in 1984.

Evans, Harold Matthew (1928–) English journalist, born in Manchester. He was the editor of the *Sunday Times* (1967–81) and a pioneer of investigative journalism during the thalidomide scandal. Then he became editor of *The Times* (1981–2) but resigned after its controversial takeover by Rupert Murdoch's News International. He moved to New York and became chief editor of *Traveler* magazine for Condé-Nast in 1986. He is married to Tina Brown, editor of the *New Yorker*.

evaporate *verb trans., intrans.* **1** to change or cause to change from a liquid into a vapour at a temperature below the boiling point of the liquid. **2** to disappear or cause to disappear. [from Latin *evaporare*, from *vapor*, steam, vapour]

evaporated milk unsweetened milk that has been concentrated by evaporation. When tinned it has a long shelf-life, and is widely used in many tropical countries.

evaporation *noun* the process of evaporating; disappearance.

evaporite *noun Geol.* a mineral deposit formed as a result of the evaporation of all or most of the water from a saline solution such as sea water or a salt lake.

evapotranspiration *noun Environ.* the loss of water from the Earth's surface as a result of both evaporation from the surface of soil, rocks, and bodies of water, and transpiration (the loss of water vapour from plants via pores in their leaves).

evasion *noun* **1** the act of evading, especially a commitment or responsibility. **2** a trick or excuse used to evade (a question, etc). [from Latin *evasio*, from *evadere*, to go out]
◆ See note at *avoidance*.

evasive *adj.* **1** having the purpose of evading, especially trouble or danger. **2** not honest or open: *an evasive answer*.

evasively *adv.* with an evasive or dishonest manner.

evasiveness *noun* being evasive or dishonest.

Eve **1** name of the first woman of the Old Testament, created from Adam's ribs. **2** a female first name. [from Hebrew *chava*, life, via Latin *Eva*]

eve *noun* **1** the evening or day before some notable event. **2** the period immediately before: *the eve of war*. [from EVEN²]

Evelyn, John (1620–1706) English diarist and author, born in Wotton, Surrey. He travelled abroad during the Civil War, was much at court after the Restoration, and became one of the Commissioners of the Privy Seal (1685–7) and treasurer of Greenwich Hospital (1695–1703). His main literary work is his *Diary*, a detailed sourcebook on life in 17c England.

Evelyn a female and male first name. [from Norman *Aveline*, itself of Germanic origin]

even¹ — *adj.* **1** smooth and flat. **2** constant or regular: *travelling at an even 50 mph*. **3** *said of a number* divisible by 2, with nothing left over. **4** designated or marked by such a number: *the even houses in the street*. **5** (**even with**) level; on the same plane or at the same height. **6** (**even with**) having no advantage or owing no debt. **7** *said of temper, character, etc* calm. **8** equal: *an even chance*. — *adv.* **1** used with a comparative to

emphasize a comparison with something else: *he's good, but she's even better.* **2** used with an expression stronger than a previous one: *he looked sad, even depressed.* **3** used to introduce a surprising piece of information: *even John was there!* **4** used to indicate a lower extreme in an implied comparison: *even a child (let alone an educated adult) would have known that!* **5** (**even if, even though**) used to emphasize that whether or not something is or might be true, the following or preceding statement is or would remain true: *he'd be unhappy even if he did get the job / even though he got the job, he's still unhappy / he got the job but, even so, he's still unhappy.* — *verb* **1** (**even something up**) to make it equal. **2** (**even something out** or **up**) to make it smooth or level. **3** (**even out**) to become level or regular. — *noun* **1** (*usually* **evens**) an even number, or something designated by one. **2** (**evens**) same as EVEN MONEY.
— **even now** still; after all that has happened. **even then** after all that had happened, will have happened, or would have happened.
get even with someone to be revenged on them.
[from Anglo-Saxon *efen*]

even² *noun old use, poetic* evening. [from Anglo-Saxon *æfen*]

even-handed *adj.* fair.

even-handedly *adv.* in an even-handed or fair way.

even-handedness *noun* being even-handed or fair.

evening — *noun* **1** the last part of the day, usually from late afternoon until bedtime. **2** a party or other social gathering held at this time: *a poetry evening.* **3** *poetic* the latter part of anything: *the evening of his life.* — *adj.* of or during the evening. [from Anglo-Saxon *æfnung*]

evening dress clothes worn on formal occasions in the evening.

evening primrose *Bot.* any of about 200 species of the genus *Oenothera*, a biennial with large scented yellow flowers that open at dusk. Evening primrose oil is claimed to have beneficial effects in the treatment of skin disorders and premenstrual tension.

evening star a planet, especially Venus, clearly visible in the west just after sunset.

Evenki — *noun* a language (formerly known as Tungus) spoken in parts of NE China and Siberia. It belongs to the Manchu-Tungus group of Altaic languages. — *adj.* relating to or spoken or written in Evenki.

evenly *adv.* **1** in an even way; uniformly. **2** in equal parts or shares: *evenly divided.*

even money gambling odds with the potential to win the same as the amount gambled.

evenness *noun* being even or uniform.

evensong *noun* the service of evening prayer in the Anglican Church. [from Anglo-Saxon *æfensang*, evening song]

event *noun* **1** something that occurs or happens; an incident, especially a significant one. **2** an item in a programme of sports, etc.
— **at all events** or **in any event** in any case; whatever happens.
in either event no matter which (of two things, possibilities, etc) happens.
in the event in the end; as it happened, happens, or may happen.
in the event of something if something occurs: *in the event of a power cut / in the event that there is a power cut.*
in that event if that occurs.
[from Latin *eventus*, result, event]

eventer *noun* a person who takes part in eventing.

eventful *adj.* full of important or significant events.

eventfully *adv.* with important or significant events.

eventide *noun poetic, old use* evening. [from Anglo-Saxon *æfentid*]

eventide home a home for old people.

eventing *noun* the practice of taking part in horse-riding events, especially the **three-day event**, a competition in jumping, cross-country riding, and dressage.

eventual *adj.* happening after or at the end of a period of time, a process, etc. [from French *éventuel*, from Latin *eventus*, result, event]

eventuality *noun* (PL. **eventualities**) a possible happening or result: *plan for every eventuality.*

eventually *adv.* after an indefinite period of time; in the end: *they came eventually.*

eventuate *verb intrans. formal* to result; to turn out.

Eve of St Agnes, The a narrative poem by John Keats (1820). It is set in medieval times and centres around Madeline's dream of her lover, Porphyro, on St Agnes's Eve.

ever *adv.* **1** at any time. **2** *formal* always; continually. **3** *colloq.* used for emphasis: *She's ever so beautiful!* [from Anglo-Saxon *æfre*]

ever- *combining form* always, continually: *ever-hopeful.*

Everdene, Bathsheba the spirited, farm-owning heroine of Thomas Hardy's *Far from the Madding Crowd*, who learns a lot about love.

Everest, Mount, Nepali **Sagarmatha**, Chinese **Qomolangma Feng** the highest mountain peak in the world. It lies in the Himalayas of central Asia on the border between Nepal and the Tibet region of China. HEIGHT 8 848m. It was named after Sir George Everest (1790–1866), a surveyor-general of India. Following attempts in 1921 and 1922, Mallory and Irvine, members of the 1924 British Expedition, climbed beyond 8 534m but failed to return. The summit was first reached via the Southeast Ridge on 29 May 1953 by Sir Edmund Hillary and Sherpa Tenzing Norgay of Nepal in a British expedition under Col John Hunt. It was reached via the West Ridge by a US team in 1963, the Southwest face by a British team in 1975, and the North Wall by a Japanese team in 1980. Claimed by China, in 1952 the Chinese banned the name Everest in favour of Qomolangma Feng ('Goddess Mother of the World').

everglade *noun* **1** a large shallow lake or marsh. **2** (**Everglades**) a large expanse of these in S Florida in the USA.

Everglades a swampy, subtropical region in S Florida, USA. AREA c.12 950sq km/5 000sq mi; length c.160km/100mi; width 80–120km/50–75mi. It covers most of the Florida peninsula, S of L Okeechobee. An area only a few metres above sea level, with heavy rainfall, it consists of saw grass savannahs and water dotted with clumps of reeds. Drainage and reclamation schemes have made a large amount of land productive, mostly in citrus fruits and sugar. It was originally occupied by Seminole Native Americans, driven out in the 1830s. Everglades National Park in the S includes much of Florida Bay, with its many keys; it is a World Heritage site.

evergreen — *adj.* **1** *Bot.* denoting plants that bear leaves all the year round, eg pines, firs. Individual leaves are shed independently of each other, and are often greatly reduced to prevent water loss. **2** always popular. — *noun* an evergreen tree or shrub.

Evergreen Bridge in the USA, a floating pontoon bridge in Seattle, Washington, built in 1963. Its longest span measures 2 293m.

everlasting — *adj.* **1** without end; continual. **2** lasting a long time, especially so long as to become tiresome. — *noun* **1** any of several kinds of flower that keep their shape and colour when dried. **2** eternity.

everlastingly *adv.* without end; continually.

evermore *adv.* **for evermore** for all time to come; eternally.

Evert, Chris(tine Marie), married name **Mill** (1954–) US lawn tennis player, born in Fort Lauderdale, Florida. She won her first Wimbledon title in 1974 at the age of 19, and later won in 1976 and 1981. She also won the US singles title in 1975–8, 1980, and 1982, the French Open in 1974–5, 1979–80, 1983, and 1985–6, and the Australian Open in 1982 and 1984. She retired from professional tennis in 1989.

every — *adj.* **1** each single, omitting none. **2** the greatest or best possible: *we're making every effort to avoid war.* — *adv.* at, in, at the end of, each stated period of time, distance, etc: *every fourth week / every six inches.*
— **every now and then** or **every now and again** or **every so often** occasionally; from time to time.
every other ... or **every second** ... one of every two repeatedly (the first, third, fifth, etc or second, fourth, sixth, etc).
[from Anglo-Saxon *æfre ælc*, ever each]

everybody *pron.* every person.

everyday *adj.* **1** happening, done, used, etc daily, or on ordinary days, rather than on special occasions. **2** common or usual: *an everyday occurrence.*

Everyman a popular early 16c morality play. It concerns the temptation and salvation of a Christian soul; hence, by association, any character whose temptations and fate may be seen as representative of common humanity.

Everyman *noun* the ordinary or common person.

Every Man in His Humour a play by Ben Jonson (1598). It is a comedy about the relationships between the old and the young, involving such characters as Knowell, who is concerned for his son's moral welfare, and Kitely, who irrationally suspects everyone of planning affairs with his young wife.

everyone *pron.* every person.

everything *pron.* **1** all things; all. **2** the most important thing: *fitness is everything in sport.*

everywhere *adv.* in or to every place.

Evesham POP (1981) 15 000, a town in Wychavon district, Hereford and Worcester, W central England. It is situated in the Vale of Evesham, in an area in which fruit and vegetables are grown.

evict *verb* to put out of a house, etc or off land by force of law. [from Latin *evincere*, to overcome]

eviction *noun* the process of evicting people, especially from a building.

evidence — *noun* **1** information, etc that gives grounds for belief; that which points to, reveals or suggests something. **2** written or spoken testimony used in a court of law. — *verb formal* to be evidence of; to prove.
— **in evidence** easily seen; clearly displayed.
[from Latin *evidentia*, clearness of speech]

evident *adj.* clear to see or understand; obvious; apparent.

evidential *adj. formal* relating to, based on, or providing evidence.

evidentially *adv.* in terms of evidence; as based on evidence.

evidently *adv.* **1** obviously; apparently: *he is evidently drunk.* **2** as it appears; so it seems: *evidently they don't believe us.*

evil — *adj.* **1** morally bad or offensive. **2** harmful. **3** *colloq.* very unpleasant: *an evil stench.* — *noun* **1** wickedness or moral offensiveness, or the source of it. **2** harm, or a cause of harm; a harmful influence. **3** anything bad or unpleasant, eg crime, disease, etc. [from Anglo-Saxon *yfel*]

evildoer *noun* a person who does evil things.

evil eye (**the evil eye**) **1** the supposed power of causing harm by a look. **2** a glare, superstitiously thought to cause harm.

evilly *adv.* with an evil manner.

evince *verb formal* to show or display (usually a personal quality) clearly. [from Latin *evincere*, to overcome]

eviscerate *verb formal* **1** to tear out the bowels of. **2** to take away the essential quality or meaning of. [from Latin *eviscerare*, to disembowel]

evisceration *noun formal* disembowelling.

evocation *noun* bringing a feeling to mind.

evocative *adj.* bringing vividly to mind.

evoke *verb* **1** to cause or produce (a response, a reaction, etc). **2** to bring into the mind. [from Latin *evocare*, to call out]

evolution *noun* **1** the process of evolving. **2** a gradual development. **3** *Biol.* the cumulative changes in the characteristics of living organisms or populations of organisms from generation to generation, resulting in the development of new types of organism over long periods of time. **4** *Chem.* the giving off of a gas. [from Latin *evolutio*, unrolling]
◇ The concept of evolution is based on the theory of natural selection (proposed jointly by Charles Darwin and Alfred Russel Wallace), according to which only those species best adapted to a particular environment will survive and reproduce. Evolution over geological time is well demonstrated by the sequence of organisms preserved as fossils in rocks, and is now generally accepted as being the means by which present-day plants and animals, including humans, have arisen, but there are different schools of thought regarding the pattern and speed of evolution. There is considerable evidence to suggest that evolution does not take place at a steady rate, but may involve periods of rapid change separated by long periods of relative stability.
It is thought that the earliest living organisms, consisting of single cells, originated on Earth about 4 000 million years ago, and that the first multicellular organisms appeared about 700 million years ago. Modern mammals and primates probably developed within the last 60 million years, and modern man (*Homo sapiens sapiens*) evolved about 100 000 years ago.

evolutionary *adj.* relating to or as a part of evolution.

evolutionism *noun Anthropol., Biol.* a widely-held 19c belief that organisms were intrinsically bound to improve themselves, that changes were progressive, and that acquired characters could be transmitted genetically. The belief was also extended to cultures and societies, and to living organisms.

evolutionist *noun* a person who believes in the theory of evolution.

evolve *verb* **1** *trans., intrans.* to develop or produce gradually. **2** *intrans.* to develop from a primitive into a more complex or advanced form. **3** *Chem.* to give off (heat, etc). [from Latin *evolvere*, to roll out, unroll]

Évora, Latin **Ebora Liberalitas Julia 1** POP (1991) 39 000, the capital of Évora district, S Portugal, situated 112km/70mi SE of Lisbon. It is an ancient walled market town; its historic centre is a World Heritage site. NOTABLE FEATURES cathedral (1186); Archbishop's Palace; Roman Temple of Diana, where the 1974 revolution was planned; Church of the Loios (15c); old university (1551). **2** a district in S Portugal with the city of Évora as its capital.

Evreux POP (1990) 52 000, the capital of Eure

department, Haute-Normandie region, NW France. It lies in the fertile Iton Valley. NOTABLE FEATURES Cathedral of Notre Dame (begun in the 11c); Bishop's Palace (15c); former Benedictine Abbey Church of St Taurin.

Ewan a male first name, largely confined to Scotland. [a Scottish Anglicization of Gaelic *Eoghan*, meaning 'born of the yew', or a form of EUGENE]

ewe *noun* a female sheep. [from Anglo-Saxon *eowu*]

ewer *noun* a large water-jug with a wide mouth. [from Old French *eviere*, from Latin *aquarius*, of water]

Ewing, (William) Maurice (1906–74) US marine geologist, born in Lockney, Texas. He taught at Lehigh University, Pennsylvania, before joining the geology department at Columbia University (1944), where he established the Lamont Geological Observatory. He pioneered marine seismic techniques which he used to show that the ocean crust is much thinner (5–8km thick) than the continental crust (around 40km thick), and discovered the global extent of mid-ocean ridges as well as the deep central rift in the Mid-Atlantic Ridge (1957). His discovery that the ocean sediment thickness increases with distance from the mid-ocean ridges gave support to modern plate tectonic theories.

ex¹ *noun* (PL. **ex's**, **exes**) *colloq.* a person who is no longer what he or she was, especially a former husband, wife, or lover.

ex² *prep. Commerce* **1** direct from: *ex warehouse*. **2** excluding: *ex dividend*. [from Latin *ex*, out of]

ex- *prefix* forming words meaning: **1** former: *ex-wife*. **2** outside: *ex-directory*. [from Latin *ex*, out of]

exacerbate *verb* to make (a bad situation, anger, pain, etc) worse. [from Latin *exacerbare*, to irritate]

exacerbation *noun* making something worse.

exact — *adj.* **1** absolutely accurate or correct. **2** insisting on accuracy or precision in even the smallest details. **3** dealing with measurable quantities or values: *psychology is not an exact science*. — *verb* **1** (**exact something from** *or* **of someone**) to demand payment from them. **2** to insist on (a right, etc). [from Latin *exigere*, to demand]

exacting *adj.* making difficult or excessive demands.

exactingly *adv.* in an exacting or demanding way.

exaction *noun formal* **1** the act of demanding payment, or the payment demanded. **2** illegal demands for money; extortion.

exactitude *noun formal* accuracy or correctness.

exactly *adv.* **1** just; quite; precisely; absolutely. **2** with accuracy; with attention to detail. **3** *said in reply* you are quite right.

exactness *noun* **1** being exact; accuracy. **2** close attention to detail.

exaggerate *verb* **1** *trans., intrans.* to regard or describe something as being greater or better than it really is. **2** to emphasize or make more noticeable: *the light emphasized the contours of the hills*. **3** to do in an excessive or affected way. [from Latin *exaggerare*, to heap up]

exaggeration *noun* exaggerating; making something seem greater than it is.

exaggerator *noun* a person who exaggerates, especially habitually.

exalt *verb* **1** to praise highly. **2** to fill with great joy. **3** to give a higher rank or position to. [from Latin *exaltare*, to raise]

exaltation *noun* **1** the act of exalting or state of being exalted. **2** a strong feeling of happiness.

exalted *adj.* **1** noble; very moral: *exalted ideals*. **2** exaggerated; too high: *an exalted opinion of one's own importance*.

exaltedly *adv.* with an exalted or noble manner.

exam *noun colloq.* an examination (sense 1).

examination *noun* **1** a set of tasks, especially in written form, designed to test knowledge or ability. **2** an inspection of a person's state of health, carried out by a doctor. **3** the act of examining, or process of being examined. **4** *Legal* formal questioning in a court of law.

examine *verb* **1** to inspect, consider, or look into closely. **2** to check the health of. **3** to test the knowledge or ability of (a person), especially in a formal examination. **4** *Legal* to question formally in a court of law. [from French *examiner*, from Latin *examinare*, to weigh or test, from *examen*, the pointer on a set of scales]

examinee *noun* a candidate in an examination.

examiner *noun* a person who sets an examination.

Examiner, The (1808–80) a Radical literary periodical (1808–81), founded and edited by John and Leigh Hunt. Published weekly, it became a focus of Liberal opinion, and promoted the work of leading men of letters, including Byron, Shelley, Keats, and Lamb.

example *noun* **1** something or someone that is a typical specimen. **2** something that illustrates a fact or rule. **3** a person, pattern of behaviour, etc as a model to be, or not to be, copied: *set a good example*. **4** a punishment given, or the person punished, as a warning to others: *make an example of someone*.
— **for example** as an example or illustration. [from Old French *example*, from Latin *exemplum*]

exasperate *verb* to make (someone) annoyed and frustrated. [from Latin *exasperare*, to make rough]

exasperation *noun* a feeling of angry frustration.

Excalibur in Arthurian legend, the name of King Arthur's sword which, in one account, he succeeded in pulling from a stone, and, in another, was given to him by the Lady of the Lake. As he lay dying he instructed Sir Bedivere to throw it back into the lake, where a hand drew it under the water.

ex cathedra — *adv.* with authority, especially the full authority of the Pope. — *adj.* (*usually* **ex-cathedra**) **1** *said of a papal pronouncement* stating an infallible doctrine. **2** made with, or as if with, authority. [from Latin *ex cathedra*, from the chair]

excavate *verb* **1** to dig up or uncover (especially historical remains). **2** to dig up (a piece of ground, etc) or to make (a hole) by doing this. [from Latin *excavare*, to make hollow]

excavation *noun* **1** the process of excavating or digging up ground, especially in archaeology. **2** an excavated area or site.

excavator *noun* **1** a person who excavates or digs up ground. **2** a machine for digging.

exceed *verb* **1** to be greater than. **2** to go beyond; to do more than is required by. [from Old French *exceder*]

exceedingly *adv.* very; extremely.

excel *verb* (**excelled, excelling**) **1** *intrans.* (**excel in** *or* **at something**) to be exceptionally good at it. **2** *trans.* to be better than.
— **excel oneself** *often ironic* to do better than usual or previously. [from Latin *excellere*, to rise up]

excellence *noun* great worth; very high or exceptional quality. [from Old French, from Latin *excellentia*]

Excellency *noun* (PL. **Excellencies**) (*usually* **His** *or* **Her** *or* **Your Excellency** *or* **Their**

Excellencies) a title of honour given to certain people of high rank, eg ambassadors.

excellent *adj.* of very high quality; extremely good.

excellently *adv.* in an excellent way; extremely well.

except — *prep.* leaving out; not including. — *verb* to leave out or exclude: *present company excepted.*
— **except for** apart from; not including or counting.
[from Latin *excipere*, to take out]

excepting *prep.* leaving out; not including or counting.

exception *noun* 1 a person or thing not included. 2 someone or something that does not, or is allowed not to, follow a general rule: *make an exception.* 3 an act of excluding.
— **take exception to** to object to; to be offended by.
[from Latin *excipere*, to take out]

exceptionable *adj.* 1 likely to cause disapproval, offence or dislike. 2 open to objection.

exceptional *adj.* 1 remarkable or outstanding. 2 being or making an exception.

exceptionally *adv.* in an exceptional way; to an exceptional or unusual degree: *it is exceptionally cold.*

excerpt — *noun* (with stress on *ex-*) a short passage or part taken from a book, film, etc. — *verb* (with stress on *-cerpt*) to select extracts from (a book, etc). [from Latin *excerptum*, from *excerpere*, to pick]

excerption *noun* selection of extracts from a book, etc.

excess — *noun* 1 the act of going, or the state of being, beyond normal or suitable limits. 2 an amount or extent greater than is usual, necessary or wise. 3 the amount by which one quantity, etc exceeds another; an amount left over. 4 (*usually* **excesses**) an outrageous or offensive act. — *adj.* 1 greater than is usual, necessary or permitted. 2 additional; required to make up for an amount lacking: *excess postage.*
— **in excess of** ... going beyond ...; more than: *in excess of 5 million.*
[from Old French *exces*, from Latin *excessus*, departure, going beyond]

excessive *adj.* too great; beyond what is usual, right or appropriate.

excessively *adv.* to an excessive degree.

excess profits tax a tax levied on a company's profits above a specified level.
◇ It was used in both World Wars to control the profits of firms producing goods for the war effort. More recently, an excess profits tax has been advocated by the British Labour Party as a means of controlling profits in privatized industries.

exchange — *verb* 1 (**exchange one thing for another**) to give, or give up, in return for something else. 2 to give and receive in return: *the two leaders exchanged gifts.* — *noun* 1 the giving and taking of one thing for another. 2 a thing exchanged. 3 a giving and receiving in return. 4 a conversation or argument, especially when brief. 5 the act of exchanging the currency of one country for that of another. 6 a place where shares are traded, or international financial deals carried out. 7 (*also* **telephone exchange**) a central telephone system where lines are connected, or the building housing this.
— **in exchange for** in return for.
[from Old French *eschangier*, from Latin *excambiare*, from EX- + *cambiare*, to barter.]

exchangeable *adj.* that may be exchanged.

exchange rate *or* **rate of exchange** the value of the currency of one country in relation to that of another country or countries.

Exchange Rate Mechanism (ABBREV. **ERM**) a system which regulates currency exchange rates in the European Monetary System. Exchange rates are allowed to fluctuate within narrow bands only, based on the European Currency Unit (ecu) rate. Sterling joined the ERM in 1990, but withdrew in Sep 1992 when it fell below the permitted ecu rate. The day it occurred came to be known as 'Black Wednesday'.

exchequer *noun* (*often* **Exchequer**) the government department in charge of the financial affairs of a nation. [from Old French *eschequier*, from Latin *scaccarium*, chessboard, from the practice of keeping accounts on a chequered cloth]

excise[1] — *noun* (with stress on *ex-*) the tax on goods, etc produced and sold within a country, and on certain licences. — *verb* (with stress on *ex-*) 1 to charge excise on (goods, etc). 2 to force (a person) to pay excise. [from Old Dutch *excijs*, from Old French *acceis*, tax]

excise[2] *verb* (with stress on *-cise*) 1 to remove (eg a passage from a book). 2 to cut out or cut off by surgery. [from Latin *excidere*, to cut out]

excision *noun* removal, especially of a passage from a text.

excitability *noun* capacity to become excited.

excitable *adj.* easily made excited, flustered, frantic, etc.

excitably *adv.* with an excitable or frantic manner.

excitation *noun Physics* the addition of energy to an atom or molecule so that it becomes raised from its ground state (its lowest energy state) to an excited state (a higher energy state).

excite *verb* 1 to cause to feel lively expectation or a pleasant tension and thrill. 2 to arouse (feelings, emotions, sensations, etc). 3 to provoke (eg action). 4 to arouse sexually. [from Old French *exciter*]

excited *adj.* aroused emotionally or sexually; thrilled.

excitedly *adv.* with an excited or aroused manner.

excitement *noun* 1 the state of being excited. 2 objects and events that produce such a state, or the quality they have which produces it: *the excitement of travel.* 3 behaviour, a happening, etc which displays excitement.

exciting *adj.* arousing a lively expectation or a pleasant tension and thrill.

excitingly *adv.* in an exciting or arousing way.

exclaim *verb trans., intrans.* to call or cry out suddenly and loudly, eg in surprise or anger. [from Latin *exclamare*]

exclamation *noun* 1 a word or expression uttered suddenly and loudly. 2 the act of exclaiming. [from Latin *exclamatio*]

exclamation mark the punctuation mark '!', used to indicate an exclamation.

exclamatory *adj.* containing or expressing exclamation.

exclude *verb* 1 to prevent (someone) from sharing or taking part. 2 to shut out or keep out. 3 to omit or leave out of consideration. 4 to make impossible. [from Latin *excludere*, to shut out]

excluding *prep.* not counting; without including.

exclusion *noun* the act of excluding, or the state of being excluded.
— **to the exclusion of** ... so as to leave out or make no time or room for ...
[from Latin *exclusio*, from *excludere*, to shut out]

exclusive — *adj.* 1 involving the rejection or denial of something else or everything else: *mutually exclusive statements.* 2 (**exclusive to some-**

one *or* **something**) limited to, given to, found in, etc only one place, group or person. 3 not including (something mentioned). 4 not readily accepting others into the group, especially because of a feeling of superiority: *an exclusive club.* 5 fashionable and expensive: *an exclusive restaurant.* — *noun* a report or story published in only one newspaper or magazine.
— **exclusive of** ... excluding ...
[from Latin *exclusivus*]

exclusively *adv.* to an exclusive degree; with exclusive right.

exclusiveness *or* **exclusivity** *noun* being exclusive; a tendency to exclude others.

excommunicate *verb Christianity* to remove (someone) from membership of a Church. [from Latin *excommunicare*, to exclude from the community]

excommunication *noun Christianity* removal from membership of a Church.

excoriate *verb* 1 *technical* to strip the skin from (a person or animal). 2 to criticize severely. [from Latin *excoriare*]

excoriation *noun technical* stripping of the skin.

excrement *noun* waste matter passed out of the body, especially faeces. [from Latin *excrementum*]

excremental *adj.* relating to or consisting of excrement or faeces.

excrescence *noun* 1 an abnormal, especially ugly, growth on a part of the body or a plant. 2 an unsightly addition. [from Latin *excrescere*, to grow up]

excreta *noun formal* excreted matter; faeces or urine. [from Latin *excernere*, to sift out]

excrete *verb, said of a plant or animal* to eliminate (waste products). [from Latin *excernere*, to sift out]

excretion *noun Biol.* in plants and animals, the removal of excess, waste, or harmful material produced during the chemical reactions that take place within living cells.
◇ In animals, the main excretory products are carbon dioxide, water, salts, ammonia, urea, and other nitrogenous compounds. The main excretory organs in vertebrates are the kidneys, which produce urine, the lungs, which release carbon dioxide when air is exhaled, and the skin, through which excess salts and water are lost during sweating. In birds and reptiles, nitrogenous products are stored in an insoluble form as uric acid until they are eliminated from the body.

excretory *adj.* relating to or having the function of excretion.

excruciating *adj.* 1 causing great physical or mental pain. 2 *colloq.* extremely bad or irritating. [from Latin *excruciare*, to torture]

excruciatingly *adv.* in an excruciating way or to an excruciating degree.

exculpate *verb formal* to remove from guilt or blame. [from EX- + Latin *culpa*, fault, blame]

exculpation *noun formal* removal from suspicion or blame.

excursion *noun* 1 a short trip, usually one made for pleasure. 2 a brief change from the usual course or pattern: *a novelist making an excursion into journalism.* [from Latin *excurrere*, to run out]

excursive *adj. formal* tending to wander from the main point. [from Latin *excursus*, a running out]

excusable *adj.* that may be excused; forgivable.

excusably *adv.* in an excusable or forgivable way; to an excusable degree.

excuse — *verb* 1 to pardon or forgive. 2 to offer justification for (a wrongdoing). 3 to free (from an obligation, a duty, etc). **4** to allow to leave (a room, etc), eg in order to go to the lavatory. — *noun* **1** an explanation for a wrongdoing, offered as an apology or justification. **2** *derog.* a very poor example: *you'll never sell this excuse for a painting!*

— **excuse me** an expression of apology, or used to attract attention.

excuse oneself to leave after apologizing or asking permission.

make one's excuses to apologize for leaving or not attending.

[from Latin *excusare*, from *ex*, from, + *causa*, cause, accusation]

ex-directory *adj.* **1** *said of a telephone number* not included in the directory at the request of the subscriber. **2** *said of a telephone subscriber* having such a number.

execrable *adj.* **1** detestable. **2** dreadful; of very poor quality. [from Latin *exsecrabilis*, detestable]

execrably *adv.* detestably; dreadfully.

execrate *verb formal* **1** to feel or express hatred or loathing of. **2** to curse. [from Latin *exsecrari*, to curse]

execration *noun formal* an expression of loathing; cursing.

execute *verb* **1** to put to death by order of the law. **2** to perform or carry out. **3** to produce, especially according to a design. **4** *Legal* to make valid by signing. **5** *Legal* to carry out instructions contained in (a will or contract). See also EXECUTOR.

execution *noun* **1** the act, or an instance, of putting to death by law. **2** the act of carrying out, or the state of being carried out.

executioner *noun* a person who carries out a sentence of death.

executive — *adj.* **1** in a business organization, etc, concerned with management or administration. **2** for the use of managers and senior staff. **3** *colloq.* expensive and sophisticated: *executive cars.* **4** *Legal, Politics* relating to the carrying out of laws: *executive powers.* — *noun* **1** a person or body of people in an organization, etc having power to direct or manage. **2** (**the executive**) *Legal, Politics* the branch of government that puts laws into effect. [from Latin *executivus*]

executive toy a gadget or object with little practical use, intended primarily as a diversion for executives.

executor *noun Legal* a male or female person appointed to carry out instructions stated in a will.

executrix *noun* (PL. **executrices, executrixes**) *Legal* a female executor.

exegesis *noun* (PL. **exegeses**) a critical explanation of a text, especially of the Bible. [from Greek *exegesis*, explanation]

exegetic *or* **exegetical** *adj.* critically explaining a text.

exemplar *noun* **1** a person or thing worth copying; a model. **2** a typical example. [from Latin *exemplum*, example]

exemplary *adj.* **1** worth following as an example. **2** serving as an illustration or warning. [from Latin *exemplaris*, from *exemplum*, example]

exemplification *noun* provision of an example or examples; illustration.

exemplify *verb* (**exemplfies, exemplified**) **1** to be an example of. **2** to show an example of, show by means of an example. [from Latin *exemplum*, example + *facere*, to make]

exempt — *verb* to free from a duty or obligation that applies to others. — *adj.* free from some obligation; not liable. [from Latin *eximere*, to take out]

exemption *noun* freeing from a duty or obligation.

exercise — *noun* **1** physical training or exertion for health or pleasure. **2** an activity intended to develop a skill. **3** a task designed to test ability. **4** *formal* the act of putting into practice or carrying out: *the exercise of one's duty.* **5** (*usually* **exercises**) *Mil.* training and practice for soldiers. — *verb* **1** *intrans., trans.* to give exercise to (oneself, or someone or something else). **2** to use or bring into use: *exercise a skill/right.* **3** to trouble, concern, or occupy the thoughts of. [from Old French *exercice*, from Latin *exercere*, to keep busy]

exert *verb* **1** to bring into use or action forcefully: *exert one's authority.* **2** to force (oneself) to make a strenuous, especially physical, effort. [from Latin *exserere*, to thrust out]

exertion *noun* making a strenuous effort.

Exeter, ancient **Isca Damnoniorum** POP (1992e) 107 000, the county town of Devon, SW England, situated in Exeter district. It lies on the R Exe, 70km/43mi NE of Plymouth. HISTORY founded by the Romans in the 1c; a stone wall was erected in the 3c against the Saxons and later the Danes; port status was partially restored in 1560 by the construction of England's first ship canal; during the Civil War it was the headquarters in the W of Royalist forces. NOTABLE FEATURES 12c cathedral (damaged by bombing in World War II); Guildhall (12c); Maritime Museum.

exeunt *verb intrans., as a stage direction* (they) leave the stage. See also EXIT.

— **exeunt omnes** all leave the stage. See also EXIT.

[from Latin *exire*, to go out; *omnis*, all, every]

ex gratia given as a favour, not in recognition of an (especially legal) obligation: *an ex gratia payment.* [from Latin *ex gratia*, as a favour]

exhalation *noun* breathing out.

exhale *verb trans., intrans.* **1** to breathe out. **2** to give off or be given off. [from Old French *exhaler*]

exhaust — *verb* **1** to make very tired. **2** to use up completely. **3** to say all that can be said about (a subject, etc). **4** *Engineering* to empty (a container), or draw off (gas). — *noun* **1** the escape of waste gases from an engine, etc. **2** the gases themselves. **3** the part or parts of an engine, etc through which the waste gases escape. [from Latin *exhaurire*, to draw off, drain away]

exhausted *adj.* made extremely tired; devoid of energy.

exhaustible *adj.* capable of being exhausted.

exhausting *adj.* extremely tiring or wearing.

exhaustion *noun* a state of being exhausted or devoid of energy.

exhaustive *adj.* complete; very thorough.

exhaustively *adv.* thoroughly; completely.

exhibit — *verb* (**exhibited, exhibiting**) **1** to present or display for public appreciation. **2** to show or manifest (a quality, etc). — *noun* **1** an object displayed publicly, eg in a museum. **2** *Legal* an object or article produced in court as part of the evidence. [from Latin *exhibere*, to produce, show]

exhibition *noun* **1** a display, eg of works of art, to the public. **2** the act, or an instance, of showing, eg a quality. **3** a scholarship awarded by a college or university.

— **make an exhibition of oneself** to behave foolishly in public.

[from Latin *exhibere*, to show]

exhibitioner *noun* a student receiving an educational exhibition.

exhibitionism *noun* **1** *derog.* the tendency to behave so as to attract attention to oneself. **2** *Psychol.* the compulsive desire to expose one's sexual organs publicly.

exhibitionist *noun* a person who behaves so as to attract attention.

exhibitionistic *adj.* characterized by or given to exhibitionism.

exhibitor *noun* a person who provides an exhibit for a public display.

exhilarate *verb* to fill with a lively cheerfulness. [from Latin *exhilarare*, from *hilaris*, cheerful]

exhilaration *noun* a feeling of extreme cheerfulness.

exhort *verb* to urge or advise strongly and sincerely. [from Latin *exhortari*, to encourage]

exhortation *noun* a strong appeal or urging.

exhumation *noun formal* digging up of a body from a grave.

exhume *verb formal* to dig up (a body) from a grave. [from French *exhumer*, from EX- + Latin *humus*, the ground]

exigency *noun* (PL. **exigencies**) *formal* **1** an urgent need. **2** an emergency. [from Latin *exigere*, to drive out]

exigent *adj. formal* **1** pressing; urgent. **2** demanding.

exiguity *or* **exiguousness** *noun* being scarce or meagre.

exiguous *adj. formal* scarce; meagre; insufficient. [from Latin *exiguus*, small, meagre]

exiguously *adv.* to a scarce or meagre degree.

exile — *noun* **1** enforced or regretted absence from one's country or town, especially for a long time, often as a punishment. **2** a person suffering such absence. — *verb* to send into exile. [from Old French *exil*, from Latin *exsilium*, banishment]

exist *verb intrans.* **1** to be, especially to be present in the real world or universe rather than in story or imagination. **2** to occur or be found. **3** to manage to stay alive; to live with only the most basic necessities of life. [from Latin *exsistere*, to stand out]

existence *noun* **1** the state of existing. **2** a life, or a way of living. **3** everything that exists.

existent *adj.* having an actual being; existing.

existential *adj.* **1** relating to human existence. **2** *Philos.* relating to existentialism.

existentialism *noun* a philosophy emphasizing freedom of choice and personal responsibility for one's own actions, which create one's own moral values and determine one's future.

existentialist *adj., noun* a person who believes in existentialism.

exit — *noun* **1** a way out of a building, etc. **2** an act of going out or departing. **3** an actor's departure from the stage. **4** a place where vehicles can leave a motorway or main road. — *verb intrans.* (**exited, exiting**) **1** *formal* to go out, leave or depart. **2** *as a stage direction* (he or she) leaves the stage. See also EXEUNT. [from Latin *exire*, to go out]

exit poll a poll of a sample of voters in an election, taken as they leave a polling-station, and used to give an early indication of voting trends in a particular election.

Exmoor a national park in Somerset and Devon, England, established in 1954. It occupies the coastline between Minehead and Combe Martin Bay, and includes the Brendon Hills in the E. The highest point is at Dunkery Beacon (520m). The park is a major tourist area and is known for its ponies. AREA 686sq km/265sq mi.

Exmouth POP (1981) 29 000, a resort town in Teignbridge district, Devon, SW England. It lies on the R Exe, 15km/9mi SE of Exeter, and is a centre for recreational sailing.

exo- *combining form* out or outside. See also ECTO-, ENDO-, ENTO-. [from Greek *exo*, outside]

exobiology *noun Astron.* the study of living organisms that may exist elsewhere in the universe, methods of detecting them, and the possible effects of extraterrestrial conditions on terrestrial life forms.

Exocet *noun* a subsonic tactile missile, launched from a ship, aircraft, or submarine, and travelling at low altitude. [French, from modern Latin *Exocoetus volitans*, the flying fish]

exocrine *noun* **1** *Physiol.* relating to external secretions, or to a pathway or structure that secretes externally. **2** *said of a gland* discharging its secretions through a duct which opens on to an epithelial surface, eg sweat gland, salivary gland. See also ENDOCRINE. [from EXO- + Greek *krinein*, to separate]

Exod. *or* **Exod** *abbrev. Biblical* Exodus.

exodus *noun* **1** a mass departure of people. **2** (**Exodus**) the departure of the Israelites from Egypt, probably in the 13c BC. [from Greek *exodos*, from *ex*, out + *hodos*, way]

Exodus, Book of the second book of the Pentateuch, in the Hebrew Bible and Old Testament. It tells of the deliverance of the Jews from slavery in Egypt under the leadership of Moses, the revelation of Israel's Law to him on Mt Sinai, and it provides instructions for building the wilderness tabernacle.

ex officio *adv.* by virtue of one's official position. [from Latin *ex officio*]

exogamy *noun Anthropol.* the practice or rule of marrying only outside one's own group. [from EXO- + Greek *gamos*, marriage]

exogenous *adj. Biol.* **1** originating outside a cell, organ, or organism. **2** growing from near the surface of a living organism.

exonerate *verb* to free from blame, or acquit of a criminal charge. [from Latin *ex*, from + *onus*, burden]

exoneration *noun* freeing from blame or guilt.

exorbitance *noun* excessiveness of prices or demands.

exorbitant *adj., said of prices or demands* very high, excessive, or unfair. [from EX- + Latin *orbita*, track]

exorbitantly *adv.* to an excessively demanding extent: *we were charged exorbitantly for the meal.*

exorcism *noun, in some beliefs* driving away of an evil spirit or influence.

exorcist *noun, in some beliefs* a person who can drive away an evil spirit or influence.

exorcize *or* **exorcise** *verb, in some beliefs* **1** to drive away (an evil spirit or influence) with prayer or holy words. **2** to free (a person or place) from the influence of an evil spirit in this way. [from Greek *exorkizein*]

exordium *noun* (PL. **exordiums**, **exordia**) *formal* an introductory part, especially of a formal speech or piece of writing. [from Latin, beginning of a speech]

exoskeleton *noun Zool.* in some invertebrates, an external skeleton which forms a rigid covering that is external to the body. In insects and crustaceans it is made of a hard material called *chitin*, and in molluscs, such as snails, it consists of a chalky shell.

exosphere *noun Astron.* the outermost layer of the Earth's atmosphere, which starts at an altitude of about 500km, and from whose outer edge rapidly moving atoms of gas (mainly hydrogen) can escape the Earth's gravitational pull.

exothermic reaction *Chem.* any process, especially a chemical reaction, that involves the release of heat.

exotic — *adj.* **1** introduced from a foreign, especially distant and tropical, country: *exotic plants.* **2** interestingly different or strange, especially colourful and rich, and suggestive of a distant land. — *noun* an exotic person or thing. [from Greek *exotikos*, from *exo*, outside]

exotica *pl. noun* strange or rare objects.

exotically *adv.* in an exotic or colourfully strange way.

expand *verb* **1** *trans., intrans.* to make or become greater in size, extent, or importance. **2** *intrans.* (**expand on** *or* **upon something**) to give additional information; to enlarge on a description, etc. **3** *intrans. formal* to become more at ease; more open and talkative. **4** *intrans., trans. formal* to fold out flat or spread out. **5** to write out in full. **6** *Maths.* to multiply out (terms in brackets). [from Latin *expandere*, to spread out]

expandable *adj.* capable of being expanded or increased.

expanse *noun* a wide area or space. [from Latin *expansum*]

expansible *adj.* able to expand or be expanded.

expansion *noun* **1** the act or state of expanding. **2** the amount by which something expands. **3** *Maths.* the result of expanding (terms in brackets). [from Latin *expandere*, to spread out]

expansionism *noun* the act or practice of increasing territory or political influence or authority, usually at the expense of other nations or bodies.

expansionist — *noun* a person who supports expansionism. — *adj.* relating to or characterized by expansionism.

expansive *adj.* **1** ready or eager to talk; open; effusive. **2** wide-ranging. **3** able or tending to expand.

expansively *adv.* in an expansive or wide-ranging way.

expansiveness *noun* an expansive or wide-ranging extent.

expat *noun colloq.* an expatriate.

expatiate *verb intrans. formal* to talk or write at length or in detail. [from Latin *exspatiari*, to digress]

expatiation *noun formal* lengthy writing or description.

expatriate — *adj.* (pronounced -ət) **1** living abroad, especially for a long but limited period. **2** exiled. — *noun* (pronounced -ət) a person living or working abroad. — *verb* (pronounced -ate) **1** to banish or exile. **2** to deprive of citizenship. [from Latin *ex*, out of + *patria*, native land]

expect *verb* **1** to think of as likely to happen or come. **2** (**expect something from** *or* **of someone**) to require it of them; to regard it as normal or reasonable. **3** *colloq.* to suppose: *I expect you're tired.*
— **be expecting** *colloq.* to be pregnant. [from Latin *exspectare*, to look out for]

expectancy *noun* (PL. **expectancies**) **1** the act or state of expecting. **2** a future chance or probability: *life expectancy.* [from Latin *exspectare*, to look out for]

expectant *adj.* **1** eagerly waiting; hopeful. **2** not yet, but expecting to be (especially a mother or father).

expectantly *adv.* in an expectant or eagerly hopeful way.

expectation *noun* **1** the state, or an attitude, of expecting. **2** (*often* **expectations**) something expected, whether good or bad. **3** (*usually* **expectations**) money, property, etc that one expects to gain, especially by inheritance.

expectorant *Medicine* — *adj.* causing the coughing up of phlegm. — *noun* an expectorant medicine.

expectorate *verb intrans., trans. Medicine* to cough up and spit out (phlegm). [from Latin *expectorare*, from EX- + *pectus*, the chest]

expedience *or* **expediency** (PL. **expediencies**) *noun* **1** suitability or convenience. **2** prac-

tical advantage or self-interest, especially as opposed to moral correctness. [from Latin *expedire*: see EXPEDITE]

expedient — *adj.* **1** suitable or appropriate. **2** practical or advantageous, rather than morally correct. — *noun* a suitable method or solution, especially one quickly thought of to meet an urgent need.

expediently *adv.* advantageously; suitably.

expedite *verb* **1** to speed up, or assist the progress of. **2** to carry out quickly. [from Latin *expedire*, set free]

expedition *noun* **1** an organized journey with a purpose, or the group making it. **2** *formal* speed, promptness. [from Latin *expeditio*]

expeditionary *adj.* of, forming, or for use on, an expedition.

expeditious *adj. formal* carried out with speed and efficiency.

expeditiously *adv.* with speed and efficiency.

expel *verb* (**expelled, expelling**) **1** to dismiss from or deprive of membership of (a club, school, etc), usually permanently as punishment for misconduct. **2** to get rid of; to force out. [from Latin *expellere*, to drive out]

expend *verb* to use or spend (time, supplies, effort, etc). [from Latin *expendere*, to weigh out]

expendable *adj.* **1** that may be given up or sacrificed for some purpose or cause. **2** not valuable enough to be worth preserving.

expenditure *noun* **1** the act of expending. **2** an amount expended, especially of money.

expense *noun* **1** the act of spending money, or money spent. **2** something on which money is spent. **3** (**expenses**) a sum of one's own money spent doing one's job, or this sum of money or an allowance paid by one's employer to make up for this.
— **at the expense of something** *or* **someone 1** with the loss or sacrifice of them. **2** causing damage to their pride or reputation. **3** with the cost paid by them. [from Latin *expensa*, from *expendere*, to weigh out]

expensive *adj.* involving much expense; costing a great deal.

expensively *adv.* with much cost.

experience — *noun* **1** practice in an activity. **2** knowledge or skill gained through practice. **3** wisdom in all matters, gained through long and varied observation of life. **4** an event which affects or involves one. — *verb* **1** to have practical acquaintance with. **2** to feel or undergo. [from Latin *experientia*, from *experiri*, to try]

experienced *adj.* having knowledge or skill gained from experience.

experiential *adj., said of knowledge or learning* based on direct experience, as distinct from theoretical knowledge.

experientially *adv. Philos.* in terms of direct experience.

experiment — *noun* **1** a trial carried out in order to test a theory, a machine's performance, etc or to discover something unknown. **2** the carrying out of such trials. **3** an attempt at something original. — *verb intrans.* (**experiment on** *or* **with something**) to carry out such an experiment. [from Latin *experimentum*, from *experiri*, to try]

experimental *adj.* **1** of the nature of an experiment. **2** relating to, or used in, experiments. **3** trying out new styles and techniques.

experimentally *adv.* in an experimental way; on an experimental basis.

experimentation *noun* the process of experimenting; experimental procedure.

experimenter *noun* a person who experiments, especially habitually.

Experiment with the Air Pump a painting by Joseph Wright (1768, London). It depicts an experiment made by candlelight.

expert — *noun* a person with great skill in, or extensive knowledge of, a particular subject. — *adj.* **1** highly skilled or extremely knowledgeable. **2** relating to or done by an expert or experts. [from Latin *expertus*, from *experiri*, to try]

expertise *noun* special skill or knowledge.

expertly *adv.* in an expert or skilful way.

expert system *Comput.* a computer program that is designed to solve problems by utilizing both knowledge and reasoning derived from human expertise in a particular field. Expert systems represent an important field of artificial intelligence research, and are used in areas such as medical diagnosis, the interpretation of the law, financial decision-making, and geological prospecting.

expiate *verb* to make amends for (a wrong). [from Latin *expiare*, to atone for]

expiation *noun* expiating; making amends for a wrong.

expiration *noun formal* **1** expiry. **2** the act of breathing out, in which the diaphragm rises and the ribcage contracts, forcing air rich in carbon dioxide out of the lungs.

expire *verb intrans.* **1** to come to an end, cease to be valid. **2** to breathe out. **3** to die. [from Latin *exspirare*, to breathe out]

expiry *noun* (PL. **expiries**) the ending of the duration or validity of something.

explain *verb* **1** to make clear or easy to understand. **2** to give, or be, a reason for. **3** to justify (oneself or one's actions).
— **explain something away** to dismiss it or lessen its importance, by explanation. [from Latin *explanare*, to make flat]

explanation *noun* **1** the act or process of explaining. **2** a statement or fact that explains.

explanatory *adj.* serving to explain.

expletive — *noun* **1** a swear-word or curse. **2** a word added to fill a gap, eg in poetry. **3** a meaningless exclamation. — *adj.* being or of the nature of such a word or exclamation. [from Latin *explere*, to fill up]

explicable *adj.* able to be explained.

explicate *verb* to explain (especially a literary work) in depth, with close analysis of particular points. [from Latin *explicare*, to fold out]

explication *noun* detailed explanation or analysis.

explicit *adj.* **1** stated or shown fully and clearly. **2** speaking plainly and openly. [from Latin *explicitus*, straightforward]

explicitly *adv.* in an explicit or openly stated way.

explicitness *noun* being explicit; open statement.

explode *verb* **1** *intrans. said of a substance* to undergo an explosion. **2** to cause (something) to undergo an explosion. **3** *intrans.* to undergo a violent explosion as a result of a chemical or nuclear reaction. **4** *intrans.* to suddenly show a strong or violent emotion, especially anger. **5** to disprove (a theory, etc) with vigour. **6** *intrans. said especially of population* to increase rapidly. [from Latin *explodere*, to force off stage by clapping]

exploded *adj.* **1** blown up. **2** *said of a theory, etc* no longer accepted; proved false. **3** *said of a diagram* showing the different parts (of something) relative to, but slightly separated from, each other.

exploit — *noun* (with stress on *ex-*) (*usually* **exploits**) an act or feat, especially a bold or daring one. — *verb* (with stress on *-ploit*) **1** to take unfair advantage of so as to achieve one's own aims. **2** to make good use of: *exploit oil resources*. [from Old French *exploiter*]

exploitation *noun* exploiting; making use of something.

exploration *noun* an exploring process or undertaking.

exploratory *adj.* **1** *said of talks, etc* serving to establish procedures or ground rules. **2** *Medicine* denoting surgery that aims to establish the nature of a complaint rather than treat it.

explore *verb* **1** to search or travel through (a place) for the purpose of discovery. **2** to examine carefully: *explore every possibility*. [from Latin *explorare*, to search out]

explorer *noun* a person who explores unfamiliar territory, especially professionally or habitually.

Explorer spacecraft *Astron.* a series of US satellites. *Explorer 1* was the first Earth satellite to be launched by the USA (in 1958). It confirmed the existence of Van Allen radiation belts around the Earth, which had previously been predicted.

explosion *noun* **1** *Chem.* a sudden and violent increase in pressure caused by an extremely rapid chemical or nuclear reaction, or a sudden change of state, that generates large amounts of heat and destructive shock waves that travel outward from the point of explosion and are heard as a loud bang. Explosions are often caused by the production of large volumes of gas, eg when chemical explosives are ignited or struck. **2** the sudden loud noise that accompanies such a reaction. **3** a sudden display of strong feelings, etc. **4** a sudden great increase.

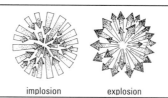
implosion   explosion

implosion and explosion

explosive — *adj.* **1** likely to, tending to, or able to explode. **2** likely to become marked by physical violence or emotional outbursts. **3** likely to result in violence or an outburst of feeling: *an explosive situation*. — *noun* any substance that is capable of producing an explosion, releasing large volumes of gas at high pressure when it is ignited or struck, eg gunpowder, dynamite, nitroglycerine, Semtex®. Explosives are used in building and construction, mining, quarrying, and military warfare.

explosively *adv.* in an explosive or violent way.

expo *noun* (PL. **expos**) *colloq.* a large public exhibition. [from EXPOSITION]

exponent *noun* **1** a person able to perform some art or activity, especially skilfully. **2** a person who explains and promotes (a theory, belief, etc). **3** *Maths.* a number that indicates how many times a given quantity, called the *base*, is to be multiplied by itself. It is usually denoted by a superscript number or symbol immediately after the quantity concerned, eg $6^4 = 6 \times 6 \times 6 \times 6$. Numbers containing exponents are multiplied by adding the exponents, and divided by subtracting them, eg $x^2 \times x^3 = x^5$ and $y^5 \div y^2 = y^3$. Any number in which the exponent is zero is equal to 1. — Also called *power*, *index*.

exponential *Maths.* — *adj.* **1** denoting a function that varies according to the power of another quantity, ie a function in which the variable quantity is an *exponent* (a symbol placed above and to the right of a mathematical expression). For example, if $y = a^x$, then y varies exponentially with x. **2** denoting a logarithmic increase or decrease in numbers of a population,

eg exponential growth of bacteria, exponential decay of radioactive isotopes. — *noun* (*also* **exponential function**) the function e^x, where e is a constant with a value of approximately 2.718. The inverse of this function, $\log_e x$, is the *natural logarithm* of x, ie natural logarithms use e as the base. [from Latin *exponere*, to set out]

exponentially *adv.* on an exponential basis; very rapidly.

export — *verb* (with variable stress) to send or take (goods, etc) to another country, especially for sale. — *noun* (with stress on *ex-*) **1** the act or business of exporting. **2** something exported. [from Latin *exportare*, to carry away]

exportation *noun* the exporting of goods.

exporter *noun* a person or business that exports goods commercially.

expose *verb* **1** to remove cover, protection, or shelter from: *exposed to wind, to criticism*. **2** to discover or make known (eg a criminal or crime). **3** to allow light to fall on (a photographic film or paper) when taking or printing a photograph. **4** (**expose someone to something**) to cause or allow them to have experience of it.
— **expose oneself** to display one's sexual organs in public.
[from Old French *exposer*, to set out]

exposé *noun* **1** a formal statement of facts, especially one introducing an argument. **2** an article or programme which exposes a public scandal, crime, etc. [from French *exposé*, from *exposer*, to expose]

exposition *noun* **1** an in-depth explanation or account (of a subject). **2** the act of presenting such an explanation, or a viewpoint. **3** a large public exhibition. [from Latin *expositio*, a setting out]

expostulate *verb intrans.* (**expostulate with someone**) to argue or reason with them, especially in protest or so as to dissuade them. [from Latin *expostulare*, to demand]

expostulation *noun* expostulating; an argument or protest.

exposure *noun* **1** the act of exposing or the state of being exposed. **2** the harmful effects on the body of extreme cold. **3** the number or regularity of appearances in public, eg on television. **4** the act of exposing photographic film or paper to light. **5** the amount of light to which a film or paper is exposed, or the length of time for which it is exposed. **6** the amount of film exposed or to be exposed in order to produce one photograph.

expound *verb* **1** to explain in depth. **2** *intrans.* (**expound on something**) to talk at length about it. [from Latin *exponere*, to set out]

express — *verb* **1** to put into words. **2** to indicate or represent with looks, actions, symbols, etc. **3** to show or reveal. **4** to press or squeeze out. **5** to send by fast delivery service. — *adj.* **1** *said of a train* travelling especially fast, with few stops. **2** of or sent by a fast delivery service. **3** clearly stated: *his express wish*. **4** particular; clear: *with the express purpose of*. — *noun* **1** an express train. **2** an express delivery service. — *adv.* by express delivery service.
— **express oneself** to put one's thoughts into words.
[from Latin *exprimere*, to press out]

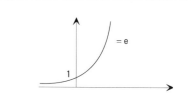
= e
1

exponential function

expressible *adj.* capable of being expressed.

expression *noun* **1** the act of expressing. **2** a look on the face that displays feelings. **3** a word or phrase. **4** the indication of feeling, eg in a manner of speaking or a way of playing music. **5** *Maths.* a symbol or combination of symbols.

Expressionism a movement in art, architecture, and literature which aims to communicate the internal emotional realities of a situation, rather than its external 'realistic' aspect. The term was first used in Germany in 1911, but the roots of the movement can be traced to Van Gogh and Gauguin in the 1880s. In this approach, traditional ideas of beauty and proportion are disregarded, so that artists can express their feelings more strongly by means of distortion, jarring colours, and exaggerated linear rhythms. The movement was also influential in literature, especially in German theatre after World War I. The use of dislocation and distortion in fiction and poetry (eg in the writing of Kafka and Joyce) has also been described as Expressionist.

Expressionist — *noun* a person, especially a painter, who practises Expressionism. — *adj.* relating to or characteristic of Expressionism.

expressionless *adj., said of a face or voice* showing no feeling.

expressive *adj.* **1** showing meaning or feeling in a clear or lively way. **2** (**expressive of something**) expressing a feeling or emotion: *words expressive of anger.*

expressively *adv.* in an expressive or openly meaningful way.

expressiveness *noun* being expressive or openly meaningful.

expressly *adv.* **1** clearly and definitely. **2** particularly; specifically.

expropriate *verb formal or Legal, said especially of the state* to take (property, etc) from its owner for some special use. [from Latin *expropriare*]

expropriation *noun* taking of property from its owner.

expropriator *noun* a person or body expropriating property.

expulsion *noun* **1** the act of expelling from school, a club, etc. **2** the act of forcing or driving out. [from Latin *expulsio*, a forcing out]

expulsive *adj.* having the power to expel or drive out.

expunge *verb* **1** to cross out or delete (eg a passage from a book). **2** to cancel out or destroy. [from Latin *expungere*, to mark for deletion]

expurgate *verb* **1** to revise (a book) by removing objectionable or offensive words or passages. **2** to remove (such words or passages). [from Latin *expurgare*, to purify]

expurgation *noun* removal from texts of items considered offensive.

exquisite *adj.* **1** extremely beautiful or skilfully produced. **2** able to exercise sensitive judgement; discriminating: *exquisite taste.* **3** *said of pain, pleasure, etc* extreme. [from Latin *exquisitus*]

exquisitely *adv.* in an exquisite or beautiful way.

ex-serviceman and **ex-servicewoman**. *noun* (PL. **ex-servicemen**, **ex-servicewomen**) a former male or female member of the armed forces.

ext. *abbrev.* **1** extension. **2** exterior. **3** external or externally.

extant *adj.* still existing. [from Latin *exstare*, to stand out]

extemporaneous *or* **extemporary** *adj.* **1** spoken, done, etc without preparation; impromptu. **2** makeshift; improvised. [from EX- + Latin *tempus*, time]

extemporaneously *or* **extemporarily** *adv., said of speaking* without preparation.

extempore *adv., adj.* without planning or preparation. [from EX- + Latin *tempus*, time]

extemporization *or* **extemporisation** *noun* speaking or performing without preparation.

extemporize *or* **extemporise** *verb trans., intrans.* to speak or perform without preparation.

extend *verb* **1** to make longer or larger. **2** *intrans., trans.* to reach or stretch in space or time. **3** to hold out or stretch out (a hand, etc). **4** to offer (kindness, greetings, etc) to someone. **5** to increase in scope. **6** *intrans.* to include or go as far as: *their kindness did not extend to lending money.* **7** to exert to the physical or mental limit: *extend oneself.* [from Latin *extendere*, to stretch out]

extendable *or* **extendible** *adj.* same as EXTENSIBLE.

extended family, the family as a unit including all relatives. See also NUCLEAR FAMILY.

extended-play *adj.* (ABBREV. **EP**) *said of a gramophone record* with each side playing for about twice the length of a single.

extensible *adj.* capable of being extended or made longer.

extensification *noun* an agricultural policy within the European Community by which land is farmed less intensively with savings in expenditure on feed, fertilizers, and pesticides balancing the loss of income from lower production. See also EXTENSIVE FARMING, INTENSIVE FARMING.

extension *noun* **1** the process of extending, or the state of being extended. **2** an added part, making the original larger or longer. **3** a subsidiary or extra telephone, connected to the main line. **4** an extra period beyond an original time limit. **5** a scheme by which services, eg those of a university or library, are made available to non-members: *an extension course.* **6** range or extent. [from Latin *extensio*]

extensive *adj.* large in area, amount, range or effect. [from Latin *extensivus*, from *extendere*, to stretch out]

extensive farming farming in which there is a relatively low level of expenditure by the farmer on expensive chemical fertilizers and sprays, and manufactured feedstuffs. The comparatively low levels of yield per hectare may be compensated for by these savings, and by farming wider areas of land, thus maintaining an acceptable level of income. See also EXTENSIFICATION, INTENSIVE FARMING.

extensively *adv.* to an extensive degree; widely.

extensor *noun Medicine* any of various muscles that straighten out parts of the body. [from Latin *extendere*, to stretch out]

extent *noun* **1** the area over which something extends. **2** amount, scope or degree. [from Old French *extente*, from Latin *extendere*, to stretch out]

extenuate *verb* to reduce the seriousness of (an offence) by giving an explanation that partly excuses it. [from Latin *extenuare*, to make thin, to lessen]

extenuating *adj., said especially of a circumstance* reducing the seriousness of an offence by partially excusing it.

extenuation *noun* lessening of an offence by extenuating circumstances.

exterior — *adj.* **1** on, from, or for use on the outside. **2** foreign, or dealing with foreign nations. — *noun* **1** an outside part or surface. **2** an outward appearance, especially when intended to conceal or deceive. **3** an outdoor scene in a film, etc. [from Latin *exterior*, from *exterus*, on the outside]

exterminate *verb* to get rid of or completely destroy (something living). [from Latin *exterminare*, to drive away, from EX- + *terminus*, boundary]

extermination *noun* total destruction of something living.

exterminator *noun* a person or thing that destroys something living.

external — *adj.* **1** of, for, from, or on, the outside. **2** of the world, as opposed to the mind: *external realities.* **3** foreign; involving foreign nations: *external affairs.* **4** *said of a medicine* to be applied on the outside of the body, not swallowed, etc. **5** taking place, or coming from, outside one's school, university, etc: *an external examination.* — *noun* **1** (*often* **externals**) an outward appearance or feature, especially when superficial or insignificant. **2** *colloq.* an external examination or examiner. [from Latin *externus*, from *exterus*, on the outside]

externalize *or* **externalise** *verb* to express (thoughts, feelings, ideas, etc) in words.

externally *adv.* outwardly; on the outside.

extinct *adj.* **1** *said of a species of animal, etc* no longer in existence. **2** *said of a volcano* no longer active. **3** *formal, said of an emotion, etc* no longer felt; dead. [from Latin *exstinguere*, to extinguish]

extinction *noun* **1** the process of making or becoming extinct; elimination, disappearance. **2** *Biol.* the total elimination or dying out of any plant or animal species, or a whole group of species, worldwide. Present-day extinctions are usually due to human activity, eg hunting, pollution, or destruction of natural habitats such as rainforests.
◇ The fossil record indicates that at certain times in the Earth's history many animal species became extinct more or less simultaneously. The largest of these mass extinctions occurred about 225 million years ago, at the end of the Palaeozoic era, when about 96 per cent of all living species died out, and only millions of years later was the former diversity of living organisms restored. The disappearance of the dinosaurs (and various marine invertebrates, including ammonites) was associated with another mass extinction about 65 million years ago. It is thought that climatic changes probably caused these mass extinctions, perhaps resulting from the collision of a large shower of asteroids or comets with the Earth.

extinguish *verb* **1** to put out (a fire, etc). **2** *formal* to kill off or destroy (eg passion). **3** *Legal* to pay off (a debt). [from Latin *exstinguere*]

extinguisher *noun* **1** a person or thing that extinguishes. **2** (*also* **fire extinguisher**) an apparatus filled with water or chemicals for putting out fires.

extirpate *verb* **1** *formal* to destroy completely. **2** *formal* to uproot. **3** to remove surgically. [from Latin *exstirpare*, to tear up by the roots]

extirpation *noun* total destruction.

extn. *abbrev.* extension.

extol *verb* (**extolled**, **extolling**) *somewhat formal* to praise enthusiastically. [from Latin *extollere*, to lift or raise up]

extolment *noun formal* enthusiastic praise.

extort *verb* to obtain (money, information, etc) by threats or violence. [from Latin *extorquere*, to twist or wrench out]

extortion *noun* the crime of obtaining money by threats.

extortionate *adj.* **1** *said of a price, demand, etc* unreasonably high or great. **2** using extortion.

extortionately *adv.* to an extortionate or unreasonable degree.

extortionist *noun* a person who practises extortion.

extra — *adj.* **1** additional; more than is usual, necessary or expected. **2** for which an additional charge is made. — *noun* **1** an additional or unexpected thing. **2** an extra charge, or an item for which this is made. **3** an actor employed temporarily in a small, usually non-speaking, part in a film. **4** a special edition of a newspaper containing later news. **5** *Cricket* a run scored other than by hitting the ball with the bat. — *adv.* unusually or exceptionally. [probably a shortening of EXTRAORDINARY]

extra- *prefix* outside or beyond: *extra-curricular*. [from Latin *extra*, outside]

extracellular *Biol.* located or taking place outside a cell.

extract — *verb* **1** to pull or draw out, especially by force or with effort. **2** to separate a substance from a liquid or solid mixture. **3** to derive (eg pleasure). **4** to obtain (money, etc) by threats or violence. **5** to select (passages from a book, etc). — *noun* **1** a passage selected from a book, etc. **2** *Chem.* a substance that is separated from a liquid or solid mixture, usually by dissolving it in a suitable solvent and then evaporating the solvent by distillation. The active ingredients of many drugs are concentrated in this way. [from Latin *extrahere*, to draw out]

extraction *noun* **1** the act of extracting. **2** the process whereby a metal is obtained from its ore. **3** the removal of a tooth from its socket. **4** the use of a solvent to separate a substance from a liquid or solid mixture. **5** family origin; descent: *of Dutch extraction.*

extractor *noun* a person or thing that extracts, especially a device for ventilating a room: *extractor fan.*

extra-curricular *adj.* not belonging to, or offered in addition to, the subjects studied in a school's, college's, etc main teaching curriculum.

extraditable *adj.*, *said of a person* liable to be extradited.

extradite *verb* to return (a person accused of a crime) for trial in the country where the crime was committed. [from EX- + Latin *tradere*, to deliver up]

extradition *noun* the procedure of returning a person accused of a crime to the country where it was committed.

extramarital *adj.*, *said especially of sexual relations* taking place outside marriage.

extramural *adj.* **1** *said of courses, etc* for people who are not full-time students at a college, etc. **2** outside the scope of normal studies. [from EXTRA- + Latin *murus*, wall]

extraneous *adj.* **1** not belonging; not relevant or related. **2** coming from outside. [from Latin *extraneus*, external]

extraneously *adv.* in an unrelated way; as a separate concern.

extraordinarily *adv.* in an extraordinary or unusual way; to an unusual degree.

extraordinary *adj.* **1** unusual; surprising; remarkable. **2** additional, not part of the regular pattern or routine: *extraordinary meeting.* **3** *formal* (often following the noun) employed to do additional work, or for a particular occasion: *ambassador extraordinary.* [from Latin *extra ordinem*, outside the usual order]

extrapolate *verb trans.*, *intrans.* **1** *Maths.* to estimate (a value that lies outside a known range of values), on the basis of those values and usually by means of a graph. **2** to make (estimates) or draw (conclusions) from known facts. [from EXTRA- + INTERPOLATE]

extrapolation *noun* the process or result of extrapolating; a conclusion from known facts.

extrasensory *adj.* achieved using means other than the ordinary senses of sight, hearing, touch, taste and smell: *extrasensory perception.*

extraterrestrial — *adj.*, *said of a being, creature, etc* coming from outside the Earth or its atmosphere. — *noun* an extraterrestrial being.

extravagance *noun* excessive or indulgent spending; lack of restraint.

extravagant *adj.* **1** using, spending, or costing too much. **2** unreasonably or unbelievably great: *extravagant claims/praise.* [from EXTRA- + Latin *vagari*, to wander]

extravagantly *adv.* in an extravagant way; to an extravagant degree.

extravaganza *noun* a spectacular display, performance or production. [from Italian *estravaganza*, extravagance]

extravert same as EXTROVERT.

Extremadura *or* **Estremadura** POP (1991) 1.1m, an autonomous region in W Spain, situated on the Portuguese frontier. AREA 41 602sq km/ 16 058sq mi. It is bounded to the N by the Sierra de Gata and the Sierra de Gredos (rising to 2 592m). CHIEF TOWNS Badajoz, Cáceres. PHYSICAL DESCRIPTION crossed by the Tagus and Guadiana rivers; the region is largely dry and covered with stony moorland. ECONOMY merino sheep, pigs, vines, figs, olives, and almonds; considerable industrial development since the 1970s through the use of hydroelectricity and irrigation channels.

extreme — *adj.* **1** very high, or highest, in degree or intensity. **2** very far, or furthest, in any direction, especially out from the centre. **3** very violent or strong. **4** not moderate; severe: *extreme measures.* — *noun* **1** either of two people or things as far, or as different, as possible from each other. **2** the highest limit; the greatest degree of any state or condition.
— **go to extremes** to take action beyond what is thought to be reasonable.
in the extreme to the highest degree.
[from Latin *extremus*, from *exterus*, on the outside]

extremely *adv.* to an extreme degree; very much: *the music was extremely loud.*

extreme unction *RC Church* the act of anointing a dying person with consecrated oil.

extremism *noun* support for extreme opinions, especially in politics.

extremist — *noun* a person who has extreme opinions, especially in politics. — *adj.* relating to, or favouring, extreme measures.

extremity *noun* (PL. **extremities**) **1** the farthest point. **2** an extreme degree; the quality of being extreme. **3** a situation of great danger. **4** (**extremities**) the hands and feet. [from Latin *extremitas*, end, farthest point]

extricable *adj.* capable of being extricated or disentangled.

extricate *verb* to free from difficulties; to disentangle. [from Latin *extricare*, from EX- + *tricae*, hindrances]

extrication *noun* extricating; disentangling.

extroversion *or* **extraversion** *noun* *Psychol.* a personality trait characterized by a tendency to be more concerned with the outside world and social relationships than with one's inner thoughts and feelings. See also INTROVERSION.

extrovert *or* **extravert** — *noun* **1** *Psychol.* a person who is more concerned with the outside world and social relationships than with his or her inner thoughts and feelings. **2** a person who is sociable, outgoing, and talkative. — *adj.* having the temperament of an extrovert; sociable, outgoing. See also INTROVERT. [from EXTRA- + Latin *vertere*, to turn]

extroverted *adj.*, *said of a person* sociable and outgoing.

extrude *verb* **1** to squeeze or force out. **2** to force or press a semisoft solid material through a shaped hole or *die* in order to mould it into a continuous length of product. [from Latin *extrudere*, to push out]

extrusion *noun* **1** *Engineering* a manufacturing process in which hot or cold semisoft solid material, especially metal, plastic, or ceramic, is forced through a shaped hole or *die* in order to produce a continuous length of product. Extrusion is used to produce metal bars, hollow pipes, sheets, wire, plastic film, etc. **2** *Geol.* an extrusive rock.

extrusive rock *Geol.* igneous rock formed from molten rock material, such as magma or volcanic lava, that has poured out on to the Earth's surface and then solidified, eg basalt.

exuberance *noun* high spirits; enthusiasm.

exuberant *adj.* **1** in very high spirits. **2** enthusiastic and energetic. **3** *said of health, etc* excellent. **4** *said of plants, etc* growing abundantly. [from Latin *exuberans*, from *uber*, rich]

exuberantly *adv.* with an exuberant or high-spirited manner.

exudate *noun* **1** *Biol.* any substance released from an organ or cell of a plant or animal to the exterior through a gland, pore, or membrane, eg resin, sweat. **2** *Medicine* the fluid containing proteins and white blood cells that is discharged through small pores in membranes, usually as a result of inflammation.

exudation *noun* exuding; giving off odour or sweat.

exude *verb* **1** to give off or give out (an odour or sweat). **2** to show or convey by one's behaviour: *exude friendliness.* **3** *intrans.* to ooze out. [from Latin *exsudare*, to sweat out]

exult *verb intrans.* **1** (**exult in** *or* **at something**) to be intensely joyful about it. **2** (**exult over something**) to show or enjoy a feeling of triumph. [from Latin *exsultare*, to jump up and down]

exultant *adj.* joyfully or triumphantly elated.

exultation *noun* a feeling or state of joyful elation.

Eyck, Jan van see VAN EYCK, JAN.

eye — *noun* **1** the sense organ, usually one of a pair, that is responsible for vision. Various forms exist, including the simple eye (ocellus) of many annelid worms, the compound eye of insects, and the highly complex organ found in cephalopod molluscs (octopus and squid) and vertebrates, including man. **2** (*often* **eyes**) sight; vision: *surgeons need good eyes.* **3** attention, gaze, or observation: *keep one's eyes on / catch someone's eye / in the public eye.* **4** the ability to appreciate and judge: *an eye for beauty.* **5** judgement; opinion: *in the eyes of the law.* **6** a look or expression: *a hostile eye.* **7** *Bot.* the bud of a tuber such as a potato. **8** an area of calm and low pressure at the centre

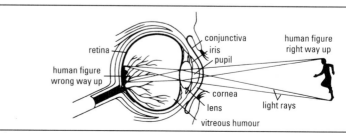

human eye

of a tornado, etc. **9** any rounded thing, especially when hollow, eg the hole in a needle or the small wire loop that a hook fits into. — *verb* (**eyed, eyeing**) **1** to look at carefully. **2** *colloq.* (*also* **eye someone** *or* **something up**) to assess their worth or attractiveness.

— **be all eyes** *colloq.* to be vigilant.

cast *or* **run an eye over something** to examine it cursorily.

clap *or* **lay** *or* **set eyes on someone** *or* **something** *colloq.* to see it, especially for the first time.

close *or* **shut one's eyes to something** to ignore or disregard it.

get *or* **keep one's eye in** to become or remain familiar with the way in which a game or sport is played.

give an eye to something *colloq.* to attend to it.

give someone the eye *or* **the glad eye** *colloq.* to look at them in a sexually inviting way.

have one's eye on something to be eager to acquire it.

have eyes for someone to be interested in them.

have an eye to something to have it as a purpose or intention.

keep one's eyes skinned *or* **peeled** *colloq.* to watch out.

make eyes at someone *colloq.* to look at them with sexual interest or admiration.

more than meets the eye more complicated, difficult, etc than appearances suggest.

my eye! *colloq.* nonsense!

one in the eye for someone *colloq.* a harsh disappointment or rebuff for them.

see eye to eye with someone to be in agreement with them.

be up to the *or* **one's eyes in something** to be busy or deeply involved in work, a commitment, etc.

with an eye to something having it as a purpose or intention.

[from Anglo-Saxon *eage*]

◇ In terrestrial vertebrates, including humans, the eye is a roughly spherical structure located in a bony socket (the *orbit*) in the skull. It is surrounded by a white fibrous outer layer (the *sclera*), which is modified at the front of the eye to form the transparent *cornea*. The sclera is lined by a vascular layer or *choroid*, which is in turn lined at the back of the eye by the *retina*, which contains millions of light-sensitive cells of two types. These are the *rods* (which function at low light levels, and are responsible for black and white vision), and the *cones* (which are responsible for colour vision).

Light enters the eye through the cornea, and passes through a watery medium (the *aqueous humour*) and then through the pupil, a small circular aperture in the *iris*. The iris is an adjustable ring of muscle that forms the coloured part of the eye, and controls the size of the pupil and thus the amount of light entering the eye. Behind the iris lies the transparent lens, whose curvature is

regulated by means of ciliary muscles that contract to make it thin, for viewing distant objects, or relax to make it thicker, for viewing nearby objects. The shape of the lens is adjusted in this way so that light is directed through the jelly-like *vitreous humour* lying between the lens and the retina, and is focused on to the retina. The light-sensitive rods and cones of the latter then transmit nerve impulses via the optic nerve to the brain, where they are interpreted as vision.

eyeball *noun* the body of the eye, which is almost spherical, and surrounded by a transparent cornea at the front and a white fibrous layer or *sclera* around the rest of the structure.

— **eyeball to eyeball** *colloq.*, *said of people* face to face and close together in a threatening confrontation.

eyebright *noun* a small annual plant belonging to the genus *Euphrasia*, so called because it is used in herbal medicine to treat sore eyes. The flowers have two lips and are usually white, with a yellow blotch and purple veins on the lower lip.

eyebrow *noun* the arch of hair on the bony ridge above each eye.

— **raise an eyebrow** *or* **one's eyebrows** to show surprise, interest, or disbelief.

eye-catcher *noun* a strikingly attractive person or thing.

eye-catching *adj.* drawing attention, especially by being strikingly attractive.

eyeful *noun colloq.* **1** an interesting or beautiful sight. **2** a look or view.

eyeglass *noun* a single lens in a frame, to assist weak sight.

eyelash *noun* any of the short protective hairs that grow from the edge of the upper and lower eyelids.

eyelet *noun* a small hole through which a lace, etc is passed, or the metal ring reinforcing it. [from Old French *oillet*, diminutive of *oil*, eye]

eyelid *noun* in many terrestrial animals, including humans, a protective fold of skin and muscle, lined with membrane, that can be moved to cover or uncover the front of the eyeball. Usually each eye has an upper and a lower eyelid.

eye-opener *noun colloq.* a surprising or revealing sight, experience, etc.

eyepiece *noun Optics* the lens or group of lenses in an optical instrument such as a telescope or microscope that is nearest to the eye of the observer.

eyesight *noun* the ability to see.

eyesore *noun derog.* an ugly thing, especially a building.

eye teeth one of the two upper canine teeth.

— **give one's eye teeth for something** to go to any lengths to obtain it.

eyewash *noun* **1** liquid for soothing sore eyes.

2 *derog. colloq.* nonsense; insincere or deceptive talk.

eyewitness *noun* a person who sees something happen, especially a crime.

Eyre, Edward John (1815–1901) English explorer, born in Hornsea, Yorkshire. He emigrated to Australia at the age of 17, where he was appointed a magistrate. In 1840 he explored part of the region between S and W Australia, and discovered L Eyre. He later became Governor of New Zealand (1847), St Vincent (1854), and Jamaica (1861), where he suppressed a revolt with great severity (1865). He was subsequently recalled to England, prosecuted, and acquitted.

Eyre, Jane see JANE EYRE.

Eyre Lakes a group of dry salt lakes situated in NE South Australia. They include L Eyre North (145km/90mi long, 65km/40mi wide, area 7 692sq km/2 969sq mi) and L Eyre South (61km/38mi long, 26km/16mi wide, and area 1 191sq km/460sq mi). L Eyre North, the largest lake in Australia, is normally a shallow pan of glistening white salt. Since European discovery, it has filled with water only three times. It lies c.15m below sea level and is fed by a series of intermittently flowing rivers, including the Finke Diamantina and Cooper Creek. Donald Campbell set a world land speed record at this site in 1964.

eyrie *noun* **1** the nest of an eagle or other bird of prey, built in a high inaccessible place. **2** any house, fortified place, etc perched high up. [from Old French *airie*]

Eysenck, Hans Jürgen (1916–) British psychologist, born in Berlin. Professor at London University (1955–83), he has frequently championed the view that genetic factors play a large part in determining the psychological differences between people, and has often held controversial views on racial differences in intelligence. He has also promoted the theory that cancer incidence is strongly related to personality type.

Ez *or* **Ezr.** *abbrev. Biblical* Ezra.

Ezek. *or* **Ezek** *abbrev. Biblical* Ezekiel.

Ezekiel *or* **Ezechiel, Book of** a major prophetic work in the Hebrew Bible and Old Testament, attributed to Ezekiel, a 6c BC priest amongst the exiles in Babylonian territories after 597 BC. The prophecies in chapters 1 to 24 warn of the impending destruction of Jerusalem (587/6 BC); chapters 25 to 32 present oracles condemning foreign nations; and chapters 33 to 48 promise the restoration of Israel.

Ezra, Book of a book of the Hebrew Bible and Old Testament, originally probably part of a work that included Chronicles and Nehemiah. It describes stages in the return to Palestine of exiled Jews from 538 BC onwards, the attempts to rebuild the Temple and city of Jerusalem, and the story of Ezra's mission under Artaxerxes I or II to restore adherence to the Jewish law.

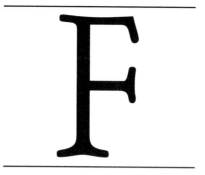

F¹ *or* **f** *noun* (PL. **Fs, F's, f's**) **1** the sixth letter of the English alphabet. **2** (**F**) *Mus.* the fourth note in the scale of C major. **3** (**F**) a musical key with this note as its base.

F² *abbrev.* **1** Fahrenheit. **2** farad. **3** faraday. **4** Fellow (of a society, etc). **5** *on pencils* fine. **6** force. **7** franc.

F³ *symbol* **1** *Chem.* fluorine. **2** *Physics* force.

f *abbrev.* **1** femto- (a prefix denoting 10⁻¹⁵ in the metric system). **2** focal length. **3** *Mus.* forte. **4** frequency.

f. *abbrev.* **1** fathom. **2** female. **3** feminine. **4** focal length. **5** folio. **6** following (page).

FA *abbrev.* Football Association.

Fa. *abbrev.* Florida.

fa same as FAH.

Fabergé, Peter Carl, originally **Karl Gustavovich Fabergé** (1846–1920) Russian goldsmith and jeweller of Huguenot descent, born in St Petersburg. In 1870 he inherited his father's establishment in St Petersburg, and moved from the design and manufacture of conventional jewellery to the creation of more elaborate and fantastic objects. He was most famous for the imperial Easter eggs, first commissioned by Alexander III for his tsarina in 1884. Fabergé's business was destroyed by the events of the Russian revolution.

Fabian — *adj.* **1** cautious; inclined to use delaying tactics. **2** of the Fabian Society, a body founded in 1884 for the gradual establishment of socialism. — *noun* a member of this society. [named after Quintus Fabius Maximus]

Fabius Maximus, Quintus, also called **Cunctator ('the Delayer')** (c.260–203 BC) Roman general and statesman whose refusal to engage Hannibal in set battle during the Second Punic War earned him his nickname. Originally a term of abuse, it became an honorific title after 216 BC, when Rome's massive and unnecessary defeat at the battle of Cannae proved that his cautious tactics had been right.

fable *noun* **1** a story with a moral, usually with animals as characters. **2** a lie; a false story. **3** a tale of wonder; myths and legends generally. [from Latin *fabula*, story]

fabled *adj.* made famous by legend.

fabliau *noun* (PL. **fabliaux**) a short comic poem or verse story popular in 12c France, and later in England. The plots usually involve deception and sex, and the subjects are amoral, frequently misogynist, and anticlerical. English examples include Chaucer's *The Miller's Tale* and *The Reeve's Tale*. [from Old French, a diminutive of FABLE]

Fabre, Jean Henri (1823–1915) French entomologist, born in St Léon, Aveyron. He isolated alizarin (a red dye used as a biological stain) from the madder plant, but is best remembered for his accounts of insect behaviour and natural history which resulted in the *Souvenirs Entomologiques* (10 vols, 1879–1907). He recognized that many behaviours, such as the wasp's method of capturing and immobilizing its prey, are inherited and not learned.

fabric *noun* **1** woven, knitted or felted cloth. **2** quality; texture. **3** the walls, floor and roof of a building. **4** orderly structure: *the fabric of society.* [from Latin *fabrica*, craft]

fabricate *verb* **1** to invent (a false story, etc). **2** to make, especially from whatever materials are available. **3** to forge (a document). [from Latin *fabricari*, to construct]

fabrication *noun* **1** something that is fabricated or invented. **2** construction. **3** manufacture. **4** a story.

fabricator *noun* a person or business that fabricates.

Fabricius, David (1564–1617) German astronomer and clergyman, born in Esens. The discoverer of the first known variable star (Mira, in the constellation Cetus) in 1596, he was pastor at Resterhaave and Osteel in East Friesland, where he was murdered by one of his parishioners.

Fabricius ab Aquapendente, Hieronymus, Italian **Girolamo Fabrici** (1537–1619) Italian anatomist, born in Acquapendente. Professor at Padua, he gave the first detailed descriptions of the placenta, larynx,. and valves of the veins. William Harvey was one of his pupils.

fabulous *adj.* **1** *colloq.* marvellous. **2** immense; amazing. **3** legendary; mythical. [from Latin *fabulosus*]

fabulously *adv.* in a fabulous way.

Façade an instrumental setting by William Walton (1923) of poems by Edith Sitwell. Gunter Hess (in 1929) and Frederick Ashton (in 1931) used the score to write ballets.

façade *or* **facade** *noun* **1** the front of a building. **2** a false appearance that hides the reality. [from French *façade*]

Face, Jeremy Lovewit's rascally housekeeper who becomes assistant to Subtle in Ben Jonson's *The Alchemist.*

face — *noun* **1** the front part of the head, from forehead to chin. **2** the features or facial expression. **3** a surface or side, eg of a mountain, gem, geometrical figure, etc. **4** the important or working side, eg of a golf-club head. **5** in a mine, the exposed surface from which coal, etc is mined. **6** the dial of a clock, watch, etc. **7** the side of a playing-card marked with numbers, symbols, etc. **8** general look or appearance. **9** an aspect. **10** impudence; cheek. **11** *literary* someone's presence: *stand before his face.* **12** *Printing* a typeface. — *verb* **1** *trans., intrans.* to be opposite to; to turn to look at or look in some direction. **2** to have before one (something unpleasant): *face ruin.* **3** to confront, brave or cope with (problems, difficulties, etc). **4** to accept (the unpleasant truth, etc). **5** to present itself to: *the scene that faced us.* **6** to cover with a surface: *bricks faced with plaster.*
— **face someone down** to confront them boldly until they give way from embarrassment, shame, etc.
face to face facing or confronting each other.
face up to something *or* **someone** to deal with them bravely; to accept an unpleasant fact, etc.
fly in the face of something to ignore a known circumstance or act contrary to it; to flout it.
in one's face right in front of one.
in the face of something in spite of a known circumstance, etc.
look someone in the face to look directly at them without shame or embarrassment.
lose face to suffer a loss of dignity or self-respect.
make *or* **pull a face** to grimace, scowl, frown, etc.
on the face of it at first glance.
put a good *or* **brave face on something** to try to hide one's disappointment, fear, etc concerning it.
save one's face to avoid losing one's dignity or self-respect.
set one's face against something to oppose an idea, course of action, etc, firmly.
show one's face to let oneself be seen.
to someone's face directly; openly, in someone's presence. See also FACIAL.
[from French *face*, from Latin *facies*]

face card a court card.

faceless *adj.* lacking identity; impersonal; anonymous.

facelift *noun* **1** *Medicine* a surgical operation to rejuvenate the appearance of the face by tightening the skin, especially around the eyes or chin, and so removing facial wrinkles. It is a form of cosmetic surgery. **2** a procedure for improving the appearance of something.

Face of the Ruling Class, The a collection of satirical drawings by George Grosz (1921).

face pack a liquid cosmetic preparation for cleaning the face, that hardens on the skin and is peeled or washed off.

facer *noun* *colloq.* a problem.

face-saving *noun, adj.* preserving one's reputation, credibility, etc, in difficult circumstances.

facet *noun* **1** any of the faces of a cut jewel. **2** an aspect, eg of a problem, topic, or personality. [from French *facette*, diminutive of *face*, face]

facetious *adj., said of a person or remark, etc* intending or intended to be amusing or witty, especially unsuitably so. [from Latin *facetus*, witty]

facetiously *adv.* in a facetious way.

facetiousness *noun* being facetious.

face value **1** the stated value on a coin, stamp, etc. **2** the apparent meaning or implication, eg of a statement.

facia same as. FASCIA

facial *adj.* of, relating to or belonging to, the face. [from Latin *facies*, face]

facile *adj.* **1** *derog.*, of *success*, *etc* too easily achieved. **2** *derog.*, said of *remarks*, *opinions*, *etc* over-simple; showing a lack of careful thought. **3** speaking or performing with fluency and ease. [from Latin *facilis*, easy]

facilely *adv.* in a facile way.

facilitate *verb* to ease (a process, etc). [from FACILITY]

facilitation *noun* **1** the process of facilitating. **2** *Physiol.* in the nervous system, the process whereby signals are transmitted more effectively by each successive nerve impulse because of an increase in the amount of *neurotransmitter* released at the synapse (junction) between two adjacent neurones (nerve cells). **3** *Zool.* in animal behaviour, an improvement in the ability of an animal to respond to a specific stimulus.

facility *noun* (PL. **facilities**) **1** skill, talent, or ability. **2** fluency; ease. **3** an arrangement, feature, attachment, etc that enables something to do something. **4** (*usually* **facilities**) a building, service or piece of equipment for a particular activity. [from Latin *facilitas*, ease]

facing *noun* **1** an outer layer, eg of stone covering a brick wall. **2** a piece of material used to back and strengthen part of a garment. **3** (**facings**) the collar and cuffs of a jacket, etc, especially if in a contrasting colour.

facsimile *noun* **1** an exact copy of a manuscript, drawing, map, photograph, etc. **2** electronic copying and telegraphic transmission of such material; fax. **3** a copy made by facsimile. [from Latin *fac simile*, make the same]

fact *noun* **1** a thing known to be true, to exist, or to have happened. **2** truth or reality, as distinct from mere statement or belief. **3** an assertion of fact; a piece of information. **4** *Legal* a crime, as in *after*, or *before the fact*.
— **as a matter of fact** *or* **in fact**, *etc* in reality; actually.
for a fact with complete certainty.
in fact *in summarizing* in short; that is to say. [from Latin *factum*, something done]

faction¹ *noun* **1** an active or trouble-making group within a larger organization. **2** argument and fighting between members of a group. [from Latin *factio*, party, side]

faction² *noun* a docudrama. [from FACT + FICTION]

factional *adj.* **1** consisting of or relating to a faction. **2** causing faction.

factitious *adj.* deliberately contrived rather than developing naturally. [from Latin *facticius*]

fact of life **1** an unavoidable truth, especially if unpleasant. **2** (**facts of life**) basic information on sexual matters and reproduction.

factor *noun* **1** a circumstance that contributes to a result. **2** *Maths.* one of two or more numbers that will divide exactly into another given number, eg 2 and 4 are factors of 8. **3** in Scotland, the manager of an estate, or other property. [from Latin *factor*, person who acts]

factor VIII *or* **factor 8** *Physiol.* one of the proteins present in the blood that controls the clotting process. Deficiency of this factor causes the disease haemophilia, in which the blood fails to clot.

factorial — *noun Maths.* the number resulting when a number and all those below it are multiplied together. — *adj.* relating to a factor or factorial.

factoring *noun* (*in full* **debt factoring**) *Commerce* the selling of a company's list of debtors to an agent (*factor*) at a discount. The factor then retrieves the sums due. Factoring can be advantageous to a firm's cash flow and reduces overheads and costs associated with the collection of debts.

factorization *or* **factorisation** *noun* the process of factorizing.

factorize *or* **factorise** *verb Maths.* to find the factors of (a number).

factory *noun* (PL. **factories**) a building or buildings with equipment for the large-scale manufacture of goods. [from Latin *factoria*]

Factory Acts legislation passed (from 1802) in Britain to regulate employment in factories. The early Acts tended to limit the hours of work of women and children in textile factories only, and the 1833 Factory Act prohibited children under nine from working in textile mills and appointed the first factory inspectors. A maximum 10-hour working day for women and older children was agreed in 1847.

factory farm, a farm in which large numbers of animals are reared indoors under controlled conditions in order to produce a standardized product. — Also called *battery farm*.

factory farming, a highly intensive form of livestock farming in which large numbers of animals are reared indoors so that their environment and feeding regimes can be strictly controlled, resulting in a standardized product. — Also called *battery farming*.
◇ In factory farming the animals are usually confined within very small areas, restricting their mobility, and drugs are often used to reduce the risk of disease. Factory farming is widely used for the production of eggs, poultry meat, pork, and veal, and the practice is opposed by many environmentalists.

factotum *noun* a person employed to do a large number of different jobs. [from Latin *fac totum*, do all]

factual *adj.* concerned with, or based on, facts.

factually *adv.* in a factual way.

facultative *adj. Biol.* able to live under different conditions, especially denoting a parasite able to live on dead or decaying organic matter as well as on its living host.

faculty *noun* (PL. **faculties**) **1** any of the range of mental or physical powers. **2** a particular talent or aptitude for something. **3** a section of a university, comprising a number of departments. **4** *North Amer.* the staff of a college, school, or university. [from Latin *facultas*, capability]

FA Cup a football competition organized by the Football Association, and held annually in England and Wales since 1872.

fad *noun derog.* **1** a shortlived fashion; a craze. **2** an especially unreasonable prejudice or dislike, usually with regard to food.

faddiness *or* **faddishness** *noun* being faddy.

faddy *or* **faddish** *adj.* (**faddier**, **faddiest**) **1** typical of a fad. **2** choosy, fussy, especially about food.

fade *verb* (*often* **fade away**) **1** *trans.*, *intrans.* to lose or cause to lose strength, freshness, or colour. **2** *intrans.* said of a sound or image to disappear gradually.
— **fade something in** *or* **out** *Cinema, Broadcasting* to cause a sound or picture to become gradually louder and more distinct, or to become fainter and disappear.
[from Old French *fade*, dull, pale]

fade-in *noun Cinema, Broadcasting* the process of fading in a picture or sound.

fade-out *noun Cinema, Broadcasting* the process of fading out a picture or sound.

faecal *adj.* of the nature of or containing faeces.

faeces *pl. noun* the solid waste matter discharged from the body through the anus. [from Latin *faex*, dregs]

Faerie Queene, The a poem by Edmund Spenser (published in six books 1590, 1596). Its primary concern is with Prince Arthur's search for Gloriana, the Queen of Fairyland, who represents Elizabeth I.

Faeroese *or* **Faroese** the N Germanic language spoken by inhabitants of the Faeroe Is. It is closely related to the other W Scandinavian languages, Norwegian and Icelandic.

faff *verb intrans. colloq.* (**faff about**) to act in a fussy, uncertain way; to dither.

fag¹ — *noun* **1** *colloq.* a cigarette. **2** *colloq.* a piece of drudgery; a bore. **3** in some schools, a young schoolboy who runs errands and does jobs for an older one. — *verb* (**fagged**, **fagging**) **1** to tire out; to exhaust. **2** *intrans.* said of a schoolboy to act as fag for an older boy. **3** *intrans.* to work hard; to toil.

fag² *noun North Amer. offensive slang* a male homosexual. [short for FAGGOT]

fag end *colloq.* **1** a cigarette end. **2** the last part of something.

faggot *noun* **1** a ball or roll of chopped liver mixed with bread and herbs. **2** a bundle of sticks. **3** *North Amer. offensive slang* a male homosexual. **4** *derog. slang* an old woman. [from Old French *fagot*, bundle of sticks]

Fagin the sly but cowardly leader of a gang of child pickpockets in Charles Dickens's *Oliver Twist*.

fah *noun* in tonic sol-fa, the fourth note of the major scale. [from the first syllable of the word *famuli* in a medieval Latin hymn, certain syllables of which were used in naming the notes of the scale]

Fahd ibn Abd al-Aziz (1923–) King of Saudi Arabia (1982–), born in Riyadh. He was effective ruler from the assassination of his older half-brother Faisal in 1975, and became king on the death of his other half-brother, Khaled.

Fahrenheit, (Gabriel) Daniel (1686–1736) German instrument-maker, born in Danzig (now Gdańsk, Poland). Working in Amsterdam, he invented an accurate alcohol thermometer (1709) and a commercially successful mercury thermometer (1714), but is best known for devising the temperature scale named after him.

Fahrenheit — *noun* a scale of temperature on which water boils at 212° and freezes at 32°. — *adj.* on or of this scale. [named after Daniel Fahrenheit]

faience *or* **faïence** *noun* glazed decorated pottery. [from French *faïence*, from *Faenza* in Italy, the place of manufacture]

fail *verb* **1** *intrans.*, *trans.* (*often* **fail in something**) not to succeed; to be unsuccessful in an undertaking. **2** to judge (a candidate) not good enough to pass a test, etc. **3** *intrans.* said of machinery, a bodily organ, etc to stop working or functioning. **4** *intrans.* not to manage (to do something). **5** not to bother (doing something). **6** to let (someone) down; to disappoint. **7** said of courage, strength, etc to desert (one) at the time of need. **8** *intrans.* to become gradually weaker. **9** *intrans.* said of a business, etc to collapse.
— **fail to see** to be unable to understand.
without fail for certain; with complete regularity.
[from Latin *fallere*, to deceive, disappoint]

failing *noun* a fault; a weakness.

fail-safe *adj. Engineering* denoting a mechanism which ensures that people operating a system, eg machinery, will not be placed at risk if that system ceases to function properly.

failure *noun* **1** the act of failing; lack of success. **2** a person or thing that is unsuccessful. **3** a stoppage in functioning. **4** a poor result. **5** the non-doing of something: *failure to turn up*.

fain *adv. old use* gladly; willingly. [from Anglo-Saxon *fægen*]

faint — *adj.* **1** pale; dim; indistinct; slight. **2** physically weak; on the verge of losing consciousness. **3** feeble; timid; unenthusiastic. — *verb intrans.* to lose consciousness; to collapse. — *noun* a sudden loss of consciousness. [from Old French *faindre*, to feign]

faint-hearted *adj.* timid; cowardly.

faintly *adv.* in a faint way; weakly.

faintness *noun* being faint.

fair¹ — *adj.* **1** just; not using dishonest methods or discrimination. **2** in accordance with the rules. **3** *said of hair and skin* light-coloured; having light-coloured hair and skin. **4** *old use* beautiful. **5** quite good; reasonable. **6** sizeable; considerable. **7** *said of the weather* fine. **8** *said of the wind* favourable. **9** *said of words* insincerely encouraging. — *adv.* **1** in a fair way. **2** *dialect* completely.
— **be fair game** to deserve to be attacked or criticized.
by fair means or foul using any possible means, even if dishonest.
fair and square 1 absolutely; exactly. **2** honest and open.
fair enough all right.
in a fair way to doing something likely to achieve it.
in all fairness *or* **to be fair** one ought to remember, if one is fair.
[from Anglo-Saxon *fæger*, beautiful]

fair² *noun* **1** a collection of sideshows and amusements, often set up temporarily on open ground and travelling from place to place. **2** *Hist.* a market for the sale of produce, livestock, etc, with or without sideshows. **3** an indoor exhibition of goods from different countries, firms, etc, held to promote trade. **4** a sale of goods to raise money for charity, etc. [from Old French *feire*, from Latin *feriae*, holiday]

Fairbanks, Douglas, originally **Douglas Elton Ulman** (1883–1939) US film actor, born in Denver, Colorado. He first appeared in stage plays (1901), but in 1915 went into films and specialized in swashbuckling hero parts, as in the *Three Musketeers* (1921) and *Robin Hood* (1922).

Fairbanks POP 31 000, a city in North Star Borough, central Alaska, USA. It was founded in 1902 after the discovery of gold, and is the terminus of the Alaska railway and highway.

fair copy a neat finished copy of a piece of writing.

fair dos *or* **fair do's** *colloq.* equal treatment for everyone.

Fairfax, Jane a quiet, pleasant character in Jane Austen's *Emma*.

Fairfax (of Cameron), Thomas Fairfax, 3rd Baron (1612–71) English Parliamentary soldier, born in Denton, Yorkshire. In the Civil War, he distinguished himself at Marston Moor (1644), and in 1645 was given command of the New Model Army, which defeated Charles I at Naseby. He was replaced by Oliver Cromwell in 1650 for refusing to march against the Scots, who had proclaimed Charles II king. In 1660 he headed the commission sent to The Hague to arrange Charles II's return from exile.

fairground *noun* the piece of land on which sideshows and amusements are set up for a fair.

fairing *noun* an external structure fitted to an aircraft or vehicle to improve streamlining and reduce drag. [from *fair*, to make smooth, to streamline]

Fair Isle a complex multicoloured type of knitting pattern. [from *Fair Isle*, Shetland, where it was first developed]

fairly *adv.* **1** justly; honestly. **2** quite; rather. **3** *colloq.* absolutely.

fairness *noun* being fair.

fair play *noun* honourable behaviour; just treatment.

Fairservice, Andrew the rascally, self-righteous gardener at Osbaldistone Hall, and some-time servant to Francis Osbaldistone in Sir Walter Scott's *Rob Roy*.

fair sex (**the fair sex**) *facetious* women.

fairway *noun* **1** *Golf* a broad strip of short grass extending from one tee to the next green. **2** a deep-water channel in a river, etc, used by shipping.

fair-weather friend a friend who deserts one when one is in trouble.

fairy *noun* (PL. **fairies**) **1** any of various supernatural beings with magical powers and more or less human shape, common in folklore. **2** *derog.* a male homosexual.
◇ The brownies in British tradition are almost wholly benevolent; pixies and elves are tiny and mischievous; goblins ugly and malicious. Some fairies, such as gnomes, Irish leprechauns, and Scandinavian trolls, traditionally guard treasure. Others, such as the Arabic jinn, inhabit stones and trees and other natural objects.

fairy godmother someone who comes unexpectedly or magically to one's aid.

fairyland *noun* **1** the home of fairies. **2** an entrancing place.

fairy lights small coloured lights used for decoration.

Fairy Queen, The a semi-opera by Henry Purcell (1692), based on Shakespeare's *A Midsummer Night's Dream*.

fairy ring a ring of dark grass at the outer edge of a growth of fungi.

fairy tale *or* **fairy story 1** a story about fairies, magic, etc. **2** *euphemistic colloq.* a lie.

Faisal I *or* **Faysal** (1885–1933) King of Iraq (1921–33), born in Ta'if, the son of Hussein-bin-Ali, King of the Hejaz. He played a major role in the Arab revolt of 1916, and was for a short while King of Syria after World War I. Installed as King of Iraq by the British, he became a leader of Arab nationalism.

Faisal II *or* **Faysal** (1935–58) King of Iraq (1939–58), born in Baghdad, the great-grandson of Hussein-bin-Ali. He succeeded his father King Ghazi and was installed as king after an English education. In Feb 1958 he concluded with his cousin King Hussein of Jordan a federation of the two countries in opposition to the United Arab Republic of Egypt and Syria. In Jul that year, he and his entire household were assassinated during a military coup, and Iraq became a republic.

Faisalabad, formerly **Lyallpur** (to 1979) POP (1990e) 1.5m, a city in Punjab province, Pakistan, W of Lahore. It is in an important cotton and wheat-growing region.

Faisal ibn Abd al-Aziz *or* **Faysal** (1904–75) King of Saudi Arabia (1964–75), born in Riyadh. Appointed Viceroy of Hejaz in 1926, he became Minister for Foreign Affairs (1930), Crown Prince (1953), and succeeded his half-brother Saud as king. He was assassinated by his nephew Faisal ibn Musaid.

fait accompli (PL. **faits accomplis**) something done and unalterable; an established fact. [from French *fait accompli*, accomplished fact]

Faith a female first name, popular among 17c Puritans. [from FAITH, ie trust or confidence (in God)]

faith *noun* **1** trust or confidence. **2** strong belief, eg in God. **3** a religion. **4** any set or system of beliefs. **5** loyalty to a promise, etc; trust: *keep/break faith with someone*.
— **in good faith** from good or sincere motives. [from Old French *feid*]

Faithful the loyal companion of Christian in John Bunyan's *The Pilgrim's Progress*.

faithful — *adj.* **1** having or showing faith. **2** loyal and true. **3** accurate. **4** loyal to one's sexual partner. **5** reliable; constant. — *noun* **1** (**the faithful**) the believers in a particular religion; loyal supporters. **2** a supporter: *party faithfuls*.
— **yours faithfully** formal wording for ending a letter.

faithfully *adv.* in a faithful way.

faithfulness *noun* being faithful.

faith healer a person who claims or is reputed to heal others by the power of religion.

faith healing the curing of illness through religious faith rather than medical treatment.

faithless *adj.* **1** disloyal; treacherous. **2** having no religious faith.

faithlessly *adv.* in a faithless way.

faithlessness *noun* being faithless.

fajitas *pl. noun* a Mexican dish of seared strips of meat, chile, onions, etc served with flour tortillas. [from Spanish, a diminutive of *faja*, bundle]

fake — *noun* a person, thing, or act that is not genuine. — *adj.* not genuine; false. — *verb* **1** to alter dishonestly; to falsify or make up. **2** *trans., intrans.* to pretend to feel (an emotion) or have (an illness).

faker *noun* a person who fakes.

fakery *noun* **1** the act of faking. **2** something that is faked.

fakir *noun* **1** a wandering Hindu or Muslim holy man depending on begging for survival. **2** a member of any Muslim religious order. [from Arabic *faqir*, poor man]

Falange Española a fascist movement, founded in 1933 by José Antonio Primo de Rivera (1903–36), the son of Miguel Primo de Rivera. It grew rapidly as disillusioned middle-class youth deserted the mainstream right-wing parties, and took part in the military rebellion of Jul 1936 and the subsequent civil war. However in 1937 Franco forcibly united the Falange with the Carlists (supporters of the claims of the descendants of Don Carlo to the Spanish throne) to become *Falange Española Tradicionalista y de las JONS*, and under his dictatorship (1937–75) it adopted a subordinate role. [Spanish, = Spanish Falange]

falcon *noun* any of several birds of prey with long pointed wings and notched beaks, capable of rapid graceful flight, eg peregrine, gyrfalcon, kestrel, merlin. They feed on the wing, taking birds, bats, and insects. [from Latin *falco*, hawk]

falconer *noun* **1** a person who breeds and trains hawks. **2** a person who takes part in the sport of hunting with hawks.

falconry *noun* the breeding and training of falcons for hunting.

Faldo, Nick (Nicholas Alexander) (1957–) English golfer, born in Welwyn Garden City, Hertfordshire. He won the British Open championship for the first time in 1987, and won it again in 1990 and 1992. Other wins include the US Masters (1989–90).

Falkirk POP (1981) 37 000, a town in Falkirk district, Central region, central Scotland, situated 37km/23mi W of Edinburgh. NOTABLE FEATURES museum; castle of the Roman Antonine Wall nearby.

Falkland Islands, Spanish **Islas Malvinas** POP (1991) 2 000, a British Crown Colony in the S Atlantic Ocean, c.650km/400mi NE of the Magellan Strait. AREA c.12 200sq km/4 700sq mi. It consists of East Falkland and West Falkland, separated by the Falkland Sound, with over 200 small islands. CAPITAL Stanley. TIME ZONE GMT −4. The population is mainly of British descent and is largely Christian. The Falkland Islands Dependencies (c.8m sq km/3m sq mi), which have no permanent population, stretch c.2 400km/1 500mi through the S Atlantic Ocean and include South Georgia, South Sandwich Islands, Shag Rocks, and Clerke Rocks. PHYSICAL DESCRIPTION deeply indented coastline; hilly terrain, rising to 705m at Mt Usborne on East Falkland and 700m at Mt Adam on West Falkland. CLIMATE strong winds; narrow temperature range, 19°C (Jan), 2°C (Jul); low annual rainfall (635mm). HISTORY seen by several early navigators, including Capt John Strong in 1689–90, who named the islands; French settlement in 1764; a British base was established in 1765; the French yielded their settlement to the Spanish in 1767; occupied in the name of the Republic of Buenos Aires in 1820; Britain asserted possession in 1833; formal annexation in 1908 and 1917; Argentina's claims to sovereignty over the whole area resulted in invasion by Argentine military forces in Apr 1982; dispatch of British Task Force led to the return of the islands to British rule in Jun 1982. GOVERNMENT external affairs and defence are the responsibility of the British government, which appoints civil and military commissioners; internal affairs are governed by executive and legislative councils. ECONOMY chiefly agricultural; oats; sheep; service industries to the continuing military presence in the islands.

Falklands War a war (Apr–Jun 1982) between Britain and Argentina, precipitated by the Argentine invasion of the Falkland Is (known to Argentina as the Malvinas). Britain had ruled the islands continuously since 1833, but Argentina claimed them by inheritance from the Spanish Empire and through their proximity. The British had been conducting talks with Argentina on sovereignty over the Falklands (involving eg a leaseback arrangement or a joint administration), but the talks broke down and the Argentinian government of General Galtieri issued a warning to the British. On the night of 1–2 Apr a full-scale invasion of the Falklands began. The 70 Royal Marines on the islands were overwhelmed, and the Governor was deported to Uruguay. The British immediately fitted out a task force to retake the islands, and the Foreign Office team, including Lord Carrington, resigned. The task force consisted of almost 70 ships, including some 40 requisitioned merchantmen, and passenger vessels (eg the *Queen Elizabeth 2*). A 200-mile maritime exclusion zone was declared around the Falklands, and on 2 May the Argentine cruiser *General Belgrano* was sunk by the nuclear submarine HMS *Conqueror*, which ended the peace initiatives conducted by the US Secretary of State Alexander Haig and the Peruvian government. South Georgia was retaken (25 Apr); the destroyer HMS *Sheffield* was sunk by an Exocet missile (4 May); 5 000 troops were landed at Port San Carlos (21 May); and more troops were landed at Bluff Cove (6–8 Jun), an operation attended by much loss of life when the Argentine air force attacked the *Sir Tristram* and *Sir Galahad*. The British forces took Darwin and Goose Green on 28 May, and after the recapture of the capital, Port Stanley, the Argentinians surrendered (14 Jun). The war cost the British £700 million and 254 British and 750 Argentine lives were lost. Some political commentators claim that it did much to restore the fortunes of the government of Margaret Thatcher.

fall — *verb intrans.* (PAST TENSE **fell**; PAST PARTICIPLE **fallen**) **1** to descend or drop by force of gravity, especially accidentally. **2** (*also* **fall over** *or* **down**) *said of a person, or something upright* to drop to the ground after losing balance. **3** *said of a building, bridge, etc* to collapse. **4** *said of rain, snow, etc* to come down. **5** *said eg of hair* to hang down. **6** *said of land* to slope down. **7** *said of a blow, glance, shadow, light, etc* to land. **8** to go naturally or easily into position: *fell open at page 61*. **9** to throw oneself; to move hurriedly or ungracefully. **10** *said of a government, etc* to lose power; to be no longer able to govern. **11** *said of a stronghold* to be captured. **12** *said of defences or barriers* to be lowered or broken down. **13** to die or be badly wounded in battle, etc. **14** to give in to temptation; to sin. **15** *said eg of value, temperature, etc* to become less. **16** *said of sound* to diminish. **17** *said eg of silence* to intervene. **18** *said of darkness or night* to arrive. **19** to pass into a certain state: *fall asleep*. **20** to be grouped or classified in a certain way: *falls into two categories*. **21** to occur at a certain time or place: *the accent falls on the first syllable*. **22** *said of someone's face* to show disappointment. — *noun* **1** an act or way of falling. **2** something, or an amount, that falls. **3** (**falls**) a waterfall. **4** a drop in eg quality, quantity, value, temperature, etc. **5** a defeat or collapse. **6** *Wrestling* a manoeuvre by which one pins one's opponent's shoulders to the ground. **7** (**the Fall**) *Biblical* the sinning of Adam and Eve. See also FALL OF MAN.
— **break someone's fall** to stop someone landing with the full impact of a free fall.
fall about *colloq.* to be helpless with laughter.
fall apart 1 to break in pieces. **2** to fail; to collapse.
fall away 1 *said of land* to slope downwards. **2** to become fewer or less. **3** to disappear.
fall back 1 to move back; to retreat. **2** (**fall back on something**) to make use of it in an emergency.
fall behind to fail to keep up with someone, with one's work, etc. (**fall behind with something**) to be late in paying instalments or doing work.
fall down *said of an argument, etc* to be shown to be invalid. (**fall down on something**) to fail in a task; to do it unsatisfactorily.
fall for someone to become infatuated with them, or fall in love with them.
fall for something to be deceived or taken in by it.
fall in 1 *said eg of a roof* to collapse. **2** *said of a soldier, etc* to take one's place in a parade. (**fall in with someone**) to chance to meet or coincide with them. (**fall in with something**) to agree to it; to support it.
fall into something to become involved in it, especially by chance.
fall off to decline in quality or quantity; to become less.
fall on *or* **upon someone 1** to attack them. **2** to embrace them passionately.
fall out 1 *said of soldiers* to come out of military formation. **2** to happen in the end; to turn out. (**fall out with someone**) to quarrel with them.
fall over oneself *or* **fall over backwards** *colloq.* to be strenuously or noticeably eager to please or help.
fall through *said of a plan, etc* to fail; to come to nothing.
fall to to begin eating.
fall to something to start it: *fall to work*.
fall to someone to become their job or duty: *it falls to me to deal with the matter*.
fall to pieces *or* **bits** to break up; to disintegrate. [from Anglo-Saxon *feallan*]

Falla, Manuel de (1876–1946) Spanish composer, born in Cadiz. He won prizes in 1905 as a pianist and for his first opera, then moved to Paris, where he published his first piano compositions. After his return to Madrid (1914), his works were enhanced by a colourful national Spanish idiom, the best-known of which is the ballet *The Three-Cornered Hat* (1919). With the outbreak of the Spanish Civil War, he settled in Argentina.

fallacious *adj.* **1** deceptive, misleading. **2** wrong. **3** disappointing.

fallaciously *adv.* so as to be fallacious.

fallacy *noun* (PL. **fallacies**) **1** a mistaken notion. **2** a mistake in reasoning that spoils a whole argument. [from Latin *fallax*, deceptive]

fallen *adj.* **1** *old use* having lost one's virtue, honour or reputation. **2** killed in battle. **3** having dropped or overturned.

fall guy *colloq.* **1** someone who is easily cheated. **2** someone who is left to take the blame for something.

fallible *adj.* capable of making mistakes. [from Latin *fallere*, to deceive]

falling-off *noun* a decline in quality or quantity.

falling star a meteor.

Fall of Man a common concept in the myths and legends of many peoples and their religious traditions, involving the fall from an original state of paradise. In Christian belief, this is the lapse into sin of Adam and Eve when they disobeyed God (by eating from the tree of knowledge) and were expelled from the Garden of Eden (Genesis 3). As a result, sin entered the world and toil and pain mark the human condition, for humanity shares the consequences of Adam's disobedience. This explains the universality of the sinful condition and the need for a second Adam (Christ) to redeem the world — God's restoration of his distorted world (Romans 5).

Fallopian tubes the two trumpet-shaped ducts through which eggs pass from a woman's ovaries into her womb. [named after the Italian anatomist Gabriel Fallopius]

Fallopius, Gabriel, Italian **Gabriello Fallopio Fallopia** (1523–62) Italian anatomist, born in Modena. Appointed professor at Pisa (1548) and Padua (1551), he made several discoveries relating to bones and to the reproductive organs. The Fallopian tube connecting the ovaries with the uterus is named after him.

fallout *noun* the particles of radioactive material that are released into the atmosphere and fall to the Earth's surface after a nuclear explosion. Fallout can cause radiation sickness, and may enter the food chain and be passed on to humans, eg via the milk and meat of grazing animals. Long-term exposure to fallout leads to a greatly increased risk of cancer and birth defects.

fallow — *noun* the period during which arable farmland is not used to grow crops. — *adj.* denoting farmland that is ploughed but then left unplanted, usually for a season, to allow it to regain its natural fertility. [from Anglo-Saxon *fealga*]

fallow deer a small deer with a reddish-brown coat, dappled with white spots in summer. Fallow deer live in open woodland in Europe, and are often kept in parks or on country estates in the UK. [from Anglo-Saxon *fealu*, tawny]

Falmouth POP (1981) 19 000, a port town linked with Penryn in Carrick district, Cornwall, SW England. It lies 12km/7mi S of Truro, on Falmouth Bay, and it is a recreational sailing centre.

false *adj.* **1** *said of a statement, etc* untrue. **2** *said of an idea, etc* mistaken. **3** artificial; not genuine. **4** *said of words, promises, etc* insincere. **5** treacherous; disloyal. **6** *Bot.*, *said of a plant* resembling, but wrongly so called: *false acacia*.
— **play someone false** to cheat or deceive them.
under false pretences by giving a deliberately misleading impression.
[from Latin *falsus*]

false alarm an alarm given unnecessarily.

false fruit *Bot.* a fruit that is formed from other parts of the flower, in addition to the ovary. It may include the receptacle (eg strawberry, apple), or a complete inflorescence or flower head (eg pineapple). — Also called *pseudocarp*.

falsehood *noun* **1** lying; dishonesty. **2** a lie.

falsely *adv.* in a false manner; with falseness.

false move a careless or unwise action that puts one in danger.

falseness *or* **falsity** *noun* being false.

false pregnancy *Medicine* a psychological disorder in which some of the physical symptoms of pregnancy, eg abdominal swelling, weight gain, morning sickness, and cessation of menstrual periods, occur in a woman who is not pregnant.

false start 1 a failed attempt to begin something. 2 an invalid start to a race, in which one competitor begins before the signal is given.

falsetto *noun* (PL. **falsettos**) an artificially high voice, especially produced by a tenor above his normal range. [from Italian *falsetto*]

falsification *noun* the act or process of falsifying.

falsify *verb* (**falsifies, falsified**) to alter dishonestly or make up, in order to deceive or mislead. [from Latin *falsus*, false + *facere*, to make]

Falstaff, Sir John the voracious, mocking buffoon who is himself an object of derision in Shakespeare's *Henry IV Part I, Henry IV Part II*, and *The Merry Wives of Windsor*.

Falstaff an opera by Giuseppe Verdi (1893), with text by Boito based on Shakespeare's *The Merry Wives of Windsor* and *Henry IV Parts I and II*. It tells of how two wives, Anna Ford and Meg Page, having compared their identical love-letters, thwart the lecherous old Falstaff's attempts to woo them, and also how Anna's daughter manages to marry her lover despite her father's plans.

falter *verb* (**faltered, faltering**) 1 *intrans.* to move unsteadily; to stumble. 2 *intrans.* to start functioning unreliably. 3 *intrans.* to lose strength or conviction; to hesitate or break down in speaking. 4 to say hesitantly.

falteringly *adv.* in a faltering way.

Falwell, Jerry L (1933–) US religious leader, born in Lynchburg, Virginia. An ordained Baptist minister, in 1956 he founded Thomas Road Baptist Church, Lynchburg, which became the centre of an extensive evangelical campaign. He was also responsible for founding Liberty University (1971) and the Moral Majority, Inc (1979–89). He has published widely, and regularly broadcasts to large audiences.

Famagusta, Greek **Ammokhostos**, Turkish **Magusa** 1 POP (1987e) 26 000, the capital of Famagusta district, E Cyprus, situated on Famagusta Bay. HISTORY the site of ancient Arsinoë (3c BC); strongly fortified by the Venetians (15c–16c); the chief port of Cyprus until the 1974 Turkish invasion; now under Turkish occupation, it has been declared closed to shipping by the Cyprus government and is an illegal port of entry. NOTABLE FEATURES old town wall; citadel (14c); ruins of Church of St George of the Latins (late 13c); cathedral of St Nicholas (early 14c French Gothic). 2 a district in E Cyprus with the city of Famagusta as its capital.

fame *noun* 1 the condition of being famous. 2 *old use* repute. [from Latin *fama*, report, rumour]

famed *adj.* famous.

familial *adj.* belonging to, typical of, or occurring in, a family.

familiar — *adj.* 1 well known or recognizable. 2 frequently met with. 3 (**familiar with something**) well acquainted with it; having a thorough knowledge of it. 4 friendly; close. 5 overfriendly; excessively informal. — *noun* 1 a close friend. 2 a demon or spirit especially in the shape of an animal, serving a witch. [from Latin *familiaris*, domestic, intimate]

familiarity *noun* being familiar.

familiarization *or* **familiarisation** *noun* the act or process of familiarizing.

familiarize *or* **familiarise** *verb* 1 (**familiarize someone with something**) to make (especially oneself) familiar with it. 2 to make well known or familiar.

familiarly *adv.* in a familiar way.

family *noun* (PL. **families**) 1 a group consisting of a set of parents and children. 2 a set of relatives. 3 a person's children. 4 a household of people. 5 all those descended from a common ancestor. 6 a related group, eg of races, languages, words, etc. 7 a related group of plant or animal genera.
— **in the family way** *colloq.* pregnant. [from Latin *familia*, household, family]

family allowance *old use* child benefit.

family credit an allowance paid to families with low incomes.

family doctor a general practitioner.

family man a married man with children, especially one fond of home life.

family name 1 a surname. 2 the family honour: *a stain on the family name*.

Family of Charles IV a group portrait of Charles IV and his family by Goya (1800, Prado, Madrid). Its realism has been criticized as being unflattering to the subjects.

family planning control over the number of children born in a family, especially through use of contraceptives.

family therapy *Psychol.* a form of psychotherapy that aims to resolve long-standing problems in communication within a family by discussing these difficulties with all family members present.

family tree the relationships within a family throughout the generations, or a diagram showing these.

famine *noun* a severe or disastrous shortage of food. [from Old French *famine*, from Latin *fames*, hunger]

famished *or* **famishing** *adj.* very hungry; starving: *famished children*. [from Latin *fames*, hunger]

famous *adj.* 1 well known; celebrated; renowned. 2 great; glorious: *a famous victory*. [from Latin *famosus*, from *fama*, report, fame]

famously *adv.* in a way that brings fame or notoriety.

fan[1] — *noun* 1 a hand-held device made of paper, silk, etc, usually semicircular and folding flat when not in use, for creating a current of air to cool the face. 2 something of a similar shape, with parts diverging from a central point. 3 a machine with revolving blades, for producing a current of air. 4 a device for winnowing grain. — *verb* (**fanned, fanning**) 1 to cool by blowing a current of air on, with or as if with a fan. 2 to kindle or stir up, with or as if with a current of air. 3 (**fan out**) to spread out in the shape of a fan. 4 to agitate (air), with or as if with a fan. 5 to winnow (grain). [from Anglo-Saxon *fann*]

fan[2] *noun* an enthusiastic supporter or devoted admirer. [from FANATIC]

fanatic — *noun* someone with an extreme or excessive enthusiasm for something. — *adj.* excessively enthusiastic. [from Latin *fanaticus*, filled with a god, frenzied]

fanatical *adj.* fanatic.

fanatically *adv.* in a fanatic way.

fanaticism *noun* wild and excessive enthusiasm, especially for a religion.

fan belt the rubber belt that drives the cooling fan in a vehicle engine.

fancier *noun* (**especially in compounds**) someone with a special interest in something, especially a breeder or grower of a certain kind of bird, animal, or plant.

fanciful *adj.* 1 indulging in fancies; imaginative or over-imaginative. 2 existing in fancy only; imaginary. 3 designed in a curious or fantastic way.

fancifully *adv.* in a fanciful way.

fancily *adv.* in a fancy way.

fan club a club of admirers of a pop star, etc.

fancy — *noun* (PL. **fancies**) 1 one's imagination. 2 an image, idea, or whim. 3 a sudden liking or desire. — *adj.* 1 elaborate. 2 *colloq.* of special, unusual, or superior quality. 3 *colloq. facetious, said of prices* too high. — *verb* (**fancies, fancied**) 1 to think or believe. 2 to have a desire for. 3 *colloq.* to be sexually attracted to. 4 to consider likely to win or do well. 5 *trans., intrans.* to take in mentally; to imagine: *fancy him getting married at last!* 6 *colloq.* to think too well of (oneself).
— **take a fancy to someone** *or* **something** to become fond of it.
take *or* **tickle the fancy of someone** to appeal to them; to intrigue or attract them. [contracted from FANTASY]

fancy dress clothes one dresses up in to represent a historical, fictional, etc character.

fancy-free *adj.* 1 not in love. 2 free to do as one pleases.

fancy goods small gifts, souvenirs, etc.

fancy man *or* **fancy woman** *old colloq. use* a lover.

fancywork *noun* fine decorative needlework.

fandango *noun* (PL. **fandangos**) an energetic Spanish dance, or the music for it. [from Spanish *fandango*]

Fanfani, Amintore (1908–) Italian politician, born in Pieve Santo Stefano. A former Professor of Political Economics, he was Prime Minister on six occasions: in 1954, 1958–9, 1960–3 (twice), 1982–3, and 1987. Nominated a life Senator in 1972, he was President of the Italian Senate in 1968–73, 1976–82, and in 1985. He is a member (and former Secretary and Chairman) of the Christian Democratic Party.

fanfare *noun* a short piece of music played on trumpets to announce an important event or arrival. [from French *fanfare*]

fang *noun* 1 one of the sharp pointed teeth by means of which a predator seizes and tears the flesh of its prey. 2 in poisonous snakes, one of the grooved teeth through which venom is injected into the prey. [from Anglo-Saxon *fang*, something caught]

Fangio, Juan Manuel (1911–) Argentine racing motorist, born in Balcarce, of Italian descent. He first took part in European Grand Prix racing in 1949, and by 1957 had won the world championship a record five times (1951, 1954–7). He won 24 Grand Prix events. After his retirement (1958) he joined Mercedes-Benz in Argentina.

fanlight *noun* a semicircular window over a door or window.

fan mail the admiring letters received by a celebrity.

fanny *noun* (PL. **fannies**) 1 *coarse slang* a woman's genitals. 2 *North Amer. slang* the buttocks.

Fanny and Alexander (Fanny och Alexander) a Swedish film directed by Ingmar Bergman (1982). Presented in a theatrical setting, it focuses on two children whose mother marries a tyrannical bishop.

Fan Si Pan the highest mountain in Vietnam, situated in the N of the country. HEIGHT 3 143m.

fantail *noun* a pigeon with a fan-shaped tail.

Fantasia a US film (1940). It consists of a fusion of classical music and Walt Disney animation.

fantasia *noun* 1 a musical composition that is free and unconventional in form. 2 a piece of music based on a selection of popular tunes. [from Italian *fantasia*, imagination]

Fantasia on a Theme by Thomas Tallis an orchestral work for strings by Ralph Vaughan Williams (1910). The theme of the title is a psalm tune ('Why fumeth in fight') composed (1597) by Tallis for Archbishop Parker's psalter.

fantasize *or* **fantasise** *verb intrans.* to indulge in pleasurable fantasies or daydreams.

fantastic *adj.* **1** *colloq.* splendid. **2** *colloq.* enormous; amazing. **3** *said of a story* absurd; unlikely; incredible. **4** strange, weird, or fanciful. [from Greek *phantastikos*, presenting to the mind]

fantastically *adv.* in a fantastic way.

fantasy *noun* (PL. **fantasies**) **1** a pleasant daydream; a longed-for but unlikely happening. **2** a mistaken notion. **3** one's imaginings. **4** the activity of imagining. **5** a product of the imagination; a fanciful piece of writing, music, film-making, etc. [from Greek *phantasia*, image in the mind, imagination]

Fanti one of the Kwa-speaking Akan peoples of S Ghana, comprising several separate traditional states, each under the authority of a royal chief (present-day population c.1m). Most are farmers and fishermen, but formerly they traded with the Europeans in coastal towns such as Elmina and Cape Coast.

Fantin-Latour, (Ignace) Henri (Jean Théodore) (1836–1904) French painter, pastellist, and lithographer, born in Grenoble. He is best known for his flower studies and portrait groups (eg *Hommage à Delacroix*, Louvre, Paris). In his later years he specialized in lithography.

fanzine *noun* a magazine written, published, and distributed by and for supporters of football or by amateur enthusiasts of science fiction, pop music, etc; also, a television programme in magazine format for football fans. [from FAN[2] + MAGAZINE]

FAO *abbrev. Agric.* Food and Agriculture Organization (of the United Nations).

far (**farther**, **farthest** *or* **further**, **furthest**) — *adv.* **1** at, to, or from a great distance. **2** to or by a great extent: *my guess wasn't far out.* **3** at or to a distant time. — *adj.* **1** distant; remote. **2** the more distant of two. **3** extreme: *the far Right of the party.*
— **as far as** ... up to (a certain place or point).
as *or* **so far as** ... to the extent that ...
as *or* **so far as I'm** *etc* **concerned** in my etc opinion.
as *or* **so far as it goes** in its own limited way.
as *or* **so far as that goes** *or* **is concerned** concerning that, etc in particular.
by far *or* **far and away** by a considerable amount; very much: *by far the most expensive item.*
far and wide extensively.
far be it from me to do something I am reluctant to do it: *far be it from me to criticize.*
a far cry from something greatly different from it.
far from ... the opposite of ...; not at all: *that is far from the truth.*
far from ... *or* **so far from** ... not only not: *so far from winning, they finished last.*
far gone in an advanced state, eg of illness or drunkenness.
go far to achieve great things.
go so far *or* **as far as to** ... to go to the extent of ...; to be prepared to ...
go too far to behave, speak, etc unreasonably.
in so far as ... to the extent that ...
[from Anglo-Saxon *feorr*]

farad *noun* (SYMBOL **F**) *Electr.* the SI unit of electrical capacitance, defined as the capacitance of a capacitor in which a charge of one coulomb produces a potential difference of one volt between its terminals. For most practical purposes the microfarad (10^{-6}F) is used. [named after the UK physicist Michael Faraday]

Faraday, Michael (1791–1867) English chemist and physicist, born in Newington, near London. In 1813 he became the assistant of Humphry Davy, succeeding him as professor at the Royal Institution in 1927. He made important studies of the condensation of gases and limits of vaporization, and was the first to isolate benzene. His great life work was the series of *Experimental Researches on Electricity* published over a period of 40 years, in which he described his many discoveries, including electromagnetic induction (1831), the laws of electrolysis (1833), and the rotation of the plane of polarized light by magnetism (1845).

faraday *noun Physics* (SYMBOL **F**) a unit of electrical charge, defined as the charge on a mole (6.02×10^{23}) of electrons, which is equal to 9.65×10^4 coulombs. [named after the UK physicist Michael Faraday]

farandole *noun* (a piece of music for) a Provençal folk dance of ancient origin and usually in 6:8 time. The dance is traditionally performed by men and women proceeding in a long chain, and accompanied by a *galoubet* (flute) and *tambourin* (drum). Georges Bizet included a famous example in his incidental music for Alphonse Daudet's play *L'Arlésienne.* [from Provençal *farandoula*]

Farange, Maisie the perceptive child heroine of Henry James's *What Maisie Knew*, whose life is thrown into turmoil by the divorce of her parents, Beale and Ida.

faraway *adj.* **1** distant. **2** *said of a look or expression* dreamy; abstracted.

farce *noun* **1** a comedy involving a series of ridiculously unlikely turns of events; comedies of this type. **2** an absurd situation; something ludicrously badly organized. [from French *farce*, stuffing]

farcical *adj.* characteristic of farce; absurdly comic.

farcically *adv.* in a farcical way.

Fardier Car a car designed by a French military engineer, Nicholas Cugnot, in 1770. It was the first automobile to use high-pressure steam without condensation. It is regarded as the first real car. The machine was basic compared to today's standards: a wooden frame mounted on three wheels with the front wheel performing both the steering and driving functions.

fare — *noun* **1** the price paid by a passenger to travel on a bus, train, etc. **2** a taxi passenger. **3** *old use, formal* food. — *verb intrans.* **1** to manage or make progress. **2** to be treated in a certain way: *fare badly.* [from Anglo-Saxon *faran*]

Far East a loosely-used term which refers to the countries of China, Japan, North Korea, South Korea, Mongolia, and East Siberia. More generally it can include the Philippines, Vietnam, Laos, Kampuchea, Thailand, Burma, Malaysia, Singapore, and Indonesia.

Far-Eastern *adj.* of or from the Far East.

Fareham POP (1992e) 101 000, a town linked with Porchester in Fareham district, Hampshire, S England. It lies 9km/6mi NW of Portsmouth, and is a sailing centre.

Farel, Guillaume (1489–1565) Swiss Protestant reformer, born in Gap, France. He was converted to Protestantism in Paris, fled to Switzerland (1524), and settled in Geneva in 1534, after twice being compelled to leave. After the Reformation was proclaimed in 1535, Farel was responsible for making Calvin stay in Geneva, but the severity of the ecclesiastical discipline which Calvin imposed caused their expulsion from the city (1538). He later returned with Calvin to Geneva, and then went to Neuchâtel (1543).

fare stage **1** each of the sections into which a bus route is divided, and for which a standard fare is charged. **2** a bus stop marking a fare stage.

farewell — *interj. old use* goodbye! — *noun* an act of saying goodbye. [from FARE *verb* + WELL[1]]

Farewell to Arms, A a novel by Ernest Hemingway (1929). It is set during the war in Italy in 1917–18 and describes the ill-fated love affair between a US ambulance driver and an English nurse.

far-fetched *adj.* unlikely; unconvincing.

far-flung *adj.* **1** extensive. **2** distant.

Far from the Madding Crowd a novel by Thomas Hardy (1874). It centres around the relationships of farm-owner Bathsheba Everdene with her various suitors.

farinaceous *adj.* like or containing flour or starch. [from Latin *farina*, flour, meal]

farm — *noun* **1** an area of land owned by a farmer, or rented by a landlord and worked by a farmer, that is used to grow crops and/or to raise livestock. It usually includes a house and various other buildings which provide shelter for animals and storage space for harvested crops, machinery, etc. **2** a place that specializes in the breeding of particular animals: *fish farm / pig farm.* — *verb* **1** *trans., intrans.* to prepare and use land to grow crops, rear livestock, etc; to run a farm. **2** to collect and keep the proceeds from (taxes, etc) in return for a fixed sum. **3** (*also* **farm something** *or* **someone out**) to give (some of one's work) to others to do; to hand over (one's children) temporarily to a carer. [from Middle English *ferme*, rented land]

farmer *noun* a person who earns a living by managing a farm, either as owner or tenant.

farmer's lung *Medicine* a lung disease caused by an allergy to fungal spores that develop in hay baled while it is still damp.

farm hand a person employed to work on a farm.

farmhouse *noun* the farmer's house on a farm.

farming *noun* the business of running a farm by growing crops and raising livestock for sale.

farmstead *noun* a farmhouse and the buildings round it.

farmyard *noun* the central yard at a farm, surrounded by farm buildings.

Farnborough POP (1981) 48 000, a town in Rushmoor district, Hampshire, S England, lying N of Aldershot. It is an air force base and aeronautical research centre. Napoleon III and the Empress Eugenie are buried nearby. EVENT biennial air displays.

Farne Islands *or* **The Staples** a group of basaltic islets in the North Sea, lying 3km/2mi NE of the mainland, Northumberland, NE England. It is a sanctuary for birds and Atlantic seals. HISTORY St Cuthbert lived and died here; the scene of the heroic rescue in 1838 of the survivors of the *Forfarshire* by Grace Darling and her father William, the lighthouse keeper.

Farnese, Alessandro (1545–92) Italian soldier, born in Rome. He fought under Philip II of Spain (his uncle), and distinguished himself against the Turks at Lepanto (1571). As Governor-General of the Spanish Netherlands (1578–92), he captured Antwerp (1585), and compelled Henry IV of France to raise the siege of Paris (1590).

Faro **1** POP (1991) 32 000, the industrial seaport capital of Faro district, S Portugal. It lies on the S coast, 219km/136mi SE of Lisbon, and is the focal point of tourism on the Algarve. NOTABLE FEATURES cathedral; Churches of the Carmo and Santo Antonio do Alto (1754). **2** a district in S Portugal with the city of Faro as its capital.

Faroes *or* **Faroe** *or* **Faero Islands**, Danish **Faerøerne** POP (1992e) 47 000, a self-governing region of Denmark consisting of a group of sparsely vegetated volcanic islands in the N Atlantic, lying between Iceland and the Shetland Is. The largest islands are Strømo and Østerø; of the 22 islands, 17 are inhabited. CAPITAL Tórshavn. LANGUAGES Faroese (a Germanic language); Danish. CURRENCY the Danish krone. HISTORY Norse settlers arrived in the 8c, the group became part of Norway in the 11c, and was passed to Denmark in 1380; became a self-governing region of Denmark in 1948. GOVERNMENT the parliament (*Lagting*), restored in 1852, consists of 34 members. ECONOMY fish; sheep; potatoes; crafts.

far-off *adj.* distant; remote.

Farouk I (1920–65) the last King of Egypt (1936–52), born in Cairo. He studied at the Royal Military Academy in Woolwich, England, and after World War II gradually adopted a life of pleasure. The defeat of Egypt by Israel (1948) and continuing British occupation led to increasing unrest, and General Neguib's coup (1952) forced his abdication and exile. In 1959 he became a citizen of Monaco.

far-out *adj. colloq.* **1** strange; weird; outlandish. **2** excellent.

farrago *noun* (PL. **farragos, farragoes**) a confused mixture; a hotchpotch. [from Latin *farrago*, mixed fodder]

far-reaching *adj.* having widespread effects.

farrier *noun* **1** a person who shoes horses. **2** *old use* a horse doctor. [from Old French *ferrier*, from Latin *ferrarius*, smith]

farrow — *noun* a sow's litter of piglets. — *verb trans., intrans., said of a sow* to give birth to (pigs). [from Anglo-Saxon *fearh*]

Farsi modern Persian, the mother tongue of some 20–30 million people in Iran, Afghanistan, Iraq, and Tadzhikistan, and the second language of a further 25–35 million people in the region. It is the official language of Iran, and belongs to the Indo-Iranian branch of the Indo-European family of languages. [from *Fars*, ('Persia'), a province of SW Iran]

far-sighted *adj.* **1** (*also* **far-seeing**) wise; prudent; forward-looking. **2** long-sighted.

far-sightedness *noun* being far-sighted.

fart *coarse slang* — *verb intrans.* **1** to emit wind from the anus. **2** (**fart about** or **around**) to fool about, waste time, etc. — *noun* **1** an act of farting. **2** a term of abuse for a person. [from Middle English *farten*]

farther same as FURTHER (with reference to physical distance).

farthest same as FURTHEST (with reference to physical distance).

farthing *noun formerly* one quarter of an old British penny, or a coin of this value. [from Anglo-Saxon *feortha*, quarter]

FAS *Medicine abbrev.* fetal alcohol syndrome.

fasces *pl. noun Roman Hist.* a bundle of rods with an axe in the middle, carried before magistrates as a symbol of authority. [from Latin *fascis*, bundle]

Fasching *noun* a period of festivity held in Munich, S Germany between Epiphany (6 Jan) and the beginning of Lent. [from German *Fasching* (Shrovetide) carnival]

fascia or **facia** *noun* **1** the board above a shop entrance, bearing the shop name. **2** the dashboard of a motor vehicle. **3** *Archit.* a long flat band or surface. **4** *Anat.* tissue sheathing a muscle or organ. [from Latin *fascia*, band]

fascial or **facial** *adj.* relating to or located in a fascia.

fascinate *verb* **1** to interest strongly; to intrigue. **2** *said of a snake* to make unable to move, from fright. **3** to hold spellbound; to enchant irresistibly. [from Latin *fascinare*, to bewitch]

fascinating *adj.* that fascinates; intriguing.

fascinatingly *adv.* in a fascinating way.

fascination *noun* **1** the act of fascinating. **2** being fascinated.

fascioliasis *noun Medicine* an infection of the bile ducts and liver of humans and other animals with the liver fluke (*Fasciola hepatica*).

fascism *noun* **1** a political movement or system in which there is, typically, state control of all aspects of society, a supreme dictator, suppression of democratic bodies such as trade unions, and emphasis on nationalism and militarism. **2** (**Fascism**) this system in force in Italy from 1922 to 1943. [from Italian *fascismo*] ◇ Fascism in Europe reached its peak in 1930–45. The original fascist movement was founded by Mussolini in Italy in 1921, and during the 1930s several such movements grew up in Europe, the most important being the German Nazi Party. Since World War II, its appeal has declined, although the 1990s have seen a revival in the fortunes of some extreme right-wing parties in countries of W Europe.

fascist — *noun* (*also* **Fascist**) a supporter of fascism. — *adj.* typical of or supporting fascism.

fashion — *noun* **1** style, especially the latest style, in clothes, etc. **2** a currently popular style or practice; a trend. **3** a manner of doing something. **4** the way something is made or constructed. — *verb* **1** to form or shape, especially with the hands. **2** to mould or influence.
— **after a fashion** in a rather inexpert way.
in or **out of fashion** currently (or no longer) fashionable.
[from Old French *fachon*]

fashionable *adj.* **1** *said of clothes or people* following the latest fashion. **2** used by, or popular with, wealthy, fashionable people.

fashionably *adv.* in a fashionable way; so as to be fashionable.

Fasil Ghebbi the royal complex of Emperor Fassilide (1632–67) in Gondar, NW Ethiopia. Gondar was the permanent capital of Ethiopia in the 17c–18c. It is a World Heritage site.

Fassbinder, Rainer Werner (1946–82) German film director, born in Bad Wöshofen. He began his career acting in fringe theatre in Munich, founding his own company. His work in cinema began in 1969, and was much influenced by Jean-Luc Godard. He completed over 40 full-length films, largely politically committed criticisms of contemporary Germany, notably *Die bitteren Tränen der Petra von Kant* (The Bitter Tears of Petra von Kant, 1972) and *Die Ehe der Maria Braun* (The Marriage of Maria Braun, 1979).

Fassett, Kaffe (1937–) US designer, born in San Francisco and brought up in Big Sur, California. The community there remains the biggest influence on his work, although his career has been made in the UK. Originally a painter, he learned to knit after moving to the UK in 1964. His colourful, highly individual designs are included in such books as *Glorious Knitting* (1985) and *Glorious Needlepoint* (1987).

fast¹ — *adj.* **1** moving, or able to move, quickly. **2** taking a relatively short time. **3** *said of a clock, etc* showing a time in advance of the correct time. **4** allowing or intended for rapid movement: *the fast lane.* **5** *said of a photographic film* requiring only brief exposure. **6** *colloq.* living a life of high excitement and expensive enjoyment. **7** *colloq.* tending to make sexual advances on rather brief acquaintance. **8** firmly fixed or caught. **9** *said of friends* firm; close. **10** *said of fabric colours* not liable to run or fade. — *adv.* **1** quickly; rapidly. **2** in quick succession: *coming thick and fast.* **3** firmly; tight. **4** deeply; thoroughly: *fast asleep.*
— **fast and furious** fast and lively; frenzied or frantic in pace.
play fast and loose to behave irresponsibly or unreliably.
pull a fast one on someone *colloq.* to cheat or deceive them.
[from Anglo-Saxon *fæst*, fixed, firm]

fast² — *verb intrans.* to abstain from food completely or to restrict one's diet, eg as a religious discipline. — *noun* abstinence from food; the day or time of fasting. [from Anglo-Saxon *fæstan*]

fast-breeder reactor a type of nuclear reactor in which the neutrons produced during nuclear fission are not slowed down by a moderator, but are used to produce (breed) more of the same nuclear fuel by converting uranium-238 to plutonium-239. At least as much fuel is produced as is consumed by the reactor.

fasten *verb trans., intrans.* (**fastened, fastening**) (*also* **fasten up**) to make or become firmly closed or fixed.
— **fasten on** or **upon something** to concentrate on it eagerly; to dwell on it.
[from Anglo-Saxon *fæstnian*]

fastener or **fastening** *noun* a device that fastens something; a clasp or catch.

fast food food that is prepared, often by frying or microwaving, and served by means of a fast production line, eg hamburgers, pizzas.

fast-forward — *noun* a facility on an audio or video cassette player for advancing a tape quickly without playing it. — *verb* **1** *trans.* to advance (a tape) quickly by this means. **2** *intrans. colloq.* to pass or move on without delay.

fastidious *adj.* **1** particular in matters of taste and detail, especially excessively so. **2** easily disgusted. [from Latin *fastidium*, disgust]

fastidiously *adv.* in a fastidious way.

fastidiousness *noun* being fastidious.

fastness *noun* **1** the quality of being firmly fixed or, with reference to fabric colours, fast. **2** *old use* a stronghold.

fast neutron *Physics* a neutron with a very high energy content, produced by nuclear fission. Fast neutrons travel too fast to cause further fission, and are used to sustain nuclear chain reactions.

fast-track *colloq.* — *noun* **1** a routine for accelerating a proposal, etc through its formalities. **2** a quick but competitive route to advancement. — *verb* to process or promote speedily.

fat — *noun* **1** any of a group of organic compounds that occur naturally in animals and plants, and have twice the energy value of carbohydrates. Fats are solid at room temperature (20°C) and insoluble in water. **2** in mammals, a layer of white or yellowish tissue that lies beneath the skin and between various organs of the body. It is composed of cells filled with lipid substances, and serves both as an insulator to prevent heat loss, and as a means of storing energy. **3** any of various greasy or oily substances derived from animals or plants and used in liquid or solid form as food or in cooking. — *adj.* (**fatter, fattest**) **1** having too much fat on the body; plump; overweight. **2** containing a lot of fat. **3** thick or wide. **4** *colloq., said of a fee, profit, etc* large. **5** fertile; profitable. **6** *facetious slang* none at all: *a fat lot of good.* — *verb* (**fatted, fatting**) *old use* to fatten.
— **the fat's in the fire** now there will be trouble.
kill the fatted calf to prepare a feast for a homecoming.
live off the fat of the land to live in luxury.
[from Anglo-Saxon *fæt*, fatted]
◇ Fats consist of carbon, hydrogen, and oxygen, and serve as a highly concentrated source of energy. Together with oils, they belong to a large class of naturally occurring compounds called *lipids*. Fat molecules consist mainly of *triglycerides* (three fatty acid chains linked to a molecule of glycerol). *Saturated fats* have chains in which the carbon atoms are linked to as many hydrogen atoms as possible, and have been associated with high levels of cholesterol in the blood and increased risk of heart disease, unlike *unsaturated* and *polyunsaturated fats*, in which fewer hydrogen

atoms are linked to the carbon atoms. Surplus carbohydrates and proteins are stored as fats in many animals and plants. Natural fats are used in the manufacture of butter, margarine, lard, candles, and soap.

Fatah, al- the popular name for the Palestine National Liberation Movement (PNLM), created in 1957 and headed by Yasser Arafat. It is the single biggest Palestinian movement, and operates under the umbrella of the PLO (Palestine Liberation Organization). [Arabic, = victory]

fatal *adj.* **1** causing death; deadly. **2** bringing ruin; disastrous. **3** destined; unavoidable. [from Latin *fatalis*, from *fatum*, fate]

fatalism *noun* the belief that fate controls everything, and humans cannot alter it.

fatalist *noun* a person who believes in fatalism.

fatalistic *adj.* characteristic of fatalism.

fatalistically *adv.* in a fatalistic way.

fatality *noun* (PL. **fatalities**) **1** an accidental or violent death. **2** the quality of being fatal. **3** the quality of being controlled by fate.

fatally *adv.* **1** so as to cause death. **2** unavoidably.

fate *noun* **1** (*also* **Fate**) the apparent power that determines the course of events, over which humans have no control. **2** the individual destiny or fortune of a person or thing; what happens to someone or something. **3** death, downfall, destruction, or doom. **4** (**the Fates**) *Mythol.* the three goddesses who determine the birth, life, and death of humans.
— **a fate worse than death** *facetious* a frightful fate, especially *old use* a woman's loss of virginity before marriage.
[from Latin *fatum*, fate]

fated *adj.* **1** destined or intended by fate. **2** doomed.

fateful *adj.* **1** *said of a remark, etc* prophetic. **2** decisive; critical; having significant results. **3** bringing calamity or disaster.

fatefully *adv.* in a fateful way.

Fatehpur Sikri *or* **Fathpur Sikri** a legendary ghost city in Uttar Pradesh, India. It was founded as the Imperial capital of the Mughal Emperor Akbar in 1569, but was abandoned within two decades because of water shortages. It contains many examples of Mughal architecture, notably the Buland Darwaza (Victory Gate). It is a World Heritage site.

Fateh Singh, Sant (1911–72) Sikh religious leader and campaigner for Sikh rights, born in the Punjab, India. Involved in religious and educational activity in Rajasthan, he founded many schools and colleges there. In 1942 he joined the Quit India Movement, and was imprisoned for his political activities. During the 1950s he agitated for a Punjabi-speaking autonomous state, which resulted in the creation of the Indian state of Punjab (1966).

Fate of the Animals, The, also called **Animal Destinies** an abstract painting by Franz Marc (1913, Basle, Switzerland).

Fates see PARCAE.

fathead *noun colloq., offensive* a fool.

fat-headed *adj.* stupid.

fat hen an annual plant (*Chenopodium album*), widespread in Europe, especially on disturbed soil and cultivated ground, that has diamond-shaped toothed lower leaves with mealy white covering, and tiny green flowers borne in densely branched clusters. If boiled, it can be eaten like spinach.

father — *noun* **1** a natural or adoptive male parent. **2** (**fathers**) one's ancestors. **3** a founder, inventor, originator, pioneer, or early leader. **4** (**Father**) a title, or form of address for a priest. **5** (**Father**) God. **6** (**fathers**) the leading or senior men of a city, etc. **7** (**Father**) used as a title in

personifying something ancient or venerable: *Father Time.* — *verb* **1** to be the father of. **2** to invent or originate. **3** (**father a child on someone**) to claim that someone is the father of the child. [from Anglo-Saxon *fæder*]

Father Christmas see SANTA CLAUS.

father figure an older man to whom one turns for help, support, advice, etc.

fatherhood *noun* being a father.

father-in-law *noun* (PL. **fathers-in-law**) the father of one's wife or husband.

fatherland *noun* one's native country.

fatherless *adj.* **1** without a living father. **2** without a known author.

fatherliness *noun* being fatherly.

fatherly *adj.* benevolent, protective, and encouraging, like a father.

Father's Day in some countries, the day on which fathers are honoured: in the USA and the UK, the third Sunday in June; in Australia, the first Sunday in September.

Fathers of the Church a title usually applied to the leaders of the early Christian Church. Recognized as eminent teachers of the faith, they were characterized by orthodoxy of doctrine and personal holiness, and were usually beatified. The study of their writings and thought is known as patristics.

fathom — *noun* a unit of measurement of the depth of water, equal to 6ft (1·8m). — *verb* (**fathomed, fathoming**) (*also* **fathom something out**) **1** to work out a problem; to get to the bottom of a mystery. **2** to measure the depth of water. [from Anglo-Saxon *fæthm*]

fathomless *adj.* **1** too deep to be measured. **2** too difficult or mysterious to understand.

fatigue — *noun* **1** a state of physical and mental tiredness, experienced as muscular weariness or discomfort, a decrease in energy and efficiency, and a strong desire for rest or sleep. It may be caused by prolonged or intense activity, inadequate food intake, disease, high temperatures, or stress. **2** permanent weakness in a material, eg a metal, due to changes in its properties resulting from repeated stresses placed on it. **3** *Mil.* a domestic task performed by a soldier. **4** (**fatigues**) uniform worn by soldiers in battle or for domestic tasks. — *verb trans., intrans.* to exhaust or become exhausted. [from French *fatigue*, from Latin *fatigare*, to weary]

Fatima (c.605–33) the youngest daughter of Muhammad, and wife of the fourth Muslim caliph, Ali. Their descendants were the Fatimids, a radical Shiite movement, who ruled over Egypt and N Africa (909–1171), and later over Syria and Palestine.

Fatima *or* **Fátima** POP (1991) 8 000, a town in Santarém district, central Portugal. It has become a town of pilgrimage following the claim of three peasant children to have seen the 'Virgin of the Rosary' here in 1917. NOTABLE FEATURE Basilica (begun in 1928, consecrated in 1953).

fatness *noun* **1** being fat. **2** richness.

fatten *verb trans., intrans.* (**fattened, fattening**) (*also* **fatten up**) to make or become fat.

fattening *adj.* that fattens.

fattiness *noun* the quality of being fat or containing fat.

fatty — *adj.* (**fattier, fattiest**) **1** containing fat. **2** greasy; oily. — *noun* (PL. **fatties**) *derog. colloq.* a fat person.

fatuity *noun* (PL. **fatuities**) **1** foolishness. **2** a fatuous act or remark; fatuous behaviour.

fatuous *adj.* foolish, especially in a self-satisfied way; empty-headed. [from Latin *fatuus*]

fatuously *adv.* in a fatuous way.

fatuousness *noun* being fatuous.

fatwa *or* **fatwah** *noun* a formal legal opinion or decision issued by a Muslim authority, eg that someone should be killed. [Arabic, = decree]

faucet *noun* **1** a tap fitted to a barrel. **2** *North Amer.* a tap on a washbasin, etc. [from Old French *fausset*, peg]

Faulkner *or* **Falkner, William (Harrison)** (1897–1962) US author, born in New Albany, Mississippi. He served with the RAF in World War I, and began his literary career with *Soldier's Pay* (1926), a novel on the aftermath of war. With *The Sound and the Fury* (1929) he began to experiment in literary form and style, and *Sartoris* (1929) was the first in a series dealing with the social and racial problems of an imaginary Southern state, Yoknapatawpha. Other major novels include *As I lay Dying* (1930), *Absalom, Absalom!* (1936) and *The Reivers* (1962). He was awarded the Nobel Prize for Literature in 1949.

fault *noun* **1** a weakness or failing in character. **2** a flaw or defect in an object or structure. **3** responsibility for something wrong: *all my fault.* **4** *Geol.* a break or fracture in the Earth's crust where one rock face has been displaced relative to another in a horizontal, vertical, or oblique direction. Abrupt movements along faults cause earthquakes. **5** *Tennis* an incorrectly placed or delivered serve. **6** *Showjumping* a penalty for refusing or failing to clear a fence.
— **at fault** blameworthy; to blame; wrong.
find fault with someone *or* **something** to criticize them, especially excessively or unfairly.
to a fault to too great an extent.
[from Old French *faute*]

faultless *adj.* having no faults; perfect.

faultlessly *adv.* in a faultless way.

faulty *adj.* (**faultier, faultiest**) having a fault or faults; not working correctly.

faun *noun* a mythical creature with a man's head and body and a goat's horns, hind legs, and tail. [from Latin *Faunus*, a rural god]

fauna *noun* (PL. **faunas, faunae**) **1** the animals that are associated with a particular habitat, region, or geological period. **2** a book or list describing the animals of a certain area. See also FLORA. [from Latin *Fauna*, goddess of living creatures]

Faunus in Roman mythology, a rural deity, sometimes associated with the Greek god Pan. He was responsible for the fertility of plants, agriculture, and woodland. He was usually depicted as half man, half goat, and annual celebrations (the Lupercalia) were held in his honour.

Faure, Edgar (Jean) (1908–88) French politician, born in Béziers. He entered politics as a radical-socialist and was Minister of Finance and Economic Affairs several times in the 1950s before becoming Prime Minister (1952, 1955–6). He was Minister of Agriculture (1966), Education (1968), and Social Affairs (1969), and President of the National Assembly (1973–8), then from 1979 a member of the European Parliament. He also published several detective novels under the pseudonym Edgar Sanday.

Fauré, Gabriel (Urbain) (1845–1924) French composer, born in Pamiers. He became organist (1896) at La Madeleine, Paris, and director of the Conservatoire (1905–20). Though he is chiefly remembered for his songs, including the evergreen *Après un rêve* (c.1865), he also wrote operas and orchestral pieces, such as *Masques et bergamasques* (1919), and a *Requiem* (1887–90).

Faust *or* **Faustus** a legendary German scholar of the early 16c (derived from a historical magician of that name), who sold his soul to the devil in exchange for knowledge, magical power, and prolonged youth. His story inspired Christopher Marlowe's *Dr Faustus* (1592), literary works by Goethe (1808, 1832), and Thomas Mann (1947), and musical works including Charles Gounod's opera *Faust* (1859).

Faust a play by Goethe in two parts (1770–1832; Part I 1808; Part II 1832), based on Christopher Marlowe's *Dr Faustus*. The disillusioned scholar, Faust, deserts his 'ivory tower' to seek happiness in real life, but his pact with Satan results in his own moral degradation.

Fauves see FAUVISM.

Fauvism *noun* an early 20c movement in painting. A group of French painters exhibiting together in 1905 were dubbed *'les Fauves'* (wild beasts) by a hostile critic. The hallmark of their work was the use of colour for its purely decorative qualities or as a means of communicating emotion, without regard to realism. The group included Henri Matisse, André Derain, and Maurice de Vlaminck, and their various styles were influenced by Vincent van Gogh, Paul Gauguin, and Paul Cézanne. [from French *fauve*, wild beast]

faux pas *noun* (PL. *faux pas*) an embarrassing blunder. [French, = false step]

favour — *noun* 1 a kind or helpful action performed out of goodwill. 2 the liking, approval, or goodwill of someone. 3 unfair preference. 4 a knot of ribbons worn as a badge of support for a particular team, political party, etc. 5 *Hist.* something given or worn as a token of affection. 6 (**favours**) *old euphemistic use* a woman's consent to lovemaking or sexual liberties. — *verb* 1 to regard with goodwill. 2 to treat with preference, or over-indulgently. 3 to prefer; to support. 4 *said of circumstances* to give an advantage to. 5 *old use* to look like (eg one's mother or father). 6 *affected* to be wearing (a colour, etc).
— **in favour of something** *or* **someone 1** having a preference for them. 2 to their benefit. 3 in support or approval of them.
in *or* **out of favour with someone** having gained or lost their approval.
[from Latin *favor*, from *favere*, to favour]

favourable *adj.* 1 showing or giving agreement or consent. 2 pleasing; likely to win approval. 3 (**favourable to someone**) advantageous or helpful to them; suitable. 4 *said of a wind* following.

favourably *adv.* in a favourable way.

favourite — *adj.* best-liked; preferred. — *noun* 1 a favourite person or thing. 2 someone unfairly preferred or particularly indulged. 3 a horse or competitor expected to win. [from Old French *favorit*]

favouritism *noun* the practice of giving unfair preference, help or support to someone or something.

Fawcett, Dame Millicent, *née* **Garrett** (1847–1929) English women's rights campaigner, born in Aldeburgh, Suffolk. Her keen interest in the higher education of women and the extension of the franchise to her sex led to her appointment as President of the National Union of Women's Suffrage Societies (1897–1919).

Fawkes, Guy (1570–1606) English conspirator, born in York. Though of Protestant parentage, he became a Catholic at an early age, and served in the Spanish army in the Netherlands (1593–1604). He crossed to England at Robert Catesby's invitation, and was a member of the Gunpowder Plot, but he was caught red-handed and hanged.

fawn[1] *noun* 1 the young of one of the small types of deer. 2 the colour of a fawn, beige. [from Old French *faon*]

fawn[2] *verb intrans.* (**fawn on someone**) 1 *said of a dog* to show affection for them by licking, nuzzling, etc. 2 to flatter them or behave over-humbly towards them, in order to win approval. [from Anglo-Saxon *fagnian*]

fawning *adj.* that fawns.

fawningly *adv.* in a fawning way.

fax — *noun* 1 facsimile transmission, a system for transmitting exact copies of printed or hand-written documents, drawings, maps, photographs, etc, using telephone networks. 2 a document transmitted in this way. — *verb* 1 to send a document via this system. 2 to send a faxed communication to. [a shortening of FACSIMILE]
◇ A document to be sent by fax is scanned by the fax machine, and the image produced is converted into electrical signals. At the other end of the telephone line used for transmission, another machine receives the signals, decodes them, and prints out a copy of the original document in horizontal chains of dots built up into lines. A modern fax machine takes less than 30 seconds to transmit a one-page document.

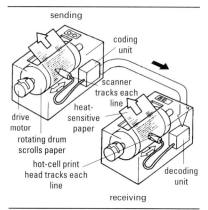

fax machine

Fay *or* **Faye** a female first name, now relatively rare. [probably from archaic *fay*, fairy]

fay *noun poetic* a fairy. [from Old French *fae*]

FBI *abbrev.* Federal Bureau of Investigation (USA).

FC *abbrev.* football club.

FD *abbrev.* (on coins) *Fidei Defensor* (Latin), Defender of the Faith.

FDA *abbrev.* Food and Drug Administration (USA).

Fe *symbol Chem.* iron. [from Latin *ferrum*]

fealty *noun Hist.* the loyalty sworn by a vassal or tenant to his feudal lord. [from Old French *fealte*, from Latin *fidelitas*, loyalty]

fear — *noun* 1 anxiety and distress caused by the awareness of danger or expectation of pain. 2 a cause of this feeling. 3 religious awe or dread. 4 *colloq.* likelihood: *no fear of winning*. — *verb* 1 to be afraid of (someone or something). 2 *intrans.* (**fear for something**) to be frightened or anxious about it: *feared for their lives*. 3 to think or expect with dread. 4 to regret; to be sorry to say.
— **for fear of something or someone** because of the danger they represent.
in fear of something *or* **someone** frightened of them.
put the fear of God into someone *colloq.* to terrify them.
without fear or favour completely impartially. [from Anglo-Saxon *fær*, calamity]

fearful *adj.* 1 afraid. 2 frightening. 3 *colloq.* very bad.

fearfully *adv.* 1 with fear. 2 in a frightening way. 3 *colloq.* very badly, terribly.

fearfulness *noun* being fearful.

fearless *adj.* without fear; brave.

fearlessly *adv.* without fear, daring.

fearlessness *noun* being fearless.

fearsome *adj.* frightening.

feasibility *noun* being feasible.

feasible *adj.* capable of being done or achieved. [from Old French *faisible*]

feasibly *adv.* possibly.

feast — *noun* 1 a large rich meal, eg to celebrate some occasion. 2 a pleasurable abundance of. 3 *Relig.* a festival or saint's day. — *verb* 1 *intrans.* (**feast on** *or* **upon something**) to eat or experience it with enjoyment. 2 to honour with a feast.
— **feast one's eyes on** *or* **upon something** to gaze at it with pleasure.
[from Old French *feste*]

Feast in the House of Levi a painting by Paolo Veronese (1573, Venice, Italy). It portrays an irreverent 'Last Supper' type of scene (featuring 'drunkards and German soldiers') which caused great controversy and resulted in Veronese being forced to defend his artistic licence to the Inquisition.

Feast of Weeks same as SHABUOTH.

feat *noun* a deed or achievement, especially a remarkable one. [from Old French *fait*]

Feather, Vic (Victor Grayson Hardie) Feather, Baron (1908–76) English trade union leader, born in Bradford, Yorkshire. He began work at 14, and joined the Shopworkers' Union. He joined the Trades Union Council in 1937, and as Assistant Secretary (1947–60) helped to reorganize trade unions in Europe after World War II. As General Secretary (from 1969), he led the union opposition to the Conservative government's Industrial Relations bill. He was also President of the European Trade Union (1973–4).

feather — *noun* 1 a rigid outgrowth of the skin of a bird, consisting of a horny material called keratin which is extremely light, and highly specialized for flight, insulation, and display purposes. 2 condition; spirits: *in fine feather*. — *verb* to provide, cover, or line with feathers, to turn (one's oar) parallel to the water, to lessen air resistance.
— **a feather in one's cap** something one can be proud of.
feather one's own nest to accumulate money for oneself, especially dishonestly.
make the feathers fly *colloq.* to cause a commotion.
[from Anglo-Saxon *fether*]
◇ An individual feather consists of a hollow central shaft bearing many slender branches or barbs which are interlocked by tiny hooked barbules. The largest feathers are the *flight feathers* of the wings and tail, which form the extensive surface area required for flight. The *contour feathers*, which resemble small flight feathers, cover the body and the front edges of the wings, providing a smooth streamlined surface. Beneath the contour feathers is a thick layer of *down feathers*, which trap warm air around the body, so providing heat insulation. Some tiny hairlike feathers (*filoplumes*) scattered among the down feathers are connected to nerves in the skin and are sensitive to ruffling of the feathers. The flight and contour feathers of the male bird are often brightly

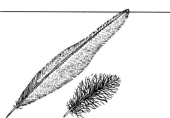

flight feather   down feather

feather

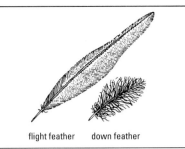

flight feather   down feather

types of feather

coloured and used for courtship displays, as in the peacock.

feather bed a mattress stuffed with feathers.

feather-bed *verb* **1** to spoil or pamper. **2** *colloq.* to give financial inducements to.

feather-brained *adj. derog.* empty-headed.

feather duster a dusting implement consisting of a stick with a head made of feathers.

feathered *adj.* **1** containing or covered with feathers or something similar. **2** like feathers.

featherweight *noun* **1** a class for boxers, wrestlers, and weight-lifters of not more than a specified weight (57 kg in professional boxing, similar weights in the other sports). **2** a boxer, etc of this weight. **3** someone who weighs very little. **4** *derog.* someone of little importance or influence.

feathery *adj.* resembling or covered with feathers, or something similar.

feature *noun* **1** any of the parts of the face, eg eyes, nose, mouth, etc; (in *pl*) the face. **2** a noticeable part or quality of something. **3** a non-news article in a newspaper. **4** a feature film. [from Old French *faiture*]

feature film a film that forms the main part of a cinema programme.

featureless *adj.* dull; with no points of interest.

Feb *or* **Feb.** *abbrev.* February.

febrile *adj.* relating to or caused by fever; feverish. [from Latin *febris*, fever]

February *noun* (PL. **Februaries**) the second month of the year. [from Latin *Februarius*, month of expiation]

February Revolution (France) the revolution in France (22–4 Feb 1848) which resulted in the abdication of King Louis Philippe, the proclamation of a republic, and the establishment of a provisional government. Although not the first of the European revolutions of 1848, it inspired subsequent revolutionary activity in Germany and Austria.

February Revolution (Russia) popular demonstrations, strikes, and military mutinies in Petrograd, Russia (Feb–Mar 1917), resulting from pre-war misgovernment and wartime privation, which led to the abdication of Tsar Nicholas II and the collapse of the tsarist government. The old regime was succeeded by a series of provisional governments composed of ostensibly liberal and moderate socialist ministers, and simultaneously by the establishment of the Soviet ('Council') of Workers' and Soldiers' Deputies.

feckless *adj.* helpless; clueless; irresponsible; aimless. [from Scot. *feck*, effect + -LESS]

fecklessly *adv.* in a feckless way.

fecklessness *noun* being feckless.

fecund *adj.* fruitful; fertile; richly productive. [from Latin *fecundus*]

fecundity *noun* fruitfulness, fertility, productiveness.

fed see FEED.

Fedayeen a term commonly used for a commando or guerilla fighter, trained by organizations such as the PLO (Palestine Liberation Organization). [from Arabic *fidai*, one who sacrifices oneself (for a cause or country)]

federal *adj.* **1** consisting of a group of states independent in local matters but united under a central government for other purposes, eg defence. **2** relating to the central government of a federal union. **3** (**Federal**) *Hist.* supporting the union government during the American Civil War. [from Latin *foedus*, treaty]

Federal Bureau of Investigation (ABBREV. **FBI**) in the USA, an organization founded in 1908 that is primarily concerned with internal security or counter-intelligence operations, such as espionage, treason, kidnapping, civil rights violations, fraud against the government, and bank robbery. It is part of the Department of Justice and is responsible to the attorney-general of the USA, who until 1986 appointed its director (now appointed by the President). The agency developed in expertise and popularity mainly under the directorship (1924–72) of J Edgar Hoover (1895–1972), being particularly successful in crime detection, though there was criticism of its apparent persecution of Communists after World War II.

federalism *noun Politics* the principles and practice of federal government, especially a system in which constitutional powers are devolved to national and regional governments.
◇ The system aims to maintain national unity while allowing for regional diversity. The key features are: two or more tiers of government enjoying their own right of existence under the constitution; separate legislative and executive powers; separate sources of revenue; an organ (normally the supreme court) to decide on disputes between the different levels; and a bicameral parliament that provides for representation in regional or state government.

federalist *noun* an advocate or supporter of federal government.

Federalist Party a political party formed in the USA in the 1790s. George Washington (in office 1789–97), who originally took a neutral stance, eventually joined it. John Adams, the second US president (in office 1797–1801), was the last Federalist president. After Jefferson's victory in the 1800 presidential election, the party gradually declined.

federalize *or* **federalise** *verb trans., intrans.* to make federal.

Federal Reserve System (ABBREV. **FRS**) the Central Bank of the USA, known as 'The Fed', set up in 1913. It divides the USA into 12 districts, each with its own Federal Reserve Bank, carries out the normal duties of a central bank, and also manages cheque clearance on behalf of member banks.

federate *verb trans., intrans.* to unite to form a federation. [from Latin *foedus*, treaty]

federation *noun* **1** a federal union of states. **2** a union of business organizations, etc. **3** the act of uniting in a league.

Fédération Internationale de Football Association see FIFA.

federative *adj.* relating to or constituted as a federation.

fee *noun* **1** a charge made for professional services, eg by a doctor or lawyer. **2** a charge for eg membership of a society, sitting an examination, entrance to a museum, etc. **3** (*usually* **fees**) a payment for school or college education, or for a course of instruction. **4** a payment made to a football club for the transfer of one of its players. **5** *Legal* an estate in the form of land that is inheritable with either restricted rights (*fee tail*) or unrestricted rights (*fee simple*). [from Old French *fie*]

feeble *adj.* **1** lacking strength; weak. **2** lacking power, influence, or effectiveness. [from Old French *feible*, from Latin *flebilis*, lamentable]

feeble-minded *adj.* **1** stupid. **2** mentally below normal.

feeble-mindedness *noun* being feeble-minded.

feebleness *noun* being feeble.

feebly *adv.* in a feeble way.

feed — *verb* (PAST TENSE AND PAST PARTICIPLE **fed**) **1** *intrans.* (**feed on something**) *said especially of animals* to eat it, especially as a regular diet. **2** to give food to or prepare food for. **3** *intrans.* (**feed on something**) to be fuelled by it. **4** to give as food. **5** to supply with fuel or other material required for continued operation or processing. **6** to strengthen or encourage (a feeling, etc). — *noun* **1** an act or session of feeding. **2** food for animals or babies. **3** *colloq.* a meal, especially a hearty one. **4** the channel or mechanism by which a machine is supplied with fuel, etc.
— **fed up** *colloq.* bored and impatient.
feed someone up to fatten them up with nourishing food.
[from Anglo-Saxon *fedan*]

feedback *noun* **1** responses and reactions, eg customers' comments on a product or service, that provide guidelines for adjustment and development. **2** the process whereby part of the output of a system or device, or of a component of a living organism, is returned to the input in order to regulate or modify subsequent output. Positive feedback increases the output, whereas negative feedback decreases it. **3** in a public-address system, etc, the partial return to the microphone of the sound output, producing a whistle or howl.

feeder *noun* **1** a baby or animal with particular eating habits: *a poor feeder*. **2** a minor road, railway line, etc leading to a main one.

feel — *verb* (PAST TENSE AND PAST PARTICIPLE **felt**) **1** to become aware of through the sense of touch. **2** *trans., intrans.* to have the sensation of; to sense. **3** *trans., intrans.* to find out or investigate with the hands, etc. **4** *intrans., trans.* to have (an emotion). **5** *trans., intrans.* to react emotionally to something: *feels the loss very deeply*. **6** *intrans.* to give the impression of being (soft, hard, rough, etc) when touched. **7** *intrans.* to be or seem. **8** to think, be of the opinion, or be under the impression that. **9** *trans., intrans.* to seem to oneself to be: *feel a fool*. — *noun* **1** a sensation or impression produced by touching. **2** an impression or atmosphere created by something. **3** an act of feeling with the fingers, etc.
— **feel around for something** to search for it with the fingers, etc.
feel for someone to feel sympathy for them.
feel for something to try to find it by feeling.
feel like something to have an inclination for it: *feel like a walk*.
feel one's way to make one's way cautiously.
feel up to something to feel fit enough for it.
get the feel of something to become familiar with it or used to it.
have a feel for something have a natural ability for, or understanding of, an activity, etc.
not feel oneself to feel unwell.
[from Anglo-Saxon *felan*]

feeler *noun* an organ of touch found in certain animals, especially one of two thread-like projections on an insect's head.
— **put out feelers** *colloq.* to test for possible reactions, before taking action.

feelgood *adj. colloq.* reinforcing or associated with pleasant feelings of comfort, security, etc: *the feelgood factor*.

feeling — *noun* **1** a sensation or emotion. **2** (**feelings**) one's attitude to something: *have strong feelings*. **3** emotion as distinct from reason. **4** strong emotion: *speak with feeling*. **5** a belief or opinion. **6** (**have a feeling for something**) a natural ability for, or understanding of, an activity, etc. **7** affection. — *adj.* sensitive; sympathetic.

feelingly *adv.* with sincerity resulting from experience.

feet see FOOT.

feign *verb* to pretend to have (eg an illness) or feel (an emotion, etc). [from Latin *fingere*, to contrive]

feigned *adj.* **1** pretended. **2** simulated. **3** imagined.

feint[1] *noun* in boxing, fencing or other sports, a movement, eg a mock attack, intended to deceive or distract one's opponent.

feint[2] *adj.*, *said of paper* ruled with faint lines. [variant of FAINT]

feisty *adj.* (**feistier, feistiest**) *colloq.* **1** spirited; lively. **2** irritable; quarrelsome. [from US dialect *fist*, an aggressive small dog]

Feldenkrais method a system of slow exercises designed to correct harmfully restrictive body movements and postures. [named after the French physicist Moshe Feldenkrais, who developed it]

feldspar *or* **felspar** *noun Geol.* any of a large group of rock-forming minerals, mainly aluminium silicates, that represent about 60 per cent of the Earth's crust. Feldspar is found in most igneous and many metamorphic rocks, eg orthoclase, plagioclase. [from Swedish *Feldt*, field + *Spat*, spar]

feldspathic *or* **felspathic** *adj.* of the nature of or containing feldspar.

felicitate *verb* to congratulate. [from Latin *felicitas*, happiness]

felicitation *noun* congratulation.

felicitations *pl. noun* congratulations.

felicitous *adj.* **1** *said of wording* elegantly apt. **2** pleasant; happy. [from Latin *felicitas*, happiness]

felicitously *adv.* aptly, appropriately.

felicitousness *noun* being felicitous.

Felicity a female first name. [from Latin *felicitas*, luck, good fortune]

felicity *noun* **1** happiness. **2** elegance or aptness of wording.

feline *adj.* of or like a cat. [from Latin *felis*, cat]

Felix a male first name, popular among the early Christians. [from Latin *felix*, lucky, happy]

Felixstowe POP (1981) 25 000, a port town and resort in Suffolk Coastal district, Suffolk, E England. It lies on the North Sea coast, 17km/11mi SE of Ipswich. There are extensive container terminals, and ferries to Europe.

fell[1] see FALL.

fell[2] *verb* **1** to cut down (a tree). **2** to knock down. **3** *Needlework* to turn under and stitch down the edges of (a seam). [from Anglo-Saxon *fyllan*, to cause to fall]

fell[3] *noun* (*often* **fells**) a hill or moor. [from Norse *fjall*]

fell[4] *adj.* old use destructive; deadly.
— **at** *or* **in one fell swoop** at a single deadly blow; in one quick operation.
[from Old French *fel*, cruel]

fellatio *noun* sexual stimulation of the penis by sucking or licking. [from Latin *fellare*, to suck]

Fellini, Federico (1920–93) Italian film director, born in Rimini. He was a cartoonist, journalist, and scriptwriter before becoming an assistant film director in 1942. His highly individual films, always from his own scripts, include *La Strada* (The Road, 1954), which won a Best Foreign Film Oscar, *Fellini's Roma* (1972), *Amarcord* (I Remember, 1974), and *La Dolce Vita* (The Sweet Life, 1960), which won him another Oscar. His later productions included *Citta della Donna* (City of Women, 1980) and *Ginger and Fred* (1986).

fellow *noun* **1** a man or boy. **2** a companion or equal. **3** a person in the same situation or condition as oneself, or having the same status, etc: *a fellow citizen.* **4** a senior member of a college or university. **5** a postgraduate research student financed by a fellowship. **6** a member of any of many learned societies. **7** *colloq.* a boyfriend. **8** one of a pair: *one sock on the chair, its fellow on the floor.* [from Anglo-Saxon *feolaga*, partner]

fellow feeling sympathy for someone with experiences similar to one's own.

fellowship *noun* **1** friendly companionship. **2** commonness or similarity of interests between people. **3** a society or association. **4** the status of a fellow of a college, society, etc; a salary paid to a research fellow.

fellow traveller someone who sympathises with a political party, especially the Communist Party, without actually joining it.

felon *noun* a person guilty of a serious crime. [from Old French *felon*, from Latin *fello*, traitor]

felonious *adj.* relating to or of the nature of a felony.

felony *noun* (PL. **felonies**) *Legal* a serious crime.

felspar same as FELDSPAR.

felt[1] see FEEL.

felt[2] — *noun* a fabric formed by matting or pressing together wool fibres, etc. — *verb* **1** *trans., intrans.* to form into felt; to mat. **2** to cover with felt. [from Anglo-Saxon *felt*]

felt-tip pen *or* **felt-tipped pen** a pen with a point made of felt.

fem. *abbrev.* **1** female. **2** feminine.

female — *adj.* **1** denoting the sex that gives birth to young, produces eggs, etc. **2** denoting the reproductive structure of a plant that contains an ovum (egg cell), such as the pistil of flowering plants. **3** of, relating to, or belonging to a woman. **4** *Engineering* denoting a piece of machinery into which another part (the male) fits. — *noun* **1** a woman or girl. **2** a female animal or plant. [from Latin *femella*, diminutive of *femina*, woman]

female condom a form of contraception that first became available in 1992, consisting of a thin polyurethane pouch that fits inside the vagina. It is a barrier method and so provides protection against sexually transmitted diseases as well as unwanted pregnancy.

female genital mutilation female circumcision.

feminine *adj.* **1** of, or typically belonging to, a woman. **2** having or denoting qualities considered suitable for a woman. **3** *Grammar, said of nouns in certain languages* belonging to the gender into which most words for females fall. [from Latin *feminina*, diminutive of *femina*, woman]

femininity *noun* being feminine.

feminism *noun* a belief or movement advocating the cause of women's rights and opportunities. [from Latin *femina*, woman]

feminist — *noun* a person who advocates or supports feminism. — *adj.* relating to or characterized by feminism.

feminist criticism literary criticism approached from a feminist standpoint.
◇ This includes the reassessment of familiar texts exposing sexist attitudes in the works themselves, and in their selection; the promotion of neglected women writers and the establishment of a clear tradition of feminine writing; and the identification of the special features (eg style, language, insight) which are found only in writing by women.

femme fatale (PL. **femmes fatales**) a woman whose irresistible charms fascinate and destroy people, usually men. [French, = fatal woman]

femoral *adj.* relating to or in the region of the thigh.

femto- *combining form* a thousand million millionth (10^{-15}). [from Danish or Norwegian *femten*, 15]

femur *noun* the thigh bone. [from Latin *femur*, thigh]

fen *noun* a waterlogged area of lowland dominated by grasses, sedges, and rushes, and having an alkaline soil, in contrast to the acid peat of a bog. [from Anglo-Saxon *fenn*]

fence — *noun* **1** a barrier eg of wood or wire, for enclosing or protecting land. **2** a barrier of any of various designs for a horse to jump. **3** *slang* a person who receives and disposes of stolen goods. **4** a guard to limit motion in a piece of machinery. **5** a guiding device on a circular saw or plane. — *verb* **1** (**fence something in** *or* **off**) to enclose or separate it with a fence, or as if with a fence. **2** *intrans.* to practise the sport of fencing. **3** *intrans.* to avoid answering directly.
— **sit on the fence** to avoid supporting either side in a dispute, etc.
[from DEFENCE]

fencer *noun* a person who fences.

fencing *noun* **1** the sport of fighting with swords. **2** material for constructing fences.
◇ Fencing was popular in the Middle Ages, and the rapier was developed by the end of the 16c. The modern competitive sport uses three weapons: the light sabre (developed in Italy in the late 19c), the foil (introduced in France as a practice weapon in the mid-17c), and the épée (developed in France in the 19c). Different target areas are designated for each weapon, and contestants wear protective clothing which is electronically wired to indicate when a successful hit has been made.

fend *verb* **1** (**fend something** *or* **someone off**) to defend oneself from (blows, questions, etc). **2** (**fend for someone**) to provide for (especially oneself). [from DEFEND]

fender *noun* **1** *North Amer.* the wing or mudguard of a car. **2** a low guard fitted round a fireplace to keep ash, coals, etc within the hearth. **3** a bundle of rope or other object hanging from a ship's side to protect it when in contact with piers, etc. [from FEND]

Fenella a female first name. [from Irish Gaelic *Fionnghuala*, formed by *fionn*, white, fair + *gualainn*, shoulder]

Fénelon, François de Salignac de la Mothe (1651–1715) French Roman Catholic prelate and writer, born in Fénelon, Périgord. He was ordained in 1675, and as tutor to Louis XIV's grandson (1689–99) he wrote such works as *Les Aventures de Télémaque* (The Adventures of Telemachus, 1699), which received the King's censure for its alleged political satire on the court. As Archbishop of Cambrai from 1695, he wrote a defence of the doctrines of the French mystic Madame Guyon (1648–1717) entitled *Explication des maximes des saints sur la vie intérieure* (Explanation of the Sayings of the Saints on the Interior Life, 1697), which was condemned by the pope.

feng shui the process of making the correct decision about the siting of a building so as to ensure the optimum happiness for the occupants. It is based on the notion that natural features in the landscape are influenced by wind and water, and that the cosmic currents resulting from the interaction between these natural elements, the five basic elements (ie earth, fire, metal, water, and wood), and the two primary elements of yin and yang will render some places more auspicious than others. [Chinese, = wind and water]

Fenians the short title of the Irish Republican Brotherhood, a nationalist organization founded in New York (1857) that advocated violence as a means of achieving its objective. It was known for committing murderous attacks (the 'Fenian

Outrages') in Manchester and London to rescue imprisoned supporters in 1867.

fennel *noun* a strong-smelling, yellow-flowered plant whose seeds, leaves, and root are used in cooking. [from Anglo-Saxon *finol*]

sweet fennel

Fens, The *or* **Fen Country** the flat marshy land surrounding the Wash, in Lincolnshire, Norfolk, Suffolk, and Cambridgeshire, E England. It extends 112km/70mi N–S and 6km/4mi E–W, and is watered by the Witham, Welland, Nene, and Ouse rivers. The Wash is a remnant of a silted-up North Sea bay. HISTORY the area was first artificially drained in the Roman era; in medieval times monasteries were built on 'islands' of dry land; there was major reclamation in the 17c. ECONOMY market gardening, fruit, vegetables; grazing.

fenugreek *noun* a white-flowered plant with strong-smelling seeds used as flavouring. [from Latin *fenum graecum*, Greek hay]

feoff same as FIEF.

feral *adj.* **1** *said of animals* wild, especially after escaping from captivity or domestication. **2** *said of a plant* uncultivated; having run wild. [from Latin *fera*, wild beast]

fer-de-lance either of two species of a New World pit viper, the commonest cause of human death by snakebite. [from French *fer de lance*, lance-head]

Ferdinand I (of the Two Sicilies) (1751–1825) King of Naples, as Ferdinand IV (1759–99, 1799–1806), and of the Two Sicilies (1816–25), born in Naples. He joined England and Austria against France in 1793, but in 1801 was forced to make a treaty with Napoleon. In 1806 he took refuge in Sicily, under English protection, and was reinstated by the Congress of Vienna (1815). In 1816 he united his two states into the Kingdom of the Two Sicilies, and despite demands for constitutional government, retained a harsh absolutism.

Ferdinand, King of Navarre the king in Shakespeare's *Love's Labour's Lost*, who immediately forgets his vow of chastity on sight of the Princess of France.

Ferdinand the son of the King of Naples in Shakespeare's *The Tempest*, who falls in love with Miranda after being shipwrecked on Prospero's island.

Ferdinand a male first name, now rare. [from Germanic elements meaning 'journey' + 'ready, prepared']

Fergus a male first name, largely confined to Scotland and Ireland. [an Anglicized form of Gaelic *Fearghus*, from Celtic elements meaning 'best' + 'choice']

Fergusson, John Duncan (1874–1961) Scottish painter, born in Perthshire. One of the group of Scottish Colourists, he acknowledged a debt to the Glasgow School of painting which emphasized colour rather than line. On trips to N Africa, Spain, and Paris, he came into contact with Mediterranean light and landscape, and

with the painting of the Post-Impressionists and Fauves. He is best known for his series of World War I paintings of naval dockyards, and his portraits of the female nude.

Fermanagh, Gaelic **Fear Manach** POP (1981) 52 000, a county in SW Northern Ireland. AREA 1 676sq km/647sq mi. It is bounded NW, W, S, and SE by the Republic of Ireland, and NE by Co Tyrone. PHYSICAL DESCRIPTION hilly in the NE and SW, rising to 667m at Cuilcagh; the Upper and Lower Lough Erne run SE–NW through the centre. CHIEF TOWN Enniskillen (county town). ECONOMY potatoes; livestock; textiles.

Fermat, Pierre de (1601–65) French mathematician, born in Beaumont. He became a lawyer before turning to mathematics, making many discoveries about the properties of numbers, probabilities, and geometry; with Descartes, he was one of the two leading mathematicians in the early 17c. In optics, 'Fermat's principle' was first stated by him in 1657.

fermata *noun* (PL. **fermatas**) *Mus.* a pause. [from Italian *fermata*, a stop, halt]

Fermat's principle the principle that light rays travels between two points in such a way that the time taken is a minimum.

ferment — *noun* a substance that causes fermentation. **1** fermentation. **2** a state of agitation or excitement. — *verb* **1** *intrans., trans.* to cause the breakdown of organic compounds such as carbohydrates in the absence of oxygen, especially by yeast or bacteria, eg during the brewing of beer. **2** to be or cause to be in a state of excitement or instability. [from Latin *fermentum*, yeast]

fermentation *noun Chem.* a biochemical process in which micro-organisms such as bacteria, yeasts, or moulds are used to break down an organic compound, usually a carbohydrate, in the absence of oxygen.
◊ Fermentation is the basic process used in the production of alcoholic beverages such as beer, wine, and cider, during which yeast breaks down sugar to form ethanol (alcohol) and carbon dioxide. It is also used to make many kinds of bread, cheese, and yoghurt, as well as antibiotics and other important drugs, eg moulds react with mixtures of inorganic salts and molasses to form penicillin. Fermentation is widely used in biotechnology.

Fermi, Enrico (1901–54) Italian–US physicist, born in Rome. Professor at Rome from 1927, he made important contributions to statistical physics and theories of nuclear decay. With colleagues he studied induced radioactivity by bombarding elements with neutrons; for this work he was awarded the 1938 Nobel Prize for Physics. Subsequently he emigrated to the USA, where he became professor at Columbia University (1939) and built the world's first nuclear reactor (1942).

fermium *noun* (SYMBOL **Fm**, ATOMIC NUMBER **100**) an artificially produced radioactive metallic element. [named after the Italian physicist Enrico Fermi]

fern *noun* any of several thousand species of seedless non-flowering plants belonging to the class Pteropsida, and related to clubmosses and horsetails. Ferns reproduce by means of spores, and include many forms that are now extinct but flourished during the Carboniferous period. [from Anglo-Saxon *fearn*]
◊ Most ferns are perennials with tough rhizomes, and several species are climbers. Some have stout erect rhizomes resembling tree trunks, and a few are genuine tree ferns with tall rigid trunks bearing a crown of fronds. The majority of fern species are found in the tropics and warm humid regions, but some also occur in temperate regions.
Ferns show alternation of generations, in which a *gametophyte* generation, which bears gametes, reproduces sexually to produce a *sporophyte* generation, which bears spores and reproduces asex-

ually. The dominant generation is the sporophyte, which is the visible plant. It usually has one or more large triangular fronds, subdivided into many leaflets, which are characteristically coiled in a crozier shape when young, unfurling as they grow. The undersides of the fertile fronds bear the sporangia (spore-bearing structures), which may be grouped into *sori* forming distinctive patterns. The sporophyte generation undergoes meiosis to produce spores which germinate and develop into a very small free-living structure, which is often heart-shaped, and is known as a *prothallus*. It bears male and female gametes, fusion of which results in the development of a new sporophyte.

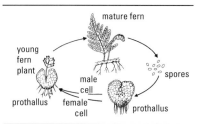

life cycle of the fern

Fernandel, stage name of **Fernand Joseph Désiré Contandin** (1903–71) French film comedian, born in Marseilles. He made his début on the stage in 1922, and from 1930 appeared in over 100 films. He established himself internationally as the country priest of *Le Petit Monde de Don Camillo* (The Little World of Don Camillo, 1953).

Fernando Póo see BIOKO.

Fernel, Jean François (c.1497–1558) French physician, born in Clermont. A popular medical teacher in Paris, his reputation as a physician soared when he saved the life of the mistress of the Dauphin (later Henri II). He was an astute observer whose many writings synthesized 16c medical orthodoxy; although he had in his early life been an advocate of astrological influences on health and disease, he later renounced these views in favour of a more naturalistic causative framework. He coined the Latin words which became 'physiology' and 'pathology'.

ferny *adj.* (**fernier, ferniest**) covered with or full of ferns.

ferocious *adj.* fierce; cruel; savage. [from Latin *ferox*, wild]

ferociously *adv.* in a ferocious way.

ferocity *or* **ferociousness** *noun* being ferocious; fierceness.

-ferous *combining form* bearing or containing: *carboniferous*. [from Latin *ferre*, to carry]

Ferranti, Sebastian Ziani de (1864–1930) English electrical engineer and inventor, born in Liverpool of Italian extraction. He conceived the idea of the large-scale generation and distribution of electricity at high voltages, and in 1887 was appointed chief electrician to the London Electric Supply Corporation, contributing to the establishment of the national electricity grid system some 40 years later. From 1882 to 1927 he took out 176 patents, and his company Ferranti Ltd, founded in 1905, was at the forefront of electrical and electronic engineering for many decades.

Ferrara POP (1991e) 141 000, the capital of Ferrara province, Emilia-Romagna region, N Italy. HISTORY the seat of the Council of Ferrara (1438) and of the 15c Renaissance court; ceded to France from 1797 until 1815; became part of the Kingdom of Sardinia in 1859. The religious reformer Savonarola was born here in 1452. NOTABLE FEATURES Castello Estense (14c–16c); Cathedral of San Giorgio (1135); university (1391).

Ferrari a type of racing car and a Grand Prix

racing team named after the Italian racing driver Enzo Ferrari (1898–1988). The first car completely designed by him was produced in 1937, and his firm (Ferrari SpA, founded 1939) began to manufacture racing and sports cars from 1946. The cars, which are renowned for their speed and high quality, have won many Grand Prix championships.

ferret — *noun* **1** a small half-tame albino type of polecat, used for driving rabbits and rats from their holes. **2** an inquisitive and persistent investigator. — *verb* (**ferreted, ferreting**) *colloq.* **1** *intrans.* (**ferret about** *or* **around**) to search busily; to rummage. **2** (**ferret something out**) to find it out through persistent investigation. [from Old French *furet*, from Latin *fur*, thief]

ferric *adj. Chem.* containing iron in its trivalent state. [from Latin *ferrum*, iron]

Ferrier, Kathleen (1912–53) English contralto singer, born in Higher Walton, Lancashire. A singing prize at a local music festival led her to study seriously (1940), and she rapidly won acclaim. One of her greatest successes was in Mahler's *Das Lied von der Erde* (The Song of the Earth) at the first Edinburgh Festival (1947).

Ferris wheel *noun* a giant fairground wheel that turns vertically, with seats hanging from its rim. [named after the US engineer G W G Ferris (1859–96)]

ferrite *noun Chem.* any of a class of ceramic materials composed of oxides of iron and some other metal, such as copper, nickel, or manganese. Ferrites have magnetic properties and a low electrical conductivity, and they are used in high-frequency electrical coils, loudspeaker magnets, and video and audio tape-recorder heads. [from Latin *ferrum*, iron]

ferro- *combining form* made of or containing iron, as in *ferromagnetic* (having the high magnetism typical of iron) or *ferroconcrete* (reinforced concrete). [from Latin *ferrum*, iron]

ferrous *adj. Chem.* containing iron in its divalent form. [from Latin *ferrum*, iron]

ferrule *noun* **1** a metal ring or cap for protecting the tip of a walking-stick or umbrella. **2** a cylindrical fitting, threaded internally like a screw, for joining pipes, etc together. [from Latin *viriola*, little bracelet]

ferry — *noun* (PL. **ferries**) a boat that carries passengers and often cars across a river or strip of water, especially as a regular service. — *verb* (**ferries, ferried**) **1** *trans., intrans.* to transport or go by ferry. **2** to convey in a vehicle. [from Anglo-Saxon *ferian*, to convey]

ferryman *noun* a person in charge of a ferry.

fertile *adj.* **1** *said of land, soil, etc* producing abundant crops, plants, etc. **2** capable of producing babies, young, or fruit. **3** *said of an egg or seed* capable of developing into a new individual. **4** *said of the mind* rich in ideas. **5** providing a wealth of possibilities: *fertile ground for research.* **6** *Physics, said of material* capable of becoming fissile or fissionable. [from Latin *fertilis*]

fertility *noun* being fertile; the ability to produce young.

fertility drug *Medicine* a drug that is used to treat infertility in women by inducing ovulation. Early fertility drugs caused multiple pregnancies, and even with newer drugs such as clomiphene, the incidence of twins is about 10 per cent of all successful pregnancies.

fertilization *or* **fertilisation** *noun* the fusion of two unlike gametes (specialized reproductive cells) to form a zygote, as occurs during sexual reproduction. The gametes are typically male (a sperm) and female (an ovum or egg). ◊ During fertilization, two gametes that are haploid (each having a single chromosome set) fuse to form a *zygote* which is diploid (having a double set of chromosomes). The zygote then divides repeatedly and develops into a new indi-

vidual. Fertilization may be internal, occurring within the body of the female, as in mammals, birds, and reptiles, or external, both gametes being released into water, as in most fishes and amphibians. In plants there may be self-fertilization, in which both gametes come from the same plant, or cross-fertilization, in which they come from different plants. In higher plants pollination is necessary for fertilization to occur.

fertilize *or* **fertilise** *verb* **1** to introduce sperm into (an egg) or pollen into (a plant) so that reproduction results. **2** to add nutrients to (soil) to make it fertile and productive.

fertilizer *or* **fertiliser** *noun* any chemical substance containing plant nutrients, especially nitrogen, potassium salts, or phosphates, that is added to the soil in order to improve the yield, size, or quality of plants, especially food crops. ◊ *Inorganic fertilizers* are the most widely used fertilizers, and may be added to the soil in the form of crystals, granules, powder, or liquid, or they may be injected directly into the ground. They include nitrogen fertilizers, produced mainly from ammonia, such as ammonium nitrate and ammonium phosphate, and potassium fertilizers, usually manufactured from naturally occurring potassium chloride. *Organic fertilizers* include animal manure, compost, bonemeal, fishmeal, and seaweed. They contain lower levels of nutrients than inorganic fertilizers, and so need to be used in large quantities, but are much less harmful to the environment. The use of large amounts of inorganic fertilizer, especially nitrates, can cause pollution of rivers, streams, lakes, and drinking water supplies, and in some countries legal limits are imposed on the total amount of fertilizer that may be applied to the land during each season.

fervent *adj.* enthusiastic; earnest or ardent. [from Latin *fervere*, to boil]

fervently *adv.* with fervour.

fervid *adj.* fervent; full of fiery passion or zeal. [from Latin *fervidus*, fiery]

fervidly *adv.* in a fervid way.

fervour *noun* passionate enthusiasm; intense eagerness or sincerity. [from Latin *fervor*, violent heat]

Fès see FEZ.

fescue *noun* a tufted grass of the genus *Festuca* with inrolled bristle-like leaves. It grows in dense tufts, and forms much of the turf on chalk downs. Upland species are often viviparous, ie the seeds germinate to form plantlets before being shed from the plant. [from Old French *festu*, from Latin *festuca*, straw]

Fessenden, Reginald Aubrey (1866–1932) Canadian-born US radio engineer and inventor, born in East Bolton, Quebec. He worked for Thomas Edison before returning to academic life, first at Purdue University and then as professor at the University of Pittsburgh, where he began to pursue his interest in radio communication. Of his many patents (over 500), the most important was his invention of amplitude modulation; in 1906, he used this to broadcast what was probably the first US radio programme from his transmitter at Brant Rock, Massachusetts.

-fest *suffix* forming ad hoc words meaning: **1** *colloq.* an indulgent spree or concentration on a particular activity or quality: *newsfest / horrorfest*. **2** a gathering for a specific purpose; a collection of articles, etc on a particular theme. [from German *Fest*, festival]

festal *adj.* relating to a festival; festive. [from Latin *festum*, holiday]

Feste the quick-witted and sometimes melancholic clown employed by Olivia in Shakespeare's *Twelfth Night*, who disguises himself as Sir Topas to get revenge on Malvolio.

fester *verb intrans.* (**festered, festering**) **1** to become infected; to go septic. **2** *said of an evil* to continue unchecked or get worse. **3** to rot or decay. **4** *said of resentment or anger* to smoulder; to become more bitter. **5** to be a continuing cause of resentment; to rankle. [from Old French *festre*, from Latin *fistula*, kind of ulcer]

festival *noun* **1** a day or period of celebration, especially one kept traditionally. **2** *Relig.* a feast or saint's day. **3** a programme of musical, theatrical, or other cultural events. [from Latin *festivalis dies*, festive day]

Festival of Britain an event held in 1951 to mark the centenary of the Great Exhibition in 1851. Despite the economic shortages of the time, it was a triumphant success and was intended to demonstrate 'the British contribution to civilization past, present, and future, in the arts, science and technology, and in industrial design'. Its central focus was the newly-built Royal Festival Hall on the south bank of the Thames.

festive *adj.* of, or suitable for, a celebration; lively and cheerful. [from Latin *festivus*]

festivity *noun* (PL. **festivities**) **1** celebration; merrymaking. **2** (**festivities**) festive activities.

festoon — *noun* a decorative chain of flowers, ribbons, etc looped between two points. — *verb* to hang or decorate with festoons. [from Italian *festone*, decoration for a feast]

feta *noun* a soft crumbly white cheese, originally from Greece, made with ewe's or goat's milk. [from modern Greek *pheta*, a slice]

fetal *or* **foetal** relating to a fetus.

fetal alcohol syndrome (ABBREV. **FAS**) a condition characterized by mental retardation, etc in a newborn baby, caused by excessive alcohol intake by its mother during pregnancy.

fetch — *verb* **1** to go and get, and bring back. **2** to be sold for (a certain price). **3** to deal (someone a blow). **4** *old use* to utter (a sigh or groan). **5** to bring forth (tears or blood). — *noun* a trick or dodge.
— **fetch and carry** to act as servant.
fetch up *colloq.* to arrive; to turn up; to end up.
fetch something up to vomit food.
[from Anglo-Saxon *feccan*]

fetching *adj. colloq.* charming; attractive.

fetchingly *adv.* charmingly, attractively.

fête *or* **fete** — *noun* an outdoor entertainment with competitions, stalls, etc usually to raise money for a charitable or other purpose. — *verb* to entertain or honour lavishly. [from French *fête*, feast]

fetid *or* **foetid** *adj.* having a disgusting smell. [from Latin *fetere*, to stink]

fetish *noun* **1** in primitive societies, an object worshipped for its magical powers. **2** a procedure or ritual followed obsessively, or an object of obsessive devotion. **3** an object that is handled or visualized as an aid to sexual stimulation; a person's attachment to such an object. [from French *fétiche*, from Portuguese *feitiço*, magic]

fetishism *noun* **1** the worship of a fetish. **2** belief in charms. **3** compulsive attachment of sexual interest to an inanimate object.

fetishist *noun* a person who believes in or is influenced by fetishism.

fetishistic *adj.* relating to or affected by fetishism or a fetish.

fetlock *noun* the projection on a horse's leg just above the hoof, or the tuft of hair growing on this. [from Middle English *fetlak*]

fetter — *noun* **1** (*usually* **fetters**) a chain or shackle fastened to a prisoner's ankle. **2** (**fetters**) tiresome restrictions. — *verb* (**fettered, fettering**) **1** to put in fetters. **2** to restrict. [from Anglo-Saxon *fetor*]

fettle *noun* spirits or condition: *in fine fettle*. [from Anglo-Saxon *fetel*, belt]

fettuccine *noun* pasta in the form of flat wide ribbons. [Italian, a diminutive (plural) of *fettuccia*, tape]

fetus *or* **foetus** 1 *Zool*. the embryo of a viviparous mammal (one giving birth to live offspring) during the later stages of development in the uterus (womb), when it has started to resemble the fully formed animal. 2 specifically, the human embryo from about 8 weeks after conception until birth. [from Latin *fetus*, offspring] ◆ The form *foetus*, although less correct in terms of its origin, is still widely used in general contexts in British English. The form *fetus* is now standard in technical contexts, and in N America generally.

fetwa same as FATWA.

feud — *noun* a long-drawn-out bitter quarrel between families, tribes, or individuals. — *verb intrans*. (**feud with someone**) to carry on a feud with them. [from Old French *feide*]

feudal *adj*. relating to the social system of medieval Europe, in which vassals or tenants were obliged to serve under their lord in battle, and were in return protected by him. [from Latin *feudum*, fee]

feudalism *noun* the medieval feudal system, or a system reminiscent of it; feudal principles.

Feuerbach, Ludwig (Andreas) (1804–72) German philosopher, born in Landshut, Bavaria. His best-known work, *Das Wesen des Christentums* (The Essence of Christianity, 1841), claims that religion rises from one's alienation from oneself, and the projection of ideal human qualities onto a fictitious supreme 'other'. His ideas influenced Karl Marx and Friedrich Engels.

fever *noun* 1 any rise in body temperature above the normal level (37°C or 98.6°F), most commonly as a result of viral or bacterial infections, or infectious diseases such as malaria. It is usually accompanied by shivering, thirst, and headache. 2 any of many usually infectious diseases in which this is a marked symptom, eg scarlet fever, yellow fever. 3 agitation or excitement. [from Latin *febris*]

fevered *adj*. feverish; affected with fever.

feverfew *noun* an aromatic perennial plant (*Tanacetum parthenium*) having yellowish-green leaves with lobed or toothed leaflets, and loose flat-topped clusters of flowers, with white outer florets and yellow inner florets. It is grown for ornament and as a medicinal herb, and is reputed to relieve the symptoms of migraine. [from medieval Latin *febrifugia*, plant for ridding fever]

feverish *adj*. 1 suffering from, or showing symptoms of, fever. 2 agitated or restless.

feverishly *adv*. in a feverish way.

fever pitch a state of high excitement.

few — *adj*. not many; hardly any. — *pron*. hardly any things, people, etc.
— **a few** a small number; some.
as few as ... no more than ...
few and far between *colloq*. rare; scarce.
a good few *or* **quite a few** a fairly large number; several.
have had a few *colloq*. to have drunk sufficient alcohol to affect one's behaviour.
no fewer than ... as many as ...
precious few *colloq*. hardly any at all.
the few the minority, or the discerning people, as distinct from *the many*.
[from Anglo-Saxon *feawa*]

fey *adj*. 1 strangely fanciful. 2 able to foresee future events. 3 *Scot*. doomed to die early. [from Anglo-Saxon *fæge*, doomed to die]

feyness *noun* being fey.

Feynman, Richard Phillips (1918–88) US physicist, born in New York City. After working on the development of the atomic bomb, he taught at Cornell University and was appointed professor at the California Institute of Technology. For important contributions to the theory of quantum electrodynamics, he shared the 1965 Nobel Prize for Physics with Julian Schwinger and Shinichiro Tomonaga. He also introduced 'Feynman diagrams', pictorial representations of particle interactions, and was one of science's most colourful characters.

Fez *or* **Fès** POP (1990e) 1m, a city in Centre-Nord province, N central Morocco, 240km/150mi NE of Casablanca. It is the oldest of Morocco's four imperial cities and a major centre of Islamic learning. HISTORY Old Fez, a World Heritage site, was founded in 808 by Moulay Idriss II; New Fez was founded in 1276 by the Merinade Dynasty. The city gave its name to a type of red felt hat worn by many Islamic followers. NOTABLE FEATURES Karaouine Mosque (first built in the 9c) became famous as a Muslim university; Sultan's Palace (Dar el Makhzen).

fez *noun* (PL. **fezzes**) a hat shaped like a flat-topped cone, with a tassel, worn by some Muslim men. [from Turkish *fes*, from *Fez* in Morocco]

Fezziwig, Mr the benevolent former employer of Scrooge in Charles Dickens's *A Christmas Carol*. Other family members include his wife and daughters.

ff *abbrev. Mus*. fortissimo.

ff. *abbrev*. and the following (pages, etc).

fiacre *noun Hist*. a small four-wheeled cab. [from French *fiacre*, from the Hôtel de St *Fiacre* in Paris, where such a vehicle was first used]

fiancé *noun* a man to whom a woman is engaged to be married. [from Old French *fiancier*, to betroth]

fiancée *noun* a woman to whom a man is engaged to be married.

Fianna Fáil an Irish political party founded in 1926 by those opposed to the 1921 Anglo-Irish Treaty. It first came to power under Eamon De Valera in 1932, and has governed for most of the period since. In the 1930s it emphasized separation from the British, and has consistently supported the unification of Ireland.

fiasco *noun* (PL. **fiascos**, **fiascoes**) 1 a ludicrous or humiliating failure. 2 a disgraceful or ludicrous affair. [from Italian *fiasco*, bottle]

fiat *noun* 1 an official command; a decree. 2 a formal authorization for some procedure. [from Latin *fiat*, let it be done]

fib *colloq*. — *noun* a trivial lie. — *verb intrans*. (**fibbed**, **fibbing**) to tell fibs.

fibber *noun* a person who fibs.

Fibonacci, Leonardo, also known as **Leonardo of Pisa** (c.1170–c.1250) Italian mathematician, the first outstanding mathematician of the Middle Ages. He was responsible for popularizing the modern decimal system of numerals in *Liber abaci* (The Book of Calculations, 1202); his greatest work, the *Liber quadratorum* (The Book of Square Numbers, 1225) contains contributions to number theory.

Fibonacci series *or* **Fibonacci sequence** *Maths*. an infinitely long series of numbers in which each term is the sum of the two preceding terms, ie 1, 1, 2, 3, 5, 8, 13 ...

fibre *noun* 1 a thin thread of a natural or artificial substance, eg cellulose, nylon. 2 an elongated cell, or a number of cells joined end to end to form a single strand of tissue, eg muscle fibre, nerve fibre. 3 *Bot*. in the stems of woody plants, a long narrow thick-walled cell that provides mechanical support. Stem fibres of many species, eg flax, jute, are economically important. 4 dietary fibre. 5 an optical fibre. 6 character; stamina. [from Latin *fibra*]

fibreboard *noun* board made from compressed wood fibres.

fibreglass *noun* a strong durable synthetic material consisting of fine flexible glass fibres. It is resistant to heat, fire, and corrosion, and is used as a strengthener in glass-reinforced plastics for boat hulls, car bodies, etc, and as an electrical insulator.

fibre-optic *adj*. containing or using fibre optics.

fibre optics *Optics* the branch of optics concerned with the behaviour of light in long thin flexible strands of glass or plastic (optical fibres), and the use of such systems to transmit telephone messages, television signals, computer data, etc, in the form of modulated light signals. See also OPTICAL FIBRE.

fibril *noun* a small fibre. [from Latin *fibrilla*, diminutive of *fibra*, fibre]

fibrillate *verb intrans. Medicine*, said of the heart to undergo fibrillation.

fibrillation *noun Medicine* the spontaneous rapid and irregular contraction of the individual muscle fibres in the muscular walls of the chambers of the heart (the atria and ventricles). *Atrial fibrillation*, usually the result of heart disease, causes a rapid and irregular heart beat. In *ventricular fibrillation*, usually caused by coronary thrombosis, drugs, or electric shock, the heart stops beating. [from Latin *fibrilla*, fibril]

fibrin *noun Biochem*. an insoluble protein that forms a network of fibres during the clotting of blood, sealing off the ruptured blood vessel.

fibrinogen *noun Biochem*. a protein, produced by the liver, that is present in blood plasma, and is converted to the insoluble protein fibrin during the clotting of blood.

fibroid — *adj*. denoting a structure composed of fibrous tissue or resembling fibres. — *noun Medicine* a benign tumour consisting of fibrous tissue, one or more of which may develop in the muscular walls of the uterus. Fibroids are usually surgically removed if they cause pain and heavy menstrual bleeding.

fibrosis *noun* the formation of an abnormal amount of fibrous tissue, eg in the lungs.

fibrositis *noun* inflammation of the fibrous tissue sheathing the muscles. [from *fibrose*, fibrous + -ITIS]

fibrous *adj*. consisting of, containing, or like, fibre.

fibula *noun* (PL. **fibulae**, **fibulas**) the outer and narrower of the two bones in the lower leg. [from Latin *fibula*, brooch]

fiche *noun* a card or strip of film containing miniaturized data; a microfiche. [from French *fiche*, a slip of paper, etc]

Fichte, Johann Gottlieb (1762–1814) German philosopher, born in Rammenau, Saxony. As Professor of Philosophy at Jena (1794), he modified Kant's doctrine of the 'thing-in-itself' as the absolute reality, substituting for it the more subjective 'Ego', the primitive act of consciousness. In 1805 he became Professor at Erlangen, where he published the more popular versions of his philosophy. His *Reden an die deutsche Nation* (Addresses to the German Nation, 1807–8), invoked a metaphysical German nationalism to resistance against Napoleon. He drew up the constitution for, and was the first Rector of, the University of Berlin (opened in 1810).

Fichtelberg a mountain in the Erzgebirge range. It lies to the S of Karl Marx Stadt, on the frontier between Germany and the Czech Republic. HEIGHT 1 214m.

Fichtelgebirge, Czech **Smrčiny** a horse-shoe-shaped mountain range in Bavaria, Germany. It rises to 1 051m at Schneeberg, and is the source of the Main, Saale, Eger, and Naab rivers. The range is largely covered with fir forests and it links the Erzgebirge and the Bohemian Forest.

fickle *adj. derog.* changeable, especially in one's loyalties. [from Anglo-Saxon *ficol*, cunning]

fickleness *noun* being fickle.

fiction *noun* **1** literature concerning imaginary characters or events. **2** a pretence; a lie. **3** *Legal* a misrepresentation of the truth, accepted for convenience. [from Latin *fictio*, from *fingere*, to mould]

fictional *adj.* relating to or of the nature of fiction.

fictionally *adv.* in a fictional way.

fictitious *adj.* **1** imagined; invented; not real. **2** of, or occurring in, fiction. [from Latin *ficticius*]

fictitiously *adv.* in a fictitious way.

fiddle — *noun* **1** *colloq.* a violin, especially when used to play folk music or jazz. **2** *colloq.* a dishonest arrangement; a fraud. — *verb* **1** *intrans.* to play about aimlessly; to tinker, toy, or meddle. **2** (**fiddle around** *or* **about**) to waste time. **3** *trans., intrans.* to falsify (accounts, etc); to manage or manipulate dishonestly. **4** *intrans., trans.* to play a violin, etc; to play (a tune) on one. — **as fit as a fiddle** in excellent health. **fiddle while Rome burns** to be preoccupied with trifles in a crisis. **on the fiddle** *colloq.* making money dishonestly. **play second fiddle to someone** to be subordinate to them. [from Anglo-Saxon *fithele*]

fiddler *noun* **1** a person who plays the fiddle. **2** a swindler. **3** a kind of small crab.

fiddlesticks *interj.* nonsense.

fiddling *adj.* unimportant; trifling.

fiddly *adj.* (**fiddlier, fiddliest**) awkward to handle or do, especially if the task requires delicate finger movements.

Fidei Defensor see DEFENDER OF THE FAITH.

fideism *noun* the doctrine that the principles of some area of inquiry cannot be established by reason, but must be accepted by faith.

Fidelio, original title **Leonore** the only opera composed by Ludwig van Beethoven (1805). Set in an 18c prison near Seville, it tells of the undeserved imprisonment of Florestan by Don Pizarro, and of the disguise (as Fidelio) adopted by Florestan's wife Leonore who hopes to rescue him.

fidelity *noun* **1** faithfulness; loyalty. **2** accuracy in reporting, describing, or copying something. **3** precision in sound reproduction. [from Latin *fidelitas*]

fidget — *verb* (**fidgeted, fidgeting**) **1** *intrans.* to move or fiddle restlessly. **2** to cause to feel nervous and uneasy. — *noun* **1** a person who fidgets. **2** (**the fidgets**) nervous restlessness. [from earlier *fidge*, to twitch]

fidgety *adj.* fidgeting, restless.

fiduciary *Legal* — *adj.* held or given in trust. — *noun* (PL. **fiduciaries**) a trustee. [from Latin *fiducia*, trust]

fie *interj. old use* for shame!

fief *noun Hist.* **1** under the feudal system, land granted to a vassal by his lord in return for military service, or on other conditions. **2** one's own area of operation or control. [from Old French *fie*]

field — *noun* **1** an area of land, usually enclosed by a fence, hedge, or ditch, that is used for growing crops, or as pasture for livestock. **2** an area marked off as a ground for a sport, etc. **3** (*in compounds*) **a** an area rich in a particular mineral, etc: *coalfield*. **b** an expanse: *snowfields*. **4** an area of knowledge, interest, or study. **5** the area included in something; the range over which a force, etc extends: *field of vision*. **6** the contestants, or a particular contestant's rivals, in a race, competition, etc. **7** a place of battle: *fell on the field*. **8** *Cricket* the fielding side. **9** the background to the design on a flag, coin, etc. — *verb* **1** *intrans.,*

trans. Cricket **a** to be the team whose turn it is to retrieve balls hit by the batting team. **b** *said of a fielder* to retrieve (the ball). **2** to put forward as (a team or player) for a match. **3** to deal with a succession of (inquiries, etc). — **hold the field** to remain supreme.

lead the field to be in the foremost or winning position.

play the field *colloq.* to try out the range of possibilities before making a choice.

take the field 1 *said of a team* to go on to the pitch ready for a match. **2** to go into battle; to begin a campaign.

field day 1 *Mil.* a day of exercises and manoeuvres. **2** *facetious* an occasion on which one has unusually wide scope for one's activities.

fielder *noun Cricket* a member of the fielding side.

field event *Athletics* a contest involving jumping, throwing, etc, as distinct from a track event. See also TRACK EVENT.

field glasses binoculars.

field gun a light cannon mounted on wheels.

field hockey *North Amer.* ordinary hockey as distinct from ice hockey.

Fielding, Henry (1707–54) English playwright and novelist, born in Sharpham Park, Glastonbury. He initially wrote theatrical comedies, including the burlesque *Tom Thumb* (1830), and became author/manager of the Little Theatre in the Haymarket (1736) until the Licensing Act (1737) closed his theatre. He was called to the Bar (1740), but his primary interests lay in journalism and fiction. His novel *Joseph Andrews* (1742) is in part a parody of Samuel Richardson's *Pamela* (1740), and other major works include *Tom Jones* (1749), which established his reputation as a founder of the English novel, and *Amelia* (1751). He was also made justice of the peace to Westminster (1748), where he helped to form the Bow Street Runners within the police force.

field magnet *Physics* a permanent magnet or electromagnet that provides the magnetic field in an electric machine.

field marshal an army officer of the highest rank.

fieldmouse *noun* a small long-tailed mouse inhabiting fields, woods, etc.

field officer an army officer between the ranks of captain and general.

Field of the Cloth of Gold the ceremonial meeting (Jun 1520) in Picardy between Henry VIII of England and Francis I of France. France was trying (in vain) to woo England away from its alliance with the Emperor Charles V. Its name derived from the pavilions of cloth of gold erected by the French.

Fields, Dame Gracie, stage name of **Grace Stansfield** (1898–1979) English singer and variety star, born in Rochdale, Lancashire. She first appeared on stage at the age of 10, made her London début in 1915, and by 1928 was firmly established in variety, singing her theme tune, 'Sally', for the first time in 1931. With her sentimental songs and broad Lancashire humour, she won a unique place in the affections of British audiences, although from the 1950s she lived mainly in Capri.

Fields, W C, originally **W(illiam) C(laude) Dukenfield** (1879–1946) US actor, born in Philadelphia. He became a vaudeville actor and juggler in the early 1900s, and appeared in the *Ziegfeld Follies* revues. He established his comic persona in silent films such as *Sally of the Sawdust* (1925), and his characteristic gravelly voice later found its full scope in sound films.

field sports the sports of hunting, shooting, and line-fishing.

fieldwork *noun* **1** practical work or research carried out away from the laboratory or place of work. **2** *Mil.* a temporary fortification.

fieldworker *noun* a person who carries out fieldwork; a practical researcher.

fiend *noun* **1** a devil; an evil spirit. **2** *colloq.* a spiteful person. **3** *colloq.* an enthusiast. [from Anglo-Saxon *feond*]

fiendish *adj.* **1** like or of a fiend. **2** devilishly cruel. **3** *colloq.* extremely difficult; most unpleasant.

fiendishly *adv.* in a fiendish way.

Fiennes, Sir Ranulph Twistleton-Wykeham- (1944–) English polar explorer, born in Windsor, Berkshire. He served with the Royal Scots Greys and the SAS, and fought with the Sultan of Oman's armed forces. Between 1979 and 1982 he organized the Transglobe expedition which traced the Greenwich Meridian across both Poles. Since then he has made several attempts to reach the North Pole unsupported, reaching the record 88°58'N in 1990. In 1993 he and Dr Michael Stroud successfully completed the first-ever unsupported crossing of the Antarctic on foot. This involved walking 2 712km/1 350mi in 88 days, dragging sleds of supplies behind them. Fiennes's publications include the autobiography *Living Dangerously* (1987) and *The Feather Men* (1991).

fierce *adj.* **1** violent and aggressive. **2** intense; strong; severe; extreme. [from Old French *fers*, from Latin *ferus*, savage]

fiercely *adv.* in a fierce way.

fierceness *noun* being fierce.

fierily *adv.* in a fiery way; angrily.

fiery *adj.* (**fierier, fieriest**) **1** consisting of fire; like fire. **2** easily enraged. **3** passionate; spirited; vigorous: *fiery oratory*. **4** *said of food* hot-tasting; causing a burning sensation.

fiesta *noun* especially in Spain or Latin America, a religious festival with dancing, singing, etc. [from Spanish *fiesta*, feast]

FIFA *abbrev. Fédération Internationale de Football Association* (French) International Association Football Federation. The world governing body of association football, it was founded in Paris in 1904. It stages its World Cup tournament every four years.

Fife *or* **Kingdom of Fife** POP (1981) 327 000, a Region in E Scotland, divided into three districts. AREA 1 307sq km/505sq mi. It is bounded by the Firth of Tay in the N, the North Sea in the E, the Firth of Forth in the S, and Central region and Tayside in the W. PHYSICAL DESCRIPTION a low-lying region, drained by the Eden and Leven rivers; the Lomond Hills rise in the W; the interior is mainly farmland. CAPITAL Glenrothes. CHIEF TOWNS Dunfermline, Cowdenbeath, Cupar, St Andrews; there are many small fishing ports.

fife *noun* a small type of flute played in military bands. [from Old German *pfifa*, pipe]

FIFO *abbrev.* first in, first out.

fifteen — *noun* **1** the number or figure 15; any symbol for this number. **2** the age of 15. **3** something, especially a garment, or a person, whose size is denoted by the number 15. **4** a set of 15 things or people, eg a Rugby team. **5** *Brit.* a film classified as suitable for people aged 15 and over. — *adj.* **1** 15 in number. **2** aged 15. [from Anglo-Saxon *fiftene*]

Fifteen Rebellion the name given to the first of the Jacobite rebellions (1715) against the Hanoverian monarchy to restore the Catholic Stuart Kings to the British throne. The rising began at Braemar (Sep) where the Earl of Mar proclaimed James Edward Stuart (the 'Old Pretender') king. Jacobite forces were defeated at Preston in November, and the rebellion collapsed early in 1716.

fifteenth *noun, adj.* **1** the position in a series corresponding to 15 in a sequence of numbers. **2** one of 15 equal parts.

fifth *noun, adj.* **1** the position in a series corresponding to 5 in a sequence of numbers. **2** one of five equal parts. **3** *Mus.* an interval of four diatonic degrees; a tone at that interval from another, or a combination of two tones separated by that interval.

Fifth Amendment an amendment (1791) to the US Constitution which protects against self-incrimination. This gained notoriety during the Cold War anti-communist investigations, when 'taking the Fifth' became synonymous with an admission of guilt. It also prohibits the deprivation of 'life, liberty, or property without due process of law', and so before the American Civil War it was used to defend slavery, and afterwards, when this clause was incorporated into the Fourteenth Amendment, it was used as an argument (known as 'substantive due process') against economic regulation.

fifth column a body of citizens prepared to co-operate with an invading enemy.

fifth columnist a person who sympathizes with and will support an enemy.

fifthly *adv.* as fifth in a series.

fifties *pl. noun* **1** the period of time between one's fiftieth and sixtieth birthdays. **2** the range of temperatures between fifty and sixty degrees. **3** the period of time between the fiftieth and sixtieth years of a century.

fiftieth *noun, adj.* **1** the position in a series corresponding to 50 in a sequence of numbers. **2** one of fifty equal parts.

fifty — *noun* (PL. **fifties**) **1** the number or figure 50; any symbol for this number. **2** the age of 50. **3** a set of 50 people or things. — *adj.* **1** 50 in number. **2** aged 50. [from Anglo-Saxon *fiftig*]

fifty-fifty — *adj., said of a chance* equal either way. — *adv., adj.* divided equally between two.

fig *noun* **1** a large shrub or small tree of the genus *Ficus* which has large shiny leaves and bears fleshy receptacles containing hundreds of tiny flowers. It is widely cultivated, especially in the Mediterranean region, for its edible fruit which contains hundreds of tiny seeds. Many species are cultivated as ornamental plants. **2** the green, brown, or purple pear-shaped fleshy fruit of this tree, which may be eaten fresh, but is usually canned or dried after harvesting.
— **not give** *or* **care a fig** *colloq.* not to care in the least
[from Latin *ficus*]

fig. *abbrev.* figure (diagram or illustration).

fight — *verb* (PAST TENSE AND PAST PARTICIPLE **fought**) **1** *trans., intrans.* to attack or engage in combat. **2** (**fight for someone** *or* **something**) to struggle or campaign on their behalf. **3** to oppose vigorously. **4** *intrans.* to quarrel. **5** to take part in or conduct (a battle, campaign, etc). **6** to make (one's way) with a struggle. — *noun* **1** a battle; a physically violent struggle; a quarrel. **2** resistance. **3** the will or strength to resist: *lost all his fight.* **4** a contest. **5** a boxing-match. **6** a campaign or crusade: *the fight for freedom.*
— **fight back** to resist an attacker.
fight something back *or* **down** to try not to show one's emotions, etc.
fighting fit *colloq.* in vigorous health.
fight someone off to repulse an attacker.
fight something off to get rid of or resist an illness.
fight it out to fight over something until one side wins.
fight shy of something to avoid it.
[from Anglo-Saxon *feohtan*, to fight]

fighter *noun* **1** a person who fights; a professional boxer. **2** a person with determination. **3** an aircraft equipped to attack other aircraft.

fighting chance a chance to succeed dependent chiefly on determination.

fighting fish a small freshwater fish, native to Thailand, that feeds on aquatic insects, especially mosquito larvae, and is up to 6cm in length. It is renowned for its aggressive behaviour, and commonly held in captivity for staged fights. Captive breeding has produced a wide variety of colour and form.

fighting fish

Fighting Téméraire, The a painting by J M W Turner (1839, National Gallery, London).

fig leaf 1 a fig-tree leaf, in art the traditional covering for the genitals in representations of nude figures. **2** any device used to cover up something embarrassing.

figment *noun* something imagined or invented. [from Latin *figmentum*]

figurative *adj.* **1** metaphorical, not literal. **2** *said of writing, etc* full of figures of speech, especially metaphor. **3** *said of art* not abstract; showing things as they look; representational; pictorial.

figuratively *adv.* in a figurative way.

figure — *noun* **1** an indistinctly seen or unidentified person. **2** the shape of one's body. **3** a symbol representing a number; a numeral. **4** a number representing an amount; a cost or price. **5** (**figures**) arithmetical calculations; statistics. **6** a well-known person: *a public figure.* **7** the impression that one makes: *cut a poor figure.* **8** a representation of the human form. **9** a diagram or illustration. **10** an image, design, or pattern. **11** a geometrical shape. **12** a set pattern of steps or movements in dancing or skating, or of notes in music. **13** a figure of speech. — *verb* **1** (**figure in something**) to play a part in a story, incident, etc. **2** *North Amer., esp. US* to think; to reckon. **3** to imagine; to envisage. **4** *intrans. colloq.* to be probable or predictable; to make sense: *that figures.* **5** to decorate (a surface) with a design; to add elaborations to (music).
— **figure on something 1** to intend to do something. **2** to make plans that depend on something happening.
figure something out to work it out; to begin to understand it.
keep one's figure to remain slim.
lose one's figure to become overweight.
[from Latin *figura*, from *fingere*, to mould]

figured bass *Mus.* a bass part with numerals added to indicate the harmonies to be played above it. Formerly known as the 'through bass' (from Italian *basso continuo*), the system originated in the early 17c and was used up to the middle of the 18c in accompaniments to one or more voices or instruments.

figurehead *noun* **1** a leader in name only, without real power. **2** *Hist.* a carved wooden figure fixed to a ship's prow.

figure of eight a pattern, movement, etc in the shape of an 8.

figure of fun someone whom others ridicule.

figure of speech any of many devices such as metaphors, similes, etc that enliven language.

figurine *noun* a little statue. [from Italian *figurina*, diminutive of *figura*, figure]

Fiji, official name **Republic of Fiji** POP (1991e) 747 000, a Melanesian island group of 844 islands and islets in the SW Pacific Ocean (c.100 permanently inhabited), forming an independent republic divided into four divisions. AREA 18 333sq km/7 076sq mi (land). It lies 1 770km/ 1 100mi N of Auckland, New Zealand. The two main islands of Viti Levu and Vanua Levu contain c.90% of the population. CAPITAL Suva. CHIEF TOWNS Lautoka, Ba, Labasa, Nadi, Nausori. TIME ZONE GMT +11. The population consists of indigenous Fijians (44%) and Indians (51%); the native Fijians are mainly Christian and the Indo-Fijians are mainly Hindu and Muslim. OFFICIAL LANGUAGE English. CURRENCY the Fijian dollar. PHYSICAL DESCRIPTION the larger islands are generally mountainous and rugged; extensive areas of flat land in the river deltas; there are fertile plains around the coastline; the highest peak, Tomaniivi (Mt Victoria) is on Vita Levu (1 324m); there are hot springs in isolated places; most smaller islands consist of limestone, with little vegetation; there is an extensive coral reef (Great Sea Reef) stretching for 500km/300mi along the W fringe; dense, tropical forest lies on the wet, windward side in the SE; mainly treeless on the dry, leeward side. CLIMATE winds are variable in the wet season between Nov and Apr, with tropical cyclonic storms likely; temperatures average 23–27°C; the annual rainfall varies from 1 900mm to 3 050mm, the higher rainfall falling in the E and SE; humidity on the windward slopes averages 74%. HISTORY visited by Tasman in 1643, and by Cook in 1774; became a British colony in 1874; gained independence within the Commonwealth in 1970; the 1987 election brought to power an Indian-dominated coalition, which led to military coups in May and Sep, and the proclamation of a republic outside the Commonwealth; a civilian government was restored in Dec; a new constitution upholding ethnic Melanesian political power was effected in 1990. GOVERNMENT a bicameral parliament of a nominated Senate of 34 members and an elected House of Representatives of 70 members. ECONOMY primarily agrarian, with sugar cane accounting for over two thirds of export earnings; copra, ginger, vegetables, fruit; livestock; tuna; timber; sugar milling, processing of coconut oil; gold mining; light industry; major tourist area; important air staging post between N America and Oceania.

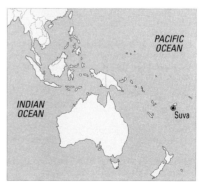

Fiji

filament *noun* **1** a fine thread or fibre. **2** *Electr.* in electrical equipment, a fine wire with a high resistance that emits heat and light when an electric current is passed through it. Filaments are used in light bulbs, heaters in thermionic valves, etc. **3** *Bot.* in a flower, the stalk of a stamen, which bears the anther. **4** *Bot.* a long strand of cells joined end to end, as in certain algae and fungi. **5** *Zool.* any of the long slender barbs of a bird's feather. [from Latin *filum*, thread]

filch *verb* to steal (something small or trivial). [from Middle English *filchen*, to take as booty]

file[1] *noun* a steel tool with a rough surface consisting of fine parallel grooves with sharp cutting edges, used to smooth metal, wood, or plastic items. [from Anglo-Saxon *fil*]

file[2] — *noun* **1** a folder or box in which to keep loose papers. **2** a collection of papers so kept, especially dealing with a particular subject. **3** a body of data stored in a computer under one reference number or name. **4** a line of people or things moving one behind the other: *single file.* — *verb* **1** to put (papers, etc) into a file. **2** *intrans.* to make a formal application to a law court: *file for divorce.* **3** *intrans.* to move along one behind the other. **4** *said of a reporter* to submit (a story) to a newspaper. — **on file** retained in a file for reference; on record. [from Latin *filum*, a thread]

file-server *noun Comput.* a computer which handles files from several computers linked in a network.

filial *adj.* of, or suitable to, a son or daughter. [from Latin *filius*, son, and *filia*, daughter]

filibuster — *noun* **1** the practice of making long speeches to delay the passing of laws. **2** a member of a law-making assembly who uses this practice. — *verb intrans.* (**filibustered, filibustering**) to obstruct legislation in this way. [from Spanish *filibustero*, freebooter]

filigree *noun* delicate work in gold or silver wire, used in jewellery, etc. [from Latin *filum*, thread + *granum*, grain]

filing cabinet a piece of furniture with drawers, etc for holding files.

filings *pl. noun* pieces of wood, metal, etc rubbed off with a file.

Filioque a dogmatic formula expressing the belief that in the operations of God, the Holy Trinity, the Holy Spirit 'proceeds' from the Son as well as from the Father. The term was inserted by the Western Church into the original Nicene-Constantinopolitan Creed, and it was considered a major cause of the breach between the Western (Roman Catholic) and Eastern (Orthodox) Churches in 1054. [Latin, = and from the Son]

fill — *verb* **1** (*also* **fill something up**) to make it full. **2** to take up the space in; to occupy completely. **3** (**be filled with feelings**, *etc*) to be profoundly affected by them. **4** *intrans.* (*also* **fill up**) to become full. **5** to satisfy (a need); to perform (a role) satisfactorily. **6** to occupy (time). **7** to appoint someone to (a position or post). **8** (**fill something in** *or* **up**) to put material into (a hole, cavity, etc) to level the surface. **9** *intrans. said of a sail* to billow out in the wind. — *noun* as much as satisfies one or as one can tolerate: *eat one's fill.* — **fill someone in** *slang* to hit or beat them. **fill something in** to write information as required on a form. **fill someone in on something** to inform them fully about it. **fill in for someone** to take over their work temporarily. **fill out** to become plumper. **fill something out** to enlarge it satisfactorily; to amplify it. **fill something out** *or* **up** to write information as required on a form. **have had one's fill of something** to have had too much of it. [from Anglo-Saxon *fyllan*]

filler *noun* a substance used for filling cracks or holes.

fillet — *noun* **1** a boneless piece of meat or fish. **2** a broad ribbon or headband. **3** *Archit.* a narrow flat band. — *verb* (**filleted, filleting**) to remove the bones from; to divide into fillets. [from Latin *filum*, thread]

filling *noun* **1** a specially prepared substance, such as amalgam, gold, or composite resin, that is inserted into a cavity that has been drilled in a decayed tooth. **2** the process whereby such a material is inserted into a drilled tooth cavity. **3** food put inside a pie, sandwich, etc.

filling-station *noun* a place where one can get petrol for one's car.

fillip *noun* **1** something that has a stimulating or brightening effect; a boost. **2** a flick made with the nail of a finger. [from Middle English *philippe*]

filly *noun* (PL. **fillies**) **1** a young female horse. **2** *old colloq. use* a young girl. [from Norse *fylja*]

film — *noun* **1** a strip of thin flexible plastic or other substance, coated so as to be light-sensitive and exposed inside a camera to produce still or moving pictures. **2** a motion picture for showing in the cinema, or on television or video. **3** (**films** *or* **the films**) the cinema in general. **4** a fine skin or coating. — *verb* **1** *trans., intrans.* to photograph with or operate a cine camera. **2** (**film over**) to become covered with a film. [from Anglo-Saxon *filmen*, membrane]
◇ Originally made of celluloid (cellulose nitrate), film was later made of the less inflammable cellulose triacetate. Motion picture film is used in long rolls, up to 300m, in widths of 16, 35, and 70mm with perforations along each edge for transport and location in the camera and other mechanisms. The amateur movie gauges of 8mm, Super-8, and 9.5mm are obsolescent. Film for still cameras is generally supplied as short rolls in various standard widths, or as cut sheets or film packs.

film festival any national or international gathering for the showing, promotion, and marketing of motion pictures. Among the most important international film festivals are those at Cannes in the S of France, and Montreux in Switzerland.

filminess *noun* being filmy.

filmsetting *noun Printing* typesetting by exposing type on to film which is then transferred by printing plates.

film star a celebrated film actor or actress.

film strip a series of photographs on a strip of film, for separate projection as slides.

filmy *adj.* (**filmier, filmiest**) *said of a fabric* thin, light, and transparent.

FILO *abbrev.* first in, last out.

filo *or* **phyllo** *noun* a type of pastry, originally from Greece, made in thin sheets and layered with oil or butter for cooking. [from Greek *phyllon*, a leaf]

Filofax *noun trademark* a small loose-leaf folder containing a diary and an interchangeable selection of maps, addresses, indexes, etc, designed to be carried in a bag or briefcase.

filoplume *noun Zool.* a small slender hairlike feather. [from Latin *filum*, thread]

filter — *noun* **1** *Chem.* a device consisting of a porous material through which a liquid or gas is passed in order to remove suspended solid particles, eg a funnel containing a cone of filter paper. **2** a plate of glass or other semi-transparent material placed over a camera lens, etc that allows only certain wavelengths of light to pass when it is placed in the path of a beam of radiation. **3** *Electr.* in electronics, a device that only allows signals of certain frequencies to pass. **4** a traffic signal at traffic lights that allows left- or right-turning vehicles to proceed while the main stream is halted. — *verb* **1** *trans., intrans.* to pass through a filter. **2** *intrans.* to pass little by little. **3** *intrans. said of a vehicle* to proceed left or right at a filter. — **filter out** *or* **through** *said of news or information* to leak out. **filter something out** to remove impurities, etc by filtering. [from Latin *filtrum*, felt used as a filter]

filter paper paper used for filtering.

filter tip a filter on the end of a cigarette that traps some of the smoke's impurities before the smoker inhales it.

filter-tipped *adj.* having a filter tip.

filth *noun* **1** repulsive dirt; disgusting rubbish. **2** obscene vulgarity. [from Anglo-Saxon *fylth*]

filthily *adv.* in a filthy way.

filthiness *noun* being filthy.

filthy — *adj.* (**filthier, filthiest**) **1** extremely dirty. **2** obscenely vulgar. — *adv. colloq.* used for emphasis, especially showing disapproval: *filthy rich.*

filthy lucre *derog. or humorous* money, profit.

filtrate — *noun Chem.* the clear liquid obtained after filtration. — *verb* to filter. [from Latin *filtrare*, to filter]

filtration *noun* the act or process of filtering.

fin *noun* **1** in fish, a wing-like projection consisting of a thin fold of skin supported by bone or cartilage, used for propelling the fish through the water, balancing, steering, display, and in some cases protection (eg the spines of the stickleback). **2** any structure of similar shape in other aquatic animals. **3** a fixed or adjustable aerofoil attached to the rear of an aeroplane, that provides increased stability. **4** a thin metal plate protruding from the cylinder of an air-cooled engine, that increases the surface area available for dissipation of heat. **5** a swimmer's flipper. [from Anglo-Saxon *finn*]

final — *adj.* **1** occurring at the end; last. **2** completed; finished. **3** *said of a decision, etc* definite; not to be altered; conclusive. — *noun* **1** the last round of a competition, or (**finals**) a round of deciding heats. **2** (**finals**) the examinations held at the end of a degree course, etc. [from Latin *finis*, end]

finale *noun* the grand conclusion to a show, etc. [from Italian *finale*, from Latin *finis*, end]

finalist *noun* a person who reaches the final round in a competition.

finality *noun* **1** being final. **2** completeness, conclusiveness. **3** something that is final.

finalization *or* **finalisation** *noun* making final; completion.

finalize *or* **finalise** *verb* **1** to decide on, or agree to, finally. **2** to complete; to finish.

finally *adv.* **1** lastly. **2** at last. **3** to conclude.

finance — *noun* (with stress on *fin-*, pronounced *fine-*) **1** money affairs; their study or management. **2** the money needed or used to pay for something. **3** (**finances**) a person's financial resources. — *verb* (with stress on *-nance*) to provide funds for. [from Old French *finer*, to settle]

financial *adj.* relating to finance.

financially *adv.* in a financial way; as regards finance.

financial year the 12-month period, in Britain starting 6 Apr, used in accounting, annual taxation, etc.

financier *noun* **1** a person engaged in large financial transactions. **2** someone who finances an operation. [from French *financier*]

finch *noun* any of several small usually colourful birds with short stout conical beaks adapted for cracking seeds, distributed worldwide, eg sparrow, crossbill, canary, chaffinch, goldfinch, bullfinch, linnet, bunting. [from Anglo-Saxon *finc*]

find — *verb* (PAST TENSE AND PAST PARTICIPLE **found**) **1** to discover through search, enquiry, mental effort, or chance. **2** to seek out and provide: *I'll find you a plumber.* **3** to realize or discover. **4** to experience as being: *find it hard to express oneself.* **5** to get or experience: *find pleasure in reading.* **6** to consider; to think. **7** to become aware of: *found her beside him.* **8** to succeed in get-

ting (time, courage, money, etc) for something. **9** to see or come across: *a bird found only in Madagascar.* **10** to reach: *find one's best form.* **11** *trans., intrans. Legal* (**find for** or **against someone**) *said of a jury* to give a verdict in favour or not in favour of the accused. — *noun* something or someone found; an important discovery. — **all found** with food and housing provided.
find it in oneself or **in one's heart** to be prepared (to do something hurtful, etc).
find oneself to find the role, etc that satisfies one.
find oneself doing something to discover or realize that one is doing it: *found themselves agreeing.*
find one's feet to establish oneself in a new situation.
find out about something to discover or get information about it.
find someone out to detect them in wrongdoing; to discover the truth about them.
[from Anglo-Saxon *findan*]

finder *noun* **1** a person or thing that finds. **2** a small telescope attached to a larger one, or a lens attached to a camera to help in positioning the apparatus.

finding *noun* (*usually* **findings**) a conclusion reached as a result of an investigation, etc.

fine¹ — *adj.* **1** of high quality; excellent; splendid. **2** beautiful; handsome. **3** *facetious* grand; superior: *her fine relations.* **4** *said of weather* bright; not rainy. **5** well; healthy. **6** quite satisfactory. **7** pure; refined. **8** thin; delicate. **9** close-set in texture or arrangement. **10** consisting of tiny particles. **11** intricately detailed: *fine embroidery.* **12** slight; subtle: *fine adjustments.* — *adv.* **1** *colloq.* satisfactorily. **2** finely; into fine pieces.
— **cut** or **run it fine** *colloq.* to leave barely enough time for something.
fine something down to make an activity, operation, etc more effective or efficient by cutting out inessentials.
get something down to a fine art to find the most efficient way of doing it.
not to put too fine a point on it to speak honestly or bluntly.
[from Old French *fin*]

fine² — *noun* an amount of money to be paid as a penalty. — *verb* to exact a fine from.
— **in fine** in total; to sum up.
[from Old French *fin*]

fine arts painting, drawing, sculpture, and architecture, the arts that appeal to the sense of beauty.

Fine Gael an Irish political party created out of the pro-Anglo-Irish Treaty (1921) wing of Sinn Féin, known as *Cummann na nGaedheal* from 1923 until it changed its name in 1933. The first government of the Irish Free State, it supports an Irish confederation and has mainly been in opposition since the 1930s.

finely *adv.* in a fine way; delicately or sensitively.

fineness *noun* **1** being fine. **2** *said of measuring gold or silver* the number of parts in a thousand.

finery *noun* splendid clothes, jewellery, etc.

fines herbes a mixture of herbs for use in cooking. [French, = fine herbs]

finespun *adj.* delicate; over-subtle.

finesse *noun* **1** skilful elegance or expertise. **2** tact and poise in handling situations. **3** *Cards* an attempt by a player holding a high card to win a trick with a lower one. [from Old French *finesse*, *fineness*]

fine-tooth comb a comb with narrow close-set teeth.
— **go over something with a fine-tooth comb** to search or examine it exhaustively.
◆ Often respelled as *fine toothcomb*.

fine-tune *verb* to make slight adjustments to (a machine, etc) to make it work perfectly.

Fingal's Cave a cave situated on the coast of Staffa in the Inner Hebrides, Scotland. The cavern is 69m deep and of volcanic origin, formed from hexagonal pillars of basalt. It is celebrated in Mendelssohn's *Hebrides* overture.

finger — *noun* **1** one of the five jointed extremities of the hand; any of the four of these other than the thumb. **2** the part of a glove that fits over a finger. **3** anything similar to a finger in shape. **4** a measure of alcoholic spirits in a glass, equal to the breadth of a finger. — *verb* **1** to touch or feel with the fingers. **2** to play (a musical instrument) with the fingers. **3** *slang* to identify (a criminal) to the police, etc.
— **be all fingers and thumbs** *colloq.* to be clumsy in handling or holding things.
keep one's fingers crossed to hope (sometimes indicated by crossing the middle finger over the index finger).
get one's fingers burnt *colloq.* to suffer for one's over-boldness or mistakes.
have a finger in every pie *colloq.* to have an interest, or be involved, in everything.
not lay a finger on someone *colloq.* not to touch or harm them.
not lift a finger *colloq.* to make no effort.
point the finger *colloq.* to blame or accuse someone.
pull or **get one's finger out** *slang* to make an effort to work effectively.
put one's finger on something *colloq.* to identify a point, difficulty, etc.
put the finger on someone *slang* to identify a criminal, etc to the police.
slip through someone's fingers to manage to escape from them.
twist someone round one's little finger *colloq.* to be able to get what one wants from them.
[from Anglo-Saxon *finger*]

fingerboard *noun* the part of a violin, guitar, etc against which the strings are pressed by the fingers to change the note.

fingerbowl *noun* a small bowl of water for cleaning one's fingers at table.

fingering *noun* the correct positioning of the fingers for playing a particular musical instrument or piece of music.

Finger Lakes a group of long, narrow, finger-like lakes in W New York State, USA. It includes (W–E) Lakes Canandaigua, Keuka, Seneca, Cayuga, Owasco, and Skaneateles.

fingermark *noun* a mark left on a surface by a finger.

fingernail *noun* the nail at the tip of one's finger.

fingerprint — *noun* **1** a mark, unique to the individual, left on a surface by a fingertip, useful as a means of identification. **2** a unique identifying feature or characteristic. — *verb* to make a record of the fingerprints of.

fingerstall *noun* a sheath for an injured finger.

fingertip *noun* the tip of one's finger.
— **have something at one's fingertips** to know a subject thoroughly.
to one's fingertips absolutely; in all ways.

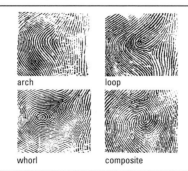

arch | loop
whorl | composite

fingerprints

finial *noun Archit.* a decorative feature on the top of a gable, spire, or pillar, often in the form of a spike or carved foliage. [from Latin *finis*, end]

finicky *adj.* **1** too concerned with detail. **2** *said of a task* intricate; tricky. **3** fussy; faddy. [from *finical*, over-precise]

finish — *verb* (*often* **finish off** or **up**) **1** *trans., intrans.* to bring or come to an end; to stop. **2** to complete or perfect. **3** to use, eat, drink, etc the last of. **4** *intrans.* (*often* **finish up**) to reach or end up in a certain position or situation. **5** (**finish something** or **someone off**) *colloq.* to exhaust them; to defeat or kill them. **6** *intrans.* (**finish with** *someone*) to end a relationship; to stop dealing with or needing. **7** to give a particular treatment to the surface of (cloth, wood, etc). — *noun* **1** the last stage; the end. **2** the last part of a race, etc. **3** perfecting touches put to a product. **4** the surface texture given to cloth, wood, etc.
— **fight to the finish** to fight till one party is dead or too severely disabled to continue.
[from Old French *finir*]

finished *adj.* **1** *colloq.* no longer useful, productive, creative, wanted, or popular. **2** *said of a performer* accomplished. **3** (**finished with something** or **someone**) having reached the end of one's need for or interest in them.

finisher *noun* **1** a person or thing that finishes. **2** a person or thing that perfects or completes something.

finishing *noun* any of the final processes in the manufacture of a fibre, fabric, or garment.

finishing-school *noun* a private school where girls are taught social skills and graces.

Finisterre, Cape a cape at La Coruña, NW Spain, and the westernmost point on the Spanish mainland. It was the scene of a British naval victory over the French in 1747.

finite *adj.* **1** having an end or limit. **2** *Grammar, said of a verb* being of a form that reflects person, number, tense, etc, as distinct from being an infinitive or participle. [from Latin *finire*, to finish]

Finland, Finnish **Suomi**, official name **Republic of Finland**, Finnish **Suomen Tasavalta**, Swedish **Republiken Finland** POP (1992e) 5.1m, a republic in N Europe, divided into 12 provinces (*lääni*). AREA 338 145sq km/ 130 524sq mi. It is bounded E by the Russian Federation, S by the Gulf of Finland, W by the Gulf of Bothnia and Sweden, and N by Norway. CAPITAL Helsinki. CHIEF TOWNS Tampere, Turku, Espoo, Vantaa. TIME ZONE GMT +2. The population consists mainly of Finns, with Swedish, Lapp, and Russian minorities; there has been slow population growth since 1950, with large numbers emigrating to Sweden. The Lutheran church is adhered to by 90% of the population. OFFICIAL LANGUAGES Finnish (94%), Swedish (6%). CURRENCY the markka. PHYSICAL DESCRIPTION a low-lying glaciated plateau, with an average height of 150m; highest peak is Haltiatunturi (1 328m) on the NW border; there are over 60 000 shallow lakes in the SE, providing a system of inland navigation; with land still rising from the sea, the area is increasing by 7sq km/2.7sq mi each year; over one third of the country lies N of the Arctic Circle; chief rivers are the Tornio, Kemi, and Oulu; the archipelago of Saaristomeri is in the SW, with over 17 000 islands and skerries; the Ahvenanmaa islands are in the W; forest land covers 65% of the country, and water 10%. CLIMATE the country's N location is ameliorated by the Baltic Sea; W winds bring warm air currents in summer; Eurasian winds bring cold spells in winter and heatwaves in summer; annual precipitation in the S is 600–700mm, and 500–600mm in the N, with half of it falling as snow; during summer the sun stays above the horizon for over 70 days. HISTORY ruled by Sweden from 1157 until its cession to Russia in

1809; became an autonomous Grand Duchy of the Russian tsar in the 19c, and a nationalist movement developed; an independent republic from 1917; its parliamentary system was created in 1928; invaded by Soviets in 1939 and 1940, lost territory to the USSR after 1944. GOVERNMENT governed by a single-chamber House of Representatives (*Eduskunta*) of 200 elected members, serving a 4-year term, and a President elected for 6 years, assisted by a Council of State. ECONOMY a traditional focus on forestry (mainly pine, spruce, and birch; paper is the chief timber product) and farming; agriculture yields hay, barley, oats, spring and autumn wheat, rye, sugar beet, potatoes, and spring oil-yielding plants; rapid economic growth since the 1950s, and a diversification of exports, such as metals, engineering, clothing, chemicals, and food processing; copper and iron ore mining; wide use of hydroelectric power; tourism.

Finland

Finland, Gulf of the E arm of the Baltic Sea, bounded N by Finland, and S and E by Estonia and Russia. It is c.4 600km/2 900mi long and 16–120km/10–75mi wide. Its shallowness and low salt-levels result in ice cover from Dec to Mar. The main ports include Helsinki, Kotka, Vyborg, St Petersburg, and Tallinn.

Finlandia a symphonic poem by Jean Sibelius (Op 26, 1899). Its similarities to Finnish folk-song have led to its performance at national events.

Finlay a male first name, after the surname. [from Gaelic *Fionnlagh*, fair warrior]

Finn, Huckleberry see HUCKLEBERRY FINN, THE ADVENTURES OF.

Finn, Phineas the young Irish barrister who appears in several of Anthony Trollope's 'Palliser' novels, most notably *Phineas Finn* and *Phineas Redux*.

Finn a male first name, largely confined to Ireland. [from Gaelic *fionn*, white, fair]

Finn *noun* a native or citizen of Finland. [from Anglo-Saxon *Finnas*, Finns]

finnan *noun* haddock cured in the smoke from peat, turf, or green wood. [probably from *Findon*, Kincardineshire]

Finnegans Wake a novel by James Joyce (1939). His last, it describes the dreams of Humphrey Chimpden Earwicker and his family during one night. It is an opaque narrative which experiments with language and style, including that of 'stream of consciousness'.

Finnish — *adj.* **1** of Finland or its inhabitants. **2** of the language spoken in Finland. — *noun* **1** the language spoken in Finland. **2** (**the Finnish**) the people of Finland. See also FINN. ◇ Finnish is spoken by about five million people in Finland, Sweden, and neighbouring parts of Russia. It belongs to the Finno-Ugric branch of the Uralic family of languages.

Finn MacCool a legendary Irish hero, the son of Cumhall and father of Ossian (Oisin). He avenged his father's murder and became leader of the troops known as the Fianna.

Finsen, Niels Ryberg (1860–1904) Danish physician and scientist, born in the Faroe Islands. Teacher of anatomy at the University of Copenhagen, he investigated the therapeutic uses of light, discovering the healing effects of infrared and ultraviolet light for certain conditions. This work was carried out despite a chronic illness; he died soon after being awarded the 1903 Nobel Prize for Physiology or Medicine.

Fiona a female first name, used initially as the pen-name of Scottish poet William Sharp (1855–1905) and now popular outside Scotland. [a Latinate derivative of Gaelic *fionn*, white, fair]

fiord same as FJORD.

fipple *noun* the piece of wood, etc that plugs the mouthpiece of a recorder or other similar wind instrument.

fir *noun* a tall evergreen tree of the pine family, with cones and thin needle-like leaves. [from Anglo-Saxon *fyrh*]

Firdausi or **Ferd(a)usi**, pseudonym **Abú Al-Qásim Mansúr** (940–c.1020) Persian poet, born near Tús, Khorassan. His major work is the epic poem *Shah Náma* (The Book of Kings, 1010), based on actual events from the annals of Persia.

fire — *noun* **1** flames coming from something that is burning. **2** an occurrence of destructive burning: *a warehouse fire*. **3** a pile of burning wood, coal, or other fuel, used for warmth or cooking. **4** a gas or electric room-heater. **5** shooting from guns. **6** heat and light produced by something burning or some other source. **7** enthusiasm; passion; ardour. **8** fever; a burning sensation. **9** sparkle; brilliance (eg of a gem). — *verb* **1** *trans., intrans.* (**fire at**, **fire on**) to shoot (a gun); to send off (a bullet or other missile) from a gun, catapult, bow, etc. **2** to launch (a rocket). **3** to detonate (an explosive). **4** to direct (eg questions) in quick succession at someone. **5** *colloq.* to dismiss from employment. **6** *trans., intrans.* to start or cause to start burning. **7** *trans., intrans.* to glow or cause to glow. **8** *intrans. said of a vehicle engine* to start working when a spark causes the fuel to burn. **9** to put fuel into (a furnace, etc). **10** to inspire or stimulate. **11** to bake (pottery or bricks) in a kiln.
— **catch fire** to begin to burn.
cease fire to stop fighting.
draw someone's fire to deliberately divert someone's gunfire, criticism, etc towards oneself.
fire away *colloq.* to say or ask what one wants to.
fire and brimstone the supposed condition or torment of hell; eternal damnation.
go through fire and water for someone or something to suffer or undergo danger for their sake.
hold one's fire to stop shooting.
in the line of fire between the guns and the target, and therefore in danger of attack.
on fire 1 burning. **2** filled with enthusiasm, love, etc.
open fire on someone or **something** to begin shooting at them.
play with fire *colloq.* to take risks; to act recklessly.
pull something out of the fire to rescue the situation at the last minute.
return someone's fire to shoot back at them.
set fire to something or **set something on fire** to cause it to begin burning.
set someone on fire to fill them with enthusiasm, love, etc.
under fire 1 being shot at. **2** being criticized or blamed.
[from Anglo-Saxon *fȳr*]

fire alarm a bell or other device activated to warn people of fire.

fire and brimstone see FIRE.

firearm *noun* a gun, pistol, revolver, or rifle.

fireball *noun* **1** a mass of hot gases at the centre of a nuclear explosion. **2** *colloq.* a lively person. **3** a ball-shaped flash of lightning. **4** a brilliant meteor.

Firebird, The a ballet by Igor Stravinsky (1910), based on Russian fairy-tales and commissioned by Sergei Diaghilev's Ballet Russes. From it Stravinsky wrote suites of five movements (1911) and ten movements (1945).

fire-bomb *noun* an incendiary bomb.

firebrand *noun* **1** a piece of burning wood. **2** someone who stirs up unrest; a troublemaker.

firebreak *noun* a cleared strip in a forest to stop the spread of a fire.

firebrick *noun* a heat-resistant brick used in furnaces, fireplaces, etc.

fire brigade a team of people trained to prevent and extinguish fires.

firebug *noun colloq.* a person who deliberately sets fire to buildings, etc.

fireclay *noun Chem.* clay that contains large amounts of alumina and silica and can withstand high temperatures. It is used for making fire-resistant pottery, firebricks, and refractory materials for lining furnaces.

firecracker *noun* a small firework that bangs repeatedly.

-fired *combining form* fuelled by: *gas-fired central heating.*

firedamp *noun* an explosive mixture of the gas methane and air, found in coalmines.

firedog *noun* an andiron.

fire drill the routine to be followed in case of fire, or a practice of this routine.

fire-eater *noun* **1** a performer who pretends to swallow fire from flaming torches. **2** an aggressive or quarrelsome person.

fire engine a vehicle carrying fire-fighting equipment.

fire escape an external metal staircase or other device by which people can escape from a burning building.

fire-extinguisher *noun* a portable device containing water, liquid carbon dioxide under pressure, foam, etc, for spraying on to a fire in order to put it out, either by cooling it or by excluding oxygen, eg by covering the fire with a thick layer of carbon dioxide gas.

fire-fighter *noun* a fireman or other person who puts out large fires.

fire-fighting *noun* the act, process, or occupation of fighting fire.

firefly *noun* any of a number of species of small winged beetles, found mainly in tropical regions, that emit light in a series of brief flashes, the pattern of flashes being unique to a particular species, so that males and females can recognize and respond to their own kind.

fireguard *noun* a protective metal or wire-mesh screen for putting round an open fire.

fire hydrant same as HYDRANT.

fire irons a set of tools for looking after a household fire, including a poker, tongs, brush and shovel.

firelighter *noun* a block of flammable material used to help light a fire.

fireman *noun* a male member of a fire brigade.

Fire of London a devastating fire which started in a baker's shop in Pudding Lane (2 Sep 1666). It engulfed c.160ha (four fifths of the city) and destroyed 13 000 houses, 89 parish churches, and most public buildings, but no more than 20 people died. The rebuilding of the capital included new churches such as Christopher Wren's St Paul's.

fireplace *noun* a recess for a fire in a room, with a chimney above it; a hearth, grate, or the structure surrounding it.

fire-power *noun Mil.* the destructive capacity of an artillery unit.

fireproof — *adj.* resistant to fire and fierce heat. — *verb* to make fireproof.

fire-raiser *noun* an arsonist.

fire-raising *noun* arson.

fireside *noun* the area round a fireplace, especially as a symbol of home.

fire station a fire brigade's headquarters, housing its fire engines, etc.

Firestone, Harvey Samuel (1868–1938) US industrialist, born in Columbiana, Ohio. He founded the Firestone Tire and Rubber Company in 1900 in Akron, Ohio. It grew to be a major US industrial corporation. He pioneered the pneumatic tyre for the Ford Model T, non-skid treads, and tyres for farm tractors and motor trucks. He also started rubber plantations in Liberia in 1924.

firetrap *noun* **1** a building without adequate escape routes in case of fire. **2** a building likely to burn easily.

firewater *noun colloq.* alcoholic spirit.

firewood *noun* wood for burning as fuel.

firework *noun* **1** a device containing combustible chemicals, designed to produce spectacular coloured sparks, flares, etc, often with accompanying loud bangs, when ignited. **2** (**fireworks**) a show at which such devices are let off for entertainment. **3** (**fireworks**) *colloq.* a show of anger or bad temper.

Fireworks Music see MUSIC FOR THE ROYAL FIREWORKS.

firing line the front line of battle. — **in the firing line** in a prominent position, liable to get shot at or criticized.

firing squad a detachment of soldiers with the job of shooting a condemned person.

firm[1] — *adj.* **1** strong; steady. **2** solid; not soft or yielding. **3** definite: *a firm offer.* **4** determined; resolute. **5** *said of a mouth or chin* suggesting determination. — *adv.* firmly: *hold firm to one's promise.* — *verb* to make firm or secure. — **firm up** to become firm or firmer. **firm something up** to make it firmer or more definite: *can we firm up the plans for your visit?* [from Latin *firmus*]

firm[2] *noun* a business company. [from Spanish *firma*, signature]

firmament *noun old literary use* the sky. [from Latin *firmamentum*]

firmly *adv.* in a firm way.

firmness *noun* being firm.

firmware *noun Comput.* software permanently held in a computer's read-only memory, eg the operating system, a particular programming language or word-processor.

first — *adj.* **1** earliest in time or order. **2** foremost in importance: *first prize.* **3** basic: *first principles.* **4** *Mus.* having the higher part. **5** denoting the lowest forward gear in a motor vehicle. — *adv.* **1** before anything or anyone else. **2** foremost: *got in feet first.* **3** before doing anything else: *first make sure of the facts.* **4** for the first time: *since I first saw her.* **5** rather; preferably: *I'd die first.* — *noun* **1** a first person or thing. **2** a first occurrence of something; something never done before. **3** first-class honours in a university degree. **4** the beginning: *from first to last.* — **at first** at the beginning. **at first hand** directly from the original source. **be the first to do something** to be most willing to do it. **first and last** essentially. **first thing** *colloq.* early; before anything else. **in the first place** firstly. **not have the first idea** *or* **know the first thing about something** *colloq.* to be completely ignorant about it.

[from Anglo-Saxon *fyrest*]

first aid immediate emergency treatment given to an injured or ill person.

first-born — *noun* the eldest child in a family. — *adj.* eldest.

first class **1** the highest grade, eg of travelling accommodation, of academic performance, etc. **2** the category of mail most speedily delivered.

first-class — *adj.* **1** of the first class. **2** excellent. — *adv.* by first-class mail or transport.

first cousin see COUSIN.

first-day cover a stamped envelope postmarked with the stamp's date of issue.

first-degree *adj.* **1** *Medicine* denoting the least serious of the three degrees of burning, with reddening of the skin. **2** *North Amer. Legal* denoting the most serious of the three levels of murder.

first floor **1** the floor above the ground floor. **2** *North Amer.* the ground floor.

first foot the first person to enter one's house in the new year.

first-foot *verb trans., intrans.* to visit as first foot.

first fruits **1** the first produce of the season. **2** the first results or proceeds from an enterprise.

first-generation *adj.* denoting the first or earliest stage in technological development: *a first-generation missile.*

first-hand *adj.* direct; from the original source.

First Lady *North Amer., esp. US* the wife of the American President.

first light dawn.

firstly *adv.* first; in the first place; to begin with.

first name one's personal name as distinct from one's family name or surname. — **be on first-name terms** to be friendly enough to address one another by first names.

first night the first public performance of a play, etc.

first offender a person found guilty for the first time of a crime.

first officer *or* **first mate** the officer second in command on a merchant ship.

first-past-the-post *adj.* of an election system in which voters have one vote only and whoever gets most votes wins.

first person see PERSON.

first-rate *adj.* **1** of the highest quality. **2** splendid; fine.

first school a primary school.

first-strike capability *Mil.* the capability of a state to launch an initial nuclear attack with long-range missiles or aircraft.

First World the richest and technologically most developed countries of the world.

firth *noun* especially in Scotland, a river estuary or an inlet. [from Norse *fjörthr*]

FIS *abbrev.* Family Income Supplement.

fiscal — *adj.* **1** relating to government finances or revenue. **2** relating to financial matters generally. — *noun Scot.* the procurator fiscal. [from Latin *fiscus*, purse, state treasury]

fiscal drag *Econ.* the effect of inflation on tax revenues. If tax allowances are not kept in line with inflation, individuals pay relatively higher amounts of tax, thereby effectively reducing net incomes; this in turn reduces demand for goods and services.

fiscally *adv.* in a fiscal way.

Fischer, Bobby (Robert James) (1943–) US chess player, born in Chicago. He was world champion from 1972–5, taking the title from Boris Spassky in a much-publicized match. He resigned his title shortly before a defence against Anatoly Karpov in 1975. In Sep 1992 he began a chess match in Montenegro with Boris Spassky, and completed his 10-5 victory over him in Nov 1992, in Belgrade.

Fischer, Emil Hermann (1852–1919) German chemist, born in Euskirchen, Prussia. Professor in Erlangen, Würzburg, and Berlin, he made important studies of the chemistry of sugars and their structures. He was awarded the 1902 Nobel Prize for Chemistry, and also made significant discoveries concerning the structures of caffeine, organic dyes, and related compounds.

Fischer, Hans (1881–1945) German chemist, born in Frankfurt. Appointed Professor of Medical Chemistry at Innsbruck (1916) and then Professor of Organic Chemistry at Munich (1921), his most important researches concerned the structure of the naturally occurring pigments haemin and chlorophyll. For the synthesis of haemin he was awarded the 1930 Nobel Prize for Chemistry.

Fischer-Dieskau, Dietrich (1925–) German baritone, born in Berlin. He studied under Georg Walter and Hermann Weissenborn, and soon after making his professional début at Freiburg in 1947 joined the Berlin Municipal Opera as a principal baritone. He soon became one of the foremost interpreters of German lieder, particularly the song-cycles of Schubert.

Fischer von Erlach, Johann Bernard (1656–1723) Austrian architect, born in Graz. He studied in Rome under Gian Lorenzo Bernini, then moved to Vienna, where he became the court architect (1687), and a leading exponent of the Baroque style. He designed many churches and palaces, notably the Karlskirche at Vienna, and the University Church at Salzburg. He also wrote a major work on architectural history (1721).

fish — *noun* (**fish**, **fishes**) **1** any cold-blooded aquatic vertebrate that has no legs, and typically possesses paired fins, breathes by means of gills, and has a bony or cartilaginous skeleton and a body covered with scales. **2** (in compounds) any of various water-inhabiting creatures: *shellfish / jellyfish.* **3** the flesh of fish as food. **4** *derog. colloq.* a person: *an odd fish.* — *verb* **1** *intrans.* to try to catch (fish). **2** to try to catch fish in (a river, etc). **3** *intrans.* to search or grope: *fished in her bag for a pen.* **4** (*also* **fish something out**) to retrieve. **5** *intrans.* (**fish for something**) to seek information, compliments etc by indirect means. — **drink like a fish** *colloq.* to be in the habit of drinking a lot of alcohol. **have other fish to fry** *colloq.* to have other, more important, things to do. **like a fish out of water** *colloq.* ill at ease in uncongenial company or surroundings. [from Anglo-Saxon *fisc*]

◇ Fishes are sometimes referred to collectively as the group Pisces, and are usually divided into three classes. The Agnatha consist of primitive

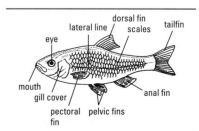

external features of a typical fish

Classification of Fishes

Order	Common name	No. of species	Order	Common name	No. of species
Class Agnatha: jawless fishes			Clenothrissiformes	macristid fish	1
Cyclostomata	lampreys and hagfishes	45	Gonorhynchiformes	milk fish	15
			Cypriniformes	carp and relatives	3 500
			Siluriformes	catfishes	2 500
Class Chondrichthyes: fishes with a cartilage skeleton			Percopsiformes	pirate perch	10
			Batrachoidiformes	toadfishes	45
Lamniformes	sharks	200	Gobiesociformes	clingfishes	100
Rajiformes	rays and skates	350	Lophiiformes	angler fishes	200
Chimaeriformes	chimaeras	25	Gadiformes	cod and relatives	800
			Beryciformes	whalefishes, squirrelfishes	150
Class Sarcopterygii: fishes with fleshy fins			Atheriniformes	flying fishes, killifishes	600
Crossopterygii	coelacanth	1	Zeiformes	John Dory	60
Dipnoi	lungfishes	5	Lampridiformes	ribbonfish	50
			Gasterostei- formes	seahorses and relatives	150
Class Actinopterygii: fishes with ray fins			Channiformes	snakeheads	5
Polypteriformes	bichirs	12	Synbranchi- formes	swamp eels and cuchias	7
Acipenseriformes	sturgeons	22	Scorpaeniformes	gurnards and relatives	700
Amiiformes	bowfin	1			
Semionotiformes	garpikes	7	Dactylopteri- formes	flying gurnards	6
Elopiformes	tarpons	12			
Anguilliformes	eels	500	Pegasiformes	sea moths, dragonfishes	4
Notacanthiformes	spiny eels	20			
Clupeiformes	herring and relatives	400	Tetraodonti- formes	triggerfishes, puffer fishes	320
Osteoglossiformes	bony tongues	16			
Mormyriformes	mormyrids	150	Pleuronectiformes	flatfishes	500
Salmoniformes	salmon, trout	1 000	Perciformes	perch and relatives	6 500
Myctophiformes	lantern fish	300			

jawless fishes, the only living representatives of which are the hagfish and lampreys. The Elasmobranchii (also called Chondrichthyes) consist of fishes with a cartilaginous skeleton, eg sharks, skates, rays. The Osteichthyes, consisting of fishes with a bony skeleton, eg cod, goldfish, is by far the largest group, with representatives in marine, estuarine, and freshwater habitats from the tropics to polar latitudes.

Fish vary widely in body shape, size, and coloration. Several species have well-developed electric organs that are used for navigation, as defence against predators, or for stunning prey. A few species are capable of breathing air, and can survive out of water on coastal mudflats. Many fish are of immense importance as a source of food.

Fishbourne a Roman palace near Chichester (*Noviomagus Regnorum*), Sussex, S England, discovered in 1960. It was erected in the AD 60s for the British client-king Cogidubnus, a noted Roman collaborator, and continued in use into the 4c.

fishcake *noun* a breadcrumb-coated flat round cake of cooked fish and potato.

Fisher, St John, also called **John of Rochester** (1469–1535) English prelate and humanist, born in Beverley, Yorkshire. He became Professor of Divinity at Cambridge (1503), zealously advocated Church reform, and resisted the Lutheran schism. In 1527 he pronounced against the divorce of Henry VIII, and on his refusal of the oath of succession was sent with Thomas More to the Tower. In 1535 Pope Paul III made him a cardinal, but soon after he was beheaded. He was canonized in 1935 and his feast day is 22 Jun.

Fisher, Sir Ronald Aylmer (1890–1962) English statistician and geneticist, born in London. A statistician at the Rothamsted Agricultural Research Institute, he developed techniques for the design and analysis of experiments which have become standard in medical and biological research. He also worked on genetics and evolution, and became Professor of

Eugenics at University College London (1933–43) and Professor of Genetics at Cambridge (1943–57).

Fisher (of Kilverstone), John Arbuthnot Fisher, 1st Baron (1841–1920) British admiral of the fleet, born in Ceylon. He joined the navy as a boy in 1854, and rose to be First Sea Lord (1904–10, 1914–15). His major reforms of the Royal Navy prepared the country for World War I and included the introduction of the 'Dreadnought' battleship and 'Invincible' cruiser.

Fisher (of Lambeth), Geoffrey (Francis) Fisher, Baron (1887–1972) English prelate and Archbishop of Canterbury, born in Higham-on-the-Hill, Warwickshire. Ordained in 1912, he was headmaster of Repton School (1914–32). His first ecclesiastical appointment was as Bishop of Chester (1932), then he became Bishop of London (1939). As Archbishop (1945–61), he crowned Elizabeth II in Westminster Abbey (1953).

fisher *noun* **1** *old use* a fisherman. **2** an animal that catches fish.

fisherman *noun* a person who fishes as a job or hobby.

fishery *noun* (PL. **fisheries**) **1** an area of sea where fishing takes place. **2** the business of catching fish.

fish-eye lens a convex camera lens giving a scope of nearly 180°.

fish finger an oblong, breadcrumb-coated piece of fish.

Fishguard, Welsh **Abergwaun** POP (1981) 4 800, a seaport in Preseli district, Dyfed, SW Wales. It lies on Fishguard Bay, 20km/12mi N of Haverfordwest. NOTABLE FEATURE Lower Fishguard fishing village.

fish hook a hook with barbs for gripping the jaw of a fish taking the bait.

fishing *noun* the sport or business of catching fish.

fishing-line *noun* a strong nylon, etc line with a fish hook.

fishing-rod *noun* a long flexible rod to which a fishing-line is attached.

fishmonger *noun* a dealer in fish.

fishnet *adj.* having an open mesh like netting.

fish slice a kitchen tool with a flat slotted head, for lifting and turning food in a frying-pan, etc.

fishwife *noun* a woman who guts or sells fish, in tradition typically loud-voiced and coarse-mannered.

fishy *adj.* (**fishier, fishiest**) **1** of or like a fish. **2** *colloq.* odd; suspicious.

fissile *adj.* capable of being split by nuclear fission. [from Latin *fissilis*, that can be split]

fission *noun* **1** a splitting or division. **2** *Biol.* the division of a cell during reproduction. **3** (*also* **nuclear fission**) the splitting of the nucleus of an atom, with a release of energy. [from Latin *fissio*, splitting]

fissionable *adj.* capable of nuclear fission.

fissure *noun* a crack, especially in rock. [from Latin *fissura*, split]

fist *noun* **1** a clenched hand. **2** *colloq.* a hand. **3** *colloq.* a person's handwriting. [from Anglo-Saxon *fyst*]

fistful *noun* (PL. **fistfuls**) an amount that can be held in a closed hand.

fisticuffs *pl. noun humorous* fighting with fists. [from *fisty*, of the fist + CUFF²]

fistula *noun Pathol.* an abnormal connection between two internal organs or body cavities, or between an internal organ or body cavity and the exterior, usually caused by infection or injury. Fistulas sometimes develop as a complication after surgery. [from Latin *fistula*, tube, ulcer]

fit¹ — *verb* (**fitted, fitting**) **1** *trans., intrans.* to be, or be made, the right shape or size for something. **2** *intrans.* (**fit in** *or* **into something**) to be small or few enough to be contained in it. **3** to be suitable or appropriate for: *a punishment that fits the crime.* **4** *trans., intrans.* to be consistent or compatible with something: *a theory that fits the facts.* **5** (**fit together** *or* **in**, *etc*) to insert or place in position. **6** to fix or install. **7** to equip. **8** (**fit someone for something**) to make them suitable: *qualities that fit her for the job.* **9** to try clothes on (someone) to see where adjustment is needed. — *noun* the way something fits: *a good fit.* — *adj.* (**fitter, fittest**) **1** (**fit for something**) suited to it; good enough for it. **2** healthy, especially because of exercise; healthy enough. **3** about to do something, or apparently so: *looked fit to drop.* — *adv.* enough to do something: *laughed fit to burst.* — **fit in** to behave in a suitable or accepted way. **fit someone** *or* **something in** to find time to deal with them. **fit something out** to equip it as necessary: *fit out the ship.* **fit something up** to equip it. **fit someone up** *colloq.* to incriminate them. **see** *or* **think fit** *ironic* to choose to do something, especially unwise. [from Middle English *fitten*]

fit² *noun* **1** a sudden attack of one or more symptoms, usually of an involuntary and relatively violent nature, eg convulsions in grand mal epilepsy (epileptic fit), or paroxysms of coughing (coughing fit). **2** a burst, spell, or bout. — **by** *or* **in fits and starts** in irregular spells; spasmodically. **in fits** *colloq.* laughing uncontrollably.

fitful *adj.* irregular, spasmodic, or intermittent; not continuous. [from FIT²]

fitfully *adv.* in a fitful way.

fitly *adv.* in a fit way.

fitment *noun* a fixed piece of equipment or furniture.

fitness *noun* being fit.

Fitt, Gerry (Gerard) Fitt, Baron (1926–) Northern Irish politician, born in Belfast. He was a merchant seaman before he entered local politics (1958) and became a Republican Labour MP (1966). He founded and led the Social Democratic and Labour Party (1970–9), but resigned to sit at Westminster as an Independent Socialist (1979–83). He had earlier been a member of the Northern Ireland Executive (1973–5), and was its Deputy Chief Executive in 1974.

fitted adj. 1 made to fit closely: fitted sheets. 2 said of a carpet covering a floor entirely. 3 fixed; built-in: fitted cupboards. 4 said of a kitchen, etc with built-in shelves, cupboards, etc.

fitter noun a person who installs, adjusts, or repairs machinery, equipment, etc.

fitting — adj. suitable. — noun 1 (usually **fittings**) a piece of fitted furniture or equipment. 2 an act of trying on a specially made piece of clothing, to see where adjustment is necessary.

fittingly adv. appropriately, suitably.

FitzGerald, Edward (1809–83) English scholar and poet, born in Bredfield House, Suffolk. He is best remembered for his English adaptation of the Rubáiyt of Omar Khayyám (1859).

Fitzgerald, Ella (1918–) US jazz singer, born in Newport News, Virginia. Discovered in 1934 at an amateur singing contest in Harlem, she joined Chick Webb's band and recorded several hits, notably A-tisket A-tasket (1938). Her lucid intonation and broad range made her a top jazz singer, and her recordings for Verve (1955–9) in multi-volume 'songbooks' are among the treasures of US popular song.

Fitzgerald, F(rancis) Scott (Key) (1896–1940) US novelist, born in St Paul, Minnesota. In 1920 he married Zelda Sayre (1900–47), and moved in 1924 to the French Riviera, where his mental breakdown and his alcoholism attracted wide publicity. He captured the spirit of the 1920s – 'The Jazz Age' – in The Great Gatsby (1925), his best-known book. Other novels include The Beautiful and the Damned (1922) and Tender is the Night (1934).

Fitzgerald, Dr Garrett (Michael) (1926–) Irish politician and Prime Minister, born in Dublin, where he became a barrister and a lecturer in political economy (1959–73). In 1969 he was elected Fine Gael member of the Irish parliament for Dublin South-East, and became Minister for Foreign Affairs (1973–7), Leader of the Fine Gael Party (1977–87), and Prime Minister (1981–2, 1982–7), when he took part in the formulation of the Ango-Irish Agreement (1985).

Fitzgerald, George Francis (1851–1901) Irish physicist, born in Dublin. Professor in Dublin from 1881, he made important discoveries in the fields of electrolysis and electromagnetic radiation. He proposed that a body moving through an electromagnetic field contracts slightly in the direction of motion.

Fitzsimmons, Bob (Robert) (1863–1917) English-born US boxer, born in Helston, Cornwall. He was brought up in New Zealand, and moved to the USA in 1890, where he won the world middleweight (1891), heavyweight (1897), and light-heavyweight championships (1903). He retired from the ring in 1914.

Fiume see RIJEKA.

Five, The, known as the **Mighty Handful** a group of 19c Russian composers (Mili Balakirev, Alexander Borodin, César Cui, Modest Mussorgsky, and Nikolaí Rimsky-Korsakov) who promoted nationalist ideals and styles in music.

five — noun 1 the number or figure 5; any symbol for this number. 2 the age of 5. 3 something,

especially a garment, or a person, whose size is denoted by the number 5. 4 5 o'clock. 5 a set of 5 people or things. 6 a playing-card with 5 pips. 7 a score of 5 points. — adj. 1 5 in number. 2 aged 5. [from Anglo-Saxon fíf]

Five Civilized Tribes the Native American tribes (Chickasaws, Creeks, Choctaws, Cherokees, Seminoles) who originally inhabited the present SE USA, so-called because they adapted relatively easily to the European way of life. Nevertheless, forced to leave the area under the Removal Act of 1830, they were relocated west of the Mississippi River. Large numbers of Native Americans died as a result of exposure, disease, and hardship suffered en route and in the new Indian Territory, and the name given to the Cherokee ordeal, the 'trail of tears', sums up the tribes' fate.

fivefold — adj. 1 equal to five times as much or many. 2 divided into, or consisting of, five parts. — adv. by five times as much.

Five Holy Mountains, Chinese **Wu Yue** the collective name for five mountains in China, regarded in Chinese legend as the gathering places of the gods. The mountains are Tai Shan in Shandong province (1 545m), Hua Shan in Shaanxi province (2 154m), Song Shan in Henan province (1 512m), Heng Shan in Hunan province (1 290m), and Heng Shan in Shanxi province (2 016m).

fiver noun colloq. a five-pound note.

fives sing. noun a game like squash, in which a gloved hand or a bat is used to hit the ball. ◇ The game is played with two or four players, and is derived from the French game jeu de paume, game of the palm. It was first recorded at Eton school in 1825; variations include Rugby and Winchester fives. The name is thought to derive from the original scoring system, in multiples of five.

5–14 Programme in Scotland, the school curriculum which details the subjects to be studied by pupils between the ages of five and fourteen.

fix — verb 1 to attach or place firmly. 2 to mend or repair. 3 to direct; to concentrate: fixed his eyes on her. 4 to transfix: fixed him with a stare. 5 to arrange or agree (a time). 6 to establish (the time of an occurrence). 7 colloq. to arrange the result of (a race, trial, etc) dishonestly. 8 colloq. to bribe or threaten into agreement. 9 colloq. to thwart, punish, or kill. 10 to make (a dye) or the image in (a photograph) permanent by the use of chemicals. 11 North Amer. to prepare (a meal, etc). 12 North Amer. to tidy. — noun 1 colloq. a difficulty; a spot of trouble. 2 slang an act of injecting a narcotic drug, etc. 3 a calculation of the position of a ship, etc.
— **fix on something** to choose it.
fix something up 1 to arrange it (eg a meeting). **2** to get a place ready for some purpose. **3** to set it up, especially temporarily. (**fix someone up with something**) to provide them with what is needed.
[from Latin fixare]

fixated adj. 1 obsessed. 2 obsessively attached.

fixation noun 1 something with which one is preoccupied or obsessed. 2 Psychol. an extreme attachment formed in early childhood, eg to one's mother. [from Latin fixare, to fix]

fixative noun 1 a liquid sprayed on a drawing, painting, or photograph to preserve and protect it. 2 a liquid used to hold eg dentures in place. 3 a substance added to perfume to stop it evaporating. [from Latin fixare, to fix]

fixed adj. 1 fastened; immovable. 2 unvarying; set or established: fixed ideas. 3 said of a gaze or expression steady; concentrated; rigid. 4 said of a point stationary. 5 permanent: a fixed address. 6 colloq. supplied, especially financially: how are you fixed for cash?

fixedly adv. steadily.

fixed star a distant star that seems almost stationary.

fixer noun 1 Photog. a solution for fixing photographic images. 2 slang a person who arranges things, especially illegally.

fixity noun the quality of being fixed, steady, unchanging, unmoving, or immovable.

fixture noun 1 a permanently fixed piece of furniture or equipment. 2 a match or other event in a sports calendar; the date for this. [from Latin fixura, from figere, to fasten]

Fizeau, Armand Hippolyte Louis (1819–96) French physicist, born in Paris. In 1849 Fizeau was the first to measure the velocity of light in a non-astronomical experiment; and later demonstrated the use of the shift in light frequency (the redshift) in determining a star's velocity along the line of sight.

fizz — verb intrans. 1 said of a liquid to give off bubbles. 2 to hiss. — noun 1 a fizzing sound or sensation; fizziness. 2 vivacity; high spirits. 3 old colloq. use champagne. [from FIZZLE]

fizziness noun being fizzy.

fizzle verb intrans. 1 to make a faint hiss. 2 (**fizzle out**) to come to a feeble end. [from Middle English fysel, to break wind]

fizzy adj. effervescent.

fjord or **fiord** noun a long narrow steep-sided inlet of the sea in a mountainous coast, eg in Norway, Greenland, or New Zealand, formed by the flooding of a previously glaciated valley. [from Norse fiörthr]

FL or **Fla.** abbrev. Florida.

flab noun colloq. excess flesh or fat on the body. [from FLABBY]

flabbergast verb colloq. to amaze; to astonish.

flabbily adv. in a flabby way.

flabbiness noun being flabby.

flabby adj. (**flabbier, flabbiest**) derog. 1 a said of flesh sagging, not firm. b said of a person having excess or sagging flesh. 2 lacking vigour; feeble; ineffective. [altered form of FLAPPY]

flaccid adj. limp and soft, not firm. [from Latin flaccidus]

flaccidity noun being flaccid.

flaccidly adv. in a flaccid way.

Flag a painting of the American flag by Jasper Johns (1954).

flag¹ — noun 1 a usually rectangular piece of cloth with a distinctive design, flown from a pole to represent a country, party, etc, or used for signalling. 2 national identity represented by a flag. 3 a small paper emblem with a pin, eg to wear in exchange for supporting a charity, or fixed as a marker to a map, etc. 4 a marker generally. 5 an adjustable plate in a taxi, raised to show that the taxi is for hire. — verb (**flagged, flagging**) 1 to mark with flag, tag, or symbol. 2 (**flag someone or something down**) to signal a vehicle or driver to stop. 3 to signal a message using flags.
— **fly the flag** or **keep the flag flying** to maintain a show of support for one's country or other affiliation.
with flags flying with flying colours; triumphantly.
◇ Flags have been used since ancient times, and some have universal significance: a white flag as a signal of truce; a yellow flag as an indication of the presence of infectious disease; a flag flown upside down as a distress signal; and one flown at half-mast as a sign of mourning. The oldest national flag (used for 700 years) is the Danish 'Dannebrog', a white cross on a red ground. The national flag of Britain, popularly known as the Union Jack, combines the three crosses of St George, St Andrew, and St Patrick (for England, Scotland, and Ireland respectively). The US flag,

popularly known as the Stars and Stripes or 'Old Glory', has 50 stars (one for each state in the Union) and 13 stripes representing the 13 original states that declared independence from Britain in 1776. The flag of the European Union has a circle of yellow stars (one for each of the member states) on a blue ground.

flag² *verb intrans.* (**flagged**, **flagging**) to grow tired or feeble; to lose vigour or enthusiasm.

flag³ — *noun* a flagstone. — *verb* (**flagged**, **flagging**) to pave with flagstones. [from Norse *flaga*, slab]

flag⁴ *noun* any of several plants of the iris family, with long blade-like leaves.

flag day a day chosen by a charity for stationing collectors in the street who distribute flags or stickers in return for donations.

flagellant *noun* a person who indulges in flagellation.

flagellate — *verb* (pronounced *-late*) to whip, as a means of religious discipline or for sexual stimulation. — *adj.* (pronounced *-lət*) *Biol.* having flagella. [from Latin *flagellum*, whip]

Flagellation, The a painting of the Flagellation of Christ by various artists including Piero della Francesca (c.1456–7, Urbino) and Sebastiano del Piombo (1516–24, St Pietro in Montorio, Rome).

flagellation *noun* the act of scourging or whipping, for religious or sexual purposes.

flagellum *noun* (PL. **flagella**) *Biol.* the long whip-like structure that projects from the cell surface of sperm, and certain bacteria, unicellular algae, and protozoans. The beating movement of the flagellum propels the cell through a liquid medium such as water. [from Latin *flagellum*, whip]

flageolet *noun* a high-pitched woodwind instrument similar to the recorder. [from French *flageolet*]

flag of convenience the flag of a foreign country in which a ship is registered to avoid taxation, etc in its real country of origin.

flag of truce a white flag flown to show willingness to stop fighting.

flagon *noun* a large bottle or jug with a narrow neck, usually with a spout and handle. [from Old French *flacon*]

flagpole *or* **flagstaff** *noun* the pole from which a flag is flown.

flagrancy *noun* being flagrant; notoriety.

flagrant *adj.*, *said of something bad* undisguised; glaring; brazen or barefaced: *a flagrant lie.* [from Latin *flagrare*, to blaze]

flagrantly *adv.* in a flagrant way.

flagship *noun* **1** the ship that carries, and flies the flag of, the fleet commander. **2** the leading ship in a shipping-line. **3** a commercial company's leading product.

Flagstad, Kirsten (1895–1962) Norwegian soprano, born in Hamar. She made her operatic début in Oslo in 1913 and excelled in Wagnerian roles (eg Sieglinde and Isolde). Acclaimed in most of the world's major opera houses, she was made director of the Norwegian State Opera in 1958.

flagstone *noun* a large flat stone for paving.

flag-waving *noun* an excessive show of patriotic feeling.

Flaherty, Robert (Joseph) (1884–1951) US pioneer documentary film-maker, born in Iron Mountain, Michigan. Trained as a mining prospector, he took a movie camera on his expeditions to Hudson Bay in 1913, and made the silent *Nanook of the North* (1922), followed by the South Seas productions *Moana* (1924) and *Tabu* (1930). His films for the commercial cinema included *Elephant Boy* (1937) and *The Louisiana Story* (1948).

flail — *noun* a threshing tool consisting of a long handle with a wooden or metal bar loosely attached to the end. — *verb* **1** (**flail about** *or* **around**) to wave about violently. **2** to beat with or as if with a flail. [from Anglo-Saxon *fligel*]

flair *noun* **1** a natural ability or talent for something. **2** stylishness; dash. [from French *flair*, sense of smell]

flak *noun* **1** anti-aircraft fire. **2** *colloq.* unfriendly criticism. [from German *Fliegerabwehrkanone*, flyer-defence-gun]

flake — *noun* (*often in compounds*) a small flat particle: *snowflakes / flakes of plaster.* — *verb* **1** *intrans.* to come off in flakes: *flaking paint.* **2** *trans.* to break (eg cooked fish) into flakes. — **flake out** *colloq.* to faint or fall asleep from exhaustion.

flak jacket a metal-reinforced jacket worn for protection by police or soldiers.

flaky *adj.* (**flakier**, **flakiest**) **1** made of or tending to form flakes. **2** *colloq.* crazy.

flambé — *adj.*, *said of food* soaked in brandy and set alight before serving. — *verb* (**flambéed**, **flambéing**) to serve (food) in this way. [from French *flamber*, to expose to flame]

flamboyance *noun* being flamboyant.

Flamboyant a style of French late Gothic architecture prevalent in the 15c, characterized by long wavy flame-like bars of stonework in the tracery. It was especially common in Normandy.

flamboyant *adj.* **1** *said of a person or behaviour* dashing, colourful, and exuberant. **2** *said of clothing or colouring* bright, bold, and striking. [from French *flamboyer*, to blaze]

flamboyantly *adv.* in a flamboyant way.

flame — *noun* **1** the luminous flickering mass of burning gases coming from something that is on fire; a tongue of this: *burst into flames / go up in flames.* **2** a strong passion: *the flame of love.* **3** a bright reddish-orange colour. — *verb intrans.* **1** to burn with flames; to blaze. **2** to shine brightly. **3** to explode with anger. **4** to get red and hot: *flaming cheeks.* — **fan the flames** *or* **add fuel to the flames** to stir up already existing feeling or unrest. [from Latin *flamma*]

flamenco *noun* (PL. **flamencos**) a rhythmical, emotionally stirring type of Spanish gypsy music; the dance performed to it. [from Spanish *flamenco*, Flemish]

flameproof *adj.* not easily damaged by fire or fierce heat.

flame retardant a material that burns very slowly if at all, and is used to make clothing, etc.

flame-thrower *noun* a gun that discharges a stream of burning liquid, used as a weapon or to clear plants from ground.

flaming *adj.* **1** blazing. **2** bright; glowing. **3** *colloq.* very angry; furious; violent. **4** *colloq.* damned: *that flaming dog!*

flamingo *noun* (PL. **flamingos**, **flamingoes**) *noun* any of several large wading birds, found in flocks of many thousands on lakes and lagoons in tropical regions, with white or pinkish plumage, a long neck and long legs, webbed feet, and a broad down-curving bill. [perhaps from Spanish, as for FLAMENCO, or from Provençal *flamenc*, flaming]

Flaminian Way the second of Rome's major trunk roads, constructed in 220 BC by Gaius Flaminius. It ran NE from Rome across the Apennines to Rimini on the Adriatic coast.

Flaminius, Gaius (d.217 BC) Roman general and statesman at the time of the Second Punic War. His name lived on in his two most popular projects: the Flaminian Way and the Circus Flaminius (the biggest arena for chariot-racing in Republican times). He died at the battle of L Trasimene after falling into Hannibal's ambush.

flammable *adj.* liable to catch fire; inflammable. [from Latin *flammare*, to blaze]

Flamsteed, John (1646–1719) English astronomer, born in Denby, near Derby. The first Astronomer Royal, he carried out an immense programme of observations on the positions of stars at the newly established Greenwich Observatory; the data was used by Isaac Newton to verify his theory of gravitation.

flan *noun* an open pastry or sponge case with a savoury or fruit filling. [from Old French *flaon*]

Flanders, Moll see MOLL FLANDERS.

Flanders, Flemish **Vlaanderen**, French **Flandre** a historical region, now occupying the provinces of East and West Flanders in NW Belgium, the French department of Nord, and part of the Dutch province of Zeeland. It is a densely populated industrial area. CHIEF TOWNS Bruges, Ghent, Sint-Niklaas, Aalst, Ronse. HISTORY autonomous from the early Middle Ages as the County of Flanders; in the 20c, the scene of heavy fighting during both World Wars. ECONOMY traditional textile industry, with linen, silk, and cotton processing; intensive farming, especially wheat, sugar-beet, oats, barley, potatoes.

flange *noun* a broad flat projecting rim, eg round a wheel, added for strength or for connecting with another object or part. [from Old French *flanche*]

flank — *noun* **1** the side of an animal or human body, between ribs and hip. **2** the side of anything, especially of a body of troops or a fleet drawn up in formation. — *verb* to be or move beside. [from French *flanc*]

flannel — *noun* **1** a soft woollen cloth used to make clothes. **2** (**flannels**) trousers made of flannel. **3** a small square of towelling for washing oneself with. **4** *colloq.* flattery, or meaningless talk intended to hide one's ignorance or true intentions. — *verb* (**flanelled**, **flanelling**) **1** *intrans.*, *trans.* to flatter, persuade by flattery, or talk flannel. **2** to rub with a flannel. [from Welsh *gwlanen*, from *gwlan*, wool]

flannelette *noun* cotton cloth with a soft brushed surface.

flap — *verb* (**flapped**, **flapping**) **1** *trans.*, *intrans.* to wave up and down or backwards and forwards. **2** *trans.*, *intrans. said of a bird* to move (the wings) in this way; to fly with pronounced wing movements. **3** *intrans. colloq.* to get into a panic or flustered state. — *noun* **1** a broad piece or part of something attached along one edge and hanging loosely: *pocket flaps.* **2** an act, sound, or impact of flapping. **3** *colloq.* a panic; a flustered state. **4** a hinged section on an aircraft wing adjusted to control speed. [imitative]

flapjack *noun* **1** a thick biscuit made with oats and syrup. **2** *North Amer.* a pancake. [from FLAP + JACK]

flapper *noun* **1** a fashionable and frivolous young woman of the 1920s. **2** something or someone that flaps.

flamingo

flappy *adj.* (**flappier**, **flappiest**) 1 tending to flap or wave up and down. 2 *colloq.* nervous, and likely to panic.

flare — *verb intrans.* 1 to burn with sudden brightness. 2 *intrans.* to explode into anger. 3 *trans., intrans.* to widen towards the edge. — *noun* 1 a sudden blaze of bright light. 2 a device composed of combustible material that produces a sudden blaze of intense light, and is activated to give warning, emergency illumination (eg on an airfield), or a distress signal (eg at sea). 3 in chemical plants and oil refineries, a device for burning off superfluous combustible gas or oil, in order to ensure its safe disposal. 4 *Astron.* (also **solar flare**) a sudden brilliant eruption on the Sun, from which a stream of charged atomic particles is ejected into space, thought to be caused by the release of magnetic energy associated with a sunspot. 5 a flared edge. 6 (**flares**) *colloq.* flared trousers.
— **flare up** 1 to blaze suddenly. 2 to explode into anger.

flare-up *noun* 1 a sudden blaze. 2 an explosion of anger or feeling.

flash — *noun* 1 a sudden brief blaze of light. 2 an instant. 3 a brief but intense occurrence: *a flash of inspiration.* 4 a fleeting look on a face. 5 a camera flashgun. 6 a brief news announcement on radio or television. 7 an emblem on a military uniform, etc indicating one's unit. — *verb* 1 *intrans., trans.* to shine briefly or intermittently. 2 *intrans., trans.* to appear or cause to appear briefly; to move or pass quickly. 3 *intrans. said of the eyes* to brighten with anger, etc. 4 to give (a smile or look) briefly. 5 to display briefly; to flourish, brandish, or flaunt. 6 to send (a message) by radio, satellite, etc. 7 *trans., intrans.* to operate (a light) as a signal. 8 *intrans. colloq., said of a man* to expose the genitals. — *adj.* 1 sudden and severe: *flash floods.* 2 quick: *flash freezing.* 3 *colloq.* smart and expensive.
— **a flash in the pan** *colloq.* an impressive but untypical success, unlikely to be repeated. [imitative]

flashback *noun* a return to the past, especially as a scene in a film, etc.

flashbulb *noun* a small light bulb used (especially formerly) to produce a brief bright light in photography.

flasher *noun* 1 a light that flashes; a device causing a light to do this. 2 *colloq.* a man who exposes his genitals in public.

flashgun *noun* 1 a device that produces brief but brilliant illumination for indoor or night photography. 2 a device that holds and operates a flashbulb.

flashily *adv.* in a flashy way.

flashiness *noun* being flashy.

flashlight *noun* North Amer. a torch.

Flashman the philandering, cowardly but irrepressible soldier in George Macdonald Fraser's series of novels, *The Flashman Papers*, derived from the character of the bully in Thomas Hughes's *Tom Brown's Schooldays*.

flashpoint *noun* 1 a stage in a tense situation at which people lose their tempers and become angry or violent. 2 an area of political unrest where violence is liable to break out. 3 *Chem.* the lowest temperature at which the vapour above a volatile liquid, eg petrol or oil, will ignite momentarily on application of a small flame. Volatile materials are stored at temperatures well below their flashpoints in order to minimize fire risks.

flashy *adj.* (**flashier**, **flashiest**) *colloq.* 1 ostentatiously smart. 2 cheap and showy.

Flask the ignorant, fearless third mate on the *Pequod* in Herman Melville's *Moby Dick*.

flask *noun* 1 (also **hip flask**) a small flat leather-cased pocket bottle for alcoholic spirits. 2 a vac-uum flask. 3 a narrow-necked bottle used in chemical experiments, etc. [from Latin *flasco*]

flat — *adj.* (**flatter**, **flattest**) 1 level; horizontal; even. 2 without hollows or prominences. 3 lacking the usual prominence: *a flat nose.* 4 not bent or crumpled. 5 *said of shoes* not having a raised heel. 6 bored; depressed. 7 dull; not lively. 8 toneless and expressionless. 9 *colloq.* definite; downright; emphatic: *a flat refusal.* 10 *said of a tyre* having too little air in it. 11 *said of a drink* having lost its fizziness. 12 *said of a battery* having little or no electrical charge remaining. 13 *said of a price, rate, fee, etc* fixed; unvarying. 14 *Mus.* lower than the correct pitch. 15 *said of paint* matt, not glossy. — *adv.* 1 stretched out rather than curled up, etc. 2 into a flat compact shape: *folds flat for storage.* 3 exactly: *in two minutes flat.* 4 bluntly and emphatically: *I can tell you that flat.* 5 *Mus.* at lower than the correct pitch. — *noun* 1 a set of rooms for living in, especially all on one floor; an apartment. 2 something flat; a flat surface or part. 3 (**flats**) an area of flat land. 4 *colloq.* a flat tyre. 5 *Mus.* a note lowered by a semitone; a sign (♭) indicating this. 6 a flat upright section of stage scenery. 7 (**the flat**) *Racing* the season of flat racing.
— **fall flat** *colloq.* to fail to achieve the hoped-for effect.
fall flat on one's face *colloq.* to fail humiliatingly.
flat broke *colloq.* completely without money.
flat out *colloq.* with maximum speed and energy.
that's flat *colloq.* that's certain or final.
[from Norse *flatr*, flat]

flatfish *noun* any of several flat-bodied fish with both eyes on one side, that lie on the sea bed.

flat foot a condition in which the arch of the instep of the foot has fallen, so that the sole lies flat against the ground.

flat-footed *adj.* 1 having flat feet. 2 *derog.* clumsy or tactless.

flatiron *noun Hist.* a clothes-pressing iron heated on the fire or stove.

flatlet *noun* a small flat.

flatly *adv.* in a flat way; firmly, definitely.

flatness *noun* being flat.

flat race a horse race over a course without jumps.

flat racing the sport of racing horses on courses with no jumps.

flat spin 1 uncontrolled horizontal spinning by an aircraft. 2 *colloq.* a state of agitated bustle.

flatten *verb* (**flattened**, **flattening**) 1 *trans., intrans.* to make or become flat or flatter. 2 *colloq.* to knock to the ground. 3 *colloq.* to overcome, crush, or subdue utterly.

flatter *verb* (**flattered**, **flattering**) 1 to compliment excessively or insincerely. 2 *said of a picture or description* to represent (someone or something) over-favourably. 3 to show off well: *a dress that flatters the figure.* 4 to cause to feel honoured; to gratify.
— **flatter oneself** to feel pleased, usually smugly and unjustifiably, about something concerning oneself.
[from Middle English *flateren*, to fawn upon]

flatterer *noun* a person who flatters.

flattery *noun* (PL. **flatteries**) excessive or insincere praise.

flatulence *noun* an accumulation of gas in the stomach or intestines, causing discomfort. [from Latin *flatus*, blowing]

flatulent *adj.* 1 suffering from or caused by flatulence. 2 causing flatulence.

flatworm *noun* a flattened worm-like animal with a definite head but without a true body cavity. Free-living flatworms typically feed on small invertebrates; parasitic forms include tapeworms and flukes.

Flaubert, Gustave (1821–80) French novelist, born in Rouen. He studied law in Paris then turned to writing, and is best-known for his novel *Madame Bovary* (1857), for which he was (unsuccessfully) prosecuted on the grounds that it was immoral. Other works include *Salammbô* (1862) and *La Tentation de St Antoine* (The Temptation of St Anthony, 1874), and the short stories *Trois contes* (Three Tales, 1877).

flaunt *verb* to display or parade, in the hope of being admired.
◆ Often confused with *flout*.

flautist *noun* a flute-player. [from Italian *flautista*, from *flauto*, flute]

flavonoid *noun Biochem.* any of a group of organic compounds containing a C_6-C_3-C_6 skeleton, where C_6 is a benzene ring. They include a large number of water-soluble plant pigments, and are responsible for most of the red, pink, and purple colours found in higher plants. [from Latin *flavus*, yellow]

flavour *noun* 1 the taste of any particular food or drink. 2 a characteristic quality or atmosphere. [from Old French *flaour*]

flavour enhancer *Food Science* any substance that improves the natural flavour of a food when added to it, without contributing any taste of its own, eg monosodium glutamate, small quantities of sugar, and salt. Some flavour enhancers can cause an allergic reaction.

flavouring *noun* any substance used to give food flavour.

flavourless *adj.* without flavour.

flavoursome *adj.* full of flavour.

flaw *noun* 1 a fault, defect, imperfection, or blemish. 2 a mistake, eg in an argument. [from Norse *flaga*, stone flag]

flawed *adj.* having flaws; imperfect.

flawless *adj.* without flaws; perfect.

flawlessly *adv.* in a flawless way; perfectly.

flax *noun* an annual plant of the genus *Linum* that has blue flowers and is cultivated in many parts of the world for the fibre in its stem, which is used to make linen thread, and the linseed oil in its seeds, which is used as a solvent for paints and varnishes. [from Anglo-Saxon *fleax*]

flaxen *adj., said of hair* very fair.

flay *verb* 1 to strip the skin from. 2 to whip or beat violently. 3 to criticize harshly. [from Anglo-Saxon *flean*]

F-layer *noun* same as APPLETON LAYER.

flea

flea *noun* any of about 1 800 species of wingless blood-sucking insects that live as parasites on mammals (including humans) and some birds.
— **a flea in one's ear** *colloq.* a severe scolding. [from Anglo-Saxon]
◇ The largest flea is about 8mm long, although most are less than half this size. They are generally brownish and flattened from side to side for easy movement through fur and feathers. The hind legs are long and powerful, enabling the insect to jump long distances, and the mouthparts are adapted for piercing and sucking. Many fleas are of medical and veterinary importance as carriers of disease.

fleabane *noun* a leafy perennial plant (*Pulicaria dysenterica*), native to marshes in Europe, N Africa, and Asia Minor, that has lance-shaped leaves with wavy margins, and yellow daisy-like flowers, so called because its dried leaves were formerly burned to repel insects.

flea bite 1 the bite of a flea, or an itchy swelling caused by it. 2 a trivial inconvenience.

flea-bitten *adj.* 1 bitten or infested with fleas. 2 dingy; squalid.

flea market *colloq.* a street market selling second-hand goods or clothes.

flea pit *colloq.* a drab cinema or other public building.

fleck *noun* a spot or speck. [from Norse *flekkr*]

flecked *adj.* spotted, dappled.

Flecker, James Elroy (1884–1915) English poet, born in London. He entered the consular service and published several volumes of verse, including *The Golden Journey to Samarkand* (1913). His best-known work is the verse drama *Hassan* (1922, staged 1923).

fled see FLEE.

Fledermaus, Die (The Bat) an operetta by Johann Strauss, the Younger (1874). Set in 19c Vienna, it is a story of comic intrigue and romance that centres around a ball and so includes many waltz tunes.

fledged *noun* 1 *said of a young bird* able to fly. 2 qualified; trained: *a fully fledged doctor*. [from Anglo-Saxon *flycge*, able to fly]

fledgling *or* **fledgeling** *noun* a young bird learning to fly. [from *fledge*, ready to fly + -LING]

flee *verb* (PAST TENSE AND PAST PARTICIPLE **fled**) 1 *intrans.* to run away; to take to flight. 2 *trans.* to escape from (danger or a dangerous place). — **flee away** *poetic* to vanish. [from Anglo-Saxon *fleon*, to fly from]

fleece — *noun* 1 a sheep's woolly coat. 2 a sheep's wool cut from it at one shearing. 3 sheepskin or a fluffy fabric for lining garments, etc. — *verb* 1 to cut wool from (sheep). 2 *slang* to rob, swindle, or overcharge. [from Anglo-Saxon *flies*]

fleecy *adj.* (**fleecier, fleeciest**) woolly, like a fleece.

fleet¹ *noun* 1 a number of ships under one command. 2 a navy. 3 a number of buses, taxis, under the same ownership or management. [from Anglo-Saxon *fleot*, ship]

fleet² *adj. poetic* swift: *fleet of foot*. [from Anglo-Saxon *fleotan*, to float]

fleeting *adj.* passing swiftly; brief; short-lived. [from Anglo-Saxon *fleotan*, to float]

fleetingly *adv.* briefly, momentarily.

fleetness *noun* swiftness.

Fleet Street a street in London, taking its name from the R Fleet. From the 16c it developed as the centre for the British press, but in recent years several major newspaper publishers have moved their offices away from the city centre.

Fleetwood POP (1981) 28 000, a port town in Wyre district, Lancashire, NW England. It lies on Morecambe Bay, at the mouth of the R Wyre, 13km/8mi N of Blackpool.

Fleming, Sir Alexander (1881–1955) Scottish bacteriologist, born in Loudoun, Ayrshire. Working at St Mary's Hospital, Paddington, he became the first to use antityphoid vaccines on humans, made early use of the new treatment salvarsan, a compound of arsenic for syphilis, and discovered the antiseptic powers of lysozyme. In 1928 he noticed a curious mould, penicillin, which he found to have unsurpassed antibiotic powers; penicillin was successfully produced as a drug around 11 years later. Appointed Professor of Bacteriology at London in 1938, he shared the 1945 Nobel Prize for Physiology or Medicine with Howard Florey and Ernst Chain.

Fleming, Ian (Lancaster) (1908–64) English novelist and journalist, born in London. He worked with Reuters in Moscow (1929–33), became a banker and stockbroker (1933–9), served with British Naval Intelligence during World War II, and was foreign manager of the *Sunday Times* (1945–59). He achieved worldwide fame as the creator of secret agent James Bond, who features in a series of spy stories and novels (many of which have been filmed) starting with *Casino Royale* (1953) and including *Dr No* (1958).

Fleming, Sir John Ambrose (1849–1945) English physicist and electrical engineer, born in Lancaster. Professor at University College London, he invented the thermionic valve and was a pioneer in the application of electricity to lighting and heating on a large scale.

Fleming, (Robert) Peter (1907–71) English travel writer and journalist, born in London, the brother of Ian Fleming. When an assistant literary editor of the *Spectator*, in 1932 he joined an expedition to explore rivers in central Brazil and ascertain the fate of Col Percy Fawcett who had disappeared in 1925. The expedition provided the material for *Brazilian Adventure* (1933), a landmark in travel literature. Other books include *One's Company* (1934) and *News From Tartary* (1936), an account of a journey from Peking to Kashmir.

Fleming *noun* a native of Flanders or of the Flemish-speaking part of Belgium. [from Anglo-Saxon *Flæming*]

Flemish — *adj.* relating to or belonging to Flanders, or to the Flemings or their language. — *noun* the language of the Flemings; Dutch. [from Old Dutch *vlaemsch*]
See also WALLOON.
◇ Flemish is a form of Dutch (Vlaams), spoken by c.5.5 million people in the N and W of Belgium, and in the Nord department of France. After Belgium became an independent kingdom in 1830, there was a strong Flemish cultural and political revival, culminating (1898) in the language being granted equal status with French.

Flemming, Walther (1843–1905) German biologist, born in Sachsenberg. Professor of Anatomy at Kiel, he is best known for his investigations of cell division which he named mitosis; he also made significant advances in microscope techniques.

flesh *noun* 1 the soft tissues covering the bones, consisting chiefly of muscle. 2 the meat of animals, as distinct from that of fish and, sometimes, birds. 3 the pulp of a fruit or vegetable. 4 the body as distinct from the soul or spirit; bodily needs. 5 *poetic* mankind. 6 excess fat; plumpness. 7 a yellowish-pink colour.
— **flesh and blood** bodily or human nature. **one's flesh and blood** one's family or relations. **flesh something out** to add descriptive detail to it. **in the flesh** in person. [from Anglo-Saxon *flæsc*]

flesh-coloured *adj.* yellowish pink.

fleshiness *noun* being fleshy.

fleshly *adj.* relating to the body as distinct from the soul; worldly.

fleshpots *pl. noun facetious* 1 luxurious living. 2 a place where bodily desires or lusts can be gratified.

flesh wound a superficial wound, not deep enough to damage bone or a bodily organ.

fleshy *adj.* (**fleshier, fleshiest**) 1 plump. 2 of or like flesh. 3 *said of leaves, etc* thick and pulpy.

Fletcher, John (1579–1625) English dramatist, born in Rye, Sussex. Many of his plays were written with other playwrights. Collaboration with Francis Beaumont resulted in such works as *Philaster* (1610), *A King and No King* (1611), and *The Maid's Tragedy* (1611). He possibly collaborated with Shakespeare for *Two Noble Kinsmen* and *Henry VIII*.

fleur-de-lis *or* **fleur-de-lys** *noun* (PL. **fleurs-de-lis, fleurs-de-lys**) a stylized three-petal representation of a lily or iris, used as a heraldic design. [from Old French *flour de lis*, lily flower]

Fleury, André-Hercule de (1653–1743) French prelate and statesman, born in Lodève. As a young priest he entered court service (1679), became almoner to Louis XIV (1683), Bishop of Fréjus (1698), and in 1715 tutor to the future Louis XV. In 1726 he replaced the Duke de Bourbon as Chief Minister and was made cardinal, and effectively controlled the government of Louis XV until 1743. A skilful diplomat, he limited French involvement in the War of the Polish Succession (1733–8), and thus restored the country's prestige as a mediator. His moderation gave France the tranquility her tangled finances demanded, and he carried out legal and economic reforms which stimulated trade.

flew see FLY².

flex¹ *verb* 1 to bend (a limb or joint). 2 to contract or tighten (a muscle) so as to bend a joint. [from Latin *flectere*, to bend]

flex² *noun* flexible insulated electric cable. [from FLEXIBLE]

flexibility *noun* the capacity to be flexible.

flexible *adj.* 1 bending easily; pliable. 2 readily adaptable to suit circumstances. [from Latin *flexibilis*]

flexibly *adv.* in a flexible way.

flexitime *noun* a system of flexible working hours operated in some organizations whereby employees may choose their time of arrival and departure, provided they work the agreed number of hours. [from FLEXIBLE]

Flexner, Simon (1863–1946) US microbiologist and medical administrator, born in Louisville, Kentucky. Working at Johns Hopkins University, Pennsylvania University, and the Rockefeller Institute for Medical Research, which thrived under his direction, he made many important contributions to bacteriology, virology, and immunology. He isolated the dysentery bacillus (1900), developed a serum for cerebrospinal meningitis (1907), and led the team that determined the cause of poliomyelitis.

flexor *noun Anat.* any muscle that causes bending of a limb or other body part.

flibbertigibbet *noun* a frivolous or over-talkative person. [imitiative of fast talking]

flick — *verb* 1 *trans., intrans.* to move or touch with a quick light movement. 2 (**flick through something**) to look quickly through a book, etc. — *noun* a flicking action. [imitative]

flicker — *verb* (**flickered, flickering**) 1 *intrans.* to burn or shine unsteadily. 2 *trans., intrans.* to move lightly to and fro; to flutter. — *noun* 1 a brief or unsteady light. 2 a fleeting appearance or occurrence. [from Anglo-Saxon *flicorian*, to flutter]

flick knife a knife whose blade is concealed in its handle and springs out at the touch of a button.

flicks *pl. noun* (**the flicks**) *old colloq. use* the cinema. [from FLICK]

flight¹ *noun* 1 the art or the act of flying with wings or in an aeroplane or other vehicle. 2 the movement of a vehicle, bird, or insect through the air, supported by aerodynamic forces. 3 a flock of birds flying together. 4 a regular air journey, numbered and at a fixed time, made by an aircraft. 5 a journey of a spacecraft. 6 a group of aircraft involved in a joint mission. 7 a set of steps or stairs leading straight up or down. 8 a rather extreme example (of fancy, imagination, etc). 9 a feather or something similar attached to the end of a dart or arrow.
— **in flight** flying. [from Anglo-Saxon *flyht*]

flight² *noun* the act of fleeing; escape.

— **put someone to flight** to cause them to flee.
take flight *or* **take to flight** to run away.
[from Middle English]

flight attendant a member of the cabin crew on a passenger aircraft.

flight crew the members of an aircraft crew whose responsibility is operation and navigation, ie the pilot, engineer, navigator, etc; as distinct from the *cabin crew*.

flight deck 1 the upper deck of an aircraft carrier where planes take off or land. **2** the forward part of an aeroplane where the pilot and crew sit.

Flight into Egypt 1 the escape (on a donkey) of Mary, Joseph and the infant Jesus, from King Herod. **2** a painting of this scene by various artists, including a series of engravings and etchings by Giandomenico Tiepolo (1753).

flightless *adj., said of birds or insects* unable to fly.

flight lieutenant the air-force rank next below squadron leader.

flight recorder an electronic instrument on an aircraft recording information about its performance in flight.

flimsily *adv.* in a flimsy way.

flimsiness *noun* being flimsy.

flimsy *adj.* (**flimsier, flimsiest**) **1** *said of clothing, etc* light and thin. **2** *said of a structure* insubstantially made; frail. **3** *said of an excuse, etc* inadequate or unconvincing. [perhaps altered from FILM]

flinch *verb intrans.* **1** to start or jump in pain or fright. **2** (**flinch from something**) to shrink from or avoid a task, duty, etc.

Flinders, Matthew (1774–1814) English explorer, born in Donington, Lincolnshire. He joined the navy in 1789, and sailed to Australia in 1795, where he explored the SE coast, and later (1801–3) circumnavigated the country. On his return he was wrecked off the Great Barrier Reef, and later kept prisoner by the French Governor of Mauritius until 1810. The Flinders R in Queensland, and the Lofty-Flinders Range in S Australia are named after him.

Flinders Ranges see LOFTY-FLINDERS RANGES, MOUNT.

fling — *verb* (PAST TENSE AND PAST PARTICIPLE **flung**) **1** to throw, especially violently or vigorously. **2** *intrans.* (**fling off** *or* **out**) to rush angrily. — *noun* **1** *colloq.* a spell of enjoyable self-indulgence. **2** a lively reel: *the Highland fling.*
— **fling something out** to throw it away or reject it.
have a fling at something attempt it; have a try at it.
[Middle English]

flint *noun* **1** *Geol.* a crystalline form of quartz, found in chalk and limestone, consisting of hard dark grey or black nodules encrusted with white, and used as an abrasive. In the Stone Age flint was used to make tools. – Also called *chert.* **2** *Archaeol.* a trimmed piece of this used as a tool. **3** a piece of a hard metal alloy from which a spark can be struck, eg in a cigarette-lighter. [from Anglo-Saxon]

flintlock *noun Hist.* a gun in which the powder was lit by a spark from a flint.

flinty *adj.* (**flintier, flintiest**) **1** made of or containing flint. **2** like flint.

flip — *verb* (**flipped, flipping**) **1** to toss (eg a coin) so that it turns over in mid air. **2** (**flip something over**) to toss or turn it with a light flick. **3** *intrans. colloq.* to go crazy. **4** (**flip through something**) to look quickly through a magazine, etc. — *noun* **1** a flipping action. **2** a somersault, especially performed in mid air. **3** an alcoholic drink made with beaten egg. **4** *colloq.* a short air trip. — *adj. colloq.* flippant; over-smart.
— **flip one's lid** *colloq.* to lose one's temper.
[imitative]

flip-flop *noun* **1** *colloq.* a rubber or plastic sandal consisting of a sole held on to the foot by a strap that separates the big toe from the other toes. **2** *Electr., Comput.* a device or circuit able to take on either of two stable states, usually 'on' or 'off'. [from FLIP]

flippancy *noun* (PL. **flippancies**) **1** being flippant. **2** a flippant act or remark.

flippant *adj.* not serious enough about grave matters; disrespectful; irreverent; frivolous. [from FLIP]

flippantly *adv.* with a flippant manner.

flipper *noun* **1** a limb adapted for swimming, eg in the whale, seal, penguin, etc. **2** a rubber foot-covering imitating an animal flipper, worn for underwater swimming. [from FLIP]

flipping *adj., adv. colloq.* used to express annoyance: *that flipping cat!* [from FLIP]

flip side *colloq.* the side of a gramophone record not containing the principal item.

flirt — *verb intrans.* **1** (**flirt with someone**) to behave amorously towards them without serious intentions. **2** (**flirt with something**) to take a fleeting interest in it; to consider it briefly; to play riskily with it. — *noun* someone who flirts.

flirtation *noun* **1** the act of flirting. **2** a brief light-hearted attachment or relationship.

flirtatious *adj.* **1** given to flirting. **2** *said of a remark, glance, etc* conveying a playful sexual invitation.

flit — *verb intrans.* (**flitted, flitting**) **1** to dart lightly from place to place. **2** *Scot. & N of England* to move house. **3** *Brit. colloq.* to move house to avoid paying debts. — *noun* an act of flitting. [from Norse *flytja*, to carry]

flitch *noun* a salted and cured side of pork. [from Anglo-Saxon *flicce*]

FLN *abbrev.* Front de Libération Nationale.

float — *verb* **1** *trans., intrans.* to rest or move, or cause to rest or move, on the surface of a liquid. **2** *intrans.* to drift about or hover in the air. **3** *intrans.* to move about in an aimless or disorganized way. **4** to start up (a company, scheme, etc). **5** to offer (stocks) for sale. **6** to allow (a currency) to vary in value in relation to other currencies. — *noun* **1** a floating device fixed to a fishing-line, that moves to indicate a bite. **2** a low-powered delivery vehicle: *milk float.* **3** a vehicle decorated as an exhibit in a street parade. **4** an amount of money set aside for giving change, etc. [from Anglo-Saxon *flotian*]

floatation see FLOTATION.

floating *adj.* **1** not fixed; moving about: *a floating population.* **2** *said of a voter* not committed to supporting any one party. **3** *said of a currency* varying in value in relation to other currencies. **4** *said of a bodily organ, eg a kidney* moving about abnormally.

flock[1] — *noun* **1** a group of creatures, especially birds or sheep. **2** a crowd of people. **3** a body of people under the spiritual charge of a priest or minister. — *verb intrans.* to gather or move in a crowd. [from Anglo-Saxon *flocc*]

flock[2] *noun* **1** a tuft of wool, etc. **2** waste wool or cotton used for stuffing mattresses, etc. **3** fine particles of wool or nylon fibre applied to paper or cloth to give a velvety surface. [from Latin *floccus*, tuft of wool]

Flodden, Battle of a victory (9 Sep 1513) for the English over the Scots, fought in Northumberland. James IV, allied with France, invaded England in August, but was defeated by English forces under Thomas Howard, Earl of Surrey, and was himself among the dead, together with 13 earls and three bishops. The battle supressed the Scottish threat for a generation.

floe *noun* a floating ice sheet. [from Norwegian *flo*, layer]

flog *verb* (**flogged, flogging**) **1** to beat; to whip. **2** *colloq.* to sell.
— **flog a dead horse** *colloq.* to waste time and energy on a lost cause.
flog something to death *colloq.* to over-use (an idea, expression, etc) so that it becomes tedious and ineffective.
[from Latin *flagellare*, to whip]

flokati *noun* a hand-woven Greek rug with a thick shaggy wool pile. [from modern Greek *phlokate*, a peasant's blanket]

Flood, Henry (1723–91) Irish statesman, who became leader of the popular party in the Irish parliament after his election in 1759. In 1775 he became Vice-Treasurer of Ireland, but was removed in 1781 as a strong Nationalist. He became MP for Winchester (1783), and for Seaford (1785), but had little influence at Westminster.

Flood, The in the Bible (Genesis 6–8), the story that in Noah's time God caused a widespread deluge to destroy all living beings (except Noah, his family, and selected animals) because the people were sinful. Similar legends are found also in other ancient near-eastern sources, such as the Babylonian Gilgamesh Epic.

flood — *noun* **1** an overflow of water from rivers, lakes, or the sea on to dry land. **2** (**the Flood**) *Biblical* see as separate entry. **3** any overwhelming flow or quantity. **4** the rising of the tide. **5** a floodlight. — *verb* **1** to overflow or submerge (land). **2** to fill too full or to overflowing. **3** (*usually* **flood someone out**) to force them to leave a building, etc because of floods. **4** to supply (a market) with too much of a certain kind of commodity. **5** to supply (an engine) with too much petrol so that it cannot start. **6** *intrans.* to become flooded, especially frequently. **7** *intrans.* to move in a great mass: *crowds flooding through the gates.* **8** *intrans.* to flow or surge.
— **in flood** overflowing.
[from Anglo-Saxon *flod*]

floodgate *noun* a gate for controlling the flow of a large amount of water.
— **open the floodgates** to remove all restraints or controls.

floodlight — *noun* a powerful light used to illuminate extensive areas, especially sports grounds or the outside of buildings. — *verb* to illuminate with floodlights.

floodlit *adj.* lit by floodlights.

flood plain *Geol.* an extensive level area beside a river, corresponding to that part of the river valley which becomes covered with water when the river floods.

floor — *noun* **1** the lower interior surface of a room or vehicle. **2** all the rooms on the same level in a building. **3** the ground in a forest or cave; the bed of the sea, etc. **4** the debating area in a parliamentary assembly; the right to speak there: *have the floor.* — *verb* **1** to construct the floor of (a room, etc). **2** *colloq.* to knock (someone) down. **3** *colloq.* to baffle completely.
— **hold the floor** to be the person who is talking while others listen.
take the floor 1 to rise to speak in a debate, etc. **2** to start dancing at a dance, etc.
wipe the floor with someone *slang* to defeat them ignominiously; to humiliate them.
[from Anglo-Saxon *flor*]

floorboard *noun* one of the boards forming a wooden floor.

flooring *noun* material for constructing floors.

floor show a series of performances at a night-club or restaurant.

floosie *or* **floozie** *noun derog. colloq.* a woman or girl, especially a disreputable or immodestly dressed one.

flop — *verb intrans.* (**flopped, flopping**) **1** to fall, drop, move or sit limply and heavily. **2** *said of eg hair* to hang or sway about loosely. **3** *colloq.*, *said of a play, etc* to fail. — *noun* **1** a flopping movement or sound. **2** *colloq.* a failure. — *adv.* with a flop. [variant of FLAP]

floppily *adv.* in a floppy way.

floppiness *noun* being floppy.

floppy *adj.* (**floppier, floppiest**) tending to flop; loose and insecure.

floppy disk *Comput.* a portable flexible plastic disc-shaped medium, coated with magnetic material and enclosed in a plastic casing, which is used to store data. It is slower in operation than a hard disk, and has a smaller storage capacity. See also HARD DISK.

Flora 1 in Roman mythology, the goddess of flowers and flowering plants, who appears with the Spring. Her spring festival was inaugurated in 238 BC. **2** a female first name, confined to Scotland until the 18c. [from Latin *flos*, *floris*, flower]

flora *noun* (PL. **floras, florae**) **1** *Bot.* the wild plants of a particular region, country, or time period. **2** *Bot.* a book or list giving descriptions of such plants. See also FAUNA. [from Latin *Flora*, goddess of flowers]

floral *adj.* **1** of or relating to flowers. **2** patterned with flowers: *floral material*. [from Latin *floralis*]

florally *adv.* like or with flowers.

Florence, Italian **Firenze** POP (1991e) 408 000, the capital of Florence province, Tuscany, Italy, on the R Arno. Its economy depends largely on tourism. HISTORY an ancient Etruscan town, it was a major trading centre by the 12c, and the cultural and intellectual centre of Italy from the Middle Ages; provisional capital of the new Kingdom of Italy from 1865 until 1871; it was badly damaged by floods in 1966; in 1993 a bomb caused the deaths of four people and the destruction of paintings in the Uffizi Galleries. NOTABLE FEATURES the city centre is a World Heritage site, famed for its many religious buildings and palaces: these include the Baptistery of San Giovanni (c.1000), the Duomo (1296); Church of Santa Croce (begun 1295), Church of Santa Maria Novella (1278–1350), Church of Santa Maria del Carmine (largely rebuilt in 1782), Church of San Lorenzo (393, rebuilt in 1425), Church of San Marco (13c, since rebuilt), Church of Santissima Annunziata (1250), Church of Or San Michele, (13c–14c); Palazzo Vecchio (1298–1314), Palazzo degli Uffizi (1560–74), Palazzo Medici-Riccardi (1444–52), Palazzo Pitti (15c and later); Ponte Vecchio (rebuilt in 1345); Boboli Gardens; the city is the seat of the Accademia della Crusca.

Florence a female first name, revived in honour of Florence Nightingale (1820–1910). [a medieval form of Latin *Florentia*, derived from *florens*, blossoming]

Florentine School a term applied to the art and artists of Florence, one of the major centres of European art during the Renaissance period. The Classical revival of the 15c began in Florence, as did the rediscovery of perspective, and the first academy of art was founded there in 1563.

floret *noun Bot.* **1** a small flower; one of the single flowers in the head of a composite flower, such as a daisy or sunflower. **2** each of the branches in the head of a cauliflower or of broccoli. [from Latin *flos floris*, flower]

Florey (of Adelaide and Marston), Howard Walter Florey, Baron (1898–1968) Australian pathologist, born in Adelaide. Professor at Oxford (1935–62), he examined and synthesized a wide range of antibacterial compounds, and in 1938 began work on penicillin, discovered in 1929 by Alexander Fleming. With colleagues, he isolated sufficient penicillin to report on its biological properties; during the early months of World War II, they started to purify penicillin for clinical use. He shared the 1945 Nobel Prize for Physiology or Medicine with Ernst Chain and Fleming.

florid *adj.* **1** over-elaborate. **2** pink or ruddy in complexion. [from Latin *floridus*, blooming]

Florida POP (1990) 13.5m, a state in SE USA, divided into 67 counties. AREA 151 934sq km/58 647sq mi. The state is one of the fastest-growing metropolitan areas in the country. It is renowned for its warm, sunny climate and is known as the 'Sunshine State'. PHYSICAL DESCRIPTION it forms a long peninsula, bounded W by the Gulf of Mexico and E by the Atlantic Ocean; rivers include the St Johns, Caloosahatchee, Apalachicola, Perdido, and St Marys; the centre of the state has many lakes, notably L Okeechobee (the fourth largest lake wholly within the USA); the highest point is in Walton County (105m); the islands of the Florida Keys stretch in a line SW from the S tip of the state, linked by a series of causeways; the NW is a gently rolling panhandle area, cut by deep swamps along the coast; the S is almost entirely covered by the Everglades; the SE coast is protected from the Atlantic Ocean by sandbars and islands, creating shallow lagoons and sandy beaches. HISTORY explored and settled by the Spanish in the 16c; ceded to Britain in 1763, and divided into East and West Florida; after the War of Independence, it was returned to Spain in 1783; West Florida was gained by the USA in the 1803 Louisiana Purchase, and East Florida in 1819; together they became the 27th state of the Union in 1845; seceded in 1861; slavery was abolished in 1865; the state was readmitted to the Union in 1868. CAPITAL Tallahassee. CHIEF TOWNS Jacksonville, Miami, Tampa, St Petersburg, Fort Lauderdale. ECONOMY the nation's greatest producer of citrus fruits, and its second largest producer of vegetables; sugar cane, tobacco; cattle and dairy products; processed foods, chemicals; electrical equipment; transportation equipment; wood products; phosphate and other minerals; tourism. NOTABLE FEATURES the Everglades National Park; Walt Disney World Entertainment Park; Universal Studios; John F Kennedy Space Center at Cape Canaveral.

Florida Keys a series of small coral islands in S Florida, USA. They curve approximately 240km/150mi SW around the tip of the Florida peninsula, about 160km/100mi NE of Havana. MAIN ISLANDS (NE–SW) Key Largo, Long Key, Key Vaca, Big Pine Key, Sugarloaf Key, Key West. The Overseas Highway (built in 1938) runs 198km/123mi from the mainland to Key West. ECONOMY tropical products (limes, pineapples, etc) in the S; tarpon fishing; tourism.

floridly *adv.* in a florid way.

florin *noun* a former name of the coin worth two shillings or 24 old pence, the equivalent of the modern ten-penny piece. [from Italian *fiorino*, a former gold coin from Florence]

Florio, John (c.1533–1625) English lexicographer, born of Italian parentage in London. He was a tutor in foreign languages at Oxford (c.1576), where his works included his Italian and English dictionary (1598). In 1603 he was appointed reader in Italian to Queen Anne, and in 1604 groom of the privy-chamber. His well-known translation of Montaigne (1603) has appeared in several modern editions.

florist *noun* a person who grows or sells flowers. [from Latin *flos*]

Florizel the son of Polixenes and prince of Bohemia in Shakespeare's *The Winter's Tale*, who falls in love with the shepherd-girl, Perdita.

floss *noun* **1** loose strands of fine silk, for embroidery, tooth-cleaning, etc. **2** the rough silk on the outside of a silkworm's cocoon. [probably from Old French *flosche*, down]

flossy *adj.* (**flossier, flossiest**) made of or like floss.

flotation *or* **floatation** *noun* the launching of a commercial company with a sale of shares to raise money. [from FLOAT]

flotilla *noun* a small fleet, or a fleet of small ships. [from Spanish *flotilla*, little fleet]

flotsam *noun* goods lost by shipwreck and found floating on the sea.
— **flotsam and jetsam 1** odds and ends. **2** homeless people; vagrants.
[from Old French *floteson*, from *floter*, to float]

Flotta an island in the Orkney group, N Scotland, situated S of Scapa Flow. It has an oil terminal, linked by a pipeline to the Piper oil field.

flounce[1] — *verb intrans.* to move in a way expressive of impatience or indignation. — *noun* a flouncing movement. [perhaps related to Norse *flunsa*, to hurry]

flounce[2] *noun* a deep frill on a dress, etc. [altered from *frounce*, plait, curl]

flounder[1] *verb intrans.* (**floundered, floundering**) **1** to thrash about helplessly, as when caught in a bog. **2** to be in difficulties or at a loss, from embarrassment, etc. [partly imitative, partly a blend of FOUNDER[2] + BLUNDER]

flounder[2] *noun* a type of edible flatfish. [from Old French *flondre*]

flour — *noun* **1** the finely ground meal of wheat or any other cereal grain. Wholemeal flour includes the bran (husk) and germ (embryo), whereas white flour contains less than 75% of the whole grain. Flour with a high gluten content is used to make bread and pasta. **2** a dried powdered form of any other vegetable material, eg potato flour. — *verb* to cover or sprinkle with flour. [from Middle English, a variant of FLOWER, in the sense 'best part']

Flourens, Pierre Jean Marie (1794–1867) French physiologist, born in Maureilhan, near Béziers. Appointed Secretary of the French Academy of Sciences (1833) and professor at the Collège de France (1835), he began working on the central nervous system from 1820, and was one of the first to demonstrate the functions of the different sections of the brain. He was later elected to the Chamber of Deputies (1838) and nominated a peer of France (1846).

flourish — *verb* **1** *intrans.* to be strong and healthy; to grow well. **2** to do well; to develop and prosper. **3** *intrans.* to be at one's most productive, or at one's peak. **4** to wave or brandish. — *noun* **1** a decorative twirl in handwriting. **2** an elegant sweep of the hand. **3** a showy piece of music; a fanfare. **4** a piece of fancy language. [from Old French *florir*, to flower]

floury *adj.* (**flourier, flouriest**) **1** covered with flour. **2** like flour.

flout *verb* to defy (an order, etc) openly; to disrespect (authority, etc). [from Middle English *flouten*, to play the flute]
◆ Often confused with *flaunt*.

flow — *verb intrans.* **1** to move along like water. **2** *said of blood or electricity* to circulate. **3** to keep moving steadily. **4** *said of hair* to hang or ripple in a loose shining mass. **5** *said of words or ideas* to come readily to mind or in speech or writing. **6** *said of the tide* to rise. — *noun* **1** the action of flowing. **2** the rate of flowing. **3** a continuous stream or outpouring. **4** the rising of the tide.
— **in full flow** speaking energetically.
[from Anglo-Saxon *flowan*]

flow chart a diagram representing the nature and sequence of operations to be carried out, especially in a computer program or an industrial process.

flower — *noun* **1** the structure in a flowering plant (angiosperm) that bears the reproductive organs, consisting of a leafy shoot in which the

leaves are modified to form four distinct whorls of parts attached to a receptacle (the swollen apex of the flower stalk). **2** a plant bearing flowers, especially if cultivated for them. **3** the best part; the cream. — *verb intrans.* **1** to produce flowers; to bloom. **2** to reach a peak; to develop to full maturity.
— **in flower** blooming or blossoming; with flowers fully out.
[from Old French *flour*]
◇ In a typical flower, a calyx of sepals surrounds a corolla of petals, which in turn encloses the stamens (collectively known as the *androecium*) which produce and store pollen containing the male gametes. At the centre of the flower are one or more carpels (collectively known as the *gynaecium*), each consisting of an ovary containing one or more ovules (the structures that contain the female gametes, and develop into seeds after fertilization). The ovary is joined by a slender stalk or *style* to a *stigma*, which receives the pollen grains and often has a sticky surface. The parts of any whorl may be fused or otherwise highly modified, or absent.
The sepals, which are often green and leaflike, but are sometimes brightly coloured, protect the developing flower bud. In insect-pollinated flowers the petals are often scented and brightly coloured, whereas in wind-pollinated flowers they are usually much reduced or absent, and the stigmas have a feathery surface and hang outside the flower to trap pollen grains carried by the wind. A flower that contains both stamens and carpels is described as *hermaphrodite*. In monoecious plants the stamens and carpels are borne in separate flowers, and in *dioecious* plants male and female flowers are borne on separate plants.

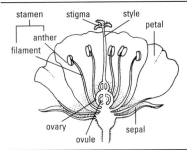

flower structure

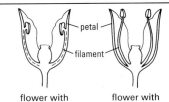

| flower with adnate petals and filaments | flower with distinct petals and filaments |

adnate and distinct flower structure

flowerpecker *noun* a name loosely applied to many small woodland birds found from India to Australia, which have a tube-like tongue. They feed on nectar and berries, especially mistletoe.

flowerpot *noun* a clay or plastic container for growing plants in.

flower power a movement in the 1960s, which rejected materialism and advocated peace and universal love.

flowery *adj.* **1** decorated or patterned with flowers. **2** *said of language or gestures* excessively elegant or elaborate.

flown see FLY[2].

fl oz *or* **fl. oz.** *abbrev.* fluid ounce.

flu *noun colloq.* influenza.

fluctuate *verb intrans.* to vary in amount, value, level, etc; to rise and fall. [from Latin *fluctus*, wave]

fluctuation *noun* **1** repeated rise and fall. **2** motion to and fro or a wave-like motion. **3** alternate variation.

flue *noun* **1** an outlet for smoke or gas, eg through a chimney. **2** a pipe or duct for conveying heat.

Fluellen the pedantic but dignified patriotic Welsh officer in Shakespeare's *Henry V*.

fluency *noun* being fluent.

fluent *adj.* **1** having full command of a language: *is fluent in French.* **2** spoken or written with ease: *speaks fluent German.* **3** speaking or writing in an easy flowing style. [from Latin *fluere*, to flow]

fluently *adv.* in a fluent way.

fluff — *noun* **1** small bits of soft woolly or downy material. **2** *colloq.* a mistake, eg in speaking or reading aloud. — *verb* **1** (*usually* **fluff something out** *or* **up**) to shake or arrange it into a soft mass. **2** *trans., intrans. said eg of an actor* to make a mistake in (one's lines, etc); to bungle (something). [from earlier *flue*, down]

fluffiness *noun* being fluffy.

fluffy *adj.* (**fluffier, fluffiest**) **1** consisting of or resembling fluff. **2** covered with fluff or something similar.

flugelhorn *noun* a brass musical instrument, like a cornet but with a larger bell. It has three pistons and the same compass as a B flat cornet, though with a fuller tone. It is a standard instrument in British brass bands, is occasionally used by jazz musicians, but is rarely found in orchestras. [from German *Flügelhorn*, from *Flügel*, wing]

fluid — *noun* a liquid or gas. — *adj.* **1** able to flow like a liquid. **2** *said eg of movements* smooth and graceful. **3** altering easily; adaptable. [from Latin *fluidus*, flowing]

fluidics *sing. noun Physics* the study of systems based on the movement of jets of fluid in pipes, used as an alternative to electronic devices to control instruments, industrial processes, etc, in cases where low sensitivity to high temperatures, radiation, and strong magnetic fields is required.

fluidity *noun* being fluid.

fluid ounce (ABBREV. **fl oz, fl. oz.**) a unit of liquid measurement, equal to 28.41cm^3 or 0.05 of a British pint.

fluke[1] *noun* a success achieved by accident.

fluke[2] *noun* **1** a flatworm infesting the liver of a sheep. **2** a flounder. [from Anglo-Saxon *floc*, plaice]

fluky *adj.* (**flukier, flukiest**) accidentally lucky.

flume *noun* a descending channel for water, used in industry, or as a chute for riding or sliding down. [from Old French *flum*, from Latin *flumen*, river]

flummery *noun* (PL. **flummeries**) **1** a jelly made with oatmeal, milk, egg, and honey. **2** pompous nonsense; empty flattery. [from Welsh *llymru*]

flummox *verb colloq.* to confuse; to bewilder.

flung see FLING.

flunk *verb North Amer. colloq.* **1** *trans., intrans.* to fail (a test, examination, etc). **2** *said eg of an examiner* to fail (a candidate).

flunkey *or* **flunky** *noun* (PL. **flunkeys, flunkys**) **1** a uniformed manservant. **2** *derog.* a slavish follower. **3** *North Amer.* a person doing a humble or menial job.

fluor see FLUORSPAR.

fluoresce *verb intrans.* to be or become fluorescent. [from FLUOR]

fluorescence *noun Physics* the emission of radiation, usually light, by an object after it has absorbed electrons, or radiation of a different wavelength, especially ultraviolet light. It ceases as soon as the energy source is removed, and is a type of luminescence. Fluorescence is exploited in dyes and in the coating of fluorescent light tubes.

fluorescent *adj., said of a material* having the property of fluorescence.

fluorescent brightener any of various special dyes used to 'whiten' textiles, paper, etc, and frequently incorporated in detergents. Their effect is based on the ability to convert invisible ultraviolet light into visible blue light, giving fabrics clean bright colours and counteracting their natural yellowness.

fluorescent light *or* **fluorescent lamp** *Electr.* a type of electric light consisting of a glass discharge tube containing mercury vapour or a chemically inert gas. The inner surface of the tube is coated with phosphors that absorb ultraviolet radiation produced by the electrical discharge, and then emit visible light (by the process of fluorescence). – Also called *strip light*.

fluoridate *or* **fluoridize** *or* **fluoridise** *verb* to add fluoride to (a water supply).

fluoridation *or* **fluoridization** *or* **fluoridisation** *noun* the addition of small amounts (about one part per million) of fluoride salts to drinking water supplies to help prevent tooth decay, a policy adopted by certain water authorities.

fluoride *noun Chem.* any chemical compound consisting of fluorine and another element, especially sodium fluoride, which is added to drinking water supplies and toothpaste to prevent tooth decay in children.

fluorine *noun Chem.* (SYMBOL **F**, ATOMIC NUMBER 9) a poisonous pale yellow gas (one of the halogens) that is highly corrosive and causes severe skin burns. It is the most electronegative and reactive chemical element, and has been used as a rocket fuel and in the manufacture of organic compounds such as fluorocarbons, which are used as refrigerants and aerosol propellants. See also AEROSOL PROPELLANT. [from FLUOR]

fluorite *noun Geol.* same as FLUORSPAR.

fluorocarbon *noun Chem.* any of various compounds of carbon and fluorine that are highly resistant to heat and chemical action, and very stable over long periods, formerly widely used as aerosol propellants and refrigerants. Recent concern about their damaging effect on the ozone layer has led many countries to sign international agreements banning their use. [from Latin *fluor*, flow]

fluorspar *noun Geol.* (FORMULA **CaF₂**) calcium fluoride, a mineral that is transparent when pure, but commonly occurs as blue or purple crystals. It is used in glass and some cements, and in the manufacture of hydrofluoric acid for the plastic industry. – Also called *fluorite*. [from Latin *fluor*, flow (from the use of fluorspar as a flux) + SPAR[2]]

flurry — *noun* (PL. **flurries**) **1** a sudden gust; a brief shower of rain, snow, etc. **2** *colloq.* a commotion; a bustle or rush. — *verb* (**flurries, flurried**) to agitate or confuse. [imitative]

flush[1] — *verb* **1** *intrans., trans.* to blush or cause to blush or go red. **2** to clean out (especially a lavatory pan) with a rush of water; to wash (something) down the lavatory. **3** (**be flushed with pride**, *etc*) to be visibly affected by it, eg by blushing. — *noun* **1** a redness or rosiness, especially of the face; a blush. **2** a rush of water that cleans a lavatory pan, or the mechanism that controls it. **3** high spirits: *in the first flush of enthusiasm.* **4** freshness; bloom; vigour: *in the first flush of youth.* [perhaps from FLUSH[4]]

flush[2] — *adj.* **1** level with an adjacent surface. **2** *colloq.* having plenty of money. — *adv.* so as to be level with an adjacent surface. [perhaps from FLUSH[1]]

flush[3] *noun Cards* a hand made up of cards from a single suit. [from Latin *fluxus*, flow]

flush[4] *verb* **1** *Hunting* to startle (game birds) so that they rise from the ground. **2** (**flush someone** *or* **something out**) to drive them out of a hiding-place. [from Middle English *flusshen*]

Flushing, Dutch **Vlissingen**, French **Flessingue** POP (1992e) 44 000, a seaport in Zeeland province, W Netherlands. It lies on Walcheren I, at the mouth of the estuary of the R Schelde. HISTORY in 1944 it was the scene of an Allied landing. NOTABLE FEATURES Grote Kerk (14c).

Flushing Meadow an international tennis ground in New York, the home of the annual US Open championship since 1978.

fluster — *noun* a state of confused agitation. — *verb* (**flustered, flustering**) to agitate or confuse. [related to Norse *flaustr*, hurry]

flute — *noun* **1** a woodwind instrument that is held horizontally out to the side of the head. **2** *Archit.* a rounded groove in wood or stone. — *verb* **1** *intrans., trans.* to speak or utter in high shrill tones. **2** *intrans., trans.* to play the flute or play (a tune, etc) on it. **3** *Archit.* to make grooves in (wood or stone). See also FLAUTIST. [from Old French *flahute*]

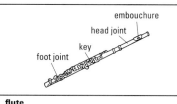

flute

fluting *noun* parallel grooves cut into wood or stone.

flutter — *verb* (**fluttered, fluttering**) **1** *trans., intrans.* to flap lightly and rapidly; to fly with a rapid wing movement or drift with a twirling motion. **2** *intrans.* to move about in a restless, aimless way. **3** *old use* to cause agitation in: *must have fluttered a few hearts in his time.* **4** *intrans.* said of the heart to race, from excitement or some disorder. — *noun* **1** agitation; excitement. **2** *colloq.* a small bet. **3** in a record-player, etc, a regularly recurring variation in loudness and pitch. [from Anglo-Saxon *floterian*, to flutter]

fluty *adj.* (**flutier, flutiest**) like a flute.

fluvial *adj.* of, relating to, or found in rivers. [from Latin *fluvialis*]

flux *noun* **1** constant change; instability. **2** any substance added to another in order to aid the process of melting. **3** in the smelting of metal ores, any substance that is added so that it will combine with impurities which can then be removed as a flowing mass of slag. **4** any substance, such as a resin, that is used to remove oxides from the surfaces of metals that are to be soldered, welded, or brazed. **5** *Physics* the rate of flow of particles, energy, mass, or some other quantity per unit cross-sectional area per unit time. **6** magnetic flux. **7** luminous flux. [from Latin *fluxus*, flow]

fly[1] *noun* (PL. **flies**) **1** a two-winged insect. **2** (*in compounds*) any of various other flying insects: *mayfly / dragonfly / butterfly.* **3** a fish hook tied with colourful feathers to look like a fly. — **drop like flies** *colloq.* to fall ill or die in large numbers.

a fly in the ointment a drawback in an otherwise satisfactory state of affairs.

a fly on the wall the invisible observer that one would like to be on certain occasions.

no flies on someone *colloq.* no lack of alertness in them.

he *etc* **wouldn't harm a fly** he, etc has a gentle nature.

[from Anglo-Saxon *fleoge*]

fly[2] — *verb* (**flies**; PAST TENSE **flew**; PAST PARTICIPLE **flown**) **1** *intrans.* **a** *said of a bird, bat, or insect* to move through the air on wings. **b** *said of an aircraft or spacecraft* to travel through the air or through space. **2** *intrans., trans.* to travel or convey in an aircraft. **3** to operate and control (an aircraft, kite, etc). **4** to cross (a stretch of water, etc) in an aircraft. **5** *trans., intrans.* to raise (a flag), or (of a flag) to blow in the wind. **6** *intrans.* to move or pass rapidly: *fly into a temper / rumours flying around.* **7** *intrans. colloq.* to depart quickly: *I must fly.* **8** *intrans.* (**fly at, fly out at**) to attack angrily. **9** *intrans., trans.* to escape; to flee (a country, etc). **10** *intrans.* to vanish: *darkness has flown.* — *noun* (PL. **flies**) **1** (**flies**) a zip or set of buttons fastening a trouser front, or the flap covering these. **2** a flap covering the entrance to a tent. **3** (**flies**) the space above a stage from which scenery is lowered.

— **fly high** to be ambitious.

let fly at someone *or* **something** to attack them.

send someone *or* **something flying** to knock them down or knock them over with considerable force.

[from Anglo-Saxon *fleogan*, to fly]

fly[3] *adj. colloq.* cunning; smart.

fly agaric a mushroom (*Amanita muscaria*) with a flattened scarlet cap covered with concentric rings of small white scales. The gills on the underside of the cap are crowded and whitish, and the stem is also white with a swollen base. It contains poisonous (though not deadly) substances and mild hallucinogens.

flyblown *noun* **1** *said of food* covered with blowfly eggs, and therefore unfit to eat; contaminated. **2** shabby, dirty, or dingy.

fly-by-night *adj. derog., said of a business, etc* not reliable or trustworthy.

flycatcher *noun* **1** a name applied to birds of three distinct groups, New World or tyrant flycatchers, Old World flycatchers, and silky flycatchers, all of which usually eat insects caught in flight. **2** any of various birds of other families.

flyer *or* **flier** *noun* **1** a creature that flies; someone or something that moves fast; an aviator or pilot. **2** an advertising leaflet.

Flyer I the plane in which Orville and Wilbur Wright made the first ever controlled manned flight on 17 Dec 1903 in Kitty Hawk, North Carolina. The first flight lasted 12 seconds and covered 37m.

fly-fish *verb intrans.* to fish using artificial flies.

fly-fishing *noun* the sport of fishing using artificial flies.

fly half *Rugby* a stand-off half.

flying — *noun* **1** flight. **2** the activity of piloting, or travelling in, an aircraft. — *adj.* **1** hasty; brief. **2** designed or organized for fast movement. **3** that flies; able to fly, or to make long gliding leaps. **4** *said eg of hair or a flag* streaming; fluttering.

flying boat a seaplane whose fuselage is shaped like a boat hull.

flying buttress a structure supporting, and forming an arch against, the outside wall of a large building, especially a church.

flying doctor especially in Australia, a doctor who travels by light aircraft to visit patients.

Flying Dutchman in sailor's folklore, a ghost ship of disastrous portent, haunting the seas around the Cape of Good Hope. Its captain had sworn a blasphemous oath when he failed to round the Cape in a storm, and was condemned to sail those waters for ever. The story inspired Richard Wagner's opera.

Flying Dutchman, The (Der Fliegende Holländer) an opera by Richard Wagner

(1843), based on the legend of the Flying Dutchman. In this version, a ghostly sailor is condemned to remain at sea for ever unless he can find a woman who loves him during one of his seven-yearly visits to port.

flying fish a tropical fish with wing-like fins that can rise above the water.

flying fox a fruit-eating bat.

flying leap a jump from a running start.

flying lemur see COLUGO.

flying lizard, also known as **flying dragon** a species of lizard native to SE Asia. It is able to glide between trees by using a semicircular membrane, which is supported by moveable ribs on either side of its body. The membrane may be folded back when not in use.

flying lizard

flying officer a Royal Air Force rank immediately below flight lieutenant.

flying phalanger a nocturnal squirrel-like marsupial, native to Australia and New Guinea, that has a gliding membrane between its front and hind limbs, and can glide for distances of up to 114m. It inhabits woodland, and feeds on plant material and animals.

flying picket a picket travelling from place to place to support local pickets during any strike.

flying saucer any of a number of unidentified circular flying objects reported in the sky from time to time, believed by some to be craft from outer space.

Flying Scotsman a steam locomotive designed by Sir Nigel Gresley (1876–1941) and manufactured by the London and Eastern Railway in 1923. It went into service on 24 Feb 1923; one of its main routes was the stretch between Peterborough and York. It is now owned by Sir William McAlpine.

flying snake a snake from SE Asia that glides between trees by launching itself in the air and

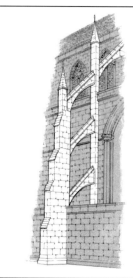

flying buttress

then flattening its body and forming several S-shaped curves. Several regions of the body are then broadside to the direction of travel and act like wings. It can glide in this manner for distances of 20m or more.

flying spot scanner *Telecomm.* a device for producing television picture signals from photographic transparencies or motion picture film by scanning the picture area with a spot of light, generated on the screen of a cathode-ray tube. The modulated transmitted light is received by a photocell or sensor tube.

flying squad a body of police specially trained for fast movement or action, or available for duty wherever the need arises.

flying squirrel any of various species of squirrel, most of which are found in SE Asia, with a large flap of skin between its front and hind legs, which it uses to glide between trees for distances of up to 450m. It hunts for food at dawn and dusk.

flying start a start to a race in which the contestants are already travelling at full speed when they cross the starting-line.
— **get off to a flying start** to begin promisingly or with a special advantage.

flyleaf *noun* a blank page at the beginning or end of a book.

Flymo *noun trademark* a type of lawnmower which hovers on a cushion of air.

Flynn, Errol (Leslie Thomson) (1909–59) Australian film actor, born in Hobart, Tasmania. He went to England to gain acting experience, and after a part in a film was offered a Hollywood contract. His first US film, *Captain Blood* (1935), established him as a hero of historical adventure films, and his good looks and athleticism confirmed him as the greatest Hollywood swashbuckler, in such films as *The Adventures of Robin Hood* (1938) and *The Sea Hawk* (1940).

flyover *noun* a bridge that takes a road or railway over another.

flypaper *noun* a strip of paper with a sticky poisonous coating that attracts, traps and kills flies.

flypast *noun* a ceremonial flight of military aircraft over a particular place.

flysheet *noun* 1 a protective outer sheet for a tent. 2 a single-sheet leaflet.

flyspray *noun* a liquid poisonous to flies, sprayed from an aerosol can.

fly-tipping *noun* unauthorized disposal of waste materials.

flyweight *noun* 1 a class for boxers, wrestlers and weight-lifters of not more than a specified weight (50.8 kg in professional boxing, similar weights in the other sports). 2 a boxer, etc of this weight.

flywheel *noun* a heavy wheel on a revolving shaft that regulates the action of a machine.

FM *abbrev.* frequency modulation.

Fm *symbol Chem.* fermium.

f-number *noun Photog.* the relative aperture of a camera lens representing its light transmission, particularly when the lens is stopped down to increase the depth of field and/or exposure time. It expresses the diameter of the lens diaphragm as a fraction of its focal length, eg f/8 or f:8 or f8.

FO *abbrev.* 1 Flying Officer. 2 *Hist.* Foreign Office.

Fo, Dario (1926–) Italian dramatist, designer, and actor, born in San Giano, Lombardy. He founded a radical theatre company (1959) with his wife, Franca Rame. His populist plays often use farce as well as surreal effects, and have political themes; best known are *Accidental Death of an Anarchist* (Morte accidentale di un anarchico, 1970) and *Can't Pay, Won't Pay!* (Non si paga! non si paga!, 1974).

foal — *noun* the young of a horse or of a related animal. — *verb intrans.* to give birth to a foal.
— **in foal** *said of a mare* pregnant.
[from Anglo-Saxon *fola*]

foam *noun* 1 a mass of tiny bubbles forming on the surface of liquids. 2 a substance composed of tiny bubbles formed by passing gas through it. 3 frothy saliva or perspiration. 4 any of many light cellular materials produced by passing gas through, and then solidifying, a liquid. 5 *poetic* the sea.
— **foam at the mouth** 1 to produce frothy saliva. 2 *colloq.* to be furiously angry.
[from Anglo-Saxon *fam*]

foam rubber rubber in cellular form, used chiefly in upholstery.

foamy *adj.* (**foamier, foamiest**) frothy.

fob[1] *verb* (**fobbed, fobbing**) 1 (**fob someone off with something**) to provide them with something inferior, eg a poor substitute, or an inadequate explanation, usually in the hope that they will be satisfied. 2 (**fob something off on someone**) to manage to sell or pass off something inferior. 3 (**fob someone off**) to dismiss or ignore them: *tried to fob off his critics.* [related to German *foppen*, to delude]

fob[2] *noun* 1 a chain attached to a watch. 2 a decorative attachment to a key ring or watch chain. 3 *Hist.* a small watch pocket in a waistcoat or trouser waistband. [perhaps related to German dialect *fuppe*, pocket]

fob watch *noun* a watch for keeping in a fob.

focaccia *noun* a flat round of Italian bread topped with olive oil and herbs or spices. [from Italian *focaccia*, cake]

focal *adj.* relating to, or at, a focus.

focal distance *or* **focal length** the distance between the surface of a mirror or centre of a lens, and its focal point.

focal point 1 the meeting-point of rays reflected by a mirror or passing through a lens. 2 a centre of attraction.

Foch, Ferdinand (1851–1929) French soldier, born in Tarbes. He taught at the Ecole de Guerre, and proved himself a great strategist at the Marne (1914), Ypres, and other World War I battles. In 1918 he became a Marshal of France and commanded the Allied armies.

fo'c'sle *noun* a spelling of **forecastle** suggested by its pronunciation.

focus — *noun* (PL. **focuses, foci**) 1 *Optics* the point on the axis of a lens or curved mirror at which parallel rays of light meet, or from which they appear to diverge. — Also called *focal point*. 2 *Geol.* in seismology, the location of the centre of an earthquake, where the subterranean fracture takes place and from which the elastic waves radiate outward. 3 a centre of interest or attention. 4 special attention paid to something: *a shift of focus.* — *verb* (**focused, focusing** *or* **focussed, focussing**) 1 *trans., intrans.* to bring or be brought into focus; to (cause to) meet or converge at a focus. 2 to adjust the thickness of the lens of the eye or to move the lens of an optical instrument so as to obtain the sharpest possible image of a particular object. 3 to cause electron beams to converge or diverge by varying the voltage or current that controls the magnetic or electric fields through which they pass. 4 *trans., intrans.* to concentrate (one's attention). [from Latin *focus*, hearth, as the centre of the home]

fodder *noun* 1 food, especially hay and straw, for cattle and other farm animals. 2 *colloq.* something that is made use of to feed a constant need: *stories about royalty are fodder for the popular press.* [from Anglo-Saxon *fodor*]

foe *noun old use, poetic* an enemy. [from Anglo-Saxon *fah*, hostile]

foetal same as FETAL.

foetid same as FETID.

foetus same as FETUS.

fog — *noun* 1 a suspension of tiny water droplets or ice crystals forming a cloud close to the ground surface, reducing visibility to less than 1km (if visibility is greater than this it is known as mist). Fog forms when air near to ground level is almost saturated with water vapour, and then cools suddenly, eg when it comes into contact with the cold ground. It is more likely to occur in areas where there is a high level of air pollution, because water vapour can then condense around the particles in the atmosphere. Fog containing smoke is often called 'smog'. 2 *Photog.* a blurred patch on a negative, print, or transparency. 3 *adj.* cloudiness. 4 a state of confusion or bewilderment. — *verb* (**fogged, fogging**) 1 *trans., intrans.* to obscure or become obscured (as if) with fog or condensation. 2 to confuse or perplex.
— **not have the foggiest idea** *colloq.* not to know at all.
[perhaps from Norse]

fog bank a thick cloud of fog.

fogbound *adj.* brought to a standstill by fog.

fogey *or* **fogy** *noun* (PL. **fogeys, fogies**) *noun derog.* someone with boring, old-fashioned ideas.

Fogg, Phileas the eccentric Englishman who, with his valet Passepartout, makes a historic journey round the globe in Jules Verne's *Around the World in Eighty Days*.

foggy *adj.* (**foggier, foggiest**) 1 covered with fog. 2 not clear; confused.

foghorn *noun* a horn that sounds a warning at regular intervals to ships in fog.

fog lamp a powerful lamp used by vehicles in fog.

Föhn wind a warm dry wind descending on the leeward side of a mountain, found in the European Alps and other mountainous areas. As moist air rises on the windward side, it cools and loses moisture before descending and warming, often causing a sudden rise in temperature. In the Rockies, N America, it is known as a *chinook* wind, in New Zealand as a *Nor-Wester*, and in Argentina as a *zonda*.

foible *noun* a slight personal weakness or eccentricity. [from Old French *foible*, variant of *faible*, feeble]

foil[1] *verb* to prevent, thwart, or frustrate (a person or attempt). [from Old French *fuler*, to trample or full cloth]

foil[2] *noun* 1 metal beaten or rolled out into thin sheets. 2 a thing or person that acts as a contrast to, and brings out, the superior or different qualities of another. [from Old French *foil*, leaf, from Latin *folium*]

foil[3] *noun* a long slender sword with its point protected by a button, used in the sport of fencing.

foist *verb* (**foist something on someone**) 1 to inflict something unwanted on them. 2 to palm off something inferior on them. [perhaps from Dutch *vuist*, fist]

Fokine, Michel, originally **Mikhail Mikhaylovich Fokine** (1880–1942) Russian-born US dancer and choreographer, born in St Petersburg. He worked as choreographer with Diaghilev's Ballets Russes in Paris from 1909, and in 1923 went to New York, where he took US citizenship (1932). He is credited with the creation of a more expressive approach to ballet than the artificial, stylized mode prevalent at the turn of the century. Among the ballets he choreographed are Chopin's *Les Sylphides* and Stravinsky's *Petrushka*.

Fokker, Anthony Herman Gerard (1890–1939) Dutch aircraft engineer, born in Kediri, Java. He built his first plane in 1911, and in 1913 founded the Fokker aircraft factory at Schwerin, Germany, to make warplanes for the

German air force in World War I. After the war he set up a factory in the Netherlands and later operated also in Britain and the USA.

fold¹ — *verb* **1** (*also* **fold something over, back, up,** *etc*) to double it over so that one part lies on top of another. **2** *intrans.* to be able to be folded: *it folds away for storage.* **3** to intertwine (one's arms) across one's chest or bend up (one's legs). **4** *said of an insect, etc* to bring in (wings) close to its body. **5** *intrans. said of flower petals* to close. **6** to wrap up. **7** to clasp (someone) in one's arms, etc. **8** to stir (an ingredient) gently into a mixture with an action like folding. **9** (*also* **fold up**) *colloq., said of a business, etc* to collapse; to fail. — *noun* **1** a doubling of one layer over another. **2** a rounded or sharp bend made by this; a crease. **3** a hollow in the landscape. **4** *Geol.* a buckling, bending, or contortion of stratified (layered) rocks as a result of movements of the Earth's crust. The most common types of fold are arch-shaped (*anticlines*) and trough-shaped (*synclines*). [from Anglo-Saxon *faldan,* to fold]

fold² *noun* **1** a walled or fenced enclosure for sheep or cattle. **2** the body of believers within the protection of a church. [from Anglo-Saxon *falod*]

-fold *suffix* **1** multiplied by a stated number: *increased threefold.* **2** having a certain number of parts: *a twofold benefit.* [from Anglo-Saxon *-feald*]

folder *noun* a cardboard or plastic cover in which to keep loose papers.

Folger Shakespeare Library a research library with holdings of over 250 000 volumes and 40 000 manuscripts largely relating to 16c–17c literature and drama. The collection of American industrialist Henry Clay Folger (1857–1930) forms the core of the library, which was founded in Washington, DC in 1932.

foliaceous *adj.* **1** consisting of or resembling leaves. **2** *Geol.* composed of thin leaflike or plate-like layers of minerals; laminated. [from Latin *foliaceus,* from *folium,* leaf]

foliage *noun* the leaves on a tree or plant. [from Old French *fueillage,* from *feuille,* leaf]

foliate *adj.* leaf-like, or having leaves. [from Latin *foliatus,* leafy]

foliation *noun* **1** *Metall.* the process of beating metal into thin sheets. **2** *Bot.* the development of leaves.

folic acid *Biochem.* a member of the vitamin B complex that is found in many foods, especially liver and green leafy vegetables, and is required for the manufacture of DNA and RNA and the formation of red blood cells. Deficiency of the vitamin causes anaemia and retarded growth. [from Latin *folium,* leaf]

Folies-Bergère a music hall opened in Paris (1869) as a venue for pantomime and opera, which became known for its performances full of scantily-clad women. It gained an international reputation under the direction (1918–66) of Paul Derval and showcased the talents of such stars as Mistinguett and Maurice Chevalier.

folio *noun* (PL. **folios**) **1** a leaf of a manuscript, etc, numbered on one side. **2** *Printing* a page number in a book. **3** *Hist.* a sheet of paper folded once; a book of the largest size, composed of such sheets: *a folio edition.* **4** *old use* a folder. [from Latin *in folio,* on (a certain numbered) leaf]

folk — *noun* **1** (*with pl. verb*) people. **2** (*with pl. verb*) (*also colloq.* **folks**) one's family. **3** a people or tribe. **4** *colloq.* folk music. — *adj.* traditional among a people; of popular origin: *folk music / a folksong.* [from Anglo-Saxon *folc*]

folk art traditional handicrafts, especially pottery, wood-carvings, textiles, and basketware, produced by local craftsmen with no formal training, usually employing techniques, patterns, and designs that have been handed down from generation to generation. The products may be functional or decorative, or have religious significance.

Folkestone POP (1981) 44 000, a seaport and resort in Shepway district, Kent, SE England. HISTORY the physician William Harvey, who discovered the circulation of blood, was born here in 1578; became a notable bathing resort in the 19c. NOTABLE FEATURE Church of St Mary and St Eanswythe (13c).

folklore *noun* the customs, beliefs, stories, traditions, etc of particular peoples, or the study of these.

folk music traditional music in Europe, N America, India, and Asia, evolved from oral transmission and usually of ancient rural or peasant origins, evoking the events of daily life.

folksy *adj.* (**folksier, folksiest**) simple and homely, especially in an over-sweet way.

follicle *noun* **1** *Anat.* a small cavity or sac within a tissue or organ, eg hair follicle, Graafian follicle. **2** *Bot.* a fruit formed from a single carpel, containing several seeds, which splits along one side when mature, eg columbine fruit. [from Latin *folliculus,* diminutive of *follis,* bellows]

follicle-stimulating hormone (ABBREV. FSH) *Physiol.* a hormone, secreted by the pituitary gland in vertebrates, that plays an important role in reproduction. In mammals it stimulates the growth of the ovarian follicles (in females) and the production of sperm (in males).

follow *verb* **1** (**follow someone** *or* **follow after someone**) to go or come after them. **2** to accompany. **3** to pursue stealthily. **4** to accept as leader or authority. **5** *intrans.* to result; to be a consequence. **6** to go along (a road, etc), alongside (a river, etc) or on the path marked by (signs). **7** to watch (someone or something) as he, she, or it moves: *her eyes followed him up the street.* **8** to pass or practise: *follow a life of self-denial / follow a trade.* **9** to conform to: *follows a familiar pattern.* **10** to obey (advice, etc). **11** *trans., intrans.* to copy: *follow her example.* **12** *trans., intrans.* to understand. **13** to read (a piece of writing or music) while listening to a performance of it. **14** to take a keen interest in (a sport, etc). — **as follows** as announced after this or shown below.

followed by ... with ... next.

follow on 1 to continue. **2** *Cricket, said of a side* to have to bat a second innings immediately after the first.

follow through *Tennis, Golf* to continue the action of a stroke after hitting the ball.

follow something through *or* **up** to investigate or test it.

follow something up to take the next step after a particular procedure: *followed up their investigations with a detailed report.* [from Anglo-Saxon *folgian*]

follower *noun* **1** a person who comes after. **2** a person who copies. **3** a supporter. **4** an attendant.

following — *noun* a body of supporters. — *adj.* **1** coming after; next. **2** about to be mentioned: *need to deal with the following points.* **3** *said of a wind* blowing in the direction in which a ship, etc is travelling. — *prep.* after.

follow-on *noun* *Cricket* following on, the batting of a second innings by the same side immediately after the first.

follow-through *noun* following through; further investigation or testing.

follow-up *noun* following up; further action or investigation.

folly *noun* (PL. **follies**) **1** foolishness; a foolish act. **2** a mock temple, castle, etc built as a romantic addition to a view. [from Old French *folie,* madness]

Folsom a prehistoric 'kill site' in New Mexico, USA, excavated in 1926. The discovery of 19 fluted spear points of 9000–8000 BC, with the skeletons of 23 extinct long-horned bison (*Bison antiquus*), established for the first time the co-existence of humans with Ice Age mammals in

the New World, and the antiquity of the Native American population.

foment *verb* to encourage or foster (ill-feeling, etc). [from Latin *fomentum,* poultice]

fomentation *noun* the act or process of fomenting.

fond *adj.* **1** (**fond of someone** *or* **something**) having a liking for them. **2** loving. **3** *said of wishes, hopes, etc* foolishly impractical. [from Middle English *fonnen,* to act foolishly]

Fonda, Henry (Jaynes) (1905–82) US actor, born in Grand Island, Nebraska. After some success on Broadway, he went to Hollywood in 1935. His performances in the *Young Mr Lincoln* (1939), *The Grapes of Wrath* (1940), and *The Oxbow Incident* (1943) established him in the role of the honest US folk hero. He won an Oscar for his role in *On Golden Pond* (1981).

Fonda, Jane (Seymour) (1937–) US actress, daughter of Henry Fonda, born in New York City. After appearances on Broadway, she married director Roger Vadim, with whom she made *La Ronde* (1964) and *Barbarella* (1968). Later roles included *Klute* (1971) and *Coming Home* (1978), for which she won Oscars, *The China Syndrome* (1978), *On Golden Pond* (1981), and *The Morning After* (1986). Noted for her anti-nuclear and feminist activities, as well as the anti-war stance which earned her the name of 'Hanoi Jane' during the Vietnam War, in the 1980s she also became involved with women's health and fitness.

fondant *noun* a soft sweet or paste made with sugar and water. [from French *fondant,* from *fondre,* to melt]

fondle *verb* to touch, stroke, or caress affectionately. [from earlier *fond,* to handle]

fondly *adv.* in a fond way.

fondness *noun* being fond.

fondue *noun* **1** an originally Swiss dish of hot cheese sauce into which bits of bread are dipped. **2** a steak dish, the pieces of meat being cooked at table by dipping briefly into hot oil. [from French *fondu(e),* from *fondre,* to melt]

Fongafale POP (1985) 3 000, the capital of Tuvalu, situated on Funafuti atoll.

font *noun* the basin in a church that holds water for baptisms. [from Anglo-Saxon *fant,* from Latin *fons,* fountain]

Fontainebleau a 16c chateau built by Italian craftsmen for Francis I on the site of an earlier royal chateau-fortress at Fontainebleau in France. It was used by Napoleon as his imperial palace. It is a World Heritage site.

fontanelle *noun* a gap between the bones of the skull in a young child or animal. [from Old French *fontanele*]

Fontenay Abbey a Cistercian abbey, founded in 1119 by Bernard of Clairvaux at Fontenay in NE France. It was abandoned by the order in the 18c, but the abbey remains were restored after 1906. It is a World Heritage site.

Fontenoy, Battle of a battle (1745) in which French forces under Louis XIV of France and Maurice, Marshal of Saxony, decisively defeated an Anglo-Dutch-Austrian army under William Augustus, Duke of Cumberland. Fought in Hainault in the Austrian Netherlands, the battle ensured the French conquest of Flanders in the War of the Austrian Succession, and was the last major military victory for a French army until the French Revolution.

Fonteyn, Dame Margot, in full Margot Fonteyn de Arias, *née* Margaret Hookham (1919–91) English ballerina, born in Reigate, Surrey. Her entire career from 1934 was spent with the Vic–Wells Ballet, which became Sadler's Wells, then the Royal Ballet. After her first solo appearance in *The Haunted Ballroom* (1939), she became one of the greatest ballerinas of the 20c, both in classic roles and in creating new roles for Frederick Ashton. A new partnership with Rudolph Nureyev in the 1960s extended her performing career.

Foochow see FUZHOU.

food *noun* **1** a substance taken in by a living organism that provides it with energy and materials for growth, maintenance, and repair of tissues. The human body requires proteins, fats, carbohydrates, vitamins, minerals, and water in order to carry out these processes. **2** solid as distinct from liquid nourishment: *food and drink*. **3** something that provides stimulation: *food for thought*. [from Anglo-Saxon *foda*]

food additive see panel p. 478.

Food and Agriculture Organization (of the United Nations) a United Nations agency established in 1945 with the aim of improving nutritional standards and the production and distribution of food and farm products, especially to developing countries, and providing financial support in emergency situations.

food chain a sequence of organisms arranged in such a way that each feeds on the organism below it in the chain, and serves as a source of food for the organism above it.
◇ All food chains begin with green plants (known as *producers*), including plant plankton, which manufacture carbohydrates from carbon dioxide and water by the process of photosynthesis. Herbivorous animals (*primary consumers*) then eat the plants, and carnivorous animals (*secondary consumers*) eat the herbivores, and may themselves be eaten by different carnivores (*tertiary consumers*). Such simple systems rarely exist in practice, and in most natural ecosystems a number of food chains interact to form complex food webs, because most consumers eat more than one type of food, and may themselves be eaten by more than one type of predator.

foodie *noun colloq.* a person who is greatly or excessively interested in the preparation and eating of food.

foodism *noun* interest in, or concern over, food.

food poisoning any of various illnesses that result from eating food or drinking water containing toxins or micro-organisms, especially species of the bacterium *Salmonella*. The main symptoms of food poisoning are vomiting and diarrhoea. Non-bacterial food poisoning may be caused by eating poisonous mushrooms, shellfish, etc.

food processor an electrical apparatus for chopping or blending food.

foodstuff *noun* a substance used as food.

food technology the application of scientific methods and engineering technology to the commercial processing, preparation, packaging, storage, and distribution of foodstuffs.
◇ Food technology employs both traditional preservation methods such as drying, smoking, salting, and pickling, and modern techniques such as canning, refrigeration, deep-freezing, freeze-drying, pasteurization, ultra-heat treatment, irradiation, and the use of a wide range of chemical additives.

food value the nutritional value of a particular food, expressed in terms of its protein, carbohydrate, fat, fibre, and energy content. In many countries it is a legal requirement for such information to be displayed on food packaging.

food web *Biol.* the interlocking patterns formed by a series of interconnected food chains.

Fool, The the loyal companion of Lear in Shakespeare's *King Lear*, who tries to point out to his master the folly of his ways.

fool[1] — *noun* **1** a person lacking common sense or intelligence. **2** someone made to appear ridiculous. **3** *Hist.* a person employed by kings, nobles, etc to amuse them; a jester. — *verb* **1** deceive (someone) so that they appear foolish.

2 (**fool someone into** *or* **out of something**) to persuade them by deception to do something or not to do it. **3** (**fool about** *or* **around**) to behave stupidly or playfully.
— **make a fool of someone** to trick them, or make them appear ridiculous.
make a fool of oneself to appear foolish.
nobody's fool too wary to be tricked or deceived.
play the fool deliberately to act in a comically foolish manner.
[from Old French *fol*]

fool[2] *noun* a dessert of puréed fruit mixed with cream or custard. [perhaps from FOOL[1]]

foolery *noun* (PL. **fooleries**) stupid or ridiculous behaviour.

foolhardiness *noun* **1** being foolhardy. **2** a foolhardy act or foolhardy behaviour.

foolhardy *adj.* taking foolish risks; rash; reckless. [from Old French *fol hardi*, foolish-bold]

foolish *adj.* **1** unwise; senseless. **2** ridiculous.

foolishly *adv.* in a foolish way.

foolishness *noun* **1** being foolish. **2** a foolish act; foolish behaviour.

foolproof *adj.* **1** *said of a plan, etc* unable to go wrong. **2** *said of a machine, etc* unable to be misunderstood or misused; simple to use.

Fools, Feast of a festival of the medieval clergy, celebrated especially in France (26–28 Dec) in which the Mass and other ecclesiastical rites were burlesqued, and a mock bishop or pope (often a boy) elected. The tradition died out with the Reformation.

foolscap *noun* a large size of printing- or writing-paper, measuring $17 \times 13\frac{1}{2}$in (432×343mm). [from the jester's cap used as a watermark]

fool's errand a pointless or unprofitable task or venture.

fool's gold see PYRITE.

fool's paradise a state of confidence based on false expectations.

Foot, Michael (Mackintosh) (1913–) English Labour politician, born in Plymouth, Devon. He joined the staff of the *Tribune* (1937), became editor there (1948–52, 1955–60), and was also acting editor of the *Evening Standard* (1942–4) and a political columnist on the *Daily Herald* (1944–64). He became an MP in 1945, and was Secretary of State for Employment (1974–6), Deputy Leader (1976–80), then Leader (1980–3) of the Labour Party, but resigned the leadership after his party's heavy defeat in the general election. He is a pacifist and has long been a CND supporter. His prolific writings include a two-volume biography of Aneurin Bevan.

foot *noun* (PL. **feet**) **1** the part of the leg on which a human being or animal stands or walks. **2** in molluscs, a muscular organ used for locomotion, which can be retracted into the animal's shell. **3** the part of a sock, stocking, etc that fits over the foot. **4** the bottom or lower part of something. **5** the end of a bed where the feet go. **6** (PL. **feet, foot**) in the imperial system, a measure of length equal to 12in (30·48cm). **7** a unit of rhythm in verse containing any of various combinations of stressed and unstressed syllables. **8** (*pl.*) *old use* infantry.
— **fall on one's feet** to be unexpectedly or undeservedly lucky.
foot it *colloq.* to walk. **2** *old use* to dance.
foot the bill to pay the bill.
get a foot in the door to gain entry into, or get accepted for the first time in, an organization, profession, etc.
get off on the wrong foot to make a bad start.
get *or* **rise to one's feet** to stand up.
have a foot in both camps to be connected with both of two opposed parties.
have one's feet on the ground to have plenty of common sense.
have one foot in the grave *colloq.* to be very old or near death.

my foot! *colloq.* used to express derisive disbelief.
not put a foot right to make many mistakes.
not put a foot wrong to make no mistakes.
on foot walking.
put one's best foot forward to set off with determination.
put one's feet up to take a rest.
put one's foot down to be firm about something.
put one's foot in it *colloq.* to cause offence or embarrassment.
set foot in *or* **on something** to arrive in or on it.
under foot beneath one's feet.
under one's feet in one's way; hindering one.

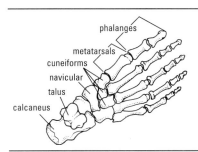

bones of the foot

footage *noun* **1** measurement or payment by the foot. **2** the length of exposed cine film measured in feet.

foot-and-mouth disease a notifiable and highly contagious viral disease of sheep, cattle, pigs, and goats, characterized by the development of blisters in the mouth and around the hooves, by weight loss, and in dairy cattle by a decline in milk yield. In the UK all diseased herds are slaughtered.

football *noun* **1** any of several team games played with a large ball that players try to kick or head into the opposing team's goal or carry across their opponents' goal line. **2** the ball used in the game. See also AMERICAN FOOTBALL, ASSOCIATION FOOTBALL, AUSTRALIAN RULES FOOTBALL, GAELIC FOOTBALL, RUGBY.

Football Association (ABBREV. **FA**) the world's first association football governing body, founded at the Freemason's Tavern, Great Queen St, London, on 26 Oct 1863. It is the governing body of the game in England.

Football League the oldest association football league in the world, formed at the Royal Hotel, Manchester on 17 Apr 1888. It now consists of four divisions comprising a total of 92 teams.

Football Players, The a painting by Henri Rousseau (1908, Guggenheim Museum, New York).

Football War a sudden war (Jul 1969) fought over several days between Honduras and El Salvador, which was rapidly halted by international pressure. Provoked by the wave of migration from overpopulated Salvador to the unoccupied territories of W Honduras, it was so named because recriminations between the two states came to a head during the qualifying matches for the 1970 World Cup.

footbridge *noun* a bridge for pedestrians.

footfall *noun* the sound of a footstep.

foothill *noun* a lower hill on the approach to a high mountain or range.

foothold *noun* a place to put one's foot when climbing.

footing *noun* **1** the stability of one's feet on the ground: *lose one's footing*. **2** basis or status. **3** relationship: *on a friendly footing*.

footlights *pl. noun* in a theatre, a row of lights set along the front edge of a stage to illuminate it.

footloose *adj.* free to go where, or do as, one likes.

Food Additives

Many additives are used in food manufacture: some to preserve the food, some to enhance its appearance, some to intensify its flavour. Those shown below are among the most commonly used; many have given rise to medical controversy regarding adverse reactions in some people.

Number	Name	Source	Function
Colours			
E102	Tartrazine	synthetic, an azo[1] dye	yellow
E104	Quinoline yellow	synthehtic 'coal tar' dye	dull yellow to greenish yellow
107	Yellow 2G	synthetic 'coal tar' dye and azo[1] dye	yellow
E110	Sunset Yellow FCF	synthetic 'coal tar' and azo[1] dye	yellow
E120	Cochineal	pregnant scale insects (*Dactilopius coccus*)	red
E122	Carmoisine	synthetic azo[1] dye	red
E123	Amaranth	synthetic 'coal tar' dye and azo[1] dye	purplish red
E124	Poncean 4R	synthetic 'coal tar' dye and azo[1] dye	red
E127	Erythrosine	the di Sodium salt of 2,4,5,7-tetraiodofluorescein; synthetic 'coal tar' dye	cherry pink to red
128	Red 2G	synthetic 'coal tar' dye and azo[1] dye	red
E131	Patent blue V	synthetic 'coal tar' dye	dark bluish-violet; diagnostic agent
E132	Indigo carmine	synthetic 'coal tar' dye	blue; diagnostic agent
133	Brilliant blue FCF	synthetic 'coal tar' dye	blue, green hues when used with tartrazine
E142	Green S	synthetic 'coal tar' dye	green
E150	Caramel colour	sugar	brown to black
E151	Black PN	synthetic 'coal tar' dye and azo[1] dye	black
154	Brown FK	synthetic mixture of six azo[1] dyes and sodium chloride and/or sodium sulphate	brown
155	Brown HT	synthetic 'coal tar' dye and azo[1] dye	brown
E160(b)	Annatto, Bixin, Norbixin	from the pericarp (seed coat) of the tropical Annatto tree (*Bixa orellana*)	yellow to peach or red
Preservatives			
E210	Benzoic acid	berries, fruits, vegetables; chemical synthesis	antifungal and antibacterial preservative (in an acid medium only)
E211	Sodium benzoate	sodium salt of benzoid acid	antifungal and antibacterial preservative (in a slightly acid medium only)
E212	Potassium benzoate	potassium salt of benzoic acid	antifungal and antibacterial preservative
E213	Calcium benzoate	calcium salt of benzoic acid	antifungal and antibacterial preservative
E214	Ethyl 4-hydroxybenzoate	benzoic acid	antifungal and antibacterial preservative
E215	Ethyl 4-hydroxybenzoate, sodium salt	benzoic acid	antifungal and antibacterial preservative
E216	Propyl 4-hydroxybenzoate	benzoic acid	antimicrobial preservative
E217	Propyl 4-hydroxybenzoate, sodium salt	benzoic acid	antimicrobial preservative
E218	Methyl 4-hydroxybenzoate	synthetic	antimmicrobial preservative
E219	Methyl 4-hydroxybenzoate, sodium salt	benzoic acid	preservative, active against fungi and yeasts, less active against bacteria
E220	Sulphur dioxide	natural; chemical production by combustion of sulphur or gypsum	preservative; bleaching agent; improving agent; stabilizer; antioxidant; used in beer and wine making
E221	Sodium sulphite	sodium salt of sulphurous acid	antimicrobial preservative; sterilizer; prevents discoloration
E222	Sodium hydrogen sulphite	sodium salt of sulphurous acid	preservative for alcoholic beverages
E223	Sodium metabisulphite	sodium salt of sulphurous acid (commercially manufactured)	antimicrobial preservative; antioxidant; bleaching agent
E224	Potassium metabisulphite	sodium salt of sulphurous acid (commercially manufactured)	antimicrobial preservative; antibrowning agent
E226	Calcium sulphite	calcium salt of sulphurous acid	preservative; firming agent; disinfectant
E227	Calcium hydrogen sulphite	calcium salt of sulphurous acid	preservative; firming agent; used in washing beer casks and to prevent secondary fermentation
E249	Potassium nitrate	potassium salt of nitrous acid	meat preservative; curing agent; prevents growth of *Clostridium botulinum* (the bacterium responsible for botulism)
E250	Sodium nitrate	chemical or bacterial action on sodium nitrate	food preservative; prevents growth of *Clostridium botulinum*; salt curing agent; red meat colour
E251	Sodium nitrate	naturally occurring mineral	preservative; salt curing agent; colour fixative
E252	Potassium nitrate	naturally occurring mineral	preservative; salt curing agent; colour fixative
Antioxidants			
E310	Propyl gallate	propyl ester of gallic acid	antioxidant in oils and fats
E311	Octyl gallate	ester of gallic acid	antioxidant
E312	Dodecyl gallate	ester of gallic acid	antioxidant
E320	Butylated hydroxyanisole (BHA)	mixture of 2- and 3-tert-butyl-4-methoxyphenol	antioxidant
E321	Butylated hydroxytoluene (BHT)	synthetic	antioxidant
Emulsifiers, stabilizers and others			
385	Calcium disodium ethylenediamine-NNN'N' tetra-acetate (EDTA)	synthetic preparation	chelating agent; antioxidant
E407	Carrageenan	red seaweeds (*Chondrus crispus* and *Gigartina*)	stabilizer; thickener; suspending and gelling agent; texture modifier
E413	Tragacanth	*Astragalus gummifer* (member of the pea family)	emulsifier; stabilizer; thickener; prevents crystallization of sugar; converts royal icing to a paste
416	Karaya gum	*Sterculia urens* trees	stabilizer; emulsifier; thickener; binding agent in meat products; prevents formation of ice crystals; filling agent; citrus and spice flavouring agent
430	Polyoxyethylene (8) stearate	stearate and ethylene oxide mixture	emulsifier; stabilizer

Food Additives (cont.)		
Number	Name	Source

Food Additives (cont.)

Number	Name	Source	Function
431	Polyoxyethylene (40) stearate	stearate and ethylene oxide mixture	emulsifier; makes bread 'feel fresh'
432	Polyoxyethylene (20) sorbitan monolaurate	sorbitol and ethylene oxide	emulsifier; stabilizer; dispersing agent
433	Polyoxyethylene (20) sorbitan monooleate	sorbitol and ethylene oxide	emulsifier; de-foamer preserves moistness; prevents oil leaking from artificial whipped cream; solubility improver
434	Polyoxyethylene (20) sorbitan monopalmitate	sorbitol and ethylene oxide	emulsifier; stabilizer; dispersing agent (flavours); defoaming agent; wetting agent
435	Polyoxyethylene (20) sorbitan monostearate	sorbitol and ethylene oxide	emulsifier; stabilizer; prevents leakage of oils; preserves moistness; wetting and dispersing agent; prevents greasy taste; foaming agent
436	Polyoxyethylene (20) sorbitan tristearate	sorbitol and ethylene oxide	emulsifier; prevents leakage of oils and water; preserves moistness; wetting and solution agent; defoaming agent; flavour dispersing agent
E450(a)	*tetra* Potassium diphosphate	potassium salt of pyrophosphoric acid	emulsifying salt; buffer; sequestrant; stabilizer
E450(b)	*penta* Sodium triphosphate	sodium salt of triphosphoric acid	emulsifying salt; texturizer; buffer; sequenstrant; stabilizer; water-binding agent; protein solubilization agent
E450(b)	*penta* Potassium triphosphate	potassium salt of triphosphoric acid	emulsifying salt; texturizer; buffer; sequestrant; stabilizer
E450(c)	Sodium polyphosphates	sodium salts of polyphosphoric acids	emulsifying salts; sequestrants; stabilizers; texturizers
Flavour enhancers			
620	L-Glutamic acid	naturally occurring amino acid; carbohydrate fermentation	dietary supplement flavour enhancer; salt substitute
621	*mono* Sodium glutamate	sodium salt of glutamic acid	flavour enhancer
622	Potassium hydrogen L-glutamate	synthetic preparation	flavour enhancer; salt substitute
623	Calcium dihydrogen di-L-glutamate	synthetic preparation	flavour enhancer; salt substitute
627	Guanosine 5'-(*di* Sodium phosphate)	sodium salt of 5'guanylic acid (synthetic preparation)	flavour enhancer
631	Inosine 5'-(*di* Sodium phosphate)	disodium salt of inosinic acid (meat extract and dried sardines)	flavour enhancer
635	Sodium 5'-ribonucleotide	*di* Sodium guanylate and *di* sodium inosinate mixture	flavour enhancer
Improving agents			
924	Potassium bromate	synthetic preparation	flour-maturing or -improving agent; used in beer making
925	Chlorine	naturally occurring gas (earth's crust, seawater)	flour bleaching; drinking water
926	Chlorine dioxide	(synthetic preparation) chlorine and sodium chloride; potassium chlorate and sulphuric acid; nitrogen dioxide passed through sodium chlorate	bleaching agent; improving agent; oxidizing agent; water purifying agent; taste and odour control of water; bactericide and antiseptic

[1]Azo dyes are derivatives of azobenzene, obtained as the reaction products of diazonum salts with tertiary amines or phenols (hydroxy-benzenes). Usually coloured yellow, red, or brown, they have acidic or basic properties.

footman *noun* a uniformed male attendant.

footnote *noun* a note at the bottom of a page.

footpath *noun* **1** a path or track for walkers. **2** a pavement.

footplate *noun* in a steam train, a platform for the driver and fireman.

footprint *noun* **1** the mark or impression of a foot or shoe. **2** *Comput.* the amount of space taken up by a computer and its hardware on a desk, etc.

footsie *noun colloq.* secret foot-touching with someone under the table, etc, especially as an indication of sexual interest.

footslog *verb intrans., trans.* to go on foot; to trudge.

footsore *adj.* having painful feet from prolonged walking.

footstep *noun* **1** the sound of a step in walking. **2** a footprint. — **follow in the footsteps of someone** to do as was done earlier by them; to copy or succeed them.

footstool *noun* a low stool for supporting the feet while sitting.

footway *noun* a passage for pedestrians.

footwear *noun* shoes, boots, socks, etc.

footwork *noun* the agile use of the feet in dancing or sport.

fop *noun* a man who is too consciously elegant in his dress and manners; a dandy.

foppery *or* **foppishness** *noun* (PL. **fopperies**) the behaviour, the concerns, or the clothes of a fop.

foppish *adj.* relating to or characteristic of a fop.

for — *prep.* **1** intended to be given or sent to. **2** towards: *heading for home.* **3** throughout (a time or distance). **4** in order to have, get, etc: *meet for a chat / fight for freedom.* **5** at a cost of. **6** as reward, payment or penalty appropriate to: *got seven months for stealing / charge for one's work.* **7** with a view to: *train for the race.* **8** representing; on behalf of: *the MP for Greenfield / speaking for myself.* **9** to the benefit of: *what can I do for you?* **10** in favour of: *for or against the proposal.* **11** proposing to oneself: *I'm for bed.* **12** because of: *couldn't see for tears.* **13** on account of: *famous for its confectionery.* **14** suitable to the needs of: *books for children.* **15** having as function or purpose: *scissors for cutting hair.* **16** on the occasion of: *got it for my birthday.* **17** meaning: *the German word for 'lazy'.* **18** in place of; in exchange with: *replacements for the breakages / translated word for word.* **19** in proportion to: *one woman for every five men.* **20** up to: *it's for me to decide.* **21** as being: *took you for someone else / know for a fact.* **22** with regard to: *can't beat that for quality.* **23** considering what one would expect: *serious for his age / warm for winter.* **24** about; aimed at: *proposals for peace / a desire for revenge.* **25** in spite of: *quite nice for all his faults.* **26** available to be disposed of or dealt with by: *not for sale.* **27** *with reference to time* **a** at or on: *an appointment for 12.00 on Friday.* **b** so as to be starting by: *7.30 for 8.00.* — *conj.* because. — **be for it** *colloq.* to be about to receive a punishment, etc.

for ever for all time. **if it hadn't been for someone** *or* **something** had they not intervened or occurred. **O for** if only I had. [from Anglo-Saxon *for*]

forage — *noun* **1** (*also* **forage crop**) *Agric.* a crop grown for consumption by livestock, eg grass, clover, kale, turnip, swede, and maize. All forage crops are either very high yielding or very fast growing, and may be grazed directly, or harvested and stored for later use when grass growth is poor. **2** the activity of foraging. — *verb* **1** *intrans.* to search around, especially for food. **2** to gather forage or provisions from (an area). **3** to find by searching. [from Old French *fourrage*]

forasmuch as *conj.* old use *Legal* since; seeing that.

foray *noun* **1** a raid or attack. **2** a venture; an attempt. [from Middle English *forrayen*, to pillage]

forbade see FORBID.

forbear[1] *verb trans., intrans.* (with stress on -*bear*) (PAST TENSE **forbore**; PAST PARTICIPLE **forborne**) (**forbear from something, or to do something**) to stop oneself going as far as that; to refrain from it: *forbear from answering / forbear to mention it.* [from Anglo-Saxon *forberan*]

forbear² (with stress on *for-*) same as FOREBEAR.

forbearance *noun* patience and self-control.

forbearing *adj.* patient and tolerant.

Forbes, Edward (1815–54) British naturalist, born in Douglas, Isle of Man. In 1841 he joined the crew of the *Beacon* as naturalist during the survey around parts of Asia Minor. He was later appointed professor at King's College in London, Curator of the Museum of the Geological Society of London, the first palaeontologist to HM Geological Survey, and then professor at the Royal School of Mines and at Edinburgh University. His work did much to advance and systematize several disciplines in natural history. He also made formative observations in oceanography; his observations of depth-related communities in the sea effectively laid the foundations for the sciences of biogeography and palaeoecology.

forbid *verb* (**forbidding**; PAST TENSE **forbade**, **forbad**; PAST PARTICIPLE **forbidden**) **1** to order (someone) not to do something. **2** to prohibit. **3** to refuse access to: *had forbidden them the orchard / forbidden territory*. **4** *trans., intrans.* to prevent or not allow: *time forbids a longer stay*. [from Anglo-Saxon *forbeodan*]

Forbidden City the Imperial Palace in Beijing (Peking). It was the residence of the imperial rulers of China from its construction by 200 000 workmen in 1420 until the fall of the Qing dynasty in 1911. The walled and moated palace complex covers 0.8sq km, and it is the best-preserved example of medieval Chinese architecture.

forbidding *adj.* threatening; grim.

forbiddingly *adv.* in a forbidding way.

forbore, forborne see FORBEAR.

force — *noun* **1** strength; power; impact or impetus. **2** compulsion, especially with threats or violence. **3** military power. **4** passion or earnestness. **5** strength or validity: *the force of her argument / come into force*. **6** meaning. **7** influence: *by force of habit*. **8** a person or thing seen as an influence: *a force for good*. **9** *Physics* any external agent that produces a change in the speed or direction of a moving object, or that causes a stationary object to move. It is equal to the rate of change of momentum of the object on which it acts, ie for an object of mass m and acceleration a, the force $F = ma$. When a force moves through some distance, it does work and uses energy. The SI unit of force is the newton (N): *the force of gravity*. **10** any irresistible power or agency: *the forces of nature*. **11** the term used in specifying wind speed: *a force-10 gale*. **12 a** a military body. **b** (**forces**) a nation's armed services. **13** any organized body or workers, etc. **14** (**the force**) the police force. — *verb* **1** to make or compel. **2** (**force someone** *or* **something back** *or* **out**) to drive them back or out, especially meeting resistance. **3** to obtain by effort, strength, threats, violence, etc: *forced an admission from them*. **4** (**force one's way**) to make progress by effort or ruthless determination. **5** to produce with an effort. **6** to inflict: *force one's opinions on people*. **7** to cause (a plant) to grow or (fruit) to ripen unnaturally quickly. **8** to strain: *force one's voice*.
— **force someone's hand** to compel them to act in a certain way.
in force 1 *said of a law, etc* valid; effective. **2** in large numbers.
join forces to come together or unite for a purpose.
[from Old French, from Latin *fortia*, strength]

forced *adj.* **1** *said of a smile, laugh, etc* unnatural; unspontaneous. **2** done or provided under compulsion: *forced labour*. **3** carried out as an emergency: *a forced landing*. **4** done with great and long effort: *forced marches*.

force-feed *verb* to force to swallow food.

forceful *adj.* powerful; effective; influential.

forcefully *adv.* in a forceful way.

forcefulness *noun* being forceful.

force majeure *Legal* any irresistible force or compulsion which will excuse a party from carrying out or completing its part of the contract. [French, = superior force]

forcemeat *noun* a mixture of sausage meat, herbs, etc used as stuffing. [from earlier *farce*, stuffing]

forceps *pl. noun* a surgical instrument like pincers, for gripping firmly. [said to be from Latin *formus*, warm + *capere*, to take]

forcible *adj.* **1** done by, or involving, force. **2** powerful: *a forcible reminder*. [from Old French, from *force*, force]

forcibly *adv.* by force.

Ford, Ford Madox, originally **Ford Hermann Hueffer** (1873–1939) English writer, born in Merton, Surrey. He collaborated with Joseph Conrad in *The Inheritors* (1901) and *Romance* (1903) and founded the *English Review* (1908). Also the founder-editor of *The Transatlantic Review* (1924, Paris), he is best known for his novel *The Good Soldier* (1915) and the war tetralogy *Parade's End* (1924–8).

Ford, Gerald R(udolph) (1913–) US politician, the 38th President, born in Omaha, Nebraska. He served in the US Navy during World War II, then became a Republican member of the House of Representatives (1949–73), and on the resignation of Spiro Agnew in 1973 was appointed Vice-President. He became President (1974–6) when Nixon resigned because of the Watergate scandal, but the full pardon he granted to Nixon (1974) made him unpopular, and he was defeated in the 1976 presidential election by Jimmy Carter.

Ford, Harrison (1942–) US film actor, born in Chicago, Illinois. While pursuing a secondary career as a carpenter, he made small appearances in various films until achieving fame in *Star Wars* (1977) and its sequels. Later successes include *Raiders of the Lost Ark* (1981), *Witness* (1985), *Presumed Innocent* (1990), and *The Fugitive* (1993).

Ford, Henry (1863–1947) US automobile engineer and manufacturer, born in Greenfield, Michigan. He produced his first petrol-driven motor car in 1893, and in 1899 founded a company in Detroit, designing his own cars. In 1903 he started the Ford Motor Company, pioneering the modern 'assembly line' mass-production techniques for his famous Model T (1908–9), 15 million of which were produced up to 1928.

Ford, John (c.1586–c.1640) English dramatist, born in Ilsington, Devon. He often collaborated with Thomas Dekker, William Rowley, and John Webster. His own plays were much influenced by Richard Burton's *Anatomy of Melancholy* (1621), which led him into the stage presentation of the melancholic, the unnatural, and the horrible, in such works as *The Lover's Melancholy* (1629) and *'Tis Pity She's a Whore* (1633).

Ford, John, originally **Sean Aloysius O'Fearna** (1895–1973) US film director, born at Cape Elizabeth, Maine. He went to Hollywood in 1913, where he worked as stunt man, actor, and assistant director. He became identified with the Western genre, through the success of *Stagecoach* (1939), among others. His four Best Director Oscars were awarded for *The Informer* (1935), *The Grapes of Wrath* (1940), *How Green Was My Valley* (1941), and *The Quiet Man* (1952).

Ford, Mistress one of the two 'merry wives' who receives a love-letter from Falstaff in Shakespeare's *The Merry Wives of Windsor*. Her jealous husband is called Frank.

ford — *noun* a shallow crossing-place in a river. — *verb* to ride, drive, or wade across (a stream, etc). [from Anglo-Saxon *ford-faran*, to go]

fordable *adj.* capable of being forded.

Ford Foundation a philanthropic foundation set up in 1936 by Henry Ford and his son, Edsel, as an international charity mainly concerned with food shortages and population control in developing nations. It has also been involved in the arts and humanities, and in public television in the USA.

Ford, Model T the first mass-produced car, launched in 1908 by Henry Ford in Detroit. At first the machine was hand-assembled by skilled mechanics and engineers which resulted in lengthy production times and very expensive automobiles. However with the introduction of the assembly line in 1913 and standardized features — 'any color you like as long as it's black' — production times were drastically reduced and cars became much cheaper. It was estimated that by 1920 roughly half of all the cars on the road in the world were Model T Fords. The last Model T was produced in 1928.

fore — *adj.* towards the front. — *noun* the front part. — *interj. Golf* ball coming!
— **fore and aft** at front and rear; at bow and stern; from bow to stern.
to the fore at or to the front; prominent; conspicuous.
[from Anglo-Saxon *fore*]

fore- *prefix* **1** before or beforehand: *forewarn*. **2** in front: *foreleg*. [from Anglo-Saxon *fore*]

fore-and-aft *adj. Naut., said of a sail or rigging* set lengthways, pointing to the bow and stern.

forearm¹ *noun* (with stress on *fore-*) the lower part of the arm between wrist and elbow.

forearm² *verb* (with stress on *-arm*) to prepare or arm beforehand.

forebear *or* **forbear** *noun* (with stress on *for-*) an ancestor. [from FORE- + BE + -ER]

forebode *verb* to foretell; to be a sign of (especially something bad).

foreboding *noun* a feeling of approaching trouble.

forebrain *noun Anat.* the largest part of the vertebrate brain, consisting of the left and right cerebral hemispheres, thalamus, and hypothalamus. In the human brain it is the region that is most strikingly different to the brain of other animals.

forecast — *verb* (PAST TENSE AND PAST PARTICIPLE **forecast**, **forecasted**) to give warning of; to predict; to gauge or estimate (weather, statistics, etc) in advance. — *noun* a warning, prediction, or advance estimate.

forecastle *noun* the bow section of a ship, formerly the quarters of the crew.

foreclose *verb intrans., said of a bank, etc* to repossess a property because of failure to pay back the loan used.

foreclosure *noun* the act or process of foreclosing.

forecourt *noun* a courtyard or paved area in front of a building, eg a filling-station.

forefather *noun* an ancestor.

forefinger *noun* the finger next to the thumb; the index finger.

forefoot *noun* either of the two front feet of a four-legged animal.

forefront *noun* **1** the very front. **2** the most prominent or active position.

foregather *verb intrans.* (**foregathered**, **foregathering**) to meet together; to assemble.

forego *or* **forgo** *verb* (PAST TENSE **forewent**; PAST PARTICIPLE **foregone**) to do without; to sacrifice or give up.

foregoing — *adj.* just mentioned. — *noun* the thing or person just mentioned.

foregone *adj.*
— **foregone conclusion** a predictable result; a certainty.

foreground *noun* **1** the part of a view or picture nearest to the viewer. **2** a position where one is noticeable.

forehand *noun Tennis, etc* a stroke made with palm facing forward. See also BACKHAND[1].

forehead *noun* the part of the face between the eyebrows and hairline; the brow.

foreign *adj.* **1** of, from, relating, or belonging to another country. **2** concerned with relations with other countries: *foreign affairs.* **3** not belonging where found: *a piece of grit or other foreign body in the eye.* **4** (**foreign to someone**) **a** unfamiliar: *the technique was foreign to them.* **b** uncharacteristic: *envy was foreign to his nature.*

foreign aid *Politics* financial or other aid given by richer to poorer nations. Foreign aid may be in the form of grants, gifts, special trading deals, cheap loans or credit terms, expertise, or goods.

Foreign and Commonwealth Office the UK government department concerned with foreign affairs, created out of the Foreign Office and Colonial Office in the mid-1960s.

foreign correspondent a newspaper or broadcasting correspondent working in a foreign country in order to report news, etc.

foreigner *noun* **1** a person from another country. **2** an unfamiliar person; a person who doesn't belong.

foreign exchange *Commerce* the amount of currency of foreign origin held in a country. It is derived from exporting and from overseas investment.

Foreign Legion, French **La Légion Étrangère** an élite formation of the French Army, which is recruited from non-French nationals. It was first raised in 1831 to control French colonies in Africa, and has seen action almost wherever French arms have been engaged. Often associated with romance and adventure (eg as in P C Wren's *Beau Geste*, 1924), the legion retains its reputation for toughness.

foreign minister *or* **foreign secretary** the government minister responsible for a country's foreign affairs.

foreign office the department of a government dealing with foreign affairs.

foreknowledge *noun* knowledge about something before it happens.

foreleg *noun* either of the two front legs of a four-legged animal.

forelock *noun* a lock of hair growing or falling over the brow.

foreman *or* **forewoman** **1** a man or woman in charge of a body of fellow workers. **2** the spokesman or spokeswoman of a jury.

foremost — *adj.* leading; best. — *adv.* leading; coming first.
— **first and foremost** essentially; most importantly.
[from Anglo-Saxon *formest*, from *forma*, first]

forenoon *noun Scot.* the morning.

forensic *adj.* **1** relating to or belonging to courts of law, or to the work of a lawyer in court. **2** concerned with the scientific side of legal investigations. [from Latin *forensis*, of the *forum*, where law courts were held in Rome]

forensically *adv.* in a forensic way.

forensic linguistics the use of linguistic techniques to investigate crime and to examine evidence relating to a crime. For example, the language used in a written version of a defendant's verbal statement to police may be compared with the defendant's normal speech style, to determine whether the written version is an accurate reflection of what he or she said.

forensic medicine the branch of medicine concerned with the production of evidence to be used in civil or criminal law cases. It is an import-

ant means of determining the cause of death in unexplained or suspicious circumstances.
◊ Forensic investigations are usually carried out by pathologists at the request of a coroner, and are based on post-mortem examinations and laboratory tests. These may include analysis of blood or other body fluids found at the scene of a crime (in order to identify the criminal), identification of bodies (eg from dental evidence), assessment of the time of death, determination of the age and cause of injuries, and analysis of any drugs and poisons present in the body. Sophisticated laboratory techniques such as DNA fingerprinting are playing an increasingly important role in forensic investigations.

foreordain *verb* to determine (events, etc) in advance; to destine.

foreplay *noun* sexual stimulation leading up to sexual intercourse.

forerunner *noun* **1** a person or thing that goes before; a predecessor; an earlier type or version. **2** a sign of what is to come. **3** an advance messenger or herald.

foresee *verb* (PAST TENSE **foresaw**; PAST PARTICIPLE **foreseen**) to see or know in advance.

foreseeable *adj.* capable of being foreseen.

foreshadow *verb* to be an advance sign or indication of.

foreshore *noun* the space on the shore between the high and low tide marks.

foreshorten *verb* (**foreshortened, foreshortening**) in photographic or artistic perspective, to give a shortening effect to: *foreshortened limbs.*
◊ In art, *foreshortening* is the distortion of the true relative proportions of a form or figure so as to convey a sense of perspective. For example, a hand stretched towards a viewer will appear large in proportion to the arm, which will appear correspondingly short or barely visible. It was a common feature in Mannerist and Baroque painting, and was used to reinforce the message in the famous World War I poster 'Your Country Needs You'.

foresight *noun* **1** the ability to foresee. **2** consideration taken or provision made for the future. **3** the front sight on a gun.

foreskin *noun Anat.* the fold of skin that covers the end (glans) of the penis. It may be surgically removed by circumcision very early in childhood for religious or other reasons.

Forest, Lee De see DE FOREST, LEE.

forest *noun* **1** *Bot.* a plant community extending over a large area and dominated by trees, the crowns of which form an unbroken covering layer or canopy. **2** a tract of country formerly owned, and used for hunting, by a sovereign. **3** a dense arrangement of objects. [from Latin *forestis silva*, unfenced woodland]

forestall *verb* to prevent by acting in advance: *issue an announcement to forestall the inevitable questions.* [from Middle English *forstallen*, to waylay]

forestation *noun Bot.* the planting of trees on land that was formerly used for other purposes.

forested *adj.* covered with, or as if with, trees.

forester *noun* a person in charge of a forest or trained in forestry.

forestry *noun* the management of forest and woodland for the commercial production of timber.
◊ Forestry includes the growing and maintenance of trees, and the felling of mature trees, usually for timber. It is also concerned with preservation of the associated wildlife and recreational resources, protection of trees from pests and diseases, and fire prevention. Most forests in the UK are planted with rapidly growing softwood conifers, which provide timber that is widely used in construction and as raw material for paper pulp.

foretaste *noun* a brief experience of what is to come.

foretell *verb* (PAST TENSE AND PAST PARTICIPLE **foretold**) to tell about beforehand; to predict or prophesy.

forethought *noun* consideration taken, or provision made, for the future.

foretold see FORETELL.

forever *adv.* **1** always; eternally. **2** continually: *forever whining.*

forewarn *verb* to warn beforehand.

forewoman see FOREMAN.

foreword *noun* an introduction to a book, often by a writer other than the author.

forfeit — *noun* something that one must surrender as a penalty. — *adj.* surrendered or liable to be surrendered as a penalty. — *verb* **1** to hand over as a penalty: *forfeit one's passport.* **2** to give up or do without voluntarily. [from Old French *forfait*, from Latin *forisfactum*, penalty]

forfeiture *noun* **1** the act of forfeiting. **2** the state of being forfeited. **3** something that is forfeited.

forgave see FORGIVE.

forge[1] — *noun* **1** a special furnace for heating metal, especially iron, prior to shaping it. **2** the workshop of a blacksmith, where metal is heated and shaped into horseshoes, tools, etc. — *verb* **1** to shape metal by heating and hammering, or by heating and applying pressure more gradually. **2** to make an imitation of (a signature, document, banknote, etc) for a dishonest or fraudulent purpose. [from Old French, from Latin *fabrica*, workshop]

forge[2] *verb intrans.* to move steadily.
— **forge ahead 1** to progress swiftly. **2** to take the lead.

forgery *noun* (PL. **forgeries**) **1** imitating pictures, documents, signatures, etc for a fraudulent purpose. **2** a copy made for a fraudulent purpose.

forget *verb trans., intrans.* (**forgetting**; PAST TENSE **forgot**; PAST PARTICIPLE **forgotten**) (*usually* **forget something** *or* **forget about something**) **1** (*also* **forget to do something**) to fail to remember it or be unable to remember it. **2** to stop being aware of: *forgot his headache in the excitement.* **3** to neglect or overlook (something). **4** to leave behind accidentally. **5** *colloq.* to dismiss from one's mind: *you can forget your proposed skiing trip.* **6** to lose control over (oneself).
— **forget it** *colloq.* it doesn't matter.
not forgetting ... and also ...; including ...
[from Anglo-Saxon *forgietan*]

forgetful *adj.* inclined to forget.

forgetfully *adv.* in a forgetful way.

forgetfulness *noun* a tendency to be forgetful.

forget-me-not *noun* a small plant with blue flowers. [a translation of Old French *ne m'oubliez mye*]

forgivable *adj.* able or likely to be forgiven.

forgivably *adv.* in a way that could be forgiven.

forgive *verb* (PAST TENSE **forgave**; PAST PARTICIPLE **forgiven**) **1** to stop being angry with (someone who has done something wrong) or about (an offence). **2** to pardon. **3** to spare (someone) the paying of (a debt). [from Anglo-Saxon *forgiefan*]

forgiveness *noun* **1** the act of forgiving or state of being forgiven. **2** readiness to forgive.

forgiving *adj.* ready to forgive; patient and tolerant.

forgot, forgotten see FORGET.

fork — *noun* **1** an eating or cooking implement with prongs, for spearing and lifting food. **2** a pronged digging or lifting tool. **3** the division of a

road, etc into two branches; one such branch. **4** something that divides similarly into two parts, eg the wheel support of a bicycle. — *verb* **1** *intrans. said of a road etc* to divide into two branches. **2** *intrans. said of a person or vehicle* to follow one such branch: *fork left*. **3** to lift or move with a fork.
— **fork something out** *or* **up** *colloq.* to pay, under pressure rather than voluntarily. [from Anglo-Saxon *forca*, from Latin *furca*]

forked *adj.* **1** dividing into two branches or parts. **2** *said of lightning* forming a zigzag.

fork-lift truck a small vehicle equipped with two horizontal prongs that can be raised or lowered to move or stack goods.

forlorn *adj.* **1** pathetically unhappy or alone. **2** deserted; forsaken. **3** desperate. [from Anglo-Saxon *forloren*, lost]

forlorn hope **1** a desperate but impractical hope. **2** a hopeless undertaking. [from Dutch *verloren hoop*, lost troop]

forlornly *adv.* in a forlorn way.

forlornness *noun* being forlorn.

form — *noun* **1** shape. **2** figure or outward appearance. **3** kind, type, variety, or manifestation. **4** a printed document with spaces for the insertion of information. **5** a way, especially the correct way, of doing or saying something. **6** structure and organization in a piece of writing or work of art. **7** one's potential level of performance, eg in sport: *soon find your form again*. **8** any of the ways that a word can be spelt or grammatically inflected. **9** a school class. **10** a bench. **11** *slang* a criminal record. **12** a hare's burrow. — *verb* **1** to organize or set up. **2** *intrans.* to come into existence; to take shape. **3** to shape; to make (a shape). **4** to take on the shape or function of. **5** to make up; to constitute. **6** to develop: *form a relationship*. **7** to influence or mould: *the environment that formed him*. **8** to construct, inflect grammatically, or pronounce (a word).
— **good** *or* **bad form** polite or impolite social behaviour.
in good form in good spirits or health.
a matter of form a case of a procedure being gone through for the sake of legality or convention.
on *or* **off form** performing well or badly.
take form to come into existence; to begin to have shape.
true to form in the usual, typical, or characteristic way.
[from Latin *forma*, shape, model]

-form *combining form* **1** having the appearance or structure of: *cuneiform*. **2** in so many forms or varieties: *multiform*. [from Latin *-formis*]

formal *adj.* **1** relating to or involving etiquette, ceremony, or conventional procedure generally: *formal dress*. **2** stiffly polite rather than relaxed and friendly. **3** valid; official; explicit: *a formal agreement / proof, etc*. **4** *said of language* strictly correct with regard to grammar, style, and choice of words, as distinct from conversational. **5** organized and methodical: *the formal approach to teaching*. **6** precise and symmetrical in design: *a formal garden*. **7** relating to outward form as distinct from content. [from Latin *formalis*]

formaldehyde *noun Chem.* (FORMULA **HCHO**) a colourless pungent gas, the simplest of the aldehydes, which is commercially available as a 40% solution known as formalin. It is widely used as a disinfectant and preservative for biological specimens, and in the manufacture of synthetic resins, eg Bakelite. — Also called *methanal*. [from FORMIC + ALDEHYDE]

formalin *noun* a clear solution of formaldehyde used as a preservative and disinfectant. [from FORMALDEHYDE; originally a trademark]

formalism *noun* concern, especially excessive concern, with outward form.

formalist *noun* a person who promotes formalism.

formality *noun* (PL. **formalities**) **1** a procedure gone through as a requirement of etiquette, ceremony, the law, etc. **2** a procedure gone through merely for the sake of correctness or legality: *the interview was a formality, as she had already been promised the job*. **3** strict attention to the rules of social behaviour.

formalization *or* **formalisation** *noun* **1** the act or process of formalizing. **2** something that is formalized.

formalize *or* **formalise** *verb* to make official, eg by putting in writing, etc; to give definite or legal form to.

formally *adv.* in a formal way.

Forman, Miloš (1932–) Czech-US film director, born in Caslav, Czechoslovakia. Two feature films, *Lásky jedné plavovlsky* (A Blonde in Love, 1965) and *Hoří, má panenko!* (The Fireman's Ball, 1967), made in Prague, brought him international recognition. *One Flew Over the Cuckoo's Nest* (1975) won five Oscar awards and was followed by his interpretations of stage presentations such as *Amadeus* (1983), which won him another Oscar.

formant *noun Phonetics* the dominant component (or components) which determines the particular sound quality of all vowels and some consonants. Formants are peaks of acoustic energy, reflecting the principal points of resonance in the vocal tract created by air flow and the alteration of the tract's shape while sounding a particular vowel or voiced consonant. [from German *Formant*, from Latin *formare*, to form]

format — *noun* **1** the size and shape of something, especially a book or magazine. **2** the style in which a television programme etc is organized and presented. **3** *Comput.* a specific arrangement of data in tracks and sectors on a disk. — *verb* (**formatted, formatting**) **1** to design, shape, or organize in a particular way. **2** to organize (data for input) into a particular computer. **3** to prepare a new disk for use by marking out the surface into tracks and sectors, so that it is capable of receiving data. [from Latin *formatus*, shaped (in a certain way)]

formation *noun* **1** the process of forming, making, developing or establishing. **2** a particular arrangement, pattern or order. **3** a shape or structure. [from Latin *formatio*, shape]

formative *adj.* **1** relating to development or growth. **2** having an effect on development. [from Old French *formatif*]

form criticism *Relig.* a method of analysing New Testament Gospel traditions, in which individual stories and sayings are studied in isolation from their Gospel contexts, and in terms of the stereotyped forms of oral folklore, in the belief that they were originally transmitted orally and individually before being strung together and given a context by Gospel writers.

Formentera POP (1990e) 5 000, an island in the Balearic Is, Spain, lying S of Ibiza. AREA 100sq km/40sq mi. It is largely formed by two high pine-clad capes (La Mola and Berberia). The central depression is edged by beaches of white sand. CAPITAL San Francisco Javier. ECONOMY tourism.

former *adj.* **1** belonging to an earlier time. **2** previous; earlier.
— **the former** the first of two things mentioned. [comparative of Anglo-Saxon *forma*, first, earliest]

formerly *adv.* previously; in the past.

Formica *noun trademark* a hard heat-resistant plastic, used for making easy-to-clean work surfaces in kitchens, laboratories, etc.

formic acid *Chem.* (FORMULA **HCOOH**) a colourless pungent liquid that is toxic and corrosive, and is largely responsible for the stinging sensation produced by ant bites and stinging nettles. It is the simplest carboxylic acid, and is used

in the dyeing of textiles, and as a fumigant and insecticide. — Also called *methanoic acid*. [from Latin *formica*, ant]

formidable *adj.* **1** awesomely impressive. **2** *said of problems, etc* enormous; difficult to overcome. [from Latin *formidabilis*, causing fear]

formidably *adv.* in a formidable way.

Formigny, Battle of the decisive defeat (1450) near Bayeux (Calvados) during the Hundred Years War of an army sent by the bankrupt English government (also bereft of allies) to stop French advances in Normandy. The English had lost their previous tactical superiority and were routed, and the reconquest of Normandy by the French was swiftly completed.

formless *adj.* lacking a clear shape or structure.

formlessly *adv.* in a formless way.

formlessness *noun* being formless.

form of address the word or words used as a title before a person's name; the form of words used in speaking to someone on a formal or ceremonial occasion.

formula *noun* (PL. **formulas, formulae**) **1** a combination of chemical symbols that represents the chemical composition of a particular substance. Subscript numbers are used to denote the number of atoms of each element that are present in a molecule of the substance, eg the formula for water is H_2O. **2** a mathematical equation or expression, or a physical law, that represents the relationship between various quantities, and is usually expressed in numerical figures and letters. **3** the combination of ingredients used in a product, etc. **4** a method or rule of procedure, especially a successful one. **5** an established piece of wording used eg in religion or law. **6** a term used for classifying racing cars according to engine size: *Formula 1 racing*. **7** *North Amer.* powdered milk for babies. [from Latin *formula*, a diminutive of *forma*, form]

formulaic *adj.* relating to or typical of a formula or formulae.

formulary *noun* (PL. **formularies**) a book or collection of especially legal or religious formulas. [from Old French *formulaire*]

formulate *verb* **1** to express in terms of a formula. **2** to express precisely and clearly.

formulation *noun* **1** the act or process of formulating. **2** something that is formulated.

fornicate *verb intrans.* to have sexual intercourse outside marriage. [from Latin *fornicari*, from *fornix*, brothel]

fornication *noun* voluntary sexual intercourse outside marriage.

Forrest, Edwin (1806–72) American actor, born in Philadelphia. He made his début there in 1820 and had successful seasons in London (1836–7), but in 1845 his Macbeth was hissed by the audience. A resentment which prompted him to hiss William Macready in Edinburgh destroyed his reputation in Britain, and the hissing of Macready's Macbeth by Forrest's sympathizers in New York in 1849 led to a riot which cost 22 lives.

forsake *verb* (PAST TENSE **forsook**; PAST PARTICIPLE **forsaken**) to desert; to abandon. [from Anglo-Saxon *forsacan*]

Forster, E(dward) M(organ) (1879–1970) English novelist, born in London. His works include *Where Angels Fear to Tread* (1905), *The Longest Journey* (1907), *A Room with a View* (1908), *Howards End* (1910), and *A Passage to India* (1924). He also wrote several volumes of essays and short stories, and in 1951 collaborated with E Crozier in the libretto of Britten's opera, *Billy Budd*. His novel *Maurice* (written 1913–14), on the theme of homosexuality, was published posthumously in 1971.

forswear *verb* (PAST TENSE **forswore**; PAST PARTICIPLE **forsworn**) *old use* **1** to give up or renounce (one's foolish ways, etc). **2** to perjure (oneself). [from Anglo-Saxon *forswerian*, to swear falsely]

Forsyte Saga a novel sequence (of nine novels) by John Galsworthy, including *The Man of Property* (1906), *In Chancery* (1920), and *To Let* (1921).

Forsyth, Bill (William David) (1948–) Scottish film-maker, born in Glasgow. He entered the film industry in 1963, making his own documentaries. His first success was *That Sinking Feeling* (1979), a comedy using actors from the Glasgow Youth Theatre. Other feature films include *Gregory's Girl* (1981) and *Local Hero* (1983). He moved to Hollywood in the mid-1980s, directing *Housekeeping* (1987).

forsythia *noun* a shrub with bright yellow flowers that appear before the leaves. [named after W Forsyth (1737–1804), British botanist]

fort *noun* a fortified military building, enclosure, or position.
— **hold the fort** to keep things running in the absence of the person normally in charge. [from Latin *fortis*, strong]

Fortaleza POP (1991) 2.3m, the port capital of Ceará state, NE Brazil, on the Atlantic coast. It is a commercial and industrial centre especially for agriculture and a centre for coastal and overseas trade. NOTABLE FEATURE cathedral.

Fort-de-France, formerly **Fort Royal** POP (1990) 102 000, the capital of Martinique, Lesser Antilles, E Caribbean Sea. It is the chief commercial and shipping centre on the island. NOTABLE FEATURE cathedral (1895).

Forte, Charles Forte, Baron (1908–) Scottish catering and hotel magnate, born in Italy. He entered the catering trade via the family ice cream business, and then became proprietor of the first milk bar in London in 1933. He built up a successful catering network, and diversified into hotels and other business interests. A merger created Trusthouse Forte in 1970, and he was Chief Executive of the new company from 1971 to 1978, becoming Chairman in 1982. The chairmanship passed to his son Rocco (1945–) in 1992, and Forte took on the role of Life President.

forte[1] *noun* something one is good at; a strong point. [from French *fort*, strong]

forte[2] *Mus.* — *adj.* played loud. — *adv.* loudly. [from Italian *forte*]

Forth, River a river in SE central Scotland, length 186km/116mi. It is formed at Aberfoyle, W Central region, by the confluence of headstreams rising on Ben Lomond. It flows generally E, widening into the estuary of the Firth of Forth (82km/51mi long, from Alloa to the North Sea, and 2.5km/1.6mi–28km/17mi wide). It is crossed by a road bridge at Kincardine, and by the Forth Road and Rail Bridges at Queensferry. The Forth and Clyde Canal connects the R Forth to the R Clyde.

forth *adv. old use* except in phrases **1** into existence or view: *bring forth children*. **2** forwards: *swing back and forth*. **3** out: *set forth on a journey*. **4** onwards: *from this day forth*.
— **and so forth** and so on.
hold forth to speak, especially at length. [from Anglo-Saxon *forth*]

forthcoming *adj.* **1** happening or appearing soon. **2** *said of a person* willing to talk; communicative. **3** available on request.

forthright *adj.* firm, frank, straightforward and decisive. [from Anglo-Saxon *forthriht*]

forthrightness *noun* being forthright.

forthwith *adv.* immediately.

forties *pl. noun* **1** the period of time between one's 40th and 50th birthdays. **2** the range of temperatures between 40° and 50°. **3** the period of time between the 40th and 50th years of a century.

— **roaring forties** the area of stormy west winds south of latitude 40°S, or north of latitude 40° N in the Atlantic.

fortieth *noun*, *adj.* **1** the position in a series corresponding to 40 in a sequence of numbers. **2** one of 40 equal parts.

fortification *noun* **1** the process of fortifying. **2** (**fortifications**) walls and other defensive structures built in preparation for an attack.

fortify *verb* (**fortifies**, **fortified**) **1** to strengthen (a building, city, etc) in preparation for an attack. **2** to add extra alcohol to (wine): *sherry is a fortified wine*. [from Latin *fortis*, strong + *facere*, to make]

fortissimo *Mus.* — *adj.* played very loud. — *adv.* very loudly. [from Italian *fortissimo*]

fortitude *noun* uncomplaining courage in pain or misfortune. [from Latin *fortitudo*, strength]

Fort Knox a US army post established in Kentucky in 1917. Since 1937, it has been the site of the US Bullion Depository.

fortnight *noun* a period of 14 days. [from Anglo-Saxon *feowertiene niht*, 14 nights]

fortnightly *adj.*, *adv.* occurring, appearing, etc once every fortnight.

FORTRAN *noun* a high-level computer-programming language widely used for mathematical, scientific, and engineering programs in the 1950s and 1960s. Many of its general principles have been absorbed into BASIC. [from *formula translation*]

fortress *noun* a fortified town, or large fort or castle. [from Old French *forteresse*, from Latin *fortis*, strong]

Fortress America a view held by many US people before World War II and during the cold war that the USA should stay out of international politics outside the W hemisphere.

Fort Stanwix, Treaties of two agreements (1768, 1784) in the USA between whites and Native American tribes, the first of which established a boundary between British Crown lands and the Iroquois confederacy. The second, forced upon the Iroquois after their defeat in the War of Independence, made them yield their lands west of the Niagara River, but it was rejected by the tribes of the Ohio County.

Fort Sumter the US federal installation in Charleston (South Carolina) harbour, bombarded (12–13 Apr 1861) in the first military engagement of the American Civil War.

fortuitous *adj.* happening by chance; accidental. [from Latin *fortuitus*]
◆ Often confused with *fortunate*.

fortuitously *adv.* in a fortuitous way; by chance.

fortuitousness *noun* being fortuitous.

Fortuna in Roman mythology, the goddess of Fortune. In the Middle Ages she was highly revered as a divine and moral figure, who redressed human pride. She is often depicted standing on a ball or wheel (indicating her changeable nature), holding a cornucopia.

fortunate *adj.* **1** lucky; favoured by fate. **2** timely; opportune. [from Latin *fortunatus*]
◆ See note at *fortuitous*.

fortunately *adv.* in a fortunate way; by good luck.

fortune *noun* **1** chance as a force in human affairs; fate. **2** luck. **3** (**fortunes**) unpredictable happenings that swing affairs this way or that: *the fortunes of war*. **4** (**fortunes**) the state of one's luck. **5** one's destiny. **6** a large sum of money.
— **make one's fortune** to become prosperous.
a small fortune a large amount of money.
tell someone's fortune to tell someone what their destiny is. [from Latin *fortuna*]

fortune-teller *noun* a person who claims to be able to tell people their destinies.

Fort William POP (1981) 11 000, the capital of Lochaber district, Highland region, W Scotland. It stands on the E side of Loch Linnhe. NOTABLE FEATURES Inverlochy Castle; in the N, Neptune's Staircase, a series of eight locks (built between 1805 and 1822) raising the Caledonian Canal by 19.5m; Ben Nevis (to the SE).

Fort Worth POP (1990) 448 000, the seat of Tarrant County, NE Texas, USA. It is an industrial city lying on the Trinity R. HISTORY established as an army post in 1847; formerly a cattle town, it is still an important livestock market centre. NOTABLE FEATURES Fort Worth Art Center; Amon Carter Museum of Western Art; Greer Island Nature Center.

forty — *noun* (PL. **forties**) **1** the number or figure 40; any symbol for this number. **2** the age of 40. **3** a set of 40 people or things. — *adj.* **1** 40 in number. **2** aged 40. [from Anglo-Saxon *feowertig*]

Forty-Five Rebellion the Jacobite rebellion (1745–6) to restore the Catholic Stuart kings to the British throne and displace the Hanoverians. It began in July 1745 when Charles Edward Stuart (the 'Young Pretender') arrived in Scotland and proclaimed his father King James III, supported mainly by the Scottish Highland Clans. The Jacobite forces reached as far south as Derby, but the rebellion lost support and was crushingly defeated at Culloden in 1746. After the '45, the Hanoverian regime brutally suppressed the clan system.

forty winks *colloq.* a short sleep.

forum *noun* **1** *Hist.* a public square or market place, especially that in ancient Rome where public business was conducted and law courts held. **2** a place, programme, or publication where opinions can be aired and discussed. [from Latin *forum*]

forward — *adv.* **1** (*also* **forwards**) in the direction in front or ahead of one. **2** (*also* **forwards**) progressing from first to last. **3** on or onward; to a later time: *put the clocks forward*. **4** to an earlier time: *bring the wedding forward a month*. **5** into view or public attention: *put forward suggestions*. — *adj.* **1** in the direction in front or ahead of one. **2** at the front. **3** advanced in development: *how far forward are the plans?* **4** concerning the future: *forward planning*. **5** *derog.* inclined to push oneself forward; over-bold in offering one's opinions. — *noun Football, Hockey* a player whose task is to score rather than defend the goal. — *verb* **1** to send (mail) on to another address. **2** to help the progress of. [from Anglo-Saxon *foreweard*]

forward-looking *adj.* planning ahead; progressive, enterprising, or go-ahead.

forwardly *adv.* in a forward way.

forwardness *noun* being forward.

forwent see FOREGO.

For Whom the Bell Tolls a novel by Ernest Hemingway (1940). It is set in the 1930s during the Spanish Civil War and focuses on the plight of Robert Jordan, a US soldier who has been sent to join the guerrillas.

fossil *noun* **1** *Geol.* the petrified remains, impression, or cast of an animal or plant preserved in a rock. Most fossils consist of hard parts, eg the internal skeleton of vertebrates, the shells of molluscs and crustaceans. **2** a relic of the past. **3** *colloq.* a curiously antiquated person. **4** (*attributive*) **a** like, or in the form of, a fossil. **b** formed naturally through the decomposition of organic matter, and dug or otherwise got from the earth: *fossil fuels*. [from Latin *fossilis*, dug up]

fossil fuel any fuel derived from the fossilized remains of plants and animals, such as coal, petroleum, and natural gas. See illustration p. 484.

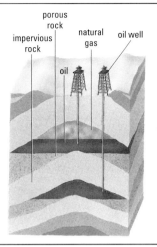

porous rock
impervious rock
natural gas
oil well
oil

location of oil and gas

fossilization *or* **fossilisation** *noun* being fossilized.

fossilize *or* **fossilise** *verb trans., intrans.* to change into a fossil or curious relic.

Foster, Jodie, originally **Alicia Christian Foster** (1962–) US film actress, born in Los Angeles. She started her career as a toddler in commercials and progressed to playing street-wise adolescent characters in films such as *Alice Doesn't Live Here Anymore* (1974) and *Taxi Driver* (1976). Her adult roles include *Hotel New Hampshire* (1984), *The Accused* (1988), for which she won an Oscar, *The Silence of the Lambs* (1991), and *Sommersby* (1992).

foster — *verb* (**fostered, fostering**) **1** to bring up (a child that is not one's own). **2** to encourage the development of (ideas, feelings, etc). — *adj.* **1** concerned with, or offering, fostering. **2** (*in compounds*) in a specified family relationship through fostering rather than by birth: *foster-mother, -brother, etc*. [from Anglo-Saxon *fostrian*, to feed]

Foucault, Jean Bernard Léon (1819–68) French physicist, born in Paris. He determined the velocity of light, showed that light travels more slowly in water than in air (1850), invented the gyroscope (1852), and improved the mirrors of reflecting telescopes (1858). In 1851, by means of a freely suspended pendulum more than 60m long, he convincingly demonstrated the rotation of the Earth to a large crowd in a Paris church.

Fouché, Joseph, Duc d'Otrante (Duke of Otranto) (1763–1829) French statesman, born in Nantes. He was elected to the National Convention in 1792 as a Jacobin, and in 1799 became Minister of Police, a post which he held successfully until 1815. A consummate intriguer, he was banished after the Bourbon restoration.

fought see FIGHT.

foul — *adj.* **1** disgusting: *a foul smell.* **2** soiled; filthy. **3** contaminated: *foul air.* **4** *colloq.* very unkind or unpleasant. **5** *said of language* offensive or obscene. **6** unfair or treacherous: *by fair means or foul.* **7** *said of weather* stormy. **8** clogged. **9** entangled. — *noun Sport* a breach of the rules. — *verb* **1** *intrans., trans. Sport* to commit a foul against (an opponent). **2** to make dirty. **3** to contaminate or pollute. **4** *trans., intrans.* **a** (*also* **foul up**) to become entangled. **b** to become entangled with (something) so as to hinder its movement or functioning. — **fall foul of** to get into trouble or conflict with. **foul something up 1** to clog it. **2** *colloq.* to mess it up; to bungle it. [from Anglo-Saxon]

foul-mouthed *adj.* using offensive or obscene language.

foulness *noun* **1** being foul. **2** something that is foul or fouled.

foul play 1 treachery or criminal violence, especially murder. **2** *Sport* a breach of the rules.

foul-up *noun colloq.* a bungled situation; a failure or disaster.

found[1] see FIND.

found[2] *verb* **1** to start or establish (an organization, institution, city, etc), often with a provision for future funding. **2** to base or establish conceptually: *a well-founded argument.* **3** to lay the foundation of (a building). [from Latin *fundare*]

found[3] *verb* **1** to cast (metal or glass) by melting and pouring into a mould. **2** to produce (articles) by this method. See also FOUNDRY. [from Latin *fundere*, to pour]

foundation *noun* **1** the act of founding or establishing an institution, etc; the institution, etc founded or the fund providing for it. **2** (*usually* **foundations**) the underground structure on which a building is supported. **3** the basis on which a theory, etc rests or depends. **4** a cream, etc smoothed into the skin as a base for additional cosmetics.

foundation course an introductory course, usually followed as a preparation for more advanced studies.

foundation stone a stone laid ceremonially as part of the foundations of a new building.

founder[1] *noun* a person who founds or endows an institution, etc.

founder[2] *verb intrans.* (**foundered, foundering**) **1** *said of a ship* to sink. **2** *said of a vehicle, etc* to get stuck in mud, etc. **3** *said of a horse* to go lame. **4** *said of a business, scheme, etc* to fail. [from Old French *fondrer*, to submerge]

foundling *noun* an abandoned child of unknown parents. [from FOUND[1] + -LING]

found object *Art* a term first used by the Dadaists and Surrealists for any everyday object incorporated in a picture. It has since been applied to any object, such as a piece of driftwood or a length of rope, picked up and exhibited as a 'work of art', whether used with others in a composition or displayed by itself. Found objects are frequently used by conceptual artists. — Also called *objet trouvé*.

foundry *noun* (PL. **foundries**) a place where metal or glass is melted and cast. [from FOUND[3]]

fount[1] *noun* **1** a spring or fountain. **2** a source of inspiration, etc. [from FOUNTAIN]

fount[2] *noun Printing* a set of printing type of the same design and size. [from Old French *fonte*, casting]

fountain *noun* **1** a jet or jets of water for drinking or for ornamental effect, or a structure supporting this. **2** a spring of water. **3** a source of wisdom, etc. [from Old French *fontaine*, from Latin *fons*, fountain]

fountainhead *noun* **1** a spring from which a stream flows. **2** the principal source of something.

fountain pen a metal-nibbed pen equipped with a reservoir of ink.

Fountains Abbey a Cistercian monastery founded in 1132 near Ripon in Yorkshire. It was once the wealthiest Cistercian house in England. The abbey ruins stand in the water gardens of Studley Royal, which were laid out in the early 18c. It is a World Heritage site.

Fouqué, Friedrich Heinrich Karl de la Motte (1777–1843) German Romantic writer, born in Brandenburg. He served as a Prussian cavalry officer and devoted himself between campaigns to literary pursuits. He published a long series of romances based on Norse Legend and Old French poetry, the best-known of which is the fairy romance *Undine* (1811).

Fouquet, Nicolas (1615–80) French statesman, born in Paris. Mazarin made him *Procureur-Général* to the parliament of Paris (1650) and Superintendent of Finance (1653). He became very rich, and was ambitious to succeed Mazarin as Chief Minister, but Louis XIV himself took over the position on Mazarin's death, and Fouquet was arrested for embezzlement (1661) and sentenced to life imprisonment.

four — *noun* **1** the number or figure 4; any symbol for this number. **2** the age of 4. **3** something, especially a garment, or a person, whose size is denoted by the number 4. **4** 4 o'clock. **5** a set of 4 things or people, eg the crew of a 4-oared boat. **6** a playing-card with 4 pips. **7** a score of 4 points. — *adj.* **1** 4 in number. **2** aged 4. — **on all fours** on hands and knees. [from Anglo-Saxon *feower*]

four-colour process *Photog., Printing* a technique for reproducing a full-colour image using only four colours of ink. The original image is photographed either by a camera using colour filters, or by an electronic scanner; single pieces of film or plates are produced, each corresponding to one of the colours of ink to be used (magenta, yellow, cyan, and black) and the final image is built up by superimposing the images from these four pieces of film or plates.

Four Corners the point in the USA where Colorado, Utah, New Mexico, and Arizona meet. This is the only place in the USA where boundaries of four states come together.

fourfold — *adj.* **1** equal to four times as much. **2** divided into or consisting of four parts. —*adv.* by four times as much.

Four Freedoms four basic human rights proclaimed by President Roosevelt in his annual message to Congress (1941). They included freedom of speech and worship, and freedom from want and fear.

Four Horsemen of the Apocalypse the symbolic biblical characters described in Revelation 6 and Zechariah 6.1–7, who signal the beginning of the messianic age. Each comes on a steed of different colour, symbolizing devastations associated with the end of the world (black=famine; red=bloodshed, war; pale=pestilence, death), except for the white horse's rider, who is given a crown and sent to conquer (Revelation 6.2).

Fourier, Jean Baptiste Joseph, Baron de (1768–1830) French mathematician, born in Auxerre. He accompanied Napoleon during the invasion of Egypt in 1798, and on his return in 1802 was made Prefect of Isère in Grenoble. While working on the flow of heat, he discovered the theorem which bears his name, that almost any mathematical function can be expressed as the sum of a series of sine waves; Fourier series are now an essential tool in mathematics and physics.

four-letter word any of several short English words referring to sex or excretion, usually considered offensive.

Four Noble Truths the summary of the central teachings of Buddha. One: all life involves suffering, and is inevitably sorrowful. Two: the cause of suffering and sorrow is craving or desire arising from ignorance. Three: there is escape from suffering, because craving and desire can end. Four: there is an Eightfold Path leading to the end of suffering and sorrow.

four-poster *noun* a large bed with a post at each corner to support curtains and a canopy.

Four Quartets a poem in four parts by T S Eliot (collectively, 1943). It is a philosophical, cyclical sequence, with each poem set in a different place but linked by the meditative consciousness of the narrator.

fourscore *adj., noun* eighty.

Four Seasons, The four paintings of the seasons by Nicolas Poussin (1660–4, Louvre, Paris).

Four Seasons, The (Le quattro sta-gioni) four violin concertos by Antonio Vivaldi (No.1 in E, No.2 in G minor, No.3 in F, No.4 in F minor, 1725), which represent the seasons of the year.

foursome *noun* **1** a set of four people. **2** *Golf* a game between two pairs.

four-square — *adj.* **1** strong; steady; solidly based. **2** *said of a building* square and solid-looking. — *adv.* steadily; squarely.

fourteen — *noun* **1** the number or figure 14; any symbol for this number. **2** the age of 14. **3** something, especially a garment, or a person, whose size is denoted by the number 14. **4** a set of 14 people or things. — *adj.* **1** 14 in number. **2** aged 14. [from Anglo-Saxon *feowertiene*]

Fourteen Points a peace programme outlined by US President Woodrow Wilson to Congress in 1918. Its offer of an acceptable peace to the Central Powers meant that Wilson was perceived as a moral leader, and it helped to effect the surrender of Germany and the beginning of peace talks, though several of the points were compromised or defeated in the actual treaty.

fourteenth *noun, adj.* **1** the position in a series corresponding to 14 in a sequence of numbers. **2** one of 14 equal parts.

Fourteenth Amendment a US constitutional amendment adopted in 1868 during Reconstruction after the American Civil War to guarantee equality to blacks and whites alike, by defining federal and state citizenship for all American-born or naturalized persons. However, judicial interpretation of the amendment soon perverted its purposes, its negative wording was taken to allow individual discrimination, and the 'separate but equal' argument even gave the amendment's sanction to formal legislative segregation.

fourth *noun, adj.* **1** the position in a series corresponding to four in a sequence of numbers. **2** one of four equal parts; a quarter. **3** *Mus.* an interval of three diatonic degrees; a tone at that interval from another, or a combination of two tones separated by that interval.

fourth dimension **1** time regarded as a dimension, as complementing the three dimensions of space (length, width, and depth). **2** anything which is beyond ordinary experience.

Fourth Estate the Press regarded as a political force. It was first coined in 1828 by Macaulay, who described the gallery of the house of Commons in which the reporters sit as 'the fourth estate of the realm', the traditional *three estates* being the lords spiritual, the lords temporal, and the commons.

fourthly *adv.* as fourth in a series.

Fourth of July a public holiday in the USA, commemorating the adoption of the Declaration of Independence in 1776.

Fourth World the poorest and technologically least developed countries of the world.

fovea *noun* (PL. **foveae**) **1** *Anat.* a shallow depression in the retina at the back of the eye in birds, lizards, and primates. It is formed only of cones, and is required for acute vision. The most accurately perceived part of an image is that which is focused on the fovea. — Also called *yellow spot*. **2** any small hollow or depression in a body structure. [from Latin *fovea*]

fowl — *noun* (PL. **fowls, fowl**) **1** a farmyard bird, eg a chicken or turkey. **2** *old use* (*in compounds*) any bird, especially if eaten as meat or hunted as game: *wildfowl*. — *verb intrans.* to hunt or trap wild birds. [from Anglo-Saxon *fugel*, bird]

Fowler, H(enry) W(atson) (1858–1933) English lexicographer, born in Tonbridge, Kent. He was a schoolmaster at Sedbergh (1882–99), then went to London to work as a freelance journalist. In 1903 he joined his tomato-growing brother, F(rank) G(eorge) (1871–1918), in Guernsey. Together they produced *The King's English* (1906) and *The Concise Oxford Dictionary* (1911). Henry later wrote the successful *Dictionary of Modern English Usage* (1926).

fowler *noun* a person who hunts wild birds.

Fowles, John (Robert) (1926–) English novelist, born in London. A former teacher, his first novel was *The Collector* (1963). His writings combine a topographical interest in Devon, a respect for the Victorian novel of social life and personal relationships, and an interest in contemporary developments in the French novel. Other works include *The Magus* (1966, revised 1977), *The French Lieutenant's Woman* (1969, a success as a film in 1981), and *A Maggot* (1985).

Fox, Charles James (1749–1806) English statesman, born in London. He became an MP at 19, and a junior Lord of the Admiralty at 21. He supported Lord North, but in 1772 resigned over American policy. He was Foreign Secretary on three occasions (1782, 1783, 1806), firstly after the downfall of North, with whom in 1783 he formed a coalition which held office for a short period. He supported the French Revolution, and strongly opposed the war with France. After the death of Pitt 'the Younger' (1806) he was recalled to office, but died soon afterwards.

Fox, George (1624–91) English religious leader and founder of the Society of Friends or 'Quakers', born in Fenny Drayton, Leicestershire. Brought up as a Puritan, he rebelled against the formalism of the established Church, and the State's control of it. He travelled about the country, attracting many followers, often interrupting sermons to expound his own teaching through which he argued for God-given inward light and against sacerdotalism and all social conventions. His life was a record of persecutions, imprisonments, and missionary travel to several parts of the world. As a writer he is remembered for his *Journal* (posthumously published), which records the birth of the Quaker movement.

Fox an Algonkian-speaking Native American group originally from N Wisconsin, who were mainly agriculturalists. They were affected by Iroquois expansionism and white settlers, and settled permanently in Iowa in 1842, where they maintain many aspects of their traditional lifestyle.

fox — *noun* **1** any of various carnivorous mammals belonging to the dog family (Canidae), especially species of the genus *Vulpes*, found in most parts of the world, and having a pointed muzzle, large pointed ears, and a long bushy tail. The fox is noted for its cunning. **2** the fur of this animal. **3** *colloq.* a cunning person. — *verb* **1** to puzzle, confuse, or baffle. **2** to deceive, trick, or outwit. **3** *trans., intrans. said of paper* to become or cause it to become discoloured with brown spots. [from Anglo-Saxon]

◇ Foxes are solitary, and remain in their burrows (known as *earths*) during the day, hunting for prey by night. The commonest species is the red fox (*Vulpes vulpes*), found throughout Europe, Asia, and N America, and having a sandy or reddish-brown coat with white underparts. Red foxes prefer woody country, and feed mainly on rodents, although birds, frogs, and plant material are sometimes eaten. Foxes occasionally take poultry and small lambs, but few become regular poultry killers. In recent years they have also become urban dwellers, living off rats and mice and scavenging in dustbins.

foxglove *noun* a biennial or perennial plant, belonging to the genus *Digitalis*, that produces tall spikes bearing many thimble-shaped purple or white flowers. The leaves are a source of digitalis, a drug that stimulates heart muscle and is used to treat heart failure.

foxhole *noun* a hole in the ground from which a soldier may shoot while protected from the enemy's guns.

foxhound *noun* a breed of dog trained to chase foxes.

foxhunting *noun* the sport of hunting foxes on horseback, with a pack of foxhounds.

◇ Foxhunting developed in the UK in the 17c, and is now regarded as a pastime of the aristocracy. The season lasts from Nov to Apr. Each hunt is controlled by a master of hounds, and the hounds are controlled by a huntsman. In recent years, animal-rights activists have attempted to disrupt hunts, and since 1949 there has been a movement to make the hunting of foxes illegal.

foxily *adv.* in a foxy way.

foxiness *noun* **1** being foxy. **2** foxy behaviour.

foxing *noun* discoloration in the form of brownish marks on paper that has been allowed to become damp.

fox terrier a breed of dog originally trained to drive foxes out of their holes.

foxtrot — *noun* a ballroom dance with gliding steps, alternating between quick and slow, or the music for this. — *verb intrans.* (**foxtrotted, foxtrotting**) to perform this dance.

foxy *adj.* (**foxier, foxiest**) **1** like a fox. **2** *North Amer. colloq., said of a woman* sexually attractive. **3** cunning; sly.

foyer *noun* **1** the entrance hall of a theatre, hotel, etc. **2** *North Amer.* the hallway of a house or apartment. [from French *foyer*, fireplace]

Foyle, Lough an inlet of the Atlantic Ocean, on the N coast of Ireland, bounded W by Donegal (Irish Republic) and E by Co Derry (Northern Ireland). It is 24km/15mi long and 16km/10mi wide; the mouth is 1.5km/0.9mi wide. It is fed by the R Foyle.

FP *abbrev.* **1** fire plug, ie a hydrant. **2** former pupil.

FPA *abbrev.* Family Planning Association.

Fr¹ *abbrev.* **1** Father, as the title of a priest. **2** (**fr**) franc. **3** French. **4** Friday.

Fr² *symbol Chem.* francium.

fracas *noun* (PL. **fracas**) a noisy quarrel; a fight or brawl. [from French *fracas*]

Fracastoro, Girolamo (1483–1553) Italian scholar and physician, born in Verona. A physician at Verona and Professor of Philosophy at Padua, he excelled as geographer, astronomer, and mathematician. He wrote a Latin poem on the 'new' venereal disease, *Syphilis sive morbus Gallicus* (Syphilis or the French Disease, 1530), from which the word 'syphilis' is derived, and his works on contagion pointed to the importance of *fomites* (clothes, bedding, etc) in the spread of certain diseases.

fractal *Maths.* an irregular curve or surface produced by repeated subdivision, eg a *snowflake curve* (resembling a snowflake in outline) produced by repeatedly dividing the sides of an equilateral triangle into three segments and adding another triangle to the middle segment. Fractals generated on a computer screen are used to construct models for processes such as coastline erosion and crystal growth, and are also used in computer art. [from Latin *fractus*, broken]

fraction *noun* **1** *Maths.* an expression that indicates one or more equal parts of a whole, usually represented by a pair of numbers separated by a horizontal or diagonal line. **2** a portion; a small part. **3** *Chem.* a group of chemical compounds whose boiling points fall within a very narrow range. The components of such a mixture can be separated by *fractional distillation*. [from Latin *fractio*, breaking]

◇ In a fraction, the lower number or *denominator* represents the number of equal parts into which the whole unit is divided, and the upper number or *numerator* indicates the number of such parts that comprise the fraction. In a *proper fraction* the numerator is less than the denominator, eg, ¼, while in an *improper fraction* the numerator is greater than the denominator, eg $\frac{5}{4}$, and can also be expressed as a *mixed number* ($1\frac{1}{4}$ in this case). In *decimal fractions* the denominator is a power of 10, but not all fractions can be expressed exactly as decimal fractions, eg $\frac{1}{3}$ = 0.333...

fractional *adj.* **1** of a fraction or fractions. **2** of the nature of a fraction. **3** tiny, insignificant

fractional distillation *Chem.* the separation by distillation of the various constituents of a mixture of liquids with different boiling points.

fractionally *adv.* to a fractional or minute degree; barely: *the train is fractionally faster.*

fractionation *noun Chem.* the separation of the components of a mixture, eg by distillation.

fractious *adj.* inclined to quarrel and complain. [from FRACTION, with its earlier meaning of rupture or dissension]

fractiously *adv.* in a fractious way.

fractiousness *noun* **1** being fractious. **2** fractious behaviour.

fracture — *noun* a break in anything hard, especially bone. — *verb trans., intrans.* to break. [from Latin *fractura*]

fragile *adj.* **1** easily broken. **2** easily damaged or destroyed. **3** delicate: *fragile beauty.* **4** in a weakened state of health. [from Latin *fragilis*, breakable]

fragility *noun* being fragile.

fragment — *noun* (with stress on *frag-*) **1** a piece broken off; a small piece of something that has broken. **2** something incomplete; a small part remaining. — *verb* (usually with stress on *-ment*) **1** *trans., intrans.* to break into pieces. **2** *intrans. Comput., said of a file* to split into sections on different parts of a floppy disk, making access slower. [from Latin *fragmentum*]

fragmentarily *adv.* in a fragmentary way; into fragments.

fragmentariness *noun* being fragmentary.

fragmentary *adj.* consisting of small pieces, not usually amounting to a complete whole.

fragmentation *noun* division into fragments.

Fragonard, Jean Honoré (1732–1806) French painter and engraver, born in Grasse. He studied at Paris, and gained the Prix de Rome in 1752. He painted genre pictures of contemporary life, the amours of the French court, and landscapes which foreshadow Impressionism.

fragrance *noun* **1** sweetness of smell. **2** a scent or odour.

fragrant *adj.* having a pleasant smell. [from Latin *fragrare*, to give out a smell]

fragrantly *adv.* in a fragrant way.

frail *adj.* **1** easily broken or destroyed; delicate; fragile. **2** in poor health; weak. **3** morally weak; easily tempted. [from Old French *fraile*, from Latin *fragilis*, fragile]

frailness *noun* being frail.

frailty *noun* (PL. **frailties**) **1** physical or moral weakness. **2** a moral failing or weakness.

frame — *noun* **1** a hard main structure round which something is built or to which other parts are added. **2** a structure that surrounds and supports. **3** something that surrounds: *her face with its frame of dark hair.* **4** a body, especially a human one, as a structure of a certain size and shape: *eased his tall frame into the chair.* **5** one of the pictures that make up a strip of film. **6** a single television picture. **7** one of the pictures in a comic strip. **8** a glass structure for protecting young plants growing out of doors. **9** a framework of bars for some purpose. **10** *Snooker* a triangular structure for confining the balls at the start of a round; a round. — *verb* **1** to put a frame round. **2** to be a frame for. **3** to compose or design. **4** *colloq.* to dishonestly direct suspicion for a crime, etc at (someone innocent). [from Anglo-Saxon *framian*, to benefit]

frame of mind a mood.

frame of reference 1 a set of facts, beliefs, or principles on the basis of which one can form opinions, make decisions, etc. **2** *Maths.* a set of three geometrical axes for defining position in space.

frame-up *noun colloq.* a plot to make an innocent person appear guilty.

framework *noun* **1** a basic supporting structure. **2** a basic plan or system. **3** a structure composed of horizontal and vertical bars or shafts.

franc *noun* the standard unit of currency in France, Belgium, Switzerland, and several other French-speaking countries. [from Old French *Francorum rex*, king of the Franks, the inscription on the first such coins]

France, Anatole, pseudonym of **Jacques Anatole François Thibault** (1844–1924) French writer, born in Paris. He worked as a publisher's reader, and published his first volume of stories in 1879. The Dreyfus case (1896) stirred him into politics as a champion of internationalism. Among his later novels are *L'Île des pingouins* (Penguin Island, 1908) and *Les Dieux ont soif* (The Gods are Athirst, 1912). He was awarded the Nobel Prize for Literature in 1921.

France, ancient **Gallia**, official name **Republic of France**, French **République Française** POP (1992e) 57.4m, a republic in W Europe, divided into 22 regions and 96 departments. AREA 551 000sq km/213 000sq mi; overseas departments 97 014sq km/37 447sq mi. It is bounded N and NE by the English Channel, Belgium, Luxembourg, and Germany, E by Switzerland, Italy, and Monaco, S by the Mediterranean Sea, Spain, and Andorra, and W by the Bay of Biscay. It includes the island of Corsica, which is in the Mediterranean Sea, and the Overseas Departments of Guadeloupe, Martinique, Guiana, and Réunion, and the Territorial Collectivities of St Pierre et Miquelon, and Mayotte. It also administers the Overseas Territories of New Caledonia, French Polynesia, Wallis and Futuna, and the Southern and Antarctic Territories. CAPITAL Paris. CHIEF TOWNS Marseilles, Lyons, Toulouse, Nice, Strasbourg. TIME ZONE GMT +1. The population is largely of Celtic and Latin origin, with several minorities; the chief religion is Roman Catholicism. OFFICIAL LANGUAGE French. CURRENCY the French franc. PHYSICAL DESCRIPTION a country of low and medium-sized hills and plateaux deeply cut by rivers; bounded S and E by large mountain ranges, notably (in the interior) the Armorican Massif, the Massif Central, the Cévennes, the Vosges, and the Ardennes; in the E the Jura and the Alps (rising to 4 807m at Mont Blanc); in the S the Pyrenees; chief rivers include the Loire, Rhône, Seine, and Garonne. CLIMATE the S has a Mediterranean climate, with warm, moist winters and hot, dry summers; in the NW the climate is maritime, with an average annual rainfall of 573mm, average temperature 3°C in winter, 18°C in summer; the E has a continental climate with an average annual rainfall of 786mm. HISTORY prehistoric settlement is revealed in Paleolithic carvings and rock paintings (eg at Lascaux) and in Neolithic megaliths (eg at Carnac); Celtic-speaking Gauls were dominant by the 5c BC; the country was part of the Roman Empire from 125 BC to the 5c AD, and was invaded by several Germanic tribes in the 3c–5c; the Franks inaugurated the Merovingian epoch in the 5c; the power of the Carolingian kings came to a peak in the 8c, with the succession of Charlemagne; a feudal monarchy was founded by Hugh Capet in 987; the Plantagenets of England acquired several French territories in the 12c; lands were gradually recovered during the Hundred Years' War (1337–1453), apart from Calais (regained in 1558); Capetian dynasty was followed by the Valois and Bourbon dynasties, from 1328 and 1589 respectively; 16c struggle between Francis I and Emperor Charles V; then

Monarchs of France	
987–996	Hugh Capet
996–1031	Robert II
1031–60	Henry I
1060–1108	Philip I
1108–37	Louis VI
1137–80	Louis VII
1180–1223	Philip II Augustus
1223–6	Louis VIII
1226–70	Louis IX
1270–85	Philip III
1285–1314	Philip IV
1314–16	Louis X
1316	John I
1316–22	Philip V
1322–8	Charles IV
1328–50	Philip VI
1350–64	John II
1364–80	Charles V
1380–1422	Charles VI
1422–61	Charles VII
1461–83	Louis XI
1483–98	Charles VIII
1498–1515	Louis XII
1515–47	Francis I
1547–59	Henry II
1559–60	Francis II
1560–74	Charles IX
1574–89	Henry III
1589–1610	Henry IV (of Navarre)
1610–43	Louis XIII
1643–1715	Louis XIV
1715–74	Louis XV
1774–92	Louis XVI
1814–24	Louis XVIII
1824–30	Charles X
1830–48	Louis-Philippe

the Wars of Religion took place from 1562 until 1595; 17c kings restored the power of the monarchy, at its peak under Louis XIV; the French Revolution of 1789 dismantled the *ancien régime* in the name of liberty, equality, and fraternity; the First Republic was declared in 1792; the First Empire (1804–14) was ruled by Napoleon, before the restoration of the monarchy for a period between 1814 and 1848; the Second Republic (1848–52) was followed by the Second Empire (1852–70), ruled by Louis Napoleon; the Third Republic lasted from 1870 to 1940; there was great political instability between the World Wars, with several governments holding office for short periods; the country was occupied by Germany from 1940 until 1944, with the pro-German government at Vichy and the Free French in London under de Gaulle; the Fourth Republic began in 1946; there was war with Indo-China (1946–54), and conflict in Algeria (1954–62); the Fifth Republic began in 1958. GOVERNMENT governed by a President, elected every seven years, who appoints a Prime Minister and presides over a Council of Ministers; the bicameral legislature consists of a National Assembly of 577 deputies elected every five years, and a 319-member Senate indirectly elected by an electoral college, triennially (a third at a time), for 9-year terms. ECONOMY W Europe's foremost producer of agricultural products, chiefly cereals, beef, sugar beet, potatoes, wine, grapes, and dairy products; there are coalfields in N France, Lorraine, and the Massif Central; metal and chemical industries are based on reserves of iron ore, bauxite, potash, salt, and sulphur; heavy industry (steel, machinery, textiles, clothing, chemicals, vehicles) is based around N coalfields; other industry includes food processing, armaments, and electronics; several nuclear power sites, providing 75 per cent of all electricity; hydroelectric power comes from the Alps; tourism and fishing are also important.

Frances a female first name. [originally used interchangably with FRANCIS, but now exclusive to females]

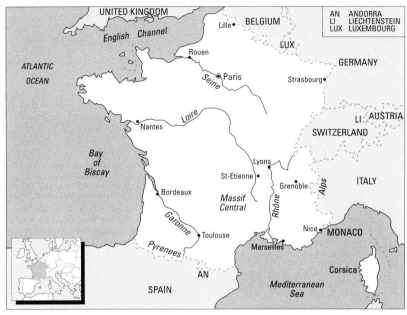

France

Francesca da Rimini (d.1285) Italian noble-woman, the daughter of Guido da Polenta, Lord of Ravenna. She was married to Gianciotto the Lame, son of Malatesta, Lord of Rimini, but she was already in love with Paolo, Gianciotto's brother. Gianciotto discovered the lovers together and killed them both. This tragic love story has often been recounted in literary and artistic works, including Dante's Inferno.

franchise — *noun* 1 the right to vote, especially in a parliamentary election. 2 a right, privilege, exemption from a duty, etc, granted to a person or organization. 3 an agreement by which a business company gives someone the right to market its products in an area; the area concerned. — *verb* to grant a franchise to. [from Old French *franchir*, to set free]

Francia, José Gaspar Rodríguez de (1766–1840) Paraguayan dictator, born in Asunción, Paraguay. He assumed a prominent role in Paraguay's movement for independence, and held absolute power from 1814 until his death. His dominant policy was to isolate Paraguay from the rest of the world.

Francis I (of France) (1494–1547) King of France (1515–47), born in Cognac. He was successor to Louis XII and had the attributes of medieval chivalry and the Renaissance prince, though he became increasingly hostile to Protestantism after 1534. His military reputation was established against the Swiss at Marignano (1515) in his first Italian campaign, but he later suffered capture at Pavia (1525) and imprisonment in Madrid. His reign was dominated by his rivalry with the Emperor Charles V, which led to a series of wars (1521–6, 1528–9, 1536–8, 1542–4).

Francis II (of France) (1544–60) King of France (1559–60), born in Fontainebleau, the eldest son of Henry II and Catherine de' Medici. In 1558 he married Mary, Queen of Scots. His short reign was dominated by the Guise family, in their struggle against the Protestants.

Francis II (Emperor), also **Francis I (of Austria)** (1768–1835) the last Holy Roman Emperor (1792–1806), the first Emperor of Austria (1804–35), and King of Hungary (1792–30) and Bohemia (1792–1836), born in Florence. Defeated on several occasions by Napoleon (1797, 1801, 1805, 1809), he made a short-lived alliance with him, and sealed the mar-

riage of his daughter, Marie Louise, to the French Emperor. Later he joined with Russia and Prussia to win the battle of Leipzig (1813), and by the Treaty of Vienna (1815), with the help of Metternich, he recovered several territories (eg Lombardy-Venetia).

Francis a male first name, and the nickname of St Francis of Assisi (baptized *Giovanni*), whose father had French business connections. [from Latin *franciscus*, frenchman]

Francis Joseph, also called **Franz Josef I** (1830–1916) Emperor of Austria (1848–1916) and King of Hungary (1867–1916), the grandson of Emperor Francis I, born near Vienna. During his reign the aspirations of the various nationalities of the empire were suppressed. He was defeated by the Prussians in 1866, and established the Dual Monarchy of Austria-Hungary in 1867. His annexation of Bosnia-Herzegovina in 1908 agitated Europe, and his attack on Serbia in 1914 precipitated World War I.

Francis of Assisi, St, originally **Giovanni Bernadone** (c.1181–1226) Italian founder of the Franciscan Order, born in Assisi. In 1205 he left a worldly life to care for the poor and the sick, and live as a hermit. By 1210 he had a brotherhood of 11 for which he drew up a rule repudiating all property. The Franciscan order grew, and by 1219 had 5 000 members. He preached widely in Europe and the Holy Land, and on returning to Italy is said to have received on his body the marks (*stigmata*) of Christ's wounds (1224). He died in Assisi, was canonized in 1228, and his feast day is 4 Oct.

Francis of Sales, St (1567–1622) French Roman Catholic prelate and writer, born in Sales, Savoy. He became a distinguished preacher, through whom the Calvinistic population of Chablais was converted. He became Bishop of Nicopolis (1599) and Bishop of Geneva (1602), where he helped to found a congregation of nuns of the Visitation. He was canonized in 1665 and his feast day is 24 Jan.

Francis Xavier, St, known as **the Apostle of the Indies** (1506–52) Spanish Roman Catholic missionary who brought Christianity to India and the Far East, born in Navarre. While studying in Paris, he became one of the first seven members of the Jesuit order (1534). He began his missionary work in Goa, India (1542), then travelled to the Malay Is (1545) and Japan

(1549). The patron saint of all missionary work, he was canonized in 1622 and his feast day is 3 Dec.

Franciscan — *noun* a member of a Christian order of nuns and friars founded by St Francis of Assisi (see FRANCISCANS). — *adj.* relating to the Franciscans. [from Latin *Franciscus*, Francis]

Franciscans the religious orders founded by St Francis of Assisi in the early 13c. The first order, of Friars Minor, is now divided into three groups: the Observants (OFM), the Conventuals (OFMConv), and the Capuchins (OFMCap). The second order is made up of nuns, known as the Poor Clares (PC). The third order is a lay fraternity. Together, they constitute the largest religious order in the Roman Catholic Church, noted for their missionary and social work.

Francistown POP (1991) 65 000, an independent township in Central district, Botswana. Originally a gold-mining settlement, it is, today, the industrial and commercial centre of Botswana.

francium *noun Chem.* (SYMBOL **Fr**, ATOMIC NUMBER **87**) the heaviest of the alkali metals, obtained by bombarding thorium with protons. It has several radioactive isotopes. [from the name *France*, where it was discovered]

Franck, César (Auguste) (1822–90) Belgian-born French composer, born in Liège. Following a period at the Liège Conservatoire, he studied in Paris, acquired French nationality, and settled there as a teacher and organist, composing in his leisure hours. His reputation rests on a few masterpieces all written after the age of 50, the best-known of which are a string quartet, a symphony, the tone poem *Le Chasseur maudit*, and the *Variations symphoniques* for piano and orchestra.

Franck, James (1882–1964) German-born US physicist, born in Hamburg. Professor at Göttingen University and later at the University of Chicago, he showed with Gustav Hertz that mercury atoms would only absorb a fixed amount of energy from bombarding electrons, demonstrating that the electron energy levels have certain fixed, discrete values. For this work they shared the 1925 Nobel Prize for Physics.

Franco (Bahamonde), Francisco (1892–1975) Spanish soldier and dictator (1936–75), born in El Ferrol, Galicia. Spain's youngest general by 1926, he repressed the revolt of the Asturias miners (1934), and during 1935 served as Chief-of-Staff. In 1936 he belatedly joined the conspiracy against the Popular Front government (elected Feb 1936) which on 17–18 Jul launched the rebellion which led to the Spanish Civil War (1936–9). Because he was leader of the Army of Africa, and had close ties with the rebels' Italian and German allies, Franco became (Sep 1936) *generalíssimo* of the rebel forces and chief of the Nationalist state. After leading the Nationalists to victory (Oct 1936–Apr 1939), he began to construct an authoritarian regime. During World War II, he initially wanted to join Germany and Italy, opting (1940) to not fight rather than be officially neutral, but in the end he kept Spain out of the war, and later distanced himself from the Axis (from 1943). During the 1950s, his anti-communism made possible a rapprochement with the Western powers. After his death the monarchy returned in the person of Juan Carlos I, grandson of Spain's last ruling king. Within two years almost every trace of his dictatorship had disappeared.

Franco- *combining form* forming words meaning 'French, French and …': *Franco-German*. [from Latin *Francus*, Frank]

Franco-German Treaty of Co-operation a treaty signed (Jan 1963) by President de Gaulle and Chancellor Adenauer that signalled the end of centuries of conflict. It made provisions for regular summit meetings, as well as co-operation and consultation in foreign, economic, and cultural affairs.

Francome, John (1952–) English jockey and trainer, born in Swindon, Wiltshire. In 1970–85 he rode a record 1 138 winners over fences. He won the 1978 Cheltenham Gold Cup, the 1981 champion hurdle, and twice won the King George VI Chase (1982, 1984). The second man to ride more than 1 000 winners, he was seven times National Hunt champion jockey (1976, 1979, 1981–5). He retired in 1985, and became a trainer, TV commentator, and novelist.

Franconian Forest, German **Frankenwald** a mountain range in Bavaria, SE Germany. It extends 36km/22mi between the R Rodach in the NW and the Fichtelgebirge in the SE. Its highest peak is the Döbraberg (795m).

francophone *noun* a French-speaking person, especially in a country where other languages are spoken. [from FRANCO- + Greek *phone*, voice]

Franco-Prussian War a conflict occasioned (1870) by the Hohenzollern candidature for the Spanish throne and the Ems telegram, and caused by the changing balance of power in Europe. It resulted in crushing defeats for France at the battles of Sedan and Metz by Moltke's reformed Prussian army, the Siege of Paris, and the humiliating Treaty of Frankfurt (1871), by which France incurred a war indemnity of five billion francs and the loss of Alsace and half of Lorraine to the new German Empire.

frangipani *noun* **1** a shrub or small tree (*Plumeria rubra*), native to tropical America, which grows up to 6m tall, and has oval leaves and large clusters of highly fragrant white, yellow, or pink flowers. It is widely cultivated in the tropics for its scented flowers, which are often placed in Buddhist temples. **2** (*also* **frangipane**) a perfume made from this, or imitating it. [from Frangipani, the name of the inventor of the perfume]

Frank, Anne (1929–45) German–Jewish concentration-camp victim, born in Frankfurt am Main. She fled from the Nazis to Holland in 1933, and after the Nazi occupation, hid with her family and four others in a sealed-off office backroom in Amsterdam from 1942 until they were betrayed in 1944. She died in Belsen concentration camp. The diary she kept during her concealment was published in 1947, dramatized, and filmed, and she came to symbolize the suffering inflicted by the Nazis.

Frank a male first name, from the name of the people; also a short form of *Francis*.

Frank *noun* a member of a Germanic people that invaded Gaul in the late 5c AD (see FRANKS). [from Anglo-Saxon *Franca*]

frank — *adj.* **1** open and honest in speech or manner. **2** bluntly outspoken. **3** undisguised; openly visible. — *verb* to mark (a letter) to show that postage has been paid. — *noun* a franking mark. [from Latin *francus*, free]

Frankenstein *or* **Frankenstein's monster** a name for a creation or creature that destroys its creator. [named after *Frankenstein* in Mary Shelley's novel]

Frankenstein a Gothic novel by Mary Shelley (1818). It describes the tragic events surrounding the creation of a man-like creature by Victor Frankenstein, a student in Geneva.

Frankfort (1990) 26 000. the capital of the state of Kentucky, USA, situated in Franklin County, N central Kentucky. A trade and shipping centre, it lies on the R Kentucky. HISTORY founded by pioneer Daniel Boone in 1770; became state capital in 1792.

Frankfurt (am Main) POP (1991e) 641 000, a manufacturing and commercial river port in Hessen state, W central Germany. It lies on the R Main, 27km/17mi N of Darmstadt. The leading German stock exchange has its headquarters in the city. Some of Germany's finest health resorts are nearby. HISTORY site of the coronation of most of the German Emperors; the poet Goethe was

born here in 1749; the first German National Assembly met in Frankfurt in 1848–9. NOTABLE FEATURES Gothic cathedral (13c–15c); the Römer (ancient town hall); Goethe House (rebuilt in 1949). EVENT International Frankfurt Fair (Aug) and many other trade fairs.

Frankfurt (an der Oder) POP (1991e) 86 000, an industrial town in Brandenburg state, NE Germany. It is 80km/50mi E of Berlin, on the R Oder, where the river follows the frontier with Poland. It was badly bombed in World War II.

frankfurter *noun* a type of spicy smoked sausage. [from German *Frankfurter Wurst*, Frankfurt sausage]

Frankfurt School, a group of philosophers, sociologists, and psychologists who belonged to the Frankfurt Institute for Social Research (1923–69) Leading figures included Max Horkheimer (1895–1973), Theodor Adorno (1903–69), Herbert Marcuse (1898–1979), and more recently Jürgen Habermas (1929–). They developed 'critical theory': an ethical, politically prescriptive critique of society inspired by the works of Marx and Freud.

frankincense *noun* a resin obtained from E African or Arabian trees, burnt to produce a sweet smell, especially during religious ceremonies. [from Old French *franc encens*, pure incense]

Frankish — *adj.* of the Franks or their language. — *noun* the W Germanic language of the Franks.

Frankland, Sir Edward (1825–99) English chemist, born near Lancaster. He taught in Manchester and London, and became professor at the Royal School of Mines (1865–85). In pure chemistry he made and studied the first organometallic compounds, which led him to the notion of 'valence' (combining power) for atoms. He also carried out important research on water and sewage purification.

Franklin, Benjamin (1706–90) US statesman, author, and scientist, born in Boston, Massachusetts. He set up a printing house in Philadelphia, bought the *Pennsylvania Gazette* (1729), and gained renown as a journalist. He became clerk of the Assembly (1736), postmaster of Philadelphia (1737), and deputy postmaster-general for the colonies (1754), and was sent on various diplomatic missions to England. In 1746 he began his research into electricity, which proved that lightning and electricity are identical and led to his suggestion that buildings should be protected by lightning conductors. Actively involved in framing the Declaration of Independence (1775), he used his negotiating skill to gain Britain's recognition of US independence (1783). He was US Minister in Paris until 1785, then three times President of the State of Pennsylvania, before he retired from public life (1788).

Franklin, Sir John (1786–1847) English Arctic explorer, born in Spilsby, Lincolnshire. He joined the navy at 14, and was present at the battles of Copenhagen (1801) and Trafalgar (1805). From 1834 to 1845 he was Governor of Van Diemen's Land (Tasmania). He then commanded an expedition to discover the Northwest Passage, but his ships were beleaguered by thick ice in the Victoria Strait, and he and his crew died. Their remains, and a record of the expedition, were found several years later. He is credited with the discovery of the Passage, because his ships came within a few miles of known American waters.

Franklin, Rosalind Elsie (1920–58) English X-ray crystallographer, born in London. Working at King's College, London, she produced excellent X-ray diffraction pictures of DNA which contributed to the discovery of the full DNA structure by James Watson and Francis Crick.

Franklin, the the well-to-do landowner in Chaucer's *The Canterbury Tales*, who tells the tale of Dorigen and Arveragus.

Franklin Institute a charitable organization founded in 1824 in Philadelphia, Pennsylvania, to further education and research in science. The centre houses a science museum and a technical library.

frankly *adv.* in a frank way.

frankness *noun* **1** being frank. **2** frank talk.

Franks Germanic peoples, originally from the lower Rhine region. In the 5c, Clovis led the Salian and Ripuarian Franks and founded a kingdom that embraced much of Gaul, the greatest ruler of which was Charlemagne (8c). They gave their name to Francia, which by the 13c stood for what is now France.

frantic *adj.* **1** desperate, eg with fear or anxiety. **2** hurried; rushed: *a frantic rush to meet the deadline.* [from Old French *frenetique*, from Greek *phrenetikos*, mad]

frantically *adv.* in a frantic way.

Franz Josef Land, Russian **Zemlya Frantsa-Iosifa** an archipelago in the Arctic Ocean, lying N of Novaya Zemlya, NW Russia. AREA 20 700sq km/8 000sq mi. It consists of over 160 islands of volcanic origin, and is uninhabited apart from occupants of scientific stations. The most northerly land of the E hemisphere, it was declared Soviet territory in 1926.

Frasch, Hermann (1851–1914) German-born US industrial chemist, born in Gailsdorf, Württemberg. In 1868 he emigrated to the USA, where he worked as a chemist and oil worker, and later founded the Union Sulphur Company, which became the largest sulphur-mining company in the world. He is best known for developing a method for extracting sulphur from deep deposits using superheated steam, now known as the Frasch process.

Fraser, Dawn (1937–) Australian swimmer, born in Balmain, near Sydney. She became the first woman swimmer to take the same individual title at three consecutive Olympics, winning the 100m freestyle in 1956, 1960, and 1964. She also won a gold medal in the 4 × 100m freestyle relay in 1956. She took six Commonwealth Games gold medals, and set 27 world records. In 1962 she became the first woman to break the one-minute barrier for the 100m. In 1964, following an over-exuberant party in Tokyo after winning her third Olympic title of that year, she was banned by the Australian association for 10 years (later reduced to 4).

Fraser a male first name, after the Scottish surname. [of Norman origin]

Fraserburgh POP (1981) 13 000, a port town in Banff and Buchan district, Grampian, NE Scotland. It lies on the North Sea, 24km/15mi NW of Peterhead, and is the main herring port in NE Scotland.

Fraser Island, also called **Great Sandy Island** an island off the SE coast of Queensland, Australia, with nature reserves and Aboriginal sites. Its economy includes yields of kauri, blackbutt, and satinay timber; sand mining ceased in 1977, when exports of the sands were banned. The island was named after Capt James Fraser who was killed there by Aborigines in 1836. It is a World Heritage site.

Fraser River a river in SW Canada, length 1 368km/850mi. Rising in the Rocky Mts, it flows NW, S, and W to enter the Strait of Georgia and the Pacific Ocean 16km/10mi S of Vancouver. The river is navigable below Yale; above Yale it flows through the canyon of the Fraser R. The 1858 gold rush along the upper reaches of the river led to independent colonial status for the mainland, and the beginnings of permanent non-native settlement.

fraternal *adj.* **1** concerning a brother; brotherly. **2** *said of twins* developed from separate ova; not identical. [from Latin *fraternus*, from *frater*, brother]

fraternally *adv.* in a fraternal way.

fraternity *noun* (PL. **fraternities**) **1** a religious brotherhood. **2** a group of people with common interests. **3** the fact of being brothers; brotherly feeling. **4** *North Amer.* a social club for male students. See also SORORITY. [from Latin *fraternitas*, from *frater*, brother]

fraternization or **fraternisation** *noun* associating as brothers; comradeship.

fraternize or **fraternise** *verb intrans.* (**fraternize with someone**) to meet or associate together as friends. [from Latin *fraternus*, brotherly]

fratricidal *adj.* relating to or of the nature of fratricide.

fratricide *noun* **1** the murder of a brother. **2** a person who murders his or her brother. [from Latin *frater*, brother + *caedere*, to kill]

fraud *noun* **1** an act of deliberate deception. **2** someone who dishonestly pretends to be something they are not. [from Latin *fraus*, trick]

fraudulence *noun* being fraudulent.

fraudulent *adj.* involving deliberate deception; intended to deceive. [from Latin *fraudulentus*, from *fraus*, trick]

fraudulently *adv.* in a fraudulent way.

fraught *adj.* **1** (**fraught with danger**, *etc*) full of danger, difficulties, problems, etc. **2** *colloq.* causing or feeling anxiety or worry. [from Dutch *vracht*, freight]

Fraunhofer, Joseph von (1787–1826) German physicist, born in Straubing, Bavaria. In 1807 he founded an optical institute at Munich, where he improved prisms and telescopes, enabling him to discover the dark lines in the Sun's spectrum now named after him. In 1823 he became professor at Munich.

fray[1] *verb intrans., trans.* **1** said of cloth or rope to wear away along an edge or at a point of friction, so that the threads come loose. **2** *said of tempers, nerves, etc* to make or become edgy and strained. [from French *frayer*, from Latin *fricare*, to rub]

fray[2] *noun* **1** a fight, quarrel, or argument. **2** any scene of lively action. [from AFFRAY]

Fray Bentos POP (1985) 20 000, the river-port capital of Río Negro department, W Uruguay, on the R Uruguay. Meat packing and canning are important to its economy. An international toll bridge crosses the R Uruguay to the Argentinian town of Puerto Unzué.

Frazer, Sir James George (1854–1941) Scottish social anthropologist, classicist, and folklorist, born in Glasgow. He spent most of his adult life as a Fellow of Trinity College, Cambridge, and became Professor of Social Anthropology at Liverpool in 1907. His major work was *The Golden Bough* (1890, rewritten in 12 vols, 1911–15).

frazzle — *noun* **1** a state of nervous and physical exhaustion. **2** a scorched and brittle state: *burnt to a frazzle.* — *verb* to tire out physically and emotionally.

FRCP *abbrev.* Fellow of the Royal College of Physicians.

FRCS *abbrev.* Fellow of the Royal College of Surgeons.

freak — *noun* **1** a person or animal of abnormal shape. **2** someone or something odd or unusual. **3** someone highly enthusiastic about something. **4** a drug addict: *an acid freak.* **5** a whim or caprice: *a freak of fancy.* — *adj.* abnormal. — *verb* (**freak out** or **freak someone out**) *colloq.* **1** to become or make mentally or emotionally over-excited, especially by taking hallucinatory drugs. **2** to become or make angry.

freakish or **freaky** *adj.* (**freakier, freakiest**) **1** very unusual; odd. **2** apt to change the mind suddenly.

freckle — *noun* a small brown mark on the skin, especially of fair-skinned people. — *verb trans., intrans.* to mark, or become marked, with freckles. [from Norse *freknur*, freckles]

freckly *adj.* (**frecklier, freckliest**) having many freckles.

Frederick I (Emperor), known as **Barbarossa** (**Redbeard**) (c.1123–90) Holy Roman Emperor, born of the Hohenstaufen family. He succeeded his uncle Conrad III in 1152 and his reign was a continuous struggle against unruly vassals at home, the city-republics of Lombardy, and the papacy. One of his campaigns in Italy resulted in defeat at Legnano (1176), but he quelled Henry the Lion of Bavaria, and asserted his feudal superiority over Poland, Hungary, Denmark, and Burgundy. He led the Third Crusade against Saladin (1189), and was victorious at Philomelium and Iconium.

Frederick I (of Prussia) (1657–1713) first King of Prussia, born in Königsberg. He succeeded to the electorate of Brandenburg in 1688 (as Frederick III) and was made the first King of Prussia in 1701 for his loyalty to the emperor Leopold against the French. He maintained a large court, established a standing army, and was a great patron of the arts and learning.

Frederick II (Emperor) (1194–1250) the last emperor of the Hohenstaufen line, born in Jesi, near Ancona, the grandson of Frederick I. He succeeded Henry VI in 1220, and was also King of Sicily (1198) and of Germany (1212). He aimed to consolidate Imperial power in Italy at the expense of the papacy, and devoted himself to organizing his Italian territories, but his plans were frustrated by the Lombard cities and by the popes. Embarking on the Fifth Crusade in 1228, he took possession of Jerusalem, and crowned himself king there (1229).

Frederick II (of Prussia), known as **the Great** (1712–86) King of Prussia, born in Berlin, the son of Frederick-William. As King (1740), he was a noted military commander in the War of the Austrian Succession (1740–8). He seized Silesia, and defeated the Austrians at Mollwitz (1741) and Chotusitz (1742). The second Silesian War (1744–5) left him with further territories which he managed to retain after fighting the Seven Years War (1756–63). In 1772 he shared in the first partition of Poland. Under him, Prussia doubled in area, gained a strong economic foundation, and became a leading European power. He was also a prolific writer on political and military subjects.

Frederick V (of the Palatinate), known as **the Winter King** (1596–1632) Elector of the Palatinate (1610–23) and King of Bohemia (as Frederick I, 1619–20), born in Amberg, Upper Palatinate. In 1613 he married Elizabeth, daughter of James I of England, put himself at the head of the Protestant union of Germany, and accepted the Crown of Bohemia. His defeat at the battle of the White Mountain (1620) by Imperialist-Spanish forces ended his short reign.

Frederick VI (of Denmark) (1768–1839) King of Denmark (1808–39) and Norway (1808–14), born in Christiansborg Castle, Denmark. During his liberal reign, feudal serfdom was abolished, the criminal code amended, and the slave trade prohibited in the Danish colonies. He refused to join Britain against Napoleon, and after the war lost Norway to Sweden (1814). Denmark then took some years to recover from bankruptcy. In 1831 he granted a liberal constitution to his subjects.

Frederick IX (of Denmark) (1899–1972) King of Denmark (1947–72), born near Copenhagen, the son of Christian X. In 1935 he married Ingrid, daughter of King Gustav VI Adolf of Sweden. They had three daughters: Margrethe (later Margrethe II), Benedikte, and Anne-Marie, who married the former King Constantine II of Greece. During World War II, he encouraged the

Danish resistance movement, and was imprisoned by the Germans (1943–5).

Frederick, Duke the usurping Duke and father of Celia, who banishes Rosalind to the Forest of Arden in Shakespeare's *As You Like It*.

Frederick a male first name, dating from the Conquest and reintroduced by George I of England, formerly Elector of Hanover. [from Germanic *fred, frid*, peace + *ric*, power]

Frederick William, known as **the Great Elector** (1620–88) Elector of Brandenburg (1640–88), born near Berlin. On his accession, he found the state exhausted by the Thirty Years War. He therefore made a treaty of neutrality with the Swedes, regulated the finances, sought to re-people the deserted towns, and reorganized the army and administrative system of the Hohenzollern state. He recovered some territory and gained E Pomerania by the Treaty of Westphalia (1648), retrieving the sovereignty of Prussia from Poland (1657), all reforms that laid the foundation of future Prussian greatness.

Frederick William III (of Prussia) (1770–1840) King of Prussia (1797–1849), the son of Frederick William II, born in Potsdam. Though at first neutral towards Napoleon's conquests, he declared war in 1806, was severely defeated at Jena and Auerstadt, and lost all territory west of the Elbe. To further Prussia's recovery, he sanctioned the reforms of Hardenburg and Stein and the military reorganization of Scharnhorst and Gneisenau, and shared in the decisive victory of Leipzig with Alexander I (1813). By the Treaty of Vienna (1815) he recovered his possessions, and thereafter tended to support the forces of conservatism.

Fredericksburg, Battle of a fruitless attempt (1862) in the American Civil War by the 113 000-strong Northern army to capture the town of Fredericksburg, Virginia, defended by a Southern army of 75 000.

Fredericton POP (1991) 45 000, the capital of New Brunswick province, E Canada, on the St John R. HISTORY originally settled by Acadians in 1731, as St Anne's Point, it was renamed in 1785 in honour of Prince Frederick, the second son of George III; became capital of the province in 1787. NOTABLE FEATURES York-Sunbury Historical Museum; Beaverbrook Art Gallery; Provincial Legislature (1880); Christ Church Cathedral (1853); Old Government House (1828), now the headquarters of the Royal Canadian Mounted Police.

Fredriksson, Gert (1919–) Swedish canoeist. He won eight Olympic medals (1948–60), including six golds, and 13 world titles, all at either kayak singles or pairs. His winning margin of 6.7 seconds in the 1948 Olympic singles final was the biggest for any kayak race other than the 10 000m. When he won his last Olympic gold in 1960, he was 40 years 292 days old — the oldest canoeing gold medallist.

free — *adj.* (**freer, freest**) **1** allowed to move as one pleases; not shut in. **2** not tied or fastened. **3** allowed to do as one pleases; not restricted, controlled, or enslaved. **4** *said of a country* independent. **5** costing nothing. **6** open or available to all. **7** not working, busy, engaged or having another appointment. **8** not occupied; not being used. **9** (**free of, free from**) without; not, or no longer, having or suffering (especially something harmful, unpleasant or not wanted). **10** (**free with**) generous, lavish, or liberal. **11** *said of a translation* not precisely literal. **12** smooth and easy: *free and relaxed body movement.* **13** without obstruction: *given free passage.* **14** *derog., said of a person's manner* disrespectful, over-familiar, or presumptuous. **15** *Chem.* not combined with anything. — *adv.* **1** without payment: *free of charge.* **2** without restriction: *wander free.* — *verb* (**free someone of something**) **1** to make them free from it; to release them. **2** to rid or relieve them of something.

— **feel free** you have permission (to do something).

for free *colloq.* without payment.

free and easy cheerfully casual or tolerant.

a free hand scope to choose how best to act.

it's a free country *colloq.* there's no objection to acting in the way mentioned.

make free with something to make too much, or unacceptable, use of something not one's own. [from Anglo-Saxon *freo*]

-free *combining form* **1** not paying: *rent-free*. **2** not having; not affected or troubled by: *fat-free / pain-free*.

freebase *slang* — *noun* cocaine refined for smoking by being heated with ether. — *verb* to smoke this.

freebie *noun colloq.* something given or provided without charge.

freeboard *noun* the distance between the top edge of the side of a boat and the surface of the water.

freebooter *noun Hist.* a pirate. [from Dutch *vrijbuiter*, from *vrij*, free + *buit*, booty]

freeborn *adj.* born as a free citizen, not a slave.

Free Church in the UK, a Protestant Church other than an established Church.

freedman *or* **freedwoman** *noun* a freed slave.

freedom *noun* **1** the condition of being free to act, move, etc without restriction. **2** liberty or independence. **3** a right or liberty: *freedom of speech*. **4** the state of being without, or exempt from, something: *freedom from pain*. **5** unrestricted access to or use of: *give someone the freedom of one's house*. **6** honorary citizenship of a place, entitling one to certain privileges. **7** frankness; candour. **8** over-familiarity; presumptuous behaviour.

freedom of conscience the right to hold religious or other beliefs without persecution.

free enterprise business done without government interference or control.

free fall 1 the fall of something acted on by gravity alone. **2** the part of a descent by parachute before the parachute opens.

free-falling *noun* **1** the process of falling by force of gravity alone. **2** in sky-diving, the part of a descent before the parachute opens (at a height of c.600m).

Freefone *noun trademark* a British Telecom service whereby calls made to a business or organization are charged to that organization rather than to the caller.

free-for-all *noun* a fight, argument, or discussion in which everybody feels free to join.

Free French Frenchmen who answered General de Gaulle's appeal in World War II (broadcast from London, 18 Jun 1940) to reject the impending armistice between France and Germany. De Gaulle became leader of the Free French forces, and the Free French 2nd Armoured Division helped liberate Paris (25 Aug 1944).

freehand *adj. adv., said of a drawing, etc* done without the help of a ruler, compass, etc.

freehold — *adj., said of land, property, etc* belonging to the owner for life and without limitations. — *noun* ownership of such land, property, etc. See also LEASEHOLD.

freeholder *noun* an owner of property by freehold.

free house a hotel or bar not owned by a particular beer-producer and therefore free to sell a variety of beers.

free kick *Football* a kick allowed to one side with no tackling from the other, as a penalty to the latter.

freelance — *noun* a self-employed person offering his or her services where needed, not under contract to any single employer. — *adj.,*

adv. of, or as, a freelance. — *verb intrans.* to work as a freelance. [term for a mercenary medieval soldier, first used by Sir Walter Scott]

freelancer *noun* a freelance.

freeload *verb intrans.* to eat, live, enjoy oneself, etc at the expense of someone else.

freeloader *noun* a sponger.

free love the practice of having sexual relations with people regardless of marriage.

freely *adv.* in a free way; openly, without restraint.

freeman *noun* a respected person who has been granted the freedom of a city.

Freemason *noun* (*also* **Mason**) a member of an international secret male society, having among its purposes mutual help and brotherly fellowship.

Freemasonry *noun* the institutions of the Freemasons.

free pardon an unconditional pardon given, eg as a result of fresh evidence, to someone convicted of a crime.

Freeport POP (1990e) 27 000, the chief town of Grand Bahama I in the Bahamas. NOTABLE FEATURE International Bazaar.

free port a port, or a free-trade zone adjacent to a port or airport, where goods may be imported free of tax or import duties, provided they are re-exported or used to make goods to be re-exported. The world's largest free ports are Hong Kong and Singapore; the UK set up six free ports in 1984, including Liverpool and Southampton.

Freepost *noun trademark* a Royal Mail service whereby postage costs for letters sent to a business or organization are charged to that organization rather than being prepaid by the sender.

free radical *Chem.* a group of atoms, containing at least one unpaired electron, that is capable of initiating a wide range of chemical reactions. Free radicals can have very damaging effects if they are formed in living organisms.

free-range *adj.* **1** *said of hens* moving about freely; not kept in a battery. **2** *said of eggs* laid by free-range hens.

freesia *noun* a plant belonging to the genus *Freesia* of the iris family, which has an underground bulb and is widely cultivated for its fragrant trumpet-shaped white, yellow, purple, or crimson flowers. It is very popular as a cut flower. [named after the Swedish botanist Elias Magnus Fries]

free speech the right to express any opinion freely.

free-standing *adj.* not attached to, or supported by, a wall or other structure.

freestyle *Sport* — *adj., said of a competition or race* in which competitors are allowed to choose their own style or programme. — *noun* a freestyle competition or race.

freethinker *noun* someone who forms his or her own, especially religious, ideas, rather than accepting the view of an authority.

free thought *Relig.* a post-Reformation movement which rejected the control of any religious authority over reason in the examination of religious issues. The term was used by the 17c and 18c deists, eg Anthony Collins (1676–1729), and is represented by the National Secularist Society (1866) and the 20c Secular Society.

Freetown POP (1985) 470 000, the seaport capital of Sierra Leone and of Freetown district. HISTORY visited by the Portuguese in the 15c; founded in the late 1790s as a settlement for freed slaves; capital of British West Africa from 1808 until 1874; W Africa's oldest university, Fourah Bay, was founded as a college in 1827; became capital of Sierra Leone in 1961. NOTABLE FEATURES fort on Bunce I.

free trade trade with foreign countries without customs, taxes, etc.

free verse poetry with no regular pattern of rhyme, rhythm, or line length.

freeware *noun Comput.* software which is in the public domain, allowing it to be copied legally, but not resold commercially.

freeway *noun North Amer., esp. US* a motorway.

freewheel *verb intrans.* **1** to travel, usually downhill, on a bicycle, in a car, etc without using mechanical power. **2** to act or drift about unhampered by responsibilities.

free will 1 the power of making choices without the constraint of fate or some other uncontrollable force, regarded as a human characteristic. **2** a person's independent choice.
◇ Philosophers have offered two major competing accounts of this faculty or condition. According to one, an action is free if the agent has the power to do it and the power to refrain from doing it. According to the other, an action is free if it accords with the agent's desires. On both accounts, free will is a necessary precondition for a person being morally responsible.

Free World (the Free World) formerly, the name used by non-communist countries for themselves.

freeze — *verb* (PAST TENSE **froze**; PAST PARTICIPLE **frozen**) **1** *trans., intrans.* to turn into ice or solidify as a result of cold. **2** (**freeze over** *or* **freeze something over**) to become covered or cover with ice. **3** (**freeze up** *or* **freeze something up**) to become blocked up or stop operating because of frost or ice. **4** *trans., intrans.* (*often* **freeze together**) to stick or cause to stick together by frost. **5** *intrans. said of the weather, temperature, etc* to be at or below freezing-point. **6** *trans., intrans. colloq.* to be or make very cold: *frozen hands*. **7** *intrans.* to die of cold: *freeze to death*. **8** *trans., intrans. said of food* to preserve, or be suitable for preserving, by refrigeration at below freezing-point. **9** *trans., intrans.* to make or become motionless or unable to move, because of fear, etc. **10** to fix (prices, wages, etc) at a certain level. **11** to prevent (money, shares, etc) from being used. **12** to stop (a moving film) at a certain frame. — *noun* **1** (*also* **freeze-up**) a period of very cold weather with temperatures below freezing-point. **2** a period of control of wages, prices, etc.
— **freeze someone out** to exclude them from an activity, conversation, etc by persistent unfriendliness or unresponsiveness.
[from Anglo-Saxon *freosan*]

freeze-dry *verb* (PAST TENSE AND PAST PARTICIPLE **freeze-dried**) to preserve (perishable material, especially food and medicines), by rapidly freezing it and then drying it under high-vacuum conditions so that ice is forced out of the material as water vapour without melting. Food preserved in this way, eg coffee and soft fruit, keeps much of its original flavour and texture.

freeze-frame *noun* a facility on a video recorder allowing the stopping of a videotape while being played to give a still view of a particular image.

freezer *noun* a refrigerated cabinet or compartment in which to preserve food at below freezing-point.

freezing point (ABBREV. **fp, f.p.**) **1** the temperature at which the liquid form of a particular substance turns into a solid. **2** (*also* **freezing**) the freezing point of water (0°C at sea level).

Frege, (Friedrich Ludwig) Gottlob (1848–1925) German mathematician and logician, born in Wismar. His *Begriffsschrift* ('Concept-script', 1879) outlined the first complete system of symbolic logic. The technical difficulties involved gave rise to his distinctive philosophical doctrines, set out in his *Grundlagen der Arithmetik*

(The Foundations of Arithmetic, 1884). His *Grundgesetze der Arithmetik* (Basic Laws of Arithmetic, 1893–1903) contained a postscript acknowledging that Bertrand Russell had spotted a contradiction in his thinking.

freight — *noun* **1** transport of goods by rail, road, sea, or air. **2** the goods transported in this way. **3** the cost of such transport. — *verb* **1** to transport (goods) by freight. **2** to load with goods for transport. [from Old Dutch *vrecht*]

freighter *noun* a ship or aircraft that carries cargo rather than passengers.

freightliner *noun* a train designed for the rapid transport of goods.

Freischütz, Der (The Freeshooter) an opera by Carl Maria von Weber (1821). Set in 18c Bohemia, the story arises from the efforts made by Max to prove himself the best marksman in a contest so that Agathe will marry him.

Fremantle POP (1990e) 24 000, a seaport city in Western Australia state, situated 10km SW of Perth, on the W coast of Australia. It lies at the mouth of the Swan R and is part of Perth metropolitan area. The city, known locally as 'Freo', was founded as a penal colony in 1829. NOTABLE FEATURES the Round House (1830), a former jail; Maritime Museum; notable sailing club; centre for the 1986–7 America's Cup yacht race.

French — *adj.* **1** relating or belonging to France or its inhabitants. **2** relating to the language of the French. — *noun* **1** the Romance language spoken in France, parts of Belgium, Luxembourg, Switzerland, and elsewhere. **2** (**the French**) the people of France.
◇ French is also spoken in many former French colonies in Africa, the Caribbean, and Oceania. It developed from the Latin spoken in Gaul and became a distinct language by the 9c. The dialect of the Ile de France became the standard from the 13c, and its literary form is still the basis of educated or 'correct' French (officially protected since 1635 by the Académie Française). See panel p. 492.

French and Indian War the last (1756–63) of the 18c wars between France and Britain for the control of N America, which culminated in France's acceptance of defeat at the Treaty of Paris (1763).

French bean a kind of green bean of which the pod and its contents are eaten.

French bread white bread in the form of long narrow loaves.

French Canadian a native of the French-speaking part of Canada.

French-Canadian *adj.* relating to French Canadians or their language.

French chalk a form of the mineral talc used to mark cloth or remove grease marks.

French Community a grouping of some former French colonies which under the Constitution of the Fifth Republic (1958) opted to stay closely associated with France. Such matters as currency, defence, and foreign affairs remained the responsibility of the Community (effectively France), until 1960 when the member states could have full independence within the Community, which eliminated its practical relevance.

French dressing a salad dressing made from oil, spices, and lemon juice or vinegar.

French fries chips.

French Guiana, French **La Guyane Française** POP (1990) 115 000, an Overseas Department of France in S America, divided into two districts. AREA 90 909sq km/35 091sq mi. It is bounded W by Suriname, E and S by Brazil and N by the Atlantic Ocean. CAPITAL Cayenne. TIME ZONE GMT −3.5. The population is comprised of Creoles, Europeans, and American Indians; Roman Catholicism is the chief religion. OFFICIAL LANGUAGE French. CURRENCY the French franc. PHYSICAL DESCRIPTION low-lying near the coast; rises in the S towards the Serra de

Tumucumaque, reaching 635m at Mont Saint Marcel; many rocky islets along the coast, notably Devil's Island. CLIMATE hot and humid tropical climate; rainy season (Dec–Jun); average daily temperatures at Cayenne, 23–33°C; monthly rainfall 551mm in May, 31mm in Sep. HISTORY area settled by Europeans in the 17c; became a territory of France in 1817; used as a penal colony in 1798–1935; became an Overseas Department of France in 1946. GOVERNMENT elects two members to the French National Assembly. ECONOMY timber is the main export; minerals are little exploited; some bauxite, kaolin, gold; shrimps; rum; essence of rosewood; only a small area is used for cultivation; some cattle, pigs, poultry.

French horn see HORN.

French leave leave taken without permission from work or duty.

French letter *slang* a condom.

Frenchman *or* **Frenchwoman** *noun* a man or woman of French nationality.

French polish a varnish for furniture.

French-polish *verb* to apply French polish to.

French Polynesia, official name **Territory of French Polynesia**, formerly **French Settlements in Oceania** POP (1992e) 207 000, an island Territory comprising five scattered archipelagoes in the SE Pacific Ocean, between the Cook Is in the W and the Pitcairn Is in the E. AREA 3 941sq km/1 521sq mi. CAPITAL Papeete. TIME ZONE GMT −6. The population is mainly Polynesian; Christianity is the chief religion. OFFICIAL LANGUAGE French; local languages are also widely spoken. PHYSICAL DESCRIPTION the island groups include the Society Is (including Tahiti and Bora-Bora), Tuamotu Archipelago, Gambier Is, Marquesas Is, and Tubuai Is; mainly volcanic, mountainous, and ringed with coral reefs; some low-lying coral atolls. CLIMATE hot and humid from Nov to Apr; tropical storms are less frequent than in the W Pacific. HISTORY French missionary activity in the 19c; French protectorates introduced from 1842; 'French Oceania' became an Overseas Territory in 1958. GOVERNMENT administered by a High Commissioner and 10-member Council of Ministers, elected by a 30-member Territorial Assembly. ECONOMY based on agricultural smallholdings (vegetables, fruit) and plantations (coconut oil, copra); cultured pearls; vanilla, citrus fruits; tourism; maintenance of the French nuclear test base.

French Republican calendar a calendar introduced during the French Revolution by the National Convention to herald a new epoch and further de-christianization, the structure and nomenclature of which were devised by a committee under the deputy, Fabre d'Eglantine. Year one dated from the abolition of the monarchy and the declaration of the Republic (22 Sep 1792), and the 12 30-day months were divided into three 10-day weeks of *decadi* (Sundays eliminated), named from nature and the seasons: Vendémiaire, Brumaire, Frimaire, Nivôse, Pluviôse, Ventôse, Germinal, Floréal, Prairial, Messidor, Thermidor, and Fructidor. The system was abolished under Napoleon (1805).

French Revolution a complex upheaval in 1789 that affected every aspect of government and society, a turning-point in French history. Conventionally the start was the summoning of the Estates General (Spring 1789). It responded to public pressure, such as the storming of the Bastille (14 Jul 1789), with wide-ranging political, social, and economic measures (1789–91). These included the abolition of feudal, aristocratic, and clerical privileges, a Declaration of the Rights of Man (1789), the establishment of a constitutional government, the confiscation of Church property, and a reorganization of Church–State relations in the Civil Constitution

of the Clergy (1790). A Legislative Assembly was elected; however, after an insurrection (10 Aug), France was declared a republic (1792) and a new assembly (the National Convention) was effected (Sep 1792). The Paris crowd, incited by demagogues, entered the prisons and massacred thousands of innocent victims in the September Massacres. Louis XVI and his queen, Marie Antoinette, were executed (1793). The Revolution then entered more dramatic phases, marked by political extremism and bitter rivalry between Girondins and Jacobins (the latter led by Robespierre). Though the Jacobins seized control of the Committee of Public Safety (Jul 1793) and instituted the dictatorship of the Reign of Terror, Robespierre's short-lived triumph ended with his execution (1794). The Convention suppressed both Jacobin and Royalist opponents with military force before establishing the government of the Directory (1795), which was in turn overthrown by Napoleon Bonaparte in the Brumaire coup (1799). The *ancien régime* was dismantled by the Revolution in the name of liberty, equality, and fraternity.

French Revolutionary Wars a series of campaigns (1792–9) between France and neighbouring European states hostile to the Revolution and to French hegemony. France declared war on Emperor Francis II, Prussia, and Sardinia, which precipitated the War of the First Coalition (1792–7). France later extended hostilities to Britain, Holland, and Spain (1793); after a successful invasion of the Netherlands (1794), the French broke the Coalition (1795–6) and isolated Britain (1797). A Second Coalition (1798) expelled French forces from Italy and the Rhinelands, before being defeated by Napoleon (1799–1800). The fighting continued in the Napoleonic Wars (1800–15).

French Southern and Antarctic Territories, French **Terres Australes et Antarctiques Françaises**. a French Overseas Territory, comprising Adélie Land in Antarctica and the islands of Kerguélen, Crozet, Amsterdam, and St Paul in the S Indian Ocean. It was established in 1955 and is governed by an administrator and a seven-member consultative council which meets twice-yearly in Paris.

French windows a pair of glass doors that open on to a garden, balcony, etc.

frenetic *adj.* frantic, distracted, hectic, or wildly energetic. [from Old French *frenetique*, from Greek *phrenitis*, delirium]

frenetically *adv.* in a frenetic way.

frenzied *adj.* in or as if in a frenzy; wild.

frenzy *noun* (PL. **frenzies**) **1** a state of violent mental disturbance. **2** wild agitation or excitement. **3** a frantic burst of activity. [from Greek *phrenesis*, madness]

frequency *noun* (PL. **frequencies**) **1** the condition of happening often. **2** the rate at which a happening, phenomenon, etc, recurs. **3** *Physics* a measure of the rate at which a complete cycle of wave motion is repeated per unit time. The SI unit of frequency is the hertz, equal to one wave cycle per second, and the frequency of a wave is inversely proportional to its wavelength. Musical notes correspond to different frequencies of sound waves, such that the higher the frequency the higher the pitch. **4** *Radio* the rate of sound waves per second at which a particular radio signal is sent out. **5** *Statistics* the number of items, values, etc, that occur within a specified category, eg the number of students with a score of 90 to 100 in a class test may be five, so for that category the frequency is five. [from Latin *frequens*, happening often]

frequency distribution *Maths.* a set of data that includes numerical values for the frequencies of different scores or results, ie the number of times that each particular score or result occurs.

French Words and Phrases Used in English

à bon marché   good market; at a good price, cheap

à deux   for two; (of a dinner or conversation) romantic, intimate

affaire   liaison, intrigue; an incident arousing speculation and scandal

agent provocateur   provocative agent; someone employed to lead others in illegal acts for which they will be punished

aide-de-camp   assistant in the field; an officer in the armed forces who acts as assistant to a senior officer

aide-mémoire   help-memory; something that helps one to remember something; a reminder

à la carte   from the menu; each dish individually priced and ordered separately

à la mode   in fashion; fashionable

ambiance   surroundings, atmosphere

amende honorable   a public apology satisfying the honour of the injured party

amour-propre   own love, self love; self-esteem

ancien régime   old regime; a superseded and outdated political system or ruling elite

à point   into the right condition; to a nicety, precisely

appellation contrôlée   certified name; used in the labelling of French wines, a guarantee of specified conditions of origin, strength, etc

après-ski   after ski; evening social activities after a day's skiing

atelier   a workshop, an artist's studio

au contraire   on the contrary

au fait   to the point; highly skilled; knowledgeable or familiar with something

au fond   at the bottom; fundamentally

au naturel   in the natural state; naked; cooked plainly, raw, or without dressing

au pair   on an equal basis; a young person from abroad who lives with a family and helps with housework, looking after children, etc, in return for board and lodging

avant-garde   front guard; using or supporting the most modern and advanced ideas in literature, art, music, etc

bain-marie   bath of Mary; a pan of hot water in which a container of food can be cooked gently or kept warm

bal costumé   a fancy-dress ball

beau geste   a beautiful gesture; a generous or unselfish act

belle époque   fine period; the time of gracious living for the well-to-do immediately preceding World War I

belles-lettres   beautiful letters; works of literature valued for their style rather than their content

bête noire   black beast; someone or something that bothers, annoys or frightens one more than anything else

blasé   cloyed; bored through over-familiarity

bon mot   good word; a short, clever remark

bonne-bouche   good mouth; a delicious morsel eaten at the end of a meal

bonvivant   good living (person); someone who lives well, particularly enjoying good food and wine

bon voyage   have a safe and pleasant journey

bourgeois   citizen; a member of the middle class; conventional, conservative

canard   duck; an untrue report; a false rumour

carte blanche   blank sheet of paper; freedom to do or organize things as one thinks best

cause célèbre   a matter that attracts attention and causes much controversy

c'est la vie   that's life; denotes fatalistic resignation

chacun à son goût   each to his own taste; implies surprise at another's choice

chambré   put into a room; (of red wine) at room temperature

chargé-d'affaires   an ambassador's deputy or substitute

chef d'oeuvre   an artist's or writer's masterpiece

cinéma-vérité   cinema truth; realism in films usually sought by photographic scenes of real life

cliché; stereotype printing block; a phrase that has become stale and feeble through repetition

comme il faut   as it is necessary; correct; genteel

cordon bleu; blue ribbon; (of a cook or cookery) of the highest standard

coup de foudre   flash of lightning; a sudden and astonishing happening; love at first sight

coupe de grâce   blow of mercy; a final decisive blow

coup d'état; blow of state; the sudden, usually violent, overthrow of a government

coupé   cut; a four-seated, two-door car with a sloping rear

crème de la crème   cream of the cream; the very best

cuisine minceur   slenderness cooking; a style of cooking characterized by imaginative use of light, simple, low-fat ingredients

cul-de-sac   bottom of the bag; a street closed at one end

décolleté   with bared neck and shoulders; (of a dress) low-cut; wearing a low-cut dress

déjà vu   already seen; the feeling or illusion of having experienced something before

de rigueur   of strictness; compulsory; strictly required

derrière   behind; the buttocks

déshabillé   undressed; only partially or casually dressed

de trop   of too much; not wanted, in the way

distingué   distinguished; with a noble or dignified appearance; striking

double entendre   double meaning; a remark with two possible meanings, one of which is sexually suggestive

doyen   dean; the most senior and most respected member of a profession, etc

droit de seigneur   the lord's right; originally the alleged right of a feudal superior to take the virginity of a vassal's bride; an excessive claim imposed on a subordinate

élan   dash, rush, bound; impressive and energetic style

embarras de richesse   embarrassment of wealth; a disconcerting amount of wealth or an abundance of any kind

embonpoint   *en bon point* in fine form; well-fed, stout, plump

éminence grise   someone who has great influence without actually occupying an official position of power

enfant terrible   terrible child; someone with a reputation for rude or embarrassing behaviour in public

ennui   boredom or discontent caused by a lack of activity or excitement

en passant   in passing; by the way, incidentally

en route   on the way, on the road

entente   understanding; a friendly agreement between nations

épater les bourgeois   shock the middle class; to disconcert the prim and proper, eg by an artistic production which defies convention

fait accompli   accomplished fact; something done and unalterable; an established fact

faute de mieux   for lack of anything better

faux ami   false friend; a word in a foreign language that does not mean what it appears to

faux-naïf   falsely naive; seeming or pretending to be unsophisticated, innocent, etc

faux pas   false step; a social blunder

femme fatale   fatal woman; a woman whose irresistible charms fascinate and destroy others, especially men

film noir   black film; style of film depicting the dark side of human nature, using stark lighting and often urban settings, etc

fin de siècle   end of the century; of the end of the 19c in Western culture or of an era

force de frappe   strike force; equivalent of the 'independent nuclear deterrent'

force majeure   superior force; an unforseeable or uncontrollable course of events, excusing one from fulfilling a legal contract

grand mal   large illness; a violently convulsive form of epilepsy

grand prix   great prize; any of a series of international motor races held to decide the world championship; a competition of similar importance in other sports

haute couture   higher tailoring; the most expensive and fashionable clothes available; the leading fashion designers or their products

haut monde   high world; high society, fashionable society

hors concours   out of the competition; not entered for a contest; unequalled

idée fixe   a fixed idea; an obsession

laissez-faire   let do; a policy of not interfering in what others are doing

lèse-majesté   injured majesty; treason

ménage à trois   household of three; a household comprised of a husband and wife and the lover of one of them

mot juste   exact word; the word which fits the context exactly

négociant   merchant, trader

noblesse oblige   nobility obliges; rank imposes obligations

nostalgie de la boue   hankering for mud; a craving for a debased physical life without civilized refinements

nouveau riche   new rich; someone who has recently acquired wealth but lacks the good taste or social graces to go with it

nouvelle cuisine   new cooking; a simple style of cookery characterized by much use of fresh produce and elegant presentation

nouvelle vague   new wave; a movement in French cinema aiming at imaginative quality films

outré   gone to excess; beyond what is customary or proper; eccentric

pied-à-terre   foot on the ground; a flat, small house, etc kept for temporary or occasional accommodation

plus ça change   abbreviated form of **plus ça change, plus c'est la même chose** the more things change, the more they stay the same

poule de luxe   luxurious hen; a sexually attractive promiscuous young woman; a prostitute

pour encourager les autres   to encourage the others (Voltaire *Candide*, on the execution of Admiral Byng); exemplary punishment

premier cru   first growth; wine of the highest quality in a system of classification

prêt-à-porter   ready to wear; (of clothes) made in standard sizes rather than being made-to-measure

prix fixe   fixed price; (of a meal) offered at a set price for a restricted choice

raison d'être   reason for existence

recherché   sought out; particularly choice; rare or exotic

reculer pour mieux sauter   move backwards in order to jump better; a strategic withdrawal to wait for a better opportunity

répondez, s'il vous plaît   reply, please; used in its abbreviated form, **RSVP**, on invitations

revenons à nos moutons   let us return to our sheep; let us get back to our subject

risqué   risky, hazardous; bordering on the rude or indecent

sang froid   cold blood; self possession; coolness under stress

savoir faire   knowing what to do; expertise; tact

succès de scandale   success of scandal; a book, film, etc that is successful because of its connection with a scandal rather than on merit

table d'hôte   host's table; a set meal at a fixed price

touché   touched; used to acknowledge a hit made in fencing, or a point scored in an argument

tour de force   turning movement; a feat of strength or skill

trompe l'oeil   deceives the eye; a painting or decoration which gives a convincing illusion of reality

vin du pays   wine of the country; a locally produced wine for everyday consumption

vis-à-vis   face to face; in relation to; with regard to

volte-face   turn-face; a sudden and complete change in opinion or in views expressed

frequency modulation *Radio* (ABBREV. **FM**) a method of radio transmission in which the frequency of the carrier wave (the signal-carrying wave) increases or decreases instantaneously in response to changes in the amplitude of the signal being transmitted. It gives a better signal-to-noise ratio than amplitude modulation (AM).

frequent *adj.* (with stress on *fre-*) **1** recurring at short intervals. **2** habitual. — *verb* (with stress on *-quent*) to visit or attend often.

frequently *adv.* often.

fresco *noun* (PL. **frescoes, frescos**) a picture painted on a wall, usually while the plaster is still damp. [from Italian *fresco*, fresh]

Frescobaldi one of several banking families in 14c–15c Florence with European-wide interests. Among their clients was the English king Edward II, whose wars with Scotland were financed in exchange for customs revenues, but the royal default on debts led to a crisis for the Frescobaldi bank in 1311.

fresh — *adj.* **1** newly made, gathered, etc. **2** having just arrived from somewhere, just finished doing something or just had some experience, etc: *fresh from university.* **3** other or another; different; clean: *a fresh sheet of paper.* **4** new; additional: *fresh supplies.* **5** original: *a fresh approach.* **6** *said of fruit or vegetables* not tinned, frozen, preserved, etc. **7** not tired; bright and alert. **8** cool; refreshing: *a fresh breeze.* **9** *said of air* cool and uncontaminated. **10** *said of water* not salt. **11** *said of the face or complexion* youthfully healthy; ruddy. **12** *colloq., said of behaviour* offensively informal. — *adv.* recently; newly: *fresh-baked bread.* [from Anglo-Saxon *fersc*, fresh, not salt]

freshen *verb* (**freshened, freshening**) **1** to make fresh or fresher. **2** (*trans, intrans.*) (*also* **freshen up** *or* **freshen someone up**) to get washed and tidy; to wash and tidy (oneself). **3** *intrans. said of a wind* to become stronger.

fresher *or* **freshman** *noun* a first-year college or university student.

freshet *noun* **1** a stream of fresh water flowing into the sea. **2** the sudden overflow of a river. [a diminutive of FRESH]

freshly *adv.* newly; with freshness.

freshness *noun* being fresh.

freshwater *adj.* denoting water that contains less than 0.2% dissolved salts, such as that found in most rivers and lakes.

Fresnel, Augustin Jean (1788–1827) French physicist, born in Broglie. Head of the department of public works in Paris, his optical investigations contributed substantially to the establishment of the wave theory of light; he invented the well-known compound lighthouse lens and produced circularly polarized light by means of a special prism (*Fresnel's rhomb*).

Fresno POP (1990) 667 000, the capital of Fresno County, central California, USA, situated c.260km/160mi SE of San Francisco. It is the centre of a wine-producing region. HISTORY founded in 1872; achieved city status in 1889.

fret¹ *verb* (**fretted, fretting**) **1** *intrans.* to worry, especially unnecessarily; to show or express anxiety. **2** to worry or agitate. **3** to wear away or consume by rubbing or erosion. [from Anglo-Saxon *fretan*, to gnaw]

fret² *noun* any of the narrow metal ridges across the neck of a guitar or similar musical instrument.

fret³ — *noun* an ornamental repeated pattern used as a border, etc. — *verb* (**fretted, fretting**) to decorate with a fret, or carve with fretwork. [from Old French *frete*, interlaced design]

fretful *adj.* anxious and unhappy; tending to fret.

fretfully *adv.* in a fretful way.

fretfulness *noun* **1** being fretful. **2** fretful behaviour.

fretsaw *noun* a narrow-bladed saw for cutting designs in wood or metal.

fretwork *noun* decorative carved openwork in wood or metal.

Freud, Anna (1895–1982) Viennese-born British psychoanalyst, the daughter of Sigmund Freud. She chaired the Vienna Psychoanalytic Society, and emigrated with her father to London in 1938, where she organized (1940–5) a residential war nursery for homeless children. A founder of child psychoanalysis, she died in London.

Freud, Sigmund (1856–1939) Austrian founder of psychoanalysis, born in Freiburg, Moravia, of Jewish parentage. He studied medicine at Vienna, then specialized in neurology and psychopathology. He became convinced of the existence of infantile sexuality, a theory which isolated him from the medical profession, and his major work, *Die Traumdeutung* (The Interpretation of Dreams, 1900), argued that dreams are disguised manifestations of repressed sexual wishes. Professor in Vienna from 1902, he was forced into exile by the Nazis in 1938, and died in London.

Freudian *adj.* relating to or suggestive of the ideas of Sigmund Freud, especially in regard to sexuality as a factor in human character and behaviour.

Freudian slip a slip of the tongue taken as revealing an unexpressed thought.

Freya *or* **Freyja** in Norse mythology, the goddess of love and fertility, especially first love. She and her brother Frey, the male fertility god, were the children of Niord, the sea god.

Freyssinet, Marie Eugène Léon (1879–1962) French civil engineer, born in Objat, Corrèze. His intuitive reinforced concrete design reached its height in his airship hangars at Orly (1916–24, destroyed 1944). He succeeded in developing practical techniques for prestressing concrete by the use of stretched steel tendons, and from 1930 was one of the leading exponents of this virtually new structural material, employing it to full advantage in various structures, including bridges and foundations.

Fri *or* **Fri.** *abbrev.* Friday.

friability *noun* being friable.

friable *adj.* easily broken; easily reduced to powder. [from Latin *friare*, to crumble]

Friar, the the corrupt, wanton Brother in Chaucer's *The Canterbury Tales*, who tells a defamatory tale about the Summoner and the Devil.

friar *noun* a member of any of various religious orders who, especially formerly, worked as teachers of the Christian religion and lived by begging. [from Old French *frere*, brother]

friar's balsam a strong-smelling compound of benzoin, used as an inhalant.

friary *noun* (PL. **friaries**) *Hist.* a building inhabited by a community of friars.

Fribourg, German **Freiburg 1** POP (1990) 34 000, the capital of Fribourg canton, W Switzerland. The medieval town stands on a peninsula on the R Sarine (Saane), 27km/17mi SW of Bern. HISTORY founded in 1178; a Catholic stronghold during the Reformation. NOTABLE FEATURES Cathedral of St Nicholas (13c–15c); Church of the Woodcutters (13c); town hall (16c). **2** a canton in W Switzerland with Fribourg as its capital.

fricassee *noun* a cooked dish usually of pieces of meat or chicken served in a sauce. [from Old French *fricasser*, to cook chopped food in its own juice]

fricative — *adj., said of a sound* produced partly by friction, the breath being forced through a narrowed opening. — *noun* a fricative consonant, eg *f* and *th*. [from Latin *fricare*, to rub]

Frick, Henry Clay (1849–1919) US industrialist, born in West Overton, Pennsylvania. He formed a company to supply the Pittsburgh steel mills with coke, and was a millionaire at the age of 30. In 1889 he became Chairman of the Carnegie Steel company, which he successfully reorganized. He was injured in a conflict with strikers at the Carnegie Steel Plant in Homestead, Pennsylvania, in 1892. He left Carnegie in 1900, and became Director of J Pierpont Morgan's United States Steel in 1901. His collection of fine art was established as the Frick Collection in a museum in New York City.

Fricker, Peter (Racine) (1920–90) English composer, born in London. He became musical director of Morley College, London (1952–64), then moved to the University of California, Santa Barbara. Influenced by Bartók and Schoenberg, he wrote several symphonies, an oratorio *The Vision of Judgment* (1957–8), and other chamber, choral, and keyboard works.

friction *noun* **1** the rubbing of one thing against another. **2** the resistance met with by an object that is moving against another or through liquid or gas. **3** quarrelling; disagreement; conflict. [from Latin *frictio*, from *fricare*, to rub]

frictional *adj.* relating to or causing friction.

Friday *noun* the sixth day of the week. [from Anglo-Saxon *Frigedæg*, (the goddess) Frig's day]

Friday, Man the indigenous islander who becomes the companion of Crusoe in Daniel Defoe's *Robinson Crusoe*.

fridge *noun colloq.* a refrigerator.

Friedan, Betty (Elizabeth Naomi), *née* **Goldstein** (1921–) US feminist leader and author, born in Peoria, Illinois. Her bestselling book *The Feminine Mystique* (1963) analyzed the role of women in US society and articulated their frustrations. She was the founder and first President of the National Association for Women (1966) and headed the National Women's Strike for Equality (1970). In *The Second Stage* (1981), she emphasized the importance of both the new and the traditional female roles. Her most recent work is *The Fountain of Age* (1993).

Friedel, Charles (1832–99) French chemist. Latterly Professor of Organic Chemistry at the Sorbonne, he worked on the production of artificial minerals (diamonds); he and the US chemist James Mason Crafts (1839–1917) gave their names to the Friedel–Crafts reaction for the synthesis of benzene-related compounds.

Friedman, Herbert (1916–) US astrophysicist, born in New York City. Working at the US Naval Research Laboratory in Washington, he carried out pioneering work in the use of rockets to study astronomical X-ray sources above the Earth's atmosphere; he produced the first X-ray and ultraviolet photographs of the Sun in 1960, and showed that an X-ray source in the constellation Taurus coincided with the Crab nebula, the luminous remnant of an exploded star.

Friedman, Milton (1912–) US economist, born in New York City. He was in US government service before becoming Professor of Economics at Chicago (1946–83). A leading monetarist, his work includes the permanent income theory of consumption, and the role of money in determining events, particularly the US Great Depression. He was awarded the Nobel Prize for Economics in 1976.

friend *noun* **1** a person whom one knows and likes. **2** a person who gives support or help: *a friend of the poor.* **3** an ally as distinct from an enemy. **4** a person or thing already encountered or mentioned: *our old friend the woodworm.* **5** (**Friend**) a member of the Religious Society of Friends; a Quaker. **6** a member of an organization giving voluntary financial support to an institution, etc: *Friends of the National Gallery.* — **be** *or* **make friends with someone** to be, or become, their friend. [from Anglo-Saxon *freond*]

friendless *adj.* lacking friends.

friendliness *noun* being friendly.

friendly — *adj.* (**friendlier, friendliest**) **1** kind; behaving as a friend. **2** (**friendly with someone**) on close or affectionate terms with them. **3** relating to, or typical of, a friend. **4** being a colleague, helper, partner, etc rather than an enemy: *friendly nations*. **5** *Sport*, said of a match, etc played for enjoyment or practice and not as part of a formal competition. — *noun* (PL. **friendlies**) *Sport* a friendly match.

-friendly *combining form* denoting things that are made easy or convenient for those for whom they are intended: *user-friendly*.

friendly fire *Mil.* accidental firing on one's own or one's allies' forces instead of the enemy.

friendly society an organization giving support to members in sickness and old age, in return for regular contributions.

Friends, Society of, also called **Quakers** a Christian movement founded by George Fox and others in mid-17c England, formally organized in 1667. Its members' popular name possibly stems from Fox's injunction 'to quake at the word of the Lord'. Persecution led William Penn to establish a Quaker colony (Pennsylvania) in 1682. Friends believe in the 'inner light', a living contact with the divine Spirit, and at worship meetings they remain in silence until He moves them to speak. They emphasize simplicity in all things, and are active reformers promoting tolerance, justice, and peace. Today most meetings have programmed orders of worship, though 'unprogrammed' silence-based meetings still take place.

friendship *noun* **1** the having and keeping of friends. **2** a particular relationship between two friends.

Friends of the Earth an international federation of environmental pressure groups with autonomous organizations in member countries. It conducts campaigns on topics such as safe energy, the recycling of waste, acid rain, tropical rainforest destruction, the preservation of endangered species, and transport.

frier another spelling of FRYER

Friese-Greene, William, originally **William Edward Green** (1855–1921) English photographer and inventor, born in Bristol. In the 1880s he designed a camera to expose a sequence of photographs for projection as a moving image by lantern slides. He is thus claimed by some as the English inventor of cinematography. However, he did not in fact propose perforated strips of film for either photography or projection.

Friesian *noun Agric.* a breed of black and white dairy cattle, originating in the Netherlands, and now the most important dairy breed in the UK on account of its very high milk yields. [variant of FRISIAN]

Friesland, ancient **Frisia** POP (1990e) 599 000, a province in N Netherlands, which includes most of the West Frisian Is. In the SW and N it borders on the Ijsselmeer and the Waddenzee. AREA (land) 3 352sq km/1 294sq mi. PHYSICAL DESCRIPTION there has been extensive land reclamation along the North Sea coast; drained by a large canal and waterway system; there are many lakes. CAPITAL Leeuwarden. CHIEF TOWNS Harlingen, Sneek. ECONOMY major livestock farming area (Friesian cattle, butter); arable farming on the coast of the Waddenzee; boat-building.

frieze *noun* **1** a decorative strip running along a wall. **2** *Archit.* a horizontal band between the cornice and capitals of a classical temple, or the sculpture filling it. [from Old French *frise*]

frigate *noun* **1** a naval escort vessel, smaller than a destroyer. **2** *Hist.* a small fast-moving sailing warship. [from Old French *fregate*]

frigate bird a large bird, native to tropical seas, the male having an inflatable coloured pouch on the throat. It steals fish from other birds, and is unable to take off from level ground, but is a good flier, covering long distances.

Frigg or **Frigga** in Norse mythology, the wife of Odin and mother of Balder, and goddess of married love (often confused with Freya).

fright *noun* **1** sudden fear; a shock. **2** *colloq.* a person or thing of ludicrous appearance. — **take fright** to become scared. [from Anglo-Saxon *fyrhto*]

frighten *verb* (**frightened, frightening**) **1** to make afraid. **2** (**frighten someone away** or **off**) to scare them away. **3** (**frighten someone into** or **out of something**) to persuade or dissuade them by threats.

frightened *adj.* afraid; scared.

frightful *adj.* **1** ghastly; frightening. **2** *colloq.* bad; awful. **3** *colloq.* great; extreme.

frightfully *adv. colloq.* very.

frightfulness *noun* being frightful.

frigid *adj.* **1** cold and unfriendly. **2** *said of a woman* not sexually responsive, especially to sexual intercourse. **3** *Geog.* intensely cold. [from Latin *frigidus*, cold]

frigidity *noun* **1** being frigid. **2** frigid behaviour.

frill *noun* **1** a gathered or pleated strip of cloth attached along one edge to a garment, etc as a trimming. **2** (*usually* **frills**) something extra serving no very useful purpose.

frilly *adj.* (**frillier, frilliest**) with frills.

Fringe cultural events (usually theatrical performances) that occur around a festival but are not central to it. The term also applies to theatre groups working on the margins of the establishment, and to unconventional theatre.

fringe — *noun* **1** a border of loose threads on a carpet, tablecloth, garment, etc. **2** hair cut to hang down over the forehead. **3** the outer area; the edge; the part farthest from the main area or centre. **4** the area of activity of people who have moved away from the conventional practices of their group, profession, etc: *fringe medicine*. — *verb* **1** to decorate with a fringe. **2** to form a fringe round. [from Old French *frenge*, from Latin *fimbriae*, threads, fringe]

fringe benefits things that one gets from one's employer in addition to wages or salary, eg a house, a car, etc.

frippery *noun* (PL. **fripperies**) showy and unnecessary finery or adornment. [from Old French *freperie*, from *frepe*, a rag]

Frisbee *noun trademark* a light plastic saucer-shaped object that spins when thrown, used for playing games. [perhaps from the surname *Frisbie*]

Frisch, Karl von (1886–1982) Austrian ethologist and zoologist, born in Vienna. Founder of the Zoological Institute in Munich (1932), his work on honey bees showed that they are able to distinguish odours, tastes and colours, and can see ultraviolet light. He also described how bees communicate the location of food by means of dances on the comb, and use the Sun as a compass even when obscured by clouds by making use of the pattern of polarized light in the sky. He shared the 1973 Nobel Prize for Physiology or Medicine with Konrad Lorenz and Nikolaas Tinbergen.

Frisch, Otto Robert (1904–79) Austrian–British physicist, born in Vienna. After working in Germany, he moved to England then to the USA, where he collaborated in the development of the atomic bomb; he was later appointed professor at Cambridge (1947–72). With his aunt, Lise Meitner, he first described 'nuclear fission', the splitting of the atom, to explain the results of experiments carried out by Otto Hahn.

Frisch, Ragnar (Anton Kittil) (1895–1973) Norwegian economist, born in Oslo. He was Professor of Economics at Oslo (1931–65). A pioneer of econometrics, he created national economic planning decision models, and advised developing countries. He was jointly awarded the first Nobel Prize for Economics in 1969.

Frisian — *noun* **1** the language of Friesland in NW Netherlands. **2** a native of Friesland. — *adj.* belonging or relating to Friesland, its people, or their language. See also FRIESIAN. [from Latin *Frisii*, a tribe of NW Germany]

Frisian Islands an island chain in the North Sea, extending along the coasts of the Netherlands, Germany, and Denmark, and politically divided between these countries. The North Frisian Is (in German *Nordfriesische Inseln*) include the German islands of Sylt, Föhr, Nordstrand, Pellworm, and Amrum, and the Danish islands of Rømø, Fanø, and Mandø. The German East Frisian Is (in German *Ostfriesische Inseln*) include Borkum, Juist, Norderney, Langeoog, Spiekeroog, and Wangerooge. The Dutch West Frisian Is (in Dutch *Friese Eilanden*) include Texel, Vlieland, Terschelling, Ameland, and Schiermonnikoog. There are several areas of reclaimed land in the island chain. ECONOMY fishing; sheep, cattle; potatoes, oats; tourism.

frisk — *verb* **1** *intrans.* to jump or run about happily. **2** *trans. slang* to search (a person) for eg weapons or drugs. — *noun* **1** a spell of prancing about. **2** an act of searching a person for weapons, etc. [from Old French *frisque*, lively]

friskily *adv.* in a frisky way.

friskiness *noun* being frisky.

frisky *adj.* (**friskier, friskiest**) lively; playful.

frisson *noun* a shiver of fear or excitement. [from French *frisson*]

fritillary *noun* **1** *Bot.* a perennial plant (*Fritillaria meleagris*), widespread in central Europe, with narrow greyish-green leaves and a drooping head bearing a single bell-shaped flower, composed of broad segments chequered pink and dull purple. It grows in woodland and in meadows subject to winter flooding, although in many areas this habitat is being destroyed and the plant is becoming increasingly rare. **2** *Zool.* any of many species of a colourful butterfly having yellowish-brown wings with black markings, and only four fully developed legs, the front pair of legs being short and brush-like, especially in the male. It lays ribbed eggs, and the caterpillars are covered with elaborate spines. [from Latin *fritillus*, dice-box]

fritter¹ *noun* a piece of meat, fruit, etc coated in batter and fried. [from French *friture*]

fritter² *verb* (**frittered, frittering**) (**fritter something away**) to waste time, money, etc on unimportant things. [from earlier *fitter*, fragment]

frivolity *noun* frivolous behaviour; being frivolous.

frivolous *adj.* **1** silly; not sufficiently serious. **2** trifling or unimportant, not useful and sensible. [from Latin *frivolus*]

frivolously *adv.* in a frivolous way.

frizz — *noun* a mass of tight curls. — *verb trans., intrans.* to form or cause to form a frizz. [from French *friser*, to curl, or from FRIZZLE²]

frizzle¹ *verb trans., intrans., said of food* to fry till scorched and brittle.

frizzle² — *verb* to frizz (hair). — *noun* **1** a curl. **2** a frizz. [perhaps related to Anglo-Saxon *fris*, curly]

frizzy *adj.* (**frizzier, frizziest**) tightly curled.

fro *adv.* old use back or from, as in **to and fro**, forwards and backwards. [from Norse *fra*, from]

Frobisher, Sir Martin (c.1535–94) English navigator, born in Altofts, Yorkshire. He made several attempts to find a Northwest Passage to Cathay (1576–8), reaching Labrador and Hudson Bay. In 1585 he commanded a vessel in Francis Drake's expedition to the West Indies. He was mortally wounded fighting the Spanish at the siege of Crozon, near Brest, France.

frock *noun* **1** a woman's or girl's dress. **2** a priest's or monk's long garment. **3** a loose smock. [from Old French *froc*, monk's garment]

frock-coat *noun Hist.* a man's knee-length coat, close-fitting round the waist.

Fröding, Gustaf (1860–1911) Swedish poet, born near Karlstad. He became a schoolmaster and journalist, and suffered several periods of mental illness. A lyric poet often compared to Robert Burns, he combines dialect and folksong rhythm in the portrayal of local characters, as in his first collection, *Guitarr och dragharmonika* (Guitar and Concertina, 1891).

Froebel, Friedrich (Wilhelm August) (1782–1852) German educationalist, born in Oberweissbach. In 1816 he put into practice his educational system whose aim (to help the child's mind grow naturally and spontaneously) he expounded in *Die Menschenerziehung* (The Education of Man, 1826). In 1836 he opened his first kindergarten school in Blankenburg, and spent the rest of his life organizing other such schools, as well as providing educational materials (eg geometrical shapes) for young children, to encourage learning through play.

frog¹ *noun* **1** a tailless amphibian belonging to the family Ranidae of the order Anura (which also includes toads), found worldwide except in Arctic and Antarctic regions, and having a moist smooth skin, protruding eyes, powerful hind legs for swimming and leaping, and webbed feet. **2** *offensive colloq.* a French person.
— **a frog in one's throat** an accumulation of phlegm on the vocal cords that interferes with one's speech.
[from Anglo-Saxon *frogga*]
◇ The best-known species of frog is the common frog (*Rana temporaria*), found in most parts of Europe and temperate Asia, although its numbers have been greatly reduced in recent years through the filling in of ponds and other breeding sites. It reaches a maximum length of about 10cm, and its colour ranges from dull green or yellow to deep brown or even red. There are always a number of dark bars on the hind legs, and there is also a dark streak extending backwards from each side of the snout and widening to enclose the ear-drum. The common frog lives in marshes and damp woodland, and in winter it hibernates, usually in the soft mud of marshes or ditches, or in the mud at the bottom of ponds. In spring the females lay large masses of eggs (known as frog spawn), from which fish-like tadpoles with long tails and feathery gills emerge. The tadpole continues to live in water while its limbs develop, and shortly before it is ready to leave the water the gills are replaced by lungs and the tail is absorbed.

frog

frog² *noun* a decorative looped fastener on a garment.

frog³ *noun* a triangular horny pad in a horse's hoof.

frogging *noun* a set of fasteners, especially on a military uniform (see FROG²).

froghopper *noun* a small hopping insect that feeds by sucking the sap of plants. Its eggs, which are laid on plants, hatch into sedentary larvae which surround themselves with foam-like *cuckoo spit* that protects them against drying out and predation.

frogman *noun* an underwater swimmer wearing a protective rubber suit and using breathing equipment.

frog-march — *verb* **1** to force (someone) forward, holding them firmly by the arms. **2** to carry in a face-downward position. — *noun* a face-downward carrying position, with all four limbs held.

Frogs, The a play by Aristophanes (c.405 BC), which skilfully parodies the tragedies of his day.

frogspawn *noun* a mass of frog's eggs encased in protective jelly.

Froissart, Jean (c.1333–c.1404) French historian and poet, born in Valenciennes, Hainault. He served Philippa of Hainault, wife of Edward III of England (1361–9), and also travelled widely in Scotland, France, and Italy. On his return to Hainault he began to compile his *Chronicles* (which cover European history from 1325 to 1400, particularly the Hundred Years War), wrote poems for noble patrons, and became private chaplain to Guy of Châtillon.

frolic — *verb intrans.* (**frolicked**, **frolicking**) to frisk or run about playfully. — *noun* **1** a spell of happy playing or frisking. **2** something silly done as a joke. [from Dutch *vrolijk*, merry]

frolicsome *adj.* playful.

from *prep.* indicating **1** a starting-point in place or time: *from London to Glasgow / crippled from birth.* **2** a lower limit: *tickets from £12 upwards.* **3** repeated progression: *trail from shop to shop.* **4** movement out of: *took a letter from the drawer.* **5** distance away: *16 miles from Dover.* **6** a viewpoint: *can see the house from here.* **7** separation; removal: *took it away from her.* **8** point of attachment: *hanging from a nail.* **9** exclusion: *omitted from the sample.* **10** source or origin: *made from an old curtain.* **11** change of condition: *translate from French into English / from being a close friend, he turned very hostile.* **12** cause: *ill from overwork.* **13** deduction as a result of observation: *see from her face she's angry.* **14** distinction: *can't tell one twin from the other.* **15** prevention, protection, exemption, immunity, release, escape, etc: *safe from harm / excused from attending / exempted from tax / released from prison.* [from Anglo-Saxon *fram*]

fromage frais a creamy low-fat cheese with the consistency of whipped cream. [French, = fresh cheese]

Frome POP (1981) 20 000, a town in Mendip district, Somerset, SW England. Standing on the R Frome, 17km/11mi S of Bath, it is a town of Anglo-Saxon origin, with narrow alleyways and old stone houses. NOTABLE FEATURE Longleat House (1568), 8km/5mi NE.

frond *noun Bot.* a large compound leaf, especially of a fern or palm. [from Latin *frons*]

Frondes, The a series of civil revolts in France during the regency of Anne of Austria, caused by economic grievances and opposition to Cardinal Mazarin and the central government. The disturbances, named after a contemporary street urchins' game, developed into two phases: the *Fronde Parlementaire* (1648–9) and that of the Princes (1650–3). After the declaration of Louis XIV's majority (1651), the Princes' opposition was slowly undermined; royal forces under Turenne recovered Paris (1652) and the provinces (1652–3), ending the most serious threat to central government during the *ancien régime*.

front — *noun* **1** the side or part of anything that is furthest forward or nearest to the viewer; the most important side or part, eg the side of a building where the main door is. **2** any side of a large or historic building. **3** the part of a vehicle

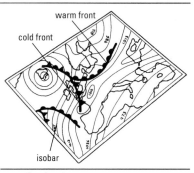

weather front

or vessel that faces, or is closest to, the direction in which it moves. **4** the auditorium of a theatre, etc. **5** the cover or first pages of a book. **6** a road in a town that runs beside the sea. **7** in war, the area where the soldiers are nearest to the enemy. **8** a matter of concern or interest: *no progress on the job front.* **9** *Meteorol.* the boundary between two air masses that have different temperatures, eg a *warm front* is the leading edge of a mass of warm air. Much weather forecasting is based on the interpretation of fronts, which are associated with changeable weather. **10** an outward appearance. **11** (*usually* **Front**) a name given to some political movements. **12** *slang* an organization or job used to hide illegal or secret activity. — *verb* **1** *trans., intrans. said of a building* to have its front facing or beside something specified: *the house fronts on to the main road.* **2** to be the leader or representative of (a group, etc). **3** to be the presenter of (a radio or television programme). **4** (**front for something**) to provide a cover or excuse for an illegal activity, etc. **5** to cover the front of (a building, etc): *the house was fronted with grey stone.*
— **in front** on the forward-facing side; ahead.
in front of someone *or* **something 1** at or to a position in advance of them. **2** to a place towards which a vehicle, etc is moving: *ran in front of a car.* **3** ahead of them: *pushed in front of her.* **4** facing or confronting them: *stood up in front of an audience.* **5** in their presence: *dare not say so in front of my mother.*
out front *colloq.* in the audience, from the performer's standpoint.
up front *colloq., said of money* paid before work is done or goods received, etc.
[from Latin *frons*, forehead]

frontage *noun* the front of a building, especially in relation to the street, etc along which it extends.

frontal *adj.* **1** relating to the front. **2** aimed at the front; direct: *a frontal assault.* **3** *Anat.* relating to the forehead. [from FRONT; sense 3 is from Latin *frontalis*, from *frons*, forehead]

frontal lobe *Anat.* the front part of each cerebral hemisphere of the brain. It includes the motor cortex, which is responsible for the control of voluntary movement, and the prefrontal lobe, which is concerned with personality, behaviour, and learning.

frontal system *Meteorol.* a system of fronts on a weather chart.

frontbench *adj.* **1** holding a position in the government or the opposition. **2** relating to this position.

frontbencher *noun* in the UK, Australia, etc, a member of Parliament holding an official position in the government or the opposition. See also BACKBENCHER.

Front de Libération Nationale (ABBREV. **FLN**) an organization founded in the early 1950s, which, led by Ahmed Ben Bella (1916–), campaigned and fought for Algerian independence from France. The war with the FLN (1954–62) led to the collapse of the Fourth French Republic

(1958) and de Gaulle's return to power. France's inability to defeat the FLN led to the Evian conference and complete Algerian independence (1962).

frontier *noun* **1** a boundary between countries. **2** (**frontiers**) limits: *the frontiers of knowledge.* **3** *North Amer. Hist.* the furthest edge of civilization, habitation or cultivation, beyond which the country is wild and deserted. [from Old French *frontier*, from *front*, opposite side]

frontispiece *noun* a picture at the beginning of a book, facing the title page. [from Latin *frons*, front + *specere*, to see]

front line 1 that area in any concern where the important pioneering work is going on. **2** in a war, the area where soldiers are closest to the enemy.

front man 1 the leader or representative of an organization. **2** the presenter of a radio or television programme.

front-page *adj.* published on the front page of a newspaper, or suitable for publication there: *front-page news.*

front projection *Cinema* the projection of an image on to an opaque screen to be viewed from the same side as the projector; the normal practice for cinema and audio-visual presentation.

front-runner *noun* the person most likely to win a competition, etc.

Frost, Robert (Lee) (1874–1963) US poet, born in San Francisco. He became a teacher, cobbler, and New Hampshire farmer before going to Britain (1912–15), where he published *A Boy's World* (1913) and *North of Boston* (1914), which gave him an international reputation. He returned to the USA and taught at Amherst, Harvard, and Michigan. He won Pulitzer Prizes for *New Hampshire* (1923), his first *Collected Poems* in 1930, *A Further Range* (1936), and *A Witness Tree* (1942) and was regarded as the premier US poet by the time of his death.

frost — *noun* **1** a white feathery or powdery deposit of ice crystals formed when water vapour comes into contact with a surface whose temperature is below the freezing point of water. **2** an air temperature below freezing-point: *12 degrees of frost.* — *verb* **1** *trans., intrans.* (also **frost up** *or* **over**) to cover or become covered with frost. **2** to damage (plants) with frost. [from Anglo-Saxon]

frostbite *noun* damage to the body tissues, usually of the extremities (eg fingers or toes), caused by exposure to very low temperatures. The affected parts become pale and numb as a result of lack of oxygen due to narrowing of the blood vessels, and amputation may be necessary if the tissues are irreparably damaged by the formation of ice crystals within them.

frostbitten *adj.* suffering from frostbite; affected by frost.

frosted *adj., said of glass* patterned or roughened as though with frost, so as to be difficult to see through.

frostily *adv.* in a frosty way.

frostiness *noun* being frosty.

frosting *noun North Amer.* cake icing.

frosty *adj.* (**frostier, frostiest**) **1** covered with frost. **2** cold enough for frost to form. **3** *said of a person's behaviour or attitude* cold; unfriendly.

froth — *noun* **1** a mass of tiny bubbles forming eg on the surface of a liquid, or round the mouth in certain diseases. **2** writing, talk, etc that has no serious content or purpose. **3** showy glamour. — *verb intrans., trans.* to produce or cause to produce froth. [from Norse *frotha*]

frothy *adj.* (**frothier, frothiest**) **1** full of or like froth. **2** insubstantial.

frottage *noun Art* a technique, analogous to

brass-rubbing, used by some modern artists, notably Max Ernst. Paper is placed over a textured surface, such as wood or fabric, and rubbed with a soft pencil or crayon to produce an impression. It is frequently combined with collage. [from French *frottage*]

Froude, James Anthony (1818–94) English writer and historian, born in Dartington, Devon. At Oxford he was part of the Oxford Movement and was awarded a fellowship, which he had to resign because his early novels (notably *The Nemesis of Faith*, 1848) were controversial. He then worked as an essayist and editor, and wrote his *History of England from the Fall of Wolsey to the Spanish Armada* (12 vols, 1856–69). He later became Rector of St Andrews (1869), and Professor of Modern History at Oxford (1892).

frown — *verb intrans.* **1** to wrinkle one's forehead and draw one's eyebrows together in worry, disapproval, deep thought, etc. **2** (**frown on** *or* **at something**) to disapprove of it. — *noun* a disapproving expression or glance. [from Old French *froignier*]

frowningly *adv.* with a frown.

frowsiness *or* **frowziness** *noun* being frowsy.

frowstiness *noun* being frowsty.

frowsty *adj.* (**frowstier, frowstiest**) stuffy; stale-smelling. [from FROWSY]

frowsy *or* **frowzy** *adj.* (**frowsier, frowsiest**) **1** *said of someone's appearance* untidy, dishevelled, or slovenly. **2** *said of an atmosphere* stuffy; stale-smelling.

froze, frozen see FREEZE.

FRS *abbrev. Brit.* Fellow of the Royal Society.

fructification *noun* **1** *Bot.* the fruit of a plant or the fruiting body (spore-producing structure) of a fungus. **2** *Bot.* the process of forming a fruit or a fruiting body. [from Latin *fructus*, fruit + *facere*, to make]

fructose *noun Biochem.* (FORMULA $C_6H_{12}O_6$) a six-carbon sugar (hexose) found in fruit, honey, and combined with glucose in sucrose (cane sugar). Its derivatives, in the form of fructose phosphates, play an important role in the chemical reactions that take place in living cells. — Also called *fruit sugar.* [from Latin *fructus*, fruit]

frugal *adj.* **1** thrifty; economical; not generous. **2** not large; costing little: *a frugal meal.* [from Latin *frugalis*]

frugality *noun* **1** being frugal. **2** economy, thrift.

frugally *adv.* in a frugal way.

fruit — *noun* **1** the fully ripened ovary of a flowering plant, containing one or more seeds that have developed from fertilized ovules, and sometimes including associated structures such as the receptacle. Many so-called 'vegetables' are in fact fruits, eg tomato, marrow. **2** an edible part of a plant that is generally sweet and juicy, especially the ovary containing one or more seeds, but sometimes extended to include other parts, eg the leaf stalk in rhubarb. **3** plant products generally: *the fruits of the land.* **4** (also **fruits**) whatever is gained as a result of hard work, etc. **5** offspring; young: *the fruit of her womb.* **6** *old colloq.* use a person: *old fruit.* — *verb intrans.* to produce fruit. — **bear fruit 1** to produce fruit. **2** to produce good results.

dried fruit fruit such as currants, raisins, sultanas, preserved by drying in the sun to remove moisture.

in fruit *said of a tree* bearing fruit.

soft fruit small fruits and berries such as blackcurrants, redcurrants, strawberries, and raspberries.

[from Old French *fruict*, from Latin *fructus*]

◇ Fruits are usually classified as either dry, eg pea pods, poppy capsules, acorn and other nuts,

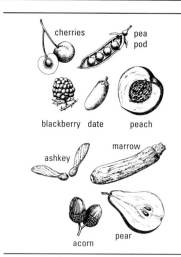

types of fruits

sycamore keys, or fleshy (succulent), eg tomato, grape. Dry fruits, which are usually dispersed by wind or water, or may be carried on the coats of animals, are either *dehiscent*, splitting open spontaneously at maturity to release their seeds, or *indehiscent*, in which case they retain the seeds and are dispersed intact.

Fleshy fruits are often edible and brightly coloured, and are usually dispersed by animals, which eat them and scatter the seed in their droppings. A *berry* is a fleshy fruit containing several to many seeds that are not surrounded by a stony protective layer, eg grape, cucumber, tomato, banana, citrus fruits. A *drupe* is a fleshy fruit containing one or more seeds that are surrounded by a stony protective layer, eg plum, cherry, peach. Raspberries and blackberries are not true berries, but clusters of very small drupes, each containing a tiny stone enclosing the seed. *False fruits* (*pseudocarps*) are formed from other parts of the flower, such as the receptacle, in addition to the ovary, eg a strawberry 'fruit' consists of tiny pips or *achenes* (the true fruits) embedded in the surface of a swollen fleshy receptacle. *Pomes*, eg apples and pears, are false fruits in which a fleshy outer layer that develops from the receptacle surrounds a central core that develops from the fused carpels and contains a number of seeds.

fruitcake *noun* **1** a cake containing dried fruits, nuts, etc. **2** *colloq.* a slightly mad person.

fruiterer *noun* a person who sells fruit.

fruit fly any of various tiny brown or yellowish flies with red eyes, mainly of tropical regions, especially those belonging to the genus *Drosophila*. They feed on sap and fermenting fruit, and can be a minor pest of orchards and stored fruit.

fruit fly

fruitful *adj.* producing good or useful results.

fruitfully *adv.* in a fruitful way.

fruitfulness *noun* being fruitful.

fruitily *adv.* in a fruity way.

fruitiness *noun* being fruity.

fruition *noun* **1** the achievement of something that has been aimed at and worked for. **2** the bearing of fruit. [from Old French *fruition*, from Latin *frui*, to enjoy]

fruitless *adj.* useless; unsuccessful; done in vain.

fruitlessly *adv.* uselessly, unsuccessfully, hopelessly.

fruitlessness *noun* being fruitless.

fruit machine a coin-operated gambling-machine with symbols in the form of fruits, that may be made to appear in winning combinations.

fruit salad a dish of mixed chopped fruits, usually eaten as a dessert.

fruit sugar fructose.

fruity *adj.* (**fruitier, fruitiest**) **1** full of fruit; having the taste or appearance of fruit. **2** *said of a voice* deep and rich in tone. **3** *colloq., said of a story, etc* containing humorous and slightly shocking references to sexual matters. **4** *colloq.* sexually aroused.

frump *noun derog. colloq.* a woman who dresses in a dowdy, old-fashioned way.

frumpish or **frumpy** *adj.* (**frumpier, frumpiest**) dowdy, unattractive.

Frunze see BISHKEK.

frustrate *verb* **1** to prevent (someone) from doing or getting something; to thwart or foil (a plan, attempt, etc). **2** to make (someone) feel disappointed, useless, lacking a purpose in life, etc. [from Latin *frustrari*, to deceive or disappoint]

frustrated *adj.* **1** disappointed; unhappy; dissatisfied. **2** unfulfilled in one's ambitions for oneself. **3** not sexually satisfied.

frustration *noun* being frustrated.
◇ A term used in contract law whereby a contract ends, through no fault of any party to the contract, because it has become impossible to perform, or illegal, or radically different in character.

Fry, C(harles) B(urgess) (1872–1956) English sportsman, born in Croydon, Surrey. He played soccer for England, and won a Football Association Cup runners-up medal with Southampton in 1902. He was a member of the Barbarians Rugby Union team, and in 1893 set a world long-jump record. At first-class cricket he scored 39 886 runs, and played for England in 26 Test Matches. He was later a journalist.

Fry, Christopher, originally **Christopher Harris** (1907–) English dramatist, born in Bristol. He was a teacher and actor before becoming director of Tunbridge Wells Repertory Players (1932–6) and of the Playhouse at Oxford (1940). His major plays in free verse, often with undertones of religion and mysticism include *The Lady's Not for Burning* (1949), *Curtmantle* (1962), and *A Yard of Sun* (1970).

Fry, Elizabeth (1780–1845) English Quaker prison reformer, born in Norwich, Norfolk. In 1810 she became a preacher in the Society of Friends, and after seeing the terrible conditions for women in Newgate prison, she devoted her life to prison reform at home and abroad. She also founded hostels for the homeless and charitable societies.

fry¹ — *verb trans., intrans.* (**fries, fried**) to cook in hot oil or fat. — *noun* (PL. **fries**) **1** a dish of anything fried, eg the offal of a pig or lamb. **2** *colloq.* (*also* **fry-up**) a mixture of fried foods; the cooking of these. [from Old French *frire*]

fry² *noun* young or newly spawned fish. See also SMALL FRY. [Middle English, = seed or descendant]

fryer or **frier** *noun* **1** a frying-pan. **2** a chicken for frying.

frying-pan or **fry-pan** *noun* a shallow long-handled pan for frying food in.
— **out of the frying-pan into the fire** from a bad situation into a worse one.

f-stop see STOP *noun* 7.

FT *abbrev.* Financial Times.

ft *abbrev.* foot or feet.

FT30 Index *abbrev.* in the UK, the Financial Times Index, a share index which records changes in the prices of shares of 30 leading British companies. It started in 1935 with a notional value of 100.

FT–SE Index, also called **Footsie** *abbrev.* in the UK, the Financial Times–Stock Exchange Index, a share index which records changes in the prices of shares of 100 leading British companies. It has been in operation since 1984, when it started with a notional value of 1 000.

Fuad I (1868–1936) King of Egypt (1922–36), born in Cairo, the son of Khedive Ismail Pasha. He was Sultan of Egypt from 1917, and became king when the British protectorate ended. In an attempt to control the ultranationalist Wafd Party, he suspended the constitution in 1931, but was forced to restore it in 1935. He was succeeded by his son Farouk I.

Fu-chou see FUZHOU.

Fuchs, Klaus (Emil Julius) (1912–88) German-born British spy and physicist, born in Rüsselsheim, Germany. He escaped from Nazi persecution to Britain in 1933, was interned during World War II, then naturalized in 1942. From 1943 he worked in the USA on the atom bomb, and in 1946 became head of the theoretical physics division at Harwell, UK. He was sentenced in 1950 to 14 years' imprisonment for disclosing nuclear secrets to the Russians, but was released (1959) and worked in the nuclear research centre of East Germany until 1979.

Fuchs, Sir Vivian Ernest (1908–) English Antarctic explorer and scientist, born in Kent. He went on expeditions to E Africa (1929–38), served in World War II, and was leader of the Falkland Islands Dependencies Survey (1947–50) and Director (1950–5). As leader of the British Commonwealth Trans-Antarctic Expedition (1955–8), he made an overland crossing from Shackleton Base via the South Pole to Scott Base (3 500km/2 200mi). He was Director of the British Antarctic Survey (1958–73).

fuchsia *noun* a shrub with purple, red or white hanging flowers. [named after the German botanist Leonard Fuchs (1501–66)]

fuck *coarse slang* — *verb trans., intrans.* to have sexual intercourse. — *noun* an act of, or partner in, sexual intercourse. — *interj.* an expression of anger, frustration, etc.
— **fuck about** or **around** to behave foolishly or waste time.

fuck all nothing; no.

fuck off *offensive* to go away.

fuck something up to ruin or spoil it.
[a 16c word of unknown origin]

fucking *adj. coarse slang, as a general term of abuse* damned; bloody.

fuck-up *noun coarse slang* a bungled or spoilt situation; a mess.

fuddle — *verb* to muddle the wits of; to stupefy. — *noun* a state of confusion or intoxication.

fuddy-duddy *colloq.* — *adj.* quaintly old-fashioned or prim. — *noun* (PL. **fuddy-duddies**) a fuddy-duddy person.

fudge¹ *noun* **1** a soft toffee made from butter and sugar. **2** *colloq.* nonsense.

fudge² *verb colloq.* **1** *intrans.* to avoid stating a clear opinion. **2** to invent or concoct (an excuse, etc). **3** to distort or deliberately obscure (figures, etc). **4** to dodge or evade. [perhaps from earlier *fadge*, to succeed or turn out]

fuel — *noun* **1** a material for burning as a source of heat or power. **2** fissile material for a nuclear reactor. **3** food, as a source of energy and a means of maintaining bodily processes. **4** something that feeds or inflames passions, etc. — *verb* (**fuelled, fuelling**) **1** to fill or feed with fuel.

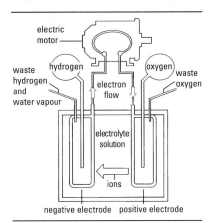

fuel cell

2 *intrans.* to take on fuel. **3** to inflame (anger or other passions). [from Old French *feuaile*, from Latin *focus*, hearth]

fuel cell *Chem.* a device in which chemical energy released by the oxidation of a liquid or gaseous fuel, eg methanol, is converted directly into electrical energy. It is more efficient than a heat engine.

fuel injection in a petrol or diesel engine, a system that injects pure fuel under pressure directly into the cylinder, the timing and amount of fuel injected being under electronic control. This eliminates the need for a carburettor and produces improved running performance.

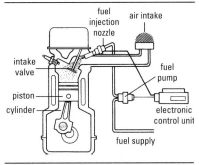

fuel injection

fug *noun* a stale-smelling stuffy atmosphere.

Fugger, Johannes (1348–1409) German weaver, who founded a family of bankers and merchants. His second son, Jacob (d.1469), carried on an extensive business, and three of his sons were ennobled by the emperor Maximilian. The house attained the height of its influence under Charles V, who made members of the family counts, gave them the rights of princes, and appointed them to high posts in the empire. The family declined towards the end of the 16c.

fuggy *adj.* (**fuggier, fuggiest**) stuffy; suffocatingly hot and airless.

fugitive — *noun* a person who is fleeing someone or something. — *adj.* **1** fleeing away. **2** lasting only briefly; fleeting: *a fugitive smile*. [from Latin *fugitivus*]

fugue *noun Mus.* a style of composition in which a theme is introduced in one part and developed as successive parts take it up. [from French *fugue*, from Italian *fuga*, flight]

Fujairah, Al POP (1985) 54 000, a member state of the United Arab Emirates, bounded E by the Gulf of Oman. AREA 1 150sq km/450sq mi. It is partly mountainous, with a fertile coastal plain and no desert. CAPITAL Al Fujairah. The people live mostly in scattered villages, depending on agriculture for their livelihood.

Fuji, Mount *or* **Fujiyama**, Japanese **Fuji-san** the highest peak in Japan, in Chubu region, 88km/55mi SW of Tokyo, central Honshu. Rising to 3 776m, the dormant volcano has an isolated peak, snow-capped from Oct to May, with an almost perfect cone and a crater of diameter c.600m. The last eruption was in 1707. Since ancient times it has been sacred.

Fujimori, Alberto Kenyo (1939–) Peruvian politician and President, born in Lima. He founded and led the conservative Cambio '90 (Change 90) Party, and, promising reform, succeeded Perez Alan García to become President of Peru (1990–). Within two years he had destroyed the apparent democracy in Peru by dismissing Congress (Apr 92), sacking senior judges, imposing order through an 'Emergency National Reconstruction Government', and changing the constitution. His administration has been dogged throughout by violence from the Maoist Sendero Luminoso (Shining Path) guerilla group.

Fujiwara style a style of art which flourished in Japan during the late Heian period (9c–12c). The aristocratic Fujiwara clan built temples and pagodas, decorated in a delicate, refined manner.

Fukuoka, formerly **Najime** POP (1991e) 1.2m, the port capital of Fukuoka prefecture, NE Kyushu, Japan. It is located 145km/90mi NE of Nagasaki. NOTABLE FEATURE Dazaifu Temman Gu nearby (10c shrine, restored in 1950).

-ful *combining form* **1** (PL. **-fuls**) forming nouns, denoting an amount held by a container, or something thought of as one: *an armful of books / two mugfuls of coffee.* **2** forming adjectives meaning. **a** full of: *meaningful / eventful.* **b** characterized by: *merciful / graceful.* **c** having the qualities of: *youthful.* **d** in accordance with: *lawful.* **e** showing an inclination to: *forgetful.* [from Anglo-Saxon *ful,* as in *handful*]

Fulbright, J(ames) William (1905–) US politician, lawyer, and author, born in Sumner, Missouri. He taught law in Washington DC and Arkansas, entered the House of Representatives as a Democrat in 1943, and the Senate in 1945. As Chairman of the Senate Committee on Foreign Relations, he became a major critic of the Vietnam War (1964–75), and he lost his Senate seat in 1974.

fulcrum *noun* (PL. **fulcrums, fulcra**) the point on which a lever turns, balances or is supported. [from Latin *fulcrum,* prop]

fulfil *verb* (**fulfilled, fulfilling**) **1** to carry out or perform (a task, promise, etc). **2** to satisfy (requirements). **3** to achieve (an aim, ambition, etc).
— **fulfil oneself** to realize one's potential through the full use of one's talents.
[from Anglo-Saxon *fullfyllan*]

fulfilment *noun* **1** being fulfilled. **2** performance. **3** achievement.

full[1] — *adj.* **1** (*also* **full of something**) holding, containing, or having as much as possible, or a large quantity. **2** complete: *do a full day's work.* **3** detailed; thorough; including everything necessary: *a full report.* **4** occupied: *my hands are full.* **5** having eaten till one wants no more. **6** plump; fleshy: *the fuller figure / full lips.* **7** said of clothes made with a large amount of material: *a full skirt.* **8** rich and strong: *a full-flavoured wine.* **9** rich and varied: *a full life.* **10** having all possible rights, etc: *a full member.* **11** said of the moon at the stage when it appears as a complete disc. **12** said of a brother or sister having the same parents or (*of a cousin*) the same grandparents, as oneself. — *adv.* **1** completely; at maximum capacity: *is the heater full on?* **2** exactly; directly: *hit him full on the nose.*
— **full of something** unable to talk about anything but it.
full of oneself having too good an opinion of oneself and one's importance.
full well perfectly well.

in full 1 completely. **2** at length; in detail: *reported in full.*
to the full to the greatest possible extent.
[from Anglo-Saxon *full*]

full[2] *verb* to shrink and beat (cloth) to thicken it. [from Latin *fullo,* fuller]

full back *Hockey, Football, Rugby* a defence player positioned towards the back of the field to protect the goal.

full-blooded *adj.* **1** of pure breed, not mixed blood. **2** enthusiastic; whole-hearted.

full-bloodedness *noun* being full-blooded.

full-blown *adj.* **1** having all the features of: *a full-blown war.* **2** said of a rose, etc completely open.

full board the provision of all meals at a hotel, etc.

full-bodied *adj.* having a rich flavour or quality: *a full-bodied wine.*

full dress the style of dress to be worn on formal or ceremonial occasions.

full-dress *adj.* relating to or wearing full dress.

full employment a situation in which all those seeking work in a community or country are able to find suitable work fairly readily, and in which the number of unfilled vacancies exceeds the number of people seeking work.
◇ Full employment does not mean that every person is employed all the time; there will usually always be some measure of unemployment because of the time taken to change from one job to another. There has not been full employment in the UK since the 1960s.

Fuller, (Richard) Buckminster (1895–1983) US inventor, designer, and philosopher, born in Milton, Massachusetts. He served in the US Navy, and later developed the Dymaxion ('dynamic and maximum efficiency') House (1927) and the Dymaxion streamlined, omnidirectional car (1932). He also designed geodesic domes, great space-frame enclosures, based on polyhedra. An enthusiastic educationalist, he was professor at Southern Illinois University (1959–75), and in 1962 became Norton Professor of Poetry at Harvard.

Fuller, (Sarah) Margaret (1810–50) US writer, feminist, and revolutionary, born in Cambridgeport, Massachusetts. She entered the Transcendentalist circle that centred on Ralph Waldo Emerson, and despite a lack of higher education became known as one of its brightest stars. Her *Woman in the Nineteenth Century* (1845) is the earliest major piece of US feminist writing. She died in a shipwreck after taking part in the abortive Italian Revolution of 1848.

Fuller, Roy (Broadbent) (1912–91) English poet and novelist, born in Oldham, Lancashire. He trained as a solicitor, served in the Royal Navy during World War II, and was Professor of Poetry at Oxford (1968–73). His first collection, *Poems,* appeared in 1939, and his war-time experiences prompted *The Middle of a War* (1942) and *A Lost Season* (1944). His later poetic works include *Retreats* (1979), *New and Collected Poems, 1934–84* (1985), and *Available for Dreams* (1989). His novels include *Image of a Society* (1956), *The Carnal Island* (1970), and *Stares* (1990).

fuller *noun* a person who fulls cloth.

fuller's earth *Geol.* a green, blue, or yellowish-brown clay, composed mainly of montmorillonite, with a high adsorptive capacity. It is used to decolourize fats and oils, to remove grease from fabrics, as a filter, and a base for paper and cosmetics. It was formerly used to remove grease from and to bleach raw wool.

full-frontal *adj.* exposing the genitals completely to view.

full house 1 a theatre or cinema audience of maximum size. **2** *Cards* especially in poker, a set of five cards consisting of three cards of one kind and two of another.

full-length *adj.* **1** complete; of the usual or standard length. **2** showing the whole body: *a full-length mirror.* **3** of maximum length; long: *a full-length skirt.*

fullness *noun* the condition of being full or complete.
— **in the fullness of time** when the proper time has elapsed.

full-scale *adj.* **1** said of a drawing, etc of the same size as the subject. **2** using all possible resources, means, etc; complete or exhaustive.

full stop, a punctuation mark (.) used to indicate the end of a sentence or to mark an abbreviation. — Also called *period.*

full time the end of the time normally allowed for a sports match, etc.

full-time *adj., adv.* occupying the whole period of working time.

fully *adv.* **1** to the greatest possible extent. **2** completely: *fully qualified.* **3** in detail: *deal with it more fully next week.* **4** quite; at least: *stayed for fully one hour.*

fully-fashioned *adj., said of knitwear or stockings* shaped so as to give a close fit.

fully-fledged *adj.* **1** said of a person completely trained or qualified. **2** said of a bird old enough to have grown feathers.

fulmar *noun* a gull-like sea bird of cold regions. [from Icelandic *ful,* foul, stinking + *mar,* gull]

fulminate *verb intrans.* to utter angry criticism or condemnation. [from Latin *fulminare,* to hurl lightning]

fulmination *noun* **1** the act of fulminating. **2** denunciation.

fulsome *adj., said of praise, compliments, etc* so overdone as to be distasteful. [from FULL[1]]

fulsomely *adv.* in a fulsome way.

fulsomeness *noun* being fulsome.

Fulton, Robert (1765–1815) US engineer, born in Lancaster Co, Pennsylvania. He became a painter of miniature portraits and landscapes, then went to London (1786) and studied mechanical engineering. His inventions included a machine for spinning flax, a dredging machine, and the torpedo, but he is best known for his development of the steamboat, which he made a commercial success in the USA.

fumble — *verb* **1** *intrans.* to handle things, or grope, clumsily. **2** *trans.* to fail to manage, because of clumsy handling: *the fielder fumbled the catch.* — *noun* an act of fumbling.

fume — *noun* (**fumes**) smoke or vapour, especially if strong-smelling or poisonous. — *verb* **1** *intrans.* to be furious; to fret angrily. **2** *intrans.* to give off fumes; to rise in fumes. **3** to treat (eg wood) with fumes. [from Latin *fumus,* smoke]

fumigant *noun* a gaseous form of a chemical compound that is used to destroy pests, especially insects and their larvae. [from Latin *fumigare,* to smoke]

fumigate *verb* to disinfect (a room, etc) with fumes.

fumigation *noun* the act or process of fumigating.

fumitory *noun* (*also* **common fumitory**) an annual plant (*Fumaria officinalis*) with slender stems and bluish-green leaves. Each flower has four pink petals with blackish-purple tips, the upper one hooded and prolonged into a short spur. It is a common weed on cultivated ground. [from Old French *fume-terre,* from Latin *fumus,* smoke + *terra,* earth]

fun — *noun* **1** enjoyment. **2** a source of amusement or entertainment. — *adj. colloq.* intended for amusement.

— **figure of fun** someone whom others ridicule.

for fun as a joke; for amusement.

fun and games 1 amusement; excitement. **2** *ironic* trouble.

in fun as a joke; not seriously.

make fun of *or* **poke fun at someone** *or* **something** to laugh at them, especially unkindly; to tease or ridicule them.
[from earlier *fon*, to make a fool of]

Funchal POP (1991) 126 000, the capital of the Portuguese island of Madeira, situated on the S coast. It is the third largest city in Portugal, and an important port and tourist resort. The famous Madeira wine is exported from here. NOTABLE FEATURES cathedral (1485); forts (17c); Chapel of Santa Catarina (15c); São Lourenço Palace (16c); Jardim de São Francisco.

function — *noun* **1** the special purpose or task of a machine, person, bodily part, etc. **2** an organized event such as a party, reception, meeting, etc. **3** *Maths.* a mathematical procedure that relates one or more variables to one or more other variables, eg in the algebraic expression $y = x + 4$, the variable y is a function of the variable x, usually written as $y = f(x)$, and a change in x will produce a change in y. — *verb intrans.* **1** to work; to operate. **2** to serve or act: *a torch that functions as a screwdriver.*

functional *adj.* **1** designed for efficiency rather than decorativeness; plain rather than elaborate. **2** in working order; operational.

functional group *Chem.* in a molecule of a substance, a combination of two or more atoms that are bonded together and tend to act as a single unit in chemical reactions, eg the hydroxyl (-OH) group. The functional group determines the chemical properties of the molecule.

functionalism *noun* the policy or practice of the practical application of ideas.
◇ In art and architecture, it is a theory that beauty is to be identified with functional efficiency. In the 18c and 19c, it was occasionally discussed by writers such as Burke and Diderot, and, in the 1920s and 1930s was applied, under Bauhaus influence, in the utilitarian designs of furniture, etc. The creed that form should be determined by function was extended to architecture, as in Le Corbusier's famous definition of a house as 'a machine for living in'.
In social anthropology and sociology, it is a theory, also known as *structural functionalism*, which developed a picture of society as a self-regulating organism in which social institutions, customs, and beliefs all have a part to play in maintaining a social system.

functionality *noun* the capacity a thing, idea, etc has to be functional or practical.

functionally *adv.* in a functional way.

functionary *noun* (PL. **functionaries**) *derog.* a person who works as a minor official in the government, etc.

function key *Comput.* any of the keys marked with an 'F' and a following numeral on a keyboard, pressed alone or in combination with other keys to perform a specific task within a program.

fund — *noun* **1** a sum of money for a special purpose. **2** a large store or supply: *a fund of jokes.* **3** (**funds**) *colloq.* money available for spending. — *verb* **1** to provide money for: *fund the project.* **2** to make (a debt) permanent, with fixed interest. — **in funds** *colloq.* having plenty of cash.
[from Latin *fundus*, bottom]

fundamental — *adj.* **1** basic; underlying: *fundamental rules of physics / her fundamental honesty.* **2** large; important: *fundamental differences.* **3** essential; necessary. — *noun* **1** (*usually* **fundamentals**) a basic principle or rule. **2** *Mus.* the lowest note of a chord. [from Latin *fundamentum*, foundation]

fundamentalism *noun* in religion, politics, etc, unquestioning faith in the traditional teach-

ings; especially, in the Protestant church, belief in the literal interpretation of the Bible.
◇ The term was originally used of the conservative US Protestant movement in the 1920s, which was characterized by a literal interpretation of the Bible, and revived to describe conservative Christian and Islamic movements in the late 20c.

fundamentalist *noun* a person who believes in fundamentalism.

fundamentally *adv.* in a fundamental way.

fundamental particle *Physics* an elementary particle.

fundamental unit *Physics* each of the units of length, mass, and time from which all other units of measurement are derived.

Fundy, Bay of a bay separating the provinces of New Brunswick and Nova Scotia, E Canada. Electricity is generated from high tides; the bay experiences tidal heights of up to 15m, which are among the highest in the world.

Fünen see FYN.

funeral — *noun* **1** the ceremonial burial or cremation of a dead person. **2** *colloq.* one's own problem. — *adj.* of or relating to funerals. [from Latin *funeralia*, funeral rites]

funeral director an undertaker.

funeral parlour an undertaker's place of business.

funerary *adj.* belonging to or used for funerals. [from Latin *funerarius*]

funereal *adj.* **1** associated with or suitable for funerals. **2** mournful; dismal. **3** extremely slow. [from Latin *funereus*]

funereally *adv.* in a funereal way.

funfair *noun* a collection of sideshows and amusements, often set up temporarily on open ground.

fungal *or* **fungous** *adj.* relating to, caused by, or resembling fungus.

fungicidal *adj.* **1** that destroys fungus. **2** relating to fungicide.

fungicide *noun Chem.* a chemical that kills or limits the growth of fungi.

fungoid *adj. Bot.* resembling a fungus in nature or consistency.

fungus *noun* (PL. **fungi**) any organism that superficially resembles a plant, but does not have leaves and roots, and lacks chlorophyll, so must obtain its nutrients from other organisms, by living either as a parasite on living organisms, or as a saprophyte on dead organic matter. Most fungi reproduce by means of spores. [from Latin *fungus*, mushroom, fungus]
◇ Fungi were formerly classified as plants, but are now usually included in a separate kingdom, Fungi. There are more than 50 000 species, mainly found in damp terrestrial habitats. Most fungi are multicellular, although some exist as single cells, eg yeasts. Multicellular fungi grow to form a mat (or *mycelium*) of thread-like filaments known as *hyphae*. Individual hyphae have rigid cell walls that differ from those of plants in that their main constituent is chitin instead of cellulose.
Fungi can be divided into four main groups. The Phycomycetes include the most primitive fungi, eg water moulds, and the Fungi Imperfecti include fungi that do not produce spores, and reproduce solely by division, eg moulds such as *Penicillium*. The Ascomycetes, which produce spores in pod-shaped structures called *asci*, include many yeasts. The Basidiomycetes often form conspicuous fruiting bodies, eg mushrooms, toadstools, bracket fungi, and they also include the rusts and smuts, which are serious pests of crop plants.
Fungi play an important ecological role in breaking down decaying plant and animal material and recycling nutrients. Many fungi are highly poiso-

nous, but some are edible, eg mushrooms, which are widely cultivated as a food crop, while others are a source of useful by-products, eg the mould *Penicillium* produces the antibiotic penicillin. Yeasts are used in brewing and baking. Some parasitic fungi cause serious diseases in animals and plants, eg potato blight.

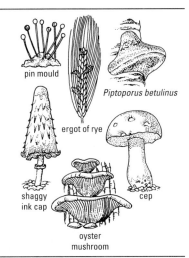

fruiting bodies of fungi

funicular — *adj.*, *said of a mountain railway* operating by a machine-driven cable, with two cars, one of which descends while the other ascends. — *noun* a funicular railway. [from Latin *funiculus*, diminutive of *funis*, rope]

funk¹ — *noun colloq.* **1** (*also* **blue funk**) a state of fear or panic. **2** a coward. — *verb* to avoid doing (something) from panic.

funk² *noun colloq.* jazz or rock music with a strong rhythm and repeating bass pattern. [from French dialect *funquer*, to give off smoke]

funky *adj.* (**funkier, funkiest**) *colloq.* **1** *said of jazz or rock music* strongly rhythmical and emotionally stirring. **2** trendy; good. **3** earthy; smelly.

funnel — *noun* **1** a tube with a cone-shaped opening through which liquid, etc can be poured into a narrow-necked container. **2** a chimney on a steamship or steam engine through which smoke escapes. — *verb* (**funnelled, funnelling**) **1** *intrans.* to rush through a narrow space: *wind funnelling through the streets.* **2** *trans.* to transfer (liquid, etc) from one vessel to another using a funnel. [from Old Provençal *fonil*, from Latin *infundere*, to pour in]

funnily *adv.* in a funny way.

funny *adj.* (**funnier, funniest**) **1** amusing; causing laughter. **2** strange; odd; mysterious. **3** *colloq.* dishonest; shady; involving trickery. **4** *colloq.* ill. **5** *colloq.* slightly crazy. [from FUN]

funny bone a place in the elbow joint where the nerve passes close to the skin.

funny farm *colloq.* a mental hospital.

fun run a long-distance race that people run in for amusement, to raise money for a charity, etc.

fur — *noun* **1** the thick fine soft coat of a hairy animal. **2** the skin of such an animal with the hair attached, used to make, line or trim garments; a synthetic imitation of this. **3** a coat, cape or jacket made of fur or an imitation of it. **4** a whitish coating on the tongue, generally a sign of illness. **5** a whitish coating that forms on the inside of water pipes and kettles in hard-water regions. — *verb intrans., trans.* (**furred, furring**) (**fur up** *or* **fur something up**) to coat or become coated with a fur-like deposit.
— **make the fur fly** *colloq.* to cause a commotion; to upset people.
[from Old French *fuerre*, sheath]

furbelow *noun* **1** a dress trimming in the form of a ruched or pleated strip, ruffle, or flounce. **2** (**furbelows**) fussy ornamentation. [from French and Italian *falbala*]

furbish *verb* (*also* **furbish something up**) to restore, decorate, or clean. [from French *fourbir*, to polish]

furcate — *adj.* forked. — *verb intrans.* to fork or divide. [from Latin *furca*, fork]

furcation *noun* a forking; a fork-like division.

Furies see ERINYES.

furioso *adj., adv. Mus.* to be played furiously. [Italian, = furious]

furious *adj.* **1** violently or intensely angry. **2** raging; stormy: *furious winds.* **3** frenzied; frantic: *furious activity.* [FROM FURY]

furiously *adv.* in a furious way.

furl *verb trans., intrans., said of flags, sails, or umbrellas* to roll up. [from Old French *fer*, firm (from Latin *firmus*) + *lier*, to bind (from Latin *ligare*)]

furlong *noun* a measure of distance used especially in horse-racing, equal to one eighth of a mile (201·2m). [from Anglo-Saxon *furh*, furrow + *lang*, long]

furlough *noun* leave of absence, especially from military duty abroad. [from Dutch *verlof*]

furnace *noun* **1** an enclosed chamber in which heat is produced, for eg smelting metal, heating water or burning rubbish. **2** *colloq.* a very hot place. [from Latin *fornax*, kiln, oven]

furnish *verb* **1** to provide (a house, etc) with furniture. **2** (**furnish someone with something**) to supply or equip them with what they require. **3** to supply (what is necessary). [from Old French *furnir*, to provide]

furnishings *pl. noun* furniture, fittings, carpets, curtains, etc.

furniture *noun* **1** movable household equipment such as tables, chairs, beds, etc. **2** the equipment needed on board ship or in a factory. **3** door fittings such as locks and handles. [from French *fourniture*, from *fournir*, to provide]

furore *noun* a general outburst of excitement or indignation in reaction to something. [from Italian *furore*, from Latin *furor*, frenzy]

furrier *noun* a person who makes or sells furs.

furrow — *noun* **1** a groove or trench cut into the earth by a plough; a rut. **2** a wrinkle, eg in the forehead. — *verb* **1** to plough (land) into furrows. **2** *intrans.* to become wrinkled. [from Anglo-Saxon *furh*]

furry *adj.* (**furrier, furriest**) **1** covered with fur. **2** made of, or like, fur.

further — *adj.* **1** more distant or remote. **2** more extended: *further delay.* **3** additional: *no further clues.* — *adv.* **1** at or to a greater distance or more distant point. **2** to or at a more advanced point: *further developed.* **3** to a greater extent or degree: *modified even further.* **4** moreover; furthermore. **5** (**further to ...**) following on from ... — *verb* (**furthered, furthering**) to help the progress of. See also FARTHER. [from Anglo-Saxon *furthra*]

furtherance *noun* the furthering, advancement or continuation of something.

further education education for school-leavers not in higher education at a university or polytechnic.

furthermore *adv.* in addition; moreover.

furthermost *adj.* most distant or remote; farthest.

furthest — *adj.* most distant or remote. — *adv.* **1** at or to the greatest distance or most distant point. **2** at or to the most advanced point; to

the greatest extent or degree. See also FARTHEST. [superlative formed from FURTHER]

futive *adj.* secretive; stealthy; sly. [from Latin *furtivus*, stolen, clandestine]

furtively *adv.* in a furtive way.

furtiveness *noun* being furtive.

Furtwängler, (Gustav Heinrich Ernst Martin) Wilhelm (1886–1954) German conductor, born in Berlin. He became conductor of the Gewandhaus concerts in Leipzig and of the Berlin Philharmonic in 1922, and established his reputation through international tours, although his highly subjective interpretations of the standard German repertory aroused controversy. His apparently ambivalent attitude to the Nazi regime caused him some unpopularity outside Germany, but after the war he quickly re-established himself.

fury *noun* (PL. **furies**) **1** violent or frenzied anger; an outburst of this. **2** violence: *the fury of the wind.* **3** a frenzy: *a fury of activity.* — **like fury** *colloq.* fast; eagerly; powerfully; like mad. [from French *furie*, from Latin *furere*, to rage]

furze *noun* gorse. [from Anglo-Saxon *fyrs*]

fuse[1] — *noun Electr.* a safety device designed to protect an electric circuit against surges of excess current, caused by overloading of the circuit, that would otherwise damage equipment or constitute a fire risk. It consists of a length of wire (usually enclosed by a small glass or ceramic tube with metal ends) that melts and breaks the circuit when the current exceeds a certain value. — *verb trans., intrans.* **1** to melt as a result of the application of heat. **2** to join by, or as if by, melting together. **3** *said of an electric circuit or appliance* to cease to function as a result of the melting of a fuse. — **blow a fuse** *colloq.* to lose one's temper. [from Latin *fusus*, melted]

fuse[2] — *noun* a cord or cable containing combustible material, used for detonating a bomb or explosive charge. — *verb* to fit with such a device. [from Latin *fusus*, spindle]

fuselage *noun* the main body of an aircraft, carrying crew and passengers. [from French *fuselé*, spindle-shaped]

fusilier *noun* **1** *Hist.* an infantryman armed with a *fusil* or light musket. **2** a member of any of several British regiments formerly armed with these. [from French *fusilier*]

fusillade *noun* **1** a simultaneous or continuous discharge of firearms. **2** an onslaught, eg of criticism. [from French *fusillade*, from *fusiller*, to shoot]

fusilli *noun* pasta shaped into short thick spirals. [from Italian]

fusion *noun* **1** *Chem.* the process of melting, whereby a substance changes from a solid to a liquid. **2** the act of joining together. **3** *Physics* the process whereby two light atomic nuclei combine to form a heavier nucleus, with the release of large amounts of energy. — Also called *nuclear fusion.* [from Latin *fusio*, melting]

fusional language *Linguistics* a language type in which words vary in their internal structure, usually by inflectional endings, which may express several grammatical meanings at once. For example, in the Latin *dominus*, 'lord', the suffix *-us* simultaneously expresses, or 'fuses', the meanings masculine, nominative, and singular. Other fusional languages include Greek and Arabic. — Also called *inflecting* or *synthetic language.* See also AGGLUTINATING LANGUAGE, ANALYTIC LANGUAGE.

fuss — *noun* **1** agitation and excitement, especially over something trivial. **2** a commotion, disturbance or bustle. — *verb intrans.* **1** to worry

needlessly. **2** to concern oneself too much with trivial matters. **3** to agitate. — **fuss over something** *or* **someone** to display a fond concern for them. **make a fuss** to complain. **make a fuss of someone** *colloq.* to give them a lot of attention. [origin unknown]

fussily *adv.* in a fussy way.

fussiness *noun* being fussy.

fusspot *noun derog. colloq.* a person who worries excessively, especially over trifles.

fussy *adj.* (**fussier, fussiest**) **1** choosy; discriminating. **2** over-concerned with details or trifles. **3** bustling and officious. **4** *said of clothes, etc* over-elaborate.

fustiness *noun* being fusty.

fusty *adj.* (**fustier, fustiest**) **1** stale-smelling; old and musty. **2** old-fashioned. [from Middle English *fust*, wine cask]

futhark *or* **futhork** *noun* the runic alphabet, so called from the names of the first six symbols: $f, u, \text{þ} (th), a$ or o, r, k.

futile *adj.* unproductive, unavailing, foolish, vain or pointless. [from Latin *futilis*, easily pouring out, unreliable]

futilely *adv.* in a futile way.

futility *noun* uselessness.

futon *noun* a cloth-filled mattress designed to be used on the floor and rolled up when not in use. [from Japanese]

future — *noun* **1** the time to come; events that are still to occur. **2** *Grammar* the future tense. **3** prospects: *must think about one's future.* **4** likelihood of success: *no future in that.* **5** (**futures**) *Stock Exchange* commodities bought or sold at an agreed price, to be delivered at a later date. The price agreed on at the earlier date remains the same whether the market price of the particular commodity has fallen or risen in the meantime. — *adj.* **1** yet to come or happen. **2** about to become: *my future wife.* **3** *Grammar, said of the tense of a verb* indicating actions or events yet to happen. — **in future** from now on. [from Latin *futurus*, about to be]

Futurism a modern art movement founded by the poet Marinetti in Milan in 1909. It expressed the dynamism of the machine age, and leading artists included Boccioni, Carrà, Balla, and Severini, working in a manner derived from the geometrical style of Cubism.

futurist *noun* **1** a person whose chief interest is what will happen in the future. **2** a person who believes in futurism.

futuristic *adj.* **1** relating to futurism. **2** *said of design, etc* so modern or original as to seem appropriate to the future.

futuristically *adv.* in a futuristic way.

futurity *noun* (PL. **futurities**) **1** the future. **2** a future event.

futurology *noun* the forecasting of future events from present tendencies.

Fuzhou *or* **Fu-chou** *or* **Foochow** POP (1990) 1.4m, the provincial capital of Fujian province, SE China. It lies on the N bank of the Min Jiang R. HISTORY founded in 202 BC; capital of an autonomous state in the 10c; established as an open port in 1842. NOTABLE FEATURES West Lake Park (imperial garden); Twin Pagodas; White Pagoda (904, rebuilt in 1548); Ebony Pagoda (941); several temples on Yushan and Wushan hills; Yongquan Si (Bubbling Spring Temple), 10km/6mi outside the city, contains a tooth of Buddha.

fuzz¹ *noun* a mass of fine fibres or hair.

fuzz² *noun slang* the police.

fuzzily *adv.* in a fuzzy way.

fuzzy *adj.* (**fuzzier**, **fuzziest**) **1** covered with fuzz. **2** forming a mass of tight curls. **3** indistinct; blurred.

fuzzy logic *Comput.* a form of logic or reasoning that is a central part of artificial intelligence, and resembles human thinking in that it is used to process information that cannot be defined precisely because it is dependent on its context. Although difficult to program, fuzzy logic is widely used in expert systems.

Fyn *or* **Funen**, German **Fünen** POP (1992e) 463 000, a Danish island lying between S Jutland and Zealand, bounded by the Little Belt in the W and the Great Belt in the E. It is the second largest island in Denmark. AREA 3 486sq km/1 346sq mi. CAPITAL Odense. CHIEF TOWNS Svendborg, Nyborg. There are some Viking remains on the island. The author Hans Christian Andersen was born in Odense in 1805. ECONOMY agriculture ('the garden of Denmark').

G

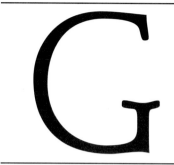

G¹ *or* **g** *noun* (PL. **Gs**, **G's**, **g's**) **1** the seventh letter of the English alphabet. **2** (**G**) *Mus.* the fifth note on the scale of C major. **3** (**G**) the musical key having this note as its base.

G² *abbrev.* **1** German. **2** *North Amer. slang* a grand, 1000 dollars.

g *abbrev.* **1** gallon. **2** gram or gramme. **3** (acceleration due to) gravity.

G7 *abbrev.* the Group of Seven, the name given to the seven countries (the UK, the USA, Canada, France, Italy, Germany, and Japan) which try to pursue a policy of co-operation on economic matters. Their heads of state and of government have met at an annual summit since 1976.

GA *or* **Ga** *abbrev.* Georgia.

Ga *symbol Chem.* gallium.

gab *colloq.* — *noun* idle talk; chat. — *verb intrans.* (**gabbed**, **gabbing**) (*also* **gab on** *or* **away**) to talk idly, especially at length.
— **the gift of the gab** *colloq.* the ability to speak with ease, especially persuasively.
[probably from Irish Gaelic *gob*, beak, mouth]

gabardine *noun* **1** a closely woven twill fabric, especially of wool or cotton. **2** a coat or loose cloak made from this. [from Old French *gauvardine*, pilgrim's garment]

gabble — *verb intrans., trans.* to talk or say quickly and unclearly. — *noun* fast indistinct talk. [from Dutch *gabbelen*]

gabbro *noun Geol.* a coarse-grained crystalline igneous rock with a low silica content. [from Italian *gabbro*]

gaberdine same as GABARDINE.

Gable, (William) Clark (1901–60) US actor, born in Cadiz, Ohio. His first leading film role was in *The Painted Desert* (1931), and he won an Oscar for *It Happened One Night* (1934). His popularity in tough but sympathetic parts labelled him the 'King of Hollywood', reaching its peak with his portrayal of Rhett Butler in *Gone With the Wind* (1939). His last performance was as an aging cowboy in *The Misfits* (1960).

gable *noun* **1** the triangular upper part of a side wall between the sloping parts of a roof. **2** a triangular canopy above a door or window. [from Norse *gafl*]

gabled *adj.* having a gable or gables.

Gabon, official name **Gabonese Republic**, French **République Gabonaise** POP (1992e) 1.2m, a republic in W equatorial Africa, divided into nine provinces. AREA 267 667sq km/ 103 319sq mi. It is bounded S, E, and NE by the Congo, N by Cameroon, NW by Equatorial Guinea, and W by the Atlantic Ocean. CAPITAL Libreville. CHIEF TOWNS Lambaréné, Franceville, Port Gentil. TIME ZONE GMT +1. The population comprises c.40 Bantu tribes (notably Fang) and c.10% expatriate Africans and Europeans; the chief religion is Christianity. OFFICIAL LANGUAGE French. CURRENCY the franc CFA. PHYSICAL DESCRIPTION on the Equator for 880km/550mi W–E; lagoons and estuaries on the coast; land rises towards the African central plateau, cut by several rivers, notably the Ogooué. CLIMATE typical equatorial climate, hot, wet, and humid; annual average rainfall is 1 250–2 000mm inland; rainfall at Libreville is 2 510mm with an average maximum daily temperature of 33–37°C. HISTORY visited by the Portuguese in the 15c; under French control from the mid 19c; a slave ship was captured by the French and the liberated slaves formed the settlement of Libreville in 1849; occupied by France in 1885; one of four territories of French West Africa in 1910; gained independence in 1960; in 1991 a new constitution was introduced allowing a multiparty system. GOVERNMENT a President elected for a five year term holds executive power; he appoints a Prime Minister who, as Head of Government, appoints the Council of Ministers; a legislative National Assembly is elected for a five year term. ECONOMY a small area of land is under cultivation but it employs 65% of the population; corn, coffee, cocoa, bananas, rice, yams, cassava; the major industry is timber extraction, notably of okoumé (world's largest producer); rapid economic growth since independence, largely because of offshore oil, natural gas, and minerals; manganese, gold, uranium; timber and mineral processing, food processing, oil refining; completion of a road-building programme and the Trans-Gabon railway system have been a stimulus to the economy.

Gabon

Gaboon viper one of the largest vipers, up to 2m in length, with the longest fangs of any viper. It has a broad flat head shaped like an arrowhead, with two small 'horns' between the nostrils. It inhabits African forest, and its body has bold markings that camouflage it well against the leaves on the forest floor. It is nocturnal, and feeds on small vertebrates.

Gabor, Dennis (1900–79) Hungarian-born British physicist, born in Budapest. He studied in Berlin, but left Germany in 1933 and in 1948 joined the staff of Imperial College, London, where he was later appointed professor. For the invention of holography, he was awarded the 1971 Nobel Prize for Physics.

Gaborone POP (1991) 134 000, the capital of Botswana. It is an independent township situated in South East district.

Gabriel 1 an angel named in both the Old and New Testaments, who helped Daniel interpret visions (Daniel 8, 9) and foretold the births of John the Baptist and Jesus (Luke 1). Gabriel is chief guardian angel in John Milton's *Paradise Lost*. **2** a male first name. [from Hebrew, = Man of God]

Gabù POP (1979) 104 000, a region in Guinea-Bissau.

Gad one of the 12 tribes of ancient Israel, descended from Jacob's seventh son (the first by Zilpah, Leah's maid). Its territory originally included the valley to the east of the R Jordan, bordered by the tribe of Manasseh in the north.

gad¹ *verb intrans.* (**gadded**, **gadding**) *colloq.* (**gad about** *or* **around**) to go from place to place busily, especially in the pursuit of amusement or pleasure. [back-formation from Anglo-Saxon *gædeling*, companion]

gad² *interj. old use* an expression of surprise or affirmation. [a form of *God*]

gadabout *noun derog. colloq., humorous* a person who gads about.

Gaddafi *or* **Qaddafi, Col Muammar (Muhammad al-)** (1942–) Libyan soldier and political leader, born into a nomadic family. He formed the Free Officers Movement which overthrew King Idris in 1969, became Chairman of the Revolutionary Command Council, promoted himself to colonel (the highest rank in the revolutionary army) and became Commander-in-Chief of the Libyan Armed Forces. As effective head of state from 1970, he set about eradicating colonialism by expelling foreigners and closing down British and US bases. He also encouraged a religious revival and return to the fundamental principles of Islam. As President of Libya since 1977, Gaddafi has openly supported violent revolutionaries in other parts of the world while ruthlessly pursuing Libyan dissidents both at home and abroad. He has waged a war in Chad, threatened other neighbours, and in the 1980s saw his territory bombed and aircraft shot down by the Americans.

gadfly *noun* (PL. **gadflies**) **1** a fly that bites horses and cattle. **2** *old derog. use* a person who deliberately and persistently annoys others. [from Anglo-Saxon *gad*, goad]

gadget *noun* any small device or appliance, especially one more ingenious than necessary.

gadgetry *noun* gadgets collectively.

gadolinium *noun Chem.* (SYMBOL **Gd**, ATOMIC NUMBER **64**) a soft silvery-white metal, belonging to the lanthanide series, which is highly magnetic at low temperatures, and also behaves as a superconductor. Two of its isotopes are the strongest neutron absorbers known, and it is used in nuclear technology, and as a constituent of ferromagnetic alloys. [named after the Finnish chemist Johan *Gadolin*]

Gadsden Purchase a strip of land in S Arizona and New Mexico bought (1853) by the USA from Mexico for US $10 000 000 as a feasible route for a southern railroad to the Pacific Ocean. It later defined the US/Mexican border.

gadwall *noun* a northern duck related to the mallard.

Gaea *or* **Gaia** *or* **Ge** in Greek mythology, 'the Earth' personified, and then the goddess of the whole Earth (not a particular piece of land). She came into being after Chaos, and was the wife of Uranus and the mother of the Titans, the Cyclops, the Erinyes, and the Gigantes. Her Roman equivalent was Tellus.

Gael *noun* a Gaelic-speaking person from the Scottish Highlands, Ireland or the Isle of Man. [from Gaelic *Gaidheal*]

Gaelic — *noun* any of the closely related Celtic languages spoken in Ireland, Scotland, and the Isle of Man. — *adj.* of or relating to these languages, the people who speak them, or their customs.
◇ The Gaelic languages are descendants of the Goidelic group of Celtic languages. The related Manx language of the Isle of Man is now extinct. Irish Gaelic (or Erse) has undergone a revival since it became one of the official languages of the Irish Republic, but the 20c has seen an overall decline in the number of native speakers of Scottish Gaelic.

Gaelic festival see MOD.

Gaelic football a game played mainly in the Republic of Ireland, a mixture of rugby, soccer, and Australian Rules football.
◇ It is played with two teams of 15 (formerly 21) players on a rectangular pitch 77–91m wide and 128–146m long, with a goal at each end resembling a set of rugby posts with a net attached to the lower part. Three points are scored by putting the ball into the net, and one point is scored for kicking the ball over the crossbar between the uprights. The principal championship is the All-Ireland Championship held on the third Sunday in September.

gaff¹ — *noun* **1** a long pole with a hook, for landing large fish. **2** a vertical spar to which the tops of certain types of sail are attached. — *verb* to seize (a fish) with a gaff. [from Provençal *gaf*, boathook]

gaff²
— **blow the gaff** *slang* to give away a secret.

gaffe *noun* a socially embarrassing action or remark. [from French *gaffe*]

gaffer *noun* **1** *colloq.* a boss or foreman. **2** the senior electrician on a film or television set. **3** *dialect, often as a form of address* an old man. [perhaps from GODFATHER]

gag¹ — *verb* (**gagged, gagging**) **1** to silence (someone) by putting something in or over their mouth. **2** to deprive of free speech. **3** *intrans.* to retch. **4** *intrans.* to choke. — *noun* something put into or over a person's mouth to impose silence. [from Middle English *gaggen*, to suffocate]

gag² *colloq.* — *noun* a joke or trick, especially as used by a professional comedian. — *verb intrans.* (**gagged, gagging**) to tell jokes.

gaga *adj. colloq.* **1** weak-minded through old age; senile. **2** silly; foolish. **3** wildly enthusiastic. [from French *gaga*]

Gagarin, Yuri (Alekseyevich) (1934–68) Russian cosmonaut, born near Gzhatsk. He joined the Soviet Air Force in 1957, and in 1961 became the first man to travel in space, completing a circuit of the Earth in the *Vostok* spaceship satellite. A hero of the Soviet Union, he was killed in a plane accident while training near Moscow.

Gage, Thomas (1721–87) English soldier, born in Firle, Sussex. He became Military Governor of Montreal (1760), Commander-in-Chief of the British forces in America (1763), and Governor of Massachusetts (1774). In 1775 (18 Apr) he sent a force to seize a quantity of arms at Concord, which was followed the next day by the skirmish at Lexington that began the Revolution. After the battle of Bunker Hill (Jun 1775) he resigned and returned to England.

gage¹ *noun* **1** an object given as security or a pledge. **2** *Hist.* something thrown down to signal a challenge, eg a glove. [from Old French *guage*]

gage² same as GREENGAGE.

gaggle *noun* **1** a flock of geese. **2** *colloq.* a group of noisy people. [imitative]

Gagnoa POP (1986e) 94 000, the capital of Gagnoa department, S central Ivory Coast.

Gaia theory a proposal, first stated by James Lovelock in 1972, and promoted by him and biologist Lynn Margulis, that Earth has a self-regulating control system, which he called Gaia. He sees Gaia as a system made up from all living things and their environment. It is a theory rejected by many scientists, but adopted by some New Age philosophers.

gaiety *noun* **1** the condition of being merry or gay. **2** attractively bright appearance. **3** fun; merry-making. [from French *gaieté*]

Gail a female first name, not in use before the mid-20c. [a short form of ABIGAIL, and now an independent name]

gaily *adv.* **1** in a light-hearted, merry way. **2** brightly; colourfully.

gain — *verb* **1** to get, obtain, or earn. **2** *intrans.* (**gain by** *or* **from something**) to benefit or profit from it. **3** to have or experience an increase in: *gain speed.* **4** *trans., intrans. said of a clock, etc* to go too fast by (an amount of time). **5** to reach (a place), especially after difficulties. **6** *intrans.* (**gain on someone** *or* **something**) to come closer to them; to catch them up. — *noun* **1** (*often* **gains**) something gained, eg profit. **2** an increase, eg in weight. **3** an instance of gaining.
— **gain ground** to make progress or win an advantage.
gain time to get extra time for something through a delay or postponement.
[from Old French *gaaignier*, to earn, gain, or till (land)]

gainful *adj.* **1** profitable. **2** *said of employment* paid.

gainfully *adv.* in a gainful way.

gainsay *verb* (PAST TENSE AND PAST PARTICIPLE **gainsaid**) *formal* to deny or contradict. [from Anglo-Saxon *gean*, against + *sayen*, to say]

Gainsborough, Thomas (1727–88) English landscape and portrait painter, born in Sudbury, Suffolk. In his youth he copied Dutch landscapes and at 14 went to London where he learnt the art of Rococo decoration. He moved to Bath in 1759, and established himself with his portrait of Earl Nugent (1760). His landscapes include *The Harvest Waggon* (1767, Birmingham) and *The Watering Place* (1777, Tate). Later works include further landscapes and portraits, notably *George III* and *Queen Charlotte* (1781, Windsor), and *Cottage Door* (1780, Pasadena).

Gaiseric *or* **Genseric** (c.390–477 AD) King of the Vandals and Alans (428–77), who led the Vandals in their invasion of Gaul. He crossed from Spain to Numidia (429), captured and sacked Hippo (430), seized Carthage (439), and made it the capital of his new dominions. He built up a large maritime power in the western Mediterranean, and in 455 he sacked Rome. He was succeeded by his son Huneric.

gait *noun* **1** a way of walking. **2** an animal's leg-movements at a particular speed, eg trotting. [variation of obsolete *gate*, manner of doing]

gaiter *noun* a leather or cloth covering for the lower leg and ankle, often with a strap fitting under the shoe. [from French *guêtre*]

Gaitskell, Hugh (Todd Naylor) (1906–63) English Labour politician, born in London. He became a socialist during the 1926 General Strike. An MP from 1945, he was Minister of Fuel and Power (1947) and of Economic Affairs (1950), and Chancellor of the Exchequer (1950–1). Elected Leader of the Opposition (1955) by a large majority over Aneurin Bevan, he retained the leadership until his sudden death. He strongly opposed Anthony Eden's Suez action (1956), and refused to accept a narrow conference vote for unilateral disarmament (1960). This caused a crisis of leadership in which he was challenged by Harold Wilson (1960) and Arthur Greenwood (1961).

Gajdusek, Daniel Carleton (1923–) US virologist, born in Yonkers, New York. He spent much time in Papua New Guinea, studying infectious diseases amongst the Fore people, especially a slowly developing lethal viral disease called *kuru*; he identified the causative agent as a 'slow virus', now implicated in many other diseases, which may take years to induce symptoms. He shared the 1976 Nobel Prize for Physiology or Medicine with Baruch Blumberg.

gal *noun old colloq. use* a girl.

gal. *abbrev.* gallon.

gala *noun* **1** an occasion of special entertainment or a public festivity of some kind, eg a carnival. **2** a meeting for sports, especially swimming, competitions. [from Old French *galer*, to make merry]

galactic *adj.* of or relating to a galaxy or the Galaxy. [from GALAXY]

galactosaemia *noun Medicine* a disorder characterized by inability to convert the sugar galactose to glucose, resulting in the accumulation of galactose in the blood, which can lead to mental retardation. It is treated by eliminating galactose from the diet. [from Greek *galaktos*, milk]

galactose *noun Biochem.* a monosaccharide (simple sugar) that occurs together with glucose in lactose (milk sugar). See also GALACTOSAEMIA. [from Greek *galaktos*, milk]

Galahad, Sir in Arthurian legend, one of King Arthur's knights, the son of Lancelot and Elaine. A pure, ideal knight, he alone was able to succeed in the adventures of the Siege Perilous and the Holy Grail.

galantine *noun* a dish of boneless cooked white meat or fish served cold in jelly. [from Old French]

Galápagos Islands, Spanish **Archipiélago de Colón** POP (1990) 10 000, an Ecuadorian island group on the Equator, 970km/600mi W of the S American mainland. AREA 7 812sq km/ 3 015sq mi. CAPITAL Baquerizo Moreno (on San Cristóbal). There are six main islands: San Cristóbal, Santa Cruz, Isabela, Floreana, Santiago, and Fernandina, and over 50 smaller islands. The highest peak is Volcán Wolf (1 707m) on Isabela I. HISTORY visited by the Spanish in 1535 but no colony was established; Ecuador took possession in 1832; became well-known after a visit by Charles Darwin in 1835. PHYSICAL DESCRIPTION volcanic origin, almost entirely composed of basaltic lava-flows with shallow, cratered cones, some of which are active; diverse vegetation and landforms, from lava deserts to tropical forests. Many unique species of flora and fauna have evolved independently of the mainland including marine iguanas on Isla Fernandina and giant tortoises, especially on Isabela and Santa Cruz. Serious fires affected wildlife in 1985 and 1994. Introduced species are presenting a threat to the survival of some indigenous species. The Charles Darwin Biological Research Station on Santa Cruz opened in 1959. The Galápagos National Park was established in 1934. The islands are a World Heritage site.

Galashiels POP (1981) 12 000, a town in Ettrick and Lauderdale district, Borders, SE Scotland. It lies on the Gala Water, 22km/14mi N of Hawick. NOTABLE FEATURE Abbotsford House (the home of Walter Scott) nearby.

Galatea in Greek mythology, a sea-nymph, wooed by Polyphemus the Cyclops with uncouth love-songs. In some versions Polyphemus destroys his rival Acis with a rock; in other versions he happily marries Galatea.

Galatians, Letter of Paul to the a New Testament writing, a letter from the apostle Paul to the Churches in some part of Galatia in central Asia Minor. It argues strongly that non-Jewish converts to Christianity were no longer subject to Jewish practices and laws.

galaxy noun (PL. **galaxies**) **1** Astron. a huge collection of stars, dust, and gas, held together by mutual gravitational attraction. **2** (**the Galaxy**) the vast spiral arrangement of stars to which our Sun belongs, known as the Milky Way, which contains about 100 000 million stars, together with vast clouds of gas and dust called nebulae. It has several long spiral arms, and rotates once every 225 million years. The Galaxy measures about 100 000 light years across, and the Sun is about 30 000 light years from the centre. **3** a fabulous gathering or array, eg of famous people. [from Greek galaktos, milk]

◊ Galaxies range from 'dwarfs', with perhaps a million stars, to 'supergiants', with perhaps a million million stars. They occur in clusters, which are thought to be moving apart from each other as the universe expands following the Big Bang. Galaxies are most often elliptical in shape, but many of them are spirals, and some have an irregular shape. They formed soon after the universe came into existence about 13 to 20 billion years ago. The stars that first formed have now cooled and dimmed, but new stars are still forming inside most galaxies. About one galaxy in a million is a radio galaxy, ie an intense source of cosmic radio waves.

Galbraith, J(ohn) Kenneth (1908–) Canadian economist and diplomat, born in Iona Station, Ontario. He was Professor of Economics at Harvard (1949–75), where he spent his career except for a short period at Princeton, wartime service in Washington, and two years (1961–3) as US Ambassador to India. He also served as advisor to Presidents Kennedy and Johnson. His many works include The Age of Uncertainty (1977).

Galdós, Benito Pérez (1843–1920) Spanish writer, born in Las Palmas, Canary Islands. Brought up in Madrid, he was deeply interested in the history of his own country. His series of 46 short novels, Episodios nacionales (1873–1912), depicts 19c Spain from the viewpoint of the people. He also wrote many longer novels, including Fortunata y Jacinta (1886–7), and several plays.

gale noun **1** a wind that blows with a speed of 63 to 87 km per hour on the Beaufort scale. **2** (usually **gales**) a sudden loud burst, eg of laughter.

Galen, properly **Claudius Galenus** (c.130–c.201 AD) Greek physician, born in Pergamum in Mysia, Asia Minor. He studied medicine there and at Smyrna, Corinth, and Alexandria, and later lived in Rome. A voluminous writer on medical and philosophical subjects, and an active experimentalist, he collated all the medical knowledge of his time, especially promoting the work of Hippocrates. For many

centuries he was venerated as the standard authority on medical matters, the man who had perfected the medical systems of antiquity.

galena noun Geol. a mineral that occurs as compact masses of very dense dark grey crystals, consisting mainly of lead sulphide. It is the most important ore of lead. [from Latin galena, lead-ore]

Galerius, in full **Gaius Galerius Valerius Maximus** (c.250–311 AD) Roman emperor (305–11) who rose from the ranks of the army to become deputy ruler of the eastern half of the empire under Diocletian (293), and chief ruler after Diocletian's abdication in 305. He was a notorious persecutor of the Christians (303–11) until near the end of his reign, when after an illness he granted them some toleration.

Galicia POP (1991) 2.7m, an autonomous region of Spain in the NW corner of the Iberian peninsula, extending S to the Portuguese border. It has a distinctive culture and language, and there is a separatist political movement. AREA 29 434sq km/11 362sq mi. PHYSICAL DESCRIPTION crossed by several rivers, reaching the sea in deep fjord-like inlets; the land is mountainous and fertile. HISTORY in the 11c Galicia was a medieval kingdom within Castile. CAPITAL Santiago de Compostela. CHIEF TOWNS Orense, La Coruña, Vigo, Pontevedra, Lugo. ECONOMY fishing; maize; wine; wolfram; tin.

Galilean telescope Physics a refracting telescope that produces an upright image using a converging (convex) lens as the objective (which collects light) and a diverging lens (concave) lens as the eyepiece (which magnifies the image formed).

Galilee, Hebrew **Galil** the N region of former Palestine and now of Israel. It is bounded W by the Mediterranean Sea, N by Lebanon, E by Syria, L Tiberias, and the Jordan Valley, and S by the Jezreel Plain. It was chiefly associated in biblical times with the ministry of Jesus and was the main centre of Judaism in Palestine after the destruction of Jerusalem in AD 70. The region was the scene of fierce fighting during the Arab invasion of Israel in 1948.

Galilee, Sea of see TIBERIAS, LAKE.

Galileo, properly **Galileo Galilei** (1564–1642) Italian astronomer, mathematician, and natural philosopher, born in Pisa. Professor at Pisa from 1589 and at Padua from 1592, he introduced the use of pendulums to measure time, showed that falling bodies of different weights fall under gravity at the same rate, and made other important discoveries in mechanics. In 1609 he reinvented the refracting telescope, which led to his many astronomical discoveries including the mountains of the Moon, four of Jupiter's satellites, sunspots, the Sun's rotation, and Saturn's appendages (though not then recognized as a ring system). A proponent of Copernicus's theory that the Sun (rather than the Earth) was the centre of the solar system, he was tried by the Inquisition for heresy, and under threat of torture recanted. For the rest of his life he continued his research under house arrest.

Galileo, The Life of (Leben des Galilei) a play by Bertolt Brecht (1938). In comparing weakness and integrity in Galileo's life, it underlines the moral that however much the intellect may be oppressed, truth will out. Charles Laughton starred in the first English-language performance (1947), which reflected the moral issues surrounding Hiroshima.

Galileo space probe Astron. a US space probe, consisting of two parts, launched from the space shuttle Atlantis in 1989, and scheduled to reach Jupiter in 1995. It is intended that one part of the probe will orbit the planet, to study its moons and clouds, while the other part descends into its atmosphere.

gall¹ noun **1** colloq. impudence; cheek. **2** bitterness or spitefulness. **3** something unpleasant. **4** old medical use a bitter liquid produced in the

liver to aid digestion; bile. [from Anglo-Saxon gealla, bile]

gall² noun Bot. a round abnormal growth on the stem or leaf of a plant, usually caused by invading parasitic fungi or bacteria, or by the presence of insects, eg gall wasps. [from Latin galla]

gall³ — noun **1** a painful swelling or sore, especially on horses, caused by chafing. **2** something annoying or irritating. **3** a state of being annoyed. — verb **1** to chafe (skin). **2** to annoy. [from Anglo-Saxon gealla, sore on a horse]

gall. abbrev. gallon.

gallant — adj. **1** brave. **2** old use, literary splendid, grand or fine. **3** said of a man courteous and attentive to women. — noun old use **1** a woman's lover. **2** a handsome young man who pursues women. [from Old French galer, to make merry]

gallantly adv. in a gallant way.

gallantry noun (PL. **gallantries**) **1** bravery. **2** old use politeness and attentiveness to women; an action or phrase demonstrating this.

gall-bladder noun the organ in which bile is stored, attached to the liver.

Galle, formerly **Point de Galle** a port and city in Sri Lanka, 116km/72mi SE of Colombo. It was a chief port under the Portuguese, then capital of the island under the Dutch (17c), until it was superseded by Colombo in 1656. The old town and its fortifications are a World Heritage site.

galleon noun a large three-masted Spanish ship used for war or trade from the 15th to the 18th century. [from Spanish galeón]

gallery noun (PL. **galleries**) **1** a room or building used to display works of art. **2** a balcony along an inside upper wall, eg of a church or hall, providing extra seating or reserved for musicians, etc: minstrels' gallery. **3** the upper floor in a theatre, usually containing the cheapest seats; the part of the audience seated there. **4** a long narrow room or corridor. **5** an underground passage in a mine or cave. **6** a covered walkway open on one or both sides. **7** the spectators in the stand at a golf, tennis, etc tournament.

— **play to the gallery** to seek mass approval or favour by crudely appealing to popular taste. [from Latin galeria]

galley noun (PL. **galleys**) **1** a long single-deck ship propelled by sails and oars. **2** the kitchen on a ship. **3** a rectangular tray holding arrangements of individual metal letters, from which a preliminary printing of part of a book, etc is made. **4** a galley proof. [from Greek galaia]

galley proof a preliminary printing of part of a book, etc in the form of a continuous sheet, on which corrections are marked.

galley slave 1 a slave forced to row a galley. **2** colloq. a person given menial tasks; a drudge.

Galliano, John, originally **Juan Carlos Galliano** (1961–) Fashion designer, born in Gibraltar of a Gibraltan father and Spanish mother. Noted for the unusual way the fabric is cut — on the bias so that it clings to the body — Galliano's designs are inspired by a range of historical and cultural references. He was Designer of the Year in 1987, and showed in Paris in 1990, the first British-based designer to show in the Louvre tent.

galliard noun a lively dance in triple time; also, a piece of music for it. It originated in the 16c and was frequently linked thematically with the stately pavan(e) to which it provided a musical contrast. See also PAVAN(E). [from French galliard, merry]

Gallic adj. **1** typically or characteristically French. **2** of ancient Gaul or the Gauls. [from Latin gallicus, Gaulish]

Gallicism noun a French word or expression used in another language.

Gallic Wars the name traditionally given to Julius Caesar's campaigns (58–51 BC) against the Celtic tribes of Gaul (ancient France). They were also the occasion of his two unsuccessful invasions of Britain.

gallinaceous adj. Biol. of or relating to birds such as grouse, pheasants and domestic poultry. [from Latin gallus, cock]

galling adj. irritating.

gallinule noun a water bird of the rail family, native to the Old World and much of S America. Its toes are often very long, enabling the bird to walk on floating vegetation. [from Latin gallinula, chicken]

Gallipoli, Turkish **Gelibolu** a narrow peninsula extending SW from the coast of Istanbul province, NW Turkey. It lies between the Dardanelles in the SE and the Aegean Sea in the W and is c.100km/62mi long. Fierce fighting took place on the peninsula in 1915–16.

Gallipoli Campaign a major campaign in World War I (1915–16). The British War Council mounted operations against the Turks to secure the Dardanelles and aid Russia, beginning with amphibious assaults on the Gallipoli Peninsula (Apr 1915) and the heavy involvement of Australian and New Zealand (ANZAC) forces (the beach where they landed is still known as Anzac Cove). It was abandoned as a costly failure: Allied casualties were 250 000 out of 480 000 engaged, but all remaining troops were successfully evacuated (Jan 1916).

gallium noun Chem. (SYMBOL **Ga**, ATOMIC NUMBER **31**) a soft silvery metal found in zinc blende, bauxite, and kaolin, and used in alloys with low melting points, and in luminous paints. Gallium arsenide is widely used as a semiconductor. [from Latin gallus, cock, from the name of its French discoverer, Le coq de Boisbaudran (1838–1912)]

gallivant verb intrans. humorous colloq., derog. to spend time idly or in search of amusement. [perhaps from GALLANT]

gallon noun **1** a unit of liquid measurement equal to four quarts or eight pints. It is equivalent to 4.546 litres (an imperial gallon) in the UK, and 3.785 litres in the USA. **2** (**gallons of something**) colloq. a large amount of liquid. [from Old French galon]

gallop — noun **1** the fastest pace at which a horse moves, with all four legs leaving the ground together. **2** a period of riding at this. **3** an unusually fast speed. — verb (**galloped, galloping**) **1** intrans. said of a horse to move at a gallop. **2** to cause (a horse) to move at a gallop. **3** intrans. colloq. to move, progress or increase very quickly: galloping inflation. [from Old French galoper]

Galloway see DUMFRIES AND GALLOWAY.

gallows sing. noun **1** a wooden frame on which criminals are put to death by hanging. **2** (**the gallows**) death by hanging. [from Anglo-Saxon gealga]

gallows humour humour derived from unpleasant subjects like death and illness; black humour.

gallstone noun a small hard mass of cholesterol and salts formed in the gall-bladder.

Gallup, George (Horace) (1901–84) US public opinion expert, born in Jefferson, Iowa. He was Professor of Journalism at Drake and Northwestern Universities until 1932, then directed research for an advertising agency, and became professor at the Pulitzer School of Journalism, Columbia University. In 1935 he founded the American Institute of Public Opinion, and developed the Gallup polls for testing public opinion.

Gallup poll a survey of the views of a representative group of people, used to assess overall public opinion, especially with regard to voting intentions. [named after George Gallup]

Galois, Évariste (1811–32) French mathematician, born in Bourg-la-Reine. He entered the École Normale Supérieure in 1829, but was expelled in 1830 due to his extreme republican sympathies. Politically active, he was imprisoned twice, and was killed in a duel. His mathematical reputation rests on fewer than 100 pages of work

of original genius; the brevity and obscurity of his writing delayed the understanding of his work, but it later came to be seen as a cornerstone of modern algebra in which the concept of a group first became of central importance.

galop noun a lively 19c dance for couples, or a piece of music for this. [from GALLOP]

galore adv. in large amounts or numbers: books galore. [from Irish Gaelic go leór, to sufficiency]

galosh noun (**golosh**) a waterproof overshoe. [from Old French galoche, from Latin gallicula, small Gaulish shoe]

Galsworthy, John (1867–1933) English novelist and playwright, born in Combe, Surrey. He was called to the Bar in 1890 but turned instead to writing. He is best known for his novel sequence The Forsyte Saga (1906–28), which records the life of the affluent British middle class before 1914. His plays, including Strife (1909), illustrate his interest in social and ethical issues. He was awarded the Nobel Prize for Literature in 1932.

Galton, Sir Francis (1822–1911) English scientist, born in Birmingham, cousin of Charles Darwin. After studying medicine, he travelled extensively in Africa. He is best known for his studies of heredity and intelligence, such as Hereditary Genius (1869), which led to the establishment of the field he called 'eugenics'.

galumph verb intrans. colloq. **1** to stride along triumphantly. **2** to walk in a heavy ungainly manner. [coined by Lewis Carroll, perhaps from GALLOP + TRIUMPH]

Galvani, Luigi (1737–98) Italian physiologist, born in Bologna, where he later became professor. In his most famous experiments he connected frog muscle to metals in various situations, and observed the twitching which took place — he attributed this to animal electricity ('galvanism'), although it was later shown that the current arose from the metals, not the frog. Galvani's name lives on in the word 'galvanized', meaning stimulated as if by electricity, and in the galvanometer, used from 1820 to detect electric current.

galvanic adj. **1** Physics **a** producing an electric current chemically. **b** said of a current produced chemically. **2** said of behaviour, etc sudden, or startlingly energetic, as if the result of an electric shock. [from GALVANISM]

galvanism noun the production of an electric current chemically, as in a battery. [named after Luigi Galvani (1738–98), Italian scientist]

galvanization or **galvanisation** noun galvanizing or being galvanized.

galvanize or **galvanise** verb **1** technical to protect a metal, especially iron or steel, from corrosion by coating it with a thin layer of zinc. **2** (**galvanize someone into something**) to stimulate or rouse them to action.

galvanized or **galvanised** adj. **1** said of a

metal coated with a thin layer of zinc. **2** coated with metal by using galvanism.

galvanometer noun an instrument for detecting or measuring small amounts of electric current. [from GALVANISM + -METER]

Galveston POP (1990) 59 000, the seat of Galveston County, SE Texas, USA. It is a port and summer resort lying on Galveston I, at the mouth of Galveston Bay. HISTORY established by privateer Jean Lafitte in 1817; the city was laid out in 1839; in 1900 a hurricane killed thousands and destroyed the city; despite building a huge sea wall (5m high, 16km/10mi long), the city was badly damaged by a hurricane in 1961. NOTABLE FEATURES Antique Doll's-house Museum; the sailing ship Elissa.

Galway, James (1939–) British flautist, born in Belfast. He played in several theatre and opera orchestras in London and in the Berlin Philharmonic (1969–75) before becoming an internationally successful professional soloist. He plays on a solid gold flute of astonishing tonal range and has made over 50 bestselling albums.

Galway, Gaelic **Na Gaillimhe** POP (1991) 130 000, a county in Connacht province, W Irish Republic. AREA 5 939sq km/2 292sq mi. It is bounded in the W by the Atlantic Ocean. CAPITAL Galway. CHIEF TOWNS Loughrea, Tuam. PHYSICAL DESCRIPTION the Twelve Bens rise to the W; the county is drained by the R Clare which joins Lough Corrib at its S end; there is agriculturally poor mountainous land in the W. ECONOMY sheep and cattle farming (in the E); craft industries; tourism.

Galway, Gaelic **Gaillimh** POP (1991) 51 000, the capital of Galway county, Connacht province, W Irish Republic. It is a seaport, lying at the head of Galway Bay and the S end of Lough Corrib. The Spanish Arch is a reminder of the former trade links with Spain in the Middle Ages. A plaque opposite the Church of St Nicholas commemorates Mayor Lynch who sentenced his own son to death and then, when the official executioner refused to carry out the sentence, hanged him himself.

Gama, Vasco da (c.1469–1525) Portuguese navigator, born in Sines in Alentejo. He led the expedition which discovered the route to India round the Cape of Good Hope (1497–9), and in 1502–3 led a squadron of ships to Calicut to avenge the murder of a group of Portuguese explorers left there by Pedro Cabral. In 1524 he was sent as viceroy to India, but he died soon after.

Gambetta, Leon (Michel) (1838–82) French Republican statesman, born in Cahors. Elected deputy in 1869, after the surrender of Napoleon III he helped to proclaim the Republic (1870), became Minister of the Interior in the Government of National Defence, made a spectacular escape from the siege of Paris in a balloon, and for five months was dictator of France. He

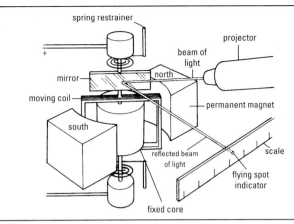

galvanometer

led the resistance to MacMahon (1877), became President of the Chamber (1879) and briefly Prime Minister (1881–2), but fell from office before implementing a programme of radical reform.

Gambia, The, official name **The Republic of The Gambia** POP (1992e) 878 000, a republic situated in W Africa. AREA 10 402sq km/4 015sq mi. It is bounded on all sides by Senegal except for the Atlantic Ocean coastline in the W. CAPITAL Banjul. CHIEF TOWNS Serrekunda, Brikama, Bakau, Waliga, Georgetown. TIME ZONE GMT. The population includes Madinka, Fula, and Wolof groups; the chief religion is Islam. OFFICIAL LANGUAGE English; Madinka, Fula, and Wolof are also spoken. CURRENCY the dalasi. PHYSICAL DESCRIPTION The Gambia is a strip of land stretching 322km/200mi E–W along the R Gambia; flat country, not rising above 90m. CLIMATE tropical; the rainy season is from Jun to Sep with rainfall decreasing inland; there is high humidity in the wet season with high night temperatures; the average annual rainfall at Banjul is 1 295mm, average temperatures range from 23°C in Jan, to 27°C in Jul, rising inland to over 40°C. HISTORY visited by the Portuguese in 1455; settled by the English in the 17c; became an independent British Crown Colony in 1843; independent member of the Commonwealth in 1965; became a republic in 1970; The Gambia and Senegal joined to form the Confederation of Senegambia between 1982 and 1989. GOVERNMENT a House of Representatives is elected for a five-year term, a President (also elected for five years), and a Cabinet. ECONOMY chiefly agriculture, especially groundnuts; cotton, rice millet, sorghum, fruit, vegetables, livestock; groundnut processing; brewing; soft drinks; agricultural machinery assembly; metal working; clothing; fishing; tourism.

The Gambia

Gambia, River, French **Gambie** a river in W Africa, rising in the Fouta Djallon Massif, Guinea. It flows c.800km/500mi W to the Atlantic Ocean and runs along the length of The Gambia for the last 470km/292mi of its course. It is navigable by ocean-going ships for 200km/125mi.

gambit *noun* **1** a chess move made early in a game, in which a pawn or other piece is sacrificed in order to gain an overall advantage. **2** an initial action or remark inviting others or establishing a point of view. **3** a piece of trickery; a stratagem. [from Italian *gambetto*, a tripping up]

gamble — *verb* **1** *trans., intrans.* to bet (usually money) on the result of a card game, horse-race, etc. **2** (**gamble on something**) to take a chance or risk on it: *gamble on the weather being fine.* **3** (*also* **gamble something away**) to lose money or other assets through gambling. — *noun* **1** an act of gambling; a bet. **2** a risk, or a situation involving risk: *take a gamble.* [from Anglo-Saxon *gamen*, to play]

gambler *noun* a person who gambles.

gambling *noun* **1** making a bet. **2** playing a game of chance. **3** taking a risk.

gamboge *noun* a gum resin obtained from various SE Asian trees, used as a yellow dye and a laxative. [from *Cambodia* in SE Asia]

gambol — *verb intrans.* (**gambolled, gambolling**) to jump around playfully. — *noun* an act of leaping around playfully; a frolic. [from Italian *gamba, leg*]

gambrel roof 1 *Brit.* a hipped roof in which the upper parts of the hipped ends take the form of a small vertical gable end. **2** *North Amer.* a roof with the lower part at a steeper pitch than the upper part (see also MANSARD).

game¹ — *noun* **1** an amusement or pastime; the equipment used for this, eg a board, cards, dice, etc. **2** a competitive activity with rules, involving some form of skill. **3** an occasion on which individuals or teams compete at such an activity; a match. **4** in some sports, a division of a match. **5** (**games**) an event consisting of competitions in various (especially sporting) activities. **6** *colloq., often derog.* a type of activity, profession, or business: *the game of politics.* **7** a person's ability or way of playing: *her backhand game.* **8** *derog.* an activity undertaken light-heartedly: *war is just a game to him.* **9** certain birds and animals which are killed for sport; also the flesh of these creatures. **10** *colloq., derog.* a scheme, trick or intention: *give the game away / what's your game?* **11** (**the game**) *slang* prostitution: *be on the game.* — *adj. colloq.* **1** (**game for something**) ready and willing to undertake it: *game for a try.* **2** *old use* having plenty of fighting spirit; plucky. — *verb intrans.* to gamble.

— **make game of something** *old use* to make fun of or laugh at it.

play the game to behave fairly. [from Anglo-Saxon *gamen*, play, amusement]

game² *adj. old use* lame. [perhaps from Irish Gaelic *cam*, crooked]

gamecock *noun* a cock trained for cock-fighting.

gamekeeper *noun* a person employed to take care of wildlife, eg on a country estate.

gamelan *noun* **1** a musical instrument of SE Asia, resembling a xylophone. **2** (*also* **gamelan orchestra**) an orchestra of SE Asia, specifically Indonesia. It is usually made up of about 30 players each performing on several instruments which include xylophones, marimbas, drums, and gongs. The music is rhythmically complex and based on a five-note scale. [from Javanese]

gamely *adv.* bravely, sportingly.

gamesmanship *noun derog.* the art or practice of winning games by trying to disturb or upset one's opponent.

gamete *noun Biol.* a specialized sex cell, especially an ovum (egg cell) or sperm, formed by *meiosis* in sexually reproducing organisms. It fuses with another gamete of the opposite type during fertilization to form a *zygote* that will develop into a new individual. [from Greek *gamete*, wife]

game theory *Maths.* the branch of mathematics that is concerned with the analysis of choices and strategies available in a range of activities involving decision-making, such as games of chance (eg chess, roulette), business conflicts, and military strategies. It attempts to predict outcomes by assuming that each 'player' will try to adopt strategies that maximize his or her chance of winning. Game theory is also used in training and selection procedures.

gametophyte *noun Bot.* in plants whose life cycle shows alternation of generations, a plant of the generation that produces gametes and reproduces sexually. [from Greek *gamete*, wife + *phyton*, plant]

gamey see GAMY.

gamine *noun* a girl or young woman with a mischievous, boyish appearance. [from French *gamin(e)*]

gaminess *noun* being gamey or high.

gamma *noun* **1** the third letter of the Greek alphabet (Γ, γ). **2** a mark indicating the third highest grade or quality.

gamma globulin *Biol.* any of various proteins in blood plasma that confer passive immunity to certain diseases, as well as disorders resulting from blood incompatibility.

gamma rays *or* **gamma radiation** *Physics* electromagnetic radiation of very high frequency, consisting of high-energy photons, often produced during radioactive decay. Gamma rays penetrate further than alpha and beta particles, and can only be stopped by a thick layer of lead or steel.

gammon *noun* **1** cured meat from the upper leg and hindquarters of a pig, usually cut into thick slices. **2** the back part of a side of bacon including the whole back leg and hindquarters. [from Old French *gambon*, from *gambe*, leg]

gammy *adj.* (**gammier, gammiest**) *old colloq. use* lame; permanently injured. [related to GAME²]

Gamow, George (1904–68) Russian-born US physicist, born in Odessa. Professor at Leningrad and later George Washington University and Colorado, he made important contributions to quantum mechanics and helped to develop the 'Big Bang' theory of the creation of the universe. In molecular biology he showed how the order of the four nucleic acid bases in DNA chains could form a 'code' capable of carrying information governing the synthesis of proteins from amino acids.

Gamp, Sarah, also called **Sairey** the vulgar, ignorant old midwife in Charles Dickens's *Martin Chuzzlewit.*

gamp *noun colloq.* an umbrella. [named after Mrs *Gamp*, a character in Dickens's novel *Martin Chuzzlewit*]

gamut *noun* **1** the whole range of anything, eg a person's emotions. **2** a scale of notes in music; the range of notes produced by a voice or instrument. [from *gamma*, the lowest note on a medieval six-note scale + *ut*, the first note (now *doh*) of an early sol-fa notation system]

gamy *or* **gamey** *adj.* (**gamier, gamiest**) *said of meat* having the strong taste or smell of game which has been kept for a long time.

Gand see GHENT.

Gandalf, the Grey the white-bearded wizard in J R R Tolkien's *The Hobbit* and *The Lord of the Rings* who helps Bilbo and Frodo, pitting his magical powers against the gathering forces of evil that threaten his country.

gander *noun* **1** a male goose. **2** *colloq.* a look: *have a gander.* [from Anglo-Saxon *gandra*]

Gandhara a region in antiquity corresponding roughly to NW Pakistan. It was occupied by the Achaemenids, conquered by Alexander the Great (327–325 BC), and was ruled in the 2c BC by the Indo-Greeks of neighbouring Bactria. It evolved a distinctive art style in which Greek and Indian elements were fused.

Gandhi, Indira (Priyadarshini) (1917–84) Indian politician, daughter of Jawaharlal Nehru, born in Allahabad. Married in 1942 to Feroze Gandhi (d.1960), she became President of the Indian Congress Party (1959–60), Minister of Information (1964), and Prime Minister (1966–77) after the death of Shastri. After her conviction for election malpractices, she declared a state of emergency (1975–7). She was Prime Minister again (1980–4) and was recognized for her work as a leader of the developing nations, but failed to suppress sectarian violence at home. She was assassinated in New Delhi by Sikh extremists who were members of her bodyguard. Her elder son Rajiv (1944–91) succeeded her, but he was forced to resign in 1989 following his party's defeat in the general election, and was killed during the 1991 election campaign.

Gandhi, (Mohandas Karamchand), known as **Mahatma** (of great soul) (1869–1948) Indian nationalist leader, born in Poorbandar, Kathiawar. He studied law in London, but in 1893 went to South Africa, where he spent 21 years opposing discriminatory legislation against Indians. In 1914 he returned to India and supported the Home Rule movement. As leader of the Indian National Congress he advocated a policy of non-violent non-co-operation to achieve independence. Following his civil disobedience campaign (1919–22), he was jailed for conspiracy (1922–4). In 1930 he led a 200-mile march to the sea to collect salt in symbolic defiance of the government monopoly. On his release from prison (1931), he attended the London Round Table Conference on Indian constitutional reform. In 1946 he negotiated with the Cabinet Mission which recommended the new constitutional structure. After independence (1947), his attempts to stop the Hindu–Muslim conflict in Bengal led to his assassination by Nathuram Godse, a Hindu fanatic.

Ganesha *or* **Ganapati** in Hindu mythology, the elephant-headed god, the son of Shiva and the brother of Skanda. He was revered as the remover of obstacles, the Lord of beginnings, and the Lord of learning who broke off his tusk to write down the epic *Mahabharata*. He is often depicted riding on a rat.

Ganesha

gang — *noun* **1** a group, especially of criminals or troublemakers. **2** a group of friends, especially children. **3** an organized group of workers. **4** a set of tools arranged so as to be used together. — *verb* to arrange (tools) for simultaneous use.
— **gang up on someone** to act as a group against them. (**gang up with someone**) to join in or form a gang with them.
[from Anglo-Saxon *gangan*, to go]

gang-bang *noun slang* an occasion on which several men successively have sexual intercourse with one woman.

Gangdisê Shan *or* **Kailas Range** a mountain range in Tibet, SW China, N of the Himalayas. It rises to 6714m at its peak, Kangrinboqê Feng. The range acts as a watershed between the inland and Indian Ocean drainage systems.

ganger *noun colloq.* the foreman of a group of workers.

Ganges, River, Hindi **Ganga** a major river in N India and Bangladesh, formed in the E Himalayas. Its length is 2510km/1560mi, flowing W through the Silwalik Range on to the Ganges Plain, continuing SE to Allahabad, then E to Benares, E through Bihar, then SE into West Bengal, where it follows the border with Bangladesh; the R Brahmaputra joins it NW of Faridpur; as the R Padma, it continues SE through Bangladesh, branches into many tributaries, and forms the vast Ganges–Brahmaputra delta in the Bay of Bengal. It is an important trade artery and irrigation source but the river can cause severe flooding. The Ganges is the most sacred Hindu river.

gangland *noun* the world of organized crime.

gangling *or* **gangly** *adj.* (**ganglier, gangliest**) tall and thin, and usually awkward in movement. [from Anglo-Saxon *gangan*, to go]

ganglion *noun* (PL. **ganglia, ganglions**) **1** *Anat.* a group of nerve cell bodies, usually enclosed by a sheath or capsule, in the central nervous system. **2** *Pathol.* a cyst or swelling that forms on the tissue surrounding a tendon, eg on the back of the hand. **3** *literary* a centre of energy or activity. [from Greek *ganglion*, cystic tumour]

gangplank *noun* a movable plank, usually with projecting cross-pieces fixed to it, serving as a gangway for a ship.

gangrene *noun* the death and subsequent decay of part of the body due to failure of the blood supply to that region as a result of disease, injury, frostbite, severe burns, arteriosclerosis, etc. The only treatment is surgical removal of the affected part. [from Greek *gangraina*]

gangrenous *adj.* **1** affected with gangrene. **2** of the nature of gangrene.

gangsta *noun* **1** a style of rap music characterized by violent lyrics or subject matter. **2** a rapper who performs in this style. [representing a colloquial pronunciation of GANGSTER]

gangster *noun* a member of a gang of usually armed criminals.

gangue *noun Geol.* rock and mineral deposits that are associated with an ore. [from French *gangue*, from German *Gang*, vein]

gangway — *noun* **1** a small movable bridge used for getting on and off a ship; the opening on the side of a ship into which this fits. **2** a passage between rows of seats, eg on a plane or in a theatre. — *interj.* make way!

ganja *noun* marijuana. [from Hindi *ganjha*]

gannet *noun* **1** a large white seabird that dives to catch fish. **2** *derog. colloq.* a greedy person. [from Anglo-Saxon *ganot*, seabird]

Gansu Corridor see HEXI CORRIDOR.

gantry *noun* (PL. **gantries**) a large metal supporting framework, eg overhead for railway signals or a travelling crane, or at the side of a rocket's launch-pad.

Ganymede 1 in Greek mythology, a beautiful Trojan prince, the son of Tros. He was carried up to Olympus by Zeus, disguised as a storm-wind, or (later and more usually) an eagle, where he became the cup-bearer. In return his father was given a stud of immortal horses (or a golden vine). **2** *Astron.* the third and largest moon of Jupiter, 5260km in diameter. It is the largest moon in the solar system, and larger than the planet Mercury.

Gao 1 POP (1987) 55000, the river-port capital of Gao region, NE Mali, situated on the R Niger. It was once the capital of the Songhai Empire. NOTABLE FEATURES Mosque of Kankan Moussa; Tomb of the Askia Dynasty. **2** POP (1987) 384000, a region in NE Mali with Gao as its capital.

gaol, and **gaoler**. See JAIL.

Gaoxiong see KAOHSIUNG.

gap *noun* **1** a break or open space, eg in a fence. **2** a break in time; an interval. **3** a difference or disparity: *the generation gap*. **4** a ravine or gorge. [from Norse *gap*, chasm]

gape — *verb intrans.* **1** to stare with the mouth open, especially in surprise or wonder. **2** to be or become wide open. **3** to open the mouth wide. — *noun* **1** a wide opening. **2** an open-mouthed stare. **3** the extent to which the mouth can be opened. [from Norse *gapa*, to open the mouth]

gaping *adj.* **1** that gapes. **2** astonished.

gappy *adj.* (**gappier, gappiest**) full of gaps.

garage *noun* **1** a building in which motor vehicles are kept. **2** an establishment where motor vehicles are bought, sold and repaired, often also selling petrol, etc. **3** a style of pop music played in a loud, energetic, and unpolished style. [from Old French *garer*, to shelter]

Garajonay National Park a national park which covers c.4ha in Gomera, one of the Canary Islands, Spain. It is a World Heritage site.

Garamba a national park established in 1938 in N Zaire, on the Sudanese border. A World Heritage site, it is noted for its unique population of heavy-jawed 'white' rhinoceroses. AREA 4480sq km/1730sq mi.

garam masala a mixture of ground spices used to make curry. [from Hindi, = hot mixture]

garb *literary* — *noun* **1** clothing, especially as worn by people in a particular job or position. **2** outward appearance. — *verb* to dress or clothe. [from Italian *garbo*, grace]

garbage *noun* **1** *North Amer., esp. US* domestic waste; refuse. **2** *derog.* worthless or poor quality articles or matter. **3** *derog.* nonsense. **4** *Comput.* unwanted meaningless information mistakenly appearing on a screen or printout.

garble *verb* **1** to unintentionally mix up the details of. **2** to deliberately distort the meaning of, eg by making important omissions. [from Arabic *ghirbal*, sieve]

Garbo, Greta, professional name of **Greta Lovisa Gustafsson** (1905–90) Swedish-born US film actress, born in Stockholm. Her first starring role was in Mauritz Stiller's *Gösta Berling's Saga* (The Story of Gösta Berling, 1924). She then followed him to the USA, where her films included *Queen Christina* (1933), *Anna Karenina* (1935) and *Ninotchka* (1939). She retired from the screen in 1941 and became a reclusive figure, living in New York.

gannet

García Márquez, Gabriel (1928–) Colombian novelist, born in Aracataca. He began writing while working as a journalist in Europe, and published his first novel, *La Hojarasca* (Leaf Storm) in 1955. His best-known novel is *Cien años de soledad* (One Hundred Years of Solitude, 1967). Other works include *El amor en los tiempos del cólera* (Love in a Time of Cholera, 1985). He was awarded the Nobel Prize for Literature in 1982.

garçon *noun* a waiter in a French restaurant or café. [from French *garçon*]

Gard, Pont du an aqueduct built by the Romans in c.1c AD to carry the water supply of the city of Nîmes in S France. It is c.275m long and its three tiers of arches reach a height of 55m above the R Gard. It is a World Heritage site.

garda *noun* (PL. **gardai**) a police officer in the Irish Republic. [from Irish Gaelic *garda*, guard]

Garda, Lake, ancient **Lacus Benacus** the largest lake in Italy, situated in the N between the regions of Lombardy and Venetia. AREA 370sq km/143sq mi; length 52km/32mi; width 5–16km/3–10mi; maximum depth 346m. It is separated from the Adige river valley to the E by the 80km/50mi-long limestone ridge of the Monte Baldo (2 218m). The N part of the lake is narrow and fjord-like. Riviera Bresciana is a fertile strip on the W side. Resort towns include Desenzano, Garda, and Sirmione.

garden — *noun* **1** a piece of ground attached to a house, on which flowers, vegetables, trees, etc are grown. **2** (*usually* **gardens**) a large area where plants are grown and displayed for public enjoyment: *botanical gardens*. **3** a similar smaller place where food and drinks are served outdoors: *tea garden*. **4** a fertile region. — *adj.* **1** *said of a plant* cultivated, not wild. **2** for use in a garden, or in gardening. — *verb intrans.* (**gardened**, **gardening**) to work at the care of a garden and its plants, usually as a hobby.
— **lead someone up the garden path** *colloq.* to mislead or deceive them deliberately.
[from Old French *gardin*]

garden centre a place where plants, seeds and garden tools are sold.

garden city a spacious modern town designed to have private gardens and numerous public parks.

gardener *noun* a person who gardens; a person employed to tend a garden.

gardenia *noun* a tropical shrub with large fragrant white or yellow flowers. [named after Dr Alexander *Garden* (1730–91), US botanist]

gardening *noun* the laying out and cultivation of gardens.

Garden of Earthly Delights, The a painting by Hieronymus Bosch (c.15c–16c, Prado, Madrid).

Garden of the Gods a park situated in central Colorado, W central USA. Its name derives from the extraordinary groups of white and red sandstone rocks and outcrops that are scattered across the area. AREA 3.1sq km/1.2sq mi.

garden party a formal party held in a large private garden.

Gardiner, Gerald Austin Gardiner, Baron (1900–90) English jurist and legal reformer. He was called to the Bar in 1925, and his cases included the *Lady Chatterley's Lover* trial, in which he acted as counsel for the defence. His support for law reform was expressed in *Capital Punishment as a Deterrent* (1956), and he was joint Chairman (with Victor Gollancz) of the National Campaign for the Abolition of Capital Punishment. In 1964 he was appointed Lord Chancellor in the government of Harold Wilson. During his six years in office, capital punishment was abolished, laws regarding abortion and homosexuality were reformed, and the Law Commission was set up. He appointed the first woman judge to the High Court, and introduced a compulsory training programme for JPs. He retired in 1970 when Labour went into Opposition, and became Chancellor of the Open University in 1973.

Gardiner, Stephen (c.1483–1555) English prelate, born in Bury St Edmunds, Suffolk. He became Thomas Wolsey's secretary (1525), then Bishop of Winchester (1531), and was sent to Rome to further Henry VIII's divorce (1527–33). He supported the royal supremacy, but opposed doctrinal reformation, and for this was imprisoned and deprived of his bishopric on Edward VI's accession. Released and restored by Mary (1553), he became a vigorous persecutor of Protestants.

Gareth a male first name, common in Wales. [of Celtic origin; perhaps related to Welsh *gwared*, gentle, benign]

Garfield, James A(bram) (1831–81) US statesman, the 20th President, born in Orange, Ohio. He was a farmworker, teacher, lay preacher, and lawyer before being elected to the Ohio State Senate in 1859. He fought in the Civil War until 1863, when he entered Congress, then became Leader of the Republican Party. After his election as President (Mar–Sep 1881), he identified himself with the cause of civil service reform, which irritated many in his own party. He was shot in Elberon, New Jersey, by a disappointed candidate for office, Charles Guiteau, and died two months later.

Gargantua a satirical work by François Rabelais (1534). It describes the life of the Giant Gargantua, the father of Pantagruel.

gargantuan *adj.* enormous; colossal. [named after *Gargantua*, the greedy giant in Rabelais' novel *Gargantua and Pantagruel*]

Gargery, Joe and Mrs the good-natured brother-in-law and vicious sister of Pip, in Charles Dickens's *Great Expectations*.

gargle — *verb intrans., trans.* to cleanse the mouth and throat by blowing air from the lungs through (a liquid) held there. — *noun* **1** an act of gargling, or the sound produced. **2** the liquid used. [from Old French *gargouille*, throat]

gargoyle *noun* a grotesque carved open-mouthed head or figure acting as a rainwater spout from a roof-gutter, especially on a church. [from Old French *gargouille*, throat]

Garibaldi, Giuseppe (1807–82) Italian patriot, born in Nice. In 1834 he joined Mazzini's 'Young Italy' movement, and was condemned to death for participating in the attempt to seize Genoa, but escaped to S America. After his return, in 1849 he joined the revolutionary government of Rome, but was again forced to leave Italy. He worked in New York until 1854, then became a farmer on the island of Caprera and returned to action with the outbreak in 1859 of Italy's war of liberation. With his 'thousand' volunteers he sailed from Genoa (May 1860) and arrived in Sicily where he assisted Mazzinian rebels to free Sicily from Neapolitan control. He then overran much of S Italy and drove King Francis of Naples from his capital (Sep 1860), thus enabling the conquest of S Italy to be completed by the Sardinians under Victor Emmanuel II.

garish *adj. derog.* unpleasantly bright or colourful; very gaudy. [from obsolete *gaurish*, from *gaure*, to stare]

garishly *adv.* in a garish way.

garishness *noun* being garish.

Garland, Judy, originally **Frances Ethel Gumm** (1922–69) US actress and singer, born in Great Rapids, Minnesota. She made stage appearances in vaudeville with her parents, and became a juvenile film star in *Broadway Melody of 1938*, then *The Wizard of Oz* (1939) and *Meet Me in St Louis* (1944), directed by Vincente Minelli, whom she later married. A demanding series of musical leads coupled with drug problems exhausted her by 1950, but after four years in variety performances she returned to film with the 1954 remake of *A Star is Born*.

garland — *noun* **1** a circular arrangement of flowers or leaves worn round the head or neck, or hung up. **2** a collection of short poems or pieces of prose. — *verb* to decorate with a garland. [from Old French *garlande*]

garlic *noun* **1** a perennial plant (*Allium sativum*) that is widely cultivated for its underground bulb, which is divided into segments (cloves) covered with white scale leaves. **2** the bulb of this plant, which contains a pungent oil and is widely used as a flavouring, especially in the form of powder or flakes, in cooking and food processing. [from Anglo-Saxon *gar*, spear + *leac*, leek]

garlicky *adj.* like garlic.

garment *noun* an article of clothing. [from Old French *garniment*, from *garnir*, to furnish]

garner *verb* (**garnered**, **garnering**) *formal, literary* to collect and usually store (information, knowledge, etc). [from Latin *granarium*, granary]

garnet *noun* Geol. any of a group of silicate minerals found mainly in metamorphic rocks. Garnet is used as an abrasive, and many of the coloured varieties are used as semi-precious stones, the best known form being deep red. [from Latin *granatum*, pomegranate]

garnish — *verb* to decorate (especially food to be served). — *noun* a decoration, especially one added to food. [from French *garnir*, to furnish]

Garonne, River, ancient **Garumna** the principal river in SW France, length 575km/357mi. Rising in the Val d'Aran, 42km/26mi inside the Spanish border, it flows from the central Pyrenees NE and NW to the Bec d'Ambes, 32km/20mi below Bordeaux. Here, it meets the R Dordogne to form the estuary of the R Gironde. It is linked to the Mediterranean Sea at Toulouse by the Canal du Midi.

garret *noun* an attic room, often a dingy one. [from Old French *garite*, refuge]

Garrick, David (1717–79) English actor, theatre manager, and playwright, born in Hereford. His first play was performed at Drury Lane in 1740, and the following year he won acting fame as Richard III. For 30 years he dominated the English stage, and as joint manager of Drury Lane (1747–76) he encouraged innovations in scenery and lighting design.

Garrison, William Lloyd (1805–79) US abolitionist, born in Newburyport, Massachusetts. Following an informal education, he emerged in 1830 as a leading voice opposing slavery in the USA. His newspaper *The Liberator* argued the case for immediate abolition, and his American Anti-Slavery Society mobilized the support of thousands.

garrison *noun* **1** a body of soldiers stationed in a town or fortress in order to defend it. **2** the building they occupy. [from Old French *garison*, from *garir*, to protect]

Garrod, Sir Archibald Edward (1857–1936) English physician, born in London. Regius Professor of Medicine at Oxford from 1920, he is best known for his studies of rare inherited diseases, such as albinism, in which he made early application of the new Mendelian genetics.

garrotte *or* **garotte** — *noun* **1** a wire loop or metal collar tightened around the neck to cause strangulation. **2** this method of execution. — *verb* to execute or kill with a garrotte. [from Spanish *garrote*]

garrulous *adj.* **1** tending to talk a lot, especially about trivial things. **2** *derog., said of a speech, etc* long and wordy. [from Latin *garrire*, to chatter]

garrulousness *or* **garrulity** *noun* being garrulous; talkativeness.

Garter, Most Noble Order of the the oldest and highest order of chivalry in Europe, founded by Edward III of England between 1344 and 1351. Its emblem is a blue garter, edged in gold and inscribed with *Honi soit qui mal y pense* (French: 'Shame on him who thinks evil of it'), traditionally the words spoken by Edward after he picked up the Countess of Salisbury's dropped garter. There are usually 25 Companions of the Order, and the sovereign.

garter *noun* a band of tight material, usually elastic, worn on the leg to hold up a stocking or sock. [from Old French *gartier*]

garter stitch a plain stitch in knitting.

Gary a male first name, after the surname, popularized by the film star Gary Cooper (1901–61).

[probably Norman, from the Germanic element *gar*, spear]

gas — *noun* **1** a form of matter that has no fixed shape, and will expand to occupy all the space available, because its molecules are in constant rapid motion, and can move around freely and independently of each other. Unlike solids and liquids, gases are light and easily compressed, and their molecules are spaced widely apart. **2** a substance or mixture of substances which is in this state at ordinary temperatures, eg hydrogen, air. **3** natural gas used as a source of fuel for heating, etc. **4** firedamp, a mixture of gases occurring naturally in coalmines, explosive in contact with air. **5** a poisonous gas used as a weapon in war. **6** *colloq. esp. North Amer., esp. US* gasoline; petrol. **7** *colloq.* an amusing or enjoyable event or situation. **8** *colloq., derog.* foolish talk; boasting. — *verb* (**gassed, gassing**) **1** to poison or kill with gas. **2** *intrans. derog. colloq.* to chat, especially at length, boastfully or about trivial things. [coined by J B van Helmont, Belgian chemist (1577–1644), after Greek *khaos*, chaos]
◇ If a liquid is heated above its boiling point, it will change into a gas, and if a gas is cooled sufficiently it will become a liquid. Gases that are compressed during cooling will become liquid at a temperature above their boiling point.
A gas that is confined within a container will exert a pressure, because its molecules will collide with the sides of the container. The pressure of a gas will double if its volume is halved and its temperature remains constant. Its pressure will also double if its temperature is doubled and its volume remains constant, because the rise in temperature causes the molecules to move more rapidly within the same space.

gasbag *noun derog. colloq.* a person who talks a lot or too much.

gas chamber a sealed room which can be filled with poisonous gas, used for killing people or animals.

gas chromatography *Chem.* a form of chromatography that is used to identify the components of a mixture of gases, and is often also used to separate them.

Gascoigne, Paul John, also called **Gazza** (1967–) English footballer, born in Gateshead. A midfielder, he was voted England's Young Player of the Year in 1988 while with his first club, Newcastle. In the same year, he was transferred to Tottenham Hotspur for a then record sum of £2 million. He played for England during the 1990 World Cup, was injured in the 1991 FA Cup Final, and was signed for £5.5 million by the Roman club Lazio in Jun 1992.

gas constant *Chem.* the constant, usually denoted as *R*, that relates the volume, pressure, and temperature of a mass of gas in the equation $pV = nRT$, where p is the pressure exerted by n moles of the gas contained in a volume V at an absolute temperature T. The gas constant has a value of about 8.3 joules per mole per kelvin.

Gascony, French **Gascogne**, Latin **Vasconia** a former province in Aquitaine region, SW France, now occupying the departments of Landes, Gers, Hautes-Pyrénées, and some adjacent areas. It is bounded S by the Pyrenees and W by the Bay of Biscay. HISTORY initially part of the Roman Empire, it was conquered by the Visigoths and later by the Franks, who made it a duchy; Gascony was joined to Guienne province in 1052; it was in the hands of the Plantagenet kings of England from 1154 to 1453.

gas-cooled reactor *Physics* a nuclear reactor in which the cooling medium is carbon dioxide or some other gas.

gas engine a specially adapted or designed internal combustion engine which uses gas as its fuel.

gaseous *adj.* of the nature of, or like, gas.

gas exchange *Biol.* the uptake and output of gases, especially of carbon dioxide and oxygen in photosynthesis and respiration.

gash — *noun* a deep open cut or wound. — *verb* to make a gash in. [from Old French *garser*, to scratch or wound]

gas holder a large expandable metal tank used for storing gas for distribution to consumers.

gasification *noun* conversion into gas.

gasify *verb* (**gasifies, gasified**) to convert into gas.

Gaskell, Mrs Elizabeth (Cleghorn), *née* **Stevenson** (1810–65) English novelist, born in London. She started to write in her middle age, publishing *Mary Barton* in 1848. Her other works include *Cranford* (1853), *Ruth* (1853), *North and South* (1854–5), *Wives and Daughters* (1865), and a biography of Charlotte Brontë.

gasket *noun* a thin flat shaped ring or sheet of rubber or paper fitting tightly in the join between two metal surfaces to form an airtight seal.
— **blow a gasket 1** *said of an engine, etc* to cause a gasket to burst or break. **2** *colloq.* to lose one's temper.
[perhaps from French *garcette*, end of a rope]

gaslight *noun* a lamp powered by gas, or the light from it.

gas mask a mask, covering the full face, which filters out poisonous gas, allowing the wearer to breathe clean air.

gas meter an instrument which measures and records the amount of gas used.

gasohol *or* **gasahol** *noun* a mixture of eight or nine parts petrol (gasoline) and one or two parts ethanol (ethyl alcohol, which must be water-free), useful as a high-octane rating fuel in internal combustion engines.

gasoline *or* **gasolene** *noun chiefly North Amer.* petrol.

gasometer *noun* a gas holder.

gasp — *verb* **1** *intrans.* to take a sharp breath in, through surprise, sudden pain, etc. **2** *intrans.* to breathe in with difficulty, eg because of illness. **3** (**gasp something out**) to say it breathlessly. **4** *intrans.* (**gasp for something**) *colloq.* to want or need it very much. — *noun* a sharp intake of breath. [from Norse *geispa*, to yawn]

Gasperi, Alcide de (1881–1954) Italian politician, born in Trentino. He entered parliament in 1911, and was imprisoned by Mussolini as an anti-fascist (1927). He worked in the Vatican library from 1929 until he became Prime Minister of the new republic (1945–53), when he headed a succession of coalition Cabinets.

gassiness *noun* being gassy.

gassy *adj.* (**gassier, gassiest**) **1** like gas; full of gas. **2** *derog. colloq.* talking a lot, especially about unimportant things.

gastarbeiter *noun* an immigrant worker granted a work permit by the host country, especially in Germany (originally in West Germany). [German, = guest-worker]

gasteropod same as GASTROPOD.

gastrectomy *noun Medicine* the surgical removal of all or part of the stomach. [from Greek *gaster*, stomach + -ECTOMY]

gastric *adj.* of the stomach. [from Greek *gaster*, belly]

gastric flu *colloq.* a disorder of the intestine, of unknown cause.

gastric juice a strongly acidic fluid produced by the gastric glands of the stomach wall during digestion of food. It is composed primarily of hydrochloric acid, mucin (the main component of mucus), and the enzymes pepsin and rennin, which function best in an acid environment.

gastric ulcer *Medicine* an ulcer on the lining of the stomach wall.

gastritis *noun Medicine* inflammation of the lining of the stomach. [from Greek *gaster*, stomach + -ITIS]

gastro- *or* **gastr-** *combining form* the stomach. [from Greek *gaster*, belly]

gastroenteritis *noun Medicine* inflammation of the lining of the stomach and intestine, usually caused by bacterial or viral infection, food poisoning, or excessive alcohol consumption. Its main symptoms are vomiting and diarrhoea. [from GASTRO- + Greek *enteron*, intestine]

gastronome *or* **gastronomer** *or* **gastronomist** *noun* a person who enjoys, and has developed a taste for, good food and wine. [from GASTRO- + Greek *nomos*, law]

gastronomic *adj.* relating to gastronomy.

gastronomy *noun* **1** the enjoyment of good food and wine. **2** the style of cooking typical of a particular country or region: *French gastronomy.*

gastropod *noun Zool.* an invertebrate animal belonging to the class Gastropoda, eg snails, slugs, whelks, and winkles, typically possessing a large flattened muscular foot. When present, the shell is in one piece and usually spirally coiled, and the head and foot can be withdrawn into it for safety. [from GASTRO- + Greek *pous podos*, foot]

Gastropoda *or* **Gasteropoda** *noun Zool.* in the animal kingdom, a class of asymmetrical molluscs.

gastroscope *noun Medicine* an instrument that is used to inspect the interior of the stomach.

gastrula *noun Zool.* in the embryonic development of animals, the stage following the blastula, during which the cells of the embryo move into the correct position for development into the various organ systems of the adult.

gas turbine an engine that passes the products of the combustion of a mixture of fuel and air over the blades of a turbine. The turbine drives an air compressor, which in turn provides the energy for the combustion process.

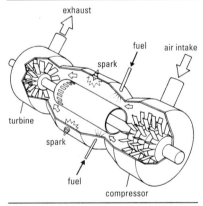

gas turbine

gasworks *sing. noun* a place where gas is manufactured from coal.

gate — *noun* **1** a usually hinged door or barrier, moved to open or close an entrance in a wall, fence, etc leading eg into a garden, field or city; the entrance itself. **2** any of the numbered exits at an airport via which passengers can board or leave a plane. **3** the total number of people attending a sports event or other entertainment. **4** (*also* **gate money**) the total money paid in admission fees. **5** any of the pairs of posts that a slalom skier passes through. **6** *technical* an electronic circuit whose output is controlled by the combination of signals at the input terminals. — *verb* to confine (pupils) to school after hours. [from Anglo-Saxon *geat*, a way]

-gate *combining form* attached to the name of a person or place to refer to an associated scandal: *Irangate*. [by analogy with WATERGATE]

gateau *or* **gâteau** *noun* (PL. **gateaux**, **gateaus**, **gâteaux**) a large rich cake, especially filled with cream and decorated with fruit, nuts, etc. [from French *gâteau*]

gatecrash *verb trans., intrans. colloq.* to gain entry to (a party, meeting, etc) uninvited or without paying.

gatecrasher *noun* a person who gatecrashes.

gatehouse *noun* a building at or above the gateway to a city, castle, etc, often occupied by the person who guards it.

gateleg *adj. said of a table* having a hinged or framed leg that can swing inwards to let down a leaf.

Gates, Horatio (1728–1806) US soldier, born in Maldon, Essex, UK. He joined the British army, served in America in the Seven Years' War (1756–63), and then settled there. In the War of Independence he sided with his adoptive country, took command of the Northern department (1777), and compelled the surrender of the British army at Saratoga. He commanded the army of the South in 1780, but was routed by Cornwallis near Camden, and was superseded in his position. He retired to Virginia until 1790, emancipated his slaves, and then settled in New York City.

Gateshead POP (1981) 92 000, an industrial town in Gateshead borough, Tyne and Wear, NE England. It lies S of the R Tyne, opposite Newcastle upon Tyne, and forms part of the Tyneside urban area.

Gates of Hell, The the unfinished bronze door made for the Musée des Arts Décoratifs by Auguste Rodin. It was commissioned in 1880 but still unfinished by his death in 1917. Many of his individual sculptures (eg *The Kiss* and *The Thinker*) had their origins in this work.

Gates of Paradise, The a pair of bronze doors made (1425–1452) for the Baptistery of Florence by Lorenzo Ghiberti. It was his second pair for the Baptistery; the first was completed in 1424.

gateway *noun* **1** an entrance, especially to a city, park, etc, with a gate across it. **2 (gateway to a place)** a way to or into it. **3 (gateway to something)** a means of acquiring it: *a gateway to success*. **4** *Comput.* a connection between computer networks, or between a computer network and a telephone line.

gather — *verb* (**gathered, gathering**) **1** *trans., intrans.* (*also* **gather together**) to bring or come together in one place. **2 (gather something in)** to collect, pick, or harvest it. **3** to increase in (speed or force). **4** to accumulate or become covered with (eg dust). **5** to learn or understand from information received. **6** to pull, and often stitch, (material) into small folds. **7** to pull (a garment) closely round the body. **8** to embrace: *she gathered the child into her arms*. **9** to wrinkle (the brow). **10 (gather something together)** to draw together or muster (strength, courage, etc) in preparation for something. **11** *intrans. said of a boil, etc* to form a head. — *noun* a small fold in material, often stitched. [from Anglo-Saxon *gaderian*]

gathering *noun* **1** a meeting or assembly. **2** a series of gathers in material.

Gatsby, Jay the enigmatic, egoistic central figure in F Scott Fitzgerald's *The Great Gatsby*.

GATT *abbrev.* General Agreement on Tariffs and Trade, an international treaty to promote trade and economic benefits, signed in 1947. Its aim is to encourage free trade by the imposition of trade rules and reduction of tariffs among its nations (now numbering 117). The 'Uruguay' or eighth round of talks involved seven years of complex negotiation (1986–93) and met much opposition, particularly from French farmers. It cut many tariffs by 40 per cent and created the World Trade Organization (WTO) to take over as the authoritative body on international commerce.

Gattopardo, Il (The Leopard) an Italian–French–US film directed by Luchino Visconti (1963). It tells of an aristocrat's view of the love of his nephew for a middle-class girl and combines nostalgia for a declining class with acceptance of the inevitability of social change, and stars Burt Lancaster and Alain Delon.

gauche *adj.* ill-at-ease, awkward in social situations. [from French *gauche*, left, left-handed]

gauchely *adv.* in a gauche way.

gaucherie *noun* social awkwardness, or an instance of this.

gaucho *noun* (PL. **gauchos**) a modern cowboy of the S American plains. [from Spanish *gaucho*]

Gaudí (I Cornet), Antonio (1852–1926) Spanish architect, born in Riudoms, Catalonia. He was the most famous exponent of Catalan 'modernisme', one of the branches of the Art Nouveau movement. Strikingly original and ingenious, he is best known for the extravagant and ornate church of the Sagrada Familia in Barcelona, which occupied him from 1884 until his death.

Casa Mila, Barcelona, designed by Gaudí

gaudily *adv.* in a gaudy way.

gaudiness *noun* being gaudy.

gaudy *adj.* (**gaudier, gaudiest**) *derog.* coarsely and brightly coloured or decorated. [from Middle English *gaude*, trinket]

gauge — *verb* **1** to measure accurately. **2** to estimate or guess (a measurement, size, etc). **3** to judge. — *noun* **1** a measuring instrument: *pressure gauge*. **2** each of a series of standard (especially diameter) sizes, eg of wire, bullets, knitting needles. **3** the distance between the rails of a railway line. **4** a standard against which other things are measured or judged. [from Old French *gauge*]

Gauguin, (Eugène Henri) Paul (1848–1903) French Post-Impressionist painter, born in Paris. He worked as a stockbroker, started exhibiting his work in 1876, and became a full-time artist in 1883. He moved to Brittany and became the leader of a group of painters there (1888). From 1891 he lived mainly in Tahiti and the Marquesas Is, and used local people as his subjects. He gradually evolved his own style, *synthétisme*, which reflects his hatred of civilization and the inspiration he found in primitive peoples. His works include *The Vision after the Sermon* (1888, Edinburgh), and the major allegorical work, *D'où venons-nous? Que sommes-nous? Où allons-nous?* (1897–8, Where Do We Come From? What Are We? Where Are We Going?, Boston).

Gaul an ancient region (Latin *Gallia*), consisting of Cisalpine Gaul (between the Alps and the Apennines) and Transalpine Gaul (north of the Alps). In Roman times, the Latin term *Gallia* was normally used for Transalpine Gaul, which was bounded by the Alps, the Rhine, and the Pyrenees. Julius Caesar completed the Roman conquest in 58–51 BC, and the impact of Romanization was felt most in the south, where Roman law remained in use until 1789. Gaul (excluding its easternmost territories) eventually developed into the medieval kingdom of France. Cisalpine Gaul lay south of the Alps and north of the Apennines. Conquered by the Romans in 201–191 BC, it was incorporated into Italy in 42 BC.

Gaul *noun* an inhabitant of ancient Gaul, especially Transalpine Gaul. [from Latin *Gallus*]

Gaulish — *noun* the language of the Gauls. — *adj.* of the Gauls or their language.

Gaulle, Charles (André Joseph Marie) de (1890–1970) French soldier and statesman, born in Lille. He fought in World War I, and became a strong advocate of mechanized warfare, but his efforts to modernize the French army had little effect. With the fall of France (Jun 1940), he fled to England to raise the standard of the 'Free French', and he entered Paris leading one of the earliest liberation forces (Aug 1944). He became head of the provisional government, then withdrew to the political sidelines, but following the troubles in N Africa he became Prime Minister (1958), and emerged as one postwar leader who could inspire confidence. In late 1958 he became the first President of the Fifth Republic, and practised a high-handed yet successful foreign policy, and repeatedly survived political crises by the free use of the referendum. His ministry was marked by the granting of independence to all French African colonies (1959–62); the development of an independent French nuclear deterrent; the signing of a historic reconciliation treaty with West Germany; and the blockading of Britain's entry into the Common Market. He had an overwhelming victory in the 1968 election, after the 'student revolution', but in 1969 resigned after the defeat of his referendum proposals for senate and regional reforms.

Gaullists members of the French political party, the *Rassemblement pour la République* (RPR) whose programmes are based on the doctrine developed by President de Gaulle in 1958–69. Nationalistic in character, Gaullists emphasize the need for a strong foreign policy, and have become one of the two main constituents of the right wing.

Gaumont, Léon (Ernest) (1864–1946) French cinema inventor, manufacturer, and producer, born in Paris. He synchronized a projected film with a phonograph in 1901, and was responsible for the first talking pictures, demonstrated in Paris in 1910. He also introduced an early form of coloured cinematography in 1912.

gaunt *adj.* **1** thin or thin-faced; lean, haggard. **2** *said of a place* barren and desolate.

gauntlet¹ *noun* **1** a metal or metal-plated glove worn by medieval soldiers. **2** a heavy protective leather glove loosely covering the wrist.
— **take up the gauntlet** to accept a challenge.
throw down the gauntlet to make a challenge. [from Old French *gantelet*, diminutive of *gant*, glove; the idioms are derived from the former practice of throwing a gauntlet on the ground when issuing a challenge to a duel]

gauntlet²
— **run the gauntlet 1** *Hist.* to suffer the military punishment of having to scramble along between two rows of men while receiving hard blows from them. **2** to expose oneself to hostile treatment or criticism. [altered from *gantlope*, from Swedish *gatlopp*, from *gata*, lane + *lopp*, course]

gauntness *noun* being gaunt.

Gauss, Carl Friedrich (1777–1855) German mathematician, astronomer, and physicist, born in Brunswick. As the Director of Göttingen Observatory, he pioneered the application of mathematics to gravitation, magnetism, and electricity, and made many contributions to pure mathematics. From 1818 to 1825 he directed the geodetic survey of Hanover, and this and his astronomical work involved him in much heavy routine calculation, leading to his study of the theory of errors of observation.

gauss *noun Physics* the cgs unit of magnetic flux density. In the SI system it has been replaced by the tesla (one gauss is equal to 10^{-4} tesla). [named after Carl Friedrich Gauss]

Gautier, Théophile (1811–72) French poet and novelist born in Tarbes. Initially an art student, he turned to literature and became an extreme Romantic. His works include the long poem, *Albertus* (1830), and the novel, *Mademoiselle de Maupin* (1835), the preface of which expounds his belief in *'l'art pour l'art'* ('art for art's sake'). His best-known collection is *Emaux et camées* (1852, Enamels and Cameos).

gauze *noun* **1** thin transparent cloth, especially cotton as used to dress wounds. **2** thin wire mesh. [from French *gaze*]

gauzy *adj.* (**gauzier, gauziest**) like gauze.

Gavaskar, Sunil (Manohar) (1949–) Indian cricketer, born in Bombay. He played 125 Test Matches, scoring a record 10 122 runs, and between 1974–5 and 1986–7 played in a record 106 consecutive Test Matches. He scored 25 834 runs in first-class cricket at an average of 51.46 per innings. His highest innings was 236 not out against the West Indies at Madras in 1983–4, the highest score by an Indian batsman in Test cricket.

gave see GIVE.

gavel *noun* a small hammer used by a judge, auctioneer, etc to call attention.

Gavin a male first name, common in Scotland, and borne by Sir Gawain (a Welsh form) of King Arthur's Round Table. [of Celtic origin, from elements meaning 'white hawk']

gavotte *noun* an old lively French country dance, or a piece of music for this. [from French *gavotte*]

Gawain *or* **Gawayne** in Arthurian legend, one of King Arthur's knights, the son of King Lot of Orkney. In the medieval verse-narrative, *Sir Gawain and the Green Knight*, he is a noble hero undergoing a test of faith. In other stories he is a jeering attacker of reputations, especially that of Lancelot.

Gawain and the Green Knight, Sir a medieval alliterative verse romance (late 14c). It is set in the time of Arthur and describes the adventures of Sir Gawain after he is set a challenge by the mysterious Green Knight.

gawk *colloq.* — *verb intrans.* to stare blankly or stupidly; to gawp. — *noun derog.* an awkward, clumsy or stupid person. [from obsolete *gaw*, to stare]

gawkiness *noun* being gawky; awkwardness.

gawky *adj.* (**gawkier, gawkiest**) *colloq., derog.* awkward-looking, ungainly, and usually tall and thin.

gawp *verb intrans. colloq.* to stare stupidly, especially open-mouthed; to gape. [from obsolete *gaw*, to stare]

Gay, John (1685–1732) English poet and dramatist, born in Barnstaple, Devon. He was apprenticed to a London silk mercer, but turned to literature, writing poems (eg *The Shepherd's Week*, 1714), pamphlets, and the first series of his popular satirical *Fables* (1727). His greatest success was *The Beggar's Opera* (1728), whose 62 performances constituted an unprecedented run.

Gay a female first name. [from GAY]

gay — *adj.* **1** happily carefree. **2** bright and attractive. **3** fun-loving or pleasure-seeking. **4** homosexual; of, frequented by, or intended for, homosexuals: *a gay bar.* — *noun* a homosexual. [from Old French *gai*]

Gay-Lussac, Joseph Louis (1778–1850) French chemist and physicist, born in Saint-Léonard, Haute Vienne. Professor of Chemistry at the École Polytechnique, the Sorbonne, and the National Museum of Natural History in Paris, he discovered independently the gas law commonly known as Charles's law, and made balloon ascents to make magnetic and atmospheric observations. In 1808 he announced his important law which states that when chemical combination occurs between gases, the volumes of those consumed and of those produced form a simple numerical ratio.

gayness *noun* the state of being gay, especially homosexual.

Gaynor a female first name, recently reintroduced from Wales. [a medieval form of *Guinevere*, Arthur's queen]

Gazankulu POP (1991) 689 000, a national state or non-independent black homeland in Transvaal province, NE South Africa. It achieved self-governing status in 1973.

Gaza Strip an Israeli-occupied district under military administration from 1967 to 1994. AREA 202sq km/78sq mi; length 50km/30mi. It is bounded NW and W by the Mediterranean Sea, SW by Egypt, and SE, E, and NE by Israel. CHIEF TOWN Gaza. It was formerly part of Egyptian Sinai, after the Arab–Israeli War in 1948–9. It contains many Palestinian refugee camps. There has been considerable tension in the area since the beginning of the uprising (*Intifada*) in 1988. In 1993 and 1994 peace agreements between Israel and the Palestine Liberation Organization were signed, setting out plans for limited Palestinian self-rule in the West Bank and the Gaza Strip.

gaze — *verb intrans.* to stare fixedly, usually for a long time. — *noun* a fixed stare. [from Middle English *gasen*]

gazebo *noun* (PL. **gazebos, gazeboes**) a small summerhouse or open hut, especially in a garden, from which a fine view can be admired. [perhaps coined from GAZE]

gazebo

gazelle *noun* (PL. **gazelles, gazelle**) a fawn-coloured antelope with a white rump and belly, and black and white face markings, found in arid plains, eg savanna, in Africa and Asia. The males have sweeping heavily ringed horns, while the females have short horns resembling spikes, or none at all. [from French, from Arabic *ghazal*, wild goat]

gazette — *noun* **1** an official newspaper giving lists of government, military and legal notices. **2** *often facetious* a newspaper. — *verb formal* to announce or publish in an official gazette. [from Venetian dialect *gazeta*, from *gazet*, a small coin, the cost of an early news-sheet]

gazetteer *noun* a dictionary of place-names, with descriptions of the places. [from GAZETTE]

gazpacho *noun* a Spanish vegetable soup, served cold. [from Spanish *gazpacho*]

gazump *verb colloq.* to go back on a verbal agreement to sell one's house to (a prospective buyer), and accept a better offer from another buyer. [perhaps from Yiddish *gezumph*, to swindle]

gazumper *noun* a person who gazumps.

gazumping *noun* **1** the act or process of gazumping. **2** being gazumped.

gazunder *verb trans., intrans. colloq., said of a buyer* to lower the sum offered to (the seller of a property) just before contracts are due to be signed. [from GAZUMP + UNDER]

GB *abbrev.* Great Britain.

GBE *abbrev.* Knight or Dame Grand Cross of the British Empire.

GBH *or* **gbh** *abbrev.* grievous bodily harm.

GC *abbrev.* George Cross, an award for bravery.

GCB *abbrev.* Knight or Dame Grand Cross of the Order of the Bath.

GCE — *abbrev.* General Certificate of Education. — *noun* a subject in which an examination is taken at this level.

GCHQ *abbrev.* Government Communications Headquarters.

GCMG *abbrev.* Knight or Dame Grand Cross of the Order of St Michael and St George.

GCSE *abbrev.* the General Certificate of Secondary Education, introduced in England and Wales in 1988. It merged what had previously been two separate examinations (the General Certificate of Education, GCE, and the Certificate of Secondary Education, CSE) for pupils aged about 16 or older. A similar examination reform, the Standard Grade, had been introduced in Scotland two years earlier.

GCVO *abbrev.* Knight or Dame Grand Cross of the Royal Victorian Order.

Gd *symbol Chem.* gadolinium.

Gdańsk, formerly German **Danzig 1** POP (1992e) 465 000, the capital of Gdańsk voivodship, N Poland. It is an industrial port lying at the mouth of the Martwa Wisła, and has the largest shipyard in Poland. It forms part of the *Tri-City* with Sopot and Gdynia. HISTORY held by Prussia (1793–1919), it became a free city within the Polish tariff area in 1919; its annexation by Germany in 1939 precipitated World War II; returned to Poland in 1945; in the 1980s the Lenin shipyard was the scene of much labour unrest in support of Solidarity. NOTABLE FEATURES High Gate; Golden Gate, Bakers' Gate, St George Fraternity Mansion (1487–94); Artus Court; Swan Tower; Royal Granary (1620); National Museum; Archaeological Museum; churches of the Virgin Mary, St John, St Elizabeth, St Catherine, and Holy Trinity. EVENT Polish Film Festival (Sep). **2** a voivodship in N Poland with the town of Gdańsk as its capital.

Gdns *abbrev.* Gardens, especially in street names.

GDP *abbrev.* gross domestic product.

GDR *abbrev.* German Democratic Republic, the former republic of East Germany.

Gdynia, German **Gdingen** POP (1992e) 252 000, a seaport in Gdańsk voivodship, N Poland. It lies on the Bay of Gdańsk, 20km/12mi NW of Gdańsk. Developed in the 1920s as a major Baltic port and naval base, the city is included with Sopot and Gdańsk as part of the *Tri-City*. NOTABLE FEATURES Oceanographic Museum; the destroyer *Błyskawica* at the S Pier.

Ge *symbol Chem.* germanium.

gear — *noun* **1** *Engineering* a toothed wheel or disc that engages with another wheel or disc having a different number of teeth, and turns it, so transmitting motion from one rotating shaft to another, the second shaft rotating at a different speed to the first one (the drive shaft). **2** the actual combination of such wheels or discs that is currently in use, eg first gear (bottom gear) in a car. **3** *colloq.* the equipment or tools needed for a

particular job, sport, etc. **4** *colloq.* clothes. — *verb* **1** to adapt or design to suit a particular need. **2** to supply with or connect by gears. **3** (**gear up** or **gear something up**) to become or make it ready or prepared.
— **in gear** *said of a motor vehicle* with a gear selected.
out of gear 1 *said of a motor vehicle* with no gear selected. **2** not working properly.
[from Middle English *gere*, from Norse *gervi*]

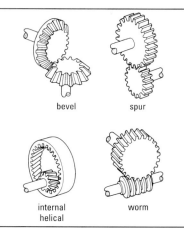

bevel   spur

internal helical   worm

types of gears

gearbox *noun* **1** the set or system of gears that transmits power from an engine (especially of a motor vehicle) to the road wheels, and allows the road speed to be varied while maintaining the engine speed at a constant high level. **2** the metal casing that encloses a system of gears.

gear lever or *North Amer.* **gear shift** a lever used in a motor vehicle to change gear.

GEC *abbrev.* General Electric Company.

gecko *noun* (PL. **geckos**, **geckoes**) any of a large family of mainly nocturnal lizards found in all warm countries, and best known for the ease with which some species can climb smooth walls, even glass, clinging by means of the hooked ridges on the underside of their toes. They feed on insects, and are the only lizards that produce specific calls, eg chirping or barking sounds. [from Malay *gekoq*, imitative of its cry]

gee¹ *interj.* (*usually* **gee up**) used to encourage a horse to move, or go faster.
— **gee someone up** *colloq.* to encourage them to work or perform better, more quickly, etc.

gee² *interj. colloq.* (*also* **gee whiz**) an expression of surprise, admiration, or enthusiasm. [a form of *Jesus*]

gee-gee *noun colloq., used especially to or by small children* a horse.

Geelong POP (1991) 145 000, a port in Barwon statistical division, S Victoria, SE Australia. It lies on the W side of Corio Bay, part of Port Phillip Bay. NOTABLE FEATURES many 19c villas with beautiful gardens; customs house (the oldest wooden building in Victoria).

geese see GOOSE.

geezer *noun colloq.* a man, especially an old man, often odd in some way. [from a dialect pronunciation of *guiser*, masked actor in mime]

gegenschein *noun Astron.* an elliptical patch of faint light that is sometimes observed in the sky directly opposite the Sun. It is caused by the reflection of sunlight from minute dust particles in space. — Also called *counterglow*. [from German *gegen* opposite + *schein* glow, shine]

Gehenna or **Gehinnom** the site of cultic child sacrifices to Baal by fire (7c BC), condemned by Jeremiah (Jeremiah 19.4–7). The name is used in Jewish and Christian eschatology for the place where the condemned live after death, usually

tormented by fire; eg in Mark 9.43, Matthew 18.9, Luke 12.5, and James 3.6 it is translated as 'hell'. [Greek form of the Hebrew *Gehinnom*, Valley of Hinnom, a ravine SW of Jerusalem]

Gehrig, Lou, properly **(Henry) Louis**, also called **Iron Horse** (1903–41) US baseball player, born in New York City. He played 2 130 consecutive games for the New York Yankees between 1925 and 1939. In a career which was cut short by illness, he had a batting average of 0.340, a score of 493 home runs, and a reputation as an outstanding first-base fielder.

Geiger, Hans Wilhelm (1882–1945) German physicist, born in Neustadt-an-der-Haardt. He worked under Ernest Rutherford at Manchester, and later in Berlin, and became professor at Kiel University in 1925. He is best known for developing with Walther Müller the particle counter used to measure radioactivity which bears his name.

Geiger counter an instrument for detecting and measuring radioactivity. [named after Hans Geiger]

Geisel, Ernesto (1908–) Brazilian soldier and politician, born in Rio Grande do Sul. When he was President (1974–9), he masterminded a return to a regime in which the military acted in their traditional role as a moderating power, and which led to the restoration of democracy in 1985.

geisha *noun* (PL. **geisha**, **geishas**) (*also* **geisha girl**) a female companion for Japanese men, trained in music, dancing, and the art of conversation. [from Japanese *gei*, art + *sha*, person]

gel — *noun* **1** *Chem.* a colloid (a state midway between a suspension and a true solution) consisting of a solid and a liquid that are dispersed evenly throughout a material and have set to form a jelly-like mass, eg gelatine. **2** (*also* **hair gel**) such a substance used to fix the hair in place. — *verb* (**gelled**, **gelling**) **1** *intrans., trans.* to form a colloid consisting of a solid and a liquid that are dispersed evenly throughout a material and have set to form a jelly-like mass. **2** *intrans.* to take on a definite form; to jell. [from GELATINE]

gelatine or **gelatin** *noun* a clear tasteless protein, formed by the partial breakdown of collagen, and extracted from animal bones and hides. It forms a stiff jelly when dissolved in water, and is used in adhesives, photographic materials, pharmaceutical capsules, and foods, eg table jellies. [from Italian *gelatina*, jelly]

gelatinize or **gelatinise** *verb trans., intrans. technical* to make or become like gelatine or jelly.

gelatinous *adj.* like gelatine or jelly.

geld *verb* to remove the testicles of (especially a horse). [from Norse *geldr*, barren]

gelding *noun* a gelded horse.

gel filtration *Chem.* a form of chromatography in which the components of a mixture of liquids are separated on the basis of differences in the size of their molecules. The mixture is passed down a tube containing a porous gel, and the smaller molecules, which can enter the pores of the gel, move more slowly down the column than the molecules that are too large to enter the pores of the gel.

gelignite *noun* a powerful explosive used especially in mining. [from GELATINE + Latin *ignis*, fire]

Gellatley, Davie the simple 'innocent' in Sir Walter Scott's *Waverley*, who recites some of Scott's most poetic lyrics.

Gell-Mann, Murray (1929–) US theoretical physicist, born in New York City. Professor at the California Institute of Technology from 1956, he explained some aspects of the properties of new subatomic particles by assigning them a property known as 'strangeness'; this theory led to the prediction and subsequent discovery of a

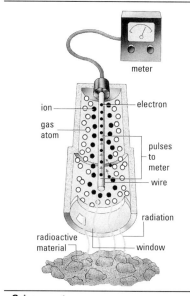

Geiger counter

new particle known as the 'hyperon'. He also introduced the concept of quarks as the basic building blocks of hadrons, the nuclear particles. For this work he was awarded the 1969 Nobel Prize for Physics.

gem *noun* **1** a precious or semi-precious stone or crystal, especially one that has been cut and polished for use in jewellery or other ornaments, eg diamond, ruby, sapphire, and emerald. **2** *colloq.* a person or thing that one values, admires or likes very much. [from Latin *gemma*, bud, precious stone]

Gemayel, Amin (1942–) Lebanese politician, son of Pierre Gemayel, who supported his brother Bashir Gemayel in the 1975–6 civil war and succeeded him as President (1982–8). Politically moderate, his policies proved no more successful in peacefully settling the problems of Lebanese government. The disorder was aggravated by the absence of a Christian successor (as the constitution required) in 1988 until the appointment of Rene Muawad and then Elias Hrawi in 1989.

Gemayel, Bashir (1947–82) Lebanese soldier and politician, youngest son of Pierre Gemayel. He joined the militia of his father's Phalangist Party, and came to be its political director in the Ashrefieh sector of E Beirut, where he was an active leader of the Christian militia in the civil war of 1975–6. By the systematic elimination of rivals he came to command the military forces of E Beirut. He distanced his party from Israeli support, and aimed to expel all foreign influence from Lebanese affairs. Having twice escaped assassination, he was killed in a bomb explosion while still President-Elect.

Gemayel, Sheikh Pierre (1905–) Lebanese politician, a member of the Maronite Christian community of Lebanon. Trained as a pharmacist, in 1936 he founded the Kataeb or Phalangist Party, modelled on the Spanish and German fascist organizations, and in 1937 became its leader. He was twice imprisoned (1937, 1943), held various ministerial posts (1960–7), and led the Phalangist militia in the 1975–6 civil war.

geminate *technical* — *adj.* (pronounced *-nət*) *said especially of leaves* arranged in pairs. — *verb trans., intrans.* (pronounced *-nate*) to arrange, or be arranged, in pairs. [from Latin *geminus*, twin]

gemination *noun* doubling, repetition.

Geminean — *noun* a person born under the sign Gemini. *adj.* relating to this sign.

Gemini *noun* **1** *Astron.* the Twins, a conspicuous zodiacal constellation that lies to the northeast of Orion. Its two brightest stars are Castor and Pollux. **2** a person born between 21 May and 20 Jun, under this sign. **3** any of a series of manned earth-orbiting space vehicles launched by the USA in 1965 and 1966 (see GEMINI PROJECT). [from Latin *geminus*, twin]

Gemini project *Astron.* a series of US spacecraft which carried two astronauts and were launched by the USA in 1965 and 1966. The flights made by these spacecraft played an important role in the development of rendezvous, docking, and other spaceflight manoeuvres in preparation for the *Apollo* Moon landings.

Gemma a female first name, introduced from Italy in the mid-20c. [originally a medieval nickname meaning 'gem, jewel']

gemstone *noun* same as GEM 1.

Gen. *abbrev.* **1** General. **2** (*also* **Gen**) Genesis.

gen *colloq.* — *noun* (**the gen**) the required information. — *verb* (**genned, genning**) (**gen up on something**) *colloq.* to obtain information about it. [from *general information*]

gen. *abbrev.* genitive.

-gen *or* **-gene** *combining form* denoting something that causes or produces: *carcinogen*. [from Greek *-genes*, born]

gendarme *noun* a member of an armed police force in France and other French-speaking countries. [from French *gens d'armes*, armed people]

gender *noun* **1** *Grammar* in some languages, the system of dividing nouns and pronouns into different classes. **2** *Grammar* any of these classes, usually two or three (masculine, feminine, and neuter) in European languages. **3** the condition of being male or female; sex. [from Latin *genus*, kind]

gender-bender *noun colloq.* someone who adopts a sexually-ambiguous image and style of dress, etc.

gene *noun* the basic unit of inheritance, consisting of a sequence of DNA that occupies a specific position or *locus* on a chromosome. Each gene is responsible for the passing on of one or more specific characteristics from parents to offspring. [from German *Gen*, from Greek *-genes*, born]

◊ There may be hundreds of genes on a chromosome, and each controls one or more characteristics of a living organism by determining which proteins are manufactured within the cells. Slight differences in genes account for many of the differences in appearance between plants or animals of the same species. This is because chromosomes and genes from both parents are mixed during sexual reproduction.

Living organisms inherit two forms of the same gene (known as *alleles*) for each characteristic. In individuals that are *homozygous* for a certain characteristic, both alleles are the same. In individuals that are *heterozygous* for that characteristic, the alleles are different, in which case one allele may be *dominant*, ie its effect will be seen in the organism, or it may be *recessive*, ie its effect will be hidden. Only if both alleles of a gene are recessive will the organism show the recessive characteristic. For example, both alleles must be recessive for blue eye colour to be manifested. If either allele is dominant, eye colour will be brown.

-gene same as -GEN.

genealogical *adj.* relating to or involving genealogy.

genealogist *noun* a person who studies or traces genealogies.

genealogy *noun* (PL. **genealogies**) **1** a person's direct line of descent from an ancestor, or a diagram or scheme showing this. **2** the study of the history and lineage of families. **3** the study of the development of plants and animals into present-day forms. [from Greek *genea*, race + *logos*, discourse]

gene probe *Genetics* a fragment of DNA that is labelled with a radioactive isotope (so that it can be easily recognized), and used to identify or isolate a gene.

genera see GENUS.

general — *adj.* **1** of, involving, or applying to all or most parts, people or things; widespread, not specific, limited, or localized: *the general opinion / general rule*. **2** not detailed or definite; rough; vague: *general description / in general terms*. **3** not specialized: *general knowledge*. **4** chief: *general manager*. — *noun* **1** a senior army officer of the rank next below Field Marshal. **2** the commander of a whole army. **3** any leader, especially when regarded as competent. **4** the head of a religious order, eg the Jesuits.
— **in general** usually; mostly.
[from Latin *generalis*, from *genus*, race, kind]

General, The a US film directed by Clyde Bruckman and Buster Keaton (1926). A silent comedy with Keaton performing daring stunts on steam trains, it combines fictional action, adventure, and romance with actual events of the Civil War.

General Agreement on Tariffs and Trade see GATT.

General Assembly the highest court, in Churches of Presbyterian order. It normally meets annually and comprises equal numbers of ministers and elders, elected by presbyteries in proportion to their size. It is presided over by a moderator, who is annually elected.

General Certificate of Education *noun* see GCSE.

General Certificate of Secondary Education (ABBREV. **GCSE**) in England and Wales, a school-leaving qualification in one or more subjects, which replaced the GCE Ordinary level and CSE qualifications in 1988.

general election a national election in which the voters of every constituency in the country elect a member of parliament.

Generalife the former summer palace of the Moorish sultans in the city of Granada, Spain. It is a World Heritage site.

generalissimo *noun* (PL. **generalissimos**) a supreme commander of the combined armed forces in some countries, often also having political power. [from Italian *generalissimo*, superlative of *generale*, general]

generality *noun* (PL. **generalities**) **1** the quality of being general. **2** a general rule or principle. **3** the majority.

generalization *or* **generalisation** *noun* **1** the act of generalizing. **2** an example of generalizing.

generalize *or* **generalise** *verb* **1** *intrans.* to speak in general terms or form general opinions, especially too general to be applied to all individual cases. **2** *trans.* to make more general, especially applicable to a wider variety of cases.

generally *adv.* **1** usually. **2** without considering details; broadly. **3** as a whole; collectively.

General Motors Corporation, commonly known as **GM**, or **GMC** an industrial corporation founded in the USA in 1908 by William C Durant (1861–1947). It became an amalgamation of several car manufacturers, including Buick, Cadillac, Oldsmobile, and Oakland. In the 1970s it was the biggest manufacturing corporation in the USA. Today, as well as cars and lorries, its major products include locomotives, engines, aerospace materials, high technology, and household appliances.

general practitioner (ABBREV. **GP**) a community doctor providing basic treatment for all common illnesses, not specializing in any one area of medicine.

general staff the officers assisting a military commander.

general strike a strike by workers in all or most of the industries in a country at one time.

◊ In Britain, the General Strike of May 1926 was organized by the Trades Union Congress (TUC) in support of the coal miners' campaign to resist wage cuts. Special constables and volunteers were mobilized by the government to counter the most serious effects of the strike, and an anti-strike journal, *The British Gazette*, was published. After the TUC had called off the strike, the miners' strike continued fruitlessly for three more months.

generate *verb* to produce or create. [from Latin *generare*, from *genus*, a kind]

generation *noun* **1** the act of producing (eg electricity). **2** all people born and living at about the same time, considered as a group: *the younger generation*. **3** the average period between a person's birth and the birth of his or her children, considered to be between 25 and 30 years: *three generations ago*. **4** a single stage in a person's descent. **5** a particular stage in the development of something: *fourth-generation computers*.

generation gap the difference in the ideas and ways of living of people from different (especially successive) generations.

generative *adj. formal* **1** able to produce or generate. **2** relating to production or creation.

generative grammar *Linguistics* a description of a language in terms of a finite set of grammatical rules able to generate an infinite number of grammatical sentences (and none of the

---

Gemstones

Nearly all gemstones are minerals, as are those in this table. The four non-mineral gems are amber, coral, jet and pearl. The hardness of solid substances is expressed on a scale called the Mohs scale. This ranges from zero, for talc, to ten, for diamond.

Mineral	Colour	Mohs of hardness
agate	brown, red, blue, green, yellow	7.0
alexandrite	green, red	8.5
amethyst	violet	7.0
aquamarine	sky blue, greenish blue	7.5
beryl	green, blue, pink	7.5
bloodstone	green with red spots	7.0
chalcedony	all colours	7.0
chrysoprase	apple green	7.0
citrine	yellow	7.0
diamond	colourless, tints of various colours	10.0
emerald	green	7.5
garnet	red and other colours	6.5–7.25
jade	green, whitish, mauve, brown	7.0
jasper	dark red, multi-coloured	7.0
lapis lazuli	deep blue	5.5
malachite	dark green banded	3.5
moonstone	whitish with blue shimmer	6.0
onyx	various colours with straight coloured bands	7.0
opal	black, white, orange-red, rainbow coloured	6.0
periodot	green	6.5
ruby	red	9.0
sapphire	blue and other colours	9.0
serpentine	red and green	3.0
soapstone	white, may be stained with impurities	2.0
sunstone	whitish red-brown flecked with golden particles	6.0
topaz	blue, green, pink, yellow, colourless	8.0
tourmaline	brown-black, blue, pink, red, violet-red, yellow, green	7.5
turquoise	greenish grey, sky blue	6.0
zircon	all colours	7.5

ungrammatical ones). Generative grammar was first devised by the US linguist Noam Chomsky in the 1950s, and developed in the 1960s by other linguists. See also TRANSFORMATIONAL GRAMMAR.

generator *noun Electr.* a machine that converts mechanical energy into electrical energy, eg a dynamo. A generator that produces alternating current, eg in a power station, is called an alternator.

generic *adj.* **1** from, or relating to, a general class or type. **2** *North Amer., esp. US* not sold as a specific brand: *generic aspirin.* **3** *Biol.* of a genus: *a generic name.* [from GENUS]

generosity *noun* **1** the quality of being generous. **2** a generous act. [from GENEROUS]

generous *adj.* **1** giving or willing to give or help unselfishly. **2** *said eg of a donation* large and given unselfishly. **3** large; ample; plentiful: *generous portions.* **4** kind; willing to forgive: *of generous spirit.* [from Latin *generosus*, of noble birth]

generously *adv.* in a generous way.

Genesis, Book of the first book of the Pentateuch, the Hebrew Bible, and the Old Testament, traditionally attributed to Moses. It depicts the creation and of the beginnings of human history (chapters 1–11), and then focuses on God's dealings with the people destined to become Israel, from Abraham to Jacob's sons.

genesis *noun* (PL. **geneses**) a beginning or origin. [from Greek *genesis*]

Genet, Jean (1910–86) French writer, born in Paris. He began to write in 1942 while serving a life sentence for theft, from which he was pardoned in 1948 after a petition by French intellectuals. His first novel, *Notre-Dame des Fleurs* (Our Lady of the Flowers, 1944) created a sensation for its portrayal of the criminal world. Other works include the plays *Les Bonnes* (The Maids, 1947) and *Les Paravents* (The Screens, 1961).

gene therapy *Genetics* the notion that genetic engineering techniques could be used to introduce a normal gene into a cell in order to alter or replace a defective gene. It is hoped that it will eventually be possible to prevent hereditary diseases such as haemophilia using such techniques.

genetic *adj.* **1** of genes or genetics; inherited: *a genetic defect.* **2** relating to origin: *a genetic study of American folk music.* [from GENE]

genetically *adv.* **1** with respect to genetics. **2** by genes; according to genetics: *a disease inherited genetically.*

genetic code the code in which genetic instructions for the manufacture of proteins in the cells of living organisms are written.
◇ The genetic code uses the four bases in the nucleic acids DNA and RNA, namely adenine, cytosine, guanine, and thymine (only in DNA) or uracil (only in RNA). A group of three bases arranged in a particular order (known as a *triplet* or *codon*) indicates that a particular type of amino acid is to be manufactured. Proteins are composed of chains of different combinations of up to 20 different amino acids. There are 64 possible triplets, so it follows that more than one triplet can code for a particular amino acid. The code is said to be *universal*, because it is the same for virtually all living organisms.

genetic counselling advice given to prospective parents by a genetics specialist in cases where there is some likelihood of their conceiving children with hereditary disorders, and the options available for their prevention or management.

genetic engineering a form of biotechnology in which the genes of an organism are deliberately altered by a method other than conventional breeding in order to change one or more characteristics of the organism.
◇ In one widely used form of genetic engineering, a specific protein-producing gene can be cut from the DNA of human or animal cells and inserted into a bacterium, which is then capable of manufacturing the protein specified by that gene, and has the advantage of being easily grown and harvested. For example, the gene for insulin production can be cut from human DNA and spliced into the nucleic acid of a virus, which then injects the nucleic acid into a bacterium. As a result, the insulin gene becomes part of the bacterium's genetic material, and is capable of producing insulin. Other biological compounds that can be produced on an industrial scale by similar methods include blood clotting factors, interferon, viral proteins for vaccines, and growth hormone.
New genes can also be incorporated into the DNA of plants, endowing them with new characteristics, such as disease resistance, the ability to fix nitrogen, or in the case of edible plants a change in flavour. Scientists hope that it will eventually be possible to excise (remove) genes responsible for hereditary diseases and replace them with normal DNA sequences. The implications of genetic engineering have led to considerable public debate, and in most countries the use of such techniques is under government control.

genetic fingerprinting *Biol.* the analysis of samples of DNA from body tissues such as blood, saliva, or semen in order to establish a person's identity in criminal investigations, paternity disputes, etc.

geneticist *noun* a person who studies or is an expert in genetics.

genetic labelling the labelling of food products in supermarkets, etc to indicate the use of gene technology in their manufacture.

genetics *sing. noun* the scientific study of heredity, and of the mechanisms whereby characteristics are transmitted from one generation to the next.

genetic variation a measure of the variation between individuals of a population due to differences in their genetic make-up.

Geneva, French **Genève**, German **Genf**, Italian **Ginevra 1** POP (1991e) 395 000, the capital of Geneva canton, W Switzerland, and of the French-speaking area of the country. It lies on the R Rhône at the W end of L Geneva. A banking and commercial centre, it is also the world capital of high-class watchmaking and jewellery. The city's cultural and artistic life is centred in the Old Town, on the left bank of the Rhône. Geneva is the headquarters of over 200 international organizations (eg International Red Cross, World Health Organization). HISTORY built on the site of a Roman town, it was a free city until the end of the 13c, and an independent republic until 1814, when it became a Swiss canton; the centre of the Reformation (16c) under the French Protestant reformer John Calvin; a university developed from the Academy founded in 1559 by Calvin to train Reformed theologians; the city was annexed to France in 1798; joined the Swiss Confederation in 1815; the seat of the League of Nations from 1920 to 1946. NOTABLE FEATURES St Peter's Cathedral (12c); a fountain, Jet d'Eau, which reaches 745m; numerous quays. **2** a canton in W Switzerland with Geneva as its capital.

Geneva, Lake, French **Lac Léman**, German **Genfersee**, ancient **Lacus Lemanus** a crescent-shaped lake in SW Switzerland and SE France. AREA 581sq km/224sq mi; maximum width 14km/9mi; maximum depth 310m. The largest of the alpine lakes, it lies on the course of the R Rhône in a wine-growing area. CHIEF TOWNS Morges, Rolle, Lausanne, Vevey.

Geneva Bible an English translation of the Bible, prepared and published (1560) in Geneva by Protestant exiles from England. Notable for its small size and legible Roman type, for its notes, and for its verse divisions, it was especially popular both in Scotland, and in England, until the Authorized Version.

Geneva Convention an international agreement on the conduct of warfare first framed in 1864 and ratified in 1906. It is chiefly concerned with the protection of wounded soldiers and the sanctity of the Red Cross; it also prohibits methods of war (eg the use of 'dumdum' bullets, which expand on impact) that might cause unnecessary suffering. The terms were extended in 1950 and again in 1978 to confirm the prohibition of attacks on non-defended civilians, reprisals against civilians, and the prisoner-of-war rights of guerrilla fighters.

Genghis Khan (1162–1227) Mongol conqueror, born in Deligun Bulduk on the R Onon. He succeeded his father at 13, and during his struggle against hostile tribes he subjugated the Naimans, conquered Tangut, and received the submission of the Turkish Uigurs. In 1206 he changed his name Temujin to Ghengis (Jingis or Chingis) Kha ('Very Mighty Ruler'). From 1211 he overran many territories, including the Empire of N China, the Kara-Chitai Empire, and the Empire of Kharezm, so that by the time he died the Mongol Empire stretched from the Black Sea to the Pacific.

genial *adj.* **1** cheerful; friendly; sociable. **2** *said of a climate* pleasantly warm or mild. [from Latin *genialis*, from *genius*, guardian spirit or deity]

geniality *noun* being genial.

genially *adv.* in a genial way.

-genic *combining form* forming words meaning 'causing or producing': *carcinogenic.*

genie *noun* (PL. **genies, genii**) in fairy stories, a spirit with the power to grant wishes. [from French *génie*]

genital *adj.* of the genitals or sexual reproduction.

genitals or **genitalia** *pl. noun* the external sexual organs. [from Latin *genitalis*, from *gignere*, to beget]

genitive *Grammar* — *noun* **1** the form, or case, of a noun, pronoun or adjective which shows possession or association, eg 'John's'. **2** a noun, etc in this case. — *adj.* of or belonging to this case. [from Latin *genitivus*]

genius *noun* (PL. **geniuses**, in sense 5 **genii**) **1** a person of outstanding creative or intellectual ability. **2** such ability. **3** a person who exerts a powerful (good or bad) influence on another. **4** in Roman mythology, a guardian spirit. **5** *formal* a quality or attitude with which something (eg a country or a period of time) is identified or typically associated: *rational inquiry was the genius of the century.* [from Latin *genius*, guardian spirit or deity]

Genoa, Italian **Genova** POP (1991e) 701 000, the seaport capital of Liguria region and of Genoa province, NW Italy, lying on the Gulf of Genoa. Its larger conurbation extends 35km/22mi along the coast. HISTORY founded as a Roman trading centre; the leading Mediterranean port by the 13c; included in the Ligurian Republic established by Napoleon in 1797 and given to the king of Sardinia in 1815; rebuilt after World War II, once again becoming a major Mediterranean port. The explorer Christopher Columbus was born in Genoa in 1451. NOTABLE FEATURES Academy of Fine Arts (1751); Verdi Institute of Music; Doge's Palace (13c); Church of San Matteo (1278); Cathedral of San Lorenzo (12–14c); Palazzo Reale (begun in 1650); Palazzo Rosso (17c); university (1471).

genocidal *adj.* relating to or involving genocide.

genocide *noun* the deliberate and systematic killing of a whole nation or people. [from Greek *genos*, race + Latin *caedere*, to kill]

genome *noun* the complete set of genetic material in the cell of a living organism. [from GENE + CHROMOSOME]

genotype *noun* the particular set of genes possessed by an organism, ie its genetic make-up. The genotype interacts with environmental factors to determine the *phenotype*, ie the observable characteristics of the organism. Thus organisms with the same genotype may have different phenotypes, and vice versa.

genre *noun* **1** a particular type or kind of literature, music or other artistic work. **2** *Art* a type of painting featuring scenes from everyday life. [from French *genre*]

genre painting paintings of scenes from everyday life, typically on a small scale. The term is most commonly applied to works by 17c Dutch masters, especially Steen and Vermeer, but may also be used for such paintings from any period. Genre painting flourished in 19c Britain when, for example, the anecdotal scenes of Scottish village life by Sir David Wilkie gained wide popularity.

Genscher, Hans-Dietrich (1927–) German politician, born in Reideburg, Germany. He became Secretary-General of the Free Democratic Party (FDP) in 1959, and was Minister of the Interior (1969–74) before he became Vice-Chancellor and Foreign Minister in Schmidt's coalition government in 1974. That year he became Chairman of the FDP (1974–85), a post to which he was re-elected in 1982 and which he retained in the coalition between the FDP and the Christian Democrats.

Gent see GHENT.

gent *noun colloq.* a gentleman.

genteel *adj.* **1** *derog.* polite or refined in an artificial, affected way approaching snobbishness. **2** well-mannered. **3** *old use, facetious* of, or suitable for, the upper classes. [from French *gentil*, well-bred]

genteelly *adv.* in a genteel way.

gentian *noun* a small plant of mountainous regions with bright (usually blue) flowers. [from Latin *gentiana*]

Gentile, Giovanni (1875–1944) Italian philosopher, born in Castelvetrano. He was Professor of Philosophy at Palermo, Pisa, and Rome, and became with Croce a leading exponent of 20c Italian idealism. He quarrelled with Croce's complex distinctions between the theoretical and practical categories of mind, arguing that nothing is real except the pure act of thought. He became Mussolini's Minister of Education (1922–4), and was assassinated by an anti-fascist in Florence in 1944.

gentile — *adj.* **1** (*often* **Gentile**) not Jewish. **2** relating to a nation or tribe. — *noun* (*often* **Gentile**) a person who is not Jewish. [from Latin *gentilis*, from *gens*, nation, clan]

gentility *noun* **1** good manners and respectability. **2** *derog.* artificial politeness. **3** *old use* noble birth; the people of the upper classes. [from Old French *gentilite*]

gentle *adj.* **1** mild-mannered, not stern, coarse or violent. **2** light and soft; not harsh, loud, strong, etc: *a gentle caress / a gentle breeze*. **3** moderate; mild: *a gentle reprimand*. **4** *said of hills, etc* rising gradually. **5** *old use* noble; of the upper classes. [from French *gentil*, well-bred]

gentlefolk *pl. noun old use* people of good breeding; members of the upper classes.

gentleman *noun* (PL. **gentlemen**) **1** a polite name for a man, used especially as a form of address. **2** a polite, well-mannered, respectable man. **3** a man from the upper classes, especially one with enough private wealth to live on without working.

gentlemanly *adj.* **1** polite and well-mannered. **2** suitable for, or typical of, a gentleman.

Gentlemen at Arms, Honourable Corps of in the UK, noncombatant troops in close attendance upon the sovereign, known as the 'nearest guard'. They provide an escort at coronations, state openings of parliament, receptions, royal garden parties, and during state visits. Instituted as the 'Gentlemen Spears' by Henry VIII in 1509, nowadays the 27 members are chosen from army or Royal Marine officers who have been decorated.

Gentlemen's Agreement an informal pact (1907) between the USA and Japan by which Japan agreed to limit Japanese migration to the USA in return for a promise by President Roosevelt not to discriminate against the Japanese.

gentlemen's agreement *or* **gentleman's agreement** an unwritten agreement to which each participant is bound only by an informal commitment not binding in law.

gentleness *noun* being gentle.

gentlewoman *noun old use* **1** a woman from the upper classes. **2** her female servant or attendant.

gently *adv.* in a gentle way.

gentrification *noun derog.* the change in the character of a traditionally working-class area following an influx of new middle-class residents. [from GENTRY]

gentrify *verb* (**gentrifies, gentrified**) **1** to convert or renovate (housing) to conform to middle-class taste. **2** to make (an area) middle-class.

gentry *pl. noun* **1** people belonging to the class directly below the nobility. **2** *derog. colloq.* people generally. [from Old French *genterise*, nobility]

gents *sing. noun* a men's public toilet.

genuflect *verb intrans.* to bend the knee, especially in worship or as a sign of respect. [from Latin *genu*, knee + *flectere*, to bend]

genuflection *or* **genuflexion** *noun* the act of genuflecting.

genuine *adj.* **1** authentic, not artificial or fake. **2** honest; sincere. [from Latin *genuinus*, natural]

genuinely *adv.* in a genuine way, sincerely.

genuineness *noun* **1** being genuine. **2** honesty.

genus *noun* (PL. **genera**) **1** *Biol.* in plant and animal classification, a group of closely related species. Related genera are in turn grouped into families. **2** a class divided into several subordinate classes. [from Latin *genus*, race or kind]

geo- *combining form* forming words associated with the Earth. [from Greek *ge*, earth]

geocentric *adj.* having the earth as the centre; measured from the centre of the earth.

geochemistry *noun Geol.* the branch of geology concerned with the scientific study of the chemical composition of the Earth.

geode *noun Geol.* a hollow cavity within a rock, lined with crystals that point inward towards its centre. [from Greek *geodes*, earthy]

geodesic *Maths.* — *noun* (*also* **geodesic line**) a line on a surface that represents the shortest distance between two points, eg a straight line on a plane, or a great circle on a sphere. — *adj.* denoting an artificial structure made up of a large number of identical components, eg a dome whose surface is composed of a large number of identical small triangles. [from GEO- + Greek *daisis*, division]

geodesy *noun Geol.* the scientific study of the Earth's surface by surveying (especially by satellite) and mapping in order to determine its exact shape and size, and to measure its gravitational field. It has applications in mapmaking, navigation, civil engineering, and geophysics.

Geoffrey a male first name. [of Germanic origin; perhaps a combination of *gaufrid*, district-peace + *walahfried*, traveller-peace]

Geoffrey of Monmouth (c.1100–54) Welsh chronicler, consecrated Bishop of St Asaph in 1152. His *Historia Regum Britanniae* (History of the Kings of Britain), composed before 1147, introduced the stories of King Lear and Cymbeline, the prophecies of Merlin, and the legend of Arthur as they are known today.

geog. *abbrev.* geographical; geography.

geographer *noun* a person who studies or is an expert in geography.

geographical *adj.* relating to or involving geography.

geographically *adv.* in a geographical way; as regards geography.

geography *noun* **1** the scientific study of the earth's surface, especially its physical features, climate, and population. **2** *colloq.* the layout of a place.

geol. *abbrev.* geological; geology.

geological *adj.* relating to or involving geology.

geologically *adv.* with regard to geology.

geological survey *Geol.* a survey of the geology of a particular area, especially in order to locate economically important rocks and minerals such as coal and oil, or to determine the past history of the area (eg its climate, or the fossil organisms associated with it).

geological time scale *Geol.* a scale in which the Earth's history is subdivided into units of time known as *eons*, which are further subdivided into *eras*, *periods*, and *epochs*. Although the Earth is estimated to be 4 600 million years old, the time scale lacks detail until the beginning of the Cambrian period about 580 million years ago.

Geological Time Scale				
Eon	Era	Period	Epoch	Million years before present
Phanerozoic	Cenozoic	Quaternary	Holocene	0.01–
			Pleistocene	2–0.01
		Tertiary	Pliocene	7–2
			Miocene	25–7
			Oligocene	38–25
			Eocene	54–38
			Palaeocene	65–54
	Mesozoic	Cretaceous		140–65
		Jurassic		210–140
		Triassic	Late Middle Early	250–210
	Palaeozoic	Permian	Late Early	290–250
		Carboniferous	Pennsylvanian Mississippian	360–290
		Devonian		410–360
		Silurian		440–410
		Ordovician		505–440
		Cambrian		580–505
Proterozoic	Precambrian			4 500–580

geologist *noun* a person who studies or is expert in geology.

geology *noun* **1** the scientific study of the Earth, including its origin, history, structure, and composition, and the changes it undergoes, especially in terms of the rocks of which it is made. **2** the history, composition, and structure of the rocks of a particular region which are relevant to such study.

geomagnetism *noun Physics* the Earth's magnetic field.

geometric *or* **geometrical** *adj.* **1** relating to, or measured using, geometry. **2** using, or consisting of, the kinds of basic forms dealt with in geometry, eg lines, circles, and triangles: *a geometrical design.*

geometric mean *Maths.* see MEAN³ 2c.

geometric progression *Maths.* a sequence of numbers in which the ratio between one term and the next remains constant, eg 1, 2, 4, 8..., where each successive term is obtained by multiplying its predecessor by 2.

geometric series *Maths.* any series of numbers or terms that forms a geometric progression.

geometry *noun* the branch of mathematics that is concerned with the properties of sets of points that form plane (two-dimensional) or solid (three-dimensional) figures in space.

geomorphology *noun Geol.* the scientific study of the nature and history of the landforms on the surface of the Earth and other planets, and of the processes that create them.

geophysics *sing. noun Physics* the study of the physical properties of the Earth, and the physical processes that determine its structure. Major subjects include seismology, geomagnetism, meteorology, and geophysical surveys to prospect for oil, gas, and mineral reserves.

geopolitics *sing. noun Politics* the study of geographical factors as a basis of the power of nations. It is a combination of political geography and political science, and its considerations include territory, resources, climate, population, social and political culture, and economic activity.

Geordie *colloq.* — *noun* **1** a person from Tyneside. **2** the Tyneside dialect. — *adj.* of or relating to Tyneside, its people, or their dialect. [diminutive of the name *George*]

George I (1660–1727) King of Great Britain and Ireland (1714–27), born in Osnabrück, Hanover, the great-grandson of James I of England. Elector of Hanover since 1698, he had commanded the Imperial forces in the Marlborough wars, and was proclaimed king on the death of Queen Anne. He divorced his wife and cousin, the Princess Dorothea of Zell, imprisoning her in the castle of Ahlde, where she died (1726). He took relatively little part in the government of Britain, for his affections remained with Hanover, where he spent much of his life.

George II (of Great Britain) (1683–1760) King of Great Britain and Ireland (1727–69), and Elector of Hanover, son of George I, born in Herrenhausen, Hanover. He married Caroline of

St George and the Dragon, Stockholm

Ansbach in 1705, and his government policy was formulated at first by Robert Walpole. George fought in the War of the Austrian Succession, and the battle of Dettingen (1743) was the last occasion on which a British sovereign commanded an army in the field. His reign also saw the crushing of Jacobite hopes at the battle of Culloden (1746), the beginning of the Seven Years' War (1756), the foundation of British India after the battle of Plassey (1757), and the capture of Quebec (1759).

George III (1738–1820) King of Great Britain and Ireland (1760–1820), Elector (1760–1815) and King (from 1815) of Hanover, born in London, the eldest son of Frederick Louis, Prince of Wales (1707–51). His father predeceased him, and so he succeeded his grandfather, George II. His eagerness to govern as well as reign caused friction, and he was particularly unpopular in the 1770s when with Lord North he was blamed for the loss of the American colonies. In 1783 he called Pitt (the Younger) to office, thus ending the supremacy of the old Whig families. In 1810 his insanity increased, and his son George, Prince of Wales, was made regent.

George IV (1762–1830) King of the United Kingdom and of Hanover (1820–30), the eldest son of George III, born in London. He became Prince Regent in 1810, because of his father's insanity. He went through a marriage ceremony with Mrs Fitzherbert, a Roman Catholic, but the marriage was not acceptable in English law. In 1795 he married Princess Caroline of Brunswick, whom he tried unsuccessfully to divorce when he became king, causing a scandal in which the people sympathized with the Queen. He was a patron of the arts and encouraged John Nash, who designed the Royal Pavilion in Brighton.

George V (1865–1936) King of the United Kingdom (1910–36), born in London, the second son of Edward VII. In 1893 he married Princess Mary of Teck. He served in the navy, travelled in many parts of the empire, and was created Prince of Wales in 1901. His reign saw the Union of South Africa (1910), World War I (1914–18), the Irish Free State settlement (1922), and the General Strike (1926).

George VI (1895–1952) King of the United Kingdom (1936–52), born at Sandringham, Norfolk, the second son of George V. He served in the Grand Fleet at the battle of Jutland (1916), was created Duke of York in 1920, and married in 1923. He played at Wimbledon in the All-England tennis championships in 1926. After ascending the throne (on the abdication of his elder brother, Edward VIII), during World War II he continued to reside in bomb-damaged Buckingham Palace, visited all theatres of war, and delivered many broadcasts, for which he mastered a speech impediment. His wife Elizabeth (1900–) was born Elizabeth Angela Marguerite Bowes-Lyon at Waldenbury, Hertfordshire. She too paid many wartime visits — to hospitals, civil defence centres, and women's organizations. In her later years, she continued to undertake a demanding programme of royal engagements at home and overseas. They had two children: Princess Elizabeth (later Queen Elizabeth II) and Princess Margaret.

George, St (early 4c AD) patron of chivalry, and guardian saint of England and Portugal. He may have been tortured and put to death (c.303) by Diocletian at Nicomedia, or he may have perished (c.250) at Lydda in Palestine, where his alleged tomb is exhibited. His name became linked with fable, such as the story by the Italian Voragine (1230–98) of his fight with a dragon to rescue a maiden. His feast day is 23 Apr.

George a male first name, popular in Britain since the succession of George I (1714). [from Greek *georgos*, farmer, from *ge*, earth + *ergein*, to work]

George-Brown, George (Alfred) Brown, Baron (1914–85) English Labour politician, born in London. He was an official of

the Transport and General Workers Union before becoming an MP (1945) and Minister of Works (1951). As Opposition spokesman on defence (1958–61), he supported Hugh Gaitskell in opposing unilateral disarmament. As Vice-Chairman and Deputy Leader of the Labour Party (1960–70), he unsuccessfully contested Harold Wilson for party leadership in 1963. As Secretary of State for Economic Affairs (1964–6), he instigated a prices and incomes policy. He was also Foreign Secretary (1966–8), but lost his seat in the 1970 election.

George Cross (ABBREV. **GC**) in the UK, an award instituted in 1940 and named after George VI. It is bestowed on civilians for acts of great heroism or conspicuous bravery, or on members of the armed forces for actions in which purely military honours are not normally granted. Inscribed 'For Gallantry' and hung from a blue ribbon, the award is second only to the Victoria Cross.

George Medal (ABBREV. **GM**) in the UK, an award instituted in 1940 by George VI and named after George I. It is the second highest award which may be bestowed on civilians for acts of bravery. The ribbon is scarlet with five narrow blue stripes.

George Town POP (1989) 13 000, a seaport and the capital of the Cayman Is, W Caribbean Sea. It is situated on Grand Cayman I. George Town is the financial and administrative centre of the island.

George Town, also **Penang**, or **Pinang** POP (1980) 248 000, the chief port in Malaysia and the capital of Penang state. It is situated on the NE coast of Penang island, W Peninsular Malaysia. The city is named after King George III of Great Britain. It has a large Chinese population. NOTABLE FEATURES Fort Cornwallis; St George's Church (oldest Anglican Church in SE Asia).

Georgetown POP (1986e) 150 000, a federal and district capital and a major port in N Guyana, founded in 1781. It is a tidal port, situated at the mouth of the R Demerara, protected by a sea wall and dykes. NOTABLE FEATURES city hall (1887); St George's Cathedral (1892); Guyana House (1852); Law Courts (1878); Botanic Gardens.

georgette *noun* a kind of thin silk material. [named after Georgette de la Plante, French dressmaker]

Georgia, Russian **Gruzinskaya**, or **Gruziya**, Georgian **Sakartvelos Respublika** POP (1991e) 5.5m, a republic in E Europe, occupying central and W Transcaucasia. AREA 69 700sq km/26 900sq mi. It is bounded SE by Azerbaijan, S by Armenia, SW by Turkey, W by the Black Sea, and N by Russia. CAPITAL Tbilisi. CHIEF TOWNS Kutaisi, Rustavi, Batumi, Sukhumi, Poti. TIME ZONE GMT +3. Most of the population are Georgian (70%) with Armenian (6%) and Russian minorities (6%); Christianity is the chief religion. OFFICIAL LANGUAGE Georgian. CURRENCY the rouble. PHYSICAL DESCRIPTION contains the Greater Caucasus in the N and the Lesser Caucasus in the S; chief rivers are the Kura and Rioni; forest covers c.39% of the republic. CLIMATE subtropical, warm and humid in the W; continental in the E with hot summers and cold winters. HISTORY proclaimed a Soviet Socialist

Georgia

Republic in 1921; formed the Transcaucasian Republic with Armenia and Azerbaijan before becoming a constituent republic of the Soviet Union in 1936; suppression of independence riots in 1989; state independence declared in 1991; deposition of the President and suspension of parliament followed unrest between supporters of the President and the National Guard; fighting between the government and provincial separatist movements; a State Council took control in 1992; fighting continues. ECONOMY manganese; coal; iron and steel; oil refining; chemicals; machines; textiles; food processing; tea; fruit; the Kakhetia region is famed for its orchards and wines; economic instability as a result of internal conflicts.

Georgia POP (1990) 6.8m, a state in SE USA, divided into 159 counties. AREA 152 571sq km/ 58 892sq mi. It is known as the 'Empire State of the South' or 'Peach State'. PHYSICAL DESCRIPTION part of the state's E border is the Atlantic Ocean; rivers include the Savannah (the SE border of the state), the Chattahoochee (part of the W border), and the Flint, which join to form the Apalachicola; the Oconee and Ocmulgee rivers join to form the Altamaha; the Blue Ridge Mts rise in the N; the highest point is Mt Brasstown Bald (1 457m); in the S, the low coastal plain is heavily forested; the fertile Piedmont Plateau, the Appalachian Plateau, and Blue Ridge Mts lie in the N. CAPITAL Atlanta. CHIEF TOWNS Columbus, Savannah, Macon. HISTORY discovered by the Spanish, but settled in 1733 as a British colony, named after George II; the last of the original 13 colonies to be founded, and the fourth of the original 13 states (the first Southern state) to ratify the Constitution in 1788; seceded from the Union in 1861; suffered much damage in the Civil War (especially during General Sherman's March to the Sea in 1864); slavery was abolished in 1865; the last state to be readmitted to the Union in 1870. ECONOMY Georgia leads the nation in the production of pulp (many local paper mills in the S); a major cotton textile producer; other leading industrial products are transportation equipment, food products, and chemicals; the state grows nearly half the US crop of peanuts; other agricultural products include tobacco, corn, cotton, poultry, livestock, and soya beans; popular tourist resorts include the Golden Isles (off the Atlantic coast) and Okefenokee Swamp.

Georgian — *adj.* **1** *said of architecture, painting, or furniture* from the reign of King George I, II, III, and IV, 1714–1830. **2** *said of literature* from the reign of King George V, especially 1910–20. **3** of the Asian republic of Georgia, its people, or their language. **4** of the US state of Georgia, or its people. — *noun* **1** a native of Georgia in E Europe, or the official language of Georgia. **2** a native of the US state of Georgia.

Georgian poetry a series of five anthologies of English poetry published (1912–22) during the reign of George V. The verse was more traditional than that of the early Modernists. Poets featured in the series included Rupert Brooke, Walter De La Mare, and Siegfried Sassoon.

Georgics a poem in four books by Virgil (c.30 BC). It presents a philosophical description of rural Italian life.

Georgina a female first name, originating in Scotland in the 18c. [a Latinate derivative of GEORGE]

geosphere *noun* **1** *Geol.* the non-living part of the Earth, including the lithosphere, hydrosphere, and atmosphere. **2** the solid part of the Earth, as opposed to the atmosphere and hydrosphere.

geostationary *adj.* same as GEOSYNCHRONOUS.

geosynchronous *adj. Astron.* denoting the orbit of an artificial satellite at such an altitude (35 900km) that it takes 24 hours to complete a circular path around the Earth (the same time

that it takes the Earth to rotate on its own axis) and therefore appears to remain stationary above a fixed point on the Earth's surface. — Also called *geostationary.*

geotaxis *noun Biol.* a change in the direction of movement of a living organism, usually an animal, in response to the force of gravity. [from GEO- + Greek *taxis*, arrangement]

geothermal *adj. Geol.* relating to or using the internal heat of the Earth.

geothermal energy *technical Geol.* the energy that can be extracted from the internal heat of the Earth, produced as a result of radioactive decay within rocks, and the slow cooling of the planet with time. It is used to generate electricity and provide domestic heating, etc, in certain parts of Italy, Iceland, California, and New Zealand, where volcanos, hot springs, or geysers serve as energy sources.

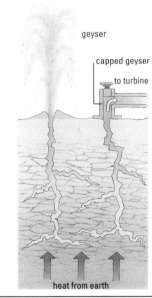

geyser

capped geyser

to turbine

heat from earth

production of geothermal energy

geotropism *noun Bot.* the growth of the roots or shoots of plants in response to gravity. Roots show positive geotropism, ie they grow in the direction of gravity, whereas shoots show negative geotropism, ie they grow in the opposite direction to gravity. [from GEO- + Greek *tropos*, a turning]

Ger. *abbrev.* German.

Gerald a male first name, revived in the 19c. [Norman, from Germanic *gar*, spear + *wald*, rule]

geranium *noun* **1** any cultivated flower of the *Pelargonium* genus, with fragrant leaves and bright red, pink, or white flowers. **2** *Bot.* a shrub or herb of the *Geranium* genus, with seed-pods shaped like a crane's bill. [from Greek *geranos*, crane]

Gerard a male first name. [Norman, from Germanic *gar*, spear + *hard*, brave, hardy]

gerbil *noun* a mouse-like desert animal with long hind legs, native to Africa and Asia. [from Latin *gerbillus*, little jerboa]

geriatric — *adj.* **1** for or dealing with old people. **2** *derog. colloq.* very old. — *noun* an old person.

geriatrician *noun* a specialist in geriatrics.

geriatrics *sing. noun Medicine* the branch of medicine concerned with the care of the elderly, and with the diagnosis and treatment of diseases and disorders associated with ageing. [from Greek *geras*, old age + *iatros*, physician]

Géricault, (Jean Louis André) Théodore (1791–1824) French painter, born in Rouen. A pupil of Guérin, he was an admirer of the 17c Flemish schools. He painted many unorthodox

and realistic scenes, notably *The Raft of the Medusa* (1819, Louvre, Paris), based on a shipwreck which had caused a sensation in France. It was harshly criticized and he left for England, where he painted racing scenes and landscapes.

Gerlachovsky *or* **Gerlachovský Štit**, formerly **Franz Josef-Spitze**, **Stalin Peak** the highest peak in the Carpathian Range and in Slovakia. It forms part of the High Tatra. HEIGHT 2 663m.

germ *noun* **1** an imprecise term for a pathogen, ie any micro-organism, such as a bacterium or virus, that causes disease. **2** formerly used to refer to any living structure that is capable of developing into a complete organism, eg a seed or a fertilized egg. **3** the embryo of a plant, especially wheat. **4** an origin or beginning: *the germ of a plan.* [from Latin *germen*, bud, sprout]

German, Sir Edward, originally **Edward German Jones** (1862–1936) English composer, born in Whitchurch, Shropshire. In 1888 he was appointed musical director of the Globe Theatre, London, and became known for his incidental music to Shakespeare. In 1901 he emerged as a light opera composer, when he completed Sullivan's *The Emerald Isle* after the composer's death. His own works include *Merrie England* (1902), *The Welsh Rhapsody* (1904), several symphonies, orchestral suites, chamber music, and songs.

German — *noun* **1** a native or citizen of Germany. **2** the official language of Germany, Austria, and parts of Switzerland. — *adj.* of Germany, its people, or their language. [from Latin *Germanus*]
◇ German has 95–100 million speakers in Germany, Austria, Switzerland, parts of E Europe, S Africa, and Latin America. The two main varieties arise from geography rather than social status: High German, the standard and literary form, originated in Central and W Germany; Low German originated in the lowlands of N Germany.

german *adj. (following the noun)* **1** having both parents the same: *brother german.* **2** having both grandparents the same on one side of the family: *cousin german.* [from Latin *germanus*, having the same parents]

germane *adj., said of ideas, remarks, etc* relevant; closely related. [see GERMAN]

Germanic — *noun* a branch of the Indo-European family of languages that includes German, English, Dutch, and the Scandinavian languages (see GERMANIC LANGUAGES). — *adj.* **1** of these languages. **2** typical of Germany or the Germans.

Germanic languages the languages, making up a branch of the Indo-European family, with a common ancestry in the language of early N European Germanic tribes. They are classified in three main groups: (1) North Germanic, including the modern Scandinavian languages, and their older forms; (2) West Germanic, including English, Frisian, German, Yiddish, Dutch (with its colonial variant, Afrikaans), and their parent languages, Anglo-Saxon and Old High German; and (3) the East Germanic languages, all of which are extinct, though there are manuscript remains of Gothic. Germanic languages are spoken as a first language by more than 500 million people, mainly because of the world-wide dissemination of English.

Germanicus, in full **Gaius Germanicus Caesar** (15 BC–AD 19) the adopted son of Emperor Tiberius, father of Caligula, brother of Claudius, and husband of Agrippina the Elder. He served as a general under Tiberius, was heir apparent from AD 14, and was appointed governor of the eastern provinces of Rome. His sudden and suspicious death in Antioch marked a turning point in Tiberius's reign, who was suspected of some degree of involvement in it.

germanium *noun Chem.* (SYMBOL **Ge**, ATOMIC NUMBER **32**) a hard greyish-white metalloid element obtained mainly as a by-product of zinc smelting, and widely used as a semiconductor in electronic devices. [from the name *Germany*, the native country of its discoverer, C A Winkler (1838–1904)]

German measles same as RUBELLA.

German shepherd an Alsatian dog.

Germany, German **Deutschland**, official name **Federal Republic of Germany**, German **Bundesrepublik Deutschland** POP (1992e) 80.6m, a central European state formed by the political unification of West Germany and East Germany in 1990, divided into 16 states (*Länder*). AREA 357 868sq km/138 137sq mi. It is bounded E by Poland and the Czech Republic, SE by Austria, SW by Switzerland, W by France, Luxembourg, Belgium, and the Netherlands, and N by the North Sea, Denmark, and the Baltic Sea. Germany also consists of the N and E Frisian Is, Heligoland, and the Sanddüne Is in the North Sea, and the Fehmarn Is in the Baltic Sea. CAPITAL Berlin. CHIEF TOWNS Bonn, Hamburg, Munich, Cologne, Essen, Leipzig, Frankfurt (am Main).

German Words Used in English

angst anxiety; a feeling of anxiety caused by the uncertainties of human existence

anschluss joining together; union, especially the political union of German and Austria in 1938

bildungsroman educational novel; a novel depicting a character's early spiritual and emotional development and education

blitzkrieg lightning war; a sudden strong attack, especially from the air; a period of hard work, etc to get something finished

doppelgänger double goer; a ghostly duplicate of a living person; someone who looks exactly like someone else

dummkopf dumb-head; a blockhead, an idiot

echt real, genuine; authentic, typical

ersatz replacement, substitute; a second-rate or cheaper substitute; substitute, imitation

führer leader, guide; someone who bossily asserts their authority

gastarbeiter guest worker; an immigrant worker, especially one who does menial work

gauleiter district leader; a chief official of a district under the Nazi regime; an overbearing wielder of petty authority

gemütlich amiable, comfortable, cosy

gestalt form, shape; a whole pattern or structure perceived as more than the sum of its parts

gesundheit health; your health, said to someone who has just sneezed

götterdämmerung twilight of the gods; the downfall of any once powerful system

jugendstil youth style; the German term for art nouveau

kaput broken, destroyed

kitsch rubbish; sentimental or vulgar tastelessness in art, design, etc

lebensraum life space; room to live; used by Hitler to justify his acquisition of land for Germany

leitmotiv leading motive; a recurrent theme associated with a particular person or thing in a piece of music, etc

putsch thrust; a sudden attempt to remove a government from power

realpolitik politics of realism; politics based on the practical needs of life, rather than moral or ethical ideas

schadenfreude hurt joy; pleasure in others' misfortunes

übermensch over-person; a superman

weltanschauung world perception; a particular philosophy of life

weltschmerz world pain; sympathy with universal misery; thoroughgoing pessimism

wunderkind wonder-child; a child prodigy, someone who shows great talent and/or achieves great success at an early age

zeitgeist time-spirit; the spirit of the age.

TIME ZONE GMT +1. The population is mainly of Germanic origin; around 5% are European 'guest workers' (*Gastarbeiter*), mainly from Turkey; Christianity is the chief religion. OFFICIAL LANGUAGE German; Sorbian (a Slavic language) is spoken by a few. CURRENCY the Deutschmark. PHYSICAL DESCRIPTION the Baltic coastline is backed by a fertile low-lying plain, low hills, and many glacial lakes; the central uplands include the Rhenish Slate Mts, the Black Forest, the Odenwald and Spessart; the land rises in the S in several ranges, notably the Bavarian Alps (highest peak is the Zugspitze, 2 962m), also the Harz Mts of the Thüringian Forest; major rivers include the Rhine (S–N), Elbe, Ems, Weser, Ruhr, Danube, Oder, and Neisse; a complex canal system links the chief rivers. CLIMATE winters are mild but stormy in the NW; elsewhere, the climate is continental (more temperate in the E); the E and S have lower winter temperatures, with considerable snowfall and some freezing of canals; average winter temperature in the N is 2°C, and in the S it is –3°C; average summer temperature in the N is 16°C, and slightly higher in the S; the average annual rainfall on the plains is 600–700mm, increasing in parts of the Alps to 2 000mm. HISTORY ancient Germanic tribes united in the 8c within the Frankish Empire of Charlemagne; after 918 the monarchy became elective and the third elected king, Otto I, became Emperor of a Holy Roman Empire divided into several hundred states; after the Congress of Vienna (1814–15), a confederation of 39 states existed under the presidency of Austria; under Bismarck, Prussia succeeded Austria as the leading German power; by 1871, Bismarck had achieved the complete union of Germany and the foundation of the Second Reich, with the King of Prussia as hereditary German Emperor; an aggressive foreign policy eventually led to World War I; after the German defeat, the Second Reich was replaced by the democratic Weimar Republic; political power passed to the Nazi Party in the 1920s; Hitler became dictator of the totalitarian Third Reich in 1933; acts of aggression led to World War II, and a second defeat for Germany resulted in the collapse of its political regime; its land area was reduced, and occupied by UK, US, French, and Soviet forces (1945–52); Berlin was partitioned into West and East Berlin, under four occupation zones; after the Berlin Airlift (1948–49), Western occupation of Germany ended with the creation of a Federal Republic of Germany (West Germany) and a socialist German Democratic Republic (East Germany); Western forces continued to occupy West Berlin, which became a province of West Germany; East Germany was governed on the communist Soviet model from 1949; anti-Soviet demonstrations were put down in 1953; both republics were recognized as sovereign states in 1954; West Germany was a founder-member of the EEC (1957); in 1961 the Berlin Wall was built; East Germany was accorded diplomatic recognition and membership of the UN after signing a treaty with West Germany in 1973; movement for democratic reform in East Germany culminated in 1989 with the opening of the Wall and other border crossings to the W; in 1990 free elections led first to economic union with West Germany and then full political unification; since 1991 the country has experienced increasing economic problems and outbreaks of racial violence by the far-right. GOVERNMENT the system of government is built around states (*Länder*) with considerable powers; there is a two-chamber legislature; a President is elected for five years by members of the *Bundesrat* and *Land* parliaments; the Chancellor is elected by the *Bundestag* from the majority party; after political unification in 1990 the five former East German *Länder*, abolished after World War II, were re-established, with the unified Berlin forming a sixth *Land*. ECONOMY a leading industrial nation, following major reconstruction after World War II; in the N and the centre there is substantial heavy indus-

---

try, especially iron and steel (in the Ruhr Valley), coal mining, cement, metal products, chemicals, textiles, machinery, electrical goods, food processing, precision and optical equipment, and vehicles; coal, iron ore, zinc, lead, and potash are mined; agriculture includes arable and livestock farming, fruit, wheat, barley, potatoes, sugar beet, and forestry; the Rhine and Mosel valleys are major wine-producing areas; tourism is increasing, especially in the S.

germ cell *Biol.* a gamete, usually a sperm or ovum (egg cell).

Germer, Lester Halbert (1896–1971) US physicist, born in Chicago, Illinois. While on the research staff of the Western Electric Co, he observed with Clinton Davisson the diffraction of electrons (1927), confirming that particles may exhibit wave-like behaviour.

germicidal *adj.* that kills germs.

germicide *noun* a substance that kills germs.

Germinal a novel by Emile Zola (1885). One of the *Rougon-Macquart* novels, it is set in a mining community and focuses primarily on the fortunes of Etienne Lantier.

germinal *adj.* **1** *technical* of or relating to germs. **2** in the earliest stage of development. [from Latin *germen*, bud, sprout]

germinate *verb trans., intrans.* **1** *Bot., said of a seed or spore* to show the first signs of development into a new individual. **2** to cause an idea to begin to grow. [from Latin *germinare*]

germination *noun Bot.* the first stages in the development of an embryo into a seedling, involving the emergence of the radicle (embryonic root) and plumule (embryonic shoot) from the seed. It is usually triggered by the presence of sufficient moisture and oxygen, and a suitable temperature.

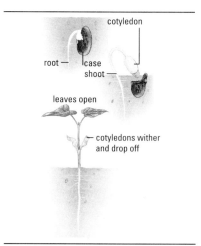

germinating seed

germ layer *Biol.* in a multicellular animal that has two or more layers of body tissue, any of the three embryonic layers of cells, ie the ectoderm, mesoderm, or endoderm.

germ warfare the use of germs to inflict disease on an enemy in war.

Geronimo, Apache name **Goyathlay** (1829–1909) Chiricahua Apache leader, born in Mexico. The best-known of all Apaches, he forcibly resisted the internment of his people on a reservation, and escaped from white control on several occasions. In later life he became a Christian and a figure in public spectacles, including President Theodore Roosevelt's inauguration parade.

gerontological *adj.* relating to gerontology.

gerontologist *noun* a person who studies or is an expert on gerontology.

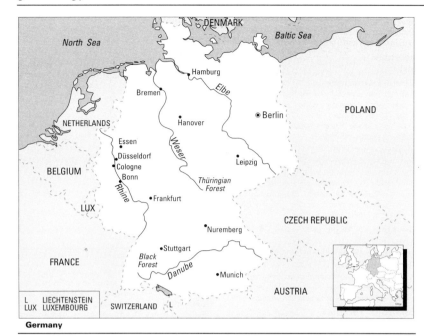

Germany

---

gerontology *noun* the scientific study of old age, the ageing process and the problems of elderly people. [from Greek *geron*, old man + -LOGY]

gerrymander *derog.* — *verb* (**gerrymandered, gerrymandering**) to arrange or change the boundaries of (an electoral constituency) so as to favour one political party. — *noun* a constituency arranged in such a way. [named after Massachusetts Governor Elbridge Gerry (1744–1814) and SALAMANDER, from the shape on the map of one of his electoral districts after manipulation]

gerrymandering *noun* the act or process of arranging the boundaries of one or more electoral constituencies to favour one political party.

Gershwin, George (1898–1937) US composer, born in New York City. Having published his first song aged 14, he became famous as a composer of Broadway musicals, often in collaboration with his lyricist brother Ira (1896–1983). Their numerous classic songs include 'Lady Be Good' (1924) and 'I Got Rhythm' (1930). He also composed extended concert works such as *Rhapsody in Blue* (1924), *An American in Paris* (1928), and the opera *Porgy and Bess* (1935), importing jazz, blues, and pop-song devices into European classical contexts.

Gertrude the mother of Hamlet, widow of old Hamlet, and wife to his murderer, Claudius, in Shakespeare's *Hamlet*, who is torn between her love for her son and her husband.

gerund *noun Grammar* a noun formed from a verb, in English ending in -ing, and describing an action, eg 'the *baking* of bread' and '*Smoking* damages your health.'. [from Latin *gerundium*, from *gerere*, to bear]

Gesamtkunstwerk *noun* a term denoting the totality of art. It was applied by Wagner to his operatic productions, in which music was combined with costume and visual effects to create a complete unified work. The idea has roots in early 19c German Romanticism, and is analogous with the modern concept of 'total theatre'. [from German, = total art work]

gesso *noun* plaster used as a medium for sculpture or as a surface for painting. [from Italian *gesso*, from Latin *gypsum*; see GYPSUM]

◇ In tempera painting, a white ground is applied to wooden panels or to canvas to prepare the surface for the paint. For wood, gesso is made by mixing whiting, size, and zinc white powder; for canvas, linseed oil is added to this mixture to prevent cracking.

Gestalt psychology *Psychol.* a school of psychology based on the concept that the whole is greater than the sum of its parts.

Gestalt therapy *Psychol.* a form of psychotherapy, derived from Gestalt psychology, which aims to make people 'whole' by increasing their awareness of aspects of their personality which have been denied or disowned. It is usually conducted in groups, and conflicts are acted out, as are the thoughts and feelings given to images in dreams.

Gestapo the political police of the German Third Reich, founded by Göring in 1933 on the basis of the Prussian political police. It extended throughout Germany, and from 1936 was under the control of Himmler, as head of the SS. [a contraction of German *Geheime Staatspolizei*, secret state police]

gestate *verb trans., intrans.* **1** *Zool.*, *said of a viviparous mammal* to carry or be carried in the uterus (womb), and to undergo physical development, during the period between fertilization and birth. In humans the gestation period corresponds to the duration of pregnancy (266 days on average). **2** to develop (an idea, etc) slowly in the mind. [from Latin *gestare*, to carry]

gestation *noun* the process or time of gestating.

gesticulate *verb* **1** *intrans.* to make (bold) gestures, especially when speaking. **2** *trans.* to express in this way. [from Latin *gesticulare*, from *gestus*, gesture]

gesticulation *noun* **1** the act of gesticulating. **2** the use of gestures.

gestural *adj.* **1** relating to or involving gestures. **2** by or using gestures.

gesture — *noun* **1** a movement of a part of the body as an expression of meaning, especially when speaking. **2** something done to communicate (especially friendly) feelings or intentions. **3** *derog.* something done simply as a formality: *asking our opinion was merely a gesture.* — *verb* **1** *intrans.* to make gestures. **2** *trans.* to express with gestures. [from Latin *gestus*]

get — *verb* (**getting**; PAST TENSE AND PAST PARTICIPLE **got**) **1** to receive or obtain. **2** to have or possess. **3** (**get across**, *or* **get someone across, away, to, through**, *etc*) to go or cause them to go, move, travel, or arrive as specified: *tried to get past him / will you get him to bed at 8? / got to Paris on Friday.* **4** (**get something down, in, out**, *etc*) to fetch, take, or bring it as specified: *get it down from the shelf.* **5** to put into a particular state or condition: *don't get it wet / got him into trouble.* **6** *intrans.* to become: *got angry.* **7** to catch (a disease, etc). **8** to order or persuade: *get him to help us.* **9** *colloq.*

to receive (a broadcast, etc): *unable to get the World Service.* **10** *colloq.* to make contact with, especially by telephone: *never get him at home.* **11** *colloq.* to arrive at by calculation. **12** *intrans.* (**get to do something**) *colloq.* to receive permission to do it: *can you get to stay out late?* **13** *colloq.* to prepare (a meal). **14** *colloq.* to buy or pay for: *got her some flowers for her birthday.* **15** *colloq.* to suffer: *got a broken arm.* **16** *colloq.* to receive as punishment: *got ten years for armed robbery.* **17** *colloq.* (**get someone** *or* **get someone back**) to attack, punish, or otherwise cause harm to: *I'll get you back for that!* **18** *trans., intrans. colloq.* (**get to someone**) to annoy them: *you shouldn't let him get to you.* **19** *colloq.* to understand. **20** *colloq.* to hear: *I didn't quite get his name.* **21** *colloq.* to affect emotionally. **22** *colloq.* to baffle: *you've got me there.* — *noun derog. slang* a stupid or contemptible person; a git.
— **be getting on for** ... *colloq.* to approach a certain time or age.

get about *or* **around** *colloq.* **1** to travel; to go from place to place. **2** *said of a rumour, etc* to circulate.

get something across to make it understood.

get along with someone *colloq.* to be on friendly terms with them.

get at something 1 to reach or take hold of it. **2** *colloq.* to suggest or imply it: *what are you getting at?*

get at someone *colloq.* **1** to criticize or victimize them persistently. **2** *colloq.* to influence them by dishonest means, eg bribery.

get away 1 to leave, or be free to leave. **2** to escape. **3** *colloq., as an exclamation* an expression of disbelief.

get away with something to commit an offence or wrongdoing without being caught or punished.

get back at someone *colloq.* to take revenge on them.

get by 1 *colloq.* to manage to live. **2** *colloq.* to be acceptable.

get someone down *colloq.* to make them sad or depressed.

get something down 1 to manage to swallow it. **2** to write it down.

get down to something to apply oneself to a task or piece of work.

get in 1 *said of a political party* to be elected to power. **2** to be accepted for entry or membership.

get something in 1 to gather or harvest it. **2** *colloq.* to succeed in doing or making it before something else occurs: *tried to get some work in before dinner.*

get in on something *colloq.* to take part in it or share in it.

get into something *colloq.* to develop a liking or enthusiasm for.

have got into someone *colloq.* to affect their behaviour: *what's got into him?*

get in with someone *colloq.* to become friendly with them, often for selfish reasons.

get it *slang* to be punished.

get it together *colloq.* to use one's energies and abilities effectively.

get nowhere *colloq.* to make no progress, or produce no results.

get off *or* **get someone off** *colloq.* to escape or cause to escape with no punishment, or with the stated punishment: *was charged but got off / managed to get him off with a warning.*

get off something *colloq.* to stop discussing it or dealing with it: *let's get off this subject.*

get off on something *colloq.* to get excitement from it.

get off with someone *colloq.* to begin a casual sexual relationship with them.

get on *colloq.* **1** to make progress or be successful. **2** *said of a person* to grow old. **3** *said of time, etc* to grow late.

get on at someone *colloq.* to pester or criticize them continually.

get on to someone to make contact with them; to begin dealing with them.

get on with someone to have a friendly relationship with them.

get on with something to continue working on it or dealing with it.

get out *said of information* to become known.

get something out to manage to say, usually with difficulty.

get out of something to avoid having to do it.

get over someone to be no longer emotionally affected by them.

get over something to recover from an illness, disappointment, etc.

get something over to explain it successfully; to make it understood.

get something over with to deal with something unpleasant as quickly as possible.

get one's own back *colloq.* to have one's revenge.

get round *colloq., said of information, a rumour, etc* to become generally known.

get round someone *colloq.* to persuade them, or win their approval or permission.

get round something to successfully pass by or negotiate a problem, etc.

get round to something *or* **someone** to deal with them eventually.

get somewhere *colloq.* to make progress.

get there *colloq.* to make progress towards, or achieve, one's final aim.

get through something 1 to complete a task, piece of work, etc. **2** to use it steadily until it is finished: *managed to get through a pound of butter in a day.* **3** *colloq.* to pass a test or examination.

get through to someone 1 to make contact with them by telephone. **2** to make them understand something: *we can't get through to him how important this is.*

get up 1 to get out of bed. **2** *said of the wind, etc* to become strong.

get someone up to make them get out of bed.

get something up to arrange, organize, or prepare it: *decided to get up a celebration.*

get up speed to increase and maintain a speed.

get up to something *colloq.* to do or be involved in something bad or unwelcome.

[from Norse *geta*, to obtain or beget]

get-at-able *adj. colloq.* able to be easily reached.

getaway an escape, especially after committing a crime.

Gethsemane a place outside Jerusalem near the Mount of Olives (described as a 'garden' in John 18.1) where Jesus prayed immediately before his betrayal and arrest (Mark 14), and agonized over whether to obey God and be sacrificed for the sins of the world.

get-together *noun colloq.* an informal meeting.

Getty, J(ean) Paul (1892–1976) US oil executive, multi-millionaire, and art collector, born in Minneapolis. He entered the oil business and made a quarter of a million dollars in his first two years. He merged his father's legacy ($15 million) with his own finances, and went on to control more than 100 companies. He founded the J Paul Getty Museum in Malibu, California, in 1954.

Gettysburg, Battle of a series of engagements (Jun–Jul 1863) that marked the turning-point in the American Civil War, fought between the army of N Virginia (Confederate) and the army of the Potomac (Union), after Robert E Lee, the Southern commander, decided to take the war into the north. The battle (1–3 Jul) was a Union victory and ended any prospect of foreign recognition for the Confederacy.

Gettysburg Address a speech given (19 Nov 1863) by President Lincoln during the American Civil War, at the dedication of a war cemetery in Pennsylvania on the site of the battle of Gettysburg. Ill-regarded at the time, it is now thought of as one of the masterpieces of US oratory.

get-up *noun colloq.* outfit or clothes, especially when considered strange or remarkable.

get-up-and-go *noun colloq.* energy.

geum *noun Bot.* a perennial plant with lobed leaves and brilliant yellow, orange, or scarlet flowers on slender stalks, often grown in rock gardens. [from Latin *geum*]

gewgaw *noun old derog. use* a brightly-coloured trinket.

Gewürztraminer *noun* **1** a variety of white grape grown especially in the Alsace region. **2** a medium-dry aromatic wine made from this grape. [from German, from *Gewürz* spice, and *Traminer* a grape variety (after *Tramin*, a wine-growing region in S Tyrol)]

geyser *noun* **1** *Geol.* in an area of volcanic activity, a type of hot spring that intermittently spouts hot water and steam into the air. In some parts of the world, eg California, geysers are used as a source of geothermal energy. **2** a domestic appliance for heating water rapidly. [from Icelandic *geysa*, from Norse *gøysa*, to gush]

Geysir a hot spring in Süurland, W Iceland, 30km/19mi NE of Laugarvatn. It is capable of sending up water columns of 40–60m.

Gezhouba Dam a dam on the R Yangtze, central China. It is situated near Yichang, at the mouth of the Yangtze Gorges. The dam is the largest water control project in the world.

Ggantija Temples a Copper Age temple complex on Gozo, NW Malta. The two well-preserved temples, built in 3600–3300 BC, were excavated in 1827. It is a World Heritage site.

Ghadamès an oasis town in NW Libya, formerly the Roman stronghold Cydamus. It is a World Heritage site.

Ghaghara *or* **Gogra** a river in W China, Nepal, and N India. It rises in the Himalayas in SW Tibet, China; then flows SE through Nepal as the R Karnali, where it is joined by the R Seti. Continuing SE, it cuts through the Siwalik Range of mountains and enters the Bihar state of India where it joins the R Ganges below Chhapra. The river is 1 030km/640mi long.

Ghana, official name **Republic of Ghana** POP (1992e) 16m, a republic in W Africa, divided into nine administrative regions. AREA 238 686sq km/ 92 133sq mi. The republic is bounded W by the Ivory Coast, N by Burkina, E by Togo, and S by the Gulf of Guinea. CAPITAL Accra. CHIEF TOWNS Sekondi-Takoradi, Kumasi, Tamale. TIME ZONE

Lincoln's Address at Gettysburg

Fourscore and seven years ago our fathers brought forth on this continent a new nation, conceived in liberty and dedicated to the proposition that all men are created equal.

Now we are engaged in a great civil war, testing whether that nation or any nation so conceived and so dedicated can long endure. We are met on a great battle field of that war. We have come to dedicate a portion of that field, as a final resting-place for those who here gave their lives that that nation might live. It is altogether fitting and proper that we should do this.

But, in a larger sense, we can not dedicate – we can not consecrate – we can not hallow – this ground. The brave men, living and dead, who struggled here, have consecrated it, far above our poor power to add or detract. The world will little note, nor long remember, what we say here, but it can never forget what they did here. It is for us the living, rather, to be dedicated here to the unfinished work which they who fought here have thus far so nobly advanced. It is rather for us to be here dedicated to the great task remaining before us – that from these honored dead we take increased devotion to that cause for which they gave the last full measure of devotion – that we here highly resolve that these dead shall not have died in vain – that this nation, under God, shall have a new birth of freedom – and that government of the people, by the people, for the people, shall not perish from the earth.

Ghana

GMT. There are c.75 tribal groups including Akan (44%), Mole-Dagbani (16%), Ewe (13%), and Ga (8%); Christianity, local beliefs, and Islam are the main religions. OFFICIAL LANGUAGE English; several African languages are also spoken. CURRENCY the cedi. PHYSICAL DESCRIPTION coastline of sand bars and lagoons; low-lying plains inland, leading to the Ashanti plateau in the W and the R Volta basin in the E, dammed to form L Volta; mountains rise in the E to 885m at Afadjado. CLIMATE tropical climate, including a warm, dry coastal belt in the SE, a hot, humid SW corner, and hot, dry savannah in the N; Kumasi has an average annual rainfall of 1 400mm. HISTORY discovered by Europeans in the 15c; centre of the slave trade in the 18c; modern state created by the union of two former British territories, British Gold Coast (Crown Colony in 1874) and British Togoland in 1957; became an independent republic within the Commonwealth in 1960; it was the first British colony in Africa to achieve independence; a multiparty constitution was approved in 1992. ECONOMY mainly agricultural; commercial reserves of oil, diamonds, gold, manganese, bauxite, wood; cocoa (world's leading producer) provides two thirds of export revenue; tobacco, rubber, cotton, peppers, pineapples, avocados, ginger; mining, lumbering, aluminium, light manufacturing, fishing. There are 40 forts and castles built along the coast dating from the late 15c onwards that have been designated World Heritage monuments.

Ghana, Kingdom of an African kingdom in the W Sudan which may have originated as early as the 5c–6c. Probably named after the title of its king (*ghana*), it bears no geographical relationship to the modern state, which lies further to the south and east. It flourished in the 8c–11c as one of a series of states between the savannah and the desert which controlled the trade of the Sahara. Its capital was sacked by the Almoravids in c.1076 and its power broken, though it remained until the 13c.

gharial *or* **gavial** *noun Zool.* a large narrow-snouted crocodile found in parts of N India. It can grow to over 6m long, and seizes fish and frogs by rapid sideways movements of its slender snout. Although considered sacred by the Hindus, it is now an endangered species. [from Hindi *ghariyal*, crocodile]

ghastliness *noun* being ghastly.

ghastly — *adj.* (**ghastlier**, **ghastliest**) **1** extremely frightening; hideous; horrific. **2** *colloq.* very bad. **3** *colloq.* very ill. — *adv. colloq.* extremely; unhealthily: *ghastly pale.* [from Middle English *gasten*, to terrify]

ghat *noun India and Pakistan* **1** a mountain pass. **2** a set of steps leading down to a river. [from Hindi *ghat*, descent]

Ghats two mountain ranges in India. The Eastern Ghats runs parallel to the Bay of Bengal, forming the E edge of the Deccan Plateau. It is made up of a series of disconnected hill ranges; Doda Betta in the Nilgiri Hills reaches 2 636m. The Western Ghats runs parallel to the Arabian Sea, forming the W boundary of the Deccan plateau. The plateau is joined to the Eastern Ghats in the Nilgiri Hills. The highest point is Anai Mudi Peak (2 695m) in the Cardamon Hills.

ghee noun butter made from cow's or buffalo's milk, purified by heating, used in Indian cooking. [from Hindi *ghi*]

Ghent, Flemish **Gent**, French **Gand** POP (1992e) 230 000, the river-port capital of East Flanders province, NW Belgium, situated at the confluence of the Scheldt and Leie rivers. The second largest port in Belgium, it is also the country's third largest urban region (with 5 suburbs). The main industrial area lies to the N of the old medieval city. Several canals connect the harbour to the North Sea and the Ghent-Terneuzen Canal. NOTABLE FEATURES Cathedral of St Bavon (begun in the 10c); town hall (15c–17c); House of Free Boatmen (1531); Abbey of St Bavon (642); castle of Gravensteen (1180–1200).

Ghent, Treaty of the treaty (1814) between the USA and Britain which ended the War of 1812, though it resolved none of the issues (eg maritime rights and military control of the Great Lakes) from which the conflict had grown.

gherkin noun a small variety of cucumber, usually pickled. [from Dutch *augurkje*]

ghetto noun (PL. **ghettos**, **ghettoes**) **1** derog. a poor area densely populated by people from a deprived social group, especially a racial minority. **2** Hist. a part of a European city to which Jews were formerly restricted. [perhaps from Italian *ghetto*, foundry, after one on the site of the first Jewish ghetto, in Venice]

giant panda

ghetto-blaster noun colloq. a large portable radio-cassette recorder, especially one playing pop music at high volume.

Ghibellines the pro-imperial party in 13c–14c Italian cities, which favoured the involvement of the Holy Roman Emperor in Italian politics, even after the decline of the Hohenstaufen state from 1266. It supported the invasion of the Holy Roman Emperor Henry VII (c.1270–1313) in 1308, although the power and status of the empire had much diminished by that date.

Ghiberti, Lorenzo (1378–1455) Italian goldsmith, bronze-caster, and sculptor, born in Florence. In 1401 he won the competition to make a pair of bronze gates for the baptistery in Florence Cathedral. When these were completed (1424), he worked on a further pair of gates, (1425–52), which were dubbed *The Gates of Paradise* by Michelangelo.

ghost — noun **1** the spirit of a dead person when visible in some form to a living person. **2** a suggestion, hint, or trace. **3** a faint shadow attached to the image on a television screen. — verb intrans., trans. to be a ghost writer for (someone), or of (some written work).
— **give up the ghost** colloq. to die.
[from Anglo-Saxon *gast*]

ghostly adj. **1** like a ghost or ghosts. **2** relating to or suggesting the presence of ghosts.

ghost town a deserted town, especially one formerly thriving.

ghost writer a person who writes books, speeches, etc on behalf of another person who is credited as their author.

ghoul noun **1** in Arab mythology, a demon that robs graves and eats dead bodies. **2** a person interested in morbid or disgusting things. [from Arabic *ghul*]

ghoulish adj. like or typical of a ghoul.

GHQ abbrev. General Headquarters.

ghyll same as GILL³.

GI noun (PL. **GIs**) colloq. a soldier in the US army, especially during World War II. [from Government Issue]

Giacometti, Alberto (1901–66) Swiss sculptor and painter, born in Stampa. He worked mainly in Paris, and joined the Surrealists in 1930. He produced many abstract constructions of a symbolic kind, and arrived finally at his characteristic 'thin man' bronzes. These long spidery statuettes include *Pointing Man* (1947, Tate, London).

giant — noun **1** in fairy stories, a huge, extremely strong, often cruel creature of human form. **2** colloq. an unusually large person or animal. **3** a person, group, etc of exceptional ability or importance: *literary giants*. — adj. **1** colloq. huge: *giant portions*. **2** of a particularly large species, in implied contrast to smaller ones: *giant tortoise*. [from Greek *gigas*]

giantess noun a female giant.

giant-killer noun colloq. a person or team that unexpectedly defeats a superior opponent.

giant panda a large bear-like mammal (*Ailuropoda melanoleuca*), about 1.8m in height, and having thick white fur, with black legs, shoulders, ears, and patches round the eyes.
◇ The giant panda is found in dense bamboo forests on the mountains of E Tibet and SW China, where it feeds on plant material such as bamboo shoots, grasses, gentians, irises, and crocuses, together with a few small rodents, and fish. The giant panda is a solitary animal, and its habitat is inaccessible, so that little is known of its habits. An endangered species, with a low success rate for breeding in captivity, it is now strictly protected, and has been adopted as the symbol of the World Wide Fund for Nature.

Giant's Causeway a volcanic basalt formation on the N coast of Co Antrim, Northern Ireland, 11km/7mi NE of Portrush. The natural 'pavement' consisting of the tops of thousands of small hexagonal basaltic columns (diameter 38–50cm) projects into the North Channel; it was formed from the cooling of a volcanic flow. A ship from the Spanish Armada was wrecked here in Spanish Bay in 1588. According to legend, the causeway, designated a World Heritage site, was built for giants to travel across to Scotland.

giant star Astron. a highly luminous star that is much larger than the Sun, and is reaching the end of its life. Giant stars lie above the main sequence on the right-hand side of the Hertzsprung-Russell diagram.

Giauque, William Francis (1895–1982) Canadian–US physical chemist, born in Niagara Falls, Ontario. Professor at the University of California, Berkeley, he took part in the discovery of the existence of isotopes of oxygen, and later developed a magnetic method for the production of very low temperatures. He was awarded the 1949 Nobel Prize for Chemistry.

gibber verb intrans. (**gibbered**, **gibbering**) **1** to talk so fast that one can not be understood. **2** derog. to talk foolishly. [imitative]

gibberellin noun Bot. any of a group of plant hormones that stimulate rapid growth by the elongation of cells as opposed to cell division. They also promote fruit and seed formation, and delay ageing in leaves. [from a fungus genus-name *Gibberella*, from Latin *gibber*, hump]

gibbering adj. that gibbers.

gibberish noun **1** fast unintelligible talk. **2** foolish talk; nonsense.

gibbet — noun Hist. **1** a gallows-like frame on which the bodies of executed criminals were hung as a public warning. **2** a gallows. — verb (**gibbeted**, **gibbeting**) **1** Hist. to hang on a gibbet. **2** to expose to public ridicule. [from French *gibet*, gallows]

Gibbon, Edward (1737–94) English historian, born in Putney, Surrey. A visit to Rome in 1764 resulted in plans for his major work, *The History of the Decline and Fall of the Roman Empire* (6 vols, 1776–88). Left money by his father, he settled in London for the task (1772), entered parliament (1774), and was made Commissioner of Trade and Plantations by Lord North. After completing his *History*, he spent much of the rest of his life with Lord Sheffield, who published his *Miscellaneous Works* (1796).

Gibbon, Lewis Grassic, pseudonym of **James Leslie Mitchell** (1901–35) Scottish novelist, born in Auchterless, Aberdeenshire. He worked as a journalist in Aberdeen, and served in the RAF until 1929. He published the historical novels *Three Go Back* (1932) and *Spartacus* (1933) under his own name, but adopted his pseudonym for his three best-known novels *Sunset Song* (1932), *Cloud Howe* (1933), and *Grey Granite* (1934), which form the trilogy *A Scots Quair*.

gibbon noun the smallest of the apes, and the only one to walk upright habitually, found in SE Asia. It feeds mainly on fruit, and swings through tree branches at great speed using its very long arms. Gibbons live in small groups, often consisting of a pair which mate for life, and up to four offspring. [from French *gibbon*]

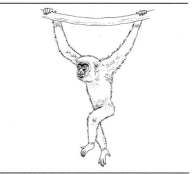

gibbon

Gibbons, Orlando (1583–1625) English composer, born in Oxford. In c.1615 he was appointed organist of the Chapel Royal, London, and then of Westminster Abbey (1623). His compositions include services, anthems, and madrigals (notably *The Silver Swan*), and also hymns, fantasies for viols, and music for virginals.

Gibbons, Stella (Dorothea) (1902–89) English writer, born in London. She worked as a journalist, and later wrote novels, poetry, and short stories. Her best-known work is the satirical novel *Cold Comfort Farm* (1933).

gibbous adj. technical **1** said of the moon or a planet not fully illuminated but more than half illuminated. **2** humpbacked. **3** swollen; bulging. [from Latin *gibbus*, hump]

Gibbs, Josiah Willard (1839–1903) US theoretical physicist, born in New Haven, Connecticut. Professor at Yale, he made important contributions to the study of thermodynamics, emphasizing the fundamental nature of the 'entropy' of a system (a measure of its disorder), and providing powerful methods for analysing the thermodynamic properties of substances. He introduced a concept of 'chemical potential', foundational for the field of physical chemistry.

gibe *or* **jibe** — *verb intrans.* to mock, scoff, or jeer. — *noun* a jeer. [from Old French *giber*, to treat roughly]

giblets *pl. noun* the heart, liver, and other edible internal organs of a chicken or other fowl. [from Old French *gibelet*, game stew, from *gibier*, game]

Gibraltar, Arabic **Jebel Tariq** POP (1991e) 31 000, a British Colony, located on a narrow rocky peninsula rising steeply from the low-lying coast of SW Spain. AREA 5.9sq km/2.3sq mi; length c.5km/3mi; width 1.2km/0.8mi, narrowing to the S. It lies at the E end of the Strait of Gibraltar and is 8km/5mi from Algeciras in Spain. Gibraltar is the gateway between the Atlantic Ocean and the Mediterranean Sea, and it is an important strategic point of control for the W Mediterranean. It is a military base, with NATO underground headquarters. TIME ZONE GMT +1. OFFICIAL LANGUAGE English; Spanish is widely spoken. Most of the population are Gibraltarians; around 17% are British. CURRENCY the British pound; the Gibraltar government also issues its own banknotes. PHYSICAL DESCRIPTION largely comprises a limestone massif, known as 'The Rock' (426m), connected to the Spanish mainland by a sandy plain; its top is a sharp ridge; the steep N side is inaccessible, as is the whole upper length of the E face; the S half of the Rock slopes down to cliffs 30m high at Europa Point; there are extensive limestone caves. CLIMATE typically Mediterranean, with dry summers; winters are wetter than S Spain due to exposure to Atlantic storms. HISTORY settled by Moors in 711, it was taken by Spain in 1462; ceded to Britain in 1713, and became a Crown Colony in 1830; played a key role in Allied naval operations during both World Wars; a proposal to end British rule was defeated by referendum in 1967; Spain closed its frontier to Gibraltar from 1969 to 1985; it continues to claim sovereignty. GOVERNMENT the British monarch is represented by a Governor, and an 18-member House of Assembly. ECONOMY largely dependent on the presence of British forces; the Royal Naval Dockyard was converted to a commercial yard in 1985; transshipment trade and fuel supplies to shipping; tourism. NOTABLE FEATURES Moorish Castle; Upper and Lower St Michael's Cave, Cathedral Cave. Gibraltar is home to the Barbary apes, the only native monkeys in Europe. [from Arab *Jebel Tariq*, the mountain of Tariq]

Gibraltar, Strait of, Arabic **Bab al Zakak**, Latin **Fretum Herculeum** a channel connecting the Mediterranean Sea to the Atlantic Ocean, length 60km/37mi. Its width range is 15–40km/9–25mi; between the Rock of Gibraltar and the Jebel Musa at Ceuta (the 'Pillars of Hercules') its width is 24km/15mi. The constant current flowing E balances evaporation from the Mediterranean Sea; the strait would otherwise become a gradually shrinking salt lake.

Gibson, Sir Alexander (Drummond) (1926–) Scottish conductor, born in Motherwell, Strathclyde. He joined Sadler's Wells Opera and became the company's youngest musical director (1957). He then returned to Scotland as the first principal conductor and artistic director of the Scottish National Orchestra (1959–84), and helped to form Scottish Opera in 1962.

Gibson, Guy (Penrose) (1918–44) British wing commander in the RAF. He led the famous 'Dambusters' raid on the Möhne and Eder Dams in 1943, an exploit for which he received the VC (Victoria Cross).

Gibson, Mel (1956–) US–Australian film actor, born in Peekskill, New York. He emigrated

to Australia in 1968 and made his film début in *Summer City* (1977), but it was *Mad Max* (1979) that brought him international recognition. Later films include *Lethal Weapon* (1989) and its sequels, *Hamlet* (1990), and *The Man Without a Face* (1993), which was also his first film as director.

Gibson, Mike, properly (**Cameron**) **Michael** (**Henderson**) (1942–) Northern Irish rugby player, born in Belfast. He played as centre and outside half with Cambridge University and the British Lions, and appeared a world record 69 times for his country (the most for any International Board nation). He toured with the British Lions in 1966, 1968, and 1971, and made 12 international appearances.

Gibson Desert the name of the central belt of the Western Australian Desert. AREA c.220 000sq km/85 000sq mi. It consists of sand dunes, scrub, and salt marshes. The desert includes the salt lakes L Disappointment and L Auld. The Rudall R National Park is also contained within its territory.

giddily *adv.* in a giddy way.

giddiness *noun* being giddy.

giddy *adj.* (**giddier**, **giddiest**) 1 suffering an unbalancing spinning sensation. 2 causing such a sensation. 3 *literary* overwhelmed by feelings of excitement or pleasure. 4 light-hearted and care-free; frivolous. [from Anglo-Saxon *gidig*, insane]

Gide, André (Paul Guillaume) (1869–1951) French writer, born in Paris. He wrote over 50 volumes of fiction, poetry, plays, criticism, biography, belles-lettres, and translations. Among his best-known works are *Les Nourritures terrestres* (Fruits of the Earth, 1897) and *Les Faux Monnayeurs* (The Counterfeiters, 1926), his translations of *Oedipus* and *Hamlet*, and his *Journal*. He was awarded the Nobel Prize for Literature in 1947.

Gideon 1 the Israelite of the Old Testament who delivered his people from the Midianites. 2 a male first name. [from Hebrew, = one who cuts down]

Gideons International an international organization, which began (1898) in Wisconsin, with the aim of spreading the Christian faith by the free distribution of copies of the Bible to public places (eg hotel rooms, hospitals, and military bases).

Gielgud, Sir (Arthur) John (1904–) English actor and producer, born in London. He made his London début in 1921, and established a reputation as Hamlet (1929) and in *The Good Companions* (1931), becoming a leading Shakespearean actor, and directing many of the Shakespeare Memorial Theatre productions. His film appearances include Disraeli in *The Prime Minister* (1940), and *Arthur* (1970), for which he received an Academy Award.

Giffard, Henri (1825–82) French engineer and inventor, born in Paris. In 1852 he built a light three horsepower steam engine, fitted it with a 3m propeller and succeeded in piloting a balloon, steered by a rudder, over a distance of 27km/17mi. This can be considered as the first powered and controlled flight ever achieved. In 1858 he patented a steam injector which became widely used in locomotives and other types of steam engine.

gift — *noun* 1 something given; a present. 2 a natural ability. 3 the act of giving: *the gift of a book.* 4 *colloq.* something easily obtained, or made easily available. — *verb formal* to give (something) as a present to (someone).

— **in someone's gift** *formal* able to be given away by someone if they wish.

look a gift-horse in the mouth to find fault with a gift or unexpected opportunity. [from Norse *gipt*]

gifted *adj.* having a great natural ability.

giftedness *noun* exceptional cleverness or ability. In children, giftedness is often defined as exceptional natural ability in a particular subject or area, such as music, art, or mathematics; or, more generally, as high intelligence.

gift tax a tax formerly levied in the UK on gifts having a substantial value. Capital transfer tax was in part a gift tax, the aim being to stop the practice of transferring property during a person's lifetime and thereby avoiding death duties. In the USA, the tax is levied on the value of property given away (payable by the donor).

gift-wrap *verb* (**gift-wrapped**, **gift-wrapping**) to wrap attractively, especially for presentation as a gift.

gig¹ *noun* 1 *Hist.* a small open two-wheeled horse-drawn carriage. 2 a small rowing boat carried on a ship. 3 a long lightweight rowing boat used for racing. [from Middle English *gigge*, whirling thing]

gig² *colloq.* — *noun* 1 a pop concert. 2 a musician's booking to play, especially for one night only. — *verb* (**gigged**, **gigging**) to play a gig or gigs.

giga- *prefix* 1 ten to the power of nine (10^9): *gigavolt.* 2 *Comput.* two to the power of thirty (2^{30}): *gigabyte.* [from Greek *gigas*, giant]

Gigantes in Greek mythology, the giant sons of Uranus and Gaea, with snake-like legs. They made war on the Olympian gods, were defeated, and are buried under various volcanic islands. The Gigantomachy ('war of the giants') was the subject of large-scale sculpture, as at Pergamum.

gigantic *adj.* huge; enormous. [from Greek *gigantikos*, from *gigas*, giant]

gigantically *adv.* hugely, enormously.

giggle — *verb intrans.* to laugh quietly in short bursts or in a nervous or silly way. — *noun* 1 such a laugh. 2 (**the giggles**) a fit of giggling. 3 *colloq.* a funny person, situation, or activity. [imitative]

giggly *adj.* (**gigglier**, **giggliest**) tending or likely to giggle.

Gigli, Beniamino (1890–1957) Italian tenor, born in Recanati. He won a scholarship to the Liceo Musicale, Rome, and made his operatic début in Ponchielli's *La Gioconda* (1914). By 1929 he had won a worldwide reputation as a lyric-dramatic tenor of great vitality, at his best in the works of Verdi and Puccini.

GIGO *abbrev.* garbage in, garbage out.

gigolo *noun* (PL. **gigolos**) 1 *derog.* the paid male companion and lover of a rich (usually older) woman. 2 a hired professional dancing partner. [from French *gigolo*]

gigot *noun* a leg of lamb or mutton. [from French *gigot*]

gigue *noun* a lively dance, usually in 16:8 or 12:8 time; also, a piece of music for it. It was probably of British origin, and became popular across Europe from the mid-17c. In the late 17c and early 18c it became the last of the four standard dances in the suite, following the sarabande. [from French *gigue*, probably related to English JIG]

Gijón POP (1991) 259 000, a seaport and industrial town in Oviedo province, Asturias region, NE Spain. It lies on the N coast, 29km/18mi N of Oviedo, and is the main outlet for the Asturian coal mines. NOTABLE FEATURE Roman Baths.

gila monster a venomous lizard, native to America, up to 60cm in length, dark with yellow mottling, and having bead-like scales, a blunt head, and a fat tail. It feeds on eggs and small invertebrates. The venom is a nerve poison, but the animal's bite is seldom fatal. [from the Gila River in Arizona]

Gilbert, Walter (1932–) US molecular biologist, born in Boston. Professor at Harvard from 1968, and founder of the genetic engineering company Biogen NV, he isolated the 'repressor molecule' which had been predicted to play a central role in controlling gene action, and he went on to describe the sequence of bases in DNA to which the repressor molecule binds. He shared the 1980 Nobel Prize for Chemistry with Frederick Sanger and Paul Berg.

Gilbert or **Gylberde, William** (1544–1603) English physician and geophysicist, born in Colchester. He settled in London, where he was physician to Queen Elizabeth. Following his own scientific research he became the first to consider the Earth as one vast spherical magnet, and he proposed that terrestrial magnetism and electricity (produced by rubbing amber) were two allied emanations of a single force; these observations were published in his *De magnete* (On the Magnet, 1600).

Gilbert, Sir W(illiam) S(chwenck) (1836–1911) English parodist and librettist of the 'Gilbert and Sullivan' light operas, born in London. Though trained as a lawyer, he failed to attract lucrative briefs and subsisted on magazine contributions to *Fun*, for which he wrote much humorous verse under his boyhood nickname 'Bab' (collected as the *Bab Ballads*, 1869), as well as fairy comedies and serious plays in blank verse. His partnership with Sir Arthur Sullivan began in 1871; together they wrote 14 popular operas, from *Trial by Jury* (1875) to *The Gondoliers* (1889).

Gilbert a male first name. [Norman, from Germanic *gisil*, pledge + *berht*, bright]

Gilbert Islands POP (1990) 68 000, an island group of Kiribati, central Pacific Ocean. AREA 264sq km/102sq mi. PHYSICAL DESCRIPTION a chain of 17 coral atolls spread over c.680km/420mi; most of the atolls are no more than 200–300m wide, but they may be 15–100km/10–60mi long; most have central lagoons. HISTORY formed part of the British colony of Gilbert and Ellice Is until 1977. CAPITAL Tarawa. ECONOMY fishing; farming; copra; phosphate.

gild verb (PAST TENSE AND PAST PARTICIPLE **gilded**, **gilt**) to cover with a thin coating of gold or something similar.
— **gild the lily** to try to improve something which is already beautiful enough, often spoiling it.
[from Anglo-Saxon *gyldan*, gold]

gilder same as GUILDER.

Giles a male first name, associated with St Giles of the 8c, famed for his miracles. [from Old French, ultimately from Greek *aigidion*, kid, young goat]

Gilgamesh a Mesopotamian hero, the tryannical King of Uruk (3rd millennium BC), and the son of the goddess Ninsun and a mortal. His battle and further adventures with the giant Enkidu are recounted in the *Gilgamesh Epic*.

Gilgamesh Epic a Babylonian epic poem, partially preserved in different versions, named after its hero the Sumerian king Gilgamesh (3rd millennium BC). It describes Gilgamesh's legendary adventures, and narrates a story of the Flood similar to the biblical account in Genesis.

Gill, (Arthur) Eric (Rowton) (1882–1940) English carver, engraver, and typographer, born in Brighton. He trained as an architect, but then took up letter-cutting, masonry, and engraving. After his first exhibition (1911) he maintained a

gila monster

steady output of engravings, type designs, and stone and wood carvings. His works include *Prospero and Ariel* (1931, Broadcasting House, London).

gill¹ noun (pronounced as in *gilt*) **1** in all fishes and many other aquatic animals, a respiratory organ that extracts dissolved oxygen from the surrounding water. **2** each of many thin vertical spore-bearing structures on the underside of the cap of mushrooms and toadstools. **3** (**gills**) *colloq.* the flesh under the ears and jaw.
— **green about the gills** *colloq.* looking or feeling sick.
[perhaps from Norse *gil*]

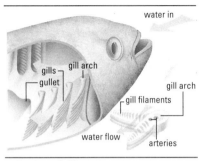

structure of gills

gill² noun (pronounced as in *jilt*) **1** in the UK, a unit of liquid measure equal to 142.1ml (a quarter of a pint). **2** *colloq.* an alcoholic drink. [from Old French *gelle*]

gill³ noun (pronounced as in *gilt*) **1** a deep wooded ravine. **2** a mountain stream. [from Norse *gil*]

Gillespie, Dizzy, originally **John Birks Gillespie** (1917–93) US jazz trumpeter, bandleader, and composer, born in Cheraw, South Carolina. He worked in prominent swing bands (1937–44), and as a leader, often with Charlie Parker on saxophone, he developed the music called 'bebop', which, with its dissonant harmonies and polyrhythms, was a reaction to swing. His own raucous big band (1946–50) was his masterpiece, and gave him scope as both soloist and showman.

Gillian a female first name. [originally a variant of JULIAN, and now an independent name]

gillie or **ghillie** noun a guide or assistant to a game-hunter or fisherman, especially in Scotland. [from Gaelic *gille*, boy]

Gillingham POP (1981) 94 000, an industrial and naval town in the Medway Towns urban area, Kent, SE England. It lies on the R Medway, 48km/30mi E of London, adjoining Chatham.

Gilman, Charlotte Anna Perkins, née **Perkins** (1860–1935) US feminist and writer, born in Hartford, Connecticut, into the same family as Catharine Beecher and Harriet Beecher Stowe. She had limited schooling, an unhappy marriage, and suffered much mental distress, then began a career as a writer, arguing in many books that women's equality required major social change. Her most notable works are *Women and Economics* (1898), *The Home* (1903), and *Man-Made World* (1911).

gilt¹ — adj. covered with a thin coating of gold; gilded. — noun **1** gold or a gold-like substance used in gilding. **2** (**gilts**) gilt-edged securities.

gilt² noun a young female pig. [from Norse *gyltr*]

gilt-edged securities government securities with a fixed rate of interest, able to be sold at face value.

gimbals pl. noun an arrangement of pivoting rings keeping navigation instruments in a horizontal position at sea or in the air. [from Old French *gemel*, double ring for a finger]

gimcrack derog. — adj. cheap, showy, and badly made. — noun a cheap and showy article. [from Middle English *gibecrake*, little ornament]

gimlet noun **1** a T-shaped hand-tool for boring holes in wood. **2** a cocktail of lime juice and gin or vodka. [from Old French *guimbelet*]

gimlet-eyed adj. having a piercing look or stare.

gimmick noun derog. a scheme or object used to attract attention or publicity, especially to bring in customers.

gimmickry noun gimmicks, or the use of gimmicks.

gimmicky adj. **1** involving a gimmick or gimmicks. **2** designed to catch attention.

gimp noun a strip of silk with a wire core, used as a decoration in dressmaking, etc. [from French *guimpe*]

gin¹ noun an alcoholic spirit made from barley, rye, or maize, flavoured with juniper berries. [from Dutch *genever*, juniper]

gin² — noun **1** a wire noose laid as a trap for animals. **2** a lifting device consisting of wire coiled round a drum turned by hand. **3** a device which turns a vertical shaft using the power from horses pulling a horizontal bar in a circle, used especially for separating seeds from raw cotton. — verb (**ginned**, **ginning**) **1** to trap with a gin. **2** to separate (cotton) with a gin. [from Old French *engin*, engine]

Ginckell or **Ginkel, Godert de** (1630–1703) Dutch soldier, born in Utrecht. He accompanied William III to England in 1688, and fought in the battle of the Boyne (1690). As Commander-in-Chief in Ireland, he defeated the remaining rebels, and he later led the Dutch troops under Marlborough.

ginger — noun **1** an aromatic spicy swollen root or rhizome, usually dried and ground to a yellow powder that is used as a flavouring in biscuits, cakes, curries, chutneys, etc, although it can also be eaten fresh or preserved in syrup. Ginger is used in some medicines. **2** the perennial plant (*Zingiber officinalis*), cultivated in many tropical regions, from which this root is obtained. **3** a reddish-brown colour. **4** *colloq.* energy; liveliness. — adj. **1** flavoured with ginger. **2** *said of hair* reddish-brown in colour. — verb (**ginger someone up**) *colloq.* to urge them to become more lively, active, or efficient. [from Latin *zingiber*, from Sanskrit *srnga*, horn + *vera*, body, from the shape of the root]

ginger ale or **ginger beer** a non-alcoholic fizzy drink flavoured with ginger.

gingerbread noun cake flavoured with treacle and ginger.

ginger group a small group within a larger (especially political) group, which urges stronger or more radical action.

gingerly adv. showing delicate caution. [perhaps from Old French *gensor*, delicate]

ginger nut or **ginger snap** a ginger-flavoured biscuit.

gingery adj. **1** ginger. **2** *said of remarks* critical.

gingham noun striped or checked cotton cloth. [from Malay *ginggang*, striped]

gingivitis noun Medicine inflammation of the gums (gingiva), which become swollen and painful and tend to bleed, usually caused by the accumulation of plaque in the region where the gums meet the teeth. [from Latin *gingiva*, gum + -ITIS]

ginkgo noun a deciduous gymnosperm (cone-bearing plant), *Ginkgo biloba*, native to SW China. Its leaves are similar to the fan-shaped leaves of the maidenhair fern, and it is the sole survivor of a formerly large and widespread family. — Also called *maidenhair tree*. [from Japanese, = silver apricot]

ginormous *adj. colloq.* exceptionally huge. [from GIGANTIC + ENORMOUS]

gin rummy *colloq.* **gin** a version of rummy allowing a finish by a player whose unmatched cards total 10 points or less.

Ginsberg, Allen (1926–) US poet, born in Newark, New Jersey. He was associated with the 'Beat' movement and his first book, *Howl and Other Poems* (1956), was a *succès de scandale*. In the 1960s he travelled widely and wrote numerous other volumes, including *Empty Mirror* (1961) and *Ankor Wat* (1968). A cult figure who coined the phrase 'flower power', his prose works include *Allen Verbatim* (1974) and *Journals* (1977). His *Collected Poems 1947–80* were published in 1984, and *White Shroud, Poems 1980–85* in 1986.

ginseng *noun* **1** either of two plant species belonging to the genus *Panax*, with yellowish-green flowers and round red fruits, cultivated in China and N America for its aromatic root, which is widely used as a tonic, stimulant, and aphrodisiac. **2** a medicinal preparation made from the root of this plant. [from Chinese *jen-shen*, image of man, from the shape of the root]

gin sling an iced drink of sweetened gin.

gintrap *noun* a powerful animal trap with teeth.

Giotto (di Bondone) (1267–1337) Italian painter and architect, born near Vespignano. He is generally regarded as the founder of the Florentine School of painting. His major work was the fresco cycle *The Lives of the Virgin and Christ* in the Arena Chapel, Padua (1305–8). From 1330 to 1333 he was employed by King Robert in Naples, and in 1334 was appointed Master of Works of the cathedral and city of Florence.

Giotto space probe *Astron.* a space probe launched by the European Space Agency in July 1985 to study Halley's comet. It passed within 600km of the nucleus of the comet in March 1986. [named after the artist Giotto, who is said to have used Halley's comet as a model for the star of Bethlehem in the fresco *The Adoration of the Magi*]

gip same as GYP.

Gippsland a district of SE Victoria, Australia. Its mountains in the N drop down to fertile plains in the S. ECONOMY lignite; dairy products; cereals; hops.

gippy tummy *colloq.* a severe stomach upset, especially as suffered by visitors to hot countries. [from EGYPTIAN]

Gipsy same as GYPSY.

giraffe *noun* a very tall mammal (*Giraffa camelopardalis*), and the tallest living animal, reaching a height of up to 5.5m. It has an extremely long neck and legs, a small head bearing two to five bony knobs, large eyes, a narrow snout, and a long tufted tail. It also has a pale buff coat boldly marked with irregular chestnut or dark brown blotches. [from Arabic *zarafah*]
◇ Giraffes live mainly in herds in the savanna of Africa south of the Sahara, but populations have been greatly reduced and the animal was once much more widespread. It is a ruminant, and feeds on the leaves of trees, especially acacia. It can survive for long periods without water, and when drinking, it moves its front legs wide apart in an ungainly manner in order to bring its head down to the level of the water. When resting, it crouches with its legs folded under its body, often laying its head along its back while sleeping.

Giralda a bell tower adjacent to Seville Cathedral, in Spain. It was built (1163–84) as an Islamic minaret, and was converted in the 16c after the mosque it served had been displaced by the present cathedral. The tower is 93m high.

Giraldus Cambrensis, also called **Gerald de Barri** (c.1147–1223) Norman-Welsh historian and churchman, born in Manorbier Castle, Pembrokeshire. Though elected Bishop of St David's in 1176, Henry II refused to confirm his election and he went to lecture in Paris. Later appointed a royal chaplain, in 1185 he accompanied Prince John to Ireland, which inspired his account of Ireland's natural history and inhabitants, and his *Expugnatio Hibernica* (History of the Conquest of Ireland, c.1189). In 1188 he travelled through Wales to recruit soldiers for the Third Crusade, and recorded his observations in the *Itinerarium Cambriae* (Itinerary of Wales, 1191).

Giraudoux, (Hippolyte) Jean (1882–1944) French writer and diplomat, born in Bellac, Limousin. He joined the diplomatic service and worked for the French Ministry of Information during World War II. His best-known works are his plays, which are mainly fantasies based on Greek myths and biblical lore satirically treated as commentary on modern life. They include *La Guerre de Troie n'aura pas lieu* (Tiger at the Gates, 1935), *Ondine* (1939), and *La Folle de Chaillot* (The Mad Woman of Chaillot, 1945).

gird *verb* (PAST TENSE AND PAST PARTICIPLE **girded**, **girt**) *literary* to encircle or fasten with a belt or something similar.
— **gird up one's loins** *literary* to prepare oneself for action.
[from Anglo-Saxon *gyrdan*]

girder *noun* a large beam of wood, iron, or steel used to support a floor, wall, road, or bridge. [from Anglo-Saxon *gyrdan*, to gird]

girdle¹ — *noun* **1** a woman's close-fitting undergarment worn to reshape the figure from waist to thigh. **2** a belt or cord worn round the waist. **3** a surrounding part, especially such a part of the body: *pelvic girdle.* — *verb* **1** to put a girdle on. **2** *literary* to surround. [from Anglo-Saxon *gyrdan*, to gird]

girdle² same as GRIDDLE.

girl *noun* **1** a female child. **2** a daughter. **3** *often offensive* a young woman, especially unmarried. **4** *often offensive* a woman of any age. **5** *colloq.* a woman's female friend or colleague. **6** a female employee, especially formerly a maid. [from Middle English *gerle, girle*, and *gurle*, child]

Girl Friday a young woman who does general office work.

girlfriend *noun* **1** a female sexual or romantic partner. **2** a female friend, especially of a woman.

Girl Guides see GUIDE ASSOCIATION.

girlhood *noun* the period of life when a person is a girl.

Girlhood of Mary Virgin, The the first major Pre-Raphaelite painting by Dante Gabriel Rossetti (1849).

girlie *or* **girly** *adj. colloq.,* said of a magazine, picture, etc featuring naked or nearly naked young women in erotic poses.

girlish *adj.* with a girlish manner; like a girl.

Girl with a Pearl Earring a painting by Jan Vermeer (17c, The Hague, Netherlands).

Giralda

giro *noun* (PL. **giros**) **1** a banking system by which money can be transferred from one account directly to another. **2** *colloq.* a social security benefit received in cheque form. [from Italian *giro*, turn or transfer]

Girondins *or* **Girondists** a group of deputies in the Legislative Assembly (1791–2) and French Convention (1792–5), led by Jean Roland, Charles Dumouriez, and Jacques Brissot. Sympathetic to the provinces rather than to Paris (their name derived from the Gironde region of SW France), they aroused the hostility of Robespierre and the 'Mountain' (a group of Jacobin extremists) in the Convention, and many were executed during the Reign of Terror (1793).

girt see GIRD.

girth *noun* **1** distance round something, eg a tree or a person's waist. **2** the strap round a horse's belly that holds a saddle in place. [from Norse *gjörth*, belt]

Gisborne POP (1991) 32 000, a port and resort town in East Coast, North I, New Zealand. It is situated at the head of Poverty Bay. Captain Cook landed at this site in 1769.

Giscard d'Estaing, Valéry (1926–) French politician, born in Koblenz, Germany. Educated in Paris, he worked for the Resistance during World War II, after which he entered the Ministry of Finance as a civil servant. He became an Assistant Director of the Cabinet (1955), Finance Minister (1962–6), and launched his own party (National Federation of Independent Republicans). He returned to the Finance Ministry in 1969, then defeated Mitterand to become President from 1974 to 1981, when Mitterand defeated him.

Giselle, in full *Giselle, ou Les Wilis* (Giselle, or The Wilis) a 'fantastic ballet' by Adolphe Adam (1841), based on a legend about ghosts of girls who have died before they are wed (the Wilis).

Gissing, George (Robert) (1857–1903) English novelist, born in Wakefield, Yorkshire. He travelled to the USA, returning to London in 1877. *Workers in the Dawn* (1880) was the first of over 20 novels which largely present realistic portraits of poverty and misery. They include his best-known work, *New Grub Street* (1891), *Born in Exile* (1892), and *The Odd Women* (1893).

gist *noun* general meaning; main point. [from Old French *gist*, from *gesir*, to lie, consist in, or reside in]

git *noun* *derog. slang* a stupid or contemptible person. [variant of GET]

Gitega POP (1989e) 100 000, the capital of Gitega province, Burundi. It lies 61km/38mi to the E of Bujumbura and was a former royal residence.

gittern *noun* a medieval musical instrument of the guitar family. It resembled a lute (but with a shorter neck which curved smoothly into the body of the instrument), and had three or four courses of strings played with a plectrum. In Tudor times, the name was loosely applied to several instruments including the Spanish guitar and cittern. [from Old French *guitern*, related to Greek *kithara*]

give — *verb* (PAST TENSE **gave**; PAST PARTICIPLE **given**) **1** to transfer ownership of; to transfer possession of temporarily: *gave him my watch / give me your bags.* **2** to provide or administer: *give advice / give medicine.* **3** to produce: *cows give milk.* **4** to perform (an action, service, etc): *give a smile, a lecture on beetles.* **5** to pay: *gave £20 for it.* **6** *intrans.* to make a donation: *please give generously.* **7** (*also* **give something up**) to sacrifice: *give one's life.* **8** to be the cause or source of: *gives me pain.* **9** *intrans.* to yield or break: *give under pressure.* **10** to organize at one's own expense: *give a party.* **11** to have as a result: *four into twenty gives five.* **12** to reward or punish by: *was given 20 years.* **13** *colloq.* to agree to or admit: *I'll give you that.* **14** to offer a toast to. **15** *Sport* to declare to be: *gave him offside*. **16** (**give into** *or* **on to some-thing**) *said of a passage, etc* to lead or be an opening to it: *a terrace giving on to the lawn*. **17** *colloq*. used to state a preference: *give me jazz any day*. — *noun* capacity to yield; flexibility.

— **give as good as one gets** *colloq*. to respond to an attack with equal energy, force, and effect.

give someone away to present a bride to a bridegroom at a wedding ceremony.

give something away 1 to hand it over as a gift. **2** to allow a piece of information to become known, usually by accident.

give in to someone *or* **something** to yield to them; to admit defeat.

give something off to produce or emit eg a smell.

give or take something *colloq*. allowing for a (stated) margin of error: *we have all the money, give or take a pound*.

give out *colloq*. to break down or come to an end: *their resistance gave out*.

give something out 1 to announce or distribute it. **2** to emit a sound, smell, etc.

give something over 1 to transfer it. **2** to set it aside or devote it to some purpose: *the morning was given over to discussing the budgets*.

give over doing something *colloq*., *usually as a command* to stop doing it: *give over shouting!*

give up to admit defeat.

give someone up to surrender a wanted person.

give something up to renounce or quit a habit, etc: *give up smoking*.

give up doing something to stop making the effort to achieve it: *gave up trying to talk sense to them*.

give someone up for dead *or* **lost**, *etc* to assume that they are dead or lost, etc, after abandoning hope.

give way 1 to give priority. **2** to collapse under pressure.

give way to something to allow oneself to be affected by it: *give way to tears*.

what gives? what is happening? [from Anglo-Saxon *gefan*]

give-and-take *noun* **1** mutual willingness to accept the other's point of view. **2** a useful exchange of views.

give-away *noun colloq*. **1** an act of accidentally revealing secrets, etc. **2** something obtained extremely easily or cheaply: *the goal was a give-away*. **3** a free gift.

given — *adj*. **1** stated or specified. **2** (**given to something**) prone to it; having it as a habit: *given to biting his nails*. — *prep*. accepting as a basis for discussion; assuming.

gizzard *noun* **1** *Zool*. in certain animals, a muscular chamber specialized for grinding up indigestible food. In birds (where it is situated behind the crop) and earthworms, it contains grit or small stones, and in insects it is lined with spines that form a tough grinding surface. **2** *colloq*. the stomach. [from Old French *guisier*, fowl's liver]

glacé *adj*. **1** coated with a sugary glaze; candied: *glacé cherries*. **2** frozen, or covered with ice. [from French *glacé*]

glacial *adj*. **1** *Geol., Geog*. of or caused by ice or glaciers. **2** *colloq*. extremely cold. **3** hostile: *a glacial stare*. [from Latin *glacialis*, icy]

glacially *adv*. **1** by glacial action. **2** in an icy way, icily.

glacial period any period during which large areas of the earth were covered with ice; an ice age.

Glaciares, Los an Andean national park in SW Santa Cruz province, Patagonia region, Argentina. Established in 1937, it includes the E parts of L Viedma and L Argentino and borders Chile in the W. The park is a World Heritage site. AREA 4 459sq km/1 721sq mi.

glaciate *verb Geol., Geog*. to cover with, or subject to the eroding action of, moving masses of ice. [from Latin *glaciare*, to freeze]

glaciation *noun Geol*. the process whereby part of the Earth's surface is covered and shaped by glaciers or ice sheets, resulting in the production of characteristic landforms after the ice has melted, eg U-shaped valleys, moraines (ridges of rock debris), and cirques.

glacier *noun* a large body of ice, formed by the compaction of snow, that occurs on land, and slowly moves down a gradient (bending under its own weight) or outward in all directions until it reaches a point where it melts or breaks up into icebergs. [from French, from *glace*, ice]
◇ There are two main types of glacier, namely the ice sheets of Antarctica, which may reach thicknesses of more than 4 000m, and the ice which accumulates in snowy and mountainous areas, and then flows slowly down valleys. When a mountain glacier melts, it leaves behind rounded hills, called *drumlins*, and narrow ridges of rock debris, called *eskers*. Hollows in the loose rock trap water, forming *meltwater lakes*. Rocks and other debris carried by the glacier are deposited as *moraines*.

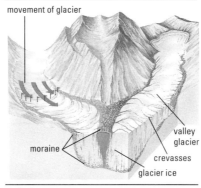

glacier

Glacier Bay National Park, formerly **Glacier Bay National Monument** a national park in SE Alaska, USA, covering c.13 000sq km/5 000sq mi, containing deep fjords and tidewater glaciers, and accessible only by air, water, or on foot. It is a World Heritage site.

Glacier National Park a national park in Montana, USA, covering 4 000sq km/1 544sq mi. It includes 50 glaciers and 200 lakes and was designated a national park in 1910.

glad *adj*. (**gladder**, **gladdest**) **1** (**glad about something**) happy or pleased about it. **2** (**glad of something**) grateful for it: *I was glad of your support*. **3** very willing: *we are glad to help*. **4** *old use* bringing happiness: *glad tidings*. [from Anglo-Saxon *glæd*]

gladden *verb* (**gladdened**, **gladdening**) to make happy or pleased.

glade *noun literary* an open space in a wood or forest.

glad eye (**the glad eye**) *old slang use* a sexually inviting look: *giving me the glad eye*.

gladiator *noun* in ancient Rome, a man trained to fight against other men or animals in an arena. [from Latin *gladiator*, swordsman]
◇ Originally an Etruscan practice, the contests were early associated with funerary rites. Under the Empire, gladiators performed for public entertainment, often fighting to the death. They were usually slaves, prisoners of war, or condemned prisoners.

gladiatorial *adj*. relating to or involving gladiators.

gladiolus *noun* (PL. **gladioli**, **gladioluses**) a garden plant with sword-shaped leaves and spiky clusters of brightly coloured flowers. [from Latin *gladiolus*, diminutive of *gladius*, sword]

gladly *adv*. with gladness, willingly.

gladness *noun* being glad.

glad rags *colloq*. one's best clothes, worn for special occasions.

Gladstone, W(illiam) E(wart) (1809–98) English Liberal statesman and Prime Minister (1868–74, 1880–5, 1886, 1892–4), born in Liverpool. He entered parliament in 1832 as a Conservative, and worked closely with Robert Peel. He served as President of the Board of Trade (1843–5), and Chancellor of the Exchequer in Lord Aberdeen's coalition (1852–5) and again under Palmerston (1859–66). In 1867 he became leader of the Liberal Party, and soon after began his first term as Prime Minister, during which he disestablished and disendowed the Irish Church and established a system of national education (1870). His later ministries were marked by parliamentary reforms that began the road to universal male suffrage, and by the question of Irish Home Rule.

Gladys a female first name, popular throughout Britain earlier in the 20c but now less common. [from Welsh *Gwladys*; perhaps a version of CLAUDIA]

glair *noun* egg-white, or a similar substance, used as a glaze or an adhesive. [from Old French *glaire*, perhaps from Latin *clarus*, clear]

Glåma *or* **Glommen** *or* **Glomma** the longest river in Norway, length 598km/372mi. Rising in Dovrefjell Plateau, E Norway, it flows S through L Øyeren to Oslo Fjord at Fredrikstad. It brings logs to the sawmills and paper-mills further downstream.

Glamorgan see MID GLAMORGAN, SOUTH GLAMORGAN, WEST GLAMORGAN.

glamorize *or* **glamorise** *verb* **1** to make glamorous. **2** to romanticize.

glamorous *adj*. full of glamour.

glamour *noun* **1** the quality of being fascinatingly, if perhaps falsely, attractive. **2** great beauty or sexual charm, especially created by make-up, clothes, etc. [a variant of GRAMMAR, arising from the medieval association of magic with learning]

glance — *verb usually intrans*. **1** (*often* **glance at something** *or* **someone**) to look quickly or indirectly. **2** (**glance off something**) to be deflected by it. **3** *trans. said of a weapon* to hit (its target) obliquely. **4** to shine in flashes; to glint: *the sunlight glanced off the table*. — *noun* **1** a brief look, often indirect. **2** a deflection. **3** *literary* a brief flash of light.

— **at a glance** at once; from one brief look: *could see at a glance that it was wrong*.

glance at *or* **over something** to read or look at it cursorily.

[from Middle English *glenten*]

gland *noun* **1** *Zool*. in animals, an organ that produces a specific chemical substance, eg a hormone, for use inside the body (by direct release into the bloodstream, or into a tubular organ via a duct), or for release to the exterior. **2** *Bot*. in plants, a specialized cell or group of cells involved in the secretion of plant products such as nectar, oils, resins, and tannins. [from Latin *glans*, acorn]

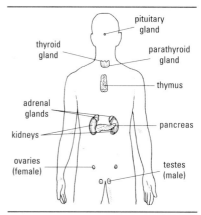

positions of the major human endocrine glands

glanders *sing. noun* an infectious, often fatal disease in horses, causing inflammation of the lungs and lymph glands. [from Latin *glans*, acorn]

glandular *adj.* of, produced by, or affecting a gland or glands. [from French *glandulaire*]

glandular fever infectious mononucleosis.

glare — *verb intrans.* **1** to stare angrily. **2** to be unpleasantly bright or shiny. — *noun* **1** an angry stare. **2** dazzling light. **3** brash colour or decoration. [from Old Dutch *glaren*, to gleam]

glaring *adj.* **1** unpleasantly bright. **2** obvious.

glaringly *adv.* in a glaring way, obviously.

Glaser, Donald Arthur (1926–) US physicist, born in Cleveland, Ohio. Professor at the universities of Michigan and California, he was awarded the 1960 Nobel Prize for Physics for inventing the 'bubble chamber' for observing the paths of elementary particles.

Glasgow POP (1992e) 684 000, the largest city in Scotland and the capital of Strathclyde region, W Scotland. It lies on the R Clyde, 66km/41mi W of Edinburgh. HISTORY expanded initially in the 17c, with trade from the Americas and, later, became important for its shipbuilding and associated engineering industries; named the European City of Culture for 1990. NOTABLE FEATURES St Mungo's Cathedral (12c); Kelvingrove Art Gallery and Museum; Burrell Collection; Hunterian Art Gallery and Museum; Museum of Transport; Victorian Tenement Museum; St Mungo's Museum of Religious Life and Art; ruins of 15c Cathcart Castle; Provand's Lordship (1471); Crookston Castle (15c); Haggs Castle (1585), now a museum of history; People's Palace (1898); Royal Exchange; Stock Exchange; University of Glasgow (1451); Royal Scottish Academy of Music (1847); Glasgow School of Art; Mitchell Library (1874). EVENT Mayfest. [from Gaelic *glas ghu*, beloved green place]

Glasgow School, also called **Glasgow Boys** a group of painters who worked in Glasgow during the late 19c. They were influenced by the Barbizon *plein air* (open air) school of painting, and were most prominent from c.1880–c.1895. Leading members included Sir James Guthrie (1859–1930), Edward Hornel (1864–1933), and George Henry (1858–1943).

Glashow, Sheldon Lee (1932–) US physicist, born in New York City. Professor of Physics at Harvard from 1967, he developed one of the first theories (the 'electroweak' theory) to describe simultaneously two of the four forces of nature; the electromagnetic and weak forces. He was also a major contributor to a theory (now known as quantum chromodynamics) of strong forces between elementary particles, which assumes that nuclear particles are made up of quarks held together by gluons. He shared the 1979 Nobel Prize for Physics with Abdus Salam and Steven Weinberg.

glasnost *noun* openness and willingness to provide information on the part of governments. [from Russian *glasnost*, speaking aloud, openness; originally used of the Soviet government under Mikhail Gorbachev]

glass — *noun* **1** a hard brittle non-crystalline material that is usually transparent or translucent.
◇ Glass does not have a specific melting point, but softens over a range of temperature. Soda glass, used in windows, bottles, and other containers, is formed by heating a mixture of dissolved silica and silicates with calcium carbonate (soda) and calcium oxide (lime). Borosilicate glass, eg Pyrex, used in cooking utensils, is stronger and more heat resistant than soda glass, because some of the silicon atoms are replaced by boron atoms. Other chemical elements, eg barium and lead, are added to glass used in lenses and optical instruments.
2 an article made from this, eg a mirror, a lens, or especially a drinking cup. **3** the amount held by a

drinking glass. **4** articles made of glass: *a collection of glass*. **5** (**glasses**) spectacles. — *adj.* made of glass. — *verb* to supply or cover with glass. [from Anglo-Saxon *glæs*]

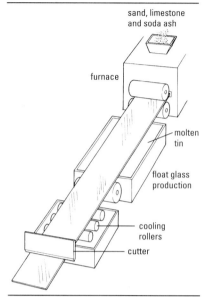

sand, limestone and soda ash

furnace

molten tin

float glass production

cooling rollers

cutter

glass production

glass-blower *noun* a person who is skilled at glass-blowing.

glass-blowing *noun* the process of shaping molten glass by blowing air into it through a tube.

glass ceiling a barrier on the career ladder beyond which certain categories of employee, especially women, can see but not progress.

glass ceramic a type of strong hard glass, composed of lithium and magnesium aluminium silicates, that has a high level of heat and shock resistance, and is used to make moulded electrical and mechanical parts, and ovenware.

glass fibre glass melted and then drawn out into extremely fine fibres. Glass fibres set in plastic resin are used to make strong lightweight structures, eg some vehicle bodies.

glasshouse *noun* **1** a greenhouse. **2** *slang* a military prison.

glasspaper *noun* paper coated with finely ground glass, used as an abrasive.

glass wool glass fibres in the form of a wool-like mass, used for insulation.

glasswort *noun* a fleshy annual plant (*Salicornia europaea*), widespread in salt marshes on European coasts, with jointed, usually branched stems often having reddish or yellowish tinges. Its leaves are reduced to fleshy translucent scales that surround the stem, and tiny greenish flowers are borne near the tip of the stem. Its young shoots may be eaten lightly boiled or pickled in vinegar.

glassy *adj.* (**glassier, glassiest**) **1** like glass. **2** expressionless: *glassy eyes*.

Glastonbury POP (1981) 6 700, a market town in Mendip district, Somerset, SW England. It lies on the R Brue, 35km/22mi SW of Bath. HISTORY a lake village in prehistoric times; according to legend, it was here that Joseph of Arimathea brought the Holy Grail, the chalice used at the Last Supper, and here that King Arthur was buried. NOTABLE FEATURES Benedictine Abbey; Glastonbury Tor (159m). EVENT Glastonbury Festival (Jun).

Glastonbury lake village a marshland settlement of the 3c–1c BC near Glastonbury, Somerset, renowned for its preservation of tim-

ber, wooden utensils, and basketry. Excavations (1892–1907) revealed an artificial island of felled trees, on which a wooden palisade enclosed c.80 reed-roofed circular huts with clay and plank floors.

Glaswegian — *noun* a native or citizen of Glasgow. — *adj.* of Glasgow or its inhabitants. [after *Norwegian*]

glaucoma *noun* an eye disease in which increasing pressure inside the eye causes gradual loss of vision. [from Greek *glaukoma*, cataract]

glaucous *adj.* **1** of a dull green or blue colour. **2** *Bot.* having a pale bluish-green waxy coating that can be rubbed off, eg the bloom of grapes. [from Greek *glaukos*, bluish-green or grey]

glaze — *verb* **1** to fit glass panes into (a window, door, etc). **2** to give a hard shiny transparent coating to (pottery). **3** (*usually* **glaze over**) *said of the eyes* to become fixed and expressionless. **4** to apply a shiny coating of milk, eggs, or sugar to (eg pastry). — *noun* **1** a hard glassy coating on pottery. **2** a shiny coating of milk, eggs, or sugar on food. [originally a variant of GLASS]

glazed *adj.* **1** fitted or covered with glass. **2** covered with a glaze. **3** stupefied: *a glazed look*.

glazier *noun* a person employed to glaze windows, doors, etc.

GLC *abbrev.* Greater London Council, abolished in 1986.

gleam — *noun* **1** a gentle glow. **2** a brief flash of (especially reflected) light. **3** a brief appearance or sign: *a gleam of excitement in his eyes*. — *verb intrans.* **1** to glow gently. **2** to shine with brief flashes of light. **3** *said of an emotion, etc* to be shown briefly. [from Anglo-Saxon *glæm*]

gleaming *adj.* shining.

glean *verb* **1** to collect (information, etc) bit by bit, often with difficulty. **2** *trans., intrans.* to collect (loose grain left on a field) after harvesting. [from Old French *glener*]

Gleaners, The a painting by Jean François Millet (1857, Louvre, Paris). It depicts a scene from rural French life.

gleanings *pl. noun* things gleaned, especially bits of information.

glebe *noun* **1** a piece of church-owned land providing income in rent, etc for the resident minister. **2** *poetic* land; a field. [from Latin *gleba*, clod]

glee *noun* **1** great delight; joy. **2** a song with different parts for three or four unaccompanied (especially male) voices. [from Anglo-Saxon *gleo*, mirth]

glee club especially in the US, a society of singers of glees.

gleeful *adj.* joyful; merry.

gleefully *adv.* with glee.

Glen a male first name, after the Scottish surname. [from Celtic *gleann*, valley]

glen *noun* a long narrow valley, especially in Scotland. [from Gaelic *gleann*]

Glenda a female first name. [from Welsh *glan*, clean, pure, holy, or a variant of GLEN]

Glendower, Owen, *or* **Glyndwr, Owain** (c.1354–1416) Welsh chief, born in Montgomeryshire. In 1401 he rebelled against Henry IV, proclaimed himself Prince of Wales, established an independent Welsh parliament, and joined the coalition with Harry Percy Hotspur, who was defeated at the battle of Shrewsbury (1403). He continued to fight for Welsh independence until his death.

glengarry *noun* (PL. **glengarries**) a narrow brimless cap creased along its middle and usually with two ribbons hanging at the back. [from *Glengarry* in Inverness-shire]

Glenn, John H(erschel) (1921–) US astronaut, the first American to orbit the Earth, born in

Cambridge, Ohio. He joined the US Marine Corps in 1943, and in 1957 completed a record-breaking supersonic flight from Los Angeles to New York. He became an astronaut in 1959, and made a three-orbit flight in the *Friendship 7* space capsule (1962). An Ohio Senator since 1975, he sought Democratic nomination for the presidency in 1984.

Glennie, Evelyn (Elizabeth Ann) (1965–) Scottish percussion player, born in Aberdeen. She experienced a gradual but total loss of hearing in her early teens but nevertheless rose to become the first full-time percussion soloist in the world, and the recipient of innumerable prizes and awards. Many leading British composers have written works for her.

Glenrothes POP (1981) 33 000, the capital of Fife region and of Kirkcaldy district, E Scotland. It was designated a 'new town' in 1948, and is a centre for electronic research.

glib *adj.* (**glibber, glibbest**) *derog.* speaking or spoken readily and persuasively, but neither sincere nor reliable: *glib politicians / glib explanations.* [from Old German *glibberich*, slippery]

glibly *adv.* in a glib way.

glibness *noun* being glib.

glide — *verb intrans.* 1 to move smoothly: *glide along the ice.* 2 *said of a bird* to sail through the air without beating the wings. 3 *said of an aircraft* to fly without engine power. 4 to fly a glider. 5 to pass gradually: *glide into sleep.* — *noun* 1 a gliding movement. 2 *Mus.* movement from one note to another with no break in sound. [from Anglo-Saxon *glidan,* to slip]

glider *noun* a small aeroplane with no engine, kept in flight by rising currents of warm air.

glimmer — *verb intrans.* (**glimmered, glimmering**) to glow faintly. — *noun* 1 a faint glow; a twinkle. 2 a hint or trace: *a glimmer of hope.* [from Middle English *glemern*]

glimpse — *noun* a very brief look. — *verb* to see momentarily. [from Middle English *glymsen*]

Glinka, Mikhail (Ivanovich) (1804–57) Russian composer, born in Novopasskoi, Smolensk. He became a civil servant, but after a visit to Italy he began to study music in Berlin and then returned to Russia to produce his opera *A Life for the Tsar* (known earlier as *Ivan Susanin,* 1836). His *Russlan and Ludmilla* (1842), based on a poem by Pushkin, pioneered the style of the Russian national school of composers.

glint — *verb intrans.* to give off flashes of bright light. — *noun* a brief flash of light. [from Middle English *glent*]

glissade — *noun* 1 a sliding ballet step. 2 *Mountaineering* an act of sliding down a snowy or icy slope. — *verb intrans.* to perform a glissade. [from French *glissade,* from *glisser,* to slide]

glissando (ABBREV. **gliss.**) *noun* (PL. **glissandi, glissandos**) *Mus.* a sliding from one note to another. The term is found on musical scores and the effect is produced on different instruments by a variety of methods. For example, on keyboard instruments the fingernail is drawn rapidly across the keys; on the harp, the finger is drawn across the strings; on instruments of the violin family, the finger slides rapidly up and down the string; and, on the trombone, the effect is produced using the slide. [from Italian *glissando,* from French *glissant,* sliding]

glisten *verb intrans.* (**glistened, glistening**) *usually said of something wet, icy, etc* to shine or sparkle. [from Middle English *glistnen*]

glitch *noun colloq.* a sudden brief irregularity or failure to function, especially in electronic equipment. [perhaps from Yiddish *glitsh,* slip]

glitter — *verb intrans.* (**glittered, glittering**) 1 to shine with bright flashes of light; to sparkle. 2 *colloq.* to be sparkingly attractive or resplendent: *a party glittering with famous film stars.* — *noun*

1 sparkle. 2 *colloq.* bright attractiveness, often superficial. 3 tiny pieces of shiny material, especially silvery paper, used for decoration. [from Middle English *gliteren*]

glitterati *pl. noun colloq.* famous, fashionable, and beautiful people. [from GLITTER, after LITERATI]

glittering *adj.* shining brightly; sparkling.

Glittertind or **Glittertinden** the highest mountain in Norway, situated in the Jotunheimen range, S central Norway. HEIGHT 2 470m.

glitz *noun* showiness, garishness.

glitzy *adj.* (**glitzier, glitziest**) *derog. slang* extravagantly showy; flashy. [perhaps from German *glitzern,* to glitter]

gloaming *noun poetic, Scot.* dusk; twilight. [from Anglo-Saxon *glomung*]

gloat — *verb intrans.* (*often* **gloat over something**) to feel or show smug or vindictive satisfaction, especially in one's own success or in another's misfortune. — *noun* an act of gloating. [perhaps from Norse *glotta,* to grin]

glob *noun colloq.* a small amount of thick liquid; a blob or dollop. [perhaps from BLOB]

global *adj.* 1 affecting the whole world. 2 total; including everything. 3 globe-shaped.

globally *adv.* in a global way.

Global Maritime Distress and Safety System an international code introduced by the International Maritime Organization in 1993 that uses satellite technology and does not require messages to be tapped out by a radio operator.

global warming a gradual increase in the average temperature of the Earth's surface and its atmosphere, attributed to the greenhouse effect.

globe — *noun* 1 (**the globe**) the earth. 2 a sphere with a map of the world on it. 3 any ball-shaped object, eg a glass lampshade. [from Latin *globus*]

globe artichoke the rounded head of the artichoke plant, with edible leaves.

globeflower *noun* a northern plant with pale (especially yellow) globe-shaped flowers.

Globe Theatre 1 a theatre constructed on Bankside (a district of Southwark), London, in 1598–9. It is thought to have originally been a polygonal wooden building comprising three tiers of seats arranged around an open yard. It was destroyed by fire (1613), rebuilt, then demolished by the Puritans (1644). Shakespeare and some of the Chamberlain's Men company of players (later called the King's Men) were shareholders, and many of Shakespeare's plays were performed there for the first time (1599–1608). A working replica of the theatre was built on the original site (1987–93) under the direction of the US actor and film producer Sam Wanamaker (1919–93). 2 a theatre on Shaftesbury Avenue, London, which was opened in 1906 as the 'Seymour Hicks' and was renamed in 1909.

globetrotter *noun colloq.* a person who travels all over the world.

globetrotting *noun* travelling the world as a sightseer.

globin *noun Biochem.* in animals, any of a group of soluble proteins that are present in the iron-containing pigments haemoglobin (in red blood cells) and myoglobin (in muscle cells). [from Latin *globus,* sphere]

globular *adj.* 1 shaped like a globe or globule. 2 consisting of globules. [from Latin *globulus,* diminutive of *globus,* globe]

globular cluster *Astron.* a spherical or nearly spherical dense cluster of hundreds of thousands to millions of very old stars that formed at an early stage in the development of the galaxies. There are more than 100 globular clusters scattered around our Galaxy.

globule *noun* a small drop, especially of liquid.

globulin *noun Biol.* any of a group of single proteins, found in blood plasma, eggs, and milk, and as storage proteins in plant seeds, that are soluble in certain salt solutions and coagulated by heat. Some globulins (*immunoglobulins*) function as antibodies in immune responses.

glockenspiel *noun* a musical instrument consisting of tuned metal plates in a frame, played with two small hammers. [from German *Glocke,* bell + *Spiel,* play]

glomerulus *noun* (PL. **glomeruli**) *Anat.* in the kidney, a small ball of blood capillaries surrounded by the cup-shaped end (*Bowman's capsule*) of a kidney tubule. There are about a million glomeruli in each kidney, and they are responsible for the initial filtration of waste products from the blood. [from Latin *glomus, glomeris,* a ball of yarn]

Glommen or **Glomma** see GLÅMA.

gloom — *noun* 1 near-darkness. 2 sadness or despair. — *verb* 1 *intrans. said of the sky* to be dark and threatening. 2 *intrans.* to behave in a sad or depressed way. 3 to make dark. 4 to make depressed or depressing. [from Middle English *gloumbe*]

gloomily *adv.* in a gloomy way.

gloomy *adj.* (**gloomier, gloomiest**) 1 dark, dimly lit. 2 causing gloom. 3 sad, depressed.

Gloria a female first name, introduced in Shaw's play *You Never Can Tell* (1898). [from Latin *gloria,* glory]

Gloriana, also known as **Tanaquil** the reigning Queen of Fairyland in Spenser's *The Faerie Queene,* who represents Queen Elizabeth I. Honourable, virtuous, and wise, her name alludes to her great power.

glorification *noun* the act of glorifying or the state of being glorified.

glorified *adj. derog.* given a fancy name or appearance.

glorify *verb* (**glorifies, glorified**) 1 to exaggerate the beauty, importance, etc of. 2 to praise or worship (God). 3 to make glorious. [from Latin *gloria,* glory + *facere,* to make]

glorious *adj.* 1 having or bringing glory. 2 splendidly beautiful. 3 *colloq.* excellent. 4 *humorous colloq.* very bad: *glorious mess.*

Glorious First of June, Battle of the a naval battle fought (1794) off the Isle d'Ouessant (near Brest) between British and French navies, which resulted in victory for Admiral Richard Howe, the capture of a third of the French ships, and confirmation of British naval supremacy.

gloriously *adv.* in a glorious way.

Glorious Revolution the name given to the events (Dec 1688–Feb 1689) during which James VII and II fled from England, effectively abdicating the throne, and William III and Mary II were established by parliament as joint monarchs. The title, coined by Whigs who in the long term benefited most, celebrates the bloodlessness of the event and the constitutional importance of parliament.

glorious twelfth (**the glorious twelfth**) 12 Aug, the opening day of the grouse-shooting season.

glory — *noun* (PL. **glories**) 1 great honour and prestige. 2 great beauty or splendour. 3 praise and thanks given to God. 4 a greatly admired asset: *patience is her crowning glory.* — *verb intrans.* (**glories, gloried**) (**glory in something**) to feel or show great delight or pride in it. [from Latin *gloria*]

glory-hole *noun colloq.* a room or cupboard where odds and ends are kept, especially in a disorganized way. [perhaps from Middle English *glory,* to defile]

Glos. *abbrev.* Gloucestershire.

gloss¹ — *noun* **1** shiny brightness on a surface. **2** a superficial pleasantness or attractiveness. **3** (*also* **gloss paint**) paint which produces a shiny finish. **4** a substance which adds shine: *lip gloss.* — *verb* **1** to give a shiny finish to. **2** to paint with gloss.
— **gloss over** to conceal, especially by treating briefly and dismissively.

gloss² — *noun* a short explanation of a difficult word, phrase, etc in a text, eg in the margin. — *verb* to provide a gloss of (a word, etc), or add glosses to (a text). [from Latin *glossa*, word requiring explanation]

glossary *noun* (PL. **glossaries**) a list of glosses, often at the end of a book.

glossily *adv.* with a gloss.

glossiness *noun* being glossy.

glossolalia *noun* 'speaking in tongues': the phenomenon of spontaneously uttering unintelligible sounds believed to form part of an unknown language or languages, and considered by certain Christians, especially Pentecostalists and charismatic Catholics, to be a manifestation of the Holy Spirit in believers and converts. See also XENOGLOSSIA. [from Greek *glossa*, tongue + *laleein*, to talk]

glossopharyngeal *adj. Anat.* denoting the ninth cranial nerve of vertebrates, which contains motor nerve fibres that supply two triangular salivary glands (known as *parotid glands*) and part of the pharynx, and sensory nerve fibres that supply the back of the tongue and the soft palate. [from Greek *glossa*, tongue + PHARYNGEAL]

glossy *adj.* (**glossier, glossiest**) **1** smooth and shiny. **2** superficially attractive. **3** *said of a magazine* printed on glossy paper.

glottal *adj. technical* of or produced by the glottis.

glottal stop *Linguistics* a sound produced when the glottis is closed and then opened sharply, eg the sound substituted for a 't' in words such as 'bottle' in some pronunciations of English.

glottis *noun* (PL. **glottises, glottides**) *Anat.* the opening through which air passes from the pharynx (back of the throat) to the trachea (windpipe), including the space between the vocal cords. [from Latin *glotta*, tongue]

glottochronology *noun Linguistics* a statistical study of vocabulary to determine the degree of relationship between two languages, how far and at what rate the languages may have diverged from a common source over the centuries, and the time-scale of their independent development. A basic word-list is used to compare languages and the time-scale of their divergence may be deduced from the percentage of words from the basic list which are common to both. [from Greek *glotta*, tongue + *chronos*, time]

Gloucester, Earl of the naively trusting father of Edgar and Edmund in Shakespeare's *King Lear*, who is brutally blinded by Cornwall and Regan because of his suspected alliance with Cordelia.

Gloucester, Humphrey, Duke of (1391–1447) youngest son of Henry IV, and Lord Protector during the minority of Henry VI (1422–9). He increased the difficulties of his brother, the Duke of Bedford, by his greed, irresponsibility, and disputes with their uncle, Cardinal Beaufort. In 1447 he was arrested for high treason and five days later was found dead in bed (apparently from natural causes). A patron of literature, he was nicknamed 'the Good Duke Humphrey'.

Gloucester, Prince Richard (Alexander Walter George), Duke of (1944–) British prince, younger son of Henry, Duke of Gloucester (the third son of George V). In 1972 he married Birgitte van Deurs; they have one son,

Alexander, Earl of Ulster (1974–) and two daughters, Lady Davina Windsor (1977–) and Lady Rose Windsor (1980–).

Gloucester, Latin **Glevum**, Anglo-Saxon **Caer Glou** POP (1992e) 105 000, the county town of Gloucestershire, SW England. It lies NE of Bristol, connected to the R Severn by canal. The Romans founded the town in the 1c AD. NOTABLE FEATURES cathedral (13c); Bishop Hooper's Lodging; Museum of Advertising and Packaging.

Gloucestershire POP (1992e) 541 000, a county in SW England, divided into six districts. AREA 2 643sq km/1 022sq mi. It is bounded N by Hereford and Worcester, NE by Warwickshire, E by Oxfordshire, S by Wiltshire and Avon, and W by Gwent in Wales. PHYSICAL DESCRIPTION drained by the R Severn; the Cotswold Hills extend NE through the county; the Forest of Dean lies to the E. CHIEF TOWNS Gloucester (county town), Cheltenham, Cirencester. ECONOMY arable farming in the Cotswolds, fruit, dairy farming; light engineering.

glove — *noun* a covering for the hand, usually with a separate sheath for each finger. — *verb* to cover with a glove or gloves.
— **fit like a glove** to fit perfectly.
the gloves are off *colloq.* the serious argument, fight, etc is about to begin.
[from Anglo-Saxon *glof*]

glover *noun* a glove-maker.

glow — *verb intrans.* **1** to give out a steady heat or light without flames. **2** to shine brightly, as if very hot: *cheeks glowing with health.* **3** to feel or communicate a sensation of intense contentment or well-being: *glow with pride.* — *noun* **1** a steady flameless heat or light. **2** bright, shiny appearance. **3** intensity of (especially pleasant) feeling. [from Anglo-Saxon *glowan*]

glower — *verb intrans.* (**glowered, glowering**) to stare angrily. — *noun* an angry stare; a scowl.

glowing *adj.* **1** which glows. **2** full of praise: *glowing report.*

glow-worm *noun* **1** a small nocturnal beetle belonging to the same family as the fireflies, and found mainly in warm climates. At night the wingless female attracts the winged male by giving out a bright greenish light from special organs on the underside of her abdomen. **2** in N America, any of various luminous insect larvae.

gloxinia *noun* any of various species of plant belonging to the genus *Siningia*, native to Brazil, and having large velvety funnel-shaped white, pink, red, or purple flowers. It is related to the African violet, and is a popular house plant. [from Gloxin, the name of a German botanist]

Glubb, Sir John Bagot, also called **Glubb Pasha** (1897–1986) English soldier, born in Preston, Lancashire. He served in World War I and became the first organizer of the native police force in the new state of Iraq (1920). In 1930 he was transferred to British-mandated Transjordan, organized the Arab Legion's Desert Patrol, and became Legion Commandant (1939). He was respected by the Bedouin, but was dismissed following Arab criticism in 1956, and later became a writer and lecturer.

glucagon *noun Biochem.* a hormone secreted by the pancreas which accelerates the conversion of glycogen to glucose in the liver, so increasing blood glucose levels. [from Greek *glykys,* sweet]

Gluck, Christoph (Willibald) (1714–87) Austro-German composer, born in Erasbach, Bavaria. He began to write operas in 1741, and collaboration with the librettist Ranieri Calzabigi produced such works as *Orfeo ed Euridice* (Orpheus and Eurydice, 1762) and *Alceste* (1767). In the late 1770s, Paris was divided into two — the Gluckists who supported Gluck's French opera style and the Piccinnists who supported the Italian style of Niccolo Piccinni (1728–1800), but Gluck finally won through with his *Iphigénie*

en Tauride (1779), and retired from Paris full of honour.

glucose *noun* **1** *Biochem.* (FORMULA $C_6H_{12}O_6$) The most abundant six-carbon sugar (hexose) in living cells. In animals it is the main form in which energy obtained from the digestion of carbohydrates is transported around the bloodstream, and in plants it is the initial product of photosynthesis. It forms the building blocks of glycogen, starch, and cellulose, and plays an important role in the chemical reactions that take place in living cells. **2** (*also* **glucose syrup**) a concentrated solution of the products of breakdown of starch, used in the confectionery industry, for canning fruit, etc. [from Greek *glykys*, sweet]

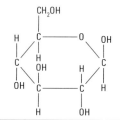

glucose

glucoside *noun Biochem.* any of various derivatives of glucose, in which the first hydroxyl (-OH) group is replaced by another group, and which on treatment with enzymes or acids yields glucose.

glue — *noun* any adhesive obtained by extracting natural substances, especially bone, in boiling water, or by dissolving synthetic substances such as rubber or plastic in a suitable solvent. — *verb* (**glueing, gluing**) **1** to use such an adhesive to stick two materials together. **2** *colloq.* to put or stay very close to; to fix on: *eyes glued to the window.* [from Latin *glus*]

glue-sniffer *noun* a person who practises glue-sniffing.

glue-sniffing *noun* the practice of breathing in fumes from some types of glue to produce hallucinatory or intoxicating effects.

gluey *adj.* (**gluier, gluiest**) containing glue; like glue, sticky.

glum *adj.* (**glummer, glummest**) in low spirits; sullen. [from Middle English *glome*, to frown]

glume *noun Bot.* an outer sterile bract which, alone or with others, encloses the spikelet in grasses and sedges. [from Latin *gluma*, husk]

glumly *adv.* in a glum way.

glumness *noun* being glum.

gluon *noun Physics* a hypothetical particle with no mass, the carrier of the force that is believed to hold quarks together.

glut — *noun* **1** an excessive supply of goods, etc. **2** an act of eating an unreasonably or unnecessarily large amount of food. — *verb* (**glutted, glutting**) **1** to feed or supply to excess. **2** to block or choke up. [from Latin *glutire*, to swallow]

glutamine *noun Biochem.* an amino acid found in proteins. [from Latin *gluten -inis*, glue]

gluten *noun Biochem.* a mixture of two plant storage proteins, *gliadin* and *glutenin*, that occurs in wheat flour. When mixed with water and kneaded, these proteins give bread dough elastic properties, and also allow it to rise as gas bubbles are trapped by the gluten. In some people the lining of the small intestine is abnormally sensitive to gluten, a condition known as *coeliac disease*, necessitating a gluten-free diet. [from Latin *gluten*, glue]

glutinous *adj.* like glue; sticky.

glutton¹ *noun* **1** *derog.* a person who eats too much. **2** a person whose behaviour suggests an

eagerness (for something unpleasant): *a glutton for hard work.*
— **a glutton for punishment** a person who is eager to undertake difficult or arduous tasks. [from Latin *gluttire*, to swallow]

glutton² same as WOLVERINE.

gluttonous *adj.* greedy.

gluttony *noun derog.* the habit or practice of eating too much.

glyceride *noun Chem.* an ester of glycerol and up to three fatty acid molecules. Triglycerides are the main components of fats and oils.

glycerine *or* **glycerin** see GLYCEROL. [from Greek *glykeros*, sweet]

glycerol *noun Chem.* a colourless viscous liquid with a sweet taste, soluble in water, that is an important constituent of fats and oils, and can be obtained from all vegetable and animal fats and oils by hydrolysis. It is used in various foodstuffs and medicines, and in the manufacture of the explosive nitroglycerine. — Also called *glycerine.*

glycine *or* **glycin** *noun Biochem.* an amino acid found in proteins. [from Greek *glykys*, sweet]

glycogen *noun Biochem.* in vertebrates, the main form in which carbohydrate is stored, especially in the liver and muscles. It is also found in invertebrates, and in some algae and fungi. Each glycogen molecule consists of a highly branched chain of glucose molecules linked end to end. — Also called *animal starch, amylum.* [from Greek *glykys*, sweet + -GEN]

glycogenic *adj.* relating to or involving the formation of sugar.

glycolysis *noun Biochem.* during respiration in the cells of living organisms, the conversion of glucose to pyruvic acid, with the release of energy in the form of ATP.

Glyndebourne Festival an annual summer festival of opera established (1934) when John Christie (1882–1962) founded the Glyndebourne Festival Opera to play in the opera house he had built on his estate (Glyndebourne) in Sussex, England. The original building was demolished in 1992, and a new, larger opera house opened in 1994.

Glynis a female first name. [from Welsh *glyn*, valley + *-is* taken from GLADYS]

GM *abbrev.* George Medal.

gm *abbrev.* gram or gramme.

GMBATU *abbrev.* General, Municipal, Boilermakers and Allied Trades Union.

GMC *abbrev.* General Medical Council.

GMT *abbrev.* Greenwich Mean Time.

GMWU *abbrev.* General and Municipal Workers Union.

gnarled *or* **gnarly** *adj., said of trees, branches, etc* twisted; with knots and lumps, usually as a result of age. [from Middle English *knarre*, knob-like protuberance]

gnash *verb trans., intrans.* to grind (the teeth) together, especially in anger. [from Middle English *gnasten*]

gnashers *pl. noun humorous slang* teeth.

gnat *noun* any of various small biting (and often bloodsucking) flies, common near stagnant water. [from Anglo-Saxon *gnætt*]

gnaw *verb (PAST PARTICIPLE* **gnawed, gnawn)** 1 (**gnaw something** *or* **gnaw at something**) to bite it with a scraping action, causing a gradual wearing away. 2 to make (eg a hole) in this way. 3 *trans., intrans.* (**gnaw someone** *or* **gnaw at someone**) *said of pain, anxiety, etc* to trouble them persistently: *is gnawed by guilt.* [from Anglo-Saxon *gnagan*]

gnawing *adj.* that gnaws.

Gneisenau, August (Wilhelm Anton), Graf Neithardt von (Count Neithardt of)

(1760–1831) Prussian soldier, born in Schildau, Prussian Saxony. He joined the Prussian army in 1786, fought at Saalfeld and Jena (1806), helped to reorganize the army after its defeat by Napoleon (1807), and gave distinguished service at Leipzig (1813) in the war of liberation. As chief of Blücher's staff in the Waterloo campaign he directed the strategy of the Prussian army.

gneiss *noun Geol.* a coarse-grained metamorphic rock that contains bands of quartz and feldspar alternating with bands of mica. [from German *Gneis*]

gnocchi *pl. noun* an Italian dish of small dumplings made with flour, cooked potato, or semolina, poached and served with various sauces. [from Italian *gnocchi*, lumps]

gnome *noun* 1 a fairy-tale creature, a small misshapen man, who lives underground, often guarding treasure. 2 a statue of such a creature, especially as a garden ornament. 3 *colloq.* a person with a secret powerful influence, especially in finance: *gnomes of Zurich.* [from Latin *gnomus*, dwarf]

gnomic *adj. formal, said of speech or writing* 1 expressing generally held views or principles. 2 *often derog.* moralizing. [from Greek *gnome*, opinion]

gnomish *adj.* like a gnome.

gnostic — *adj.* 1 relating to knowledge, especially mystical or religious knowledge. 2 (*usually* **Gnostic**) relating to Gnosticism. — *noun* (*usually* **Gnostic**) an early Christian heretic believing in redemption of the soul from the world of matter through special religious knowledge. [from Greek *gnosis*, knowledge]

Gnosticism a system of belief prominent within 2c Christianity, but which may have had earlier, non-Christian roots. It emphasized salvation through the acquisition of secret revealed knowledge about cosmic origins and the true destiny of the spirit within people; in later forms, this knowledge was imparted by a heavenly redeemer figure. Gnosticism was considered a heresy by the early Church Fathers, particularly for its appeal to secret traditions, its deprecatory view of the Creator God, and its Docetic view of Christ (a heretic claim that his body was a semblance or ethereal).

GNP *abbrev.* gross national product.

gnu *noun* (PL. **gnus, gnu**) a type of large African deer with a buffalo-like head and horns. [from Hottentot]

go¹ — *verb usually intrans.* (**goes;** PAST TENSE **went;** PAST PARTICIPLE **gone**) 1 (*often* **go about, by, down**, *etc*) to walk, move, or travel in the direction specified. 2 to lead or extend: *a path going across the field / the road goes all the way to the farm.* 3 (**go to somewhere**) to visit or attend it, once or regularly: *go to the cinema / go to school.* 4 to leave or move away. 5 to be destroyed or taken away; to disappear: *the old door had to go / the peaceful atmosphere has gone.* 6 to proceed or fare: *the scheme is going well.* 7 to be used up: *money going on drink.* 8 to be given or sold for a stated amount: *went for £20.* 9 to leave or set out for a stated purpose: *go for a ride / go on holiday / gone fishing.* 10 *intrans., trans.* to perform (an action) or produce (a sound): *go like this / go bang.* 11 to break, break down, or fail: *the old TV finally went / his eyes have gone.* 12 to work or be in working order: *get it going.* 13 to become; to pass into a certain condition: *go mad.* 14 to belong; to be placed correctly: *where does this go?* 15 to fit, or be contained: *my foot won't go into the shoe / four into three won't go.* 16 to continue in a certain state: *go hungry.* 17 *said of time* to pass. 18 to run in words or notes: *as the story goes.* 19 (*often* **go for someone** *or* **something**) to apply to them; to be valid or accepted for them: *the same goes for you / in this office, anything goes.* 20 *colloq.* to carry authority: *what she says goes.* 21 (*often* **go with something**) *said of colours, etc* to match or blend. 22 (**go with**

something) to co-exist with it: *goodness doesn't always go with beauty.* 23 (**go by something**) to be guided by it: *don't go by what he says.* 24 to subject oneself: *go to much trouble.* 25 to adopt a system: *go metric.* 26 *trans.* to bet, especially at cards: *went five pounds.* 27 *colloq.* to be in general, for the purpose of comparison: *as girls go, she's quite naughty.* 28 to exist or be on offer: *the best offer going at the moment.* 29 *trans. colloq.* to welcome or enjoy: *I could go a cup of tea.* 30 *trans. colloq., usually with quoted speech* to say. — *noun* (PL. **goes**) 1 a turn or spell: *it's my go.* 2 an attempt: *have a go.* 3 energy; liveliness: *she lacks go.* 4 a verbal attack: *really had a go at me.* 5 *colloq.* busy activity: *it's all go.* 6 *colloq.* a success: *make a go of it.* — *adj. colloq.* working properly; in operation: *all systems go.*
— **be going on for** (**a stated age**) *colloq.* to be approaching it: *she's going on for 60.*

go about 1 to circulate: *a rumour going about.* 2 *Naut.* to change course.

go about something 1 to busy oneself with it. 2 to attempt or tackle it: *how to go about doing this.*

go against something to be contrary to it.

go against someone to be decided unfavourably for them: *the court case went against him.*

go ahead to proceed.

go all out for something to make a great effort to obtain or achieve it.

go along with someone *or* **something** to agree with and support them.

go and ... to be so unwise or unfortunate as to: *they've gone and got lost.*

go back on something to break an agreement, etc.

go down 1 to decrease. 2 *colloq.* to be accepted or received: *the joke went down well.*

go down with something to contract an illness.

go for someone *or* **something** *colloq.* 1 to attack them. 2 to be attracted by them. 3 to choose them: *went for the red shoes instead.*

go in for something *colloq.* 1 to take up a profession. 2 to enter a contest. 3 to be interested or attracted by something, as a rule.

go into something 1 to take up or join a profession. 2 to discuss or investigate something: *cannot go into that now.*

go it alone *colloq.* to manage or try to manage without help, especially in difficulties.

go off 1 to explode. 2 *said of perishables, eg food* to become rotten. 3 to proceed or pass off: *the party went off well.*

go off someone *or* **something** to stop liking them.

go on 1 to continue or proceed. 2 *colloq.* to talk too much.

go on at someone *colloq.* to criticize them or complain to them persistently.

go out 1 *said of a fire or light* to become extinguished. 2 to be broadcast. 3 to no longer be fashionable.

go out to someone to feel sympathy for them: *my heart went out to him.*

go out with someone to spend time with someone socially or especially romantically.

go over to pass off or be received: *the play went over well.*

go over something 1 to examine it. 2 to revise or rehearse it.

go over to someone to transfer support or allegiance: *go over to the enemy.*

go round to be enough for all.

go slow to work slowly so as to encourage an employer to negotiate or meet a demand.

go through to be approved.

go through something 1 to use it up. 2 to revise or rehearse it. 3 to examine it. 4 to suffer from it: *went through hell.* 5 to search it: *went through all our bags.*

go through with something to carry it out to the end.

go under *colloq.* to fail or be ruined.

go up 1 to increase. 2 *said of a building, etc* to be erected. 3 *colloq.* to be destroyed by fire or explosion.

go with someone *colloq.* to have a close romantic friendship with them.
go with something to agree with or support it.
go without something to suffer a lack of an essential thing or things.
have something going for one *colloq.* to have as an attribute or advantage: *you have a lot going for you.*
no go *colloq.* not possible; in vain.
on the go *colloq.* busily active.
to be going on with *colloq.* for the moment: *enough to be going on with.*
[from Anglo-Saxon *gan*]

go² *noun* a Japanese board game for two players, played with black and white pieces. The object is to capture one's opponent's pieces and control the larger part of the board. [from Japanese]

Goa POP (1991) 1.2m, a state in W India. AREA 3 701sq km/1 429sq mi. HISTORY conquered by the Muslims in 1312; taken by Portugal in 1510; Old Goa became a prosperous port city in the 16c.

goad — *verb* (**goad someone into something** *or* **to do something**) to urge or provoke. — *noun* **1** a sharp-pointed stick used for driving cattle, etc. **2** anything that provokes or incites. [from Anglo-Saxon *gad*]

go-ahead *colloq.* — *adj.* energetically ambitious and far-sighted. — *noun* (**the go-ahead**) permission to start.

goal *noun* **1** a set of posts with a crossbar, through which the ball is struck to achieve a score in various sports, especially football; also more generally, the area in which the goal stands. **2** an act of scoring in this way; the point or points scored. **3** an aim or purpose: *one must have a goal in life.* [perhaps from Middle English *gol*, boundary]

goalie *noun colloq.* a goalkeeper.

goalkeeper *noun* the player guarding the goal in various sports, with the task of preventing the opposition from scoring.

goal-line *noun* the line marking each end of the field of play in some sports.

goalpost *noun* each of two upright posts forming the goal in some sports.
— **move the goalposts** to change the accepted rules or aims of an activity during its course, to suit new conditions.

goat *noun* **1** any of a number of species of herbivorous mammal (*Capra hircus*) belonging to the family Bovidae, related to the sheep, and characterized by the presence of a beard in the male. **2** *derog. colloq.* a man, especially if old, who makes unwanted sexual advances to women. **3** *derog. colloq.* a foolish person.
— **get someone's goat** *colloq.* to annoy or irritate them.
[from Anglo-Saxon *gat*]
◇ Wild goats, found in rocky and mountainous regions of S Europe, the Middle East, and Central Asia, are noted for their physical agility and sure-footedness (they frequently climb trees). They live in herds and feed on grass and leaves. The males are larger than the females, and the horns of the males are sweeping and scimitar-shaped. The coat is typically reddish-brown in summer and greyish-brown in winter, with black markings on the body and limbs. Domestic goats, descended from a Persian species, feed on shrubs and trees, and also graze on pasture. Goats are kept worldwide for their milk (which is also used to make cheese), and the hides of young kids are used to make leather. Some goats are a source of excellent wool.

goatee *noun* a pointed beard growing on the front of the chin only, like a goat's.

goatherd *noun* a person who looks after goats.

goatish *adj.* **1** like a goat. **2** stupid. **3** lustful.

gob — *noun* **1** *coarse slang* the mouth. **2** a soft wet lump. **3** *coarse slang* spit. — *verb intrans.*

(**gobbed**, **gobbing**) *coarse slang* to spit. [from Old French *gober*, to gulp down]

gobbet *noun* **1** a lump or chunk. **2** *colloq.* an extract from a text. [from Old French *gobet*, diminutive of *gobe*, mouthful]

Gobbi, Tito (1915–84) Italian baritone, born in Bassano del Grappa. He studied law, but took up singing in Rome, and made his operatic début in Gubbio (1935). A regular performer with the Rome Opera from 1938, he soon made an international reputation, especially in Verdian roles such as Falstaff and Don Carlos.

gobble — *verb* **1** *trans., intrans.* (*usually* **gobble something up** *or* **down**) to eat it hurriedly and noisily. **2** *intrans. said of a turkey* to make a loud swallowing noise in the throat. — *noun* the gobbling sound made by a turkey. [from Old French *gober*, to gulp down]

gobbledygook *or* **gobbledegook** *noun colloq. usually. derog.* **1** official jargon, meaningless to ordinary people. **2** nonsense; rubbish. [imitative, after GOBBLE]

gobbler *noun North Amer., esp. US* a male turkey.

Gobbo, Launcelot the clown, attendant to Shylock, in Shakespeare's *The Merchant of Venice*. His father is called Old Gobbo.

Gobelins, Manufacture Nationale des a tapestry factory on the Left Bank of the R Seine in Paris. It was established in 1440 by Jean Gobelin as a dye works, and in the 17c a number of tapestry workshops were brought together here. The term *Gobelins* has become synonymous with the art of tapestry making.

Go-Between, The a novel by L P Hartley (1953). It describes an old man's remembrance of the significant events of a summer holiday during his adolescence.

go-between *noun* a messenger between two people or sides; an intermediary.

Gobi Desert a desert in central Asia. AREA c.1 295 000sq km/500 000sq mi. It stretches c.1 600km/1 000mi E–W across SE Mongolia and N China. The desert lies on a plateau, at an altitude of 900–1 500m. PHYSICAL DESCRIPTION a series of shallow, alkaline basins; completely sandy in the W. There are some nomadic Mongolian tribes on grassy margins. NOTABLE FEATURES many fossil finds, including dinosaur eggs, and prehistoric implements.

goblet *noun* a drinking-cup with a base and stem but no handles, often made from metal or glass. [from Old French *gobelet*, diminutive of *gobel*, cup]

goblin *noun* in folk-tales, an evil or mischievous spirit in the form of a small man. [from Old French *gobelin*, perhaps from Greek *kobalos*, mischievous spirit]

gobsmacked *adj. colloq.* astonished; dumbfounded.

gobstopper *noun colloq.* a large round sweet for sucking.

goby *noun* (PL. **gobies**) a small fish whose lower fins are joined to form a sucker. [from Latin *gobius*, gudgeon]

go-by
— **give someone the go-by** *colloq.* to ignore or snub them.

god *noun* **1** in many beliefs, a divine or superhuman being with power over nature and the human race, and often an object of worship. **2** (**God**) in the Christian and other religions, the supreme being and creator of the universe and the human race, an object of worship. **3** a man greatly admired, especially for his fine physique or wide influence. **4** *often derog.* an object of excessive worship or influence: *he made money his god.*
— **the gods** the area of the balcony or upper circle in a theatre.
[from Anglo-Saxon *god*]

◇ In some world religions (eg Christianity, Judaism, Islam) there is one God only (*monotheism*), who is transcendent, all-powerful, and related to the cosmos as creator. In other religions (eg Hinduism, Classical Greek and Roman religions, and primitive religions) many gods may be recognized (*polytheism*), and individual gods have particular properties and powers.
In the Judaeo-Christian tradition, God, though transcendent and invisible, revealed himself in history through the life and response of the people of Israel, and, in the Christian tradition, supremely and finally in the life, death, and resurrection of Jesus of Nazareth, the Christ, all as testified to in the Scriptures of the Old and New Testaments of the Bible.
From the time of the ancient Greeks, philosophers have tried to prove the existence of a supreme being by reason alone (ie not by divine revelation); of these attempts the 'ontological' arguments of St Anselm and Descartes, the 'Five Ways' of St Thomas Aquinas, and Kant's moral argument are among the more famous and abiding.

Godard, Jean-Luc (1930–) French film director, born in Paris. His first major film *A Bout de Souffle* (Breathless, 1960) established him as a leader of the Nouvelle Vague cinema. He wrote his own filmscripts on contemporary themes, such as *Vivre sa Vie* (It's My Life, 1962). Later feature films include *Sauve Qui Peut* (Slow Motion, 1980), *Détective* (1984), *Je Vous Salue, Marie* (Hail Mary, 1985) and *Hélas Pour Moi* (Woe is me, 1993).

godchild *noun* a child for whom a godparent is responsible.

Goddard, Robert Hutchings (1882–1945) US physicist, rocket engineer, and inventor, born in Worcester, Massachusetts. Professor at Clark University, Worcester, he developed the first successful liquid-fuelled rocket, launched in 1926, and developed the first instrument-carrying rocket able to make observations in flight (1929); he was granted over 200 patents.

Goddard Space Flight Center *Astron.* a large NASA establishment at Greenbelt, Maryland, USA, responsible for the operation of the Hubble Space Telescope and other unmanned artificial satellites, and for astronomical research, and the design and development of Earth-orbiting spacecraft. It is also the site of the National Space Science Data centre. [named after the US physicist Robert Hutchings Goddard]

goddaughter *noun* a female godchild.

goddess *noun* **1** a superhuman feminine being with power over nature and man, an object of worship. **2** a woman greatly admired for her great beauty or wide influence.

Godfather, The a US film directed by Francis Coppola (1972). It is a drama focusing on the power and influence of a Mafia dynasty, starring Marlon Brando and Al Pacino, and had two sequels.

godfather *noun* **1** a male godparent. **2** the head of a criminal group, especially in the Mafia.

God-fearing *adj.* respectful of God's laws; pious.

God-forsaken *adj. derog.* remote and desolate.

Godfree, Kitty, *née* McKane (1896–1992) English tennis player, born in London. As Kitty McKane, she lost to Suzanne Lenglen in the 1923 Wimbledon singles final. She won the title in 1924, defeating Helen Wills, and in 1926, as Kitty Godfree, regained it after defeating Lili de Alvarez. In 1986 she presented a silver salver to Martina Navratilova when the latter won her seventh title.

Godfrey a male first name. [Norman, from Germanic *god*, good + *fred, frid*, peace]

Godhead *noun* **1** the divine state attributed to God or a god. **2 (the Godhead)** God.

Godiva, Lady (d.1080) English noblewoman and religious benefactress. According to tradition, she rode naked through Coventry marketplace in order to persuade her husband Leofric to reduce a heavy tax imposed upon the townsfolk (1040). The story is documented by Roger of Wendover (1235).

godless *adj.* **1** not religious; not believing in God. **2** wicked; immoral.

godlessness *noun* **1** wickedness. **2** lack of faith.

godlike *adj.* like a god.

godliness *noun* piety.

godly *adj.* (**godlier, godliest**) religious; pious.

godmother *noun* a female godparent.

Godolphin, Sidney Godolphin, 1st Earl of (1645–1712) English statesman, born near Helston, Cornwall. He entered parliament (1668), visited Holland (1678), and was made head of the Treasury (1684). He supported James when William of Orange landed (1688), and voted for a regency, yet William reinstated him as First Commissioner of the Treasury (1689–96). Queen Anne made him Lord High Treasurer (1702) and his able management of the finances helped Marlborough in the War of the Spanish Succession.

Godoy, Manuel de (1767–1851) Spanish court favourite and chief minister (1792–1808) under Charles IV. From being a guards officer, he achieved dictatorial power at the age of 25 as the lover of the Queen, Maria Luisa. In 1795 he assumed the title 'Prince of the Peace', following Spain's defeat by Revolutionary France. His alliance with France against England in 1796 was a disastrous move that made Spain into a virtual French satellite and contributed to the loss of Spain's American Empire. In 1808 he was overthrown, and went into exile.

godparent *noun* a person with responsibility for the religious education of another, especially a child, or, loosely, for a child's upbringing in the event of the death of its parents.

God Save the Queen *or* **God Save the King** the British national anthem, written anonymously in the 18c. Its music has also been used by other countries, and is still used for the national anthem of Liechtenstein.

godsend *noun* a person or thing whose arrival is unexpected but very welcome.

godson *noun* a male godchild.

Godspeed *interj. old use* an expression of wishes for a person's safety on a journey.

Godunov, Boris Fyodorovich (1552–1605) Tsar of Russia (1598–1605), previously Regent (from 1584) for Fyodor, the imbecilic elder son of Ivan IV (the Terrible). Ivan's younger son Dimitry had been banished to the upper Volga, where he died in 1591 (allegedly murdered at Boris's command). Later, a pretender who claimed to be Dimitry started a revolt, overcame Boris's troops, and after the sudden death of Boris in Moscow, was crowned in 1605.

Godwin (d.1053) Earl of Wessex, probably son of the South Saxon Wulfnoth. Having become powerful under King Canute, in 1042 he helped to raise Edward the Confessor, who married his daughter Edith, to the throne. However, he then led the struggle against the King's foreign favourites, which Edward revenged by confining Edith in a monastery, and banishing Godwin and his sons (1051). In 1052 Godwin landed in England, received the support of the people, and was reinstated. After his death, his son was for a few months Edward's successor as Harold II.

Godwin, William (1756–1836) English political writer and novelist, born in Wisbech, Cambridgeshire. His major work of social philosophy is *An Enquiry Concerning Political Justice* (1793), and his best-known novel is *The Adventures of Caleb Williams* (1794). He married Mary Wollstonecraft in 1797.

Godwin-Austen, Mount see K2.

godwit *noun* a large wading bird of northern regions, with an upturned bill.

Goebbels, (Paul) Joseph (1897–1945) German Nazi politician, born in Rheydt. Absolved from military service because of a deformed foot, he became an enthusiastic supporter of Hitler and was appointed head of the Ministry of Public Enlightenment and Propaganda (1933). A bitter anti-Semite, his skilful mob oratory made him a powerful exponent of the more radical aspects of Nazi philosophy. Wartime conditions greatly expanded his responsibilities and power, and by 1943, while Hitler was running the war, Goebbels was virtually running the country. He retained Hitler's confidence to the last, and in the Berlin bunker he and his wife committed suicide, after taking the lives of their six children.

Goeppert-Mayer, Maria, née **Maria Goeppert** (1906–72) German-born US physicist, born in Kattowitz (now Katowice in Poland). She studied at Göttingen before emigrating to the USA, where she taught at Johns Hopkins University, and became professor at the University of California in 1960. Following her discovery that certain nuclei are very stable, having 'magic numbers' of protons and neutrons, she developed a complete shell model of the nucleus. She shared the 1963 Nobel Prize for Physics with Eugene Wigner and Hans Jensen.

goer *noun* **1** (*usually in compounds*) a person who makes (especially regular) visits: *cinema-goer*. **2** *colloq.* a sexually energetic person, especially a woman. **3** *colloq.* something that travels fast, or makes fast progress.

Goering *or* **Göring Hermann (Wilhelm)** (1893–1946) German soldier and politico-military leader, born in Rosenheim, Bavaria. He fought on the Western Front in World War I, then transferred to the Air Force and commanded the famous 'Death Squadron'. In 1922 he joined the Nazi Party and was given command of the Hitler storm troopers. He became President of the Reichstag in 1932, and joined the Nazi government in 1933, then founded the Gestapo and set up the concentration camps for political, racial, and religious suspects. In 1940 he became economic dictator of Germany, and was made Marshal of the Reich, the only holder of the rank. In 1944 he attempted a palace revolution and was condemned to death, but he escaped and was captured by US troops. He was sentenced to death at the Nuremberg War Crimes Trial (1946), but committed suicide before his execution could take place.

Goesler, Madame Max the rich widow in the 'Palliser' novels of Anthony Trollope, who marries Phineas Finn.

Goethe, Johann Wolfgang von (1749–1832) German poet, dramatist, and scientist, born in Frankfurt-am-Main. He captured the spirit of German nationalism with his drama, *Götz von Berlichingen* (1773), following this with the novel *Leiden des jungen Werther* (The Sorrows of Young Werther, 1774). He then wrote much lyric poetry, and his plays *Iphigenie auf Tauris* (1789) and *Torquato Tasso* (1790) show a preoccupation with poetical form. His later works include the poems *Römische Elegien* (Roman Elegies, 1795), the play *Wilhelm Meisters Lehrjahre* (Wilhelm Meister's Apprentice Years, 1796), and his two-part version of *Faust*, on which he worked for most of his life (1808, 1832).

gofer *noun North Amer., esp. US* an office junior who runs errands. [from *go for*]

Gog and Magog the biblical names applied to future foes of the people of God. Ezekiel 38.2–6 predicted that a ruler (Gog) of the land in the north (Magog) would battle against Israel in the days before its restoration. Revelation 20.8 and rabbinic literature treat Gog and Magog as paired figures representing Satan in the final conflict against God's people. In British folklore, they refer to the survivors of a race of giants annihilated by Brutus, the founder of Britain.

go-getter *noun colloq.* an ambitious, enterprising person.

go-getting *adj.* ambitious, pushy.

goggle — *verb* **1** *intrans.* to look with wide staring eyes. **2** to roll (the eyes). **3** *intrans. said of the eyes* to stick out. — *noun* a wide-eyed stare. [perhaps Middle English *gogelen*, to look aside]

goggle-box *noun colloq.* a television set.

goggles *pl. noun* protective spectacles with edges fitting closely against the face.

go-go dancer a female erotic dancer, especially in a club or bar. [from French *à gogo*, galore, aplenty]

Gogol, Nikolai (Vasilievich) (1809–52) Russian novelist and dramatist, born in Sorochinstsi, Poltava, Ukraine. In 1829 he settled in St Petersburg, and later lived abroad for many years, mainly in Rome (1836–46). Also the author of several short stories, he is best-known for the play *The Inspector General* (1836), a satire exposing the corruption and vanity of provincial officials, and the novel *Dead Souls* (1842).

Goiânia POP (1991) 921 000, the capital of Goiás state, W central Brazil, SW of Brasília. Founded in 1933, it became state capital of Goiás Velho in 1937. notable features Parque Mutirama (with an Educational Park); racecourse; motor racetrack.

Goidelic — *noun* one of two distinct branches of the early Celtic language of Britain. Goidelic (or Gaelic) arose from the 4c BC with the first wave of Celtic-speaking people from Europe who settled first in Ireland, later reaching Scotland and the Isle of Man. See also BRYTHONIC, CELTIC, GAELIC.

going — *noun* **1** an act of leaving; a departure. **2** the condition of the track in horse-racing. **3** progress: *made good going.* **4** *colloq.* general situation or conditions: *when the going gets tough.* **5** (*in compounds*) the act or practice of making (especially regular) visits to: *theatre-going.* — *adj.* **1** working, especially bringing in business: *a going concern.* **2** usual or accepted: *the going rate.*

going-over *noun colloq.* **1** a beating. **2** a close inspection.

goings-on *pl. noun colloq.* events or happenings, especially if strange or disapproved of.

goitre *noun Medicine* abnormal enlargement of the thyroid gland, often resulting in a large swelling in the neck. It may be caused by hypothyroidism (in which there is too little thyroid hormone, and the gland swells in an attempt to increase the output of hormone), hyperthyroidism (overactivity of the thyroid gland), or a tumour. [from French *goître*, from Latin *guttur*, throat]

go-kart *noun* a low racing vehicle consisting of a frame with wheels, engine, and steering gear.

Gokhale, Gopal Krishna (1866–1915) Indian social reformer and nationalist, born in Kotluk, Bombay. He founded the Servants of India Society (1905) to work for the relief of the underprivileged, and the same year was elected President of the Indian National Congress. He advocated moderate and constitutional methods of agitation and gradual reform.

Gokstad ship a Viking oak-built sailing ship found in 1881 beneath a burial mound at Gokstad, 80km/50mi SE of Oslo, Norway. It measured 23.3m long, with a 5.2m beam, and was c.50 years old when buried in the late 9c. A replica crossed the Atlantic successfully in 1893.

Golan *or* **Golan Heights**, Arabic **Al Jawlan** POP (1988e) 24 000, an Israeli-occupied area of Syria, administered as part of Northern district, N Israel. It lies E of the Sea of Galilee. AREA 1 176sq km/454sq ml, rising to 1 204m at Mt Avital. The Golan area, which is of great strategic importance, was occupied by Israel in 1967, and annexed in 1981. Several Jewish settlements were founded in the area.

Gold, Thomas (1920–) Austrian-born US astronomer, born in Vienna. Having left Austria during Hitler's rise to power in central Europe, he became Director of the Center for Radiophysics and Space Research at Cornell University in 1959. He developed the steady-state theory of the origin of the universe (1948), which proposes that the universe is uniform in space and unchanging in time; although later displaced through new evidence, it was a valuable contribution to cosmological debate. He later proposed the currently accepted theory that 'pulsars' are rapidly rotating neutron stars, dense collapsed stars which produce beams of radio waves from their poles which appear as radio pulses on Earth.

gold — *noun* **1** (SYMBOL **Au**, ATOMIC NUMBER **79**) a soft dense yellow precious metal that is chemically unreactive, so does not tarnish, and highly malleable, so can be beaten into very thin sheets known as *gold leaf*. **2** articles made from it, especially jewellery and coins. **3** its value, used as a standard for the value of currency. **4** its deep yellow colour. **5** *colloq.* a gold medal. **6** precious or noble quality: *heart of gold*. **7** monetary wealth. — *adj.* **1** made of gold. **2** gold-coloured. [from Anglo-Saxon]
◇ Gold occurs naturally as small particles of the free metal in gravel, quartz veins, and some lead and copper ores. It is usually hardened by alloying it with silver or copper, and the gold content of an alloy is expressed in carats, pure gold being equivalent to 24 carats. It is used in jewellery, ornaments, dental fillings, and electronic devices (it is a good conductor of electricity), and was formerly used to make coins. Most gold is held for investment purposes as it is thought to have a more stable value than many currencies.

Goldberg, Whoopi (1949–) US film actress, born in New York City. Acting on stage from childhood, she made her major film début with an acclaimed performance in *The Color Purple* (1985). Later successes include *Ghost* (1990), for which she won a Best Supporting Actress Oscar, and *Sister Act* (1992).

Goldberg Variations thirty variations on an original theme for harpsichord by J S Bach (c.1741), named after the harpsichordist J G Goldberg (1727–56), for whom they may have been written.

Gold Coast POP (1991) 158 000, an urban area in Moreton statistical division, Queensland, E Australia. It is situated S of Brisbane, partly overlapping New South Wales. The largest resort region in Australia, it has beaches stretching for 32km/20mi, including Southport, Surfers' Paradise, Broadbeach, Mermaid Beach, Burleigh Heads, and Coolangatta. NOTABLE FEATURES Dreamworld; Sea World; bird sanctuary; Air Museum.

gold-digger *noun* **1** a person who digs for gold. **2** *derog. slang* a person who starts love affairs with rich people in order to get at their money.

gold dust gold in the form of a very fine powder.

golden *adj.* **1** gold-coloured. **2** made of or containing gold. **3** happy; prosperous or thriving: *golden years, age*. **4** excellent; extremely valuable: *golden opportunity*. **5** greatly admired or favoured: *golden girl*. **6** denoting a 50th anniversary.

Golden Ass, The, also called *Metamorphoses* a Latin novel by Lucius Apuleius (2c). It is a picaresque description of the adventures of an ass, satirizing the vices of the age, particularly those of the priesthood.

Golden Bough, The a definitive and influential work by Sir J G Frazer (published in 12 vols, 1890–1915). It is a comparative study of the evolution of the religious beliefs of humankind.

Golden Bowl, The a novel by Henry James (1904). It is set mainly in London and describes the various relationships of three Americans and an Italian prince.

Golden Bull any document whose importance was stressed by authentication with a golden seal. Specifically, it refers to the edict promulgated by Emperor Charles IV in 1356 to define the German constitution, which formally affirmed that election of an emperor was by a college of seven princes, whom it recognized as virtually independent rulers. [from Latin *bulla*, stud]

Golden Cockerel, The (Zolotoy Petushok) an opera by Rimsky-Korsakov (1907), based on a story by Pushkin, and banned until after the composer's death because of his revolutionary sympathies. It tells of King Didon, who is given a golden cockerel by an astrologer to warn him of impending danger, but finds that the beauty of the Queen of Shemakha is unconquerable and that he cannot meet the demands of the astrologer.

golden eagle a large eagle found in mountainous regions of the northern hemisphere, with dark brown plumage, a golden nape, and a wingspan of up to 2m. Golden eagles feed mainly on small mammals, birds, snakes, and occasionally carrion, and they pair for life.

golden eagle

Golden Fleece in Greek mythology, the fleece of a ram which had saved Phrixus from sacrifice by carrying him through the air to Colchis. The fleece was placed in a sacred grove there, and guarded by a dragon. Its retrieval was the mission undertaken by Jason and the Argonauts, at the command of King Pelias. Jason obtained the fleece with Medea's help.

Golden Gate Bridge a major steel suspension bridge across the Golden Gate, a channel connecting San Francisco Bay with the Pacific Ocean. Completed in 1937, it has a main span of 1 280m.

golden handshake *noun colloq.* a large sum received from an employer on retirement, or in compensation for compulsory redundancy.

Golden Horde a feudal state that at its height (mid-13c to end 14c) constituted the western part of the Mongol Empire and occupied most of central and S Russia and W Siberia. Its capital was first at Sarai Batu and then at Sarai Berbe on the R Volga. The state was weakened by the Black Death (1346–7) and then overthrown by the Grand Princes of Moscow.

Golden Journey to Samarkand, The a collection of poems by James Elroy Flecker (1913).

golden jubilee the 50th anniversary of a significant event.

golden mean the midpoint between two extremes.

Golden Notebook, The a novel by Doris Lessing (1962). It is a multiple narrative which focuses on the experiences of Anna Wulf, a female writer. It is generally considered to be a landmark in women's writing.

goldenrod *noun* a plant with a rod-like stem and spikes of yellow flowers.

golden rule 1 any essential principle or rule. **2** the name given to Christ's command concerning one's duty to others: 'Do to others as you would have them do to you' (Luke 6.31; Matthew 7.12), a rule also found in earlier Jewish and Greek ethical teaching.

golden share a large share in a company held by an institution, or often a government, which prevents takeover by another company.

golden syrup *noun* light golden-coloured treacle.

goldfield *noun* an area where gold is mined.

goldfinch *noun* any of a number of species of finch, found in Europe and Asia, so called because of the broad yellow bar across each wing, only clearly visible when the bird is in flight. The head is covered with bold red, black, and white markings.

goldfish *noun* (PL. **goldfishes**, **goldfish**) a freshwater fish belonging to the carp family, which is green or brown in its wild form, although most of the varieties that have been bred from it are yellow, orange, or golden-red in colour. It is widely used to stock aquariums and artificial ponds.

Golding, William (Gerald) (1911–93) English novelist, born near Newquay, Cornwall. He became a teacher, served in the navy in World War II, then returned to teaching until 1960. His first novel was *Lord of the Flies* (1954), which was followed by *The Inheritors* (1955), *Pincher Martin* (1956), *Free Fall* (1959), and *The Spire* (1964). Later novels include *Rites of Passage* (1980, Booker Prize) and *The Paper Men* (1984). He was awarded the Nobel Prize for Literature in 1983.

gold leaf gold rolled or beaten into very thin sheets used to decorate books, etc.

Goldman, Emma (1869–1940) US anarchist, feminist, and advocate of birth control, born in Kaunas, Lithuania. To avoid anti-Jewish persecution, her family left Russia for Germany, and in 1885 she migrated to the USA, where she began her anarchist career. She was imprisoned during World War I for opposing government policy, then deported to the Soviet Union, but she eventually settled in France.

Golden Gate Bridge

gold medal a medal awarded to the winner of a sporting contest, or in recognition of excellence, eg of a wine.

gold mine 1 a place where gold is mined. 2 *colloq.* a source of great wealth.

gold plate 1 a thin coating of gold, especially on silver. 2 articles, eg spoons and dishes, made of gold.

gold-plate *verb* to coat (another metal) with gold.

gold-plated *adj.* plated with gold.

Gold Rush, The a US film directed by Charles Chaplin (1925). A silent comedy depicting the struggle for survival in the frozen wastes of Alaska, in which the little tramp (Chaplin) feasts on his boots but eventually strikes it rich in the boom town.

gold rush a frantic settlement of masses of people in a newly-discovered goldfield.

Goldschmidt, Victor Moritz (1888–1947) Swiss-born Norwegian geologist and crystallographer, born in Zurich. Professor in Oslo and Göttingen, World War II politics forced his return Norway and subsequent moves to Sweden and the UK. His earliest work was on the petrology of southern Norway. He made important contributions to X-ray crystallography studies of the binary compounds of the elements and the theory of crystal structures, and investigated the distribution of the elements in the Earth.

Goldsmith, Oliver (1728–74) Irish playwright, novelist, and poet, born in Kilkenny West. He practised as a physician in London, held several temporary posts, and took up writing and translating. *The Vicar of Wakefield* (1766) secured his reputation as a novelist, *The Deserted Village* (1770) as a poet, and *She Stoops to Conquer* (1773) as a dramatist.

goldsmith *noun* a person who makes articles out of gold.

gold standard *Finance* a monetary standard or system according to which the unit of currency has a precise value in gold.

Goldwater, Barry M(orris) (1909–) US politician and author, born in Phoenix, Arizona. He became a US Senator for his home state in 1952, but gave up his Senate seat in 1964 to become Republican nominee for the presidency. Overwhelmingly defeated by the Democrat Lyndon Johnson however, he returned to serve in the Senate (1969–87), and was one of the architects of the conservative revival within the Republican Party. *The Conscience of a Conservative* (1960) is his most notable book.

Goldwyn, Samuel, originally **Samuel Goldfish** (1882–1974) US film producer, born in Warsaw, Poland. An orphan, he ran away to London and the USA, where he helped to found a film company, producing *The Squaw Man* in 1913. In 1917 he founded the Goldwyn Pictures Corporation, in 1919 the Eminent Authors Pictures and finally in 1925 the Metro-Goldwyn-Mayer Company, allying himself with the United Artists from 1926. His 'film-of-the-book' policy included *Wuthering Heights* (1939). *The Best Years of our Lives* (1946) won a Best Picture Oscar.

golem *noun* in Jewish folklore, an image or automaton endowed with life, typically the servant and protector of a rabbi. [from Hebrew *gōlem*, a shapeless or embryonic thing]

golf — *noun* a game played on a large outdoor course, the object being to hit a small ball into each of a series of (nine or eighteen) holes using a set of long-handled clubs, taking as few strokes as possible. — *verb intrans.* to play golf. [perhaps from Old Dutch *colf*, club]

◊ A hole consists of three distinct areas: the *tee*, a flat starting area where the player strikes the ball off a small plastic or wooden support; the *fairway*, a long stretch of mown grass with obstacles such as bunkers, water, and trees placed on

or around it at various points; and the *green*, an area of smooth grass where the actual hole is situated. The expected number of strokes that a good player would play for any given hole is known as *par*. If a player holes the ball in one stroke below par, this is known as a *birdie*; two strokes below par is an *eagle*.
There are 14 clubs in a standard set of golf clubs, each club being used for a specific type of shot. The origins of the game are uncertain, although there is evidence that *gouf* (as it was then known) was played in Scotland in the 15c. It is believed that the Dutch played a similar game with a stick and ball in the 14c.
The ruling body of the game in Britain is the Royal and Ancient Club at St Andrews, Scotland.

golf club *noun* 1 any of the set of long-handled clubs used to play golf. 2 an association of players of golf, or its premises with a golf course attached.

golfer *noun* a person who plays golf.

golf links *noun* a golf course, especially by the sea.

Golgi, Camillo (1843–1926) Italian cytologist, born in Corteno, Lombardy. Professor at Pavia, he developed a technique, still known by his name, of impregnating particular nerve cells with silver salts; this allowed them to be closely examined under the microscope and opened up a new field of research into the fine structure of the central nervous system, sense organs, muscles, and glands. He shared the 1906 Nobel Prize for Physiology or Medicine with Santiago Ramón y Cajal.

Golgi apparatus *Biol.* any of various structures found within plant and animal cells, consisting of a stack of flattened discs, each of which is surrounded by a membrane. It is involved in the storage and transport of secretory products such as enzymes and hormones. [named after the Italian histologist Camillo Golgi]

goliard *noun* any of a band of wandering scholars and students of the 12–13c, renowned for their riotous behaviour, and for the satirical Latin verses lampooning the Church which they wrote and performed. [from Old French *golart, golard,* drunkard, glutton, from Latin *gūla,* gluttony]

Goliath a biblical character described in 1 Samuel 17 as a giant from Gath in the Philistine army who entered into single combat with the young David and was slain by a stone from David's sling, resulting in Israel's victory. Some confusion exists over a similar name in 2 Samuel 21.19 (also 1 Chronicles 20.5).

goliath *noun colloq.* 1 an unusually large or tall person. 2 a person or organization of great importance or influence. [named after *Goliath,* the Old Testament Philistine giant killed by David]

Gollancz, Sir Victor (1893–1967) English publisher, author, and philanthropist, born in London. He became a teacher, then entered publishing, founding his own firm in 1928, but also becoming known for his campaigns. In 1936 he founded the Left Book Club, which had a great influence on the growth of the Labour Party, and after World War II founded the Jewish Society for Human Service.

golliwog *or* **gollywog** *noun* a child's cloth doll with a black face and bristling hair and bright clothes. [from *Golliwogg,* the name of a character in children's books in the US, published from 1895]

golly¹ *interj. old use* an expression of surprise or admiration. [a euphemistic form of *God*]

golly² *noun* (PL. **gollies**) *colloq.* a golliwog.

golosh see GALOSH.

Gomateswara, statue of the tallest monolith statue in the world, sculpted in 983 at Sravanabelagola, Karnataka, India. The statue,

which is 17m high, represents Gomateswara, a Jain holy man, and is the focus of a major Jain festival every 12 years.

Gompers, Samuel (1850–1924) US labour leader, born in London, UK. After migrating to the USA in 1863, he followed his father's trade as a cigar maker and joined a union the following year. Self-educated, he studied and rejected Marxian socialism, and developed instead the US practice of non-political trade unionism. He was founder (1886) and long-time President of the American Federation of Labor, and as the AFL gained recognition as the main force in organized labour, he became a major public figure.

Gomułka, Władysław (1905–82) Polish communist leader, born in Krosno, SE Poland. A professional trade unionist, in 1943 he became Secretary of the outlawed Communist Party. He was Vice-President of the first postwar Polish government (1945–8), but his criticism of the Soviet Union led to his arrest (1951–4). He returned to power as Party First Secretary in 1956, but resigned office in 1971, following a political crisis.

-gon *combining form Maths.* forming words denoting a shape with a given number of sides: *polygon.* [from Greek *gonia,* angle]

gonad *noun Biol.* an organ in which gametes (eggs or sperm) are produced, especially the ovary or testis. It may also secrete sex hormones. [from Greek *gone,* generation]

gonadotrophic hormone *Physiol.* any of various hormones that stimulate the gonads (the ovaries and testes), and are responsible for the production of sex hormones, the onset of sexual maturity, and the control of the menstrual cycle in humans. Gonadotrophic hormone is also used to treat infertility in women. – Also called *gonadotrophin.* [from Greek *gone,* generation]

gonadotrophin *Physiol.* gonadotrophic hormone.

Goncourt, Edmond de (1822–96) and **Jules de** (1830–70) French brothers and novelists, born respectively in Nancy and Paris. Primarily artists, in 1849 they travelled across France doing watercolour sketches. They then collaborated in studies of history and art, and took to writing novels, notably *Germinie Lacerteux* (1865) and *Madame Gervaisais* (1869). They are also remembered for their *Journal,* begun in 1851, a detailed record of French social and literary life which Edmond continued for over 40 years. Edmond also founded in his will the Goncourt Academy which awards the annual Prix Goncourt for fiction.

gondola *noun* 1 a long narrow flat-bottomed boat with pointed upturned ends, used on the canals of Venice. 2 the passenger cabin suspended from an airship, balloon or cable-railway. [from Venetian dialect]

gondolier *noun* a person who rows a gondola on a canal.

Gondomar, Diego Sarmiento de Acuña, Conde de (Count of) (1567–1626) Spanish diplomat, who as Ambassador in England (1613–18, 1620–22) worked to arrange the marriage of Prince Charles (later Charles I) with the Infanta. He had much influence over Charles's father James I, but caused public hostility in England. He was recalled to Spain (1622), and lost influence after the Anglo-Dutch alliance (1624).

Gondwanaland *Geol.* the hypothetical southern supercontinent thought to have broken away from the single land mass Pangea about 200 million years ago. It is believed to have drifted apart to form parts of the present continents of Africa, Australia, S America, India, and Antarctica.

gone — *verb* past participle of GO. — *adj.* 1 departed. 2 lost. 3 dead. 4 *colloq.* pregnant: *four months gone.* 5 *colloq.* in ecstasy. 6 *colloq.* (**gone on**

someone *or* **something**) infatuated or obsessed with them.

goner *noun colloq.* a person or thing beyond hope of recovery.

Goneril the callous, selfish eldest daughter of Lear in Shakespeare's *King Lear*, who is married to Albany and poisons her sister, Regan, in an attempt to win the affections of Edmund.

Gone with the Wind 1 a novel by Margaret Mitchell (1936). It is set on a plantation in Georgia during the American Civil War and focuses on the passionate life of Scarlett O'Hara and her involvement with dashing rogue Rhett Butler. **2** a US film directed by Victor Fleming (1939), based on the novel. It stars Vivien Leigh as Scarlett O'Hara and Clark Gable as Rhett Butler.

gonfalon *noun* a banner hung from a horizontal bar. [from Italian *gonfalone*, from Old German *gund*, battle+ *fano*, flag]

gong *noun* **1** a hanging metal plate which sounds when struck. **2** *slang* a medal. [from Malay]

Góngora y Argote, Luis de (1561–1627) Spanish lyric poet, born in Córdoba. He studied law, but in 1606 took orders and eventually became chaplain to Philip III. His earlier writings were sonnets, romances, and satirical verses, but he is best known for his later, longer poems, including *Solidades* and *Polifemo* (both 1613), executed in an affected style which came to be called 'gongorism'.

gonorrhoea *noun Medicine* a sexually transmitted disease characterized by inflammation of the genital mucous membranes as a result of infection with the bacterium *Neisseria gonorrhoeae*. Its symptoms include the discharge of pus, and pain on passing urine. If left untreated gonorrhoea may cause sterility, arthritis, and inflammation of the heart. [from Greek *gonos*, seed, semen + *rheein*, to flow]

González, Felipe (1942–) Spanish politician, born in Seville. A practising lawyer, in 1962 he joined the Spanish Socialist Workers' Party (PSOE), an illegal organization at the time. He became Secretary-General in 1974 and the Party regained legal status in 1977. He persuaded the PSOE to adopt a more moderate policy, and in the 1982 elections they won a substantial majority. As Prime Minister (1982–), he formed the first left-wing administration since 1936.

Gonzalo the 'honest old Counsellor' in Shakespeare's *The Tempest*, who remains loyal to Prospero despite his banishment.

goo *noun colloq.* **1** any sticky substance. **2** *derog.* excessive sentimentality.

Gooch, Graham (1953–) English cricketer, born in Leytonstone. He made his début for Essex in 1973, and was first capped for England in 1975. He has since played in over 100 Test matches, and recorded his highest score of 333 runs against India at Lord's in 1990. In Jul 1993 he resigned as captain of England after their eighth defeat in nine Test matches. He became England's highest-scoring Test player in Aug 1993 when he reached a career total of 8 293 runs.

good — *adj.* (**better**, **best**) **1** having desirable or necessary (positive) qualities; admirable. **2** (**good at something**) competent with it; talented. **3** morally correct; virtuous. **4** (**good for someone** *or* **something**) beneficial to them. **5** kind and generous. **6** bringing happiness or pleasure: *good news.* **7** well-behaved. **8** wise; advisable: *a good buy.* **9** thorough. **10** finest among others: *my good cups.* **11** adequate; satisfactory: *a good supply.* **12** enjoyable: *having a good time.* **13** valid. **14** well-respected. **15** sound; giving use; serviceable: *the roof is good for another winter.* **16** considerable; at least: *waited a good while / lasted a good month.* **17** certain to provide the desired result: *good for a laugh.* — *noun* **1** moral

correctness; virtue. **2** benefit; advantage: *do you good / £20 to the good.* **3** (**the good**) good people. — *interj.* an expression of approval or satisfaction. — *adv. colloq. North Amer., esp. US* well. — **as good as** ... almost ...; virtually ... **for good and all** for ever; permanently. **good and** ... *colloq.* very ...; completely or absolutely: *good and ready.* **good for** *or* **on someone** an expression of approval or congratulation. **good morning, afternoon,** *etc* expressions of greeting or farewell. **make good** to be successful. **make something good 1** to repair it. **2** to carry it out or fulfil it. [from Anglo-Saxon *god*]

goodbye — *interj.* an expression of farewell. — *noun* an act of saying goodbye.

Goodbye, Mr Chips a novel by James Hilton (1934). It is a sentimental tale of a retired English schoolmaster.

good-for-nothing — *adj.* lazy and irresponsible. — *noun* a lazy and irresponsible person.

Good Friday *noun* a Christian festival on the Friday before Easter, in memory of Christ's crucifixion.

goodies *pl. noun colloq.* things considered pleasant or desirable. See also GOODY.

goodliness *noun* being goodly.

goodly *adj.* (**goodlier**, **goodliest**) *old use* **1** quite large. **2** physically attractive; fine.

Goodman, Benny (Benjamin David) (1909–86) US clarinettist and bandleader, born in Chicago, the 'King of Swing' in the big-band era. In 1934 he formed a big band and made live network broadcasts. The sensation the band caused on tour at the Palomar Ballroom in Los Angeles is said to mark the beginning of the Swing Era. Their hit recordings include 'Let's Dance', 'Stompin' at the Savoy', and 'One O'Clock Jump'. Goodman's performances also featured trios and quartets, sometimes with Lionel Hampton and from 1938 they included classical music as well as jazz.

goodness — *noun* **1** the state or quality of being good; generosity; kindness; moral correctness. **2** *euphemistic, used in exclamations* God: *goodness knows.* **3** nourishing quality: *all the goodness of the grain.* — *interj.* an expression of surprise or relief.

goods *pl. noun* **1** articles for sale; merchandise. **2** freight: *goods train.* **3** *colloq.* the required result: *deliver the goods.* **4** *old use* personal possessions. — **have the goods on someone** *colloq.* to have proof of wrongdoings or crimes committed by them.

goodwill *noun* **1** a feeling of kindness towards others. **2** the good reputation of an established business, seen as having an actual value.

goody *colloq. noun* (PL. **goodies**) a hero in a film, book, etc. See also GOODIES.

goody-goody *colloq.* — *adj.* virtuous in an ostentatious or self-satisfied way. — *noun* an ostentatiously virtuous person.

gooey *adj.* (**gooier**, **gooiest**) sticky.

goof *chiefly North Amer. colloq.* — *noun* **1** a silly or foolish person. **2** a stupid mistake. — *verb intrans.* **1** to make a stupid mistake. **2** (**goof around**) to spend time idly or foolishly. [perhaps from Old French *goffe*, clumsy]

goofy *adj.* (**goofier**, **goofiest**) *colloq.* silly; crazy.

googly *noun* (PL. **googlies**) *Cricket* a ball bowled so as to change direction unexpectedly after bouncing.

goon *noun* **1** *colloq.* a silly person. **2** *slang* a hired thug. [from US cartoon character Alice the *Goon*, created by E C Segar (1894–1938)]

Goons, The a group of four British comedians (Spike Milligan, Peter Sellers, Harry Secombe,

and Michael Bentine) who created the much-loved radio *Goon Show* (1951–9). Known for its mixture of surrealism and slapstick, and anarchic humour, the show achieved worldwide popularity and influence. The members of the group later developed individual careers.

goosander *noun* a large duck with a serrated bill, native to Europe and N America. [perhaps from GOOSE + Norse *ander*, plural of *önd*, duck]

goose — *noun* (PL. **geese**, sense 5 **gooses**) **1** any of numerous species of large wild or domesticated waterfowl related to ducks and swans, with a stout body, long neck, webbed feet, and a broad flat bill, found in all parts of the world except Antarctica. They are mainly terrestrial, despite being strong swimmers, and many species migrate south in winter, usually flying in V-formation and making characteristic honking sounds as they fly. **2** the female of this bird, as opposed to the gander, which is the male. **3** the flesh of a goose cooked as food. **4** *old colloq. use* a silly person. **5** *colloq.* a poke or pinch on the buttocks. — *verb colloq.* to poke or pinch (someone) on the buttocks. — **cook someone's goose** *colloq.* to ruin their plans or chances. [from Anglo-Saxon *gos*]

gooseberry *noun* (PL. **gooseberries**) **1** a thorny shrub that produces an edible yellowish-green or reddish-purple berry. **2** one of these berries. — **play gooseberry** *colloq.* to be an unwanted third person.

goosefish *noun* same as ANGLERFISH.

Goose Green POP (1980) 100, the second largest settlement in the Falkland Is. It is situated on East Falkland at the head of Choiseul Sound, on the narrow isthmus that joins the N half of East Falkland to Lafonia in the S. It was invaded by Argentina during the Falklands War in 1982, but was re-taken by the British on 28 May 1982.

goose pimples *or* **goose flesh** *or* **goose bumps** a condition of the skin caused by cold or fear, in which the body hairs become erect, causing pimples to appear on the surface and causing a bristling feeling.

goose-step — *noun* a military marching step in which the legs are kept rigid and swung very high. — *verb intrans.* to march with this step.

Goossens, Sir Eugene (1893–1962) English composer and conductor, born in London. He became associate conductor to Sir Thomas Beecham, then worked in the USA (1923–45) as conductor of orchestras in Rochester (New York) and Cincinnati. As conductor of the Sydney Symphony Orchestra and director of the New South Wales Conservatory (1947–56), he became a major influence on Australian music. His compositions include two operas, a ballet, an oratorio, and two symphonies.

Goossens, Léon (1897–1988) English oboist, born in Liverpool. He held leading posts in most of the major London orchestras before he devoted himself to solo playing and teaching. He was the brother of the conductor Eugene; his sisters Marie (1894–1991) and Sidonie (1899–) became well-known harpists.

gopher *noun* **1** any of various burrowing rat-like animals found in Europe, Asia, and N and Central America. **2** a burrowing N American tortoise.

gopher *or* **pocket gopher** *noun North Amer.* any of various hamster-like rodents found only in N America, and having two external fur-lined cheek pouches. They are burrowing animals with thick-set bodies and short powerful legs. [said to be from French *gaufre*, honeycomb (a reference to its burrows)]

Gorazde a Muslim town in E Bosnia-Herzegovina, situated on the Drina R. Before the Civil War in Yugoslavia (1992–3) it had a population of 37 000, but by Jun 1993 the influx of

Muslim refugees had raised this to 60 000. It became a symbol of Muslim resistance to attack by Bosnian Serbs. Designated a UN 'safe area', it remained under attack from Serb artillery. NATO planes bombed the Serb portions in Apr 1994 with the aim of protecting UN personnel. The incident heightened tensions and threatened the peace negotiations.

Gorbachev, Mikhail (Sergeyevich) (1931–) Russian politician, General Secretary of the Communist Party of the Soviet Union (1985–) and President of the Supreme Soviet of the USSR (1988–90), born in Privolnoye. He joined the Communist Party in 1952 and held a variety of senior posts in the Stavropol city and district Party organization (1956–70), and was elected a deputy to the USSR Supreme Soviet (1970) and a member of the Party Central Committee (1971). He became Central Committee Secretary for Agriculture (1979–85), full member (1980–) of the Politburo of the Central Committee (1979–80) and, on the death of Chernenko, General Secretary of the Central Committee (1985–91). In 1988 he became Chairman of the Presidium of the Supreme Soviet, (ie head of state), and in 1990, the first executive President of the USSR. On becoming Party General Secretary he launched a radical programme of *perestroika* (reform and restructuring) of the Soviet economic and political system. A greater degree of civil liberty, public debate, journalistic and cultural freedom, and a reappraisal of Soviet history were allowed under the policy of *glasnost* (openness of information). In foreign and defence affairs he reduced military expenditure, pursued a policy of detente and nuclear disarmament with the West, and ended the Soviet military occupation of Afghanistan (1989). Growing dissatisfaction at home and opposition to his policies led to an attempted coup on 19 Aug 1991. Gorbachev tried in vain to form a new Union of Sovereign States to replace the USSR, but by this time the republican leaders had gained power and the Communist Party was disbanded by Boris Yeltsin, the Russian President. Despite Gorbachev's historic achievements as the 'father' of *glasnost* and *perestroika*, which included the ending of the Cold War and the bringing down of the walls across E Europe, he was forced to resign on 25 Dec 1991. With the Soviet Union officially broken up into constituent states and Russia in economic chaos, Gorbachev has remained in the public eye. He became head of the International Foundation for Social and Economic and Political Research in 1991 and has undertaken tours worldwide. He was awarded the Nobel Peace Prize in 1990.

Gorbals a district of Glasgow, Scotland. It was originally a village on the S bank of the R Clyde; by the end of the 19c it had become infamous as an area of overcrowding and deprivation. The redevelopment of the area started in the late 1950s with the construction of high-rise buildings designed by Sir Basil Spence. The demolition of one of these buildings took place in 1993 despite protests from some architects.

Gorboduc a legendary king of Britain, first heard about in Geoffrey of Monmouth's *History*. When he grew senile, his two sons Ferrex and Porrex quarrelled over the inheritance. He was the subject of an early Elizabethan tragedy in the Senecan style, written by Norton and Sackville (1561).

Gordian knot a difficult problem or dilemma. — **cut the Gordian knot** to resolve a difficulty by decisive and often evasive action. [named after Gordius, king of ancient Phrygia in Asia Minor, who tied a complicated knot that no one could untie; Alexander the Great solved the problem by cutting the knot with a sword]

Gordimer, Nadine (1923–) South African novelist, born in Springs, Transvaal. She has lived in Johannesburg since 1948, and taught in the

USA during the early 1970s. Her novels focus on race and repression both in her native country and in other African states. They include *A Guest of Honour* (1970), *The Conservationist* (1974, joint Booker Prize), *Burger's Daughter* (1979), *A Sport of Nature* (1987), and *My Son's Story* (1990). She was awarded the Nobel Prize for literature in 1991.

Gordon, Charles George (1833–85) English soldier, born in Woolwich, near London. In 1855–6 he fought in the Crimean War, then in 1860 went to China, where his suppression of the Taiping Rebellion earned him the nickname 'Chinese Gordon'. Appointed Governor General of the Sudan (1877), he resigned in poor health in 1880, but returned in 1884 to relieve Egyptian garrisons which lay in rebel territory. He was besieged at Khartoum for 10 months by the Mahdi's troops, and was killed there two days before a relief force arrived.

Gordon, John (Rutherford) (1890–1974) Scottish journalist, born in Dundee. He left school at the age of 14 to join a local newspaper, and worked as a sub-editor in London. Appointed editor of the *Sunday Express* in 1928, he increased its circulation from 450 000 to 3 200 000. He introduced the first crossword puzzle and the first astrology column in a British newspaper.

Gordon a male first name, after the Scottish surname and place-name.

Gordon Riots anti-Catholic riots in London which caused a breakdown of law and order in parts of the capital for several days in early Jun 1780. They occurred after the leader of the Protestant Association Lord George Gordon (1751–93) had failed in his attempt to have clauses in the 1778 Catholic Relief Act (which furthered Catholic emancipation) repealed.

gore¹ *noun* blood from a wound, especially when clotted. [from Anglo-Saxon *gor*, filth]

gore² *verb* to pierce with horn or tusk. [from Anglo-Saxon *gar*, spear]

gore³ — *noun* a triangular piece of material, eg a section of an umbrella or a tapering piece in a garment. — *verb* to construct from, or shape with, gores. [from Anglo-Saxon *gara*, triangular piece of land]

Gorée Island a small island off the Cape Verde Peninsula, Senegal. During the 18–19c when it was first a French, and then a British, colony, it was a major storage centre for slaves who were being shipped to the Americas. Today it is a museum of slave trade history, and a World Heritage site.

Göreme a valley in Cappadocia region, central Turkey. Noted for its cave dwellings, the area is a World Heritage site.

gorge — *noun* 1 a deep narrow valley, usually containing a river. 2 the contents of the stomach. 3 a spell of greedy eating. 4 *old use* the throat or gullet. — *verb* 1 *intrans., trans.* to eat or swallow greedily. 2 (*usually* **gorge oneself**) to stuff oneself with food. — **make one's gorge rise** to disgust or sicken one; to fill one with resentment. [from Old French *gorge*, throat]

gorgeous *adj.* 1 extremely beautiful or attractive; magnificent. 2 *colloq.* excellent; extremely pleasant. [from Old French *gorgias*, fine, elegant]

gorgeously *adv.* in a gorgeous way.

gorgeousness *noun* being gorgeous.

Gorgias (c.485–c.380 BC) Greek sophist, sceptical philosopher, and rhetorician, born in Leontini, Sicily. He went to Athens as ambassador in 427 BC, and became well-known as a teacher of eloquence. In his work *On Nature* he argued that nothing exists; even if something did exist, it could not be known, and even if it could be known, it could not be communicated. Plato's dialogue *Gorgias* is written against him.

gorgon *noun* 1 (*usually* **Gorgon**) *Mythol.* each of three monstrous sisters with live snakes for hair, capable of turning to stone anything that met its gaze. 2 *derog. colloq.* a fierce, frightening, or very ugly woman. [from Greek *gorgos*, terrible] ◇ Of the three Gorgons (Medusa, Stheno, and Euryale) only Medusa was mortal. Perseus killed her to rescue Andromeda from a sea-monster, using her severed head to turn the monster to stone. The head was later carried in the centre of Athena's shield.

Gorgonzola *noun* a blue-veined Italian cheese with a sharp flavour. [from *Gorgonzola*, a town near Milan]

gorilla *noun* 1 the largest of the apes (*Gorilla gorilla*), native to the rainforests of W and Central Africa, and reaching a height of up to 1.8m. It has a heavily built body, broad chest, long arms, strong hands and feet, and jet black skin covered with dense fur. 2 *colloq.* a brutal-looking man, especially a hired thug. [from Greek *Gorillai*, a tribe of hairy African women] ◇ Gorillas live in troops consisting of one or more adult males with several females and their young. They normally walk on all fours, with their knuckles on the ground, and the adults seldom climb trees. Gorillas in lowland forests feed on fruit and leaves, often raiding banana plantations, while those living in mountainous regions feed on bark, stems, and roots. They are peaceful gentle animals that never attack unless provoked, and are highly intelligent.

Gorky, Maxim, pseudonym of **Aleksei Maksimovich Peshkov** (1868–1936) Russian novelist, born in Nizhniy Novgorod, renamed Gorky (1932–90), Russia. He held a variety of posts before becoming a writer, as described in his autobiographical trilogy (1913–23). Involved in strikes and imprisoned in 1905, he was an exile in Italy until 1914, and then engaged in revolutionary propaganda for the new regime. His writings include several Romantic short stories, and social novels and plays, notably the drama *The Lower Depths* (1902). He was the first President of the Soviet Writers Union, and a supporter of Stalinism.

gormless *adj. derog. colloq.* stupid; dim. [variant of obsolete *gaumless*, from *gaum*, understanding]

gormlessly *adv.* in a gormless way.

gorse *noun* a wild thorny evergreen shrub with yellow flowers. [from Anglo-Saxon *gorst*]

gorsy *adj.* covered with gorse.

gory *adj.* (**gorier, goriest**) 1 causing or involving bloodshed. 2 *colloq.* unpleasant: *gory details*. 3 covered in gore. [from GORE]

gosh *interj. colloq.* a mild expression of surprise. [euphemistic form of GOD]

goshawk *noun* a large bluish-grey hawk native to Europe, Asia and N America. [from Anglo-Saxon *gos*, goose + *hafoc*, hawk]

Goslar a town in Lower Saxony state, Germany. It was founded in the early 10c, after

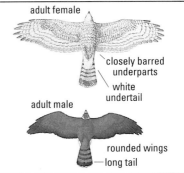

northern goshawk

silver was discovered at Rammelsberg. The mines, and the historical remains of the town (eg 11c imperial palace) form a World Heritage site.

gosling *noun* a young goose. [from Anglo-Saxon *gos*, goose + -LING]

go-slow *noun* working slowly to encourage an employer to negotiate.

gospel *noun* 1 the life and teachings of Christ: *preach the gospel*. 2 (*usually* **Gospel**) each of the New Testament books describing the life of Christ ascribed to Matthew, Mark, Luke, and John. 3 (**gospel truth**) *colloq.* the absolute truth. 4 a set of closely followed principles or rules. 5 (*also* **gospel music**) lively religious music of Black American origin. [from Anglo-Saxon *god-spel*, from *god*, good + *spel*, story]

Gospels, apocryphal several writings from the early Christian era which are often somewhat similar to the canonical gospels in title, form, or content, but which have not been widely accepted as canonical themselves. They include popular infancy stories about Christ (eg *Infancy Gospel of Thomas*, *Protoevangelium of James*), apocryphal accounts of Christ's final suffering (*Gospel of Peter*, *Gospel of Nicodemus*), gnostic collections of sayings and stories (*Gospel of Thomas*, *Gospel of Philip*), and Judaeo-Christian works (*Gospel of the Hebrews*). Many are known from citations in the early Church Fathers or from recent Nag Hammadi discoveries.

Gospels, canonical four books of the New Testament, known as the Gospels according to Matthew, Mark, Luke, and John, and named 'gospels' by the 2c Church. Each provides a perspective on the ministry and teaching of Jesus of Nazareth, and concludes with the account of his arrest, crucifixion, and resurrection. Three of the four (Matthew, Mark, Luke) seem to have a literary interrelationship, the nature of which is debated as the *synoptic* problem. John's Gospel is different in character and is usually dated as the latest because of the extent of theological reflection. [from Greek *euangelion*, good news]

Gosport POP (1981) 77 000, a town in Gosport district, Hampshire, S England. Part of the Portsmouth urban area, it lies at the entrance to Portsmouth Harbour.

Gossaert, Jan, also called **Mabuse** (c.1478–1532) Flemish painter, born (possibly) in Maubeuge, Hainault. He registered as a master in the Antwerp guild in 1503, and went to Rome (c.1508–9). He then introduced Italianate details including Classical architecture, putti, and nude figures into his otherwise traditional early Netherlandish pictures. His works include *Adoration of the Magi* (National Gallery, London) in his pre-Italian style, and *Hercules* (Barber Institute, Birmingham) in his later 'Romanist' style.

gossamer *noun* 1 fine filmy spider-woven threads seen on hedges or floating in the air. 2 any soft fine material. [from Middle English *gossomer*, goose summer, a period in November when goose was traditionally eaten, and these cobwebs often seen]

gossip — *noun* 1 *derog.* talk or writing about the private affairs of others, often spiteful and untrue. 2 *derog.* a person who engages in or spreads such talk. 3 casual and friendly talk. — *verb intrans.* (**gossiped**, **gossiping**) 1 to engage in, or pass on, malicious gossip. 2 to chat. [from Anglo-Saxon *godsibb*, godparent, hence a familiar friend one chats to]

gossipy *adj.* 1 involving gossip. 2 likely to gossip.

got see GET.

Go Tell It on the Mountain a novel by James Baldwin (1953). It focuses on one day in the life of various Harlem churchgoers.

Goth *noun* 1 a member of a Scandinavian people who invaded parts of the Roman Empire

between the 3c and 5c AD (see GOTHS). 2 a crude or uncivilized person. [from Anglo-Saxon *Gotan*]

Gothenburg, Swedish **Göteborg** POP (1992e) 432 000, the seaport capital of Göteborg och Bohus county, SW Sweden, and the second largest city in the country. It lies at the mouth of the R Göta on the Kattegat. The Göta Canal provides a link to the Baltic Sea. HISTORY founded in 1619; became a free port in 1921. NOTABLE FEATURES cathedral (1633, restored in 1956–7); town hall (1750).

Gothic — *adj.* 1 of the Goths or their language. 2 of a style of architecture featuring high pointed arches, popular in Europe between the 12c and 16c. 3 of a type of literature dealing with mysterious or supernatural events in an eerie setting, popular in the 18c. 4 of a modern style of literature, films, etc which imitates this. 5 of various styles of heavy black printed letter. — *noun* 1 Gothic architecture or literature. 2 Gothic lettering. 3 the extinct Germanic language of the Goths.

Gothic Letters				
Letter	Usual trans-literation		Letter	Usual trans-literation
𝔄 a	a		𝔒 o	o
𝔄̈ ä	ae		𝔒̈ ö	oe
𝔅 b	b		𝔓 p	p
ℭ c	c		𝔔 q	q
𝔇 d	d		ℜ r	r
𝔈 e	e		𝔖 ſ s	s
𝔉 f	f		𝔗 t	t
𝔊 g	g		𝔘 u	u
𝔥 h	h		𝔘̈ ü	ue
𝔍 i	i		𝔙 v	v
𝔍 j	j		𝔚 w	w
𝔎 k	k		𝔛 x	x
𝔏 l	l		𝔜 y	y
𝔐 m	m		𝔷 z	z
𝔑 n	n			

Gothic novel a type of fiction, written in reaction to 18c rationalism, which reclaims mystery and horror and licenses extreme emotions. Examples include *The Monk* (1797) by M G Lewis and *The Mysteries of Udolpho* (1794) by Mrs Radcliffe.

Gothic Revival a movement to revive Gothic architecture, prevalent during the late 18c and 19c, popular in England, France, Germany, and N America. It often displayed ideological associations with the spiritual and social conditions of the Middle Ages, particularly with the writings of Pugin and Ruskin. The style was applied to many different types of buildings, but particularly to churches (eg St Denys-de-l'Estrée, 1864–7, by Viollet-le-Duc).

Goths a Germanic people who by the end of the 1c AD had moved south from the Baltic area (Gotland) to the lower Vistula valley. By the 3c they had expanded into the Black Sea region and divided into two confederations, Ostrogoths and Visigoths. Displaced by the Huns, they created two kingdoms in the 5c out of the ruins of the Roman Empire in the west.

Gotland *or* **Gottland** *or* **Gothland** POP (1992e) 58 000, an island county lying off the SE coast of Sweden, in the Baltic Sea. AREA (land) 3 140sq km/1 212sq mi. It comprises the islands of Gotland (the largest), Fårö, and Karlsö. CAPITAL Visby. HISTORY colonized by Germans in the 12c; taken by Sweden in 1280, by Denmark in 1361, and again by Sweden in 1645. ECONOMY cattle, sheep; tourism. NOTABLE FEATURE spectacular rock formations at Raukar.

gotten *North Amer., esp. US* past participle of GET.

Gottfried von Strassburg (13c) German mediaeval epic poet. No facts are known about his life, but he is referred to by other poets, and is known as the author of the German version of Tristan and Isolde. He also wrote appraisals of poets of the period.

gouache *noun* 1 a painting technique using a blend of watercolour and a glue-like substance, giving an opaque matt surface. 2 a painting done in this way. [from French *gouache*]
◊ Gouache was used by medieval manuscript illuminators, and was especially popular with 17c European artists. It is commonly combined with pencil, watercolour, and ink.

Gouda POP (1992e) 67 000, a city in South Holland province, W Netherlands. It lies at the confluence of the Gouwe and Ijssel rivers, 23km/14mi NE of Rotterdam, in a fertile polder area. It is famous for its cheese market; the mild cheese Gouda originated here. NOTABLE FEATURES town hall (1449–59); Janskerk (rebuilt in the 16c).

Gouda *noun* a flat round mild Dutch cheese. [from *Gouda* in Holland]

gouge — *noun* 1 a chisel with a rounded hollow blade, used for cutting grooves or holes in wood. 2 a groove or hole made using this. — *verb* 1 to cut it out with or as if with a gouge. 2 (*also* **gouge something out**) to force or press it out of position: *gouged his eye out*. [from Old French, from Latin *gubia*, chisel]

goujons *pl. noun* small strips of fish or chicken coated in seasoned flour, egg, and breadcrumbs, and deep-fried. [from French *goujon*, gudgeon (the fish)]

goulash *noun* a thick meat stew heavily seasoned with paprika, originally from Hungary. [from Hungarian *gulyas hus*, herdsman's meat]

Gould, Stephen Jay (1941–) US palaeontologist, born in New York City. Professor at Harvard, he proposed the theory of 'punctuated equilibrium', that most evolutionary change occurs rapidly and that species then persist for long periods with little or no change. His ideas on evolution have been published in many popular books such as *Ever Since Darwin* (1977).

Gounod, Charles (François) (1818–93) French composer, born in Paris. After studying at the Paris Conservatoire and in Rome, he became organist of the Church of the Missions Etrangères, Paris, where his earliest compositions, chiefly polyphonic in style, were performed. His major works include the comic opera *Le Médecin malgré lui* (The Mock Doctor, 1858) and his masterpiece *Faust* (1859). He also published masses, hymns and anthems, and was popular as a songwriter.

gourd *noun* 1 any of various mostly climbing plants belonging to the cucumber family (Cucurbitaceae) that produce a large fruit with a hard woody outer shell, which varies widely in colour and is usually pear- or bottle-shaped, eg members of the genus *Lagenaria*, which includes the calabash and bottle gourds. 2 the hard durable shell of the fruit of such a plant, which can be hollowed out, dried, and used as an ornament, cup, bowl, or other utensil. [from Old French *gourde*]

gourmand *noun* 1 a greedy eater; a glutton. 2 a gourmet. [from French *gourmand*]

gourmandise *or* **gourmandism** *noun* 1 indulgence in good eating. 2 discerning appreciation of good food and wines.

gourmet *noun* a person with expert knowledge of, and a passion for, good food and wine. [from French *gourmet*]

gout *noun* a disease in which excess uric acid accumulates in the bloodstream and is deposited as crystals of sodium urate in the joints. It causes recurrent attacks of acute arthritis, most commonly of the big toe. [from Old French *goute*, a drop, the disease having formerly been thought of as caused by drops of humours]

gouty *adj.* afflicted with gout.

Gov. *or* **gov.** *abbrev.* **1** government. **2** governor.

govern *verb* **1** *trans., intrans.* to control and direct the affairs of (a country, state, or organization). **2** to guide or influence; to control or restrain: *govern his temper.* **3** *Grammar* to determine the form, or case, taken by (a word). [from Latin *gubernare*, from Greek *kybernaein*, to steer]

governable *adj.* capable of being governed.

governance *noun* **1** the act of governing. **2** system of government. **3** authority or control.

governess *noun Hist.* a woman employed to teach, and perhaps look after, children, usually resident in their home.

governing *adj.* that governs.

government *noun* **1** (*often* **the Government**) a body of people, usually elected, with the power to control the affairs of a country or state. **2** the way in which this is done; the particular system used. **3** the act or practice of ruling. **4** *Grammar* the power of one word to determine the form, or case, of another.

governmental *adj.* relating to or involving government.

Government Communications Headquarters (ABBREV. **GCHQ**) in the UK government, a self-governing department (in Cheltenham, Gloucester) under the Secretary of State for Foreign and Commonwealth Affairs, where the government's electronic surveillance affairs are organized and monitored.

Government Inspector, The (or The Inspector General) a play by Nikolai Gogol (1836). It is a wild and boisterous satire exposing the corruption and vanity of provincial officials.

Government of India Acts legislation passed (1883–1935) by the British parliament to regulate the government of India. It included the 1858 Act, which transferred British East India Company powers to the British Crown, and the 1919 and 1935 Acts which introduced constitutional change and helped pave the way for Indian independence.

governor *noun* **1** (*also* **Governor**) the elected head of a US state. **2** the head of an institution, eg a prison. **3** a member of a governing body of a school, hospital, college, etc. **4** (*also* **Governor**) the head of a colony or province, especially the monarch's representative. **5** *colloq* (*often* **guvnor** or **guv'nor** or **guv**) one's boss or father; a respectful form of address used to any man. **6** a device for maintaining or controlling uniform speed in an engine or vehicle.

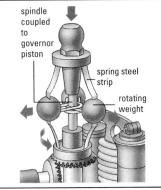

spindle coupled to governor piston

spring steel strip

rotating weight

governor

Governor-General *noun* (PL. **Governors-General, Governor-Generals**) the official representative of the British monarch in a Commonwealth country or British colony.

Govt. *abbrev.* Government.

Gower, John (c.1325–1408) English medieval poet, born in Kent. A friend of Chaucer, his works include many French ballads, and the Latin *Vox Clamantis* (c.1382–4). His best-known work is the long English poem, *Confessio Amantis* (c.1383), comprising over 100 stories from various sources on the theme of Christian and courtly love.

Gowers, Sir Ernest (Arthur) (1880–1966) English civil servant, and author of an influential work on English usage. He was called to the Bar in 1906. After a distinguished career in the civil service, he wrote *Plain Words* (1948) and *ABC of Plain Words* (1951) in an attempt to maintain standards of clear English, especially in official prose.

gown *noun* **1** a woman's long formal dress. **2** an official robe worn by clergymen, lawyers and academics. **3** a protective overall worn by a surgeon and surgical staff in a hospital. **4** *formal* the members of a university, especially as opposed to *town*, the residents of the university town. [from Latin *gunna*, garment made of fur or leather]

goy *noun* (PL. **goys, goyim**) *slang* a Jewish word for a non-Jewish person. [from Hebrew *goy*, people, nation]

Goya (y Lucientes), Francisco (José) de (1746–1828) Spanish artist, born in Fuendetodos. He designed for the Royal Tapestry factory in Spain. In 1798 he produced a series of frescoes, incorporating scenes from contemporary life, in the Church of San Antonio de la Florida, Madrid, and in 1799 issued over 80 satirical etchings, *Los caprichos* (The Caprices). He became famous for his portraits, was made court painter to Charles IV (1799), and produced the *Family of Charles IV* (1800, Prado, Madrid). Other works include *Maja nude* and *Maja clothed* (c.1797–1800, Prado, Madrid).

Gozo, Maltese **Ghaudex**, ancient **Gaulus** POP (1991e) 26 000 (with Comino), an island in the Maltese group, often called the 'Isle of Calypso', 6km/4mi NW of the main island of Malta. AREA 67sq km/26sq mi the shoreline length is 43km/27mi. CHIEF TOWN Victoria. The island is largely given over to agriculture. NOTABLE FEATURES prehistoric temples; the Ta' Pinu Church, a centre of pilgrimage to the Virgin Mary.

GP *abbrev.* **1** Gallup poll. **2** general practitioner.

GPO *abbrev.* General Post Office.

Gr *abbrev.* Greek.

gr *or* **gr** *abbrev.* **1** grain. **2** gram or gramme. **3** gross.

Graaff, Robert Jemison Van de see VAN DE GRAAFF, ROBERT JEMISON.

Graafian follicle *Anat.* in the ovary of female mammals, one of many small spherical sacs within which an ovum (egg cell) develops. Periodically a mature follicle swells until it reaches the surface of the ovary, where it bursts and releases the ovum during the process of *ovulation.* – Also called *ovarian follicle.* [named after the Dutch anatomist Regnier de Graaf]

grab — *verb* (**grabbed, grabbing**) **1** *trans., intrans.* (**grab something** *or* **grab at something**) to seize it suddenly and often with violence. **2** to take greedily. **3** to take hurriedly or without hesitation: *grab a snack* / *grab an opportunity.* **4** *colloq.* to impress or interest: *how does that grab you?* — *noun* **1** an act of taking suddenly or greedily. **2** a mechanical device with scooping jaws, used eg for excavation.

— **up for grabs** *colloq.* available, especially easily or cheaply.
[from Old German dialect or Old Dutch *grabben*]

graben *noun Geol.* a rift valley, usually a very large one, formed when a block of the Earth's crust, usually much longer than it is wide, drops down between two faults. [from German *Graben*, ditch]

Gracchi, The, in full **Tiberius Sempronius Gracchus** (c.168–133 BC) and **Gaius Sempronius Gracchus** (c.159–121 BC) Roman politicians of aristocratic lineage who were appointed Tribunes in 133 BC and 123 BC respectively (and Gaius again in 122 BC). They attempted to force sweeping land reforms, to create a class of small independent farmers, in an attempt to counteract the growing landlessness of the Roman peasantry and the consequent decline in army recruitment. Tiberius was killed at the instigation of a group of senators opposed to his methods. Gaius committed suicide 10 years later.

Grace, W(illiam) G(ilbert) (1848–1915) English cricketer and physician, born in Downend, near Bristol. In his career in first-class cricket which began in 1864 for Gloucester County and lasted until 1908, he scored 126 centuries, 54 896 runs, and 2 876 wickets. In 1876 he scored the first triple century. He toured Canada, the USA, and Australia, and twice captained the English team against Australia in 1880 and 1882.

Grace a female first name, popularized by the film star Grace Kelly (1929–82). [from Latin *gratia*, grace]

grace — *noun* **1** elegance and beauty of form or movement. **2** decency; politeness: *had the grace to offer.* **3** a short prayer of thanks to God said before or after a meal. **4** a delay allowed, especially to a debtor, as a favour. **5** a pleasing or attractive characteristic: *social graces* / *a saving grace.* **6** *Relig.* the mercy and favour shown by God to mankind. **7** *Relig.* the condition of a person's soul of being made free from sin and evil by God. **8** (**His Grace** *or* **Your Grace**) a title used of or to a duke, duchess, or archbishop. **9** (**the Graces**) *Greek Mythol.* see separate entry. — *verb* **1** *often facetious* to honour, eg with one's presence. **2** to add beauty or charm to.

— **airs and graces** behaviour meant to impress others or to show that one considers oneself superior to them.
with a good *or* **bad grace** willingly or unwillingly.
[from Latin *gratia*, favour]

grace-and-favour *adj. Brit., said of a property* owned by the monarch and let rent-free.

graceful *adj.* having or showing elegance and beauty of form or movement.

gracefully *adv.* in a graceful way.

gracefulness *noun* being graceful.

graceless *adj.* **1** awkward in form or movement. **2** bad-mannered.

gracelessly *adv.* in a graceless way.

gracelessness *noun* being graceless.

Graces, the, Greek **Charites** in Greek mythology, three daughters of Zeus and Hera, embodying beauty and social accomplishments. They were usually called Aglaia, Euphrosyne, and Thalia.

gracious — *adj.* **1** kind and polite. **2** *said of God* merciful. **3** having qualities of luxury, elegance, comfort, and leisure. **4** *formal* used out of polite custom to describe a royal person or their actions. — *interj.* an expression of surprise. [from Latin *gratiosus*]

graciously *adv.* in a gracious way.

graciousness *noun* being gracious.

gradate *verb* **1** to shade off; to change imperceptibly. **2** to arrange according to grades.

gradation *noun* **1** a series of gradual and successive stages or degrees, or one step in this. **2** the act or process of forming grades or stages. **3** the gradual change or movement from one state, musical note, colour, etc to another. [from GRADE]

gradational *adj.* involving or characterized by gradation.

Grade, Lew, Baron Grade of Elstree, originally **Louis Winogradsky** (1906–) British theatrical impresario, born near Odessa, Russia, the eldest of three brothers who were to dominate British showbusiness for over 40 years. He arrived in Britain in 1912 with his parents and brothers Boris (later named Bernard, Baron Delfont of Stepney) and Leslie. He became a dancer then a theatrical agent, and later as an impresario he helped establish such stars as Norman Wisdom and Morecambe and Wise. An early entrant to the world of commercial television, he became managing director of ATV in 1962, and has headed several large film entertainment and communications companies.

Grade, Michael (Ian) (1943–) English broadcasting executive, born in London. After training and working for the *Daily Mirror* (1960–6) he was a theatrical agent for his family's Grade Organization, and he entered television administration as Deputy Controller of London Weekend Television (1973–7). He was Controller of BBC1 (1984–6), Director of Programmes (1986–8) and in 1988 became Chief Executive Officer of Channel 4.

grade — *noun* **1** a stage or level on a scale of quality, rank, size, etc. **2** a mark indicating this. **3** *North Amer., esp. US* a particular class or year in school, or the level of work taught in it. **4** a slope or gradient. — *verb* **1** to arrange in different grades. **2** to award a mark indicating grade to. **3** to produce a gradual blending or merging of (especially colours).
— **make the grade** *colloq.* to succeed; to reach the required or expected standard.
[from Latin *gradus*, step]

Gradgrind, Thomas the dictatorial, inflexible father of Tom and Louisa in Charles Dickens's *Hard Times*.

gradient *noun* **1** the steepness of a slope. **2** *formal* a slope. **3** *Maths.* the gradient of a line, or the slope of a tangent to a curve at a particular point. **4** *Physics* the rate of change of a variable quantity over a specified distance, eg the temperature gradient in a metal bar is the rate of change of temperature along the bar. [from Latin *gradiens*, stepping]

gradual *adj.* **1** developing or happening slowly, by degrees. **2** *said of a slope* not steep; gentle. [from Latin *gradualis*, from *gradus*, step]

gradualism *noun* the process of, or support for, gradual progress or change, especially in politics.

gradualist — *noun* a supporter of gradual action. — *adj.* involving gradualism.

gradually *adv.* in a gradual way, slowly, steadily.

graduand *noun* a person who is about to be awarded a higher-education degree. [from Latin *graduare*, to take a degree]

graduate — *verb* (pronounced -*ate*) **1** *intrans.* to receive an academic degree from a higher-education institution. **2** *intrans. North Amer.* to receive a diploma at the end of one's course of study at a high school. **3** *intrans.* to move up from a lower to a higher level, often in stages. **4** to mark (eg a thermometer) with units of measurement or other divisions. **5** to arrange into regular groups, according to size, type, etc. — *noun* (pronounced -*ot*) a person with a higher-education degree or *North Amer.* a high-school diploma. [from Latin *graduare*, to take a degree, from *gradus*, step]

graduation *noun* **1** the act of receiving a higher-education degree or *North Amer.* a high-school diploma. **2** the ceremony marking this. **3** a unit of measurement or other division marked on a ruler, thermometer, etc; the process of marking such divisions.

Graeco- *combining form* forming words relating to Greece or Greek: *Graeco-Roman*.

Graf, Steffi (1969–) German lawn tennis player, born in Bruehl. In 1982 she became the youngest person to receive a World Tennis

Association ranking, aged 13, and reached the semifinal of the US Open in 1985. In 1988 she took all four major Grand Slam titles and an Olympic gold. She retained the Wimbledon singles title in 1989, and won again in 1991–3. Other singles wins include the French Open (1987, 1993), the Australian Open (1989–90), and the US Open (1989, 1993). She has also won various doubles titles.

graffiti *pl. noun* (SING. **graffito**) words or drawings, usually humorous or political slogans, scratched or painted on walls, etc in public places. [from Italian *graffiti*]

graffito **1** *Art* same as SGRAFFITO. **2** see GRAFFITI.

graft[1] — *noun* **1** *Bot.* a piece of plant tissue (the *scion*) that is inserted into a cut in the outer stem of another plant (the *stock*), resulting in fusion of the tissues and growth of a single plant. **2** *Medicine* the transfer or transplantation of an organ or tissue from one individual to another, or to a different site within the same individual, usually to replace diseased or damaged tissue, eg skin graft, kidney transplant. — *verb* **1** to attach a graft in; to attach as a graft. **2** *intrans.* to attach grafts. [from Old French *graffe*, from Greek *graphein*, to write]

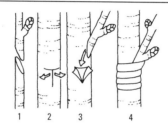

1: a cutting
2: T-shape cut through bark of stock
3: cutting inserted in the graft
4: cutting held in place with tape

graft

graft[2] — *noun* **1** *colloq.* hard work. **2** *slang* the use of illegal or unfair means to gain profit, especially by people in the public eye; the profit gained. — *verb intrans.* **1** *colloq.* to work hard. **2** *slang* to gain profit through corruption.

grafter *noun colloq.* a hard worker.

Graham, Billy (William Franklin) (1918–) US evangelist, born in Charlotte, North Carolina. Ordained a minister of the Southern Baptist Church in 1940, he quickly gained a reputation as a preacher. Since the 1950s he has conducted a series of highly organized revivalist crusades in the USA, the UK, S America, and all over Europe.

Graham, Martha (1894–1991) US dancer, teacher, and choreographer, born in Pittsburgh. She first appeared on stage in vaudeville and revue, started the Martha Graham School of Contemporary Dance in 1927, and became the most famous exponent of expressionist modern dance in the USA — her dance training methods have been adopted worldwide. Her works display an interest in Native American life, as in *Appalachian Spring* (1944), Greek myths, as in *Clytemnestra* (1958), and psychological drama.

Graham, Thomas (1805–69) Scottish chemist, born in Glasgow. Professor in Glasgow and London, and later Master of the Mint, he is most famous for his research on the diffusion of gases and related phenomena; 'Graham's law' states that the velocity of 'effusion' of a gas as it passes through small holes is inversely proportional to the square root of its density. His studies of diffusion in liquids led him to distinguish between crystalloids and colloids, and to devise the process of dialysis for their separation.

Graham or **Grahame** a male first name, after the surname. [from Anglo-Saxon *grand*, gravel + *ham*, homestead]

Grahame, Kenneth (1859–1932) Scottish writer, born in Edinburgh, He entered the Bank of England in 1879, became its secretary in 1898, and retired for health reasons in 1908. He wrote several stories for children, the best known of which is *The Wind in the Willows* (1908), dramatized in 1930 by A A Milne as *Toad of Toad Hall*.

Graham Land a mountainous Antarctic peninsula. It rises to c.3 600m at Mt Jackson. The Weddell Sea lies to the E.

Graham's law *Chem.* a law which states that the rate of diffusion of a gas is inversely proportional to the square root of its density, so a light gas will diffuse more rapidly than a heavy one.

Graiae in Greek mythology, three sisters with the characteristics of extreme old age, who had one eye and one tooth between them. Perseus took the eye and made them tell him how to get to the Gorgons, who were their sisters.

Graian Alps, Italian **Alpi Graie**, French **Alpes Graian** the N division of the W Alps in SE France and NW Italy, situated on the French–Italian border. It extends in an arc from the Alpes Cottiennes at Mont Cenis to the St Bernard Pass and Dora Baltea Valley. The highest peak is Grand Paradis/Gran Paradiso (4 061m).

Grail, Holy, also called **Sangreal** in Arthurian legend, the chalice sought after by the Knights of the Round Table. It was associated with the chalice used by Christ at the Last Supper, in which Joseph of Arimathea later collected some drops of Christ's blood before bringing it to Glastonbury. It appeared at Pentecost at King Arthur's table and the Knights (eg Galahad, Percival) set out to find it.

grain — *noun* **1** a single seed of a cereal plant. **2** cereal plants or their seeds as a whole. **3** a small hard particle of anything. **4** a very small amount: *a grain of truth*. **5** a small unit of weight, equal to 0·065 grams. **6** the direction or arrangement of the lines of fibre in wood, paper, or leather, or of the layers in rock; the pattern they form. **7** the tiny light and dark particles which form the image on a photograph. — *verb* **1** *trans., intrans.* to form into grains. **2** to give a rough appearance or texture to. **3** to paint or stain with a pattern like the grain of wood or leather.
— **go against the grain** to be against one's principles or natural character.
[from Latin *granum*, seed]

Grainger, (George) Percy (Aldridge) (1882–1961) Australian composer and pianist, born in Melbourne. He studied under Pabst and Busoni, then in 1914 settled in the USA. He championed the revival of folk music in such works as *Molly on the Shore* and *Shepherd's Hey* (1911), which make skilful use of traditional dance themes. He often returned to Australia, and in 1935 founded the Grainger Museum in Melbourne.

grainy *adj.* (**grainier**, **grainiest**) *said of a photograph* having a large grain size, and therefore not sharp or distinct.

Gram, Hans Christian Joachim (1853–1938) Danish bacteriologist, born in Copenhagen. In 1884 he developed an important staining technique in microbiology, which divides bacteria into two groups (Gram-positive and Gram-negative), based on the structure of their cell walls. He became Professor of Medicine at Copenhagen in 1900.

gram or **gramme** *noun* (ABBREV. **g**, **gr**) the basic unit of mass in the metric system, equal to 10^{-3} (one thousandth) of a kilogram. It is also the fundamental unit of mass in the centimetre-gramme-second (c.g.s.) system of measurement. [from Greek *gramma*, small weight]

gram. *abbrev.* grammar or grammatical.

-gram *combining form* denoting something written or recorded in a specified way: *diagram / telegram*. [from Greek *gramma*, letter]

Graminae *pl. noun Bot.* in the plant kingdom, the large family of flowering plants that consists of the grasses, including cereals such as wheat and rice, and the bamboos. [from Latin *gramen graminis*, grass]

grammar *noun* **1** the accepted rules by which words are formed and combined into sentences. **2** the branch of language study dealing with these. **3** a description of these rules as applied to a particular language; a book containing this. **4** a person's understanding or use of these rules: *bad grammar*. [from Greek *gramma*, letter]
◇ The term *grammar* embraces many aspects of language. The study of the structure of words is also known as *morphology*, and the study of the structure of phrases, clauses, and sentences is known as *syntax*. A *prescriptive grammar* is one in which rules of 'correct' usage are laid down; a *descriptive grammar* describes the language as it is used, without making value judgements. A *comparative grammar* compares the grammatical features of related languages, and a *universal grammar* investigates those grammatical features shared by the structure of all language.

grammarian *noun* an expert on grammar.

grammar school *noun* especially formerly, a secondary school emphasising the study of academic rather than technical subjects.

grammatical *adj.* **1** relating to grammar. **2** correct according to the rules of grammar. [from Greek *grammatikos*, from *gramma*, letter]

grammatically *adv.* in a grammatical way; as regards grammar.

gramme see GRAM.

gramophone *noun* a record player, especially an old-fashioned one. [from Greek *gramma*, letter, record + *phone*, sound]

Grampian POP (1992e) 522 000, a region in NE Scotland, divided into five districts. AREA 8 704sq km/3 360sq mi. It is bounded N and E by the North Sea, W by Highland Region, and S by Tayside. PHYSICAL DESCRIPTION drained by the Spey, Dee, Don, Ythan, and Deveron rivers; part of the Cairngorms and part of the Grampian Mts lie in the SW. CAPITAL Aberdeen. CHIEF TOWNS Peterhead, Stonehaven, Fraserburgh, Elgin. ECONOMY fishing; farming; oil-related industries; whisky; tourism. NOTABLE FEATURE Balmoral Castle.

Grampians *or* **Grampian Mountains** a mountain system extending SW–NE across Scotland. Its S edge forms the natural border between the Highlands and the Lowlands. Rising to 1 344m at Ben Nevis (Britain's highest peak), the Grampians have gentle slopes in the S and steep slopes in the N. Several smaller chains, eg the Cairngorms, are contained within the Grampian range. The Grampians are the source of the Dee, Don, Spey, Findhorn, Esk, Tay, and Forth rivers.

Grampians a mountain range in SW central Victoria, SE Australia. It extends c.64km/40mi NW from Ararat and forms the SW spur of the Great Dividing Range. Mt William is the highest point at 1 167m.

grampus *noun* **1** a grey blunt-nosed dolphin that blows out air and water noisily. **2** a killer whale. **3** a person who breathes heavily. [from Old French *graspois*, from *gras*, fat + *pois*, fish]

Gram's stain *Biol.* an important staining procedure used to distinguish between two major groups of bacteria. Gram-positive bacteria stain deep purple and Gram-negative bacteria stain red, owing to differences in cell wall structure. [named after the Danish bacteriologist Hans Christian Joachim Gram]

gran *noun colloq.* a grandmother.

Granada POP (1991) 254 000, the capital of Granada province, Andalusia, S Spain. It lies at the foot of the Sierra Nevada on the R Genil, 434km/270mi S of Madrid, and at an average altitude of 720m. HISTORY founded by the Moors in the 8c, it became capital of the Kingdom of Granada in 1238; it was the last Moorish stronghold in Spain before its capture by the Spanish in 1492. The poet and dramatist Federico Garcia Lorca was born here in 1899. NOTABLE FEATURES cathedral (16c), with the tombs of Ferdinand and Isabella of Castile; the Generalife Palace and the Alhambra have been designated a World Heritage site.

granary — *noun* (PL. **granaries**) **1** a building where grain is stored. **2** a region that produces large quantities of grain. — *adj., said of bread* containing whole grains of wheat. [from Latin *granarium*, from *granum*, grain]

Granby, John Manners, Marquis of (1721–70) English soldier, the eldest son of the Duke of Rutland. He made his reputation in the Seven Years' War (1756–63), by leading the British cavalry to a major victory over the French at Warburg (1760). He became a popular hero, and in 1763 was appointed Master-General of the Ordnance.

Gran Chaco a lowland plain covering part of N Argentina, W Paraguay, and S Bolivia. Drained by the R Paraná and R Paraguay, it is an area of scrub forest and grassland, with a tropical savannah climate. The region, which has a sparse population, is noted for cattle raising. It was a disputed area in the Chaco War between Paraguay and Bolivia from 1932 until 1935.

grand — *adj.* **1** large or impressive in size, appearance or style. **2** *sometimes derog.* dignified; self-important. **3** intended to impress or gain attention: *a grand gesture*. **4** complete; in full: *grand total*. **5** *colloq.* very pleasant; excellent. **6** greatest; highest ranking: *Grand Master*. **7** highly respected: *grand old man*. **8** main; principal: *the grand entrance*. — *noun* **1** *slang* a thousand dollars or pounds. **2** *colloq.* a grand piano. [from French *grand*, from Latin *grandis*, great]

grand- *combining form* indicating a family relationship that is one generation more remote than that of the base word.

grandad *noun colloq.* **1** a grandfather. **2** *offensive* an old man.

Grand Alliance, War of the a phase (1805–7) in the Napoleonic Wars, when a Third Coalition of states (Britain, Austria, Russia, Sweden, and Prussia) attacked France by land and sea. Despite Britain's success at Trafalgar (1805), the coalition was weakened by spectacular French victories at Ulm, Austerlitz (1805), and Jena and Auerstädt (1806). Hostilities were ended by the Treaties of Pressburg (1805) and Tilsit (1807).

Grand Bahama POP (1990) 41 000, an island in the NW Bahamas and the fourth largest island in the group. AREA 1 372sq km/530sq mi. CHIEF TOWN Freeport-Lucaya. The island is a popular tourist resort.

Grand Banks a major fishing ground in the N Atlantic Ocean. It lies off the coast of Newfoundland, Canada, formed by an extensive underwater plateau on the continental shelf. The plankton-rich shallow waters provide an important breeding area for fish.

Grand Canal, Chinese **Da Yunhe** a canal connecting Beijing municipality to Hangzhou in Zhejiang province of E China. It is the longest artificial waterway in the world (1 794km/1 115mi). HISTORY begun in the 5c BC to carry tribute rice from the Yangtze Plain to the imperial government in Beijing; opened in 610. A major transport artery between N and S China from the 13c until the 19c, its use declined with silting and the coming of railways.

Grand Canary, Spanish **Gran Canaria** a volcanic Atlantic island in the Canary Is, Spain. AREA 1 532sq km/591sq mi. PHYSICAL DESCRIPTION there are steep cliffs in the N and W, and wide beaches in the S; the highest point is Pozo de las Nieves (1 980m). CHIEF TOWN Las Palmas de Gran Canaria. ECONOMY sugar cane; tobacco; distilling; chemicals; light engineering; tourism.

Grand Canyon an enormous gorge in NW Arizona, USA, located in Grand Canyon National Park. It is one of the main tourist attractions in the USA. AREA 349km/217mi long; 8–25km/5–15mi wide, from rim to rim; maximum depth c.1 900m. The gorge resulted from large-scale erosion by the Colorado R, exposing 1 500 million years of geological formations. Parts of the side walls have formed isolated towers ('temples') due to stream erosion; the best known are Vishnu Temple, Shiva Temple, and Wotan's Throne.

Grand Canyon of the Snake see HELL'S CANYON.

Grand Cayman POP (1989) 24 000, the largest of the Cayman Is, W Caribbean Sea. AREA 197sq km/76sq mi. The island is flat and surrounded by coral reefs. It is 45km/28mi long and measures 13km/8mi at its widest point. CAPITAL George Town. The only commercial turtle farm in the world is based on the island. Tourist development is concentrated along the Seven Mile Beach Peninsula.

grandchild *noun* a child of one's son or daughter.

Grand Coulee a valley in Douglas County, NE Washington, USA. The Grand Coulee Dam (1933–42) is a major gravity dam on the Columbia R; it holds Lake Franklin D Roosevelt as a reservoir. The dam is 168m high, 1 272m long, and is able to generate 6 180 megawatts of hydroelectricity.

granddaughter *noun* a daughter of one's son or daughter.

grand duchess *noun* **1** the wife or widow of a grand duke. **2** a high-ranking noblewoman who rules a grand duchy.

grand duchy *noun* a small European country or state having a grand duke or grand duchess as its sovereign.

grand duke *noun* a high-ranking nobleman who rules a grand duchy.

Grande Comore *or* **Njazidja** POP (1990e) 249 000, the largest island of the Comoros group, in the Mozambique Channel. AREA 1 148sq km/443sq mi. CHIEF TOWN Moroni. PHYSICAL DESCRIPTION steep mountains rise to the peak of Kartala, an active volcano (2 361m).

Grande Dixence Dam a major gravity dam (285m high) on the R Dixence, Switzerland, completed in 1962. It has the capacity to generate 840 megawatts of hydroelectricity.

grandee *noun* **1** a Spanish or Portuguese nobleman of the highest rank. **2** any well-respected or high-ranking person. [from Spanish *grande*]

Grande Odalisque, La a painting by Jean Auguste Dominique Ingres (1814, Louvre, Paris). It is one of his best-known female nudes.

Grande-Terre POP (1990) 178 000, an island of the French Overseas Department of Guadeloupe, Lesser Antilles, E Caribbean Sea. AREA 585sq km/226sq mi. CHIEF TOWN Pointe-à-Pitre. PHYSICAL DESCRIPTION one of the two main islands of Guadeloupe, it is of coral formation, rising to only 150m.

grandeur *noun* **1** greatness of character, especially dignity or nobility. **2** impressive beauty; magnificence. **3** *derog.* self-importance; pretentiousness. [from French *grandeur*]

grandfather *noun* the father of one's father or mother.

grandfather clock *noun* a clock built into a tall free-standing wooden case, operated by a long pendulum.

Grand Guignol short sensational shows, popular in late-19c Paris, which depicted violent crimes in a style designed to shock and titillate. Guignol was originally a puppet in the French marionette theatre.

grandiloquence *noun* being grandiloquent.

grandiloquent *adj. derog.* speaking, or spoken, or written, in a pompous, self-important style. [from Latin *grandis*, great + *loqui*, to speak]

grandiloquently *adv.* in a grandiloquent way.

grandiose *adj.* 1 splendid; magnificent; impressive. 2 *derog.* exaggeratedly impressive or imposing, especially on a ridiculously large scale. [from Italian *grandioso*, from *grande*, great]

Grandison, Sir Charles see Sir Charles Grandison.

grand jury *noun* in the US, a jury which decides whether there is enough evidence for a person to be brought to trial.

grandly *adv.* in a grand way.

grandma *colloq.* a grandmother.

grand mal *Medicine* a serious form of epilepsy, commonly known as an epileptic fit, in which there is sudden loss of consciousness followed by convulsions, which subside after a period of a few seconds to several minutes. [French, = great illness]

grandmother *noun* the mother of one's father or mother.

Grand National a British horserace, generally viewed as the most famous steeplechase in the world, first held at Maghull near Liverpool in 1836. The race moved to its present course at Aintree in 1839. It is raced over 7.2km/4mi, in which the competitors have to negotiate 31 severe fences, including the hazardous Becher's Brook. In 1993, the race was declared void after many of the riders failed to realize they had been recalled, and completed the course.

grand opera *noun* serious opera of the 19c, based on grand themes and using large forces and elaborate staging, with all the dialogue usually sung.

grandpa *noun colloq.* a grandfather.

grandparent *noun* either parent of one's father or mother.

grand piano *noun* a large piano in which the strings are arranged horizontally, used especially for concerts.

Grand Prix (PL. **Grands Prix**) the name applied to automobile racing on closed circuits, which began in France in 1906, and is controlled by the FIA (Fédération Internationale de l'Automobile). The premier class of Grand Prix racing-car is Formula One. The World Championship of Drivers comprises more than 15 Grand Prix races held annually in many different countries. The term 'Grand Prix' is also used in other sports (eg horse-racing, tennis) in which a series of events decides the overall champion. [from French *grand prix*, great prize]

grand slam *noun* 1 *Sport* the winning in one season of every part of a competition, or of all major competitions. 2 *Cards* especially in bridge, the winning of all thirteen tricks by one player or side, or the contract to do so.

◇ In tennis, Grand Slam events are the Australian Open, the French Open, Wimbledon (the All England Championships), and the US open. In rugby union, the Five Nations' Championship is contested between England, France, Ireland, Scotland, and Wales; the Grand Slam is achieved by beating all four opponents.

grandson *noun* a son of one's son or daughter.

grandstand *noun* the largest covered stand at a sports ground, providing the best view.

grandstand finish 1 a close and rousing finish to a sporting contest. 2 a supreme effort to win at the close of a sporting contest.

Grand St Bernard an alpine mountain pass on the Italian-Swiss border. It lies in the SW Pennine Alps, E of the Mont Blanc group, and connects the Rhône Valley with the Valle d'Aosta in Italy. The road is the highest in the Swiss Alps (2 469m) after the Umbrail Road, and is usually open only from Jun to Oct. Following the construction of the 5 828m-long St Bernard Tunnel (1959–63), the route is passable throughout the year.

grand tour *noun* 1 a tour of the major cities of Europe, considered essential to the education of a rich young person, especially in the 18c. 2 *colloq.* any extended tour or inspection.

grange *noun* a country house with farm buildings attached. [from Old French *grange*, barn]

Grangemouth POP (1981) 22 000, an industrial port in Falkirk district, Central region, central Scotland. It lies on the S shore of the Firth of Forth, 5km/3mi E of Falkirk. NOTABLE FEATURES petrochemicals, oil refining; Grangemouth Museum.

granite *noun Geol.* a hard coarse-grained igneous rock, generally grey, pink, yellow, or green in colour, consisting mainly of quartz and feldspar, with small amounts of mica. It is widely used in the construction of buildings and roads. [from Italian *granito*, grained]

granny *or* **grannie** *noun* (PL. **grannies**) *colloq.* a grandmother.

granny flat *noun colloq.* a flat for an elderly relative or parent, built on to or contained in a house.

granny knot *noun* a reef knot with the ends crossed the wrong way, allowing it to slip or undo easily.

Granny Smith *noun* a crisp green variety of eating apple, originally Australian.

Grant, Cary, originally **Archibald Leach** (1904–86) English-born US actor, born in Bristol. He went to Hollywood in 1928, played opposite Marlene Dietrich and Mae West, and played leading comedy roles, such as in *Bringing Up Baby* (1938) and *His Girl Friday* (1940). His performances for Hitchcock included *Suspicion* (1941), *Notorious* (1946), *To Catch a Thief* (1955), and *North by North-West* (1959).

Grant, Ulysses S(impson) (1822–85) US soldier and statesman, the 18th President, born in Point Pleasant, Ohio. He fought in the Mexican War (1846–8), then settled as a farmer in Missouri, but on the outbreak of the Civil War (1861) he rejoined the army, rose rapidly, and led Union forces to victory, first in the Mississippi Valley, then in the final campaigns in Virginia. He accepted the Confederate surrender at Appomattox Court House (1865), and was made a full general in 1866. Elected to two terms as President (1869–77), he presided over the reconstruction of the South, but his administration was marred by scandal and corruption.

Grant, William (1863–1946) Scottish lexicographer, born in Elgin. He studied in France, Belgium, and Germany, and became a lecturer at Aberdeen University. He published various works on Scottish dialects, and was until his death the editor of the *Scottish National Dictionary*.

Grant a male first name, after the Scottish surname. [from a Norman nickname *grand*, large]

grant — *verb* 1 to give, allow, or fulfil. 2 to admit to be true. — *noun* 1 something granted, especially an amount of money from a public fund for a specific purpose. 2 *Legal* the transfer of property by deed. 3 (**granted**) an admission that

Grapes for Wine-making

Red

Cabernet Sauvignon	used in Bordeaux, for claret, important in Australia and Chile
Carignan	commonest grape in France, much used in Spain and California
Gamay	used for Beaujolais and rose
Merlot	used in Medoc blended with Cabernet; softer
Pinot Noir	used in Burgundy, and for champagne
Sangiovese	principal grape of Chianti
Syrah/Shiraz	used in the Rhône, very important in Australia
Zinfandel	peculiar to California, lively and fruity

White

Chardonnay	used for white Burgundy, very successful in Australia, California, New Zealand
Chenin Blanc	used in the Loire and California
Gewurztraminer	speciality of Alsace
Muscat	used for light fragrant wine in Alsace, sweet in Australia, E Europe, France
Riesling	used extensively in Germany, California, Australia, New Zealand
Sauvignon Blanc	used in white Bordeaux, the Loire, and in California, Australia, New Zealand
Semillon	used extensively for sauternes (Bordeaux), and in Australia
Sylvaner	used extensively in Germany, and in Alsace, N Italy, California

something is true or valid: *granted you gave it back later.*

— **take someone for granted** to treat them casually and without appreciation.

take something for granted to assume it to be true or valid; to accept it without question. [from Old French *granter* or *greanter*, variant of *creanter*, to promise]

Granth *noun* (*also* **Granth Sahib**) the sacred scripture of the Sikh religion. [from Hindi *granth*, book]

Grantham POP (1981) 31 000, a town in South Kesteven district, Lincolnshire, E central England. It lies on the R Witham, 35km/22mi E of Nottingham, and is the market town for a rich agricultural region. NOTABLE FEATURES Grantham House (14c); Church of St Wulfram (14c).

Grantly, Archdeacon the son-in-law of the Rev Septimus Harding in Anthony Trollope's *The Warden* and other titles in the 'Barsetshire' novels. His daughter Griselda marries Lord Dumbello.

granular *adj. technical* 1 made of, or containing, tiny particles or granules. 2 *said of appearance or texture* rough. [see GRANULE]

granularity *noun* being granular.

granulate *verb* 1 to break down into small particles or granules. 2 to give a rough appearance or texture to.

granulation *noun* 1 forming into grains. 2 a granulated texture.

granule *noun* a very small particle or grain. [from Latin *granulum*, diminutive of *granum*, grain]

Granville-Barker, Harley (1877–1946) English actor, playwright, and producer, born in London. He began with an acting career, then entered theatre management at the Court Theatre (1904) and the Savoy (1907). His own plays included *The Voysey Inheritance* (1905). He also collaborated in translations and wrote a well-known series of prefaces to Shakespeare's plays (1927–45).

grape *noun* **1** a pale green or purplish-black juicy edible berry, which may be eaten fresh, pressed to make wine, or dried to form currants, raisins, and sultanas. Grape varieties used for wine production are usually relatively acidic, whereas those cultivated for dessert fruit are sweeter and often seedless. **2** a perennial climbing vine of the genus *Vitis*, widely cultivated in warm temperate regions for these edible berries, which are borne in clusters. **3** *literary* (**the grape**) wine. [from Old French *grape*, bunch of grapes]

grapefruit *noun* (PL. **grapefruit**, **grapefruits**) a large round citrus fruit with thick yellow skin and slightly sour flesh.

grape hyacinth a plant belonging to the genus *Muscari*, native to Europe, and having grass-like leaves, and dense spikes of drooping urn-shaped blue flowers, each with six small lobes. The upper flowers are often sterile and more brightly coloured, and serve to attract insect pollinators. The plant is widely cultivated for ornament.

Grapelli, Stephane (1908–) French jazz violinist, born in Paris. He and the guitarist Django Reinhardt were the principal soloists in the Quintet of the Hot Club of France (1934–9), the first European jazz band to exert an influence in the USA. Since World War II he has performed all over the world, continuing to be active in his eighties.

grapeshot *noun* ammunition in the form of small iron balls, spreading when fired in bunches from a cannon.

Grapes of Wrath, The 1 a novel by John Steinbeck (1939). It describes the fate of the Joad family who travel to California after being evicted from their Oklahoma farm. **2** a US film directed by John Ford adapted from John Steinbeck's novel. Henry Fonda stars as Tom Joad.

grape sugar *Biochem.* glucose.

grapevine *noun* **1** a vine on which grapes grow. **2** (**the grapevine**) *colloq.* informal conversation between people, regarded as a network through which information is spread: *I heard on the grapevine that you're leaving.*

graph — *noun* **1** a diagram that illustrates the way in which one quantity varies in relation to another. It usually consists of two axes, one horizontal and the other vertical, which cross each other at a point called the origin. Points representing different sets of data are plotted in the areas between the axes. **2** a symbolic diagram. — *verb* to represent with a graph. [from Greek *graphein*, to write]

-graph *combining form* forming words denoting: **1** an instrument that records or records: *telegraph*. **2** something written or recorded: *autograph*. [from Greek *graphein*, to write]

grapheme *noun Linguistics* **1** the letters or combination of letters used together to form a phoneme. **2** a letter of an alphabet. [from Greek *graphema*, letter]

graphic *adj.* **1** described or shown vividly and in detail. **2** of the branch of the arts concerned with drawing, printing and lettering: *graphic design*. **3** relating to graphs; shown using a graph.

-graphic *or* **graphical** *combining form* forming adjectives corresponding to nouns in -*graph* and -*graphy*: *telegraphic / geographical*.

graphically *adv.* in a graphic way.

graphic equalizer *Electron.* a device for boosting or cutting frequencies of an audio signal using a type of sliding control.

graphic novel a full-length story, often of science fiction or some other form of fantasy, told in comic strip form and published as a book.

graphics *noun* **1** (*sing.*) the art or science of drawing according to mathematical rules. **2** (*pl.*) the photographs and illustrations used in a magazine; the non-acted visual parts of a film or television programme, eg the credits.

graphics tablet *Comput.* an input device which translates the movements of a pen over a sensitive pad to a corresponding pattern on the screen.

graphite *noun* a soft black allotrope of carbon that is a good conductor of heat and electricity, and is greasy and slippery to the touch. It is used as a lubricant, an electrical contact, and a constituent of paints, and is mixed with clay to form the 'lead' in pencils. – Also called *black lead*, *plumbago*. [from Greek *graphein*, to write]

graphologist *noun* a person skilled in or practising graphology.

graphology *noun* the study of handwriting, especially as a way of analysing the writer's character. [from Greek *graphein*, to write + -LOGY]

graph paper paper covered in small squares, used for drawing graphs.

-graphy *combining form* **1** a type of writing or method of representing: *biography / lithography*. **2** a descriptive science or art: *geography / choreography*. [from Greek *graphein*, to write]

grapnel *noun* **1** a large multi-pointed hook on the end of a rope, used for securing a heavy object on the other end. **2** a light anchor for small boats. [from Old French *grapin*, diminutive of *grape*, hook]

grappa *noun* a brandy distilled from the fermentable residue (grape skins and stalks) from a wine-press. Originally Italian, it is now made in California, Uruguay, and elsewhere. [from Italian *grappa*, grape stalk]

grapple — *verb* **1** (**grapple with someone**) to grasp and struggle or fight. **2** (**grapple with something**) to struggle mentally with a difficult problem. **3** to secure with a hook, etc. — *noun* **1** a hook or other device for securing. **2** an act of gripping, as in wrestling; a way of gripping. [from Old French *grappelle*, diminutive of *grape*, hook]

grappling-iron *or* **grappling-hook** *noun* a grapnel.

graptolite *noun Geol.* any of a group of extinct marine animals that were common in the Palaeozoic era, and are thought to be related to present-day coelenterates (eg jellyfish, corals). Their fossilized skeletons have been found in Palaeozoic rocks worldwide, and they are so common in rocks of the Ordovician and Silurian periods that they are used as 'index fossils' to date the rocks in which they are found. [from Greek *graptos*, written + *lithos*, stone]

Grasmere POP (1981) 1 100, a scenic resort village in Cumbria, NW England. It is by L Grasmere, 23km/14mi N of Kendal. NOTABLE FEATURES Dove Cottage, home of William Wordsworth (1799–1808), and of Samuel Taylor Coleridge and Thomas de Quincey; Church of St Oswald, where Wordsworth is buried.

grasp — *verb* **1** to take a firm hold of; to clutch. **2** (**grasp at something**) to make a movement as if to seize it. **3** to understand. — *noun* **1** a grip or hold. **2** power or control; ability to reach, achieve, or obtain: *in one's grasp*. **3** ability to understand: *beyond their grasp*. [from Middle English *graspen*]

grasping *adj. derog.* greedy, especially for wealth.

Grass, Günter (Wilhelm) (1927–) German writer and political activist, born in Danzig. He moved to Paris in 1956, and made his name with his first novel, *Die Blechtrommel* (The Tin Drum, 1959, filmed 1979). This was followed by other political novels, including *Hundejahre* (Dog Years, 1963), and various prose works, including *Die Rättin* (The Rats, 1986) and *Der Bürger und seine Stimme* (The Citizen and his Vote, 1974), a collection of speeches and essays.

grass — *noun* **1** any flowering plant belonging to the family Gramineae, typically having long narrow leaves with parallel veins, a jointed upright hollow stem, and flowers with no petals borne alternately on both sides of an axis known as a spikelet, eg wheat, maize, rye, sugar-cane, bamboo. **2** an area planted with or growing such plants, eg a lawn or meadow. **3** lawn or pasture. **4** *slang* marijuana. **5** *slang* a person who betrays others, especially to the police. — *verb* **1** to plant with grass or turf. **2** to feed with grass; to provide pasture for. **3** *slang* (*often* **grass on someone**) to inform, especially to the police.

— **let the grass grow under one's feet** to delay or waste time.

put something *or* **someone out to grass 1** to give a life of grazing to an old animal, eg a racehorse. **2** *colloq.* to put someone into retirement. [from Anglo-Saxon *gærs, græs*]

◇ There are about 9 000 species of grass, with representatives in most parts of the world except

1: sugar   2: maize   4: timothy
cane   3: wheat   5: bamboo

grasses

the polar regions. All grasses are monocotyledons, ie the embryo contains a single cotyledon or seed leaf, and most of them are perennial. Their fruits, often loosely referred to as 'seeds', are rich in carbohydrate, and many grasses are economically important, cultivated grasses or *cereals* such as wheat, rice, and oats being an important human food source. Grasses form the main food for grazing animals, eg sheep, and differ from most other plants in that the growing points are close to ground level, so that even when the grass blades are constantly grazed, the plant continues to grow.

grasshopper *noun* a large brown or green jumping insect belonging to the same order (Orthoptera) as the crickets, but distinguished from them by its short antennae. Grasshoppers have long powerful hind legs, and some species have reduced wings or none at all. They feed on plants, and the males produce a characteristic chirping sound by rubbing the hind legs against the wings.

grass roots 1 ordinary people, as opposed to those in a position of (especially political) power. **2** bare essentials; fundamental principles.

grass-roots *adj.* relating to or involving ordinary people.

grass snake a small harmless European snake with a brownish-green body.

grass widow *or* **grass widower** a person whose husband or wife is absent from home for long periods of time.

grassy *adj.* (**grassier, grassiest**) like or covered with grass.

grate¹ *noun* **1** a framework of iron bars for holding coal, etc in a fireplace or furnace. **2** the fireplace or furnace itself. [from Latin *grata*]

grate² *verb* **1** to cut into shreds by rubbing

against a rough surface. **2** *trans., intrans.* to make or cause to make a harsh grinding sound by rubbing. **3** (**grate on someone**) to irritate or annoy them. [from Old French *grater*, to scrape]

grateful *adj.* **1** feeling thankful; showing or giving thanks. **2** *formal* pleasant and welcome: *grateful sleep*. See GRATITUDE. [from Latin *gratus*, pleasing, thankful]

gratefully *adv.* in a grateful way; with gratitude.

grater *noun* a device with a rough surface for grating food.

gratification *noun* **1** a pleasing. **2** that which pleases. **3** satisfaction.

gratify *verb* (**gratifies, gratified**) **1** to please. **2** to satisfy or indulge (eg a desire). [from Latin *gratus*, pleasing, thankful + *facere*, to make]

grating¹ *noun* a framework of metal bars fixed into a wall eg over a window, or into a pavement eg over a drain. [from GRATE¹]

grating² — *adj.* **1** *said of sounds, etc* harsh. **2** irritating. — *noun* a grating sound.

gratis *adv., adj.* free; without charge. [from Latin *gratis*, from *gratia*, favour]

gratitude *noun* the state or feeling of being grateful; thankfulness. [from Latin *gratus*, thankful]

Grattan, Henry (1746–1820) Irish statesman, born in Dublin. He entered the Irish parliament in 1775 and became the leading spokesman for the patriotic party, and managed to secure Irish free trade in 1779, and legislative independence in 1782. Returned for Dublin in 1790, in 1805 he was elected to the House of Commons, where he fought for Catholic emancipation.

gratuitous *adj.* **1** done without good reason; unnecessary or unjustified. **2** given or received without charge; voluntary. [from Latin *gratuitas*, from *gratia*, favour]

gratuitously *adv.* in a gratuitous way.

gratuity *noun* (PL. **gratuities**) **1** a sum of money given as a reward for good service; a tip. **2** a sum of money given to a soldier, etc on retirement, in recognition of long service. [from Latin *gratus*, thankful]

grave¹ *noun* **1** a deep trench dug in the ground for burying a dead body. **2** the site of an individual burial. **3** (**the grave**) *literary* death. — **dig one's own grave** to be the cause of one's own downfall.
turn in one's grave *said of a dead person* to be thought likely to be distressed or offended when alive by circumstances such as those in question. [from Anglo-Saxon *græf*, grave or trench, from *grafan*, to dig]

grave² *adj.* **1** giving cause for great concern; very dangerous. **2** very important; serious. **3** solemn and serious in manner. [from Latin *gravis*]

grave³ *noun* (pronounced as in *halve*) (*also* **grave accent**) a mark placed over a vowel (eg *à è*) in some languages to indicate a particular pronunciation or extended length of the vowel. [from French *grave*]

gravel — *noun* **1** a mixture of small stones and coarse sand, used for the surface of paths and roads. **2** *Medicine* stone-like masses of mineral salts in the kidneys or bladder. — *verb* (**gravelled, gravelling**) to cover (eg a path) with gravel. [from Old French *gravele*]

gravelly *adj.* **1** full of, or containing, small stones. **2** *said of a voice* rough and usually deep.

Gravelotte, Battle of a critical engagement (1870) in the Franco-Prussian War. The French Army of the Rhine under Marshal Bazaine inflicted heavy casualties on the Germans but failed to break von Moltke's troops and had to retreat to nearby Metz. This led to MacMahon's attempt to relieve Metz, and to the disastrous French defeat at the battle of Sedan.

gravely *adv.* in a grave way.

graven *adj.* **1** *old use* carved or engraved. **2** firmly fixed in the mind. [from old word *grave*, to carve or engrave]

Gravenhage, 's- see HAGUE, THE.

graven image *Biblical* a carved idol used in worship.

Graves, Robert (Ranke) (1895–1985) English poet and novelist, born in London. He was Professor of English at Cairo, Professor of Poetry at Oxford (1961–6), but lived most of his life in Majorca. His best-known novels are *I, Claudius* and its sequel, *Claudius the God* (both 1934), which were adapted for television in 1976. His non-fiction works include the autobiography *Goodbye to All That* (1929), the treatise on poetic inspiration, *The White Goddess* (1948), and *Greek Myths* (1955). His volumes of *Collected Poems* were published in 1955 and 1975.

Gravesend POP (1981) 54 000, an industrial town in Gravesham district, Kent, SE England. It lies on the R Thames, c.40km/25mi E of London, and is the Port of London customs and pilot station.

gravestone *noun* a stone marking a grave, usually having the dead person's name and dates of birth and death engraved.

Gravettian a European archaeological culture of the Upper Palaeolithic Age, c.26 000–18 000 BC (sometimes referred to as the Later Aurignacian/Later Perigordian). It is named after the cave at La Gravette, Dordogne, SW France, notable for its associations with carved Venus figurines.

graveyard *noun* a burial place; a cemetery.

gravid *adj.* *Medicine* pregnant. [from Latin *gravis*, heavy]

gravimeter *noun* *Geol.* an instrument for measuring variations in the magnitude of the gravitational field at different points on the Earth's surface. It is used to prospect for mineral deposits, eg petroleum, which produce local variations in the force of gravity. [from Latin *gravis*, heavy + Greek *metron*, measure]

gravimetric *adj.* relating to measurement by weight.

gravimetry *noun* *technical* measurement of weight.

gravitas *noun* *literary* seriousness of manner; solemnity. [from Latin *gravitas*]

gravitate *verb intrans.* **1** to fall or be drawn under the force of gravity. **2** to move or be drawn gradually, as if attracted by some force. [from GRAVITY¹]

gravitation *noun* **1** the force of attraction existing between two objects; gravity. **2** the process of moving or being drawn, either by this force or some other attracting influence.

gravitational *adj.* relating to or involving gravity.

gravitational field *Physics* that region of space in which one object, by virtue of its mass, exerts a force of attraction on another object.

graviton *noun* *Physics* the hypothetical carrier of gravitational force.

gravity¹ *noun* **1** the observed effect of the force of attraction that exists between two massive bodies. The magnitude of the force is proportional to the product of the masses of the two bodies, and inversely proportional to the square of the distance between them. The force of attraction that exists between the planets and the Sun on account of their masses maintains the planets in their orbits around the Sun. The gravitational force exerted by the Moon moves water around in the oceans on the Earth's surface, producing tides. **2** the name commonly used to refer to the force of attraction between any object that

is situated within the Earth's gravitational field, and the Earth. Objects feel heavy, and are pulled down towards the ground, because of this force. [from Latin *gravitas*, heaviness]

gravity² *noun* **1** seriousness; dangerous nature. **2** serious attitude; solemnity. [from Latin *gravitas*, seriousness]

gravlax *or* **gravadlax** *noun* a Scandanavian dish of salmon dry-cured with herbs (usually dill), sugar, salt, and pepper, sliced on the slant to serve. [from Swedish *gravlax*, Norwegian *gravlaks*, buried salmon]

gravure *noun* **1** a form of intaglio printing in which the image is engraved or etched into the surface of a metal cylinder; after inking, surplus ink is removed from the surface of the cylinder, and the ink retained in the engraved recesses is transferred to paper. **2** an image produced by this process (see also PHOTOGRAVURE).

gravy *noun* (PL. **gravies**) **1** the juices released by meat as it is cooking. **2** a sauce made by thickening and seasoning these juices; a similar sauce made with an artificial substitute. **3** *slang* easily obtained money. [perhaps from French *gravé*, mistaken reading of *grané*, cooking spice]

gravy boat a small boat-shaped container with a handle, for serving gravy and other sauces.

gravy train *slang* a job or scheme from which a lot of money is gained for little effort.

Gray, Asa (1810–88) US botanist, born in Sauquoit, New York. Professor of Natural History at Harvard (1842–73), he was the first paid professional botanist in the US and eventually the leading 19c plant taxonomist. A strong Darwinian, he used Charles Darwin's theory of evolution to explain the distribution of plants occurring in both E Asia and eastern N America. His total output numbered some 780 works, including *Manual of Botany of the Northern United States* (known as 'Gray's Manual', 1848).

Gray, Stephen (1666–1736) English physicist, born in Canterbury. His first scientific paper (1696) described a microscope made of a water droplet, similar to the simple glass bead microscopes which became famous in the following decade. He was also one of the first experimenters in static electricity, using frictional methods to prove conduction.

Gray, Thomas (1716–71) English poet, born in London. In 1742 he wrote his 'Ode on a Distant Prospect of Eton College' (1747), and began his best-known work, 'Elegy written in a Country Churchyard' (1751). He then settled in Cambridge, where he wrote his two *Pindaric Odes* (1757). He declined the laureateship in 1757, and became Professor of History and Modern Languages at Cambridge in 1768.

gray¹ *North Amer., esp. US* same as GREY.

gray² *noun* *Physics* (ABBREV. **Gy**) the SI unit used to express the amount of radiation absorbed, equal to one joule of energy per kilogram. [named after the UK radiobiologist Louis H Gray]

grayling *noun* (PL. **grayling, graylings**) a silver-grey freshwater fish of the salmon family. [from GREY]

Graz POP (1991) 232 000, the capital of Styria state, SE Austria, and the second-largest city in the country. It lies on the R Mur, at the foot of the Schlossberg (473m), and is the economic and commercial focus of the whole region. The outskirts of the city are heavily industrialized. NOTABLE FEATURES opera house; Renaissance Landhaus (1557–65); Landeszeughaus (Provincial Arsenal); Gothic cathedral (15c); 28m-high clock tower (1561); Piber Stud Farm (3.5km/2mi NE), where Lippizaner horses are bred for the Spanish Riding School in Vienna; Austrian Open-air Museum at Stübing (15km/9mi N).

graze¹ *verb* **1** *intrans. said of animals* to eat grass. **2** *trans.* to feed (animals) on grass. [from Anglo-Saxon *grasian*, from *græs*, grass]

graze² — *verb* **1** to suffer a break in the skin of (eg a limb), through scraping against a hard rough surface. **2** to brush against lightly in passing. — *noun* **1** an area of grazed skin. **2** the action of grazing skin.

grazing *noun* land with grass for animals to feed on; pasture.

grease — *noun* **1** animal fat softened by melting or cooking. **2** any thick oily substance, especially a lubricant for the moving parts of machinery. — *verb* **1** to lubricate or dirty with grease. **2** to ease the progress of.
— **grease someone's palm** or **hand** *colloq.* to bribe them.
grease the wheels *colloq.* to make progress easier.
[from Old French *graisse*]

greasepaint *noun* waxy make-up used by actors.

greaser *noun* **1** a person whose job it is to grease machinery. **2** *slang* a member of a gang of usually long-haired motorcyclists. **3** *North Amer. offensive slang* a Mexican or Spanish American.

greasiness *noun* being greasy.

greasy *adj.* (**greasier, greasiest**) **1** containing, or covered in, grease. **2** having an oily appearance or texture. **3** slippery, as if covered in grease. **4** *colloq.* insincerely friendly or flattering.

great — *adj.* **1** outstandingly talented, and much admired and respected. **2** very large in size, quantity, intensity, or extent. **3** (*also* **greater**) *Biol.* larger in size than others of the same kind, species, etc. **4** *colloq.* very enjoyable; excellent or splendid. **5** *colloq.* (**great at something**) clever at it; talented. **6** *colloq.* (**great for something**) very suitable or useful for it. **7** most important: *the great advantage of it*. **8** enthusiastic; keen: *a great reader*. **9** *colloq.* used to emphasize other adjectives describing size, especially *big*: *a great big dog*. **10** (**the Great**) in names and titles, indicating an importance or reputation of the highest degree: *Alfred the Great*. **11** *old use* used in various expressions of surprise: *Great Scott!* — *noun* a person who has achieved lasting fame, deservedly or not: *all-time greats*. [from Anglo-Saxon *great*]

great- *combining form* indicating a family relationship that is one generation more remote than that of the base word: *great-grandmother / great-great-grandson*. [from Anglo-Saxon *great*]

great-aunt *noun* an aunt of one's father or mother.

Great Australian Bight an area of the Southern Ocean off the S coast of Australia, between Cape Pasley in the W and Port Lincoln in the E. It covers a distance of c.1 450km/900mi and depths range from 70m over the continental shelf to c.5 600m over the Great Bight abyssal plain.

Great Awakening in the USA, the widespread 18c Christian revival movement, which reached its high point in the 1740s in New England. Jonathan Edwards and George Whitefield were among its leaders.

Great Barrier Reef a coral reef in the Coral Sea off the NE coast of Australia. It forms part of the Australian Coral Sea Islands Territory. The reef lies c.50–150km/30–90mi offshore and is 2 000km/1 200mi long. It is the largest accumulation of coral known, yielding trepang, pearl-shell, and sponges. The surf is violent and dangerous, but the intervening channel, clustered with atolls, forms a safe, shallow passage connected by several navigable channels with the deeps of the Coral Sea. The area is a major tourist attraction.

Great Basin a vast interior region in W USA. It lies between the Sierra Nevada and the Cascade Range in the W and the Wasatch Range and Colorado Plateau to the E. The region includes parts of Oregon and Idaho, most of Nevada, W Utah, and part of SE California. PHYSICAL DESCRIPTION rugged mountain ranges run N–S; with a semi-arid climate, the region has few streams (the largest are the Humboldt and Carson rivers); these drain into saline lakes or sinks; the biggest lakes are the Great Salt, Utah, Sevier, Pyramid, and Walker, as well as the remnants of the enormous prehistoric lakes, Bonneville and Lahontan; there are several deserts, eg Great Salt Lake, Mojave, Colorado, Black Rock, Smoke Creek, Death Valley, and Carson Sink. ECONOMY agriculture (possible only with irrigation), grazing land; minerals.

Great Bear (the Great Bear) same as URSA MAJOR.

Great Bear Lake a lake in Northwest Territories, NW Canada. It lies on the Arctic Circle to the E of the Franklin Mts. AREA 31 153sq km/12 025sq mi; length 320km/200mi; width 40–177km/25–110mi; maximum depth 413m. It is drained in the SW by the Great Bear R, and is navigable for only four months each year because of ice.

Great Bitter Lake, Arabic **Buheiret Murrat El Kubra** a lake on the Suez Canal between Ismailiya in the N and Suez in the S.

Great Britain a name for the combined kingdoms of England and Scotland, and the principality of Wales, which, together with Northern Ireland, make up the United Kingdom.

Great Britain an Atlantic liner, the first to be built of iron, launched in 1845, at which time it was the largest ship in the world (98m). It was designed by Isambard Kingdom Brunel. It was scuttled in 1937, and later restored and exhibited in Bristol.

greatcoat *noun* a heavy overcoat.

Great Dane a very large breed of smooth-haired dog.

Great Depression the worldwide slump in output and prices, and increase in unemployment levels (1929–34), precipitated by the collapse of the US stock market (the Wall Street crash, Oct 1929). American loans to Europe ended, business confidence decreased worldwide, and the collapse of a major Austrian bank meant destabilization in much of central and E Europe.

Great Divide see CONTINENTAL DIVIDE.

Great Dividing Range a mountain range in Queensland, New South Wales, and Victoria, E Australia. It extends c.3 600km/2 200mi from Cape York Peninsula to the Victoria–South Australia border, rising to 2 228m at Mt Kosciusko. Included in the Great Dividing Range are the McPherson and New England ranges, the Australian Alps, the Blue Mts, and the Grampians.

Great Eastern a steamer designed by Isambard Kingdom Brunel and J Scott Russell, launched in 1858, at which time it was the largest ship in the world (211m). It originally sailed on a cargo route between England and New York, and was sold to the Great Eastern Steamship Company in 1864. Its functions included laying the first transatlantic telegraph cable. It was destroyed in 1889.

Greater Manchester POP (1992e) 2.6m, a metropolitan county area in NW England. Its metropolitan county council was abolished in 1986. AREA 1 287sq km/497sq mi. It consists of 10 boroughs: Manchester (county town), Bolton, Bury, Oldham, Rochdale, Salford, Stockport, Tameside, Trafford, and Wigan. NOTABLE FEATURES Manchester Ship Canal; Old Trafford Cricket Ground.

Great Exhibition an exhibition held (May–Oct 1851) in Hyde Park, London. Intended to celebrate the 'Works of Industry of all Nations', in reality it symbolized Britain's mid-19c industrial supremacy. Prince Albert helped to organize the Exhibition, for which the Crystal Palace was constructed.

Great Expectations **1** a novel by Charles Dickens (1860–1). It describes the life of the orphan Pip as he attempts to become a gentleman. **2** a British film directed by David Lean (1946). Adapted from Charles Dickens's classic text, it features John Mills as Pip, whose anonymous benefactor is the escaped convict Magwitch (Finlay Currie).

Great Gatsby, The a novel by F Scott Fitzgerald (1925). It is set in Long Island and describes the tragic events surrounding the central character Jay Gatsby.

Great-heart, Mr the courageous escort of Christiana and her children in Part II of John Bunyan's *The Pilgrim's Progress*.

Great Indian Desert see THAR DESERT.

Great Lakes the largest group of freshwater lakes in the world, in central N America, on the Canada–USA border. It consists of Lakes Superior, Michigan (the only one entirely in the USA), Huron, Erie, and Ontario; sometimes L St Clair is included. The total water surface is c.245 300sq km/94 700sq mi, of which c.87 270sq km/33 690sq mi are in Canada. All the lakes are connected by navigable straits and canals (St Mary's R and the Soo Canals, Strait of Mackinac, the St Clair R and L St Clair, Detroit R, Niagara R, Welland Canal, and the St Lawrence R and Seaway). From May to Dec an enormous volume of coal, ore, grain, and other products passes through the lakes (and ship canals) to the St Lawrence. Water pollution has recently become a problem.

greatly *adv.* in a great way, much, very.

Great Malvern see MALVERN.

Rulers of Great Britain	
House of Stuart	
1603–25	James I
	(VI of Scotland)
1625–49	Charles I
Commonwealth and Protectorate	
1649–53	*Council of State*
1653–8	Oliver Cromwell
	Lord Protector
1658–9	Richard Cromwell
	Lord Protector
House of Stuart (restored)	
1660–85	Charles II
1685–8	James II
	(VII of Scotland)
1689–94	William III
	(I of Scotland)
	(*jointly with* Mary II)
1694–1702	William III (*alone*)
	(I of Scotland)
1702–14	Anne
House of Hanover	
1714–27	George I
1727–60	George II
1760–1820	George III
1820–30	George IV
1830–7	William IV
	(II of Scotland)
1837–1901	Victoria
House of Saxe-Coburg	
1901–10	Edward VII
	(I of Scotland)
House of Windsor	
1910–36	George V
1936	Edward VIII
	(II of Scotland)
1936–52	George VI
1952–	Elizabeth II
	(I of Scotland)

great-nephew *noun* a son of one's nephew or niece.

greatness *noun* being great.

great-niece *noun* a daughter of one's nephew or niece.

Great Northern War a war (1700–21) between Russia and Sweden for the mastery of the Baltic coastal region. Charles XII of Sweden defeated Peter I 'the Great' of Russia at Narva (1700), but failed to pursue his advantage and was later defeated by him at the battle of Poltava (1709). By 1718 (when Charles died) Sweden had lost most of its Baltic possessions and by various treaties (eg Nystadt, 1721) Russia became the leading Baltic power.

Great Plains a region of central N America. It borders the E base of the Rocky Mts from Alberta in Canada to the Llano Estacado in New Mexico and Texas, USA. The plains include the E parts of Montana, Wyoming, Colorado, and New Mexico, and the W parts of North Dakota, South Dakota, Nebraska, Kansas, Oklahoma, and Texas as well as parts of Alberta and Saskatchewan in Canada. PHYSICAL DESCRIPTION a sloping plateau, generally 650km/400mi wide; it has limited rainfall, short grass, and large level tracts, with some highlands (Black Hills, in South Dakota), badlands (South Dakota), sand hills (Nebraska), and lowlands; drained by the headwaters of the Missouri and by the Platte, Republican, Arkansas, Kansas, and Canadian rivers. HISTORY dry farming and overpasturing led to the dust storms of the drought years (1930s); this created the Dust Bowl, semi-arid regions where wind storms carry off large quantities of topsoil. ECONOMY used chiefly for stock grazing and grain growing; mineral resources of oil, natural gas, coal, and lignite.

Great Red Spot *Astron.* the Red Spot of Jupiter.

Great Rift Valley see RIFT VALLEY.

Great Salt Lake a large inland salt lake in NW Utah, USA, lying NW of Salt Lake City. AREA length 120km/75mi; width 80km/50mi; maximum depth 11m. Fed by the Jordan, Weber, and Bear rivers, it has no outlet and fluctuates greatly in size; it includes Antelope I and Fremont I. Sodium chloride is extracted from the lake for commercial use; the water is 20–27% saline, several times more salty than ocean water. The lake is a remnant of the enormous prehistoric L Bonneville.

Great Salt Lake Desert an arid region in NW Utah, USA, to the W of the Great Salt Lake. It extends 177km/110mi S from the Goose Creek Mts. Near the Nevada border are the Bonneville Salt Flats, where world speed car records were established in the 1930s.

Great Sandy Desert the N belt of the Western Australian Desert, situated to the N of the Gibson Desert. AREA c.450 000sq km/ 175 000sq mi. It extends W as far as the Indian Ocean and consists mostly of sand dune, scrub, and salt marsh.

Great Sandy Desert an arid region in S Oregon, USA. It is 240km/150mi long and 48–80km/30–50mi wide. A largely volcanic area, its foundation is formed from porous mantle rock into which surface waters disappear.

Great Slave Lake a lake in W Northwest Territories, central Canada. It is situated near the Alberta border, N of the Caribou Mts. AREA 28 570sq km/11 028sq mi; length 483km/300mi; width 48–225km/30–140mi; maximum depth is over 600m. It contains numerous islands, and is drained in the W by the Mackenzie R. The town of Yellowknife, capital of the province, lies on the N shore.

Great Smoky Mountains a mountain range in the Appalachians, on the Tennessee–North Carolina state frontier, USA. It

rises to 2 025m at Clingmans Dome. The range is a national park, protecting the largest tract of red spruce and the largest area of hardwood in the USA.

Great Smoky Mountains National Park a national park on the Tennessee–North Carolina state frontier, USA. The park covers c.210 000ha, and was founded in 1934 to protect the primeval forests. It is a World Heritage site.

Great Society a legislative programme called for by US President Lyndon B Johnson on 19 Jan 1965, which committed his administration to vigorous action on health insurance, education, housing, and urban renewal.

Great Train Robbery the largest train robbery ever accomplished (8 Aug 1963). The night mail train transferring High Value Packages from Glasgow to London was stopped by a gang of robbers (which included Ronald Biggs) at Sears Crossing in Buckinghamshire. They escaped with 120 mailbags, containing over £2.5m, but were traced and arrested after their fingerprints were found in a farm hideout.

Great Trek the migration of 12 000 to 14 000 Boers (*Voortrekkers*) in separate trekking groups from Cape Colony (where they objected to British suzerainty) that began in 1836. Two parties were wiped out by African resistance and malaria on the way to Delagoa Bay in Mozambique. Some settled in the Transvaal, where they were threatened by the Ndebele. A party in Natal was massacred by the Zulus, an event avenged by the battle of Blood River (1838). When the British annexed Natal (1843), the majority of the Boers returned to the interior, where they mastered large areas of land. The British made several unsuccessful attempts to resolve the divisions in the area, but when the region was reunited it was largely under Boer control.

great-uncle *noun* an uncle of one's father or mother.

Great Victoria Desert *or* **Victoria Desert** the S belt of the Western Australian Desert, N of the Nullarbor Plain. AREA c.325 000sq km/125 000sq mi. It consists of sand dunes and salt marsh and there are three national parks.

Great Wall of China a defensive frontier stretching 4 100km/2 150mi across N China from the Yellow Sea to the central Asian desert. Under Qin Shihuangdi, it was built from 221 BC to repel attacks from the Jung and Ti nomads to the north. It was improved during later dynasties by extension to Yumen in the W and the addition of 25 000 turrets. The conserved stretch of stone-faced wall now seen by visitors at Badeling Pass, N of Beijing, dates to the Ming dynasty (1368–1644). The wall is c.7.6m high and 3.7m broad, and made of earth and stone with a facing of bricks. It is a World Heritage site.

Great War (the Great War) World War I, 1914–18.

Great Western a British transatlantic steamer, which made its maiden voyage from Bristol to New York City in 1838. It was designed by Isambard Kindgdom Brunel.

Great Yarmouth *or* **Yarmouth** POP (1992e) 89 000, a resort and port town in Great Yarmouth district, Norfolk, E England. It lies on a peninsula between the North Sea and the confluent mouths of the Bure, Yare, and Waveney rivers. It was once an important herring port and is today a base for North Sea oil and gas exploration. NOTABLE FEATURES town walls (13c–14c); Church of St Nicholas (12c); Elizabethan Museum.

Great Zimbabwe a group of drystone enclosures near Fort Victoria, SE Zimbabwe, capital of a prosperous African chiefdom in the 14c–15c. The largest valley enclosure incorporates a 9m

drystone tower. The population of the city was c.10 000–18 000. It is a World Heritage site.

greave *noun* (*usually* **greaves**) armour for the legs below the knee. [from Old French *greve*, shin]

grebe *noun* any of a family of large waterfowl with short wings, long individually webbed toes, a pointed bill, vestigial tail, and in most species colourful plumes on the head. They are found on lakes, marshes, and reservoirs worldwide, and are best known for their complex courtship dances. [from French *grèbe*]

Grecian *adj.*, *said of a design*, *etc* in the style of ancient Greece. [from Latin *Graecus*, Greek]

Grecian nose an uncurved nose forming a straight line with the forehead.

Greco, El, pseudonym of **Domenikos Theotokopoulos** (1541–1614) Spanish painter, born in Candia, Crete. He studied in Italy, probably as a pupil of Titian, and settled in Toledo (c.1577). He became a portrait painter whose reputation fluctuated because of the suspicion which greeted his characteristically distorted figures. His works include *The Assumption of the Virgin* (1577, Chicago) and *The Burial of Count Orgaz* (1586, Church of San Tomé, Toledo).

Greco- same as GRAECO-.

Greece, ancient **Hellas**, Greek **Ellás**, official name **The Hellenic Republic**, Greek **Elliniki Dimokratia** POP (1992e) 10.3m, a republic in SE Europe, occupying the S part of the Balkan Peninsula and numerous islands in the Aegean and Ionian seas. It is divided into 10 geographical regions, which are subdivided into departments (*nomoi*). AREA 131 957sq km/50 935sq mi. It is bounded N by Albania, Macedonia, and Bulgaria, E by Turkey and the Aegean Sea, S by the Mediterranean Sea, and W by the Ionian Sea. CAPITAL Athens. CHIEF TOWNS Thessaloniki, Patras, Heraklion, Volos, Larisa, Piraievs. TIME ZONE GMT +2. The population is mainly of Greek origin (98%); Greek Orthodox is the chief religion. OFFICIAL LANGUAGE Greek. CURRENCY the drachma. PHYSICAL DESCRIPTION the country consists of a large area of mainland including the Peloponnese in the S, linked to the rest of the mainland by the narrow Isthmus of Corinth; there are over 1 400 islands, notably Crete, Euboea, Lesbos, Rhodes, Chios, Cephalonia, Corfu, Lemnos, Samos, and Naxos; nearly 80% of the country is mountainous or hilly; main ranges are the Pindhos Mts in the N, the Rhodope Mts in the NE, and the E coast range, which includes Mt Olympus (2 917m), the highest point in Greece; there are several rivers and small lakes. CLIMATE Mediterranean on the coast and islands, with mild, rainy winters and hot, dry summers; rainfall occurs almost entirely in the winter months; average annual rainfall in Athens is 414mm. HISTORY prehistoric civilization culminated in the Minoan-Mycenean culture of Crete; the Dorians invaded from the N in the 12c BC; Greek colonies were established along the N and S Mediterranean coasts and on the shores of the Black Sea; there were many city states on the mainland, notably Sparta and Athens; Persian

Greece

invasions in the 5c BC were repelled at Marathon, Salamis, Plataea, and Mycale; Greek literature and art flourished in the 5c BC; conflict between Sparta and Athens (the Peloponnesian War) weakened the country, which was taken by the Thebans and then the Macedonians (4c BC); military expeditions under Alexander the Great penetrated Asia and Africa, but Macedonian power was broken by the Romans in 197 BC; Greece then formed part of the Byzantine Empire of Rome; it was ruled by the Turks in the 15c–19c; a national reawakening began in 1821 and by 1828 Greece was a free state; the Greek Republic was established in 1924 and the monarchy restored in 1935; German occupation in World War II was followed by Civil War (1944–9); a military coup in 1967 led to a series of military governments; the monarchy was abolished in 1969; in 1974 democracy was restored; became a member of the EEC in 1981. GOVERNMENT governed by a Prime Minister, Cabinet, and unicameral Parliament of 300 deputies, elected for four years; a President (head of state) is elected by Parliament for a five-year term; Mount Athos in Macedonia region is a self-governing community of 20 monasteries. ECONOMY the service sector accounts for c.55% of the national income; agricultural sector is based on cereals, cotton, tobacco, fruit, figs, raisins, wine, olive oil, vegetables; ores and minerals include iron, magnesite, bauxite, lignite; there is little coal, and some oil; manufacturing is based on the production of processed foods, textiles, metals, chemicals, electrical equipment, cement, glass, transport equipment, and petroleum products; tourism is important, especially on the islands.

The Greek Alphabet					
Letter	Name	Usual transliteration	Letter	Name	Usual transliteration
A α	alpha	a	N ν	nu	n
B β	beta	b	Ξ ξ	xi	x
Γ γ	gamma	g	O o	omicron	o
Δ δ	delta	d	Π π	pi	p
E ε	epsilon	e	P ϱ	rho	r
Z ζ	zeta	z	Σ σ,ς	sigma	s
H η	eta	e, ē	T τ	tau	t
Θ θ	theta	th	Y υ	upsilon	y
I ι	iota	i	Φ φ	phi	ph
K κ	kappa	k	X χ	chi	ch, kh
Λ λ	lambda	l	Ψ ψ	psi	ps
M μ	mu	m	Ω ω	omega	o, ō

Greed a US film directed by Erich Von Stroheim (1924). It is a study of avarice, murder, and betrayal in the lives of a young miner, his wife, and friend.

greed *noun* **1** an excessive desire for, or consumption of, food. **2** selfish desire in general, eg for money. [back-formation from GREEDY]

greedily *adv.* in a greedy way; with greed.

greedy *adj.* (**greedier, greediest**) filled with greed. [from Anglo-Saxon *grǣdig*]

Greek — *noun* **1** the official language of Greece. **2** a native or inhabitant of Greece. **3** *colloq.* any language, jargon, or subject one cannot understand. — *adj.* of Greece, its people, or their language. [from Latin *Graecus*]

Greek Orthodox Church the self-governing ('autocephalous') Orthodox Church of Greece. After the schism of 1054, the Orthodox Church in Greece remained under the Patriarch of Constantinople, but was declared independent in 1833. The governing body is the Holy Synod, which comprises 67 metropolitan bishops, presided over by the archbishop of all Greece in the head see of Athens. In doctrine, it shares the beliefs of Orthodox Churches, and in worship uses the Byzantine liturgy.

Greek-Persian Wars see PERSIAN WARS.

Greek War of Independence the struggle (1821–8) of the Greeks to gain independence from the Ottoman Turks, who were aided in the War by Egyptian forces. Until 1825 Greece fought unaided, but was then joined by Britain, Russia, and later France, and achieved the destruction of the Egyptian fleet at Navarino Bay (1827). Greek independence was guaranteed by its allies in the Treaty of Adrianople (1829), and formally recognized by the Ottoman Porte (imperial government) in the Treaty of Constantinople (1832).

Greeley, Horace (1811–72) American editor and politician, born in Amherst, New Hampshire. He worked as a printer, went to New York in 1831, and started the weekly *New Yorker* (1834) and the daily *Tribune* (1841), of which he was editor. A zealous opponent of slavery during the 1860s, he was an unsuccessful candidate for the presidency in 1872.

Green, Lucinda, *née* **Prior-Palmer** British three-day eventer, born in London. She won the Badminton Horse Trials a record six times (1973, 1976–7, 1979, 1983–4), and the Burghley Horse Trials in 1977 and 1981. At the European championships she won an individual gold medal in 1975 and 1977, a team gold in 1977, 1985, and 1987, and an individual and team silver in 1983. She was the 1982 world champion on *Regal Realm*, when she also won a team gold medal.

Green, George (1793–1841) English mathematician and physicist, born in Sneinton, near Nottingham. Largely self-taught, in 1828 he published a pamphlet containing what are now known as Green's theorem and Green's functions, valuable in solving physical problems and partial differential equations. He entered Cambridge University in 1833, and published several papers on wave motion and optics.

green — *adj.* **1** of the colour of the leaves of most plants, between yellow and blue in the spectrum. **2** covered with grass, bushes, etc: *green areas of the city.* **3** consisting mainly of leaves: *green salad.* **4** *said of fruit* not yet ripe. **5** *colloq., said of people* young, inexperienced, or easily fooled. **6** showing concern for, or designed to be harmless to, the environment. **7** *said of a person's face* pale; showing signs of nausea. **8** not dried or dry: *green bacon / green timber.* **9** extremely jealous or envious. **10** healthy, vigorous, or flourishing: *green old age.* — *noun* **1** the colour of the leaves of most plants, between yellow and blue in the spectrum. **2** something of this colour. **3** an area of grass, especially in a public place. **4** an area of specially prepared turf: *bowling-green.* **5** (**greens**) vegetables with edible green leaves and stems. **6** a person who supports actions or policies designed to protect or benefit the environment, especially (*often* **Green**) one belonging to or supporting a green party. — *verb trans., intrans.* to make or become more green. [from Anglo-Saxon *grene*]

green alga *Bot.* any alga belonging to the class Chlorophyceae, characterized by possession of the green pigment chlorphyll, the storage of starch as a food reserve, and the presence of cell walls composed of cellulose.

green audit *Environ.* an investigation of a company's accounts in order to determine the effects on the environment of that company's activities, eg the effects of a particular process, or of a product that is being manufactured, the possibility of recycling raw materials, etc.

Greenaway, Kate (1846–1901) English artist and book illustrator, born in London. She became well known in the 1880s for her colour portrayals of childhood life, in such works as *The Birthday Book* (1880). The Greenaway Medal is awarded annually for the best British children's book artist.

Greenaway, Peter (1942–) English filmmaker and painter, born in London. He gained an international reputation for originality with such works as *A Walk Through H* (1978) and *The Falls* (1980) before *The Draughtsman's Contract* (1982) won him critical acclaim. Characterized by stunning visual composition, a painterly sense of colour, and the distinctive music of Michael Nyman, and exploring such preoccupations as sex, death, decay, and gamesmanship, his films include *The Belly of An Architect* (1987), *Drowning By Numbers* (1988), *The Cook, The Thief, His Wife and Her Lover* (1989), and *Prospero's Books* (1991).

greenback *noun colloq.* a US currency note (often printed in green on the back), first issued in 1862.

green bean any variety of bean of which the unripe pod and contents are eaten whole.

green belt open land surrounding a town or city, where building or development is strictly controlled.

Greene, (Henry) Graham (1904–91) English novelist, born in Berkhamsted, Hertfordshire. He converted from Anglicanism to Catholicism in 1926, and moved to London, where he worked for *The Times* (1926–30), *The Spectator,* (1937–41), and served with the Foreign Office (1941–4). His early novels or 'entertainments', which include *Stamboul Train* (1932), use the melodramatic technique of the thriller. In his major novels, central religious issues emerge, first apparent in *Brighton Rock* (1938), and more explicit in *The Power and the Glory* (1940), *The End of the Affair* (1951), and *A Burnt-Out Case* (1961). He also wrote several plays, film scripts (notably, *The Third Man*, 1950), short stories, and essays, as well as three volumes of autobiography.

Greene, Sir Hugh (Carleton) (1910–87) English journalist and television executive, born in Berkhamsted, Hertfordshire, brother of Graham Greene. His first job was in Germany, working as a foreign correspondent for the *Daily Herald* and later the *Daily Telegraph* (1934–9). In 1940 he joined the BBC to work on propaganda broadcasts and he later rebuilt the country's peacetime radio service. He worked with the BBC's Overseas Service (1952–6) and was also the BBC's first director of news and current affairs (1958–60) before being chosen as director-general (1960–9).

Greene, Nathanael (1742–86) US soldier, born in Warwick, Rhode Island. In the American Revolution he fought (1775–6) at Boston, Trenton, Brandywine, and Germanton, and in 1780 took command of the Southern army, which had just been defeated by Cornwallis. Considered to be a general second only to Washington, he got his army into better condition by much effort, and though Cornwallis defeated him at Guilford Courthouse, the victory was so costly that Greene was able to recover S Carolina and Georgia, thus paving the way to American victory in the South.

Greene, Robert (1558–92) English dramatist, born in Norwich, Norfolk. He moved to London (c.1585) and wrote many plays and romances, including the comedy *Friar Bacon and Friar Bungay* (c.1591). He helped to lay the foundations of English drama, and his *Pandosto* (1588) was a source for Shakespeare's *The Winter's Tale*.

greenery *noun* green plants or their leaves, either when growing or when cut for decoration.

green-eyed *adj. colloq.* jealous or envious.

greenfinch *noun* a bird belonging to the finch family, native to S Europe and S Asia, that inhabits forests and cultivated land, and feeds on seeds and insects.

green fingers *colloq.* natural skill at growing plants successfully.

greenfly *noun* (PL. **greenfly, greenflies**) a small green insect which feeds on garden plants and crops.

greengage *noun* a type of greenish-yellow plum; the tree that bears it.

greengrocer *noun* a person or shop selling fruit and vegetables.

greengrocery *noun* the produce sold by a greengrocer.

Greenham Common formerly the site of a US military base in Berkshire, England. In the 1980s it was subjected to continuous picketing by the Women's Peace movement, opposed in particular to the siting of Cruise missiles in Britain, and in general to nuclear weaponry.

greenhorn *noun colloq.* an inexperienced person; a novice.

greenhouse *noun* a building with walls and a roof made of glass, used for growing plants which need special protection or conditions.

greenhouse effect the warming of the Earth's surface as a result of the trapping of long-wave radiation by carbon dioxide, ozone, and certain other gases in the Earth's atmosphere, so called because the atmosphere has a similar effect to the glass panels of a greenhouse.
◇ The atmosphere allows short-wave radiation from the Sun to pass through it and heat the surface of the Earth, which then reflects much of the heat energy back into the atmosphere as long-wave radiation. However, a large proportion of this long-wave radiation cannot escape back into space because it is absorbed by carbon dioxide and certain other gases (including methane, chlorofluorocarbons (CFCs), nitrogen oxides, and ozone, often referred to collectively as 'greenhouse gases'), and then reflected back to Earth. As a result, the temperature of the Earth's surface is about 38°C warmer than it would be in the absence of the greenhouse effect, which is beneficial in that it serves to insulate the Earth.
Since the Industrial Revolution, carbon dioxide levels in the atmosphere have increased significantly as a result of the burning of fossil fuels, large-scale deforestation, pollution from vehicle exhaust fumes, etc. Many scientists consider that if the greenhouse effect continues to increase at its present rate, it may change the climate over the next 100 years or so, and it has been suggested that melting of the polar ice caps could lead to a rise in sea level which could flood large areas of coastal land.

greenhouse gas any of various gases such as carbon dioxide, methane, or chlorofluorocarbons, which are present in the lower atmosphere and act like a pane of glass in a greenhouse, trapping solar radiation reflected from the Earth's surface and redirecting it back towards the Earth. Increased emissions of greenhouse gases from burning fossil fuels are causing a slow increase in the average temperature of the Earth's surface, resulting in the so-called *greenhouse effect.*

greenkeeper *noun* a person responsible for the maintenance of a golf course or bowling-green.

Greenland, Inuit **Kalâtdlit-Nunât**, Danish **Grønland** POP (1991e) 56 000, the second-largest island in the world (after Australia), lying NE of N America in the N Atlantic and Arctic oceans. It is a self-governing province of Denmark. AREA 2 175 600sq km/839 780sq mi. CAPITAL Nuuk. TIME ZONES GMT 0, −1, −4. The population is largely Inuit, but with Danish admixtures. The main religions are Lutheran Christianity and Shamanism. OFFICIAL LANGUAGES Inuit, Danish. PHYSICAL DESCRIPTION largely covered by an ice-cap (up to 4 300m thick); the coastline is deeply indented; coastal mountains rise to 3 702m at Gunnbjørn Fjeld in the SE; natural vegetation includes mosses, lichens, grasses, and sedges; there are dwarf trees on the SW coast; major animal species include polar bear, musk ox, polar wolf, Arctic hare, lemming, and reindeer; less than 5% of the island is inhabitable. HISTORY AND GOVERNMENT settled by seal-hunting Eskimos from N America in c.2500 BC; Norse settlers occupied the SW in the 12c–15c; English navigators Frobisher and Davis explored the territory in the 16c; became a Danish colony in 1721; granted home rule in 1979 as a Self-Governing Province of Denmark; an elected Provincial Council sends two members to the Danish Parliament. ECONOMY largely dependent on inshore and deep-water fishing from ice-free ports in the SW; some sheep farming in the SW; cryolite is mined at Iviglut; there are reserves of lead, zinc, molybdenum, uranium, and coal.

Greenland Sea a gulf connecting the Atlantic Ocean and the Arctic Ocean, bounded W by Greenland and E by the island group of Svalbard. Depths range from c.180m on the continental shelf to 3 535m in the abyssal plain.

green light 1 a signal to move forward. 2 *colloq.* (**the green light**) permission to proceed: *we've got the green light.*

Green Line the dividing line between Muslim W Beirut and Christian E Beirut, Lebanon, during the 1975–6 Civil War. It continues to be recognized.

greenmail *noun* the practice of buying sufficient shares in a company to threaten takeover and force the company to buy back its shares at a premium. [from GREEN (of paper money) + BLACKMAIL]

Green Man in European folklore, a leaf-clad figure taking various forms, associated with spring festivals, and sometimes found depicted on inn-signs.

Greenmantle a novel by John Buchan (1916). It is a thriller featuring Richard Hannay.

Green Mountain Boys the movement of landowners and speculators that created the state of Vermont from territory disputed between New York and New Hampshire. Of many rural insurrections in early America, the Green Mountain Boys was the only one that succeeded. During the American Revolution, they helped capture the British fort at Ticonderoga on L Champlain (1775) for the colonists.

Greenock POP (1981) 59 000, the chief town in Inverclyde district, Strathclyde, W central Scotland. It is a port lying on the S shore of the Firth of Clyde, 3km/2mi W of Glasgow. The inventor James Watt was born in the town in 1736. NOTABLE FEATURE McLean Museum.

green paper (*often* **Green Paper**) in the UK, a written statement of the Government's proposed policy on a particular issue, for discussion. See also COMMAND PAPER, WHITE PAPER.

green party (*also* **Green Party**) a political party concerned with promoting policies for the protection and benefit of the environment.
◇ In the UK, a political party was founded in 1973 under the name *People*. This was changed to the *Ecological Party* in 1975, and to its present name in 1985. Its policies are based on the principles that people must live within the limitations of the Earth's finite supply of resources.

Greenpeace an international environmental pressure group which began in Canada and the USA in 1971, and was set up in the UK in 1976. It campaigns by direct action (non-violent passive resistance) against commercial whaling and seal culling, the dumping of toxic and radioactive waste at sea, the testing of nuclear weapons etc. In 1985 the Greenpeace ship *Rainbow Warrior* was sunk by French intelligence agents in Auckland Harbour, New Zealand, an event which provoked an international outcry.

green pepper, a green unripe sweet pepper, eaten as a vegetable. See also RED PEPPER.

green pound the pound's value compared with that of the other European currencies used in trading EC farm produce.

Green Revolution a popular term for the recent improvements in agricultural productivity in some Third World countries that resulted from the development of new high-yielding strains of cereal crops, and the use of fertilizers and pesticides.
◇ The Green Revolution, which occurred in some developing countries in the 1960s and 1970s, was largely the result of Norman Borlaug's plant breeding research in Mexico, which produced high-yielding dwarf wheat varieties, and work at the International Rice Research Institute in the Philippines, which produced similarly improved strains of rice. Success with these new varieties depended on an integrated crop management system, the application of high levels of fertilizers and pesticides, and adequate water supplies. For this reason it tended to benefit only the most prosperous farmers, and was too costly for farmers living in poorer areas where an increase in agricultural productivity was most urgently needed.

greenroom *noun* a backstage room in a theatre where actors, musicians, etc can relax and receive visitors.

greensand *noun Geol.* a greenish sand or sandstone, consisting mainly of grains of glauconite (a green mineral closely related to the micas).

Greensleeves a well-known English tune first referred to in 1580, and mentioned in Elizabethan writings.

greenstick fracture *Medicine* an incomplete fracture of a long bone, in which the bone is bent but only part of it is broken, most common in children, whose bones are more flexible than those of adults.

green tea a sharp-tasting light-coloured tea made from leaves that have been dried quickly without fermenting.

Greenwich, Anglo-Saxon **Grenawic** POP (1987e) 217 000, a borough in E central Greater London, England, S of the R Thames. It is the site of the original Royal Greenwich Observatory (founded in 1675). Meridians of longitude are reckoned from this point which is also the source of the world time standard, Greenwich Mean Time (GMT). Henry VIII, Elizabeth I, and Mary I were born here. NOTABLE FEATURES Greenwich Hospital (1694); Royal Naval College; National Maritime Museum, including Inigo Jones' Queen's House (1637); the clipper *Cutty Sark* and Francis Chichester's *Gypsy Moth IV* are at Greenwich Pier. [from Anglo-Saxon *grenawic*, green habitation on the bank of a river]

Greenwich Mean Time (ABBREV. **GMT**) the local time at the line of 0° longitude, passing through Greenwich in England, used to calculate times in most other parts of the world.

Greenwich Village a residential district of Manhattan, New York City, which became famous during the 20c as the quarter of writers, artists, intellectuals, and bohemians.

Greenwood, Walter (1903–74) English writer, born in Salford, Lancashire. His best-known novel is *Love on the Dole* (1933), inspired

Greenland

International Time Differences

The time zones of the world are conventionally measured from longitude 0 at Greenwich Observatory (Greenwich Mean Time, GMT).

Each 15° of longitude east of this point is one hour ahead of GMT (eg when it is 2 pm in London it is 3 pm or later in time zones to the east). Hours ahead of GMT are shown by a plus sign, eg +3, +4–8.

Each 15° west of this point is one hour behind GMT (eg 2 pm in London would be 1 pm or earlier in time zones to the west). Hours behind GMT are shown by a minus sign, eg −3, −4–8.

Some countries adopt time zones that vary from standard time. Also, during the summer, several countries adopt Daylight Saving Time (or Summer Time), which is one hour ahead of the times shown below.

Afghanistan	+4	Egypt	+2	Lesotho	+2	Saudi Arabia	+3
Albania	+1	El Salvador	−6	Liberia	0	Senegal	0
Algeria	0	Equatorial	+1	Libya	+1	Seychelles	+4
Angola	+1	Guinea		Liechtenstein	+1	Sierra Leone	0
Antigua	−4	Ethiopia	+3	Luxembourg	+1	Singapore	+8
Argentina	−3	Falkland Is	−3	Madagascar	+3	Solomon Is	+11
Australia	+8-10	Fiji	+12	Malawi	+2	Somalia	+3
Austria	+1	Finland	+2	Malaysia	+8	South Africa	+2
Bahamas	−5	France	+1	Maldives	+5	South West	+2
Bahrain	+3	Gabon	+1	Mali	0	Africa	
Bangladesh	+6	Gambia, The	0	Malta	+1	Spain	+1
Barbados	−4	Germany	+1	Mauritania	0	Sri Lanka	+5
Belgium	+1	Ghana	0	Mauritius	+4	Sudan	+2
Belize	−6	Gibraltar	+1	Mexico	−6-8	Suriname	−3
Benin	+1	Greece	+2	Monaco	+1	Swaziland	+2
Bermuda	−4	Greenland	−3	Morocco	0	Sweden	+1
Bolivia	−4	Grenada	−4	Mozambique	+2	Switzerland	+1
Botswana	+2	Guatemala	−6	Nauru	+12	Syria	+2
Brazil	−2-5	Guinea	0	Nepal	+5	Taiwan	+8
Brunei	+8	Guinea–Bissau	0	Netherlands	+1	Tanzania	+3
Bulgaria	+2	Guyana	−3	New Zealand	+12	Thailand	+7
Burkina Faso	0	Haiti	−5	Nicaragua	−6	Togo	0
Burma	+6	Honduras	−6	Niger	+1	Tonga	+13
Burundi	+2	Hong Kong	+8	Nigeria	+1	Trinidad and	−4
Cameroon	+1	Hungary	+1	Norway	+1	Tobago	
Canada	−3-9	Iceland	0	Oman	+4	Tunisia	+1
Cape Verde	−1	India	+5	Pakistan	+5	Turkey	+3
Central African	+1	Indonesia	+7-9	Panama	−5	Tuvalu	+12
Republic		Iran	+3	Papua New	+10	Uganda	+3
Chad	+1	Iraq	+3	Guinea		United Arab	+4
Chile	−4	Iceland	0	Paraguay	−3-4	Emirates	
China	+8	Israel	+2	Peru	−5	UK	0
Colombia	−5	Italy	+1	Philippines	+8	Uruguay	−3
Comoros	+3	Ivory Coast	0	Poland	+1	USA	−5-11
Congo	+1	Jamaica	−5	Portugal	0	USSR (former)	+3-13
Costa Rica	−6	Japan	+9	Qatar	+3	Vanuatu	+11
Cuba	−5	Jordan	+2	Romania	+2	Venezuela	−4
Cyprus	+2	Kampuchea	+7	Rwanda	+2	Vietnam	+7
Czechoslovakia	+1	Kenya	+3	St Christopher	−4	Yemen	+3
Denmark	+1	Kiribati	+12	and Nevis		Yugoslavia	+1
Djibouti	+3	Korea, North	+9	St Lucia	−4	Zaire	+1-2
Dominica	−4	Korea, South	+9	St Vincent	−4	Zambia	+2
Dominican	−4	Kuwait	+3	Samoa	−11	Zimbabwe	+2
Republic		Laos	+7	San Marino	+1		
Ecuador	−5	Lebanon	+2	Sao Tomé	0		

by his experiences of unemployment and depression in the early 1930s, which was subsequently dramatized (1934) and filmed (1941).

Greer, Germaine (1939–) Australian feminist and author, born in Melbourne. She lectured in English at Warwick University (1968–73) and was director of the Tulsa Center for the Study of Women's Literature (1979–82). Her controversial and highly successful book *The Female Eunuch* (1970) portrayed marriage as a legalized form of slavery for women, and attacked the misrepresentation of female sexuality by a male-dominated society. Her more recent works include *The Change* (1991).

greet¹ *verb* **1** to address or welcome, especially in a friendly way. **2** to react to in a certain way: *remarks greeted with dismay*. **3** to be immediately noticeable to: *smells of cooking greeted me*. [from Anglo-Saxon *gretan*]

greet² *Scot. & N of England dialect.* — *verb intrans.* (PAST TENSE **grat**; PAST PARTICIPLE **grutten**) to cry. — *noun* a spell of crying. [from Anglo-Saxon *gretan*]

greeting *noun* **1** a friendly expression or gesture used on meeting or welcoming someone.

2 (**greetings**) a good or fond wish; a friendly message.

greetings card a decorated card used to send greetings.

gregarious *adj.* **1** *said of a person* liking the company of other people; sociable. **2** *said of an animal* tending to live in groups. [from Latin *gregarius*, from *grex*, flock]

gregariousness *noun* being gregarious.

Gregorian calendar, the system introduced by Pope Gregory XIII in 1582, and still widely in use, in which an ordinary year is divided into 12 months or 365 days, with a leap year of 366 days every four years. See also JULIAN CALENDAR.

Gregorian chant the monophonic and (in its purest form) unaccompanied chant of the Roman Catholic liturgy. The earliest musical sources date from the late 9c and 10c, and the compilation of the repertory has been credited to Pope Gregory the Great.

Gregory I (the Great), St (c.540–604) Italian pope (590–604) and saint, the fourth Latin Doctor of the Church, born in Rome. Appointed praetor of Rome, he left this office (c.575), distributed his wealth among the poor, and with-

drew into a monastery in Rome. It was there that he saw some Anglo-Saxon youths in the slave market, and was seized with a longing to convert their country to Christianity, a mission to which he appointed Augustine. As pope he reformed all public services and ritual, and systematized the sacred chants. In his writings the whole dogmatic system of the modern Church is fully developed. He was canonized on his death and his feast day is 12 Mar.

Gregory VII, originally **Hildebrand** (c.1020–85) Italian pope (1073–85), born near Soana, Tuscany. He worked to change the secularized condition of the Church, but this resulted in conflict with the German emperor Henry IV, who declared Gregory deposed in a diet at Worms (1076), but then yielded to him after excommunication. In 1080 Henry resumed hostilities by appointing an antipope (Clement III), and after a siege took possession of Rome (1084). Gregory was freed by Norman troops, but was forced to withdraw to Salerno. He was canonized in 1606 and his feast day is 25 May.

Gregory XIII, originally **Ugo Buoncompagni** (1502–85) Italian pope (1572–85), born in Bologna. After being Professor of Law at Bologna for several years, he settled in Rome (1539), took part in the Council of Trent, and became a cardinal (1565). As pope, he zealously promoted education, and endowed many of the colleges in Rome. He also corrected the errors of the Julian calendar, and in 1582 introduced the calendar that bears his name.

Gregory, Lady Isabella Augusta, *née* **Persse** (1852–1932) Irish playwright, born in Roxborough, Galway. She became an associate of W B Yeats in the foundation of the Abbey Theatre and the Irish players, for whom she wrote a number of short plays, notably *Spreading the News* (1904) and *The Rising of the Moon* (1907). She also wrote Irish legends in dialect and translated Molière.

Gregory, James (1638–75) Scottish mathematician, born in Drumoak, Aberdeenshire. He invented the Gregorian reflecting telescope in 1661, and published a book giving convergent infinite sequences for the areas of circles and hyperbolas. He was professor at St Andrews and Edinburgh, and much of his later work was concerned with infinite series, a term which he introduced into the language.

Gregory a male first name, popular with the early Christians; the Scots form *Gregor* gave rise to the patronymic surname Macgregor. [from Greek *gregorein*, to watch or be vigilant]

gremlin *noun* an imaginary mischievous creature blamed for faults in machinery or electronic equipment. [origin unknown; there are many anecdotal accounts, but none is historically sound]

◇ The term came into general use after World War II, when it was widely used by RAF personnel as a humorous explanation for any defects in their aircraft. One common explanation of the word's origin is that the imaginary sprite came out of Fremlin's beer bottles; there are many other such stories.

Grenada POP (1992e) 91 000, an independent constitutional monarchy and the most southerly of the Windward Is, E Caribbean Sea. AREA 344sq km/133sq mi. It lies c.240km/150mi SW of Barbados and is divided into six parishes. CAPITAL St George's. CHIEF TOWNS Gouyave, Victoria, Grenville. TIME ZONE GMT −4. The population is mainly of Black African descent; Roman Catholicism is the chief religion. OFFICIAL LANGUAGE English. CURRENCY the E Caribbean dollar. PHYSICAL DESCRIPTION comprises the main island of Grenada (34km/21mi long and 19km/12mi wide) and the S Grenadines (including Carriacou), an arc of small islands extending from Grenada N to St Vincent; Grenada is of volcanic origin, with a ridge of mountains along its entire length; the highest point is Mt St Catherine, which rises to 843m. CLIMATE subtropical; the average annual temperature is 23°C; the annual rainfall varies from 1 270mm on the coast to 5 000mm in the interior. HISTORY discovered by Columbus in 1498, and named Concepción; settled by the French in the mid-17c; ceded to Britain in 1763; retaken by France in 1779; ceded again to Britain in 1783; became a British Crown Colony in 1877; gained independence in 1974; a popular people's revolution was successfully mounted in 1979; Prime Minister Maurice Bishop was killed during a further uprising in 1983; a group of Caribbean countries requested US involvement, and troops invaded the island in Oct 1983 to restore stable government. GOVERNMENT the 1973 constitution of Grenada recognizes the British Monarch as head of state; a bicameral legislature comprises an appointed 13-member Senate and an elected 15-member House of Representatives; a Prime Minister heads a Cabinet of 15 ministers. ECONOMY based on agriculture, notably fruit, vegetables, cocoa, nutmegs, bananas, mace; diversification policy, introducing guavas, citrus fruits, avocados, plums, mangoes, cashew nuts; processing of agricultural products and their derivatives (sugar, rum, coconut oil, lime juice, honey).

Grenada

Grenada Invasion the 'police' action by the USA in the Caribbean (25 Oct 1983), provoked by the fear that the lives of 1 000 US citizens were at risk following the murder of Prime Minister Maurice Bishop and the subsequent army takeover. It was claimed that the USA had been asked for help by the Organization of East Caribbean States. This invasion of a member of the British Commonwealth of Nations received widespread criticism from the USA's Western allies.

grenade *noun* a small bomb thrown by hand or fired from a rifle. [from Spanish *granada*, pomegranate]

grenadier *noun* a member of a regiment of soldiers formerly trained in the use of grenades.

grenadine *noun* a syrup made from pomegranate juice, used to flavour (especially alcoholic) drinks. [related to GRENADE]

Grenadines, The a group of 600 small islands and islets in the Windward Is, E Caribbean Sea. The N Grenadines are administered by St Vincent and the S Grenadines are administered by Grenada. MAIN ISLANDS Carriacou, Union, Mustique, Bequia, Canouan, Mayreau. ECONOMY some agriculture; tourism.

Grenoble, ancient **Gratianopolis** POP (1990) 400 000, the capital of Isère department, Rhône-Alpes region, E France, situated at the confluence of the Isère and Drac rivers. An ancient fortified city, Grenoble lies in a striking Alpine setting, with Mont Blanc to the NE. It is an important sports and tourist centre, with several ski slopes nearby. HISTORY achieved prosperity in the French colonial period due to trade with the French African colonies and the opening of the Suez Canal; it was a pioneer in the generation of hydroelectric power. The writer Stendhal was born here in 1783. NOTABLE FEATURES World Trade Centre; Industrial Science Park (the Zirst); Cathedral of Notre-Dame (12c–13c); brick church of St André (13c); Palais de Justice (partly 15c); university (1339).

Grenville, Sir Richard (1542–91) English naval commander. He fought in Hungary and Ireland (1566–9) and in 1585 commanded the seven ships that carried his cousin Walter Raleigh's first colony to Virginia. In 1591, as commander of the *Revenge*, he fought alone against a large Spanish fleet off the Azores, but died of his wounds.

Grenville (of Wotton-under-Bernewood), William Wyndham Grenville, 1st Baron (1759–1834) English statesman, the son of Prime Minister George Grenville (1712–70). He entered parliament in 1782, and became Paymaster-General (1783), Home Secretary (1790), and Foreign Secretary (1791). He resigned (with Pitt 'the Younger') on George III's refusal to agree to Catholic emancipation (1801). In 1806–7 he formed the coalition government of 'All the Talents', which abolished the slave trade.

Gretna Green a village in Dumfries and Galloway region, Scotland, on the border between Scotland and England. From 1754, when English matrimonial law was constricted, Gretna Green became renowned as a wedding destination for runaway couples from south of the border; in Scotland, 'marriages of declaration', announced before indiscriminate witnesses, were legal until 1 Jul 1940, from which time they have had to be performed before a minister or registrar. After 1856, one of the couple had to reside in Scotland for a minimum of 21 days before they were legally allowed to marry.

Gretzky, Wayne (1961–) Canadian ice hockey player, born in Brantford, Ontario. He scored a record 92 goals in the National Hockey League (NHL) in 1981–2, and a record 215 points in 1985–6. In 1988–9 he surpassed Gordie Howe's record of 1 890 points in a career. Known as 'the Kid', he won the NHL Most Valuable Player Award nine times (1980–7, 1989). A member of four Stanley Cup winning teams with Edmonton, in 1988 he was transferred to Los Angeles Kings for a record $15m.

grew see GROW.

Grey, Lady Jane (1537–54) Queen of England for nine days in 1553, born in Broadgate, Leicestershire, the great-granddaughter of Henry VII and eldest daughter of Henry Grey, Marquis of Dorset. In 1553 the Duke of Northumberland wanted to ensure that a Protestant would succeed the ailing Edward VI, rather than the Catholic Mary, and Jane (against her wish) was married to his fourth son, Lord Guildford Dudley. Declared queen three days after Edward's death (9 Jul), she was soon forced to abdicate in favour of Mary, and imprisoned. Following a rebellion in her favour, she was beheaded.

Grey, Charles Grey, 2nd Earl (1764–1845) English statesman and Prime Minister (1830–4), born in Fallodon, Northumberland. He became a Whig MP in 1786, and was a leading supporter of parliamentary reform in the 1790s. In 1806 he became First Lord of the Admiralty, Foreign Secretary, and also Leader of the House of Commons. In 1830 he formed a government promising peace and reform, and after much difficulty the 1832 Reform Bill was passed, and he later carried the Act for the abolition of slavery in the colonies, but was forced to resign over the Irish question.

Grey, Zane, originally **Pearl Grey** (1875–1939) US novelist, born in Zanesville, Ohio. He first worked as a dentist, but after a trip out west in 1904 began to write westerns. The best known of his 54 books was *Riders of the Purple Sage* (1912), which sold nearly 2 million copies.

grey — *adj.* **1** of a colour between black and white, the colour of ash and slate. **2** *said of the weather* dull and cloudy. **3 a** *said of a person's hair* turning white. **b** *said of a person* having grey hair. **4** *derog.* anonymous or uninteresting; having no

distinguishing features: *a grey character.* **5** *literary* aged, mature, or experienced. — *noun* **1** a colour between black and white. **2** grey material or clothes: *dressed in grey.* **3** dull light. **4** an animal, especially a horse, that is grey or whitish in colour. — *verb trans., intrans.* to make or become grey. [from Anglo-Saxon *græg*]

grey area an unclear situation or subject, often with no distinct limits or identifiable characteristics.

Grey Friar a Franciscan friar.

greyhound *noun* a tall thin sharp-sighted breed of dog capable of great speed. [from Anglo-Saxon *grighund*, probably bitch-dog]

greylag *noun* a large grey Eurasian goose.

greylag goose a goose native to Europe and Asia, where it is the most numerous and widespread goose species. It has mainly grey plumage, and inhabits estuaries and flood plains, feeding on vegetation in water or on land. It is the ancestor of the domestic goose. [*lag* may be because of its lateness in migrating]

grey matter 1 *Anat.* the tissue of the brain and spinal cord that consists mainly of nerve cell bodies which give it a grey colour, especially the cerebral cortex of the brain. **2** *colloq.* intelligence or common sense.

greyness *noun* being grey.

grey squirrel a grey-furred squirrel native to America and now the most common squirrel in Britain.

greywacke *or* **graywacke** *noun Geol.* a type of hard sandstone, dark grey or greenish-grey in colour, and composed of angular grains of quartz and feldspar embedded in a matrix of clay. [from German *Grauwacke*, partly translated and partly adopted]

grid *noun* **1** a set of numbered squares on a map, etc by which precise points are located. **2** a network of cables, pipes, etc bringing a supply to a large area. **3** a framework of metal bars, especially one covering the opening to a drain. **4** an arrangement of lines marking the starting-points on a motor racing track. **5** *technical* a fine wire mesh controlling the flow of electrons between the electrodes in an electronic valve. [back-formation from GRIDIRON]

griddle *or* **girdle** *noun* a flat iron plate, either loose with a handle or set into the top of a stove, heated for baking or frying. [from Old French *gridil*]

gridiron *noun* **1** a frame of iron bars used for grilling food over a fire. **2** the field of play in American football. [from Middle English *gredire*]

grief *noun* **1** great sorrow and unhappiness, especially at a person's death. **2** an event causing this. **3** *colloq.* trouble or bother.
— **come to grief** *colloq.* to end in failure; to have an accident.
[from Old French *grever*, to grieve]

Grieg, Edvard (Hagerup) (1843–1907) Norwegian composer, born in Bergen. He studied in Leipzig, where he was much influenced by Schumann's music, then worked in Copenhagen (1863–7) and developed into a strongly national Norwegian composer. After some years teaching and conducting in Christiania, the success of his incidental music for Ibsen's *Peer Gynt* (1876) and the award of a state pension enabled him to settle near Bergen. His other works include the A minor Piano Concerto, orchestral suites, violin sonatas, and numerous songs and piano pieces.

grievance *noun* **1** a real or perceived cause for complaint, especially unfair treatment at work. **2** a formal complaint, especially made in the workplace. [from Old French *grevance*]

grieve *verb* **1** *intrans.* to feel grief, especially at a death. **2** *trans.* to upset or distress. [from Old French *grever*, to grieve, from Latin *gravare*, to burden]

grievous *adj.* **1** very severe or painful. **2** causing or likely to cause grief. **3** showing grief. **4** extremely serious or evil. [from Old French *grevos*]

grievous bodily harm (ABBREV. **GBH**) *Legal* severe injury caused by a physical attack; the criminal charge of causing such injury.

griffin *or* **gryphon** *noun Mythol.* a winged monster with an eagle's head and a lion's body. [from Old French *grifon*]

Griffith, Arthur (1872–1922) Irish nationalist politician, born in Dublin. He worked as a compositor, then as a miner and journalist in South Africa (1896–8), before he edited *The United Irishman*. He also founded and edited *Sinn Féin* (1905–15). He was twice imprisoned, became an MP (1918–22), signed the peace treaty with Great Britain, and was a moderate President of Dáil Éireann (1922).

Griffith, D(avid) W(ark) (1875–1948) US pioneer film director, born in Floydsfork, Kentucky. He began with literary ambitions, then turned to film-making, where he experimented with new techniques in photography and production, and brought out two masterpieces: *The Birth of a Nation* (1915) and *Intolerance* (1916).

Griffith a male first name, which gave rise to the surname. [an Anglicization of Welsh *Gryffydd*, perhaps meaning 'ruddy, rufous']

Griffith-Joyner, Florence (Delores), *née* **Griffith** (1959–) US track athlete, born in Los Angeles. She won three gold medals at the 1988 Olympics, in the 100m, 200m, and 4 × 100m relay. She set world record times in the 100m and 200m (1988).

griffon *noun* **1** a small coarse-haired terrier-like dog. **2** a large pale-coloured vulture with black wings. [variant of GRIFFIN]

Grigson, (Heather Mabel) Jane (1928–90) English cookery writer. She worked as an editorial assistant (1953–5) and as a translator from Italian (1956–67) before she wrote her first book, *Charcuterie and French Pork Cookery* (1967), which acknowledged Elizabeth David's influence on her work. She became cookery correspondent for the *Observer* magazine, and continued to write books, much influenced by her country lifestyle, including the three now regarded as cookery classics: *English Food* (1974), *Jane Grigson's Vegetable Book* (1978) and *Jane Grigson's Fruit Book* (1982). Her husband was the poet Geoffrey Grigson (1905–85).

grill — *verb* **1** to cook under radiated heat. **2** *colloq.* to interrogate, especially at length. — *noun* **1** a device on a cooker which radiates heat downwards. **2** a metal frame for cooking food over a fire; a gridiron. **3** a dish of grilled food. **4** (*also* **grillroom**) a restaurant or part of a restaurant specializing in grilled food. [from French *griller*, to grill]

grille *or* **grill** *noun* a protective framework of metal bars or wires, eg over a window or a car radiator. [from French *gril*]

grilling *noun colloq.* an interrogation.

grilse *noun* (PL. **grilse**, **grilses**) a young salmon returned to fresh water after its first journey to the sea.

grim *adj.* (**grimmer**, **grimmest**) **1** stern and unsmiling. **2** terrible; horrifying. **3** resolute; dogged: *grim determination*. **4** depressing; gloomy. **5** *colloq.* unpleasant. **6** *colloq.* ill. [from Anglo-Saxon *grimm*]

grimace — *noun* an ugly twisting of the face, expressing pain or disgust, or for amusement. — *verb intrans.* to make a grimace. [from French *grimace*]

Grimaldi, Joseph (1779–1837) English comic actor, singer, and acrobat, born in London. From 1800 to 1828 he dominated the Sadler's Wells stage as the pantomime clown (or 'Joey')

griffin

and many of his innovations became the character's distinctive characteristics. His memoirs were edited by Charles Dickens.

grime — *noun* thick ingrained dirt or soot. — *verb* to soil heavily; to make filthy. [from Middle English]

Grimes Graves prehistoric flint mines lying on the Norfolk Breckland, E England, in use c.3000–2500 BC. About 400 shafts up to 15m deep and 5m wide, with radial shafts at the bottom following the flint seams, are spread over 14ha.

griminess *noun* being grimy.

Grimké, Sarah Moore (1792–1873) and **Angelina Emily** (1805–79) US abolitionists and feminists, born into a major slaveholding family in Charleston, South Carolina. Rejecting their family's way of life, the sisters joined the Quakers, who were officially anti-slavery. They moved to Philadelphia and lived quietly until in 1835 Angelina had a letter published in the anti-slavery newspaper, *The Liberator*. They became public figures, and Angelina undertook an unprecedented speaking tour. She resisted efforts to silence her, but gave up public life when she married the abolitionist Theodore Weld (1803–95), after which Sarah lived with the couple and the two remained committed to social change.

grimly *adv.* in a grim way.

Grimm, Jacob Ludwig Carl (1785–1863) and **Wilhelm Carl** (1786–1859) German brothers who were folklorists and philologists, both born in Hanau, Hesse-Kassel. Between 1812 and 1822 they published the three volumes known as *Grimm's Fairy Tales* (*Kinder-und Hausmärchen*). Jacob also wrote the philological work *Deutsche Grammatik* (Germanic Grammar, 1819, revised 1822–40) and formulated 'Grimm's Law' of consonant sound changes. In 1854 they began work on their historical dictionary, the *Deutsches Wörterbuch*, which was completed by scholars in 1961.

grimness *noun* being grim.

Grimond, Jo(seph) Grimond, Baron (1913–93) Scottish Liberal politician, born in St Andrews, Fife. Called to the Bar in 1937, he entered parliament in 1950 and was elected Leader of the Liberal Party (1956–67). Largely responsible for the modernizing of both the Party and Liberalism, he called for a 'realignment of the left' of British politics. He served again as Party Leader for a short period following the resignation of Jeremy Thorpe (1976), and was active in the Lords from 1983 until the week before he died.

Grimsby, formerly **Great Grimsby** POP (1992e) 91 000, a port town in Great Grimsby district, Humberside, NE England. It lies on the S side of the estuary of the R Humber and is the largest fishing port in England. It is also a leading centre of the food industry.

grimy *adj.* (**grimier**, **grimiest**) covered with grime, dirty.

grin — *verb* (**grinned**, **grinning**) **1** *intrans.* to smile broadly, showing the teeth. **2** *trans.* to express (eg pleasure) in this way. — *noun* a broad smile, showing the teeth.

— **grin and bear it** *colloq.* to endure something unpleasant without complaining. [from Anglo-Saxon *grennian*]

grind — *verb* (PAST TENSE AND PAST PARTICIPLE **ground**) **1** to crush into small particles or powder between two hard surfaces. **2** to sharpen or polish by rubbing against a hard surface. **3** *trans.*, *intrans.* to rub together with a jarring noise. **4** to press hard with a twisting action: *ground his heel into the dirt*. **5** to operate by turning a handle: *organ-grinding*. **6** (**grind down**) to crush the spirit of; to oppress. — *noun* **1** *colloq.* steady, dull, and laborious routine. **2** the act or sound of grinding. **3** the size or texture of crushed particles. **4** *colloq.* an erotic circling movement of the hips when dancing.

— **grind something out** to produce it mechanically or routinely.

grind to a halt to stop completely and abruptly. [from Anglo-Saxon *grindan*]

grinder *noun* **1** a person or machine that grinds. **2** a molar tooth.

grindstone *noun* a revolving stone wheel used for sharpening and polishing.

— **have** *or* **keep one's nose to the grindstone** *colloq.* to work hard and with commitment.

gringo *noun* (PL. **gringos**) *derog.* an English-speaking foreigner in Latin America, especially Mexico. [from Spanish *gringo*, from *griego*, a Greek, a foreigner]

grinningly *adv.* with a grin.

grip — *verb* (**gripped**, **gripping**) **1** to take or keep a firm hold of. **2** to capture the imagination or attention of. — *noun* **1** a firm hold; the action of taking a firm hold. **2** a way of gripping. **3** a handle or part that can be gripped. **4** a U-shaped wire pin for keeping the hair in place. **5** *North Amer., esp. US* a holdall. **6** *colloq.* understanding. **7** *colloq.* control; mastery: *lose one's grip of the situation.* **8** *technical* a stagehand who moves scenery. **9** *technical* a person who manoeuvres a film camera.

— **get to grips with something** to begin to deal successfully with it. [from Anglo-Saxon *gripe*, a grasp]

gripe — *verb* **1** *intrans. colloq.* to complain persistently. **2** *trans., intrans.* to feel or cause to feel intense stomach pain. — *noun* **1** *colloq.* a complaint. **2** (*usually* **gripes**) *old colloq.* use a severe stomach pain. [from Anglo-Saxon *gripan*]

Gripe Water *trademark* medicine given to babies to relieve colic and stomach complaints.

gripping *adj.* holding the attention.

Griqualand a region in Cape province, South Africa, mostly in the homeland of Transkei. It is bounded to the N by Lesotho. East Griqualand was joined to Cape Colony in 1879 and West Griqualand, including the diamond fields of Kimberley, joined in 1880. CHIEF TOWNS Kokstad, Kimberley.

grisaille *noun* a painting executed in shades of grey. The term applies to a style of painting, in imitation of sculpture or bas-relief, used as a decorative feature on walls, pottery, or glass; and to a method of painting by Renaissance painters, in which the subject was modelled in light grey before colour was applied. A reduced grisaille copy of a painting was often made for an engraver to work from. [from French *grisaille*, from *gris*, grey]

Griselda, Patient the paragon of wifely virtue who endures without complaint all the hardships imposed on her by her husband in 'The Clerk's Tale', in Chaucer's *The Canterbury Tales*.

griseofulvin *noun Medicine* an antibiotic obtained from the fungus *Penicillium griseofulvum*, administered by mouth as a treatment for fungal infections of the skin, hair, and nails. [from Latin *griseus*, grey + *fulvus*, reddish yellow]

grisliness *noun* being grisly.

grisly *adj.* (**grislier**, **grisliest**) horrible; ghastly; gruesome. [from Anglo-Saxon *grislic*]

grist *noun* **1** cereal grain that is to be, or that has been, ground into flour in a mill. **2** malt that has been crushed in preparation for brewing.
— **grist to the mill** anything useful or profitable; a useful contribution.
[from Anglo-Saxon]

gristle *noun* cartilage, especially in meat. [from Anglo-Saxon *gristle*]

gristly *adj.* full of gristle.

grit — *noun* **1** *Geol.* small particles or grains of a rock or mineral, especially sand. **2** *colloq.* courage and determination. — *verb* (**gritted**, **gritting**) **1** to spread grit on (icy roads, etc). **2** to clench (the teeth), eg to overcome pain. [from Anglo-Saxon *greot*]

grits *noun* **1** (*pl.*) coarsely ground grain, especially oats, with the husks removed. **2** (*sing.*) a dish of these, boiled and eaten for breakfast in the southern USA. [from Anglo-Saxon *grytta*]

gritty *adj.* (**grittier**, **grittiest**) **1** full of or covered with grit. **2** of the nature of grit. **3** determined.

Grivas, Georgeios (Theodoros) (1898–1974) the leader of EOKA (the 1950s Cypriot terrorist organization that fought for the union of Cyprus with Greece), born in Trikomo, Cyprus. He commanded a Greek Army division in the Albanian campaign of 1940–1, and led a secret organization called 'X' during the German occupation of Greece. In 1955 he became head of the underground campaign against British rule in Cyprus, and called himself 'Dighenis' after a legendary Greek hero. In 1959, after the Cyprus settlement, he left Cyprus and was promoted general in the Greek army. In 1971 he returned secretly to Cyprus and, as leader of EOKA-B, directed a second terrorist campaign for *enosis* (union with Greece).

grizzle *verb intrans. colloq.* **1** *especially of a young child* to cry fretfully. **2** to sulk or complain.

grizzled *adj. literary* **1** *said of the hair* grey or greying. **2** *said of a person* having such hair. [from Middle English *grisel*, from Old French *gris*, grey]

grizzly — *adj.* (**grizzlier**, **grizzliest**) grey or greying; grizzled. — *noun* (PL. **grizzlies**) *colloq.* a grizzly bear. [etymology as for GRIZZLED]

grizzly bear the largest of the bears, so called because its dark brown fur is frosted with white. It is found in Alaska, Canada, and western N America.

groan — *verb* **1** *intrans., trans.* to make, or utter with, a long deep sound in the back of the throat, expressing pain, distress, disapproval, etc. **2** *intrans.* to creak loudly. **3** *intrans.* to be weighed down or almost breaking: *a table groaning under heaps of food / a system groaning under inefficiency.* — *noun* an act, or the sound, of groaning. [from Anglo-Saxon *granian*]

groat *noun* an obsolete British silver coin worth four old pennies. [from Old Dutch *groot*, thick]

groats *pl. noun* crushed grain, especially oats, with the husks removed. [from Anglo-Saxon *grot*, particle]

grocer *noun* **1** a person selling food and general household goods. **2** a grocer's shop. [from Middle English *grosser*, wholesale merchant, from French *grossier*; see GROSS]

grocery *noun* (PL. **groceries**) **1** the trade or premises of a grocer. **2** (**groceries**) merchandise, especially food, sold in a grocer's shop.

Grodno *or* **Gardinas** POP (1991e) 285 000, the capital city and river port of Grodno region, E Belorussia. It is situated on the R Sozh.

grog *noun* **1** a mixture of alcoholic spirit, especially rum, and water, as formerly drunk by sailors. **2** *Austral., New Zealand colloq.* any alcoholic drink. [from Old Grog, nickname of British admiral Edward Vernon, who in 1740 issued the naval ration of rum diluted with water]

groggily *adv.* in a groggy way.

grogginess *noun* being groggy.

groggy *adj.* (**groggier**, **groggiest**) *colloq.* weak, dizzy and unsteady on the feet, eg from the effects of illness or alcohol.

grogram *noun* a coarse fabric made from a mix of silk and wool or mohair. [from Old French *gros grain*, coarse grain]

groin — *noun* **1** the part of the body where the lower abdomen joins the upper thigh. **2** *euphemistic* the male sex organs. **3** *Archit.* the edge formed by the joining of two vaults in a roof. — *verb Archit.* to build with groins. [perhaps from Anglo-Saxon *grynde*, abyss]

grommet same as GRUMMET.

Gromyko, Andrei Andreevich (1909–89) Soviet politician, born near Minsk. He was a research scientist at the Soviet Academy of Sciences, then in 1939 joined the staff of the Russian embassy in Washington. He became Ambassador in 1943, and after World War II was permanent delegate to the UN Security Council (1946–9). As longest-serving Foreign Minister (1957–85), he was responsible for conducting Soviet relations with the West during the Cold War, and his austere and humourless demeanour became notorious in diplomatic circles. He became President in 1985, but retired from office following the 19th Party Conference (1988) and was replaced by Gorbachev.

Groningen POP (1990e) 554 000, the capital of Groningen province, Netherlands, and the most important city in the N of the country. It lies at the confluence of the Drentse Aa (Hoornse Diep) and Winschoter Diep, and is connected to its outer port, Delfzijl, by the Eems Canal. There is a large market and the city is the headquarters of the Dutch Grain Exchange. NOTABLE FEATURES Martinkerk (13c); town hall (1777–1810).

groom — *noun* **1** a person who looks after horses and cleans stables. **2** a bridegroom. **3** a title given to various officers in a royal household. — *verb* **1** to clean, brush, and generally smarten (animals, especially horses). **2** to keep (a person) clean and neat, especially regarding clothes and hair. **3** to train or prepare for a specific purpose or job. [from Middle English *grom*, manservant]

groove — *noun* **1** a long narrow channel, especially cut with a tool. **2** the long spiral cut in a gramophone record. **3** *colloq.* a set routine, especially when monotonous. **4** *colloq.* a state of performing excellently; top form: *the champion is really in the groove.* — *verb* **1** to cut a groove in. **2** *intrans. old slang use* to enjoy oneself. [from obsolete Dutch *groeve*, furrow]

groovy *adj.* (**groovier**, **grooviest**) **1** *old slang use* excellent, attractive, or fashionable. **2** *slang* no longer fashionable; dated.

grope — *verb* **1** *intrans.* to search by feeling about with the hands, eg in the dark. **2** *intrans.* to search uncertainly or with difficulty: *groping for answers.* **3** to find (one's way) by feeling. **4** *colloq.* to touch or fondle (someone) sexually. — *noun colloq.* an act of sexual fondling. [from Anglo-Saxon *grapian*]

Gropius, Walter (Adolph) (1883–1969) German architect, born in Berlin. After World War I, he was appointed Director of the Grand Ducal group of schools of art in Weimar, which he reorganized to form the Bauhaus. His revolutionary architectural methods and bold use of unusual building materials were condemned in Weimar, and the Bauhaus was transferred to Dessau in 1925. When Hitler came to power, he moved to London (1934–7) and designed factories and housing estates, and then to the USA, where he was Professor of Architecture at Harvard (1937–52).

grosbeak *noun* any of various finches with a strong thick beak. [from French *grosbec*, thick beak]

Gros Morne a national park on the W coast of Newfoundland, E Canada, established in 1970. A World Heritage site, it is noted for its landscape of forests and fjords, and for its wildlife, which includes caribou, moose, arctic hares, pine martens, seals, and whales. AREA 2 000sq km/772sq mi.

Gross, Michael, also called **the Albatross** (1964–) German swimmer, born in Frankfurt. A butterfly and freestyle swimmer, in 1981–7 he won a record 13 gold medals for West Germany at the European championships. He was the world 200m freestyle and 200m butterfly champion in 1982 and 1986, and has won three Olympic gold medals: the 100m butterfly and 200m freestyle in 1984, and the 200m butterfly in 1988.

gross — *adj.* **1** total, with no deductions, as opposed to *net*: *gross weight.* **2** very great; flagrant; glaring: *gross negligence.* **3** *derog.* vulgar; coarse. **4** *derog.* unattractively fat. **5** *derog. colloq. chiefly North Amer.* very unpleasant. **6** dense; lush: *gross vegetation.* **7** *derog.* dull; lacking sensitivity or judgement. **8** solid; tangible; concrete; not spiritual or abstract. — *noun* **1** (PL. **gross**) 12 dozen, 144. **2** (PL. **grosses**) the total amount or weight, without deductions. — *verb* to earn as a gross income or profit, before tax is deducted. [from French *gros*, large, fat]

gross domestic product (ABBREV. **GDP**) the total value of all goods produced and all services provided by a nation in one year.

Grossglockner the highest peak in Austria, situated in the Hohe Tauern Range, S central Austria. HEIGHT 3 797m. It was first climbed in 1800. The Grossglocknerstrasse at 2 505m is Austria's highest pass.

grossly *adv.* extremely and flagrantly.

Grossmith, George (1847–1912) English comedian and entertainer, born in London. From 1877 to 1889 he took leading parts in Gilbert and Sullivan's operas, and with his brother, Weedon, he wrote *Diary of a Nobody* in *Punch* (1892). His son George (1874–1935) was a well-known musical-comedy actor, songwriter, and manager of the Gaiety Theatre.

gross national product (ABBREV. **GNP**) gross domestic product plus the value of income from investments abroad.

grossness *noun* extreme rudeness or vulgarity.

Grosz, George (1893–1959) German-born US artist, born in Berlin. He was associated with the Berlin Dadaists (1917–18), and produced a series of bitter, ironical drawings attacking German militarism and the middle classes (eg *The Face of the Ruling Class*, 1921). He fled to the USA in 1932, was naturalized in 1938, and subsequently produced many oil paintings of a symbolic nature.

grotesque — *adj.* **1** very unnatural or strange-looking, so as to cause fear or laughter. **2** exaggerated; ridiculous; absurd. — *noun* **1** (**the grotesque**) a 16c style in art which features animals, plants, and people mixed together in a strange or fantastic manner. **2** a work of art in this style. [from Italian *pittura grottesca*, cave painting, from *grotta*, cave]
◇ In art, the term was first applied to fanciful murals found in ancient Roman buildings. It was revived in the Renaissance and was a popular form of ornament throughout 16c Europe, and in the 18c Gothic revival.

grotesquely *adv.* in a grotesque way.

grotesqueness *noun* being grotesque.

Grotowski, Jerzy (1933–) Polish theatre director, teacher, and drama theorist, born in Rzeszów. He founded the Theatre of 13 Rows in Opole (1956–64), which moved to Wrocław as the Laboratory Theatre (1965–84). His work had a major impact on experimental theatre and actor training in the West during the 1960s and 1970s.

grottiness *noun* being grotty.

grotto *noun* (PL. **grottos, grottoes**) **1** a cave, especially small and picturesque. **2** a man-made cave-like structure, especially in a garden or park. [from Italian *grotta*, cave]

grotty *adj.* (**grottier, grottiest**) *colloq.* **1** *derog.* unpleasantly dirty or shabby. **2** ill. [short form of GROTESQUE]

grouch *colloq.* — *verb intrans.* to grumble or complain. — *noun* **1** a complaining person. **2** a bad-tempered complaint; the cause of it. [from Old French *grouchier*, to complain]

grouchy *adj.* (**grouchier, grouchiest**) bad-tempered, likely to grumble.

ground[1] — *noun* **1** the solid surface of the earth, or any part of it; soil; land. **2** (*often* **grounds**) an area of land, usually extensive, attached to or surrounding a building. **3** an area of land used for a specific purpose: *football ground*. **4** the substance of discussion: *cover a lot of ground*. **5** a position or standpoint, eg in an argument: *stand/shift one's ground*. **6** progress relative to that made by an opponent; advantage: *lose/gain ground*. **7** (*usually* **grounds**) a reason or justification. **8** background colour in a painting. **9** (**grounds**) sediment or dregs, especially of coffee. **10** the bottom of the sea. — *verb* **1** to base (an argument, complaint, etc): *an argument grounded on logic*. **2** (**ground someone in something**) to give basic instruction to them. **3** *trans., intrans.* to hit or cause (a ship) to hit the seabed or shore and remain stuck. **4** to refuse to allow (a pilot or aeroplane) to fly. **5** to lay (eg weapons) on the ground. — *adj.* on or relating to the ground: *ground forces*.

— **cut** *or* **take the ground from under someone's feet** to act in anticipation of someone's plan, etc, destroying its effect.

down to the ground *colloq.* absolutely; completely: *suits me down to the ground*.

get something off the ground to make a start on it.

go to ground 1 *said of an animal* to go into a burrow to escape from hunters. **2** to go into hiding, eg from the police.

into the ground to the point of exhaustion; to a position of total defeat.

on the ground amongst ordinary people: *opinion on the ground*.

[from Anglo-Saxon *grund*]

ground[2] see GRIND.

ground bait bait which drops to the river bed, attracting fish to a general area.

ground bass *Mus.* a short bass part constantly repeated throughout a changing melody.

ground control the people or equipment on the ground that direct and monitor the flight of an aircraft or spacecraft.

ground elder a perennial plant (*Aegopodium podagraria*), widespread in Europe, with creeping underground stems that send up new shoots some distance from the parent plant. Its leaves are divided into groups of three oval toothed leaflets, and it has white flowers. It grows in woodland, along roadsides, and on waste ground, and often becomes a persistent weed in gardens.

ground floor the floor of a building at or nearest to the level of the ground outside.

— **be** *or* **get in on the ground floor** *colloq.* to be or become involved at the beginning of an enterprise or undertaking.

Groundhog Day in the USA, a name given to 2 Feb (Candlemas) when, according to popular tradition, the groundhog or woodchuck (American marmot) is supposed to emerge from hibernation, marking the end of winter.

grounding *noun* a foundation of basic knowledge or instruction.

groundless *adj.* having no reason or justification.

groundling *noun* **1** a fish that lives close to the bottom of a river, etc. **2** a low-growing plant. **3** *colloq.* a person who lives or works on the ground, as opposed to a pilot, etc. **4** *Hist.* a person standing in the pit, the cheapest area, of an Elizabethan theatre. **5** *derog.* a person of inferior tastes.

groundnut *noun* **1** a fleshy rounded edible underground stem, or tuber, of a N American climbing plant. **2** a peanut.

ground plan 1 a plan of the ground floor of a building. **2** any general, undetailed plan.

ground rent rent paid to the owner of land leased for building on.

ground rule a basic principle.

groundsel *noun* a weed with small yellow flowers. [from Anglo-Saxon *gundeswilge*, from *gund*, pus + *swelgan*, to swallow, from its use in poultices]

groundsheet *noun* a waterproof sheet spread on the ground, eg in a tent, to give protection against damp.

groundsman *noun* a person who maintains a sports field.

ground squirrel any of various small burrowing rodents resembling rats or squirrels, eg the chipmunk.

ground state *Physics* the lowest energy state of an atom. If an atom in its ground state absorbs energy, one of its electrons will be raised to a higher energy level, and the atom is then said to be in an excited state.

groundswell *noun* **1** a spell of forceful but smooth waves at sea caused by a distant storm or earth tremor. **2** a sudden and rapid growth, especially of public opinion.

groundwater *noun Geol.* water which is distributed in the rocks beneath the surface of the Earth, and provides water for many springs. It collects in a layer of porous material (an *aquifer*), which usually lies between layers of impermeable rocks that do not hold water. Wells are drilled down into aquifers to bring the groundwater to the surface. The level corresponding to the surface of groundwater is known as the *water table*.

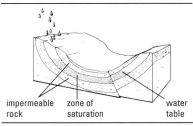

groundwater

groundwork *noun* essential preparatory work.

group — *noun* **1** a number of people or things gathered, placed, or classed together. **2** a number of business companies under single ownership and central control. **3** a band of musicians and singers, especially playing pop music. **4** a subdivision of an air force, consisting of two or more wings. **5** *Chem.* in the periodic table, a vertical column representing a series of chemical elements with similar chemical properties, eg the rare (noble) gases. **6** (*in full* **functional group**) *Chem.* a combination of two or more atoms that are bonded together and tend to act as a single unit in chemical reactions, eg the hydroxyl (-OH) group. The group determines the chemical prop-

erties of the molecule to which it is attached. **7** a blood group. — *verb trans.* to form or make into a group. [from French *groupe*]

group captain an air force officer of the rank above wing commander and below air commodore, equivalent to an army colonel.

groupie *noun colloq., often derog.* an ardent follower of a touring pop star or group, often a young woman seeking a sexual relationship with them.

Group of Seven see G7.

Group Theater a New York theatre company founded in 1931, the importance of which extends beyond the 23 plays it produced during its 9 years of existence. It concentrated on group work and emphasized the social importance of a theatre independent of commercialism, enabling many of those involved (eg Clurman, Strasberg, Kazan, Odets, Carnovsky) to be associated with the best of US theatre for some time afterwards.

group theory *Maths.* the study of the properties of mathematical groups, ie sets of elements (such as real numbers) that can be combined by an operation (such as addition).

group therapy a form of psychotherapy that involves the joint participation of several people (under the guidance of a trained therapist) who discuss their problems and possible ways of overcoming them or changing undesirable mental states or behaviour, eg alcoholism.

grouse[1] *noun* (PL. **grouse, grouses**) any of a family of mainly ground-living gamebirds found in the colder regions of the N hemisphere, with a plump body, short wings, feathered legs, and a short curved bill, eg red grouse, black grouse, ptarmigan, capercaillie. Game species are protected during the breeding season in the UK.

grouse[2] *colloq.* — *verb intrans.* to complain. — *noun* a complaint or spell of complaining.

grout — *noun* thin mortar applied to the joints between bricks or especially ceramic tiles, as a decorative finish. — *verb* to apply grout to the joints of. [from Anglo-Saxon *grut*]

Grove, Sir George (1820–1900) English civil engineer, musicologist, and biblical scholar, born in London. His work as an engineer included erecting two cast-iron lighthouses in the West Indies and assisting with the Britannia tubular bridge. He was secretary to the Society of Arts (1849) and became director of the Crystal Palace Company (1852), but his major work was as editor of the *Dictionary of Music and Musicians* (1878–89). He also edited *Macmillan's Magazine* (1868–83) and contributed to William Smith's *Dictionary of the Bible*. Knighted in 1883 on the opening of the Royal College of Music, he was director there until 1895.

Grove, Sir William Robert (1811–96) Welsh physicist and jurist, born in Swansea. He was educated at Oxford in law, but then turned to science, particularly electrochemistry; he invented a 'gas battery' (the first fuel cell, 1842), and the earliest form of filament lamp intended for use in mines. Professor at the London Institution (1841–64), he studied electrolytic decomposition and demonstrated the dissociation of water; thereafter he turned to the law, becoming a judge in the High Court of Justice (1875–87).

grove *noun* **1** *literary* a small group of trees. **2** an area planted with fruit trees. [from Anglo-Saxon *graf*]

grovel *verb intrans.* (**grovelled, grovelling**) **1** to act with exaggerated (and usually insincere) respect or humility, especially to gain the favour of a superior. **2** to lie or crawl face down, in fear or respect. [back-formation from Middle English *groveling*, prone]

groveller *noun* a person who grovels.

grow *verb* (PAST TENSE **grew**; PAST PARTICIPLE

grown) 1 *intrans. said of a living thing* to develop into a larger more mature form. 2 *intrans., trans. said of hair, nails, etc* to increase or allow to increase in length. 3 *intrans.* to increase in size, intensity, or extent. 4 to cultivate (plants). 5 (**grow into something**) to develop to become that form: *tadpoles grow into frogs.* 6 to become gradually: *over the years they grew very lazy.* 7 (**grow to do something**) to come gradually: *grew to hate him.* 8 (**grow from** or **out of something**) to originate in it: *the scheme grew from an idea they had at school.*
— **grow into something** to become big enough to wear clothes that were originally too large.
grow on someone to gradually come to be liked by them.
grow out of something 1 to become too big to wear clothes that were originally the right size. 2 to lose a liking for it, or the habit of doing it, with age: *grew out of reading comics.*
grow up 1 to become, or be in the process of becoming, an adult. 2 to behave in an adult way. 3 to come into existence; to develop. [from Anglo-Saxon *growan*]

growing pains 1 muscular pains, especially in the legs, sometimes experienced by growing children. 2 temporary problems or difficulties encountered in the early stages of a project or enterprise.

growl — *verb* 1 *intrans. said of animals* to make a deep rough sound in the throat, showing hostility. 2 *intrans., trans. said of people* to make a similar sound showing anger or displeasure; to speak or say angrily. — *noun* an act or the sound of growling. [from Old French *grouller*, to grumble]

grown *adj.* 1 mature: *grown woman.* 2 developed to a certain degree: *fully grown.*

grown-up *colloq.* — *adj.* adult. — *noun* an adult.

growth *noun* 1 the process or rate of growing; specifically, the increase in size, weight, and complexity of a living organism, associated with cell division, that takes place as it develops to maturity. When an organism has reached its maximum size, cell division serves merely to replace existing old or damaged cells. Growth is controlled by a combination of genetic factors and hormones, which together determine the pattern of cell division. 2 an increase. 3 an increase in economic activity or profitability: *a growth industry.* 4 a benign or malignant tumour formed as a result of the uncontrolled multiplication of cells.

growth hormone *Biochem.* 1 a hormone, secreted by the anterior lobe of the pituitary gland, that controls growth and development in vertebrates. — Also called *somatotrophin.* 2 any artificially manufactured substance used for the same purpose.

growth industry 1 *Commerce* an industry or branch of industry which is developing and expanding. 2 an area of human activity which is not necessarily a commercial enterprise but which is expanding in a similar way.

groyne *noun* a low broad wall built like a pier from a shore to reduce the force of waves and so check land erosion. [from Old French *groign*, snout]

Grozny POP (1991e) 401 000, the capital of Chechenia, SE Russia. The city lies on a tributary of the R Terek, in the N foothills of the Greater Caucasus. It was founded as a fortress in 1818.

grub — *noun* 1 the worm-like larva of an insect, especially a beetle. 2 *colloq.* food. — *verb* (**grubbed, grubbing**) 1 (*usually* **grub about**) to dig or search in the soil. 2 to search generally. 3 to clear (ground) by digging up roots and stumps. [from Middle English *grobe*]

grubbily *adv.* in a grubby way.

grubbiness *noun* being grubby.

grubby *adj.* (**grubbier, grubbiest**) *colloq.* dirty. [from GRUB]

Grub Street *slang* the profession, lifestyle, or standards of writers of low-grade literature.

grudge — *verb* 1 to feel a sense of unfairness or resentment at. 2 to be unwilling to give or do; to do or give unwillingly. — *noun* a long-standing feeling of resentment: *bear a grudge.* [from Old French *grouchier*, to grumble]

grudging *adj.* 1 resentful. 2 unwilling.

grudgingly *adv.* in a grudging way.

gruel *noun* thin porridge. [from Old French *gruel*, groats]

gruelling *adj.* exhausting; punishing. [from old word *gruel*, to punish]

gruesome *adj.* inspiring horror or disgust; sickening; macabre. [from dialect *grue*, shiver, shudder + -SOME]

gruff *adj.* 1 *of a voice* deep and rough. 2 rough, unfriendly, or surly in manner. [from Dutch *grof*, coarse]

gruffly *adv.* in a gruff way.

gruffness *noun* being gruff.

grumble — *verb intrans.* 1 to complain in a bad-tempered way. 2 to make a low rumbling sound. — *noun* 1 a complaint. 2 a rumbling sound. [from Old German *grommelen*]

grumbler *noun* a person who grumbles.

grumbling *adj., said of the human appendix* intermittently painful.

grummet *noun* a rubber or plastic ring around a hole in metal, to protect a tube or insulate a wire passing through. [perhaps Old French *grommette*, jaw strap on a bridle]

grump *noun colloq.* 1 a grumpy person. 2 a fit of bad temper or sulking.

grumpily *adv.* in a grumpy way.

grumpiness *noun* being grumpy.

grumpy *adj.* (**grumpier, grumpiest**) surly bad-tempered; [from old word *grump*, surly remark]

Grünewald, Matthias, originally **Mathis Gothardt** (c.1470–1528) German artist, architect, and engineer, born (probably) at Würzburg. He was the court painter at Mainz (1508–14) and Brandenburg (1515–25), and in c.1516 completed the Isenheim altarpiece (now in Colmar Museum).

grunge *noun colloq.* 1 dirt, grime, trash. 2 any unpleasant or nasty substance. 3 a crude style of dress, rejecting current fashions. [probably imitative]

grunt — *verb* 1 *intrans. said of animals, especially pigs* to make a low rough sound in the back of the throat. 2 *intrans. said of people* to make a similar sound, eg indicating disgust or unwillingness to speak fully. 3 to express with this sound. — *noun* an act or the sound of grunting. [from Anglo-Saxon *grunian*]

Gruyère *noun* a pale yellow cheese with holes, originally made in *Gruyère*, in Switzerland.

gryke or **grike** *noun Geol.* any of the clefts or fissures formed by the widening of joints between the blocks of limestone in limestone pavement (a flat expanse of exposed limestone). See also CLINT. [from Old Norse *kriki*, a crack]

gryphon see GRIFFIN.

G7 *abbrev.* Group of Seven, a group of seven leading industrial nations (Canada, France, Germany, Italy, Japan, the UK, and the USA), established in 1986 as a basis for economic summit meetings.

G-string or **gee-string** *noun* a thin strip of cloth covering the genital area, attached with a string round the waist.

G-suit or **g-suit** *noun* a close-fitting suit with cells that inflate to prevent the flow of blood away from the head, worn by astronauts and military pilots as a defence against blackout due to high acceleration.

GT *noun* a name given to certain fast but comfortable sports cars. [abbreviation of Italian *gran turismo*, grand touring]

Gt *abbrev., in place-names* Great.

guacamole *noun* a traditional Mexican dish of mashed avocado, tomatoes, and onions, eaten cold. [from Aztec *ahuacatl*, avocado + *molli*, sauce]

Guadalajara POP (1990) 2.8m, the second-largest city in Mexico and the capital of Jalisco state. It is situated in the W central area of the country, 535km/332mi NW of Mexico City. The city was founded in 1530. NOTABLE FEATURES many colonial buildings; cathedral (1561–1618); Government Palace (1643); Jalisco State Museum; Santa Mónica Church (1718), San Francisco Church (1550); Museo Taller José Clemente Orozco.

Guadalcanal POP (1991e) 61 000, the largest of the Solomon Is, SW Pacific Ocean. AREA 5 302sq km/2 047sq mi. It is 144km/89mi long and has a maximum width of 56km/35mi. The island rises to 2 477m at Mt Makarakomburu. It was the scene of the first World War II Allied Pacific invasion northward, in 1942. CAPITAL Honiara. ECONOMY copra; rice; rubber; oil palms; gold.

Guadalcanal, Battle of a battle in the South Pacific in 1942, during World War II. Following the attacks on Pearl Harbor and Singapore (7–8 Dec 1941), Japan advanced into the South Pacific, reaching Guadalcanal in the Solomon Islands in May 1942. US forces again invaded and after six months of bitter fighting, in one of the crucial actions of the War, they halted the Japanese advance.

Guadalquivir, River, ancient **Baetis,** Arabic **Vad-el-kebir** a river in S Spain, length 657km/408mi. Rising in the Sierra de Cazorla, Andalusia, it flows W then SW to enter the Atlantic Ocean at Sanlúcar de Barrameda. The river, which is navigable to Seville, provides reservoirs used for irrigation and hydroelectric power. [from Arabic *vad-el-kebir*, large river]

Guadalupe Hidalgo an agreement (1848) that settled the Mexican War. Mexico yielded all of Texas, Arizona, Nevada, California, and Utah, and some parts of New Mexico, Colorado, and Wyoming, and in return the USA paid $15m and assumed Mexican debts worth $3.25m.

Guadeloupe POP (1990) 378 000, an Overseas Department of France. AREA 1 779sq km/687sq mi. It comprises a group of seven islands in the central Lesser Antilles, E Caribbean Sea. CAPITAL Basse-Terre. CHIEF TOWN Pointe-à-Pitre. TIME ZONE GMT –4. OFFICIAL LANGUAGE French. CURRENCY the French franc. PHYSICAL DESCRIPTION the main islands of Grand-Terre and Basse-Terre make up 80% of the total land area and accommodate over 90% of the population. CLIMATE warm and humid, with an average annual temperature of 28°C. HISTORY visited by Columbus in 1493; occupied by France in 1635; later held by Britain and Sweden; returned to France in 1816. GOVERNMENT two senators and three deputies are sent to the National Assembly in Paris; a Commissioner advised by a 36-member general council and a 41-member elected regional council. ECONOMY mainly agricultural processing, especially sugar refining and rum distilling; the chief crops are sugar cane, bananas, aubergines, and sweet potatoes.

Guadiana, River, ancient **Anas** a river in Spain and Portugal, length 578km/359mi. Rising in S central Spain, it flows 338km/210mi W to Portugal, then S to the Gulf of Cadiz at Vila Real de Santo Antonio.

Guam POP (1992e) 139 000, a Unincorporated Territory of the USA and the largest and southernmost island of the Mariana Is, W Pacific Ocean. AREA 541sq km/209sq mi. Guam lies 2 400km/1 500mi E of Manila. CAPITAL Agaña.

TIME ZONE GMT +10. The population consists largely of Chamorros (42%), Caucasians (24%), and Filipinos (21%); Roman Catholicism is the chief religion. OFFICIAL LANGUAGES Chamorro, English. PHYSICAL DESCRIPTION Guam is a volcanic island, fringed by a coral reef; it is c.48km/30mi long and rises to 406m at Mt Lamlam. CLIMATE tropical maritime; temperatures range between 24°C and 30°C; most of the average annual rainfall of 2 125mm falls during the wet season, the period from Jul to Dec. HISTORY occupied by Japan from 1941 until 1944. GOVERNMENT elected Governor and a unicameral legislature of 21 members. ECONOMY highly dependent on government activities; military installations cover 35% of the island; diversifying industrial and commercial projects; oil refining; dairy products; garments; printing; furniture; watches; copra; palm oil; processed fish; rapidly growing tourist industry.

Guanajuato a city, the capital of Guanajuato state, central Mexico. It was founded in 1554, and became a major silver-mining centre. Its major thoroughfare, the Subterraneo, runs underground, and was formerly the town sewer. It is a World Heritage site.

Guan Di or **Kuan Ti** in Chinese mythology, the god of war, based on a historical person who died in the 3c AD. He was made a god in 1594, and greatly revered.

Guangxi or **Kwangsi Chuang** POP (1990) 42.3m, an autonomous region in S China. It is bordered in the S by Vietnam and the Gulf of Tongking. AREA 220 400sq km/85 100sq mi. PHYSICAL DESCRIPTION mountainous with a low central river basin. CAPITAL Nanning. CHIEF TOWNS Beihai, Guilin. ECONOMY agriculture; fishing; mining; the Hongshui He R is the site for hydroelectric power stations.

Guangzhou or **Canton** or **Kwangchow** POP (1990) 3.7m, the capital of Guangdong province, S China. It lies on the delta of the Pearl R. The city has been designated a special economic zone and is an important industrial and foreign trade centre in S China. HISTORY founded in 200 BC; opened to foreign trade following the Opium War of 1839–42; occupied by Japan from 1938 until 1945. NOTABLE FEATURES Yuexiu Public Park, containing the Guangdong Historical Museum and Five Goats Statue; Huaisheng Mosque (627), National Peasant Movement Institute (1924); Mausoleum of the 72 Martyrs; Sun Yatsen Memorial Hall.

guanine noun Biochem. a base derived from purine that occurs in the nucleic acid DNA. [from GUANO]

guano noun the accumulated droppings of large colonies of bats, fish-eating seabirds, or seals. It is rich in nitrogen and used as a fertilizer. [from Spanish guano, huano, from Quechua huanu, dung]

Guaraní a Tupian-speaking S American Indian group, who lived in Brazil, Paraguay, and Argentina, practising slash-and-burn agriculture, hunting, and fishing. A few scattered groups still live in the forests of Paraguay and Brazil. Guaraní is spoken by c.1m Paraguayans.

Guaranis, Jesuit Missions of the religious settlements established in the 17c–18c by Spanish Jesuit missionaries to convert the Guarani Indians of Latin America to Christianity. Five of these missions, São Miguel das Missões in Brazil, and San Ignacio Mini, Santa Ana, Nuestra Señora de Loreto, and Santa Maria Mayor in Argentina, are World Heritage sites.

guarantee — noun 1 a formal and usually written promise, especially by a manufacturer, to repair or replace an article found to be faulty within a stated period of time. 2 (also **guaranty**) an agreement, usually written, to take on another person's responsibility or debt if they neglect it. 3 a person making such an agreement; a guarantor.

4 (also **guaranty**) something undertaken to be handed over if a contract or agreement is broken; a security or pledge. — verb 1 to act as, or give, a guarantee for. 2 to promise; to state as unquestionably true. 3 to ensure. [from Old French garantie, from garant, warrant]

guarantor noun a person who gives a guarantee.

guaranty noun (PL. **guaranties**) a guarantee (see GUARANTEE 2, 4).

guard — verb 1 to protect from danger or attack. 2 to prevent from escaping. 3 (**guard against something**) to take precautions to prevent it. 4 to control or check: guard your tongue. — noun 1 a person or group whose job is to provide protection, eg from danger or attack, or to prevent escape. 2 a person in charge of a railway train. 3 a state of readiness to give protection or prevent escape: on guard / keep guard. 4 on alert or in a wary state: on one's guard against thieves / caught you off guard. 5 a defensive position, eg in boxing or cricket. 6 (especially in compounds) anything that gives protection from something: fireguard. 7 the act or duty of protecting. 8 (often **Guard**) a soldier in any of certain army regiments originally formed to protect the sovereign. — **stand guard** to act as a guard or sentry. [from Old French garder, to protect]

guard cell Bot. either of two semicircular cells that surround each of the specialized pores, known as stomata, present on the aerial parts of a plant, especially the undersurface of the leaves. The guard cells control the opening and closing of the stomata in response to the plant's need to conserve water.

guarded adj. cautious.

guardedly adv. in a guarded way.

guardedness noun being guarded.

guardhouse or **guardroom** noun a building or room for guards on duty, especially at the gate of a military camp, often also housing prisoners.

guardian noun 1 a person legally responsible for the care of another, especially an orphaned child. 2 a guard, defender or protector. [from Old French gardein]

guardianship noun the position or state of being a guardian.

guardsman noun 1 a member of a regiment of guards. 2 a guard.

Guareschi, Giovanni (1908–68) Italian writer and journalist, born in Parma. He became editor of the Milan magazine Bertoldo, and after World War II he continued in journalism. He achieved fame with his humorous stories of a village priest, beginning with The Little World of Don Camillo (1950).

Guarnieri or **Guarneri** (17c–18c) a celebrated Italian family of violin-makers from Cremona. The most important were Andrea (fl.1650–95), his sons Giuseppe (fl.1690–1730) and Pietro (fl.1690–1725), and Giuseppe's famous son Giuseppe (fl.1725–45), who was commonly known as 'Giuseppe del Gesù', because he signed his violins with 'I H S' (derived from 'Jesus') after his name.

Guatemala, official name **Republic of Guatemala**, Spanish **República de Guatemala** POP (1992e) 9.8m, the northernmost of the central American republics, divided into 22 departments. AREA 108 889sq km/42 031sq mi. It is bounded N and W by Mexico, SW by the Pacific Ocean, E by Belize and the Caribbean Sea, and SE by Honduras and El Salvador. CAPITAL Guatemala City. CHIEF TOWNS Quezaltenango, Escuintla, Antigua, Mazatenango. TIME ZONE GMT −6. The chief ethnic groups are S American Indian (41%) and mestizo; Roman Catholicism is the chief religion. OFFICIAL LANGUAGE Spanish; several Indian languages are also spoken. CURRENCY the quetzal.

PHYSICAL DESCRIPTION over two thirds mountainous with large forested areas; from the narrow Pacific coastal plain, the highlands rise steeply to heights of between 2 500m and 3 000m; there are many volcanoes on the S edge of the highlands; rivers flow to both the Pacific Ocean and the Caribbean Sea; the low undulating tableland of El Petén lies to the N. CLIMATE humid and tropical on the lowlands and the Caribbean coast; rainy season from May to Oct; Guatemala City average temperatures are 17°C in Jan and 21°C in Jul; average annual rainfall is 1 316mm; much higher rainfall on exposed slopes; the area is subject to hurricanes and earthquakes, which have caused great damage (eg 1976). HISTORY Mayan and Aztec civilizations flourished before the Spanish conquest of 1523–4; gained independence as part of the Federation of Central America in 1821; the Federation dissolved in 1840; thereafter, a series of dictatorships broken by short periods of representative government. GOVERNMENT the 1985 Constitution provides for the election of a President (who appoints a Cabinet), and a National Assembly of 100 Deputies elected for five-year terms; a claim is still made over the territory of Belize to the E. ECONOMY agricultural products account for c.65% of exports, chiefly coffee, bananas, cotton, sugar; wheat, maize, beans on higher ground; cotton, sugar cane, rice, beans on the Pacific coastal plain; cattle raising and beef production; forestry; foodstuffs; chemicals; textiles; construction materials; tyres; pharmaceuticals; newer industries include the manufacture of electrical goods, plastic sheet, and metal furniture; reserves of nickel, lead, silver, oil.

Guatemala

Guatemala City or **Guatemala** POP (1992e) 1.1m, the capital of Guatemala. It is situated on a plateau in the Sierra Madre Range, at an altitude of 1 500m. HISTORY founded to serve as the capital in 1776 after the earlier capital, Antigua, was destroyed by earthquake in 1773; Guatemala City has been rebuilt since its almost total destruction by earthquakes in 1917–18. NOTABLE FEATURES cathedral (1782–1815); the churches of Santo Domingo and San Francisco; Mayan Ruins of Kaminal Juyú to the W.

guava noun 1 a tropical American tree which bears a pear-shaped fruit with yellow skin and pink edible flesh. 2 the fruit of this tree. [from Spanish guayaba]

Guayaquil POP (1990) 1.5m, the capital of Guayas province, W Ecuador. Founded in 1537, it is, today, a major seaport and commercial city, on the W bank of the R Guayas. The city is the world's chief exporter of bananas and the location of the world's first submarine trial. NOTABLE FEATURES municipal and government palaces, museum, House of Culture, San Francisco Church (1603, rebuilt 1968), Santo Domingo Church (1548).

gubbins sing. noun colloq. 1 derog. a worthless object. 2 a device or gadget. 3 derog. rubbish. [from old word gobbon, portion]

gubernatorial adj. formal of or relating to a governor. [from Latin gubernator, steersman]

gudgeon¹ noun 1 a small European freshwater fish often used as bait by anglers. 2 colloq. a gullible person. [from Old French goujon]

gudgeon² *noun* **1** a pivot or pin of any kind. **2** the socket part of a hinge or rudder, into which the pin part fits. [from Old French *goujon*, pin of a pulley]

Gudrun in Norse mythology, the wife of Sigurd the Volsung. After his death she married Atli (the legendary Attila) who put her brothers to death; in revenge she served up his sons in a dish, and then destroyed him by fire. In the similar German story (*Niebelungenlied*) she is known as Kriemhild.

guelder rose a deciduous shrub producing bunches of white flowers. [from *Gelder* land, province of the Netherlands]

Guelfs the pro-papal, anti-imperial party in Italian cities in the 13c–14c, who were opposed to the power of the Holy Roman Emperors, and successful in resisting the authority of the Hohenstaufen Dynasty, whose power was eclipsed after 1266. Allied with the papacy, the Guelfs resisted the claims of potential successors, and dominated Florentine politics.

Guelph POP (1991) 88 000, an industrial town in SE Ontario, S Canada. It lies on the Speed R, 43km/27mi NW of Hamilton, and was founded in 1827 by the Scottish novelist John Galt. NOTABLE FEATURES Church of Our Lady, modelled on Cologne Cathedral; Waterfowl Park; Electric Railway Museum.

Guernica POP (1987e) 18 000, a Basque town in Vizcaya province, NE Spain. It lies on an inlet of the Bay of Biscay, 25km/16mi NE of Bilbao. German planes bombed the town in 1937 during the Spanish Civil War. This event was recalled in a famous painting by Picasso (now in Madrid).

Guernica a painting by Pablo Picasso (1937, Madrid). It depicts the destruction of the town of Guernica during the Spanish Civil War.

Guernsey POP (1991) 59 000, the second largest of the Channel Is, lying NW of Jersey and W of Normandy. AREA 63sq km/24sq mi. Together with Alderney, Sark, and some smaller islands, it forms the Bailiwick of Guernsey. The island was occupied by German forces during World War II. CAPITAL St Peter Port. ECONOMY horticulture; dairy farming; tourism. Guernsey gives its name to a sailor's knitted garment and a breed of dairy cattle.

guernsey *noun* (PL. **guernseys**) **1** a tight-fitting woollen pullover, especially worn by sailors. **2** (**Guernsey**) *Agric.* a breed of dairy cattle, similar to Jersey cattle but larger, that has a golden-red coat, often with distinct white markings, and short curved horns. It produces high yields of rich creamy milk with a characteristic yellow colour, which is widely used for butter-making.

guerrilla *or* **guerilla** *noun* a member of a small, independent, often politically motivated armed force making surprise attacks, eg against government troops. [from Spanish *guerrilla*, diminutive of *guerra*, war]
◊ The term was first applied in the Peninsular War to Spanish and Portuguese resistance fighters. Guerrilla techniques were used during World War II (eg by the Chetniks and Partisans in Yugoslavia, and the National Liberation Front in Greece), and in the Vietnam War (by the Viet Cong). National liberation groups, militant extremists, and freedom fighters in many countries have favoured guerrilla warfare, both the traditional method of harrying and attacking the enemy in open countryside, and the more recent tactic of mounting attacks in built-up areas (the so-called urban guerrilla).

guess — *verb* **1** *trans., intrans.* to make an estimate or form an opinion about something, based on little or no information. **2** to estimate correctly. **3** *chiefly North Amer.* to think or suppose. — *noun* an estimate based on little or no information.
— **anybody's guess** *colloq.* something impossible to know or determine.

[from Middle English *gessen*]

guesstimate *or* **guestimate** *colloq.* — *noun* (pronounced -mət) a rough estimate, based on scant knowledge. — *verb* (pronounced -mate) to make such an estimate of. [from GUESS + ESTIMATE]

guesswork *noun* the process or result of guessing.

guest — *noun* **1** a person who receives hospitality in the home of, or at the expense of, another. **2** a person staying at a hotel, boarding-house, etc. **3** a person specially invited to take part: *guest star / guest speaker.* — *verb intrans.* to appear as a guest, eg on a television show. [from Anglo-Saxon *gest*]

guesthouse *noun* a private home offering accommodation to paying guests; a boarding-house.

Guevara, Che, originally **Ernesto Guevara (de la Serna)** (1928–67) Argentine revolutionary leader, born in Rosario. He trained as a doctor (1953), and played an important part in the Cuban revolution (1956–9), after which he held government posts under Castro. He left Cuba in 1965 to become a guerrilla leader in S America, but was captured and executed in Bolivia.

guff *noun colloq., derog.* nonsense.

guffaw — *noun* a loud coarse laugh. — *verb intrans.* to make this sound. [imitative]

Guggenheim Museum a modern US art gallery in New York City, endowed by Solomon R Guggenheim (1861–1949) in 1937. The concrete building was designed by Frank Lloyd Wright in 1947 and built between 1956 and 1959. It takes the form of a continuous spiral ramp around a central courtyard.

GUI *abbrev. Comput.* graphic user interface, the combination of windows, icons, pull-down menus, etc, presented to the user by a particular software program.

Guiana Highlands a mountainous tableland mainly in S and SE Venezuela, but extending into Brazil and Guyana. The tableland, a forested plateau, covers half of Venezuela, rising to 2 875m at Mt Roraima. The vast plateaux are separated by deep valleys with major waterfalls, including the Angel Falls, considered to be the highest waterfall in the world.

Guicciardini, Francesco (1483–1540) Italian historian, lawyer, and diplomat, born in Florence. He served as Florentine Ambassador to the court of Ferdinand of Aragon (1512–14), then travelled widely in papal service, acting as Governor of Modena (1516) and Reggio (1517) before he retired in 1534. He secured the election of Cosimo de' Medici as Duke of Florence, then withdrew to Arcetri, where he wrote *Storia d'Italia* (History of Italy), an account of events in Italy in the period 1494–1534.

guidance *noun* **1** help, advice, or counselling; the act of guiding. **2** direction or leadership. **3** the process of directing a missile to its target: *guidance system.*

guide — *verb* **1** to lead, direct, or show the way to. **2** to control or direct the movement or course of: *guided missile.* **3** to advise or influence: *be guided by your parents.* — *noun* **1** a person who leads the way for eg tourists or mountaineers. **2** any device used to direct movement. **3** same as GUIDEBOOK. **4** (**Guide**) a member of a worldwide youth organization for girls. **5** a person or thing, especially a quality, which influences another person's decisions or behaviour: *let truth be your guide.* [from Old French *guider*]

Guide Association an organization for girls, similar to the Boy Scouts, founded as the Girl Guides in 1910 by Robert Baden-Powell and his sister Agnes. In the UK, its three classes of membership are Brownie Guides (aged 7–10), Guides (10–16), and Ranger Guides (14–20). In the USA, the groups are Brownies (7–8), Juniors (9–11),

Cadettes (12–14), and Seniors (15–17). Its name was changed to the Guide Association in 1994.

guidebook *noun* a book containing information on a particular subject or place.

guide dog a dog specially trained to guide a blind person safely.

guideline *noun* (*also* **guidelines**) an indication of what future action is required or recommended.

Guido d'Arezzo *or* **Guido Aretino** (c.990–1050) Italian Benedictine monk and musical theorist, probably born in Arezzo. He was a monk at Pomposa, and is supposed to have died prior of the Camaldolite monastery of Avellana. He contributed much to musical science: ascribed to him are the invention of the staff and the introduction of the system of using syllables to name the notes of a scale.

Guienne see GUYENNE.

guild *noun* **1** a medieval association of merchants or craftsmen, maintaining standards and providing mutual support. **2** a name used by various modern societies, clubs, and associations. [from Anglo-Saxon *gield*]
◊ First formed for devotional and charitable purposes, their functions increasingly split, from c.1300, into the economic and the spiritual. Trading and craft guilds controlled economic life in medieval towns; religious guilds flourished in cities and villages.

guilder *noun* **1** (PL. **guilder**, **guilders**) the standard unit of currency of the Netherlands, divided into 100 cents. **2** (PL. **guilders**) an old German and Dutch gold coin. [from Dutch *gulden*]

Guildford POP (1992e) 127 000, a city in Guildford district, Surrey, SE England, situated 45km/28mi SW of London. It was originally a ford over the R Wey. The author Lewis Carroll is buried here. NOTABLE FEATURES Royal King Edward VI Grammar School (1557); cathedral (1964); ruins of a Norman castle; Archbishop Abbot's Hospital; Women's Royal Army Corps Museum.

guildhall *noun* **1** a hall where members of a guild or other association meet. **2** a town hall.

Guildhall School of Music and Drama a London conservatory founded in 1880 as the Guildhall School of Music, renamed in 1935. Originally a school for amateurs, it began professional training in 1892, and moved to the Barbican Arts Centre in 1977.

guile *noun* the ability to deceive or trick; craftiness or cunning. [from Old French *guile*, deceit]

guileful *adj.* crafty, deceitful.

guileless *adj.* without guile.

Guilin *or* **Kweilin** POP (1990) 364 000, a town in Guangxi autonomous region, S China. It is situated on the W bank of the Li R. The majority of China's Muslim population live in Guilin. It served as a US air base in World War II and was badly damaged. NOTABLE FEATURES Reed Flute Cave, with Shuiqinggong (Crystal Palace) Grotto; Zengpiyan Cave (Stone Age Village); Seven Star Park, with Forest of Tablets (stelae from the Tang and Ming dynasties).

Guillaume de Machaut (c.1300–1377) French poet and musician, born possibly in Rheims. One of the creators of the harmonic art, he wrote a mass, motets, songs, and ballads. His poetry greatly influenced Chaucer.

guillemot *noun* a northern diving sea-bird with black and white plumage and a long bill. [from French *Guillaume*, William, perhaps from Breton *gwelan*, gull]

guilloche *noun* an ornamental border or moulding in the form of interlacing or plaited bands in a continuous repeated pattern enclosing roundels. It appears in the decoration of pottery,

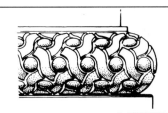

guilloche

manuscripts, textiles, and in architecture, in many styles and periods, and is particularly characteristic of Celtic and Anglo-Saxon art. [from French, a tool used to make a curved line, said to be from the proper name *Guillot*]

Guillotin, Joseph (Ignace) (1738–1814) French physician and revolutionary, born in Saintes. A deputy of the Constituent Assembly, he suggested using a decapitating instrument as a means of execution. This was adopted in 1791 and named after him, though a similar apparatus had already been used in Scotland, Germany, and Italy.

guillotine — *noun* **1** an instrument for beheading, consisting of a large heavy blade sliding rapidly down between two upright posts. **2** a device with a large blade moved lever-like to cut paper or metal. **3** a time limit set to speed up discussion of, and voting on, a parliamentary bill. — *verb* to behead, cut, or speed up progress of, with a guillotine. [named after Joseph Guillotin]

guilt *noun* **1** a feeling of shame or remorse resulting from a sense of having done wrong. **2** the state of having done wrong or having broken a law. **3** blame. [from Anglo-Saxon *gylt*]

guiltily *adv.* in a guilty way.

guiltiness *noun* being guilty.

guiltless *adj.* innocent.

guilty *adj.* (**guiltier**, **guiltiest**) (*often* **guilty of something**) **1** responsible for a crime or wrongdoing, or judged to be so. **2** feeling, showing, or involving guilt: *a guilty look*. **3** able to be justly accused of something: *guilty of working too hard*.

Guimar— POP (1991) 48 000, a fortified city in Braga district, N Portugal, 21km/13mi SE of Braga. It was Portugal's first capital, and the birthplace of the country's earliest king, Alfonso I (c.1110). NOTABLE FEATURES castle (10c); Ducal Palace and the Chapel of São Miguel (1105).

Guinea, French **Guinée**, formerly **French Guinea**, official name **The Republic of Guinea**, French **République de Guinée** POP (1992e) 6.1m, a republic in W Africa, divided into four administrative regions. AREA 246 048sq km/ 94 974sq mi. It is bounded NW by Guinea-Bissau, N by Senegal and Mali, E by the Ivory Coast, S by Liberia and Sierra Leone, and SW by the Atlantic Ocean. CAPITAL Conakry. CHIEF

Guinea

TOWNS Kankan, Kindia, Labé. TIME ZONE GMT. Ethnic groups include Fulani (40%), Malinké (25%), and Susu (11%); Islam is the chief religion. OFFICIAL LANGUAGE French; several local languages are also spoken widely. CURRENCY the franc. PHYSICAL DESCRIPTION the coast is characterized by mangrove forests, rising to a forested and widely cultivated narrow coastal plain; the Fouta Djallon massif beyond lies c.900m above the coastal plain; higher peaks near the Senegal frontier include Mt Tangue (1 537m); savannah plains in the E are cut by rivers flowing towards the upper basin of the R Niger; the Guinea Highlands in the S are forested and generally rise above 1 000m. CLIMATE tropical climate (wet season May–Oct); the average temperature in the dry season on the coast is 32°C, dropping to 23°C in the wet season; cooler inland; the average annual rainfall at Conakry is 4 923mm. HISTORY part of the Mali empire in the 16c; became a French protectorate in 1849; governed with Senegal as Rivières du Sud; became a separate colony in 1893; became a constituent territory within French W Africa in 1904; reverted to separate colonial status as an Overseas Territory in 1946; became an independent republic in 1958; a coup in 1984 established a Military Committee for National Recovery; a multiparty system was introduced in 1992. GOVERNMENT a president and a 10-member Council of Ministers. ECONOMY largely agricultural country, growing rice, maize, yams, cassava, sugar cane, groundnuts, coffee, bananas, palm kernels, pineapples, timber; rich in minerals, with a third of the world's bauxite reserves; iron ore, diamonds, gold, uranium; independence brought a fall in production and a deterioration in the infrastructure as a result of the withdrawal of French expertise and investment.

Guinea, Gulf of an arm of the Atlantic Ocean, lying in the great bend of the W African coast. It is bounded to the N by the Ivory Coast, Ghana, Togo, and Benin and to the E by Nigeria, Cameroon, Equatorial Guinea, and Gabon. The Bight of Benin and the Bight of Biafra are the major inlets. The Equator lies to the S.

guinea *noun* **1** an obsolete British gold coin worth 21 shillings (£1.05). **2** its value, still used as a monetary unit in some professions, especially horse-racing. [named after Guinea in W Africa, where the gold for the coin was obtained]

Guinea-Bissau, formerly **Portuguese Guinea** (to 1974), official name **Republic of Guinea-Bissau**, Portuguese **Republica da Guiné-Bissau** POP (1992e) 1m, a republic in W Africa, divided into eight administrative regions and the capital. AREA 36 260sq km/14 000sq mi. It is bounded SE by Guinea, N by Senegal, and SW by the Atlantic Ocean. CAPITAL Bissau. CHIEF TOWNS Bafatá, Bolama, Mansôa. TIME ZONE GMT. The chief ethnic groups are Balanta (30%), Fula (20%), Manjaca (14%), and Mandingo (13%); local beliefs and Islam are the main religions. OFFICIAL LANGUAGE Portuguese; many African languages are also spoken. CURRENCY the peso. PHYSICAL DESCRIPTION an indented coast typified by islands and mangrove-lined estuaries, backed by forested coastal plains; chief rivers are the Cacheu, Geba, and Corubal; a low-lying country with savannah-covered plateaux in the S and E, rising to 310m on the Guinea border; includes the heavily-forested Bijagos archipelago. CLIMATE tropical climate with a wet season (Jun–Oct); average annual rainfall at Bissau is 1 950mm and the temperature range is 24–27°C. HISTORY discovered by the Portuguese in 1446; became a Portuguese colony in 1879; became an Overseas Territory of Portugal in 1952; gained independence in 1973; military coup in 1980; a multiparty system was introduced in 1991. GOVERNMENT a President is head of state; a National People's Assembly has 150 Representatives. ECONOMY based on agriculture, especially rice, maize, sorghum, cassava, beans, yams, peanuts, coconuts, palm oil, groundnuts, timber; cattle,

Guinea-Bissau

sheep, shrimps, fish; construction, food processing, brewing, soft drinks; reserves of petroleum, bauxite, phosphate.

guinea fowl (PL. **guinea fowl**) any of a family of ground-living birds related to pheasants and chickens, with a naked head and greyish plumage speckled with white. Guinea fowl are native to Africa and Madagascar, and have also been domesticated worldwide for food.

guinea pig 1 a domesticated species of cavy, a small burrowing S American rodent unrelated to the pig, with a rounded body, short legs and ears, and a large head. The coat is black, brown, golden, or white, or a combination of these colours. The most common varieties are the short-haired, the Abyssinian, of which the fur is arranged in rosettes, and the Peruvian, which has long soft fur. Guinea pigs are kept as domestic pets throughout the world, and are also used as laboratory animals. **2** (*in full* **human guinea pig**) a person used as the subject of an experiment.

Guinevere in Arthurian legend, King Arthur's queen, and lover of Sir Lancelot, originally called Guanhamara in Geoffrey of Monmouth's *History*. In Thomas Malory's epic poem (*Morte d'Arthur*) she survives Arthur's death and enters a nunnery.

Guinness, Sir Alec (1914–) English actor, born in London. He began acting in 1934, and joined the Old Vic company in 1936. His stage performances include Hamlet (1938) and Macbeth (1966) and his notable films are *Kind Hearts and Coronets* (1949), *The Lavender Hill Mob* (1951), *The Bridge on the River Kwai* (1958), for which he won an Oscar, and *Little Dorrit* (1987). He also played Ben Kenobi in the *Star Wars* series and Smiley in the television versions of John Le Carré's novels (1979, 1982).

Guinness, Sir Benjamin Lee (1798–1868) Irish brewer, born in Dublin, the grandson of Arthur Guinness (1725–1803) who founded Guinness's Brewery (1759). He became sole owner of the firm on his father's death in 1855, and under him the brand of stout became famous. He was the first Lord Mayor of Dublin in 1851, and he was responsible for restoring St Patrick's Cathedral (1860–5).

guipure *noun* heavy lace having a large open pattern with no background. [from French *guipure*, from *guiper*, to cover with cloth]

Guisborough POP (1981) 19 000, a town in Langbaurgh district, Cleveland, NE England, situated 9km/6mi S of Redcar. NOTABLE FEATURES Augustinian Monastery (12c); Church of St Nicholas (15c).

Guiscard, Robert (c.1015–85) Norman adventurer, the son of Tancred de Hauteville, who campaigned with his brothers against the Byzantine Greeks, and created a duchy comprising S Italy and Sicily. In 1059 the papacy recognized him as Duke of Apulia, Calabria, and Sicily. He ousted the Byzantines from Calabria by 1060, then conquered Bari (1071) and captured Salerno (1076). In 1081 he crossed the Adriatic, seized Corfu, and defeated the Byzantine emperor, Alexius Comnenus, at Durazzo.

Guise (16c–17c) French ducal house of Lorraine, named after the town of Guise. Its members were leaders of the Catholic Party during the 16c civil wars, due to their relationship with the Stuart and Valois royal houses. The first duke was Claude de Lorraine (1496–1550), who served under Francis I in Italy and was given the ducal title in 1528. Henry, the third duke, instigated the murder of Gaspard II de Coligny in the St Bartholomew's Day Massacre (1572). On the death of the seventh duke, Francis Joseph (1675), the estates reverted to Mary of Lorraine, the last of the line.

guise *noun* 1 assumed appearance; pretence: *under the guise of friendship*. 2 external appearance in general. [from Old French *guise*]

guiser *noun Scot.* a person, especially a child, who goes from house to house in disguise, especially at Hallowe'en, entertaining with songs, etc and receiving small gifts in return.

guitar *noun* a musical instrument with a body generally shaped like a figure of eight, a long fretted neck, and (usually six) strings that are plucked or strummed. [from French *guitare*]
◇ Modern electric guitars are of two types: the first (semi-acoustic) type has a hollow body, and the second, more common, type has a solid body. The standard instrument has six strings; the bass guitar has four strings tuned one octave below the four lowest strings of the standard instrument. The acoustic guitar has been associated with folk music since its earliest days, especially with Spanish flamenco, and its popularity as a recital and concerto instrument owes much to the example and influence of virtuoso performers such as Andrés Segovia.

guitar fish a bottom-dwelling ray-like fish with a flattened head, broad pectoral fins, and a slender body resembling a guitar or violin.

guitarist *noun* a person who plays the guitar.

Guiyang *or* **Kuei-yang** POP (1990) 1.6m, the capital of Guizhou province, S China.

Guizot, François (Pierre Guillaume) (1787–1874) French historian and statesman, born in Nîmes. In 1812 he became Professor of Modern History at the Sorbonne, then was a member of the Doctrinaires under Louis XVIII, and was elected to the Chamber (1830), became Minister of the Interior (1830), and then of Public Instruction (1832). As the King's chief adviser (1840), he relapsed into reactionary methods of government, and was forced to escape to London with Louis Philippe (1848). After 1851 he devoted himself to his historical publications.

Gujarat POP (1991) 41.3m, a state in W India, bounded N by Pakistan, SW, S, and SE by the Arabian Sea. AREA 195 984sq km/75 650sq mi. HISTORY independent sultanate in 1401; part of the Mongol Empire in 1572; retained its own princely rulers under British control; part of Bombay state in 1947; created in 1960 from the N and W Gujarati-speaking areas of Bombay state. CAPITAL Gandhinagar. GOVERNMENT 182-member Legislative Assembly. ECONOMY highly industrialized; textiles, electrical engineering, petrochemicals, machine tools, cement, oil refining, fertilizers; cotton, rice, groundnuts; reserves of crude oil, and gas. It was the scene of a flood disaster in 1983, after the Fodana Dam burst.

Gujarati *or* **Gujerati** — *noun* an Indo-Aryan language spoken by c.20–35 million people in the state of Gujarat, NW India, and surrounding areas. — *adj.* relating to or spoken or written in Gujarati.

Gujranwala POP (1981) 659 000, a city in NE Punjab province, Pakistan, 67km/42mi NW of Lahore. It was formerly a Sikh capital. The Sikh ruler Ranjit Singh was born here in 1780.

Gujrat POP (1981) 155 000, a city in Punjab province, E Pakistan, 109km/68mi N of Lahore, between the Jhelum and Chenab rivers. It was founded in the 16c.

gulag *noun* 1 a network of political prisons or labour camps that existed formerly in the Soviet Union; one of these prisons or camps. 2 the government department responsible for their administration. [from Russian *glavnoe upravlenie ispravitelno-trudovykh lagerei*, main administration for corrective labour camps]
◇ Many Soviet dissidents were punished by forced labour in the camps. Aleksandr Solzhenitsyn's novel *The Gulag Archipelago* (1973) is an exposé of the camp system.

Gulbenkian, Calouste (Sarkis) (1869–1955) British financier, industrialist, and diplomat, born in Scutari, of Ottoman-Turkish nationality. He entered his father's oil business in 1888. A major figure in international oil negotiations for over 50 years, he left art collections and $70m to finance an international Gulbenkian Foundation.

gulch *noun North Amer., esp. US* a narrow rocky ravine with a fast-flowing stream running through it.

Guldberg, Cato Maximilian (1836–1902) Norwegian mathematician and chemist, born in Christiania (now Oslo). Professor in his home town from 1869, he formulated with his brother-in-law Peter Waage the law of mass action, which states that the rate of a homogeneous chemical reaction is proportional to the concentrations of the reacting substances (1864).

gulden same as GUILDER.

Gulf see ARABIAN GULF.

gulf *noun* 1 a very large inlet of the sea extending far into the land, much more deeply indented and more enclosed than a bay. 2 a vast difference or separation, eg between viewpoints. 3 a deep hollow in the ground; a chasm. [from Old French *golfe*, from Greek *kolpos*, bosom]

Gulf Intracoastal Waterway see INTRACOASTAL WATERWAY.

Gulf of Tonkin Resolution the US constitutional authorization (1964) to escalate the Vietnam War, passed at the request of President Johnson by an overwhelming majority in Congress, after two US destroyers had reportedly been attacked by N Vietnamese torpedo boats. Its repeal in 1970 (due to growing opposition to the war and uncertainty about giving such discretion to the President) was unopposed by President Nixon, who believed that he had authority enough to achieve US aims in the war by virtue of being Commander-in-Chief.

Gulf States 1 the oil-producing countries around the Persian Gulf, ie Iran, Iraq, Kuwait, Bahrain, Saudi Arabia, Oman, Qatar, and the United Arab Emirates. 2 the US states around the Gulf of Mexico, ie Florida, Texas, Alabama, Mississippi, and Louisiana.

Gulf Stream an ocean current which flows out of the Gulf of Mexico (after which it is named), past Florida, and along the E coast of the USA. Near Newfoundland the current is deflected NE across the Atlantic Ocean and becomes known as the North Atlantic Drift. Its warm water has an important moderating effect on the climate of NW Europe.

Gulf War 1 see IRAN–IRAQ WAR. 2 a war (16 Jan–27 Feb 1991) which followed the invasion of Kuwait by Iraq in Aug 1990. A rapid air and land campaign was mounted by a US-led United Nations coalition based in Saudi Arabia, including forces from 29 countries. Iraqi forces were expelled from Kuwait and a large part of Iraq's military resources was destroyed.

gull[1] *noun* any of various species of sea-bird with predominantly white plumage. [probably from Welsh *gwylan*]

gull[2] *old use* — *verb* to cheat or deceive. — *noun* an easily fooled person. [perhaps from dialect *gull*, unfledged bird]

gullet *noun* the oesophagus or throat. [from Old French *goule*, throat, from Latin *gula*]

gullibility *noun* being gullible.

gullible *adj.* easily tricked or fooled. [from GULL[2]]

Gulliver, Lemuel see GULLIVER'S TRAVELS.

Gulliver's Travels a prose satire by Jonathan Swift (1726). It describes the shipwreck (on Lilliput) and subsequent voyages into strange countries of Lemuel Gulliver, a ship's surgeon.

gully *or* **gulley** (PL. **gullies**, **gulleys**) *noun* 1 a small channel or cutting with steep sides, formed by running water, especially after heavy rainstorms in tropical and semi-arid regions. 2 *Cricket* a position around 9m from the batsman and at a level slightly behind the wicket; also, a fielder in this position.

gulp — *verb* 1 *trans., intrans.* (*also* **gulp down**) to swallow (food, drink, etc) eagerly or in large mouthfuls. 2 *intrans.* to make a swallowing motion, eg because of fear. 3 (**gulp something back** *or* **down**) to stifle (tears, etc). — *noun* 1 a swallowing motion. 2 an amount swallowed at once; a mouthful. [from Old Dutch *gulpen*]

gum[1] *noun Anat.* the firm fibrous flesh surrounding the roots of the teeth. [from Anglo-Saxon *goma*, palate]

gum[2] — *noun* 1 *Bot.* one of various substances found in the stems and branches of certain plants, mainly trees, that produce a sticky solution or gel when added to water. Gums are widely used in confectionery, and in stationery items, eg gummed envelopes. 2 this or any similar substance used as glue. 3 same as GUMDROP. 4 *colloq.* chewing-gum. — *verb* (**gummed**, **gumming**) to glue with gum.
— **gum up the works** *colloq.* to prevent a machine, scheme, etc from working properly. [from Old French *gomme*, from Latin *gummi*]

gum arabic gum produced by some acacia plants, used in foods, pharmaceuticals, and inks.

gumbo *noun* (PL. **gumbos**) 1 a thick soup or stew made from meat or fish, okra, and other vegetables. 2 okra. [from Louisiana French *gombo*, from a Bantu language]

gumboil *noun* a small abscess on the gum.

gumboot *noun* a long rubber waterproof boot, a wellington boot.

gumdrop *noun* a sweet made from transparent hard jelly.

gummy[1] *adj.* (**gummier**, **gummiest**) having prominent gums; toothless.

gummy[2] *adj.* (**gummier**, **gummiest**) 1 sticky. 2 producing gum.

gumption *noun colloq.* 1 common sense; initiative. 2 courage.

gumshoe *noun* 1 a rubber overshoe, a galosh. 2 *slang* a detective, especially a private detective.

gum tree any gum-producing tree, especially eucalyptus.
— **up a gum tree** *colloq.* in a difficult position, especially with no chance of escape.

gun — *noun* 1 any weapon which fires bullets or shells from a metal tube. 2 any instrument which forces something out under pressure: *spray gun*. 3 *colloq.* a gunman. 4 a member of a party of hunters. 5 the signal to start, eg a race. — *verb* (**gunned**, **gunning**) (**gun someone down**) to shoot them with a gun.
— **go great guns** *colloq.* to function or be carried out with great speed or success.
be gunning for someone to be searching determinedly for them, usually with hostile intent.

be gunning for something to try to obtain it: *we're gunning for a pay rise.*

jump the gun to do something before the proper time.

stick to one's guns to maintain one's position firmly, in an argument, etc. [from Middle English *gonne*]

gunboat *noun* a small warship with large mounted guns.

gunboat diplomacy diplomacy consisting of threats of military attack.

gun cotton a highly explosive cellulose material containing nitric acid.

gun dog a dog specially trained to find and retrieve birds or small animals shot by hunters.

gunfire *noun* **1** the act of firing guns. **2** the bullets fired. **3** the sound of firing.

Gunga Din a poem by Rudyard Kipling in *Barrack Room Ballads* (1892). It describes Gunga Din, a much-abused but loyal Indian water-carrier.

gunge *colloq.* — *noun* any messy, slimy, or sticky substance. — *verb* (*also* **gunge something up**) to cover or block it with gunge. [perhaps from GOO + SPONGE]

gung-ho *adj. derog.* excessively or foolishly eager, especially to attack an enemy. [from Chinese *gong*, work + *he*, together]

gungy *adj.* (**gungier, gungiest**) of or like gunge.

gunk *noun colloq.* any slimy or oily semi-solid substance. [originally a trademark of a grease-solvent]

gunman *noun* **1** an armed criminal. **2** an assassin.

gunmetal *noun* **1** an alloy of copper, zinc and tin, originally used to make cannons. **2** any similar metal, especially one formerly used to make toys. **3** a dark grey colour.

Gunn, Ben the marooned English pirate with a craving for cheese in Robert Louis Stevenson's *Treasure Island*.

Gunn, Thom(son William) (1929–) English poet, born in Gravesend, Kent. He moved to California (1954) and taught English at Berkeley (1958–66), returning as Senior Lecturer in 1990. His first collection *Fighting Terms* (1954), labelled him a 'Movement' poet. Other volumes include *My Sad Captains* (1961), *The Passages of Joy* (1982), and *The Man with Night Sweats* (1992).

Gunnbjørn Fjeld the highest mountain in Greenland, near the SE coast. HEIGHT 3 702m.

gunnel see GUNWALE.

Gunnell, Sally (Jane Janet) (1966–) English track and field athlete, born in Chigwell, Essex. Her first national title was in the long jump at the WAAA (Women's Amateur Athletic Association) junior championships in 1980. She later won a gold medal in the 100m at the Commonwealth Games in 1986, and silver in 1990. She made her début in the 400m hurdles in 1987, came fifth at the Olympics in 1988, and won gold medals at the Commonwealth Games in 1990, and at the Olympic Games in 1992. In 1993, she became world champion and set a new

world record in the 400m hurdles in Stuttgart, and also won that event in the European Cup.

gunner *noun* **1** any member of an armed force who operates a heavy gun. **2** a soldier in an artillery regiment.

gunnery *noun* **1** the use of guns. **2** the science of designing guns.

gunny *noun* (PL. **gunnies**) **1** thick coarse jute cloth, used especially for sacking. **2** a sack made from this. [from Hindi *goni*]

gunpoint

— **at gunpoint** threatening, or being threatened, with a gun.

gunpowder *noun* the oldest known explosive, and the only one in wide use until the mid-19c, consisting of a mixture of potassium nitrate, sulphur, and charcoal. It is still used in fireworks and for quarry blasting.

Gunpowder Plot a conspiracy by Catholic gentry, led by Robert Catesby, to blow up the English Houses of Parliament. The plot failed because one conspirator, Francis Tresham, warned his brother-in-law Lord Monteagle not to attend parliament. He reported the matter and Guy Fawkes was arrested placing the explosives (5 Nov 1605). The scheme reflected Catholic desperation that had been increased by the failure of previous plots to remove James I in 1603, the peace with Spain (1604) that had ended the prospect of foreign support, and by new sanctions against recusant Catholics that had resulted in 5 000 convictions in the spring of 1605.

gunrunner *noun* a person who smuggles guns.

gunrunning *noun* the act of smuggling arms into a country, often to help terrorists, etc.

gunshot *noun* **1** bullets fired from a gun. **2** the distance over which a gun can fire a bullet: *within gunshot.* **3** a sound of firing.

gunslinger *noun slang* an armed fighter in the lawless days of the American West.

gunwale *or* **gunnel** *noun* the upper edge of a ship's side.

— **full to the gunwales** completely full.
[from GUN + WALE]

guppy *noun* (PL. **guppies**) a small brightly-coloured W Indian freshwater fish, often kept in aquariums. [named after R J L Guppy, who sent the first specimens to the British Museum in the 19c]

Gupta Empire a decentralized state system (320–540) that covered most of N India, with provinces (*desa*) and districts (*pradesa*). Materially prosperous, especially in urban areas, it is known as India's 'Classical' or 'Golden' Age, when the literature, art, architecture, and philosophy of India were established, and Hinduism underwent revival.

Gur Amir *or* **Gur Emir** the mausoleum of Timur (Tamerlane), Ulugh Beg, and others of the house of Timur, built in Samarkand (in present-day Uzbekistan) in the 15c and restored in 1967. The interior of the mausoleum is decorated with turquoise and gold designs, while the exterior is dominated by a ribbed dome.

gurdwara *noun Relig.* a Sikh place of worship which includes a place where the scripture is housed. In addition, it should include a hostel and an area for serving meals. [from Punjabi *gurduārā*, from Sanskrit *guru*, teacher + *dvāra*, door]

gurgle — *verb* **1** *intrans. said of water* to make a bubbling noise when flowing. **2** *intrans., trans.* to make, or express with, a bubbling noise in the throat. — *noun* the sound of gurgling. [from Latin *gurgulare*]

Guri Dam a major earth- and rock-fill gravity dam on the R Caroni in Venezuela, built in the late 1980s. It is 162m high and 9.4km/5.84mi long, and has the capacity to generate over 10 000 megawatts of hydroelectricity.

Gurkha *noun* a member of a Hindu people of Nepal, from whom whole regiments in the British and Indian armies are formed.

Gurkhali *noun* the Indo-European language spoken by Gurkhas.

Gurney, Edmund (1847–88) English psychical researcher, born in Hersham, Surrey. One of the founding members of the Society for Psychical Research, he conducted important experimental studies of hypnosis and telepathy, and a statistical survey of hallucinations. His investigation of apparitions, telepathy, and other such phenomena culminated in his classic *Phantasms of the Living* (with F W H Myers and F Podmore, 1886).

Gurney, Ivor (1890–1937) English composer and poet, born in Gloucester. Gassed and shell-shocked in 1917, he published two volumes of poems from hospital: *Severn and Somme* (1917) and *War's Embers* (1919), and later *Five Elizabethan Songs* (1920). He studied in London with Ralph Vaughan Williams and published his first songs *5 Elizabethan Songs* (1920), but from 1922 he was confined in an asylum. Considered his best work, some 300 of his songs survive, and there are also c.900 poems.

guru *noun* **1** a Hindu or Sikh spiritual leader or teacher. **2** *sometimes facetious* any greatly respected and influential leader or adviser. [from Hindi *guru*, from Sanskrit, venerable]

gush — *verb* **1** *intrans., trans. said of a liquid* to flood out or cause it to flood out suddenly and violently. **2** *intrans. derog.* to speak or act with an affected and exaggerated emotion or enthusiasm. — *noun* **1** a sudden violent flooding-out. **2** *derog. colloq.* exaggerated emotion or enthusiasm. [from Middle English *gosshe* or *gusche*]

gusher *noun* an oil-well from which oil flows without the use of pumps.

gushing *adj.* that gushes.

gusset *noun* a piece of material sewn into a garment for added strength, or to allow for freedom of movement, eg at the crotch. [from Old French *gousset*]

gust — *noun* **1** a sudden blast or rush, eg of wind or smoke. **2** an emotional outburst. — *verb intrans., said of the wind* to blow in gusts. [from Norse *gustr*, blast]

Gustavus I *or* **Gustav Vasa** (1496–1560) King of Sweden (1523–60), founder of the Vasa dynasty, born in Lindholmen, Upland. In 1518 he was taken to Denmark as a hostage, but he escaped and led a peasant rising against the occupying Danes, captured Stockholm (1523), and drove the enemy from Sweden. He was elected king by the Diet and, despite several rebellions, his 40-year reign left Sweden peaceful.

Gustavus II *or* **Gustavus Adolphus** (1594–1632) King of Sweden (1611–32), born in Stockholm, the son of Charles IX. He reorganized the government with the assistance of Chancellor Oxenstierna and recovered his Baltic provinces from Denmark. He ended wars with Russia (1617) and Poland (1629), and carried out major military and economic reforms at home. In 1630 he entered the Thirty Years War, leading the German Protestants against the Imperialist forces under Wallenstein, and won several victories, notably at Breitenfeld (1631), and at Lützen, where he was killed.

gusto *noun* enthusiastic enjoyment; zest; vigour. [from Italian *gusto*, from Latin *gustus*, taste]

gusty *adj.* (**gustier, gustiest**) **1** blowing in gusts, stormy. **2** fitfully irritable or upset.

gut — *noun* **1** the alimentary canal, or part of it. **2** (**guts**) *colloq.* the insides of a person or animal. **3** *colloq.* the stomach or abdomen. **4** *colloq.* a fat stomach; a paunch. **5** (**guts**) *colloq.* courage or determination. **6** (**guts**) *colloq.* the inner or essen-

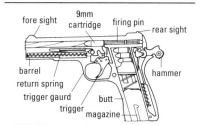

fore sight | 9mm cartridge | firing pin | rear sight
barrel | return spring | trigger gaurd | hammer | butt | trigger | magazine

handgun

tial parts: *the guts of the scheme.* **7** a strong thread made from animal intestines, used for violin and racket strings; catgut. — *verb* (**gutted, gutting**) **1** to take the guts out of (especially fish). **2** to destroy the insides of; to reduce to a shell: *fire gutted the building.* — *adj.* **1** based on instinct and emotion, not reason: *a gut reaction.* **2** essential; basic: *the gut problem.*

— **hate someone's guts** *colloq.* to have a violent dislike for them.

work, sweat, slave, *etc* **one's guts out** *colloq.* to work extremely hard.

[from Anglo-Saxon *gutt*]

Gutenberg, Beno (1889–1960) German-born US geophysicist, born in Darmstadt. Following studies of the waves generated by earthquakes, he made the first correct determination of the depth to the Earth's core, which he concluded is liquid (1914). In 1929 he moved to the USA, where he became professor at the California Institute of Technology in 1930.

Gutenberg, Johannes (Gensfleisch) (1400–68) German printer, regarded as the inventor of printing from movable type, born in Mainz. He may have begun printing when in Strasbourg (1830–44), and he set up a printing press (1848) in Mainz, financed by Johann Fust. His best-known book is the 42-line Bible, often called 'Gutenberg's Bible' (c.1455).

Guthrie, Chris the heroine of Lewis Grassic Gibbon's trilogy *A Scots Quair*, who bears witness to the enduring nature of the land.

Guthrie, Sir (William) Tyrone (1900–71) English theatrical producer, born in Tunbridge Wells, Kent. After being director of the Scottish National Players and the Cambridge Festival Theatre, he produced many successful Shakespeare plays at the Old Vic during the 1930s, becoming director of the Old Vic and Sadler's Wells (1939–45), and director of the Old Vic (1950–1). He often worked abroad, and founded the Tyrone Guthrie Theatre in Minneapolis, USA, in 1963.

Guthrie, Woody (Woodrow Wilson) (1912–67) US folksinger and songwriter, born in Okemah, Oklahoma. During the Great Depression he took to the road, singing for his meals. He wrote hundreds of songs, often in praise of migrant workers, pacifists, and underdogs of all kinds, including 'So Long, It's Been Good to Know You' and 'This Land Is Your Land'. By the time he died, a new generation (including Joan Baez and Bob Dylan) had adopted his causes and his songs.

Gutland *or* **Pays Gaumais** a geographical region of S Luxembourg, occupying nearly 70 per cent of the country. It forms part of the fertile uplands of Lorraine and includes an important wine-producing area along the R Mosel. The city of Luxembourg lies on the less fertile Jurassic sandstone table in the centre of the region.

gutless *adj. derog.* cowardly; lacking determination.

gutsy *adj.* (**gutsier, gutsiest**) *colloq.* **1** courageous and determined. **2** gluttonous.

gutta-percha *noun* a white rubber-like substance obtained from Malaysian trees, used as insulation for electrical cables, and in dentistry. [from Malay *getah*, gum + *percha*, the tree producing it]

gutted *adj. colloq.* extremely shocked or disappointed.

gutter — *noun* **1** a channel for carrying away rainwater, fixed to the edge of a roof or built between a pavement and a road. **2** (**the gutter**) a state of poverty and social deprivation, or of coarse and degraded living. **3** *Printing* the inner margins between two facing pages. — *verb* (**guttered, guttering**) **1** *intrans. said of a candle* to melt away with wax forming channels down the side. **2** to wear away channels in. **3** *intrans.* to trickle. [from Old French *goutiere*, from *goute*, drop]

guttering *noun* **1** gutters collectively. **2** material for making roof-gutters.

gutter press *derog.* newspapers dealing largely with scandal and gossip reported in a sensational style.

guttersnipe *noun old derog. use* a raggedly dressed or ill-mannered person, especially a child.

guttural *adj.* **1** *said of sounds* produced deep in the throat. **2** *said of a language or style of speech* having or using such sounds; harsh-sounding. [from Latin *guttur*, throat]

gutturally *adv.* in a guttural way.

guv, guvnor and **guv'nor** see GOVERNOR (under GOVERN).

Guy a male first name. [from Norman, from *witu*, wood or *wit*, wide; with Norman French *w*-changed to *gu*-]

guy[1] — *noun* **1** *colloq.* a man or boy. **2** a crude model of Guy Fawkes, burnt on a bonfire on Guy Fawkes Day. — *verb* to make fun of. [named after Guy Fawkes]

guy[2] — *noun* a rope or wire used to hold something, especially a tent, firm or steady. — *verb* to secure with guys. [named after Old French *guie*, guide]

Guyana, official name **Co-operative Republic of Guyana**, formerly (to 1966) **British Guiana** POP (1992e) 808 000, a republic on the N coast of S America, divided into nine districts. AREA 214 969sq km/82 978sq mi. It is bounded E by Surinam, W by Venezuela, S by Brazil, and N by the Atlantic Ocean. CAPITAL Georgetown. TIME ZONE GMT –3.5. The population is mainly East Indian (51%) and mixed Afro-S American Indian (43%); the majority follow Christian or Hindu religions. OFFICIAL LANGUAGE English; Hindi, Urdu, and local dialects are also spoken. CURRENCY the Guyana dollar. PHYSICAL DESCRIPTION inland forest covers c.85% of the land area; grass-

Guyana

covered savannah in the hinterland; the coastal plain, below sea level at high tide, is protected by sea defences, dams, and canals; main rivers are the Essequibo, Demerara, and Berbice, with many rapids and waterfalls in the upper courses; the highest peak is Mt Roraima, rising to 2 875m in the Pakaraima Mts to the W. CLIMATE equatorial climate in the lowlands, hot, wet, with constant high humidity; Georgetown, representative of the coastal lowland area, has minimum temperatures of 23°C, maximum 34°C and two seasons of high rainfall (May–Jul, Nov–Jan); lower temperatures and less rainfall on the high plateau

inland. HISTORY sighted by Columbus in 1498; settled by the Dutch in the late 16c; several areas ceded to Britain in 1815; consolidated as British Guiana in 1831; racial disturbances in 1962; gained independence in 1966; became a republic in 1970. GOVERNMENT a president and a unicameral 65-member National Assembly, elected every five years. There is high unemployment, influenced by labour unrest, low productivity, and a high foreign debt. The International Monetary Fund made Guyana ineligible for further credits due to lack of repayment in 1985. ECONOMY largely based on sugar, rice, bauxite; shrimps, livestock, cotton, molasses, timber, rum.

Guyenne *or* **Guienne**, Latin **Acquitania** a former province of Aquitaine region, SW France, bounded W by the Bay of Biscay. It is now occupied by the departments of Gironde, Dordogne, Lot, Aveyron, Tarn-et-Garonne, and Lot-et-Garonne. HISTORY initially a medieval duchy (including Gascony), with Bordeaux as its capital; a possession of the English crown after Normandy and other French territories were lost in 1204–5; the claim of the kings of England to be independent rulers of Guyenne was one of the causes of the Hundred Years War; finally conquered by the French in 1453.

Guy Fawkes Day 5 Nov, the anniversary of the discovery of the Gunpowder Plot, a plot to blow up Parliament in 1605 of which Guy Fawkes was the leader, celebrated with firework displays.

Guyon, Sir the worthy, self-restrained knight of Temperance in Spenser's *The Faerie Queene*, whose duty it is to defend helpless maidens.

Guzmán Blanco, Antonio (1829–99) Venezuelan dictator, born in Carácas. Vice-President from 1863 to 1868, he was driven from office, but headed a revolution which restored him to power (1870). He became dictator and held the presidency on three occasions (1873–7, 1879–84, 1886–8), then retired to Paris.

guzzle *verb trans., intrans.* to eat or drink greedily. [perhaps from French *gosier*, throat]

guzzler *noun* a person who guzzles.

Gwalior POP (1991) 693 000, a city and former princely state in Madhya Pradesh, central India. HISTORY founded in the 8c; famous cultural centre in the 15c; Mughal city in the 15c–16c; taken by the British in 1780. NOTABLE FEATURES fort on Gwalior Rock, with several palaces, temples, and shrines.

Gwendolen a female first name; its short form *Gwen* is often regarded as an independent name. [from Welsh *gwen*, white, fair, holy + *dolen*, ring, bow]

Gwent POP (1992e) 449 000, a county in SE Wales, which is divided into five districts. AREA 1 376sq km/531sq mi. It is bounded W by W Glamorgan, NW by Powys, NE by Hereford and Worcester, E by Gloucestershire, and S by the Bristol Channel. The county is drained by the Usk and Wye rivers. CHIEF TOWNS Cwbran (county town), Abergavenny, Newport, and Tredegar. ECONOMY market gardening, dairy farming; coal mining, aluminium, tinplate; chemicals; food processing; tourism. NOTABLE FEATURES Wye Valley; Tintern Abbey; castles at Chepstow and Raglan; Roman remains at Caerleon.

Gweru, formerly **Gwelo** POP (1982) 79 000, the capital of Midlands province in Zimbabwe, 155km/96mi NE of Bulawayo. It is an important communications and administrative centre.

Gwyn, Eleanor, known as **Nell** (c.1650–87) English actress and mistress of Charles II of Scotland and England. Of humble parentage, she lived precariously as an orange girl before establishing herself as a comedienne at Drury Lane. She had at least one son by the King — Charles Beauclerk, Duke of St Albans — and James Beauclerk is allegedly a second.

Gwynedd POP (1992e) 240 000, a county in NW Wales, divided into five districts, and including the island of Anglesey separated from the mainland by the Menai Strait. AREA 3 869sq km/1 493sq mi. It is bounded N, W, and SW by the Irish Sea, E by Clwyd, and S by Powys. The county operates a bilingual language policy. PHYSICAL DESCRIPTION rises to 1 085m at Mt Snowdon in Snowdonia National Park; drained by the R Conwy; Llyn Tegid (Bala) is the largest Welsh lake. CHIEF TOWNS Caernarfon (administrative centre), Bangor, Pwllheli, Barmouth, Holyhead. ECONOMY livestock; slate quarrying; textiles; electronics; light engineering; tourism. NOTABLE FEATURES castles at Caernarfon, Beaumaris, Conwy, Criccieth, and Harlech.

Gwyneth a female first name, not common outside Wales. [from Welsh *gwynaeth*, luck, prosperity]

gybe — *verb trans., intrans. Naut.* (*also* **gibe**) **1** *said of a sail* to swing or cause it to swing over from one side of a boat to the other. **2** *said of a boat* to change or cause it to change course in this way. — *noun* an act of gybing. [from JIB]

Gyda Peninsula, Russian **Gydanskiy Poluostrov** a peninsula in Russia, lying between the mouths of the rivers Taz in the W and Yenisei in the E. It is bounded in the N by the Kara Sea, in the W by Ob Bay, and in the NE by the Yenisei Gulf. The land is generally low-lying, poorly drained, and tundra-covered.

Gylberde, William see GILBERT, WILLIAM.

gym *noun colloq.* **1** gymnastics. **2** a gymnasium.

gymkhana *noun* **1** a local public event consisting of competitions in various sports, especially horse-riding. **2** formerly, in India under British rule, an athletics meeting, or a public place providing athletics facilities. [from Hindi *gend-khana*, racket-court, remodelled on GYMNASIUM]

gymnasium *noun* (PL. **gymnasiums**, **gymnasia**) **1** a building or room with equipment for physical exercise. **2** in various European countries, a top-grade secondary school preparing pupils for university. [from Greek *gymnasion*, from *gymnazein*, to exercise naked]

gymnast *noun* a person skilled in gymnastics. [from Greek *gymnastes*, trainer of athletes]

gymnastic *adj.* relating to or involving gymnastics.

gymnastics *sing. noun* **1** physical exercises designed to strengthen the body and improve agility, usually using special equipment. **2** difficult exercises that test or demonstrate ability of any kind: *mental gymnastics.*
◇ In modern competitive gymnastics, disciplines include: for men, parallel bars, pommel horse, horse vault, horizontal bars, rings, and floor exercise; and, for women, horizontal beam, asymmetrical bars, horse vault, and floor exercise.

gymnosperm *Bot.* any plant belonging to the subdivision Gymnospermae, a large group of woody plants which produce seeds that are not

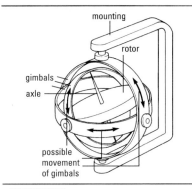

gyrocompass

enclosed in an ovary or fruit, but are usually borne on the surface of overlapping scale-like leaves (*sporophylls*) in cones, eg conifers, cycads. Together with the angiosperms, the gymnosperms belong to the subdivision Spermatophyta (seed-bearing plants) of the plant kingdom. [from Greek *gymnos*, naked + *sperma*, seed]

gym shoe a light, canvas, usually rubber-soled, shoe.

gym slip a belted sleeveless dress or tunic, worn (especially formerly) by schoolgirls as part of their uniform.

gynaecium *or* **gynoecium** *noun Bot.* the female reproductive parts of a flower, consisting of the carpels. [from Greek *gynaikeion*, women's apartments]

gynaecological *adj.* relating to or involving gynaecology.

gynaecologist *noun* a doctor who specializes in gynaecology.

gynaecology *noun* the branch of medicine concerned with the diagnosis and treatment of diseases and disorders that affect the reproductive organs of the female body, eg cervical cancer, menstrual disorders, and the effects of the menopause. [from Greek *gyne*, woman + -LOGY]

Győr, German **Raab**, Latin **Arrabona** POP (1991e) 130 000, the industrial capital of Győr-Sopron county, NW Hungary. It lies at the junction of the Rába and Repce rivers with an arm of the R Danube, and is linked to L Fertő by canal. NOTABLE FEATURES Carmelite Convent (18c); cathedral (12c, rebuilt in the 18c); city hall (18c).

gyp¹
— **give someone gyp** *slang* to cause them pain or discomfort.
[perhaps a contraction of *gee up*; see GEE¹]

gyp² *slang* — *verb* (**gypped**, **gypping**) to cheat or swindle. — *noun* a cheat. [a back-formation from GYPSY]

gypsophila *noun Bot.* an annual or perennial plant with dainty branching heads of small flowers, usually white, but sometimes pink or

crimson. It is widely used by florists. [from Greek *gypsos*, chalk + *phileein*, to love]

gypsum *noun Geol.* a soft mineral composed of calcium sulphate, used to make plaster of Paris, cement, rubber, and paper. Alabaster is a fine-grained variety of gypsum. [from Latin, from Greek *gypsos*, chalk]

Gypsy *or* **Gipsy** *noun* (PL. **Gypsies**, **Gipsies**) **1** a member of a dark-skinned travelling people, originally from NW India, now scattered throughout Europe and N America. See also ROMANY. **2** (**gypsy**) a person resembling or living like a Gypsy. [from *Egyptian*, because they were originally thought to have come from Egypt]

gyrate *verb intrans.* to move with a circular or spiralling motion. [from Greek *gyros*, circle]

gyration *noun* **1** a whirling motion. **2** a whirl or twist. **3** a whorl.

gyre *noun Geol.* a circular movement of water that occurs in all of the major ocean basins, and is caused by the Earth's rotation, convection currents of warm surface water, and the prevailing winds. The heat transported by gyres often influences the weather and climate of the surrounding land areas. [from Latin *girus*, from Greek *gyros*, circle, ring]

gyrfalcon *noun* a large rare northern and arctic falcon. [from Old French *gerfaucon*]

gyrocompass *noun* a non-magnetic compass operated by means of a motor-driven gyroscope.

gyroscope *noun Engineering* a device consisting of a small flywheel with a heavy rim, mounted in such a way that it can rotate at high speed in any direction, but once in motion it resists any changes in the direction of rotation. Gyroscopes are used in ship stabilizers, and in the automatic steering systems of aircraft, missiles, etc. [from Greek *gyros*, circle + -SCOPE]

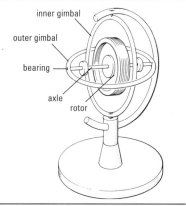

gyroscope

gyroscopic *adj.* relating to or of the nature of a gyroscope.

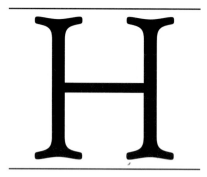

H¹ *or* **h** *noun* (**Hs**, **H's**, **h's**) the eighth letter of the English alphabet.

H² *abbrev.* **1** *on a pencil* hard. **2** hospital.

H³ *symbol Chem.* hydrogen.

h *abbrev.* **1** hecto-. **2** height.

ha *or* **ha.** *abbrev.* hectare.

ha! *interj.* an expression of surprise, happiness, triumph, etc.

Haakon IV, also called **the Old** (1204–63) King of Norway (1217–63). He annexed Greenland (1261) and Iceland (1262), and in 1263 attempted to assert Norway's traditional rights over the Hebrides. He died in Orkney, after his defeat at Largs by Alexander III of Scotland.

Haakon VII (1872–1957) King of Norway (1905–57), born in Charlottenlund. He became king when Norway voted for independence from Sweden in 1905. Dispensing with regal pomp, he emerged as the 'people's king'. During World War II, after the German invasion of Norway (1940) he continued his resistance to Nazi occupation from England and returned in triumph in 1945.

Ha'apai POP (1986) 9 000, an island group of central Tonga, S Pacific. AREA 109sq km/42sq mi. CHIEF TOWN Pangai (on Lifuka). The famous mutiny on *HMS Bounty* took place in Ha'apai waters.

Habakkuk *or* **Habacuc Book of** one of the 12 so-called 'minor' prophetic writings of the Hebrew Bible and Old Testament, attributed to the prophet Habakkuk (possibly late 7c BC).

habeas corpus *noun Legal* a writ requiring a prisoner to be brought into court for a judge to decide if his or her imprisonment is legal. [from Latin *habeas corpus*, have the body (brought before the judge)]

◇ The person or authority detaining the individual is required to justify the detention to the court. If no good reason is provided, release is ordered. In England and Wales, the writ is issued by either the Divisional Court of the Queen's Bench Division, or a High Court judge. The term is not used in Scots law.

Haber, Fritz (1868–1934) German physical chemist, born in Breslau (now Wrocław, Poland). Professor at Karlsruhe and Berlin, he is best known for developing a method of synthesis of ammonia from nitrogen and hydrogen gases (the 'Haber process') – this led to the large-scale production of ammonia. He was awarded the 1918 Nobel Prize for Chemistry.

haberdasher *noun* a person who deals in small items used for sewing, such as ribbons, needles, buttons, etc. [from Old French *hapertas*]

haberdashery *noun* (PL. **haberdasheries**) **1** a haberdasher's shop, business or department. **2** the ribbons, etc sold by a haberdasher.

Habermas, Jürgen (1929–) German philosopher and sociologist, born in Düsseldorf. He became Professor of Philosophy and Sociology at Frankfurt (1964) and was director of the Max Planck Institute, Starnberg (1971–80). The central theme of his work is the possibility of a rational political commitment to socialism in societies in which science and technology are dominant. His books include *Erkenntnis und Interesse* (Knowledge and Human Interests, 1968) and *Theorie des kommunikatives Handelns* (Theory of Communicative Action, 1982).

Haber process *or* **Haber–Bosch process** *Chem.* an industrial process by which ammonia is manufactured from hydrogen and atmospheric nitrogen under conditions of high temperature and pressure, and in the presence of a catalyst consisting of powdered iron. [named after the German chemist Fritz Haber]

Habima a Hebrew theatre company originally formed in Poland (1912), then re-established in Moscow after the Revolution. After touring widely as one of the studios of the Moscow Art Theatre, it moved to Palestine in 1931, and in 1953 became Israel's National Theatre.

habit *noun* **1** a usual or regular practice or tendency. **2** a practice, often bad, which is hard to give up. **3** mental attitude or constitution: *habit of mind*. **4** a long loose garment worn by monks and nuns. [from Latin *habitus*, practice]

habitability *noun* being habitable.

habitable *adj.* suitable for living in. [from Latin *habitabilis*]

habitat *noun Biol.* that part of the environment in which a particular plant or animal species (either an individual or a population) normally lives. It is usually defined in terms of its physical features or the dominant plant types, eg stream, pond, woodland, grassland. [from Latin *habitat*, it inhabits]

habitation *noun* **1** the act of living in a building, etc. **2** a house or home. [from Latin *habitatio*]

habitat loss *Environ.* the loss of distinct parts of the environment in which plants or animals normally live. Destruction or disturbance of such areas by human activity, eg the widespread felling of rainforest, may threaten the continued existence of wildlife, and result in the extinction of some species.

habit-forming *adj., said of a drug, activity, etc* likely to become a habit or addiction.

habitual *adj.* **1** seen, done, etc regularly. **2** done, or doing something, by habit. [from Latin *habitualis*, from *habitus*, habit]

habitually *adv.* usually, regularly.

habituate *verb* (**habituate to**) to make (someone) used to something. [from Latin *habituare*]

habituation *noun* accustoming or becoming accustomed.

habitué *noun* a regular or frequent visitor to a place, eg a restaurant. [from French *habitué*]

Habsburg Dynasty a major European dynasty whose origins lie in the Upper Rhine region. From the medieval period they were the sovereign rulers of Austria, and extended their territories and influence to secure the title of Holy Roman Emperor (1452–1806). The zenith of Habsburg power was reached under Charles V, who presided over an empire stretching from the Danube to the Caribbean (1519–56). After he abdicated his inheritance was divided between his son and brother, which created the Spanish Habsburg line, rulers of Spain until 1700, and the German line, whose members adopted the title of Emperor of Austria in 1804 and ruled the Habsburg possessions in central Europe until 1918. [from German *Habichtsburg*, Hawk's Castle (in what is now Switzerland)]

hachure *noun* **1** (**hachures**) a system of parallel lines on a map to show the contours of hills, the closeness of the lines indicating steepness. **2** any of these lines. [from French *hachure*]

hacienda *noun* in Spanish-speaking countries, a ranch or large estate with a house on it. [from Spanish *hacienda*]

hack¹ — *verb* **1** (*often* **hack something down, away**, *etc*) to cut or chop roughly. **2** (*often* **hack something out**) to cut (a path, etc) roughly. **3** *colloq.* (**hack into something**) to obtain access to computer files without authority. **4** *slang* to be able to bear or suffer. **5** *intrans.* to cough. **6** to kick (an opponent) on the shins, especially in football. — *noun* **1** a kick on the shins. **2** a wound or rough cut, especially from a kick. **3** a miner's pick. [from Anglo-Saxon *tohaccian*]

hack² — *noun* **1** a horse kept for general riding, especially one for hire. **2** a ride on horseback. **3** a writer, journalist, etc who produces dull, mediocre or routine work. — *verb intrans.* to travel on horseback at a leisurely pace, usually for pleasure. [abbreviation of HACKNEY]

hacker *noun colloq.* **1** a person who gains access to computer files without permission. **2** a computer enthusiast.

hacking — *noun colloq.* the act of gaining access to computer files without permission. — *adj., said of a cough* rough and dry.

hacking jacket a tweed jacket with slits at the sides, worn when hacking.

hackles *pl. noun* the hairs or feathers on the back of the neck of some animals and birds, raised when they are angry.
— **make someone's hackles rise** to make someone very angry.
[from Middle English *hechele*]

hackney *noun* (PL. **hackneys**) a horse for general riding. [named after Hackney in E London, where horses used to be pastured]

hackney cab *or* **hackney carriage**
1 *Hist.* a horse-drawn carriage for public hire.
2 *formal* a taxi.

hackneyed *adj.*, *said of a word, phrase, etc*
meaningless and trite through too much use.
[from HACKNEY, in the sense of 'for general use']

hacksaw *noun* a saw for cutting metals.

had see HAVE.

Hadamard, Jacques Salomon (1865–
1963) French mathematician, born in Versailles.
Professor at the Collège de France and the École
Polytechnique in Paris, he was a leading figure in
French mathematics throughout his career,
working in complex function theory, differential
geometry, and partial differential equations. In
1896 he proved the definitive form of the 'prime
number theorem', a long-standing problem in
number theory.

Haddington POP (1981) 8 100, the chief town
in East Lothian district, Lothian region, E
Scotland. It lies on the R Tyne, 26km/16mi E of
Edinburgh. Haddington is one of the best-preserved towns in Scotland, with an almost complete medieval street plan. It is the birthplace of
John Knox. NOTABLE FEATURES town house (1748);
Nungate Bridge (17c); St Mary's Church
(14c–15c).

haddock *noun* (PL. **haddock**) a commercially
important food fish related to but smaller than
the cod, found close to the sea-bed on both sides
of the North Atlantic. Haddock populations are
becoming depleted as a result of overfishing.
[from Middle English *haddok*]

Hades in Greek mythology, the god of the
dead; also, by association, the name of the
Underworld (hell) itself. Hades was the brother
of Zeus and Poseidon, and he married
Persephone, whom he kidnapped. He was identified by the Romans as Pluto.

Hadfield, Sir Robert Abbott (1858–1940)
English metallurgist and steel manufacturer, born
in Sheffield. As chairman of his family's steelmaking firm, he discovered several important
steel alloys and investigated their properties.

Hadith the Islamic tradition on a variety of subjects, traced to the prophet Muhammad or one of
his companions. It provides guidance for
Muslims on all aspects of life, and is second in
authority to the Koran.

hadj, hadji same as HAJJ, HAJJI.

Hadlee, Sir Richard (John) (1948–)
New Zealand all-round cricketer, born in
Christchurch. He started his first-class career
with Canterbury in 1971–2, and has also played
for Nottinghamshire and Tasmania. In England
in 1984 he made 1 000 runs and took 100 wickets. He made his Test début for New Zealand in
1973, surpassed Ian Botham's record of 373 Test
wickets in 1988, and went on to set a new world
record of 431 wickets in 1990; he retired in the
same year. His world record was surpassed in
Feb 1994 by Kapil Dev.

hadn't *contr.* had not.

Hadrian, originally **Publius Aelius
Hadrianus** (AD 76–138) Roman emperor
(117–38), ward, protégé, and successor of the
emperor Trajan. He came to power in ambiguous
circumstances on the death of Trajan and suppressed a conspiracy in Rome against him (118).
He spent little of his reign at Rome, and instead
toured the empire, consolidating the frontiers (as
in Britain, where he initiated the building of the
wall named after him), and visiting the provinces.
The last years of his life were spent in Rome,
where he rebuilt the Pantheon.

Hadrian's Wall the principal N frontier of the
Roman province of Britain. It was built
(AD 122–8) on the orders of the emperor Hadrian
(117–138) and ran 117km/73mi from the Solway
Firth to the R Tyne. The wall itself was 4.5m high
(probably with a 2m timber parapet), and had a

forward defensive ditch of c.8.5m wide and 3m
deep. It incorporated 16 forts (the best preserved
at Housesteads and Chesters), 80 milecastles, and
numerous signal turrets. It was overrun several
times by Picts and N tribes, and finally abandoned in c.400–410. It is a World Heritage site.

hadron *noun Physics* one of a class of subatomic
particles, including baryons and mesons, that
interact strongly with other subatomic particles.
[from Greek *hadros*, heavy]

hadst *verb old use* the form of the past tense of
the verb *have* used with *thou*.

**Haeckel, Ernst Heinrich Philipp
August** (1834–1919) German naturalist, born
in Potsdam. Profoundly influenced by Charles
Darwin's *Origin of Species* (1859), he abandoned
medical studies and became Professor of Zoology
at Jena (1862–1909). Known as the 'German
Darwin', he was a charismatic and enthusiastic
ambassador for evolution, his books becoming
bestsellers; he was also the first to attempt a
genealogical tree of all animals.

haem *noun Medicine* the iron compound which
is combined with the protein globin in the respiratory pigment haemoglobin, and which gives
the red blood cells their colour.

haem- *or* **haemato-** *or* **haemo-** *combining
form Medicine* forming words relating to blood.
[from Greek *haima*, blood]

haematite *or* **hematite** *noun Geol.* a dense
and relatively hard mineral containing iron oxide
(Fe_2O_3), often occurring as dark brown nodules,
that is the most important ore of iron. Powdered
haematite is used as a pigment (red ochre) and as
an abrasive and polishing agent.

haematology *noun Medicine* the branch of
medicine concerned with the diagnosis and treatment of diseases and disorders of the blood, and
of the tissues in which the blood cells are formed.

haematuria *noun Medicine* the presence of
blood in the urine. [from HAEM- + Greek *ouron*,
urine]

haemodialysis *noun Medicine* the purification
of the blood by means of an artificial kidney
machine that removes waste products such as
urea or excess salts, while blood cells and proteins are retained. It is used in cases of kidney
failure. See also DIALYSIS.

haemoglobin *noun Biol.* the oxygen-carrying
pigment that is the main constituent of the red
blood cells (erythrocytes) in all vertebrates and
some invertebrates, and contains the iron compound *haem* combined with the protein *globin*.
Haemoglobin takes up oxygen in the lungs and
combines with it to form *oxyhaemoglobin*, which
is transported via the bloodstream to the body
tissues, where the oxygen is released for use by
the cells. [from HAEM- + Latin *globus*, ball]

haemolysis *noun Biol.* the abnormal destruction of red blood cells, accompanied by the
release of the pigment haemoglobin, eg as a
result of malaria, poisoning, the presence of
abnormal types of haemoglobin or red blood
cells, or mis-matching of blood groups in a blood
transfusion.

haemophilia *noun* an inherited disorder in
which normal blood clotting is impaired, owing
to a deficiency of factor VIII, one of the proteins
that is essential for clotting. [from HAEM- + Greek
philia, friendship]
◇ Haemophilia is a sex-linked disorder caused
by a defective gene on the X-chromosome, so it
is almost entirely restricted to males. Women can
carry the disease without being affected by it, but
there is a 50 per cent chance that they will pass it
on to their male offspring, and that their female
offspring will become carriers. The disorder has
in the past afflicted several European royal
households.
Haemophiliacs experience prolonged bleeding
after even minor injury, as well as painful spontaneous bleeding, mainly into muscles and joints.

The end result may be crippling deformity due to
severely damaged joints. Bleeding may be treated
with transfusions of plasma, or with concentrated preparations of factor VIII.

haemophiliac — *noun* a person who suffers
from haemophilia. — *adj.* affected with
haemophilia.

haemorrhage — *noun* an escape of large
amounts of blood, especially from a ruptured
blood vessel. — *verb intrans.* to suffer a haemorrhage. [from HAEM- + Greek *rhegnynai*, to burst]

haemorrhoid *noun* (*usually* **haemorrhoids**) a
swollen vein around the inside or outside of the
anus. Haemorrhoids often cause itching or bleeding, and may be painful. They are usually associated with prolonged constipation. [from HAEM- +
Greek *rheein*, to flow]

Haerbin *or* **Haerhpin** see HARBIN.

Hafiz *or* **Hafez**, pseudonym of **Shams ed-
Din Mohammad** (c.1326–c.1390) Persian lyrical
poet, born in Shiraz. A member of the mystical
sect of Sufi philosophers, his short poems (*ghaz-
als*), all on sensuous subjects, such as love, wine,
and flowers, contain an esoteric signification to
the initiated.

hafnium *noun Chem.* (SYMBOL **Hf**, ATOMIC NUM-
BER **72**) a silvery metal found mainly in zirconium minerals, and used in tungsten alloys for
light bulb filaments and electrodes. It is also a
strong neutron absorber and is used to make control rods for nuclear reactors. [from Latin *Hafnia*,
Copenhagen, where it was discovered]

haft *noun* a handle of a knife, axe, etc.
[from Anglo-Saxon *hæft*]

hag — *noun* 1 *offensive* an ugly old woman. 2 a
witch. [from Anglo-Saxon *hægtes*]

Haganah the Jewish underground militia in
Palestine, founded during the period of the
British Mandate in the 1920s. Following its major
role in the War of Independence and the declaration of the State of Israel (1948), the Haganah
became the Israel Defence Force, the official
Israeli army. [from Hebrew, = self defence]

Hagen, Walter (Charles), also called **the
Haig** (1892–1969) US golfer, born in Rochester,
New York. The first US-born winner of the
British Open, he won the title four times (1922,
1924, 1928–9), the US Open twice (1914, 1919),
the US Professional Golfers' Association championship a record five times (1921, 1924–7), and
captained the first six US Ryder Cup teams
(1927–37).

Hagen POP (1991e) 214 000, an industrial city in
North Rhine-Westphalia state, W central
Germany. It lies at the junction of important traf-
fic routes, 48km/30mi NE of Düsseldorf. NOTABLE
FEATURE Westphalian Open-air Museum of
Technology.

hagfish *noun* a primitive marine fish lacking
true jaws, vertebrae, paired fins, and scales, and
having an eel-like body covered in copious slime.
It feeds on invertebrates and fish.

Haggai, Book of one of the 12 so-called
'minor' prophetic writings of the Hebrew Bible
and Old Testament, attributed to the prophet
Haggai.

Haggard, Sir H(enry) Rider (1856–1925)
English novelist, born in Bradenham Hall,
Norfolk. He travelled widely in government service in South Africa, before taking up a literary
life in England in 1881. His best-known work is
King Solomon's Mines (1885), and other works
include *She* (1887) and *Allan Quatermain* (1887).

haggard *adj.* looking very tired and thin-faced,
because of pain, worry, etc. [from Old French
hagard]

haggis *noun* a Scottish dish made from sheep's
or calf's offal mixed with suet, oatmeal and
seasonings and then boiled in a bag made from
the animal's stomach, or something similar.
[from Old Scot. *haggeis*]

haggish *adj.* like a hag; old and ugly.

haggle *verb intrans.* (**haggle over** *or* **about something**) to bargain over or argue about a price, etc. [from Norse *höggva*, to hew]

haggler *noun* a person who haggles.

Hagia Sophia *or* **Santa Sophia** a Byzantine domed basilica built (532–7) for Emperor Justinian I in Constantinople (now Istanbul) by Anthemius of Tralles and Isidore of Miletus. The Ottoman Turks, who took Constantinople in 1453, converted it into a mosque, and since 1935 it has been a museum. It is a World Heritage site.

hagiographer *noun* **1** a writer of saints' lives. **2** one of the writers of certain parts of the Old Testament.

hagiography *noun* (PL. **hagiographies**) the writing of the stories of saints' lives. [from Greek *hagios*, holy + -GRAPHY]

hagiology *noun* (PL. **hagiologies**) literature about the lives of, and legends about, saints. [from Greek *hagios*, holy + -LOGY]

hag-ridden *adj.* troubled or unhappy, as if cursed by a witch.

Hague, The, Dutch **'s-Gravenhage**, or **Den Haag** POP (1992e) 445 000, the capital of South Holland province, W Netherlands, and the seat of the Dutch government. Lying 3km/2mi from the North Sea, it is part of the Randstad conurbation and is the third largest city in the Netherlands. Industry plays a subordinate role in this cultural, administrative, and political city, which is often called the 'City of the Arts'. Several international organizations have their headquarters here, notably the International Court of Justice and the Permanent Court of Arbitration. Many Dutch painters have lived in The Hague; it is also noted for its furniture, gold and silverware, and pottery craftwork. HISTORY the States-General met here in 1527; the centre of European diplomacy from the 17c (many treaties were signed here); the Hague Convention (1907) formulated much of the law governing international warfare. NOTABLE FEATURES Gothic Hall of the Knights (13c); Palace of Peace (1913); Nieuwe Kerk (1641); the royal residence 'House in the Wood' (1647); town hall (16c); the seaside resort of Scheveningen is nearby.

Hague Agreement the convention of 1899 for the Pacific Settlement of International Disputes. It established a Permanent Court of Arbitration — the forerunner of the World Court.

Hague Peace Conferences two conferences (1899, 1907) in The Hague, Netherlands. They first met to discuss the limitation of armaments, but the 26 countries represented made little progress. A permanent court of arbitration was set up for states in dispute wishing to use its services. The second met on the initiative of President Theodore Roosevelt and produced a series of conventions to try to limit the horrors of war.

Hague School a group of Dutch landscape and peasant genre painters who worked in The Hague (c.1860–c.1900). They were influenced by the Barbizon School, and produced realistic paintings of their locale, with particular attention paid to light effects. Leading members included Josef Israëls (1824–1911), Johannes Bosboom (1817–91), and Anton Mauve (1838–88).

ha-ha[1] *or* **ha ha** *interj.* a standardised way of representing the sound of laughter. [imitative]

ha-ha[2] *noun* a ditch, often with a low wall inside it, which divides areas of land and forms a barrier or obstacle without interrupting the view. [from French; possibly from the supposed cry made when discovering one]

Hahnemann, (Christian Friedrich) Samuel (1755–1843) German physician, born in Meissen. He studied at Leipzig, and for 10 years practised medicine. The founder of homeo-pathy, his experiments led him to the conclusion that drugs produce a very similar condition in healthy persons to that which they relieve in the sick; this was the origin of his famous principle, *similia similibus curantur* (like cures like). His methods caused him to be prosecuted in every town in which he tried to settle, although during retirement in Paris he pursued a very lucrative practice.

Haida a Pacific Northwest Coast Native American group in Queen Charlotte Island, British Columbia, famous for their wood carvings, totem poles, and canoes. They traditionally lived by fishing and hunting, and held potlatch ceremonies, distributing ceremonial goods. The present-day population (including the Tlingit) is c.7 500.

Haidar Ali *or* **Hyder Ali** (1722–82) Indian Muslim ruler of Mysore, born in Budikote, Mysore. Having conquered Calicut and fought the Marathas, he waged two wars against the British, in the first of which (1767–9) he won several victories. In 1779 he and his son Tippoo again attacked the British, initially with great success, but in 1781–2 he was defeated.

Haifa *or* **Hefa** **1** POP (1990e) 224 000, the third largest city in Israel and an industrial centre and seaport. It is situated in Haifa district, in the NW part of the country. NOTABLE FEATURES Bahai Shrine; Persian Gardens. **2** a district in NW Israel with Haifa as its capital.

Haig, Alexander (Meigs) (1924–) US soldier and politician, born in Philadelphia. He held a number of army staff and field positions, served in the Vietnam War, and was a full general by 1973. He then retired from the army to become White House Chief of Staff during the last days of the Nixon presidency. After returning to active duty he became Supreme NATO Commander, but went back to civilian life as President of United Technologies Corporation. He served President Reagan as Secretary of State in 1981–2, and unsuccessfully sought the Republican nomination for the presidency in 1988.

Haig, Douglas, 1st Earl Haig of Bemersyde (1861–1928) Scottish soldier, born in Edinburgh. He obtained a commission in the 7th Hussars, and served in Egypt, South Africa, and India. In 1914 he led the 1st Army Corps in France, and in 1915 became Commander of the British Expeditionary Force. He waged a costly and exhausting war of attrition, for which he was much criticized, but led the final successful offensive (Aug 1918). In postwar years he devoted himself to the care of ex-servicemen and set up the Royal British Legion.

haiku *noun* (PL. **haiku**) a Japanese poem with three lines of three, five and three syllables. [from Japanese]

hail[1] — *noun* **1** a form of precipitation that consists of roughly spherical pellets of ice, with diameters ranging from 5mm to several centimetres in some cases. **2** a large number or amount of words, questions, missiles, etc. — *verb* **1** *intrans. said of hail* to fall. **2** *intrans., trans.* to shower with words, questions, missiles, etc or come down on in great numbers. [from Anglo-Saxon *hagol*]

hail[2] — *verb* **1** to call out to in order to attract attention, eg to signal to (a taxi) to stop. **2** to greet. **3** to recognize or describe as being or representing: *was hailed as emperor* / *was hailed a hero*. **4** *intrans.* to come from or belong to a place: *hails from Manchester.* — *interj. old use* expressing greeting.
— **within hail** *or* **within hailing distance** close enough to hear when called to.
[from Norse *heill*, healthy]

Haile Selassie I, originally **Prince Ras Tafari Makonnen** (1891–1975) Emperor of Ethiopia (1930–6, 1941–74), born near Harer. He led the revolution in 1916 against Lij Yasu, and as regent and heir to the throne, began to westernize the institutions of Ethiopia. After the Italian conquest of Abyssinia (1935–6) he settled in England, but was restored in 1941 following British liberation. In the early 1960s he helped to establish the Organization of African Unity. The disastrous famine of 1973 led to economic chaos, industrial strikes, and mutiny among the armed forces, and he was deposed in favour of the Crown Prince (1974). Despite accusations of corruption he is still revered by certain groups, notably the Rastafarians.

hail-fellow-well-met *adj.* overpoweringly hearty and friendly.

Hail Mary, Latin **Ave Maria**, also known as the **Angelic Salutation** a prayer to the Virgin Mary, used devotionally since the 11c in the Roman Catholic Church (often sung in Latin), officially recognized in 1568. The first two parts are from scripture (Luke 1.28, 42), and the third was added later.

Hailsham, Quintin (McGarel) Hogg, Baron Hailsham of St Marylebone, 2nd Viscount (1907–) English Conservative politician, born in London. Called to the Bar in 1932, he became an MP (1938), succeeded to his title (1950), and was First Lord of the Admiralty (1956–7), Minister of Education (1957), Lord President of the Council (1957–9, 1960–4), Chairman of the Conservative Party (1957–9), Minister for Science and Technology (1959–64), and Secretary of State for Education and Science (1964). In 1963 he renounced his peerage and re-entered the House of Commons in an unsuccessful bid to become Leader of the Conservative Party. He also held the post of Lord Chancellor (1970–4, 1979–87).

hailstone *noun* a single grain of hail.

hailstorm *noun* a storm during which hail falls heavily.

Hailwood, Mike (Stanley Michael Bailey) (1940–81) English motorcyclist, born in Oxford. He took nine world titles: the 250cc in 1961 and 1966–7, the 350cc in 1966–7, and the 500cc in 1962–5, all using Honda or MV Augusta machines. In addition, he won a record 14 Isle of Man Tourist Trophy (TT) races between 1961 and 1979, and during the 1960s he also had a career in motor racing. He was killed in a car accident.

Hainan Island an island off the S coast of China and a prefecture of Guangdong province. AREA 34 000sq km/13 000sq mi. It is separated from the mainland by the Hainan Strait and rises to 1 879m at Wuzhi Shan. It was opened to tourism and foreign trade in 1982. CHIEF TOWNS Haikou, Dongfang, Yulin. There are reserves of many minerals, including limestone, marble, quartz, china clay, and iron ore.

Haiphong POP (1989) 1.5m, the third largest city in Vietnam. It is a seaport in the N area of the country, in the Red R delta, 88km/55mi SE of Hanoi. The city, which was founded in 1874, was badly bombed in the Vietnam War.

Hair a US rock musical by Galt MacDermot, Gerome Ragni, and James Rado (1967), which shocked with its scene featuring nudity. It was a great success at the time, symbolizing social revolution, but failed when a revival was attempted in 1993.

hair *noun* **1** each of many long threadlike structures that grow out from the skin of mammals, including humans. Hairs contain the fibrous protein keratin, and are produced from bulb-shaped hair follicles within the dermis of the skin. They serve to regulate the body temperature by reducing heat loss from the skin and trapping warm air next to the body, and they also provide camouflage in many animals. **2** a mass of these, especially on a person's head. **3** anything resembling a hair. **4** a thread-like cell growing from the surface of a plant. **5** a hair's-breadth.
— **get in someone's hair** *colloq.* to annoy or irritate them.

a hair of the dog *colloq.* an alcoholic drink taken as a cure for a hangover.

keep one's hair on *colloq.* to remain calm and not get angry.

let one's hair down *colloq.* to enjoy onself without restraint.

make someone's hair curl *colloq.* to shock them.

make someone's hair stand on end *colloq.* to terrify them.

not turn a hair to remain calm.

split hairs to make small or unimportant distinctions or quibbles.

[from Anglo-Saxon *hær*]

hairbrush *noun* a brush for smoothing and arranging one's hair.

haircut *noun* the cutting of a person's hair; the shape or style in which it is cut.

hairdo *noun* (PL. **hairdos**) *colloq.* a style or process of hairdressing; a woman's haircut or style.

hairdresser *noun* **1** a person who cuts, washes and styles hair. **2** a hairdresser's shop.

hairdressing *noun* the art or occupation of a hairdresser.

hairdrier *or* **hairdryer** *noun* an electrical apparatus which dries a person's hair by blowing hot air over it.

hair-grip *noun* a small wire clasp for holding the hair in place.

hairiness *noun* being hairy.

hairless *adj.* **1** having no hair. **2** *colloq.* very angry.

hairline *noun* the line along the forehead where the hair begins to grow.

hairnet *noun* a fine-meshed net, usually with an outer band of elastic for fitting around the head, worn to keep the hair in place.

hair-piece *noun* a piece of false hair worn over a bald area on one's head, or to make one's own hair appear thicker.

hairpin *noun* a thin flat U-shaped piece of wire for keeping the hair in place.

hairpin bend a sharp and often U-shaped bend, especially on a mountain road.

hair-raising *adj.* extremely frightening.

hair's-breadth *noun* a very small distance or margin.

hair shirt a shirt made of a thick, coarse, uncomfortable cloth woven from hair, worn by religious people as a penance.

hair-slide *noun* a small metal or plastic clip, used to keep the hair in place.

hair-splitting *noun* the act of insisting on considering small, unimportant distinctions.

hairspray *noun* liquid sprayed from a can as a fine mist, used to keep the hair in place.

hair-spring *noun* a very small spring which regulates a watch.

hairstyle *noun* the way in which a person's hair is cut or shaped.

hairy *adj.* (**hairier**, **hairiest**) **1** covered in hair. **2** *colloq.* dangerous, frightening and exciting.

Haiti, official name **Republic of Haiti**, French **République d'Haiti** POP (1992e) 6.8m, a republic in the West Indies, divided into five departments. AREA 27 750sq km/10 712sq mi. It occupies the W third of the island of Hispaniola in the Caribbean Sea, 80km/50mi E of Cuba. CAPITAL Port-au-Prince. CHIEF TOWNS Port-de-Paix, Cap-Haïtien, Gonaïves, Les Cayes, Jacmel, Jérémie. TIME ZONE GMT –5. The population is mainly of African descent (95%); Roman Catholicism and voodoo are the chief religions. OFFICIAL LANGUAGES French, Creole. CURRENCY the gourde. PHYSICAL DESCRIPTION consists of two mountainous peninsulas (the Massif du Nord in the N and the Massif de la Hotte in the S), separated by a deep structural depression, the Plaine du Cul-de-

Sac; to the E is the Massif de la Selle, with Haiti's highest peak, La Selle (2 680m); Haiti includes the islands of Gonâve off the W coast and Tortue off the N coast. CLIMATE tropical maritime; average monthly temperatures range from 24°C to 29°C; annual average rainfall for the N coast and mountains is 1 475–1 950mm, but only 500mm on the W side; the wet season is May–Sep; hurricanes are common. HISTORY Hispaniola was discovered by Columbus in 1492; Haiti was created when the W third of the island was ceded to France in 1697; a slave rebellion was followed by independence in 1804 with an emperor until 1859, when it became a republic; united with Santo Domingo (Dominican Republic) from 1822 until 1844; under US occupation from 1915 until 1934; the Duvalier family had absolute power from 1957 until 1986, their rule being enforced by a civilian militia known as the Tonton Macante; following a military coup in 1991 the UN imposed a trade embargo on Haiti which has had a severe effect on the economy; under military rule the Tonton Macante were revived under the name *attachés*. ECONOMY based on agriculture; large plantations grow coffee, sugar, sisal; rice, bananas, corn, sorghum, cocoa; sugar refining; textiles; flour milling; cement; bauxite; light assembly industries; lobster fishing; tourism.

Haiti

Hajj one of the Five Pillars of Islam, it is a formal pilgrimage to the holy city of Mecca during the Islamic month of Dhu-ul-Hijja. [from Arabic *hajj*, pilgrimage]

hajji *noun* a Muslim who has been on pilgrimage to Mecca.

hake *noun* (PL. **hake**, **hakes**) a sea-fish like cod, used for food.

Hakluyt, Richard (c.1552–1616) English geographer, born in Hertfordshire. He became the first ordained lecturer in geography at Oxford. He wrote widely on exploration and navigation, including his major three-volume work, *Principal Navigations, Voyages, and Discoveries of the English Nation* (1598–1600). He also introduced the use of globes into English schools. The *Hakluyt Society* was instituted in 1846.

Halakhah the complete body of laws and decrees contained in the Talmudic and Rabbinic literature of Judaism, which governs religious or civil practice in the Jewish community. It is distinguished from the *Haggadah*, which is not concerned with religious law and which includes fables and prayers. [Hebrew, = the way]

halal *noun* meat from an animal which has been killed in a way approved of by Muslim holy law. [from Arabic *halal*, lawful]

halation *noun* **1** *Photog.* the spread and blurring of a photographic image of a bright object, caused by light scattered in the photographic emulsion and reflected from the rear surface of the base material. In some films, this rear surface is coated with a thin black layer to reduce the effect. **2** a bright area around a bright spot on a fluorescent screen. [from HALO]

halberd *noun Hist.* a long spear with an axe-blade and a pick at one end. [from Old German *helm*, handle + *barde*, hatchet]

halcyon *adj.* peaceful, calm, and happy: *halcyon days*. [from Greek *halkyon*, kingfisher, from the

ancient belief that it nested on the sea and that the sea remained calm while it did so]

Halcyone *or* **Alycone** in Greek mythology, a daughter of Aeolus, who married Ceyx, son of the Morning Star. Either for impiety, or because she mourned his death at sea, both were changed into sea-birds (halcyons, or kingfishers), who are fabled to calm the sea. The name is sometimes applied to one of the Pleiades.

Haldane, J(ohn) B(urdon) S(anderson) (1892–1964) British–Indian biologist, born in Oxford. He was professor in London from 1933 until 1957, when he emigrated to India. He wrote widely on biology and genetics, and was well known for his popularizations; he was also Chairman of the editorial board of the *Daily Worker* (1940–9), but left the Communist Party in 1956 following the Lysenko controversy.

Haldane, Richard Burdon Haldane, 1st Viscount (1856–1928) Scottish politician, philosopher, and lawyer, born in Edinburgh. Called to the Bar in 1879, he entered parliament that year as a Liberal. As Secretary of State for War (1905–12), he remodelled the army, founded the Territorial Army, and made the plans by which British mobilization took place (1914). He was Lord Chancellor (1912–15, and, under Labour, in 1924) and ranked high as a judge. He also wrote on the philosophical aspects of relativity, and helped to found the London School of Economics (1895).

Hale, George Ellery (1868–1938) US astronomer, born in Chicago. Professor at the University of Chicago and Director of the Yerkes and Mount Wilson observatories, he initiated the construction of some of the world's largest telescopes. His scientific work at Mount Wilson included his discovery and measurement of magnetic fields in sunspots.

hale *adj.* strong and healthy: *hale and hearty*. [from Anglo-Saxon *hal*]

Haleakala Crater *or* **Kolekole** a dormant volcano on E Maui I, Hawaii, USA. HEIGHT 3 055m. It contains the largest inactive crater in the world, with an area of 49sq km/19sq mi, length 12km/8mi, width 4km/2mi, circumference 32km/20mi, and depth 600m. The volcano is part of Haleakala National Park.

Hales, Stephen (1677–1761) English botanist and chemist, born in Beaksbourn, Canterbury. Perpetual curate of Teddington from 1709, his *Vegetable Staticks* (1727) was the foundation of plant physiology, setting standards in the methodology of biological experimentation. In *Haemastaticks* (1733) he discussed the circulation of the blood and blood pressure; his other writings covered a wide range of fields, and he was credited with a number of inventions.

half — *noun* (PL. **halves**) **1** one of two equal parts which together form a whole. **2** the fraction equal to one divided by two. **3** *colloq.* a half pint, especially of beer. **4** one of two equal periods of play in a match. **5** a half-price ticket, especially for a child or old person. — *adj.* forming or equal to half. — *adv.* **1** to the extent or amount of one half: *half finished*. **2** almost; partly; to some extent: *half dead with exhaustion*. **3** 30 minutes past the hour stated.

— ... and a half *colloq.* a very good...: *she's a singer and a half*.

by half *colloq.* excessively: *too clever by half*.

by halves without being thorough.

go halves to share the cost or expenses.

not half *colloq.* very; very much.

one's better half *colloq.* one's husband, wife, or partner.

[from Anglo-Saxon *healf*]

half-and-half *adv., adj.* in equal parts.

halfback *noun* in football, hockey, etc, a player or position immediately behind the forwards.

half-baked *adj. colloq.*, said of an idea, scheme, etc not properly or completely thought out; hasty and unrealistic.

half-board *noun Brit.* the provision of a bed, breakfast, and one other meal in a hotel or boarding house.

half-breed *often offensive — noun* a person having parents of different races, especially one black parent and one white. — *adj.* concerning or relating to half-breeds. See also HALF-CASTE.

half-brother *or* **half-sister** *noun* a brother or sister with whom one has only one parent in common.

half-caste *often offensive — noun* a person having parents of different races, especially an Indian mother and a European father. — *adj.* concerning or relating to half-castes. See also HALF-BREED.

half-cell *noun Chem.* half of an electrolytic cell, consisting of one electrode (a positively charged anode or a negatively charged cathode) immersed in an electrolyte consisting of a solution of ions.

half-crown *or* **half-a-crown** *noun Hist.* a British coin worth two shillings and sixpence (12½p).

half-cut *adj. slang* drunk.

half-day *noun* a day on which one only works, etc in the morning or in the afternoon.

half-hearted *adj.* not eager; without enthusiasm.

half-heartedly *adv.* in a half-hearted way.

half-heartedness *noun* being half-hearted.

half-hitch *noun* a simple knot or noose formed by passing the end of the rope through a loop made in the rope.

half-hour *noun* a period of thirty minutes.

half-hourly *adj., adv.* done, occurring, etc every half-hour.

half-life *noun Physics* the period of time required for half the original number of atoms of a radioactive substance to undergo spontaneous radioactive decay. Some materials have half-lives of a few seconds, whereas others (eg some isotopes of plutonium) have half-lives of millions of years.

half-light *noun* dull light, especially at dawn or dusk.

half-marathon *noun* a long-distance race over 21km (13mi), half the distance of a modern marathon.

half mast the position half way up a flagpole, where flags are flown as a mark of respect for a dead person.

half measures actions which are not sufficient or thorough enough to deal with a problem.

half-moon *noun* 1 the moon when only half of it can be seen from the Earth. 2 the time when this occurs. 3 anything shaped like a half-moon.

half nelson a hold in wrestling in which one puts one's arm under one's opponent's arm from behind, and pushes on the back of his or her neck with one's palm.

halfpenny *or* **ha'penny** *noun Hist.* a British coin worth half a penny.

halfpennyworth *or* **hap'orth** *noun Brit.* 1 *Hist.* an amount of something costing a halfpenny. 2 *colloq.* a very small amount: *not make a hap'orth of difference.*

half-price *adj., adv.* at half the usual price.

half-sister see HALF-BROTHER.

half-term *noun Brit.* a short holiday halfway through a school term.

half-timbered *adj.,* said of a house, *etc* built with a timber frame with brick or plaster filling.

half-time *noun* an interval between the two halves of a match.

half-tone *noun* an illustration produced using a method of printing in which black and white

dots of different sizes create various shades of grey.

half-track *noun* a usually military vehicle with wheels in front and caterpillar tracks behind.

half-truth *noun* a statement which is only partly true.

half volley *Cricket, Tennis* a stroke in which the ball is hit immediately after it bounces or as it bounces.

halfway *adj., adv.* 1 of, at, or to a point equally far from two others: *halfway between France and England.* 2 in, of, or into an incomplete manner. — **meet someone halfway** to compromise with someone.

halfway house 1 *Hist.* an inn where one can rest halfway through a journey. 2 *colloq.* something which is between two extremes, and which has some features of each. 3 a home where former prisoners or patients with mental illnesses stay so they may get used to life outside the prison or hospital.

halfwit *noun* a foolish or stupid person.

halfwitted *adj.* foolish, stupid.

halfwittedly *adv.* stupidly, foolishly.

half-yearly *adj., adv.* done, occurring, etc every six months.

halibut *noun* (PL. **halibut**) either of two species of very large flatfish found in the cold deep waters of the North Atlantic and North Pacific, respectively. It is a commercially important food fish. [from Middle English *halybutte,* from *haly, holy + butt,* flat fish, so-called because it was eaten on holy days]

Halicarnassus an ancient Greek city-state founded by the Dorians on the coast of SW Asia Minor, now Bodrum in Turkey. It was the birthplace of Herodotus, the Greek historian, and the site of the Tomb of Mausolus.

halide *noun Chem.* a chemical compound consisting of a halogen and another chemical element (eg hydrogen) or functional group (eg a hydrocarbon group). Halides may be fluorides (containing fluorine), chlorides (containing chlorine), bromides (containing bromine), or iodides (containing iodine). [from Greek *hals,* salt]

Halidon Hill, Battle of a battle (1333) between England and Scotland during the Scottish Wars of Independence. Edward III of England turned from besieging Berwick-upon-Tweed, and inflicted a massive defeat on the Scottish relief army.

Halifax, Charles Montagu, 1st Earl of (1661–1715) English Whig statesman, born in Horton, Northamptonshire. He became MP for Maldon (1688) and a Lord of the Treasury (1692), and he established the National Debt and the Bank of England (1694). As Chancellor of the Exchequer (1694–5), he introduced a new coinage. In 1697 he was First Lord of the Treasury and Leader of the House of Commons, but resigned when the Tories came to power in 1699. On Queen Anne's death he became a member of the Council of Regency, and on George I's arrival (1714) was made an earl and Prime Minister. He was also a patron of letters and a poet.

Halifax, Edward Frederick Lindley Wood, 1st Earl of (1881–1959) English Conservative politician, born at Powderham Castle, Devon. He became an MP in 1910, and held a range of political posts before he was Viceroy of India (1926–31). He was Foreign Secretary (1938–40) under Neville Chamberlain, whose 'appeasement' policy he implemented, and Ambassador to the USA (1941–6).

Halifax, George Savile, 1st Marquis of (1633–95) English statesman, born in Thornhill, Yorkshire. He was created viscount (1668) for his share in the Restoration, and in 1672 was made a marquis and Lord Privy Seal.

On the accession of James II (1685) he became President of the Council, but he was dismissed soon after for opposing the repeal of the Test and Habeas Corpus Acts. He was one of the three Commissioners appointed to negotiate with William of Orange after he landed in England (1688). He gave allegiance to William and resumed the office of Lord Privy Seal, but joined the Opposition and resigned his post in 1689.

Halifax POP (1981) 77 000, a town on the R Calder in West Yorkshire, N England, lying 11km/7mi SW of Bradford. In medieval times it was noted for its cloth manufacturing and textiles remain an important industry in the town.

Halifax POP (1991) 115 000, the seaport capital of Nova Scotia province, SE Canada. It is a major transatlantic port and rail terminus, joined to Dartmouth by two suspension bridges. British forces founded the port as a military and naval base in 1749 and used it notably in the American Revolution and the War of 1812. A British garrison was stationed here until 1906. In both World Wars it again served as a naval base and convoy terminal, and was the scene of harbour disasters in 1917 and 1945. Victims of the *Titanic* disaster were buried here in 1912. NOTABLE FEATURES the Historic Properties area (built in the 1800s) includes Collins Bank and the Privateers' Warehouse; Citadel Hill is a National Historic Park from where a cannon is fired daily at noon; Maritime Museum of the Atlantic.

halite *noun Geol.* the mineral form of sodium chloride. — Also called *rock salt.*

halitosis *noun* unpleasant-smelling breath. [from Latin *halitus,* breath + -OSIS]

Hall, Sir Peter (Reginald Frederick) (1930–) English theatre, opera, and film director, born in Bury St Edmunds, Suffolk. His many positions in the theatre world include artistic director of the Elizabethan Theatre Company (1953), founder of the International Playwrights' Theatre (1957), and director of the Royal Shakespeare Company, where he remained as managing director of the company's theatres in Stratford and London until 1968, making his name by giving many of the classics a social context. He was also director of the Covent Garden Opera (1969–71) and of the National Theatre (1973–88), before founding the Peter Hall Company (1988).

hall *noun* 1 a room or passage just inside the entrance to a house, usually allowing access to other rooms and the stairs. 2 a building or large room, used for concerts, public meetings, etc. 3 a large country house. 4 *Brit.* (**hall of residence**) a building where university or college students live. 5 *Brit.* the dining-room in a college or university; dinner in such a dining-room. [from Anglo-Saxon *heall*]

Halle *or* **Halle an der Saale** POP (1991e) 310 000, a town in Saxony-Anhalt state, SE Germany. It lies on the R Saale, NW of Leipzig. The composer George Frideric Handel was born here in 1685.

Hallé, Sir Charles (1819–95) German-born British pianist and conductor, born in Hagen, Westphalia. From 1840 he studied in Paris, where his reputation was established by his concerts of classical music. Driven to England by the Revolution of 1848, he settled in Manchester, where in 1858 he founded his famous orchestra.

hallelujah see ALLELUIA.

Hallé Orchestra a British orchestra, founded (1858) by Sir Charles Hallé. Based in Manchester, it became an international success under Sir John Barbirolli.

Haller, (Viktor) Albrecht von (1708–77) Swiss anatomist, botanist, physiologist, and poet, born in Bern. As professor at the University of Göttingen, he organized a botanical garden, an anatomical museum and theatre, and an obstetrical school; he also helped to found the Academy of Sciences, wrote anatomical and physiological works, and took an active part in the literary movement. In 1753 he resigned and returned to Bern, where he became a magistrate and director of a saltworks.

Halles, Les the former wholesale food-markets and, by association, the district in central Paris in which they were situated for over 700 years. In 1969 the markets were moved to the suburbs, and a multilevel shopping complex (Forum des Halles) was constructed on the site.

Halley, Edmond (1656–1742) English astronomer and mathematician, born in London. His calculations of the orbits of comets enabled him to predict correctly the return of a comet that had been observed in 1583, and is now named after him. He made many further significant discoveries about the Earth and the solar system, and funded the publication of Isaac Newton's *Principia* (1687). He was appointed professor at Oxford (1703), and in 1720 became Astronomer Royal of England.

Halley's comet *Astron.* a large bright comet that takes about 76 years to orbit the Sun (in the opposite direction to the planets). It was first recorded in 239 BC, and last appeared in 1986. [named after Edmond Halley]

halliard see HALYARD.

hallmark — *noun* 1 an official mark on a gold or silver article guaranteeing its quality. 2 a typical or distinctive feature, especially of quality. — *verb* to stamp with a hallmark.
◇ Hallmarks are struck on all modern and much old English, Scottish, and Irish silver and gold, and since 1975 on platinum. They date from 1300, when a decree was made that no silver or gold items should leave the smith until they had been assayed (tested for standard and quality) and marked with a leopard's head. British hallmarks have four elements: the standard mark indicating the purity of the metal, the assay office's mark, the date mark, and the maker's mark.

Jonathon Reid, Boston USA 1725–40 | Edinburgh | Florence 17th–18th c | Lille 1750

London | Rome late 17th c | Stockholm 1500–1600 | Vienna 1570–1674

hallmarks

hallo see HELLO.

halloo — *noun, interj.* a cry encouraging hunting dogs or calling for attention. — *verb intrans.* to cry halloo, especially to dogs at a hunt. [imitative]

hallow — *verb* to make or regard as holy. — *noun old use* a saint. See HALLOWE'EN. [from Anglo-Saxon *halgian*]

hallowed *adj.* holy, revered.

Hallowe'en *noun* the evening of 31 October, the eve of All Saints' Day. [from *all hallow even*, all saints' eve]

hallstand *noun* a piece of furniture in the hall of a house, on which coats, hats, etc are hung.

Hallstatt POP (1991) 1 000, a small market town in Oberösterreich state, N Austria, lying on the SW shore of Hallstätter See, 50km/30mi SE of Salzburg. It gave its name to the Hallstatt period, the first phase of the European Iron Age (8c–4c BC). This period is characterized by goods

from the prehistoric burial tombs found in the area.

hallucinate *verb intrans.* to seem to see or hear something which does not really exist. [from Latin *hallucinari*, to wander in the mind]

hallucination *noun* the apparent perception of something that is not actually present, ie that has no objective reality. Hallucinations may involve any of the senses, and may be caused by mental disorders (eg schizophrenia), drugs (eg LSD or cannabis), extreme fatigue, fever, hypothermia, or sensory deprivation.

hallucinatory *adj.* characterized by or involving hallucinations.

hallucinogen *noun* a drug that causes hallucinations. [from HALLUCINATE + -GEN]

hallucinogenic *adj.* causing hallucinations.

hallway *noun* an entrance hall.

halma *noun* a game for two players played on a board of 256 squares, in which each player attempts to move pieces into vacant squares immediately behind the opposing pieces. [from Greek *halma*, jump, leap]

Halmahera, formerly **Djailolo** POP (1980) 93 895, the largest island in the Moluccas, Indonesia. AREA 17 936sq km/6 923sq mi. It lies on the Equator, SW of the Philippines. PHYSICAL DESCRIPTION forested mountain chains, including active volcanoes. ECONOMY hunting; fishing; rice; coconuts.

halo — *noun* (PL. **halos, haloes**) 1 a ring of light around the head of a saint, angel, etc in paintings, etc. 2 the glory or glamour attaching to a person or thing. 3 *Astron.* a luminous white or rainbow-coloured ring sometimes seen around a celestial body, especially the Sun or Moon, caused by the reflection or refraction of light by ice crystals in the Earth's atmosphere. — *verb* (**haloes, haloed**) to put a halo round. [from Greek *halos*, circular threshing floor]

halogen *noun Chem.* any of the five chemical elements in group VII of the periodic table, ie fluorine, chlorine, bromine, iodine, or astatine. Halogens are non-metallic substances that react with most metals to form salts, and also form a wide range of organic compounds. [from Greek *hals*, salt + -GEN]

halogenation *noun Chem.* any chemical reaction in which an atom of a halogen (fluorine, chlorine, bromine, or iodine) is introduced into a compound.

halophyte *noun Bot.* a plant that can tolerate a very salty environment, such as a salt marsh or mudflat. [from Greek *hals* salt]

Hals, Frans (c.1580–1666) Dutch portrait and genre painter, born probably in Antwerp. He painted several portraits of militia groups, notable for their lively facial expressions, and bold use of colour (eg *The Banquet of the Officers of the St George Militia Company*, Haarlem, 1616). After 1640, his mood became more contemplative and sombre, as in *Man in a Slouch Hat* (c.1660–6, Kassel). Other works include *The Laughing Cavalier* (1624, Wallace Collection, London), *Gypsy Girl* (c.1628–30, Louvre), and the group portraits *Regents* and *Regentesses of the Old Men's Alms House* (1664, Haarlem).

Hal Saflieni Hypogeum a prehistoric rock-cut catacomb for multiple burial in Paola, SE Malta. The excavation, which was in use throughout the Copper Age, consists of three layers of tomb-chambers dug into a mound of soft limestone and linked by halls and corridors. It was discovered in 1902. It is a World Heritage site.

Hälsingborg see HELSINGBORG.

Halstaat a lakeside village 50km/30mi E of Salzburg, upper Austria, excavated from 1846 to 1864. It is notable for its prehistoric cemetery of 3 000 graves spanning the transition between the

central European Bronze and Iron Ages. Since 1872, the term *Halstaat* has been used to describe the European early Iron Age, 7c–6c BC.

halt — *noun* 1 a short or temporary stop. 2 *Brit.* a small railway station without a building. — *verb intrans., trans.* to stop or cause to stop. — **call a halt to something** to put an end to it. [from German *Halt*, stoppage]

halter — *noun* a rope or strap for holding and leading a horse by its head. — *verb* to put a halter on. [from Anglo-Saxon *hælfter*]

halterneck *noun* a woman's top or dress held in place by a strap which goes round her neck, leaving the shoulders and back bare.

Haltia or Halti, Mount, Finnish **Haltiatunturi**, Swedish **Hadefjall** a mountain in Lapland province, NW Finland, on the Norwegian frontier. HEIGHT 1 328m.

halting *adj.* pausing a lot; hesitant. [from Anglo-Saxon *healt*, lame]

haltingly *adv.* 1 hesitatingly. 2 lamely.

halva or halvah *noun* a sweetmeat, of E Mediterranean and Middle Eastern origin, containing sesame seeds, honey, nuts, rosewater, and saffron. [from Yiddish *halva*; ultimately from Arabic *halwa*, sweetmeat]

halve *verb* 1 to divide into two equal parts or halves. 2 to reduce (costs, problems, etc) by half. 3 *Golf* to draw a hole or match with one's opponent.

halves see HALF.

halyard or halliard *noun* a rope for raising or lowering a sail or flag on a ship. [from Middle English *halier*]

Ham a biblical character, one of Noah's three sons, the brother of Shem and Japheth, and father of Canaan. He helped Noah to build the ark, but after the Flood his son Canaan was cursed by God because Ham had seen his father Noah asleep naked (Genesis 9.22). This curse may be an attempt to explain the later subjugation of the Canaanites to Israel due to Canaanite sexual perversion.

ham[1] *noun* 1 the top part of the back leg of a pig, salted and smoked and used as food. 2 the back of the thigh. [from Anglo-Saxon *hamm*]

ham[2] *colloq.* — *noun* 1 a bad actor, especially one who overacts and exaggerates. 2 an amateur radio operator. — *verb intrans., trans.* (**hammed, hamming**) (*also* **ham something up**) to overact or exaggerate. [from *hamfatter*, a third-rate minstrel]

hamadryad *noun* 1 *Greek and Roman Mythol.* a nymph who lives in a tree and dies when it dies. 2 a king cobra. [from Greek *hama*, together + *drys*, oak tree]

hamadryas baboon, a baboon native to NE Africa and SW Arabia, having silver-brown fur (which is long and thick over the male's head and shoulders), a naked face, and a long tail. It inhabits rocky hillsides, and was sacred to the ancient Egyptians.— Also called *sacred baboon*.

Hamas (Islamic Resistance Movement) a militant Islamic organization which opposes the attempted peaceful settlement between Israeli and PLO leaders.

Hamburg 1 POP (1991e) 1.6m, the capital of Hamburg state, N Germany. It lies on the R Elbe, 109km/68mi from its mouth, and has an area of 755sq km/291sq mi (which includes the islands of Neuwerk and Scharhörn). After Berlin, it is the second largest city in Germany, and it is the country's largest port. HISTORY founded by Charlemagne in the 9c; an alliance was formed with Lübeck in the 12c, leading to the Hanseatic League; the city was badly bombed in World War II. It was the birthplace of the composers Mendelssohn (1809) and Johannes Brahms (1833). NOTABLE FEATURES St Michael's Church

(1750–62); town hall (1886–97); art gallery; opera house. **2** a state in N Germany.

hamburger *noun* a flat, round cake of finely chopped beef, usually fried and served in a soft roll. [named after Hamburg in Germany]

Hamersley Range a mountain range in NW Western Australia, S of the Fortescue R. It extends for 257km/160mi from the Robe R as far as Newman and rises to 1 244m at Mt Meharry. The area is a great source of iron. A national park is contained within the range.

ham-fisted *or* **ham-handed** *adj. colloq.* clumsy.

Hamilton, Alexander (1757–1804) US statesman, born on the West Indian island of Nevis. He fought in the American Revolution and became Washington's aide-de-camp (1777–81). After the war he studied law, and in 1782 entered Congress, where he was instrumental in the movement to establish the USA in its present political form. As Secretary of the Treasury (1789–95), he restored the country's finances, and he was Leader of the Federalist Party until his death. His efforts to suppress the ambition of his rival Aaron Burr led to a duel in New York City, in which Hamilton was killed.

Hamilton, Lady Emma, originally **Emily Lyon** (c.1765–1815) mistress of Lord Nelson, born (probably) in Ness, Cheshire. In 1782 she accepted the protection of Charles Greville, but in 1786 accepted that of his uncle, Sir William Hamilton (1730–1803), whom she married (1791). She first met Nelson in 1793, and bore him a daughter (1801). After his death she squandered her inheritance from her husband and was arrested for debt (1813).

Hamilton, James Hamilton, 1st Duke of (1606–49) Scottish Royalist soldier, who commanded during the English Civil War. He fought during the Thirty Years War, leading an army in support of Gustavus Adolphus (1631–2), and later took part in the contest between Charles I and the Covenanters. He led a Scottish army into England (1643), but was defeated by Cromwell at Preston, and beheaded.

Hamilton, Sir William Rowan (1805–65) Irish mathematician, born in Dublin. In 1827, while still an undergraduate, he was appointed professor at Dublin and Irish Astronomer Royal. After working on optics, he developed a new approach to dynamics which became of considerable importance in the 20c development of quantum mechanics. In 1843 he introduced 'quaternions', a generalization of complex numbers for which the commutative law does not hold (ie A×B does not equal B×A); this discovery was the forerunner of much modern algebra.

Hamilton POP (1981) 52 000, the capital of Hamilton district, Strathclyde, W central Scotland, 17km/11mi SE of Glasgow. NOTABLE FEATURES Cameronians Regimental Museum; Hamilton District Museum; Old Parish Church (1734); Strathclyde Country Park is nearby, containing Hamilton Mausoleum (built in the 1840s).

Hamilton POP (1991) 319 000, a town in SE Ontario, SE Canada. It lies on Hamilton Harbour at the head of L Ontario, 58km/36km SW of Toronto. It was founded in 1813 and the Battle of Stoney Creek took place here in the same year.

Hamilton POP (1991) 149 000, a city on North I, New Zealand. It is situated on the R Waikato and is New Zealand's largest inland city. The area is noted for horse breeding and agricultural research. NOTABLE FEATURES Waikato Art Museum; Turangawaewae Marae (home of the Maori Queen) to the N.

Hamilton POP (1991e) 1 000, the capital of Bermuda, on Great Bermuda I. It is a resort and port with a deep harbour approached by a long, intricate channel through Two Rock Passage. The port has modern berthing and container facilities. Hamilton was founded in 1612 and has

been the capital since 1815. NOTABLE FEATURE cathedral.

Hamina, Swedish **Fredrikshamn** POP (1990) 10 000, a major port in Kymi province, SE Finland. It is situated on a peninsula in the bay of Vehkalahti, in the Gulf of Finland. The town was established in 1653, and named after King Fredrik I of Sweden in 1753. In 1809 the Treaty of Hamina ceded the whole of Finland to Russia.

Hamish a male first name, usually confined to Scotland. [derived from the vocative case *Sheumais* of the Gaelic for JAMES]

Hamitic — *noun* a group of N African languages, including ancient Egyptian and Berber. *adj.* relating to this group of languages. [named after *Ham*, one of Noah's sons, supposed founder of a race of people in N Africa]

hamlet *noun* a small village. [from Old French *hamelet*]

Hamlet, Prince of Denmark a play by William Shakespeare (1600–1). It is a tragedy (considered by many to be Shakespeare's greatest) focusing on Hamlet's desire for vengeance following the murder of his father and his mother's remarriage to his uncle, the suspected killer. It has been filmed five times; Laurence Olivier played the title role and directed the 1948 version, winning an Oscar for best actor and another for best film. The most recent version (1990) was directed by Franco Zeffirelli and starred Mel Gibson.

Hammarskjöld, Dag (Hjalmar Agne Carl) (1905–61) Swedish politician, born in Jönköping. After teaching at Stockholm University, he was secretary (1935) then Chairman (1941–8) of the Bank of Sweden, and Swedish Foreign Minister (1951–3). As Secretary-General of the United Nations (1953–61), he helped to set up the Emergency Force in Sinai and Gaza (1956), and worked for conciliation in the Middle East (1957–8). He was awarded the 1961 Nobel Peace Prize after his death in an air crash in Zambia, while involved in negotiations over the Congo crisis.

Hammer, Armand (1899–1990) US business executive, born in New York. He served with the US Army Medical Corps (1918–19). He later turned to business, and exported grain to the former USSR in exchange for furs. In 1925 he founded the A Hammer Pencil Company, operating in New York, London, and Moscow, and in 1957 he bought the Occidental Petroleum Corporation of California. He acted as intermediary between the USSR and US governments on a number of occasions (eg the Soviet troop withdrawal from Afghanistan in 1987).

hammer — *noun* **1** a tool with a heavy metal head on the end of a handle, used for driving nails into wood, breaking hard substances, etc. **2** the part of a bell, piano, clock, etc that hits against some other part, making a noise. **3** the part of a gun, attached to the trigger, which causes the bullet to be fired. **4** a metal ball on a long, flexible steel chain, thrown in competitions; the sport of throwing this. **5** an auctioneer's gavel. — *verb* (**hammered**, **hammering**) **1** *trans.* to hit with a hammer. **2** *trans., intrans.* (**hammer something** *or* **hammer at** *or* **on something**) to strike it loudly and repeatedly. **3** (**hammer something in**) to drive or force it in with, or as if with, a hammer. **4** *Brit. colloq.* to criticize or beat severely. **5** *colloq.* to defeat. **6** *intrans.* (**hammer at** *or* **away at something**) to work constantly at it: *hammer away at the problem.*
— **come** *or* **go under the hammer** to be sold at auction.

hammer and tongs *colloq.* with a lot of noise and violence.

hammer something out to produce an agreement, etc with a great deal of effort and discussion.

[from Anglo-Saxon *hamor*]

◇ The athletics field event (hammer throw) uses a 7.6kg hammer, which is thrown with both

hands from within the confines of a 2.13m circle. In competition, six throws are allowed, the aim being to throw it as far as possible. Because of the dangers, the throwing circle is protected by a wire cage.

hammer and sickle *noun* the sign of a hammer and a sickle laid across each other, used as a symbol of communism.

hammer-beam roof *Archit.* a type of timber roof consisting of arched ribs, supported on hammer beams at their feet, and carrying the principal rafters. Hammer beams are short cantilevered beams projecting inwards from the junction of wall and roof and strengthened by curved struts underneath. An example of an elaborately ornamented hammer-beam roof is the Great Hall of Hampton Court Palace built by Henry VIII in 1531–6.

hammerhead *noun* a shark with a hammer-shaped head.

hammering *noun Brit. colloq.* a severe beating.

Hammerklavier Sonata Beethoven's Piano Sonata No.29 in B flat (Op 106, 1818). [from 19c German, = pianoforte]

Hammerstein II, Oscar (1895–1960) US librettist, born in New York City. With composer Jerome Kern, he wrote *Show Boat* (1928), a landmark of musical theatre, with such songs as 'Ol' Man River' and 'Only Make Believe'. Later, with composer Richard Rodgers (1902–79), he wrote such great musicals as *Oklahoma!* (1943), *South Pacific* (1949), *The King and I* (1951), and *The Sound of Music* (1959).

hammer-toe *noun* a condition in which a toe is permanently bent.

Hammett, (Samuel) Dashiell (1894–1961) US writer, born in St Mary's County, Maryland. His early career was spent with the Pinkerton Detective Agency in New York, after which he became the first US author of authentic 'private eye' crime stories. The best-known of his novels (all of which have been filmed) are *The Maltese Falcon* (1930) and *The Thin Man* (1934).

hammock *noun* a piece of canvas or a net hung by the corners and used as a bed, eg in a ship. [from Spanish *hamaca*]

Hammond, Dame Joan (1912–) New Zealand-born Australian soprano, born in Christchurch. Originally a violinist, she was also a champion golfer and swimmer (up to 1935), but when an arm injury forced her to give up playing, she turned to singing. She made her operatic début in 1939 and toured widely, receiving acclaim particularly for her Puccini roles. Following her retiral from singing (1971), she became artistic director of the Victoria Opera Company (1971–6) and head of vocal studies at the Victorian College of the Arts.

Hammurabi (18c BC) Amorite king of Babylon (c.1792–1750 BC), best-known for his Code of Laws. He is also famous for his military conquests that increased Babylonian power in Mesopotamia.

Hamnett, Katharine (1952–) English fashion designer, born in Gravesend, Kent. She studied fashion at art school in London, then worked as a freelance designer, and set up her own company in 1979. She is environmentally concerned, and draws inspiration for her designs from workwear, and from social movements such as the peace movement, which she supports. She made her début in theatrical design for a production of Japanese writer Yukio Mishima's *Madame de Sade* in 1991.

Hampden, John (1594–1643) English Parliamentarian and patriot, born in London. An MP from 1621, his opposition to Charles II's financial measures led to his imprisonment (1627–8), and in 1634 he became famous for refusing to pay Charles's imposed levy for outfitting the navy ('ship money'). A member of both the Short and the Long Parliaments, he was one of the five members whose attempted seizure by Charles (1642) precipitated the Civil War.

Hampden Park a football ground in Glasgow, Scotland, the home of the Scottish national team, and of Queen's Park FC. The current Hampden Park, the third to bear that name, was opened on 31 Oct 1903.

hamper[1] *verb* (**hampered, hampering**) to hinder the progress or movement of. [from Middle English *hampren*]

hamper[2] *noun* **1** a large basket with a lid, used especially for carrying food. **2** *Brit.* the food and drink packed in such a basket. [from Middle English *hanypere*, wicker basket]

Hampi the site of the former Hindu capital of Vijayanagar, near the SW Indian village of Hampi. The city was founded in the 14c, and remained the centre of a Hindu empire until 1565, when it was sacked. It is a World Heritage site.

Hampshire POP (1992e) 1.6m, a county in S England, divided into 13 districts. AREA 3 777sq km/1 458sq mi. It is bounded S by the English Channel, E by West Sussex and Surrey, N by Berkshire, and W by Wiltshire and Dorset; the North Downs cross it in the NW and W, and it is drained by the Test and Itchen rivers; the New Forest lies to the W of Southampton. CHIEF TOWNS Winchester (county town), Portsmouth, Southampton. ECONOMY agriculture; livestock; shipbuilding; oil refining; chemicals; pharmaceuticals; electronics; tourism. NOTABLE FEATURES New Forest; Winchester Cathedral (11c).

Hampton Court the royal residence situated by the R Thames near London. It was built by Cardinal Wolsey, who occupied it until 1529, when it became the residence of British monarchs for over two centuries. Queen Victoria declared it open to the public in 1851, and its gardens and maze are a major tourist attraction.

hamster *noun* any of a family of short-tailed burrowing nocturnal rodents native to Europe and Asia, similar to voles and gerbils, with large cheek pouches in which they store cereal, fruits, roots, leaves, etc, before returning to their underground burrows. The golden hamster is a popular domestic pet and laboratory animal. [from Old German *hamstra*, weevil]

hamstring — *noun Anat.* any of the tendons at the back of the knee which are attached to muscles in the thigh. — *verb* (PAST TENSE AND PAST PARTICIPLE **hamstringed, hamstrung**) **1** to make powerless or hinder. **2** to lame by cutting the hamstring. [from HAM[1]]

Hamsun, Knut, pseudonym of **Knut Pederson** (1859–1952) Norwegian writer, born in Lom in the Gudbrandsdal. He had a variety of jobs before his novel *Hunger* (1890) brought him fame. His best-known book is the novel *Growth of the Soil* (1917). He was awarded the Nobel Prize for Literature in 1920.

hand — *noun* **1** in humans, the extremity of the arm below the wrist, consisting of a thumb, four fingers and a palm; any corresponding member in the higher vertebrates. **2** (*often* **hands**) control, agency, or influence. **3** help; assistance. **4** a part or influence in an activity: *had a hand in the victory.* **5** a needle or pointer on a clock, watch, or gauge. **6** *colloq.* applause. **7** a manual worker or assistant, especially in a factory, on a farm, or on board ship. **8** a person skilful in some activity: *a dab hand at baking.* **9** a way of doing something: *have a light hand at pastry.* **10** the cards dealt to a player in one round of a card game. **11** one round of a card game. **12** a position in relation to an object or (*in compounds*) to a point in time: *on the right hand / behindhand.* **13** a source of information considered in terms of closeness to the original source: *hear the news at first hand.* **14** a person's handwriting or its style. **15** a promise or agreement to marry: *ask for her hand.* **16** a unit of

measurement, equal to four inches, used for measuring the height of horses. — *verb* (**hand something back, out, round**, *etc*) to deliver or give it using the hands.

— **at hand** near by; about to happen.

by hand 1 with a person's hand or tools held in the hands. **2** delivered by messenger, not by post.

from hand to mouth with only enough money and food for one's immediate needs.

get one's hands on something *or* **someone** *colloq.* to catch or find someone or obtain something.

hand something down to pass an heirloom, tradition, etc on to the next generation.

hand something in to deliver something to someone entitled to hold it, eg lost property.

hand in glove very closely associated.

hand in hand 1 holding a person's hand. **2** in close association.

hand it to someone *colloq.* to give them due credit.

hand something on to give it to the next person in succession.

hand something over to give possession of it to someone else, especially to someone entitled to it.

hand over fist *colloq.* in large amounts and very quickly.

have one's hands full *colloq.* to be very busy.

in hand 1 under control. **2** being done or prepared.

keep one's hand in *colloq.* to practise a skill, etc so as to remain competent at it.

off one's hands *colloq.* no longer one's responsibility.

on hand near; available for use.

on one's hands *colloq.* **1** left over; not sold or used. **2** remaining as one's responsibility.

on one's hands and knees 1 in a position with one's hands knees and feet on the ground. **2** begging.

on the one hand... on the other hand ... from one point of view... from another point of view ...

out of hand 1 *said of a person, especially a child* unable to be controlled. **2** immediately and without thinking.

to hand within reach.

the upper hand the advantage or position of greatest power or strength.

[from Anglo-Saxon *hand*]

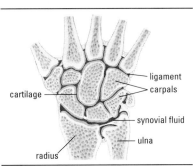

bone structure of the human hand

Handa an island and nature reserve in Sutherland district, Highland region, NW Scotland. Lying 5km/3mi NW of Scourie, it is a seabird sanctuary noted for its vast numbers of fulmars, gulls, kittiwakes, shags, and skuas.

handbag *noun* a woman's small bag, often with a strap for carrying, for money, make-up, etc.

handball *noun* a game in which players hit a small ball with their hands.

handbill *noun* a small printed notice or advertisement given out by hand.

handbook *noun* a short manual or guidebook.

handbrake *noun* a brake on a motor vehicle which is operated by the driver's hand.

handcart *noun* a small light cart which can be moved by hand.

handclap *noun* a clap of the hands.

handcrafted *adj.* made by handicraft.

handcuff — *verb* to put handcuffs on (a person). — *noun* (**handcuffs**) a pair of steel rings, joined by a short chain, for locking round the wrists of prisoners.

Handel, George Frideric, originally **George Frideric Händel** (1685–1759) German–English composer, born in Halle. He was organist of Halle Cathedral at the age of 17, while also studying law, and worked as a violinist and keyboard player in the Hamburg opera orchestra (1703–6). Appointed in 1710 to the court of the Elector of Hanover (later George I), he wrote his *Water Music* in c.1717. In London in 1720 he produced a stream of operas, and then developed a new form, the English oratorio, which proved to be highly popular. After a stroke in 1737, he recovered and afterwards wrote some of his most memorable work, such as *Saul* (1739), *Israel in Egypt* (1739), and *Messiah* (1742). His output included 46 operas, 32 oratorios, cantatas, sacred music, concerti grossi, and other orchestral, instrumental, and vocal works.

handful *noun* (PL. **handfuls**) **1** as much as can be held in one hand. **2** a small amount or number. **3** *colloq.* a person who is difficult to control; a difficult task.

hand-grenade *noun* a grenade to be thrown by hand.

handgun *noun* a gun that can be held and fired in one hand, eg a pistol.

handicap — *noun* **1** a physical or mental disability that results in partial or total inability to perform social, occupational, or other normal everyday activities. **2** a disadvantage given to a superior competitor in a contest, race, etc. **3** a race or competition in which some competitors are given a handicap. **4** the number of strokes by which a golfer usually exceeds par for the course. — *verb* (**handicapped, handicapping**) **1** to give a handicap to. **2** to make something difficult for (someone). [from *hand i' cap*, an old sporting lottery]

handicapped — *adj.* physically or mentally disabled. — *pl. noun* handicapped people.

handicraft *noun* **1** an activity which requires skilful use of the hands, eg pottery or model making. **2** (*usually* **handicrafts**) any object produced by such craft. [from Anglo-Saxon *handcræft*]

handily *adv.* in a handy way or position.

handiness *noun* being handy.

handiwork *noun* **1** work, especially skilful, done by the hands. **2** something bad done or caused by a particular person. [from Anglo-Saxon *handgeweorc*]

handkerchief *noun* (PL. **handkerchiefs, handkerchieves**) a small, usually square piece of cloth or soft paper used for wiping one's nose, face, etc. [from HAND + KERCHIEF]

handle — *noun* **1** the part of an object by which it is held so that it may be used or operated. **2** an advantage or opening given to an opponent. **3** *slang* a person's name. — *verb* **1** to touch, hold, move or operate with the hands. **2** to deal with or manage, especially successfully or in the correct way. **3** to buy, sell, or deal in (goods). **4** to write about or discuss (a subject). **5** *intrans.* to respond to control in the way stated. — **fly off the handle** *colloq.* to become suddenly angry. [from Anglo-Saxon *handle*]

handlebar moustache a wide, thick moustache which curls up at the ends.

handlebars *pl. noun* a usually curved metal bar with handles at each end, for steering a bicycle or motorcycle.

handler *noun* **1** a person who trains and controls an animal, especially a dog. **2** a person who handles something: *a baggage handler*.

handless *adj. old use* awkward or clumsy.

Handley, Tommy (Thomas Reginald) (1892–1949) English comedian, born in Liverpool. After working in variety, he became a regular broadcaster in the infancy of radio. In 1939 he achieved nationwide fame through the wit and satire of his weekly programme *ITMA* (It's That Man Again), which helped to boost wartime morale.

handling *noun* **1** touching, moving, holding, or turning with the hand. **2** packaging and transportation of goods. **3** treatment or management.

handmade *adj.* made with a person's hands or with tools held in the hands, not by machine.

handmaiden *or* **handmaid** *noun old use* a female servant.

hand-me-down *noun colloq.* a second-hand garment, toy, etc.

handout *noun* **1** money, food, etc given to people who need it. **2** a leaflet, statement containing information, etc, given eg to students before a lecture, to newspaper reporters, etc.

handover *noun* the transfer of power from one person or group of people to another.

hand-pick *verb* to choose carefully, especially for a particular purpose.

hand-picked *adj.* carefully chosen.

handrail *noun* a narrow rail running along stairs, etc for support.

handsaw *noun* a saw worked by hand, especially one with a handle at one end.

handset *noun* a telephone mouthpiece and earpiece together in a single unit.

handshake *noun* the act of holding or shaking a person's hand, especially as a greeting.

hands-off *adj.* not touched or operated by the hands.

handsome *adj.* **1** *said of a man* good-looking. **2** *said of a woman* attractive in a strong, healthy, imposing way. **3** *said of a building* large and imposing. **4** substantial; generous: *a handsome donation*. [from HAND + -SOME; originally meaning 'easy to handle']

handsomely *adv.* in a handsome way.

handsomeness *noun* being handsome.

hands-on *adj.* involving practical experience rather than just information or theory.

handspring *noun* a somersault or cartwheel in which one lands first on one's hands and then on one's feet.

handstand *noun* an act of balancing one's body upside down on one's hands.

hand-to-hand *adj., said of fighting* involving direct physical contact with the enemy.

handwriting *noun* **1** writing with a pen or pencil. **2** the characteristic way a person writes.

handwritten *adj.* written using a pen or pencil, not printed or typed.

handy *adj.* (**handier, handiest**) **1** ready to use and conveniently placed. **2** easy to use or handle. **3** clever with one's hands.

handyman *noun* a person skilled at, or employed to do, odd jobs around the house.

hang — *verb* (PAST TENSE AND PAST PARTICIPLE **hung**, in senses 3 and 12 **hanged**) **1** *trans., intrans.* to fasten or be fastened from above, especially with the lower part free. **2** *trans., intrans. said eg of a door* to fasten or be fastened with hinges so that it can move freely. **3** *trans., intrans.* to suspend or be suspended by a rope or something similar around the neck until dead. **4** (**hang over**) to remain without moving, especially in the air or in a threatening way. **5** *trans., intrans.* to

droop or cause to droop: *hang one's head in shame*. **6** to fix (wallpaper) to a wall. **7** *trans., intrans. said of a painting, etc* to place or be placed in an exhibition. **8** to decorate (a room, wall, etc) with pictures or other hangings. **9** (**hang something on someone**) *colloq.* to blame them for it. **10** (**hang on something**) to depend on it: *it all hangs on the weather*. **11** (**hang on something**) to listen closely to it: *hanging on her every word*. **12** *trans., intrans. colloq.* to damn. **13** *intrans. said of a piece of clothing* to sit in a stated way when worn: *a coat which hangs well*. **14** to suspend (game) from a hook until it is mature. — *noun* the way something hangs, falls, or droops.

— **get the hang of something** *colloq.* to learn or begin to understand how to do it.

hang about *or* **around** *colloq.* **1** to stand around doing nothing. **2** (**hang about** *or* **around with someone**) to spend a lot of time with them.

hang back to be unwilling or reluctant to do something.

hang fire 1 to delay taking action. **2** to cease to develop or progress.

hang in the balance to be uncertain or in doubt.

hang loose *North Amer. colloq.* to stay calm and in control of oneself.

hang on *colloq.* **1** to wait. **2** to carry on bravely, in spite of problems or difficulties.

hang on to something to keep a hold or control on it.

hang out 1 to lean or bend out. **2** *colloq.* to spend much time in a place: *hangs out in local bars*.

hang together 1 to be united and support each other. **2** *said of ideas, etc* to be consistent.

hang up 1 to finish a telephone conversation by replacing the receiver.

hang something up to hang it on a hook or hanger.

let it all hang out *colloq.* to be totally uninhibited and relaxed.
[from Anglo-Saxon *hangian*]

hangar *noun* a large shed in which aircraft are kept. [from French *hangar*]

Hangchow see HANGZHOU.

hangdog *adj.* ashamed or guilty.

hanger *noun* **1** a metal, wooden or plastic frame on which jackets, dresses, etc are hung up to keep their shape. **2** a person who hangs something.

hanger-on *noun* (PL. **hangers-on**) a fan or follower, especially one who is not wanted.

hang-glider *noun* **1** a large, light, metal frame with cloth stretched across it, which flies using air currents, with a harness hanging below it for the pilot. **2** the pilot of a hang-glider.

hang-gliding *noun* the sport of flying supported by a hang-glider.

hanging *noun* **1** an execution by hanging. **2** (*usually* **hangings**) curtains, tapestries, etc hung on walls for decoration.

hangman *noun* an official who hangs criminals.

hangnail *noun* a piece of loose skin that has been partly torn away from the base or side of a fingernail.

hang-out *slang* a place one lives in or spends much time in.

hangover *noun* **1** a collection of unpleasant physical symptoms that may follow a period of heavy drinking, such as headache, nausea, excessive thirst, dizziness, fatigue, and sensitivity to light and noise. Many of these effects are caused by dehydration. **2** something which remains from an earlier time.

Hang Seng Index the indicator of relative prices of stocks and shares on the Hong Kong stock exchange.

hang-up *noun colloq.* an emotional or psychological problem.

Hangzhou *or* **Hangchow** POP (1990) 1.4m, the capital of Zhejiang province, E China. It lies

on the Qiantang R at the S end of the Grand Canal. HISTORY founded in 2 200 BC; from the 6c BC it grew rapidly as a trade and administration centre; served as capital of several kingdoms and dynasties from the 8c until the 12c. NOTABLE FEATURE Spirits' Retreat (Buddhist temple founded in AD 326).

Hanif Mohammad (1934–) Pakistani cricketer, born in Junagadh, India. One of five Test-playing brothers, he made his first-class début for Karachi at the age of 16. He took 970 minutes to amass 337 runs against Australia in 1957–8, and established a world record score of 499 against Bahawalpur in 1959. He made his Test début at the age of 17, and played in 55 Tests, scoring 3 915 runs. He captained Pakistan 11 times between 1964 and 1967.

hank *noun* a length of wool, string, rope, etc gathered in a loop. [from Old Norse *hanki*, a hasp]

hanker *verb intrans.* (**hankered, hankering**) (**hanker after** *or* **for something**) to long for or crave it.

hankering *noun* a craving, a yearning.

hankie *or* **hanky** *noun* (PL. **hankies**) *colloq.* a handkerchief. [abbreviation]

Han-kou *or* **Han-kow** see WUHAN.

hanky-panky *noun colloq.* **1** slightly improper sexual behaviour. **2** dishonest dealing.

Hannah a female first name, and mother of the prophet Samuel in the Old Testament. [from the Hebrew name *Chana* meaning 'He (God) has favoured me' (with a child)]

Hannay, Richard the adventurous hero in novels by John Buchan, including *The Thirty-Nine Steps*, *Greenmantle*, and *The Island of Sheep*.

Hannibal (247–182 BC) Carthaginian general and statesman, the son of Hamilcar Barca. He served in Spain under Hamilcar and Hasdrubal, and as general reduced most of S Spain (221–219 BC). When he was a child, his father made him swear eternal enmity to Rome. In the Second Punic War, he left New Carthage (218 BC), defeated the Gauls, and crossed the Alps in fifteen days. He marched on Rome, and defeated the Romans at L Trasimene (217 BC) and at Cannae (216 BC). He was denied support by his countrymen, but fought on for several years, until recalled to Africa in 203 BC. He was finally defeated by Scipio at Zama (202 BC), leaving Carthage to the mercy of Rome. After making peace, he turned to political reform, but raised such opposition that he voluntarily exiled himself, first to Syria, then Crete and finally Bithynia, where he committed suicide to avoid Roman capture.

Hannover see HANOVER.

Hanoi POP (1989) 3.1m, the capital of Vietnam, on the Red R, 88km/55mi NW of Haiphong. HISTORY capital of the Vietnamese Empire from the 11c until the 17c; capital of French Indo-China from 1887 until 1946; occupied by the Japanese in World War II; severely damaged by bombing during the Vietnam War. NOTABLE FEATURES surviving sites include Co Loa Citadel (3c BC); Temple of Literature (11c); Mot Cot Pagoda (11c); several museums.

Hanover, German **Hannover** POP (1991e) 510 000, the commercial and industrial capital of Lower Saxony state, NW Germany. It lies on the R Leine, 56km/35mi NW of Brunswick. HISTORY chartered in 1241; in the early 17c it became the home of the Dukes of Brunswick-Lüneburg (later the electors of Hanover); in 1714, Elector George Louis became George I of Great Britain; badly bombed in World War II. NOTABLE FEATURES Neoclassical opera house (1845–52); Leine Palace; Gothic Old Town Hall (15c).

Hanover, House of a dynasty of British monarchs (1714–1901), encompassing George I, George II, George III, George IV, William IV, and

Queen Victoria, though only the Georges and William are usually referred to as 'Hanoverians'. The dynasty secured the Protestant succession after the death of Queen Anne, and was descended through the female line from Princess Elizabeth, the sister of Charles I.

House of Hanover	
1714–27	George I
1727–60	George II
1760–1820	George III
1820–30	George IV
1830–7	William IV
1837–1901	Victoria

Hanoverian — *adj.* of British sovereigns from George I (1714) to Victoria (1901), George I being also the Elector of Hanover in N Germany. — *noun* a member of this dynasty.

Hansard, Luke (1752–1828) English printer, who entered the office of Hughes, printer to the House of Commons, becoming acting manager in 1774, and in 1798 succeeding as sole proprietor. The parliamentary reports were printed by his family from 1774 to 1889 and still bear his name.

Hansard in the UK, the official transcript of speeches made in the House of Commons, published from 1774 by the Hansard family, and since 1909 by the Stationery Office.

Hanseatic League, also called **Hansa** a late medieval association of 150 N German towns, including Bremen, Hamburg, and Lübeck, which had origins in the merchants' practice of travelling together for safety. It dominated trade from the Atlantic to the Baltic, and fought successful wars against neighbours between 1350 and 1450. It declined because of internal divisions, English and Dutch competition, and the growth of princely power. [from Old German *hansa*, a band of men]

Hansel and Gretel (Hänsel und Gretel) an opera by Englebert Humperdinck (1893), based on the Grimm Brothers' fairy tale. It tells of the adventures of two small children lost in a forest, where they are lulled to sleep by the Sandman, woken by the Dew Fairy, and imprisoned in a gingerbread house by the Wicked Witch.

hansom *or* **hansom cab** *noun Hist.* a small, two-wheeled, horse-drawn carriage with a fixed roof and the driver's seat high up at the back, used as a taxi. [named after J A Hansom (1803–82), its inventor]

Hanson, James Edward Hanson, Baron (1922–) English business executive, born in Huddersfield. Following army service (1939–46), he inherited the family transport business, and started a successful greetings-card business with his partner, Gordon White. He became Chairman of Hanson Trust in 1965, and was Chairman of Trident Television in 1974. He built up a diversified conglomerate of businesses under the umbrella of Hanson Trust. Since 1984 he has been a director of Lloyds Bank.

Hants. *abbrev.* Hampshire.

Hanukkah *noun* an eight-day Jewish festival held annually in December, commemorating the re-dedication of the Temple at Jerusalem in 165 BC. [from Hebrew *hanukkah*, consecration]

Hanuman a popular Hindu deity, the monkey-god (represented as half-human, half-monkey) of the *Ramayana* epic, who is the courageous and loyal supporter of Rama.

ha'penny see HALFPENNY at HALF.

haphazard — *adj.* done by chance; random. — *adv.* at random. [from Norse *happ*, good luck + HAZARD]

haphazardly *adv.* in a haphazard way.

hapless *adj.* unlucky; unfortunate. [from Norse *happ*, good luck]

haploid *adj.* **1** describing a cell nucleus that contains only a single set of chromosomes. **2** describing a living organism, or stage of its life cycle, that has only a single set of chromosomes in its cell nuclei. [from Greek *haploos*, single, simple]

hap'orth see HALFPENNYWORTH at HALF.

happen — *verb intrans.* (**happened, happening**) **1** to take place or occur. **2** (**happen to someone**) *said especially of something unwelcome* to be done to them, or be experienced by them. **3** to have the good or bad luck to: *happened to meet him on the way.* **4** (**happen on something**) to discover or encounter it, especially by chance. — *adv. dialect* perhaps. [from Norse *happ*, good luck]

happening *noun* **1** an event. **2** a public performance, especially one which takes place in the street, which has not been fully planned, and in which the audience is invited to take part.

happily *adv.* **1** in a happy way. **2** luckily.

happiness *noun* being happy.

happy *adj.* (**happier, happiest**) **1** feeling or showing pleasure or contentment: *a happy smile.* **2** causing pleasure: *a happy day for the company.* **3** suitable; fortunate: *a happy coincidence.* [from Norse *happ*, good luck]

happy event *euphemistic* the birth of a child.

happy-go-lucky *adj.* carefree.

happy medium a reasonable middle course between two extreme positions.

hara-kiri *noun* ritual suicide by cutting one's belly open with a sword, formerly practised in Japan to avoid dishonour. [from Japanese *hara*, belly + *kiri*, cut]

harangue — *noun* a loud, forceful speech either to attack people or to try to persuade them to do something. — *verb* to address such a speech to. [from Old French *arenge*]

Harappa a prehistoric city on the dried-up course of the R Ravi in the Pakistani Punjab, c.800km/500mi S of Islamabad, occupied c.2300–1750 BC. It was discovered in 1826, and excavated from 1921.

Harare, formerly **Salisbury** (to 1982) POP (1987e) 863 000, the capital of Zimbabwe and the largest city in the country. It is situated 370km/230mi NE of Bulawayo at an altitude of 1 473m. The city was founded in 1890 and was named after the then British Prime Minister, Lord Salisbury. NOTABLE FEATURES international conference centre; horse-racing and trotting tracks; motor-racing circuit; Queen Victoria Museum; National Gallery; National Archives; National Botanical Garden; two cathedrals.

harass *verb* **1** to annoy or trouble (a person) constantly or frequently. **2** to make frequent sudden attacks on (an enemy). [from Old French *harasser*, to harry]

Hanuman

harassed *adj.* troubled, worried, overburdened.

harassment *noun* **1** harassing. **2** being harassed.

Harbin *or* **Haerhpin** *or* **Haerbin**, formerly **Pinkiang** POP (1990) 3m, the capital of Heilongjiang province, NE China. It is an industrial centre situated on the Songhua R. HISTORY founded in the 12c; developed as a fishing village; c.500 000 White Russians fled here in 1917. NOTABLE FEATURES Stalin Park; Harbin Zoo (1954).

harbinger *noun* a person or thing which is a sign of something that is to come. [from Old French *herbergere*, host]

harbour — *noun* **1** a place of shelter for ships. **2** a refuge. — *verb* **1** to give shelter or protection to (eg a criminal). **2** to have (thoughts) in one's head: *harbour a grudge.* [from Anglo-Saxon *herebeorg*, lodgings]

harbour master a person officially in charge of a harbour.

hard — *adj.* **1** *said of a substance* resistant to scratching or indentation. **2** difficult to do, understand, solve or explain. **3** using, needing, or done with a great deal of effort. **4** harsh; cruel. **5** *said of weather* severe. **6** causing or suffering hardship: *hard times.* **7** harsh and unpleasant to the senses: *a hard light.* **8** *said of information, etc* proven and reliable. **9** *said of water* containing calcium or magnesium salts, and tending to produce an insoluble scum instead of a lather with soap. **10** *said of a drug* highly addictive. **11** *said of an alcoholic drink* strong; being a spirit rather than beer or wine. **12** politically extreme: *hard right.* **13** *said of the sounds of certain letters* produced as a stop rather than a fricative, as eg the *c* in *cat* and the *g* in *got.* **14** *said of currency* with a stable value and exchange rate. **15** *said of pornography* sexually explicit. — *adv.* **1** with great effort or energy: *work hard.* **2** with difficulty; as a result of great effort: *a hard-won victory / hard-earned results.*
— **be hard going** to be difficult to do.
be hard put to do something to have difficulty doing it.
go hard with someone to be unpleasant or difficult for them.
hard at it working hard.
hard by close by.
hard done by *colloq.* unfairly treated.
hard of hearing partially deaf.
hard on someone *or* **something** close behind them.
hard up *colloq.* short of something, especially money.
[from Anglo-Saxon *heard*]

hard-and-fast *adj., said of a rule or principle* permanent or absolute; that can never be changed.

Hardanger Plateau *or* **The Vidda**, Norwegian **Hardangervidda** an extensive mountain plateau in SW Norway, extending 160km/100mi between the head of Hardanger Fjord and the Hallingdal Valley. It is a barren, bedrock area with an average elevation of 1 000m, rising to 1 862m at Hardangerjøkulen. The plateau is a popular winter sports and tourist area.

hardback — *noun* a book with a hard cover. — *adj.* having a hard cover.

hard-bitten *adj. colloq., said of a person* tough and ruthless, especially through difficult experience.

hardboard *noun* light, strong board made by compressing wood pulp.

hard-boiled *adj.* **1** *said of eggs* boiled until the yolk is solid. **2** *said of a person* tough; cynical.

hard case *colloq.* a tough, often violent person.

hard cash coins and bank-notes, as opposed to cheques and credit cards.

hard copy information from a computer printed on paper.

hardcore *noun* **1** pieces of broken brick, stone, etc used as a base for a road. **2** (*also* **hard core**) the central, most important group within an organization.

hard-core *adj.* **1** having long-lasting, strong, unchanging beliefs. **2** denoting pornography that is sexually explicit.

hard currency **1** money in the form of coins or notes. **2** a currency with a high, stable, or improving exchange rate, not subject to depreciation. **3** a currency backed by bullion.

hard disk *Comput.* a rigid aluminium disk, coated with magnetic material and normally permanently sealed within the disk drive, that is used to store data. It is much faster in operation than a floppy disk, and can store large amounts of data. See also FLOPPY DISK.

Harden, Sir Arthur (1865–1940) English chemist, born in Manchester. He worked in the Jenner (later Lister) Institute from 1897, and was appointed professor at London University in 1912. For his studies of fermentation and enzymes, he shared the 1929 Nobel Prize for Chemistry with Hans von Euler-Chelpin.

harden *verb* (**hardened**, **hardening**) **1** *trans.*, *intrans.* to make or become hard or harder. **2** *trans.*, *intrans.* to become or make less sympathetic or understanding: *hardened his heart to her tears.* **3** *intrans. said of prices* to stop falling.

hardened *adj.* toughened through experience and not likely to change: *a hardened criminal.*

hardening of the arteries same as ARTERIOSCLEROSIS.

hard-headed *adj.* clever and not influenced by emotion.

hard-hearted *adj.* feeling no pity or kindness.

hard-heartedly *adv.* in a hard-hearted way.

hard-heartedness *noun* being hard-hearted.

hard-hitting *adj.* direct; frankly critical.

Hardicanute, also called **Harthacnut** (c.1018–42) King of Denmark (1035–42), and the last Danish King of England (1040–2), the only son of Canute and Emma of Normandy. Canute had intended that Hardicanute should succeed him in both Denmark and England simultaneously, but he was unable to secure his English inheritance until his stepbrother, Harold I, died (1040). Hardicanute's death without children led to the restoration of the Old English royal line in the person of his half-brother Edward the Confessor, the only surviving son of Emma and Ethelred the Unready.

Hardie, (James) Keir (1856–1915) Scottish Labour politician, one of the founders of the Labour Party, born near Holytown, Lanarkshire. He worked in the mines from age seven, was victimized as the champion of the miners, then became a journalist and, as the first Labour candidate, entered parliament (1892). He founded and edited the *Labour Leader*, and was Chairman of the Independent Labour Party (founded 1893). Instrumental in the establishment of the Labour Representation Committee, he served as Chairman of the Labour Party (1906–8). A strong pacifist, he lost his seat through opposing the Boer War.

hardihood *noun* courage and daring.

hardiness *noun* being hardy.

Harding, the Rev Septimus the unassuming clergyman who finds himself at the centre of a public scandal in Anthony Trollope's *The Warden.*

Harding, Warren G(amaliel) (1865–1923) US politician, the 29th President, born in Blooming Grove, Ohio. A successful journalist, he gained a seat in the Ohio State Senate (1899) and the lieutenant-governorship (1902), after which he returned to journalism until 1914, when he was elected to the US Senate. He

emerged as a power in the Republican Party, won its nomination and became President (1920–3), when he campaigned against US membership of the League of Nations.

hard labour heavy physical work, eg breaking rocks, especially as a punishment in prison.

hardline *adj.* **1** *said of an attitude or policy* definite and unyielding. **2** having such an attitude or policy.

hard line a strong opinion, decision, or policy which is not likely to be changed.

hardliner *noun* a person who supports or promotes a hardline attitude or policy.

hardly *adv.* **1** only with difficulty; scarcely: *could hardly keep her eyes open.* **2** probably not: *they'll hardly come now.* **3** harshly.

hardness *noun* being hard.

hard-nosed *adj. colloq.* determined; influenced by reason, not emotion.

hard nut *colloq.* a person or thing that is tough or difficult to deal with.

hard-on *noun coarse slang* an erection of the penis.

hardpad *noun* a symptom of distemper in dogs, causing hardness of the pads of the feet.

hard palate *Anat.* the bony front part of the palate, which separates the mouth from the nasal cavities.

hard-pressed *or* **hard-pushed** *adj.* having problems; in difficulties.

hard sell an aggressive and insistent way of promoting, selling, or advertising.

hardship *noun* severe suffering and pain, or a cause of this.

hard shoulder a hard verge along the side of a motorway, on which vehicles can stop if in trouble.

hardtack *noun* hard biscuits formerly given to sailors as food on long journeys.

hardtop *noun* **1** a rigid roof on a motor vehicle. **2** a vehicle, especially a motor car, with such a roof.

hardware *noun* **1** metal goods such as pots, cutlery, tools, etc. **2** *Comput.* the electronic, electrical, magnetic, and mechanical components of a computer system, as opposed to the programs that form the software. See also SOFTWARE. **3** heavy military equipment, eg tanks.

hard water *Chem.* water that contains dissolved calcium or magnesium salts, which prevent it forming a lather with soap, and are responsible for the 'furring up' of hot-water pipes and kettles. Hard water forms a scum with soap.

hard-wearing *adj.* that will last a long time and stay in good condition.

hard-wired *adj., said of a computer* having functions which are controlled by hardware and cannot be altered by software programs.

hardwood *noun* **1** *Bot.* the wood of a slow-growing deciduous tree, eg oak, mahogany, teak. It is dense and has a fine grain. **2** *Bot.* any tree which produces such wood. See also SOFTWOOD.

Hardy, Bert (1913–) English photojournalist, born in London. He started as a general assistant in a photographic agency, and was one of the first Fleet Street newsmen to use a 35mm camera in the 1930s. He portrayed the life of ordinary people, eg during the London Blitz in World War II. As an army photographer (1942–5) he recorded the horrors of the concentration camps, and on the staff of *Picture Post* he covered the Korean and Vietnam Wars. In later years he produced much creative work for advertising until his retirement in 1967.

Hardy, Godfrey Harold (1877–1947) English mathematician, born in Cranleigh. Professor at Oxford and Cambridge, he was an

internationally important figure in mathematical analysis, working in many areas such as number theory and Fourier series. With Srinivasa Ramanujan, he found an exact formula for the partition function, which expresses the number of ways a number can be written as a sum of smaller numbers.

Hardy, Thomas (1840–1928) English novelist and poet, born in Upper Bockhampton, Dorset. He studied as an architect before taking up writing as a profession. His first success was with his fourth novel *Far from the Madding Crowd* (1874), and other major titles include *The Return of the Native* (1878), *The Mayor of Casterbridge* (1886), *Tess of the D'Urbervilles* (1891), and *Jude the Obscure* (1896), all of which are tragedies. Thereafter he returned to poetry and produced several volumes of lyrics, which express his love of rural life, and the epic drama, *The Dynasts* (1903–8).

Hardy, Oliver, originally **Norvell Hardy Junior** (1892–1957) US comedian, born near Atlanta, Georgia. He left college to join a troupe of minstrels before drifting into the film industry. From 1926 he worked with Stan Laurel (see also LAUREL AND HARDY).

hardy *adj.* (**hardier**, **hardiest**) **1** tough; strong; able to bear difficult conditions. **2** *said of a plant* able to survive outdoors in winter. [from Old French *hardi*, made bold]

Hare, David (1947–) English dramatist, director, and film-maker, born in London. He was resident dramatist at the Royal Court (1969–71) and elsewhere before becoming associate director at the National Theatre (1984). Among his stage plays are *Slag* (1970), *Plenty* (1978), *Pravda* (1985, written with Howard Brenton), *The Secret Rapture* (1988), and *Racing Demon* (1990). His other work includes the films *Wetherby* (1985) and *Paris By Night* (1988).

hare — *noun* a herbivorous mammal belonging to the same family as the rabbit, found in Europe, Asia, Africa, and N and Central America, and having a brown or greyish coat which becomes white during the winter in northern species. It differs from the rabbit in that it is larger, has longer ears, often with black tips, longer hind legs, and does not form burrows, but spends the day lying in a hollow in the ground (a form). In spring, male hares buck, bound, kick, and stand on their hind legs to box with one another, giving rise to the expression *mad as a March hare*. — *verb intrans. colloq.* to run very fast. [from Anglo-Saxon *hara*]

harebell *noun* a wild plant with violet-blue, bell-shaped flowers.

hare-brained *adj., said of people, actions, etc* foolish; done without considering the consequences.

Hare Krishna movement a religious movement founded (1965) in the USA by His Divine Grace A C Bhaktivedanta Swami Prabhupada (1896–1977) as The International Society for Krishna Consciousness. One of the best known of the new religious movements from the East, it is based on the ancient Vedic texts of India, and promotes 'Krishna Consciousness' (the original human relationship with Krishna). Its shaven-headed and saffron-robed young people are sometimes seen chanting on city streets. In their pursuit of spiritual advancement they do not eat meat or use intoxicants, do not gamble, and are celibate outside marriage.

hare lip *Medicine* a deformity of the upper lip, present from birth, in which there is a cleft on one or both sides of the centre, caused by incomplete merging of the embryonic tissues beneath one or both nostrils. It is often associated with a cleft palate, and can be corrected by plastic surgery during childhood.

hare-lipped *adj.* having a hare-lip.

harem *noun* **1** a separate part of a traditional Muslim house in which the women live. **2** the women living in this. [from Arabic *harim*, forbidden]

Harewood, George Henry Hubert Lascelles, 7th Earl of (1923–) English nobleman and arts patron, elder son of the Princess Royal, and cousin of Elizabeth II, born in Harewood, near Leeds. He served in the Grenadier Guards in World War II, and was a prisoner of war. Since the 1950s he has been much involved in the direction of operatic and arts institutions, (eg the Edinburgh Festival, Covent Garden, and Leeds), and has held such positions as managing director of English National Opera (1972–85). He is the editor of *Kobbé's Complete Opera Book* (1957) and *Kobbé's Illustrated Opera Book* (1989).

haricot *or* **haricot bean** *noun* a small, white, dried bean, used as food. [from French *haricot*]

Harimandir, also called **Golden Temple** the centre of the Sikh religion at Amritsar, Punjab, India. The temple dates from 1766 and stands in a sacred lake. It is faced with copper-gilt plates bearing inscriptions from the Granth Sahib, the holy book of the Sikhs, which is housed within.

hark *verb intrans. literary* (**hark at** *or* **to something** *or* **someone**) to listen to them attentively. — **hark back to something** to refer to or remind one of past experiences: *hark back to one's childhood.* [from Anglo-Saxon *heorcnian*, to hearken]

harken same as HEARKEN.

Harlech, William David Ormsby Gore, 5th Baron (1918–85) English Conservative politician and businessman. He entered parliament in 1950, and became Minister of State at the Foreign Office in 1956. During the Kennedy administration in the USA he served as British Ambassador (1961–5) in Washington. Meanwhile, he had succeeded to his father's title (1964), and on his return to the UK he obtained the franchise for Harlech Television (1967). He was President of the British Board of Film Censors at a time of increasing permissiveness regarding what was displayed on screen.

Harlem, Dutch **Haarlem** POP (1992e) 150 000, the capital of North Holland province, W Netherlands. It lies on the R Spaarne, 7km/4mi from the North Sea coast. Part of the Randstad conurbation, Harlem was founded in the 10c and received its charter in 1245. The Spaniards sacked the city in 1573. It is a well-known export centre for tulip, hyacinth, and crocus bulbs. NOTABLE FEATURES town hall (13c–17c); Grote Kerk (1472); Frans Hals Museum.

Harlem Globetrotters a professional US touring basketball team, formed in 1927 in Harlem, New York City, by London-born immi-

grant Abraham Saperstein (1903–66). They developed a comedy routine to add to their skills, and now tour worldwide, giving exhibitions.

harlequin — *noun* (*also* **Harlequin**) a humorous character from traditional Italian plays who wears a black mask and a brightly coloured, diamond-patterned costume. — *adj.* in varied bright colours. [from French *harlequin*, probably from Old French *Hellequin*]

Harley, Robert, 1st Earl of Oxford (1661–1724) English statesman, born in London. A Whig MP from 1689, he became Secretary of State in 1704. He soon joined the Tories, and when in 1710 Godolphin was dismissed, Harley became Chancellor of the Exchequer, and (1711) Earl of Oxford and Lord High Treasurer. As Chief Minister to Queen Anne (1711–14), his administration included the Treaty of Utrecht (1713), but he was dismissed and imprisoned for two years for alleged treasonable activity.

harlot *noun old use* a prostitute. [from Old French *herlot*, rascal]

harlotry *noun* prostitution.

Harlow POP (1992e) 75 000, a town co-extensive with Harlow district, Essex, SE England. It is 33km/21mi NE of London and was designated a 'new town' in 1947.

Harlowe, Clarissa see CLARISSA.

harm — *noun* physical, mental, or moral injury or damage. — *verb* to cause harm to.
— **out of harm's way** in a safe place, not able to be harmed or cause harm.
[from Anglo-Saxon *hearm*]

harmful *adj.* causing harm.

harmfully *adv.* in a harmful way.

harmfulness *noun* being harmful.

harmless *adj.* not able or likely to cause harm.

harmlessly *adv.* in a harmless way.

harmlessness *noun* being harmless.

harmonic — *adj.* of or relating to harmony; harmonious. — *noun* a note produced on a stringed instrument by touching one of the strings lightly at one of the points which divide the string into exact fractions. [from Greek *harmonikos*, from *harmos*, joint]

harmonica *noun* **1** a mouth organ; a small, rectangular, musical instrument with metal reeds along one side, played by being held against the mouth, blown through, and moved from side to side to change the notes. **2** (*in full* **glass harmonica**) a musical instrument consisting of drinking-glasses (or revolving glass bowls in Benjamin Franklin's mechanized version) filled to different levels with water, and touched on the rims with a damp finger to produce sounds of different pitch. Several 18c composers, including Mozart and Johann A Hasse (1699–1783), wrote music for glass harmonica. **3** a musical instrument made up of a sound-box with hanging strips of glass or metal, struck with a hammer.

harmonic motion *Physics* same as SIMPLE HARMONIC MOTION.

harmonic progression *Maths.* a series of terms in which there is a constant difference between the reciprocals of the terms, eg $\frac{1}{4}, \frac{1}{2}, \frac{1}{3}, \frac{1}{4}, \ldots$

harmonics *sing. noun* the science of musical sounds.

harmonic series *Mus.* the combination or series of notes produced when a string or column of air is vibrated. A principal note, eg C, has a complex of such notes known as overtones or partials, which have the effect of enriching the quality of the principal note. The tone quality of musical instruments depends on the presence or absence of these overtones and their relative intensity.

harmonious *adj.* **1** pleasant-sounding and tuneful. **2** forming a pleasing whole: *a harmonious*

arrangement of colours. **3** without disagreement or bad feeling. [from HARMONY]

harmoniously *adv.* in a harmonious way.

harmoniousness *noun* being harmonious.

harmonium *noun* a musical instrument with a keyboard, in which air from bellows pumped by the feet makes the reeds vibrate to produce sound. [from HARMONY]
◇ The instrument was patented in 1842 by the French instrument-maker A F Debain (1809–77). The name is also applied to reed organs in general.

harmonization *or* **harmonisation** *noun* the act of harmonizing.

harmonize *or* **harmonise** *verb* **1** *intrans., trans.* to be or bring into musical harmony. **2** *intrans., trans.* to form or be made to form a pleasing whole. **3** to add notes to (a simple tune) to form harmonies.

harmony *noun* (PL. **harmonies**) **1** *Mus.* a pleasing combination of notes or sounds produced simultaneously. **2** a pleasing arrangement of parts or things: *harmony of colour.* **3** agreement in opinions and feelings. [from Greek *harmonia*, from *harmos*, joint]

Harmsworth, Alfred (Charles William), 1st Viscount Northcliffe (1865–1922) Irish journalist and newspaper magnate, born in Chapelizod, Co Dublin, and brought up in London. One of the pioneers of mass circulation journalism, in 1894 he took over the *London Evening News* and sponsored the Jackson Arctic expedition. He published some Sunday magazine papers and in 1896 revolutionized Fleet Street with his US-style *Daily Mail*. With his brother Harold, he also pioneered the first newspaper for women, the *Daily Mirror* (1903) and founded the Amalgamated Press for periodical and popular educational literature. In 1908 he became proprietor of *The Times*, and made its editorial policy a vehicle for his political ambitions. However he came into conflict with Lloyd George throughout World War I, and his attack on Lord Kitchener in the *Daily Mail* reduced its circulation by nearly 300 000.

Harmsworth, Harold (Sydney), 1st Viscount Rothermere (1868–1940) English newspaper magnate, born in London. Closely associated with his brother Alfred (later Lord Northcliffe), he founded the Glasgow *Daily Record* and in 1915 the *Sunday Pictorial*. He became Air Minister (1917–18), and after Northcliffe's death acquired control of the *Daily Mail* and *Sunday Dispatch*.

harness — *noun* **1** a set of leather straps used to attach a cart to a horse, and to control the horse's movements. **2** a similar set of straps for attaching to a person's body, eg to hold a child who is just learning to walk. — *verb* **1** to put a harness on (a horse, person, etc). **2** to control and make use of (especially natural resources), especially to produce power.
— **in harness** occupied with one's daily work or routine.
[from Old French *herneis*, equipment]

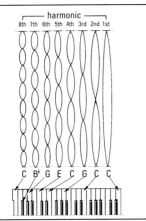

harmonic series

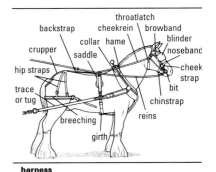

harness

Harold I, also called **Harefoot** (c.1016–40) King of England (1037–40), the younger son of Canute and Aelfgifu of Northampton. Canute had intended that Hardicanute, his only son by Emma of Normandy, should succeed him in Denmark and England simultaneously, but due to Hardicanute's absence in Denmark, Harold was accepted in England, first as regent (1035–6), and from 1037 as king.

Harold II (c.1022–66) the last Anglo-Saxon King of England (1066), and second son of Earl Godwin. By 1045 he was Earl of East Anglia, and in 1053 succeeded to his father's earldom of Wessex. After the death of Edward the Confessor (Jan 1066), Harold was crowned king as Harold II. He defeated his brother Tostig and Harold Hardrada, King of Norway, at Stamford Bridge (Sep 1066), but Duke William of Normandy then invaded England, and defeated and killed Harold near Hastings (14 Oct 1066).

Harold III, also called **Hardrada (the Ruthless)** (1015–66) King of Norway (1047–66). Until 1045 he served in Constantinople as captain of the Scandinavian bodyguard of the Greek emperors, and defeated the Saracens in Sicily and Italy. On his return to Norway, he divided the kingdom with his nephew Magnus, and then became sole ruler (1047). He waged war against Denmark until 1064, then in 1066 landed in England to aid Tostig against the English King Harold II, but fell at Stamford Bridge.

Harold a male first name, revived in the 19c. [from Anglo-Saxon *here*, army + *weald*, rule]

harp — *noun* a large three-sided musical instrument with a series of strings stretched vertically across it, played by plucking the strings with the fingers. — *verb* (**harp on about something**) *colloq.* to talk or write repeatedly and tediously about it. [from Anglo-Saxon *hearpe*]
◇ The modern concert harp, designed in 1810 by the French pianoforte maker Sébastien Érard (1752–1831), has a single row of 46 or 47 strings tuned to the major scale of C♭, and seven pedals used to raise a pitch by either a semitone or a tone.

Harpers Ferry Raid an attack (1859) on the Federal arsenal in Virginia, led by abolitionist John Brown, who intended to launch a slave insurrection. The raiders were captured, and Brown was executed amidst great publicity.

Harpies in Greek mythology, (usually) three malicious creatures with women's features and birds' wings and claws. They were originally thought of as ghosts or winds that carried people away. In the legend of Jason and the Argonauts, they plagued Phineus until they were chased away by the Argonauts.

harpist *noun* a person who plays the harp.

Harpocrates see HORUS.

harpoon — *noun* a barbed spear fastened to a rope, used for catching whales. — *verb* to strike (a whale, etc) with a harpoon. [from Greek *harpe*, hook]

harpsichord *noun* a keyboard instrument in which the strings are plucked mechanically (and not struck with hammers as in a piano) when the player presses the keys. [from Latin *harpa*, harp + *chorda*, string]
◇ Harpsichords were in use from the 14c, and were especially popular in the Baroque period.

harpy *noun* (PL. **harpies**) **1** an evil creature in Greek mythology (see HARPIES). **2** a cruel, grasping woman. [from Greek *harpyia*, snatcher]

harridan *noun* a bad-tempered, scolding old woman.

harrier¹ *noun* **1** a cross-country runner. **2** a hound used originally for hunting hares. [from HARE]

harrier² *noun* **1** a bird of prey with long wings. **2** any person or thing which harries. [from HARRY]

Harriet a female first name, dating from the 17c. [an Anglicization of French *Henriette*, a feminine diminutive of HENRY]

Harriman, W(illiam) Averell (1891–1986) US statesman and diplomat, born in New York City. He became Ambassador to the USSR (1943) and to Britain (1946), Secretary of Commerce (1946–8), and special assistant to President Truman (1950–1), when he helped to organize NATO. He was Director of Foreign Aid (1951–3), Governor of New York (1955–8), ambassador-at-large (1961, 1965–9), and US representative at the Vietnam peace talks in Paris (1968). He negotiated the partial nuclear test-ban treaty between the USA and USSR in 1963, and continued to visit the USSR on behalf of the government until the age of 91.

Harris, Sir Arthur Travers, known as **Bomber Harris** (1892–1984) English airman, born in Cheltenham, Gloucestershire. He served in the Royal Flying Corps in World War I, and as Commander-in-Chief of Bomber Command in World War II (1942–5) successfully organized the mass 'carpet bombing' of industrial Germany, a policy later criticized by some because it resulted in many civilian deaths.

Harris, Joel Chandler (1848–1908) US author, born in Eatonton, Georgia. He was in turn printer, lawyer, and journalist, and is remembered for his stories of *Uncle Remus* (1880), and several other children's books.

Harris the S part of the island district of Lewis with Harris, Western Isles, Scotland. AREA c.500sq km/200sq mi. A narrow isthmus links Harris to Lewis. Harris is known for its tweed manufacture.

Harrisburg POP (1990) 52 000, the capital of the state of Pennsylvania, USA, in Dauphin County in the S. It lies on the Susquehanna R. HISTORY scene of many important conventions, especially the Harrisburg Convention (1788); site of Camp Curtin, the first Union camp in the Civil War; in 1979 there was a nuclear power station accident nearby on Three Mile Island.

Harrison, Rex, originally **Reginald Carey Harrison** (1908–90) British actor, born in Houghton, Lancashire. His first leading film role was in *Storm in a Teacup* (1937) and his charming, somewhat blasé style attracted many star comedy parts, such as Charles in *Blithe Spirit* (1945) and Professor Higgins in *My Fair Lady* (1964), for which he won an Oscar.

Harrison, William Henry (1773–1841) US soldier and statesman, the ninth President, born in Charles City Co, Virginia. He fought against the Native Americans, and when Indiana Territory was formed (1800) he was appointed Governor. He tried to avoid further wars with them, but was compelled to suppress Tecumseh's outbreak, which led to the battle of Tippecanoe (1811). In the war of 1812–14 he defeated the British in the battle of the Thames (1813). He was elected to Congress (1816) and became a Senator (1824) and later President (1841), but died a month after his inauguration. His grandson was Benjamin Harrison, the 23rd US President.

Harrogate POP (1992e) 146 000, a spa town in Harrogate district, North Yorkshire, N England, situated 20km/12mi N of Leeds. It developed in the 17c as an important spa town after the discovery of 88 sulphur, saline, and chalybeate springs. Today, Harrogate is largely a tourist centre and a popular location for conferences and trade fairs. NOTABLE FEATURES Royal Pump Room; the Stray.

harrow — *noun Agric.* a farm implement consisting of a heavy metal frame bearing a row of spikes or discs, which is dragged over the surface of ploughed soil in order to level it and reduce the soil to fine particles prior to seed sowing. It is also used to cover the seeds with soil after sowing. — *verb* **1** to level the surface of ploughed soil, or to cover seeds with soil after sowing, using such an implement. **2** (*usually* **be harrowing**) to distress greatly. [from Middle English *harwe*]

harrowing *adj.* distressing.

Harry a male first name, and a common variant of *Henry* during the Middle Ages. In modern use, it is often an independent name.

harry *verb* (**harries, harried**) **1** to ravage or destroy. **2** to annoy or worry (a person). See also HARRIER². [from Anglo-Saxon *hergian*]

Harsa (c.590–c.647) ruler of the large N Indian Empire. His influence extended from Gujarat to Assam, but he made no attempt to build a centralized empire. Instead, he ruled according to the traditional pattern of leaving kings on their thrones and receiving tribute and homage. He was also a patron of learning and a convert to Buddhism. Following his death, a period of anarchy led to the splintering of his empire.

harsh *adj.* **1** rough; grating; unpleasant to the senses. **2** strict, cruel or severe. [from Middle English *harsk*]

harshly *adv.* in a harsh way.

harshness *noun* being harsh.

hart *noun* a male deer, especially one over five years old, when the antlers begin to appear. [from Anglo-Saxon *heorot*]

Harte, (Francis) Bret(t) (1836–1902) US writer, born in Albany, New York. He settled in San Francisco (1860) where he worked as a compositor and journalist, and was Secretary of the US Mint (1864–70). He was US consul at Krefeld (1878–80) and at Glasgow (1880–5). In 1868 he founded and edited the *Overland Monthly*, to which he contributed several short stories, notably those later collected in *The Luck of Roaring Camp and Other Sketches* (1870). Among his best-known poems is 'John Burns of Gettysburg'.

hartebeest *noun* a large African antelope with curved horns. [from Afrikaans *hartebeest*, hart beast]

Hartford POP (1990) 768 000, the capital of the state of Connecticut, USA. It lies on the Connecticut R, in Hartford County, central Connecticut. The city holds the world's largest concentration of insurance companies. HISTORY founded by Dutch settlers in 1633; achieved city status in 1784. NOTABLE FEATURES Old State House; Wadsworth Atheneum; Museum of Connecticut History.

Hartford Convention a gathering (1814–15) in Hartford, Connecticut, of New England states delegates to oppose the War of 1812 and to propose changes in the US Constitution. The Treaty of Ghent ending the war, and US victory at New Orleans discredited both the Convention and the Federalist Party, with which the Convention was associated.

Hartlepool POP (1992e) 92 000, a port town in Hartlepool district, Cleveland, NE England. It is situated 11km/7mi N of Middlesbrough. An advanced gas-cooled nuclear reactor started commercial operation here in 1984. NOTABLE FEATURE 12–13c St Hilda's Church.

Hartley, L(eslie) P(oles) (1895–1972) English writer, born near Peterborough. He started out writing macabre short stories, including *Night Fears* (1924), but is best known for his novel *The Go-Between* (1953). Other novels include *The Shrimp and the Anemone* (1944), *The Boat* (1950), and *The Hireling* (1957).

Hartnell, Sir Norman (1901–78) English couturier and court dressmaker. He started his own business in 1923 and received the Royal Warrant in 1940. He was President of the Incorporated Society of London Fashion designers (1946–56). His work included costumes for leading actresses, wartime 'utility' dresses, the WRAC uniform, and Princess Elizabeth's wedding and coronation gowns.

Hartono, Rudy, properly **Rudy Hartono Kurniawan** (1948–) Indonesian badminton player. The winner of a record eight All-England titles (1968–74, 1976), he was also a member of Indonesia's Thomas Cup winning teams in 1970, 1973, 1976, and 1979. He was world champion in 1980.

hart's tongue fern *Bot.* a fern belonging to the genus *Asplenium*, and having bright green strap-shaped undivided fronds.

harum-scarum — *adj.* wild and thoughtless; reckless. — *adv.* recklessly. — *noun* a wild, thoughtless person.

haruspex *noun* (PL. **haruspices**) in ancient Rome, a practitioner of the Etruscan system of divination foretelling events by examination of the entrails of sacrificial animals. Though less prestigious than the augurs, they were widely employed, and their art survived well into the Christian era. [perhaps from an Etruscan word + Latin *specere*, to view]

Harvard University in the USA, a university in Cambridge, Massachusetts, founded in 1636, the oldest in the USA. It is named after a Puritan minister, John Harvard (1607–38), who was its first benefactor. Originally intended as a religious training centre for ministers, it gradually expanded and by the late 19c had become a major educational institution. The affiliated college for women is called Radcliffe College (founded in 1879).

harvest — *noun* **1** the gathering in of ripened crops, usually in late summer or early autumn. **2** the season when this takes place. **3** the crops gathered. **4** the product or result of some action. — *verb trans., intrans.* to gather as a harvest; to reap. [from Anglo-Saxon *hærfest*]

harvester *noun Agric.* a machine that harvests a crop, eg a combine harvester or potato lifter.

harvest festival *or* **harvest thanksgiving** a Christian religious service to thank God for the crops gathered in the harvest.

harvestman *noun* an extremely long-legged arthropod, having a compact body and four pairs of long legs, typically a predator of small insects, molluscs, or worms. Some are scavengers.

harvest moon the full moon nearest to the autumnal equinox, usually 22 or 23 September.

harvest mouse a very small mouse that nests in the stalks of corn.

Harvest Waggon, The a landscape painting by Thomas Gainsborough (1767, Birmingham).

Harvey, William (1578–1657) English physician, born in Folkestone. In 1602 he set up in practice in London as a physician; he later held appointments at St Bartholomew's Hospital and the College of Physicians, and served as physician to James I (from 1618) and Charles I (from 1640). In 1628 he published a celebrated treatise in which he described his discovery of the circulation of the blood; he concluded that the heart was a muscle functioning as a pump, and that it effected the movement of the blood through the body via the lungs by means of the arteries, the blood then returning through the veins to the heart.

Harwich POP (1981) 17 000, a port in Tendring district, Essex, SE England. It lies on the North Sea coast, 26km/16mi E of Colchester.

has see HAVE.

has-been *noun colloq.* a person who is no longer successful, important or influential.

Hasdrubal the name of several Carthaginian leaders, notably Hamilcar Barca's son-in-law and successor in Spain (murdered 221 BC) and his son (Hannibal's younger brother), who died in battle with the Romans at the R Metaurus (207 BC).

Hašek, Jaroslav (1883–1923) Czech novelist and short-story writer, born in Prague. He is best known for his novel *The Good Soldier Svejk*

(1920–3), a satire on military life and bureaucracy, four volumes of which were completed by his death.

Haselrig *or* **Heselrige, Sir Arthur** (d.1661) English Parliamentarian, who in 1640 sat in the Long and Short Parliaments for his native county, Leicestershire. He was one of the five members whose attempted seizure by Charles I (1642) precipitated the Civil War. He commanded a Parliamentary regiment, and in 1647 became Governor of Newcastle. After the Restoration, he died imprisoned in the Tower.

hash¹ — *noun* **1** a dish of cooked meat and vegetables chopped up together and recooked. **2** a re-using of old material. **3** *colloq.* a mess: *make a hash of something.* — *verb* to make into a hash. — **settle someone's hash** *colloq.* to silence or subdue them. [from Old French *hacher*, to chop]

hash² *noun slang* hashish. [abbreviation]

hash browns a dish of potato (sometimes mixed with onion) cut into thin strips, fried to form a flat, browned cake, and eaten hot.

hashish *noun* a drug in the form of a resin, made from the dried leaves and flowers of hemp, smoked or chewed for its intoxicating effects. [from Arabic *hashish*, dry leaves]

Hashman, Judy (Judith), *née* **Devlin** (1935–) US badminton player, born in Winnipeg, Canada. The winner of the singles title at the All-England championships a record ten times (1954, 1957–8, 1960–4, 1966–7), she also won seven doubles titles (six with her sister, Susan Peard (1940–). She was a member of the US Uber Cup winning teams in 1957, 1960, and 1963.

Hasidim *or* **Chasidim** *or* **Hasideans** originally, those Jews in the 2c BC who resisted Greek and pagan influences on Israel's religion and adhered strictly to the Jewish law; probably the ancestors of the Pharisees. They supported the early Maccabean revolt against the Hellenistic Seleucids until the legitimate high priesthood had been restored. [Hebrew, = faithful ones]

Hasidism a movement of Jewish mysticism that began in 18c Poland, characterized by an ascetic pattern of life, strict observance of the commandments, and loud ecstatic forms of worship and prayer. It was originally opposed to rabbinic authority and traditional Jewish practices, stressing prayer rather than study of the Torah as the means of communicating with God, but as it spread through the Ukraine, E Europe, and eventually W Europe and America, it was finally accepted as a part of Orthodox Judaism.

Haskalah *or* **Haskala** a late 18c and 19c Jewish movement in central and E Europe which advocated the modernization and secularization of Judaism, and the promotion of enlightenment.

Haslemere POP (1981) 11 000, a residential town in Waverley district, Surrey, SE England. It is 20km/12mi SW of Guildford.

hasn't *contr.* has not.

hasp *noun* a metal fastening for a door, box, etc consisting of a flat metal strip with a narrow slit in it, which fits over a small curved metal bar and is held shut by a pin or padlock fastened through the bar. [from Anglo-Saxon *hæpse*]

hassle *colloq.* — *noun* **1** trouble, annoyance, or inconvenience, or a cause of this. **2** a fight or argument. — *verb* **1** to annoy or bother, especially repeatedly. **2** *intrans.* to argue or fight.

hassock *noun* **1** a firm cushion for kneeling on in church. **2** a tuft of grass. [from Anglo-Saxon *hassuc*]

hast *verb old use* the form of the present tense of the verb *have* used with *thou.*

haste *noun* **1** urgency of movement. **2** too much speed. — **in haste** in a hurry; quickly.

make haste to hurry. [from Old French *haste*]

hasten *verb* **1** *trans., intrans.* to move or cause to move with speed. **2** (**hasten to do something**) to do it eagerly and promptly: *he hastened to admit we were right.*

hastily *adv.* in a hasty way.

hastiness *noun* **1** hurry. **2** rashness. **3** irritability.

Hastings, Warren (1732–1818) English administrator in India, born in Churchill, Oxfordshire. He joined the East India Company in 1750, and by 1774 was Governor-General of Bengal, where he carried out several reforms, making the Company's power paramount in many parts of India. However, wars (1778–84) interfered with trade and damaged his reputation, and on his return to England in 1784 he was charged with corruption. He was acquitted after a seven-year trial, and the Company made provision for his retirement.

Hastings POP (1992e) 84 000, a resort town in Hastings district, East Sussex, SE England. It lies on the English Channel, 52km/32mi E of Brighton. The scene of the Battle of Hastings (1066) is 9km/5mi to the NW. Hastings was one of the Cinque Ports and the former base of the Royal Fleet. The port went into decline as the inland harbour silted up; the harbour was abandoned in the late 13c. NOTABLE FEATURES castle (1066), built by William the Conqueror; St Clement's and All Saints Church (14c); Fisherman's Museum; St Clement's sandstone caves; White Rock Pavilion with tapestry depicting the Battle of Hastings; Bateman's (17km/10mi NW), the 17c home of Rudyard Kipling (1902–36).

Hastings, Battle of the most decisive battle fought (14 Oct 1066) on English soil, which led to the Norman Conquest of England. Norman cavalry defeated the Anglo-Saxon army fighting on foot, and Harold II's death in battle cleared the way for Duke William of Normandy's coronation. However, the Normans did not master all England until 1092 (the capture of Carlisle).

hasty *adj.* (**hastier, hastiest**) **1** hurried; done or acting too quickly. **2** done without enough thought or preparation.

hat *noun* **1** a covering for the head, usually worn out of doors. **2** *colloq.* a role or capacity: *wearing her vet's hat.* — **keep something under one's hat** *colloq.* to keep it secret. **old hat** *colloq.* so well-known, familiar, etc as to be tedious and uninteresting. **pass the hat round** to collect money for a cause. **take one's hat off to someone** *colloq.* to admire or praise them, especially for some achievement. **talk through one's hat** *colloq.* to talk nonsense. [from Anglo-Saxon *hæt*]

hatband *noun* a band of cloth or ribbon around a hat just above the brim.

hatbox *noun* a large, rounded, cardboard box for storing or carrying hats.

hatch¹ *noun* **1** a door covering an opening in a ship's deck. **2** a hatchway. **3** a door in an aircraft or spacecraft. **4** an opening in a wall between a kitchen and dining-room, used especially for serving food. [from Anglo-Saxon *hæc*]

hatch² — *verb* **1** (*also* **hatch out**) *said of an animal or bird* to break out of an egg. **2** *intrans. said of an egg* to break open, allowing young animals or birds to be born. **3** to produce (young animals or birds) from (eggs). **4** (**hatch something up**) to plan or devise a plot, scheme, etc, especially in secret. — *noun* **1** an act of hatching. **2** a brood hatched. [from Middle English *hacchen*]

hatch³ *verb* to shade (eg the surface of a map, drawing, or engraving) with close parallel or crossed lines. [from Old French *hacher*, to chop]

hatchback *noun* a car with a sloping door at the back which opens upwards, allowing access to the rear compartment.

hatchery *noun* (PL. **hatcheries**) a place where eggs, especially fish eggs, are hatched in controlled conditions.

hatchet *noun* a small axe held in one hand. [from Old French *hachette*, from *hacher*, to chop]

hatchet-faced *adj.* with a long thin face and sharp profile.

hatchet job *colloq.* a severe written or spoken critical attack on a person or his or her good reputation.

hatchet man *colloq.* a person employed to injure, kill, or ruin a person, his or her reputation, or some thing.

hatching *noun* shading with fine lines.
◇ In art, it is a technique for producing tonal and shading effects by drawing or painting a series of lines or brush strokes side by side. When these lines are crossed and recrossed in many directions the technique is known as *cross-hatching*. Both techniques are used in pencil, charcoal, and ink drawings, pastels, acrylics, and tempera.

hatchway *noun* an opening in a ship's deck for loading cargo through.

hate — *verb* **1** to dislike very much. **2** *colloq.* to regret: *I hate to bother you.* — *noun* **1** great dislike. **2** *colloq.* a greatly disliked person or thing. [from Anglo-Saxon *hatian*]

hateful *adj.* causing or deserving great dislike.

hatefully *adv.* in a hateful way.

hatefulness *noun* being hateful.

hate mail correspondence containing an abusive or threatening message, especially sent to a celebrity or person in the news.

Hathor in Egyptian religion, the goddess of love, fertility, and pleasure. She is often represented by a cow, or has cow-like features. She was identified by the Greeks with Aphrodite.

hatpin *noun* a long metal pin, often decorated, pushed through a woman's hat and hair to keep the hat in place.

Hatra an ancient Parthian fortress city located between the Tigris and Euphrates rivers in N Iraq. It was founded in the 1c BC, and flourished as a trading and religious centre for four centuries before being razed by the Persian Sassanids. It is a World Heritage site.

hatred *noun* great dislike or ill-will. [from Middle English]

Hatshepsut (c.1540–c.1481 BC) Queen of Egypt of the 18th dynasty, the daughter of Thothmes I. She was married to her half-brother Thothmes II, on whose accession (1516 BC) she became the real ruler. On his death (1503 BC) she acted as regent for his son, Thothmes III, then had herself crowned as Pharaoh and took on the regular pharaonic attributes, including a false beard. She re-established trade and communications with Punt.

hatstand *noun* a piece of furniture with pegs for hanging hats, coats, umbrellas, etc on.

hatter *noun* a person who makes or sells hats.
— **mad as a hatter** extremely mad or eccentric.

Hattersley, Roy (Sydney George) (1932–) English Labour politician. He was a journalist and local authority politician before he entered parliament (1964). A supporter of Britain's membership of the EEC, he was a Minister at the Foreign Office (1974–6), then Secretary of State for Prices and Consumer Protection in the government of James Callaghan (1976–9). He was Opposition spokesman on the environment and on home affairs, shadow Chancellor, then Deputy Leader of the Labour Party (1983–92).

hat trick 1 the taking of three wickets in cricket with three balls following each other.

2 the scoring of three points, goals, etc in a single period of time or match. **3** the winning of three victories in a row.

Hattusas or **Hattusha** the ancient capital of the Hittites, now Bogazkoy in central Turkey. It was originally an Assyrian trading colony, which was taken by the Hittites in the 17c BC. It was destroyed in 1200 BC by marauders known as the Sea Peoples. Its ruins (discovered in 1834) are a World Heritage site.

hauberk *noun Hist.* a long coat of chain-mail. [from Old French *hauberc*]

Haughey, Charles (James) (1925–) Irish politician and Prime Minister, born in Castlebar, Co Mayo. Called to the Bar in 1949, he became a Fianna Fáil MP (1957), and from 1961 held posts in justice, agriculture, and finance, until his dismissal in 1970 after a quarrel with the Prime Minister, Jack Lynch. Later he spent two years as Minister of Health and Social Welfare, then became Prime Minister (1979–81, 1982, 1987–92); he was succeeded by Albert Reynolds in 1992.

haughtily *adv.* in a haughty way.

haughtiness *noun* being haughty.

haughty *adj.* (**haughtier**, **haughtiest**) very proud; arrogant. [from Latin *altus*, high]

haul — *verb* **1** *trans., intrans.* to pull with great effort or difficulty. **2** to transport by road, eg in a lorry. — *noun* **1** the distance to be travelled: *a short haul.* **2** the act of pulling with effort or difficulty. **3** an amount gained at any one time, eg of fish caught in a single net or of something stolen. [from Old French *haler*, to drag]

haulage *noun* **1** the business of transporting goods by road, especially in lorries. **2** the money charged for this.

haulier *noun* a person or company which transports goods by road, especially in lorries.

haulm *noun Bot.* the stalk or stem of potatoes, peas, beans, or grasses. [from Anglo-Saxon *healm*]

haunch *noun* **1** the fleshy part of the buttock or thigh. **2** the leg and loin, especially of a deer, as a cut of meat. [from Old French *hanche*]

haunt *verb* **1** *said of a ghost or spirit* to be present in (a place) or visit (a person or place) regularly. **2** *said of unpleasant thoughts, etc* to keep coming back to a person's mind: *haunted by the memory of his death.* **3** *colloq.* to visit (a place) frequently. [from Old French *hanter*]

haunted *adj.* **1** frequented or infested by ghosts, etc. **2** worried.

haunting *adj., said of a place, memory, piece of music, etc* making a very strong and moving impression.

hauntingly *adv.* in a haunting way.

Hauptmann, Gerhart (Johann Robert) (1862–1946) German writer, born in Obersalzbrunn, Silesia. He established a reputation with his first play, *Von Sonnenaufgang* (Before Dawn, 1889). This was followed by several other social dramas, including *Die Weber* (The Weavers, 1892). He also wrote poetry and novels, and was awarded the Nobel Prize for Literature in 1912.

Hausa a Chadic-speaking (African-Asiatic), predominantly Muslim people of Nigeria and Niger, the largest ethnic group in the area (present-day population c.12m). They are an agricultural people, also famed for their crafts. Most Hausa were conquered by the Fulani in the early 19c, and today form the populations of the Muslim emirates of Nigeria. The Hausa language has c.25m mother-tongue speakers, and is the only Chadic language to be written, now in a Roman alphabet which has displaced an Arabic one used from the 16c.

Hauser, Kaspar (c.1812–33) German foundling, a 'wild boy', found in the marketplace

of Nuremberg in May 1828. Though apparently 16 years old, his mind was a blank, and his behaviour that of a little child. He later gave an account of himself as having lived in a hole, looked after by a man who had brought him to the place where he was found. Many have regarded him as an imposter but others regarded him as a person of noble birth who was the victim of a crime.

Haussmann, Georges Eugène, Baron (1809–91) French financier and town planner, born in Paris. Under Napoleon III he became prefect of the Seine (1853) and improved Paris by widening streets, laying out boulevards and parks, and building bridges. He was made baron and senator, was dismissed in 1870, and was elected to the Chamber of Deputies in 1881.

hautboy *noun old use* an oboe. [from French *haut*, high + *bois*, wood]

haute couture the most expensive and fashionable clothes available; the leading fashion designers or their products. [from French *haute couture*]

haute cuisine cookery (especially French) of a very high standard. [from French *haute cuisine*]

hauteur *noun* haughtiness; arrogance. [from French *hauteur*]

Haüy, René Just (1743–1822) French crystallographer and mineralogist, born in St Just. Professor at the Ecole Normale and the Museum of Natural History, and Curator of the Ecole des Mines in Paris, his initial observation that calcite crystals of different form always break to produce rhomboidal fragments led him to the discovery of basic laws of crystallography, allowing crystal form to be used as an important aid in the identification of minerals.

Havana, Spanish **La Habana 1** POP (1990e) 2.1m, the capital of Cuba, situated on the N coast. The city was founded in 1519. It is the chief port in the country and is situated on a fine, natural harbour. NOTABLE FEATURES cathedral (1704); Presidential Palace (1920); several old fortresses including La Fuerza (1538), the oldest building in Cuba; castles of El Morro (1589–1630) and La Punta (late 16c). The old city centre is a World Heritage site. **2** a province in Cuba with Havana as its capital.

have — *verb* (**has**; PAST TENSE AND PAST PARTICIPLE **had**) **1** to possess. **2** to receive, obtain, or take: *have a drink / have a look.* **3** to think of or hold in the mind: *have an idea.* **4** to experience, enjoy, or suffer: *have a good time / have a headache / had my car stolen.* **5** to be in a state: *have a page missing.* **6** to take part in or hold: *have a party.* **7** to cause, order, or invite someone to do something or something to be done: *have your hair cut / had him fired.* **8** (**have to be** or **do something**) to be required to be or do it: *had to run fast / had to be gentle.* **9** to eat or drink. **10** to gain an advantage over: *you have me on that point.* **11** *colloq.* to cheat or deceive: *you've been had.* **12** to show or feel: *have pity / have the goodness to leave.* **13** to accept or tolerate: *I won't have any of that!* **14** to receive as a guest: *have people to dinner.* **15** to be pregnant with or give birth to: *be having a baby.* **16** *coarse slang* to have sexual intercourse with. — *verb aux.* used with past participles of verbs to show that an action has been completed: *have made the cake / has been there many times.* — *noun* **1** (**haves**) *colloq.* people who have wealth and the security it brings: *the haves and the have-nots.* **2** *slang* a trick or swindle.
— **have had it** *colloq.* **1** to be dead, ruined, or exhausted. **2** to have missed one's opportunity.
have it coming *colloq.* to deserve the bad luck, punishment, etc that one will get.
have it in for someone *colloq.* to feel hostile towards them.
have it off or **away with someone** *coarse slang* to have sexual intercourse with them.
have someone on *colloq.* to trick or tease them.
have something on 1 to be wearing it. **2** to have an engagement or appointment.

have something on someone to have information about them, especially when adverse or incriminating.

have it out to settle a disagreement by arguing or discussing it frankly.

have someone up *Brit. colloq.* to bring them to court to answer a charge.

have what it takes *colloq.* to have the required qualities or ability.
[from Anglo-Saxon *habban*]

Havel, Vaclav (1936–) Czech dramatist and political leader, born in Prague. He was resident writer for the Prague 'Theatre on the Balustrade' (1960–9) but his work was later judged subversive, and he was imprisoned (1979–83), his plays being performed abroad but not at home. These include *Zahradni slavnost* (The Garden Party, 1963), *Spiklenci* (The Conspirators, 1970), and *Temptation* (1987). He was imprisoned again in 1989, but was elected President by direct popular vote (Dec 1989) following the resignation of the hardline Communist Party leadership. However, due to opposition from Slovak nationalists, he failed to achieve re-election in 1992.

haven *noun* 1 a place of safety or rest. 2 a harbour. [from Anglo-Saxon *hæfen*]

haven't *contr.* have not.

haversack *noun* a canvas bag carried over one shoulder or on the back. [from German *Habersack*, from *Haber*, oats + *Sack*, bag]

Havilland, Sir Geoffrey de see DE HAVILLAND, SIR GEOFFREY.

Havisham, Miss the skeletal man-hater, and mentor of Estella, in Charles Dickens's *Great Expectations*.

havoc *noun* 1 great destruction or damage. 2 *colloq.* chaos.
— **play havoc with something** to cause damage or confusion to it.
[from Old French *havot*, plunder]

haw¹
— **hum and haw** see HUM.

haw² *noun* a hawthorn berry. [from Anglo-Saxon *haga*]

Hawaii POP (1990) 1.2m, a state of the USA in the Pacific Ocean, divided into five counties. AREA 16 759sq km/6 469sq mi. It consists of a group of eight major islands (Hawaii, Kahoolawe, Kauai, Lanai, Maui, Molokai, Niihau, and Oahu) and numerous islets in the central Pacific Ocean. It is known as the 'Aloha State'. The population of Hawaii is of diverse origin with a large proportion of Japanese descent. PHYSICAL DESCRIPTION the islands are of volcanic origin, with offshore coral reefs; the highest point is Mauna Kea (4 201m), a dormant volcano on Hawaii I, and a major astronomical site; Mauna Loa (4 169m) and Kilauea are active volcanoes; the islands are generally fertile and highly vegetated, although Kahoolawe is arid; over 90 per cent of its flora and fauna is unique to the islands. HISTORY reached by the Polynesians over 1 000 years ago; visited by Captain Cook in 1778, and named by him the Sandwich Is; King Kamehameha I united the islands in 1810, and encouraged trade with the USA; arrival of Christian missionaries in 1820; Polynesian monarchy overthrown in 1893; request for annexation to the USA rejected by President Cleveland, then accepted by President McKinley in 1898; became a territory in 1900; an attack by Japanese planes on the US naval base at Pearl Harbor on Oahu (1941) brought the USA into World War II; remained the chief US Pacific base throughout the war, and was under martial law until March 1943; admitted to the Union as the 50th state in 1959. CAPITAL Honolulu (on Oahu). ECONOMY pineapples, coffee, macadamia nuts, sugar cane; cattle; dairy produce; fishing (especially tuna); food processing; defence installations at Pearl Harbor; major tourist area, with Haleakala and Hawaii Volcanoes National Parks and Waikiki Beach.

Hawaii POP (1988e) 118 000, the largest island and a county in the US state of Hawaii, situated SE of Maui. AREA 10 488sq km/4 048sq mi. CHIEF TOWN Hilo. The island, a popular tourist destination, is known as the 'orchid isle'. NOTABLE FEATURE Volcanoes National Park in which lie the volcanoes Mauna Loa and Kilauea.

Hawaiian guitar a type of guitar developed in Hawaii in the 19c. It has a straight body which is placed across the player's knees, and metal strings that are 'stopped' with a movable steel bar to produce the characteristic glissando sound. Electric Hawaiian (or 'steel') guitars, sometimes free-standing, have been manufactured since the 1930s.

Hawaii Volcanoes National Park a volcanic area and national park in the SE of Hawaii I, USA. It was founded in 1961 and covers c.229 200ha, an area which includes two active volcanoes, Kilauea, and Mauna Loa. It is a World Heritage site.

hawfinch *noun* a type of finch with a large beak.

hawk¹ — *noun* 1 a relatively small bird of prey with short rounded wings and very good eyesight, belonging to the family Accipitridae. Hawks include sparrowhawks, harriers, kites, and buzzards (as opposed to eagles, the large members of this family). Most hawks hunt by pouncing on their prey, often flying in a series of short dashes followed by a long glide. Their prey includes small birds and mammals. 2 in the USA, any of various falcons. 3 *Politics* a person favouring force and aggression rather than peaceful means of settling disputes. See also DOVE. — *verb intrans.* to hunt with a hawk.
— **watch someone like a hawk** watch them closely.
[from Anglo-Saxon *hafoc*]

hawk² *verb* to carry (goods) round, usually from door to door, trying to sell them. [from Old German *haker*, retail dealer]

hawk³ *verb* 1 *intrans.* to clear the throat noisily. 2 *trans.* to bring (phlegm) up from the throat. [imitative]

Hawke (of Towton), Edward Hawke, 1st Baron (1705–81) English admiral, born in London. As a young commander, he fought against the French and Spanish, and his major victory was against the French at Quiberon Bay (1759), which caused the collapse of their invasion plan. He later became First Lord of the Admiralty (1766–71).

hawker¹ *noun* a person who hunts with a hawk.

hawker² *noun* a person who goes from house to house offering goods for sale from his vehicle.

hawk-eyed *adj.* having very keen eyesight.

Hawking, Stephen William (1942–) English theoretical physicist, born in Oxford. Professor at Cambridge from 1980, his research on relativity made his major contributions to the theory of the 'Big Bang' when the universe was created, and black holes, which sometimes result when stars collapse at the end of their lives; current knowledge of the physics of black holes owes much to his mathematical work. His book *A Brief History of Time* (1988) is a bestselling popular account of modern cosmology. From the 1960s he has suffered from a highly disabling and progressive neuromotor disease.

Hawkins, Coleman (1901–69) US tenor saxophonist, born in St Joseph, Missouri. In 1923 he joined Fletcher Henderson's jazz orchestra, where his performances on lively swing tunes such as 'The Stampede' (1926) and on slow ballads such as 'One Hour' (1929) irrevocably altered the way the tenor saxophone was played. After playing widely in Europe (1934–9), he returned to New York and recorded the jazz landmark 'Body and Soul'.

Hawkins, Jim the young narrator and hero of Robert Louis Stevenson's *Treasure Island*, who goes to sea in search of treasure.

hawkish *adj.* like a hawk.

hawkishness *noun* in a hawkish way.

hawk moth a medium to large moth, most abundant in the tropics, typically with long triangular wings and an elongated body. It is a fast flier, capable of hovering flight, and often has a long proboscis, used to suck nectar.

Hawks, Howard (1896–1977) US film director, born in Indiana. He wrote and directed his first feature film, *The Road to Glory* (1926). Success followed in such varied genres as airforce dramas (eg *The Dawn Patrol*, 1930), detection and crime (eg *The Big Sleep*, 1946), westerns (eg *Rio Lobo*, 1970), and comedy (eg *Man's Favorite Sport*, 1962).

hawkweed *noun Bot.* a perennial plant, belonging to the genus *Hieracium*, found mainly in the northern hemisphere, having leaves arranged spirally around the stem, or forming a rosette at the base, and yellow flower heads that may be solitary or borne in loose clusters.

Hawkyns, Sir John (1532–95) English sailor, born in Plymouth. He was the first Englishman to traffic in slaves (1562) between W Africa and the West Indies, but on his third expedition his fleet was destroyed by the Spanish (1567). He was knighted for his services against the Armada (1588), and in 1595, with his kinsman Francis Drake, he commanded an expedition to the Spanish Main, but died in Puerto Rico.

hawser *noun* a thick rope or a steel cable for tying ships to the quayside. [from Old French *haucier*]

hawthorn *noun* a thorny tree or shrub with pink or white flowers and red berries. [from Anglo-Saxon *haguthorn*]

Hawthorne, Nathaniel (1804–64) US novelist and short-story writer, born in Salem, Massachusetts. He lived in seclusion in Salem for many years writing stories and sketches. His first success was a collection of short stories, *Twice-told Tales* (1837), which was acclaimed in London, but his best-known works are his New England novels, notably *The Scarlet Letter* (1850) and *The House of the Seven Gables* (1851).

Hay, John (Milton) (1838–1905) US statesman and writer, born in Salem, Indiana. Trained as a lawyer, he became private secretary to President Lincoln, after whose death (1865) he served as a diplomat in Paris, Vienna, and Madrid. He returned to the USA and to journalism in 1870, and went on to write poetry, fiction, and a multi-volume biography of Lincoln. He became Assistant Secretary of State (1878), Ambassador to Britain (1897), and Secretary of State (1898), when he served under Presidents McKinley and Roosevelt.

hay *noun* grass that has been cut and allowed to dry in the field before being baled and stored for use as winter fodder for animal livestock.
— **hit the hay** *slang* to go to bed.
make hay while the sun shines to take advantage of an opportunity while one has the chance. [from Anglo-Saxon *hieg*]

Hay–Bunau-Varilla Treaty an agreement (1903) between the USA and Panama that created the Panama Canal Zone under US sovereignty. It gave the USA the right to build and operate the canal in return for a $10 000 000 fee and $250 000 annual rent. The chief parties involved were US Secretary of State John Hay, and the Panamanian representative Philippe Bunau-Varilla.

haycock *noun* a small, cone-shaped pile of hay in a field.

Haydn, (Franz) Joseph (1732–1809) Austrian composer, born in Rohrau, Lower Austria. Educated at the Cathedral Choir School of St

Stephen's, Vienna, he earned his living initially by playing in street orchestras and teaching. He became musical director (1759–60) for Count von Morzin's court musicians, then entered the service of the Esterházy family as musical director (1761–90). He was given great scope for composition, and among his innovations were the four-movement string quartet and the 'classical' symphony. His prolific output earned him a major international reputation and includes 104 symphonies, about 50 concertos, 84 string quartets, 24 stage works, 12 masses, orchestral divertimenti, keyboard sonatas, and diverse chamber, choral, instrumental, and vocal pieces.

Hayes, Rutherford B(irchard) (1822–93) US Republican statesman, the 19th President, born in Delaware, Ohio. He practised as a lawyer in Cincinnati (1849–61), served in the Civil War, entered Congress (1865–7), and became Governor of Ohio (1868–76). Under his presidency (1877–81), the country recovered commercial prosperity, and his policy included the reform of the civil service and the conciliation of the Southern states.

Hay Fever a play by Noël Coward (1925). Filled with satiric humour and witty dialogue, it depicts an eccentric family's weekend house party.

hay fever an allergic response to the pollen of grasses, trees, or other plants, characterized by sneezing, itching and watering of the eyes, and a running or blocked nose. Most of the symptoms are caused by the release of histamines, and are relieved by treatment with antihistamines.

hayfork *noun* a long-handled long-pronged fork for tossing and lifting hay.

Hay–Herrán Treaty an agreement (1903) between the USA and Colombia that gave the USA the right to build a canal across the isthmus of Panama, then part of Colombia. Its rejection by the Colombian Senate led to the US-sponsored Panamanian revolt for independence. The chief parties involved were US Secretary of State John Hay, and the Colombian chargé d'affaires in Washington DC, Tomás Herrán.

Hayley a female first name, after the surname. Popularized by the actress Hayley Mills in the 1960s. [probably from Anglo-Saxon *heg*, hay + *leah*, clearing]

Haymarket Square Riot a clash (4 May 1886) between police and demonstrators at a labour union rally in Chicago at which a bomb exploded, killing seven police and injuring some 70 others. Four people were executed by the state of Illinois for their involvement and public support for the union movement waned.

Hay–Pauncefote Treaties agreements (1901) between the USA and Britain that ended the British claim to joint rights to build and operate a canal across Central America. The chief parties involved were US Secretary of State John Hay and British Ambassador Lord Pauncefote.

haystack *or* **hayrick** *noun* a large firm stack of hay built in the open field and protected by plastic sheets or, more rarely, by thatching. Haystacks tend to be confined to small farms and hilly areas.
— **look for a needle in a haystack** to try to find something which is lost or hidden in a pile of things and so is almost impossible to find.

Haystacks a series of paintings by Claude Monet (1890–1, Musée d'Orsay, Paris). Each painting is done under different aspects of light.

Hay Wain, The a landscape painting by John Constable (1821, National Gallery, London).

haywire *adj. colloq.* out of order; in a state of confusion.

Haywood, William D(udley), known as **Big Bill** (1869–1928) US labour leader, born in Salt Lake City, Utah. After working as a miner, homesteader, and cowboy, he joined the

Western Federation of Miners (1896) and quickly became prominent. In 1905 he helped to found the Industrial Workers of the World, which was committed to revolutionary labour politics and to the organization of all workers in one big union. An active socialist, he was convicted of sedition in 1917 for his opposition to World War I, then he fled from the USA (1921) and took refuge in the Soviet Union.

hazard — *noun* **1** a risk of harm or danger. **2** something which is likely to cause harm or danger. **3** an obstacle on a golfcourse. — *verb* **1** to put forward (a guess or suggestion). **2** to risk. [from Old French *hasard*]

hazardous *adj.* damaging to safety or health; dangerous.

hazardously *adv.* in a hazardous way.

hazardousness *noun* being hazardous.

hazardous substance any chemical substance that is potentially damaging to health, and that can cause pollution of the environment.
◊ Hazardous substances may be toxic (eg arsenic, cyanide compounds, heavy metals), corrosive (eg strong acids or alkalis), oxidizing (eg nitrates or chromates), or flammable (eg petroleum). They also include radioactive waste produced during the generation of nuclear power. Special provisions are made for their disposal if this is particularly difficult or dangerous, but even so the effect on the environment of disposal of such substances is a source of major concern in many countries.

haze — *noun* **1** a thin mist, vapour, or shimmer which obscures visibility. **2** a feeling of confusion or not understanding. — *verb intrans.* (*also* **haze over**) to become covered in a thin mist.

Hazel a female first name, dating from the late 19c.

hazel — *noun* a small tree or shrub on which nuts grow; its wood. — *adj.* of a greenish-brown colour. [from Anglo-Saxon *hæsel*]

hazelnut *noun* the edible nut of the hazel, with a smooth, shiny shell.

hazily *adv.* **1** in a hazy way. **2** dimly, not clearly.

haziness *noun* being hazy.

Hazlitt, William (1778–1830) English essayist, born in Maidstone, Kent. He abandoned his studies for the ministry and took up painting before, on Coleridge's encouragement, he turned to writing and produced *Principles of Human Action* (1805) and further essays. In 1812 he found employment in London as a journalist, and contributed essays on many subjects including literary criticism to numerous periodicals, including the *Edinburgh Review*. His best-known essay collections are *Table Talk* (1821) and *The Spirit of the Age* (1825).

hazy *adj.* (**hazier, haziest**) **1** misty. **2** vague; not clear.

HB *abbrev., on a pencil* hard black.

H-bomb *noun* a hydrogen bomb.

HDTV *abbrev.* high-definition television.

HE *abbrev.* **1** His Eminence. **2** high explosive. **3** His or Her Excellency.

He *symbol Chem.* helium.

he — *pron.* **1** a male person or animal already referred to. **2** a person or animal of unknown or unstated sex. — *noun* (PL. **hes**) a male person or animal: *a he-goat.* [from Anglo-Saxon *he*]

head — *noun* **1** the uppermost or foremost part of an animal's body, containing the brain and the organs of sight, smell, hearing, and taste. **2** the head thought of as the seat of intelligence, imagination, ability, etc: *use your head / a good head for heights.* **3** something like a head in form or function, eg the top of a tool. **4** the person with the most authority in an organization, country, etc. **5**

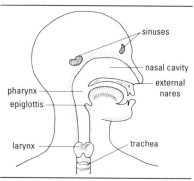

human head

the position of being in charge. **6** *colloq.* a headmaster, headmistress, or principal teacher. **7** the top or upper part of something, eg a table or bed. **8** the front or forward part of something, eg a queue. **9** the foam on top of a glass of beer. **10** the top part of a plant which produces leaves or flowers. **11** a crisis: *come to a head.* **12** the pus-filled top of a boil or spot. **13** (PL. **head**) a person, animal, or individual considered as a unit: *600 head of cattle.* **14** *colloq.* a headache. **15** the source of a river, lake, etc. **16** the height or length of a head, used as a measurement: *win by a head.* **17** a headland: *Beachy Head.* **18** the amount of pressure produced by water or steam in an enclosed space. **19** an electromagnetic device in a tape recorder, video recorder, computer, etc for converting electrical signals into the recorded form on tapes or disks, or vice versa, or for erasing recorded material. **20** the side of a coin bearing the head of a monarch, etc. **21** a headline. — *verb* **1** to be at the front of or top of: *head the queue.* **2** to be in charge of. **3** *intrans.* to move in a certain direction: *head for home.* **4** to put or write (a title or headline) at the beginning of a chapter, top of a letter, etc. **5** *Football* to hit (the ball) with the head.
— **above one's head** too difficult for one to understand.
give someone his *or* **her head** to allow someone to act freely and without restraint.
go to one's head 1 *said of alcoholic drink* to make one slightly intoxicated. **2** *said of praise, success, etc* to make one conceited.
have one's head in the clouds 1 to be inattentive to what is said. **2** to have impractical or unrealistic thoughts, ideas, etc.
head someone off to get ahead of them so as to intercept them and turn them back.
head over heels 1 rolling over completely with the head first. **2** completely.
head and shoulders by a considerable amount; to a considerable degree: *is head and shoulders above his competitors.*
keep one's head to remain calm and sensible in a crisis.
lose one's head to become angry, excited, or act foolishly in a crisis.
not make head or tail of to not understand.
off one's head *colloq.* mad, crazy.
off the top of one's head *colloq.* without much thought or calculation.
on your *etc* **own head be it** you, etc will bear the full responsibility for your, etc actions.
over one's head 1 to a higher authority. **2** too difficult for one to understand.
put our *or* **your** *or* **their heads together** to consult together.
take it into one's head 1 to decide to do something, usually foolishly. **2** to come to believe something, usually wrongly.
turn someone's head to make them vain and conceited.
[from Anglo-Saxon *heafod*]

headache *noun* **1** any continuous pain felt deep inside the head, usually caused by fatigue or anxiety, but sometimes associated with migraine, ear infections, eye disorders, toothache, alcohol consumption, drug abuse, head injury (eg concussion), serious disorders such as meningitis, or brain disease. **2** *colloq.* a person or thing that causes worry or annoyance.

headachy *adj.* **1** suffering or tending to suffer from headaches. **2** likely to cause a headache.

headband *noun* a band worn round the head, especially for decoration.

headbanger *noun slang* **1** a young person who shakes violently to the beat of pop or rock music. **2** a stupid or fanatical person.

headboard *noun* a board at the top end of a bed.

head cold a cold which affects one's eyes, nose, and head, rather than one's throat and chest.

head count a count of people present.

headdress *noun* a covering for the head, especially one which is highly decorative and is used in ceremonies.

headed *adj.* having a heading: *headed notepaper.*

header *noun* **1** *colloq.* a fall or dive forwards. **2** *Football* the hitting of the ball with the head.

headfirst *adv.* **1** moving especially quickly with one's head in front or bent forward. **2** without thinking; rashly.

headgear *noun* anything worn on the head.

headhunter *noun* a person whose occupation is headhunting.

headhunting *noun* **1** the practice of taking the heads of one's dead enemies as trophies. **2** the practice of trying to attract people away from their present jobs to work for one's own company, by offering them more money.

heading *noun* **1** a title at the top of a page, letter, section of a report, etc. **2** a horizontal tunnel in a mine.

Headingley a cricket ground in Leeds, England, the home of Yorkshire County Cricket Club and a regular Test venue. It was founded in 1890.

headlamp same as HEADLIGHT.

headland *noun* a strip of land which sticks out into the sea.

headless *adj.* lacking a head.

headlight *noun* a powerful light on the front of a vehicle.

headline *noun* **1** the title or heading of a newspaper article, written above the article in large letters. **2** (**headlines**) the most important points in a television or radio news broadcast. — **hit the headlines** *colloq.* to be an important or dramatic item of news.

headlong *adj., adv.* **1** moving especially quickly with one's head in front or bent forward. **2** quickly and usually without thinking.

headman *noun* a tribal chief or leader.

headmaster *or* **headmistress** *noun* the principal teacher in charge of a school.

head-on *adv., adj.* **1** head to head; with the front of one vehicle hitting the front of another: *a head-on crash.* **2** in direct confrontation.

headphones *or* **earphones** *pl. noun* an apparatus, consisting of two small sound receivers which are held over the ears by a metal strap passed over the head, which can be connected to a radio or record-player so that the sound is heard only by the person wearing the headphones.

headquarters *sing. or pl. noun* the centre of an organization or group, eg in the army, from which activities are controlled.

headrest *noun* a cushion which supports the head, fitted to the top of a car seat, etc.

headroom *noun* the space between the top of a vehicle and the underside of a bridge.

headscarf *noun* a scarf worn over the head and tied under the chin.

headset *noun* a pair of headphones, often with a microphone attached.

headship *noun* the position of, or time of being, head or leader of an organization, especially a school.

headshrinker *noun colloq.* a psychiatrist.

Head-Smashed-In Buffalo Jump an archaeological site in the Porcupine Hills of SW Alberta, Canada. From c.4000 BC until the early 19c, indigenous peoples slaughtered herds of buffalo here by stampeding them over the edge of the 'jump', a 10m high cliff. It is a World Heritage site.

headstall *noun* the part of a bridle which fits round a horse's head.

Head Start in the USA, a project begun in the early 1960s to help pre-school children from a disadvantaged background prepare for schooling. The main emphasis was on language and social development, with attention also paid to health care and parent education.

head start an advantage at the beginning of a race or competition.

headstone *noun* an inscribed stone at the head of a grave.

headstrong *adj., said of a person* difficult to persuade; determined; obstinate.

head teacher a headmaster or headmistress.

headwaters *pl. noun* the small streams flowing from a river's source.

headway *noun* **1** progress: *make no headway with the backlog.* **2** a ship's movement forwards. **3** same as HEADROOM.

headwind *noun* a wind which is blowing towards one, in the opposite direction to which one is travelling.

headword *noun* a word forming a heading, especially for a dictionary or encyclopedia entry.

heady *adj.* (**headier**, **headiest**) **1** tending to make one drunk quickly. **2** very exciting. **3** rash; impetuous.

heal *verb* **1** to cause (a person, wound, etc) to become healthy again. **2** *intrans.* (*also* **heal up** *or* **over**) *said of a wound* to become healthy again. **3** to make (sorrow) less painful. **4** to settle or put right (disputes, etc). [from Anglo-Saxon *hælan*]

healer *noun* a person who heals another.

Healey, Denis (Winston) Healey, Baron (1917–) English politician, born in Keighley, Yorkshire. For seven years after World War II he was secretary of the Labour Party's International Department before he became MP for Leeds (1952). In Harold Wilson's governments he was Secretary of State for Defence (1964–70), and later became Chancellor of the Exchequer (1974–9). Unsuccessful in the Labour leadership contests of 1976 and 1980, he became Deputy Leader (1980–3), and was shadow Foreign Secretary until he resigned from the shadow Cabinet (1980–7).

healing *noun* the action or process of restoring to a healthy state.

health *noun* **1** a state of physical, mental, and social well-being accompanied by freedom from illness or pain. **2** a person's general mental or physical condition: *be in poor health.* **3** the soundness, especially financial, of an organization, country, etc: *the economic health of the nation.* [from Anglo-Saxon *hælth*]

health centre a centre where a group of doctors and nurses provide health care for a community.

health education teaching, advice, and the provision of information to schoolchildren and the population at large, on healthy living.

◇ In schools, health education may include sex education; advice on nutrition and on drugs, smoking, alcohol, and other hazards to health; and the promotion of physical exercise. Government health education programmes are usually targeted at particular areas, such as the prevention of heart disease and cancer, the promotion of vaccination, and advice on how to prevent the spread of diseases such as AIDS.

health farm a place, usually in the country, where people go to improve their health through diet and exercise.

health food any food that is considered to be natural, free of additives, and particularly beneficial to one's health, eg whole-grain cereals, honey, organically grown fruit and vegetables.

healthful *adj.* causing or bringing good health.

healthily *adv.* in a healthy way.

healthiness *noun* being healthy.

health screening *Medicine* the performance of various tests on a large population of apparently healthy people in order to identify the presence of certain diseases or disorders, eg cervical smears to detect early stages of cancer of the cervix (neck of the womb).

health service a public service providing medical care, usually without charge.

health visitor a nurse trained in midwifery, preventive medicine, and health education, who is notified of all births in his or her area, and is responsible for visiting pre-school children and educating parents and relatives about childcare, as well as visiting the elderly and chronically ill on a regular basis.

healthy *adj.* (**healthier**, **healthiest**) **1** having or showing good health. **2** causing good health. **3** in a good state: *a healthy economy.* **4** wise: *a healthy respect for authority.*

Heaney, Seamus (1939–) Irish poet, born in Londonderry, Northern Ireland. Brought up on a farm, he moved to Dublin in 1976, and since 1989 has been Professor of Poetry at Oxford. His early volumes include *Death of a Naturalist* (1966), *Door into the Dark* (1969), and *North* (1975). Recent poetic works include *The Haw Lantern* (1987, Whitbread Award), *Seeing Things* (1991), and *Sweeney's Flight* (1992), his version of the Irish odyssey of Mad Sweeney. He has also written various critical essays, and his first play, *The Cure at Troy* (a version of Sophocles' *Philoctetes*), was published in 1990. His *New Selected Poems 1966–1987* appeared in 1990.

heap — *noun* **1** a collection of things in an untidy pile or mass. **2** (*usually* **heaps**) *colloq.* a large amount or number. **3** *colloq.* something, especially a motor vehicle, that is very old and not working properly. — *verb* **1** *trans., intrans.* (*also* **heap up** *or* **heap something up**) to collect it or be collected together in a heap. **2** (**heap something on someone**) to give it to them in large amounts: *heaped insults on his ex-wife.* [from Anglo-Saxon *heap*]

heaped *adj.* denoting a spoonful that forms a rounded heap on the spoon.

heaps *adv. colloq.* very much: *heaps better.*

hear *verb* (PAST TENSE AND PAST PARTICIPLE **heard**) **1** *trans., intrans.* to perceive (sounds) with the ear. **2** to listen to. **3** (**hear about** *or* **of something**) to be told about it or informed of it: *heard about his problems.* **4** (**hear from someone**) to be contacted by them, especially by letter or telephone. **5** *said of a judge* to listen to and judge (a case). — **hear! hear!** an expression of agreement or approval.

hear someone out to allow them to finish speaking or explaining.

not hear of something not to allow it to happen: *they would not hear of it.* [from Anglo-Saxon *hieran*]

Heard and McDonald Islands an island group in the S Indian Ocean, about

4 000km/2 500mi SW of Fremantle, Australia. AREA 412sq km/159sq mi. It is an Australian external territory comprising Heard I, Shag I, and the McDonald Is. The group was transferred from UK to Australian control in 1947. Heard I, which rises to over 2 000m, is actively volcanic and has a weather station.

hearer *noun* a person who hears.

hearing *noun* 1 the sense that involves the perception of sound. The main organ of hearing is the cochlea of the inner ear, which relays nerve impulses via the auditory nerve to the brain, where they are interpreted as sound. 2 the distance within which something can be heard. 3 an opportunity to state one's case: *give him a hearing.* 4 a court case.

hearing aid a small electronic device, consisting of a miniature sound receiver, an amplifier, and a power source, worn in or just behind the ear to aid the hearing of a person who is totally or partially deaf.

hearken *verb intrans.* (**hearken to something** *or* **someone**) *old use* to listen or pay attention to them. [from Anglo-Saxon *heorcnian*]

Hearns, Thomas, also called **Hit Man**, and **Motor City Cobra** (1958–) US boxer, born in Memphis, Tennessee. In 1987 he became the first man to win world titles at four different weights, and in 1988 the first to win titles at five different weights. His WBA championship title wins include welterweight (1980) as well as super-welterweight (1982); WBC title wins include junior-middleweight (1984), light-heavyweight and middleweight (1987), and super-middleweight (1988).

hearsay *noun* rumour; gossip.

hearse *noun* a car used for carrying a coffin at a funeral. [from Latin *hirpex*, harrow]

Hearst, William Randolph (1863–1951) American newspaper owner, born in San Francisco. He took over the San Francisco *Examiner* from his father (1887) and revolutionized journalism by introducing banner headlines and lavish illustrations. He then took over the New York *Journal* (1895), and headed a chain of newspapers and periodicals. His career inspired the film *Citizen Kane* (1941).

heart *noun* 1 in vertebrates, the hollow muscular organ that contracts and pumps blood through the blood vessels of the body. 2 this organ considered as the centre of a person's thoughts, emotions, conscience, etc. 3 ability to feel tenderness or pity: *have no heart.* 4 courage and enthusiasm: *take heart / lose heart.* 5 the central or most important part: *the heart of the problem.* 6 the breast: *hold her to her heart.* 7 the compact inner part of some vegetables, eg cabbages and lettuces. 8 a usually red symbol representing the heart, with two rounded lobes at the top curving down to meet in a point at the bottom. 9 a a playing-card with a red heart-shaped symbol on it. b (**hearts**) a suit of cards with such shapes on them.
— **at heart** really; basically.
break someone's heart to cause them great sorrow.
by heart by or from memory.
change of heart a change of decision, attitude, etc, usually to a kinder one.
have one's heart in one's mouth to be very frightened, worried, or anxious.
heart and soul completely; with all one's attention and energy.
lose heart to become discouraged.
lose one's heart to someone to fall in love with them.
not have the heart to do something to be too kind (to do something unpleasant).
set one's heart on something to want it very much.
take heart to become encouraged or more confident.

take something to heart to pay great attention to it or be very affected by it.
to one's heart's content as much as one wants.
wear one's heart on one's sleeve to show one's deepest feelings openly.
with all one's heart very willingly or sincerely. [from Anglo-Saxon *heorte*]
◇ In mammals, the heart is divided into four chambers, namely the right and left *atria* (sometimes called auricles), and the right and left *ventricles*. Blood that has been oxygenated in the lungs enters the left atrium of the heart and passes to the left ventricle, contraction of which pumps oxygenated blood into the aorta, a major blood vessel that leads to the arteries and thence to all the tissues of the body. Deoxygenated blood from the body tissues is returned to the heart via the veins, which lead into the superior vena cava and inferior vena cava, two major blood vessels. These convey the blood to the right atrium of the heart, and from there to the right ventricle, which pumps blood on to the lungs, where it is oxygenated and then returned to the heart so that the cycle can begin again. The presence of several valves within the heart ensures that the blood can only flow in one direction.
The muscular contractions of the heart are self-sustaining, because it consists of a special type of muscle, known as *cardiac muscle*, which does not become fatigued, and continues to contract rhythmically even when it is disconnected from the nervous system. The average rate of contraction, measured as the pulse rate, is about 72 beats per minute in men and about 80 beats per minute in women.

heartache *noun* great sadness or mental suffering.

heart attack a sudden severe chest pain, which may spread to the left arm, caused by death of part of the heart muscle (known as *myocardial infarction*) after its blood supply has been interrupted by blockage of a coronary artery, usually by a blood clot (*coronary thrombosis*). About half of all heart attacks result in death, but people who survive a heart attack are usually able to resume a full and active life.

heartbeat *noun* 1 the regular throb or pulsation of the heart, measured as the pulse, caused by the alternate contraction and relaxation of the heart muscle as it pumps blood around the body. *Diastole*, during which the atria contract and the ventricles relax, alternates with *systole*, when both ventricles contract. 2 a single pumping action of the heart.

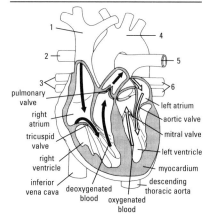

1: superior vena cava (deoxygenated blood from cells)
2: right pulmonary artery (deoxygenated blood to lungs)
3: right pulmonary veins
4: ascending aorta (oxygenated blood to body's cells)
5: left pulmonary artery
6: left pulmonary veins (oxygenated blood from lungs)

human heart

heartbreak *noun* very great sorrow or grief.

Heartbreak House a play by George Bernard Shaw (1919). A comedy set during World War I, and partly inspired by Chekhov's *The Cherry Orchard*, it presents an attempt to analyse in an English social environment the causes of contemporary moral and political discontents.

heartbreaking *adj.* causing great sorrow or grief.

heartbroken *adj.* grieving; severely disappointed.

heartburn *noun* a feeling of burning in the chest caused by indigestion.

hearten *verb trans., intrans.* (**heartened, heartening**) to make or become happier, more cheerful or encouraged.

heartening *adj.* cheering, encouraging.

hearteningly *adv.* in a heartening way.

heart failure a condition in which the ventricles of the heart fail to pump enough blood to meet the requirements of the body.
◇ The main symptoms of heart failure are congestion of the lungs and liver with blood, swelling of the veins in the neck, oedema (accumulation of fluid in the tissues), and breathlessness. The condition is most commonly caused by coronary thrombosis, hypertension (high blood pressure), or disease of the valves of the heart (which may become narrow or leak). It is usually treated with rest and a low-salt diet.

heartfelt *adj.* sincere.

hearth *noun* 1 the floor of a fireplace, or the area surrounding it. 2 the home. [from Anglo-Saxon *heorth*]

hearthrug *noun* a rug placed on the floor in front of the hearth.

heartily *adv.* in a hearty way.

heartiness *noun* being hearty.

heartland *noun* a central or vitally important area or region.

heartless *adj.* cruel; very unkind.

heartlessly *adv.* in a heartless way.

heartlessness *noun* being heartless.

heart-lung machine an apparatus that takes over the pumping action of the heart, together with the breathing action of the lungs, used especially so that the heart can be stopped and operated on. The blood is circulated by roller pumps through special plastic tubes; oxygen is put into the blood, and carbon dioxide removed, in a bubble oxygenator; and the blood is filtered and kept at the correct temperature as it passes through the machine.

Heart of Darkness, The a short story by Joseph Conrad (in *Youth: A Narrative*, 1902). It is narrated by the sailor Marlow, who describes his disturbing involvement with an ivory trader, Mr Kurtz.

Heart of Midlothian, The a novel by Sir Walter Scott (1818). It is set against the historical background of the Porteous Riots (1736) and describes Jeanie Deans's journey to London to plead for her sister's life.

Heart of the Matter, The a novel by Graham Greene (1948). It is set in a W African wilderness during World War II and focuses on the ill-fated life of Scobie, the Deputy Commissioner of police.

heart-rending *adj.* causing great sorrow or pity.

heart-rendingly *adv.* in a heart-rending way.

heart-searching *noun* the close examination of one's deepest feelings and conscience.

heartsease *noun* an annual, biennial, or perennial plant (*Viola tricolor tricolor*), native to Europe, with tufted stems, heart-shaped to lance-shaped leaves, and multicoloured flowers, usually yellow, violet, and white. — Also called *wild pansy*.

heartsick *adj.* very sad or disappointed.

heartstrings *pl. noun* deepest feelings of love, sympathy, or pity: *tug at her heartstrings*.

heart-throb *noun colloq.* a person whom a lot of people find very attractive, especially a male actor or singer.

heart-to-heart — *adj., said of a conversation* intimate, sincere, and candid. — *noun* an intimate and candid conversation.

heart-warming *adj.* pleasing; emotionally moving.

heartwood *noun Bot.* the hard wood at the centre of a tree trunk or branch, which provides structural support. It consists of dead cells containing oils, gums, and resins which give it a distinct dark colour.

hearty *adj.* (**heartier, heartiest**) **1** very friendly and warm in manner. **2** strong, vigorous, or enthusiastic: *hale and hearty*. **3** *said of a meal, or an appetite* large.

heat — *noun* **1** a form of energy that is stored as the energy of vibration or motion (kinetic energy) of the atoms or molecules of a material. The amount of vibration determines the temperature, and large objects contain more heat energy than smaller ones at the same temperature. Heat can travel by electromagnetic radiation, by conduction through a material, or by convection, which involves the circulation of a liquid or gas which carries heat with it. **2** a high temperature. **3** hot weather. **4** warmth of feeling, especially anger or excitement: *the heat of the argument*. **5** the most intense part of: *in the heat of the battle*. **6** in a sports competition, etc, a preliminary race or contest which eliminates competitors. **7** oestrus, a period of sexual receptivity in some female mammals: *on heat*. **8** redness of the skin, especially when sore, with a feeling of heat: *prickly heat*. — *verb trans., intrans.* to make or become hot or warm. [from Anglo-Saxon *hætu*]

heat capacity *or* **specific heat capacity** *Physics* the quantity of heat that is required to raise the temperature of unit mass of a substance by one kelvin (or 1°C). Loosely, it measures the ability of a substance to get hot while it is absorbing energy.

heated *adj.* **1** having been made hot or warm. **2** angry or excited.

heatedly *adv.* angrily, passionately.

heatedness *noun* being heated.

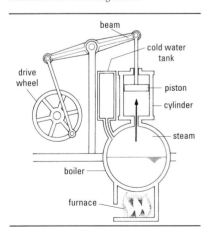

heat engine

heat engine *Engineering* any device that transforms heat energy into useful mechanical work.

heater *noun* an apparatus for heating a room, building, water in a tank, etc.

heat exchanger *Physics* a device that transfers heat from one stream of fluid (gas or liquid)

to another, without allowing the two fluids to come into contact, eg a car radiator.

Heath, Sir Edward (Richard George), also called **Ted** (1916–) English Conservative politician and Prime Minister, born in Broadstairs, Kent. He became an MP (1950), worked in the Whip's office (1951–9), then was Minister of Labour (1959–60), Lord Privy Seal (1960–3), and the chief negotiator for Britain's entry into the European Common Market. Elected Leader of the Conservative Party in 1965, he was Leader of the Opposition until he became Prime Minister (1970–4). After a confrontation with the miners' union in 1973, he narrowly lost the two elections of 1974, and in 1975 was replaced as leader by Margaret Thatcher, whose extreme policies he openly criticised.

heath *noun* **1** an area of open land, usually with dry sandy acidic soil, dominated by low-growing evergreen shrubs, especially heathers. **2** a low evergreen shrub of the genus *Erica*, with needle-like leaves and white, pink, or yellow bell-shaped flowers, found in northern and alpine regions, especially on open moors and heaths with acid soil. [from Anglo-Saxon *hæth*]

Heathcliff the tempestuous hero of Emily Brontë's *Wuthering Heights*.

heathen — *noun* **1** a person who is not a Christian, Jew, or Muslim, but who follows another religion, especially one with many gods. **2** *colloq.* an ignorant or uncivilized person. **3** (**the heathen**) heathens as a group. — *adj.* of heathens; having no religion. [from Anglo-Saxon *hæthen*]

heathenish *adj.* involving or characteristic of heathens.

Heather a female first name, dating from the late 19c but only recently common.

heather *noun* **1** a low evergreen shrub of the genus *Calluna*, with many side shoots bearing small scale-like leaves, and small pink or purple bell-shaped flowers, found in northern and alpine regions, and usually the predominant plant on open moors and heaths with acid soil. — Also called *ling*. **2** loose term for a heath. [from Middle English *hathir*]

Heath-Robinson *adj., said of a machine or device* peculiarly or ludicrously complicated and impractical in design, especially in relation to its function. [named after William Heath Robinson (1872–1944), the cartoonist who drew such machines]

heating *noun* any of various systems for maintaining the temperature inside a room or building at a level higher than that of the surroundings.

heat pump *Engineering* a device that is used to transfer heat from a cooler object or space to a warmer one, ie in the opposite direction to the natural flow of heat, so that an input of energy is required. Heat pumps are used to maintain low temperatures in refrigerators and freezers.

heat-seeking *adj., said of a missile, etc* able to detect heat from its target and use this as a guide to hitting it.

heat shield an apparatus or substance which protects a spacecraft from the extreme heat it experiences when returning to the Earth's atmosphere.

heatstroke *noun* a severe and sometimes fatal condition in which continuous exposure to unaccustomed heat results in failure of the mechanism that regulates the internal temperature of the body. The main symptoms are a high body temperature (without sweating), exhaustion, headache, nausea, and eventual loss of consciousness. – Also called *sunstroke*.

heatwave a prolonged period of unusually hot dry weather.

heave — *verb* (PAST TENSE AND PAST PARTICIPLE **heaved**, in sense 6 and for *heave to* **hove**) **1** to lift

or pull with great effort. **2** *colloq.* to throw (something heavy). **3** to utter: *heave a sigh*. **4** *intrans.* to rise and fall heavily or rhythmically. **5** *intrans.* to retch or vomit. **6** *intrans. said of a ship* to move: *heave into sight*. — *noun* an act of heaving.
— **get the heave** *colloq.* to be dismissed or rejected.
give someone the heave *colloq.* to dismiss or reject them.
heave to *said of a ship* to stop or cause it to stop while at sea.
[from Anglo-Saxon *hebban*]

heaven *noun* **1** the place believed to be the abode of God, angels, and the righteous after death. **2** (*usually* **heavens**) the sky. **3** great happiness or bliss. **4** *often used in exclamations* God or Providence: *heaven forbid*. [from Anglo-Saxon *heofon*]
◇ In the Bible, heaven is usually conceived as high above the Earth. In modern theology, the emphasis is more on the quality, transformation, or fulfilment of life, the fully revealed presence of God, and the perfection of the divine-human relationship, than on a place. In Islam, heaven is usually symbolized as paradise, a garden so wonderful it is beyond human imagination to fully conceive it.

heavenliness *noun* being heavenly.

heavenly *adj.* **1** *colloq.* very pleasant; beautiful. **2** of or from heaven or the sky.

heavenly bodies *pl. noun* the sun, moon, planets, stars, etc.

heavens *interj.* an expression of surprise, anger, dismay, etc.

heaven-sent *adj.* very lucky or convenient; timely.

heavily *adv.* **1** in a heavy way; with or as if with weight. **2** intensely, severely, violently.

heaviness *noun* being heavy.

Heaviside, Oliver (1850–1925) English physicist, born in London. A telegrapher by training, he spent much of his life living reclusively in Devon. He made various important advances in the study of electrical communications, and in 1902 predicted the existence of an ionized gaseous layer in the Earth's atmosphere capable of reflecting radio waves, the *Heaviside layer* (also known as the ionosphere), which was verified 20 years later.

Heaviside layer *Physics* in the Earth's atmosphere, a layer of the ionosphere that reflects medium-frequency radio waves, and is most effective during daylight hours. [from Oliver Heaviside]

heavy — *adj.* (**heavier, heaviest**) **1** having great weight. **2** having a great or relatively high density: *a heavy metal*. **3** great in size, amount, force, power, etc: *heavy traffic / a heavy crop*. **4** severe, intense, or excessive: *heavy fighting / a heavy sleep*. **5** hard to bear or endure: *a heavy fate*. **6** *said of the sky* dark and cloudy. **7** needing a lot of physical or mental effort. **8** *said of literature* serious in tone and content. **9** *said of food* difficult to digest. **10** *said of breathing* loud, because of excitement, exhaustion, etc. **11** striking or falling with force; powerful: *heavy rain / a heavy sea*. **12** sad or dejected: *with a heavy heart*. **13** ungraceful and coarse: *heavy features*. **14** physically and mentally slow. **15** fat; solid. **16** *said of soil* wet and soft because containing a lot of clay. **17** *colloq.* strict; severe: *don't be heavy on him*. **18** *said of guns* large and powerful. **19** *said of cakes and bread* dense through not having risen enough. — *noun* (PL. **heavies**) **1** *slang* a large, violent, and usually not very intelligent man. **2** a villain in a play, film, etc. **3** *Scot.* a beer like bitter but darker in colour and gassier. **4** (*usually* **heavies**) a serious newspaper. — *adv.* heavily: *time hangs heavy on my hands*.
— **heavy going** difficult or slow progress.
make heavy weather of something to exaggerate the difficulties involved in it.

[from Anglo-Saxon *hefig*]

heavy-duty *adj.* made to resist very hard wear or use.

heavy-handed *adj.* **1** clumsy. **2** too severe or strict.

heavy-handedly *adv.* in a heavy-handed way.

heavy-handedness *noun* being heavy-handed.

heavy-hearted *adj.* sad.

heavy hydrogen same as DEUTERIUM.

heavy industry an industry or the industries involving the use of large or heavy machines or producing large or heavy products, such as coal-mining, ship-building, etc.

heavy metal 1 loud, repetitive rock music with a strong beat. **2** large guns.

heavy water see DEUTERIUM OXIDE.

heavyweight — *noun* **1** the class for the heaviest competitors in boxing, wrestling, and weight-lifting. **2** (**light heavyweight**) a class between heavyweight and middleweight. **3** a boxer, etc of this weight. **4** *colloq.* an important, powerful, or influential person. **5** a person who is heavier than average. — *adj.* of the specified weight.

hebdomadal *adj.* weekly. [from Greek *hebdomas*, week]

hebdomadally *adv.* weekly.

Hebe in Greek mythology, the goddess of youth, the daughter of Zeus and Hera. She became cup-bearer to the Olympians, and was married to Heracles after he was deified.

Hébert, Jacques René (1757–94) French revolutionary extremist who represented the aspirations of the sans-culottes, born in Alençon. A popular political journalist, he assumed the psuedonym 'Le père Duchesne' after launching a satirical newspaper of that name (1790), and joined both the Cordelier and Jacobin Clubs. One of the Revolutionary Council, he was active in the September Massacres and the overthrow of the monarchy. After denouncing the Committee of Public Safety for its failure to help the poor, he tried to incite a popular uprising, but he incurred the suspicion of Danton and Robespierre and was guillotined with 17 of his followers ('Hébertists').

Hebraic *adj.* of Hebrews or the Hebrew language. [from Greek *hebraikos*]

Hebrew — *noun* **1** the ancient Semitic language of the Hebrews, revived and spoken in a modern form by Jews in Israel. **2** a member of an ancient Semitic people, originally based in Palestine. — *adj.* of the Hebrew language or people. [from Greek *Hebraios*, from Aramaic *Ibhraij*, one from the other side of the river]
◇ Classical Hebrew is the language of the Old Testament and Judaism. Modern Hebrew is the official language of Israel, and is spoken by c.4 million people worldwide. Classical Hebrew has an alphabet of 19 characters, Modern Hebrew has 23, and both are written from right to left.

Hebrews, Letter to the a New Testament writing of unknown authorship and recipients, sometimes attributed to Paul. It emphasizes how Jesus Christ, as Son of God, is superior to the angels and the prophets (including Moses), and how he acts as the perfect heavenly high priest. The main instructions are against spiritual lethargy and falling back into sin.

Hebrides a group of over 500 islands lying off the W coast of Scotland. They are divided into the Inner Hebrides (notably Skye, Eigg, Coll, Mull, Iona, Staffa, Islay, and Jura) and the Outer Hebrides (notably Lewis with Harris, and the Uists), separated by the Minch. HISTORY the Hebrides became part of the Kingdom of

Scotland in 1266, when they were ceded to Alexander III by Magnus of Norway. ECONOMY farming; fishing; Harris tweed; tourism.

Hebrides Overture, also called ***Fingal's Cave***, in full ***Die Hebriden; Fingals Höhle*** a tone poem by Felix Mendelssohn (Op 26, 1832). It is based on his *Die Einsamer Insel* (The Lonely Island, 1829), and is thought to have been inspired also by a visit to the Hebrides and Isle of Staffa. See also FINGAL'S CAVE.

Hebron, Arabic **El Khalil**, Hebrew **Hevron 1** POP (1984e) 75 000, the capital city of Hebron governorate (Jordan), in the Israeli-occupied West Bank, W Jordan, 29km/18mi SW of Jerusalem. One of the oldest cities in the world, it was built in 1730 BC. The city is a religious centre of Islam and was the home of Abraham. NOTABLE FEATURES Shrine of Haram El-Khalil over the Cave of Machpelah. **2** a governorate in the Israeli-occupied West Bank, W Jordan, with Hebron as its capital.

Hecate in Greek mythology, the goddess associated with witchcraft and magic. She appears in Hesiod, where she seems to represent the powerful mother-goddess of Asia Minor. She was worshipped at crossroads because of her assistance in the search for Persephone, whom she saw being abducted into the Underworld.

heck *interj. colloq.* a mild exclamation of anger, annoyance, surprise, etc; hell.

heckle *verb trans., intrans.* to interrupt (a speaker) with critical or abusive shouts, especially at a public meeting. [from Middle English *hekelen*]

heckler *noun* a person who heckles.

hectare *noun* a metric unit of land measurement, equivalent to 100 acres, or 10 000 square metres. [from HECTO- + ARE²]

hectic *adj.* very busy, confused, and excited. [from Greek *hektikos*, habitual]

hectically *adv.* in a hectic way.

hecto- *combining form* one hundred: *hectometre*. [from Greek *hekaton*, one hundred]

Hector 1 in Greek legend, the son of King Priam of Troy and Hecuba. He was married to Andromache, and led the Trojan army into war. Achilles killed him in revenge for the death of Patroclus, and dragged his body behind his chariot. Priam begged for the return of the body, which received a ceremonial burial. **2** a male first name. [from Greek *ekhein*, to check, restrain; also taken as an Anglicization of Gaelic *Eachdonn*, horse + brown]

hector — *verb* (**hectored, hectoring**) to bully, intimidate, or threaten. — *noun* a bully. [named after Greek *Hektor*, the Trojan hero in Homer's *Iliad*]

The Hebrew Alphabet					
Letter	Name	Usual trans-literation	Letter	Name	Usual trans-literation
א	'aleph	'	מ ם	mem	m
ב	beth	b	נ ן	nun	n
ג	gimel	g	ס	samekh	s
ד	daleth	d	ע	'ayin	'
ה	he	h	פ ף	pe	p, f
ו	waw	w	צ ץ	saddhe	s
ז	zayin	z	ק	qoph	q
ח	heth	h	ר	resh	r
ט	teth	t	שׁ	shin	sh, ś
י	yodh	y, j	שׂ	śin	ś
כ ך	kaph	k	ת	taw	t
ל	lamedh	l			

Hecuba *or* **Hecabe** in Greek legend, the wife of Priam, King of Troy, and mother of 18 children, including Hector and Cassandra. She was sent into slavery after the Greeks took Troy, and in revenge for the murder of her son Polydorus, she blinded Polymestor, King of Thrace, and murdered his two sons.

he'd *contr.* **1** he had. **2** he would.

Hedda Gabler a play by Henrik Ibsen (1890). It depicts female protagonists who pursue disastrous missions and analyses Hedda Gabler Tesman's inability to bear the banality of her life.

hedge — *noun* **1** a fence or boundary formed by bushes and shrubs planted close together. **2** a barrier or protection against loss, criticism, etc. — *verb* **1** *intrans.* to avoid making a decision or giving a clear answer. **2** to enclose (an area of land) with a hedge. **3** to protect oneself from possible loss or criticism (eg in a bet or argument) by backing both sides: *hedge one's bets.* [from Anglo-Saxon *hecg*]

hedgehog *noun* an insectivorous mammal belonging to the family Erinaceidae, native to Europe, Africa, and Asia, and having a body covered with spines, and a short tail.
◇ The common or European hedgehog (*Erinaceus europaeus*) is about 25cm long, and has small eyes, short ears and legs, a short tail, and a long snout. The back of the body and top of the head are covered with sharply pointed spines, each spine standing almost at right angles to the skin, and when threatened by a predator the hedgehog curls into a prickly ball. It sometimes eats plants, but its diet consists mainly of snails, slugs, insects, and worms. Occasionally hedgehogs eat lizards, mice, frogs, and snakes, and have also been seen to eat bird's eggs. They sleep during the day and search for food at night, using their acute hearing and sense of smell (they have very poor eyesight). In winter they hibernate completely or intermittently.

hedge-hop *verb intrans.* (**hedge-hopped, hedge-hopping**) to fly at a very low altitude, eg when crop-spraying.

hedgerow *noun* a row of bushes forming a hedge.

hedge-sparrow *noun* a small, grey-brown song-bird.

hedonism *noun* the belief that pleasure is the most important aim in life. [from Greek *hedone*, pleasure]

hedonist *noun* a person whose chief concern is pleasure.

hedonistic *adj.* relating to hedonists or hedonism.

heebie-jeebies *pl. noun colloq.* feelings of nervousness or anxiety. [origin unknown]

heed — *verb* to pay attention to or take notice of (advice, a warning, etc). — *noun* attention; notice: *take heed of what she says.*

heedful *adj.* (**heedful of something** *or* **someone**) paying careful attention to a warning, advice, etc.

heedless *adj.* (**heedless of something** *or* **someone**) careless; taking no notice of a warning, advice, etc. [from Anglo-Saxon *hedan*]

heedlessly *adv.* in a heedless way.

heedlessness *noun* being heedless.

hee-haw — *noun* the bray of a donkey. — *verb intrans.* to bray. [imitative]

heel¹ — *noun* **1** the rounded back part of the foot. **2** the part of a sock, stocking, etc that covers the heel. **3** the part of a shoe, boot, etc which supports the heel. **4** anything shaped or functioning like the heel, eg that part of the palm near the wrist. **5** *slang* a person very much disliked, or not considered trustworthy. — *verb* **1** to put a new heel on (a shoe, etc). **2** *intrans. Rugby* to kick the ball backwards with the heel. **3** *intrans.* said of a

dog to walk at, or go to, a person's side. **4** *intrans.* to touch the ground with the heel, eg in dancing.
— **cool** *or* **kick one's heels** to be kept waiting indefinitely.
dig one's heels in to behave stubbornly.
down at heel untidy; in poor condition.
lay *or* **set someone by the heels** *old colloq. use to* put them in prison.
on the heels of someone following close behind.
take to one's heels to run away.
to heel close behind; under control.
turn on one's heel to turn round suddenly or sharply.
[from Anglo-Saxon *hela*]

heel² *verb intrans.* (*often* **heel over**) *said of a ship* to lean over to one side. [from Anglo-Saxon *hieldan*, to slope]

heelball *noun* a black waxy substance used for blacking the heels and soles of shoes and doing brass rubbings.

Heenan, John Carmel (1905–75) English Roman Catholic Archbishop of Westminster, born in Ilford, Essex. Ordained in 1930, he became a parish priest in E London, and during World War II worked with the BBC, when he was known as the 'Radio Priest'. He was Bishop of Leeds (1951), and Archbishop of Liverpool (1957), then of Westminster (1963–75). A convinced ecumenist, he was created a cardinal in 1975.

Heep, Uriah the obsequious but scheming clerk of Mr Wickfield in Charles Dickens's *David Copperfield*.

heftily *adv.* in a hefty way, vigorously, strongly.

heftiness *noun* being hefty.

hefty *adj.* (**heftier, heftiest**) *colloq.* **1** *said of a person* big and strong. **2** *said of an object, blow, etc* large, heavy, or powerful. **3** large in amount: *a hefty sum of money.* [from HEAVE]

Hegel, Georg Wilhelm Friedrich (1770–1831) German idealist philosopher, born in Stuttgart. He was a headmaster in Nuremberg (1808–16), Professor at Heidelberg, and in 1818 he became Professor at Berlin. In his first major work *Phänomenologie des Geistes* (The Phenomenology of the Mind, 1807), he attacked the romantic intuitionism of Friedrich Schelling. Other works include *Wissenschaft der Logik* (Science of Logic, 1812–16) and *Enzyklopädie der philosophischen Wissenschaften* (Encyclopedia of the Philosophical Sciences, 1817), in which he set out his tripartite system of logic, philosophy of nature, and mind. His approach rejects the reality of finite and separate objects and minds in space and time, and establishes an underlying, all-embracing unity, the Absolute. His works exerted considerable influence on subsequent European and US philosophy.

Hegelianism a philosophical movement begun in the 1820s, inspired by Hegel. It split into the Hegelian Right and the Hegelian Left: the Right adhered to Hegel's rationalism and idealism, while the Left (including Marx) adopted Hegel's dialectic to attack his commitment to idealism, Christianity, monarchy, and bourgeois ideals.

hegemony *noun* (PL. **hegemonies**) leadership or control by one state within a group of states or alliance. [from Greek *hegemonia*, from *hegemon*, leader]

Hegira *noun Relig.* the flight of the Prophet Muhammad from Mecca to Yathrib (thereafter known as Medina, 'The City of the Prophet'), in Jul 622. The departure marks the beginning of the Muslim era. [from Arabic *hejira*, flight]

Heidegger, Martin (1889–1976) German philosopher, born in Messkirch, Baden. He was Professor of Philosophy at Marburg (1923–8) and Freiburg (1929–45), when he was retired for his connections with the Nazi regime. In his uncom-

pleted main work *Sein und Zeit* (Being and Time, 1927), he presents an exhaustive ontological classification of 'Being'.

Heidelberg POP (1991e) 137 000, an industrial city in Baden-Württemberg state, SW Germany. It lies on the R Neckar, 18km/11mi SE of Mannheim. Its university is the oldest in Germany, dating from 1386. During the 16c Heidelberg was the centre of German Calvinism. NOTABLE FEATURES castle (1583–1610); Holy Ghost Church (15c); town hall (18c).

Heidelberg, University of the oldest university in Germany, founded in 1386 by Elector Rupert I in Heidelberg. It lost much of its former importance during the Thirty Years' War (1618–48) and the Napoleonic Wars (1796–1815), but regained its prestige as a centre of learning during the 19c.

heifer *noun* a female cow over one year old that has not calved, or that has calved only once. [from Anglo-Saxon *heahfore*]

Heifetz, Jascha (1901–87) US violinist, born in Vilna, Lithuania. He began studying at the St Petersburg Conservatory in 1910, and toured Russia, Germany, and Scandinavia at the age of 12. After the Russian Revolution he settled in the USA and took US citizenship (1925). William Walton's violin concerto is among other works commissioned by him from leading composers.

height *noun* **1** the distance from the bottom of something to the top. **2** a distance above the ground from a recognized point, especially above sea level. **3** relatively great altitude. **4** a high place or rising ground. **5** the highest point; the summit. **6** the most intense part: *the height of battle.* **7** a very good, bad, or serious example: *the height of stupidity.* [from Anglo-Saxon *hiehthu*]

heighten *verb trans., intrans.* (**heightened, heightening**) to make or become higher, greater, stronger, brighter, etc.

Heilong Jiang see AMUR RIVER.

Heimdall *or* **Heimdal** in Norse mythology, the watchman of the gods. He lived outside Asgard (the home of the gods), and guarded the rainbow bridge Bifrost. It was believed that at the end of the world (Ragnarok) he would blow on the Giallar Horn to call the gods to a council.

Heine, (Christian Johann) Heinrich (1797–1856) German poet and essayist, born in Düsseldorf of Jewish parents. He studied banking and law, and in 1821 began to publish poetry. His best-known works include the 4-volume prose *Reisebilder* (Pictures of Travel, 1826–7, 1830–1), and the influential *Das Buch der Lieder* (The Book of Songs, 1827). He became a Christian in 1825, but his revolutionary opinions rendered him unemployable in Germany. He went into voluntary exile in Paris after the 1830 revolution, and became leader of the cosmopolitan democratic movement, writing widely on French and German culture.

heinous *adj.* very evil or wicked. [from Old French *haineus*, from *hair*, to hate]

heinously *adv.* in a heinous way.

heinousness *noun* being heinous.

Heinz, H(enry) J(ohn) (1844–1919) US food manufacturer and packer, born of German parents in Pittsburgh, Pennsylvania. In 1876 he became co-founder, with his brother and cousin, of F & J Heinz. The business was reorganized as the H J Heinz Company in 1888, and he was its President from 1905 to 1919. He invented the slogan '57 varieties' in 1896, promoted the pure food movement in the USA, and was a pioneer in staff welfare work.

heir *noun* a person who by law receives wealth, a title, etc when the owner or holder dies. [from Latin *heres*]

heir apparent (PL. **heirs apparent**) **1** *Legal* an heir whose claim cannot be set aside by the birth

of another heir. **2** *colloq.* the probable next leader of an organization, especially a political party.

heiress *noun* a female heir, especially a woman who has inherited or will inherit great wealth when some person dies.

heirloom *noun* an object that has been handed down in a family from parents to children over many years.

heir presumptive (PL. **heirs presumptive**) *Legal* an heir whose claim can be set aside by the birth of another heir whose claim is more valid.

Heisenberg, Werner Karl (1901–76) German theoretical physicist, born in Würzburg. He was professor at Leipzig University (1927–41), and later moved to Berlin, Göttingen, and then Munich. For developing and applying the theory of quantum mechanics using matrix methods, he was awarded the 1932 Nobel Prize for Physics. His revolutionary principle of indeterminacy or uncertainty principle (1927) showed that there is a fundamental limit to the accuracy with which certain pairs of variables (such as the position and momentum of an electron) can be determined.

heist *noun North Amer. slang* a robbery. [variant of HOIST]

Hejira same as HEGIRA.

Hel *or* **Hela** in Norse mythology, originally the Underworld, later the goddess of death herself. She was the youngest child of Loki and half her body was living human flesh, the other half decayed. She was assigned by Odin to rule Niflheim (the Underworld).

held see HOLD.

Heldenleben, Ein (A Hero's Life) a tone poem for orchestra by Richard Strauss (Op 40, 1897–8).

Helen 1 in Greek legend, the daughter of Zeus and Leda, and wife of Menelaus of Sparta. She was famous for her beauty, and her abduction by Paris the Trojan led to the Trojan War. She returned to Menelaus after the capture of Troy. **2** a female first name. [probably related to Greek *helios*, sun]

Helena 1 one of the two heroines in Shakespeare's *A Midsummer Night's Dream*, in love with Demetrius. **2** The heroine of Shakespeare's *All's Well that Ends Well*, in love with Bertram.

Helga a female first name, reintroduced from Scandinavia and Germany in the 20c. [from Old Norse *haelga*, holy]

helical *adj.* of or like a helix; coiled. [from HELIX]

helical scan *Electron.* a system of magnetic tape recording in which the tape is wrapped in a partial helix around a drum carrying two or more rotating heads which trace a series of tracks diagonally across its width. Very high frequencies may be recorded economically, as the relative head-to-tape speed is greater than the rate at which the tape itself advances. It is used in video tape recording and in the production of compact high-quality audio tracks.

Helicon the largest mountain in Boeotia. In Greek mythology, it was the sacred hill of the Muses, whose temple was found there, along with the fountains of Aganippe and Hippocrene.

helicopter *noun* an aircraft, lifted and propelled by rotating blades, which takes off and lands vertically, and can hover above the ground. [from Greek *helix*, screw + *pteron*, wing]

Heligoland, German **Helgoland** POP (1990e) 2 000, a rocky North Sea island in Heligoland Bay, Schleswig-Holstein state, Germany. It lies 64km/40mi NW of Cuxhaven. AREA 2.1sq km/ 0.8sq mi. HISTORY captured from Denmark by the UK in 1807; ceded to Germany in 1890 in exchange for Zanzibar; a German naval base in both World Wars. Popular with tourists, it is also a centre for the study of birds.

heliocentric *adj. Astron.* denoting a system with the Sun at its centre. [from Greek *helios*, sun + *kentron*, centre]

heliograph *noun* an instrument which uses mirrors to reflect light from the sun in flashes, as a way of sending messages in Morse code. [from Greek *helios*, sun + -GRAPH]

Heliopolis the name given in antiquity to the Egyptian city which was the centre of the cult of the Sun-god, Re. It is also the ancient name for Baalbek in Lebanon. [Greek, = city of the sun]

Helios in Greek mythology, the Sun-god, represented as a charioteer with four horses. In early times he was worshipped at Rhodes; later, he became associated with other gods (eg Apollo).

heliosphere *Astron.* a spherical region of space surrounding the Sun, whose outer boundary (the *heliopause*), thought to lie about 100 astronomical units from the Sun, represents the zone where the solar wind merges with the interstellar gas. [from Greek *helios*, sun + SPHERE]

heliotrope *noun* **1** a garden plant with small, fragrant, lilac-blue flowers which grow towards the sun. **2** the colour of these flowers. [from Greek *helios*, sun + *trepein*, to turn]

helipad *noun* a landing place for a helicopter, usually a square marked with a cross or a large H.

heliport *noun* a place where helicopters take off and land. [contraction of HELICOPTER + AIRPORT]

helium *noun Chem.* (SYMBOL **He**, ATOMIC NUMBER **2**) a colourless odourless inert gas found in uranium and thorium ores and some natural gas deposits, and formed in stars by nuclear fusion. It is one of the rare or noble gases, and is used to fill balloons and airships, to provide inert atmospheres for welding, and is also used together with oxygen in 'air' mixtures for divers. Liquid helium is used as a refrigerant for superconductors. [from Greek *helios*, sun, so called because it was first identified in the sun's atmosphere]

helix *noun* (PL. **helices**, **helixes**) **1** a spiral or coiled structure, eg the thread of a screw. **2** *Geom.* a spiral-shaped curve that lies on the lateral surface of a cylinder or cone. [from Greek *helix*]

hell — *noun* **1** the abode of evil spirits and the place or state of punishment for the wicked after death. **2** the abode of the dead. **3** any place or state which causes pain and misery. — *interj. colloq.* an exclamation of annoyance.
— **beat** *or* **knock the hell out of someone** *colloq.* to beat them severely.
come hell or high water *colloq.* in spite of whatever problems or difficulties may arise.
for the hell of it *colloq.* just for fun.
give someone hell *colloq.* **1** to scold or punish them severely. **2** to make things extremely difficult for them.
hell for leather *colloq.* extremely fast.
a hell *or* **one hell of a ...** *colloq.* a very great or significant: *one hell of a row.*
[from Anglo-Saxon *hel*]
◊ In traditional Christian thought, hell is the eternal abode and place of torment of the damned, developed out of Hebrew *sheol* and Greek *hades* as the place of the dead. Much contemporary Christian thought rejects the idea of vindictive punishment as incompatible with belief in a loving God.

he'll *contr.* he will; he shall.

hell-bent *adj.* (**hell-bent on something**) *colloq.* determined about it.

hellebore *noun* a plant with white, greenish-white, or purplish flowers. [from Greek *helleboros*]

Hellen in Greek mythology, the grandson of Prometheus and eponymous ancestor of the

Greeks, who were called Hellenes. The Dorian, Ionian, Aeolian, and Achean branches of the Greek race were named after his sons and grandsons.

Hellene *noun* a Greek. [from Greek *Hellen*]

Hellenic *adj.* Greek.

Hellenism *noun* Greek character or culture, especially that of ancient Greece.

Hellenist *noun* an admirer of or expert in Greek language and culture.

Hellenistic *adj.* relating to the people, language, or culture of the ancient Greek world after the death of Alexander the Great in 323 BC.

Hellenistic Age the period from the death of Alexander the Great (323 BC) to the beginning of the Roman Empire (31 BC). It was politically and culturally dominated by various Greek or Hellenized dynasties (eg the Ptolemies and Seleucids), who ruled the entire area from Greece to the N of India.

Hellenistic philosophy a philosophical speculation which was centred in Athens (c.300 BC–c.200 AD), and dominated by Stoicism, Epicureanism, and scepticism. Two of its chief concerns were the possibility of developing an empiricist account of knowledge, and the description of the ideal human life.

Hellenists a group referred to in Acts (6.1, 9.29) contrasted with the Hebrews, and usually interpreted as Greek-speaking Jewish Christians who were critical of the Temple worship and who prepared for the Christian mission to convert non-Jews. Stephen may have been a Hellenist.

Hellenization the process in antiquity by which Greek language and culture were spread among non-Greek (usually oriental) peoples by Alexander the Great and his successors. They established Greek city-states throughout their dominions to produce cultural unification.

Heller, Joseph (1923–) US novelist, born in New York City. He served with the US Air Force in World War II, and his wartime experience forms the background for his successful first novel, *Catch-22* (1961). Other novels include *Something Happened* (1964) and *Picture This* (1988).

Hellespont see DARDANELLES.

hell-fire *noun* the fire of, or punishment in, hell.

hellish *adj. colloq.* very bad; very unpleasant.

hellishly *adv.* in a hellish way.

hellishness *noun* being hellish.

hello *or* **hallo** *or* **hullo** *interj.* a word used as a greeting, to attract attention, to start a telephone conversation, or to express surprise.

hell's angel a member of a motorcycle gang, especially one whose behaviour is violent and anti-social.

Hell's Canyon *or* **Grand Canyon of the Snake** a gorge on the Snake R, north-west USA, where it follows the Oregon–Idaho state frontier. With a depth of c.2 450m, it is one of the deepest gorges in the world; its length is 65km/40mi.

Hellyer, Arthur George Lee (1902–93) English horticulturalist, writer, and journalist, born in London. When sent for a period of convalescence to a tomato farm, he began a career in horticulture. He was editor of *Amateur Gardening* for 21 years and also wrote 10 books, including the *Popular Encyclopedia of Flowering Plants* (1957).

helm *noun* the wheel or tiller by which a ship is steered.
— **at the helm** in a controlling position; in charge.
[from Anglo-Saxon *helma*]

Helmand River the longest river in Afghanistan, length 1 125km/700mi. It flows SW into the marshy lake of Hamu-e-Saberi and rises

in the Hindu Kush Mts. Genghis Khan (13c) and Timur (14c) destroyed the ancient irrigation and river control system.

helmet *noun* a hard, protective covering for the head. [from Anglo-Saxon *helm*]

Helmholtz, Hermann von (1821–94) German physiologist and physicist, born in Potsdam. Professor at Königsberg, Bonn, Heidelberg, and Berlin, his significant contributions to physiology were principally connected with the eye, the ear, and the nervous system. He was also important for his research on the spectrum, conservation of energy, and the development of electric current within a galvanic battery.

helmsman *noun* a person who steers a ship.

helot *noun* a serf, especially in ancient Sparta. [from Greek *heilotes*, inhabitants of *Helos*, a town in ancient Laconia (the area around Sparta)]

help — *verb* **1** *trans., intrans.* to assist. **2** *trans., intrans.* to contribute towards making (difficulties, pain, etc) less severe; to improve (a situation). **3** *trans., intrans.* to refrain from: *couldn't help laughing.* **4** to prevent or control: *I can't help the bad weather.* **5** (**help someone to something**) to serve a person: *help him to potatoes.* — *noun* **1** an act of helping. **2** a person or thing that helps. **3** a domestic servant; servants in general. **4** a remedy or relief.
— **cannot help oneself** is not able to refrain from doing something.
help oneself to something 1 to take (food, etc) for oneself, without being served. **2** to take something without authority or permission.
help out *or* **help someone out** to offer help, usually for a short time, and especially by sharing a burden or the cost of something.
[from Anglo-Saxon *helpan*]

helper *noun* a person who helps.

helpful *adj.* giving help; useful.

helpfully *adv.* in a helpful way.

helpfulness *noun* being helpful.

helping *noun* a single portion of food.

helpless *adj.* **1** unable to do anything for oneself. **2** weak and defenceless.

helplessly *adv.* in a helpless way.

helplessness *noun* being helpless.

Helpmann, Sir Robert (Murray) (1909–86) Australian dancer, actor, and choreographer, born in Mount Gambier. He made his début in Adelaide in 1923, studied with Anna Pavlova's touring company in 1929, and in 1931 went to Britain to study under Ninette de Valois. As first dancer of the new Sadler's Wells Ballet (1933–50), he was noted for his dramatic roles in de Valois's works, and he also danced in many films. His choreographic work includes *Hamlet* (1942) and *Miracle in the Gorbals* (1944).

helpmate *noun* a friend or partner, especially a husband or wife.

Helsingborg, Swedish **Hälsingborg** POP (1992e) 110 000, a seaport and commercial town on the W coast of Malmöhus county, SW Sweden. It lies on The Sound opposite Helsingör, Denmark. The town was part of Denmark until 1658. NOTABLE FEATURES town hall (1897); St Mary's Church (13c).

Helsingfors see HELSINKI.

Helsingør see ELSINORE.

Helsinki, Swedish **Helsingfors** POP (1992e) 496 000, the capital of Finland and of Uudenmaa province, S Finland. It is a seaport on the Gulf of Finland, lying on a peninsula surrounded by islands. The heart of the city is the harbour, where the dominant style of architecture is 19c neoclassical. The residential garden city of Tapiola, 6km/4mi from the city centre, is a model of modern town planning (built in the 1950s). HISTORY founded by Gustavus Vasa of Sweden in 1550, N of the present site; became capital in

1812; heavily bombed in World War II. NOTABLE FEATURES cathedral (completed in 1852); Olympic Stadium; Rock Church (Tempeliaukio); Ateneum Museum; National Museum; Open-air Museum on the nearby island of Seurasaari.

Helsinki Conference a conference (1975) on security and co-operation in Europe, attended by the heads of 35 states, including the USA and USSR, with the objective of forwarding the process of détente through agreements on economic and technological co-operation, security, and disarmament.

helter-skelter — *adj.* careless and confused. — *adv.* in a careless and confused manner. — *noun Brit.* a spiral slide down the outside of a tower in an amusement park.

Helvellyn a mountain in the Lake District, Cumbria, NW England. It is situated between two lakes, Ullswater and Thirlmere. HEIGHT 950m. Striding Edge descends to the E.

Helvetiia Celtic people forced south by Germanic tribesmen in the 2c BC into modern Switzerland. In 58 BC Germanic pressure prompted Helvetian migration into Gaul, but Julius Caesar drove them back to their Swiss lands, and they later became allies then subjects of Rome (until c.400 AD). The official names for Switzerland derive from this source: *Helvetia* and *Confederatio Helvetica.*

hem¹ — *noun* a bottom edge of a piece of clothing, folded over and sewn down. — *verb* (**hemmed, hemming**) to make a hem on.
— **hem something** *or* **someone in** to surround them closely, preventing movement.
[from Anglo-Saxon *hemm*]

hem² — *interj.* a slight clearing of the throat or coughing to show hesitation or call for attention. — *noun* such a sound. — *verb intrans.* (**hemmed, hemming**) to clear the throat or cough slightly. [imitative]

he-man *noun colloq.* a very strong, virile man.

Hemel Hempstead POP (1981) 80 000, a town in Dacorum district, Hertfordshire, SE England. It lies on the R Gade and the Grand Union Canal, 11km/7mi NW of Watford. Part of the Greater London urban area, it was designated a 'new town' in 1946.

hem-, hemat-, hemo- *North Amer., esp. US* same as HAEM-, HAEMA1-, HAEMU-.

hemi- *combining form* forming words meaning 'half': hemisphere. [from Greek *hemi*]

Hemingway, Ernest (Miller) (1899–1961) US novelist and short-story writer, born in Oak Park, Illinois. He served in World War I as an ambulance driver in Italy and in World War II as a war correspondent, and worked as a journalist in France and then in Spain during the Civil War. His major novels include *A Farewell to Arms* (1929), *For Whom the Bell Tolls* (1940), and *The Old Man and the Sea* (1952, Pulitzer Prize). He was awarded the Nobel Prize for Literature in 1954. He committed suicide in Ketchum, Idaho.

Hemiptera *pl. noun Zool.* in the animal kingdom, an order of insects, commonly known as bugs, that includes aphids, mealy bugs, water boatmen, etc. [from HEMI- + Greek *pteron*, wing]

hemipterous *adj. Zool.* denoting an insect that belongs to the order Hemiptera, members of which have an oval flattened body and mouthparts modified into a beak for piercing and sucking. [from HEMI- + Greek *pteron*, wing]

hemisphere *noun* 1 one half of a sphere. 2 each half of the Earth's sphere, traditionally divided by the equator into the northern hemisphere and the southern hemisphere.

hemispherical *adj.* having the shape of a hemisphere.

hemline *noun* the level at which the bottom of a garment or its hem hangs.

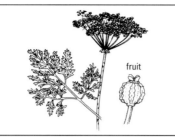

hemlock

hemlock *noun* 1 a poisonous plant with small white flowers and a spotted stem. 2 a poisonous potion made from this. [from Anglo-Saxon *hymlic*]

hemp *noun* 1 a tall annual plant (*Cannabis sativa*) that bears clusters of tiny green flowers, native to Asia. It is grown commercially for its stem fibres (hemp), which are used to make rope, and for its leaves and flowers, which are used (usually illicitly) to prepare a narcotic drug. 2 the common name for any narcotic drug obtained from this plant, eg cannabis or marijuana. 3 the coarse tough fibre obtained from the stem of this plant, and used to make rope, cord, coarse cloth, etc. [from Anglo-Saxon *hænep*]

hemp

hemstitch *noun* a decorative stitch used when sewing hems.

hen *noun* a female bird of any kind, especially of the domestic fowl. [from Anglo-Saxon *henn*]

henbane *noun* a poisonous wild plant with hairy leaves, light green flowers, and an unpleasant smell. [from HEN + BANE, so-called because it is especially poisonous to domestic fowl]

Henbury Crater a meteorite crater at Henbury, Northern Territory, Australia. It lies c.100km/60mi SW of Alice Springs.

hence *adv.* 1 for this reason. 2 from this time. 3 *old use* from this place. [from Middle English *hennes*]

henceforth *or* **henceforward** *adv.* from now on.

Henchard, Michael the central figure in Thomas Hardy's *The Mayor of Casterbridge*, whose fluctuating fortunes reflect his varying consumption of alcohol.

henchman *noun* (PL. **henchmen**) a faithful supporter, especially one who obeys without question. [from Anglo-Saxon *hengest*, horse + *man*, man]

Henderson, Arthur (1863–1935) Scottish Labour politician, born in Glasgow. An MP from 1903, he was Chairman of the Labour Party (1908–10, 1914–17, 1931–2), served in the coalition Cabinets (1915–17), and became Home Secretary (1924) and Foreign Secretary (1929–31). He was President of the World Disarmament

Conference in 1932, won the Nobel Peace Prize in 1934, and also helped to establish the League of Nations.

Henderson Island one of the islands forming the Pitcairn Islands group (a British colony) in the central S Pacific Ocean. An uninhabited coral atoll, it is a World Heritage site.

Hendrix, Jimi (1942–70) US rock guitarist, singer, and songwriter, born in Seattle, Washington. He learnt blues techniques as a sideman for Little Richard and the Isley Brothers. Later he explored electronic tricks on his guitar at maximum amplitude, to which he added such stage gimmicks as playing behind his back or with his teeth, and developed a raucous blues style that influenced heavy metal bands. He died young after taking barbiturates and alcohol.

Hendry, Stephen (1969–) Scottish snooker player, born in Edinburgh. He turned professional at the age of 16 and became the youngest winner of a professional title with his 1987 victory in the Rothmans Grand Prix. In 1990 he became the youngest winner of the world championship, which he won again in 1992, 1993 and 1994.

Hengduan Shan a mountain range in SW China. It is a series of parallel ranges running N–S, with an average height of 3 000–4 000m. The range rises to 7 556m at Gongga Shan Peak.

henge *noun* a circular, prehistoric monument consisting of large upright stones or wooden posts. [from *Stonehenge*, a famous stone circle in S England]

Hengist and Horsa in British folklore, two brothers, leaders of the first Anglo-Saxon settlers in Britain. According to the *Anglo-Saxon Chronicle*, Horsa was killed in AD 455 and Hengist ruled in Kent until his death in AD 488.

Henie, Sonja (1912–69) Norwegian figure skater, born in Oslo. The winner of three Olympic gold medals (1928, 1932, 1936), she also won a record 10 individual world titles (1927–36). She retired from competitive skating in 1936, and then appeared in films. She became a US citizen in 1941. She died in an aeroplane ambulance while flying to Oslo.

Henley-on-Thames POP (1981) 11 000, a residential town in South Oxfordshire district, Oxfordshire, S central England. It lies on the R Thames, 10km/6mi NE of Reading. EVENT Royal Regatta (Jul).

Henley Royal Regatta a series of rowing races which take place annually in July on the R Thames, Henley-on-Thames, UK, inaugurated in 1839. The Diamond Sculls and the Grand Challenge Cup are the most coveted events.

henna — *noun* reddish-brown dye obtained from a tropical shrub, used for colouring the hair and decorating the skin. — *verb* (**hennaed, hennaing**) to dye or stain using henna. [from Arabic *hinna*]

hen party a party for a group of women only, especially one to celebrate the future marriage of one woman in the group.

henpecked *adj. colloq., usually said of a man* constantly harassed and criticized, especially by a wife, girlfriend, etc.

Henrietta Maria (1609–69) queen-consort of Charles I of England, born in Palace of the Louvre, Paris, the youngest child of Henry IV of France. She married Charles in 1625, but her French attendants and Roman Catholic beliefs made her unpopular. In 1642, under the threat of impeachment, she fled to Holland and raised funds for the Royalist cause. A year later she returned and met Charles near Edgehill (the site of the first battle of the Civil War). In 1644, shortly after giving birth to Henrietta Anne, she fled to France (1644). She paid two visits to England after the Restoration (1660–1, 1662–5).

Henry I (**of England**) (1068–1135) King (1100–35) and Duke of Normandy (1106–35), the youngest son of William the Conqueror. Henry conquered Normandy from his brother, Robert Curthose, at the battle of Tinchebrai (1106), and exercised varying degrees of authority over the King of Scots, the Welsh princes, the Duke of Brittany, and the Counts of Flanders, Boulogne, and Ponthieu. He governed England and Normandy with the aim of financing warfare and alliances, and of consolidating the unity of the two countries as a single cross-Channel state. Following the death of his only legitimate son, William Adelin (1120), in 1127 he nominated his daughter Empress Matilda, widow of Emperor Henry V of Germany (and wife of Geoffrey Plantagenet, Count of Anjou from 1128) as his heir, but after his death the Crown was seized by Stephen, son of his sister, Adela.

Henry II (**of England**) (1133–89) King of England (1154–89), born in Le Mans, Maine-et-Loire, the son of Empress Matilda, Henry I's daughter and acknowledged heir, and her second husband Geoffrey Plantagenet, Count of Anjou. Already established as Duke of Normandy (1150) and Count of Anjou (1151), and as Duke of Aquitaine by marriage to Eleanor of Aquitaine (1152), he invaded England in 1153 to succeed Stephen, founding the Angevin or Plantagenet dynasty of English kings, and ruling England as part of a wider Angevin Empire. He restored and transformed English governance after the disorders of Stephen's reign, but his efforts to restrict clerical independence caused conflict with his former chancellor, Thomas Becket, Archbishop of Canterbury, which ended only with Becket's murder (1170). He led a major expedition to Ireland (1171), which resulted in its annexation. The most serious challenge to his power came in 1173–4 when his son the young Henry, encouraged by Queen Eleanor, rebelled in alliance with Louis VII of France, William I of Scotland, and Count Philip of Flanders. In 1189 he faced further disloyalty from his family when his sons John and Richard allied with Philip II of France and overran Maine and Touraine. Henry agreed a peace which recognized Richard as his sole heir for the Angevin Empire.

Henry II (**of France**) (1519–59) King of France (1547–59), born near Paris, the second son of Francis I. He married Catherine de' Medici in 1533 and became heir to the throne in 1536. Soon after his accession, he began to oppress his Protestant subjects. Through the influence of the Guises he formed an alliance with Scotland, and declared war against England, which ended in 1558 with the taking of Calais. He continued the long-standing war against the emperor Charles V, gaining Toul, Metz, and Verdun, but suffered reverses in Italy and the Low Countries, which led to the Treaty of Cateau-Cambrésis (1559).

Henry III (**of England**) (1207–72) King (1216–72), the elder son and successor of John. He declared an end to his minority in 1227, and asserted his royal rights in a way that annoyed the barons and conflicted with the principles of Magna Carta. Although he failed to recover Poitou (N Aquitaine) in 1242, he accepted the Kingdom of Sicily (1254). When Henry sought the barons' support, led by the King's brother-in-law Simon de Montfort, they imposed the Provisions of Oxford (1258), reforms that gave them a definite say in government. On his attempt to restore royal power, they rebelled and captured the King at Lewes (1264), but were defeated at Evesham (1265). The Dictum of Kenilworth (1266), though favourable to Henry, urged him to observe Magna Carta. Henry was succeeded by his elder son, Edward I.

Henry III (**of France**) (1551–89) King of France (1574–89), born in Fontainebleau, the third son of Henry II, and the last of the Valois line. He gained victories over the Huguenots (1569), and was active in the St Bartholomew's Day Massacre (1572). In 1573 he ascended the throne of Poland,

but soon after succeeded his brother, Charles IX, as King of France, commencing a reign marked throughout by civil war between Huguenots and Catholics. In 1588 he engineered the assassination of the Duke of Guise, which enraged the Catholic League. He then joined forces with his brother-in-law, the Huguenot Henry of Navarre, who succeeded him on his assassination by a fanatical priest.

Henry IV (**of England**) (1366–1413) the first King of England (1399–1413) from the House of Lancaster, the son of John of Gaunt, who was the fourth son of Edward III. He was surnamed Bolingbroke, after his birthplace in Lincolnshire. In 1397 he supported Richard II against the Duke of Gloucester. Banished in 1398, the following year Henry successfully persuaded the deserted and betrayed Richard to abdicate in his favour. His reign featured rebellion and lawlessness, and he was constantly hampered by lack of money. Under Owen Glendower the Welsh maintained their independence, and Henry was defeated when he attacked Scotland (1400). Henry Percy (Hotspur) and his house then joined with the Scots and the Welsh against him, but they were defeated at Shrewsbury (1403).

Henry IV, Parts I and II two historical plays by William Shakespeare (1697), which with *Henry V* form a trilogy based on Henry V's life. Part I deals with Henry IV's displeasure with his son's dissolute lifestyle, and Prince Hal's success in defeating a rebellion led by Hotspur. The prince's riotous friendship with Falstaff leads to some deceitful schemes and to the latter's expectation of Hal's continuing favour. Part II depicts further rebellions, the accession of Hal to the throne, and his rejection of the anarchic Falstaff.

Henry IV (**of France**), known as **Henry of Navarre** (1553–1610) the first Bourbon King of France (1589–1610), born in Pau, the third son of Antoine de Bourbon. Brought up a Calvinist, he led the Huguenot army at the battle of Jarnac (1569), and became leader of the Protestant Party. After the St Bartholomew's Day Massacre (1572), he was spared by professing himself a Catholic, and spent three years virtually a prisoner at the French court. In 1576 he escaped, revoked his conversion, and resumed command of the army in continuing opposition to the Guises and the Catholic League. After the murder of Henry III, he succeeded to the throne. In 1593 he became a Catholic, thereby unifying the country, but by the Edict of Nantes Protestants were granted liberty of conscience. His economic policies, implemented by his minister Sully, gradually brought new wealth to the country. He was assassinated in Paris by a religious fanatic.

Henry V (**of England**) (1387–1422) King of England (1413–22), born in Monmouth, the eldest son of Henry IV. He fought against Glendower and the Welsh rebels (1402–8), and became constable of Dover (1409) and captain of Calais (1410), all during a period illustrated by stories of his allegedly wild youth. His reign was marked by his claim, through his great-grandfather Edward III, to the French Crown. In 1415 he invaded France, won the battle of Agincourt against great odds, and by 1419 Normandy was again under English control. The 'perpetual peace' of Troyes was made (1420), under which Henry was recognized as heir to the French throne and Regent of France, and married to Charles VI's daughter, Catherine of Valois.

Henry V 1 a historical play by William Shakespeare (1599), which forms a trilogy with *Henry IV* Parts I and II. The new King Henry begins by impressing the court with his competence and piety and then invades France, which leads to his 'St Crispin's Day' speech and victory at Agincourt. This patriotic play ends with an act devoted to his wooing of Catherine of France. 2 a British film directed by Laurence Olivier (1944). A depiction of a contemporary performance of Shakespeare's play, starring Olivier,

which expands into the countryside. 3 a British film directed by Kenneth Branagh (1989). Director/actor Branagh's version focuses on the price of conflict.

Henry VI (**of England**) (1421–71) King (1422–61, 1470–1), the only child of Henry V and Catherine of Valois, born in Windsor, Berkshire. During Henry's minority, his uncle John, Duke of Bedford, was Regent in France, and another uncle, Humphrey, Duke of Gloucester, was Lord Protector of England. Henry was crowned in England in 1429, and as King of France in 1431, but Henry V's French conquests were progressively eroded; by 1453 the English retained only Calais. Henry had few kingly qualities, and from 1453 suffered from bouts of insanity. Richard, Duke of York, seized power as Lord Protector in 1454, and defeated the King's army at St Albans (1455), the first battle of the Wars of the Roses. York himself was killed at Wakefield (1460), but his heir was proclaimed king as Edward IV after Henry's deposition (1461). In 1464 Henry returned from exile in Scotland to lead the Lancastrian cause, but was captured and imprisoned (1465–70). Richard Neville, Earl of Warwick, restored him to the throne (Oct 1470), but his nominal rule ended on Edward IV's return to London (Apr 1471). After the Yorkist victory at Tewkesbury (May 1471), where his only son was killed, Henry was murdered in the Tower.

Henry VII (**of England**) (1457–1509) the first Tudor King of England (1485–1509), born in Pembroke Castle, Wales, the grandson of Owen Tudor, who married Queen Catherine, the widow of Henry V. After the Lancastrian defeat at Tewkesbury (1471), Henry was taken to Brittany, where several Yorkist attempts on his life and liberty were frustrated. In 1485 he landed unopposed at Milford Haven, and defeated Richard III at Bosworth. As King, his policy was to restore peace and prosperity to the country, which was helped by his marriage of reconciliation with Elizabeth of York, but he dealt firmly with Yorkist plots (eg the one led by Perkin Warbeck). His financial and administrative policies were successful, peace was concluded with France, and the marriage of his heir (Henry VIII) to Catherine of Aragon cemented an alliance with Spain.

Henry VIII (**of England**) (1491–1547) King of England (1509–47), born in Greenwich, London, the second son of Henry VII. A very popular prince, he succeeded his father Henry VII and married Catherine of Aragon, his brother Arthur's widow. As a member of the Holy League, he invaded France (1512) and won the battle of The Spurs (1513), and during his absence the Scots were defeated at Flodden. At this time Thomas Wolsey rose to prominence as his advisor. In 1521 Henry published a book on the Sacraments in reply to Luther, and received from the pope the title 'Defender of the Faith'. From 1527 he determined to divorce Catherine, whose children, except for Mary (later Mary I), had died in infancy. The pope failed to grant his wish and Wolsey fell from favour. Henry tried to put pressure on the pope by humbling the clergy, and in defiance of Rome was privately married to Anne Boleyn (1533). In 1534 it was enacted that his marriage to Catherine was invalid, and that the king was the sole head of the Church of England. The policy of suppressing the monasteries, begun under Wolsey, proceeded in earnest under Thomas Cromwell. In 1536 Catherine died, and Anne Boleyn was executed for infidelity. Henry then married Jane Seymour (c.1509–37), who died leaving a son (who later succeeded him as Edward VI). In 1640 he made Anne of Cleves his fourth wife, in the hope of gaining Protestant support in Germany, but he disliked her appearance and soon divorced her. He then married Catherine Howard (1540), who two years later was executed on a charge of infidelity (1542). In 1543 his last marriage was to Catherine Parr, who survived him. His later years saw further war with France and Scotland, before peace was concluded with France (1546). His reign saw an ecclesiastical revolution as well as the judicial murder of those like Sir Thomas More and Henry Howard, Earl of Surrey, who dared to oppose his will.

Henry VIII a portrait of Henry VIII, his third wife Jane Seymour, and his mother and father by Hans Holbein the Younger (1537, destroyed 1698). There are numerous copies of this representation of Henry, but the only portrait of him which is definitely by Holbein himself is in the Thyssen collection in Lugano.

Henry, known as **the Lion** (1129–95) Duke of Saxony (1142–80) and Bavaria (1156–80), the head of the Guelfs, who encouraged commerce and founded the city of Munich. For a time the most powerful prince in Germany, his ambitions aroused the opposition of a league of princes (1166), but he retained power through an alliance with Emperor Frederick I Barbarossa. After breaking with Frederick in 1176, he lost most of his lands and was exiled, but was later reconciled to Frederick's successor, Henry VI.

Henry, known as **the Navigator** (1394–1460) Portuguese prince, the third son of John I, King of Portugal, and Philippa, daughter of John of Gaunt, Duke of Lancaster. He set up court at Sagres, and founded an observatory and school of scientific navigation at Cape St Vincent. He sponsored many exploratory expeditions along the W African coast, which prepared the way for the discovery of the sea route to India.

Henry a male first name, borne by eight kings of England since the Norman Conquest. French influence brought about the vowel change from Norman *Harry*. [ultimately from Germanic *haim*, home + *ric*, power]

Henry of Navarre see HENRY IV (OF FRANCE).

Henry, Joseph (1797–1878) US physicist, born in Albany, New York. Professor at Albany Academy and Princeton University, he independently discovered electrical induction, and constructed the first electromagnetic motor (1829). He appreciated the effects of resistance on current and demonstrated the oscillatory nature of electric discharges (1842); he also introduced a system of weather forecasting. The SI unit of inductance is named after him.

Henry, Lenny (1958–) English comedian, born in Dudley, West Midlands. He made his television début as a winning contestant on *New Faces* (1975) and developed a career as a stand-up comedian and impressionist. Working mainly on television, his series include *Tiswas* (1975), *Three of a Kind* (1982), and *Chef* (1993), and he is a leading figure in the charity Comic Relief.

Henry, O, pseudonym of **William Sydney Porter** (1862–1910) US short-story writer, born in Greenboro, North Carolina. Brought up during the depression in the South, he began to write short stories while in jail for embezzlement. In 1902 he moved to New York City, and produced *Cabbages and Kings* (1904), the first of many volumes noted for their use of coincidence and their humorous treatment of everyday life.

Henry, Patrick (1736–99) American revolutionary and statesman, born in Hanover Co, Virginia. He trained as a lawyer and entered the colonial Virginia House of Burgesses, where his oratory won him fame. He was an outspoken opponent of British policy towards the colonies, particularly concerning the Stamp Act (1765), and he made the first speech in the Continental Congress (1774). In 1776 he became Governor of independent Virginia, and was four times re-elected.

Henry, William (1774–1836) English physician and chemist, born in Manchester. He gave up medicine due to ill-health and turned to chemistry, formulating the generalization that has become known as 'Henry's law', that the solubil-

ity of a gas at a given temperature is proportional to its pressure (1803).

henry *noun* (SYMBOL **H**) (PL. **henries**) the SI unit of electrical inductance, defined as the inductance that produces an electromotive force of one volt when the electric current in a closed circuit changes at the rate of one ampere per second. [named after Joseph Henry]

Henryson, Robert (c.1425–1508) Scottish medieval poet. Thought to have been a 'schoolmaster of Dunfermline', his best-known works include the narrative poem *Testament of Cresseid* (written as a sequel to Chaucer's *Troilus and Criseyde*), *Robene and Makyne*, the earliest Scottish specimen of pastoral poetry, and a metrical version of 13 *Morall Fabels of Esope*.

Henslowe, Philip (c.1550–1616) English theatre manager, born in Lindfield, Sussex. He became lessee of the Rose Theatre on the Bankside, London, in 1584, and from 1591 until his death he was in partnership with Edward Alleyn. Henslowe's business diary contains invaluable information about the stage of Shakespeare's day.

Henzada POP (1983) 284 000, a city in Irrawaddy division, S central Burma (Myanma), situated on the Irrawaddy R.

heparin *noun Biochem.* a chemical substance that prevents the clotting of blood, and in an extracted and purified form is used as an anticoagulant drug in medicine, eg to prevent thrombosis (formation of clots in blood vessels). [from Greek *hepar hepatos*, liver]

hepatic *adj.* of the liver.

hepatitis *noun* inflammation of the liver, usually caused by a viral infection, but sometimes occurring as a reaction to toxic substances such as alcohol or drugs, or as a complication of diseases such as amoebic dysentery. Typical symptoms include jaundice (yellowing of the skin), weakness, fever, loss of appetite, and nausea. [from Greek *hepar*, liver + -ITIS]
◇ *Hepatitis A* (infectious hepatitis) is spread via contaminated food, and often occurs in areas with poor sanitation. *Hepatitis B* (serum hepatitis), which can be fatal, is usually transmitted by infected blood or blood products, eg during blood transfusions. It is also common among drug addicts who use contaminated needles.

Hepburn, Audrey, originally **Edda Van Heemstra Hepburn-Ruston** (1929–93) Belgian-born US film actress, born in Brussels. She studied ballet and appeared on the London stage, on Broadway, and in minor film roles before winning an Oscar for *Roman Holiday* (1953). A major star for two decades, her successes included *Funny Face* (1956) with Fred Astaire, *Breakfast at Tiffany's* (1961), and *My Fair Lady* (1964). She later travelled as a goodwill ambassodor for UNICEF.

Hepburn, Katharine (Houghton) (1909–) US actress, born in Hartford, Connecticut. She acted on stage at Baltimore and on Broadway, but from 1932 attained international fame as a film actress, notably in *Morning Glory* (1933), *Guess Who's Coming to Dinner* (1967), *The Lion in Winter* (1968), and *On Golden Pond* (1981), all of which gained her Academy Awards. She was also acclaimed in *The Philadephia Story* (1940), *The African Queen* (1951), and in the series of witty farces with Spencer Tracy, which included *Adam's Rib* (1949) and *Pat and Mike* (1952). Her personal and professional partnership with Tracy lasted for 25 years, until his death.

Hephaestus in Greek mythology, the god of fire and craftsmen, the lame son of Zeus and Hera. He was associated with volcanic sites, and was assisted in his work as a blacksmith by the Cyclopes. He was identified by the Romans with Vulcan.

Hepplewhite, George (d.1786) English cabinet-maker, who came from Lancaster to set up

business in London. His designs, characterized by the free use of inlaid ornament and shield shape, are mainly found in his major work, the *Cabinet-maker and Upholsterer's Guide* (1788).

hepta- *combining form* forming words meaning 'seven'. [from Greek *hepta*, seven]

heptagon *noun* a plane figure with seven sides. [from Greek *hepta*, seven + *gonia*, angle]

heptagonal *adj.* having seven angles and seven sides.

heptarchy *noun* (PL. **heptarchies**) **1** government by a group of seven, or a country governed in this way. **2** *Hist.* a once supposed system of seven English kingdoms, Wessex, Sussex, Kent, Essex, East Anglia, Mercia, and Northumbria.

heptathlon *noun* an athletic contest consisting of seven events, 100 metres hurdles, shotput, javelin, high jump, long jump, and races over 200 and 800 metres. [from HEPTA- + Greek *athlon*, contest]

Hepworth, Dame (Jocelyn) Barbara (1903–75) English sculptor, born in Wakefield, Yorkshire. She became one of the foremost nonfigurative sculptors of her time, notable for the strength and formal discipline of her carving, as in her *Contrapuntal Forms* exhibited at the Festival of Britain (1951). Other works include *Pierced Form* (1931), *The Unknown Political Prisoner* (1953), and *Single Form* (1963).

her — *pron.* the form of *she* used as the object of a verb or after a preposition: *we all like her / send it to her.* — *adj.* of or belonging to a female person or animal, or a thing personified or thought of as female, eg a ship: *went to her house / give the cat her milk.*
— **be her** *colloq.* to be suited to her: *that hat isn't her at all.*
[from Anglo-Saxon *hire*]

Hera in Greek mythology, the daughter of Cronus, sister and wife of Zeus, and goddess of women and marriage. She was traditionally jealous of the many lovers of Zeus, and also of their children. In her anger at Paris, she took sides against the Trojans and made herself the protector of Achilles and Menelaus. She was identified by the Romans with Juno.

Heracles see HERCULES.

Heraclitus (d.460 BC) Greek philosopher, born in Ephesus. Only fragments of his writings survive. He seems to have thought that all things are composed of opposites (eg hot/cold, wet/dry), and because the opposites are constantly at strife with one another, all things are in perpetual change. The change is governed by *Logos*, a principle of order and intelligibility.

Heraion of Samos the scant ruins of the sanctuary of Hera, one of the seven wonders of the ancient world. It is a World Heritage site.

Heraklion, Greek **Iráklion**, Italian **Candia** POP (1991) 128 000, the seaport capital of Heraklion department, Crete region, S Greece. It lies on the N coast of Crete and is the island's chief town and foremost port. NOTABLE FEATURES Church of St Titos; Cathedral of St Minas (19c); old city within the circuit of Venetian walls (begun in 1538); Archaeological Museum.

herald — *noun* **1** a person who announces important news. **2** a person or thing that is a sign of what is to come. **3** *Hist.* an officer responsible for keeping a record of the genealogies and coats of arms of noble families. — *verb* to be a sign of the approach of; to proclaim: *dark clouds heralding a storm.* [from Old French *herault*]

heraldic *adj.* of or concerning heraldry.

heraldry *noun* the art of recording genealogies and studying and preparing coats of arms.
◇ The pictorial devices borne on the shields of knights in armour served to identify them in battle. In the early 12c these devices became hereditary in Europe through the male line of descent.

Arms are regarded as insignia of honour and their use is regulated by the College of Arms in England, and by the court of the Lord Lyon King of Arms in Scotland.

In England, the College of Arms is the body responsible for regulating the use of arms and for granting new coats of arms: the equivalent body in Scotland is the Lord Lyon King of Arms.

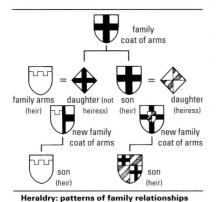

Heraldry: patterns of family relationships

Herat, ancient **Harat** or **Heroiva** POP (1981) 808 000, a province in W Afghanistan. AREA 61 315sq km/23 668sq mi. It is bounded W by Iran, N by Turkmenistan and is crossed by the Hindu Kush and the Hari Rud. It is situated in a fertile river valley noted for its fruit, especially grapes. CAPITAL Herat. ECONOMY textiles (carpets), trade in dried fruits, nuts, wool. The city lies on the old trade route from Persia to India and on the caravan route from China to Europe. NOTABLE FEATURE Great Mosque (12c).

herb *noun* 1 *Bot.* a flowering plant in which the stems contain very little permanent woody tissue, and the aerial parts die back at the end of the growing season. 2 any flowering plant that has aromatic leaves or other parts, used for flavouring food, or as a source of essential oils for use in herbal medicine or perfumery, eg mint, parsley, thyme, sage. [from Latin *herba*, grass, green plant]

herbaceous *adj.*, *said of a plant* having a stem which is soft, not hard and woody. [from Latin *herba*, grass, green plant]

herbaceous border a garden border containing mainly perennial plants and flowers.

herbage *noun* green plants in general, especially those on which cattle graze. [from Latin *herba*, grass, green plant]

herbal — *adj. Bot.* relating to herbs. — *noun Bot.* a book describing the use of plants, or substances extracted from them, to treat medical disorders. [from Latin *herbalis*]

herbalism *noun Medicine* the use of herbs for medicinal purposes.

herbalist *noun* a person who prescribes and uses plant extracts and their derivatives for medical purposes.

herbarium *noun* (PL. **herbaria**) 1 *Bot.* a collection of dried pressed plants, mounted on sheets of card labelled with the plant's name, the place and date of collection, and usually the collector's name. The larger herbaria are centres for research on the classification of plants. 2 a room or building housing such a collection.

Herbert a male first name, dating from the Norman Conquest, which gave rise to the surname. [Norman, from Germanic *heri*, army + *berht*, famous]

herbicide *noun* a chemical that kills plants, either non-selectively, destroying all vegetation, or selectively, eg killing only weeds and leaving crops unharmed. The widespread use of herbicides in agriculture has led to a sustained increase in crop yield, but also to soil and water pollution,

and the destruction of natural habitats. [from Latin *herba*, grass, green crops]

herbivore *noun* an animal that feeds exclusively or mainly on plants, eg rabbit, cow, horse.

Culinary Herbs	
English name/Species	Origin
basil	
Ocimum basilicum	Middle East
borage	
Borago officinalis	Mediterranean
celery	
Apium graveolens	Europe
chervil	
Anthnius cerefolium	Europe, Asia
chicory	
Chicoium intybus	Europe
chives	
Allium schoenoprasum	Europe, America
coriander	
Coriandrum sativum	N Africa, W Asia
dandelion	
Taraxacum officinale	Europe
dill	
Anethum graveolens	S Europe
epazote	
Chenopodium ambrosioides	C and S America
fennel, Florentine	
Foeniculum dulce	Mediterranean
garlic	
Allium sativum	Asia
horseradish	
Armoracia rusticana	SE Europe, W Asia
juniper	
Juniperus communis	Mediterranean
leek	
Allium porrum	Europe
lemon	
Citrus limon	Asia
lemon balm	
Melissa officinalis	S Europe
lime	
Tilia cordata	Europe
lovage	
Levisticum officinale	W Asia
marjoram	
Majorana hortensis	Africa, Mediterranean, Asia
nasturtium	
Tropaelom majus	Peru
onion	
Allium cepa	Asia
oregano	
Origanum vulgare	Mediterranean
parsley	
Petroselinum crispum	Mediterranean
peppermint	
Menthaxpiperita	Europe
rosemary	
Rosmarinus officinalis	Mediterranean
saffron	
Crocus sativus	Asia Minor
sage	
Salvia officinalis	N Mediterranean
sorrel	
Rumex acetosa	Europe
spearmint	
Mentha spicata	Europe
tarragon, French	
Artemesia dracunculus	Asia, E Europe
thyme	
Thymus serpyllum	Mediterranean
watercress	
Nasturtium officinale	Europe, Asia

[from Latin *herba*, grass, green plant + *vorare*, to swallow]

herbivorous *adj.* feeding on grass and other plants.

Herculaneum a town in ancient Italy situated near Mt Vesuvius in SW Italy. The ancient town was destroyed in the volcanic eruption of AD 79.

herculean *adj.* having, showing or needing great strength or effort: *a herculean task.* [named after Greek *Heracles* (in Latin *Hercules*), mythical Greek hero famous for his great strength]

Hercules, Greek **Heracles** in Greek mythology, a hero famous for his strength, the son of Zeus and Alcmene. He undertook Twelve Labours for Eurystheus of Tiryns. These were: (1) to kill and flay the Nemean Lion, (2) to kill the monster Hydra, (3) to capture the Hind of Ceryneia, (4) to capture the Boar of Erymanthus, (5) to clean out the stables of King Augeas of Elis, (6) to remove the man-eating birds from the Stymphalian Lake, (7) to capture the Cretan Bull, (8) to capture the four savage mares of the Thracian king Diomedes, (9) to steal the golden girdle worn by the Amazonian queen Hipployte, (10) to capture the oxen of the giant Geryon, (11) to fetch the golden apples of the Hesperides; (12) to capture Cerberus, the guardian of Hades. His wife Deianira killed him by mistake with a shirt smeared with the poison of Nessus; after his body was burnt on a pyre he was received into Olympus, and became the subject of a cult.

Hercules *Astron.* a large constellation of the northern hemisphere, which is the fifth largest constellation but contains no prominent stars.

herd — *noun* 1 a group of animals, especially cattle, that are kept together on a farm. 2 a person who looks after a herd. 3 a large group of people, especially when behaving noisily. 4 (**the herd**) the mass of people in general when seen as behaving in an unthinkingly conventional way. — *verb* 1 *trans.*, *intrans.* to gather or be gathered together in a group or herd. 2 *trans.* to look after a herd of animals, or to group animals together. [from Anglo-Saxon *heord*]

Herder, Johann Gottfried von (1744–1803) German critic and poet, born in Mohrungen, East Prussia. Court preacher at Bückeburg (1770), and Weimar (1776), he was a major influence on Goethe and German Romanticism. He collected folk-songs, wrote on poetry and mythology, and published a philosophy of history *Ideen zur Geschichte der Menschheit* (Outlines of a Philosophy on the History of Man, 1784–91).

herd instinct the instinct to associate with and act like a group of similar people or animals.

herdsman *noun* a person who looks after a herd of animals.

here — *adv.* 1 at, in, or to this place. 2 at this time; at this point in an argument. 3 used after a noun for emphasis: *this book here.* 4 *colloq.*, *dialect* used between a noun and *this*, *that*, etc for emphasis: *this here book.* — *noun* this place. — *interj.* 1 calling for someone's attention. 2 calling attention to one's own presence.

— **here and now** at this time; immediately.

here and there in, or to, various places.

here goes! an expression used when about to start something difficult or challenging.

here's to ... an expression used as a toast when drinking: *here's to the President / here's to gambling.*

neither here nor there of no importance. [from Anglo-Saxon *her*]

hereabouts or **hereabout** *adv.* near this place.

hereafter — *adv. formal* after this; from now on. — *noun* (**the hereafter**) the future; life after death.

hereby *adv. formal* by means of; as a result of this.

Heredia 1 POP (1984) 27 000, the capital town of Heredia province, NE Costa Rica. 2 POP (1983e) 172 000, a province in NE Costa Rica. AREA 2 656sq km/1 025sq mi. CAPITAL Heredia. It is bounded in the N by Nicaragua. The S part of the province is crossed by the Cordillera Central with peaks rising to over 2 000m.

hereditable *adj.* that may be inherited. [from Latin *hereditas*, inheritance]

hereditarily *adv.* in a hereditary way.

hereditary *adj.* **1** relating to or determined by heredity. **2** denoting a characteristic that can be genetically transmitted from parents to offspring. [from Latin *hereditas*, inheritance]

heredity *noun* (PL. **heredities**) **1** the transmission of genetically based characteristics from one generation to the next. **2** the genetic constitution of a living organism. [from Latin *hereditas*]

Hereford POP (1992e) 51 000, a town in Hereford district, Hereford and Worcester, W central England. It lies on the R Wye in the centre of a farming region. NOTABLE FEATURE 11c Cathedral of St Mary and St Ethelbert, with the largest chained library in the world and the famous *Mappa Mundi*, a medieval map of the world.

Hereford and Worcester POP (1992e) 690 000, a county in W central England, divided into nine districts. AREA 3 926sq km/1 515sq mi. It is bounded W and SW by Wales, S by Gloucestershire, E by Warwickshire, NE by the West Midlands, and N by Staffordshire and Shropshire. PHYSICAL DESCRIPTION drained by the Severn, Wye, and Teme rivers; the Malvern Hills rise SW of Worcester. CHIEF TOWNS Worcester (county town), Hereford, Kidderminster, Malvern, Evesham. ECONOMY horticulture (hops, soft fruit, vegetables), especially in the Vale of Evesham; cattle (Herefords); high technology; food processing.

Hereford cattle a breed of cattle with a white face and a red coat, originating in Herefordshire.

herein *adv. Legal formal* in this place, document, or matter.

hereinafter *adv. Legal formal* from this point on.

hereof *adv. Legal formal* of or concerning this.

Herero a group of Bantu-speaking peoples of Namibia and neighbouring areas, once pastoralists, but today mostly settled farmers. They were severely treated during German colonial rule, and after their defeat in 1907 their numbers greatly declined.

heresy *noun* (PL. **heresies**) **1** an opinion or belief which is contrary to official doctrine held by the religious community to which one belongs. **2** an opinion contrary to that which is normally accepted. [from Greek *hairesis*, choice]

heretic *noun* a person who is guilty of especially religious heresy.

heretical *adj.* of heresy or heretics.

hereto *adv. Legal formal* to this place, document or matter.

heretofore *adv. Legal formal* before this time; formerly.

hereupon *adv. Legal formal* after or as a result of this.

Hereward, also called **the Wake** (d.c.1080) Anglo-Saxon thane and rebel who returned from exile to lead the last organized English resistance against the Norman invaders, when he held the Isle of Ely against William I (the Conqueror) for nearly a year (1070–1). He was the hero of Charles Kingsley's romance *Hereward the Wake* (1866).

herewith *adv. Legal formal* with this; enclosed with this letter.

heritable *adj.* **1** *said of property* that may be passed on from parent to child. **2** *said of people* able to inherit property. **3** denoting a characteristic that can be transmitted from one generation to the next. [from Old French *heriter*, to inherit]

heritage *noun* **1** that which is inherited. **2** the characteristics, qualities, property, etc that one inherits at birth. **3** a nation's historic buildings, countryside, cultural traditions, etc seen as the

nation's wealth to be passed on to future generations. [from Old French *heritage*]

Her Majesty's Stationery Office *or* **His Majesty's Stationery Office** (ABBREV. **HMSO**) the UK government publisher, which has some 40 000 titles in print and 8 000 new titles every year, and has responsibility for publishing Hansard, Acts, Bills, White Papers, and the Highway Code.

hermaphrodite — *noun* **1** a plant or animal possessing both male and female reproductive organs, eg earthworm, many plants. **2** an animal, especially a mammal, possessing both male and female reproductive organs as a result of an abnormality in development. — *adj.* possessing both male and female reproductive organs. [from Greek Hermaphroditos, in Greek mythology the son of Hermes and Aphrodite, who grew into one person with the nymph Salmacis]

hermaphroditic *adj.* **1** belonging to or typical of a hermaphrodite. **2** combining two opposites.

Hermaphroditus in Greek mythology, a minor god with bisexual characteristics, the son of Hermes and Aphrodite. The nymph Salmacis, unloved by him, prayed to be united with him; this was granted by combining them in one body.

hermeneutics *sing. noun* **1** the theory of the interpretation and understanding of texts. Its origins lie in ancient Greek philosophy, and it received fresh impetus in 18c discussion of the problems of biblical interpretation. In the 20c the discussion has expanded to include all aspects of the understanding of texts and has embraced many fields, including literary theory, the social sciences, social philosophy, and aesthetics. **2** *Psychol.* methods which go beyond mere experimentation in an attempt to understand the reason behind human actions. [from Greek *hermēneutikos*, from *hermēneus*, an interpreter, from *Hermēs*]

Hermes in Greek mythology, the ambassador of the gods, the son of Zeus and Maia, and the inventor of the lyre. He was thought of as the god of riches, good luck, and dreams, and the protector of travellers and thieves. As Hermes Psychopompus, he guided the souls of the dead to Hades. He was identified by the Romans as Mercury.

Hermes Carrying the Infant Dionysus a sculpture in marble by Praxiteles (4c BC)

Hermes Trismegistos the Greek name for the Egyptian god Thoth. In late Classical times the name was also applied to the supposed author of alchemical texts, which were passed down secretly and revived in the 17c. The name means 'Hermes the thrice great'.

hermetic *adj.* closed very tightly so that no air gets in or out. [named after Greek Hermes Trismegistos]

hermetically *adv.* in a hermetic way.

Hermia one of the two heroines in Shakespeare's *A Midsummer Night's Dream*, in love with Lysander.

Hermione the faithful wife of Leontes in Shakespeare's *The Winter's Tale*, who is imprisoned by her husband on the charge of infidelity.

hermit *noun* a person who lives alone, especially for religious reasons. [from Greek *eremos*, solitary]

Hermitage an art gallery in St Petersburg, Russia, built in the 18c–19c to house the art collection of the Czars, and opened to the public in 1852. The complex also includes the Winter Palace, built for Czarina Elizabeth Petrovna by Bartolomeo Rastrelli (1754–62). After the deposition of the Czar, this became the headquarters of Kerensky's provisional government, but was stormed by the Bolsheviks in Nov 1917.

hermitage *noun* **1** the place where a hermit lives. **2** any retreat or secluded place.

hermit crab a small crab, common in shallow coastal waters, with a soft, unprotected abdomen, that inhabits the cast-off shells of other animals, from which only the hard front end of its body protrudes. When it has outgrown its shell it searches for a larger one and moves into it.

hermit crab

Hermite, Charles (1822–1901) French mathematician, born in Dieuze. Professor at the École Normale and the Sorbonne, he proved that the base of natural logarithms (e) is transcendental, ie cannot be a solution of a polynomial equation with rational coefficients. He published works on the theory of numbers, elliptic functions, and invariant theory.

hernia *noun* a medical condition in which an organ (especially part of the bowel) protrudes through an opening or weak spot in the wall of its surroundings. [from Latin *hernia*]

Hero the dutiful daughter of Leonato in Shakespeare's *Much Ado About Nothing*, who is accused of unchastity by her future husband, Claudio.

hero *noun* (PL. **heroes**) **1** a person who is admired for bravery, courage, noble qualities, etc. **2** the main male character in a story, play, etc. See also HEROINE. [from Greek *heros*]

Hero and Leander in Greek legend, lovers whose story is recounted in Ovid and Musaeus. They lived on opposite sides of the Hellespont; Hero was the priestess of Aphrodite at Sestos, and Leander, who lived at Abydos, swam across each night guided by her light. When this was extinguished in a storm, he was drowned; whereupon Hero threw herself into the sea.

Herod Agrippa I (10 BC–AD 44) King of Judaea (41–4), the grandson of Herod the Great.

Hermitage, St Petersburg, Russia

He was reared at the court of the Emperor Augustus after his father was executed by Herod the Great. Caligula gave him two thirds of the former kingdom of Herod the Great, while Claudius added the remaining third, the kingdom of Judaea (41). He was popular with the Jews but repressed the Christians; he executed St James and imprisoned St Peter.

Herod Antipas (21 BC–AD 39) the son of Herod the Great and ruler (tetrarch) of Galilee and Peraea (4–39), after Herod's death. He enjoyed a good relationship with the Emperor Tiberias, but fell foul of his successor, Caligula, largely through the machinations of his nephew, Herod Agrippa. In the Christian tradition, he is notorious as the murderer of John the Baptist.

Herod the Great (c.73–4 BC) King of Judea (37–4 BC), the younger son of the Idumaean chieftain, Antipater. He owed his initial appointment as Governor of Galilee (47 BC) to Julius Caesar, his elevation to the kingship of Judea (37 BC) to Mark Antony, and his retention in that post after Actium (31 BC) to Octavian. He was a loyal Roman client king who ruthlessly kept all his subjects in check, but he also founded cities and fortresses and did much to develop the economic potential of his kingdom. Life at court was marked by constant and often bloody infighting between his sister, his various wives, and their many offspring. Just before his death he ordered the slaughter of the infants of Bethlehem (the biblical Massacre of the Innocents).

Herodotus (c.485–425BC) Greek historian, born in Halicarnassus, Asia Minor. He travelled widely in Asia Minor and the Middle East, and in 443 BC joined the colony of Thurii, from where he visited Sicily and Lower Italy. On his travels, he collected material for his great narrative history, which included a record of the wars between the Greeks and the Persians. Cicero called him 'the father of history'.

heroic — *adj.* **1** very brave. **2** of or about heroes or heroines. — *noun* (**heroics**) over-dramatic speech or behaviour.

heroically *adv.* in a heroic way.

heroic couplet *Poetry* a pair of rhymed 10-syllable lines, usually in iambic pentameters; one of the commonest metrical forms in English poetry. First found in Old French, it was used by Chaucer, and became firmly established in English verse by the 16c. It was used by Spenser, Shakespeare, and Donne, and was developed with particular mastery by Dryden and Pope. It is occasionally used for special effect in modern poetry.

heroin *noun* a powerful, habit-forming drug formed from morphine, used in medicine to stop pain, and illegally for pleasure. [from German *Heroin*, from Greek *heros*, hero]

heroine *noun* **1** a woman admired for her bravery, courage, noble abilities, etc. **2** the main female character in a play, story, etc. [from Greek *heros*, hero]

heroism *noun* the qualities of a hero, especially great bravery.

heron *noun* **1** a large wading bird, with grey and white feathers, long legs and a long neck. **2** any of a number of related birds. [from Old French *hairon*]

Hero of Alexandria (1c AD) Greek mathematician. He wrote on mechanics and invented many machines, including the aeolipile (the earliest known steam engine), a fire engine pump, and coin-operated devices. He also formulated an expression for the area of a triangle in terms of the lengths of its sides.

Herophilus (fl. 300 BC) Greek anatomist, born in Chalcedon, Asia Minor, founder of the school of anatomy in Alexandria. He was probably the first to dissect the human body, to compare it with those of other animals. He described the liver, spleen, sexual organs, brain and nervous

systems, distinguishing between sensory and motor nerves; he also emphasized the dissimilarity between arteries and veins, and in defiance of received opinion, maintained that the arteries contain blood rather than spirit.

Héroult, Paul Louis Toussaint (1863–1914) French metallurgist, born in Thury-Harcourt, Normandy. He invented the method of extracting aluminium by electrolysis of cryolite, and a furnace for producing steel.

hero-worship — *noun* **1** the worship of heroes in antiquity. **2** great or excessive fondness and admiration for someone. — *verb* have a great fondness and admiration for (someone).

herpes *noun* any of several infectious skin diseases caused by a virus, which gives rise to watery blisters. [from Greek *herpein*, to creep]

Herrick, Robert (1591–1674) English poet, born in London. The son of a goldsmith, he was ordained in 1623 and worked in Devon, until deprived of his living in 1647 because he was a Royalist. His writing, both secular and religious, is mainly collected in *Hesperides* and *Noble Numbers* (both 1648), and includes such well-known lyrics as 'Cherry ripe'. He resumed his living after the Restoration.

herring *noun* (PL. **herring, herrings**) the most important of all food fishes, found in very large shoals in the surface waters of the Atlantic and Pacific oceans, and migrating north in the summer. It is eaten fresh, and also cured for marketing as kippers, bloaters, roll-mops, etc. In many areas herring stocks are becoming depleted by overfishing. [from Anglo-Saxon *hæring*]

herringbone *noun* a zigzag pattern woven into cloth.

herring gull a large gull with white feathers and black-tipped grey wings.

hers *pron.* the one or ones belonging to her. — **of hers** of or belonging to her.

Herschel, Sir John Frederick William (1792–1871) English astronomer, born in Slough, son of William Herschel. He continued his father's research, completing a survey of nebulae and clusters in the southern skies, and discovering over 1 200 pairs of double stars. He was also a pioneer photographer.

Herschel, Sir (Frederick) William (1738–1822) German-born British astronomer, born in Hanover. He moved in 1755 to England where he built up a successful career in music, eventually settling in Bath in 1766 and later working in Slough. He built his own telescopes, and in 1781 he discovered the planet Uranus. He later discovered two satellites of Uranus (1787) and two of Saturn (1789). He also drew up important star and nebulae catalogues, and produced a model of the Milky Way.

herself *pron.* **1** the reflexive form of *her* and *she*: *she made herself a dress.* **2** used for emphasis: *she did it herself.* **3** her normal self: *she isn't feeling herself.* **4** also **by herself** alone; without help. [from Anglo-Saxon *hire self*]

Hershey, Alfred Day (1908–) US biologist, born in Owosso, Michigan. He worked at the Carnegie Institution in Washington, and in research on bacteriophages (the viruses which infect bacteria) in the early 1950s, he provided the first firm evidence that the DNA of this organism is the genetic information-carrying component; he and others later confirmed that the DNA of other organisms fulfils the same role. He shared the 1969 Nobel Prize for Physiology or Medicine with Salvador Luria and Max Delbrück.

Hertford POP (1981) 22 000, the county town of Hertfordshire, SE England, in East Hertfordshire district. It lies on the R Lea, 32km/20mi N of London. NOTABLE FEATURES 12c Hertford Castle; Waltham Abbey (20km/12mi SE).

Hertfordshire POP (1992e) 994 000, a county in SE England, divided into 10 districts. AREA

1 634sq km/631sq mi. It is bounded S by Greater London, W by Buckinghamshire, N by Bedfordshire and Cambridgeshire, and E by Essex. PHYSICAL DESCRIPTION drained by the Colne and Lee rivers and the Grand Union Canal; a part of the Chiltern Hills lies in the SW of the county. CHIEF TOWNS Hertford (county town), St Albans, Harpenden, Welwyn Garden City. ECONOMY wheat; cattle; horticulture; brewing; paper; printing; electronics; pharmaceuticals; aerospace.

Herts. *abbrev.* Hertfordshire.

Hertz, Heinrich Rudolf (1857–94) German physicist, born in Hamburg. Professor of Physics at Karlsruhe and Bonn, he discovered 'Hertzian waves', now known as radio waves, in 1887.

hertz *noun* (PL. **hertz**) (ABBREV. **Hz**) the SI unit of frequency, equal to one cycle per second. One kilohertz (kHz) is equal to 1 000 hertz, and one megahertz (MHz) is equal to 1 000 000 hertz. Radio waves have frequencies in the range 200kHz to 100 MHz. [named after the German physicist Heinrich Hertz]

Hertzog, J(ames) B(arry) M(unnik) (1866–1942) South African statesman, born in Wellington, Cape Colony. He was a Boer general (1899–1902), and in 1910 became Minister of Justice in the first government of the Union of South Africa. In 1913 he founded the Nationalist Party, which advocated complete independence from the British Empire for South Africa. As Prime Minister (1924–39), in coalition with Labour (1924–9), and with Jan Smuts in a United Party (1933–9), he pursued a legislative programme which destroyed the African franchise, created reservation for whites, and tightened land segregation. He renounced his earlier secessionism, but at the outbreak of World War II declared for neutrality. When this was rejected, he left office and in 1940 retired.

Hertzsprung, Ejnar (1873–1967) Danish astronomer, born in Fredriksberg, a suburb of Copenhagen. He held posts in Copenhagen, Göttingen, Potsdam, and Leiden, and in 1905 published the principle of the Hertzsprung–Russell diagram, which illustrates the relationship between luminosity and type of spectrum for different kinds of stars; this was essential to subsequent theories of stellar evolution.

Hertzsprung–Russell diagram *Astron.* a graph in which the surface temperature (or the colour) of stars (on the horizontal axis) is plotted against their luminosity (on the vertical axis). The temperature is always shown decreasing from left to right along the horizontal axis. [named after the Danish astronomer Ejnar Hertzsprung and the US astronomer Henry Norris Russell]

◇ Most stars, including the Sun, fall within a broad band, known as the *main sequence*, running diagonally from the top left-hand side to the bottom right-hand side of the graph. This zone contains normal stars that are burning hydrogen fuel. White stars (faint stars which have begun to collapse) form a cluster on the bottom left-hand side of the graph, and giants (large highly luminous stars) and supergiants (the largest and most luminous of all stars) form two clusters on the upper right-hand side of the graph. The Hertzsprung–Russell diagram forms the basis of the theory of development of stars, from their formation to their extinction.

Herzberg, Gerhard (1904–) German-Canadian physicist, born in Hamburg. He emigrated to Canada in 1935. Professor at the University of Saskatchewan and later Director of the physics division of the National Research Council, Ottawa, he is best known for his applications of spectroscopic methods, particularly for study of energy levels in atoms and molecules, and the detection of unusual molecules, including those in interstellar space. He was awarded the 1971 Nobel Prize for Chemistry.

Herzog, Werner, originally **Werner Stipetic** (1942–) German film director, screenwriter, actor, and producer, born in Sachrang. Following numerous shorts in the 1960s, he became recognized as a leading member of the New Cinema in Germany with his feature film *Aguirre, der Zorn Gottes* (Aguirre, Wrath of God, 1973). Later films include *Nosferatu the Vampyre* (1979) and *Fitzcarraldo* (1982).

Herzog a novel by Saul Bellow (1964). It describes the activities and mental disintegration of scholarly Moses Herzog as he tries to come to terms with his two failed marriages.

he's *contr.* **1** he is. **2** he has.

Heseltine, Michael (Ray Dibdin) (1933–) British Conservative politician, born in Swansea, S Wales. He built up a publishing business before entering parliament (1966), then held junior posts in Transport (1970), Environment (1970–2), and Aerospace and Shipping (1972–4). After being Secretary of State for the Environment (1979–83), he became Defence Secretary (1983), but resigned dramatically over the takeover of Westland Helicopters (1986). He was unsuccessful in the leadership contest following Margaret Thatcher's resignation (Nov 1990), and under John Major again became Secretary of State for the Environment (1990–2) and Secretary of State for Trade and Industry (1992–).

Hesiod (8c BC) Greek poet, born in Ascra. He is best known for the epics, *Works and Days*, which deals with the farmer's life, and the *Theogony*, which teaches the origin of the universe and the history of the gods.

hesitance *or* **hesitancy** *noun* hesitating, doubt, delay.

hesitant *adj.* uncertain; holding back; hesitating.

hesitantly *adv.* in a hesitant way.

hesitate *verb intrans.* **1** to be slow in speaking or acting, especially because of uncertainty. **2** to be unwilling to do or say something, eg because one is not sure it is right. [from Latin *haesitare*, to remain stuck]

hesitation *noun* hesitating, doubt, delay.

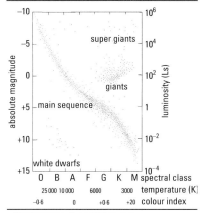

Hertzsprung–Russell diagram

Hesperides in Greek mythology, the daughters of the evening star (Hesper), who guarded the Golden Apples together with the dragon, Ladon. Heracles was commanded to steal the apples as one of his Twelve Labours.

Hess, Germain Henri (1802–50) Swiss-born Russian chemist, born in Geneva. Professor in St Petersburg, he formulated Hess's law (1838–40), which states that the heat developed in a given chemical change is constant, independent of whether the change is carried out in one or several stages.

Hess, Harry Hammond (1906–69) US marine geophysicist and geologist, born in New York City. Professor at Princeton University, he is best known for his theory of seafloor spreading, the process by which the ocean floor is pushed away from the midocean ridges through convection in the Earth's mantle, carrying the continental plates with it; this is thought to provide the power for continental drift.

Hess, Dame Myra (1890–1965) English pianist, born in London. She studied under Tobias Mathay and was an immediate success on her first public appearance in 1907. She worked as a chamber musician, recitalist and virtuoso, and achieved fame in N America and Britain. During World War II she organized the lunchtime concerts in the National Gallery, for which she was awarded the DBE.

Hess, (Walter Richard) Rudolf (1894–1987) German politician, born in Alexandria, Egypt. He fought in World War I, joined the Nazi Party (1920), and became Hitler's close friend and deputy Party Leader (1934). In 1941, on the eve of Germany's attack on Russia, he flew alone to Scotland supposedly to plead the cause of a negotiated Anglo-German peace. After being temporarily imprisoned in the Tower of London, he was placed under psychiatric care near Aldershot. At the Nuremberg Trials (1946) he was sentenced to life imprisonment, and he spent the rest of his life in Spandau prison, Berlin, where after 1966 he was the only prisoner.

Hess, Victor Francis (1883–1964) Austrian-born US physicist, born in Waldstein. Working at Vienna University, he discovered cosmic rays, and later made important discoveries concerning radioactive emission of alpha particles from radium. He shared the 1936 Nobel Prize for Physics with Carl Anderson, and in 1938 emigrated to the USA to become professor at Fordham University, New York.

Hess, Walter Rudolf (1881–1973) Swiss physiologist, born in Frauenfeld. Professor at the University of Zurich, he allowed major advances in the study of brain function by developing methods of stimulating localized areas of the brain using electrodes, and demonstrated the role of the hypothalamus in regulating the activity of certain organs. He shared the 1949 Nobel Prize for Physiology or Medicine with António Egas Moniz.

Hesse, Hermann (1877–1962) German novelist and poet, born in Calw, Württemberg. He worked as a bookseller and antiquarian before turning to writing in 1904. His major novels include *Rosshalde* (1914), *Siddhartha* (1922), *Steppenwolf* (1927), and the visionary *Das Glasperlenspiel* (The Glass Bead Game, 1943). He was awarded the Nobel Prize for Literature in 1946.

hessian — *noun* a coarse cloth similar to sacking, made from jute. — *adj.* made of hessian. [from *Hesse*, in Germany]

Hester a female first name. [a variant of ESTHER]

Hestia in Greek mythology, the goddess of the hearth, the daughter of Cronus and Rhea. Zeus granted her the privilege of keeping her virginity forever. She looked after the family fire, and also had a public cult in the centre of the city, where her flame burned ceaselessly. She was identified by the Romans with Vesta.

Heston, Charlton, originally **John Charlton Carter** (1923–) US film actor, born in Evanston, Illinois. His first Hollywood film was *Dark City* (1950) but his major early successes were the De Mille films *The Greatest Show on Earth* (1952), *The Ten Commandments* (1956), and *Ben Hur* (1959), for which he won an Oscar. He continued acting on screen, stage, and television for the next four decades.

het
— **het up** *colloq.* angry; over-anxious; over-excited.

[dialect for *heated*]

hetero- *combining form* forming words meaning 'other, different': *heterosexual*. [from Greek *heteros*, other]

heterodox *adj.* having a religious or other belief that is different from the one commonly accepted. [from Greek *heteros*, other + *doxa*, opinion]

heterogeneity *noun* **1** being heterogeneous. **2** something which is heterogeneous.

heterogeneous *adj.* made up of parts, people, things, etc of very different kinds. [from Greek *heteros*, other + *genos*, sort]

heteromorphic *adj.* **1** *Biol.* denoting an organism that has different forms at different stages of its life cycle, eg many insects, or whose form differs from one season to the next, or from one generation to the next, eg fern. **2** *Genetics* denoting a pair of chromosomes that differ in size and shape, eg the X and Y chromosome pair. [from HETERO- + Greek *morphe*, form]

heteromorphism *noun* being heteromorphic.

heterosexual — *adj.* **1** sexually attracted to people of the opposite sex. **2** *said of a relationship* between a man and a woman. — *noun* a heterosexual person.

heterosexuality *noun* being heterosexual.

heterotrophic *adj.* *Biol.* describing a living organism that must obtain nutrients by taking in organic material from the environment, because it is unable to manufacture such material from simple compounds. All animals, fungi, and many bacteria, and a few flowering plants are heterotrophic.

heterozygous *adj.* describing an individual that contains two different alleles for a particular gene, and may therefore produce offspring that differ from the parent with respect to that gene. [from HETERO- + Greek *zygon*, yoke]

Heuneberg, The a prehistoric hillfort of the Halstaat Iron Age on a spur overlooking the R Danube near Binzwagen, Württemburg, S Germany. There were five building periods (7c–5c BC), of which the second (early 6c BC) is notable for its defensive wall of unbaked clay bricks, clearly constructed under Greek influence.

heuristic *adj.* **1** *said of a teaching method* encouraging learners to find their own solutions. **2** *Comput.* proceeding through trial and error. [from Greek *heuriskein*, to find]

heuristically *adv.* in a heuristic way.

Heuss, Theodor (1884–1963) German statesman, born in Brackenheim, Württemberg. He was editor of the political magazine *Hilfe* (1905–12), professor at the Berlin College of Political Science (1920–33), and an MP (1924–8, 1930–2). A prolific author and journalist, he wrote two books denouncing Hitler, and when the latter came to power (1933), he was dismissed from his chair and his books publicly burnt. In 1946 he was a founder-member of the Free Democratic Party, helped to draft the new federal constitution, and became the first President of the Federal Republic of Germany (1949–59).

Hevesy, George Charles von (1885–1966) Hungarian chemist, born in Budapest. Working in Copenhagen, he was involved in the discovery of the element hafnium. Later he became professor at Freiburg and Stockholm, and from 1934 he pioneered the use of radioactive tracers to study chemical processes, particularly in living organisms; this work revealed that chemical changes are continually taking place in all living tissue and brought him the 1943 Nobel Prize for Chemistry.

hew *verb* (PAST TENSE **hewed**; PAST PARTICIPLE **hewn**) **1** *trans., intrans.* to cut or hit (a person or thing) with an axe, sword, etc. **2** to carve or shape (figures, etc) out of wood or stone. [from Anglo-Saxon *heawan*]

Hewish, Antony (1924–) English radio astronomer, born in Fowey. Professor at Cambridge, he discovered with his student Jocelyn Bell the first radio sources (now known as 'pulsars') emitting radio signals in regular pulses; they are believed to be very small and dense rotating neutron stars. He shared the 1974 Nobel Prize for Physics with Martin Ryle.

hexa- *combining form* forming words meaning 'six'. [from Greek *hex*, six]

hexadecimal *adj. Comput.* relating to or using a number system with a base of 16.

hexagon *noun* a plane figure with six sides. [from Greek *hex*, six + *gonia*, angle]

hexagonal *adj.* having six sides and angles.

hexagram *noun* a star-shaped figure formed by extending the lines of a hexagon until they meet at six points. [from HEXA- + Greek *gramma*, line]

hexameter *noun Poetry* a line or verse with six measures or feet. [from Greek *hex*, six + *metron*, measure]

hexane *noun Chem.* (FORMULA C_6H_{14}) a toxic flammable colourless liquid belonging to the alkane series of hydrocarbons, used as a solvent. [from Greek *hex*, six]

Hexi Corridor *or* **Gansu Corridor** a natural corridor from central China through Gansu province to Xinjiang autonomous region. It is c.1 200km/750mi long and forms a major part of the ancient Silk Road. The Hexi Corridor was the scene of numerous battles from the 3c BC.

hexose *noun Biochem.* a sugar that has a molecule consisting of six carbon atoms, and has the general formula $C_6H_{12}O_6$, eg glucose, fructose. Hexoses belong to the simplest group of carbohydrates, known as monosaccharides.

hey *interj. colloq.* a shout expressing joy, surprise, a question, dismay, or used to attract attention. — **hey presto!** a conjuror's phrase, usually used at the successful completion of a trick. [from Middle English *hei*]

heyday *noun* a time of most success, power, importance, strength, popularity, etc. [from Old German *heida*, hey there]

Heyerdahl, Thor (1914–) Norwegian anthropologist, born in Larvik. In 1947 he set out to prove, by sailing a balsa raft (the *Kon-Tiki*) from Peru to Tuamotu I in the S Pacific Ocean, that the ancient Peruvian peoples could have settled in Polynesia. His success in this venture, and his archaeological expedition to Easter I, won him popular fame and several awards. In 1970 he sailed from Morocco to the West Indies in a papyrus boat, *Ra II*, and in 1977–8 made the journey from Iraq to Djibouti in a reed boat, the *Tigris*.

Heysel stadium a sports stadium in Brussels, Belgium, opened in 1930. It was the scene of a riot at the 1985 European Cup football final between Liverpool and Juventus, where 39 people were crushed to death after a wall collapsed.

Hf *symbol Chem.* hafnium.

Hg *symbol Chem.* mercury. [from Latin *hydrargyrum*]

HGV *abbrev.* heavy goods vehicle.

HH *abbrev.* `1 *on a pencil* double hard. **2** His Holiness. **3** His or Her Highness.

HI *abbrev.* Hawaii.

hi *interj.* a word used as a greeting or to attract attention. [from HEY]

hiatus *noun* (PL. **hiatuses**) **1** a break or gap in something which should be continuous. **2** a break between two vowels coming together but not in the same syllable. [from Latin *hiare*, to gape]

Hiawatha the name of a legendary Iroquois chief of the 16c, used by Longfellow for his hero in *The Song of Hiawatha*. Hiawatha is educated by his grandmother Nokomis, and marries Minnehaha.

Hiawatha, Song of a narrative poem by Henry Wadsworth Longfellow (1855). It describes the life of the Native American leader, Hiawatha, and his marriage to Minnehaha.

hibernate *verb intrans., said of certain animals* to pass the winter in a sleep-like state. [from Latin *hibernare*, from *hibernus*, wintry]

hibernation *noun* hibernating; a period of hibernating.

Hibernia *noun literary* Ireland. [from Latin *Hibernia*]

Hibernian *literary* — *adj.* of Ireland. — *noun* a native of Ireland.

hibiscus *noun* (PL. **hibiscuses**) a usually tropical tree or shrub with large, brightly coloured flowers. [from Greek *hibiskos*, marsh-mallow]

hiccup *or* **hiccough** — *noun* **1** a sudden breathing in of air caused by a spasm in the diaphragm, or the sound caused by this. **2** (**hiccups**) the frequent repetition of this, at intervals of a few seconds. **3** *colloq.* a minor and usually temporary problem or interruption. — *verb* (**hiccuped**, **hiccuping**) **1** *intrans.* to make a hiccup or hiccups. **2** *trans.* to say with a hiccup. [imitative]

hick *noun chiefly North Amer. colloq.* an unsophisticated person from the country. [a familiar form of *Richard*]

hickory *noun* (PL. **hickories**) **1** a N American tree related to the walnut, with edible nuts. **2** the tough heavy wood produced by it. [from an American Indian language]

hidden *adj.* difficult to see or find.

hidden agenda a set of motions or goals kept secret from those who might object to them or until it is too late to object.

hide[1] — *verb* (PAST TENSE **hid**; PAST PARTICIPLE **hidden**) **1** to put (a person, thing, etc) in a place where one cannot easily see or find him, it, etc. **2** *intrans.* to go to or be in a place where one cannot be seen or found easily. **3** to keep (information, feelings, etc) secret. **4** to make (something) difficult to see; to obscure: *trees hiding the house*. — *noun* a concealed shelter used for watching birds and wild animals. [from Anglo-Saxon *hydan*]

hide[2] *noun* **1** the skin of an animal, either raw or tanned. **2** *colloq.* the human skin. — **not** *or* **neither hide nor hair** not the slightest trace. [from Anglo-Saxon *hyd*]

hide-and-seek *noun* a children's game in which one child searches for the others who have hidden themselves.

hideaway *or* **hideout** *noun* a hiding-place or refuge.

hidebound *adj.* unwilling to accept new ideas or opinions, especially because of a petty or conservative attitude. [from HIDE[2] + BOUND[1]]

hideous *adj., said of a person or thing* repulsively ugly or unpleasant. [from Old French *hideus*]

hideously *adv.* in a hideous way.

hideousness *noun* being hideous.

Hideyoshi, Toyotomi, known as the **Napoleon of Japan** (1536–98) Japanese soldier, who became the second of the three great historical unifiers of Japan (the others were Nobunaga and Ieyasu Tokugawa). Unusually, he was an ordinary soldier who rose to become Nobunaga's foremost general. His law forbade all except samurai to carry swords (1588), and he banned Christianity for political reasons (1597). His armies invaded Korea (1592–8), but withdrew after his death.

hiding[1] *noun* the state of being hidden or concealed.

hiding[2] *noun colloq.* a severe beating. [from HIDE[2]]

hiding-place *noun* a place of concealment.

hie *verb intrans.* (**hieing**, **hying**) *old use* to go quickly. [from Anglo-Saxon *higian*]

Hierapolis, modern **Pamukkale**, English **Cotton Castle** an archaeological site, the remains of an ancient Phrygian city in SW Turkey, abandoned in the 14c. It is famed for its thermal springs, which have formed crystalline shelves down the side of the plateau. It is a World Heritage site.

hierarchical *adj.* relating to or involving a hierarchy.

hierarchy *noun* (PL. **hierarchies**) **1** an arrangement (especially of people or things in a group) in order of rank or importance. **2** the people who control an organization. [from Greek *hieros*, sacred + *archein*, to rule]

hieroglyph *noun* a picture or symbol used to represent a word, syllable, or sound, especially in ancient Egyptian. [from Greek *hieros*, sacred + *glyphein*, to carve]

hieroglyphic *adj.* relating to or written in hieroglyphs or hieroglyphics.

hieroglyphics *pl. noun* **1** a form of writing using hieroglyphs, used in ancient Egypt. **2** *colloq.* writing that is difficult to read.

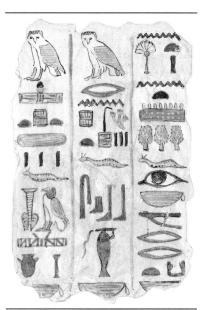

Egyptian hieroglyphics

hi-fi — *adj. colloq.* high fidelity. — *noun* an electronic system that gives such faithful reproduction of recorded music or speech that it is virtually indistinguishable from the original sound, with minimal distortion and background noise. Modern hi-fi systems often include a compact disc player, tape deck, record turntable, radio tuner, amplifier, and loudspeakers. [a shortening of *high fidelity*]

Higgins, Alex (**Alexander Gordon**), also called **Hurricane Higgins** (1949–) Northern Irish snooker player, born in Belfast. He won the world championship title at his first attempt in 1972, and again in 1982. Also in 1982, he defeated Steve Davis to win the Coral UK championship. Renowned for his tempestuous nature, he was banned during 1990-1 after confrontations with the authorities.

Higgins, Professor Henry the bachelor phoneticist in George Bernard Shaw's *Pygmalion* who, while teaching Eliza to speak correctly, completely disregards her sensibilities in his desire to win a wager.

higgledy-piggledy *adv., adj. colloq.* in confusion; in a muddle.

Higgs, Peter Ware (1929–) British theoretical physicist, born in Newcastle upon Tyne. Professor at Edinburgh University, he developed a theory of the way fundamental particles interact, in which the interactions which constitute the fundamental forces of nature take place via the exchange of particles, known as gauge bosons, with mass. This requires the existence of an as yet undiscovered family of particles known as the 'Higgs bosons'.

high — *adj.* 1 reaching up to a relatively great distance from the bottom: *high buildings.* 2 of a particular height: *three feet high.* 3 situated at a relatively great distance from the ground or from sea level: *a high branch.* 4 great; intense: *a high wind.* 5 greater than average height: *a high-necked sweater.* 6 at its peak: *high summer.* 7 very important or exalted: *high art.* 8 *said of sound* acute in pitch. 9 extremely emotional: *high drama.* 10 *said of meat* beginning to go bad. 11 elated. 12 *colloq.* under the influence of drugs or alcohol. — *adv.* at or to a height; in or into a raised position. — *noun* 1 a high point. 2 an area of high pressure; an anticyclone. 3 *colloq.* a state of great excitement or happiness, often produced by drugs or alcohol: *on a high.*
— **high and dry 1** *said of boats* out of the water. **2** stranded or helpless.
high and low 1 everywhere. **2** everyone, rich and poor alike.
high and mighty *colloq.* arrogant.
on high at or to a high place or position; in or to heaven.
on one's high horse *colloq.* behaving arrogantly or condescendingly.
[from Anglo-Saxon *heah*]

high altar the main altar in a large church which has more than one altar.

highball *noun North Amer.* an alcoholic drink of spirits and soda served with ice in a long glass.

high-born *adj.* of noble birth.

highbrow *often derog.* — *noun* an intellectual or cultured person. — *adj., said of art, literature, etc* intellectual or cultured.

high-chair *noun* a baby's or young child's tall chair, used especially at mealtimes.

High Church a section of the Church of England which places great importance on ceremony and priestly authority.

high-class *adj.* of high quality or high social class.

High Commission an embassy representing one member country of the Commonwealth, situated in another.

High Commissioner *noun* the senior diplomat at the head of such an embassy.

High Court *noun* the supreme court for civil cases in England and Wales.

High Court of Justice a court established for England and Wales by the Judicature Acts (1873), principally a trial court for civil cases. It hears appeals on points of law from magistrates' courts in both civil and criminal cases, and also undertakes judicial review. The court has three divisions: Queen's Bench Division (for commercial, maritime, and some civil law cases), Chancery Division (for probate, bankruptcy, and equity cases), and Family Division (for matters of family law).

high-definition television (ABBREV. **HDTV**) an advanced television system in which the image is composed of more than 1 000 scanning lines, nearly twice the number in the standard system, which affords much improved picture quality.

higher education *noun* education beyond secondary-school level, eg at university or college.

Higher grade in Scotland, an examination taken by (usually) school and college students which qualifies them for entrance to higher education and the professions. It is a single-subject examination at a level representing one further year of study beyond the Ordinary/Standard grades.

high explosive — *noun* a very powerful explosive, such as dynamite. — *adj.* exploding with very great effect.

high-falutin or **high-faluting** *adj. colloq.* pompous or pretentious.

high fidelity the reproduction of sound with great accuracy.

high-five *noun* a sign of greeting or celebration, consisting of slapping together raised palms.

high-flier or **high-flyer** *noun* 1 an ambitious person who is likely to be successful. 2 a person with great ability in his or her career.

high-flown *adj., usually said of language* sounding grand but lacking real substance; rhetorical, extravagant.

high-flying *adj.* extremely ambitious.

high frequency a radio frequency between 3 and 30 megahertz.

High German the standard form of the German language.

high-handed *adj.* acting or done without thought or consideration for others.

high-handedly *adv.* in a high-handed way.

high-handedness *noun* being high-handed.

highjack same as HIJACK.

high jinks *colloq.* boisterous fun; mischief.

high jump *noun* 1 an athletic event in which competitors jump over a bar which is raised higher as the event progresses. 2 *colloq.* a severe punishment: *be for the high jump.*

Highland POP (1992e) 206 000, a large region in N Scotland divided into eight districts, including Skye and the Inner Hebrides. AREA 25 391sq km/9 801sq mi. The region is bounded N and E by the North Sea, SE by Grampian Region, S by Tayside, SW by Strathclyde, and W by the Minch and the Little Minch. It is sparsely inhabited and of great scenic beauty, dominated by the Grampian, Monadhliath, and Cairngorm Mts. The Grampians rise to 1 344m at Ben Nevis, Britain's highest mountain. The region is crossed by many rivers, and SW–NE by lochs (notably Linnhe, Lochy, Oich, Ness); this is also the route of the Caledonian Canal. CAPITAL Inverness. CHIEF TOWNS Wick, Dingwall, Thurso, Nairn. ECONOMY forestry, livestock, oil, winter skiing, fishing, fish farming, game hunting, tourism. NOTABLE FEATURES Eas Coul Aulin in the NW, the highest waterfall in the UK (drop of 200m); John o' Groats (in the extreme NE); Glencoe in the SE, the site of the 1692 battle; Dounreay Nuclear Research Station.

highland — *noun* 1 (*often* **highlands**) a high mountainous area. 2 (**the Highlands**) the mountainous area of northern and western Scotland. — *adj.* of highlands or (**Highland**) the Scottish Highlands.

Highland cattle *noun* a Scottish breed of cattle with a long, shaggy coat and long horns.

highlander *noun* a person who comes from a mountainous area, especially (**Highlander**) that of Scotland.

Highland fling *noun* a lively solo dance from the Scottish Highlands.

Highland Games the name applied to athletics meetings originally held in the highlands of Scotland; the first Games were organized by the St Fillans (Perthshire) Highland Society in 1819. A range of athletic events takes place, in addition to specifically Scottish events, such as tossing the caber, Highland dancing, and bagpipe-playing competitions.

high-level *adj.* conducted by or involving people at a high level of management, etc: *high-level discussions.*

high-level language *Comput.* a programming language that allows the user to write programs using English-like commands, mathematical equations, etc, rather than actual computer instructions. The programs produced are relatively slow because each statement corresponds to several computer instructions. See also LOW-LEVEL LANGUAGE.

highlight — *noun* 1 the best or most memorable event, experience, part of something, etc. 2 a lighter patch in one's hair, usually made artificially. 3 the brightest part of a photograph. — *verb* to draw attention to or emphasise.

highlighter *noun* a broad-tipped felt pen run over parts of a text to highlight the content.

highly *adv.* 1 very: *highly gratified.* 2 with approval: *speak highly of her.*

highly-strung *adj.* very nervous and easily upset or excited.

High Mass especially in the Roman Catholic Church, an elaborate and usually sung form of the mass.

high-minded *adj.* having or showing noble ideals and principles, etc.

high-mindedness *noun* being high-minded.

highness *noun* 1 (**Highness**) a title used when addressing or speaking about a member of a royal family: *Your Highness.* 2 the state or quality of being high.

High Noon a US film directed by Fred Zinneman (1952). A Western, it tells of a retired marshal (played by Gary Cooper) whose integrity forces him to face an outlaw bent on revenge who arrives during his wedding celebrations.

high-octane *adj., said of petrol* having a high octane rating, and therefore good antiknock qualities.

high-pitched *adj.* 1 *said of sounds, voices, etc* high in tone. 2 *said of a roof* steeply angled.

high point the best state reached.

high-powered *adj.* very powerful or energetic; very efficient.

high-pressure *adj.* 1 having, using, etc air, water, etc at a high pressure. 2 *colloq.* very forceful and persuasive. 3 involving considerable effort or stress.

high priest or **high priestess** the priest or priestess who is the head of a cult.

high-rise *adj., said of a building* having many storeys.

high-risk *adj.* dangerous: *high-risk sports.*

high road *noun* a main road.

high school *noun* a secondary school.

high seas the open sea not under the control of any country.

high season the busiest time of year at a holiday resort or destination.

Highsmith, Patricia (1921–) US novelist, born in Fort Worth, Texas. Her first novel, *Strangers on a Train* (1949), became famous as a source of Hitchcock's 1957 film of that name. Her best novels are generally held to be those describing the criminal adventures of her psychotic hero Tom Ripley, beginning with *The Talented Mr Ripley* (1956).

high-sounding *adj.* pretentious; pompous.

high-spirited *adj.* lively, cheerful and vivacious.

high street the main shopping street of a town.

high tea *Brit.* a meal consisting usually of cooked food with bread, cakes, and tea, served in the late afternoon.

high tech or **hi-tech** *colloq.* **1** involving or using advanced, especially electronic equipment. **2** *said of interior decoration, designs, etc* based on styles or elements found in industry. [a shortening of *high technology*]

high-tension *adj.* carrying high-voltage electrical currents.

high tide the time when the tide is farthest up the shore; the highest level reached by the water at this time.

high time *colloq.* the time by which something ought to have been done.

high treason treason against one's sovereign or country.

high water the time at which the tide, river, etc is at its fullest.

high-water mark the highest level reached by a tide, river, etc.

highway *noun North Amer.* a public road that everyone may use, especially a large or main road.

Highway Code *Brit.* an official booklet containing rules and guidance for road-users.

highwayman *noun Hist.* a robber, usually on horseback, who attacks and robs people travelling on public roads.

high wire a tightrope high above the ground.

High Wycombe, formerly **Chepping Wycombe** POP (1981) 70 000, a market town in Wycombe district, Buckinghamshire, S central England. It lies on the R Wye, 45km/28mi NW of London. NOTABLE FEATURES Local History Museum; Hughenden Manor (the home of Benjamin Disraeli).

hijack *verb* **1** to take control of (a moving vehicle, especially an aircraft) and force it to go to a different destination. **2** to stop and rob (a vehicle). **3** to steal (goods) in transit. **4** *colloq.* to seize control of (an organization, event, etc).

hijacker *noun* a person who hijacks.

hijacking *noun* **1** being attacked or taken over by a hijacker. **2** the action of a hijacker.

hike — *noun* a long walk, usually in the country, often carrying equipment on one's back. — *verb* **1** *intrans.* to go on a hike. **2** (**hike something up**) to pull up or raise it with a jerk. **3** to increase (prices) suddenly. [originally a dialect word, of unknown origin]

hiker *noun* a person who walks long distances for pleasure.

hilarious *adj.* very funny. [from Greek *hilaros*, cheerful]

hilariously *adv.* in a hilarious way.

hilariousness *noun* being hilarious.

hilarity *noun* merriment, laughter.

Hilary a female first name, formerly given to males. [from Latin *hilaris*, cheerful]

Hilary (of Poitiers), St (c.315–68 AD) French prelate and one of the Doctors of the Church, born of pagan parents in Limonum (Poitiers). Converted to Christianity quite late in life, in c.350 he was elected Bishop of Poitiers and soon became a leading opponent of Arianism. His principal work was on the Trinity. His feast day (13 Jan) marks the beginning of a term at Oxford and Durham Universities, and English law sittings, to which his name is applied.

Hilbert, David (1862–1943) German mathematician, born in Königsberg (now Kaliningrad, Russia). Professor at Göttingen (1895–1930), he critically examined the foundations of geometry; he also made important contributions to the theory of numbers, the theory of invariants, and the application of integral equations to physical problems.

Hilda a female first name. [Norman, from Germanic + Anglo-Saxon *hild*, battle]

Hildesheim POP (1991e) 105 000, an industrial port in Lower Saxony state, NW Germany. Founded in 1300, it lies in the fertile valley of the R Innerste, 29km/18mi SE of Hanover. NOTABLE FEATURES St Michael's Church (11c) and Romanesque St Mary's Cathedral (1054–79), both of which are World Heritage sites.

Hill, Sir (Austin) Bradford (1897–1991) English medical statistician. Working at the National Institute for Medical Research, Mill Hill, and the London School of Hygiene and Tropical Medicine, he studied occupational hazards, the value of immunization against whooping cough and poliomyelitis, and the effects of smoking. Renowned for his carefully controlled and unbiased studies, he concluded that smoking was an important cause of lung cancer.

Hill, David Octavius (1802–70) Scottish painter and pioneer photographer, born in Perth. He studied art at Edinburgh, and with the technical collaboration of Robert Adamson (1821–48) was one of the first to make use of Fox Talbot's Calotype process. He created many portraits of his contemporaries in the period 1843–8.

Hill, Geoffrey (1932–) English poet, born in Bromsgrove, Worcestershire. He taught at the Universities of Leeds and Cambridge before becoming Professor of Literature and Religion at Boston University in 1988. His poetic works include *For the Unfallen* (1959), *King Log* (1968), *Mercian Hymns* (1971), *Tenebrae* (1978), and *The Mystery of the Charity of Charles Peguy* (1983).

Hill, (Norman) Graham (1929–75) English motor racing driver, born in London. He won 14 races from a record 176 starts (since surpassed) between 1958 and 1975, and was world champion in 1962 and 1968. He won the Monaco Grand Prix five times (1963–5, 1968–9). In 1975 he started his own racing team, Embassy Racing, but was killed when the plane he was piloting crashed.

Hill, Octavia (1838–1912) English housing reformer and founder of the National Trust, born in London. She worked among the London poor, and in 1864, supported by John Ruskin, commenced her project to improve the homes of working men in the slums. Her methods were imitated in Europe and the USA.

hill *noun* **1** a piece of high land, smaller than a mountain. **2** a slope on a road. **3** a heap or mound.
— **over the hill** *colloq.* past one's best; too old. [from Anglo-Saxon *hyll*]

Hillary, Sir Edmund (Percival) (1919–) New Zealand mountaineer and explorer, more recently author and lecturer, born in Auckland. As a member of John Hunt's Everest expedition he reached, with Sherpa Tenzing, the summit of Mt Everest in 1953, for which he was knighted. With a New Zealand party led by Vivian Ernest Fuchs, he reached the South Pole in 1958. He was appointed New Zealand High Commissioner to India in 1984.

hillbilly *noun* (PL. **hillbillies**) *North Amer., esp. US* **1** *derog.* an unsophisticated person from a remote, mountainous country area. **2** country and western music.

Hillel I or **Hillel the Elder**, surnamed **Hababli** (**the Babylonian**), or **Hazaken** (**the Elder**) (1c BC–1c AD) Jewish sage, born (probably) in Babylonia, and one of the most respected doctors of the Jewish law. He went to Palestine (when he was about 40), where he was chosen President of the Sanhedrin as an authority on biblical law.

hilliness *noun* being hilly.

hillock *noun* a small hill.

Hillsborough a football stadium in Sheffield, England, the scene of the worst disaster in British sporting history at the FA Cup semi-final match between Liverpool and Nottingham Forest (15 Apr 1989). Due mainly to crushing at the perimeter fences, 95 Liverpool fans died and 400 people were injured.

hillside *noun* the sloping side of a hill.

hilly *adj.* (**hillier, hilliest**) having many hills.

hilt *noun* the handle of a sword, dagger, knife, etc.
— **up to the hilt** completely; thoroughly. [from Anglo-Saxon *hilte*]

Hilton, Conrad Nicholson (1887–1979) US hotelier, born in San Antonio, New Mexico. By 1915 he was President of A H Hilton and Son, General Store. He took over the family inn in 1918, bought his first hotel in Cisco, Texas, in 1919, and built up a chain of hotels in the major cities of the USA. He formed Hilton Hotels Corporation in 1946, and Hilton International in 1948. His son Barron Hilton succeeded him as President in 1966.

Hilton, James (1900–54) English novelist and Hollywood scriptwriter, born in Leigh, Lancashire. His first novel, *Catherine Herself* appeared in 1920, and his best-known novels, many of which were filmed, include *Lost Horizon* (1933) and *Goodbye Mr Chips* (1934).

hilum *noun* (PL. **hila**) *Bot.* a scar on the seed or ovule of a plant marking the point at which it was attached to the wall of the fruit or ovary, respectively. [from Latin *hilum*, a little thing]

Hilversum POP (1992e) 85 000, a city in SE North Holland province, W Netherlands. It is a fashionable residential and commuter district of Amsterdam which has become famous for its radio and television stations.

him *pron.* a male person or animal, the object form of *he*.
— **be him** *colloq.* to be suited to him: *jackets and ties aren't really him.*
[from Anglo-Saxon *him*]

Himalayas a gigantic wall of mountains in central Asia, N of the Indus and Brahmaputra rivers. There is a series of parallel ranges, generally rising towards the N with a length of over 2 400km/1 500mi from the Pamirs in the NW to the borders of Assam and China in the E. The three main ranges are the Outer, Middle, and Inner Himalayas, which become five ranges in Kashmir: the Lesser and the Great Himalayas, the Zāskār Range, the Ladākh Range, and the Karakorams. Mt Everest rises to 8 848m on the Nepal–Tibet border. Other major peaks include K2 in the Karakorams (8 611m), Kangchenjunga (8 586m), Makalu (8 475m), Dhaulagiri (8 167m), Nanga Parbat (8 126m), and Annapurna (8 091m). In Hindu mythology the mountains are highly revered.

Himmler, Heinrich (1900–45) German Nazi leader and chief of police, born in Munich. He joined the Nazi Party in 1925, and in 1929 was made head of the SS, which he developed from Hitler's personal bodyguard into a powerful party weapon. He also directed the Gestapo (secret police) and initiated the systematic killing of Jews. In 1943 he became Minister of the Interior, and in 1944 Commander-in-Chief of the home forces. He was captured by the Allies, and committed suicide at Lüneburg.

himself *pron.* **1** the reflexive form of *him* and *he*: *he taught himself to dance.* **2** used for emphasis: *he did it himself.* **3** his normal self: *be feeling himself again after the operation.* **4** also **by himself** alone; without help.

Hinault, Bernard (1954–) French cyclist, born in Yffignac, Brittany. He was French pursuit champion in 1974, and turned professional in 1977. He won the Tour de France in 1978–9, 1981–2, and 1985, joining Eddy Merckx and Jacques Anquetil as a five-times winner. He has also won the Tour of Italy three times and the Tour of Spain twice.

hind¹ *noun* a female deer, especially a red deer, usually after three years of age. [from Anglo-Saxon *hind*]

hind² *adj.* at the back: *hind legs*. [from Middle English *hinde*]

Hindemith, Paul (1895–1963) German composer, born in Hanau, near Frankfurt. He played violin in the Rebner Quartet and the Opera Orchestra (1915–23), and wrote operas (eg the contoversial *Mathis der Maler*, 1933–5), concertos, and a wide range of instrumental pieces. He also pioneered *Gebrauchsmusik*, pieces written for specific purposes (eg newsreels and community singing), but his music was banned by the Nazis in 1934.

Hindenburg, Paul (Ludwig Hans Anton von Beneckendorff und) von (1847–1934) German soldier and statesman, born in Posen, Prussia. He fought in the Franco-Prussian War (1870–1), rose to the rank of general (1903), and retired in 1911. Recalled at the outbreak of World War I, he won victories over the Russians (1914–15), but was forced to direct the German retreat on the Western Front (to the 'Hindenburg line'). A national hero, he was the second President of the German Republic (1925–34), and in 1933 appointed Hitler as Chancellor.

Hindenburg a zeppelin airship built by the German government in 1936. It was of rigid-frame construction, and capable of carrying 72 passengers. After 63 successful flights, most of which were across the Atlantic Ocean, the Hindenburg caught fire and was destroyed in May 1937 whilst coming in to moor in New Jersey. The fire was probably due to hydrogen leaks being ignited by atmospheric electricity.

hinder¹ *verb* (pronounced *hind-*) (**hindered**, **hindering**) to delay or keep back; to prevent progress. [from Anglo-Saxon *hindrian*]

hinder² *adj.* (pronounced *hined-*) at the back: *the hinder part*.

Hindi *noun* **1** one of the main languages of India, a literary form of Hindustani. **2** a group of languages spoken in N India, including Hindustani. [from Persian *Hind*, India]
◊ Hindi is an Indo-Aryan language. It is spoken by 130–200 milllion people as a first language in N and central India, and by a further 100–500 million as a second language throughout India and elsewhere. It has close links with Sanskrit, and is written in Devangari script (from left to right).

Hindlish *or* **Hinglish** — *noun* a language consisting of a mixture of Hindi and English. — *adj.* written or spoken in this language. [from HINDI + ENGLISH]

hindmost *adj.* last; farthest behind.

hindquarters *pl. noun* the back legs and buttocks of a four-legged animal.

hindrance *noun* **1** a person or thing that hinders. **2** the act of hindering. [from HINDER¹]

hindsight *noun* wisdom or knowledge after the event.

Hindu — *noun* a person who practises Hinduism. — *adj.* of Hindus or Hinduism. [from Persian *Hind*, India]

Hinduism *noun* the main religion of India, which includes worship of many gods, a belief in reincarnation, and the arrangement of people in society in social castes.
◊ Hinduism developed over several thousand years and intertwined with the country's history and social system. It has no set creed, has no prophets, and no particular institutional structure. It embraces diverse religious beliefs and practices, and there are significant variations between different regions of India in the deities worshipped, the scriptures used, and the festivals observed. Common to most forms is the idea of reincarnation or transmigration; *samsara* is the

process of birth and rebirth continuing for life after life; *mohsha* is the ultimate spiritual goal, or release from the cycle of samsara. Hinduism has a rich and varied religious literature: the earliest extant texts are from the Vedic period (c.1200–500 BC) and are known as the Vedas. Later religious law books (c.500 BC–AD 500), the *dharma sutras* and *dharma shastras*, codified the classes of society (*varna*) and the four stages of life (*ashrama*) and were the basis of the Indian caste system. There are also the great epics, the Ramayana and the Mahabharata (which includes the most influential Hindu scripture, the Bhagavadgita). The chief gods are Brahma, Vishnu, and Shiva.

Hindu Kush, ancient **Paropamisus** a mountain range in central Asia, an extension of the Himalayan system, covering c.800km/500mi. It is the world's second highest range, running SW, and rising to 7 690m in Tirich Mir. There are four subsidiary ridges. The peaks are permanently snow-covered and have little vegetation. Several passes cross the range. The Salang Tunnel allows Kabul to be linked to the N area and Tajikistan. Alexander the Great and Timur followed these passes in their invasions of India.

Hindustani — *noun* a form of Hindi with elements from Arabic and Persian, used as a lingua franca in much of the Indian subcontinent. — *adj.* relating to or spoken or written in Hindustani.

Hindustani music see CARNATIC MUSIC.

Hines, Earl, also called **Fatha** ('**Father**') (1905–83) US jazz pianist and bandleader, born in Duquesne, Pennsylvania. Part of the jazz immigration to Chicago in the 1920s, his first recordings with Louis Armstrong in 1928 (eg 'Weather Bird' and 'West End Blues') revolutionized jazz piano. He improvised single-note lines in the treble clef and punctuated them with internal rhythms in the bass, a style later known as 'trumpet piano'. His popularity waned with the end of the Swing Era, but was renewed following an appearance at a New York concert (1965).

hinge — *noun* **1** the movable joint by means of which a door is fastened to a door-frame, a lid is

Hindu Festivals	
Chaitra S 9	Ramanavami (Birthday of Lord Rama)
Asadha S 2	Rathayatra (Pilgrimage of the Chariot at Jagannath)
Sravana S 11–15	Jhulanayatra ('Swinging the Lord Krishna')
Sravana S 15	Rakshabandhana ('Tying on lucky threads')
Bhadrapada K 8	Janamashtami (Birthday of Lord Krishna)
Asvina S 7–10	Durga-puja (Homage to Goddess Durga) (Bengal)
Asvina S 1–10	Navaratri (Festival of 'nine nights')
Asvina S 15	Lakshmi-puja (Homage to Goddess Lakshmi)
Asvina K 15	Diwali, Dipavali ('String of Lights')
Kartikka S 15	Guru Nanak Jananti (Birthday of Guru Nanak)
Magha K 5	Sarasvati-puja (Homage to Goddess Sarasvati)
Magha K 13	Maha-sivaratri (Great Night of Lord Shiva)
Phalguna S 14	Holi (Festival of Fire)
Phalguna S 15	Dolayatra (Swing Festival) (Bengal)

S: Sukla 'waxing fortnight'.
K: Krishna 'waning fortnight'.

fastened to a box, etc and on which the door, lid, etc turns when it opens or closes. **2** a principle or fact on which anything depends. — *verb* **1** *intrans.* to hang or turn on. **2** *intrans.* (**hinge on something**) to depend on it: *it all hinges on their decision.* **3** to fit with a hinge. [from Middle English *henge*]

hinged *adj.* having a hinge or hinges.

hinge joint *Anat.* in vertebrates, a joint between two or more bones that allows free movement in one plane only, eg elbow and knee joint.

Hinkley Point a nuclear power station in Somerset, England, on the coast of Bridgwater Bay, W of Stolford. Its gas-cooled, graphite-moderated reactors came into commercial operation in 1965, and its advanced gas-cooled reactors in 1976 and 1978.

hinny *noun* (PL. **hinnies**) the offspring of a stallion and a female donkey or ass. [from Greek *hinnos*, mule]

hint — *noun* **1** a statement that passes on information without giving it openly or directly. **2** a helpful piece of advice. **3** a very small amount; a slight impression or suggestion of: *a hint of perfume.* — *verb intrans.* (**hint at something**) to suggest or imply it, especially slightly or indirectly.
— **take a hint** *colloq.* to understand what a person is hinting at, and do what that person wants. [from Anglo-Saxon *hentan*, to seize]

hinterland *noun* **1** the district lying inland from the coast or the banks of a river. **2** an area dependent on a nearby port, commercial centre, etc. [from German *hinter*, behind + *Land*, land]

hip¹ *noun* the haunch, or upper fleshy part of the thigh just below the waist; the joint of the femur (thigh bone) with the pelvis. [from Anglo-Saxon *hype*]

hip² *noun* the large red cup-shaped fruit produced by members of the genus *Rosa*, eg dog-rose and other roses. [from Anglo-Saxon *heope*]

hip³ *interj.* an exclamation used to call for a united cheer: *hip, hip hooray!*

hip⁴ *adj.* (**hipper**, **hippest**) *colloq.* interested in, knowing about, and following current fashions in music, fashion, etc.

hip bath *noun* a portable bath for sitting in.

hip-hop *noun* a popular culture movement originating in the USA in the 1980s, incorporating rap music, breakdancing, and graffiti, and the wearing of characteristically baggy clothing. [from HIP⁴]

Hipparchos (c.180–125 BC) Greek astronomer, born in Nicaea, Bithynia. He made his observations from Rhodes, and may also have lived in Alexandria. Among a multitude of important discoveries he compiled the first star catalogue (containing 850 stars), discovered the precession of the equinoxes (ie the shifting of the point of intersection of the Sun's annual path with the celestial equator), estimated the relative distances of the Sun and Moon, and developed trigonometry.

Hipparchos *noun Astron.* the first astrometry satellite, launched by the European Space Agency in 1989 to obtain data that will eventually provide highly accurate positions for thousands of stars, together with details of their colour, brightness, etc. [a shortening of *high precision parallax collecting satellite*, and associated with the Greek astronomer Hipparchos]

hipped roof *Archit.* a pitched roof consisting of two or more sloping roof ends with the walls finishing at the eaves instead of forming an angled gable.

hippie *or* **hippy** *noun* (PL. **hippies**) *colloq.* especially in the 1960s, a young person typically wearing brightly coloured casual clothes and long hair, advocating freedom of thought and expression, and rejecting many of the more conservative standards and values of society.

hippo *noun* (PL. **hippos**) *colloq.* a hippopotamus. [abbreviation]

hippocampus (PL. **hippocampi**) *noun* **1** *Anat.* in the vertebrate brain, a structure consisting of two ridges, one over each of the fluid-filled cavities in the cerebral hemispheres. It it thought to be associated with short-term memory in human beings. **2** (*Hippocampus*) a genus of small fishes with a horse-like head and neck. — Also called *sea horse*. [from Greek *hippokampos*, from *hippos* a horse, and *kampos* a sea-monster]

Hippocrates (d.377 or 359 BC) Greek physician, known as the 'father of medicine'. The most celebrated physician of antiquity, he was born and practised on the island of Cos; skilled in diagnosis and prognosis, he gathered together all the work of his predecessors which he believed to be sound, and laid the early foundations of scientific medicine. His followers developed the theories that four fluids or 'humours' of the body are the primary seats of disease. His name is remembered in the 'Hippocratic oath'.

Hippocratic oath an oath taken by doctors by which they agree to observe a code of medical ethics. [named after Hippocrates]

hippodrome *noun* **1** a variety theatre or circus. **2** in ancient Greece and Rome, an open-air racecourse for horses and chariots. [from Greek *hippos*, horse + *dromos*, course]

Hippolytus in Greek legend, the son of Theseus and Hippolyta. Theseus' new wife, Phaedra, made advances to Hippolytus, which were refused; she then falsely accused Hippolytus of rape. Theseus invoked a curse of Poseidon, who sent a frightening sea-monster, and Hippolytus was thrown from his chariot and killed.

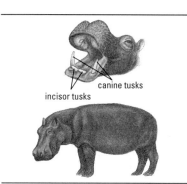

hippopotamus

hippopotamus (PL. **hippopotamuses**, **hippopotami**) either of two species of mammal, especially *Hippopotamus amphibius*, which is found in rivers and lakes in certain parts of Africa, and having a thick hairless body, massive head, and short stout legs. Its enormous mouth contains large canine tusks which may be over 1.5m long. [from Greek *hippos*, horse + *potamos*, river] ◊ *Hippopotamus amphibius* is nearly 4.3m long and weighs about 4 tonnes. It was once found throughout Africa, but is now extinct north of Khartoum, in the Sudan, and south of the Zambezi R, except in protected areas. Its eyes are situated on the top of its large flat head, and it has small ears, and slit-like nostrils high up on its muzzle, so that it is able to see and breathe while basking below the surface of the water. It emerges on to dry land at night to feed, mainly on grass. The smaller pygmy hippopotamus (*Choeropsis liberiensis*) is only about 150cm long, and is found in swamps and forests in Liberia, Sierra Leone, and S Nigeria. It is less aquatic than the other species.

hippy see HIP⁴.

hipsters *pl. noun* trousers which hang from the hips rather than the waist. [from HIP¹]

hiragana see KANA.

hire — *verb* **1** to get the temporary use of (something which belongs to someone else) in exchange for payment. **2** (**hire something out**) to give someone the temporary use of it for payment. **3** to employ (a servant, workman, etc) for wages. — *noun* **1** an act of hiring. **2** payment for hiring something.
— **for hire** ready for hiring.
on hire hired out.
[from Anglo-Saxon *hyr*]

hireling *noun derog.* a person who works for another for payment. [from Anglo-Saxon *hyrling*]

Hireling, The a novel by L P Hartley (1957). It focuses on the relationship between a widow, Lady Franklin, and her driver.

hire-purchase *noun Brit.* a way of buying an article by paying for it in several weekly or monthly parts after one has taken possession of it.

Hirohito (1901–89) Emperor of Japan (1926–89), the 124th in direct lineage, born in Tokyo. His reign was marked by rapid militarization and the aggressive wars against China (1931–2, 1937–45) and Britain and the USA (1941–5), which ended after the atomic bombs were dropped on Hiroshima and Nagasaki by the USA. Under American occupation, in 1946 Hirohito renounced his 'divinity' and most of his powers, and became a democratic constitutional monarch.

Hiroshige, Ando, originally **Ando Tokutaro** (1797–1858) Japanese artist and wood engraver born in Edo (modern Tokyo). He was a leading exponent of the *ukiyo-e* (passing of the floating world) school and it is estimated that he created more than 5 000 original prints in his lifetime. He created a distinctive landscape style, freer than that of his contemporary Hokusai, and shown at its greatest in his series *Fifty-three Stages on the Tokaido* (1832). His masterpieces are striking compositions of snow or rain and mist.

Hiroshima POP (1991e) 1.1m, the capital of Hiroshima prefecture, S Honshu, Japan. It is located on the S coast, on the delta of the R Ota. HISTORY founded as a castle in 1594; site of the military headquarters in the Sino-Japanese War (1894–5) and the Russo-Japanese War (1904–5); an atomic bomb was dropped here on 6 Aug 1945 which resulted in c.150 000 people killed or wounded and 75 per cent of buildings being destroyed or severely damaged; the town was rapidly rebuilt. NOTABLE FEATURES the Peace Memorial Park featuring the Cenotaph, Eternal Flame, Fountain of Prayer, Peace Memorial Museum, and shell of the Industrial Exhibition Hall which is the only major building to survive the holocaust and is now known as the Atom Dome; the Ri jô Castle (rebuilt in 1958).

Hiroshima, Atomic Bombing of on 6 Aug 1945 Hiroshima, the capital of Hiroshima prefecture, South Honshu I, Japan, was chosen (because of its importance as a centre of military and supply bases, shipyards, and industrial plants) as the target for Little Boy, the first atomic bomb ever dropped. Approximately 150 000 people were killed or wounded as a result, and 75 per cent of the city's buildings were destroyed or severely damaged.

hirsute *adj.* hairy; shaggy. [from Latin *hirsutus*]

His, Wilhelm (1831–1904) Swiss biologist, born in Basle. Professor in Basle and Leipzig, he investigated developmental processes and embryonic growth, developed the microtome (1866) for cutting very thin serial sections for microscopy, and gave the first accurate description of the human embryo.

his — *adj.* of or belonging to a male person or animal. — *pron.* the one or ones belonging to him. [from Anglo-Saxon *his*]

Hispanic — *adj.* of Spain, the Spanish, or other Spanish-speaking countries and peoples, eg Mexican. — *noun North Amer., esp. US* a Spanish-speaking American of Latin-American descent. [from Latin *Hispania*, Spain]

Hispanic American any person resident in the USA who comes from, or whose parents came from, Spanish-speaking countries in Central and S America, including the Caribbean. Hispanic Americans are the fastest-growing ethnic group in the USA and are thought to number around 12 million. The main groups are Mexican Americans (c.7 million), Puerto Ricans (1.6 million), and Cuban (0.6 million). Most migrated to the USA to find work, and there are many illegal immigrants, particularly from Mexico. Cubans, on the other hand, are given automatic entry into the USA, as political refugees from Castro's communist regime.

Hispaniola, formerly **Santo Domingo** the second-largest island of the Greater Antilles, E Caribbean Sea. It is situated between Cuba in the W and Puerto Rico in the E. The W third is occupied by Haiti, the remainder by the Dominican Republic. It was named La Isla Espanola by Columbus in 1492. PHYSICAL DESCRIPTION predominantly mountainous, traversed NW–SE by several forested ranges, notably the Cordillera Central, where the highest peak in the Caribbean is Pico Duarte at 3 175m.

Hiss, Alger (1904–) US State Department official, born in Baltimore. He reached high office as a State Department official, then stood trial twice (1949, 1950) on a charge of perjury, having denied before a Congressional Un-American Activities Committee that he had passed secret state documents to Whittaker Chambers, an agent for an international communist spy ring. The Alger Hiss Case roused great controversy, but he was convicted at his second trial and sentenced to five years' imprisonment, after which he returned to private life as a lawyer, with continuing dispute over the justice of his conviction.

hiss — *noun* a sharp sound like that of a prolonged *s*. — *verb* **1** *intrans. said of a person or animal, eg a snake* to make a hiss, especially as a sign of disapproval or anger. **2** *trans.* to show one's disapproval (of a person, etc) by hissing. [imitative]

histamine *noun Biochem.* a chemical compound present in most body tissues, and released from connective tissue during allergic or inflammatory reactions. It causes dilation of capillaries and contraction of the smooth muscle of the bronchi, and is responsible for many of the symptoms in conditions such as hay fever and asthma. [from Greek *histos*, web + AMINE]

histidine *noun Biochem.* an amino acid found in proteins. [from Greek *histos*, web]

histogram *noun* a chart in which vertical rectangles of differing sizes are used to represent the class intervals (eg age range) and relative frequencies of a given variable, eg height. [from Greek *histos*, web + -GRAM]

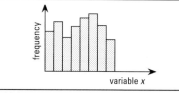

histogram

histology *noun* the scientific study of the structure and organization of cells and tissues of living organisms by light and electron microscopy combined with special staining techniques. [from Greek *histos*, web + -LOGY]

histone *noun Biochem.* any of the soluble basic proteins that tend to form complexes with nucleic acids (DNA and RNA), and are present in large amounts in chromosomes. [from Greek *histos*, web]

historian *noun* a person who studies or writes about history.

historiated *adj.* decorated with elaborate ornamental designs and figures of humans and animals. In Romanesque architecture, the capitals of columns were frequently carved with secular and religious subjects forming a narrative decoration, often with the same theme continued in a series of columns. [related to HISTORY]

historic *adj.* famous or important in history; significant.

historical *adj.* **1** of or about history; of or about people or events from history. **2** *said of the study of a subject* based on its development over a period of time. **3** that actually happened or existed; authentic.

historically *adv.* in a historical way.

historical novel a fictional prose narrative based on historical characters and/or events. Sir Walter Scott's series of romantic adventures, beginning with *Waverley*, greatly enhanced the appeal of the historical novel. Other notable examples include: Dickens's *Barnaby Rudge* and *A Tale of Two Cities*; C S Forester's 'Hornblower' series, set at the time of the Napoleonic Wars; and Robert Graves's novels about the Roman emperor Claudius, *I, Claudius* and *Claudius the God*.

historicism *noun* **1** the belief that historical events are governed by natural laws. **2** too much emphasis on or respect for the past, past styles, etc.

historicity *noun* historical truth or authenticity.

historiographer *noun* a writer of history, especially the official historian of a group.

historiography *noun* the study of the writing of history.

history *noun* (PL. **histories**) **1** the study of events, etc that happened in the past. **2** a record or account of past events and developments: *a history of the computer.* **3** everything that is known about past events connected with a particular nation, the world, a person, etc: *kings and queens are part of our history.* **4** a past full of events and of more than usual interest: *a house with an interesting history.* **5** a play which represents historical events.
— **make history** to do something important or memorable, especially to be the first person to achieve something.
[from Greek *historia*, from *histor*, knowing]

History of England a historical work by Thomas Macaulay (5 vols, 1848–61, the last unfinished).

histrionic — *adj.* **1** *said of behaviour, etc* theatrical; showing too much emotion. **2** of actors or acting. — *noun* (**histrionics**) theatrical or dramatic behaviour which shows excessive emotion and is insincere. [from Latin *histrionicus*, from *histrio*, actor]

histrionically *adv.* in a histrionic way.

hit — *verb* (**hitting**; PAST TENSE AND PAST PARTICIPLE **hit**) **1** to strike (a person or thing) with a blow, missile, etc. **2** to knock (something) against something, especially hard or violently: *hit one's head on the door.* **3** to cause to suffer or affect badly: *the bad news hit her hard.* **4** *intrans.* to direct a blow; to strike: *hit as hard as you can.* **5** *colloq.* to find (especially an answer) by chance: *you've hit it!* **6** to reach or arrive at: *hit an all-time low.* **7** to drive (a ball) with a stroke of a bat, etc. — *noun* **1** a blow, stroke or shot. **2** a shot that is successful. **3** *colloq.* something which is popular or successful.
— **hit back** to retaliate.
hit it off with someone to get on well with them.

hit on *or* **upon something** to think of an idea or find an answer, etc by chance.
hit out at *or* **against something** *or* **someone** to attack them physically or verbally.
make *or* **score a hit with someone** to be successful or popular with them.
[from Anglo-Saxon *hittan*]

hit-and-miss *or* **hit-or-miss** *adj. colloq.* without any system, planning or care; random.

hit-and-run *adj., said of a motor-vehicle accident* in which the driver leaves the scene immediately, without stopping, reporting the accident, or helping the victim.

hitch — *verb* **1** to fasten with a piece of rope, etc; to tether. **2** (*also* **hitch something up**) to pull it up with a jerk: *hitched up his trousers.* **3** *intrans., trans. colloq.* to hitchhike; to obtain (a lift) by hitchhiking: *hitch a ride.* — *noun* **1** a minor, temporary delay or difficulty. **2** a slight jerk. **3** a knot for attaching two pieces of rope together.
— **get hitched** *colloq.* to get married.
[from Middle English *hytchen*]

Hitchcock, Sir Alfred (Joseph) (1899–1980) English film producer, born in London. He began as a technician in 1920, directed his first film in 1925, and rose to become a master of suspense. His British films included *The Thirty-Nine Steps* (1935) and *The Lady Vanishes* (1938). His first film in the USA, *Rebecca* (1940), won a Best Picture Oscar. Later films included *Psycho* (1960), *The Birds* (1963), and *Frenzy* (1972).

hitchhike *verb intrans.* to travel by means of free rides in other people's vehicles. [from HITCH + HIKE]

hitchhiker *noun* a person who hitchhikes.

hi-tech see HIGH TECH.

hither *adv. old use* to this place.
— **hither and thither** in different directions.
[from Anglo-Saxon *hider*]

hitherto *adv.* up to this or that time.

Hitler, Adolf, originally **Schicklgrüber**, also called **der Führer** (**the Leader**) (1889–1945) German dictator, born in Braunau, Upper Austria, the son of a minor customs official. He seized control in Germany at a time when social conditions were ripe to receive his brand of extreme nationalism, and as Leader of the Third Reich for 12 years, during which 30 million people died as a result of his policies, he wielded power unequalled in modern times. Originally wishing to be an artist, he attended an art school in Munich, but twice failed to pass into the Vienna Academy. In 1914 he served in a Bavarian regiment, became a corporal, and was wounded in the last stages of the war. In 1919 he joined a small political party which in 1920 he renamed as the National Socialist German Workers' Party. In 1923, with other extreme right-wing factions, he attempted to overthrow the Bavarian government, but was imprisoned for nine months in Landsberg jail, during which time he dictated his political testament, *Mein Kampf* (My Struggle, 1925), to Rudolf Hess. He expanded his Party greatly in the late 1920s, and though he was unsuccessful in the presidential elections of 1932 against Hindenburg, he was made Chancellor in 1933. He then exploited successfully the burning of the *Reichstag* building, which he denounced as a communist plot, and brought the Nazi Party to power. The Enabling Acts gave him absolute power and he crushed all opposition – several of his opponents within his own Party were murdered by his bodyguard, the SS, in the Night of the Long Knives (1934). He openly rearmed the country (1935), and claiming a need for living space (*Lebensraum*) he sent troops into the demilitarized Rhineland. He established the Rome–Berlin 'axis' with Mussolini (1936), created 'Greater Germany' by the union with Austria (*Anschluss*, 1938), and absorbed the German-populated Sudeten region of

Czechoslovakia, an act to which Britain and France acquiesced at Munich (1938). He then demanded from Poland the return of Danzig and free access to E Prussia. Poland's refusal precipitated World War II (3 Sep 1939). His domestic policy was one of total Nazification, enforced by the Gestapo (Secret State Police). Political opponents, Jews, and all people he considered socially undesirable were imprisoned in concentration camps, which resulted in the murder of over six million people in the course of World War II. After his early war successes, he increasingly ignored the advice of military experts. The supposedly invincible Luftwaffe was defeated in the Battle of Britain (1940). His attack on Russia, which had taken his army to Moscow and Leningrad, faltered after defeat at Stalingrad (1942), and Rommel's army was defeated at El Alamein. Having miraculously survived the explosion of the bomb placed at his feet by Col Stauffenburg (Jul 1944), Hitler purged the army of all suspects, including Rommel. When Germany was invaded, he retired to his bunker, an air-raid shelter under the Chancellory building in Berlin. With the Russians only several hundred yards away, he went through a marriage ceremony with his mistress, Eva Braun, in the presence of the Goebbels family, who then poisoned themselves. All available evidence suggests that Hitler and his wife committed suicide and that their bodies were cremated (30 Apr 1945). The full horror of his forced labour camps, concentration camps, and policies of genocide was revealed when the Allies took control of Germany.

hit list *noun colloq.* a list of people, organizations, etc to be killed, closed down, etc.

hit man *noun colloq.* a hired assassin.

hit parade *noun* the best-selling records.

Hittites a people of uncertain origin who inhabited central Asia Minor in the first part of the second millennium BC. They spoke an Indo-European language, known as Hittite. At its height (1450–1200 BC), the Hittite Empire covered most of Anatolia and parts of N Syria (eg Carchemish). It was destroyed by marauding invaders, known as the Sea Peoples, in c.1200 BC.

HIV *abbrev.* human immunodeficiency virus, the virus responsible for the disease AIDS.
◇ HIV, first identified in 1983 and now known to be a retrovirus, is transmitted in blood, semen, and vaginal fluids. It destroys the immune system, in particular T-helper cells (which manufacture antibodies) and macrophages (which engulf invading bacteria), leaving the body susceptible to potentially fatal infections such as pneumonia and Kaposi's sarcoma (an otherwise rare skin tumour). Individuals are regarded as 'HIV-positive' if they test positive for antibodies to the virus (it usually takes up to 12 weeks for antibodies to develop after infection). HIV may remain inactive in its host for several years without causing any symptoms, but can still be transmitted to others.

hive *noun* **1** a box for housing bees. **2** the bees that live in such a place. **3** a place where people are working very busily: *a hive of activity.*
— **hive something off 1** to separate (a company, etc) from a larger group or organization. **2** to transfer (the assets, especially of a nationalized company) to other ownership, especially private ownership. **3** to give (work) to another, subsidiary, company.
[from Anglo-Saxon *hyf*]

hives *pl. noun* sore, itchy skin caused by contact with certain plants; nettlerash.

HIV-positive *Medicine* denoting a person who has tested positively for the presence of the human immunodeficiency virus (HIV), and may therefore be assumed to be carrying the virus.

Hizbullah *or* **Hezbollah** *or* **Hizbollah** the umbrella organization in S Beirut of militant Shiite Muslims with Iranian links. It came to world attention after the TWA hijacking in Cairo in 1985 and the subsequent hostage-taking. [from Arabic, = party of God]

HM *abbrev.* Her or His Majesty or Majesty's, used in the titles of some British government organizations.

HMI *abbrev.* Her or His Majesty's Inspector, a British government official who checks on schools.

HMS *abbrev.* Her or His Majesty's Ship.

HMSO *abbrev.* Her or His Majesty's Stationery Office.

HNC *abbrev.* Higher National Certificate, a qualification in a technical subject recognized by many professional institutions.

HND *abbrev.* Higher National Diploma, a qualification in a technical subject, recognized by many professional institutions as equivalent to a degree.

Ho *symbol Chem.* holmium.

hoar *adj.* white or greyish-white, especially with age. [from Anglo-Saxon *har*]

hoard — *noun* an often secret store of money, food, treasure, usually hidden away for use in the future. — *verb trans., intrans.* to store (food, money, etc), often in secret and especially for use in the future. [from Anglo-Saxon *hord*]

hoarder *noun* a person who hoards.

hoarding *noun* 1 a temporary fence of light boards, especially round a building site. 2 a large, flat, wooden surface on which advertisements, posters, etc are displayed. [from Old French *hourd*, palisade]

Hoare, Sir Samuel (John Gurney), 1st Viscount Templewood (1880–1959) British conservative politician. He was Secreatry of State for Air (1922–9), and as Secretary of State for India (1931–5) he piloted the 1935 India Act through the Commons. In 1935, as Foreign Secretary, he was criticized for his part in the Hoare–Laval Pact and resigned the following year. As Home Secretary (1937–9), he was a strong advocate of penal reform. His Criminal Justice bill never became law because of the outbreak of World War II, but much of it was embodied in the Act of 1948.

Hoare–Laval Pact an agreement concluded in 1935 by the British Foreign Secretary Samuel Hoare and the French Prime Minister Pierre Laval to settle a dispute between Italy and Abyssinia, whereby large parts of Abyssinia were ceded to Italy. Public outcry against the pact led to its repudiation by Britain and to Hoare's resignation.

hoar-frost *noun* the white frost on grass, leaves, etc in the morning after a cold night.

hoariness *noun* being hoary.

hoarse *adj.* 1 *said of the voice* rough and croaking, especially because of a sore throat or too much shouting. 2 *said of a person* having a hoarse voice. [from Anglo-Saxon *has*]

hoarsely *adv.* in a hoarse way.

hoarseness *noun* being hoarse.

hoary *adj.* (**hoarier, hoariest**) 1 white or grey with age. 2 ancient.

hoax — *noun* a trick done to deceive people, done either humorously or spitefully. — *verb* to trick or deceive with a hoax. [probably from *hocus*, to trick]

hoaxer *noun* a person who hoaxes.

hob *noun* 1 the flat surface for heating pots, etc on top of a cooker. 2 a small shelf next to a fireplace on which pots, etc may be kept hot.

Hobart POP (1990) 184 000, a seaport and the state capital of Tasmania, Australia. It is situated in the SE of the state, in Hobart statistical division, and lies on the Derwent R at the foot of Mt Wellington. HISTORY founded as a penal colony in

1804; became state capital in 1812; achieved city status in 1842. NOTABLE FEATURE Hobart Theatre Royal.

Hobbema, Meindert (1638–1709) Dutch landscape painter, born (probably) in Amsterdam. He studied under Jacob van Ruysdael, and eventually became collector of the city's wine customs. His paintings deal mainly with placid woodland and watermill scenes. His best-known work is *The Avenue at Middelharnis* (1689, National Gallery, London).

Hobbes, Thomas (1588–1679) English political philosopher, born in Malmesbury. He wrote several works on government, and in 1646 became mathematical tutor to the Prince of Wales at the exiled English court in Paris, where he wrote his major work on political philosophy, the *Leviathan* (1651). In 1652 he returned to England, submitted to Cromwell, and settled in London.

Hobbit, The a fantasy novel by J R R Tolkien (1937). It describes the adventures of hobbit Bilbo Baggins.

hobble *verb* 1 *intrans.* to walk with difficulty, taking short unsteady steps. 2 *trans.* to tie the legs of (a horse) together loosely, to stop it straying. [from Middle English *hobelen*]

Hobbs, Sir John Berry, also called **Jack** (1882–1963) English cricketer, born in Cambridge. He played in county cricket for Cambridgeshire (1904) and Surrey (1905–34), and for England (1908–30), when he and Herbert Sutcliffe (1894–1978) established themselves as an unrivalled pair of opening batsmen. He made a record number of 197 centuries and 61 167 runs in first-class cricket.

hobby *noun* (PL. **hobbies**) 1 an activity or occupation done in one's spare time for pleasure or relaxation. 2 a small species of falcon. [from Middle English *hobyn*, a pet form of the name *Robin*]

hobby-horse *noun* 1 a child's toy consisting of a long stick with a horse's head at one end. 2 a figure of a horse used in Morris dancing. 3 a subject which a person talks about frequently.

hobgoblin *noun* a mischievous or evil spirit. [from Middle English *Hob*, pet form of *Robin* + GOBLIN]

Hobhouse, Leonard (Trelawney) (1864–1929) English social philosopher and journalist, born in St Ives, Cornwall. He worked on the *Manchester Guardian* (1897–1903), then was editor of the *Sociological Review* (1903–5), during which time he was also secretary of the Free Trade Union, and became political editor of *Tribune* (1906–7). From 1907 he was Professor of Sociology at London University. His best-known works are *Labour Movement* (1893), *Theory of Knowledge* (1896), *Morals in Evolution* (1906) and *Development and Purpose* (1913).

hobnail *noun* a short nail with a heavy head for protecting the soles of boots and shoes: *hobnail boots*. [from an old meaning of HOB, peg or pin]

hobnailed *adj.* fitted with hobnails.

hobnob *verb intrans.* (**hobnobbed, hobnobbing**) (**hobnob with someone**) to spend time with them socially. [from the phrase *hab or nab*, have or have not]

hobo *noun* (PL. **hobos, hoboes**) North Amer. a tramp; a wandering worker.

HOBS *abbrev. Brit.* home and office banking service or system.

Hobson's choice *noun* the choice of taking what is offered, or nothing at all. [named after Thomas Hobson (died 1631), a Cambridge carrier who hired out his horses on the basis that customers had to take the one nearest the door]

Hochdorf a prehistoric chariot-burial of c.550–500 BC near Ludwigsburg, S Germany, intact when excavated in 1978–9. The 60m diam-

eter barrow concealed a timber-lined tomb 5m square, containing various artefacts and clothing.

Hochhuth, Rolf (1931–) German dramatist, born in Eschwege. His controversial play *Der Stellvretreter* (The Representative, 1963) which focuses on the role of the pope in World War II, introduced the fashion for 'documentary drama'. Later plays include *Soldaten* (Soldiers, 1967), on the war morality of the Allies, and *Juristen* (The Legal Profession, 1979), on collaboration with the Nazis. His novel *Eine Liebe in Deutschland* (German Love Story, 1978) deals with Nazi atrocities.

Ho Chi Minh, originally **Nguyen That Thanh** (1892–1969) Vietnamese politician, born in central Vietnam. Between 1912 and 1918 he visited London and the USA, then lived in France, where he was a founder-member of the Communist Party, and from 1922 was often in Moscow. He led the Viet Minh independence movement in 1941, directed the successful military operations against the French (1946–54), became Prime Minister (1954–5) and President of North Vietnam (from 1954), and was a leading force in the war between North and South Vietnam during the 1960s.

Ho Chi Minh City, formerly **Saigon** (to 1976) POP (1992e) 4.1m, the largest city in Vietnam, on the R Saigon, 54km/34mi from the S China Sea. It is jointly administered with Cholon city. HISTORY capital of French Indo-China from 1887 until 1902; former capital of South Vietnam; occupied by the USA in the Vietnam War.

hock¹ *noun* in horses and other hoofed mammals, the joint corresponding to the ankle bone on the hind leg. [from Anglo-Saxon *hoh*, heel]

hock² *noun* a German white wine from the Rhine valley. [from German *Hochheimer*, from *Hochheim*, a town on the Main]

hock³ *verb colloq.* to pawn.
— **in hock** *colloq.* 1 in pawn. 2 in debt. 3 in prison.
[from Dutch *hok*, prison, debt]

hockey *noun* 1 a game for two teams of eleven players in which each team tries to score goals, played with long clubs which are bent at one end and a small, hard ball. 2 North Amer. same as ICE HOCKEY.
◇ In outdoor hockey, the pitch is 91m/100yd long and 54m/60yd wide with a goal at either end. A game lasts for 70 minutes, in two 35-minute halves. The modern game dates from 1875, when the English Hockey Association was formed and rules of play were standardized.

Hockney, David (1937–) English artist, born in Bradford, Yorkshire. He was associated with the Pop Art movement from his earliest work, and became internationally known with his series of etchings *The Rake's Progress* (1963). He taught in the USA at the University of California (1964–7) and has also worked in printmaking and photography, and designed sets and costumes.

hocus-pocus *noun colloq.* trickery; words, actions, etc which are intended to deceive or mislead; a formula used in conjuring. [sham Latin]

hod *noun* 1 a V-shaped box on a pole, used for carrying bricks. 2 a container for coal used in the home, usually near a fireplace. [from Middle English *hot*, basket]

hodgepodge *noun North Amer.* same as HOTCHPOTCH.

Hodgkin, Sir Alan Lloyd (1914–) English physiologist, born in Banbury. Professor at Cambridge, he described in mathematical terms the mechanisms by which nerves conduct electrical impulses by the movement of electrically charged particles across the nerve membrane. He shared the 1963 Nobel Prize for Physiology or Medicine with John Eccles and Andrew Huxley.

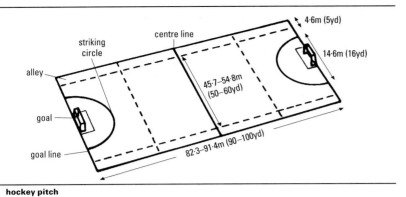

hockey pitch

Hodgkin, Dorothy Mary, née **Dorothy Crowfoot** (1910–) British crystallographer, born in Cairo, Egypt. Professor at Oxford, she used X-rays to analyse the structure of many biologically important molecules, including penicillin, cholesterol, insulin, and her greatest triumph, vitamin B_{12}. She was awarded the 1964 Nobel Prize for Chemistry.

Hodgkin, Thomas (1798–1866) British pathologist, born in Tottenham, Middlesex. Educated at Edinburgh, he held various posts at Guy's Hospital, London, and described the glandular disease later named after him in which spleen, liver, and lymph nodes become enlarged. He died while travelling in Palestine.

Hodgkin's disease or Hodgkin's lymphoma *Medicine* a malignant disease of the lymphatic tissue, which causes painless progressive enlargement of the lymph nodes, and may then spread to the spleen, liver, bones, and bone marrow. The main symptoms are weight loss, anaemia, fever, itching, fatigue, and sweating at night. [named after Thomas Hodgkin, who first described the disease]

hoe — *noun* **1** a farm implement pulled by a tractor and consisting of horizontal blades that turn the soil between rows of a crop, in order to destroy weeds. **2** a long-handled tool with a metal blade at one end, used to loosen soil, control weeds, etc. — *verb* **1** to use a hoe to loosen soil and remove weeds from (crops, flower-beds, etc). **2** *intrans.* to use a hoe. [from Old French *houe*]

Hofburg the official residence of the Austrian President in Vienna. From 1279 until 1918 it was the seat of the Habsburg rulers of Austria. It houses the Austrian National Library, the Spanish Riding School, and several museums. Parts of the building, including the Redoutensaal hall, were destroyed by fire in 1992.

Hoffman, Dustin (1937–) US actor, born in Los Angeles. His first leading film role was in *The Graduate* (1967). Similar antihero roles followed in *Midnight Cowboy* (1969), *Little Big Man* (1970), and *Marathon Man* (1976). He found wider scope in *All The President's Men* (1976), returned to comedy in *Tootsie* (1982), and won Oscars for *Kramer Vs Kramer* (1979) and *Rain Man* (1988).

Hoffmann, E(rnst) T(heodor) W(ilhelm), known as **Amadeus** (1776–1822) German composer, writer, and music critic, born in Königsberg. He trained in law but was more interested in the romantic arts. As a composer his most important opera was *Undine* (1816), a precursor of the scores of Weber and Wagner. He also wrote vocal, chamber, orchestral, and piano works. Three of his stories provided the basis for Jacques Offenbach's *Tales of Hoffmann* (1881), and another for Léo Delibes's *Coppelia* (1970).

Hofmann, August Wilhelm von (1818–92) German chemist, born in Giessen. Professor at the College of Chemistry in London

and later in Berlin, he extracted aniline from coal tar, and discovered and explored the chemistry of many organic compounds, preparing the way for the development of the dyestuffs industry. He devoted much labour to the theory of chemical 'types', later discredited.

Hofmannsthal, Hugo von (1874–1929) Austrian poet and dramatist, born in Vienna. His early work includes the 'lyrical dramas' *Gestern* (Yesterday, 1891) and *Der Tod des Tizian* (The Death of Titian, 1892). Among his plays are *Electra* (1903), the morality play *Jedermann* (1912), and the comedy *Der Schwierige* (The Difficult Man, 1921). He also wrote the libretti for Richard Strauss's operas, including *Der Rosenkavalier* (1911), and with Strauss and Max Reinhardt he founded the Salzburg Festival.

Hofmeister, Wilhelm Friedrich Benedikt (1824–77) German botanist, born in Leipzig. Working in his home town, he carried out fundamental work on plant embryology, and discovered alternation of generations (in which a generation that reproduces sexually alternates with one that reproduces asexually). He was one of the first to observe chromosomes, although he did not appreciate their significance.

Hofstadter, Robert (1915–) US physicist, born in New York City. Professor at Stanford University from 1954, he developed an X-ray detector (1948) and later investigated nuclear structure; he showed that charge is constant within the core of the nucleus, but decreases sharply at the nuclear surface, and that protons and neutrons also contain inner structure (now known to be due to 'quarks'). He shared the 1961 Nobel Prize for Physics with Rudolph Mössbauer.

hog — *noun* **1** a castrated male pig. **2** *North Amer., esp. US* a pig. **3** *colloq.* a greedy, and often bad-mannered or dirty person. — *verb* (**hogged, hogging**) *colloq.* to take, use or occupy selfishly. [from Anglo-Saxon *hogg*]

Hogan, Ben, properly **William Benjamin** (1912–) US golfer, born in Dublin, Texas. In 1948 he became the first man in 26 years to win all three US major titles; despite a bad car accident in 1949, he returned to win three of the four 'major' golf titles in 1953 (US Open, US Masters, and British Open). He won the US Open four times (1948, 1950–1, 1953) before retiring in 1970.

Hogarth, William (1697–1764) English painter and engraver, born in London. By 1720 he had his own business as an engraver, and by the late 1720s as a portrait painter. His sequences of moral paintings include the crowded canvases of *A Rake's Progress* (1733–5, Soane Museum, London), and *Marriage à la Mode* (1743–5, London). Other works include several prints of low life (eg the *Industry and Idleness* series, 1747), and the portrait *A Shrimp Girl* (c.1759, National Gallery, London).

Hogg, James (1770–1835) Scottish poet and novelist, born near Ettrick, Selkirkshire. He

tended sheep in his youth, and became known as the 'Ettrick Shepherd', gaining recognition as a poet with *The Queen's Wake* (1813). He eventually settled in Edinburgh, was a regular contributor to *Blackwood's Magazine*, and wrote several works in verse and prose, the best-known of which is the novel *Private Memoirs and Confessions of a Justified Sinner* (1824).

Hoggar or Ahaggar Mountains a mountain range in the central Sahara, S Algeria. It rises to 2 918m at Mt Tahat, the highest point in Algeria. The peaks include the 'mountain of goblins', Garet el Djenoun (2 327m), which according to legend is a holy mountain.

Hogmanay *noun Scot.* New Year's Eve, the last day of the year, when children traditionally demanded gifts or *hogmanay* of oatcake or white bread. [possibly from Old French *aguillaneuf*, a gift at New Year]

hogshead *noun* a large cask.

hogwash *noun colloq.* nonsense.

hogweed *noun* a robust perennial plant (*Heracleum sphondylium*), native to north temperate regions, with ribbed hairy stems and large coarse leaves divided into irregularly lobed and toothed leaflets. It has white or pinkish flowers arranged in large almost flat-topped heads up to 15cm across, which attract many types of insect, including beetles.

Hohenlinden, Battle of a confused but crucial battle (1800) in the closing stage of the French Revolutionary War, fought near Munich between the French under General Moreau and Austrian forces under Archduke John. The Austrians suffered heavy casualties and had to abandon the Second Coalition by the Armistice of Steyr.

Hohenstaufen *noun* a German dynasty, dukes of Swabia from 1079, who ruled as German kings, or Holy Roman Emperors (1138–1254), and as kings of Sicily (1194–1266). The most notable member of the dynasty was Conrad III, Emperor Frederick I Barbarossa.

Hohenzollerns the German ruling dynasty of Brandenburg-Prussia (1415–1861) and Imperial Germany (1871–1918), which originated in Swabia in the 9c. One branch of the family became Burgraves of Nuremberg, and a descendant, Frederick VIII, was rewarded by the emperor with the title of Elector of Brandenburg (1415). After the Thirty Years War, the Hohenzollern policy was one of state expansion and consolidation. This generated a long-standing rivalry with the Habsburg Dynasty (1740–1871), but Bismarck ensured the Hohenzollerns emerged successfully with the imperial title (1871). World War I ruined Hohenzollern militarism, and forced the abdication of the last emperor, William II (1918).

ho! ho! *interj.* an expression used to show amusement or disbelief.

Hohokam the prehistoric inhabitants of the S Arizona desert (c.300 BC– AD 1400), ancestors of the modern Pima and Papago Native Americans. From c.500 AD , they adopted a system of maize cultivation, and from c.1000 sophisticated irrigation engineering and intensive agriculture allowed a population spread over c.26 000sq km/ 10 000sq mi, stimulating the development of an extended trade network.

hoi same as HOY.

hoick *verb colloq.* to lift up sharply.

hoi polloi (*usually* **the hoi polloi**) the masses; the common people. [from Greek *hoi polloí*]

hoisin *noun* a thick sweet slightly hot Chinese sauce made with soya beans, sugar, vinegar, chilli, and sesame oil. [from Chinese]

hoist — *verb* **1** to lift or heave up (especially something heavy). **2** to raise or lift using ropes and pulleys. — *noun* **1** equipment for hoisting heavy objects. **2** *colloq.* an act of hoisting.

— hoist with one's own petard caught in the trap one set to catch someone else.
[past tense of the old verb *hoise*, to hoist; *petard*, small bomb]

hoity-toity *adj. colloq.* arrogant; haughty.
[from old word *hoit*, to romp]

Hokan languages a group of about 30 N American Indian languages spoken by small numbers in W and SW USA, and E Mexico; the only Hokan language with more than 20 000 speakers is Tlapanec. It is one of the groups of languages that create a bridge between the indigenous languages of North, central, and South America.

Hokkaido, formerly **Yezo Ezo** POP (1990) 5.7m, the northernmost and second largest island of the Japanese archipelago. AREA 83 513sq km/ 32 236sq mi. It is bounded by the Sea of Japan in the W, the Pacific Ocean in the E, and the Sea of Okhotsk in the NE. The Tsugaru-kaikyo Strait separates the island from Honshu I in the S, and the La Pérouse (Soya-kaikyo) Strait separates it from Sakhalin I in the N. The island measures 418km/260mi N–S, 450km/280mi E–W, and has an irregularly shaped peninsula in the SW. PHYSICAL DESCRIPTION largely mountainous with active and inactive volcanic cones in the central area; there are numerous hot springs in the SW; it rises to 2 290m at Mt Asahi-dake. The Ainu originally populated the island. CAPITAL Sapporo. ECONOMY rice, rye, sugar beet; grazing; forestry; fishing; iron, gold, chrome; oil, natural gas; popular as a winter sports resort.

hokum *noun North Amer. slang* **1** nonsense. **2** over-sentimental and over-sensational material in a play, film, etc. [probably from HOCUS-POCUS + BUNKUM]

Hokusai, Katsushika (1760–1849) Japanese artist and wood engraver, born in Edo (modern Tokyo). He abandoned traditional styles of engraving for the coloured woodcut designs of the *ukiyo-e* ('floating world') school. His 15 volumes of *Manga* or *Random Sketches* depict most facets of Japanese life. His best-known works include his *36 Views of Mount Fuji* (c.1826–33).

Holbein, Hans, also called **the Younger** (1497–1543) German painter, born in Augsburg, the son of the painter Hans Holbein the Elder (c.1460–1524). He worked in Basle, where he settled in 1520. His notable paintings of that period include the *Madonna of Burgomaster Meyer* (1526) and his woodcuts include the two series *The Dance of Death* and the *Old Testament Cuts* (issued 1538). Other works include *The Ambassadors* (1533, National Gallery, London) and various portraits of eminent people including *Erasmus* (1523, Louvre, Paris) and Henry VIII, to whom he was appointed painter in 1536.

Holberg, Ludvig, Baron (1684–1754) Norwegian poet, playwright, and philosopher, born in Bergen. He was Professor of Metaphysics (1717), Eloquence (1720), and History (1730) at Copenhagen University. His poetical works include the satirical epics, *Peder Paars* (1719–20), and *Nicolai Klimii Iter Subterraneum* (Niels Klim's Subterranean Journey). He also wrote historical books about Denmark, the Church, and the Jews.

hold¹ — *verb* (PAST TENSE AND PAST PARTICIPLE **held**) **1** to have or keep in one's hand, or in something else stated. **2** (**hold something down, up**, etc) to support or keep in a particular position. **3** *trans., intrans.* to keep or stay in a particular state: *hold firm*. **4** *intrans.* to remain in position, fixed and unbroken, especially when under pressure. **5** to detain or restrain. **6** to contain or be able to contain: *a bottle holding three pints*. **7** to cause to take place; to conduct: *hold a conversation / hold a meeting*. **8** to have (a position of responsibility, job, etc): *hold office*. **9** to have or possess: *hold the world record*. **10** to keep (a person's attention). **11** *intrans. said of good weather* to continue. **12** to consider to be; to think or believe. **13** *intrans.* to continue to be valid or apply.

14 (**hold someone to something**) to compel them to keep a promise, etc: *hold him to his word*. **15** to defend from the enemy. **16** to be able to drink (alcohol) without feeling any bad effects. **17** to stop: *hold fire*. **18** to continue to sing or play (a musical note). **19** *intrans. said of a telephone caller* to wait without hanging up while the person being called comes to the telephone. **20** *trans., intrans. said of the future, regarded as a force* to have in readiness: *no knowing what the future holds*. — *noun* **1** the act of holding; a grasp. **2** power; influence: *have a hold over him*. **3** a way of holding someone, especially in certain sports. **4** a thing to hold on to.
— get hold of someone *colloq.* to manage to speak to them.
get hold of something to buy or obtain it.
hold something against someone to regard them as responsible for it, especially to their discredit.
hold back to hesitate; to restrain oneself.
hold someone back to restrain them from doing something.
hold something back to keep it in reserve.
hold court to be surrounded by a group of admirers.
hold someone down to control their freedom; to repress them.
hold something down to manage to keep it: *hold down a job*.
hold forth to give one's opinions about something, usually loudly and at great length.
hold good or **hold true** to be true or valid; to apply.
hold something in to restrain or check it.
hold off or **hold off doing something** to delay or not begin: *I hope the rain holds off / hold off making a start*.
hold someone off to keep an attacker at a distance.
hold on *colloq.* to wait, especially during a telephone conversation.
hold on to something 1 to keep it. **2** to keep a firm hold on it.
hold out 1 to continue to stand firm, resist difficulties, etc: *held out against the enemy*. **2** to last.
hold something out to offer it, especially as a promise or inducement: *held out the prospect of a pay rise*.
hold out for something to continue to demand or fight for it.
hold out on someone *colloq.* to keep back money, information, etc from them.
hold something over to postpone or delay it.
hold someone up to stop and rob them.
hold something up 1 to support it. **2** to delay or hinder it. (**hold something** or **someone up as something**) to exhibit it or point to it, as an example of some quality, attribute, etc: *held them up as models of integrity*.
keep hold of something or **someone** to continue to hold on to them.
no holds barred not observing any rules; with no restrictions.
not hold with something decline to endorse or approve of it.
[from Anglo-Saxon *healdan*]

hold² *noun* the place where cargo is stored in ships and aeroplanes. [variant of HOLE]

holdall *noun* a large, strong bag for carrying clothes, etc when travelling.

Holden in Australia, the brand name of the first mass-produced car designed and built for Australian conditions. Holdens were first produced in 1948 by General Motors-Holden Ltd, which was the leading Australian car manufacturer until 1982.

holder *noun* a person or thing that holds.

Hölderlin, (Johann Christian) Friedrich (1770–1843) German poet, born in Lauffen. He trained as a Lutheran minister, then became a family tutor in Frankfurt (1796–98). With the help of Johann Schiller, he began to publish; his best-known work is the philosophical novel,

Hyperion (1797–9). He became increasingly schizophrenic, and spent a period in an asylum (1806–7).

holding *noun* **1** land held by lease. **2** the amount of land, shares, etc which a person or company owns.

holding company a company which owns and controls all or part of at least one other company.

hold-up *noun* **1** a delay or setback. **2** an attack with a view to robbery.

hole — *noun* **1** an opening or gap in or through something: *a hole in the wall*. **2** a hollow area in something solid. **3** an animal's burrow. **4** *colloq.* an unpleasant or gloomy place. **5** *colloq.* an awkward or difficult situation. **6** *colloq.* a fault or mistake: *a hole in the argument*. **7** *Golf* a round can-shaped hollow in the middle of each green, into which the ball is hit; also, each of the (usually 18) sections of a golf course extending from the tee to the green. — *verb* **1** to make a hole in. **2** to hit (a ball, etc) into a hole.
— hole up *colloq.* to hide.
make a hole in something *colloq.* to use a large amount of a resource, eg money.
pick holes in something to find fault with it. [from Anglo-Saxon *hol*]

hole-and-corner *adj.* secretive; underhand.

hole in the heart a congenital defect in the heart in which there is an opening in the wall between the left and right sides.

holey *adj.* (**holier, holiest**) full of holes.

Holi *noun* the Hindu 'Festival of Fire' in honour of Krishna, held in February or March and characterized by boisterous revelry, including the throwing of coloured water over people. It is also celebrated by Sikhs with sports competitions. [from Hindi *holī*, from Sanskrit *holikā*]

Holiday, Billie, originally **Eleanora Fagan** (1915–59) US singer, born in Baltimore, Maryland, who created many memorable ballads, such as 'Easy Living' (1937), 'Yesterdays' (1939), and 'God Bless the Child' (1941). Her troubled life (raped as a child, jailed for prostitution as a teenager, addicted to heroin as an adult) made sensational reading in her 1956 'autobiography' (actually written by William Dufty), *Lady Sings the Blues*.

holiday — *noun* **1** (often **holidays**) a period of time taken as a break from work, etc and during which one may go away from home. **2** a day when one does not have to work, eg a religious festival. — *verb intrans.* to spend a holiday. [from Anglo-Saxon *haligdæg*, holy day]

holiday camp a place, usually near the sea, which organizes games and other activities for the people staying there on holiday.

holidaymaker *noun* a person who is on holiday away from home.

holier-than-thou *adj. derog.* thinking oneself to be morally superior.

holily *adv.* in a holy way.

holiness *noun* **1** the state of being holy. **2** (**Holiness**) a title of the Pope and certain other religious leaders.

Holinshed, Raphael (d.c.1580) English chronicler, born apparently of a Cheshire family. He went to London early in Elizabeth's reign, and became a translator. His compilation of *The Chronicles of England, Scotland, and Ireland* (1577), was a major source for many of Shakespeare's plays.

holism *noun Philos.* the thesis that some wholes cannot be fully understood solely by reference to the self-sufficient elements which make up their parts. The doctrine is found in such disparate fields as political philosophy, social science, psychology, and biology. [from Greek *holos*, whole]

holistic *adj.* denoting of a method of treating disease that considers a person as a whole and takes social and psychological factors into account as well as the physical symptoms. [from Greek *holos*, whole]

holistically *adv.* in a holistic way.

Holland a name often used to mean The Netherlands. The provinces of North Holland and South Holland are adjacent to one another, situated in the W of The Netherlands.

holland *noun* a smooth, hard-wearing linen cloth, usually unbleached or dyed brown. [originally made in *Holland*]

holler (**hollered, hollering**) — *verb intrans., trans. colloq.* to shout or cry loudly. — *noun* a shout. [from French *holà*, stop!]

Hollerith, Herman (1860–1929) US inventor and computer scientist, born in Buffalo, New York. Working as a statistician for the US census of 1880, he devised a system for recording and processing large masses of data, initially based on punched cards using electrical contacts. He developed the system while employed at the Massachusetts Institute of Technology and the US Patent Office, and in 1896 established his own company, which later merged to form IBM.

Holles (of Ifield), Denzil Holles, 1st Baron (1599–1680) English statesman, born in Houghton, Nottinghamshire. He became an MP in 1624, and in 1642 was one of the five whose attempted seizure by Charles I precipitated the Civil War. During the War he advocated peace, was accused of treason, and fled to Normandy. In 1660 he was the spokesman of the commission delegated to recall Charles II at Breda.

Monument to the Holocaust, Warsaw

Holliger, Heinz (1939–) Swiss oboist and composer. An internationally renowned soloist and ensemble player, he has experimented with various new effects on the oboe, and this has led several avant-garde composers (eg Karlheinz Stockhausen) to write works for him. His own compositions, both vocal and instrumental, also use experimental techniques.

hollow — *adj.* **1** containing an empty space; not solid. **2** sunken: *hollow cheeks.* **3** *said of a sound* echoing as if made in a hollow place. **4** worthless; insincere. — *noun* **1** hollow or sunken space in something. **2** a small valley or depression in the land. — *adv. colloq.* completely: *beat the other team hollow.* — *verb* (**hollow something out**) to make a hole or hollow in it; to form it by making a hollow. [from Anglo-Saxon *holh*]

hollow-eyed *adj.* having sunken eyes, usually because of tiredness.

hollowly *adv.* **1** in a hollow way. **2** with a hollow sound.

hollowness *noun* **1** being hollow. **2** a cavity. **3** insincerity.

Holly a female first name, dating from the beginning of the 20c. [from the plant name, Anglo-Saxon *holegn*]

holly *noun* (PL. **hollies**) a tree or shrub with dark, shiny evergreen leaves, usually with prickly edges, and red berries, used for Christmas decorations. [from Anglo-Saxon *holen*]

hollyhock *noun* a tall garden plant with colourful flowers. [from Middle English *holi*, holy + *hoc*, mallow]

Hollywood Bowl a natural amphitheatre covering 24ha in a canyon in California. Built in 1919, it has seating capacity for c.25 000, and has been the venue of the 'Symphonies under the Stars' summer music festival since 1922.

Holmes, Arthur (1890–1965) English geologist, born in Hebburn-on-Tyne. Professor at the universities of Durham and Edinburgh, he determined the ages of rocks by measuring their radioactive constituents, and was an early scientific supporter of the theory of continental drift. His *Principles of Physical Geology* (1944) has been one of the most successful geological textbooks ever written.

Holmes, Larry, also called **the Easton Assassin** (1949–) US boxer, born in Cuthbert, Georgia. He beat Ken Norton for the World Boxing Council heavyweight title in 1978, and held it until 1985, when he lost to Michael Spinks. He lost the return contest with Spinks, and in 1988 challenged Mike Tyson for the title, but was defeated in four rounds.

HOLMES *abbrev.* in the UK, Home Office Large Major Enquiry System, a computer system introduced in the 1980s for crime detection in the UK. It gives the police immediate access to large databases containing information about crimes, thereby saving time and reducing the risk of human error in carrying out investigations.

Holmes, Sherlock the pipe-smoking, violin-playing master of deduction in Arthur Conan Doyle's *A Study in Scarlet* and other stories.

holmium *noun* a soft, silver-white metallic element (symbol **Ho**). [from Latin *Holmia*, Stockholm]

Holocaust the attempt by Nazi Germany to systematically destroy European Jews. From the inception of the Nazi regime in 1933 Jews were deprived of civil rights, persecuted, imprisoned, and murdered. During the gradual conquest of Europe by Germany, the death toll increased, and a meeting at Wannsee (Jan 1942) made plans for the so-called 'final solution'. Jews were herded into concentration camps, labour camps, and extermination camps. By the end of World War II (1945), more than six million Jews (three million from Poland) had been murdered out of a total Jewish population of eight million in those countries occupied by the Nazis. Other minorities (eg Gypsies, some religious sects, homosexuals) were also subject to Nazi persecution.

holocaust *noun* **1** large-scale destruction and loss of life. **2** (**Holocaust**) see as separate entry. [from Greek *holos*, whole + *kaustos*, burnt]

Holocaust Museum in the USA, a museum in Washington, DC, opened in Apr 1993. It contains registers, archives, and 24 000 artefacts which detail the attempted genocide by the Nazis of Jews living in Europe during World War II.

Holocene *Geol.* relating to the most recent epoch of the Quaternary period, from 10 000 years ago to the present time. During this epoch modern human beings appeared and civilization began. [from Greek *holos*, whole + *kainos*, new]

Holofernes the pedantic schoolmaster in Shakespeare's *Love's Labour's Lost*.

hologram *noun Photog.* a three-dimensional image of an object recorded on a photographic plate by the process of holography. [from Greek *holos*, whole + -GRAM]

holograph — *adj., said of a document* completely in the handwriting of the author. — *noun* a holograph document. — *verb* to make a hologram of. [from Greek *holos*, whole + *graphein*, to write]

holographic *adj.* relating to or involving holographs.

holographically *adv.* **1** in a holographic way. **2** by means of holography.

holography *noun Photog.* a photographic technique that uses beams of laser light to produce a three-dimensional image of an object.
◊ To produce a three-dimensional image, a beam of laser light is split into two separate beams. One part of the beam is aimed at the object to be photographed, and is then reflected back from the object on to a photographic plate. The other part of the beam is aimed directly at the photographic plate. Interference between the two beams produces a pattern on the plate that is known as a hologram, but is not recognizable as a photograph (except in the case of *reflection holograms*, which produce images in ordinary light, eg on credit cards). When the hologram is illuminated by a laser beam, it produces a three-dimensional image of the original object. Holograms are used in advertisements and decorative items, and to record very small changes in the size of objects, eg to detect stresses within industrial materials.

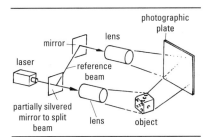

holography

holophrase *noun* a one-word utterance used by young children in the earliest stages of language-learning to express meaning which in more mature speech would normally be contained in more complex grammatical structure, such as a phrase or sentence. A single word may be used, with variations of intonation, to express a question, command, or simple statement, for example, *in*, *dada*, or *allgone*. [from Greek *holos*, whole + PHRASE]

hols *pl. noun colloq.* holidays. [abbreviation]

Holst, Gustav (Theodore), originally **Gustav (Theodore) von Holst** (1874–1934) English composer, born of Swedish origin in Cheltenham, Gloucestershire. He studied under Charles Stanford but neuritis in his hand prevented him from becoming a concert pianist. He taught music at St Paul's School, Hammersmith (1905–7), and then became musical director at Morley College (1907) and at Reading College (1919). He emerged as a major composer with the seven-movement suite *The Planets* (1914–16). Among his other major works are *The Hymn of Jesus* (1917), his comic operas *The Perfect Fool* (1922) and *At the Boar's Head* (1924), and his orchestral tone poem, *Egdon Heath* (1927).

holster *noun* a leather case for a pistol, usually worn attached to a belt round a person's hips. [from Dutch *holster*]

holt *noun* an otter's den. [from HOLD¹]

holy *adj.* (**holier, holiest**) **1** belonging to or associated with God or gods; sacred. **2** morally pure and perfect; saintly. [from Anglo-Saxon *halig*]

Holy Communion see COMMUNION.

Holy Ghost see HOLY SPIRIT.

Holy Grail see GRAIL.

Holyhead, Welsh **Caergybi** POP (1981) 13 000, a port and the chief town in Anglesey district, Gwynedd, NW Wales. It lies on the N coast of Holyhead I, which lies SW of the island of Anglesey. NOTABLE FEATURES Holyhead Mountain (Mynydd Twr), height 216m; breakwater (1845–73), length 2.4km/1.5mi; St Cybi's Church (founded in the 6c) within 3c Roman walls.

Holy Innocents' Day a Christian festival on 28 Dec commemorating the massacre ordered by Herod the Great of the male children of Bethlehem at the time of the birth of Christ.

Holy Island *or* **Lindisfarne** an island lying off the NE coast of England, 15km/9mi SE of Berwick-upon-Tweed. AREA 10sq km/4sq mi. At low water it is accessible from the mainland by a causeway. The island's famous monastery was founded from Iona by St Aidan in 634, burnt by Danish Vikings in 793, and ultimately abandoned in c.875. A notable centre of early English Christianity and learning, its most famous bishop was the ascetic St Cuthbert. The Lindisfarne Gospels were illuminated here, probably in the 690s.

Holy Land W Palestine, especially Judaea; the scene of Christ's ministry in the New Testament.

Holy League **1** (1510) an alliance of the papacy under Julius II with Venice, Aragon, and England against France. **2** (1571) an alliance of the three Catholic powers, Venice, Spain, and the Papacy, to counter Turkish supremacy in the E Mediterranean. The league's fleet commanded by Don John of Austria smashed the Turks at the battle of Lepanto (1571). **3** (1576) an association of militant French Catholics, led by Henry, 3rd Duke of Guise, until his death in 1588. One of its members, a monk, assassinated Henry III (of France), after which the League proclaimed the Cardinal de Bourbon king as 'Charles X'. However, Henry IV managed to impose himself as king by renouncing Protestantism ('Paris is worth a mass'). **4** (1684) the union of the empire, Poland, Venice, and the Papacy against Turkey, following the imperial repossession of Vienna (1683). After several years' fighting (1683–99) the league recovered most of Hungary for the Habsburgs, and began the reconquest of Greece (1685–7).

Holyoake, George (Jacob) (1817–1906) English social reformer, born in Birmingham. He taught mathematics, lectured on Robert Owen's socialist system, edited the *Reasoner*, and promoted the legalization of secular affirmations. He was the last person imprisoned in England on a charge of atheism (1842). He wrote histories of the co-operative movement and of secularism.

Holy of Holies the innermost and most sacred part of the Jewish tabernacle, and later of the Jerusalem Temple, cubic in shape, which housed the Ark of the Covenant. Only the High Priest was permitted to enter, once yearly on the Day of Atonement.

holy of holies any place or thing regarded as especially holy.

holy orders the office of an ordained member of the Christian clergy: *take holy orders*.

Holy Roman Empire the revived medieval title of the Roman Empire, which dated from the 9c when Charlemagne, King of the Franks, was granted the title by the papacy. After Charlemagne, imperial power was greatest under the Hohenstaufen Dynasty in the 12c–13c, when the full title 'Holy Roman Empire' (*sacrum Romanum imperium*) was used from the reign of Frederick I ('Barbarossa'), and Frederick II came close to consolidating territories in much of cen-

tral Europe and Italy. The House of Luxemburg and the Habsburg Dynasty also received the title. From the 14c, the empire's power declined with the rise of princely power and city-states, and the title was dropped in 1806.

Holyrood House a palace in Edinburgh, the official residence in Scotland of the reigning British monarch. It was built in the 16c and reconstructed in the 1670s by the architect Sir William Bruce (d.1710).

Holy See the see of Rome, the pope's see.

Holy Shroud see TURIN, SHROUD OF.

Holy Spirit a term used to denote the presence or power of God, often imbued with quasi-personal characteristics; in Christian thought, considered the third person of the Trinity, alongside the Father and the Son. Doctrinal differences exist between Western churches, which regard the Spirit as 'proceeding from' both the Father and the Son, and Eastern Christianity, which accepts procession from the Father only. In the Old Testament, the Spirit is depicted as an agent in creation, and of inspiration to the prophets. In Acts, the early Christians received the Spirit at Pentecost, from which time it continued to direct the Church's missionary activities. Paul not only considered the 'gifts of the Spirit' as empowering various ministries in the Church, but also as associated with speaking in tongues and prophesying (1 Corinthians 12–14), practices which continue among Christians today (particularly in the Pentecostal Church).

holy war *Relig.* a war waged for the eradication of heresy or a rival religion, eg Christian Crusades and jihad (in defence of Islam).

Holy Week in the Christian Church, the week before Easter Sunday, beginning on Palm Sunday and including Maundy Thursday and Good Friday.

Holywell, Welsh **Treffynnon** POP (1981) 11 000, a town in Delyn district, Clwyd, NE

Wales, lying 6km/4mi NW of Flint. Known as the 'Welsh Lourdes', it has been a place of pilgrimage since the 7c, when St Winefride was beheaded. NOTABLE FEATURE 15c St Winefride's Chapel, standing above a healing spring.

Holy Writ holy writings, especially the Bible.

homage *noun* **1** a display of great respect towards someone or something. **2** *Hist.* a vassal's formal public acknowledgement that he is his feudal lord's servant. [from Old French *homage*]

Homage to Clio a collection of poems by W H Auden (1960). It includes many examples of his light verse.

home — *noun* **1** the place where one lives. **2** the country or area one originally comes from. **3** a place where a thing first occurred or was first invented. **4** an institution where people who need care or rest live, eg orphans, the aged, etc. **5** a match won by a team playing on their own ground. **6** the finishing point in some games and races. — *adj.* **1** of one's home, country, or family. **2** made or done at home or in one's own country. **3** *said of a sporting event* played on one's own ground. — *adv.* **1** at or to a person's home. **2** to the place, position, etc aimed at: *hit the point home*. **3** as far as possible: *hammer the nail home*. **4** *said of a sporting event* on one's own ground, etc. — *verb intrans.* **1** *said of a bird* to return home safely. **2** (**home in on something**) to be directed towards a destination or target.
— **at home 1** in one's home, country, sports ground, etc. **2** feeling at ease or familiar with a place. **3** prepared to receive visitors.
bring something home to someone to make it clear or obvious to them.
home and dry having arrived home or achieved one's goal.
home from home a place where one feels as comfortable, relaxed, and happy as one feels at home.
make oneself at home to behave as one would in one's own home.

Holy Roman Emperors			
800–14	Charlemagne (Charles I)	1247–56	William, Count of Holland[2][4]
814–40	Louis I, 'the Pious'	1250–4	Conrad IV[4]
840–3	Civil War	1254–73	Great Interregnum
843–55	Lothair I	1257–72	Richard[2][4]
855–75	Louis II	1257–75	Alfonso (Alfonso X of Castile)[2][4]
875–7	Charles II, 'the Bald'	1273–91	Rudolf I[4]
877–81	Interregnum	1292–8	Adolf[4]
881–7	Charles III, 'the Fat'	1298–1308	Albert I[4]
887–91	Interregnum	1308–13	Henry VII
891–4	Guido of Spoleto	1314–26	(Frederick (III)[3][4]
892–8	Lambert of Spoleto[1]	1314–46	Louis IV, 'the Bavarian'
896–9	Arnulf[2]	1346–78	Charles IV
901–5	Louis III	1378–1400	Wenceslas[4]
911–18	Conrad I[2][4]	1400–10	Rupert I[4]
905–24	Berengar I	1410–37	Sigismund
919–36	Henry I, 'the Fowler'[4]	1438–9	Albert II[4]
936–73	Otto I, 'the Great'	1440–93	Frederick III
973–83	Otto II	1493–1519	Maximilian I[4]
983–1002	Otto III	1519–56	Charles V[4]
1002–24	Henry II	1556–64	Ferdinand I[4]
1024–39	Conrad II	1564–76	Maximilian II[4]
1039–56	Henry III	1576–1612	Rudolf II[4]
1056–1106	Henry IV	1612–19	Matthias[4]
1077–80	Rudolf of Rheinfelden[2][4]	1619–37	Ferdinand II[4]
1081–93	Hermann[2][4]	1637–57	Ferdinand III[4]
1093–1101	Conrad[2][4]	1658–1705	Leopold I[4]
1106–25	Henry V	1705–11	Joseph I[4]
1125–37	Lothair II	1711–40	Charles VI[4]
1138–52	Conrad III[4]	1740–2	Interregnum
1152–90	Frederick I, 'Barbarossa'	1742–5	Charles VII[4]
1190–7	Henry VI	1745–65	Francis I[4]
1198–1208	Philip of Swabia[2][4]	1765–90	Joseph II[4]
1198–1214	Otto IV	1790–2	Leopold II[4]
1215–50	Frederick II	1792–1806	Francis II[4]
1246–7	Henry Raspe[2][4]		

[1]Co-Emperor [2]Rival [3]Co-Regent
[4]Ruler not crowned at Rome; therefore, strictly speaking, only King of Germany

nothing to write home about *colloq.* not very exciting or attractive.
[from Anglo-Saxon *ham*]

home banking a banking service allowing customers to access information about their account, transfer funds, etc using a computer link from their home or office to the bank's own system.

home-coming *noun* the return home of a person who has been away for a long time.

Home Counties the counties which border London, and into which the city has expanded. They are Essex, Kent, Surrey, Hertfordshire, and the former county of Middlesex, which is now included in Greater London.

home farm a farm, usually one of several on a large estate, set aside to produce food, etc for the owner of the estate.

Home Guard *Brit. Hist.* a volunteer army formed to defend Britain from invasion during World War II.
◇ When first formed in May 1940, the force was known as the *Local Defence Volunteers*: its name was changed at Winston Churchill's urging to the more evocative title of *Home Guard*. It was made up of men aged from 17 to 65 who had not been called up, and by 1944 was over two million strong. It was disbanded in December 1945.

home help *Brit.* a person who is paid, often by the local authority, to help people who are ill or old with their cleaning, cooking, etc.

homeland *noun* 1 the country where a person is born, or from where his or her ancestors come. 2 in South Africa, land set aside by the government for the native black population.

homeless — *adj., said of people* without a home; having nowhere to live. — *pl. noun* (**the homeless**) people without a place to live.

homelessness *noun* being homeless.

homeliness *noun* being homely.

homely *adj.* (**homelier, homeliest**) 1 simple but pleasant. 2 making someone feel at home. 3 *North Amer., esp. US, said of a person* plain and unattractive.

home-made *adj., said of food, clothes, etc* made at home.

home movie a motion picture made by an amateur, using equipment such as a cine camera or a camcorder, and usually intended for domestic viewing.

Home Office *Brit.* the government department which deals with law and order within the country, immigration, etc.

Home (of the Hirsel), Alec (Alexander Frederick) Douglas-Home, 14th Earl of Home, Baron (1903–) English Conservative politician and Prime Minister, born in London. He became an MP in 1931 and was Neville Chamberlain's secretary during the negotiations with Hitler (1937–40). He succeeded to the peerage as 14th Earl (1951), was Commonwealth Relations Secretary (1955–60), and Foreign Secretary (1960–3). When Harold Macmillan's resignation, to general surprise he emerged as Prime Minister (1963–4), renounced his peerage and fought a by-election, during which, although Prime Minister, he technically belonged to neither House. After the 1964 defeat by the Labour Party, he was Leader of the Opposition until replaced in 1965 by Edward Heath, under whom he was Foreign Secretary (1970–4).

homeopathy *or* **homoeopathy** *noun* a system of alternative medicine developed by the German physician Samuel Hahnemann (1755–1843). It is based on the principles that like cures like, and that the activity of a drug is enhanced by dilution. Thus a drug that in large doses would induce particular symptoms of an illness is used in minute doses to cure the same symptoms. The emphasis is on treatment of the

patient as a whole, rather than the eradication of a single symptom. [from Greek *homoios*, similar + *patheia*, suffering]

homeostasis *or* **homoeostasis** *noun Biol.* the maintenance by a living organism, usually a higher animal, of a constant internal environment that is independent of fluctuations in the external environment, eg constant body temperature, blood sugar levels, etc. [from Greek *homos*, same + *stasis*, a standing still]

Homer, Greek **Homeros** (c.8c BC) Greek poet regarded in Greek and Roman antiquity as the author of the *Iliad* and the *Odyssey*. It is now believed that the works were developed from orally translated poems, which were much modified and extended by several hands. They are usually dated to the 8c BC, although the *Odyssey* is probably later than the *Iliad*. The ancient Greeks regarded Homer as a blind poet, and several places claimed to be his birthplace, notably Chios and Smyrna. The 33 'Homeric Hymns' are almost certainly from a later age, and are no longer attributed to Homer.

Homer, Winslow (1836–1910) US marine and genre painter, born in Boston, Massachusetts. He was apprenticed to a lithographer and during the Civil War was illustrator for *Harper's Weekly*. He painted watercolours of rural and domestic scenes and specialized in seascapes, which he mainly painted after 1881 while staying at Prout's Neck on the Maine coast.

Homeric *adj.* 1 relating to the Homer or the poems attributed to him. 2 relating to Bronze Age Greece.

home rule government of a country by its own citizens.
◇ Home rule is normally associated with separatism, but the term may also be applied to the devolution of certain legislative powers and administrative functions from a higher authority to an elected body located in a country or province, as in Northern Ireland, which had its own parliament at Stormont Castle until 1972.

Home Secretary *Brit.* the government minister in charge of the Home Office.

homesick *adj.* sad and depressed at being away from one's home and family.

homesickness *noun* being homesick.

homespun *adj.* 1 *said of advice, thinking, etc* simple and straightforward. 2 *old use, said of cloth* woven at home.

homestead *noun* 1 a house, especially a farmhouse, with the land and other buildings which belong to it. 2 *North Amer., esp. US* an area of land (usually 65ha) granted to a settler for development as a farm.

Homestead Act a US law (1862) aimed at increasing the agricultural development of the West. It granted 65ha of public land to settlers, who agreed to stay and cultivate their land for five years. Homesteaders had to be US citizens or to have filed for citizenship, and either heads of families or over 21 years of age.

home straight *or* **home stretch** the last part of a racecourse just before the finish.

home truth (*usually* **home truths**) frank but unwelcome information about oneself, usually told directly.

homeward — *adj.* going home. — *adv.* (*also* **homewards**) towards home.

homework *noun* work or study done at home, especially by school pupils.

homicidal *adj., said of a person* psychologically disposed to commit murder.

homicide *noun* 1 the killing of one person by another. 2 a person who kills another person. [from Latin *homo*, man + -CIDE]
◇ In England, Scotland, N. Ireland and Wales, unlawful homicide includes the crimes of murder, manslaughter, and infanticide; in certain circum-

stances, homicide may be lawful, such as in self-defence, but only where the action is seen to be reasonable in the circumstances. In the USA, criminal homicide usually includes murder, manslaughter, and negligent homicide (where the death is caused by an omission but where there was a duty to act).

homiletic *adj.* 1 relating to or involving a homily or sermon. 2 characteristic of the art of writing or giving sermons.

homily *noun* (PL. **homilies**) 1 a sermon. 2 a long, boring talk, usually telling someone how to behave. [from Greek *homilia*, assembly, sermon]

homing *adj.* 1 *said of a pigeon* able to find its way home after being released a long way away. 2 *said of a missile* able to guide itself to its target.

homing instinct *Biol.* the navigational behaviour that occurs in a number of animal species, ranging from returning home after a daily foraging and other excursions, to the more complex navigational task involved in large migrations.

hominid *noun, adj.* a primate belonging to the primate family Hominidae, which includes modern man (*Homo sapiens*) and his fossil ancestors. [from Latin *homo*, man]

hominoid — *adj.* of man; manlike. — *noun* any animal resembling man. [from Latin *homo*, man + -OID]

hominy *noun North Amer., esp. US* coarsely ground maize, boiled with milk or water to make porridge. [an American Indian word]

homo- *combining form* forming words meaning 'same': *homosexual*. [from Greek *homos*, same]

homoeopath *noun* a person who practises homoeopathy.

homoeopathic *adj.* relating to or involving homoeopathy.

homoeopathically *adv.* in a homoeopathic way.

homoeopathy *noun* the system of medicine in which an illness is treated by giving the patient very small doses of drugs which induce the same symptoms as the disease. [from Greek *homoios*, similar + *patheia*, suffering]

homogeneity *noun* being homogeneous.

homogeneous *adj.* made of parts that are all of the same kind. [from Greek *homos*, same + *genos*, kind]

homogeneously *adv.* in a homogeneous way.

homogenize *or* **homogenise** *verb* 1 to break up the fat droplets of a liquid, especially milk, into smaller particles that are evenly distributed throughout the liquid. 2 to make homogeneous. [from Greek *homos*, same + *genos*, kind]

homogenous *adj.* similar owing to common descent.

homogeny *noun* a likeness owing to common descent or origin. [from Greek *homos*, same + *genos*, kind]

homograph *noun* a word with the same spelling as another, but with a different meaning and origin and sometimes a different pronunciation, eg *like* (similar) and *like* (be fond of), and *entrance* (a way in; stressed on *en*-) and *entrance* (to bewitch; stressed on *-trance*). [from Greek *homos*, same + -GRAPH]

homoiothermic *adj. Zool.* denoting an animal that maintains its internal body temperature at a relatively constant level, independent of fluctuations in the temperature of its environment. Higher vertebrates, such as mammals and birds, are homoiothermic. – Also called *warm-blooded*.

homologous *adj.* 1 having a related or similar function or position. 2 *Biol.* denoting plant or animal structures that have a common origin, but that have evolved in such a way that they may no longer perform the same functions or resemble each other in appearance, eg human arm and bird's wing. See also ANALOGOUS. **3** *Biol.* denoting two chromosomes in a cell, usually of the same size and shape, that contain genes for the same set of characteristics, but are derived from different parents. [from Greek *homos*, same + *logos*, proportion]

homologous series *Chem.* a series of organic chemical compounds that have the same functional group, each member of the series differing from the next by the presence of an extra -CH_2 group in its molecules. For example, the alkane series of hydrocarbons includes methane (CH_4), ethane (C_2H_6), propane (C_3H_8), etc.

homology *noun* the state of being homologous.

homonym *noun* a word having the same sound and spelling as another word, but a different meaning, eg *kind* (helpful) and *kind* (sort). [from Greek *homos*, same + *onoma*, name]

homophobia *noun* an intense dislike or fear of homosexuals. [from HOMOSEXUAL + PHOBIA]

homophone *noun* a word which has the same sound as another word but has a different spelling and meaning, eg *bear bare*. [from Greek *homos*, same + *phone*, voice]

homophony *noun Mus.* a style of musical composition in which one part or voice carries the melody with other parts or voices adding texture with simple chordal accompaniment. See also POLYPHONY. [from Greek *homos*, same + *phone*, a voice, sound]

Homo sapiens *noun* the species of modern man. [from Latin *homo sapiens*, wise man]

homosexual — *noun* a person who is sexually attracted to people of the same sex. — *adj.* of or concerning a homosexual or homosexuals. [from Greek *homos*, same]

homosexuality *noun* **1** being homosexual. **2** a homosexual character or nature. **3** homosexual activity or behaviour.

◇ There are both clinical and sociological theories to account for homosexuality. It is widely believed that those people who become permanently homosexual do so as a result of some genetic predisposition combined with emotional influences during early childhood, or in early adolescence.

homozygous *adj. Genetics* describing an individual that contains two identical alleles for a particular gene, and will therefore produce offspring that are identical to the parent with respect to that gene.

Homs *or* **Hims**, ancient **Emesa** POP (1990e) 1.1m, the industrial capital city of Hims governorate, W central Syria, on the R Orontes, 160km/100mi N of Damascus. It is a commercial centre in a well-irrigated area. NOTABLE FEATURE Crusader Fortress.

homy *adj.* (**homier**, **homiest**) like a home, especially in being warm and comfortable.

Hon. *abbrev.* Honourable.

Honan see LUOYANG.

Honda, Soichiro (1906–91) Japanese motorcycle and car manufacturer, born in Iwata Gun. He started as a garage apprentice in 1922, and opened his own garage in 1928. By 1934 he had started a piston-ring production factory. He began producing motorcycles in 1948, and was President of Honda Corporation (1948–73). He was 'supreme adviser' from 1983.

Honduras, official name **Republic of Honduras**, Spanish **República de Honduras** POP (1992e) 5.5m, a republic in Central America, divided into 18 departments. AREA 112 088sq km/43 266sq mi. It is bounded SW by El Salvador, W by Guatemala, E and SE by Nicaragua, N by the Caribbean Sea, and S by the Pacific Ocean. CAPITAL Tegucigalpa. CHIEF TOWNS San Pedro Sula, Choluteca, La Ceiba, El Progreso. TIME ZONE

Honduras

GMT –6. The population is mainly of Spanish–S American Indian origin (90%). The chief religion is Roman Catholicism. OFFICIAL LANGUAGE Spanish; English is also spoken. CURRENCY the lempira. PHYSICAL DESCRIPTION coastal lands in the S are separated from the Caribbean coastlands by mountains running NW–SE; S plateau rises to 2 849m at Cerro de las Minas; the Bay Is in the Caribbean Sea and a group of nearly 300 islands in the Gulf of Fonseca also belong to Honduras; the Laguna Caratasca lies in the extreme NE. CLIMATE tropical climate in coastal areas, temperate in the centre and W; two wet seasons in upland areas (May–Jul, Sep–Oct); variable temperatures in the interior, 15–24°C; on the coastal plains the average is c.30°C. HISTORY centre of Maya culture in the 4c–9c; settled by the Spanish in the early 16c, and became a province of Guatemala; gained independence from Spain in 1821 and joined the Federation of Central America; became an independent sovereign state in 1838; several military coups in the 1960s and 1970s. During the 1980s it was the base for rebels (Contras) fighting against the government of Nicaragua. Honduras became dependent on help from the USA, which supported the rebels. The Contra war ended in 1990. GOVERNMENT an executive President and a National Assembly are elected for four-year periods. It is the least developed country in Central America, dependent largely on agriculture (providing one third of the national income). ECONOMY forestry (nearly half the land area), mining, and cattle raising; bananas, coffee, beef, cotton, tobacco, sugar; gold, silver, lead, zinc; offshore oil exploration in the Caribbean; cement, textiles, wood products, cigars, light manufacturing, fishing.

hone — *noun* a smooth stone for sharpening tools and knives. — *verb* to sharpen with or as if with a hone. [from Anglo-Saxon *han*]

Honecker, Erich (1912–) German politician, born in Neunkirchen. Active in the communist youth movement from an early age, he was involved in underground resistance to Hitler, and was imprisoned for 10 years. Released by Soviet forces, he became the first Chairman of the Free German Youth in the German Democratic Republic (1946–55). He entered the Politburo (1958), was elected Party Chief (1971), and became head of state (1976–89), but was dismissed because of the anti-communist revolution, and in 1990 was arrested on charges of manslaughter and treason. In 1991 he escaped to Moscow in a Soviet military aircraft, but returned to face trial after about 18 months in hiding. Terminally ill with liver cancer, in Jan 1993 he was judged too sick to attend trial. Acquitted, he retired to Chile.

Honegger, Arthur (1892–1955) French composer, born in Le Havre of Swiss parentage. After World War I he became one of the group of Parisian composers known as *Les Six*. His dramatic oratorio *King David* established his reputation in 1921, and *Pacific 231* (1923), a musical picture of a locomotive, won considerable popularity. His other works include five symphonies and a second dramatic oratorio *Joan of Arc at the Stake* (1930).

honest — *adj.* **1** truthful; trustworthy; not likely to steal, cheat, or lie. **2** just or fair: *an honest wage*. **3** sincere and respectable: *an honest attempt*.

4 ordinary and undistinguished: *an honest wine*. — *adv. colloq.* honestly: *I do like it, honest*. [from Latin *honestus*]

honestly *adv.* **1** in an honest way. **2** truly.

honesty *noun* **1** the state of being honest and truthful. **2** a common garden plant with silvery leaf-like pods.

honey *noun* (PL. **honeys**) **1** a sweet viscous fluid, white to dark yellow in colour, manufactured by bees from the nectar of flowers, and stored in honeycombs as food for the developing larvae. It consists mainly of simple sugars such as glucose and fructose, and is used as a food and sweetener. **2** a dark dull yellow colour resembling that of honey. **3** *North Amer. colloq.* a word used when speaking to a person one loves. **4** *colloq.* a person or thing which is excellent of its kind. [from Anglo-Saxon *hunig*]

honey bee a species of bee (*Apis mellifera*), native to tropical Asia, that has been semi-domesticated for centuries in most parts of the world as a source of honey.

◇ There are many different strains, or races, of honey bee, most of which live in hives provided by bee keepers, although there are many 'wild' bees which have escaped and established nests in hollow trees. Honey bees form colonies, each colony being dominated by a fertile female bee (the *queen*). There may be up to 60 000 sterile females, known as *workers*, in the colony in midsummer. They build the wax combs of the nest, collect nectar and pollen from flowers, and feed the young. The workers 'dance' on the combs when they return to the hive, the speed and direction of the dance indicating to the other bees the distance and direction of the nearest food source. Much of the harvested pollen and nectar is used to feed the developing grubs, and the remaining nectar is converted to honey and stored in the cells, together with excess pollen. If the hive becomes too crowded, the queen leaves with a swarm of workers to start a new nest.

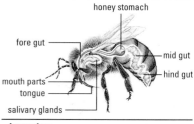

honey stomach
fore gut
mid gut
hind gut
mouth parts
tongue
salivary glands

honey bee

honeycomb *noun* **1** the structure formed by the rows of wax cells in which bees store honey. **2** anything like a honeycomb.

honeyed *adj.*, *said of a voice, words, etc* pleasing, flattering, or soothing.

honey guide *Bot.* any of various markings on the petal of a flower, said to show the way to the nectaries.

honeymoon — *noun* **1** a holiday taken by a newly married couple. **2** a period of goodwill and enthusiasm at the beginning, eg of a new business relationship. — *verb intrans.* to spend a honeymoon.

honeymooner *noun* a person taking a honeymoon, a newly married person.

honeysuckle *noun* a climbing garden shrub with sweet-smelling white, pale yellow, or pink flowers. [from Anglo-Saxon *hunigsuge*]

Hong Kong POP (1992e) 5.8m, a British Crown Colony off the coast of SE China, on the South China Sea, lying E of the estuary of the Pearl R. It is divided into Hong Kong I, Kowloon, and New Territories (includes most of the colony's 235 islands). AREA 1 067sq km/412sq mi. TIME ZONE GMT +8. The population is mainly Chinese

(98%), but there are many illegal immigrants from China and refugees from Vietnam; the chief religions are Buddhism and Taoism. OFFICIAL LANGUAGES English, Cantonese. CURRENCY the Hong Kong dollar. CLIMATE subtropical with hot, humid summers and cool, dry winters; average monthly temperatures are 16°C in Jan, 29°C in Jul. HISTORY ceded to Britain in 1842; New Territories leased to Britain in 1898; occupied by the Japanese in World War II. GOVERNMENT a Governor represents the British Crown, advised by a 14-member Executive Council and a 56-member Legislative Council. ECONOMY based on banking, import-export trade, tourism, shipbuilding, and a diverse range of light industry; textiles, electronic goods, watches, jewellery, cameras, footwear, toys, plastic goods; imports c.80% of its food; an important freeport acting as a gateway to China for the West. In 1997, Britain's 99-year lease of the New Territories will expire, whereupon, under the Sino-British Declaration initialled in 1984, Hong Kong will be restored to China in July. China has designated Hong Kong a special administrative region from 1997, and has stated it will allow regional independence in domestic affairs. Hong Kong will stay a freeport and separate customs zone. Foreign markets will be retained, and the Hong Kong dollar will remain as official currency. However, anxiety about the colony's political future grew in 1989, in the aftermath of the shootings in Tiananmen Square, Beijing (Peking), followed by controversy over the UK's refusal to guarantee Hong Kong's British residents a home in Britain, should conditions prove unacceptable to them.

Hong Kong

Hong Kong Island an island within Hong Kong colony. AREA 75sq km/29sq mi. It is bounded on all sides by the S China Sea and contains the city of Hong Kong. The highest point is Victoria Peak at 554m.

Honiara POP (1990e) 35 000, the port capital of the Solomon Is. It lies on the R Mataniko, on the NW coast of Guadalcanal I. The town developed after World War II around the site of the US military headquarters.

honk — *noun* **1** the sound made by a car horn. **2** the cry of a wild goose. — *verb trans., intrans.* to make or cause to make a honking noise. [imitative]

honky or **honkie** *noun* (PL. **honkies**) *North Amer. Black slang* a white person.

honky-tonk *noun colloq.* **1** a style of popular piano music based on ragtime. **2** a cheap, seedy nightclub.

Honolulu POP (1990) 836 000, the seaport capital and largest city of the state of Hawaii, USA. It lies on Mamala Bay, Oahu I, in Honolulu County. The headquarters of the US Pacific Fleet, Honolulu is also a noted tourist resort, with tropical vegetation and a famous beach at Waikiki. HISTORY the harbour was entered by William Brown, an English captain, in 1794; became capital of the Kingdom of Hawaii in 1845; an attack

by the Japanese in 1941 on the US naval base at adjacent Pearl Harbor brought the USA into World War II. NOTABLE FEATURES Bishop Museum; Pearl Harbor; Iolani Palace (the only royal palace in the USA); Aloha Tower; Diamond Head Crater.

honorarium *noun* (PL. **honorariums, honoraria**) a gift, usually money, given to someone in return for professional services which would normally be free. [from Latin *honorarium*, honorary]

honorary *adj.* **1** given to a person as a mark of respect, and without the usual functions, etc. **2** *said of an official position* not having any payment. [from Latin *honorarius*]

honorific *adj.* showing or giving respect. [from Latin *honor*, honour + *facere*, to do]

honour — *noun* **1** great respect or public regard. **2** the quality of doing what is right and having a high standard of moral behaviour. **3** fame or glory; distinction for bravery, etc. **4** a source of fame, glory, or distinction (for one's country, etc). **5** a pleasure or privilege. **6** *old use* a woman's chastity or her reputation for this. **7** (**honours**) *said of a university degree* a higher grade of distinction for specialized or advanced work. **8** (**Honour**) a title of respect given to judges, mayors, etc. **9** (**honours**) a mark of respect, especially at a funeral. **10** in some card games, any of the top four or five cards. **11** *Golf* the right to play from the tee first. — *verb* **1** to respect greatly. **2** to give (someone) an award, title, or honour as a mark of respect for (an ability or achievement, etc). **3** to pay (a bill, debt, etc) when it falls due. **4** to keep (a promise).
— **do the honours** to perform the task of host towards one's guests, eg offering them drinks, etc.
on one's honour under a moral obligation.
word of honour a solemn promise.
[from Latin *honor*]

honourable *adj.* **1** deserving or worthy of honour. **2** having high moral principles. **3** (**Honourable**) a courtesy title, given to some high officials, the children of some peers, and MPs. See also RIGHT HONOURABLE.

honourably *adv.* in an honourable way.

honour-bound *adj.* obliged to do something not by law, but from duty or from moral considerations.

Honshu POP (1990) 99.3m, the largest of the four main islands of Japan. It is bounded W by the Sea of Japan and E by the Pacific Ocean. The Tsugaru-kaikyo Strait separates it from Hokkaido I in the N; it is separated from Shikoku I in the S by the Seto Naikai Sea, and from Kyushu I in the SW by the Suo-nada Sea and the Kammon-kaikyo Tunnels. AREA 230 897sq km/89 126sq mi; c.1 290km/800mi long, 48–240km/30–150mi wide. PHYSICAL DESCRIPTION broadest in the centre, rising to the Japan Alps; the highest peak is Mt Fuji (3 776m); Lake Biwa in the W is the largest lake in Japan. The coastal lowlands contain most of the population and several major cities, including Tokyo, the capital of Japan. Earthquakes are common. ECONOMY silk; rice, tea, cotton, fruit; oil; zinc, copper; a wide range of industries centred on the cities.

Hooch or **Hoogh Pieter de** (c.1629–c.1684) Dutch painter, born in Rotterdam. He lived in Delft and Amsterdam, and painted domestic interior, garden, and courtyard scenes. His *Interior of a Dutch House* (National Gallery, London) is one of the best-known examples of the 17c Dutch School. Other works include *Courtyard of a House in Delft* (1658, National Gallery, London).

hooch *noun North Amer. colloq.* strong alcoholic drink, especially when distilled illegally. [from a Native American word]

hood¹ *noun* **1** a usually loose covering for the whole head, often attached to a coat at the collar. **2** a folding, usually removable, roof or cover on a

car, cooker, push-chair, etc. **3** *North Amer.* a car bonnet. **4** a piece of cloth worn as part of academic dress. [from Anglo-Saxon *hod*]

hood² *slang* a hoodlum.

-hood *suffix* **1** denoting a state or condition: *manhood*. **2** denoting a collection or group: *priesthood*. [from Anglo-Saxon -*had*]

Hood, Thomas (1799–1845) English poet and humorist, born in London. He achieved recognition when, with John Hamilton Reynolds (1794–1852), he published *Odes and Addresses to Great People* (1825). In his *Whims and Oddities* (1826) he showed his graphic talent in 'picture-puns', of which he seems to have been the inventor. In 1844 he started *Hood's Monthly Magazine*.

Hood (of Whitley), Samuel Hood, 1st Viscount (1724–1816) English admiral, born in Thorncombe, Dorset. He joined the navy in 1741, and fought during the American Revolution, when he defeated the French in the West Indies (1782). In 1784 he became an MP, and in 1788 a Lord of the Admiralty. In 1793 he directed the occupation of Toulon and the operations in the Gulf of Lyons.

hooded *adj.* having, covered with, or shaped like a hood.

hooded crow a crow with a grey body and black head.

hoodlum *noun* **1** *North Amer., esp. US* a criminal. **2** a young, violent, destructive, or badly behaved person.

hoodoo — *noun* **1** voodoo. **2** bad luck, or the thing or person which brings it. — *verb* to bring bad luck to. [variant of VOODOO]

hoodwink *verb* (**hoodwink someone into something**) to trick or deceive them to do it. [from HOOD¹ + WINK]

hooey *noun slang* nonsense.

hoof — *noun* (PL. **hoofs, hooves**) in horses and other mammals that walk on the tips of their digits (toes), the horny structure that grows beneath and covers the ends of the digits. — *verb* (**hoof it**) *slang* to go on foot.
— **on the hoof** *said of cattle, horses, etc* alive.

hoo-ha *noun colloq.* excited and noisy talk; a commotion. [probably from Yiddish *hu-ha*, uproar]

Hook, Capt the wicked pirate leader in J M Barrie's *Peter Pan*.

hook — *noun* **1** a small piece of metal, etc shaped like a J, used for catching and holding things. **2** a curved tool for cutting grain, branches, etc. **3** a sharp bend or curve, eg in land or a river. **4** *Boxing* a swinging punch with the elbow bent. **5** *Cricket, Golf* a shot that sends the ball to the right-handed player's left. — *verb* **1** to catch with or as if with a hook. **2** *trans., intrans.* (*also* **hook up** or **hook something up**) to fasten or be fastened to something else by means of a hook or hooks. **3** *Golf, Cricket* to hit (the ball) out round the other side of one's body, ie to the left if one is right-handed. **4** in a rugby scrum, to catch (the ball) with the foot and kick it backwards. **5** to make into the shape of a hook.
— **by hook or by crook** by some means or another.

hook and eye a small metal hook and the loop it fits into, used to fasten clothes.

hook, line, and sinker *colloq.* completely.

off the hook 1 *colloq.* no longer in trouble; excused of the blame for something. **2** *said of a telephone receiver* not on its rest so not able to receive incoming calls.
[from Anglo-Saxon *hoc*]

hookah *noun* an oriental tobacco-pipe consisting of a tube which passes through water, used for cooling the smoke before it is drawn into the mouth. [from Arabic *huqqah*, bowl]

Hooke, Robert (1635–1703) English chemist and physicist, born in Freshwater, Isle of Wight.

Curator of Experiments and later secretary at the newly founded Royal Society, and professor at Gresham College, London, he made a multitude of diverse scientific discoveries. He anticipated the development of the steam engine, discovered the relationship between the stress and strain in elastic bodies known as Hooke's law, and invented the balance-spring of watches; many of his microscopic discoveries appeared in his classic *Micrographia* (1665). He also anticipated Newton's inverse square law of gravitation (1678), and constructed the first Gregorian or reflecting telescope.

hooked *adj.* **1** curved like a hook. **2** *colloq.* (**hooked on something**) addicted to a drug or activity; obsessively interested in something or committed to it.

Hooker, Sir Joseph Dalton (1817–1911) English botanist and traveller, born in Halesworth, Suffolk. His first post was as assistant surgeon and naturalist on HMS *Erebus* in the Southern Ocean; later he worked for the Geological Survey and at Kew, where he succeeded his father as director in 1865. He explored Sikkim, Darjeeling, E Nepal, and Assam, and introduced many species to cultivation; his *Flora of British India* (7 vols, 1872–97) remains the standard Flora for the whole Indian subcontinent.

Hooker, Richard (1554–1600) English theologian, born near Exeter. He took orders in 1581, and became rector of a parish near Tring. After engaging in doctrinal controversy, he resolved to set forth the basis of Church government, and in 1591 accepted the living of Boscombe near Salisbury, where he began his eight-volume work *Of the Laws of Ecclesiastical Polity* (1594, 1597, 1648, 1662). It is mainly to this work that Anglican theology owes its tone and direction.

hooker *noun* **1** *colloq.* a prostitute. **2** *Rugby* the forward whose job is to hook the ball out of a scrum.

Hooke's law *Physics* the law which states that, for an elastic material within its elastic limit, the extension produced by stretching the material is proportional to the force that is producing the extension (above the elastic limit permanent deformation occurs). [named after the UK physicist Robert Hooke]

hookey *or* **hooky**
— **play hookey** *North Amer. colloq.* to be absent from school without permission.

Hook of Holland, Dutch **Hoek van Holland** a cape on the SW coast of South Holland province, SW Netherlands. It lies N of the mouth of the Nieuwe Maas R. The name also belongs to a port 27km/17mi NW of Rotterdam.

hook-up *noun* a temporary linking up of different broadcasting stations, especially the radio and a television channel, for a special broadcast.

hookworm *noun* a parasitic worm with hook-like parts in its mouth, which affects animals and humans and causes a type of anaemia.

hooligan *noun* a violent, destructive or badly-behaved young person.

hooliganism *noun* **1** characteristic behaviour of hooligans. **2** an instance of such behaviour.

hoop — *noun* **1** a thin ring of metal, wood, etc, especially those used round casks. **2** a large ring, especially one made of light wood or plastic, rolled along the ground as a toy, whirled round the body, or for circus performers, etc to jump through. **3** an iron arch that the ball is hit through in croquet. — *verb* to bind or surround with a hoop or hoops.
— **go** *or* **be put through the hoops** *colloq.* to undergo a thorough and difficult test.
[from Anglo-Saxon *hop*]

hoop-la *noun* a fairground game in which small rings are thrown at objects, with the thrower winning any objects he or she manages to throw a hoop over.

hoopoe *noun* a bird with salmon-coloured feathers, black and white striped wings and fan-like feathers on top of its head. [from Latin *upupa*, imitative of its cry]

hoopoe

hooray *or* **hoorah** same as HURRAH.

Hooray Henry *noun slang* a young middle- or upper-class man with a loud voice and immature and ineffectual manner.

hoot — *noun* **1** the call of an owl. **2** the sound of a car horn, siren, steam whistle, etc. **3** a loud shout of laughter, scorn, or disapproval. **4** *colloq.* an amusing person, event, or thing. — *verb* **1** *intrans.* to make a hoot. **2** to sound (a car horn, etc). **3** *intrans.* to shout or laugh loudly expressing disapproval, scorn, etc. **4** to force (a performer) off stage by hooting.
— **not care** *or* **give a hoot** *or* **two hoots** *colloq.* not to care at all.
[from Middle English *houten*, perhaps imitative]

hooter *noun* **1** an instrument which makes a hooting sound. **2** *Brit. colloq.* a nose.

Hoover, Herbert (Clark) (1874–1964) US Republican politician, the 31st President, born in West Branch, Iowa. During and after World War I he was associated with relief of distress in Europe, and he then became Secretary of Commerce (1921). As President (1929–33), his opposition to direct governmental assistance for the unemployed after the world slump of 1929 made him unpopular, and he was defeated by Roosevelt in 1932. He assisted Truman with the various American European economic relief programmes which followed World War II.

Hoover, William Henry (1849–1932) US industrialist, born in Ohio. He ran a tannery business (1870–1907), then bought the patent of an electric cleaning machine and formed the Electric Suction Sweeper Co in 1908 to manufacture and market it throughout the world. The company was renamed Hoover in 1910.

Hoover — *noun* trademark a vacuum cleaner. — *verb trans., intrans.* (**hoover**) (**hoovered, hoovering**) to clean (a carpet, etc) with a vacuum cleaner.

Hoover Dam, formerly **Boulder Dam** (**1936–47**) a dam on the Colorado River, Arizona, USA, impounding L Mead. It was built between 1931 and 1936, has a height of 221m and a length of 379m, and can generate 1 345 megawatts of hydroelectricity.

hooves see HOOF.

hop¹ — *verb* (**hopped, hopping**) **1** *intrans. said of a person* to jump on one leg, especially repeatedly as a form of movement. **2** *intrans. said of certain small birds, animals, and insects* to jump on both or all legs simultaneously. **3** to jump over. **4** *intrans.* (**hop in, out, etc**) *colloq.* to move in a sprightly or lively way. **5** (*usually* **hop over**) *colloq.* to make a short journey, especially by air. — *noun* **1** an act of hopping; a short jump. **2** *colloq.* a distance travelled in an aeroplane without landing; a short journey by air. **3** *old colloq. use* an informal dance.
— **catch someone on the hop** *colloq.* to catch them unprepared or unawares.

hop it *Brit. colloq.* to go away.
hopping mad *colloq.* very angry.
keep someone on the hop to keep someone busy, active, or alert.
[from Anglo-Saxon *hoppian*, to dance]

hop² — *noun* **1** a tall perennial climbing plant (a vine) of the genus *Humulus*, widely cultivated for its green cone-shaped female flowers, which are used to give a bitter flavour to beer. **2** (*usually* **hops**) the female flower of this plant, which contains bitter resins and essential oils used in brewing. — *verb* (**hopped, hopping**) **1** *intrans.* to pick hops. **2** to flavour (beer) with hops. [from Middle English *hoppe*]

Hope, Anthony, pseudonym of **Sir Anthony Hope Hawkins** (1863–1933) English novelist, born in London. He was called to the Bar in 1887, but after the success of his 'Ruritanian' romance *The Prisoner of Zenda* (1894) he turned entirely to writing.

Hope, Bob, originally **Leslie Townes Hope** (1903–) US comedian, born in Eltham London, England. He began as a dancer and comedian on the US stage and made his first film appearance in *The Big Broadcast of 1938*. In partnership with Bing Crosby and Dorothy Lamour he appeared in the six highly successful *Road to . . .* comedies (1940–52). During World War II and the Korean and Vietnam Wars he spent time entertaining the troops in the field. He received a Special Academy Award on five occasions.

Hope a female first name, invented by the 17c Puritans. [from HOPE]

hope — *noun* **1** a desire for something, with some confidence of obtaining it. **2** a person, thing, or event that one is relying on for help, or that gives one a good reason for hope. **3** a reason for believing that the thing desired will still happen. **4** that which is desired or hoped for. — *verb* **1** *trans., intrans.* (**hope for something**) to wish or desire that something may happen, especially with some reason to believe that it will. **2** *intrans. old use* to have confidence.
— **hope against hope** to continue hoping when all reason for it has gone.
some hope *colloq.* no hope at all.
[from Anglo-Saxon *hopa*]

Hopeful the companion of Christian in the latter stages of his journey in John Bunyan's *The Pilgrim's Progress*.

hopeful — *adj.* **1** feeling hope. **2** giving a reason for hope; likely to succeed. — *noun* a person, especially a young person, who is ambitious or expected to do well.

hopefully *adv.* **1** in a hopeful way. **2** *colloq.* it is to be hoped.

hopefulness *noun* being hopeful.

hopeless *adj.* **1** not likely to be successful. **2** *colloq.* (**hopeless at something**) not competent to do it. **3** unable to be stopped or cured.

hopelessly *adv.* in a hopeless way.

hopelessness *noun* being hopeless.

Hopewell a Native American Woodland culture of the SE USA (c.100 BC– AD 400), with its focus the Scioto River valley of S Ohio. It is notable for its geometric ceremonial earthworks (eg at Newark, Ohio) and richly furnished burial mounds averaging 30m in diameter and 12m in height. The enclosure at Hopewell itself, excavated in the 1890s, included the largest such mound in the USA.

Hopi a Shoshonean-speaking Pueblo group living in Arizona, USA. They farmed corn and other crops and became famous for their basketry and pottery. They were peaceful and democratic, and lived in houses of stone and adobe. Today many work in cities, but several features of their traditional life survive (present-day population c.7 000).

Hopkins, Anthony (1937–) Welsh film and stage actor, born in Port Talbot, Wales. Very successful on stage since 1964, he had leading cinema roles in *Audrey Rose* (1977) and *The Elephant Man* (1980). Following some work in television (eg *The Hunchback of Notre Dame*, 1982) and on stage (eg *Pravda*, 1985) he won an Oscar for *The Silence of the Lambs* (1991), following which he was critically acclaimed for his performances in *Howards End* (1992), *The Remains of the Day* (1993), and *Shadowlands* (1993).

Hopkins, Sir Frederick Gowland (1861–1947) English biochemist, born in Eastbourne. Professor at Cambridge from 1914, he was a pioneer in the study of accessory food factors, now called vitamins. He shared the Nobel Prize for Physiology or Medicine in 1929.

Hopkins, Gerard Manley (1844–89) English poet, born in London. He became a Catholic in 1866, was ordained a Jesuit in 1877, and in 1884 became Professor of Greek at Dublin. None of his poetry was published in his lifetime, the first edition of his *Poems* being published by his friend Robert Bridges in 1918. His best-known poems include 'The Wreck of the Deutschland' and 'The Windhover', in which he experimented with what he called 'sprung rhythm'.

Hopkinson, Sir Tom (Henry Thomas) (1905–90) British writer and journalist who was involved in setting up *Picture Post* in 1938. He became its editor two years later and encouraged the craft of photo-journalism. He left after a dispute with its owner, Edward Hulton, and later became a teacher. His publications include the novel *Shady City* (1987).

hopper[1] *noun* **1** a person, animal, or insect which hops. **2** *Agric.* a large container with a hole in the bottom that is used to feed grain, fertilizer, etc, into another container below it, into seed drills, or on to the ground.

hopper[2] *noun* a person or machine that picks hops.

Hoppe-Seyler, (Ernst) Felix (Immanuel) (1825–95) German physiological chemist, born in Freiburg. Professor at Tübingen and Strassburg, he discovered and named haemoglobin (1862), and showed that the haemoglobin in red blood cells binds oxygen which is subsequently delivered to the tissues. He also investigated the chemical composition and functions of chlorophyll as well as the chemistry of putrefaction.

hopscotch *noun* a children's game in which players take turns at throwing a stone into one of a series of squares drawn on the ground and hopping in the others around it.

Horace, in full **Quintus Horatius Flaccus** (65–8 BC) Roman poet and satirist, born near Venusia, Italy. He served in Brutus's army (44–42 BC) and fought at the battle of Philippi, then returned to Italy where he began to write for a living. Through the influence of Virgil he came under the patronage of Maecenas, who gave hima a house in the Sabine Hills. His works include the *Satires* (c.35 BC), the *Odes* (c.23 BC), the *Epistles* (c.19 BC), and the poetic epistle, *Ars Poetica* (c.19 BC).

Horace a male first name, now less common. [from Roman Family name *Horatius*]

Horae in Greek mythology, the goddesses of the seasons and natural order. In Hesiod, they were the children of Zeus, and were called Eunomia (good order), Dike (justice), and Eirene (peace). They later became the four seasons, daughters of the sun-god Helios, and the moon-goddess Selene.

Horatio Hamlet's friend in Shakespeare's *Hamlet*, who is clear-thinking, loyal, and level-headed.

Horatti and Curiatii in Roman legend, two groups of three brothers, from Rome and Alba respectively, whose story was used to justify legal appeals. Under Tullus Hostilius there was war between Rome and Alba, and it was agreed

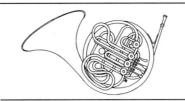

French horn

that the opposing brothers would fight to decide the battle. All were killed except one Horatius. When his sister, who was betrothed to a Curiatius, berated him, he murdered her, but was acquitted after appealing to the Roman people.

horde *noun* **1** *often derog.* a crowd or large group, especially one which is noisy. **2** a group of nomads. [from Turkish *ordu*, camp]

Hore-Belisha (of Devonport), (Isaac) Leslie Hore-Belisha, 1st Baron (1893–1957) English barrister and politician, born in Devonport. He became a London journalist, and in 1923 was called to the Bar and became a Liberal MP. In 1934, as Minister of Transport, he gave his name to the 'Belisha' beacons, drafted a new highway code, and inaugurated driving tests for motorists. As Secretary of State for War (1937–40) he carried out several army reforms, and introduced conscription (1939).

horizon *noun* **1** the line at which the earth and the sky seem to meet. **2** the limit of a person's knowledge, interests, or experience. [from Greek *horizein*, to limit]

horizontal — *adj.* **1** at right angles to vertical; parallel to the horizon; level or flat. **2** applying equally to all members of a group or aspects of a situation. — *noun* a horizontal line or position.

horizontally *adv.* in a horizontal way or position.

Horkheimer, Max (1895–1973) German philosopher and social theorist, born in Stuttgart. A leading figure (with Theodor Adorno and Herbert Marcuse) at the Frankfurt School, he moved with it to New York City when the Nazis came to power (1933), and returned to Frankfurt in 1950 as professor of the university. His articles collected in *Kritische Theorie* (1968) expound the basic principles of the school in their critique of industrial civilization and epistemology and the key tenets of their 'critical theory'. He also wrote *Eclipse of Reason* (1947).

hormonal *adj.* **1** relating to or involving hormones. **2** that is or behaves as a hormone.

hormone *noun* **1** a substance that is manufactured and secreted in minute amounts by a specialized gland, known as an endocrine gland, in one part of the body, and carried via the bloodstream to organs or tissues located elsewhere in the body, where it causes specific biological changes. Examples of hormones include insulin, adrenaline, thyroxine, and the sex hormones (androgens and oestrogens). **2** an artificially manufactured chemical compound which has the same effects as such a substance. **3** a plant growth substance that influences the growth and development of plant tissue. [from Greek *horman*, to stimulate]

hormone replacement therapy (ABBREV. **HRT**) *Medicine* a treatment for post-menopausal women that involves the administration (either by mouth or by injection) of the oestrogenic hormones that are not produced naturally after the menopause, in order to relieve some of the more undesirable menopausal symptoms, such as hot flushes, vaginal dryness, osteoporosis (thinning of the bones), and emotional disturbances.

Hormuz, Strait of a passage linking the Arabian Gulf to the Arabian Sea. It is 50–80km/30–50mi wide and situated between the S coast of Iran and the Musandam Peninsula

of Oman. It is a strategic route controlling ocean traffic to the oil terminals of the Gulf and was a major point of international tension during the Iran–Iraq War. Qeshm I is separated from the coast of Iran by the Clarence Strait.

horn — *noun* **1** one of a pair of hard hollow structures, usually pointed, that grow on the head of many ruminant animals, eg cattle, sheep. In male deer the horns are known as antlers. **2** any similar structure growing on the head of another animal, eg rhinoceros, or one of the two tentacles borne on the head of a snail. **3** the bony substance of which horns are made. **4** something which looks like a horn in shape. **5** a musical wind instrument originally made from horn but now usually made of brass. **6** (*in full* **French horn**) a coiled brass wind instrument. **7** an apparatus for making a warning sound, especially on a vehicle. — *verb* **1** to fit with a horn or horns. **2** to injure or gore with horns.
— **horn of plenty** cornucopia.
on the horns of a dilemma having to make a choice between two equally unwelcome alternatives.
[from Anglo-Saxon]

hornbeam *noun* a tree with hard, tough wood.

hornbill *noun* a tropical bird with a horn-like growth on its beak.

hornbill

hornblende *noun Geol.* a dark green or black mineral that is a major component of many metamorphic and igneous rocks, including granite. [from German]

Hornblower, Horatio the insecure but intelligent and much-admired hero of C S Forester's *The Happy Return* and other novels.

horned *adj.* having a horn or horns or something shaped like a horn.

hornet *noun* any of several large social wasps, similar in habits and life cycle to the common wasp, but with a brown and yellow striped body (as opposed to black and yellow), and up to 3.5cm in length. The sting of some tropical species can be fatal.
— **stir up a hornet's nest** to cause a strong or hostile reaction.
[from Anglo-Saxon *hyrnet*]

hornet

hornfels *noun Geol.* any of various hard fine-grained metamorphic rocks that originate from sedimentary rocks. [from German *Hornfels*, from *Horn*, horn + *Fels*, rock]

hornpipe *noun* **1** a lively, solo, sailor's jig. **2** the music for this dance.

horntail *noun* a large member of the wasp family, typically with a long cylindrical body without a distinct waist, black in colour and banded with yellow or red. It lays its eggs in wood, and the larvae burrow deep into the timber.

horny *adj.* (**hornier, horniest**) **1** of or like horn, especially in being hard. **2** *slang* sexually excited.

horological *adj.* **1** relating to horology. **2** measuring time.

horologist *noun* an expert in horology; a maker of clocks and watches.

horology *noun* the art of measuring time or making clocks and watches. [from Greek *hora*, hour + -LOGY]

horoscope *noun* **1** a description of a person's future based on the position of the stars and planets at the time of his or her birth. **2** a diagram showing the positions of the stars and planets at a particular moment in time, eg at the time of a person's birth. [from Greek *hora*, hour + *skopein*, to observe]

Horowitz, originally **Gorowicz Vladimir** (1904–89) Russian pianist, born in Kiev. He made his concert début aged 17, toured widely, and settled in the USA. There were long periods of retirement from concert life, but in 1986 he played again in Russia. A highly accomplished musician, his mastery ranged from Scarlatti to Liszt, Scriabin, and Prokofiev.

horrendous *adj.* causing great shock, fear, or terror; horrifying. [from Latin *horrere*, to shudder]

horrendously *adv.* in a horrendous way.

horrendousness *noun* being horrendous.

horrible *adj.* **1** causing horror, dread, or fear. **2** *colloq.* unpleasant. [from Latin *horribilis*]

horribly *adv.* **1** in a horrible way. **2** badly, very: *the plot went horribly wrong.*

horrid *adj.* **1** revolting; detestable. **2** *colloq.* unpleasant; disagreeable. [from Latin *horridus*]

horridly *adv.* in a horrid way.

horridness *noun* being horrid.

horrific *adj.* **1** causing fear, disgust, or horror; terrible. **2** *colloq.* very bad. [from Latin *horror*, horror + *facere*, to make]

horrifically *adv.* in a horrific way.

horrify *verb* (**horrifies, horrified**) to shock greatly. [from Latin *horror*, horror + *facere*, to make]

horrifying *adj.* causing horror.

horrifyingly *adv.* in a horrifying way.

Horrocks, Sir Brian (Gwynne) (1895–1985) British general, born in Ranikhet, India. He joined the army in 1914, served in France and Russia, and in 1942 commanded the 9th Armoured Division and then the 13th and 10th Corps in N Africa, where he helped to defeat Rommel. Wounded in Tunis, he headed the 30th Corps during the Allied invasion (1944). He later became well known as a military journalist and broadcaster.

horror *noun* **1** great fear, loathing, or disgust. **2** great dislike. **3** a person or thing causing horror. **4** *colloq.* a bad or ridiculous person or thing. **5** (*attributive*) *said of literature, films, etc* based on horrifying or frightening themes. — **the horrors** *colloq.* a fit of anxiety and fear. [from Latin *horror*, a shudder with fear]

horror-stricken *or* **horror-struck** *adj.* shocked; horrified.

hors d'oeuvre *noun* a savoury appetiser served at the beginning of a meal. [from French *hors d'œuvre*]

horse *noun* **1** any of many domestic and wild breeds of a large hoofed mammal of the genus *Equus* belonging to the same family (Equidae) as asses and zebras, and having a slender head, a long neck covered with a mane of hair, and long legs. Horses are used in many countries for

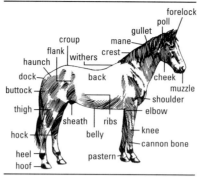

forelock
poll
gullet
croup mane
flank crest
haunch withers
dock back
buttock cheek
muzzle
thigh shoulder
elbow
sheath ribs
knee
hock belly
cannon bone
heel pastern
hoof

horse

pulling loads, carrying goods, and for riding. **2** an adult male horse. **3** cavalry. **4** a piece of apparatus used for vaulting over and other gymnastic exercises. **5** (*also* **clothes-horse**) a frame on which clothes, etc are hung to dry. — **horse about** *or* **around** *colloq.* to fool about. **straight from the horse's mouth** directly from a well-informed and reliable source. [from Anglo-Saxon *hors*]

◇ Horses were first domesticated about 5 000 years ago, and are now found worldwide. Wild horses belong to the same family as asses and zebras, and were widespread in Europe and Asia in prehistoric times, but their numbers were subsequently reduced through hunting and domestication. The domesticated horse (of which there are about 300 breeds) is probably descended from either the tarpan (a small shy swift-running animal, now extinct) or Przewalski's horse (a stocky horse of central Asia, with a sandy-brown coat and an erect black mane). Wild horses live in herds consisting of mares (adult females), foals, and colts (male animals up to four years of age) led by a stallion (adult male). As male colts reach maturity, the stallion drives them to the outside of the herd. Horses commonly live to 20 years of age or more, the record being 62 years.

horseback
— **on horseback** on the back of a horse.

horse-box *noun* a closed trailer fixed to or pulled by a motor vehicle and used for carrying horses.

horse chestnut see CHESTNUT.

horseflesh *noun* **1** the meat of a horse. **2** horses as a group.

horsefly *noun* a large fly that bites horses and cattle.

Horse Guards *or* **Royal Horse Guards**, also called the **Blues** an élite regiment of the British Army, first raised in 1661. Amalgamated in 1969 with the Royal Dragoon Guards, the 'Blues and Royals' form, with the Life Guards, the British Sovereign's Household Cavalry.

Horsehead nebula *Astron.* a dark nebula that protrudes into a bright nebula in the constellation Orion, so called because it resembles the silhouette of a horse's head.

Horse Latitudes the two belts of ocean calm at 30° N and S of the Equator, where conditions of high atmospheric pressure exist almost permanently. Trade Winds constantly blow from these belts towards the Doldrums.

horse laugh a loud, coarse laugh.

horseman *or* **horsewoman** *noun* **1** a rider. **2** a skilled rider.

horsemanship *noun* the art of riding, training, and managing horses.

Horse of the Year Show an international showjumping competition, held annually in Wembley Arena, London. It includes various categories of competition for both adults and children.

horseplay *noun* rough and noisy play.

horsepower *noun* (ABBREV. **HP, hp**) the imperial unit of power, which in the SI system has been replaced by the watt. One horsepower is equal to 745.7 watts.

horse-racing *noun* racing of horses against each other, each ridden by a jockey.
◇ Modern races fall into two categories: *flat races*, over a predetermined distance (without jumps), which can be between 5 furlongs (1km) and 4km; and *national hunt races*, over distances up to 6.5km and including a series of hurdles or fixed fences which the horses must negotiate. In Britain, the sport has been supported by most monarchs and has thereby become known as the 'sport of kings'. The oldest course in Britain is Chester, and some of the most prestigious races include the five English Classics and the Grand National.

horseradish *noun* a plant with a long, white, sharp-tasting root which is used to make a sauce usually eaten with beef.

horse sense plain good sense.

horseshoe *noun* **1** a piece of curved iron nailed to the bottom of a horse's hoof to protect the foot. **2** something in the shape of a horseshoe, especially as a symbol of good luck.

horsetail *noun* **1** the tail of a horse. **2** a primitive spore-bearing plant of the genus *Equisetum*, related to the ferns and clubmosses, and having a hollow green jointed stem bearing whorls of small scale-like leaves at regular intervals. It is the only living representative of a group of much taller plants that flourished during the Carboniferous period.

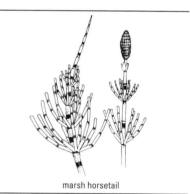

marsh horsetail

horsetail

horse-trading *noun* hard bargaining.

horse trials a training competition combining the three main equestrian disciplines: dressage, showjumping, and cross-country.

horsewhip — *noun* a whip for encouraging horses. — *verb* (**horsewhipped, horsewhipping**) to whip, especially severely, and usually as a punishment.

horsewoman see HORSEMAN.

horsey *or* **horsy** *adj.* (**horsier, horsiest**) **1** of or relating to horses. **2** like a horse. **3** *Brit. colloq.* very interested in or devoted to horses.

Horst-Wessel-Lied the song of the Nazi Party, sung in Germany (1933–45) in conjunction with the official national anthem, 'Deutschland, Deutschland über alles'. The words were written by Horst Wessel (1907–30), who died for the Nazi cause.

hortative *or* **hortatory** *adj.* encouraging. [from Latin *hortari*, to incite to action]

Horthy (de Nagybánya), Miklós (1868–1957) Hungarian politician, born in Kenderes. He commanded the Austro-Hungarian fleet (1918), and was Minister of War in the counter-revolutionary 'white' government (1919), opposing

Bela Kun's communist regime, which he suppressed (1920). He became regent (1920–44) and presided over a resolutely conservative, authoritarian regime. In World War II he supported the Axis Powers until Hungary was overrun by the Germans in 1944, who imprisoned him until he was released by the Allies in 1945.

horticultural *adj.* relating to or involving horticulture.

horticulture *noun* the intensive cultivation of fruit, vegetables, flowers, and ornamental shrubs, usually conducted on a smaller scale than agriculture. [from Latin *hortus*, garden + *cultura*, cultivation]
◇ Horticulture is concerned mainly with the production of fresh fruit and vegetables for sale, but also includes the production of seeds and plants for sale to gardeners, and the breeding of new and improved varieties of garden plant, as well as the development of new methods for the control of garden pests.

horticulturist *noun Bot.* a person who specializes in horticulture; an expert gardener.

Hortobagy a national park in E central Hungary, established in 1973. It is noted for its wild birds, plants, and stock breeding. The nine-arched bridge in the park is the longest stone bridge in Hungary. AREA 520sq km/200sq mi.

Horus in Egyptian religion, the god of the sky, usually depicted with a falcon's head. He was the son of Isis and Osiris, and the ancestor of the dynasties of the pharoahs. He became universal king of the earth after defeating Set, who had seized power after murdering Osiris.

Horyuji Temple a Buddhist complex built in Nara, Japan, for Prince Shotoku in the 7c. It comprises 45 buildings (of which 17 are national treasures) and houses many works of art.

hosanna *noun, interj.* a shout of adoration or praise to God. [from Hebrew *hoshiah nna*, save now, I pray]

hose — *noun* 1 (*also* **hosepipe**) a flexible tube for directing water, eg for watering plants. 2 (*as pl.*) stockings, socks, and tights. 3 *Hist.* breeches. — *verb* (**hose something down**) to direct water at or clean with a hose. [from Anglo-Saxon *hosa*]

Hosea *or* **Osee, Book of** the first of the 12 so-called 'minor' prophetic writings of the Hebrew Bible and Old Testament, attributed to the prophet Hosea, who was active in the N kingdom of Israel (c.750–725 BC) during a period of Assyrian military invasions. It contains a warning of judgement for Israel's defection to the Canaanite Baal cult, but affirms God's love in seeking to restore Israel.

hosepipe *noun* a flexible tube for directing water, eg for watering plants.

hosier *noun* a person who makes or sells hosiery.

hosiery *noun* stockings, socks, tights and knitted underwear. [from HOSE]

hospice *noun* 1 an institution that specializes in the care of the terminally ill and provides support for their families. Most hospices specialize in one particular condition, such as AIDS or cancer, and are run as charities. 2 *old use* a house offering lodging for travellers, especially one kept by a religious order. [from Latin *hospes*, guest]

hospitable *adj.* showing kindness to guests or strangers. [from Latin *hospes*, guest]

hospitably *adv.* in a hospitable way.

hospital *noun* an institution, staffed by doctors and nurses, for the treatment and care of people who are sick or injured, either as *in-patients*, who receive treatment while residing at the hospital, or as *out-patients*, who attend clinics in various areas of speciality. Some hospitals cater for the needs of a single category of patient, eg psychiatric, maternity, or paediatric hospitals. General hospitals accept all categories of patient, but treat them in specialized wards or units. [from Latin *hospes*, guest]

hospitality *noun* a friendly welcome for guests or strangers, which usually includes offering them food and drink. [from Latin *hospes*, guest]

hospitalization *or* **hospitalisation** *noun* being hospitalized.

hospitalize *or* **hospitalise** *verb* to take or admit (a person) to hospital for treatment.

hospitaller *noun* a member of a religious order which does work for charity, especially in hospitals. [from Latin *hospes*, guest]

Hospitallers members (priests or brother knights subject to monastic vows) of the Order of the Hospital of St John of Jerusalem. Originally a charitable organization to care for sick pilgrims to the Holy Land, from the 12c they played a prominent role in the Crusades as an international religious-military order. After the loss of Acre in 1291, they moved their headquarters to Limassol, Cyprus (1292), then Rhodes (1309), but were expelled by the Ottoman Turks (1523). They moved to Malta (1530), which they held until dislodged by Napoleon I (1798). Now based in Rome, the Sovereign Order is also known as the Order of the Hospital of St John of Jerusalem, the Knights of Rhodes, Knights of Malta, or Knights of St John of Jerusalem.

host¹ — *noun* 1 a person who receives and entertains guests or strangers in his or her own home. 2 *old use* an innkeeper. 3 *Biol.* a plant or animal on which a parasite lives and feeds for all or part of its life. 4 a person who introduces performers, etc on a television or radio show. 5 *Medicine* the recipient of a tissue graft or organ transplant. — *verb* to act as a host to (people) or be the host of (an event or programme). [from Latin *hospes*, guest]

host² *noun* 1 a very large number. 2 *old use* an army. [from Latin *hostis*, enemy]

host³ *noun* the bread or wafer used in a Holy Communion service. [from Latin *hostia*, victim]

hosta *noun* a perennial plant of the genus *Hosta*, native to China and Japan, and having conspicuous lance-shaped or broadly oval leaves, often variegated or bluish in colour, and spikes of tubular white or violet flowers. [named after the Australian botanist N T Host]

hostage *noun* a person who is held prisoner as a guarantee that demands, the conditions of an agreement, etc will be carried out. [from Latin *obses*]

hostel *noun* 1 a building which provides overnight accommodation as a charity, especially for the homeless. 2 a residence for students or nurses. 3 a youth hostel. 4 *old use* an inn. [from Old French *hostel*, from Latin *hospes*, guest]

hostelry *noun* (PL. **hostelries**) *old use, facetious* an inn or public house.

hostess *noun* 1 a female host. 2 a woman employed to act as a man's companion for the evening at a night club. 3 an air hostess.

hostile *adj.* 1 unfriendly; aggressive. 2 of or belonging to an enemy. 3 (**hostile to something**) strongly opposed to it. [from Latin *hostis*, enemy]

hostility *noun* (PL. **hostilities**) 1 unfriendliness; opposition; aggression. 2 (**hostilities**) acts of war; battles.

hot — *adj.* (**hotter, hottest**) 1 having or producing a great deal of heat. 2 having a higher temperature than is normal or desirable. 3 *said of food* spicy; causing a burning sensation on the tongue. 4 easily made angry; excitable. 5 feeling intense emotion or sexual desire. 6 *said of a contest or fight* intense; animated. 7 *said of news* recent; fresh. 8 strongly favoured: *a hot favourite*. 9 *said of music* having strong and exciting rhythms. 10 *said of red colours* bright and fiery. 11 *slang, said of goods* stolen, especially recently stolen. 12 *said of a scent in hunting* fresh and strong, suggesting the quarry is not far ahead. 13 *slang, said of information* up to date and reliable: *a hot tip*. 14 *colloq., said of a situation* difficult, unpleasant, or dangerous: *make life hot for him*. 15 *slang* radioactive. 16 in a game, etc, very close to guessing correctly or finding the thing sought. — *adv.* hotly. — *verb* (**hotted, hotting**)
— **hot up** *or* **hot something up** to become or make gradually hotter, more exciting, more dangerous, etc.
have *or* **get the hots for someone** *coarse slang* to have a strong sexual desire for them.
hot and bothered *colloq.* anxious and confused.
hot on something very interested in or well informed about.
in hot pursuit chasing as fast or as closely as one can.
[from Anglo-Saxon *hat*]

hot air *colloq.* empty or boastful talk, promises that will not be kept, etc.

hotbed *noun* a place which allows something, especially something bad, to grow quickly: *a hotbed of discontent.*

hot-blooded *adj.* having strong, especially sexual, feelings.

hotchpotch *noun* 1 a confused mass or jumble. 2 a mutton stew with many different vegetables in it. [from Old French *hochepot*, from *hocher*, to shake + *pot*, pot]

hot cross bun a fruit bun marked with a cross on top, traditionally eaten on Good Friday.

hot dog a hot sausage in a long, soft, bread roll.

hotel *noun* a large house or building providing accommodation, meals, and other services, usually with a high level of comfort, to visitors for payment. [from Old French *hostel*, hostel, from Latin *hospes*, guest]

hotelier *noun* a person who owns or manages a hotel.

hotfoot *colloq.* — *adv.* in haste. — *verb* (**hotfoot it**) to rush.

hothead *noun* a person who is easily made angry.

hotheaded *adj.* easily angered, impetuous.

hotheadedness *noun* being hotheaded.

hothouse — *noun* 1 a greenhouse which is kept warm for growing tender or tropical plants. 2 (*attributive*) *said of a plant* suitable for growing in a greenhouse. — *verb* to subject (a young child) to intensive education to boost its intellectual or artistic development.

hot key *Comput.* a key which activates a terminate-and-stay-resident program when pressed, either alone or in combination with other keys.

hot line 1 a direct exclusive telephone line, especially for use in emergencies by political leaders. 2 an emergency telephone number for inquiries about a particular incident or accident.

hotly *adv.* 1 with great heat. 2 excitedly, keenly, passionately.

hot money money transferred from one country to another to take advantage of exchange rates and trading conditions, and make a quick profit.

HOTOL *abbrev.* horizontal take-off and landing.

hotplate *noun* 1 the flat top surface of a cooker on which food is cooked and kept warm. 2 a portable heated metal surface for keeping food, dishes, etc hot.

hotpot *noun* meat and vegetables, with a layer of sliced potato on top, cooked slowly in a closed pot.

hot potato *colloq.* a difficult problem or situation.

hot rod a motor car modified to have extra speed.

hot seat 1 *colloq.* an uncomfortable or difficult position. **2** *North Amer. slang* the electric chair.

hot spot 1 *colloq.* an area where there is likely to be trouble, especially political or military. **2** an area where there is evidence of volcanic activity occurring underground.

hot spring *Geol.* a spring of hot or warm groundwater that emerges from the Earth's surface and often contains dissolved minerals or sulphur. Such springs were formerly used as health spas, especially in Victorian Britain. Very hot springs emerge as geysers, and are sometimes used as sources of geothermal energy.

Hotspur, properly **Henry Percy** the brave, chivalrous but impetuous eldest son of the Earl of Northumberland, in Shakespeare's *Richard II* and *Henry IV Part I*.

hot stuff *colloq.* **1** a person who has outstanding ability. **2** a person who is sexually exciting.

hot-tempered *adj.* quick to get angry.

Hottentot *noun* **1** a member of a pale-brown-skinned race of people in SW Africa. **2** the language spoken by this people. [from Afrikaans *Hottentot*]

hotting *noun slang* the performing of stunts and skilful manoeuvre at high speed in a stolen car.

hot water *colloq.* trouble; bother: *get into hot water*.

hot-water bottle a rubber container for hot water, used to warm beds.

hot-wire *verb slang* to restart (a vehicle engine) by touching together electrical wires, rather than using the ignition switch.

Houdini, Harry, originally **Erich Weiss** (1874–1926) American magician, born in Budapest, Hungary. After his family emigrated to the USA, he became a trapeze performer, then gained an international reputation as an escape artist, freeing himself from handcuffs, shackles, and other devices, even while imprisoned in a box underwater or in mid-air. He died from peritonitis following a stomach injury incurred by being punched when he was unprepared.

hound — *noun* **1** (*often in compounds*) a hunting-dog: *wolfhound*. **2** (**hounds**) a pack of foxhounds. **3** *colloq.* a man one despises or feels contempt for. — *verb* to chase or bother relentlessly. [from Anglo-Saxon *hund*]

Hounsfield, Sir Godfrey Newbold (1919–) English electrical engineer, born in Newark. Working for Thorn/EMI, he led the team which developed the technique of computer-assisted tomography (CAT scanning), which produces detailed X-ray pictures of the human body. For this major breakthrough in the non-invasive diagnosis of disease, he shared the 1979 Nobel Prize for Physiology or Medicine with Allan Cormack.

hour *noun* **1** sixty minutes, a twenty-fourth part of a day. **2** any of the points on a clock or watch that shows the hour. **3** a point in time: *an early hour*. **4** the time allowed or fixed for some activity: *office hours*. **5** the distance travelled in an hour: *two hours away from the airport*. **6** a special occasion: *his finest hour*. **7** a time for action: *the hour has come*. **8** (**hours** or **canonical hours**) *Relig.* seven set times for prayer during the day and night, or the prayers to be said at these times. — **after hours** after closing-time.

at all hours at irregular times, especially late at night.

out of hours before or after usual working hours.

[from Greek *hora*]

hourglass — *noun* an instrument that measures time in hours, consisting of one glass container on top of and joined to another by a narrow glass tube, filled with as much sand as will pass from one container into the other in the space of one hour. — *adj.* curving in at the waist or middle like an hourglass.

houri *noun* a beautiful young woman, especially in the Muslim Paradise. [from Arabic *haura*, gazelle-eyed]

hourly — *adj.* **1** happening or done every hour. **2** measured by the hour. **3** frequent; continual: *live in hourly fear of discovery*. — *adv.* **1** every hour. **2** at any hour: *expect news hourly*. **3** by the hour. **4** frequently.

house — *noun* **1** a building in which people, especially a single family, live. **2** the people living in such a building. **3** (*in compounds*) a building used for a particular purpose: *an opera-house*. **4** (**House**) the body of people who govern a country and make laws, or the place where they meet. **5** a business firm: *a publishing house*. **6** the audience in a theatre, a theatre, or a performance given there. **7** a family, especially an important or noble one: *the House of Hanover*. **8** *Astrol.* one of the twelve divisions of the heavens. **9** *Brit.* one of several divisions of pupils at a large school. **10** a building in which students or members of a religious community live. **11** a style of dance music produced electronically, incorporating edited fragments of other recordings. — *verb* **1** to provide with a house or similar shelter. **2** to store. **3** to protect (a part) by covering.

— **bring the house down** *colloq.* to produce loud applause in a theatre.

keep house to manage a household.

like a house on fire *colloq.* **1** very well. **2** very quickly.

on the house *said of food, drink, etc* free; paid for by the manager or owner.

put or **set one's house in order** to organize or settle one's affairs.

[from Anglo-Saxon *hus*]

house agent a person who arranges the buying, selling, or renting of houses.

house arrest confinement in one's own home rather than prison.

houseboat *noun* a boat, usually with a flat bottom and usually stationary, which is built to be lived in.

housebound *adj.* unable to leave one's house because of illness, young children, etc.

housebreaker *noun* a person who breaks into a house to steal.

housebreaking *noun* unlawful breaking into a building to steal.

housecoat *noun* a woman's long, loose garment like a dressing-gown, worn at home.

housefly *noun* a common fly of the family Muscidae, often found in houses.

household — *noun* the people who live together in a house and make up a family. — *adj.* of the house or family living there.

householder *noun* **1** the person who owns a house or pays the rent for it. **2** the head of a family.

household name or **household word** a name or saying known to everyone.

house husband a husband who does the work usually done by a housewife.

housekeeper *noun* a person who is paid to look after the management of a usually large house and household.

housekeeping *noun* **1** the management of a house and household. **2** money set aside to pay for the expenses of running a house.

house lights the lights in the part of a cinema, theatre, etc where people sit.

housemaid *noun* a maid employed to keep a house clean and tidy.

housemaid's knee inflammation of the knee, caused by prolonged kneeling.

houseman *noun* a recently qualified doctor who is living in a hospital while working there to complete his or her training.

house martin a black and white bird with a short forked tail, that builds nests on house walls.

housemaster or **housemistress** *noun* in Britain, a teacher in charge of a house in a school, especially a boarding-school.

House of Bernarda Alba, The (La Casa de Bernarda Alba) a play by Federico García Lorca (1936). The last of a trilogy of folk tragedies (preceded by *Blood Wedding*, 1933, and *Yerma*, 1934), it is about four frustrated sisters forced by their mother's sense of decorum to remain confined in mourning.

House of Commons in the UK, the lower elected assembly in parliament, or the building where this meets.

◇ It contains 650 members, elected by universal adult suffrage, each representing a particular constituency. The Commons is elected for a maximum period of five years, and the government is drawn from the party that wins a majority of seats. The ascendancy of the House of Commons over the House of Lords began in the 16c, and was completed with the passage of the Parliament Acts of 1911 and 1949. The Commons is presided over by the Speaker.

House of Keys in the Isle of Man, the elected chamber of the Manx parliament, the Tynwald.

House of Lords in the UK, the upper assembly in parliament, made up of peers and bishops.

◇ It is non-elected, and consists of hereditary and life peers, and the two archbishops (of Canterbury and York) and certain bishops of the Church of England. It can no longer veto bills passed by the House of Commons, with the exception of a bill to prolong the duration of a parliament. It also constitutes the highest court in the UK.

House of Representatives in the USA, one of the two chambers of the bicameral legislature, in which all legislative power is vested. The 435 members of the House are elected from Congressional districts according to population, although each state has at least one representative. Although many bills are acted on by both the Senate and the House, all revenue bills must originate in the House.

house party a group of guests staying in a country house for several days.

house-proud *adj.* taking a lot of, often too much, pride in the condition and appearance of one's house.

Houses of Parliament the Palace of Westminster in London. The first palace on the site was built by King Canute in the 11c, and was finally destroyed by fire in 1834. The present structure was begun in 1839, and was occupied by the Commons and Lords in 1852.

housetop *noun* (*usually* **housetops**) the roofs of houses, especially seen as a row against the skyline.

— **shout something from the housetops** to announce it loudly and publicly.

housetrain *verb* to train (a pet) to be clean in the house and to urinate and defecate outside or in a special tray, etc.

house-warming *noun* a party given to celebrate moving into a new house.

housewife *noun* **1** a woman who looks after her house, her husband and her family, and who sometimes does not have a job outside the home. **2** a pocket sewing-kit.

housewifely *adj.* **1** thrifty and neat and tidy. **2** like or suitable for a housewife.

housework *noun* the work of keeping a house clean and tidy.

housing *noun* **1** houses as a group. **2** the act or job of providing housing for people. **3** the hard cover round a machine.

Housman, A(lfred) E(dward) (1859–1936) English scholar and poet, born near Bromsgrove,

Worcestershire. Despite having failed his degree, he became Professor of Latin at London in 1892, and at Cambridge in 1911. He is best known for his own poetry, notably *A Shropshire Lad* (1896) and *Last Poems* (1922).

Houston POP (1990) 3.3m, the seat of Harris County, SE Texas, USA, and the country's third busiest port. It is situated near Galveston Bay, on the deep-water Houston Ship Channel (1914), which allows ocean-going vessels to reach the city. Settled in 1836, it was capital of the Republic of Texas in 1837–9 and 1842–5. Now the fifth largest city in the USA, this major oil centre has huge refineries and the largest petrochemical complex in the world. Numerous energy companies have their corporate headquarters in the city, which is also the base for several space and science research firms. NOTABLE FEATURES National Space Hall of Fame; San Jacinto battleground; Astroworld; Sam Houston Historical Park; NASA's Lyndon B Johnson Space Center at nearby Clear Lake City; the battleship *Texas*.

Houyhnhnms a race of wise and noble creatures in Jonathan Swift's *Gulliver's Travels*, who are shaped as horses but endowed with speech and the power of reason.

Hove POP (1992e) 90 000, a resort and residential suburb in East Sussex, SE England. It adjoins Brighton to the W.

hove see HEAVE.

hovel *noun* a small, dirty, dismal dwelling. [from Middle English *hovell*]

hover — *verb intrans.* (**hovered, hovering**) 1 *said of a bird, helicopter, etc* to remain in the air without moving in any direction. 2 to move around while still remaining near a person or thing. 3 (**hover between**) to be undecided. — *noun* an act or state of hovering or waiting to make a decision. [from Middle English *hoveren*]

hovercraft *noun* a vehicle which is able to move over land or water, supported by a cushion of air.
◇ The first hovercraft was designed by Christopher Cockerell in 1950, and the first operational model (the SR-N1) was demonstrated in 1959. The craft is propelled by an airscrew, and rides on a cushion of air trapped between the hull and the surface of the water (or land) by a flexible skirt, which is usually made of heavy-duty neoprene. The first regular hovercraft service operated across the Dee estuary in summer 1962; today there is a car-ferry service across the English Channel between Dover and Calais.

hoverfly *noun* a medium to large fly often found hovering over flowers. The adults resemble wasps, and feed on pollen and nectar.

how — *adv.* 1 in what way; by what means: *how did it happen?* 2 to what extent: *how old is he?* 3 in what condition, especially of health: *how is she feeling now?* 4 to what extent is something good, successful, etc: *how was your holiday?* 5 using whatever means are necessary: *do it how best you can.* — *conj. colloq.* that: *told me how he'd done it on his own.* — *noun* a manner or means of doing something: *the how and why.*
— **and how** *colloq.* very much indeed.
how about? would you like?; what do you think of?: *how about another piece of cake?*
how come? *colloq.* for what reason?
how do you do? a formal greeting, especially to a person one is meeting for the first time.
how's that? 1 what is your opinion of that? 2 an appeal to the umpire in cricket to give the batsman out.
[from Anglo-Saxon *hu*]

Howard, Catherine (d.1542) fifth wife of Henry VIII, a granddaughter of the 2nd Duke of Norfolk. She became queen in the same month as Anne of Cleves was divorced (Jul 1540). A year later she was charged by Cranmer with intercourse before her marriage with a musician and a kinsman, and was beheaded for treason.

Howard, Sir Ebenezer (1850–1928) English founder of the garden city movement, born in London. He emigrated to Nebraska in 1872, but returned to England in 1877. His *Tomorrow* (1898) envisaged self-contained communities with both rural and urban amenities and green belts, and led to the laying out of Letchworth (1903) and Welwyn Garden City (1919) in Hertfordshire.

Howard, John (1726–90) English prison reformer, born in London. While travelling in Europe he was captured and imprisoned by the French. In 1773 he became high sheriff for Bedfordshire, and began to investigate the conditions of prisons and prisoners. Two Acts resulted (1774): one provided for fixed salaries to jailers, and the other enforced cleanliness. Whilst in Kherson, Russia, he died from camp fever after attending a prisoner.

Howard, Thomas, 3rd Duke of Norfolk (1473–1554) English statesman, the brother-in-law of Henry VII, who held several high offices under Henry VIII. He was the uncle of Anne Boleyn and Catherine Howard; after Catherine's execution (1542) he lost power. The father of the Earl of Surrey, who was executed for treason by Henry VIII, he escaped being executed as an accessory but remained in prison during the reign of Edward VI, until his release by the Catholic Queen Mary.

Howard a male first name, after the surname. [probably from Old Norse elements *ha*, high + *ward*, guard]

Howard League for Penal Reform a charity dedicated to the cause of international penal reform, formed in 1921 by the amalgamation of the Howard Association with the Prison Reform League, and named after John Howard. It urges the UN to enforce the minimum standards for the treatment of prisoners, and campaigns for the abolition of corporal and capital punishment.

Howards End 1 a novel by E M Forster (1910). It focuses on the problematic relationships between the cultured Schlegel sisters and the business-orientated Wilcox family. 2 a British film produced by Ismail Merchant and directed by James Ivory (1992), based on the novel. The Schlegel sisters are played by Emma Thompson (who won a Best Actress Oscar for the part) and Helena Bonham-Carter, with Anthony Hopkins as Henry Wilcox and Vanessa Redgrave as his first wife.

howdah *noun* a seat, usually with a sun-shade, used for riding on an elephant's back. [from Arabic *hawdaj*]

howdy *interj. North Amer. slang* hello. [a corrupt form of *how do you do?*]

Howe, Richard Howe, 1st Earl (1726–99) English admiral, born in London. He entered the navy at 13, and distinguished himself in the Seven Years' War (1756–63). His positions included Treasurer of the Navy (1765) and First Lord of the Admiralty (1783). In 1778 he defended the American coast against a superior French force, and in the French Revolutionary Wars defeated the French at 'the glorious first of June' (1794).

Howe, William Howe, 5th Viscount (1729–1814) British soldier who commanded the army in N America during the American Revolution. He joined the army in 1746, served under Wolfe at Louisburg (1758) and Quebec, where he led the famous advance to the Heights of Abraham, and became an MP in 1758. In the American War of Independence his victories included Bunker's Hill (1775), Brandywine Creek (1777), and the capture of New York City (1776).

Howe (of Aberavon), (Richard Edward) Geoffrey Howe, Baron (1926–) English Conservative politician. Called to the Bar in 1952, he became an MP in 1964, and was Solicitor-General (1970–2), Minister for Trade and Consumer Affairs (1972–4), Chancellor of

the Exchequer (1979–1983), and Foreign Secretary (1983–9). In 1989 he was made Deputy Prime Minister, Lord President of the Council, and Leader of the House of Commons, but he resigned (Nov 1990) over Margaret Thatcher's hostility towards European Monetary Union, a move that was instrumental in bringing about her downfall.

however *adv.* 1 in spite of that; nevertheless. 2 *colloq., especially implying surprise* in what way?; by what means?: *however did you do that?* 3 by whatever means: *do it however you want to.* 4 to no matter what extent: *you must finish this however long it takes.* [from Middle English]

howitzer *noun* a short heavy gun which fires shells high in the air. [from Czech *houfnice*, sling, catapult]

howl — *noun* 1 the long, loud, sad cry of a wolf or dog. 2 a long, loud cry made eg by the wind. 3 a cry of pain or distress. 4 a loud yell of laughter. — *verb* 1 *intrans.* to make a long, loud, sad cry or similar wailing noise. 2 *intrans.* to cry or laugh loudly. 3 to shout or shriek (instructions, orders, etc).
— **howl someone down** to prevent a speaker from being heard by shouting loudly and angrily. [from Middle English *houlen*]

howler *noun colloq.* a glaring mistake.

howler monkey the largest of the S American monkeys, having black, brown, or reddish fur, and so called because it often howls at dawn in order to warn others off its territory.

howling *adj. colloq.* very great.

howsoever *adv.* in whatever way; to whatever extent. [from Middle English]

howzat *interj.* an appeal to the umpire in cricket to give the batsman out. [a contraction of *how's that*]

Hoxha or **Hodja Enver** (1908–85) Albanian politician, born in Gjirokastër. He founded and led the Albanian Communist Party (1941) in the fight for national independence. In 1946 he deposed King Zog (who had fled in 1939), and became head of state, first as Prime Minister (1946–54), then as Party Secretary (1954–85).

hoy *interj.* a word used to attract someone's attention. [a variant of HEY]

hoyden *noun* a wild, lively girl. [from Dutch *heyden*, boor]

hoydenish *adj.* like a hoyden; boisterous.

Hoyle, Edmond (1672–1769) English writer on card games, called the 'father of whist'. His popular *Short Treatise on Whist* (1742) ran into many editions, and was ultimately incorporated with his manuals on backgammon, brag, quadrille, piquet, and chess into an omnibus volume (1748).

Hoyle, Sir Fred (1915–) English astronomer and mathematician, born in Bingley, Yorkshire. Professor at Cambridge University and later at Cornell, he was one of the developers of the influential but now discredited 'steady state' theory of the universe, which proposes that the universe is uniform in space and unchanging in time. He also suggested the currently accepted scenario of the build-up to supernovae, in which a chain of nuclear reactions in a star is followed by a massive explosion, in which the matter is ejected into space, and recycled in second-generation stars which form from the remnants.

HP or **hp** *abbrev.* 1 high pressure. 2 *Brit.* hire purchase. 3 horsepower.

HQ or **hq** *abbrev.* headquarters.

hr *abbrev.* hour.

HRH *abbrev.* His or Her Royal Highness.

HRT *abbrev.* hormone replacement therapy.

Hua Guofeng or **Hua Kuo-feng** (1920–) Chinese statesman and Prime Minister

(1976–80), born in Hunan province. He was Vice-Governor of Hunan (1958–67), but came under attack during the Cultural Revolution (1966–76). A member of the Central Committee of the Party from 1969 and of the Politburo from 1973, he became Deputy Prime Minister and Minister of Public Security (1975–6), and in 1976 was made Prime Minister and Chairman of the Central Committee. Under him China adopted closer relations with Western and Third World countries. He resigned as Chairman in 1981.

Huangguoshu Falls a waterfall on the Bai Shui R, in W Guizhou province, S central China. It is the largest waterfall in the country, 84m wide, with a drop of 67m. At the side of the falls is Waterfall Cave, a 100m-long cavern set in the cliff face.

Huang He see YELLOW RIVER.

Huang Ho see YELLOW RIVER.

Huang, Mount, Chinese **Mount Huangshan** a mountain in the Huang (Huangshan) Mountains, S Anhwei province, China. It is 1 402m high, and is noted for its scenery (eg pine trees, waterfalls, caves, hot springs). It is a World Heritage site.

Huang-ti in Chinese mythology, the third emperor of China, and the patron saint of Taoism. He was also the founder of civilization, and the inventor of chariots, ships, and houses. On his death he was believed to have become an immortal. [Chinese, = yellow emperor]

Huari an ancient Andean city near Ayacucho, the capital (c.650–800) of a powerful pre-Inca empire which controlled much of Peru N of Cuzco. Its art and pottery styles are similar to those in evidence at Tiahuanaco.

Huascarán a national park in W Peru. It consists of the Cordillera Blanca, part of the Andean Cordillera Occidental. It rises to 6 768m at the Nevado de Huascarán, the highest peak in Peru. The park, established in 1975, is a World Heritage site. AREA 3 400sq km/1 312sq mi.

hub noun **1** the centre of a wheel. **2** the main point of activity, interest, etc. [perhaps a variant of HOB]

Hubbard, Ron (Lafayette Ronald) (1911–86) US writer and founder of the Church of Scientology, born in Tilden, Nebraska. He wrote science-fiction before his best-selling work, *Dianetics: The Modern Science of Mental Health* (1950) became the basic text of the scientology movement. Hubbard, who claimed to have visited heaven twice, was banned (1968) from re-entering Britain amid public concern over his aims and methods. In the 1980s he went into seclusion and returned to fiction writing.

Hubble, Edwin Powell (1889–1953) US astronomer, born in Marshfield, Missouri. Working at Mount Wilson Observatory, he determined the distance to the Andromeda nebula (1923), and recognized that spiral nebulae are independent stellar systems, often similar to our own Milky Way galaxy. In 1929 he announced his discovery that galaxies recede from us with speeds which increase in direct proportion to their distance (Hubble's law), confirming that our universe is expanding. The Hubble Space Telescope launched in 1990 was named in his honour.

hubble-bubble noun **1** a bubbling sound. **2** confusion; confused talk. **3** a simple type of hookah. [a fanciful elaboration of BUBBLE]

Hubble's constant or **Hubble constant** Astron. a constant that describes the rate at which the universe is expanding by relating the speed at which a galaxy is moving away from us to its distance. [named after Edwin Hubble]
◇ The exact value of the constant is not known, but the galaxies have been estimated to be moving away at a speed of 49-95km s^{-1} for each million parsecs of distance. The reciprocal of Hubble's constant corresponds approximately to

the age of the universe (which according to the Big Bang theory began at one point), and suggests that it is now 10 to 20 billion years old.

Hubble's law Astron. the law which states that the speed at which a galaxy is moving away increases as it becomes more distant (as measured by the redshift), due to the uniform expansion of the universe.

Hubble space telescope an optical telescope that was launched into orbit around the Earth in Apr 1990 in the space shuttle *Discovery*, as a joint project of the European Space Agency and NASA.
◇ The Hubble space telescope has a reflecting mirror 2.4m in diameter, and was designed to allow astronomers to observe the stars without the distortion caused by the Earth's atmosphere. It was expected to produce sharper images of objects than telescopes on Earth, and to detect fainter sources. However, following the launch, the mirror was found to have a defect which meant that it could not be focused properly, and in Dec 1993 a maintenance mission, *Endeavour*, was sent to install instruments that would counteract the effect of the defect in the mirror. Spacewalking astronauts also replaced a camera, installed new solar panels, and made various other repairs, and much more sharply focused images have been obtained subsequently.

hubbub noun **1** a confused noise of many sounds, especially voices. **2** uproar. [probably of Irish origin]

hubby noun (PL. **hubbies**) colloq. a husband. [abbreviation]

hub-cap noun the metal cover over the hub of a wheel.

Hubel, David Hunter (1926–) Canadian-born US neurophysiologist, born in Windsor, Ontario. Professor at Harvard, his investigations of the mechanisms of visual perception provided a complex picture of the analysis of visual information by brain cells. He shared the 1981 Nobel Prize for Physiology or Medicine with Roger Sperry and Torsten Wiesel.

hubris noun arrogance or over-confidence, especially when likely to end in disaster or ruin. [from Greek *hybris*]

huckleberry noun Bot. **1** either of two species of plant belonging to the genus *Gaylussacia*, native to woodlands and swamps of eastern N America. **2** the round fruit of this plant, which is either bluish or black, depending on the species. **3** sometimes used incorrectly to refer to blueberry.

Huckleberry Finn, The Adventures of a novel by Mark Twain (1884). It describes the adventures on the Mississippi River of the narrator Huck with Jim, a runaway slave.

huckster noun **1** old use a street trader. **2** an aggressive seller. [from Middle English *huccstere*]

Huddersfield POP (1981) 149 000, an industrial town in Kirklees borough, West Yorkshire, N England. It lies on the R Colne, 17km/10mi S of Bradford. In the 18c it was a centre of the textile industry, especially wool.

huddle — verb **1** trans., intrans. (**huddle together** or **up**) to heap or crowd together closely. **2** intrans. to sit curled up. **3** to curl (oneself) up. — noun **1** a confused mass or crowd. **2** a secret or private conference: *go into a huddle.* [probably related to HIDE^1]

Huddleston, Trevor (1913–) English Anglican missionary and human rights campaigner. Ordained in 1937, he entered the Community of the Resurrection, and in 1943 went to Johannesburg, where he became provincial of the order (1949–55). After working in England (1956–60), he became Bishop of Masasi, Tanzania (1960–8), Bishop Suffragan of Stepney until 1978, then Bishop of Mauritius and Archbishop of the Indian Ocean. He retired and

returned to London to become Chairman of the Anti-Apartheid Movement (1981). His books include *Naught for your Comfort* (1956), which arose from his experience of the racial problems in South Africa, *God's World* (1966), and *I Believe: Reflections on the Apostles' Creed* (1986).

Hudson, Henry (c.1550–1611) English navigator, who explored the NE coast of N America. He sailed in search of a passage across the North Pole in 1607. He reached Novaya Zemlya in 1608, and in 1609, on his third voyage, he discovered the Hudson River. In 1610, he travelled through the strait and bay which now bear his name. During the winter there, food fell short, the men mutinied, and he and eight others were cast adrift to die.

Hudson, William (1734–93) English botanist and apothecary, born in Kendal. Demonstrator to the Apothecaries' Company at Chelsea Physic Garden (1765–7), his *Flora Anglica* (1762) was the first British botanical work to adopt the Linnaean classification system and its binomial nomenclature, and contained much original work; he also studied insects and molluscs. See LINNAEUS, CAROLUS.

Hudson Bay a large inland sea in Northwest Territories, Canada. It is connected to the Arctic Ocean via the Foxe Basin and Channel, and to the Atlantic Ocean by the 800km/500mi-long Hudson Strait. AREA c.1 230 250sq km/ 475 000sq mi; maximum length c.1 600km/ 1 000mi, including James Bay in the S; maximum width c.1 000km/650mi. It is slowly becoming shallower, and is generally ice-clogged (but open to navigation mid-Jul–Oct). The E shore is rocky, fringed by small islands. English navigator Henry Hudson was the first to explore the bay (1610) during his search for the Northwest Passage.

Hudson River a river in NE USA, length 560km/350mi. Rising in the Adirondack Mts, New York State, it flows S past New York City to meet the Atlantic Ocean. It is navigable for large craft as far as Albany and is tidal for 240km/150mi. English navigator Henry Hudson explored the river in 1609.

Hué POP (1989) 211 000, a town in Binh Tri Thien province, central Vietnam. It is situated near the mouth of the R Hué, 8km/5mi from the South China Sea. An ancient town, it was part of the Chinese Empire and the former capital of Annam and of the Vietnamese Empire. Many of the town's historical sites were destroyed in the Vietnam War.

hue^1 noun **1** a colour or shade. **2** the feature of a colour which makes it different from other colours. **3** aspect. [from Anglo-Saxon *hiw*]

hue^2 noun
— **hue and cry** a loud public protest. [from Old French *huer*]

Huelva, Latin **Onuba** POP (1991) 141 000, the river-port capital of Huelva province, Andalucia, SW Spain. It lies in the delta of the Odiel and Tinto rivers, 632km/393mi SW of Madrid.

huff — noun a fit of anger or annoyance: *in a huff.* — verb **1** intrans. to blow or puff loudly. **2** trans., intrans. to give or take offence. **3** *Draughts* to remove an opponent's man for failing to capture one's own man.
— **huffing and puffing** loud empty threats. [imitative]

huffily adv. in a huffy way.

huffiness noun being huffy.

huffy or **huffish** adj. (**huffier**, **huffiest**) **1** offended. **2** easily offended; touchy.

hug — verb (**hugged**, **hugging**) **1** to hold tightly in one's arms, especially to show love. **2** to keep close to: *a ship hugging the shore.* **3** to hold (a belief, etc) very firmly. — noun a tight grasp with the arms, especially to show love. [perhaps from Norse *hugga*, to soothe]

huge *adj.* very large. [from Old French *ahuge*]

hugely *adv.* very; very much.

hugeness *noun* being huge.

hugger-mugger — *noun* **1** secrecy. **2** confusion. — *adj., adv.* **1** secret; in secret. **2** confused; in confusion or disorder. [from Middle English *hokeren*, to hoard]

Huggins, Sir William (1824–1910) English astronomer, born in London. Working at his private observatory near London, his studied the spectra of many astronomical objects, including comets, stars and nebulae, and revealed that certain nebulae were composed of luminous gases. He used the Doppler shift in the spectra of stars as a means of measuring their radial motion, and with his wife pioneered dry plate photography in astronomy.

Hugh *or* **Huw** a male first name, particularly popular in Wales. [Norman, from Germanic *hug*, heart, mind, spirit; in Ireland, sometimes taken as an Anglicization of *Aodh*, fire]

Hughes, Howard (Robard) (1905–76) US millionaire businessman, film producer and director, and aviator, born in Houston, Texas. He inherited his father's oil-drilling equipment company at 18, and in 1926 began to involve himself in Hollywood, producing several films. He became known as an eccentric, left Hollywood in 1932, and began to design, build, and fly aircraft. He broke most of the world's air speed records (1935–8), then returned to film-making, producing and directing *The Outlaw* (1943). After severe injuries in an air crash (1946), his eccentricity increased. He eventually became a recluse, and lived in complete seclusion from 1966.

Hughes, Ted (Edward James) (1930–) English poet, born in Mytholmroyd, Yorkshire. Best known for his animal poems, his first collection was *The Hawk in the Rain* (1957). He married the US poet, Sylvia Plath, in 1956, and after her death edited her collected poems (1981). Other works include *Wodwo* (1967), *Crow* (1970), and *Rain-charm for the Duchy* (1992). He also writes for children, his publications in that genre including the story *The Iron Man* (1968). His *Selected Poems, 1957–81* appeared in 1982, and he was made Poet Laureate in 1984.

Hughes, Thomas (1822–96) English novelist, born in Uffington, Berkshire. He was called to the Bar in 1848 and became a county court judge in 1882. A Liberal MP (1865–74), he was closely associated with the Christian Socialists and helped to found the Working Men's College (1854), of which he became principal (1872–83). He is primarily remembered as the author of the public-school novel *Tom Brown's Schooldays* (1856).

Huguenot *Hist.* — *noun* a French Protestant (see HUGUENOTS). — *adj.* relating to the Huguenots. [from French *Huguenot*]

Huguenots French Calvinist Protestants whose political rivalry with Catholics (eg the House of Guise) led to the French Wars of Religion (1562–98). Their leader, Henry of Navarre (Henry IV), succeeded to the throne (1589) and granted them important concessions on his conversion to Catholicism (Edict of Nantes, 1598), but these were later revoked by Louis XIV (1685), which resulted in persecution and emigration.

Huguenots, The an opera by Giacomo Meyerbeer (1836) to a libretto by Eugène Scribe (1791–1861) and Emile Deschamps (1791–1871). It is a story of love and conflict between the opposing parties of aristocratic Catholics and Huguenots in 16c France.

huh *interj. colloq.* an expression of disgust, disbelief or inquiry. [imitative]

Huila Peak an Andean volcanic peak in S central Colombia. Rising to 5 750m, it is Columbia's second highest peak.

Huis Clos (In Camera; Vicious Circle; No Exit) a play by Jean-Paul Sartre (1943). It is a tale of three people in Hell who discover that they are assigned to be each other's perpetual tormentors.

Huitzilopochtli Aztec god of the Sun and of war, depicted as a hummingbird or as a warrior adorned in hummingbird feathers. The Aztecs believed that at the time of death a warrior was changed into a hummingbird. He was also credited with founding Tenochtitlan, the Aztec capital, in 1325 in the Valley of Mexico.

Huitzilopochtli

hula *noun* a Hawaiian dance in which the dancer sways his or her hips and moves his or her arms gracefully. [from Hawaiian *hula*]

hulk *noun* **1** the body of an old ship from which everything has been taken away. **2** a ship which is or looks difficult to steer. **3** *derog. colloq.* a large, awkward person or thing. **4** *Hist.* the body of an old ship used as a prison. [from Anglo-Saxon *hulc*]

hulking *adj. derog. colloq.* large and awkward.

Hull, Cordell (1871–1955) US politician, born in Overton, Tennessee. He became Secretary of State under Theodore Roosevelt in 1933, and served for the longest term in that office until he retired in 1944, having attended most of the great wartime conferences. He was a strong advocate of maximum aid to the Allies, and helped to organize the United Nations, for which he received the Nobel Peace Prize in 1944.

Hull, properly **Kingston-upon-Hull** POP (1992e) 269 000, a seaport in Humberside, NE England. It lies at the junction of the Hull and Humber rivers, 35km/22mi from the North Sea and 330km/205mi N of London. Hull was granted city status in 1897 and is now a major container port. NOTABLE FEATURES William Wilberforce house; Holy Trinity Church; Humber Bridge.

Hull POP (1991) 61 000, a town in S Quebec, SE Canada, lying on the Ottawa R, NW of Ottawa. It was founded in 1801 by settlers from the USA.

hull[1] — *noun* the frame or body of a ship or airship. — *verb* to pierce the hull of. [perhaps from HULL[2]]

hull[2] — *noun* the outer covering of certain fruit and vegetables, especially the pod of beans and peas and the green leaves and stem at the bottom of a strawberry. — *verb* to remove the hulls from (fruit and vegetables). [from Anglo-Saxon *hulu*, husk]

hullabaloo *noun colloq.* an uproar. [from Scot. *baloo*, lullaby]

hullo see HELLO.

Hulton, Sir Edward (George Warris) (1906–88) English magazine proprietor and journalist, born in Harrogate. He succeeded to his father's newspaper interests and became Chairman of Hulton Press Ltd. He was founder of

Picture Post, a brilliant experiment in journalism (1938–57).

hum — *verb* (**hummed, humming**) **1** *intrans.* to make a low, steady murmuring sound like a bee. **2** *trans., intrans.* to sing (a tune) with one's mouth shut. **3** *intrans.* to speak indistinctly or stammer, especially through embarrassment. **4** *intrans. colloq.* to be full of activity. **5** *intrans. slang* to give off an unpleasant smell. — *noun* **1** a humming sound. **2** *slang* a bad smell. — *interj.* an expression of hesitation.
— **hum and haw** to make sounds which express doubt, uncertainty or hesitation; to hesitate.

human — *adj.* **1** of or belonging to people. **2** having or showing the qualities, especially the weaknesses, of people as opposed to God, animals, or machines. **3** having the better qualities of people, eg in being kind, thoughtful, etc. — *noun* a human being. [from Latin *humanus*, from *homo*, man]

human being *noun* a person.

Human Comedy, The see COMÉDIE HUMAINE, LA.

Human Condition, The two paintings by René Magritte (1934, 1935).

humane *adj.* **1** kind; sympathetic. **2** *said of a killing* done with as little pain and suffering as possible. **3** *said of a branch of learning* likely to civilize or make more elegant. [a variant of HUMAN]

humanely *adv.* in a humane way.

humaneness *noun* being humane.

Humanism a philosophical and literary movement which stresses the importance of people and their capabilities. The movement arose in the Renaissance, and emphasized the liberation of humanity from the control of the medieval Church and State. Thinkers and writers who have been described as humanists include Boccaccio, Erasmus, and Thomas More.

humanism *noun* a non-religious system of thought which holds that humans are responsible and intelligent beings, capable by themselves of solving the problems of the world and deciding what is or is not correct moral behaviour.

humanist — *noun* **1** a follower of humanism. **2** *Hist.* a student of Greek and Roman culture during the Renaissance. — *adj.* of humanism or humanists.

humanistic *adj.* relating to or involving humanism.

humanitarian — *adj.* concerned about improving, or likely to improve, people's lives: *humanitarian aid for the war-zone.* — *noun* a person who tries to improve the quality of people's lives by means of reform, charity, etc.

humanitarianism *noun* humanitarian principles, system, or practice.

humanity *noun* (PL. **humanities**) **1** the human race. **2** the nature of human beings. **3** the qualities of human beings, especially in being kind or showing mercy. **4** (**humanities**) subjects involving the study of human culture, especially language, literature, and philosophy.

humanization *or* **humanisation** *noun* the act or process of humanizing.

humanize *or* **humanise** *verb* to make more caring, more thoughtful, less brutal, etc.

humankind *noun* human beings as a race.

humanly *adv.* within human power.

humanoid — *noun* an animal or machine with human characteristics. — *adj., said of an animal or machine* having human characteristics. [from HUMAN + -oid, from Greek *eidos*, form]

human rights the rights of every person to justice and freedom.
◇ First formally incorporated into the US Declaration of Independence (1776), a Declaration of the Rights of Man and the Citizen

was adopted by the French National Assembly (1789). The UN General Assembly adopted a Universal Declaration of Human Rights in 1948, detailing individual and social rights and freedoms. Under the European Convention of Human Rights (1953), the Council of Europe established the European Commission of Human Rights which together with the European Court of Human Rights (established 1959) investigates and examines complaints by states or individuals.

human shield *Mil.* a non-combatant person or group of people deployed in strategic sites during hostilities, in order to deter enemy attack on those sites.

Humber, River a river estuary in Humberside, NE England, length 64km/40mi. It is formed by the Ouse and Trent rivers, and its entrance is dominated by Spurn Head. Hull is on the N shore of the estuary, Immingham and Grimsby on the S. The Humber Bridge, the largest single-span suspension bridge in the world, was completed in 1981.

Humber Bridge the longest single-span suspension bridge in the world, built (1973–81) across the R Humber, England. It has a main span of 1 410m and its total length is 2 220m.

Humberside POP (1992e) 881 000, a county in NE England, divided into nine districts. AREA 3 512sq km/1 356sq mi. It is bounded E by the North Sea, N and NW by North Yorkshire, SW by South Yorkshire, and S by Nottinghamshire and Lincolnshire. PHYSICAL DESCRIPTION drained by the R Humber which flows into the North Sea; the county is divided by the Humber Estuary. CHIEF TOWNS Hull (county town), Beverley, Scunthorpe, Grimsby, Goole, Immingham. ECONOMY cereals; sugar beet; livestock; fishing; iron and steel; chemicals; petrochemicals.

Humbert, Humbert the psycopathic Swiss literary historian, obsessed with the adolescent Lolita, in Vladimir Nabokov's *Lolita*.

humble¹ — *adj.* **1** having a low opinion of oneself and one's abilities, etc; not proud. **2** having a low position in society. **3** lowly; modest. — *verb* to make humble, modest or of less importance. HUMILITY [from Latin *humilis*, low]

humble²
— **eat humble pie** to be forced to make a humble apology.
[a variant of *numbles*, the offal of a deer]

humbleness *noun* being humble.

humbly *adv.* in a humble way.

Humboldt, (Friedrich Wilhelm Heinrich) Alexander, Baron von (1769–1859) German naturalist and geographer, born in Berlin. From 1799 he spent five years with Aimé Bonpland (1773–1858) exploring S America. He worked mainly in France until 1827, then explored central Asia. From 1830 he was employed in political service. His major work, *Kosmos* (1845–62), endeavours to provide a comprehensive physical picture of the universe. The ocean current off the west coast of S America is named after him.

humbug *noun* **1** a trick; something done to deceive. **2** nonsense; rubbish. **3** a person who pretends to be something he or she is not. **4** *Brit.* a hard, stripy, peppermint-flavoured sweet.

humdinger *noun slang* an exceptionally good person or thing. [a fanciful elaboration of HUM + DING]

humdrum *adj.* dull; ordinary. [probably from HUM]

Hume, Cardinal (George) Basil (1923–) English Roman Catholic Benedictine monk and cardinal, born in Newcastle-upon-tyne. Ordained in 1950, he became Magister Scholarum of the English Benedictine Congregation (1957–63), and then abbot of Ampleforth, where he remained until created Archbishop of Westminster and a

cardinal in 1976. His books include *Searching for God* (1977) and *In Praise of Benedict* (1981).

Hume, David (1711–76) Scottish philosopher and historian, born in Edinburgh. In 1734 he went to La Flèche in Anjou, where he wrote his major work, *A Treatise of Human Nature* (1739–40), in which he consolidated and extended the empiricist legacy of John Locke and George Berkeley. His views became widely known only when he wrote two volumes of *Essays Moral and Political* (1741–2). He wrote the posthumously published *Dialogues concerning Natural Religion* in the 1750s. His atheism thwarted his applications for professorships at Edinburgh and Glasgow, and he became a tutor, secretary, and keeper of the Advocates' Library in Edinburgh, where he published his popular *Political Discourses* (1752), and his six-volume *History of England* (1754–62).

Hume, Joseph (1777–1855) Scottish radical politician, born in Montrose, Tayside. Trained in medicine, he was assistant surgeon under the East India Company (1797–1808). He returned to England, and sat in parliament (1812, 1819–55), where his arguments for reform included the legalizing of trade unions, freedom of trade with India, and the abolition of army flogging, naval impressment (seizure for service), and imprisonment for debt.

humeral *adj.* relating to or in the region of the humerus or shoulders.

humerus *noun* (PL. **humeri**) the bone in the upper part of the arm. [from Latin *umerus*, shoulder]

humid *adj.* damp; moist. [from Latin *humidus*]

humidifier *noun* an apparatus for maintaining or increasing the humidity of a room, etc.

humidify *verb* (**humidifies, humidified**) to make (the air or atmosphere) damp or humid.

humidity *noun* **1** *Meteorol.* a measure of the amount of water vapour in the atmosphere, usually expressed as a percentage. **2** dampness.

humiliate *verb* to make (someone) feel ashamed or look foolish, especially in the presence of others. [from Latin *humilis*, humble]

humiliating *adj.* shaming, humbling, embarrassing.

humiliatingly *adv.* in a humiliating way.

humiliation *noun* **1** the act of humiliating. **2** being humiliated.

humility *noun* **1** the state or quality of being humble. **2** lowliness of mind; modesty. [from Latin *humilis*, humble]

hummingbird *noun* a small bird with brilliant plumage, often with iridescent patches, found mainly in the forests of S America, and so called because its wings beat so rapidly that they produce a low humming sound. Its fast wing-beats enable the bird to hover, and to fly backwards, sideways, upwards, or downwards. It feeds constantly on nectar, which it extracts from flowers using its long tubular tongue while hovering in mid-air. The bee hummingbird is the world's smallest bird.

hummock *noun* a low hill.

hummus or **hoummos** or **houmus** *noun* a Middle Eastern hors d'oeuvre or dip consisting of pureed cooked chickpeas and tahini paste, flavoured with lemon juice and garlic. [from Turkish *humus*]

humongous or **humungous** *adj. colloq.* huge, enormous. [perhaps a mixture of HUGE and MONSTROUS]

humorist *noun* a person who writes or tells humorous stories, jokes, etc.

humorous *adj.* containing humour; funny; amusing.

humorously *adv.* in a humorous way.

humorousness *noun* being humorous.

humour — *noun* **1** the quality of being amusing. **2** the ability to amuse or be amused. **3** a state of mind: *good humour*. **4** writing, plays, speech, etc that are amusing or funny. **5** any of various fluids in the body. **6** *Hist.* any of the four bodily fluids (blood, choler, melancholy, and phlegm) which were formerly believed to govern a person's physical health and character. — *verb* to please (someone) by doing what they wish. [from Latin *humor*]

humourless *adj.* without humour.

hump — *noun* **1** a large rounded lump of fat on the back of a camel that serves as an energy store when food is scarce. **2** an abnormal outward curvature of the spine, giving the back a hunched appearance, caused by a deformity of the spine, in some cases present at birth. **3** a rounded lump on a road. **4** *Brit. colloq.* a feeling of unhappiness or annoyance. — *verb* **1** (**hump something about** or **around**) to carry (especially something awkward or heavy) with difficulty. **2** *trans., intrans. coarse slang* to have sexual intercourse with (someone).

humpback — *noun* **1** a back with a hump. **2** a hunchback. **3** a whale with a fin on its back which forms a hump. — *adj.* (also **humpbacked**) rising and falling in the shape of a hump; having a hump.

humpback bridge a bridge with steep slopes on either side.

Humperdinck, Engelbert (1854–1921) German composer, born in Siegburg, near Bonn. He studied music, travelled widely in Europe as a teacher, and gained fame for the highly successful fairy opera *Hänsel und Gretel* (1893). *Schneewittchen, Königskinder* (opera, 1910), *The Miracle* (pantomime, 1912), and others followed.

humph *interj.* an expression of doubt or displeasure. [imitative]

Humphrey, Doris (1895–1958) US dancer, choreographer, and teacher, born in Oak Park, Illinois. She studied a range of dance forms, including ballroom, before turning to become one of the founders of modern dance. She and Charles Weidman (1901–75) formed a group in 1928, and toured with performances of her own choreography, which were often concerned with form and based on musical structures, eg *With my Red Fires* (1935–6) and *Day on Earth* (1947). She also wrote *The Art of Making Dances* (1959), the key text on dance composition in modern dance.

Humphrey, Hubert H(oratio) (1911–78) US Democratic politician, born in Wallace, South Dakota. He became Mayor of Minneapolis in 1945, and was elected Senator in 1948. He built up a strong reputation as a liberal, particularly concerning the civil rights issue, but as Lyndon B Johnson's Vice-President (from 1964), he alienated many by his apparent support of the continuation of the war in Vietnam. Although he won the Democratic presidential nomination in 1968, a substantial minority of Democrats opposed him and he was narrowly defeated by Richard Nixon, after which he returned to the Senate.

Humphrey a male first name, now less common. [Norman, from Germanic *hun*, bear-cub, warrior + *fred, frid*, peace]

Humphry Clinker, The Expedition of an epistolary novel by Tobias Smollett (1771). It chronicles the comic adventures which befall the various characters on a round journey from Wales to London and Scotland and back.

Humpty Doo POP (1981) 1 000, a town in Northern Territory, Australia. NOTABLE FEATURES Graeme Gow's Reptile Park, a collection of Australia's most venomous snakes and reptiles; bird sanctuary.

Humpty-Dumpty an egg-shaped nursery-rhyme character prone to falling off walls, who also features as a crotchety figure in Lewis Carroll's *Through the Looking-Glass*.

humus *noun* dark brown organic material that is produced in the topmost layer of soil as a result of the decomposition of plant and animal matter by fungi and bacteria. [from Latin *humus*, soil]

Hun *noun* **1** *Hist.* a member of a powerful and warlike people who invaded Europe in the 4c and 5c. **2** *offensive colloq.* a German. [from Anglo-Saxon *Hune*]

hunch — *noun* **1** an idea or belief based on one's feelings, suspicions, or intuition rather than on clear evidence. **2** a hump. — *verb* **1** to bend or arch. **2** *intrans.* (*also* **hunch up**) to sit with one's body curled up or bent.

hunchback *noun* a person with a large rounded lump on his or her back, usually caused by a problem with the spine.

hunchbacked *adj.* having a deformed back.

Hunchback of Notre Dame, The a US film directed by William Dieterle (1939). Charles Laughton plays the hunchbacked bellringer Quasimodo who saves the life of beautiful gypsy girl Esmeralda (Maureen O'Hara) in 15c Paris.

hundred — *noun* (PL. **hundreds**, after another number **hundred**) **1** the number which is 10 times 10. **2** a numeral, figure or symbol representing this, eg *100°C*. **3** a set of 100 people or things: *one hundred pounds*. **4** a score of 100 points. **5** (*usually* **hundreds**) *colloq.* very many: *hundreds of people.* **6** (**hundreds**) *in cmpds* the 100 years of a particular century: *the thirteen-hundreds.* **7** *Hist.* a division of an English county. — *adj.* totalling 100. [from Anglo-Saxon *hundred*]

Hundred Days an interlude (Mar–Jun 1815) between Napoleon I's escape from Elba and his defeat at the battle of Waterloo, during which he returned to Paris and tried to reconstitute the First Empire. He was finally exiled to St Helena.

hundredfold — *adj.* **1** equal to 100 times as much. **2** divided into or consisting of 100 parts. — *adv.* by 100 times as much.

hundreds and thousands tiny balls of coloured sugar used to decorate cakes.

hundredth *noun, adj.* **1** the position in a series corresponding to 100 in a sequence of numbers. **2** one of 100 equal parts.

hundredweight *noun* (PL. **hundredweight**, **hundredweights**) **1** (*also* **long hundredweight**) *Brit.* a measure of weight equal to 112 pounds (50·8kg). **2** (*also* **short hundredweight**) *North Amer.* a measure of weight equal to 100 pounds (45·4kg). **3** (*also* **metric hundredweight**) a metric measure of weight equal to 50kg.

Hundred Years' War a series of wars between England and France. Conventionally dated 1337–1453, they formed part of a longer contest which began when England was linked first with Normandy (1066), and then Anjou and Aquitaine (1154). In the 13c, the Capetians aimed to rule all France, but when Edward III claimed the French throne and styled himself 'King of England and France' (from 1340), traditional rivalries became a dynastic struggle. Under Henry V (1415–22) the English turned from raiding to territorial conquest, a task ultimately beyond their resources. Only the Channel Is were retained after Calais was lost (1588) but the title of King of France was not relinquished until 1801.

hung — *verb* see HANG. — *adj.*, *said of a parliament or jury* with no one side having a majority.
— **hung over** *colloq.* suffering from a hangover.
hung up on something *colloq.* extremely anxious about it, especially needlessly.

Hungarian — *adj.* of Hungary or its official language. — *noun* **1** a citizen of or person from Hungary. **2** the official language of Hungary.

Hungarian Uprising a national insurrection (Oct–Nov 1956) centred on Budapest following the denunciation of Stalin at the 20th Congress of the Soviet Communist Party for his oppressive rule. Rioting students and workers demolished statues of Stalin and demanded radical reform, and when the new Prime Minister Imre Nagy announced his plans (eg for Hungary's withdrawal from the Warsaw Pact), Soviet troops and tanks crushed the uprising. Many were killed, thousands fled abroad, and Nagy was executed.

Hungary, Hungarian **Magyarország**, official name **Hungarian People's Republic**, Hungarian **Magyar Népköztársasg** POP (1993e) 10.3m, a landlocked state in the Danube basin, central Europe, divided into 19 counties. AREA 93 036sq km/35 912sq mi. It is bounded N by Slovakia, E by the Ukraine and Romania, S by Yugoslavia, SW by Croatia, and W by Slovenia and Austria. CAPITAL Budapest. CHIEF TOWNS Miskolc, Debrecen, Szeged, Pécs, Györ. TIME ZONE GMT +1. The population is mainly Magyar (92%), with several minorities; Roman Catholicism and Calvinism (20%) are the chief religions. OFFICIAL LANGUAGE Magyar. CURRENCY the forint. PHYSICAL DESCRIPTION drained by the R Danube (flowing N–S) and its tributaries; there is frequent flooding, especially in the Great Plains, E of the Danube; a low spur of the Alps crosses Hungary in the W, separating the Little Hungarian Plain from the Transdanubian downlands; the highest peak is Kékes (1 014m). CLIMATE the landlocked position gives a fairly extreme continental climate with a marked difference between summer and winter; it is wettest in spring and early summer; winters are cold with snow lying for 30–40 days and the R Danube is sometimes frozen over for long periods; fog is frequent during settled winter weather. HISTORY a kingdom was formed under St Stephen I in the 11c; conquered by Turks in 1526; became part of the Habsburg Empire in the 17c; Austria and Hungary were reconstituted as a dual monarchy in 1867; after World War I Hungary became a republic, but a communist revolt introduced a new regime in 1919; a monarchical constitution was restored in 1920; a new republic under communist government was formed in 1949; Soviet forces crushed an uprising in 1956; in 1989 pressure for political change was led from within the Communist Party; the same year Hungary was declared a democratic state and in 1990 multiparty elections were held. GOVERNMENT governed by a unicameral legislature (National Assembly), elected every five years; this elects the executive 21-member Presidential Council and the 17-member Council of Ministers. ECONOMY large-scale nationalization took place in 1946–9 as part of the centralized planning strategy of the new republic; greater independence was given to individual factories and farms from 1968; agriculture includes grain, potatoes, sugar beet, fruit, and wine; coal, bauxite, and lignite are mined; main industries are metallurgy, engineering, chemicals, textiles, and food processing.

Hungary

hunger — *noun* **1** the desire or need, especially very great, for food. **2** a strong desire: *hunger for affection.* — *verb intrans.* (**hungered, hungering**) (**hunger for** *or* **after something**) to have a strong desire for it. [from Anglo-Saxon *hungor*]

hunger strike a prolonged refusal to eat, usually by a prisoner as a form of protest.

hunger striker a person protesting by means of a hunger strike.

hungrily *adv.* **1** in a hungry way. **2** eagerly.

hungriness *noun* being hungry.

hungry *adj.* (**hungrier, hungriest**) **1** wanting or needing food. **2** (**hungry for something**) having a great desire for it. **3** greedy; eager: *hungry eyes.* [from Anglo-Saxon *hungrig*]

hunk *noun* **1** a lump broken or cut off from a larger piece. **2** *colloq.* a strong, muscular, sexually attractive man. [perhaps a variant of HAUNCH]

hunky *adj.* (**hunkier, hunkiest**) *colloq.*, *said of a man* strong, muscular, and sexually attractive.

hunky-dory *adj. colloq.*, *said of a situation* quite satifactory; excellent.

Huns an Asiatic people who in AD 375 overran the Gothic tribes of S Russia, and precipitated the great Germanic migration into the Roman Empire. Feared throughout the Empire for their brutality, under Attila they laid waste parts of Gaul and Italy (451–2), but were then forced to retreat.

Hunt, Geoff(rey) (1947–) Australian squash rackets player, born in Victoria. He was the Australian amateur champion at age 17, the world amateur champion in 1967, 1969, and 1971, and the world Open champion in 1976–7 and 1979–80.

Hunt, Henry, also called **Orator Hunt** (1773–1835) English radical agitator, born in Upavon, Wiltshire. A wealthy farmer, in 1800 he became a staunch radical, and spent the rest of his life advocating the repeal of the Corn Laws, democracy, and parliamentary reform. In 1819, on the occasion of the Peterloo massacre, he delivered a speech which earned him three years' imprisonment.

Hunt, James (Simon Wallis) (1947–93) English motor racing driver. He drove with the Hesketh and McLaren teams (1973–9), and was world motor racing Grand Prix champion in 1976. He retired in 1979 and was a BBC television broadcaster from 1980 until his death.

Hunt, (William) Holman (1827–1910) English painter, born in London. With John Millais and Dante Gabriel Rossetti he was co-founder of the Pre-Raphaelite Brotherhood. His works in this vein include *The Light of the World* (1854, Keble College, Oxford) and *The Scapegoat* (1856).

Hunt, (James Henry) Leigh (1784–1859) English poet and essayist, born in Southgate, Middlesex. From 1808 he edited (with his brother) *The Examiner*, which became a focus of Liberal opinion and attracted leading men of letters, including Byron, Percy Bysshe Shelley, and Charles Lamb. His own works include his *Autobiography* (1850).

Hunt (of Llanfair Waterdine), (Henry Cecil) John Hunt, Baron (1910–) English mountaineer, born in Marlborough, Wiltshire. After military and mountaineering service in India and Europe, he led the first successful expedition to Mt Everest in 1953, for which he was knighted. He also led the British party in the British-Soviet Caucasian mountaineering expedition (1958). He has since become known as a social reformer.

hunt — *verb* **1** *trans., intrans.* to chase and kill (animals) for food or for sport. **2** *intrans. Brit.* to hunt foxes using hounds, and on horseback. **3** *intrans.* (**hunt for something**) to search for it: *hunt for a new house.* **4** (**hunt someone** *or* **something down** *or* **out**) to search for them and find or capture them. — *noun* **1** an act or instance of hunting. **2** a group of people meeting together on horses to hunt foxes. **3** the area where such a group of people hunts. [from Anglo-Saxon *huntian*]

Hunter, John (1728–93) Scottish physiologist and surgeon, born in Long Calderwood, East

Kilbride. A surgeon for the army, St George's Hospital in London, and to George III, he built up huge collections of specimens to illustrate the processes of plant and animal life, and elucidate comparative anatomy. Among much important work he developed new methods of treating aneurysm (a bulge appearing at a weak point in an artery wall), and succeeded in grafting animal tissues; he also studied the habits of bees and silkworms, hibernation, egg incubation, and the electrical discharges of fish.

hunter *noun* **1** a person who hunts. **2** an animal that hunts, usually other animals for food. **3** a horse used in hunting, especially fox-hunting. **4** a watch with a hinged metal cover to protect the glass over its face.

Hunterston a port facility in Cunninghame district, Strathclyde, Scotland. Its gas-cooled nuclear reactors came into commercial operation in 1964, and its advanced gas-cooled reactors in 1976–7.

hunting *noun* the activity or sport of pursuing and capturing or killing wild animals.

Huntingdon, Selina Hastings, Countess of, *née* **Shirley** (1707–91) English Methodist leader, born in Staunton Harold, Leicestershire. In 1728 she married the Earl of Huntingdon (d.1746). She joined the Methodists in 1739, became their 'elect lady' in 1946, made George Whitefield her chaplain, and assumed a leadership among his followers, who became known as 'The Countess of Huntingdon's Connexion'. She built a training school for ministers, and many chapels, most of which have survived under Congregational management.

Huntingdon POP (1981) 18 000 (including Godmanchester), a town linked with Godmanchester in Huntingdon district, Cambridgeshire, E central England. It lies on the Great Ouse R, 24km/15mi NW of Cambridge. Oliver Cromwell was born here in 1599. NOTABLE FEATURES Hinchingbrooke House (13c); Church of St Mary the Virgin (13c); Cromwell Museum; Buckden Palace, 8km/5mi SW.

Huntingdonshire a former county of E central England; it has been part of Cambridgeshire since 1974.

Huntington's chorea *or* **Huntington's disease** *Medicine* an inherited brain disorder, which appears in early adulthood, characterized by slowly developing dementia accompanied by uncontrolled jerking or slow writhing movements. [named after the US physician George Summer Huntington (d.1916), who described it]

huntress *noun* a female hunter.

Huntsman, Benjamin (1704–76) English inventor, born in Barton-on-Humber. He was apprenticed to a clock-maker and in 1725 established a business in Doncaster making clocks, locks, and scientific instruments. By 1742 he had developed the crucible process for steel manufacture at a foundry he opened in Sheffield.

huntsman *noun* **1** a person who hunts. **2** an official who manages the hounds during a fox-hunt.

Huntsville POP (1990) 239 000, the seat of Madison County, N Alabama, USA, situated 39km/24mi NE of Decatur. It is a major US space research centre. NOTABLE FEATURE Alabama Space and Rocket Center (NASA), the world's largest space museum.

Hunyady, János Corvinus, *or* **John** (c.1387–1456) Hungarian statesman and warrior, apparently a Wallach (modern Romanian) by birth, who was knighted and in 1409 given the Castle of Hunyad in Transylvania by Emperor Sigismund. He spent most of his life crusading against the Turks, whom he defeated notably in the storming of Belgrade (1456). During the minority of Ladislaus V he acted as Governor of the Kingdom (1446–53). One of his sons, Matthias, became King of Hungary.

Hupa an Athapascan-speaking Native American people of the Pacific Coast, NW California (present-day population c.1 000). They lived in villages along Trinity River, where they hunted, trapped, gathered, and fished. They were renowned for their basketry.

Hurd, Douglas (Richard) (1930–) English Conservative politician. After a career in the Diplomatic Corps (1952–66), he moved to the Conservative Research Department (1966–70), and became an MP (1974). He became Northern Ireland Secretary (1984), Home Secretary (1985), and Foreign Secretary (1989–), and was unsuccessful in the leadership contest following Margaret Thatcher's resignation (Nov 1990).

hurdle — *noun* **1** one of a series of light frames or hedges to be jumped in a race. **2** (**hurdles**) a race with hurdles. **3** a problem or difficulty. **4** a light frame with bars or wire across it, used as a temporary fence. — *verb trans., intrans.* to jump (hurdles) in a race. [from Anglo-Saxon *hyrdel*]

hurdler *noun* **1** a person or horse that runs hurdle races. **2** a person who makes hurdles.

hurdling *noun* racing over hurdles.
◇ It is an athletics field event which involves foot racing while clearing obstacles (*hurdles*) en route. Race distances are 100m and 400m for women, 110m and 400m for men. The height of a hurdle varies according to the type of race: 2ft 9in (84cm) for the 100m; 3ft (91.4cm) for the 400m; and 3ft 6in (106.7cm) for the 110m. Hurdles are also included in the steeplechase.

hurdy-gurdy *noun* (PL. **hurdy-gurdies**) a musical instrument with strings which make a droning sound when they are sounded by a wheel turned by a handle. [a variant of Scot. *hirdy-girdy*, uproar]

hurl *verb* **1** to throw violently. **2** to speak (especially words of abuse or insults) with force and spite. [from Middle English *hurlen*]

hurling *or* **hurley** *noun* a traditional Irish game resembling hockey, played by two teams of 15 players each. [from HURL]
◇ The striking face of the hurling stick is broader than that of a hockey stick, and the (lighter) ball may be played above shoulder height. A ball struck into the goal under the crossbar scores three points; one hit above the crossbar and between the posts scores one point. Standardization of the rules occurred with the formation of the Gaelic Athletic Association in 1884, and the Irish Hurling Union was formed in 1879. The premier competition is the All-Ireland Championships, held since 1887.

hurly-burly *noun* the noisy activity of crowds of people; uproar. [from obsolete *hurling*, uproar]

Huron an Iroquoian-speaking Native American people, who settled in large towns and farming villages in Quebec and Ontario in the 16c. They were defeated by the Iroquois in 1648–50, and many were forced to the west, where they settled on land in Ohio and Michigan, before being driven by the whites to Oklahoma. Their descendants use the name Wyandot.

Huron, Lake the second-largest of the N American Great Lakes, situated on the US–Canadian frontier. AREA 59 570sq km/22 994sq mi; length 330km/205mi; width 294km/183mi; maximum depth 229m. Around 60% of the lake is in Canada; it is linked to Lake Superior in the NW via St Mary's R, and to L Michigan in the W via the Straits of Mackinac; it empties into L Erie in the SE via the St Clair R, L St Clair, and the Detroit R; Georgian Bay lies to the NE and Saginaw Bay to the SW. Ports include Bay City, Alpena, Cheboygan, and Midland. The lake is generally ice-bound in winter months. It was probably the first of the Great Lakes to be visited by Europeans, in c.1612.

hurrah *noun, interj.* a shout of joy, enthusiasm or victory. [from German *hurra*]

Hurrians an ancient, non-Semitic, non-Indo-European people who lived in the Caucasus area in the latter part of the third millennium BC. From there they migrated to N Mesopotamia, Syria, and E Anatolia, where in the next millennium they influenced the Hittites.

hurricane *noun* an intense, often devastating, cyclonic tropical storm with average wind speeds in excess of 118kph, or force 12 on the Beaufort scale. The winds spiral around a central calm area (the 'eye') of low pressure and light winds. Most hurricanes originate over warm tropical seas, but their high winds may cause major destruction of buildings, etc, on adjacent coastal land. [from West Indian *hurakán*]

hurricane lamp an oil lamp in which the flame is enclosed in glass to protect it from the wind.

hurried *adj.* done or forced to act quickly, especially too quickly.

hurriedly *adv.* in a hurry.

hurriedness *noun* being hurried.

hurry — *verb* (**hurries, hurried**) **1** *intrans., trans.* to move or cause to move or act quickly. **2** to cause to progress too quickly. — *noun* **1** great haste or speed. **2** the need for haste or speed. **3** eagerness.
— *also* **hurry up** *or* **hurry someone up** to move or cause to move more quickly than before.
in a hurry 1 hurrying; rushed. **2** readily; willingly: *they won't eat all that in a hurry / I shan't do that again in a hurry.*
[probably imitative]

hurt — *verb* (PAST TENSE AND PAST PARTICIPLE **hurt**) **1** to injure or cause physical pain to. **2** to upset or cause mental or emotional pain to. **3** *intrans.* to be injured or painful. — *noun* **1** an injury or wound. **2** mental pain or suffering. — *adj.* **1** injured. **2** upset; distressed. [from Old French *hurter*, to knock against]

hurtful *adj.* causing mental or emotional pain.

hurtfully *adv.* in a hurtful way.

hurtfulness *noun* being hurtful.

hurtle *verb trans., intrans.* to move or throw very quickly and violently. [from Middle English *hurtlen*]

husband — *noun* a man to whom a woman is married. — *verb* to use (money, resources, etc) wisely and with economy. [from Anglo-Saxon *husbonda*]

husbandry *noun* **1** farming. **2** the management, especially careful, of one's money and resources.

hush — *interj.* be quiet; be still. — *noun* silence, especially after noise. — *verb trans., intrans.* to make or become quiet, calm, or still.
— **hush something up** to prevent it becoming known; to keep it secret.
[imitative]

hushed *adj.* silent, very quiet, still.

hush-hush *adj. colloq.* secret.

hushkit *noun colloq.* a device fitted to an aircraft engine to reduce noise.

hush money *colloq.* money paid to someone in return for his or her agreeing to keep certain facts secret.

husk — *noun* the thin dry covering of certain fruits and seeds. — *verb* to remove the husk of. [from Middle English *huske*]

huskily *adv.* in a husky way.

huskiness *noun* being husky.

husky[1] *adj.* (**huskier, huskiest**) **1** *said of a voice* rough and dry in sound. **2** *colloq., usually said of a man* big and strong. [from HUSK]

husky[2] *noun* (PL. **huskies**) a medium-sized, thickset dog with a thick coat and curled tail, used as a sled dog in the Arctic. [from Inuit]

Huss, John, also called **Jan Hus** (c.1369–1415) Bohemian religious reformer, born in Husinetz, from which his name derives. In 1398 he lectured on theology at Prague, where he was influenced by the writings of John Wycliffe. In 1408 he defied a papal bull by continuing to preach, and was excommunicated (1411). After writing his main work, *De Ecclesia* (On the Church, 1413), he was called before a General Council at Constance, but refused to recant and was burned at the stake. The anger of his followers in Bohemia led to the Hussite Wars, which lasted until the mid-15c.

hussar *noun* a soldier in a cavalry regiment who carries only light weapons. [from Hungarian *huszar*]

Hussein or **Husain, Saddam** (1937–) Iraqi politician, born in Tikrit, near Baghdad. He joined the Arab Baath Socialist Party in 1957, and was sentenced to death in 1959 for the attempted execution of General Kassem, but escaped to Egypt. He played a prominent part in the 1968 revolution in Iraq, and became Vice-President of the Revolutionary Command Council (1969) that had ousted the civilian government. When his colleague President al-Bakr retired, Hussein became sole President. His attack on Iran in 1980, to gain control of the Strait of Hormuz, led to the Iran–Iraq War (1980–8), and his invasion of Kuwait in Aug 1990 led to the 1991 Gulf War, but by Feb that year he had been defeated by an Allied Force backed by the UN and commanded by General Norman Schwarzkopf. However he defied UN ceasefire resolutions imposed on Iraq and made further raids on Iran in 1993.

Hussein (ibn Talal) (1935–) King of Jordan since 1952, born in Amman. In the face of political upheavals inside and outside his country, he steered a middle course that favoured the Western powers, particularly Britain, and attempted to pacify Arab nationalism. After the 1967 war with Israel, the PLO made increasingly frequent raids into Israel from Jordan. Their power developed to such an extent that he ordered the Jordanian army to move against them, resulting in a short civil war (1970) that put the PLO leadership to flight. His decision to cut links with the West Bank (1988) prompted the PLO to establish a government in exile. The longest-serving Arab leader, and pro-Western in attitude, he has made steps towards democracy in Jordan, such as the introduction of political parties (although this led to the joining together of fundamentalist Islamic groups against him). He has been married four times; his heir, Abdullah (1962–) is the son of his second wife Antoinette Gardiner.

Husserl, Edmund (Gustav Albrecht) (1859–1938) German philosopher, founder of the school of phenomenology, born in Prossnitz, Austrian Empire. He taught at Halle (1887), Göttingen (1901), and Freiburg (1916). His works include the two-volume *Logische Untersuchungen* (Logical Investigations, 1900–1). He developed phenomenology (a philosophy concerned with describing personal experiences without seeking to arrive at metaphysical explanations of them) while at Göttingen – an approach which was particularly influential in Germany and the USA, and gave rise to *Gestalt* psychology.

Hussites the followers of John Huss who in the early 15c formed a movement for the reform of the Church in Bohemia (Czechoslovakia). They anticipated the 16c Reformation by demanding the moral reform of the clergy, free preaching of the Word of God, and the administration of the Eucharist in two kinds (ie bread and wine).

hussy *noun* (PL. **hussies**) *derog.* an immoral or immodest girl or woman. [a contraction of HOUSEWIFE]

hustings *pl. noun* **1** the platform, etc from which speeches are made during a political election campaign. **2** the speeches, etc made during an election campaign. [from Anglo-Saxon *husting*, tribunal, from *hus*, house + *thing*, assembly]

hustle — *verb* **1** to push quickly and roughly; to jostle. **2** *colloq.* to coerce (someone) to act or deal with something quickly: *hustled us into agreeing.* **3** *intrans. slang* to work as a prostitute. — *noun* **1** lively activity. **2** *slang* a swindle. [from Dutch *huselen*, to shake]

hustler *noun slang* **1** a swindler. **2** a prostitute.

Huston, John (Marcellus) (1906–87) US film director, born in Nevada, Missouri. He came to Hollywood in 1930 as a scriptwriter, and in 1941 directed *The Maltese Falcon*, then some wartime documentaries. A series of successful films followed, including *The Treasure of the Sierra Madre* (1948), for which he won an Oscar, *The Asphalt Jungle* (1950), *The African Queen* (1951), *Moulin Rouge* (1952) and *Night of the Iguana* (1964). In 1982 he made the musical *Annie*.

hut *noun* a small house or shelter, usually made of wood. [from Old German *hutta*]

hutch *noun* a box with a wire front in which small animals, eg rabbits, are kept. [from Old French *huche*]

Hutton, James (1726–97) Scottish geologist, born in Edinburgh. In *A Theory of the Earth*, published in the late 18c, he emphasized the igneous origin of many rocks and proposed the 'uniformitarian' principle, that the features of the Earth have formed from processes still observable, such as erosion and deposition, rather than from any catastrophic events in the past.

Hutton, Len, properly **Sir Leonard Hutton** (1916–90) English cricketer, born in Fulneck, Yorkshire. He first played for England in 1937, and in 1938, while playing against Australia at the Oval, he scored a (then) world record of 364 runs. He captained the English team which regained the Ashes from Australia in 1953. Between 1937 and 1955 he scored 6971 Test runs at an average of 56.67, and his first-class career (1934–60) included 129 centuries.

Hutu, also called **Bahutu**, **Wahutu** a Bantu-speaking people who form the majority population in Burundi and Rwanda. Their culture has been integrated with that of the Tutsi, but since the 1960s there has been a struggle between the different tribal elements for control of government in both countries.

Huxley, Aldous (Leonard) (1894–1963) English novelist and essayist, born in Godalming, Surrey. His early writing includes poetry, short stories, and literary journalism, but it was his satirical novels *Crome Yellow* (1921) and *Antic Hay* (1923) that made his reputation. Later novels include *Point Counter Point* (1928) and, his best-known work, *Brave New World* (1932). His later writing is more mystical in character, as in *Eyeless in Gaza* (1936) and *Time Must Have a Stop* (1944).

Huxley, Hugh Esmor (1924–) English biophysicist, born in Birkenhead. He worked in London and Cambridge before becoming professor at Brandeis University in Massachusetts (1987). From the 1950s he was a central figure in developing the model of muscle action in which muscle filaments slide past each other to produce contraction; during this work he also devised important X-ray diffraction and electron microscopy techniques.

Huxley, Sir Julian Sorell (1887–1975) English biologist and humanist, grandson of T H Huxley. He was professor at King's College in London and the Royal Institution, Secretary to the Zoological Society of London, and the first Director-General of UNESCO. Extending the application of his scientific knowledge to political and social problems, he formulated a pragmatic ethical theory of 'evolutionary humanism', based on the principle of natural selection.

Huxley, T(homas) H(enry) (1825–95) English biologist, born in Ealing, Middlesex, the son of a schoolmaster. Professor at the Royal School of Mines in London, he made significant contributions to palaeontology and comparative anatomy, including studies of dinosaurs, and the relationship between birds and reptiles. He was best known as the foremost scientific supporter of Charles Darwin's theory of evolution by natural selection during the heated debates which followed its publication. Later he turned to theology and philosophy, and coined the term 'agnostic' for his views.

Huygens, Christiaan (1629–93) Dutch physicist, born in the Hague. He constructed the first pendulum clock and a refracting telescope, with which he discovered the rings and fourth satellite of Saturn (1655). In optics he first propounded the wave theory of light, devising a technique for predicting the shape of an evolving wavefront (Huygens' principle), and discovered polarization. He later lived in Paris (1666–81), but as a Protestant he encountered religious hostility, and returned to the Hague.

Huysmans, Joris Karl (1848–1907) French novelist of Dutch origin, born in Paris. His works reflect many aspects of the spiritual and intellectual life of late 19c France. The best-known of these include *À rebours* (Against the Grain, 1884), a study of aesthetic decadence (which influenced Oscar Wilde); the controversial *Là-Bas* (Down There, 1891), which deals with devil-worship; and *En Route* (1892), an account of his return to Catholicism.

Hvannadalshnjúkur the highest mountain in Iceland. It is situated at the S edge of Vatnajökull glacier, in SE Iceland. HEIGHT 2 119m.

hyacinth *noun* a plant which grows from a bulb and has sweet-smelling flowers, grown either in the garden or in pots indoors. [named after Greek *Hyakinthos*, in Greek mythology a youth from whose blood sprang a blue flower when he was killed by Apollo]

hyaena same as HYENA.

hybrid — *noun* **1** an animal or plant produced by crossing two species, varieties, or breeds. **2** anything produced by combining elements from different sources. — *adj., said of an animal or plant* produced by crossing two species, varieties, or breeds.

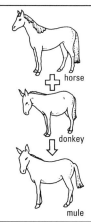

hybridization

hybridism *noun* being hybrid.

hybridization or **hybridisation** *noun* the production of hybrids; cross-breeding.

hybridize or **hybridise** *verb* **1** to cause (different species, etc) to breed together. **2** *intrans.* to produce hybrids.

hybrid vigour the increased size and vigour relative to its parents often found in a hybrid.

Hyde, Douglas, Irish **Dubhighlas de Hide** (1860–1949) Irish author and philologist, born in

Frenchpark, Co Roscommon. He was founder and first President (1893–1915) of the Gaelic League, Professor of Irish in the National University (1909–32), and first President (1938–45) of Eire. His works include *A Literary History of Ireland* (1889), poems, plays, and works on history and folklore in both Irish and English.

Hyde, Mr see Dr JEKYLL AND MR HYDE.

Hyde Park a royal park in central London, covering 255ha, separated from Kensington Gardens by the Serpentine Lake. It was first opened to the public during the reign of James I, and became a popular place for horse-riding until the end of World War I. The Albert Memorial, Speaker's Corner, and Marble Arch are situated in the park.

Hyderabad POP (1991) 4.3m, the capital of Andhra Pradesh, S India, on the R Musi, 611km/380mi SE of Bombay. HISTORY founded in 1589 as the capital of the Kingdom of Golconda; former capital of Hyderabad state; joined with India in 1948. NOTABLE FEATURES ruins of Golconda fort; tombs of the Qutb Shahi Kings; mosque modelled on the Great Mosque of Mecca, the Charminar (1591).

Hyderabad, also **Haidarabad** POP (1981) 752 000, the second-largest city in Sind province, SE Pakistan. It lies 164km/102mi NE of Karachi, on the E bank of the R Indus, c.190km/120mi N of its mouth. It was the provincial capital from 1768 until it was captured by the British in 1843.

hydr- see HYDRO-.

Hydra, Greek **Ìdhra** POP (1982) 3 000, a Greek island in the Aegean Sea, lying off the E coast of the Peloponnese. AREA 50sq km/20sq mi. The island is a popular resort. CHIEF TOWN Hydra.

Hydra 1 in Greek mythology, a many-headed monster, the child of Typhon and Echnida, which lived in a swamp at Lerna. Two heads grew each time one was struck off, but Heracles managed to kill it with the assistance of Iolaos, who cauterized the places where the heads grew. **2** *Astron.* the Water Snake, a constellation in the S hemisphere, and the largest constellation in the sky (by area). Despite its size it contains only one moderately bright star, Alphard.

hydra *noun* **1** a freshwater polyp with a tube-like body and tentacles round the mouth. **2** anything which is hard to finish, get rid of, or destroy.

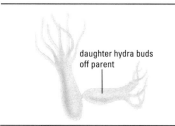
daughter hydra buds off parent

budding hydra

hydrangea *noun* a garden shrub with clusters of pink or blue flowers. [from HYDR- + Greek *angeion*, vessel]

hydrant *noun* a pipe connected to the main water supply especially in a street, with a nozzle for attaching a hose when fighting fires. [from Greek *hydor*, water]

hydrate — *noun* (with stress on *hyd-*) *Chem.* any crystalline chemical compound that contains a fixed number of molecules of water of crystallization. — *verb* (with stress on *drate-*) **1** to form such a compound. **2** to cause a substance to absorb water. See also WATER OF CRYSTALLIZATION. [from Greek *hydor*, water]

hydration *noun Chem.* the process whereby water molecules become attached to the con-

stituent ions of a solute (a soluble compound) as it is being dissolved in water.

hydraulic *adj.* **1** worked by the pressure of water or some other liquid carried in pipes: *hydraulic brakes*. **2** relating to hydraulics. [from HYDR- + Greek *aulos*, pipe]

hydraulically *adv.* with hydraulic power or equipment.

hydraulics *sing. noun Engineering* the branch of engineering concerned with the mechanical properties of fluids, especially water, at rest or in motion, and their practical applications, eg the flow of liquids in pipes, the effects of water pressure on dams.

hydride *noun* a chemical compound of hydrogen plus another element, especially a metal. [from Greek *hydor*, water]

hydro¹ *noun* (PL. **hydros**) *old use* a hotel or clinic providing hydropathic treatment. [from HYDRO-PATHIC]

hydro² *noun* (PL. **hydros**) a plant producing hydroelectric power. [from HYDROELECTRIC]

hydro- *or* **hydr-** *combining form* forming words meaning: **1** of or by means of water: *hydroelectricity*. **2** combined with hydrogen. [from Greek *hydor*, water]

hydrocarbon *noun Chem.* any of a very large group of organic chemicals that contain only carbon and hydrogen, eg methane, natural gas, kerosene. The main source of hydrocarbons is unrefined petroleum (crude oil).

hydrocephalic *adj.* **1** relating to or characteristic of hydrocephalus. **2** suffering from hydrocephalus.

hydrocephalus *noun Medicine* an abnormal condition in which excessive amounts of cerebrospinal fluid are present within the ventricles (hollow cavities) of the brain. In children it causes enlargement of the head, and in adults (who have rigid skulls) it causes compression of the brain, leading to drowsiness, vomiting, mental deterioration, and convulsions. [from HYDR- + Greek *kephale*, head]

hydrochloric acid *Chem.* (FORMULA **HCl**) a strong corrosive acid that is formed by dissolving hydrogen chloride in water. It reacts with most metals, releasing hydrogen and forming the metal salt, which is known as a *chloride*. It is an important laboratory reagent, and is widely used in the manufacture of other chemicals, and for cleaning (*pickling*) metal surfaces before they are electroplated or galvanized.

hydrodynamics *sing. noun* the science of the movement and power of liquids.

hydroelectric *adj.* generating electricity by means of water power.

hydroelectrically *adv.* by means of hydro-electricity.

hydroelectricity *noun* (also **hydroelectric power**) electricity produced by generators linked to turbines that are driven by the force of falling water. About 20 per cent of the world's electricity is generated in this way.
◇ In a hydroelectric power station, some of the water stored in a reservoir behind a dam is allowed to escape by means of valves, and this rapidly flowing water rotates turbines that are linked to an electricity generators. While the hydroelectric generators are operating the water level in the reservoir falls. In *pumped-storage* systems water flows from a high-level reservoir through the turbines to a low-level reservoir during the day. At night, when the demand for electricity is low, water is pumped from the low-level reservoir back to the high-level reservoir, ensuring that power can be generated the next day.

hydrofoil *noun* **1** a device on a boat which lifts it out of the water as its speed accelerates. **2** a boat fitted with such a device. [from HYDRO- + AEROFOIL]

◇ Lift is provided by a set of foils fitted at a depth greater than the draft of the boat's hull; it develops in much the same way as that of an aeroplane's wing. Successful trials were first held in Italy in 1906 but it was 50 years before the first hydrofoil was operated commercially: they are used extensively for inland water transport.

hydrogen *noun* (SYMBOL **H**, ATOMIC NUMBER **1**) a colourless, odourless, tasteless gas that burns readily in air. It is the first and lightest element in the periodic table, and by far the most abundant element in the universe. [from HYDR- + Greek *gennaein*, to produce]
◇ Hydrogen is a major constituent of water (H_2O) and all organic compounds, so is present in all living organisms, and in coal, petroleum, and other hydrocarbons. It is chemically reactive and forms compounds with most elements, and it is also the main fuel for the nuclear fusion reactions that produce heat and light in the Sun and other stars. Hydrogen is used in the production of ammonia, the hydrogenation (solidification) of vegetable oils to produce margarine, etc, and the manufacture of a wide range of organic chemicals. It is also used in liquid form as a rocket fuel, and in a mixture with oxygen to produce a hot flame for welding, and for melting glass. Hydrogen has two other isotopes, deuterium (heavy hydrogen) and tritium, both of which are used as radioactive tracers and in nuclear weapons.

hydrogenate *verb Chem.* to undergo or cause to undergo hydrogenation.

hydrogenation *noun Chem.* any chemical reaction in which hydrogen is combined with another substance, especially in many industrial processes, such as the formation of solid fats, eg margarine, from liquid oils, eg vegetable oil.

hydrogen bomb *Mil.* the most powerful form of nuclear bomb, that releases vast amounts of energy as a result of the nuclear fusion of deuterium and tritium, which are isotopes of hydrogen. – Also called *H-bomb*. See also THERMONU-CLEAR BOMB.

hydrogen bond *Chem.* a strong chemical bond that is formed when a hydrogen atom that is already bonded to another atom in a molecule forms an additional bond with an atom in the same or another molecule.

hydrogencarbonate *noun Chem.* a salt of carbonic acid that contains the HCO_3^- ion. — Also called *bicarbonate*.

hydrogen chloride *Chem.* (FORMULA **HCl**) a fuming poisonous colourless gas that is prepared by treating a chloride with concentrated sulphuric acid. It readily dissociates in water to form

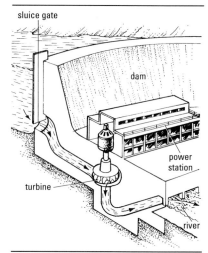
sluice gate
dam
power station
turbine
river

hydroelectric plant

hydrochloric acid, and is used in the manufacture of polyvinyl chloride (PVC).

hydrogen ion *Chem.* a hydrogen atom carrying a positive charge. – Also called *proton*.

hydrogenous *adj.* relating to or consisting of hydrogen.

hydrogen peroxide *Chem.* (FORMULA H_2O_2) an unstable colourless viscous liquid that is a strong oxidizing agent and soluble in water. It is used as an oxidant in rocket fuel, and in antiseptics, disinfectants, and bleaches for hair and textiles. – Also called *peroxide*.

hydrogen sulphide *Chem.* (FORMULA H_2S) a colourless poisonous gas with a characteristic smell of bad eggs, produced by decaying organic matter, and also found in natural gas (from which it is removed) and volcanic emissions. It is used as a source of sulphur, in the purification of certain acids, and in stink bombs.

hydrographer *noun* an expert in hydrography.

hydrographic *adj.* relating to or involving hydrography.

hydrography *noun* the science of charting seas, rivers, and lakes. [from HYDRO- + -GRAPHY]

hydrology *noun* the scientific study of the occurrence, movement, and properties of water on or near the Earth's surface, and in the atmosphere. Its practical applications include flood control, irrigation schemes, control of industrial and domestic water supplies, and the generation of hydroelectric power.

hydrolysis *noun* the decomposition of organic compounds by the action of water. [from HYDRO- + Greek *lysis*, a loosening]

hydrometer *noun Physics* a floating instrument, consisting of a weighted glass bulb with a long calibrated stem, that is used to measure the density of a liquid as indicated by the depth of immersion of the bulb. Hydrometers are widely used in brewing.

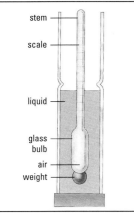

stem
scale
liquid
glass bulb
air
weight

hydrometer

hydropathic *adj.* relating to or involving hydropathy.

hydropathy *noun* a way of treating disease or illness using water both internally and externally. [from HYDRO- + Greek *patheia*, suffering]

hydrophilic *adj. Chem.* denoting a substance that has an affinity for, absorbs, or attracts water.

hydrophobia *noun* **1** the fear of water. **2** the inability to swallow water, especially as a symptom of rabies. **3** rabies.

hydrophobic *adj.* **1** *Chem.* denoting a substance that repels or does not absorb water. **2** relating to or suffering from hydrophobia.

hydroplane *noun* **1** a light, flat-bottomed motorboat which, at high speeds, skims along the surface of the water. **2** a fin-like device on a

submarine which allows it to rise and fall in the water.

hydroponic *adj.* relating to or involving hydroponics.

hydroponics *sing. noun Bot.* a technique for growing certain commercially important plants (especially glasshouse crops) without soil, by immersing the roots in water that contains essential nutrients, and using an inert substance such as sand or gravel to provide support. [from HYDRO- + Greek *ponos*, work]

hydrosphere *noun* the water, eg seas and rivers, on the surface of the earth. [from HYDRO- + SPHERE]

hydrostatic *adj.* relating to or involving hydrostatics.

hydrostatics *sing. noun* the science of the behaviour and power of liquids which are not moving. [from HYDRO- + Greek *-states*, causing to stand]

hydrotherapy *noun Medicine* the treatment of diseases and disorders by the external use of water, especially as a comparatively weightless form of exercise in physiotherapy, such as the rehabilitation of partially paralysed patients in remedial swimming pools.

hydrous *adj.*, *said of a substance* containing water. [from Greek *hydor*, water]

hydroxide *noun Chem.* any chemical compound that contains the hydroxide (OH^-) ion or the hydroxyl (–OH) group.

hydroxyl group *Chem.* in a chemical compound, the (-OH) group, consisting of a hydrogen atom and an oxygen atom bonded together, as for example in alcohols, organic acids, phenols, and hydroxides. [from HYDROGEN + OXYGEN + Greek *hyle*, matter]

Hydrus *Astron.* the Lesser Water Snake, an inconspicuous constellation in the southern hemisphere.

hyena *noun* a mainly nocturnal dog-like mammal with strong shoulders that are higher than its hindquarters, powerful jaws, and strong teeth. Hyenas are found in open country in Africa and SW Asia, and feed mainly on carrion, although they also hunt prey such as zebra and wildebeest. They are known for their shrill cries which resemble maniacal laughter. [from Greek *hys*, pig]

Hyères, Iles d' or **Les Iles d'Or** an island group in the Mediterranean Sea, SE France, lying SE of Toulon. The chief islands are (from E to W) Levant (occupied partly by the French Navy, partly by a nudist colony), Port-Cros (a nature reserve), and the fortified island of Porquerolles. The Allies briefly occupied the island group in 1944.

Hygeia in Greek mythology, the goddess of health, the daughter or, in later literature, wife of Asclepius.

hygiene *noun* the practice or study of staying healthy and preventing the spread of disease, especially by keeping oneself and one's surroundings clean. [from Greek *hygieia*, health]

hygienic *adj.* promoting and preserving health, sanitary.

hygienically *adv.* in a hygienic way.

hygrometer *noun Meteorol.* an instrument for measuring the relative humidity of the air, ie the amount of water vapour in the atmosphere. [from Greek *hygros*, wet + -METER]

hygroscope *noun* an instrument which indicates changes in air humidity without measuring it. [from Greek *hygros*, wet + -SCOPE]

hygroscopic *adj.* **1** of a hygroscope. **2** *said of a substance* able to absorb moisture from the air.

Hyksos a tribe of desert nomads from Palestine, who founded a dynasty in ancient Egypt in c.1670 BC. The Egyptians called them

'shepherd kings' or 'the princes from foreign parts'.

Hymen in Greek mythology, the god of marriage and the son of Apollo or of Dionysus and Aphrodite. He is depicted as a youth with a torch.

hymen *noun Anat.* a thin membrane that covers the opening of the vagina at birth. It may be broken the first time a woman has sexual intercourse, but is usually at least partially ruptured before puberty. [from Greek *hymen*, membrane]

Hymenoptera *pl. noun Zool.* in the animal kingdom, a diverse order of insects that includes the ants, bees, wasps, and sawflies. The adults typically have two pairs of membranous wings, and their mouthparts are adapted for chewing or for sucking nectar. The ovipositor (egg-laying tube) is often adapted for stinging. [from Greek *hymen*, membrane + *pteron*, wing]

hymenopterous *adj.* denoting an insect that belongs to the order Hymenoptera, including ants, bees, wasps, and sawflies. [from Greek *hymen*, membrane + *pteron*, wing]

hymn *noun* a song of praise, especially to God. [from Greek *hymnos*]

hymnal *or* **hymnary** (PL. **hymnaries**) *noun* a book containing hymns.

hymnody *noun* **1** the writing of hymns. **2** hymns as a group.

hymnologist *noun* a person who composes or studies hymns.

hymnology *noun* the study or writing of hymns.

Hypatia (c.375–415 AD) Greek Neoplatonist philosopher, born in Alexandria, the daughter of Theon. An astronomer and mathematician, she became head of the Neoplatonist school in Alexandria; her philosophy was an attempt to combine Neoplatonism with Aristotelianism. She was associated by many Christians with paganism, and was murdered by a fanatical mob in Alexandria.

hype¹ *colloq.* — *noun* intensive, exaggerated, and usually misleading publicity or advertising. — *verb* (**hype something up**) to promote or advertise it intensively.

hype² *verb intrans. slang* (*usually* **hype up**) to inject oneself with a drug.
— **hyped up** *slang* highly excited, especially as if by drugs.
[abbreviation of HYPODERMIC]

hyper *adj. colloq.*, *said of a person* over-excited; over-active. [abbreviation of HYPERACTIVE]

hyper- *combining form* forming words meaning 'over, beyond, more than normal': *hyperactive*. [from Greek *hyper*, over]

hyperactive *adj.*, *said especially of a child* more active than is normal.

hyperactivity *noun Psychol.* a condition characterized by overactive, poorly controlled behaviour and lack of concentration, most frequently seen in children.

hyperbola *noun* (PL. **hyperbolas**, **hyperbolae**) *Geom.* the curve produced when a

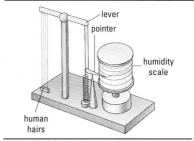

lever
pointer
humidity scale
human hairs

hygrometer

plane (flat surface) cuts through a cone in such a way that the angle between the base of the cone and the plane is greater than the angle between the base and the sloping side of the cone. It is one type of *conic section*. [from Greek *hyperbole*, excess]

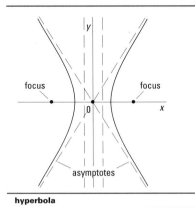

hyperbola

hyperbole *noun* the use of an overstatement or exaggeration to produce an effect. [from Greek *hyperbole*, excess]

hyperbolic¹ *adj.* relating to or in the form of a hyperbola.

hyperbolic² *or* **hyperbolical** *adj.* involving hyperbole.

Hyperboreans in Greek mythology, an unvisited people of fabled virtue and prosperity who lived in a land beyond the North Wind (Boreas). In Herodotus, they worshipped Apollo and sent offerings to Delos.

hypercritical *adj.* over-critical.

hypercritically *adv.* in a hypercritical way.

hyperglycaemia *noun Medicine* a condition in which the glucose (sugar) concentration in the blood is abnormally high. It is most commonly associated with diabetes mellitus. [from HYPER- + Greek *glykys*, sweet]

Hyperion in Greek mythology, one of the Titans, the son of Uranus and Gaea, and father of Eos (the Dawn), Helios (the Sun), and Selene (the Moon). Later, as in Shakespeare and Keats, he was identified with the Sun.

hypermarket *noun* a very large supermarket. [a translation of French *hypermarché*]

hypermetropia *Medicine* the condition of being long-sighted, in which parallel rays of light entering the eye are brought to a focus behind the retina, so that nearby objects appear blurred. It usually occurs because the distance between the lens and the retina is too short, and is corrected by wearing contact lenses or spectacles with convex (converging) lenses. [from HYPER- + Greek *metron*, measure + *ops*, eye]

hyperon *noun Physics* any of a class of elementary particles with masses greater than that of a neutron.

hypersensitive *adj.* very sensitive, or more sensitive than is normal.

hypersensitivity *noun* being hypersensitive.

hypersonic *adj.* **1** *Aeron.* denoting a speed greater than Mach number 5 (about five times the speed of sound in the same medium). **2** denoting an aircraft or rocket capable of flying at such speeds. **3** denoting sound waves with a frequency greater than 1 000 million hertz.

hypertension *noun Medicine* a condition in which the blood pressure is abnormally high. It may be caused by obesity, stress, ageing, disease of the heart, arteries, or kidneys, or hormonal disorders, or it may have no identifiable cause. Hypertension itself may increase the risk of heart failure, atherosclerosis, kidney failure, or stroke.

hypertext *noun Comput.* computer-readable text in which cross-reference links have been inserted, enabling the user to call up relevant data from other files, or parts of the same file, by clicking on a coded word or symbol, etc.

hyperthyroidism *noun Medicine* overproduction of thyroid hormones by the thyroid gland, which may result in goitre (swelling of the neck due to enlargement of the thyroid gland), weight loss, rapid heartbeat, tremor, and increased appetite.

hypertonic *adj. Chem.* denoting a solution that has a higher osmotic pressure than another solution with which it is being compared.

hypertrophy *noun* (PL. **hypertrophies**) *Biol.* an abnormal increase in the size of an organ as a result of the enlargement of its individual cells, rather than an increase in the total number of cells. Muscles undergo hypertrophy in response to a long-term increase in exercise. [from HYPER- + Greek *-trophia*, nutrition]

hyperventilation *noun Medicine* a condition in which breathing while at rest becomes abnormally rapid and deep, causing dizziness, a feeling of suffocation, and sometimes loss of consciousness. It is usually caused by anxiety, but may also occur when oxygen uptake is impaired by shallow breathing, eg in pneumonia.

hypha *noun Biol.* in fungi, any of many thread-like filaments that form a dense network known as a mycelium. [from Greek *hyphe*, web]

hyphen — *noun* a punctuation mark (-) used to join two words to form a compound (*booby-trap*, *double-barrelled*) or, especially in printing, to split a word between the end of one line and the beginning of the next. — *verb* (**hyphened**, **hyphening**) to hyphenate. [from Greek *hypo*, under + *hen*, one]

hyphenate *verb* to join (two words or parts of words) with a hyphen.

hyphenation *noun* the use of a hyphen or hyphens.

hypnosis *noun* (PL. **hypnoses**) a sleep-like state in which a person is deeply relaxed and unusually receptive to external suggestion, and may by questioning be induced to recall memories of past events, thought to have been forgotten. It is used to treat mental illnes, addictions, and psychosomatic disorders, and for the relief of pain, eg during childbirth or dental treatment. [from Greek *hypnos*, sleep]

hypnotherapy *noun* the treatment of illness or habits such as smoking by hypnosis. [from *hypno-*, of hypnosis]

hypnotic — *adj.* **1** of, causing, or caused by, hypnosis. **2** causing sleepiness. — *noun* **1** a drug that produces sleep or hypnosis. **2** a person in a state of hypnosis.

hypnotically *adv.* in a hypnotic way.

hypnotism *noun* the science or practice of hypnosis.

hypnotist *noun* a person who practises hypnotism.

hypnotize *or* **hypnotise** *verb* **1** to put (someone) in a state of hypnosis. **2** to fascinate or bewitch.

hypo *noun* (PL. **hypos**) *colloq.* a hypodermic syringe or injection. [abbreviation of HYPODERMIC]

hypo- *combining form* forming words meaning 'under, beneath, inadequate': *hypotension*. [from Greek *hypo*, under]

hypocaust *noun* a hollow space under a floor or between double walls in ancient Roman houses, into which hot air was passed as a form of heating. [from Latin *hypocaustum*, from Greek *hypo*, under + *kaiein*, to burn]

hypochlorite *noun Chem.* a salt of hypochlorous acid (a weak acid that is only stable in solution), containing the ClO⁻ ion, and used as a disinfectant and bleach.

hypochondria *noun* a condition, often associated with anxiety or depression, characterized by excessive concern about one's health. It often involves belief in the existence of a serious illness, for which treatment is sought, and may become a handicapping neurosis that dominates a person's life. [from Greek *hypochondrion*, abdomen, formerly believed to be the source of melancholy]

hypochondriac — *noun* a person suffering from hypochondria. — *adj.* of or relating to hypochondria or hypochondriacs.

hypochondriacal *adj.* relating to or affected by hypochondria.

hypocrisy *noun* (PL. **hypocrisies**) the act or state of pretending to have feelings or beliefs which one does not actually have, or of hiding one's true character. [from Greek *hypokrisis*, play-acting]

hypocrite *noun* a person who pretends to have feelings or beliefs he or she does not actually have, or who hides his or her true character.

hypocritical *adj.* **1** practising hypocrisy. **2** of the nature of hypocrisy.

hypocritically *adv.* in a hypocritical way.

hypodermic — *adj.*, *said of an instrument or drug* for injecting under the skin. — *noun* **1** a hypodermic syringe. **2** an injection of a drug under the skin. [from HYPO- + Latin *dermis*, skin]

hypodermic syringe a syringe with a fine hollow needle, used for injecting drugs under the skin or taking blood samples.

hypoglycaemia *or* **hypoglycemia** *noun Medicine* an abnormal reduction in glucose (sugar) content of the blood, most commonly occurring in diabetics after an overdose of insulin. Symptoms include muscular weakness, sweating, mental confusion, faintness, and even coma in severe cases. It is treated by giving glucose by mouth.

hyponym *noun Linguistics* one of a group of specific terms whose meanings are included in a more general term: for example, *oak* and *cedar* are hyponyms of *tree* and of *wood*, and *dog* and *alligator* are hyponyms of *animal*. [from HYPO- + Greek *onyma*, *onoma*, a name]

hypotension *noun* abnormally low blood-pressure.

hypotenuse *noun Maths.* the longest side of a right-angled triangle, opposite the right angle. [from Greek *hypoteinousa*, subtending]

hypothalamus *noun Anat.* the region of the vertebrate forebrain that lies below the thalamus and above the pituitary gland. It is linked to both, and so acts as a centre for coordination of nervous system and hormonal activity. In mammals it is involved in the control of body temperature, heartbeat, breathing rate, blood pressure, water balance, hunger, thirst, and sleep patterns. It also influences emotional activity and libido in humans.

hypothermia *noun* **1** *Medicine* a condition in which the body temperature falls below normal as a result of exposure to cold. It most commonly occurs in babies and the elderly, especially during a long spell of exceptionally cold weather. **2** a decrease in body temperature that is deliberately induced, eg to reduce a patient's oxygen requirements during heart surgery. [from HYPO- + Greek *therme*, heat]

hypothesis *noun* (PL. **hypotheses**) a statement or proposition assumed to be true and on which an argument, etc may be based. [from Greek *hypothesis*, supposition]

hypothesize *or* **hypothesise** *verb* **1** *intrans.* to form a hypothesis. **2** *trans.* to assume as a hypothesis.

hypothetical *adj.* based on hypothesis; assumed.

hypothetically *adv.* in a hypothetical way.

hypothyroidism *noun Medicine* a deficiency in the production of thyroid hormones by the thyroid gland, which may result in slowing of the heartbeat, extreme sensitivity to cold, an increase in weight, and a slowing down of physical and mental activity. If present at birth and left untreated it can lead to cretinism.

hypotonic *adj. Chem.* describing a solution that has a lower osmotic pressure than another solution with which it is being compared.

hypsometer *noun* an instrument for measuring the height of positions on the Earth's surface by observing the effect of altitude on the boiling point of water; the boiling point, dependent on incumbent pressure, decreases with increasing altitude. [from Greek *hypsos*, height + -METER]

Hyracotherium *noun* same as EOHIPPUS.

hyrax *noun* a mammal, native to Africa and Arabia, related to the elephant and aardvark, and superficially resembling a large guinea pig, with a pointed muzzle and round ears. [from Greek *hyrax*, shrew]

hyssop *noun* a small shrubby perennial plant (*Hyssopus officinalis*), native to S Europe and W Asia, and having narrow leaves and long loose one-sided spikes of two-lipped bluish-violet flowers. It was formerly cultivated as a medicinal herb. [from Greek *hyssopos*]

hyssop

hysterectomy *noun* (PL. **hysterectomies**) the surgical removal of the uterus (womb), after which menstruation ceases and pregnancy is no longer possible. The operation is usually performed to treat conditions such as cancer or fibroids, and has no effect on the libido. [from Greek *hystera*, womb + -ECTOMY]

hysteresis *noun Physics* the delay or lag between the cause of an effect, and the appearance of that effect. It occurs, for example, when a magnetic material becomes magnetized. [from Greek *hysteresis*, deficiency, delay]

hysteria *noun* **1** *Psychol.* a mental disorder characterized by mental and physical symptoms such as hallucinations, uncontrolled weeping, amnesia, or paralysis. This condition is a form of neurosis. **2** any uncontrolled emotional state caused by acute stress or a traumatic experience. [from Greek *hystera*, womb, from the former belief that disturbances in the womb caused emotional imbalance]

hysteric *noun* a person suffering from hysteria.

hysterical *adj.* **1** of or suffering from hysteria. **2** *colloq.* very funny.

hysterically *adv.* in a hysterical way.

hysterics *pl. noun* **1** a fit of hysteria. **2** *colloq.* uncontrollable laughter.

Hz *abbrev.* hertz.

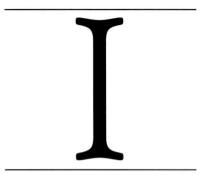

I

I¹ *or* **i** *noun* (PL. **Is**, **I's**, **i's**) the ninth letter of the English alphabet.

I² *pron.* used by the speaker or writer to refer to himself or herself as the subject of an actual or implied verb. [from Anglo-Saxon *ic*]

I³ *abbrev.* **1** Institute. **2** Island. **3** Isle.

I⁴ *symbol* **1** *Chem.* iodine. **2** the Roman numeral for one.

IA *or* **Ia** *abbrev.* Iowa.

IAAF *abbrev.* International Amateur Athletic Federation.

Iachimo the cunning villain in Shakespeare's *Cymbeline*, who makes a wager with Posthumus.

Iacocca, Lee, properly **Lido Anthony** (1924–) US businessman, and head of Chrysler Corporation, born in Allentown, Pennsylvania. He worked for the Ford Motor Company (1946–78), of which he was President from 1970. He joined Chrysler Corporation as President and Chief Executive Officer when the company was in serious financial difficulties, with declining market share. He has been Chairman of the board since 1979.

IAEA *abbrev.* International Atomic Energy Agency.

Iago the villainous soldier in Shakespeare's *Othello*, whose jealous desire to wreak vengeance on Cassio results in tragedy.

-ial *suffix* **1** forming adjectives meaning 'of, relating to': *managerial*. **2** forming nouns meaning 'the action of': *tutorial*. [from Latin *-ialis*]

iambic — *adj.* of or using iambuses. — *noun* an iambus.

iambus *or* **iamb** *noun* (PL. **iambuses**, **iambi**) *Poetry* a metrical foot containing one short or unstressed syllable followed by one long or stressed one. [from Greek *iambos*, from *iaptein*, to lampoon, this verse form being first used by satirists]
◇ The iambus is the most common measure in English verse, and corresponds with the general pattern of English words and phrases. The following example is from Gray's *Elegy in a Country Churchyard*: And leaves the world to darkness, and to me.

Ian a male first name, originally a Scottish version of *John* (Gaelic *Iain*), but now an independent name, common throughout Britain.

-ian *suffix* **1** forming adjectives meaning 'relating to, similar to': *Dickensian*. **2** forming nouns meaning 'a person interested or skilled in': *historian*.

Iapetus in Greek mythology, one of the Titans, the father of Prometheus, Epimetheus, Atlas, and Menoetius.

ib. *abbrev.* ibidem.

IBA *abbrev. Brit.* Independent Broadcasting Authority.

Ibadan POP (1992e) 1.3m, the capital of Oyo state, Nigeria, and the country's second largest city. It is situated 113km/70mi NE of Lagos. The city was founded in the 1830s and came under British control in 1896. It is regarded as the intellectual centre of the country.

Ibáñez, Vicente Blasco (1867–1928) Spanish novelist, born in Valencia. He dealt in realistic fashion with provincial life and social revolution, as in *Sangre y arena* (Blood and Sand, 1909). His depiction of World War I, *Los cuatro jinetes del Apocalipsis* (The Four Horsemen of the Apocalypse, 1916) brought him international fame.

Ibárruri (Gómez), Dolores, known as **la Pasionaria** (**the Passionflower**) (1895–1989) Spanish communist orator and politician, born into a poor mining family in Gallarta. A member of the Central Committee of the Spanish Communist Party from 1930, she served as Spanish delegate to the Third International (1933, 1935), and was elected deputy to the Spanish Cortes (1936). With the outbreak of the Civil War (1936), she became the Republic's most emotional and effective propagandist. When Franco took power after the War, she took refuge in the USSR (1939), and became President of the Spanish Communist Party in exile. In 1977 she returned to Spain as Communist deputy for Asturias.

Iberian — *adj.* relating to the Iberian Peninsula, or its inhabitants, languages, and culture. — *noun* a person from the Iberian Peninsula; a Spaniard or Portuguese. [from Latin *Iberia*]

Iberian Peninsula the region of Europe SW of the Pyrenees comprising Portugal and Spain. AREA c.593 000sq km/229 000sq mi. The name is probably derived from Iberus, the Roman name for the R Ebro; Iberia is an ancient name for Spain.

Iberians a group of Iron Age peoples inhabiting the southern and eastern periphery of present-day Spain (Andalusia, Valencia, Aragon, and Catalonia), and extending north into present-day France as far as the Rhône valley.

ibex *noun* (PL. **ibex**, **ibexes**, **ibices**) a wild mountain goat with large, ridged, backward-curving horns, found in Europe, N Africa and Asia. [from Latin *ibex*]

ibid. *abbrev.* ibidem.

ibidem *adv.* in the same place in a book, article, passage, etc previously mentioned or cited. [from Latin *ibidem*, in the same place]

-ibility *suffix* forming nouns corresponding to adjectives in *-ible*: *possibility*.

ibis *noun* (PL. **ibis**, **ibises**) a wading bird with a long slender downward-curving beak. [from Greek *ibis*, from Egyptian]

Ibiza *or* **Iviza**, ancient **Ebusus** POP (1990e) 81 000, the third-largest island of the

Mediterranean Balearic Is, Spain. It lies 88km/55mi SW of Majorca, surrounded by islets. AREA 572sq km/221sq mi. CAPITAL Ibiza. It was founded by the Carthaginians in 645 BC. ECONOMY almonds, figs, olives, apricots; it is a major tourist destination. NOTABLE FEATURE on the W coast is Roman Portus Magnus, now San Antonio Abad, with its chapel-catacomb of Santa Ines (a national monument).

-ible *suffix* forming adjectives meaning 'that may be or is capable of being': *possible* / *expressible*. See also -ABLE. [from Latin *-ibilis*]

Iblis the Islamic name for the archangel Lucifer, who rebelled against God and was banished from heaven to become Satan, the tempter.

-ibly *suffix* forming adverbs corresponding to adjectives in *-ible*: *possibly* / *inexpressibly*.

Ibn Saud, properly **Ibn Abd al-Rahman al-Saud** (1880–1953) the first King of Saudi Arabia (1932–53), born in Riyadh. He followed his family into exile in 1890 and was brought up in Kuwait. In 1901 he succeeded his father, and set out to reconquer the family domains from the Rashidi rulers, an aim which he achieved with British recognition in 1927. He changed his title from Sultan of Nejd to King of Hejaz and Nejd in 1927, and in 1932 to King of Saudi Arabia. After the discovery of oil (1938) he granted substantial concessions to US oil companies. His son Saud (1902–69) had been Prime Minister for three months when he succeeded his father (1953). In 1964 Saud was peacefully deposed by the Council of Ministers, succeeded by his half-brother Faisal as king, who also remained Prime Minister and Minister of Foreign Affairs.

IBRD *abbrev.* International Bank for Reconstruction and Development (World Bank).

IBS *Medicine abbrev.* irritable bowel syndrome.

Ibsen, Henrik (Johan) (1828–1906) Norwegian dramatist and poet, born in Skien. His first major play was *The Pretenders* (Konsemnerne, 1857). His theatre having gone bankrupt, and angry at Norway's aloofness in Denmark's struggle with Germany, he went into voluntary exile in Rome, Dresden, and Munich (1864–92). His international reputation began with *Brand* and *Peer Gynt* (1866–7) and continued with the social plays *A Doll's House* (Et Dukkehjem, 1879) and the controversial *Ghosts* (Gengangere, 1881). Latterly, apart from the realism of *Hedda Gabler* (1890), he turned more to symbolism, as in *The Wild Duck* (Vildanden, 1884), *Rosmersholm* (1886), and *The Master Builder* (Bygmester Solness, 1892).

-ic *suffix* **1** (*also* **-ical**, often with some difference in meaning) forming words meaning 'relating to': *historic* / *historical* / *photographic* / *political*. **2** *Chem.* forming words meaning 'formed with an element in its higher valency': *sulphuric*. See also -ICS. [from French *-ique*]

-ically *suffix* forming adverbs corresponding to adjectives in *-ic* or *-ical*: *historically* / *graphically*.
◆ All adjectives ending in *-ic* and *-ical* that form adverbs form them in *-ically*, except *public*, which forms *publicly*.

Icaria, Greek **Ikaría** a Greek island in the Aegean Sea, SW of Samos. AREA 255sq km/ 98sq mi. Ayios Kyrikos is a popular resort; there are medicinal springs at Thermai. [named after the legendary Icarus]

Icarus 1 in Greek mythology, the son of Daedalus. His father made him wings to escape from Crete, but he flew too near the Sun. The wax holding the wings melted, and he fell into the Aegean at a point now known as the Icarian Sea. **2** *Astron.* an Apollo asteroid, about 1.5km in diameter, with a highly elliptical orbit that takes it closer to the Sun than the planet Mercury.

ICBM *abbrev.* intercontinental ballistic missile.

ICD *abbrev.* interactive compact disc; CD-i.

ice — *noun* **1** water in its solid frozen state. Pure water freezes at 0°C (32°F), and unlike other liquids it expands and becomes less dense when it freezes. For this reason it floats on water, and frozen water may cause pipes to burst. Ice may also be formed by the condensation of water vapour in the atmosphere directly into crystals, or by the compaction of fallen snow. **2** a sheet of frozen water, eg on the surface of a road. **3** ice-cream or water ice, or a portion of this. **4** *slang* diamonds. **5** *slang* an illicit drug, a highly synthesized form of metamphetamine. **6** coldness of manner; reserve. — *verb* **1** to cool with ice. **2** *intrans.* (*usually* **ice over** *or* **up**) to become covered with ice; to freeze. **3** to cover (a cake) with icing.
— **break the ice** to relax feelings of reserve, shyness, or formality, especially between strangers.
cut no ice to count for nothing.
on ice in readiness or reserve, either to be used later, or awaiting further attention.
skate on thin ice to be in a difficult, delicate, or potentially embarrassing situation.
[from Anglo-Saxon *is*]

Ice Age 1 any of several periods of time in the Earth's history when the average temperature of the atmosphere decreased to such an extent that ice sheets and glaciers advanced from polar regions to cover large areas of the Earth that had previously had a temperate climate. **2** (**the Ice Age**) a popular name for the Pleistocene epoch.

ice-axe *noun* an axe used by mountain-climbers to cut holes in the ice for their hands and feet.

iceberg *noun* a huge mass of ice floating in the sea, only a small part of which projects above the surface. Icebergs are broken off from a glacier or polar ice sheet, and commonly drift for up to two years before melting.
— **the tip of the iceberg** the initial visible or perceived part of a much larger problem or commitment which remains to be discovered.

iceberg lettuce a crisp, light-green type of lettuce.

icebox *noun* **1** a refrigerator compartment where food is kept frozen and ice is made. **2** a container packed with ice, for keeping food cold. **3** *North Amer.* a refrigerator.

icebreaker *noun* a ship designed to cut channels through floating ice.

ice-bucket *noun* a small bucket for ice cubes, used for keeping bottles of wine cold.

icecap *noun* a permanent covering of ice, eg on top of a mountain, or at the North or South Poles.

ice cream a sweet, creamy frozen dessert, made either from cream or a substitute, and flavoured.

ice cube a small block of ice used for cooling drinks, etc.

iced *adj.* **1** covered with or affected by ice. **2** *said of a cake, etc* covered with icing.

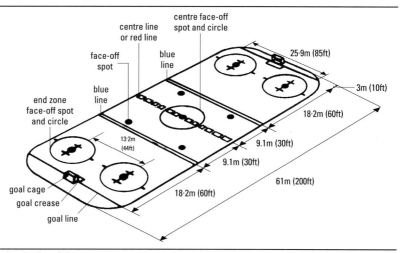

ice hockey rink

ice field a large flat area of land covered with ice, or an area of sea covered with floating ice.

ice floe a large sheet of ice floating on the sea.

ice hockey a form of hockey played on ice by skaters, and with a puck instead of a ball.
◇ Each team has six players on the ice, and all players (especially the goal tender) wear protective clothing to guard against injury from falls and collisions. The sport is thought to have originated in Canada in the 1850s. The National Hockey League (NHL) is contested by 21 teams from Canada and the USA.

Iceland, Icelandic **Ìsland**, official name **Republic of Iceland**, Icelandic **Lýdhveldidh Ìsland** POP (1992e) 260 000, an island state lying between the N Atlantic Ocean and the Arctic Ocean, SE of Greenland and 900km/550mi W of Norway. It is divided into eight regions. AREA 103 000sq km/40 000sq mi. CAPITAL Reykjavík. CHIEF TOWNS Akureyri, Húsavík, Akranes, Keflavík, Ìsafjördur. TIME ZONE GMT. OFFICIAL LANGUAGE Icelandic. The population is almost entirely of Norse stock, descended from Norwegians and Celts; Lutheran Protestantism is the chief religion. CURRENCY the krónur. PHYSICAL DESCRIPTION a volcanic island of relatively recent geological origin, at the N end of the mid-Atlantic Ridge, with several active volcanoes (eg Hekla); famous for its geysers, notably *Geysir* from which the term is derived; many towns are heated by subterranean hot water; there is a geothermal power station at Krafla; the coastline is heavily indented, with many long fjords; high ridges rise to 2 119m at Hvannadalshnjúkur in the SE; large snowfields and glaciers cover much of the land area. CLIMATE changeable climate, with relatively mild winters; average daily temperatures are minimum −2°C (Jan), maximum 14°C (Jul–Aug); Reykjavík is generally ice-free throughout the year; summers are cool and cloudy; average monthly rainfall reaches 94mm (Oct). HISTORY settled by the Norse in the 9c; the world's oldest parliament, the *Althing*, was established in the 10c; united with Norway in 1262, and with Denmark in 1380; in 1918 Iceland became an independent kingdom with the same sovereign as Denmark; since 1944 it has been an independent republic; extension of the fishing limit around Iceland in 1958 and 1975 precipitated the 'Cod War' disputes with the UK. GOVERNMENT governed by a 63-member Parliament, which includes a 21-member Upper House; a President appoints a Prime Minister and Cabinet. ECONOMY largely based on inshore and deep-water fishing (75% of the national income); stock farming, dairy farming, potatoes, and greenhouse vegetables are important; there is also production of aluminium and diatomite; tourism.

Icelandic — *adj.* of Iceland or the Germanic language spoken in Iceland. — *noun* the language of Iceland.
◇ The geographical isolation of Iceland from the other W Scandinavian-speaking countries led to the separate development of Old Icelandic; its literary form, Old Norse, was used from medieval times to transcribe the poetry and stories of the oral tradition, notably the Icelandic sagas. Icelandic has c.250 000 speakers in Iceland and parts of the USA.

Iceland spar *Geol.* a pure transparent form of calcite, noted for its ability to split a single incident ray of light into two refracted rays.

ice lolly *Brit. colloq.* flavoured water or ice-cream, frozen on a small stick.

Iceman Cometh, The a play by Eugene O'Neill (1946). It is a tragic parable about the dangers of shattering illusions, played out by drinkers discussing their dreams until disturbed by the ice-delivery man, the personification of death.

Iceni an ancient British tribe that occupied what is now Norfolk and NW Suffolk. They rebelled in AD 47 and again in AD 60, when their queen, Boadicea, led them and other tribes in a major revolt that briefly threatened the Roman administration in Britain.

ice pack 1 a bag packed with crushed ice, used in medicine eg to reduce a swelling or to reduce a patient's temperature. **2** an area of pack ice.

ice pick 1 a tool with a pointed end used by rock and mountain climbers for splitting ice. **2** a similar smaller tool for breaking ice into small pieces for drinks.

ice skate a skate with a metal blade for use on ice.

ice-skate *verb intrans.* to skate on ice.

ice-skater *noun* a person who skates on ice.

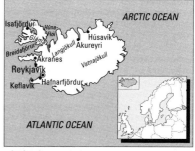

Iceland

ice-skating *noun* skating on ice.

◇ *Figure skating* is artistic dancing on ice. Competitions are held for individual, pairs, and ice dancing. The first known skating club was formed in the mid-18c in London, and the first artificial rink was opened in Baker Street in 1876. In *speed skating*, one competitor races against another on an oval ice track over distances of 500–10 000m.

ICFTU *abbrev.* International Confederation of Free Trade Unions.

Ichkeul a national park in Tunisia, established in 1978. The area is occupied by many kinds of wildfowl and is a World Heritage site. AREA 108sq km/42sq mi.

ichneumon *noun* 1 any of several winged insects which lay their larvae in or on the larvae of other insects, especially caterpillars. 2 a mongoose, especially the Egyptian species which destroys crocodile eggs. [from Greek *ichneumon*, tracker]

ichthyological *adj.* relating to or involving ichthyology.

ichthyologist *noun* an expert in ichthyology.

ichthyology *noun* the study of fishes. [from Greek *ichthys*, fish + -LOGY]

ICI *abbrev.* Imperial Chemical Industries.

icicle *noun* a long hanging spike of ice, formed by water freezing as it drops. [from Anglo-Saxon *isgicel*]

icily *adv.* in an icy way.

iciness *noun* being icy.

icing *noun* 1 a mixture of sugar, egg whites, water and sometimes lemon juice or other flavouring, used to form a hard coating on cakes. 2 the forming of ice on a ship or aircraft.
— **the icing on the cake** *colloq.* a desirable although unnecessary addition to something which is already satisfactory.

icing sugar sugar in the form of a very fine powder used to make icing, sweets, etc.

Icknield Way a neolithic track linking Salisbury Plain in SE England to the E coast. It was gravelled by the Romans and used as a secondary road.

Ickx, Jacky (1945–) Belgian racing driver, born in Brussels. He won eight races from 116 starts in Formula One. He won 34 world sports car championship races, and was world champion in 1982–3 (both Porsche). He won the Le Mans 24-hour race a record six times (1969, 1975–7, and 1981–2).

ICL *abbrev.* International Computers Ltd.

icon *or* **ikon** *noun* 1 an image of Christ, the Virgin Mary or a saint, usually painted on wood or done as a mosaic, especially in the Orthodox church. 2 a picture, image or representation. 3 *Comput.* an image on a computer screen which represents a function, operation, file, etc which is available, and which may be selected using the cursor rather than a typed command. [from Greek *eikon*, image]

iconoclasm *noun* the beliefs or actions of an iconoclast.

iconoclast *noun* 1 a person who destroys religious images and is opposed to their use in worship. 2 a person who is opposed to and attacks traditional and cherished beliefs and superstitions. [from Greek *eikon*, image + *klastes*, breaker]

iconoclastic *adj.* relating to iconoclasts or iconoclasm.

iconography *noun* the branch of art history that is concerned with the form and representation of the subject. Originally it was concerned with the identification of portraits, for example those depicted on coins. From the mid-19c it has been extended to cover the whole science of description of subject-matter and symbolism in the figurative arts, especially under the influence of Aby Warburg (1866–1929) and his followers. [from Greek *eikon*, an image + -GRAPHY]

iconology *noun* 1 the historical study of the social, political, and religious meanings of works of art. The method was laid down by the German art historian Edwin Panofsky (1892–1968). 2 the study of icons. [from Greek *eikon*, an image + -LOGY]

iconostasis *noun* a screen dividing the sanctuary from the main part of a Greek Orthodox or Byzantine church. It is usually covered with icons arranged in rows. [from Greek *eikon*, an image + *stasis*, placing]

icosahedron *noun* (PL. **icosahedrons**, **icosahedra**) a solid figure with twenty faces. [from Greek *eikosi*, twenty + *hedra*, seat]

-ics *suffix* forming singular or plural nouns denoting subjects of study or activities: *acoustics / athletics / mathematics*. [from French *-iques*, from Greek *-ika*]

Ictinus (5c BC) Greek architect, who with Callicrates designed the Parthenon at Athens (438 BC). He was also architect of temples at Eleusis and near Phigalia.

ICU *abbrev.* intensive care unit.

icy *adj.* (**icier**, **iciest**) 1 very cold. 2 covered with ice. 3 *said of someone's manner, behaviour, etc* unfriendly; hostile.

ID *abbrev.* 1 (*also* **Id**) Idaho. 2 identification.

I'd *contr.* 1 I had. 2 I would.

id *noun Psychol.* in psychoanalysis, the part of the unconscious mind that is regarded as the source of primitive biological instincts and urges for survival and reproduction. It governs the unconscious. The effects of the id on behaviour are limited by the *ego* and *superego*. See also EGO, SUPEREGO. [from Latin *id*, it]

Idaho POP (1990) 1.1m, a state in NW USA, divided into 44 counties, and bounded N by British Columbia, Canada. AREA 216 422sq km/ 83 564sq mi. PHYSICAL DESCRIPTION rivers include the Snake (forms part of the W border) and Salmon; the Bitterroot Range lies along much of the Montana border; in the centre and the N are the Sawtooth Mts, Salmon River Mts, and Clearwater Mts; the highest point is Borah Peak (3 860m); the state consists of largely rugged, mountainous country, with nearly half under national forest (mostly in the N); includes part of the Northern and Middle Rockies; the Snake R Plain is one of the largest irrigated areas in the USA; river dams also generate hydroelectric power; Hell's Canyon, on the Snake R, is one of the deepest gorges in the world. HISTORY the first European exploration was made by Lewis and Clark in 1805; held jointly by Britain and the USA until 1846; discovery of gold in 1860 led to an influx of settlers; the Territory of Idaho was established in 1863; admitted to the Union as the 43rd state in 1890; Idaho is known as the 'Gem State'. CAPITAL Boise. CHIEF TOWNS Pocatello, Idaho Falls. ECONOMY mainly an agricultural state; wheat, potatoes, hay, sugar-beets; cattle; dairy produce; industrial manufactures include wood products, processed foods, and chemicals; silver and antimony are mined; tourism and winter sports.

'Id-al-Adha the Muslim 'Feast of Sacrifice' celebrating the faith of Abraham who was willing to sacrifice his son, Isaac, at Allah's request. Sheep and goats are killed as a reminder of the sheep Allah provided as a substitute for the boy, and the meat is shared with the poor. [from Arabic *'Id al-Adha*]

'Id-al-Fitr a Muslim festival, the 'Feast of Breaking Fast' on the first day after Ramadan, celebrated with festive meals, the wearing of new clothes, and giving gifts to charity. [from Arabic *'Id al-Fitr*]

IDD *abbrev.* International Direct Dialling.

-ide *suffix Chem.* denoting a compound of an element with some other element, etc, eg *chloride*, a compound of chlorine. See also -ATE, -ITE.

idea *noun* 1 a thought, image, notion or concept formed by the mind. 2 a plan or intention. 3 a main aim, purpose, or feature: *the idea of the game is to win as many cards as possible*. 4 an opinion or belief: *he's got the idea that no one likes him*. 5 a vague notion or fancy: *have no idea of the work required*. 6 a person's conception of what is the best or perfect example of something: *not my idea of fun*. 7 in Plato's philosophy, a universal model of which all existing examples are imperfect copies.
— **get ideas** *colloq.* to have ideas which are over-ambitious or undesirable.
put ideas into someone's head to cause them to have over-ambitious or impractical ideas. [from Latin and Greek *idea*, form, pattern]

ideal — *adj.* 1 perfect; highest and best possible. 2 existing only in the mind; imaginary; visionary. — *noun* 1 the highest standard of behaviour, perfection, beauty, etc. 2 a person or thing considered to be perfect. [from Latin *idealis*]

ideal gas *Physics* a hypothetical gas in which atoms do not interact with one another. Such a gas would obey the gas laws, such as Boyle's law and Charles's law, exactly. – Also called *perfect gas*.

idealism *noun* 1 a tendency to show or present things in an ideal or idealized form rather than as they really are. 2 the practice of forming, and living according to, ideals. 3 *Philos.* the theory that material objects and the external world do not really exist but are products of the mind. See also REALISM.

idealist *noun* 1 a person who lives or tries to live according to ideals. 2 an impractical person. 3 *Philos.* a believer in idealism.

idealistic *adj.* involving or characterized by idealism.

idealistically *adv.* in an idealiztic way.

idealization *or* **idealisation** *noun* idealizing or being idealized.

idealize *or* **idealise** *verb* 1 to regard or treat (a person, etc) as perfect or ideal. 2 *intrans.* to form ideas.

ideally *adv.* in an ideal way; in ideal circumstances.

idée fixe *noun* (PL. **idées fixes**) an idea which dominates the mind; an obsession. [French, = fixed idea]

idem — *pron.* the same author, place, etc as previously mentioned. — *adv.* in the same place as previously mentioned. [from Latin *idem*, the same]

identical *adj.* 1 being very similar or exactly alike in every respect. 2 being the very same. 3 *said of twins* developed from a single fertilized egg which subsequently divided into equal halves to give two separate fetuses. They are always of the same sex and virtually identical genetically, closely resembling each other both physically and mentally. [from Latin *identicus*, from *idem*, the same]

identically *adv.* in an identical way.

identifiable *adj.* capable of being identified.

identification *noun* 1 an act of identifying or process of being identified. 2 something which allows a person or thing to be identified.

identification parade *Brit.* a line of people containing one person who is suspected of a crime and others who are innocent of it, from which a witness will try to identify the criminal.

identify *verb* (**identifies**, **identified**) 1 to recognize (someone or something) as being a particular person or thing; to establish the identity of. 2 to associate (one person, thing or group) with another. 3 (**identify with someone**) to feel sympathy and understanding for a real or fictional person because of shared personal characteristics or experiences. **4** to see clearly or pinpoint (a problem, method, solution, etc). [from Latin *idem*, the same + *facere*, to make]

Identikit *noun trademark* a series of transparent strips, each one showing a different typical facial feature, from which an impression or rough picture of a criminal or suspect can be put together from witnesses' descriptions.

identity *noun* (PL. **identities**) **1** the state or quality of being a specified person or thing; who or what a person or thing is: *the winner's identity is not yet known.* **2** the individual characteristics by which a person or thing can be identified; individuality; personality. **3** the state of being exactly the same. **4** *Maths.* **a** same as IDENTITY ELEMENT. **b** an equation which remains true whichever way it is written or expressed, and whichever values are substituted for the letters used. [from Latin *identitas*, from *idem*, the same]

identity card a card bearing information about, and often a photograph of, the holder, taken as proof of a person's identity.

identity crisis *Psychol.* a mental conflict involving loss of a person's sense of self, and inability to accept or adopt the role he or she believes is expected by society. Identity crises are common in adolescence, and in situations where rapid social, educational, or technological changes occur. Typical symptoms include withdrawal or rebelliousness.

identity element *Maths.* an element which when combined with another element in a certain mathematical operation gives that second element as the product of the operation, *0* in addition (as $a + 0 = a$) and *1* in multiplication (as $a{\times}1 = a$).

identity parade same as IDENTIFICATION PARADE.

ideogram *or* **ideograph** *noun* a written symbol designed to convey an abstract concept, or which stands for a real object without being a direct representation of it. Ideograms are seen as a development of the early pictographs in ancient writing systems, and are found in early Egyptian, Hittite, and Sumerian inscriptions. Modern ideograms may be found on signs and the manufacturer's care labels on garments, etc. See also LOGOGRAPH, PICTOGRAPH. [from Greek *idea*, idea + *gramma*, drawing]

ideograph *noun* an ideogram. [from Greek *idea*, idea + -GRAPH]

ideographic *adj.* of the nature of or made up of ideographs.

ideographically *adv.* in an ideographic way.

ideological *adj.* relating to or involving ideology.

ideologically *adv.* in an ideological way.

ideologist *noun* **1** a person who supports a particular ideology. **2** a theorist. **3** a person who studies or is an expert in ideologies.

ideology *noun* (PL. **ideologies**) **1** the body of ideas and beliefs which form the basis for a social, economic, or political system. **2** the opinions, beliefs, and way of thinking characteristic of a particular person, group of people or nation. [from Greek *idea*, idea + -LOGY]

Ides *pl. noun* (in the ancient Roman calendar) the fifteenth day of March, May, July, and October and the thirteenth day of the other months. [from Latin *idus*]

idiocy *noun* (PL. **idiocies**) **1** the state of being an idiot or extremely retarded mentally. **2** a foolish action or foolish behaviour.

idiolect *noun* a person's individual and distinctive way of speaking. [from Greek *idios*, own + dia*lect*]

idiom *noun* **1** an expression with a meaning which cannot be guessed at or derived from the

meanings of the individual words which form it. **2** the syntax, grammar and forms of expression peculiar to a language or a variety of language. **3** the language, vocabulary, forms of expression, etc used by a particular person or group of people. **4** the characteristic style or forms of expression of a particular artist, musician, artistic or musical school, etc. [from Greek *idios*, own]

idiomatic *adj.* **1** characteristic of a particular language. **2** tending to use idioms.

idiomatically *adv.* in an idiomatic way.

idiosyncrasy *noun* (PL. **idiosyncrasies**) any personal way of behaving, reacting or thinking; a personal peculiarity or eccentricity. [from Greek *idios*, own + *syn*, together + *krasis*, mixing]

idiosyncratic *adj.* involving idiosyncrasy; individual, eccentric.

idiosyncratically *adv.* in an idiosyncratic way.

Idiot, The a novel by Fyodor Dostoevsky (1868). It describes the life of the Christ-like hero Myshkin who eventually goes insane.

idiot *noun* **1** *colloq.* a foolish or stupid person. **2** a person who is severely mentally retarded. [from Greek *idiotes*, person lacking skill or expertise]

idiotic *adj.* stupid, foolish.

idiotically *adv.* in an idiotic way.

idle — *adj.* **1** not in use; not being used; unoccupied. **2** not wanting to work; lazy; indolent. **3** having no effect, result, purpose or value: *idle gossip.* **4** without cause, basis or good reason; unnecessary: *idle rumour.* — *verb* **1** (*usually* **idle away time**, *etc*) to spend time doing nothing or being idle. **2** *intrans.* to do nothing or be idle. **3** *intrans. said of an engine, machinery, etc* to run gently without doing any work. **4** to cause (an engine, etc) to idle. [from Anglo-Saxon *idel*, worthless]

idleness *noun* being idle; doing nothing.

idler *noun* a person who wastes time or is reluctant to work.

idly *adv.* in an idle way.

idol *noun* **1** an image or symbol, especially of a god, used as an object of worship. **2** an object of excessive love, honour or devotion. [from Greek *eidolon*]

idolater *noun* **1** a person who worships idols. **2** a person who is a passionate and devoted admirer of someone or something.

idolatress *noun* a female idolater.

idolatrous *adj.* relating to or involving the worship of idols.

idolatrously *adv.* in an idolatrous way.

idolatry *noun* (PL. **idolatries**) **1** the worship of idols. **2** excessive, love, honour, admiration or devotion.

idolization *or* **idolisation** *noun* idolizing or being idolized.

idolize *or* **idolise** *verb* **1** to love, honour, admire, etc (a person) too much. **2** to make an idol of.

idolizer *or* **idoliser** *noun* a person who idolizes.

Idomeneus in Greek legend, the leader of the Cretans who assisted the Greeks at Troy, the grandson of Minos. He was caught in a storm at sea and vowed to sacrifice the first thing he met on his safe return. This was his son, and after carrying out the sacrifice he was driven into exile.

idyll *or* **idyl** *noun* **1** a short poem or prose work describing a simple, pleasant, usually rural or pastoral scene. **2** a story, episode or scene suitable for such a work, eg one of happy innocence or love. [from Greek *eidyllion*]

idyllic *adj.* **1** relating to or typical of an idyll. **2** charming, picturesque.

idyllically *adv.* in an idyllic way.

Idylls of the King a sequence of 12 connected poems by Alfred Lord Tennyson (1859–85). They tell the legend of King Arthur from his meeting with Guinevere to his death.

ie *or* **i.e.** *abbrev.* for Latin *id est*, that is to say.

Ieper see YPRES.

if — *conj.* **1** in the event that; on condition that; supposing that. **2** although; even though. **3** whenever. **4** whether. **5** used to express a wish: *if only it would stop raining.* **6** used to make a polite request or suggestion: *if you wouldn't mind stopping just a minute.* **7** used to express surprise or annoyance: *well, if it isn't that book I'd thought I'd lost!* — *noun* a condition or supposition: *too many ifs and buts.*

— **if anything** perhaps; on the contrary. [from Anglo-Saxon *gif*]

Ife a Yoruba ceremonial and trading centre in SW Nigeria, occupied from the 11c, from which the Yoruba dispersed to found their kingdoms. It is noted for its naturalistic figures in brass and terracotta (possibly from the late 14c or early 15c). The related Benin tradition may also derive from Ife.

iffy *adj.* (**iffier, iffiest**) *colloq.* uncertain; doubtful; dubious.

Igbo *or* **Ibo** a people of E Nigeria, living in many small and traditionally autonomous communities, with a common culture (present-day population c.13m); the Igbo language is a member of the Kwa branch of the Niger–Congo family. They dominated agricultural trade in Nigeria, and produced the earliest bronze art in the region. They established the short-lived state of Biafra (1960–70), during which time the genocide of Igbo living in other parts of Nigeria occurred.

igloo *noun* a dome-shaped Inuit house built with blocks of snow and ice. [from Inuit *iglu*, house]

Ignatius Loyola, St, originally Iñigo López de Recalde (1491–1556) Spanish soldier and founder of the Jesuits, born in his ancestral castle of Loyola in the Basque province of Guipúzcoa. He was wounded in action, and while convalescing read the lives of Jesus Christ and the saints, following which he renounced military life and went on a pilgrimage to Jerusalem (1522). In 1534 with Frances Xavier and four other associates he founded the Society of Jesus, a missionary order. After the rule was approved by the pope (1540), he sent out missionaries to Japan, India, and Brazil, and founded schools. He wrote the influential *Spiritual Exercises*, was canonized in 1622, and his feast day is 31 Jul.

igneous *adj.* **1** of or like fire. **2** *Geol.* denoting any of a group of rocks that are formed by the solidification of molten magma either beneath the Earth's surface, producing *intrusive* (plutonic) rocks, eg granite, or after it has been extruded on to the surface, producing *extrusive* (volcanic) rocks, eg basalt. See also METAMORPHIC, SEDIMENTARY. [from Latin *ignis*, fire]

ignis fatuus (PL. **ignes fatui**) a will-o'-the-wisp. [from Latin *ignis fatuus*, foolish fire]

ignitable *or* **ignitible** *adj.* capable of being ignited.

ignite *verb* **1** to set fire to. **2** *intrans.* to catch fire. **3** to heat to the point at which combustion occurs. **4** to excite (feelings, emotions, etc). [from Latin *ignis*, fire]

ignition *noun* **1** *Chem.* the point at which combustion of a chemical substance begins. **2** *Engineering* a system that initiates such combustion, especially by producing a spark which ignites an explosive mixture of fuel and air in an internal combustion engine, such as the petrol engine of a car. See illustration p. 624.

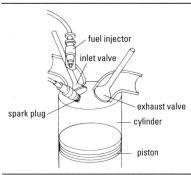

ignition system — petrol engine

Labels: fuel injector, inlet valve, spark plug, exhaust valve, cylinder, piston

ignition temperature *Chem.* the temperature to which a substance must be heated before it will burn in air.

ignobility *or* **ignobleness** *noun* being ignoble.

ignoble *adj.* **1** causing shame; dishonourable; mean. **2** of humble or low birth. [from Latin *ignobilis*]

ignobly *adv.* in an ignoble way.

ignominious *adj.* causing shame or dishonour; humiliating.

ignominiously *adv.* in an ignominious way.

ignominiousness *noun* being ignominious.

ignominy *noun* **1** public shame, disgrace or dishonour. **2** dishonourable conduct. [from Latin *ignominia*]

ignoramus *noun* (PL. **ignoramuses**) an ignorant person. [from Latin *ignoramus*, we do not know]

ignorance *noun* **1** lack of knowledge or awareness. **2** being ignorant.

ignorant *adj.* **1** knowing very little; uneducated. **2** (**ignorant of something**) knowing little or nothing about it. **3** rude; ill-mannered. [from Latin *ignorare*, not to know]

ignorantly *adv.* in an ignorant way.

ignore *verb* to take no notice of deliberately; to refuse to pay attention to. [from Latin *ignorare*, not to know]

Iguaçu a national park on the border between Argentina and Brazil. It is noted for its spectacular scenery, particularly the 82m-high Iguaçu Falls. The park is a World Heritage site. AREA 1 950sq km/750sq mi.

iguana *noun* (PL. **iguanas**, **iguana**) any of a family of large insectivorous lizards with a crest of spines along its back. The common iguana is bright green and lives in tree branches in tropical Central and S America. Ground-dwelling iguanas and the marine iguana (the only lizard that swims underwater to browse on seaweed) are found on the Galapagos Islands. [from Carib (S American Indian language) *iwana*]

iguana

Iguvine Tablets a set of seven inscribed bronze tablets, relating to the period c.400–90 BC, discovered in 1444 near Iguvium (modern Gubbio), Italy. They contain rules for the ceremonies of a brotherhood of priests, with much information about the cults of Roman gods and goddesses (eg Jupiter and Pomona).

Ikaría see ICARIA.

ikebana *noun* the Japanese art of flower arranging, in which blooms (or a single bloom), leaves, and other materials, are arranged formally and in careful relationship with one another to create a correct balance. [Japanese, = living flowers]

ikon see ICON.

IL *abbrev.* Illinois.

il- a form of *in-* used before words beginning in *l*: *illogical*.

ileostomy *noun Medicine* a surgical operation in which the ileum (the lowest part of the small intestine) is brought through an artificial opening in the abdominal wall, so that the contents of the ileum can be discharged directly to the outside of the body, bypassing the colon.

ileum *noun* (PL. **ilea**) the lower part of the small intestine leading into the large intestine. [from Latin *ilia*, groin, guts]

iliac *adj.* relating to or in the region of the ilium.

Iliad, The an epic poem by Homer (c.8c BC). It describes the siege and sack of Troy following the abduction by Paris of Menelaus's queen, Helen. It focuses particularly on the wrath of Achilles during the campaign and gives a detailed description of many battles, including Achilles' slaying of Hector in revenge for the death of his friend Patroclus.

ilium *noun* (PL. **ilia**) one of a pair of large bones that form the upper part of each side of the pelvis; commonly called the hip bone. [from Latin *ilia*, groin, guts]

ilk — *noun* type; kind; class. — *adj. Scot.* same. — **of that ilk 1** of that type or kind. **2** *Scot.* of that same, ie of the estate or place of the same name (as the person's family name). [from Anglo-Saxon *ilca*]

Ill. *abbrev.* Illinois.

I'll *contr.* I will or I shall.

ill — *adj.* (**worse, worst**) **1** not in good health; sick. **2** *said of health* not good. **3** bad or harmful: *ill effects / ill-treatment.* **4** hostile; unfriendly: *ill-will.* **5** causing bad luck: *an ill omen.* **6** *said of manners* incorrect; improper. — *adv.* (**worse, worst**) **1** not easily; with difficulty. **2** hardly, scarcely: *be ill able to afford the money.* **3** badly; wrongly: *ill-matched.* **4** unfavourably: *it went ill with them.* **5** harshly: *speak ill of someone.* — *noun* **1** evil; harm. **2** injury; ailment.
— **ill at ease** uneasy; embarrassed.
ill become one to do one no credit; not to be to one's advantage.
take it ill to be offended.
[from Norse *illr*]

ill-advised *adj.* foolish; done, or doing things, with little thought or consideration.

Illampu, Nevado de *or* **Mount Sorata** the highest mountain in the Andean Cordillera Oriental, situated in W central Bolivia in the Cordillera de la Paz Range. It consists of two peaks – Illampu (6 485m) and Ancohuma (6 388m).

ill-assorted *adj.* badly matched; not going well together.

ill-bred *adj.* badly brought up or educated; rude.

ill-considered *adj.* badly thought out; not well planned.

ill-disposed *adj.* unfriendly; unsympathetic; unwilling to be supportive or helpful.

illegal *adj.* against the law; not legal. [from Latin *illegalis*]

illegality *noun* (PL. **illegalities**) an illegal state or action.

illegally *adv.* in an illegal way.

illegibility *noun* being illegible.

illegible *adj.* difficult or impossible to read; not legible.

illegibly *adv.* in an illegible way.

illegitimacy *noun* being illegitimate.

illegitimate *adj.* **1** born of parents not married to each other at the time of birth. **2** unacceptable or not allowed, especially illegal. **3** *Logic* not properly inferred or reasoned. **4** improper.

illegitimately *adv.* in an illegitimate way.

ill-equipped *adj.* poorly provided with the necessary tools, abilities, etc.

ill-fated *adj.* ending in or bringing bad luck or ruin.

ill-favoured *adj.* not attractive, especially in appearance; objectionable.

ill-feeling *noun* bad or hostile feeling; animosity.

ill-founded *adj., said of an argument, theory, suspicion, etc* having no sound basis or reason.

ill-gotten *adj.* obtained dishonestly: *ill-gotten gains.*

ill-humoured *adj.* bad-tempered; quick-tempered.

illiberal *adj.* **1** having strict opinions about morality, behaviour, etc; narrow-minded; prejudiced. **2** not generous; mean. **3** uncultured; unrefined. [from Latin *illiberalis*]

illiberality *noun* being illiberal.

illiberally *adv.* in an illiberal way.

illicit *adj.* not permitted by law or by social custom. [from Latin *illicitus*]

illicitly *adv.* in an illicit way.

illicitness *noun* being illicit.

ill-informed *adj.* lacking knowledge or information.

Illinois POP (1990) 11.6m, a state in N central USA, divided into 102 counties. AREA 145 928sq km/56 328sq mi. The Mississippi R forms the W border, the Ohio R follows the Kentucky border, the Wabash R forms the lower part of the Indiana border, and the Illinois R flows SW across the state to meet the Mississippi R. The land is mostly flat prairie and Illinois is known as the 'Prairie State'. HISTORY first European exploration in 1673 by Jolliet and Marquette, then settled by the French who established Fort St Louis in 1692; included in French Louisiana, the area was ceded to the British in 1763 and by the British to the USA in 1783; in 1818 it was the 21st state to join the Union; use of its more than 275 rivers for exploration and transportation, and the completion of the Erie Canal, aided the settlement of the prairies. CAPITAL Springfield. CHIEF TOWNS Chicago, Rockford, Peoria. ECONOMY an important agricultural state; maize, soya beans, wheat; cattle, hogs; coal mining; diverse manufacturing is centred on the Chicago area.

illiteracy *noun* being illiterate; the inability to read and write.

illiterate — *adj.* **1** unable to read and write. **2** uneducated or ignorant, especially in a particular field or subject. — *noun* an illiterate person. [from Latin *illiteratus*]

illiterately *adv.* in an illiterate way.

ill-judged *adj.* poorly advised; done without proper consideration.

ill-mannered *adj.* having bad manners; rude; uncouth.

ill-natured *adj.* spiteful; mean; surly.

illness *noun* **1** a disease. **2** the state of being sick or unwell.

illogical *adj.* **1** not based on careful thinking or reason. **2** not following the principles of logic.

illogicality *noun* (PL. **illogicalities**) being illogical, or an instance of this.

illogically *adv.* in an illogical way.

ill-omened *adj.*, *said of a plan, course of action, etc* likely to end badly.

ill-starred *adj.* marked by bad luck; bound to fail.

ill-tempered *adj.* bad-tempered; spiteful and surly.

ill-timed *adj.* said or done at an unsuitable time; inopportune.

ill-treat *verb* to treat badly or cruelly; to abuse.

ill-treatment *noun* abuse, cruelty, misuse.

illuminant — *noun* something that gives off light. — *adj.* giving off light. [from Latin *illuminare*, from *lumen*, light]

illuminate *verb* 1 to light up or make bright. 2 to decorate with lights. 3 to decorate (a manuscript) with elaborate designs and initial letters in gold, silver or bright colours. 4 to make clearer and more easily understood. 5 to enlighten spiritually or intellectually. [from Latin *illuminare*, from *lumen*, light]

illuminating *adj.* that clarifies, explains, or informs.

illumination *noun* 1 the act of illuminating or state of being illuminated. 2 any source of light; lighting. 3 (**illuminations**) coloured decorative lights hung in streets and towns. 4 the art or skill of decorating manuscripts with elaborate designs and initial letters in gold, silver and bright colours. 5 such a design or initial letter in a manuscript.

illuminative *adj.* illuminating, lighting.

illumine *verb poetic*, *literary* to illuminate. [from Old French *illuminer*]

illusion *noun* 1 a deceptive or misleading appearance. 2 a false or misleading impression, idea, belief or understanding; delusion. 3 *Psychol.* a false perception of an object or experience due to misinterpretation by the mind of evidence relayed to it by the senses, eg the overheard conversations of others may be interpreted as voices conspiring to destroy the listener. [from Latin *illusio*, irony, mocking]
♦ Often confused with *allusion*.

illusionism *noun Art* the use of perspective, foreshortening, light and shade, and other pictorial devices to produce an illusion of reality. Ancient Roman wall-paintings (such as at Pompeii), Renaissance stage-scenery, and Baroque ceiling-decoration are examples of illusionism.

illusionist *noun* a conjurer who plays tricks on the eyes.

illusive *or* **illusory** *adj.* 1 seeming to be or having the characteristics of an illusion. 2 deceptive; unreal.

illustrate *verb* 1 to provide (a book, text, lecture, etc) with pictures and diagrams. 2 to make (a statement, etc) clearer, especially by providing examples. 3 to be an example of. [from Latin *illustrare*, to light up]

illustrated *adj.* having or using illustrations.

illustration *noun* 1 a picture or diagram that helps make a text, book, lecture, etc clearer, or decorates it. 2 an example which makes something clear. 3 the act of illustrating or state of being illustrated.

illustrative *adj.* being or acting as an illustration, explanation or example.

illustratively *adv.* in an illustrative way.

illustrator *noun* a person who provides illustrations.

illustrious *adj.* distinguished; renowned; celebrated; noble. [from Latin *illustris*, bright, lustrous]

illustriously *adv.* famously.

ill-will *noun* bad or unfriendly feeling; the urge or wish to do harm: *bear him no ill-will*.

Illyria in antiquity, the E coast of the Adriatic and its mountainous hinterland on the NW part of the Balkan peninsula. It was inhabited from the 10c BC by the Illyrians and other tribes. It was eventually conquered by the Romans, and became the Roman province of Illyricum in 167 BC.

ilmenite *noun Geol.* a black or dark brown mineral composed of iron, titanium, and oxygen, found in igneous rocks, and in metamorphic rocks such as gneiss and schist. It is the principal ore of titanium. [named after the Ilmen Mountains in the Urals]

Ilyushin, Sergei Vladimirovich (1894–1977) Soviet aircraft designer, born in Dilialevo, Vologda province. After working as an aviation mechanic, he graduated in engineering, and in 1931 took charge of the design of both military and civil aircraft, including the Il–4 long-range bomber, which was important in World War II. Later his passenger aeroplanes became the basic Soviet carriers.

I'm *contr.* I am.

im- a form of *in-* (see IN-[1], IN-[2]) used before words beginning in *b*, *m*, and *p*: *immature / implode*.

image — *noun* 1 a likeness of a person or thing, especially in the form of a portrait or statue. 2 a person or thing that resembles another person or thing closely. 3 an idea or picture in the mind. 4 an optical reproduction of a physical object formed by light reflected in a mirror or refracted through a lens. It may be upright or inverted, and magnified or reduced in size. A *real* image, eg one produced by a convex lens, can be projected on to a screen, whereas a *virtual* image, eg one produced by a plane mirror, does not in fact exist, but only appears to the observer to do so. 5 *Physics* any reproduction of a physical object formed by sound waves or electromagnetic radiation originating from or reflected by the object, eg ultrasound scan, X-ray photograph. 6 the visual display reproduced by a television receiver. 7 *Psychol.* a mental view of another person, eg a child's image of its mother. 8 (*in full public image*) the impression that people in general have of someone's character, behaviour, etc. 9 a typical example or embodiment. 10 a simile or metaphor. — *verb* 1 to form an image of. 2 to form a likeness of in the mind; to imagine. 3 to mirror. 4 to be a typical example of. [from Latin *imago*]

imagery *noun* (PL. **imageries**) 1 the use of figures of speech in writing, literature, etc. 2 the making of images, especially in the mind. 3 mental images. 4 statues, carvings, etc.

imaginable *adj.* capable of being imagined.

imaginary *adj.* existing only in the mind or imagination; not real.

imaginary number *Maths.* the square root of a negative number.

imagination *noun* 1 the ability to form or the process of forming mental images of things, etc one has not seen or of which one has no direct perception or knowledge. 2 the creative ability of the mind. 3 the ability to cope resourcefully with unexpected events or problems.

imaginative *adj.* 1 showing, done with or created by imagination. 2 having a lively imagination.

imaginatively *adv.* in an imaginative way.

imaginativeness *noun* being imaginative.

imagine *verb* 1 *trans.*, *intrans.* to form a mental picture of something. 2 to see or hear, etc something which is not true or does not exist: *imagine things*. 3 to think, suppose, or guess: *I can't imagine where she's got to*. 4 *intrans.* to use the imagination. 5 *intrans.*, *trans.* used as an exclamation of surprise: *imagine that!* [from Latin *imaginari*, from *imago*, image]

imaginings *pl. noun* things seen or heard which do not exist; fancies, fantasies.

Imagism an early 20c poetic movement which sought to return (and confine) poetry to its essential ingredient, the image. Examples of Imagist poetry can be seen in the work of Ezra Pound and Amy Lowell.

imago *noun* (PL. **imagos**, **imagines**) the final stage in the life cycle of an insect, when it is a sexually mature adult. [from Latin *imago*, image]

imam *noun* 1 a leader of prayers in a Mosque. 2 (**Imam**) a title given to various Muslim leaders, eg a Shiite religious leader believed to be a direct successor of the prophet Mohammed, or a learned Muslim theologian. [from Arabic *imam*, chief, leader]

IMAX *noun trademark* a system of large widescreen motion-picture presentation, developed in Canada in 1968, using 70mm film running horizontally with a frame size 70×46 mm. It is projected on a screen, usually 18–23m wide and 14–18m high; the audience is seated comparatively close to the screen so that the picture fills their field of vision. [from IMAGE + MAXIMUM]

imbalance *noun* a lack of balance or proportion; inequality.

imbecile — *noun* 1 a person of very low intelligence, especially someone who is capable only of keeping himself or herself out of danger and of performing simple tasks under supervision. 2 a stupid person; a fool. — *adj.* mentally weak; stupid; foolish. [from Latin *imbecillus*]

imbecility *noun* (PL. **imbecilities**) 1 being an imbecile. 2 extreme stupidity, or an instance of this.

imbed *verb* (**imbedded**, **imbedding**) same as EMBED.

imbibe *verb* 1 *trans.*, *intrans.* to drink (especially alcoholic drinks). 2 to take in or absorb (ideas, etc). [from Latin *imbibere*]

imbricate *adj.* Biol., *said of fish scales, leaves, layers of tissue, teeth, etc* overlapping like roof tiles. [from Latin *imbricare*, to cover with overlapping tiles, from *imbrex* a tile]

imbroglio *noun* (PL. **imbroglios**) 1 a confused mass or heap. 2 a confused and complicated situation. 3 a misunderstanding or disagreement. [from Italian *imbroglio*, confusion]

imbue *verb* 1 (**imbue someone with something**) to fill or inspire them, especially with ideals or principles. 2 to soak or saturate, especially with dye. [from Latin *imbuere*, to saturate]

IMF *abbrev.* International Monetary Fund.

imitable *adj.* capable of being imitated.

imitate *verb* 1 to copy the behaviour, manners, appearance, etc of; to take as a model. 2 to mimic. 3 to make a copy of; to reproduce or duplicate. [from Latin *imitari*]

imitation — *noun* 1 an act of imitating. 2 that which is produced by imitating; a copy or counterfeit. 3 *Mus.* the repeating of a passage, phrase, theme, etc which has already been heard, often at a different pitch or in a different voice. — *adj.* cheaply made to look or function like something which is more expensive.

Imitation of Christ, The (De Imitatione Christi) a Latin devotional book by Thomas A Kempis. It describes the steady advancement of the soul towards a state of Christian harmony.

imitative *adj.* 1 imitating, copying, or mimicking. 2 copying a more expensive original. 3 *said of a word* imitating the sound (eg *sizzle*) or trying to represent the appearance, movement or general impression (eg *flash*) of a thing or action.

imitatively *adv.* in an imitative way.

imitativeness *noun* being imitative.

imitator *noun* a person or creature that imitates.

immaculate *adj.* **1** perfectly clean and neat; perfectly groomed. **2** free from blemish, flaw or error; pure. [from IM- + Latin *macula*, spot, stain]

Immaculate Conception the belief that the Virgin Mary was free from sin from the moment of her conception. This was promulgated as a dogma of the Roman Catholic Church by Pope Pius IX in 1854. It was always rejected by Protestants as unbiblical, and in 1854 was rejected also by the Orthodox Church.

immaculately *adv.* in an immaculate way.

immanence *or* **immanency** *noun* the concept of a supreme being present throughout the universe.

immanent *adj.* **1** existing or remaining within; inherent. **2** *said of a supreme being or power* present everywhere. [from IM- + Latin *manere*, to remain]

Immanuel *or* **Emmanuel** in the Hebrew Bible and Old Testament, a name mentioned in Isaiah (eg 7.14), where the birth of a son of this name to a young woman is a sign to King Ahaz of Judah's security against her northern enemies. In the New Testament, this text is cited in Matthew 1.23 where an angel appears to Joseph and prophesies the birth of Jesus the Messiah. [Hebrew, = God with us]

immaterial *adj.* **1** not important. **2** not formed of matter. [from Latin *immaterialis*]

immature *adj.* **1** not fully grown or developed; not ripe. **2** not fully developed emotionally or intellectually and therefore childish. [from Latin *immaturus*]

immaturely *adv.* in an immature way.

immaturity *noun* being immature.

immeasurable *adj.* too great to be measured; very great; immense.

immeasurably *adv.* greatly, in a way that cannot be measured.

immediacy *noun* (PL. **immediacies**) **1** the quality of being immediate or appealing directly to the emotions, understanding, etc. **2** an immediate problem, requirement, or necessity.

immediate *adj.* **1** happening or done at once and without delay. **2** nearest or next in space, time or relationship: *the immediate family / the immediate vicinity.* **3** of the current time; urgent: *deal with the immediate problems first.* **4** having a direct effect and without anything coming in between: *the immediate cause of death.* [from Latin *immediatus*]

immediately — *adv.* at once or without delay; without anything coming in between. — *conj.* as soon as.

immemorial *adj.* extending far back in time beyond anyone's memory or written records: *a custom since time immemorial.* [from Latin *immemorialis*]

immemorially *adv.* far back in time.

immense *adj.* **1** very or unusually large or great. **2** *colloq.* very good. [from Latin *immensus*, immeasurable]

immensely *adv.* very greatly.

immenseness *or* **immensity** *noun* great size, immeasurable extent.

immerse *verb* **1** to dip into or under the surface of a liquid completely. **2** to baptize by submerging the whole body in water. **3** (**be immersed in something**) to be occupied or involved deeply in it; to be absorbed: *became immersed in the book.* [from Latin *immergere*, to dip]

immersible *adj.* capable of being immersed.

immersion *noun* **1** immersing or being immersed. **2** baptism.

immersion heater an electric heating element that is immersed directly in a tank of water, and controlled by a thermostat. Immersion heaters are used to provide a supply of hot water for domestic purposes.

immigrant — *noun* **1** a person who immigrates. **2** *Biol.* an animal or plant which becomes established in an area where it was previously not found. — *adj.* **1** *said of a person* having recently immigrated. **2** concerning or relating to immigrants. See also EMIGRANT.

immigrate *verb intrans.* to come to a foreign country with the intention of settling in it. See also EMIGRATE. [from Latin *immigrare*]

immigration *noun* immigrating; settling in a foreign country.

imminence *noun* **1** being imminent. **2** something imminent.

imminent *adj.*, *said especially of something unwelcome* likely to happen in the near future. [from Latin *imminere*, to project over]

Immingham POP (1981) 12 000, an important port situated in Holderness district, Humberside, NE England.

immiscible *adj. Chem.* denoting two or more liquids that when shaken together form separate layers and do not mix, eg oil and water.

immobile *adj.* **1** not able to move or be moved. **2** not moving; motionless. [from Latin *immobilis*]

immobility *noun* being immobile; stability, lack of movement.

immobilization *or* **immobilisation** *noun* immobilizing or being immobilized.

immobilize *or* **immobilise** *verb* to make or keep immobile.

immoderacy *noun* lack of restraint.

immoderate *adj.* going far beyond normal or reasonable limits; extreme; excessive. [from Latin *immoderatus*]

immoderately *adv.* extravagantly, without restraint.

immoderateness *noun* being immoderate.

immodest *adj.* **1** lacking modesty; shameful; indecent; improper. **2** boastful and conceited; forward. [from Latin *immodestus*]

immodestly *adv.* without modesty, indecently.

immodesty *noun* lack of modesty, indecency.

immolate *verb* to kill or offer in sacrifice. [from Latin *immolare*, to sprinkle with meal before sacrificing]

immolation *noun* **1** an act of immolating, a sacrifice. **2** something that is sacrificed.

immoral *adj.* **1** morally wrong or bad; evil. **2** not conforming to the sexual standards of society; promiscuous. See also AMORAL.

immorality *noun* (PL. **immoralities**) **1** being immoral. **2** an immoral act or activity. **3** promiscuity.

immorally *adv.* in an immoral way.

immortal — *adj.* **1** living forever and never dying. **2** lasting forever; perpetual. — *noun* **1** a person who will live forever, or who will always be remembered. **2** (**the immortals**) the ancient Greek and Roman gods. [from Latin *immortalis*]

immortality *noun* being immortal.

immortalize *or* **immortalise** *verb* to make (a person, event, etc) famous for ever, especially by inclusion in a work of art.

immovability *noun* being immovable.

immovable *adj.* **1** impossible to move; not meant to be moved. **2** steadfast; unyielding. **3** incapable of feeling or showing emotion, especially sorrow or pity. **4** *Legal, said of property* consisting of land or houses.

immovably *adv.* in an immovable way; so as to be immovable.

immune *adj.* **1** (**immune to something**) protected by inoculation from, or having a natural resistance to, a particular disease: *is immune to German measles.* **2** (**immune from something**) free, exempt, or protected from it: *was immune from prosecution.* [from Latin *immunis*]

immune response *Physiol.* the response of the body to the introduction of an antigen (a foreign substance), especially the formation of antibodies, but also including the development of cellular immunity, hypersensitive reactions, etc.

immune system *Physiol.* the tissues and cells of the body that recognize and attack the antigens (foreign substances) associated with different diseases.

immunity *noun* (PL. **immunities**) an immune state; protection.

immunization *or* **immunisation** *noun* making immune, especially to a disease.

immunize *or* **immunise** *verb* to produce artificial immunity to a disease in (a person) by injecting an antiserum (containing antibodies formed in another organism), which confers *passive immunity*, or a treated antigen (eg dead or weakened viruses or bacteria), which confers *active immunity* by stimulating the body to produce its own antibodies.

immunodeficiency *noun* (PL. **immunodeficiencies**) a deficiency or breakdown in the body's ability to fight infection.

immunoglobulin *noun Biol.* one of a group of proteins found in blood plasma, acting as antibodies.

immunological *adj.* relating to or involving immunology.

immunologist *noun* an expert in immunology.

immunology *noun* the scientific study of resistance to, and protection against, infection.

immunosuppressive *or* **immunosuppressant** — *noun Medicine* a drug or other agent that suppresses the body's normal immune response and so lowers its resistance to infection. Immunosuppressive drugs are used to ensure that transplanted organs and tissues are not rejected. — *adj.* denoting such a drug or agent.

immure *verb* **1** to enclose or imprison within, or as if within, walls. **2** to shut (someone or oneself) away. [from IM- + Latin *murus*, wall]

immutability *noun* being unchangeable.

immutable *adj.* that cannot be changed or will not change. [from Latin *immutabilis*]

immutably *adv.* unalterably.

Imogen **1** the virtuous daughter and heroine of Shakespeare's *Cymbeline*, who remains loyal to her husband Posthumus despite the knowledge that he is plotting her death. **2** a female first name, after Shakespeare's character. [from the Celtic name *Innogen*, related to Gaelic *ingean*, girl, maiden]

imp *noun* **1** a small mischievous or evil spirit. **2** a mischievous or annoying child. [from Anglo-Saxon *impa*, shoot]

impact — *noun* (with stress on *im-*) **1** the act of an object hitting or colliding with another object; a collision. **2** the force of such a collision. **3** a strong effect or impression. — *verb* (with variable stress) **1** to press (two objects) together with force or to force (one object) into (another). **2** *intrans.* to come into contact with force. **3** *intrans.* to have an impact or effect on someone or something. [from Latin *impingere*, to strike against]

impacted *adj.* **1** *said of a tooth* unable to grow because of being wedged between the jawbone and another tooth. **2** *said of a fracture* with the two broken ends of bone crushed together.

impair *verb* to damage or weaken, especially in quality or strength. [from Old French *empeirer*]

impairment *noun* damage, weakening.

impala noun (PL. **impalas**, **impala**) noun a graceful African antelope with lyre-shaped horns, capable of long high leaps. [from Zulu]

impale verb **1** to pierce with or as if with a long pointed object or weapon. **2** to put (two coats-of-arms) on a shield divided vertically into two. [from IM- + Latin palus, stake]

impalement noun impaling or being impaled.

impalpability noun being impalpable.

impalpable adj. **1** not able to be felt or perceived by touch. **2** difficult to understand or grasp. [from Latin impalpabilis]

impalpably adv. not palpably.

impanel verb (**impanelled**, **impanelling**) same as EMPANEL.

impart verb **1** to make (information, knowledge, etc) known; to communicate (news, etc). **2** to give or transmit (a particular quality). [from Latin impartire]

impartation noun imparting, communication.

impartial adj. not favouring one person, etc more than another; fair and unbiased; not partial.

impartiality noun being impartial, fairness.

impartially adv. in an impartial way.

impassability or **impassableness** noun being impassable.

impassable adj. not able to be passed through or travelled along.

impassably adv. in an impassable way.

impasse noun a situation in which progress is impossible and from which there is no way out. [from French impasse]

impassion verb (**impassioned**, **impassioning**) to move with or fill with passion. [from Italian impassionare]

impassioned adj. moved by or showing very strong feelings.

impassive adj. **1** incapable of feeling and expressing emotion. **2** showing no feeling or emotion.

impassively adv. in an impassive way.

impassiveness or **impassivity** noun being impassive.

impasto noun in painting and pottery, the technique of laying the paint or pigment on thickly. [from Italian impasto]
◇ Traditionally, painters in oils, such as Titian and Rembrandt, worked with a mixture of smooth underpainting, thinly executed shadows, and thick (impasted) lights, overpainted with transparent glazing. Modern artists frequently use impasto to create texture or three-dimensional effect and may apply the paint directly from the tube or pot.

impatience noun lack of patience or tolerance.

impatiens noun any of 500 to 600 species of annual and perennial plants belonging to the genus Impatiens, native to Europe, Asia, most of Africa, and N America, and having translucent stems and oval toothed leaves. The flowers hang from a slender stalk, and either have five flat petals and a slender curved spur, or are two-lipped with a funnel-shaped tube and spur. Hybrids between Impatiens holstii and Impatiens sultanii, with red, pink, or white flowers, are popular ornamentals, commonly known as 'busy Lizzie'.

impatient adj. **1** unwilling to wait or delay. **2** intolerant. **3** restlessly eager and anxious. [from Latin impatiens]

impatiently adv. without patience.

impeach verb **1** Brit. to charge with a serious crime, especially a crime against the state or treason. **2** North Amer. to accuse (a public or government official) with misconduct while in office. **3** to call into question; to cast doubt upon (eg a

person's honesty). [from Latin impedicare, to fetter]

impeachable adj. **1** capable of being impeached. **2** said of an offence making a person liable to be impeached.

impeachment noun Politics the legal process of removing an undesirable person from office.

impeccable adj. **1** free from fault or error. **2** not liable to sin. [from Latin impeccabilis]

impeccably adv. in an impeccable way.

impecunious adj. having little or no money; poor; penniless. [from IM- + obsolete pecunious, wealthy]

impecuniously adv. without funds.

impecuniousness noun lack of funds.

impedance noun (SYMBOL Z) **1** Electr. the effective resistance of an electric circuit or circuit component to the passage of an electric current. For an a.c. circuit it is due to the combined effect of resistance and reactance, and for a d.c. circuit it is due to the resistance alone. **2** anything that impedes.

impede verb to prevent or delay the start or progress of (an activity, etc); to obstruct or hinder. [from Latin impedire, to snare the foot]

impediment noun **1** a thing or person that delays or prevents the start or progress of something; an obstacle or hindrance. **2** a minor defect in a person's speech, eg a lisp. [from Latin impedimentum]

impedimenta pl. noun any objects which impede progress or movement, especially military baggage and equipment.

impel verb (**impelled**, **impelling**) **1** to push, drive or urge forward; to propel. **2** to force or urge into action. [from Latin impellare]

impend verb intrans. **1** to be about to happen. **2** said of a danger, etc to threaten; to hover threateningly. [from Latin impendere, to hang over]

impending adj. about to happen.

impenetrability noun being inpenetrable.

impenetrable adj. **1** incapable of being entered or passed through. **2** not capable of receiving or being touched by intellectual ideas and influences. [from Latin impenetrabilis]

impenetrably adv. in an impenetrable way.

impenitence noun being impenitent.

impenitent adj. not sorry for having done something wrong; unrepentant. [from Latin impaenitens]

impenitently adv. in an impenitent way.

imperative — adj. **1** absolutely essential; urgent. **2** having or showing authority; commanding. **3** Grammar of or being the mood of a verb used to give orders. — noun **1** Grammar the imperative mood. **2** a verb in the imperative mood. **3** that which is imperative, especially a command or order. [from Latin imperativus, from imperare, to command]

imperatively adv. in an imperative way.

imperceptibility noun being imperceptible.

imperceptible adj. **1** too small or slight to be seen, heard, noticed, etc. **2** not able to be perceived by the senses. [from Latin imperceptibilis]

imperceptibly adv. in an imperceptible way.

imperfect — adj. **1** having faults; spoilt; not perfect. **2** lacking the full number of parts; incomplete. **3** Grammar of or being the verb tense expressing a continuing state or incomplete action, usually in the past. — noun Grammar **1** the imperfect tense. **2** a verb in the imperfect tense. [from Latin imperfectus]

imperfection noun **1** the state of being imperfect. **2** a fault, weakness or blemish.

imperfectly adv. in an imperfect way.

imperial adj. **1** of or suitable for an empire, emperor, or empress. **2** having supreme authority. **3** commanding; august. **4** regal; magnificent. **5** Brit., said of the non-metric measure or system conforming to standards fixed by parliament. [from Latin imperialis]

Imperial British East Africa Company a British company founded (1888) and chartered to rule a large area of E Africa. Though designed to ward off the German and French threats to the area and maintain British access to L Victoria, Uganda, and the upper Nile, it was unable to find the resources to develop the region, create an infrastructure, or withstand African resistance. When it was wound up (1894), its territories became the protectorates (later Crown Colonies) of Kenya and Uganda.

Imperial Diet or **Reichstag** the Diet was the assembly of the Holy Roman Empire (c.1100–1806). After 1489, the Diet was divided into three chambers or colleges. Seven lay and ecclesiastical princes (electors) formed the electoral college and were charged with electing a new emperor. The second college, also of princes, was composed of the other noble rulers, lay and ecclesiastical. The third college represented delegates from the Imperial towns. With the collapse of central authority during the Thirty Years War the Diet lost its legislative powers and became a largely ceremonial body.

imperialism noun **1** rule by an emperor or empress. **2** the policy or principle of having and extending control over the territory of other nations, or of extending one's country's influence through trade and diplomacy, etc.
◇ The main era of imperialism was in the 1880s to 1914, when many European powers sought to gain territories in Africa and Asia. The term is now often applied to any attempts by developed countries to interfere in underdeveloped countries.

imperialist — noun a believer in or supporter of imperialism. — adj. relating to or characterized by imperialism.

imperialistic adj. **1** involving imperialism. **2** according to an imperial system.

imperially adv. with an imperial manner.

Imperial Palace the former palace, in Beijing, China, of the emperors of the Ming and Qing dynasties. The main buildings are now a museum. It is a World Heritage site.

Imperial War Museum the Museum of British and Commonwealth military operations since 1914, founded in London in 1917 as a memorial to those who died in World War I. It was housed in the Crystal Palace until 1924, when it was moved to the former Imperial Institute and then to the former Royal Bethlehem Hospital.

imperil verb (**imperilled**, **imperilling**) to put in peril or danger.

imperilment noun endangering, being imperilled.

imperious adj. arrogant, haughty and domineering. [from Latin imperiosus]

imperiously adv. with an imperious manner.

imperiousness noun being imperious.

imperishable adj. which will not decay and will last forever.

impermanence or **impermanency** noun lack of permanence.

impermanent adj. not lasting or remaining; transient.

impermeability noun being impermeable.

impermeable adj. not allowing especially liquids to pass through or penetrate. [from Latin impermeabilis]

impermissible adj. not permitted or allowed.

impersonal *adj.* **1** having no reference to any particular person; objective. **2** without or unaffected by personal or human feelings, warmth, sympathy, etc; cold. **3** without personality. **4** *Grammar, said of a verb* used without a subject, or with a formal one, usually *it*, as in *it's snowing*. **5** *Grammar, said of a pronoun* not referring to a definite person; indefinite. [from Latin *impersonalis*]

impersonality *noun* being impersonal, lack of personality.

impersonally *adv.* in an impersonal way.

impersonate *verb* to pretend to be, or copy the behaviour and appearance of (another person), especially to entertain or deceive. [from IM- + Latin *persona*, person]

impersonation *noun* impersonating.

impersonator *noun* a person who impersonates.

impertinence *noun* **1** impertinent language or behaviour. **2** an impertinent act.

impertinent *adj.* **1** rude; not showing respect where it is due; insolent. **2** *old use Legal* not relevant. [from Latin *impertinens*]

impertinently *adv.* in an impertinent way.

imperturbability *noun* being imperturbable.

imperturbable *adj.* not easily worried or upset; always calm. [from Latin *imperturbabilis*]

imperturbably *adv.* in an inperturbable way.

impervious *adj.* (**impervious to something**) **1** not allowing fluids to pass through or penetrate. **2** not influenced or affected by it: *they seem impervious to criticism.* [from Latin *impervius*]

imperviously *adv.* so as to be impervious.

imperviousness *noun* being impervious.

impetigo *noun* a contagious skin disease causing pustules and yellow sores. [from Latin *impetigo*, from *impetere*, to attack]

impetuosity *or* **impetuousness** *noun* being impetuous; an impetuous act.

impetuous *adj.* **1** acting or done hurriedly and without thinking. **2** moving or acting forcefully or with great energy. [from Latin *impetuosus*]

impetuously *adv.* in an impetuous way.

impetus *noun* (PL. **impetuses**) **1** the force or energy with which something moves. **2** a driving force. **3** an incentive or encouragement. [from Latin *impetus*, attack]

impi *noun* (PL. **impis**, **impies**) a group of Zulu warriors. [from Zulu]

impiety *noun* (PL. **impieties**) **1** lack of piety or devotion. **2** an act of impiety: *committed many impieties.* [from Latin *impietas*]

impinge *verb intrans.* (**impinge against** *or* **on something** *or* **someone**) **1** to interfere with or encroach on them. **2** to come into contact with them. **3** to make an impression on them. [from Latin *impingere*]

impingement *noun* impinging.

impious *adj.* lacking respect or proper reverence, especially for a divine being. [from Latin *impius*]

impiously *adv.* in an impious way.

impiousness *noun* being impious.

impish *adj.* like an imp; mischievous.

impishly *adv.* in an impish way.

impishness *noun* being impish; mischief.

implacability *or* **implacableness** *noun* being implacable.

implacable *adj.* not able to be calmed, satisfied or appeased. [from Latin *implacabilis*]

implacably *adv.* in an implacable way.

implant — *verb* (with stress on *-plant*) **1** to fix or plant securely. **2** to fix (ideas, beliefs, etc) permanently in a person's mind. **3** to put (tissue, hormones, etc) permanently into the body. — *noun* (with stress on *im-*) anything implanted, especially tissue, a capsule containing a hormone, etc in the body.

implantation *noun* the process of implanting or being implanted.

implausibility *noun* being implausible.

implausible *adj.* not plausible or easy to believe; not likely to be true.

implausibly *adv.* in an implausible way.

implement — *noun* a tool or utensil; a necessary piece of equipment. — *verb* to carry out, fulfil, or perform. [from Latin *implementum*]

implementation *noun* implementing, performance, fulfilment.

implicate *verb* **1** to show or suggest that (a person) is involved, especially in a crime. **2** to imply. [from Latin *implicare*, to interweave]

implication *noun* **1** the act of implicating or state of being implicated. **2** the act of implying or state of being implied. **3** that which is implied. — **by implication** by suggestion and without being stated directly.

implicit *adj.* **1** implied or meant, although not stated directly. **2** present, although not explicit or immediately discernible: *there was a disappointment implicit in her words.* **3** unquestioning; complete. [from Latin *implicitus*, involved]

implicitly *adv.* in an implicit way.

implicitness *noun* being implicit.

implied *adj.* hinted at, suggested.

implode *verb intrans., trans. Physics* to undergo or cause to undergo a sudden reduction in pressure as a result of a chemical reaction, or to collapse or burst inward in a violent manner. [from IM- + EXPLODE]

implore *verb* **1** to entreat or beg (a person). **2** to beg for earnestly. [from Latin *implorare*]

imploring *adj.* begging, pleading.

imploringly *adv.* in an imploring way.

implosion *noun Physics* a violent collapse or bursting inward, eg when the seal of a vacuum-filled glass vessel is broken, or when material capable of nuclear fission is compressed by ordinary explosives in a nuclear weapon; the opposite of an explosion.

implosive *adj.* formed by implosion.

imply *verb* (**implies**, **implied**) **1** to suggest or express indirectly; to hint at. **2** to suggest or involve as a necessary result or consequence. [from Latin *implicare*, to interweave]

impolite *adj.* not polite; rude, disrespectful.

impolitely *adv.* in an impolite way.

impoliteness *noun* being impolite, rudeness.

impolitic *adj.* unwise; not to be advised.

imponderable — *adj.* having an influence or importance which cannot be measured or determined. — *noun* something that is imponderable. [from Latin *imponderabilis*]

import — *verb* (with variable stress) **1** to bring (goods, etc) in from another country. **2** to signify, imply, or portend. — *noun* (with stress on *im-*) **1** something imported. **2** the act or business of importing goods. **3** importance. **4** meaning. [from Latin *importare*]

importance *noun* being important, significance.

Importance of Being Earnest, The a play by Oscar Wilde (1895). His finest play, it is a comedy of assumed identities and verbal repartee, focusing on two young men, Jack and Algy, whose double lives lead to much confusion during their courtship of Gwendolen and Cecily.

important *adj.* **1** having great value, influence or effect. **2** (**important to someone**) of great significance or value to them: *their happiness is important to me.* **3** of high social rank or status; eminent. **4** pompous. [from Latin *importare*, to be of consequence]

importantly *adv.* in an important way.

importation *noun* **1** importing. **2** something that is imported.

importer *noun* a person or organization that imports.

importunate *adj.* **1** persistent or excessively demanding. **2** extremely urgent. [from Latin *importunus*, inconvenient]

importunately *adv.* in an importunate way.

importune *verb trans., intrans.* **1** to make persistent and usually annoying requests (of someone). **2** to solicit for immoral purposes, eg prostitution. [from Latin *importunus*, inconvenient]

importunity *noun* (PL. **importunities**) being importunate.

impose *verb* **1** (**impose something on** *or* **upon someone**) to make payment of a tax, fine, etc or performance of a duty compulsory; to enforce it. **2** (**impose oneself on** *or* **upon someone**) to force oneself, one's opinions and company, etc on them. **3** (**impose on** *or* **upon someone**) to take advantage of them; to set unreasonable burdens or tasks on them: *it's easy impose on his good nature.* **4** (**impose something on** *or* **upon someone**) to palm it off on them surreptitiously or dishonestly. **5** to arrange (pages) in the proper order for printing. [from Old French *imposer*]

imposing *adj.* impressive, especially because of large size, dignity, handsome appearance, etc.

imposingly *adv.* in an imposing way.

imposition *noun* **1** the act of imposing or process of being imposed. **2** something imposed, especially a tax, or an unfair or excessive demand or requirement. **3** *Brit.* work given as a punishment at school. **4** the arranging of pages in the proper order for printing. [from Latin *impositio*]

impossibility *noun* (PL. **impossibilities**) **1** the state of being impossible. **2** something which is impossible.

impossible *adj.* **1** that cannot be done or cannot happen. **2** that cannot be true; difficult to believe. **3** *colloq.* unacceptable, unsuitable, or difficult to bear; intolerable. [from Latin *impossibilis*]

impossibly *adv.* not possibly, in an impossible way.

impostor *or* **imposter** *noun* a person who pretends to be someone else in order to deceive others. [from Latin *imponere*, to impose]

imposture *noun* **1** deception, especially by pretending to be someone else. **2** an act of imposture.

impotence *noun* **1** weakness. **2** usually said of men inability to perform sexual intercourse.

impotent *adj.* **1** powerless; lacking the necessary strength. **2** said of a man unable to sustain a sexual erection and therefore unable to perform sexual intercourse. [from Latin *impotentia*, lack of self-control]

impotently *adv.* in an impotent way.

impound *verb* **1** to shut (eg an animal) up in, or as if in, a pound; to confine. **2** to take legal possession of; to confiscate. **3** *said of a reservoir, dam, etc* to collect and hold (water).

impoverish *verb* **1** to make poor. **2** to reduce the quality or fertility of (eg soil). [from Middle English *empoverishen*]

impoverished *adj.* **1** made poor. **2** weakened, in poor condition.

impoverishment *noun* **1** impoverishing. **2** being impoverished. **3** loss of wealth.

impracticability *noun* being impracticable.

impracticable *adj.* not able to be done, put into practice or used.

impracticably *adv.* in an impracticable way.

impractical *adj.* lacking common sense; not practical. See also UNPRACTICAL.

impracticality *noun* (PL. **impracticalities**) being impractical.

impractically *adv.* in an impractical way.

imprecate *verb formal* **1** to call down by prayer (especially something evil). **2** to call down evil upon (someone); to curse. [from Latin *imprecari*, to pray to or for]

imprecation *noun* **1** imprecating. **2** a curse.

imprecatory *adj.* expressing or using imprecation, cursing.

imprecise *adj.* not precise; inaccurate.

imprecision *noun* lack of precision.

impregnability *noun* being impregnable.

impregnable *adj.* **1** not able to be seized, defeated, or taken by force. **2** not able to be affected by criticism, doubts, etc. [from Old French *imprenable*, from Latin *prehendere* to take]

impregnably *adv.* in an impregnable way.

impregnate *verb* **1** to permeate completely or saturate. **2** to fill or imbue. **3** to make pregnant or fertilize. [from Latin *impraegnare*, to fertilise]

impregnation *noun* impregnating or being impregnated.

impresario *noun* (PL. **impresarios**) an organizer of public entertainments, eg concerts, or the manager of an opera or theatre company. [from Italian *impresario*]

impress — *verb* (with stress on *-press*) **1** *trans.*, *intrans.* to produce a strong, lasting and usually favourable impression on (someone). **2** (**impress on** *or* **upon someone**) to make very clear or emphasize to them. **3** to make or stamp (a mark) on by applying pressure. **4** (**impress something on** *or* **upon someone**) to fix a fact, etc firmly in their mind or memory. — *noun* (with stress on *im-*) **1** the act of impressing. **2** that which is made by impressing or being impressed, such as a mark or impression. [from Latin *imprimere*, to press into or on]

impression *noun* **1** an (especially favourable) idea or effect produced in the mind or made on the senses. **2** a vague or uncertain idea, notion or belief. **3** an act of or the process of impressing. **4** a mark or stamp produced by, or as if by, impressing or pressure. **5** an imitation, especially a caricature, of a person, or an imitation of a sound, done for entertainment. **6** the number of copies of a book, newspaper, etc printed at one time. **7** the pressing of a prepared inked plate or type on to the paper, etc being printed, or a copy made in this way.

impressionability *noun* susceptibility to being influenced by impressions.

impressionable *adj.* easily impressed or influenced.

impressionably *adv.* in an impressionable way.

Impressionism a 19c style of art, music, or literature which aims to give a general impression of feelings and events rather than a formal or structural treatment of them.
◇ In art, the movement arose in France in the 1860s; the name, coined by a hostile critic, was taken from Claude Monet's picture, *Impression: soleil levant* (Impression: Rising Sun, 1872). The Impressionists, who included Pissarro, Sisley, and Renoir, rejected the dark tones of 19c studio painting and set up their easels out-of-doors. Impressionist pictures are typically bright and cheerful and avoid the sort of social realism favoured earlier by Gustave Courbet (1819–77) and others.
In literature, the term signifies the conveying of a subjective impression of the world rather than its

objective appearance. It relates primarily to the work of the Symbolist poets and the psychological or stream-of-consciousness novel, drawing attention to the blurred outlines, shifting categories, and uncertain truth-values of the modern world.
In music, it denotes a style of harmony and instrumentation which blurs the edges of tonality and generally aims for veiled suggestion and understatement rather than a detailed picture. The term is used with particular reference to music by Debussy and some of his French contemporaries.

Impressionist — *noun* **1** a painter, writer, or composer in the style of Impressionism. **2** (**impressionist**) a person who imitates or gives impressions of others. — *adj.* relating to or characteristic of Impressionism.

impressionistic *adj.* based on impressions or personal observation as distinct from definite facts or particular knowledge.

impressionistically *adv.* in an impressionistic way.

Impression: soleil levant (Impression: Rising Sun) a painting by Claude Monet (1872). It gave its name to the whole Impressionist movement after being exhibited at their first exhibition.

impressive *adj.* capable of making a deep impression on a person's mind, feelings, etc; causing admiration, wonder or approval.

impressively *adv.* in an impressive way.

impressiveness *noun* being impressive.

imprimatur *noun* **1** a licence or permission to print or publish a book, granted especially by the Roman Catholic church. **2** approval; permission. [from Latin *imprimatur*, let it be printed]

imprint — *noun* (with stress on *im-*) **1** a mark or impression made by pressure. **2** a permanent effect, eg on the mind, produced by some experience or event. **3** a publisher's name and address, printed at the bottom of a book's title page. — *verb* (with stress on *-print*) **1** to mark or print an impression of (something). **2** to fix firmly in the mind.

imprinting *noun Zool.* the process by which animals rapidly learn the appearance, sound, or smell of significant individual members of their own species (eg parents, offspring, suitable mates) through being exposed to them. Imprinting to parent or offspring usually results in attachment or following behaviour.

imprison *verb* (**imprisoned**, **imprisoning**) to put in prison.

imprisonment *noun* **1** being imprisoned. **2** imprisoning.

improbability *noun* (PL. **improbabilities**) *noun* **1** being improbable. **2** something that is improbable.

improbable *adj.* **1** unlikely to happen or exist; not probable. **2** hard to believe.

improbably *adv.* in an improbable way.

improbity *noun* (PL. **improbities**) dishonesty; wickedness. [from IM- + PROBITY]

impromptu — *adj.* made or done without preparation; improvised; spontaneous. — *adv.* without preparation; spontaneously. — *noun* **1** something that is impromptu. **2** a piece of music which suggests improvisation. [from Latin *in promptu*, in readiness]

improper *adj.* **1** not conforming to accepted standards of modesty and moral behaviour; unseemly; indecent. **2** not correct; wrong. **3** not suitable. [from Latin *improprius*]

improper fraction, a fraction in which the numerator (upper part) has a value which is equal to or higher than that of the denominator (lower

part), eg ⅘. Therefore it is always equal to or greater than 1. See also PROPER FRACTION.

improperly *adv.* in an improper way.

impropriety *noun* (PL. **improprieties**) **1** an improper act or improper use of a word. **2** the state of being improper; indecency. [from Latin *improprietas*]

improve *verb* **1** *trans.*, *intrans.* to make or become better, of higher quality or value; to make or cause to make progress. **2** (**improve on something**) to produce something better, of higher quality or value than a previous example. **3** to increase the value or beauty of (land or property) by cultivation, laying out gardens, building, etc. [from Old French *emprower*, from *prou*, profit]

improvement *noun* **1** the act of improving or state of being improved. **2** something that adds beauty, quality, value, etc. **3** something which has been improved.

improvidence *noun* being improvident.

improvident *adj.* **1** not provident; not considering or providing for likely future needs; lacking foresight. **2** careless; thoughtless.

improvidently *adv.* in an improvident way.

improvisation *noun* **1** the process of improvising. **2** an instance of improvising.

improvise *verb* **1** *trans.*, *intrans.* to compose, recite or perform (music, verse, etc) without preparing it in advance. **2** to make or provide quickly, without preparing in advance and using whatever materials are to hand. [from Latin *improvisus*, not foreseen]

improviser *noun* a person who improvises.

imprudence *noun* **1** being imprudent. **2** an instance of this.

imprudent *adj.* not having or showing good sense or caution; rash; heedless. [from Latin *imprudens*, rash]

imprudently *adv.* in an imprudent way.

impudence *noun* **1** being impudent. **2** impudent behaviour or language.

impudent *adj.* rude, insolent, or impertinent. [from Latin *impudens*, shameless]

impudently *adv.* in an impudent way.

impugn *verb* to call into question or raise doubts about (a person's honesty, integrity, a claim, etc), to criticize. [from Latin *impugnare*, to attack]

impugnable *adj.* capable of being questioned or criticized.

impugnment *noun* questioning, criticizing.

impulse *noun* **1** a sudden push forwards; a force producing sudden movement forwards. **2** the motion or movement produced by such a force or push. **3** a sudden desire or urge to do something without thinking of the consequences: *bought the dress on impulse.* **4** an instinctive or natural tendency. **5** *Physiol.* (also **nerve impulse**) an electrical signal that travels along a nerve fibre, and in turn causes excitation of other nerve, muscle, or gland cells, so relaying information throughout the nervous system. **6** *Physics* for two objects that briefly collide with each other, the product of the force produced and the time for which it acts. It is equal to the change in momentum of either object. [from Latin *impulsus*, pressure]

impulse buying the buying of goods on the basis of an impulse or whim.

impulsion *noun* **1** an act of urging, forcing, or pushing forwards, into motion or into action, or the state of being so urged. **2** a force which urges, etc forwards, into motion, etc. **3** a sudden desire or urge.

impulsive *adj.* **1** likely to act suddenly and without considering the consequences. **2** done without such consideration. **3** having the power to urge or push forwards, into motion or into action.

impulsively *adv.* in an impulsive way.

impulsiveness *noun* **1** being impulsive. **2** impulsive behaviour.

impunity *noun* freedom or exemption from punishment, injury, loss, or other ill consequences. **— with impunity** without having to suffer the normal consequences. [from Latin *impunitas*]

impure *adj.* **1** mixed with something else; adulterated. **2** dirty. **3** immoral; not chaste. **4** ritually unclean. [from Latin *impurus*]

impurity *noun* (PL. **impurities**) **1** the state of being impure. **2** an impure or unclean thing or constituent.

imputation *noun* the act of imputing; something imputed.

impute *verb* (**impute something to someone**) **1** to regard something unfavourable or unwelcome as being brought about by them. **2** to believe something to be caused by a person or thing: *imputed his failure to laziness.*

I'm Talking about Jerusalem see ROOTS.

IN *abbrev.* Indiana.

In *symbol Chem.* indium.

in — *prep.* **1** used to express the position of a person or thing with regard to what encloses, surrounds or includes it, him, etc. **2** into: *get in the car.* **3** after (a period of time): *come back in an hour.* **4** during; while: *lost in transit.* **5** used to express arrangement or shape: *in a square / in alphabetical order.* **6** from; out of: *two in every eight.* **7** by the medium or means of; using: *sung in Italian / in code.* **8** wearing. **9** used to describe a state or manner: *in a hurry.* **10** used to state an occupation: *a job in local government.* **11** used to state a purpose: *a party in his honour.* **12** *said of some animals* pregnant with: *in calf.* — *adv.* **1** to or towards the inside; indoors. **2** at home or work. **3** so as to be added or included: *beat in the eggs.* **4** so as to enclose or conceal, or be enclosed or concealed. **5** in or into political power or office. **6** in or into fashion. **7** in a good position; in favour. **8** *in certain games* batting. **9** into a proper, required or efficient state: *run a new car in.* **10** *said of the tide* at its highest point; as close to the shore as it gets. **11** (*in compounds*) expressing prolonged activity, especially by large numbers of people: *a sit-in.* — *adj.* **1** internal; inside; inwards. **2** fashionable. **3** in power or office. **4** used for receiving things coming in: *an in-tray.* **5** (*also in compounds*) shared by a group of people: *an in-joke.* **— be in for it** *colloq.* be likely to experience some trouble or difficulty.

have it in for someone *colloq.* to cause them trouble, especially because of dislike.

in as far as *or* **in so far as** ... to the degree that ...

in as much as ... because ...; considering that ...

in on something *colloq.* knowing about it and sharing in it.

ins and outs the complex and detailed facts of a matter.

in with someone *colloq.* friendly with them. [from Anglo-Saxon *in*]

in. *abbrev.* inch.

in-¹ *prefix* (*also* **il-** before words beginning in *l*, **im-** before words beginning in *b, m,* and *p,* **ir-** before words beginning in *r*) forming words that are the negative or opposite of the root word, or that denote a lack of the quality implied by the root word: *inhospitable / illogical / immature / irrelevant.* [from Latin *in-*]

in-² *prefix* (*also* **il-** before words beginning with *l*, **im-** before words beginning with *b, m,* and *p,* **ir-** before words beginning with *r*) forming words meaning 'in, on, towards': *intrude / imprison.* [from Latin *in-* and Old French *en-*, in, into]

inability *noun* (PL. **inabilities**) the lack of sufficient power, means or ability. [from Latin *inhabilitas*]

in absentia in his, her, or their absence. [Latin, = in absence]

inaccessibility *noun* **1** being inaccessible. **2** unapproachability.

inaccessible *adj.* **1** difficult or impossible to approach, reach, or obtain. **2** *said of a person* difficult to understand or influence; unapproachable. [from Latin *inaccessibilis*]

inaccessibly *adv.* in an inaccessible way; so as to be inaccessible.

inaccuracy *noun* (PL. **inaccuracies**) **1** the state of not being inaccurate. **2** a mistake or error.

inaccurate *adj.* containing errors; not correct or accurate.

inaccurately *adv.* in an inaccurate way.

inaction *noun* lack of action; sluggishness.

inactive *adj.* **1** taking little or no exercise; idle. **2** no longer operating or functioning. **3** *said of members of a group, especially members of the armed forces* not taking part in or available for eg military duties. **4** *Chem.* showing little or no reaction.

inactively *adv.* not actively, passively.

inactivity *noun* **1** being inactive. **2** lack of activity.

inadequacy *noun* (PL. **inadequacies**) insufficiency.

inadequate *adj.* **1** not sufficient or adequate. **2** *said of a person* not able to cope; not competent or capable.

inadequately *adv.* in an inadequate way; so as to be inadequate.

inadmissibility *noun* being inadmissible.

inadmissible *adj.* not allowable or able to be accepted.

inadmissibly *adv.* in an inadmissible way.

inadvertence *noun* negligence, oversight.

inadvertent *adj.* **1** *said of an act* not done deliberately; unintentional. **2** not paying proper attention; heedless. [from Latin *inadvertentia*, inadvertence]

inadvertently *adv.* unintentionally, carelessly.

inadvisability *noun* being inadvisable.

inadvisable *adj.* not wise; not to be advised.

inalienable *adj.* not capable of being taken or given away (eg to another person).

inamorata *noun* (PL. **inamoratas**) a woman who is in love or who is beloved. [from Italian *inamorata*, from *innamorare*, to inflame with love]

inamorato *noun* (PL. **inamoratos**) a man who is in love or who is beloved.

inane *adj.* without meaning or point; silly. [from Latin *inanis*]

inanely *adv.* in an inane way.

inanimate *adj.* **1** without life; not living: *inanimate objects.* **2** dull; spiritless. [from Latin *inanimatus*]

inanition *noun* emptiness or exhaustion, especially physical from lack of food. [from Latin *inanitio*]

inanity *noun* (PL. **inanities**) **1** the state of being inane. **2** an inane remark, action, etc.

inapplicability *noun* **1** being inapplicable. **2** unsuitability.

inapplicable *adj.* not applicable or suitable.

inapplicably *adv.* not applicably, unsuitably.

inapposite *adj.* not suitable or appropriate; out of place.

inappositely *adv.* in an inapposite way.

inappositeness *noun* being inapposite.

inappropriate *adj.* not suitable or appropriate.

inappropriately *adv.* in an inapproriate way.

inappropriateness *noun* **1** being inappropriate. **2** unsuitability.

inapt *adj.* **1** not suitable or appropriate. **2** lacking skill; unqualified.

inaptly *adv.* in an inapt way, inappropriately.

inaptness *noun* being inapt.

inarticulate *adj.* **1** unable to express oneself clearly or to speak distinctly. **2** badly expressed; not spoken or pronounced clearly. **3** not jointed or hinged. [from Latin *inarticulatus*]

inarticulately *adv.* in an inarticulate way.

inarticulateness *noun* **1** being inarticulate. **2** lack of clarity of sound or expression in speaking.

inartistic *adj.* **1** not following the rules or principles of art. **2** not able to appreciate art.

inartistically *adv.* in an inartistic way.

inasmuch as see IN.

inattention *or* **inattentiveness** *noun* lack of attention.

inattentive *adj.* not paying proper attention; neglectful.

inattentively *adv.* in an inattentive way; without attention.

inaudibility *noun* being inaudible.

inaudible *adj.* not audible; not loud enough to be heard.

inaudibly *adv.* so that nothing is heard.

inaugural — *adj.* **1** relating to or describing a ceremony officially marking the beginning of something. **2** *said of a speech, lecture, etc* given by a person on taking office. — *noun* an inaugural speech or lecture. [from Latin *inaugurare*, to inaugurate]

inaugurate *verb* **1** to place (a person) in office with a formal ceremony. **2** to mark the beginning of (some activity) with a formal ceremony. **3** to mark the opening of (a new building or service), especially by being the first person to try it out. [from Latin *inaugurare*]

inauguration *noun* **1** being inaugurated, especially formally into office. **2** inaugurating.

inaugurator *noun* a person who inaugurates.

inauspicious *adj.* not promising future success; not auspicious; unlucky.

inauspiciously *adv.* in an inauspicious way.

inauspiciousness *noun* being inauspicious.

in-between *adj.* coming between in space, time, style, etc; neither one thing nor the other.

inboard *adj., adv.* **1** *said of a boat's motor or engine* situated inside the hull. **2** situated within or close to an aircraft's fuselage. See also OUTBOARD.

inborn *adj., said of a human attribute or characteristic* possessed or apparently possessed by a person from birth; innate or hereditary.

inbound *adj., said of a vehicle, flight, etc* coming towards its destination; arriving.

inbred *adj.* **1** inborn. **2** denoting a plant or animal that is the result of inbreeding.

inbreed *verb* (PAST TENSE AND PAST PARTICIPLE **inbred**) to allow reproduction between closely related plants or animals within a species.

inbreeding *noun* breeding within a closely related group. Inbreeding eventually results in an increase in the frequency of abnormalities, eg certain mental defects in humans.

Inc. *abbrev.* North Amer., esp. US Incorporated.

Incahuasi, Cerro an Andean volcano on the Chile–Argentina border, 200km/124mi NE of Copiapó, Chile. HEIGHT 6 709m.

incalculability *noun* being incalculable.

incalculable *adj.* **1** not able to be estimated or reckoned in advance; unpredictable. **2** too great to be measured.

incalculably *adv.* in an incalculable way; so as to be incalculable.

in camera *adv.* **1** *Legal* in a judge's private room. **2** in secret; in private. [Latin, = in a chamber]

incandesce *verb trans., intrans.* to glow or cause to glow white with intense heat.

incandescence *noun* the light produced by a body that is being heated, or the production of such light.

incandescent *adj.* **1** white or glowing with intense heat. **2** shining brightly. **3** of, relating to, or being light produced by heating a substance until it glows white with intense heat. [from Latin *incandescere*, to glow]

incandescent lamp *Electr.* an electric lamp consisting of an evacuated glass bulb containing an inert gas and a filament of highly resistive wire (usually tungsten) that becomes white hot and emits visible light when a current passes through it.

incandescently *adv.* in an incandescent way.

incantation *noun* **1** words said or sung as a spell; a magical formula. **2** the use of spells and magical formulae. [from Latin *incantare*, to put a spell on]

incantatory *adj.* of the nature of or using incantation.

incapability *noun* being incapable.

incapable *adj.* (**incapable of something**) **1** not capable of doing it. **2** lacking the necessary ability to do something. **3** unable or unfit to do anything, especially look after one's own affairs. [from Latin *incapabilis*]

incapably *adv.* in an incapable way.

incapacitate *verb* **1** to take away (a person's) strength, power, or ability; to make (someone) unfit (for). **2** to disqualify legally. [from INCAPACITY]

incapacitated *adj.* **1** disabled; deprived of power or strength. **2** disqualified by law.

incapacitation *noun* **1** being incapacitated. **2** incapacitating.

incapacity *noun* (PL. **incapacities**) **1** a lack of the necessary strength, power, or ability. **2** legal disqualification. [from Latin *incapacitas*]

incapsulate same as ENCAPSULATE.

incapsulating language same as POLYSYNTHETIC LANGUAGE.

incarcerate *verb* to shut in or keep in prison. [from Latin *incarcerare*]

incarceration *noun* **1** being incarcerated. **2** incarcerating.

incarnate — *adj.* **1** in bodily, especially human, form: *God incarnate.* **2** personified; typified. — *verb* **1** to give bodily, especially human, form to. **2** to personify or typify. [from Latin *incarnare*, to make flesh]

Incarnation in Christianity, the union of the divine and human natures in Jesus Christ: 'the Word (of God) became flesh' (John 1.14). In other religions (eg Hinduism) it refers to a life-spirit being given a material form.

incarnation *noun* **1** the bodily, especially human, form taken by a spirit or god. **2** a person who personifies, or thing that typifies, a quality or idea. **3** the taking of bodily, especially human, form by a spirit or god. **4** any of a succession of periods spent in a particular bodily form or state.

Incas originally a small group of Quechua-speaking Indians living in the central Andean highlands which became, during the 15c, one of the world's major civilizations, and was the largest Precolumbian state in the New World,

with an estimated population of 5–10m. In the 11c, they established their capital at Cuzco, the Sacred City of the Sun. During the 15c, their empire stretched along the entire western length of South America, from near the present Ecuador–Colombia border to S central Chile, and into the Andean regions of Bolivia as well. The Incas used former rulers as regional administrators but these were denied any independence, and Inca culture, language (Quechua), and the cult of the Sun were forcibly imposed. Their society was hierarchical, ruled by a noble class presided over by a despotic emperor who was a quasi-religious figure believed to have descended from the Sun-god Inti. They had a system of more than 15 000km of roads that provided an essential infrastructure for communication, conquest, and control. In 1523, Spanish invaders under Pizarro encountered the Incas, captured the emperor Atahualpa, and took control of the empire. The present descendants of the Incas, 3 million Quechua-speaking peasants of the Andes, comprise 45% of Peru's population.

incautious *adj.* acting or done without thinking; heedless.

incautiously *adv.* in an incautious way.

incautiousness *noun* being incautious.

incendiarism *noun* arson.

incendiary — *adj.* **1** of or relating to the deliberate and illegal burning of property or goods. **2** *said eg of a bomb* designed to start fires. **3** tending to cause trouble or violence. — *noun* (PL. **incendiaries**) **1** a person who deliberately and illegally sets fire to buildings or property. **2** a device, eg a bomb, for starting fires. **3** a person who stirs up trouble or violence. [from Latin *incendere*, to kindle]

incense¹ (with stress on *in*-) — *noun* **1** a spice or other substance which gives off a pleasant odour when burned, used especially during religious services. **2** the odour or smoke given off by burning spices, etc. — *verb* **1** to offer incense to (a god). **2** to perfume or fumigate with incense. [from Latin *incensum*, thing burnt, from *incendere*, to kindle]

incense² *verb* (with stress on *-cense*) to make (someone) very angry. [from Latin *incendere*, to kindle]

incentive — *noun* something that motivates or encourages an action, work, etc, such as extra money paid to workers to increase output. — *adj.* serving to motivate or encourage. [from Latin *incentivus*, provocative]

inception *noun* a beginning. [from Latin *incipere*, to begin]

incertitude *noun* uncertainty; doubt. [from Latin *incertitudo*]

incessant *adj.* going on without stopping; continual. [from Latin *in*-, not + *cessare*, to cease]

incessantly *adv.* without stopping, endlessly.

incest *noun* sexual intercourse between people who are too closely related to be allowed to marry, eg between brother and sister. [from Latin *incestum*, from *in*-, not + *castus*, chaste]

◇ Incest is the most powerful taboo of family life, which occurs in all societies composed of family groups related by kinship, to avoid inbreeding or to prevent disruptive sexual jealousy.

incestuous *adj.* **1** of, guilty of, or involving incest. **2** *said of a relationship or group of people* closed to outside influences or other people.

incestuously *adv.* in an incestuous way.

incestuousness *noun* **1** being incestuous. **2** incestuous behaviour.

inch — *noun* **1** a measure of length equal to one twelfth of a foot (2·54 centimetres). **2** the amount of rain or snow that will cover a surface to the depth of one inch. **3** a small amount or distance. **4** (**inches**) stature. — *verb trans., intrans.* to

move or be moved slowly, carefully, and by degrees.

— **every inch** completely; in every way.

inch by inch gradually; by small degrees.

within an inch of something almost as far as it.

within an inch of one's life almost as far as death; thoroughly: *beat him within an inch of his life.* [from Anglo-Saxon *ynce*]

-in-chief *combining form* highest in rank; supreme: *commander-in-chief.*

inchoate *adj.* **1** at the earliest stage of development; just beginning. **2** not fully developed; unfinished; rudimentary. [from Latin *inchoare*, to begin]

inchoately *adv.* so as to be inchoate.

Inchon *or* **Jinsen** *or* **Chemulpo** POP (1990) 1.8m, a special city in W South Korea. It is situated W of Seoul, on the coast of the Yellow Sea. HISTORY the scene of a battle between Japanese and Russian navies in 1904; UN forces landed at Inchon during the Korean War in 1950. It is a major port for Seoul. Songdo leisure resort lies to the S.

incidence *noun* **1** the frequency with which something happens or the extent of its influence. **2** the way in which something moving in a line, eg a ray of light, comes into contact with a surface. [from Latin *incidentia*]

incident — *noun* **1** an event or occurrence. **2** an event or occurrence which is dependent on, related to, or a consequence of something else. **3** a relatively minor event or occurrence which might have serious consequences. **4** a brief violent conflict or disturbance, eg a bomb explosion. — *adj.* **1** (**incident to something**) belonging naturally to it or being a natural consequence of it. **2** *Legal* (**incident to something**) dependent on it. **3** *Physics, said of light rays, etc* falling or striking. [from Latin *incidens*, from *in*, on + *cadere*, to fall]

incidental — *adj.* **1** happening, etc by chance in connection with something else, and of secondary or minor importance: *incidental expenses.* **2** occurring or likely to occur as a minor consequence. — *noun* **1** anything that occurs incidentally. **2** (**incidentals**) minor expenses.

incidentally *adv.* **1** by the way; parenthetically. **2** in an incidental manner.

incidental music music which accompanies the action of a film, play, etc.

incinerate *verb* to burn to ashes. [from Latin *in*, in + *cinis*, ashes]

incineration *noun* burning completely; reduction to ashes.

incinerator *noun* a furnace or machine for burning rubbish, etc to ashes.

incipience *or* **incipiency** *noun* **1** being incipient. **2** a beginning.

incipient *adj.* beginning to exist; in an early stage. [from Latin *incipere*, to begin]

incipiently *adv.* in an incipient way.

incise *verb* **1** to cut into. **2** to engrave (an inscription, stone, etc). [from Latin *incidere*, to cut into]

incision *noun* **1** a cut, especially one made by a surgeon. **2** an act of cutting, especially by a surgeon.

incisive *adj.* clear and sharp; to the point; acute.

incisively *adv.* in an incisive way.

incisiveness *noun* being incisive.

incisor *noun* one of the eight (in humans) sharp cutting teeth in the front of the mouth.

incite *verb* (**incite someone to something**) to stir them up or provoke them, eg to action. [from Latin *incitare*, to urge forward]

incitement *noun* **1** inciting. **2** something which incites, a stimulus.

incivility *noun* (PL. **incivilities**) **1** rudeness. **2** a rude act or remark. [from Latin *incivilitas*]

incl. *abbrev.* **1** included. **2** including. **3** inclusive.

inclemency *noun* severity of weather.

inclement *adj.*, *said of the weather* stormy or severe; harsh. [from Latin *inclemens*]

inclination *noun* **1** a particular tendency or disposition, especially a liking. **2** an act of inclining or bowing (the head, etc); a bow or nod. **3** a slope. **4** the degree at which an object slopes away from a horizontal or vertical line or plane.

incline — *verb* (with stress on *-cline*) **1** *trans.*, *intrans.* (**incline to** or **towards something**) to lean or cause to lean towards a particular opinion or conduct; to make or be disposed towards it. **2** *trans.*, *intrans.* to slope or cause to slope from a horizontal or vertical line or direction. **3** to bow or bend (the head, one's body) forwards or downwards. — *noun* (with stress on *in-*) a slope; an inclined plane. [from Latin *inclinare*, to bend towards]

inclined plane a plane surface at an angle to a horizontal surface, used especially as a mechanism for lessening the force needed to raise or lower heavy objects.

include *verb* **1** to take in or consider along with others as part of a group. **2** to contain or be made up of. [from Latin *includere*]

inclusion *noun* **1** the act of including or state of being included. **2** something which is included.

inclusive *adj.* **1** comprehensive; including everything. **2** including the stated limits: *March to August inclusive.*

inclusively *adv.* in an inclusive way.

incognito — *adv.*, *adj.* keeping one's identity a secret, eg using a disguise and a false name. — *noun* (PL. **incognitos**) **1** a person who is incognito. **2** the disguise and false name of a person who wishes to keep his or her identity secret. [from Latin *incognitus*, unknown]

incognizance or **incognisance** *noun* failure to recognize.

incognizant or **incognisant** *adj.* not aware; not knowing.

incoherence *noun* **1** being incoherent. **2** lack of clarity in speech or writing. **3** difficulty in expressing oneself.

incoherent *adj.* **1** *said of speech or writing* not expressed clearly or logically; difficult to understand and follow. **2** *said of a person* unable to speak clearly and logically.

incoherently *adv.* in an incoherent way.

incombustible *adj.* incapable of being set alight or burned. [from Latin *incombustibilis*]

income *noun* money received over a period of time as payment for work, etc or as interest or profit from shares or investment. [from Middle English *income*, that which has come in]

incomer *noun* a person who comes to live in a place, not having been born there.

incomes policy a government policy designed to curb inflation by controlling wages. Full legal backing is necessary if the policy is to be effective, and this step is opposed by some economists (who see it as interfering with market mechanisms), and trade unionists.

income support a state benefit paid to people on low incomes and to the unemployed.

income tax a personal tax levied on income. ◇ Income tax is often set as a fixed percentage of income, with increasing percentages being levied on higher levels of income. In the UK, tax payers in paid employment have tax deducted from their wages and salaries by the employer, who acts as tax gatherer for the Revenue service; people who are self-employed or who derive income from investments, etc pay tax direct to the Revenue, usually on an annual basis. Rates of income tax vary from time to time, and are fixed by a government in its budgetary statement.

incoming *adj.* **1** which is coming in; approaching. **2** next or following.

incommensurability *noun* being incommensurable.

incommensurable *adj.* (**incommensurable with something**) having no common standard or basis and not able to be compared. [from Latin *incommensurabilis*]

incommensurate *adj.* **1** (**incommensurate with** or **to something**) out of proportion to it; inadequate for it. **2** incommensurable.

incommensurately *adv.* in an incommensurate way.

incommensurateness *noun* being incommensurate.

incommode *verb* to cause bother, trouble, or inconvenience to. [from Latin *incommodare*]

incommodious *adj.* inconvenient or uncomfortable, especially because too small. [from Latin *incommodus*]

incommodiously *adv.* in an incommodious way.

incommodiousness *noun* being incommodious.

incommunicado *adv.*, *adj.* not allowed to communicate with other people, especially because of being in solitary confinement. [from Spanish *incomunicado*]

incomparability or **incomparableness** *noun* inability to be compared; an incomparable state or standard.

incomparable — *adj.* **1** without equal. **2** not to be compared. [from Latin *incomparabilis*]

incomparably *adv.* in an incomparable way; to an incomparable extent.

incompatibility *noun* being incompatible.

incompatible *adj.* **1** *said of people* unable to live and work together in harmony. **2** (**incompatible with something**) *said of statements, etc* not in agreement; inconsistent. **3** *said eg of drugs* not able to be combined; mutually intolerant. [from Latin *incompatibilis*]

incompatibly *adv.* in an incompatible way.

incompetence *noun* being incompetent.

incompetent *adj.* **1** lacking the necessary skill, ability, or qualifications. **2** not legally qualified. [from Latin *incompetens*]

incompetently *adv.* in an incompetent way.

incomplete *adj.* not complete or finished. [from Latin *incompletus*]

incompletely *adv.* in an incomplete way.

incompleteness *noun* being incomplete.

incomprehensibility *noun* being incomprehensible.

incomprehensible *adj.* difficult or impossible to understand. [from Latin *incomprehensibilis*]

incomprehensibly *adv.* in an incomprehensible way.

incomprehension *noun* inability or failure to understand.

inconceivability *noun* being inconceivable.

inconceivable *adj.* unable to be imagined, believed, or conceived by the mind.

inconceivably *adv.* in an inconceivable way; so as to be inconceivable.

inconclusive *adj.* not leading to a definite conclusion, result, or decision.

inconclusively *adv.* in an inconclusive way.

inconclusiveness *noun* being inconclusive.

incongruity *noun* (PL. **incongruities**) **1** the state of being incongruous. **2** something which is incongruous.

incongruous *adj.* out of place; unsuitable; inappropriate. [from Latin *incongruus*]

incongruously *adv.* in an incongruous way.

incongruousness *noun* being incongruous.

inconsequent *adj.* **1** not following logically or reasonably; illogical. **2** irrelevant. **3** not connected or related. [from Latin *inconsequens*]

inconsequential *adj.* **1** of no importance or value. **2** illogical.

inconsequentiality *noun* an inconsequential character or quality.

inconsequentially *adv.* in an inconsequential way; so as to be inconsequential.

inconsiderable *adj.* not worth considering; small in amount, value, etc. [from Latin *inconsiderabilis*]

inconsiderably *adv.* insignificantly.

inconsiderate *adj.* thoughtless, especially in not considering the feelings, rights, etc of others. [from Latin *inconsideratus*]

inconsiderately *adv.* in an inconsiderate way.

inconsiderateness or **inconsideration** *noun* lack of consideration.

inconsistency *noun* (PL. **inconsistencies**) lack of consistency, or an instance of this.

inconsistent *adj.* **1** (**inconsistent with something**) not in agreement or accordance with it. **2** *of a single thing* having contradictory or incompatible elements. **3** *said of a person* not always thinking, speaking, behaving, etc in accordance with the same principles; not consistent in thought, speech, behaviour, etc.

inconsistently *adv.* in an inconsistent way.

inconsolable *adj.* not able to be comforted. [from Latin *inconsolabilis*]

inconsolably *adv.* in an inconsolable way.

inconspicuous *adj.* not easily noticed; attracting little attention. [from Latin *inconspicuus*]

inconspicuously *adv.* in an inconspicuous way.

inconspicuousness *noun* being inconspicuous.

inconstancy *noun* changeability.

inconstant *adj.* **1** *said of a person* having feelings which change frequently; fickle; unfaithful. **2** subject to frequent change; variable. [from Latin *inconstans*]

incontestability *noun* being incontestable.

incontestable *adj.* too clear or definite to be disputed. [from Latin *incontestabilis*]

incontestably *adv.* in an incontestable way.

incontinence or **incontinency** *noun* being incontinent.

incontinent *adj.* **1** unable to control one's bowels or bladder or both. **2** unable to control oneself, especially one's sexual desires. **3** (**incontinent of something**) lacking control over it. [from Latin *incontinens*]

incontrovertible *adj.* not able to be disputed or doubted. [from IN-[1] + *controvert*, to oppose]

incontrovertibly *adv.* in an incontrovertible way.

inconvenience — *noun* trouble or difficulty, or a cause of this. — *verb* to cause trouble or difficulty to. [from Latin *inconvenientia*]

inconvenient *adj.* not convenient, especially causing trouble or difficulty.

inconveniently *adv.* in an inconvenient way; at an inconvenient time.

incorporate — *verb* (pronounced *-rate*) **1** to contain as part of a whole. **2** *trans.*, *intrans.* to include or be included as part of a whole. **3** *trans.*, *intrans.* to combine or be united thoroughly in a single mass. **4** to admit to membership of a legal corporation. **5** to form into a legal corporation. **6** *intrans.* to form a legal corporation. — *adj.* (pronounced *-rət*) (*also* **incorporated**) **1** united in one body or as a single whole. **2** forming or formed into a legal corporation. [from Latin *incorporare*, from *in-*, + *corpus*, body]

incorporating language same as POLYSYN-THETIC LANGUAGE.

incorporation *noun* **1** incorporating. **2** being incorporated.

incorporeal *adj.* **1** without bodily or material form or substance. **2** *Legal* having no material existence or value in itself, but attached as a right or profit to something else. [from Latin *incorporeus*, from *in-*, not + *corpus*, body]

incorporeally *adv.* in an incorporeal way.

incorporeity *noun* being incorporeal.

incorrect *adj.* **1** not accurate; wrong. **2** not in accordance with normal or accepted standards; improper. [from Latin *incorrectus*]

incorrectly *adv.* in an incorrect way, wrongly.

incorrectness *noun* being incorrect.

incorrigibility *noun* being incorrigible.

incorrigible *adj.*, *said of a person, behaviour, or habit* not able to be improved, corrected, or reformed, usually because too bad. [from Latin *incorrigibilis*]

incorrigibly *adv.* in an incorrigible way.

incorruptibility *noun* being incorruptible.

incorruptible *adj.* **1** incapable of being bribed or morally corrupted. **2** that cannot decay. [from Latin *incorruptibilis*]

incorruptibly *adv.* in an incorruptible way.

increase — *verb trans.*, *intrans.* (with stress on *-crease*) to make or become greater in size, intensity, or number. — *noun* (with stress on *in-*) **1** the act or process of increasing or becoming increased; growth. **2** the amount by which something increases or is increased. — **on the increase** increasing in number, size, or frequency. [from Latin *increscere*, to grow]

increasingly *adv.* so as to increase; more and more.

incredibility *noun* being incredible.

incredible *adj.* **1** difficult or impossible to believe. **2** *colloq.* amazing; unusually good. [from Latin *incredibilis*]

incredibly *adv.* in an incredible way; so as to be incredible.

incredulity *noun* **1** being incredulous. **2** disbelief.

incredulous *adj.* **1** unwilling to believe or accept something as true. **2** showing or expressing disbelief. [from Latin *incredulus*]

incredulously *adv.* in an incredulous way; sceptically.

incredulousness *noun* **1** being incredulous. **2** unbelieving, sceptical.

increment *noun* **1** an increase, especially of one point or level on a fixed scale, eg a regular increase in salary. **2** the amount by which something is increased. **3** *Maths.* a small increase in the value of a variable quantity. [from Latin *incrementum*]

incremental *adj.* involving or based on increments.

incrementally *adv.* in an incremental way; in terms of increments.

incriminate *verb* **1** to show that (someone) was involved in especially a crime. **2** to involve in especially a crime. **3** to charge with a crime or fault. [from Latin *incriminare*, to accuse of a crime]

incriminating *or* **incriminatory** *adj.* that incriminates; implying or suggesting guilt.

incrimination *noun* **1** incriminating. **2** being incriminated.

incrust same as ENCRUST.

incubate *verb* **1** *trans.*, *intrans. said of birds* to hatch (eggs) by sitting on them to keep them warm. **2** to cause (germs, bacteria, etc) to develop by creating favourable and controlled conditions, eg in a laboratory. **3** *intrans. said of germs, bacteria, etc* to develop gradually and slowly before signs of disease begin to appear. [from Latin *incubare*, to lie on]

incubation *noun* **1** an act of incubating. **2** the period between infection with bacteria, germs, etc and the appearance of the actual disease these cause.

incubative *or* **incubatory** *adj.* relating to or involving incubation.

incubator *noun* **1** a transparent box-like container in which a prematurely born baby can be reared under controlled conditions and protected from infection. **2** a cabinet or room that can be maintained at a constant preset temperature, used for culturing bacteria and other microorganisms, hatching eggs, etc.

incubus *noun* (PL. **incubuses**, **incubi**) **1** an evil male spirit which is supposed to have sexual intercourse with sleeping women. See also SUCCUBUS. **2** something which oppresses or weighs heavily upon one, especially a nightmare. [from Latin *incubus*, nightmare]

inculcate *verb* (**inculcate something in** *or* **upon someone**) to teach or fix ideas, habits, a warning, etc firmly in their mind by constant repetition. [from Latin *inculcare*, to tread in]

inculcation *noun* inculcating.

inculpate *verb* to blame or show to be guilty of a crime; to incriminate. [from Latin *inculpare*, to blame]

incumbency *noun* (PL. **incumbencies**) the period of office of an incumbent.

incumbent — *adj.* **1** (**incumbent on** *or* **upon someone**) imposed as a duty on them. **2** occupying a specified position. — *noun* a holder of an office, especially a church office or benefice. [from Latin *incumbere*, to lie on]

incunabulum *noun* (PL. **incunabula**) an early printed book, especially one printed before 1501. [from Latin *incunabula*, swaddling-clothes]

incur *verb* (**incurred**, **incurring**) to bring (something unpleasant) upon oneself; to become liable for (debts, etc). [from Latin *incurrere*, to run into]

incurability *noun* being incurable.

incurable — *adj.* unable to be cured or corrected. — *noun* an incurable person or thing. [from Latin *incurabilis*]

incurably *adv.* in an incurable way; so as to be incurable.

incurious *adj.* showing no interest; lacking a normal curiosity; indifferent.

incuriously *adv.* without curiosity; in an uninterested way.

incursion *noun* **1** a brief or sudden attack made into enemy territory. **2** a using up of something: *unexpected expenses which made an incursion into their savings*. [from Latin *incursio*]

incursive *adj.* aggressive, invasive.

incus *noun* (PL. **incudes**) *Anat.* a small anvil-shaped bone in the middle ear. Together with two other bones, the malleus and stapes, it transmits sound waves from the eardrum to the inner ear. [from Latin *incus*, anvil]

Ind. *abbrev.* **1** Independent. **2** India; Indian. **3** Indiana.

indaba *noun* **1** an important conference or discussion between members of South African tribes. **2** *colloq.* a concern or problem for discussion. [from Zulu, = affair]

indebted *adj.* (*often* **indebted to someone**) **1** having reason to be grateful or obliged to them. **2** owing them money.

indebtedness *noun* being indebted.

indecency *noun* (PL. **indecencies**) **1** indecent behaviour or character. **2** an indecent act.

indecent *adj.* **1** offensive against accepted standards of morality or sexual behaviour. **2** in bad taste; improper; unseemly. [from Latin *indecens*]

indecent assault a sexual attack which falls short of being rape.

indecent exposure the crime of indecently showing parts of one's body, especially one's sexual organs, in public.

indecently *adv.* in an indecent way.

indecipherability *noun* being indecipherable.

indecipherable *adj.* that cannot be read or understood.

indecipherably *adv.* in an indecipherable way.

indecision *noun* the state of not being able to decide; uncertainty.

indecisive *adj.* **1** not producing a clear or definite decision or result. **2** unable to make a firm decision; hesitating.

indecisively *adv.* in an indecisive way.

indecisiveness *noun* being indecisive.

indecorous *adj.* not decorous; in bad taste; improper. [from Latin *indecorus*]

indecorously *adv.* in an indecorous way.

indecorousness *noun* being indecorous.

indecorum *noun* improper or unseemly behaviour; lack of decorum.

indeed — *adv.* **1** without any question; in truth. **2** in fact; actually. **3** used for emphasis: *very wet indeed*. — *interj.* an expression of irony, surprise, disbelief, etc or acknowledgement. [from Middle English]

indefatigable *adj.* **1** never becoming tired. **2** never stopping; unremitting. [from Latin *indefatigabilis*]

indefatigably *adv.* in an indefatigable way.

indefensibility *noun* being indefensible.

indefensible *adj.* that cannot be defended or justified.

indefensibly *adv.* in an indefensible way.

indefinable *adj.* that cannot be clearly, fully, or exactly defined or described.

indefinably *adv.* in an indefinable way.

indefinite *adj.* **1** without fixed or exact limits. **2** uncertain; vague; imprecise. [from Latin *indefinitus*]

indefinite article *Grammar* a word (*a* or *an* in English) used before a noun to denote an example that is not definite or specific: *a cat in the road* / *a new government* / *half a pound*. See also DEFINITE ARTICLE.

indefinitely *adv.* in an indefinite way; without limit.

indefiniteness *noun* being indefinite.

indehiscent *adj. Bot.* denoting a fruit that does not split open but is dispersed intact.

indelible *adj.* **1** *said of a mark, writing, etc* unable to be removed or rubbed out. **2** *said of a pen, etc* making indelible marks. [from Latin *indelebilis*]

indelibly *adv.* so as to be indelible; permanently.

indelicacy *noun* (PL. **indelicacies**) embarrassing or offensive language or behaviour.

indelicate *adj.* **1** tending to embarrass or offend; in poor taste; immodest. **2** slightly coarse; rough.

indelicately *adv.* in an indelicate way.

indemnification *noun* the process of indemnifying; protection against loss or misfortune.

indemnify *verb* (**indemnifies, indemnified**) **1** (**indemnify someone against something**) to provide them with security against loss or misfortune. **2** (**indemnify someone for something**) to pay them money in compensation for especially loss or damage; to reimburse them. [from Latin *indemnis*, without loss, unhurt]

indemnity *noun* (PL. **indemnities**) **1** compensation for loss or damage, or money paid in compensation. **2** security from loss or damage. **3** legal exemption from liabilities or penalties incurred.

indent¹ — *verb* (with stress on *-dent*) **1** *trans., intrans.* to begin (a line or paragraph) from the margin. **2** to divide (a document drawn up in duplicate in two columns) along a zigzag line. **3** to draw up (a document, deed, etc) in duplicate. **4** *trans., intrans. Brit.* to make out a written order (for especially foreign goods). **5** to indenture as an apprentice. **6** to make a notch in. — *noun* (with stress on *in-*) **1** *Brit.* a written order for especially foreign goods. **2** an indented line or paragraph. **3** a notch. **4** an indenture. [from Latin *indentatus*]

indent² *verb* (with stress on *-dent*) to form a dent in or mark with dents.

indentation *noun* **1** a cut or notch. **2** a deep inward curve or recess, eg in a coastline. **3** the act of indenting.

indention *noun* **1** the indenting of a line or paragraph. **2** the blank space at the beginning of a line caused by indenting a line or paragraph.

indenture — *noun* **1** (*usually* **indentures**) a contract binding an apprentice to a master. **2** an indented document, agreement, or contract. — *verb* to bind (eg an apprentice) by indentures or by an indented contract or agreement.

independence *noun* an independent state or condition.

Independence, US War of see AMERICAN REVOLUTION.

Independence, War of see NETHERLANDS, REVOLT OF THE.

Independence Day a public holiday celebrating the anniversary of a country's declaration of independence, eg held on 4 July in the US.

Independence Hall a building in Independence National Historical Park, Philadelphia, where the Declaration of Independence was proclaimed. The Liberty Bell, rung at the proclamation, is kept here. It is a World Heritage centre.

independent *adj.* **1** not under the control or authority of others, especially (of a country or state) self-governing. **2** not relying on others for financial support, care, help, or guidance. **3** thinking and acting for oneself and not under an obligation to others. **4** not dependent on something else for value, purpose, or function. **5** *said of two or more people or things* not related to or affected by the others. **6** *said of private income or resources* large enough to make having to work for a living unnecessary: *independent means.* **7** not belonging to a political party. **8** *said of a school or broadcasting company* not paid for with public money.

independent clause *Grammar* a clause which is grammatically correct and complete and has meaning even when it is taken out of the sentence in which it is found, eg *she picked it up* in *she picked it up and ran off*; a main clause.

Independent Group a group of artists, architects, and critics who met during the 1950s in the Institute of Contemporary Arts in London. They were instrumental in the emergence of Pop Art in Britain. Leading members included the sculptor Eduardo Paolozzi, the painter and sculptor William Turnbull, and the architects Peter and Alison Smithson.

Independent Labour Party (ABBREV. **ILP**) a British political party formed in 1893 with the objective of sending working men to parliament. Keir Hardie was one of its leading figures, many of whom played a major part in founding the Labour Representation Committee (1900), which became the Labour Party in 1906. The ILP was affiliated to the Labour Party, disaffiliated in 1932, and had a few MPs until 1950.

independently *adv.* in an independent way.

in-depth *adj.* thorough, exhaustive: *an in-depth study of the problem.*

indescribable *adj.* that cannot be described, often because too extreme or too vague.

indescribably *adv.* in an indescribable way.

indestructibility *noun* being indestructible.

indestructible *adj.* that cannot be destroyed.

indestructibly *adv.* in an indestructible way.

indeterminable *adj.* **1** not able to be fixed, decided, or measured. **2** *said of an argument, etc* that cannot be settled. [from Latin *indeterminabilis*]

indeterminacy *noun* being indeterminate.

indeterminate *adj.* **1** not precisely or exactly fixed, determined, or settled. **2** doubtful; vague. **3** *Maths.* not having a fixed or definite value. [from Latin *indeterminatus*]

indeterminately *adv.* in an indeterminate way.

indeterminateness *noun* **1** being indeterminate. **2** lack of determination. **3** absence of direction.

index — *noun* (PL. **indexes,** *technical* **indices**) **1** an alphabetical list of names, subjects, etc dealt with in a book, usually given at the end of that book, and with the page numbers on which each item appears. **2** a catalogue or set of reference cards, eg in a library, which lists each book, magazine, etc alphabetically, usually by author or title, and gives details of where it is shelved. **3** anything which points to, identifies, or highlights a particular trend or condition. **4** a scale of numbers which shows changes in price, wages, rates of interest, etc: *retail price index.* **5** a hand or pointer on a dial or scale. **6** *Maths.* an exponent or power, usually denoted by a superscript number or symbol which indicates the number of times a given value is to be multiplied by itself (see also EXPONENT). **7** *Physics* a numerical quantity, usually lacking units, that indicates the magnitude of a particular physical effect, eg refractive index. **8** *Geol.* a fossil or mineral that characterizes a particular type of rock. **9** (**Index**) *RC Church* an official list of prohibited books. — *verb* **1** to provide (a book) with an index. **2** to list in an index. **3** to relate (prices, wages, etc) to the cost-of-living index, so that they may rise or fall accordingly. [from Latin *index*, informer]

indexation *or* **indexing** *noun* the linking of prices, wages, rates of interest, etc to changes in an index showing the cost of living.

indexer *noun* a person who compiles an index.

index finger the finger next to the thumb; the forefinger.

Index Librorum Prohibitorum a list of books which members of the Roman Catholic Church were forbidden to read. It originated with the Gelasian Decree (496), and was frequently revised until 1948 (the last revision). Although the Church still claims the right to prevent its members reading material harmful to their faith or morals, it was decided in 1966 to publish no further editions. [Latin, = index of forbidden books]

index-linked *adj., said of prices, wages, rates of interest, etc* calculated so as to rise or fall by the same amount as the cost of living.

India, Hindi **Bharat**, official name **Republic of India** POP (1992e) 879.6m, a federal republic in S Asia, divided into 22 states and nine union territories. AREA 3 166 829sq km/1 222 396sq mi. It is bounded NW by Pakistan, N by China, Nepal, and Bhutan, E by Burma (Myanma) and Bangladesh, SE by the Bay of Bengal, and SW by the Arabian Sea. CAPITAL New Delhi. CHIEF TOWNS Ahmadabad, Bangalore, Bombay, Calcutta, Hyderabad, Jaipur, Kanpur, Lucknow, Madras, Nagpur, Poona. TIME ZONE GMT +5.5. The chief ethnic groups are Indo-Aryan (72%) and Dravidian (25%); Hinduism is the main religion. OFFICIAL LANGUAGES Hindi,English, and 14 others. CURRENCY the Indian rupee. PHYSICAL DESCRIPTION the second largest state in Asia, bordered to the N by the Himalayas; folded mountain ridges and valleys lie to the N; the highest peaks are over 7 000m in the Karakoram Range and the Ladakh Plateau; the central river plains of the Ganges, Yamuna, Ghaghari, and Brahmaputra are to the S; the best agricultural land is in the E; control measures are needed to prevent flooding; the Thar Desert NW of Rajasthan is bordered by semi-desert areas; the Deccan Plateau in the S peninsula, with hills and wide valleys, is bounded by the Western and Eastern Ghats; the coastal plains are important areas of rice cultivation. CLIMATE dominated by the Asiatic monsoon; rains come from the SW (Jun–Oct); rainfall decreases (Dec–Feb) as winds blow in from the N, followed by drought until Mar or May; temperatures in the N mountains vary greatly with altitude; rainfall decreases E–W on the N plains, with desert conditions in the extreme W; temperatures vary with altitude on the Deccan Plateau, although towards the S of the plateau region the climate is tropical, even in the cool season; the W coast is subject to rain throughout the year, particularly in the S, where humidity is high; cyclones and storms on the SE coast (especially Oct–Dec), with high temperatures and humidity during the monsoon season. HISTORY the Indus civilization, which emerged in c.2500 BC, was destroyed in 1500 BC by the Aryans, who developed the Brahmanic caste system; the Mauryan Emperor Asoka unified most of India, and established Buddhism as the state religion in the 3c BC; spread of Hinduism in the 2c BC; Muslim influences during the 7c–8c, with a sultanate established at Delhi; Delhi captured by Timur in 1398; a Mughal Empire was established by Babur in 1526, extended by Akbar and Aurangzeb; Portuguese, French, Dutch, and British footholds in India in the 18c; conflict between France and Britain in 1746–63; development of British interests represented by the East India Company; British power was established after the Indian Mutiny was crushed in 1857; movement for independence in the late 19c; the Government of India Act in 1919 allowed the election of Indian ministers to share power with appointed British governors; a further Act in 1935 allowed the election of independent provincial governments; passive resistance campaigns led by Mahatma Gandhi began in the 1920s; independence was granted in 1948, on the condition that a Muslim state be established (Pakistan); Indian states were later reorganized on a linguistic basis; Pakistan–India war over disputed territory in Kashmir and Jammu in 1948; Hindu–Muslim hostility, notably in 1978, and further India–Pakistan conflict in 1965 and 1971; separatist movements continue, especially relating to Sikh interests in the Punjab; the suppression of the militant Sikh movement in 1984 led to the assassination of Indira Gandhi; a major gas leak in 1984 at the city of Bhopal caused c.2 500 deaths; Rajiv Gandhi, leader of the Congress (I)

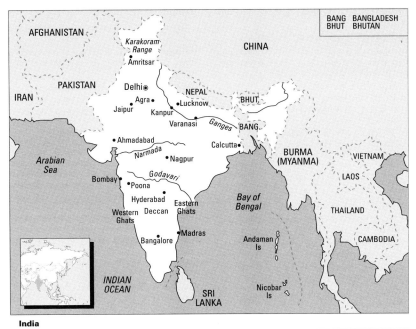

India

Party, was assassinated in 1991 during the general election; torrential rainstorms in 1992 resulted in many people being killed in the S states; increasing tension resulted in inter-communal violence and the declaration in 1993 of a national state of emergency. GOVERNMENT a federal democratic republic within the Commonwealth since 1950; each of the 25 states is administered by a Governor appointed by the President for five years; each state has an Assembly (numbers range from 30 to 425 members); each of the seven union territories is administered by the President who is elected for a five-year term; the President, advised by a Council ofMinisters, appoints a Prime Minister; Parliament comprises the President, an Upper House (*Rajya Sabha*) of no more than 250 members, and a 544-member House of the People (*Lok Sabha*). ECONOMY over two thirds of the work force is employed in agriculture; tea, rice, wheat, coffee, sugar cane, cotton, jute, oilseed, maize, pulses, milk; floods and drought cause major problems; fishing, forestry; considerable increase in industrial production since independence; iron, steel, aluminium; vehicles; oil products; cement; chemicals; fertilizers; paper; jute goods; textiles; sugar; coal, iron, mica, manganese, bauxite, limestone, chromite, barites, oil, natural gas.

India Acts see GOVERNMENT OF INDIA ACTS.

Indiaman *noun* (PL. **Indiamen**) *Hist.* a merchant ship trading with India or the East Indies.

Indian — *noun* **1** a native or citizen of India. **2** a person whose ancestors were born in India. **3** a member of any of the various native peoples of N, Central, and S America (but not including the Inuit). **4** any of the languages spoken by the native peoples of America. — *adj.* **1** relating to India or the Indian subcontinent (India, Bangladesh, and Pakistan), or its inhabitants, languages, and culture. **2** relating to the native peoples of America, or their languages and culture. [from Greek *India*, from *Indos*, the Indus river]

Indiana POP (1990) 5.7m, a state in E USA, S of L Michigan, divided into 92 counties. It is known as the 'Hoosier State'. AREA 93 716sq km/ 36 185sq mi. PHYSICAL DESCRIPTION there are many hills in the S; there are fertile plains in the centre; flat, glaciated land lies to the N. HISTORY visited by La Salle in 1679 and 1681; occupied by the French, who ceded the state to the British in 1763; the scene of several battles; in 1816 it was the 19th state to join the Union. CAPITAL Indianapolis. CHIEF TOWNS Fort Wayne, South Bend, Gary, Evansville. ECONOMY grain, soya beans; pigs, cattle; meat packing; bituminous coal, limestone; steel and iron; chemicals; motor vehicles; electrical goods.

Indianapolis POP (1990) 1.3m, the capital of the state of Indiana, USA. It lies on the White R, in Marion County, central Indiana. Founded in 1820, it became state capital in 1825. NOTABLE FEATURES State Museum; Museum of Art; City Market Internationale; major medical centre at the Indiana–Purdue Universities Campus (1969); Motor Speedway. EVENT 'Indianapolis 500' motor race.

Indianapolis 500 see INDY 500.

Indian club one of a pair of heavy, bottle-shaped clubs swung to develop the arm muscles.

Indian corn same as MAIZE.

Indian file single file.

Indian hemp same as HEMP 1.

Indian ink or *North Amer.* **India ink** black ink made from lampblack.

Indian Mutiny see INDIAN UPRISING.

Indian National Congress a broad-based political organization (founded 1885), which became a nationwide political party in 1920. It spearheaded the nationalist movement for independence from Britain under the leadership of charismatic figures such as M K Gandhi and Jawaharlal Nehru. It has been the dominant political party in India since 1947, except in 1977–80 when the Janata Party ruled, and 1989–91 when the Janata Dal and one of its factions, Janata Dal (S) ruled.

Indian Ocean, ancient **Erythræan Sea** the third largest ocean in the world, bounded W by Africa, N by Asia, E by Australia and the Malay archipelago, and S by the Southern Ocean. AREA 73 427 000sq km/28 343 000sq mi. The width is c.6 400km/4 000mi at the Equator and the maximum depth is 7 125m in the Java Trench. There is a link to the Mediterranean via the Suez Canal. The ocean floor is divided into E and W sections by the Mid-Oceanic Ridge. A rift valley runs along the ridge axis and is the centre of seafloor spreading. MAIN ISLAND GROUPS Andaman Is, Nicobar Is, Chagos Is, and Seychelles. The largest islands are Madagascar and Sri Lanka.

Indian summer 1 a period of unusually warm, dry weather in late autumn or early winter. **2** a period of happiness and success towards the end of a person's life.

Indian Territory land set aside in the USA as a 'permanent' home for Native Americans removed from the area east of the Mississippi River between 1825 and 1840. Originally it included most of Oklahoma and parts of Kansas and Arkansas, but by the end of the 19c most of it had been opened to whites.

Indian Uprising a serious rebellion (1857–8) against British rule, triggered off partly by the belief among Indian troops in British service that new cartridges had been greased with animal fat — a notion abhorrent to both Hindus and Muslims. At the same time there was resentment among the old governing class over both the reduction in their power and also Western innovations. The uprising at Meerut (10 May 1857) spread throughout N India, leading quickly to the fall of Delhi and the siege of Kanpur and Lucknow garrisons. The British finally regained full control (mid-1858) and government was transferred from the British East India Company to the British Crown (1858). The uprising is also known as the Indian Mutiny or the 1st National War of Independence.

Indian Wars the process (1622–1890) of invasion and conquest by which white people settled the present USA. By the end of the 18c, the native population of N America had been reduced from roughly one million to c.250 000. This decline in numbers was caused by European diseases to which the Native Americans had no natural resistance, the imposition of white culture, and warfare. There were many specific Indian wars, most of them skirmishes between a local tribe and the white settlers usurping their land as they moved their frontier westward. They are generally accepted to have begun with the revolt of the Powhatan Confederacy against settlers at Jamestown, Virginia (1622), and to have ended with the massacre at Wounded Knee (1890). Specific early conflicts include the Pequot War (1637) and King Philip's War (1676) in New England and the Pueblo Revolt (1680–92) led by Popé against Spanish settlements in what is now New Mexico and Arizona. From 1689 to 1763 Indian warfare was bound up with the struggle between France and Britain for control of the continent (the French and Indian War). The Algonkin tribes sided with the French. The English, eventually victorious, enjoyed the support of the Iroquois Confederacy of W New York, important both for their internal strength and for their control of the Mohawk Valley and L Ontario plain, which formed the only natural break in the Appalachian Mountains. Further west, the Ottawa chief, Pontiac, seized almost all the British fur trading posts from upper Michigan to New York state before the French cut off their supplies. By 1830 the US government had formalized a policy of denying Native American rights and removing tribes from the lands east of the Mississippi to unsettled lands in the west. Despite resistance, the Five Civilized Tribes of the southeast and others were forced to move west and settle in Indian Territory. The Seminole people of Florida, whose number included escaped black slaves, fought for over 30 years, accepting defeat in 1842 when nearly all had been killed. Some finally moved west, but a small group survived by living in the Everglades. On the plains, the US cavalry fought the Sioux and the Cheyenne, under such leaders as Sitting Bull and Crazy Horse. These 'Sioux Wars' lasted over 30 years until finally ended by the incident at Wounded Knee (1890). In the southwest, the Navajo conflict ended with their mass imprisonment (1864–8) at Fort Sumpter, while the Apache under such leaders as Cochise and Geronimo fought on until 1900. At the same time Nez Percé under Chief Joseph and the Modoc fought for their lands in the northwest until their eventual defeat. Throughout these wars, the Native Americans fought at material and numerical disadvantage and they were handicapped by their own lack of unity.

India paper 1 a thin, soft, absorbent paper originally made in China and Japan. **2** a very thin, strong, opaque paper, used eg for printing Bibles.

India rubber same as RUBBER[1] 2.

Indic — *adj.* of the Indian branch of the Indo-European languages, made up of Sanskrit, and modern languages such as Hindi, Gujarati and Urdu. — *noun* the languages forming this group. [from Greek *Indikos*, Indian]

indicate *verb* **1** to point out or show. **2** to be a sign or symptom of. **3** *said of a gauge, dial, etc* to show as a reading. **4** to state briefly. **5** to point to as a suitable treatment or desirable or required course. [from Latin *indicare*]

indication *noun* **1** an act of indicating. **2** something which serves to indicate; a sign. **3** something which is indicated. **4** a reading on a gauge, dial, etc.

indicative — *adj.* **1** (**indicative of something**) being a sign or indication of it. **2** *Grammar* being the mood, or in the mood, used to state facts, describe events, or ask questions. — *noun* **1** the indicative mood. **2** a verb in the indicative mood.

indicator *noun* **1** an instrument, or a needle or pointer on a device, that shows the level of temperature, fuel, pressure, etc. **2** any of the flashing lights on a motor vehicle which show that the vehicle is about to change direction. **3** any sign, condition, situation, etc which shows or illustrates something. **4** a board or diagram giving information, eg in a railway station. **5** *Chem.* a substance, eg litmus, that changes colour reversibly depending on the pH of a solution, and that indicates when a chemical reaction is complete, eg during chemical titrations. **6** *Biol.* (also **indicator species**) a plant or animal species whose presence or absence indicates the levels of a particular environmental factor in an area, eg certain lichens are sensitive to air pollutants.

indicatory *adj.* giving a sign or symptom.

indices see INDEX.

indict *verb* to accuse of or charge formally with a crime, especially in writing. [from Old French *enditer*, with spelling influenced by Latin *indicere*, to announce]

indictable *adj.* **1** *said of a person* liable to be indicted for a crime. **2** *said of a crime* liable to cause a person to be indicted.
◇ In England and Wales, certain indictable offences must be tried in the Crown Court, for example murder and rape. Indictable offences such as theft may be tried in a magistrates' court or in the Crown Court, although all criminal cases start in a magistrates' court, where the venue for trial is determined.

indictment *noun* **1** a formal written accusation or charge. **2** an act of indicting. **3** something which deserves severe criticism or censure.

indie *noun colloq.* a small, independent, and usually non-commercial record or film company. [abbreviation of INDEPENDENT]

indifference *noun* **1** being indifferent. **2** lack of quality. **3** lack of importance.

indifferent *adj.* **1** (**indifferent to something** *or* **someone**) showing no interest in them or concern for them. **2** neither good nor bad; average; mediocre. **3** fairly bad; inferior. **4** without importance. **5** neutral. [from Latin *indifferens*]

indifferently *adv.* in an indifferent way.

indigence *noun* poverty.

indigenous *adj.* belonging naturally to or occurring naturally in a country or area; native. [from Latin *indigena*, original inhabitant]

indigenously *adv.* in an indigenous way.

indigent *adj.* very poor; needy. [from Latin *indigens*]

indigestibility *noun* being indigestible.

indigestible *adj.* **1** *said of food* difficult or impossible to digest. **2** not easily understood; complicated. [from Latin *indigestibilis*]

indigestion *noun* discomfort or pain in the abdomen or lower region of the chest, especially after eating, caused by difficulty in digesting or inability to digest food.

Indigirka a river in NE Siberia, Russia, length 1 779km/1 095mi. The river discharges into the E Siberian Sea where it forms a large, swampy delta.

indignant *adj.* feeling or showing anger or a sense of ill-treatment. [from Latin *indignans*]

indignantly *adv.* with an indignant manner.

indignation *noun* anger caused by a feeling of having been ill-treated.

indignity *noun* (PL. **indignities**) **1** any act or treatment which causes someone to feel shame; disgrace or dishonour. **2** a feeling of shame, disgrace, or dishonour. [from Latin *indignitas*]

indigo — *noun* (PL. **indigos**, **indigoes**) **1** a violet-blue dye either obtained naturally from a plant or made synthetically. **2** any of several leguminous plants whose leaves yield a violet-blue dye. **3** the violet-blue colour of this dye. — *adj.* violet-blue. [from Greek *indikon*, Indian]

indirect *adj.* **1** *said of a route, course, line, etc* not straight or direct. **2** not going straight to the point; devious. **3** not directly aimed at or intended: *indirect consequences*. [from Latin *indirectus*]

indirectly *adv.* in an indirect way.

indirectness *noun* being indirect.

indirect object *Grammar* a noun, noun phrase, or pronoun which is affected indirectly by the action of a verb, usually standing for the person or thing to whom something is given or for whom something is done, eg *him* in *give him a kiss*. See also DIRECT OBJECT.

indirect speech *Grammar* a speaker's words reported by another person with change of person and tense, eg *we will come* becomes *they said they would come* in indirect speech.

indirect tax a tax levied on goods and services as opposed to a person's income. See also DIRECT TAX

indirect taxation see TAXATION.

indiscernible *adj.* that cannot be noticed or recognized as being distinct, especially because too small: *indiscernible differences*.

indiscipline *noun* lack of discipline.

indisciplined *adj.* lacking discipline.

indiscreet *adj.* **1** giving away too many secrets or too much information; not discreet. **2** not wise or cautious; injudicious. [from Latin *indiscretus*]

indiscreetly *adv.* in an indiscreet way.

indiscretion *noun* **1** lack of discretion or caution; rashness. **2** an act or remark showing this.

indiscriminate *adj.* **1** making no distinctions; not making or showing careful choice and discrimination. **2** confused; not differentiated.

indiscriminately *adv.* in an indiscriminate way.

indiscriminateness *noun* being indiscriminate.

indispensability *noun* being indispensable.

indispensable *adj.* necessary; essential; that cannot be done without. [from Latin *indispensabilis*]

indispensably *adv.* in an indispensable way.

indisposed *adj.* **1** slightly ill. **2** (**indisposed to do something**) reluctant or unwilling to do it.

indisposition *noun* being indisposed.

indisputable *adj.* certainly true; beyond doubt.

indisputably *adv.* as cannot be disputed or denied; unquestionably: *indisputably the finest singer in Italy*.

indissolubility *noun* being indissoluble.

indissoluble *adj.* incapable of being dissolved or broken; permanent; lasting. [from Latin *indissolubilis*]

indissolubly *adv.* so as to be lasting; permanently.

indistinct *adj.* not clear to a person's eye, ear or mind; confused; dim. [from Latin *indistinctus*]

indistinctly *adv.* in an indistinct way.

indistinctness *noun* being indistinct.

indistinguishable *adj.* not able to be distinguished or told apart.

indistinguishably *adv.* in an indistinguishable way.

indium *noun Chem.* (SYMBOL **In**, ATOMIC NUMBER 49) a soft silvery-white metal that is used in the manufacture of mirrors, semiconductor devices, metal bearings, and certain alloys. [from Latin *indicium*, indigo, because of the indigo-coloured lines in its spectrum]

individual — *adj.* **1** intended for or relating to a single person or thing. **2** particular to one person; showing or having a particular person's unique qualities or characteristics. **3** separate; single. — *noun* **1** a particular person, animal, or thing, especially in contrast to the group to which it belongs. **2** *colloq.* a person: *a most offensive individual*. [from Latin *individualis*, from *individuus*, indivisible]

individualism *noun* **1** behaviour governed by the belief that individual people should lead their lives as they want and should be independent. **2** the theory that the state should in no way control the actions of the individual. **3** egoism; self-centredness.

individualist — *noun* **1** a person who thinks and acts with independence or great individuality, sometimes for the sake of being different. **2** a person who supports individualism. — *adj.* (also **individualistic**) of individualists or individualism.

individualistically *adv.* in an individualistic way.

individuality *noun* (PL. **individualities**) **1** the qualities and character which distinguish one person or thing from others. **2** a separate and distinct existence.

individualization *or* **individualisation** *noun* making individual.

individualize *or* **individualise** *verb* **1** to give (someone or something) a distinctive character or personality. **2** to make suitable for a particular person, thing, or situation.

individually *adv.* in an individual way; one by one.

indivisibility *noun* being indivisible.

indivisible *adj.* **1** not able to be divided or separated. **2** *Maths.* leaving a remainder. [from Latin *indivisibilis*]

indivisibly *adv.* in an indivisible way.

Indo- *combining form* Indian; India: *Indo-European*. [from Greek *Indos*]

Indo-Aryan a group of some 500 languages, also known as Indic languages, spoken by c.500 million people in the N and central region of the Indian subcontinent. They form a subgroup of the Indo-Iranian branch of the Indo-European family, and include Hindu and Urdu, Assamese and Bengali, Panjabi, and Romany. Their early forms, from c.1000 BC, are known as Sanskrit; and the later Buddhist and Jainist literary forms are known as Prakrits.

indoctrinate *verb* to teach (an individual or group) to accept and believe a particular teaching or set of beliefs uncritically. [from Latin *indoctrinare*, to teach]

indoctrination *noun* the process of indoctrinating or being indoctrinated.

Indo-European — *adj.* denoting the family of languages which are spoken throughout Europe and in many parts of Asia, including most of the European languages and many Asian ones, such as Hindi and Persian. — *noun* **1** the languages forming this family. **2** the hypothetical language which all of the languages in the Indo-European family come from.
◇ The principal branches of the Indo-European family of languages are: Germanic, Celtic, Balto-Slavic, Indo-Iranian, Greek (or Hellenic), Albanian, Armenian, Italic (including Latin and the Romance languages), Anatolian (now extinct), and Tocharian (an extinct language spoken in Chinese Turkistan, c.1000).

Indo-Iranian the easternmost branch of the Indo-European family of languages made up of two major subgroups, the Indo-Aryan (or Indic) languages and the Iranian languages.

indolence *noun* laziness, idleness.

indolent *adj.* **1** lazy; disliking and avoiding work and exercise. **2** *Medicine* causing no pain. [from Latin *indolens*, not suffering pain]

indolently *adv.* in an indolent way.

indomitability *noun* in an indomitable way.

indomitable *adj.* that cannot be conquered or defeated. [from Latin *indomitabilis*]

indomitably *adv.* in an indomitable way.

Indonesia, official name **Republic of Indonesia**, Bahasa Indonesian **Republik Indonesia**, formerly **Netherlands Indies**, **Dutch East Indies**, **Netherlands East Indies**, **United States of Indonesia** POP (1992e) 191.2m, a republic in SE Asia comprising the world's largest island group, divided into 27 provinces. AREA 1 906 240sq km/735 809sq mi. The republic is made up of five main islands: Sumatra, Java, Kalimantan (two thirds of Borneo I), Sulawesi (Celebes), and Irian Jaya (the W half of New Guinea I). CAPITAL Jakarta. TIME ZONES GMT +7 to GMT +9. Chief ethnic groups are Javanese, Sundanese, Madurese, and coastal Malays. Islam is the main religion. OFFICIAL LANGUAGE Indonesian; English, Dutch, and Javanese are also widely spoken. CURRENCY the rupiah. PHYSICAL DESCRIPTION five main islands and 30 smaller archipelagos totalling 13 677 islands and islets, of which c.6 000 are inhabited; over 100 volcanic peaks on Java, of which 15 are active. CLIMATE hot and humid equatorial climate; dry season (Jun–Sep), rainy season (Dec–Mar), apart from the Moluccas (Jun–Sep); the average temperature is 27°C on island coasts, falling inland and with altitude. HISTORY settled in early times by Hindus and Buddhists whose power lasted until the 14c; Islam introduced in the 14c–15c; Portuguese settlers arrived in the early 16c; the Dutch East India Company was established in 1602; Japanese occupation in World War II; independence proclaimed in 1945, under Dr Sukarno; the 1945 constitution established a 1000-member People's Consultative Assembly; the federal system was replaced by unified control in 1950; the expulsion of Dutch citizens led to a breakdown of the economy, causing hardship and unrest; Sukarno's rule became increasingly authoritarian and was opposed by the Communist Party; there was a military coup in 1966; East Timor became the 27th province of Indonesia in 1976 but the United Nations refuses to recognize Indonesian sovereignty in East Timor and continues to regard it as a Portuguese Colony; protesters for independence were massacred by the Indonesian army in Dili, the East Timor capital, in 1991, provoking international condemnation. GOVERNMENT governed by a President elected for a five-year

term, advised by a Cabinet and several advisory agencies; separatist movements in Irian Jaya and East Timor. ECONOMY mainly agrarian, notably rice; maize, cassava, sugar, sweet potatoes, bananas, coffee, tobacco, tea, rubber, coconuts, palm oil; fishing, timber; oil, natural gas, and petroleum products from Borneo and Sumatra account for nearly 60% of national income; tin, nickel, bauxite, copper, manganese; small manufacturing industry, based on textiles, paper, cement, chemicals, fertilizers, motorcycles, household goods.

Indonesia

Indonesian — *noun* **1** a native or citizen of Indonesia or the Malay archipelago. **2** the languages spoken in the Malay archipelago, especially the official language of the Republic of Indonesia. — *adj.* relating to Indonesia or its people, languages, and culture. [from Greek *Indos*, Indian + *nesos*, island]

indoor *adj.* used, belonging, done, happening, etc inside a building. [earlier *within-door*]

indoors *adv.* in or into a building.

Indo-Pacific — *adj.* denoting a group of c.700 languages spoken in New Guinea and nearby islands to the W and E. These languages are located in the middle of the Austronesian group, but are linguistically independent. The group as a whole has fewer than 3 million speakers; there has been no comprehensive study of the languages, and many tribes have never been contacted. — *noun* the languages forming this group.

indorse same as ENDORSE.

Indra in Hinduism, the Vedic king of the gods, to whom many of the prayers of the Rig Veda are addressed.

indrawn *adj.* **1** *said especially of the breath* drawn or pulled in. **2** *said of a person* aloof.

indri *or* **indris** *noun* a leaping lemur, the largest primitive primate, having a dark coat with white legs and hindquarters, fluffy round ears, a very short tail, and a loud far-reaching cry. It inhabits tree tops and feeds on leaves. [from Malagasy *indry!*, look!; the exclamation was mistaken for the animal's name]

indubitable *adj.* that cannot be doubted; certain. [from Latin *indubitabilis*]

indubitably *adv.* as cannot be doubted; certainly.

induce *verb* **1** to persuade, influence, or cause to do something. **2** to cause to happen or appear. **3** *Medicine* to cause (labour) to begin, especially by the use of drugs; to cause labour in (a pregnant woman). **4** to produce or transmit (an electrical current or magnetism) by induction. **5** *Logic* to infer or come to (eg a general conclusion) from particular cases. [from Latin *inducere*, to lead in]

inducement *noun* that which induces, especially something which is persuasive or which influences or encourages certain behaviour.

inducible *adj.* capable of being induced.

induct *verb* **1** to place (eg a priest) formally and often ceremonially in an official position. **2** to initiate as a member of eg a society or profession.

3 *North Amer., esp. US* to enrol for military service or training. [from Latin *inducere*, to lead in]

inductance *noun* the property of an electric circuit or circuit component that causes an electromotive force to be generated in it in the presence of a changing current.

induction *noun* **1** the act or process of inducting or being inducted, especially into office. **2** *Medicine* during childbirth, the initiation of labour by artificial means, often involving the use of drugs such as oxytocin. It is used to stimulate uterine contractions if continuation of the pregnancy would jeopardize the life or well-being of the mother or baby. **3** *Logic* the process of forming or coming to a general conclusion from particular cases. See also DEDUCTION. **4** *Electr.* the production of an electric current in a conductor as a result of its close proximity to a varying magnetic field. **5** *Electr.* the production of magnetization in an unmagnetized material as a result of its close proximity either to a magnetic field, or to the electromagnetic field of a current-carrying conductor. **6** *Engineering* the drawing in of steam or an explosive mixture of fuel and air into the cylinder of an engine.

induction coil a type of transformer that can produce a high-voltage alternating current from a low-voltage direct current source. Induction coils are used to produce short bursts of high voltages, eg to form a spark across the terminals of a spark plug in the internal combustion engine of a motor vehicle.

induction motor *Engineering* an alternating-current motor in which an electric current is supplied to a stationary coil, which creates a magnetic field and induces an electric current in a moving coil (known as the *rotor*). The magnetic field interacts with the induced current, causing the rotor to turn.

inductive *adj.* **1** *Logic* of or using induction. **2** of electric or magnetic induction. See also DEDUCTIVE.

inductively *adv.* by an inductive method or process.

inductor *noun* **1** *Electr.* a component of an electrical circuit that shows the property of inductance. **2** *Chem.* any substance that accelerates a reaction between two or more chemical substances by reacting rapidly with one of them.

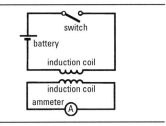

inductor

indue same as ENDUE.

indulge *verb* **1** *trans., intrans.* (**indulge in something** *or* **indulge someone in something**) to allow oneself or someone else pleasure or the particular pleasure of something. **2** to allow (someone) to have anything they want; to pamper or spoil. **3** not to restrain or ignore (a desire, taste, wish, etc): *indulge a whim*. **4** *intrans. colloq.* to drink alcohol, especially freely or without restraint. [from Latin *indulgere*, to be kind or indulgent to]

indulgence *noun* **1** an act of indulging a person, desire, etc. **2** the state of being indulgent; generosity; favourable or tolerant treatment. **3** a pleasure that is indulged in. **4** in the Roman Catholic church, remission from the punishment which remains due after the sin has been absolved.

indulgent *adj.* too quick to overlook or forgive faults or gratify the wishes of others; too tolerant or generous.

indulgently *adv.* in an indulgent way.

Indus *Astron.* the Indian, an inconspicuous constellation in the southern hemisphere that does not contain any particularly bright stars.

Indus, River, Sanskrit **Sindhu** a river in Asia, mostly in NW India, the longest of the Himalayan rivers. Its length is 3 000km/1 900mi, rising in the Kalias Range in Tibet region and flowing NW through Tibet, Jammu, and Kashmir, then turning S into Pakistan. Within Pakistan the flow is generally SW in a broad braided channel and it enters the Arabian Sea SE of Karachi. The river delta is a muddy area supporting little cultivation. A barrage at Sukkur, in N Sind province, supplies water for an extensive irrigation system and power project. Relics of the Indus civilization which flourished in 4000–2000 BC have been excavated at Mohenjo-daro and Harappa.

industrial *adj.* **1** relating to or concerned with industry. **2** used in industry. **3** *said of a country, city, etc* having highly developed industry.

industrial action *Brit.* action, eg strikes, taken by workers as a protest.

industrial democracy a form of industrial management in which workers' representatives are appointed to the board of a company, or actively participate in the management in some other capacity.

industrial design a term referring to the design of anything made by machine or by an industrial process, from Coke® bottles to Volkswagens. Early examples included Wedgwood pottery and Sheffield plate.

industrial espionage the practice of obtaining or attempting to obtain trade secrets or other confidential information about a company's activities by underhand or dishonest means. The information so obtained may be used, for example, to negate a company's competitive advantage, or to deal in the company's shares.

industrial estate an area in a town which is developed for industry and business.

industrialism *noun* a social system in which industry (rather than agriculture) is dominant and forms the basis of commerce and the economy.

industrialist *noun* a person who owns a large industrial organization or who is involved in its management at a senior level.

industrialization *or* **industrialisation** *noun* the process of industrializing.

industrialize *or* **industrialise** *verb trans., intrans.* to make or become industrially developed; to introduce industry, or have industry introduced.

industrially *adv.* in an industrial way; as regards industry: *industrially advanced nations.*

industrial relations relations between management and workers, especially in manufacturing industries.

Industrial Revolution the rapid development of a country's industry characterized by a change from small-scale production to increased mechanization and mass production in factories, especially in 18c Britain.
◇ The process developed in Britain in the last quarter of the 18c with the mechanization of the cotton and woollen industries of Lancashire, central Scotland, and the West Riding of Yorkshire.
After the harnessing of steam power, cotton and woollen factories were increasingly concentrated in towns, and there were hugely increased rates of urbanization, as well as a rapid population increase stimulated by greater economic opportunities for early marriage.

industrial tribunal *Industry* a tribunal set up to hear complaints and make judgements in disputes between employers and employees on matters such as industrial relations and alleged unfair dismissal.

industrious *adj.* busy and hard-working; diligent.

industriously *adv.* diligently; busily.

industriousness *noun* being industrious.

industry *noun* (PL. **industries**) **1** the business of producing goods; all branches of manufacturing and trade. **2** a branch of manufacturing and trade which produces a particular product: *the coal industry.* **3** organized commercial exploitation or use of natural or national assets, such as historical buildings, famous people, etc: *the tourist industry.* **4** hard work or effort; diligence. [from Latin *industria*]

Indus Valley Civilization the earliest known S Asian civilization, which flourished c.2300–1750 BC across 1.1 million sq km/0.5 million sq mi around the R Indus in Pakistan. Over 100 sites have been identified, with important urban centres at Mohenjo-daro and Harappa (Pakistan), and Kalibangan and Lothal (W India). There were uniform principles of urban planning, with streets set out in a grid pattern and public drainage systems. A common writing system was used, which remains only partly deciphered. There is no firm explanation for the decline of the civilization.

Indy 500, properly **Indianapolis 500** an automobile race held annually since 1911 at Indianapolis Motor Speedway in Indianapolis, Indiana. It is supervised by the United States Auto Club and involves the fastest 33 cars from earlier four-lap time trials. They race over 200 laps of the 4km/2.5mi circuit.

-ine *suffix* forming words meaning 'like, relating to': *crystalline / Alpine.* [from Latin *-inus*]

inebriate — *verb* (pronounced *-ate*) **1** to make drunk. **2** to exhilarate greatly. — *adj.* drunk, especially habitually. — *noun* (pronounced *-ət*) a person who is drunk, especially habitually. [from Latin *inebriare*]

inebriation *or* **inebriety** *noun* drunkenness, intoxication.

inedibility *noun* being inedible.

inedible *adj.* not fit or suitable to be eaten; not edible.

ineducability *noun* being ineducable.

ineducable *adj.* not capable of being educated, especially because mentally retarded.

ineffability *noun* being ineffable.

ineffable *adj.* **1** that is too great to be described or expressed in words. **2** that should not be said or uttered. [from Latin *ineffabilis*]

ineffably *adv.* in an ineffable way; to an ineffable degree.

ineffective *adj.* **1** having no effect; not producing a result or the result intended. **2** *said of a person* incapable of achieving results.

ineffectively *adv.* in an ineffective way; so as to be ineffective.

ineffectiveness *noun* being ineffective.

ineffectual *adj.* **1** not producing any result or the intended result. **2** *said of a person* lacking the ability and confidence needed to achieve results; weak. [from Latin *ineffectualis*]

ineffectually *adv.* in an ineffectual way.

ineffectualness *noun* being ineffectual.

inefficacious *adj.*, *said especially of a medicine* not having the desired or intended effect.

inefficaciously *adv.* in an inefficacious way.

inefficacy *noun* lack of efficacy.

inefficiency *noun* (PL. **inefficiencies**) lack of efficiency; an inefficient practice.

inefficient *adj.* not working or producing the required results, etc in the best way, thus wasting time, energy, resources, etc; not efficient.

inefficiently *adv.* in an inefficient way.

inelegance *noun* lack of grace or refinement.

inelegant *adj.* not graceful; awkward; lacking elegance or good taste. [from Latin *inelegans*]

inelegantly *adv.* in an inelegant way.

ineligibility *noun* being ineligible.

ineligible *adj.* (**ineligible for something**) not qualified, not worthy, or not allowed.

ineluctable *adj.* that cannot be avoided, resisted, or escaped from. [from Latin *ineluctabilis*]

ineluctably *adv.* unavoidably.

inept *adj.* **1** awkward; done without, or not having, skill. **2** not suitable or fitting; out of place. **3** silly; foolish. [from Latin *ineptus*]

ineptitude *or* **ineptness** *noun* **1** awkwardness, incapacity. **2** silliness.

ineptly *adv.* in an inept way.

inequable *adj.* not fair or just. [from Latin *inaequabilis*, uneven]

inequality *noun* (PL. **inequalities**) **1** a lack of equality, fairness, or evenness. **2** an instance of this. **3** any dissimilarity or disparity. **4** *Maths.* a statement that two quantities or expressions are not equal. [from Latin *inaequalitas*]

inequitable *adj.* not fair or just.

inequitably *adv.* in an unfair or unjust way.

inequity *noun* (PL. **inequities**) **1** lack of fairness. **2** an unjust action.

ineradicable *adj.* not able to be removed completely or rooted out. [from IN-[1] + Latin *eradicare*, to root out]

ineradicably *adv.* so as to be ineradicable.

inert *adj.* **1** without the power to move. **2** not wanting to move, act, or think; indolent; sluggish. **3** without active chemical, biological, etc properties. [from Latin *iners*, unskilled, idle]

inert gas *Chem.* same as NOBLE GAS.

inertia *noun* **1** the tendency of an object to remain at rest, or to continue to move in the same direction at constant speed unless it is acted on by an external force. The magnitude of an object's inertia is determined by its mass. **2** the state of not wanting to move, act, or think; indolence; sluggishness. [from Latin *iners*, unskilled, idle]

inertial *adj.* relating to or involving inertia.

inertial control guidance *or* **navigation** an automatic gyroscope guidance system for aircraft, submarines, missiles, etc, which depends on the tendency of an object to continue in a straight line (*inertia*). Any changes in the direction and magnitude of motion are sensed, using data computed from the rate of acceleration and the physical properties of the Earth, and corrected automatically. The system dispenses with the magnetic compass and is independent of ground-based radio aids.

inertia-reel seat belt a vehicle seat belt on a reel which allows the wearer to move freely in normal conditions but which locks tight under impact or sudden movement.

inertia selling *Brit.* the illegal practice of sending unrequested goods to people followed by a bill if the goods are not returned.

inertly *adv.* in an inert way; idly, inactively.

inertness *noun* being inert.

inescapable *adj.* that cannot be avoided.

inescapably *adv.* unavoidably.

inessential — *adj.* not essential or necessary. — *noun* an inessential thing.

inestimable *adj.* too great, or of too great value, to be estimated, measured, or fully appreciated. [from Latin *inaestimabilis*]

inestimably adv. to an inestimable degree; certainly.

inevitability noun being inevitable.

inevitable — adj. 1 that cannot be avoided; certain to happen. 2 colloq. tiresomely regular or predictable. — noun that which is certain to happen and is unavoidable. [from Latin inevitabilis]

inevitably adv. so as to be inevitable; certainly.

inexact adj. not quite correct, exact, or true.

inexactitude or **inexactness** noun lack of exactitude, or an instance of this.

inexactly adv. in an inexact way.

inexcusable adj. too bad to be excused, justified, or tolerated. [from Latin inexcusabilis]

inexcusably adv. in an inexcusable way.

inexhaustibility noun being inexhaustible.

inexhaustible adj. incapable of being used up (especially because too big) or exhausted. [from Latin inexhaustus, not exhausted]

inexhaustibly adv. in an inexhaustible way.

inexorability noun being inexorable.

inexorable adj. 1 that cannot be moved by entreaty or persuasion; unrelenting. 2 that cannot be altered or avoided. [from Latin inexorabilis]

inexorably adv. in an inexorable way.

inexpedience or **inexpediency** noun being inexpedient.

inexpedient adj. not wise, suitable, or appropriate.

inexpensive adj. not costing much; cheap.

inexpensively adv. without great expense; cheaply.

inexpensiveness noun being inexpensive.

inexperience noun lack of experience, or of skill or knowledge gained from experience. [from Latin inexperientia]

inexperienced adj. lacking experience; or unskilled.

inexpert adj. not skilled; not expert. [from Latin inexpertus]

inexpertly adv. in an inexpert way.

inexplicability noun being inexplicable.

inexplicable adj. impossible to explain, understand or account for. [from Latin inexplicabilis]

inexplicably adv. in an inexplicable way.

inexplicit adj. not clearly and exactly stated. [from Latin inexplicitus, not straightforward]

inexplicitly adv. in an inexplicit way.

inexpressible adj. that cannot be expressed or described, especially because too strong.

inexpressibly adv. as cannot be expressed in words; indescribably.

inexpressive adj., said especially of a person's face expressing little or no emotion.

inextinguishable adj. that cannot be put out or destroyed.

in extremis in desperate or extreme circumstances, especially at or as if at the point of death. [Latin, = in the last]

inextricable adj. 1 that cannot be escaped from. 2 that cannot be disentangled or untied. [from Latin inextricabilis]

inextricably adv. so as to be inextricable.

infallibility noun being infallible.

infallible adj. 1 said of a person never making a mistake; incapable of error. 2 RC Church, said of the pope unable to err when pronouncing officially on dogma. 3 always successful; not likely to fail. [from Latin infallibilis]

infallibly adv. in an infallible way.

infamous adj. 1 having a very bad reputation; notoriously bad. 2 evil; vile. [from Latin infamis]

infamously adv. notoriously.

infamy noun (PL. **infamies**) 1 bad reputation; notoriety; shame. 2 an infamous act.

infancy noun (PL. **infancies**) 1 the state or time of being an infant. 2 an early period of existence, growth, and development. 3 Legal the state of being under the legal age of maturity (in Britain, usually eighteen).

infant noun 1 a very young child in the first period of life. 2 Legal a person who is under the legal age of maturity (in Britain, usually eighteen). 3 Brit. a schoolchild under the age of seven or eight. [from Latin infans, not able to speak, from in, not + fari, to speak]

infanta noun Hist. 1 the eldest daughter of the king of Spain or Portugal. 2 the wife of an infante.

infante noun Hist. a son of the king of Spain or Portugal who is not heir to the throne. [from Spanish and Portuguese infante, from Latin infans, infant]

infanticide noun 1 the murder of a young child or infant. 2 a person who murders a young child or infant. [from Latin infans, infant + caedere, to kill]

infantile adj. 1 of infants or infancy. 2 very childish; immature. [from Latin infantilis]

infantile paralysis old medical use poliomyelitis.

infantilism noun the presence of childish characteristics in an adult or older child.

infantry — noun (PL. **infantries**) a body of soldiers trained and equipped to fight on foot. — adj. relating to or for the infantry. [from Italian infanteria]

infantryman noun a soldier in the infantry.

infant school Brit. a school for children aged between five and seven or eight.

infarction noun Medicine the death of a localized area of tissue as a result of the blocking of its blood supply, usually by a blood clot (thrombus), air bubble, or fragment of tissue or foreign material. Myocardial infarction (infarction of part of the heart muscle) causes heart attack. [from Latin infarcire, to stuff]

infatuate verb to cause to feel a passionate, foolish, and unreasonable love or admiration. [from Latin infatuare]

infatuated adj. (infatuated with someone) filled with passion for them; besotted with them.

infatuation noun 1 being infatuated. 2 someone or something one is infatuated with.

infect verb 1 to contaminate (a living organism) with a pathogen, such as a bacterium, virus, or fungus, and thereby cause disease. 2 to pass a feeling or opinion, especially an adverse or negative one, to (someone). [from Latin inficere, to stain]

infection noun 1 the process of infecting or state of being infected. 2 the invasion of a human, animal, or plant by pathogenic (disease-causing) micro-organisms, such as bacteria, viruses, fungi, or protozoa, which then multiply rapidly and usually cause symptoms of disease, sometimes after an incubation period during which no symptoms appear. 3 a disease caused by such a micro-organism. 4 the passing on of feelings, opinions, etc.

infectious adj. 1 said of a disease capable of being transmitted by air, water, etc. 2 causing infection. 3 said of a feeling, opinion, etc likely to be passed on to others.

infectiously adv. in an infectious way.

infectious mononucleosis Medicine an infectious disease, mainly affecting adolescents, caused by the Epstein-Barr virus (a herpes virus).

Its symptoms include swelling of the lymph nodes, fever, a sore throat, and headache, and it usually lasts for several weeks, although it may cause fatigue and depression for several months afterwards. — Also called glandular fever.

infectiousness noun being infectious.

infelicitous adj. 1 not happy, fortunate, or lucky. 2 not suitable, fitting, or apt.

infelicity noun (PL. **infelicities**) 1 bad luck; misfortune; unhappiness. 2 something, especially an expression, phrase, choice of word, etc, that is not suitable or fitting. [from Latin infelicitas]

infer verb (**inferred**, **inferring**) 1 to conclude or judge from facts, observation, and deduction. 2 colloq. to imply or suggest. [from Latin inferre, to bring in]
◆ Use in sense 2 is often regarded as incorrect, and it is usually advisable to use imply.

inferable or **inferrable** adj. capable of being inferred or deduced.

inference noun 1 an act of inferring, especially of reaching a conclusion from facts, observation and careful thought. 2 that which is inferred, especially a conclusion.

inferential adj. of or based on inference.

inferentially adv. in an inferential way.

inferior — adj. (often **inferior to something** or **someone**) 1 poor or poorer in quality. 2 low or lower in value, rank, or status. 3 low or lower in position. 4 said of letters or figures printed or written slightly below the line. 5 said of a planet revolving within the Earth's orbit; nearer the Sun. — noun a person who is inferior in some way to another. [from Latin inferior, lower]

inferiority noun the state of being inferior.

inferiority complex Psychol. a constant feeling that one is not as good as others in some way, which may lead to shyness or, in an attempt to compensate for this feeling, aggressive behaviour.

inferior planet Astron. a planet whose orbit around the Sun lies within the orbit of the Earth, ie Mercury or Venus.

infernal adj. 1 of hell. 2 wicked; evil. 3 colloq. extremely annoying or unpleasant. [from Latin infernalis, from inferus, low]

infernally adv. 1 in an infernal way. 2 colloq. dreadfully.

inferno noun (PL. **infernos**) 1 (often **Inferno**) hell. 2 a place or situation of horror and confusion. 3 a raging fire. [from Italian inferno, from Latin infernus, hell]

infertile adj. 1 said of soil, etc not fertile or producing good crops. 2 said of a person or animal unable to have young. [from Latin infertilis]

infertility noun the inability to produce offspring.
◇ Human infertility may be due to inability of a woman to conceive, eg as a result of failure to ovulate, or damage to or blockage of the Fallopian tubes; or it may be due to inability of a man to induce conception, eg as a result of a low sperm count or the production of defective sperm. Infertility treatments include the induction of ovulation by means of drugs, the repair of damaged Fallopian tubes by surgery, artificial insemination by partner or donor, and in-vitro fertilization (IVF).

infest verb, said of parasites such as fleas, lice, and certain fungi to be present in large numbers on the surface of or within an animal or plant. [from Latin infestare, to disturb]

infestation noun 1 infesting. 2 an attack, especially by parasites.

infidel — noun 1 a person who rejects a particular religion, especially Christianity or Islam. 2 a person who rejects all religions; an unbeliever.

3 a person who rejects a theory. — *adj.* of unbelievers; unbelieving. [from Latin *infidelis*]

infidelity *noun* (PL. **infidelities**) **1** unfaithfulness to someone, especially a husband, wife, or partner. **2** an instance of this. **3** lack of belief in a religion. [from Latin *infidelitas*]

infield *noun* **1** *Cricket* the area of the field close to the wicket, or the players positioned here. **2** *Baseball* the diamond-shaped area of the pitch formed by the four bases, or the players positioned here. See also OUTFIELD.

infielder *noun* a player who stands in the infield.

in-fighting *noun* fighting or competition between members of the same group, company, or organization.

infill — *noun* (*also* **infilling**) **1** the act of filling or closing gaps, holes, etc. **2** the material used to fill a gap, hole, etc. — *verb* to fill in (a gap, hole, etc).

infiltrate *verb* **1** *trans., intrans. said of troops, agents, etc* to pass into (territory or an organization held by the enemy or rivals) secretly, to gain influence, control, or information. **2** to filter (eg liquid or gas) through (a substance). **3** *intrans. said eg of liquid or gas* to filter in. **4** *trans., intrans.* to permeate gradually in (a substance). [from IN-² + FILTRATE]

infiltration *noun* infiltrating or being infiltrated.

infiltrator *noun* someone who infiltrates a group or organization.

infinite — *adj.* **1** having no boundaries or limits in size, extent, time, or space. **2** too great to be measured or counted. **3** very great; vast. **4** *Maths.* having an unlimited number of elements, digits, or terms. — *noun* anything which has no limits, boundaries, etc, especially (**the Infinite**) God. [from Latin *infinitus*]

infinitely *adv.* to an infinite degree; without limit.

infiniteness *noun* **1** being infinite. **2** infinity. **3** vastness.

infinitesimal — *adj.* **1** infinitely small; with a value close to zero. **2** *colloq.* extremely small. — *noun* an infinitesimal amount. [from Latin *infinitesimus*]

infinitesimally *adv.* to an infinitesimal degree; minutely.

infinitive — *noun Grammar* a verb form which expresses an action but which does not refer to a particular subject or time, in English often used with *to*, eg *tell him to go*, but used without *to* after certain verbs, eg *let her go*. — *adj., said of a verb* having this form. [from Latin *infinitivus*]

infinitude *noun* **1** the state or quality of being infinite. **2** something infinite, especially an infinite quantity, degree, amount. [from INFINITE + MAGNITUDE]

infinity *noun* **1** the quality or state of being infinite. **2** space, time, distance, or quantity that is without limit or boundaries, or *loosely* is too great to be measured. **3** *Maths.* a number that is larger than any finite value, symbol ∞, that can be approached but never reached, because the sequence of natural numbers continues indefinitely. It is considered to be the reciprocal of zero, ie ⅟₀. [from Latin *infinitas*]

infirm *adj., said of a person* weak or ill, especially from old age. [from Latin *infirmus*]

infirmary *noun* (PL. **infirmaries**) **1** a hospital. **2** a room or ward where the sick and injured are treated, especially in a school or monastery. [from Latin *infirmaria*]

infirmity *noun* (PL. **infirmities**) **1** the state or quality of being sick, weak, or infirm. **2** a disease or illness.

infix — *verb* (with stress on *-fix*) **1** to fix firmly in (something, the mind, etc). **2** *Grammar* to

insert (an affix) into the main part of a word as opposed to adding it as a prefix or suffix. — *noun* (with stress on *in-*) an affix inserted into the main part of a word, as opposed to a prefix or suffix. [from Latin *infigere*]

infixation *noun* the process of infixing or being infixed.

in flagrante delicto in the very act of committing a crime. [Latin, = in the blazing crime]

inflame *verb* **1** to arouse strong or violent emotion in. **2** *intrans.* to begin to feel strong or violent emotion; to become excited or angry. **3** *trans., intrans.* to burst or cause to burst into flames. **4** to make more heated or intense; to exacerbate. **5** *trans., intrans.* to cause (part of the body) to become, or (of part of the body) to become, affected by inflammation. [from Latin *inflammare*, to kindle]

inflammability *noun* an inflammable quality.

inflammable — *adj.* **1** easily set on fire. **2** easily excited or angered. — *noun* an inflammable substance. [from Latin *inflammabilis*]

inflammation *noun* **1** a protective response of the body tissues to disease, injury, infection, or the presence of an allergen. The affected part becomes red, heated, swollen, and painful. **2** an act of inflaming or state of being inflamed. [from Latin *inflammatio*]

inflammatory *adj.* **1** likely to cause strong or violent emotion, especially anger. **2** of, causing, or caused by inflammation of part of the body. [from Latin *inflammare*, to kindle]

inflatable — *adj., said of a cushion, ball, etc* that can be filled with air for use. — *noun* an inflatable object.

inflate *verb* **1** *trans., intrans.* to swell or cause to swell or expand with air or gas. **2** to exaggerate the importance or value of. **3** to increase (prices generally) artificially or to increase (the volume of money in circulation). See also DEFLATE, REFLATE. [from Latin *inflare*, to blow into]

inflated *adj.* **1** *said of prices* artificially increased to a high level. **2** *said especially of language or opinions* showing too great a sense of one's importance. **3** blown up or filled with air or gas; distended.

inflation *noun* **1** the process of inflating or being inflated. **2** a general increase in the level of prices accompanied by a fall in the purchasing power of money, caused by an increase in the amount of money in circulation and credit available. See also DEFLATION, REFLATION, STAGFLATION.

inflationary *adj.* relating to or involving inflation.

inflect *verb* **1** *Grammar* to change the form of (a word) to show eg tense, number, gender, grammatical case, etc. **2** *intrans. Grammar, said of a word* to change, or be able to be changed, to show tense, number, gender, grammatical case, etc. **3** to vary the tone or pitch of (the voice). **4** to bend inwards. [from Latin *inflectere*, to curve]

inflection *or* **inflexion** *noun* **1** an act of inflecting or state of being inflected. **2** *Grammar* **a** the change in the form of a word which shows tense, number, gender, grammatical case, etc. **b** an inflected form of a word. **c** a suffix which is added to a word to form an inflected form, eg *-s*, *-ing*. **3** a change in the tone, pitch, etc, of the voice. **4** a change in a curve from being convex to concave, or vice versa.

◇ The English language has relatively few inflections, mainly used to indicate plurality, eg *box/boxes, button/buttons*, and for certain forms of verbs, eg I *buy*, he *buys*, he *bought*. Highly inflected languages, such as Latin, have many word endings indicating a wide variety of grammatical functions including tense, mood, voice, person, and plurality.

inflectional *or* **inflexional** *adj. Grammar* relating to or involving inflection.

inflective *adj. Grammar* of or subject to inflection.

inflexibility *or* **inflexibleness** *noun* being inflexible.

inflexible *adj.* **1** incapable of being bent; rigid. **2** *said of a person* never giving way; unyielding; obstinate. **3** that cannot or may not be changed; fixed. [from Latin *inflexibilis*]

inflexibly *adv.* in an inflexible way.

inflexion see INFLECTION.

inflict *verb* (**inflict something on someone**) to impose on or cause to suffer something unpleasant, eg a blow, defeat, or pain. [from Latin *infligere*, to strike against]

infliction *noun* **1** an act of inflicting. **2** something that is inflicted.

in-flight *adj.* provided during an aircraft flight.

inflorescence *noun* **1** *Bot.* the complete flower-head of a flowering plant, including the stem. **2** *Bot.* any of a number of different arrangements of the flowers on the main stem of a flowering plant. [from Latin *inflorescere*, to begin to blossom]

inflow *noun* **1** the act or process of flowing in. **2** something that flows in.

inflowing — *noun* the process of flowing in. — *adj.* that flows in.

influence — *noun* (*often* **influence on** *or* **over someone** *or* **something**) **1** the power that one person or thing has to affect another. **2** a person or thing that has such a power: *be a good influence on him*. **3** power resulting from political or social position, wealth, ability, standards of behaviour, etc. — *verb* to have an effect, especially an indirect or unnoticed one, on (a person, events, etc). — **under the influence** *colloq.* affected by alcohol; drunk. [from Latin *influentia*, from *influere*, to flow into]

influential *adj.* **1** having influence or power. **2** (**influential in something**) making an important contribution to it.

influentially *adv.* in an influential way.

influenza *noun* an infectious illness caused by a virus, whose symptoms include headache, fever, a sore throat, catarrh and muscle pains. See also FLU. [from Italian *influenza*, influence, from the belief that stars caused epidemics]

influx *noun* **1** a continual stream or arrival of large numbers of people or things. **2** a flowing in. [from Latin *influere*, to flow into]

info *noun colloq.* information. [abbreviation]

infomercial *noun* a short informational film promoted for commercial purposes.

inform *verb* **1** *trans., intrans.* (**inform someone about** *or* **of something**) to give them knowledge or information on it. **2** (**inform against** *or* **on someone**) to give incriminating evidence about them to the authorities. **3** to animate, inspire, or give life to. **4** to give an essential quality to. [from Latin *informare*, to give form to]

informal *adj.* **1** without ceremony or formality; relaxed and friendly. **2** *said of language, clothes, etc* suitable for and used in relaxed, everyday situations.

informality *noun* (PL. **informalities**) lack of formality, or an instance of this.

informally *adv.* in an informal way.

informant *noun* someone who informs, eg against another person, or who gives information.

information *noun* **1** knowledge gained or given; facts; news. **2** the communicating or receiving of knowledge. **3** an accusation made before a court or magistrate. **4** a signal or character which represents data, especially in telecommunications and computing.

informational *adj.* relating to or involving information.

information retrieval the storing, sorting, and finding of information stored especially in a computer.

information technology *Comput.* (ABBREV. **IT**) the use of a range of technologies, especially computer systems, digital electronics, and telecommunications, to store, process, and transmit information.

◇ Information technology developed very rapidly in the 1970s and 1980s when inexpensive electronic hardware became available, together with improved methods of communication, especially via satellite or optical fibres. It has many applications, including word processing, data processing, information storage and retrieval, electronic mail, stock control (eg in supermarkets), banking services (eg automatic cash withdrawal), retailing services (eg automatic reading of bar codes), the control of manufacturing and production processes (eg by robots), desk-top publishing, and expert systems.

information theory *Maths.* the mathematical analysis of the efficiency of communication channels, especially with regard to the coding and transmission of information. It uses statistical methods to determine the quantity and speed of information transmission that can be achieved by computers and telecommunication systems.

informative *adj.* giving useful or interesting information; instructive.

informatively *adv.* in an informative way.

informativeness *noun* being informative.

informed *adj.* having or showing knowledge, especially in being educated and intelligent.

informer *noun* a person who informs against another, especially to the police and usually for money or some other reward.

infotainment *noun* the presentation of serious subjects or current affairs as entertainment.

infra *adv.* below; lower down on the page or further on in the book. [from Latin *infra*]

infra- *combining form* forming words meaning 'below, beneath'. [from Latin *infra*, below]

infraction *noun* the breaking of a law, rule, etc. [from Latin *infringere*, to break]

infra dig *colloq.* abbreviation of Latin *infra dignitatem*, beneath one's dignity.

infrared — *adj.* of, using, producing, or sensitive to radiation with a wavelength just beyond the red end of the visible spectrum, usually felt as heat. — *noun* infrared radiation.

infrared astronomy *Astron.* the study of infrared radiation produced by celestial bodies, or by gas or dust in space, used to detect comets, star formation in galaxies, dust clouds, etc. Such observations are made from aircraft, satellites, or high mountain sites, because infrared radiation is absorbed by the lower layers of the Earth's atmosphere.

infrasonic *adj.* of or having a frequency below the range which can normally be heard by the human ear.

infrasound *noun Physics* sound having a frequency of less than 20Hz. Such sound waves cannot be heard by humans, but may be felt. Infrasound waves are produced by explosions and by an unsteady airflow past an object.

infrastructure *noun* **1** the basic structure of a society, organization or system. **2** the permanent services and equipment, eg the roads, railways, bridges, factories, and schools needed for a country to be able to function properly. **3** the permanent services and equipment, eg roads, railways and bridges, needed for military purposes.

infrequency *noun* **1** being infrequent. **2** rarity.

infrequent *adj.* not frequent; occurring rarely or only occasionally. [from Latin *infrequens*]

infrequently *adv.* to an infrequent extent; not often.

infringe *verb* **1** to break or violate (eg a law or oath). **2** to interfere with (a person's rights). **3** *intrans.* (**infringe on** *or* **upon something**) to affect a person's rights, freedom, etc in such a way as to limit or reduce them; to encroach or trespass. [from Latin *infringere*, to break]

infringement *noun* **1** infringing. **2** a breach.

infuriate *verb* to make very angry. [from Latin *infuriare*]

infuriating *adj.* causing great anger or annoyance.

infuriatingly *adv.* so as to infuriate.

infuse *verb* **1** (**infuse something into someone** *or* **infuse someone with something**) to inspire them with a positive feeling, quality, etc. **2** *trans., intrans.* to soak or cause (leaves, eg tea) to be soaked in hot water to release their flavour or other qualities. [from Latin *infundere*, to pour into]

infusion *noun* **1** the act of infusing. **2** being infused.

-ing[1] *suffix* forming nouns, especially from verbs, usually expressing the action of the verb, its result or product, etc: *building / driving.* [from Anglo-Saxon *-ing, -ung*]

-ing[2] *suffix* used to form the present participle of verbs: *charming / walking.* [from Anglo-Saxon *-ende*]

-ing[3] *suffix* forming nouns meaning 'one belonging to' or 'one of the same kind of': *gelding.* [from Anglo-Saxon *-ing*]

◇ No longer an active suffix.

Ingen-Housz, Jan (1730–99) Dutch physician and plant physiologist, born in Breda. He practised as a doctor in England and was physician to the Holy Roman Empress Maria Theresa. In 1779 he discovered that carbon dioxide is absorbed by plants in the day and given out at night. He also devised a method for comparing heat conductivities.

ingenious *adj.* marked by, showing or having skill, originality and inventive cleverness. [from Latin *ingenium*, common sense, cleverness]

ingeniously *adv.* in an ingenious way.

ingeniousness *noun* being ingenious.

Ingénue *noun* **1** a naïve and unsophisticated young woman. **2** an actress playing the role of an *ingénue.* [French, from Latin *ingenuus*, native]

ingenuity *noun* inventive cleverness, skill or originality; ingeniousness. [from Latin *ingenuitas*, ingenuousness]

ingenuous *adj.* innocent and childlike, especially in being frank, honest, and incapable of deception. [from Latin *ingenuus*, native]

ingenuously *adv.* in an ingenuous way.

ingenuousness *noun* being ingenuous.

ingest *verb* **1** to take (eg food or liquid) into the body. **2** *said of a jet engine* to suck in (an object, eg a bird). [from Latin *ingerere*, to carry in]

ingestible *adj.* capable of being ingested.

ingestion *noun* **1** ingesting. **2** being ingested.

inglenook *noun* a corner or alcove in a large open fireplace. [from Scots Gaelic *aingeal*, fire + NOOK]

inglorious *adj.* **1** ordinary; not glorious or noble. **2** bringing shame. [from Latin *inglorius*]

ingloriously *adv.* in an inglorious way.

ingloriousness *noun* being inglorious.

ingoing *adj.* going in; entering.

ingot *noun* a brick-shaped mass of metal, especially of gold or silver. [from Middle English *ingot*, something poured in, from Anglo-Saxon *goten* cast in metal]

ingrained *adj.* fixed firmly; difficult to remove or wipe off or out. [from the phrase *dyed in grain*]

Ingrams, Richard (Reid) (1943–) English journalist, born in Westcliffe-on-Sea, Essex. He founded the satirical magazine *Private Eye* in 1962 and became its editor (1963–86). He has also written for the *Spectator* and the *Observer* and he founded the *Oldie* in 1992.

ingrate — *noun* an ungrateful person. — *adj.* ungrateful. [from Latin *ingratus*]

ingratiate *verb* (**ingratiate oneself with someone**) to gain or try to gain their favour or approval. [from Latin *in*, into + *gratia*, favour]

ingratiating *adj.* trying to gain favour.

ingratiatingly *adv.* in an ingratiating way.

ingratitude *noun* the quality of being ungrateful; lack of proper gratitude. [from Latin *ingratitudo*]

ingredient *noun* one of several things that goes into a mixture, especially in cooking. [from Latin *ingrediens*, going into]

Ingres, Jean Auguste Dominique (1780–1867) French painter, born in Montauban. Regarded as the leading exponent of the Classical tradition in France in the 19c, he was Professor at the Ecole des Beaux-Arts, Paris, and Director of the French Academy in Rome. He lived in Rome (1806–20), where he painted many of his famous nudes, including *La Grande Odalisque* (1814, Louvre, Paris), *Baigneuse, La Source* (completed 1859, Louvre), and *The Turkish Bath* (1859–62, Louvre).

ingress *noun* the act of going in or entering, or power or right to do so. [from Latin *ingredi*, to go into]

Ingrid a female first name, popularized by the film actress Ingrid Bergman (1915–82). [from the Old Norse fertility god *Ing* + *fridr*, fair, beautiful]

ingrowing *adj., said especially of a toenail* growing inwards, usually into the flesh.

ingrown *adj.* that has grown inwards.

inhabit *verb* (**inhabited, inhabiting**) to live in or occupy (a place). [from Latin *inhabitare*, to live in]

inhabitable *adj.* fit to be lived in.

inhabitant *noun* a person or animal that lives permanently in a place.

inhalant *noun* a medicine (eg one for relieving congestion in the chest) which is inhaled.

inhalation *noun* the act of breathing in, or that which is breathed in.

inhale *verb trans., intrans.* to breathe in (air, gas, etc). [from Latin *inhalare*]

inhaler *noun* a small portable device used for inhaling certain medicines.

inharmonious *adj.* **1** not sounding well together; lacking harmony. **2** not agreeing or going well together; not compatible.

inharmoniously *adv.* in an inharmonious way.

inhere *verb intrans.* (*often* **inhere in something** *or* **someone**) *said of character, a quality, etc* to be an essential or permanent part. [from Latin *inhaerere*, to stick in]

inherent *adj.* (**inherent in someone** *or* **something**) *said of a quality, etc* belonging naturally or being an essential or permanent part.

inherently *adv.* by virtue of being an essential part; in its nature: *an inherently difficult topic.*

inherit *verb* (**inherited, inheriting**) **1** *trans., intrans.* to receive (property, a title, position, etc) from a member of one's family on his or her death, or through legal descent from a predecessor. **2** to receive genetically transmitted characteristics from the previous generation. [from Latin *inhereditare*]

inheritable *adj.* **1** capable of being passed by heredity from one generation to another. **2** capable of being inherited.

inheritance *noun* **1** something (eg property, a title, physical or mental characteristics) that is or may be inherited. **2** the act of inheriting or right to inherit. **3** heredity.

inheritance tax a tax levied on inheritors according to their relationship to the person from whom they have inherited.

inheritor *noun* an heir.

inhibit *verb* (**inhibited**, **inhibiting**) **1** to hold back, restrain or prevent (an action, desire, progress, etc). **2** to make (a person) feel nervous or frightened about acting freely or spontaneously, eg by causing him or her to doubt his or her abilities. **3** to prohibit or forbid (someone) from doing something. **4** *Chem.* to decrease the rate of a chemical reaction, or to stop it altogether, by means of a substance known as an inhibitor. [from Latin *inhibere*, to keep back]

inhibited *adj.* held back by inhibition.

inhibitedly *adv.* in an inhibited way.

inhibition *noun* **1** a feeling of fear or embarassment, caused by emotional or psychological factors, which prevent one from acting, thinking, etc freely or spontaneously in some way: *sexual inhibitions*. **2** an act of inhibiting or process of being inhibited. **3** something which inhibits, prevents progress, holds back or forbids, etc. **4** *Chem.* a decrease in the rate of a chemical reaction, or of a biochemical reaction (catalyzed by enzymes) in living cells, that is brought about by a substance known as an inhibitor.

inhibitor *or* **inhibiter** *noun* **1** something that inhibits. **2** *Biochem.* a substance that interferes with a chemical or biological process.

inhospitable *adj.* **1** *said of a person* not friendly or welcoming. **2** *said of a place* offering little shelter (eg from harsh weather); barren. [from Latin *inhospitabilis*]

inhospitably *adv.* in an inhospitable way.

inhuman *adj.* **1** without human feeling; cruel and unfeeling; brutal. **2** not human. [from Latin *inhumanus*]

inhumane *adj.* showing no kindness, sympathy, or compassion; cruel; unfeeling. [a variant of INHUMAN]

inhumanely *adv.* in an inhumane way; cruelly.

inhumanity *noun* (PL. **inhumanities**) **1** the state of being inhuman or inhumane; cruelty; lack of feeling or pity. **2** an inhuman, inhumane, cruel, etc act.

inhumanly *adv.* in an inhuman way; cruelly.

inimical *adj.* (*often* **inimical to someone**) **1** tending to discourage; unfavourable. **2** not friendly; hostile. [from Latin *inimicalis*]

inimically *adv.* in an inimical way.

inimitable *adj.* too good, skilful, etc to be satisfactorily imitated by others; unique. [from Latin *inimitabilis*]

inimitably *adv.* in an inimitable way.

iniquitous *adj.* **1** grossly unjust or unreasonable. **2** wicked.

iniquitously *adv.* in an iniquitous way.

iniquity *noun* (PL. **iniquities**) **1** the state of being unfair, unjust, wicked, or sinful. **2** an unfair, unjust, wicked, or sinful act. [from Latin *iniquitas*]

initial — *adj.* of or at the beginning. — *noun* the first letter of a word, especially of a proper name. — *verb* (**initialled**, **initialling**) to mark or sign with the initials of one's name, especially as a sign of approval. [from Latin *initialis*]

initially *adv.* **1** as a beginning. **2** at first.

Initial Teaching Alphabet (**i.t.a.** *or* **ITA**) an alphabet of 44 characters devised in 1959 by James Pitman (1901–85), in which each character corresponds to a single sound or phoneme in English. It has been used in the teaching of reading, though its popularity has declined in recent years.

initiate — *verb* (pronounced -*ate*) **1** to cause to begin. **2** (**initiate someone into something**) to accept a new member into a society, organization, etc, especially with secret ceremonies. **3** (**initiate someone in something**) to give them instruction in the basics or rudiments of a skill, science, etc. — *noun* (pronounced -*ət*) a person who has recently been or is soon to be initiated. — *adj.* (pronounced -*ət*) having been recently initiated or soon to be initiated. [from Latin *initiare*]

initiation *noun* **1** initiating or being initiated. **2** the formal introduction of a new member into an organization or society.

initiation rites ceremonies effecting or marking a transition from one social condition or role to another, especially from childhood to adulthood: one of a number of rites of passage or *passage rites*. For example, in certain E African tribes, a youth on reaching puberty, will make the transition from boyhood to junior warrior in a series of ceremonies which include circumcision, ritual slaughter of an ox, cutting of his hair, and painting of his body with red ochre to indicate his new status.

initiative — *noun* **1** the ability or skill to initiate things, take decisions or act resourcefully. **2** a first step or move towards an end or aim. **3** the right or power to begin something. **4** the right of voters to originate legislation. — *adj.* serving to begin; introductory.

— **on one's own initiative** as a result of one's own action; without needing to be prompted by others.

initiator *noun* **1** someone who initiates. **2** *Chem.* a substance which starts a chain reaction.

inject *verb* **1** to introduce (a liquid, eg medicine) into the body of (a person or animal) using a hypodermic syringe. **2** to force (fuel) into an engine. **3** to introduce (a quality, element, etc): *inject a note of optimism*. [from Latin *injicere*, to throw in]

injection *noun* **1** an act of injecting or forcing in or the process of being injected. **2** that which is injected, eg a liquid medicine.

injection moulding *Engineering* a process used in the manufacture of plastics, in which plastic is heated until it is soft enough to inject through a nozzle into a mould in the shape of the desired articles.

injudicious *adj.* not wise; showing poor judgement.

injudiciously *adv.* in an injudicious way.

injudiciousness *noun* being injudicious.

injunction *noun* **1** *Legal* an official order from a court forbidding something, or commanding that something should be done. **2** any authoritative order or warning. [from Latin *injungere*, to enjoin]

injunctive *adj.* enjoining.

injure *verb* **1** to do physical harm or damage to. **2** to harm, spoil, or weaken. **3** to do an injustice or wrong to. [from Latin *injuria*, injury]

injurious *adj.* causing injury or damage; harmful.

injuriously *adv.* so as to harm or injure.

injury *noun* (PL. **injuries**) **1** physical harm or damage. **2** a wound. **3** a wrong or injustice.

injury time playing time added to the end of a football, rugby, etc match to make up for time taken to treat injured players during the match.

injustice *noun* **1** unfairness or lack of justice. **2** an unfair or unjust act.

— **do someone an injustice** to judge them unfairly.

[from Latin *injustitia*]

ink — *noun* **1** a liquid, paste, or powder, consisting of a pigment or a dye, that is used for writing, drawing, or printing on paper and other materials. **2** a dark liquid ejected by certain cephalopods, eg octopus, squid, in order to confuse predators by forming a smokescreen. — *verb* **1** to mark with ink. **2** to cover (a surface to be printed) with ink.

— **ink something in** to write over a rough design in pencil using ink.

[from Old French *enque*]

Inkatha *noun* a South African Zulu cultural and political movement, originally a paramilitary organization, which sought liberation from white minority rule. [from Zulu, = a plaited grass coil used for carrying loads on the head]

inkblot test same as RORSCHACH TEST.

inkiness *noun* being inky.

inkjet printer *Comput.* a printer which produces characters on paper by spraying a fine jet of ink which is vibrated, electrically charged, and deflected by electrostatic fields.

inkling *noun* a hint; a vague or slight idea or suspicion. [from Middle English *inclen*, to hint]

inkpad *noun* a pad of inked cloth inside a box, used for putting ink on rubber stamps.

inkstand *noun* a container for ink bottles and pens on a desk.

inkwell *noun* a small container for ink, especially one which fits into a hole in a desk.

inky *adj.* (**inkier**, **inkiest**) **1** covered with ink. **2** like ink, especially in being black or very dark.

INLA *abbrev.* Irish National Liberation Army.

inlaid *adj.* **1** *said of a design* set into a surface. **2** *said of an object* having a design set into its surface.

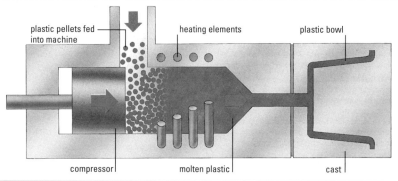

injection moulding

inland — *adj.* **1** of or in that part of a country which is not beside the sea. **2** *Brit.* done, operating, etc inside one country and not abroad; domestic. — *noun* those parts of a country that are not beside the sea. — *adv.* in or towards the inner regions of a country away from the sea. [from Anglo-Saxon *inland*, domain]

Inland Revenue *Brit.* the government department responsible for assessing and collecting taxes.

in-law *noun* (PL. **in-laws**) *colloq.* a relative by marriage.

inlay — *verb* (PAST TENSE AND PAST PARTICIPLE **inlaid**) **1** to set in or embed (eg pieces of wood, metal, etc in another material) so that the surfaces are flat. **2** to decorate (eg a piece of furniture) by setting flat pieces of different coloured wood, ivory, metal, etc in the surface. — *noun* **1** a decoration or design made by inlaying. **2** the pieces used to create an inlaid design. **3** a filling shaped to fit a cavity in a tooth.

inlaying *noun* a method of decorating furniture and other wooden objects by cutting away part of the surface of the solid material and replacing it with a thin sheet of wood in another colour or texture. Occasionally, slivers of ivory, bone, or shell are used in this way.

inlet *noun* **1** a narrow arm of water running inland from a sea-coast or lake-shore, or forming a passage between two islands. **2** a place of entry, eg for liquid or gas in a machine. **3** an extra piece of material sewn into a garment to make it larger. [from Middle English]

in loco parentis *said of those responsible for children* in the role or position of a parent. [Latin, = in the place of a parent]

inmate *noun* any of several people living in an institution, especially a prison or a hospital.

inmost *adj.* **1** farthest in; most in towards the centre. **2** most secret or private. [from Middle English]

inn *noun* a public house or small hotel providing food and accommodation, especially (*formerly*) one for travellers. [from Anglo-Saxon *inn*, dwelling]

innards *pl. noun colloq.* **1** the inner organs of a person or animal, especially the stomach. **2** the inner workings of a machine. [a variant of INWARDS]

innate *adj.* belonging to or existing in a person from birth; natural rather than learnt or acquired; inherent. [from Latin *innatus*]

innately *adv.* in an innate way.

innateness *noun* being innate.

innateness hypothesis *Linguistics* a controversial hypothesis proposed by the US linguist Noam Chomsky, which claims that a child is born with an inbuilt knowledge of at least some of the structures of language, and that it is this genetic predisposition which enables the child to acquire language with such speed and efficiency in its early years.

inner *adj.* **1** further in; situated inside or close to the centre. **2** *said of thoughts, feelings, etc* secret, hidden, and profound. [from Anglo-Saxon *innera*]

inner city the central area of a city, often densely populated and very poor, with bad housing, roads, etc.

inner ear *Anat.* the innermost part of the ear in vertebrates, located in a bony cavity in the skull. It contains the cochlea and the semicircular canals, which are responsible for the sense of hearing and the maintenance of balance, respectively.

inner man *or* **inner woman** **1** the mind or soul. **2** *humorous* the stomach.

Inner Mongolia, Chinese **Nei Mongol** POP (1990) 21.5m, an autonomous region in N China. AREA 450 000sq km/173 700sq mi. It is bordered N by Mongolia and Russia. Part of the S border is formed by the Great Wall of China. PHYSICAL DESCRIPTION two thirds of the area is grassland and the remainder is desert; the Greater Khingan Range in the NE rises to over 1 000m; the Hetao Plain is a fertile area N of the Yellow R; several deserts lie further S. CAPITAL Hohhot. CHIEF TOWN Baotou. ECONOMY horse breeding, cattle and sheep rearing; wheat is grown in irrigated areas; forestry; iron and steel, coal mining.

innermost *adj.* **1** furthest within. **2** most secret or hidden.

inner tube an inflatable rubber tube inside a tyre.

inning *noun North Amer., esp. US* a division of a baseball match during which each team has an opportunity to bat. [see INNINGS]

innings *pl. noun* **1** *Cricket* a team's or a player's turn at batting. **2** *Cricket* the runs scored, or the quality of batting, during such a turn. **3** *Brit.* a period during which a person has an opportunity for action or achievement.

— **have had a good innings** *colloq.* to have lived a long and eventful life.

[from Anglo-Saxon *innung*, contents]

innkeeper *noun* a person who owns or manages an inn.

innocence *noun* being innocent.

Innocent III, originally **Lotario de' Conti di Segni** (1160–1216) Italian pope, born in Agnagni. His pontificate (1198–1216) is regarded as the high point of the temporal and spiritual supremacy of the Roman see. He judged between rival emperors in Germany, and had Otto IV deposed. He put England under an interdict and excommunicated King John for refusing to recognize Stephen Langton as Archbishop of Canterbury.

innocent — *adj.* (*often* **innocent of something**) **1** free from sin; pure. **2** not guilty (eg of a crime). **3** not intending to cause or not causing harm. **4** lacking, free, or deprived of something. **5** simple and trusting; guileless; artless. — *noun* an innocent person, especially a young child or simple and trusting adult. [from Latin *innocens*, harmless]

innocently *adv.* in an innocent way.

innocuous *adj.* harmless; inoffensive. [from Latin *innocuus*]

innocuously *adv.* in an innocuous way.

innocuousness *noun* being innocuous.

Inn of Court *Brit. Legal* **1** any of the four societies which call lawyers to the bar. See INNS OF COURT. **2** any of the sets of buildings that these societies occupy.

innovate *verb* **1** *intrans.* to make changes; to introduce new ideas, methods, etc. **2** *trans.* to introduce (something) as new. [from Latin *innovare*, to renew]

innovation *noun* **1** an act of innovating. **2** something new which is introduced.

innovative *or* **innovatory** *adj.* innovating.

innovator *noun* a person who innovates.

Innsbruck POP (1991) 115 000, the capital of Tirol state, W Austria. It lies in the valley of the R Inn, surrounded by mountains. Its medieval old town has narrow and irregular streets and tall houses in late Gothic style. The city is a popular tourist and winter skiing centre. NOTABLE FEATURES Goldenes Dachl ('golden roof', 1494–6); cathedral (1717–22); Hofburg (15–16c palace); Hofkirche (Court Church, 1553–63); Altes Landhaus (1725–8); Alpine Zoo. [from German *Innsbruck*, inn bridge]

Inns of Court voluntary unincorporated societies having the exclusive right to confer the rank of barrister in England, Wales, and Northern Ireland. For England and Wales, the Inns (which have existed in London since the 14c) are the Inner Temple, the Middle Temple, Lincoln's Inn, and Gray's Inn. The Inn of Court of Northern Ireland was established in Belfast in 1926. Each Inn is governed by its Benchers (Masters of the Bench).

innuendo *noun* (PL. **innuendos**, **innuendoes**) **1** an indirect, and usually slightly unpleasant, critical, spiteful or rude remark, especially about someone's reputation or character; an oblique allusion or insinuation. **2** the act of making such remarks. [from Latin *innuendo*, by nodding at]

Innuit same as INUIT.

innumerable *adj.* too many to be counted; a great many. [from Latin *innumerabilis*]

innumerably *adv.* to an innumerable extent.

innumeracy *noun* being innumerate.

innumerate *adj.* having no knowledge or understanding of mathematics or science. [from IN-[1] + NUMERATE, modelled on *illiterate*]

inoculate *verb* **1** to produce a mild form of a particular infectious disease in (a person or animal), followed by immunity to it, by injecting a harmless form of an antigen (eg dead or weakened viruses or bacteria) which stimulates the body to produce its own antibodies (same as VACCINATE). **2** to introduce a micro-organism, eg a bacterium or virus, into (a sterile medium) in order to start a culture, or into another organism, eg a rabbit, in order to produce antibodies to that micro-organism. **3** to imbue or instil (someone) with ideas. [from Latin *inoculare*, to graft a tree bud]

inoculation *noun* the process of inoculating against a disease.

inoffensive *adj.* harmless; not likely to offend.

inoffensively *adv.* in an inoffensive way.

inoffensiveness *noun* being inoffensive.

Inönü, Ismet, originally **Ismet Paza** (1884–1973) Turkish soldier and politician, born in Izmir, Asia Minor. He fought in World War I, then became Atatürk's Chief-of-Staff in the war against the Greeks (1919–22), whom he defeated twice at Inönü. As the first Prime Minister of the new republic (1923–37) he introduced many political reforms and was elected President on Atatürk's death (1938). From 1950 he was Leader of the Opposition, but was premier again in 1961–5, with General Gürsel as President.

inoperable *adj.* **1** *said of a disease or condition* unable to be removed by surgery or operated on successfully. **2** *said of a plan, idea, etc* not workable.

inoperative *adj.* not working or functioning; having no effect.

inopportune *adj.* not suitable or convenient; badly timed. [from Latin *inopportunus*]

inopportunely *adv.* in an inopportune way, at a bad time.

inordinate *adj.* greater than is reasonable; beyond acceptable limits. [from Latin *inordinatus*]

inordinately *adv.* to an inordinate degree.

inorganic *adj.* **1** not made of or found in living (ie animal or plant) material; mineral. **2** not caused by natural growth. **3** not produced naturally.

inorganically *adv.* in an inorganic way.

inorganic chemistry, the branch of chemistry concerned with the properties and reactions of the elements, and of compounds that do not contain chains or rings of carbon atoms. It therefore deals mainly with compounds of mineral origin, and includes only the simpler compounds of carbon, such as carbon oxides, carbonates, carbides, and cyanides. See also ORGANIC CHEMISTRY.

inorganic fertilizer *Agric.* a fertilizer containing a mixture of chemical compounds, mainly of nitrogen, potassium, and phosphorus, that are added to the soil in order to improve its fertility. The use of large amounts of inorganic fertilizers can be harmful to the environment.

in-patient *noun* a patient temporarily living in hospital while receiving treatment there.

input — *noun* **1** *Comput.* the data that is transferred from a disk, tape, or input device, such as the keyboard, into the main memory of a computer. **2** something which is put or taken in, eg a contribution to a discussion. **3** an act or process of putting something in. **4** the money, power, materials, labour, etc required to produce something, especially the power put into a machine. — *verb* (**inputting**; PAST TENSE AND PAST PARTICIPLE **input**, **inputted**) to transfer (data) from a disk, tape, or input device into the main memory of a computer.

input device *Comput.* any piece of equipment used to transfer data into memory, such as a keyboard, mouse, or light pen.

input-output analysis *Econ.* an analysis which demonstrates how materials and goods flow between industries, and identifies where additional value is created. It enables economists to examine how the various sectors of an economy interrelate.

inquest *noun* **1** an official investigation into an incident, especially an inquiry into a sudden and unexpected death in a coroner's court before a jury. **2** *colloq.* any discussion after an event, game, etc, especially one which analyses its result and discusses mistakes made. [from Latin *inquesta*]

inquietude *noun* physical or mental restlessness or uneasiness. [from Latin *inquietudo*]

inquire *or* **enquire** *verb* **1** *trans., intrans.* to ask for information about something. **2** (**inquire after someone**) to ask about their health or happiness. **3** (**inquire for someone**) to ask to see or talk to them. **4** (**inquire for something**) to ask for goods, a service, etc. **5** (**inquire into something**) to try to discover the facts of a crime, etc, especially formally. **6** (**inquire of someone**) to ask them for information. [from Latin *inquirere*]
◆ Some people use *inquire* (and *inquiry*) for more formal investigating, and *enquire* (and *enquiry*) for more simple asking; but the two words are commonly regarded as alternative spellings.

inquirer *or* **enquirer** *noun* a person who inquires; an investigator, a questioner.
◆ See note at *inquire*.

inquiring *or* **enquiring** *adj.* **1** eager to discover or learn things. **2** *said eg of a look* appearing to be asking a question.
◆ See note at *inquire*.

inquiringly *or* **enquiringly** *adv.* with an inquiring manner.
◆ See note at *inquire*.

inquiry *or* **enquiry** *noun* (PL. **inquiries**) **1** an act of asking for information or inquiring. **2** an investigation, especially a formal one.
◆ See note at *inquire*.

Inquisition a papal tribunal for the prosecution of heresy, and such things as witchcraft and alchemy, originally of the medieval Christian Church. Pope Gregory IX (13c) gave it special responsiblity to counter the threat to political and religious unity from heretical groups. The Spanish Inquisition, which continued until the 19c, was notorious for the tortures and punishments that had come to characterize inquisitors' activities.

inquisition *noun* **1** a searching or intensive inquiry or investigation. **2** an official or judicial inquiry. [from Latin *inquisitio*]

inquisitional *adj.* relating to or in the nature of inquiry.

inquisitive *adj.* **1** over-eager to find out things, especially about other people's affairs. **2** eager for knowledge or information. [from Latin *inquisitivus*]

inquisitively *adv.* in an inquisitive way.

inquisitiveness *noun* being inquisitive.

inquisitor *noun* **1** a person carrying out an inquisition or inquiry, especially harshly or intensively. **2** (**Inquisitor**) a member of the Spanish Inquisition. [from Latin *inquisitor*]

inquisitorial *adj.* **1** of or like an inquisitor. **2** unnecessarily or offensively curious about other people's affairs. **3** *Legal, said of a trial or legal system* in which the judge is also the prosecutor.

inquisitorially *adv.* in an inquisitorial way.

in re *formal* in the matter of; about. [Latin, = in the matter]

INRI the first letters of the Latin inscription placed on the Cross of Jesus at Pilate's command (John 19.19–20): *Iesus Nazarenus, Rex Iudaeorum* (Jesus of Nazareth, King of the Jews).

inroad *noun* **1** (*usually* **inroads into something**) a large or significant using up or consumption: *make inroads into my savings*. **2** a hostile attack or raid.

inrush *noun* a sudden crowding or rushing in.

insalubrious *adj., said of a place* unhealthy; sordid. [from Latin *insalubris*]

insane — *adj.* **1** not of sound mind; mentally ill. **2** extremely foolish; stupid. **3** of or for the mentally ill. — *noun* people who are insane. [from Latin *insanus*]

insanely *adv.* in an insane way; to an insane degree.

insanitariness *noun* an insanitary state or condition.

insanitary *adj.* so dirty as to be dangerous to health.

insanity *noun* (PL. **insanities**) **1** the state of being insane. **2** extreme folly or stupidity.

insatiability *noun* being insatiable.

insatiable *adj.* not able to be satisfied; extremely greedy. [from Latin *insatiabilis*]

insatiably *adv.* to an insatiable degree.

inscribe *verb* **1** to write, print, or engrave (words) on (paper, metal, stone, etc), often as a lasting record. **2** to enter (a name) on a list or in a book; to enrol. **3** (**inscribe something to someone**) to dedicate or address a book, etc to them, usually by writing in the front of it. **4** *Geom.* to draw (a figure) within another figure so as to touch all or some of its sides or faces. See also CIRCUMSCRIBE. [from Latin *in*, on + *scribere*, to write]

inscription *noun* **1** words written, printed, or engraved, eg as a dedication in the front of a book or as an epitaph on a gravestone. **2** the act of inscribing, especially of writing a dedication in the front of a book or of entering a name on a list. [from Latin *inscriptio*, from *inscribere*, to inscribe]

inscriptional *adj.* relating to or characteristic of inscriptions.

inscrutability *noun* being inscrutable.

inscrutable *adj.* hard to understand or explain; mysterious; enigmatic. [from Latin *inscrutabilis*]

inscrutably *adv.* in an inscrutable way.

insect *noun* **1** *Zool.* any invertebrate animal belonging to the class Insecta, the largest and most diverse class of living organisms, containing more than a million species, eg fly, beetle, ant, bee, wasp, butterfly. **2** *loosely* any other small invertebrate, eg a spider. **3** an insignificant or worthless person. [from Latin *insectum*, cut, notched]
◊ Insects typically have a segmented body divided into three sections, the head, thorax, and abdomen, and are covered with a hard casing or *exoskeleton* made of chitin. The thorax bears three pairs of legs and usually two pairs of wings, and the head bears a pair of compound eyes (each consisting of thousands of tiny lenses), a pair of

antennae, and three pairs of mouthparts variously adapted for chewing, biting, sucking, or piercing. Insects breathe by means of tiny tubes or tracheae that carry air to all parts of the body from external holes called spiracles on the body surface.
Many insects display metamorphosis, often having a life cycle that consists of four different stages: egg, larva, pupa, and adult. Many important pests of crops and animal livestock, as well as vectors of disease, are insects, eg the malaria mosquito. Some species are beneficial to humans, eg bees, which pollinate plants and produce honey.

Insecta *pl. noun Zool.* in the animal kingdom, the largest and most diverse class of living organisms, containing more than a million identified species, although this is thought to represent only a small fraction of the total number of insect species in the world.

insecticidal *adj.* that kills insects.

insecticide *noun* any naturally occurring or artificially manufactured substance that is used to kill insects, usually to protect crops and animal livestock on farms, but also used in homes, hospitals, restaurants, etc.
◊ The most commonly used insecticides are synthetic organic compounds, often applied as liquid sprays by farmers, but they may also be used in the form of granules or powder. There is much concern about the fact that these substances enter the food chain and have a detrimental effect on wildlife, and possibly on humans as well. DDT was one of the most widely used insecticides in the post-war period, but is now banned in many countries because of its persistence in the environment. Insects eventually become resistant to each new insecticide that is developed, so there is a continual need for new products.

insectivore *noun* **1** a living organism that feeds mainly or exclusively on insects, eg anteater. **2** an animal belonging to the order Insectivora, a group of small placental mammals that feed mainly although not necessarily exclusively on insects, eg moles, hedgehogs. [from Latin *insectum*, insect + *vorare*, to devour]

insectivorous *adj.* feeding on insects.

insecure *adj.* **1** not firmly fixed; unstable. **2** *said of a person* lacking confidence; anxious about possible loss or danger. **3** under threat or in danger or likely to be so. [from Latin *insecurus*]

insecurely *adv.* in an insecure way.

insecurity *noun* (PL. **insecurities**) **1** being insecure. **2** anxiety, lack of confidence.

inseminate *verb* **1** to introduce semen into (a female) by a natural or artificial method. **2** to sow (seeds, ideas, etc). [from Latin *inseminare*]

insemination *noun* inseminating or being inseminated.

insensate *adj.* **1** not able to perceive physical sensations or experience consciousness; inanimate. **2** insensitive and unfeeling. **3** having little or no good sense; stupid. [from Latin *insensatus*]

insensately *adv.* in an insensate way.

insensateness *noun* being insensate.

insensibility *noun* being insensible.

insensible *adj.* **1** not able to feel pain or experience consciousness; unconscious. **2** (**insensible of** *or* **to something**) unaware of it; not caring about it. **3** not capable of feeling emotion; callous. **4** too small or slight to be noticed; imperceptible. [from Latin *insensibilis*]

insensibly *adv.* in an insensible state.

insensitive *adj.* (*often* **insensitive to something**) **1** not aware of or not capable of responding sympathetically, especially to other people's feelings. **2** not reacting to stimulation, eg touch or light.

insensitively *adv.* in an insensitive way.

insensitivity *noun* **1** being insensitive. **2** insensitive behaviour or language.

inseparability *noun* being inseparable.

inseparable *adj.* **1** incapable of being separated. **2** *said of friends, siblings, etc* unwilling to be apart and constantly together. [from Latin *inseparabilis*]

inseparably *adv.* in an inseparable way; so as not be separated.

insert — *verb* (with stress on *-sert*) **1** to put or fit (something) inside something else. **2** to introduce (text, words, etc) into the body of other text, words, etc. — *noun* (with stress on *in-*) something inserted, especially a loose sheet in a book or magazine, or piece of material in a garment. [from Latin *inserere*]

insertion *noun* **1** an act of inserting. **2** something inserted, especially a piece of lace or embroidery inserted in a garment or an advertisement in a newspaper. **3** *Medicine* the place where, or the way in which, a muscle is attached to a bone.

in-service *adj.* carried on while a person is employed.

inset — *noun* (with stress on *in-*) **1** something set in or inserted, eg a piece of lace or cloth set into a garment, or a leaf or leaves set in into a book. **2** a small map or picture put in the corner of a larger one. — *verb* (with stress on *-set*) (**insetting**; PAST TENSE AND PAST PARTICIPLE **inset**) to put in, add, or insert.

inshore *adv., adj.* in or on the water but near or towards the shore.

inside — *noun* **1** the inner side, surface, or part of something. **2** the part of a path away from the road. **3** the lower part of a double-decker bus. **4** the lane of a running track-that is nearest the centre; the equivalent part of any racetrack. **5** (**insides**) *colloq.* the inner organs, especially the stomach and bowels. **6** *colloq.* a position which gains one the confidence of and otherwise secret information from people in authority. — *adj.* **1** being on, near, towards, or from the inside. **2** *colloq.* coming from, provided by, or planned by someone within an organization: *the robbery was an inside job.* — *adv.* **1** to, in, or on the inside or interior. **2** indoors. **3** *colloq.* in or into prison. — *prep.* (also *colloq.* **inside of**) **1** to or on the inside of; within. **2** in less than: *be back inside an hour.* — **inside out 1** with the inside surface turned out. **2** *colloq.* thoroughly; completely, knows it all inside out. [from Middle English]

insider *noun* a recognized or accepted member of an organization or group who has access to secret information about it.

insider dealing *or* **insider trading** the illegal buying and selling of shares by people who work on the stock exchange, based on their having access to information which has not been made public.

inside track 1 the inside lane of a race track, slightly shorter than the other lanes because of the curve. **2** a position of strength, power or advantage.

insidious *adj.* **1** developing gradually without being noticed but causing very great harm. **2** attractive but harmful; treacherous. [from Latin *insidiae*, ambush]

insidiously *adv.* in an insidious way.

insidiousness *noun* being insidious.

insight *noun* **1** the ability to gain a relatively rapid, clear, and deep understanding of the real, often hidden, and usually complex nature of a situation, problem, etc. **2** an instance or example of this. [from Middle English]

insightful *adj.* characterized by insight.

insignia *noun* (PL. **insignia**, **insignias**) badges or emblems of office, honour, or membership. [from Latin *insignia*, badges]

insignificance *noun* being insignificant.

insignificant *adj.* **1** of little or no meaning, value, or importance. **2** relatively small in size or amount.

insignificantly *adv.* in an insignificant way.

insincere *adj.* not sincere or genuine; false; hypocritical. [from Latin *insincerus*]

insincerely *adv.* in an insincere way.

insincerity *noun* (PL. **insincerities**) being insincere, or an instance of this.

insinuate *verb* **1** to suggest or hint (something unpleasant) indirectly. **2** to introduce (eg an idea) in an indirect or devious way. **3** (**insinuate someone into something**) to gain acceptance or favour for (especially oneself) by gradual, careful, and often cunning means. [from Latin *insinuare*]

insinuatingly *adv.* with an insinuating manner.

insinuation *noun* **1** an unpleasant, devious or indirect suggestion, reference or hint. **2** an act of insinuating.

insipid *adj.* **1** without interest or liveliness; boring. **2** without taste or flavour. [from Latin *insipidus*]

insipidly *adv.* in an insipid way.

insipidness *noun* being insipid.

insist *verb* **1** *intrans., trans.* to maintain, state, or assert firmly: *insisted that we were right.* **2** (**insist on** *or* **upon something**) to demand it firmly: *insisted on a fair hearing.* [from Latin *insistere*]

insistence *noun* insisting; determination.

insistent *adj.* **1** making continual, forceful demands; insisting. **2** demanding attention; compelling.

insistently *adv.* in an insistent way.

in situ done, carried out, etc while remaining in place; in the natural or original position. [Latin, = in the place]

insofar as see IN.

insole *noun* **1** a loose inner sole which can be put in a shoe or boot for extra warmth, or to make it slightly smaller. **2** a fixed inner sole in a shoe or boot.

insolence *noun* being insolent; insolent behaviour or language.

insolent *adj.* rude or insulting; showing a lack of respect. [from Latin *insolens*, departing from custom]

insolently *adv.* in an insolent way.

insolubility *noun* being insoluble.

insoluble *adj.* **1** *said of a substance* not able to be dissolved in a particular solvent, especially water, to form a solution. **2** *said of a problem or difficulty* not able to be resolved. [from Latin *insolubilis*]

insolvency *noun* being insolvent.

insolvent — *adj.* **1** not having enough money to pay one's debts. **2** of or relating to insolvent people or the state of being insolvent. — *noun* an insolvent person.

insomnia *noun* regular or habitual inability to sleep. [from Latin *insomnia*, from *in-*, not + *somnus*, sleep]

insomniac — *noun* a person who suffers from insomnia. — *adj.* **1** suffering from insomnia. **2** causing or caused by insomnia.

insomuch *adv.* (**insomuch that** ... *or* **as** ...) **1** to such an extent. **2** given that; because of the fact that.

insouciance *noun* lack of concern; indifference; carelessness.

insouciant *adj.* without cares or worries; light-hearted. [from French *insouciant*, from *in*, not + *soucier*, to worry]

inspect *verb* **1** to look at or examine closely, often to find faults or mistakes. **2** to look at or examine officially or ceremonially. [from Latin *inspicere*, to look into]

inspection *noun* inspecting, examination.

inspector *noun* **1** a person employed to inspect something, especially officially. **2** *Brit.* a police officer below a superintendent and above a sergeant in rank.

inspectorate *noun* **1** a body of inspectors. **2** the office or post of inspector.

Inspector Calls, An a play by J B Priestley (1946). It is a psychological drama depicting an evening at a family home which is interrupted by a mysterious inspector investigating a suicide.

inspiration *noun* **1** a supposed power which stimulates the mind, especially to artistic activity or creativity. **2** a similar supposed divine power or influence which leads to the writing of Scripture. **3** a person or thing that inspires, or the state of being inspired. **4** a brilliant or inspired idea. **5** the act of drawing breath into the lungs, or a breath so taken.

inspirational *adj.* involving or arising from inspiration; inspiring, inspired.

inspire *verb* **1** to stimulate (a person) to activity, especially artistic or creative activity. **2** to fill (a person) with a feeling of confidence, encouragement and exaltation. **3** (**inspire someone with something** *or* **something into someone**) to create a particular feeling in them. **4** to be the origin or source of (a poem, piece of music, etc). **5** *said of supposed divine power or influence* to guide (someone). **6** *trans., intrans.* to breathe (air, etc) in. [from Latin *inspirare*, to breathe into]

inspired *adj.* so good, skilful, accurate, etc as to seem to be the result of inspiration, especially divine inspiration.

inspiring *adj.* that inspires.

inspiringly *adv.* in an inspiring way.

inst. *abbrev.* instant (= in the current month).

instability *noun* lack of physical or mental steadiness or stability. [from Latin *instabilitas*]

install *verb* **1** to put (equipment, machinery, etc) in place and make it ready for use. **2** to place (a person) in office with a formal ceremony. **3** to place (something, oneself, etc) in a particular position, condition or place. [from Latin *installare*]

installation *noun* **1** the act or process of installing. **2** a piece of equipment, machinery, etc that has been installed ready for use. **3** a military base.

instalment *noun* **1** one of a series of parts into which a debt is divided for payment. **2** one of several parts published, issued, broadcast, etc at regular intervals. [from Old French *estaler*, to fix, set, probably influenced by INSTALL]

instalment plan *noun* payment for goods purchased by instalments; hire-purchase.

instance *noun* **1** an example, especially of a particular condition or circumstance. **2** a particular stage in a process or a particular situation: *in this instance.* **3** *formal* request; urging: *at the instance of.* **4** *Legal* a process or suit. — **for instance** for example. [from Latin *instantia*, from *instare*, to be present]

instant — *adj.* **1** immediate. **2** *said of food, etc* quickly and easily prepared. **3** urgent; pressing. **4** of or occurring in the current month. **5** present; current. — *noun* **1** a particular moment in time, especially the present: *this instant.* **2** a very brief period of time. [from Latin *instare*, to be present]

instantaneous *adj.* done, happening, or occurring at once, very quickly or in an instant; immediate. [from Latin *instantaneus*, from *instare*, to be present]

instantaneously *adv.* in an instant; immediately.

instantly *adv.* at once; immediately.

instar *noun Zool.* the form of an insect at any stage of its physical development between two successive moults, before it has become fully mature. [from Latin *instar*, image]

instead *adv.* as a substitute or alternative; in place of something or someone.
— **instead of something** *or* **someone** in place of them or as an alternative to them.
[from Middle English *in stead*, in place]

instep *noun* **1** the inside of the arched middle section of the human foot. **2** the part of a shoe, sock, etc that covers this.

instigate *verb* **1** to urge on or incite (someone) especially to do something wrong or evil. **2** to set in motion or intitiate (eg an inquiry). [from Latin *instigare*, to goad on]

instigation *noun* **1** instigating; inciting. **2** something that instigates, a stimulus.

instigator *noun* a person who instigates, an inciter.

instil *verb* (**instilled, instilling**) **1** (**instil something into someone**) to impress ideas, feelings, etc gradually into a person's mind. **2** to pour (a liquid) into something drop by drop. [from Latin *instillare*, to drip into]

instillation *or* **instilment** *noun* **1** instilling. **2** something that is instilled or infused.

instiller *noun* a person who instills or infuses.

instinct *noun* **1** in animal behaviour, an inherited and usually fixed pattern of response to a particular stimulus, common to all members of a particular species, that has not been learned but is based on a biological need, especially for survival or reproduction, eg the alarm call of a bird. It can be modified by learning or environmental stimuli. **2** in humans, a basic drive that urges a person towards a specific goal such as survival or reproduction. **3** intuition. [from Latin *instinctus*, prompting]

instinctive *adj.* prompted by instinct or intuition; involuntary; automatic.

instinctively *adv.* in an instinctive way, by instinct.

institute — *noun* **1** a society or organization which promotes research, education or a particular cause. **2** a building or group of buildings used by an institute. **3** an established law, principle, rule, or custom. **4** (**institutes**) a book of laws or principles. — *verb* **1** to set up, establish, or organize. **2** to initiate or cause to begin. **3** to appoint to or install in a position or office. [from Latin *instituere*, to establish]

institution *noun* **1** an organization or public body founded especially for charitable or educational purposes, or as a hospital. **2** *derog.* a hospital, old people's home, etc, regarded as an impersonal or bureaucratic organization. **3** a custom or tradition. **4** a familiar and well-known object or person. **5** the act of instituting or process of being instituted. [from Latin *instituere*, to establish]

institutional *adj.* of or like an institution, especially in being dull or regimented.

institutionalism *noun* **1** the characteristics or system of institutions, or life in institutions. **2** belief in the merits of such a system.

institutionalize *or* **institutionalise** *verb* **1** to place in an institution. **2** to cause (someone) to lose his or her individuality and ability to cope with life by keeping him or her in an institution (eg a long-stay hospital or prison) for too long. **3** to make into an institution.

instruct *verb* **1** to teach or train (a person) in (a subject or skill). **2** to direct or order. **3** *Legal* to give (a lawyer) the facts concerning a case. **4** *Legal* to engage (a lawyer) to act in a case. [from Latin *instruere*, to equip, train]

instruction *noun* **1** (*often* **instructions**) a direction, order, or command. **2** (**instructions**) a set of detailed guidelines, eg on how to operate a machine or piece of equipment. **3** a command or code in a computer program that activates a particular function. **4** teaching.

instructive *adj.* giving knowledge or information.

instructively *adv.* in an instructive way.

instructiveness *noun* an instructive quality.

instructor *noun* **1** a person who gives instruction. **2** *North Amer.* a college or university teacher ranking below a professor.

instructress *noun* a female instructor.

instrument — *noun* **1** a tool, especially one used for delicate scientific work or measurement. **2** (*also* **musical instrument**) any of several devices which can be made to produce sounds and music. **3** any thing or person used as a means of achieving or doing something. **4** any of several devices inside a vehicle or aircraft which measure, show, and control speed, temperature, direction, etc. **5** a formal or official legal document. — *verb* **1** to arrange (music). **2** to equip with instruments for measuring, etc. [from Latin *instrumentum*, equipment, tool]

instrumental — *adj.* **1** (*often* **instrumental in** *or* **to something**) being responsible for it or an important factor in it. **2** performed by or written or arranged for musical instruments (as opposed to voices). **3** of or done with an instrument or tool. **4** *Grammar* denoting the grammatical case which shows how or by what means an action is performed. — *noun* **1** a piece of music performed by or written or arranged for musical instruments. **2** *Grammar* the instrumental case.

instrumentalist *noun* a person who plays a musical instrument.

instrumental learning *Psychol.* an elementary learning process in which an individual comes to perform a certain action more or less frequently or intensively than before, by virtue of the action having produced positive or negative consequences.

instrumentally *adv.* **1** in an instrumental way, or with an instrument. **2** on or with a musical instrument. **3** *Grammar* in the instrumental case.

instrumentation *noun* **1** the particular way in which a piece of music is written or arranged to be played by instruments. **2** the instruments used to play a particular piece of music. **3** the use, design or provision of instruments or tools.

insubordinate *adj.* disobedient; refusing to take orders.

insubordinately *adv.* in an insubordinate way.

insubordination *noun* being insubordinate; defiance of authority.

insubstantial *adj.* **1** not solid, strong, or satisfying; flimsy. **2** not made up of solid material; not real. [from Latin *insubstantialis*]

insubstantiality *noun* being insubstantial, lack of substance.

insubstantially *adv.* to an insubstantial degree.

insufferable *adj.* too unpleasant, annoying, etc to bear; intolerable.

insufferably *adv.* in an insufferable way, unbearably.

insufficiency *noun* **1** being insufficient. **2** *Pathol.* the failure of an organ to function.

insufficient *adj.* not enough or not adequate; not sufficient. [from Latin *insufficientia*]

insufficiently *adv.* inadequately; so as to be insufficient.

insular *adj.* **1** of or belonging to an island or the inhabitants of an island. **2** *said of a person, opin-*

ions, etc not influenced by or responsive to contact with other people, cultures, etc; narrow-minded; prejudiced. [from Latin *insularis*, from *insula*, island]

insularity *noun* being insular.

insulate *verb* **1** to prevent the passing of heat, sound, electricity, etc from (a body), especially by covering it with some special material. **2** to remove or set (someone or something) apart; to isolate. [from Latin *insula*, island]

insulating tape adhesive tape used to cover bare or exposed electrical wires, to protect people from electric shocks.

insulation *noun* **1** material used in insulating, especially material which does not conduct heat or electricity. **2** the process of insulating or being insulated.

insulator *noun* any material that is a poor conductor of heat and electricity, eg plastics, glass, ceramics, and most non-metallic elements except for carbon.

insulin *noun* a hormone produced in the pancreas which controls the amount of sugar in the blood, a lack of this hormone being the cause of diabetes. [from Latin *insula*, island, because it is obtained from a part of the pancreas known as the islet of Langerhans]

insult — *verb* to behave rudely or offensively to; to speak rudely or offensively to or about. — *noun* **1** a rude and offensive remark or action. **2** an affront. **3** *Medicine* injury or damage to the body, or a cause of this.
— **add insult to injury** to treat with further discourtesy someone one has already harmed. [from Latin *insultare*, to jump on]

insulting *adj.* that insults.

insultingly *adv.* in an insulting way.

insuperability *noun* being insuperable.

insuperable *adj.* too difficult to be overcome, defeated, or dealt with successfully. [from Latin *insuperabilis*]

insuperably *adv.* in an insuperable way.

insupportable *adj.* **1** that is too unpleasant, severe, annoying, etc to be tolerated. **2** that cannot be justified. [from Latin *insupportabilis*]

insurable *adj.* capable of being insured.

insurance *noun* **1** an agreement by which one party promises to pay another party money in the event of loss, theft, or damage to property, personal injury or death, etc. **2** (*also* **insurance policy**) the contract for such an agreement. **3** the protection offered by such a contract. **4** money, usually paid regularly, in return for such a contract; an insurance premium. **5** the sum which will be paid in the event of loss, theft, or damage to property, personal injury or death, etc. **6** the business of providing such contracts for clients. **7** anything done, any measure taken, to try to prevent possible loss, disappointment, problems, etc. **8** an act or instance of insuring.
◇ Insurance is taken out to guard against an event which may happen. In this respect, it is distinguished from *assurance*, which provides for an event which is certain. The insured pays a fee (the *premium*) to the insurer, the size of which is calculated to reflect the size of the risk at stake, the number of premiums to be received, and the risk of the event actually occurring. Insurance may be obtained against most events; the four main classes are marine, fire, life, and accident.

insure *verb* (*often* **insure against something**) **1** *trans., intrans.* to arrange for the payment of an amount of money in the event of the loss or theft of or damage to (property) or injury to or the death of (someone), etc by paying regular amounts of money to an insurance company. **2** to take measures to try to prevent (an event leading to loss, damage, difficulties, etc). **3** *intrans. chiefly North Amer.* to provide insurance; to underwrite. [from Old French *enseurer*, to ensure]

insured *adj.* (**the insured**) a person whose life, health, or property is covered by insurance.

insurer *noun* a person or company that provides insurance.

insurgence *or* **insurgency** *noun* an uprising or rebellion.

insurgent — *adj.* opposed to and fighting against the government of the country; rebellious. — *noun* a rebel. [from Latin *in surgere*, to rise up]

insurmountability *noun* being insurmountable.

insurmountable *adj.* too difficult to be dealt with successfully; impossible to overcome.

insurrection *noun* an act of rebellion against authority. [from Latin *insurgere*, to rise up]

insurrectionist *noun* a person who takes part in or supports an insurrection.

int. *abbrev.* **1** interior. **2** internal. **3** international.

intact *adj.* whole; not broken or damaged; untouched. [from Latin *intactus*]

intaglio *noun* (PL. **intaglios**) **1** a stone or gem which has a design engraved in its surface (cf. CAMEO). **2** the art or process of engraving designs into the surface of objects, especially jewellery; also, an engraved design. **3** a technique of printmaking in which the design is incised into a metal plate, ink is forced into the cut lines and wiped off the rest of the surface, damp paper is laid on top, and both plate and paper are rolled through a press. [from Italian *intaglio*, from *intagliare*, to cut into]

intake *noun* **1** a thing or quantity taken in or accepted. **2** an opening through which liquid or gas enters a pipe, engine, etc. **3** an act of taking in.

intangibility *noun* being intangible.

intangible *adj.* **1** not able to be felt or perceived by touch. **2** difficult to understand or for the mind to grasp. **3** *said of part of a business, eg an asset* not having a solid physical existence, but having some value or worth. [from Latin *intangibilis*]

intangibly *adv.* in an intangible way.

integer *noun* any of the positive or negative whole numbers, or zero, eg 0, 8, –12. [from Latin *integer*, untouched]

integral — *adj.* **1** being a necessary part of a whole. **2** forming a whole; supplied or fitted as part of a whole. **3** whole; complete. **4** *Maths.* denoting a number that is an integer. — *noun* *Maths.* the result of integrating a function. [from Latin *integralis*]

integral calculus *Maths.* the branch of calculus concerned with *integration*, ie the summing of a very large number of extremely small quantities. It can be used to solve differential equations, and to calculate the area enclosed by a curve, or the volume enclosed by an irregular surface.

integrand *noun* *Maths.* a function that is to be integrated. [from Latin *integrandus*]

integrate *verb* **1** to fit (parts) together to form a whole. **2** *trans., intrans.* to mix or cause to mix freely with other groups in society, etc. **3** to end racial segregation in. **4** *Maths.* **a** to find the integral of. **b** to find the total or mean value of. [from Latin *integrare*, to renew]

integrated circuit *Electron.* a miniature solid-state circuit formed on a single paper-thin chip of semiconductor material, usually silicon, and ranging in size from about one millimetre to one centimetre square.
– Also called *silicon chip*.
◇ An integrated circuit may contain up to 1m circuit components such as transistors, capacitors, and resistors. Fine wires are attached to the ends of the circuit so that it can be connected to other components of an electronic device such as

a pocket calculator, watch, etc. The most important type of integrated circuit is the *microprocessor*, which forms the calculating and control centre of a microcomputer and is the main reason for the dramatic reduction in the size of such computers in recent years.

integration *noun* **1** the process of integrating. **2** *Maths.* a method used in calculus to sum the effects of a continuously varying quantity or function, by treating it as a very large number of infinitely small quantities that represent the difference between two values of a given function.
◇ Integration is the opposite process to differentiation. It can be used to calculate the area beneath a curve between two particular values of a variable, or the volume enclosed by an irregular surface, and it is also used to solve differential equations. The integration of a function $f(x)$ is written as $\int f(x)dx$, and the result of such integration is called the *integral*. In an *indefinite integral* the interval over which the integration takes place is not specified, whereas in a *definite integral* the interval is specified, eg $\int_{-a}^{a} f(x)dx$ signifies that the function $f(x)$ is to be integrated between the values $x = a$ and $x = -a$.

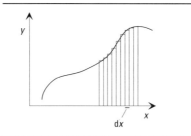

integration

integrity *noun* **1** strict adherence to moral values and principles; uprightness. **2** the quality or state of being whole and unimpaired. [from Latin *integritas*]

integument *noun* any natural outer covering, eg a shell, skin, husk, etc. [from Latin *integumentum*]

integumental *or* **integumentary** *adj.* relating to or in the region of the integument.

intellect *noun* **1** the part of the mind that uses both memory and intelligence in order to think, reason creatively, and understand concepts. **2** a person who has a highly developed intellect and great mental ability. [from Latin *intelligere*, to understand]

intellectual — *adj.* **1** of, involving or appealing to the intellect. **2** having a highly developed ability to think, reason and understand. — *noun* a person with a highly developed intellect and great mental ability.

intellectualize *or* **intellectualise** *verb* **1** to think about or analyse (eg a problem) intellectually or rationally. **2** *intrans.* to think rationally or intellectually; to philosophize.

intellectually *adv.* in an intellectual way; as regards intellect (as distinct from emotion).

intelligence *noun* **1** the ability to use memory, knowledge, experience, understanding, reasoning, imagination, and judgment in order to solve problems and adapt to new situations. **2** news or information. **3** the gathering of secret information about an enemy. **4** the government department or group of people, eg in the army, responsible for gathering such information. [from Latin *intelligentia*, from *intelligere*, to understand]

intelligence quotient (ABBREV. **IQ**) a measure of a person's intellectual ability in relation to that of the rest of the population. It is expressed as the ratio of mental age to actual age, multiplied by 100, and is based on the scores achieved in an *intelligence test*.

intelligence test *Psychol.* any standardized assessment procedure to determine an individual's intellectual ability, or the age at which his or her ability would be normal. The score produced is usually expressed as an *intelligence quotient*.

intelligent *adj.* **1** having or showing highly developed mental ability; clever. **2** *said of a machine, computer, weapon, etc* able to vary its behaviour according to the situation.

intelligently *adv.* in an intelligent way.

intelligentsia *noun* (*usually* **the intelligentsia**) the most highly educated and cultured people in a society, especially when considered as a political class. [from Russian, from Latin *intelligentia*]

intelligibility *noun* being intelligible.

intelligible *adj.* **1** able to be understood; clear. **2** only able to be understood by the intellect and not by the senses or feelings. [from Latin *intelligibilis*]

intelligibly *adv.* in an intelligible way.

intemperance *noun* excess, lack of moderation.

intemperate *adj.* **1** going beyond reasonable limits; not controlled or restrained. **2** habitually drinking too much alcohol. **3** *said of a climate or region* having extreme and severe temperatures. See also TEMPERATE. [from Latin *intemperatus*]

intemperately *adv.* in an intemperate way; severely, excessively.

intend *verb* **1** to plan or have in mind as one's purpose or aim. **2** (**intend something for someone** *or* **something**) to set it aside or destine it to some specified person or thing. **3** to mean. [from Latin *intendere*, to stretch towards]

intended — *adj.* meant, done on purpose or planned. — *noun colloq.* one's future husband or wife.

intense *adj.* **1** very great or extreme. **2** feeling or expressing emotion deeply. **3** very deeply felt: *intense happiness*. [from Latin *intendere*, to stretch towards]

intensely *adv.* in an intense way; deeply, extremely.

intensification *noun* **1** intensifying. **2** being intensified.

intensifier *noun* *Grammar* an adverb or adjective which adds emphasis to or intensifies the word or phrase which follows it.

intensify *verb trans., intrans.* (**intensifies**, **intensified**) to make or become intense or more intense.

intensity *noun* (PL. **intensities**) **1** the quality or state of being intense. **2** *Physics* the measurable amount of some force or quality, eg heat, light or sound.

intensive — *adj.* **1** (*often in compounds*) using, done with, or requiring considerable amounts of thought, effort, time, etc within a relatively short period: *labour-intensive*. **2** thorough; intense; concentrated. **3** using large amounts of capital and labour (rather than more land or raw materials) to increase production. **4** *Grammar, said of an adverb or adjective* adding force or emphasis, eg *extremely*, *quite*. — *noun* *Grammar* an intensive adverb or adjective. [from Latin *intensivus*, from *intendere*, to stretch towards]

intensive care **1** the care of critically ill patients who require continuous attention, eg following severe injury or major surgery. **2** (*in full* **intensive-care unit**) a hospital unit that specializes in intensive care. Such units contain special equipment for monitoring body temperature, blood pressure, heart rate, and other vital body functions.

intensive farming farming in which the use of high levels of chemicals, and manufactured or supplementary feedstuffs, produces a higher level of yield per hectare, thus enabling the farmer to generate an acceptable income from a limited area. See also EXTENSIVE FARMING, FACTORY FARMING.

intensively *adv.* in an intensive way.

intensiveness *noun* being intensive.

intent — *noun* **1** something which is aimed at or intended; a purpose. **2** the purpose of committing a crime: *loitering with intent.* — *adj.* **1** (**intent on** *or* **upon something**) firmly determined to do it. **2** (**intent on something**) having one's attention firmly fixed on it; concentrating hard on it. **3** showing concentration; absorbed: *an intent look.* — **to all intents and purposes** in every important respect; virtually. [from Latin *intendere*, to stretch towards]

intention *noun* **1** that which one plans or intends to do; an aim or purpose. **2** (**intentions**) *colloq.* someone's, especially a man's, purpose with regard to marriage. **3** *RC Church* (also **special** *or* **particular intention**) the purpose or reason for prayers being said or mass celebrated. [from Latin *intendere*, to stretch towards]

intentional *adj.* said, done, etc on purpose; deliberate.

intentionally *adv.* so as to be intentional; deliberately.

intently *adv.* earnestly, diligently.

intentness *noun* **1** being intent. **2** close attention.

inter *verb* (**interred**, **interring**) to bury (a dead person, etc) in the earth or a tomb. [from Latin *in*, into + *terra*, earth]

inter- *combining form* forming words meaning: **1** between or among. **2** mutual or reciprocal. [from Latin *inter*, among]

interact *verb intrans.* to act with or on one another.

interaction *noun* action or influence of people or things on each other.

interactive *adj.* **1** in which the people, things, etc interact. **2** involving or allowing a continuous exchange of information between a computer and its user.

interactively *adv.* in an interactive way.

inter alia among other things. [Latin]

interbreed *verb intrans., trans.* (PAST TENSE AND PAST PARTICIPLE **interbred**) to breed or cause to breed with an animal or plant that is a member of a different variety or species.

interbreeding *noun* breeding together.

intercalary *adj.* **1** *said of a day* added to a calendar month to make the calendar year match the solar year, eg the day added to February every leap year. **2** *said of a year* containing such a day or days. **3** coming between two layers; intervening. [from Latin *intercalarius*]

intercede *verb intrans.* **1** to act as a peacemaker between (two parties, countries, etc). **2** (**intercede for someone**) to plead or make an appeal on their behalf. See also INTERCESSION. [from Latin *inter*, between + *cedere*, to move]

intercellular *adj. Biol.* situated or occurring between cells.

intercept — *verb* **1** to stop or catch (eg a person, missile, aircraft, etc) on his, its, etc way from one place to another; to prevent (a missile, etc) from arriving at its destination, often by destroying it. **2** *Maths.* to mark off (a space, line, curve, etc) between two points. — *noun Maths.* that part of a line that is intercepted. [from Latin *inter*, between + *capere*, to seize]

interception *noun* intercepting.

interceptive *adj.* intercepting.

interceptor *noun* a person or thing that intercepts, especially a small light aircraft used to intercept approaching enemy aircraft.

intercession *noun* **1** an act of interceding or making an appeal on behalf of another. **2** *Christianity* a prayer or request to God on behalf of someone else. [from Latin *intercessio*]

intercessional *adj.* relating to or involving intercession.

intercessor *noun* a person who intercedes; a mediator.

interchange — *verb intrans., trans.* to change or cause to change places with something or someone. — *noun* **1** an act of interchanging; an exchange. **2** a road junction, especially leading to or from a motorway, consisting of a series of roads and bridges designed to prevent streams of traffic from directly crossing one another. [from Middle English *entrechaungen*]

interchangeability *noun* being interchangeable.

interchangeable *adj.* capable of being interchanged.

interchangeably *adv.* in an interchangeable way.

intercity *adj. Brit., said of transport* denoting an express service between major cities.

intercom *noun* a system consisting of microphones and loudspeakers which allow communication within a building, aircraft, ship, etc. [abbreviation of INTERCOMMUNICATION]

intercommunicate *verb intrans.* **1** to communicate mutually or together. **2** *said of adjoining rooms* to have a connecting door; to interconnect. [from Latin *intercommunicatus*, intercommunicating]

intercommunication *noun* mutual communication.

interconnect *verb trans., intrans.* to connect (two things) or be connected together or with one another.

interconnection *noun* mutual connection.

intercontinental *adj.* travelling between or connecting different continents.

intercontinental ballistic missile a ballistic missile which can travel great distances and which can therefore be fired at a target in another continent.

intercourse *noun* **1** sexual intercourse. **2** communication, connection or dealings between people, groups of people, countries, etc. **3** communion, eg between people and God. [from Latin *intercursus*, a running between, communication]

intercropping *Agric.* the practice of growing two or more crops in a field at the same time, in alternate rows.

interdenominational *adj.* happening between or involving (members of) different religious denominations.

interdepartmental *adj.* happening between or involving (members of) different departments within a single organization, etc.

interdependence *noun* mutual dependence.

interdependent *adj.* depending on one another.

interdependently *adv.* in an interdependent way.

interdict — *noun* **1** an official order forbidding someone to do something. **2** *RC Church* a sentence or punishment removing the right to most sacraments (including burial but not communion) from the people of a place or district. — *verb* to place under an interdict; to forbid or prohibit. [from Latin *interdictum*, prohibition]

interdiction *noun* **1** interdicting. **2** being interdicted.

interdictory *adj.* interdicting.

interdisciplinary *adj.* involving two or more subjects of study.

interest — *noun* **1** the desire to learn or know about someone or something; curiosity. **2** the power to attract a person's attention and curiosity. **3** something which arouses a person's attention and curiosity; a hobby or pastime. **4** money paid as a charge for borrowing money or using credit, usually in the form of a percentage of what is borrowed or owed. **5** (*often* **interests**) advantage, benefit, or profit, especially financial: *it is in your own interests to be truthful.* **6** a share or claim in a business and its profits, or a legal right to property. **7** (*also* **interest group**) a group of people or organizations with common, especially financial, aims and concerns: *the banking interest.* — *verb* **1** to attract the attention and curiosity of. **2** (**interest someone in something**) to cause them to take a part in or be concerned about some activity. — **in the interest** *or* **interests of something** in order to achieve or contribute to an objective: *in the interests of good industrial relations.* [from Latin *interest*, it concerns]
◇ The sum lent, on which interest is calculated, is known as the *principal*. The rate of interest will depend on the amount of the principal, the length of time the loan is outstanding, and the risk involved. Interest rates generally vary according to the state of the economy.

interested *adj.* **1** (*often* **interested in something** *or* **someone**) showing or having a concern or interest in them. **2** personally involved and therefore not impartial or disinterested. See also DISINTERESTED, UNINTERESTED.

interestedly *adv.* in an interested way.

interesting *adj.* attracting interest; holding the attention.

interestingly *adv.* in an interesting way.

interface — *noun* **1** a surface forming a common boundary between two regions, things, etc which cannot be mixed, eg oil and water. **2** a common boundary or meeting-point between two different systems or processes. **3** *Physics* boundary between two adjacent phases, ie between gas and liquid, gas and solid, liquid and liquid, liquid and solid, or solid and solid. **4** *Comput.* a device consisting of hardware together with software programs to drive it, that links a computer to a peripheral device such as a printer. **5** *Comput.* the physical connection between a computer and the user. — *verb trans., intrans.* to connect (a piece of equipment, etc) with another by means of an interface.

interfacing *noun* a piece of stiff fabric sewn between two layers of material to give shape and stiffness.

interfere *verb intrans.* **1** (**interfere in** *or* **with something**) to involve oneself in matters which do not concern one and where one is not wanted. **2** (**interfere with something**) to get in the way of a process; to slow down or hinder the progress of something. **3** (**interfere with someone**) *euphemistic* to assault or molest them sexually. **4** *Physics, said of sound waves, rays of light, etc* to combine together to cause disturbance or interference. [from Old French *s'entreferir*, to strike each other]

interference *noun* **1** the act of interfering. **2** *Physics* the interaction between two or more waves of the same frequency. If the peaks of two such waves arrive at the same point together, they will combine to give a larger wave, but if a peak of one wave coincides with a trough of the other, the waves cancel each other out and there is no wave motion. With light of a single wavelength, interference produces patterns of light and dark bands. **3** *Telecomm.* the distortion of transmitted radio or television signals by an external power source, eg machinery near to the receiver.

interfering *adj.* that interferes.

interferometer *noun Physics* an instrument that splits a beam of light into two or more parts which are then recombined to form an interference pattern. Interferometers are used to measure wavelengths, to test optical surfaces, and to measure accurately small angles and distances, eg the distance between two close stars. Radio interferometers are used in many radio telescopes.

interferon *noun* any of various proteins, secreted by animal cells that have been infected with a virus, which are capable of preventing the multiplication of that virus in non-infected cells. Interferon can be used to treat certain herpes virus infections, and it is thought that it may prove effective in the treatment of certain forms of leukaemia. [from INTERFERE]

interfuse *verb* **1** to mix (with something). **2** *trans., intrans.* to blend or fuse together. [from Latin *interfundere*, to pour between]

interfusion *noun* **1** interfusing. **2** being interfused.

intergalactic *adj.* happening or situated between different galaxies.

interim *adj.* not intended to be final or to last; provisional, temporary.
— **in the interim** in the time between two events; in the meantime.
[from Latin *interim*, in the meantime]

interior — *adj.* **1** on, of, suitable for, happening or acting in, or coming from the inside; inner. **2** away from the shore or frontier; inland. **3** concerning the domestic or internal, rather than foreign, affairs of a country. **4** of or existing in the mind or spirit; of mental or spiritual life. — *noun* **1** an internal or inner part; the inside. **2** the part of a country or continent that is furthest from the coast. **3** the internal or home affairs of a country. **4** a picture or representation of the inside of a room or building, especially with reference to its decoration or style: *a typical southern French interior*. [from Latin *interior*, further inward, from *inter*, inward]

interior angle an angle between two adjacent sides of a polygon.

interior decoration *or* **interior design 1** the decoration, design and furnishings of a room or building. **2** the art or job of designing the insides of rooms, including selecting colours and furnishings.

interior decorator *or* **interior designer** a person whose occupation is interior decoration or design.

interj. *abbrev.* interjection.

interject *verb* to say or add abruptly; to interrupt with. [from Latin *interjicere*, to throw between]

interjection *noun* **1** a word, phrase or sound used as an exclamation to express surprise, sudden disappointment, pain, etc. **2** an act of interjecting.

interjectional *adj.* of the nature of an interjection.

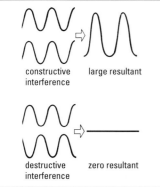

constructive interference large resultant

destructive interference zero resultant

wave interference

interlace *verb* **1** *trans., intrans.* to join by lacing or by crossing over. **2** to mix or blend with: *a story interlaced with graphic descriptions*. [from Middle English *entrelacen*]

interlacement *noun* **1** interlacing. **2** being interlaced.

interlard *verb* to add foreign words, quotations, unusual phrases, etc to (a speech or piece of writing), often excessively. [from Old French *entrelarder*]

interleaf *noun* (PL. **interleaves**) a usually blank leaf of paper inserted between the leaves of a book.

interleave *verb* to insert a usually blank leaf of paper between.

interleukin *noun* a protein produced by white blood cells which fights infection. [from INTER- + LEUCOCYTE]

interline[1] *verb* to insert (words) between the lines of (a document, book, etc). [from Latin *interlineare*]

interline[2] *verb* to put an extra lining between the first lining and the fabric (of a garment), especially for stiffness.

interlinear *adj., said of words* inserted between the lines of a document, book, etc.

interlineation *noun* **1** inserting a word or words between lines or writing. **2** the word or words inserted.

interlining *noun* a piece of material used as an extra lining.

interlink *verb trans., intrans.* to join or connect together.

interlock — *verb trans., intrans.* to fit, fasten or connect together, especially by the means of teeth or parts which fit into each other. — *noun* a device or mechanism that connects and co-ordinates the functions of the parts or components of eg a machine. — *adj., said of a fabric or garment* knitted with closely locking stitches.

interlocking *adj.* that interlocks.

interlocution *noun* dialogue, conversation.

interlocutor *noun* a person who takes part in a conversation or dialogue. [from Latin *interloqui*, to speak between]

interlocutory *adj.* **1** of conversation or dialogue. **2** *Legal, said of a decree* given during legal proceedings and only provisional.

interloper *noun* a person who meddles or interferes with other people's affairs, or goes to places where he or she has no right to be; an intruder.

interlude *noun* **1** a short period of time between two events, or a short period of a different activity. **2** a short break between the acts of a play or opera, or between items of music. **3** a short piece of music, or short item of entertainment, played during such a break. [from Latin *interludium*]

intermarriage *noun* **1** intermarrying. **2** marriage between people of different groups, races, or nations etc. **3** marriage of people closely related.

intermarry *verb intrans.* (**intermarries, intermarried**) **1** *said of different races, social and religious groups, etc* to become connected by marriage. **2** to marry someone from one's own family.

intermediary *noun* (PL. **intermediaries**) **1** a person who mediates between two people or groups, often to try to settle a dispute between them or bring them into agreement. **2** any intermediate person or thing. [from Latin *intermedium*, intervening place]

intermediate — *adj.* (pronounced -*ət*) in the middle; placed between two points, stages, or extremes in place or time or skill. — *noun* (pronounced -*ət*) **1** an intermediate thing. **2** *Chem.* a short-lived chemical compound that is formed

during one of the middle stages of a complex series of chemical reactions. **3** *Chem.* a chemical compound that is the precursor of a particular end-product, eg a dye, and must undergo a number of chemical changes to give the finished product. — *verb intrans.* (pronounced -*ate*) to act as an intermediary. [from Latin *intermediatus*, from *intermedium*, intervening place]

intermediately *adv.* in an intermediate position or condition.

Intermediate Nuclear Force Treaty a treaty signed (Dec 1987) in Washington by US President Reagan, and USSR General Secretary Gorbachev. It involved the elimination of 1 286 missiles from Europe and Asia, and over 2 000 warheads, and was regarded as a major break in the arms race.

intermediate technology technology involving the adaptation of highly sophisticated scientific inventions and techniques for use in the Third World, using local materials and methods of manufacture in order to reduce overhead costs and minimize environmental damage. It has been used to introduce or adapt technologies for agriculture, food processing, energy generation, and industry, in order to enable less industrialized countries to develop economically.

intermediation *noun* intermediating.

interment *noun* a burial.
◆ Sometimes confused with *internment*.

intermezzo *noun* (PL. **intermezzi, intermezzos**) *Mus.* a short instrumental piece usually performed between the sections of a symphonic work, opera, or other dramatic musical entertainment. From the 16c to the 18c the term was applied specifically to a short dramatic interlude with music performed on stage between the acts of a serious opera: an example of this was Pergolesi's *La serva padrona* ('The Maidservant turned Mistress', 1733) originally performed between the acts of his opera *Il Prigionier superbo*. [from Italian, from Latin *intermedium*, intervening place]

interminable *adj.* having or seeming to have no end, especially because of being extremely dull and tedious. [from Latin *interminabilis*]

interminableness *noun* being interminable.

interminably *adv.* endlessly, on and on.

intermingle *verb trans., intrans.* to mingle or mix together.

intermission *noun* a short pause between two things, eg between two parts of a film, play, etc or between two serious attacks of disease. [from Latin *intermissio*, interruption]

intermittence *noun* intermitting.

intermittent *adj.* happening occasionally; stopping for a while and then starting again; not continuous. [from Latin *intermittere*, to leave a space between]

intermittently *adv.* in an intermittent way; at intervals.

intern[1] *verb* (with stress on -*tern*) to confine within a country, restricted area or prison, especially during a war. [from French *interner*]

intern[2] *or* **interne** *noun* (with stress on *in*-) *North Amer.* an advanced student or graduate who is gaining practical professional experience by working, especially a medical graduate working as an assistant physician or surgeon in a hospital. [from Latin *internus*, internal]

internal *adj.* **1** of, on, in, or suitable for the inside; inner. **2** of, on, in, or suitable for the inside of the body. **3** of a nation's domestic affairs as opposed to its relations with foreign countries. **4** of, for, or coming from within an organization. **5** of the inner nature or feelings of the mind or soul. [from Latin *internalis*, from *internus*, inward]

internal combustion engine an engine that produces power by the combustion (burn-

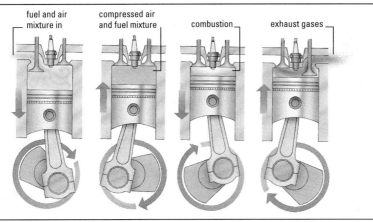

four-stroke engine cycle

fuel and air mixture in   compressed air and fuel mixture   combustion   exhaust gases

ing) of a mixture of fuel and air within an enclosed space inside the engine. The hot gas produced is used to drive a moving piston, rotor, or turbine.

◇ Internal combustion engines, used in modern motor vehicles, ships, and aircraft, are of three main types: petrol, diesel, and gas-turbine (jet) engines. In all cases air is heated and caused to expand by the burning of fuel. In petrol and diesel engines, the air expands inside a cylinder and pushes downward on a piston, which turns a crankshaft connected to the wheels of the vehicle. Motor engines usually have four, six, or eight cylinders which fire one after another. In petrol engines the fuel is ignited by an electric spark, but in diesel engines it is ignited by compressing the air drawn into the cylinder until it reaches a high temperature. The type of engine normally used to drive motor cars is the four-stroke with one in every four strokes of the piston being the power-stroke.

A gas-turbine (jet) engine has no cylinders, and air flows through it from front to rear, being compressed by fans and heated on its way through the engine. Forward thrust is produced by the stream of rapidly expanding hot gases ejected from the rear of the vehicle.

internalization *or* **internalisation** *noun* internalizing or being internalized.

internalize *or* **internalise** *verb* **1** to make (a type of behaviour, characteristic, etc) part of one's personality. **2** to keep (an emotion) inside oneself rather than express it.

internally *adv.* **1** in, on, or concerned with the inside or interior. **2** with respect to the inner state of anything, especially the internal affairs of a state or country.

International a shortening originally of International Working Men's Association, the name given to attempts to establish international co-operative organizations of socialist, communist, and revolutionary groups. The First International was created in 1848 by Marx, and inspired the Communist Manifesto. The Second International was formed in Paris in 1889, but collapsed in 1914 as socialist parties took sides in World War I. The Third International (Comintern) was founded by Lenin in 1919, and represented mainly communist parties until abolished in 1943. There was a brief attempt in the 1930s by Trotsky to launch a Fourth International, but it became merely an umbrella for unimportant socialist groups.

international — *adj.* involving, affecting, used by, or carried on between two or more nations. — *noun* **1** a sports match between two national teams. **2** a player who takes part in, or has taken part in, such a match.

International Amateur Athletic Federation (ABBREV. **IAAF**) the governing body which controls athletics worldwide, founded in Stockholm, Sweden, in 1912. The IAAF is responsible for ratifying world records in all track and field events.

International Atomic Energy Agency an international agency, founded in 1957, which promotes research into and development of the non-military uses of nuclear energy, and oversees a system of safeguards and controls that restrict the use of nuclear materials for military purposes.

International Baccalaureate a two-year award accepted in many countries as a qualification for entry to higher education. The examination covers a spread of subjects including languages, mathematics, science, humanities, and the arts.

International Bank for Reconstruction and Development (ABBREV. **IBRD**) also called the **World Bank** a bank that was founded in 1945 after the Bretton Woods Conference, to help raise standards of living in developing countries. It is affiliated to the United Nations, and based in Washington, DC.

International Brigades in the Spanish Civil War (1936–9), foreign volunteer forces recruited by the Comintern and by individual communist parties to assist the Spanish Republic. Almost 60 000 volunteers, mostly workers, fought in Spain between October 1936 and the brigades' withdrawal in October 1938, and were instrumental in the defence of Madrid (1936–7).

International Commodity Agreement (ABBREV. **ICA**) an association of producers of a commodity (eg cocoa, sugar, tin) to cope with widely fluctuating prices. It can fix a floor price for a commodity in times of excessive output, when otherwise the price would fall to below the cost of production.

International Confederation of Free Trade Unions (ABBREV. **ICFTU**) an association of 154 trade union federations from 109 countries in W Europe, USA, and the British Commonwealth, located in Brussels, Belgium, founded in 1949. It was created after withdrawing from the World Federation of Trade Unions because of differences with the communist unions. Its aim is collaboration between free and democratic trade unions throughout the world.

International Court of Justice a court established by the United Nations for the purpose of hearing international law dispute, known widely as the *World Court*. The court sits at The Hague, Netherlands, and is presided over by 15 judges. Nation states must consent to the jurisdiction of the court with regard to contentious proceedings.

International Date Line an imaginary line on the earth's surface running N to S across the middle of the Pacific Ocean, the date in countries on the W of it being one day ahead of the date in countries on the E.

International Development Association (ABBREV. **IDA**) an organization affiliated to, but distinct from, the International Bank for Reconstruction and Development, based in Washington, DC. It was set up in 1960 to provide help to the world's 50 poorest countries by giving them aid on easier terms than the IBRD.

Internationale, L' a revolutionary socialist song composed by Pierre Degeyter (1848–1932), with words by Eugène Pottier. Used (in translation) by left-wing groups in many countries, it was also the national anthem of Soviet Russia (1917–44).

Internationale same as INTERNATIONAL. [from French *internationale*, international]

International Gothic a style of art which flourished in W Europe (c.1375–c.1425), characterized by jewel-like colour, graceful shapes, and realistically-observed details. The style was seen especially in miniature paintings, drawings, and tapestries, often representing secular themes from courtly life.

internationalism *noun* the view that the nations of the world should co-operate politically, economically, culturally, etc and work towards greater mutual understanding.

internationalist *noun, adj.* **1** a person who favours internationalism. **2** a person chosen to represent a country at international level in sport.

internationality *noun* the state of being international.

internationalization *or* **internationalisation** *noun* making international.

internationalize *or* **internationalise** *verb* to make international, especially to bring under the control of two or more countries.

International Labour Organization an autonomous agency associated with the League of Nations, founded in 1919, which became a specialized agency of the United Nations in 1946. A tripartite body representing governments, employers, and workers, it is concerned with industrial relations and the pay, employment, and working conditions of workers.

international law the law that governs relationships between states (*public international law*), or the law that determines which nation's law shall in any particular case govern the relations of private persons (*private international law*). There is no worldwide international legislature and international law is principally based on custom.

internationally *adv.* **1** in an international way. **2** among or between nations.

International Monetary Fund an international financial organization set up to promote trade by keeping currencies stable and having a fund of money from which member states may borrow.

International Monetary Fund (ABBREV. **IMF**) a financial agency affiliated to the United Nations, and located in Washington, DC. It was formed in 1945 to promote international monetary co-operation, the expansion of international trade, and exchange rate stability, and to give financial assistance to states in need.

International Phonetic Alphabet (ABBREV. **IPA**) a system of signs and letters able to represent all of the speech sounds of every language.

International Standard Book Number see ISBN.

International Style 1 a term sometimes used by art historians to refer to the more or less homogeneous Gothic style which flourished throughout Europe (c.1400). **2** a term first used in the USA to describe a new style of architecture developed principally in Europe in the 1920s, also known as the Modern Movement. It is characterized by geometric shapes and an absence of decoration and was at first particularly concerned with low-income, standardized housing projects.

International Telecommunication Union (ABBREV. **ITU**) an agency of the United Nations, which since 1947 has promoted worldwide co-operation in all aspects of telecommunications (eg radio frequency regulation).

International Union for the Conservation of Nature and Natural Resources (ABBREV. **IUCN**) an international organization, founded in 1948, which exists to promote sustainable use and conservation of natural resources. It publishes Red Data books which list endangered species of plants and wildlife, and administers the Convention on International Trade in Endangered Species.

International Youth Hostel Federation see YOUTH HOSTEL FEDERATION, INTERNATIONAL.

interne see INTERN[2].

internecine *adj.* 1 *said of a fight, war, etc* destructive and damaging to both sides. 2 involving or being a conflict or struggle within a group or organization: *an internecine feud.* [from Latin *internecinus*, murderous]

internee *noun* a person who is interned.

Internet *noun* an international computer network linking both business and private users.

internment *noun* interning or being interned.
◆ Sometimes confused with *interment*.

internode *noun Bot.* the part of a plant stem that lies between two successive nodes (points where leaves are attached, or may develop from buds). [from Latin *internodium*, from *inter*, between + *nodus*, knot]

internship *noun* the position of an intern.

interpellate *verb* to question (eg a government minister) about policy during the course of, and as an interruption to, a debate. [from Latin *interpellare*, to disturb by speaking]

interpellation *noun* a question raised during a debate, especially in parliament.

interpellator *noun* a person who interpellates.

interpenetrate *verb* 1 to penetrate thoroughly. 2 *intrans.* to penetrate mutually.

interpenetration *noun* penetrating among or in; thorough penetration.

interpersonal *adj.* concerning or involving the relationships between people.

interphase *noun Biol.* the period between successive divisions of a living cell by mitosis.

interplanetary *adj.* 1 relating to the Solar System. 2 happening or existing in the space between the planets.

interplanetary matter *Astron.* matter in the solar system other than the planets and their satellites (moons). It includes dust particles, and gas that flows continuously outward from the Sun as the solar wind, consisting of streams of charged particles, mainly protons and electrons.

interplay *noun* the action and influence of two or more things on each other.

Interpol *noun* an international organization through which police forces in different countries can communicate and co-operate with each other in fighting crime. [from *Inter*national *Criminal Police Organization*]

interpolate *verb* 1 to add (words) to a book or manuscript, especially so as to make the text misleading or corrupt. 2 to alter (a text) in this way. 3 to interrupt a conversation, a person speaking, etc with (a remark or comment). 4 *Maths.* to estimate (values) from others in the same series which are already known. [from Latin *interpolare*, to refurbish or touch up]

interpolation *noun* 1 interpolating. 2 something that is interpolated.

interpose *verb* 1 *trans., intrans.* to put (something), or come, between two other things. 2 to interrupt a conversation or argument with (a remark, comment, etc). 3 *intrans.* to act as mediator; to intervene. [from Old French *interposer*]

interposition *noun* 1 the act of placing something or oneself between others. 2 intervention. 3 interference.

interpret *verb* (**interpreted, interpreting**) 1 to explain the meaning of (a foreign word, dream, etc). 2 *intrans.* to act as an interpreter. 3 to consider or understand (behaviour, a remark, etc): *interpret her silence as disapproval.* 4 to bring out one's idea of the meaning of (eg a dramatic role, piece of music) in one's performance. [from Latin *interpretari*]

interpretation *noun* 1 an act of interpreting or the sense given as a result. 2 the representing of one's idea of the meaning of a dramatic role, piece of music, etc in one's performance.

interpretative *or* **interpretive** *adj.* 1 interpreting, explanatory. 2 of or using interpretation.

interpretatively *or* **interpretively** *adv.* in an interpretative way.

interpreter *noun* 1 a person who translates speech in a foreign language as the words are spoken, relaying the translation orally as it is done. 2 a computer program that translates instructions one by one and executes them immediately.

interracial *adj.* between different races of people.

interracially *adv.* in an interracial way.

interregnum *noun* (PL. **interregnums, interregna**) 1 the time between two reigns when the throne is unoccupied, eg between the death of one monarch and the coronation of the next. 2 the period between the end of rule by one government and the beginning of rule by the next. 3 any interval or pause in a continuous sequence of events. [from Latin *inter*, between + *regnum*, reign]

interrelate *verb trans., intrans.* to be in or be brought into a mutually dependent or reciprocal relationship.

interrelated *adj.* mutually related or connected.

interrelation *noun* being interrelated.

interrelationship *noun* mutual relationship.

interrogate *verb* 1 to question closely and thoroughly, or examine by asking questions and sometimes with threatening behaviour. 2 *said of a radar set, etc* to send out signals to (a radio beacon) to work out a position. [from Latin *interrogare*]

interrogation *noun* 1 the act or process of interrogating. 2 a question.

interrogative — *adj.* 1 like a question; asking or seeming to ask a question. 2 *Grammar, said of an adjective or pronoun* used to ask a question. — *noun* an interrogative word, sentence or construction. [from Latin *interrogativus*]

interrogatively *adv.* in an interrogative way.

interrogator *noun* 1 a person who interrogates. 2 a transmitter used to send out interrogating signals.

interrogatory — *adj.* being or expressing a question. — *noun* (PL. **interrogatories**) a question or inquiry. [from Latin *interrogatorius*]

interrupt *verb* 1 *trans., intrans.* to break into (a conversation or monologue) by asking a question or making a comment. 2 to make a break in the continuous activity of (an event). 3 to destroy (a view eg of a clear sweep of land) by getting in the way. [from Latin *interrumpere*, to break apart]

interrupter *or* **interruptor** *noun* 1 a person who interrupts. 2 a device for interrupting, especially for opening and closing an electric circuit.

interruption *noun* 1 the act of interrupting or state of being interrupted. 2 something that interrupts, such as a question or remark. 3 a short pause or break.

interruptive *adj.* tending to interrupt.

intersect *verb* 1 to divide (lines, an area, etc) by passing or cutting through or across. 2 *intrans. said especially of lines, roads, etc* to run through or cut across each other. [from Latin *intersecare*, to cut through]

intersection *noun* 1 a place where things meet or intersect, especially a road junction. 2 the act of intersecting. 3 *Geom.* the point or line where two lines or plane surfaces intersect. 4 *Maths.* the set of elements which two or more sets have in common.

intersectional *adj.* relating to or involving intersection.

interspace — *noun* a space between two things; an interval. — *verb* to put a space or intervals between.

intersperse *verb* 1 to scatter or insert (something) here and there. 2 *intrans.* to diversify or change slightly with scattered things. [from Latin *interspergere*, to strew here and there]

interspersion *noun* 1 interspersing. 2 being interspersed. 3 dispersion.

interstate — *adj.* between two or more states, especially in the USA or Australia. — *noun North Amer., esp. US* a major road crossing a state boundary.

interstellar *adj.* happening or existing in the space between individual stars within galaxies.

interstice *noun* 1 a very small gap or space between two things. 2 *Physics* any of the spaces between atoms in a crystal. [from Latin *interstitium*]

intertwine *verb trans., intrans.* to twist or be twisted together.

interval *noun* 1 a period of time between two events. 2 a space or distance between two things. 3 *Brit.* a short break between the acts of a play or opera, or between parts of a concert or long film. 4 *Mus.* the difference in pitch between two notes or tones.
— **at intervals** 1 here and there; now and then. 2 with a stated distance in time or space between: *at intervals of ten minutes.* [from Latin *intervallum*, space between pallisades]

intervene *verb intrans.* 1 (**intervene in something**) to involve oneself in something which is happening in order to affect the outcome. 2 (**intervene in something** *or* **between people**) to involve oneself or interfere in a dispute between other people in order to settle it or prevent more serious conflict. 3 to come or occur between two things in place or time. 4 *Legal* to become involved in a lawsuit as a third party. [from Latin *intervenire*, to come between]

intervention *noun* an act of intervening, especially in the affairs of other people or other countries.

interventionism *noun* the belief that the government of a country should be allowed to interfere, or should interfere, in the economic affairs of the country or in the internal affairs of other countries or states.

interventionist — *noun* a person who supports interventionism. — *adj.* relating to or characteristic of interventionism.

interview — *noun* 1 a formal meeting and discussion with someone, especially one at which an employer meets and judges a prospective employee. 2 a conversation or discussion which aims at obtaining information, especially one in which a journalist asks questions of a famous or important person and which is broadcast or published. — *verb* to hold an interview with. [from Old French *entrevue*, from *entrevoir*, to glimpse]

interviewee *noun* a person who is interviewed.

interviewer *noun* a person who interviews.

interweave *verb trans., intrans.* (PAST TENSE **interwove**; PAST PARTICIPLE **interwoven**) to weave or be woven together.

intestacy *noun* the state of dying without making a valid will.

intestate *Legal — adj., said of a person* dying without having made a valid will. — *noun* a person who dies without making a valid will. [from Latin *intestatus*]

intestinal *adj.* relating to or in the region of the intestines.

intestine *noun* the tube-like part of the alimentary canal leading from the stomach to the anus, divided into the *small intestine* (comprising the duodenum, jejunum, and ileum) and the *large intestine* (comprising the caecum, colon, and rectum). [from Latin *intestinus*, internal]

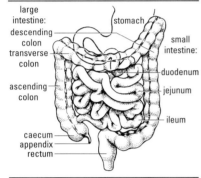

human intestines

intifada the name for the Palestinian uprising against the Israelis in Gaza which began in Dec 1987, and also for the militant group of Palestinians involved in it. [Arabic, = shaking off]

intimacy *noun* (PL. **intimacies**) **1** a warm, close personal friendship. **2** an intimate or personal remark. **3** sexual intercourse. **4** the state or quality of being intimate.

intimate[1] (pronounced *-mət*) — *adj.* **1** marked by or sharing a close and affectionate friendship. **2** very private or personal. **3** *said of a place* small and quiet with a warm, friendly atmosphere promoting close personal relations. **4** (**intimate with someone**) sharing a sexual relationship with them. **5** *said of knowledge* deep and thorough. — *noun* a close friend. [from Latin *intimus*, innermost]

intimate[2] *verb* (pronounced *-mate*) **1** to announce or make known. **2** to hint or suggest indirectly. [from Latin *intimare*, to impress upon]

intimately *adv.* in an intimate way.

intimation *noun* **1** an indication, a hint. **2** an announcement.

Intimations of Immortality (from Recollections of Early Childhood) an ode by William Wordsworth (1807). It is a reflection on life and the importance, particularly in the natural world, of childhood experience, which is interpreted as a kind of pre-existence.

intimidate *verb* (**intimidate someone into something**) to coerce or frighten them into doing what one wants, especially with threats. [from Latin *intimidare*, from *timidus*, frightened]

intimidating *adj.* that intimidates.

intimidation *noun* **1** intimidating. **2** being intimidated.

intimism *or* **intimisme** *noun* Art a genre of French Impressionist painting that flourished c.1890. The term was applied to the representation of everyday subjects, such as domestic interiors, portrayal of close family members and friends in their home or working environment, and small-scale landscapes of local areas. Vuillard's studies of his mother at home, his views from his studio window in Montmartre, and Bonnard's colourful nudes and family scenes typify the style.

into *prep.* **1** to or towards the inside or middle of. **2** against; into contact or collision with. **3** *expressing a change of state or condition* so as to be: *change into a suit / get into difficulties / form into groups.* **4** up to a certain point in time. **5** *Maths.* used to express division: *divide four into twenty.* **6** *colloq.* involved with, interested in or enthusiastic about. [from Anglo-Saxon]

intolerable *adj.* which is too bad, difficult, painful, etc to be put up with. [from Latin *intolerabilis*]

Intolerable Acts the American name for laws (1774) passed by the British Parliament to punish Massachusetts for the Boston Tea Party (1773) — the Boston Port Act, the Massachusetts Government Act, the Administration of Justice Act, and a Quartering Act.

intolerably *adv.* in an intolerable way; to an intolerable degree.

intolerance *noun* **1** being intolerant. **2** an inability to tolerate.

intolerant *adj.* (*often* **intolerant of something**) refusing or unwilling to accept ideas, beliefs, behaviour, etc different from one's own. [from Latin *intolerans*, impatient]

intolerantly *adv.* in an intolerant way.

intonate *verb trans., intrans.* to intone. [from Latin *intonare*, to intone]

intonation *noun* **1** the rise and fall of the pitch of the voice in speech. **2** the opening phrase of a plainsong melody. **3** an act of intoning. **4** the correct pitching of musical notes.

intone *verb trans., intrans.* **1** to recite (a prayer, etc) in a solemn, monotonous voice or in singing tones. **2** to say (something) with a particular intonation or tone. [from Latin *intonare*]

in toto totally, completely; in sum. [Latin, = in total]

intoxicant — *noun* something that causes intoxication, especially an alcoholic drink. — *adj.* intoxicating. [from Latin *intoxicare*, to poison]

intoxicate *verb* **1** to make drunk. **2** to excite or elate to the point at which self-control is lost.

intoxicating *adj.* having the power to intoxicate.

intoxication *noun* a condition in which certain centres in the brain are affected as a result of poisoning by ingestion of alcohol (or other drugs), gases, heavy metals, or other toxic substances. It is characterized by impaired intellectual ability and confusion, and alcoholic intoxication also causes severe dehydration.

intra- *prefix* forming words meaning 'within, inside, on the inside'. [from Latin *intra*, within]

intracellular *adj. Biol.* situated or occurring within cells.

Intracoastal Waterway a shipping route extending 4 989km/3 100mi from Boston, Massachusetts to Key West, Florida (the Atlantic Intracoastal Waterway) and from Apalachee Bay, Florida, to Brownsville, Texas (the Gulf Intracoastal Waterway). The waterway is composed of natural water routes, such as bays and rivers, which are linked by canals. It is used by both commercial and pleasure craft.

intractability *noun* being intractable.

intractable *adj.* **1** *said of a person* difficult to control or influence; obstinate. **2** *said of a problem, illness, etc* difficult to solve, cure, or deal with. [from Latin *intractabilis*]

intractably *adv.* in an intractable way.

intramural *adj.* **1** within or amongst the people in an institution, especially a school, college, or university. **2** within the scope of normal studies. **3** situated within walls. [from INTRA- + Latin *murus* wall]

intramurally *adv.* within the boundaries or walls; inside a particular community or organization, etc.

intransigence *noun* being intransigent.

intransigent — *adj.* holding firmly to one's (often extreme) beliefs and refusing to change or compromise; stubborn. — *noun* an intransigent person. [from Spanish *intransigente*, from Latin *in-*, not + *transigere*, to come to an agreement]

intransigently *adv.* in an intransigent way.

intransitive *adj. Grammar, said of a verb* not having a direct object, such as the verb *run* in the phrase *run as fast as you can.* See also TRANSITIVE. [from Latin *intransitivus*]

intransitively *adv.* in an intransitive way.

intrapreneur *noun* someone who initiates commercial ventures within a large organization. [from INTRA- + ENTREPRENEUR]

intrauterine *adj.* within the uterus.

intrauterine device *or* **intrauterine contraceptive device** (ABBREV. **IUD**, **IUCD**) a contraceptive device consisting of a plastic or metal coil, loop, or other shape that is inserted into the uterus (womb) to prevent implantation of a fertilized egg (and thus pregnancy) by causing mild inflammation of the lining of the uterus. — Also called *coil*.

intravenous *adj.* in or into a vein or veins.

intravenously *adv.* into or through a vein or veins.

intrepid *adj.* bold and daring; fearless; brave. [from Latin *intrepidus*]

intrepidity *noun* being intrepid, courage.

intrepidly *adv.* in an intrepid way.

intricacy *noun* (PL. **intricacies**) **1** being intricate, complexity. **2** a complication.

intricate *adj.* full of complicated, interrelating, or tangled details or parts and therefore difficult to understand, analyse, or sort out. [from Latin *intricare*, to perplex]

intricately *adv.* in an intricate way.

intrigue — *noun* **1** secret plotting or underhand scheming. **2** a secret plot or plan. **3** a secret illicit love affair. — *verb* **1** to arouse the curiosity or interest of; to fascinate. **2** *intrans.* to plot secretly. [from French *intrigue*]

intriguing *adj.* arousing curiosity or interest.

intriguingly *adv.* in an intriguing way.

intrinsic *adj.* (**intrinsic to something**) **1** belonging to it as an inherent and essential part of its nature. **2** *Anat.* denoting a muscle that is entirely contained within the organ or body part on which it acts, eg the muscles of the tongue. [from Latin *intrinsecus*, inwardly]

intrinsically *adv.* in an intrinsic way.

intro *noun* (PL. **intros**) *colloq.* an introduction. [abbreviation]

intro- *prefix* forming words meaning 'within, into, inwards'. [from Latin *intro*, to the inside]

introduce *verb* **1** (**introduce one person to another**) to make them known by name to each other, especially formally. **2** to announce or present (eg a radio or television programme) to an audience. **3** to bring (especially something new) into a place, situation, etc for the first time. **4** to bring into operation, practice, or use. **5** to put forward or propose (a possible law or bill) for attention, consideration, or approval. **6** (**introduce someone to something**) to cause (a person) to experience or discover something for the first time. **7** to start or preface: *introduce the play with a brief analysis of the plot.* **8** (**introduce one**

thing into another) to insert or put (something) into something else. [from Latin *introducere*]

introducible *adj.* capable of being introduced.

introduction *noun* **1** the act of introducing or process of being introduced. **2** a presentation of one person to another or others. **3** a section at the beginning of a book which explains briefly what it is about, why it was written, etc. **4** a book which outlines the basic principles of a subject. **5** a short passage of music beginning a piece or song, or leading up to a movement. **6** something which has been introduced.

introductorily *adv.* in an introductory way.

introductory *adj.* giving or serving as an introduction; preliminary.

introit *noun* a hymn, psalm, or anthem sung at the beginning of a service or, in the RC Church, as the priest approaches the altar to celebrate Mass. [from Latin *introitus*]

intron *noun Genetics* any segment of a gene that does not carry coded instructions for the manufacture of a protein. [from *intervening sequence*]

introspection *noun* the (sometimes excessive or morbid) examination of one's own thoughts, feelings, and intuitions, etc. [from Latin *introspicere*, to look within]

introspective *adj.* looking within oneself; examining one's own emotions, thoughts, and intuitions, or having a tendency to do so.

introspectively *adv.* in an introspective way.

introversion *noun* a personality trait characterized by a tendency to be more interested in the self and inner feelings than in the outside world and social relationships. See also EXTROVERSION.

introvert *or* **intravert** — *noun* **1** *Psychol.* a person who is more concerned with his or her thoughts and inner feelings than with the outside world and social relationships. **2** a person who tends not to socialize and who is uncommunicative and withdrawn. — *adj.* (*also* **introverted**) concerned more with one's own thoughts and feelings than with other people and outside events. — *verb* **1** to turn (one's thoughts) inward to concentrate on oneself. **2** to withdraw (eg a part of the body) into the main part, eg as a tortoise can withdraw its head into its shell. See also EXTROVERT. [from Latin *intro*, within + *vertere*, to turn]

intrude *verb trans., intrans.* (**intrude** *or* **intrude oneself into** *or* **on someone** *or* **something**) to force or impose oneself, one's presence or the presence of something, where it is unwanted and unwelcome. [from Latin *intrudere*, to thrust in]

intruder *noun* a person who enters premises secretly or by force in order to commit a crime.

intrusion *noun* **1** an act of intruding or process of being intruded, especially on someone else's property. **2** *Geol.* the forcing of molten magma under pressure into pre-existing rock. **3** a mass of igneous rock formed by the solidification of molten magma beneath the Earth's surface, after it has been forced into pre-existing rock. [from Latin *intrusio*, from *intrudere*, to thrust in]

intrusive *adj.* **1** tending to intrude. **2** *said of rock* being an intrusion.

intrusively *adv.* in an intrusive way.

intrusiveness *noun* being intrusive.

intrusive rock *Geol.* igneous rock formed by the cooling and solidification of magma beneath the Earth's surface, eg granite.

intrust same as ENTRUST.

intuit *verb* (**intuited**, **intuiting**) to become aware of (something) by intuition.

intuition *noun* **1** the power of understanding or realizing something without conscious rational thought or analysis. **2** something understood or realized in this way. **3** immediate, instinctive

understanding or belief. [from Latin *intuitio*, from *in*, in + *tueri*, to look]

intuitive *adj.* having, showing or based on intuition.

intuitively *adv.* in an intuitive way.

intuitiveness *noun* being intuitive.

Inuit a native people of the Arctic and sub-Arctic regions of Canada, Greenland, Alaska, and Siberia (also known as Eskimos), closely related to the Aleut. Despite geographical separation, the way of life in different Inuit groups was very similar, determined largely by climatic considerations — living on the coast during the winter months, and moving inland for the brief summers to hunt and to fish. After contact with Europeans in the 18c, their way of life was radically altered, from hunting for food to hunting for furs, which they exchanged for European manufactured goods. By the late 20c, many had settled in villages, and while some continue to hunt and fish, most have at least seasonal employment in the countries where they live. The combined populations of Inuits and Aleuts in Russia is c.1 300, with 33 000 in Alaska, 24 000 in Canada, and 43 000 in Greenland.

Inuktitut *noun* the form of the Inuit language spoken in the Canadian Arctic. [Inuit, from *inuk*, person]

inundate *verb* to overwhelm with or as if with water. [from Latin *inundare*, to flow over]

inundation *noun* **1** a flood. **2** an act of inundating.

inure *verb* (**inure someone to something**) to accustom someone or oneself to something unpleasant or unwelcome. [from Old French *en ure*, in use]

inurement *noun* **1** inuring. **2** being inured.

invade *verb* **1** *trans., intrans.* to enter (a country) by force with an army. **2** *trans., intrans.* to attack or overrun. **3** to interfere with (a person's rights, privacy, etc). See also INVASION. [from Latin *invadere*]

invader *noun* a person who invades.

invalid¹ (with stress on *in-*) — *noun* a person who is constantly ill or who is disabled. — *adj.* suitable for or being an invalid. — *verb* (**invalided**, **invaliding**) (**invalid someone out**) to discharge (a soldier, etc) from service because of illness. [from French *invalide*, from Latin *invalidus*, weak]

invalid² *adj.* (with stress on -*val*-) **1** *said of a document, agreement, etc* having no legal force. **2** *said of an argument, reasoning, etc* based on false reasoning or a mistake and therefore not valid, correct, or reliable. [from Latin *invalidus*, weak]

invalidate *verb* to make (a document, agreement, argument, etc) invalid.

invalidation *noun* invalidating or being invalidated.

Invalides, Hôtel des a hospital for the care of old and disabled soldiers, founded in Paris by Louis XIV and built between 1671 and 1676. The main building, which is now mainly given over to a museum, was designed by Libéral Bruant (c.1635–97). Hardouin-Mansart's St Louis Church stands in the courtyard, where Napoleon's tomb has rested since 1840.

invalidity¹ *noun* being an invalid.

invalidity² *noun* being invalidated.

invalidly *adv.* so as to be invalid.

invaluable *adj.* having a value that is too great to be measured.

invaluably *adv.* in an invaluable way.

invariable *adj.* which does not change and is always the same. [from Latin *invariabilis*]

invariably *adv.* consistently, constantly.

invariant *noun Maths.* a property of a mathematical equation, geometric figure, etc, that is unaltered by a particular procedure.

invasion *noun* an act of invading or process of being invaded, eg by a hostile country or by something harmful. [from Latin *invasio*]

invasive *adj.* **1** invading, aggressive. **2** entering, penetrating.

invective *noun* **1** angry attacking words, often including abuse and swearing. **2** an attack using such words. [from Latin *invectivus*, abusive]

inveigh *verb intrans.* to speak strongly or passionately against someone or something, especially in criticism or protest. [from Latin *invehi*, to attack with words]

inveigle *verb* (**inveigle someone into something**) to trick or deceive them into doing something. [from Old French *enveogler*, to blind]

inveiglement *noun* trickery, enticement.

invent *verb* **1** to be the first person to make or use (a machine, game, method, etc). **2** to think or make up (an excuse, false story, etc). [from Latin *invenire*, to find]

invention *noun* **1** something invented, especially a device, machine, etc. **2** the act of inventing. **3** the ability to create and invent things; inventiveness. **4** *colloq.* a lie. **5** *Mus.* a short piece of keyboard music based on a single, simple idea.

inventive *adj.* skilled at inventing; creative; resourceful.

inventiveness *noun* the quality of being inventive; creativity.

inventor *noun* a person who invents.

inventory — *noun* (PL. **inventories**) **1** a formal and complete list of the articles, goods, etc found in a particular place, eg of goods for sale in a shop, or of furniture and possessions in a house. **2** the items included in such a list. **3** the making of such a list of articles, goods, etc. — *verb* (**inventories**, **inventoried**) to make an inventory of; to list in an inventory. [from Latin *inventorium*, list of things found]

Inverness POP (1981) 40 000, the capital of Highland region and of Inverness district, NE Scotland. It lies at the mouth of the R Ness, 180km/112mi NW of Edinburgh, and is the NE terminus of the Caledonian Canal. NOTABLE FEATURES Inverness Museum and Art Gallery; castle (Victorian); the battle site of Culloden Moor (1746), 8km/5mi E.

inverse — *adj.* opposite or reverse in order, sequence, direction, effect, etc. — *noun* **1** a direct opposite. **2** the state of being directly opposite or reversed. **3** *Maths.* describing a mathematical function that is opposite in effect or nature to another function. [from Latin *inversus*, from *invertere*, to invert]

inversely *adv.* **1** in an inverse way, condition, or state. **2** by inversion.

inversion *noun* **1** the act of turning upside down or inside out, or otherwise inverting. **2** the state of being turned upside down, inside out, or otherwise inverted. **3** a reversal of position, order, direction, form, effect, etc. **4** something achieved by inverting. [from Latin *inversio*]

invert *verb* **1** to turn upside down or inside out. **2** to reverse in order, sequence, direction, effect, etc. **3** *Mus.* to change (eg a chord) by placing the lowest note an octave higher. [from Latin *invertire*]

invertase *noun Biochem.* an enzyme found in plants that breaks down sucrose to form glucose and fructose.

invertebrate — *noun Zool.* any animal that does not possess a backbone, such as an insect, worm, snail, or jellyfish. — *adj.* **1** relating to an animal that does not possess a backbone. **2** having no strength of character. [from Latin *in-*, no + *vertebra*, spinal joint]. See panel p. 654.

Classification of Invertebrates

Phylum	Common name, if any	No. of species
Mesozoa	none	c.50
Porifera	sponges	c.5000
Coelenterata	jellyfish and relatives	c.9500
Ctenophora	comb jellies	c.100
Platyhelminthes	flatworms	c.15000
Nemertea	ribbonworms	750
Nematoda	roundworms	10000
Rotifera	rotifers	2000
Gastrotricha	hairy backs	175
Kinorhyncha	none	100
Acanthocephala	thorny-headed worms	300
Bryozoa	moss animals	4000
Brachiopoda	lamp shells	260
Annelida	earthworms and relatives	c.7000
Arthropoda	spiders, insects, crustaceans	1150000
Sipunculoidea	peanut worms	250
Echiuroidea	echiurid worms	60
Pentastomida	tongue worms	70
Tardigrada	water bears	180
Mollusca	molluscs	more than 65000
Chaetognatha	arrow worms	65
Pogonophora	beard worms	c.80
Echinodermata	starfish and relatives	c.5500
Hemichordata	acorn worms and relatives	90
Chordata	chordates	c.2000 plus back-boned animals

This list includes only the major phyla of invertebrates.

inverted comma same as QUOTATION MARK.

invert sugar *Biochem.* a mixture of glucose and fructose, found in many fruits, and formed as a result of the breakdown of sucrose (cane-sugar).

invest *verb* **1** *trans., intrans.* to put (money) into a company or business, eg by buying shares in it, in order to make a profit. **2** (**invest in something**) *colloq.* to buy it: *decided to invest in some new socks.* **3** *trans., intrans.* to devote (time, effort, energy, etc) to something: *invested all their energies in animal welfare.* **4** (**invest someone with something**) to give them the symbols of power, rights, rank, etc officially. See also INVESTITURE. **5** (**invest something in someone**) to place power, rank, a quality or feeling, etc in someone. **6** to clothe or adorn. **7** *Mil.* to besiege (a stronghold). [from Latin *investire*, to clothe]

investigate *verb trans., intrans.* to carry out a thorough, detailed and often official inquiry into or examination of (something or someone). [from Latin *investigare*, to track down]

investigation *noun* the act or process of investigating.

investigative *or* **investigatory** *adj.* relating to or involving investigation.

investigative journalism journalism involving the investigation and exposure of corruption, crime, inefficiency, etc. A notable example was the exposure of the Watergate affair by journalists of the Washington Post in the USA, which ultimately led to the resignation of President Nixon.

investigator *noun* a person who investigates.

investiture *noun* a formal ceremony giving a rank or office to someone. See also INVEST. [from Latin *investitura*]

investment *noun* **1** a sum of money invested. **2** something, such as a business, house, etc in which one invests money, time, effort, etc. **3** the act of investing.

investment bank a US bank handling new share issues, often in a syndicate with others. It may buy all the shares on offer and then resell them to the general public, in effect underwriting the issue. Its function is similar to that of a British merchant bank.

investment company *or* **investment trust** a company which holds a portfolio of shares in other companies, aimed at obtaining a reasonable dividend yield, growth, and balanced risk. Such companies are often of value to inexperienced investors who wish to invest in the stock market.

investment trust an organization which invests money in different companies or financial concerns on behalf of its members.

investor *noun* a person who invests.

inveterate *adj.* **1** *said of a habit, practice, etc* firmly established. **2** *said of a person* firmly fixed in a habit by long practice. [from Latin *inveteratus*, long continued]

inveterately *adv.* in an inveterate way.

invidious *adj.* likely to cause envy, resentment, or indignation, especially by being or seeming to be unfair. [from Latin *invidia*, envy]

invidiously *adv.* in an invidious way.

invidiousness *noun* being invidious.

invigilate *verb trans., intrans. Brit.* to keep watch over people sitting (an examination), especially to prevent cheating. [from Latin *invigilare*, to keep watch over]

invigilation *noun* invigilating.

invigilator *noun* a person who invigilates.

invigorate *verb* to give fresh life, energy, and health to; to strengthen or animate. [from Latin *in*, in + *vigor*, strength]

invigorating *adj.* having the power to invigorate.

invigoration *noun* being invigorated.

invincibility *or* **invincibleness** *noun* being invincible.

invincible *adj.* that cannot be defeated. [from Latin *invincibilis*]

invincibly *adv.* in an invincible way.

inviolability *noun* being inviolable.

inviolable *adj.* that must not be broken or violated; sacred. [from Latin *inviolabilis*]

inviolably *adv.* in an inviolable way.

inviolate *adj.* which has not been broken, violated, or injured. [from Latin *inviolatus*, unhurt]

invisibility *noun* being invisible.

invisible *adj.* **1** not able to be seen. **2** unseen. **3** *Econ.* relating to services (eg insurance, tourism) rather than goods: *invisible earnings / invisible exports.* **4** not shown in regular statements: *invisible assets.* [from Latin *invisibilis*]

◇ Invisibles, such as tourism, shipping, air freight, banking, insurance, and other financial services, make a major contribution to the balance of payments in many countries.

Invisible Man, The 1 a science fiction novel by H G Wells (1897). It recounts the events surrounding a scientist's discovery of how to become invisible. **2** (*Invisible Man*) a novel by Ralph Ellison (1952). It describes the life of an unidentified black man in New York City.

invisibly *adv.* without being seen.

invitation *noun* **1** a request to a person to come or go somewhere, eg to a party, meal, etc. **2** the form such a request takes, either verbally or written on a card. **3** an act of inviting. **4** encouragement; enticement; inducement.

invite — *verb* **1** to request the presence of (someone) at one's house, at a party, etc, especially formally or politely. **2** to ask politely or formally for (eg comments, advice, etc). **3** to bring on or encourage (something unwanted or undesirable). **4** to attract or tempt. — *noun colloq.* an invitation. [from Latin *invitare*]

inviting *adj.* attractive or tempting.

invitingly *adv.* in an inviting way.

in vitro *Biol.*, said of biological techniques or processes performed outside a living organism in an artificial environment created by means of scientific equipment, eg in a test-tube: *in-vitro fertilization.* See also IN VIVO. [Latin, = in glass]

in-vitro fertilization (ABBREV. **IVF**) a technique whereby a human embryo is conceived outside the mother's body. A mature ovum (egg cell) is removed from the ovary of a woman who is unable to conceive normally, and it is placed in a culture medium in a laboratory and fertilized with sperm from the father. After an egg has been fertilized and has divided several times, it is reimplanted in the mother's uterus (womb), and the pregnancy proceeds in the normal manner thereafter.

in vivo *Biol.*, said of biological techniques or processes performed within a living organism. See also IN VITRO. [Latin, = in a living thing]

invocation *noun* **1** an act of invoking. **2** a prayer calling on God, a saint, etc for blessing or help. **3** an opening prayer at the beginning of a public service or sermon. **4** any appeal to supernatural beings, spirits, etc, such as an appeal to a Muse for inspiration at the beginning of a poem. [from Latin *invocatio*]

invocatory *adj.* making an invocation.

invoice — *noun* a list of goods supplied, delivered with the goods and giving details of price and quantity, usually treated as a request for payment. — *verb* **1** to send an invoice to (a customer). **2** to provide an invoice for (goods). [from obsolete *invoyes*, from Old French *envoyer*, to send]

invoke *verb* **1** to make an appeal to (God, some deity, a Muse, authority, etc) for help, support, or inspiration. **2** to appeal to (a law, principle, etc) as an authority or reason for eg one's behaviour. **3** to make an earnest appeal for (help, support, inspiration, etc). **4** to conjure up (a spirit) by reciting a spell. **5** to put (a law, decision, etc) into effect. See also INVOCATION. [from Latin *invocare*]

involuntarily *adv.* in an involuntary way.

involuntary *adj.*, *said of an action, movement, muscle action, etc* done without being controlled by the will; not able to be controlled by the will; unintentional. [from Latin *involuntarius*]

involuntary muscle *Anat.* muscle that is not under conscious control, eg muscle of the heart, blood vessels, stomach, and intestines. — Also called *smooth muscle.*

involve *verb* **1** to require as a necessary part. **2** (**involve someone in something**) to cause them to take part or be implicated in it. **3** to have an effect on. **4** (**involve oneself in something**) to become emotionally concerned in it. **5** to complicate. [from Latin *involvere*, to roll up]

involved *adj.* **1** concerned, implicated. **2** complicated.

involvement *noun* **1** involving. **2** being involved.

invulnerability *noun* being invulnerable.

invulnerable *adj.* that cannot be hurt, damaged, or attacked. [from Latin *invulnerabilis*]

invulnerably *adv.* in an invulnerable way or condition.

inward — *adj.* **1** placed or being within. **2** moving towards the inside. **3** of or relating to the mind or soul. — *adv.* (*also* **inwards**) **1** towards the inside or the centre. **2** into the mind, inner thoughts, or soul. [from Anglo-Saxon *inweard*]

inwardly *adv.* **1** on the inside; internally. **2** in one's thoughts; secretly.

inwards see INWARD.

Inyangani, Mount the highest peak in Zimbabwe, near the Mozambique frontier. HEIGHT 2 592m.

in-your-face *adj. colloq., of a style, production, etc* aggressively assertive; demanding attention.

Io 1 in Greek mythology, the daughter of Inachos of Argos. She was a priestess of Hera, and beloved by Zeus, who turned her into a heifer to allay Hera's jealousy. Hera was not fooled however, and had her watched by hundred-eyed Argus, but she escaped with Hermes' help. She arrived finally in Egypt, where Zeus changed her back into human shape, and she gave birth to Epaphus, ancestor of many peoples. **2** *Astron.* the third largest natural satellite of Jupiter, 3 630km in diameter, and the closest moon to Jupiter. It has a yellow surface covered with sulphur produced by volcanoes.

IOB *abbrev.* Institute of Building.

IOC *abbrev.* International Olympic Committee.

iodide *noun* a chemical compound containing iodine.

iodine *noun* **1** *Chem.* (SYMBOL **I**, ATOMIC NUMBER **53**) a non-metallic element consisting of dark violet crystals that sublime to a violet vapour when heated. It is obtained from Chile saltpetre, seaweed, and seawater, and is used as an antiseptic, in the production of dyes, and as a catalyst and chemical reagent. Silver iodide is used in photography. Iodine is essential for the normal functioning of the thyroid gland. **2** *Medicine* (also **tincture of iodine**) a solution of iodine in ethanol (alcohol), used as an antiseptic. [from Greek *ioeides*, violet-coloured]

iodize *or* **iodise** *verb* to treat with iodine.

IOM *abbrev.* Isle of Man.

ion *noun Chem.* an atom or group of atoms that has acquired a net positive charge as a result of losing one or more electrons, or a net negative charge as a a result of gaining one or more electrons. [from Greek, = going]

-ion *suffix* forming nouns denoting a process, state, result, etc: *completion / contrition\pollution*. See also -ATION. [from French *-ion*]

Iona an island off Mull, W Scotland, the site of a monastery established in 563 by the Irish missionary St Columba and 12 companions to convert the inhabitants of N Britain to Christianity. The monastery flourished until the onset of Viking attacks (c.800), then declined until c.1200, when a Benedictine abbey was founded on the site. The Iona Community (a religious group) was founded in 1938.

ion engine *Engineering* an engine, used to propel spacecraft or satellites, in which the thrust is produced by a stream of ionized (charged) particles.

Ionesco, Eugène (1912–94) French playwright, born in Slatina, Romania. He settled in Paris before World War II and after the success of

La Cantatrice chauve (The Bald Soprano, 1950), he became a prolific writer of one-act plays which came to be seen as typical examples of the Theatre of the Absurd eg *Les Chaises* (The Chairs, 1952). His later, full-length plays centre around a semi-autobiographical figure, Berenger. From 1970 his writing was mainly non-theatrical, including essays, children's stories, and a novel.

ion exchange *Chem.* a chemical reaction in which ions which have the same charge are exchanged between a solution and a porous granular solid, such as a synthetic resin, in contact with the solution. It is used to remove undesirable salts during the processes of water softening and sugar refining, and in desalination plants. It also occurs when soil particles absorb and retain potassium ions from water-soluble fertilizers.

Ionia in antiquity, the central part of the W coast of Asia Minor. The name came from the occupation of the area by Ionian Greeks around the beginning of the first millennium BC. It was the birthplace of Greek philosophy and science.

Ionian Islands, Greek **Iónioi Nesoi** *or* **Eptánisos** POP (1991) 191 000, a region and island group in W Greece, situated in the Ionian Sea, and extending from the Albanian frontier to the Peloponnese. AREA 2 307sq km/890sq mi. The chain of c.40 islands includes Corfu, Cephalonia, and Zacynthus. The islands are mountainous, with fertile plains and valleys. They were under British control from 1815 to 1864. ECONOMY wine, olives, fruit; tourism.

Ionian Sea a body of water forming part of the Mediterranean Sea, lying W of the Greek islands and S of Italy. It is linked to the Adriatic Sea by the Strait of Otranto, and to the Aegean Sea by the Sea of Crete.

Ionic *adj.* denoting an order of classical architecture, characterized by slim and usually fluted shafts and capitals with spiral scrolls known as *volutes*. See also CORINTHIAN, DORIC. [from Greek *Ionikos*]

ionic *adj.* relating to or using ions.

ionic bond *Chem.* a chemical bond formed by the transfer of one or more electrons from one atom to another, resulting in the conversion of electrically neutral atoms to positively and negatively charged ions.

ion implantation *noun Electron.* the introduction of impurities into a semiconductor crystal, in order to modify its electronic properties, by directing a beam of ions at its surface.

ionization *or* **ionisation** *noun Chem.* the formation of ions from atoms as a result of chemical reactions, dissociation of atoms of a molecule in solution, electrolysis, exposure to ionizing radiation (eg alpha particles) or short-wavelength electromagnetic radiation (eg X-rays), or passage through a discharge tube. Very high temperatures can also cause ionization.

ionize *or* **ionise** *verb trans., intrans. Chem.* to produce or cause to produce ions.

ionizer *or* **ioniser** *noun* a device that produces negatively charged ions, considered to relieve headaches, fatigue, and other symptoms said to be caused by the accumulation of positive ions in rooms and buildings where electrical machinery, computers, etc, are in frequent use.

ionizing radiation *Physics* any radiation that can cause ionization (formation of ions).

ionomer *noun Chem.* a thermoplastic polymer which has both organic components (mainly ethylene) and inorganic components (such as sodium, potassium, magnesium, or zinc). Ionomers are tough, resilient, and highly transparent, and are used to make goggles, shields, bottles, refrigerator trays, toys, and electrical parts.

ionosphere *noun Meteorol.* the layer of the Earth's atmosphere that extends from about 50km to about 500km above the Earth's surface. It contains many ions and free electrons produced by the ionizing effects of solar radiation, and it plays an important role in the transmission of radio waves. [from ION + SPHERE]

ionospheric *adj.* relating to the ionosphere.

Ios an island in the Cyclades, Greece, situated in the Aegean Sea, SW of Naxos. AREA 108sq km/42sq mi. The port of Ormos Iou is on the W coast. Homer is said to have died on the island.

iota *noun* **1** the ninth letter of the Greek alphabet (I, ι). **2** a very small amount. [from Greek *iota*]

IOU *noun* (PL. **IOUs, IOU's**) *colloq.* a written and signed note of a debt. [pronunciation of *I owe you*]

IOW *abbrev.* Isle of Wight.

Iowa POP (1990) 2.8m, a state in N central USA, which is divided into 99 counties. It is known as the 'Hawkeye State'. AREA 145 747sq km/56 275sq mi. PHYSICAL DESCRIPTION the Mississippi R follows the E border; the Des Moines R flows SE across the central state before emptying into the Mississippi R; the Big Sioux R forms the border with South Dakota, emptying into the Missouri R, which then follows the Nebraska state border; Ocheyedan Mound (511m) is the highest point; the state consists almost entirely of prairieland with rich soil, but few areas of original grassland remain. HISTORY became part of the USA with the Louisiana Purchase in 1803; became a territory in 1838 and a state in 1846; in the same year it was the 29th state to be admitted to the Union; its capital was Iowa City until 1857; in 1993 the Mississippi flooding caused severe damage. CAPITAL Des Moines. CHIEF TOWNS Cedar Rapids, Davenport, Sioux City, Iowa City. ECONOMY the chief crops are corn and soya beans; over half the corn grown is used for feeding pigs and cattle; Iowa leads the nation in corn and pig production; industry, dominated by food processing and machinery manufacture, also includes chemicals and electrical equipment.

Iowa City POP (1990) 96 000, the seat of Johnson County, E Iowa, USA. It lies on the Iowa R, 40km/25mi S of Cedar Rapids. Founded in 1838, it was capital of Iowa territory from 1839 and then of Iowa state (1846–57).

IPA *abbrev.* International Phonetic Alphabet.

IPCS *abbrev.* Institution of Professional Civil Servants.

ipecacuanha *noun* the dried root of several Latin American plants, used as a purgative or emetic. [from Portuguese *ipecacuanha*, from Tupi (S American Indian language) *ipekaaguene*, from *ipeh*, low + *kaa*, leaves + *guene*, vomit]

Iphigeneia in Greek mythology, the daughter of Agamemnon and Clytemnestra. At the start of the Trojan War, she was demanded as a sacrifice by the goddess Artemis before the Greek fleet would have a favourable wind to sail from Aulis to Troy. In Euripides' plays, she was spared by

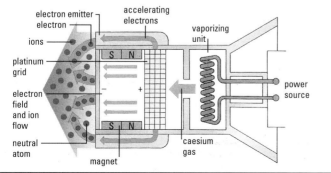

ion engine

Artemis at the last moment, and made a priestess in Tauris (the Crimea).

IPM *abbrev.* Institute of Personnel Management.

Ipoh POP (1980) 301 000, the capital of Perak state, W Peninsular Malaysia. It was originally settled by Chinese miners. The town replaced Taiping as state capital in 1937. NOTABLE FEATURES State Mosque; rock paintings in the limestone caves nearby; Perak Tong and Sam Poh Tong Buddhist temples, 6km/4mi S.

IPPF *abbrev.* International Planned Parenthood Federation.

ipso facto by or because of that very fact; thereby. [Latin, = by the fact itself]

Ipswich, Anglo-Saxon **Gipeswic** POP (1992e) 116 000, the county town of Suffolk, E England. It is a port at the head of the estuary of the R Orwell, 106km/66mi NE of London. Ipswich was a major wool port in the 16c. It was the birthplace of Cardinal Wolsey in c.1475 and the home of Thomas Gainsborough. NOTABLE FEATURES Church of St Mary-le-Tower; Church of St Margaret; Ipswich Museum.

IQ *abbrev.* (PL. **IQs**, **IQ's**) *colloq.* intelligence quotient.

Iqbal, Sir Muhammad (1875–1938) Indian poet and philosopher, born in Sialkot (now in Pakistan). He worked as a lawyer but achieved fame through his poetry, whose mysticism and nationalism caused him to be regarded almost as a prophet by Muslims. His efforts to establish a separate Muslim state were influential in the formation of Pakistan.

Iquique 1 POP (1991e) 152 000, the port capital of Iquique province, N Chile. It is a free port, S of Arica. HISTORY founded in the 16c; partly destroyed by an earthquake in 1877; it was the scene of a naval battle in the War of the Pacific in 1879. NOTABLE FEATURES Naval Museum; Palacio Astoreca (1903). **2** a province in N Chile with Iquique as its capital.

Iquitos POP (1990e) 270 000, the capital of Loreto department, NE Peru, a fast-developing city lying on the W bank of the Amazon, 3 700km/2 300mi from its mouth. The city is accessible only by air and river and is the limit of navigation for ocean vessels. It is the chief town in Peru's jungle region and the centre for oil exploration in Peruvian Amazonia.

Ir *symbol Chem.* iridium.

ir- *prefix* a form of *in-* used before words beginning in *r*: *irrelevant.*

IRA *abbrev.* the Irish Republican Army, an anti-British paramilitary guerrilla force established in 1919 by Irish nationalists to combat British forces in Ireland. In 1969 a major split in its ranks led to the formation of the Provisional IRA alongside the Official IRA. The Official IRA has been virtually inactive since 1972, and generally supports political action to achieve Irish unity. The Provisionals have become the dominant republican force, responsible for shootings and bombings in Northern Ireland, Britain, and W Europe. Targets have mainly been security and military personnel and establishments, although there have been many sectarian killings and attempts to disrupt civilian life. Responsible over the past 25 years for over 1 740 killings, the IRA continued its violence into the 1990s. This was augmented by escalating terrorist activity against Catholics by Loyalist groups. In late 1993 the British government invited the IRA to take part in peace talks, and an attempt at reconciliation was made in the Downing Street Declaration (see ANGLO-IRISH AGREEMENT, SINN FÉIN).

Iran, formerly **Persia** (to 1935), official name **Islamic Republic of Iran**, Persian **Jomhori-e-Islami-e-Iran** POP (1992e) 60m, a republic in SW Asia, divided into 24 provinces. AREA 1 648 000sq km/636 128sq mi. It is bounded N by Armenia, Azerbaijan, Turkmenistan, and the Caspian Sea,

E by Afghanistan and Pakistan, S by the Gulf of Oman and the Arabian Gulf, SW by Iraq, and NW by Turkey. CAPITAL Tehran. CHIEF TOWNS Mashhad, Isfahan, Tabriz, Shiraz, Abadan. TIME ZONE GMT +3.5. Most of the population are of Persian (63%) or Turkic (18%) origin; Islam is the main religion. OFFICIAL LANGUAGE Farsi, with several minority languages spoken. CURRENCY the rial. PHYSICAL DESCRIPTION largely composed of a vast arid central plateau, average elevation of 1 200m, with many salt and sand basins; rimmed by mountain ranges that drop down to narrow coastal lowlands; bounded N by the Elburz Mts, rising to 5 670m at Mt Demavend; the Zagros Mts in the W and S rise to 3 000–4 600m. CLIMATE mainly a desert climate, with annual rainfall below 300mm; average temperatures at Tehran are 2°C (Jan), 29°C (Jul), average annual rainfall is 246mm; the Caspian coastal strip is much wetter (800–2 000mm) than the interior and rain is more widely distributed throughout the year; hot and humid on the shores of the Arabian Gulf; frequent earthquakes. HISTORY an early centre of civilization, dynasties including the Achaemenids and Sassanids; ruled by the Arabs, Turks, and Mongols until the Sasavid Dynasty in the 16c–18c and the Qajar Dynasty in the 19c–20c; a military coup in 1921 led to independence under Reza Shah Pahlavi in 1925; protests against the Shah's regime in the 1970s led to a revolution in 1978; exile of the Shah and proclamation of an Islamic Republic under Ayatollah Khomeini in 1979; occupation of the US embassy in Tehran in 1979–81; the Iran–Iraq War took place from 1980 until 1988; a major earthquake in 1990 killed thousands of people in the NW; several provinces suffered severe flooding in 1993. GOVERNMENT governed by a President, elected for a four-year term, who appoints a Prime Minister and other ministers; the Ayatollah is the appointed religious leader with the authority to protect the constitution; there is a 270-member National Consultative Assembly; since the death of Khomeini in 1989, there has been a political struggle for power. ECONOMY the world's fourth largest oil producer, but production was severely disrupted by the 1978 revolution and the Iran–Iraq War; natural gas, iron ore, copper, manganese, chromite, coal, salt; textiles; sugar refining, food processing; petrochemicals, iron and steel; cement; fertilizers; machinery; traditional handicrafts (especially carpets); one third of the population are involved in agriculture and forestry; wheat, rice, tobacco, barley, sugar beet, cotton, dates, raisins, tea; sheep, goats; silkworms.

Iran

Iran–Contra Affair a major US political scandal (1986). It grew out of efforts made by the Reagan administration to obtain the release of US hostages held in Lebanon by secretly supplying arms to Iran's strongly anti-American government. National Security officials (notably Col Oliver North) had been involved in the diversion of the proceeds of such arms sales to support the anti-government Contra rebels in Nicaragua, even though Congress had banned the supplying of arms to the Contras. Congressional hearings in 1987 centred on the legality of the arms-for-hostages deal and on whether Col North had

acted on his own as the administration claimed, or whether top governement officials, including President Reagan himself, were involved. The issues have not been satisfactorily resolved.

Irangate see IRAN–CONTRA AFFAIR.

Iran Hostage Crisis a crisis that involved the holding of 52 US hostages (1979–81), after the US Embassy in Tehran, Iran, was seized on 4 Nov 1979. The action was approved by the Ayatollah Khomeini who had been angered by the role of the CIA in the overthrow of the Mossadegh government (1953) and by the US training of Shah Muhammad Reza Pahlavi's secret police. The price demanded for the hostages' release was the return of the Shah and all his wealth. UN appeals and President Jimmy Carter's move to freeze all Iranian assets failed to induce Iran to release the hostages; this may have contributed to Carter's defeat by Ronald Reagan in the 1980 election. After 444 days of captivity, the hostages were released, and Iranian assets were unfrozen.

Iranian — *noun* 1 a native or citizen of Iran. 2 a branch of the Indo-European family of languages (see IRANIAN LANGUAGES). — *adj.* relating to the Iranians or their language, history, or culture.

Iranian languages a subgroup of the Indo-Iranian branch of the Indo-European family of languages, spoken in the area of present-day Afghanistan and Iran. The group includes Avestan and Old Persian, with written records dating from the 6c BC, and the modern languages Farsi (modern Persian), Tadzhik, Pashto, Kurdish, and Baluchi.

Iranian Revolution the revolution (1979) in Iran which deposed the Shah (15 Jan) and led to the triumphant return (1 Feb) of the Ayatollah Khomeini (from exile in France). Dr Mehdi Bazargan was appointed Prime Minister (1979–80), although real power remained with Khomeini's 15-man Islamic Revolutionary Council. Revolutionary forces took control of the country, and Khomeini announced the establishment of the Islamic Republic.

Iran–Iraq War, also called **Gulf War** (**1980–8**) although Iraq's Kurdish revolt had ended with a peace agreement with Iran (1975), Iraq still wanted to readjust its borders. Following the Islamic Revolution in Iran, the Iranians accused Baghdad of fomenting demands for autonomy by the Arabs of Iran's Khuzestan province. In addition, Iraq feared Iranian provocation of its own 60 per cent Shiite population. Border fighting broke out (1980), and then Iraqi forces advanced into Iran (22 Sep). A peace was not agreed until 1988, by which time half a million lives on both sides had been lost, and shipping in the Gulf had been seriously threatened. Iraq accepted Iran's terms in Aug 1990.

Iraq, official name **Republic of Iraq**, Arabic **Al Jumhouriya al Iraquia** POP (1992e) 19.3m, a republic in SW Asia, divided into 18 governorates. AREA 434 925sq km/167 881sq mi. It is bounded E by Iran, N by Turkey, NW by Syria, W by Jordan, SW and S by Saudi Arabia, and SE by Kuwait and the Arabian Gulf. CAPITAL Baghdad. CHIEF TOWNS Basra, Kirkuk, Mosul. TIME ZONE GMT +3. The majority of the population are of Arab (79%) or Kurd (16%) origin; Islam is the chief religion. OFFICIAL LANGUAGE Arabic. CURRENCY the dinar. PHYSICAL DESCRIPTION largely comprises the vast alluvial tract of the Tigris–Euphrates lowland (which is equal to ancient Mesopotamia); both rivers are separated in their upper courses by the plain of Al Jazirah, rising to 1 547m; about 190km/118mi from the Arabian Gulf they join to form the navigable Shatt al-Arab; the lowland here has swamp vegetation; mountains in the NE rise to over 3 000m; desert in other areas. CLIMATE mainly arid; summers are very hot and dry; winters are often cold; average temperatures at Baghdad are 10°C in Jan and 35°C in Jul, with an average annual rainfall of

140mm; rainfall is highest in the NE, where the average is 400–600mm. HISTORY part of the Ottoman Empire from the 16c until World War I; captured by British forces in 1916; became a British-mandated territory in 1921; gained independence under the Hashemite Dynasty in 1932; the monarchy was replaced by military rule in 1958; since the 1960s, Kurdish nationalists in the NE have been fighting to establish a separate state; the invasion of Iran in 1980 led to the Iran–Iraq War lasting until 1988; the invasion of Kuwait in 1990 led to UN sanctions, the Gulf War in 1991, and Iraqi withdrawal; tension in the area remains, Iraqi attacks on Kurdish settlements and Shiite refugees continue, and UN sanctions remain in place. GOVERNMENT a President, elected from and by the Revolutionary Command Council, is head of state and appoints the Council of Ministers; Legislative power rests with the National Assembly and the Revolutionary Command Council; the Kurdish regional assembly has various limited powers of legislation. ECONOMY the world's second largest producer of oil, but production was severely disrupted during the Iran–Iraq War and the Gulf War with several oil installations destroyed; natural gas, oil refining, petrochemicals; cement; textiles; dates, cotton, rice, winter wheat, barley, lentils; sheep; cattle; major irrigation schemes under way; rich archaeological remains, especially along the Euphrates Valley; the economy has suffered from trade sanctions first imposed by the UN in 1990.

Iraq

irascibility *noun* being irascible.

irascible *adj.* easily made angry; irritable. [from Latin *irascibilis*, from *ira*, anger]

irascibly *adv.* with an irascible manner.

irate *adj.* very angry; enraged. [from Latin *iratus*, from *ira*, anger]

irately *adv.* furiously, angrily.

irateness *noun* being irate, fury.

Irbid 1 POP (1990e) 315 000, the capital town of Irbid governorate, East Bank, N Jordan, 64km/40mi N of Amman. 2 a governorate of the East Bank, N Jordan, with Irbid as its capital.

ire *noun* anger. [from Latin *ira*]

ireful *adj.* 1 angry. 2 resentful.

Ireland, Latin **Hibernia** an island on the W fringe of Europe, separated from Great Britain by the Irish Sea. Its maximum length is 486km/302mi and its maximum width is 275km/171mi. Since 1921, it has been divided politically into the independent Irish Republic and Northern Ireland, part of the UK. It is known poetically as *Erin*, derived from Strabo's name for the island, *Ierne*; from the 6c until the 13c Ireland was often known as *Scotia*. The name, Ireland, is in widespread use for the Irish Republic.

Irene 1 in Greek mythology, one of the Horae, or 'seasons', a personification of Peace. 2 a female first name. [from Greek *eirene*, peace]

Ireton, Henry (1611–51) English soldier, born in Attenborough, Nottingham. At the outbreak of the Civil War he fought for Parliament, and served at the battles of Edgehill, Naseby, and the

siege of Bristol. Cromwell's son-in-law from 1646, he was an ardent enemy of the king, and signed the warrant for his execution. He accompanied Cromwell to Ireland, and in 1650 became Lord Deputy.

Irgun (Zvai Leumi) the terrorist organization that operated in Palestine during the British Mandate and sought to establish a Jewish state. Formed in 1931 after disagreement with the Haganah and reconstituted in 1937, it engaged in armed conflict with Arabs and the British. Led by Menachem Begin from 1943, Irgun bombed Jerusalem's King David Hotel (1946), hanged two British sergeants (1947), and attacked the Arab village of Deir Yassin (1948), after which it became the nucleus for the Herut Party in Israel. [from Hebrew, = National Military Organization]

Irian Jaya, English **West Irian**, formerly **Dutch New Guinea** POP (1990) 1.6m, a province in Indonesia, comprising the W half of New Guinea and the islands adjacent to it. AREA 421 981sq km/162 885sq mi. It is forested and mountainous with the Pegunungan Maoke Range rising to 5 029m at Jaya Peak. The province became a part of Indonesia in 1963; there is a separatist guerrilla movement. CAPITAL Jayapura. ECONOMY copra, maize, groundnuts; tuna; pepper; gold, oil, coal, phosphate.

iridescence *noun* an iridescent quality.

iridescent *adj.* having many bright rainbow-like colours which seem to shimmer and change constantly. [from Greek *iris*, rainbow]

iridescently *adv.* in an iridescent way.

iridium *noun* Chem. (SYMBOL **Ir**, ATOMIC NUMBER 77) a silvery metal that is resistant to corrosion, and is mainly used in hard alloys with platinum or osmium to make surgical instruments, pen nibs, bearings, electrical contacts, and crucibles. The radioactive isotope iridium-192 is used in radiotherapy to treat cancer. [from Greek *iris*, rainbow, from the colourful appearance of some solutions of its salts]

Iris 1 in Greek mythology, the goddess of the rainbow and messenger of the gods, especially of Zeus and Hera. She is usually portrayed with wings, carrying a herald's staff and a vase. 2 a female first name. [from Greek *iris*, rainbow]

iris *noun* 1 (PL. **irises**, **irides**) a perennial plant of the genus *Iris*, having an underground rhizome or corm, flattened sword-shaped leaves, and large brilliantly coloured flowers consisting of equal numbers of upright and hanging petals. Wild irises (flags) are found in most N temperate regions, and there are also many ornamental varieties. 2 *Anat.* an adjustable pigmented ring of muscle, lying in front of the lens of the eye and surrounding a small circular aperture (the pupil). By contraction or relaxation of its muscle fibres it increases or decreases the size of the pupil, and so controls the amount of light entering the eye. Eye colour is determined by the amount of melanin pigment in the iris. 3 (**iris diaphragm**) a device consisting of a series of thin overlapping crescent-shaped plates surrounding a central circular aperture. By adjustment of the plates the diameter of the aperture can be continuously varied, eg to control the amount of light entering the lens of a camera. [from Greek *iris*, rainbow]

Irish — *adj.* 1 of Ireland, its inhabitants, history, culture, Celtic language, or dialect of English. 2 *colloq.* amusingly contradictory or inconsistent. — *noun* 1 (**the Irish**) the people of Ireland as a group. 2 (*in full* **Irish Gaelic**) the Celtic language of Ireland. 3 whiskey made in Ireland. [from Anglo-Saxon *Iras*, people of Ireland]

Irish coffee coffee served with a dash of Irish whiskey and cream on top.

Irish elk a giant fossil deer that ranged through open woodland from Ireland to Siberia and China during the Pleistocene epoch.

Irish Famine the widespread starvation of Irish peasantry which followed the potato blight (1845–7) that had destroyed the crop. Due to starvation and emigration (to Britain and the USA), the population of Ireland fell by almost 25 per cent between 1845 and 1851. The British government was widely blamed by the emigrants for the scale of disaster.

Irishman *noun* a man who is Irish by birth or descent.

Irish moss an edible red seaweed found in the N Atlantic Ocean, used for making soup.

Irish National Liberation Army (ABBREV. **INLA**) the military wing of the Irish Republican Socialist Party, a small paramilitary group which commits few terrorist attacks, but is noted for the ruthless nature of those it does carry out. Probably created by members of the Official IRA disenchanted with the 1972 ceasefire, it was responsible for the killing of the Conservative MP Airey Neave (Mar 1979).

Irish Republic *or* **Ireland**, Irish **Éire**, official name **Republic of Ireland** POP (1992e) 3.5m, a republic occupying S, central, and NW Ireland, divided into 26 counties grouped into the four provinces of Ulster, Munster, Leinster, and Connacht. AREA 70 282sq km/27 129sq mi. It is separated from Great Britain by the Irish Sea and St George's Channel, and is bounded in the NE by Northern Ireland, part of the UK. CAPITAL Dublin. CHIEF TOWNS Cork, Limerick, Waterford, Galway, Drogheda, Dundalk, Sligo. TIME ZONE GMT. The population is largely Celtic; Roman Catholicism is the most common religion. OFFICIAL LANGUAGES English, Irish Gaelic; the Gaelic-speaking areas, mostly in the W, are known as the *Gaeltacht*. CURRENCY the Irish pound (*punt*). PHYSICAL DESCRIPTION the mountainous landscapes in the W are part of the Caledonian system of Scandinavia and Scotland, with quartzite peaks weathered into conical mountains such as Croagh Patrick (765m); a younger mountain system in the S, rising W towards Macgillycuddy's Reeks, creates a landscape of ridges and valleys; the lowlands in the E are drained by slow-moving rivers such as the Shannon, Liffey, and Slaney; there are long E–W valleys in the S. CLIMATE mild and equable, with few extremes of temperature; rainfall is heaviest in the W, often over 3 000mm; it is drier in the E, the Dublin annual average being 785mm. HISTORY occupied by Goidelic-speaking Celts during the Iron Age; a high kingship was established c.AD 200, its capital being at Tara (Meath); following conversion to Christianity by St Patrick in the 5c, Ireland became a centre of learning and missionary activity; the SE was attacked by Vikings from c.800; Henry II of England declared himself Lord of Ireland in 1171, but English influence was restricted to the area round Dublin (the Pale); Henry VIII took the title 'King of Ireland' in 1542; a Catholic rebellion was suppressed by the barbarous campaign of Oliver Cromwell (1649–50) during the English Civil War; supporters of the deposed Catholic King James II were defeated by William III at the battle of the Boyne (1690); following a century of suppression, the struggle for

Ireland

Irish freedom developed in the 18c–19c, including such revolutionary movements as Wolfe Tone's United Irishmen (1796–8), and later Young Ireland (1848) and the Fenians (1866–7); the Act of Union, uniting Ireland and Britain, was passed in 1801; the Catholic Relief Act (1829) enabled Catholics to sit in Parliament; Land Acts (1870–1903) attacked Irish poverty; prior to these acts, famine in 1846 had reduced the population by half; two Home Rule Bills were introduced by Gladstone (1886, 1893); a third Home Rule Bill was passed in 1914, but never came into effect because of World War I; in 1916 there was an armed rebellion against British rule; a republic was proclaimed by Sinn Féin in 1919; a partition proposed by Britain in 1920 was largely ignored by the Irish Republic; a treaty signed in 1921 gave Ireland dominion status, subject to the right of Northern Ireland to opt out; this right was exercised, and a frontier was agreed in 1925; it was renamed Éire in 1937; all constitutional links between the Irish Republic and the UK were severed by 1948; in 1949 it left the Commonwealth; since 1973 the Irish Republic has been a member of the EC. GOVERNMENT a President (head of state) is elected for seven years; the National Parliament (*Oireachtas*) includes a House of Representatives (*Dáil Éireann*) of 166 elected members, and a 60-member Senate (*Seanad Éireann*); a Prime Minister is head of government. ECONOMY two thirds of the country is covered by improved agricultural land, sheep and cattle grazing on much of the remainder; mainly mixed pastoral farming with some arable cropping; forestry has been developed since the 1950s; fishing is important; manufacturing includes metals, food, drink, tobacco, and textiles; there has been recent growth in light engineering, synthetic fibres, electronics, pharmaceuticals, and plastics; hydroelectricity is generated on the main rivers; there are several peat-fired power stations, and the Kinsale natural gas field near Cork; tourism.

Irish Republican Army see IRA.

Irish Republican Socialist Party a political party formed (1974) largely as a breakaway group from the official Sinn Féin, which disagreed with its political strategy and the ceasefire. Its most prominent member was Bernadette McAliskey. Following a feud with the Official IRA in the 1970s, it moved closer to the Provisional Sinn Féin.

Irish Sea the arm of the Atlantic Ocean between Ireland and Great Britain. AREA 103 600sq km/39 990sq mi; 210km/130mi long by 225km/140mi at its widest point. It is linked to the Atlantic Ocean by the North Channel, St George's Channel, and the Celtic Sea.

Irish stew a stew made from mutton, potatoes, and onions.

Irish wolfhound the tallest domestic breed of dog, a very old breed, used for hunting by the Celts, and having a long, usually grey, coat, and soft ears.

Irishwoman *noun* a woman who is Irish by birth or descent.

irk *verb* to annoy or irritate, especially persistently. [from Middle English *irken*]

irksome *adj.* annoying, irritating, or boring.

irksomely *adv.* in an irksome way.

Irkutsk 1 POP (1991e) 641 000, the capital of Irkutsk oblast, S Siberia, Russia, lying at the confluence of the Irkut and Angara rivers. Founded as a fortress in 1661, the city is one of the larger economic centres in Siberia, specializing in fur-purchasing and gold transshipment. 2 an oblast in S Siberia, Russia, with the city of Irkutsk as its capital.

iron — *noun* 1 (SYMBOL **Fe**, ATOMIC NUMBER **26**) a strong hard silvery-white metallic element that is naturally magnetic, and is thought to be the main component of the Earth's core. 2 a tool, weapon, or other implement made of iron. 3 a

triangular, flat-bottomed, now usually electrical, household tool used for smoothing the creases out of and pressing clothes. 4 a golf club with an angled iron head. 5 (*in full* **branding-iron**) a metal instrument with a long handle and shaped end which can be heated and used to mark animals for identification. 6 great physical or mental strength. 7 (**irons**) chains; fetters. 8 (**irons**) supports for a weak or lame leg or legs. — *adj.* 1 made of iron. 2 like iron, especially in being very strong, inflexible, unyielding, etc. — *verb* (**ironed, ironing**) 1 to smooth the creases out of or press (eg clothes) with an iron. 2 (*also* **iron something out**) to remove creases in it by ironing. 3 *intrans. said of clothing or fabric* to react or respond in the way specified to being ironed: *shiny material which irons badly.*

— **iron something out** to remove or put right difficulties, problems, etc so that progress becomes easier.

have several *or* **too many irons in the fire** to be have several or too many commitments at the same time.

strike while the iron is hot to act while the situation is to one's advantage.

[from Anglo-Saxon *isen*]

◇ Iron is mainly obtained from ores such as haematite and magnetite. It is malleable and ductile, a good conductor of heat and electricity, and chemically fairly reactive, forming compounds with non-metallic elements, and rusting readily in moist air to produce iron oxide. It is extracted by heating iron ore, coke, and limestone in a blast furnace to yield *pig iron*, which can then be processed further to give wrought iron or cast iron, but in most cases is alloyed with carbon and other elements to make different types of steel. Iron compounds are used as pigments in paints, dyes, and inks. Iron is an important trace element in plants and animals, and is a component of the respiratory pigment haemoglobin in the red blood cells of vertebrates. Dietary deficiency of iron is one cause of anaemia.

Iron Age the period in history following the Bronze Age, when weapons and tools were made of iron, from about 1000 BC.

Ironbridge a historic industrial town in the Severn River gorge, 21km/13mi SE of Shrewsbury, Shropshire, regarded as the birthplace of England's Industrial Revolution. In 1709 iron was first smelted with coke nearby at Coalbrookdale, and in 1778–9 Europe's first iron bridge was cast and erected here. Since 1968 the bridge has been the focus of an open-air museum. Ironbridge Gorge is a World Heritage site.

ironclad — *adj.* covered with protective iron plates. — *noun Hist.* a 19c warship covered with protective iron plates.

Iron Cross a military decoration (an iron cross edged with silver) instituted in Prussia in 1813 and reinstated by Hitler as a German medal in 1939. The ribbon is black, white, and gold.

Iron Curtain from 1945 to 1989, a notional barrier between countries in W Europe and the communist countries of E Europe, which hindered trade and communications.

◇ The term was first used by Nazi propaganda minister Goebbels in 1943, and became widely known after Winston Churchill used it in a speech in 1946.

iron-grey *adj.* dark grey.

iron hand see VELVET GLOVE.

ironic *or* **ironical** *adj.* 1 containing, characterized by, or expressing irony. 2 *said of a person* given to frequent use of irony.

ironically *adv.* in an ironic way.

ironing *noun* clothes and household linen, etc which need to be or have just been ironed.

ironing board a collapsible, narrow wooden or metal table with a thick fitted cover, used for ironing clothes.

iron lung an apparatus consisting of a long metal case which covers the body up to the neck and which by means of rhythmically varying air pressure helps the person in it to breathe.

ironmaster *noun* the owner of an ironworks.

ironmonger *noun Brit.* a person who sells articles made of metal, eg tools, locks, etc and other household hardware.

ironmongery *noun* (PL. **ironmongeries**) *Brit.* the business of, or the goods sold by, an ironmonger.

iron pyrites see PYRITE.

iron rations small quantities of food with a high energy value, carried for emergencies by climbers, walkers, military personnel, etc.

Irons, Jeremy (John) (1948–) English film actor, born in Cowes, Isle of Wight. His début film *Nijinsky* (1980) was followed by success in the television series *Brideshead Revisited* (1981) and in the film *The French Lieutenant's Woman* (1981). Other films include *Betrayal* (1983), *The Mission* (1986), *Reversal of Fortune* (1990), for which he won an Oscar, and *The House of the Spirits* (1993).

Ironside, William Edmund Ironside, 1st Baron (1880–1959) Scottish soldier, born in Ironside, Aberdeenshire. He served as a secret agent disguised as a railwayman in the Boer War, held several staff appointments in World War I, and then commanded the Archangel expedition against the Bolsheviks (1918). He was Chief of the Imperial General Staff at the outbreak of World War II, and as field marshal commanded the Home Defence Forces (1940). The 'Ironsides', fast light-armoured vehicles, were named after him.

Ironsides *pl. noun Hist.* Oliver Cromwell's cavalry during the English Civil War (1642–9).

ironstone *noun* 1 *Geol.* a sedimentary rock, at least 15 per cent of which comprises iron minerals such as haematite and pyrite. 2 hard, white earthenware.

ironware *noun* things made of iron, especially household hardware.

ironwork *noun* 1 things made of iron, especially iron which has been specially shaped for decoration, such as gates and railings. 2 (**ironworks**) a factory where iron is smelted and made into goods.

irony *noun* (PL. **ironies**) 1 a linguistic device or form of humour that takes its effect from stating or implying the opposite of what is the case or what is intended; eg *you have done well* might be used to refer to someone who has done badly. 2 a dramatic device by which information is given to the audience that is not known to all the participants in the drama, or in which the same words are meant to convey different meanings to the audience and to other participants; eg the fact that one of the characters being discussed in the drama is in fact dead. 3 awkward or perverse circumstances applying to a situation that is in itself satisfactory or desirable. [from Greek *eironeia, dissimulation*]

◇ The term was originally applied to the Socratic method of discussion a subject by claiming ignorance of it (*Socratic irony*). As a mode of literary expression, irony may be extremely subtle and complex, involving not only awareness of the ambiguity of language, but also of the incongruity between actions and their results, or between appearance and reality.

Iroquois a Native American people of the NE region, concentrated in the Great Lakes area. They lived in longhouse villages; the women farmed, and the men hunted, traded, and defended the communities from attack. They fought many wars with their neighbours, enslaving captives or absorbing them into the community. Five (and after 1772, six) of their tribes formed the Iroquois League in the 16c (see

Iroquois Confederacy). The present-day population is c.21 500.

Iroquois Confederacy, also called **Iroquois League**, or **Six Nations** a confederation of Iroquois tribes during the 17c–18c in N New York State, consisting of the Mohawk, Oneida, Onondaga, Cayuga, and Seneca, later joined by the Tuscarora, united largely for control of the fur trade and war. They numbered almost 16 000 and dominated the area, but the league broke up during the American Revolution when the tribes took sides. Most of the Iroquois now live in upstate New York, although some live on reservations elsewhere in the USA and Canada.

irradiate *verb* **1** to expose a part of the body to electromagnetic radiation or a radioactive source for diagnostic or therapeutic purposes. **2** to preserve food by exposing it to electromagnetic radiation or a radioactive source in order to destroy bacteria and other micro-organisms. **3** to shed light on; to light up. **4** to make bright or clear intellectually or spiritually. [from Latin *irradiare*]

irradiation *noun* **1** *Medicine* exposure of part of the body to electromagnetic radiation, eg X-rays, or a radioactive source, for diagnostic or therapeutic purposes, eg the use of certain radioactive isotopes to treat cancerous tumours. **2** *Optics* an optical illusion that causes bright objects to appear larger than their actual size when viewed against a dark background. It is a result of spreading of excitation of the retina. **3** a highly effective method of preserving food by exposing it to either ultraviolet radiation, which sterilizes the food surface, or ionizing radiation from radioactive isotopes, which destroys micro-organisms. Food preserved in this way does not become radioactive, but some vitamins, eg vitamin C, are destroyed. **4** the use of microwaves (high-energy electromagnetic radiation) to heat food.

irrational — *adj.* **1** not the result of clear, logical thought. **2** not able to think logically and clearly. **3** *Maths.*, said of a root, expression, etc involving irrational numbers. — *noun* an irrational number. [from Latin *irrationalis*]

irrationality *noun* being irrational.

irrationally *adv.* in an irrational way.

irrational number *Maths.* a real number that cannot be expressed as a fraction in the form m/n, where m and n are integers. Irrational numbers can be expressed to any degree of accuracy, but their exact value can never be calculated, eg π (the ratio of the circumference of a circle to its diameter, equal to approximately 3.141592...), and surds such as $\sqrt{2}$.

Irrawaddy, River a major river dissecting Burma (Myanma) N–S, formed in Kachin state in the N of the country by the meeting of the Mali Hka and Nmai Hka. It is c.1 600km/1 000mi long and is navigable to Bhamo (1 300km/800mi inland). The river flows S through gorges, then W and S to form a delta beginning 290km/180mi from the sea. It empties into the Andaman Sea in a broad front of tidal forests spreading for 260km/160mi. The E arm of the delta is linked to Rangoon by canal. The chief tributary is the R Chindwin.

irreconcilability *noun* being irreconcilable.

irreconcilable *adj.* **1** not agreeing or able to be brought into agreement; inconsistent; incompatible. **2** hostile and opposed; unwilling to be friendly.

irreconcilably *adv.* so as to be irreconcilable.

irrecoverable *adj.* not able to be recovered.

irrecoverably *adv.* so as to be irrecoverable.

irredeemable *adj.* **1** *said of a person* too evil to be saved; beyond help. **2** incapable of being recovered, repaired, or cured. **3** *said of shares, etc* which the issuing company does not have the right to buy back from the shareholder for the

sum originally paid. **4** *said of paper money* which cannot be exchanged for coin.

irredeemably *adv.* so as to be irredeemable.

irredentism *noun* the policy or activities of the irredentists.

irredentist *noun* a person, especially in 19c Italy, who is in favour of his or her country recovering territory which belonged to it in the past. [from Italian *Italia irredenta*, unredeemed Italy]

irreducible *adj.* **1** that cannot be reduced or made simpler. **2** that cannot be brought from one state into another, usually desired, state.

irreducibly *adv.* so as to be irreducible.

irrefutable *adj.* not able to be denied or proved false. [from Latin *irrefutabilis*]

irrefutably *adv.* in an irrefutable way.

irregular — *adj.* **1** not happening or occurring at regular or equal intervals. **2** not smooth, even, or balanced. **3** not conforming to rules, custom, accepted or normal behaviour, or to routine. **4** *Grammar, said of a word, especially a verb or noun* not changing its form (eg to show tenses or plurals) according to the usual patterns in the language. **5** *said of troops* not belonging to the regular army. — *noun* an irregular soldier. [from Latin *irregularis*]

irregularity *noun* (PL. **irregularities**) **1** being irregular. **2** an act or behaviour not conforming to expected standards. **3** a bump or patch of roughness on an otherwise smooth surface.

irregularly *adv.* in an irregular way.

irrelevance or **irrelevancy** *noun* (PL. **irrelevancies**) *noun* being irrelevant, lack of relevance.

irrelevant *adj.* not connected with or applying to the subject in hand; not relevant.

irrelevantly *adv.* in an irrelevant way.

irreligion *noun* **1** lack of religion. **2** lack of respect for or opposition or hostility towards religion.

irreligious *adj.* **1** lacking a religion. **2** lacking in respect for or hostile or opposed to religion. [from Latin *irreligiosus*]

irremediable *adj.* which cannot be made better, cured, or corrected. [from Latin *irremediabilis*]

irremediably *adv.* so as to be irremediable.

irremovable *adj.* not able to be removed.

irremovably *adv.* so as to be irremovable, permanently.

irreparability *noun* being irreparable.

irreparable *adj.* not able to be restored or put right. [from Latin *irreparabilis*]

irreparably *adv.* so as to be irreparable.

irreplaceable *adj.* not able to be replaced, especially because too rare or valuable.

irreplaceably *adv.* so as to be irreplaceable.

irrepressibility *noun* being irrepressible.

irrepressible *adj.* not able to be controlled, restrained, or repressed, especially because of being too lively and full of energy or strength.

irrepressibly *adv.* in an irrepressible way.

irreproachable *adj., said especially of behaviour* free from faults; blameless.

irreproachably *adv.* in an irreproachable way.

irresistibility or **irresistibleness** *noun* being irresistible.

irresistible *adj.* too strong, tempting, or attractive to be resisted; overpowering. [from Latin *irresistibilis*]

irresistibly *adv.* in an irresistible way.

irresolute *adj.* hesitating or doubtful; not able to take firm decisions; showing that no firm decision has been taken.

irresolutely *adv.* in an irresolute way.

irresoluteness or **irresolution** *noun* being irresolute.

irrespective *adj.* (**irrespective of something**) without considering or taking it into account.

irresponsibility *noun* **1** being irresponsible. **2** lack of responsibility.

irresponsible *adj.* **1** done without or showing no concern for the consequences; reckless; careless. **2** not able to bear responsibility; not reliable or trustworthy.

irresponsibly *adv.* in an irresponsible way.

irretrievable *adj.* not able to be recovered or put right.

irretrievably *adv.* so as to be irretrievable.

irreverence *noun* **1** lack of reverence, disrespect. **2** a disrespectful act or remark.

irreverent *adj.* lacking respect or reverence (eg for things considered sacred, or important people). [from Latin *irreverentia*]

irreverently *adv.* in an irreverent way.

irreversible *adj.* not able to be changed back to a former or original state; permanent.

irreversible reaction *Chem.* a chemical reaction which takes place in one direction only, and therefore proceeds to completion.

irreversibly *adv.* so as to be irreversible.

irrevocability *noun* being irrevocable.

irrevocable *adj.* that cannot be changed, stopped, or undone. [from Latin *irrevocabilis*]

irrevocably *adv.* in an irrevocable way.

irrigable *adj.* capable of being irrigated.

irrigate *verb* **1** *said of a river, etc* to provide (land) with a supply of water. **2** to supply water to (agricultural land) by channels or other artificial means. **3** *Medicine* to wash out (the eye, or a wound, body cavity, or hollow organ, eg the colon), with a continuous flow of water or antiseptic solution. [from Latin *irrigare*]

irrigation *noun* the supply of water to agricultural land by artificial means, such as channels, dams, or sprinklers, especially to enable crops to be grown in dry regions.

irritability or **irritableness** *noun* being irritable.

irritable *adj.* **1** easily annoyed, angered, or excited. **2** extremely or excessively sensitive. **3** *Biol.* denoting a living organism that is capable of responding to an external stimulus, such as light, heat, or touch.

irritable bowel syndrome *Medicine* a condition in which the mucous membrane lining the colon becomes inflamed, causing abdominal pain, with constipation or diarrhoea, in otherwise healthy individuals. Its cause is unknown, but the disease is often associated with stress and anxiety. Treatment is based on a change of diet and removal of the cause of anxiety.

irritably *adv.* in an irritable way.

irritant — *noun* **1** any chemical, physical, or biological agent that causes irritation of a tissue, especially inflammation of the skin or eyes, eg nettles. **2** something that causes physical or mental irritation. — *adj.* irritating.

irritate *verb* **1** to make angry or annoyed. **2** to make (part of the body, an organ, etc) sore and swollen or itchy. **3** *Biol.* to stimulate (eg an organ) to respond. [from Latin *irritare*]

irritating *adj.* that irritates.

irritatingly *adv.* in an irritating way.

irritation *noun* **1** something that irritates. **2** irritating. **3** being irritated.

irrupt *verb intrans.* (**irrupt into a place**) to burst into it or enter it suddenly with speed and violence. [from Latin *irrumpere*]

irruption *noun* entering violently, violent entry.

irruptive *adj.* **1** irrupting or tending to irrupt. **2** relating to or causing irruption.

IRS *abbrev.* Internal Revenue Service (USA).

Irtysh, River the chief tributary of the R Ob, mainly in Kazakhstan and Siberia, Russia, length 4 248km/2 640mi. Rising in N China on the W slopes of the Mongolian Altai Mts, it flows W to enter L Zaysan, then generally NW to join the R Ob at Khanty Mansiysk.

Irvine, Andy (Andrew Robertson) (1951–) Scottish rugby player, born in Edinburgh. A fullback, he played club rugby for Heriot's Former Pupils, and played for Scotland 51 times. He toured with the British Lions in 1974, 1977, and 1980, and during his international career he scored a world record total of 301 points for Scotland and the Lions.

Irving, Sir Henry, originally **John Henry Brodribb** (1838–1905) English actor and theatre manager, born in Keinton-Mandeville, Somerset. He went on stage in 1856, developing a reputation as a great English actor. He had an acclaimed theatrical partnership (1878–1902) with Ellen Terry and was the first actor to receive a knighthood (1895).

Irving, Washington (1783–1859) US man of letters, born in New York City. He began writing in 1807, lived largely in Europe (1815–32), and was later appointed Ambassador to Spain (1842–6). Under the pseudonym of Geoffrey Crayon he wrote *The Sketch Book* (1819–20), a miscellany which includes the tales 'Rip Van Winkle' and 'The Legend of Sleepy Hollow'.

is see BE.

Isaac 1 a biblical character, son of Abraham and Sarah. He was nearly sacrificed by Abraham at God's command (Genesis 22) but survived for God's promises to Abraham to continue through his descendants. Rebecca gave birth to his sons Esau and Jacob, and the latter deceived his blind father into blessing him instead of Esau (Genesis 27). **2** a male first name, most common among Jews.

Isaacs, Alick (1921–67) Scottish biologist, born in Glasgow. He joined the virology division of the National Institute for Research in London (1950), and in 1957 isolated a substance now known as interferon; this protein is produced as part of the body's response to a viral infection, and has been shown to be of therapeutic use in some viral diseases and several forms of cancer.

Isabella I (of Castile), also called **Isabella the Catholic** (1451–1504) Queen of Castile (1474–1504), the daughter of John II, King of Castile and Leon. In 1469 she married Ferdinand V of Aragon, with whom she ruled jointly from 1479. During her reign, the Inquisition was introduced (1478), the reconquest of Granada completed (1482–92), and the Jews expelled (1492), and she sponsored the voyage of Christopher Columbus to the New World.

Isabella the virginal heroine of Shakespeare's *Measure for Measure*, who refuses to compromise her chastity in pleading for her brother's life.

Isabella of France (1292–1358) daughter of Philip IV of France. In 1308 she married Edward II of England but then became the mistress of Roger Mortimer, with whom she overthrew and murdered the King (1327). Her son, Edward III, had Mortimer executed in 1330, and Isabella was sent into retirement.

Isabella, or The Pot of Basil a narrative poem by John Keats (1820). It is a romance based on Boccaccio's *Decameron*.

Isaiah, Hebrew **Jeshaiah** (8c BC) Old Testament prophet, son of Amoz. A citizen of Jerusa-lem, he began to prophesy c.747 BC, and wielded much influence in the kingdom of Judah until the Assyrian invasion of 701 BC. According to tradition, he was martyred.

Isaiah, Book of *or* **Isaias** a major prophetic work in the Hebrew Bible and Old Testament, ostensibly from the prophet Isaiah.

ISBN *abbrev.* International Standard Book Number, a system of 10-digit numbers allocated individually to books on publication since 1971.

ischaemia *or* **ischemia** *noun Medicine* an inadequate flow of blood to a part of the body, caused by blockage or constriction of a blood vessel. [from Greek *ischein*, restrain + *haima*, blood]

-ise see -IZE.

Isenheim Altar an altarpiece by Matthias Grünewald (completed c.1516, now in Colmar Museum, France). It is a series of paintings depicting scenes from the New Testament and the life of St Anthony.

Isfahan *or* **Esfahan** *or* **Aspadana 1** POP (1990e) 1.5m, the third-largest city in Iran and the capital of Isfahan district in Isfahan province. It is situated in the W central area of the country, on the R Zaindeh, 336km/209mi S of Teheran. NOTABLE FEATURES Lutfullah Mosque, Royal Mosque (17c); Ali Kapu Gate; Chihil Satun; Jolfa Cathedral. **2** a mountainous province in central Iran with Isfahan as its capital.

-ish *suffix* forming adjectives meaning **1** slightly; fairly; having a trace of: *reddish / autumnish*. **2** like; having the qualities of: *childish*. **3** having as a nationality: *Swedish*. **4** approximately; about; roughly: *fiftyish*. [from Anglo-Saxon *-isc*]

Isherwood, Christopher (William Bradshaw) (1904–86) English novelist, who was born in Disley, Cheshire. He collaborated with W H Auden in three prose-verse plays with political overtones, travelled in China with him in 1938, and wrote *Journey to a War* (1939). In 1940 he went to California as a Hollywood scriptwriter, and took US citizenship in 1946. His best-known works, *Mr Norris Changes Trains* (1935) and *Goodbye to Berlin* (1939), were based on his experiences as an English tutor (1930–3) in the decadence of post-slump Berlin. These stories were adapted into a play, *I am a Camera*, and later inspired *Cabaret* (musical, 1966; film, 1972).

Ishmael a biblical character, the son of Abraham and Hagar (his wife Sarah's maid). After the birth of Isaac, Ishmael and his mother were expelled into the desert from Abraham's household. Purported to have fathered 12 princes, he is considered the ancestor of the Bedouin tribes of the Palestinian deserts (the Ishmaelites). Muhammad considered Ishmael and Abraham to be ancestors of the Arabs, and therefore associated with the construction of the Kaba at Mecca.

Ishmael the narrator, and sole survivor of the shipwreck, in Herman Melville's *Moby Dick*.

Ishtar, also called **Astarte** in Mesopotamian religion, the mother goddess of love and war, later the goddess of love, identified with the planet Venus. She travelled to the Underworld to rescue her lover Tammuz, an event commemorated in annual ceremonies.

Isidore of Seville *or* **Isidorus Hispalensis, St** (c.560–636) Spanish prelate and scholar, born in Seville or Carthagena. A Doctor of the Church, and the last of the Latin Fathers of the Church, he was Archbishop of Seville in c.600, and his episcopate included the Councils at Seville (618 or 619) and Toledo (633). A voluminous writer, he is best known for his vast encyclopedia of knowledge, *Etymologiae*. He was canonized in 1598 and his feast day is 4 Apr.

isinglass *noun* **1** the purest form of animal gelatine, made from the dried swim bladders of certain fish, eg sturgeon. It has strong adhesive properties, and is used in glues, cements, and printing inks. **2** thin transparent sheets of mica used in furnace and stove doors. [from Old Dutch *huizenblas*, sturgeon's bladder]

Isis in Egyptian religion, a goddess and protector, the wife of Osiris and mother of Horus. She represented the rich plains of Egypt made fruitful by the flooding of the Nile (represented by Osiris) and was sometimes portrayed crowned with horns and the Sun's disc. In Hellenistic and Roman times, she was a central figure in mystery religions, identified with Demeter, Hera, and Selene, and was associated with magical beliefs.

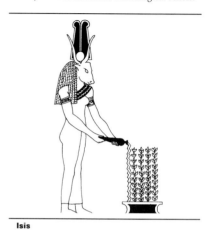

Isis

ISIS *abbrev.* Independent Schools Information Service.

Isla a Scottish female first name. [probably after the island *Islay*]

Islam the religion that originated in Arabia during the 7c AD through the prophet Muhammad. Followers of Islam are known as Muslims, or Moslems, and their religion embraces every aspect of life. They believe that individuals, societies, and governments should all be obedient to the will of God as it is set forth in the Koran, which they regard as the Word of God revealed to his Messenger, Muhammad. On the Day of Resurrection they will be judged and those who have obeyed God's commandments will dwell for ever in paradise, but those who have sinned against God and have not repented will be condemned eternally to the fires of hell. Since the beginning of creation God has sent prophets, including Moses and Jesus (whose divinity Islam does not recognize). There are five essential religious duties known as the 'Pillars of Islam'. One: the *shahada* (profession of faith) is the sincere recitation of the two-fold creed, 'There is no god but God' and 'Muhammad is the Messenger of God'. Two: the *salat* (formal prayer) must be performed at fixed hours five times a day while facing towards the holy city of Mecca. Three: alms-giving through the payment of *zakat* ('purification') is regarded primarily as an act of worship, and is the duty of sharing one's wealth out of gratitude for God's favour, according to the uses laid down in the Koran. Four: there is a duty to fast (*saum*) during the hours of daylight of the month of Ramadan. Five: the *Hajj* or pilgrimage to Mecca is to be performed if at all possible at least once during one's lifetime. *Shari'a* is the sacred law of Islam, and applies to all aspects of life, not just religious practices. It describes the Islamic way of life, and prescribes the way for a Muslim to fulfil the commands of God and reach heaven. There is an annual cycle of festivals, including Hijra, the beginning of the Islamic year, and Ramadan. There is no organized priesthood, but great respect is accorded the Hashim family, descendants of Muhammad, and other publicly acknowledged holy men, scholars, and teachers, such as mullahs and ayatollahs. There are two basic groups within Islam. Sunni Muslims are in the majority, and they recognize the first four caliphs as Muhammad's legitimate successors. The Shiites comprise the largest minority group, and regard the imam as the principal religious authority. There are a number of subsects, including the Ismailis (one group of which, the Nizaris, regard the Aga Khan as their imam), and the Wahhabis, a reform movement begun in the 18c. [from Arabic *múslim*, from *sálma*, to submit (to the will of God)]

Islamic Festivals

1 Muharram	New Year's Day; starts on the day which celebrates Muhammad's departure from Mecca to Medina in AD 622.
12 Rabi I	Birthday of Muhammad (Mawlid al-Nabi) AD 572; celebrated throughout month of Rabi I.
27 Rajab	'Night of Ascent' (Laylat al-Miraj) of Muhammad to Heaven.
1 Ramadan	Beginning of month of fasting during daylight hours.
27 Ramadan	'Night of Power' (Laylat al-Qadr); sending down of the Koran to Muhammad.
1 Shawwal	'Feast of breaking the Fast' (Id al-Fitr): marks the end of Ramadan.
8–13 Dhu-I-Hijja	Annual pilgrimage ceremonies at and around Mecca; month during which the great pilgrimage (Hajj) should be made.
10 Dhu-I-Hijja	Feast of the Sacrifice (Id al-Adha).

Islamabad POP (1990e) 537 000, the capital city of Pakistan, on the R Jhelum. It is a modern planned city, built since 1961. Lying on an upper tributary of the R Jhelum, it is the head of navigation for larger vessels in the Vale of Kashmir. NOTABLE FEATURES Shrine of Bari Imam; Museum of Folk and Traditional Heritage.

Islamic *adj.* relating to Islam, Muslim.

Islamicist *adj.* a person who studies Islam, Islamic law or Islamic culture.

Islamicize *or* **Islamicise** *verb* to Islamize.

Islamization *or* **Islamicization** *noun* the process of making Islamic.

Islamize *or* **Islamise** *verb* to cause to become a follower of or conform to Islam.

island *noun* 1 a piece of land completely surrounded by water. 2 anything which is like an island, especially in being isolated or detached. 3 (*in full* **traffic island**) a small raised traffic-free area in the middle of a street on which people may stand when crossing the road. [from Anglo-Saxon *iegland*, with the *s* from Old French *isle*]

island arc *Geol.* an arc-shaped (curved) chain of oceanic islands, eg the islands of Japan, that usually contain active volcanoes. The side of the islands facing the ocean is convex in shape, and often associated with deep ocean trenches.

islander *noun* a person who lives on an island.

isle *noun* an island, especially a small one. [from Old French *isle*]

Isle of Man see MAN, ISLE OF.

Isle of Wight see WIGHT, ISLE OF.

islet *noun* 1 a small island. 2 a small area of tissue which has a different nature and structure to the tissue surrounding it.

islets of Langerhans *Anat.* in vertebrates, small groups of specialized cells scattered throughout the pancreas. They control the level of glucose (sugar) in the blood by secreting the hormones insulin (which decreases the amount of glucose) and glucagon (which increases it). [named after the German anatomist Paul Langerhans who described them in 1869]

ism *noun colloq.* usually. *derog.* a distinctive and formal set of ideas, principles, or beliefs. [from -ISM, regarded as a separate word]

-ism *suffix* forming nouns meaning 1 a formal set of beliefs, ideas, principles, etc: *feminism*. 2 a quality or state: *heroism*. 3 an activity or practice,

or its result: *criticism*. 4 discrimination or prejudice on the grounds of: *ageism*. 5 an illness caused by, causing resemblance to, or named after (something or someone stated): *alcoholism / dwarfism*. 6 a characteristic of (a specified language or type of language): *regionalism*. [from Greek *-ismos* or *-isma*]. See panel p. 662.

Ismailis, also known as the **Seveners** the adherents of a secret Islamic sect, one of the main branches of the Shiites, which developed from an underground movement (c.9c), and reached political power in Egypt and N Africa in the 10c–12c. It criticized Islamic law, and claimed that in the eventual new age of the seventh imam, a kind of universal religion would emerge that was independent of the laws of all organized religions.

Ismailiya *or* **Ismailia** 1 POP (1986) 213 000, the capital of Ismailiya governorate, NE Egypt. It is situated on the W bank of the Suez Canal by L Timsah, 72km/45mi NW of Suez. The city was founded in 1863 as a base for constructing the canal. 2 a governorate in NE Egypt with Ismailiya as its capital.

Ismail Pasha (1830–95) Khedive (viceroy) of Egypt, born in Cairo, the second son of Ibrahim Pasha. He became deputy of the Ottoman Sultan (1863) and was granted the title of khedive in 1866. His massive development programme included the building of the Suez Canal (opened 1869). The accumulation of a large foreign debt led to European intervention, and when he declined to abdicate, he was deposed by the Sultan and replaced by his eldest son Tewfik Pasha.

isn't *contr.* is not.

ISO *abbrev.* 1 Imperial Service Order. 2 International Standards Organization.

iso- *combining form* forming words meaning 'same, equal'. [from Greek *isos*, equal]

isobar *noun* 1 a line drawn on a weather chart connecting points that have the same atmospheric pressure at a given time. Different pressure systems produce different weather conditions, so they can be used to make forecasts, eg closely packed isobars are associated with strong winds. 2 *Physics* either of two atoms which have

Largest Islands

Name	Area	
---	sq km	sq mi
Australia	7 692 300	2 969 228
Greenland	2 175 600	839 780
New Guinea	790 000	305 000
Borneo	757 050	292 220
Madagascar	592 800	228 821
Sumatra	473 606	182 812
Baffin	318 186	122 820
Honshu (Hondo)	230 897	89 126
Great Britain	219 000	84 400
Victoria, Canada	217 300	83 900
Ellesmere, Canada	196 236	75 747
Sulawesi	174 000	67 400
South I, New Zealand	153 978	59 435
Java	132 187	51 024
North I, New Zealand	114 834	44 326
Newfoundland	109 000	42 000
Cuba	110 860	42 792
Luzon	108 130	41 738
Iceland	103 000	40 000
Mindanao	99 040	38 229
Ireland	84 100	32 500
Hokkaido	83 513	32 236
Novaya Zemlya (two islands)	81 279	31 374
Hispaniola	77 200	29 800
Sakhalin	74 066	28 589
Tierra del Fuego	73 746	28 467
Tasmania	67 800	26 200

the same total number of protons and neutrons in their nuclei, but have different numbers of protons and therefore different atomic numbers and chemical properties. [from Greek *isobares*, of equal weight]

isobaric *adj.* 1 relating to or measured in isobars. 2 having equal atmospheric pressure.

Isobel *or* **Isabel** a female first name. [originally a Spanish version of ELIZABETH, and now an independent name]

isochronal *or* **isochronous** *adj.* 1 having the same length of time. 2 performed or happening at the same time. 3 happening at equal or regular intervals. [from Greek *isochronos*, equal in age or time]

Isocrates (436–338 BC) Greek orator and prose writer, born in Athens. In his youth, he joined the circle of Socrates, but abandoned philosophy for speech-writing. He was an influential teacher of oratory (c.390 BC), and presented rhetoric as an essential foundation of education. In speeches and writings, he urged the Greek city-states to unite against the Persians. His style employs complex sentence structure and the frequent use of antithesis. It influenced Demosthenes and Marcus Tullius Cicero, through whom the example of Isocrates was passed on to European literature.

isolate *verb* 1 to separate from others; to cause to be alone. 2 to place in quarantine. 3 to separate or detach, especially to allow closer examination: *isolate a problem*. 4 to separate so as to obtain in a pure or uncombined form. [from Italian *isolare*, from Latin *insula*, island]

isolated *adj.* 1 placed or standing alone or apart. 2 separate. 3 solitary.

isolation *noun* 1 isolating. 2 being isolated. 3 separation.

isolationism *noun* the policy of not joining with other countries in international political and economic affairs.

isolationist — *noun* a person who supports or promotes isolationism. — *adj.* relating to isolationism or isolationists.

isoleucine *noun Biochem.* an essential amino acid found in proteins.

isomer *noun* 1 *Chem.* one of two or more chemical compounds that have the same chemical formula, ie the same molecular composition, but different three-dimensional structures. As a result they may have different physical and chemical properties. 2 *Physics* one of two or more atomic nuclei with the same atomic number and mass number, but with different energy states and radioactive properties, eg different half-lives. [from Greek *isomeres*, having equal parts]

isomeric *adj. Chem.* identical in every way except in the arrangement of atoms.

isometric *adj.* 1 having equal size or measurements. 2 *said of muscle movement* with the muscle tense and with an increase of muscle strength and tone but without the muscle being contracted or shortened (eg without causing a limb to bend). 3 *said of a three-dimensional drawing* in which the three faces shown are drawn at the same angle to the drawing surface so that all of the lines are equally foreshortened. [from ISO- + Greek *metron*, measure]

isometrics *sing. or pl. noun* a system of physical exercises for strengthening and toning the body in which the muscles are pushed either together or against an immovable object and are not contracted or flexed or made to bend limbs.

isomorph *noun* an individual, chemical, or set, etc in an isomorphic relation with another.

isomorphic *or* **isomorphous** *adj.* showing isomorphism.

isomorphism *noun* 1 *Biol.* apparent similarity of form between individuals belonging to different races or species. 2 *Chem.* the existence of two

-Isms

Most of the words included here denote beliefs and practices. Some, however, denote aspects of discrimination; these include **ageism** and **sexism**.

ageism discrimination on the grounds of age

agnosticism belief in the impossibility of knowing God Greek *agnostos* unknown, unknowable

alcoholism addiction to alcohol

altruism unselfish concern for the welfare of others Latin *alteri huic* to this other

atavism reversion to an earlier type Latin *atavus* ancestor

atheism belief that God does not exist Greek *atheos* without god

barbarism state of being coarse or uncivilized Greek *barbaros* foreign, stammering

behaviourism basis of psychology in behaviour of people and animals

cannibalism practice of eating human flesh Spanish *Canıbal* Carib

capitalism economic system based on the private ownership of wealth and resources

communism political and economic system based on collective ownership of wealth and resources

conservatism inclination to preserve the status quo

consumerism economic policy of encouraging spending and consuming

Cubism artistic movement using geometrical shapes to represent objects

cynicism belief in the worst in others Greek *kynikos* doglike

defeatism belief in the inevitability of defeat

dogmatism tendency to present statements of opinion as if unquestionable Greek *dogma* opinion

dynamism state of having limitless energy and enthusiasm

egoism principle that self-interest is the basis of morality Latin *ego* I

elitism belief in the natural superiority of some people Latin *eligere* to elect

empiricism theory that knowledge can only be gained through experiment and observation Greek *empeiria* experience

environmentalism concern to protect the natural environment

escapism tendency to escape from unpleasant reality into fantasy

evangelism practice of trying to persuade someone to adopt a particular belief or cause Greek *evangelion* good news

exhibitionism tendency to behave so as to attract attention to oneself

existentialism philosophy emphasizing freedom of choice and personal responsibility for one's actions

Expressionism artistic movement emphasizing expression of emotions over representation of external reality

extremism adherence to fanatical or extreme opinions

fanaticism excessive enthusiasm for something Latin *fanaticus* filled with a god, frenzied

fatalism belief that fate is predetermined and unalterable

fascism political system based on dictatorial rule and suppression of democracy Italian *fascio* bundle, group

favouritism practice of giving unfair preference to a person or group

feminism advocacy of equal rights and opportunities for women

feudalism social system based on tenants' allegiance to a lord

functionalism theory that the intended use of something should determine its design

hedonism belief in the importance of pleasure above all else Greek *hedone* pleasure

heroism quality of showing great courage in one's actions

holism theory that any complex being or system is more than the sum of its parts Greek *holos* whole

humanism philosophy emphasizing human responsibility for moral behaviour

hypnotism practice of inducing a hypnotic state in others Greek *hypnos* sleep

idealism practice of living according to ideals

imperialism principle of extending control over other nations' territory Latin *imperium* sovereignty

Impressionism artistic movement emphasizing artists' impressions of nature

individualism belief in individual freedom and self-reliance

liberalism belief in tolerance of different opinions or attitudes

magnetism state of possessing magnetic attraction

mannerism excessive use of an individual artistic style

Marxism philosophy that political change is brought about by struggle between social classes

masochism derivation of pleasure from one's own pain or suffering named after Sacher-Masoch

materialism excessive interest in material possessions and financial success

monarchism support of the institution of monarchy

monetarism economic theory emphasizing the control of a country's money supply

mysticism practice of gaining direct communication with a deity through prayer and meditation Greek *mystes* initiate

narcissism excessive admiration for oneself or one's appearance

nationalism advocacy of national unity or independence

naturalism realistic and non-idealistic representation of objects

nihilism rejection of moral and religious principles Latin *nihil* nothing

objectivism tendency to emphasize what is objective

opportunism practice of taking advantage of opportunities regardless of principles

optimism tendency to expect the best possible outcome Latin *optimus* best

pacifism belief that violence and war are unjustified Latin *pax* peace, and *facere* to make

paganism belief in a religion which worships many gods Latin *paganus* peasant, civilian

pantheism doctrine that equates all natural forces and matter with god Greek *pas* all, *theos* god

parochialism practice of being narrow or provincial in outlook Latin *parochia* parish

paternalism practice of benevolent but over-protective management or government Latin *pater* father

patriotism devotion to one's country Greek *patriotes* compatriot

pessimism tendency to expect the worst possible outcome Latin *pessimus* worst

plagiarism practice of stealing an idea from another's work and presenting it as one's own Latin *plagiarius* kidnapper

pluralism co-existence of several ethnic and religious groups in a society Latin *plus* more

Pointillism artistic movement using small dabs of unmixed colour to suggest shapes French *pointille* dot

polytheism belief in more than one god Greek *polys* many, *theos* god

pragmatism a practical, matter-of-fact approach to dealing with problems Greek *pragma* deed

professionalism practice of showing professional competence and conduct

racism or **racialism** discrimination on the grounds of ethnic origin

realism tendency to present things as they really are

regionalism devotion to or advocacy of one's own region

sadism derivation of pleasure from inflicting pain on others named after Marquis de Sade

Satanism belief in and worship of the devil

scepticism tendency to question widely-accepted beliefs Greek *skeptikos* thoughtful

sexism discrimination on the grounds of sex

socialism doctrine that a country's wealth belongs to the people as a whole

spiritualism practice of communicating with the spirits of the dead through a medium

stoicism tendency to accept misfortune or suffering without complaint Greek *Stoa Poikile* Painted Porch (where Zeno taught)

Surrealism artistic movement emphasizing use of images from the unconscious

symbolism use of symbols to express ideas or emotions

terrorism practice of using violence to achieve political ends

Thatcherism political system based on privatization and monetarism advocated by Margaret Thatcher

tokenism practice of doing something once or with minimum effort to appear to comply with a law or principle

tourism practice of travelling to and visiting places for pleasure and relaxation

vandalism practice of inflicting indiscriminate damage on others' property

vegetarianism practice of not eating meat or animal products

ventriloquism practice of making one's voice appear to come from another source Latin *ventri* belly, *loqui* to speak

voyeurism practice of watching private actions of others for pleasure or sexual gratification

---

or more chemical compounds with the same crystal structure. **3** *Maths.* a one-to-one correspondence between the elements of two or more sets and between the sums or products of the elements of one set and those of the equivalent elements of the other set or sets. [from ISO- + Greek *morphe,* from]

isoprene *noun Chem.* (FORMULA C_5H_8) a colourless liquid hydrocarbon that is the basic unit of natural rubber, and can be polymerized to form synthetic rubber. [from ISO- + *propyl,* the name of an alkyl group, + *-ene*]

isosceles *adj., said of a triangle* having two sides of equal length. [from Greek *isos,* equal + *skelos,* leg]

isostasy *noun Geol.* a theoretical state of equilibrium in which the Earth's crust, which is considered to consist of large blocks of material of relatively low density, floats on the surface of the much denser semi-solid material of the Earth's mantle. [from Greek *isos,* equal + *stasis,* setting]

isotherm *noun* a line on a weather map connecting places where the temperature is the same

at a particular time or where the average is the same for a particular period of time. [from Greek *isos,* equal + *therme,* heat]

isotonic *adj. Chem.* denoting a solution that has the same osmotic pressure as another solution with which it is being compared. [from ISO- + Greek *tonos,* tension, tone]

isotope *noun Chem.* one of two or more atoms of the same chemical element that contain the same number of protons but different numbers of neutrons in their nuclei. Isotopes of an element have the same atomic number and chemical properties, but different mass numbers and physical properties. [from ISO- + Greek *topos*, place (ie on the periodic table)]

isotopic *adj.* relating to or involving an isotope or isotopes.

isotropic *adj., said of a substance, material, etc* having physical properties (eg magnetism and elasticity) which do not vary with direction. [from ISO- + Greek *tropos*, turn]

Israel, Hebrew **Yisrael**, official name **State of Israel**, Hebrew **Medinat Israel** POP (1992e) 5.2m, a state in the Middle East, divided into six districts, plus the occupied territories of Judaea-Samaria and Gaza. AREA 20 770sq km/8 017sq mi (within the boundaries defined by 1949 armistice agreements). It is bounded to the W by the Mediterranean Sea, N by Lebanon, NE by Syria, E by Jordan, and SW by Egypt. CAPITAL Jerusalem. CHIEF TOWNS Tel Aviv-Jaffa, Haifa, Beersheba, Acre, Holon. TIME ZONE GMT +2. The population is mainly Jewish (83%), and Arab (11%); Judaism is the chief religion, with Islam, Christianity, and other religions, followed by minorities. OFFICIAL LANGUAGES Hebrew, Arabic. CURRENCY the shekel. PHYSICAL DESCRIPTION extends 420km/260mi N–S; width varies from 20km/12mi to 116km/72mi; the narrow coastal plain is crossed by several rivers; mountainous interior, rising to 1 208m at Mt Meron; mountains in Galilee and Samaria, dissected by faults, dropping E to below sea level in the Jordan–Red Sea Rift Valley; the R Jordan forms part of the E border; the Negev Desert in the S occupies c.60% of the country's area. CLIMATE typically Mediterranean in the N and central area, with hot, dry summers and warm, wet winters; average temperatures at Tel Aviv-Jaffa are 14°C in Jan and 27°C in Jul; average annual rainfall is 550mm; rainfall is heavier inland, with occasional snow; low rainfall in Negev, decreasing in the S. HISTORY the Zionist movement was founded by Theodor Herzl at the end of the 19c; thousands of Jews returned to Palestine, then part of the Ottoman Empire; Britain was given the League of Nations mandate to govern Palestine and establish a Jewish national home there in 1922; Nazi persecution of Jews in the 1930s greatly increased Jewish immigration; the British evacuated Palestine, and Israel proclaimed independence in 1948; invasion by Arab nations resulted in an armistice in 1949; the Six-Day War in 1967 brought Israeli control of the Gaza Strip, the Sinai Peninsula as far as the Suez Canal, the West Bank of the R Jordan including the E sector of Jerusalem, and the Golan Heights in Syria; Camp David conference between Egypt and Israel in 1978; Israeli withdrawal from Sinai in 1979; invasion of Lebanon, forcing the PLO to leave Beirut in 1982–5; renewed tension began in 1988, with the uprising of Arabs in occupied territories (the *intifada*); peace agreements between Israel and the PLO, signed 1993–4, set out the introduction of limited self-rule for the Palestinians; the peace plans were opposed by extremists on both sides, and damaged by the killings in Hebron (West Bank) and Afula (N Israel). GOVERNMENT a parliamentary democracy

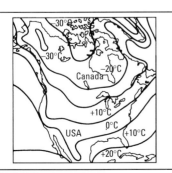

isotherms

with a Prime Minister, a Cabinet, and a unicameral 120-member Parliament (*Knesset*), elected for a four-year term; the President is elected for a maximum of two five-year terms. ECONOMY over 90% of exports are industrial products, including polished diamonds, transportation equipment, plastics, processed foods, textiles, chemicals, electronics, medical engineering, agricultural equipment, computers, alternative energy sources; major tourist area, primarily to the religious centres; copper, potash, phosphates; citrus fruits, melons, avocados, flowers, cotton, sugar beet, vegetables, olives, tobacco, bananas, beef and dairy products; a world leader in agro-technology, with areas of intensive cultivation; major irrigation schemes, including the 'National Water Carrier' project to transfer water from L Tiberias in the N to the Negev Desert in the S; the *kibbutz* system produces c.40% of food output, but in recent years has turned increasingly towards industry.

Israel

Israel, Tribes of in the Bible, a confederacy of 12 tribes generally traced to Jacob's 12 sons — six by Leah (Reuben, Simeon, Levi, Judah, Issachar, Zebulun), two by Rachel (Joseph, Benjamin), two by Rachel's maid Bilhah (Dan, Naphtali), and two by Leah's maid Zilpah (Gad, Asher). Jacob had received the name Israel (Genesis 32.28) when he wrestled with a divine being. During the settlement of Canaan and the Transjordan, the tribes were allocated portions of land (Joshua 13–19), but the Levites, a priestly class, had no allocation, and Joseph's 'tribe' actually comprised two tribes, traced to his two sons Ephraim and Manasseh (Genesis 48). Once the monarchy was established in Israel (c.10c BC), the tribal confederation effectively ended, although it continued in Jewish religious thought.

Israeli — *adj.* of the modern state of Israel or its inhabitants. — *noun* a person born or living in the modern state of Israel. [from Hebrew *Yisrael*, God perseveres]

Israelite — *noun Hist.* a person born or living in the ancient kingdom of Israel (922 BC–721 BC), especially a Jew claiming descent from Jacob. — *adj.* of the ancient kingdom of Israel or its inhabitants.

Issachar, Tribe of one of the 12 tribes of ancient Israel, descended from Issachar, one of Jacob's sons by his wife Leah. Its territory included the central plain of Jezreel between Mt Tabor and Mt Gilboa.

Issigonis, Sir Alec (Alexander Arnold Constantine) (1906–88) Turkish-born automobile designer, born in Smyrna. He settled in Britain in 1923, and as an enthusiastic sports driver became familiar with all aspects of car design. During his long association with Morris (later British Motor Company) he designed the Morris 'Minor', launched in 1948 and produced until

1971, and the revolutionary 'Mini' launched in 1959.

issue — *noun* 1 the giving out, publishing, or making available of something, eg stamps, a magazine, etc. 2 that which is given out, published, or made available, eg stamps, a magazine, book, etc. 3 one item in a regular series: *the December issue of the magazine.* 4 a subject for discussion or argument. 5 a result or consequence. 6 *formal* children; offspring. 7 an act of going or flowing out. 8 a way out, outlet, or outflow, eg where a stream begins. — *verb* 1 to give or send out, distribute, publish, or make available, especially officially or formally. 2 (**issue someone with something**) to supply them with something required, eg an official document. 3 *intrans.* (often **issue forth** *or* **out**) to flow or come out, especially in large quantities. 4 (**issue in something**) to end or result in it. 5 (**issue from someone** *or* **something**) to come or descend from them; to be produced or caused by them.
— **at issue** 1 in dispute or disagreement. 2 under discussion.
force the issue to act so as to force a decision to be taken.
join *or* **take issue with someone** to disagree with them.
make an issue of something to make it the explicit subject of an argument or disagreement. [from Old French *issue*, from Latin *exitus*, exit]

issuing house a merchant bank which specializes in the issue of shares and bonds on the stock market. Over 50 banks belong to the Issuing Houses Association in the UK.

Issyk Kul, Lake a lake in Issyk Kul region, NE Kirghizia, situated in the N Tien Shan Range. AREA 6 280sq km/2 424sq mi. The lake is 178km/111mi long and 60km/37mi at its widest point; its maximum depth is 702m. It is one of the largest mountain lakes in the world.

-ist *suffix* forming words denoting 1 a believer in some formal system of ideas, principles or beliefs: *feminist.* 2 a person who carries out some activity or practises some art: *novelist.* [from Greek *-istes*]

Istanbul *or* **Stamboul** 1 formerly **Byzantium** (c.660 BC–AD 330), **Constantinople** (AD 330–1930) POP (1990) 6.6m, the chief city and seaport of Turkey and the capital of Istanbul province, NW Turkey. It lies on the Golden Horn and on both sides of the Bosporus. It is the only city in the world to be situated on two continents; suspension bridges link the European and Asian sections. The part corresponding to historic Constantinople is on the European side; it was founded by Constantine I in AD 330 on the site of ancient Byzantium, and became the new capital of the Roman Empire. It is today a commercial and financial centre, and the see of the patriarch of the Greek Orthodox Church and of the Armenian Church. It was once noted as the E rail terminus of the Orient Express. Istanbul is a major tourist area, and the remains of ancient Constantinople are a World Heritage site. NOTABLE FEATURES Topkapi Palace (15c); Hagia Sophia Basilica (6c); Blue Mosque of Sultan Ahmet Camii; Mosque of Süleyman the Magnificent (16c); Roman cisterns; covered bazaar. 2 a province in NW Turkey with the city of Istanbul as its capital. See illustration p. 664.

Isthmian Games in ancient Greece, a biennial Pan-Hellenic contest, held near the Isthmus of Corinth. They were in honour of the god Poseidon, and consisted of athletic contests, horse-racing, and poetical and musical competitions.

isthmus *noun* (PL. **isthmuses**) 1 a narrow strip of land, bounded by water on both sides, joining two larger areas of land. 2 *Anat.* a narrow or constricted region of an organ or tissue. [from Greek *isthmos*]

Istria, Serbo-Croatian **Istra** a peninsula at the N end of the Adriatic Sea, in Croatia and Slovenia. AREA 3 160sq km/1 220sq mi. CHIEF TOWN Pula. Formerly part of the Italian province of Venezia

Blue Mosque, Istanbul

Giulia, it was ceded to Yugoslavia in 1947 (apart from Trieste). It became part of the Republic of Croatia in 1991.

IT *abbrev.* information technology.

it¹ — *pron.* **1** the thing, animal, small baby, or group already mentioned. **2** the person in question: *who is it?* **3** used as the subject with impersonal verbs and when describing the weather or distance or telling the time. **4** used as the grammatical subject of a sentence when the real subject comes later: *it's not a very good idea running away.* **5** used to refer to a general situation or state of affairs: *how's it going?* **6** used to emphasize a certain word or phrase in a sentence: *when is it her train is due to arrive?* **7** exactly what is needed, suitable or available: *that's it!* **8** used with many verbs and prepositions as an object with little meaning: *run for it.* — *noun* **1** the person in a children's game who has to oppose all the others, eg by trying to catch them. **2** *old colloq. use* sex appeal. **3** *colloq.* sexual intercourse. [from Anglo-Saxon *hit*]

it² *noun old colloq. use* Italian vermouth. [abbreviation]

ITA *abbrev.* Independent Television Authority (now IBA).

i.t.a. or **ITA** *abbrev.* Initial Teaching Alphabet.

Itaipu Dam a major earth- and rock-fill gravity buttress dam (189m high) on the R Paraná at the Brazil–Paraguay frontier, completed in 1985. With the capacity to generate 12 600 megawatts of hydroelectricity, it is said to be the largest hydroelectric complex in the world.

Italian — *adj.* of Italy, its inhabitants, culture, history, or the Romance language spoken there. — *noun* **1** a person born or living in Italy. **2** the Romance language spoken in Italy and in parts of Switzerland. [from Latin *Italianus*, from *Italia*, Italy]

◇ Italian is spoken by c.60 million people in Italy, Switzerland, San Marino, the Vatican City, Sardinia, and in parts of the USA, former Yugoslavia, and Africa. The standard form derives from the dialect spoken in medieval Tuscany with many borrowings from Latin.

Italianate *adj.* of or in an Italian style, especially of decoration, architecture, or art.

Italian Wars a series of conflicts lasting from 1494 to 1559 (Treaty of Cateau-Cambrésis) between the French Valois monarchs and the Habsburgs for the control of Italy. Both houses laid claim to the throne of the Kingdom of Naples, but after seven phases of warfare, involving a host of different monarchs and states, Spain emerged victorious.

italic — *adj.* **1** of or in a typeface with characters which slope upwards to the right. **2** (**Italic**) of ancient Italy. — *noun* (*usually* **italics**) a typeface, first used in Italy, with characters which slope upwards to the right or a letter printed or written in this typeface. [from Greek *Italikos*]

italicization *or* **italicisation** *noun* putting or being in italics.

italicize *or* **italicise** *verb* to print or write in italics.

Italo- *combining form* of Italy, the Italians, etc.

Italy, Italian **Italia**, official name **Italian Republic**, Italian **Repubblica Italiana** POP (1992e) 57.8m, a republic in S Europe, comprising the boot-shaped peninsula extending S into the Mediterranean Sea, as well as Sicily, Sardinia, and some smaller islands. The country is divided into 20 regions. AREA 301 225sq km/ 116 273sq mi. It is bounded W by the Tyrrhenian Sea, NW by France, N by Switzerland and Austria, NE by Slovenia, E by the Adriatic Sea, and S by the Ionian Sea. CAPITAL Rome. CHIEF TOWNS Milan, Turin, Genoa, Naples, Bologna, Palermo, Florence, Venice. TIME ZONE GMT +1. The chief religion is Roman Catholicism. OFFICIAL LANGUAGE Italian; German is also spoken in the Trentino-Alto Adige, French in Valle d'Aosta, and Slovene in Trieste-Gorizia. CURRENCY the lira. PHYSICAL DESCRIPTION the Italian peninsula extends c.800km/500mi SE from the Lombardy plains; the Apennines rise to peaks above 2 000m; the Alps in the N form an arc from Nice in France to Fiume, and the highest peaks along the Swiss–French frontier are at Mt Blanc (4 807m) and the Matterhorn (4 477m); the broad, fertile Lombardo–Venetian plain is in the basin of the R Po; there are several lakes at the foot of the Alps, including Maggiore, Como, and Garda; it is flat and marshy on the Adriatic coast in the N; on the Riviera to the W, coastal mountains descend steeply to the Ligurian Sea; chief rivers include the Po, Tiber, Arno, Volturno, Liri, and Adige; the island of Sicily, separated from the mainland by the Strait of Messina, includes the limestone massifs of Monti Nebrodi and the volcanic cone of Mt Etna (3 323m), one of three active volcanos in the country; the others are Vesuvius (1 277m) and Stromboli (926m); Sardinia rises to 1 835m at Monti del Gennargentu. CLIMATE there is great variation with relief and latitude; rainfall on the R Po plain is well distributed throughout the year with hot sunny summers and short cold winters; the higher areas of peninsular Italy are cold, wet, often snowy; coastal regions have a Mediterranean climate, with warm wet winters and hot dry summers; the W coast is warmer than the Adriatic coast and receives more rainfall; there are long hours of sunshine in the extreme S during summer. HISTORY in pre-Roman times, Italy was inhabited by Etruscans in the N, Latins in the centre of the country, and Greeks in the S; most regions were part of the Roman Empire by the 3c BC; barbarian tribes invaded in the 4c, and the last Roman emperor was deposed in AD 476; it was later ruled by the Lombards and by the Franks under Charlemagne, who was crowned Emperor of the Romans in 800; it became part of the Holy Roman Empire under Otto in 962, and conflict

between popes and emperors continued throughout the Middle Ages; there were disputes between Guelfs and Ghibellines in the 12c; Italy was divided among five powers in the 14c–15c (Kingdom of Naples, Duchy of Milan, the republics of Florence and Venice, and the papacy); the country contributed greatly to European culture through the Renaissance; numerous republics were set up after the French Revolution; Napoleon was crowned King of Italy in 1805; the 19c saw the upsurge of liberalism and nationalism (the *Risorgimento*); unification was achieved by 1870 under Victor Emmanuel II of Sardinia, aided by Cavour and Garibaldi; colonies were established in Eritrea (1870–89) and in Somaliland (1889); the attempt to secure a protectorate over Abyssinia was defeated at Adowa in 1896; Italy fought alongside the Allies in World War I; the Fascist movement brought Mussolini to power in 1922; conquest of Abyssinia (1935–6) and Albania (1939); the alliance with Hitler in World War II led to the end of the Italian Empire; political instability has resulted in over 45 governments in power since the formation of the republic; growing disillusionment with the political parties following a series of corruption scandals in the early 1990s led to voting reforms; in the 1994 elections the right-wing Forza Italia party won the most seats, causing fears in Europe about a resurgence of the extreme right. GOVERNMENT a democratic republic since 1946, when the monarchy was abolished; Parliament consists of a 630-member Chamber of Deputies and a 315-member Senate, both bodies elected for five years; a President serves a seven-year term, and appoints a Prime Minister; over 45 governments have been in power since the formation of the republic; following corruption scandals, a right-wing government was elected in 1994. ECONOMY industry is largely concentrated in the N while the poorer agricultural region is in the S; agriculture, wine, machine tools, vehicles, textiles, foodstuffs, chemicals, footwear, tourism.

ITC *abbrev.* Independent Television Commission.

itch — *noun* **1** an unpleasant irritation on the surface of the skin which makes one want to scratch. **2** *colloq.* a strong or restless desire. **3** a skin disease or condition which causes a constant unpleasant irritation, especially scabies. — *verb* **1** *intrans.* to have an itch and want to scratch. **2** *trans., intrans.* to cause (someone) to feel an itch. **3** *intrans. colloq.* to feel a strong or restless desire. [from Anglo-Saxon *giccan*]

itchiness *noun* being itchy.

itchy *adj.* (**itchier**, **itchiest**) causing or affected with an itch or itching.

itchy feet *colloq.* the strong desire to leave, move, or travel.

itchy palm *or* **itching palm** greed for money.

it'd *contr.* **1** it had. **2** it would.

-ite *suffix* forming nouns denoting: **1** a place, origin, or national group: *Israelite.* **2** a follower of or believer in: *pre-Raphaelite / anti-semite.* **3** a fossil: *ammonite.* **4** a mineral: *graphite.* **5** a salt of a certain formula: *nitrite.* See also -ATE, -IDE. **6** an explosive: *dynamite.* [from Greek *-ites*]

item *noun* **1** a separate item, object, or unit, especially one on a list. **2** a separate piece of information or news. [from Latin *item*, likewise]

itemization *or* **itemisation** *noun* listing or being listed item by item.

itemize *or* **itemise** *verb* to list (things) separately, eg on a bill.

iterate *verb* to say or do again; to repeat. [from Latin *iterare*, from *iterim*, again]

iteration *noun* repetition.

iterative *adj.* repeating.

itinerant — *adj.* travelling from place to place, eg on business. — *noun* an itinerant person. [from Latin *iter*, journey]

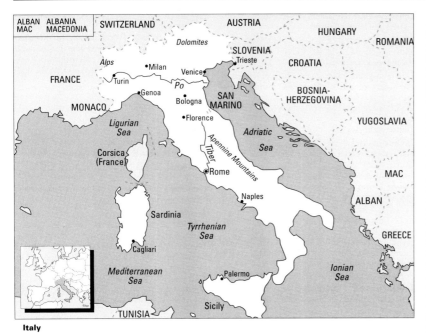

Italy

itinerary *noun* (PL. **itineraries**) **1** a plan of one's route for a journey or trip. **2** a diary or record of a journey. **3** a guidebook. [from Latin *iter*, journey]

-itis *combining form* **1** *in the names of diseases* denoting inflammation: *appendicitis*. **2** *colloq.* in ad hoc formations, denoting distress or suffering caused by an excess: *jazzitis*. [from Greek *-itis*]

it'll *contr.* **1** it will. **2** it shall.

ITN *abbrev.* Independent Television News.

Ito, Hirobumi (1838–1909) Japanese statesman, born in Choshu province. As Prime Minister (1885–8, 1892–6, 1898, 1900–1), he visited Europe and the USA on several occasions, drafted the Meiji constitution (1889), and played a major role in abolishing Japanese feudalism and building up the modern state. He was assassinated in Harbin by a supporter of Korean independence.

its — *adj.* belonging to it. — *pron.* the one or ones belonging to it.
◆ Note that there is no apostrophe; *it's* means 'it is' or 'it has'.

it's *contr.* **1** it is. **2** it has.

itself *pron.* **1** the reflexive form of *it*. **2** used for emphasis. **3** (*also* **by itself**) alone; without help.

itsy-bitsy *or* **itty-bitty** *adj. colloq.* very small. [a rhyming compound based on *little bit*]

ITT *abbrev.* International Telephone and Telegraph Corporation.

ITU *abbrev.* International Telecommunication Union.

Itúrbide, Agustín de (1783–1824) Mexican general, born in Morelia. He became prominent in the movement for Mexican independence, and made himself Emperor as Agustín I (1822–3). He was forced to abdicate, travelled in Europe, and was executed on his return to Mexico.

ITV *abbrev. Brit.* Independent Television.

-ity *suffix* forming words denoting a state or quality, or an instance of it: *authority / irregularity*. [from French *-ité*]

IUD *abbrev.* intrauterine device.

Iuppiter see JUPITER.

Ivan III, known as **the Great** (1440–1505) Grand Prince of Moscow (1462–1505), born in Moscow. He ended his city's subjection to the Tartars, and gained control over several Russian

principalities. In 1472 he assumed the title of 'Sovereign of all Russia', and adopted the emblem of the two-headed eagle of the Byzantine Empire.

Ivan IV, known as **the Terrible** (1530–84) Grand Prince of Moscow (1533–84), born near Moscow, the first to assume the title of 'tsar' (Latin *Caesar*). He subdued Kazan and Astrakhan, made the first inroads into Siberia, and established commercial links with England. In 1564 the treachery of one of his counsellors caused him to see treachery everywhere, and he embarked on a reign of terror, directed principally at the feudal aristocracy (princes and boyars), but he nonetheless encouraged Russian culture and commerce.

Ivanhoe a novel by Sir Walter Scott (1819). It describes the career of Wilfred of Ivanhoe at the time of Richard I.

Ivanovo, formerly **Ivanovo-Voznesensk** (1871–1932) **1** POP (1991e) 482 000, the capital of Ivanovo oblast, W Russia. It is situated on the R Uvod, 318km/198mi NE of Moscow. Founded in 1871, the city was noted for its revolutionary activities in the 1880s, 1905, and 1917. It is also the historic centre of Russia's cotton-milling industry. **2** an oblast in W Russia with the city of Ivanovo as its capital.

Ivanovo churches a series of cells, chapels, and churches cut out of the rock face on the banks of the Rusenski Lom River, near the village of Ivanovo in NE Bulgaria. The complex was constructed by monks during the 13c and 14c. It is a World Heritage site.

I've *contr.* I have.

-ive *suffix* forming words denoting a quality, action, etc, or a person associated with it: *creative / detective*. [from French *-if*]

IVF *abbrev.* in-vitro fertilization.

Iviza see IBIZA.

Ivor a male first name, found especially in Wales. [from Old Norse *yr*, yew, bow + *herr*, army]

ivory — *noun* **1** a hard white material that forms the tusks of the elephant, walrus, etc, formerly used to make ornaments, art objects, and piano keys. **2** the creamy-white colour of this substance. **3** an article made from this substance. **4** (**ivories**) *colloq.* the keys on a piano. — *adj.* of or resembling this material, especially in colour. [from Latin *ebur*]

◇ The main source of ivory, the African elephant, is now an endangered species, and plastic or ceramic substitutes for ivory are increasingly used. There is still an extensive illegal trade in ivory.

Ivory Coast, French **Côte d'Ivoire**, official name **Republic of the Ivory Coast**, French **République de Côte d'Ivoire** POP (1992e) 12.9m, a republic in W Africa, divided into 26 departments. AREA 320 633sq km/123 764sq mi. It is bounded SW by Liberia, NW by Guinea, N by Mali and Burkina, E by Ghana, and S by the Gulf of Guinea. CAPITAL Yamoussoukro. CHIEF TOWNS Abidjan, Bouaké, Daloa, Man, Korhogo, Gagnoa. TIME ZONE GMT. The population consists of several ethnic groups, including the Agni, Baoule, Krou, Senoufou, and Mandingo; most of the population follows local beliefs and the remainder are Muslim and Christian. OFFICIAL LANGUAGE French; many local languages are also spoken. CURRENCY the franc CFA. PHYSICAL DESCRIPTION sandy beaches and lagoons, backed by a broad forest-covered coastal plain; the land rises towards savannah at 300–350m; the Mt Nimba massif in the NW is 1 752m; rivers generally flow N–S. CLIMATE tropical, varying with distance from the coast; rainfall decreases towards the N; the average annual rainfall at Abidjan is 2 100mm; average temperatures are 25–27°C. HISTORY explored by the Portuguese in the 15c; French influence from 1842; declared a French protectorate in 1889 and a French colony in 1893; territory within French West Africa in 1904; gained independence in 1960; student demonstrations and opposition followed the disputed electoral results of 1992. GOVERNMENT governed by a 175-member National Assembly and an executive President (both elected for five-year terms), with a Council of Ministers. ECONOMY largely based on agriculture, which employs c.82% of the population; the world's largest cocoa producer and third-largest coffee producer; bananas, rice, pineapples, cotton, coconuts, palm oil, sugar, cassava, corn; livestock; fishing; food processing; timber; textiles; clothing; vehicle assembly; small shipyards; fertilizers; battery production; oil refining; cement.

Ivory Coast

ivory tower a place where one can be secluded from the unpleasant realities of life.

Ivy a female first name, introduced at the end of the 19c, after the plant-name.

ivy *noun* (PL. **ivies**) **1** an evergreen shrub with dark leaves with five points which climbs on walls and trees. **2** any of several other climbing plants, such as poison ivy.

Ivy League a group of long-established colleges and universities in NE USA. The league, which includes Harvard, Yale, Princeton, Columbia, Dartmouth, Cornell, Brown, and the University of Pennsylvania, was formally established in 1956 to oversee inter-collegiate sports.

Iwo Jima the most important and largest of the Japanese Volcano Is, situated in the W Pacific Ocean, 1 222km/759mi to the S of Tokyo. It is 8km/5mi long and measures 4km/2.5mi at its widest point. Suribachi-yama, an extinct volcano, is the highest point at 167m. A major battle of World War II took place on the island in 1944–5, when the heavily fortified Japanese air base was taken in a three-month campaign. The island was occupied by the USA from 1945 and returned to Japan in 1968. ECONOMY sugar; sulphur.

IWW *abbrev.* Industrial Workers of the World, a radical US labour organization movement, whose members were known as Wobblies. An offshoot of the Western Federation of Miners, it was founded (1905) by a group who opposed the craft unionism of the AFL (American Federation of Labor) and proposed instead a union of both skilled and unskilled workers. The movement splintered because of the radical anti-capitalist ideology of its leader, 'Big Bill' Haywood, who preferred striking and sabotage to negotiation. Lack of organization and funds soon meant the IWW had few successes in industrial conflicts, depite its membership of 60 000. It declined rapidly after the Red Scare of 1919 (a period of anticommunist repression, aimed mostly at foreigners and labour unions).

ixia *noun* a plant of the iris family with large showy flowers, originally found in S Africa. [from Greek *ixos*, mistletoe]

Ixion in Greek mythology, a king of Thessaly, the father of the Centaurs. He murdered his father-in-law, was pardoned by Zeus, but then attempted to rape Hera, for which he was bound to a wheel of fire, usually located in the Underworld.

Ixtaccihuatl, Aztec **Iztaccihuatl** a dormant volcano in central Mexico, 56km/35mi SE of Mexico City. HEIGHT 5 286m. It is an irregular-shaped, snow-capped volcano which has three summits and is situated in Ixtaccihuatl-Popocatépetl National Park.

Izabal, Lake the largest lake in Guatemala. AREA 1 000sq km/400sq mi; length 48km/30mi; width 24km/15mi. It is situated in Izabal department, in the E part of the country. The lake drains into an inlet of the Caribbean Sea, via the R Dulce. It is an important commercial waterway.

Izanagi and Izanami in Japanese mythology, respectively, the male and female gods who created Japan and the other gods. Izanami died when she gave birth to the fire god, and went to the land of the dead (Yomi). Izanagi followed her there, but she turned against him and pursued him. Finally he had to block the exit from Yomi with a large rock. Izanami then became the goddess of the underworld.

-ization *or* **-isation** *suffix* forming nouns of action corresponding to verbs in *-ize* or *-ise*.

-ize *or* **-ise** *suffix* forming verbs meaning **1** to make or become: *equalize*. **2** to treat or react to (in a stated way): *criticize*. **3** to engage in (a stated activity): *theorize*. [from Latin *-izare*]

Izhevsk, formerly **Ustinov** (until 1991) POP (1991e) 647 000, the capital of Udmurtia, W central Russia. Founded in 1760, it is a cultural and educational centre.

Izmir, formerly **Smyrna 1** POP (1990) 2.7m, the seaport capital of Izmir province, W Turkey, lying on an inlet of the Aegean Sea. It is the third-largest city in Turkey and a commercial and industrial centre. NATO's SE Command has its headquarters here. NOTABLE FEATURES Kadifekale Fortress (4c BC); Roman remains. EVENT annual international fair. **2** a province in W Turkey with the city of Izmir as its capital.

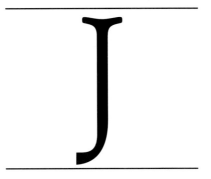

J¹ *or* **j** *noun* (PL. **Js, J's, j's**) the tenth letter of the English alphabet.

J² *abbrev.* joule.

jab — *verb trans., intrans.* (**jabbed, jabbing**) (**jab something** *or* **jab at something**) to poke or prod it. — *noun* **1** a poke or prod. **2** *colloq.* an injection or inoculation. **3** *Boxing* a short straight punch. [from Middle English *jobben*]

jabber — *verb intrans., trans.* (**jabbered, jabbering**) to talk or utter rapidly and indistinctly. — *noun* rapid indistinct speech. [imitative]

Jabberwock, the the terrifying, fictitious monster whose story is told in the poem 'Jabberwocky' in Lewis Carroll's *Through the Looking-Glass.*

Jabneh *or* **Jamnia** an ancient city on the coastal plain east of Jerusalem and south of modern Tel Aviv, referred to occasionally in writings of the biblical and Maccabean periods. It achieved special prominence in early Judaism after the fall of Jerusalem (AD 70), when Rabban Johanan ben Zakkai asked the Roman emperor for the city, and it became a centre of Jewish learning. [Hebrew, = God builds]

jabot *noun* a lace ruffle for a shirt front, worn especially with full Highland dress. [from French *jabot*]

Jack, in full **Jack Martin** the natural leader of the three shipwrecked boys in R M Ballantyne's *The Coral Island.*

Jack a male first name, originally a pet form of *John,* but also taken to be an anglicization of French *Jacques.*

jack — *noun* **1** a device for raising heavy objects off the ground. **2** *Cards* the court card of least value, bearing a picture of a page (also called KNAVE). **3** *Bowls* the small white ball that players aim at. **4** a small national flag flown at the bows of a ship. **5** one of the playing-pieces used in the game of jacks. **6** *Electr.* (also **jack socket**) a socket taking a single-pronged plug (see JACK PLUG). **7** the male of certain animals, eg the donkey. — *verb* (often **jack something up**) to raise it with a jack.

— **every man jack** everybody.
jack something in *or* **up** *slang* to give it up. [from the name *Jack*]

jackal *noun* a mainly nocturnal carnivorous mammal, closely related to the dog and wolf, that lives in deserts, grassland, and woodland in Asia and Africa, and is often found scavenging and feeding on refuse in urban areas. Jackals feed on carrion and also prey on gazelles, hunting in pairs or small packs. [from Persian *shagual*]

jackanapes *noun old use* a mischievous or impertinent person. [from Middle English *Jakken apes,* or 'jack of the apes', ie the Duke of Suffolk (1396–1450), whose badge was an ape's ball and chain]

jackass *noun* **1** a male ass. **2** *colloq.* a foolish person.

jackboot *noun* a tall leather knee-high military boot, especially as a symbol of oppressive military rule.

jackdaw *noun* a bird of the crow family having a reputation for stealing bright objects. [from JACK + old word *daw,* jackdaw]

jacket *noun* **1** a short coat, especially a long-sleeved hip-length one. **2** something worn over the top half of the body: *a life jacket.* **3** same as DUST JACKET. **4** an outer casing for a boiler, etc, for preventing heat loss; any protective casing. **5** the skin of a potato that has been cooked without being peeled. **6** an animal's natural coat. [from Old French *jaquet*]

Jack Frost in story books, etc, a being personifying frost.

jack-in-office *noun derog.* a self-important minor official.

jack-in-the-box *noun* (PL. **jack-in-the-boxes**) a box containing a doll attached to a spring, that leaps out when the lid is opened.

jackknife — *noun* **1** a large pocket knife with a folding blade. **2** a dive in which the body is bent double and then straightened before entering the water. — *verb intrans., said of an articulated vehicle* to go out of control in such a way that the trailer swings round against the cab.

Jacklin, Tony (Anthony) (1944–) English golfer, born in Scunthorpe, Humberside. He won the 1969 British Open at Royal Lytham (the first British winner for 18 years), and in 1970 won the US Open at Hazeltine (the first British winner for 50 years). He turned professional in 1962, and won the Jacksonville Open in 1968, the first Briton to win on the US Tour. A former Ryder Cup player, he was captain of the European team from 1983 to 1989.

jack-of-all-trades *noun* (PL. **jacks-of-all-trades**) a handyman used to a variety of jobs.

jack plug *Electr.* an electrical plug with a single prong.

jackpot *noun* the maximum win, especially consisting of the accumulated stakes, to be made in a lottery, card game, etc.
— **hit the jackpot** *colloq.* to have a remarkable financial win or stroke of luck.

jack rabbit a long-eared N American hare.

Jack Robinson
— **before you can say Jack Robinson** *colloq.* very suddenly or quickly; in a trice.
[18c; various origins have been suggested, but none is certain]

jacks *or* **jackstones** *noun* a game in which playing-pieces (originally small bones or pebbles) are tossed and caught on the back of the hand.

Jackson, Andrew, known as **Old Hickory** (1767–1845) US statesman, the seventh President, born in Waxhaw, North Carolina. He trained as a lawyer, became a member of Congress for Tennessee (1796), Senator (1797), a judge of its supreme court (1798–1804), and then won fame in the war of 1812 against Britain, when he was given command of the South and achieved the famous defence of New Orleans (1815). His election as President (1829–37) was the result of a campaign in which he gained the support of the majority of voters — a development in US politics which came to be part of the new 'Jacksonian Democracy'.

Jackson, Glenda (1936–) English actress and MP, born in Birkenhead, Merseyside. She was a leading member of the Royal Shakespeare Company before appearing in films from 1967, winning Oscars for *Women in Love* (1969) and *A Touch of Class* (1973). Later films include *Stevie* (1978), *Beyond Therapy* (1985), and *Business as Usual* (1987). She continued to portray complex characterizations on stage and screen, and made several television appearances, before she turned to a career in politics, and became Labour MP for Hampstead and Highgate in 1992.

Jackson, Jesse (Louis) (1941–) US clergyman and politician, born in Greenville, North Carolina. Ordained a Baptist minister in 1968, he was an active participant in the civil rights movement, and organized Operation PUSH (People United to Save Humanity) in 1971. In 1984 and 1988 he sought the Democratic nomination for the presidency, won considerable support, and became the first black American to be considered a serious candidate for the office.

Jackson, Michael (1958–) US pop singer, born in Gary, Indiana. With his brothers, Jackie, Tito, Marlon, and Jermaine in the vocal/instrumental pop group The Jacksons, he knew stardom from the age of 11, and sang on four consecutive number-one hits. Between 1972 and 1975 he also had six solo hits on the Motown record label. In 1977 he played the scarecrow in *The Wiz,* a black remake of the film *The Wizard of Oz.* His first major solo album was *Off the Wall* (1979) and he consolidated his career with *Thriller* (1982) which sold over 35 million copies and which helped to establish him as one of the major pop superstars of the 1980s. Having been a celebrity since childhood, he developed a reclusive lifestyle in adulthood. He cancelled a world tour in 1993 following allegations of child abuse. No legal charges were laid.

Jackson, Reggie (Reginald) (1946–) US baseball player, born in Wyncote, Pennsylvania. In the 1977 World Series he equalled Babe Ruth's 51-year-old record for hitting three home runs in one game. He started his League career with Kansas City in 1967, and also played for Oakland, the Yankees, and (from 1982) the California Angels.

Jackson, Thomas Jonathan, also called **Stonewall Jackson** (1824–63) US soldier, born in Clarksburg, West Virginia. In 1851 he became a professor at the Virginia Military Institute. During the American Civil War, he took command of the Confederate troops at Harper's Ferry on the secession of Virginia, and commanded a brigade at Bull Run, where his firm stand gained him his nickname. He showed tactical superiority in the campaign of the Shenandoah valley (1862), and gained several victories, notably at Cedar Run, Manassas, and Harper's Ferry. He was accidentally killed by his own troops at Chancellorsville.

Jackson (of Lodsworth), Baroness, previously **Dame Barbara Mary Ward** (1914–81) English economist, journalist, and conservationist, born in Sussex. She became foreign editor of the *Economist* in 1939 and later lectured in the USA. She was President of the International Institute for Environment and Development (1973–80). Her books include *The International Share Out* (1936), *The Rich Nations and the Poor Nations* (1962), *Spaceship Earth* (1966) and *Only One Earth — the Care and Maintenance of a Small Planet* (1972).

Jackson POP (1990) 395 000, the capital of the state of Mississippi, USA. It lies on the Pearl R, in Hinds County, central Mississippi, and is the largest city in the state. HISTORY established as a trading post (Le Fleur's Bluff) in 1792; became state capital in 1821; much of the city was destroyed by Sherman's forces during the Civil War (1863); there were many civil rights demonstrations in the 1960s. 'Casey' Jones is buried here. [named after President Andrew Jackson]

Jack tar *old use* a sailor.

Jack the Ripper (19c) an unidentified and undiscovered British murderer, who between Aug and Nov 1888 mutilated and murdered six prostitutes in the East End of London. The affair roused much public disquiet, provoked a violent press campaign against the CID and the Home Secretary, and resulted in some reform of police methods.

Jacob 1 a biblical character, son of Isaac, patriarch of the nation Israel. He pretended to be his elder brother Esau to obtain his father Isaac's special blessing (Genesis 27), and so was seen as the inheritor of God's promises. He was re-named *Israel* (perhaps meaning 'God strives' or 'he who strives with God') after his struggle with a divine being. By his wives Leah and Rachel and their maids he fathered 12 sons, to whom the 12 tribes of Israel are traced. 2 a male first name. [Hebrew, = supplanter]

Jacobean *adj.* 1 relating or belonging to the reign of James I of England (VI of Scotland) (1603–25). 2 *said of furniture, drama, etc* typical of the style current in his reign. 3 denoting a style of English architecture characterized by a symmetry of façades, large windows and, in the case of manor houses such as Hatfield (1608–12), E- or H-shaped plans. [from Latin *Jacobus*, James]

Jacobi, Carl Gustav Jacob (1804–51) German mathematician, born in Potsdam. Professor at the University of Königsberg, his *Fundamenta nova* (1829) was the first definitive book on some important mathematical functions, of which he was the joint discoverer. He also made important advances in the study of differential equations, the theory of numbers, and determinants.

Jacobins a radical political group in the French Revolution. Originally the Club Breton in Versailles, it was renamed after moving to the premises of the Dominican or 'Jacobin' fathers in Paris (1789). After successive purges, the club became the instrument of the Reign of Terror under Robespierre's dictatorship (1793–4), and thereafter the name was associated with left-wing extremism.

Jacobite *Brit. Hist.* — *noun* a member or supporter of the Jacobites. — *adj.* relating to the Jacobites. [from Latin *Jacobus*, James]

Jacobites those who supported the claim of the Catholic James II and VII, and his successors, to the British throne. The Jacobites launched two major rebellions (the Fifteen Rebellion, 1715, and the Forty-Five Rebellion, 1745) against the Protestant Hanoverian succession, and in the period 1714–60 some British Tory politicians had Jacobite sympathies.

Jacobsen, Arne (1902–71) Danish architect and interior designer, born in Copenhagen. Appointed Professor of Architecture at the Royal Danish Academy in 1956, his theory was 'economy plus function equals style'. He designed many private houses, including those for Bellevue seaside resort near Copenhagen. His later works include the SAS building, Copenhagen (1959) and St Catherine's College, Oxford (1964).

Jacquard, Joseph Marie (1752–1834) French silk-weaver, born in Lyons. His invention (1801–8) of the Jacquard loom, which uses perforated cards for controlling the movement of the warp threads, enabled the production of highly intricate weaving patterns. Napoleon rewarded him with a small pension, but the silk weavers themselves were long opposed to his machine. By the time of his death, his machine was in almost universal use.

Jacqueline a female first name. [a French feminine diminutive of *Jacques*, the French equivalent of JAMES]

Jacuzzi *noun trademark* a large bath equipped with underwater jets that massage and invigorate the body.

jade¹ *noun* 1 *Geol.* a very hard green, white, brown, or yellow semi-precious stone consisting of either of two minerals, *jadeite* and *nephrite*, used to make vases and carved ornaments. The most highly prized variety is a translucent green form of jadeite. 2 the intense green colour of jade. [from Spanish *piedra de ijada*, colic(-curing) stone]

jade² *noun old use* 1 a disreputable or ill-natured woman. 2 a worn-out old horse.

jaded *adj.* fatigued; dull and bored.

jadeite *noun Geol.* a tough fibrous mineral with a slightly greasy lustre, consisting of a silicate of aluminium and sodium that forms in compact waxy masses, principal sources occurring in Burma and Guatemala. A translucent green form of jadeite is the most highly prized form of jade.

Jaffa see TEL AVIV-JAFFA.

Jaffna POP (1990e) 129 000, the capital of Jaffna district, Northern Provence, Sri Lanka. It is the financial and cultural centre of the Tamil-Hindu dominated north. The area was of great importance to the Portuguese and Dutch colonial powers. There has been fighting between Tamil separatists and Sri Lankan forces in the Jaffna Peninsula since the early 1980s. NOTABLE FEATURES Dutch Fort (1680); many Hindu temples and shrines; beaches, coralline coast, and sand dunes of Manalkadu.

jag¹ — *noun* 1 a sharp projection. 2 *Scot.* an injection or inoculation. — *verb* (**jagged**, **jagging**) to prick, sting, or pierce.

jag² *noun slang* 1 a bout of heavy drinking or drug-taking. 2 a bout of indulgence in anything.

Jagannātha a Hindu deity equated with Vishnu. His temple is in Puri in E India, and is noted for its annual festival. [from Sanskrit *Jagannātha*, lord of the world]

jagged *adj.* having a rough or sharp uneven edge. [from JAG¹]

jaggedly *adv.* in a jagged way.

jaggedness *noun* being jagged.

Jaguar *trademark* a luxury car first produced in Coventry in 1936 by S S Cars. The company was renamed Jaguar Cars Ltd in 1945. It was sold to Ford in 1989.

jaguar *noun* the largest of the American cats, with a deep yellow or tawny coat covered with black spots, more heavily built than a leopard and with larger spots, found mainly in tropical forests, especially near water. Jaguars are strong swimmers, and often catch fish, as well as being capable of stalking prey along tree branches. They feed on capybaras, peccaries, alligators, turtles, and domestic cattle, and are hunted in areas where they prey on domestic animals. They are also shot for their skins. [from S American Indian (Tupí) *jaguara*]

jail *or* **gaol** — *noun* prison. — *verb* to imprison. [from Old French *gaole*]

jailbird *or* **gaolbird** *noun colloq.* a person in prison, especially regularly so.

jailbreak *or* **gaolbreak** *noun* an escape, especially by several prisoners, from jail.

jailer *or* **gaoler** *noun* a person who is in charge of prisoners in a jail.

Jain *noun* an adherent of Jainism.

Jainism an indigenous religion of India which regards Vardhamana Mahavir (599–527 BC) as its founder. Jains believe that salvation consists in conquering material existence through adherence to a strict ascetic discipline, thus freeing the soul from the working of karma to enter eternal all-knowing bliss. An essential practice is Ahimsa, non-injury to living beings. [from Hindi *jina*, conquerer, title of the teachers]

Jaipur POP (1991) 1.5m, the capital of Rajasthan state, NW India, lying SW of Delhi. It was founded in 1727 and has been known as the 'pink city' since 1875, when Sawai Ram Singh had all the buildings of the bazaar painted pink. NOTABLE FEATURES Maharaja's Palace; Sawai Man Singh Museum; Hawa Mahal 'Hall of the Winds' (1799); Jantar Mantar Observatory (1726).

Jakarta *or* **Djakarta**, formerly **Batavia** (until 1949) POP (1990e) 9.3m, the seaport capital of Indonesia and the largest city, situated on the NW coast of Java, at the mouth of the R Liwung on Jakarta Bay. HISTORY developed as a trading post in the 15c; headquarters of the Dutch East India Company in the 17c; became capital in 1949. NOTABLE FEATURES Istiqlal Mosque; 90m-high National Monument; Taman Mini Park.

Jakobson, Roman (1896–1982) Russian theoretician of linguistics, born in Moscow. The founder of the Moscow Linguistic Circle (which generated Russian Formalism), he moved in 1920 to Czechoslovakia and started the Prague Linguistic Circle, and finally in 1941 to the USA, where he taught at Harvard and the Massachusetts Institute of Technology. Many of his influential books and papers on language are included in *Selected Writings* (8 vols, 1962–88).

jalopy *noun* (PL. **jalopies**) *colloq.* a worn-out old car.

jam¹ *noun* a thick sticky food made from fruit boiled with sugar, used as a spread on bread, etc. — **jam tomorrow** *colloq.* something agreeable constantly promised but never provided. **money for jam** *colloq.* money easily made. **want jam on it** *colloq.* to expect more than is reasonable. [perhaps from JAM²]

jam² *verb* (**jammed, jamming**) 1 to stick or wedge so as to be immovable. 2 *trans., intrans. said of machinery, etc* to stick or cause it to stick and stop working. 3 to push or shove; to cram, press, or pack. 4 (*also* **jam something up**) to fill (eg a street) so full that movement comes to a stop. 5 *trans.* to cause interference to (a radio signal, etc), especially deliberately. 6 *intrans. colloq.* to play jazz in a jam session. [probably imitative]

Jamaica POP (1992e) 2.5m, an island nation in the Caribbean Sea. AREA 10 957sq km/ 4 229sq mi. Jamaica is situated 160km/100mi W of Haiti, 144km/89mi S of Cuba and is divided into three counties. CAPITAL Kingston. CHIEF

TOWNS Montego Bay, Spanish Town. TIME ZONE GMT −5. The population are of African (76%) and Afro-European (15%) origin; Christianity is the chief religion. OFFICIAL LANGUAGE English; Jamaican Creole is also spoken. CURRENCY the Jamaican dollar. PHYSICAL DESCRIPTION the third-largest island in the Caribbean Sea with a maximum length of 234km/145mi and width varying from 35km/22mi to 82km/51mi; mountainous and rugged particularly in the E, where the Blue Mts rise to 2 256m; over 100 small rivers, several of which are used for hydroelectric power. CLIMATE humid and tropical climate at sea level, more temperate at higher altitudes; coastal temperatures range from 21°C to 34°C, with an average annual rainfall of 1 980mm; virtually no rainfall on the S and SW plains; the island lies within the hurricane belt. HISTORY visited by Columbus in 1494; settled by the Spanish in 1509; W African slave labour imported for work on sugar plantations from 1640; British occupation in 1655; self-government was introduced in 1944; gained independence in 1962. GOVERNMENT a Governor-General appoints a Prime Minister and a Cabinet; a bicameral Parliament consists of an elected 60-member House of Representatives and a nominated 21-member Senate. ECONOMY plantation agriculture still employs about a third of the workforce; sugar, bananas, citrus fruits, coffee, cocoa, ginger, coconuts, pimento; second-largest producer of bauxite in the world; alumina; gypsum; cement; fertilizer; textiles; foodstuffs; rum; chemical products; tourism is the biggest earner of foreign currency.

Jamaica

jamb *noun* the vertical post at the side of a door, window, or fireplace. [from Old French *jambe*, leg]

jamboree *noun* **1** *colloq.* a large and lively gathering. **2** a large rally of Scouts, Guides, etc.

James I (of Scotland) (1394–1437) King of Scots (1406–37), the third son of Robert III, born in Dunfermline. He was sent for safety to France, but was captured at sea (1406) and imprisoned in England, unable to rule until his release in 1424. An accomplished poet, he wrote *The Kingis Quair* to celebrate his romance with Joan Beaufort, a cousin of Henry V of England. His ruthlessness towards the Stuarts led to his murder at Perth.

James I (of England) (1566–1625) the first Stuart King (1603–25), also King of Scotland (1567–1625) as James VI, the son of Mary, Queen of Scots, and Henry, Lord Darnley, born in Edinburgh Castle. On his mother's forced abdication, he was proclaimed king, and brought up by several regents. At first he ruled through his favourites, which caused a rebellion and a period of imprisonment. He hated Puritanism, and in 1600 managed to establish bishops in Scotland. On Elizabeth I's death, he ascended the English throne by right of his descent (great-grandson) from Margaret, daughter of Henry VII (and sister of Henry VIII).

James II (of Scotland) (1430–60) King of Scots (1437–60), the son of James I, whom he succeeded at the age of six. He took control of the government in 1449, and during the early years tried to curb the power of the mighty Black Douglases, whom he eventually defeated in 1455 at Arkinholm, Dumfriesshire. He was killed during an attempt to recover Roxburgh Castle from the English.

James II (of England) (1633–1701) King of England and Ireland (1685–8), also King of Scotland, as James VII, the second son of Charles I, born in London. Nine months before his father's execution he escaped to Holland. At the Restoration (1660) he was made Lord High Admiral of England, and commanded the fleet in the Dutch Wars, but when he converted to Catholicism he was forced to resign his post. The furore occasioned by the Popish Plot in 1678 (a scare begun by Titus Oates's allegations that there was a plan to murder Charles II and establish Catholicism in England) forced him to retire to the Continent, but attempts made to exclude him from the succession were unsuccessful. When his brother Charles II died without legitimate heirs, he succeeded to the throne. During his reign his actions in favour of Catholicism raised general indignation, and William, Prince of Orange, his son-in-law and nephew, was formally asked by leading clerics and landowners to invade. He made an ineffectual attempt to regain his throne in Ireland, which ended in the battle of the Boyne (1690).

James III (of Scotland) (1452–88) King of Scots (1460–88), the eldest son of James II, whom he succeeded at the age of eight. He took control of the government in 1469, the year of his marriage to Margaret of Denmark, which led to the incorporation of Orkney and Shetland within the Scottish realm (1472). He was defeated and killed by rebel nobles at the Battle of Sauchieburn, near Stirling.

James IV (of Scotland) (1473–1513) King of Scots (1488–1513), the eldest son of James III. He ascended the throne at the age of 15 and was soon active in government. In 1503 he married Margaret Tudor, the eldest daughter of Henry VII — an alliance which led ultimately to the union of the crowns. He nevertheless adhered to the French alliance when Henry VIII joined the League against France, which led to his invasion of England, and his defeat and death at the battle of Flodden, Northumberland.

James V (of Scotland) (1512–42) King of Scots (1513–42), whose father, James IV, died when he was an infant, leaving him to grow up among the quarrelling pro-French and pro-English factions in his country. In 1536 he visited France, and married first Magdeleine, the daughter of Francis I (1537), and, after her death, Mary of Guise (1538). After the French alliance (1542) he warred with England, and an attempted invasion ended in defeat at Solway Moss. He retired to Falkland Palace where his daughter Mary (later Mary, Queen of Scots) was born shortly before his death.

James, also known as **St James** (**the Just**) (1c AD) an early Christian, listed with Joseph, Simon, and Judas (Matthew 13.55) as a 'brother' of Jesus of Nazareth, and identified as the foremost leader of the Christian community in Jerusalem (Galatians 1.19, 2.9; Acts 15.13), not to be confused with James son of Alphaeus or James son of Zebedee. Although he was not one of Jesus' 12 Apostles, he did witness the resurrected Christ (1 Corinthians 15.7). According to Josephus, he was martyred by stoning (c.62 AD). His feast day is 1 May.

James (son of Alphaeus), also known as **St James** (**the Less**) (1c AD) one of the 12 Apostles of Jesus Christ, possibly the James whose mother Mary is referred to at the crucifixion of Christ.

James (son of Zebedee), also known as **St James** (**the Great**) (1c AD) one of the 12 Apostles of Jesus Christ, often listed with John (his brother) and Peter in the group closest to Jesus, who were among the first to be called, and who were with him at the Transfiguration and at Gethsemane. James and John were also called *Boanerges* ('sons of thunder'). According to Acts

12.2, James was martyred under Herod Agrippa I (c.44 AD). His feast day is 25 Jul.

James a male first name, borne by two of Christ's disciples and several kings of Scotland and England. [originally from JACOB]

James, Clive (Vivian Leopold) (1939–) Australian broadcaster and writer, born in Sydney. He began his career as a television critic with the *Observer* (1972–82), later publishing some of his work and writing other non-fiction, fiction, and verse, and three volumes of memoirs. Known as a perceptive cultural commentator, his clever turn of phrase was later heard on television in his *Postcard From . . .* series (1989–) and his late-night chat shows.

James, Henry (1843–1916) US novelist, born in New York City. He travelled widely in the USA and Europe, and studied law at Harvard, before he began to write literary reviews and short stories. His work as a novelist can be divided into three periods. In the first, he is mainly concerned with the impact of American life on the older European civilization, as in *Roderick Hudson* (1875), *Portrait of a Lady* (1881), and *The Bostonians* (1886). He lived in England from 1869, and his second period is devoted to purely English subjects, such as *The Tragic Muse* (1890) and *The Spoils of Poynton* (1897). He reverted to Anglo-American attitudes in his last period, which includes *The Wings of a Dove* (1902) and *The Ambassadors* (1903).

James, Jesse (Woodson) (1847–82) US Wild West outlaw, born in Clay County, Missouri. After fighting with a guerilla group in the American Civil War, he led numerous bank and train robberies before being murdered by one of his associates. He has been the subject of many Hollywood westerns.

James, P(hyllis) D(orothy) see JAMES (OF HOLLAND PARK), BARONESS.

James, William (1842–1910) US psychologist and philosopher, born in New York City, the brother of the novelist Henry James. He began teaching anatomy and physiology (1873), and philosophy (1879) at Harvard. His books include *The Principles of Psychology* (1890), *The Will to Believe and Other Essays in Popular Philosophy* (1897), and *The Varieties of Religious Experience* (1902). He helped found the American Society for Psychical Research.

James (of Holland Park), P(hyllis) D(orothy) James, Baroness, originally **Phyllis Dorothy White** (1920–) English detective-story writer, born in Oxford. She was a National Health Service administrator (1949–68), then worked in the Home Office (1968–9), first in the Police Department, then in the children's division of the Criminal Law Department. Her first novel was *Cover Her Face* (1962). Other novels include *Death of an Expert Witness* (1977), *A Taste for Death* (1986), *Devices and Desires* (1991), and *The Children of Men* (1992).

James, Letter of a New Testament writing attributed to James, who was considered in early tradition to be the brother of Jesus, but who is now often considered a late 1c author, because the writing shows little similarity to Pauline theology and polemic. The letter emphasizes a variety of ethical teachings, but was sometimes criticized (most notably by Martin Luther) for lacking a distinctively Christian message and for its un-Pauline emphasis on 'works' rather than 'faith'.

Jameson, Sir Leander Starr, 1st Baronet (1853–1917) South African politician, born in Edinburgh, Scotland. Trained in medicine, 'Dr Jim' engaged in pioneer work, was in 1891 made administrator for the South Africa Company, and was very popular among the whites. He invaded the Transvaal (the Jameson Raid) on 29 Dec 1895, but the rising he had expected failed to materialize. At Krugersdorp Jameson and his men were overpowered by Boers, and were compelled to surrender (2 Jan

1896). Handed over to the British authorities (Jul), Jameson was condemned in London to 15 months' imprisonment, but was released in Dec. In 1900 he was elected to the Cape Legislative Assembly, and in 1904–8 was (Progressive) premier of Cape Colony.

Jameson Raid an expedition against the South African Republic (Dec 1895–Jan 1896), which was supposed to link up with a revolt by white workers on the Rand and topple the government of President Kruger. Leander Starr Jameson, administrator for the South Africa Company at Fort Salisbury, led a detachment of British South Africa Police into the Transvaal, but they were easily defeated and arrested. The German Kaiser Wilhelm II sent a telegram of congratulation to Kruger, and the incident caused a major government crisis in Britain as well as contributing to the tensions that led to the Boer War.

Jamestown POP (1992e) 2 000, the seaport capital and the only town on the British island of St Helena in the S Atlantic Ocean.

Jamestown a deserted town, 24km/15mi inland from Chesapeake Bay, Virginia, the site of the first successful British settlement in the USA. It was founded in 1607 as James Fort, but after 1699 was superseded as the capital of Virginia by Williamsburg, and abandoned. It was excavated archaeologically from 1934 to 1956.

Jammu-Kashmir POP (1981) 7.7m, a state in the extreme N of India. AREA 101 283sq km/ 39 095sq mi. The state is bounded N by the July 1972 line of control (separating territory claimed by both India and Pakistan), W by Pakistan, E by China, and is crossed by several mountains and rivers. HISTORY became part of the Mughal Empire in 1586; Afghan rule in 1786; annexed to the Sikh Punjab in 1819; Kashmir asked for agreements with both India and Pakistan under the Indian Independence Act of 1947; attacked by Pakistan and acceded to India in 1947; further hostilities in 1965 and 1971; unrest continues. CAPITAL Srinagar (summer), Jammu (winter). GOVERNMENT governed by a 36-member Legislative Council and a 76-member Legislative Assembly. ECONOMY rice, wheat, maize, fruit; forestry; crafts; manufacturing industry largely in Jammu; horticulture widespread in Kashmir.

jammy *adj.* (**jammier, jammiest**) **1** covered, or filled, with jam. **2** *colloq.*, *said of a person* lucky. **3** *colloq.*, *said of a job, etc* profitable, especially at little cost in effort.

jam-packed *adj. colloq.* packed tight.

jam session *slang* a session of live, especially improvised, jazz or popular music.

Jan *or* **Jan.** *abbrev.* January.

Janáček, Leoš (1854–1928) Czech composer, born in Hukvaldy, Moravia. At 16 he was choirmaster in Brno and he became devoted to the Czech folksong tradition. He matured late as a composer, principally of operas, which include *Osud* (1904), *Jenufa* (1904), *Kátya Kabanov* (1921), *The Cunning little Vixen* (1924), and *From The House of the Dead* (1928); it was only after the Prague première of *Jenufa* in 1916 that his reputation was secured. He also wrote a mass, instrumental chamber pieces, and song cycles.

Jane, Frederick Thomas (1865–1916) English naval author, journalist, and artist, born in Upottery, Devon. He worked first as an artist, then as a naval correspondent. He founded and edited *Jane's Fighting Ships* (1898) and *All the World's Aircraft* (1909), wrote fictional works including the novel *A Royal Bluejacket* (1908), and invented the naval war-game.

Jane a female first name, the most popular feminine equivalent of *John*, and often used in combination with another name, eg *Mary-Jane*. [from Old French *Je(h)anne*]

Jane Eyre a novel by Charlotte Brontë (1847). It describes the life of the narrator Jane Eyre, a

plain but passionate orphan, as she journeys towards independence and true love.

JANET *abbrev.* Joint Academic Network, a computer network linking UK universities and research bodies.

Janet a female first name, and until the 20c confined to Scotland. [a Middle English diminutive of JANE]

jangle *verb* **1** *trans., intrans.* to make or cause to make a discordant ringing noise. **2** to upset or irritate. [from Old French *jangler*]

jangly *adj.* (**janglier, jangliest**) making a jangling sound.

Janice a female first name, introduced at the end of the 19c. [a derivative of JANE, with suffix *-ice*]

janissary *or* **janizary** *noun* (PL. **janissaries, janizaries**) *Hist.* a soldier of the Turkish sultan's personal guard. [from Turkish *yeniçeri*, new troops]

janitor *noun* **1** *North Amer., Scot.* a caretaker. **2** a doorkeeper. [from Latin *janitor*, from *janua*, door]

Jan Mayen formerly English **Hudson's Tutches** a Norwegian volcanic island in the Arctic Ocean, lying 480km/298mi E of Greenland and 576km/358mi NE of Iceland. AREA 380sq km/147sq mi; length 53km/33mi. The highest point is Beerenberg at 2 277m. HISTORY discovered by Henry Hudson in 1608; annexed to Norway in 1929. There are radio and meteorological stations on the island.

Jansen, Cornelius (Otto) (1585–1638) Dutch Roman Catholic theologian, founder of the reform movement known as Jansenism, born in Acquoi. He became Professor of Theology at Louvain (1630) and Bishop of Ypres (1636), where he died after completing his four-volume work, *Augustinus* (published 1640). This sought to prove that St Augustine's teaching on grace, free will, and predestination was opposed to the teaching of the Jesuit schools. The book was condemned by Pope Urban VIII (1642), but the controversy raged in France for nearly a century, until a large number of Jansenists emigrated to the Netherlands.

Jansenism a heretical movement in the Roman Catholic Church in France and Holland in the 17c and 18c, formed by Cornelius Jansen, who adopted the theology of St Augustine, particularly concerning predestination, and promulgated a rigorous and ascetic way of life.

Condemned in France, where its adherents included Antoine Arnauld and Blaise Pascal, it survived into the 20c in Holland.

Jansky, Karl Guthe (1905–50) US radio engineer, born in Norman, Oklahoma. While investigating the sources of interference on short-wave radio telephone transmissions at Bell Telephone Laboratories, he accidentally made the first discovery of an astronomical radio source (1932), in the direction of the centre of our galaxy.

January *noun* the first month of the year. [from Latin *Januarius mensis*, month of the god Janus]

Janus in Roman mythology, the god of gates, doorways, and beginnings. He is the first god named in a list, and the god of the first month (January). He is usually depicted with a two-faced head.

Japan, Japanese **Nippon**, or **Nihon** POP (1992e) 123.5m, an island state off the E coast of Asia. AREA 381 945sq km/147 431sq mi. It comprises the four large islands of Hokkaido, Honshu, Kyushu, Shikoku, and many small islands. The country is divided into nine regions and is bounded in the W by the Sea of Japan, Korea Strait, and East China Sea, in the E by the Pacific Ocean, and in the N by the Tsugaru-kaikyo Strait. CAPITAL Tokyo. CHIEF TOWNS Yokohama, Osaka, Nagoya, Sapporo, Kyoto, Kobe. TIMEZONE GMT +9. Over 99% of the population are Japanese; the chief religions are Shinto and Buddhism. OFFICIAL LANGUAGE Japanese. CURRENCY the yen. PHYSICAL DESCRIPTION the islands consist mainly of steep mountains with many volcanoes; the northernmost island, Hokkaido, has a central range which runs N–S, rising to over 2 000m, falling to coastal uplands and plains; Honshu, the largest island, comprises parallel arcs of mountains bounded by narrow coastal plains and includes the sacred Mt Fuji rising to 3 776m; the heavily populated Kanto plain lies in the E; the islands of Shikoku and Kyushu in the SW consist of clusters of low cones and rolling hills, mostly at 1 000–2 000m high; to the S of this, the country tails off into the Ryukyu chain of volcanic islands, of which Okinawa is the largest; earthquakes occur frequently. CLIMATE an oceanic climate, influenced by the Asian monsoon; there is heavy winter rainfall on the W coasts of N Honshu and in Hokkaido; in the N there are short, warm summers, and severe winters, with heavy snow; Akita in N Honshu has an average daily temperature of −5–2°C in Jan,

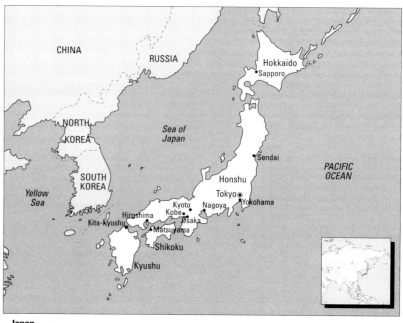

Japan

Japanese Emperors

The first 14 emperors (to Chuai) are regarded as legendary, and the regnal dates for the 15th to the 28th emperor (Senka), taken from the early Japanese chronicle, *Nihon shoki* are not considered to be authentic.

Date	Name	Date	Name	Date	Name
660–585BC	Jimmu	724–49	Shomu	1246–59	Go-Fukakusa
581–549BC	Suizei	749–58	Koken	1259–74	Kameyama
549–11BC	Annei	758–64	Junnin	1274–87	Go-Uda
510–477BC	Itoku	764–70	Shotoku	1287–98	Fushimi
475–393BC	Kosho	770–81	Konin	1298–1301	Go-Fushimi
392–291BC	Koan	781–806	Kammu	1301–8	Go-Nijo
290–215BC	Korei	806–9	Heizei	1308–18	Hanazono
214–158BC	Kogen	809–23	Saga	1318–39	Daigo II (Go-Daigo)
158–98BC	Kaika	823–33	Junna	1339–68	Go-Murakami
97–30BC	Sujin	833–50	Nimmyo	1368–83	Chokei
29BC–AD70	Suinin	850–8	Montoku	1383–92	Go-Kameyama
71–130	Keiko	858–76	Seiwa		Northern Court
131–190	Selmu	876–84	Yozei	1331–3	Kogon
192–200	Chuai	884–7	Koko	1336–48	Komyo
270–310	Ojin	887–97	Uda	1348–51	Suko
313–99	Nintoku	897–930	Daigo	1352–71	Go-Kogon
400–5	Richu	930–46	Suzaku	1371–82	Go-Enyu
406–10	Hanzel	946–67	Murakami	1382–1412	Go-Komatsu
412–53	Ingyo	967–9	Reizei	1412–28	Shoko
453–6	Anko	969–84	En'yu	1428–64	Go-Hanazono
456–79	Yuryaku	984–6	Kazan	1464–1500	Go-Tsuchimikado
480–4	Seinei	986–1011	Ichijo	1500–26	Go-Kashiwabara
485–7	Kenzo	1011–16	Sanjo	1526–57	Go-Nara
488–98	Ninken	1016–36	Go-Ichijo	1557–86	Ogimachi
498–506	Buretsu	1036–45	Go-Suzako	1586–1611	Go-Yozei
507–31	Keitai	1045–68	Go-Reizei	1611–29	Go-Mizunoo
531–5	Ankan	1068–72	Go-Sanyo	1629–43	Meisho
535–9	Senka	1072–86	Shirakawa	1643–54	Go-Komyo
539–71	Kimmei	1086–1107	Horikawa	1654–63	Go-Sai
572–85	Bidatsu	1107–23	Toba	1663–87	Reigen
585–7	Yomei	1123–41	Sutoku	1687–1709	Higashiyama
587–92	Sushun	1141–55	Konoe	1709–35	Nakamikado
592–628	Suiko	1155–8	Goshirakawa	1735–47	Sakuramachi
629–41	Jomei	1158–65	Nijo	1747–62	Momozono
642–5	Kogyoku	1165–8	Rokujo	1762–70	Go-Sakuramachi
645–54	Kotuko	1168–80	Takakura	1770–9	Go-Momozono
655–61	Saimei	1180–3	Antoku	1779–1817	Kokaku
662–71	Tenji	1183–98	Go-Toba	1817–46	Ninko
671–2	Kobun	1198–1210	Tsuchimikado	1846–66	Komei
673–86	Temmu	1210–21	Juntoku	1867–1912	Meiji
686–97	Jito	1221	Chukyo	1912–26	Taisho
697–707	Mommu	1221–32	Goshirakawa	1926–89	Hirohito
707–15	Gemmei	1232–42	Shijo	1989–	Akihito
715–24	Gensho	1242–6	Go-Saga		

19–28°C in Aug, and rainfall in this area is a minimum of 104mm in Feb–Mar and a maximum of 211mm in Sep; there is variable winter weather throughout Japan, especially in the N and W; typhoons occur in summer and early autumn; there are mild and almost subtropical winters, with light rainfall, in S Honshu, Shikoku, and Kyushu; the summer heat is often oppressive, especially in the cities. HISTORY originally occupied by the Ainu; in the 4c the country developed from individual communities into small states; by the 5c, the Yamato dynasty was the most dominant; culture was strongly influenced by China in the 8c–12c; it was ruled by feudal shoguns for many centuries; little contact was made with the West until the Meiji Restoration in 1868; successful wars were waged with China in 1894–5, and Russia in 1904–5; Korea was annexed in 1910; occupied Manchuria in 1931–2; entered World War II with a surprise attack on the US fleet at Pearl Harbor, Hawaii, in 1941; occupied British and Dutch possessions in SE Asia in 1941–2; was pushed back during 1943–5; atomic bombs were dropped on Hiroshima and Nagasaki in 1945; there was strong economic growth in 1960s; affected severely by the international oil crisis in the 1970s; investment in other countries led to increased economic success and a trade surplus with most trading partners. GOVERNMENT a constitutional monarchy with an Emperor as head of state, and a Prime Minister and Cabinet; bicameral Diet (*Kokkai*), with a 512-member House of Representatives (*Shugiin*) elected every four years and a 252-member House of Councillors (*Sangiin*) elected every six years. ECONOMY natural resources are limited, with less than 20% of the land under cultivation; there is intensive crop production, principally of rice; timber, fishing; metallurgy; engineering; electrical goods; electronics industries; vehicles; petrochemicals; ship-building; textiles; chemicals.

Japan, Sea of an arm of the Pacific Ocean, bounded by South Korea and North Korea to the SW, Russia to the N and W, and the islands of Japan to the E and S. AREA 1 012 900sq km/390 900sq mi. The NE-flowing warm current keeps coastal conditions ice-free as far N as Vladivostok in Russia, the only major port in the N Pacific which is open all year.

japan — *noun* a hard glossy black lacquer, originally from Japan, used to coat wood and metal. — *verb* (**japanned, japanning**) to lacquer with japan. [from JAPAN]

Japanese — *noun* 1 (PL. **Japanese**) a native or citizen of Japan. 2 the language of Japan. — *adj.* relating or belonging to Japan, or its people or language.
◊ Japanese is an isolated language spoken by c.118 million people in Japan and a further 2 million people elsewhere. It may be related to the Altaic family, although the connection is uncertain. It has been strongly influenced by Mandarin Chinese: one of its three integrated writing systems (*kanji*) is based on Chinese ideograms, and it has a large vocabulary of foreign loan words (*gairaigo*) which are written in the syllabic system (*katagana*). Japanese has an extensive literature, including religious writings and the poetic form *haiku*.

jape *noun old use* a trick, prank, or joke. [from Middle English *japen*]

Japheth a biblical character, one of the sons of Noah who survived the Flood, the brother of Shem and Ham. He was the ancestor of peoples in the area of Asia Minor and the Aegean (Genesis 10).

Japonaiserie a term used for the imitation of Japanese motifs, patterns, and compositions by European artists from the mid-19c to the early 20c. James McNeill Whistler and Vincent van Gogh were among those inspired, in particular by coloured woodcuts.

japonica *noun* 1 a red-flowered shrub of the quince family, originally from Japan. 2 another name for the oriental plant camellia. [from Latin *japonica*, Japanese]

Jaquenetta the country wench pursued by Don Adriano de Armado in Shakespeare's *Love's Labour's Lost*.

Jaques one of the exiled Duke's lords, of a melancholic, philosophical temperament, in Shakespeare's *As You Like It*.

Jaques-Dalcroze, Emile (1865–1950) Swiss music teacher and composer, born in Vienna. He was the founder of eurhythmics, a method of expressing the rhythmical aspects of music by physical movement. He taught at Dresden and Geneva, where he was Professor at the Conservatory, and composed operas and other works.

jar¹ *noun* 1 a wide-mouthed cylindrical container, usually of glass; the contents of this. 2 *colloq.* a glass of beer. [from Old French *jarre*, from Arabic *jarrah*, earthenware vessel]

jar² — *verb* (**jarred, jarring**) 1 *intrans.* to have a harsh effect; to grate. 2 *trans., intrans.* to jolt or vibrate. 3 *trans., intrans.* to make or cause to make a harsh sound. 4 *intrans.* (**jar with something**) to clash or conflict with it: *buildings that jar with the environment.* — *noun* a jarring sensation, shock, or jolt. [imitative]

Jarash, ancient **Gerasa** a village in Irbid governorate, East Bank, NW Jordan, 35km/22mi N of Amman. It is built on the site of the old city of Gerasa. NOTABLE FEATURES colonnades; triumphal arch; temples; theatres; baths.

jardinière *noun* 1 an ornamental pot or stand for flowers. 2 *Cookery* an accompaniment of mixed vegetables for a meat dish. [from French *jardinière*, feminine of *jardinier*, gardener]

jargon *noun* 1 the specialized vocabulary of a particular trade, profession, group, or activity. 2 *derog.* confusing or meaningless talk. [from Old French *jargon*]

Jarman, Derek (1942–94) English painter and film-maker, born in Northwood, Middlesex. He studied painting at the Slade School, London (1963–7). He did costume and set design for the Royal Ballet and first worked in the cinema as a production designer for Ken Russell's *The Devils* (1970). He directed his first feature film, *Sebastiane*, in 1976 and transferred his painterly instincts to the cinema in a succession of often controversial works exploring the decline of modern Britain, his homosexual sensibilities, and artistic idols. His films include *Jubilee* (1977), *Caravaggio* (1985), *The Last of England* (1987), *Edward II* (1991), an adaptation of Christopher Marlowe's 1594 play, and *Wittgenstein* (1993).

jarring *adj.* that jars.

jarringly *adv.* 1 harshly. 2 with a shock or jolt.

Jarrow POP (1981) 31 000, a port town in South Tyneside borough, Tyne and Wear, NE England. It lies on the R Tyne, 8km/5mi E of Newcastle, and forms part of the Tyneside urban area. The Jarrow March to London took place in 1936.

NOTABLE FEATURE 7c monastery, home of the Venerable Bede.

Jarrow March a march (Oct 1936) to London by unemployed workers. The Durham shipbuilding and mining town Jarrow was among the worst affected by the Depression, and the march to put the case for the unemployed took place at a time when the economy was recovering in much of the rest of the country. It alerted the more prosperous South and Midlands to the intractable problems of depressed areas.

Jarry, Alfred (1873–1907) French writer, born in Laval. His satirical play, *Ubu-Roi*, was first written when he was 15 and later revised; it was produced in 1896. He wrote short stories, poems, and other plays in a Surrealist style, and invented a logic of the absurd which he called *pataphysique*.

Jaruzelski, General Wojciech (Witold) (1923–) Polish soldier and politician, born near Lublin. He became Chief of General Staff (1965), Minister of Defence (1968), a member of the Politburo (1971), and Prime Minister (1981–5). Later in 1981, in an attempt to ease the country's economic problems and to counteract the increasing political influence of the free trade union Solidarity, he declared a state of martial law, which was lifted in 1982. He was head of state (1985–9), and President of the Polish People's Republic in 1989, when he relinquished his leadership of the Polish United Workers' Party (PUWP), and President of the Polish Republic until Dec 1990, when he was succeeded by Lech Walesa, the leader of Solidarity.

Jarvie, Baillie Nicol the level-headed Glasgow merchant who accompanies Francis Osbaldistone to the Highlands in Sir Walter Scott's *Rob Roy*.

Jasmine *or* **Jasmin** a female first name, after the flower.

jasmine *noun* a shrub or vine of the genus *Jasminium* with fragrant white or yellow flowers, native to Asia, but widely cultivated as an ornamental plant and as a source of jasmine oil for use in perfumery. The flowers are used to scent tea. [from Persian *yasmin*]

Jason 1 in Greek mythology, the leader of the Argonauts and son of Aeson, King of Iolcos. When Pelias usurped the kingdom, Jason was taken away and educated by the Centaur Chiron. He returned to the city to claim the throne, and was sent by Pelias on the quest of the Golden Fleece. After many adventures, he led the Argonauts to Colchis, where he obtained the fleece with the assistance of Medea, whom he married. He later deserted her for Glauce, and died sitting under the wreck of the *Argo*, whose stern-post fell on him. **2** a male first name. [probably from Greek *iasthai*, to heal]

jasper *noun Geol.* a usually red semi-precious gemstone that is an impure form of chalcedony (a variety of the mineral quartz) containing iron oxides, used to make jewellery and ornaments. [from Greek *iaspis*]

Jaspers, Karl (Theodor) (1883–1969) German existentialist philosopher, born in Oldenburg. He joined the psychiatric clinic (1909–15) at Heidelberg, and became Professor of Psychology in 1916 and of Philosophy in 1921. His main work is the three-volume *Philosophie* (1932), a systematic exposition of existential philosophy. With the advent of Nazism, he was removed from his Chair (1937) and had his work banned, but he nonetheless stayed in Germany, and was awarded the Goethe Prize in 1947. From 1948 until his death he was professor at Basle.

jaundice *noun* a condition in which there is an excess of the bile pigment *bilirubin* in the blood, as a result of which the skin and the whites of the eyes take on a yellowish appearance. It is often a symptom of liver disease, anaemia, malaria, or obstruction of the bile duct by gallstones. [from Old French *jaunisse*, from *jaune*, yellow]

jaundiced *adj.* **1** suffering from jaundice. **2** *said of a person or attitude* bitter or resentful; cynical.

jaunt — *noun* a short journey for pleasure. — *verb intrans.* to go for a jaunt.

jauntily *adv.* with a jaunty manner.

jauntiness *noun* being jaunty.

jaunty *adj.* (**jauntier**, **jauntiest**) **1** *said of a person's manner or personality* breezy and exuberant. **2** *said of dress, etc* smart; stylish. [from French *gentil*, noble, gentle]

Jaurès, (Auguste Marie Joseph) Jean (1859–1914) French socialist leader, writer, and orator, born in Castres. He lectured on philosophy at Toulouse, became a deputy (1885), cofounded the socialist paper *L'Humanité* (1904), and was the main figure in the founding of the French Socialist Party. He was assassinated in Paris.

Java, Indonesian **Jawa** POP (1990) 96.4m, an island of Indonesia, in the Greater Sunda group, SE of Sumatra and S of Borneo. AREA 132 187sq km/51 024sq mi. It is one of the most densely populated island in the world. This mountainous island, covered with dense rainforest, has 115 volcanic peaks, of which 15 are still active. The mountains rise to 3 371m at Gunung Sumbung and drop sharply into the Java Sea in the S. CHIEF TOWNS Jakarta (capital of Indonesia), Bandung, Surabaya. ECONOMY textiles; timber; rubber, tea, tobacco, rice, maize, sugar. The island is noted for its batik method of cloth decoration. NOTABLE FEATURES Siva temple Prambanan (9c); Buddhist temple; Hindu temple.

Java Man the first known fossil of *Homo erectus*, found in Java in 1891 by the Dutch anatomist Eugène Dubois (1858–1940). It was long known by the name he gave it: *Pithecanthropus erectus*.

Javanese the largest ethnic group of Java, Indonesia (present-day population c.65m). Their language (Javanese), a member of the Indo-Pacific family, is spoken throughout Java and in parts of Indonesia, and has a literary tradition dating from the 8c. The people are Muslim with some Hindu traditions retained from an earlier period.

Java Sea a sea in SE Asia, bounded N by Borneo, S by Java, and W by Sumatra. It is linked to the Celebes Sea in the E by the Makassar Strait.

javelin *noun* **1** a light spear for throwing as a weapon or in sport. **2** throwing the javelin as an athletic event. [from Old French *javeline*]
◇ The athletics field event involves throwing a spear-like javelin which consists of three parts: the pointed metal head, the shaft, and the grip. The men's javelin is 2.6–2.7m in length, and weighs 800g; the women's javelin is 2.2–2.3m in length, and weighs at least 600g. With the javelin in one hand, the competitor runs to a specified mark and throws it; for the throw to count, the metal head must touch the ground before any other part. The mark made by the head is the point used for measuring the distance achieved.

jaw — *noun* **1** either of the two hinged parts of the skull in which the teeth are set. **2** the lower part of the face round the mouth and chin. **3** (**jaws**) the mouth, especially of an animal. **4** (**jaws**) a threshold, especially of something fearful: *the jaws of death*. **5** (**jaws**) the gripping parts of a tool, etc. **6** *colloq.* a long conversation; a talking-to; talk; chatter. — *verb intrans. colloq.* to chatter, gossip, or talk. [from Old French *joue*, cheek]

jawbone *noun* the bone that forms the lower jaw.

jay *noun* a noisy bird of the crow family, with pinkish-brown plumage and blue, black, and white bars on its wings. [from Old French *jai*]

Jayawardene, Junius Richard (1906–) Sri Lankan politician, born in Colombo. A member of the State Council (1943) and the House of Representatives (1947), he became Honorary Secretary of the Ceylon National Congress (1940–7), Minister of Finance (1947–53), Vice-President of the United National Party, Deputy Leader of the Opposition (1960–5), Opposition Leader (1970–7), Prime Minister (1977–8), and finally President (1978–89).

Jay's Treaty an agreement (1794) between the USA and Britain to end the British occupation of military posts in the north-western parts of US territory, and to alter the terms of US commerce with Britain and its colonies. Negotiated by American jurist John Jay (1745–1829), it was very unpopular with the US public, largely because of the restrictions it imposed on US trade with the West Indies.

jaywalk *verb intrans.* to cross streets at will, without regard to traffic. [from JAY, with the meaning 'fool']

jaywalker *noun* a pedestrian who jaywalks.

jaywalking *noun* crossing the road carelessly, or disregarding pedestrian crossing signals.

jazz — *noun* **1** popular music of Black American origin, with strong, catchy rhythms, performed with much improvisation. **2** *colloq.* talk; nonsense; business, stuff, etc. — *verb* (*usually* **jazz something up**) *colloq.* **1** to enliven or brighten it. **2** to give it a jazzy rhythm.
— **... and all that jazz** *colloq.* ... and all that sort of thing: *philosophy and all that jazz.*
◇ Jazz originated in the southern states of the USA at the beginning of the 20c. The music was a fusion of ragtime and the blues, influenced by European military (especially marching) tunes. It was characterized by strongly accented rhythms conflicting with a driving basic pulse (syncopation) and collective improvisation, exploiting the unusual timbres and extreme ranges of instruments such as the trumpet or cornet, clarinet, trombone, and piano. The 1930s saw the development of the style known as swing, with large bands in which brass and reed sections predominated. From the 1940s, there was a return to collective improvisation in smaller ensembles, and greater emphasis on individual virtuosity. Modern jazz has developed into various styles, though at least one of the elements of traditional jazz is usually present.

jazzily *adv.* in a jazzy way.

jazz poetry poetry which is recited to the accompaniment of jazz music, popular in the 1960s in Britain (especially London) and the USA. One of the principal UK exponents was the poet and dramatist Christopher Logue (1926–).

Jazz Singer, The a US film directed by Alan Crosland (1927). The first film with synchronized music and dialogue, it is the story of a jazz entertainer (played by Al Jolson) torn between his profession and his father's condemnation of it as sacrilegious.

jazzy *adj.* (**jazzier**, **jazziest**) **1** in the style of, or like, jazz. **2** *colloq.* showy; flashy; stylish.

JCB *noun* a vehicle or machine used in the building industry, with a digging shovel at the front and a digging arm at the back. [named after Joseph Cyril Bamford, the manufacturer]

JCR *abbrev.* junior common room.

J-curve *noun Econ.* a J-shaped curve on graphs showing balance-of-trade statistics over a period of time after a currency has been devalued. After a small initial decrease, there is a large sustained increase as the effect of cheaper exports and more expensive imports is felt.

jealous *adj.* (*often* **jealous of someone** *or* **something**) **1** envious of someone else, his or her possessions, success, talents, etc. **2** suspicious and resentful of possible rivals; possessive. **3** anxiously protective of something one has.

4 *Biblical, said of God* intolerant of unfaithfulness. **5** caused by jealousy: *a jealous fury*. [from Old French *gelos*, from Greek *zelos*, rivalry, jealousy]

jealously *adv.* in a jealous way.

jealousy *noun* (PL. **jealousies**) **1** the emotion of envy or suspicious possessiveness. **2** (*usually* **jealousies**) an occurrence of this.

Jean a female first name, until the 20c largely confined to Scotland. [a medieval variant of JANE, close to the French source of *Je(h)anne*]

Jean De Florette a French film directed by Claude Berri (1986). The first part of a lavishly beautiful period drama, starring Gérard Depardieu, it is about a peasant farmers' dispute over a spring; the sequel is *Manon Des Sources*.

Jeans, Sir James Hopwood (1877–1946) English physicist and astronomer, born in Ormskirk, near Southport. He taught at Princeton University and Cambridge before becoming a research associate at Mt Wilson Observatory in Pasadena. He made important contributions to the theory of gases, stellar evolution, and quantum theory, and was renowned as a popularizer of science for works such as *The Universe Around Us* (1929).

jeans *pl. noun* casual denim trousers, especially blue. [from *jean*, a strong cotton from *Gênes* (French, Genoa)]

Jeddah *or* **Jedda** *or* **Jiddah** POP (1991) 1.8m, the commercial centre and largest port in Saudi Arabia. It is situated in Mecca province, in the W central area of the country, on the E shore of the Red Sea, 64km/40mi W of Mecca. It is a port of entry on the pilgrimage route to Mecca.

Jeep *noun trademark* a light military vehicle capable of travelling over rough country. [from *GP*, general-purpose vehicle]

jeer — *verb* **1** to mock or deride (a speaker, performer, etc). **2** *intrans.* (**jeer at**) to laugh unkindly: *jeered at his accent*. — *noun* a taunt, insult, or hoot of derision.

Jeeves, Reginald the noble, intelligent manservant who tends Bertie Wooster like a guardian angel, displaying no emotion, in the stories and novels of P G Wodehouse.

Jefferson, Thomas (1743–1826) US statesman, the third President, born in Shadwell, Virginia. He became a lawyer (1767), joined the revolutionary party, took a prominent part in the first Continental Congress (1774), and drafted the Declaration of Independence. He was Governor of Virginia (1779–81), Minister in France (1785), Secretary of State (1789), Vice-President under Adams (1797–1801), and then became President (1801–9). His administration was marked by the war with Tripoli, the Louisiana Purchase (1803), and the prohibition of the slave trade. He retired in 1809, but continued to advise as an elder statesman.

Jefferson City POP (1990) 36 000, the capital of the state of Missouri, USA. It lies on the Missouri R, in Cole County, central Missouri. It achieved city status in 1839.

Jeffreys, Sir Harold (1891–1989) English mathematician, geophysicist, and astronomer, born in Fatfield, Durham. Professor at Cambridge, he discovered the discontinuity between the Earth's upper and lower mantle, found evidence for the fluid nature of the core, and did much pioneering theoretical work on the shape and strength of the Earth. He also made important contributions to planetary astronomy, and devised a theory of probability applicable to a wide range of sciences.

Jeffreys (of Wem), George Jeffreys, 1st Baron (1648–89) English judge, born near Wrexham. He was active in the Popish Plot prosecutions and rose to become Chief Justice of the King's Bench (1683). In every state trial he proved a willing tool of the Crown, and was raised to the peerage by James II (1685). His journey to the

west country to try the followers of Monmouth earned the name of the 'bloody assizes' for its severity. He was Lord Chancellor (1685–8), but on James's flight was imprisoned in the Tower.

Jeffries, John (1744–1819) US balloonist and physician, born in Boston. He settled in England after the American Revolution, and made the first balloon crossing of the English Channel with the French aeronaut, François Blanchard, in 1785.

jehad see JIHAD.

Jehovah a term used since the 11c as a form of the Hebrew name for Israel's God 'Yahweh'. It combines the Latinized consonants of the Hebrew word *YHWH* with the vowels of the Hebrew word *Adonai* ('Master, Lord').

Jehovah's Witness *noun* a member of a fundamentalist sect of Christians.

Jehovah's Witnesses a millennialist sect organized (1884) in the USA by Charles Taze Russell (1852–1916). Previously called 'Millennial Dawnists' and 'International Bible Students', they adopted the name Jehovah's Witnesses in 1931. They have their own translation of the Bible, which they interpret literally. They believe in the imminent second coming of Christ, avoid worldly involvement, and refuse to obey any law which they see as a contradiction of the law of God (eg refusing to take oaths, enter military service, or receive blood transfusions). They publish *The Watchtower*, meet in churches called Kingdom Halls, and 'witness' through regular house-to-house preaching.

jejune *adj. derog.* **1** *said of writing, ideas, etc* dull, banal, unoriginal, and empty of imagination. **2** childish; naïve. [from Latin *jejunus*, hungry, empty]

jejunum *noun Anat.* the part of the small intestine between the duodenum and the ileum. [from Latin *jejunum intestinum*, empty intestine]

Jekyll and Hyde a person with two distinct personalities, one good, the other evil (see DR JEKYLL AND MR HYDE).

jell *or* **gel** *verb intrans.* (**jelled, jelling**) **1** to become firm; to set. **2** to take definite shape. [from JELLY]

Jellicoe, John Rushworth, 1st Earl (1859–1935) English admiral, born in Southampton. He became Third Sea Lord (1908), and was Commander-in-Chief at the outbreak of World War I, in which his main engagement was the battle of Jutland (1916). Promoted First Sea Lord, he organized the defences against German submarines, and was made Admiral of the Fleet (1919). He later served as Governor of New Zealand (1920–4).

jellied *adj.* set in jelly: *jellied eels*.

jelly *noun* (PL. **jellies**) **1** a wobbly, transparent, fruit-flavoured dessert set with gelatine. **2** a clear jam made by boiling and straining fruit. **3** meat stock or other savoury medium set with gelatine. **4** any jelly-like substance. [from Old French *gelee*, from Latin *gelare*, to freeze]

jelly baby *or* **jelly bean** a soft fruit-flavoured sweet in the shape of a baby, or a bean made with gelatine.

jellyfish *noun* (PL. **jellyfish, jellyfishes**) the common name for the free-swimming stage (medusa) of invertebrate animals belonging to the phylum Coelenterata. Its body is usually umbrella-shaped, with tentacles containing stinging cells dangling from the margin. Most jellyfish live in marine surface waters and feed on plankton.

Jemima a female first name, borne by the eldest daughter of Job in the Old Testament. [from Hebrew, = dove]

jemmy *noun* (PL. **jemmies**) a small crowbar used by burglars for forcing open windows, etc. [from the name *James*]

Jenkins, Winifred the illiterate servant of Tabitha Bramble, who marries Humphry in Tobias Smollett's *Humphry Clinker*.

Jenkins (of Hillhead), Roy (Harris) Jenkins, Baron (1920–) Welsh Labour politician, born in Abersychan, Monmouthshire. He became an MP in 1948, and was Minister of Aviation (1964–5), Home Secretary (1965–7), Chancellor of the Exchequer (1967–70), Deputy Leader of the Opposition (1970–2), and again Home Secretary (1974–6). Following his presidency of the European Commission (1977–81), he co-founded the Social Democratic Party in Britain (1981), and became its first leader in 1982, but stood down in 1983 in favour of David Owen. He represented Glasgow (Hillhead) from 1982 until defeated in 1987, when he became Chancellor of Oxford University.

Jenkins' Ear, War of a war between Britain and Spain that began in 1739 and merged into the War of the Austrian Succession (1740–8). Some of the violent anti-Spanish indignation in Britain that provoked the war was due to Capt Robert Jenkins, who claimed to have had an ear cut off by Spanish coastguards in the Caribbean.

Jenner, Edward (1749–1823) English physician, born in Berkeley vicarage, Gloucestershire. He practised medicine at Berkeley from 1773, and in 1796 made the revolutionary discovery of vaccination. He inoculated a child with cowpox, then later with smallpox, and found that the child failed to develop the disease; although violently opposed at first, within five years vaccination was being practised in many parts of the world.

Jennifer a female first name, popular since the beginning of the 20c. [a Cornish form of *Guinevere*, Arthur's queen]

Jennings, Pat(rick) (1945–) Northern Irish footballer, born in Newry, Co Down. He started his career with Newry Town then joined Watford. He moved to Tottenham Hotspur in 1974, and became their regular goalkeeper for over 10 years before joining Arsenal in 1977. He played 119 games for Northern Ireland, made a total of 747 Football League appearances, and won several cup winner's medals. He retired in 1986.

jenny *noun* (PL. **jennies**) **1** a name given to the female of certain birds, eg the wren, or animals, eg the donkey. **2** a spinning-jenny. [from the name *Jenny*]

Jensen, Johannes V(ilhelm) (1873–1950) Danish poet, novelist, and essayist, born in Farsö, Jutland. He began as a writer of tales, many of which are based on his extensive travels in the Far East and USA. His best-known work is the novel sequence *Den Lange Rejse* (The Long Journey, 1908–22). He was awarded the Nobel Prize for Literature in 1944.

jeopardize *or* **jeopardise** *verb* to put at risk of harm, loss, or destruction.

jeopardy *noun* danger of harm, loss, or destruction. [from Old French *jeu parti*, a divided or even (ie uncertain) game]

jerbil same as GERBIL.

jerboa *noun* a small rat-like animal of N Africa and Asia, with long hind legs adapted for jumping. [from Arabic *yarbu*]

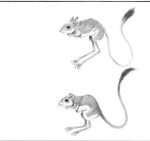

jerboa

jeremiad *noun colloq.* a lengthy and mournful tale of woe. [from French *jérémiade*, from *The Lamentations of Jeremiah* in the Old Testament]

Jeremiah *or* **Jeremias, Book of** a major prophetic work of the Hebrew Bible and Old Testament, attributed to the prophet Jeremiah, who was active in Judah c.627–587 BC. The work is a record of the prophet's inner struggles, persecution, and despair.

Jeremiah, Letter of in the Roman Catholic Bible, chapter 6 of the Book of Baruch, or for Protestants, a separate work in the Old Testament Apocrypha. It is ostensibly a letter from the prophet Jeremiah to Jewish captives in Babylon (c.597 BC) warning them against idolatry.

Jeremy a male first name. [an Anglicized form of the Hebrew name *Jeremiah*, meaning 'appointed by God']

Jerez (de la Frontera) *or* **Xeres** POP (1991) 183 000, a picturesque town a few miles inland from Cádiz, Andalusia, S Spain. It gave its name to the drink sherry; the town is also a noted centre for wine and brandy. Jerez horses are bred here.

Jericho, Arabic **Eriha**, Hebrew **Yeriho** an oasis town in Jerusalem governorate, in the Israeli-occupied West Bank, W Jordan, 36km/22mi NE of Jerusalem. It is the site of the world's earliest known town, continuously occupied from c.9000–1850 BC. Archaeological excavations of the mound of Tell es Sultan, begun in the 20c, have revealed 20 successive settlement layers. The town was the scene of a famous siege during the Israelite conquest of Canaan, when it is said that the walls fell down at the shout of the army under Joshua (Joshua 6.20). Agreement was reached in 1993 between Israel and the Palestine Liberation Organization that limited Palestinian self-rule would be phased in. NOTABLE FEATURES Mount of the Temptation in the NW; ruins of the palace of Qirbat al-Mafyar (724).

jerk — *noun* **1** a quick tug or pull. **2** a sudden movement; a jolt. **3** *derog. slang* a stupid person. — *verb* **1** to pull or tug sharply. **2** *intrans.* to move with sharp suddenness.

jerkily *adv.* in a jerky way.

jerkin *noun* a short close-fitting especially sleeveless jacket.

jerky *adj.* (**jerkier, jerkiest**) moving in or with jerks.

jeroboam *noun* a large wine bottle holding the equivalent of six standard bottles (or four of champagne). [from *Jeroboam* in the Old Testament, I Kings 11.28]

Jerome, St, originally **Eusebius Hieronymus** (c.342–420 AD) Christian ascetic and scholar, one of the four Latin Doctors of the Church, born in Stridon, Dalmatia. He lived as a hermit, then was ordained (379), and became secretary to Pope Damasus (reigned 366–84). In 386 he moved to Bethlehem, where he wrote many letters, treatises, and commentaries on the Bible. He was the first to translate the Bible from Hebrew into Latin (the *Vulgate*). His feast day is 30 Sep.

Jerome, Jerome K(lapka) (1859–1927) English humorous novelist, and playwright, born in Walsall, Staffordshire. He was successively a clerk, schoolmaster, reporter, actor, and journalist, then became joint editor of *The Idler* (1892) and started his own weekly, *To-Day*. His humorous novel *Three Men in a Boat* (1889) is the work for which he is best known.

Jerome a male first name, borne by the saint who translated the Bible into Latin. [an anglicized form of the Greek name *Hieronymous*, from *hieros*, holy + *onoma*, name]

Jerry *noun* (PL. **Jerries**) *Brit. war slang* a German or German soldier; the Germans collectively. [alteration of GERMAN]

jerry *noun* (PL. **jerries**) *old colloq. use* a chamber pot. [from JEROBOAM]

jerry-builder *noun* a person who puts up flimsy buildings cheaply and quickly.

jerry-building *noun* the act or process of putting up cheap and flimsy buildings.

jerry-built *adj., said of buildings, etc* built cheaply, hastily and incompetently.

jerry can a flat-sided can used for carrying water, petrol, etc. [from JERRY]

Jersey POP (1991) 84 000, the largest of the Channel Is, lying W of Normandy. AREA 116sq km/45sq mi. CAPITAL St Helier. The chief language spoken is English, with some Norman-French. ECONOMY noted for its dairy farming (Jersey cattle) and potatoes; tourism. The island gave its name to the woollen garment. NOTABLE FEATURES Jersey Zoological Park (founded by Gerald Durrell in 1959); underground German Headquarters from World War II.

jersey *noun* (PL. **jerseys**) **1** a knitted garment worn on the upper part of the body, pulled on over the head; a pullover. **2** a fine knitted fabric used for clothing. **3** (**Jersey**) a breed of dairy cattle. [named after *Jersey* in the Channel Islands]

Jerusalem, Hebrew **Yerushalayim** POP (1990e) 508 000, the capital of the State of Israel and of Jerusalem district. It is a holy city of Christians, Jews, and Muslims, situated on the E slope of the Judean Range. The old city is a World Heritage site, surrounded by a fortified wall and divided into four quarters (Armenian, Muslim, Christian, and Jewish). HISTORY part of the Roman Empire in 1c BC; under Turkish rule until conquered by the Crusaders, and the Kingdom of Jerusalem was established in 1099; retaken by the Turks in 1187, and held again in the 16c until 1917; capital of Palestine from 1922 until 1948; divided between Israel and Jordan by the 1949 armistice; W Jerusalem was declared the capital of Israel in 1950; E Jerusalem was annexed after the Six-Day War in 1967; united Jerusalem became the nation's capital in 1980 although not recognized as such by the United Nations. NOTABLE FEATURES citadel (24 BC); 12c Cathedral of St James; Temple Mount; El Aqsa Mosque (705–15); Dome of the Rock (685–705); Western Wall known as the 'Wailing Wall'; Antonia Fortress (37–4 BC); Church of the Holy Sepulchre; Garden of Gethsemane; Tomb of the Kings; Mount of Olives.

Jerusalem, in full *Jerusalem, The Emanation of the Giant Albion* a prophetic poem by William Blake (1804–20). Its main theme, presented in mystic terms, is the spiritual regeneration of England.

Jerusalem artichoke a plant related to the sunflower; its potato-like roots can be eaten as a vegetable. [a corruption of Italian *girasole*, sunflower]

Jesse **1** a biblical character, father of King David. **2** a male first name, now confined to America. [from Hebrew, = gift]

Jessica **1** the daughter of Shylock in Shakespeare's *The Merchant of Venice*, who is disinherited for marrying Lorenzo. **2** a female first name. [from Hebrew, = God is looking]

jest *noun* a joke or prank. — **in jest** as a joke; not seriously. [from Old French *geste*, deed, from Latin *gesta*, things done]

jester *noun Hist.* a colourfully dressed professional clown employed by a king or noble to amuse the court. [from Middle English *gester*, from *gest*, exploit]

jestingly *adv.* as a joke, with jesting.

Jesuit — *noun* a member of the Society of Jesus (see JESUITS). — *adj.* relating to the Jesuits.

jesuitical *adj.* **1** *said of an argument* over-subtle; cleverly misleading. **2** *said of a plan* crafty; cunning.

jesuitically *adv.* in a jesuitical way.

Jesuits, in full the **Society of Jesus** (ABBREV. **SJ**) a male religious order, founded in 1540 by Ignatius de Loyola. It is non-contemplative and demands strict obedience, compliance with Ignatius's Spiritual Exercises, and special loyalty to the pope. Its wide-ranging ministry to society has included the foundation of several colleges and universities throughout the world. Jesuits have been leading apologists for the Roman Catholic Church, particularly at the time of the Counter-Reformation.

Jesus 1 see JESUS CHRIST. **2** *offensive* an exclamation of surprise, anger, etc. [from Hebrew *Yeshua*]

Jesus Christ *or* **Jesus of Nazareth** (1c AD) the central figure of the Christian faith, which is based on the fundamental belief that he was the Son of God who was sacrificed and raised from the dead to redeem humanity from the consequences of sin and death. In Islam, he is considered a prophet second only to Muhammad. 'Christ' was added to the name when he was perceived to be the Messiah promised to the Jews. He was born in Bethlehem c.6–5 BC (before the death of Herod the Great in 4 BC) and brought up in Nazareth by Mary and Joseph. He began his ministry (mainly recorded in the New Testament Gospels) with baptism by John in the R Jordan (Luke 3.1) when he was about 30. The Gospels record his temptations by the Devil in the wilderness, after which he gathered a group of 12 close followers or Apostles whom he taught about God and his own purpose on earth, so that they could continue to spread the Gospel ('good news') after his death. He was mainly active for about three years in the villages and country of Galilee rather than in towns and cities, healing the sick and demon-possessed, performing miracles, and proclaiming the coming of the kingdom of God. Conflict with the Pharisees often arose, especially over his pronouncing forgiveness of sins, which they said was God's right alone (they did not believe that Jesus was divine). Jesus was executed by crucifixion under the order of the Roman procurator Pontius Pilate, after he said that he was in fact King of the Jews (AD 30 or 33). Accounts of his resurrection from the dead are found in the Gospels, Pauline writings, and in Acts; Acts and the Gospel of John also refer to his subsequent ascension into heaven. Limited references to Jesus can also be found in works of the Jewish historian Josephus and the Roman historians Tacitus and Suetonius. There are other noncanonical Christian traditions circulated about Jesus, many of which are late and probably spurious.

jet¹ *noun Geol.* a hard black variety of lignite (a low-grade coal) that can be cut and polished and was formerly a popular gemstone, used to make jewellery and ornaments. It will burn because it is a form of coal. [from Old French *jaiet*]

jet² — *noun* **1** a strong fast stream (of liquid, gas, etc) forced under pressure from a narrow opening. **2** the opening through which a jet is forced. **3** (*also* **jet aircraft**) an aircraft powered by a jet engine. — *verb* (**jetted, jetting**) **1** *intrans., trans. colloq.* to travel or transport by jet aircraft. **2** *intrans.* to come out in a jet; to spurt. [from French *jeter*, to throw]

jet-black *adj.* deep glossy black.

jet engine a type of gas turbine engine used in aircraft, in which air taken in from outside is compressed to a high pressure, mixed with fuel, and ignited. A stream of rapidly expanding hot gases is ejected to the rear of the aircraft, and is used to drive a turbine (coupled to the compressor). As it finally passes at very high speed from the rear of the aircraft it produces a powerful forward thrust.

jetfoil *noun* an advanced form of hydrofoil propelled by waterjets. Water is sucked in from the sea and expelled at great pressure through the after foils. Originally developed by Boeing, jet-foils have been in commercial service since 1975.

jet lag the tiredness and lethargy that result from the body's inability to adjust to the rapid changes of time zone that go with high-speed, long-distance air travel.

jet-lagged *adj.* affected by jet-lag.

jet plane an aircraft powered by a jet engine.

jet-propelled *adj.* **1** driven by jet propulsion. **2** *colloq.* fast.

jet propulsion the forward thrust effected as air sucked into the front of an engine is forced out behind.

jetsam *noun* goods jettisoned from a ship and washed up on the shore. See also FLOTSAM. [contracted from JETTISON]

jet set *colloq.* (**the jet set**) wealthy people who lead a life of fast travel and expensive enjoyment.

jet-setter *noun* a member of the jet set.

jet-setting — *noun* the lifestyle of a jet-setter. — *adj.* relating to jet-setters, or their way of life.

jet stream *Geol.* a narrow current of rapidly moving air blowing in a westerly direction at speeds ranging from 60kph in summer to 125kph in winter, and found in both hemispheres at or just below the top of the troposphere. Jet streams have a significant effect on air travel, increasing or decreasing journey times according to the direction of flight across the Atlantic and Pacific Oceans.

jettison *verb* (**jettisoned, jettisoning**) **1** to throw (cargo) overboard to lighten a ship, aircraft, etc in an emergency. **2** to abandon, reject, or get rid of. [from Old French *getaison*, from Latin *iactatio*, a tossing]

jetty *noun* (PL. **jetties**) **1** a stone or wooden landing-stage. **2** a stone barrier built out into the sea to protect a harbour from currents and high waves. [from Old French *jetee*, from *jeter*, to throw]

Jeune Peinture Belge an association of mainly abstract artists founded in Brussels in 1945. The *Prix de la Jeune Peinture Belge* is awarded annually to painters under the age of 40.

Jew *noun* **1** a member of the Hebrew race. **2** someone who practises Judaism. **3** *old offensive use* a miser; an unrelenting bargainer. [from Old French *Juiu*, from Latin *Judaeus*]

jewel *noun* **1** a precious stone. **2** a personal ornament made with precious stones and metals. **3** a gem used in the machinery of a watch. **4** someone or something greatly prized. [from Old French *joel*]

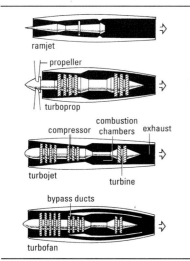

ramjet

propeller

turboprop

combustion
compressor chambers exhaust

turbojet turbine

bypass ducts

turbofan

types of jet engine

jewelled *adj.* set or decorated with jewels.

jeweller *noun* a person who deals in, makes or repairs jewellery, watches, and objects of gold and silver.

jewellery or *North Amer., esp. US* **jewelry** *noun* articles worn for personal adornment, eg bracelets, necklaces, brooches, rings, etc.

Jewess *noun offensive* a Jewish woman or girl.

Jewish *adj.* relating or belonging to the Jews or to Judaism.

Jewish Cemetery, The a painting by Jacob van Ruisdael (17c, two versions, in Dresden and Detroit).

Jewish liturgical music an extensive repertory of monodic chant that parallels and influences that of the early Christian Church (which, though there are many references to music in the Old Testament, had been lost with the destruction of the Temple in AD 70). Transmitted orally, as instruments were excluded from the synagogue, it began to be transcribed and studied in the 20c.

Jew of Malta, The a play by Christopher Marlowe (c.1592). Written in blank verse, it is a melodramatic story and comment on religious attitudes which focuses on a rich, violent, and villainous Jew, Barabas.

Jewry *noun old use* Jews collectively.

Jew's harp a tiny lyre-shaped musical instrument held between the teeth, with a narrow metal tongue that is twanged with the finger.

Jezebel *noun derog.* a shameless or scheming woman. [named after Ahab's wife in the Old Testament, 1 Kings 21; 2 Kings 9.30]

Jhelum, River a river in Asia, the most westerly of the five rivers of the Punjab, Pakistan. It is 725km/450mi long, rising in the Himalayas and flowing NW through the Vale of Kashmir, then W and generally S to meet the R Chenab SW of Jhang Maghiana. The river is the source of many canals and irrigation systems in the Punjab Plain. The famous battle between Alexander the Great and Porus was fought on its banks in 326 BC.

Jiang Jieshi *or* **Chiang Kai-shek** (1887–1975) revolutionary leader of 20c China, the effective head of the Nationalist Republic (1928–49), and later of the emigré Nationalist Party regime in Taiwan. Born into a merchant family in Zhejiang, he interrupted his military education in Japan to return to China and join the Nationalist revolution. In 1918 he joined the separatist revolutionary government of Sun Yixian (Sun Yat-sen) in Canton, where he was appointed Commandant of the new Whampoa Military Academy. After Sun's death (1925), he launched an expedition against the warlords and the Beijing (Peking) government, entering Beijing in 1928, but fixed the Nationalist capital at Nanjing (Nanking). During the ensuing decade the Nationalist Party steadily lost support to the Communists. When Japan launched a campaign to conquer China (1937), Nationalist resistance was weak. Defeated by the Communist forces, he was forced to retreat to Taiwan (1949), where he presided over the beginnings of Taiwan's 'economic miracle'. His son, Jiang Jingguo (Chiang Ching-kuo, 1918–), became Prime Minister in 1971 and President in 1978.

Jiang Qing *or* **Chiang Ch'ing** (1914–) Chinese politician, born in Zhucheng, Shandong province. She trained in drama and literature, and became an actress in Shanghai. In 1936 she went to Yenan to study Marxist–Leninist theory, met Mao Zedong (Mao Tse-tung), and became his third wife in 1939. She was attached to the Ministry of Culture (1950–4), and in the 1960s began her attacks on bourgeois influences in the arts and literature. One of the leaders of the Cultural Revolution (1966–76), she was elected to the Politburo (1969), but after Mao's death (1976) was arrested with three others — the

'Gang of Four' — imprisoned, expelled from the Communist Party, and tried in 1980. She was sentenced to death, though the sentence was later suspended.

jib[1] — *noun* a small three-cornered sail in front of the mainsail of a yacht. — *verb* (**jibbed, jibbing**) (*often* **jib at something**) **1** *intrans. said of a horse* to refuse a jump, etc. **2** *intrans. said of a person* to object to it. **3** *intrans., trans. Naut.* to gybe. [17c, origin unknown]

jib[2] *noun* the projecting arm of a crane from which the lifting gear hangs. [from GIBBET]

jib boom *Naut.* an extension to the bowsprit on which the jib is spread.

jibe another spelling of GIBE or GYBE.

Jiddah see JEDDA.

jiffy *or* **jiff** *noun* (PL. **jiffies**) *colloq.* a moment.

Jiffy bag *trademark* a padded envelope.

jig — *noun* **1** a lively country dance or folk dance; music for this. **2** *Mech.* a device that holds a piece of work in position and guides the tools being used on it. — *verb* (**jigged, jigging**) **1** *intrans.* to dance a jig. **2** *intrans.* to jump up and down. **3** *Mech.* to work on (something under construction) using a jig.

jigger[1] *noun* **1** a small quantity of alcoholic spirits, or a glass for measuring this. **2** *Billiards colloq.* a cue rest. **3** *Golf* an iron-headed club. **4** *North Amer. colloq.* an all-purpose term for a gadget when its name is not known or not remembered. [from JIG *noun*]

jigger[2] *noun* a variant of CHIGGER.

jiggered *adj. colloq.* exhausted. — **I'll be jiggered** *colloq.* an expression of astonishment. [possibly euphemistic for *buggered*]

jiggery-pokery *noun colloq.* trickery or deceit. [from Scot. *joukery-pawkery*, from *jouk*, to dodge + *pawk*, trick]

jiggle — *verb trans., intrans.* to jump or cause to jump up and down or jerk about. — *noun* a jiggling movement. [from JIG 1]

jigsaw *noun* **1** (*also* **jigsaw puzzle**) a picture mounted on wood or cardboard and sawn into irregularly shaped interlocking pieces, taken apart for later re-assembly into the picture. **2** a fine-bladed saw for cutting intricate patterns. [from JIG + SAW[1]]

jihad *or* **jehad** *noun* a holy war fought by Muslims on behalf of Islam. [from Arabic *jihad*, struggle]
◊ According to the Koran, Muslims have a duty to oppose those who reject Islam, by armed struggle if necessary, and jihad has been invoked to justify both the expansion and defence of Islam. Islamic states pledged a jihad against Israel in the Mecca declaration of 1981.

Jilong see KEELUNG.

jilt *verb old use* to discard (a lover). [contracted from *jillet*, a flirt]

Jima, Italian **Gimma** POP (1984e) 61 000, the capital of Kefa region, SW Ethiopia. It was occupied by the Italians in 1936.

Jim Crow *North Amer. slang* **1** *offensive* a black person. **2** the policy of segregating blacks from whites. [from the title of a black minstrel song]

Jim Crow Laws a term used to characterize US state laws passed from the 1890s onwards to segregate blacks from whites in the South. They were gradually abolished from the mid-20c, largely because of the civil rights movement, which led to Supreme Court decisions and changes in federal policies.

Jiménez, Juan Ramón (1881–1958) Spanish lyric poet, born in Moguer, Huelva. His *Platero y Yo* (Platero and I, 1914), about a young poet and his donkey (and set in his home town) is regarded as one of the classics of modern Spanish literature. Other works include *Sonetos espirituales* (Spiritual Sonnets, 1916). In 1936 he left Spain because of the Civil War and settled in Florida. He was awarded the Nobel Prize for Literature in 1956.

jimjams *pl. noun* **1** *colloq.* a state of nervous excitement. **2** *slang* delirium tremens. **3** *colloq.* pyjamas.

Jimmu Tenno in the Shinto religion, the first emperor of Japan. He is said to be descended from the sun goddess Amaterasu, and to have reigned 660–585 BC, and died at the age of 127.

Jinan *or* **Tsinan** *or* **Chi-nan**, also called **City of Springs** POP (1990) 2.4m, the capital of Shandong province, E China. There are over 100 natural springs at Daming L. A dam is on the Yellow R for flood control and irrigation. HISTORY founded in the 8c BC; commercial centre in the Tang Dynasty (618–907).

jingle — *noun* **1** a ringing or clinking sound, as of small bells, coins, or keys. **2** a simple rhyming verse or song. — *verb trans., intrans.* to make or cause to make a ringing or clinking sound. [imitative]

jingoism *noun* over-enthusiastic or aggressive patriotism. [from 'By jingo!' (ie by God!), from a chauvinistic British song of 1878]

jingoist *noun* an over-enthusiastic patriot.

jingoistic *adj.* characteristic of jingoism.

Jinja POP (1991) 70 000, the second-largest city in Uganda, in Busoga province. It is situated on the N shore of L Victoria at the outflow of the Victoria Nile R, 33km/20mi E of Kampala.

jinja *noun Relig.* a Shinto shrine or sanctuary. It may be a small shrine by the roadside, a larger building surrounded by smaller buildings, or a large group of temple buildings surrounded by a wooded area. Its central feature is the *honden*, the main dwelling of the deity, containing a single chamber in which the sacred symbol is housed.

jink — *verb intrans., trans.* to dodge. — *noun* a dodge. See also HIGH JINKS. [imitative]

Jinnah, Muhammad Ali (1876–1948) Indian Muslim politician and founder of Pakistan, born in Karachi. A practising Bombay lawyer, he became a member of the Indian National Congress (1906) and the Muslim League (1913), and supported Hindu–Muslim unity until 1930, when he resigned from the Congress in opposition to Mahatma Gandhi's policy of civil disobedience. His advocacy of a separate state for Muslims led to the creation of Pakistan in 1947, and he became its first Governor-General.

jinni *or* **jinnee** *or* **djinni** *noun* (PL. **jinn, djinn**) in Muslim folklore, a supernatural being able to adopt human or animal form. [from Arabic *jinni*]

jinx — *noun* an evil spell or influence, held responsible for misfortune. — *verb* to put a jinx on. [from *jynx*, the wryneck, a bird used in spells; hence a spell or charm]

jitter *colloq.* — *verb intrans.* (**jittered, jittering**) to shake with nerves. — *noun* (**jitters**) an attack of nervousness. [variant of *chitter*, to shiver]

jitterbug — *noun* **1** an energetic dance like jive, popular in the 1940s. **2** an alarmist or scaremonger. — *verb intrans.* (**jitterbugged, jitterbugging**) to dance the jitterbug. [from JITTER]

jittery *adj.* nervous.

Jivaro a S American Indian people living in the tropical forests of Ecuador, Peru, and the Montana (E slopes of Andes), growing cassava, sweet potatoes, and corn, and foraging, fishing, and hunting. They destroyed the Spanish community in Montana in 1599, and became well known for their shrunken heads (*tsantsas*) of victims captured in war.

jive — *noun* a lively style of dancing to jazz music, popular in the 1950s. — *verb* to dance in this style.

Jnr *abbrev.* Junior.

Joad, C(yril) E(dwin) M(itchinson) (1891–1953) English philosopher and controversialist, born in Durham. He was a civil servant (1914–30), then joined the philosophy department at Birkbeck College, London. He wrote 47 highly personal books, notably *Guide to Philosophy* (1936), and was a fashionable atheist until his last work, *Recovery of Belief* (1952). He is also remembered for his BBC Brains Trust radio programme and his catchphrase, 'It all depends what you mean by ...'.

Joan, Pope (800–900) a fictitious person long believed to have been pope as John VII (855–58). One legend claims she was born in Mainz, and elected pope while in male disguise. Her reign is said to have ended abruptly when she died giving birth to a child during a papal procession.

Joan a female first name, revived in the 20c. [a Middle English feminine form of JOHN, relating to Old French *Jo(h)anne*]

Joan of Arc, St, French **Jeanne d'Arc**, also called **the Maid of Orleans** (1412–31) French patriot and martyr, born in Domrémy. At the age of 13 she heard the voices of saints Michael, Catherine, and Margaret bidding her rescue France from English domination during the Hundred Years War. She was taken to the Dauphin, and eventually allowed to lead the army assembled for the relief of Orleans. Clad in white armour and flying her own standard, she entered Orleans (1429), forced the English to retire, and took the Dauphin to be crowned Charles VII at Rheims. She then set out to relieve Compiègne, but was captured and sold to the English by John of Luxembourg. Put on trial (1431) for heresy and sorcery, she was found guilty by an English-dominated court, and burned. She was canonized in 1920 and her feast day is 30 May.

Job, Book of a major book of the wisdom literature of the Hebrew Bible and Old Testament, named after its main character. It is composed of narrative and speeches in which the poet tackles the question of the meaning of undeserved suffering and of faith; despite the advice of his friends, Job persists in his struggles, refusing to blame God, until he is presented with the inscrutable majesty of God.

job — *noun* **1** a person's regular paid employment. **2** a piece of work. **3** a completed task: *made a good job of the pruning.* **4** a function or responsibility. **5** *colloq.* a problem; difficulty: *had a job finding it.* **6** a crime, especially a burglary: *an inside job.* **7** an underhand scheme: *a put-up job.* **8** *colloq.* a do, affair, business, etc: *the wedding was a proper church job.* **9** *colloq.* a surgical operation, usually involving plastic surgery: *a nose job.* **10** *colloq.* a manufactured product, or other object: *smart little jobs, these calculators.* — *verb* (**jobbed, jobbing**) **1** *intrans.* to do casual jobs. **2** *trans., intrans.* to buy and sell (stocks) as a stockjobber; to act as stockjobber. **3** *trans., intrans.* to bring about by, or practise, jobbery. **4** to hire or let out for a period or a job.
— **do the job** to succeed in doing what is required.
give something up as a bad job to abandon a task, etc as impossible or not worthwhile.
a good job *colloq.* fortunate; lucky: *it's a good job I was early.*
jobs for the boys *derog.* superfluous work created as employment for one's supporters and friends.
just the job exactly what is required.
make the best of a bad job to do one's best in difficult circumstances.
[16c, origin unknown]

jobber *noun Stock Exchange* a stockjobber. [from JOB]

jobbery *noun* the abuse of public office for private gain. [from JOB]

job centre *or* **Jobcentre** *Brit.* a government office displaying information on available jobs.

job club *or* **Jobclub** an association aimed at helping the jobless find work through learning and using the necessary skills of presentation, etc.

job description *Industry* a systematic and detailed listing of all the duties, responsibilities, activities, etc necessary to a specific job.

job evaluation *Industry* a method of assessing the relative position and appropriate salary for the different jobs in an organization by allocating points for the various aspects of each job as listed in a job description.

jobless — *adj.* having no paid employment; unemployed. — *noun* (**the jobless**) unemployed people.

job lot a mixed collection of objects sold as one item at an auction, etc.

Job's comforter a person whose attempts at sympathy have the effect of adding to one's distress. [from *Job* in the Old Testament]

job-sharing *noun* the practice of sharing the tasks of one full-time job between two or more part-time workers.

Jocasta in Greek mythology, the wife of King Laius of Thebes and mother of Oedipus, who later unwittingly became the wife of her son; she is called Epikaste in Homer. She bore Oedipus four children — Eteocles, Polynices, Antigone, and Ismene — and killed herself when she discovered her incest.

Jocelyn a male and now largely female first name, after the surname. [Norman, of Germanic origin]

Jock *noun colloq.* a Scotsman, especially a soldier. [Scots form of *Jack*]
◆ now usually regarded as offensive.

jockey — *noun* (PL. **jockeys**) a rider, especially professional, in horse races. — *verb* **1** to ride (a horse) in a race. **2** *trans., intrans.* (**jockey someone into something, out of something**, etc) to manipulate them deviously.
— **jockey for position** to seek an advantage over rivals, especially unscrupulously. [diminutive of JOCK]

Jockey Club the controlling body for horse racing in Britain, founded in c.1750 at the Star and Garter Coffee House, Pall Mall, London. In 1968 the Jockey Club and National Hunt Committee amalgamated.

jockstrap *noun* a garment for supporting the genitals, worn by male athletes. [from dialect *jock*, penis]

jocose *adj.* playful; humorous. [from Latin *jocosus*]

jocosely *adv.* in a humorous way, merrily.

jocosity *noun* being playful or humorous.

jocular *adj.* **1** given to joking; good-humoured. **2** *said of a remark* intended as a joke. [from Latin *joculus*, a little joke]

jocularity *noun* merriment, being jocular.

jocularly *adv.* in a jocular way.

jocund *adj.* cheerful; merry; good-humoured. [from Latin *jocundus*, agreeable]

jocundity *noun* a cheerful condition or state.

jodhpurs *pl. noun* riding-breeches that are loose-fitting over the buttocks and thighs and tight-fitting from knee to calf. [from *Jodhpur* in India]

Jodl, Alfred (1890–1946) German soldier, born in Aachen. An artillery subaltern in World War I, he became general of artillery in 1940. Considered to be the planning genius behind the German High Command, he was Hitler's chief adviser. He was found guilty of war crimes at Nuremburg (1946) and executed.

Jodrell Bank *Astron.* the location in Cheshire, UK, of the Nuffield Radio Astronomy Laboratories of the University of Manchester.

Joel, Book of one of the 12 so-called 'minor' prophetic writings of the Hebrew Bible and Old Testament, attributed to Joel, who is thought to have lived in the period (c.400–350 BC) after the exile of Israel.

jog — *verb* (**jogged, jogging**) **1** to knock or nudge slightly. **2** to prompt (the memory). **3** *intrans.* (**jog along**) to progress slowly and steadily; to plod. **4** *intrans.* to run at a gentle, steady pace, for exercise. — *noun* **1** a spell of jogging. **2** a nudge, knock, or jolt. [variant of *shog*, to shake]

jogger *noun* a person who jogs, especially on a regular basis.

joggers *or* **jog pants** loose trousers of a warm material, fitting tightly round the waist and ankles.

jogger's nipple *colloq.* painful inflammation of the nipples caused by friction against clothing while running or jogging.

jogging *noun* running at a gentle or steady pace.

joggle — *verb trans., intrans.* to jolt, shake, or wobble. — *noun* a shake or jolt. [from JOG]

jog-trot *noun* an easy pace like that of a horse between walking and trotting.

Johanan ben Zakkai, Rabban (1c AD) Jewish teacher and leader of the reformulation of Judaism after the fall of Jerusalem (70), who helped to found rabbinic Judaism. His early career was apparently in Galilee, although tradition relates legal disputes he had with the Sadducees in Jerusalem before its fall. Afterwards he helped to reconstitute the Sanhedrin council in Jabneh.

Johannesburg, abbreviated **Jo'burg** POP (1990e) 1.7m (metropolitan area), the largest city in South Africa, 50km/31mi SW of Pretoria. It is the commercial, financial, and industrial centre of the Transvaal. The city, which lies at an altitude of 1 665m, was founded in 1886 after the discovery of gold in the Witwatersrand. It was originally laid out by the surveyor Josais de Villiers and is now the hub of a populous conurbation of municipalities. NOTABLE FEATURES Carlton Panorama; Gold Reef City; art gallery.

Johanson, Donald Carl (1943–) US palaeoanthropologist, born in Chicago, Illinois. His spectacular finds of fossil hominids 3–4 million years old at Hadar in the Afar triangle of Ethiopia included 'Lucy', a female specimen, and the 'first family', a scattered group containing the remains of 13 individuals. He suggested that these remains belong to a previously undiscovered species, which he named *Australopithecus afarensis* (Afar ape-man). In 1981 he became Director of the Institute of Human Origins in Berkeley, California.

John, also called **John Lackland** (1167–1216) King of England (1199–1216), the youngest son of Henry II, born in Oxford. He tried to seize the Crown during Richard I's captivity in Germany (1193–4), but was nevertheless nominated successor by Richard, despite the superior claim of Arthur, the son of John's elder brother Geoffrey. Arthur's claims were supported by Philip II of France, and after Arthur was murdered on John's orders (1203), Philip marched against him and conquered all but a portion of Aquitaine (1204–5). In 1206 John refused to receive Stephen Langton as Archbishop of Canterbury, and in 1208 his kingdom was placed under papal interdict. He was then excommunicated (1209) until he finally conceded (1213). His oppressive government, and failure to recover Normandy, provoked baronial opposition, which led to demands for constitutional reform. The barons met the King at Runnymede, and forced him to seal the Great Charter (Magna Carta) (Jun 1215),

the basis of the English constitution, which he later repudiated, precipitating the first Barons' War (1215–17).

John II, known as **the Good** (1319–64) King of France (1350–64), the son of Philip VI, born near Le Mans. At the battle of Poitiers in 1356 he was captured by Edward the Black Prince, and taken to England, but after the treaty of Brétigny (1360) he returned home, leaving his second son, the Duke of Anjou, as a hostage. When the duke broke his parole and escaped (1363), John chivalrously returned to London, and died there.

John XXII, originally **Jacques Duèse** (c.1245–1334) French pope (1316–34), the second Pope of Avignon, born in Cahors. Following his persecution of the Franciscan Spirituals who did not agree with his support of the Franciscan Conventuals, he intervened in the contest for the Crown of the Holy Roman Empire between Louis of Bavaria and Frederick of Austria, in support of the latter. A long conflict ensued both in Germany and Italy between the Guelf (papal) Party and the Ghibelline (imperial) Party. In 1327 Louis entered Italy, was crowned Emperor at Rome, deposed John, and set up an antipope, Nicholas V (1328).

John, St (1c AD) one of the 12 Apostles of Jesus Christ, son of Zebedee and the younger brother of James. Formerly a Galilean fisherman, he was one of those closest to Christ, among the first to be called, and with him at the Transfiguration and at Gethsemane. In Acts and Galatians he is described as one of the 'pillars' of the early Jerusalem Church. Some traditions claim he was slain by the Jews or Herod Agrippa I, but from the 2c he apparently spent his closing years at Ephesus. He wrote the Revelation, the Gospel, and the three Epistles which bear his name (although his authorship of these works has been disputed by modern scholars).

John, St, also called **John the Baptist**, or **Baptizer** (1c AD) a prophetic and ascetic figure referred to in the New Testament Gospels and in Josephus's *Antiquities*, the son of a priest named Zechariah. His life was roughly contemporary with Jesus of Nazareth, and his mother was Elizabeth, cousin of Mary the mother of Jesus (Luke 1). He baptized Jesus and others at the R Jordan, and preached about the coming of the Lord and the consequent need for repentance. He was executed by Herod Antipas, but the circumstances differ in the accounts of Josephus and the Gospels. In the New Testament he is portrayed as Christ's forerunner, and sometimes as a returned Elijah (Matthew 11.13–14). His feast day is 24 Jun.

John a male first name, borne by several Christian saints, and the most common name given to boys thoughout the Christian world. [from Hebrew *Johanan*, = God is gracious]

John of the Cross, St, originally **Juan de Yepes y Álvarez** (1542–91) Spanish Christian mystic and poet, born in Fontiveros, Ávila. He was a Carmelite monk, and founded the Discalced Carmelites with St Teresa (1568). Imprisoned in Toledo (1577), he wrote a number of poems, such as *Canto espiritual* (The Spiritual Canticle), which are highly regarded in Spanish mystical literature. After escaping, he became Vicar Provincial of Andalusia (1585–7). He was canonized in 1726 and his feast day is 14 Dec.

John of Austria, Don, Spanish **Don Juan** (1547–78) Spanish soldier, the illegitimate son of the emperor Charles V, born in Regensburg, Germany. He defeated the Moors in Granada (1570) and the Turks at Lepanto (1571). In 1573 he took Tunis, and was then sent to Milan and (1576) to the Netherlands as Viceroy. He planned to marry Mary, Queen of Scots, but died of typhoid in Namur.

John of Gaunt (1340–99) Duke of Lancaster, the fourth son of Edward III, and ancestor of Henry IV, V, and VI, born in Ghent, Flanders. He

married his cousin Blanche of Lancaster (1359), and was created duke (1362). After her death (1369), he married Constance, daughter of Pedro the Cruel of Castile, and assumed the title of King of Castile, though he failed to oust his rival, Henry of Trastamare. In England he was an influential peacemaker during the troubled reign of Richard II, who made him Duke of Aquitaine (1390). On his second wife's death (1394) he married his mistress Catherine Swynford, and their eldest son was the ancestor of Henry VIII.

John of Leyden, originally **Jan Beuckelson** *or* **Bockhold** (1509–36) Dutch Anabaptist leader, born in Leiden. He worked as a tailor, merchant, and innkeeper, and became noted as an orator. He turned Anabaptist and went to Münster, where he headed the movement and set up a 'kingdom of Zion', with polygamy and community of goods. In 1535 the city was taken by the Bishop of Münster, and John and his accomplices were executed.

John, Augustus (Edwin) (1878–1961) Welsh painter, born in Tenby, Pembrokeshire. He made an early reputation with his etchings (1900–14). His favourite themes were gypsies, fishing folk, and naturally regal women, as in *Lyric Fantasy* (1913). He also painted portraits of several political and artistic contemporary figures, including George Bernard Shaw, Thomas Hardy, and Dylan Thomas.

John, Don the villainous illegitimate brother of Don Pedro in Shakespeare's *Much Ado About Nothing*, who contrives to prevent the marriage of Claudio and Hero.

John, Elton, originally **Reginald Kenneth Dwight** (1947–) English rock singer and pianist, born in Pinner, Middlesex. He played the piano by ear from the age of four, and studied at the Royal Academy of Music at the age of 11. In 1967, he and Bernie Taupin began writing songs such as 'Rocket Man', 'Honky Cat', and 'Goodbye Yellow Brick Road'. Pressed by their publisher to perform them, John developed a flamboyant stage image and rose to achieve stardom, which continued into the 1980s with numerous albums, eg *Too Low For Zero* (1983) and *Breaking Hearts* (1984). In 1976 he became owner and Chairman of the Watford Football Club, but sold most of his shares in Aug 1990. He returned as Director until 1993, when he became Life President.

John, Otto (1909–) German lawyer, the defendant in a major postwar treason case. He was involved in the plot against Hitler in 1944, after which he escaped to Britain. In 1950 he was appointed to the West German Office for the protection of the constitution, but in 1954 mysteriously disappeared from West Berlin, and later broadcast for the East German communists. In 1956 he returned to the West, was arrested for treasonable falsification and conspiracy, tried, and imprisoned. His defence was that he had been drugged, driven to the communist sector, held prisoner, and forced to make broadcasts until he managed to escape. Released in 1958, he still protests his innocence.

John, Gospel according to, also known as the **Fourth Gospel** a New Testament book, distinct from the other three ('synoptic') gospels because of its unique theological reflections on Christ as the Son of God and the divine Word, and its record of Christ's sayings and deeds. Though it is anonymous, John 21.24 associates it with 'the disciple whom Jesus loved', traditionally held to be John the son of Zebedee.

John, Letters of three short New Testament writings; the first lacks reference to its writer or recipients, but the others are in the form of a letter from 'the Elder'. Traditionally they were considered the work of the author of the Fourth Gospel, but are now thought to be later.

john *noun North Amer. colloq.* (*usually* **the john**) a lavatory. [from the name JOHN]

John Birch Society a moderately-sized, extreme right-wing pressure group in the USA which promotes conservative ideas and policies, and is strongly patriotic and anti-communist. Founded in 1958, it was named after a US missionary and intelligence officer who was killed by Chinese communists on 25 Aug 1945 and considered the first hero of the cold war.

John Bull the personification of the typical Englishman, or of England itself, first depicted in John Arbuthnot's *The History of John Bull* (1712). In many 18c and 19c political cartoons, he is drawn as a short stocky figure, often wearing a Union Jack waistcoat.

johnny *noun* (PL. **johnnies**) *colloq.* a chap; a fellow. [diminutive of *John*]

John Paul I, originally **Albino Luciani** (1912–78) Italian pope (Aug–Sep 1978), born near Belluno. Ordained in 1935, he became a parish priest and teacher in Belluno, vicar general of the diocese of Vittorio Veneto (1954), a bishop (1958), Patriarch of Venice (1969), and a cardinal (1973). The first pope to use a double name (from his two immediate predecessors, John XXIII and Paul VI), his was the shortest pontificate of modern times, lasting only 33 days.

John Paul II, originally **Karol Jozef Wojtyla** (1920–) Polish pope (from 1978), born in Wadowice, the first non-Italian pope in 456 years. He was ordained in 1946, and became Professor of Moral Theology at Lublin and Cracow, Archbishop and Metropolitan of Cracow (1964–78), and Cardinal (1967). Noted for his energy and analytical ability, he has travelled widely and preached to huge audiences, championing economic justice and outspokenly defending the Church in communist countries. Though criticized by some for his conservatism, he has remained uncompromising on such issues as artificial birth control, women priests, and the marriage of priests.

Johns, Jasper (1930–) US painter and sculptor, born in Allendale, South Carolina. One of the forerunners of Pop Art in the USA, he became a painter in New York City in 1952, and was influenced by the Dadaist ideas of Marcel Duchamp. He challenged the relationship between art and reality, painting ordinary objects (eg flags, targets, maps) in a style deliberately clumsy and banal (eg *Flag*, 1954). He later began to attach real objects (eg coathangers, rulers) to his paintings.

Johns Hopkins University a private university endowed by financier Johns Hopkins (1795–1873) and established at Baltimore, Maryland, in 1876. It was the first US educational establishment to offer both undergraduate and graduate degrees, with an emphasis on graduate study. It is renowned for its medical school, endowed by a group of women in 1893.

Johnson, Amy (1903–41) English aviator, born in Hull, Yorkshire. She flew solo from England to Australia (1930), to Japan via Siberia (1931), and to Cape Town (1932), making new records in each case. She joined the Air Transport Auxiliary as a pilot in World War II, and was drowned after baling out over the Thames estuary.

Johnson, Andrew (1808–75) US statesman, the 17th President, born in Raleigh, North Carolina. With little formal schooling, he became Alderman and Mayor in Greenville, Tennessee, a member of the Legislature (1835), State Senate (1841), and Congress (1843), and was Governor of Tennessee (1853) and a Senator (1857). During the Civil War he was made Military Governor of Tennessee (1862) and Vice-President (1865). On Lincoln's assassination (1865) he became Democratic President (1865–9). The Republican Congress however, who wished to keep the Southern states under military government, opposed his reconstruction policies; after he vetoed the Civil Rights Act (1866), he was

impeached, brought to trial, and acquitted by one vote.

Johnson, Ben (1961–) Canadian track athlete, born in Falmouth, Jamaica. He won gold in the 100m at the Commonwealth Games in 1986, and at the world championships in 1987. At the 1988 Olympics, he finished first in the 100m in a world record time of 9.79 seconds, but later had his medal withdrawn, was stripped of his world record, and was suspended after allegations that he had used steroids. His life ban from the Canadian team was lifted in 1990 but in Mar 1993 he was banned for life by the IAAF after he failed a drugs test in Montreal.

Johnson, Dame Celia (1908–82) English actress, born in Richmond, Surrey. She became well-established on the stage, and had leading roles in Noël Coward's films *In Which We Serve* (1942) and *This Happy Breed* (1944). She is best remembered for her performance in *Brief Encounter* (1945). Later film appearances were infrequent, among them *The Prime of Miss Jean Brodie* (1968), but she continued in the theatre and on television until shortly before her death.

Johnson, Earvin, also called **Magic Johnson** (1959–) US basketball player, born in Lansing, Michigan. He played for the LA Lakers (1979–91) and was a member of the gold medal-winning US Olympic basketball team in 1992. He was a member of the National Basketball Association All-Star Team (1980, 1982–92), and was named the Most Valuable All-Star Player in 1990 and 1992. He retired from the game after revealing that he had been diagnosed HIV positive; his attempt to make a competitive comeback in 1993 was abandoned. His publications include *Magic* (1983), and *What You Can Do to Avoid AIDS* (1992).

Johnson, Lyndon B(aines), also called **LBJ** (1908–73) US politician, the 36th President, born in Stonewall, Texas. He was a teacher and congressman's secretary before being elected a Democrat representative (1937). He became a senator in 1948, and an effective leader of the Democratic majority. Vice-President under Kennedy (1960), he became President (1963–9) after Kennedy's assassination, and achieved a huge majority when he was returned to the post in 1964. His administration passed the Civil Rights Act (1964) and the Voting Rights Act (1965), which helped the position of blacks in US society. However, the escalation of the war in Vietnam caused him to lose popularity, and he decided not to seek re-election in 1968.

Johnson, Pamela Hansford (1912–81) English novelist, born in London. She is best known for her portrayal of her native postwar London. Her books include *An Avenue of Stone* (1947), *The Unspeakable Skipton* (1958), *A Bonfire* (1981), and several works of non-fiction, such as her study of the Moors murders, *On Iniquity* (1967).

Johnson, Samuel, also called **Dr Johnson** (1709–84) English lexicographer, critic, and poet, born in Lichfield. He became a teacher and went to London in 1737 where he worked as a journalist. From 1747 he worked for eight years on his *Dictionary of the English Language*. He started the moralistic periodical, *The Rambler*, in 1750, and in 1759 wrote his prose tale of Abyssinia, *Rasselas*. In 1762 he was given a Crown pension, and in 1764 he became a founder member of The Literary Club. He produced his edition of Shakespeare in 1765, and from 1772 engaged in political pamphleteering. In 1773 he went with James Boswell on a tour of Scotland, and wrote *A Journal to the Western Isles of Scotland* (1775). Other works include *Lives of the English Poets* (1779–81).

Johnson Space Center *Astron.* in the USA, the mission control centre for NASA crewed space missions, located at Houston, Texas. [named after US president Lyndon B Johnson]

Johnstone POP (1981) 43 000, a town in Renfrew district, Strathclyde, W Scotland. It is situated 6km/4mi W of Paisley.

Johnston Island POP (1980) 327, a coral atoll enclosing four islets in the central Pacific Ocean. AREA 2.5sq km/1sq mi. It is situated 1 150km/715mi SW of Honolulu. The atoll is used as a store for poisonous gas. HISTORY discovered in 1807; claimed by Hawaii in 1858; taken over by the US Navy in 1934.

Johor *or* **Johore** POP (1990) 2.1m, a state in S Peninsular Malaysia, occupying the entire S tip of the peninsula. AREA 18 985sq km/7 328sq mi. It is bounded W by the Strait of Malacca, E by the S China Sea, and is separated from Singapore in the S by the Johor Strait. CAPITAL Johor Baharu. ECONOMY tin; bauxite; rubber; oil palm; pineapple; pepper; timber.

Johor Baharu POP (1980) 246 000, the capital of Johor state, S Peninsular Malaysia, 365km/227mi SE of Kuala Lumpur. It is connected to Singapore by a causeway. NOTABLE FEATURES Grand Palace (19c); Abu Bakar Mosque; Johor Safariworld; Fiesta Village.

joie de vivre enthusiasm for living; exuberant spirits. [French, = joy of life]

join — *verb* 1 (*often* **join one thing to another**, *or* **join things up**) to connect, attach, link, or unite. 2 *trans., intrans.* to become a member of (a society, firm, etc). 3 *intrans., trans. said of roads, rivers, etc* to meet. 4 to come together with; to enter the company of: *joined them for supper.* 5 *trans., intrans.* (*also* **join on**) to add oneself: *join the queue.* 6 to take part in. 7 to do the same as, for companionship: *who'll join me in a drink?* — *noun* a seam or joint.
— **join in** to participate in; to take part.
join up to enlist as a member of an armed service.
join up with someone to come together for joint action, etc.
[from Old French *joindre*]

joiner *noun* 1 a craftsman who makes and fits wooden doors, window frames, stairs, shelves, etc. 2 *colloq.* a sociable person who likes joining clubs and being a member of a group.

joinery *noun* the trade or work of a joiner.

joint — *noun* 1 the place where two or more pieces join. 2 in vertebrates, the point of contact or articulation between two or more bones, together with the ligaments that surround it. 3 a piece of meat, usually containing a bone, for cooking or roasting. 4 *slang* a cheap, shabby cafe, bar, nightclub, etc. 5 *slang* a cannabis cigarette. 6 *Geol.* a crack in a mass of rock. — *verb* 1 connect by joints. 2 to divide (a bird or animal) into, or at, the joints, for cooking. — *adj.* 1 owned, done, etc in common; shared. 2 working together.
— **case the joint** *slang* to look over premises with a view to burgling them.
out of joint 1 *said of a bone* dislocated. 2 in disorder.
[from Old French *joint(e)*, from *joindre*, to join]
◇ In the human body, some joints, eg those between the bones of the skull, are rigidly fixed, but many have a complex structure that allows them to move freely. The bones of such joints are held in position by flexible strands of ligament, and the ends of the bones are capped with rubbery cartilage, which cushions the shocks caused by walking and other movements, and also provides a slippery bearing surface. In many joints there is a flexible capsule, containing synovial fluid, between the ends of the bones, which allows the joint to move without any friction and so plays a similar role to a lubricant. The structure of a joint varies according to the type of movement that is required. The knee and elbow are typical *hinge joints*, which permit movement in one plane only, whereas the hip and shoulder, known as *ball-and-socket joints*, allow circular limb movement in any direction.

jointly *adv.* together; in combination.

joint-stock company a business whose capital is owned jointly by the shareholders.

jointure — *noun* property settled on a woman by her husband for her use after his death. — *verb* to provide with a jointure. [from Old French, from Latin *junctura*, joining]

joint venture a business activity undertaken by two or more companies acting together, sharing the costs, risks, and profits.

joist *noun* any of the beams supporting a floor or ceiling. [from Old French *giste*, from *gesir*, to lie]

jojoba *noun* a N American shrub whose seeds contain a wax similar to spermaceti and which is used as a substitute for it in cosmetics, etc. [from Mexican Spanish *jojoba*]

joke — *noun* **1** a humorous story: *crack a joke.* **2** anything said or done in jest. **3** an amusing situation. **4** something or someone ludicrous. — *verb intrans.* **1** to make jokes. **2** to speak in jest, not in earnest.
— **the joke's on him, her,** *etc colloq.* he, she, etc has become the victim of his or her own joke.
joking apart *or* **aside** to be serious; seriously.
no joke *colloq.* a serious matter.
play a joke on someone to trick them.
see the joke *colloq.* to see the funny side of a situation.
take a joke to be able to laugh at a joke played on one.
[from Latin *jocus*, joke]

joker *noun* **1** *Cards* an extra card in a pack, usually bearing a picture of a jester, used in certain games. **2** a cheerful person, always full of jokes. **3** *colloq.* an irresponsible or incompetent person. **4** *colloq.* a person.
— **joker in the pack** a person or thing whose effect on a situation is unpredictable.

jokey *adj.* **1** given to joking, good humoured. **2** as or in a joke.

jokiness *noun* being jokey.

jokingly *adv.* as a joke.

Joliot-Curie, Frédéric, originally **Jean-Frédéric Joliot** (1900–58) French physicist, born in Paris. He joined the Radium Institute under Marie Curie, and married her daughter Irène in 1926; in joint research they produced the first artificial radioactive isotope and for this work they shared the 1935 Nobel Prize for Chemistry. He became professor at the Collège de France in 1937. During World War II he was a strong supporter of the Resistance movement; also an active member of the Communist Party, he was awarded the Stalin Peace Prize in 1951.

Joliot-Curie, Irène, née **Curie** (1897–1956) French physicist, born in Paris, daughter of Marie Curie. She worked at the Radium Institute in Paris from 1918, and in 1926 married Frédéric Joliot. Together they made the first artificial radioisotope by bombarding aluminium with alpha particles to produce a radioactive isotope of phosphorus (1933–4). They shared the 1935 Nobel Prize for Chemistry. Similar methods led them to make a range of radioisotopes, some of which have proved indispensable in medicine, scientific research, and industry.

jollification *noun* **1** merriment; fun. **2** (**jollifications**) cheerful celebrations. [a fanciful elaboration of JOLLY]

jolliness *noun* being jolly.

jollity *noun* (PL. **jollities**) **1** merriment. **2** (**jollities**) festivities. [from Middle English *jolite*, from Old French *jolif*, pretty, merry]

jolly — *adj.* (**jollier, jolliest**) **1** good-humoured; cheerful. **2** happy; enjoyable; convivial. — *adv. Brit. colloq.* very. — *verb* (**jollies, jollied**) **1** (*also* **jolly someone up**) to make them more cheerful. **2** (**jolly someone into** *or* **out of something**) to coax or cajole them. **3** (*also* **jolly someone along**) to keep them cheerful and co-operative.
— **jolly well** *Brit. colloq.* used for emphasis: *you jolly well deserved it.*
[from French *jolif*, pretty, merry]

jollyboat *noun* a small boat carried on a larger ship.

Jolly Roger *Hist.* the black flag of a pirate ship bearing a white skull-and-crossbones.

Jolson, Al, originally **Asa Yoelson** (1886–1950) US singer, born in St Petersburg, Russia, and raised in Washington and New York. His sentimental songs, such as 'Mammy', 'Sonny Boy', and 'Swanee', delivered on one knee with arms outstretched, moved vaudeville audiences in the 1920s, but he is best known for his starring role in *The Jazz Singer* (1927), the first motion picture with sound. Later, the films *The Jolson Story* (1946) and *Jolson Sings Again* (1949) briefly revived his career.

jolt — *verb* **1** *intrans.* to move along jerkily. **2** *trans.* to shake, jog, or jar. — *noun* **1** a jarring shake. **2** an emotional shock. [blend of dialect *jot* and *joll*, to bump]

Jonah, Book of *or* **Jonas** one of the 12 so-called 'minor' prophetic writings of the Hebrew Bible and Old Testament. Though probably from the period following Israel's exile, it is set in the mid-8c BC and tells of the prophet Jonah's reluctance to preach to the city of Nineveh, and also how he was reputedly swallowed by and saved from a 'great fish'.

Jonah *noun* a person who seems to bring bad luck. [named after Jonah in the Old Testament, who almost brought disaster on the ship on which he was sailing]

Jonathan (c.11c BC) **1** a biblical character, the son and heir of Saul (the first King of Israel), and friend of David. He was a cunning soldier (1 Samuel), but faced conflicting loyalties when he continued his friendship with David despite his father's mounting hostility. Jonathan was killed in the battle of Gilboa against the Philistines, and David succeeded Saul as King of Israel. **2** a male first name. [from Hebrew elements meaning 'God' and 'gift']

Jones, Bobby (Robert Tyre) US golfer, born in Atlanta, Georgia. An amateur throughout his career, he won the British Open three times (1926–7, 1930) and the US Open four times (1923, 1926, 1929–30). He also won the US amateur title five times and the British amateur title once. In 1930 he took the amateur and Open titles of both countries, the game's most successful Grand Slam. He was responsible for the founding of the US Masters in Augusta.

Jones, Daniel (1881–1967) English phonetician. He became lecturer (1907) and Professor (1921–49) of Phonetics at London. He wrote phonetic readers for several languages, compiled the *English Pronouncing Dictionary* (1917), and produced several influential textbooks. His 'cardinal vowels' act as a reference system for the description of the vowels of real languages.

Jones, Sir Harold Spencer (1890–1960) English astronomer, born in Kensington, London. Astronomer at the Royal Observatory, Greenwich, and at the Cape of Good Hope, he organized an international project to improve the value of the Earth–Sun distance. He discovered long-term and irregular variations in the rate of the Earth's rotation (1939), and this led to the concept of 'ephemeris time' (1950).

Jones, Henry, also called **Cavendish** (1831–99) English physician and writer on whist and other games, born in London. The author of manuals on several games, he is mainly remembered for his codification of the rules of whist (1862). His pseudonym derives from the name of the first whist club he went to in London.

Jones, Inigo (1573–1652) English architect, born in London. He introduced the Palladian style into England from Venice. In 1606 James I employed him in arranging the masques of Ben Jonson, and he introduced the proscenium arch and moveable scenery to the English stage. In 1615 he became surveyor-general of the royal buildings, and designed the Queen's House at Greenwich, the Banqueting House in Whitehall, and laid out Covent Garden and Lincoln's Inn Fields.

Jones, Jack (James Larkin) (1913–) English trade unionist, born in Liverpool. As General Secretary of the Transport and General Workers Union (1969–78), he favoured the decentralization of trade union power to the local branch and had some influence on the Labour government's policies of 1974–6.

Jones, Mary Harris, known as **Mother Jones** (1830–1930) US labour agitator, born in Co Cork, Ireland. She migrated to the USA via Canada, and lost her family to an epidemic in 1867, and her home to the Chicago fire of 1871 (which destroyed 18 000 buildings and made nearly 100 000 homeless). Thereafter, she devoted herself to the cause of labour, travelled to areas of labour strife, especially in the coal industry, and was imprisoned in W Virginia on a charge of conspiracy to murder in 1912, aged 82. Freed by a new governor, she returned to labour agitation, which she continued almost until her death.

Jones, (John) Paul, originally **John Paul** (1747–92) US naval commander, born in Kirkbean, Kirkcudbrightshire, Scotland. Apprenticed as a sailor boy, he made several voyages to America, and in 1773 inherited a property in Virginia. He joined the navy at the outbreak of the War of Independence, and performed a number of daring exploits off the British coast, where he captured and sank several ships.

Jones, Tom see TOM JONES, THE HISTORY OF.

Jones, Sir William (1746–94) English Orientalist, born in London. He was called to the Bar (1774), and became a judge in the Supreme Court in Bengal (1783). He devoted himself to Sanskrit, and in 1787 pointed out its resemblance to Latin and Greek.

Jönköping 1 POP (1992e) 112 000, the industrial capital of Jönköping county, S Sweden, situated at the S end of L Vättern. It received its charter in 1284, and is the industrial centre for an agricultural and forestry region. **2** a county in S Sweden with Jönköping as its capital.

jonquil *noun* a European and Asian plant of the narcissus family, with sweet-smelling white or yellow flowers. [from French *jonquille*]

Jonson, Ben (Benjamin) (1572–1637) English dramatist, born in London. His major plays were *Every Man in His Humour* (1598), *Volpone* (1606), and *The Alchemist* (1610). He also wrote several masques and was a major influence on 17c poets (known as the 'tribe of Ben').

Joplin, Scott (1868–1917) US composer and pianist, born in Texarkana, Arkansas. He gained fame as a pianist in Chicago and St Louis in the 1890s, but longed for recognition as a serious composer. Ragtime music became a national craze following his 'Maple Leaf Rag' (1899), and during its revival in the 1970s Joplin's music (especially 'The Entertainer') became more widely known.

Jordan, (Marie-Ennemond) Camille (1838–1922) French mathematician, born in Lyons. Professor at the Ecole Polytechnique and the Collège de France, he applied group theory to geometry and linear differential equations, and attempted to derive the important, intuitively obvious, but elusive proof (today called the 'Jordan curve theorem') that every closed curve that does not cross itself has an inside and an outside. He also gave an account of the theory of certain important mathematical functions.

Jordan, Dorothy, née **Bland** (1762–1816) Irish actress, born near Waterford. She made her début in Dublin in 1777, moved to London in 1785, and played mainly comic tomboy roles for nearly 30 years. From 1790 to 1811 she had a liaison with the Duke of Clarence, afterwards William IV, by whom she had 10 of her 15 children.

Jordan, Michael (1963–) US basketball player, born in Brooklyn. He played for Chicago Bulls from 1984 holding the record for the most points in an NBA (National Basketball Association) playoff game (63). He was a member of the US Olympic gold medal-winning teams in 1984 and 1992. A member of the NBA All-Star team (1985–92), he has received numerous awards, including being named the NBA Most Valuable Player in 1988, 1991, and 1992.

Jordan, (Ernst) Pascual (1902–) German theoretical physicist, born in Hanover. Professor at Rostock, Berlin, and Hamburg, he helped to develop the theory of quantum mechanics, showing how light could be interpreted as being composed of discrete quanta of energy; he also contributed to the theories (now known as 'quantum electrodynamics') which laid the foundations for the theory of electromagnetism.

Jordan, official name **Hashemite Kingdom of Jordan**, Arabic **Al Mamlaka al Urduniya al Hashemiyah** POP (1992e) 4.3m, a kingdom in the Middle East, divided into eight governorates (*muhafazas*). AREA 96 188sq km/37 129sq mi (including 6 644sq km/2 565sq mi in the West Bank). It is bounded N by Syria, NE by Iraq, E and S by Saudi Arabia, and W by Israel. CAPITAL Amman. CHIEF TOWNS Irbid, Zarqa, Salt, Karak, Aqaba. TIME ZONE GMT +2. The population is mainly of Arab descent. Islam is the chief religion, with Christian and other minorities. OFFICIAL LANGUAGE Arabic. CURRENCY the Jordanian dinar. PHYSICAL DESCRIPTION divided N–S by the Red Sea–Jordan rift valley, much of which lies below sea level; the lowest point is –400m at the Dead Sea; the main area of irrigated cultivation is at El Ghor in the N; the sides of the rift rise steeply through undulating hill country to heights above 1 000m; land levels out to the Syrian desert in the E, sandy in the S, hard and rocky further N; the highest point is Mt Ram (1 754m). CLIMATE c.90% of Jordan is desert, annual rainfall is below 200mm; summers there are uniformly hot and sunny; typically Mediterranean climate elsewhere, with hot, dry summers and cool, wet winters; temperatures at Amman are 7°C (Jan), 25°C (Jul); average annual rainfall is 290mm. HISTORY part of the Roman Empire; under Arab control in the 7c; centre of Crusader activity in the 11c–12c; part of the Turkish Empire from the 16c until during World War I; area divided into Palestine (W of the R Jordan) and Transjordan (E of the R Jordan), administered by Britain; Transjordan gained independence in 1946; the British mandate over Palestine ended in 1948, with newly-created Israel fighting to control the West Bank area; an armistice in 1949 left Jordan in control of the West Bank; the West and East Banks united within Jordan in 1951; Israel took control of the West Bank after the Six-Day War in 1967; Civil War, following attempts by the Jordanian army to expel Palestinian guerrillas from the West Bank in 1970–1; an amnesty was declared in 1973; claims to the West Bank ceded to the Palestine Liberation Organization in 1974; legal and administrative links with the West Bank were cut in 1988, prompting the PLO to establish a government in exile; in 1991, a ban on political parties was ended. GOVERNMENT the monarch is head of state and of government; parliament consists of a 30-member Senate and an elected 80-member House of Representatives. ECONOMY oil, cement, potash, phosphate (world's third largest exporter); light manufacturing; cereals, vegetables, citrus fruits, olives; major investment in Jordan valley agricultural development.

Jordan, River a river in the Middle East. It rises in several headstreams in the Anti-Lebanon

Mts, on the Lebanon–Syria border and flows over 320km/200mi S through L Tiberias and El Ghor to the Dead Sea. The N half of the river forms part of the Israel–Jordan and Israel–Syria borders. The S half separates the East Bank of Jordan from the Israeli-occupied West Bank.

Joseph II (1741–90) Holy Roman Emperor (1765–90), the son of Francis I and Maria Theresa, born in Vienna. Until his mother's death (1780) he was co-regent, with power over the army and foreign affairs. He became known as 'the revolutionary emperor' for his programme of modernization. He was determined to assert Habsburg leadership, but some of his ambitious plans were thwarted – by the diplomatic obstruction of France, Prussia, the United Provinces, and Britain, by war (with Prussia in 1778–9 and Turkey in 1788) and by insurrection (in the Netherlands in 1787, Hungary 1789, and the Tyrol 1790).

Joseph, St (1c BC) the husband of Mary the mother of Christ. A carpenter in Nazareth, he last appears in the Gospel account when Christ is 12 years old, so must be assumed to have already died by the time of Christ's ministry. His feast day is 19 Mar.

Joseph a biblical character and subject of many stories in Genesis 37–50; the eleventh son of Jacob, but the first by his wife Rachel. He is depicted as Jacob's favourite son (marked by the gift of a multicoloured coat), but was sold into slavery by his jealous brothers. The stories show him using his wisdom and God's help to rise to high office in Pharaoh's court, and he was reconciled with his brothers when they arrived in Egypt seeking food during a famine. His sons, Ephraim and Manasseh, were blessed by Jacob, and became ancestors of two of the tribes of Israel.

Joseph a male first name, more common in N America. [from Hebrew, = (God) shall add (another son)]

Joseph of Arimathea, St (1c AD) a New Testament figure who was a wealthy councillor and a secret follower of Jesus. He begged Pontius Pilate for the body of Jesus, which he buried in his own rock-hewn tomb. He is referred to in later Christian literature, and supposedly travelled to England with the Holy Grail after the Crucifixion. His feast day is 17 Mar (W) or 31 Jul (E).

Joseph, Keith (Sinjohn) Joseph, Baron (1918–) English Conservative politician, born in London. Called to the Bar in 1946, he became an MP in 1956. A former Secretary of State for Social Services (1970–4) and Industry (1979–81), he then held the Education and Science portfolio (1981–6). He was given an overall responsibility for Conservative policy and research in 1975, and was also a close political advisor to Margaret Thatcher, with whom he founded the Centre for Policy Studies.

Joseph, Père, also called **Eminence Grise** (**Grey Eminence**), originally **François Joseph le Clerc du Tremblay** (1577–1638) French

diplomat and mystic, born in Paris. He became a Capuchin in 1599, and secretary to Cardinal Richelieu in 1611. His byname derives from his contact with Richelieu (the 'Red Eminence'), for whom he went on important diplomatic missions, notably during the Thirty Years War.

Joseph, Tribes of the descendants of Joseph, the eleventh son of Jacob. Instead of being a single tribe of Joseph, one of the 12 tribes of Israel, they were represented by two tribes — Manasseh and Ephraim, from Joseph's two sons who were blessed by Jacob (Genesis 48–9).

Joseph Andrews, in full ***The History of the Adventures of Joseph Andrews, and of his Friend Mr Abraham Adams*** a novel by Henry Fielding (1742). It describes the comic adventures of Joseph as he travels around England with various companions.

Joséphine, *née* **Marie Josèphe Rose Tascher de la Pagerie** (1763–1814) first wife of Napoleon Bonaparte, born in Trois-Ilets, Martinique. In 1779 she married the Vicomte de Beauharnais, who was executed during the French Revolution (1794). She then married Napoleon (1796), and accompanied him on his Italian campaign, but soon returned to Paris. At Malmaison, and afterwards at the Luxembourg and the Tuileries, she gathered round her the most brilliant society of France. The marriage, being childless, was dissolved in 1809, but she retained the title of Empress.

Josephson, Brian David (1940–) Welsh physicist, born in Cardiff. Professor at Cambridge, he deduced theoretically the possibility of the 'Josephson effect' on electric currents in superconductors separated by a very thin insulator; he demonstrated that a current can flow between the superconductors with no applied voltage, and that when a constant voltage is applied, an alternating current of frequency proportional to the voltage is produced. This effect has been utilized in computers and scientific instruments. He shared the 1973 Nobel Prize for Physics with Leo Esaki and Ivar Giaever.

josh *North Amer. colloq.* — *verb trans., intrans.* to tease. — *noun* a bit of teasing.

Joshua, Hebrew **Yehoshua** a biblical character, the son of Nun, of the tribe of Ephraim. During the 40 years' wanderings of the Israelites he acted as 'minister' of Moses, and on Moses' death was appointed to lead the people into Canaan. The Book of Joshua is named after him.

Joshua *or* **Josue, Book of** a book of the Hebrew Bible and Old Testament, named after its main hero (originally Hoshea, but renamed by Moses). Continuing the stories of the Pentateuch, it begins with the death of Moses, and tells of Israel's conquest of the land west of the R Jordan from the Canaanites after 40 years in the desert. It ends with the death of Joshua after the apportionment of land among the tribes of Israel.

Joshua Commanding the Sun to Stand Still a painting by John Martin (1816).

joss-stick *noun* a stick of dried scented paste, burnt as incense. [from *joss* (pidgin Chinese), household god, from Portuguese *deos*, god]

Jostedalsbreen *or* **Jostedalsbre** the largest ice field in Europe, on the Jostedalsbreen Plateau, W Norway, 160km/100mi NE of Bergen. AREA 486sq km/188sq mi; length 96km/60mi; width 24km/15mi. HEIGHT 2 044m. The field is 300m thick and the village of Jostedal lies at its E foot.

jostle *verb* **1** *intrans., trans.* to push and shove; to push against (someone) roughly. **2** *intrans.* to compete aggressively. [formed from JOUST]

jot — *noun* (*usually* **not** *or* **never a jot**) the least bit: *not a jot of sympathy*. — *verb* (**jotted, jotting**) (*often* **jot something down**) to write it down hastily. [from *iota*, the Greek letter *i*]

jotter *noun Scot.* a school notebook for rough work and notes.

Jordan

jotting noun (usually **jottings**) something jotted down.

Jotunheimen or **Jotunheim** the highest mountain range in Europe, situated in S central Norway. It extends c.112km/70mi between Sogne Fjord and the upper Gudbrandsval, and rises to 2 470m at Glittertind. There are more than 250 peaks over 1 900m and over 60 glaciers. The range has many associations with folk legends and is also the scene of Ibsen's *Peer Gynt*.

Joule, James Prescott (1818–89) British natural philosopher, born in Salford. He studied chemistry, and in a series of experiments showed that heat is a form of energy, and established the mechanical equivalent of heat; this became the basis of the theory of the conservation of energy. He also worked with Lord Kelvin on temperature changes in gases.

joule noun Physics (ABBREV. **J**) the SI unit of work and energy, equal to the work done when a force of one newton moves through a distance of one metre in the direction of the force. [named after James Joule]

journal noun **1** a magazine or periodical, eg one dealing with a specialised subject. **2** a diary in which one recounts one's daily activities. **3** Mech. the part of an axle or rotating shaft within the bearing. [from Latin *diurnalis*, daily]

journalese noun derog. the language, typically shallow and full of clichés and jargon, used by less able journalists.

journalism noun the profession of writing for newspapers and magazines, or for radio and television.

journalist noun a person whose profession is journalism.

journalistic adj. relating to or involving journalism or journalists.

Journal of a Tour to the Hebrides, The an account by James Boswell of his tour of the Highlands and the Western Isles (1785), made with Samuel Johnson in 1773. It gives a record of the journey and describes Johnson's reactions to Highland life.

Journal of the Plague Year, A a historical fiction by Daniel Defoe (1722). It claims to be the account by a London dweller of the events of the Great Plague (1664–5).

journey — noun (PL **journeys**) **1** a process of travelling from one place to another. **2** the distance covered by, or time taken for, a journey. — verb intrans. (**journeys, journeyed**) to make a journey. [from Old French *journee*, day]

journeyman noun (PL. **journeymen**) **1** a craftsman qualified in a particular trade and working for an employer. **2** an experienced and competent but not outstanding worker. [from JOURNEY, in the old sense of a day's work]

journo noun (PL. **journos, journoes**) colloq. a journalist.

joust — noun Hist. a contest between two knights on horseback armed with lances. — verb to take part in a joust. [from French *jouster*, to joust, from Latin *juxta*, near]

Jouvet, Louis (1887–1951) French actor and theatre/film director, born in Crozon. Director from 1924 of the Comédie des Champs Elysées, he was the first to recognize Jean Giraudoux, all but one of whose plays he produced. In 1934 his company transferred to the Théâtre de l'Athénée, and he became professor at the Paris Conservatoire.

Jove see JUPITER.
— **by Jove!** Brit. old colloq. use an exclamation of surprise or emphasis.

jovial adj. good-humoured; merry; cheerful. [from Latin *jovialis*, of the planet Jupiter, believed to be a lucky influence]

joviality noun being cheerful.

jovially adv. in a cheerful way.

Jowett, Benjamin (1817–93) English scholar of Greek, born in London. He became a tutor at Oxford in 1840, was Professor of Greek (1855–93), and was elected Master of Balliol College in 1870. He was ordained an Anglican priest in 1845. His main works include *The Epistles of St Paul* (1855), which was received controversially, and his translation of Plato's *Dialogues* (1871).

jowl¹ noun **1** the lower jaw. **2** the cheek. [from Anglo-Saxon *ceafl*, jaw]

jowl² noun (usually **jowls**) **1** loose flesh under the chin; a heavy double chin. **2** an animal's dewlap. [from Anglo-Saxon *ceole*, throat]

Joy a female first name, popular in the 17c. [from JOY]

joy noun **1** a feeling of happiness. **2** a cause of this. **3** Brit. colloq. satisfaction; success: *any joy at the enquiry desk?* [from Old French *joie*]

Joyce, James (Augustine Aloysius) (1882–1941) Irish writer, born in Dublin. He went to Paris in 1903 to study medicine, and then took up voice training for a concert career. He returned to Dublin and published a few stories but was unable to make a living from his writing and found the Catholic society too bigoted. He spent five years in Zürich before settling in Paris (1920–40). His early work includes the short stories, *Dubliners* (1914), and the autobiographical novel, *A Portrait of the Artist as a Young Man* (1914–5). His best-known work, *Ulysses*, appeared in Paris in 1922, but was banned in the UK and USA until 1936. *Work in Progress* began to appear in 1927, and finally emerged as *Finnegans Wake* (1939). His work revolutionized the novel form, partly through the abandonment of ordinary plot for 'stream of consciousness', but more fundamentally through his unprecedented exploration of language.

Joyce, William, known as **Lord Haw-Haw** (1906–46) British traitor, born in New York City. He founded the fanatical British National Socialist Party in England in 1937, and fled to Germany before the outbreak of World War II. With Radio Hamburg throughout the war, he broadcast propaganda against Britain, gaining his nickname from his accent. He was captured by the British at Flensburg, and tried and executed in London.

Joyce a female first name, originally given to males. [from *Jodocus*, a Latinized form of a Celtic name meaning 'lord']

joyful adj. **1** happy; full of joy. **2** expressing or causing joy.

joyfully adv. with joy; gladly.

joyless adj. without joy, not giving joy.

joyous adj. filled with, causing, or showing joy.

joyously adv. in a joyous way.

joyousness noun being joyous.

joyride — noun a jaunt, especially a reckless drive in a stolen vehicle. — verb intrans. to go for such a jaunt.

joyrider noun a person who joyrides, especially in a stolen vehicle.

joystick noun colloq. a controlling lever, eg for a computer or an aircraft.

JP abbrev. Justice of the Peace.

J Paul Getty Museum a museum in Malibu, California, founded in 1954 by J Paul Getty. Its exhibits include paintings, sculptures, and decorative arts from various European countries, and ancient Greek and Roman works of art. They are housed in a building which is almost an exact copy of an ancient Roman villa.

Jr abbrev. (used after a name) Junior: *John Smith, Jr.*

Juan Carlos I (1938–) King of Spain (1975–), born in Rome, the son of Don Juan de Borbón y Battenberg, Count of Barcelona (1913–), and the grandson of Spain's last ruling monarch, Alfonso XIII (1886–1941). He was educated in Switzerland, and, by agreement between his father and General Franco, in Spain from 1948. After earning commissions in the army, navy, and air force, and attending Madrid University, he married Princess Sophia of Greece (1962), who bore him three children. In 1969 Franco named him as his eventual successor, and he was proclaimed king on the death of Franco (1975), who had intended him to uphold the dictatorship. However he decisively presided over Spain's democratization, helped to defeat a military coup (1981), and assumed the role of a constitutional monarch.

Juan Fernández Islands a group of three volcanic islands in Valparaíso province, Chile, situated in the Pacific Ocean, 640km/398mi W of the mainland. They are Más a Tierra, Más Afuera, and Santa Clara. AREA 181sq km/70sq mi (total). Alexander Selkirk was shipwrecked on Más a Tierra in 1704 for four years and his experiences were the basis of Daniel Defoe's novel *Robinson Crusoe*.

Juan-les-Pins a fashionable resort on the Cap d'Antibes, in Alpes-Maritimes department, Provence-Alpes-Côte d'Azur region, SE France. It lies on the Mediterranean coast between Nice and Cannes, 8km/5mi from Antibes. The resort is noted for its beaches and casinos.

Juárez, Benito (Pablo) (1806–72) Mexican national hero and statesman, born of Zapotec Indian parents near Oaxaca. His ideas for reform forced him to live in exile (1853–5), but he then joined the new Liberal government. During the civil war of 1857–60, he assumed the presidency, and was elected President on the Liberal victory (1861–72). The French invasion under Maximilian forced him to the far north, from where he directed resistance until the defeat of Maximilian (1867).

jubilant adj. showing and expressing triumphant joy. [from Latin *jubilare*, to shout for joy]

jubilantly adv. with great joy.

jubilation noun **1** triumphant rejoicing. **2** (**jubilations**) celebrations. [from Latin *jubilatio*]

jubilee noun a special anniversary, especially the 25th (*silver jubilee*), 50th (*golden jubilee*), or 60th (*diamond jubilee*) of a significant event, eg the succession of a monarch. [from Old French *jubile*, from Latin *jubilaeus annus*, the Jewish celebration of emancipation and restoration held every 50 years; ultimately from Hebrew *yobhel*, the ram's horn or trumpet used to announce this]

Jud. abbrev. Biblical **1** Judges. **2** Judith (Apocrypha).

Judaeo- or **Judeo-** combining form forming words meaning 'Jewish, Jewish and ...': *Judaeo-Hispanic*.

Judah, Kingdom of an ancient Jewish state which incorporated the tribal areas of Judah and Benjamin, established when the united monarchy split into the kingdoms of Judah (in the south) and Israel (in the north) in the late 10c BC after the reign of Solomon. Jerusalem was in the kingdom of Judah; both fell to the Babylonians in 587/6 BC.

Judah, Tribe of one of the 12 tribes of ancient Israel, descended from Jacob's fourth son by his wife Leah. Its territory originally extended south of Jerusalem, bounded on the west by the Mediterranean and on the east by the Dead Sea, but later it was restricted.

Judaic adj. relating to the Jews or Judaism.

Judaism the religion of the Jews, central to which is the belief in one God, the transcendent creator of the world who delivered the Israelites out of their bondage in Egypt, revealed his law (*Torah*) to them, and chose them to be a light to all humankind. The Hebrew Bible is the primary source of Judaism. Next in importance is the *Talmud*, which consists of the *Mishnah* (the codification of the oral *Torah*) and a collection of extensive early rabbinical commentary. Various later commentaries and the standard code of Jewish law and ritual (halakhah) produced in the late Middle Ages have been important in shaping Jewish practice and thought. All Jews see themselves as members of a community whose origins lie in the patriarchal period, a past that lives on in rituals; their beliefs and attitudes are more readily expressed through ritual than through abstract doctrine. The family is the basic unit of Jewish ritual, though the synagogue has come to play an increasingly important role. The Sabbath, which begins at sunset on Friday and ends at sunset on Saturday, is the central religious observance. The synagogue, the centre for community worship and study, houses the 'ark' (a cupboard), which contains the hand-written scrolls of the Pentateuch. The rabbi is primarily a teacher and spiritual guide. Today most Jews are the descendants of either the *Ashkenazim* or the *Sephardim*, each with their marked cultural differences. There are also several religious branches of Judaism. *Orthodox* Judaism (19c) seeks to preserve traditional Judaism. *Reform* Judaism (19c) represents an attempt to interpret Judaism in the light of modern scholarship — a process carried further by *Liberal* Judaism. *Conservative* Judaism attempts to modify orthodoxy through an emphasis on the positive historical elements of Jewish tradition. Anti-Semitic prejudice and periods of persecution have been a feature of the Christian culture of Europe, and increased with the rise of European nationalism, culminating in the Nazi Holocaust. [from Latin *Juda*, a son of Jacob]

Judas *noun* a traitor, especially to one's friends. [named after Judas Iscariot]

Judas Iscariot (1c AD) one of the 12 Apostles of Christ, usually named last in the lists in the synoptic Gospels (Mark 3.19). He had a role as treasurer (John 13.29), and is identified as the one who betrayed Christ for 30 pieces of silver by helping to arrange for his arrest at Gethsemane by the Jewish authorities (Mark 14.43–6). His later repentance and suicide is related in Matthew 27.3–5. *Iscariot* may mean 'man of Keriot', 'assassin', or 'man of falsehood'.

judder — *verb intrans.* (**juddered, juddering**) *said of a vehicle* to jolt, shake, shudder, or vibrate. — *noun* a shuddering vibration. [perhaps from SHUDDER + JAR?]

Jude, St (1c AD) one of the 12 Apostles of Jesus Christ, probably the Judas who was one of the 'brethren of the Lord', perhaps a brother of St James 'the Just'. A New Testament letter bears his name, but its authorship is disputed. According to tradition he was martyred in Persia with St Simon, who shares his feast day (28 Oct (W) and 19 Jun or 21 Aug (E)).

Jude, Letter of a short New Testament writing, considered one of the 'catholic' or 'general' letters, attributed to Jude the brother of James. The work warns an unspecified readership about false teachers, who are portrayed as immoral, intemperate, and divisive, and who perhaps represent libertine, gnostic views.

Judea POP (1992e) 974 000, the Roman–Greek name for S Palestine, the area now occupied by SW Israel and W Jordan. It was the southernmost of the Roman divisions of Palestine, rising to 1 020m in the S near Hebron. CHIEF TOWN Jerusalem. Following the 1948–9 war, the W region became part of Israel, and the E region part of Jordan. The West Bank and E Jerusalem have been occupied by Israel since 1967 but a peace agreement between Israel and the Palestinian Liberation Organization was signed in 1993. See also HEBRON.

Judea-Samaria see WEST BANK.

Jude the Obscure a novel by Thomas Hardy (1895). His last, it describes the ill-fated life of aspiring student, Jude Fawley.

judge — *noun* 1 a public officer who hears and decides cases in a law court. 2 a person appointed to decide the winner of a contest. 3 someone who assesses something; a connoisseur: *a good judge of character*. 4 the person who decides or assesses: *let me be the judge of that*. — *verb* 1 to try (a legal case) in a law court as judge. 2 to decide the winner of (a contest). 3 to act as judge or adjudicator. 4 *trans., intrans.* to assess; to form an opinion. 5 to estimate. 6 to consider or state: *judged her fit to travel*. 7 to criticize, especially severely; to condemn. [from Old French *juge*]

judgement *or* **judgment** *noun* 1 the decision of a judge in a court of law. 2 the act or process of judging. 3 the ability to make wise or sensible decisions; good sense. 4 an opinion: *in my judgement*. 5 (**judgement on someone**) *old use* punishment regarded as sent by divine providence: *his sickness was a judgement on him*.
— **against one's better judgement** contrary to what one believes to be the sensible course.
pass judgement on someone to condemn them.
pass judgement on someone *or* **something** to give an opinion or verdict about them.
reserve judgement to postpone one's verdict.
sit in judgement on someone to assume the responsibility of judging another person. [from Old French *jugement*]

judgemental *or* **judgmental** *adj.* 1 involving judgement. 2 apt to pass judgement.

Judgement of Paris, The a painting by Pierre Auguste Renoir (c.1914).

Judges, Book of a book of the Hebrew Bible and Old Testament; 'judges' refers to the tribal heroes (eg Deborah, Gideon, and Samson) whose acts of leadership are described. It relates to the unstable period between the initial conquest of Palestine by the Israelites and the establishment of the monarchy over Israel, and draws moral lessons from contrasting examples of good and bad leadership.

judicature *noun* 1 the administration of justice by legal trial. 2 the office of judge. 3 a body of judges. 4 a court or system of courts. [from Latin *judicare*, to judge]

judicial *adj.* of, or relating to, a court of law, judges, or their decisions. [from Latin *judicialis*, from *judicium*, judgement]

judicially *adv.* in a judicial way.

judiciary *noun* (PL. **judiciaries**) 1 the branch of government concerned with the legal system and the administration of justice. 2 a country's body of judges. [from Latin *judiciarius*, of the law courts]

judicious *adj.* shrewd, sensible, wise or tactful. [from Latin *judicium*, judgement]

judiciously *adv.* in a judicious way.

judiciousness *noun* being judicious.

Judith a female first name, borne by a wife of Esau in the Old Testament. [probably from Hebrew, = Jewess]

Judith, Book of a book of the Old Testament Apocrypha (or deuterocanonical writings recognized by the Catholic Church), possibly from the Maccabean period (mid-2c BC). It relates how Judith, an attractive and pious Jewish widow, saved the city of Bethulia from siege by the Assyrian army (c.6c BC) by beheading its general Holofernes in his tent, once she had beguiled and intoxicated him.

Judith and Holofernes a statue in bronze by Donatello (c.mid-15c).

judo *noun* a Japanese form of wrestling using minimum physical effort, developed from jujitsu. [from Japanese *ju*, gentleness + *do*, art]

◇ The modern-day sport dates from the end of the 19c. Contestants wear a loose-fitting suit known as a *judogi*, and compete on a mat to break their falls. They are graded by ability from 5th to 1st Kyn, then from 1st to 12th Dan; coloured belts are worn to indicate a fighter's grade.

jug — *noun* 1 a deep container for liquids with a handle and a shaped lip for pouring. 2 the amount that a jug can hold. 3 *slang* prison. — *verb* (**jugged, jugging**) to stew (hare) in an earthenware container.

jugful *noun* (PL. **jugfuls**) the amount a jug will hold.

juggernaut *noun* 1 a mighty force sweeping away and destroying everything in its path. 2 *Brit. colloq.* a large articulated commercial road vehicle. [named after the gigantic chariot of the Hindu god: see JAGANNĀTHA]

juggle *verb* 1 *intrans.* to keep several objects simultaneously in the air by skilful throwing and catching. 2 *trans., intrans.* (usually **juggle with something**) to adjust facts or figures to create a misleading impression. [from Old French *jogler*, to act as jester]

juggler *noun* a person who juggles.

Jugoslavia see YUGOSLAVIA.

jugular — *adj.* relating to the neck or throat. — *noun Anat.* (in full **jugular vein**) any of several veins that carry deoxygenated blood from the head to the heart in vertebrates. [from Latin *jugulum*, throat]

juice *noun* 1 liquid from fruit or vegetables. 2 (*usually* **juices**) the body's natural fluids: *digestive juices*. 3 *slang* power or fuel, especially electricity or petrol. [from Old French *jus*]

juiciness *noun* being juicy.

juicy *adj.* (**juicier, juiciest**) 1 full of juice; rich and succulent. 2 *colloq., said of a problem, etc* challenging; meaty. 3 *colloq., said of gossip* intriguing; spicy. 4 *colloq.* profitable; lucrative.

Juilliard School a US conservatory of music, dance, and drama in New York City. It began as the Institute of Musical Art (1905), then in 1946 merged formally with the Juilliard Graduate School (formed in 1923 with a $20m legacy left by Augustus D Juilliard) to become the Juillard School of Music. It moved to the Lincoln Centre in 1968.

jujitsu *or* **jiu-jitsu** *noun* a martial art founded on the ancient Japanese system of combat and self-defence without weapons, developed by the Samurai. It is the basis for many modern forms of combat sports, such as judo, aikido, and karate. [from Japanese *ju*, gentleness + *jutsu*, art]

juju *noun* 1 a charm or fetish used by W African tribes. 2 the magic contained in such a charm. [from Hausa (W African language) *djudju*, fetish]

jujube *noun* 1 a soft fruit-flavoured sweet made with gelatine. 2 *Hist.* the fruit of a spiny shrub of the buckthorn family, dried and eaten as a sweet. [from Latin *jujuba*, from Greek *zizyphon*]

jukebox *noun* a coin-operated machine that plays whatever gramophone record one selects. [from Gullah (W African language) *juke*, disorderly]

Jul *or* **Jul.** *abbrev.* July.

julep *noun* especially in N America, an iced drink of spirits and sugar, flavoured especially with mint. [from Persian *gulab*, rosewater]

Jules et Jim a French film directed by François Truffaut (1961). An emotional story of a triangular relationship, it was a landmark in the development of the New Wave genre. It stars Jeanne Moreau, Oskar Werner, and Henri Serre.

Julia 1 the determined lover of Proteus in Shakespeare's *The Two Gentlemen of Verona*, who disguises herself as a page, Sebastian, to win back his love. 2 a female first name, introduced to

Britain in the 18c. [a feminine form of the Roman family name *Julius*]

Julian a male (and earlier also female) first name. [from the Roman family name *Julius*]

Juliana, Louise Emma Marie Wilhelmina (1909–) Queen of the Netherlands (1948–80), born in The Hague. She became a lawyer, and in 1937 married Prince Bernhard zur Lippe-Biesterfeld; they have four daughters. On the German invasion of Holland (1940), Juliana escaped to Britain and later resided in Canada. She returned to Holland in 1945, and became queen on the abdication of her mother, Wilhelmina. She in turn abdicated in favour of her eldest daughter, Beatrix.

Julian Alps, Slovenian **Julijske Alpe** a mountain range in NW Slovenia and NE Italy. It is a SE extension of the alpine system, bounded to the N by the Karawanken Alps. The range rises to 2 863m at Triglav, the highest peak in Slovenia.

Julian calendar, the calendar introduced by Julius Caesar in 46 BC, with a year of 365 days and 366 every leap year or centenary year. See also GREGORIAN CALENDAR.

Julian of Norwich (c.1342–1413) English mystic who probably lived in isolation outside St Julian's Church, Norwich. Her work, *Sixteen Revelations of Divine Love*, based on her own religious experiences, has had lasting influence on theologians stressing the power of the love of God.

Julie a female first name, continuously popular since its introduction to Britain in the 1920s. [a French variant of JULIA]

Juliet the tragic young heroine of Shakespeare's *Romeo and Juliet*, who defies her parents for her love of Romeo.

Julius Caesar a historical play by William Shakespeare (1599). It follows the events surrounding Julius Caesar's assassination, focusing on the guilt-racked Brutus and his accomplices.

Julunggul see RAINBOW SNAKE.

July noun the seventh month of the year. [from *Julius mensis*, the month of Julius Caesar]

July Days anti-government demonstrations (2–5 Jul 1917) in Petrograd, Russia, that marked growing popular dissatisfaction with the provisional government's record since the beginning of the Revolution. Demonstrators demanded the withdrawal of Russia from World War I, the overthrow of the provisional government, and the transfer of 'All power to the soviets', but nothing was achieved except a slight swing to the right in the provisional government.

July Revolution a three-day revolt (1830) in Paris which ended the Bourbon Restoration and forced the abdication of the reactionary Charles X. It resulted in the establishment of a more liberal regime dominated by the wealthy bourgeoisie, the so-called 'July Monarchy', under the Orléanist Louis Philippe, 'King of the French'.

Jumblat, Kemal (1919–77) Lebanese socialist politician and hereditary Druze chieftain, born in the Chouf Mts. He founded the Progressive Socialist Party (1949), held several Cabinet posts (1961–4), and was Minister of the Interior (1969–70). The increasing power of his authority in partnership with the Palestinians resulted in the Syrian intervention on the side of the Christians (1976). He was assassinated in an ambush outside the village of Baaklu in the Chouf Mts, after which his son Walid became leader of the Druze.

jumble — verb (often **jumble things up** or **together**) **1** to mix or confuse them, physically or mentally. **2** to throw them together untidily. — noun **1** a confused mass. **2** unwanted possessions collected, or suitable, for a jumble sale. [probably imitative]

jumble sale a sale of unwanted possessions, eg used clothing, usually to raise money for charity.

jumbo *colloq.* — adj. extra-large. — noun (PL. **jumbos**) a jumbo jet. [origin unknown; popularized as the name of an elephant exhibited in London in the 1880s]

jumbo jet *colloq.* the largest size of passenger jet airliner.

Jumna, River see YAMUNA, RIVER.

jump — verb **1** *intrans.* to spring off the ground, pushing off with the feet. **2** *intrans.* to leap or bound. **3** to get over or across by jumping. **4** to make (especially a horse) leap. **5** *intrans. said of prices, levels, etc* to rise abruptly. **6** *intrans.* to make a startled movement. **7** *intrans.* to twitch, jerk, or bounce. **8** *intrans.* to pass directly from one point to another, omitting intermediate matter or essential steps: *jump straight to the mad scene / jump to conclusions.* **9** to omit; to skip: *jump the next chapter.* **10** *colloq.* to pounce on. **11** *North Amer. colloq.* to board and travel on (especially a train) without paying. — noun **1** an act of jumping. **2** an obstacle to be jumped, especially a fence by a horse. **3** the height or distance jumped. **4** a jumping contest: *the high jump / the long jump.* **5** a sudden rise in amount, cost, or value. **6** an abrupt change or move. **7** a startled movement; a start: *gave a jump of surprise.*

— **be** or **stay one jump ahead of someone** *colloq.* to anticipate the moves of rivals, and so maintain an advantage over them.

have the jump on someone *colloq.* to have an advantage over them.

jump at something to take or accept it eagerly.

jump down someone's throat *colloq.* to snap at them impatiently.

jump on someone to attack them physically or verbally.

jump to it to hurry up.

jumped-up *adj. derog. colloq.* having an inflated view of one's importance; cocky, arrogant.

jumper¹ noun **1** a knitted garment for the top half of the body. **2** *North Amer.* a pinafore dress. [from old word *jump*, a short coat]

jumper² noun **1** a person or animal that jumps. **2** *Electr.* a wire used to make a temporary connection.

jumpily *adv.* in a nervous way.

jumpiness noun nervousness.

jump jet a jet aircraft that can take off and land vertically.

jump lead one of the two electric cables used to recharge one battery from another.

jump-off noun *Showjumping* an extra round held in the event of a tie.

jump start the act of jump-starting a vehicle.

jump-start verb to start the engine of (a motor vehicle) that has a weak or flat battery by using leads to attach it to a charged battery.

jumpsuit noun a one-piece garment combining trousers and top.

jumpy *adj.* (**jumpier, jumpiest**) **1** nervy; anxious. **2** moving jerkily.

Jun or **Jun.** *abbrev.* **1** June. **2** Junior.

junction noun **1** a place where roads or railway lines meet; an intersection. **2** a point of exit from, and access to, a motorway. **3** *Electr.* a point at which wires or cables are connected. **4** the process, an instance, or a point, of joining. [from Latin *junctio*, joining]

junction box the casing for an electrical junction.

juncture noun a point in time, especially if critical. [from Latin *junctura*, connection]

June a female first name, dating from the early 20c. [from Latin *Junius*]

June noun the sixth month of the year. [from *Junius mensis*, the month of the goddess Juno]

Juneau POP (1990) 27 000, the seaport capital of the state of Alaska, USA. It lies on Gastineau Channel, in the Alaskan Panhandle, SE Alaska. It developed as a gold-rush town after 1880, and is now a trade centre. The harbour is ice-free. NOTABLE FEATURE House of Wickersham.

June Days a violent episode (1848) in the French February Revolution, when working-class radicals resisted the dissolution of the National Workshops in Paris and were crushed by the National Guard and troops of the Republican government under the direction of General Louis Eugène Cavaignac (1802–57).

Jung, Carl (Gustav) (1875–1961) Swiss psychiatrist, born in Kesswil. After collaborating with Sigmund Freud, he went on to develop his own theories of 'analytical psychology'. Professor at Basle and Zürich, his approach included a description of psychological types ('extraversion/introversion'); the exploration of the 'collective unconscious'; and the concept of the psyche as a 'self-regulating system' expressing itself in the process of 'individuation'.

Jungfrau a mountain peak in the Bernese Alps, S central Switzerland. HEIGHT 4 158m. It was first ascended in 1811. A mountain railway runs almost to the summit.

jungle noun **1** an area of dense vegetation in an open area of tropical rainforest, eg on the site of former tree clearings, along a river bank, or at the forest edge. **2** a popular name for a tropical rainforest. **3** a mass of complexities difficult to penetrate: *the jungle of building regulations.* **4** a complex or hostile environment where toughness is needed for survival: *the blackboard jungle.* [from Hindi *jangal*]

Jungle Book, The a collection of short stories and poems by Rudyard Kipling (1894). They all feature animals, and most of them focus on the life of the boy Mowgli as he grows up in the jungle of India. *The Second Jungle Book* was published in 1895.

junglefowl noun a pheasant native to E India and SE Asia, that inhabits forest and scrub, and feeds on grain, shoots, berries, and insects. It is the ancestor of the domestic fowl.

junglefowl

jungly *adj.* (**junglier, jungliest**) characteristic of or like jungle.

junior — adj. **1** (often **junior to someone**) **a** low or lower in rank. **b** younger. **2** of or for schoolchildren aged between 7 and 11: *junior schools.* **3** *North Amer., esp. US* of third-year college or university students. **4** younger; used after the name of a person with the same name as his or her parent. — noun **1** a person of low, or lower, rank in a profession, organization, etc. **2** a pupil in a junior school. **3** *North Amer., esp. US* a third-year college or high-school student. **4** a person younger than the one in question: *she's three years his junior.* **5** (**Junior**) a name used for referring to the son of a family: *have you seen Junior?* [from Latin *junior*, younger]

juniper noun an evergreen shrub of northern regions with purple berries used as a medicine and for flavouring gin. [from Latin *juniperus*]

junk¹ — noun *colloq.* **1** worthless or rejected material; rubbish. **2** old or second-hand articles sold cheaply: *a junk shop.* **3** nonsense. **4** *slang* narcotic drugs, especially heroin. — adj. cheap and worthless: *junk jewellery.* [from Middle English *jonke*, pieces of old rope]

junk² *noun* a Far-Eastern flat-bottomed square-sailed boat. [from Portuguese *junco*, from Malay *jong*]

junk

Junkers Prussian aristocrats whose power rested on their large estates, mainly to the east of the R Elbe, and on their traditional role as army officers and civil servants. Their position came increasingly under threat in late 19c Germany as a result of industrialization, but they jealously safeguarded their privileges and power, until the confiscation of their estates in East Germany after World War II.

junket — **1** *noun* a dessert made from sweetened and curdled milk. **2** a feast or celebration. **3** a trip made by a government official and paid for out of public funds. — *verb intrans.* (**junketed**, **junketing**) to feast, celebrate, or make merry. [from Old French *jonquette*, a rush basket for holding cheeses, etc]

junk food food with little nutritional value.

junkie or **junky** *noun* (PL. **junkies**) *slang* a drug addict or drug-pusher. [from JUNK¹ 4]

Juno in Roman mythology, the supreme goddess, and the wife of Jupiter. Originally an ancient Italian deity associated with the Moon and the life of women, she was later identified with Hera.

Juno and the Paycock a play by Sean O'Casey (1924). Set in the Dublin slums during the Civil War after the 1921 Settlement, it tells of the resultant disintegration of the Boyle family.

junta *noun derog.* a group, clique or faction, usually of army officers, in control of a country after a coup d'état. [from Spanish *junta*, meeting]

Jupiter or **Iuppiter** in Roman mythology, the chief Roman god, equivalent to the Greek Zeus, originally a sky-god with the attributes of thunder and the thunderbolt. He was worshipped by Roman generals in his temple on the Capitoline Hill. — Also called *Jove*.

Jupiter *Astron.* the fifth planet from the Sun, and the largest planet in the solar system. Its orbit lies between those of Mars and Saturn.
◇ Jupiter is about 778 million km from the Sun, and has a diameter of 142 700km at the equator. It rotates so rapidly on its axis that its 'day' is only 9h 50min long, but it takes 11.9 years to orbit around the Sun. The rapid rotation of the planet has caused its equator to bulge outwards. Jupiter is thought to have a solid rocky core, surrounded by liquid hydrogen and helium. Its atmosphere consists mainly of hydrogen and helium gases, and white bands of frozen ammonia crystals move rapidly through the cloudy surface of the planet.
The Great Red Spot, a large oval feature south of the equator, varies in colour from pale pink to orange-red. It is larger than the Earth, and is thought to represent the top of a long-lasting swirling storm, consisting of a cloud of gases that rise upward and then revolve in an anticlockwise direction. Although the temperature of the planet's outer layers is about -150°C, the centre of the planet is believed to be hotter than the surface of the Sun.
Jupiter has 16 natural satellites, of which four (Callisto, Ganymede, Europa, and Io) are at least as large as our own Moon, and are visible from Earth with good binoculars. The space probes *Voyager 1* and *Voyager 2* have shown that Callisto and Ganymede are covered with craters similar to those on the Moon, Europa is a smooth ball of ice, and Io (nearest to Jupiter) has a yellow sulphur-covered surface and volcanoes that eject material 100km into space.

Jupiter Symphony Mozart's Symphony No.41 in C (K551, 1788), allegedly named by the violinist J P Salomon (1745–1815).

Jura Mountains a limestone mountain range in E France and W Switzerland. It lies on the French–Swiss border, forming a plateau 250km/155mi long and 50km/31mi wide. The highest point of the range in France is Crêt de la Neige (1 718m); in Switzerland the highest point is Mt Tendre (1 682m). Slopes are forested, with poor pasture. The range provides opportunities for caving and winter sports.

Jurassic — *noun Geol.* in the Mesozoic era, the period of geological time between the Triassic and Cretaceous periods, lasting from about 210 to 140 million years ago. — *adj.* belonging or relating to this period. [from the name *Jura*, a limestone mountain range in E France]
◇ During this time reptiles, and especially dinosaurs, were the dominant vertebrates, and the first flying reptiles (*pterosaurs*) appeared together with the first bird (*Archaeopteryx*). Plants included conifers, cycads, club mosses, ferns, and rushes, and the climate was warm and humid.

juridical *adj.* of or relating to the law or the administration of justice. [from Latin *juridicus*, of justice]

jurisdiction *noun* **1** the right or authority to apply laws and administer justice. **2** the district or area over which this authority extends. **3** authority generally. [from Latin *jurisdictio*, administration of justice]

jurisprudence *noun* **1** the science and philosophy of law. **2** a specialty within law: *medical jurisprudence*. [from Latin *jurisprudentia*, from *jus*, law + *prudentia*, wisdom]

jurisprudential *adj.* relating to or involving jurisprudence.

jurist *noun* an expert in law. [from French *juriste*]

juristic *adj.* **1** relating to jurists. **2** relating to law or the study of it.

juror *noun* **1** a member of a jury in a court of law. **2** a person taking an oath. [from Latin *jurare*, to swear]

jury¹ *noun* (PL. **juries**) **1** a body of usually 12 people sworn to give an honest verdict on the evidence presented to a court of law on a particular case. **2** a group of people selected to judge a contest. [from Old French *juree*, something sworn]

jury² *adj. Naut.* makeshift; temporary: *a jury mast*.

jury-box *noun* the enclosure in which the jury sit in a law court.

just¹ *adj.* **1** fair; impartial. **2** reasonable; based on justice. **3** deserved. [from Latin *justus*, just, upright, equitable]

just² *adv.* **1** exactly; precisely. **2** a short time before: *he had just gone.* **3** at this or that very moment: *was just leaving.* **4** and no earlier, more, etc: *only just enough.* **5** barely; narrowly: *just missed his ear.* **6** only; merely; simply: *just a brief note.* **7** *colloq.* used for emphasis: *just not true.* **8** *colloq.* absolutely: *just marvellous.*
— **just about** almost: *am just about ready.*

just about to do something on the point of doing it.

just as well 1 fortunate; lucky: *it's just as well you came.* **2** advisable: *it would be just as well to wait.*

just in case as a precaution.

just a minute or **second, etc** an instruction to wait a short while.

just now at this particular moment.

just so 1 a formula of agreement. **2** neat and tidy: *they like everything just so.*

just then 1 at that particular moment. **2** in the next moment.

just the same nevertheless.

not just yet not immediately, but soon.
[from Latin *justus*, right, proper]

justice *noun* **1** the quality of being just; just treatment; fairness. **2** the quality of being reasonable. **3** the law, or administration of or conformity to the law: *a miscarriage of justice.* **4** (**Justice**) the title of a judge. **5** a justice of the peace. **6** *North Amer., esp. US* a judge.
— **bring someone to justice** to arrest and try them.

do justice to someone or **something 1** to treat them fairly or properly. **2** to show their full merit, etc.

do justice to oneself to fulfil one's potential.

in justice to someone or **something** to be fair to them.
[from Latin *justitia*, from *justus*, just]

justice of the peace (PL. **justices**) a person authorized to judge minor criminal cases.

justiciary *noun* (PL. **justiciaries**) an administrator of justice; a judge. [from Latin *justiciarius*]

justifiable *adj.* that can be justified.

justifiably *adv.* in a justifiable way.

justification *noun* **1** justifying. **2** something which justifies.

justify *verb* (**justifies**, **justified**) **1** to prove or show to be right, just, or reasonable. **2** *Printing* to arrange (text) so that the margins are even-edged. [from Latin *justus*, just + *facere*, to make]

Justin a male first name, borne by several early saints. [from Latin *justus*, just or fair]

Justinian, in full **Flavius Petrus Sabbatius Justinianus** (c.482–565 AD) Roman emperor (527–65), the protégé of his uncle, the Byzantine emperor, Justin (518–27). He was at first co-emperor with Justin, and on his death became sole ruler, along with his wife Theodora. Through his generals, Belisarius and Narses, he recovered N Africa, Spain, and Italy. He is noted for his administrative reforms and his major codification of the Roman law.

Justinian Code the emperor Justinian's codification of Roman law, carried out under the direction of Tribonian and published in four sections between 529 and 565. Also known as the *Corpus Juris Civilis*, it is regarded as the pinnacle of Roman Law.

justly *adv.* in a just way.

justness *noun* being just.

Just So Stories, in full *Just So Stories for Little Children* a collection of tales and poems by Rudyard Kipling (1902). The majority of them give humorous accounts of how various animals came by their distinguishing features eg 'How the Camel got his Hump'.

jut *verb intrans.* (**jutted**, **jutting**) (*also* **jut out**) to stick out; to project. [variant of JET²]

Jute *noun* a member of a Germanic people (see JUTES). [from Anglo-Saxon *Iotas*, the Jutes]

jute *noun* fibre from certain tropical barks used for making sacking, ropes, etc. [from Bengali *jhuta*]

Jutes a Germanic people whose original homeland was the northern part of the Danish peninsula (Jutland). The tradition preserved by Bede, that Jutes participated in the 5c Germanic invasions of Britain and settled in Kent and the Isle of Wight, is confirmed by archaeological evidence.

Jutland, Danish **Jylland** the Danish peninsula extending N from the German mainland and bounded by the North Sea, Skagerrak, and Kattegat. Its S border with Germany is Denmark's only land frontier. Along the W coast are massive dykes, designed to protect the land from devastating storm tides. The major entry port of Esbjerg lies on the W coast.

Jutland, Battle of a sea battle (1916) in World War I, in which Admiral Jellicoe led the British Grand Fleet from Scapa Flow, Orkney and intercepted the German High Seas Fleet off the west coast of Jutland, Denmark. Though the battle itself was inconclusive, the Germans withdrew their fleet to port and turned to submarine warfare to challenge British command of the sea.

Juvenal, in full **Decimus Junius Juvenalis** (c.55–c.130 AD) Roman lawyer and satirist, born in Aquinum, Italy. He served as tribune in the army, and under Domitian was banished to Egypt for some years on account of his satirical writing. His 16 verse satires (c.100–128) deal with a wide range of subjects, notably the corruption and immorality of the times. These poems had great influence on British 17c–18c writers such as John Dryden and Alexander Pope.

juvenile — *adj.* **1** young; youthful. **2** suitable for young people. **3** *derog.* childish; immature. — *noun* **1** a young person. **2** a young animal. **3** an actor playing youthful parts. [from Latin *juvenilis*, youthful]

juvenile delinquency criminal or antisocial acts or behaviour of juvenile delinquents.

juvenile delinquent a young person who is guilty of a crime.

juvenile hormone *Zool.* a hormone that is required for growth and development of the immature stages in the life cycle of an insect, but inhibits development into the adult form.

juvenilia *pl. noun* the works produced by a writer or artist during his or her youth. [from Latin *juvenilis*, youthful]

juxtapose *verb* to place side by side. [from Latin *juxta*, beside + POSITION]

juxtaposition *noun* placing or being placed together.

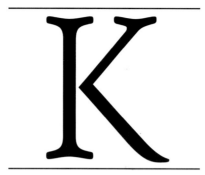

K¹ *or* **k** *noun* (PL. **Ks, K's, k's**) the eleventh letter of the English alphabet.

K² *noun* (PL. **K**) **1** *colloq.* one thousand, especially £1000. **2** *Comput.* a unit of memory equal to 1024 bits, bytes, or words. [from KILO-]

K³ *abbrev.* **1** kelvin. **2** kilo-. **3** *Chess, Cards* king. **4** *Knitting* knit (a plain stitch). **5** krona, króna, or krone.

K⁴ *symbol Chem.* potassium. [from Latin *kalium*]

K2 *or* **Mount Godwin-Austen**, also known as **Chogori** the second highest mountain in the world and highest in the Karakoram Range, NE Pakistan. HEIGHT 8 611m. [named K2 because it was the second peak to be measured in the Karakoram Range]

Kaa the friendly rock python in Rudyard Kipling's *The Jungle Book*.

Kaba *or* **Kaaba** *or* **Kabah** a shrine situated in the Great Mosque at Mecca, Saudi Arabia, considered by Muslims to be the most sacred site in Islam. It is a small cube-shaped building, unadorned except for the sacred Black Stone, a meteorite, set into the eastern corner of its walls. Earlier shrines on this spot were important centres of pilgrimage even in pre-Islamic times, but in 630 Muhammad stripped the Kaba of its pagan decorations and it became the spiritual centre of Islam. The stone, or *qibla*, is the focus-point to which Muslims turn when they pray. [from Arabic *ka'bah*, from *ka'b*, cube]

kabaddi *noun* an Asian version of tag played barefoot by two teams of seven. Players in turn make 'raids' on the opposing team's court with the aim of touching a specific member of the opposing team, who is shielded and defended by the other members, and then escaping.

Kabbalah a form of Jewish religious teaching originally transmitted orally, predominantly mystic in nature, and ostensibly consisting of secret doctrines. It developed along two lines: the 'practical', centring on prayer, meditation, and acts of piety, and the 'speculative' or 'theoretical', centring on the discovery of mysteries hidden in the Jewish Scriptures by special methods of interpretation. [Hebrew, = tradition]

Kabbalists the name applied to followers of the ancient Jewish mystical tradition of Kabbalah. Their way of life was characterized by devout ascetism. Important Kabbalists included Moses de Léon (1250–1305), Isaac ben Solomon Luria (1534–72), and Hayyim ben Joseph Vital (1543–1620).

Kabuki a type of theatre that originated as a city entertainment in Japan. Especially popular from 1650 to 1850, it was performed for commercial gain during the five seasonal festivals and consisted of a play in numerous acts, designed to last from dawn to dusk and presented in a manner that allowed an audience to watch, talk, and picnic during the performance. Men play both male and female parts. [from Japanese]

Kabul 1 POP (1992e) 1.3m, the capital of Afghanistan and of Kabul province, in the E of the country. It is situated on the R Kabul in a high mountain valley, commanding the approaches to the Khyber Pass. HISTORY capital of the Mughal Empire (1504–1738); modern state capital in 1773; captured in 1839 and 1879 by the British during the Afghan Wars; from 1979 until 1989 the city was occupied by Soviet forces; faction-fighting in 1992–3. **2** a province in E Afghanistan with Kabul as its capital.

kachina *noun Relig.* any of the ancestral spirits invoked by the Pueblo Indians of N America at ritual ceremonies; also, a dancer representing one of these. [from Hopi *qachina*, supernatural]

Kaddish an ancient Jewish prayer mostly in Aramaic, which is said at the close of daily public worship, praising the name of God and seeking the coming of his kingdom. Usually recited while standing and facing Jerusalem, it has affinities with the Christian Lord's Prayer. [Aramaic, = holy]

Kádr, János (1912–89) Hungarian politician and premier, born in Kapoly. He joined the (illegal) Communist Party in 1931, and was arrested several times. He became a member of the Central Committee (1942) and the Politburo (1945), and Minister of the Interior (1949), but was arrested for anti-Stalinist views (1951–3). When the anti-Soviet uprising broke out in 1956, he was a member of the 'national' government of Imre Nagy, but then formed and led a puppet government which repressed the uprising. He resigned in 1958, but was premier again (1961–5) and First Secretary of the Central Committee (1956–88).

Kaédi POP (1988) 31 000, the capital of Gorgol region, S Mauritania. It is located on the right bank of the R Sénégal.

Kaffir *noun* **1** *South Afr. offensive* a black African. **2** *old use* the Xhosa language, a Bantu language of South Africa. [from Arabic *kafir*, unbeliever]

Kafka, Franz (1883–1924) Austrian novelist, born of German–Jewish parents in Prague, Czechoslovakia. He studied law, and became an official in an insurance company (1907–23), and moved to Berlin. His short stories and essays, including *Die Verwandlung* (Metamorphosis, 1916), appeared in his lifetime, but his three unfinished novels were published posthumously by his friend Max Brod. They include *Ein Prozess* (The Trial, 1925), *Das Schloss* (The Castle, 1926), and *Amerika* (1927). His vision of society (often called 'Kafkaesque') as a pointless organization with tortuous bureaucratic and totalitarian procedures has influenced many writers.

kaftan see CAFTAN.

Kahlo, Frida (1907–54) Mexican artist, born in Coyoicoán, Mexico City, the daughter of a Jewish German immigrant photographer and a Catholic Mexican mother. She was seriously injured in a road accident at the age of 15 but during her convalescence she started painting, and sent her work to the painter Diego Rivera, whom she married in 1928. Many of her pictures are striking self-portraits, characterized by vibrant imagery. Pain, which dogged her all her life, and the suffering of women are recurring themes in her surrealistic and often shocking pictures. The Frida Kahlo Museum was opened in her house in Coyoicoán in 1958.

Kahuzi-Biega National Park a national park in Zaire, notable for its mountain gorillas. It is a World Heritage site.

Kaieteur Falls a waterfall in central Guyana, on the R Potaro. It is nearly five times the height of Niagara, with a sheer drop of 226m from a sandstone tableland (c.100m wide) into a broad basin where the water drops a further 22m. The falls are set in the Kaieteur National Park.

Kaikoura Ranges a set of mountain ranges in NE South I, New Zealand. There are two parallel ranges, the Inland Kaikoura and the Seaward Kaikoura. They extend 40km/25mi and are separated by the Clarence R. Mt Tapuaenuku, in the Inland Kaikoura, is the highest peak at 2 885m.

Kailasa Temple the most famous of the 34 Hindu, Buddhist, and Jain cave temples and monasteries at Ellora, Maharashtra, India. The edifice, which was built in the 8c, represents Shiva's Himalayan home of Mt Kailasa, and is renowned for its sculptures and friezes.

Kailas Range see GANGDISE SHAN.

Kairouan 1 POP (1984) 72 000, the capital of Kairouan governorate, NE Tunisia, 130km/80mi S of Tunis. Founded in 671, it became the capital of the Aglabite Dynasty in the 9c. It is an important Muslim holy city. NOTABLE FEATURES Great Mosque, the oldest in the Maghreb (7c, since rebuilt); Carpet Museum; archaeological site of Reqqada nearby. **2** a governorate in NE Tunisia with Kairouan as its capital.

Kaiser, Georg (1878–1945) German dramatist, born at Magdeburg. He wrote plays which established him as a leader of the German Expressionist movement, such as *Von Morgens bis Mitternachts* (From Morn to Midnight, 1916), *Gas I* (1918), and *Gas II* (1920), but his work was banned by the Nazis, and he left Germany in 1938.

Kaiser the title assumed (Dec 1870) by the Prussian king, William (Wilhelm) I, following the unification of Germany and the creation of the German Empire. He was succeeded on his death (1888) by his son Frederick (Friedrich) III, who survived him by only three months, and then by his grandson William (Wilhelm) II, who ruled until his enforced abdication (1918). [from German *Kaiser*, from *Caesar*, family name of the earliest Roman emperors]

kaiser *noun Hist.* the emperor of Germany, Austria or the Holy Roman Empire.

Kakadu a national park in Arnhem Land, Northern Territory, Australia, established in 1979. It is bordered to the N by the Van Diemen Gulf. Included within its territory are the Jim Jim and Twin Falls, and Aboriginal rock paintings which are 18 000 years old. The landscape is the product of continual weather erosion over the past 2m years. AREA 6 144 sq km/2 372sq mi. The park is a World Heritage site.

kakemono *noun* a Japanese wall hanging made of silk or paper with a roller at the bottom. It may be a painting, print, or calligraphic inscription and is normally placed in a special alcove called a *tok-on-oma*. [from Japanese *kake*, to hang + *mono*, thing]

Kakopetria POP (1987e) 1 000, a summer resort town in Nicosia district, Cyprus. NOTABLE FEATURES tomb of Archbishop Makarios III; nearby are the Byzantine churches of Lagoudhera and Stavros tou Ayiasmati.

Kalahari a desert region in the S area of Africa between the Orange and Zambezi rivers. AREA c.260 000sq km/100 000sq mi. PHYSICAL DESCRIPTION elevation is generally 850–1 000m; although it is called a desert, the Kalahari is mainly covered with grass and woodland but there is bare sand in the extreme SW, where annual rainfall is below 200mm; higher rainfall in the N gives rise to savannah woodland. The region is sparsely inhabited by nomads. There is a game reserve in the S.

kalanchoe *noun* a succulent herb or shrub of the genus *Kalanchoe*, native to tropical Africa and Madagascar. The leaves often have brown markings, and in many species the leaf margins bear plantlets which drop off and grow into new plants. [from Mandarin]

kalashnikov *noun* a type of submachine-gun manufactured in the Soviet Union. [from Russian *Kalashnikov*; the name of the inventor]

kale *noun* **1** a variety of cabbage that does not form a head, and has loose wrinkled or curled leaves, widely cultivated in Europe as a vegetable and fodder crop. **2** *Scot.* cabbage. [from Anglo-Saxon *cawl*]

kaleidoscope *noun* **1** a tubular device inside which loose fragments of coloured glass, etc are reflected in mirrors, usually two set at 45° or 60°, so as to form constantly changing symmetrical patterns as the tube is shaken or rotated. **2** any colourful and constantly changing scene or succession of events. [from Greek *kalos*, beautiful, *eidos*, form + -SCOPE]

kaleidoscopic *adj.* **1** relating to or characteristic of a kaleidoscope. **2** showing constant change.

kaleidoscopically *adv.* in a kaleidoscopic way.

kalends same as CALENDS.

Kalevala (Land of Heroes) a compilation of Finnish legends (1835). It is regarded as the national epic poem of Finland.

kaleyard *noun Scot.* a vegetable garden.

Kalgoorlie *or* **Kalgoorlie-Boulder** POP (1991) 25 000, a gold-mining town in Western Australia state, Australia. It lies 550km/340mi E of Perth. Gold was discovered here in 1887–8. Around 60% of Australia's gold is mined in the suburb of Boulder. Kalgoorlie and Boulder amalgamated in 1966. A square mile of ground rich in gold, known as the 'Golden Mile', lies between them. As the town is located in the middle of infertile desert, water has to be piped in from Mundaring Weir near Perth. Kalgoorlie is a Flying Doctor centre.

Kali the Hindu goddess of destruction, who is also represented as the Great Mother, the giver of life. She is the consort of Shiva.

Kalimantan POP (1990) 9.1m, a group of four provinces in the Indonesian part of Borneo. AREA c.540 000sq km/208sq mi. PHYSICAL DESCRIPTION mountainous in the N areas but generally low-level. CHIEF TOWNS Pontianak, Banjarmasin, Palangkaraya, Samarinda, Balikpapan. ECONOMY pepper; coffee; timber; petroleum; copra; rubber. There is an active guerrilla separatist movement.

Kalinin, Mikhail Ivanovich (1875–1946) Soviet politician, born in Tver. He was formal head of state after the 1917 Revolution and during the years of Stalin's dictatorship (1919–46). A peasant and metal-worker, he entered politics and won great popularity as a champion of the peasant class. He became President of the Soviet Central Executive Committee (1919–38) and of the Presidium of the Supreme Soviet (1938–46).

Kalmar *or* **Calmar** POP (1992e) 57 000, the capital of Kalmar county, SE Sweden, situated on the Kalmar Sound, opposite Öland I. It was the site of the Union of Kalmar, which united Denmark, Sweden, and Norway under a single monarchy (1397–1523). NOTABLE FEATURE castle (11c).

Kama the Hindu god of love. It also refers to the pursuit of love or pleasure, one of the four aims of life in Hindu tradition, which is necessary but should be regulated by considerations of dharma.

Kama Sutra an erotic Sanskrit exposition on the art of loving (4c–7c). It was translated into English by Sir Richard Francis Burton (1883).

Kamchatka 1 a large peninsula in Kamchatka oblast, E Siberia, Russia, separating the Sea of Okhotsk in the W from the Bering Sea in the E. AREA 270 033sq km/104 233sq mi. It extends c.1 200km/750mi S from the Koryakskiy Khrebet to Cape Lopatka; it is 130–480km/80–300mi wide. The Sredinnyy Range runs down the centre of the peninsula. Beyond the R Kamchatka to the E, volcanic cones rise above lava plateaux; several cones are still active. Klyuchevskaya Sopka (4 750m) is the highest peak. Hot springs are abundant. The chief population centre is Petropavlovsk-Kamchatskiy on the SE coast. **2** an oblast in E Siberia, Russia.

Kamehameha (1758–1819) a chief of the island of Hawaii. He extended his power until by 1810 he had united all the Hawaiian group under his rule. The royal dynasty he founded lasted until the death of Kamehameha V in 1872, although the Hawaiian monarchy endured until 1895, when Queen Liliuokoalani renounced her claim to the throne.

Kami in Japanese religion, objects of worship and sacred powers. Traditionally, there are millions of kami, both celestial and earthly; they can be present in animate and inanimate objects, and in aspects of nature (eg Mount Fujiyama). The kami sun-goddess, Amaterasu, was believed to be responsible for establishing the imperial line of Japan.

kamikaze — *noun* in World War II, a Japanese plane loaded with explosives deliberately crashed by its pilot on an enemy target; the pilot himself. — *adj. colloq., said of exploits, missions, etc* suicidally dangerous. [from Japanese, = divine wind]

Kammersee see ATTERSEE.

Kampala POP (1991) 774 000, the capital of Uganda, close to the N shore of L Victoria. Founded in the late 19c, it became the capital in 1962.

Kampong Saom see SIHANOUKVILLE.

Kampuchea see CAMBODIA.

Kan. *abbrev.* Kansas.

kana *noun* either of two Japanese syllabic writing systems based on spoken language: *katagana*, based on Chinese cursive ideograms, with 75 basic graphemes used to transcribe words borrowed from foreign languages (other than Chinese); and *hiragama* or 'flat kana', with rounded graphemes, each of which represents the various grammatically distinct elements expressed. Kana is distinguished from the form of Japanese writing based on Chinese characters known as *Kanji*. See also SYLLABARY.

Kananga, formerly **Luluabourg** (to 1966) POP (1991e) 372 000, the capital of Kasai Occidental region, W central Zaire, on the R Lulua. It was the scene of a mutiny by Congo Free State troops in 1895.

Kanchenjunga see KANGCHENJUNGA.

Kandahar 1 POP (1988e) 225 000, the capital of Kandahar province, S Afghanistan. It was situated on the ancient trade routes of central Asia, and was fought over by India and Persia. HISTORY capital of Afghanistan from 1748 until 1773; occupied by the British during the Afghan Wars (1839–42, 1879–81). **2** a province in S Afghanistan with Kandahar as its capital.

Kandinsky, Wasily, or **Vasily (Vasilyevich)** (1866–1944) Russian-born French painter, born in Moscow. He is generally regarded as the founder of Abstract painting, and he became head of the Museum of Modern Art in Russia in 1919 and founded the Russian Academy in 1921. He taught at the Weimar Bauhaus, (1922–33) then moved to Paris. He had a great influence on young European artists, and was a leader of the Blaue Reiter group.

Kandy, known as **City of the Five Hills** POP (1990e) 104 000, the capital of Kandy district, Central province, Sri Lanka, looped by the R Mahaweli, 116km/72mi NE of Colombo. It was a royal city until 1815. The city is a commercial centre for the tea-growing area and the focal point of the Buddhist Sinhalese culture. NOTABLE FEATURES Dalada Maligawa (Temple of the Tooth), where the eye tooth of Buddha is enshrined; Peradeniya Botanical Gardens.

kangaroo *noun* any of various herbivorous marsupials native to Australia, Tasmania, and New Guinea, and having strong hind legs with elongated feet, short front legs, and a thick muscular tail. [from *gangurru*, an Australian Aboriginal word]
◇ Kangaroos move on all four feet when grazing, but can travel at considerable speed (up to 48kph/30mph over short distances) by taking enormous leaps with their powerful hind legs, using the tail for balance. When stationary, the animal sits up on its hind legs, and is supported by its tail. The young kangaroo or *joey* is born at a very early stage of development, and crawls to its mother's pouch, where it remains for about six months. Even after leaving the pouch the joey will return to it for some time in order to suckle. The great grey kangaroo (*Macropus giganteus*), which stands up to 1.8m high, and has a grey coat with whitish patches on the legs and underparts, lives mainly in open forest, where it browses on vegetation.

kangaroo court an unofficial court of eg strikers to try strikebreakers, or prisoners to try fellow prisoners.

Kangchenjunga *or* **Kanchenjunga, Mount**, Tibetan **Gangchhendzönga**, Nepali **Kumbhkaran Lungur** the third highest mountain in the world, on the border between Nepal and the Sikkim state of India, in the Himalayan Range. It comprises five peaks, the highest of which is 8 586m. The Zemu glacier on the E slope reaches down into Sikkim state.

KaNgwane POP (1991) 446 000, a national state or non-independent black homeland in Natal province, South Africa. It received self-governing status in 1971. CHIEF TOWN Eerstehoek.

Kankan POP (1983) 89 000, the second largest town in Guinea and the capital of Haute-Guinée region, E Guinea. Situated on the R Milo, 280km/175mi SW of Banako (Mali), it is a commercial and transportation centre.

Kano 1 POP (1992e) 700 000, the capital of Kano state, N Nigeria, 1 130km/700mi NE of Lagos. An ancient Hausa settlement, the modern city was founded in the 19c, becoming a major terminus for trans-Saharan trade. The city walls are nearly 18km/11mi long, 12m thick at the base, and up to 12m high. **2** a state in N Nigeria with Kano as its capital.

Kanpur, formerly **Cawnpore** POP (1991) 2.1m, a city in Uttar Pradesh, N India, on the R Ganges, 185km/115mi NW of Allahabad. It was ceded to the British in 1801. The entire British garrison was massacred during the Indian Mutiny in 1857. Today the city is a major trade and industrial centre.

Kans. *abbrev.* Kansas.

Kansas POP (1990) 2.5m, a state in central USA, divided into 105 counties. AREA 213 089sq km/ 82 252sq mi. PHYSICAL DESCRIPTION the Missouri R forms part of the E state border; the Republican and Smoky Hill rivers join to form the Kansas R, which meets the Missouri at Kansas City; the Arkansas R also crosses the state; the highest point is Mt Sunflower (1 227m); land rises steadily from the prairies in the E to the semi-arid high plains in the W; severe land erosion occurred during the 1930s (Kansas forms part of the Dust Bowl); Kansas is known as the 'Sunflower State'. HISTORY part of the 1803 Louisiana Purchase; there was virtual civil war in 1854–6 over whether Kansas should be a free or slave state; in 1861 it was the 34th state to be admitted to the Union (as a free state). CAPITAL Topeka. CHIEF TOWNS Wichita, Kansas City. ECONOMY the nation's leading wheat producer; other major crops are grain sorghum, corn, and hay; a major cattle state; petroleum; natural gas; industries include aircraft, chemicals, processed foods, and manufacturing.

Kansas City POP (1990) 1.6m, the seat of Wyandotte County, E Kansas, USA. It is a port at the junction of the Kansas and Missouri rivers, adjacent to its sister city, Kansas City, Missouri. Settled by Wyandotte Native Americans in 1843, it was sold to the US government in 1855. It is a major commercial and industrial centre, together with its sister city, and provides the market for the surrounding agricultural region. NOTABLE FEATURE Agricultural Hall of Fame.

Kansas City POP (1990) 435 000, a river-port city in Jackson County, W Missouri, USA. It lies on the S bank of the Missouri R, adjacent to its sister city, Kansas City, Kansas. HISTORY the Town of Kansas was established in 1838, achieved city status in 1853, and adopted its present name in 1889; it was a jazz centre in the 1930s and 1940s. It has the nation's leading winter-wheat market. NOTABLE FEATURES Nelson Art Gallery; Atkins Museum of Fine Arts.

Kansas–Nebraska Act a bill passed (1854) by the US Congress to establish the territories of Kansas and Nebraska. Since it opened up the problem of extending slavery into western territories, by allowing popular sovereignty, it led to bitter debates. The ensuing protests contributed to the formation of the Republican Party, which was hostile to the expansion of slavery.

Kant, Immanuel (1724–1804) German philosopher, born in Königsberg. He became Professor of Logic and Metaphysics at Königsberg in 1770. His major work is the *Kritik der reinen Vernunft* (Critique of Pure Reason, 1781), in which he provided a response to the empiricism of Hume. His views on ethics are set out in the *Grundlagen zur Metaphysik der Sitten* (Foundations of the Metaphysics of Morals, 1785) and the *Kritik der praktischen Vernunft* (Critique of Practical Reason, 1788), in which he elaborates on the Categorical Imperative as the supreme principle of morality. Other works include his third and last Critique, the *Kritik der Urteilskraft* (Critique of Judgment, 1790).

Kanto earthquake the worst Japanese earthquake (1923) of modern times. It occurred in E Japan during the day, when lunch was cooking over open fires. Strong winds spread the flames, c.100 000 people were killed, and Old Tokyo and Yokohama were destroyed.

Kantorovich, Leonid (Vitaliyevich) (1912–86) Soviet economist, born in St Petersburg. He was a professor at Leningrad State University (1934–60) and later held senior administrative posts. He was jointly awarded the Nobel Prize for Economics in 1975 for his work on the optimum allocation of resources.

KANU *abbrev.* Kenya African National Union.

Kaohsiung *or* **Gaoxiong**, Japanese **Takao** POP (1992e) 1.4m, a special municipality and seaport in SW Taiwan, situated on the SW coast, facing the Taiwan Strait. It is the largest seaport and industrial city in Taiwan, the world's largest shipbreaking centre, and the second largest dry dock. It was occupied by the Japanese from 1895 until 1945. NOTABLE FEATURES Cheng Ching Lake Resort; Kenting National Park; Fo Kuang Shan (Buddha Torch Mountain), with a 25m-tall statue of Buddha on a 12m-high pedestal.

Kaolan see LANZHOU.

kaolin *noun* china clay, a fine white clay used for making pottery, and medically in poultices and medicines. [named after Chinese *Kao-ling* or *Gao-ling* ('high ridge'), a mountain where it was mined]

kaolinite *noun Geol.* a white, grey, or yellowish clay mineral consisting of hydrated aluminium silicate formed as a result of the alteration of feldspars by heated water or weathering. [from the mountain Kao-ling (high ridge) in China]

Kapil Dev (Nihanj) (1959–) Indian cricketer, born in Chandigarh, Punjab. An all-rounder, he made his first-class début for Haryana at the age of 16, and played county cricket in England for Northamptonshire and Worcestershire. He led India to victory in the 1983 World Cup, and set a competition record score of 175 not out against Zimbabwe. In 1983 he became the youngest player (at 24 yrs 68 days) to perform a Test double of 2 000 runs and 200 wickets (surpassing Ian Botham). In Feb 1992 he became only the second player in Test history to take 400 wickets. In Feb 1994 he set a new world record of 432 Test wickets, surpassing the record (431 wickets) held by Sir Richard Hadlee.

Kapitza, Peter (Pyotr Leonidovich) (1894–1984) Russian physicist, born in Kronstadt. He became Assistant Director of Magnetic Research at Cambridge, and was later Director of the Moscow Institute for Physical Problems; he was dismissed from this post in 1946 for refusing to work on the atomic bomb, but reinstated in 1955. He achieved the production of unprecedentedly strong magnetic fields for research, engineered a helium liquefier, and investigated some of liquid helium's extraordinary properties. He shared the 1978 Nobel Prize for Physics with Arno Penzias and Robert Wilson.

kapok *noun* a light cotton-like fibre obtained from the pods of a tropical tree and used as padding or as stuffing for toys, etc. [from Malay *kapoq*]

kappa *noun* the tenth letter of the Greek alphabet (κ).

kaput *adj. colloq.* **1** broken. **2** ruined; destroyed. [from German *kaputt*]

Karachi POP (1990e) 7.7m, the principal seaport in Pakistan and the provincial capital of Sind province, in the SE of the country. It is situated on the Arabian Sea coast, NW of the mouths of the Indus. HISTORY founded in the 18c; under British rule from 1843; capital from 1947 until 1959. NOTABLE FEATURES tomb of Quaid-i-Azam, Muhammad Ali Jinnah, founder of Pakistan; National Museum.

Karadzic *or* **Karadjic, Radovan** (not known–) Bosnian-Serb politician, formerly a psychiatrist and poet. Born in Montenegro, he came to Sarajevo as a teenager after World War II. He emerged in 1990 on the creation of the Serbian Democratic Party (SDS), the main Serbian party in Bosnia. With the aim of uniting all the Serbs in the former Yugoslavia into one Greater Serbia, his militias have driven over one million Muslims from their homes, killing many thousands. He signed the Vance–Owen Peace Plan in May 1993, and a cease-fire began to operate in 1994.

Karageorge, Turkish **Karadjordje**, also **Czerny George**, originally **George Petrović** (1766–1817) leader of the Serbs in their struggle for independence, born in Viševac, Serbia, known as 'Black George' because of his dark complexion. He led a revolt against Turkey, and in 1808 was elected Governor and recognized as Prince of Serbia by the Sultan. When Turkey regained control of Serbia (1813) he was exiled, and on his return was murdered at the instigation of his rival, Prince Milosch.

Karagoz (Black Eye) an anti-hero who has given his name to Turkish shadow theatre. He has a black beard and contrasting bald head, and wears a large turban. He is considered stupid and thoroughly amoral, but cunning.

Karajan, Herbert von (1908–89) Austrian conductor, born in Salzburg. His career began at the opera houses of Ulm (1928–33) and Aachen (1934–8), and his fame grew when he was conductor at the Berlin Staatsoper (1938–42). He joined the Nazi Party in 1933 and after World War II was not permitted to work until 1947, but in 1955 was made principal conductor of the Berlin Philharmonic, the orchestra with which he was mainly associated. He also conducted frequently elsewhere, and was artistic director of the Salzburg Festival (1956–60) and of the Salzburg Easter Festival (from 1967).

karakul *noun* an Asian sheep whose lambs have a dark curly fleece; fur made from, or in imitation of, this fleece. [named after *Kara-Kul*, a lake in Tajikistan, central Asia, near which the sheep were originally bred]

Kara Kum an extensive desert in Turkmenistan. AREA c.300 000sq km/ 115 000sq mi. It is bounded S by the Khrebet Kopet-Dag Range, W by the Caspian Sea, and N and E by the R Amudarya.

Karamanlis *or* **Caramanlis Konstantinos** (1907–) Greek politician, born in Próti, Macedonia. Elected to parliament in 1935, he became Minister of Public Works (1952), then Prime Minister (1955–63), when he formed the National Radical Union Party. During his administration, Greece signed a Treaty of Alliance with Cyprus and Turkey. After election defeat he left politics and lived abroad, but

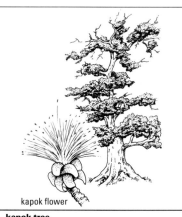

kapok flower

kapok tree

returned to become premier again in 1974–80, when he supervised the restoration of civilian rule after the collapse of the military government. He then served as President (1980–5, 1990–).

karaoke *noun* an originally Japanese form of entertainment in which amateur performers sing pop songs to the accompaniment of pre-recorded music from a machine. [from Japanese, = 'empty orchestra']

karate *noun* an originally Japanese system of unarmed self-defence, using blows and kicks. [from Japanese, = empty hand]
◇ Dating from the 17c, and developed in Japan in the 19c and 20c, the name karate was adopted in the 1930s. The aim is to be in total control of the muscular power of the body, so that it may be used with maximum force and accuracy at any instant. This is often demonstrated by breaking thick blocks of wood by blows from the hands or feet. Levels of prowess are indicated by coloured belts, as in other martial arts.

Karate Belts

Junior grades (Kyu)
in rising proficiency (subject to some variation in different styles)
white
yellow
green
brown
black (1st Dan)

Senior grades (Dans)
1 to 8 (all wear black belts)

karate chop *noun* a sharp downward blow with the side of the hand.

Karawanken Alps, Serbo-Croatian **Karavanke** a mountain range in the E Alps, situated on the border between Slovenia and Austria, mostly in the Austrian state of Kärnten. It is an extension of the Carnic Alps. Hochstuhl (2 238m) is the highest peak in the range.

karbovanets *noun* (PL. **karbovantsi**) the unit of currency of the Republic of the Ukraine. [Ukrainian]

Karelia, Russian **Karelskaya** POP (1989) 270 000, an autonomous republic in NW Russia, bounded W by Finland and E by the White Sea. AREA 172 400sq km/66 550sq mi. It is heavily forested, with many lakes and rivers. HISTORY in medieval times, it was an independent state with strong Finnish associations; under Swedish domination in the 17c; annexed by Russia in 1721; constituted as a Soviet Socialist Republic in 1923; territory was extended during World War II when the Finnish-Soviet border was altered. ECONOMY based on mining, timber, cereals, and fishing.

Karen various Sino-Tibetan-speaking, ethnically-diverse groups of S Burma (Myanma). Following Burmese independence (1948), fighting broke out between the government and groups identifying themselves as Karen, who wanted autonomy. Sometimes divided into White Karen and Red Karen, they have united in common opposition to Burmese control. In the late 1980s many fled to refugee camps in Thailand. In 1993, Karen leaders voted to hold talks with Burma's military government.

Karen a female first name. [the Danish form of KATHERINE]

Kariba Dam a major concrete arch dam on the Zambezi R at the Zambia–Zimbabwe border, completed in 1959. It is 128m high and 579m long, and has the capacity to generate 705 megawatts of hydroelectricity.

Karisimbi a dormant volcano in the Virunga Range, situated on the Rwanda–Zaire frontier.

Rising to 4 507m, it is the highest point of the range.

Karloff, Boris, originally **William Henry Pratt** (1887–1969) English film actor, born in London. He emigrated to Canada in 1909 and spent 10 years in repertory companies, then went to Hollywood. After several silent films, he played the monster in *Frankenstein* (1931), which led to a career mostly spent in popular horror films, such as *The Bodysnatchers* (1945), but he returned to the stage in 1941.

Karlovy Vary, German **Karlsbad** POP (1991) 56 000, a town in Západočeský region, NW Czech Republic, lying on the R Ohre, W of Prague. It is a famous health resort with hot, alkaline springs.

Karlsbad see KARLOVY VARY.

Karlsruhe POP (1991e) 275 000, a river port in Baden-Württemberg state, SW Germany. It lies on the R Rhine in the foothills of the Black Forest, 56km/35mi S of Mannheim. NOTABLE FEATURE palace (1752–85).

karma *noun Buddhism, Hinduism* one's lifetime's actions, seen as governing one's fate in one's next life. [from Sanskrit *karma*, act, deed]

Karnak *or* **al-Karnak** a village in Qina, Upper Egypt, which dates to c.3200 BC. The name is used to refer to the ruins of Thebes on the E bank of the Nile, which contain the Great Temple of Amun, built c.1570–1085 BC.

Karnataka, formerly **Mysore** POP (1991) 45m, a state in SW India, bounded W by the Arabian Sea. AREA 191 773sq km/74 024sq mi. CAPITAL Bangalore. OFFICIAL LANGUAGE Kannada. PHYSICAL DESCRIPTION numerous rivers cross the state, including the Karanja, Benithora, and Bhima. HISTORY formed as Mysore under the States Reorganization Act of 1956, bringing the Kannada-speaking population of five states together; renamed as Karnataka in 1973. GOVERNMENT a bicameral legislature comprises a 63-member Legislative Council and an elected 225-member Legislative Assembly. ECONOMY rice, groundnuts, cotton, coffee, bamboo, sandalwood, silk; gold, silver, iron ore, manganese, limestone, chromite; iron and steel; engineering; electronics; chemicals; textiles; cement; sugar; paper.

Karnische Alpen see CARNIC ALPS.

Karoo the dry steppe country of Cape province, South Africa, extending from the Orange R down to the Cape. The Karoo National Park, established in 1979, covers 180sq km/70sq mi of the arid region called the Great Karoo.

Kárpathos, Italian **Scarpanto**, ancient **Carpathus** POP (1981e) 5 000, a mountainous, elongated island in the Dodecanese, E Greece. It lies in the Aegean Sea, between Rhodes and the E end of Crete. AREA 301sq km/116sq mi; length 48km/30mi. It rises to 1 216m. CAPITAL Pigadhia. There are numerous bathing beaches.

Karst, Slovenian **Kras**, Italian **Carso** a barren, stony limestone plateau in the Dinaric Alps of Bosnia-Herzegovina. It extends c.80km/50mi from the R Isonzo in the NW to the Kvarner Gulf in the SE. There are notable caves at Postojna. The name has come to be used in geography to describe limestone topography of this kind.

kart *noun colloq.* a go-kart.

karyotype *noun Genetics* **1** the number, size, and structure of the chromosomes in the nucleus of a cell, characteristic of all the diploid cells of a particular individual, strain, or species. **2** the representation of this in a diagram or photograph. [from Greek *karyon*, kernel]

kasbah *noun* a castle or fortress in a N African town or the area around it, especially in Algiers. [from Arabic dialect *kasba*]

Kasbah of Algiers a fortress in the Muslim section of Algiers, which was the residence of the

last two Turkish governors of Algiers. It is a World Heritage site.

Kashmir see JAMMU-KASHMIR.

Kasparov, Gary (Kimovich) (1963–) Azerbaijani chess player, born in Baku. He beat Anatoliy Karpov for the World title in Nov 1985, becoming the youngest world champion, at the age of 22 years 210 days. He has successfully defended his title, in 1993 against Nigel Short, and is the highest-ranked active player.

Kassala a town in Eastern Region, Sudan, situated on the R Gash. HISTORY founded by the Egyptian military in 1834; held by the Madhists between 1885 and 1894; held by the Italians from 1894 to 1897 and from 1940 to 1941 during World War II.

Kassel POP (1991e) 194 000, a town in Hessen state, central Germany. It lies on the R Fulda, 114km/71mi NW of Erfurt. It was badly bombed in World War II. NOTABLE FEATURES Wilhelmshöhe (health resort); Gallery of Old Masters in the Schloss Wilhelmshöhe; Schloss Wilhelmsthal (11km/7mi NW); Grimm Brothers Museum.

Kassites a people, possibly of Iranian origin, who were the dominant power in Babylonia and Lower Mesopotamia after the Hittite destruction of Babylon in 1595 BC. They were conquered by the Assyrians and Elamites around 1150 BC.

Katanga see SHABA.

Kathakali epic theatre from the south-west coastal region of India. Troupes of actors, in stylized make-up and costume, enact dramas based on the Ramayana and Mahabharata, using song, dance, and an elaborate system of hand symbols instead of speech. [from Malayalam, from *katha*, story + *kali*, drama]

Katharina *or* **Kate** the rude, aggressive 'shrew' of the title in Shakespeare's *The Taming of the Shrew*, who marries Petruchio and meets her match.

Katharine, Princess of France the dutiful daughter of the King of France who is married off to Henry V in Shakespeare's *Henry V*.

Katherine *or* **Katharine** *or* **Catherine** a female first name. [from Greek *aikaterine*, of unknown origin, later assimilated to *katharos*, pure; many variants are recorded]

Katherine Gorge a national park in Northern Territory, Australia, established in 1963. There are spectacular gorges along the Katherine R up to 60m high and many Aboriginal rock drawings. AREA c.1 800sq km/700sq mi.

Kathmandu *or* **Katmandu**, formerly **Kantipur** POP (1981) 235 000, the capital and principal city in Nepal, 121km/75mi from the Indian frontier in the Kathmandu Valley. It is situated on the ancient pilgrim and trade route from India to Tibet, China, and Mongolia. HISTORY built in its present form in 723; Gurkha capital in 1768; British seat of administration in the 18c. Today the city is a commercial and religious centre, popular with tourists. NOTABLE FEATURES Machendra Nath Temple, Kasthamanadap Temple, Swayambhunath (Buddhist shrine), Pashupatinath Temple (centre of an annual pilgrimage); Hanuman Dhoka Palace; Natural History Museum. The Vale of Kathmandu is a World Heritage site.

Katowice, German **Kattowitz 1** POP (1992e) 367 000, the industrial capital of Katowice voivodship, S Poland, and the centre of the Upper Silesian Industrial Region. NOTABLE FEATURES Kościuszko Park; cathedral. **2** a voivodship in S Poland with Katowice as its capital.

katydid *noun* a large N American grasshopper. [imitative]

Katyn massacre the massacre (May 1940) of more than 10 000 Polish army officers in the Katyn forest near Smolensk, Belorussia, whose mass graves were discovered by German occupying forces in 1943. Soviet authorities denied responsibility and blamed the Germans, but in 1989 the Soviet-Polish historical commission (set up in 1987 to establish the truth) reported that the massacre was most probably committed by the Soviet security service (NKVD), a fact later confirmed by the Soviet authorities.

Katz, Sir Bernard (1911–) British biophysicist, born and educated in Leipzig, Germany. He left Nazi Germany in 1935, and spent most of his career at University College London, where he became professor in 1952. He discovered how the neurotransmitter acetylcholine is released by neural impulses, and shared the 1970 Nobel Prize for Physiology or Medicine with Julius Axelrod and Ulf von Euler.

Kauai, formerly **Kaieiewaho** POP (1988e) 49 000, an island in the US state of Hawaii, lying in the Pacific Ocean, NW of Oahu. AREA 1 692sq km/653sq mi. Together with Niihau, it forms Kauai County. The chief town is Lihue; tourism is important to the economy.

Kaunas, formerly **Kovno** POP (1991e) 433 000, an ancient town and river port in Lithuania, lying on the R Neman at its confluence with the R Vilnya. One of the ancient centres of artistic trades, it was the capital of independent Lithuania from 1920 to 1940. The town was the scene of nationalistic riots in 1972. NOTABLE FEATURES castle (13c–17c); Massalski Palace (17c); Vytautas Church (1400).

Kaunda, Kenneth (David) (1924–) Zambian nationalist leader and politician, born in Lubwa. He became a teacher, founded the Zambian African National Congress (1958), and was subsequently imprisoned (1959–60). Elected President of the United National Independence Party (UNIP) in 1960, he played a leading part in his country's independence negotiations, and became the country's first President (1964–91). He made the UNIP the sole legitimate party but was forced by internal and international pressures to call an election in 1991, when he was defeated.

Kaunitz(-Rietberg), Wenzel Anton, Fürst von (Prince of) (1711–94) Austrian statesman, born in Vienna. He distinguished himself at the Congress of Aix-la-Chapelle (1748), and as Austrian Ambassador at the French court (1750–2). As Chancellor (1753–92), he instigated the Diplomatic Revolution and directed Austrian politics under Maria Theresa and Joseph II. He was also a liberal patron of arts and sciences.

kauri *noun* a coniferous tree of New Zealand grown for its wood and resin. [from Maori]

Kawabata, Yasunari (1899–1972) Japanese writer, born in Osaka. He experimented with various Western forms of the novel but by the mid 1930s had returned to traditional Japanese ones. His best-known novels include *Snow Country* (1947), *Thousand Cranes* (1949) and *The Sound of the Mountain* (1949–54). He was awarded the Nobel Prize for Literature in 1968. He committed suicide in Zushi, Japan.

Kawasaki POP (1991e) 1.2m, the capital of Kanagawa prefecture, Kanto region, E Honshu, Japan. It is situated S of Tokyo, on the W shore of Tokyo-wan Bay.

kayak *noun* **1** a sealskin-covered canoe used by the Inuit. **2** a similar canvas-covered or fibreglass craft used in the sport of canoeing. [from Inuit *qayaq*]

Kaye, Danny, professional name of **Daniel Kominski** (1913–87) US stage, radio, and film actor, born in New York City. His first film, *Up in Arms* (1943), was followed by *Wonder Man* (1944), which made his reputation as a film comedian. He had international success in *The Secret Life of Walter Mitty* (1946). Other films included *The Inspector General* (1950) and *Hans Christian Andersen* (1952). He received an Honorary Oscar in 1955, and in later years

worked for international childrens' charities, especially UNICEF.

Kayes POP (1984e) 67 000, **1** the river-port capital of Kayes region, W Mali. **2** a region in W Mali. AREA 119 813sq km/46 248sq mi. CAPITAL Kayes. CHIEF TOWNS Nioro du Sahel, Bafoulabé, Kita, Yélimané, Kéniéba. ECONOMY iron ore; marble; alabaster; gold and diamond mining; cement processing. NOTABLE FEATURE Boucle de Baoulé National Park to the E.

Kazakhstan, Russian **Kazakhskaya**, or **Kazakh** POP (1992e) 17m, a republic in W Asia. AREA 2 717 300sq km/1 048 878sq mi. It is bounded N by Russia, S by Turkmenistan, Uzbekistan, and Kirghizia, E by China, and W by the Caspian Sea. PHYSICAL DESCRIPTION steppeland in the N gives way to desert in the S; the lowest elevation is near the E shore of the Caspian Sea (132m below sea level); mountain ranges are situated in the E and SE; the chief rivers are the Irtysh, Syr-Darya, Ural, Emba, and Ili; the largest lake is L Balkhash; the Aral Sea is located on the S border with Uzbekistan. CAPITAL Alma-Ata. CHIEF TOWNS Karaganda, Semipalatinsk, Chimkent, Petropavlovsk. The population consists mainly of Kazakhs (40%), Russians (38%), Germans (6%), and Ukrainians (5%); Sunni Muslim is the chief religion. OFFICIAL LANGUAGE Kazakh. CURRENCY the tenge. HISTORY became a constituent republic of the Soviet Union in 1936; became an independent republic in 1991. GOVERNMENT a President may appoint important ministerial positions but does not have the power to dissolve the Government and the Government does not have power to impeach the President. ECONOMY coal, iron ore, bauxite, copper, nickel, oil; oil refining, metallurgy, heavy engineering, chemicals, leatherwork, footwear, food processing; cotton, fruit, grain, sheep.

Kazakhstan

Kazan, Elia, originally **Elia Kazanjoglous** (1909–) US stage and film director, born in Constantinople (now Istanbul), Turkey. Resident in the USA from 1913, he acted in minor roles before becoming a theatre director. He produced many plays by Arthur Miller and Tennessee Williams, and co-founded the Actors Studio (1947). He began as a film director in 1944, and won Oscars for *Gentleman's Agreement* (1948) and *On the Waterfront* (1954).

Kazan POP (1990e) 1.1m, the river-port capital of Tatarstan, Russia, lying on the R Volga at its confluence with the R Kazanka. Founded in the 13c, it is one of the most important industrial and cultural centres of the Volga region. NOTABLE FEATURES Cathedral of the Annunciation (19c); Governor's Palace (1845–8).

Kazanlak tomb a 4c BC Thracian tomb located near Kazanlak in the department of Stara Zagora, Bulgaria. It was discovered in 1944, and is noted for the frescoes which decorate the burial chamber and vaulted corridor within. It is a World Heritage site.

Kazantzakis, Nikos (1883–1957) Greek writer, born in Heraklion, Crete. He is best

known for the novel *Zorba the Greek* (1946, filmed 1964) and the long autobiographical narrative poem, *The Odyssey, a Modern Sequel* (1938).

Kaziranga a national park on the S bank of the Brahmaputra R in Assam, India. It was established in 1908 to protect the great Indian rhino and the swamp deer. AREA 430sq km/166sq mi. The park is a World Heritage site.

kazoo *noun* a crude wind instrument consisting of a short metal tube into which one hums, causing a strip of parchment, etc stretched across a hole in its upper surface, to vibrate with a buzzing effect. [imitative]

KB *abbrev.* King's Bench.

KBE *abbrev.* Knight Commander of the British Empire.

KBS *abbrev. Comput.* knowledge-based systems, software systems which aim to store and effectively utilize large amounts of specialist knowledge.

KC *abbrev.* King's Counsel.

KCB *abbrev.* Knight Commander of the (Order of the) Bath.

KCMG *abbrev.* Knight Commander of (the Order of) St Michael and St George.

KCVO *abbrev.* Knight Commander of the (Royal) Victorian Order.

Kean, Edmund (c.1789–1833) English actor, born in London. He became a strolling player, and made his first appearance at Drury Lane as Shylock (1814). A period of great success followed as a tragic actor, but his popularity ended when he was successfully sued for adultery in 1825.

Keating, Tom (1918–84) English artist and forger, born in London. A self-confessed 'art imitator', he claimed to have produced some 2 000 fakes in 25 years. His activity came to light in 1976, when a group of 13 drawings in imitation of Samuel Palmer came on to the market and aroused suspicions. He was arrested but charges against him were dropped when his health declined. He became a celebrity, made a television series, and wrote (with Geraldine and Frank Norman) *The Fake's Progress*.

Keaton, Buster, originally **Joseph Francis Keaton** (1895–1966) US film comedian, born in Piqua, Kansas. He joined his parents in vaudeville at the age of three, developing great acrobatic skill. His Hollywood film début was in *The Butcher Boy* (1917), the start of a prolific career. Renowned for his 'deadpan' expression in all circumstances, he starred in and directed such classics as *The Navigator* (1924) and *The General* (1926). He received a Special Academy Award in 1959.

Keats, John (1795–1821) English poet, born in London. He became a medical student in London (1815–17), but was introduced to other young Romantics by Leigh Hunt, who published his first sonnets in the *Examiner* (1816). His first book of poems (1817) was followed by the long mythological poem, *Endymion* (1818), which was fiercely criticized on publication. *Lamia and Other Poems* (1820) was much better received. It contains his well-known romances 'The Eve of St Agnes' and 'Lamia', the epic 'Hyperion', and his major odes. He is also remembered for his *Letters*, published in 1848 and 1878. He died in Rome of tuberculosis.

kebab *noun* a dish of small pieces of meat and vegetable, especially (*shish kebab*) grilled on a skewer. [from Arabic *kabab*; from Turkish şiş, skewer]

Keble, John (1792–1866) English Anglican churchman and poet, born in Fairford, Gloucestershire. Ordained in 1816, he became a college tutor (1818–23) and Professor of Poetry (1831–41) at Oxford. In 1827 his book of poems *The Christian Year* was widely circulated. The

Oxford Movement was inspired by his sermon on 'National apostasy' (1833), which encouraged a return to High Church ideals, and his circle issued the 90 *Tracts for the Times*. Keble College, Oxford, was founded in his memory (1870).

Kebnekaise the highest peak in Sweden, situated in the Kjölen Mts, NW Sweden, 40km/25mi from the Norwegian frontier. HEIGHT 2 111m. It has several glaciers.

Kedah POP (1990) 1.4m, a state in NW Peninsular Malaysia. AREA 9 425sq km/ 3 638sq mi. It is bounded E by Thailand and W by the Strait of Malacca. The state was governed by Thailand from the early 19c until 1909, when it came under British rule. CAPITAL Alor Setar. ECONOMY rice, rubber, tin, tungsten.

kedge — *verb trans., intrans.*, *said of a ship* to manoeuvre by means of a hawser attached to a light anchor. — *noun* a light anchor used for kedging. [related to Middle English *caggen*, to fasten]

kedgeree *noun* an originally E Indian dish, now usually a mixture of rice, fish and eggs. [from Hindi *khichri*]

Kee, Robert (1919–) English broadcaster and writer. He spent four years in a POW camp during World War II, an experience reflected in his first novel, *A Crowd is Not Company* (1947). After some time as a print journalist he joined the BBC, working on *Panorama* (1958–62). His other major television work includes the series *Ireland* (1981) and co-founding the breakfast programme *TV-am* (1983). His publications include the novel *A Sign of the Times* (1955) and the non-fiction *Trial and Error* (1986).

keek *Scot.* — *noun* a peep. — *verb intrans.* to take a peep. [from Middle English *kiken*]

keel — *noun* the timber or metal strut extending from stem to stern along the base of a ship, from which the hull is built up. — *verb* (**keel over**) 1 *said of a ship* to tip over sideways. 2 *colloq.* to fall over, eg in a faint. — **on an even keel** calm and steady. [from Middle English *kele*, from Old Dutch *kiel*, ship]

keelhaul *verb* to drag (someone) under the keel of a ship from one side to the other, as a naval punishment.

Keeling Islands see COCOS ISLANDS.

keelson same as KELSON.

Keelung, also **Jilong**, or **Chi-lung**, Japanese **Kirun**, formerly Spanish **Santissima Trinidad** POP (1992c) 356 000, an independent municipality and the second largest seaport in Taiwan, situated on the N coast of Taiwan I, overlooking the E China Sea. HISTORY occupied by the Spanish and Dutch in the 17c; occupied by the Japanese from 1895 until 1945; destroyed by an earthquake in 1867.

keen[1] *adj.* 1 eager; willing. 2 (**keen on someone** *or* **something**) enthusiastic about them; fond of them. 3 *said of competition, rivalry, etc* fierce. 4 *said of the wind* bitter. 5 *said of a blade, etc* sharp. 6 *said of the mind or senses* quick; acute. 7 *said of prices* low; competitive. [from Anglo-Saxon *cene*, bold, fierce]

keen[2] — *verb intrans., trans.* especially in Ireland, to lament or mourn in a loud wailing voice. — *noun* a lament for the dead. [from Irish *caoine*, lament]

keenly *adv.* in a keen way; with enthusiasm.

keenness *noun* being keen.

keep[1] — *verb* (PAST TENSE AND PAST PARTICIPLE **kept**) 1 to have; to possess. 2 to continue to have; not to part with; to save. 3 to maintain or retain: *keep one's temper*. 4 to store. 5 *trans., intrans.* to remain or cause to remain in a certain state, position, place, etc. 6 *intrans.* to continue or be frequently (doing something): *keep smiling /*

keep fainting. 7 *said of a shopkeeper, etc* to have regularly in stock. 8 to own (an animal, etc) for use or pleasure: *keep hens*. 9 to own or run (a shop, boarding-house, etc). 10 to look after: *keep house / keep this for me*. 11 *intrans. said of food* to remain fit to be eaten. 12 to maintain (a record, diary, accounts, etc). 13 (**keep from something**) to hold back or delay doing it. 14 to obey (the law, etc). 15 to preserve (a secret). 16 to stick to (a promise or appointment). 17 to celebrate (a festival, etc) in the traditional way; to follow (a custom). 18 to support financially. 19 to protect: *keep them from harm*. 20 to guard (the goal) in football or (the wicket) in cricket. 21 to remain firm on: *managed to keep his feet despite the strong wind*. — *noun* the cost of one's food and other daily expenses: *earn one's keep*.
— **for keeps** *colloq.* permanently; for good.
keep at something to persevere at or persist in it.
keep something back 1 to conceal information, etc. 2 to suppress laughter, tears, etc.
keep someone down to oppress them; to prevent their development, progress, etc.
keep something down 1 to control or limit prices, etc. 2 to manage not to vomit food, etc.
keep someone from something to prevent them from doing something.
keep something from someone to prevent it from reaching them: *tried to keep the news from him.*
keep going to persevere in spite of problems.
keep someone going to help them survive difficulties, etc.
keep in with someone to remain on good terms with them, especially for selfish reasons.
keep off something to avoid a harmful food, awkward topic, etc.
keep on doing something to continue with it.
keep someone on to continue to employ them.
keep on 1 to continue renting or using it: *we had a flat in town but decided not to keep it on.* 2 to continue to wear a piece of clothing.
keep on about something *or* **someone** to talk continually and repetitively about them.
keep on at someone to nag or harass them.
keep to something not to leave it: *keep to the path.*
keep someone to something to make them adhere to a promise, decision, etc: *I'll keep you to that.*
keep to oneself to avoid the company of others.
keep something to oneself not to reveal it to others.
keep someone under to subdue, repress, or crush them.
keep something up 1 to prevent eg spirits, morale, etc from falling. 2 to maintain a habit, friendship, pace, etc. 3 to go on making payments, etc. 4 to maintain a house, garden, etc in good condition. (**keep up with someone**) not to be left behind; to maintain the pace or standard set by someone else.
keep up with the Joneses *colloq.* to compete with one's neighbours in a display of material prosperity.
[from Anglo-Saxon *cepan*, to guard, observe, watch]

keep[2] *noun* the central tower or stronghold in a Norman castle. [from KEEP[1]]

keeper *noun* 1 a person who looks after something, eg animals in a zoo or a collection in a museum. 2 *colloq.* a goalkeeper or wicketkeeper.

keep-fit *noun* a series or system of exercises, especially for women, intended to improve suppleness, stamina, etc.

keeping *noun* care or charge.
— **in** *or* **out of keeping with something** in, or not in, harmony with it.

keepsake *noun* something kept in memory of the giver.

Keetmanshoop POP (1990e) 14 000, a town in S Namibia. It is situated 450km/280mi SE of Windhoek and 355km/220mi NW of Upington

(South Africa). The town is the centre of the karakul (sheepskin) industry.

Keflavik POP (1991e) 8 000, a fishing port in Suðurland region, SW Iceland, situated 48km/30mi SW of Reykjavík. Iceland's international airport is nearby. HISTORY an important trade centre since the 16c; first modern freezing plant started here in 1929; became a NATO base in 1951.

keg *noun* a small barrel for transporting and storing beer. [from Old Norse *kaggi*]

Keitel, Wilhelm (1882–1946) German soldier, born in Helmscherode. He joined the army in 1901, and was an artillery staff officer in World War I. An ardent Nazi, he was made Chief of the Supreme Command of the Armed Forces (1938). In 1940 he signed the Compiègne armistice with France, and in 1945 was one of the German signatories of surrender in Berlin. Convicted of war crimes at Nuremberg, he was executed.

Keith a male first name, after the Scottish surname or place-name. [probably from a Celtic word meaning 'wood']

Kékes, Mount the highest peak in Hungary, lying in the Matra range in the N of the country. HEIGHT 1 014m.

Kekulé von Stradonitz, Friedrich August (1829–96) German chemist, born in Darmstadt. Professor at Ghent and Bonn, he greatly advanced knowledge of the structure of organic molecules, proposing that they consist of atoms linked together by bonds according to the valency or combining power of each atom. He recognized that carbon atoms are often linked together in chains, determined the cyclic nature of the benzene molecule, and suggested the existence of delocalized electrons which interact with a number of atomic nuclei rather than fixed double bonds.

Kelantan POP (1990) 1.2m, a state in NE Peninsular Malaysia. AREA 14 796sq km/ 5 711sq mi. It is bounded N by Thailand and E by the S China Sea. The state is drained by the R Kelantan and its tributaries. It was governed by Thailand from the early 19c until 1909, when it came under British rule. CAPITAL Kota Baharu. ECONOMY rice, rubber, copra; tin.

Keldysh, Mstislav Vsevoldvich (1911–78) Soviet mathematician and space programme leader, born in Riga, Latvia. Educated in Moscow, he conducted aeronautical research at Zhukovskii Aero-Hydrodynamics Institute (from 1934) and at Steklow Mathematics Institute (from 1939). He was a leading figure in the development of the theory of rocketry and in the emergence of the USSR in space exploration.

Keller, Gottfried (1819–90) Swiss writer, born near Zurich. He studied landscape painting at Munich (1840–2), and then took up literature. He lived in Berlin (1850–5), and then returned to Zurich, where he became clerk of his canton (1861–76). His chief works are the autobiographical novel *Der grüne Heinrich* (Green Henry, 1854), and his volumes of short stories, including *Sieben Legenden* (Seven Legends, 1872).

Kellogg–Briand Pact the result of a proposal made (1927) by French Foreign Minister Aristide Briand to US Secretary of State Frank B Kellogg (1856–1937) to sign a pact renouncing war as an instrument of national policy. A Paris conference (27 Aug 1928) formally condemned recourse to war, and the pact was subsequently signed by 65 states (the Pact of Paris), but no provision was made for the punishment of aggressors.

Kells, Gaelic **Ceanannus Mór** POP (1991) 4 000, an urban district in Meath county, Leinster province, E Irish Republic. Lying on the R Boyne, NW of Dublin, it is noted for its monastery (founded by St Columba) and the remains of five

Celtic crosses. The Book of Kells (now in Trinity College, Dublin) was produced there in c.800.

Kelly, Gene (1912–) US actor, dancer, and film director, born in Pittsburgh. His stage success in *Pal Joey* led to a Hollywood début in *For Me and My Gal* (1942), followed by many musicals which he often co-directed and choreographed, such as *An American in Paris* (1951), and *Singin' in the Rain* (1952). In 1951 he received a Special Academy Award for his versatility. From the 1960s he worked mainly as a director.

Kelmscott Press a private printing press founded by William Morris in 1890. It issued Morris's own works and reprints of classics, including an edition of the works of Chaucer (1896).

kelp *noun* **1** the common name for any large brown seaweed that grows below the low-tide mark. Most kelps have long strap-like fronds. **2** the ash obtained by burning kelp, used as an agricultural fertilizer and a source of iodine. [a variant of Middle English *culp*]

kelpie *noun* *Scot. Folklore* a malignant water spirit in the form of a horse.
◊ It was believed to haunt fords and river crossings and to delight in luring travellers to their deaths by drowning. A kelpie may also do a miller a good turn by keeping his waterwheel working through the night.

Kelso POP (1981) 5 700, a market town in Roxburgh district, Borders, SE Scotland, at the junction of the Teviot and Tweed rivers. NOTABLE FEATURES Kelso Abbey (1128); Floors Castle (1721), 3km/2mi NW.

kelson *or* **keelson** *noun* a timber fixed along a ship's keel for strength. [from Old German *kielswin*, keel swine]

Kelt same as CELT.

kelt *noun* a salmon or sea trout that has just spawned.

Kelvin, William Thomson, 1st Baron of Largs (1824–1907) British natural philosopher, born in Belfast. He went to university at the age of 10, and became professor at Glasgow in 1846. In a versatile career of international distinction, he invented many instruments, made important contributions to electromagnetism, investigated hydrodynamics, and played a major role in the establishment of the first transatlantic telegraph cable. In thermodynamics he helped to develop the law of conservation of energy, established the second law of thermodynamics, and introduced the absolute (Kelvin) scale of temperature (1848).

kelvin *noun* *Physics* the SI unit of thermodynamic temperature, equal to one degree Celsius. [named after William Thomson Kelvin]

Kemble the name of a famous British acting family of the 18c. The founding member was Roger (1721–1802), a travelling manager, whose children were Sarah (1755–1831), John Philip (1757–1823), Stephen (1758–1822), and Charles (1775–1854). Charles's daughter, Frances Ann, known as Fanny (1809–93), became one of the leading actresses of the 19c.

Kemi, River, Finnish **Kemijoki,** Swedish **Kemiä** the longest river in Finland, length 480km/300mi. Rising in Lappi province, N Finland, near the Russian border, it flows S, then W to meet the Gulf of Bothnia at Kemi.

Kempe, Rudolf (1910–76) German conductor, born near Dresden. He played the oboe in orchestras in Dortmund and Leipzig before his début as a conductor in 1935. Although he worked mainly in Germany, he later appeared frequently at Covent Garden, London, and was principal conductor of the Royal Philharmonic Orchestra (1961–75) and then of the BBC Symphony Orchestra.

Kempe, Will(iam) (c.1550–c.1603) English comic actor, a leading member of Shakespeare's company. When the Chamberlain's Men moved to the Globe, he left the stage, and in 1600 performed a nine-day Morris dance from London to Norwich.

Kempis, Thomas à, also called **Thomas Hemerken** (1379–1471) German religious writer, named after his birthplace, Kempen. In 1400 he entered the Augustinian convent of Agnietenberg near Zwolle, was ordained in 1413, chosen sub-prior in 1429, and died there as superior. His many writings include the influential devotional work *Imitatio Christi* (The Imitation of Christ, c.1415–24).

Ken. *abbrev.* Kentucky.

ken — *verb* (**kenning**; PAST TENSE AND PAST PARTICIPLE **kent, kenned**) *Scot. dialect* to know. — *noun* one's range of knowledge: *beyond/within one's ken.* [from Anglo-Saxon *cennan*]

Kendal POP (1981) 24 000, a town in South Lakeland district, Cumbria, NW England. It lies on the R Kent, 30km/19mi N of Lancaster. Catherine Parr was born here in 1512. NOTABLE FEATURES Church of the Holy Trinity (13c); castle (12c); Abbott Hall (1759); Levens Hall (8km/5mi S); Sizergh Castle (5km/3mi S).

Kendall, Edward Calvin (1886–1972) US chemist, born in South Norwalk, Connecticut. Professor at the Mayo Foundation, Rochester, he isolated thyroxine (the hormone of the thyroid gland); in collaboration, he also isolated the adrenal hormone cortisone (around 1936), and demonstrated some of its therapeutic properties. He shared the 1950 Nobel Prize for Physiology or Medicine with Philip Hench and Tadens Reichstein.

kendo *noun* a Japanese form of fencing using bamboo swords. [from Japanese *kendo*, sword way]

kendo

Keneally, Thomas (Michael) (1935–) Australian novelist, born in Sydney. His novels are frequently historical, and include *Gossip from the Forest* (1975), about the armistice negotiations in Nov 1918, and *Schindler's Ark* (1982, Booker Prize), the story of a German industrialist who saved the lives of Polish Jews during World War II. Other books include *A Family Madness* (1985) and *The Playmaker* (1987), in which a group of young convicts in a remote penal colony stage the first-ever play in that part of the universe.

Kenilworth POP (1981) 19 000, a residential town in Warwick district, Warwickshire, central England. It is situated 8km/5mi SW of Coventry. NOTABLE FEATURE 12c Kenilworth Castle (depicted in Walter Scott's novel *Kenilworth*).

Kenilworth a novel by Sir Walter Scott (1821). It is set in the time of Elizabeth I and reinterprets the tragic life of Amy Robsart.

Kennedy, Edward M(oore) (1932–) US politician, son of Joseph Kennedy, and brother of John and Robert, born in Brookline, Massachusetts. He was called to the Bar in 1959, and elected a Democratic Senator in 1962. In 1969 he became the youngest-ever majority whip in the US Senate, but his involvement the same year in a car accident at Chappaquiddick, in which a girl companion was drowned, dogged his subsequent political career, and the revival of the scandal caused his withdrawal as a presidential candidate in 1979.

Kennedy, Helena Ann (1950–) Scottish barrister, broadcaster, and writer, born in Glasgow. She set up practice in London, where her clients have included a member of the Guildford Four and Myra Hindley. She achieved public recognition with her appearance on the BBC documentary series *The Heart of the Matter* (1987) and with *Blind Justice* (1988), a television drama loosely based on her own legal experiences. Overtly left-wing and feminist, she has hastened changes in attitudes within the English legal profession. In 1991 she was made a QC and was appointed to the Bar Council.

Kennedy, John F(itzgerald) (1917–63) US politician, the 35th President, son of Joseph Kennedy, and brother of Robert and Edward, born in Brookline, Massachusetts. He joined the navy (1941) and became a torpedo-boat commander in the Pacific. He wrote *Profiles in Courage* (1956), which won the Pulitzer Prize. Elected Democrat Representative (1947) and Senator (1952) for Massachusetts, in 1960 he was the first Catholic, and the youngest person, to be elected President (1961–3). His 'new frontier' in social legislation involved a federal desegregation policy in education and civil rights reform. He displayed firmness and moderation in foreign policy, which enabled him to induce Russia to withdraw its missiles from Cuba (1962), and to achieve a partial nuclear test-ban treaty with Russia (1963). On 22 Nov he was assassinated by rifle fire (allegedly by Lee Harvey Oswald) while being driven in an open car through Dallas, Texas. In 1953 Kennedy had married Jacqueline Lee Bouvier (1929–94), who in 1968 married Aristotle Onassis.

Kennedy, Joseph P(atrick) (1888–1969) US businessman and diplomat, father of John, Robert, and Edward Kennedy, born in Boston, Massachusetts. The grandson of an Irish Catholic immigrant, by the 1920s he was a multimillionaire. During the 1930s he strongly supported Roosevelt and the 'New Deal', and was rewarded with minor administrative posts and the ambassadorship to Britain (1938–40). In 1914 he married a local politician's daughter Rose Fitzgerald, also of Irish immigrant descent, and they had five daughters and four sons, at whose political disposal he placed his fortune. The eldest son, Joseph Patrick (1915–44), was killed in a flying accident while on naval service in World War II, but the others achieved international political fame.

Kennedy, Nigel (Paul) (1956–) English violinist, born in Brighton. He made his début in 1977 and won international acclaim for his concert appearances and recordings, notably the Elgar *Violin Concerto* in 1985. His recordings include concertos by Tchaikovsky, Sibelius, Bruch, Mendelssohn, Walton, Brahms, Beethoven, and Vivaldi, such as the best-selling *The Four Seasons*. Through his own punk-like image he tried to change the image of classical music, making it accessible to a wider audience, but in 1992 he decided to concentrate instead on chamber music and music by living composers, and to develop his interest in jazz and rock.

Kennedy, Robert F(rancis) (1925–68) US politician, son of Joseph Kennedy, born in Brookline, Massachusetts. He served at sea (1944–6), was admitted to the Bar (1951), and became a member of the staff of the Senate Select Committee on Improper Activities (1957–9). An efficient manager of his brother John's presidential campaign, he became an energetic Attorney-General (1961–4), notable in his dealings with civil rights problems, and Senator for New York from 1965. On 5 Jun 1968, after winning the California primary election, he was shot, and died the following day. His assassin was Sirhan Bishara Sirhan, a 24-year-old Jordanian-born immigrant, who was sentenced to death in the gas chamber (1969).

Kennedy Space Center, John F US space centre situated on Merrit I and Cape Canaveral (known as Cape Kennedy 1963–73) off the E coast of Florida. Since the late 1950s Cape Canaveral has been used as the principal launch site for the US space exploration programme conducted by NASA from its headquarters on Merrit I.

kennel — *noun* **1** a small shelter for a dog. **2** (**kennels**) an establishment where dogs are boarded or bred. — *verb* (**kennelled, kennelling**) to put or keep in a kennel. [from Latin *canis*, dog]

Kennelly, Arthur E(dwin) (1861–1939) US electrical engineer, born in Bombay, India. In 1894 he founded a consultancy firm in Philadelphia, where he developed new mathematical analyses of electrical circuits, and in 1902 he discovered the ionized layer in the atmosphere, sometimes named after him.

Kenneth I, also called **MacAlpin** (d.858) King of the Scots (from 841) and King of the Picts (from c.843). He combined the territories of both peoples in a united kingdom of Scotia (Scotland north of the Forth–Clyde line), and also moved the centre of the Church from Iona to Dunkeld.

Kenneth a male first name. [from the Gaelic names *Cinaed*, born of fire + *Cainnech*, handsome]

Kensington and Chelsea POP (1987e) 133 000, a borough of central Greater London, England, lying N of the R Thames. Kensington was granted the designation 'Royal Borough' by Edward VII in 1901. NOTABLE FEATURES Kensington Palace; Kensington Gardens; Chelsea Royal Hospital; Victoria and Albert Museum; Science Museum; British Museum (Natural History); Nottingham House, birthplace of Queen Victoria. EVENTS Crufts Dog Show (Feb); Chelsea Antiques Fair (Mar, Sep); Ideal Home Exhibition (Mar); Chelsea Flower Show (May); Royal Tournament (Jul); Smithfield Agricultural Show (Dec).

Kent, Earl of the faithful follower of Lear in Shakespeare's *King Lear*, who serves him in disguise after being banished from his kingdom.

Kent, Prince Edward (George Nicholas Paul Patrick), Duke of (1935–) British prince, the eldest son of Duke George Edward Alexander Edmund (1902–42), who was the fourth son of King George V and Queen Mary. He served in the army (1955–76), and in 1961 married Katharine Worsley (1933–). They have three children: George Philip Nicholas, Earl of St Andrews (1962–), Helen Marina Lucy, Lady Helen Windsor (1964–), and Nicholas Charles Edward Jonathan, Lord Nicholas Windsor (1970–).

Kent, Prince Michael of (1942–) British prince, the younger brother of Edward, Duke of Kent. In 1978 he married Baroness Marie-Christine von Reibniz; their children are Frederick Michael George David Louis, Lord Frederick Windsor (1979–) and Gabriella Marina Alexandra Ophelia, Lady Gabriella Windsor (1981–).

Kent, William (1685–1748) English painter, landscape gardener, and architect, born in Bridlington, Yorkshire. He studied in Rome, and became one of the principal exponents of the Palladian style of architecture in England. His best-known works include Holkham Hall in Norfolk (begun 1734) and the Horse Guards block in Whitehall.

Kent POP (1992e) 1.5m, a county in SE England, divided into 14 districts. AREA 3 731sq km/ 1 440sq mi. The county is bounded S by East Sussex, W by Surrey, NW by Greater London, N by the R Thames estuary, and E by the English Channel. PHYSICAL DESCRIPTION rises to 251m in the North Downs; The Weald lies to the SW; Kent is drained by the Thames, Medway, and Stour rivers; there are high chalk cliffs, especially at Dover. CHIEF TOWNS Maidstone (county town), Dover, Folkestone, Ramsgate, Canterbury, Tunbridge Wells. ECONOMY cross-Channel transport; fruit and hops ('the Garden of England'); cattle and sheep; grain; vegetables; cement; paper; shipbuilding; fishing; electronics; pharmaceuticals; oil; tourism.

Kentucky POP (1990) 3.8m, a state in E central USA, divided into 120 counties. AREA 104 658sq km/40 410sq mi. PHYSICAL DESCRIPTION rivers include the Mississippi (part of the SW border), Ohio (part of the NW and N border), Tennessee, Cumberland, Kentucky, and Big Sandy with its tributary, the Tug Fork (part of the E border); the Cumberland Mts lie to the SE; Mt Black (1 263m) is the highest point; the central plain is known as Bluegrass country; to the W and E are rough uplands with vast coal reserves; in the SW corner are floodplains bounded by the Ohio, Mississippi, and Tennessee rivers; Kentucky is known as the 'Bluegrass State'. HISTORY part of the territory was ceded by the French in 1763; explored by Daniel Boone from 1769; the first permanent British settlement was founded in 1775 at Boonesborough; originally part of Virginia, it was admitted to the Union as a separate state (the 23rd) in 1792; Kentucky is known as the 'Bluegrass State'. CAPITAL Frankfort. CHIEF TOWNS Louisville, Lexington. ECONOMY famous for the distilling of Bourbon whiskey, and for the breeding of thoroughbred racehorses; chief agricultural products are tobacco, cattle, dairy produce, and soya beans; major industrial manufactures are machinery, electrical equipment, processed foods, chemicals, and fabricated metals; natural resources include coal (the nation's leading producer), petroleum, and natural gas. NOTABLE FEATURE Mammoth Cave National Park; Fort Knox. EVENT the Kentucky Derby for three-year-olds (the nation's oldest continuously-held classic horse race).

Kentucky and Virginia Resolutions statements made (1798 and 1799) by two state legislatures claiming that the Alien and Sedition laws violated the US Constitution. This later led to the development of the doctrine of 'state sovereignty' and the state's right to nullify federal law. The resolutions were written by Thomas Jefferson (Kentucky) and James Madison (Virginia).

Kenya, official name **Republic of Kenya** POP (1992e) 27m, a republic in E Africa, divided into eight provinces. AREA 564 162sq km/217 766sq mi. The republic is bounded S by Tanzania, W by Uganda, NW by Sudan, N by Ethiopia, NE by Somalia, and E by the Indian Ocean. CAPITAL Nairobi. CHIEF TOWNS Mombasa, Kisumu, Nakuru, Malindi. TIME ZONE GMT +3. The chief population groupings are Kikuyu (21%), Luhya (14%), Luo (13%), Kalejin (11%), and Kamba (11%); the majority are Protestant or Roman Catholic. OFFICIAL LANGUAGES English and Swahili, with many tribal languages spoken. CURRENCY the Kenya shilling. PHYSICAL DESCRIPTION crossed by the Equator; the SW plateau rising to 600–3 000m includes Mt Kenya (5 200m) and the Aberdare range; the Great Rift Valley in the W runs N–S; dry, arid semi-desert in the N, generally under 600m; L Turkana, the largest body of water, is situated in the N; the Chalbi desert lies SE of the lake; the coastal strip S of the R Tana is typified by coral reefs, mangrove swamps, and small island groups. CLIMATE tropical climate on the coast, with high temperatures and humidity; in Mombasa the average annual rainfall is 1 200mm, the average daily temperatures are 27–31°C; annual rainfall decreases from 500mm in the S to 250mm in the far N; frost and snow lie in the high mountains. HISTORY very early fossil hominids found in the region by anthropologists; coast settled by Arabs in the 7c; Portuguese control in the 16c–17c; British control as East African Protectorate in 1895; British colony in 1920; an independence movement led to the Mau Mau rebellion in 1952–60; gained independence in 1963; in 1991 a multiparty system was legalized; in 1992 there was unrest in many areas, leading to the Rift Valley being regarded as a War Zone. GOVERNMENT governed by a president elected for a five-year term, with a unicameral National Assembly of 202 members. ECONOMY agriculture accounts for one third of the national income; coffee, tea, sisal, pyrethrum, cashew nuts, rice, wheat, maize, sugar cane; food processing, textiles; chemicals; cement; steel; paper; metal products; car assembly; oil refining; consumer goods; tobacco; rubber; reserves of soda ash, fluorspar, salt, diatomite, limestone, lead, gemstones, silver, gold. NOTABLE FEATURES 14 national parks attract a large numbers of tourists.

Kenya

Kenya, Mount the second highest mountain in Africa. It is an extinct volcano cone in central Kenya, 112km/70mi NE of Nairobi. The mountain comprises three peaks, Batian (5 199m), Nelion (5 188m), and Lenana (4 985m). Many lakes and glaciers are in the area. It is often possible to view the summit of Kilimanjaro 323km/201mi away, one of the longest confirmed lines of sight on Earth. Thick forest extends to a high level with varied wildlife; a national park was established in 1949.

Kenya African National Union (ABBREV. KANU) the party which led Kenya to independence (1963), founded in 1960 to succeed the Kikuyu Central Association of 1929 and the Kenya African Union of 1947. The Kenya African Democratic Union (KADU) was a rival body which represented mainly non-Kikuyu groups. KANU won the first Kenyan election and President Kenyatta became the leader of independent Kenya, although he tried to bring KADU into a coalition.

Kenyatta, Jomo, originally **Kamau Ngengi** (c.1889–1978) Kenyan nationalist and politician, born in Mitumi. He joined the Young Kikuyu Association (1922) and played a leading role in representing black Kenyan opinion. He attended the Fifth Pan-Africanist Conference in Manchester (1945) and on his return to Kenya was elected President of the Kenyan African Union, which advocated total independence in a unitary state. Charged with leading the Mau Mau terrorist organization (a charge he denied), he was sentenced to seven years' hard labour in 1952, released in 1958, then exiled. In 1960 he was elected President of the new Kenya African National Union Party, and he became an MP (1961), Prime Minister (1963), and President of the Republic of Kenya (1964–78). He adopted moderate social and economic policies, and succeeded in conciliating many members of the Kenyan white community.

Kenzo, originally **Kenzo Takada** (1940–) Japanese fashion designer, born in Kyoto. He studied art in Japan and moved to Paris in 1964, where he started producing freelance collections. He started a shop called Jungle Jap in 1970, and is known for his innovative ideas and use of traditional designs. He creates clothes showing both Oriental and Western influences, and is a trend-setter in the field of knitwear.

Keoladeo, also known as **Bharatpur** a national park in Rajasthan, India. AREA 29sq km/11sq mi. It provides breeding grounds for thousands of migrating birds from Siberia and China, including herons, storks, and cranes.

kepi *noun* a French military cap with a flat circular crown and horizontal straight-edged peak. [from French *képi*, from Swiss German *Käppi*, diminutive of German *Kappe*, cap]

Kepler, Johannes (1571–1630) German astronomer, born in Weilderstadt, Württemberg. Professor at Graz from 1594, he succeeded Tycho Brahe as imperial mathematician in Prague in 1601. In studies of the planets, he broke with the tradition of more than 2 000 years by demonstrating that the planets do not move uniformly in circles, but in ellipses with the Sun at one focus. The (imaginary) line from the Sun to the planet sweeps equal areas of the ellipse in equal times (Kepler's first and second laws). His third law connected the periods of revolution of the planets with their mean distances from the Sun.

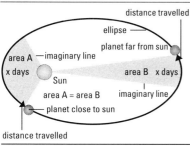

Kepler's second law

kept 1 past tense and past participle of KEEP. **2** *said of a man or woman* supported financially by someone in return for being available to them for sexual relations.

Kerala POP (1991) 29.1m, a state in S India, bounded W by the Arabian Sea and crossed by several rivers. AREA 38 864sq km/15 001sq mi. CAPITAL Trivandrum. PHYSICAL DESCRIPTION three physical regions include densely forested, hilly tracts running W to E, a cultivated plain and an indented coastal region with coconut plantations and rice fields. HISTORY the state was created out of the former state of Travancore–Cochin under the 1956 States Reorganization Act. GOVERNMENT governed by a 140-member unicameral legislature. ECONOMY rice, tapioca, coconut, oilseeds, sugar cane, pepper, rubber, tea, coffee; teak, sandalwood, ebony, blackwood; textiles; ceramics; fertilizer; chemicals; glass; electrical goods; paper; weaving; copper and brass ware; furniture.

keratin *noun Biol.* a tough fibrous protein produced by the outer layer of the skin (the epidermis) of vertebrates. It is the main component of hair, nails, claws, horns, feathers, and the dead outer layers of skin cells. [from Greek *keras -atos*, horn]

kerb *noun* the row of stones forming the edging of a pavement. [variant of CURB]

kerb-crawler *noun* a person who practises kerb-crawling.

kerb-crawling *noun* the practice of driving slowly alongside the kerb in order to lure potential sexual partners into one's car.

kerbstone *noun* one of the stones forming a kerb.

kerchief *noun old use* **1** a cloth or scarf for wearing over the head or round the neck. **2** a handkerchief. [from Old French *cuevrechief*, from *covrir*, to cover + *chef*, head]

Kerensky, Alexandr Fyodorovich (1881–1970) Russian socialist, born in Simbirsk. He was a leader in the 1917 Revolution, and became Minister of Justice (Mar), War (May), and Premier (Jul) in the provisional government. He crushed Kornilov's military revolt (Aug), but was deposed (Oct) by the Bolsheviks, and fled to France. He went to Australia (1940) and to the USA (1946), and wrote several books on the Revolution.

kerfuffle *noun colloq.* a commotion or fuss. [from Gaelic prefix *car-* + Scot. *fuffle*, to disorder]

Kérkira see CORFU.

Kerkuane a Punic town in N Tunisia, founded in the 5c BC and abandoned c.140 BC after the destruction of Carthage. A necropolis was discovered nearby in 1968. It is a World Heritage site.

Kermit *noun Comput.* a public-domain program used to transfer files between different computer systems, eg between a PC and a mainframe. [named after *Kermit the Frog*, a character in the US television show 'The Muppet Show']

Kermode, Frank (1919–) British literary critic, born in the Isle of Man. He served in the Royal Navy (1940–6), and has since held posts at several universities in England and the USA. His works include *Romantic Image* (1957), *The Sense of an Ending* (1967), *The Genesis of Secrecy* (1979), and *Forms of Attention* (1985).

Kern, Jerome (David) (1885–1945) US songwriter, born in New York City. His first complete score for a musical play was *The Red Petticoat* (1912), followed by several successful Broadway shows. *Show Boat* (1928, book and lyrics by Hammerstein) is considered his greatest musical, and *Roberta* (1933) included three of his finest songs: 'Smoke Gets in Your Eyes', 'Yesterdays', and 'The Touch of Your Hand'.

kernel *noun* **1** *Bot.* the inner part of a seed, eg the edible part of a nut. **2** *Bot.* in cereal plants such as corn, the entire grain or seed. **3** the important, essential part of anything. [from Anglo-Saxon *cyrnel*, diminutive of *corn*, a grain]

kerosene *noun* **1** paraffin oil distilled from petroleum or obtained from coal or shale, used for heating and lighting, and as an aircraft fuel. **2** *North Amer.* paraffin. [from Greek *keros*, wax]

Kerouac, Jack, originally **Jean Louis** (1922–69) US author, born in Lowell, Massachusetts. His first novel, *The Town and the City* (1950), was written in a conventional style which he abandoned in *On the Road* (1957), a spontaneous work which expresses the youthful discontent of the 'Beat' generation. Later works in this vein, all autobiographical in character, include *The Subterraneans* (1958) and *Big Sur* (1962).

Kerr, John (1824–1907) Scottish physicist, born in Ardrossan. In 1876 he discovered the effect named after him, concerning the behaviour of polarized light in electric and magnetic fields.

Kerry, Gaelic **Chiarraighe** POP (1991) 122 000, a county in Munster province, SW Irish Republic, bounded W by the Atlantic Ocean. AREA 4 701sq km/1 815sq mi. PHYSICAL DESCRIPTION rises to the Slieve Mish Mts on the N side of Dingle Bay and to Macgillycuddy's Reeks on the S side; watered by the Feale and Blackwater rivers; the Blasket and Skellig islands lie offshore. CAPITAL Tralee. CHIEF TOWNS Killarney (notable

lakeland area), Listowel. ECONOMY fishing; textiles; tourism.

Kerry a male and female first name, of recent Australian origin, probably after the name of the Irish county.

kerygma *noun Relig.* the preaching of the Christian gospel, especially in the way of the early Christian Church, specifically the apostles' announcement of the saving nature of Christ's death and resurrection, so that Christ becomes not just the proclaimer of salvation but that which is proclaimed. [from Greek *kerygma*, proclamation, that which is announced]

Kesey, Ken (1935–) US novelist, born in Colorado. Associated with the 'Beat' movement, his reputation is based on his first novel *One Flew Over the Cuckoo's Nest* (1962, filmed 1975). It is a black comedy set in a mental institution and based on the author's experience as an aide on the psychiatric ward of a veterans' hospital. He served a prison sentence for marijuana possession and formed the 'Merry Pranksters', whose weird exploits are described at length in Tom Wolfe's *The Electric Kool-Aid Acid Test* (1967).

Kesselring, Albert (1885–1960) German airman, born in Markstedt, Bavaria. During World War II he led the Luftwaffe attacks on France and (unsuccessfully) on Britain. He was made Commander-in-Chief in Italy (1941), and in the West (1945). Condemned to death as a war criminal in 1947, he had his sentence commuted to life imprisonment, but was released in 1952.

kestrel *noun* a small type of falcon. [from Old French *quercerelle*]

Keswick POP (1981) 5 700, a resort and market town in Allerdale district, Cumbria, NW England. It lies at the N end of Derwent Water, on the R Greta, 26km/16mi W of Penrith. NOTABLE FEATURES 16c Church of St Kentigern; Greta Hall, home of Robert Southey; Castle Rigg stone circle (3km/2mi E); St Herbert's Island on Derwent Water, a 7c hermitage.

ketch *noun* a small two-masted sailing boat. [from Middle English *cache*, related to CATCH]

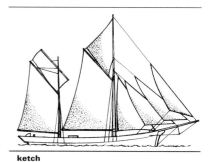

ketch

ketchup *noun* a thick sauce made from tomatoes, vinegar, spices, etc. [from Malay *kechap*]

ketone *noun Chem.* any member of a class of organic chemical compounds that are formed by the oxidation of secondary alcohols, and contain a carbonyl (C=O) group attached to two hydrocarbon groups, eg acetone. [from German *Keton*, from *Aketon*, acetone]

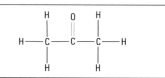

ketone: propanone (acetone)

kettle *noun* a kitchen vessel with a spout, lid and handle, for boiling water.
— **a different kettle of fish** *colloq.* an entirely different matter.

a pretty kettle of fish *colloq.* an awkward situation.
[from Anglo-Saxon *cetel*]

kettledrum *noun* a large copper or brass cauldron-shaped drum mounted on a tripod.

Kettlewell, Henry Bernard David (1907–79) English geneticist and entomologist, born in Howden, Yorkshire. He started a career in medicine, but from 1952 held various posts in genetics at Oxford University. He is best known for his work on industrial melanism, in which he discovered a rapid mechanism of natural selection occurring in moths, to adapt to live in areas where industry causes atmospheric carbon pollution.

Kevin a male first name of Irish origin. It was the name of a 7c saint, the patron saint of Dublin. [from the Gaelic name *Caoimhin*, comely birth]

Kew Gardens the Royal Botanical Gardens in Kew, Surrey. The gardens, which were inherited by George III from his mother, expanded and flourished under the direction of Sir Joseph Banks (1743–1820) and were given to the nation in 1841. They were severely damaged, with hundreds of trees destroyed, by a hurricane in Oct 1987.

key¹ — *noun* **1** an instrument designed to turn a lock, wind a clock, grip and turn a nut, etc. **2** one of a series of buttons or levers pressed to sound the notes on a musical instrument, or to print or display a character on a computer, typewriter, calculator, etc. **3** a system of musical notes related to one another in a scale. **4** pitch, tone or style: *spoke in a low key.* **5** something that provides an answer or solution. **6** a means of achievement: *the key to success.* **7** a set of answers, eg at the back of a book of puzzles, exercises, etc. **8** a table explaining signs and symbols used on a map, etc. **9** *Electr.* a switch for completing or breaking a circuit. **10** the winged seed of the sycamore or ash tree. **11** roughness given to a surface by sandpapering, etc, so as to take paint, etc more readily. **12** a fret pattern. **13** a pin or wedge for fixing something. — *adj.* centrally important: *key questions.* — *verb* **1** to enter (data) into a computer by operating keys. **2** to fasten or fix with a key. **3** (**key one thing to another**) to adjust or harmonize it.
— **keyed up** *colloq.* excited; tense; anxious.
under lock and key 1 safely stored. **2** in prison.
[from Anglo-Saxon *ceg*]

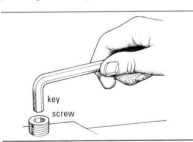

Allen key and screw

key² *or* **cay** *noun* a small low island or reef formed of sand, coral, rock, or mud, especially such islands off the coast of Florida. [Spanish *cayo*]

keyboard — *noun* **1** the set of keys on a piano, etc or the bank of keys for operating a typewriter or computer. **2** especially in jazz, a musical instrument with a keyboard, eg a synthesizer. — *verb* **1** *intrans.* to operate the keyboard of a computer. **2** *trans.* to set (text) using a computer keyboard.

keyboarder *noun* a person who enters data, especially text, by means of a keyboard.

keyboardist *noun* **1** a person who plays music on a keyboard. **2** same as KEYBOARDER.

keyhole *noun* the hole through which a key is inserted into a lock.

keyhole surgery *Medicine* surgery using miniature instruments, performed through tiny holes in the outer tissue.

Keynes (of Tilton), John Maynard, 1st Baron (1883–1946) English economist, born in Cambridge. He became one of the 'Bloomsbury group', and lectured in economics. In both World Wars he was an adviser to the Treasury. The unemployment crises inspired his two major works, *A Treatise on Money* (1930) and the revolutionary *General Theory of Employment, Interest and Money* (1936). His views on a planned economy influenced Roosevelt's 'New Deal' administration.

Keynesian *adj.* relating to the economic theories of J M Keynes, advocating government funding of public works to maintain full employment.

keynote *noun* **1** the note on which a musical scale or key is based. **2** a central theme of a speech, feature of an occasion, etc.

key pad a small panel of keys or buttons. eg for dialling a telephone number, operating a calculator, adjusting a television, etc.

key punch a device operated by a keyboard for transferring data on to punched cards.

key-ring *noun* a ring for keeping keys on.

key signature *Mus.* the sharps and flats shown on the stave at the start of a piece of music, indicating its key.

Keystone a production company of silent films (1912–19) founded by Mack Sennett. It specialized in knock-about comedy shorts, especially those featuring the Keystone Kops.

keystone *noun* **1** the central supporting stone at the high point of an arch. **2** the point in a theory or argument on which the rest depends.

keystroke *noun* a single press of a key on a typewriter, computer, etc.

keyword *noun* **1** in text, a word that sums up or gives an indication of the nature of the passage in which it occurs. **2** a word indexed or highlighted in a concordance or VDU display.

KG *abbrev.* Knight of the Order of the Garter.

kg *abbrev.* kilogram.

KGB *abbrev. Komitet Gosudarstvennoi Bezopastnosti* (Russian), Committee of State Security, the Russian and former Soviet secret police.

Khajuraho a group of 20 Hindu temples in Madhya Pradesh, India. The temples were constructed, mainly of sandstone, in 950–1050. They are renowned for the erotic sculptures which embellish their internal and external walls. It is a World Heritage site.

khaki *noun* **1** a brownish-green colour. **2** cloth of this colour, or military uniforms made of it. [from Urdu and Persian *khaki*, dusty]

Khalid *or* **Khaled, ibn Abdul Aziz** (1913–82) King of Saudi Arabia (1975–82), the fourth son of the founder of the Saudi dynasty. He ascended the throne after the assassination of his brother Faisal, and his moderation was a stabilizing factor in the Middle East. His personal influence was seen in the halting of the Lebanese Civil War (1975–6), and in his country's disagreement with the other members of OPEC over oil-price increases.

khalif see CALIPH.

Khama, Sir Seretse (1921–80) Botswanian statesman, born at Serowe, Bechuanaland (now Botswana). He became a lawyer in England, and after marrying an Englishwoman, Ruth Williams (1948), was banned from the chieftainship and the territory of the Bamangwato. Permitted to return as a private citizen in 1956, he became active in politics, and was restored to the chieftainship in 1963. He was the first Prime Minister

of Bechuanaland in 1965, and first President of Botswana (1966–80).

Khan, (Muhammad) Ayub (1907–74) Pakistani soldier and politician, born in Abbottabad. He served in World War II and was the first Commander-in-Chief of Pakistan's army (1951). He became President after a bloodless coup in 1958, and introduced a system of 'basic democracies' (a system of self-governing local bodies). Following widespread civil disorder, he resigned in 1969, and martial law was re-established.

Khan, (Niazi) Imran (1952–) Pakistani cricketer. He played county cricket for Worcestershire and Sussex, and made his Test début in 1971. In 1983, he became the second player to score a century and take 10 wickets in a Test match. He captained Pakistan on several occasions (1982–3, 1985–7, 1988–92), and led them to victory in the World Cup in 1992. He scored over 3 000 Test runs, and took over 325 wickets in Test matches, before announcing his retirement from cricket in 1992.

Khan, Jahangir (1963–) Pakistani squash rackets player, born in Karachi. He won three world amateur titles (1979, 1983, 1985), a record six World Open titles (1981–5, 1988), and nine consecutive British Open titles (1982–90). He was undefeated from Apr 1981 to Nov 1986, when he lost to Ross Norman (Australia) in the World Open final.

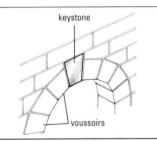

position of the keystone

Khan, Sir Sayyid Ahmad, or **Syed Ahmed** (1817–1898) Indian Muslim educationist, jurist, and author, born in Delhi. After a traditional Muslim education, he was employed by the British (1837), became a subordinate judge in Bijnor (1850), and received a special pension for his loyal services during the 1857 uprising. In 1875, to encourage Western education among Indian Muslims, he set up the Mohammedan Anglo-Oriental School in Aligarh. Opposed to the Indian National Congress, he formed the All-India Muhammadan Educational Conference in 1886. Through his educational and religious reforms, he was the main motivating force behind the late-19c revival of Indian Islam.

khan *noun* **1** the title of a ruler or prince in central Asia. **2** in ancient Persia, a governor. [related to Turkish *kagan*, ruler]

Kharga, El *or* **Al Kharijah** the capital of Al-Wadi Al-Jadid governorate, S central Egypt. It is situated in the Great Oasis, Egypt's largest oasis. NOTABLE FEATURES ruins of the Temple of Hibis (now a Christian necropolis, c.500 BC) and Nadura (Christian convent, c.150 AD).

Kharkov 1 POP (1991e) 1.6m, the capital city of Kharkov region, NE Ukraine. It is situated on several tributaries of the R Severskiy Donets. The city was founded in 1655–56 as a fortress to protect Russia's S border. The Krivoy Rog iron mines and the Donets coal basin nearby provided the basis for engineering industries that produce a wide variety of heavy metal goods. NOTABLE FEATURES Pokrovskii Cathedral (1689); Uspenskii Cathedral (1821–41). **2** a region in NE Ukraine with the city of Kharkov as its capital.

Khartoum *or* **El Khartûm** POP (1990e) 2m, the capital of Sudan, near the junction of the

White Nile and the Blue Nile rivers, 1 600km/1 000mi S of Cairo in Egypt. Khartoum is regarded as the economic link between the Arab countries in the N and the African countries in the S. HISTORY founded in the 1820s; garrison town in the 19c; scene of the British defeat against the Mahdi, in which General Gordon was killed in 1885; the city was regained by Lord Kitchener in 1898. NOTABLE FEATURES three cathedrals, mosques, Sudan National Museum.

Khatchaturian, Aram (1903–78) Russian composer, born in Tiflis. He was a student of folk-song, and an authority on oriental music. His compositions include symphonies, concertos, ballets, instrumental and film music.

khedive *noun* an ancient Persian title conferred on Ismail Pasha, Viceroy of Egypt in 1866, by the Ottoman Sultan, and used by his successors until 1914, when Egypt became a British protectorate. [from French *khédive*, from Turkish *khidiv*, from Persian *khidīw*, prince]

Khmer — *noun* an Austro-Asiatic language spoken by five million people in Cambodia and parts of neighbouring countries. The official language of Cambodia (formerly Kampuchea and the Khmer Republic): also known as Cambodian. — *adj.* relating to or spoken or written in Khmer.

Khmer Empire an empire in SE Asia, founded in the 7c, with its capital at Angkor from 802 onwards. In the 11c–12c it included S Laos, a large part of Thailand, and Cambodia. It was overthrown by the Thais in the 15c.

Khmer Rouge a Cambodian communist guerrilla force which opposed the right-wing government that deposed Prince Sihanouk in 1970, and after the subsequent US invasion of Cambodia. After gaining control in 1975, its government, led by Pol Pot, set about a drastic transformation of the state, renamed 'Democratic Kampuchea'. This involved mass forced evacuation from the towns to the countryside, the creation of agricultural co-operatives, and the execution of thousands of people. In 1978, Vietnam invaded Cambodia, and the Khmer Rouge were ousted, retiring to the Thai-Cambodian border region. Following the Vietnamese withdrawal in 1989, they mounted a major offensive, especially in the W and S provinces. In 1991 they agreed to a ceasefire and signed a peace agreement with the other factions in Cambodia. However, they refused to accept the authority of the UN peacekeeping force UNTAC, and fighting continued throughout 1992. Following their exclusion from the government which was formed after the general election (May 1993), the Khmer Rouge continued their guerrilla attacks (especially against the Vietnamese population in Cambodia), and in Aug 1993 government forces launched a major military offensive against them.

Khoisan a collective term for the San (Bushmen) and Khoi (Hottentot) peoples of southern Africa. The San were formerly hunter-gatherers who populated most of E central and southern Africa, but today are marginalized in the Kalahari Desert of Botswana. Many now work for African or white cattle-farmers. The Khoi were traditionally pastoralists, but they were devastated by a smallpox epidemic in 1713, and their culture collapsed. Today they are represented only by groups of mixed ancestry in Namibia, where their population is c.100 000.

Khoisan languages the smallest distinct language family in Africa, consisting of less than 50 so-called 'click languages' spoken mainly in the area of the Kalahari Desert in Botswana, and parts of Angola and South Africa. The family includes the languages of the Bushmen and Hottentots, and the related click languages of Tanzania, Sandawe, and Kwadi.

Khomeini, Ayatollah Ruhollah (1900–89) Iranian religious and political leader, born in Khomeyn, Iran. A Shiite Muslim who was bitterly opposed to the pro-Western regime of

Shah Mohammed Reza Pahlavi, he was exiled to Turkey and Iraq in 1964, and from Iraq to France in 1978. He returned to Iran amid great popular acclaim in 1979 after the collapse of Shah Mohammed Reza Pahlavi's government and became virtual head of state. Under his leadership, Iran underwent a turbulent 'Islamic Revolution' in which a return was made to the strict observance of Muslim principles and traditions. A new Islamic constitution was sanctioned in 1979, into which was incorporated his leadership concept of the Vilayet-i faqih (Trusteeship of the Jurisconsult), a supreme religious and political position that was recognized as belonging to Khomeini, as was the title Rabhar (leader).

Khorana, Har Gobind (1922–) Indian-born US molecular chemist, born in Raipur (now in Pakistan). He studied in the Punjab and in Britain, before moving to Vancouver, Wisconsin, and the Massachusetts Institute of Technology, where he has been professor since 1970. Among many major contributions to the elucidation of the genetic code, he became in the early 1970s one of the first to artificially synthesize a gene. He shared the 1968 Nobel Prize for Physiology or Medicine with Marshall Nirenberg and Robert Holley.

Khrushchev, Nikita Sergeyevich (1894–1971) Soviet politician, born in Kalinovka. He joined the Bolshevik Party (1918), fought in the Russian Civil War, and rose rapidly in the Party organization until in 1939 he was made a full member of the Politburo and of the Presidium of the Supreme Soviet. On the death of Stalin, he became First Secretary of the Communist Party of the Soviet Union (1953–64), and three years later at the 20th Party Congress denounced Stalinism, a speech which had far-reaching results. His administration was marked by the 1956 Poznan riots and Hungarian uprising, and the failed attempt to install missiles in Cuba (1962). Also Prime Minister from 1958, he was deposed in 1964, replaced by Brezhnev and Kosygin, and went into retirement.

Khwarizmi, Abu Ja'far Muhammad ibn Musa al- (c.800–c.850) Arab mathematician. He lived in Baghdad where he wrote highly influential works on astronomy, geography, and mathematics, including an early Arabic treatise on the solution of quadratic equations, synthesizing Babylonian solution methods with Greek-style proofs of their correctness for the first time. The word 'algorithm' is derived from a corrupted form of his name; 'algebra' comes from the word *al-jabr* in the title of his book on the subject.

Khyber Pass a defile through the Safed Koh mountain range on the frontier between Pakistan and Afghanistan. A route favoured through history by both traders and invaders, it is 45km/28mi long, and reaches heights of 1 280m.

KHz *abbrev.* kilohertz.

kibbutz *noun* (PL. **kibbutzim**) in Israel, a farm or other concern owned and run jointly by its workers. [from Modern Hebrew *kibus*]

kibosh *noun*
— **put the kibosh on something** *colloq.* to put an end to it; to ruin it.

kick — *verb* **1** to hit (a person, etc) or propel (a ball, etc) with the foot. **2** *intrans., trans.* to swing or jerk (the leg) vigorously. **3** *intrans. said of a gun* to recoil when fired. **4** *intrans.* (**kick against something**) to resist it: *kick against discipline.* **5** to get rid of (a habit, etc). **6** to score (a goal) with a kick. — *noun* **1** a blow with the foot. **2** a swing of the leg: *high kicks.* **3** Swimming any of various leg movements. **4** the recoil of a gun after firing. **5** *colloq.* a thrill of excitement. **6** *colloq.* a strong effect; power: *a drink with quite a kick.* **7** *colloq.* a brief enthusiasm: *we're on a culture kick.*
— **kick about** *or* **around** *colloq.* **1** to lie around unused. **2** to be idle; to go about aimlessly.
kick someone about *or* **around** *colloq.* to treat them badly or roughly.

kick something about *or* **around** *colloq.* to discuss an idea, etc informally among several people.
a kick in the teeth *colloq.* a humiliating snub.
kick someone in the teeth *colloq.* to inflict a snub on them.
kick off 1 to start a football game by kicking the ball away from the centre. **2** *colloq.* to begin a discussion or other activity involving several people.
kick something off *colloq.* to begin a discussion.
kick something *or* **someone out** *colloq.* to dismiss or get rid of them, especially using force.
kick up a fuss *or* **stink** *colloq.* to complain or disapprove strongly.
kick someone upstairs *colloq.* to promote them to a position of higher rank but less influence. [from Middle English *kiken*]

kickback *noun* money paid for help or favours, especially if illegally given.

kicker *noun* a person or animal that kicks.

kick-off *noun* **1** the start or re-start of a football match. **2** *colloq.* the start of anything.
— **for a kick-off** *colloq.* for a start.

kick pleat a small pleat at the back of a skirt.

kick-start — *noun* **1** (*also* **kick-starter**) a pedal on a motor cycle that is kicked vigorously downwards to start the engine. **2** the starting of an engine with this. — *verb* to start (a motor cycle) using this.

kid[1] — *noun* **1** *colloq.* a child; a young person. **2** a young goat. **3** soft leather made from its skin. — *adj. colloq.* younger: *my kid sister.*
— **handle someone with kid gloves** to treat them with special care or caution. — *verb intrans.* (**kidded, kidding**) *said of a goat* to give birth to young.
[related to Norse *kith*, young goat]

kid[2] *verb* (**kidded, kidding**) *colloq.* **1** to fool or deceive, especially light-heartedly or in fun. **2** *intrans.* to bluff; to pretend. **3** *trans., intrans.* to tease.
— **kid oneself** to fool oneself about something: *kidding himself all was well.*
[perhaps from KID[1]]

Kidd, William, also called **Capt Kidd** (c.1645–1701) Scottish privateer and pirate, born (probably) in Greenock. He made his name as a courageous privateer, and in 1696 when he was commissioned to suppress piracy he reached Madagascar, but then turned pirate himself. After a two-year cruise he returned to the West Indies, but he then ventured to Boston, and was arrested, sent to England, and hanged.

kidder *noun* a person who deceives, a joker.

Kidderminster POP (1981) 51 000, a market and industrial town in Wyre Forest district, Hereford and Worcester, W central England. It lies on the R Stour, 25km/15mi N of Worcester. Carpets have been manufactured here since the 18c.

kiddie *or* **kiddy** *noun* (PL. **kiddies**) *colloq.* a small child. [from KID[1]]

Kiddush a prayer usually recited by the head of the family over a cup of wine at the start of a meal in the home on the eve of a Sabbath or festival, sometimes used also in synagogues to consecrate the Sabbath or a festival. A 'minor' Kiddush is often said before the first meal the following morning. [from Hebrew *kiddush*, sanctification]

kidnap *verb* (**kidnapped, kidnapping**) to seize and hold (someone) prisoner illegally, usually demanding a ransom for his or her release. [from KID[1] + NAP, variant of *nab*]

Kidnapped a novel by Robert Louis Stevenson (1886). It is set in the aftermath of the 1745 Jacobite Rebellion and describes the adventures of David Balfour and Alan Breck Stewart.

kidney *noun* (PL. **kidneys**) **1** in vertebrates, one of a pair of organs that are concerned with the removal of waste products, especially nitrogenous compounds, from the blood, and the excretion of such waste material, usually in the form of urine. **2** animal kidneys as food. [from Middle English *kidnei*; *-ei* is perhaps related to EGG (from the shape of the organ)]

◇ In humans, the kidneys are situated at the back of the abdominal cavity on either side of the spine. Each kidney filters waste products from the blood by means of millions of tiny tubular filtration devices, known as *nephrons*. Blood enters the kidneys via capillaries (very small blood vessels) and then passes through a tiny ball of capillaries (the *glomerulus*) which is enclosed by the cup-shaped end (*Bowman's capsule*) of a nephron. Water and nitrogenous products are filtered from the blood by the glomerulus, drain into the nephron, and are carried down into the kidney along a twisted tube (known as a *kidney tubule*). During this process most of the water and many useful dissolved salts are reabsorbed into the blood, leaving concentrated urine (containing urea), which passes from the kidneys via two tubes known as *ureters* to the bladder, where it is stored before being excreted from the body. The kidneys also regulate the balance of water and salts (such as sodium, potassium, and phosphate ions) in the blood, and play a vital role in maintaining the blood pressure.

kidney bean a dark red kidney-shaped bean eaten as a vegetable.

kidney machine an apparatus used, when the kidney has failed, to remove harmful substances from the blood by dialysis.

Kiel POP (1991e) 246 000, the port capital of Schleswig-Holstein state, Germany. It is a naval base at the S end of the Kieler Förde, an arm of the Baltic Sea. It was badly bombed in World War II. NOTABLE FEATURE Schloss (13c).

Kielder Water a reservoir in Northumberland, NE England, and one of the largest artificial lakes in Europe. Built in 1974–82 by damming the North Tyne R, it is the first regional water grid system in the UK. It supplies water to the industrial NE. The planting of nearby Kielder Forest began in 1922; its area (with other Border forests) of 650sq km/ 250sq mi constitutes the largest area of planted forest in Europe.

Kieran a male first name, an Anglicized version of an Irish saint's name, *Ciaran*. [from *Ciar*, dark]

Kierkegaard, Sören (Aabye) (1813–55) Danish philosopher and theologian, one of the founders of existentialism, born in Copenhagen. He criticized purely speculative systems of thought, such as Hegel's, as irrelevant to existence-making choices, and tried to reinstate the central importance of the individual. His works include *Enten-Eller* (Either/Or, 1843), and *Afsluttende uvidenskabelig Efterskrift* (Concluding Unscientific Postscript, 1846).

kieselguhr *noun Geol.* a soft whitish powdery deposit containing silica, and consisting mainly of the remains of cell walls of diatoms. It is used as an abrasive, filler, and insulator, and as an absorbent material in dynamite. — Also called *diatomite*. [from German *Kieselguhr*, from *kiesel*, flint + *Ghur*, fermentation]

Kiesinger, Kurt Georg (1904–88) German statesman, born in Ebingen. During World War II he served at the Foreign Office on radio propaganda, then was interned until 1947. Exonerated of Nazi crimes, in 1949 he became a member of the *Bundestag*, and succeeded Erhard as Chancellor (1966–9). He was a convinced supporter of Adenauer's plans for European unity, and formed a government that combined Willy Brandt's Christian Democratic Union and the Social Democrats, until Brandt succeeded him as Chancellor.

Kiev *or* **Kiyev**, Ukrainian **Kiyiv** POP (1990e) 2.6m, the capital of Ukraine, lying on the R Dnieper. The city is a major industrial, cultural, and scientific centre. HISTORY founded in the

6c–7c, it was the earliest centre of Slavonic culture and learning; in the 9c it was capital of medieval Kievan Russia; became capital of Ukraine Soviet Socialist Republic in 1934; besieged and occupied by Germany during World War II; Ukrainean independence was declared in 1991 with Kiev as capital. NOTABLE FEATURES St Sofia Cathedral (1037); Zabrovsky Gate (1746); Monastery of the Caves (1051); fivedomed All Saints Church (17c); Vydubetsky Monastery (1070–7); Kiev Opera; Kiev Ballet.

Kiev Dam a dam built (1964) on the R Dnieper in Ukraine. At 256m high and 412km long, it is the longest dam in the world.

Kigali 1 POP (1991) 233 000, the capital of Rwanda and of Kigali prefecture. It lies 80km/50mi E of L Kivu. **2** a prefecture in Rwanda with Kigali as its capital.

Kikuyu a Bantu-speaking agricultural people of the central highlands of Kenya, the country's largest ethnic group (population c.3.5m). During the 1950s they were involved in the Mau Mau uprising against European colonialists, and after Kenya's independence (1963) they provided many of the country's political leaders.

Kildare, Gaelic **Chill Dara** POP (1991) 123 000, a county in Leinster province, E Irish Republic, SW of Dublin county. AREA 1 694sq km/ 654sq mi. PHYSICAL DESCRIPTION Kildare is watered by the Liffey and Barrow rivers and the Grand and Royal canals; the low-lying central plain is known as the Curragh. CAPITAL Naas. CHIEF TOWNS Kildare, Athy, Droichead Nua. ECONOMY farming, cattle, horse breeding. NOTABLE FEATURES national stud at Tully; racecourse at the Curragh.

Kilimanjaro, Mount a mountain on the frontier between Tanzania and Kenya. HEIGHT 5 895m. The highest point on the African continent, it is a glaciated double-peaked massif of volcanic origin, capped by the dormant cone of Kibo peak and the jagged extinct Mawenza peak. Kilimanjaro National Park is a World Heritage site.

Kilkenny, Gaelic **Chill Choinnigh** POP (1991) 74 000, a county in Leinster province, SE Irish Republic. AREA 2 062sq km/796sq mi. It is a fertile county watered by the R Nore; the Slieve Ardagh Hills rise in the W. CAPITAL Kilkenny. ECONOMY agriculture, livestock; coal.

Kilkenny, Gaelic **Cill Choinnigh** POP (1991) 18 000, the capital of Kilkenny county, Leinster, SE Irish Republic, lying on the R Nore. NOTABLE FEATURES cathedrals; town hall (Tholsel); Kilkenny Castle (18c); Bishop Rothe's House.

kill — *verb* **1** to cause the death of. **2** *colloq.* to cause pain to: *my feet are killing me.* **3** *colloq.* to cause to fail; to put an end to: *how to kill a conversation.* **4** to defeat (a parliamentary bill). **5** *colloq.* to destroy the effect of: *the turquoise kills the green.* **6** *colloq.* to deaden (pain, noise, etc). **7** to pass (time), especially aimlessly or wastefully, while waiting for some later event. **8** *colloq.*, *usually ironic* to exhaust or put a strain on: *don't kill yourself.* — *noun* **1** an act of killing. **2** the prey killed by any creature.
— **be in at the kill** *colloq.* to be present at someone's dramatic downfall, or some other kind of confrontation.
dressed to kill *facetious* captivatingly or impressively dressed.
kill someone *or* **something off** to destroy them completely, or on a large scale.
kill oneself *colloq.* to be reduced to helpless laughter.
[from Middle English *cullen* or *killen*]

Killarney, Gaelic **Cill Airne** POP (1991) 10 000, a resort town in Kerry county, Munster province, SW Irish Republic. It lies in the centre of a scenic lakeland area.

killer *noun* **1** a person who kills. **2** a substance or thing that can cause or has caused death. **3** *colloq.* a gruelling activity or task.

killer whale a toothed whale found worldwide in cool coastal waters, 9m to 10m in length, black with white underparts, and having white patches on its head, and a narrow vertical dorsal fin. It feeds on marine mammals, fish, and squid.

killifish *noun* a small colourful carp-like freshwater fish widespread in tropical and warm temperate regions, and having jaws bearing small teeth. It is a popular aquarium fish. [from dialect *kill*, stream]

killing *colloq.* — *noun* an act of slaying. — *adj.* **1** exhausting. **2** highly amusing.
— **make a killing** *colloq.* to make a large amount of money, especially unexpectedly or in a quick transaction.

killingly *adv.* overpoweringly, exhaustingly.

killjoy *noun* someone who spoils others' pleasure.

Killy, Jean Claude (1943–) French alpine skier, born in Val d'Isère. He left school at 16 to join the French ski team, and won all three alpine skiing titles (slalom, giant slalom, and downhill) at the 1968 Olympics. He was combined world champion in 1966 and 1968, and downhill champion in 1966. Winner of the inaugural World Cup overall title in 1967, he retained the title the following year, when he won 12 races. He retired after the 1968 Olympics.

Kilmarnock POP (1981) 52 000, a town in Kilmarnock and Loudoun district, Strathclyde, W Scotland. It is situated 31km/19mi SW of Glasgow. The first book of poetry by Robert Burns was published here in 1786. NOTABLE FEATURES Dick Institute Museum and Art Gallery; Burns Monument and Museum; Dean Castle (14c).

kiln *noun* an oven for baking pottery or bricks or for drying grain. [from Anglo-Saxon *cylen*, from Latin *culina*, kitchen]

kilo *noun* (PL. **kilos**) a kilogram or kilometre.

kilo- *combining form* forming words meaning 'one thousand'. [from Greek *chilioi*, thousand]

kilobyte *noun Comput.* a unit of 1 024 bytes.

kilocalorie *noun* (ABBREV. **kcal**) the amount of heat required to raise the temperature of one kilogram of water by 1°C (1K). It is often used to express the energy content of food, but has been replaced in SI units by the joule (1kcal = 4.18kJ). — Also called *calorie*, *large calorie*.

kilocycle *noun* old use a kilohertz.

kilogram *or* **kilogramme** *noun* (ABBREV. **kg**) the SI unit of mass, equal to 1 000 grams (2.2 pounds).

kilohertz *noun* (PL. **kilohertz**) a unit of frequency of sound and radio waves equal to 1000 cycles per second.

kilolitre *noun* a unit of liquid measure equal to 1000 litres.

kilometre *noun* a unit of distance equal to 1000 metres.

kiloton *or* **kilotonne** *noun* a unit of explosive force equal to that of 1000 tons of TNT.

kilowatt *noun* a unit of electrical power equal to 1000 watts.

kilowatt hour (ABBREV. **kWh**) a unit of electricity consumption, equal to the energy used when an electrical appliance with a power of one kilowatt is run for one hour.

kilt *noun* a pleated tartan knee-length skirt, traditionally worn by men as part of Scottish Highland dress. [related to Danish *kilte*, to tuck up]

kilted *adj.* wearing a kilt.

Kim a novel by Rudyard Kipling (1901). It is set mainly in India and describes the life of the Irish orphan, Kimball O'Hara.

Kimberley POP (1985) 74 000, a city in Cape province, South Africa, 450km/280mi SW of

Johannesburg. It has been a major diamond-mining centre since its foundation in 1871. The city was under siege in the Boer War (1899–1900). The Big Hole (formerly, Kimberley Mine), said to be the biggest artificial hole on Earth, is 800m deep and 500m across. NOTABLE FEATURES two cathedrals; Bantu Gallery.

Kimberley, Siege of one of the three sieges (Oct 1899–Feb 1900) in the second Boer War, in which Boer forces penned up their British opponents and secured control of vital lines of communication, until the town was relieved by General John French (later Earl of Ypres, 1852–1925).

Kimberley a first name, originally male, now more commonly female. [after Kimberley in South Africa; it was brought to public attention in the late 19c after the Boer War]

Kim Il-sung, originally **Kim Song-ju** (1912–   ) North Korean soldier and politician, born near Pyongyang. He founded the Korean People's Revolutionary Army in 1932, and led a long struggle against the Japanese. He proclaimed the Democratic People's Republic of Korea in 1948, and has since been effective head of state. (Prime Minister, 1948–72; President, 1972–   ). He was re-elected President for a fifth four-year term in 1990. His son, Kim Jong II, has been named as his eventual political successor.

kimono noun (PL. **kimonos**) **1** a long loose wide-sleeved Japanese garment fastened by a sash at the waist. **2** a dressing-gown imitating this. [from Japanese kimono, clothing]

kin — noun one's relations. — adj. related: kin to the duke.
— **next of kin** one's nearest relative. [from Anglo-Saxon cynn]

-kin suffix indicating a diminutive: catkin / lambkin. [from Old Dutch]

Kinabalu Mount, Malay **Gunong** the highest peak in SE Asia. It is situated in Sabah state, E Malaysia, in the Crocker Range. HEIGHT 4 094m. The mountain lies within the Kinabalu National Park.

kind¹ noun **1** a group, class, sort, or type. **2** nature, character, or distinguishing quality: differ in kind.
— **a kind of** ... something like a ...: a kind of magazine.
in kind 1 said of payment in goods instead of money. **2** said of repayment or retaliation in the same form as the treatment received.
kind of ... colloq. somewhat ...; slightly: kind of old-fashioned.
nothing of the kind not at all; completely the reverse.
of a kind 1 of the same sort: three of a kind. **2** derog. of doubtful worth: an explanation of a kind.
[from Anglo-Saxon gecynd, nature]

kind² adj. **1** friendly, helpful, well-meaning, generous, benevolent, or considerate. **2** warm; cordial: kind regards.
— **be so kind as to** ... or **be kind enough to** ... a polite formula of request.
[from Anglo-Saxon gecynde, natural]

kindergarten noun a school for young children, usually ones aged between four and six. [from German Kindergarten, children's garden]

kind-hearted adj. kind; generous; good-natured.

kind-heartedly adv. in a kind-hearted way.

kind-heartedness noun being kind-hearted.

Kind Hearts and Coronets a British film directed by Robert Hamer (1949). It is a black comedy about a dispossessed haberdasher (played by Dennis Price) who murders his way through an aristocratic family to attain the dukedom.

kindle verb trans., intrans. **1** to start or cause to start burning. **2** said of feelings to stir or be stirred. [related to Norse kyndill, torch]

kindliness noun **1** being kindly. **2** a kindly act.

kindling noun dry wood, leaves, etc for starting a fire.

kindly — adv. **1** in a kind manner. **2** please. adj. (**kindlier, kindliest**) kind, friendly, generous, or good-natured.
— **look kindly on someone** or **something** to approve of them.
not take kindly to something to be unwilling to put up with it.
think kindly of someone or **something** to have a good opinion of it.

kindness noun **1** being kind. **2** a kind act.

kindred — noun **1** one's relations. **2** relationship by blood. — adj. **1** related. **2** having qualities in common: kindred arts. [from Anglo-Saxon cynred]

kindred spirit someone who shares one's tastes, opinions, etc.

kine pl. noun old use cattle. [from Anglo-Saxon cyna, of cows]

kinematic adj. relating to or involving kinematics.

kinematics sing. noun Physics the branch of mechanics that deals with the motion of objects, but unlike dynamics is not concerned with the forces that act to produce such motion. [from Greek kinema, movement]

kinesics noun Psychol. the study of visual body language as communication. It is concerned with the conventional movements and gestures that convey deliberate messages, and also with the way in which facial expressions, body movements, and posture provide patterns of involuntary clues as to the emotional state of the person being observed, and the nature of social interactions. [from Greek kinesis, movement]

kinesis noun Zool. the movement of a living organism or cell in response to a simple stimulus (eg light, humidity), the rate of movement being dependent on the intensity as opposed to the direction of the stimulus.

kinetic adj. of or relating to motion. [from Greek kinetikos, from kineein, to move]

kinetically adv. in a kinetic way.

kinetic art or **kinetic sculpture** art or sculpture of which movement (produced by air currents, electricity, etc) is an essential feature.

kinetic energy Physics the energy possessed by an object because of its motion. The kinetic energy of an object of mass m moving with velocity v is equal to $\frac{1}{2}mv^2$.

kinetics sing. noun **1** Chem. the scientific study of the rates of chemical reactions. **2** Physics the branch of mechanics concerned with the relationship between moving objects, their masses, and the forces acting on them.

kinetic theory Physics a theory which attempts to account for the physical properties of matter, especially gases, in terms of the movement of the atoms or molecules of which they are composed.

King, Billie Jean, née **Moffatt** (1943–   ) US lawn tennis player, born in Long Beach, California. She won the ladies doubles title at Wimbledon in 1961 (with Karen Hantze) at her first attempt, and between 1961 and 1979 won a record 20 Wimbledon titles, including the singles in 1966–8, 1972–3, and 1975. She also won 13 US titles (including four singles in 1967, 1971–2, and 1974), four French titles (one singles in 1972), and two Australian titles (one singles in 1968).

King, Cecil (Harmsworth) (1901–87) British newspaper proprietor, nephew of the Harmsworth brothers. He joined the Daily Mirror in 1926, became Chairman of Daily Mirror Newspapers Ltd and Sunday Pictorial Newspapers Ltd (1951–63), and Chairman of International Publishing Corporation and Reed Paper Group (1963–8).

King, Martin Luther (1929–68) US black minister, born in Atlanta, Georgia. His first ministry was in Montgomery, Alabama, and he became a leader of the civil rights movement. In 1964 he received the Kennedy Peace Prize and the Nobel Peace Prize. His greatest successes came in challenging the segregation laws of the South, but after 1965 he turned his attention to social conditions in the North, which he found less tractable. He was assassinated in Memphis, Tennessee, by James Earl Ray, who was apprehended in London, and in 1969 given a 99-year sentence in Memphis.

king noun **1** a male, especially hereditary, ruler of a nation. **2** a ruler or chief. **3** a creature considered supreme in strength, fierceness, etc: the lion, king of beasts. **4** a large, or the largest, variety of something: king penguins / king prawns. **5** a leading or dominant figure in some field, eg a wealthy manufacturer or dealer: the diamond king. **6** Cards the court card bearing a picture of a king. **7** Chess the most important piece, which must be protected from checkmate. **8** Draughts a piece that, having crossed the board safely, has been crowned, and may move both forwards and backwards.
— **live like a king** colloq. to live in great luxury. [from Anglo-Saxon cyning]

King Charles spaniel a small black and tan spaniel, made popular by Charles II.

king cobra the world's largest venomous snake, up to 5.5m in length, native to India and SE Asia. It inhabits forests, especially near water, and feeds on snakes (including venomous species) and monitor lizards. The female builds a nest on the ground and coils on top to incubate the eggs. — Also called hamadryad.

King Cophetua and the Beggar Maid a painting by Sir Edward Burne-Jones (1884).

kingcup noun the marsh marigold.

kingdom noun **1** a country or organized community ruled by a king or queen. **2** Biol. the highest rank in the classification of plants and animals. Five kingdoms are now widely accepted, namely the Animalia (animals), Plantae (plants), Fungi, Protista (protozoans), and Monera (bacteria and blue-green algae). **3** the domain in which something is thought of as existing or operating: the kingdom of the imagination.
— **to kingdom come** colloq. as if into the next world: blow them all to kingdom come.
till kingdom come for ever; indefinitely: wait till kingdom come.

kingfisher noun any of a large family of brightly coloured birds with long stout bills. The common kingfisher of Europe, N Africa, and Asia has iridescent blue plumage and is often found by rivers and streams, where it catches fish with a single swooping dive, swallowing them head first and whole when it has returned to its perch. [originally king's fisher]

King James Version same as AUTHORIZED VERSION.

King Kong a US film directed by Ernest B Schoesdsack and Merian C Cooper (1933). An actress (played by Fay Wray) is abducted by island inhabitants for their gargantuan ape-god Kong, who is in turn captured by her colleagues and taken to New York.

King Lear a play by William Shakespeare (1605–6). It is a tragedy that begins with Lear's division of his kingdom between his two power-hungry daughters and his rejection of the third (the youngest and most loyal), Cordelia. The wisdom he gains from the resultant breakdown of his world comes too late. See also LEAR, KING.

kingliness noun with a kingly manner.

kingly adj. (**kinglier, kingliest**) **1** suitable for a king. **2** royal.

kingmaker noun someone who has influence over the choice of people for high office.

king of arms or **king at arms** the most senior rank in heraldry; the chief herald.

King Philip's War an attempt (1675–6) by the Native Americans of central New England to stop further white expansion, led by Metacom, King Philip, or Chief of the Wampanoags, who tried to build an inter-tribe coalition. The defeated Native Americans were killed or enslaved, but not before killing hundreds of colonists.

kingpin noun **1** the most important person in an organization, team, etc. **2** Mech. a bolt serving as a pivot.

kingpost noun Archit. a perpendicular beam in the frame of a roof rising from the tie-beam to the ridge and shaped near the base to bear a strut on either side which support the principal rafters.

King Priam an opera by Michael Tippett (1962), based on Homer's Iliad. King Priam and his wife Hecuba reluctantly order the death of their baby, Paris, because they believe a prophesy that he will cause his father's death. He is spared by the guard and is later welcomed back, but he quarrels with his brother Hector and goes travelling, only to return with Helen, wife of the Greek king Menelaus. War between Greece and Troy inevitably ensues; Hector kills Patroclus, friend of the Greek hero Achilles, and is in turn killed by Achilles, to the intense sorrow of Priam, who berates Paris and goes to Achilles' tent to ask for Hector's body. Paris kills Achilles, and is briefly reconciled with his father before Priam perishes at the hands of Achilles's son and he too is sent to his death.

Kings, Books of two books of the Hebrew Bible and Old Testament. They comprise a compilation of stories about the kings and prophets of Judah and Israel from the enthronement of Solomon to the fall of the kingdom of Israel in c.721 BC, and the final collapse of Judah and Jerusalem in c.587/6 BC. It is strongly critical of idolatry, apostasy, and religious fragmentation away from the Jerusalem Temple cult.

King's Bench see QUEEN'S BENCH.

King's Counsel see QUEEN'S COUNSEL.

King's English see QUEEN'S ENGLISH.

King's evidence see QUEEN'S EVIDENCE.

King's evil old use scrofula, ie tuberculosis of the neck glands, once believed curable by the touch of a monarch.

kingship noun the position and authority of a king; royalty.

king-size or **king-sized** adj. of a large, or larger-than-standard, size.

Kingsley, Charles (1819–75) English author, born in Holne vicarage, Dartmoor, Devon. He was ordained in 1842, and lived as curate and rector of Eversley, Hampshire. In 1860 he was appointed Professor of Modern History at Cambridge, and in 1873 Chaplain to the Queen. A 'Christian Socialist', he was involved in schemes for the improvement of working-class life, and his influential social novels include Alton Locke (1850). His best-known works include Westward Ho! (1855), Hereward the Wake (1866), and his children's book, The Water Babies (1863).

King's Lynn or **Lynn Regis** or **Lynn** or **Bishop's Lynn** POP (1981) 38 000, a port and market town in West Norfolk district, Norfolk, E England. It lies S of the Wash on the R Ouse, 63km/39mi W of Norwich. NOTABLE FEATURES Chapel of St Nicholas (1146); Guildhall of the Holy Trinity (1421); Castle Rising; royal residence of Sandringham (1867–70).

Kingston POP (1991) 644 000, the capital and commercial centre of Jamaica. It is a port situated on the SE coast. HISTORY founded in 1693; became the capital in 1870. NOTABLE FEATURES St Peter's Church (1725); Coin and Note Museum; National Gallery; Hope Botanical Gardens; Tuff

Gong International Studio built by reggae star Bob Marley.

Kingston POP (1991) 57 000, a town in SE Ontario, SE Canada, situated at the NE end of L Ontario, where it joins the St Lawrence R. HISTORY site of a former fort (Fort Frontenac); founded in 1784 by United Empire Loyalists; a Canadian naval base in the War of 1812; capital of United Canada from 1841 until 1844. NOTABLE FEATURES Royal Military College (1876); Pump House Steam Museum; Fort Henry.

Kingston-upon-Hull see HULL.

Kingstown POP (1991) 27 000, the capital and main port of St Vincent, Windward Is. It is situated on the SW coast of the island. NOTABLE FEATURES beach resorts nearby; Botanical Gardens (1763); St George's Cathedral; courthouse.

King William's War the first (1689–97) of the great wars between France and England for the control of N America. Known in Europe as the War of the League of Augsburg, it was settled by the Treaty of Ryswick (1697).

kinin noun **1** Physiol. any of a group of peptides, found in blood, that are associated with inflammation (eg as a result of insect stings), and cause contraction of smooth muscles, dilation of blood vessels, and an increase in the permeability of capillaries. **2** Bot. any of a group of plant growth substances that stimulate cell division. — Also called cytokinin. [from Greek kinesis, movement]

kink — noun **1** a bend or twist in a string, rope, wire, etc. **2** colloq. an oddness of personality; an eccentricity; a strange sexual preference. — verb trans., intrans. to develop or cause to develop a kink. [from Dutch kink]

Kinkakuji, also called **Golden Pavilion** a three-tiered gilded pavilion built in 1394 by Ashikaga Yoshimits (1358–1408) as a retirement villa in a lakeside setting in Kyoto, Japan. The present building (a temple) dates from 1955; it is a faithful reconstruction of the original which was burnt down.

kinkiness noun being kinky.

kinky adj. (**kinkier**, **kinkiest**) colloq. intriguingly odd or eccentric, especially in some sexual way.

Kinnock, Neil (Gordon) (1942–) Welsh Labour politician, born in Tredegar, Monmouthshire. He became MP for Bedwellty in 1970, joined the Labour Party's National Executive Committee (1978), and was chief Opposition spokesman on education (1979–83). In 1983 he succeeded Michael Foot as Party leader, and united the Party under moderate policies, but resigned following the 1992 election defeat.

kinnor noun a musical instrument of the ancient Hebrews: a type of lyre plucked with a plectrum or the fingers. The word is also the modern Hebrew name for the violin.

Kinsey, Alfred Charles (1894–1956) US zoologist and social scientist, born in Hoboken, New Jersey. He was Professor of Zoology at Indiana from 1920, and in 1942 was the founder Director of the Institute for Sex Research there. He is best known for his controversial studies of human sexual behaviour published in Sexual Behavior in the Human Male (1948) and Sexual Behavior in the Human Female (1953).

kinsfolk noun one's relations.

Kinshasa, formerly Belgian **Léopoldville** (to 1964) POP (1991e) 3.8m, the river-port capital of Zaire, on the Zaire R, opposite Brazzaville (Congo). HISTORY founded by the explorer Henry Stanley in 1887; became capital of the Belgian colony in 1926; US troops were stationed here during World War II.

kinship noun family relationship.
◇ In every human society, relationships between people of common descent differ from

relationships with non-kin. In primitive societies, kinship relationships may provide the primary basis for association, and the society as a whole is often conceived as a body of kin, with the family having a social, political, and ritual role to play as well as being the centre of economic life.

kinsman or **kinswoman** noun one's male or female relation.

Kintai Bridge, also called **Bridge of the Brocade Sash** a bridge built of wood, bronze, and iron at Iwakuni, Japan in 1673, famous for its five graceful arches. The present bridge is a replica of the original structure, which was swept away in 1950.

Kintyre a peninsula in Strathclyde, SW central Scotland. It is 64km/40mi long with an average width of 13km/8mi. It is bounded in the W by the North Channel and the Atlantic Ocean and in the E by the Firth of Clyde. From a narrow isthmus, it runs S to the Mull of Kintyre. CHIEF TOWN Campbeltown.

kiosk noun **1** a booth or stall for the sale of sweets, newspapers, etc. **2** a public telephone box. [from French kiosque, stand in a public park, from Turkish köşk, villa]

kip slang — noun **1** sleep or a sleep. **2** somewhere to sleep; a bed. — verb intrans. (**kipped**, **kipping**) **1** to sleep. **2** (**kip down**) to go to bed; to doss down. [originally 'brothel']

Kipling, (Joseph) Rudyard (1865–1936) British writer, born in Bombay, India. He was educated in England and returned in 1880 to India, where he worked as a journalist. He established himself in England (to which he returned in 1889) with his satirical verses and short stories, including Plain Tales from the Hills (1888) and Soldiers Three (1889). He is best known for his popular verse collections Barrack Room Ballads (1892) and The Seven Seas (1896), the two Jungle Books (1894–5), Kim (1901), and the Just So Stories (1902). He was awarded the Nobel Prize for Literature in 1907.

kipper — noun **1** a herring split open, salted, and smoked. **2** a male salmon in the spawning season. — verb (**kippered**, **kippering**) to cure (herring) by salting and smoking. [from Anglo-Saxon cypera, spawning salmon]

Kipping, Frederick Stanley (1863–1949) English chemist, born in Manchester. He worked at Imperial College, London, before becoming professor at University College in Nottingham (1897). He is best known for producing many polymeric materials which he called 'silicones', soon after recognized by others as important commercial materials.

Kirbigrip noun trademark a hair-grip. [named after Kirby, the manufacturer's name]

Kirchhoff, Gustav Robert (1824–87) German physicist, born in Königsberg (now Kaliningrad, Russia). While still a student, he devised 'Kirchhoff's laws' for electrical circuits. Professor at Breslau, Heidelberg, and Berlin, he distinguished himself in electricity, heat, optics, and especially spectrum analysis, which led to the discovery of caesium and rubidium (1859), and many important theoretical results concerning radiation.

Kirghizia, Russian **Kirgizskaya**, or **Kirgiziya** POP (1992e) 4.5m, a mountainous republic in NE Middle Asia. AREA 198 500sq km/76 621sq mi. It is bounded N by Kazakhstan, W by Uzbekistan, S and SW by Tajikistan and SE and E by China. CAPITAL Bishkek. CHIEF TOWNS Osh, Przhevalsk, Kyzyl-Kiya. Nomadic Kirgiz people comprise one third of the population; Sunni Muslim is the main religion. OFFICIAL LANGUAGE Kirgiz. CURRENCY the rouble. PHYSICAL DESCRIPTION the republic is largely occupied by the Tien Shan Mts and the highest point is at Pik Pobedy (7 439m); the chief river is the Naryn and L Issyk-Kul is the largest lake. HISTORY proclaimed a constituent republic within the USSR in 1936 and became independent in 1991. GOVERNMENT a constitution introduced in 1993 advocated respect for the international and moral principles of law and human rights and for the beliefs of Islam. ECONOMY metallurgy; machines; coal; natural gas; textiles; food processing; gold; wheat, cotton, tobacco, animal husbandry.

Kirghizia

Kiribati, formerly **Gilbert Islands**, official name **Republic of Kiribati** POP (1992e) 74 000, a group of 33 low-lying coral islands scattered over c.3m sq km/1.2m sq mi of the central Pacific Ocean. AREA 717sq km/277sq mi. It comprises the Gilbert Group, Phoenix Is, eight of the 11 Line Is, and Ocean I. CAPITAL Bairiki (on Tarawa). TIME ZONE GMT −12. The population is chiefly Micronesian; Christianity is the chief religion. LANGUAGES Gilbertese, English. CURRENCY the Australian dollar. PHYSICAL DESCRIPTION the islands seldom rise to more than 4m and usually consist of a reef enclosing a lagoon; Banaba, a solid coral outcrop with a fringing reef, rises to 87m. CLIMATE maritime equatorial climate in the central islands; the islands further N and S are tropical; the average annual temperature is 27°C; the average annual rainfall varies from 1 020mm near the Equator to 3 050mm in the extreme N and S; the rainy season is from Nov to Apr; some islands suffer from periodic drought. HISTORY the Gilbert and Ellice Is were proclaimed a British protectorate in 1892; annexed in 1915; the Ellice Is severed links with the Gilbert Is to form a separate dependency called Tuvalu in 1975; Gilbert achieved independence as Kiribati in 1979. GOVERNMENT a sovereign and democratic republic, with a President and an elected 39-member House of Assembly. ECONOMY phosphates; copra, coconuts, bananas, pandanus, breadfruit, papaya; sea fishing.

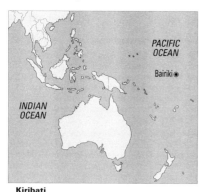

Kiribati

Kiritimati see CHRISTMAS ISLAND.

Kirk a male first name, after the surname. It has been popularized by the film actor Kirk Douglas. [from Old Norse *kirkja*]

kirk *noun* Scot. **1** a church. **2** (**the Kirk**) the Church of Scotland. [from Old Norse *kirkja*]

Kirkby POP (1981) 53 000, a town in Knowsley borough, Merseyside, NW England, situated 10km/6mi NE of Liverpool. Kirkby industrial estate lies to the E.

Kirkcaldy POP (1981) 47 000, the capital of Kirkcaldy district, Fife, E Scotland. It lies on the N shore of the Firth of Forth, 17km/11mi N of Edinburgh. The economist Adam Smith and the architect Robert Adam were born here in 1723 and 1728 respectively. NOTABLE FEATURES Kirkcaldy Museum and Art Gallery; John McDouall Stuart Museum at Dysart.

Kirkcudbright POP (1981) 3 400, the capital of Stewartry district, Dumfries and Galloway Region, S Scotland. It lies on the estuary of the R Dee. NOTABLE FEATURES MacLellan's Castle (1582); Tolbooth (16c); Stewartry Museum.

Kirkintilloch POP (1981) 33 000, a town in Strathkelvin district, Strathclyde, W central Scotland. It lies 11km/7mi NE of Glasgow, on the Forth and Clyde Canal, and is part of the Clydeside urban area. It is the site of a fort on the Antonine Wall.

kirk session the governing body of a Presbyterian congregation, consisting of the minister and elders.

Kirkwall POP (1981) 6 000, the port capital of Orkney, N Scotland. It lies on the island of Mainland, between Wide Firth to the N and Scapa Flow to the S. NOTABLE FEATURES Earl Patrick's Palace (1607); St Magnus Cathedral (1137–1200); Tankerness House (1574), now a museum of Orkney life.

Kirov, Sergey Mironovich (1886–1934) Russian revolutionary and politician, born in Urzhun. He was active in the October Revolution and Civil War, and during the 1920s held a number of leading provincial party posts. In 1934 he became a full member of the central Politburo and at the 17th Party Congress was elected a Secretary of the Central Committee. Later that year he was assassinated at his Leningrad headquarters, possibly at the instigation of Stalin, and his death was used as the pretext for a campaign of reprisals.

Kirov Ballet (Balet imeni kirova) a Russian ballet company, based at the Kirov Theatre in St Petersburg. Originally a dancing academy (founded 1735), its 20c traditions were established by choreographers such as Marius Petipa, and dancers such as Vaclav Nijinsky, Anna Pavlova, and Michel Fokine.

kirsch *noun* a clear liqueur distilled from black cherries. [from German *Kirschwasser*, cherry water]

Kisalföld, English **Little Alföld** a flat, lowland geographical region in NW Hungary. It is bounded by the R Danube, the Hungarian Alps, and the Transdanubian Central Mountain Range.

Kisangani, formerly **Stanleyville** (to 1966) POP (1991e) 374 000, the capital of Haut-Zaire region, N central Zaire. It is situated on the Zaire R, 1 250km/775mi NE of Kinshasa. The city was founded by the explorer Henry Stanley in 1882.

Kishinev POP (1991e) 677 000, the capital of Moldavia. It lies on the R Byk, in central Moldavia. The city was founded in 1420 as a monastery town. NOTABLE FEATURE Cathedral of the Nativity (1836).

Kismaayo, Italian **Chisimaio** POP (1981) 70 000, a port in Jubbada Hoose province, Somalia. It is situated on the Indian Ocean coast near the mouth of the R Juba. HISTORY founded in 1872 by the Sultan of Zanzibar; taken by British forces in 1887; subsequently became part of Jubaland which was ceded to the Italians in 1925; occupied again by the British during World War II.

kismet *noun* **1** fate. **2** one's destiny. [from Turkish *qismet*]

Kiss, The a sculpture by Auguste Rodin (1898).

kiss — *verb* **1** to touch with the lips, as a greeting or sign of affection. **2** *intrans.* to kiss each other on the lips. **3** to express by kissing: *kissed them goodbye*. **4** *poetic* to pass over with a gentle touch; to caress: *sun-kissed peaches*. — *noun* **1** an act of kissing. **2** a gentle touch.
— **kiss hands** to kiss the sovereign's hands on acceptance of high office. [from Anglo-Saxon *cyssan*]

kissable *adj.* **1** that can be kissed. **2** desirable.

kiss curl a flat curl pressed against the cheek or forehead.

kisser *noun* **1** one who kisses. **2** *slang* the mouth or face.

Kissinger, Henry A(lfred) (1923–) US academic and statesman, born in Fürth, Germany. His family emigrated to the USA in 1938 to escape the Nazi persecution of Jews during World War II. After war service he worked for a number of public agencies before he joined the Harvard faculty (1962–71). He became President Nixon's adviser on national security affairs (1969), was the main American figure in the negotiations to end the Vietnam War (for which he shared the 1973 Nobel Peace Prize), and was Secretary of State (from 1973) under Nixon and Ford. His 'shuttle diplomacy' was aimed at bringing about peace between Israel and the Arab states, and resulted in a notable improvement in Israeli-Egyptian relations. After leaving public office (1977), he became Professor of Diplomacy at Georgetown, and established Kissinger Associates, a consulting firm.

kiss of death *colloq.* something that brings failure or ruin on some enterprise; a fatal move.

kiss of life 1 in first aid, a mouth-to-mouth method of restoring the breathing. **2** a means of restoring vitality or vigour.

kissogram *or* **kissagram** *noun* **1** a greetings service by means of which one may employ someone to deliver a kiss to someone else on a special occasion. **2** the kiss or greeting thus delivered. **3** the person delivering it. [from KISS + TELEGRAM]

Kistna, River see KRISHNA, RIVER.

kit[1] — *noun* **1** a set of instruments, equipment, etc needed for a purpose, especially if kept in a container. **2** a set of special clothing and personal equipment, eg for a soldier, footballer, etc. **3** a set of parts ready for assembling. — *verb* (**kitted**, **kitting**) (*also* **kit someone out**) to provide them with the clothes and equipment necessary for a particular occupation, assignment, etc. [from Old Dutch *kitte*, tankard]

kit[2] *noun* a kitten. [shortened form]

Kita-Kyushu POP (1991e) 1m, a city in Fukuoka prefecture, N Kyushu, Japan. It comprises the former towns of Tobata, Kokura, Moji, Wakamatsu, and Yawata. The city is Japan's leading centre for chemicals and heavy industry.

Kitasato, Shibasaburo (1852–1931) Japanese bacteriologist, born in Oguni. He studied in Tokyo and Berlin, and later founded in Japan an institute for infectious diseases. He discovered the bacillus which caused bubonic plague, and isolated the bacilli of tetanus, symptomatic anthrax, and dysentery. His work on immunity led to the development of treatments and immunization for tetanus and diphtheria.

kitbag *noun* a soldier's or sailor's bag, usually cylinder-shaped, for holding kit.

Kit-cat *noun* a portrait painted on a canvas 36 × 28in (c.90 × 70cm) or, more generally, any canvas of this size. It derives from the series of life-size, half-length portraits of members of the Kit-cat dining-club, London, painted by Kneller c.1700–17 and now in the National Portrait Gallery in London.

kitchen *noun* a room where food is prepared and cooked. [from Anglo-Saxon *cycene*, from Latin *coquina*]

kitchen cabinet an informal unelected group of advisors to a political office-holder, particularly a US president. The term was first used in the mid-19c in the administration of President Jackson.

Kitchener (of Khartoum and of Broome), (Horatio) Herbert Kitchener, 1st Earl (1850–1916) British soldier and statesman, born near Ballylongford, Kerry, Ireland. He joined the Royal Engineers in 1871, and served in Palestine (1874), Cyprus (1878), and the Sudan (1883), and won back the Sudan for Egypt by the final rout of the Khalifa at Omdurman (1898). Successively Chief-of-Staff and Commander-in-Chief in South Africa (1900–2), he brought the Boer War to an end, then became Commander-in-Chief in India (1902–9), Consul-General in Egypt (1911), field marshal (1914) and Secretary for War (1914), when he organized manpower (the 'Kitchener armies') on a vast scale for World War I. He was lost with HMS *Hampshire*, mined off the Orkney Is.

kitchenette *noun* a small kitchen, or a section of a room serving as a kitchen.

kitchen garden a garden, or a section of one, in which vegetables are grown.

Kitchen-Sink *adj.* a term coined in the 1950s and used, often in a derogatory sense, to describe a style of British contemporary drama and painting which dealt with domestic themes. The banality and sordidness of the settings, and the realism with which they were portrayed, were characteristic of the work of playwrights such as John Osborne, Arnold Wesker, and Alun Owen.

pale wing patches — forked tail — pale head

red kite

kite *noun* **1** a long-tailed bird of prey of the hawk family. **2** a light frame covered in paper or some other light material, with a long holding string attached to it, for flying in the air for fun, etc.
— **fly a kite** to spread a rumour or suggestion intended to provoke reaction and so test public opinion.
high as a kite *colloq.* in an elated state brought on by drugs or alcohol.
[from Anglo-Saxon *cyta*]

Kitemark *noun* a kite-shaped mark on goods indicating that they conform to the specification of the British Standards Institution.

kith *noun* friends, as in **kith and kin**, friends and relations. [from Anglo-Saxon *cythth*, from *cunnan*, to know]

kithara *noun* a musical instrument of classical antiquity: the national instrument of the ancient Greeks. It resembled a lyre with a square wooden resonator from which two hollow arms extended upwards: these were connected by a crossbar from which up to eleven gut strings were stretched to the base of the resonator. It was held upright, supported against the body,

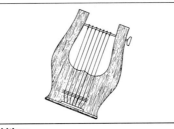

kithara

and plucked with a plectrum. [from Greek *kithara*]

kitsch *noun* sentimental or vulgar tastelessness in art, design, writing, film-making, etc. [from German *kitsch*]

kitschy *adj.* (**kitschier, kitschiest**) like kitsch; bright and gaudy.

kitten *noun* **1** a young cat. **2** the young of any of several small furry mammals, eg the rabbit.
— **have kittens** *colloq.* to become extremely agitated.

kittenish *adj.* like a kitten, playful.

kittiwake *noun* a long-winged type of seagull. [imitative of its cry]

kitty¹ *noun* (PL. **kitties**) **1** a fund contributed to jointly, for communal use by a group of people. **2** *Cards* a pool of money used in certain games.

kitty² *noun* (PL. **kitties**) an affectionate name for a cat or kitten.

Kitwe POP (1990) 338 000, the second largest town in Zambia. It is a modern mining city in Copperbelt province, 50km/31mi NW of Ndola. The city was extended in 1970 to include several townships.

Kitzbühel POP (1991) 8 000, a winter sports resort and capital of Kitzbühel district, Tirol state, central Austria. It lies in the Kitzbüheler Alps on the route to the Thurn Pass. Copper and silver were mined here in the 16c–17c.

Kivu, Lake a lake in E central Africa, the highest in the Albertine Rift. It lies on the frontier between Zaire and Rwanda. AREA 2 700sq km/1 000sq mi; length c.95km/60mi, width 50km/30mi. It drains into L Tanganyika via the Ruzizi R; Idiwi I is to the S.

Kiwanis International a worldwide civilian service club, founded in 1915 in Detroit, Michigan, for men and women to perform volunteer community service. [from a Native American term, = we make ourselves known]

kiwi *noun* **1** any of three species of nocturnal flightless bird about the size of a chicken, found only in pine forests in New Zealand, with hair-like body feathers, no tail, vestigial wings, short stout legs, and a long slender bill with slit-like nostrils at its tip. **2** *colloq.* a New Zealander. [from Maori]

kiwi

kiwi fruit an oval edible fruit with pale green juicy flesh, rich in vitamin C, enclosed by a brown hairy skin, produced by a climbing plant (*Actinidia chinensis*) native to China, and so called because the fruit is exported to Europe and the USA from New Zealand.

Kizil Irmak, ancient **Halys** the longest river in Turkey, length 1 355km/842mi. Rising in the Kizil Dağ, N central Turkey, it flows in a wide arc

SW, then generally N to enter the Black Sea N of Bafra. It is an important source of hydroelectric power. [from Turkish *Kizil Irmak*, red river]

kJ *abbrev.* kilojoule.

Kjölen Mountains *or* **Kolen Mountains** a mountain range along the boundary between NE Norway and NW Sweden. It rises to 2 111m at Kebnekaise, Sweden's highest peak, and is the source of many rivers flowing SE to the Gulf of Bothnia.

KKK *abbrev.* Ku-Klux Klan.

kl *abbrev.* kilolitre.

Klammer, Franz (1953–) Austrian alpine skier, born in Mooswald. He was the Olympic downhill champion in 1976, and the World Cup downhill champion five times (1975–8, 1983). In 1974–84 he won a record 25 World Cup downhill races.

Klaproth, Martin Heinrich (1743–1817) German analytical chemist, born in Wernigerode. From 1792 he held various lectureships, becoming Germany's leading chemist and the first Professor of Chemistry at Berlin University. He devised important new analytical methods, discovered zirconium and uranium, and named tellurium.

klaxon *noun* a loud horn used as a warning signal on ambulances, fire engines, etc. [originally a tradename]

Klee, Paul (1879–1940) Swiss artist, born in Münchenbuchsee, near Bern. He settled in Munich and became a member of the Blaue Reiter group (1911–12). He then taught at the Bauhaus (1920–32), but after he returned to Bern (1933) many of his works were confiscated by the Nazis, as degenerate. His early work consists of bright watercolours, but after 1919 he worked in oils, producing small-scale, mainly abstract pictures (eg *Twittering Machine*, New York).

Klein, Calvin (Richard) (1942–) US fashion designer, born in New York City. He graduated from the Fashion Institute of Technology in 1962, and set up his own firm (Calvin Klein Ltd) in 1968. He quickly achieved recognition, becoming known for understatement, and for the simple but sophisticated style of his clothes, including 'designer jeans'.

Klein, (Christian) Felix (1849–1925) German mathematician, born in Düsseldorf. Professor at Göttingen (1886–1913), he did much to make the university a world centre for mathematics. His 'Erlanger Programm', which was published in 1872, showed how different geometries could be classified in terms of group theory. His subsequent work on geometry included studies of non-Euclidean geometry and function theory.

Klein, Melanie (1882–1960) British psychoanalyst, born in Vienna. Educated in Berlin before moving to London, she pioneered the now widely used techniques of 'play therapy', and was the first to apply psychoanalysis to small children, developing the controversial view that neuroses are fixed in the earliest months of life.

Klemperer, Otto (1885–1973) German conductor, born in Breslau. He first appeared as a conductor in 1906, became known as a champion of modern music, and was appointed director of the Kroll Opera in Berlin (1927–31). Nazism drove him to the USA, where he directed the Los Angeles Symphony Orchestra (1933–9). He was also musical director of Budapest Opera (1947–50). In his later years he concentrated mainly on the German classical composers, and was renowned for his interpretation of Beethoven. He also composed six symphonies, a mass, and lieder.

kleptomania *noun* Psychol. an irresistible urge to steal, especially objects that are not desired for themselves, and are of little monetary value. It is sometimes associated with depression or stress. [from Greek *kleptein*, to steal + -MANIA]

kleptomaniac — *noun* a person suffering from kleptomania. — *adj.* relating to or affected by kleptomania.

Klimt, Gustav (1862 1918) Austrian painter, born in Baumgarten, Vienna. A prominent member of the Vienna Sezession, he was influenced by Impressionism, Symbolism, and Art Nouveau. He painted murals for the University of Vienna (1900–3) which were considered pornographic and aroused official condemnation. His portraits, mainly of women, combine realistically-painted figures with elaborate and decorative backgrounds.

Klinger, Friedrich Maximilian von (1752–1831) German playwright and romance writer, born in Frankfurt am Main. He became an actor, joined the Russian army and rose to the rank of general, held various government posts, and became curator of the University of Dorpat (1803–17). The 'Sturm-und-Drang' school was named after his tragedy *Der Wirrwarr, oder Sturm und Drang* (1776).

klipspringer *noun* a dwarf antelope, native to Africa south of the Sahara, and having a thick yellowish-grey speckled coat, short vertical horns, rounded ears with dark radiating lines, and black feet. It stands on the points of its small peg-like hooves, and inhabits rocky outcrops in scrubland. [from Dutch *klip*, rock + *springer*, jumper]

Klitzing, Klaus von see VON KLITZING.

KLM *abbrev. Koninklijke Luchtvaart Maatschappij* (Dutch) Royal Dutch Airlines.

Klopstock, Friedrich Gottlieb (1724–1803) German poet, born in Quedlinburg. Inspired by Virgil and Milton, he began his religious epic, *Der Messias* (The Messiah), as a student at Jena in 1745, and completed it in 1773. He is also remembered for his odes (collected in *Oden*, 1771) and lyrics.

Klosters an alpine winter skiing resort in Graubünden canton, E Switzerland. It lies on the R Landquart, NE of Davos resort town, with which it shares snowfields. The resort comprises the villages of Platz, Dörfli, and Brücke; there is also a children's ski school. Kloster Pass (12km/7mi E) leads to Austria.

Kluane a national park in SW Yukon Territory, NW Canada, established in 1972. It contains part of the St Elias Mts, rising to 5 950m at Mt Logan. Along with the Wrangell–St Elias Park, the area forms the world's largest nature reserve, lying on both sides of the US–Canadian border. Both parks are World Heritage sites. AREA 22 015sq km/8 498sq mi.

KM *abbrev.* Knight of Malta.

km *abbrev.* kilometre.

kn *abbrev. Naut.* knot.

knack *noun* 1 the ability to do something effectively and skilfully: *has a knack of tying knots*. 2 a habit or tendency. [probably related to *knack*, sharp blow or sound]

knacker — *noun* a buyer of worn-out old horses for slaughter. — *verb* (**knackered, knackering**) *colloq.* to exhaust.

knapsack *noun* a hiker's or traveller's canvas bag for food, clothes, etc, carried on the back or over the shoulder. [from Old German *knappen*, eat + *sack*, bag]

knapweed *noun* a plant of the daisy family, with purple thistle-like flowers. [from Middle English *knopwed*]

knave *noun old use* 1 *Cards* the jack. 2 a mischievous young man; a scoundrel. [from Anglo-Saxon *cnafa*]

Knave of Diamonds an avant-garde association of artists founded in Moscow in 1910. It was also responsible for staging numerous exhibitions (until 1918).

knavery *noun* (PL. **knaveries**) mischief; trickery.

knavish *adj. old use* rascally.

knavishly *adv. old use* in a knavish way.

knead *verb* 1 to work (dough) with one's fingers and knuckles. 2 to massage (flesh) with firm finger movements. [from Anglo-Saxon *cnedan*]

knee — *noun* 1 the joint between the femur (thigh bone) and the tibia (shin bone). It is protected by the patella (knee-cap). 2 the upper surface of a sitting person's thigh; the lap: *sat with the child on her knee*. 3 the part of a garment covering the knee. — *verb* (**kneed**) to strike or nudge with the knee.
— **at one's mother's knee** as a small child.
bring someone to his or **her knees** to defeat, prostrate or ruin someone utterly.
go weak at the knees *colloq.* to be overcome by emotion.
on one's knees 1 kneeling. 2 exhausted; prostrated.
[from Anglo-Saxon *cneow*]

knee-breeches *pl. noun* knee-length breeches.

kneecap — *noun* a triangular plate of bone covering the front of the knee joint. — *verb* (**kneecapped, kneecapping**) to shoot or otherwise damage the kneecaps of (a person) as a form of revenge or unofficial punishment.

kneecapping *noun* being kneecapped.

knee-deep *adj., adv.* up to the knees.

knee-high *adj.* tall enough to reach the knees: *knee-high grass*.

knee-jerk — *noun* an involuntary kick of the lower leg, a reflex response to a tap on the tendon below the knee. — *adj., said of a response or reaction* automatic; unthinking.

kneel *verb intrans.* (PAST TENSE **knelt**; PAST PARTICIPLE **kneeled**) (*also* **kneel down**) to support one's weight on, or lower oneself on to, one's knees. [from Anglo-Saxon *cneowlian*]

knee-length *adj.* coming down, or up, as far as the knees.

kneeler *noun* a cushion for kneeling on, especially in church.

knees-up *noun colloq.* a party or dance.

knell — *noun* 1 the tolling of a bell announcing a death or funeral. 2 something that signals the end of anything. — *verb* to announce or summon by or as if by tolling. [from Anglo-Saxon *cnyll*]

knelt see KNEEL.

Knesset the 120-member Israeli parliament, which has a four-year term of office, and which elects the country's president for five years.

knew see KNOW.

knickerbockers *pl. noun* baggy trousers tied just below the knee or at the ankle. [named after Diedrich *Knickerbocker*, the supposed author of Washington Irving's *History of New York*, 1809]

knickers *pl. noun* an undergarment for women and girls, covering the lower abdomen and buttocks, with separate legs or leg holes. [short for KNICKERBOCKERS]

knick-knack *noun* a little trinket or ornament. [from KNACK, with the old meaning 'toy']

knife — *noun* (PL. **knives**) a cutting instrument or weapon, typically in the form of a blade fitted into a handle. — *verb* to stab or kill with a knife.
— **have one's knife into someone** *colloq.* to be constantly spiteful to them.
the knives are out *colloq.* the argument has taken a savage turn.
twist the knife in the wound to deliberately increase someone's distress or embarrassment by constant reminders of the circumstances that caused it.
under the knife *colloq.* having a surgical operation.

[from Anglo-Saxon *cnif*]

knife-edge *noun* the cutting edge of a knife.
— **on a knife-edge** in a state of extreme uncertainty.

knife pleat a flat narrow pleat.

Knight, Dame Laura, *née* **Johnson** (1877–1970) English artist, born in Long Eaton, Derbyshire. She studied in Nottingham and married her fellow student, portrait painter Harold Knight (1874–1961). She produced a series of oil paintings of the ballet, the circus, and gipsy life, and also executed a number of watercolour landscapes.

Knight, the the apparent paragon of chivalric virtue who begins the story-telling in Chaucer's *The Canterbury Tales* with the tale of Palamon and Arcite.

knight — *noun* 1 *Hist.* a man-at-arms of high social standing, usually mounted, serving a feudal lord. 2 *Hist.* the armed champion of a lady, devoted to her service. 3 a man who has been awarded the highest or second highest class of distinction in any of the four British orders of chivalry, ie honours for service or merit awarded by the Queen or the Government. See also DAME. 4 *Chess* a piece shaped like a horse's head. — *verb* to confer a knighthood on. [from Anglo-Saxon *cniht*, boy, servant, warrior]

knight errant (PL. **knights errant**) *Hist.* a knight travelling about in search of opportunities for daring and chivalrous deeds.

knighthood *noun* the rank of a knight, just below that of a baronet, conferring the title 'Sir'.

Knightly, Mr George the perceptive and sensible landowning bachelor who marries Emma in Jane Austen's *Emma*.

knightly *adj.* (**knightlier, knightliest**) relating to or suitable for a knight.

knit *verb* (**knitting**; PAST TENSE AND PAST PARTICIPLE **knitted**, *old use* **knit**) 1 *trans., intrans.* to produce a fabric composed of interlocking loops of yarn, using a pair of knitting-needles or a machine; to make (garments, etc) by this means. 2 to make (a stitch) in plain knitting. 3 to unite: *a close-knit family* / *a loosely-knit alliance*. 4 *trans., intrans. said of broken bones* to grow or cause them to grow together again. 5 to draw (one's brows) together in a frown. 6 *poetic* to intertwine. [from Anglo-Saxon *cnyttan*, to tie]

knitter *noun* a person who knits (by hand or machine).

knitting *noun* knitted work or the art of producing it.

knitting-needle *noun* an implement like a long stout pin, made of wood, plastic or metal.

knitwear *noun* knitted garments.

knives see KNIFE.

knob *noun* 1 a hard rounded projection. 2 a handle, especially rounded, on a door or drawer. 3 a button on mechanical or electrical equipment, pressed or rotated to operate it. 4 a small roundish lump: *a knob of butter*. [from Old German *knobbe*, knot in wood]

knobbly *adj.* (**knobblier, knobbliest**) covered with knobs. [from KNOB]

knobby *adj.* (**knobbier, knobbiest**) having or full of knobs.

knock — *verb* 1 *intrans.* to tap or rap with the knuckles or some object. 2 (**knock something down, over**, *etc*) to strike and so push it, especially accidentally. 3 to put into a certain condition by hitting: *knocked him senseless*. 4 to make by striking. 5 *trans., intrans.* (**knock against** or **into something** *or* **someone**) to strike, bump, or bang against them. 6 *colloq.* to find fault with or criticize, especially unfairly. 7 *intrans. Engineering, said of an internal combustion engine* to make a metallic knocking sound caused by the explosion of an unburned mixture of fuel vapour and air before it is ignited by the spark. Knocking can be prevented by using petrol that contains lead additives, but the use of unleaded petrol is becoming increasingly widespread in an attempt to reduce environmental pollution. See also PINK[3]. — *noun* **1** an act of knocking. **2** a tap or rap. **3** *colloq.* a personal misfortune, blow, setback, calamity, etc. **4** a metallic knocking sound caused by the explosion of an unburned mixture of fuel vapour and air before it is ignited by the spark.

— **knock about** *or* **around** *colloq.* **1** *said of a person* to wander about casually or aimlessly; to be idle. **2** *said of a thing* to lie about unused or not needed.

knock someone about *or* **around** to treat them roughly; to hit or batter them.

knock about with someone *colloq.* to associate or go about with them.

knock something back *colloq.* to eat or drink it rapidly and with relish.

knock someone back 1 to cost them a specified amount: *knocked them back twenty pounds.* **2** to surprise, dismay, or disappoint them.

knock someone down to strike them to the ground.

knock something down 1 to demolish a building, etc. **2** *colloq.* to reduce a price.

knock something down to someone *colloq.* to sell them goods at an auction.

knocking on ... *colloq.* nearly ..., especially with reference to a person's age: *must be knocking on 60 by now.*

knock something into someone *colloq.* to teach it to them vigorously: *has had some sense knocked into him.*

knock off *colloq.* to stop working.

knock off doing something *colloq.* to stop doing it.

knock someone off *colloq.* to kill them.

knock something off *colloq.* **1** to produce it quickly or in large quantities. **2** to deduct it from a price or charge: *knocked £15 off.* **3** to steal it.

knock on *Rugby* to commit the foul of sending the ball forward with the hand.

knock something on the head *colloq.* to put an end to it.

knock someone out 1 to hit them unconscious; in boxing, to hit an opponent so as to be incapable of rising in the required time. **2** to defeat an opponent in a knockout competition. **3** *colloq.* to amaze them; to impress them hugely.

knock something out *colloq.* to cause it to stop functioning.

knock someone sideways *colloq.* to come as a severe shock to them.

knock something together *colloq.* to assemble it hurriedly.

knock up *Tennis* to exchange practice shots with one's opponent before a match.

knock someone up 1 *colloq.* to wake or disturb them suddenly, especially by loud knocking. **2** *colloq.* to exhaust them. **3** *North Amer. coarse slang* to make someone pregnant.

knock something up *colloq.* to assemble it hurriedly.

[from Anglo-Saxon *cnucian*]

knockabout *adj.*, *said of comedy, etc* boisterous; slapstick.

knockdown *adj. colloq.* **1** low; cheap: *knockdown prices.* **2** *said of furniture* able to be taken to pieces easily. **3** *said of an argument* overwhelmingly strong.

knocker *noun* **1** (*also* **door knocker**) a heavy piece of metal, usually of a decorative shape, fixed to a door by a hinge and used for knocking. **2** (**knockers**) *coarse slang* a woman's breasts.

knocking-shop *noun slang* a brothel.

knock-kneed *adj.* having knock knees.

knock knees *noun* a condition of the legs in which the knees are close together but the feet splayed out.

knock-on *noun Rugby* the foul of sending the ball forward with the hand.

knock-on effect *noun* a secondary or indirect effect of some action, etc.

knockout *noun* **1** *colloq.* someone or something stunning. **2** a competition in which the defeated competitors are dropped after each round. **3** *Boxing* the act of knocking out.

knoll *noun* a small round hill. [from Anglo-Saxon *cnoll*]

Knossos an Aegean Bronze Age town at Kephala, Crete, which was noted for the sophistication of its art and architecture. It flourished c.1900 BC–1400 BC, and was dominated by the Minoan palace discovered in 1899, and later partly reconstructed by Sir Arthur Evans. It is associated in legend with Minos, the labyrinth of Theseus, and the Minotaur.

Snake goddess, Knossos

knot — *noun* **1** a join or tie in string, etc made by looping the ends around each other and pulling tight. **2** a bond or uniting link. **3** a coil or bun in the hair. **4** a decoratively tied ribbon, etc. **5** a tangle in hair, string, etc. **6** a difficulty or complexity. **7** a hard mass in a tree trunk where a branch has grown out from it; the resultant cross-grained patch in timber. **8** a small gathering or cluster of people, etc. **9** a unit of speed at sea, a nautical mile (1·85km) an hour. **10** a tight feeling, eg in the belly, caused by nervousness. — *verb* (**knotted**, **knotting**) **1** to tie in a knot. **2** *trans., intrans.* to tangle. **3** *intrans.* to become tight with nervousness, etc.

— **at a rate of knots** *colloq.* very fast.

get knotted *offensive slang* an expression of disagreement, refusal, or dismissiveness. — **tie someone in knots** to confuse or perplex them.

tie the knot *colloq.* to get married.

[from Anglo-Saxon *cnotta*]

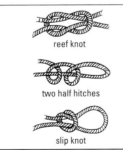

reef knot

two half hitches

slip knot

knots

Knot Garden, The an opera by Michael Tippett (1970). It tells of a meeting, overlooked by the analyst, Mangus, of six unfulfilled people in a walled garden: Thea who enjoys gardening as release from her husband Faber; their ward Flora and the homosexual Dov, both of whom Faber finds attractive; Dov's black lover Mel; and the campaigner Denise, sister of Thea.

knotgrass *or* **knotweed** *noun* an annual plant (*Polygonum aviculare*), widespread throughout most of Europe, that usually forms low mats up to 100cm across. It has slender branched

stems bearing small narrow leaves, and tiny white or pink flowers are borne in the angles between the leaf stalks and the stem. It grows in waste areas, on seashores, and on disturbed soil.

knothole *noun* a hole left in a piece of wood where a knot has fallen out.

knotty *adj.* (**knottier**, **knottiest**) **1** full of knots. **2** *said of a problem, etc* difficult, complex or intricate.

know *verb* (PAST TENSE **knew**; PAST PARTICIPLE **known**) **1** *trans., intrans.* (**know something** *or* **know of** *or* **about something**) to be aware of it; to be certain about it. **2** to have learnt and remember. **3** to have an understanding or grasp of. **4** to be familiar with: *know her well.* **5** to be able to recognize or identify. **6** to be able to distinguish or tell apart: *wouldn't know him from Adam.* **7** *intrans.* to have enough experience or training: *knew not to question him further.* **8** to think of (someone or something) in a certain way: *knew him as a kindly man.* **9** to experience or be subject to: *know poverty / happiness knew no bounds.* **10** *old use* to have sexual intercourse with.

— **be known as** ... be called ...; have ... as one's name.

Heaven *or* **God knows** *colloq.* a formula admitting ignorance.

in the know *colloq.* having information not known to most.

know a thing or two *colloq.* to be pretty shrewd.

know something backwards *colloq.* to know it thoroughly.

know what's what to be shrewd, wise, or hard to deceive.

let it be known to reveal, especially indirectly.

make oneself known to introduce oneself.

there's no knowing it's impossible to predict.

what do you know? *colloq.* an expression of surprise.

you never know *colloq.* it's not impossible.

[from Anglo-Saxon *cnawan*]

knowable *adj.* that can be known.

know-all *noun derog.* a person who seems, or claims, to know more than others.

know-how *noun colloq.* skill; ability; adroitness.

knowing *adj.* **1** shrewd; canny; clever. **2** *said of a glance, etc* signifying secret awareness.

knowingly *adv.* **1** in a knowing manner. **2** on purpose; deliberately.

knowingness *noun* being knowing, cunning.

knowledge *noun* **1** the fact of knowing; awareness; understanding. **2** what one knows; the information one has acquired through learning or experience. **3** learning; the sciences: *a branch of knowledge.*

— **to the best of one's knowledge** as far as one knows.

[from Middle English *knouleche*]

knowledgeable *adj.* well-informed.

knowledgeably *adv.* in a knowledgeable way.

known see KNOW.

Knox, John (c.1513–72) Scottish Protestant reformer, born near Haddington, Lothian. As a Catholic priest he was notary in Haddington (1540–3), until in 1544 he was influenced by George Wishart to work for the Lutheran Reformation. After Wishart was burned (1546), Knox joined the Reformers defending the castle of St Andrews, and became a minister. When the castle fell to the French, he was imprisoned until 1549, then became a chaplain to Edward VI, and contributed to the Second Book of Common Prayer. On Mary I's accession (1553), he fled to Dieppe, and then to Geneva, where he was much influenced by Calvin. He returned to Scotland in 1555 to preach, and then again in 1559, where he gathered a strong party in favour of reform, and founded the Church of Scotland (1560). He played a major part in the composition of *The Scots Confession*, *The First Book of Discipline*, and *The Book of Common Order*.

knuckle *noun* **1** a joint of a finger, especially the one at its base. **2** the knee or ankle joint of an animal, especially with the surrounding flesh, as food.

— **knuckle down to something** to begin to work hard at it.

knuckle under *colloq.* to submit, yield, or give way.

near the knuckle *colloq.* bordering on the indecent or obscene.

[from Middle English *knokel*]

knuckle-duster *noun* a set of metal links or other metal device worn over the knuckles as a weapon.

KO *colloq.* — *noun* a knockout. — *verb* (**KO's**, **KO'd**, **KO'ing**) to knock out. [abbreviation]

koala *noun* (*also* **koala bear**) a nocturnal marsupial found only in Australia and resembling a very small bear, with thick grey fur, whitish underparts, no tail, large ears, and a black nose. It feeds exclusively on the shoots of a few species of eucalyptus tree, and has been hunted for fur and food to the extent that it is now considered to be an endangered species. [from Aboriginal *koolah*]

Kobe POP (1991e) 1.5m, the port capital of Hyogo prefecture, central Honshu, Japan, situated W of Osaka. It is Japan's leading commercial port. The town is gradually expanding due to land reclamation on the seaward side of the city. NOTABLE FEATURES the Harbour and Naval Museum; Museum of Namban Art; Minatogawa Shrine.

Koblenz see COBLENZ.

Koch, Ed(ward) (1924–) US politician, born in New York City. He practised law and became a member of the City Council (1967). Elected to Congress as a Democrat in 1969, he became Mayor of New York in 1978, and in the 1980s was a widely known political figure in the USA.

Koch, (Heinrich Hermann) Robert (1843–1910) German physician and pioneer bacteriologist, born in Klausthal. He practised medicine at Hanover and elsewhere, and discovered the bacillus that causes tuberculosis (1882); the drug he produced to prevent the development of tuberculosis was found to be ineffective as a cure, but later proved useful in diagnosis. In 1883 he led an expedition to Egypt and India where he discovered the cholera bacillus. He became professor at Berlin and Director of the Institute of Hygiene in 1885, and first Director of the Berlin Institute for Infectious Diseases in 1891. He was awarded the 1905 Nobel Prize for Physiology or Medicine.

Köchel, Ludwig Ritter von (1800–77) Austrian musicologist, born in Stein. A botanist by training, he compiled the catalogue of Mozart's works, which he arranged in chronological order, giving them the 'K' numbers now commonly used to identify them.

Kodály, Zoltán (1882–1967) Hungarian composer, born in Kecskemét. He studied at the Budapest Conservatory, where he became professor. Among his best-known works are the *Háry Jnos* suite (1926) and several choral compositions, especially his *Psalmus Hungaricus* (1923) and *Te Deum* (1936). He also published editions of folk songs with Bartók, carried out important reforms in musical education, and developed an evolutionary system of training and sight-singing.

Kodiak Island POP (1990) 16 000, an island in the Gulf of Alaska, USA, 160km/100mi long. It constitutes the northernmost section of the Coast Range Mts. HISTORY scene of the first settlement in Alaska (by the Russians in 1784); until 1804 the centre for Russian interests in the USA. ECONOMY dairying; cattle and sheep raising; fur

trapping; fishing; farming. The island is the home of the Kodiak brown bear (grizzly), the largest living carnivore.

Koechlin-Smythe, Pat(ricia Rosemary) (1928–) British show jumper, born in Switzerland. She was a member of the British show jumping team from 1947 to 1964. She won the European championship four times on Flanagan (1957, 1961–3), and in 1956 was the first woman to ride in the Olympic Games, winning a bronze medal in the team event. Her numerous wins include the Queen Elizabeth II Cup on *Mr Pollard* in 1958.

Koestler, Arthur (1905–83) Hungarian-born British writer and journalist, born in Budapest. His major work is the political novel *Darkness at Noon* (1940), and his non-fiction books and essays include works on politics, scientific creativity, and parapsychology, notably *The Act of Creation* (1964). He and his wife were active members of the Voluntary Euthanasia Society and after he developed a terminal illness they committed suicide.

Kofun the burial-mounds characteristic of early historic Japan, which have given their name to the archaeological period c.300–700 AD. The biggest measure over 400m in length. Large hollow clay *haniwa* models of heavily armed warriors were often placed on top or inside.

Kohl, Helmut (1930–) German politician, born in Ludwigshafen am Rhein. He became a lawyer, joined the Christian Democrats, became Leader of the Opposition, and his Party's candidate for the Chancellorship. After the collapse of the Schmidt coalition in 1982, Kohl was installed as interim Chancellor, and in the elections of 1983 he formed a government which has since adopted a central course between political extremes. He played a decisive part in the integration of the former East Germany into the Federal Republic.

kohl *noun* an oriental cosmetic in the form of a powder, used to darken the eyelids. [from Arabic *koh'l*]

kohlrabi *noun* a kind of cabbage whose thick turnip-like stem is eaten as a vegetable. [from Italian *cavolrape*, cabbage turnip]

kola see COLA.

Kola Peninsula, Russian **Kol'skiy Poluostrov** a peninsula in NW Russia. It forms the NE extension of Scandinavia and separates the Barents Sea in the N from the White Sea in the S; length, 400km/250ml; width, 240km/150mi. There are numerous rivers and small lakes. The NE is tundra-covered and the SW is forested but the forests have been affected by pollution from the processing of the peninsula's rich mineral deposits.

Kolchak, Alexander Vasilevich (1870–1920) Russian admiral and leader of counter-revolutionary (White) forces during the Russian Civil War, born in the Crimea. He fought in the Russo-Japanese War (1904–5), and in 1916 became Commander of the Black Sea fleet. After the 1917 Revolution he established an anti-Bolshevik government in Siberia, and proclaimed himself 'Supreme Ruler' of Russia. He was killed by Red Army forces in Irkutsk.

Koldewey, Robert (1855–1925) German archaeologist, born in Blankenburg am Harz, Brunswick. He excavated several sites in Asia Minor and Turkey, including Baalbek in E Lebanon. His major work was his excavations of the remains of the city of Babylon (1899–1917), where his discoveries included the Processional Street, the Ishtar Gate, and the site of the Tower of Babel.

Kolding POP (1992e) 58 000, a seaport on the inlet of the Little Belt, Vejle county, SE Jutland, Denmark. It was founded in the 10c. NOTABLE FEATURE the oldest stone church in Denmark (13c).

Kolekole see HALEAKALA CRATER.

Kolen Mountains see KJÖLEN MOUNTAINS.

kolkhoz *noun* a large-scale collective farm in the former Soviet Union. [from Russian]

Kolmogorov, Andrei Nikolaevich (1903–87) Russian mathematician, born in Tambov. Professor at Moscow State University from 1931, he worked on a wide range of topics in applied and pure mathematics, and is particularly remembered for his work on probability theory. The partial differential equations which bear his name found wide application in physics and chemistry.

Köln see COLOGNE.

Kolyma a gold-producing area around the valley of the R Kolyma, used in Stalin's time as a forced labour camp, where about four million people died.

Kolyma, River a river in E Russia, length 2 513km/1 562mi. Rising in the SE Cherskogo Range, N of the Sea of Okhotsk, it flows generally N and NE to enter the E Siberian Sea, forming a delta W of Ambarchik. Swamps and small lakes are numerous in the lower floodplain of the river; its upper course crosses the rich Kolyma gold fields.

Komodo a small island in Nusa Tenggara Timur province, Indonesia. It is part of the Lesser Sunda Is. A national park was established in 1980. The island is the home of the Komodo dragon, the world's largest lizard.

Komodo dragon *or* **Komodo lizard** a rare SE Asian monitor lizard, native to the islands of Komodo, Flores, Pintja and Padar (Indonesia). It is the world's largest lizard, up to 3m in length, and it climbs and swims well. It inhabits grassland, often kills pigs and deer, and is capable of killing an adult water buffalo. It occasionally attacks and kills people.

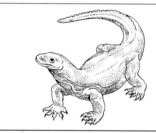

Komodo dragon

Kompong Saom see SIHANOUKVILLE.

Kompong Som see SIHANOUKVILLE.

Komsomol the Russian name for the Soviet All-Union Leninist Communist League of Youth, founded (1918) for all people aged 14 to 28 – a recruiting ground for Communist Party membership.

Konev, Ivan Stepanovich (1897–1973) Soviet military commander and Marshal of the Soviet Union (1944), born in Lodeyno. He was drafted into the Tsarist army in 1916, and joined the Red Army in 1918. During World War II he commanded several different fronts against the Germans, and then became Commander-in-Chief, Ground Forces (1946–50), first Deputy Minister of Defence, and Commander-in-Chief of the Warsaw Pact forces (1956–60).

Kongo, Kingdom of an African kingdom situated to the south of the R Congo which by the 15c had a coastline of 250km/150ml, reached inland for 400km/250ml, and traded in ivory, copper, and slaves. When the Portuguese arrived in the area (1482), some of its kings accepted Christianity, but it was disrupted by the growth of the slave trade, and declined during the 18c when the Portuguese turned their attention southwards to Angola.

Konstanz see CONSTANCE.

Kon Tiki a balsa wood raft built in 1947 by Thor Heyerdahl. He and five others sailed 6 000km/3 800mi from S America to Polynesia in the 13.7m long raft to prove his theories on the migration of early man. The vessel is now preserved in an Oslo museum.

Konya, ancient **Iconium** POP (1990) 1m, a holy city and the capital of Konya province, S central Turkey, 260km/162mi S of Ankara. It is the trade centre of a rich agricultural and livestock-raising region and has notable Seljuk architecture. HISTORY visited by St Paul; order of the Whirling Dervishes was founded here by the Islamic mystical poet, Mevlana. NOTABLE FEATURE Mevlana Mausoleum.

kook *noun North Amer. colloq.* a crazy or eccentric person. [perhaps from CUCKOO]

kookaburra *noun* either of two species of large bird of the kingfisher family, found in Australia and New Guinea in open forests, especially gum trees, and more recently in parks and gardens. It feeds on large insects, crabs, fish, birds, and even snakes, and is known for its chuckling cry. — Also called *laughing jackass*. [from Aboriginal *gugubarra*]

kooky *or* **kookie** *adj.* (**kookier, kookiest**) *North Amer., esp. US* crazy, eccentric, foolish.

kopeck *or* **kopek** *noun* a coin or unit of currency of the former Soviet Union worth a hundredth of a rouble. [from Russian *kopeika*]

Koran *noun* the holy book of Islam, believed by Muslims to be composed of the revelations of Allah to Muhammad. [from Arabic *qur'an*, book]

Koranic *adj.* relating to the Koran.

Korda, Sir Alexander, originally **Sándor Laszlo Kellner** (1893–1956) Hungarian-born British film producer, born in Pusztatúrpáztó. He was a film producer in Budapest, Vienna, Berlin, and Hollywood, where he directed for First National, before moving to the UK, where he founded the London Film Productions and Denham studios (1932). His many films as producer include *The Private Life of Henry VIII* (1932), which he also directed, *The Thief of Baghdad* (1940), *The Third Man* (1949), and *Richard III* (1956).

Kordestan see KURDISTAN.

kore *noun* (PL. **korai**) *Art* a term conventionally applied by art historians to the draped, standing, female figure commonly represented by Greek sculptors working in the Archaic style. See also KOUROS. [from Greek *kore*, maiden]

Korea POP (1992e) 22.6m, see NORTH KOREA, SOUTH KOREA.

Korean — *noun* **1** a native or citizen of N or S Korea. **2** a language spoken by some 50–60 million people in North and South Korea (where it is the official language), and parts of China, Japan, and the former USSR. The language is of uncertain origin and may have developed independently, though it shows some resemblances to the Altaic family and to Japanese. — *adj.* relating to Korea or its people or language.

Korean War a war (1950–3) between communist and non-communist forces in Korea, which had been partitioned along the border of the 38th parallel (the latitude line of 38°N) in 1945 after the defeat of Japan. The communist North invaded the South in 1950 after a series of border clashes, and a UN force intervened. China then entered the war, and together with the N Koreans occupied Seoul. The UN forces counterattacked, and by 1953, when an armistice was signed, had retaken all territory south of the 38th parallel.

Kórinthos see CORINTH.

Kornberg, Arthur (1918–   ) US biochemist, born in New York City. Working at Washington University, he discovered DNA polymerase, the enzyme that synthesizes new DNA from a mixture of the triphosphate bases and a DNA template; for this work he shared the 1959 Nobel Prize for Physiology or Medicine with Severo Ochoa. As professor at Stanford University from 1959, he became the first to synthesize viral DNA (1967).

Korolyov, Sergei Pavlovich (1907–66) Soviet rocketry pioneer and aerospace engineer, born in Zhitomir. He was the leader of the team that developed and launched the first Soviet liquid-fuelled rocket (1933), and during World War II worked on aircraft jet-assisted take-off systems. Later he developed the first Soviet intercontinental ballistic missile, and led the Soviet space programme.

Koror POP (1990) 9 000, the capital town of Palau, W Pacific Ocean, on Koror I. NOTABLE FEATURE Palau National Museum.

Koryo the name given to Korea by Wang Kon, founder of the Koryo dynasty (918–1392) which had its capital at Kaesong (Songdo). It was an abbreviation of the ancient name Koguryo.

Kós see COS.

Kosciusko, Mount the highest mountain in Australia, located in the Snowy Mts of the Australian Alps, New South Wales. HEIGHT 2 228m. It is situated within a national park and is a popular winter sports area.

Köseg POP (1990) 12 000, a historic town in Vas county, W Hungary, situated at the foot of the Alps, close to the Austrian frontier. It is the highest town in Hungary. NOTABLE FEATURES Jurisich Square; Castle with Jurisich Miklós Museum.

kosher — *adj.* **1** in accordance with Jewish law. **2** *said of food* prepared as prescribed by Jewish dietary laws. **3** *colloq.* genuine; legitimate. — *noun* kosher food, or a shop selling it. [from Yiddish *kosher*, from Hebrew *kasher*, right, fit]

Košice, German **Kaschau**, Hungarian **Kassa** POP (1991) 235 000, the industrial capital of Východoslovenský region, Slovakia, lying on the R Hornad. It was formerly part of Hungary. NOTABLE FEATURE St Elizabeth Cathedral (13c).

Kosovo POP (1991e) 2m, a province in S Serbia, Yugoslavia. AREA 10 887sq km/4 202sq mi. CAPITAL Priština. The population is mainly of Albanian origin. The province effectively lost its autonomous status to Serbia in 1990. In 1992 ethnic Albanians held parliamentary and presidential elections which were declared invalid by the Serbs. ECONOMY agriculture; livestock; minerals.

Kosovo, Battle of a battle (28 Jun 1389) in which the Ottoman Turks defeat of the Serbs on the Kosovo plain marked the end of the medieval kingdom of Serbia. The battle was the subject of Serbian ballads in the oral tradition including the celebrated *Maiden of Kosovo*.

Kosrae, formerly **Kusaie** POP (1990e) 7 000, an island group, one of the Federated States of Micronesia. AREA 100sq km/40sq mi. CAPITAL Lelu. It formed part of the Trust Territory of the Pacific Is until 1977.

Kossuth, Lajos (1802–94) Hungarian statesman, a leader of the 1848 Hungarian Revolution, born in Monok. He was a political journalist, for which he was imprisoned (1837–40), and in 1847 became Leader of the Opposition in the Diet. In 1848 he demanded an independent government for Hungary. At the head of the Committee of National Defence, he was appointed Provisional Governor of Hungary (1849), but internal dissensions led to his resignation, and he fled to Turkey, and then to England.

Kosygin, Alexei Nikolayevich (1904–80) Soviet politician, born in Leningrad. He joined the army in 1919, and the Communist Party in 1927. Elected to the Supreme Soviet (1938), he held a variety of industrial posts, and became a member of the Central Committee (1939–60) and the Politburo (1946–52). Chairman of the State Economic Planning Commission (1959–60), and first Deputy Prime Minister (with Mikoyan) from 1960, he became premier when he succeeded Khrushchev as Chairman of the Council of Ministers (1964–80).

Kota Kinabalu, formerly **Jesselton** POP (1980) 56 000, the capital of Sabah state, E Malaysia. It is situated on the W coast, between the mountains and the S China Sea. The islands of the Tun Abdul Razak National Park lie offshore. [named after SE Asia's highest mountain, Mt Kinabalu]

Kotor a region of both natural and culturo-historical interest, located on the Gulf of Kotor on the coast of the former Yugoslavia. The area is noted for its plant and marine life, and for its historic settlements. It is a World Heritage site.

Koulouri see SALAMIS (GREECE).

kouros *noun* (PL. **kouroi**) *Art* a term conventionally applied by art historians to the naked, standing, youthful male figure commonly represented by Greek sculptors working in the Archaic style (7c–5c BC). See also KORE. [from Greek *kouros*, young man]

Kowalski, Stanley the hot-blooded macho husband of Stella in Tennessee Williams's *A Streetcar Named Desire*, who rapes his sister-in-law, Blanche Dubois.

Kowloon *or* **Jiulong** a peninsula and region of Hong Kong. AREA 11sq km/4sq mi. It is one of the most densely populated areas in the world. Victoria Harbour lies between the peninsula and Hong Kong I.

kowtow — *verb* **1** *intrans.* (**kowtow to someone**) *colloq.* to defer to them, especially in an over-submissive or obsequious way. **2** to touch the forehead to the ground in a gesture of submission. — *noun* an act of kowtowing. [from Chinese *k'o t'ou*, strike the head]

Kozhikode, formerly **Calicut** POP (1991) 420 000, a port city in Kerala, SW India, on the Malabar Coast of the Arabian Sea, 530km/330mi SW of Madras. It has been a trade centre since the 14c. It was the Portuguese navigator, Vasco da Gama's first Indian port of call in 1498. The city gave its name to calico cotton.

KP *abbrev.* Knight of (the Order of) St Patrick.

kph *abbrev.* kilometres per hour.

Kr *symbol Chem.* krypton.

kraal *noun* **1** in S Africa, a village of huts surrounded by a fence. **2** *South Afr.* an enclosure for cattle, sheep, etc. [from Afrikaans *kraal*, from Portuguese *curral*, pen]

krai any of six territories in Russia.

Kraków *or* **Cracow**, German **Krakau**, ancient **Cracovia** POP (1992e) 751 000, the industrial capital of Kraków voivodship, S Poland, lying on the R Vistula. It is the third largest city in Poland and was the country's capital from 1305 until 1609. Its Jagiellonian University, dating from 1364, is one of the oldest in Europe. NOTABLE FEATURES cathedral (14c); Royal Castle; City Museum; Churches of St Andrew, Sts Peter and Paul, St Barbara, and the Virgin Mary; Market Square, with 14c buildings including the clothier's hall, is a World Heritage site.

Krasnoyarsk POP (1991e) 924 000, the fast-growing river-port capital of Krasnoyarsk krai, W Siberia, Russian Federation, lying on the R Yenisei. HISTORY founded as a fortress in 1628; grew rapidly after the discovery of gold in the area in the 19c. The city is the site of a huge hydroelectric station.

Krebs, Sir Hans Adolf (1900–81) German-born British biochemist, born in Hildesheim. He emigrated to the UK in 1934, and worked at the University of Sheffield before becoming professor at Oxford (1954–67). For his work on metabolic processes, especially his discovery of the tricarboxylic acid cycle or Krebs cycle, a series of energy-generating reactions which occurs in living cells, he shared the 1953 Nobel Prize for Physiology or Medicine with Fritz Lipmann.

Krebs cycle *Biochem.* in the cells of living organisms, a sequence of biochemical reactions in which pyruvic acid formed in the process of glycolysis is broken down to form carbon dioxide and water, with the release of large amounts of energy in the form of ATP (the chemical that serves as an energy store in cells). The Krebs cycle can only take place if oxygen is available. [named after Hans Krebs]

kremlin *noun* **1** the citadel of a Russian town, especially (**Kremlin**) that of Moscow. **2** (**Kremlin**) the government of the former Soviet Union. [from Russian *kreml*]
◇ The Kremlin in Moscow was built in the 12c, and later altered and extended. It was the residence of the Tsars until 1712, and in 1918 became the political and administrative headquarters of the USSR.

krill *noun* a tiny shrimp-like shellfish, eaten by whales, etc. [from Norwegian *kril*, fry, ie young fish]

kris *noun* a Malay or Indonesian dagger with a wavy blade. [from Malay]

Krishna according to Hindu tradition, the eighth incarnation, in human form, of the deity Vishnu. He was a great hero and ruler, whose youthful amorous adventures are told in the *Mahabharata*. His story reaches its climax when, disguised as a charioteer in an eve-of-battle dialogue with Arjuna, he delivers the great moral discourse of the *Bhagavadgita*.

Krishna

Krishna *or* **Kistna, River** a river in S India, length 1 300km/800mi. It rises in the Western Ghats, 65km/40mi E of the Arabian Sea and flows generally SE through Maharashtra and Andhra Pradesh to enter the Bay of Bengal. The source of the river is sacred to Hindus.

Krishna Menon, V(engalil) K(rishnan) (1896–1974) Indian politician and diplomat, born in Calicut, Malabar. He was a history teacher and barrister, and in 1929 became Secretary of the India League and the mouthpiece of Indian nationalism in Britain. He was India's first High Commissioner in London (1947), and the leader of the Indian delegation to the United Nations (1952).

Krishnamurti, Jiddu (1895–1986) Indian theosophist, born in Madras. He was educated in England by Annie Besant, who in 1925 proclaimed him the Messiah. Later he rejected this persona, dissolved the World Order of the Star in the East (founded by Besant), and travelled the world teaching and advocating a way of life and thought unconditioned by the narrowness of nationality, race, and religion.

Kristiansen, Ingrid, *née* **Ingrid Christensen** (1956–) Norwegian athlete. A former cross-country skiing champion, and now a long-distance runner, in 1985–6 she ran world best times for the 5 000m, 10 000m (surpassed in 1993 by Wang Junxia of China), and marathon. In 1986 she knocked 45.68 seconds off the world 10 000m record, and won the European title. She has won most of the world's major marathons, including London (1984–5, 1987–8), and was the world cross-country champion in 1988.

Kristianstad 1 POP (1992e) 72 000, the seaport capital of Kristianstad county, S Sweden, lying on the R Helge. HISTORY founded by Denmark in 1614; ceded to Sweden in 1658; taken by the Danes in 1676; recaptured by Sweden in 1678. It is the earliest example of Renaissance town-planning in N Europe. **2** a county in S Sweden with Kristianstad as its capital.

Krogh, (Schack) August (Steenberg) (1874–1949) Danish physiologist, born in Grenaa, the son of a brewer. Professor at Copenhagen University, he demonstrated that blood flow through capillaries is determined by the activity of the surrounding muscle, rather than simply by blood pressure. He was awarded the 1920 Nobel Prize for Physiology or Medicine for this discovery, and later showed that the capillaries are under nervous and hormonal control.

krona *noun* **1** (PL. **kronor**) the standard unit of Swedish currency. **2** (PL. **kronur**) the standard unit of Icelandic currency. [from Swedish and Icelandic *krona*, crown]

krone *noun* (PL. **kroner**) the standard unit of Danish and Norwegian currency. [from Danish & Norwegian *krone*, crown]

Kronecker, Leopold (1823–91) German mathematician, born in Liegnitz. An active member of the Academy of Sciences in Berlin, where he conducted his private research, he worked in algebraic number theory, elliptic functions and the foundations of analysis, and lectured widely. He strongly rejected the use of the infinite, as well as any irrational or imaginary numbers, believing that mathematics should be essentially based on the arithmetic of the whole numbers.

Kronstadt rebellion an uprising (Mar 1921) of sailors from the Balic fleet stationed at Kronstadt in the Gulf of Finland. Protesting against the dictatorial Bolshevik policy of 'war communism', the mutineers demanded political and economic reforms under the slogan of 'free soviets', and established a revolutionary commune on the orders of Lenin. The rising was crushed by Red Army units after fierce fighting and heavy losses on both sides.

Kropotkin, Knyaz (Prince) Peter, Russian **Pyotr Alekseyevich** (1842–1921) Russian revolutionary and geographer, born in Moscow. In 1872 he associated himself with the extremist section of the International, and was imprisoned (1874). He escaped to England (1876), then to Switzerland and to France, where he was imprisoned again for anarchism (1883–6). He settled in England, and wrote on anarchism, social justice, and many topics in biology, literature, and history, then returned to Russia in 1917.

Kru a Kwa-speaking people of Liberia and the Ivory Coast, famous as fishermen and stevedores throughout W Africa from Senegal to Cameroon. Land shortages have forced many into cities, and the largest settlement of Kru is now in Monrovia, Liberia (present-day population c.1.2m).

Kruger, Paul (Stephanus Johannes Paulus), also called **Oom** (**Uncle**) **Paul** (1825–1904) Afrikaner statesman, born in Colesberg, Cape Colony. He took part in the Great Trek of the 1830s, and became leader of the independence movement when Britain annexed Transvaal (1877). In the first Boer War (1881), he was head of the provisional government; afterwards he was President of Transvaal, or the South African Republic (1883–1902).

Kruger National Park a game reserve in Transvaal, S Africa. It was founded in 1898 as the Sabi Game Reserve, and in 1926 it was renamed in honour of the Afrikaner statesman, Paul Kruger. The sanctuary covers about 20 700sq km/8 000sq mi and is one of the largest national parks in the world.

krugerrand *noun* a South African one-ounce (or 28-gram) gold coin bearing a portrait of Paul Kruger, Boer statesman. [from RAND]

krummhorn *or* **krumhorn** *noun* a musical instrument used widely throughout Europe in the Middle Ages and the Renaissance. It consisted of a wooden tube curved at the end like a hockey stick, with a double reed enclosed in a wind capsule through which the player directed the breath without making contact with the reed. [from German *Krummhorn*, curved horn]

Krupp, Friedrich (1787–1826) German industrialist, the founder of an armaments business. He built a steel factory at Essen in 1810. His son, Alfred (1812–87) established the first Bessemer steel plant, and became the foremost arms supplier to the world. In 1906, Alfred's daughter, Bertha (1886–1957), married Gustav von Bohlen und Halbach (1870–1950), who during World War I manufactured the long-range gun nicknamed 'Big Bertha'. He supported Hitler financially, and connived in secret rearmament. He was succeeded by his son, Alfried (1907–67), who became head of the firm in 1943. He was arrested (1945) and convicted (1947) by a US Military Tribunal for war crimes, but released under an amnesty in 1951. After the War, the Krupp empire was split up by the Allies, but the company survived to play a prominent part in the West German 'economic miracle'.

krypton *noun* Chem. (SYMBOL **Kr**, ATOMIC NUMBER **36**) a colourless odourless gas, representing 0.0001% of the air by volume. It is one of the rare or noble gases, but forms a few unstable compounds. It is used in lasers, and with other inert gases to fill fluorescent lamps and discharge tubes. [from Greek *kryptos*, hidden, secret]

KS *or* **Ks.** *abbrev.* Kansas.

KT *abbrev.* Knight of the Thistle.

Kt *abbrev.* Knight.

Kuala Lumpur POP (1990e) 1.8m, the capital of Malaysia, in Wilayah Persekutuan territory, E Peninsular Malaysia. It has a large Chinese and Indian population. The city was the capital of the Federated Malay States in 1895 and is the former capital of the state of Selangor in the E of the country. NOTABLE FEATURES National Mosque, Sri Mahamariamman (Hindu temple, 1873); National Museum; National Museum of Art; Selangor Turf Club; Mimaland Recreational Complex. [from Malay, meaning 'muddy estuary']

Kubitschek (de Oliveira), Juscelino (1902–76) Brazilian politician, born in Diamantina, Minas Gerais. When he was President (1956–61), his government sponsored rapid economic growth and the dramatic building of a new capital, Brasília.

Kublai Khan (c.1216–94) Mongol Emperor of China (1279–94), the grandson of Genghis Khan. An energetic prince, he suppressed his rivals, adopted the Chinese mode of civilization, encouraged men of letters, and made Buddhism the state religion. The first foreigner ever to rule in China, he established himself at Cambaluc (modern Beijing), where the splendour of his court was legendary, and ruled an empire extending as far as the R Danube.

Kubla Khan, in full *Kubla Khan, or, A Vision in a Dream* a fragmentary poem by Samuel Taylor Coleridge (1816). It is a vision of an exotic garden, reputedly composed during a drug-induced dream.

Kubrick, Stanley (1928–) US screenwriter, film producer, and director, born in New York City. After directing *Paths of Glory* (1957) and *Spartacus* (1960), he worked mainly in the UK. His unusual and varied feature films include *Lolita* (1962), *Dr Strangelove* (1964), *2001: A Space Odyssey* (1965), *A Clockwork Orange* (1971), *Barry Lyndon* (1975), *The Shining* (1980), and *Full Metal Jacket* (1987).

Kuching POP (1980) 74 000, the capital of Sarawak state, E Malaysia. It is situated on the R Sarawak where it meets the S China Sea. The city was formerly associated with the Brooke Dynasty of 'white rajahs'. NOTABLE FEATURES Fort Margherita, now a police museum; Sarawak Museum, built in the style of a Normandy town house in 1891.

kudos *noun colloq.* credit, honour or prestige. [from Greek *kudos*, glory]

Kuei-yang see GUIYANG.

Kuhn, Richard (1900–67) German chemist, born in Vienna-Döbling. Professor in Heidelberg from 1929, he did important work on the structure and synthesis of vitamins A and B, and studied the carotenoids. He was awarded the 1938 Nobel Prize for Chemistry, but forbidden by the Nazi government to accept it, although it was presented to him after World War II.

Kühne, Wilhelm (1837–1900) German physiologist, born in Hamburg. Professor at Heidelberg from 1871, he was noted for his studies of digestion. He proposed the expression *enzyme* (Greek for *in yeast*) to describe ferments and other organic substances that actuate chemical changes. He also investigated vision, making important discoveries about the way the retina functions.

Kuiper, Gerard Peter (1905–73) Dutchborn US astronomer, born in Harenkarspel. Educated in Leiden, he worked at various observatories in the USA from 1933. He discovered a satellite of Uranus (Miranda) and of Neptune (Nereid), and proposed that there is a belt of comets (the Kuiper belt) just beyond the orbit of Pluto. He was also the first to confirm that a planetary satellite had an atmosphere, detecting methane on Titan, and was involved with the early US space flights, including the Ranger and Mariner missions.

Ku Klux Klan the name of successive secret societies in the USA. The first was founded after the American Civil War (1861–5) to oppose Reconstruction and the new rights being granted to blacks. Its members, disguised in robes and hoods, terrorized blacks and their sympathizers in the country areas of the South. Later, after World War I, its targets were Catholics, foreigners, Jews, and organized labour, as well as blacks. The movement was revived in the 1950s by the fear of communism, and again in the 1960s by opposition to civil rights movements. [probably from Greek *kyklos*, circle + *klan* as variant of clan]

kukri *noun* a heavy curved knife or short sword used by Gurkhas. [from Hindi *kukri*]

kulak *noun Hist.* a wealthy, property-owning Russian peasant. [from Russian *kulak*, literally 'fist']

Kumasi, bynames **Garden City**, **City of the Golden Stool** POP (1988) 385 000, the second largest city in Ghana and the capital of Ashanti region. It is situated in S central Ghana, 180km/112mi NW of Accra. The city, headquarters of the Ashanti kingdom from the 17c, is the centre of the Ghanaian transport network. NOTABLE FEATURES National Cultural Centre, including zoo, art gallery, open-air theatre; Bonwire, nearby, is a woodcarving and cloth centre.

kümmel *noun* a German liqueur flavoured with cumin and caraway seeds. [from German *Kümmel*, from *kumin*, cumin]

kumquat *noun* a citrus fruit resembling a miniature orange. [from Chinese dialect *gamgwat*, golden citrus fruit]

Kun, Béla (1886–c.1939) Communist leader, born in Szilágycseh, Transylvania. He was a journalist, soldier, and prisoner in Russia (1916), where he joined the Bolsheviks. In 1919 he set up a Soviet republic in Hungary, but his policy of nationalization alienated much of the population. His regime was overthrown after only five months, and he fled to Vienna. On his return to Russia he was killed in one of the Stalinist purges of the late 1930s.

kung fu *noun* a Chinese martial art with similarities to karate and judo. [from Chinese]
◇ It dates from the 16c and has various forms. It is generally characterized by flowing movements designed to anticipate and respond to the moves of an opponent. The best known form is *wing chun*, 'beautiful springtime', practised by the actor Bruce Lee in several popular films.

Kunlun Mountains a mountain range in W China. It extends 2 500km/1 500mi along the border of Xinjiang province and Tibet autonomous region and rises to a peak of 7 723m at Muztag. The range divides E to form the Altun Shan and Hoh Xil Shan ranges.

Kunming, formerly **Yunnan** POP (1990) 1.7m, the capital of Yunnan province, S China, lying on the Yunnan Plateau at an altitude of 1 894m. Kunming became a major market and transport centre in 279 BC. It is known as the 'City of Eternal Spring' because of its spring-like weather and scenery. NOTABLE FEATURES Qiongzhu Si (Bamboo Temple) lies 11km/7mi W; the Stone Forest is located 126km/78mi SE.

Kunsthistorisches Museum an art museum in Vienna. Its collection is mainly derived from those of various rulers of the Habsburg empire from the 16c onwards, and contains many Renaissance and Baroque paintings.

Kurdistan *or* **Kordestan** POP (1986) 1.1m, a province in NW Iran. AREA 24 998sq km/ 9 649sq mi. It is bounded to the W by Iraq. CAPITAL Sanandaj. The province is inhabited by Kurds, who also occupy parts of NE Iraq, SE Turkey, and NE Syria. In 1920 a Kurdish autonomous state was agreed at the Treaty of Sèvres, but the terms were never carried out.

Kurds a nationalistic West Iranian-speaking ethnic group settled in neighbouring mountainous areas of Anatolia, Iraq, Iran and Turkey (including some in Syria and Armenia), an area which they themselves call Kurdistan. They were originally pastoral nomads with some agriculture, but the creation of national boundaries after World War I restricted their seasonal migrations, and most are now urbanized. They have been Sunni Muslims since the 7c. They are politically oppressed in Turkey, and have suffered religious persecution in Iran, especially after the Iranian revolution of 1979. In Iraq, the Kurds' failure to achieve autonomous status for Kurdistan during the 1970s resulted in hostilities between Kurds and government forces. After the allied victory over Iraq in Kuwait in Feb 1991, the Kurds revolted against the government but were suppressed. Following continued Iraqi attacks on the Kurdish population in northern Iraq, the UN created a security zone there to protect them. In Jul 1992, Kurds in northern Iraq formed their first government, which was not acknowledged by the central government in Baghdad. In Mar 1993, in the face of continued hardship caused partly by an economic embargo imposed by Iraq, the first Kurdish government resigned and was replaced.

Kurgan culture the semi-nomadic population of the S Russian steppes in the fourth millennium BC, characterized archaeologically by burials sprinkled with red ochre beneath a barrow mound or *kurgan*.

Kuril Islands *or* **Kurils**, Russian **Kurilskiye Ostrova** an archipelago off the E Russian coast, between the N Pacific Ocean to the E and the Sea of Okhotsk to the W. AREA 15 600sq km/ 6 000sq mi. The archipelago of over 50 islands extends c.1 200km/750mi from the S tip of Kamchatka Peninsula to the NE coast of Hokkaido I, Japan. PHYSICAL DESCRIPTION actively volcanic with hot springs; the highest point is 2 339m. HISTORY visited in 1634 by the Dutch; divided between Russia and Japan in the 18c; all ceded to Japan in 1875; occupied by Soviet troops in 1945; became part of the Soviet Union in 1947; continuing dispute over the S Kurils, claimed by Japan.

Kurosawa, Akira (1910–) Japanese film director, born in Tokyo. His first feature film was *Sanshiro Sugata* (1943). He often adapts the techniques of the Noh theatre, such as in *Rashomon* (1951) and *The Seven Samurai* (1954). Also characteristic are his literary adaptations, such as *The Throne of Blood* (1957, from Shakespeare's *Macbeth*). Later films include *Kagemushi* (1980), *Ran* (1985), and *Rhapsody in August* (1991).

Kush, Kingdom of an independent kingdom on the Nile which emerged from the Egyptian province of Nubia in the 11c BC. In the 8c BC Kush conquered Egypt and established the 25th dynasty, which ruled until the Assyrian conquest in 671–666 BC. The Kush kings became Egyptianized, but after their withdrawal from Egypt in the 7c BC they moved to the more southerly capital of Meroe, where the good supplies of iron ore and timber made it an important iron smelting centre; large slag heaps can still be seen there.

Kutaisi POP (1991e) 238 000, a city in central Georgia. It is situated on the R Rioni, where it leaves a ravine to flow over the Colkhidian Plateau. NOTABLE FEATURES cathedral (1003).

Kutch *or* **Kachh** *or* **Cutch, Rann of**, a region of salt marsh in the Indian state of Gujarat and the Sind province of Pakistan. AREA 9 000sq km/3 500sq mi. It is bounded N by the Thar Desert and W by the Arabian Sea, of which it was once a shallow arm. Extensive mud flats have great accumulations of salt on the surface when dry, but are inundated during the SW monsoon season. The region was the scene of Indo-Pakistani fighting in 1965.

Kutuzov, Mikhail Ilarionovich, Knyaz (Prince) (1745–1813) Russian soldier, born in St Petersburg. He distinguished himself in the Turkish war, and in 1805 commanded against the French, but was defeated at Austerlitz. In 1812, as Commander-in-Chief, he fought Napoleon at Borodino, and achieved a major victory over Davout and Ney at Smolensk.

Kuwait, official name **State of Kuwait**, Arabic **Dowlat al Kuwait** POP (1992e) 2m, an independent state at the head of the Arabian Gulf. AREA 17 818sq km/6 878sq ml. It is bounded N and W by Iraq, S by Saudi Arabia, and E by the Arabian Gulf. CAPITAL Kuwait City. CHIEF TOWNS Shuwaikh, Mina al Ahmadi. TIME ZONE GMT +3. The population is 42% Kuwaiti, 40% other Arab nationalities; Sunni Muslim is the chief religion. OFFICIAL LANGUAGE Arabic; English is also widely spoken. CURRENCY the dinar. PHYSICAL DESCRIPTION consists of the mainland and nine offshore islands; the terrain is flat or gently undulating, rising in the SW to 271m; the Wadi al Batin runs along the W border with Iraq; terrain is generally stony with a sparse vegetation. CLIMATE hot, dry climate, with an average annual rainfall of 111mm; summer temperatures are very high, often above 45°C (Jul–Aug); winter daytime temperatures often exceed 20°C; humidity is generally high; sandstorms are common throughout the year. HISTORY port founded in the 18c; Britain became responsible for Kuwait's foreign affairs in 1899; British protectorate in 1914; became fully independent in 1961; the invasion and annexation by Iraq in Aug 1990 led to the Gulf

War in Jan–Feb 1991, with severe damage to Kuwait City and the infrastructure of the country; the Kuwait government went into exile in Saudi Arabia until the country was liberated in 1991; major post-war problems included large-scale refugee emigration, the burning of oil wells by Iraq (all capped by Nov 1991), and the pollution of Gulf waters by oil; in 1992 the port of Umm Quasr and part of an oilfield were passed to Kuwait when the boundary between Iraq and Kuwait was moved by 600m. GOVERNMENT the Amir is head of state, governing through an appointed Prime Minister and Council of Ministers. ECONOMY traditionally pearl diving, seafaring, boatbuilding, fishing, nomadic herding; oil discovered in 1938 has made Kuwait a wealthy country but it has suffered economically from the effects of the Gulf War; petrochemicals, fertilizers, construction materials, asbestos, batteries; active programme of economic diversification, creating a post-oil high-technology state; agriculture gradually expanding; dates, citrus fruits, timber, livestock, poultry.

Kuwait

Kuwait City, Arabic **Al Kuwayt**, formerly **Qurein** POP (1993e) 400 000, the capital city of Kuwait, on the S shore of Kuwait Bay. It expanded considerably in the 1940s as a result of the discovery of oil and it is an important banking and investment centre. During the Iraqi occupation of Kuwait in 1990–91, the city was pillaged. The suburban port of Shuwaikh lies to the SW.

Kuznets, Simon (Smith) (1901–85) US economist and statistician, born in Pinsk, Russia. He went to the USA as a young man, worked with the National Bureau of Economic Research (1927–71), and was Professor in Economics at Pennsylvania (1930–54), then Johns Hopkins (1954–60), and Harvard (1960–71). He combined a concern for facts and measurement with creative and original ideas on economic development and social change, such as the 20-year 'Kuznets cycle' of economic growth. He was awarded the Nobel Prize for Economics in 1971.

Kuznetsk Basin the basin of the Tom R, situated in Kemerovo oblast, Russia. Stretching SE from Tomsk to Novokuznetsk, it is a major industrial zone, with rich deposits of coal and iron ore.

kvass *noun* a weak rye beer made in countries of E Europe. [from Russian *kvas*]

kW *abbrev.* kilowatt.

Kwakiutl a N Pacific Coast Native American group living on the coast of British Columbia as fishermen and traders. They are famed for their woodwork, frequently painted in bright colours, including masks, totem poles, war canoes, whale hunting vessels, and decorative boxes.

KwaNdebele POP (1991) 299 000, a national state or non-independent black homeland in Transvaal province, NE South Africa. AREA 2 860sq km/1 104sq mi. It is situated NE of Johannesburg and E of Pretoria. In 1981 it achieved self-governing status. CHIEF TOWN Moutjana.

Kwang-chow see GUANGZHOU.

kwashiorkor *noun* a disease of children caused by lack of protein in the diet. [a Ghanaian name]

KwaZulu POP (1991) 4.5m, a national state or non-independent black homeland in Natal province, E South Africa. It is situated close to the Indian Ocean between the Transkei and Durban. In 1971 it achieved self-governing status.

kWh *abbrev.* kilowatt hour.

KWIC *abbrev.* keyword in context, with reference to a concordance or VDU text display in which a selected keyword is highlighted.

KWOC *abbrev.* keyword out of context.

KY *or* **Ky** *abbrev.* Kentucky.

Kyd, Thomas (1558–94) English dramatist, born in London. His reputation rested on his tragedies, especially *The Spanish Tragedy* (c.1589). Credited with a share in several plays, he may have written an earlier version of *Hamlet*.

Kyle a male first name, after the Irish and Scottish surname. [from Gaelic *caol*, narrow]

kyle *noun Scot.* a channel, strait or sound. [from Gaelic *caol*, narrow]

Kyoga, Lake a lake in central Uganda, N of Kampala. AREA 4 427sq km/1 709sq mi. The Victoria Nile R passes through it from L Victoria.

Kyoto POP (1991e) 1.5m, the capital of Kyoto prefecture, central Honshu, Japan. It lies to the SW of Lake Biwa. The city was founded in the 8c and was the capital of Japan from 794 until 1868. NOTABLE FEATURES over 2 000 temples and shrines; Nijo-jo Castle (1603); Imperial Palace; Kinkakuji, containing the Golden Pavilion (1394); Ryoanji Temple (1450, later rebuilt); Daitokuji Monastery (14c); Kiyomizu Dera Temple (8c); Sanjusangen do (12c).

Kyrie eleison an early Christian petition for divine mercy used in various forms in the liturgical worship of both Eastern and Western Christianity, dating at least to the 4c AD . In the Roman Catholic Mass it may be part of a ninefold petition in which the Kyrie is recited three times, followed by a threefold variant *Christe eleison* ('Christ, have mercy') and then a final threefold Kyrie. [Greek, = Lord, have mercy]

Kyushu POP (1990) 13.3m, an island region in Japan. AREA 42 084sq km/16 244sq mi. It is the southernmost and most densely populated of the four main islands. There are four volcanic ranges, rising to 1 935m at Mt Miyanoura-dake on Yakushima I to the S. The region is heavily forested apart from the NW, which is an extensive rice-growing area. Many spas are located on Kyushu. CLIMATE subtropical. CHIEF TOWNS Fukuoka, Kita-Kyushu, Oita, Kagoshima, Nagasaki. ECONOMY rice, grain, sweet potatoes; fruit; silk; timber; fishing; porcelain.

Kyzyl-Kum, Russian **Peski Kyzylkum** an extensive desert in Kazakhstan and Uzbekistan, between the Amudarya R in the W and the Syr Darya in the E. AREA 300 000sq km/ 115 000sq mi. It extends SE from the Aral Sea and rises to 922m in the centre. The desert is partially covered with sand dunes.

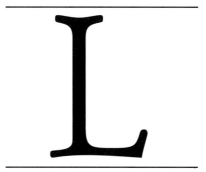

L¹ *or* l *noun* (PL. **Ls, L's, l's**) the twelfth letter of the English alphabet.

L² *abbrev.* **1** lake. **2** learner driver. **3** Liberal. **4** licentiate. **5** lira or lire.

L³ *symbol* the Roman numeral for 50.

l *abbrev.* **1** left. **2** length. **3** line. **4** lira or lire. **5** litre.

LA *abbrev.* **1** Los Angeles. **2** Louisiana.

La *symbol Chem.* lanthanum.

La. *abbrev.* Louisiana.

la *or* **lah** *noun Mus.* in tonic sol-fa, the sixth note of the major scale. [from the first syllable of the word *labii* in a medieval Latin hymn, certain syllables of which were used in naming the notes of the scale]

Laâyoune POP (1982) 94 000, the capital of Western Sahara and of Laâyoune province, NW Africa.

Lab *abbrev.* Labour.

lab *noun colloq.* a laboratory.

Laban, Rudolf von (1879–1958) Hungarian dancer, choreographer, and dance theoretician, born in now Bratislava, Austria-Hungary (now in Czechoslovakia). He studied painting, acting, and dancing in Paris, toured Europe and N Africa as a dancer, founded a school in Munich in 1910, worked in many German cities as a choreographer and teacher, then went to England (1938). As the leader of the central European dance movement he was instrumental in the development of modern dance as a theatre form, and his dance notation system, which was widely influential, is now known as Labanotation.

Labé POP (1983) 65 000, the capital of Moyenne-Guinée region, W central Guinea. It is situated near the source of the R Gambia, 260km/162mi NE of Conakry.

label — *noun* **1** a small written note attached to a parcel, object, etc, giving details of its contents, owner, destination, etc. **2** a word or short phrase which describes only part of a person's or thing's character but which comes to be used as a general description. **3** a small strip of material inside a garment, giving the maker's or designer's name. **4** a record company's trademark. — *verb* (**labelled, labelling**) **1** to attach a label to. **2** to call by a certain name or describe in a certain way: *were labelled as rebels.* [from Old French *label*, ribbon]

labial — *adj.* **1** relating to the lips. **2** *said of a sound* made with the lips almost or completely closed. — *noun* a sound made with the lips almost or completely closed, eg *b, m.* [from Latin *labium*, lip]

labiate *Bot.* — *noun* any flowering plant belonging to the family Labiatae, in which the stems are usually square, and the corolla of petals is divided into two lips, eg various aromatic herbs, including mint and thyme. — *adj.* **1** of this family of plants. **2** *Anat.* having or resembling lips. [from Latin *labium*, lip]

Labiche, Eugène (Marin) (1815–88) French playwright, born in Paris. He wrote over 100 comedies, farces, and vaudevilles, such as *Le Chapeau de paille d'Italie* (The Italian Straw Hat, 1851) and *Le Voyage de M Perrichon* (The Journey of M Perrichon, 1860).

labile *adj.* **1** unstable. **2** *Chem.* denoting a chemical compound that can be readily altered by heat, etc. [from Latin *labilis*, from *labi*, to slip]

labium *noun* (PL. **labia**) a lip or lip-like structure, especially one of the folds of the vulva. [from Latin *labium*, lip]

laboratory *noun* (PL. **laboratories**) a room or building specially equipped for scientific experiments, research, the preparation of drugs, etc. [from Latin *laborare*, to work]

laborious *adj.* **1** requiring hard work or much effort. **2** not looking or sounding natural; not fluent. [from Latin *laboriosus*]

laboriously *adv.* in a laborious way; at tedious length.

labour — *noun* **1** strenuous and prolonged physical or mental work. **2** (*usually* **labours**) a difficult task or job. **3** working people or their efforts regarded collectively as a resource or as a political force. **4** the process of giving birth, especially from the point where contractions of the uterus begin. **5** (**Labour**) in the UK, a shortened name for the Labour Party: *Labour won the seat with an increased majority.* — *verb* **1** *intrans.* to work hard or with difficulty. **2** *intrans.* to progress or move slowly and with difficulty: *the old man laboured slowly up the path.* **3** *intrans.* to strive earnestly to do something: *laboured hard to get results.* **4** *trans.* to deal with (a subject or issue) at excessive length or in too much detail, especially tediously and repetitively: *I have no wish to labour the point.*
— **labour under a misapprehension** to persist in some activity or notion while unknowingly mistaken about it.
[from Latin *labor*]

labour camp a prison camp where prisoners are made to do hard labour.

Labour Day a public holiday in honour of working people, often celebrated with marches. It is held on 1 May in many countries and on the first Monday in September in the USA and Canada.

laboured *adj.* **1** showing signs of effort or difficulty. **2** not natural or spontaneous.

labourer *noun* a worker employed to do heavy and usually unskilled physical work.

labour exchange *Brit.* a former term for a job centre, still used informally.

labour force the body of people available for work, especially in a particular company or area, or in a country as a whole.

labour-intensive *adj., said of an industry or enterprise* requiring a large resource of people as distinct from machinery. See also CAPITAL-INTENSIVE.

labour of love an undertaking made mainly for personal satisfaction or pleasure rather than for profit or material advantage.

Labour Party in the UK, a political party originally formed in 1900 as the Labour Representation Committee to represent the interests of working people. The name was changed to Labour Party in 1906, when 26 MPs were elected. In 1922 it overtook the Liberals as the main opposition party, and the first minority Labour government held office in 1924 (for 11 months) and in 1929–31. The first majority Labour government under Clement Attlee (1945–51) established the welfare state and carried out an extensive nationalization programme. After just over seven years in opposition under Hugh Gaitskell (1955–63), the Labour Party was in office again in 1964–70 and 1974–9 under Harold Wilson and (from 1976) James Callaghan. In 1981 the 'Gang of Four' (Roy Jenkins, David Owen, William Rodgers, and Shirley Williams) left the Labour Party to found the Social Democratic Party (SDP). The Leader and Deputy Leader are elected annually when in opposition by an electoral college composed of trade unions, constituency parties, and the Parliamentary Labour Party. The annual conference and the National Executive Committee share in forming policy. Leaders since 1979 have been Michael Foot (1980–3), Neil Kinnock (1983–92), and John Smith (1992–4).

labour-saving *adj.* serving to reduce the amount of work or effort needed: *labour-saving devices.*

Labrador POP (1991) 30 000, a part of Newfoundland province, E Canada, bounded E by the Labrador Sea and separated from Newfoundland by the Strait of Belle Isle. AREA 285 000sq km/110 000sq mi. PHYSICAL DESCRIPTION mainly a barren plateau, part of the Canadian Shield; the E coast is heavily indented by bays and fjords; there are many lakes. The award of the interior region to Newfoundland in 1927 is disputed by Quebec. CHIEF TOWN Labrador City. ECONOMY fishing; iron ore; hydroelectric power (from the Churchill and Twin falls).

Labrador *noun* a breed of large dog with a short black or golden coat. [named after *Labrador* in Canada]

Labrador Sea the arm of the Atlantic Ocean between Newfoundland and Greenland, connected to Baffin Bay by the Davis Strait. The cold SE-flowing Labrador Current brings icebergs, while the warm Greenland Current flowing NW helps modify the climate of the SW shore of Greenland.

La Bruyère, Jean de (1645–96) French writer, born in Paris. He helped in the education of the Dauphin and became tutor to the Duc de Bourbon. His major work is the satirical *Caractères de Théophraste...* (Characters of Theophrastus..., 1688), which made his reputation but also gained him many enemies.

laburnum *noun* a small garden tree of the pea family, with hanging yellow flowers and poisonous seeds. [from Latin *laburnum*]

labyrinth *noun* **1** a complicated network of passages through which it is very difficult to find one's way. **2** a complicated arrangement. **3** *Anat.* in the inner ear of vertebrates, the complex arrangement of membranous and bony structures that form the organs of hearing and balance. [from Greek *labyrinthos*]

labyrinthine *adj., said of an arrangement or system* extremely complex and confusing.

lac *noun* a resinous substance produced by certain Asian insects, used in making varnish. [from Hindi *lakh*]

Laccadive Islands see LAKSHADWEEP.

lace — *noun* **1** a delicate material made from fine thread woven into net-like patterns. **2** a string or cord drawn through holes, used for fastening shoes, etc. — *verb* **1** *trans., intrans.* (also **lace up**) to fasten or be fastened with a lace or laces. **2** to flavour or strengthen with alcohol: *bitter lemon laced with gin*. **3** to trim with lace. **4** to weave in and out of; to intertwine.
— **lace into someone** *colloq.* to attack them physically or with words.
[from Latin *laqueus*, noose]

Lacedaemon in antiquity, the official name for the Spartan state. It comprised the districts of Laconia and Messenia.

lacerate *verb* **1** to tear or cut (flesh) roughly. **2** to wound or hurt (a person's feelings). [from Latin *lacerare*, to tear]

laceration *noun* the process or an act of lacerating or cutting.

Lacerta *Astron.* the Lizard, a small faint constellation in the N hemisphere.

lace-up — *noun* a shoe fastened with a lace. — *adj., said of shoes* fastened with a lace or laces.

Lachesis see MOERAE.

Lachlan a male first name. It is said to have referred originally to a settler from Norway, the 'land of the lochs'.

Lachlan River a river in New South Wales, SE Australia. It rises in the Great Dividing Range, N of Canberra and flows 1 484km/922mi to join the Murrumbidgee R.

lachrymal *adj. literary* relating to or producing tears. [from Latin *lacrima*, tear]

lachrymal gland the tear-producing gland at the outer edge of the eye.

lachrymose *adj. literary* **1** crying very easily and very often. **2** very sad; likely to make a person cry. [from Latin *lacrima*, tear]

lack — *noun* something missing or in short supply; a deficiency or want. — *verb* **1** to be completely without or to have too little of. **2** (**lack for something**) to be in need of something: *did not lack for money*.
— **no lack of something** a plentiful supply of it. [from Middle English *lak*]

lackadaisical *adj.* **1** without energy, interest, or enthusiasm. **2** sentimental in a feeble dreamy way. [from archaic *alack the day*, alas the day]

lackadaisically *adv.* without energy; feebly.

lackey *noun* (PL. **lackeys**) **1** *derog.* a grovelling or servile follower. **2** *old use* a male servant. [from Old French *laquais*]

lacking *adj.* absent; deficient: *is lacking in energy*.

lacklustre *adj.* lacking in energy or brightness; dull.

Laconia in ancient Greece, the SE portion of the Peloponnese, of which Sparta was the principal city.

laconic *adj.* using few words; terse, concise. [from Greek *lakonikos*, of Laconia or Sparta in ancient Greece, so called from the Spartans' reputedly terse style of speech]

laconically *adv.* tersely; with few words.

lacquer — *noun* **1** a usually clear substance made by dissolving natural or man-made resins in alcohol, used to form a hard, shiny covering on wood and metal. **2** the sap from some trees, used as a varnish for wood. **3** a clear, sticky substance sprayed on to hair to keep it place. — *verb* (**lacquered, lacquering**) to cover with lacquer. [from Portuguese *laca, lac*]

lacrimal same as LACHRYMAL.

Lacroix, Christian (1951–) French couturier, born in Arles, Provence. He studied fashion history from 1973, intending to become a museum curator, but then joined Hermès, the leather firm (1978–9), and worked with the ready-to-wear designer Guy Paulin (1980–1). In 1981 he joined Jean Patou as Artistic Director, which showed his first collection in 1982. In 1987 he left Patou and, with other partners, opened the House of Lacroix in Paris. He made his name with ornate and frivolous clothes.

lacrosse *noun* a game in which two teams use long sticks with rigid triangular nets at one end to throw a small ball into their opponents' goal-net. [from French *la*, the + *crosse*, hooked stick]
◊ Derived from the N American Indian game *baggataway*, it was brought to Europe in the early part of the 19c, and introduced into Britain in 1867. It is played on a pitch 100–110m (110–120yd) long by 55–75m (60–85yd) wide, by two teams of 10 or 12 players.

lactate — *verb intrans.* (with stress on -*tate*) *Zool.*, *said of the mammary glands of a mammal* to secrete milk. — *noun* (with stress on *lac*-) *Biochem.* a salt or ester of lactic acid. [from Latin *lac*, milk]

lactation *noun Zool.* in mammals, the secretion of milk by the mammary glands, under the control of hormones, in order to feed a baby or young animal until it is weaned.

lactic *adj.* of or derived from milk. [from Latin *lac*, milk]

lactic acid *Biochem.* (FORMULA $CH_3CHOHCOOH$) an organic acid produced during the souring of milk by bacterial fermentation of lactose (milk sugar), a process that is of commercial importance in the manufacture of cheese, yoghurt, and other dairy products. Lactic acid is also produced in the muscles of animals when all the available oxygen has been used to break down carbohydrate to release energy, eg during strenuous exercise.

lactose *noun Biochem.* (FORMULA $C_{12}H_{22}O_{11}$) a white crystalline disaccharide sugar, found only in milk, consisting of a molecule of glucose and a molecule of galactose. It is used as a food for infants, and as a laxative and diuretic. — Also called *milk sugar*. [from Latin *lac*, milk]

lactovegetarian *or* **lactarian** — *noun* a vegetarian whose diet includes milk and other dairy products. — *adj.* relating to such a person or diet.

lacuna *noun* (PL. **lacunae, lacunas**) a gap or a space where something is missing, especially in printed text. [from Latin *lacuna*, pool]

lacy *adj.* (**lacier, laciest**) of or like lace, especially in being fine and delicate.

lad *noun* **1** a boy or youth. **2** (*usually* **the lads**) *colloq.* a group of regular male acquaintances: *one of the lads*. **3** *Brit.* a person working in stables,

regardless of age or sex. [from Middle English *ladde*]

ladder — *noun* **1** a piece of equipment consisting of a set of horizontal rungs or steps between two long vertical supports, used for climbing up or down. **2** a long narrow flaw, especially in a stocking or tights, where a row of stitches has broken. **3** a means or route of progress or advancement: *the social ladder*. **4** anything like a ladder in arrangement, eg a list of names of players in a competition on which names are moved up or down depending on whether the players win or lose. — *verb* (**laddered, laddering**) **1** *intrans. said of stockings, etc* to develop a ladder. **2** to cause a ladder in stockings, etc. [from Anglo-Saxon *hlæder*]

laddie *noun dialect, colloq.* a young boy or lad.

laden *adj.* **1** *said of a ship* loaded with cargo. **2** *said of a person, animal, or vehicle; or something comparable* heavily loaded: *trees heavily laden with fruit*. **3** *said of one's mind, conscience, etc* oppressed with guilt, worry, etc. [from Anglo-Saxon *hladan*, to load]

la-di-da *or* **lah-di-dah** *adj. colloq.* behaving or speaking in a pretentious or affected way. [imitating an affected manner of speech]

ladies *sing. noun* a women's public lavatory.

lading *noun* **1** a cargo or load carried. **2** the act of loading cargo or goods. See also BILL OF LADING. [from Anglo-Saxon *hladan*, to load]

ladle — *noun* a large spoon with a long handle and deep bowl, for serving or transferring liquid. — *verb* to serve or transfer with a ladle.
— **ladle something out** to serve or distribute praise, blame, etc generously or excessively. [from Anglo-Saxon *hlædel*]

ladleful *noun* (PL. **ladlefuls**) the amount held in a ladle.

Ladoga, Lake, Russian **Ozero Ladozhskoye**, Finnish **Laatokka** the largest lake in Europe, situated in Russia, close to the Finnish border. AREA 17 700sq km/6 830sq mi; length 219km/136mi; maximum depth 230m. It receives the R Svir and the R Vuoksa; over 90% of the outflow is via the R Neva into the Gulf of Finland. The lake contains c.660 islands, mostly located along the NW coast. Navigation is difficult in winter because of ice and storms. An extensive network of canals has developed.

lady *noun* (PL. **ladies**) **1** a woman regarded as having good manners and elegant or refined behaviour. **2** a polite word for a woman generally. **3** *Hist.* a woman belonging to the upper classes by birth. **4** (**Lady**) in the UK, a title of honour used for peeresses (but not duchesses), the wives and daughters of peers and knights, and for some women of importance, eg mayoresses. **5** a woman in a position of authority or control: *lady of the house*. **6** (*attributive*) female: *a lady doctor*.
— **Our Lady** *RC Church* the Virgin Mary. [from Anglo-Saxon *hlæfdige*, kneader of bread]

ladybird *noun* any of thousands of species of small beetle with an oval body that is usually bright red or yellow with black spots, a colouration that serves to warn birds and other predators of its unpleasant taste. Ladybirds feed mainly on aphids and scale insects, and play an important role in controlling the numbers of plant pests.

Lady Chapel *RC Church* a chapel dedicated to the Virgin Mary. It is usually built behind the main altar, and forms an extension to the main building.

Lady Chatterley's Lover a novel by D H Lawrence (1928). It describes the life and loves of Connie Chatterley, the wife of a landowner disabled in World War I. Its language and sexual explicitness caused it to be prohibited in Britain until 1960 when, after publishing a complete edition, Penguin Books were unsuccessfully prosecuted in a highly publicized obscenity trial.

Lady Day 25 Mar, the feast of the Annunciation.

lady-in-waiting noun (PL. **ladies-in-waiting**) a woman attending a queen or princess.

lady-killer noun colloq. a man who habitually pursues or seduces women.

ladylike adj. like or appropriate to a lady in manners, appearance, or behaviour, especially in being polite and elegant.

Lady Macbeth of Mtsensk (Ledi Makbet Mtsenskovo uyezda), later revised as *Katerina Ismailova* by Dmitri Shostakovich (1934). The story, set in 19c Russia, arises from Katerina's affair with Sergey during her husband's absence.

Lady of Shalott, The a poem by Alfred, Lord Tennyson (1832, revised 1842). It is set in Arthurian times and describes the fate of a lonely lady who can only look on the outside world via its reflection in a mirror.

Lady of the Lake, The a poem in six cantos by Sir Walter Scott (1810). Set in the Trossachs of Scotland during the early 16c, it is a romantic tale based on a true story.

Ladyship noun (usually **Your** or **Her Ladyship**) a title used to address peeresses (but not duchesses) and the wives and daughters of peers and knights.

Ladysmith, Siege of one of the three sieges (1899–1900) in the second Boer War, around which much of the War's action took place. An attempt to relieve the town was frustrated at the battle of Spion Kop (Jan 1900), but then General Sir Redvers Buller (1839–1908) succeeded in raising the siege (28 Feb 1900).

Lady's Not For Burning, The a play by Christopher Fry (1949). Set in the Middle Ages, it is a comedy about a woman unfairly accused of witchcraft, and is noted for its eloquent wordplay.

lady's-slipper noun an orchid with a large yellow slipper-like lip.

Lady Windermere's Fan a play by Oscar Wilde (1892). It is a comedy in which the heroine's reputation rests on a credible explanation of why her fan should have been found in Lord Darlington's apartments.

Lae POP (1990) 81 000, a seaport and industrial city in Morobe province, Papua New Guinea. It is situated on the S coast of Huon Peninsula, E New Guinea, c.320km/200mi N of Port Moresby. The city was occupied by the Japanese in World War II.

Laënnec, René Théophile Hyacinthe (1781–1826) French physician, born in Quimper, Brittany. An army doctor from 1799, in 1814 he became physician to the Salpêtrière, and in 1816 Chief Physician to the Hôpital Necker, where he invented the stethoscope in the same year. In 1819 he published outstanding clinical and pathological descriptions of many chest diseases, such as tuberculosis, pneumonia, and bronchitis.

Laertes the cynical but ultimately noble brother of Ophelia in Shakespeare's *Hamlet*, who is manipulatively drawn into the plot to kill Hamlet.

La Fayette, Marie Madeleine (Pioche de Lavergne), Comtesse (1634–93) French novelist and reformer of French Romance writing, born in Paris. She married the Comte de La Fayette in 1655, and at 33 formed a liaison with La Rochefoucauld, which lasted until his death in 1680. Her major novel is *La Princesse de Clèves* (1678), which depicts the court life of her day.

Lafayette, Marie Joseph (Paul Yves Roch Gilbert du Motier), Marquis de (1757–1834) French soldier, politician, and reformer, born in Chavagniac into an ancient noble family. He fought in America against the British during the War of Independence (1777–9,

1780–2), and became a friend of George Washington. A liberal aristocrat, in the National Assembly of 1789 he presented a draft of a declaration of the Rights of Man, based on the US Declaration of Independence. Hated by the Jacobins for his moderation, he defected to Austria, but returned to France during the Consulate. During the Restoration he sat in the Chamber of Deputies (1818–24), became a radical leader of the Opposition (1825–30), and commanded the National Guard in the 1830 Revolution.

La Fontaine, Jean de (1621–95) French poet, born in Château-Thierry. His *Contes et nouvelles en vers* (Tales and Novels in Verse, 1665) was followed by his major work, *Fables choisies mises en vers* (Selected Fables in Verse), published between 1668 and 1694.

Laforgue, Jules (1860–87) French poet, born in Montevideo, Uruguay. He published only two volumes, *Les Complaintes* (The Complaints, 1885) and *L'Imitation de Notre-Dame la lune* (The Imitation of Our Lady the Moon, 1886), and left the posthumous *Derniers Vers* (Last Poems, 1890). His work influenced Modernist poets, especially Ezra Pound and T S Eliot.

lag[1] — verb intrans. (**lagged, lagging**) (often **lag behind**) to move or progress too slowly and become left behind. — noun **1** a lagging behind; a delay. **2** the amount by which one thing is delayed behind another. [origin uncertain: perhaps a corruption of *last* in a children's game]

lag[2] — verb (**lagged, lagging**) to cover (a boiler, water pipes, etc) with a thick covering to keep the heat in. — noun same as LAGGING.

lag[3] noun slang a convict or former convict. [origin unknown]

lager noun a light beer. [from German *Lagerbier*, beer for storing]

Lagerkvist, Pär (Fabian) (1891–1974) Swedish writer, born in Växjö. He began his literary career as an Expressionist poet with *Angest* (Anguish, 1916) which emphasizes the catastrophe of war. His novels include *The Hangman* (1934), *The Dwarf* (1944), and *Barabbas* (1951). He was awarded the Nobel Prize for Literature in 1951.

Lagerlöf, Selma (Ottiliana Lovisa) (1858–1940) Swedish novelist, born in Värmland. She became a schoolteacher, and sprang to fame with *Gösta Berling's Saga* (1891). The author of many fairy tales and romances, she was awarded the 1909 Nobel Prize for Literature — the first woman to receive the distinction.

lager lout a man, especially a youth, who behaves in a boorish, aggressive, or unruly manner after drinking lager, beer, etc.

laggard noun a person or thing that lags behind.

lagging an insulating cover for pipes, boilers, etc.

lagoon noun a relatively shallow body of water, often brackish, that is more or less separated from the open sea by a barrier such as a reef or a narrow bank of sand or shingle. [from Italian *laguna*]

Lagos POP (1992e) 1.3m, the chief port and former capital of Nigeria, situated 120km/75mi SW of Ibadan, on Lagos I. HISTORY settled by Yoruba peoples in c.1700; a slave-trade centre until the mid-19c; occupied by the British in 1851; the Colony of Lagos was created in 1862; became part of the S Nigeria protectorate in 1906; capital of Nigeria from 1960 until 1982. NOTABLE FEATURES National Museum; palace; racecourse.

Lagrange, Joseph Louis de, Comte (1736–1813) Italian–French mathematician, born in Turin. Director of the mathematical section of the Berlin Academy from 1766, he gained a Europe-wide reputation for his work on calculus, celestial mechanics, the nature of sound, and

algebraic equations. He returned to Paris in 1787 at the invitation of Louis XVI. Under Napoleon I he became a senator and a count, and taught at the École Normale and the École Polytechnique. His greatest work was *Traité de mécanique analytique* (Treatise on Analytic Mechanics, 1788).

La Guardia, Fiorello H(enry) (1882–1947) US lawyer and politician, born in New York City, where he spent the whole of his career. He became Deputy Attorney-General (1915–17), and sat in Congress as a Republican (1917–21, 1923–33). A popular Mayor of New York (1933–45), he initiated housing and labour safeguards schemes. One of the city airports is named after him.

Laguna, La POP (1991) 110 000, the second-largest town and former capital of Tenerife I, Canary Is, Spain. NOTABLE FEATURES cathedral (16c), Church of the Conception (1502).

lah see LA.

Lahore POP (1990e) 4.1m, the second-largest city in Pakistan and the capital of Punjab province. It lies between the Ravi and the Sutlej rivers, 1 030km/640mi from Karachi. The city was taken in 1849 by the British, who made it the capital of Punjab. It is considered to be the cultural capital of Pakistan. NOTABLE FEATURES museum; Badshahi Mosque; Wazir Khan Mosque; Shalimar Gardens; Royal Fort of Akbar. The city is a World Heritage site.

laid past participle of LAY[1].
— **laid back** colloq. relaxed.
laid up 1 colloq. confined to bed because of illness. **2** *said of a boat* in dock or on shore.

laid paper paper with fine lines running across the surface.

lain past participle of LIE[2].

Laing, Ronald David (1927–89) Scottish psychiatrist, born in Glasgow. He worked at the Tavistock Clinic in London and the Tavistock Institute for Human Relations, and became Chairman of the Philadelphia Association in 1964. His *The Divided Self* (1960) suggested that psychiatrists should not attempt to cure or ameliorate the symptoms of mental illness (itself a term which he repudiated), but rather should encourage patients to view themselves as going through an enriching experience. He also implied that the primary responsibility for psychiatric breakdown lies with society and/or with the patient's immediate family.

lair noun **1** a wild animal's den. **2** colloq. a place of refuge or hiding. [from Anglo-Saxon *leger*]

laird noun Scot. a landowner, especially of a large estate.

laissez-faire or **laisser-faire** noun a policy of not interfering in what others are doing. [from French *laissez faire*, let do]

laity noun (usually **the laity**) ordinary people who are not members of a particular profession, especially people who are not members of the clergy. [from LAY[3]]

Laius in Greek mythology, a king of Thebes, son of Labdacus and father of Oedipus. He married Jocasta, and was warned by an oracle that their son would destroy him. This happened when Oedipus, assumed to be dead, returned from Corinth and accidentally killed Laius during a quarrel on the road.

lake[1] noun a large area of still fresh or salt water, surrounded by land and lying in a depression in the Earth's surface, which receives water from rivers, streams, springs, direct rainfall, or melting snow. Many lakes are used as reservoirs, and for the generation of hydroelectricity. [from Middle English *lac*]

lake[2] noun **1** a reddish dye, originally obtained from lac. **2** a substance made from dye and a mordant, used in dyeing fabrics to make the dye insoluble. [from LAC]

Lake District (*usually* **the Lake District**) a part of Cumbria, NW England, noted for its scenery. AREA c.1 800sq km/700sq mi. It consists of a system of glaciated valleys and ribbon lakes. The lakes include Windermere (largest lake in England), Derwent Water, Ullswater, Bassenthwaite, Thirlmere, Buttermere, and Coniston Water. Mountains include Scafell (highest peak in England), Skiddaw, and Helvellyn. Chief towns are Keswick, Windermere, Ambleside, and Grasmere. The area has associations with William Wordsworth, Samuel Taylor Coleridge, Robert Southey, and John Ruskin. A national park, established in 1951, protects 866sq km/334sq mi of the Lake District. The area is popular for walking, climbing, and water sports; it is supported by farming, quarrying, and forestry.

lake dwellings *Archaeol.* Stone Age villages built on supports on marshy ground around lakes, or on piling driven into the bottom of lakes. There are numerous examples in W Africa, S America, and on Pacific islands. In Europe, a 3c–1c BC marshland settlement of some 80 reed-roofed huts built on an artificial island of felled trees has been excavated near Glastonbury, England, and some 200 similar communities have been found around the Swiss lakes.

Lake Placid POP (1984e) 3 000, a winter sports resort in Essex County, N New York State, USA. It lies in the Adirondack Mts, 65km/40mi SW of Plattsburg on Mirror Lake.

Lake poets a term referring to the poets who took up residence in the English Lake District in the early 19c. They include William Wordsworth, Samuel Taylor Coleridge and Robert Southey.

Laker, Jim (James Charles) (1922–86) English cricketer, born in Saltaire, Yorkshire. He made test cricket history at Old Trafford in 1956 when he took 19 of the 20 Australian wickets for 90 runs, including 10 in one innings. Earlier in that season, playing for his county (Surrey) against the Australians, he had also taken all 10 Australian wickets in an innings. He took 193 wickets in 46 test matches and during his career (1946–64) took 1 944 wickets (average 18.41). He retired in 1959, but made a comeback with Essex.

Lakota — *noun* **1** a Native American people comprising the westernmost branch of the Sioux. **2** a member of this people. **3** the Siouan language of this people. — *adj.* relating to this people or their langauge. [a native American name]

Lakshadweep, formerly (to 1973) **Laccadive Islands** POP (1991) 52 000, a union territory in India. AREA 32sq km/12sq mi. It comprises 10 inhabited and 17 uninhabited coral islands in the Arabian Sea, 320km/200mi off the Malabar Coast of Kerala. Kavaratti is the administrative centre. The Malayalam language is spoken widely, although Mahl is spoken on Minicoy; Muslim is the main religion. HISTORY discovered by Vasco da Gama in 1498; the British took the N islands in 1792 and those in the S in 1877; ceded to India in 1956. ECONOMY coconuts, coir, bananas; fishing; tourism.

Lakshmi, also called the **lotus-goddess** the Hindu goddess of prosperity, and the consort of Vishnu. She is associated with Diwali, the autumn festival of lights.

Lalibela churches a group of 11 churches in the holy city of Lalibela, central Ethiopia. Each of the buildings, which date from c.13c BC, is hewn from a single rock, hollowed and sculpted to look as if it were constructed from separate stones. It is a World Heritage site.

Lalique, René (1860–1945) French jeweller and glassware designer, born in Ay. He founded his own business in Paris in 1885. His glass designs, decorated with relief figures, animals, and flowers, were an important contribution to the Art Nouveau movement.

Lalla Rookh a sequence of four oriental tales in verse connected by a tale in prose by Thomas Moore (1817). The framework for the verse tales is the marriage-journey of Lalla Rookh, the emperor's daughter.

Lally, Thomas Arthur, Comte de (Count of) (1702–66) French soldier, the son of an Irish Jacobite, born in Romans. He accompanied Prince Charles Edward Stuart to Scotland in 1745, and in 1756 became Commander-in-Chief in the French East Indies. Active against the British in the Seven Years' War, he was defeated, and capitulated in 1761. On his return to France, he was accused of treachery, and executed.

lam *verb* (**lammed**, **lamming**) *slang* to beat or thrash. [from Norse *lemja*, to beat until lame]

lama *noun* a Buddhist priest or monk in Tibet or Mongolia. [from Tibetan *blama*]

Lamaism, also called **Tibetan Buddhism** the religion of Tibet, a form of Mahayana Buddhism. When Buddhism entered Tibet in the 7c, the traditional Bon religion opposed it, but the following century the Indian missionary Padmasambhava combined elements of both religions and Lamaism developed. Later the reformer Tsong Kha Pa (1357–1419) founded a school called the Gelu, the heads of which acquired the title of Dalai Lama. When a reigning Lama dies, an infant is sought who is his reincarnation.

Lamarck, Jean-Baptiste Pierre Antoine de Monet, Chevalier de (1744–1829) French naturalist and evolutionist, born in Bazentin. After serving in the French army, he studied medicine and botany, and in 1773 published the successful *Flore française* (French Flora), the first key to French flowers. He was later appointed to posts at the royal garden and the Natural History Museum. The originator of the taxonomic distinction between vertebrates and invertebrates, his *Histoire des animaux sans vertèbres* (Natural History of Invertebrates) appeared in 1815–22. He foreshadowed Charles Darwin's theory of evolution, but became best known for his theory that the development or degeneration of organs by 'use or disuse' can be inherited by later generations.

Lamarckism *Biol.* one of the earliest theories of evolution, proposed by Jean-Baptiste Lamarck during the early 19c. He suggested that characteristics acquired during the lifetime of an organism, eg a change in the size of one of its parts as a result of use or disuse, could be transmitted to parents to offspring. The theory was discredited when the true principles of heredity were established, and it was superseded by Darwinism.

Lamartine, Alphonse (Marie Louis) de (1790–1869) French poet and politican, born in Mâcon. He was a diplomat in Naples and

Lakshmi

Florence, and in the 1848 Revolution became a member of the provisional government in which he served as Minister of Foreign Affairs. His best-known work is his first volume of lyrical poems, *Méditations poétiques* (1820). His historical works include the *Histoire de la Révolution de 1848* (1849).

Lamb, Charles (1775–1834) English essayist, born in London. He worked as a clerk for the East India Company (1792–1825), and achieved success as a writer through the joint publication with his sister of *Tales from Shakespeare* (1807), which was followed by other works for children. In 1818 he published his collected verse and prose, and was invited to join the staff of the new *London Magazine*. This led to his best-known works, the series of essays under the pen name Elia.

lamb — *noun* **1** a young sheep. **2** the flesh of a lamb or sheep, eaten as food. **3** a person who is kind, gentle, and good. **4** (**the Lamb** *or* **the Lamb of God**) a name for Christ (John 1.29). — *verb intrans.* **1** *said of a ewe* to give birth to a lamb or lambs. **2** *said of a shepherd* to tend lambing ewes. [from Anglo-Saxon *lamb*]

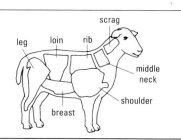

lamb cuts

lambada *noun* a style of dance with sinuous hip movements to salsa-like music, originating in Brazil and popularized in the late 1980s. [from Portuguese *lambada*, whip-crack]

lambaste *or* **lambast** *verb* **1** to thrash or beat severely. **2** to scold severely. [from LAM + BASTE³]

lambency *noun* a state of sparkling or flickering.

lambent *adj.* **1** *said of a flame or light* flickering over a surface. **2** *said of eyes, etc* gently sparkling. **3** *said of wit* light and brilliant. [from Latin *lambere*, to lick]

Lambert, John (1619–84) English soldier, born in Calton, Yorkshire. He joined the Parliamentary army in the English Civil War, and commanded the cavalry at Marston Moor (1644). He headed the cabal which overthrew Richard Cromwell (1659), and virtually governed the country with his officers as the 'Committee of Safety'. At the Restoration (1661) he was tried, and imprisoned on Drake's I, Plymouth, until his death.

Lambeth Conferences the meetings of a consultative body of bishops of the Anglican Communion. They gather at the personal invitation of the Archbishop of Canterbury to consider issues of common concern, but have no legislative powers. Normally convened every 10 years, the most recent meetings have lasted for about a month, and have considered not only internal Anglican matters (such as the ordination of women) and theological issues, but also social issues (such as race relations and human rights).

lambing *noun* the time when ewes give birth to lambs.

lambskin *noun* the skin of a lamb, usually with the wool left on it, used to make slippers, coats, etc.

lambswool *noun* fine wool obtained from a lamb.

LAMDA *abbrev.* London Academy of Music and Dramatic Art.

lame — *adj.* **1** not able to walk properly, especially because of an injury or defect. **2** *said of an excuse, etc* not convincing; weak. — *verb* to make lame. [from Anglo-Saxon *lama*]

lamé *noun* a fabric which has gold and silver threads woven into it. [from French *lamé*]

lame duck 1 a person who can do nothing without the help of others. **2** an official in the final months of office, after the election of a successor. **3** a company with financial problems.

lamella *noun* (PL. **lamellae**) **1** *Anat.* a thin sheet or plate of tissue, especially one of the many thin layers of which compact bone is formed. **2** *Bot.* any of the thin sheet-like membranes that are present within the chloroplasts of plant cells. **3** *Biol.* in a mushroom or toadstool, any of the vertical spore-bearing structures or gills that radiate outwards from the stalk on the underside of the cap. [from Latin *lamella*]

lamely *adv.* in a weak or ineffectual manner; feebly.

lameness *noun* a lame state; weakness.

lament — *verb trans., intrans.* to feel or express regret or sadness. — *noun* **1** an expression of sadness, grief, regret, etc. **2** a poem, song, etc which expresses great grief, especially following someone's death. [from Latin *lamentum*]

lamentable *adj.* (with stress on *lam*-) regrettable, shameful, deplorable.

lamentably *adv.* (with stress on *lam*-) regrettably; shamefully: *they are lamentably behind the times.*

lamentation *noun* an act of lamenting; a lament.

Lamentations, Book of a book of the Hebrew Bible and Old Testament, probably dated shortly after the Babylonian conquest of Jerusalem (587/6 BC), traditionally attributed to the prophet Jeremiah, but not of the same style as the Book of Jeremiah. It consists of five poems which lament the destruction of Jerusalem, express the distress of its people, and petition God for its restoration.

lamented *adj.*, *said of a dead person* mourned for.

lamina *noun* (PL. **laminae**) **1** a thin plate or layer of a material of uniform thickness, eg bone, rock, or metal. **2** *Bot.* the flattened part of a leaf blade. [from Latin *lamina*]

laminate — *verb* (pronounced -*nate*) **1** to beat (metal) into sheets. **2** to make by bonding thin sheets of material on top of each other. **3** to cover with a thin sheet of plastic or other material. **4** *trans., intrans.* to split or be split into layers. — *noun* (pronounced -*nət*) material or a structure made by bonding thin layers of material together. — *adj.* (pronounced -*nət*) in thin plates or layers. [from Latin *lamina*, thin plate]

laminated *adj.*, *said of metal* beaten into thin sheets; made into laminate.

lamination *noun* the process of laminating or making metal into thin sheets.

Lammas *noun* 1 Aug, an old feast celebrating the first crops from the harvest. [from Anglo-Saxon *hlafmæsse*, from *hlaf*, loaf + *mæsse*, mass]

lammergeyer *noun* a large rare vulture, found in the remote moutain regions of Europe, Africa, and Asia (especially the Himalayas), that has a wingspan of nearly 3m, a feathered neck, and dark tufts of feathers on either side of its beak. It feeds on carrion, but is relatively timid and will not approach a carcase until other vultures have eaten their fill. [from German *Lämmergeier*, lamb vulture]

Lammeter, Nancy a no-nonsense character who is wooed, and eventually won, by Godfrey Cass in George Eliot's *Silas Marner.*

Lamont, Norman (Stewart Hughson) (1942–) Scottish Conservative politician, born in Lerwick, Shetland. He entered parliament in 1972 and in the Thatcher administrations rose to be Under-Secretary of State for Energy (1979–81) and Trade and Industry Minister (1981–5), before he entered the Treasury. As Financial Secretary (1986–9), then Chief Secretary, he supported the then Chancellor, John Major, in his successful bid for the premiership (1990), and was appointed Chancellor in the new government. With the economy increasingly troubled, he decided to withdraw Britain from the European Exchange Rate Mechanism (Sep 1992), which led to the effective devaluation of sterling. He resigned in 1993.

lamp *noun* **1** an appliance for producing a steady light, especially in the form of bulb-holder and shade. **2** an appliance with a glass case covering a flame produced by burning oil, etc, as a source of light. **3** an appliance producing ultraviolet or infrared radiation for treating certain medical complaints. [from Greek *lampe*, torch]

lampblack *noun* soot obtained from burning carbon, used as a pigment.

Lampedusa, Giuseppe (Tomasi), Duke of Palma (1896–1957) Italian writer, born in Palermo, Sicily. He is remembered for his only complete work, *Il gattopardo* (The Leopard), published posthumously in 1958, and filmed in 1963. A collection of autobiographical and fictional pieces, *Racconti*, was published in 1961.

lampoon — *noun* a personal satirical attack. — *verb* to attack or laugh at in lampoons. [from French *lampon*, thought to be from *lampons*, let us drink, the refrain of a drinking-song]

lampooner *or* **lampoonist** *noun* a person who composes lampoons.

lamppost *noun* a tall post supporting a street-lamp.

lamprey *noun* (PL. **lampreys**) *Zool.* any of about 30 species of primitive jawless fish, resembling an eel in shape, and belonging to the same class (Agnatha) as the hagfish. Lampreys lack scales, and have a skeleton of cartilage. [from Old French *lampreie*, from medieval Latin *lampreda*]

◇ Lampreys vary in size, the largest being about 1m in length. They are found in the sea and in freshwater in temperate and subarctic regions, and all species swim up rivers in order to breed. Young lampreys are blind, and spend up to eight years on muddy river-beds before migrating to the sea as adults. Lampreys feed by clinging to other fishes with their sucker-like mouths, and sucking the blood of their hosts after they have rasped away the flesh with their horny teeth. They also eat carrion, and their well-developed eyes suggest that they hunt by sight, and not by smell as the hagfish does.

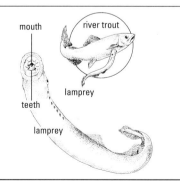

lamprey

lampshade *noun* a shade placed over a lamp or light-bulb to soften or direct the light coming from it.

LAN *abbrev. Comput.* local area network, a computer network operating over a small area, such as an office or group of offices.

Lanai POP (1988e) 2 000, an island of the US state of Hawaii. It lies in the Pacific Ocean, W of Maui and S of Molokai. AREA 365sq km/ 140sq mi. Part of Maui county, its chief town is Lanai City. ECONOMY pineapples.

Lanark POP (1981) 9 900, the capital of Clydesdale district, Strathclyde, S central Scotland. It is a market town, lying on the R Clyde, 18km/11mi SE of Motherwell. The former mill village of New Lanark, 2km/1mi S, was founded in 1784 and was the setting for the experimental social ideas of Robert Owen.

Lancashire POP (1992e) 1.4m, a county in NW England, divided into 14 districts. AREA 3 063sq km/1 182sq mi. It is bounded W by the Irish Sea, N by Cumbria, E by North and West Yorkshire, and S by Greater Manchester and Merseyside. PHYSICAL DESCRIPTION the county is drained by the Lune and Ribble rivers; to the E lie the Pennines. CHIEF TOWNS Preston (county town), Lancaster, Blackpool, Blackburn, Burnley; ports at Heysham and Fleetwood. It was a world centre for cotton manufacture in the 19c. ECONOMY textiles; footwear; fishing; mining; tourism; aerospace; electronics. NOTABLE FEATURE Forest of Bowland.

Lancaster, Sir Osbert (1908–86) English cartoonist and writer. He worked on the *Architectural Review* (1934–9). He began drawing cartoons for the *Daily Express* in 1939 and created Maudie Littlehampton and other characters. He also worked as a theatrical designer (from 1951).

Lancaster POP (1981) 45 000, a city in Lancaster district, Lancashire, NW England, lying on the R Lune, 32km/20mi N of Preston. It was chartered in 1193 and became a city in 1937. Its port trade declined because of river silting. NOTABLE FEATURES 12c castle, on the site of a Roman fort; Priory Church of St Mary (15c).

Lancaster, Duchy of see DUCHY OF LANCASTER.

Lancaster, House of a branch of the Plantagenet dynasty, founded by Edmund 'Crouchback', the younger son of Henry III and 1st Earl of Lancaster (1267–96). From this branch came three kings of England: Henry IV, Henry V, and Henry VI.

Lancaster House Agreement an agreement that ended the war in Zimbabwe and created a new constitution under which independence would be given in Apr 1980. An election, held under British supervision, was won by the Zimbabwe African National Union under the leadership of Robert Mugabe.

Lancastrian — *noun* **1** a person from Lancaster or Lancashire. **2** *Hist.* a supporter of the House of Lancaster in the Wars of the Roses. See also YORKIST. — *adj.* relating to Lancaster, the House of Lancaster, or Lancashire.

Lance a male first name, a short form of various compound names beginning *Land*-, meaning 'land' or 'territory'. [from the Old French name *Lance*, the weapon, and the Germanic name *Lanzo*]

lance — *noun usually Hist.* a long spear with a hard pointed head at one end and sometimes a small flag at the other, used as a weapon by charging horsemen. — *verb* **1** to cut open (a boil, etc) with a lancet. **2** to pierce with, or as if with, a lance. [from Latin *lancea*]

lance corporal in the British army, a soldier holding the lowest rank of non-commissioned officer, between private and corporal.

Lancelot, Sir *or* **Launcelot du Lac** in Arthurian legend, one of the Knights of the Round Table, the son of King Ban of Benoic, the courtly lover of Guinevere, and the father of Galahad by Elaine. In spite of his near-perfection as a knight, he failed in the quest for the Holy Grail because of his adultery with Guinevere; he arrived too late to help Arthur in the last battle.

lanceolate *adj.* shaped like a spearhead, being much longer than it is wide, and tapering to a point at each end. [from Latin *lanceola*, small lance]

lancer *noun Hist.* a cavalry soldier belonging to a regiment armed with lances.

lancers *sing. noun* a set of quadrilles, or the music for it.

lancet *noun* 1 a small surgical knife with a point and both edges sharpened. 2 (*in full* **lancet arch** *or* **window**) *Archit.* a high and narrow pointed arch or window, typical of Early English architecture of the 13c. [from Old French *lancette*, a small lance]

Lancs. *abbrev.* Lancashire.

Land, Edwin Herbert (1909–91) US inventor and physicist, born in Bridgeport, Connecticut. Before graduating from Harvard he left to set up his own laboratory (1932), and developed the polarizing film 'Polaroid®', which he used to manufacture camera filters and sunglasses. He founded the Polaroid Corporation in 1937, and invented the one-step Polaroid Land camera (1947), which developed pictures inside the camera within one minute; he also contributed to the theoretical understanding of colour vision.

land — *noun* 1 the solid part of the earth's surface, not covered by water. 2 the ground or soil, especially in terms of its use or quality: *building land.* 3 land used for agriculture: *farmland.* 4 a country, state, or region: *one's native land.* 5 (**lands**) estates. — *verb* 1 *intrans., trans.* to come or bring to rest on the ground or water, or in a particular place, after flight through the air. 2 to bring on to land from a ship. 3 (**land someone** *or* **oneself in something**) *colloq.* to put someone or find oneself in a given position or situation, usually unwelcome or unfavourable: *landed themselves in trouble.* 4 (**land someone with something**) *colloq.* to give or pass something unpleasant or unwanted to someone: *landed us with all the bills to pay.* 5 to bring (a fish caught on a line) to land. 6 *colloq.* to succeed in acquiring (a job, prize, etc). 7 *colloq.* to give (a blow) to (someone): *landed him one on the ear.* — **land up** *colloq.* to come to be in a given position or situation: *likely to land up married.* **see how the land lies** to find out what the situation is, especially before making a decision. [from Anglo-Saxon *land*]

Land Acts, Irish a succession of British Acts passed in 1870, 1881, 1903, and 1909 which aimed first to give tenants greater security and compensation for improvements, and later to enable them to buy the estates they farmed. The Acts also aimed to reduce nationalist agitation.

land agent a person who manages a large estate for the owner.

landau *noun* a four-wheeled, horse-drawn carriage with a removable front cover and a back cover which folds down. [from *Landau* in Germany, where they were first made]

landed *adj.* 1 owning land or estates: *landed gentry.* 2 consisting of or derived from land: *landed estates.*

landfall *noun* an approach to land, or the land approached, after a journey by sea or air.

land-girl *noun* a woman who works on a farm, especially during a war.

landing *noun* 1 the process of coming to shore or to ground. 2 a place for disembarking, especially from a ship. 3 the level part of a staircase between flights of steps, or at the very top.

landing-craft *noun* (PL. **landing-craft**) *Mil.* a low open vessel for landing troops and equipment on beaches.

landing-gear *noun* the wheels and supporting structure which allow an aircraft to land and take off.

landing-stage *noun* a platform, either fixed or floating, for disembarking passengers and goods from a ship.

landlady *noun* 1 a woman who owns property which is let to a tenant. 2 a woman who keeps a public house or hotel.

Land League an association formed (1879) in Ireland by Michael Davitt to agitate for tenant rights, in particular the '3 Fs': *fair rents*, to be fixed by arbitration if necessary; *fixity of tenure* while rents were paid; and *freedom* for tenants to sell rights of occupancy. William Gladstone conceded the essence of these demands in the 1881 Land Act.

landlocked *adj., said of a country* almost or completely enclosed by land.

landlord 1 a man who owns property which is let to a tenant. 2 a man who keeps a public house or hotel.

landlubber *noun derog. Naut.* a person who lives and works on the land and has no experience of the sea.

landmark *noun* 1 a conspicuous or well-known object on land, especially one that serves as a guide to sailors and travellers. 2 an event of importance, especially in marking a significant stage in the history or development of something.

landmass *noun* a large area of land unbroken by seas.

land mine a mine laid on or near the surface of the ground, detonated when disturbed from above.

Land of Youth, Irish **Tir na n-Og** in Irish mythology, the name for a land of shining beauty and comely women, free from suffering and death, which lies across the sea or in the burial mound. It is visited by kings and heroes, who find Lug, the god of the Sun, reigning there.

Landor, Walter Savage (1775–1864) English writer, born in Warwick. He was expelled from both Rugby and Oxford, and lived for many years on the Continent. He wrote poems, plays, and essays, but is mainly remembered for his prose dialogues, *Imaginary Conversations* (1824–9).

landowner *noun* a person who owns extensive areas of land.

landrace *noun* a type of domestic pig, originating from Denmark, that has a long pale body, white hair, and large pendulous ears. It is reared mainly for bacon.

Landrover *noun trademark* a strong motor vehicle used for driving over rough ground.

landscape *noun* 1 the area and features of land that can be seen in a broad view. 2 a picture showing a view of the countryside. 3 the genre of landscape painting.
◇ The representation of unified scenes from nature, for their own sake, did not develop until the 16c. Isolated natural elements, such as trees, rivers, and mountains, had featured in the backgrounds of pictures since ancient times, but were generally incidental to the main theme. From the 16c onwards, paintings with landscape as the principal theme developed in various modes: ideal, heroic, pastoral, and naturalistic. It flourished in the 18c and 19c with, for example, John Constable, Joseph Turner, and the Barbizon School, and reached the peak of its popular appeal with the Impressionists.

landscape gardener a person who practises landscape gardening, especially professionally.

landscape gardening the art or business of planning and laying out gardens and parks, especially on a large scale and so as to resemble natural scenery.

Landseer, Sir Edwin (Henry) (1802–73) English artist, born in London. He was trained by his father to sketch animals from life, and he exhibited at the Royal Academy at the age of 13. His paintings, several of which are set in the Scottish Highlands, are mainly of dogs and deer (eg the *Monarch of the Glen*, 1851). His sculptures include the bronze lions in Trafalgar Square (1867).

Land's End, ancient **Bolerium** a granite headland, situated in Cornwall, SW England. It forms the westernmost extremity of England. Offshore lies the Longships Lighthouse.

Land's End to John o' Groats by Car a trip made for the first time on four motorized wheels by Henry Sturmey, the editor of *Autocar*, in 1897. He took just over 93 hours to complete the 1 495km/929mi journey at an average speed of 16kph/10mph and described the trip as being 'trouble free'.

landslide *noun* 1 (*also* **landslip**) the sudden downward movement of a mass of soil and rock material, especially in mountainous areas, under the influence of gravity, eg as a result of heavy rain or snow, earthquakes, or blasting operations. 2 a victory in an election by an overwhelming majority.

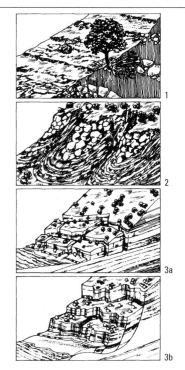

1: soil creeps slowly downhill, pulled by gravity
2: a shock causes clay to liquefy to form a mudflow
3: material may fall from a break along a plane (a) or curved surface (b)

landslide formation

landslip same as LANDSLIDE 1.

Landsteiner, Karl (1868–1943) Austrian-born US pathologist, born in Vienna. Professor at the University of Vienna from 1909, he later worked at the Rockefeller Institute in New York (1922–43). He discovered the four major blood groups (A, B, AB, and O) in 1901, and the M and N groups in 1927. This led to the development of safe blood transfusions and brought him the 1930 Nobel Prize for Physiology or Medicine.

landward — *adj.* lying or facing toward the land. — *adv.* (**landward** *or* **landwards**) towards land: *then turned landward.*

Lane, Sir Allen, originally **Allen Lane Williams** (1902–70) English publisher and pioneer of paperback books, born in Bristol. In 1919 he was apprenticed to The Bodley Head, where he eventually became Chairman. In 1935 he formed the revolutionary Penguin Books Ltd, where he began by reprinting novels in paper covers at 6d (2½p) each, later expanding to nonfictional Pelicans and children's Puffins.

lane *noun* **1** a narrow road or street. **2** a division of a road for a single line of traffic. **3** a regular course across the sea taken by ships, or through the air by aircraft. **4** a lengthways division of a running track or swimming pool, for one competitor. **5** a passage through a crowd. [from Anglo-Saxon *lanu*]

Lang, Fritz (1890–1976) US film director, born in Vienna. After World War I he moved to Berlin, where he began to make films, notably *Metropolis* (1926). He settled in America and his later films include his portrayal of mob rule, *Fury* (1936), as well as several thrillers and westerns.

Lange, David (Russell) (1942–) New Zealand politician, born in Auckland. A lawyer by profession, he entered parliament in 1977, became Leader of the Labour Party in 1983, and Prime Minister (1984–9) in the fourth Labour government.

Langevin, Paul (1872–1946) French physicist, born in Paris. Professor at the Sorbonne, he made important studies of the magnetic properties of materials, and worked on the molecular structure of gases; during World War I he pioneered the application of sonar techniques to the detection of submarines. Imprisoned by the Nazis after the occupation of France, he was later released, and although kept under surveillance, managed to escape to Switzerland. After the liberation he returned to Paris.

Langland *or* **Langley, William** (c.1332–c.1400) English poet, born (probably) in Ledbury, Herefordshire. He is thought to have been a clerk and a minor cleric who lived for many years in London. He is credited with the authorship of *Piers Plowman*, the medieval alliterative poem on the theme of spiritual pilgrimage.

Langley, Samuel Pierpont (1834–1906) US astronomer and aeronautical pioneer, born in Roxbury, Massachusetts. He worked as an engineer and architect before becoming Professor of Astronomy at Western University, Pennsylvania, in 1867. He invented the bolometer to measure the Sun's radiant heat (1880), and was the first to build a heavier-than-air flying machine.

Langmuir, Irving (1881–1957) US physical chemist, born in New York City. He worked at the General Electric Company (1909–50), where he became associate director of research in 1932, the year in which he was awarded the Nobel Prize for Chemistry for his work on solid and liquid surfaces. His many inventions included the gas-filled tungsten lamp and an improved vacuum pump.

Langton, Stephen (c.1150–1228) English prelate and Archbishop of Canterbury. Pope Innocent III made him a cardinal (1206) and Archbishop (1207), but King John refused to accept his appointment, and Langton was kept out of the see until 1213. He took sides with the barons against John, and his name is the first of the subscribing witnesses of Magna Carta.

Langtry, Lillie, *née* **Emilie Charlotte Le Breton**, known as the **Jersey Lily** (1853–1929) British actress, born in Jersey, Channel Is. One of the most noted beauties of her time, she made her first major stage appearance in 1881, managed the Imperial Theatre, and was also a racehorse owner.

language *noun* **1** the system of human communication, both spoken and written, using words in combinations according to established principles. **2** the speech and writing of a particular nation or social group. **3** the faculty of speech. **4** a style of speech or expression with words: *ele-*

gant language. **5** any other way of communicating or expressing meaning: *sign language.* **6** professional or specialized vocabulary: *legal language.* **7** (**language** *or* **bad language**) the use of rude and offensive words: *mind one's language.* **8** a system of signs and symbols used to write computer programs.
— **speak the same language** to have the same way of thinking or similar tastes.
[from Old French *langage*]

Language Families

Estimates of the numbers of speakers in the main language families.

Indo-European	2 000 000 000
Sino-Tibetan	1 040 000 000
Niger-Congo	260 000 000
Afro-Asiatic	230 000 000
Austronesian	200 000 000
Dravidian	140 000 000
Japanese	120 000 000
Altaic	90 000 000
Austro-Asiatic	60 000 000
Korean	60 000 000
Tai	50 000 000
Nilo-Saharan	30 000 000
Amerindian	25 000 000
(North, Central, South America)	
Uralic	23 000 000
Miao-Yao	7 000 000
Caucasian	6 000 000
Indo-Pacific	3 000 000
Khoisan	50 000
Australian aborigine	50 000
Palaeosiberian	25 000

---

language laboratory a room with separate cubicles equipped with tape recorders and prerecorded tapes, used for language learning.

Languedoc a former province of France, situated between the R Rhône, the Mediterranean, and the former provinces of Guyenne and Gascogne, S France. The area is a centre of wine production. To the E lie the Cévennes Mts. [the name is derived from the local variety of language, *langue d'oc* (Provençal).]

languid *adj.* **1** lacking in energy or vitality; listless. **2** slow-moving; sluggish. [from Latin *languere*, to languish]

languidly *adv.* in a listless or sluggish way.

languish *verb intrans.* **1** to grow weak; to lose energy or vitality. **2** to look sorrowful. **3** to pine: *the old dog was languishing for its master.* [from Latin *languere*, to be faint]

languishing *adj.* growing weak; pining.

languor *noun* **1** a feeling of dullness or lack of energy. **2** tender softness or sentiment. **3** a stuffy suffocating atmosphere or stillness. [from Latin *languor*]

languorous *adj.* lacking in energy; dull, idle.

lank *adj.* **1** long and thin. **2** *said of hair* long, straight, and limp. [from Anglo-Saxon *hlanc*]

lankiness *noun* being lanky.

lankness *noun* a lank state; being long and thin.

lanky *adj.* (**lankier, lankiest**) thin and tall, especially in an awkward and ungainly way.

lanolin *noun* fat obtained from sheep's wool, used in ointments and cosmetics. [from Latin *lana*, wool + *oleum*, oil]

Lansbury, George (1859–1940) English politician, born near Lowestoft. Active as a radical since boyhood, he became a convinced socialist in 1890 and a Labour MP in 1910, but resigned in 1912 to stand in support of women's suffrage. Defeated and not re-elected until 1922, he meanwhile founded and edited the *Daily Herald* (1912–22), which became the official paper of the

Labour Party. He later became the first Commissioner of Works (1929), and Leader of the Labour Party (1931–5).

Lansdowne Road a rugby stadium in Dublin, the home venue for Ireland since 1878.

L'Anse aux Meadows an isolated Norse settlement of nine turf-built houses on Epaves Bay, Newfoundland, Canada, discovered in 1961. It was dated by radiocarbon to c.970–1000, which proved that the Vikings reached N America in pre-Columbian times. It is a National Park and a World Heritage site.

Lansing POP (1990) 127 000, the capital of the state of Michigan, USA. It lies on the Grand R, in Ingham County, S central Michigan and is a carand truck-manufacturing centre.

lantern *noun* **1** a lamp or light contained in a transparent case, usually of glass, so that it can be held or carried. **2** a fixed lamp or light in this style. **3** the top part of a lighthouse, where the light is kept. **4** a structure with windows or open sides, built over an opening in the top of a roof or dome, for letting in light or air. [from Old French *lanterne*]

lantern-jawed *adj., said of the face* hollow and drawn.

lantern jaws long thin jaws giving the face a hollow drawn appearance.

lanthanide series *Chem.* any of a group of 15 chemical elements in the periodic table with atomic numbers ranging from 57 (lanthanum) to 71 (lutetium). They are silvery, highly reactive metals that share similar chemical properties. — Also called *rare earths*.

lanthanum *noun Chem.* (SYMBOL **La**, ATOMIC NUMBER **57**) a silvery-white metal (one of the lanthanide series) that ignites spontaneously in air, and is used in rocket propellants, electronic devices, alloys for lighter flints, and as a catalyst for the cracking of petroleum. [from Greek *lanthanein*, to escape notice, because it was hidden in rare minerals until 1839]

lanyard *noun* **1** a cord for hanging a knife, whistle, etc round the neck, worn especially by sailors. **2** *Naut.* a short rope for fastening rigging, etc. [from Old French *laniere*]

Lanza, Mario, Alfredo Arnold Coccozza (1921–59) US tenor and actor, born in Philadelphia. He studied singing under Enrico Rosati and took part in opera and recitals before appearing in such films as *The Toast of New Orleans* (1950), which includes the song 'Be My Love', and he took the title role in *The Great Caruso* (1951). An alcohol problem and obesity contributed to his early death.

Lanzhou *or* **Lanchow** *or* **Kaolan** POP (1990) 1.6m, the capital of Gansu province, N central China. It lies on the upper Yellow R. The city has been the centre of China's atomic energy industry since 1960. NOTABLE FEATURE Gansu Province Museum.

Laocoon in Greek mythology, a Trojan prince and a priest of Apollo, who opposed the plan to admit the Wooden Horse into Troy. He and his two sons were crushed to death by two sea serpents sent by Apollo.

Laocoon a statue of Laocoon and his two sons being killed by serpents (2c BC).

Laoighis *or* **Leix**, formerly **Queen's County** POP (1991) 52 000, a county in Leinster province, S central Irish Republic. AREA 1 720sq km/ 664sq mi. PHYSICAL DESCRIPTION the county is watered by the R Nore; the Slieve Bloom Mts rise in the NW. CAPITAL Portlaoighise. ECONOMY agriculture; livestock; huge tracts of peat are used to fuel power stations.

Laos, official name **Lao People's Democratic Republic**, Lao **Sathalanalat Paxathipatai Paxaxôn Lao** POP (1992e) 4.5m, a republic in SE Asia, divided into 13 provinces (khouèng). AREA

236 800sq km/91 405sq mi. It is bounded E by Vietnam, S by Cambodia, W by Thailand and Burma (Myanma), and N by China. CAPITAL Vientiane. CHIEF TOWNS Luang Prabang, Pakse, Savannakhét. TIME ZONE GMT +7. Most of the E area has been largely depopulated by war. The population is 60% Laotian and 35% hill tribes; Buddhism is the main religion. OFFICIAL LANGUAGE Lao. CURRENCY the new kip. PHYSICAL DESCRIPTION a landlocked country on the Indochinese Peninsula; dense jungle and rugged mountains in the E, rising to 2 751m; the Mekong R flows NW–SE, following much of the W frontier with Thailand. CLIMATE monsoonal with heavy rain in May–Sep; hot and dry Feb–Apr; average annual temperatures in Vientiane are 14–34°C. HISTORY discovered by Europeans in the 17c; dominated by Thailand in the 19c; French protectorate in 1893; occupied by the Japanese in World War II; gained independence from France in 1949; Civil War in 1953–75, between the Lao government, supported by the USA, and the communist-led Patriotic Front (Pathet Lao), supported by North Vietnam; the monarchy was abolished and a communist republic was established in 1975. GOVERNMENT headed by a President and governed by a Prime Minister, who is also secretary-general of the Central Committee of the Lao People's Revolutionary Party. ECONOMY agricultural economy suffered severely in the Civil War; rice, coffee, tobacco, cotton, spices, opium; tin, iron ore, potash; forestry, rubber; cigarettes, matches, textiles, foodstuffs, energy.

Laos

Lao Zi or **Lao-tzu** (6c BC) Chinese philosopher and sage, traditionally the founder of Taoism. Probably a legendary figure, he is represented as the older contemporary of Confucius, against whom most of his teaching is directed. The *Tao Te Ching* (The Way of Power), the most venerated of the three classical texts of Taoism, is attributed to him, though it dates from 300 years after his death. [Chinese, = old master]

lap¹ — *verb* (**lapped, lapping**) **1** *usually said of an animal* to drink (liquid) by scooping it up with the tongue. **2** *trans., intrans. said of water* to wash or flow against a shore or other surface with a light splashing sound. — *noun* **1** the act of lapping or the amount lapped up. **2** the sound of waves gently splashing or lapping.
— **lap something up 1** to drink something by lapping, especially eagerly or greedily. **2** to listen eagerly to (praise, gossip, information, etc). [from Anglo-Saxon *lapian*]

lap² *noun* **1** the front part of the body, from waist to knees, when sitting. **2** the part of clothing, especially of a skirt or dress, which covers this part of the body.
— **drop** or **land in someone's lap** to make or become someone's responsibility, especially suddenly or unexpectedly.
in the lap of the gods *said of a situation* beyond human control.
in the lap of luxury in very luxurious conditions.

[from Anglo-Saxon *læppa*]

lap³ — *noun* **1** one circuit of a racecourse or other track. **2** one section of a journey. **3** a part which overlaps or the amount it overlaps by. **4** the amount of thread or material wound once round a reel, etc. — *verb* (**lapped, lapping**) **1** to get ahead of (a competitor) in a race by one or more laps. **2** (**lap something round someone**) to fold a piece of clothing etc round someone. **3** (**lap someone in something**) to wrap a person in clothing etc, especially protectively. **4** to cause to overlap. **5** *intrans.* to lie with an overlap. [from Middle English *lappen*]

laparoscope *Medicine* a surgical instrument, consisting of a narrow flexible illuminated tube with an eyepiece, that is inserted through a small incision in the abdominal wall, enabling the abdominal cavity to be examined without the need for invasive surgery. [from Greek *lapara*, flank + -SCOPE]

La Paz **1** POP (1990e) 1.2m, the regional and government capital of Bolivia. It is situated in Murillo province, La Paz department, in the W of the country. Mt Illimani (6 402m) towers above it to the SE. The city is the highest capital in the world, with an altitude of 3 665m. It was founded in 1548 by the Spanish. NOTABLE FEATURES cathedral; Presidential Palace (Palacio Quemado); National Congress; National Art Museum; Monastery of San Francisco; the world's highest ski run at nearby Mt Chacaltaya. **2** a department in W Bolivia with La Paz as its capital.

lapdog *noun* a small pet dog.

lapel *noun* the part of a coat or jacket joined to the collar and folded back across the chest. [a diminutive of LAP²]

lapidary — *noun* (PL. **lapidaries**) a person who cuts and polishes gemstones. — *adj.* **1** relating to stones. **2** engraved on stone. **3** *said of writing* concise and to the point, as in inscriptions. [from Latin *lapis*, stone]

lapis lazuli **1** *Geol.* a deep blue gemstone, consisting of *lazurite* (a deep blue mineral) embedded in a matrix of white calcite, together with dark specks of pyrite. It is used as a semi-precious stone and ornamental material. **2** the bright blue colour of this material. [from Latin *lapis*, stone + *lazuli*, azure]

Lapiths in Greek mythology, a people of Thessaly, mentioned in several legends. Perithous, King of the Lapiths, invited the Centaurs to his wedding with Hippodameia. A terrible fight took place between the two groups, in which the Centaurs were defeated.

lap joint a joint formed in rails, timbers, etc, by reducing their thickness at the ends and overlapping them.

Laplace, Pierre Simon, Marquis de (1749–1827) French mathematician and astronomer, born in Beaumont-en-Auge. As professor at the École Militaire he gained fame by his astronomical researches, especially on the stability of planetary orbits. In 1799 he entered the senate. His greatest work was *Mécanique céleste* (Celestial Mechanics, 1799–1825). His famous nebular hypothesis of planetary origin proposed that the solar system originated as a massive cloud of gas which collapsed to form the Sun and planets. He also formulated the fundamental differential equation in physics which bears his name, and the modern form of probability theory.

Lapland, Finnish **Lappi**, Swedish **Lappland** POP (1992e) 202 000, a province in N Finland, bounded W by Sweden, NW by Norway, and E by Russia. AREA 98 938sq km/38 190sq mi. It lies mainly within the Arctic Circle. There has been considerable emigration to the S in recent years. PHYSICAL DESCRIPTION largely tundra in the N, forest in the S, and mountainous in the W; occupies c.30% of the total area of Finland; Mt Haltia

(Finland's highest peak) is situated on the frontier with Norway. PROVINCIAL CAPITAL Rovaniemi. ECONOMY chromium; iron mining; farming; fishing; trapping. The larger area generally called Lapland also includes large parts of Norway, Sweden, and Russia.

La Plante, Lynda (1946–) English stage and television actress and writer, born in Formby, Liverpool. She began her career touring with Brian Rix in 1972, and working on both stage and television (eg in *The Sweeney*, 1974–8 and *Minder*, 1979–86). Among her successes are the screenplays *Prime Suspect* (1991) and *Civvies* (1992), a violent story of soldiers returning to civilian life.

La Plata POP (1991) 543 000, the capital of Buenos Aires province, Litoral, E Argentina. It is a port situated on the R Plate, SW of Buenos Aires. The city was founded in 1882 and during the period between 1946 and 1955 it was named Eva Perón. NOTABLE FEATURES Museum of Natural History; Zoological Gardens; observatory; Garden of Peace, with each country in the world represented by one flower.

lap of honour a ceremonial circuit of a racecourse or sports pitch by the winner to acknowledge the applause of the audience.

Lapp — *noun* **1** a member of a nomadic people living in N Scandinavia. **2** (**Lapp** or **Lappish**) the language spoken by this people. — *adj.* (**Lapp** or **Lappish**) relating to this people or their language or culture.

lappet *noun* **1** a small flap or fold in material, a piece of clothing, etc. **2** a piece of loose hanging flesh. [a diminutive of LAP²]

Lapplander same as LAPP *noun¹*.

lapse — *noun* **1** a slight mistake or failure: *a lapse of memory.* **2** a decline in standards of behaviour. **3** a passing of time: *after a lapse of two years.* **4** *Legal* the loss of a right or privilege by failing to renew a claim to it. — *verb intrans.* **1** to fail to behave properly or in a morally sound way. **2** (**lapse into something**) to pass into or return to a bad or less welcome state: *showed signs of lapsing into carelessness.* **3** to turn away from a faith or belief. **4** *Legal, said of a right or privilege* to be no longer valid because the claim to it has not been renewed. [from Latin *lapsus*, slip]

lapsed *adj.* **1** having fallen into error or former bad ways. **2** no longer practising a religion, etc: *a lapsed Catholic.* **3** no longer used or valid.

laptop *noun Comput.* a portable personal computer that is small enough to be used on a person's lap and can be operated from batteries or mains power. It has a lid which folds back to form a flat screen, and it uses a liquid crystal or gas plasma display with a very low power consumption.

lapwing *noun* a plover with greenish-black and white feathers and a crest. [from Anglo-Saxon *hleapewince*]

Lara a female first name. More common in Russia, it became popular in Britain through the character *Lara* in the film version (1965) of Boris Pasternak's novel *Dr Zhivago* (1957). [a form of *Larunda*, a nymph of Roman mythology, or a diminutive of Greek *Larissa*]

larcenist *noun old use Legal* a person who committed larceny.

larceny *noun* (PL. **larcenies**) *old use Legal* theft of personal property. [from Old French *larcin*]

larch *noun* **1** a coniferous tree with needle-like leaves and cones, which loses its leaves in the winter. **2** the wood of this tree. [from Latin *larix*]

lard — *noun* soft white fat from pigs, used in cooking. — *verb* **1** to put lard on. **2** to stuff (meat) with bacon or pork. **3** to fill (a piece of writing, etc) with details, technical or elaborate words, etc. [from Latin *laridum*, bacon fat]

larder *noun* **1** a cool room or cupboard for storing food. **2** a store of food kept for winter by a wild animal. [from Old French *lardier*, from Latin *laridum*, bacon fat]

Lardner, Ring(gold) (Wilmer) (1885–1933) US writer, born in Michigan. He earned his living as a sports columnist in Chicago and New York and published his first collection of short stories *You Know Me, Al* (about baseball) in 1916. Between then and 1929 he wrote many novels, plays, satirical verse (eg *Bib Ballads*, 1915), and an autobiography, *The Story of a Wonder Man* (1927), but remains best known for his short stories.

Lares in Roman mythology, minor Roman gods. They included the guardians of the household (*lar familiares*), of the crossroads (*lares compitales*), and of the state (*lares praestites*). The household gods ruled in conjunction with the Penates, the gods of the storeroom.

large — *adj.* **1** occupying much space; great in size, extent, or amount. **2** broad; wide-ranging. **3** generous. **4** in a big way; extensive. — *adv.* importantly; prominently.
— **at large 1** *said of prisoners, etc* free and threatening. **2** in general; as a whole: *people at large.* **3** at length and with full details. [from Latin *largus*, plentiful]

largely *adv.* **1** mainly or chiefly. **2** to a great extent.

largeness *noun* a large state or size.

largesse *or* **largess** *noun* **1** generosity. **2** gifts, money, etc given generously. [from Old French *largesse*, from Latin *largus*, plentiful]

largo *Mus.* — *adv.* slowly and with dignity. — *adj.* slow and dignified. — *noun* (PL. **largos**) a piece of music to be played in this way. [from Italian *largo*, broad]

lariat *noun* a lasso or rope used for tethering animals. [from Spanish *la reata*, the lasso]

lark¹ *noun* any of several kinds of songbirds, especially the skylark. [from Anglo-Saxon *lawerce*]

lark² *noun colloq.* **1** a joke or piece of fun. **2** *Brit.* a job or activity. — *verb intrans.* (**lark about** *or* **around**) *colloq.* to play or fool about frivolously. [origin uncertain]

Larkin, Philip (1922–85) English poet and novelist, born in Coventry, Warwickshire. He worked in various libraries, and eventually became librarian at the University of Hull (1955). His collections of poems include *The Less Deceived* (1955), *The Whitsun Weddings* (1964), and *High Windows* (1974), and his *Collected Poems* appeared in 1988. His other writings include the novels *Jill* (1946) and *A Girl in Winter* (1947), and a book on jazz, *All What Jazz?* (1970). He also edited the *Oxford Book of Twentieth Century English Verse* (1973).

Lark Quartet (Lerchenquartett) Joseph Haydn's String Quartet in D (Op 64, No.5, 1790), named after the soaring violin melody at the beginning.

larkspur *noun* a plant with spur-like calyces and blue, white, or pink flowers. [from LARK¹ + SPUR]

Larnaca, Greek **Larnax**, Turkish **Larnaka, Iskele 1** POP (1991e) 60 000, the capital of Larnaca district, S Cyprus. It is a port town lying on Larnaca Bay. NOTABLE FEATURE old Turkish fort (1625), now a museum. **2** a district in S Cyprus with Larnaca as its capital.

La Rochefoucauld, François, 6th Duke (1613–80) French writer, born in Paris. An active member of the opposition to Cardinal Richelieu, he was forced to live abroad (1639–42). He then joined in the Fronde revolts (1648–53), and was wounded at the siege of Paris. He retired to the country in 1652 and returned to the court on Jules Mazarin's death in 1661. His major works include *Mémoires* (1664) and the epigrammatic collection, *Réflexions*, commonly known as the *Maximes* (Maxims, 1665).

Larousse, Pierre (Athanase) (1817–75) French publisher, lexicographer, and encyclopedist, born in Toucy. He became a teacher in Toucy, and began his linguistic research in Paris in 1840. In 1852 he founded a publishing house and bookshop in Paris. He produced several grammars, dictionaries, and other textbooks, notably his *Grand dictionnaire universel du XIXᵉ siècle* (15 vols, 1865–76).

Lartet, Edouard Arman Isidore Hippolyte (1801–71) French palaeontologist, born in St Guiraud, Gers. He discovered the fossil jawbone of an ape, *Pliopithecus*, in the Tertiary formations of Sansan, Gers (1836) — this refuted the assertion of many scientists that neither men nor apes could be found in a fossil state. His later studies yielded conclusive proof of the contemporaneity of man and extinct animal species.

larva *noun* (PL. **larvae**) *Zool.* in the life cycle of many insects, amphibians, and fish, the immature stage which hatches from the fertilized egg and is capable of independent existence, eg the caterpillar of butterflies, the tadpole of frogs. [from Latin *larva*, ghost, mask]

larva

larval *adj.* like or in the form of a larva.

laryngeal *adj.* relating to the larynx.

laryngitis *noun* inflammation of the larynx, causing pain and making it difficult to speak.

larynx *noun* a hollow organ in the throat, forming the upper end of the windpipe and containing the vocal cords. [from Greek *larynx*]

La-sa see LHASA.

lasagne *noun* pasta in the form of thin flat sheets, often cooked in layers with a mixture of meat and tomatoes, and a cheese sauce. [from Italian *lasagne* (plural)]

La Salle, (René) Robert Cavelier, Sieur de (1643–87) French explorer, born in Rouen. He settled in Canada in 1666, and descended the Ohio and Mississippi rivers to the sea (1682), naming the area Louisiana (after Louis XIV of France). In 1684 he fitted out an expedition to establish a French settlement on the Gulf of Mexico. He spent two years in fruitless journeys and was murdered near the Brazos River, Texas.

La Scala *or* **Teatro Alla Scala** the world's most famous opera house, built (1776–8) on the site of the Church of Santa Maria della Scala in Milan, Italy. [Italian, = theatre at the stairway]

Las Casas, Bartolomé de, known as **the Apostle of the Indians** (1474–1566) Spanish Dominican missionary priest, born in Seville. He sailed in the third voyage of Columbus (1498), went to Hispaniola (1502), was ordained (1512), and travelled to Cuba (1513). His ardent desire to protect the natives from slavery led him to visit the Spanish court on several occasions. Appointed Bishop of Chiapa, he was received (1544) with hostility by the colonists, returned to Spain, and resigned his see (1547), but continued to campaign in favour of the natives until his death.

Las Casas, Emmanuel (Augustin Dieudonné Joseph) (1766–1842) French historian, born in Las Casas, Languedoc. A lieutenant in the royal French navy, at the Revolution he fled to England, where he wrote his *Atlas his-*

torique (1803–4). Though a Royalist by birth, he supported Napoleon during the Hundred Days and chose to share his exile on St Helena. There he recorded their conversations. His complaint to the British government about Napoleon's treatment led to his own deportation, but he returned to France (1822) and published the *Mémorial de Sainte-Hélène* (1823).

cave painting, Lascaux

Lascaux a small cave near Montignac, Dordogne, SW France, richly-decorated with illustrations from the Palaeolithic era, c.15000 BC. It is renowned for its naturalistic mural cave paintings and engravings of animals — cows, bulls, horses, bison, ibex, musk-ox, and reindeer. It was found by schoolboys in 1940, opened to the public in 1947, and closed permanently in 1963 when humidity changes threatened the paintings. A replica was opened nearby in 1984.

lascivious *adj.* feeling, expressing, or causing sexual desire. [from Latin *lascivus*, playful, wanton]

lasciviously *adv.* in a lascivious or sensuous way.

Las Cruces POP (1990) 136 000, the seat of Dona Ana County, S New Mexico, USA. It lies on the R Grande, 66km/41mi NW of El Paso, Texas, and was founded in 1848. Nearby is the White Sands Missile Range, a major military and NASA testing site where the first atomic bomb was tested. [from Spanish *las cruces*, the crosses; the name commemorates the massacre of 40 travellers by Apaches in 1830]

laser *noun* a device that produces a very powerful narrow beam of coherent light of a single wavelength by stimulating the emission of photons from atoms, molecules, or ions. [from *light amplification by stimulated emission of radiation*]
◇ Lasers do not generate light, but amplify it. Within a laser, light from an external source is trapped between semi-silvered mirrors, and is then reflected to and fro through an energized crystal or gas. The atoms in the crystal or gas absorb photons of light, become excited, and when they collide with other photons release light energy. The light produced is of a single wavelength or frequency, and is said to be *coherent*, different kinds of laser producing different wavelengths of light.
Lasers are used for cutting metal, concrete, etc, for drilling holes (eg in diamonds), welding, measuring minute distances, satellite tracking, printing, and reading compact discs, bar codes, and other forms of digital information. They are also used in eye surgery, holography, and optical communications, and as entertainment in light shows.

laser mass spectrometer a mass spectrometer which uses a laser to convert a sample for analysis into a form which can pass through the analysing system. Because mass spectrometry requires a pure and uncontaminated source of matter propelled to the system, lasers can be used particularly for the non-destructive evaporation of the sample without disturbing the mounting or medium.

laser printer *Comput.* a fast high-quality printer that projects a laser beam on to a rotating drum coated with a material that becomes electrically charged and attracts a metallic powder. The powder image is then transferred to paper and fixed to it by heat.

lash — *noun* **1** a stroke or blow with a whip. **2** the flexible part of a whip. **3** (*usually* **lashes**) an eyelash. — *verb* **1** to hit or beat with a lash. **2** *trans., intrans.* (of waves or rain) to beat or strike with great force: *waves lashing the shore / rain lashing against the window*. **3** (*often* **lash something down** *or* **together**) to fasten with a rope or cord. **4** *intrans. said of something resembling a whip* to make a sudden whip-like movement. **5** *said of an animal* to move (the tail) with a sudden or restless movement. **6** to attack with harsh scolding words or criticism. **7** to urge on as if with a whip. — **lash out** to hit out or complain violently.
lash out on something *colloq.* to spend money extravagantly on it.
[from Middle English *lashe*]

lashing *noun* **1** a rope for tying things fast. **2** a beating with a whip.

lashings *pl. noun colloq.* a large amount.

Lasker, Emmanuel (1868–1941) German chess player and mathematician, born in Berlinchen, Prussia. He won the world championship in 1894 and retained it until 1921, when he was defeated by José Capablanca (1888–1942). He left Germany in 1933, and finally settled in the USA.

Laski, Harold (Joseph) (1893–1950) English political scientist and socialist, born in Manchester. He lectured at several US universities before joining the London School of Economics (1920), where he became Professor of Political Science (1926). The development of his political philosophy, a modified Marxism, can be seen in his many books, eg *Authority in the Modern State* (1919) and *A Grammar of Politics* (1925).

Laski, Marghanita (1915–88) English novelist and critic, born in Manchester. Her first novel, *Love on the Supertax*, appeared in 1944, and later novels include *Little Boy Lost* (1949) and *The Victorian Chaise-longue* (1953). She wrote extensively for newspapers and reviews, and also published a number of critical works.

Las Palmas POP (1991) 342 000, a Spanish province in the Canary Is, comprising the islands of Gran Canaria, Lanzarote, and Fuerteventura. AREA 4 072sq km/1 572sq mi. CHIEF TOWNS Las Palmas de Gran Canaria (capital), Puerto de la Luz (seaport resort). ECONOMY shipyards; mineral water; cement; livestock; textiles; metal products; food processing; trade in sugar, tomatoes, and bananas; tourism.

lass *noun dialect, poetic* a girl or young woman (now often used as a general term of affection). [from Middle English *lasce*, from Old Norse *laskwa*, unmarried]

Lassalle, Ferdinand (1825–64) German social democrat, born in Breslau. He studied philosophy, and in 1846 engaged in eight years of divorce litigation on behalf of the Countess Hatzfeld, for which he received a pension. Active in the revolution of 1848, he was imprisoned for six months for an inflammatory speech. Much influenced by Karl Marx, he developed his theories of socialism, and in 1863 in Leipzig founded the Universal German Workers' Association to agitate for universal suffrage. He was killed in a duel over a love affair.

lassi *noun* an Indian cold drink of yoghurt mixed with water, flavoured with salt or sugar. [from Hindi]

lassie *noun Scot.* a young girl.

lassitude *noun* a feeling of physical or mental tiredness; lack of energy and enthusiasm. [from Latin *lassus*, faint]

lasso — *noun* (PL. **lassos**, **lassoes**) a long rope with a loop which tightens when the rope is pulled, used for catching animals, etc. — *verb* (**lassoes**, **lassoed**) to catch with a lasso. [from Spanish *lazo*, from Latin *laqueus*, noose]

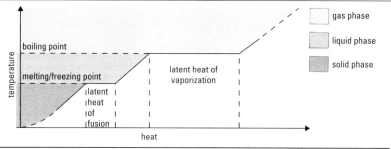

latent heat

last[1] — *adj.* **1** coming at the end of a series or after all others. **2** most recent; next before the present: *last week*. **3** coming or remaining after all the others. **4** least likely or suitable: *the last person to expect help from*. **5** lowest in rank; worst. **6** (used for emphasis) single: *broke every last one of the plates*. — *adv.* **1** after all others. **2** most recently. **3** lastly. — *noun* **1** the person or thing that is last. **2** the end or last moment. **3** (**the last**) the final appearance or mention: *we haven't heard the last of him*.
— **at long last** in the end, especially after a long delay.
last thing after doing everything else, especially before leaving or going to bed.
on one's last legs worn out; exhausted.
to the last until the very end, especially until death.
[from Anglo-Saxon *latost*, latest]

last[2] *verb intrans.* **1** to continue for a long time, or for a specified time: *the journey lasts for three days*. **2** to remain adequate or in good condition: *enough water to last us a week / but the bread will only last one more day*.
— **last out** to survive for a given or implied length of time.
[from Anglo-Saxon *læstan*]

last[3] *noun* a foot-shaped piece of wood or metal on which shoes are made and repaired.
— **stick to one's last** to avoid interfering in things one does not understand.
[from Anglo-Saxon *læste*]

last-ditch *adj.* done as a last resort.

lasting *adj.* existing or continuing for a long time or permanently.

Last Judgement see DAY OF JUDGEMENT.

Last Judgement, The a painting of the Last Judgement by various artists including Michelangelo (1536–41, Sistine Chapel, Rome) and (as a triptych) Lucas van Leyden (1526, Leyden).

lastly *adv.* as the last item; finally; at the end.

last-minute *adj.* made, done, or given at the latest possible moment: *a last-minute birthday present*.

last name a surname.

Last of England, The a painting by Ford Madox Brown (1855, Birmingham).

Last of the Mohicans, The a novel by James Fenimore Cooper (1826). The second of the Leather-Stocking Tales, it centres on the fate of an English party in 1757, during the Seven Years War with the French and the Native Americans.

last rites (**the last rites**) religious rites for a dying person.

last straw (**the last straw**) an often insignificant addition to a mounting difficulty or burden, which finally makes all of it intolerable: *losing my keys was the last straw*.

Last Supper in the New Testament Gospels, the last meal of Christ with his disciples on the eve of his arrest and crucifixion. In the three synoptic gospels, this is a Passover meal, significant for Christ's declaration concerning the bread and wine: 'This is my body' and 'This is my blood of the covenant which is poured out for many' (Mark 14.22–4). The event is commemorated in the early Church's celebration of the Lord's Supper (1 Corinthians 11), and subsequently in the sacrament of Holy Communion.

Last Supper, The a painting of the Last Supper by various artists including Leonardo da Vinci (completed c.1498, Santa Maria delle Grazie, Milan), Tintoretto (two versions, 1547 and c.1592–4, Venice), and Paolo Veronese (titled *Feast in the House of Levi*, 1573, Venice).

last word (the last word) **1** the final or definitive remark in an argument or debate. **2** the final decision. **3** the most up-to-date or fashionable thing: *the last word in elegance*.

Last Year at Marienbad (L'Année Dernière à Marienbad) a French–Italian film directed by Alain Resnais (1961). A romance with a puzzling style of shifting between truth, fantasy, past, present, and future, it is a landmark in modernist cinema.

Las Vegas POP (1990) 741 000, the seat of Clark County, SE Nevada, USA, and the largest city in the state. A commercial centre for a mining and ranching area, it is noted for its casinos and 24-hour entertainment. HISTORY settled by Mormons in 1855–7; purchased by a railway company in 1903; became a city in 1911. NOTABLE FEATURES Mormon Fort; Liberace Museum. [from Spanish *las vegas*, the meadows; these served as camping sites on early trails to the W]

Lat *or* **Lat.** *abbrev.* Latin.

lat. *abbrev.* latitude.

Latakia, Arabic **Al Ladhiqiyah** **1** POP (1992) 284 000, the commercial seaport capital of Latakia governorate, W Syria, situated on the Mediterranean Sea. The city is famous for its tobacco (Latakia). **2** a governorate in W Syria with Latakia as its capital.

latch — *noun* **1** a door-catch consisting of a bar which is lowered or raised from its notch by a lever or string. **2** a door-lock by which a door may be opened from the inside using a handle, and from the outside by using a key. — *verb trans., intrans.* to fasten or be fastened with a latch.
— **latch on** *colloq.* to understand: *took them a moment to latch on*.
latch on to someone *colloq.* to follow or observe them closely.
on the latch *said of a door* shut but not locked; able to be opened by the latch.
[from Anglo-Saxon *læccan*]

latchkey *noun* a key for an outer door with a latch.

latchkey child a child who returns home from school while the parents are still out at work.

late — *adj.* **1** coming, arriving, etc after the expected or usual time. **2** far on in the day or night; nearly at the end: *late afternoon*. **3** occurring, ripening, etc at a relatively advanced time in the season: *late potatoes*. **4** having died, especially recently: *his late father*. **5** former: *the late prime minister*. **6** most recent. — *adv.* **1** after the expected or usual time. **2** far on in the day or night. **3** at an advanced time: *flower late in the season*. **4** recently: *the letter was sent as late as this morning*. **5** formerly, but no longer: *late of Glasgow*.

— **late in the day** at a late stage, especially too late to be of any use.

of late lately; recently.

[from Anglo-Saxon *læt*]

lateen *adj. Naut., said of a ship* having a triangular sail on a long, sloping yard. [from French *voile latine*, Latin sail: so called because they are common on the Mediterranean]

lately *adv.* in the recent past; not long ago.

latency *noun* the state of being latent or hidden.

La Tène a prehistoric site on the shores of L Neuchâtel, Switzerland, excavated from 1858. Its name is commonly used to describe the later European Iron Age that succeeded Halstaat culture from c.500 BC and survived until the coming of the Romans. The period was characterized by hill-forts, increasing trade and warfare, the development of towns and coinage, and a curvilinear art style.

lateness *noun* a late state or time.

latent *adj.* present but hidden and not yet developed. [from Latin *latere*, to lie hidden]

latent heat *Physics* the amount of heat energy that is required to change a solid to a liquid, or a liquid to a gas, without a change in temperature. The same amount of energy is released when the liquid changes back to a solid, or the gas changes back to a liquid.

latent image the invisible image formed in a photographic emulsion by its exposure to light. It is made visible in the development process when the light-affected silver halide grains are converted to black metallic silver.

latent period 1 *Biol.* the period of time between a stimulus and a response. **2** *Medicine* the time between the contracting of a disease and the appearance of symptoms.

later *adj., adv.* at some time after, or in the near future: *they are coming here later*.

lateral — *adj.* at the side; to or from the side. — *noun* a side part, especially a branch. [from Latin *latus*, side]

laterality *or* **lateralization** *noun* **1** the state of being lateral or to the side; physical one-sidedness, either right or left. **2** *Physiol.* a characteristic of the human brain, in which the left and right cerebral hemispheres are specialized for different functions. In the majority of both left- and right-handed people, the left hemisphere is specialized for language functions, eg reading, writing, speaking, understanding, and the right hemisphere is specialized for the perception of complex patterns.

lateral line *Zool.* in fishes, a line of specialized receptor cells along the sides of the body that is sensitive to vibrations and water pressure.

laterally *adv.* on or to a side.

lateral thinking a form of thinking which seeks new and unusual ways of approaching and solving problems, and does not merely proceed by logical steps from the starting point of what is known or believed.

Lateran Councils a series of councils of the Church held at the Lateran Palace, Rome, between the 7c and the 18c. Those held in 1123, 1139, 1179, and especially 1215 are the most significant. The Fourth or Great Council defined the word transubstantiation in Eucharistic doctrine, and marked the culmination of medieval papal legislation.

Lateran Pacts agreements (1929) between the Italian fascist state and the papacy which ended a Church–State conflict that dated from the Risorgimento (c.1870). By them, Italy recognized

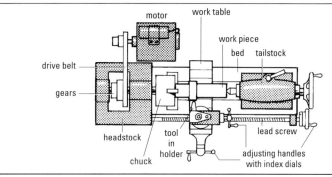

lathe

the sovereignty of Vatican City, gave compensation for the loss of papacy territories during the Risorgimento, and guaranteed religious education at all levels of state schooling. In return, the Church recognized the Italian state for the first time. The treaty was confirmed in the 1948 constitution.

laterite *noun Geol.* a deposit that may consist of soft porous soil or hard dense rock, often occurring as a thick reddish layer, and formed as a result of the weathering of igneous rocks in humid tropical climates. It is composed mainly of hydroxides of iron (which gives the clay its red colour) and aluminium, and is often used as a building material. [from Latin *later*, brick]

latest — *adj.* most recent. — *noun* (**the latest**) the most recent news, occurrence, fashion, etc.

— **at the latest** not later than a time stated: *be home by 10 at the latest*.

latex *noun* (PL. **latexes**, **latices**) **1** a thick milky juice of some plants, especially of the rubber tree, used in commercial applications. **2** a rubber-like synthetic product. [from Latin *latex*, liquid]

lath *noun* a thin narrow strip of wood, especially one of a series used to support plaster. [from Anglo-Saxon *lætt*]

lathe *noun* a machine tool that is used to cut, drill, or polish a piece of metal, wood, or plastic, which is rotated against the cutting edge of the lathe. [from Middle English, = frame, stand]

lather — *noun* **1** a foam made by mixing water and soap. **2** foamy sweat, especially of a horse. — *verb* (**lathered, lathering**) **1** *intrans.* to form a lather. **2** to cover with lather. **3** *colloq.* to beat or thrash.

— **in a lather** *colloq.* extremely agitated or excited. [from Anglo-Saxon *leathor*, soap]

lathery *adj.* like lather; foamy.

Latimer, Hugh (c.1485–1555) English Protestant reformer and martyr, born in Thurcaston, Leicestershire. He was appointed a university preacher at Cambridge in 1522. Converted to Protestantism, he was one of the divines appointed to examine the lawfulness of Henry VIII's marriage to Catherine of Aragon; he declared on the King's side and was made chaplain to Anne Boleyn. In 1535 he was made Bishop of Worcester, but opposed the Six Articles of Henry VIII, for which he was imprisoned in 1536, 1546, and 1553. He became known as a preacher under Edward VI, but under Mary I was tried for heresy and burned in Oxford.

Latin — *noun* **1** the language of ancient Rome and its empire. **2** an inhabitant of ancient Latium in Central Italy. — *adj.* **1** relating to or in the Latin language. **2** *said of a language* ultimately derived from Latin, as Italian and Spanish are. **3** *said of a person* having a passionate or excitable character. **4** relating to the Roman Catholic Church. [from Latin *latinus*, of Latium]

◇ Latin was the most important of the Italic group of extinct languages, and is the parent of the Romance languages. From its centre in ancient Rome it spread throughout the Roman Empire; it was adopted as the liturgical language of the Roman Catholic Church and as the lan-

guage of culture, science, and law throughout W Europe from the Middle Ages to the Renaissance. See panel p. 720.

Latin America the 18 Spanish-speaking republics of the W hemisphere, together with Portuguese-speaking Brazil (the largest Latin-American country) and French-speaking Haiti. The name first came into use in France just before 1860.

Latin American *noun* an inhabitant of Latin America. — *adj.* relating to Latin America.

Latino *or* **Latina** *noun* a man or woman of Latin American descent, especially in N America.

Latinus in Roman legend, the ancestor and eponymous King of the Latins. He was either descended from Circe (according to Hesiod) or from Faunus (according to Virgil). In Virgil's *Aeneid*, his daughter Lavinia marries Aeneas.

latitude *noun* **1** any of a series of imaginary circles drawn around the Earth parallel to the Equator. All points on the Equator have a latitude of 0°, and the distance between the Equator and the poles is divided into 90° of latitude, ie the North and South Poles correspond to 90°N and 90°S, respectively. Latitude is used together with longitude to specify any position on the Earth's surface. See also LONGITUDE. **2** (*usually* **latitudes**) a region or area in terms of its distance from the equator or its climate: *warm latitudes*. **3** scope for freedom of action or choice. [from Latin *latus*, broad]

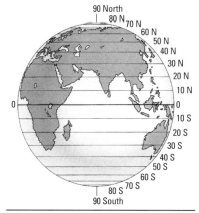

lines of latitude

latitudinal *adj.* relating to latitude; measured by latitude.

latitudinally *adv.* as regards latitude; in terms of latitude.

Latium in antiquity, the area SE of Rome between the Apennine Mts and the sea. It was the territory of the Latini, Latin-speaking peoples of whom the Romans are the best known. It became the recreation area of the Roman rich who filled it with luxurious villas.

Látrabjarg the westernmost point of Iceland, and one of the highest cliff faces in the world, situated in Vestfirðir region, W Iceland. The British trawler *Dhoon* ran aground below the cliff in 1947, the entire crew being saved by men lowered down the cliff on ropes.

latrine *noun* a communal lavatory, especially in a barracks. [from Latin *lavatrina*, bath]

latter — *adj.* **1** (**the latter**) nearer to the end: *the latter part of the holiday.* **2** being the second of two people or things mentioned, or (loosely) the last of several mentioned. **3** recent; modern. — *noun* (**the latter**) the second of two people or things mentioned, or (loosely) the last of several mentioned. [from Anglo-Saxon *lætra*]

latter-day *adj.* recent or modern.

Latter-day Saints the Mormons' preferred name for themselves.

latterly *adv.* **1** recently. **2** towards the end.

lattice *noun* **1** (*also* **lattice-work**) an open frame made from crossed narrow strips of wood or metal, used especially for gates and fences. **2** (*also* **lattice window**) a window with small diamond-shaped panels of glass formed by strips of lead. **3** *Chem.* the regular three-dimensional arrangement of atoms, ions, or molecules that forms the structure of a crystalline solid. [from Old French *lattis*, from *latte*, lath]

latticed *adj.* containing or made up of lattice.

Latvia, Latvian **Latvija**, Russian **Latviskaya** POP (1993e) 2.6m, a republic in NE Europe. AREA 63 700sq km/24 600sq mi. It is bounded W by the Baltic Sea, NW by the Gulf of Riga, N by Estonia, E by Russia, and SE by Belorussia and Lithuania. CAPITAL Rīga. CHIEF TOWNS Daugavpils, Liepāja. OFFICIAL LANGUAGE Latvian. The population is mainly Latvian (52%) with a large Russian minority (34%); most of the population are Christian. CURRENCY the rouble. PHYSICAL DESCRIPTION a flat, glaciated area; the NW coast is indented by the Gulf of Riga; the chief river is the Daugava; over 40% of Latvia is forested. HISTORY incorporated into Russia in 1721; became an independent state in 1918, but was proclaimed a Soviet Socialist Republic in 1940; occupied by Germany during World War II; there was growth of a new nationalist movement in the 1980s; in 1990 independence talks began with the Soviet Union, and independence was declared in 1991. The Latvians have a well-developed folklore, which found particular national expression in the 1860s after the founding of a Latvian theatre in Rīga. GOVERNMENT Parliament elects a President who, with Parliament's agreement, appoints a Prime Minister; the Prime Minister and Parliament exercise executive power within a democratic system. ECONOMY machines, metalworking, instruments, electrical engineering, electronics; chemicals; furniture; knitwear; food processing; fishing; cattle, pigs, oats, barley, rye, potatoes, flax.

Latvian — *noun* **1** a native or citizen of Latvia. **2** the Baltic language of Latvia. — *adj.* relating to Latvia or its people or language.

Latynina, Larissa (Semyonovna), *née* **Diril** (1935–) Soviet gymnast, born in Kharsan, the Ukraine. In 1956 and 1964 she collected 18

Latin Phrases Used in English

ab initio from the beginning

ab ovo from the egg; from the beginning

absit omen a superstitious formula; may there be no ill omen (as in a reference just made

ad hoc towards this; for one particular purpose

ad hominem to the man; appealing not to logic or reason but to personal preference or feelings

ad infinitum to infinity; for ever; without limit

ad litem for the lawsuit; used of a guardian appointed to act in court (eg because of insanity or insufficient years of the litigant)

ad nauseam to the point of sickness; excessively

ad referendum for reference; to be further considered

ad valorem to value; according to what it is worth, often used of taxes, etc

a fortiori from the stronger (argument); for a stronger reason

anno Domini in the year of the Lord; used in giving dates since the birth of Christ

ante meridiem before midday; between midnight and noon, abbreviated to **am**

a posteriori from the later; based on observation or experience

a priori from the previous; working from cause to effect

ave atque vale hail and farewell

bona fide genuine or sincere

carpe diem seize the day; enjoy the pleasures of the present moment while they last

caveat emptor let the buyer beware; warns the buyer to examine carefully the article he is about to purchase

compos mentis having control of one's mind; of sound mind; rational

contra mundum against the world; denotes defiant perseverance despite universal criticism

cum grano salis with a grain (pinch) of salt

de facto from the fact; actually, though not necessarily legally, so

de gustibus non est disputandum (often in English shortened for convenience to *de gustibus*) there is no disputing about tastes; there is no sense in challenging people's preferences

de jure according to law; denotes the legal or theoretical position, which may not correspond with reality

deo volente God willing; a sort of good-luck talisman

eheu fugaces opening of a quotation (Horace *Odes* II, XIV, 1–2) alas! the fleeting years slip away; bemoans the brevity of human existence

et al. *et alii* and other things; used to avoid giving a complete and possibly over-lengthy list of all items eg of authors

et tu, Brute you too, Brutus (Caesar's alleged exclamation when he saw Brutus among his assassins); denotes surprise and dismay that a supposed friend has joined in a conspiracy against one

ex cathedra from the chair; with authority

ex gratia as a favour; given as a favour

ex officio from office, by virtue of office; by virtue of one's official position

ex parte from (one) part; on behalf of one side only in legal proceedings; partial, prejudiced

fidus Achates the faithful Achates (Aeneas' friend); a loyal follower

fons et origo the source and origin

habeas corpus have the body; requiring a prisoner to be brought into court

hic jacet here lies; the first words of an epitaph; memorial inscription

honoris causa for the sake of honour; a token of respect; used to designate honorary university degrees

in absentia in absence; in a person's absence

in camera in the chamber; in a private room; in secret

in extremis in the last; in desperate circumstances; at the point of death

in flagrante delicto in the blazing crime; in the very act of committing the crime

infra dig below dignity; beneath one's dignity

in loco parentis in the place of a parent

inter alia among other things

in vitro in glass; in a test tube

ipso facto by the fact itself; thereby

mea culpa through my fault; I am to blame

mens sana in corpore sano a sound mind in a sound body (Juvenal X, 356); the guiding rule of the 19th-c English educational system

mirabile dictu wonderful to tell (Virgil, *Georgics* II, 30); an expression of (sometimes ironic) amazement

multum in parvo much in little; a large amount in a small space

mutatis mutandis having changed what needs to be changed

ne plus ultra not more beyond; extreme perfection

non sequitur it does not follow; an illogical step in an argument

nota bene observe well, note well; often abbreviated **NB**

O tempora! O mores! O the times! O the manners! (Cicero *In Catalinam*) a condemnation of present times, as contrasted with a past which is seen as golden

panem et circenses bread and circuses, or food and the big match (Juvenal *Satires* X, 80); amusements which divert the populace from unpleasant realities

per capita by heads; for each person

post meridiem after noon

prima facie at first sight; on the evidence available

primus inter pares first among equals

pro bono publico for the public good; something done for no fee

quid pro quo something for something; something given or taken as equivalent to another, often as retaliation

quod erat demonstrandum which was to be shown; often used in its abbreviated form **qed**

reductio ad absurdum reduction to absurdity; originally used in logic to mean the proof of a proposition by proving the falsity of its contradictory; the application of a principle so strictly that it is carried to absurd lengths

rus in urbe the country in the town (Martial XII, 57, 21); the idea of country charm in the centre of a city

salus populi suprema est lex let the welfare of the people be the chief law (Cicero *De Legibus* III, 3)

sic transit gloria mundi so passes away earthly glory

sine die without a day; with no future time fixed

sine qua non without which not; an essential condition or requirement

sub judice under a judge; under consideration by a court

sub rosa under the rose; in secret, privately

summa cum laude with the highest praise; with great distinction; the highest class of degreee that can be gained by a US college student

summum bonum the chief good

tempus fugit time flies; delay cannot be tolerated

ultra vires beyond strength, beyond powers; beyond one's power or authority

urbi et orbi to the city and the world; used of the Pope's pronouncements; to everyone

Latvia

Olympic medals, a record for any sport, winning nine golds. During her 13-year career she won 24 Olympic, World, and European titles, including that of individual world champion in 1958 and 1962. She retired in 1966.

Laud, William (1573–1645) English prelate and Archbishop of Canterbury, born in Reading, Berkshire. Ordained in 1601, his antipathy to dominant Puritanism made him unpopular among the university authorities, but his learning and industry brought him many patrons, and he became King's Chaplain (1611), Bishop of St David's (1621), Bishop of Bath and Wells and a Privy Councillor (1626), Bishop of London (1628), and Archbishop of Canterbury (1633). With Thomas Strafford and Charles I, he worked for absolutism in Church and State. In Scotland, his attempt (1635–7) to anglicize the Church led to the Bishops' Wars, which in turn led to his being impeached for treason by the Long Parliament (1640), and executed.

laud — verb formal to praise (a deity), especially in hymns. — noun formal praise for a deity. See also LAUDS. [from Latin laus, praise]

Lauda, Niki (1949–) Austrian racing driver, born in Vienna. He was three times world champion, in 1975, 1977 (both Ferrari), and 1984 (Marlboro–McLaren). He survived a horrific crash at the Nurburgring, Germany, in 1976, and despite bad burns returned and was runner-up in the world championship in that year. He retired in 1979, but made a comeback in 1984, when he won his third world title. He retired again in 1985 after 25 career wins, and became the proprietor of Lauda–Air.

laudability noun being laudable or praiseworthy.

laudable adj. worthy of praise; commendable.

laudably adv. in a worthy or commendable way.

laudanum noun Medicine a solution of morphine in alcohol, prepared from raw opium, and formerly often taken by mouth as an analgesic (painkiller). [a Latinized name used by Paracelsus (16c) for an expensive medicine containing opium]

laudatory adj. containing or expressing praise. [from Latin laus, praise]

Lauder, Sir Harry (MacLennan) (1870–1950) Scottish comic singer, born near Edinburgh. He began on the music-hall stage as an Irish comedian, but made his name as a singer of Scottish songs, many of which he wrote himself, such as 'Roamin' in the Gloamin'.

Lauderdale, John Maitland, Duke of (1616–82) Scottish statesman, born in Lethington (now Lennoxlove), East Lothian. He ardently supported the Covenanters (1638), and in 1643 became a Scottish Commissioner at Westminster. He was taken prisoner at Worcester (1651) and imprisoned, but at the Restoration (1660) he became Scottish Secretary of State. A Privy Councillor, he was an adviser in the cabal under Charles II, and was created duke in 1672.

lauds pl. noun RC Church the customary first morning prayers.

Laue, Max Theodor Felix von see VON LAUE.

laugh — verb 1 intrans. to make spontaneous sounds associated with happiness, amusement, scorn, etc. 2 (**laugh oneself silly** etc) to bring oneself into a certain state (often figuratively) through laughing. 3 to express by laughing: laughed his contempt. — noun 1 an act or sound of laughing. 2 colloq. a person or thing that is amusing or causes laughter.
— **have the last laugh** to win or succeed in the end, especially after setbacks, or be finally proved right.
laugh at someone or **something** to make fun of or ridicule them.
laugh something off to treat (an injury, embarrassment, etc) trivially.
laugh up one's sleeve to be secretly or gleefully amused.
[from Anglo-Saxon hlæhhan]

laughable adj. deserving to be laughed at; absurd, ludicrous.

laughably adv. in a laughable or absurd way.

laughing noun laughter.
— **no laughing matter** a very serious matter.

Laughing Cavalier, The a painting by Frans Hals (1624, Wallace Collection, London).

laughing gas nitrous oxide used as an anaesthetic. It can cause a feeling of exhilaration when inhaled without oxygen.

laughing jackass see KOOKABURRA.

laughingly adv. in a laughing or derisory manner.

laughing-stock noun someone who is laughed at or ridiculed.

laughter noun the act or sound of laughing.

Laughton, Charles (1899–1962) English actor, born in Scarborough, Yorkshire. He first appeared on the stage in 1926, and gave many renowned Shakespearean performances. He began to act in films in 1932, and portrayed Henry VIII in The Private Life of Henry VIII (1933) and Capt Bligh in Mutiny on the Bounty (1935).

Launce the clownish servant of Proteus in Shakespeare's The Two Gentlemen of Verona, who is the owner of the sour-natured dog, Crab.

Launcelot Gobbo see GOBBO.

Launceston POP (1991) 67 000 (Greater Launceston), a city in N statistical division, Tasmania, Australia. It is situated at the confluence of the N Esk, S Esk, and Tamar rivers. The city is the second largest in Tasmania. NOTABLE FEATURE Cataract Gorge.

launch¹ — verb 1 to send (a boat or ship) into the water, especially for the first time. 2 to send (a spacecraft, missile, etc) into the air. 3 to start (a person, project, etc) off on a course. 4 to bring (a new product) on to the market, especially with promotions and publicity. 5 (**launch into something**) **a** to begin an undertaking with vigour and enthusiasm. **b** to begin a story or speech, especially a long one. — noun a launching of a ship or spacecraft. [from Latin lanceare, to wield a lance]

launch² noun 1 a large powerful motorboat. 2 Hist. the largest boat carried by a man-of-war. [from Spanish lancha, perhaps via a Malay word meaning 'swift']

launcher noun a device used for launching a spacecraft or missile.

launching-pad or **launch pad** noun a platform for launching a spacecraft or rocket.

launch vehicle Astron. a rocket-propelled vehicle that is used to carry a spacecraft (eg a satellite or space probe) from the Earth's surface into space.

launch window Astron. the period of time during which the launching of a spacecraft must take place if it is to put a satellite, space probe, etc, in the right orbit or on the right flight path.

launder verb (laundered, laundering) 1 to wash and iron (clothes or linen). 2 colloq. to transfer (money obtained illegally) through banks or legitimate businesses to hide its origins. [from Latin lavanda, things to be washed, from lavare, to wash]

launderette or **laundrette** noun an establishment with coin-operated machines for customers to wash and dry clothes. [originally a trademark]

laundress noun a woman who washes and irons clothes and linen, especially professionally.

laundry noun (PL. laundries) 1 a place where clothes and linen are washed. 2 clothes and linen for washing or newly washed.

Laura a female first name. [a form of the Latin male name Laurus, Laurel]

Laurasia noun Geol. the ancient landmass or 'supercontinent' that is thought to have existed in the N hemisphere during the Mesozoic era. It subsequently split to form the present-day landmasses of N America, Greenland, Europe, and N Asia. Together with the landmass known as Gondwanaland in the S hemisphere, it is thought to have been derived from a single original landmass, known as Pangaea. [named after Laurentia, the ancient N American landmass, from Laurentian strata of the Canadian Shield, and Eurasia]

laureate adj. crowned with laurel leaves as a sign of honour or distinction. — noun a person honoured for artistic or intellectual achievement, especially a poet laureate. [from Latin laureatus, from laurus, laurel]

Laurel, Stan, originally **Arthur Stanley Jefferson** (1890–1965) US comedian, born in Ulverston, England. He began in a British touring company, went to the USA in 1910, and worked in silent films from 1917. From 1926 he worked with Oliver Hardy (see also LAUREL AND HARDY).

laurel noun 1 a small evergreen tree with smooth, dark, shiny leaves used for flavouring in cooking. 2 a crown of laurel leaves worn as a symbol of victory or mark of honour. 3 (**laurels**) honour; praise.
— **look to one's laurels** beware of losing one's reputation by being outclassed.
rest on one's laurels to be satisfied with one's past successes and not try to achieve anything more.
[from Latin laurus]

Laurel and Hardy US comedians Stan Laurel (the 'thin one') and Oliver Hardy (the 'fat one'), who formed the first Hollywood film comedy team. They came together in 1926 and made many shorts (1927–32), such as The Music Box (1932), which won an Oscar, and some full-length feature films, including Bonnie Scotland (1935) and Way Out West (1937). Their contrasting personalities, general clumsiness, and disaster-packed predicaments made them a universally popular comedy duo.

Laurence a male and sometimes female first name. [from a French form of Latin Laurentius, man from Laurentum]

Laurence, Friar the friar in Shakespeare's Romeo and Juliet, who marries the lovers and concocts the potion which temporarily puts Juliet to sleep.

Laurie a rich, charming, and slightly spoilt character who marries Amy in Louisa May Alcott's Little Women.

Lausanne POP (1990e) 263 000, the capital of Vaud canton, W Switzerland. It lies on the N shore of L Geneva, 51km/32mi NE of Geneva. The city is a tourist resort, a convention centre, and the seat of the International Olympic Committee. NOTABLE FEATURES Mon Repos Park, with Olympic Museum; Gothic cathedral (1275); town hall (17c); Bishop's Palace.

LAUTRO *abbrev.* Life Assurance and Unit Trust Regulatory Organization.

lav *noun colloq.* a lavatory.

lava *noun* **1** *Geol.* hot molten rock material (*magma*) that has erupted from a volcano or fissure and flowed on to the Earth's surface or the ocean floor. **2** the solid rock that forms as a result of cooling and solidification of this material. [from Italian *lava*, from Latin *labes*, a sliding down]

Laval, Pierre (1883–1945) French politician, born in Châteldon. He was a lawyer, deputy (1914), and senator (1926), before serving as Premier (1931–2, 1935–6). From a Socialist position, he moved to the right during the late 1930s, and in the Vichy government was Pétain's deputy (1940), rival, and Prime Minister (1942–4), when he collaborated with the Germans. After the liberation he fled to Germany and Spain, but was brought back, charged with treason, and executed.

La Vallière, Louise Françoise de la Baume le Blanc, Duchesse de (Duchess of) (1644–1710) mistress of Louis XIV of France (1661–7), born in Tours. She was maid of honour to Henrietta Anne of England, Duchess of Orleans, before becoming the royal mistress. She bore the King four children, and reluctantly remained at court after Mme de Montespan superseded her. She eventually retired to a Carmelite nunnery in Paris (1674).

lavatorial *adj.*, *said especially of humour* relating to lavatories and excretion.

lavatory *noun* (PL. **lavatories**) **1** a piece of equipment for receiving urine and faeces, and with a mechanism for flushing this away into a sewer. **2** a room containing one or more of these. [from Latin *lavare*, to wash]

lavender *noun* **1** a plant or shrub with sweet-smelling pale bluish-purple flowers. **2** the dried flowers from this plant, used to perfume clothes or linen. **3** the pale bluish-purple colour of the flowers. [from Latin *lavendula*]

lavender water a light perfume containing lavender oil.

Lavengro a fictionalized autobiography by George Borrow (1851). It describes the vagrant lifestyle of a young man in the early 19c. 'Lavengro' means 'philologist' in Romany language.

La Venta an Olmec ceremonial centre in Tabasco province, Mexico, occupied c.900–400 BC but now destroyed by oil operations. Its linear complex of platforms, plazas, and 34m-high Great Pyramid covered 5sq km/2sq mi. It was noted for its stone pavements, and sculptures in basalt, serpentine, and jade, now displayed at Parque La Venta, near the original site.

Laver, Rod(ney George), also called **the Rockhampton Rocket** (1938–) Australian lawn tennis player, born in Rockhampton, Queensland. He was the first person to achieve the Grand Slam twice (1962, 1969), and in all he won four singles titles at Wimbledon (1961–2, 1968–9). He also won the Australian Open in 1960, and had several doubles wins. He turned professional in 1963, and was the first person to win at Wimbledon when it was opened to professionals in 1968.

laver *noun* any of several edible seaweeds. [from Latin *laver*, water plant]

Laveran, Charles Louis Alphonse (1845–1922) French physician and parasitologist, born in Paris. Professor at the military college of Val de Grâce, his studies of malaria in Algeria revealed the blood parasite which causes the disease; for this work he was awarded the 1907 Nobel Prize for Physiology or Medicine. He also carried out important work on other tropical diseases such as sleeping-sickness. From 1896 until his death he worked at the Pasteur Institute in Paris.

laver bread a Welsh dish made from boiled laver dipped in oatmeal and fried.

Lavinia a female first name, and the name of the second wife of Aeneas. [origin unknown]

lavish — *adj.* **1** *said of a person* spending or giving generously. **2** gorgeous or luxurious: *lavish decoration*. **3** too generous; extravagant or excessive. — *verb* to spend (money) or give (praise, etc) freely or generously: *lavished all kinds of honours on them*. [from Old French *lavasse*, deluge of rain]

lavishly *adv.* in a lavish or generous way.

lavishness *noun* a lavish or generous state or condition.

Lavoisier, Antoine Laurent (1743–94) French chemist, born in Paris. He showed that air is a mixture of gases, identifying both oxygen and nitrogen. His major work, *Traité élémentaire de chimie* (Elementary Treatise on Chemistry, 1789), contained many of the ideas which set chemistry on its modern path. He also devised the modern method of naming chemical compounds, and helped to introduce the metric system. From the mid-1760s he had also been involved in finance and politics and despite his introduction of reforms, he was guillotined in revolutionary Paris for his role as a government tax-collector.

Law, (Andrew) Bonar (1858–1923) Canadian-born British politician and Prime Minister, born in New Brunswick. An iron merchant in Glasgow, he became a Unionist MP (1900), and in 1911 succeeded Arthur Balfour as Unionist leader. He acted as Colonial Secretary (1915–16), a member of the War Cabinet, Chancellor of the Exchequer (1916–18), Lord Privy Seal (1919), and from 1916 Leader of the House of Commons. He retired in 1921 through ill health, but returned to serve as Prime Minister in 1922–3.

law *noun* **1** a customary rule recognized as allowing or prohibiting certain actions. **2** a collection of such rules according to which people live or a country or state is governed. **3** the control which such rules exercise: *law and order*. **4** a controlling force: *their word is law*. **5** a collection of laws as a social system or a subject for study. **6** a group of laws relating to a particular activity: *commercial law*. **7** (**the law**) people skilled in law, especially professionally. **b** *colloq.* the police or a member of the police. **8** (**laws**) jurisprudence. **9** the legal system as a recourse; litigation: *go to law*. **10** a rule in science, philosophy, etc, based on practice or observation, which says that under certain conditions certain things will always happen. **11** (**the Law**) the first five books of the Old Testament, which contain Jewish law. — **be a law unto oneself** to act as one wants and not according to laws or custom. **have the law on someone** *colloq.* (usually as a threat) to ensure that legal action is taken against them. **lay down the law** to assert one's opinions and orders forcefully and domineeringly. **take the law into one's own hands** to get justice in one's own way, without involving the law or the police. [from Anglo-Saxon *lagu*]

law-abiding *adj.* obeying the law.

law centre *Brit.* a legal advisory service available to the public free of charge.

Law Commission a body established by the Law Commissions Act (1965) for England and Wales and (separately) for Scotland, appointed by the Lord Chancellor. Its function is to examine the law with a view to reform and codification, and to suggest the removal of obsolete and anomalous laws.

lawcourt *noun* (*also* **court of law**) a place where people accused of crimes are tried and legal disagreements settled.

Lawes, Sir John Bennet (1814–1900) English agriculturist, born in Rothamstead, near St Albans. After a series of experiments he developed artificial fertilizers, and in 1843 began to manufacture these 'superphosphates' at his factory at Deptford Creek. In the same year he founded the famous agricultural research station at Rothamstead.

lawful *adj.* **1** allowed by or according to law. **2** just or rightful.

lawfully *adv.* justly; in accordance with law.

lawfulness *noun* being lawful or just; a just state.

lawless *adj.* **1** ignoring or breaking the law, especially violently. **2** having no laws.

lawlessly *adv.* without regard to the law.

lawlessness *noun* a lawless state; lack of laws.

Law Lord 1 a peer in the House of Lords who holds or has held high legal office, and who sits in the highest court of appeal. **2** *Scot.* a judge of the Court of Session.

lawn¹ *noun* an area of smooth mown grass, especially as part of a garden. [from Middle English *launde*, glade]

lawn² *noun* fine linen or cotton. [probably from *Laon* in France, where linen-making was once important]

lawnmower *noun* a machine for cutting grass on lawns.

lawn tennis, the usual form of tennis, played on grass-covered or hard courts. See also REAL TENNIS.

◇ Developed from real tennis, lawn tennis is now played on a variety of surfaces: grass, clay, shale, concrete, wood, and suitable man-made material. The most famous lawn tennis championship is the All-England Championships held at Wimbledon each year.

Lawn Tennis Association (ABBREV. **LTA**) in Britain, the governing body in tennis, formed in 1888. The equivalent body in the USA is the US Tennis Association (USTA), originally founded in 1881, and given its present name in 1975.

law of averages the theory that if something happens, its opposite is likely to happen also, so that balance may be maintained.

law of the jungle the principle that one should protect one's own interests ruthlessly and competitively.

Lawrence, D(avid) H(erbert) (1885–1930) English poet and novelist, born in Eastwood, Nottinghamshire. The son of a miner, he worked as a schoolmaster and became a full-time writer after the success of his first novel, *The White Peacock* (1911). In 1912 he eloped with Frieda von Richthofen and travelled in Europe. He achieved fame with *Sons and Lovers* (1913), but was prosecuted for obscenity after publishing *The Rainbow* (1915). In 1919 he left England, lived in Italy, Australia, the USA, and Mexico, and returned to Italy for health reasons in 1921. He was further prosecuted over the publication in Florence of *Lady Chatterley's Lover* (1928), and over an exhibition of his paintings in London in the same year. His collected poems were also published in 1928. Other major novels include *Women in Love* (1921) and *The Plumed Serpent* (1926). He also wrote many short stories, short novels, and travel books, and over 5 000 letters.

Lawrence, Ernest Orlando (1901–58) US physicist, born in Canton, South Dakota. Professor at Berkeley, California, and the first Director of the Berkeley Radiation Laboratory, he built the first cyclotron accelerator for the production of high-energy particles. For this work he was awarded the 1939 Nobel Prize for Physics.

Lawrence, T(homas) E(dward), also called **Lawrence of Arabia** (1888–1935) Anglo-

Irish soldier and author, born in Tremadoc, N Wales. Before World War I he travelled in the Middle East, where he studied Crusader castles and participated in the excavation of Carchemish. In 1914 he joined military intelligence and became a member of the Arab Bureau in Cairo. From 1916 he was British liaison officer to the Arab Revolt, led by Feisal, the son of the Sherif of Mecca, and was present at the taking of Aqaba (1917) and of Damascus (1918). His account of the Revolt, *Seven Pillars of Wisdom*, abridged as *Revolt in the Desert*, became a war literature classic. His exploits made him a legendary figure, and his attempts to escape his fame included enlisting in the ranks of the RAF (1922) as J H Ross and in the Royal Tank Corps (1923) as T E Shaw. He is the subject of David Lean's film *Lawrence of Arabia* (1962).

Lawrence of Arabia a British film directed by David Lean (1962), based on the life of T E Lawrence (played by Peter O'Toole).

lawrencium *noun Chem.* (SYMBOL **Lr**, ATOMIC NUMBER **103**) a synthetic radioactive metallic element formed by bombarding californium with boron ions. [named after Ernest Orlando Lawrence]

Law Society the professional body for solicitors in England and Wales; separate Law Societies exist for Scotland and Northern Ireland. It has disciplinary powers relating to solicitors' conduct, prescribes the rules governing their admission to practice, and promotes the interests of the profession as a whole.

Lawson (of Blaby), Nigel Lawson, Baron (1932–) English Conservative politician. He worked for various newspapers and for television (1956–72), and also edited the *Spectator* (1966–70). Elected to parliament in 1974, when the Conservatives took office he became Financial Secretary to the Treasury (1979–81), Energy Secretary (1981–3), and Chancellor of the Exchequer (1983–9). In these six years, Britain's economy experienced one of the greatest booms of the 20c, despite high interest rates and record trade deficits. Disagreement with Margaret Thatcher over his advocacy of lower interest rates and membership of the European monetary system led to Lawson's dramatic resignation and replacement by John Major.

lawsuit *noun* an argument or disagreement taken to a court of law to be settled.

lawyer *noun* a person whose work it is to know about the law, and give legal advice and help, especially a solicitor.

lax *adj.* **1** lacking care or concern in one's behaviour or morals. **2** loose, slack, or flabby. [from Latin *laxus*, loose]

laxative *noun* a medicine or food that stimulates movement of the bowels. — *adj.* having this effect. [from Latin *laxare*, to loosen]

laxity *or* **laxness** *noun* being lax; a lax state.

laxly *adv.* in a lax or slack way.

Laxness, Halldór (Gudjónsson Kiljan) (1902–) Icelandic writer, born in Reykjavik. He travelled in Europe and the USA after World War I, became a Catholic, and converted to Socialism in 1927. His works include *Salka Valka* (1934), a story of Icelandic fishing folk, and the epic *Independent People* (1934–5). He was awarded the Nobel Prize for Literature in 1955.

lay¹ — *verb* (PAST AND PAST PARTICIPLE **laid**) **1** to place on a surface, especially in a lying or horizontal position: *laid the letter on the table*. **2** to put or bring into the proper or stated position or condition: *laid her hand on his arm*. **3** to design, arrange, or prepare: *lay plans*. **4** to put plates and cutlery, etc on (a table) ready for a meal. **5** to prepare (a fire) by putting coal, etc in the grate. **6** *trans., intrans. said of a female bird* to produce (eggs). **7** to present: *lay one's case before the court*. **8** to deal with or remove: *lay a fear*. **9** to locate or attribute: *laid the blame on his friends*. **10** *trans. col-*

loq. to place (a bet). **11** *offensive, slang* to have sexual intercourse with (especially a woman). — *noun* **1** the way or position in which something is lying. **2** *offensive, slang* **a** a partner in sexual intercourse. **b** an act of sexual intercourse.

— **lay about one** to strike blows in all directions.

lay something aside 1 to put it to one side, especially for later use or treatment. **2** to discard or abandon it.

lay something bare to reveal or explain a plan or intention that has been kept secret.

lay something by to put it away for future use.

lay something down 1 to put it on the ground. **2** to give up or sacrifice something: *lay down one's life*. **3** to formulate or devise something: *lay down a plan*. **4** to store (wine) in a cellar. **5** to begin to build (a ship or railway).

lay one's hands on something *colloq.* **1** to find or be able to get it. **2** to catch something.

lay something in to get and store a supply of it.

lay into someone *colloq.* to attack or scold them severely.

lay someone low 1 *said of an illness* to affect them severely. **2** to make them feel humble.

lay people off to dismiss (employees) when there is no work available. See also LAY-OFF.

lay off doing something *colloq.* to stop doing something annoying or unwelcome.

lay something on to provide a supply of something: *we'll bring the food if you'll lay on some drinks*.

lay it on thick *colloq.* to exaggerate, especially praise or flattery.

lay oneself open to expose oneself to criticism or attack.

lay something open 1 to uncover or reveal something. **2** to cut or wound something.

lay someone out 1 *colloq.* to knock them unconscious. **2** to prepare a dead body for burial.

lay something out 1 to plan and arrange (land or natural features): *the next stage was to lay out the new park*. **2** to spread out or display something. **3** *colloq.* to spend (money). See also LAYOUT.

lay someone to rest to bury a dead body.

lay someone up *colloq., said of an illness* to force them to stay in bed or at home.

lay something up to keep or store something, to put a ship out of use, especially for repairs.

lay waste to destroy or devastate completely. [from Anglo-Saxon *lecgan*]

lay² see LIE².

lay³ *adj.* **1** relating to or involving people who are not members of the clergy. **2** not having specialized or professional knowledge of a particular subject. [from Greek *laos*, the people]

lay⁴ *noun* a short narrative or lyric poem, especially one intended to be sung. [from Old French *lai*]

layabout *noun* a lazy or idle person.

Layamon (early 13c) English poet and priest, who lived at Ernley (now Areley), on the River Severn, Worcestershire. He wrote an amplified imitation of Robert Wace's *Brut d'Angleterre*, which recounts the history of England from the arrival of a legendary Trojan, Brutus, to the 7c. It is one of the first poems written in Middle English.

Layard, Sir Austen Henry (1817–94) British archaeologist and politician, born in Paris. He carried out excavations (1845–7, 1849–51) at Nimrud near Mosul in Iraq, which he identified as the ancient city of Nineveh, where he found the remains of four palaces of the 7c–9c BC. He was an MP in 1852, Under-Secretary of Foreign Affairs (1861–6), Chief Commissioner of Works (1868–9), and British Ambassador in Spain (1869) and Istanbul (1877–80).

lay-by *noun* (PL. **lay-bys**) *Brit.* an area at the side of a road for drivers to stop out of the way of the traffic.

layer — *noun* **1** a thickness or covering, especially one of several on a surface. **2** a person or thing that lays: *carpet-layer*. **3** a hen regularly lay-

ing eggs. **4** a shoot from a plant which is fastened into the soil to root while still attached to the parent plant. — *verb* **1** to arrange or cut in layers. **2** to produce (a new plant) by preparing a layer from the parent plant.

layette *noun* a complete set of clothes, blankets, etc for a baby. [from Old French *laiete*, small chest]

lay figure 1 a jointed adjustable model of the human body, used as a guide by painters and sculptors. **2** a person or a character in a novel who lacks individuality or is unrealistic. [from Dutch *leeman*, from *led*, jointed + *man*, man] ◇ The lay figure is most frequently used to study the effects of drapery. Life-size versions are especially useful to portrait painters as they may be dressed in the sitter's clothes, enabling work to proceed on a picture in the sitter's absence.

layman *or* **layperson** *or* **laywoman** *noun* **1** a person who is not a member of the clergy. **2** a person who does not have specialized or professional knowledge of a particular subject. See also LAITY.

lay-off a dismissal of employees when there is no work available.

layout *noun* **1** an arrangement or plan of how land, buildings, pages of a book, etc are to be set out. **2** the things displayed or arranged in this way. **3** the general appearance of a printed page.

lay reader an unordained person licensed to undertake some religious duties.

Lays of Ancient Rome, The a series of poems by Thomas Macaulay (1842). They describe specific events from the traditional history of Rome.

Lazarists, properly the **Congregation of the Mission (CM)**, also called the **Vincentians** a religious order, founded (1625) in France at the priory of St Lazare, Paris, by St Vincent de Paul. Originally missionaries to rural districts and educators of the clergy, they now have foundations worldwide.

Lazarus a New Testament character (in John's Gospel only), the brother of Mary and Martha. The miracle of his being raised from the dead by Christ contributed significantly to the Jewish leaders' decision to put Christ to death (John 11, 12.9–11).

laze — *verb intrans.* to be idle or lazy. — *noun* a period of time spent lazing.

— **laze around** to spend one's time doing nothing. [a back-formation from LAZY]

lazily *adv.* in a lazy or idle manner.

laziness *noun* a lazy state; a spell of idleness.

lazy *adj.* (**lazier, laziest**) **1** disinclined to do work or anything requiring effort; idle. **2** of or causing idleness. **3** *said of a river* slow-moving, sluggish.

lazy-bones *noun colloq.* a lazy person.

lb *abbrev.* pound (weight). [from Latin *libra*]

lbw *or* **l.b.w.** *abbrev. Cricket* leg before wicket.

lc *or* **l.c.** *abbrev.* **1** *loco citato* (Latin), in the place cited. **2** *Printing* lower case.

LCD *abbrev.* **1** liquid crystal display. **2** (*also* **lcd**) lowest common denominator.

LCDT *abbrev.* London Contemporary Dance Theatre.

LCM *or* **lcm** *abbrev.* lowest common multiple.

L/Cpl *abbrev.* Lance Corporal.

LEA *abbrev. Brit.* Local Education Authority.

lea *noun poetic* a field, meadow, or piece of arable or pasture land. [from Anglo-Saxon *leah*]

Leach, Johnny (John) (1922–) English table tennis player, born in Romford, Essex. He won the world singles title in 1949 and 1951, and was a member of England's winning Swaythling

Cup team in 1953. During 12 years as an England international (1947–59), he represented his country 152 times. He became England's non-playing captain upon retirement, and was team manager from 1968 to 1970.

leach *verb* **1** *Chem.* to wash a soluble substance out of a solid by allowing a suitable liquid solvent to percolate through it. **2** to make liquid seep through (bark, ash, or soil) to remove certain substances from (the bark, etc). **3** *trans., intrans. (also* **leach away** *or* **out**) to remove (soluble substances) or be removed by having liquid seep through. [probably from Anglo-Saxon *leccan*, to water]

leaching 1 *Chem.* the process of washing a soluble substance out of a solid by allowing a suitable liquid solvent to percolate through it. **2** *Geol.* the natural removal of soluble substances, eg certain mineral salts, from a layer of soil or rock as a result of the action of water percolating through it. Mineral salts are often re-deposited in a lower layer as a result of this process.

lead¹ (pronounced *leed*) — *verb* (PAST AND PAST PARTICIPLE **led**) **1** *trans., intrans.* to guide by going in front. **2** to guide or cause to go in a certain direction by holding or pulling with the hand, etc. **3** *trans., intrans.* to direct or be in control (of). **4** to cause to act, feel, or think in a certain way: *what led you to say that?* **5** to pass or experience: *lead a miserable existence.* **6** *trans., intrans.* to go or take in a certain direction: *the road leads to the village.* **7** *intrans.* to have as an end or consequence: *this will lead to problems.* **8** *trans., intrans.* to be foremost or first; to be the most important or influential person (in a group) in a particular field: *they lead the world in engineering.* **9** *intrans. said of a newspaper* to have a particular story as its most important article: *the tabloids all lead with the royal separation.* **10** *Brit.* to play the principal violin in (an orchestra). **11** to conduct (liquid) along a channel or course. **12** *trans., intrans.* to begin a round of cards by playing (the first card, especially of a particular suit). — *noun* **1** an instance of guidance given by leading: *we're waiting for you to give a lead.* **2** the first, leading, or most prominent place; leadership. **3** the amount by which a person, etc is in front of others in a race, contest, etc. **4** a strap or chain for leading or holding a dog, etc. **5** a clue or piece of information, especially at the beginning of an inquiry, which might help solve a problem, mystery, etc. **6** the principal part in a play, film, etc, or the actor playing this role. **7** the most important story in a newspaper. **8** an act of playing the first card in a card game, or the first card played. **9** a wire or conductor taking electricity from a source to an appliance.
— **lead off** to begin.
lead someone on 1 to persuade them to go further than intended. **2** to deceive or mislead them.
lead up to something 1 to prepare to do something, for something to happen, etc by gradual steps or stages: *all that flattery was leading up to a request for money.* **2** to be an underlying cause of something.
lead the way to go first, especially to guide others.
[from Anglo-Saxon *lædan*]

lead² (pronounced *led*) — *noun* **1** (SYMBOL **Pb**, ATOMIC NUMBER **82**) a soft heavy bluish-grey metallic element that is highly toxic, malleable, ductile, resistant to corrosion, and a poor conductor of heat and electricity. **2** graphite. **3** a thin stick of graphite, or some other coloured substance, used in pencils. **4** a lump of lead used for measuring the depth of the water, especially at sea. **5** (*usually* **leads**) a sheet of lead for covering roofs; a roof covered with lead sheets. **6** a lead frame for a small window-pane, eg in stained glass windows. **7** a lead weight or piece of lead shot used at the end of a fishing line and in cartridges. **8** (**leading**) a thin strip of metal used formerly in printing to produce a space between lines. — *adj.* made of lead. — *verb* to cover, weight, fit, or surround with lead. [from Anglo-Saxon *lēad*]
◊ Lead is mainly obtained from its sulphide ore, galena. The metal is used in the building and roofing trades, as a protective shielding against radiation (eg in nuclear reactors), and in lead-acid storage batteries, high-quality glass, and as a protective covering for cables. Lead alloys are used to make bearings and ammunition, and also include solder and pewter. Lead compounds have been widely used as antiknock additives in petrol, and as pigments in paints, but their use is now strictly regulated. In order to reduce the risk of lead poisoning and environmental pollution, most modern cars are designed to run on lead-free petrol, and lead pipes are being replaced by plastic or copper ones.

lead-acid accumulator *Chem.* a rechargeable electrolytic cell consisting of a negatively charged electrode made of lead, and a positively charged electrode coated with lead(II) oxide, both of which are immersed in dilute sulphuric acid. Lead-acid accumulators are used in car batteries.

Leadbelly, originally **Huddie Ledbetter** (1888–1949) US folk and blues singer and guitarist, born in Mooringsport, Louisiana. By 16 he could play 6- and 12-string guitars, accordion, harmonica, and piano, and had become a wandering musician in the US South. At 17 he killed a man in a fight and was sentenced to 36 years in prison, but after six years he sang for the warden and was pardoned. He was sentenced to 10 years in 1930 for stabbing a man, but folklorist Alan Lomax got him a pardon after five years, and took him to New York City where he made several recordings.

leaded *adj. said of petrol* having added lead, which acts as an antiknock agent.

leaden *adj.* **1** made of lead. **2** dull grey in colour. **3** heavy or slow. **4** depressing; dull.

leader *noun* **1** a person, animal, or thing that leads or guides others. **2** a person who organizes or is in charge of a group. **3** *Brit.* the principal violinist in an orchestra. **4** *Brit. (also* **leading article**) an article in a newspaper, etc written to express the opinions of the editor. **5** *Brit.* (**Leader** or **Leader of the House**) a member of the government officially responsible for introducing business in Parliament. **6** *Photog.* a short blank strip at the beginning and end of a film or tape, used for loading the film or tape on to a spool. **7** a horse or dog in front place in a team or pair. **8** *Bot.* a long shoot growing from the stem or branch of a plant.

leadership *noun* **1** the state of being a leader. **2** the ability to lead others. **3** leaders as a group.

lead-in *noun* **1** an introduction to an article, discussion, piece of music, etc. **2** a cable connecting a television or radio with an outside aerial.

leading — *adj.* acting as leader; guiding; directing. — *noun* guidance, leadership.

leading aircraftman or **leading aircraftwoman** a man or woman with the rank above aircraftman or aircraftwoman.

leading article see LEADER 4.

leading light a very important and influential person in a particular field or subject.

leading note *Mus.* the seventh note of the diatonic scale in any key.

leading question a question asked in such a way as to suggest the answer wanted.

lead pencil a pencil with a thin stick of graphite in the middle.

lead poisoning poisoning caused by the absorption of lead into the body.
◊ Acute lead poisoning, usually caused by inhalation of lead fumes, causes severe abdominal pain, vomiting, diarrhoea, anaemia, and convulsions. Chronic poisoning, caused by the absorption of lead or lead salts over long periods of time, causes bluish coloration of the gums, nerve damage, and mental disturbances. The use of lead in paint, pencils, water pipes, etc, is now strictly controlled, and most modern cars are designed to run on lead-free petrol.

lead time 1 the time necessary between the conception or design of a product and its production. **2** the time taken for delivery of goods after an order has been placed.

lead-up something that introduces or causes something else, or the process involved.

leaf — *noun* (PL. **leaves**) **1** an expanded outgrowth, usually green and flattened, from the stem of a plant, that contains the pigment chlorophyll and is the main site of photosynthesis in green plants. **2** anything like a leaf. **3** leaves as a group. **4** the condition of having leaves: *in leaf.* **5** a single sheet of paper forming two pages in a book. **6** a metal, especially gold, that has been beaten into very thin sheets, usually so that it can be stamped on to another material, such as a book cover: *gold leaf.* **7** a hinged or sliding extra part or flap on a table, door, etc. — *verb* **1** *trans., intrans.* to turn the pages of a book quickly, and usually only glancing at the contents. **2** *intrans. said of plants* to produce leaves.
— **turn over a new leaf** to resolve to do or behave better.
[from Anglo-Saxon *lēaf* or *lāf*]
◊ A leaf typically consists of a flattened *lamina* (the leaf blade), which presents a large surface area for trapping sunlight for use in photosynthesis. It is borne on a stalk or *petiole* that grows from a node on the stem. The upper surface of the lamina is covered with a waxy cuticle that is largely impervious to water and gases, and the lower surface contains many specialized pores, called *stomata*. These allow the exchange of air and carbon dioxide between the plant and the surrounding atmosphere, and the loss of water vapour from the plant during the process of *transpiration*. Leaves vary widely in size and shape, and may be lobed or toothed. *Simple* leaves, eg oak, have a single leaf blade, whereas *compound* leaves, eg horse chestnut, are divided into separate leaflets. The lamina contains a network of veins that strengthen it and serve as a conducting tissue for the transport of water to the leaf, and for the movement of carbohydrates (mainly sugars), formed during photosynthesis, out of the leaf. *Deciduous* plants, eg horse chestnut, shed their leaves at a certain time of year, usually the autumn in temperate regions, whereas *evergreen* plants, eg pine, bear leaves all the year round because individual leaves are shed independently of each other.

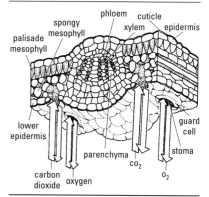

longitudinal section through a leaf

leafage *noun* the leaves of plants.

leafcutter bee a solitary bee that cuts pieces of leaf to line or close its nest. It can be an important pollinator of plants such as alfalfa.

leafless *adj.* without leaves.

leaflet — *noun* **1** a single sheet of paper, or several sheets of paper folded together, giving information, advertising products, etc. **2** *Bot.* a small leaf. **3** *Bot.* one of the individual leaf-like parts of a compound leaf. — *verb trans., intrans.* (**leafleted**, **leafleting**) to distribute leaflets to.

leaf mould earth formed from rotted leaves, used as a compost for plants.

leafy *adj.* (**leafier**, **leafiest**) **1** having or covered with leaves. **2** like a leaf.

league[1] — *noun* **1** a union of persons, nations, etc formed for the benefit of the members. **2** a group of sports clubs which compete over a period for a championship. **3** a class or group, considered in terms of ability, importance, etc: *they're not in the same league.* — *verb trans., intrans.* to form or be formed into a league.
— **in league with someone** acting in concert with them, usually for some unfavourable purpose.
[from Latin *ligare*, to bind]

league[2] *noun old use* a unit for measuring distance travelled, usually about 4·8km/3mi. [from Latin *leuga*, a Gaulish unit of distance]

League of Nations a former international organization, the constitution of which was drafted at the Paris Peace Conference (1919) and incorporated into the Treaty of Versailles. The main aims were to preserve international peace and security by the prevention or swift settlement of disputes and the promotion of disarmament. It had its headquarters in Geneva and operated through a Council, which met several times a year, and an annual Assembly. Its original members included the victorious Allies of World War I, except the USA, which refused to join, and most of the neutral nations. Germany joined in 1926, and the USSR in 1934, but Germany and Japan withdrew in 1933, and Italy in 1936. The League became increasingly ineffective in the later 1930s, when it failed to stop major acts of aggression by Japan, Italy, and Germany, and in 1946 transferred its functions to the United Nations.

League of Rights in Australia, a populist right-wing organization, founded in 1960. It operates on the fringe of conservative politics and supports God, Queen, the Commonwealth of Nations, apartheid, and private enterprise.

league table 1 a table in which clubs in a league are placed according to their performance.

compound palmate

palmate

simple peltate

variegated

compound pinnate

needles

simple lanceolate pinnate

lanceolate parallel

leaf shapes

2 any grouping made to reflect relative success, importance, etc.

leak — *noun* **1** an unwanted crack or hole in a container, pipe, etc which allows liquid or gas to pass in or out. **2** liquid or gas which has escaped in this way: *can you smell a leak?* **3** a loss of electricity from a conductor, etc, usually because of faulty insulation. **4** a divulging of secret information, especially when unauthorized. **5** *slang* an act of urinating. — *verb* **1** *intrans. said of liquid, gas, etc* to pass accidentally in or out of an unwanted crack or hole. **2** to allow (liquid, gas, etc) to leak. **3** to divulge (secret information) without authorization. **4** *intrans. said of secret information* to become known. [from Anglo-Saxon *hlec*, leaky]

leakage *noun* **1** an act or instance of leaking. **2** something that enters or escapes through a leak.

Leakey, Louis Seymour Bazett (1903–72) Kenyan anthropologist, born in Kabete. Educated at Cambridge, he took part in archaeological expeditions in E Africa, and became Curator of the Corydon Memorial Museum at Nairobi (1945–61). Among many great early hominid fossil discoveries, he unearthed, with his wife Mary, the skull of the hominid *Zinjanthropus* (1959), now thought to be about 1.7 million years old; the first remains of *Homo habilis*, a smaller species some two million years old, were found the following year. In 1967 he discovered fossilized remains of an ape around 14 million years old.

Leakey, Mary Douglas, née **Nicol** (1913–) English anthropologist, born in London. In 1948 she discovered *Proconsul africanus*, a 1.7 million year old primitive ape that brought her and her husband Louis Leakey international attention. In 1959 they discovered the hominid *Zinjanthropus* of around the same age. She also found solid evidence that our ancestors already walked upright 3.6 million years ago.

Leakey, Richard (Erskine Frere) (1944–) Kenyan palaeoanthropologist, born in Nairobi, son of Louis and Mary Leakey. He organized several African research expeditions, and discovered well-preserved hominid remains that drew worldwide publicity, such as *Homo habilis* (1972), around 1.9 million years old. He resigned as head of Kenya's Wildlife Service in 1994.

leakiness *noun* a leaky state.

leaky *adj.* (**leakier**, **leakiest**) **1** having a leak or leaks. **2** habitually divulging secrets.

Leamington Spa *or* **Leamington** *or* **Royal Leamington Spa** POP (1981) 57 000, a town in Warwick district, Warwickshire, central England. It lies on the R Leam, 13km/8mi S of Coventry and has been a Royal Spa since 1838, following a visit by Princess Victoria.

Lean, Sir David (1908–91) English film director, born in Croydon. Noël Coward and the Cineguild group gave him co-direction of *In Which We Serve* (1942), and for them he directed and co-scripted *This Happy Breed* (1944), *Blithe Spirit*, and *Brief Encounter* (both 1945). His interpretations of Dickens in *Great Expectations* (1946) and *Oliver Twist* (1948) were acclaimed as classics. Later films included *The Bridge Over the River Kwai* (1957), *Lawrence of Arabia* (1962), *Doctor Zhivago* (1965), *Ryan's Daughter* (1970), and *A Passage to India* (1984).

lean[1] — *verb* (PAST AND PAST PARTICIPLE **leant**, **leaned**) **1** *intrans., trans.* to slope or be at an angle in a sloping position. **2** *intrans., trans.* to rest or be rested against (something) for support. **3** to have an inclination or preference for or tendency towards: *they were leaning towards the moderate view.* — *noun* an act or condition of leaning.
— **lean on someone** *or* **something 1** to rely on or be supported by them. **2** *colloq.* to put pressure on someone to persuade them to act in a certain way.

[from Anglo-Saxon *hlinian*]

lean[2] *adj.* **1** *said of a person or animal* thin; having no superfluous fat. **2** *said of meat* containing little or no fat. **3** producing very little food, money, etc; unfruitful: *lean years.* [from Anglo-Saxon *hlæne*]

Leander see HERO AND LEANDER.

leaning *noun* a liking or preference.

leanness *noun* a lean state; thinness.

lean production the business practice of cutting costs and improving efficiency by streamlining production lines, keeping only minimum stocks, etc.

leant see LEAN[1].

lean-to *noun* (PL. **lean-tos**) a shed or light construction built against another building or wall.

leap — *verb* (PAST AND PAST PARTICIPLE **leapt**, **leaped**) **1** *intrans.* to jump suddenly or with force. **2** to jump over: *then they must leap the fence.* **3** (**leap at something**) to accept it eagerly. **4** *intrans. said of prices* to go up suddenly and quickly. — *noun* **1** an act of leaping or jumping. **2** the distance leaped.
— **by leaps and bounds** extremely rapidly and successfully.
a leap in the dark an action, decision, etc whose results cannot be guessed in advance.
[from Anglo-Saxon *hleapan*]

leap-frog — *noun* a game in which one player bends over for another player to vault over with legs parted. — *verb trans., intrans.* **1** to jump over a person's back in this way. **2** *said of two or more people, vehicles, etc* to move forward by passing each other one after the other.

leap year a year of 366 days, with 29 Feb being taken as the extra day.
◇ Any year exactly divisible by 4 is a leap year, except for a year ending in 00, which must be divisible by 400. The extra day is added every four years to accommodate the difference between the year of 365 days and the actual time it takes the Earth to circle the Sun (approximately 365¼days).

Lear, King a legendary king of Britain, first recorded by Geoffrey of Monmouth, and later in Spenser and Shakespeare. He ruled for sixty years before dividing his kingdom between his three daughters. Goneril and Regan conspired against him, but the third daughter, Cordelia, saved him and became queen after his death The story is changed by Shakespeare, so that she died before his eyes. See also KING LEAR.

Lear, Edward (1812–88) English artist and writer, born in London. From the age of 15 he lived by his drawing, and after 1837 lived mainly abroad, where he painted many landscapes. He is remembered more for his illustrated books of travels, and for his books of nonsense verse, which begin with the *Book of Nonsense* (1846).

learn *verb* (PAST AND PAST PARTICIPLE **learnt**, **learned**) **1** *trans., intrans.* to gain knowledge of or skill in through study, teaching, or experience. **2** to get to know by heart; to memorize. **3** (**learn of** *or* **about something**) to acquire information about something: *we've learned of a new plan to increase efficiency.* **4** *old use or slang* to teach. [from Anglo-Saxon *leornian*]

learned *adj.* (pronounced as two syllables) **1** having great knowledge or learning, especially through years of study. **2** showing or needing great learning. **3** of or relating to learned people; scholarly.

learnedly *adv.* in a learned or scholarly way.

learner *noun* **1** a person who is learning or being taught something. **2** a person who is learning to drive a motor vehicle, and has not passed a driving test.

learning *noun* knowledge gained through study.

learning curve 1 a graph used in education and research to represent progress in learning. **2** the rate at which knowledge and practical skill is acquired (over a given period or time) by an individual or group: *a steep learning curve*.

learning support, teaching intended to help pupils with learning difficulties. See also REMEDIAL.

lease — *noun* a contract by which the owner of a house, land, etc agrees to let another person use it for a stated period of time in return for payment. — *verb* to give or borrow (a building or land) on lease.
— **a new lease of life** the prospect of renewed life or health, or of use of something after repair. [from Old French *lais*]

leaseback *noun Commerce* a method of converting property into cash while still being able to use it. For example, a business may sell a property and lease it back from the buyer. The cost of leasing is a permitted business expense for which tax relief can be obtained, and the business also benefits from the cash it receives for the sale.

leasehold — *noun* **1** the holding of land or buildings by lease. **2** the land or building held by lease. — *adj.* held by lease. See also FREEHOLD.

leaseholder *noun* a holder of a lease.

leash — *noun* a strip of leather or chain used for leading or holding a dog or other animal. — *verb* **1** to put a leash on. **2** to control or restrain.
— **straining at the leash** impatient or eager to begin.
[from Old French *laisser*, to let a dog run on a leash]

least — *adj.* smallest; slightest. — *adv.* in the smallest or lowest degree. — *pron.* the smallest amount.
— **at least 1** at all events; anyway. **2** not less than.
at the least as a minimum.
not in the least *or* **not the least bit** not at all. [from Anglo-Saxon *læst*]

leather — *noun* **1** the skin of an animal made smooth by tanning. **2** a small piece of leather for polishing or cleaning. **3** the leather part of something. — *verb trans.* (**leathered**, **leathering**) **1** to cover or polish with leather. **2** *colloq.* to thrash. [from Anglo-Saxon *lether*]

leather-jacket *noun* a grub of the crane-fly, with a skin which is tough like leather.

Leather-Stocking Tales a series of five novels by James Fenimore Cooper set during the early years of the American frontier. They include *The Pioneers* (1823), *The Last of the Mohicans* (1826), *The Prairie* (1827), *The Pathfinder* (1840), and *The Deerslayer* (1841). The series title comes from the nickname of the hero, Natty Bumppo.

leathery *adj.* tough like leather.

leave¹ *verb* (PAST AND PAST PARTICIPLE **left**) **1** *trans., intrans.* to go away (from); to move out (of). **2** (*also* **leave behind**) to go without taking; to cause to remain behind. **3** to allow to remain in a particular state or condition: *leave the window open*. **4** *trans., intrans.* to stop going to, belonging to, or working at: *decided to leave the company*. **5** to deliver to or deposit with: *I'll leave the keys with a neighbour*. **6** (**leave something to someone**) to allow or cause someone to do something without help: *leave the cleaning to me*. **7** to have as a remainder: *three minus one leaves two*. **8** to make a gift of (something) in one's will when one dies. **9** to cause: *it may leave a scar*.
— **leave someone or something alone** to avoid disturbing, upsetting, worrying, or interfering with them.
leave off doing something to stop doing it; to come or bring to an end.
leave something out to exclude or omit it. [from Anglo-Saxon *læfan*]

leave² *noun* **1** permission to be absent, especially from work or military duties. **2** the length of time this lasts. **3** permission to do something.
— **on leave** officially absent from work.
take one's leave of to say goodbye to.
[from Anglo-Saxon *leaf*]

leaven — *noun* (*also* **leavening**) **1** a substance, especially yeast, added to dough to make it rise. **2** anything which is an influence and causes change. — *verb* **1** to cause (dough) to rise with leaven. **2** to influence or cause change in. [from Latin *levare*, to lift]

leaves see LEAF.

Leaves of Grass a collection of poems by Walt Whitman (first published 1855). It was a ground-breaking collection of initially 12 free-verse poems which was constantly revised throughout the author's lifetime. The final edition appeared in 1891–2.

leavings *pl. noun colloq.* things which are left; rubbish.

Leavis, F(rank) R(aymond) (1895–1978) English critic, born in Cambridge. After service in World War I, he became a lecturer in English at Emmanuel College (1925), and was later a Fellow of Downing College (1936–52). He edited the journal *Scrutiny* (1932–53), and wrote several major works of literary criticism, notably *New Bearings in English Poetry* (1932), *The Great Tradition* (1948), and *The Common Pursuit* (1952).

Lebanon, French **Liban**, official name **Republic of Lebanon**, Arabic **Al-Jumhouriya al-Lubnaniya** POP (1992e) 2.8m, a republic on the E coast of the Mediterranean Sea, SW Asia, divided into five regional governments (moafazats). AREA 10 452sq km/4 034sq mi. It is bounded N and E by Syria, and S by Israel. CAPITAL Beirut. CHIEF TOWNS Tripoli, Saida, Zahle. TIME ZONE GMT +2. The population is mainly Arab (93%), with several minorities; Islam and Christianity are the main religions. OFFICIAL LANGUAGE Arabic. CURRENCY the Lebanese pound. PHYSICAL DESCRIPTION the narrow Mediterranean coastal plain rises gradually E to the Lebanon Mts, which extend along most of the country; peaks include the Qornet es Saouda (3 087m); the arid E slopes fall abruptly to the fertile El Beqaa plateau (c.1 000m); the Anti-Lebanon range lies in the E; the R Litani flows S between the ranges. CLIMATE Mediterranean, varying with altitude, with hot, dry summers and warm, moist winters; average rainfall at Beirut is 920mm and average temperatures are 13°C–27°C. It is much cooler and drier in the Beqaa valley and irrigation is essential. HISTORY part of the Ottoman Empire from the 16c; after the massacre of Roman Catholic Maronites by Muslim Druzes in 1861, the Maronite area around Jabal Lubnan was granted special autonomous status; following the collapse of the Ottoman Empire after World War I the State of Greater Lebanon, based upon Maronite Christian Jabal Lubnan, was created in 1920 under French mandate; the Muslim coastal regions were incorporated in this new state despite great opposition; became a constitutional republic in 1926; gained independence in 1941; Palestinian resistance units were established in Lebanon by the late 1960s, despite government opposition; Palestinian raids into Israel were followed by Israeli reprisals; several militia groups developed in the mid-1970s, notably the Shiite Muslim Afwaj al-Muqawama al-Lubnaniya (AMAL) and the Muslim Lebanese National Movement (LNM); Palestinian firepower was used to back up the political struggle of the LNM against the Maronite Christian and Sunni Muslim establishment; Muslim and Christian differences grew more intense and from 1975 Lebanon was beset by civil disorder as rival political and religious factions sought to gain control; Palestinian commandos joined the predominantly leftist Muslim side; the Syrian-dominated Arab Deterrent Force (ADF) was created to pre-vent Palestinian fighters gaining control; in 1976, Palestinian forces moved from Beirut to S Lebanon where the ADF was unable to deploy; W Beirut, also outside government control, was the scene of frequent conflict between opposing militia groups. Meanwhile, Christian militias, backed by Israel, sought to regain control in E Beirut and areas to the N; following Palestinian terrorist attacks, Israel invaded S Lebanon in 1978 and 1982; the Israeli siege of Palestinian and Syrian forces in Beirut led to the withdrawal of Palestinian forces in 1982; unilateral withdrawal of Israeli forces brought clashes between the Druze (backed by Syria) and the Christian Lebanese militia; a ceasefire was announced in late 1982 but was broken many times; international efforts to achieve a political settlement were unsuccessful; in the mid-1980s rival groups began taking foreigners as hostages; Syrian troops entered Beirut in 1988 in an attempt to restore order; in the early 1990s the foreign hostages were gradually released, the Lebanese army extended government control, and government elections took place; plans were made to rebuild the economy. GOVERNMENT the constitution (in semi-suspension since 1988) provides for a Council of Ministers, a President (a Maronite Christian elected for a six-year term), a Prime Minister (a Sunni Muslim), a Cabinet, and a 108-member Parliament equally divided between Christians and Muslims; a timetable for militia disarmament was introduced in 1991. ECONOMY the commercial and financial centre of the Middle East until the Civil War, which severely damaged the enonomic infrastructure and reduced industrial and agricultural production; oil refining; cement; textiles; chemicals; food processing; service industries; citrus fruits, apples, grapes, bananas, sugar beet, olives, wheat; the tourist industry has virtually collapsed; irrigation projects are under way to harness the waters of the Litani R.

Lebanon

Lebanon Mountains, Arabic **Jebel Liban** a mountain range in Lebanon, extending c.160km/100mi NE–SW, parallel to the Mediterranean coast. It is separated from the Anti-Lebanon range to the E by the fertile El Beqaa Valley. The range rises to 3 087m at Qornet es Saouda. Grapes, olives, and apples grow on the lower slopes.

Lebensraum an expansionist concept developed by the Nazis from the early 1920s to explain the planned extension of German control into E Europe. Hitler argued that Germany was over-populated and needed more agriculturally productive land to guarantee future food supplies for an expanded German population. [from German *Lebensraum*, living space]

Lebesgue, Henri Léon (1875–1941) French mathematician, born in Beauvais. He taught at Rennes, Poitiers, the Sorbonne, and the Collège de France, and developed an indispensable theory of integration which bears his name. He applied it to many problems of analysis, in particular the theory of Fourier series, and also wrote widely on the history of mathematics.

Lebowa POP (1991) 2.1m, a non-independent black state in N Transvaal province, NE South

Africa. The state, which is situated NE of Pretoria, achieved self-governing status in 1972.

Le Carré, John, pseudonym of **David John Moore Cornwell** (1931–) English novelist, born in Poole, Dorset. He taught at Eton, entered the British Foreign Service in Bonn and Hamburg, and resigned in 1964 to become a full-time writer. His first published novel, *Call for The Dead* (1961) introduced his 'anti-hero' George Smiley, who appears in most of his works. Among his successes are *The Spy Who Came In From The Cold* (1963), *Tinker, Tailor, Soldier, Spy* (1974), and *The Perfect Spy* (1986). Many of his novels have been successfully filmed or televised.

Le Chatelier, Henri Louis (1850–1936) French chemist and metallurgist, born in Paris. Professor at the Ecole des Mines, the Collège de France, and the Sorbonne, he is best known for the principle named after him (1884), which states that if a change is made in pressure, temperature, or concentration of a system in chemical equilibrium, the equilibrium will be displaced in such a direction as to oppose the effect of this change. He also devised several scientific instruments.

Le Chatelier's principle *Physics* the principle that if any change of conditions (eg temperature or pressure) occurs in a system that is at equilibrium, then the system will tend to alter in such a way as to counteract the effect of that change. [named after Henri Le Chatelier]

lecher *noun* a lustful or lecherous man. [from Old French *lecheor*, from *lechier*, to lick]

lecherous *adj.* having or showing great or excessive sexual desire, especially in ways which are offensive.

lecherously *adv.* with a lecherous or excessively sensuous manner.

lechery *noun* excessive sexual desire.

Lechtal Alps, German **Lechtaler Alpen** a mountain range of the E Alps in Tirol state, W Austria. It rises to 3 036m at Parseierspitze. There are numerous lakes, including the Spullersee. The Arlberg to the W is a major skiing area.

lecithin *noun Biochem.* a chemical compound that is a major component of cell membranes in higher animals and plants. It is a *phosphoglyceride*, ie it contains both glycerol and a phosphate group. Lecithin is used in foods, pharmaceuticals, cosmetics, and paints. [from Greek *lekithos*, egg-yolk]

Leclanché, Georges (1839–82) French chemist, born in Paris. An engineer by training, he is remembered for the galvanic cell invented by him and given his name.

Leconte de Lisle, Charles Marie René (1818–94) French poet, born in Saint-Paul, Réunion. He settled in Paris, where he headed the group called *Parnassiens*. His *Poésies complètes* appeared in 1858, and other volumes include *Poèmes barbares* (1862), and *Pòemes tragiques* (1884).

lectern *noun* a stand with a sloping surface for holding a book to be read from, especially in a lecture-hall or church. [from Latin *legere*, to read]

lecture — *noun* **1** a formal talk on a particular subject given to an audience. **2** a long and tedious scolding or warning. — *verb* **1** *trans., intrans.* to give or read a lecture (to a group of people). **2** to scold (someone) at length. [from Latin *legere*, to read]

lecturer *noun* a person who lectures, especially to students at a college or university.

lectureship *or* **lecturership** *noun* a position or post held by a lecturer.

LED *abbrev.* light-emitting diode.

led see LEAD[1].

Leda in Greek mythology, the wife of Tyndareus, and mother, either by him or Zeus, of

Castor and Pollux, Helen, and Clytemnestra. A frequent subject in art is Zeus in the form of a swan courting Leda; Helen (and sometimes Pollux) was believed to have been hatched from an egg.

Lederberg, Joshua (1925–) US biologist and geneticist, born in Montclair, New Jersey. Professor at Wisconsin and Stanford, and President of Rockefeller University (1978–90), he showed that bacteria can reproduce by a sexual process; he went on to initiate the fields of bacterial genetics and genetic engineering. He shared the 1958 Nobel Prize for Physiology or Medicine with Edward Tatum and George Beadle.

ledge *noun* a narrow horizontal shelf or shelf-like part. [from Middle English *legge*, perhaps from *leggen*, to lay]

ledger *noun* the chief book of accounts of an office or shop, in which details of all transactions are recorded. [probably from Middle English *leggen*, to lay]

ledger line a short line added above or below a musical stave on which to mark a note higher or lower than the stave allows for.

Lee, Laurie (1914–) English writer, born in Slad, Gloucestershire. He worked as a scriptwriter for documentary films during the 1940s, and travelled widely. A nature poet of great simplicity, he is best known for his autobiographical stories of childhood and country life, including the trilogy *Cider With Rosie* (1959), *As I Walked Out One Midsummer Morning* (1969), and *A Moment of War* (1991), as well as *I Can't Stay Long* (1975).

Lee, Robert E(dward) (1807–70) US soldier, born in Stratford, Virginia. He received a commission in the engineers, and in 1861 was made Commander-in-Chief of the Virginia forces. As a Confederate general in the Civil War, he was in charge of the defences at Richmond, and defeated Federal forces in the Seven Days' battles (1862). His strategy in opposing General Pope, and his invasion of Maryland and Pennsylvania, are among his achievements central to the war's history. He surrendered his army to General Grant at Appomattox Courthouse, Virginia (1865), and later became President of Washington College in Lexington.

Lee, Tsung-Dao (1926–) Chinese-born US physicist, born in Shanghai. He taught at the University of California, and from 1956 was professor at Columbia University. He shared the 1957 Nobel Prize for Physics with Chen Ning Yang for work on quantum physics.

Lee a male and female first name, after the surname. [from Anglo-Saxon *leah*, wood, clearing]

Lee (of Asheridge), Jennie Lee, Baroness (1904–88) Scottish Labour politician, born in Lochgelly, Fife. The daughter of a Scottish miner, she was an ardent socialist and rose in left-wing politics to become the youngest elected woman MP (1929–31). She married Aneurin Bevan in 1934. Re-elected to parliament in 1945, she became the first Minister for the Arts (1967–70), and was instrumental in establishing the Open University.

lee *noun* **1** shelter given by a neighbouring object. **2** (*also* **lee side**) the sheltered side, away from the wind. [from Anglo-Saxon *hleo*, shelter]

leech *noun* **1** any of various annelid worms with a cylindrical or flattened body consisting of 33 segments, and bearing suckers at each end which are used as anchors during movement. Most species live in ponds and streams, where they feed on worms, insect larvae, snails, etc, while others are parasitic and suck the blood from larger animals. The medicinal leech was once used for blood-letting as a treatment for many ailments. **2** a person who befriends another in the hope of personal gain. [from Anglo-Saxon *læce*]

Leeds POP (1992e) 722 000, a town in Leeds borough, West Yorkshire, N England. It lies on the R Aire, 315km/196mi NW of London. HISTORY there was a ford across the R Aire here in Roman times; in the 18c Leeds became an important centre of cloth manufacture; incorporated by Charles I in 1626; the world's first railway line was opened here in 1758; Leeds is today the sixth largest city in England. NOTABLE FEATURES civic hall (1933); town hall (1858); art gallery; Churches of St John (1634) and St Peter (1841); Kirkstall Abbey (1147); Temple Newsam, birthplace of Lord Darnley.

leek *noun* a long thin vegetable with broad flat dark green leaves and a white base, closely related to the onion. It is used as the national emblem of Wales. [from Anglo-Saxon *leac*]

leer — *noun* a lecherous grin or sneer. — *verb intrans.* to grin or sneer lecherously at someone. [from Anglo-Saxon *hleor*, face, cheek]

leering *adj.* grinning lecherously.

leeringly *adv.* with a lecherous grin or sneer.

leery *adj.* (**leerier, leeriest**) **1** sly; cunning. **2** (**leery of someone**) not having great trust in them; suspicious of them.

lees *pl. noun* the sediment that settles at the bottom of wine. [from Old French *lie*]

leet *noun Scot.* a selected list of candidates for an office.

Leeuwarden, Frisian **Liouwert** POP (1992e) 86 000, the capital of Friesland province, N Netherlands, lying on the River Ee. Before the draining of the Middelzee fenlands, the city was a port. It developed into a centre for gold and silverware. It now has the largest cattle market in the Netherlands. The dancer and spy Mata Hari was born here in 1876. NOTABLE FEATURES Grote Kerk (13c–16c); Frisian Museum.

Leeuwenhoek, Antoni van (1632–1723) Dutch scientist, born in Delft. A clerk for a cloth merchant in Amsterdam until around 1650, he subsequently returned to Delft and became a famous microscopist, the first to observe bacteria, protozoa, spermatozoa, and features of the blood.

leeward *Naut.* — *adj., adv.* in or towards the direction in which the wind blows. — *noun* the sheltered side.

Leeward Islands, Spanish **Islas de Sotavento** an island group of the Lesser Antilles in the Caribbean Sea, N of the Windward Is. HISTORY the Leeward Islands were a division of the West Indies Federation (1958–62); the name was formerly used by the Spanish to include the Greater Antilles.

Leeward Islands, French **Iles sous le Vent** POP (1988) 22 000, an island group of the Society Is, French Polynesia. AREA 507sq km/196sq mi. It comprises the volcanic islands of Huahine, Raiatea, Tahaa, Bora-Bora, and Maupiti, with four small, uninhabited atolls. CHIEF TOWN Uturoa on Raiatea. ECONOMY copra; vanilla; pearls.

leeway *noun* **1** *Naut.* a ship's drift sideways, away from its true course. **2** scope for freedom of movement or action.

— **make up leeway** to make up for lost progress or time.

Le Fever, Lt a character in a sentimental story told in Laurence Sterne's *Tristram Shandy*.

left[1] see LEAVE[1].

left[2] — *adj.* **1** relating to the side of a person or thing which is towards the west when that person or thing is facing north. **2** on or close to a spectator's left side: *stage left*. **3** *said of a river bank* on the left hand of a person going downstream. **4** relating to the political left. — *adv.* on or towards the left side. — *noun* **1** the left side, part, direction, etc. **2** the members of any political party holding the most socialist views (from the practice of European parliaments in which members holding the most radical views sat on the president's left). **3** (**the Left**) people, political parties, etc, in favour of socialism. **4** *Boxing* the left hand, or a punch with this. [from Anglo-Saxon *left*, weak]

Left Bank the south bank of the River Seine in Paris, an area occupied by numerous educational establishments, including part of the University of Paris and the Ecole des Beaux Arts. It is noted as a haunt of writers and intellectuals.

left-field *adj. North Amer. slang* out of the ordinary, bizarre. [from the area so designated on a baseball field, to the left facing from the plate]

left-hand *adj.* **1** on or towards the left. **2** done with the left hand.

left-handed *adj.* **1** having the left hand stronger and more skilful than the right. **2** for use by left-handed people, or the left hand. **3** awkward, clumsy. **4** *said of compliments, etc* dubious, ambiguous; only seeming to be sincere.

left-handedly *adv.* with the left hand; awkwardly.

left-handedness *noun* being left-handed; awkwardness.

left-hander *noun* a left-handed person.

left-hand rule *Physics* in an electric motor, a rule which relates the direction of movement, the direction of the magnetic field, and the direction of flow of electric current, so called because it can be represented by holding the left hand with the thumb and first and second fingers at right angles. The thumb represents the direction of movement, the first finger represents the direction of the magnetic field, and the second finger represents the direction of flow of current. See also RIGHT-HAND RULE.

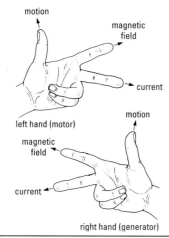

left- and right-hand rules

leftism *noun* the principles and policies of the political left.

leftist *noun* a supporter of the political left, a socialist. — *adj.* relating to or characteristic of the political left.

left-luggage office an office at a railway or coach station where travellers may leave luggage in return for payment.

left-over *adj.* not used up, eaten, etc.

leftovers *noun* food that remains uneaten at the end of a meal.

left wing **1** the members of a political party who hold the most socialist opinions. **2 a** the left side of a team in a field game. **b** a player playing on this side. **3** the left side of an army.

left-wing *adj.* relating to or supporting the political left.

left-winger *noun* a member of a political left wing.

lefty *noun* (PL. **lefties**) *colloq.* a left-winger.

leg *noun* **1** one of the limbs on which animals, birds, and people walk and stand. **2** an animal's or bird's leg used as food. **3** the part of a piece of clothing that covers one of these limbs. **4** a long narrow support of a table, chair, etc. **5** one stage in a journey. **6** a section of a competition or lap of a race. **7** *Cricket* **a** the side of the field that is to the left of a right-handed batsman facing the bowler or to the right of a left-handed batsman. **b** a fielder on this side of the field. **8** a branch or limb of a forked object. — *verb* (**legged**, **legging**) (*usually* **leg it**) *colloq.* to walk or run quickly.

— **a leg up** *colloq.* help in climbing up or over something.

leg before wicket *Cricket, said of a batsman* given out because of stopping with any part of the body other than the hand a ball which would otherwise have hit the wicket.

not have a leg to stand on *colloq.* to have no way of excusing one's behaviour or supporting one's arguments with facts.

on one's last legs near to being no longer usable; near to death or total collapse.

pull someone's leg *colloq.* to try to make them believe something which is not true, especially as a joke.

shake a leg *colloq.* to hurry up.
[from Norse *leggr*]

Legacy in Australia, an organization (formerly called the Remembrance Club) founded in 1922 by Major-General Sir John Gellibrand. It cares for the families of servicemen who have died as a result of war.

legacy *noun* (PL. **legacies**) **1** an amount of property or money left in a will. **2** something handed on or left unfinished by a past owner or predecessor: *a legacy of mismanagement.* [from Latin *legare*, to leave by will]

legal *adj.* **1** lawful; allowed by the law. **2** of or relating to the law or lawyers. [from Latin *legalis*]

legal aid financial assistance from public funds given to people who cannot afford to pay for legal advice.

◇ In the UK, the scheme provides the public with advice and assistance from solicitors, and aid with representation at civil and criminal trials. Civil legal aid is administered by the Legal Aid Board (since 1989) under general guidance from the Lord Chancellor; help is means-tested, and a contribution may be required. A person seeking criminal legal aid applies to the court (in Scotland, to the Legal Aid Board), which may grant such aid if it is both needed and in the interests of justice to grant it; the court may order a contribution.

legalism *noun* strict adherence to the law.

legalist *noun* a person who adheres strictly to the law.

legalistic *adj.* adhering strictly to the law.

legality *noun* the state of being legal; lawfulness.

legalization *or* **legalisation** *noun* the process of making legal or lawful.

legalize *or* **legalise** *verb* to make legal or lawful.

legally *adv.* in accordance with or as regards the law: *they were not acting legally / legally, you are entitled to compensation.*

legal tender currency which legally must be accepted in payment.

legate *noun* an ambassador or representative, especially from the pope. [from Latin *legare*, to send a commission]

legatee *noun* a person who is left a legacy by the terms of a will. [from Latin *legare*, to leave by will]

legation *noun* **1** a diplomatic mission or group of delegates. **2** the official residence of such a mission or group. [from Latin *legare*, to send a commission]

legato *Mus.* — *adv.* smoothly, with the notes running into each other. — *adj.* smooth and flowing. — *noun* (PL. **legatos**) **1** a piece of music to be played in this way. **2** a legato style of playing. [from Italian *legato*, bound]

legend *noun* **1** a traditional story which is popularly regarded as true but is not confirmed as such. **2** such stories collectively: *the realm of legend.* **3** a famous person about whom popularly believed stories are told: *a legend in her own lifetime.* **4** words accompanying a map or picture, etc, which explain the symbols used. **5** an inscription on a coin, medal, or coat of arms. [from Latin *legenda*, to be read]

legendary *adj.* **1** relating to or in the nature of legend. **2** described or spoken about in legend. **3** *loosely* very famous.

Legend of the Holy Cross, The a series of frescoes by Piero della Francesca (c.1452–c.1466, San Francesco, Arezzo).

Legendre, Adrien-Marie (1752–1833) French mathematician, born in Paris. Professor at the Ecole Militaire and the Ecole Normale, he independently proposed the method of least squares in 1806, and made important contributions to the study of elliptic functions and number theory. His works reintroduced rigour to the teaching of elementary geometry in France.

legerdemain *noun* (pronounced like *ledger domain*, with stress on -*main*) **1** skill to deceive or conjure with the hands. **2** trickery. [from French *léger*, light + *de*, of + *main*, hand]

leger line same as LEDGER LINE.

leggings *pl. noun* outer coverings for the lower legs.

leggy *adj.* (**leggier, leggiest**) **1** *said especially of a woman* having attractively long slim legs. **2** *said of a plant* having a long stem.

Leghorn, Italian **Livorno** POP (1991e) 171 000, a city in W Tuscany, Italy. It is situated on the low-lying coast of the Tyrrhenian Sea, SW of Pisa. HISTORY developed into an important commercial centre by the Medici family; much of the city was rebuilt after extensive damage in World War II. NOTABLE FEATURES cathedral (17c); Italian Naval Academy.

legibility *noun* being legible; the capacity to be read.

legible *adj.* (especially of handwriting) clear enough to be read. [from Latin *legibilis*]

legibly *adv.* so as to be readable: *please write legibly.*

legion — *noun* **1** *Hist.* a unit in the ancient Roman army, containing between 3 000 and 6 000 soldiers. **2** a very great number. **3** the name of certain military forces: *the French Foreign Legion.* — *adj.* great in number: *books on this subject are legion.* [from Latin *legere*, to choose]

◇ A typical legion was subdivided into 10 cohorts, each of which were divided into six centuries. Augustus established the military system of which the senior part was a citizen army of some 30 legions (around 165 000 men), each commanded by a middle-ranking senator. This army was largely deployed in the provinces and frontier areas of the Empire.

legionary — *noun* (PL. **legionaries**) *Hist.* a soldier in an ancient Roman legion. — *adj.* relating to legions.

Légion d'Honneur in France, a decoration instituted by Napoleon I in 1802 to reward civil and military service. The president of the Republic is grand master, and the five grades are chevalier, officer, commander, grand officer, and grand cross. The ribbon is scarlet. [French, = legion of honour]

legionnaire *noun* a member of a legion, especially of the French Foreign Legion.

Legionnaires' disease *Medicine* a severe and sometimes fatal disease caused by infection of the lungs with the bacterium *Legionella pneumophila*. It is characterized by muscle pain, fever, coughing, breathlessness, chest pain, and sometimes kidney failure and pneumonia. [named after the American Legion Convention in Philadelphia, Pennsylvania, where an outbreak of the disease occurred in 1976]

legislate *verb intrans.* **1** to make laws. **2** (**legislate for something**) make provision for it. [from Latin *lex*, law + *latio*, bringing, proposing]

legislation *noun* **1** the process of legislating. **2** a group of laws.

legislative *adj.* **1** relating to or concerned with law-making. **2** having the power to make laws: *a legislative assembly*.

legislator *noun* a person who makes laws, especially a member of a legislative body.

legislature *noun* the part of the government which has the power to make laws.

legitimacy *noun* being legitimate; a legitimate state.

legitimate — *adj.* (pronounced -mət) **1** lawful. **2** born to parents who are married to each other. **3** *said of an argument or conclusion, etc* reasonable or logical. **4** *said of a sovereign* ruling according to strict hereditary right. — *verb* (pronounced -mate) to make lawful or legitimate. [from Latin *legitimus*]

legitimately *adv.* lawfully; with justification: *they felt they could legitimately complain.*

legitimization *or* **legitimisation** *noun* making legitimate or lawful.

legitimize *or* **legitimise** *verb* **1** to make lawful or legal. **2** to make (an illegitimate child) the legal heir to its parents.

legless *adj.* **1** having no legs: *a legless amphibian.* **2** *colloq.* very drunk.

Lego *noun trademark* a children's toy construction system consisting of small plastic bricks which can be fastened together. [from Danish *lege*, to play]

Legoland see VEJLE.

leg-pull *noun colloq.* a joking attempt to make someone believe something which is not true.

Legree, Simon the barbaric, drunken planter in Harriet Beecher Stowe's *Uncle Tom's Cabin*, who buys Tom as a slave and is the instigator of his murder.

legroom *noun* space for one's legs, especially in a vehicle, aircraft, etc.

legume *noun Bot.* **1** any plant belonging to the pulse family (Leguminosae), which produces a dry dehiscent fruit in the form of a pod, including many important vegetable crops (eg pea, bean, lentil, peanut, soya bean), several fodder crops (eg clover, alfalfa), and ornamental plants (eg sweet pea). Legumes are the only flowering plants that possess root nodules containing bacteria that can take up atmospheric nitrogen and convert it to other nitrogenous compounds that can be used by the plant. **2** the dry dehiscent fruit of this plant, containing one to many often edible seeds rich in protein. It splits into two valves when ripe, thereby releasing the seeds. **3** the edible seed of this plant, which may be cooked and eaten when green and immature (eg pea, bean), or harvested when mature and then dried (eg chickpea, lentil). [from Latin *legumen*, that which is picked by hand]

leguminous *adj. Bot.* producing fruit or seeds in pods.

Lehár, Franz (1870–1948) Hungarian composer, born in Komárom. He became a military band conductor in Vienna and wrote a violin concerto, but is best known for his operettas which include *The Merry Widow* (1905) and *The Count of Luxembourg* (1909).

Le Havre, formerly **Le Havre-de-Grace** POP (1990) 254 000, a commercial seaport in Seine-Maritime department, Haute-Normandie region, NW France. It lies on the English Channel, on the N side of the estuary of the R Seine, 176km/109mi NW of Paris. HISTORY founded by François I in 1517 to replace the silted-up port of Harfleur; it was a naval base under Napoleon I; in World War I, it was an Allied base; after heavy damage in World War II, it was largely rebuilt. It is the biggest port in Europe and the second most important in France after Marseilles; oil forms 80% of the commodities handled. NOTABLE FEATURES medieval town of Harfleur to the E; Church of St Joseph.

Lehmann, Lotte (1888–1976) German soprano, born in Perleberg. After making her début in Hamburg (1910), she sang at the Vienna Staatsoper (1914–38), appeared frequently at Covent Garden and at the New York Metropolitan, and became noted particularly for her performances in operas by Richard Strauss, including two premières. She later took US nationality, and in 1951 retired to Santa Barbara.

lei *noun* a Polynesian garland of flowers worn round the neck. [from Hawaiian *lei*]

Leibniz, Gottfried Wilhelm (1646–1716) German mathematician and philosopher, born in Leipzig. In 1667 he obtained a legal position at the court of the Elector of Mainz, and at the same time absorbed the philosophy, science, and mathematics of the day. He published his theory of calculus in 1684, but became involved in a priority dispute over this with Isaac Newton; in 1676 he became librarian to the Duke of Brunswick at Hanover. He initiated the founding in 1700 of the Prussian Academy of Sciences in Berlin, of which he became the first president, but died in Hanover without real recognition. He made important and diverse contributions to physics, statistics, logic, and probability theory; he built calculating machines, and contemplated a universal language; he also wrote on history, law, and political theory, and his philosophy was the foundation of 18c rationalism.

Leicester, Robert Dudley, Earl of (c.1532–88) English nobleman, the favourite and possibly the lover of Elizabeth I. He became Master of the Horse, Knight of the Garter, a Privy Councillor, and Earl of Leicester (1564). Despite unpopularity at court and a secret marriage to the Dowager Lady Sheffield (1573), he retained Elizabeth's favour, and she was only temporarily offended when in 1578 he bigamously married the widow of Walter, Earl of Essex. Sent in 1585 to command the expedition to the Low Countries, he was recalled for incompetence (1587), but was nonetheless appointed to lead the forces against the Spanish Armada in 1588.

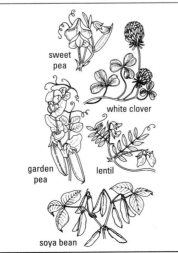

legumes

Leicester, Latin **Ratae Coritanorum** POP (1992e) 285 000, a city and the county town of Leicestershire, central England. It lies 160km/99mi N of London. In medieval times it was an important royal residence; its charter was granted in 1589 by Elizabeth I. NOTABLE FEATURES many Roman remains; Cathedral of St Martin (14c), Churches of St Margaret, St Mary de Castro, and St Nicholas; Guildhall (17c); Belgrave Hall Museum.

Leicestershire POP (1992e) 902 000, a county in central England, divided into nine districts. AREA 2 553sq km/985sq mi. It includes the former county of Rutland, and is bounded N by Nottinghamshire, NE by Lincolnshire, NW by Derbyshire, SW by Warwickshire, and S by Northamptonshire. It is drained by the R Soar. CHIEF TOWNS Leicester (county town), Market Harborough, Loughborough. ECONOMY agriculture; livestock; cheese (Stilton); coal mining; limestone; engineering; hosiery; footwear. NOTABLE FEATURES Charnwood Forest; Vale of Belvoir.

Leics. *abbrev.* Leicestershire.

Leiden see LEYDEN.

Leif Eriksson, also called **the Lucky** Icelandic explorer, the son of Erik the Red, the first European to reach America. He Christianized Greenland, and in c.1000 discovered land which he named Vinland after the vines he found growing there. The precise location of Vinland is still uncertain; possibly Labrador, Newfoundland, or Massachusetts.

Leigh, Vivien, originally **Vivian Mary Hartley** (1913–67) British actress, born in Darjeeling, India. After RADA, her first contract was with Alexander Korda, playing in *Fire Over England* (1936) with Laurence Olivier, whom she later married (1940–60). In Hollywood she played Scarlett O'Hara in *Gone With the Wind* (1939), for which she was awarded an Oscar. Other major roles were in *Anna Karenina* (1948) and *A Streetcar Named Desire* (1951), which gained her another Oscar.

Leila a female first name. [of Arabic origin, = night]

Leinster POP (1991) 1.9m, a province in the E Irish Republic. AREA 19 633sq km/7 578sq mi. CAPITAL Dublin. It comprises the counties of Louth, Meath, Westmeath, Longford, Offaly, Kildare, Dublin, Laoighis, Wicklow, Carlow, Kilkenny, and Wexford.

Leipzig, ancient **Lipsia** POP (1991e) 514 000, a city in Saxony, E Germany, 103km/64mi NW of Dresden. It is a centre for commerce, education, and music (particularly associated with Bach and Mendelssohn). NOTABLE FEATURES Church of St Thomas, with the tomb of J S Bach; Museum of Fine Art; Battle of the Nations Monument; Renaissance town hall; Lenin Memorial; Dimitrov Museum; Karl Marx University (1409).

Leipzig, Battle of, also called **Battle of the Nations** the overwhelming defeat (1813) of Napoleon's forces, who were heavily outnumbered by the armies of the Fourth Coalition — an Allied force of Austrians, Prussians, Russians, and Swedes. Napoleon tried to withdraw, but his troops were badly mauled and he effectively surrendered French control of the territory E of the Rhine.

leisure *noun* time when one is free to relax and do as one wishes.
— **at leisure 1** not occupied. **2** without hurrying.
at one's leisure at a time convenient to one. [from Latin *licere*, to be allowed]

leisure centre a centre providing a wide variety of recreational facilities.

leisured *adj.* having ample leisure time.

leisurely — *adj.* not hurried; relaxed. — *adv.* without hurrying and taking plenty of time.

leitmotiv *or* **leitmotif** *noun* a theme associated with a particular person, idea, etc which recurs throughout a piece of music, novel, etc. [from German *Leitmotiv*, from *leiten*, to lead + *Motiv*, motif]

Leitrim, Gaelic **Liathdroma** POP (1991) 25 000, a county in Connacht province, Irish Republic, stretching SE from Donegal Bay. AREA 1 526sq km/589sq mi. It is bounded NE by Northern Ireland. CAPITAL Carrick-on-Shannon. ECONOMY cattle, sheep; potatoes, oats; coarse angling (on the R Shannon and L Allen).

Lemaître, Georges Henri (1894–1966) Belgian astrophysicist, born in Charleroi. Ordained as a Catholic priest, he studied at the Universities of Louvain, Cambridge, Harvard, and the Massachusetts Institute of Technology, and became professor at Louvain in 1927. From 1945 he developed the notion of the 'primeval atom' which is unstable and explodes, instituting the theory of what is now called the 'Big Bang', the beginning of the expanding universe.

Léman, Lac see GENEVA, LAKE.

Le Mans, ancient **Oppidum Suindinum** POP (1990) 189 000, the commercial capital of Sarthe department, Pays de la Loire region, NW France. It lies on the R Sarthe, 187km/116mi SW of Paris. HISTORY the ancient capital of Maine; fortified by the Romans in the 3c–4c. NOTABLE FEATURES Cathedral of St Julien (11c–15c); Notre-Dame-de-la-Coiture (11c); well-preserved Roman wall. EVENT annual 24-hour motor race (Jun).

lemming *noun* a northern and Arctic rodent, reputed to rush into the sea in large numbers and drown during migration. [from Norwegian *lemming*]

Lemminkäinen Finnish hero in the *Kalevala*, who has to undertake impossible tasks, such as shooting the swan of Tuonela. This causes his death, and his mother has to reanimate him. His ride through a land of horrors inspired the symphonic poems of the composer Jean Sibelius.

Lemnos, Greek **Límnos** POP (1981) 16 000, a Greek island in the N Aegean Sea, off the NW coast of Turkey. AREA 476sq km/184sq mi; length 40km/25mi. It rises to 430m. CAPITAL Kastron. NOTABLE FEATURE several Neolithic remains.

lemon — *noun* 1 a small oval citrus fruit with pointed ends and a tough yellow outer skin or rind enclosing membranous segments filled with sour-tasting acidic juicy flesh rich in vitamin C. It is squeezed for its juice, and used as a source of citric acid, essential oils, pectin, and food flavourings. 2 *Bot.* the small evergreen tree (*Citrus limon*) that bears this fruit, widely cultivated in S Europe, California, and Florida. 3 a pale yellow colour. 4 *colloq.* a person or thing thought of as worthless. — *adj.* 1 pale yellow in colour. 2 tasting of or flavoured with lemon. [from Persian *limun*]

lemonade *noun* a fizzy or still drink flavoured with or made from lemons.

lemon curd *or* **lemon cheese** a thick creamy paste made from lemons, sugar, butter, and egg.

lemon sole a European flatfish used as food. [from French *limande*]

lemon squash a concentrated drink made from lemons.

lemur *noun* any of various species of nocturnal tree-dwelling primate, related to but more primitive than monkeys, and once widespread but now confined to Madagascar. Lemurs have large eyes and long bushy tails, and feed mainly on fruit and insects. Some lemurs produce weird ghostly cries. [from Latin *lemures*, ghosts]

Lemures in Roman mythology, ghosts who wandered about outside their relatives' houses on 9, 11, and 13 May – the Lemuri.

Lena, River a river in Siberia, Russia, length 4 400km/2 700mi. Rising in the Baykalskiy

Khrebet near L Baikal, it flows generally NE and N to enter the Laptev Sea in a wide swampy delta, NW of Tiksi. Coal, oil, and gold are obtained on the banks of the Lena and its tributaries.

Lenard, Philipp Eduard Anton (1862–1947) German physicist, born in Pozsony, Hungary (now Bratislava, Slovakia). Professor at Heidelberg and Kiel, he made early observations of the photoelectric effect, and discovered many properties of cathode rays. On the basis of this work he suggested that atoms contain units of both positive and negative charge. He was awarded the 1905 Nobel Prize for Physics.

Lenclos, Anne, known as **Ninon de Lenclos** (1620–1705) French courtesan, born of a good family in Paris. Her lovers included several prominent members of the aristocracy, as well as political and literary figures. She was celebrated almost as much for her manners as for her beauty, and respectable women sent their children to her to learn taste, style, and politeness.

lend *verb* (PAST TENSE AND PAST PARTICIPLE **lent**) 1 to give (someone) the use of (something) on the understanding that it is to be returned. 2 to allow (someone) the use of (money), especially in return for interest paid on it. 3 to give or add (interest, beauty, etc) to (something or someone). — **lend a hand** to help.

lend an ear to listen.

lend itself to something to be suitable for a purpose.

lend oneself to something to adapt oneself to a purpose or policy. [from Anglo-Saxon *lænan*]

lender *noun* a person who lends, especially money.

Lendl, Ivan (1960–) Czech lawn tennis player, born in Ostrava, Czechoslovakia. He won the singles title at the US Open (1985–7), French Open (1984, 1986–7), and Australian Open (1989), and was the Masters champion (1986–7) and the World Championship Tennis champion (1982, 1985). He was runner-up at Wimbledon in 1986–7.

Lend-Lease Agreement the means by which the USA lent or leased war supplies and arms to Britain and other countries during World War II. The Lend-Lease Act was passed by Congress in March 1941, when British reserves were almost exhausted. Up to the end of the agreement (Aug 1945), the Allies had received materials worth about £5 000 million.

Leng, Virginia, *née* **Holgate** (1955–) British three-day eventer, born in Malta. The European junior champion in 1973, she won the team gold at the senior championship in 1981, 1985, 1987, and individual titles in 1985, 1987, and 1989. She won the world championship team gold in 1982 and 1986, and the individual title in

lemur

1986 on *Priceless*. She has also won at Badminton (1985, 1989) and at Burghley (1983–6, 1989).

Lenglen, Suzanne (1899–1938) French lawn tennis player, born in Compiègne. She won the French singles title (1920–3, 1925–6), and the women's and mixed doubles (1925–6). Her Wimbledon championship wins were the women's singles and doubles (1919–23, 1925), and the mixed doubles (1920, 1922, 1925). In 1920 she was Olympic singles and mixed doubles champion. She became a professional in 1926, toured the US, and retired in 1927 to found the Lenglen School of Tennis in Paris.

length *noun* 1 the distance from one end of an object to the other, normally the longest dimension. 2 the distance a thing extends: *an arm's length*. 3 a period of time. 4 the quality of being long. 5 a long piece of something or a stated amount of something long, eg cloth, hair, or tubing. 6 the extent from end to end of a horse, boat, etc, as a unit by which a lead in a race is measured. 7 (*usually* **lengths**) trouble or effort; action taken: *go to great lengths*. 8 Phonetics, Mus. the amount of time a vowel, syllable, note, etc sounds.
— **at length** 1 in detail. 2 at last. [from Anglo-Saxon *lengthu*]

lengthen *verb trans., intrans.* to make or become longer.

lengthily *adv.* at great length; tediously: *spoke lengthily about the war*.

lengthiness *noun* a lengthy state; being excessively long.

lengthways *or* **lengthwise** *adv., adj.* in the direction of a thing's length; longways.

lengthy *adj.* (**lengthier, lengthiest**) 1 of great, often excessive, length. 2 *said of speech, etc* long and tedious.

lenience *or* **leniency** *noun* being lenient or mild.

lenient *adj.* mild and tolerant, especially in punishing; not severe. [from Latin *lenis*, soft]

leniently *adv.* mildly; with tolerance.

Lenin, Vladimir Ilyich, originally **V I Ulyanov** (1870–1924) Russian Marxist revolutionary and politician, born in Simbirsk. A graduate in law, from 1897 to 1900 he was exiled to Siberia for participating in underground revolutionary activities. At the Second Congress of the Russian Social Democratic Labour Party (1903) he caused the split between the Bolshevik and Menshevik factions. Following the February 1917 revolution, he returned to Petrograd (now St Petersburg) from Zurich, and urged the immediate seizure of political power by the proletariat under the slogan 'All Power to the Soviets'. In Oct 1917 he led the Bolshevik revolution and headed the first Soviet government. At the end of the ensuing Civil War (1918–21) he introduced the New Economic Policy, which his critics in the Party saw as a 'compromise with capitalism' and a retreat from strict socialism. On his death, his body was embalmed and placed in a mausoleum in Red Square, Moscow. However, under President Boris Yeltsin signs of the Lenin cult began to disappear: in Oct 1993 the goose-stepping honour guard was dismissed from outside the mauseoleum, in Nov 1993 the Lenin Museum was closed, and in Jan 1994 (the seventieth anniversary of his death) the body was removed from the mausoleum and buried in St Petersburg.

Lenin Mausoleum the former tomb of Lenin, designed by Aleksey V Shchusev and built between 1924 and 1930 in Red Square, Moscow.

Lenin Peak, Russian **Lenina Pik**, formerly **Mt Kaufmann** the highest peak in the Alayskiy Khrebet, on the border between Tajikistan and Kirghizia. HEIGHT 7 134m.

lenity *noun literary* mildness; mercifulness. [from Latin *lenis*, soft]

Lennon, John (Winston) (1940–80) English songwriter, vocalist, and rhythm guitarist, born in Liverpool. He first saw fame as a member of the Beatles, and pursued a solo career after the group disbanded in 1970. His marriage to Japanese conceptual artist Yoko Ono (1933–) sharpened his social conscience and refocused the surreal wit that was part of his Lancashire Catholic inheritance. Their work together produced songs of mild protest like 'Give Peace a Chance' (1969); others included 'Cold Turkey' (1969) and 'Working Class Hero' (1970), a rare balance of the personal and political. His most successful albums were *Imagine* (1971) and *Mind Games* (1973). On 8 Dec 1980 he was shot dead in New York.

Lenoir, Jean Joseph Étienne (1822–1900) French inventor and engineer, born in Luxembourg. He invented the first practical internal combustion gas engine (around 1859) and later built the first car to use it (1860). He also constructed a boat driven by his engine (1886).

lens *noun* 1 an optical device consisting of a piece of glass, clear plastic, etc, curved on one or both sides, that changes the direction of a beam of light by the process of refraction. Biconvex lenses cause parallel rays to converge, and biconcave lenses cause them to diverge, in both cases producing an image of an object. Optical lenses are used in cameras, binoculars, telescopes, microscopes, etc, and in spectacles and as contact lenses. **2** any similar device that focuses a beam of electrons, eg an electromagnet in an electron microscope. **3** in the eyes of many vertebrates, including humans, a transparent biconvex structure lying between the iris and the vitreous humour. It focuses light from an object on to the retina, forming an image, and its curvature is controlled by means of ciliary muscles. [from Latin *lens*, lentil (because of the shape)]

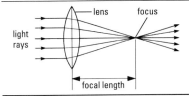

focal length of a lens

Lent in the Christian Church, the weeks before Easter; a period of prayer, penance, and abstinence commemorating Christ's 40-day fast in the wilderness. In Western Churches, it begins on Ash Wednesday; in Eastern Orthodox Churches, it begins eight weeks before Easter. [from Anglo-Saxon *lencten*, spring]

lent see LEND.

Lenten *adj.* relating to or during Lent.

lenticel *noun Bot.* a small pore, on the surface of a woody stem or root, that allows gases to pass to and from tissues. [from Latin *lenticula*, a diminutive of *lens lentis*, lentil]

lentil *noun* a small orange, brown, or green seed from a pod-bearing plant, used as food. [from Latin *lens, lentis*]

lento *Mus.* — *adv.* slowly. — *adj.* slow. — *noun* (PL. **lentos**) a piece of music to be performed in this way. [from Italian *lento*]

Lenya, Lotte, originally **Karoline Wilhelmine Blamauer** (1898–1981) Austrian actress and cabaret singer, born in Vienna. She studied dancing in Zurich (1914–20), and then moved to Berlin, where she took up acting and married Kurt Weill (1926). She made an international reputation as Jenny in Weill's *Die Dreigroschenoper* (The Threepenny Opera, 1928). The couple fled to Paris in 1933 and then settled in the USA (1935), where her stage appearances included *The Firebrand of Florence* (1945) and *Mother Courage* (1972).

Lenz, Heinrich Friedrich Emil (1804–65) Russian-born German physicist and geophysicist, born in Dorpat (now Tartu). Professor at St Petersburg from 1836, he formulated 'Lenz's law' governing induced current, and is credited with discovering the dependence of electrical resistance on temperature.

Leo III (Emperor) (c.680–741) Byzantine emperor (717–41), born in Syria. He reorganized the army and financial system, and in 718 repelled a major attack on Constantinople by the Arabs. In 726 he prohibited the use of images in public worship, which led to more than a century of controversy. In 740 his defeat of the Arabs at Amorium halted their forays into Asia Minor.

Leo X, originally **Giovanni de' Medici** (1475–1521) Italian pope (1513–21), born in Florence. He was a noted patron of the arts. His vast project to rebuild St Peter's, and consent in the preaching of an indulgence in order to raise funds, provoked the Reformation and led to Martin Luther's excommunication (1520).

Leo *noun* 1 *Astron.* the Lion, a large conspicuous northern constellation of the zodiac, lying between Cancer and Virgo. It contains numerous galaxies, and the outline of some of its brighters stars bears some resemblance to the profile of a lion. **2** *Astrol.* the fifth sign of the zodiac, the Lion. **3** a person born between 21 July and 22 August, under this sign. **4** a male first name. [from Latin *leo*, lion]

León POP (1990) 144 000, the capital of León province, Castilla-León region, NW Spain. It lies at the junction of the Torio and Bernesga rivers, 333km/207mi NW of Madrid. It was the capital of a medieval kingdom. NOTABLE FEATURES cathedral (13c–14c); town walls; San Isidore; Monastery of St Mark.

León POP (1990) 873 000, a town in Guanajuato state, S central Mexico. It is situated 200km/120mi N of Morelia.

Leonard a male first name. [a French name of Germanic origin, = lion-hard]

Leonardo da Vinci (1452–1519) Italian painter, sculptor, architect, and engineer, born in Vinci. He entered the studio of Andrea del Verrochio (1470) then settled in Milan (1472), where he painted his *Last Supper* (completed c.1498) on the refectory wall of Santa Maria delle Grazie. In 1500 he entered the service of Cesare Borgia in Florence as architect and engineer, and with Michelangelo decorated the Sala del Consiglio in the Palazzo della Signoria with historical compositions. He was employed by Louis XII of France in 1506. His best-known painting is the *Mona Lisa* (c.1504, Louvre, Paris). Other works include the (unfinished) *Adoration of the Magi* (1481–2, Uffizi, Florence), *The Virgin and Child with St Anne* (cartoon, c.1499, National Gallery, London; painting, c.1501–12, Louvre, Paris), and *St John The Baptist* (c.1515, Louvre, Paris).

Leoncavallo, Ruggiero (1857–1919) Italian composer, born in Naples. Possibly encouraged by Richard Wagner while travelling in Europe, he wrote *I Pagliacci* (The Clowns, 1892) followed by some less successful operas, including a *La Bohème* which failed where that of Giacomo Puccini, on the same theme, was a success.

Leonidas (d.480 BC) King of Sparta (c.491–480 BC) and hero of the Persian Wars. He commanded a small force which, in an attempt to halt the Persian advance into central Greece, held the pass of Thermopylae for three days before being defeated by the Persians.

leonine *adj.* of or like a lion. [from Latin *leo*, lion]

Leonora No.3 Overture an overture by Beethoven written for the first revision of his opera *Fidelio* in 1806.

Leontes the jealously irrational king of Sicilia in Shakespeare's *The Winter's Tale*, who is obsessed by the idea that his wife has had an affair with his friend Polixenes.

Leontief, Wassily (1906–) Russian-born US economist, born in St Petersburg, Russia. He has been Professor at Harvard (1946–75) and New York (1983–), and was Director of the Institute of Economic Analysis at New York University (1975–84). He was awarded the Nobel Prize for Economics in 1973 for developing the input-output method of economic analysis, used in more than 50 industrialized countries for planning and forecasting.

Leopard, The (Il Gattopardo) a novel by Giuseppe Tomasi Di Lampedusa (1958, trans. 1960). It focuses on a noble family in Sicily in the aftermath of Garibaldi's annexation (1860).

leopard *noun* **1** a large cat (*Panthera pardus*) belonging to the same family (Felidae) as the lion, tiger, and jaguar. It is found in forest, bush, and scrub, or on rocky hillsides of Africa and S Asia, and has tawny yellow fur covered with small black spots (many of which are arranged in rosettes), and whitish underparts. **2** the male of this animal, as opposed to the female. [from Greek, *leon*, lion + *pardos*, panther] ◇ Leopards are generally solitary outside the breeding season, and in areas where they are hunted they are nocturnal. They feed mainly on small and medium-sized antelopes, and often ambush their prey. Individuals sometimes develop a taste for just one kind of prey, which may account for the occasional man-killers and cattle raiders. The leopard is now an endangered species, as countless numbers have been hunted for their skins, or because they are regarded as farm pests. At one time 50 000 leopards were poached annually in E Africa alone.

leopardess *noun* a female leopard.

Leopardi, Giacomo (1798–1837) Italian poet, born in Recanati. Despite poor health, he travelled extensively and lived successively in Bologna, Florence, Milan, Pisa, and Naples. His works express a pessimistic view of life. He is best known for his lyrics, collected under the title *I Canti* (1831, Songs).

Leopold I (Emperor) (1640–1705) Holy Roman Emperor (1658–1705), born in Vienna, the second son of Ferdinand III and the Infanta Maria Anna. He was elected to the crowns of Hungary (1655) and Bohemia (1657), before he succeeded to the Imperial title. By his third wife Eleonore of Palatinate-Neuburg (1676) he had two sons, the future emperors Joseph I and Charles VI. Throughout his reign he strove to defend the power and unity of the House of Habsburg, particularly against the Ottoman Turks, the King of France, and the hostility of the Hungarian nobility. Treaties of neutrality (1667, 1671) between Leopold and Louis XIV of France gave way to military conflict over the Rhine frontier (1674–9, 1686–97), as the issue of the Spanish inheritance loomed closer. To enforce the rights of his son Charles against the French claimant, Leopold took the empire into the Grand Alliance (1701). He died in Vienna while his armies were still deeply involved in the War of the Spanish Succession (1701–13) and the Hungarian revolt of Rákóczi (1703–11).

Leopold I (of Belgium) (1790–1865) first King of the Belgians (1831–65), son of Francis, Duke of Saxe-Coburg and uncle of Queen Victoria, born in Coburg, Germany. In 1816 he married Charlotte, daughter of the future George IV of England, and lived in England after her death (1817). He declined the Crown of Greece (1830), but was then elected King of the Belgians. His second marriage to Marie Louise of Orleans, daughter of Louis Philippe, ensured French support for his new kingdom against the Dutch, and his policies did much to keep Belgium free from European conflicts.

Leopold II (1835–1909) King of the Belgians (1865–1909), born in Brussels, the son of Leopold

I. His chief interest was the expansion of Belgium abroad. In 1879 he founded a company to develop the Congo, and in 1885 became King of the Congo Free State, which was annexed to Belgium in 1908.

Leopold III (1901–83) King of the Belgians (1934–51), born in Brussels, the son of Albert I. On his own authority he ordered the capitulation of the Belgian army to the Germans (1940), which opened the way to Dunkirk. He was then a prisoner in his own palace at Laeken until 1944, and afterwards in Austria, and following his return to Belgium (1945) he was forced to abdicate in favour of his son Baudouin.

Leopold a male first name. [of Germanic origin, from *liut*, people + *bold*, bold]

Léopoldville see KINSHASA.

leotard *noun* a tight-fitting one-piece garment worn for dancing and exercise. [from Jules Léotard (1830–70), French trapeze artist]

Lepanto, Battle of a naval battle (7 Oct 1571) off the coast of Greece in which the forces of the Christian Holy League, commanded by Don John of Austria, defeated those of the Ottoman Empire, under Ali Pasha. It ended the Turks' long-standing domination of the E Mediterranean and increased the security of W Europe which was threatened by successful Ottoman expansion.

Lepenski Vir a small prehistoric fishing settlement on the banks of the R Danube in the Iron Gates Gorge, in the former Yugoslavia. Seven phases of occupation (c.6500–5500 BC) have been identified since excavations began in 1965. It is particularly renowned for its abstract and representational sandstone sculptures of humans and animals.

leper *noun* **1** a person who has leprosy. **2** a person who is avoided, especially on moral grounds.

Lepidoptera *pl. noun Zool.* a large order of insects, found mainly in the tropics, comprising butterflies and moths. The adult insect typically has two pairs of wings, often brightly coloured and patterned, and mouthparts that have been modified to form a long narrow coiled proboscis for sucking up nectar. The wings, legs, and body are covered with small overlapping scales. [from Greek *lepis*, scale + *pteron*, wing]

lepidopterist *noun* a person who studies butterflies and moths.

lepidopterous *adj.* relating to the order Lepidoptera, including butterflies and moths.

Lepidus, Marcus Aemilius (d.c.13 BC) Roman politician of the civil war era (49–31 BC), who became deputy to Julius Caesar. After the death of Caesar, he formed the second triumvirate with Antony and Octavian (43 BC). He retired from active politics after being outmanoeuvred by Octavian in the power struggle of the 30s BC, but remained head of state religion (Pontifex Maximus) until his death.

leprechaun *noun* a small mischievous elf in Irish folklore. [from Old Irish *lúchorpán*, from *lú*, small + *corp*, body]

◇ Traditionally a tiny old man occupying himself with cobbling, and the guardian of a crock of gold whose whereabouts he could be persuaded to reveal by threats of violence.

leprosy *noun Medicine* an infectious disease of the skin, mucous membranes, and nerves. It occurs mainly in tropical regions, and is caused by infection with the bacterium *Mycobacterium leprae*.

◇ The symptoms of leprosy include thickening of the skin, swelling of the nerves, muscular weakness, and loss of sensation over large areas of skin. In the past, severe cases have led to paralysis, disfigurement, and deformity, eg loss of fingers and toes, but the disease can now be successfully treated with antibacterial drugs.

[see LEPER]

leprous *adj.* suffering from leprosy.

Leptis Magna an ancient seaport of N Libya, now the site of Roman remains. It was founded by the Phoenicians as a trading post in the c.7c BC, and was at its height in the 3c AD, after one of its citizens, Septimius Severus, became Roman emperor. It is a World Heritage site.

lepton *noun* **1** *Physics* any subatomic particle that participates only in weak interactions with other particles. Leptons include electrons, muons, and tau particles, and their respective neutrinos and antiparticles. **2** *Physics* originally used to refer to any light particle (eg an electron), as opposed to a heavy one. [from Greek *leptos*, small, thin]

leptotene *Biol.* the first stage of prophase in the first cell division of meiosis, during which the chromosomes become visible as thin threads. [from Greek *leptos*, slender]

Lermontov, Mikhail (Yurevich) (1814–41) Russian writer, born in Moscow. He started writing at an early age, but much of his work was not published until his later years. He is best known for his novel *A Hero of Our Time* (1840).

Lerner, Alan Jay (1918–86) US librettist, lyricist, and playwright, born in New York City. With Frederick Loewe, whom he met in 1942, he collaborated to produce several successful Broadway musicals, including *Brigadoon* (1947), *Paint Your Wagon* (1951), and *My Fair Lady* (1956), and the film *Gigi* (1958). Lerner also wrote the script for the film *An American in Paris* (1951) and (with composer Burton Lane) produced the musical *On a Clear Day You Can See Forever* (1965, filmed 1970).

Lerwick POP (1981) 8 000, the capital of the Shetland Is, N Scotland. It is situated on E Mainland, by Bressay Sound. NOTABLE FEATURES museum; Fort Charlotte (1665); Clickhimin Broch (Iron Age).

lesbian — *noun* a woman who is sexually attracted to other women. — *adj.* relating to lesbians. [from *Lesbos*, Aegean island and home of the 7c BC Greek poetess Sappho, whose works deal with homosexual relations between women]

lesbianism *noun* female homosexuality.

Lesbos, Greek **Lesvos** POP (1991) 104 000, the third largest island in Greece, situated in the E Aegean Sea, off the NW coast of Turkey. AREA 1 630sq km/629sq mi; length 61km/38mi. It is hilly, rising to 969m. CHIEF TOWN Mitilini. In classical times, the island was a centre of Greek lyric poetry and home of Sappho. ECONOMY cereals; grapes; olives; fishing; tourism.

Lescot, Pierre (c.1510–78) French Renaissance architect, born in Paris. Among his works are the screen of St Germain l'Auxerrois, the Fontaine des Innocents, and the Hôtel de Ligneris, all in Paris. He is best known for his work on the Louvre, one wing of which he completely rebuilt.

lese-majesty *noun* an insult to a sovereign; treason. [from French *lèse-majesté*, from Latin *laesa majestas*, injured majesty]

lesion *noun* **1** an injury or wound. **2** *Medicine* an abnormal change in the structure of an organ or tissue as a result of disease or injury, eg a scar, ulcer, or abscess. [from Latin *laesio*, from *laedere*, to injure]

Leskovac or **Leskovats** POP (1991e) 161 000, a town in SE Serbia, Yugoslavia, situated 37km/23mi S of Niš. NOTABLE FEATURE nearby 6c Byzantine ruins of Caračin Grad.

Leslie or **Lesley** a first name, after the Scottish surname or place-name; the male form is usually *Leslie*, and the female form *Lesley*.

Lesotho, official name **Kingdom of Lesotho** POP (1992e) 1.8m, an African kingdom completely bounded by South Africa. AREA 30 460sq km/11 758sq mi. CAPITAL Maseru. CHIEF TOWNS Mafeteng, Quthing. TIME ZONE GMT +3. The population is mainly Bantu (Basotho); the majority are Christian. OFFICIAL LANGUAGES Sesotho, English; Zulu and Xhosa are also spoken. CURRENCY the loti (maloti). PHYSICAL DESCRIPTION 230km/140mi E–W, 200km/120mi N–S; the Drakensberg Mts lie in the NE and E and include Lesotho's highest peak, Thabana-Ntlenyana (3 482m); the Mulati Mts run SW from the NE border forming a steep escarpment; the population mainly lives W of the highlands at an altitude of 1 500–1 800m; serious soil erosion, especially in the W; the main rivers are the Orange and the Caledon. CLIMATE mild, dry winters; the warm summer season is Oct–Apr; the lowland summer maximum temperature is 32°C, the winter minimum is –7°C; annual average rainfall is 725mm. HISTORY originally inhabited by hunting and gathering bushmen; Bantu peoples arrived in the 16c and the Basotho nation was established; incorporated into Orange Free State in 1854; came under British protection as Basutoland in 1869; the Kingdom of Lesotho gained independence as a hereditary monarchy within the Commonwealth in 1966. GOVERNMENT a hereditary monarchy dedicated to a multiparty democratic constitution; the monarchy lost effectve power in 1990 in the transition to democracy. ECONOMY based on intensive agriculture and male contract labour working in South Africa; maize, sorghum, wheat, peas, beans, barley, cattle; diamonds; food processing; textiles; electrical consumer goods; carpets; pharmaceuticals; jewellery; crafts; tractor assembly; wool, mohair.

Lesotho

less — *adj.* **1** smaller in size, duration, etc. **2** *colloq.* fewer in number: *smoke less cigarettes.* — *adv.* not so much; to a smaller extent. — *noun* a smaller amount or number. — *prep.* without; minus. [from Anglo-Saxon *læssa* (adj.), *læs* (adv.)]

-less *combining form* forming words meaning: **1** free from; lacking; without: *heartless / godless.* **2** not subject to the action of the verb: *countless.* [from Anglo-Saxon *leas*]

lessee *noun* (with stress on second syllable) a person granted the use of property by lease.

lessen *verb trans., intrans.* to make or become less.

Lesseps, Ferdinand Marie, Vicomte de (1805–94) French engineer, born in Versailles. After holding several diplomatic posts in Europe, in 1854 he began to plan the Suez Canal, which was finally built in 1860–9. In 1881 work began on his scheme for a Panama Canal, but in 1892–3 the management was charged with breach of trust, and Lesseps was found guilty.

lesser *adj.* smaller in size, quantity, or importance.

Less Favoured Areas (LFAs) areas established in 1975 under a European Community directive to provide assistance to farmers in order to conserve the countryside, protect coastlines, and preserve areas of tourist potential. In the UK, most LFAs are in upland regions, where capital grants are available for such work as land drainage.

Lessing, Doris (May) (1919–) South African writer, born in Kermanshah, Iran. Her family moved to Southern Rhodesia in 1924, where she began to write while living on the family farm. In 1952 *Martha Quest* appeared, the first novel in her 5-book sequence *The Children of Violence*, which was completed in 1969 with *The Four-Gated City*. *The Golden Notebook*, her best-known novel, appeared in 1962. Other works include the novel *The Good Terrorist* (1985), numerous collections of short stories, and a number of science-fiction works.

Lessing, Gotthold (Ephraim) (1729–81) German writer and man of letters, born in Kamenz, Saxony. He studied theology at Leipzig, then moved to Berlin and Wittenberg. While secretary to the governor of Breslau, he wrote *Laokoon* (Laocoön, 1766), a critical treatise which defines the limits of poetry and the plastic arts. His major dramatic work is the comedy *Minna von Barnhelm* (1767).

lesson *noun* **1** an amount taught or learned at one time. **2** a period of teaching. **3** (**lessons**) instruction in a particular subject given over a period of time: *have singing lessons.* **4** an experience or example which one should take as a warning or encouragement: *let that be a lesson to you.* **5** a passage from the Bible read during a church service. [from French *leçon*, from Latin *legere*, to read]

lessor *noun* a person who rents out property by lease.

lest *conj. formal, literary* **1** for fear that: *speak quietly lest they hear us.* **2** that: *worried lest we are late.* [from Anglo-Saxon *thy læs the*, the less that]

Lester a male first name, after the surname, which is derived from the place-name *Leicester*.

let¹ *verb* (**letting**; PAST TENSE AND PAST PARTICIPLE **let**) **1** to allow, permit, or cause to do something. **2** (**let someone** *or* **something in** *or* **out**) to allow or cause them to pass in or out: *will someone let the cat in?* **3** *Brit.* to give the use of (rooms, a building, or land) in return for payment. **4** (*usually in imperative*) to give orders, requests, warnings, permission, etc and to show assumptions: *let him go* / *let him just try!* / *let 'D' be the distance travelled.*
— **let alone** not to mention; without considering: *they have no radio, let alone a television.*
let someone alone *or* **let someone be** to avoid disturbing or worrying them.
let someone or something down 1 to lower them. **2** to disappoint or fail to help someone when necessary. **3** to allow the air to escape from something inflated: *let down the tyres.* **4** to make longer: *let the hem down.*
let something drop to make secret information, etc known, especially unintentionally.
let fly at someone to attack them physically or verbally.
let go of something to release or stop holding it.
let someone in for something *colloq.* to involve them in something difficult or unpleasant.
let someone in on something *colloq.* to share a secret, etc with them.
let something loose to release it.
let someone off 1 to allow them to go without punishment, etc. **2** to release them from work, duties, etc.
let something off 1 to fire a gun or explode a bomb. **2** to release liquid or gas.
let up 1 to become less strong or violent. **2** to stop or relax.
to let *said of property* available for rent. [from Anglo-Saxon *lætan*, to permit]

let² *noun Tennis, Squash* an obstruction of the ball (eg by the net), requiring the ball to be served again.
— **without let or hindrance** without anything hindering or preventing action or progress. [from Anglo-Saxon *lettan*, to hinder]

-let *suffix* denoting a small or young example of the thing specified: *piglet* / *leaflet.*

Letchworth POP (1981) 38 000, a town linked with Baldock in North Hertfordshire district, Hertfordshire, SE England. It lies 9km/5mi N of Stevenage and was the first English 'garden city', founded in 1903.

let-down *noun* a disappointment.

lethal *adj.* causing or enough to cause death. [from Latin *letum*, death]

lethally *adv.* so as to cause death.

lethargic *adj.* lacking in energy or vitality.

lethargically *adv.* without energy or vitality.

lethargy *noun* **1** lack of interest, enthusiasm, or energy. **2** *Medicine* a state of abnormal drowsiness and inactivity caused by inadequate rest, insomnia, boredom, depression, anxiety, anaemia, lack of food, recent illness (eg glandular fever), or any of various disorders (eg diabetes mellitus). [from Greek *lethargos*, drowsy]

Lethe in Greek and Roman mythology, the name of a slow-moving river in the Underworld. When the souls of the dead drank from it, they forgot their lives on Earth.

Leto *or* **Latona** in Greek mythology, a Titaness, the mother by Zeus of the twins Apollo and Artemis. They were born on the barren floating island of Delos because, in her jealousy, Hera, the wife of Zeus, would not allow any land to offer sanctuary to Leto.

letter — *noun* **1** a conventional mark, usually part of an alphabet, used to express a speech sound. **2** a written or printed message normally sent by post in an envelope. **3** (**the letter**) the strict, literal meaning of words: *the letter of the law.* **4** (**letters**) literature; knowledge of books: *a woman of letters.* — *verb* (**lettered, lettering**) to write or mark letters on.
— **to the letter** exactly; in every detail. [from Latin *littera*, letter of the alphabet]

letter bomb a device concealed in an envelope that explodes when the envelope is opened.

letter box *Brit.* **1** a slot in a door, sometimes with a box behind it, by which letters are delivered to a building. **2** a large metal box with a slot in the front, for people to post letters.

letterboxing *noun* the screening of films on television in their original wide-screen format, producing a black band at the top and bottom of the screen.

lettered *adj.* **1** well educated; literary. **2** marked with letters.

letterhead *noun* a printed heading on notepaper, giving a person's or company's name, address, etc.

lettering *noun* **1** the act of forming letters or the way in which they are formed. **2** letters which have been written, painted, or inscribed.

letter of credit a letter authorizing a bank to issue credit or money to the bearer.

letterpress *noun* **1** the printed words in an illustrated book. **2** a technique of printing by which ink on raised surfaces is pressed on to paper.

letters patent an official document giving a patent to an inventor, etc.

lettuce *noun* a green plant with large edible leaves used as a salad vegetable. [from Latin *lactuca*, from *lac*, milk, because of the milky juice from the leaves]

leucine *or* **leucin** *noun Biochem.* an essential amino acid found in proteins. [from Greek *leukos*, white]

leucocyte *or* **leukocyte** *noun Anat.* a white blood cell. [from Greek *leukos*, white + -CYTE]

Leuctra, Battle of a battle (371 BC) in which the Thebans under Epaminondas defeated the invading Spartans in Boeotia. It signalled the end of Sparta's hegemony in Greece.

leukaemia *noun Medicine* any of a group of malignant diseases which affect the bone marrow and other blood-forming organs so that there is a permanent increase in the number of white blood cells produced. It tends to be progressive and fatal. [from Greek *leukos*, white + *haima*, blood]
◊ Leukaemia is characterized by the overproduction of white blood cells which are immature or in some way abnormal, and suppress the production of normal white cells, red blood cells, and platelets. As a result the body becomes extremely susceptible to infection, due to the absence of much of the normal immune system. Other symptoms include anaemia, failure of the blood to clot, and enlargement of the lymph nodes, liver, and spleen. The cause is unknown, although the disease has been associated with exposure to ionizing radiation. There is no certain cure, but promising results are being obtained using chemotherapy to suppress the proliferation of abnormal cells, radiotherapy, and bone-marrow transplantation.

Leuven, French **Louvain**, German **Lowen** POP (1992e) 85 000, a town in Brabant province, central Belgium, lying on both banks of the R Dijle. The oldest university town in Belgium, it has a famous Catholic University (1425). HISTORY the old town, circular in shape, was once surrounded by moats; centre of the cloth trade in the Middle Ages; largely destroyed in World War I. NOTABLE FEATURES town hall (1448–63); Church of St Peter (15c–16c); Church of St Michael (1650–6); Premonstratensian Abbey of the Park, to the SW (1129).

Levant, The a general name formerly given to the E shores of the Mediterranean Sea, from W Greece to Egypt. The Levant States were Syria and Lebanon, during the period of their French mandate in 1920–41. [from Old French *levaunt*, place where the sun rises]

Levantine *adj.* **1** of the Levant. **2** *said of ships* trading to the Levant.

levee¹ *noun* **1** *Hist.* a sovereign's official meeting on rising from bed. **2** *old use* an official reception of guests or visitors in the morning or relatively early in the day. [from French *levée*, from *lever*, to raise]

levee² *noun* **1** the natural embankment of silt and sand that is deposited along the banks of a river or stream during flooding. **2** an artificial embankment contructed along a water course in order to protect the surrounding land from flooding, or to control the flow of water in irrigation channels. **3** a quay. [from French *levée*, raised, from *lever*, to raise]

level — *noun* **1** a horizontal plane or line. **2** a height, value, or extent. **3** position, status, or importance in a scale of values: *discussions at government level.* **4** a stage or degree of progress. **5** an aspect or way: *provide help on a practical level.* **6** a flat area of land. **7** same as SPIRIT LEVEL. — *adj.* **1** having a flat smooth even surface. **2** horizontal. **3** having the same height (as something else): *a chair level with the bed.* **4** having the same standard (as something else); equal to it. **5** steady; constant; regular: *keep one's body temperature level.* **6** denoting a spoonful that forms a flat heap on the spoon. — *verb* (**levelled, levelling**) **1** to make flat, smooth, or horizontal. **2** to make equal. **3** (**level something at someone**) to point (a gun, etc) at them. **4** to pull down or demolish. **5** (**level something at** *or* **against someone**) to direct (an accusation, criticism, etc). **6** *intrans.* (**level with someone**) *colloq.* to speak honestly to them.
— **do one's level best** *colloq.* to make the greatest possible effort.

find one's level to find one's proper place, rank, etc among others, or a comfortable rate of work, etc.

level off *or* **something off** to make or become flat, even, steady, regular, etc.

level out *or* **level something out** to make or become level.

level pegging equality of scores and accomplishments among rivals.

on the level *slang* fair; honest; genuine.

[from Latin *libella*, little scale]

level crossing *Brit.* a place where a road crosses a railway on the same level.

level-headed *adj.* sensible; well-balanced.

Levellers a radical political movement during the English Civil Wars and the Commonwealth, which called for the extension of manhood franchise to all but the poorest, religious toleration, and the abolition of the monarchy and the House of Lords. Led by John Lilburne (c.1614–57), Richard Overton (c.1631–64), and William Walwyn (1600–80), it was supported by 'agitators' in the Parliamentary army from 1647, and defeated at Burford (May 1649).

levelness *noun* a level state; being level.

level pegging equality of scores or accomplishments among rivals.

Leven, Loch the largest freshwater loch in lowland Scotland, situated in Perth and Kinross district, Tayside. AREA 14sq km/5sq mi. It is drained by the R Leven to the SE. A nature reserve, it is famous for its trout fishing and also for its associations with Mary, Queen of Scots, who was compelled to abdicate the throne during her imprisonment at Loch Leven in 1567–8. It should be distinguished from a loch of the same name in Lochaber district, Highland region.

lever — *noun* **1** a rigid bar that is supported by and pivots about a fulcrum at some point along its length, so that an *effort* applied at one point can be used to move an object (the *load*) at another point. There are three classes of levers. In a first-class lever, the fulcrum is between the load and the effort, eg pliers, crowbar, seesaw. In a second-class lever, the load is between the fulcrum and the effort, eg wheelbarrow. In a third-class lever, the effort is between the fulcrum and the load, eg sugar tongs, mechanical digger. **2** a strong bar for moving heavy objects, prising things open, etc. **3** a handle for operating a machine. **4** anything that can be used to gain an advantage. — *verb* (**levered**, **levering**) to move or open using a lever. [from Latin *levare*, to raise]

leverage *noun* **1** the mechanical power or advantage gained by using a lever. **2** the action of a lever. **3** power or advantage over someone.

leveret *noun* a young hare. [from Latin *lepus*, hare]

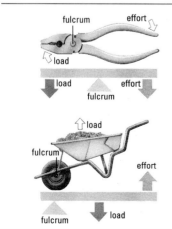

first- and second-class levers

Leverhulme (of the Western Isles), William Hesketh Lever, 1st Viscount (1851–1925) English soap manufacturer, born in Bolton, Lancashire. He founded (with his brother James) the Lever Brothers company, making soap from vegetable oils instead of tallow, and turned it into an international business. In 1888 he developed Port Sunlight as a model industrial village.

Levi, Primo (1919–87) Italian novelist, born in Turin. One of the survivors of Auschwitz, he returned to Italy in 1945. All of his novels are attempts to understand the nature of Nazi barbarity and the variety of responses to it shown by its victim. The first of these is *Si questo i un Uomo* (If this is a Man, 1947), a graphic account of life in a concentration camp. Other works include its sequel *La tregua* (The Truce, 1963), and *The Periodic Table* (1985).

Levi a biblical character, the third son of Jacob and his wife Leah (Genesis 35.23). It is debated whether his descendants ever formed one of the 12 tribes of Israel descended from Jacob's sons. Although they were called a tribe, no territory was apparently allocated to them (Joshua 13.14), and they seem to have been a kind of priestly class. Moses is later depicted as a descendant of Levi.

leviathan *noun* anything which is large or powerful.

Leviathan a work on political philosophy by Thomas Hobbes, written 1651.

Leviathan a rare Hebrew loan-word of uncertain derivation, used in the Bible to refer to a kind of sea or river monster (Psalms 74.14 and 104.26; Isaiah 27.1). In Job 41, it seems more like a crocodile, but Ugaritic parallels suggest it may have been a mythical supernatural figure, a sea dragon, perhaps symbolic of chaos or evil.

Levi-Montalcini, Rita (1909–) Italian neuroscientist, born in Turin. She graduated in medicine, and during World War II worked in a home laboratory; in 1947 she moved to the USA, where she became professor at Washington University. There she isolated and analysed a substance (now called *nerve growth factor*) that promotes the development of sympathetic nerves (those that prepare the body for action) providing new insights into the mechanisms and possible therapy of certain diseases. She shared the 1986 Nobel Prize for Physiology or Medicine with Stanley Cohen.

Levis *pl. noun trademark* heavy, close-fitting jeans with points of particular strain made stronger by rivets.

Lévi-Strauss, Claude (1908–) French social anthropologist, born in Brussels, Belgium. In 1950 he became Director of Studies at the Ecole Pratiques des Hautes Etudes in Paris, and in 1959 Professor of Social Anthropology at the Collège de France. He has been a major influence on contemporary anthropology, establishing a new method for analysing various collective phenomena such as kinship, ritual, and myth. His major 4-volume study *Mythologiques* (1964–72) studies the systematic ordering behind codes of expression in different cultures.

levitate *verb trans., intrans.* to float or cause to float in the air, especially through supernatural power or spiritualism. [from Latin *levis*, light, on the model of *gravitate*]

levitation *noun* the act or process of levitating; floating in the air.

Levites in the Old Testament, the descendants of Jacob's son Levi. Originally one of the 12 tribes of ancient Israel, they had no land allocation and became a class of auxiliary ministers dedicated to the care of the Tabernacle and eventually the Jerusalem Temple (Numbers 3.5–10).

Leviticus, Book of a book of the Hebrew Bible and Old Testament, the third book of the Pentateuch, traditionally attributed to Moses but probably compiled during the exile from earlier

material. Concerned with the priestly traditions of the Levites, it continues from the end of the Book of Exodus, and contains directions about offerings (chapters 1–7), priesthood (8–10), purity laws (11–15), and the Day of Atonement (16), a section called the 'holiness code' (17–26), and an appendix (27).

levy — *verb* (**levies**, **levied**) to raise or collect, especially an army or a tax. — *noun* **1** the act of levying. **2** soldiers or money collected by order. [from Latin *levare*, to raise]

lewd *adj.* feeling or expressing crude sexual desire or lust; obscene, indecent. [from Anglo-Saxon *læwede*, unlearned]

lewdly *adv.* in a lewd or indecent way.

lewdness *noun* being lewd; indecency.

Lewes POP (1981) 15 000, the county town of East Sussex, SE England, lying on the R Ouse, 13km/8mi NE of Brighton. It was the site of the battle of Lewes (1264) in which Henry III was defeated by Simon de Montfort. NOTABLE FEATURES Churches of St Anne (12c), St John the Baptist (12c–18c), and St Michael; Glyndebourne Estate nearby (annual opera festival).

Lewis, Carl (1961–) US track and field athlete, born in Birmingham, Alabama. He won the long jump gold medal at the 1981 World Cup, three golds in the inaugural world championships in 1983, and gold in the long jump at the 1987 world championships. He equalled Jesse Owens's record by winning four gold medals in track and field events at the 1984 Olympic Games, and won two more at the 1988 Olympics. In 1991 he set a world record of 9.86 seconds for the 100m.

Lewis, C(live) S(taples) (1898–1963) British medievalist and Christian apologist, born in Belfast, Northern Ireland. He served in World War I, was a lecturer at Oxford (1925–54), and became Professor of Medieval and Renaissance English at Cambridge in 1954. His works include the critical study *The Allegory of Love* (1936), and *The Screwtape Letters* (1942), one of several works which expound issues of Christian belief and practice. He is also known for his children's stories of the land of Narnia which begin with *The Lion, the Witch, and the Wardrobe* (1950), and for his science fiction books which include *Out of the Silent Planet* (1938).

Lewis, Gilbert Newton (1875–1946) US physical chemist, born in Weymouth, Massachusetts. He spent most of his career at the University of California. His best-known work, published during World War I, developed the notions of chemical bonding between atoms and introduced the idea of sharing of electrons in covalent bonds.

Lewis, Lennox (1965–) British boxer, born in London. He won a gold medal at the 1988 Olympics for Canada, his home country since he was a young boy. Having turned professional in 1989, he returned to Britain and became European heavyweight champion in 1990. In 1991, he took the British heavyweight title from Gary Mason, and in late 1992, after a victory over Donovan 'Razor' Ruddock, was established as the number-one challenger for the World title. In Dec 1992, he was awarded the WBC title by default (thus becoming Britain's first world heavyweight champion of the century), when Riddick Bowe, the then champion, refused to fight him and was stripped of the title.

Lewis, Matthew Gregory, also called **Monk Lewis** (1775–1818) English novelist, born in London. In 1794 he went as an attaché to The Hague, where he wrote the Gothic novel *The Monk* (1795), the work for which he is chiefly remembered.

Lewis, Meriwether (1774–1809) US explorer, born in Charlottesville, Virginia. He grew up in the wilderness, served in the army, and in 1801 became private secretary to President

Thomas Jefferson for two years. With William Clark he was joint leader of the first overland transcontinental expedition to the Pacific coast and back (1804–6). From 1808, he was Governor of Louisiana Territory.

Lewis, (Harry) Sinclair (1885–1951) US novelist, born in Sauk Center, Minnesota. He became a journalist and wrote several minor works before he made his name with *Main Street* (1920), the first of a series of best-selling novels satirizing the materialism and intolerance of American small-town life. *Babbitt* (1922) still lends its title as a synonym for middle-class American philistinism. Other works of this period include *Martin Arrowsmith* (1925), *Elmer Gantry* (1927), and *Dodsworth* (1929). He was awarded the Nobel Prize for Literature in 1930.

Lewis, (Percy) Wyndham (1884–1957) British artist, writer, and critic, born on a yacht in the Bay of Fundy, Maine, USA. He studied art in London, and with Ezra Pound founded *Blast*, the magazine of the Vorticist school. His writings include the satirical novel *The Apes of God* (1930), the multi-volume *The Human Age* (1955–6), literary criticism (eg *Men Without Art*, 1934), and autobiographical works (eg *Blasting and Bombardiering*, 1937). His paintings include works of abstract art, a series of war pictures, and portraits.

Lewis a male first name. [from Norman and French *Louis*]

Lewis with Harris an island in the Western Isles, NW Scotland, the largest and northernmost of the Hebrides. AREA 2 134sq km/824sq mi. It is separated from the mainland to the W by the North Minch and from Skye to the SE by the Little Minch. Lewis in the N is linked by a narrow isthmus to Harris in the S. CHIEF TOWNS Stornoway, Tarbert. ECONOMY fishing; crofting; tweeds.

lexeme *noun Linguistics* a word or other essential unit of vocabulary in a language which represents the constant semantic element in a set of related forms, as in *buy, buyer, buying, bought*. [from LEXICON + -*eme* as in PHONEME]

lexical *adj.* **1** relating to the words of a language. **2** relating to a lexicon. [from Greek *lexis*, word]

lexically *adv.* as regards words; in terms of words.

lexicographer *noun* a writer or editor of dictionaries.

lexicographic *adj.* relating to lexicography or to dictionaries.

lexicography *noun* the writing of dictionaries. [from Greek *lexis*, word]

lexicology *noun* the study of the vocabulary of a language, both historical and modern, and the investigation of the similarities and differences between vocabularies of different languages.

lexicon *noun* **1** a dictionary. **2** the vocabulary of an individual person, branch of knowledge, or language. [from Greek *lexikon*, from *lexis*, word]

Lexington POP (1990) 29 000, a town in Middlesex County, NE Massachusetts, USA, situated 16km/10mi NW of Boston. The US War of Independence started here in 1775.

Lexington and Concord, Battles of the first armed conflicts (19 Apr 1775) of the US War of Independence, fought in Massachusetts after British troops tried to seize supplies stored in the village of Concord and were confronted by colonial militia (minutemen).

lexis *noun* **1** the way in which a piece of writing is expressed in words; diction. **2** the total stock of words in a language. [from Greek *lexis*, word]

ley *or* **lea** *noun Agric.* an area of arable land that is temporarily under grass (eg for hay or silage production) or pasture, and will eventually be ploughed and used to grow crops.

Leyden, Dutch **Leiden** POP (1992e) 113 000, a university city in South Holland province, W Netherlands, lying on the R Oude Rijn. HISTORY received its charter in 1266; famous for its weaving in the 14c; the city was besieged for a year by the Spaniards in 1573 but was relieved when William the Silent ordered the dykes to be cut enabling the Dutch fleet to sail to the city walls: as a reward for their bravery the citizens were given Holland's first university in 1575. Several 16c and 17c painters, notably Rembrandt, were born here. NOTABLE FEATURES Gemeenlandshuis van Rijn (1596); Weighhouse (1658); Church of St Pancras (15c); Church of St Peter (1315); town hall (17c); Municipal Museum (1869).

Leyden jar *noun* a glass jar coated inside and out with layers of metal foil, used as an early form of electricity condenser. [from the name *Leyden* in the Netherlands, where it was invented in the 18th century]

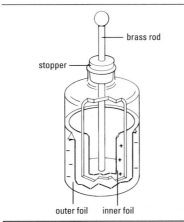

brass rod — stopper — outer foil — inner foil

Leyden jar

Leyden, University of the first Dutch university, founded in Leyden in 1575 by William the Silent (1533–84). It was an important centre of learning during the 16c–17c, and in the 18c became highly regarded for its science and medical faculties.

Leyte Gulf, Battle of a battle (1944) in World War II, when the Japanese fleet converged on the US 3rd and 7th Fleets protecting Allied landings on Leyte in the central Philippines. The Japanese suffered irreplaceable losses of 300 000 tonnes of combat ships, compared to US losses of 37 000 tonnes. It paved the way for further US gains in the Philippines and on islands nearer Japan.

Lhasa *or* **La-sa**, also called **The Forbidden City** POP (1990) 107 000, the capital of Tibet autonomous region, SW China. It stands at an altitude of 3 600m. The city is an ancient centre of Tibetan Buddhism, with many temples and holy sites. HISTORY closed to foreigners in the 19c; Chinese occupation began in 1951; many monks fled Chinese rule (including the Dalai Lama), especially the uprising in 1959. NOTABLE FEATURES Potala Fortress (17c), including Red Palace, the former home of the Dalai Lama; Drepung Monastery (1416), still an active lamisary; Jokhang Temple (6c), containing the Sakyamuni Buddha.

Li *symbol Chem.* lithium.

liability *noun* (PL. **liabilities**) **1** the state of being legally liable or responsible for something. **2** a debt or obligation. **3** a person or thing one is responsible for. **4** a person or thing which is or causes a problem.

liable *adj.* **1** legally bound or responsible. **2** (**liable to something**) likely to have, get, suffer from it, etc. **3** (**liable to do something**) likely to do it: *they are liable to act childishly*. [from Old French *lier*, to bind]

liaise *verb intrans.* (**liaise between** *or* **with**) to have or establish a close working relationship with or between other people. [back-formation from LIAISON]

liaison *noun* **1** communication or co-operation between groups. **2** a sexual or romantic relationship which is kept secret, especially when illicit or adulterous. [from French *liaison*]

liana *noun* a climbing, twisting plant found in tropical forests. [from French *liane*]

liar *noun* a person who tells lies, especially habitually.

Lib *abbrev.* Liberal.

lib *noun colloq.* liberation, used especially in the names of movements: *gay lib*.

libation *noun* **1** the pouring out of wine, etc in honour of a god. **2** the drink poured. [from Latin *libare*, to pour]

Libby, Willard Frank (1908–80) US chemist, born in Grand Valley, Colorado. He worked at the University of California, Berkeley, and on the development of the atomic bomb during World War II, before becoming professor at the University of Chicago and later at the University of California in Los Angeles. He was awarded the 1960 Nobel Prize for Chemistry for his development of the radiocarbon dating technique, which has found extensive applications in estimating the age of archaeological remains and rocks.

libel — *noun* **1** *Legal* the publication of a false statement which damages a person's good reputation (see also SLANDER). **2** any false, damaging, or unflattering description of a person. — *verb* (**libelled, libelling**) **1** *Legal* to commit a libel against (someone). **2** to accuse wrongly and spitefully. [from Latin *libellus*, little book]

◇ Any defamatory statement published in permanent form may constitute libel, including one broadcast on radio or television, or made during the public performance of a play. A libel need not take the form of words; for example, a painting or sculpture may be libellous. Libel is not recognized in Scots law, where both slander and libel come under defamation.

libellous *adj.* containing or forming a libel; damaging to a person's reputation.

libellously *adv.* in a libellous way; so as to damage a person's reputation.

liberal — *adj.* **1** given or giving generously, freely, or abundantly. **2** tolerant of different opinions; open-minded. **3** in favour of social and political reform. **4** (**Liberal**) of the Liberal Party. **5** *said of education* aiming at developing general cultural interests and broadening the mind. **6** free from restraint: *a liberal translation*. **7** free from dogma, etc. — *noun* **1** a liberal person. **2** (**Liberal**) a member or supporter of the Liberal Party in the UK; a member or supporter of any other Liberal Party. [from Latin *liberalis*, from *liber*, free]

liberalism *noun* liberal moral, religious, or political views.

◇ As a political philosophy, liberalism developed in the 18c–19c associated with the new middle classes who challenged the traditional monarchical, aristocratic, and religious views of the state. Classical liberalism argues for limited government, and the values traditionally espoused are those of freedom (of the individual, religion, trade and economics, and politics). In the 20c, it has come to occupy the centre ground in the political spectrum.

liberality *noun* **1** the quality of being generous. **2** the quality of being open-minded and free from prejudice.

liberalization *or* **liberalisation** *noun* the act or process of liberalizing.

liberalize *or* **liberalise** *verb trans., intrans.* to make or become more liberal or less strict.

liberally *adv.* freely, generously.

Liberal Party 1 a British political party originating in the 1860s, and one of the two major parties until 1922, when it was overtaken by the Labour Party. In 1988, it combined with the Social Democrats to form the Social and Liberal Democrats (later to be known as the Liberal Democrats), occupying the centre ground in the political spectrum. **2** in Australia, the largest conservative political party, formed by R G Menzies in 1944 from existing conservative groups. It built up a mass following in the late 1940s, and was victorious in 1949. It stayed in power until 1966, and was then in coalition with the Country Party until 1972, and again from 1975 to 1983, when the Labor Party came to power.

liberate *verb trans.* **1** to set free. **2** to free (a country) from enemy occupation. **3** *Chem.* to give off (a gas).

liberated *adj.* **1** not bound by traditional ideas about sexuality and morality. **2** freed from enemy occupation.

liberation *noun* the act or process of liberating.

liberation theology a development of Christian doctrine which emphasizes a commitment to liberation from social, political, and economic oppression.

liberator *noun* a person who liberates, especially from oppression.

Liberia, official name **Republic of Liberia** POP (1992e) 2.6m, a republic in W Africa. AREA 113 370sq km/43 760sq mi. It is bounded NW by Sierra Leone, N by Guinea, E by the Ivory Coast, and S by the Atlantic Ocean. CAPITAL Monrovia. CHIEF TOWNS Harper, Greenville, Buchanan, Robertsport. TIME ZONE GMT. The majority of the population is made up of indigenous tribes (95%), the remainder being descendants of repatriated slaves from the USA (Americo-Liberians). The population mainly follow local beliefs, the rest are either Muslim (15%) or Christian (10%). OFFICIAL LANGUAGE English; many local languages are also spoken. CURRENCY the Liberian dollar. PHYSICAL DESCRIPTION low coastal belt with lagoons, beaches, and mangrove marshes; a rolling plateau (500–800m) with grasslands and forest; land rises inland to mountains, reaching 1 752m at Mt Nimba; rivers cut SW down through the plateau. CLIMATE equatorial climate, with high temperatures and abundant rainfall; rainfall declines from S to N; high humidity during the rainy season (Apr–Sep), especially on the coast; the average annual rainfall at Monrovia is 4 150mm. HISTORY mapped by the Portuguese in the 15c; created as a result of the activities of several US philanthropic societies wishing to establish a homeland for former slaves; founded in 1822; constituted as the Free and Independent Republic of Liberia in 1847; a military coup and the assassination of the President in 1980 established a People's Redemption Council, with a chairman and a cabinet; the National Democratic Party of Liberia formed the government in the mid 1980s under a new constitution; Civil War was followed by the arrival of a West African peacekeeping force in 1991; a peace agreement was signed in 1993. ECONOMY based on minerals, especially iron ore; gold, diamonds, platinum group metals, barite, titanium, zirconium, rare-earth metals, clay; two thirds of the population rely on subsistence agriculture; rubber, timber, palm oil, rice, cassava, coffee, cocoa, coconuts; the largest merchant fleet in the world, including the registration of many foreign ships.

Liberia POP (1984) 29 000, the capital town of Guanacaste province, NW Costa Rica.

libertarianism *noun* **1** a metaphysical doctrine, held by Jean-Paul Sartre and others, which attempts to vindicate free will and responsibility of action by denying causal determinism in respect of many human actions and responses. **2** a political philosophy, held by Russo-US novelist Ayn Rand (1905–82) and others, which claims that the only justified function of the state is to

Statue of Liberty

provide protection; the promotion of other goals is an intrusion on individual rights.

libertine — *noun old use* a person, especially a man, who leads a life not bound by the generally accepted rules of morality. — *adj.* leading such a life; dissolute; promiscuous. [from Latin *libertinus*, freed-man]

liberty *noun* (PL. **liberties**) **1** freedom from captivity or from slavery. **2** freedom to act and think as one pleases. **3** (*usually* **liberties**) a natural right or privilege. **4** an action or utterance thought of as over-familiar or presumptuous. — **at liberty 1** free from prison or control. **2** allowed or permitted (to). **take liberties with someone** to treat them with too much freedom or familiarity. **take the liberty** to do or venture to do something, usually without permission. [from Latin *libertas*]

Liberty, Statue of a statue on Liberty Island in New York City harbour, representing a woman holding aloft a torch. The idea for 'Liberty Enlightening the World' was conceived in France; it was designed by the French sculptor Bartholdi, and shipped to New York to be assembled and dedicated in 1886. The statue is 40m high (92m including its pedestal). It is a World Heritage site.

libidinal *adj.* concerning or characteristic of libido.

libidinous *adj.* lustful. [from Latin *libido*, desire]

libido *noun* (PL. **libidos**) **1** the intensity of sexual desire, which varies from one person to another, and even within the same person at different times. **2** *Psychol.* in psychoanalysis, the sexual drive which, like the death instinct, is said to be a fundamental source of energy for mental events and behaviour. [from Latin *libido*, desire]

Li Bo *or* **Li Po** *or* **Li T'ai Po** (c.700–62) Chinese poet, born in Szechwan. He led a dissi-

Liberia

pated life at the Emperor's court, and later became a member of a wandering band calling themselves 'The Eight Immortals of the Wine Cup'. He wrote verse about wine, women, and nature, and it is said that he was drowned while attempting to kiss the Moon's reflection.

Libra *noun* **1** *Astron.* the Balance, a dim southern constellation and one of the least conspicuous in the zodiac, lying between Virgo and Scorpius. **2** the seventh sign of the zodiac, the Scales. **3** a person born between 23 Sep and 22 Oct, under this sign. [from Latin *libra*, pound weight]

Libran — *noun* a person born under the sign Libra. — *adj.* relating to this sign.

librarian *noun* a person who is employed in or in charge of a library.

librarianship *noun* the business of a librarian.

library *noun* (PL. **libraries**) **1** a collection of books, either for public or private use. **2** the room or rooms or building housing a collection of books. **3** a similar collection of films, records, etc, or the place where it is kept. **4** a group of books published as a series. **5** *Comput.* a collection of related computer files. **6** *Comput.* a collection of programs that can be accessed by a computer programmer when required. [from Latin *librarium*, book-case]
◇ Libraries date from the earliest times, with examples being known in ancient Babylonia and Egypt. There were famous libraries at Alexandria, Athens, and Rome. In Christian Europe, libraries were usually attached to monasteries; secular collections emerged during and after the Renaissance, several of which have provided the basis for major modern libraries, such as the Bodleian at Oxford. In the UK, there is a countrywide network of public libraries, as well as those attached to educational and other institutions. There is now an international library network.

Library of Congress the US depository and largest library in the world, founded in 1800 in Washington, DC. The library provides bibliographical and cataloguing services for libraries throughout the world; its main function is the provision of reference materials for the US Congress.

library science the study of all aspects of library functions, including selection and acquisition policy, classification systems, cataloguing, bibliography, and library administration. Library science as a discipline in its own right developed in the late 19c.

librettist *noun* the writer of an opera libretto.

libretto *noun* (PL. **libretti**, **librettos**) the words or text of an opera, oratorio, or musical. [from Italian *libretto*, little book]

Libreville POP (1988e) 352 000, the capital of Gabon, at the mouth of the R Gabon, 520km/ 325mi NW of Brazzaville (Congo). HISTORY founded in 1849 as a refuge for slaves freed by the French; it was attacked and occupied by the

British and the Free French in 1940; until 1946 it was the main port of what was then French Equatorial Africa; the discovery of oil has resulted in rapid development since the 1970s. NOTABLE FEATURES Cathedral of Sainte-Marie; museum; art gallery.

Libya, official name **Socialist People's Libyan Arab Jamahiriya** POP (1992e) 4.9m, a N African state divided into 10 provinces. AREA 1 758 610sq km/678 823sq mi. It is bounded NW by Tunisia, W by Algeria, SW by Niger, S by Chad, SE by Sudan, E by Egypt, and N by the Mediterranean Sea. CAPITAL Tripoli. CHIEF TOWNS Misurata, Benghazi, Tobruk. TIME ZONE GMT +1. The main ethnic groups are Berber and Arab (97%); Islam (mainly Sunni) is the chief religion. OFFICIAL LANGUAGE Arabic. CURRENCY the Libyan dinar. PHYSICAL DESCRIPTION mainly low-lying Saharan desert or semi-desert; the land rises in the S to over 2 000m in the Tibesti massif; the highest point, Pic Bette (2 286m), lies on the Chad frontier; surface water is limited to infrequent oases. CLIMATE Mediterranean climate on the coast; Tripoli, representative of the coastal region, has an average annual rainfall of 385mm with average maximum daily temperatures of 16–30°C; annual rainfall in the desert seldom exceeds 100mm; temperatures in the S are over 40°C for three months of the year. HISTORY controlled at various times by Phoenicians, Carthaginians, Greeks, Vandals, and Byzantines; Arab domination during the 7c; Turkish rule from the 16c until the Italians gained control in 1911; named Libya by the Italians in 1934; heavy fighting during World War II, followed by British and French control; became the independent Kingdom of Libya in 1951; a military coup established a republic under Muammar Gaddafi in 1969; governed by a Revolutionary Command Council; foreign military installations closed down in the early 1970s; government policy since the revolution has been based on the promotion of Arab unity and the furtherance of Islam; relations with other countries have been strained by controversial activities, including the alleged organization of international terrorism; diplomatic relations were severed by the UK after the murder of a policewoman in London in 1984; Tripoli and Benghazi were bombed by the US Air Force in response to alleged terrorist activity in 1986; two Libyan fighter planes were shot down by aircraft operating with the US Navy off the N African coast in 1989; sanctions were imposed against Libya in 1992 following its refusal to extradite for trial suspects for the Lockerbie bomb. ECONOMY once a relatively poor country, with an agricultural economy based on barley, olives, fruit, dates, almonds, and tobacco; the economy was transformed by the discovery of oil and natural gas in 1959; natural gas liquefaction plant, iron ore, gypsum, sulphur; cement, petroleum processing, iron, steel, aluminium,

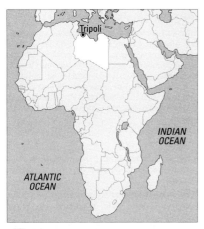

Libya

food processing, textiles, crafts; cattle, sheep, goats, with nomadic farming in the S.

lice see LOUSE.

licence or North Amer., esp. US **license** noun **1** a document giving official permission to own a dog, gun, television, etc, or to do something such as sell alcohol. **2** permission or leave. **3** excessive freedom of action or speech. **4** a departure from a rule or convention, especially by writers and artists, for effect: poetic licence. [from Latin licentia, from licere, to be allowed]

license verb to give a licence or permit for (something) or to (someone).

licensed adj., said of a shop, hotel, etc legally allowed to sell alcohol.

licensee noun (with stress on -see) a person to whom a licence is given, especially to sell alcohol.

licentiate noun **1** a person who holds a certificate of competence to practise a profession. **2** a person licensed to preach in the Presbyterian church. [from Latin licentia, licence]

licentious adj. immoral or promiscuous. [from Latin licentia, licence]

licentiously adv. in a licentious or immoral way.

licentiousness noun being licentious or immoral.

lichee same as LYCHEE.

lichen noun Bot. the common name for any plant belonging to the division Lichenes, consisting of composite organisms formed by the symbiotic association between a fungus, which represents most of the plant body or thallus, and a green or blue-green alga, the cells of which are distributed throughout the threads or hyphae of the fungus. [from Greek leichen]
◇ Lichens grow in the form of an encrusting scale-like or leafy thallus, yellow or grey in colour, usually on rocks, walls, or tree trunks, especially in regions where environmental conditions are extreme. Some species are very sensitive to air pollution, and can be used as pollution indicators. The alga carries out photosynthesis and manufactures carbohydrates, both for itself and for the fungus, which in turn protects the algal cells and provides them with water. Lichens reproduce by means of fungal spores.

Lichfield POP (1981) 26 000, a town in Lichfield district, Staffordshire, central England, situated 20km/12mi SW of Burton-upon-Trent. Samuel Johnson was born here in 1709. NOTABLE FEATURES Cathedral of St Mary and St Chad, with three spires; Johnson Museum; Staffordshire Regiment Museum.

lichgate noun a gate with a roof over it in a wall around a church, where originally a coffin would wait for the arrival of a member of the clergy. [from Anglo-Saxon lic, corpse + GATE]

licit adj. lawful; permitted. [from Latin licitus].

licitly adv. in a lawful way.

lick — verb **1** to pass the tongue over to moisten, taste, or clean. **2** to flicker over or around. **3** colloq. to defeat. **4** colloq. to beat or hit repeatedly. — noun **1** an act of licking with the tongue. **2** colloq. a small amount. **3** colloq. a quick speed: at a lick. **4** colloq. a sharp blow.
— **a lick and a promise** colloq. a short and not very thorough wash.
lick into shape colloq. to make more efficient or satisfactory.
lick one's wounds to recover after having been thoroughly defeated or humiliated.
[from Anglo-Saxon liccian]

licorice North Amer., esp. US same as LIQUORICE.

lictor noun in ancient Rome, an officer who attended a magistrate, and whose duties included binding the hands and feet of criminals before

sentence was executed. [from Latin ligo, I bind or tie]

lid noun **1** a removable or hinged cover for a pot, box, etc. **2** an eyelid. [from Anglo-Saxon hlid, covering]

lidded adj. having a lid.

lido noun (PL. **lidos**) **1** a fashionable beach. **2** a public open-air swimming pool. [from Italian Lido, an island in the Venice lagoon which has a fashionable beach]

Lie, (Marius) Sophus (1842–99) Norwegian mathematician, born in Nordfjordeide. He studied at Christiania (now Oslo) University, and later became professor there and at Leipzig. He developed an extensive theory of continuous families of transformations, now known as 'Lie groups'; these have become a central part of 20c mathematics, with important applications in quantum mechanics and theories of elementary particles.

Lie, Trygve (Halvdan) (1896–1968) Norwegian lawyer and politician, born in Oslo. A Labour member of the Norwegian parliament, he held several posts before fleeing with the government to Britain (1940), where he acted as its Foreign Minister until 1945. Elected the first Secretary-General of the United Nations in 1946, he resigned in 1952 over Soviet opposition to his policy of intervention in the Korean War.

lie¹ — noun **1** a false statement made with the intention of deceiving. **2** anything misleading; a fraud: live a lie. — verb intrans. (**lying**) **1** to say things which are not true with the intention of deceiving. **2** to give a wrong or false impression: the camera never lies.
— **give the lie to someone** or **something 1** to accuse someone of lying. **2** to show a statement, etc to be false. See also LIAR.
[from Anglo-Saxon lyge]

lie² — verb intrans. (**lying**; PAST TENSE **lay**; PAST PARTICIPLE **lain**) **1** to be in or take on a flat or more or less horizontal position on a supporting surface. **2** said of subjects for discussion to remain undiscussed: let matters lie. **3** to be or remain in a particular, especially hidden, state: lie dormant. **4** (**lie with someone**) to apply to or rest with them: the responsibility lies with you. **5** to be situated. **6** to stretch or be spread out to view: the harbour lay before us. **7** (**lie in something**) to consist in or have as an essential part: success lies in hard work. — noun **1** the way or direction in which something is lying. **2** an animal's or bird's hiding-place.
— **lie back 1** to lean back on a support. **2** to rest, especially after a period of hard work.
lie down to take a flat or horizontal position, especially to sleep or have a short rest.
lie in 1 to stay in bed later than usual in the morning. **2** old use to be in bed giving birth to a child.
lie in wait or **lie in wait for someone** to wait in ambush.
lie low to stay quiet or hidden.
the lie of the land the current state of affairs.
see how the land lies to find out all the facts before taking a decision which will affect one.
take something lying down to accept a rebuke or disappointment, etc meekly and without protest (usually in uses with not, refuse, etc): refused to take it lying down.
[from Anglo-Saxon licgan]

Liebig, Justus von (1803–73) German chemist, born in Darmstadt. Professor at the universities of Giessen and Munich, he was one of the most illustrious chemists of his age. He developed improved procedures for the elemental analyses of organic compounds, investigated many aspects of animal and agricultural chemistry, and developed new equipment such as the distillation aparatus known as Liebig's condenser.

Liebknecht, Wilhelm (1826–1900) German social democrat, born in Giessen. He became a lawyer (1847) and developed an interest in Socialism. For his part in the Baden insurrection of 1848–9, he had to take refuge in Switzerland and in England, where he worked closely with Karl Marx. He returned to Germany (1862) and during a two-year imprisonment was elected to the Reichstag (1874). He co-founded the German Social Democratic Party (1891) and became one of its leading spokesmen.

Liechtenstein, official name **Principality of Liechtenstein**, German **Fürstentum Liechtenstein** POP (1990e) 29 000, an independent alpine principality in central Europe, lying between the Austrian state of Voralberg to the E and the Swiss cantons of St Gallen and Graubünden to the W. AREA 160sq km/62sq mi. It is the fourth smallest country in the world, with a land boundary of 76km/47mi, and is divided into the districts of Oberland (Upper Country) and Unterland (Lower Country). CAPITAL Vaduz. TIME ZONE GMT +1. The population is of Alemannic origin; Roman Catholicism is the chief religion. OFFICIAL LANGUAGE German, spoken in the form of an Alemannic dialect. CURRENCY the Swiss franc. PHYSICAL DESCRIPTION bounded W by the R Rhine, its valley occupying c.40% of the country; much of the rest of Liechtenstein consists of forested mountains, rising to 2 599m in the Grauspitz. CLIMATE mild, influenced by a warm S wind (the *Föhn*); average high temperature of 20–28°C in summer; average annual rainfall is 1 050–1 200mm. HISTORY formed in 1719, Liechtenstein was part of the Holy Roman Empire until 1806. GOVERNMENT a constitutional monarchy ruled by the hereditary princes of the House of Liechtenstein; the country is governed jointly by the Prince, head of state, and Parliament, consisting of a Prime Minister, four Councillors, and a unicameral Parliament (*Landtag*) of 25 members elected for four years. ECONOMY agriculture includes vegetables, corn, wheat, potatoes, grapes, and timber; the industrial sector, developing since the 1950s, is export-based, and centred on specialized and high-tech production; major industries are metal-working, engineering, chemicals, pharmaceuticals, textiles, ceramics, and foodstuffs; revenue comes from international banking and finance, postage stamps, and tourism.

Liechtenstein

lied *noun* (PL. **lieder**) a German song, usually romantic in theme, for solo voice and piano. [from German *Lieder*, songs]

lie detector a machine which is connected to a person's body during questioning to measure changes in blood pressure and pulse. These symptoms are thought to indicate an internal discomfort caused by lying.

lie-down *noun* a short rest taken lying down.

Lied von der Erde, Das (The Song of the Earth) a song-symphony by Gustav Mahler (1908–9), comprising six songs for tenor and alto or baritone soloists and orchestra.

Liège, Flemish **Luik**, German **Lüttich** 1 POP (1992e) 196 000, the river-port capital of Liège province, E Belgium, situated at the confluence of the Ourthe and Meuse rivers. The fifth largest city in Belgium, and one of Europe's biggest river ports, it is associated with the earliest coal-mining in Europe. NOTABLE FEATURES Church of St Jacques (11c, rebuilt 1513–1538); Palace of Justice (1526–40); Gothic St Paul's Cathedral. 2 a province in E Belgium with the city of Liège as its capital.

liege *Hist.* — *adj.* 1 entitled to receive feudal service or homage from a vassal. 2 bound to give feudal service or homage to a superior. — *noun* 1 (*also* **liege lord**) a feudal superior, lord, or sovereign. 2 a feudal subject or vassal. [from Old French *lige*]

lie-in a long stay in bed in the morning.

lien *noun Legal* a right to keep another person's property until the owner pays a debt. [from Old French *loien*, from Latin *ligamen*, bond]

lieu
— **in lieu of** in place of or instead of. [from French *lieu*, place]

Lieut *or* **Lieut.** *abbrev.* Lieutenant.

lieutenancy *noun* (pronounced *left*-) (PL. **lieutenancies**) the rank of lieutenant.

lieutenant *noun* (pronounced left-) 1 a deputy acting for a superior. 2 an officer in the British army with the rank next below captain. 3 an officer in the British navy with the rank next below lieutenant commander. 4 *North Amer., esp. US* a police officer or fireman with the rank next below captain. [from French *lieutenant*, from *lieu*, place + *tenant*, holding]

lieutenant colonel an officer with the rank next below colonel.

lieutenant commander an officer with the rank next below commander.

lieutenant general an officer with the rank next below general.

Lif and Lifthrasir in Norse mythology, the mother and father of the new race of human beings after Ragnarok (the last battle).

Lifar, Serge (1905–86) Russian-born French dancer and choreographer, born in Kiev. A student and friend of Diaghilev, he joined the Ballets Russes in 1923, and danced successfully with Anna Pavlova, among others. As a choreographer he scored his first triumph in 1929 with *Créatures de Promethée*, the year he became artistic director and guiding genius of the Paris Opéra (1929–58).

life *noun* (PL. **lives**) 1 the quality or state which distinguishes living animals and plants from dead ones and from matter such as rocks, stones, etc which have never been alive, including the ability to grow, develop, and change. 2 the period between birth and death, between birth and the present time, or between the present time and death. 3 the length of time a thing exists or is able to function: *a battery with a long life.* 4 living things as a group: *marine life.* 5 the condition of being alive as a living person: *many lives lost in war.* 6 a way or manner of living: *a joyless life.* 7 an aspect of one's life: *love-life.* 8 liveliness; energy; high spirits: *full of life.* 9 a source of liveliness, energy, or high spirits: *the life and soul of the party.* 10 a written account of a person's life. 11 *colloq.* a prison sentence for life, now usually taken to mean about 15 years. 12 any of a number of opportunities of remaining in a game: *each player starts with four lives.*
— **as large as life** *colloq.* in person; real and living.
bring to life to make lively or interesting.
come to life to become lively or interesting.
for life until death.
a matter of life and death an extremely important or urgent matter.

not on your life *colloq.* on no account.
take one's life in one's hands to take a very important decision which will have serious consequences for oneself; to put one's life at risk.
to the life exactly like the original.
[from Anglo-Saxon *lif*]

life-and-death *adj.* extremely serious or critical, deciding or as if deciding whether someone will live or die.

Life and Death of Colonel Blimp, The a British film directed by Michael Powell and Emeric Pressburger (1943). A Nazi attack during World War II causes an experienced soldier (played by Roger Livesey) to contemplate his gentlemanly conduct in previous wars.

life assurance *or* **life insurance** insurance which will be paid to the policy-holder on reaching a certain age, or to the policy-holder's dependants in the case of his or her death.

Life Assurance and Unit Trust Regulatory Organization (ABBREV. **LAUTRO**) a self-regulating organization set up to supervise certain aspects of investment business in the UK's financial markets, and thus to protect the investor. Recognized by the Securities and Investments Board (SIB), it was authorized by the Financial Servies Act (1986).

lifebelt *noun* a ring or belt which floats in water, used to support people in danger of drowning.

lifeblood *noun* 1 the blood necessary for life. 2 anything which is an essential part or factor.

lifeboat *noun* 1 a boat for rescuing people in trouble at sea. 2 a small boat, usually one of several, carried on a larger ship for use in emergencies.
◇ The first sea-going lifeboat, in 1786, was based at Bamburgh Head, Northumberland. The British Royal National Lifeboat Institution (RNLI), founded in 1824, is a voluntary-manned service, and has been the model for similar services in many other countries. The standard RNLI lifeboat used for rescues out at sea is a 16m long, self-righting vessel; inflatable boats are used for most inshore rescues.

lifebuoy *noun* a float for supporting a person in the water until help is available.

life cycle 1 the sequence of different stages through which a living organism passes, from the fusion of male and female gametes (specialized reproductive cells) to form a zygote (fertilized egg), until the same stage is reached in the next generation. The life cycle is often complex, eg in animals in which there are several stages that differ markedly from the mature adult form, such as insects, amphibians, or in plants in which a sexually reproducing generation alternates with an asexually reproducing generation, eg ferns, mosses. 2 in vertebrates, the sequence of stages between the fusion of male and female gametes to form a zygote, and the eventual death of the organism.

life expectancy 1 the average length of time for which a person from a particular location might be expected to live if general health and living standards are not affected by disease, dietary factors, stress, war, famine, etc. In the UK the average life expectancy is 75 years. 2 the length of time for which any living organism can reasonably be expected to remain alive.

lifeguard *noun* an expert swimmer employed at a swimming-pool or beach to rescue people in danger of drowning.

Life Guards a British army regiment which guards the monarch, especially on ceremonial occasions.

life imprisonment a sentence in which the convicted person is to be imprisoned for the remainder of his or her life. In the UK, it is the usual sentence for murder, and the maximum sentence for such crimes as manslaughter and rape. In practice, the sentence is often not for life; a prisoner may be released on licence by the Home Secretary on the recommendation of a Parole Board, after serving 10 or 15 years. While the trial judge may recommend a minimum term of imprisonment, this is not binding on the Home Secretary.

life interest an interest in property that entitles the holder to income (eg rents, interest, and dividends) only; the capital or land is preserved for the benefit of those that follow.

life-jacket *noun* an inflatable sleeveless jacket for supporting a person in the water until help is available.

lifeless *adj.* **1** dead. **2** unconscious. **3** having no energy or vivacity; dull.

lifelessly *adv.* with no sign of life: *lay lifelessly on the floor.*

lifelessness *noun* being without signs of life; lack of vitality.

lifelike *adj.*, *said of a portrait etc* very like the person or thing represented.

lifeline *noun* **1** a rope for support in dangerous operations or for saving lives. **2** a vital means of communication or support.

lifelong *adj.* lasting the whole length of a life: *their lifelong wish.*

Life of Galileo, The see GALILEO, THE LIFE OF.

Life of Samuel Johnson, The a biography by James Boswell (1791). It has been regarded by many as a supreme example of biographical writing.

life peer *or* **life peeress** a peer whose title is not hereditary.

lifer *noun slang* a person sent to prison for life.

life raft a raft kept on a ship, for use in emergencies.

life-saver *noun* a person or thing that saves lives, or that saves a person from difficulty.

life-saving *noun* the act or skill of rescuing people who are in danger of drowning.

life sciences the sciences concerned with living animals, plants, or organisms, such as biology and zoology.

life-size *or* **life-sized** *adj.*, *said of a copy, drawing, etc* as large as the original.

lifestyle *noun* a person's or group's way of living.

life-support *adj.*, *said of equipment* allowing a person to remain alive, eg in an unfavourable environment such as space, or when seriously ill.

life-support machine a device or system designed to keep a person alive in adverse conditions, as in space, or to maintain vital functions such as breathing and heartbeat in a seriously ill person.

lifetime *noun* the duration of a person's life.

Liffey, River a river in the E Irish Republic, length 80km/50mi. Rising in N Wicklow county, it flows W, NE, and E through Dublin to meet the Irish Sea at Dublin Bay. It is crossed by the Grand Canal.

LIFO *abbrev.* last in, first out.

lift — *verb* **1** *trans., intrans.* to raise or rise to a higher position. **2** to move (especially one's eyes or face) upwards. **3** to take and carry away. **4** to raise to a better or more agreeable level: *lift one's spirits.* **5** *intrans. said of cloud, fog, etc* to clear. **6** to remove (a barrier or restriction). **7** to dig up (crops growing in the ground, eg potatoes). **8** *colloq.* to plagiarize from someone else's work or from published material. — *noun* **1** an act of lifting. **2** the upward force of the air on an aircraft, etc. **3** *Brit.* a device for moving people and goods between floors of a building, consisting of a compartment which moves up and down in a vertical

shaft. **4** a ride in a person's car or other vehicle. **5** a boost to the spirits or sudden feeling of happiness.
— **lift off** *said of a spacecraft* to rise, especially vertically, from the ground.
[from Norse *lypta*]

lift-off *noun* the vertical launching of a spacecraft or rocket.

ligament *noun Anat.* a band of tough fibrous connective tissue that holds two bones together at a joint, thereby limiting the number of directions in which it can move. [from Latin *ligare*, to bind]

ligature — *noun* **1** anything that binds or ties. **2** a thread, etc for tying, especially for sealing blood vessels during surgery. **3** *Mus.* a smooth link between a sequence of notes. **4** *Printing* a character formed from two or more characters joined together. — *verb* to bind with a ligature. [from Latin *ligare*, to bind]

Ligeti, György (Sándor) (1923–) Hungarian-born Austrian composer, born in Dicsöszentmárton. He studied and later taught at the Budapest Academy of Music. After leaving Hungary (1956), he worked at the electronics studio in Cologne, and settled in Vienna, where he developed an experimental approach to composition. His first large orchestral work, *Apparitions* (1958–9), made his name widely known. In *Aventures* (1962) he uses his own invented language of speech sounds. He has also written a choral requiem, a cello concerto, and music for harpsichord, organ, and wind and string ensembles.

light¹ — *noun* **1** a form of electromagnetic radiation that travels freely through space, especially visible light, which is that part of the electromagnetic spectrum that can be seen, and that has wavelengths ranging from about 390 to 780 nanometres. Light energy can be absorbed and reflected, and like other electromagnetic waves it is thought to consist of particles of energy called photons. **2** any source of light, such as the sun, a lamp, a candle, etc. **3** an appearance of brightness; a shine or gleam: *see a light away in the distance.* **4** daylight; dawn. **5** a particular quality or amount of light: *a good light for taking photographs.* **6** (*usually* **lights**) a traffic light: *turn left at the lights.* **7** a flame or spark for igniting. **8** a means of producing a flame for igniting, such as a match. **9** a way in which something is thought of or regarded: *see the problem in a new light.* **10** a glow in the eyes or on the face as a sign of energy, liveliness, happiness, or excitement. **11** sudden understanding or spiritual insight: *see the light.* **12** an eminent person: *a leading light.* **13** (**lights**) a person's mental ability, knowledge, or understanding: *act according to one's lights.* **14** an opening in a wall that lets in light, such as a window. — *adj.* **1** having light; not dark. **2** *said of a colour* pale; closer to white than black. — *verb* (PAST TENSE AND PAST PARTICIPLE **lit**, **lighted**) **1** to bring light to: *light the stage.* **2** *trans., intrans.* to begin or cause to begin to burn: *light the fire.* **3** to guide or show (someone) the way, or (someone's way), using a light or torch.
— **bring something to light** to make it known or cause to be noticed.
come to light to be made known or discovered.
in the light of something taking it into consideration.
light up 1 to become bright. **2** *said of a person* to become lively and excited. **3** *colloq.* to light a cigarette, etc and begin smoking.
light something up 1 to illuminate it or make it bright. **2** to light (a cigarette, etc).
see the light of day 1 to be born, discovered, or produced. **2** to come to public notice.
shed *or* **throw light on something** to make it clear or help to explain it.
[from Anglo-Saxon *leoht*]

light² — *adj.* **1** of little weight; easy to lift or carry. **2** low in weight, amount, or density: *light rain.* **3** easy to bear, suffer, or do: *light work.* **4** of

less weight than is correct or proper. **5** having only light weapons or equipment: *light infantry.* **6** without problems, sorrow, etc; cheerful: *a light heart.* **7** graceful and quick; nimble: *a light skip.* **8** not serious or profound, but for amusement only: *light reading.* **9** thoughtless or trivial: *a light remark.* **10** not thinking clearly or seriously; giddy: *a light head.* **11** *said of food* easily digested. **12** *technical, said of wine* with an alcohol content of between 5·5% and 15% by volume. **13** *loosely, said of wine* with a delicate, fresh flavour. **14** *said of cakes, etc* spongy and well risen. **15** *said of soil* loose and sandy. **16** *said of a vehicle or ship* designed to carry light loads only. **17** *said of a ship* unloaded. — *adv.* **1** in a light manner. **2** with little luggage: *travel light.*
— **make light of something** to treat it as unimportant or trivial.
[from Anglo-Saxon *leoht*]

light³ *verb* (PAST TENSE AND PAST PARTICIPLE **lit**, **lighted**) **1** (**light on** *or* **upon**) to come upon or find by chance. **2** *said especially of birds* to come to rest after flight. [from Anglo-Saxon *lihtan*, to alight]

light bulb an airtight glass envelope surrounding the electric filament of an incandescent lamp. The filament becomes white hot and emits visible light when a current is passed through it.

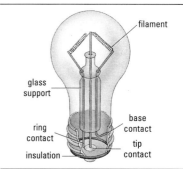

light bulb

light-emitting diode *Electron.* (ABBREV. **LED**) a semiconductor diode that gives out light when an electric current is passed through it, used to display numerals and letters in calculators, watches, and other electronic instruments that require a self-luminous display.

lighten¹ *verb* **1** *trans., intrans.* to make or become brighter. **2** to cast light on. **3** *intrans.* to shine or glow.

lighten² *verb* **1** *trans., intrans.* to make or become less heavy. **2** *trans., intrans.* to make or become happier or more cheerful. **3** to make (a problem, unhappy mood, etc) less: *tried to lighten her sadness.*

lighter¹ *noun* a device for lighting cigarettes, etc.

lighter² *noun* a large, open boat used for transferring goods between ships, or between a ship and a wharf. [from Anglo-Saxon *lihtan*, to relieve of a weight]

lighter-than-air *adj.*, *said of an aircraft* weighing less than the air it displaces.

light-fingered *adj.* having a tendency to steal habitually.

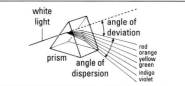

dispersion of light

light-headed *adj.* **1** having a dizzy feeling in the head. **2** thoughtless and silly; frivolous.

light-headedly *adv.* in a light-headed or frivolous way.

light-headedness *noun* being light-headed or frivolous.

light-hearted *adj.* **1** *said of a person* happy and carefree. **2** not serious; cheerful and amusing: *a light-hearted entertainment.*

light-heartedly *adv.* in a light-hearted or carefree way.

light-heartedness *noun* being light-hearted or carefree.

lighthouse *noun* a building on the coast with a flashing light to guide ships or warn them of rocks, etc.

lighting *noun* **1** equipment for providing light. **2** the quality or type of light produced.

lighting-up time the time of day at which road vehicles must have their lights turned on.

lightly *adv.* in a light or frivolous manner.
— **get off lightly** escape without serious rebuke or punishment.

light meter a meter for measuring the amount of light present, used especially when taking photographs.

lightness *noun* being light; lack of weight.

lightning — *noun* a gigantic spark produced by the discharge of static electricity from a charged cloud to the Earth's surface, from one charged cloud to another, or between different parts of the same cloud. It is accompanied by a bright flash of light, and thunder resulting from the sudden expansion of air that has been rapidly heated by the flash. — *adj.* very quick and sudden.

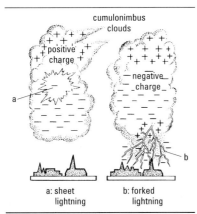

cumulonimbus clouds

positive charge

negative charge

a: sheet lightning

b: forked lightning

lightning

lightning conductor a metal rod, usually projecting above the roof of a building, that is connected by a wire or cable to another rod buried beneath the ground. It prevents structural damage to tall buildings by diverting lightning directly to earth.

Light of the World, The a painting by William Holman Hunt (1854, Keble College, Oxford).

light pen **1** *Comput.* a light-sensitive device resembling a pen that can be used to select objects on a computer screen to which it is connected, or to draw shapes and move them about on the screen using a suitable graphics program. Light pens are used when great precision is needed, eg in computer-aided design. **2** a loose term for a bar code reader.

light pollution an excessive amount or degree of artificial lighting, especially in large cities.

lights *pl. noun* the lungs of an animal, used for food. [a Middle English use of LIGHT² as a noun]

lightship *noun* a ship with a beacon, which acts as a lighthouse.

lightweight — *adj.* **1** light in weight. **2** having little importance or authority. — *noun* **1** a person or thing having little importance or authority. **2** a person or thing of little physical weight. **3** a class for boxers, wrestlers, and weight-lifters of not more than a specified weight (61·2 kg in professional boxing, different but similar weights in amateur boxing and the other sports). **4** a boxer, etc of this class.

light-year *noun* the distance light travels in a year, nearly 10 million million miles.

ligneous *adj. technical* made of or like wood. [from Latin *lignum*, wood]

lignin *noun Biochem.* a complex polymer that cements together the fibres of cellulose within the cell walls of plants, making them woody and rigid. [from Latin *lignum*, wood]

lignite *noun Geol.* a soft brown low-grade form of coal, intermediate between peat and bituminous coal, with a high moisture content. It burns with a smoky flame and gives out little heat. – Also called *brown coal.* [from Latin *lignum*, wood]

Ligurian Sea an arm of the Mediterranean Sea, bounded N and E by NW Italy and S by Corsica and Elba. The Gulf of Genoa lies to the N.

like¹ — *adj.* **1** similar; resembling. **2** typical of: *it's just like them to forget.* **3** in the correct state or mood for: *we feel like a drink.* — *prep.* in the same manner as; to the same extent as: *run like a deer.* — *adv.* **1** *old use, dialect* likely: *she'll be on time, like as not.* **2** *old use* in the same manner. — *conj.* **1** *colloq.* as if: *look like you've been awake all night.* **2** as: *not pretty like you are.* — *noun* the equal of a person or thing: *compare like with like.*
— **the like** a thing or things of the same kind: *hills, mountains, and the like.*
the likes of people or things such as. [from Anglo-Saxon *gelic*, alike]

like² — *verb* **1** to be pleased with; to find pleasant or agreeable. **2** to be fond of. **3** to prefer: *she likes her tea without sugar.* **4** to wish, or wish for: *would you like to help?* — *noun* (*usually* **likes**) a thing liked: *likes and dislikes.* [from Anglo-Saxon *lician*, to please]

-like *combining form* forming words meaning 'resembling, suitable for, or characteristic of': *childlike.*

likeable *or* **likable** *adj.* easy to like; lovable; pleasant.

likelihood *noun* probability.
— **in all likelihood** very probably.

likely — *adj.* **1** probable. **2** suitable or useful for a particular purpose: *a likely spot for a picnic.* — *adv.* probably.
— **as likely as not** probably.
not likely! *colloq.* an exclamation of refusal or denial.

like-minded *adj.* having similar opinions, tastes, or purpose.

liken *verb* (**likened**, **likening**) (**liken one thing to another**) to think or speak of them as comparable.

likeness *noun* **1** a similarity. **2** a person or thing which is like someone or something else. **3** a portrait: *have one's likeness taken.*

likewise *adv.* **1** in the same or a similar manner. **2** also.

liking *noun* **1** a taste or preference: *a liking for chocolates.* **2** satisfaction.

lilac — *noun* a small tree or shrub which has bunches of white or pale pinkish-purple, sweet-smelling flowers. — *adj.* pale pinkish-purple in colour. [from Persian *nilak*, bluish, from *nil*, blue]

Lilburne, John (c.1614–57) English revolutionary, born near London, who became a leading figure in the Levellers during the English Civil War. Imprisoned by the Star Chamber in 1638, he rose in the Parliamentary army, but resigned from it in 1645. He then became an indefatigable agitator, and was repeatedly imprisoned for his pamphlets.

Lilienthal, Otto (1849–96) German aeronautical inventor, born in Anklam. He studied bird flight in order to build heavier-than-air flying machines resembling the birdman designs of Leonardo da Vinci. He made many short flights in his machines, but crashed to his death near Berlin in 1896.

Lilith in Jewish legend, a female demon believed to have been the first wife of Adam who, after quarrelling with him, resolved to slay children.

Lille, formerly Flemish **Lisle Ryssel**, ancient **Insula** POP (1990) 950 000, the industrial and commercial capital of Nord-Pas-de-Calais region and of Nord department, N France. It lies near the Belgian frontier, 208km/129mi NE of Paris. In both World Wars it was badly damaged. Lille forms part of the industrial urban metropolis of Lille-Roubaix-Tourcoing, the largest economic and industrial centre of N France. NOTABLE FEATURES Gothic Church of St-Maurice; Church of Ste-Catherine (16c); cathedral (begun in 1854); old exchange (17c); citadel (16c); Palais des Beaux-Arts.

Lillie, Beatrice (Gladys) (1898–1989) Canadian revue singer, born in Toronto. Renowned from 1914 in music hall and the new vogue of 'intimate revue', she later worked also in international revues and in films, such as *Thoroughly Modern Millie* (1967).

Lilliputian — *noun* a very small person or thing. — *adj.* very small.

Lilliputians the small, politically incompetent inhabitants of Lilliput in Jonathan Swift's *Gulliver's Travels*, who represent the moral and mental absurdity of humankind.

LILO *abbrev.* last in, last out.

Lilo *noun trademark* a type of inflatable mattress.

Lilongwe POP (1987) 223 000, the capital of Malawi, situated in Central region, on the R Lilongwe. It has been the capital since 1975, when it replaced Zomba.

lilt — *noun* **1** a light, graceful, swinging rhythm. **2** a tune, song, or voice with such a rhythm. **3** a springing, swinging quality when walking. — *verb intrans.* to speak, sing, or move with a lilt. [from Middle English *lulte*]

lilting *adj., said of a tune* graceful and with a gentle rhythm.

lily — *noun* (PL. **lilies**) **1** any of various perennial plants belonging to the genus *Lilium,* native to north temperate regions, that have underground bulbs, narrow leaves, and white or brightly coloured flowers, often spotted, with long protruding stamens, borne on a tall stem, eg Easter lily, tiger lily. **2** any of a large number of perennial plants belonging to the family Liliaceae, which in addition to true lilies of the genus *Lilium* includes the hyacinth, bluebell, tulip, onion, etc. **3** any flowering plant that superficially resembles a lily, eg water lily. **4** any person or thing considered exceptionally pure. — *adj.* pale; white. [from Latin *lilium*]

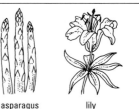

asparagus   lily   tulip

the lily family

lily-livered *adj.* morally feeble; cowardly.

lily-of-the-valley *noun* a spring plant with small white bell-shaped flowers having a sweet smell.

lily-white *adj.* pure white; faultless.

Lima POP (1990e) 6.4m, the federal capital of Peru. It lies on both sides of the R Rímac, at the foot of the Cerro San Cristóbal. history founded by the Spanish conqueror, Francisco Pizarro, in 1535; it was the chief city of Spanish S America until independence in the early 19c; devastated by an earthquake in 1746. NOTABLE FEATURES cathedral (16c); Palacio del Gobierno, Archbishop's Palace; Unity Hall; Santo Domingo Church (1549), San Francisco Church (1674); National Museum of Art, Museum of Peruvian Culture; Parque de las Leyendas.

lima bean a flat white edible bean from tropical America. [named after Lima in Peru]

Limassol, Greek **Lemesos**, Turkish **Limasol** POP (1991e) 130 000, the port capital of Limassol district, S Cyprus, lying on Akrotiri Bay, NE of Akrotiri. An influx of Greek Cypriot refugees since the 1974 Turkish invasion has dramatically increased the population. NOTABLE FEATURE castle (14c).

limb[1] *noun* **1** an arm, leg, or wing. **2** a main branch on a tree. **3** a branch or section of a larger organization.
— **out on a limb** exposed or isolated, especially as regards an opinion or attitude.
[from Anglo-Saxon *lim*]

limb[2] *noun* **1** an edge of the disk of the sun or moon or a planet as specified: *the northern limb.* **2** *Bot.* the expanded, blade-like part of a leaf or petal. [from Latin *limbus*, border]

Limbe a town in Southern region, S Malawi. It is situated in a hilly region 8km/5mi SE of Blantyre. In 1909 it became a township.

limbed *adj.* having limbs.

limber[1] *adj.* flexible and supple. — *verb* (**limbered, limbering**) (**limber up**) *trans., intrans.* to stretch and warm up (oneself or a part of the body) before exercise. [perhaps from LIMB[1]]

limber[2] — *noun* the detachable front part of a gun carriage, consisting of an axle, pole, and two wheels. — *verb* (**limbered**; LIMBERING) to attach (a gun) to a limber. [from Middle English *lymour*, the pole of a vehicle]

limbic system *Physiol.* that part of the central nervous system, including the hippocampus and parts of the midbrain, that is associated with emotions such as fear, pleasure, and happiness, and with various autonomic functions. [from Latin *limbus*, border]

limbless *adj.* having no limbs.

limbo[1] *noun* (PL. **limbos**) **1** an area between heaven and hell, reserved for the unbaptised dead. **2** a state of uncertainty or waiting: *in limbo.* **3** a place of oblivion or neglect. [from Latin *in limbo*, from *in*, in + *limbus*, border]

limbo[2] *noun* (PL. **limbos**) a West Indian dance in which the dancer leans backwards to dance under a rope or bar which is moved lower and lower towards the floor. [from Jamaican English *limba*, to bend]

lime[1] — *noun* *Chem.* a loose term for calcium oxide (quicklime) or calcium hydroxide (slaked or hydrated lime), also often used incorrectly to refer to limestone. — *verb* to apply ground limestone as a fertilizer to soil in order to reduce its acidity and increase its calcium content. [from Anglo-Saxon *lim*]

lime[2] *noun* **1** a small round green citrus fruit having a sour taste. **2** (*also* **lime green**) the green colour of this fruit. [from Persian *limun*]

lime[3] *noun* **1** a tree with rough bark, heart-shaped leaves and sweet-smelling yellow blossom. – Also called *linden*. **2** the wood from this tree. [from Anglo-Saxon *lind*, linden]

limekiln *noun* a kiln for heating limestone to produce lime.

limelight *noun* **1** a bright white light produced by heating a block of lime in a flame, used formerly in theatres. **2** the glare of publicity: *in the limelight.*

Limerick, Gaelic **Luimneach** POP (1991) 75 000, the capital of Limerick county, Munster, SW Irish Republic. It is an industrial city and river port at the head of the estuary of the R Shannon. Founded in 1197, it was the scene of major sieges by Cromwell and William III. NOTABLE FEATURES Belltable Arts Centre; St Mary's Cathedral (12c); St John's Cathedral (19c); remains of city walls; King John's Castle; Treaty Stone.

Limerick, Gaelic **Luimneach** POP (1991) 110 000, a county in Munster province, SW Irish Republic. AREA 2 686sq km/1 037sq mi. It is bounded N by the R Shannon. CAPITAL Limerick. ECONOMY dairy farming; hydroelectric power (Ardnacrusha); lace.

limerick *noun* a humorous poem of five lines with an *aabba* rhyme-scheme. [said to be from the refrain *Will you come up to Limerick?*, sung between comic verses at a party]

limestone *noun* *Geol.* any of a group of sedimentary rocks composed mainly of calcium carbonate. and in most cases of organic origin, eg chalk, which is formed from the calcareous skeletons and shell fragments of marine invertebrates. Limestone is used as a building material, and in iron smelting and the manufacture of cement. Large caves are often associated with weathered limestone rock formations.

lime water *Chem.* an alkaline solution of calcium hydroxide in water, sometimes used as an antacid.

limey *noun* (PL. **limeys**) *North Amer. slang* a British person, originally a British sailor or ship. [from LIME[2] because of the use of lime-juice on British navy ships to prevent scurvy]

limit — *noun* **1** a point, degree, or amount beyond which something does not or may not pass. **2** (*often* **limits**) the boundary or edge of an area. **3** the greatest or smallest extent, degree, etc allowed. **4** (**the limit**) *colloq.* an intolerable or extremely annoying person or thing. **5** *Maths.* in calculus, a value that is approached more and more closely, but never reached. — *verb* (**limited, limiting**) to be a limit or boundary to; to restrict.
— **within limits** with a moderate degree of freedom only.
[from Latin *limes*, boundary]

limitation *noun* **1** an act of limiting or the condition of being limited. **2** (*often* **limitations**) a person's weakness, lack of ability, etc which sets a limit on what he or she can achieve: *know one's limitations.* **3** *Legal* a period of time within which an action must be brought.

limited *adj.* **1** having a limit or limits. **2** restricted; incomplete: *a limited understanding of the problem.*

limited company *or* **limited liability company** a business company owned by shareholders who are responsible for its debts only to the extent of the money they have put into it.

limited edition an edition of a book, art print, etc of which only a certain number of copies are printed or made.

limitless *adj.* having no limit; endless.

limning *noun* a term applied by the Elizabethans to the technique of painting 'pictures in little', ie miniature paintings, especially portraits. Nicholas Hilliard's treatise *The Art of Limning* (c.1600) describes the highly specialized techniques required for these paintings, which were often so small they were mounted and worn as lockets or cameos. The term was originally applied to the illumination of manuscripts in the Middle Ages, a painter of miniature por-

traits. [from Old French *eluminer*, to illuminate (a manuscript)]

limo *noun* (PL. **limos**) *colloq.* a limousine.

Limoges, ancient **Augustoritum Lemovicensium**, later **Lemovices** POP (1990) 170 000, the capital of Limousin region and of Haute-Vienne department, central France. It lies in the R Vienne Valley, 176km/109mi NE of Bordeaux. HISTORY a Gallic tribal capital, destroyed in the 5c; sacked by the English in 1370; famed for the manufacture of enamels and porcelain since the 18c; rapid post-War expansion (due largely to mining of uranium near Ambazac). NOTABLE FEATURES Gothic Cathedral of St Etienne (begun in 1273); Church of St Pierre du Queyroix (13c belfry, 16c facade); Church of St Michel des Lions (14c–16c).

limonite *noun* *Geol.* any of a group of brown or yellowish-brown amorphous iron oxides, formed by the oxidation of iron minerals, or by direct precipitation from water in bogs, shallow seas, or lagoons. It is a minor source of iron, and is also used as the pigment yellow ochre. [from Greek *leimon*, a meadow]

limousine *noun* a large, luxurious motor car, especially one with a screen separating the driver and passengers. [from French *limousine*: originally a cloak worn in *Limousin*, a province in France]

limp[1] — *verb intrans.* **1** to walk with an awkward or uneven step, because one leg is weak or injured. **2** *said of a damaged ship or aircraft* to move with difficulty. — *noun* the walk of a person who limps. [from Anglo-Saxon *lemphealt*]

limp[2] *adj.* **1** not stiff or firm; hanging loosely. **2** without energy or vitality; drooping. **3** *said of a book* with a soft cover not stiffened by boards.

limpet *noun* **1** a small shellfish with a cone-shaped shell, which fastens itself very firmly to rocks. **2** a person it is difficult to get rid of. [from Anglo-Saxon *lempedu*]

limpet

limpet mine a mine which attaches itself to its target with a magnet.

limpid *adj., said of water, the air, eyes, etc* clear, transparent. [from Latin *limpidus*]

limpidity *or* **limpidness** *noun* a limpid state; clarity.

limpidly *adv.* clearly, transparently.

limping *noun, adj.* involving a limp; halting: *a limping walk.*

limpingly *adv.* with a limp.

limply *adv.* **1** flexibly. **2** feebly: *answered limply that he didn't know.*

limpness *noun* being limp; lacking firmness or vitality.

Limpopo *or* **Crocodile, River** a river in SE Africa, length c.1 600km/1 000mi. Rising in South Africa in the S Transvaal, N of Johannesburg, it follows the Botswana–Transvaal and Transvaal–Zimbabwe borders. It enters Mozambique at Pafuri and flows into the Indian Ocean 130km/80mi NE of Maputo. Vasco da Gama named it the Rio do Espiritu Santo in 1497.

Limp Watches see PERSISTENCE OF MEMORY.

limy[1] *adj.* (**limier, limiest**) like or having the consistency of lime (calcium oxide).

limy² *adj.* (**limier**, **limiest**) tasting of lime (the fruit).

Linacre, Thomas (c.1460–1524) English humanist and physician, born in Canterbury, Kent. He travelled widely in Italy (1485–97), and became a tutor to Henry VII's son, Arthur in c.1501. He was King's Physician to Henry VII and Henry VIII, and founded the Royal College of Physicians in 1518. He took Catholic orders in 1520.

linage *noun* **1** the number of lines to a page. **2** payment by the line.

Lin Biao *or* **Lin Piao** (1907–71) one of the leaders of the Chinese Communist Party and a Marshal of the Red Army, born in Hupeh province. He became Minister of Defence in 1959, and in 1968 replaced the disgraced Liu Shaoqi as heir apparent to Mao Zedong (Mao Tse-tung). He was one of the promoters of the Cultural Revolution of 1966. In 1971, after a political struggle, he was killed in a plane crash in Mongolia, apparently in the course of an attempt to seek refuge in the USSR.

linchpin *noun* **1** a pin-shaped rod passed through an axle to keep a wheel in place. **2** a person or thing essential to a business, plan, etc. [from Anglo-Saxon *lynis*]

Lincoln, Abraham (1809–65) US Republican statesman, the 16th President, born near Hodgenville, Kentucky. Elected to the Illinois legislature in 1834, he became a lawyer in 1836. He was elected to a single term in Congress 10 years later, where he spoke against the extension of slavery. In 1860 he was elected on a platform of opposition to the expansion of slavery, and as President (1861–5) when the Civil War began (1861), he defined the issue in terms of national integrity, not anti-slavery, a theme he restated in the Gettysburg Address of 1863. Nonetheless, the same year he proclaimed freedom for all slaves in areas of rebellion. Re-elected in 1864, after the final Northern victory he intended to reunite the former warring parties on the easiest possible terms, but on 14 Apr 1865 he was shot at Ford's Theatre, Washington, by John Wilkes Booth, an actor, and died next morning.

Lincoln POP (1992e) 86 000, the county town of Lincolnshire, E central England. It lies on the R Witham, 230km/143mi N of London and 64km/40mi from the North Sea. The city was an important centre of the wool trade in the Middle Ages. NOTABLE FEATURES parts of the 3c Roman wall; Lincoln Castle; cathedral (1073), including Wren Library (contains an original Magna Carta manuscript).

Lincoln, formerly **Lancaster** POP (1990) 214 000, the capital of the state of Nebraska, USA. It is situated in Lancaster County, SE Nebraska, 82km/51mi SW of Omaha. In 1867 it became state capital and was renamed after President Lincoln. NOTABLE FEATURES planetarium; art gallery; sculpture garden.

Lincoln Center for the Performing Arts a group of theatres and recital halls erected to the west of Broadway, New York City. The complex, completed in 1969, comprises the New York State Theater, Avery Fisher Hall, the Metropolitan Opera House, Vivien Beaumont Theater, Alice Tully Hall, the Juilliard School for the Performing Arts, and the Library and Museum of the Performing Arts.

Lincoln Memorial a monument in Washington, DC, dedicated in 1922 to President Abraham Lincoln. The building (designed on the plan of a Greek temple by Henry Bacon) houses the statue of Lincoln (6m high) by Daniel Chester French (1850–1931).

Lincolnshire POP (1987e) 575 000, a flat agricultural county in E central England, divided into seven districts. AREA 5 915sq km/2 283sq mi. It is bounded E by the North Sea, N by Humberside, W by Nottinghamshire, SW by Leicestershire, S

by Cambridgeshire, and SE by Norfolk. PHYSICAL DESCRIPTION the Welland, Witham, and Trent rivers flow through Lincolnshire; the Fens area in the SE was drained in the 17c. CHIEF TOWNS Lincoln (county town), Grantham, Gainsborough, Spalding. ECONOMY intensive farming; horticulture; tourism. NOTABLE FEATURES Belton House; Lincoln Wolds.

Lincs. *abbrev.* Lincolnshire.

linctus *noun* (PL. **linctuses**) *Brit.* a syrup-like medicine which helps soothe a sore throat. [from Latin *linctus*, licking]

Lind, James (1716–94) Scottish physician, born in Edinburgh. He first served in the navy, then after qualifying in medicine at Edinburgh, became physician at the Royal Naval Hospital at Haslar. His experimental results on the cure and prevention of scurvy allowed the incidence of the disease within the navy to be substantially reduced; he also stressed the importance of cleanliness in the prevention of fevers.

Lind, Jenny, originally **Johanna Maria Lind** (1820–87) Swedish soprano, born in Stockholm. At the age of nine she entered the court theatre school of singing, and after lessons in Paris, made her début in Stockholm (1838) and attained international popularity. Known as the 'Swedish nightingale', she founded and endowed musical scholarships and charities in Sweden and in England, where she lived from 1856, and became Professor of Singing at the Royal College of Music (1883–6).

Linda a female first name. [of Germanic origin, from the feminine name-ending *-lind*, weak, tender, soft]

Lindbergh, Charles A(ugustus) (1902–74) US aviator, born in Detroit. He made the first solo nonstop transatlantic flight (New York–Paris, 1927), in the monoplane *The Spirit of St Louis*. His book of that name won the Pulitzer Prize in 1954. His young son was kidnapped and murdered in 1932 in what became a highly publicized crime. He later became an aeronautics consultant.

linden same as LIME³.

Linde process *Chem.* a process for the liquefaction of air and the subsequent extraction of liquid oxygen and liquid nitrogen from it. [named after the German engineer Carl von Linde]

Lindisfarne, also called **Holy Island** an island off the NE coast of Northumberland, renowned for its monastery founded by St Aidan from Iona in 634. It was a notable centre of early English Christianity and learning, and its most famous bishop was the ascetic St Cuthbert. The Lindisfarne Gospels were illuminated here, probably in the 690s, by Eadfrith (Bishop, 698–721).

Lindrum, Walter (1898–1960) Australian billiards player, born in Kalgoorlie. In 1932, at Thurston's Hall, London, he set the current world break record of 4 137 while playing Joe Davis. He competed in only two world championships (1933–34), and won both. He retired from competitive play in 1950.

Lindsay a male and female first name, after the Scottish surname.

line¹ — *noun* **1** a long narrow mark, streak, or stripe. **2** the use of such lines in art. **3** a length of thread, rope, wire, etc, especially for a specified purpose: *a fishing-line*. **4** a wrinkle or furrow, especially on the skin. **5** the path which a moving object is considered to leave behind it, having length but no breadth. **6** (often **lines**) an outline or shape, especially as part of the design: *a car noted for its clean lines*. **7** a row. **8** a row of words. **9** (**lines**) the words of an actor's part. **10** (**lines**) an amount of text to be written as a punishment at school. **11** any one of the five horizontal marks forming a musical stave. **12** a series of notes forming a melody. **13** *colloq.* a short letter or note: *drop him a line*. **14** a series or group of people which come one after the other, espe-

cially in the same family or profession: *come from a long line of doctors*. **15** a field of activity, interest, study, or work: *one's line of business*. **16** a course or way of acting, behaving, thinking, or reasoning: *think along different lines*. **17** the rules or limits of acceptable behaviour: *toe the line*. **18** a group or class of goods for sale. **19** the manufacturing process: *a production line*. **20** *North Amer., esp. US* a boundary: *the county line*. **21** a point of change or development: *the dividing line between genius and madness*. **22** one of several white marks showing a pitch, race-track, etc on a field. **23** a single track for a railway or trams; a branch or route of a railway system. **24** a route, track, or direction of movement: *line of fire*. **25** a continuous system, eg of telephone cables, connecting one place with another. **26** a telephone connection: *trying to get a line to Manchester*. **27** a company running regular services of ships, buses, or aircraft between two or more places. **28** an arrangement of troops or ships side by side and ready to fight. **29** a connected series of military defences: *behind enemy lines*. **30** the regular army. **31** one of several narrow horizontal bands forming a television picture. **32** *North Amer.* a queue. **33** (**lines, marriage lines**) a marriage licence. — *verb* **1** to mark or cover with lines. **2** to form a line along.
— **all along the line** at every point.
get a line on *colloq.* to get information about.
hard lines! *colloq.* bad luck!
in line for likely to get: *in line for promotion*.
lay it on the line to speak frankly.
lay *or* **put (something) on the line** to risk one's reputation or career on.
line up 1 *trans., intrans.* to bring into or form a line. **2** *trans., intrans.* to organize or be organized: *lined herself up a new job*. **3** *intrans.* (**line up for** *or* **against something**) to make a stand in support of or against it.
read between the lines to understand something implied but not actually stated.
[from Old French *ligne*, combined with Anglo-Saxon *line*, rope]

line² *verb* **1** to cover the inside of (a garment, box, etc) with some other material. **2** to cover as if with a lining: *line the walls with books*. **3** *colloq.* to fill, especially with large amounts. [from Anglo-Saxon *lin*, flax]

lineage *noun* ancestry. [from Latin *linea*, *line¹*]

lineal *adj.* **1** *said of family descent* in a direct line. **2** of or in lines. [from Latin *linealis*, from *linea*, *line¹*]

lineally *adv.* in a direct line.

lineament *noun* (*usually* **lineaments**) a feature or distinguishing mark, especially of the face. [from Latin *linea*, *line¹*]

linear *adj.* **1** of, consisting of, or like a line or lines. **2** relating to length. **3** *Maths.* involving one dimension only. **4** *Maths.* denoting an equation of a graph that is a straight line, of the general form $y = mx + c$, where x and y are variables, m is the gradient of the line, and c is the value of y at the point where the line crosses the vertical axis. [from Latin *linea*, line]

Linear A a syllabic script used for writing an as yet undeciphered pre-Greek language in Minoan Crete. Examples have been found at the palace sites in Crete, eg at Phaestos in the S, and are preserved on clay tablets.

Linear B a syllabic script found on clay tablets at Mycenaean palace sites, adapted from Minoan Linear A and used by the Mycenaeans to write an early form of Greek. Unlike Linear A it has been deciphered (by Michael Ventris in the 1950s), and from the archaeological evidence appears to have been used extensively for business and administration, eg for inventories.

linearity *noun* a linear state.

linear momentum *Physics* the product of the mass *m* and the velocity *v* of a moving object.

linear motor *Engineering* a type of induction motor in which the stator (the stationary part of the motor) and the rotor are straight and parallel to each other, rather than being cylindrical and one inside the other. Linear motors are used in automatic sliding doors, in which the rotor travels along a rail that acts as the stator.

lineation *noun* **1** the act of marking with lines. **2** an arrangement of lines.

lined *adj.* having lines.

line drawing a drawing in pen or pencil using lines only.

line-engraving *noun* a technique used in intaglio print-making, in which the metal plate is cut with a burin. It originated in 15c Germany and Italy, and its greatest early master was Martin Schongauer (c.1430–91). Developed to a masterly degree by Dürer, it largely fell into disuse from the 17c, as other methods of engraving were developed. It was revived in the 20c by graphic artists of the Atelier 17 workshop established in Paris in 1927.

Line Islands POP (1990) 5 000, a coral island group of Kiribati, central and S Pacific Ocean. The largest of the N Line Is are Christmas I (Kiritimati), Fanning I, and Washington I. They are inhabited by coconut plantation workers. The S Line Is have been worked for guano in the past but are now uninhabited. Three of the N group are US territories.

Lineker, Gary (Winston) (1960–) English footballer and commentator, born in Leicester. He turned professional with Leicester City in 1978, and made his début for England in 1984. He moved to Everton in 1985, then played for Barcelona, Tottenham Hotspur, and finally Grampus Eight of Nagoya, Japan. He was the top scorer in the 1986 World Cup, and by the time he retired from international football in 1991 had scored 48 goals for England.

linen — *noun* **1** cloth made from flax. **2** household articles such as sheets, tablecloths, tea-towels, etc originally made from linen, now more likely to be made from cotton, nylon, etc. **3** underclothes, originally made from linen. — *adj.* of or like linen. — **wash one's dirty linen in public** to let one's personal problems and quarrels become generally known. [from Anglo-Saxon, from *lin*, flax]

line printer a printer attached to a computer which prints a line at a time rather than a character at a time.

liner[1] *noun* a large passenger ship or aircraft.

liner[2] *noun* something used for lining: *bin-liner*.

linesman or **lineswoman** *noun* an official at a boundary line in some sports, eg football, whose job is to indicate when the ball has gone out of play.

line-up *noun* **1** an arrangement of things or people in line. **2** a list of people selected for a sports team, or appearing in a show. **3** an identity parade.

ling[1] *noun* (PL. **ling**, **lings**) a fish of the cod family with a long, slender body. [Middle English]

ling[2] *noun* heather. [from Norse *lyng*]

-ling *suffix* forming words meaning: **1** a young, small, or minor person or thing: *duckling / princeling*. **2** *sometimes derog.* a person: *weakling / earthling*.

linga or **lingum** *noun* the principal symbolic representation of the Hindu deity Shiva, a phallic emblem. The female equivalent is the *yoni*, the shaped image of the female genitalia. [from Sanskrit]

linger *verb intrans.* (inferred, **inferring**) **1** to be slow to depart; to delay. **2** *said of a dying person* to die very slowly. **3** (**linger over something**) to spend a long time with it or doing it. [from Anglo-Saxon *lengan*, to lengthen]

lingerer *noun* a person who lingers or delays unduly.

lingerie *noun* women's underwear and nightclothes. [from French *lingerie*, from Latin *linum*, flax]

lingering *adj.*, *said especially of a memory or thought* staying in the mind, persisting.

lingeringly *adv.*, *said especially of a memory or thought* persistently.

lingo *noun* (PL. **lingos**) *colloq.*, often *derog.* **1** language. **2** the specialized vocabulary used by a particular group of people or profession: *medical lingo*. [from Latin *lingua*, tongue, language]

lingua franca (PL. **lingua francas**) **1** a language, or often a simplified form of it, used as a means of mutual communication by speakers of other languages. **2** any system or set of conventions which are readily and easily understood. **3** *Hist.* Italian with a mixture of French, Spanish, Greek, and Arabic words, used in the eastern part of the Mediterranean for trade. [from Italian *lingua franca*, Frankish language]

lingual *adj.* **1** of the tongue; pronounced using the tongue. **2** of speech or languages. [from Latin *lingua*, tongue, language]

lingually *adv.* **1** with the tongue. **2** as regards speech or language.

linguist *noun* **1** a person who has a good knowledge of languages. **2** a person who studies linguistics, especially professionally. [from Latin *lingua*, tongue, language]

linguistic *adj.* of language or linguistics.

linguistically *adv.* as regards language or linguistics.

linguistics *sing. noun* the scientific study of language.

liniment *noun* a kind of thin oily cream for rubbing into the skin to ease muscle pain. [from Latin *linimentum*]

lining *noun* a piece of material used to line garments, boxes, etc.

link — *noun* **1** a ring of a chain. **2** any person or thing that connects. **3** a means of communication or travel. **4** a cuff-link. **5** a unit of measurement, equal to one hundredth of a surveyor's chain, 7·92 in (c.20 cm). — *verb* **1** to connect or join. **2** *intrans.* to be or become connected. — **link up** or **link something up** to join or be joined closely or by a link. [from Norse *link*]

linkage *noun* *Genetics* the association between two or more genes that occur close together on the same chromosome and therefore tend to be inherited together.

linkage politics *Politics* a method of analysis which attempts to explain the behaviour of a political system by reference to phenomena occurring in a wider international context.

Linklater, Eric (Robert) (1899–1974) Scottish novelist, born in Penarth, Wales. He served in World War I, became a journalist in Bombay (1925–7), and an English lecturer at Aberdeen. While in the USA (1928–30) he wrote *Poet's Pub* (1929), the first of a series of satirical novels which include *Juan in America* (1931) and *Private Angelo* (1946).

links *noun* **1** (*pl.*) a stretch of more or less flat ground along a shore near the sea. **2** (*sing., pl.*) a golf course by the sea. [from Anglo-Saxon *hlinc*, ridge]

link-up *noun* a connection or union, especially of two different systems.

Linlithgow POP (1981) 9 600, a town in West Lothian district, Lothian region, E central Scotland. It is situated 26km/16mi W of Edinburgh. NOTABLE FEATURES ruins of Linlithgow Palace (15c), birthplace of Mary Queen of Scots; Canal Museum.

Linnaeus, Carolus, Swedish **Carl von Linné** (1707–78) Swedish naturalist and physician, born in Råshult. He travelled widely for botanical exploration in Europe, and in the late 1730s published his so-called 'sexual system' of classification based on the number of flower parts, for long the dominant system; names consisted of generic and specific elements, with plants grouped hierarchically into genera, classes, and orders. He later practised as a physician in Stockholm, and in 1741 became Professor of Medicine and Botany at Uppsala.

linnet *noun* a small brown songbird. [from Old French *linette*, from Latin *linum*, flax, so called because it feeds on flax seeds]

lino *noun* (PL. **linos**) *colloq.* linoleum.

linocut *noun* **1** a design cut in relief in linoleum. **2** a print made from this.

linoleum *noun* a smooth hard-wearing covering for floors, made of canvas coated with linseed oil and cork. [from Latin *linum*, flax + *oleum*, oil]

linseed *noun* the seed of flax. [from Anglo-Saxon *linsǽd*]

linseed oil a pale yellow oil, extracted from flax seed, which hardens on exposure to air, and is used in paints, varnishes, enamels, etc.

lint *noun* **1** linen or cotton with a raised nap on one side, for dressing wounds. **2** fine, very small pieces of wool, cotton, etc; fluff. [from Middle English *lynt*]

lintel *noun* a horizontal wooden or stone beam placed over a doorway or window. [from Old French *lintel*, threshold, from Latin *limes*, boundary, border]

Linton, Edgar the insubstantial husband of Catherine in Emily Brontë's *Wuthering Heights*.

Linz POP (1991) 203 000, the industrial capital of Oberösterreich state, N Austria, situated on both banks of the R Danube. The third largest city in Austria, it is the centre of a rich agricultural region, and has extensive port installations. NOTABLE FEATURES many historical buildings, including an early 16c castle; Martinskirche (oldest preserved church in Austria); Landhaus (former seat of the state assembly); Minoritenkirche (1758); opera house; museums; art galleries; theatres.

lion *noun* **1** a large carnivorous cat (*Panthera leo*) with a tawny coat and tufted tail, belonging to the same family (Felidae) as the leopard, jaguar, and tiger, and now confined to Africa and a wildlife reserve in India. **2** the male of this animal, as opposed to the female. **3** a brave or celebrated person. (**the Lion**) the constellation and sign of the zodiac Leo. — **the lion's share** the largest share. [from Greek *leon*]

◇ The male lion is up to 2.7m long (including the tail), weighs up to 250kg, and its head, neck, and shoulders are covered with a characteristic long thick tawny or black mane. The female (lioness) is smaller and has no mane. Lions live in open country where there is scrub, and their tawny coats camouflage them well among the tall tropical grasses of savanna lands. They live in groups called prides of up to 20 animals, each pride containing one or more mature lions and a number of lionesses with their cubs. Members of a pride co-operate in the stalking and ambushing of prey, and the lionesses usually kill the prey, which consists mainly of wildebeest, antelope, and zebra, although almost any animal is taken, from cane rat to elephant. Old or injured lions often seek easier prey, such as porcupines, smaller rodents, sheep, goats, and occasionally humans. They have no natural enemies apart from humans.

Lionel a male first name. [a diminutive form of the Old French name *Leon*, young lion]

lioness *noun* **1** a female lion. **2** a brave or celebrated woman.

lion-hearted *adj.* very brave.

lionize or **lionise** *verb* to treat as a celebrity or hero.

Lions Clubs, International Association of a worldwide civilian service club, founded in 1917 in Dallas, Texas, for men and women to perform volunteer community service, and to encourage such things as 'generous consideration' and good citizenship among peoples.

Liouville, Joseph (1809–82) French mathematician, born in St Omer. He taught at the École Polytechnique, the Collège de France, and the University of Paris. He studied algebraic function theory, the theory of differential equations, mathematical physics, and celestial mechanics. In number theory he introduced new methods of investigating transcendental numbers (numbers which cannot be solutions of algebraic equations with rational coefficients), showing for the first time that there are infinitely many of them.

lip *noun* 1 either of the folds of flesh which form the edge of the mouth. 2 the edge or rim of something, especially a container for liquid. 3 *slang* insolence.
— **bite one's lip** to control or smother one's feelings, tears, anger, etc.
curl one's lip to sneer scornfully.
keep a stiff upper lip to show no emotion or worry when faced with difficulties.
lick *or* **smack one's lips** to lick or part one's lips noisily as a sign of relish or in anticipation of pleasure.
[from Anglo-Saxon *lippa*]

lipase *noun Biochem.* an enzyme that catalyses the breakdown of lipids (fats and oils) in living cells. [from Greek *lipos*, fat]

lipid *noun Biochem.* any of a group of organic compounds, mainly oils and fats, that occur naturally in living organisms, and are generally insoluble in water. [from Greek *lipos*, fat]

lipogram *noun* a composition in words from which a specific letter of the alphabet (and any word containing it) has been intentionally omitted. Lipograms are usually made to demonstrate the author's verbal ingenuity, and famous examples include: an epic in 24 books by the 5c Greek poet Tryphiodorus, each book omitting a letter of the Greek alphabet; five novels by Lope de Vega, each omitting one vowel; and the novel *Gadsby* (1939) by Earnest Wright, written entirely without the letter 'e'. [from Greek *leipein*, to want, leave + *gramma*, a letter]

liposculpture *noun* the practice of using liposuction to reshape the body. [from Greek *lipos*, fat + SCULPTURE]

liposome *noun Biol.* 1 a droplet of fat in a living cell. 2 a microscopic spherical vesicle or sac, surrounded by a membrane, that is made artificially in a laboratory, and can be incorporated into living cells and used to study the transport of substances across membranes, or to deliver relatively toxic drugs to diseased cells, eg to treat cancer. [from Greek *lipos*, fat + *soma*, body]

liposuction *noun* a process for removing excess fat from the body by sucking it out mechanically through an incision in the skin. [from Greek *lipos*, fat]

lipped *adj., said especially of a container* having a lip.

Lippi, Filippino (c.1458–1504) Italian painter, born in Prato, near Florence. He completed (c.1484) the frescoes in the Brancacci Chapel in the Carmine, Florence, left unfinished by Masaccio. His easel pictures include *The Vision of St Bernard* (c.1480).

Lippi, Fra Filippo, also called **Lippo** (c.1406–69) Italian religious painter, born in Florence. He became a Carmelite monk but later abducted, and was eventually allowed to marry, a nun, Lucrezia, who was the model for many of his Madonnas. His major work includes a series of frescoes on the choir walls of Prato cathedral, begun in 1452. His later works are deeply religious and include a series of *Nativities*.

Lippmann, Walter (1899–1974) US journalist, born in New York City. He joined the editorial staff of the *New York World* until 1931, then became a special writer for the *Herald Tribune*. His daily columns became internationally famous, and he won many awards, including the Pulitzer Prize for International Reporting (1962). He also wrote several books including *Public Opinion* (1922) and *The Cold War* (1947).

lip-read *verb intrans., said especially of a deaf person* to understand what a person is saying by watching the movement of the lips.

lip-reader *noun* a person who lip-reads or is lip-reading.

lip-reading *noun* the process by which a person lip-reads.

lip-service
— **pay lip-service to someone or something** to pretend to agree with (someone) or approve of (an idea, etc) without really doing so.

lipstick *noun* a stick of cosmetic colouring for the lips.

liquefaction *noun* the process of liquefying.

liquefy *verb trans., intrans.* (**liquefies, liquefied**) to make or become liquid. [from Latin *liquere*, to be liquid + *facere*, to make]

liqueur *noun* any of several strong sweet heavily perfumed alcoholic drinks, drunk especially at the end of a meal. [from French *liqueur*, liquor]

liquid — *noun* 1 a substance in a water-like state. 2 *Phonetics* the sound of *l* or *r*. — *adj.* 1 *said of a substance* able to flow and change shape; in a state between solid and gas, like water. 2 like water in appearance, especially in being clear: *liquid blue eyes*. 3 flowing and smooth. 4 *said of sounds* harmonious. 5 *said of assets* able to be easily changed into cash. [from Latin *liquidus*, liquid, clear]

liquidate *verb* 1 to bring the trading of (a person or company) to an end, and have its debts and assets calculated. 2 to turn (assets) into cash. 3 to pay off (a debt). 4 *slang* to get rid of by violence; to kill. [from Latin *liquidare*, to make clear]

liquidation *noun* 1 the bringing to an end of a company's trading. 2 *slang* killing.
— **go into liquidation** *said of a company, etc* to stop trading and have its debts and assets calculated.
◇ The liquidation or winding-up of a company is the process by which it ceases to trade and its property is distributed to its creditors and members. Liquidation may be compulsory if a company is trading insolvently or may be initiated by its members who pass a resolution to close it down.

liquidator *noun* an official called in to wind up a company's trading.

liquid crystal *Chem.* a chemical compound that flows like a liquid but resembles solid crystalline substances in its optical properties, because large clusters of its molecules retain some order in their arrangement.

liquid crystal display *Electron.* (ABBREV. **LCD**) a display unit with a very low power consumption and requiring an external light source, used in digital watches, calculators, laptop computers, etc.
◇ A liquid crystal display consists of a group of segments from which individual numerical or alphabetical characters can be formed, each segment being composed of a liquid crystal solution sandwiched between two transparent electrodes. When an electric field is applied across the electrodes individual segments are selectively darkened, forming the shapes of different characters.

liquidize *or* **liquidise** *verb* to make (food, etc) into a liquid or purée.

liquidizer *or* **liquidiser** *noun* a machine used in cookery to liquidize food.

liquor *noun* 1 strong alcoholic, especially distilled, drink. 2 water or liquid produced in cooking. 3 a solution of a drug or chemical in water. [from Latin *liquor*, from *liquere*, to be liquid]

liquorice *noun* 1 a Mediterranean plant with sweet roots used in medicine and confectionery. 2 a black sticky sweet made from the juice of the roots of this plant. [from Greek *glykys*, sweet + *rhiza*, root]

liquorice plant

lira *noun* (PL. **lire, liras**) the standard unit of currency in Italy and Turkey. [from Italian *lira*, from Latin *libra*, pound]

lira organizzata an 18c musical instrument, a development of the medieval hurdy-gurdy incorporating a set or sets of organ pipes. Haydn wrote several concertos for the instrument in the 1780s. It was also known by the French name *vielle organizée*.

Lisbon, Portuguese **Lisboa**, ancient **Olisipo Felicitas Julia** POP (1991) 1.9m, 1 the seaport capital of Portugal and of Lisbon district, lying on the N bank of the R Tagus in the W of the country. It is the largest Portuguese city. HISTORY settled during the time of the Roman Empire; occupied by Moors in the 8c; became Portuguese capital in 1256; reached its peak of prosperity in the 16c; devastated by an earthquake in 1755; the Chiado shopping district of the old town was destroyed by fire in 1988. NOTABLE FEATURES 16c Tower of Belém, built to protect the Restelo harbour from which many of the voyages of discovery set out; Jerônimos Monastery, a World Heritage site; Monument of the Discoveries (1960); cathedral (1344); Church of São Roque; São Jorge Castle; National Museum of Art; botanical garden. 2 a district in W Portugal with the city of Lisbon as its capital.

Lisdoonvarna POP (1991) 842, a spa town in Clare county, Munster, W Irish Republic, situated 37km/23mi NW of Ennis. It is Ireland's leading sulphur spring health centre. EVENTS Lisdoonvarna fair (Oct), with its famous mating game when shy bachelors go in search of a wife; three-day folk festival (Jul).

lisle *noun* (pronounced lile) fine smooth cotton thread used for making gloves, stockings, and underwear. [from *Lisle* (now Lille), a town in N France where it was first made]

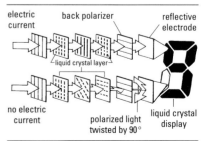

liquid crystal display

Lismahago, Obadiah the quarrelsome, colourful Scot who marries Tabitha Bramble in Tobias Smollett's *Humphry Clinker*.

LISP *noun Comput.* a high-level computer programming language, designed to manipulate complex lists of operations and data, and used mainly in artificial intelligence research. [a contraction of *list processing*]

lisp — *verb* **1** *intrans.* to pronounce *s* as *th* in *thin* and *z* as *th* in *this*, as a speech defect. **2** to say or pronounce in this way. — *noun* the act or habit of lisping. [from Anglo-Saxon *wlisp*, lisping]

lispingly *adv.* with a lisp.

lissom *or* **lissome** *adj.* graceful and supple in shape and movement. [from LITHE + -SOME]

list¹ — *noun* **1** a series of names, numbers, prices, etc written down or said one after the other: *shopping list*. **2** (**lists**) *Hist.* the barriers enclosing an area used for jousting and tournaments. **3** (**lists**) any scene of combat or conflict. — *verb* **1** to make a list of. **2** to add to a list.
— **enter the lists** to give or accept a challenge; to start or become involved in a fight or controversy.
[from Anglo-Saxon *liste*, border]

list² — *verb intrans.*, *said especially of ships* to lean over to one side. — *noun* the act of listing or a listing position.

listed building a building of particular architectural or historical interest, which may not be destroyed or changed.

listen — *verb intrans.* (**listened, listening**) **1** (*also* **listen out**) to give attention so as to hear something: *will you listen out for the milkman.* **2** to follow advice: *I warned him but he wouldn't listen.* — *noun* an act or period of listening.
— **listen in 1** to listen deliberately to a telephone conversation, radio message, etc intended for someone else. **2** to listen to a radio broadcast. [from Anglo-Saxon *hlysnan*]

listener *noun* a person who listens, especially to radio programmes.

Lister, Joseph, Lord (1827–1912) English surgeon, born in Upton, Essex. Professor in Glasgow, Edinburgh, and London, his greatest work was the introduction of the antiseptic system (1867), which revolutionized modern surgery.

listeria *noun* a bacterium sometimes found in certain foods, eg chicken and soft cheese, which if not killed in cooking may cause *listeriosis*, a serious disease which can cause death and miscarriage. [named after Joseph Lister]

listless *adj.* restlessly tired and lacking energy or interest. [from Middle English *listen*, to please]

listlessly *adv.* in a listless way; without energy or interest.

listlessness *noun* being listless; lack of energy or interest.

list price a price for an article recommended by the maker.

Liszt, Franz (1811–86) Hungarian composer and pianist, born in Raiding. He first played in public aged nine, then studied and played in Vienna and Paris, and toured widely in Europe as a virtuoso pianist. In the late 1830s he lived with the Comtesse d'Agoult, by whom he had three children (one, Cosima, married Richard Wagner), and in 1847 met Princess Carolyne zu Sayn-Wittgenstein with whom he lived until his death. In 1848 he went to Weimar, where he directed opera and concerts, composed, and taught, making it the musical centre of Germany. He later received minor orders in the Catholic Church (1865) and was known as Abbé. His works include 12 symphonic poems, masses, two symphonies, and a large number of piano pieces.

lit see LIGHT¹, LIGHT².

litany *noun* (PL. **litanies**) **1** a series of prayers or supplications with a response which is repeated several times by the congregation. **2** a long tedious list: *a litany of jobs to be done.* [from Greek *litaneia*, prayer]

litchi same as LYCHEE.

liter *North Amer., esp. US* same as LITRE.

literacy *noun* the ability to read and write.

literal — *adj.* **1** following the exact meaning of words or a text (ie without allegorical or metaphorical interpretation). **2** *said of a translation* exactly following the words of the original. **3** *said of a person* unimaginative and matter-of-fact. **4** true; exact: *the literal truth.* — *noun Printing* a misprint of one letter. [from Latin *literalis*, from *litera*, letter]

literalism *noun* strict adherence to the literal meaning of words.

literalist *noun* an advocate of literalism.

literally *adv.* **1** in a literal interpretation of the words. **2** as an intensifying word in figurative contexts: *they literally flew down the road.*
◆ Sense 2 is often regarded as incorrect, but is the more common use.

literalness *noun* being literal; direct interpretation.

literary *adj.* **1** of, relating to, or concerned with literature or the writing of books. **2** *said of a person* knowing a great deal about literature. **3** *said of a word* formal; used in (especially older) literature. [from Latin *literarius*, from *litera*, letter]

literate *adj.* **1** able to read and write. **2** (*in combination*) competent and experienced in something specified: *computer-literate.* [from Latin *literatus*, from *litera*, letter]

literati *pl. noun* learned people; those who are knowledgeable about literature. [from Latin *literatus*, literate]

literature *noun* **1** written material of high quality, valued for its language and content, such as novels, poems and plays. **2** the whole body of written works of a particular country or period in time: *Elizabethan literature.* **3** the whole body of information published on a particular subject: *the literature on growing vegetables.* **4** the art or works produced by a writer. **5** *colloq.* any printed matter, especially advertising leaflets. [from Latin *literatura*, from *litera*, letter]

litharge *noun Chem.* lead monoxide, a bright yellow solid compound, insoluble in water, used in pigments and paints, and in the manufacture of glass and ceramics. [from Greek *lithargyros*, from *lithos*, stone + *argyros*, silver]

lithe *adj.* bending easily; supple and flexible. [from Anglo-Saxon *lithe*, gentle, soft]

lithely *adv.* supplely; flexibly.

litheness *noun* being supple or flexible.

lithification *noun Geol.* the process whereby an unconsolidated sediment is converted into solid rock, eg as a result of compaction, desiccation, or crystallization. [from Greek *lithos*, stone]

lithium *noun Chem.* (SYMBOL **Li**, ATOMIC NUMBER **3**) a soft silvery reactive metal, and the lightest of all solid chemical elements, used in batteries and certain alloys. Its compounds are used in lubricants, glass, ceramics, and drugs such as lithium carbonate for treating certain psychiatric disorders. [from Greek *lithos*, stone]

litho — *noun* (PL. **lithos**) **1** a lithograph. **2** lithography. — *adj.* lithographic. — *verb* (**lithoes, lithoed**) to lithograph.

lithograph — *noun* a picture or print made using lithography. — *verb* to print (images, etc) using lithography.

lithographer *noun* a person who makes lithographs.

lithographic *adj.* relating to or using lithography.

lithographically *adv.* by means of lithography.

lithography *noun* a method of printing using a stone or metal plate which has been treated so that the ink adheres only to the design or image to be printed. [from Greek *lithos*, stone + *graphein*, to write]
◇ The traditional method, invented by Aloys Senefelder in 1796, uses a porous limestone block on which the design or image is executed using a greasy crayon; the stone is then dampened and printing ink applied (which adheres to the greasy areas and is repelled by the areas of damp stone). The image is then printed directly on to paper. Most modern lithography is done with flexible metal plates of zinc or aluminium, although the principle remains the same.

lithosphere *noun Geol.* the rigid outer layer of the Earth, consisting of the crust and the solid outermost layer of the upper mantle, and extending to a depth of about 100km. It is composed of a wide range of different rock types. [from Greek *lithos*, stone + *sphaira*, sphere]

Lithuania, Lithuanian **Lietuva**, Russian **Litovskaya**, or **Litva** POP (1993e) 3.6m, a republic in NE Europe, bounded SW by Poland and W by the Baltic Sea. AREA 65 200sq km/25 167sq mi. CAPITAL Vilnius. CHIEF TOWNS Kaunas, Klaipeda, Šiauliai. TIME ZONE GMT +2. Most of the population are Lithuanian (80%) with a small minority of Russians (9%) and Poles (7%); Christianity is the chief religion. OFFICIAL LANGUAGE Lithuanian. CURRENCY the rouble. PHYSICAL DESCRIPTION glaciated plains cover much of the area; the chief river is the Neman. HISTORY united with Poland from 1385 to 1795; intensive russification led to revolts in 1905 and 1917; occupied by Germany in both World Wars; proclaimed a republic in 1918; annexed by the USSR in 1940; growth of nationalist movement in the 1980s led to declaration of independence in 1990. GOVERNMENT a Prime Minister is appointed by a President and approved by a 141-member parliament; the Prime Minister forms a cabinet. ECONOMY electronics; electrical engineering; computer hardware; instruments; machine tools; shipbuilding; synthetic fibres; fertilizers; plastics; food processing; oil refining; agricultural activity centres on cattle, pigs, and poultry.

Lithuania

Lithuanian — *noun* **1** a native or citizen of Lithuania. **2** the Baltic language of Lithuania. — *adj.* relating to Lithuania or its people or language.

litigant *noun* a person involved in a lawsuit.

litigate *verb* **1** *intrans.* to be involved in a lawsuit; to go to law. **2** to contest (a point, claim, etc) in a lawsuit. [from Latin *litigare*, from *lis*, lawsuit + *agere*, to do]

litigation *noun* action at law; legal contest.

litigious *adj.* **1** relating to litigation or lawsuits. **2** often taking legal action over arguments, problems, etc. **3** disputable in a court of law. [from Latin *litigium*, quarrel]

litigiously *adv.* **1** as regards litigation. **2** with frequent recourse to legal action.

litmus — *noun Chem.* a dye obtained from certain lichens, widely used as an indicator to distinguish between acid solutions, in which it turns red, and alkaline ones, in which it turns blue. It is used either in solution or as strips of absorbent paper (litmus paper). — *adj.* relating to this dye. [from Norse *litmosi*, dyeing-moss]

litmus paper paper treated with litmus, used to test liquids for acidity and alkalinity.

litmus test 1 a chemical test using litmus paper. **2** a definitive test or trial of something.

litotes *noun* (pronounced lie-tote-eez) understatement used for effect, as in *not a little angry* meaning *furious*. [from Greek *litotes*, simplicity]

litre *noun* (ABBREV. **l**) the basic unit of volume in the metric system, equal to 1dm³ (1 000 cm³) or 1.76 pints, and formerly defined as the volume of 1kg of distilled water at 4°C. [from Greek *litra*, pound]

litter — *noun* **1** a mess of paper, rubbish, etc in a public place. **2** a scattered or confused collection of objects. **3** straw, hay, etc used as bedding for animals. **4** a number of animals born to the same mother at the same time. **5** a framework consisting of a cloth stretched tight between two long poles, used to carry the sick or wounded. **6** a framework consisting of a couch covered by curtains, with poles on either side, for transporting a single passenger. — *verb* (**littered**, **littering**) **1** to make (a place) untidy by spreading litter or objects: *they seemed to have littered the room with books and sweet wrappings.* **2** *said of objects* to lie untidily around (a place): *books littered the room.* **3** *trans., intrans. said of animals* to give birth to (a number of young). **4** to give bedding litter to (animals). [from Old French *litiere*, from Latin *lectus*, bed]

litterbug *noun North Amer. colloq.* same as LITTER-LOUT.

litter-lout a person who drops litter in public places.

little — *adj.* (usually having connotations of affection or emotion not present in *small*) **1** small in size, extent, or amount. **2** young or younger: *a little girl / her little brother.* **3** small in importance; trivial; petty: *funny little ways.* **4** small-minded or mean: *he's a little liar.* — *noun* anything small in size, amount, or extent: *do a little to help out.* — *adv.* **1** (**a little**) to a small degree or extent: *run around a little to keep warm.* **2** not much or at all: *they little understood the implications.*
— **in a little** soon, shortly: *he'll be here in a little.*
little by little gradually or by degrees.
make little of something 1 to treat it as unimportant or trivial. **2** to understand only a little of it.
think little of something *or* **someone** to have a low opinion of them; to disapprove of them. [from Anglo-Saxon *lytel*]

Little Bighorn, Battle of the, also called **Custer's Last Stand** a famous battle (26 Jun 1876) between US cavalry under General Custer, and the Sioux and Cheyenne under Sitting Bull and Crazy Horse. It was precipitated by Custer's bloody dawn attack on a Cheyenne village at the Washita (1868), and the white invasion of the Black Hills, sacred to the Sioux. Custer's force was destroyed by the Native Americans.

Little Dorrit a novel by Charles Dickens (1855–7). It focuses primarily on the varying fortunes of Amy ('Little Dorrit'), the daughter of an inmate in a debtor's prison.

little end the smaller end of a main connecting rod in a car engine.

Little Entente a system of alliances between Czechoslovakia and Yugoslavia (1920), Czechoslovakia and Romania (1921), and Yugoslavia and Romania (1921), consolidated into a single treaty signed in Belgrade (1929). The alliances aimed to maintain post-1919 boundaries in central Europe, and to prevent a Habsburg restoration.

Little Lord Fauntleroy a children's novel by Frances Hodgson Burnett (1886). It describes

the life in America and England of young Cedric Errol, the heir to Dorincourt.

little people a fanciful name for fairies.

Little Rock POP (1990) 176 000, the capital of the state of Arkansas, USA, and the state's largest city. It is a port on the Arkansas R, in Pulaski County, central Arkansas, first settled in 1821. In 1957 Federal troops were sent to the city to enforce a 1954 ruling of the US Supreme Court against segregation in schools. NOTABLE FEATURES Territorial Restoration; old statehouse.

little slam *Cards, especially in Bridge* the winning of all but one trick, or the contract to do so.

Little Women a novel by Louisa May Alcott (1868–9). It describes the varying fortunes of the four March sisters as they grow to maturity.

Littlewood, Joan (Maud) (1914–) English theatre director, born in London. A pioneer in left-wing, popular theatre, she co-founded the Theatre Union (1935) in Manchester, which became the Theatre Workshop (1945). After she moved to the Theatre Royal Stratford East in 1953, her productions included *The Hostage* (1958) and *Oh What A Lovely War* (1963).

littoral — *adj.* on or near the shore of a sea or lake. — *noun* an area of land on a shore or coast. [from Latin *littoralis*, from *litus*, shore]

liturgical *adj.* relating to liturgy or public worship.

liturgically *adv.* as regards the liturgy or public worship: *a concept that is not liturgically sound.*

liturgy *noun* (PL. **liturgies**) **1** the standard form of service in a church. **2** the service of Holy Communion in the Eastern Orthodox Church. [from Greek *leitourgia*, public service]

Litvinov, Maxim Maximovich (1876–1951) Soviet diplomat, born in Bielostok, Russian Poland. He was Bolshevik Ambassador in London (1917–18), Deputy Commissar (1921) then Commissar (1930) for Foreign Affairs, Ambassador to the USA (1941), and Vice-Minister of Foreign Affairs (1942–6). He strongly advocated co-operation between the USSR and the West, and world disarmament.

Liupanshui *or* **Suicheng** POP (1990) 364 000, a city in Guizhou province, S China, situated W of Guiyang.

Liu Shaoqi *or* **Liu Shao-ch'i** (1898–1969) a leading figure in the Chinese communist revolution, born in Hunan. He was educated in the USSR, returned to China in 1922, and became a communist trade-union organizer. In 1939 he joined Mao Zedong (Mao Tse-tung) at Yanan, where he emerged as the chief party theorist on questions of organization. In 1943 he became Party Secretary, and succeeded Mao in 1959. After the Cultural Revolution (1966–76), the extreme left made Liu their principal target, and in 1968 he was stripped of all his posts and dismissed from the Party.

live¹ *verb usually intrans.* (pronounced *liv*) **1** to have life; to be alive. **2** to continue to be alive; to survive or to escape death. **3** (**live on**) to continue or last: *memories live on.* **4** (**live with something**) to continue to suffer from or be haunted by the memory of; to put up with: *will live with the mistake for the rest of his life.* **5** to have a home or dwelling: *we live in a small flat.* **6** to lead one's life in a certain way: *live well.* **7** (**live by** *or* **on** *or* **off**) to support one's life; to get a living: *live by farming / live on rice / live off the land.* **8** to pass or spend: *live a happy life in the country.* **9** to enjoy life passionately or to the full: *they really know how to live.* **10** *trans.* to express in one's life or live according to: *live a lie / live one's religion.*
— **live and let live** to be tolerant and expect toleration from others.
live something down to cause (a mistake, guilt, etc in one's past) to be forgotten by living a normal and blameless life: *a blunder he could never live down.*

live in to have one's home where one works. See also LIVE-IN.

live it up *colloq.* to fill one's life with excitement and pleasure, often excessively.

live together *said of an unmarried couple* to live as man and wife.

live up to someone to behave in a manner worthy of them: *could never live up to her parents' expectations.* [from Anglo-Saxon *lifian*, *libban*]

live² (pronounced like *hive*) — *adj.* **1** having life; not dead. **2** *said of a radio or television broadcast* heard or seen as the event takes place and not from a recording. **3** *said of a record, etc* recorded during a performance. **4** *said of a wire* connected to a source of electrical power. **5** *said of coal, etc* still glowing or burning. **6** *said of a bomb, etc* still capable of exploding. — *adv.* at, during, or as a live performance: *they had to perform live on stage.*

liveable *adj.* **1** *said of a house, etc* fit to live in. **2** *said of a person* friendly and easy to live with. **3** *said of life* worth living.

Live Aid two charity concerts organized by the rock musician Bob Geldof (1954–) in response to appeals for Ethiopian famine relief. In 1985 £48m was raised through the simultaneous staging of pop concerts in London and Philadelphia, and their transmission throughout the world.

lived-in *adj.* **1** *said of a room, etc* having a comfortable homely feeling. **2** *said of a face* showing a life's experiences by its expression.

live-in *adj.* **1** *said of a worker* living where one works. **2** *said of a sexual partner* living in the same house, etc as one's partner.

livelihood *noun* a means of living, especially of earning enough money for the basic requirements of life. [from Anglo-Saxon *liflad*, from *lif*, life + *lad*, course]

liveliness *noun* being lively or full of energy.

livelong *adj. poetic, said of the day or night* in all its pleasant or excessive length. [from Middle English *lief*, dear + *longe*, long]

lively *adj.* (**livelier**, **liveliest**) **1** active and full of life, energy, and high spirits. **2** brisk. **3** vivid, bright. [from Anglo-Saxon *liflic*]

liven *verb trans., intrans.* (**livened**, **livening**) (*usually* **liven up**) to make or become lively.

liver¹ *noun* a person who lives life in a specified way: *a fast liver.*

liver² — *noun* **1** in vertebrates, the largest gland in the body, a dark red flattened organ situated in the abdominal cavity just below the diaphragm. Its main function is to regulate the chemical composition of the blood. **2** this organ in certain animals used as food. — *adj.* dark reddish-brown in colour. [from Anglo-Saxon *lifer*]
◊ In human adults the liver weighs about 1.5 to 2kg, and it consists of four lobes, each composed of thousands of lobules (small collections of liver cells surrounded by tiny blood vessels). It receives two separate blood supplies, one of which transports oxygen to the liver and removes waste products. The other conveys blood directly from the intestine to the liver via the *hepatic portal vein*, which carries the dissolved products of the digestion of food. These substances are then processed by the liver. It converts excess glucose and other sugars, produced by the digestion of carbohydrates, into *glycogen*, a storage carbohydrate that functions as a food reserve. Surplus amino acids, produced by the digestion of proteins, are converted to *urea*, a nitrogenous waste product that is excreted via the kidneys.
The liver also secretes *bile*, a digestive fluid that accumulates in the gall bladder and passes down the bile duct to the intestine, where it helps to break down fats. The products of the digestion of fats are also processed in the liver, and surplus fats are sent to fat deposits in various parts of the body. The liver breaks down toxins (eg alcohol) in the blood by a process known as *detoxification*,

and its other functions include the removal of damaged red blood cells, the manufacture of vitamins A and D, the production of *prothrombin* and *fibrinogen* (both of which are needed for normal blood clotting), and the storage of iron.

liver fluke a leaf-like parasitic flatworm with a mouth-sucker on its cone-shaped front end. It has a complex life cycle, involving a snail as an intermediate host in which it reproduces asexually. Its final host is a vertebrate, often a sheep, and it can be a serious pest of domesticated animals.

liver fluke

liveried *adj.* wearing or covered in livery.

liverish *adj.* **1** *old use* suffering from a disordered liver. **2** easily annoyed or made angry.

Liverpool, Robert Banks Jenkinson, 2nd Earl of (1770–1828) English statesman and Tory Prime Minister (1812–27), born in London. He entered parliament in 1790, and was a member of the India Board (1793–6), Master of the Royal Mint (1799–1801), Foreign Secretary (1801–4), Home Secretary (1804–6, 1807–9), and Secretary for War and the Colonies (1809–12). As Prime Minister, he oversaw the final years of the Napoleonic Wars and the War of 1812–14 with the USA.

Liverpool POP (1992e) 479 000, a seaport in Merseyside, NW England. It lies on the right bank of the estuary of the R Mersey, 5km/3mi from the Irish Sea and 312km/194mi NW of London. The city is a major world trading centre and the UK's most important seaport for Atlantic trade. HISTORY founded in the 10c, it became a borough in 1207 and a city in 1880; port trade developed in the 16c–17c; Liverpool's importance was enhanced in the 18c by the slave trade and the Lancashire cotton industry. NOTABLE FEATURES Catholic cathedral, a modern design by Frederick Gibberd on an earlier Classical foundation by Edward Lutyens (consecrated in 1967), Anglican cathedral, designed by Giles Gilbert Scott (begun in 1904, completed in 1980); Royal Liver Building (landmark at Pier Head); St George's Hall; Albert Dock redevelopment; Maritime Museum; Tate in the North (1987); Walker Art Gallery; Merseyside Innovation Centre; Speke Hall; Beatles Museum (1984); Royal Liverpool Philharmonic Orchestra. EVENT Grand National steeplechase at Aintree (Apr).

Liverpudlian — *noun* a native or citizen of Liverpool. — *adj.* relating to Liverpool or its inhabitants.

liver sausage a sausage containing liver.

liverwort *noun Bot.* the common name for any plant belonging to the class Hepaticae, which consists of small spore-bearing bryophytes without a vascular system, closely related to mosses, and typically growing in moist shady conditions, eg on damp ground, rocks, or tree trunks. [from LIVER[2] + WORT]

liverworts

◇ Liverworts, like all bryophytes, show *alternation of generations*. A free-living *gametophyte* (which bears gametes) alternates with a *sporophyte* (which bears spores). In *thalloid* liverworts the gametophyte consists of a flattened green lobed or branched structure or *thallus* that grows very close to the ground. In *leafy* liverworts the gametophyte has slender creeping stems with many leaflike lobes. All liverworts have single-celled root-like structures or *rhizoids* that anchor the plant to the ground but do not absorb water. The sporophyte is usually parasitic on the thallus, and consists of a leafless stalk bearing a star-shaped capsule that contains spores. When mature, the spores are released and develop into new plants.

livery *noun* (PL. **liveries**) **1** a distinctive uniform worn by male servants belonging to a particular household or the members of a trade guild. **2** *literary* distinctive markings or outward appearance: *the trees in their autumn livery*. **3** the distinctive colours and decoration used to identify the buses, aircraft, etc operated by a particular company. **4** the feeding, care, stabling, and hiring out of horses for money. [from Old French *livree*, from Latin *liberare, to free*]

livery company any of several trade guilds in the City of London whose members formerly wore distinctive clothes.

liveryman *noun* a member of a livery company.

livery stable a place where people may keep their horses or where horses may be hired.

lives see LIFE.

livestock *noun* domesticated animals, especially sheep, cattle, horses, pigs, and poultry, that are kept for the production of meat, milk, wool, etc, or for breeding purposes.

liveware *noun* the users and controllers of a computer system; personnel as distinct from hardware or software.

live wire *colloq.* a person who is full of energy and enthusiasm.

Livia, later called **Julia Augusta** (58 BC–AD 29) the third wife of Augustus (39 BC– AD 14) and a key influence in the early days of the Roman Empire. The mother of Tiberius by her first husband, Tiberius Claudius Nero, she plotted to ensure his succession (she had no offspring from her marriage to Augustus). Augustus adopted her into his family on his death (AD 14) and she received the name Julia Augusta.

livid *adj.* **1** having the greyish colour of lead. **2** *said of a bruise* black and blue. **3** white or very pale. **4** *colloq.* extremely angry. [from Latin *lividus*, lead-coloured]

living — *adj.* **1** having life; alive. **2** currently in existence, use, or activity. **3** *said of a likeness* exact. — *noun* **1** livelihood or means of subsisting. **2** a manner of life: *riotous living*. **3** *Church of E.* a position as a vicar or rector which has an income or property attached to it. **4** (**the living**) people who are alive.

— **within living memory** within a period of time remembered by people who are still alive.

living-room *noun* a room in a house, etc for sitting and relaxing in.

Livingstone, David (1813–73) Scottish missionary and traveller, born in Low Blantyre, Lanarkshire. He trained as a physician in Glasgow, and was ordained in the London Missionary Society in 1840. He worked for several years in Bechuanaland (now Botswana), then travelled north (1852–6) and discovered L Ngami and the Victoria Falls. He led an expedition to the Zambezi (1858–63), and discovered L Shirwa and L Nyasa. In 1866 he returned to Africa to establish the sources of the Nile, but the river he encountered proved later to be the Congo. On his return after severe illness to Ujiji, he was found there in 1871 by Henry Morton Stanley,

sent to look for him by the *New York Herald*. He again set out to find the Nile, but died at Chitambo (now in Zambia).

Livingston POP (1981) 39 000, a town in West Lothian district, Lothian Region, E central Scotland. It is situated 21km/13mi W of Edinburgh and was designated a 'new town' in 1962. It is a centre for industrial research and development.

living stone a perennial plant of the genus *Lithops*, native to Southern Africa, and adapted to dry desert conditions. It consists of a single annual pair of succulent leaves, grossly swollen with water, and more or less fused together. The daisy-like flower appears between the leaves. Each species is associated with a particular kind of rock, which its leaves resemble in colour.

living wage a wage which can support a wage-earner and family.

Livorno see LEGHORN.

Livy, originally **Titus Livius** (c.59BC–AD17) Roman historian, born in Patavium (Padua). He went to Rome, and was admitted to the court of Augustus, but took no part in politics. His history of Rome, from its foundation to the death of Drusus (9BC), comprised 142 books, of which 35 have survived. The work was a great success during his lifetime, and was a major influence on subsequent historical writing.

lizard *noun* any of numerous small and very active reptiles belonging to the same order (Squamata) as snakes, but differing from them in having an outer ear opening, movable eyelids, much less flexible jaws, and four well-developed limbs. Most lizards live in warm climates, controlling their body temperature by basking in the sun, and then burrowing or lying in the shade. They include the iguanas, geckos, skinks, chameleons, monitor lizard, and Komodo dragon. [from Latin *lacerta*]

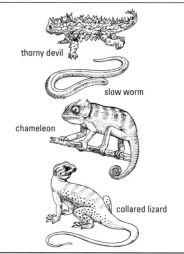

thorny devil

slow worm

chameleon

collared lizard

types of lizard

Lizard Point The southernmost point on the UK mainland, near Lizard Town, Cornwall, England.

Ljubljana, Italian **Lubiana**, ancient **Emona** POP (1991) 323 000, the capital of Slovenia, lying on the Sava and Ljubljanica rivers. It was founded in 34 BC. The city was badly damaged by an earthquake in 1895. NOTABLE FEATURES Tivoli Sports Park; National Museum; castle; cathedral; Ursuline Church.

ll *or* **ll.** *abbrev.* lines.

'll *contr.* (usually with a pronoun) shall; will: *I'll* / *they'll*.

llama *noun* a domesticated hoofed mammal of S America, related to the camel, and having a long shaggy white, brown, or black coat, a long neck, and large ears. It is used as a pack animal, as it is well adapted to working at high altitudes, and is also kept for its meat, milk, wool, and hide. [from Quechua *llama*]

llama

Llanfairpwllgwyngyll, in full **Llanfairpwllgwyngyllgogerychwyrndrobwllllantysiliogogogoch** a village in Anglesey district, Gwynedd, NW Wales, lying W of the Menai Bridge. It achieved fame through the extension of its name (to 58 letters) by a poetic cobbler in the 18c, probably to attract visitors. The first Women's Institute in Britain was founded here in 1915. NOTABLE FEATURES Marquis of Anglesey's Column (1816); Plas Newydd stately home nearby. [from Welsh, = St Mary's Church in the hollow of the white hazel near a rapid whirlpool and the Church of St Tysilio by the red cave]

Llangefni POP (1981) 4 600, a town in Anglesey district, Gwynedd, NW Wales, lying on the R Cefni. It is the administrative centre for Anglesey.

Llangollen POP (1981) 3 100, a town in Glyndŵr district, Clwyd, NE Wales. It lies on the R Dee, 15km/9mi SW of Wrexham. NOTABLE FEATURES St Collen's Church (14c); bridge (14c); Valle Crucis Abbey (c.1200) and Eliseg's Pillar (8c–9c cross) are nearby; Plâs Newydd, headquarters of the Welsh National Theatre since 1943. EVENT annual international *Eisteddfod* (since 1947).

Llano Estacado a vast semi-arid S portion of the Great Plains, in E New Mexico and W Texas, USA. It consists of flat, windswept grasslands broken by streams. The region was formerly devoted to cattle raising but there are now also natural gas and oilfields as well as irrigated farming. [from Spanish *llano estacado*, staked plain]

llanos the savannah grasslands of the plains and plateaux of the Orinoco region (Colombia, Venezuela), northern S America. Traditionally it was an important livestock farming area, and there have been recent schemes to re-establish cattle ranching following a decline in the early 20c.

LLB *abbrev.* Bachelor of Laws. [from Latin *legum baccalaureus*]

LLD *abbrev.* Doctor of Laws. [from Latin *legum doctor*]

Llewellyn, Richard, pseudonym of **Richard Dafydd Vivian Llewellyn Lloyd** (1907–83) Welsh writer, born in St David's, Pembrokeshire. After service with the regular army and a short spell as a film director, he became a best-selling novelist with *How Green was my Valley* (1939). His later works include *Up, into the Singing Mountain* (1963) and *I Stand On A Quiet Shore* (1982).

Llewelyn a male first name. [a Welsh name, = doubtful]

Lleyn Peninsula a peninsula in Dwyfor county, Gwynedd, NW Wales. It separates Cardigan Bay and Tremadog Bay in the S from

Caernarfon Bay in the N. CHIEF TOWNS Pwllheli, Porthmadog. ECONOMY agriculture; tourism.

Llosa, Mario Vargas see VARGAS LLOSA, MARIO.

Lloyd, Harold (1893–1971) US film comedian, born in Burchard, Nebraska. He started as a film extra in 1913, and subsequently made hundreds of short silent comedies, featuring as the unassuming 'nice guy' in horn-rimmed glasses and a straw hat. His few full-length features include *Safety Last* (1923) and *Welcome Danger* (1929).

Lloyd, Marie, originally **Matilda Alice Victoria Wood** (1870–1922) English music hall entertainer, born in London. She first appeared in 1885, and became a very popular music hall performer, with songs including 'Oh, Mr Porter' and 'My Old Man Said Follow the Van'.

Lloyd a male first name. [originally a Welsh nickname meaning 'grey(-haired)']

Lloyd-George (of Dwyfor), David Lloyd George, 1st Earl (1863–1945) British Liberal politician and Prime Minister, born in Manchester of Welsh parentage. In 1890, a strong supporter of Home Rule for Ireland, he became an MP for Caernarvon Boroughs (a seat he was to hold for 55 years). He was President of the Board of Trade (1905–8), and Chancellor of the Exchequer (1905–15). His 'people's budget' of 1909–10 was rejected by the House of Lords, and led to a constitutional crisis and the Parliament Act of 1911, which removed the Lords' power of veto. He became Minister of Munitions (1915), Secretary for War (1916), and superseded H H Asquith as coalition Prime Minister (1916–22). After World War I, he continued as head of a coalition government dominated by Conservatives. He negotiated with Sinn Féin, and conceded the Irish Free State (1921), a measure which brought his downfall. Following the 1931 general election, he led a group of Independent Liberal MPs.

Lloyd's an international association of insurance underwriters, based in London. It originated from 1688 in Edward Lloyd's coffee house in the City of London. Anyone wishing to insure a ship or its cargo would seek out individuals willing to 'underwrite the risk' – or pay for any losses sustained to the items insured. It became a private club, and in 1871 the Lloyd's Act was passed, setting a legal framework on its activities. All kinds of insurance are now handled worldwide, with some three-quarters of all business from outside the UK. The members (underwriters, or 'Names') of Lloyd's are organized into syndicates, and risks are spread among the members of the syndicate. There is, however, no limit to a member's liability. In 1994, Lloyd's faced legal action after its Names rejected a £900 million out-of-court settlement designed to compensate them for record losses suffered by them in recent years. *Lloyd's List* and *Lloyd's Shipping Index* provide daily information on shipping matters.

Lloyd's Register of Shipping a publication which catalogues information about the construction and characteristics of individual vessels, to help insurance underwriters. Known as the Underwriters' Register, or 'Green Book', it was first published in 1760, but has been published by a separate organization from Lloyd's since 1834. 'A1 at Lloyd's' refers to the top grade of the classification made by the Register, indicating that the vessel is in first-class order.

Lloyd Webber, Sir Andrew (1948–) English composer, born in London. In 1965 he met Tim Rice, with whom he wrote a 'pop oratorio' *Joseph and the Amazing Technicolour Dreamcoat* (1968) which was extended and staged in 1973. Their greatest success was the 'rock opera' *Jesus Christ Superstar* (staged 1971, filmed 1973). His later musicals include *Evita* (1978), *Cats* (1981), *Starlight Express* (1983), *The Phantom of the Opera* (1986), and *Aspects of Love* (1989). His brother Julian (1951–) is a cellist.

Llull *or* **Lull Ramón**, English **Raymond Lully**, also called **the Enlightened Doctor** (c.1232–1315) Spanish theologian and mystic, born in Palma, Majorca. He served as a soldier and led a dissolute life, but from 1266 turned to asceticism, became a Franciscan, and went on a spiritual crusade to convert the Muslims. His major work, the *Ars Magna* (The Great Art), was condemned in 1376 for its attempt to link faith and reason, but later was viewed more sympathetically. He travelled widely, and was allegedly killed on missionary work in Bugia (Bougie), Algeria. His followers, known as Lullists, combined religious mysticism with alchemy.

Llullaillaco, Cerro a snow-capped extinct volcano on the Chile–Argentina border. HEIGHT 6 723m. It is situated 300km/190mi W of Salta (Argentina).

Llywelyn the name of two Welsh princes. Llywelyn ap Iorwerth or Llywelyn the Great (d.1240) successfully maintained his independence against King John and Henry III, and gained recognition of Welsh rights in the Magna Carta (1215). Llywelyn ap Gruffydd (d.1282) helped the English barons against Henry III, and opposed Edward I, who forced his submission. On his death Wales lost her political independence.

lo *interj. old use* look, see.
— **lo and behold** an expression indicating surprise, etc at something unexpected.
[from Anglo-Saxon *la*]

loach *noun* a slender-bodied freshwater fish found in rivers and lakes throughout Europe and Asia, usually less than 10cm in length. It is a popular aquarium fish. [from French *loche*]

load — *noun* **1** something that is carried; a burden. **2** something that is or can be carried at one time: *a coach-load of children*. **3** (**loads**) *colloq.* a large amount: *loads of money*. **4** work, duties, feelings, etc which are oppressive and heavy to bear. **5** an amount or number of things to be dealt with at one time, especially of clothes to be washed. **6** the power carried by an electric circuit. **7** the power produced by an engine. — *verb* **1** to put (a load of something) on or in (a ship, vehicle, washing-machine, etc). **2** *intrans.* (**load up**) to take or pick up a load. **3** to be a weight on or burden to; to oppress. **4** (**load someone with something**) to give something lavishly or in great amounts to someone. **5** to put (film, audio or video tape, etc) into a (camera, tape or video recorder, etc). **6** *Comput.* **a** to put (a disk, computer tape, etc) into a drive, so that it may be used. **b** to transfer (a program or data) to a main memory, so that it may be used. **7** to put (ammunition) into a gun. **8** to give weight or bias to (dice, a roulette wheel, etc).
— **get a load of something** *slang* to pay attention to, listen to, or look at it.
load the dice against someone to deprive someone of a fair chance.
[from Anglo-Saxon *lad*, course, journey]

loaded *adj.* **1** carrying a load; with a load in place. **2** *said of a gun* containing bullets. **3** *said of a camera* containing film. **4** *said of a person colloq.* having much money; rich. **5** *said of a question* intended to elicit a particular response by the way it is phrased or by an implicit assumption contained in it.
◆ An example of a loaded question is the type *Have you given up cheating yet?*, to which a direct answer either way has to admit to former cheating.

loader *noun* (*in combination*) a gun or machine, etc loaded in a specified way: *front-loader*.

loadstar same as LODESTAR.

loadstone same as LODESTONE.

loaf¹ *noun* (PL. **loaves**) **1** a mass of bread for baking or when baked. **2** a quantity of food formed into a regular shape, eg meat or sugar. **3** *slang* the head or brains: *use one's loaf*. [from Anglo-Saxon *hlaf*]

loaf² *verb* **1** *intrans.* (**loaf about** *or* **around**) to pass time or stand about idly. **2** *trans.* (**loaf away**) to spend or pass idly: *loaf away one's life.*

loafer *noun* **1** a person who loafs about. **2** a light casual shoe like a moccasin.

loam *noun* a dark fertile easily worked soil consisting of sand, silt, small amounts of clay, and humus. [from Anglo-Saxon *lam*]

loamy *adj.* (**loamier**, **loamiest**) containing much loam.

loan — *noun* **1** anything lent, especially money lent at interest. **2** the act of lending or state of being lent. — *verb* to lend (especially money). — **on loan** given as a loan. [from Norse *lan*]

loan shark *colloq.* a person who lends money at exorbitant rates of interest.

loanword *noun* a word taken into one language from another.
◇ Examples of loanwords in English are: (from French) *blasé, café,* and *gauche,* (from German) *echt* and *leitmotif,* and (from Russian) *glasnost* and *sputnik.* Usually loanwords retain the form (in some cases transliterated from another alphabet) of the original language; sometimes they also retain their original cultural associations.

loath *adj.* unwilling; reluctant: *were loath to admit it.*
— **nothing loath** willing or willingly. [from Anglo-Saxon *lath*, hated]

loathe *verb* to feel intense dislike or disgust for. [from Anglo-Saxon *lathian*, to hate]

loathing *noun* intense dislike or disgust.

loathsome *adj.* causing intense dislike or disgust.

loaves see LOAF¹.

lob — *noun* **1** *Tennis* a ball hit in a high overhead path. **2** *Cricket* a slow high underhand ball. — *verb trans.* (**lobbed**, **lobbing**) to hit or throw (a ball) in this way. [from Anglo-Saxon *lobbe*, spider]

Lobachevski, Nikolai Ivanovich (1793–1856) Russian mathematician, born in Makariev. He was educated at Kazan, where he became Professor of Mathematics (1816) and Rector (1827). In 1829 he published the first geometry on non-Euclidean principles, but the significance of his work was not appreciated until after his death.

lobar *adj.* relating to or affecting a lobe, especially in the lungs.

lobate *adj.* having lobes.

lobby — *noun* (PL. **lobbies**) **1** a small entrance-hall, passage, or waiting-room from which several rooms open. **2** *Brit.* either of two corridors in the House of Commons which members pass into when they vote. **3** *Brit.* a hall in the House of Commons where members of the public may meet politicians. **4** a group of people who try to influence the government, politicians, etc in favour of a particular cause. — *verb* (**lobbies**, **lobbied**) to try to influence (the government, politicians, etc) in favour of a particular cause. [from Latin *lobia*]

lobbying *noun* *Politics* the process by which attempts are made to influence elected representatives through personal contacts in the 'lobbies' of legislative buildings. Originating in the USA, the practice is now universal in all liberal democracies, with many special-interest groups employing professional lobbyists.

lobbyist *noun* a person employed to lobby politicians, etc on behalf of a particular cause.

lobe *noun* **1** the soft, broad, lower part of the ear. **2** a division of an organ or gland in the body, especially the lungs or brain. **3** a broad, usually rounded division or projection of a larger object. [from Greek *lobos*]

lobed *adj.* having a lobe or lobes.

lobelia *noun* a garden plant with red, white, purple, blue, or yellow flowers. [from Matthias de *Lobel* (1538–1616), Flemish botanist]

lobotomy *noun* (PL. **lobotomies**) *Medicine* the surgical operation of cutting into a lobe of an organ or gland, especially the front lobes in the brain to cure certain mental disorders. [from Greek *lobos*, lobe + *tomia*, cutting]

lobster *noun* **1** any of various large crustaceans belonging to the order Decapoda, and typically having four pairs of walking legs, and a pair of large claws or pincers that reach out in front and are used for capturing prey. **2** the flesh of this animal used as food. [from Anglo-Saxon *loppestre*]
◇ Lobsters are found mainly around rocky shores in N coastal waters. They hide among rocks and emerge at night to feed on crabs, small fish, molluscs, and even other lobsters. They can escape from predators by shedding a limb that is being held, and they can also dart rapidly backwards to avoid attack. The hard outer shell or exoskeleton, which is bluish-black in colour, is moulted at intervals to allow growth. When cooked the shell turns bright red.

lobster pot a basket for catching lobsters.

local — *adj.* **1** of or belonging to a particular place. **2** of or belonging to one's home area or neighbourhood. **3** *said of a train or bus* stopping at all the stations or stops in a neighbourhood or small area. **4** *Medicine* affecting or confined to a small area or part: *a local anaesthetic.* — *noun* **1** a person living in a particular area. **2** one's nearest and most regularly visited public house. **3** a local bus or train. **4** an anaesthetic affecting only a particular part of the body. [from Latin *localis*, from *locus*, place]

local authority the elected local government body in an area.

local colour details in a story, etc which are characteristic of the time or place in which it is set.

locale *noun* the scene of some event or occurrence. [from French *local*, local]

local education authority (**LEA**) a regional government organization responsible for education in its area. In the UK, this is usually a city, county, or regional council, and comprises elected members (local politicians), and professional officers, responsible for the day-to-day running of the education system in their area.

local government government of town or county affairs by a locally elected authority, as distinct from national or central government.

Local Group *Astron.* the name of the group of about 30 galaxies to which our own Galaxy, the Milky Way, belongs.

locality *noun* (PL. **localities**) **1** a district or neighbourhood. **2** the scene of an event. **3** the position of a thing. [from Latin *localitas*, from *locus*, place]

localization *or* **localisation** *noun* the act of process of localizing.

localize *or* **localise** *verb* **1** to restrict to a place or area. **2** to mark with the characteristics of a particular place.

localized *or* **localised** *adj.* restricted to or characterized by a particular place.

locally *adv.* within or in terms of a particular area or the people living in it: *important issues to be decided locally.*

Locarno Pact an international agreement (Oct 1925) held in Locarno, Italy, that guaranteed post-1919 frontiers between France, Belgium, and Germany, and the demilitarization of the Rhineland. The treaty was guaranteed by Britain and Italy and signed by the three states concerned — France, Germany, and Belgium. Germany also agreed to arbitration conventions with France, Belgium, Poland, and Czecho-slovakia, and France signed treaties of mutual guarantee with Poland and Czechoslovakia.

locate *verb* **1** to set in a particular place or position. **2** to find the exact position of. **3** to establish in its proper place or position. **4** to describe or state the position of (something). **5** *intrans. North Amer.* to establish oneself in business or residence in an area. [from Latin *locare*, from *locus*, place]

location *noun* **1** a position or situation. **2** the act of locating or process of being located. **3** an authentic place or natural setting for making a film or broadcast, as distinct from an artificial setting in a studio: *made on location in Spain.* **4** *South Afr.* any of the townships or other areas where black or coloured people were obliged to live. **5** *Comput.* a position in a memory which can hold a unit of information.

loc. cit. *abbrev.* for *loco citato* (Latin), in the passage just quoted.

loch *noun* *Scot.* **1** a lake. **2** (*also* **sea loch**) a long narrow arm of the sea surrounded by land on three sides. [from Gaelic *loch*]

Lochinvar the gallant hero of a ballad in Canto V of Sir Walter Scott's *Marmion*, who carries off his beloved Ellen in dramatic fashion.

loci see LOCUS.

lock¹ — *noun* **1** a mechanical device that provides security by fastening a door, lid, machine, item of movable property, etc. Most locks consist of a cylinder containing a sliding bolt that is moved by turning a key, dial, or some other device. **2** an enclosed section of a canal or river in which the water level can be raised or lowered by means of gates, enabling boats to move from a higher section of the waterway to a lower one, or vice versa. **3** a state of being jammed or locked together, and completely immovable. **4** the part of a gun which explodes the charge. **5** *Wrestling* a tight hold which prevents one's opponent from moving. **6** the full amount by which the front wheels of a vehicle will turn. **7** (*in full* **lock forward**) a Rugby player in the second row of a scrum. **8** an airlock. — *verb* **1** to fasten (a door, box, bag, etc) with a lock. **2** *intrans. said of a door, etc* to become locked or have the means of becoming locked. **3** to shut up or secure (a building) by locking all the doors and windows. **4** *trans., intrans.* to jam or cause to jam. **5** *trans., intrans.* to fasten or cause to be fastened so as to prevent movement. **6** to hold closely in an embrace or tussle.
— **lock someone in** to prevent them from leaving a building or room by locking the doors while they are inside.
lock someone out 1 to prevent them from entering a building or room by locking the doors while they are outside. **2** to prevent employees from entering a factory, etc during industrial action.
lock, stock, and barrel completely; the whole thing.
lock up to lock all the doors and windows of a building, especially when leaving it empty or unoccupied.
lock someone up to confine them or prevent them from leaving by locking them in somewhere; to put them in prison.
lock something up to lock a building, etc securely.
under lock and key securely locked up; in prison. [from Anglo-Saxon *loc*]

lock² *noun* **1** a section or curl of hair. **2** (**locks**) hair. [from Anglo-Saxon *locc*]

lockable *adj., said especially of a room or building* able to be locked.

Locke, John (1632–1704) English empiricist philosopher, born in Wrington, Somerset. In his major work, the *Essay Concerning Human Understanding* (1690), he accepts the existence of God, but denies the idea of innateness, maintaining that at birth the mind is a blank, and that 'all knowledge is founded on and ultimately derives itself from sense...or sensation'. His two treatises *On Government* (1689) were also influential, and his sanctioning of rebellion was an inspiration for both American and French revolutionaries.

locker *noun* a small lockable cupboard for personal, temporary use, eg for sports equipment.

Lockerbie a town in the Scottish Borders, the scene of Britain's worst air disaster, when a Pan Am Boeing 747 flying from Frankfurt to New York via London crashed (21 Dec 1988). There were no survivors, and the death toll of 270 included townspeople killed by falling debris which demolished houses. Terrorists associated with Libya, Syria, or Iran have been alleged at various times to be the perpetrators, but no one has yet been brought to trial.

locket *noun* a small ornamented case for holding a personal photograph or memento, worn on a chain round the neck. [from Old French *loquet*, latch]

Lockhart, John Gibson (1794–1854) Scottish biographer and critic, born near Wishaw, Lanarkshire. He was called to the Scottish Bar in 1816, but turned increasingly to writing and journalism. He became one of the main contributors to *Blackwood's Magazine*, wrote four novels and several biographies, notably his life of Sir Walter Scott, and was editor of the *Quarterly Review* (1825–53).

Lockit the crooked jailer in John Gay's *The Beggar's Opera*. His daughter Lucy is seduced by Capt MacHeath.

lockjaw *noun* 1 tetanus. 2 difficulty in opening the mouth caused by spasm of the jaw muscles. It may be a symptom of tetanus, or associated with hysteria or dental disease.

lockout *noun* the exclusion of employees by the management from their place of work during an industrial dispute, as a means of imposing certain conditions. See also LOCK OUT.

locksmith *noun* a person who makes and mends locks.

lockup *noun* 1 a cell for locking up prisoners. 2 *Brit.* a small shop with no living quarters attached. 3 the action or time of locking up a building, etc. 4 (*attributive*) *Brit.* denoting a building, etc that can be locked up: *a lockup garage*.

Lockyer, Sir (Joseph) Norman (1836–1920) English astronomer, born in Rugby. In studies of the Sun he designed a spectroscope for observing prominences (1868), and in the same year detected an unknown element which he named helium (the 'Sun element'), not found on Earth until 1895. He was also the founder (1869) and first editor of the scientific periodical *Nature*.

loco[1] *noun* (PL. **locos**) *colloq.* a locomotive.

loco[2] *adj. slang* crazy; mad. [from Spanish *loco* insane]

locomotion *noun* the process or capacity of moving from one place to another. [from Latin *locus*, place + *motio*, motion]

locomotive — *noun* a railway engine for pulling trains. — *adj.* relating to or causing locomotion.

locomotory or **locomotor** *adj.* relating to or involving locomotion.

locum *noun* (*in full* **locum tenens**) a person who temporarily takes the place of someone else, especially a doctor or dentist. [from Latin *locus*, place + *tenere*, to hold]

locus *noun* (PL. **loci**) 1 an exact place or location. 2 *Maths.* the set of points or values that satisfy an equation or a particular set of conditions. 3 *Biol.* the position of a particular gene on a chromosome. [from Latin *locus*, place]

locust *noun* 1 any of various large grasshoppers belonging to the same family (Acrididae) as ordinary grasshoppers, but distinguished from them by their tendency to form dense swarms and migrate, eating all the vegetation in their path and causing extensive destruction of crops. 2 (*in full* **locust tree**) an alternative name for the carob (*Ceratonia siliqua*), an evergreen tree native to the Mediterranean region. See CAROB. 3 (*in full* **locust bean**) a carob pod. [from Latin *locusta*, lobster, locust]

◇ There are several species of locust in the warmer parts of the world. The migratory locust (*Locusta migratoria*) ranges from S Europe to Japan and Australia, although major plagues of the insect seem to occur only in West Africa. The most destructive species is the desert locust (*Schistocerca gregaria*), which inhabits dry regions from West Africa to India.

For long periods locusts are solitary like grasshoppers, but from time to time they congregate in particularly favourable areas, perhaps attracted by a plentiful food supply. Once they become crowded, their behaviour changes and they form dense swarms. Eggs are laid, and the resulting *nymphs* (called hoppers) group together in thousands and move across the land, eating almost all the vegetation in their path, and developing into adults that differ slightly in shape and colour from solitary locusts. This phase may last for several generations, during which time swarms of more than 100 million insects cover vast areas, blackening the sky as they fly. Eventually the swarms decline and the locusts return to the solitary phase.

locution *noun* 1 a style of speech. 2 a word, phrase, or sentence. [from Latin *locutio*, from *loqui*, to speak]

lode *noun* a thin band or strip of rock containing metallic ore. [from Anglo-Saxon *lad*, course, journey]

lodestar *noun* 1 a star used as a guide by sailors and astronomers, especially the Pole Star. 2 any guide or guiding principle.

lodestone or **loadstone** *noun* 1 (FORMULA Fe₃O₄) a black naturally occurring variety of the mineral magnetite (iron oxide), which has strong magnetic properties. Small pieces of this material will point towards the Earth's magnetic poles if allowed to rotate freely. 2 an elongated piece of this material used as a magnet. 3 any person or thing that attracts.

Lodge, David (1935–) English novelist and critic, born in Dulwich, Greater London. From 1976 to 1987 he was Professor of Modern English Literature at the University of Birmingham. His best-known novels include *Changing Places* (1975) and its sequel, *Small World* (1984), both of which are set in the academic world, and *Nice Work* (1988, adapted for television 1989), which has an industrial setting. *Paradise News* (1991) moves the scene to Honolulu. He has also written several works of literary criticism, including *The Novelist at the Crossroads* (1971).

Lodge, Henry Cabot (1850–1924) US Republican Senator, historian, and biographer, born in Boston, Massachusetts. He was assistant editor of the *North American Review*, but from 1878 his career was mainly political. A Senator from 1893, he led the opposition to the Treaty of Versailles (1919) and prevented the USA joining the League of Nations (1920).

Lodge, Thomas (c.1558–1625) English dramatist, romance writer, and poet, born in London. His best-known work is the pastoral romance, *Rosalynde* (1590), which was the source of Shakespeare's *As You Like It*.

lodge — *noun* 1 a small house at the gate to the grounds of a large house. 2 a small house in the country for sportsmen: *a hunting-lodge*. 3 a porter's room in a university or college. 4 the meeting-place of a local branch of some societies, or the members of this branch. 5 a beaver's nest, made of sticks that are usually plastered with mud, and having an underwater entrance. In winter the roof freezes and becomes sufficiently hard to deter predators. — *verb* 1 *intrans.* to live

in rented accommodation, especially in someone else's home and usually temporarily. 2 to provide with rented, usually temporary accommodation, especially in one's home. 3 to bring (a charge or accusation) against someone; to make (a complaint) officially. 4 (**lodge something in** or **with someone**) to deposit money or valuables for safety with them. 5 *trans., intrans.* to become or cause to become firmly fixed. 6 (**be lodged in** or **with someone**) *said of power, authority, etc* to be attributed to them. [from Old French *loge*, shelter]

lodger *noun* a person who rents accommodation in someone else's home, often temporarily.

lodging *noun* 1 (*usually* **lodgings**) a room or rooms rented in someone else's home. 2 temporary accommodation.

Łódź POP (1992e) 847 000, 1 the industrial capital of Łódź voivodship, central Poland, and the second largest city in the country. It received its charter in AD 500, but owes its development from 1820 to the textile industry. NOTABLE FEATURES Museum of Art; Archaeological and Ethnographical Museum; Central Textile Industry Museum; film studios; botanical gardens. 2 a voivodship in central Poland with Łódź as its capital.

loess *noun Geol.* a loose fine-grained highly fertile soil consisting of particles of quartz, feldspar, hornblende, mica, and clay, thought to have been deposited by the wind during the Pleistocene period. [from Swiss German *lösch*, loose]

Loess Plateau, Chinese **Huangtu Gaoyuan** a plateau in N central China. AREA 400 000sq km/154 000sq mi. It lies at an altitude of 800–2 000m and is covered with a layer of wind-blown loamy deposit (*loess*), generally 100m deep, but much deeper in places. The plateau has suffered serious soil erosion. Trees and grass have been planted to help conserve soil and water.

Loewe, Frederick (1904–88) US composer, born in Berlin. He went to the USA in 1924, and worked as a composer on a number of Broadway musicals. Those he wrote in collaboration with Alan Jay Lerner (1918–86), including *Brigadoon* (1947) and *My Fair Lady* (1956), were particularly successful, as also was his film score for *Gigi* (1958).

Lofoten Islands a mountainous island group in the Norwegian Sea, off the NW coast of Norway, separated from the mainland by Vest Fjord. AREA 1 425sq km/550sq mi. The islands are administered by Nordland county. There are major fishing grounds nearby. ECONOMY fish processing.

loft — *noun* 1 a room or space under a roof. 2 a gallery in a church or hall. 3 a room used for storage, especially one over a stable for storing hay. 4 a loft in a house used for keeping pigeons in. 5 a backward slope on the head of a golfclub. 6 a stroke that causes a golfball to rise up high. — *verb* to strike, kick, or throw (a ball, etc) high up in the air. [from Anglo-Saxon, from Norse *lopt*, sky, upper room]

loftily *adv.* imposingly; proudly, haughtily.

loftiness *noun* 1 great height. 2 haughtiness.

lofty *adj.* (**loftier, loftiest**) 1 of great or imposing height. 2 of high or noble character: *lofty ideals*. 3 haughty or proud.

Lofty-Flinders Ranges, Mount the mountain ranges of SE South Australia state, Australia. They extend 800km/500mi N from Cape Jervis to the N end of L Torrens. The Flinders Ranges in the N include a national park and rise at St Mary Peak to 1 166m. The Mt Lofty Ranges in the S are comparatively low with Mt Lofty rising to 727m. NOTABLE FEATURES unusual basins (including Wilpena Pound) with multicoloured rock faces and wild flowers; numerous examples of Aboriginal art, some 10 000 years old. Copper, coal, and gold have been mined in the ranges, which form a popular tourist area.

log¹ — *noun* **1** part of a tree trunk or thick bare branch, especially when cut for firewood. **2** a detailed record of events occurring during the voyage of a ship or aircraft, etc. **3** a logbook. **4** a float attached by a line to a ship, used for measuring its speed. — *verb* (**logged**, **logging**) **1** to record (distances covered on a journey, events, etc) in a book or logbook. **2** to cut (trees, etc) into logs. **3** *intrans.* to cut logs.
— **log in** *or* **on** *Comput.* to gain access to a computer system by keying in an appropriate command.
log out *or* **off** *Comput.* to relinquish access to a computer system by keying in a closing command.
sleep like a log to sleep very soundly.
[from Middle English *logge*]

log² *noun colloq.* a logarithm.

Logan, Mount the highest mountain in Canada, and the second highest in N America. It is situated in the St Elias Mts, in SW Yukon Territory. HEIGHT 5 950m. It lies within Kluane National Park, to the N of the Seward Glacier.

loganberry *noun* (PL. **loganberries**) **1** a large dark red berry eaten as a fruit. **2** the plant which produces it, thought to be a cross between a raspberry and a blackberry. [from J H Logan (1841–1928), the American judge in whose garden it first grew]

logarithm *noun Maths.* the power to which a number *a* must be raised in order to give another number *b*. It is usually referred to as the logarithm to the base *a* of *b*, eg because $10^2 = 100$, the logarithm of 100 to the base 10 is 2 (written $\log_{10} 100 = 2$). [from Greek *logos*, ratio + *arithmos*, number]
◇ The logarithmic function is the inverse of the exponential, which means that numbers can be multiplied by adding their logarithms, and divided by subtracting their logarithms. Before the advent of electronic calculators and computers, such calculations were made using tables of logarithms and antilogarithms to convert numbers into logarithms, and vice versa. Logarithms to the base *e* are called *natural* or *Napierian* logarithms, denoted by ln *x* or $\log_e x$. Logarithms to the base 10 are called *common logarithms*, denoted by lg *x* or $\log_{10} x$.

logarithmic *adj.* in the nature of logarithms; relating to logarithms and their principles.

logarithmically *adv.* by or according to the principles of logarithms: *solved the problem logarithmically.*

logarithmic scale *Maths.* a scale of measurement that varies logarithmically with the quantity being measured, eg a scale in which an increase of one unit on the scale represents a tenfold increase in the quantity being measured. The decibel scale used to express noise level is a logarithmic scale.

logbook *noun* **1** a book containing an official record of the voyage of a ship, aircraft, etc including details of crew and any incidents which occur. **2** *Brit.* the registration documents of a motor vehicle.

loggerhead
— **at loggerheads** arguing or disagreeing fiercely.
[possibly from dialect *logger*, a block of wood for hobbling a horse + HEAD]

loggia *noun* a roofed gallery or arcade on the side of a building, open to the garden. [from Italian *loggia*, lodge]

logging *noun* the work of cutting trees and preparing timber.

logic *noun* **1** the science of reasoning. **2** correct or incorrect use of reasoning; the ability to reason soundly. **3** an individual, personal, or particular way of reasoning: *feminine logic.* **4** the convincing and compelling force of a thing; the inevitability

of a consequence of a thing: *the inescapable logic of events.* **5** *Electron., Comput.* the arrangement of circuit elements which allows specified arithmetical functions to be performed. [from Greek *logike techne*, logical art]

logical *adj.* **1** of or according to logic. **2** correctly reasoned or thought out. **3** able to reason correctly. **4** following reasonably or necessarily from facts or events.

-logical *or* **-logic** *combining form* forming adjectives corresponding to nouns in *-logy*: *archaeological / pathological.*

logicality *noun* the condition of being logical.

logically *adv.* according to the rules of logic; rationally.

logical positivism *Philos.* a philosophical movement, beginning with 'the Vienna Circle' in the 1920s, concerned with determining whether or not statements are meaningful. It rejected traditional philosophy insofar as it did not possess scientific rigour; metaphysical, ethical, and religious pronouncements were branded as meaningless because their truth or falsity was unverifiable.

logician *noun* a person who is skilled in or studies logic.

logistic *or* **logistical** *adj.* relating to or in terms of logistics.

logistically *adv.* in terms of logistics: *it is logistically impossible to arrive by ten o'clock.*

logistics *sing. or pl. noun* **1** the art of moving and supplying troops and military equipment. **2** the organizing of everything needed for any large-scale operation. [from French *logistique*, quartermaster's work, from *loger*, to lodge]

log jam 1 a jam caused by logs being floated down a river. **2** a complete stopping of movement or progress.

logo *noun* (PL. **logos**) a small design used as the symbol of an organization. [from *logotype*, from Greek *logos*, word]

logograph *or* **logogram** *noun* a symbol which represents a whole word or phrase (or, in some cases, parts of words), used in certain writing systems such as shorthand and scientific notation. Chinese (and its Japanese derivative script, *kanji*) now uses logographs which stand for whole words or syllables rather than referring directly to concepts or things (ideograms). [from Greek *logos*, word + *graphein*, to write]

Logroño, Latin *Juliobriga*, ancient **Varela** POP (1991) 121 000, the capital of Rioja region and of Logroño province, N Spain. It is a market town lying on the R Ebro, 336km/209mi N of Madrid, and is the centre of a wine-growing region. NOTABLE FEATURES Churches of St Bartholomew and St Mary.

-logy *or* **-ology** *combining form* forming words denoting: **1** a science or study: *geology.* **2** writing or speech: *trilogy.* [from Greek *logos*, word, reason]. See panel p. 752.

Lohengrin an opera by Richard Wagner (1848), based on the legend of the Knights of the Holy Grail. Set in 10c Antwerp, the story begins with Elsa of Brabant, who is accused of murdering her brother (revealed later to be the swan pulling Lohengrin's boat), but is defended by a mysterious knight. They marry, but he has to leave after she asks him to reveal his identity, which he has vowed never to do.

loin *noun* **1** (**loins**) the waist and lower back area, between the ribs and the hips. **2** (**loins**) *poetic* the genitals, especially when thought of as the source of life: *fruit of one's loins.* **3** a cut from the lower back area of an animal. [from Old French *loigne*]

loincloth *noun* a piece of material worn round the hips, especially as the only garment of primitive peoples.

Loire, River, ancient **Liger** the longest river in France, length 1 020km/634mi. Rising in the Massif Central, SE France, it flows N and NW to Orléans, then turns W past Blois, Tours, and

Nantes to empty into the Bay of Biscay by a wide estuary below St Nazaire. There is a canal link to the R Seine. The Loire Valley is known for its vineyards and its chateaus.

loiter *verb intrans.* (**loitered**, **loitering**) **1** to work slowly and idly. **2** to stand around or pass one's time doing nothing. [from Middle English *loteren*]

loiterer *noun* a person who loiters or is loitering.

Loki in Norse mythology, a mischievous god, originally a Giant, who was able to change his shape and sex. He played tricks on the gods until, after contriving the death of Balder, he was tied to a rock.

Lola a female first name. [from the Spanish name DOLORES]

Lolita a novel by Vladimir Nabokov (1958). It focuses on the relationship between Humbert Humbert, a psycopathic Swiss historian, and Lolita (Dolores Haze), an adolescent girl.

loll *verb intrans.* **1** (**loll about**) to lie or sit about lazily; to lounge or sprawl. **2** *said of the tongue* to hang down or out. [from Middle English *lollen*]

Lollards a derisive term applied to the followers of the English theologian John Wycliffe in the 14c. The movement, through which the Bible was translated into the vernacular, was suppressed, but it continued among the enthusiastic but less literate of society (who were generally anticlerical in attitude), and paved the way for the Reformation in England. [from Middle Dutch *lollaert*, mumbler]

lollipop *noun* a large round boiled sweet on a stick. [from dialect *lolly*, tongue + POP¹]

lollipop man *or* **lollipop lady** a man or woman whose job it is to see children safely across busy roads, recognized by carrying a pole with a circular sign on top.

lollop *verb intrans.* (**lolloped**, **lolloping**) *colloq.* to move about in a lively but ungainly manner. [possibly from LOLL]

lolly *noun* (PL. **lollies**) *colloq.* **1** a lollipop. **2** (*also* **ice lolly**) a frozen ice cream or flavoured water ice on a stick. **3** money. [from LOLLIPOP]

Loman, Willy the bemused, disillusioned travelling salesman suffering from delusions in Arthur Miller's *Death of a Salesman.* His understanding wife is Linda, and his sons are Biff and Happy.

Lombard League a coalition of N Italian cities, established (1167) to assert their independence as communes (city-republics) confronting the German emperor, Frederick I, 'Barbarossa'. The League set a model for inter-city alliances, and underlined the rising political importance of urban communities in the medieval West.

Lombards a Germanic people settled in Hungary who invaded N Italy in AD 568 under their king, Alboin. They founded a new capital at Milan, and in time controlled most of the peninsula except for the S and the area around Ravenna. Their kingdom was annexed by Charlemagne in 774, but the Lombard duchies (Benevento, Spoleto) survived as autonomous entities until the 11c. [from Latin *langobardus*, long beard]

Lombardy, Italian **Lombardia** POP (1991) 8.9m, a region in N Italy. AREA 23 833sq km/ 9 199sq mi. CAPITAL Milan. CHIEF TOWNS Brescia, Pavia, Varese. S Lombardy, in the plain of the R Po, is one of Italy's most highly developed industrial and agricultural regions. Tourism is important around the alpine lakes and in the mountains.

Lomé POP (1987e) 500 000, the capital of Togo. It is a seaport and an important market centre, noted for its marble, gold, and silver crafts.

Lomond, Loch the largest loch in Scotland, and the largest stretch of inland water in the UK.

-logies

This list is of words ending in -logy (often -ology) that denote areas of knowledge and study. Other words having the same form, eg apology and eulogy, are not included.

anthropology study of human societies and cultures Greek *anthropos* man
archaeology study of ancient civilizations Greek *archaiologia* ancient history
astrology study of planetary influences on human life Greek *astron* star
bacteriology study of bacteria Greek *bacterion* little stick
biology study of living things Greek *bios* life
campanology study of bells Latin *campana* bell
chronology study of historical dates Greek *chronos* time
climatology study of climates Greek *klima* latitude, region
cosmology study of the universe Greek *kosmos* universe
criminology study of crime and criminals Latin *crimen* crime
cytology study of plant and animal cells Greek *kytos* vessel
deltiology study of picture postcards Greek *deltion* writing-tablet
demonology study of demons Latin *daemon* evil spirit
dendrochronology study of dating from tree-rings Greek *dendron* tree, *chronos* time
dermatology study of the skin and skin diseases Greek *derma* skin
ecology study of living things in relation to their environment Greek *oikos* house
embryology study of embryos Greek *embryon* embryo
entomology study of insects Greek *entomon* insect
epistemology study and theory of human knowledge Greek *episteme* knowledge
escapology study of methods of escape Old French *escaper* escape
ethnology study of peoples and cultures Greek *ethnos* nation
etymology study of word origins and development Greek *etymos* true
gemmology study of gems Latin *gemma* bud
genealogy study of family history Greek *genea* race
geology study of the earth's structure Greek *ge* earth
gynaecology study of diseases relating to women Greek *gyne* woman
haematology study of blood and blood diseases Greek *haima* blood
histology study of plant and animal tissues Greek *histos* web
horology study of clocks and time-keeping Greek *hora* hour
ideology study of ideas Greek *idea* idea
immunology study of the immune system Latin *immunis* exempt from service

lexicology study of word meanings Greek *lexikon* dictionary
meteorology study of the earth's atmosphere and weather
microbiology study of micro-organisms Greek *mikros* little, *bios* life
mineralogy study of minerals French *miner* to mine
musicology study of music Latin *musica* music
mycology study of fungi Greek *myketes* mushroom
mythology study of myths Greek *mythos* myth
neurology study of the nervous system Greek *neuron* nerve
oenology study of wines Greek *oinos* wine
oncology study of tumours Greek *onkos* tumour
ontology study of the nature of being Greek *einai* to be
ophthalmology study of the eye Greek *ophthalmos* eye
ornithology study of birds Greek *ornis* bird
palaeontology study of fossils Greek *palaios* old, *einai* to be
parapsychology study of psychic phenomena Greek *para* beside, *psyche* soul
pathology study of human diseases Greek *pathos* suffering
petrology study of rocks Greek *petra* rock
pharmacology study of medicines and drugs Greek *pharmakon* drug
phonology study of speech sounds Greek *phone* sound, voice
physiology study of life processes Greek *physis* nature
psephology study of election results and trends Greek *psephos* pebble
psychology study of the human mind and behaviour Greek *psyche* soul
radiology study of radioactivity and radiation Latin *radius* spoke, ray
Sinology study of Chinese language and culture Greek *Sinai* Chinese
seismology study of earthquakes Greek *seismos* shaking
sexology study of human sexuality Latin *sexus* sex
sociology study of human society Latin *socius* companion
theology study of religions Greek *theos* god
toxicology study of poisons Greek *toxikon* poison for arrows
ufology study of UFOs
urology study of the urinary system Greek *ouron* urine
vinology study of (grape-)vines Old French *vine* vine
virology study of viruses Latin *virus* poison

It is situated 32km/20mi NW of Glasgow. AREA 70sq km/27sq mi; 34km/21mi long; narrow in the N, opening out to 8km/5mi at the S end; up to 190m deep. The outlet is the R Leven at the S end of the loch; in the NW is the Loch Sloy hydroelectric power scheme. Loch Lomond is a major tourist area.

London, Fritz Wolfgang (1900–54) German-born US physicist, born in Breslau (now Wrocław, Poland). In early work he developed the theory of the 'covalent' chemical bond. Forced to leave Germany in 1933 with his brother Heinz, he moved to Oxford, where they made important contributions to the theory of superconductivity. He later worked at Duke University in the USA (1939–54).

London, Jack, pseudonym of **John Griffith Chaney** (1876–1916) US novelist, born in San Francisco. He was successively sailor, tramp, and gold miner in the Klondyke Gold Rush before he took to writing. His best-known novels include *Call of the Wild* (1903), *Sea-Wolf* (1904), and *White Fang* (1906). Other works include the more serious political novel, *The Iron Heel* (1907), and an autobiographical tale of alcoholism, *John Barleycorn* (1913).

London, Latin **Londinium** (in the 4c, **Augusta**) POP (1992e) 6.9m (Greater London); (1987e) 4 700 (City of London), the capital of the UK and of England, lying on the R Thames in SE England. Greater London consists of 32 boroughs and the City of London; its area is 1 579sq km/609sq mi. HISTORY from the 1c until the 5c the site was a Roman town (founded c.43 AD), situated where the Thames narrowed to its lowest convenient crossing; sacked by Boadicea (c. AD 61); later surrounded by a defensive wall, fragments of which remain; developed as the leading trade and administrative centre of England; received charter privileges in 1067; mayoralty established in 1191; major building programmes in the Middle Ages, and then extension to the W, especially in the 16c; the Great Plague (1665) and the Great Fire (1666) were followed by major reconstruction; many squares were laid out in the 17c–18c; in the 17c London developed into a major trade centre and became one of the world's largest cities; during the Blitz of World War II there was severe damage especially to the City and East End, with much subsequent rebuilding. London was administered by London County Council from 1888 until 1963 and then by the Greater London Council until 1986; its functions then transferred to the boroughs and other bodies. The City Corporation, independent of the local authority administration in some respects, retains its ancient electoral system in which a great part is played by the livery companies, successors of the medieval trade guilds. It comprises the Lord Mayor, 24 Aldermen, and 132 Common Councilmen. The City of London, occupying the site of the old medieval city N of the Thames, is the financial and business centre, including the Bank of England, Stock Exchange, and Royal Exchange; the National Westminster Building (1977) is the tallest building in London (183m). The City of Westminster is the administrative and judicial centre, including the Houses of Parliament, Buckingham Palace, and government departments within its bounds. The West End is the main shopping and entertainment centre, around Oxford Street, Piccadilly, and Regent Street. Outer boroughs comprise mixed residential and industrial developments, and there is extensive dockland, much of it now being redeveloped. Major railway terminuses exist at Euston, King's Cross, Paddington, St Pancras, Victoria, and Waterloo; the extensive underground system, known as 'the Tube', is the oldest in the world; there are main airports at Heathrow and Gatwick, also at London City, Luton, and Stansted. The central bridges across the R Thames include Westminster (1750), Blackfriars (1769), Waterloo (1817), and Southwark (1819); there are markets at Billingsgate, Smithfield, and Nine Elms at Vauxhall (replacing Covent Garden, now a tourist centre); there are zoological gardens at Regent's Park. NOTABLE FEATURES London is a leading cultural centre, with many theatres, museums (British/London/Natural History/Science/ Victoria and Albert), galleries (National/ National Portrait/Tate Galleries, Courtauld Institute), concert halls (Albert/Queen Elizabeth/ Royal Festival/Wigmore Halls, Barbican Centre), churches and cathedrals (Saint Paul's/Westminster Cathedrals; Westminster Abbey and St Margaret's Church, a World Heritage site); BBC Symphony/London Philharmonic/London Symphony/Royal Philharmonic Orchestras; Royal Shakespeare Company/Opera House (Covent Garden)/Ballet (Sadler's Wells)/Academy of Music/College of Music/Guildhall/ Academy of Dramatic Art; it is a centre for radio, television, and the press; Central Criminal Court (Old Bailey); leading medical centre, with several major hospitals, and Harley Street (private practices); leading educational centre, with several constituent colleges of London University, and many other institutions; Madame Tussaud's; Planetarium; Battersea/Hyde/Regent's/St James's Parks; Kensington Gardens; Zoological Gardens at Regent's Park; Tower of London; Covent Garden. EVENTS Trooping of the Colour on the Queen's official birthday (Jun); procession to the Royal Courts of Justice (Lord Mayor's Show).

London Bridge a bridge over the R Thames linking Southwark with the City of London. Early wooden structures were replaced in the 12c by a 19-arch stone bridge bearing shops and houses. This was superseded in 1831 by a 5-arch bridge, which in 1968 was dismantled and sold to Lake Havasu City, Arizona, and replaced by a concrete structure (1973).

London Contemporary Dance Theatre a dance company founded in London in 1967 by the philanthropist Robin Howard, under the artistic direction (1967–83) of Robert Cohan, who created many works for it. Since the 1980s its repertoire has included popular works based on jazz steps and street dance.

Londonderry, also known as **Derry**, Gaelic **Doire** POP (1981) 135 000, a county of N Northern Ireland. AREA 2 067sq km/798sq mi. It is bounded N by Lough Foyle and the Atlantic Ocean, E by Co Antrim, SE by Lough Neagh, S and SW by Co Tyrone, and NW by the Republic of Ireland. PHYSICAL DESCRIPTION a hilly area, with part of the Sperrin Mts rising in the S; drained by the Bann, Roe, and Foyle rivers. CHIEF TOWNS Derry (county town), Coleraine, Portstewart. ECONOMY seed potatoes, flax, dairy produce; fishing; textiles; light engineering.

Londonderry, also known as **Derry** POP (1991) 72 000, the county town of Co Londonderry, NW Northern Ireland. It lies on a hill above the R Foyle, 8km/5mi above its mouth into Lough Foyle, and is 122km/76mi NW of Belfast. HISTORY a monastery was founded here by St Columba in c.546 and the Celtic settlement of Derry was built around it; James I proclaimed the city of Derry to be part of the Corporation of London in 1613; renamed London-Derry, and settled by a Protestant colony; it resisted a siege by James II for 105 days in 1689, during which time 7 000 inhabitants died. NOTABLE FEATURES old town walls and gates; St Columba's Cathedral (Protestant, 1628–33); St Columba's Church (Catholic, 1873); Guildhall (1912).

Londonderry Air an Irish folk tune by an anonymous composer, first recorded in a collection in 1855. Used in Stanford's First Irish Rhapsody, its associations now include the song 'Danny Boy' and various hymns (eg 'I cannot tell why He whom angels worship').

London Festival Ballet see ENGLISH NATIONAL BALLET.

London Group a society of British artists founded in 1913 by Nash, Epstein, Fry, and others; its first President was Harold Gilman (1878–1919). It held regular exhibitions for half a century.

London Museum a museum at London Wall in the City of London, created from the former London and Guildhall museums and opened in 1975. It covers the history of London from prehistoric times to the present day.

London Palladium a variety theatre in Argyll Street, London, opened in 1910. The Royal Variety Show is usually staged here, in addition to many revues and musicals, including *Barnum* (1981).

London Philharmonic Orchestra (ABBREV. **LPA**) a English orchestra founded (1923) by Thomas Beecham.

London pride a plant of the saxifrage family with pink flowers.

London Symphony Orchestra (ABBREV. **LSO**) an English orchestra founded (1904) by musicians from Henry Wood's Queen's Hall Orchestra. Hans Richter was its first conductor (until 1911), and it enjoyed a long association with Elgar and his music.

London University a federation of colleges, medical schools, and research institutions established as a university in London in 1836. In addition to the medical schools of the London teaching hospitals, several major institutions form part of the university.

lone *adj.* 1 *said of a person* alone; without a companion. 2 *said of a place* isolated and unfrequented.

loneliness *noun* being lonely or solitary.

lonely *adj.* (**lonelier**, **loneliest**) 1 *said of a person* sad because without companions or friends. 2 solitary and without companionship: *a lonely existence*. 3 *said of a place* isolated and unfrequented.

lonely heart a lonely person, especially one who is seeking a loving relationship.

loner *noun* a person who prefers to be alone and who avoids close relationships.

lonesome *adj. North Amer.* 1 sad and lonely. 2 causing feelings of loneliness.

lone wolf a person who prefers to live or act alone.

long¹ — *adj.* 1 measuring a great distance from one end to the other in space or time. 2 measuring a specified amount in space or time: *six centimetres long*. 3 having a large number of items: *a long list*. 4 measuring more in space or time than the average or more than is expected or wanted. 5 greater in value, amount, etc than is usual or expected. 6 lasting for an extended period of time. 7 *said of a dress, trousers, curtains, etc* reaching down to or close to the ground, floor, etc; full-length. 8 *said of a cold drink* large and thirst-quenching. 9 *said of stocks* bought in large amounts in expectation of a rise in prices. 10 *Phonetics, said of a vowel or syllable* having the greater of two recognized lengths, such as the *a* in *bake* and the *i* in *pile*, as distinct from the short *a* in *back* and the short *i* in *pill*. 11 *said of betting odds* showing a low level of probability. — *adv.* 1 for, during, or by a long period of time: *long ago* / *long-lasting*. 2 throughout the whole time: *all night long*. — *noun* anything that is long, especially a long period of time, or a long vowel or syllable.

— **as long as** *or* **so long as** 1 provided that. 2 while; during the time that.

before long in the near future; soon.

in the long run in the end.

long on something *colloq.* having a lot of it: *not too long on brains*.

the long and the short of it the most important facts in a few words.

no longer not now as it was in the past.

so long *colloq.* goodbye.

[from Anglo-Saxon *lang*]

long² *verb intrans.* (**long for something** or **someone**) to want them intensely. [from Anglo-Saxon *langian*, to yearn after]

Long Beach POP (1990) 429 000, a city in Los Angeles County, SW California, USA. It lies on San Pedro Bay, 32km/20mi S of Los Angeles. After the discovery of oil in 1921, its industry developed rapidly. The city is a tourist centre. NOTABLE FEATURES a long bathing beach; British cruise liner *Queen Mary*, now a museum-hotel-convention centre; Long Beach Marine Stadium.

longboat *noun* the largest small boat carried by a ship.

longbow *noun* a large bow drawn by hand.

Longchamp a horse racecourse in the Bois de Boulogne, Paris, France.

Long Count calendar a calendar for recording historical events used by the Olmec and Maya of Mexico from the 1c BC to the 9c AD .

Long Day's Journey Into Night a play by Eugene O'Neill (1941, Pulitzer Prize). Probably his masterpiece, and closely based on

London University	
College	Founded
Royal Veterinary College	1791
Birkbeck College	1823
University College	1827
King's College, London	1831
(merged with Queen Elizabeth College and Chelsea College 1985)	
Goldsmiths' College	1904
London School of Economics and Political Science	1895
Imperial College of Science, Technology and Medicine	1907
School of Oriental and African Studies	1916
Royal Holloway and Bedford New College	1985
(founded through merger of Bedford College (1849) and Royal Holloway College (1886))	
Queen Mary and Westfield College	1989
(founded through merger of Queen Mary College (1887) and Westfield College (1882))	

O'Neill's early life, it is a realist study of the tragic Tyrone family: actor father James, drug-addict mother Mary, alcoholic son Jamie, and sickly son Edmund (who represents O'Neill).

long-distance *adj.* covering, travelling, operating, etc between or over long distances: *a long-distance runner* / *long-distance telephone calls*.

long division a division of numbers in which the working is shown in full.

long-drawn-out *adj.* taking a longer time than is normal or expected.

longevity *noun* great length of life. [from Latin *longus*, long + *aevum*, age]

long face a dismal or disappointed expression.

Longfellow, Henry Wadsworth (1807–82) US poet, born in Portland, Maine. He spent three years in Europe, and became Professor of Modern Languages and Literature at Harvard (1836–54). His works include *Voices of the Night* (1839), *Evangeline* (1847, a narrative poem on the French exiles of Acadia), and *The Song of Hiawatha* (1855).

Longford, Gaelic **Longphuirt** POP (1991) 30 000, a county in NW Leinster province, central Irish Republic. AREA 1 044sq km/403sq mi. PHYSICAL DESCRIPTION drained by the R Shannon and its tributaries; crossed by the Royal Canal; hilly in the NW. CAPITAL Longford. ECONOMY sheep, cattle; oats, potatoes.

Longford, Gaelic **Longphort** POP (1991) 7 000, the capital of Longford county, NW Leinster, central Irish Republic. It lies on the R Camlin and a branch of the Royal Canal. NOTABLE FEATURES St Mel's Cathedral; Tullynally Castle at Castlepollard.

longhand *noun* ordinary writing as opposed to shorthand.

long haul 1 the carrying of cargo or passengers over a long distance. 2 any work requiring great effort or considerable time.

longing *noun* an intense desire or yearning: *a longing for freedom*. — *adj.* having this feeling.

longingly *adv.* with intense desire or yearning: *looked longingly out of the window*.

Longinus, Dionysius (c.213–73 AD) Greek Neoplatonic rhetorician and philosopher. He taught rhetoric in Athens, settled in Palmyra, and became chief counsellor to Queen Zenobia, for which Emperor Aurelian beheaded him. He is the supposed author of the treatise on excellence in literature, *On the Sublime*, which influenced many neoclassical writers, including Dryden and Pope.

Long Island an island in SE New York State, USA, to the E of New York City. AREA 3 600sq km/1 400sq mi; length 190km/118mi. Bounded N by Long Island Sound, it is separated from the Bronx and Manhattan by the East R, and from Staten I by the Narrows. It is made up of four counties: Kings, Queens, Nassau, and Suffolk. Kings and Queens form part of New York City. There are many residential towns and resort beaches. HISTORY settled by the Dutch in 1623, and by the English in c.1640; site of the Battle of Long Island (1776) in the US War of Independence, when British forces under Howe defeated US forces under Washington. NOTABLE FEATURE John F Kennedy Airport.

longitude *noun* any of a series of imaginary circles that pass around the Earth through both poles, crossing circles of latitude at right angles. All points on the *prime meridian*, which passes through Greenwich, UK, have a longitude of 0°, and the distance E or W of this is divided into 180° of longitude. Longitude is used together with latitude to specify any position on the Earth's surface. See also LATITUDE. [from Latin *longus*, long]. See illustration p.754.

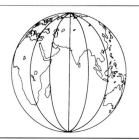

lines of longitude

longitudinal *adj.* **1** relating to longitude; measured by longitude. **2** lengthways.

longitudinally *adv.* as regards longitude; in terms of longitude.

longitudinal wave *Physics* a wave in which particles are displaced in the same direction as that in which the wave is being propagated, eg sound waves.

long johns *colloq.* long underpants.

long jump an athletics contest in which competitors jump as far as possible along the ground from a running start.

long-lived *adj.* having a long life.

Longman, Thomas (1699–1755) English publisher, born in Bristol. He bought a bookselling business in Paternoster Row in 1724, and shared in publishing such works as Ephraim Chambers's *Cyclopaedia* and Samuel Johnson's *Dictionary*. He was the founder of the British publishing house that bears his name.

Long March in China, the long trek (c.8 000km) made by 100 000 communists under Mao Zedong to reach their base in Shaanxi from the Jiangxi Soviet, which had been encircled by nationalist government troops. It began in Oct 1934 and lasted about a year.

Long Parliament an English parliament called (Nov 1640) by Charles I after his defeat by the Scots in the second of the Bishops' Wars. In being until 1660, though it did not meet continuously, it attacked prerogative rights and alleged abuses of power by the King and his ministers, and abolished the Court of Star Chamber, the Councils of the North and for Wales, and the Ecclesiastical Court of High Commission (1641), the bishops and the Court of Wards (1646), and the monarchy and the House of Lords (1649). Moderates were eliminated in Pride's Purge (Dec 1648), and the remaining Rump was dismissed by Cromwell (1653), but it was recalled in the death-throes of the Protectorate (May 1659), as were all members (Dec 1659).

long-playing *adj.*, *said of a gramophone record* with each side playing for 20 to 30 minutes.

long-range *adj.* **1** *said of a missile or vehicle* able to reach to remote or far-off targets or destinations. **2** *said of a weather forecast* covering a period of several weeks or more.

longship *noun Hist.* a long narrow Viking warship propelled by rowers.

longshore *adj.* found on or employed along the shore. [from the phrase *along shore*]

longshoreman *noun North Amer.* a person who loads and unloads ships at a sea-port.

long shot *colloq.* a guess, attempt, etc which is unlikely to be successful.

— **not by a long shot** not by any means.

long-sighted *adj.* **1** *said of a person* affected by hypermetropia, and only able to see distant objects clearly. **2** wise and prudent as to the future; far-sighted.

long-sightedness *noun* the condition of being long-sighted.

long-standing *adj.* having existed or continued for a long time.

long-suffering *adj.* patiently tolerating difficulties and hardship.

long-term *adj.*, *said of a plan, etc* occurring in or concerned with the future.

longtime *adj.* lasting for a long time; longstanding.

long wave a radio wave using wavelengths over 1000 metres.

longways *adv.*, *adj.* in the direction of a thing's length; lengthways.

long-winded *adj.*, *said of a speaker or speech* verbose and tedious.

long-windedly *adv.* in a long-winded way; verbosely.

long-windedness *noun* being long-winded or verbose.

Lonsdale, Dame Kathleen, née **Kathleen Yardley** (1903–71) Irish crystallographer, born in Newbridge, County Kildare. She worked at University College London (UCL), where she later became professor, and at the Royal Institution. Of her many contributions to crystallography, the most celebrated was her X-ray analysis in 1929 of hexamethylbenzene and hexachlorobenzene, which showed that the carbon atoms in a benzene ring are on the same plane and hexagonally arranged.

Lonsdale Belt in boxing, a championship belt awarded to a fighter who wins a British title fight, named after the 5th Earl of Lonsdale who presented the first belt to the National Sporting Club in 1909. If he wins three fights (not necessarily in succession) in one weight division, he is allowed to keep the belt permanently. The British heavyweight boxer Henry Cooper (1934–) won three Lonsdale Belts outright.

loo *noun Brit. colloq.* a lavatory. [of uncertain origin]

loofah *or* **loofa** *noun* the long thin dried inner part of a tropical gourd-like fruit, used as a sponge. [from Arabic *lufah*]

look — *verb usually intrans.* **1** (**look at**) to turn the eyes in a certain direction so as to see; to use one's sight. **2** (**look at** *or* **to something**) to consider, examine, or give attention to. **3** to seem to be or appear. **4** to face or be turned towards: *a window looking south.* **5** (**look for something**) to search for it. **6** (**look to someone**) to rely on or turn or refer to them: *we look to you for support.* **7** (**look into something**) to investigate it: *please look into the matter for him.* **8** *trans.* to direct one's sight towards in a particular way: *look her in the eyes.* **9** *trans.* to express by a look: *she was looking daggers at him.* **10** *trans.* to consider or realize: *just look where we are now!* — *noun* **1** an act of looking; a glance or view: *have a good look.* **2** the general appearance of a thing or person. **3** (**looks**) beauty; attractiveness. — *interj.* used to call for attention or to express protest.

— **look after someone or something** to attend to or take care of them.

look ahead to consider what will happen in the future.

look down on *or* **look down one's nose at someone** to consider them as not good enough or not as good as oneself.

look forward to something to wait for something or anticipate it with pleasure.

look here! used to call for attention or to express protest.

look in on someone to visit them briefly and often uninvited.

look on to watch without taking part.

look on someone *or* **something** to think of or consider in a certain way: *you should look on me as a friend.*

look oneself to appear one's normal healthy self: *he doesn't look quite himself yet, does he?*

look out to keep watch and be careful.

look something out to find it by searching: *looked out all her old clothes.* See also LOOKOUT.

look something over to check it cursorily.

look sharp *colloq.* to act quickly.

look up to show signs of improving: *the weather's looking up at last.*

look someone up *colloq.* to visit them.

look something up to search for an item of information in a reference book.

look up to someone to respect their behaviour, opinions, etc.

never look back to continue to make progress or prosper.

[from Anglo-Saxon *locian*]

lookalike *noun* a person who looks very much like someone else; a double.

look and say, a method of teaching reading through the recognition of whole words, rather than 'sounding' their constituent parts, as used in the phonics approach. The aim of look-and-say is to facilitate the reading of longer sentences and more complex words using frequently-occurring words such as *go, to, see, my, the,* etc, as links between the more difficult words (for which a pictorial or visual 'clue' is given). Those who advocate this method maintain that it is less rigid and more stimulating for young children. See also PHONICS.

Look Back in Anger a play by John Osborne (1956). The 'hero', Jimmy Porter, is the prototype 'Angry Young Man', who echoes the author's uncompromising hatred of outworn social and political institutions and attitudes.

looker *noun colloq.* an attractive person.

looker-on a person who looks on.

look-in *noun* **1** a chance of joining in, being included, or doing something: *never get a look-in.* **2** a short visit.

looking-glass *noun old use* a mirror.

lookout *noun* **1** a careful watch. **2** a place from which such a watch can be kept. **3** a person set to watch, eg on board ship. **4** *colloq.* a personal concern or problem: *that's your lookout.* **5** prospect or outlook: *a dim lookout.*

look-see *noun colloq.* a brief look around or inspection.

loom[1] *noun* a machine for weaving thread into fabric. [from Anglo-Saxon *loma*, tool]

loom[2] *verb intrans.* **1** (**loom up**) to appear indistinctly and usually in some enlarged or threatening form. **2** *said of an event* to be imminent, especially in some menacing or threatening way.

loon *noun North Amer.* a diving bird with a slender body and sharp beak; a diver. [from Norse *lomr*]

loony *slang* — *noun* (PL. **loonies**) a mad person; a lunatic. — *adj.* (**loonier, looniest**) crazy; mad. [a shortening of LUNATIC]

loony-bin *noun slang* a mental home or hospital.

loop — *noun* **1** an oval-shaped coil in a piece of rope, chain, etc, formed as it crosses over itself. **2** any similar oval-shaped or U-shaped bend, eg in a river. **3** a manoeuvre in which an aircraft describes a complete vertical circle in the sky. **4** a strip of magnetic tape or film forming a loop, allowing the sound or images on it to be continually repeated. **5** *Electron.* a closed ciruit which a signal can pass round. **6** *Comput.* a sequence of instructions in a program that are repeated all the time a given condition exists. **7** a branch of a railway, telegraph line, etc that leaves the main line and then rejoins it. **8** a contraceptive coil. — *verb trans.* **1** to fasten with or enclose in a loop. **2** to form into a loop or loops.

— **loop the loop** *said of an aircraft, etc* to make a loop in the sky.

[from Middle English *loupe*, loop of cloth]

loophole *noun* a means, usually based on a legal weakness or oversight, of avoiding obeying a rule or law or fulfilling a contract, without formally breaking it. [from Middle English *loop*, window + HOLE: it was originally a narrow slit in a wall for shooting arrows through and for letting in light, without undue risk from opponents' weapons]

loopy *adj.* (**loopier, loopiest**) *slang* mad; crazy.

loose — *adj.* **1** not or no longer tied or held in confinement; free. **2** not tight or close-fitting. **3** not held together; not fastened or firmly fixed in place; not packeted. **4** not tightly-packed or compact: *loose soil.* **5** vague or inexact: *a loose translation.* **6** immoral or promiscuous. **7** indiscreet: *loose talk.* **8** *Sport, said of a ball, etc* in play but not under a player's control. — *noun Rugby* the part of play where the players are not in scrums or close together round the ball. — *verb* **1** to release or set free. **2** to unfasten or untie. **3** to make less tight, compact, or dense. **4** to relax: *loose one's hold.* **5** to discharge (a gun, bullet, arrow, etc). — **at a loose end** having nothing to do. **on the loose** free from confinement or control. [from Norse *lauss*]

loose box a part of a stable or horse-box where horses are kept untied.

loose change coins kept in one's pocket or bag, for small expenses.

loose-leaf *adj., said of a folder, binder, etc* having clips or rings which open to allow pages to be removed and inserted.

loosely *adv.* **1** in a loose manner. **2** roughly; approximately; without precision.

loosen *verb trans., intrans.* (**loosened, loosening**) **1** to make or become loose or looser. **2** (**loosen up**) to make or become less tense, rigid, or stiff.

looseness *noun* being loose (often in the sense 'immoral'); freedom from restraint.

Loot a play by Joe Orton (1965). It is an outrageous black farce on the theme of corruption, involving a comic detective, huge amounts of money, and a corpse, which was originally considered a scandalous prop to use for comic effect.

loot — *noun* **1** stolen goods, especially those stolen from an enemy in wartime. **2** *colloq.* money. — *verb* **1** to steal (money or goods) or to steal them from (someone, especially an enemy in wartime, or some place). **2** *intrans.* to rob and plunder. [from Hindi *lut*]

looter *noun* a person who loots or is looting.

looting *noun* the activity of people who loot; stealing from an enemy.

lop[1] *verb* (**lopped, lopping**) **1** (**lop off**) to cut off, especially the branches of a tree. **2** (**lop something off** *or* **away**) to cut away unnecessary or superfluous parts of something. [from Middle English *loppe*, parts cut off]

lop[2] *verb intrans.* (**lopped, lopping**) to hang down loosely.

lope — *verb intrans.* to run with long bounding steps. — *noun* a bounding leap. [from Norse *hlaupa*]

lop-eared *adj., said of animals* having ears that droop.

lopsided *adj.* **1** with one side smaller, lower, or lighter than the other. **2** leaning over to one side; unbalanced.

loquacious *adj. formal* highly talkative. [from Latin *loquax*, from *loqui*, to speak]

loquaciously *adv. formal* in a loquacious or talkative way.

loquacity *or* **loquaciousness** *noun formal* talkativeness.

Lorca, Federico García (1899–1936) Spanish poet and playwright, born in Fuente Vaqueros. His gypsy songs *Canciones* (1927) and *Romancero Gitano* (1928 abd 1935) reveal a classical control of imagery, rhythm, and emotion. He also wrote the successful trilogy of folk tragedies: *Bodas de Sangre* (Blood Wedding, 1933), *Yerma* (1934), and *La Casa de Bernarda Alba* (The House of Bernarda Alba, 1936). He was killed early in the Spanish Civil War.

lord — *noun* **1** a master or ruler. **2** *Hist.* a feudal superior. **3** *Brit.* a male member of the nobility. **4** (**Lord**) a title used to address some noblemen, eg earls, viscounts, the younger sons of dukes. **5** (**Lord** *or* **Our Lord**) God or Christ. — *interj.* (**Lord**) an expression of surprise or dismay. — **live like a lord** to live in luxury.
lord it over someone *colloq.* to behave in a haughty and domineering manner. [from Anglo-Saxon *hlaford*, from *hlaf*, bread + *weard*, guardian]

Lord Chamberlain in the UK, the chief official of the royal household, who oversees all aspects of its management, and bears responsibility for matters ranging from the care of works of art to the appointment of royal tradesmen. This office is not the same as that of Lord Great Chamberlain, whose duties are largely ceremonial (eg he presents the sovereign to the people at coronations).

Lord Chancellor *or* **Lord High Chancellor** in the UK, a high officer of state whose office combines the judicial, executive, and legislative functions of government. The Lord Chancellor is head of the judiciary, advises the Crown on senior appointments, appoints magistrates, and is also a government Minister and Speaker of the House of Lords.

Lord Chief Justice in England and Wales, and (separately) in Northern Ireland, the head of the Queen's Bench Division of the High Court; also the President of the Criminal Division of the Court of Appeal.

Lord High Chancellor see LORD CHANCELLOR.

Lord Howe Island POP (1989e) 320, an Australian volcanic island in the Pacific Ocean, 702km/436mi NE of Sydney. AREA 17sq km/6sq mi. It was discovered in 1788 and now forms part of New South Wales. Mt Gower is the highest point at 866m. The island is a popular resort area and a World Heritage site.

Lord Jim a novel by Joseph Conrad (1900). It describes the ill-fated life of sailor Jim as he tries to redeem himself for an early mistake.

Lord Lieutenant in the UK, the sovereign's permanent representative in a county or county borough of England, Wales, or Northern Ireland, and in several parts of each of the Scottish regions. The office is now primarily one of honour.

lordliness *noun* being lordly or haughty.

lordly *adj.* (**lordlier, lordliest**) having the attributes popularly associated with lords, especially in being grand or haughty.

Lord Lyon King of Arms in Scotland, the person who presides over the Court of the Lord Lyon, which is the Scottish Court of Chivalry, with a similar function to the College of Arms in England. It establishes pedigrees, rights to existing arms, and the succession of clan or family chiefship.

Lord Mayor the title of the mayor in the City of London and some other cities.

Lord of the Flies a novel by William Golding (1954). It describes the descent into savagery of a party of schoolboys after they are stranded on a desert island.

Lord of the Rings, The a trilogy of novels by J R R Tolkien (1954–5). It describes the fantastic adventures of the hobbit Frodo as he reluctantly sets out to save the world from evil.

Lord Privy Seal a senior British cabinet minister without official duties.

Lord Provost the title of the mayor of certain Scottish cities.

Lords a cricket ground in London, England, the home of Middlesex Cricket Club, and the headquarters of cricket's governing body, the Marylebone Cricket Club (MCC). It was originally developed in Dorset Square in 1787 by Thomas Lord (1757–1832), and was moved to its present site in St John's Wood in 1814.

Lords, House of the non-elected house of the UK legislature. Its membership (currently c.1 200) includes hereditary peers and life peers (including judicial members–the *Lords of Appeal in Ordinary*); also the two archbishops and certain bishops of the Church of England. The House, whose powers were limited in 1911 and 1949, can no longer veto bills passed by the House of Commons, with the exception of a bill to prolong the duration of a parliament. It constitutes the most senior court in the UK, and hears appeals on matters of law.

lords-and-ladies, a perennial plant (*Arum maculatum*), widespread in Europe, with large leaves shaped like arrow-heads, often with dark blotches. A pale green spathe partially surrounds a club-shaped reddish-purple *spadix*, which becomes warm to the touch as a result of the breakdown of starch within it just before pollination. At that time it emits a fetid odour which attracts pollinating insects, and it subsequently develops into a spike of poisonous orange-red berries. — Also called *cuckoo pint*.

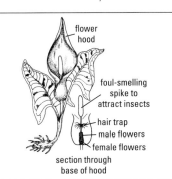

flower hood
foul-smelling spike to attract insects
hair trap
male flowers
female flowers
section through base of hood

lords-and-ladies

Lord's Day (the Lord's Day) Sunday, regarded as a day of Christian worship.

Lordship *noun* (**His** *or* **Your Lordship**) a title used to address bishops, judges, and all peers except for dukes.

Lord's Prayer, also known as the *Pater Noster* (**Our Father**) a popular prayer of Christian worship, derived from Matthew 6.9–13 and (in different form) Luke 11.2–4, where Jesus taught his followers how to pray. In Matthew, it consists of three petitions praising God and seeking his kingdom, followed by four petitions concerning the physical and spiritual needs of people. The closing doxology ('For thine is the kingdom ...') was apparently added later in Church tradition.

lords spiritual the archbishops and bishops in the House of Lords.

Lord's Supper (the Lord's Supper) *Christianity* the Eucharist.

lords temporal the members of the House of Lords who are not archbishops or bishops.

lore *noun* the whole body of knowledge, especially traditional knowledge, on a subject. [from Anglo-Saxon *lar*]

Lorelei the name of a precipitous rock in the Rhine near St Goar, Germany, dangerous to boatmen and celebrated for its echo. The story of the siren of the rock whose songs lure sailors to their death dates only from 1800.

Loren, Sophia, originally **Sofia Scicolone** (1934–) Italian film actress, born in Rome and brought up in poverty near Naples. As a film extra she became the protégée of the producer Carlo Ponti, who later married her. Through him she gained the lead in *The Pride and the Passion* (1957) and other US productions. She won an Oscar for her performance in De Sica's *La Ciociara* (Two Women, 1961) and in *Sophia, Her Own Story* (1981) she played the part of her mother as well as herself.

Lorentz, Hendrik Antoon (1853–1928) Dutch physicist, born in Arnhem. He was professor at Leiden from 1878, and later Director of the Teyler's Institute in Haarlem. With his electron theory, which proposed that atoms contain small particles with either a positive or negative charge, he formulated a new theory of light. In 1904 he derived a mathematical transformation, the 'Fitzgerald–Lorentz contraction', which prepared the way for Einstein's theories of relativity. He shared the 1902 Nobel Prize for Physics with Pieter Zeeman.

Lorenz, Konrad Zacharias (1903–89) Austrian zoologist, born in Vienna. A founder of ethology, he advocated the observation of animal behaviour under natural conditions rather than in the laboratory. He was the first to describe 'imprinting'. He shared the 1973 Nobel Prize for Physiology or Medicine with Nikolaas Tinbergen and Karl von Frisch.

Lorenzo a Christian character in Shakespeare's *The Merchant of Venice*, who elopes with Jessica and marries her.

lorgnette *noun* eyeglasses or opera-glasses held on a long handle. [from French *lorgnette*, from *lorgner*, to peer at]

loris *noun* a primitive primate, native to forests in S Asia, and having a pale face with dark rings around its eyes, and no tail. [from French *loris*, possibly from Dutch]

Lorna a female first name, first appearing as the heroine of R D Blackmore's novel *Lorna Doone* (1869).

Lorna Doone a novel by R D Blackmore (1869). It is set in Exmoor during the 17c and focuses on the lives of Lorna Doone, a kidnapped heiress, and John Ridd, a young farmer.

Lorraine, German **Lothringen** POP (1991e) 2.3m, a region and former province in NE France, comprising the departments of Meurthe-et-Moselle, Meuse, Moselle, and Vosges. AREA 23 547sq km/9 089sq mi. It is bordered by the Plaine de Champagne to the W, the Vosges to the E, the Ardennes to the N, and Monts Faucilles to the S. HISTORY a frequent source of French–German conflict; it was a duchy in the 10c, and became part of France in 1766; ceded to Germany as part of Alsace-Lorraine in 1871; returned to France after World War I. CAPITAL Metz. CHIEF TOWNS Nancy, Luneville, Epinal. ECONOMY corn; fruit; cheese; iron ore, coal; salt; mineral springs.

Lorraine a female first name, after the surname and French regional name.

Lorraine, Cross of a cross with two horizontal crosspieces. The symbol of Joan of Arc, it was adopted by the free French forces leader (Charles de Gaulle) in 1940.

Lorris, Guillaume de (c.1200–?) French poet, born in Lorris-en-Gatinais. He wrote the first 4 000 lines of the allegorical *Roman de la Rose* (c.1235, Romance of the Rose) which was continued by Jean de Meung.

lorry *noun* (PL. **lorries**) *Brit.* a large heavily built road vehicle for transporting heavy loads.

Lorsch, Abbey and Altenmünster of the ruins of a medieval abbey in Lorsch, central Germany. It is a World Heritage site.

Los Alamos POP (1980) 11 000, a community in Los Alamos County, N New Mexico, USA. It is situated in the Jemez Mts, 56km/35mi NW of Santa Fe. Since 1943 it has been a nuclear research centre; during World War II the first nuclear weapons were developed here. Government control of the site ended in 1962.

Los Angeles, originally **Nuestra Señora Reina de Los Angeles** POP (1990) 8.9m, the seaport capital of Los Angeles County, California, USA. It is the third largest US city and has absorbed several towns, villages, and independent cities. The city is a major cultural, artistic, and financial centre. It is also an important industrial area and there is a high density of road traffic, leading to the serious problem of smog developing. HISTORY founded by the Spanish in 1781; captured from Mexico by the US Navy in 1846; it was incorporated as a town in 1850, and grew after the arrival of the Southern Pacific Railroad and the discovery of oil nearby in 1894; racial tension resulted in serious rioting in 1992; the city suffered earthquake damage in 1994. NOTABLE FEATURES the glamorous district of Hollywood is a major centre of the US film and television industry; Los Angeles County Museum of Art; 28-storey City Hall; Old Mission Church (c.1818), now a museum; La Brea Tar Pits; Hollywood Bowl; Hollywood Wax Museum; Universal Film Studios; Disneyland.

lose *verb* (PAST TENSE AND PAST PARTICIPLE **lost**) **1** to stop having; to fail to keep or obtain, especially in error or through carelessness. **2** to suffer the loss of or be bereaved of (especially a parent or unborn baby) through death. **3** to leave accidentally or be unable to find: *lose one's way*. **4** to fail to use or get; to miss: *lose a good opportunity*. **5** *trans., intrans.* to fail to win (a game, battle, etc). **6** to fail or cease to hear, see, or understand: *lost the thread of his argument*. **7** to waste (time, money, etc); to use to no purpose. **8** to escape or get away from. **9** to prevent the gaining or achieving of. **10** *trans., intrans. said of a clock or watch* to become slow (by a specified amount). **11** *intrans.* to be in a worse position or suffer as the result of something. **12** to cause to disappear or die.
— **lose oneself in something** to have all one's attention taken up by an activity.
lose out *colloq.* **1** to suffer loss or be at a disadvantage. **2** to fail to get something one wants.
lose out on something *colloq.* to be at a disadvantage in some way: *he really lost out on the bonus scheme*.
[from Anglo-Saxon *losian*, to be lost]

loser *noun* **1** a person who loses. **2** *colloq.* a person who is habitually unsuccessful.

Losey, Joseph (Walton) (1909–84) US film director, born in La Crosse, Wisconsin. His first feature film was the pacifist allegory *The Boy with Green Hair* (1945). Blacklisted as a suspected communist by the McCarthy Committee, he went to England in 1952, where he made *The Servant* (1963) and *The Go-Between* (1971). From the mid-1970s he worked mostly in France, where he made *La Truite* (1982, The Trout).

losing *adj.* failing; never likely to be successful: *a losing battle*.

loss *noun* **1** the act or fact of losing or being lost. **2** the thing, amount, etc lost. **3** the disadvantage or detriment resulting from losing: *be a great loss to the company*.
— **at a loss 1** puzzled and uncertain. **2** *said of an article sold, etc* for less than was paid for it originally. **3** *said of a company, etc* losing more money than it is making.
[from Anglo-Saxon *los*]

Lossiemouth POP (1981) 6 900, a port town in Moray district, Grampian region, NE Scotland. It lies on the coast, 8km/5mi N of Elgin. NOTABLE FEATURE air force base nearby (often involved in air-sea rescue).

loss-leader *noun* an item on sale at a lower price than normal, as a means of attracting custom for a wider range of goods.

lost past participle of LOSE. — *adj.* **1** missing; no longer to be found. **2** unable to find one's way. **3** confused, puzzled. **4** (**lost on someone**) not properly appreciated by them: *good music is lost on them*. **5** morally fallen: *lost women*. **6** damned: *lost souls*.
— **be lost in something** to have one's attention completely engrossed in something.
get lost *slang* to go away and stay away.
lost to someone to be no longer open or available to someone.
lost to something to be no longer capable of feeling an emotion, etc.

lost cause an aim, ideal, person, etc that has no chance of success.

lost generation a term applied by Gertrude Stein to a group of US expatriate writers living in Paris in the 1920s, including herself, Ezra Pound, Ernest Hemingway, and F. Scott Fitzgerald. Their work reflects the breakdown of order and values after World War II.

Lost World a name given by novelist Arthur Conan Doyle to an imaginary range of mountains where prehistoric animals survived into the 20c. It was based on Col Percy Fawcett's description of the Ricardo Franco Hills in the Mato Grosso state of W Brazil.

Lot a biblical character, the nephew of Abraham who separated from him and settled in Canaan, near Sodom (Genesis 13), a place of wickedness from which he was rescued by two angels. Lot's wife, who looked back during this escape and was turned into a pillar of salt (Genesis 19.26), has come to symbolize backsliding. Lot was the ancestor of the Moabites and Ammonites.

lot *noun* **1** *colloq.* (often **a lot of** or **lots of**) a great number or amount. **2** (**the lot**) the total; the whole number or amount. **3** any of a set of objects, eg a slip of paper, drawn from among a group, as a way of reaching a decision by chance: *draw lots / cast lots*. **4** this way of making a decision. **5** a person's fortune or destiny. **6** a separate part. **7** an item or set of items for sale by auction. **8** *North Amer.* an area of land: *parking lot*.
— **a bad lot** a person with a bad character or bad reputation.
cast *or* **throw in one's lot with someone** to decide to share their fortunes.
[Anglo-Saxon *hlot*, portion, choice]

loth same as LOATH.

Lothian POP (1992e) 751 000, a region in E Scotland, divided into four districts. AREA 1 755sq km/677sq mi. It is bounded N by the Firth of Forth, NE by the North Sea, S by Borders Region, SW by Strathclyde, and W by Central Region. PHYSICAL DESCRIPTION the Pentland and Moorfoot Hills lie in the S; to the SW are the Lammermuir Hills. CAPITAL Edinburgh. CHIEF TOWNS Linlithgow, Livingston, Musselburgh, Haddington, Dalkeith, Penicuik.

lotion *noun* a liquid for healing or cleaning the skin, as either a medicine or a cosmetic. [from Latin *lotio*, from *lavare*, to wash]

Lotophagi see LOTUS-EATERS.

lottery *noun* (PL. **lotteries**) **1** a system of raising money by selling tickets and giving prizes for those tickets drawn at random. **2** anything which is thought of as being a matter of chance. [from Dutch *loterie*, related to LOT]

lotto *noun* a game like bingo, with numbers drawn instead of called. [from Italian *lotto*]

lotus *noun* **1** the jujube shrub (*Zizyphus lotus*), native to the Mediterranean region, whose fruit was used by the ancient Greeks to make bread and wine, thought to produce a state of blissful and dreamy forgetfulness. **2** a species of water lily (*Nymphaea lotus*) known as the sacred lotus of Egypt, often depicted in Egyptian art. **3** either of two species of water lily of the genus *Nelumbo*. The sacred lotus (*N.nucifera*), native to Asia, has pink flowers and is traditionally associated with Buddhism and Hinduism. The American lotus (*N.lutea*), native to southern USA, has yellow flowers. Both are widely cultivated as ornamental plants. **4** *Greek Mythol.* a fruit which causes the eater to enter a state of blissful and dreamy forgetfulness. **5** a representation of a water-lily in architecture or art, especially symbolically in ancient Egyptian or Hindu art. [from Greek *lotos*]

lotus flower

lotus-eater *noun* a person who lives a lazy and indulgent life.

Lotus-eaters *or* **Lotophagi** in Homer and Tennyson, a fabulous people encountered by Odysseus, who lived on 'a flowery food' which made those who ate it forget their own country, and wish to live always in a dreamy state.

lotus position *Yoga* a seated position with the legs crossed and each foot resting on the opposite thigh.

Lotus Sutra one of the most popular scriptures in Mahayana Buddhism, especially in China and Japan. Written in India c.200 AD, it emphasizes the cosmic body of Buddha which is equivalent to a kind of eternal and real Buddha of whom the historical Buddhas are merely manifestations. Through the *Lotus Sutra* and the eternal Buddha, Buddhahood is open to everyone.

Louangphrabang see LUANG PRABANG.

louche *adj.* shady, sinister, shifty or disreputable. [from French *louche*, squinting]

loud — *adj.* **1** making a great sound; noisy. **2** capable of making a great sound: *a loud horn*. **3** shrill and insistent: *loud complaints*. **4** *said of colours or a design* too bright; gaudy. **5** *said of behaviour* aggressively noisy and coarse. — *adv.* in a loud manner.
— **out loud** aloud; loudly.
[from Anglo-Saxon *hlud*]

loudhailer *noun* a portable electronic device which amplifies the voice.

loudly *adv.* in a loud way; with great sound.

loud-mouthed *adj. colloq.* noisily and aggressively boastful.

loudness *noun* being loud; much noise or sound.

loudspeaker *noun Electron.* an electronic device that converts electrical signals into audible sound waves, used in radio, television, telephone receivers, hi-fi systems, etc.

Louganis, Greg(ory) (1960–) US diver, born in El Cajon, California, of Samoan and Swedish ancestry. In the 1983 world championships, he was the first man to achieve a score of more than 700 points for 11 dives. He won two Olympic gold medals in 1984 and 1988, and was World Diving champion in platform (1978, 1982, 1986), and springboard (1982, 1986).

lough *noun Irish* same as LOCH. [from Irish Gaelic *loch*, Middle English *lough*]

Loughborough POP (1981) 46 000, a town in Charnwood district, Leicestershire, central England, situated 16km/10mi N of Leicester. It was formerly famous for its lace. NOTABLE FEATURE War Memorial Tower, with a chime of 47 bells.

Louis IX, also called **St Louis** (1214–70) King of France (1226–70), born in Poissy, near Paris, the son of Louis VIII. By his victories he compelled Henry III of England to acknowledge French suzerainty in Guienne (1259). He led the Seventh Crusade (1248), but was defeated in Egypt, taken prisoner, and ransomed. After returning to France (1254), he carried out legal reforms, and encouraged learning, the arts, and literature. He embarked on a new Crusade in 1270, but died of plague in Tunis. He was canonized in 1297 (feast day 25 Aug).

Louis XII (1462–1515) King of France (1498–1515), born in Blois, the son of Charles, Duke of Orléans. He commanded the French troops at Asti during Charles's invasion of Italy (1494–5) before he succeeded him to the French throne (1498) and married his widow, Anne of Brittany. He proved a popular ruler, concerned to provide justice and avoid oppressive taxation. His Italian ambitions brought him into diplomatic and military involvement with Ferdinand II of Castile (1500–12), who finally outmanoeuvred Louis by his part in the Holy League (1511). Meanwhile, Louis caused the emperor Maximilian's dynastic designs on Brittany to be unsuccessful, but in return his forces were driven from Italy (1512) and then defeated by an Anglo-Imperial alliance at the battle of Guinegate (1513). To guarantee peace, Louis married Mary Tudor, sister of Henry VIII (1514).

Louis XIII (1601–43) King of France (1610–43), born in Fontainebleau, the eldest son of Henry IV of France and Marie de Médici. He succeeded to the throne on the assassination of his father (1610), but even after he came of age (1614) the Queen Regent excluded him from power. She arranged Louis's marriage to Anne of Austria, daughter of Philip III of Spain (1615). In 1617 Louis took over government, and exiled Marie de Médici to Blois (1619–20). He became dependent upon Cardinal Richelieu, his Chief Minister from 1624, whose domestic and foreign policies suited the royal ambitions. Louis's later years were enhanced by French military victories in the Thirty Years War against the Habsburgs, and by the birth of his son, the future Louis XIV (1638).

Louis XIV, known as **the Great**, or **le Roi Soleil** (**the Sun King**) (1638–1715) King of France (1643–1715), born in St Germain-en-Laye, the son of Louis XIII, whom he succeeded. During his minority (1643–51) France was ruled by his mother, Anne of Austria, and her Chief Minister, Cardinal Mazarin. In 1660 Louis married the Infanta Maria Theresa, elder daughter of Philip IV of Spain, through whom he later claimed the Spanish succession for his second grandson (Philip I). In 1661 he assumed sole responsibility for government, advised by various royal councils. Obsessed with the greatness of France, his foreign and commercial policies were aggressive, particularly against the Dutch, and his patronage of the Catholic Stuarts led to the hostility of England after 1689. However his major political rivals were the Austrian Habsburgs (particularly Leopold I). From 1665 Louis tried to take possession of the Spanish Netherlands, but later desired the whole Spanish inheritance. His attempt to create a Franco-Spanish Bourbon bloc led to the formation of the Grand Alliance of England, the United Provinces, and the Habsburg Empire, and resulted in the War of the Spanish Succession (1701–13). He was determined to preserve the unity of the French state and the independence of the French Church, which led to conflict with the Jansenists, the Huguenots, and the papacy. Although his old age saw military disaster and the financial rav-

ages of prolonged warfare, Louis is considered a great monarch, who established the parameters of successful absolutism. His long reign also marked the cultural ascendancy of France within Europe, symbolized by the Palace of Versailles. He was succeeded by his great-grandson Louis XV.

Louis XV, known as **le Bien-Aimé** (**the Well-Beloved**) (1710–74) King of France (1715–74), born in Versailles, the son of Louis, Duc de Bourgogne and Marie-Adelaide of Savoy, and the great-grandson of Louis XIV, whom he succeeded. His reign coincided with the great age of decorative art in the Rococo mode (the Louis XV style). Until he came of age (1723) he was guided by the regent, Philippe d'Orléans, and then by the Duc de Bourbon, who negotiated a marriage alliance with Maria Leczczynska, daughter of the deposed King Stanislas I of Poland. In 1726 Bourbon was replaced by the King's former tutor, the elderly Fleury, who skilfully steered the French state until his death (1744). Thereafter Louis vowed to rule without a Chief Minister, but allowed the government to drift into the hands of ministerial factions, while he indulged in secret and unofficial diplomatic activity. This system (*le secret du roi*) brought confusion to French foreign policy in the years prior to the Diplomatic Revolution (1748–56) and obscured the country's interests overseas, leading to a trio of continental wars and culminating in the loss of the French colonies in America and India (1763). His attempt to introduce reforms in 1771 came too late and the decline in royal authority continued. He was succeeded by his grandson, Louis XVI.

Louis XVI (1754–93) King of France (1774–93), born in Versailles, the third son of the Dauphin Louis and Maria Josepha of Saxony, and the grandson of Louis XV, whom he succeeded in 1774. He was married in 1770 to the Archduchess Marie Antoinette, daughter of the Habsburg Empress Maria Theresa, to strengthen the Franco-Austrian alliance. His reign saw the country decline into social and economic crisis, but he failed to support the ministers (eg Turgot and Necker) who tried to reform its outmoded financial and social structures. He also allowed France to become involved in the costly War of American Independence (1778–83), and the monarchy was further discredited by Marie Antoinette's propensity for scandalous behaviour. In 1789 he agreed to summon the Estates General, but, encouraged by the Queen, he resisted demands from the National Assembly reform, and in Oct was brought with his family from Versailles to Paris as a hostage to the Revolutionary movement. Louis reluctantly approved the new constitution (Sep 1791), but by then his moral authority had collapsed. In Aug an insurrection suspended Louis's constitutional position, and in Sep the monarchy was abolished. He was tried before the National Convention for conspiracy with foreign powers, and was guillotined in Paris.

Louis (Charles) XVII (1785–95) titular King of France (1793–5), born in Versailles, the second son of Louis XVI. On his father's execution (Jan 1793) he remained in the Temple prison in Paris, where he died, dashing the hopes of Royalists and constitutional monarchists. The secrecy surrounding his last months led to rumours of his escape and produced several claimants to his title.

Louis XVIII *or* **Louis Stanislas Xavier, Comte de (Count of) Provence** (1755–1824) King of France in name from 1795 and in fact from 1814, born in Versailles, the younger brother of Louis XVI. He fled from Paris in Jun 1791, and eventually took refuge in England, where he became the focal point for the Royalist cause. On Napoleon's downfall (1814) he re-entered Paris, and promised a Constitutional Charter. His restoration was interrupted by Napoleon's return from Elba, until after Waterloo

(1815). His reign was marked by the introduction of parliamentary government with a limited franchise.

Louis, Joe, properly **Joseph Louis Barrow**, also called **the Brown Bomber** (1914–81) US boxer, born in Lexington, Alabama. He was the US amateur light-heavyweight champion in 1934, and turned professional the same year. He beat James J Braddock (1905–74) for the world heavyweight title in 1937, and held the title for a record 12 years, making a record 25 defences. He retired in 1949, but made a comeback in 1950. He lost the world title fight to Ezzard Charles (1921–75), and had his last fight against Rocky Marciano in 1951. He won 63 of his 66 contests.

Louisiade Archipelago POP (1980) 17 000, a mountainous island group of Papua New Guinea, SE of New Guinea. AREA 1 553sq km/ 599sq mi. The group comprises the islands of Tacuta, Rossel, and Misima, with numerous other small islands and coral reefs. Gold has been worked on Tacuta. [named in 1768 after Louis XIV of France]

Louisiana POP (1990) 4.3m, a state in S USA, divided into 64 parishes, and bounded S by the Gulf of Mexico. AREA 123 673sq km/47 738sq mi. It is known as the 'Pelican State'. The state's population includes groups of Creoles (of French descent) and Cajuns (descendants of French Acadians driven from Canada by the British in the 18c). PHYSICAL DESCRIPTION rivers include the Mississippi (its large delta area is in the S), Red, Sabine, and Pearl; the highest point is Mt Driskill (162m); there are vast coastal areas of marsh, lagoon, and fertile delta lands; further inland are plains and low, rolling hills; over half the land area is forested, supporting a major lumber and paper industry. HISTORY the name (after Louis XIV of France) was originally applied to the entire Mississippi R basin, which was claimed for France by La Salle in 1682; most of the E region was ceded to Spain in 1763, then to the USA in 1783; the W region was acquired by the USA in the Louisiana Purchase in 1803; it was admitted to the Union as the 18th state in 1812; it seceded from the Union in 1861 and joined the Confederacy; in 1868 it was readmitted to the Union; the state experienced economic revolution in the early 1900s when large oil and natural gas deposits were discovered; the state is world famous for the jazz music which grew up in and around New Orleans. CAPITAL Baton Rouge. CHIEF TOWNS New Orleans, Shreveport. ECONOMY highly productive in agriculture, with soya beans, rice, sugar cane, sweet potatoes, cotton; cattle, dairy products; fishing, particularly for shrimps and oysters; second only to Texas in oil and natural gas production (mainly offshore); several cities have oil refineries and petrochemical plants; Louisiana leads the nation in salt and sulphur production; manufactures foods, clay, glass, and transportation equipment; tourism is increasing.

Louisiana Purchase the sale (1803) by France to the USA of an area between the Mississippi River and the Rocky Mts for $15m, by which the USA gained full control of the Mississippi Valley.

Louis period styles a range of Classical, Baroque, and Rococo stylistic variations used in the 17c and 18c, and particularly associated with the reign of Louis XIV of France. They are broadly characterized by lavish and ornate internal decoration and comparatively restrained façades and formal gardens (eg Palais de Versailles, 1661-1756).

Louis Philippe, known as **the Citizen King** (1773–1850) King of the French (1830–48), born in Paris, the eldest son of the Duke of Orléans, Philippe Egalité. At the Revolution he entered the National Guard, and with his father renounced his titles to demonstrate his progressive sympathies. He joined the Jacobin Club (1790), fought in the Army of the North, and deserted to the

Austrians (1793). He lived in Switzerland (1793–4), the USA, and England (1800–9), and in 1809 moved to Sicily and married Marie Amélie, daughter of Ferdinand IV of Naples and Sicily. He returned to France in 1814, but fled to England again in the Hundred Days. On the eve of Charles X's abdication (1830) he was elected Lt-General of the kingdom, and after the Revolution was given the title of King of the French. He steered a powerful middle course helped by the upper bourgeoisie, but political corruption and industrial and agrarian depression (1846) caused discontent, and united the radicals in a cry for electoral reform. When the Paris mob rose (1848), he abdicated and escaped to England.

Louisville POP (1990) 953 000, the seat of Jefferson County, NW Kentucky, USA, and the largest city in the state. It lies at the Falls of the Ohio R. Louisville is a major horse breeding centre and an important shipping point for coal. The University of Louisville (1798) is the oldest municipal university in the USA. HISTORY settled in 1778, the port was named after Louis XVI of France and achieved city status in 1828. NOTABLE FEATURES JB Speed Art Museum; Kentucky Railway Museum; Kentucky Derby Museum. EVENT Kentucky Derby (May) at Churchill Downs.

lounge — *verb usually intrans.* **1** to lie or recline comfortably. **2** (**lounge around**) to be idle or lazy. **3** *trans.* (**lounge away**) to pass (time) idly. — *noun* **1** a sitting-room in a private house. **2** a large room in a public building, eg in a hotel for sitting in, or in an airport for waiting in, often providing refreshment facilities. **3** (*also* **lounge bar**) *Brit.* a smarter and more expensive bar in a public house. **4** an act or spell of lounging. [thought to be from obsolete *lungis* lout]

lounger *noun* **1** a person who lounges. **2** a comfortable chair for lounging on. **3** a woman's loose garment, worn when relaxing at home.

lounge suit *Brit.* a man's formal suit for ordinary everyday wear.

lour *or* **lower** *verb intrans.* (**loured, louring**) *said of the sky or elements* to become dark or threaten rain or storms. [from Middle English *louren*, to frown]

Lourdes a town and important site of Roman Catholic pilgrimage in Hautes-Pyrénées department, S France. In 1858 Bernadette Soubirous, a French peasant girl, was led by a vision of the Virgin Mary to the springs at the Grotte de Massabielle. NOTABLE FEATURES include the Basilica of the Rosary (1885–9), and the Church of St-Pie-X (completed 1958).

louring *or* **lowering** *adj.* menacing; threatening.

louse — *noun* **1** (PL. **lice**) a wingless insect with a flat body and short legs, which sucks the blood of the animal or person it is living on. **2** (PL. **louses**) *slang* a general term of abuse for a person. — *verb* to remove lice from. — **louse something up** *slang* to spoil or ruin it. [from Anglo-Saxon *lus*]

lousily *adv.* badly; disgustingly.

lousiness *noun* a lousy state; being unpleasant.

lousy *adj.* (**lousier, lousiest**) **1** having lice. **2** *slang* very bad, unpleasant, or disgusting. **3** (**lousy with something**) *slang* having a great deal of something unwelcome: *the place was lousy with police.*

lout *noun* an aggressively rough and coarse boy or man. [of uncertain origin]

Louth, Gaelic **Lughbhaidh** POP (1991) 91 000, a county in NE Leinster province, Irish Republic. AREA 821sq km/317sq mi. It is bounded N by Northern Ireland and E by the Irish Sea. CAPITAL Dundalk. ECONOMY cattle; oats; potatoes.

Loutherbourg, Philip James de (1740–1812) French scene designer, born in Strasbourg. After working in Paris, he was

employed by David Garrick at the Drury Lane Theatre (1771–81). His innovations in scene design and particularly in stage lighting led to the development of pictorial illusion and the picture-frame concept in stagecraft.

loutish *adj.* characteristic of louts; aggressively rough and coarse.

Louvain see LEUVEN.

Louvois, François Michel le Tellier, Marquis de (1641–91) French statesman, born in Paris. An energetic war minister under Louis XIV from the War of Devolution (1668), his work reforming and strengthening the army bore fruit in the Dutch War, which ended with the Peace of Nijmegen (1678). Recognized as a brilliant administrator, he was the King's most influential minister in the years 1683–91.

Louvre the national museum and art gallery of France, situated in Paris. It was built for Francis I in 1546 on the site of an earlier building, and added to by successive French monarchs. The Grande Galerie of the Louvre was officially opened to the public in 1793. It houses a rich collection of paintings, sculpture, and antiquities, including an unrivalled collection of French paintings. The complex was remodelled in the 1980s, with the addition of a steel and glass pyramid at the entrance in the Cour Napoléon.

louvre *or* **louver** *noun* **1** any one of a set of horizontal, sloping, overlapping slats in a door, etc, which let air in but keep rain and light out. **2** a dome-like structure on a roof for letting smoke out and air in. [from Old French *lovier*]

louvred *or* **louvered** *adj.* having or equipped with louvres.

lovable *or* **loveable** *adj.* worthy of or inspiring love or affection.

lovage *noun* a herb with small, greenish-yellow flowers, used for flavouring. [from Old French *luvesche*]

love — *noun* **1** a feeling of great affection for and devotion to another person. **2** strong sexual attraction. **3** a strong liking for something. **4** sexual passion; sexual relations. **5** *often used as a term of address* a person one loves. **6** *Brit. colloq.* a term of address used for anyone regardless of affection. **7** *Tennis, Squash* no score. — *verb* **1** to feel great affection for. **2** to enjoy very much; to like. — **fall in love with someone** to develop feelings of love and sexual attraction for someone. **in love with someone** feeling love and sexual attraction for them. **make love to** *or* **with someone 1** to have sexual intercourse with someone. **2** *old use* to woo. **not for love or money** under no circumstances. [from Anglo-Saxon *lufu*]

love affair a romantic and sexual relationship, especially a transitory one.

lovebird *noun* a small African parrot that shows strong attachment to its mate.

love-child *noun* an illegitimate child.

Love for Love a play by William Congreve (1695). It is a satiric comedy about an agreement between an extravagant son whose father offers to pay his debts if he will sign away his inheritance, and his sweetheart's subsequent plot to obtain the bond.

love-in-a-mist *noun* a garden plant with pale blue or white flowers and feathery leaves.

Lovelace, (Augusta) Ada, Countess of, née **Ada Byron** (1815–52) English mathematician and writer, daughter of the poet Lord Byron. She taught herself geometry, was trained in astronomy and mathematics, and wrote extensively on the work of the computer pioneer Charles Babbage. The high-level universal computer programming language ADA was named in her honour.

Lovelace, Richard (1618–57) English Cavalier poet, born (possibly) in Woolwich, near

entrance to the Louvre

London. He was twice imprisoned during the Civil War, and spent his estate in the King's cause. In 1642 he wrote 'To Althea, from Prison' ('Stone walls do not a prison make...'), and in 1649 published his best-known work, *Lucasta*.

Lovelace, Robert the charming but profligate libertine in Samuel Richardson's *Clarissa*.

loveless *adj.* without love.

love-letter *noun* a letter expressing feelings of sexual love.

love-lies-bleeding *noun* a garden plant with drooping spikes of reddish-purple flowers.

love life a person's sexual activity.

loveliness *noun* being lovely or attractive; striking beauty.

Lovell, Sir (Alfred Charles) Bernard (1913–) English astronomer, born in Oldham Common, Gloucestershire. In 1951 he became professor at Manchester University and Director of Jodrell Bank Experimental Station. An energetic pioneer of radio astronomy, he initiated the establishment of the 250ft steerable radio telescope at Jodrell Bank, and has made important contributions to the study of the physics of radio sources.

Lovelock, James (Ephraim) (1919–) British scientist, originator of the Gaia theory. After attending the Universities of London and Manchester he went to the USA in 1954, working at Harvard and Yale. He first stated his ideas on Gaia in 1972, and they were adopted by some environmentalists and New Age thinkers, but remain controversial.

lovelorn *adj.* left by or pining for the person one is in love with.

lovely — *adj.* (**lovelier, loveliest**) **1** strikingly attractive; beautiful. **2** *colloq.* delightful or pleasing. — *noun* (PL. **lovelies**) *colloq.* a pretty woman.

love-making *noun* sexual activity between lovers.

love-match *noun* a marriage based on love.

lover *noun* **1** a person in love with another, especially a person having a romantic and sexual relationship. **2** (**lovers**) two people who are in love with one another or who are sharing a sexual relationship. **3** (*in combination*) a person who enjoys or is fond of something specified: *a dog-lover*.

lovesick *adj.* sad or pining because of love.

Lovesong of J Alfred Prufrock, The a poem by T S Eliot (1917). It is a dramatic monologue describing the lonely life of the middle-aged Prufrock.

Lovewit the employer of Face, whose house is used as a fraudulent alchemist's practice in his absence, in Ben Jonson's *The Alchemist*.

lovey-dovey *adj. colloq.* affectionate in a silly or sentimental way.

loving *adj.* feeling and showing affection or love.

loving-cup *noun* a large two-handled drinking cup passed round at the end of a banquet.

lovingly *adv.* with love or affection.

low¹ — *adj.* **1** less than average in height; not reaching to a high level. **2** situated close to the ground, to sea-level, or to the horizon. **3** (**low in something**) containing less than average amount, etc: *low in fat.* **4** *said of numbers* small or reduced in amount. **5** with little value or quality. **6** (**low on something**) not having much left of it: *running low on petrol.* **7** of humble rank or position; common. **8** *said of clothes* cut so as to expose the neck and part of the chest. **9** making little sound; soft: *a low voice.* **10** *said of sounds, notes, etc* produced by slow vibrations and having a deep pitch. **11** not physically or mentally strong; weak; with no energy or vitality: *be feeling low after the operation.* **12** unfavourable: *a low opinion.* **13** coarse, rude, and vulgar. **14** *said of latitudes* near the equator. **15** *said of a gear* giving a relatively slow engine speed. — *adv.* **1** in or to a low position, state, or manner. **2** in a small quantity or to a small degree. **3** with a low voice; quietly. **4** at or in a low pitch. — *noun* **1** the position, level, etc which is low or lowest: *the pound has reached a new low.* **2** *Meteorol.* an area of low atmospheric pressure. [from Norse *lagr*]

low² — *verb intrans., said of cattle* to make a low, gentle, mooing sound. — *noun* (*also* **lowing**) the low, gentle mooing sound made by cattle. [from Anglo-Saxon *hlowan*]

low-born *adj.* of humble birth.

lowbrow — *adj.* having or involving tastes that are relatively popular and unintellectual. — *noun* a lowbrow person.

Low Church a group within the Church of England which puts little value on ceremony and the authority of priests and which stresses evangelical theology.

low comedy comedy which borders on the farcical and absurd.

Low Countries a term used to refer to the Netherlands and Belgium. It derives its name from the low-lying coastal plain of both countries. Luxembourg is often included as one of the Low Countries.

low-down *colloq.* — *adj.* mean and dishonourable. — *noun* information about someone or something, especially when disreputable or acquired surreptitiously: *I've got the low-down on your brother.*

Lowell, Amy (1874–1925) US Imagist poet, born in Brookline, Massachusetts. After travelling with her parents in Europe, she began to produce volumes of free verse in which she experimented with what she called 'unrhymed cadence' and 'polyphonic prose', as in *Sword Blades and Poppy Seed* (1914). She was posthumously awarded the Pulitzer Prize in 1926 for the collection *What's O'Clock* (1925). She also wrote several critical works, and a biography of John Keats.

Lowell, Robert (Traill Spence, Jr) (1917–77) US poet, born in Boston, Massachusetts. A conscientious objector, he was jailed during World War II (1944). His early poems (eg *Land of Unlikeness*, 1944, *Lord Weary's Castle*, 1946, Pulitzer Prize) show a preoccupation with his conversion to Catholicism. His status as a 'confessional' poet was confirmed with *Life Studies* (1959), *Notebook* (1969), *The Dolphins* (1973, Pulitzer Prize), and *Day by Day* (1977).

Lower, Richard (1631–91) English physician and physiologist, born in Tremeer, near Bodmin. He set up in medical practice in London, and carried out early experiments on blood transfusion between dogs. Following William Harvey, he recognized that the heart acts as a muscular pump; from investigations of the colour change between dark venous blood and red arterial blood, he deduced that the red colour resulted from the mixing of dark blood with air in the lungs.

lower¹ — *adj.* **1** not as high as something else in position, status, height, etc. **2** *said of an animal or plant* less highly developed than other species. — *adv.* in or to a lower position. — *verb* (**lowered, lowering**) **1** *trans., intrans.* to make or become lower in amount, value, status, sound, etc. **2** to close; to pull or let down: *we'd better lower the blinds.*

lower² (*low-* pronounced like *now*) same as LOUR.

lower case *Printing* small letters as opposed to capitals.

lower-case *adj.* consisting of small letters.

lower class the social class including manual workers and their families.

lower-class *adj.* belonging or relating to the lower class.

lower house *or* **lower chamber** the larger and normally elected part of a two-chamber (bicameral) parliament, such as the House of Commons in the United Kingdom.

lowest common denominator *Maths.* (ABBREV. **LCD**) in a group of fractions, the lowest common multiple of all the denominators, eg the LCD of ⅓ and ¼ is 12. Fractions must be expressed in such a form if they are to be added or subtracted.

lowest common multiple *Maths.* (ABBREV. **LCM**) the smallest number into which every member of a group of numbers will divide exactly, eg the LCM of 2, 3, and 4 is 12.

Lowestoft POP (1981) 60 000, a port town and resort in Waveney district, Suffolk, E England. It lies on the North Sea coast, 61km/38mi NE of Ipswich. Lowestoft Ness is the easternmost point in England. NOTABLE FEATURE Royal Naval Patrol Service Memorial.

low frequency a radio frequency between 30 and 300 kilohertz.

low-key *adj.* **1** restrained and subdued. **2** *said of a person* not easily excited.

lowland — *noun* **1** (*usually* **lowlands**) land which is low-lying in comparison with other areas. **2** (**Lowlands**) the less mountainous region of Scotland lying to the south and east of the Highlands. — *adj.* (*also* **Lowland**) of or relating to lowlands or the Scottish Lowlands.

Lowlander *noun* a person who lives in lowlands, especially the Scottish Lowlands.

low-level language *Comput.* a programming language in which each instruction represents a single machine-code operation. Programs written in low-level languages can usually only be run on computers using the same type of processor. See also HIGH-LEVEL LANGUAGE.

lowliness *noun* a lowly or humble state or rank.

lowly *adj.* (**lowlier, lowliest**) **1** humble in rank, status, or behaviour. **2** simple, modest, and unpretentious.

lowness *noun* a low state or condition.

low-pitched *adj.* **1** *said of a sound* low in pitch. **2** *said of a roof* having a gentle slope.

low-pressure *adj., said of steam and steam-engines* using or creating little pressure.

low profile a deliberate avoidance of publicity and attention.

Lowry, L(aurence) S(tephen) (1887–1976) English artist, born in Manchester. From the 1920s he produced many pictures of the Lancashire industrial scene, mainly in brilliant whites and greys, peopled with scurrying 'matchstick' men and women. A major retrospective exhibition of his work was held at the Royal Academy in the year of his death.

Lowry, (Clarence) Malcolm (1909–57) English novelist, born in New Brighton, Merseyside. His reputation rests on *Under the Volcano* (1947), a novel set in Mexico, where he lived from 1936 to 1937. He also wrote *Ultramarine* (1933), based on his first sea voyage, and several other novels which were published posthumously, including *Dark is the Grave Wherein my Friend is Laid* (1968).

low-spirited *adj.* dejected or depressed.

low tech *colloq.* simple, unsophisticated technology used to make basic products. [a shortening of *low technology*]

low tide *or* **low water** the minimum level reached by a falling tide.

loyal *adj.* 1 faithful and true. 2 personally devoted to a sovereign, government, leader, friend, etc. 3 expressing or showing loyalty: *the loyal toast to the Queen.* [from Old French *loial*]

loyalist *noun* 1 a loyal supporter, especially of a sovereign or an established government. 2 (**Loyalist**) (in Northern Ireland) a supporter of the British Government.

loyally *adv.* with loyalty; faithfully.

loyalty *noun* (PL. **loyalties**) 1 the state or quality of being loyal. 2 (*often* **loyalties**) a feeling of loyalty or duty towards a person or institution.

Loyalty Islands, French **Iles Loyauté** POP (1989) 18 000, a group of coral islands in the SW Pacific Ocean, 128km/79mi E of New Caledonia. AREA 1 981sq km/765sq mi. It comprises Ouvéa, Lifu, Mare, Tiga, and many small islets. They are a dependency of the French Territory of New Caledonia. CAPITAL We (Lifu I). ECONOMY coconuts; sandalwood; copra.

lozenge *noun* 1 a small sweet or tablet which dissolves in the mouth. 2 a rhombus. [from Old French *losenge*]

LP *abbrev.* a long-playing gramophone record.

L-plate *noun* a small square sign with a red letter *L* on a white background, displayed by law at each end of cars being driven by learners.

Lr *symbol Chem.* lawrencium.

LRAM *abbrev.* Licenciate of the Royal Academy of Music.

LRCP *abbrev.* Licenciate of the Royal College of Physicians.

LRCS *abbrev.* Licenciate of the Royal College of Surgeons.

LSD *abbrev.* lysergic acid diethylamide, a drug which causes hallucinations.

L.S.D. or **l.s.d.** or **£.s.d.** *abbrev.* pounds, shillings, pence (with reference to pre-decimal coinage in the UK). [from Latin *librae, solidi, denarii*]

LSE *abbrev.* London School of Economics.

LSO *abbrev.* London Symphony Orchestra.

Lt *or* **Lt.** *abbrev.* Lieutenant.

Ltd *or* **Ltd.** *abbrev.* Limited, used in the names of limited liability companies.

Lu *symbol Chem.* lutetium.

Luanda, formerly also **Loanda**, Portuguese **São Paulo de Loanda** 1 POP (1990e) 1.8m, the capital of Angola, situated on the Bay of Bengo. It is a seaport lying on the estuary of the R Cuanza. HISTORY founded in 1575; the centre of Portuguese administration from 1627; a major slave trading centre with Brazil in the 17c–18c.

NOTABLE FEATURES cathedral; Governor's Palace; São Miguel Fortress (17c). 2 a province in NW Angola with Luanda as its capital.

Luang Prabang *or* **Louangphrabang** 1 POP (1985) 68 000, a town in W Laos, on the R Mekong, at its limit of navigation. It is the centre of an agricultural region. HISTORY capital of the kingdom of Luang Prabang; capital of Laos from 1946 until 1975. NOTABLE FEATURES Buddhist pagodas dating from the 16c. 2 a province in N Laos with Luang Prabang as its capital.

Luba-Lunda Kingdoms a succession of African states occupying territory in what is now Zaire. Powerful by the 17c, they were involved in slave and ivory trading with the Portuguese and later with Zanzibar. The Luba states were relatively unstable, but the Lunda Empire seems to have consolidated its power through trade, though its central state did not survive the ending of the Angolan slave trade in the 1840s, and the others fell to European imperialism.

lubber *noun* a big awkward and clumsy person. [from Middle English *lobre*]

lubberly *adj., adv.* like a lubber; clumsy or clumsily.

Lubbock, Sir John, 1st Baron Avebury (1834–1913) English politician and biologist, born in London. He became an MP in 1870, and passed more than a dozen important measures, including the Bank Holidays Act (1871). Scientifically, he is best known for his researches on primitive man and on the habits of bees and ants, for which he devised new methods of study.

Lübeck POP (1991e) 215 000, a commercial and manufacturing seaport in E Schleswig-Holstein province, Germany. It lies on the R Trave, 56km/35mi NE of Hamburg. Formerly a major city of the Hanseatic League, it is today Germany's most important Baltic port. Lübeck is also noted for its red wine trade and its marzipan. The novelist Thomas Mann was born here in 1875. NOTABLE FEATURES Holstentor (1477); town hall (13c–15c); St Mary's Church (13c–14c); Holy Ghost Hospital (13c); cathedral (1173); the Hanseatic City is a World Heritage site.

Lubitsch, Ernst (1892–1947) German film director, born in Berlin. In Hollywood from 1923, he established himself as the creator of sophisticated light comedies. The availability of sound enabled the full development of 'the Lubitsch touch' (wit, urbanity, visual elegance) throughout the 1930s, from *The Love Parade* (1929) to *Ninotchka* (1939). He received a Special Academy Award in 1947.

Lublin 1 POP (1992e) 352 000, the capital of Lublin voivodship, E Poland. It is situated c.160km/100mi SE of Warsaw, on a plateau crossed by the R Bystrzyca. HISTORY a castle town, gaining urban status in 1317; the Act of Union between Poland and Lithuania was signed here in 1569; Poland's first Council of Workers' Delegates was formed here in 1918. NOTABLE FEATURES castle; Kraków Gate; cathedral (16c); St Brigittine's Convent; Bernardine Monastery. 2 a voivodship in E Poland with Lublin as its capital.

lubricant — *noun* oil, grease, etc used to reduce friction. — *adj.* lubricating.

lubricate *verb* 1 to cover with oil, grease, or some other such substance, to reduce friction. 2 to make smooth, slippery, or greasy. [from Latin *lubricus*, slippery]

lubrication *noun* the act or process of lubricating.

lubricator *noun* a person or thing that lubricates.

lubricious *adj. literary* lewd. [from Latin *lubricus*, slippery]

lubricity *noun literary* lewdness.

Lubumbashi, formerly (to 1966) **Elisabethville** POP (1991e) 739 000, the capital of

Shaba region, SE Zaire. It lies on the R Lualaba, close to the Zambian frontier. The city was founded in 1910. NOTABLE FEATURE cathedral.

Lucas van Leyden, also called **Lucas Jacobsz** (1494–1533) Dutch painter and engraver, born in Leyden. He practised almost every branch of painting, and as an engraver ranks with Dürer, by whom he was much influenced. His notable works include the triptych *The Last Judgement* (1526, Leyden).

Luce, Henry R(obinson) (1898–1967) American magazine publisher and editor, born in Shandong province, China, to a missionary family. He co-founded and edited *Time* (1923), which aimed to present news in narrative style, and later founded *Fortune* (1930), *Life* (1936), and *Sports Illustrated* (1954). In the 1930s he inaugurated the radio programme 'March of Time', which was developed into cinema newsreels in 1935.

Lucerne, German **Luzern** 1 POP (1990) 150 000, the resort capital of Lucerne canton, central Switzerland. Situated on the W shore of L Lucerne, 40km/25mi SW of Zürich, it developed as a trade centre on the St Gotthard route. NOTABLE FEATURES Lion Monument (to the Swiss Guards); wooden-roofed footbridge (16c); cathedral (17c); town hall (17c); lake steamers. 2 a canton in central Switzerland with Lucerne as its capital.

lucerne *noun Brit.* same as ALFALFA. [from French *luzerne*]

Lucerne, Lake, German **Vierwaldstätter See** an irregular and indented lake in central Switzerland, and the fourth largest of the Swiss lakes. AREA 114sq km/44sq mi; length 38km/24mi; maximum depth 214m. The main arm runs E and SE from Lucerne, then in a narrower arm, the Urner See, it runs S. The R Reuss feeds the lake from the S, and drains it from the NW to the Aare and Rhine rivers. Resorts on its shores include Weggis, Gersau, Brunnen, and Vitznau. L Lucerne is associated with the origins of the Swiss Confederation and the legend of William Tell.

Lucia di Lammermoor an opera by Gaetano Donizetti (1835), based on Scott's *The Bride of Lammermoor*. Set in 16c Scotland, it tells of Enrico, Lord Ashton of Lammermoor who picks a husband for his sister Lucia in the hope of procuring money and allies. Though Lucia loves Edgardo, the exiled heir of the estate that Enrico has just taken over, she is told of Edgardo's infidelity and complies, an act which leads to madness, murder, and suicide.

Lucian (c.117–180 AD) Greek rhetorician, born in Samosata, Syria. He practised as an advocate in Antioch, and travelled widely in Asia Minor, Greece, Italy, and Gaul. He then settled in Athens, where he devoted himself to philosophy, and produced a new form of literature – humorous dialogue. His satires include *Dialogues of the Gods* and *Dialogues of the Dead*.

Luciana the sister of Adriana in Shakespeare's *The Comedy of Errors*, who mistakenly believes herself to be being courted by her brother-in-law.

lucid *adj.* 1 easily understood; expressed, or expressing something, clearly. 2 *said of a person's mind* sane and not confused, especially between periods of insanity. 3 bright, shining. [from Latin *lucidus*, full of light]

lucidity *noun* being lucid; clarity.

lucidly *adv.* with clear expression; so as to be understood easily.

Lucifer *noun* Satan. [from Latin *lucifer*, light-bringer]

Lucius a male first name. [a Roman name, probably connected with Latin *lux*, light]

luck *noun* 1 chance, especially when thought of as bringing good fortune. 2 good fortune.

3 events in life which cannot be controlled and seem to happen by chance: *bad luck.*

— down on one's luck experiencing problems or suffering hardship.

push one's luck *colloq.* to risk total failure by trying to gain too much when one has already been partly successful.

worse luck *colloq.* unfortunately. [from Old Dutch *luc*]

luckily *adv.* (applying to a whole sentence or phrase) as a piece of good fortune: *luckily, they were at home when we called.*

luckiness *noun* a lucky or fortunate state or situation.

luckless *adj.* unlucky, especially habitually; unfortunate.

Lucknow POP (1991) 1.6m, the capital of Uttar Pradesh, N central India. It is situated 410km/255mi SE of Delhi, on the R Gomati. HISTORY centre of the Mogul Empire during the 16c; capital of the Kingdom of Oudh from 1775 until 1856; became capital of the United Provinces in 1877; the British garrison was besieged here for five months in 1857 during the Indian Mutiny. The city was the focal point of the movement for an independent Pakistan betwen 1942 and 1947. NOTABLE FEATURES Imamabara Mausoleum (1784); British Residency (1800); palaces; royal tombs.

Lucky a character, oppressed by Pozzo, in Samuel Beckett's *Waiting for Godot.*

lucky *adj.* (**luckier, luckiest**) **1** having good luck. **2** bringing good luck. **3** fortunate: *a lucky coincidence.*

lucky dip a tub or container full of paper, bran, etc, from which prizes are drawn at random.

Lucky Jim a novel by Kingsley Amis (1954). His first, it describes the disaster-prone life of history lecturer, Jim Dixon.

lucrative *adj.* affording financial gain; profitable. [from Latin *lucrativus*]

lucratively *adv.* so as to provide financial gain; profitably.

lucre *noun derog.* profit or financial gain. [from Latin *lucrum*, gain]

Lucretia **1** in Roman legend, the wife of Collatinus. She was raped by Sextus, son of Tarquinius Superbus, and after telling her story, she committed suicide. The incident led to the expulsion of the Tarquins from Rome. **2** (*also* **Lucrece**) the virtuous wife of Collatinus in Shakespeare's *The Rape of Lucrece.*

Lucretius, in full **Titus Lucretius Carus** (1c BC) Roman poet and philosopher. Little is known of his life, though he is rumoured to have committed suicide after drinking a love potion. His major work is the 6-volume hexameter poem *De Natura Rerum* (On the Nature of Things).

Lucretius Brutus the noble father of Lucretia in Shakespeare's *The Rape of Lucrece.*

Lucullus, Lucius Licinius (c.110–57 BC) Roman politician and general. He is noted for his victories over Mithridates VI (74–67 BC), and also for his wealth, luxurious lifestyle ('Lucullan' banquets), and patronage of the arts.

Lucy Poems, The a series of poems by Wordsworth (published in *Lyrical Ballads,* 1801). They focus with a lyrical intensity on the pure and innocent character of Lucy.

Lud a legendary king of Britain recorded by Geoffrey of Monmouth. He was the first to wall the principal city of the country, which was then called Kaerlud after him, and eventually London.

Luddite — *noun* **1** *Hist.* a member of a band of 19c artisans (see LUDDITES). **2** any person opposed to new technology or industrial change. — *adj.* relating to or characteristic of the Luddites.

Luddites the name given to the group of workers who in 1811–12 destroyed newly-introduced textile machinery in Nottingham, Yorkshire, and Lancashire. Their fear was that the output of the equipment was so much faster than the output of a hand-loom operator that many jobs would be lost. Known as 'the Luds', after their leader, Ned Ludd, the movement ended with a mass trial in York in 1813 after which many were hanged or transported to Australia.

Lüderitz, formerly **Angra Pequena** POP (1990e) 6 000, a seaport in SW Namibia, on Lüderitz Bay, an inlet of the Atlantic Ocean. HISTORY the Portuguese navigator, Bartholomew Diaz, landed here in 1486; it was the first German settlement in SW Africa in 1883; taken by South African forces during World War I. [named after the German merchant who acquired the area in 1883]

ludicrous *adj.* completely ridiculous; laughable. [from Latin *ludicrus*]

ludicrously *adv.* in a ludicrous way; to a ludicrous extent: *the price is ludicrously high.*

Ludlow POP (1981) 8 000, a historic market town in Shropshire, W central England. Lying on the R Teme, 38km/24mi S of Shrewsbury, it developed in the 12c around a Norman fortress. NOTABLE FEATURES Ludlow Castle (11c); Church of St Lawrence (12c–14c); Reader's House.

ludo *noun* a simple game in which counters are moved on a board according to the numbers shown on a dice. [from Latin *ludo*, I play]

Ludwig, Karl Friedrich Wilhelm (1816–95) German physiologist, born in Witzenhausen. Professor mainly in Leipzig, he did much to create the foundations of modern physiology, devising methods to illuminate respiration, the function of the blood, and the action of the kidneys and heart.

Ludwigshafen *or* **Ludwigshafen am Rhein** POP (1991e) 162 000, a commercial and manufacturing river port in E Rhineland-Palatinate state, Germany. It lies on the W bank of the R Rhine, opposite Mannheim.

luff *verb* **1** *trans., intrans.* to turn (a ship) towards the wind. **2** *trans.* to move (the jib of a crane or derrick) in and out or up and down, in order to move a load. [from Old French *lof*]

Luftwaffe the correct name for the German Air Force, re-established in 1935 under Hermann Göring, in contravention of the Treaty of Versailles. It was dominant during the early years of World War II, but had all but ceased to exist by 1945, having lost some 100 000 aircraft. The Federal Republic of Germany's air force, also known as the Luftwaffe, was re-established in 1956, and today is a critical element in NATO, operating over 600 combat aircraft.

Lug *or* **Lugh** *or* **Lugus** in Irish mythology, the god of the Sun. He was skilled in many arts and was the divine leader of the Tuatha De Danann, who led his people to victory over the Formorians.

lug¹ *verb trans.* (**lugged, lugging**) to pull or drag (something bulky or heavy) with difficulty. [from Middle English *luggen*]

lug² *noun* **1** *dialect or colloq.* an ear. **2** a projection on a thing, especially one by which it may be carried or turned.

Lugano POP (1990) 114 000, a resort town in Ticino canton, S Switzerland. It lies on the N shore of L Lugano on the N–S road and rail route over the St Gotthard Pass. It is the third largest financial centre in Switzerland. NOTABLE FEATURES town hall (1844); Cathedral of St Lawrence (13c).

Lugansk, formerly **Voroshilovgrad** (1935–58, 1970–1989) POP (1991e) 504 000, the industrial capital of Lugansk region, E Ukraine. It lies on a tributary of the R Severskiy Donets and was founded in 1795.

luge — *noun* a type of light toboggan on which the rider adopts a sitting rather than a prone position. The competition luge is approximately 1.5m (5ft) in length and is steered with the feet and a hand rope. — *verb intrans.* to travel across snow or ice on a luge. [from Swiss French *luge*]

◇ The first official comptetition was at Klosters, Switzerland in 1881. The International Luge Federation was formed in 1957, and it became an Olympic sport in 1964, with competitions for single- and two-seater luges.

Luger pistol a model of automatic pistol associated with the German armed forces in two World Wars. It was designed by the Austrian Georg Luger in 1899, and subsequently manufactured in large quantities.

luggage *noun* suitcases, bags, etc, used in travelling. [from LUG¹]

lugger *noun* a small vessel with square sails attached to yards hanging obliquely to the mast. [from Middle English *lugge*, pole]

lughole *noun colloq.* the ear.

Lugo, Latin **Lucus Augusti** POP (1989e) 408 000, the capital of Lugo province, Galicia, NW Spain. It lies on the R Minho, 511km/317mi NW of Madrid. NOTABLE FEATURES town walls; cathedral (12c); hot springs nearby.

lugubrious *adj.* sad and gloomy; mournful. [from Latin *lugere*, to mourn]

lugubriously *adv.* with a lugubrious manner; mournfully.

lugworm *noun* a worm which lives in the sand on a sea-shore, often used as bait.

Luik see LIEGE.

Lukács, Georg, or **György** (1885–1971) Hungarian Marxist philosopher and critic, born in Budapest. He was a major figure in the articulation of the Marxist theory of literature and Socialist Realism, especially through his work on the novel, as in *Die Theorie des Romans* (1920, The Theory of the Novel). His major work on Marxism *History and Class Consciousness* (1923) was repudiated as heretical by the Russian Communist Party and later by Lukács himself.

Luke, St (1c AD) a New Testament evangelist, possibly the 'beloved physician' and companion of St Paul (Colossians 4.14, Philippians 24). Church tradition made him a native of Antioch in Syria, and a martyr. He was first named as author of the third Gospel in the 2c, and tradition has ever since ascribed to him both that work and the Acts of the Apostles. His feast day is 18 Oct.

Luke a male first name, popular in the Christian world because it was borne by the evangelist. [a Middle English form of *Lucas*, derived from the post-classical Greek name *Loukas*]

Luke, Gospel according to a New Testament writing, one of the four canonical Gospels, and the first part of a two-fold narrative that includes the Acts of the Apostles. It is anonymous, but is traditionally attributed to Luke, a Gentile convert, physician, and friend of Paul. The Gospel is noteworthy for its stories of the births of Jesus and John the Baptist (Luke 1–2), Jesus's promises to the poor and oppressed, the extensive 'travel narrative' (Luke 9–19) which contains many parables and sayings, and its accounts of Jesus's passion and resurrection.

lukewarm *adj.* **1** moderately warm. **2** *said of interest, support, etc* not enthusiastic; indifferent. [from Middle English *luke*, tepid + *warme*, warm]

lukewarmly *adv.* without enthusiasm; indifferently: *they responded lukewarmly to our suggestions.*

lull — *verb trans., intrans.* **1** to make or become calm or quiet. **2** *trans.* to deceive (someone) into feeling secure and not suspicious. — *noun* a period of calm and quiet. [from Middle English *lullen*, imitative]

lullaby *noun* (PL. **lullabies**) a soothing song to lull children to sleep.

Lully, Jean Baptiste, originally **Giovanni Battista Lulli** (1632–87) French composer of Italian parentage, born in Florence. He came as a boy to Paris, and, after much ambitious intriguing, was made operatic director by Louis XIV (1672). His works include many operas, in which he made the ballet an essential part, church music, dance music, and pastorals.

Luluabourg see KANANGA.

lumbago noun Medicine chronic pain in the lower (lumbar) region of the back, which is usually caused by a strained muscle or ligament, arthritis, a slipped disc, or a trapped nerve. [from Latin lumbago, from lumbus, loin]

lumbar adj. relating to the lower part of the back between the lowest ribs and the pelvis. [from Latin lumbus, loin]

lumbar puncture Medicine the insertion of a needle into the lower (lumbar) region of the spine, either to remove cerebrospinal fluid (eg to diagnose a disease or disorder of the nervous system), or to inject a drug (eg an anaesthetic).

lumber[1] — noun **1** useless and disused articles of furniture, etc which have been stored away. **2** North Amer. timber, especially when partly cut up ready for use. — verb **1** (**lumber someone with something**) colloq. to burden (someone) with an unwanted or difficult responsibility or task. **2** to fill with lumber or other useless items. **3** intrans. esp. North Amer. to fell trees and saw the wood into timber for transporting. [perhaps from LUMBER[1]]

lumber[2] verb intrans. (**lumbered, lumbering**) to move about heavily and clumsily. [from Middle English lomeren]

lumbering adj. moving about awkwardly and clumsily.

lumberjack noun a person employed to fell, saw up, and move trees.

Lumbini a town and centre of pilgrimage in the W Terai region of Nepal, 431km/268mi SW of Kathmandu. It was the birthplace of Buddha. NOTABLE FEATURES the broken Ashokan Pillar, the remains of a monastery, and images of Maya Devi (Buddha's mother) are preserved here.

lumen noun (PL. **lumina, lumens**) **1** Physics (SYMBOL **lm**) the SI unit of luminous flux, defined as the amount of light emitted by a point source of intensity one candela within a solid angle of one steradian. **2** Biol. in living organisms, the space enclosed by the walls of a vessel or tubular organ, eg within a blood vessel or intestine. [from Latin lumen, light]

Lumière, Auguste (Marie Louis) (1862–1954) French inventor of photographic equipment, born in Besançon. With his brother, Louis Jean (1864–1948), in 1893 he developed a cine camera, the cinématographe. They showed the first motion pictures using film projection in 1895. They also invented the Autochrome screen plate for colour photography in 1903.

luminaire noun **1** the British Standards Institution term for any sort of electric-light fitting. **2** a general term for any artificial light source (with its mountings and controls) used in photography and video production, such as flood lights, directional spot lights, etc. [from French]

luminance Physics noun **1** (SYMBOL **L**) the measure of brightness of a surface, measured in candela per square centimetre of the surface radiating normally. **2** the component controlling the brightness of a colour television picture; its point-to-point image brightness, as distinct from its colour. [from Latin lumen, -inis, light]

luminary — noun (PL. **luminaries**) **1** a famous or prominent member of a group. **2** a person considered as an expert or authority, and therefore able to enlighten or instruct others: one of the luminaries of the British theatre. **3** literary a source of light, such as the sun or moon. — adj. of or relat-

ing to light or enlightenment. [from Latin luminaria, lamp]

luminescence noun Physics the emission of light by a substance, usually a solid, in the absence of a rise in temperature. It is caused when electrons in the solid return to a lower energy state (ground state) after having been raised (excited) to a higher energy state, the surplus energy being emitted as light. The main types of luminescence are fluorescence and phosphorescence. [from Latin lumen, light]

luminescent adj. giving out light by luminescence.

Luminism an art term formerly applied to the brilliant, high-key effects of light found in the work of painters such as the Impressionists. Since the 1960s, however, the term has been used for moving patterns of light projected mechanically to create 'light spectacles'.

luminosity noun **1** the property of emitting light. **2** Astron. the brightness of a celestial object, eg a star, which is influenced by its surface area and temperature, and is equal to the total energy radiated per unit time.

luminous adj. **1** full of or giving out light. **2** giving out light in the dark; phosphorescent. [from Latin lumen, light]

luminous intensity Physics the amount of visible light capable of causing illumination that is emitted from a point source per unit solid angle. It is independent of the distance from the source. The SI unit of luminous intensity is the candela.

luminously adv. in a luminous way; so as to give out light.

Lummer, Otto Richard (1860–1925) German physicist, born in Breslau (now Wrocław, Poland), where he was later appointed professor. He was one of the discoverers of an interference effect in optics which became known as the 'Lummer fringes' (1884), and designed a number of instruments for research on light. His investigation of certain properties of black-body radiation was an essential step on the road to Max Planck's quantum theory.

lump[1] — noun **1** a small solid shapeless mass. **2** a swelling or tumour. **3** a feeling of tightening or swelling, especially in the throat. **4** the total number of things taken as a single whole. **5** a considerable quantity or heap. **6** a heavy dull or awkward person. **7** Brit. (**the lump**) self-employed casual workers especially in the building trade, paid in lump sums to evade tax. — verb **1** trans., intrans. to form or collect into a lump. **2** trans. (**lump something together**) to treat or consider as a single whole, especially without good reason. [from Middle English lumpe]

lump[2] verb colloq. to accept or put up with: like it or lump it.

lumpectomy noun (PL. **lumpectomies**) the surgical removal of a lump, especially a cancerous tumour, from the breast.

lumpfish or **lumpsucker** noun a heavy-bodied fish widespread in the N Atlantic and Arctic Oceans, up to 60cm in length, which has a rounded body bearing rows of spiny plates, and a large sucker on the underside of the body. It feeds on invertebrates and small fish, and is marketed commercially, salted or smoked, in some areas. Its eggs are dyed black and used as a substitute for caviar.

lumpily adv. in a lumpy way; with lumps.

lumpiness noun being lumpy; a lumpy quality.

lumpish adj., said of a person heavy, dull, or awkward.

lump sugar sugar in small lumps or cubes.

lump sum a large single payment instead of several smaller ones spread out over a period of time.

lumpy adj. (**lumpier, lumpiest**) full of lumps.

Lumumba, Patrice (Hemery) (1925–61) Congolese politician, born in Katako Kombe. He helped form the Mouvement National Congolais (1958) to challenge Belgian rule and became Prime Minister (1960–1) when the Congo became an independent republic (now Zaire). Almost immediately the country suffered chaos through warring factions. He opposed the secession of Katanga, but was arrested by his own army, handed over to the Katangese, and killed.

lunacy noun (PL. **lunacies**) **1** insanity. **2** great foolishness or stupidity.

lunar adj. **1** resembling the moon. **2** relating to or caused by the moon. **3** for use on the surface of the moon or in connection with travel to the moon: lunar vehicle. [from Latin luna, moon]

lunate adj. crescent-shaped [from Latin luna, moon]

lunatic — adj. **1** insane. **2** foolish, stupid, or wildly eccentric. — noun an insane or highly eccentric person; (more loosely) a foolish person. [from Latin lunaticus, moonstruck, from luna, moon, from the belief that intermittent insanity was caused by the phases of the moon]

lunatic asylum Hist. a home or hospital for people regarded as insane.

lunatic fringe the most extreme, fanatical, or eccentric members of any group.

lunch — noun a meal eaten in the middle of the day. — verb intrans. to eat lunch. [a shortening of LUNCHEON]

luncheon noun a lunch, especially a formal one. [from Middle English noneschench, from none, noon + schench, drink]

luncheon meat a type of pre-cooked meat, processed and mixed with cereal, usually bought tinned and served cold.

luncheon voucher Brit. a voucher of a specified value given to employees by their employers and used to pay for lunches at restaurants and shops.

lunchtime noun the time set aside for lunch.

Lund POP (1992e) 90 000, an ancient city in Malmöhus county, SW Sweden, lying NE of Malmö. It was intermittently under Danish rule until 1658. NOTABLE FEATURE cathedral (1080).

Lundy Island an island in the Bristol Channel. It lies off the NW coast of Devon, SW England, 19km/12mi NW of Hartland Point. AREA 9.6sq km/3.7sq mi. At one time the island was a refuge for pirates. A National Trust area since 1969, it is noted for its interesting flora and birdlife. It has two lighthouses.

Luneburg Heath, German **Lüneburger Heide** a region of moorland and forest lying between the R Aller and R Elbe in Germany, where Field Marshal Montgomery accepted the capitulation of the German Army (4 May 1945).

lung noun **1** in the chest cavity of air-breathing vertebrates, a large spongy respiratory organ, usually one of a pair, which removes carbon dioxide from the blood and replaces it with oxygen. **2** a simple respiratory organ found in some terrestrial molluscs, eg slugs and snails. [from Anglo-Saxon lungen]
◇ In mammals, the surface area of the lungs is greatly increased by the presence of millions of tiny air sacs, known as alveoli. For example, in humans the total surface area of the alveoli is about 70m². Air containing oxygen is drawn into the lungs through the trachea (windpipe), which divides at its lower end to form two bronchi, which in turn divide into many fine tubes known as bronchioles. Each bronchiole terminates in a cluster of alveoli, which are lined with a thin moist membrane richly supplied with capillaries (very small blood vessels). Oxygen from the air on one side of the membrane passes through the thin walls of the alveoli into the capillaries, while

carbon dioxide passes out of the capillaries into the lungs in the same way. Air is forced in and out of the lungs as a result of movements of the diaphragm (a sheet of muscle that separates the thorax from the abdomen). During inhalation the diaphragm is lowered, and the lungs expand to fill with air. During exhalation, the diaphragm is raised, and air is forcibly expelled from the lungs.

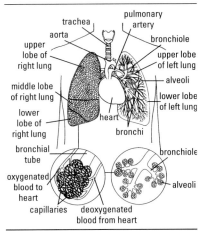

human lungs

lunge — *noun* **1** a sudden plunge forwards. **2** *Fencing* a sudden thrust with a sword. — *verb intrans.* to make a sudden strong or thrusting movement forwards, in Fencing with a sword in one's hand. [from French *allonger*, to lengthen]

lungfish *noun* a fish that has a lung as well as gills.

Luoyang *or* **Honan** POP (1990) 1.2m, a town in Henan province, N central China. It was the capital of ancient China during the E Zhou Dynasty (770–256 BC). NOTABLE FEATURES Wangcheng (Royal Town) Park; Luoyang Museum; Baimasi (White Horse) Temple (founded in AD 75) is 8km/5mi to the NE; the Longmen Caves, with c.100 000 images and statues of Buddha (5c–7c) lie 14km/9mi to the S.

Lupercalia an ancient festival of purification and fertility. It was held on 15 Feb every year in ancient Rome, in a cave on the Palatine Hill called the Lupe.

lupin *noun* a garden plant with long spikes of brightly coloured flowers. [from Latin *lupinus*, wolfish]

lupin

lupine *adj.* relating to or like a wolf. [from Latin *lupinus*, from *lupus*, wolf]

Lupus *Astron.* the Wolf, a small constellation in the southern hemisphere, containing bright stars and lying next to the Milky Way.

lupus *noun* a skin disease characterized by the formation of ulcers and lesions. [from Latin *lupus*, wolf; it is so called because it eats away the skin]

lurch¹ — *verb intrans.* to move or stagger unsteadily, especially rolling slightly to one side. — *noun* a sudden roll to one side.

lurch²
— **leave someone in the lurch** *colloq.* to leave them in a difficult situation and without help. [from Old French *lourche*, a game like backgammon]

lurcher *noun Brit.* a cross-bred dog, usually a cross between a sheepdog or a golden retriever and a greyhound, used for hunting. [from Middle English *lorchen*, to lurk]

lure — *verb trans.* (**lure someone away** *or* **into something**) to tempt, attract, or entice (someone), often by offering some reward. — *noun* **1** a person or thing which tempts, attracts, or entices. **2** (**the lure of something**) its attractive or tempting qualities: *the lure of the chase.* **3** *Angling* a metal or plastic bait with hooks attached. **4** a bunch of feathers to which meat may be attached, used by falconers to recall a hawk. [from Old French *luere*, bait]

lurid *adj.* **1** glaringly bright: *lurid colours.* **2** horrifying or sensational: *lurid details.* **3** pale or wan. [from Latin *luridus*, pale yellow, wan]

luridly *adv.* in a lurid or glaring way.

luridness *noun* a lurid or glaring quality or state.

lurk *verb intrans.* **1** to lie in wait, especially in ambush, with some sinister purpose in mind. **2** to linger unseen or furtively; to be latent: *a lurking suspicion.* [from Middle English *lurken*]

Lusaka POP (1990) 982 000, the capital of Zambia, situated in the centre of the country, 370km/230mi NE of Livingstone and the Victoria Falls. It replaced Livingstone as the capital of former Northern Rhodesia in 1935 and became capital of independent Zambia in 1964. NOTABLE FEATURES cathedral (1957); Geological Survey Museum; National Archives; Munda Wanga Gardens; zoo.

luscious *adj.* **1** richly sweet; delicious. **2** attractive in a voluptuous way. [from Middle English *lucius*, perhaps a variant of DELICIOUS]

lusciously *adv.* in a luscious or delicious way.

lusciousness *noun* being luscious or delicious.

lush¹ *adj.* **1** *said of grass or foliage, etc* green and growing abundantly. **2** luxurious. [from Middle English *lusch*, slack]

lush² *noun North Amer. slang* a drunkard or alcoholic. [perhaps from LUSH¹]

lushness *noun* a lush or luxurious state or quality.

Lusitania a British (Cunard) passenger liner that was sunk, with great loss of life, by a German U-boat in the Irish Sea in 1915. The Germans claimed she was carrying armaments, but this was officially denied by the British. Its sinking caused worldwide anger, and was instrumental in bringing the USA into World War I.

lust — *noun* **1** strong sexual desire. **2** enthusiasm; relish: *a lust for life.* — *verb intrans.* (**lust after** *or* **for someone**) to have a strong, especially sexual, desire for (someone). [from Anglo-Saxon *lust*, desire, appetite]

lustful *adj.* having or showing strong sexual desire; characterized by lust.

lustfully *adv.* with a lustful manner.

lustfulness *noun* a lustful state or quality.

lustily *adv.* with a lusty or vigorously loud manner.

lustiness *noun* a lusty or loud state or quality.

lustre *noun* **1** the shiny appearance of a surface in reflected light. **2** shine, brightness, or gloss. **3** splendour and glory, on account of beauty or accomplishments, etc. **4** a thin metallic glaze for pottery. [from Latin *lustrare*, to light up]

lustrous *adj.* having a lustre; bright and shining.

lustrously *adv.* with a lustre; brightly.

lusty *adj.* (**lustier, lustiest**) **1** vigorous or loud: *a baby's lusty cries.* **2** strong and healthy.

lute *noun* a medieval and Renaissance stringed instrument with a pear-shaped body and a long neck. [from Arabic *al ud*]
◇ The European instrument was descended from an Arabian instrument, and was in use from the Middle Ages to the 18c. By the 16c, it normally had six courses of stopped strings (strung from a pegbox at right angles to the neck) which the player plucked with the right hand: lower 'open' strings were added later.

luteinizing hormone *Physiol.* (ABBREV. **LH**) a hormone secreted by the pituitary gland in vertebrates, which stimulates ovulation and the formation of the corpus luteum in females, and the secretion of testosterone by the testes in males. [from Latin *luteum*, eggyolk]

lutenist *noun* a person who plays the lute.

lutetium *noun Chem.* (SYMBOL **Lu**, ATOMIC NUMBER **71**) a very rare soft silvery metal, belonging to the lanthanide series, that is usually obtained by the processing of other metals. It is used as a catalyst and in nuclear technology. [from Latin *Lutetia*, Paris, where it was discovered in 1907]

Luther, Martin (1483–1546) German religious reformer, born in Eisleben. He spent three years in an Augustinian monastery and was ordained in 1507. His career as a reformer began after a visit to Rome in 1510–11, where he was angered by the sale of indulgences. In 1517 he drew up 95 theses on indulgences, denying the pope the right to forgive sins, which he nailed on the church door at Wittenberg. Violent controversy followed, and he was summoned to Rome to defend his theses, but did not go. He then began to attack the papal system more boldly, and publicly burned the papal bull issued against him. An order was issued for the destruction of his books; he was summoned to appear before the Diet at Worms, and was put under the ban of the Empire. The drawing up of the Augsburg Confession, where he was represented by Melanchthon, marks the culmination of the German Reformation (1530). His translation of the Bible became a landmark of German literature.

Luther a male first name; its popularity derives from the ecclesiastical reformer Martin Luther and more recently from the civil rights leader Martin Luther King. [from the Germanic surname, composed of two elements, *liut*, people + *heri*, army, warrior]

Luther a play by John Osborne (1961). It focuses mainly on Martin Luther's early life, and the physical problems and psychological development that preceded his religious struggles.

Lutheran — *noun* a follower of the German Protestant reformer Martin Luther, or a member of the Lutheran Church based on his teaching. — *adj.* relating to Martin Luther or his teaching.

Lutheranism the doctrine and the churches derived from the Reformation of Martin Luther. Lutheran Churches originally flourished in Germany and Scandinavia, then spread throughout Europe, the USA, and, through missionary activity, into Africa and Asia. The doctrine emphasizes justification by faith alone, the importance of Scripture, and the priesthood of all believers. Three sacraments are recognized: Baptism, Eucharist, and penance. The Lutheran World Federation, a free association of Lutheran Churches, was founded in 1947, and is the largest of the Protestant confessional families.

Luthuli *or* **Lutuli, Albert (John Mvumbi)** (⁇1899–1967) African resistance leader, born in Rhodesia. He spent 15 years as a teacher before being elected tribal chief of Groutville, Natal. Deposed for anti-apartheid activities, he became

President-General of the African National Congress, and dedicated himself to a campaign of non-violent resistance, for which he was awarded the Nobel Peace Prize (1960).

Lutine bell a bell formerly rung in Lloyd's, the London shipping insurers, to announce the loss or safe arrival of a ship. It is now rung only on ceremonial occasions. [the bell originally belonged to the frigate *Lutine*, which was lost at sea in 1799]

Luton POP (1992e) 176 000, an industrial town in Bedfordshire, S central England. It lies 45km/28mi NW of London. NOTABLE FEATURES Church of St Mary (13c–15c); Luton Hoo Mansion (3km/2mi S), in a park laid out by Capability Brown.

Lutyens, Sir Edwin (Landseer) (1869–1944) English architect, born in London. He became known as a designer of country houses. His best-known projects are the Cenotaph, Whitehall (1919–20), and the layout and Viceroy's House of New Delhi (1912–30). His project for a Roman Catholic cathedral in Liverpool was incomplete at his death.

Lützen, Battle of 1 a battle (1632) during the Thirty Years War, fought near Leipzig in Saxony between forces led by King Gustav II Adolf of Sweden (who was killed) and an Imperial army under Wallenstein. **2** a battle (1873) during the Napoleonic Wars between Napoleon I's advance guard and Russo-Prussian armies, which resulted in heavy casualties but was inconclusive.

lux *noun Physics* the SI unit of illumination, equal to one lumen per square metre. [from Latin *lux*, light]

luxe see DE LUXE.

Luxembourg *or* **Luxemburg**, official name **Grand Duchy of Luxembourg**, French **Grande-Duché de Luxembourg**, German **Gross-Herzogtum Luxemburg**, Letzeburgish **Grousherzogdem Lëtzebuerg** POP (1992e) 370 000, an independent constitutional monarchy in NW Europe, divided into three districts. AREA 2 586sq km/998sq mi. It is bounded E by Germany, W by Belgium, and S by France. CAPITAL Luxembourg. CHIEF TOWNS Esch-sur-Alzette, Dudelange, Differdange. TIME ZONE GMT +1. OFFICIAL LANGUAGES French, German, Letzeburgish. Most of the population is descended from the Mosel Franks, but one quarter is foreign; the chief religion is Roman Catholicism. CURRENCY the franc. PHYSICAL DESCRIPTION divided into the two natural regions of Ösling in the N (wooded, hilly land, of average height 450m) and the flatter, more fertile Gutland (average height 250m); water resources have been developed by canalization of the R Mosel, by hydroelectric dams on the R Our, and by reservoirs on the R Sûre. CLIMATE it is drier and sunnier in the S, but winters can be severe; in the sheltered Mosel Valley, summers and autumns are warm enough for cultivation of vines. HISTORY made a Grand Duchy by the Congress of Vienna in 1815, after 400 years of domination by various European powers; granted political autonomy in 1838; recognized as a neutral independent state in 1867; occupied by Germany in both World Wars; joined Benelux economic union in 1948; abandoned neutrality on joining NATO in 1949. GOVERNMENT a hereditary monarchy with the Grand Duke or Grand Duchess as head of state; Parliament has a Chamber of Deputies with 64 members elected every five years and a State Council with 21 members appointed for life; the head of government is the Minister of State. ECONOMY the city of Luxembourg is an important international centre; iron and steel (c.25% of the national income); food processing; chemicals; tyres; metal products; engineering; mixed farming; dairy farming; wine; forestry; tourism.

Luxembourg 1 POP (1991e) 75 000, the capital of Luxembourg, lying on the Alzette and Petrusse rivers. It is the residence of the Grand Duke of Luxembourg, and the seat of government. Luxembourg also houses the Court of Justice of the European Communities, the General Secretariat of the European Parliament, the Consultative Committee, the European Investment Bank, the European Monetary Fund, and the Coal and Steel Union. It was built originally on an impregnable, defensive location as a fortress controlling the route between France and Germany. NOTABLE FEATURES Musée de l'Etat with the 8c Echternach Stone; cathedral (17c); fortress. **2** a district in the S of Luxembourg. **3** a canton in the S of Luxembourg, in central Luxembourg district. **4** a province in SE Belgium with Arlon as its capital.

Luxembourg, Palais du the seat of the French Senate in Paris since 1958. The palace was built in 1613–14 by Salomon de Brosse (1565–1626) for Henri IV's Florentine widow, Marie de Medicis. Its design was based on that of the Pitti Palace, and it was altered and enlarged in the 19c.

Luxemburg, Rosa (1871–1919) German revolutionary, born in Russian Poland. A German citizen from 1895, she emigrated to Zürich in 1889, where she studied law and political economy. With the German politician Karl Liebknecht (1871–1919), she formed the Spartacus League, which later became the German Communist Party. She was arrested and murdered during the Spartacus revolt in Berlin.

Luxor, Arabic **El Uqsor** *or* **Al-Uqsur** POP (1986) 125 000, a winter resort town in Qena governorate, E central Egypt. It lies on the E bank of the R Nile, 676km/420mi S of Cairo. The city was the capital of Upper Egypt for 1500 years. It was Homer's 'city of a hundred gates'. NOTABLE FEATURES on the W bank, 700 tombs (including the Valley of the Kings) and Theban ruins; Temple of Luxor (built by Amenhotep III who reigned in 1390–53 BC); one of the obelisks was removed to the Place de la Concorde in Paris. [from Arabic, meaning 'the palaces']

luxuriance *noun* being luxuriant; lushness of vegetation.

luxuriant *adj.* **1** *said of plants, etc* growing abundantly; lush. **2** very elaborate; extravagant; flowery. [from Latin *luxuria*, luxury]
◆ Often confused with *luxurious*.

luxuriantly *adv.* in a luxuriant or abundant way.

luxuriate *verb intrans.* **1** (**luxuriate in something**) to enjoy it greatly or revel in it. **2** to live in great comfort or luxury. **3** to grow richly or abundantly. [from Latin *luxuria*, luxury]

luxurious *adj.* **1** supplied or furnished with luxuries. **2** enjoying or providing luxury. [from Latin *luxuriosus*, from *luxus*, excess]

◆ Often confused with *luxuriant*.

luxuriously *adv.* in a luxurious way; with luxury.

luxuriousness *noun* a luxurious state or quality.

luxury *noun* (PL. **luxuries**) **1** expensive, rich, extremely comfortable surroundings and possessions. **2** habitual indulgence in or enjoyment of luxurious surroundings. **3** something that is pleasant and enjoyable but not essential. **4** (*attributive*) relating to or providing luxury: *luxury hotels*. [from Latin *luxuria*, from *luxus*, excess]

Luzon POP (1980) 23.9m, the largest island of the Philippines. AREA 108 130sq km/41 738sq mi. It is bounded in the W by the South China Sea, in the E by the Philippine Sea, and in the N by the Luzon Strait. The island forms an irregular shape with its many bays and offshore islets. The Sierra Madre rises in the NE and the Cordillera Central rises to 2 929m in the NW at Mt Puog. Laguna de Bay is the largest lake. Japanese troops occupied the island in World War II. CHIEF TOWN Manila. ECONOMY grain; sugar cane; timber; hemp; chromite; tourism.

LV *abbrev.* luncheon voucher.

Lvov, Giorgiy Yevgenievich, Knyaz (Prince) (1861–1925) Russian liberal politician, born in Popovka. He was head of the first and second provisional governments after the February Revolution of 1917, but his moderate policies and popular opposition to Russia's war effort led to the collapse of his government. He was succeeded by Kerensky, and arrested by the Bolsheviks, but escaped to Paris.

Lvov, Polish **Lwow**, German **Lemberg**, Ukrainian **Lwiw** POP (1991e) 802 000, a city in the Ukraine, close to the Polish border and near the R Poltva. It is a centre for Ukrainian culture. HISTORY founded in 1256; became an important centre on the Black Sea–Baltic trade route; ceded to Poland after World War I; ceded to the Soviet Union in 1939; the scene of nationalistic demonstrations in 1989. NOTABLE FEATURES St Yuri's Uniate Cathedral; Church of the Assumption (16c).

Lw *symbol Chem.* formerly used for lawrencium (now generally replaced by *Lr*).

-ly an element used: **1** to form adverbs: *cleverly / hopefully*. **2** to form adverbs and adjectives with the sense of 'at intervals of': *daily*. **3** to form adjectives with the sense 'in the manner of, like': *brotherly*. [from anglo-Saxon forms]

Lyallpur see FAISALABAD.

lycanthropy *noun Relig.* in popular superstition, the power of changing from human shape into that of an animal, usually the most dangerous beast of the area. In Europe and N Asia it is usually a wolf or bear, in India and other parts of Asia a tiger, and in Africa a leopard. Also, a kind of madness, in which the patient has fantasies of being a wolf. [from Greek *lykos*, wolf + *anthropos*, man]

lyceum *noun* **1** (**Lyceum**) the garden in Athens where Aristotle taught. **2** a place or building devoted to teaching, especially literature and philosophy. [from Greek *Lykeion*, from *lykeios*, an epithet of Apollo. Apollo's temple stood near the Lyceum and gave it its name]

Lyceum Theatre the Royal Lyceum and English Opera House in Wellington Street, London, built in 1834 on a site occupied by theatres since 1772. When the Lyceum was managed by Sir Henry Irving from 1878 to 1902, Ellen Terry was his leading lady, and it dominated the English stage for a quarter of a century. Its demolition was postponed by World War II, when it was used as a dance hall.

lychee *noun* a small fruit with sweet, white, juicy flesh, originally from China. [from Chinese *lichi*]

lychgate same as LICHGATE.

BELGIUM

Diekirch •

GERMANY

Luxembourg
Esch-sur-
Alzette
Differdange •
Dudelange

FRANCE

Mosel

Luxembourg

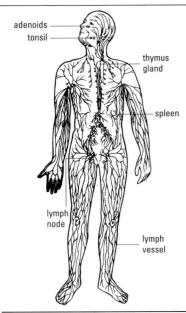

adenoids
tonsil
thymus gland
spleen
lymph node
lymph vessel

the lymphatic system

Lycidas a poem by John Milton (1638). It is a pastoral elegy on the death of Edward King, a contemporary of Milton's at Cambridge, who was drowned in 1637.

Lycra *noun trademark* fabric made from a lightweight synthetic elastomeric fibre, often used to make skintight clothing.

Lycurgus the legendary founder of the Spartan constitution, first mentioned in Herodotus. The name also refers to various other Greeks, including in mythology, the King of Thrace who opposed Dionysus and was blinded.

Lydgate, John (c.1370–c.1451) English poet, born in Lydgate, Suffolk. He travelled in Europe as a Benedictine monk, and became prior of Hatfield Broadoak in 1423. Influenced by Chaucer, his major works are the narrative poems, *The Troy Book* (1412–20), *The Siege of Thebes* (1420–22), and the *Fall of Princes* (1431–8).

Lydia an ancient region of W Asia Minor lying inland of Ionia, with its capital at Sardis. At the height of its power (7c–6c BC) it was the centre of an empire which stretched from the Aegean to central Turkey. It was conquered by the Persians in 546 BC and was successively ruled by Persians, Seleucids, Attalids, and Romans.

Lydia a female first name. [from Greek, = woman from Lydia]

lye *noun* **1** a caustic solution made by passing water through wood ash. **2** a strong solution of sodium or potassium hydroxide. [from Anglo-Saxon *leag*]

Lyell, Sir Charles (1797–1875) Scottish geologist, born in Kinnordy, Forfarshire. During travel in Europe in 1828 he decided to give up a law career and became immersed in geological research; he soon published his authoritative *Principles of Geology* (1830–3), and was appointed professor at King's College, London. His established the 'uniformitarian' principle already stated by James Hutton, asserting that the greatest geological changes have been produced by the forces in operation now, and later became an enthusiastic supporter of the theories of Charles Darwin, who had drawn heavily on Lyell's work.

lying see LIE[1], LIE[2].

Lyly, John (c.1554–1606) English writer, born in the Weald of Kent. An MP from 1597 to 1601, he is chiefly remembered for the style of his writing, as seen in his two-part prose romance, *Euphues* (1578, 1580). It led to the term

'euphuism', referring to an artificial and extremely elegant language, with much use made of complex similes and antithesis.

Lymington POP (1981) 12 000, a resort town in New Forest district, Hampshire, S England, situated 25km/15mi E of Bournemouth. It is a recreational sailing centre.

lymph *noun* in animals, a colourless fluid, derived from blood, that bathes all the tissues, cleansing them of cellular debris and bacteria. It contains lymphocytes and antibodies which prevent the spread of infection, and it drains into the vessels of the lymphatic system. [from Latin *lympha*, water]

lymphatic *adj.* **1** relating to or carrying lymph. **2** *said of a person* slow and lethargic.

lymphatic system the network of vessels that carries lymph throughout the body.

lymph node *or* **lymph gland** *Anat.* one of a number of small rounded bodies found in the lymphatic system. It produces antibodies in immune responses, and filters bacteria and foreign bodies from the lymph before it rejoins the bloodstream, so preventing the spread of infection. There are large clusters of lymph nodes in the neck, armpit, and groin of the human body.

lymphocyte *noun Medicine* a type of white blood cell with a dense nucleus and clear cytoplasm, present in large numbers in lymphatic tissues such as the lymph nodes and spleen, and involved in immune responses in the body, such as the production of antibodies.

lymphoma *noun Medicine* a tumour of the lymph nodes, especially a malignant one.

Lynch, Jack (John) (1917–) Irish politician and Prime Minister, born in Cork. Following a career in the Department of Justice (1936), he was called to the Bar (1945) and became an MP (1948). He held ministerial posts in Lands (1951), the Gaeltacht (1957), Education (1957–9), Industry and Commerce (1959–65), and Finance (1965–6), then became Prime Minister (1966–73, 1977–9). Perceived as a strong supporter of the Catholic minority in Ulster, he drew criticism from both Ulster and mainland Britain. In 1979 he resigned both the premiership and the leadership of Fianna Fáil.

lynch *verb, said of a body of people* to condemn and put to death, usually by hanging, without a legal trial. [named after William Lynch (1742–1820), who presided over self-instituted tribunals in Virginia, USA]

lynching *noun* the activity of people who lynch others; an occurrence of this.

Lynette a female first name. [a medieval French form of Welsh *Eluned*]

Lynx *Astron.* a faint constellation in the northern hemisphere.

lynx *noun* any of several bobtailed members of the cat family (Felidae), found in Europe, Asia, and N America, especially in pine forests, and having yellowish-grey or reddish fur, long legs with wide paws, a short stubby tail with a black tip, tufted ears, and a ruff of fur around the face. It feeds on hares, rabbits, badgers, foxes, birds, and small deer, and also catches fish. [from Greek *lynx*]

lynx

lynx-eyed *adj.* sharp-sighted.

Lyon, John (1962–) English boxer, born in St Helens, Merseyside. He is the only man to win eight Amateur Boxing Association titles — the light-flyweight title (1981–4) and the flyweight title (1986–9). He also won the 1986 Commonwealth Games flyweight title.

Lyons, Sir Joseph (1848–1917) English business man, born in London. He joined with three friends to establish what was to become J Lyons and Co Ltd. He started in Piccadilly with a teashop, and became head of one of the largest catering businesses in Britain.

Lyons, French **Lyon**, ancient **Lugdunum** POP (1990) 1.3m, the manufacturing and commercial capital of Rhône-Alpes region, S central France, at the confluence of the Rhône and Saône rivers. The city centre is on a peninsula between the rivers, linked to their banks by many bridges. In Roman times it was the walled city of Lugdunum, the capital of Gaul, and the centre of a military highway network. Now the third largest city in France, it is the principal centre of the French textile industry, particularly silk production. NOTABLE FEATURES international exhibition hall (Eurexpo); Palais St-Pierre (17c); Church of St-Nizier (rebuilt in the 15c); Hôtel de Ville (1646–72); Cathedral of St-Jean (12c–15c); Basilica of Notre-Dame-de-Fourvière (19c).

lyophilic *adj. Chem.* denoting a substance that has an affinity for liquid solvents. [from Greek *lye*, separation + *phileein*, to love]

lyophobic *adj. Chem.* describing a substance that tends to repel liquid solvents.

Lyot, Bernard Ferdinand (1897–1952) French astronomer, born in Paris. He trained as an engineer before joining the staff of the Paris Observatory at Meudon (1920), where his studies of the polarization of light from the Moon and planets led to new information about their surfaces. In 1930 he invented the coronagraph, allowing observations of the solar corona without the need for a solar eclipse.

Lyra *Astron.* the Lyre, a small but obvious constellation in the northern hemisphere. Its brightest star is Vega, the fifth brightest star in the sky.

lyre

lyre *noun* a U-shaped harp-like instrument plucked with a plectrum. It was used, especially in ancient Greece, to accompany poetry. [from Greek *lyra*]
◇ The body of the classical instrument was made of tortoiseshell or wood, and had from three to twelve gut strings. It was a simplified form of the kithara, which was larger and was made of wood.

lyre-bird *noun* either of two Australian pheasant-like birds, the male of which has lyre-shaped tail feathers displayed during courtship.

lyric — *adj.* **1** *said of poems or poets* expressing personal, private, or individual emotions. **2** having the form of a song; meant to be sung, originally to the lyre. — *noun* **1** a short lyric poem or a song. **2** (*usually* **lyrics**) the words of a song. [from Greek *lyrikos*, from *lyra*, lyre]

lyrical *adj.* **1** lyric; song-like. **2** full of enthusiastic praise.

Lyrical Ballads a collection of poems by William Wordsworth and Samuel Taylor Coleridge (1798, 2nd ed. 1801, 3rd ed. 1802). It challenged the traditional view of poetry by taking its main inspiration from the life and language of the rural class.

lyrically *adv.* in a lyrical or song-like way.

lyricism *noun* **1** the state or quality of being lyrical. **2** a pouring out of emotions.

lyricist *noun* **1** a person who writes the words to songs. **2** a lyric poet.

Lyric Theatre **1** a theatre in Hammersmith, London, opened in 1888 as the Lyric Hall. It was a leading influence in the 1920s. The present theatre, opened in 1979, has developed a reputation for serious theatre, complemented by the Lyric Studio Theatre. **2** the oldest surviving theatre in Shaftesbury Avenue, London, opened in 1888. It had a reputation for comic operas but this developed to focus on serious theatre and popular musicals.

Lysander **1** Spartan naval commander (d.395 BC). He commanded the Spartan navy in the final years of the Peloponnesian War and defeated the Athenian fleet in 407 BC. A further victory at the Battle of Agospotami (405 BC) ended the war. He was killed in Boeotia, leading the Spartan army. **2** one of the two heroes in Shakespeare's *A Midsummer Night's Dream*, in love with Hermia.

Lysenko, Trofim Denisovich (1898–1976) Soviet geneticist and agronomist, born in Karlovka, the Ukraine. He promoted agricultural techniques which gained him enthusiastic political support, and developed a theory of genetics which suggested that environment can alter the hereditary material. As Director of the Institute of Genetics of the Soviet Academy of Sciences (1940–65), he declared Gregor Mendel's theory of heredity to be erroneous, and ruthlessly silenced scientists who opposed him. Following Stalin's death, he increasingly lost support and was forced to resign 1965.

lysergic acid diethylamide see LSD.

lysine *noun Biochem.* an essential amino acid that is found in proteins. [from Greek *lysis*, dissolution]

lysis *noun Biol.* any process that causes the destruction of a living cell by the disruption of the cell membrane and release of the cell contents. It may occur naturally in the case of damaged or worn out cells, or it may be caused by an antibody or bacterial toxin. [from Greek *lysis*]

Lysistrata a play by Aristophanes (411 BC). It is a comedy about the women of Greece who decide on a 'sex strike' to force their men to end the Athens–Sparta war.

lysosome *noun Biol.* a specialized membrane-bound structure (organelle), found mainly in animal cells, that contains a range of digestive enzymes which can break down proteins and other biochemical compounds. Lysosomes play an important role in the destruction of foreign particles (eg bacteria), and the breakdown of damaged or worn out cells.

lysozyme *noun Biochem.* an enzyme that breaks down bacterial cell walls and is present in many body fluids and secretions, including saliva, tears, and mucus, as well as egg white. [from Greek *lysis*, dissolution]

Lytham St Anne's POP (1981) 40 000, a resort town in Blackpool urban area and Fylde district, Lancashire, NW England. It lies on the estuary of the R Ribble, 20km/12mi W of Preston. NOTABLE FEATURE championship golf course.

Lyttelton, Humphrey (Richard Adeane) (1921–) English jazz trumpeter and bandleader, born in Eton, Berkshire. He played with George Webb's Dixielanders before forming his own band in 1948. A leading figure in the British revival of traditional jazz, he was one of the first 'trad' bandleaders to move towards the mainstream, replacing the banjo with the guitar and introducing an alto saxophone into the line-up.

M

M¹ *or* **m** *noun* (PL. **Ms**, **M's**, **m's**) the thirteenth letter of the English alphabet.

M² *abbrev.* **1** Majesty. **2** mark (German currency). **3** Master. **4** (French) Monsieur. **5** Motorway.

M³ *symbol* the Roman numeral for 1 000.

m *abbrev.* **1** male. **2** married. **3** masculine. **4** *meridiem* (Latin), noon. **5** metre. **6** mile. **7** million. **8** minute. **9** month.

'm *contr.* am: *I'm going.*

MA *abbrev.* **1** Massachusetts. **2** Master of Arts.

ma *noun colloq.* a mother.

ma'am *noun* madam, used as a polite form of address, eg to female royalty.

Maastricht, ancient **Traieclum ad Mosam, Traiectum Tungorum** POP (1992e) 118 000, the capital of Limburg province, S Netherlands, lying on the R Maas. The city, noted for its vegetable and butter markets, is the commercial hub of an area extending well into Belgium. The Maastricht summit between EC leaders was held here in 1991. NOTABLE FEATURES St Pietersburg underground gallery; Church of St Servatius (6c); Romanesque basilica (10c–11c).

Maastricht, Treaty of an agreement signed (7 Feb 1992) in Maastricht, Netherlands, by the 12 nations of the EC to create the European Union. The EU has a common foreign, security, interior, and justice policy, which will be implemented when the Treaty is ratified by all 12 governments. Particularly controversial sections have been the Social Chapter and European Monetary Union (EMU). Britain 'opted out' of the former when it was signed (Dec 1989) by the other 11 countries, and will not be obliged to agree to all three stages of EMU.

Maazel, Lorin (1930–) US conductor, born in Neuilly, France. His family moved to the USA when he was a child, and he made his début as a violinist in 1945 and as a conductor in 1953. He directed the Deutsche Oper Berlin (1965–71), the Cleveland Orchestra (1972–82), and the Vienna Staatsoper (1982–4). More recently he was appointed musical director of the Orchestre National de France (1988–90) and of the Pittsburgh Symphony Orchestra (1988–), and chief conductor of the Bavarian State Radio Orchestra (1992–).

Mabinogion, The the name given to a group of Welsh prose tales published in English by Lady Charlotte Guest (1838–49). The four main tales come from two 14c manuscripts and are set in 11c, pre-Norman Wales.

Mabuse see GOSSAERT, JAN.

MAC *abbrev.* Multiplex Analogue Components.

mac *noun colloq.* a mackintosh.

macabre *adj.* **1** dealing with death. **2** ghastly or horrific. [from French *macabre*]

macadam *noun* **1** a road-making material consisting of layers of compacted broken stones, usually bound with tar. **2** a road surface made with this. See also TARMACADAM. [from John McAdam, Scottish engineer]

macadamize *or* **macadamise** *verb* to build or cover (a road) with macadam.

Macao, Portuguese **Macáu** POP (1992e) 374 000, an Overseas Territory of Portugal. AREA 16sq km/6sq mi. It comprises a flat, maritime tropical peninsula on the SE coast of China and the nearby islands of Taipa and Colôane, on the Pearl R delta, 64km/40mi W of Hong Kong. CAPITAL Nome de Deus de Macau. The population is largely Chinese (99%); Buddhism and Roman Catholicism are the chief religions. OFFICIAL LANGUAGE Portuguese; Cantonese is spoken generally. CURRENCY the pataca. Macao is under Portuguese administration but this will end in 1999 when it is returned to Chinese sovereignty. GOVERNMENT a governor is appointed by Portugal with a 23-member Legislative Assembly. ECONOMY textiles; electronics; toys; tourism; gambling; fishing. NOTABLE FEATURES several fortresses; Jaialai Palace.

Macao

macaque *noun* any of various short-tailed or tailless monkeys of Asia and Africa, with large cheek-pouches. [from French *macaque*, from Portuguese *macaco*, monkey]

macaroni *noun* (PL. **macaronis, macaronies**) **1** pasta in the form of short tubes. **2** in 18c Britain, a dandy. [from Italian *maccaroni*]

macaroon *noun* a sweet cake or biscuit made with sugar, eggs, and crushed almonds or coconut. [from French *macaron*]

MacArthur, Douglas (1880–1964) US soldier, born in Little Rock, Arkansas. He joined the US army engineers, served with distinction in France in World War I, and in 1930 was promoted general and army chief of staff. In World War II he became commanding general of the US armed forces in the Far East (1941), and from Australia directed the recapture of the SW Pacific (1942–5). He formally accepted the Japanese surrender, and commanded the occupation of Japan (1945–51), where he introduced a new constitution. In 1950 he led the UN forces in the Korean War, defeated the North Korean army, but was relieved of command when he tried to continue the war against China.

MacArthur, Robert Helmer (1930–72) Canadian-born US ecologist, born in Toronto. Professor at Princeton University from 1965, he developed quantitative analysis of the relative abundances of species in different habitats, and distinguished two groups of species: those exhibiting rapid growth followed by catastrophic decline which have fast rates of population increase and development ('r-selected' species, eg lemmings), and 'K-selected' species having stable populations with slow growth rates (eg tigers).

Macassar see MAKASSAR STRAIT; UJUNG PADANG.

Macaulay, Dame (Emilie) Rose (1889–1958) English novelist, essayist, and poet, born in Rugby, Warwickshire. Her first book appeared in 1906, following which she won a considerable reputation as a social satirist with such novels as *Dangerous Ages* (1921). Her best-known novel is *The Towers of Trebizond* (1956). Two posthumous volumes, *Letters to a Friend* (1961–2), describe her return to the Anglican faith.

Macaulay (of Rothley), Thomas Babington Macaulay, 1st Baron (1800–59) English essayist and historian, born in Rothley Temple, Leicestershire. He became a Fellow at Cambridge and was called to the Bar (1826), but disliked his profession and turned to literature. An MP from 1830, he proved to be a skilful orator in the Reform Bill debates. After a period in Bengal (1834–8), he became Secretary of War (1839–41), and wrote the highly popular *Lays of Ancient Rome* (1842). His major work, the *History of England from the Accession of James II*, was published between 1848 and 1861, the fifth volume unfinished.

macaw *noun* any of numerous large brilliantly coloured parrots with long tails and strong beaks, found mainly in the tropical forests of Central and S America, where they feed on fruit, seeds, and nuts. Their bright colours and social habits make them easy prey for hunters, and several species have become extinct in the West Indies. Some macaws are popular cage birds. [from Portuguese *macao*]

Macbeth (c.1005–1057) King of Scots (1040–57), probably a grandson of Malcolm II. The mormaer (provincial ruler) of Moray, he overthrew and killed Duncan I in battle near Elgin. He was a benefactor of the Church and in 1050 went on pilgrimage to Rome. He was defeated and killed by Duncan's son, Malcolm III

(Canmore), after an invasion from England aided by Earl Siward of Northumbria.

Macbeth, Lady the ambitious wife of Macbeth in Shakespeare's *Macbeth*, who is driven to insanity after colluding with her husband in the murder of Duncan.

Macbeth a tragedy by William Shakespeare (1605–6). It is about the ambitious Macbeth who, encouraged by his wife, kills the King of Scotland in an attempt to fulfil a witches' prophesy. It depicts his subsequent fall from power and guilt-induced disintegration.

Maccabees, also known as the **Hasmoneans** a priestly Jewish family who initially resisted the influences of Greek culture on Israel during Syrian rule over Palestine. Judas Maccabeus (or ben Mattathias) led a revolt in 166–4 BC, which was continued by his brothers Jonathan and Simon in a kind of guerrilla warfare. The Hasmonean dynasty of high priestly rulers lasted until the rise of Herod the Great under Roman patronage (c.37 BC). [from Hebrew, = hammerer]

MacCaig, Norman (Alexander) (1910–) Scottish poet, born in Edinburgh. He worked for many years as a primary school teacher, and lectured in English Studies at Stirling University (1970–9). His collections include *Rings on a Tree* (1968), *The Equal Skies* (1980), *Voice-Over* (1988), and *Collected Poems* (1985).

Macchiaioli a group of Italian painters who worked mainly in Florence (c.1855–c.1865). They used patches of colour (*macchie*) in their paintings to portray the effects of light.

Macclesfield POP (1981) 48 000, a town in Macclesfield district, Cheshire, NW central England. It lies on the R Bollin, 17km/11mi S of Stockport.

MacDiarmid, Hugh, pseudonym of **Christopher Murray Grieve** (1892–1978) Scottish poet, born in Langholm, Dumfriesshire. He served in both World Wars, worked as a journalist in the 1920s, and was a founder-member of the National Party of Scotland (later the SNP) in 1928, from which he was later expelled. He joined the Communist Party in 1934 but was also expelled, four years later, from that. At the forefront of the movement known as the Scottish Renaissance, he dedicated himself to the regeneration of Scots as a literary language. He founded and edited the *Scottish Chapbook* (1922–3), and his early lyrics in Scots appeared in *Sangschaw* (1925) and *Penny Wheep* (1926). His best-known work is *A Drunk Man Looks at the Thistle* (1926), and his later publications include *In Memoriam James Joyce* (1955), and *The Kind of Poetry I Want* (1961). His *Complete Poems 1920–1976* were published posthumously in 1978.

Macdonald, Flora (1722–90) Scottish heroine, born in South Uist. After the rebellion of 1745, she led the Young Pretender, Prince Charles Edward Stuart, in disguise as 'Betty Burke', to safety in Skye. Consequently she was imprisoned in the Tower of London, but released in 1747.

MacDonald, (James) Ramsay (1866–1937) Scottish politician and first British Labour Prime Minister, born in Lossiemouth, Morayshire. Despite little formal education, he joined the Independent Labour Party in 1894, entered parliament (1906), and became Party Leader (1911–14, 1922–31). He was Prime Minister and Foreign Secretary of the first British Labour government (1924, 1929–31). He met the financial crisis of 1931 by forming a largely Conservative 'National' coalition government (opposed by most of his Party), which he reconstructed and led after a general election (1931–5). In 1935 Stanley Baldwin took over the premiership and Macdonald became Lord President. He died shortly after his retirement, on his way to S America.

MacDonnell Ranges the mountain ranges in S Northern Territory, central Australia. They

extend 320km/200mi W from Alice Springs and rise to 1 524m at Mt Liebig, the highest point in the state.

Macduff the Thane of Fife in Shakespeare's *Macbeth*, who is the eventual slayer of Macbeth. His wife, Lady MacDuff, is murdered, along with her children, by Macbeth.

mace[1] *noun* **1** a heavy club, usually with a spiked metal head, used as a weapon in medieval times. **2** a ceremonial rod carried as a symbol of authority. [from Old French *mace*]

mace[2] *noun* a spice ground from the dried fleshy covering around the nutmeg seed. [from Middle English *macis*]

Macedonia, Greek **Makedhonia** POP (1991) 2.3m, a region in N Greece, extending from the Albanian frontier in the W to the R Nestos in the E, and from frontier of the Macedonian Republic in the N to Mt Olympus in the S. It is mountainous with fertile plains watered by the Struma and Vardar rivers. AREA 34 177sq km/13 192sq mi. CAPITAL Salonica. CHIEF TOWNS Kavalla, Drama, Edhessa, Kastoria. There are several important ancient sites in the region, notably Pella (formerly capital of the region) and Vergina. ECONOMY livestock; cereal, tobacco, olives, grapes.

Macedonia *or* **Macedon** the ancient region between the Balkans and the Greek peninsula. Its economic and military power was established by Philip II (359–336 BC), and extended by his son Alexander the Great, who conquered the Persian Empire. After the death of Alexander (323 BC), Macedonia was ruled by a dynasty founded by Alexander's general Antigonus. In the 3c–2c, Philip V and Perseus were conquered by the Romans, and Macedonia became a Roman province in 146 BC.

Macedonia, Serbo-Croatian **Makedonija**, in full **Former Yugoslav Republic of Macedonia** POP (1991) 2m, a republic in S Europe, bounded W by Albania, S by Greece, E by Bulgaria, and N by Serbia and Kosovo, Yugoslavia. AREA 25 713sq km/9 925sq mi. CAPITAL Skopje. CHIEF TOWNS Bitola, Gostivar, Tetovo, Kumanovo. PHYSICAL DESCRIPTION to the SW are L Ohrid and L Prespa. LANGUAGE Macedonian. CURRENCY the denar. The chief religions are Macedonian Eastern Orthodoxy and Islam. HISTORY incorporated into Serbia after the Balkan Wars; independence was declared in 1991; UN and US peacekeeping forces arrived in 1992 and 1993 to maintain borders and prevent the conflict in Bosnia spreading to Macedonia. The towns are of varied origin, some are early Byzantine and some are from the more recent Turkish colonial period. ECONOMY market gardening.

Macedonia

macerate *verb technical* **1** *intrans., trans.* to break up or cause to break up or become soft by soaking. **2** *intrans.* to waste away as a result of fasting. [from Latin *macerare*, to soak]

maceration *noun* the act or process of macerating or being macerated.

MacEwen, Sir William (1848–1924) Scottish neuro-surgeon, born in Glasgow, where

he worked throughout his life. He adopted and then extended Joseph Lister's antiseptic surgical techniques, and pioneered operations on the brain for tumours, abscesses, and trauma. He also operated on bones, introducing methods of implanting small grafts to replace missing portions of bones in the limbs.

Macgillycuddy's Reeks a mountain range in Kerry county, Munster, SW Irish Republic. It rises to 1 041m at Carrantuohill, the highest peak in the Irish Republic.

MacGregor, Rob Roy see ROB ROY.

Mach, Ernst (1838–1916) Austrian physicist and philosopher, born in Chirlitz-Turas, Moravia. He became Professor of Mathematics at Graz, of Physics in Prague, and of Philosophy in Vienna. Following his experiments on air flow and wave propagation, his name became associated with the ratio of the speed of a body, or of the flow of a fluid, to the speed of sound in the same medium (the *Mach number*). His writings greatly influenced Einstein and laid the foundations of the philosophy known as 'logical positivism'.

Mach *noun* (*also* **Mach number**) *Aeron.* the ratio of the speed of an object such as an aircraft to the speed of sound in the same medium, eg Mach 2 is twice the speed of sound. Speeds above Mach 1 are *supersonic*, and speeds above Mach 5 are *hypersonic*. [named after Ernst Mach]

MacHeath, Capt the womanising leader of a gang of thieves who marries Polly Peachum in John Gay's *The Beggar's Opera*.

machete *noun* a long, heavy, broad-bladed knife used as a weapon or cutting tool, especially in S America and the W Indies. [from Spanish *machete*]

Machiavelli, Niccolò (di Bernardo dei) (1469–1527) Italian politician and political theorist, born in Florence. He travelled on several missions in Europe to promote the republic (1498–1512) but after the restoration of the Medici, he was arrested on a charge of conspiracy (1513), and although pardoned, was obliged to withdraw from public life. He devoted himself to literature, and wrote historical treatises, poetry, short stories, and comedies. His masterpiece is *Il Principe* (The Prince, 1532), which has as its main theme the idea that all means may be used in order to maintain authority, and that the worst acts of the ruler are justified by the treachery of the governed. It was condemned by the pope, and its viewpoint gave rise to the term *Machiavellian*. His writings were not published until 1782.

Machiavellian *adj.* politically cunning and unscrupulous, seeking power or advantage at any price; amoral and opportunist.

Machiavellianism *noun* **1** the principles described by Niccolò Machiavelli. **2** political cunning and unscrupulousness.

machinate *verb intrans.* to plot or scheme, usually for doing harm.

machination *noun* (*usually* **machinations**) *formal* a crafty scheme or plot, usually sinister. [from Latin *machinari*, from Greek *mechane*, contrivance]

machine — *noun* **1** a device with moving parts, and usually powered, designed to perform a particular task. **2** a group of people or institutions, or a network of equipment, under a central control: *the party's political machine*. **3** *colloq.* a motor vehicle, especially a motorcycle. **4** *colloq.* a person with no initiative, capable only of following orders; a tireless or mechanically efficient worker. — *verb* **1** to make, shape, cut, etc with a machine. **2** to stitch with a sewing-machine. [from Latin *machina*, from Greek *mechane*, contrivance]

machine code *or* **machine language** a numerical (eg binary) code used for writing instructions in a form which a computer can understand.

machine-gun — *noun* any of various portable guns mounted on stands, that fire a continuous stream of bullets. — *verb* to shoot with a machine-gun.

machinery *noun* **1** machines in general. **2** the working or moving parts of a machine. **3** the combination of processes, systems or people that keeps anything working.

machine tool any stationary power-driven machine that is used to shape or finish metal, wood, or plastic parts by cutting, planing, drilling, polishing, etc.

machinist *noun* **1** a person who operates a machine. **2** a person who makes or repairs machines.

machismo *noun* exaggerated manliness. [from Spanish, from *macho*, male]

macho — *adj.* exaggeratedly or aggressively manly. — *noun* (PL. **machos**) **1** *colloq.* a man of this type. **2** machismo. [from Spanish *macho*, male]

Machu Picchu a ruined Inca city in S central Peru located on the saddle of a high precipitous mountain. It is comparatively well-preserved, as it was never found by the Spanish, and was discovered in 1911 by US explorer Hiram Bingham. The ruins consist of staircases, temples, terraces, palaces, towers, fountains, and a well-known sundial. It is a World Heritage site.

macintosh same as MACKINTOSH.

MacIvor, Fergus, also called **Vich Ian Vohr** the young Highland chieftain and Jacobite sympathizer in Sir Walter Scott's *Waverley*. Flora MacIvor is his beautiful, loyal sister who rejects the advances of Edward Waverley.

mack *noun colloq.* a mackintosh.

Mackenzie, Sir (Edward Montague) Compton (1883–1972) British writer, born in West Hartlepool, county Durham. He served at Gallipoli in World War I, and in 1917 became director of the Aegean Intelligence Service in Syria. His best-known works include the semi-autobiographical *Sinister Street* (1913–14) and the novel *Whisky Galore* (1947). He lived in Scotland from 1928, and was one of the founders of the Scottish National Party.

Mackenzie, Sir James (1853–1925) Scottish physician and cardiologist, born in Scone. He practised in Burnley before moving to London as a consultant cardiologist in 1907, and later established the Institute of Clinical Research at St Andrews. He developed a 'polygraph' for recording the pulse and investigated the heartbeat, distinguishing between harmless irregularities and those associated with heart disease.

Mackenzie Range a mountain range in Northwest Territories, NW Canada. It extends c.800km/500mi SE–NW and rises to 2 972m at Keele Peak. It is the watershed for the tributaries of the Mackenzie and Yukon rivers. Nahanni Nature Park lies in the S.

Mackenzie River a river in Northwest Territories, NW Canada, length 1 802km/ 1 120mi. It issues from the W end of Great Slave Lake and flows NW to enter the Beaufort Sea through a wide delta near the boundary with Yukon Territory. Navigable in summer (Jun–Oct), the river is used for oil and mineral transportation and for hydroelectricity.

mackerel *noun* (PL. **mackerels**, **mackerel**) **1** an important food fish belonging to the same family as the tuna and bonito, with a streamlined body that is blue-green above and silvery below. It is found on both sides of the N Atlantic Ocean, and in the Mediterranean, often swimming in large shoals in the surface waters, where it feeds on small fish and crustaceans. **2** the oily edible flesh of this fish. [from Old French *maquerel*]

mackerel shark a large powerful shark found in open ocean waters of the N Atlantic and Mediterranean. It feeds mainly on fish and squid, is not normally aggressive, and is a popular sport fish. It is caught commercially on long lines.

mackerel sky *Geol.* a sky that is patterned with cirrocumulus (thin white ripples of cloud) or altocumulus (wavy rounded masses of cloud), so called because it resembles the markings on a mackerel.

Mackinac Bridge a major steel suspension bridge built (1954–7) across the Straits of Mackinac in Michigan, USA, which has a main span of 1 158m.

Mackintosh, Charles Rennie (1868–1928) Scottish architect and designer, born in Glasgow. He became a leader of the 'Glasgow Style', a movement related to Art Nouveau. As well as interiors, furniture, and jewellery, his designs include the Glasgow School of Art (1896–9 and 1906–9) and Hill House, Helensburgh (1902–3). In his later years he lived in France and painted watercolours.

mackintosh *noun* **1** a waterproof raincoat. **2** material waterproofed with rubber. [named after from Charles Macintosh (1766–1843), a Scottish chemist who patented the waterproofing process]

Maclean, Alistair (1922–87) Scottish writer, born in Glasgow. He served in the Royal Navy (1941–6), and worked as a teacher. His first novel *HMS Ulysses* (1955) was an immediate bestseller, and he followed it with *The Guns of Navarone* (1957), and turned to full-time writing. His novels (which he called 'adventure stories') include *Ice Station Zebra* (1963), *Where Eagles Dare* (1967), and *San Andreas* (1984). Most of them have been made into successful films.

Maclean, Donald (Duart) (1913–83) British traitor, born in London. He studied at Cambridge at the same time as Anthony Blunt, Guy Burgess and Kim Philby, and was similarly influenced by communism. He joined the diplomatic service in 1935, and from 1944 acted as a Soviet agent, but managed to become head of the American Department of the Foreign Office. By 1951 he was a suspected traitor, and after Philby's warning in May of that year, he disappeared with Burgess to the USSR, where he became a respected citizen.

MacLeish, Archibald (1892–1982) US poet, born in Glencoe, Illinois. He was librarian of Congress (1939–44), Assistant Secretary of State (1944–5), and Professor of Rhetoric at Harvard (1949–62). His early work includes *The Pot of Earth* (1925), and he won Pulitzer Prizes for *Conquistador* (1932), *Collected Poems 1917–52* (1952), and his verse drama *J.B.* (1958).

MacLeod, Iain (Norman) (1913–70) English Conservative politician, born in Skipton, Yorkshire. He became an MP in 1950, and was Minister of Health (1952–5), Minister of Labour (1955–9), Secretary of State for the Colonies (1959–61), and Chairman of the Conservative Party (1961–3). He refused to serve under Lord Home (having supported R A Butler's claim for the leadership), so spent two years editing the *Spectator*. When Edward Heath became leader, MacLeod was appointed shadow Chancellor (1965–70), and after the Conservative victory (1970) became Chancellor of the Exchequer, but he died a month later.

MacMahon, Marie Edme Patrice Maurice de, Duc de (Duke of) Magenta (1808–93) French soldier and statesman, born in Sully, descended from an Irish Jacobite family. He was a commander in the Crimean War (1854–6), and for his services in the Italian campaign (1859) was made Marshal and a duke. In the Franco-Prussian War (1870–1) he was defeated at Wörth and surrendered at Sedan. He then suppressed the Commune (1871) and succeeded Thiers as second President of the Third Republic (1873), but he failed to gain dictatorial powers and resigned in 1879.

Macmillan, Daniel (1813–57) Scottish bookseller and publisher, born in Upper Corrie, Arran. In 1843 he and his brother opened a bookshop in London and then moved to Cambridge. There they branched out into publishing, first educational and religious works, and then English classics, and the company became one of the world's largest publishing houses.

Macmillan, Sir (Maurice) Harold, 1st Earl of Stockton (1894–1986) English Conservative politician and Prime Minister, born in London. He became an MP in 1924, and was Minister of Housing (1951–4) and Defence (1954–5), Foreign Secretary (1955), Chancellor of the Exchequer (1955–7), and succeeded Anthony Eden as Prime Minister (1957–63). He gained unexpected popularity with his infectious enthusiasm, effective domestic policy ('most of our people have never had it so good'), and resolute foreign policy, and was re-elected in 1959. After several political setbacks, he resigned through ill health in 1963.

Macmillan, Sir Kenneth (1929–92) Scottish ballet-dancer and choreographer, born in Dunfermline. He was one of the original members of the Sadler's Wells Theatre Ballet (1946–8), and began to choreograph with the Royal Ballet in 1953 (with *Somnambulism*). After directing the Berlin opera (1966–9), he became artistic director of the Royal Ballet (1970), and its principal choreographer (1977). His works include *Romeo and Juliet* (1965), *Manon* (1974), *Mayerling* (1978), and *The Judas Tree* (1992).

MacNeice, Louis (1907–63) Irish poet, born in Belfast. He lectured at Birmingham (1930–6) and London (1936–40), and was closely associated with the British left-wing poets of the 1930s, especially W H Auden. His books of poetry include *Letters from Iceland* (1937, with Auden), *Autumn Journal* (1939), *The Burning Perch* (1963), and *Collected Poems* (1966). He also wrote radio plays, notably *The Dark Tower* (1947).

Mâcon, ancient **Matisco** POP (1990) 39 000, a manufacturing city and the capital of Saône-et-Loire department, central France. It lies on the W bank of the R Saône and is the commercial centre of a major wine area. The city is the birthplace of Alphonse de Lamartine. HISTORY episcopal see from the 6c until the Revolution. NOTABLE FEATURES remains of a 12c cathedral; prehistoric site at Solutre, 8km/5mi W.

Maconchy, Dame Elizabeth (1907–) English composer, born in Broxbourne, Hertfordshire. She studied under Ralph Vaughan Williams and in 1929 went to Prague, where her first major work, a piano concerto, was performed in 1930, the year her suite *The Land* was performed at the London Proms. She has written much chamber music, and also choral, operatic, and ballet music, as well as orchestral works and songs. Her daughter Nicola LeFanu (1947–) is also a composer.

Macquarie Island an island lying 1 345km/835mi SW of Tasmania, Australia. It is a Tasmanian dependency. AREA 123sq km/ 47sq mi. NOTABLE FEATURES meteorological and geological research stations; nature reserve (1933); breeding ground of the royal penguin; colony of fur seals (re-established here in 1956).

macramé *noun* **1** the art of weaving and knotting string or coarse thread into patterns. **2** articles produced in this way. [from Turkish *maqrama*, towel]

Macready, William Charles (1793–1873) English actor and theatre manager, born in London. He made his acting reputation with Shakespearean roles and then became manager of Covent Garden (1837) and of Drury Lane (1841). His last visit to the USA (1849) was marked by riots which followed the hissing of his Macbeth by supporters of a rival American actor, Edwin Forrest.

macro *noun* (PL. **macros**) *Comput.* (*also* **macro-instruction**) a single instruction that brings a set of instructions into operation.

macro- *or* **macr-** *combining form* forming words meaning: **1** large, long, or large-scale: *macroeconomics.* **2** *Pathol.* abnormally large or overdeveloped: *macrocephaly.* [from Greek *makros*, long, great]

macrobiotic *adj.* **1** relating to macrobiotics. **2** relating to long life. **3** prolonging life. **4** long-lived.

macrobiotics *sing. noun* the science of devising diets using whole grains and organically-grown fruit and vegetables; the practice of following such a diet, thought to prolong life. [from MACRO- + Greek *biotos*, life]

macrocephaly *noun* *Pathol.* the condition of having a relatively large head. [from MACRO- + Greek *kephale*, head]

macrocosm *noun* **1** (**the macrocosm**) the universe as a whole. **2** any large or complex system or structure made up of similar smaller systems or structures. [from MACRO- + Greek *kosmos*, world]

macroeconomics *sing. noun* the study of economics on a large scale or of large economic units, especially the nation as a whole, and taking into account aspects such as trade, monetary policy, prices, national income, output, exchange rates, growth, and forecasting (*econometrics*).

macro-instruction see MACRO.

macromolecule *noun* *Chem.* a very large molecule, usually consisting of a large number of relatively simple structural units, eg proteins, DNA, natural and synthetic polymers such as rubber and plastics.

macron *noun* a mark (ˉ) placed over a letter to show it is a long vowel. See also BREVE. [from Greek *makros*, long or great]

macrophotography *noun* also known as *photomacrography*: the photography of small objects or details in extreme close-up using normal camera lenses, resulting in an image size as large or larger than the actual subject. Macro lens settings permit focusing down to a subject distance of 1–2cm.

macroscopic *adj.* **1** large enough to be seen by the naked eye. **2** considered in terms of large units or elements.

macula *noun* (PL. **maculae**) *technical* a spot or blemish, eg a freckle on the skin, a sunspot on the Sun. [from Latin *macula*]

mad *adj.* (**madder**, **maddest**) **1** mentally disturbed; insane. **2** foolish or senseless; extravagantly carefree. **3** *colloq.* (*often* **mad at** *or* **with someone**) very angry. **4** *colloq.* (**mad about something**) extremely enthusiastic; fanatical; infatuated. **5** marked by extreme confusion, haste or excitement: *a mad dash for the door.* **6** *said of a dog* infected with rabies.
— **like mad** *colloq.* frantically; very energetically. [from Anglo-Saxon *gemæded*, made insane]

Madagascar, official name **Democratic Republic of Madagascar**, Malagasy **Repoblika Demokratika n'i Madagaskar** POP (1992e) 12.8m, an island republic in the Indian Ocean, separated from E Africa by the Mozambique Channel. It is the world's fourth-largest island, divided into six provinces. AREA 592 800sq km/ 228 821sq mi; length (N–S) 1 580km/982mi. CAPITAL Antananarivo. CHIEF TOWNS Toamasina, Mahajanga, Fianarantsoa, Antsiranana, Toliara. TIME ZONE GMT +3. The population is mainly made up of Malagasy tribes; Christianity is followed by the majority with the remainder following either Muslim or local beliefs. OFFICIAL LANGUAGE Malagasy; French is also widely spoken. CURRENCY the Malagasy franc. PHYSICAL

DESCRIPTION dissected N–S by a ridge of mountains rising to 2 876m at Maromokotra; cliffs to the E drop down to a coastal plain through tropical forest; a terraced descent to the W through savannah to the coast which is heavily indented in the N. CLIMATE temperate climate in the highlands; the average annual rainfall is 1 000–1 500mm; tropical coastal region with an annual rainfall at Toamasina in the E of 3 500mm. HISTORY settled by Indonesians in the 1c AD and by African traders in the 8c; the French established trading posts in the late 18c and claimed the island as a protectorate in 1885; became an autonomous overseas French territory (Malagasy Republic) in 1958; gained independence in 1960; became Madagascar in 1977; a new constitution reducing the powers of the President was approved in 1992. GOVERNMENT governed by a president, elected for seven years, who appoints a Council of Ministers and is guided by a 20-member Supreme Revolutionary Council; a 137-member National People's Assembly is elected every five years. ECONOMY chiefly agricultural; coffee, sugar, vanilla, cloves, rice, manioc, cotton, peanuts, sisal, tobacco, livestock; food processing, tanning, cement, soap, glassware, paper, textiles, oil products; graphite, chrome, coal, bauxite, ilmenite, semi-precious stones.

Madagascar

madam *noun* (PL. **madams**, **mesdames** in sense 1) **1** a polite form of address to a woman. **2** a form of address to a woman in authority, often prefixed to an official title: *Madam Chairman.* **3** *colloq.* an arrogant or spoiled girl or young woman. **4** a woman who manages a brothel. [see MADAME]

Madama Butterfly an opera by Giacomo Puccini (1904). It is the story of a young geisha Cio-Cio-San (Madam Butterfly) in early 20c Nagasaki. Deeply in love, she renounces her faith and marries US Lt Pinkerton. Recalled soon afterwards to the USA, he abandons her but later returns (a bigamist) and requests custody of their son Trouble, which destroys her.

Madame *noun* (PL. **Mesdames**) (ABBREV. **Mme**) a title equivalent to Mrs, used especially of a French or French-speaking (usually married) woman. [from French, originally *ma*, my + *dame*, lady]

Madame Bovary a novel by Gustave Flaubert (1857). It describes the adulterous, tragic life of a doctor's wife in Normandy.

Madara Rider an 8c bas-relief, carved out of the cliff face in the village of Madara, E Bulgaria. The near life-size sculpture depicts a man on horseback trampling a lion beneath his horse's hooves. It is a World Heritage site.

madcap — *adj.* foolishly impulsive or reckless.
— *noun* a foolishly impulsive person.

mad cow disease *colloq.* BSE.

madden *verb* (**maddened**, **maddening**) to make mad, especially to enrage.

maddening *adj.* so as to madden.

madder *noun* **1** a Eurasian herbaceous plant with yellow flowers and a red root; any of various related plants. **2** a dark red dye, originally made from the root of this plant. [from Anglo-Saxon *mæddre* or *mædere*]

made past tense and past participle of MAKE. —
adj. **1** artificially produced. **2** composed of various ingredients put together: *a made dish.*
— **have it made** *colloq.* to enjoy or be assured of complete success or happiness.

made for someone *or* **something** ideally suited to or for them.

-made *combining form* forming words meaning 'produced, constructed or formed in the stated way': *handmade.*

Madeira *or* **Funchal Islands**, Portuguese **Ilha de Madeira** POP (1991) 263 000, the main island in a Portuguese archipelago off the coast of N Africa, 990km/615mi SW of Lisbon. The name is often given to the group as a whole; several of its islands are uninhabited. The islands constitute an autonomous region of Portugal. PHYSICAL DESCRIPTION highest point is Pico Ruivo de Santana (1 861m); in the W is the Paul da Serra Plateau, in the E the smaller plateau of Santo Antonio da Serra. CAPITAL Funchal. ECONOMY sugar cane; fruit; farming; fishing; wine; embroidery; crafts; tourism. [from Portuguese *ilha de madeira*, island of timber]

Madeira, River a river in NW Brazil. It is the longest tributary of the R Amazon, and the third-longest river in S America. The length with its headstream, the Mamoré, is over 3 200km/2 000mi. It flows N along the Bolivia–Brazil border, then NE to join the Amazon 152km/94mi E of Manaus.

Madeira *noun* a strong white dessert wine made on the island of Madeira.

Madeira cake a kind of rich sponge cake.

made-up *adj.* **1** wearing make-up. **2** not true; invented. **3** *slang* extremely pleased.

Mad Hatter, the a fantastic, rude character encountered by Alice in Lewis Carroll's *Alice's Adventures in Wonderland.*

madhouse *noun* **1** *old use* a mental hospital. **2** *colloq.* a place of great confusion and noise.

Madhya Pradesh POP (1991) 66.2m, the largest state in India. AREA 442 841sq km/170 937sq mi. It is situated in the central part of the country, between the Deccan and the Ganges plains and is crossed by numerous rivers. HISTORY ruled by the Gonds in the 16c–17c and the Mahrattas in the 18c; occupied by the British in 1820; called the Central Provinces and Berar in 1903–50; the state was formed under the States Reorganization Act in 1956; over 2 000 people died following a poisonous gas escape at Bhopal in 1984. CAPITAL Bhopal. GOVERNMENT governed by a 90-member Upper House and an elected 320-member Lower House. ECONOMY major irrigation schemes; sugar cane, oilseed, cotton, forestry; steel; electrical engineering; aluminium; paper; textiles; machine tools; food processing; handicrafts; coal, iron ore, manganese, bauxite.

Madison POP (1990) 367 000, the capital of the state of Wisconsin, USA, situated in Dane County. It lies on L Mendota and L Monona. It has been state capital since 1836 and it became a city in 1856. Madison is the trading and manufacturing centre in an agricultural region.

Madison Avenue a street in Manhattan, New York City, which extends N to the R Harlem from Madison Square. It is seen as the centre of the advertising industry.

madly *adv.* **1** in a mad way. **2** *colloq.* passionately: *I love you madly.*

madman *or* **madwoman** *noun* an insane or foolish man or woman.

madness *noun* **1** insanity. **2** extreme anger, excitement, or silliness.

Madonna *noun* **1** (**the Madonna**) a title for the Virgin Mary, the mother of Christ. **2** a picture or statue of the Virgin Mary. [from Italian, originally *ma donna*, my lady]

Madonna, properly **Madonna Louise Ciccone** (1958–) US pop singer, born in Rochester, Michigan. She trained as a dancer at Michigan University before moving to New York where she began her professional career as a backing singer and then sang with a number of New York groups. She hired Michael Jackson's manager prior to releasing *Madonna* (1983), an album which included five US hit singles. Subsequent albums have included *Like A Virgin* (1984), *True Blue*, and *You Can Dance* (1987). She has also acted in films, including *Desperately Seeking Susan* (1985) and *Shanghai Surprise* (1986). Her success has been greatly enhanced by clever promotion and image-making, a feature which helped to make her book *Sex* (1993), which included nude photographes of her, a bestseller.

Madonna and Child two unfinished marble sculptures (*tondi*) by Michelangelo (c.1503, Pitti Palace, Florence and Royal Academy, London).

Madonna del Prato a painting by Raphael (c.1505).

Madonna of Burgomaster Meyer a painting by Hans Holbein the Younger (1526).

Madonna of the Goldfinch a painting by Raphael (c.1505, Uffizi, Florence).

Madonna of the Long Neck a painting by Parmigiano (c.1535, Uffizi, Florence).

Madras POP (1991) 5.4m, the capital and chief port of Tamil Nadu, SE India. It is the fourth-largest city in India and is situated on the R Coom, 1 360km/845mi SW of Calcutta. The city was founded by the British in the 17c. NOTABLE FEATURES Fort St George (1639); Kapaleeswara Temple, Pathasarathy Temple (8c); San Thome Cathedral, St Mary's Church (1680), thought to be the oldest Anglican church in Asia. Mount St Thomas, nearby, is the traditional site of martyrdom of the Apostle Thomas.

Madrid POP (1991) 3m, the capital of Spain and of Madrid province, Castilla-La Mancha region. It is an industrial city lying on the R Manzanares, central Spain. Madrid is Spain's largest city and the seat of government; at an altitude of 655m, it is also the highest capital city in Europe. HISTORY site of a Moorish fortress until the 11c; under siege for nearly three years in the Civil War; became capital in 1561, replacing Valladolid. NOTABLE FEATURES El Escorial, a World Heritage site; Plaza Major; Royal Palace (18c); Prado Museum; Lazaro Galdiano Museum; El Retiro Park; Archaeological Museum; National Library.

madrigal *noun* a 16c or 17c unaccompanied song with different parts sung together, typically about love or nature. [from Italian *madrigale*]

Madurai POP (1991) 1.1m, a city in Tamil Nadu, S India. It is situated on the R Voigai, 425km/264mi SW of Madras. HISTORY capital of the Pandyan Kingdom and the Nayak Dynasty; occupied by the British in 1801. NOTABLE FEATURE large Dravidian temple complex (built in the 14c–17c).

maelstrom *noun* **1** a violent whirlpool. **2** *literary* a place or state of uncontrollable confusion, especially one to which one is inevitably drawn. [from Dutch (now *maalstroom*), whirlpool]

maenad *noun* **1** *Mythol.* a female participant in orgies and rites in honour of Bacchus or Dionysus, the god of wine. **2** *literary* a woman who behaves in a frenzied or uncontrolled way. [from Greek *mainas*, raving]

maenadic *adj.* **1** relating to drinking or drunken revels. **2** furious.

Maes Howe a chambered tomb of the early third millennium BC in Orkney, N Scotland. The mound (35m in diameter) conceals a long drystone-walled entrance passage which gives on to a cross-shaped burial chamber with a corbelled vault. Inside are 24 runic inscriptions scratched by Viking raiders in the mid-12c.

maestro *noun* (PL. **maestros**, **maestri**) *often used as a title* a man regarded as the master of an art, especially a distinguished musical composer, performer, or teacher. [from Italian *maestro*, master]

Maeterlinck, Count Maurice (1862–1949) Belgian writer, born in Ghent. He became a disciple of the Symbolist movement, and in 1889 produced his first volume of poetry, *Les Serres chaudes* (Hot House Blooms). His plays include *Pelléas et Mélisande* (1892), on which Claude Debussy based his opera. *La Vie des abeilles* (The Life of the Bee, 1901) is one of many popular expositions of scientific subjects, and he also wrote several philosophical works. He was awarded the Nobel Prize for Literature in 1911.

Maeve a female first name. [from Celtic *Meadhbh*, intoxicating, making drunk; name of the legendary queen of Connaught]

Mae West *noun* an inflatable life-jacket worn by pilots. [named after Mae West, a US actress famous for her large bust]

Mafeking, Siege of an action (Oct 1899–May 1900) of the second Boer War during which Col Robert Baden-Powell and a detachment of British troops were besieged by the Boers. The news of their relief aroused hysterical celebrations (known as 'mafficking') in Britain, but the truth about the siege differed from the heroic action depicted by the British press. It is now known that the white garrison survived in reasonable comfort as the result of appropriating the rations of the blacks, who were faced either with starvation or with running the gauntlet of the Boers by escaping from the town.

MAFF *abbrev.* Ministry of Agriculture, Fisheries, and Food.

Mafia *noun* **1** (**the Mafia**) a secret international criminal organization controlling numerous illegal activities worldwide, especially in the USA. **2** any group exerting a secret and powerful influence, especially one operating unscrupulously. [from Sicilian Italian *mafia*, hostility to the law]

Mafioso *noun* (PL. **Mafiosi**) a member of the Mafia.

mag *noun colloq.* a magazine or periodical.

Magallanes-La Antártica Chilena a region in S Chile. It comprises the provinces of Ultima Esperanza, Magallanes, Tierra del Fuego, and Antártica Chilena, the slice of Antarctica to which Chile lays claim. The region has several national parks. CAPITAL Punta Arenas. ECONOMY sheep, cattle; forestry; oil, natural gas; food canning. NOTABLE FEATURES Cueva de Miladón, where the remains of several *Mylodon listai* (a Prehistoric giant sloth-like animal), were found: they are c.8 000 years old.

magazine *noun* **1** a paperback periodical publication containing articles, stories, etc by various writers, usually heavily illustrated. **2** a regular broadcast presenting reports on a variety of subjects. **3** a metal container for several cartridges, used in some automatic firearms. **4** a storeroom for ammunition, explosives, etc. **5** a container from which photographic slides are automatically fed through a projector. [from Italian *magazzino*, from Arabic *makhzan*, storehouse]

Magdalen a female first name. [from *Magdala*, on the sea of Galilee]

Magdalena, River a major river in Colombia, rising in the Cordillera Central. It flows N 1 600km/1 000mi to enter the Caribbean Sea 14km/9mi NW of Barranquilla in a wide delta. The river is navigable for most of its course. Its fertile valley in the upper and mid course produces coffee, sugar cane, tobacco, cacao, and cotton.

Magdeburg POP (1991e) 279 000, the river-port capital of Saxony-Anhalt state, central Germany. It lies on the R Elbe SW of Berlin, and provides access to the Ruhr and Rhine rivers via the Mittelland Canal (1938). HISTORY former capital of Saxony, and an important medieval trading town at the centre of the N German plain; badly bombed in World War II; became state capital upon West and East German reunification in 1990. NOTABLE FEATURE cathedral (13c–16c).

Magellan, Ferdinand, Portuguese **Magalhães** (c.1480–1521) Portuguese navigator, born near Villa Real. He served in the East Indies and Morocco, then offered his services to Spain. He sailed from Seville (1519) around the foot of S America (Cape of the Virgins), to reach the ocean which he named the Pacific Ocean (1520). He was killed in the Philippines, but his ships continued back to Spain (1522), thus completing the first circumnavigation of the world. The Strait of Magellan is named after him.

Magellan project *Astron.* a US space mission, managed by NASA, which aimed to map the surface of Venus (which is obscured by clouds) using radar. In 1992 the space probe *Magellan* mapped 95 per cent of the planet's surface.

Magendie, François (1783–1855) French physiologist, born in Bordeaux. Physician to the Hôtel-Dieu, the hospital for the poor in Paris, and later professor at the Collège de France, he studied nerve physiology, the veins, and the physiology of food. He also introduced into medicine the range of plant-derived compounds now known as alkaloids.

magenta — *adj.* having a dark purplish-red colour. — *noun* this colour. [from *Magenta*, an Italian town and scene of a bloody battle in 1859]

Magersfontein, Battle of an engagement (1899) in the second Boer War in which British forces were defeated by the Boers, which closely followed the defeat of the British at Modder River. Both battles issued from British attempts to relieve the besieged town of Kimberley.

Maggie the passionate 'cat' in Tennessee Williams's *Cat on a Hot Tin Roof*, who energetically pursues her desires.

Maggiore, Lake, ancient **Verbanus Lacus** the second-largest of the N Italian lakes. Its N end is in the Swiss canton of Ticino. AREA 212sq km/82sq mi; length 60km/37mi; width 3–5km/2–3mi; maximum depth 372m. It is a major tourist area, surrounded by mountains to the W, mostly wooded. Lake resorts include Ispra, Stresa, Arona, and (Swiss) Locarno. The Borromean Is are on the west arm of the lake.

maggot *noun* the worm-like larva of various flies, especially the housefly. [from Middle English *maddok* or *mathek*]

maggoty *adj.* full of maggots.

Maghreb, English **Maghrib** an area in NW Africa including the countries of Morocco, Algeria, and Tunisia. AREA c.9m sq km/4m sq mi. It is largely occupied by sedentary and nomadic Berbers of the Kabyle, Shluh, and Tuareg groups. In Arabic, it refers to Morocco only. The Maghreb Union is an economic union of Maghreb countries formed in 1989.

Magi **1** a Greek term used in antiquity to refer to members of the priestly clan of the Persians, or used by Classical Greek and Roman writers in a derogatory sense to refer to sorcerers and quacks. **2** a group who came from 'the East' guided by a star (Matthew 2.1–12) to visit the infant Jesus in Bethlehem. Origen suggested they were three because of their three gifts: gold, frankincense, and myrrh. Tertullian deduced that they were kings. Later Christian tradition named them as Gaspar, Melchior, and Balthasar.

magi see MAGUS.

magic — *noun* **1** the supposed art or practice of using the power of supernatural forces to affect people, objects, and events. **2** the art or practice of performing entertaining illusions and conjuring tricks. **3** the quality of being wonderful, charming, or delightful. — *adj.* **1** of, used in, or using sorcery or conjuring. **2** *colloq.* excellent. — *verb* (**magicked, magicking**) (**magic something away, up**, *etc*) to produce, transform, or otherwise affect it using, or as if using, sorcery or conjuring.
— **like magic 1** mysteriously. **2** suddenly and unexpectedly. **3** excellently.
[from Greek *magike*]

magical *adj.* **1** relating to the art or practice of magic. **2** fascinating; wonderful; charming.

magically *adv.* in a magical way.

magic bullet a drug which is capable of destroying bacteria, cancer cells, etc without adversely affecting the host.

magic carpet a mythical carpet that can carry people through the air.

magic eye a light-sensitive electric switch; a photoelectric cell.

Magic Flute, The (Die Zauberflöte) an opera by Wolfgang Amadeus Mozart (1791). The quest of Tamino and Papageno is to rescue Pamina from the allegedly evil Sarastro, only to find that the evil one is really her mother, the Queen of the Night. With the help of a magic flute, Tamino and Pamina survive various trials, Papageno finds Papagena, light conquers darkness, and love conquers all.

magician *noun* **1** a performer of illusions; a conjurer. **2** a person with supernatural powers.

magic lantern an early form of slide projector.

Magic Mountain, The (Der Zauberberg) a novel by Thomas Mann (1924). It is set mainly in a sanatorium and describes the experiences of the central character, Hans Castorp.

magic square a square filled with rows of figures so arranged that the sums of all the rows (vertical, horizontal, diagonal) will be the same.

10	1	16	7
15	8	9	2
3	12	5	14
6	13	4	11

magic square

Maginot Line French defensive fortifications stretching from Longwy to the Swiss border, named after the French Minister of Defence André Maginot (1877–1932). The line was constructed (1929–34) to protect against German invasion, but Belgium refused to extend it along its frontier with Germany. The German attack (1940) through the Low Countries largely bypassed the Maginot Line, the name of which became synonymous with passive defence and defeatism.

magisterial *adj.* **1** of, or administered by, a magistrate. **2** authoritative; commanding; dictatorial. **3** of, or suitable to, a teacher, instructor or master. [from Latin *magister*, master]

magisterially *adv.* in a magisterial way.

magistracy *noun* (PL. **magistracies**) **1** the rank or position of a magistrate. **2** magistrates as a whole. [from Latin *magister*, master]

magistrate *noun* **1** a judge in a lower court of law dealing with minor offences; a justice of the peace. **2** any public official administering the law. [from Latin *magister*, master]

maglev *noun* a high-speed transport system in which magnetism is used to keep an electrically powered train gliding above a track. [a shortening of *magnetic levitation*]

magma *noun* (PL. **magmas, magmata**) **1** *Geol.* hot molten rock material generated deep within the Earth's crust or mantle, and consisting of a mixture of silicates, water, and dissolved gases. On cooling it solidifies to form igneous rock. Lava is magma that has reached the Earth's surface as a result of volcanic activity. **2** a pasty or doughy mass. [from Greek *magma*, thick ointment]

Magna Carta a charter imposed (Jun 1215) by rebellious barons on King John of England, designed to prohibit arbitrary royal Acts by declaring a body of defined law and custom which the king must respect. Although the principle that kings should rule justly was not new, this was the first systematic attempt to distinguish between kingship and tyranny. Despite its failure to resolve all the problems inherent in the relations between the English Crown and the community, Magna Carta endured as a symbol of the sovereignty of the rule of law, and was of fundamental importance to the constitutional development of England and other countries whose legal and governmental systems were modelled on English conventions. [from Latin *magna charta*, great charter]

magnanimity *noun* generosity.

magnanimous *adj.* having or showing admirable generosity of spirit not spoiled by petty feelings. [from Latin *magnus*, great + *animus*, mind]

magnate *noun* a person of high rank or great power, especially in industry. [from Latin *magnas*, from *magnus*, great]

magnesia *noun* **1** *Chem.* the common name for magnesium oxide (MgO), a white powder obtained from the mineral magnesite, used to line furnaces, and as a component of semiconductors, insulators, cosmetics, antacids, laxatives, and reflective coatings for optical instruments. **2** (*also* **milk of magnesia**) a suspension of magnesium hydroxide in water, used as an antacid. [from the name *Magnesia* in Asia Minor (modern Turkey)]

magnesite *noun* *Geol.* the mineral form of magnesium carbonate ($MgCO_3$), which occurs as compact white or grey masses, and is produced as a result of the alteration of magnesium-rich rocks by fluids. It is an important ore of magnesium, and is also used as a refractory for lining furnaces.

magnesium *noun* *Chem.* (SYMBOL **Mg**, ATOMIC NUMBER **12**) a reactive silvery-grey metal found in seawater and several minerals, eg dolomite, talc, and asbestos, that burns with a brilliant white flame when ignited. It is used in lightweight alloys for aircraft components, and in fireworks, flares, and batteries. It is an essential trace element for plants and animals, and an important component of the pigment chlorophyll. [see MAGNESIA]

magnesium sulphate *Chem.* (FORMULA **MgSO₄**) a white soluble compound used for fireproofing cotton and silk, and in ceramics, cosmetics, fertilizers, and explosives. One of the hydrated crystalline forms, known as Epsom salts, is used in mineral waters and as a laxative.

magnet *noun* **1** a piece of metal, especially iron, with the power to attract and repel iron, and the tendency to point in an approximate north–south direction when freely suspended. **2** a person or thing that attracts. [from Greek *magnetis lithos*, Magnesian stone, from *Magnesia*, in Asia Minor]

magnetic *adj.* **1** of, having the powers of, or operating by means of a magnet or magnetism. **2** able to be made into a magnet. **3** extremely charming or attractive.

magnetically *adv.* in a magnetic way, like a magnet.

magnetic disk *Comput.* a flat circular sheet of material coated with a magnetic oxide, used to store programs and data.

magnetic domain *Physics* in a ferromagnetic material (one in which magnetism persists after the removal of a magnetic field), a region in which individual magnetic moments are all aligned parallel to each other.

magnetic drum *Comput.* a computer storage device consisting of a rapidly rotating drum covered with magnetic material (eg iron oxide) on which data can be read or written by a set of read-write heads. Magnetic drums are used on large computers to allow very fast access to data.

magnetic field *Physics* the region of physical space surrounding a permanent magnet, electromagnetic wave, or current-carrying conductor, within which magnetic forces may be detected.

magnetic flux *Physics* a measure of the size of the magnetic field from the north pole to the south pole of a magnet, or around a current-carrying wire. The SI unit of magnetic flux is the weber.

magnetic induction *Physics* the production of magnetic properties in a previously unmagnetized material, eg as a result of stroking it with another magnet, or placing it in the electromagnetic field of a current-carrying conductor.

magnetic ink character recognition *Comput.* the reading of characters formed in magnetic ink, which contains a magnetic powder that activates an electronic character-reading device, so enabling the characters to be identified, eg during banking procedures such as the processing of numbered cheques.

magnetic mine a mine detonated when it detects a magnetic field created by the presence of a large metal object, eg a ship.

magnetic moment *Physics* a measure of the magnetic strength of a permanent magnet, or of a current-carrying coil, moving charge, or individual atom in a magnetic field. It is equal to the maximum torque (turning force) exerted on such a magnet, coil, moving charge, or individual atom in a magnetic field, divided by the strength of the field.

magnetic north the direction in which a magnetic needle of a compass always points, slightly east or west of true north.

magnetic pole 1 *Physics* either of two regions, usually at opposite ends of a magnet and referred to as north and south, from which the lines of force of a magnetic field appear to radiate. Like poles of two magnets repel each other, and unlike poles attract each other. **2** *Geol.* either of two points on the Earth's surface where the magnetic field is vertical, and to or from which a magnetized compass needle points. The magnetic poles do not coincide with the geographic poles, and their exact positions vary with time.

magnetic storm a sudden, severe disturbance of the earth's magnetic field, caused by streams of particles from the sun.

magnetic tape *Electron.* a medium consisting of narrow plastic ribbon, coated with a magnetizable material such as iron oxide powder, which is used to record and store data in audio and video tape recorders and computers. Information in the form of electronic signals magnetizes the iron oxide particles, providing a permanent record of the data.

magnetism *noun* **1** the properties of attraction possessed by magnets, or the scientific study of these. **2** strong personal charm.

magnetite *noun* *Geol.* a shiny black mineral form of iron oxide (Fe_2O_3) that is an important ore of iron. It is strongly magnetic, and some forms of magnetite, known as lodestone, are natural magnets. See also LODESTONE.

magnetization *or* **magnetisation** *noun* the act or process of making or becoming magnetic.

magnetize *or* **magnetise** *verb* **1** to make magnetic. **2** to attract strongly.

magneto *noun* (PL. **magnetos**) *Electr.* a simple electric generator consisting of a rotating magnet that induces an alternating current in a coil surrounding it, and is used to provide the spark in the ignition system of petrol engines that have no batteries, eg in lawn mowers, outboard motors, and some motor cycles. [short for *magnetoelectric generator*]

magnetosphere *noun* **1** *Astron.* the region of space surrounding the Earth that contains charged particles held around the Earth by its magnetic field. It extends about 100 000km towards the Sun and about one million km away from it, and contains the Van Allen belts. **2** a similar region around any other planet that has a magnetic field.

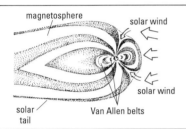

magnetosphere

magnetron *noun Physics* a device for generating microwaves, developed during the 1940s for use in radar transmitters, and now widely used in microwave ovens.

magnificat *noun* **1** (**Magnificat**) *Relig.* the Virgin Mary's hymn of praise to God, sung in services in certain branches of the Christian Church. **2** any song of praise. [from the opening word of the hymn in the Latin New Testament (Luke 1.46–55)]

magnification *noun* **1** a measure of the extent to which an image of an object produced by a lens or optical instrument is enlarged or reduced. **2** an appearance enlarged by a stated amount. [from Latin *magnificare*, to magnify]

magnificence *noun* being magnificent.

magnificent *adj.* **1** splendidly impressive in size or extent. **2** *colloq.* excellent; admirable. [from Latin *magnificens*, doing great things]

Magnificent Ambersons, The a US film directed by Orson Welles (1942). It is the story of the decline and fall of an aristocratic family seen through the eyes of a prosperous social inferior (played by Joseph Cotten).

magnificently *adv.* in a magnificent way.

Magnificent Seven, The a US film directed by John Sturges (1961). A remake of the Japanese *Seven Samurai* (1954) as a Western, it tells of a group of mercenaries (whose leader is played by Yul Brynner) protecting a town from marauding bandits (led by Eli Wallach).

magnifier *noun* **1** an instrument which magnifies. **2** a person who magnifies, or who praises highly.

magnify *verb* (**magnifies**, **magnified**) **1** to cause to appear larger, eg using a microscope or telescope. **2** to exaggerate. [from Latin *magnus*, great + *facere*, to make]

magnifying glass a convex (especially hand-held) lens through which objects appear larger.

magniloquence *noun* being magniloquent.

magniloquent *adj.* speaking or spoken in a grand or pompous style. [from Latin *magnus*, great + *loqui*, to speak]

Magnitogorsk, formerly **Magnitnaya** POP (1991e) 445 000, an industrial town in Chelyabinsk oblast, SW Siberia, Russia, lying on the R Ural. It was built between 1929 and 1931 on the site of iron and magnetite deposits. NOTABLE FEATURE Palace of Metallurgists (1936).

magnitude *noun* **1** importance or extent. **2** size; largeness. **3** *Astron.* the degree of brightness of a star. [from Latin *magnitudo*, from *magnus*, great]

magnolia — *noun* **1** a tree or shrub with large sweet-smelling white or pink flowers; one of its flowers. **2** a pale pinkish-white colour. — *adj.* of the colour magnolia. [from Pierre Magnol (1638–1715), French botanist]

magnum *noun* a wine bottle holding twice the normal amount, approximately 1·5 litres. [from Latin *magnum*, big]

magnum opus *literary* a great work of art or literature, especially the greatest produced by a particular artist or writer. [from Latin *magnum opus*, great work]

Magnus a male first name. [from Latin *magnus*, great, usually as a title as in *Pompeius Magnus*]

magpie *noun* **1** a black-and-white bird of the crow family, known for its chattering call and its habit of collecting shiny objects. **2** a person who hoards things, especially useless trinkets. **3** a chattering person. [from *Mag*, diminutive of *Margaret* + *pie*]

Magritte, René (François Ghislain) (1898–1967) Belgian painter, born in Lessines. He became a commercial artist, and in 1924 was a leading member of the Belgian Surrealist group. Apart from a brief Impressionist phase in the 1940s, he remained constant to Surrealism. His works include *The Menaced Assassin* (1926, New York), *The Wind and the Song* (1928–9), *On the Threshold of Liberty* (1930), and *The Human Condition* (1934, 1935).

Magua the traitorous Native American in James Fenimore Cooper's *Last of the Mohicans*, one of the novels in the 'Leather-Stocking Tales'.

magus *noun* (PL. **magi**) **1** an ancient Persian priest. **2** an ancient sorcerer or astrologer. **3** (**Magus**) each of the three wise men from the East who brought gifts to the infant Jesus. [from Old Persian *magus*, magician] see also MAGI.

Magwitch, Abel the convict father of Estella, and anonymous benefactor of Pip, in Charles Dickens's *Great Expectations*.

Magyar — *noun* **1** a member of the predominant race of people in Hungary, also found in NW Siberia. **2** the Hungarian language. — *adj.* of the Magyars or their language.

Mahabalipuram monuments a collection of Hindu monolithic temples and cave temples at Mahabalipuram in Tamil Nadu, S India. The temples (7c–8c) are noted for their rich carvings, particularly the rock sculpture known as 'The Descent of the Ganges' or 'Arjuna's Penance'. It is a World Heritage site.

Mahabharata an epic Hindu poem dating back to the first millennium BC which was first printed in the 19c. The longest epic in the world, it is the sacred book of the Hindus, centring on the conflict between the Kurus (spirits of evil) and Pandus (spirits of good).

Mahajanga, Swahili **Majunga**, formerly **Port-Bergé** POP (1990e) 122 000, a port on the NW coast of Madagascar, situated 618km/384mi NW of Antananarivo. The port was the former capital of the Boina Kingdom.

Mahamuni Pagoda *or* **Arakan Pagoda** a temple built near Mandalay, Burma, by King Bodawpaya in 1784 to house the 'Mahamuni', a

4m high image of Buddha probably cast in Arakan in the 2c. The statue has been covered with gold leaf by Buddhist pilgrims.

maharajah *or* **maharaja** *noun, also used as a title* an Indian prince, especially any of the former rulers of the states of India. [from Hindi, from Sanskrit *mahat*, great + *rajan*, king]

maharani *or* **maharanee** *noun, also used as a title* **1** the wife or widow of a maharajah. **2** a woman of the same rank as a maharajah in her own right. [from Hindi, from Sanskrit *mahat*, great + *rani*, queen]

Maharashtra POP (1991) 78.9m, a state in W central India. AREA 307 762sq km/118 796sq mi. It is bounded W by the Arabian Sea and crossed by several mountain ranges and rivers. HISTORY ruled by the Muslims in the 14c–17c; came under British control in the early 19c; became a state in 1960. CAPITAL Bombay. GOVERNMENT governed by a 78-member Legislative Council and an elected 287-member Legislative Assembly. ECONOMY rice, sugar cane, groundnuts, cotton; textiles; electrical equipment; machinery; chemicals; oil products; coal, chromite, iron ore, bauxite; industry is largely in Bombay, Poona, and Thana.

Maharishi a Hindu title for a guru or spiritual leader, such as the Maharishi Mahesh Yogi (b.c.1911), the founder of Transcendental Meditation, which became popular in the West in the 1950s and 1960s. [from Hindi, from Sanskrit *mahat*, great + *rishi*, sage]

mahatma *noun* a wise and holy Hindu leader. [from Hindi, from Sanskrit *mahat*, great + *atman*, soul]

Mahayana the form of Buddhism commonly practised in China, Tibet, Mongolia, Nepal, Korea, and Japan, which dates from about the 1c. It emphasizes various forms of popular devotion based on its theory of the bodhisattvas. [Sanskrit, = greater vehicle]

Mahdi in Islam, the name given by Sunni Muslims to the messianic deliverer who will eventually establish a reign of justice on Earth. Shiites identify the Mahdi with the messianic Imam. Among the many Muslim leaders who have claimed the title is Muhammad Ahmed, who established a theocratic state in the Sudan (1882). [Arabic, = divinely guided one]

Mahé POP (1987) 60 000, the main island of the Seychelles, lying in the Indian Ocean. AREA 153sq km/59sq mi. Victoria, the capital of the Seychelles, lies on the NW coast. NOTABLE FEATURE Morne Seychelles National Park.

Mahfouz, Naguib (1911–) Egyptian novelist, born in the Gamaliyya quarter of Cairo. His novels include *The Cairo Trilogy* (1956–7), and his descriptions of Cairo have been compared to Charles Dickens's work on London or Emile Zola's on Paris. He was awarded the Nobel Prize for Literature in 1988.

mahi-mahi *noun* the dolphin fish, especially its flesh prepared as food. [from Hawaiian, from *mahi*, strong]

mah-jong *or* **mah-jongg** *noun* an originally Chinese game for four players, played with small patterned tiles of wood or bone, with rules similar to rummy. [from Chinese dialect *mah-jong*, sparrows]

Mahler, Gustav (1860–1911) Austrian composer, born in Kalist, Bohemia. After studying at the Vienna Conservatory he worked as a conductor, and became artistic director of the Vienna State Opera House in 1897, where he established its high standards. He resigned after 10 years to concentrate on composition and the concert platform, which later resulted in songs and nine large-scale symphonies, with a tenth left unfinished. He is best known for the song-symphony *Das Lied von der Erde* (The Song of the Earth, 1908–9).

mahlstick *or* **maulstick** *noun* a stick or rod, with a pad on one end, used by painters to steady the painting hand while executing delicate brushwork in their pictures. The stick is held with the pad resting on the canvas or its frame. Mahlsticks are sometimes seen in artists' self-portraits. [from Dutch *malen*, to paint]

mahogany — *noun* (PL. **mahoganies**) 1 any of various tall evergreen trees found in tropical Africa and America, especially species of the genus *Swietenia*, grown commercially for timber. 2 the highly prized hard reddish-brown wood of this tree, which has attractive markings and takes a high polish. It is used for furniture-making, cabinetwork, and boat-building. 3 the colour of the wood, a reddish-brown. — *adj.* 1 made from this wood. 2 reddish-brown.

Mahomet see MUHAMMAD.

mahout *noun* a person who drives, trains, and looks after elephants, especially in India. [from Hindi *mahaut*]

maid *noun* 1 a female servant. 2 *old use, literary* an unmarried woman. [short form of MAIDEN]

maiden — *noun* 1 *old use, literary* a young unmarried woman. 2 *old use, literary* a virgin. 3 a horse that has never won a race. 4 *Cricket* a maiden over. — *adj.* 1 first ever: *maiden voyage*. 2 *literary* unused; fresh. 3 *said of a horse race* open to maidens only. [from Anglo-Saxon *mægden*]

Maiden Castle an Iron Age hillfort near Dorchester, Dorset, UK. It covers 18ha, and was constructed after 350 BC on the site of an earlier Neolithic camp. It was the capital of the native tribe of the Durotriges, and was thought to have been captured by Vespasian's Second Legion following the Roman invasion of Britain in AD 43, and abandoned.

maidenhair *noun* any of various tropical ferns with delicate fan-shaped leaves.

maidenhair tree ginkgo.

Maidenhead POP (1981) 61 000, a town in Windsor and Maidenhead district, Berkshire, S England. It is situated on the R Thames, 8km/5mi W of Slough. NOTABLE FEATURE railway bridge (1838), with the largest brick-built arches in the world.

maidenhead *noun old use, literary* 1 virginity. 2 the hymen.

maidenhood *noun* the state or time of being a maiden.

maiden name a married woman's surname before her marriage.

maiden over *Cricket* an over from which no runs are scored.

maid of honour (PL. **maids of honour**) 1 an unmarried female servant of a queen or princess. 2 the principal bridesmaid at a wedding, if unmarried. See also MATRON OF HONOUR.

maidservant *noun old use* a female servant.

Maidstone POP (1992e) 138 000, the county town of Kent, SE England, situated in Maidstone district. It lies on the R Medway, S of Chatham. The essayist William Hazlitt was born in the town in 1778. NOTABLE FEATURES All Saints Church (14c); Archbishop's Palace (14c); Chillington Manor; Tyrwhitt Drake Museum of Carriages.

Maigret, Jules the pipe-smoking inspector in the crime stories of Georges Simenon, which include *Introducing Inspector Maigret*, *The Triumph of Inspector Maigret*, and *Maigret and the Coroner*, many of which have been filmed and televised.

mail¹ — *noun* 1 the postal system. 2 letters, parcels, etc sent by post. 3 a single collection or delivery of letters, etc. 4 a vehicle carrying letters, etc. — *verb* to send by post. [from Old French *male*, bag or trunk]

mail² *noun* flexible armour for the body, made of small linked metal rings. [from Old French *maille*, mesh]

mailbag *noun* a large strong bag in which mail is carried.

mailed *adj.* covered in or protected by mail, armoured.

Mailer, Norman (1923–) US writer, born in Long Branch, New Jersey. He served as an infantryman (1944–6), and in 1948 published his first novel, *The Naked and the Dead*. Other novels include *American Dream* (1964), *Ancient Evenings* (1983), and *Tough Guys Don't Dance* (1984). Identified with many of the US liberal protest movements, he has also written political studies, including *The Armies of the Night* (1968, Pulitzer Prize).

mailing list a list of the people to whom an organization regularly sends information.

mailmerge *noun Comput.* 1 the process of producing a series of letters addressed to individuals by merging a file of names and addresses with a file containing the text of the letter. 2 a computer program which carries out this process.

mail order a system of buying and selling goods by post.

mail-order *adj.* bought or sold by mail order, or dealing with mail order.

mailshot — *noun* an unrequested item of post, especially a piece of advertising material. — *verb* to send unsolicited advertising material to (a person or organization).

maim *verb* to wound seriously, especially to disable or cripple. [from Old French *mahaignier*, to wound]

Maiman, Theodore Harold (1927–) US physicist, born in Los Angeles. After studying engineering physics, he joined the Hughes Research Laboratories, Miami, in 1955. He made improvements to the maser, and in 1960 constructed the first working laser. Later he founded companies to develop and exploit the device.

Maimonides, Moses, originally **Moses ben Maimon** (1135–1204) Jewish philosopher, born in Córdoba, Spain. He studied Aristotelian philosophy and Greek medicine, and migrated to Egypt, where he became physician to Saladin. A major influence on Jewish thought, he wrote an important commentary on the Mishna, and a philosophical work, the *Guide to the Perplexed*, which argued for the reconciliation of Greek philosophy and religion.

main — *adj.* 1 most important; chief. 2 *literary* extreme; utmost: *main force*. — *noun* 1 (**mains**) the chief pipe or cable in a branching system. 2 (**mains**) the network by which power, water, etc is distributed. 3 *old use* the open sea: *the Spanish main*. 4 *old use* great strength, now especially in the phrase *with might and main*. — **in the main** mostly; on the whole. [from Anglo-Saxon *mægen*, strength, and Norse *meginn*, strong]

Mainbocher, properly **Main Rousseau Bocher** (c.1890–1976) US fashion designer, born in Chicago. He studied and worked in Chicago and Paris, eventually becoming a fashion artist with *Harper's Bazaar* and, later, editor of *French Vogue* until 1929. He started his couture house in Paris in 1930; one of his creations was the wedding dress of Mrs Wallis Simpson, the Duchess of Windsor. He opened a salon in New York City in 1940, which continued until 1971.

mainbrace *noun Naut.* the rope controlling the movement of a ship's mainsail.

main clause *Grammar* a clause which can stand alone as a sentence.

Maine POP (1990) 1.2m, a New England state in the NE corner of the USA, divided into 16 counties. AREA 86 153sq km/33 255sq mi. It is bounded N and E by Canada. PHYSICAL DESCRIPTION the Kennebec and Penobscot rivers run S to the Atlantic Ocean; the state is crossed by the Appalachian Mts which rise to 1 605m at Mt Katahdin in Baxter State Park; dotted with over 1 600 lakes, the largest of which is L Moosehead; the S coastal strip is mainly arable and the northern 80% of the state is forested; Maine is known as the 'Pine Tree State'. HISTORY explored by the Cabots in the 1490s; settled first by the French in 1604, and by the English in 1607; separated from Massachusetts in 1820, when it was admitted to the Union as the 23rd state. CAPITAL Augusta. CHIEF TOWN Portland. ECONOMY agriculture (especially potatoes and blueberries); forestry; fishing.

mainframe *noun* a large computer, to which many smaller computers can be linked, that is capable of handling very large amounts of data at high speed, and can usually several programs simultaneously. Mainframes are used by large organizations, eg banks, universities.

mainland *noun* (**the mainland**) a country's principal mass of land, as distinct from a nearby island or islands forming part of the same country.

mainline *verb trans., intrans. slang* to inject (a drug) into a principal vein, so that it has the quickest possible effect.

main line the principal railway line between two places.

mainliner *noun slang* a person who mainlines drugs.

mainlining *noun slang* the practice of injecting drugs into the veins.

mainly *adv.* for the most part; largely.

mainsail *noun* the largest and lowest sail on a sailing ship.

Main Sequence *Astron.* in the Hertzsprung–Russell diagram (a graph in which the surface temperature of stars is plotted against their luminosity), a broad diagonal band within which most stars lie, including the Sun. See also HERTZSPRUNG–RUSSELL DIAGRAM.

mainspring *noun* 1 the chief spring in a watch or clock. 2 a chief motive, reason or cause.

mainstay *noun* 1 *Naut.* a rope stretching forward and down from the top of the principal mast of a sailing ship. 2 the chief support.

mainstream *noun* 1 the principal current of a river. 2 the chief trend or direction of development in an activity.

mainstreaming *noun* the introduction of children with special educational needs (eg those formerly described as 'handicapped') into ordinary schools.
◇ In the late 1970s and early 1980s, in both the USA and UK, it was decided to reduce the number of children who attended special schools. It was felt that many special schools set targets which were too low, and that many of their pupils would derive benefit from being educated alongside so-called 'normal' children.

maintain *verb* 1 to continue; to keep in existence. 2 to keep in good condition. 3 to pay the expenses of; to support financially. 4 to continue to argue; to assert. [from Old French *maintenir*, from Latin *manu tenere*, to hold in the hand]

maintenance *noun* 1 the process of keeping something in good condition. 2 money paid by one person to support another, as ordered by a court of law, eg following a divorce. See also ALIMONY. 3 the process of continuing something or keeping something in existence. [from Old French *maintenir*, from Latin *manu tenere*, to hold in the hand]

Maintenon, Françoise d'Aubigné, Marquise de, known as **Madame de Maintenon** (1635–1719) second wife of Louis XIV of France, born in Niort. In 1652 she married the crippled poet Paul Scarron, and on his death was reduced to poverty. In 1669 she became governess to the King's two sons by his mistress Mme de Montespan, and moved with them to the court (1673). By 1674 the King's generosity enabled her to purchase the estate of Maintenon, near Paris, which was converted to a marquisate. After the queen's death (1683) Louis married her secretly, and when he died (1715) she retired to the educational institution for poor girls which she had founded at St-Cyr (1686).

Mainz, French **Mayence** POP (1991e) 180 000, the commercial capital of Rhineland–Palatinate state, Germany. An old Roman city, it lies on the left bank of the R Rhine opposite the mouth of the R Main. Mainz is the centre of the Rhine wine trade and the headquarters of radio and television corporations. The printer Johannes Gutenberg was born in 1400 in Mainz; here in c.1448 he invented the art of printing with movable type. NOTABLE FEATURE cathedral (mostly 11c–13c).

Maipó *or* **Maipú, Battle of** a decisive battle (1818) in the Spanish–American Wars of Independence, fought near Santiago, Chile. A notable victory for the Argentine general, José de San Martín, it secured the liberation of Chile from Spanish rule.

Mairi a female first name. [a Scottish Gaelic form of MARY]

maisonette *or* **maisonnette** *noun* a flat within a larger house or block, especially on two floors, usually with its own separate entrance. [from French diminutive of *maison*, house]

maître d'hôtel (PL. **maîtres d'hôtel**) **1** a head waiter. **2** the manager of a hotel or restaurant. [French, = master of the hotel]

maize *noun* **1** a cereal (*Zea mays*) belonging to the grass family (Gramineae), and the only cereal native to the New World. Maize was developed as a major food crop by the Indians of Central America, especially Mexico, and it is now cultivated mainly in the tropics and subtropics, although some modern strains are suitable for temperate regions. The male flowers are borne in a terminal tassel, and the female flowers form a woody cob, which bears rows of plump white, yellow, red, or purple grains, which are eaten as a vegetable (sweet corn). The grains and foliage are also used for animal fodder. **2** the grain of this plant, eaten ripe or unripe as a vegetable (sweet corn). It also yields oil, flour, starch, and syrup. — Also called *sweetcorn, Indian corn.* [from Spanish *maíz*, from Taino (extinct S American Indian language) *mahiz*]

Maj. *abbrev.* Major.

Maja clothed a painting by Goya (c.1797–1800, Prado, Madrid).

Maja nude a painting by Goya (c.1797–1800, Prado, Madrid).

majestic *adj.* having or exhibiting majesty; stately, grand.

majestically *adv.* in a majestic way.

majesty *noun* (PL. **majesties**) **1** great and impressive dignity. **2** splendour. **3** (**His** *or* **Her** *or* **Your Majesty**) a title used when speaking of or to a king or queen. [from Latin *majestas*]

Majlis *noun* **1** the parliament of Iran. **2** (**majlis**) an assembly or council in various N African and Middle Eastern countries. [from Persian *majlis*]

majolica *noun* colourfully glazed or enamelled earthenware, especially popular in Italy from the 14c to the 16c. [from Italian, from Latin *Majorica*, Majorca, where it was originally made]

Major, John (1943–) English Conservative politician and Prime Minister, born in Merton, SW London. The son of a trapeze performer, after beginning a career in banking, he became MP for Huntingdonshire (1979). He rose quickly under Margaret Thatcher to become Treasury Chief Secretary (1987), Foreign Secretary (1989), and, to general surprise, Chancellor of the Exchequer (on Nigel Lawson's dramatic resignation, 1989). He remained loyal to Thatcher in the first round of the 1990 Conservative party leader-

ship election, but when she stood down, ran successfully against Michael Heseltine and Douglas Hurd to become Prime Minister, thus completing one of the swiftest rises to power of recent times. Despite the country's deepening recession and Labour's improved showing in the opinion poles, his government was re-elected in the 1992 general election.

major — *adj.* **1** great, or greater, in number, size, importance, etc. **2** *said of a musical key or scale* having two full tones between the first and third notes. — *noun* **1** an army officer of the rank above captain and below lieutenant-colonel. **2** a major key, chord, or scale. **3** *North Amer., esp. US* a student's main subject of study; a student studying such a subject. **4** a person who has reached the age of full legal responsibility. — *verb intrans.* (**majored, majoring**) *North Amer., esp. US* to specialize in a particular subject of study. [from Latin, comparative of *magnus*, great]

Major Barbara a play by George Bernard Shaw (1905). Through the dilemma of a salvation army major tempted to accept money from manufacturers of weapons and alcohol, social conscience is contrasted with amoral social reform.

Majorca, Spanish **Mallorca**, ancient **Balearis Major** POP (1990e) 171 000, the largest of the Balearic Is of Spain, situated in the W Mediterranean Sea 240km/150mi to the N of Algiers. AREA 3 640sq km/1 400sq mi. PHYSICAL DESCRIPTION the tree-covered Sierra del Alfabia rises to 1 445m at Puig Mayor and to the E the smaller Sierra de Levante Hills rise to 500m; between these ranges there is a flat plain indented by the bays of Alcudia and Pollensa in the N and Palma Bay in the S. CLIMATE rainfall is low and the fields of the plain are watered with the aid of windmills. CHIEF TOWNS Palma, Manacor. HISTORY Majorca was taken in 1229 by James I of Aragón. There are many Roman, Phoenician, and Carthaginian remains on the island. In the Middle Ages, Majorca was famous for its porcelain. ECONOMY pottery; brandy; jewellery; mining; sheep; timber; fishing; tourism is very important.

major-domo *noun* (PL. **major-domos**) a chief servant in charge of the management of a household. [from Spanish *mayor-domo*]

majorette *noun* (also **drum majorette**) each of a group of girls who march in parades performing elaborate displays of baton-twirling.

major-general *noun* an army officer of the rank above brigadier and below lieutenant-general.

majority *noun* (PL. **majorities**) **1** the greater number; the largest group; the bulk. **2** the winning margin of votes in an election. **3** the age at which a person legally becomes an adult. — **in the majority** forming the larger group or greater part. [from Latin *majoritas*]

majority rule *Politics* government by members, or by a body including members, of the largest racial, ethnic, or religious group(s) in a country, as opposed to a political system which excludes them.

Majuba Hill, Battle of an engagement (1881) which ended the first Boer War. In 1877 the British plan to federate the British and Boer territories of South Africa commenced with the successful annexation of the Transvaal, but after the British victory at Ulundi in the Zulu War of 1879, which effectively removed the Zulu threat, the Boers resolved to re-establish their independence and finally defeated the British at Majuba Hill. William Ewart Gladstone's government restored a limited independence to the Orange Free State and the Transvaal under the Pretoria Convention, subsequently modified by the London Convention of 1884, but disagreements over the interpretation of these conventions increased tensions later in the 19c.

Makale see MEKELE.

Makarios III, Cyprus Enosis, originally **Mihail Khristodoulou Mouskos** (1913–77) Cypriot Orthodox Archbishop and statesman, born in Pano Panayia. He was ordained priest (1946), elected Bishop of Kition (1948), and Archbishop (1950). He reorganized the *Enosis* movement (which aimed towards union with Greece), was arrested and detained in 1956, but returned to a tumultuous welcome in 1959 to become chief Greek–Cypriot Minister in the new Greek–Turkish provisional government. Later that year he was elected the first President of Cyprus (1960–77).

Makassar see UJUNG PADANG.

Makassar *or* **Macassar Strait**, Indonesian **Selat** a stretch of water lying between the islands of Borneo in the W and Sulawesi (Celebes) in the E, linking the Java Sea in the S to the Celebes Sea in the N. It is 720km/447mi long.

make — *verb* (PAST TENSE AND PAST PARTICIPLE **made**) **1** to form, create, manufacture, or produce by mixing, combining, or shaping materials. **2** to cause to be or become. **3** to cause, bring about, or create by one's actions. **4** to force, induce, or cause. **5** to cause to change into something else; to transform or convert: *make a man of him / made the barn into a cottage.* **6** to be suitable for; to have or develop the appropriate qualities for: *this material will make a nice dress / he'll never make a singer.* **7** to appoint. **8** to cause to appear; to represent as being: *long hair makes her look younger / the film makes him a hero.* **9** to gain, earn, or acquire: *make a fortune.* **10** to add up to or amount to; to constitute: *4 and 4 makes 8 / the book makes interesting reading.* **11** to calculate, judge, or estimate to be: *I make it three o'clock.* **12** to arrive at or reach; to succeed in achieving, reaching or gaining. **13** to score (points). **14** to ensure the success of: *made my day.* **15** to propose: *make an offer.* **16** to engage in; to perform, carry out, or produce: *make war / make a speech / make a decision.* **17** to tidy (a bed) after use. **18** (**make to do something**) to show an intention of doing it; to make an attempt or start to do it: *made to stand up, then sat down again.* **19** *slang* to succeed in having sexual intercourse with. — *noun* **1** a manufacturer's brand. **2** the way in which something is made.
— **make away with someone** to kill them.
make away with something to steal it.
make believe to pretend.
make do with something to make the best use of a second or inferior choice.
make do without something to manage without it.
make for something *or* **someone 1** to move rapidly or suddenly towards them. **2** to have a specific result: *fine weather made for an enjoyable holiday.*
make it *colloq.* **1** to be successful. **2** to survive.
make like ... *colloq. North Amer., esp. US* to act or behave as if ...
make of something *or* **someone** to understand them to mean or signify: *what do you make of their comments? / they did not know what to make of us.*
make off to leave, especially hurriedly or secretly.
make off with something *or* **someone** to run off with them; to steal or kidnap them.
make or break to bring the success or failure of.
make out 1 to pretend: *made out that he was ill.* **2** *colloq.* to make progress: *how did they make out?* **3** *colloq. chiefly North Amer.* to manage, succeed, or survive: *we'll make out.*
make something out 1 to begin to discern it, especially to see or hear it: *could make out a vague figure in the distance.* **2** to write or fill in a document, etc: *make out a cheque for £20.*
make something *or* **someone out to be something** to cause them to seem what they are not: *they made us out to be liars.*
make out a case for something to support or justify it with argument.

make something over 1 to transfer ownership of it. **2** *North Amer., esp. US* to convert it.

make up to resolve a disagreement with someone.

make someone up to apply cosmetics to their face.

make something up 1 to fabricate or invent it. **2** to prepare or assemble it. **3** to constitute it; to be the parts of it: *the three villages together make up a district.* **4** to form the final element in something; to complete it: *another player to make up the team.* **5** to settle differences.

make up for something to compensate or serve as an apology for it.

make up to someone *colloq.* to seek their friendship or favour; to flirt with them.

on the make *colloq.* seeking a large or illegal profit.

[from Anglo-Saxon *macian*]

make-believe — *noun* pretence, especially when playful or innocent. — *adj.* pretended; imaginary.

make-or-break *adj.* determining success or failure.

maker *noun* **1** *combining form* a person who makes. **2** (**Maker**) God.

makeshift *adj.* serving as a temporary and less adequate substitute.

make-up *noun* **1** cosmetics applied to the face, etc. **2** the combination of characteristics or ingredients that form something, eg a personality.

makeweight *noun* **1** a small quantity added to a scale to get the required weight. **2** a person or thing of little value or importance, included only to make up for a deficiency.

making *noun, combining form* the process of producing or forming something.
— **be the making of someone** to ensure their success.
have the makings of ... to have the ability to become ...; to show signs of becoming ...
in the making in the process of being made, formed, or developed.
of one's own making caused by one's own actions.

mal see GRAND MAL, PETIT MAL.

mal- *combining form* forming words meaning: **1** bad or badly: *maladapted.* **2** incorrect or incorrectly: *malfunction.* [from Latin *male*, badly]

Malabo, formerly **Clarencetown, Port Clarence**, and later **Santa Isabel** POP (1986e) 10 000, the seaport capital of Equatorial Guinea. It is situated on the island of Bioko in the Gulf of Guinea. The city was founded by the British in 1827.

malabsorption *noun Medicine* the impaired absorption of one or more nutrients from digested food material in the small intestine, which can cause anaemia, weight loss, and symptoms of specific vitamin deficiencies. The most important cause of malabsorption in the UK is coeliac disease.

Malacca or **Melaka** POP (1990) 584 000, a state in SW Peninsular Malaysia. AREA 1 657sq km/640sq mi. It is bounded W by the Strait of Malacca and was one of the former Straits Settlements. CAPITAL Malacca. HISTORY the centre of a great trading empire since the 15c; Islam spread from here throughout the Malay Peninsula; held at various times by the Portuguese, Dutch, and British. The state has a large Chinese population. ECONOMY rubber; tin; rice. NOTABLE FEATURES State Museum; St John's Fort; St Peter's Church (1710); Cheng Hoon Teng Temple (oldest Chinese temple in Malaysia); Kampung Kling Mosque; Vinayagar Moorthi Temple.

Malacca, Strait of the channel between Peninsular Malaysia and the Indonesian island of Sumatra. It is 800km/500mi long and 50–320km/30–200mi wide. The strait which links the Andaman Sea to the S China Sea is an important shipping lane. Singapore is the largest port.

Malachi *or* **Malachias, Book of** the last of the 12 so-called 'minor' prophetic writings of the Hebrew Bible and Old Testament, possibly the work of a 'cult prophet' in view of the strong criticism of priestly neglect of cultic requirements. [Hebrew, = my messenger]

malachite *noun Geol.* a bright green copper mineral that is used as a gemstone and as a minor ore of copper. [from Greek *malakhe*, mallow, whose leaves are a similar shade of green]

Malade Imaginaire, Le (The Imaginary Invalid; The Hypochondriac) a play by Molière (1673). It is a comedy about a hypochondriac father who wants his daughter to marry a doctor. Ironically, Molière himself died suddenly after performing the title role.

maladjusted *adj.* psychologically unable to deal with everyday situations and relationships, usually as a result of an emotionally disturbing experience.

maladjustment *noun* **1** poor or bad adjustment. **2** inability to cope with day-to-day life.

maladminister *verb* (**maladministered, maladministering**) to manage or administer badly.

maladministration *noun* incompetent or dishonest management, especially of public affairs.

maladroit *adj.* clumsy; tactless. [from French *maladroit*]

maladroitly *adv.* in a maladroit way.

maladroitness *noun* being maladroit.

malady *noun* (PL. **maladies**) *old use, formal* an illness or disease. [from French *maladie*, from Latin *male habitus*, in bad condition]

Málaga, ancient **Malaca** POP (1991) 512 000, the port capital of Málaga province, Andalusia, S Spain. It is situated at the mouth of R Guadalmedina 544km/338mi S of Madrid and is the air arrival point for visitors to the popular tourist region, the Costa del Sol. HISTORY founded by the Phoenicians in the 12c BC; taken by the Moors in the 8c; became part of Spain in 1487. NOTABLE FEATURES birthplace of Pablo Picasso; Moorish Alcazaba; cathedral (16c–18c); Roman theatre; Fine Arts Museum.

Malagasy the peoples of the island of Madagascar, comprising about 50 ethnic groups, of diverse origins, of which the strongest element is from Indonesia (present-day population c.9m). Malagasy languages belong to the Malayo–Polynesian family of languages. Before colonial rule, groups were politically autonomous, and mostly lacking centralized organization, except for the Merina of the central highlands, who established a powerful kingdom in the 16c.

malaise *noun* **1** a feeling of uneasiness or discontent. **2** a general feeling of ill health, not attributable to any particular disease. [from French, from *mal*, ill + *aise*, ease]

Malamud, Bernard (1914–86) US novelist and short-story writer, born in New York City. His early novels *The Natural* (1952) and *The Assistant* (1957) combine realistic descriptions of life among poor Jewish immigrants in New York City with an element of fantasy that reappears in his short stories (eg *The Magic Barrel*, 1958). *The Fixer* (1967) is a more directly serious depiction of Jewish life in Tzarist Russia. Later novels include *Pictures of Fidelman* (1965) and *Dubin's Lives* (1979).

Malan, Daniel F(rançois) (1874–1959) South African politician, born in Riebeek West, Cape Province. In 1905 he joined the ministry of the Dutch Reform Church, but in 1915 left to be editor of the Nationalist newspaper *Die Burger*. An MP from 1918, in 1924 he held the portfolios of the Interior, Education, and Public Health in the Hertzog administration. He left the government in 1934 and founded the Purified Nationalist Party, which became the official opposition to the new merger of J B M Hertzog's National Party and Jan Smuts's South African Party. Later reconciled with Hertzog, he formed the reunited National Party with him in 1939, and was Leader of the Opposition, Minister for External Affairs, and Prime Minister (1948–54), when he introduced the controversial apartheid policy.

Malaprop, Mrs the aunt of Lydia Languish in Richard Brinsley Sheridan's *The Rivals*, famous for her hilarious misuse of words which gave rise to the term 'malapropism'.

malapropism *noun* the misuse of a word, usually with comic effect, through confusion with another which sounds similar but has a different meaning; a word misused in this way. [from Mrs Malaprop; associated with French *mal à propos* inappropriate]

malaria *noun* an infectious disease, mainly of tropical and subtropical regions, caused by a parasitic protozoan (of the genus *Plasmodium*) that is transmitted to humans by the bite of the *Anopheles* mosquito. Its main symptoms are anaemia and recurring bouts of fever, and similar drugs are used for both preventive and curative treatment of the disease. [from Italian *mal' aria*, bad air, formerly thought to be the cause of the disease]

malarial *adj.* **1** infected with malaria. **2** belonging to or of the nature of malaria.

malarkey *noun colloq.* nonsense; rubbish.

Mälar, Lake, Swedish **Mälaren** a lake in SE Sweden, extending 113km/70mi inland from the Baltic Sea. AREA 1 140sq km/440sq mi. The city of Stockholm lies on both sides of the strait which connects the lake with the Baltic Sea.

Malatesta lords of the state of Rimini in NE Italy from the 13c to the 16c, who were among the most durable of several families of *signori* who dominated political life in the Italian Renaissance. Originally the political 'vicars' of the papacy, the Malatesta state was overthrown in 1500 by a coalition of the papacy and the French.

Malawi, official name **Republic of Malawi** POP (1992e) 8.8m, a republic in SE Africa, divided into three regions and 24 districts. AREA 118 484sq km/45 735sq mi. It is bounded SW and SE by Mozambique, E by L Nyasa (L Malawi), N by Tanzania, and W by Zambia. CAPITAL Lilongwe. CHIEF TOWNS Blantyre, Zomba, Limbe, Salima. TIME ZONE GMT +2. The population is largely Bantu and chief religions are Protestantism (55%), Roman Catholicism (20%), and Islam (20%). OFFICIAL LANGUAGES English, Chichewa. CURRENCY the kwacha. PHYSICAL

Malawi

DESCRIPTION crossed N–S by the Great Rift Valley in which lies Africa's third-largest lake, L Nyasa (L Malawi); high plateaux on either side (900–1 200m); Shire highlands in the S rise to nearly 3 000m at Mt Mulanje. CLIMATE tropical climate in the S, with high year-round temperatures, 28–37°C; average annual rainfall, 740mm; more moderate temperatures in centre; higher rainfall in the mountains overlooking L Nyasa (1 500–2 000mm). HISTORY discovered by the Portuguese in the 17c; European contact was established by David Livingstone in 1859; Scottish church missions were established in the area; claimed as the British Protectorate of Nyasaland in 1891; it was established as a British colony in 1907; in the 1950s it joined with N and S Rhodesia to form the Federation of Rhodesia and Nyasaland; gained independence in 1964; became a republic in 1966; as a result of international pressure and growing unrest within the country a referendum was held in 1993 in which the population voted for a multiparty system. ECONOMY based on agriculture, which employs 90% of the population; tobacco, sugar, tea, cotton, groundnuts, maize; textiles, matches, cigarettes, beer, spirits, shoes, cement.

Malawi, Lake see NYASA, LAKE.

Malay — *noun* **1** a member of a people inhabiting Malaysia, Singapore, and Indonesia. **2** their language, the official language of Malaysia. — *adj.* relating to the Malays or their language. [from Malay *malayu*]

◇ The Malays are a group of Austronesian peoples of the Malay Peninsula (where they form 54% of the population) and neighbouring islands and territory, including parts of Borneo and Sumatra. Most became Hindu before being converted to Islam in the 15c, and Hindu Indian influence on their culture is still strong. Most Malay villages are along the rivers and coasts, and rice and rubber are the main crops.

Malay Peninsula see PENINSULAR MALAYSIA.

Malaysia POP (1992e) 18.2m, an independent federation of states situated in SE Asia, AREA 329 749sq km/127 283sq mi. It comprises 11 states and a federal territory in Peninsular Malaysia, and the E states of Sabah and Sarawak on the island of Borneo. CAPITAL Kuala Lumpur. CHIEF TOWNS George Town, Ipoh, Malacca, Johor Baharu, Kuching, Kota Kinabalu. TIME ZONE GMT +8. The population is mainly Malay (59%) with Chinese (32%) and Indian (9%); Islam is the chief religion. OFFICIAL LANGUAGE Bahasa Malaysia (Malay); Chinese, English, and Tamil are also spoken. CURRENCY the Malaysian ringgit. PHYSICAL DESCRIPTION Peninsular Malaysia consists of a mountain chain of granite and limestone running N–S, rising to Mt Tahan (2 189m); there are narrow E and broader W coastal plains; the peninsula length is 700km/435mi and its width is up to 320km/200mi; mostly tropical rainforest and mangrove swamp; a coastline of long, narrow beaches; the chief river is the Pahang (456km/283mi long). Sarawak, on the NW coast of

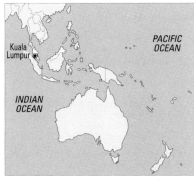

Malaysia

Borneo, has a narrow, swampy coastal belt backed by foothills rising sharply towards mountain ranges on the Indonesian frontier; Sabah, in the NE corner of Borneo, has a deeply indented coastline and a narrow W coastal plain, rising sharply into the Crocker Range, reaching 4 094m at Mt Kinabalu, Malaysia's highest peak. CLIMATE a tropical climate, with highest temperatures in coastal areas; it is strongly influenced by monsoon winds; humidity is high. HISTORY part of the Srivijaya Empire in the 9c–14c; Hindu and Muslim influences in the 14c–15c; Portugal, the Netherlands, and Britain vied for control from the 16c; Singapore, Malacca, and Penang were formally incorporated into the British Colony of the Straits Settlements in 1826; British protection which extended over Perak, Selangor, Negeri Sembilan, and Pahang was constituted into the Federated Malay States in 1895; protection treaties with several other states (Unfederated Malay States) were agreed in 1885–1930; occupied by the Japanese in World War II; after the war, Sarawak became a British colony, Singapore became a separate colony, the colony of North Borneo was formed, and the Malay Union was established, uniting the Malay states and the Straits Settlements of Malacca and Penang; the Federation of Malaya was created in 1948; gained independence in 1957; the constitutional monarchy of Malaysia came into existence in 1963; Singapore withdrew from the Federation in 1965. GOVERNMENT governed by a bicameral Federal Parliament, consisting of a 69-member Senate elected for six years and a 180-member House of Representatives elected for five years; the head of state is a monarch elected for five years by sultans; a Prime Minister and a Cabinet advise. ECONOMY the discovery of tin in the late 19c brought European investment; rubber trees introduced from Brazil; rice, palms, timber, fishing; iron ore, ilmenite, gold, bauxite, oil, natural gas; textiles, rubber and oil products, chemicals, electronic components, electrical goods, tourism.

Malcolm III, also called **Malcolm Canmore** ('large headed') (c.1031–1093) King of Scots (1058–93), the son of Duncan I. He returned from exile (1054) and conquered S Scotland, but did not become king until 1058, when he had defeated and killed Macbeth (who had killed his father), and disposed of Macbeth's stepson, Lulach. He married (as his second wife) the English princess Margaret (later St Margaret), sister of Edgar the Atheling, and launched five invasions of England (1061–93).

Malcolm IV, also called **the Maiden** (c.1141–65) King of Scots (1153–65), the grandson and successor of David I. He was compelled to restore the N English counties to Henry II in return for the earldom and honour of Huntingdon (1157), then served on Henry's expedition to Toulouse (1159). He defeated Fergus, Lord of Galloway, in 1161, and in 1164 Somerled, Lord of Argyll, was vanquished and slain at Renfrew. His nickname was coined in the 15c, in recognition of his reputation for chastity.

Malcolm a male first name. [from the Scottish Gaelic name *Mael Coluim*, servant of Columba]

malcontent — *adj.*, *said of a person* dissatisfied and inclined to rebel. — *noun* a dissatisfied person. [from Old French *malcontent*]

Maldives, formerly **Maldive Islands**, official name **Republic of Maldives**, Divehi **Divehi Jumhuriya** POP (1992e) 231 000, a republic consisting of an island archipelago in the Indian Ocean, divided into 19 administrative atolls, situated 670km/416mi SW of Sri Lanka. AREA 300sq km/120sq mi. It comprises 1 190 islands, of which 202 are inhabited. CAPITAL Malé. TIME ZONE GMT +5.5. The population is mostly of Aryan origin; Islam (Sunni) is the official religion. OFFICIAL LANGUAGE Divehi; English is spoken widely. CURRENCY the Maldivian rupee (*rufiyaa*). PHYSICAL DESCRIPTION small, low-lying islands, with sandy beaches fringed with coconut palms.

CLIMATE generally warm and humid; affected by SW monsoons in Apr–Oct; the average annual rainfall is 2 100mm and the average daily temperature is 22°C. HISTORY a former dependency of Ceylon; a British protectorate from 1887 until 1965 when it gained independence. GOVERNMENT governed by a President, elected every five years, a Ministers' Cabinet, and a Citizens' Cabinet of 48 members elected for five years. ECONOMY breadfruit, banana, coconut, mango, cassava, sweet potato, millet; fishing; shipping; tourism.

Maldives

Malé, Divehi **Daviyani** POP (1990) 55 000, the capital and chief atoll of the Maldives. AREA 2sq km/0.8sq mi. There is a developing tourist industry on Malé.

male — *adj.* **1** denoting the sex that produces sperm and fertilizes the ovum (egg cell). **2** denoting the reproductive structure of a plant that produces the male gamete. **3** of or characteristic of men; masculine. **4** for or made up of men or boys. **5** *Engineering* denoting a piece of machinery that fits into another part (the female). — *noun* a male person, animal, or plant. [from Old French *masle*]

male chauvinism a self-interested prejudice shown by men against women.

male chauvinist or **male chauvinist pig** *derog.* a man who is prejudiced against women and is primarily concerned to promote the interests of men.

malediction *noun* a curse; an act of cursing. [from MAL- + Latin *dicere*, to speak]

maledictory *adj.* using or full of curses.

malefaction *noun* evil-doing, wrongdoing.

malefactor *noun old use, formal* a criminal; an evil-doer; a wrongdoer. [from MAL- + Latin *facere*, to do]

male fern a common woodland fern (*Dryopteris filix-mas*) that has fronds up to 150cm long. Each frond is divided into many tapering lobes called pinnae, and each pinna is divided into a number of smaller toothed lobes called pinnules, although these are not all completely separated. On the underside of each pinnule are the spore-bearing structures or *sori*, each of which is covered by a heart-shaped flap which shrivels as the spores ripen.

male menopause *colloq.* a crisis of confidence identified in middle-aged men, regarded as comparable with the menopause in women but caused by psychological factors such as fear of ageing.

maleness *noun* a male state or quality.

Malenkov, Giorgiy Maksimilianovich (1901–79) Soviet politician, born in Orenburg. He joined the Communist Party in 1920 and was involved in the collectivization of agriculture and the purges of the 1930s under Stalin. He became a member of the Politburo and deputy premier in 1946, and succeeded Stalin as Party First Secretary and premier (1953–5). When he resigned he admitted responsibility for the failure of Soviet agricultural policy, and in 1957 was sent to Kazakhstan as manager of a hydroelectric plant.

Malesherbes, Chrétien (Guillaume de Lamoignon) de (1721–94) French statesman, born in Paris. In 1744 he became a counsellor of the Parlement of Paris, and in 1750 was made chief censor of the press. On Louis XVI's accession (1774) he was made Secretary of State for the royal household. He brought about prison and legal reforms alongside Anne-Robert-Jacques Turgot's economic improvements, but resigned on the eve of Turgot's dismissal (1776). Despite his reforming zeal, he was mistrusted as an aristocrat during the Revolution, arrested as a Royalist in 1794, and guillotined.

Malevich, Kasimir Severinovich (1878–1935) Russian painter and designer, born near Kiev. He was interested in developing a totally non-objective style of art, and in Moscow in c.1913 he launched the Suprematist movement, in which art is based on geometric shapes. The movement culminated in his *White on White* series (a white square painted onto a white background) in 1918–19. After this he concentrated on expounding his theories through writing and teaching, first in Vitebsk and later in Leningrad (now St Petersburg). His theories are outlined in *Die gegenstandlose Welt* (The Non-Objective World, 1926).

malevolence *noun* **1** being malevolent. **2** ill will.

malevolent *adj.* wishing to do evil to others; malicious. [from MAL- + Latin *velle*, to wish]

malfeasance *noun Legal* an unlawful act, especially committed by a public official. [from French *malfaisance*]

malfeasant *adj.* that commits evil deeds.

malformation *noun* **1** the state or condition of being badly or wrongly formed or shaped. **2** a badly or wrongly formed part; a deformity.

malformed *adj.* badly or wrongly formed.

malfunction — *noun* the act or state of working imperfectly or not at all. — *verb intrans.* to work imperfectly; to fail to work.

Malherbe, François de (1555–1628) French poet, born in Caen. He became court poet to Henry IV (1605) and, in opposition to the school of Ronsard, advocated a refined, regular, and prosaic style with an emphasis on strict form, which anticipated Classicism. He produced odes, songs, epigrams, epistles, translations, and works of criticism.

Mali, official name **Republic of Mali**, French **République de Mali** POP (1992e) 9.8m, a republic in W Africa, divided into six regions. AREA 1 240 192sq km/478 714sq mi. It is bounded NE by Algeria, NW by Mauritania, W by Senegal, SW by Guinea, S by the Ivory Coast, SE by Burkina, and E by Niger. CAPITAL Bamako. CHIEF TOWNS Ségou, Mopti, Sikasso, Kayes, Gao, Timbuktu. TIME ZONE GMT. The majority of the population belongs to the Mande tribes; Islam is the main religion. OFFICIAL LANGUAGE French; local languages are spoken widely. CURRENCY the Mali franc. PHYSICAL DESCRIPTION a landlocked country on the fringe of the Sahara; the lower part of the Hoggar massif is located in the N; arid plains lie between 300m and 500m; there is featureless desert land in the N with sand dunes; mainly savannah land in the S; the main rivers are the Niger and Sénégal. CLIMATE hot, dry climate with rainfall increasing from N–S; in the S the rainfall season lasts for five months (Jun–Oct); the annual average rainfall is c.1 000mm in the S, decreasing to almost zero in the Saharan N. HISTORY a medieval state of Mali in the area controlled the trade routes between the savannah and Sahara, reaching its peak in the 14c; important in the Islamicization of W Africa; governed by France from 1881 to 1895; it was a territory of French Sudan (part of French W Africa) until 1959; part-

nership with Senegal as the Federation of Mali in 1959; achieved separate independence in 1960; a new multiparty constitution was approved in a referendum in 1992. ECONOMY mainly subsistence agriculture; sorghum, millet, rice, maize, cotton, groundnuts; crops severely affected by drought conditions; small amounts of marble, limestone, bauxite, nickel, manganese; fishing, livestock, food processing, textiles, leather, cement; some tourism.

Mali

malice *noun* **1** the desire or intention to harm or hurt others. **2** mischievousness. [from French, from Latin *malus*, bad]

malice aforethought *Legal* a firm intention to commit a crime, especially against a person.

malicious *adj.* feeling, or motivated by, hatred or a desire to cause harm.

malign — *verb* to say or write unpleasant things about. — *adj.* **1** evil in nature or influence; displaying ill-will. **2** *said of a disease* harmful; malignant. [from Latin *malignus*, of evil disposition]

malignancy *noun* (PL. **malignancies**) **1** being malignant. **2** a cancerous growth.

malignant *adj.* **1** feeling or showing hatred or the desire to do harm; malicious or malevolent. **2** *Medicine* denoting any disorder that, if left untreated, may cause death, especially a cancerous tumour, ie one that invades and destroys the surrounding tissue, and may spread to more distant parts of the body via the bloodstream or lymphatic system. See also BENIGN. [from Latin *malignare*, to act maliciously]

malignity *noun* **1** being malign, evil, or deadly. **2** a malicious act. **3** hatred.

malinger *verb intrans.* (**malingered, malingering**) to pretend to be ill, especially in order to avoid work. [from French *malingre*, sickly]

malingerer *noun* a person who malingers.

Malinowski, Bronisław (Kasper) (1884–1942) Polish-born British anthropologist, born in Kraków. He travelled to London in 1910 and taught at the London School of Economics, where he became a professor in 1927. In 1938 he went to the USA, where he accepted a post at Yale. He was the pioneer of 'participant observation' as a method of fieldwork (notably, in the Trobriand Is), and a major proponent of functionalism in anthropology.

mall *noun* **1** a public promenade, especially tree-lined. **2** a shopping precinct closed to vehicles. [from The Mall, a street in London]

Mallard a steam locomotive designed by Sir Nigel Gresley and built at Doncaster Works in 1938. In the same year it became the fastest steam locomotive in the world, when it momentarily reached a speed of 203kph/126mph. It is on display in the National Railway Museum in York, England.

mallard *noun* (PL. **mallard, mallards**) the most widespread species of wild duck, that breeds on

lakes, ponds, etc, throughout most of Europe, Asia, and N America, migrating south of these regions in the autumn. The male has a dark green glossy head and neck with a white collar and dark brown breast, while the female is mottled brown. Most domestic ducks are descended from wild mallards. [from Old French *mallart*]

Mallarmé, Stéphane (1842–98) French Symbolist poet, born in Paris. He taught English, mainly in Paris, translated the poems of Edgar Allan Poe, and in his own writing became a leader of the Symbolist school. His works include *Hérodiade* (1864), *L'Après-midi d'un faune* (1865, published 1876), which inspired Debussy's prelude, and the experimental poem, *Un Coup de dés* (A Dice-Throw, 1914).

malleability *noun* being malleable.

malleable *adj.* **1** *Chem.* denoting certain metals and alloys that can be beaten into a different shape, hammered into thin sheets, and bent without fracture. **2** easily influenced. [from Latin *malleabilis*, from *malleus*, hammer]

mallet *noun* **1** a hammer with a large wooden head. **2** a long-handled wooden hammer for playing croquet or polo. [from Old French *maillet*, wooden hammer]

malleus *noun Anat.* a small hammer-shaped bone in the middle ear. Together with two other bones, the incus and stapes, it transmits sound waves from the eardrum to the inner ear. [from Latin *malleus*, hammer]

mallow *noun* any of various European plants with pink, purple, or white flowers and fine hairs on the leaves and stem. [from Anglo-Saxon *mealwe*]

Malmö POP (1992e) 235 000, the fortified seaport capital of Malmöhus county, SW Sweden. It lies on The Sound opposite Copenhagen, Denmark, and is the third-largest city in Sweden. In 1658 the city, which was under Danish rule, was conquered and made a part of Sweden by Charles X. NOTABLE FEATURES town hall (16c); Church of St Peter (14c).

malmsey *noun* a strong sweet wine originally from Greece, but now usually from Madeira. [from Latin *Malmasia*, from Greek *Monembasia*, the Greek port from which it was shipped]

malnutrition *noun* any of various disorders resulting from inadequate food intake, an unbalanced diet (eg lack of protein or vitamins), or inability to absorb nutrients from food. It results in fatigue, susceptibility to infection, and slow physical deterioration, and is particularly prevalent in countries that are affected by famine or war, and in areas of extreme poverty.

malodorous *adj. formal* foul-smelling.

Malory, Sir Thomas (d.1471) English writer, known for his work, *Le Morte d'Arthur* (The Death of Arthur). From William Caxton's preface, we are told that Malory was a knight, that he finished his work in the ninth year of the reign of Edward IV (1469–70), and that he 'reduced' it from some French book. It is probable that he was the Sir Thomas Malory (d.1471) of Newbold Revel, Warwickshire, whose quarrels with a neighbouring priory and (probably) Lancastrian politics brought him imprisonment.

Malpighi, Marcello (1628–94) Italian anatomist and microscopist, born near Bologna. He became a professor at Pisa, Messina, and Bologna, and from 1691 he served as Chief Physician to Pope Innocent XII. An early pioneer of histology, plant and animal, his microscopic studies led to many discoveries, including important new information on blood circulation, the development of embryos, and insect physiology.

Malpighian body *Anat.* in the mammalian kidney, the end of the kidney tubule, consisting of the *glomerulus* enclosed by a cup-shaped *Bowman's capsule*. Its function is to filter waste products from the blood. [named after the Italian anatomist Marcello Malpighi]

Malplaquet, Battle of a bitter engagement (1709) in the War of the Spanish Succession between the French army led by Marshals Claude-Louis-Hector Villars (1653–1734) and Louis-François Boufflers (1644–1711) and the Grand Alliance army commanded by the Duke of Marlborough and Prince Eugene of Savoy. A costly victory for the Allies, Malplaquet stiffened French resistance and swung English opinion behind the Tories' peace policy.

malpractice *noun* **1** improper, careless, or illegal professional conduct; an example of this. **2** any wrong or illegal act.

Malraux, André (Georges) (1901–76) French statesman and novelist, born in Paris. He spent much time in China, where he worked for the Guomindang and was active in the 1927 revolution. He also fought in the Spanish Civil War, and in World War II escaped from a prison camp to join the French resistance. From 1945 to 1946 he was Minister of Information in Charles de Gaulle's government, and Minister of Cultural Affairs from 1960 to 1969. His best-known novels include *La Condition humaine* (Man's Fate, 1933, Prix Goncourt) and *L'Espoir* (Man's Hope, 1937).

malt — *noun* **1** a mixture prepared from barley or wheat grains that have been soaked in water, allowed to sprout, and then dried in a kiln. Malt is used in brewing and distilling to make beer and whisky. **2** malt whisky. — *verb* to make into malt; to treat or combine with malt. [from Anglo-Saxon *mealt*]

Malta, official name **Republic of Malta**, Maltese **Repubblika ta' Malta**, ancient **Melita** POP (1992e) 360 000, an archipelago republic in the central Mediterranean Sea, comprising the islands of Malta (246sq km/95sq mi), Gozo, Comino, and some uninhabited islets. It is situated 93km/58mi S of Sicily, and 290km/180mi E of Tunisia. AREA 316sq km/122sq mi. CAPITAL Valletta. CHIEF TOWNS Sliema, Birkirkara, Qormi, Victoria (Rabat). TIME ZONE GMT +2. The population is of European origin; the chief religion is Apostolic Roman Catholicism. OFFICIAL LANGUAGES English, Maltese; there are many Arabic words in the local vocabulary. CURRENCY the Maltese pound. PHYSICAL DESCRIPTION the islands are generally low-lying, rising to 253m; there are no rivers or mountains; well-indented coastline. CLIMATE dry summers and mild winters; average annual rainfall is c.400mm; average daily winter temperature is 13°C. HISTORY controlled at various times by Phoenicia, Greece, Carthage, and Rome; conquered by Arabs in the 9c; given to the Knights Hospitallers in 1530; became a British Crown Colony in 1815; an important strategic base in both World Wars; in 1942 Malta was awarded the George Cross for its resistance to heavy air attacks; achieved independence in 1964, and became a republic in 1974; British Military Facilities agreement expired in 1979. GOVERNMENT governed by a President, Prime Minister, Cabinet, and a 65-member House of Representatives elected for five years. ECONOMY tourism and ship repair are the major industries; naval dockyards are now converted to commercial use; developing as a transshipment centre for

Malta

the Mediterranean; exports include tobacco, canned foods, light engineering products, textiles, paints, detergents, and plastic and steel goods; main crops are potatoes, tomatoes, onions, wheat, barley, grapes, oranges, and cut flowers; large numbers of cattle, sheep, goats, and poultry.

Malta, Knights of see HOSPITALLERS.

maltase *noun Biochem.* an enzyme, found in animals and plants, that breaks down maltose (malt sugar) into glucose.

Maltese — *noun* **1** (PL. **Maltese**) a native or citizen of Malta. **2** an official language of Malta, a Semitic language with a strong Italian influence. **3** a small toy spaniel developed in Italy, uniform in colour with straight hair and a long thick coat that reaches the ground, and conceals its short legs. — *adj.* relating to Malta or its people or language. [from Latin *Melita*]

Maltese cross a cross with four arms of equal length tapering towards the centre, each with a V cut into the end.

Maltese Falcon, The a US film directed by John Huston (1941), based on Dashiell Hammett's classic detective story. It is about the pursuit of an ultimately illusory black falcon statuette, and stars Humphrey Bogart as private detective Sam Spade.

Malthus, Thomas Robert (1766–1834) English economist, born near Dorking. He was ordained in 1797, and in 1798 published anonymously his *Essay on the Principle of Population*. This argued that the population has a natural tendency to increase faster than the means of subsistence, and that efforts should be made to cut the birth rate — a view later represented under the name of Malthusianism. In 1805 he became Professor of Political Economy in the East India College in Haileybury, where he wrote *Principles of Political Economy* (1820).

Malthusian — *adj.* relating to or supporting the theory of economist Thomas Malthus, that increases in populations tend to exceed the capacity to sustain them, and that there should therefore be restraint or control of sexual activity. — *noun* a supporter of this theory.

maltose *noun Biochem.* a disaccharide sugar that occurs in starch and glycogen, and is composed of two glucose molecules linked together.

maltreat *verb* to treat roughly or cruelly.

maltreatment *noun* bad, cruel, or rough treatment.

malt whisky whisky made entirely from malted barley.

Malvern or Great Malvern POP (1981) 31 000, a town in Malvern Hills district, Hereford and Worcester, W central England. It lies in the Malvern Hills, 11km/7mi SW of Worcester, and is a popular health resort. The composer Edward Elgar lived and was buried here.

malversation *noun formal* corruption in public affairs; illegal use of public funds. [from French, from MAL- + Latin *versari*, to occupy oneself]

Malvinas see FALKLAND ISLANDS.

Malvolio the pompous, humourless steward of Olivia in Shakespeare's *Twelfth Night*, who is tricked into believing that Olivia is in love with him.

mama or mamma *noun* a child's word for mother. [from the reduplication of a baby's babbled syllable *ma*]

Mamaev Kurgan or Mamai Hill an area in the heart of Volgograd, Russia, and the scene of the most severe conflict during the battle of Stalingrad (1942–3). The Soviet victory is commemorated by the Motherland monument, a 52m-high statue which dominates the hill.

mamba *noun* a large poisonous black or green African snake. [from Zulu *imamba*]

mambo *noun* (PL. **mambos**) a Latin American rhythmic dance, or a piece of music for this. [from American Spanish *mambo*]

Classification of Mammals

There are about 4 000 species of mammals, grouped into 19 orders and about 120 families.

Order	Animals	No. of species
Monotremata	egg-laying mammals – the platypus and echidnas	6
Marsupialia	pouched mammals, including kangaroos, opossums, koalas	238
Insectivora	insect-eating animals including hedgehogs, moles and shrews	293
Chiroptera	bats, the only mammals that can really fly	690
Primates	lemurs, monkeys, apes, humans	171
Edentata	anteaters, armadillos, sloths	30
Pholidota	pangolins (scaly anteaters)	7
Dermoptera	flying lemurs	2
Rodentia	rodents, gnawing animals, including beavers, capybara, hamsters, mice, porcupines, rats, squirrels	1 792
Lagomorpha	hares, pikas, rabbits	64
Cetacea	whales, dolphins, porpoises	82
Carnivora	flesh-eating animals such as bears, cats, dogs, pandas, raccoons	245
Pinnepedia	seals, sea lions, walrus	32
Artiodactyla	hoofed mammals with an even number of toes, including antelopes, camels, cattle, deer, giraffe, hippopotamuses, pigs	377
Perissodactyla	hoofed mammals with an odd number of toes – rhinoceroses, horses and zebras, tapirs	15
Sirenia	water mammals – dugong, manatees	4
Tubulidentata	the aardvark	1
Hyracoidea	hyraxes	6
Proboscidea	elephants	2

Mamluks or Mamelukes slave soldiers who constituted the army of the Ayyubid sultanate established in Egypt by Saladin in the 1170s. Their commanders (*amirs*) created a professional army of high quality, which overthrew the Ayyubids (1250) and established Muslim dynasties until conquered by the Turks in 1516–17. They continued to rule in Egypt with Ottoman blessing until their massacre by Mohammed Ali (1811).

mamma see MAMA.

mammal *noun Zool.* any warm-blooded vertebrate animal belonging to the class Mammalia, which contains about 4 000 species, characterized by the possession in the female of mammary glands which secrete milk to feed the young, eg humans, monkeys, apes, whales, elephants, hoofed mammals, dogs and other carnivores, mice and other rodents, and bats. [from Latin *mammalis*, of the breast, from *mamma*, breast]

◊ Other typical features of mammals are an insulating covering of body hair, which is very sparse in some mammals (eg whales), a four-chambered heart, sweat glands, a muscular diaphragm, and a lower jaw consisting of only two bones. Most mammals are terrestrial, but bats are capable of flight, and the whales and sea cows are entirely confined to water.
Mammals are divided into three groups. In *placental mammals* (the most advanced group), the young develop inside the mother's body in a uterus (womb), where they are nourished. Food from the mother's bloodstream passes into the embryo's bloodstream via the placenta, a specialized organ in which the two sets of blood vessels

meet. While placental mammals are born at an advanced stage of development, in *marsupials* (eg kangaroos, koalas) the young are born in a very immature state and develop outside the mother's body in a pouch (marsupium). In *monotremes* (the most primitive group), eg duck-billed platypus, the young hatch from an egg laid by the mother, and are then suckled with the mother's milk. Present-day mammals are more highly developed than any other group of animals, and placental mammals have spread to all parts of the world.

Mammalia *noun Zool.* in the animal kingdom, the class of warm-blooded vertebrates, including humans, that have a body covering of hair, and give birth to live young, which they suckle with secreted milk.

mammalian *adj. Biol.* relating to or typical of mammals.

mammary *adj. Biol., Medicine* of the breasts or other milk-producing glands. [from Latin *mamma*, breast]

mammary gland the milk-producing gland of a mammal, eg woman's breast or cow's udder.

mammography *noun Medicine* the process whereby an X-ray photograph of the breast is taken, usually in order to detect any abnormal or malignant growths at an early stage.

Mammon the savage, cave-dwelling miser in Edmund Spenser's *The Faerie Queene*, who represents the fact that God and riches cannot be simultaneously served.

mammon *noun* wealth when considered a source of evil and immorality, personified in the New Testament as a false god (**Mammon**). [from Aramaic *mamon*, wealth]

mammoth — *noun* any of various prehistoric hairy elephants belonging to the same order (Proboscoidea) as present-day elephants. — *adj.* huge. [from Old Russian *mammot*]
◇ Mammoths first appeared in Africa three million years ago during the Pliocene epoch, and spread through tundra regions of Europe, Asia, and N America during the early Pleistocene epoch, becoming extinct about 10 000 years ago. They differed from modern elephants in having shaggy hair, and larger curved tusks (up to 4m long). Some of them were larger and some smaller than present-day elephants.

Mammoth Cave National Park a system of subterranean passages and caverns created by limestone erosion, extending over 484km/301mi in W Kentucky, USA. The area is a National Park and a World Heritage site.

Mamoudzan POP (1985) 6 000, the chief town of Mayotte.

Man 1 POP (1975) 279 000, a department in W Ivory Coast. AREA 7 050sq km/2 720sq mi. CAPITAL Man. CHIEF TOWN Logoualé. ECONOMY iron ore. **2** the capital of Man department, W Ivory Coast.

Man, Isle of POP (1993e) 71 000, a British Crown Dependency in the Irish Sea, W of England and E of Northern Ireland. AREA 572sq km/221sq mi. The island rises to 620m at Snaefell. CAPITAL Douglas. CHIEF TOWNS Castletown, Peel, Ramsey. HISTORY ruled by the Welsh from the 6c until the 9c, then by the Scandinavians, Scots, and English; it was purchased by the British Government partly in 1765 and wholly in 1828. Manx survived as an everyday language until the 19c. GOVERNMENT the island has its own Parliament, the bicameral Court of Tynwald, which consists of the elected House of Keys and the Legislative Council (composed of the Lieutenant-Governor, the President, the Lord Bishop of Sodor and Man, the Attorney-General, and seven members elected by the House of Keys); Acts of the British Parliament do not generally apply to the I of Man. ECONOMY tourism; agriculture; light engineering; used as a tax haven. NOTABLE FEATURE Tynwald Hill, where all

acts of the Manx Parliament must be proclaimed. EVENT annual Tourist Trophy motorcycle races.

man — *noun* (PL. **men**) **1** an adult male human being. **2** human beings as a whole; the human race. **3** an adult male human being displaying typical masculine qualities: *a real man.* **4** *colloq.* a husband or boyfriend. **5** an ordinary employee, worker, or member of the armed forces, not a manager or officer. **6** one of the movable pieces in various board games. **7** a male member of a team. **8** *old use* any male servant, especially a valet. **9** *colloq.* used as a form of address in various contexts, eg indicating friendship or impatience: *damn it, man!* — *verb* (**manned**, **manning**) **1** to provide with sufficient (especially male) workers. **2** to operate: *man the pumps.* — *interj. colloq.* used to intensify a following statement: *man, is she gorgeous!*
— **as one man** simultaneously; together.
man and boy from childhood to manhood.
man to man openly or frankly.
to a man without exception.
men in grey suits unseen establishment figures holding the ultimate power in an organization, political party, etc.
[from Anglo-Saxon *mann*]

-man *combining form* forming words denoting: **1** a man associated with a specified activity: *postman.* **2** a man who is a native of a specified country or place: *Yorkshireman.*

man-about-town *noun* (PL. **men-about-town**) a fashionable and sophisticated male socialiser.

manacle — *noun* a handcuff. — *verb* to handcuff. [from Latin *manicula*, from *manus*, hand]

manage *verb* **1** to be in overall control or charge of. **2** to deal with or handle successfully or competently: *manage my own affairs.* **3** *trans., intrans.* to succeed in doing or producing (something). **4** to have enough room, time, etc for. **5** to handle (a tool or weapon). **6** to control (an animal). [from Italian *maneggiare*, from Latin *manus*, hand]

manageable *adj.* that can be managed.

management *noun* **1** the skill or practice of controlling something, especially a commercial enterprise. **2** the managers of a company, etc, as a group.

Management and Budget, Office of the office used by the US president to control the financial operations of government, created in 1970 out of the Bureau of the Budget. An important political arm of the presidency and not just a technical budget advisory office, it has been used more recently (eg under Presidents Reagan and Clinton) as an instrument of policy, for the control of domestic spending.

management buyout *Commerce* the purchase of the majority of the shares in a company by members of its management, especially in order to forestall an outside takeover.

manager *noun* a person in overall charge, especially of a commercial enterprise.

manageress *noun sometimes offensive* a female manager.

managerial *adj.* of a manager or management.

Managua 1 POP (1985e) 682 000, the capital city and commercial centre of Nicaragua, situated on the S shore of Lago de Managua, 45km/28mi inland from the Pacific Ocean. It was badly damaged by earthquakes in 1931 and 1972, and by Civil War in the late 1970s. NOTABLE FEATURE archaeological site of Huellas de Acahualinca nearby. **2** a department in W Nicaragua with Managua as its capital.

Manama, Arabic **Al Manamah** POP (1988e) 152 000, the seaport capital of Bahrain. It is connected by a causeway with Muharraq I to the NE. The city is a free trade port and an oil refining centre.

mañana *noun, adv. colloq.* tomorrow; some later time. [from Spanish *mañana*, tomorrow]

Man and Superman a play by George Bernard Shaw (1902). One of his greatest philosophical comedies, it argues through the relationship of Tanner and Anne that women are dominant over men, and stresses through Don Juan the importance of man's unceasing creative urge for world-improvement.

Mana Pools a national park in N Zimbabwe, established in 1963. AREA 2 196sq km/848sq mi. It is partly bordered in the NW by the R Zambezi, which forms the frontier with Zambia. The park contains extensive wildlife which migrate towards the river in huge numbers in the dry season. It is a World Heritage site.

Manasseh, Tribe of one of the 12 tribes of ancient Israel, but said to be descended from Joseph's elder son, who with Ephraim was adopted by Jacob to share in his blessing (Genesis 48–9). Its territory in central Palestine extended on both sides of the R Jordan, located between the tribes of Ephraim and Issachar in the west.

man-at-arms *noun* (PL. **men-at-arms**) *Hist.* a soldier, especially heavily armed and mounted.

manatee *noun* a large plant-eating marine mammal of the tropical waters of America, Africa, and the West Indies. [from Spanish *manatí*, from Carib (a West Indian language)]

Manaus or **Manáos** POP (1991) 1m, the river-port capital of Amazonas state, N Brazil, situated on the N bank of the R Negro just above its influx into the Amazon. Although the city, which was founded in 1660, lies 1 600km/1 000mi from the Atlantic Ocean, it is accessible to ocean-going vessels. It is the collecting point for produce from a vast area, including parts of Peru, Bolivia, and Colombia. A free zone was established in 1967. NOTABLE FEATURE the Teatro Amazonas Opera House (originally 1896).

Manchester, Latin **Mancunium** POP (1992e) 435 000, a city in Greater Manchester urban area, NW England. It is situated on the R Irwell, 256km/159mi NW of London, and is connected to the Irish Sea by the Manchester Ship Canal. It is the UK's second-largest commercial centre and a cultural centre for the NW. HISTORY the Roman town was located at a major crossroads; became the centre of the local textile industry in the 17c, and the focal point of the English cotton industry during the Industrial Revolution; it became a city in 1853. NOTABLE FEATURES art gallery; Royal Exchange (theatre); Cotton Exchange (leisure centre); Hallé Orchestra; Royal Northern College of Music; cathedral (15c); Chetham's Hospital and Library, the oldest public library in England; Free Trade Hall (1843); Liverpool Road Station, the world's oldest surviving passenger station; Museum of Science and Industry.

Manchester Ship Canal an artificial waterway in the UK linking Manchester with the Mersey estuary. The canal, which is 57km/35mi long, was opened in 1894 and allowed the city to develop as a sea port.

Manching a hillfort of the Middle La Tène period (2c–1c BC) near Ingolstadt, Bavaria, S Germany. It was one of Europe's earliest towns.

Manchuria a former region of NE China. It is a mountainous area, sparsely populated by nomadic tribes. The area has vast natural resources of timber and minerals (coal, iron, magnesite, oil, uranium, gold). HISTORY Manchus overthrew the Ming Dynasty to become the last Chinese emperors (Qing Dynasty, 1644–1911); under Russian military control in 1900; captured by Japan in 1932 and became part of the puppet state of Manchukuo; Russian control was reasserted in 1945; Chinese sovereignty was recognized in 1950, but the border area with Russia is a continuing focus of political tension.

Mancunian — *noun* a native or citizen of Manchester in NW England. — *adj.* relating to

Manchester or its inhabitants. [from Latin *Mancunium*, Manchester]

mandala *noun Buddhism, Hinduism* a circular symbol representing the universe. [from Sanskrit *mandala*]

Mandalay 1 POP (1983) 533 000, the river-port capital of Mandalay division, central Burma (Myanma). It lies on the R Irrawaddy. The city was founded by King Mindon in 1857 and was the capital of Burma from 1860 until 1885. NOTABLE FEATURES the Kuthodaw Pagoda contains 729 marble slabs on which are inscribed the entire Buddhist canons; Shwenandaw Kyaung Monastery; the old city of Pagan to the W, founded in AD 109, contains the largest concentration of pagodas and temples in Burma (Myanma), which are mainly 11c–13c. 2 a division in central Burma (Myanma) with Mandalay as its capital.

mandarin *noun* 1 (**Mandarin** *or* **Mandarin Chinese**) the official spoken language of China since 1917. 2 *Hist.* a senior official in the Chinese empire. 3 any high-ranking official, especially one thought to be outside political control. 4 a person of great influence, especially in the literary world. 5 a small citrus fruit similar to the tangerine; the tree that bears it. [from Portuguese *mandarim*, from Malay *mantri*, counsellor]

mandate — *noun* 1 a right given to a nation, person, or political party to act on behalf of others. 2 an order given by a superior. 3 *Hist.* (*also* **mandated territory**) a territory administered by a country on behalf of the League of Nations. — *verb* 1 to give authority or power to. 2 to assign (territory) to a nation under a mandate. [from Latin *mandare*, from *manus*, hand + *dare*, to give]

mandatory *adj.* 1 not allowing any choice; compulsory. 2 of the nature of, or containing, a mandate.

Mandela, Nelson (1918–) African Nationalist leader, born in Transkei, South Africa. After becoming a lawyer in Johannesburg, he joined the African National Congress (ANC) in 1944 and for the next 20 years directed a campaign of defiance against the South African government and its racist policies. He organized a three-day national strike in 1961 and in 1964 was sentenced to life imprisonment for political offences. However, he continued to be such a potent symbol of black resistance that there was a co-ordinated international campaign for his release in the 1980s, and he was released from prison in Feb 1990, after President F W de Klerk had unbanned the ANC, removed restrictions on political groups, and suspended executions. He was elected President (1991) of the ANC. In 1993 he was jointly awarded the Nobel Peace Prize with F W De Klerk, and in 1994 he became South Africa's first black President.

Mandela, Winnie, originally **Nomzamo Winifred** (1934/6–) South African social worker and black activist, wife of Nelson Mandela. She trained in social work, began working with Mandela in 1956, and married him in 1958. When he was put in prison by the South African government (1962–90), she too was banned, imprisoned (1969–70), and forced into internal exile (1977–85). Her popularity declined in 1988–9 when her bodyguards were implicated in the beating and murder of a black youth. She and Nelson Mandela separated in 1992.

Mandeville, Jehan de *or* **Sir John** (14c) The name assigned to the compiler of a famous book of travels, published around 1366, and translated from the French into many languages. It is thought to have been written by a physician, Jehan de Bourgogne, or Jehan à la Barbe, who died at Liège in 1372. He is said to have revealed on his death-bed his real name of Mandeville, explaining that he had had to flee from his native England following a homicide. Some scholars attribute it to Jean d'Outremeuse, a Frenchman.

mandible *noun Zool.* 1 the lower jaw of a vertebrate. 2 the upper or lower part of a bird's beak. 3 one of a pair of jaw-like mouthparts in insects, crustaceans, etc, used for cutting food. [from Latin *mandibula*, from *mandere*, to chew]

mandolin *or* **mandoline** *noun* a musical instrument like a small guitar, with four pairs of metal strings and a rounded back. [from Italian *mandolino*, diminutive of *mandora*, lute]

mandrake *noun* a Eurasian plant with purple flowers and a forked root, formerly thought to have magical powers; the root, formerly used to make sleep-inducing drugs. [from Latin *mandragora*]

mandrel *or* **mandril** *noun technical* 1 the rotating shaft on a lathe, to which the object being worked on is fixed. 2 the axle of a circular saw or grinding wheel. [from French *mandrin*, lathe]

mandrill *noun* a large W African baboon with a red and blue muzzle and hindquarters. [probably from MAN + DRILL⁴]

mane *noun* 1 the long hair growing from the neck of horses, lions, and other animals. 2 a long bushy or flowing head of human hair. [from Anglo-Saxon *manu*]

man-eater *noun* 1 a wild animal that attacks, kills, and eats people. 2 *colloq.* a woman who is domineering or aggressive in her relations with men.

manège *or* **manege** *noun technical* 1 the skill or practice of training or handling horses; the movements taught to a horse. 2 a riding-school. [from French, from Italian *maneggiare*, to manage]

Manes in Roman religion, 'the dead'. The concept developed from (1) the spirits of the dead in general, to (2) the Gods of the Underworld, Di Manes, (3) the ancestors of the family, and (4) the spirits of individuals in gravestone inscriptions.

Manet, Edouard (1832–83) French painter, born in Paris. Originally destined for a legal career, he became a painter and was influenced by the Spanish masters, especially Velázquez, and later helped to form the group out of which the Impressionist movement arose. He achieved fame with the *Spanish Guitar-Player* (Salon, 1861). Other early works (eg *Le Déjeuner sur l'herbe*, 1863, and *Olympia*, exhibited 1865) scandalized the traditional classicists with their provocative portrayal of women. Other works include *Absinthe Drinker* (1859) and *Un Bar aux Folies-Bergères* (1881–2, Courtauld Institute, London).

man Friday a junior male worker given various duties.

manful *adj.* brave and determined; manly.

manfulness *noun* being manful.

Manga, also called **Random Sketches** a collection of drawings by Hokusai (15 vols, from 1814). They give an illustrated insight into most areas of Japanese life.

manga *noun* a type of Japanese adult comic book, or animated film in the same style. [from Japanese]

manganese *noun Chem.* (SYMBOL **Mn**, ATOMIC NUMBER **25**) a hard brittle pinkish-grey metal obtained from the mineral pyrolusite, and widely used to make alloys, including manganese steels, that are very hard and resistant to wear, and are used in railway lines, etc. It is an essential trace element for plants and animals. [from Latin *magnesia*]

mange *noun* a skin disease of hairy animals, causing itching and loss of hair. [from Old French *mangeue*, itch]

mangel-wurzel *noun* a variety of beet with a large yellow root, used as cattle food. [from German *Mangold*, beet + *Wurzel*, root]

manger *noun old use* an open box or trough from which cattle or horses feed. [from Old French *mangeoire*, from *mangier*, to eat]

mangetout *noun* a variety of garden pea of which the whole pod is eaten. [from French *mange tout*, eat all]

mangily *adv.* in a mangy way.

manginess *noun* being mangy.

mangle¹ *verb* 1 to damage or destroy by cutting, crushing, or tearing. 2 to spoil, ruin, or bungle. [from Old French *mangler*, from *mahaigner*, to maim]

mangle² — *noun* a hand-operated device with two large rollers between which wet laundry is drawn to be squeezed dry. — *verb* to pass through a mangle. [from Dutch *mangel*]

mango *noun* (PL. **mangos, mangoes**) 1 a large evergreen tree (*Mangifera indica*) with glossy leaves and small fragrant yellow or red flowers, native to India but cultivated throughout the tropics for its edible fruit. 2 the heavy oblong fruit of this tree, which is slightly larger than an apple and contains a central stone surrounded by soft juicy orange flesh and a thick green, yellow, or red skin. It is eaten raw when ripe, and the green fruit is used to make chutneys and pickles. [from Portuguese *manga*]

mangrove *noun* any of several unrelated tropical and subtropical evergreen trees, especially species of *Rhizophora*, that grow in salt marshes and on mudflats along tropical coasts and tidal estuaries, mainly in Asia, Africa, and the SW Pacific. They send out aerial roots from their trunks, which mingle with the roots of adjacent mangrove plants to form a tangled network that traps sediment, aerates the roots, and provides physical support for the trees. In many species the seeds germinate in the fruit while still attached to the parent plant, enabling the seedlings to become quickly established in the shifting tidal environment. Mangroves often cover very large areas, forming a distinct vegetation type known as a mangrove swamp. [earlier *mangrow*, from Portuguese *mangue*]

mangrove swamps

mangy *adj.* (**mangier, mangiest**) 1 suffering from mange. 2 *derog.* shabby; seedy.

manhandle *verb* 1 to treat roughly. 2 to move or transport using manpower, not machinery.

Manhattan POP (1990) 1.5m, an island forming one of the five boroughs of the City of New York, New York State, E USA. Co-extensive with New York County, it lies at the N end of New York Bay, bounded W by the Hudson R. AREA 57sq km/22sq mi. It is a major financial and commercial centre based around Wall Street and the World Trade Center. The United Nations has its headquarters here. HISTORY bought from local Native Americans for trinkets and cloth worth c.$24, the island was settled by the Dutch as part of the New Netherlands in 1626; taken by the British in 1664. NOTABLE FEATURES Broadway; Empire State Building; Greenwich Village; Wall

Street; Central Park; Carnegie Hall; Madison Square Garden. [named after a local tribe of Native Americans]

Manhattan project the codename for the most secret scientific operation of World War II, the development of the atomic bomb, undertaken in the USA from 1942 onwards. The project culminated in the detonation of the first atomic weapon at Alamogordo, New Mexico (16 Jul 1945).

manhole *noun* an opening large enough to allow a person through, especially in a road, usually leading to a sewer.

manhood *noun* **1** the state of being an adult male. **2** manly qualities. **3** men collectively.

man-hour *noun* a unit of work equal to the work done by one person in one hour.

manhunt *noun* a concentrated and usually large-scale search for a person, especially a criminal.

mania *noun* **1** *Medicine* a mental disorder characterized by great excitement or euphoria, rapid and incoherent thought and speech, hyperactivity, grandiose delusions, and domineering behaviour which may become violent. It is usually treated with drugs, and severe cases require hospitalization. **2** a great desire or enthusiasm; a craze. [from Latin, from Greek *mainomai*, to be mad]

-mania *combining form* forming words denoting: **1** an abnormal or uncontrollable desire: *kleptomania*. **2** (often as ad hoc formations) great enthusiasm: *balletomania* (= great enthusiasm for ballet).

maniac *noun* **1** *colloq.* a person who behaves wildly. **2** an extremely keen enthusiast: *a video maniac*. **3** *old medical use* a person suffering from mania.

-maniac *combining form* forming nouns denoting a person affected with a -mania: *kleptomaniac*.

maniacal *adj.* **1** affected with or typical of mania. **2** typical of or like a maniac.

manic *adj.* **1** *Medicine* of, relating to, or suffering from mania. **2** *colloq.* very energetic or active.

manic-depressive — *adj.* affected by or suffering from an illness which produces alternating phases of extreme elation and severe depression. — *noun* a person suffering from this kind of depression.

Manichaeism *or* **Manichaeanism** a religious sect founded by the prophet Manes (or Mani) (c.216–76) who began teaching in Persia in 240. He taught that in the primeval conflict between the realms of light and darkness, the material world represents an invasion of the realm of light by the powers of darkness, from which it had to be released (eg through adherence to a strictly ascetic life), with the help of Buddha, the Prophets, Jesus, and finally Manes. The Zoroastrians condemned the sect and executed Manes, but it spread rapidly in the West, and survived until the 10c.

manicure — *noun* a cosmetic treatment of the hands, especially the fingernails, usually carried out by a trained professional. — *verb* to carry out a manicure on (a person or hand). [from Latin *manus*, hand + *cura*, care]

manicurist *noun* a person who gives manicures.

manifest — *verb* **1** to show or display clearly. **2** to be evidence or proof of. **3** to reveal or declare (itself). — *adj.* easily seen; obvious. — *noun* **1** a customs document giving details of a ship or aircraft, its cargo and its destination. **2** a passenger list. [from Latin *manifestare*]

manifestation *noun* **1** the act of disclosing or demonstrating. **2** display. **3** public demonstration.

manifestly *adv.* obviously, undoubtedly.

manifesto *noun* (PL. **manifestos**, **manifestoes**) a written public declaration of policies

or intentions, especially by a political party or candidate. [from Italian, from Latin *manifestare*, to manifest]

manifold — *adj.* **1** many and various; of many different kinds. **2** having many different features or functions. — *noun* **1** *formal* a thing with many different forms or functions. **2** *technical* a pipe with several inlets and outlets. [from MANY + -FOLD]

manikin *or* **mannikin** *noun* **1** *old use* an abnormally small person; a dwarf. **2** a model of the human body, used in teaching art and anatomy. [from Dutch *manneken*, double diminutive of *man*, man]

Manila POP (1990) 7.9m, the capital of the Philippines, on the R Pasig, Manila Bay, SW Luzon I. HISTORY founded in 1571, it became an important trade centre under the Spanish; occupied by the British in 1762–3; taken by the USA during the Spanish–American War in 1898; badly damaged in World War II.

manila *or* **manilla** *noun* a type of thick strong brown paper, originally made from the fibre of a Philippine tree.

manipulate *verb* **1** to handle, especially skilfully. **2** to control or influence cleverly and unscrupulously, especially to one's own advantage. **3** to apply treatment with the hands to (a part of the body). [from Latin *manipulus*, handful]

manipulation *noun* the act or process of manipulating.

manipulative *adj.*, *said of a person* given to or skilled in manipulating or exploiting people or circumstances.

Manipur POP (1991) 1.8m, a state situated in NE India and bounded E by Burma (Myanma). AREA 22 356sq km/8 629sq mi. CAPITAL Imphal. HISTORY under British rule in 1891; administered from the state of Assam until 1947, when it became a union territory; became a state in 1972. GOVERNMENT governed by a 60-member Legislative Assembly. ECONOMY weaving; cement; wheat, maize, pulses, fruit, sugar, bamboo, teak.

Manitoba, formerly **Red River Settlement** (to 1870) POP (1991) 1.1m, a province in central Canada. AREA 649 950sq km/250 945sq mi. It is bounded by Hudson Bay in the NE and the USA in the S. PHYSICAL DESCRIPTION as a result of glaciation, Manitoba is known as the 'land of 100 000 lakes', notably lakes Winnipeg, Winnipegosis, and Manitoba; drained by several rivers flowing into L Winnipeg or Hudson Bay; land gradually rises in the W and S to 832m at Mt Baldy; around half of the land in the province is forested. HISTORY trading rights given to Hudson's Bay Company in 1670; several forts established because of English–French conflict, including Fort Rouge in 1738 (the site of Winnipeg); French claims were ceded to the British under the 1763 Treaty of Paris; settlement on the Red R from 1812, with many Scottish and Irish settlers; Manitoba joined the confederation in 1870, provoking insurrection under Louis Riel; boundaries extended in 1881 and 1912; major development of the area took place after the railway reached Winnipeg in the 1880s. GOVERNMENT governed by a Lieutenant-Governor and an elected 57-member Legislative Assembly. CAPITAL Winnipeg. CHIEF TOWN Brandon. ECONOMY cereals (especially wheat), livestock, vegetables; fishing; timber; hydroelectric power; food processing; mining (oil, gold, nickel, silver, copper, zinc); machinery; tourism.

Manizales POP (1992e) 328 000, the capital of Caldas department, central Colombia. It is situated in the Cordillera Central, 2 153m above sea level. The city, which was founded in 1848, is the centre of a coffee-growing area. NOTABLE FEATURES Teatro de los Fundadores; cathedral (unfinished).

mankind *noun* the human race as a whole.

Mankind, Museum of a museum in London which houses the ethnographical collections of the British Museum. The collections include works of art and everyday artefacts from the (ancient to contemporary) cultures of many different peoples.

Mankowitz, (Cyril) Wolf (1924–) British author, playwright, and antique dealer, born in London. An authority on Wedgwood®, his publications in the art domain include *The Concise Encyclopedia of English Pottery and Porcelain* (1957). His fiction includes the novel *A Kid for Two Farthings* (1953), the play *The Bespoke Overcoat* (1954), and the films *The Millionairess* (1960), *The Long, the Short, and the Tall* (1961), and *Casino Royale* (1967).

manky *adj.* (**mankier**, **mankiest**) *colloq.* **1** dirty. **2** of poor quality; shoddy. [from obsolete Scots *mank*, defective]

manliness *noun* being manly.

manly *adj.* (**manlier**, **manliest**) displaying qualities considered admirable in a man, usually strength, determination, courage, etc; suitable for a man.

man-made *adj.* artificial or synthetic, not natural or naturally produced.

Mann, Thomas (1875–1955) German novelist, born in Lübeck. He lived in Italy, Germany, Switzerland, and the USA, and returned finally to Switzerland in 1947. His best-known works include the novel *Buddenbrooks* (1901), which traces the decline of a family over four generations, the novella *Der Tod in Venedig* (Death in Venice, 1913), and the novels *Der Zauberberg* (The Magic Mountain, 1924), and *Doktor Faustus* (1947), a modern version of the medieval legend. He was awarded the Nobel Prize for Literature in 1929.

manna *noun* **1** in the Old Testament, the food miraculously provided by God for the Israelites in the wilderness. **2** any unexpected gift or windfall: *manna from heaven*. [from Aramaic, possibly from Hebrew *man*, gift]

mannequin *noun* **1** a fashion model. **2** a life-size dummy of the human body, used in the making or displaying of clothes. [from French *mannequin*; see MANIKIN]

manner *noun* **1** way; fashion. **2** (**manners**) behaviour towards others: *bad manners*. **3** (**manners**) polite social behaviour: *have no manners*. **4** style: *dressed in the Chinese manner*. **5** kind or kinds: *all manner of things*.
— **to the manner born** accustomed since birth (to a particular occupation, activity, etc).
by no manner of means *or* **not by any manner of means** under no circumstances; certainly not.
in a manner of speaking in a way; to some degree; so to speak.
[from Old French *maniere*, from Latin *manuarius*, of the hand]

mannered *adj.* *formal usu. derog.* unnatural and artificial; affected.

-mannered *combining form* forming adjectives denoting a specified kind of social behaviour: *bad-mannered*.

Mannerheim, Carl Gustav (Emil), Baron von (1867–1951) Finnish soldier and politician, born in Villnäs. When Finland declared independence (1918), he became Supreme Commander and Regent. Defeated in the presidential election of 1919, he retired into private life, but returned as Commander-in-Chief against the Russians in the Winter War of 1939–40 and continued to command the Finnish forces until he became President of the Finnish Republic (1944–6).

Mannerism a form of art and architecture prevalent in France, Spain, and especially Italy during the 16c. It is characterized by the playful use of Classical elements and *trompe l'oeil* effects in bizarre or dramatic compositions. Giorgio

Vasari (1550) used the word *maniera* for a type of refined and artificial beauty (eg as in Raphael's *St Cecilia*). The style is apparent in the architectural design of Michelangelo's Laurentian Library vestibule, Florence (1526), and in the work of the artists Giulio Romano, Jacopa da Pontormo, and Parmigiano, and the sculptor Benvenuto Cellini.

mannerism *noun* **1** an individual characteristic, eg a gesture or facial expression. **2** *derog.* excessive use of an individual style in art or literature.

mannerliness *noun* courtesy.

mannerly *adj. old use* polite.

Mannheim POP (1991e) 310 000, a commercial and manufacturing river-port in Baden-Württemberg state, SW Germany. It lies on the right bank of the R Rhine, at the outflow of the canalized R Neckar, 70km/43mi SW of Frankfurt, and it is one of the largest inland harbours in Europe. HISTORY seat of the Electors Palatine in 1720; became a cultural centre in the 18c, particularly noted for its composers of the Mannheim school; badly bombed in World War II. NOTABLE FEATURES castle; town hall; National Theatre; Reiss Museum.

mannikin see MANIKIN.

mannish *adj., usually said of a woman* having an appearance or qualities regarded as more typical of a man.

manoeuvrability *noun* being manoeuvrable.

manoeuvrable *adj.* that can be manoeuvred.

manoeuvre — *noun* **1** a movement requiring, or performed with, considerable skill. **2** a clever handling of affairs, often involving deception. **3** (**manoeuvres**) military exercises, especially on a large scale. — *verb* **1** *trans., intrans.* to move (something) accurately and with skill: *manoeuvred the car into the space.* **2** *trans., intrans.* to use ingenuity, and perhaps deceit, in handling (something or someone). **3** *intrans.* to carry out military exercises. [from French, from Latin *manu*, by hand + *opera*, work]

Man of Law, the the self-interested, money-making lawyer in Chaucer's *The Canterbury Tales*, who tells the tale of Constance.

man of the world a man who is mature and widely experienced.

man-of-war or **man-o'-war** *noun* (PL. **men-of-war**) *Hist.* an armed sailing ship used as a warship.

manometer *noun Physics* an instrument for measuring the difference in pressure between two fluids (liquids or gases), especially by determining the difference in height between two columns of liquid, eg mercury, in a U-shaped glass tube when, for example, a gas whose pressure is to be measured is fed to one arm of the tube, while the other arm is left open to the atmosphere. [from Greek *manos*, rare, thin + -METER]

manometric *adj.* involving or made with a manometer.

manor *noun* **1** in medieval Europe, an area of land under the control of a lord. **2** (*also* **manorhouse**) the principal residence on a country estate, often the former home of a medieval lord. **3** *slang* the area in which a particular person or group, especially a police unit or a criminal, operates. [from Old French *manoir*, from Latin *manere*, to stay]

manorial *adj.* relating to or associated with a manor.

manpower *noun* **1** number of employees. **2** human effort, as opposed to mechanical power.

Manpower Services Commission (ABBREV. **MSC**) a UK quango, established in 1974, with responsibility for the provision of employment and training services. In 1988 the employ-

ment and training service functions were returned to the Department of Employment, and the MSC ceased to exist.

manqué *adj. literary (used following a noun)* having once had the ambition or potential to be something, without achieving it: *an artist manqué.* [from French *manqué*, having missed]

mansard *noun* a four-sided roof, each side of which is in two parts, the lower part sloping more steeply. [from François Mansart (1598–1666), French architect]

manse *noun* the house of a religious minister, especially in Scotland. [from Latin *mansus*, dwelling]

Mansell, Nigel (Ernest James) (1953–) English motor-racing driver, born in Solihull. He made his Grand Prix début in 1980, and had his first win in 1985, with the Williams team. He finished second in the 1986 world championship, after being forced to withdraw in the last race, and became world champion in 1992. He left Formula One racing for the Indycar circuit, and in 1993 became the first man to win the Indycar world series championship in his rookie year.

manservant *noun* (PL. **menservants**) *old use* a male servant, especially a valet.

Mansfield, Katherine, pseudonym of **Kathleen Middleton Murry**, née **Beauchamp** (1888–1923) British short-story writer, born in Wellington, New Zealand. In 1908 she settled in Europe, and married the writer John Middleton Murry in 1918. Her major works include *Bliss* (1920), *The Garden Party* (1922), and *Something Childish* (1924).

Mansfield POP (1981) 72 000; 156 000 (urban area), a town in Mansfield district, Nottinghamshire, central England. It lies on the R Maun, 22km/14mi N of Nottingham.

Mansfield Park a novel by Jane Austen (1814). It is set in a country mansion and focuses mainly on the interplay between the Bertrams, the Crawfords, and the heroine, Fanny Price.

mansion *noun* **1** a large and usually luxurious house. **2** a manor-house. **3** (**mansions**) *Brit.* a large building divided into luxury apartments. [from Latin *mansio*, remaining]

manslaughter *noun* the crime of killing someone without intending to do so.

Manson, Sir Patrick (1844–1922) Scottish physician, born in Aberdeenshire. He practised medicine in China and Hong Kong, where he helped establish a school of medicine that became the University of Hong Kong; he was later one of the founders of the London School of Tropical Medicine. He was the first to argue that the mosquito is host to the malaria parasite (1877).

manta ray a giant ray that may exceed 9m in width and 2 tonnes in weight, and has a broad mouth situated across the front of the head. It feeds on plankton and small fish filtered from water that passes over the gill arches. [from Spanish *manta*]

Mantegna, Andrea (1431–1506) Italian painter, born near Vicenza. He worked in Padua then settled in Mantua (1460), where he was appointed court painter. His major works include nine tempera pictures representing the *Triumph of Caesar* (begun c.1486, Hampton Court, near London). Other works include *Agony in the Garden* (c.1450).

mantel *noun old use* a mantelpiece or mantelshelf. [related to MANTLE]

Mantell, Gideon Algernon (1790–1852) English palaeontologist, born in Lewes, Sussex, where he later became a practising surgeon; he moved to Brighton in 1833, and later to London (1844). Interested in geology, he built up an important fossil collection and discovered several dinosaur types, including the first to be fully

described; noting the similarity between the fossil teeth and those of the living iguana, he named it 'Iguanodon' (1825).

mantelpiece *noun* the ornamental frame around a fireplace, especially the top part which forms a shelf.

mantelshelf *noun* the shelf part of a mantelpiece.

mantilla *noun* **1** a scarf of lace or silk, worn by women over the hair and shoulders, especially in Spain and S America. **2** a short lightweight cape or cloak. [from Spanish *mantilla*, diminutive of *manta*, from *manto*, cloak]

mantis *noun* (PL. **mantises**, **mantes**) (*also* **praying mantis**) an insect-eating insect with a long body, large eyes, and a tendency to carry its two front legs raised as if in prayer. [from Greek *mantis*, prophet]

mantissa *noun Maths.* the part of a logarithm comprising the decimal point and the figures following. See also CHARACTERISTIC. [from Latin *mantissa*, something added]

Mantle, Mickey (Charles) (1931–) US baseball player, born in Spavinaw, Oklahoma. He was an outfielder and batter in the New York Yankees team of the 1950s. He was the American League's Most Valuable Player in 1956, and once hit a home run measured at a record 177m.

mantle — *noun* **1** a fireproof mesh round a gas or oil lamp that glows when the lamp is lit. **2** a cloak or loose outer garment. **3** *literary* a position of responsibility: *given the leader's mantle.* **4** *literary* a covering: *a mantle of snow.* **5** *Geol.* the part of the Earth between the crust and the core. — *verb literary* to cover or conceal. [from Latin *mantellum*, diminutive of *mantum*, cloak]

man-to-man *adj., said especially of personal discussion* open and frank.

mantra *noun* **1** a word or sound repeated as an aid to concentration when meditating. **2** any of the hymns of praise in the ancient sacred Hindu scriptures, the Vedas. [from Sanskrit *mantra*, instrument of thought]

mantrap *noun* **1** a trap or snare for catching trespassers, poachers, etc. **2** any source of potential danger.

Mantua, Italian **Mantova** POP (1990e) 54 000, the capital of Mantua province, Lombardy, N Italy. Situated SW of Verona, it lies on the lower course of the R Mincio which surrounds the town on three sides. It was founded in Etruscan times. The birthplace of the poet Virgil is nearby. NOTABLE FEATURES ringed by ancient walls and bastions; Church of Sant'Andrea (1472–94); cathedral (10c–18c); Palazzo Ducale; Castello San Giorgio (1395–1406).

Manu in Hindu mythology, the forefather of the human race, to whom the Manu Smirti ('Lawbook of Manu') is attributed.

Manú a national park in SE Peru, founded in 1968. AREA 15 328sq km/5 917sq mi. It is a World Heritage site.

manual — *adj.* **1** of the hand or hands. **2** using the body, rather than the mind; physical: *manual worker.* **3** worked, controlled or operated by hand; not automatic. — *noun* **1** a book of instructions, eg for repairing a car. **2** an organ keyboard. [from Latin *manualis*, from *manus*, hand]

manually *adv.* in a manual way; by hand.

manufacture — *verb* **1** to make from raw materials, especially in large quantities using machinery. **2** to invent or fabricate: *manufacture evidence.* **3** *derog.* to produce in a mechanical fashion. — *noun* the practice or process of manufacturing. [from Latin *manu*, by hand + *facere*, to make]

manufacturer *noun* **1** a person or business that manufactures. **2** a person who makes or invents.

manufacturing — *adj.* relating to or engaged in manufacture. — *noun* the action, practice, or process of making or inventing.

manumission *noun* **1** the act of manumitting. **2** being manumitted.

manumit *verb* (**manumitted, manumitting**) *formal* to release from slavery; to set free. [from Latin *manu*, by hand + *mittere*, to send]

manure — *noun* any substance, especially animal dung, used on soil as a fertiliser. — *verb* to apply manure to. [from Old French *manouvrer*, to work by hand]

manuscript (ABBREV. **MS**) *noun* **1** an author's handwritten or typed version of a book, etc, before it has been printed. **2** a book or document written by hand. [from Latin *manuscriptus*, written by hand]

Man with a Glove a painting by Titian (c.1520, Louvre).

Manx — *adj.* relating to the Isle of Man or its inhabitants. — *noun* an almost extinct Celtic language, formerly spoken widely on the Isle of Man. [from an earlier form *Maniske*, Man-ish]

Manx cat a breed of tailless cat, originally from the Isle of Man.

Manxman *noun* a man who is a native of the Isle of Man.

Manxwoman *noun* a woman who is a native of the Isle of Man.

many — *adj.* **1** great in number; numerous. **2** being one of numerous: *many a man*. — *pron.* a great number of people or things: *many of the victims were children*. — *noun* (**the many**) the majority; ordinary people, not nobility or royalty. — **in as many** in the same number of. [from Anglo-Saxon *manig*]

Manzini, formerly **Bremersdorp** (to 1960) POP (1986) 52 000, a town in Manzini district, Swaziland, SE of Mbabane. It is the country's main industrial, commercial, and agricultural centre and was Swaziland's first administrative capital from 1890 until 1902. NOTABLE FEATURE cathedral.

Manzoni, Alessandro (1785–1873) Italian novelist and poet, born in Milan. He published his first poems in 1806, and spent several years in writing sacred lyrics. He achieved European fame with his historical novel, *I Promessi Sposi* (The Betrothed, 1825–7).

Maoism *noun* the policies and theories of Mao Zedong (or Mao Tse-tung) (1893–1976), the first leader of Communist China.

Maoist — *noun* a follower of Chinese communism as expounded by Mao Zedong. — *adj.* relating to or characteristic of Maoism or a Maoist.

Maori — *noun* (PL. **Maori, Maoris**) **1** a member of the aboriginal Polynesian people of New Zealand. **2** the language of this people. — *adj.* of this people or their language. [from Maori]

Maori Wars a succession of conflicts (1843–7 and 1860–72) in which the Maori people attempted, unsuccessfully, to resist the occupation of New Zealand by British settlers. Time and numbers were on the side of the Europeans; Maori resistance was worn down, and they were forced to surrender or retreat to the wilder central North Island. An uneasy stand-off was reached by the early 1870s but peace was not formalized until 1881.

Mao Zedong or **Mao Tse-tung** (1893–1976) leader and leading theorist of the Chinese Communist revolution which won national power in China in 1949. He was born in Hunan province, the son of a farmer; at the age of 12 he sought an education in Changsha. After graduating from a teachers' training college there, he went to Beijing (Peking) where he came under the influence of Li Dazhao. He became a Marxist and was a founding member of the Chinese Communist Party (1921). During the first united front with the Nationalist Party, he concentrated on political work among the peasants of his native province, creating a rural Soviet in Jiangxi province in 1928. After the break with the Nationalists in 1927, the Communists were driven from the cities, and he evolved the guerilla tactics of the 'people's war'. In 1934 the Nationalist government was at last able to destroy the Jiangxi Soviet, and in the subsequent Long March the Communist forces retreated to Shaanxi to set up a new base. When in 1936, under the increasing threat of Japanese invasion, the Nationalists renewed their alliance with the Communists, Mao restored and vastly increased the political and military power of his Party. His claim to share in the government led to civil war; the regime of Jiang Jieshi (Chiang Kai-shek) was forced from the Chinese mainland, and the new People's Republic of China was proclaimed (1 Oct 1949) with Mao as both Chairman of the Chinese Communist Party and President of the Republic. He followed the Soviet model of economic development and social change until 1958, then launched his Great Leap Forward, which encouraged the establishment of rural industry and the use of surplus rural labour to create a new infrastructure for agriculture. The failure of the Great Leap lost him most of his influence, but by 1965, with China's armed forces securely in the hands of his ally Lin Piao, he launched a Cultural Revolution (1966–76). After his death a strong reaction set in against the excessive collectivism and egalitarianism which had developed, but his emphasis on rural industry and on local initiative was retained by his successors.

map — *noun* **1** a diagram of any part of the earth's surface, showing geographical and other features, eg the position of towns and roads. **2** a similar diagram of the surface of the moon or a planet. **3** a diagram showing the position of the stars in the sky. **4** a diagram of the layout of anything. — *verb* (**mapped, mapping**) to make a map of.
— **map something out** to plan a route, course of action, etc, in detail.
put something on the map *colloq.* to cause it to become well-known or important.
[from Latin *mappa*, napkin, painted cloth]

maple *noun* **1** (*also* **maple tree**) any of various broad-leaved deciduous trees of northern regions, whose seeds float by means of wing-like growths. **2** the hard light-coloured wood of these trees, used to make furniture, etc. [from Anglo-Saxon *mapul*]

maple syrup syrup made from the sap of the sugar maple tree.

Maputo, formerly **Lourenço Marques** (to 1976) **1** POP (1991e) 1.2m, the seaport capital of Mozambique, on Delagoa Bay in the S of the country. It acts as an outlet for several SE African countries. HISTORY discovered by the Portuguese in 1502; explored by the trader Lourenço Marques; became capital of Portuguese E Africa in 1907. **2** a province in S Mozambique with Maputo as its capital.

maquette *noun* a model made by a sculptor as a preliminary study for a full-size work. A maquette is usually made in clay, wax, or plaster. [from French *maquette*]

Maquis *noun* **1** (**the Maquis**) the French resistance movement that fought against German occupying forces during World War II. **2** (**maquis**) a member of this movement. [from French *maquis*, from Italian *macchia*, thicket, referring to a type of thick shrubby vegetation found in coastal areas of the Mediterranean, which provided cover for those hiding in the hills]

Mar or **Mar.** *abbrev.* March.

mar *verb* (**marred, marring**) **1** to spoil. **2** to injure or damage. [from Anglo-Saxon *merran*]

marabou *noun* **1** a large black-and-white African stork. **2** its feathers, used to decorate clothes, trim hats, etc. [from Arabic *murabit*, hermit, holy man, the stork being considered holy in Islam]

maraca *noun* a musical instrument consisting of a hollow shell filled with beans, pebbles, etc, held by a handle and shaken, usually in pairs, originally used in Latin America. [from Portuguese *maraca*]

Maracaibo POP (1990e) 1.4m, the second-largest city in Venezuela and the capital of Zulia state. It is situated in the NW part of the country, on the NW shore of L Maracaibo. The city is an important oil production and processing centre.

Maracaibo, Lake a lake in NW Venezuela. AREA 13 000sq km/5 000sq mi; length c.210km/130mi. It is linked to the Gulf of Venezuela through narrows and the Tablazo Bay. The lake contains an important oilfield, discovered in 1917.

Maradi 1 POP (1988) 1.4m, a department in S central Niger. AREA 38 581sq km/14 892sq mi. It is a low-lying region with extensive seasonal floodplains. The R Gada flows NW from its source in Nigeria across the SW corner of the region. **2** the capital of Maradi department, S central Niger.

Maradona, Diego (1960–) Argentine footballer, born in Lanus, near Buenos Aires. He became Argentina's youngest-ever international player in 1977, transferred to Boca Juniors as a teenager, and in Jun 1982 became the world's most expensive footballer when he joined Barcelona for £5m. He then played for Naples (1984–91), and captained Argentina to their second World Cup in 1986. He left Naples in 1991 after being suspended for 15 months following a drugs test, and in Jun 1993 he returned to Argentina after being released by his club Seville.

Maralinga a ghost town on the E Nullarbor Plain, South Australia. The area was used by the British as a nuclear testing site in the 1950s.

Marañón, River a river in Peru. One of the Amazon's major headstreams, its estimated length is 1 600km/1 000mi and it is navigable as far as the Pongo de Manseriche Gorge. The river rises in the Andes 137km/85mi E of the Pacific and joins the R Ucayali to form the Amazon 88km/55mi SW of Iquitos.

maraschino *noun* (PL. **maraschinos**) a liqueur made from cherries, with a taste like bitter almonds. [from Italian, from *amarasca*, sour cherry]

maraschino cherry a cherry preserved in maraschino or a similar liqueur, used for decorating cocktails, cakes, etc.

Marat, Jean Paul (1743–93) French physician and revolutionary politician, born in Boudry, Switzerland. He joined the Cordelier Club and established the radical paper *L'Ami du Peuple* (The Friend of the People), which incited the *sans-culottes* to violence. Forced several times into hiding by the hatred he engendered, he was later elected to the National Convention, became a leader of the Mountain, and advocated radical reforms. After Louis XVI's death he quarrelled violently with the Girondins, and was fatally stabbed in his bath by a Girondin supporter, Charlotte Corday.

Maratha or **Mahratta** a Marathi-speaking people of Maharashtra, W India (though sometimes the name refers only to the Maratha caste in the region). They are mainly peasant farmers, soldiers, and landowners, who were historically known as warriors and promoters of Hinduism. The Maratha kingdom in the 17c rivalled that of the Mughals. In the 18c a military confederacy was formed to resist the British in three wars (1775–82, 1803–5, 1817–18), but ultimately the confederacy was defeated and its territory annexed. The present-day population is c.41m.

Marathi — *noun* an Indo-Aryan language spoken by c.30–50 million people in the state of

Maharashtra, W India, and surrounding areas. — *adj.* relating to or spoken or written in Marathi.

Marathon, Battle of a battle (490 BC) on the E coast of Attica, in which the Athenians, with allies from Plataea, defeated a much larger force of invading Persians.

marathon — *noun* **1** a long-distance race on foot, usually 42.195km (26 mi 385 yd). **2** any lengthy and difficult task. — *adj.* **1** relating to a marathon race. **2** requiring or displaying great powers of endurance: *a marathon effort.* [from *Marathon*, in Greece, from where a messenger is said to have run to Athens with news of victory over the Persians in 490 BC; the length of the race is based on this distance, although in the more authentic accounts (eg Herodotus) the runner went to Sparta to appeal for help before the battle]
◇ The distance of the modern race was standardized in 1924, having first been used at the London Olympics in 1908. Marathons are now held annually in many of the world's major cities, including London and New York. They are open to amateur enthusiasts as well as to competitive athletes.

maraud *verb* to wander in search of people to attack and property to steal or destroy. [from French *marauder*, to prowl]

marauder *noun* a raider.

marauding *adj.* raiding.

Maravi, Kingdom of an African kingdom situated north of the Zambesi and south of L Malawi, which has given its name to modern Malawi. It consisted of a loose confederation of chiefdoms that occupied territory in Malawi, Zambia, and Mozambique, and was involved in long-distance trade. In the 17c its power reached the E African coast, but it was disrupted by the migrations of the Ngoni in the early 19c.

Marbella POP (1991) 77 000, a port and resort lying on the Costa del Sol, Málaga province, Andalusia, in S Spain. There are large bathing beaches and watersports are popular.

marble *noun* **1** *Geol.* a metamorphic rock, white when pure, but often mottled or streaked with red or grey, consisting of recrystallized limestone or dolomite. It can be cut and polished, and is widely used as an ornamental stone in the building industry. The pure white form is used by sculptors. **2** a general term for any rock that can be polished and used for decorative purposes. **3** a small hard ball originally of this rock, now of glass, used in children's games. [from Old French *marbre*]

marbled *adj.* having irregular streaks of different colours, like marble.

marbles *noun* **1** any of several children's games played with marbles. **2** *colloq.* mental faculties; wits: *have all one's marbles / lose one's marbles.*

Marburg POP (1991e) 74 000, a city in Hessen state, W central Germany. It lies on the R Lahn, 74km/46mi N of Frankfurt. NOTABLE FEATURES St Elizabeth's Church (1235–83); Gothic castle (15c–16c); university (1527).

Marc, Franz (1880–1916) German artist, born in Munich. He helped to found the Blaue Reiter group in Munich in 1911. Most of his paintings were of animals (eg *Blue Horses*, 1911, and *The Fate of the Animals*, 1913) portrayed in forceful colours. He was killed at Verdun during World War I.

marc *noun* the left-over skins and stems of grapes used in wine-making, or a kind of brandy made from these. [from French *marc*]

marcasite *noun Geol.* a pale yellow sulphide mineral formerly used to make jewellery, and now mined for use in the manufacture of sulphuric acid. [from Latin *marcasita*]

marcato *adj., adv. Mus.* stressed or accented; emphatic, distinct. A term used in musical scores

to indicate the tempo and/or expression required for a particular passage or section. [from Italian, from *marcare*, to mark]

Marceau, Marcel (1923–) French mime artist, born in Strasbourg. He founded and directed (1948–64) the Compagnie de Mime Marcel Marceau in Paris, and was head of the Ecole Mimodrame Marcel Marceau from 1978. The leading exponent of the art of mime, his white-faced character, 'Bip', became famous worldwide from his appearances on stage and television.

March, Amy, Beth, Jo, and **Meg** the sisters at the heart of Louisa May Alcott's *Little Women.*

March *noun* the third month of the year. [from Latin *Martius*, of Mars]

march¹ — *verb* **1** *intrans.* to walk in a stiff upright formal manner, usually at a brisk pace and in step with others. **2** to force (especially soldiers) to walk in this way. **3** *intrans.* to walk in a purposeful and determined way. **4** *intrans.* to advance or continue steadily: *events marched on.* — *noun* **1** an act of marching; a distance travelled by marching. **2** a brisk walking pace. **3** a procession of people moving steadily forward. **4** a piece of music written in a marching rhythm. **5** unstoppable progress or movement: *the march of time.*
— **steal a march on someone** to get an advantage over them, especially by trickery. [from French *marcher*, to walk]

march² *noun* **1** a boundary or border. **2** a border district, especially (**Marches**) those around the English–Welsh and English–Scottish borders, fought over continuously from the 13c to the 16c. [from French *marche*]

marcher *noun* **1** a person who marches. **2** a person who takes part in a march.

March hare **1** a hare during its breeding season in March, proverbially mad because of its excitable behaviour. **2** one of the mad characters encountered by Alice in Lewis Carroll's *Alice's Adventures in Wonderland.*

marching orders **1** orders to march in a certain way, given to soldiers, etc. **2** *colloq.* dismissal from a job, etc.

marchioness *noun* **1** the wife or widow of a marquis. **2** a woman of the same rank in her own right. [from Latin *marchionissa*, from *marchio*, marquis]

March on Rome a march (Oct 1922), largely symbolic, on the Italian capital made by several thousand fascists. Though later portrayed by Mussolini as a seizure of power, he had already successfully negotiated his way into office as premier.

March Through Georgia a campaign (1864) in the American Civil War by the Northern army under General Sherman. It resulted in devastation of the area between Atlanta and the ocean, and in military terms completed the task of splitting the Confederacy on an east–west line.

Marciano, Rocky, originally **Rocco Francis Marchegiano** (1923–69) US heavyweight boxing champion, born in Brockton, Massachusetts. He became a professional in 1947, and made his name by defeating the former world champion, Joe Louis, in 1951. He won the world title from Jersey Joe Walcott the following year, and when he retired in 1956 was undefeated as world champion, with a professional record of 49 bouts and 49 victories. He died in an air crash in Newton, Iowa.

Marconi, Guglielmo, Marchese (1874–1937) Italian physicist and inventor, born in Bologna. He successfully experimented with wireless telegraphy in Italy and England, and succeeded in sending signals across the Atlantic in 1901. He shared the 1909 Nobel Prize for Physics with Ferdinand Braun.

Marcos, Ferdinand (Edralin) (1917–89) Filipino politician, born in Ilocos Norte. He trained as a lawyer, and as an anti-communist politician obtained considerable US support. His regime as President (1965–86) was marked by increasing repression, misuse of foreign financial aid, and political murders (eg the assassination of Benigno Aquino, 1983). He declared martial law in 1972, but was overthrown in 1986 by a popular front led by Corazon Aquino. He went into exile in Hawaii, where he and his wife Imelda fought against demands from US courts investigating charges of financial mismanagement and corruption.

Marcus Aurelius see AURELIUS.

Marcuse, Herbert (1898–1979) US Marxist philosopher, born in Berlin. He became an influential figure of the Frankfurt School, fled to Geneva in 1933, and after World War II moved to the USA, where he worked in intelligence. His books include *Reason and Revolution* (1941), *Eros and Civilization* (1955), and *One Dimensional Man* (1964).

Mar del Plata POP (1991) 415 000, a port on the Atlantic coast in SE Buenos Aires province, E Argentina. It was founded in 1874 and is one of the prime holiday resorts in S America, with 8km/5mi of beaches. NOTABLE FEATURES museums; casino.

Mardi Gras *noun* **1** Shrove Tuesday, celebrated with a festival in some places, especially famously in Rio de Janeiro, Brazil. **2** the festival. [from French *Mardi Gras*, fat Tuesday]

Marduk in Babylonian mythology, originally the patron deity of the city of Babylon. He later became the supreme god of Babylonia, taking over the functions of Enlil after defeating Tiamat, the sea monster representing chaos.

Marduk

mare¹ *noun* an adult female horse or zebra. [from Anglo-Saxon *mere*]

mare² *noun* (PL. **maria**) any of numerous large flat areas on the surface of the Moon or Mars, seen from Earth as dark patches and originally thought to be seas. [from Latin *mare*, sea]

Marengo, Battle of a narrow French victory (1800) over the Austrians, fought in N Italy during the War of the Second Coalition. It enabled Napoleon I to ensure his restored hegemony in N Italy, to guarantee the re-establishment of the Cisalpine Republic, and to assert his political authority in France.

mare's nest a discovery that proves to be untrue or without value.

Marey, Etienne-Jules (1830–1904) French physiologist, born in Beaune. He had a passion for ingenious mechanical devices, and used his skill to study and measure heart action. From the 1860s he introduced scientific photography, devising by 1881 a cine camera to analyse rapid movements through 'slow motion', and using time lapse to speed up slow changes.

marg *or* **marge** *noun colloq.* margarine.

Margaret (1353–1412) Queen of Denmark, Norway, and Sweden, born in Søborg, Denmark. She became Queen of Denmark in 1375, on the death of her father, Waldemar IV, and ruled Norway from the death of her husband, Haakon VI (1380). In 1388 she aided a rising of Swedish nobles against their king, Albert of Mecklenburg, and became Queen of Sweden. She had her infant cousin, Eric of Pomerania, crowned king of the three kingdoms at Kalmar in 1397, but remained the real ruler of Scandinavia until her death.

Margaret (Rose), Princess (1930–) British princess, second daughter of George VI and sister of Elizabeth II, born in Glamis Castle in Scotland. She was married (1960–78) to Antony Armstrong-Jones, who was created Viscount Linley and Earl of Snowdon in 1961. The former title devolved upon their son, David Albert Charles (1961–). They also have a daughter, Sarah Frances Elizabeth (1964–).

Margaret, St (c.1045–1093) Scottish queen, born in Hungary. She went to England, but after the Norman Conquest fled to Scotland with her mother and young brother, Edgar the Atheling. She married the Scottish king, Malcolm Canmore (1069), and did much to civilize the realm, and to assimilate the old Celtic Church to the rest of Christendom. She was canonized in 1250 and her feast day is 10 Jun or (in Scotland) 16 Jun.

Margaret a female first name. [from Greek *margaron*, pearl]

Margaret of Anjou (1429–82) the queen-consort of Henry VI of England from 1445, and daughter of René of Anjou. Because of Henry's madness, she became involved in political life, and during the Wars of the Roses was a leading Lancastrian. Defeated at Tewkesbury (1471), she was imprisoned in the Tower for four years, until ransomed by Louis XI. She then retired to France.

Margaret Tudor (1489–1541) Queen of Scotland, the eldest daughter of Henry VII, born in London. She married James IV of Scotland (1503) and was the mother of James V, for whom she acted as regent. After James IV's death in 1513 she was married to the Earl of Angus (1514) and then to Lord Methven (1527). She was much involved in the political intrigues between the pro-French and pro-English factions in Scotland, but she lacked Tudor shrewdness and was discredited (1534) when James discovered that she had betrayed state secrets to her brother, Henry VIII of England.

margarine *noun* a food product that is used as a substitute for butter. It is usually made from vegetable oils (although some margarines are made from animal fats), and also contains water, flavourings, and colourings. Margarine is usually fortified with vitamins A and D. [from French, from Greek *margaron*, pearl]

Margate, formerly **Mergate** POP (1981) 55 000, a resort town in Thanet district, Kent, SE England. It is situated on the I of Thanet, N of Ramsgate.

margin *noun* **1** the blank space around a page of writing or print. **2** any edge or border. **3** something extra, beyond what should be needed; an amount by which one thing exceeds another: *allow a margin for error / win by a large margin*. **4** an upper or lower limit, especially beyond which it is impossible to exist or operate. [from Latin *margo*, border]

marginal — *adj.* **1** small and unimportant. **2** appearing in the margin of a page of text. **3** *said of a political constituency* whose current MP or other representative was elected by only a small majority of votes. — *noun* a marginal constituency.

marginal cost *Econ.* the cost of producing one extra unit, or the total cost saved if one less unit is produced. In accountancy, it is the variable cost of producing a unit. Those costs, which remain unchanged whatever the volume produced (*fixed costs*), are not included in the calculation of marginal costs.

marginally *adv.* in a marginal way; to a marginal degree: *is only marginally longer*.

Margrethe II (1940–) Queen of Denmark, born in Copenhagen, the daughter of Frederick IX, whom she succeeded in 1972. She trained and qualified as an archaeologist, then in 1967 married a French diplomat, Count Henri de Laborde de Monpezat (now Prince Henrik of Denmark). Their children are the heir apparent Prince Frederik André Henrik Christian (1968–) and Prince Joachim Holger Waldemar Christian (1969–).

marguerite *noun* any of various garden plants whose large flowers have pale yellow or white petals round a yellow centre. [from French *marguerite*, daisy]

Mari the most important city on the middle Euphrates in the third and second millennia BC until its destruction c.1759 BC by the Babylonians. It was once the centre of a vast trading network in NW Mesopotamia. Since 1933, c.20 000 cuneiform tablets dating from c.18c BC have been discovered, which provide much information about the period, including interesting parallels to practices in the patriarchal period of Israel's history.

Maria the witty, devious lady-in-waiting to Olivia in Shakespeare's *Twelfth Night*, who writes a fake letter to Malvolio and eventually marries Sir Toby Belch.

Maria, Mad a pathetic character in Laurence Sterne's *Tristram Shandy*, who also appears in *A Sentimental Journey*.

Mariana the rejected fiancée of Angelo in Shakespeare's *Measure for Measure*, whose continuing faithfulness to him is finally rewarded in marriage.

Mariana a poem by Alfred Lord Tennyson (1830). It describes a downcast woman waiting in vain for her lover. It was the inspiration for John Millais's painting of the same name (1851).

Mariana Islands, in full **Commonwealth of the Northern Mariana Islands** POP (1990) 43 000, an Overseas Territory of the USA comprising a group of 14 islands in the NW Pacific Ocean, c.2 400km/1 500mi to the E of the Philippines. AREA 471sq km/182sq mi. CAPITAL Saipan. The islands are mainly volcanic, with three still active. Saipan, Tinian, Rota, Pagan, and Guguan are included in the group. HISTORY from 1947 held by the USA under UN mandate as part of the US Trust Territory of the Pacific Is; they became a self-governing commonwealth of the USA in 1978. ECONOMY sugar cane; coconuts; coffee; tourism.

Mariana Trench an oceanic trench running SW to N off the island of Guam and the Mariana Is, in the Pacific Ocean. Its deepest point, Challenger Deep, at 11 034m, is the Earth's maximum ocean depth.

Maria Theresa (1717–80) Archduchess of Austria, Queen of Hungary and Bohemia (1740–80), and Holy Roman Empress, the daughter of Emperor Charles VI, born in Vienna. In 1736 she married Francis, Duke of Lorraine (who became Holy Roman Emperor in 1745), and in 1740 succeeded her father in the hereditary Habsburg lands, but this claim led to the War of the Austrian Succession (1741–8), during which she lost Silesia to Frederick II of Prussia. Although her Foreign Minister, Kaunitz-Rietberg, tried to isolate Prussia by diplomatic means, military conflict was renewed in the Seven Years' War (1756–63), which confirmed her loss of Silesia. During her later years she strove to maintain international peace, and reluctantly accepted the partition of Poland (1772). Of her 10 surviving children, the eldest son, Joseph II, succeeded her.

Marie Antoinette (Josèphe Jeanne) (1755–93) Queen of France, born in Vienna, the daughter of Maria Theresa and Francis I, and sister of Leopold II. She was married to the Dauphin (later Louis XVI, 1770), to strengthen the Franco-Austrian alliance. Capricious and frivolous, she was criticized for her extravagance, disregard for convention, devotion to the interests of Austria, and opposition to reform. From the outbreak of the French Revolution, she resisted the advice of constitutional monarchists (eg Comte de Mirabeau), and helped to alienate the monarchy. In Jun 1791 she and Louis tried to escape from the Tuileries to her native Austria, but they were apprehended at Varennes, imprisoned in Paris, and guillotined.

Marie de France (12c) French poet, born in Normandy. She spent much of her life in England, and is best known for her *Lais*, a series of romantic Celtic narratives dedicated to 'a noble king' (probably Henry II).

Marie de Médicis, Italian **Maria de' Medici** (1573–1642) queen-consort of Henry IV of France, born in Florence, the daughter of Francesco de' Medici, Grand Duke of Tuscany. She married Henry in 1600, following his divorce from his first wife, Margaret, and gave birth to a son (later Louis XIII) in 1601. After Henry's assassination (1610) she acted as regent, but her capricious behaviour led to her confinement in Blois

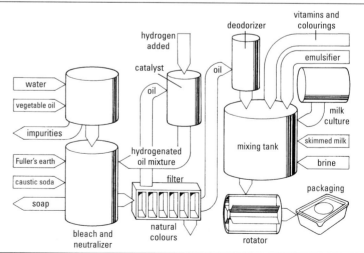

margarine production

when Louis assumed royal power (1617). She continued to scheme against Louis and her former protégé, Cardinal Richelieu, the King's adviser, and was banished to Compiègne, but escaped to Brussels (1631), and spent her last years in poverty.

Marie Louise (1791–1847) Empress of France, born in Vienna, the daughter of Francis I of Austria. She married Napoleon in 1810 (after his divorce from Josephine), and in 1811 bore him a son, who later became King of Rome and Napoleon II. On Napoleon's abdication she returned to Austria. By the Treaty of Fontainebleau (1814) she was awarded the Duchies of Parma, Piacenza, and Guastalla in Italy.

Mariette (Pasha), Auguste (Ferdinand François) (1821–81) French Egyptologist, born in Boulogne. In 1849 he joined the Louvre, and in 1850 was sent to Egypt to acquire Coptic manuscripts. His excavations brought to light numerous monuments and inscriptions, notably around Sakkara, and in 1858 he entered the service of the Shedive Saïd to found the Egyptian Museum and Antiquities Service. He was made a Pasha in 1879.

Marigold a female first name, after the flower.

marigold *noun* any of various garden plants with bright orange or yellow flowers and strongly scented leaves. [from (the Virgin) *Mary* + *gold*, an obsolete name for the plant]

marijuana *or* **marihuana** *noun* **1** a narcotic drug prepared from the dried leaves and flowers of the hemp plant (*Cannabis sativa*). When swallowed, or smoked in the form of a cigarette (a 'joint'), it produces euphoria or mild hallucinations. Its use is illegal in many countries. — Also called *cannabis*, *hashish*, *pot*[2]. **2** the hemp plant from which this drug is obtained. [from Mexican Spanish]

marimba *noun* an originally African type of xylophone consisting of a set of hardwood strips which, when struck with soft hammers, vibrate metal plates underneath, producing musical sound. [from a W African language]

Marina a female first name. [from the Latin word *marinus*, of the sea]

marina *noun* a harbour for private pleasure boats. [from Latin *marinus*; see MARINE]

marinade — *noun* any liquid mixture in which food, especially meat or fish, is soaked to add flavour before cooking. — *verb trans., intrans.* to marinate. [from French *marinade*, from Spanish *marinar*, to pickle in brine]

marinate *verb trans., intrans.* to soak in a marinade. [from Spanish *marinar*, to pickle in brine]

marine — *adj.* **1** of, concerned with, or found in the sea. **2** of ships, shipping trade, or the navy. — *noun* **1** a soldier trained to serve on land or at sea. **2** the merchant or naval ships of a nation collectively. [from Latin *marinus*, from *mare*, sea]

mariner *noun old use* a seaman.

Marines the name applied to soldiers, under naval command, who are also equipped and organized to make war on land. They were originally posted in small units aboard warships but have also been used as combat forces in their own right, specializing in such operations as commando raiding and amphibious assault.

Marinetti, Filippo Tommaso (Emilio) (1876–1944) Italian dramatist, novelist and poet, born in Alexandria, Egypt. He published his influential manifesto for Futurism in *Figaro* in 1909, and became a fascist in 1919. In his writings he glorified war, the machine age, speed, and 'dynamism', and condemned all traditional forms of literature and art.

Marini, Marino (1901–80) Italian sculptor, born in Pistoia. He worked first as a painter, and then mainly in bronze in a traditional figurative style. His subjects included horses and riders, and dancers, and he also painted many portraits.

Marino, Dan (1961–) US footballer, born in Pittsburgh. He plays as quarterback with the Miami Dolphins, and in the 1984 season he gained 5 084 yards passing to create a National Football League record. He completed a record 29 passes in the 1985 Super Bowl, and in 1986 established a record for the most passes completed in a season (378).

Marion *or* **Marian** a female first name. [a combination of MARY + ANN]

marionette *noun* a puppet with jointed limbs moved by strings. [from French *marionette*, diminutive of *Marion*, woman's name]

marital *adj.* of or relating to marriage. [from Latin *maritus*, married]

maritally *adv.* as regards marriage.

maritime *adj.* **1** of the sea or ships. **2** living or growing near the sea. **3** *said of a climate* having relatively small temperature differences between summer and winter. [from Latin *maritimus*, of the sea]

Maritime Trust in the UK, a national organization founded in 1969 to restore, maintain, and display ships of historic or technical importance. It has preserved many ships including HMS *Warrior*, and Capt Scott's *Discovery*.

Maritsa *or* **Marica, River**, Greek **Hevros, Everos**, or **Hebros**, Turkish **Meric** a river in Bulgaria, Greece, and Turkey, length 480km/ 298mi. Rising on Musala Peak in the Rila Mts, it flows E and SE in Bulgaria, then follows the Bulgaria–Greece and Greece–Turkey borders. It turns S and SW to the Aegean Sea, where it forms a delta on the Gulf of Enos.

Mariupol, formerly **Zhdanov** (1948–89) POP (1991e) 522 000, an industrial seaport in Donetsk region, Ukraine. It lies at the mouth of the R Kalmius, on the Sea of Azov, and was founded in the 18c. It is a noted mud-bath resort.

Marius, Gaius (157–86 BC) Roman general and politician from Arpinum, who was consul seven times. He reformed the Roman army and had victories over Jugurtha in Numidia (105 BC), the Teutones (102 BC), and the Cimbri (101 BC). His final years were dominated by his rivalry with the Roman dictator Sulla over the command against Mithridates. He captured Rome for the Roman politician Cinna from the forces backing Sulla (87 BC) but died soon after.

marjoram *noun* a purple-flowered Mediterranean plant whose sweet-smelling leaves are used to season food. [from Old French *marjorane*]

Mark *or* **John Mark, St** (1c AD) a New Testament evangelist, described as 'John whose surname was Mark' (Acts 12.12, 25), and commended in Colossians 4.10 and 2 Timothy 4.11. He helped the apostles Barnabas and Paul during their first missionary journey, but caused a split between Barnabas and Paul over the question of his loyalty. Traditionally the author of the second Gospel, he was also described as the 'disciple and interpreter' of Peter in Rome. His feast day is 25 Apr.

Mark a male first name, borne by the evangelist and by many saints. [from the Latin name *Marcus*, probably derived from *Mars*, the god]

Mark, Gospel according to the second book of the New Testament canon, the shortest and perhaps the earliest of the four Gospels, traditionally attributed to John Mark. Since it contains less teaching material than the other Gospels, it places relatively greater emphasis on Christ's passion, and constitutes a dynamic account of his role and activities.

mark[1] — *noun* **1** a visible blemish, eg a scratch or stain. **2** a patch, stripe, spot, etc forming part of a larger pattern. **3** a grade of a student's, competitor's, etc proficiency, or a number or letter used to denote this. **4** a sign or symbol: *a question mark*. **5** an indication or representation: *a mark of respect*. **6** the position from which a competitor starts in a race: *on your marks*. **7** an object or thing aimed at; a target: *wide of the mark*. **8** a required standard: *up to the mark*. **9** influence: *your work bears his mark*. **10** a cross or other sign used instead of a signature. **11** (*often* **Mark**) a type of design, or model, especially of vehicles. — *verb* **1** *trans., intrans.* to make or become spoiled by a mark. **2** to award a grade to. **3** to show; to be a sign of: *X marks the spot / events marking a new era*. **4** to make a note of. **5** to pay close attention to: *mark my words*. **6** *Sport* to stay close to (an opposing player), limiting his or her influence on the game. **7** to characterize or label: *this incident marks him as a criminal*.

— **leave** *or* **make one's mark** to make a strong or permanent impression.

mark something down 1 to note it. **2** to reduce the price of it.

mark something off *or* **out** to fix its boundaries or limits.

mark time 1 to move the feet up and down as if marching, but without going forward. **2** to merely keep things going while waiting to speed up or progress.

mark something up to increase its price, to provide profit for the seller.
[from Anglo-Saxon *merc*, boundary, limit]

mark[2] *noun* **1** the standard unit of currency in Germany. **2** a unit of weight for gold and silver. [from Anglo-Saxon *marc*]

Mark Antony see ANTONIUS, MARCUS.

mark-down *noun* a reduction in price, especially in determining level of profit.

marked *adj.* **1** obvious or noticeable. **2** watched with suspicion; selected as the target for an attack: *a marked man*.

markedly *adv.* noticeably.

marker *noun* **1** a person who takes notes, eg of the score in a game. **2** anything used to mark the position of something. **3** (*also* **marker pen**) a pen with a thick point, for writing signs, etc.

market — *noun* **1** a periodic gathering of people to buy and sell various goods. **2** the building or other public place in which this takes place. **3** a particular region or section of the population considered as a potential customer: *the teenage market*. **4** a level of trading: *the market is slow*. **5** opportunity to trade; demand: *no market for these goods*. — *verb* (**marketed, marketing**) **1** to offer for sale; to promote. **2** *intrans.* to trade or deal.

— **be in the market for something** to wish to buy it.

on the market on sale; able to be bought.
[from Anglo-Saxon, from Latin *mercatus*, trade, market]

marketable *adj.* saleable, suitable for sale.

market economy an economic system where prices, wages, products, and services are determined by market forces of supply and demand, with no state interference. The contrast is with a *command economy*, where the state takes all economic decisions. Most Western economies are mixed, with varying degrees of state control.

market forces the willingness of customers to buy goods or services that suppliers are willing to offer at a particular price; supply and demand.

market-garden *noun* an area of land, usually near a large town or city, that is used to grow produce, especially vegetables, salad crops, soft fruit, and flowers, for immediate sale at a market.

market-gardener *noun* the owner of or person who tends a market-garden.

marketing *noun* the business techniques or processes by which anything may be sold.

market leader a company that sells more goods of a specific type than any other company; also, a brand of goods that sells more than any other of its kind.

market-place *noun* **1** the open space in a town in which a market is held. **2** (**the market-place**) the commercial world of buying and selling.

market price the price at which a thing is being sold at a particular time.

market research investigation of the habits, needs and preferences of customers.

market town a town, often at the centre of a farming area, where a market is regularly held.

Markievicz, Constance (Georgine), Countess (1868–1927) Irish nationalist, and first British woman MP, born in London. In 1900 she married the Polish Count Casimir Markievicz, with whom she moved to Dublin (1903), but her husband deserted her (1913). She joined Sinn Féin (1908), fought in the Easter Rising (1916), and was sentenced to death but reprieved. Elected the first British woman MP in 1918, she refused to take her seat, but was a member of the Dáil from 1923.

marking *noun* (*often* **markings**) a distinctive pattern of colours on an animal or plant.

Markov, Andrei Andreyevich (1856–1922) Russian mathematician, born in Ryazan. He was professor at St Petersburg from 1893 to 1905, before he went into a self-imposed exile in the town of Zaraisk. He is best known for introducing the concept of the Markov chain, a series of events in which the probability of a given event occurring depends only on the immediately previous event; this has since found many applications in physics and biology.

Markova, Dame Alicia, originally **Lilian Alicia Marks** (1910–   ) English ballerina, born in London. She joined Sergei Diaghilev's Ballets Russes (1924–9), then returned to England to the Vic–Wells (later Sadler's Wells and Royal) Ballet, and later founded the Markova–Dolin Ballet Company in 1935 with Anton Dolin (1904–83). Their partnership was acclaimed especially for its interpretations of *Giselle*, and their touring group developed into the London Festival Ballet (the English National Ballet from 1988). She became director of the Metropolitan Opera Ballet for three years in 1963.

Marks (of Broughton), Simon Marks, 1st Baron (1888–1964) English businessman, born in Leeds. In 1907 he inherited the 60 Marks and Spencer 'penny bazaars', which his father, Michael Marks, and Thomas Spencer had built up from 1884. In collaboration with his brother-in-law Israel (later Lord) Seiff (1899–1972), he expanded Marks and Spencer into a major retail chain. The 'Marks and Sparks' brand label (St Michael®) became a guarantee of high quality at a reasonable price.

marksman *noun* a person able to shoot a gun or other weapon accurately, especially a trained soldier or policeman.

marksmanship *noun* the skill of a marksman.

mark-up *noun* an increase in price, especially in determining level of profit.

marl — *noun Geol.* a mixture of clay and limestone, formerly added to light sandy soil to improve its texture and fertility and to increase its water-holding capacity, this process being known as marling. — *verb* to apply marl to. [from Old French *marle*]

Marlborough, John Churchill, 1st Duke of (1650–1722) English soldier, born in Ashe, Devon. He was commissioned in the Guards (1667), and fought in the Low Countries. In 1678 he married Sarah Jennings (1660–1744), a close friend and attendant of Princess (later Queen) Anne, and was further promoted. On James II's accession (1685), he achieved the rank of general. He quelled the Duke of Monmouth's rebellion at Sedgemoor but, concerned for the integrity of the Anglican Church under James, deserted to the Prince of Orange in 1688, and served the Protestant cause in campaigns in Ireland and Flanders. Under Queen Anne he was Supreme Commander of the British forces in the War of the Spanish Succession, and he became Capt-General of the Allied armies. His military and organizational skills resulted in the great victories of Donauwörth and Blenheim (1704), Ramillies (1706), Oudenarde, and the capture of Lille (1708), for which he was rewarded with Blenheim Palace and a dukedom. Following his political interests, he sided with the Whig War Party (1708), but his influence waned with theirs after 1710, and when his wife fell from royal favour, the Tories pressed for his downfall. He was dismissed on charges of embezzling, and left England for continental Europe (1712), but returned after the accession of George I (1714).

Marlene a female first name, borne by the German actress Marlene Dietrich. [a contracted form of *Maria Magdalene*]

Marley, Bob (Robert Nesta) (1945–81) Jamaican singer, guitarist, and composer of reggae music, born near Kingston. In 1965, tourists started returning with records and stories of Bob Marley and his band, the Wailers. Their music (reggae) developed political themes with an artless lyricism and infectious rhythms, and spread worldwide during the 1970s. A disciple of Rastafarianism, Marley was a charismatic spokesman not only for his religion but also his culture and generation.

Marley, Jacob the deceased partner of Scrooge, whose ghost haunts Scrooge into repentance in Charles Dickens's *A Christmas Carol*.

marlin *noun* (PL. **marlin, marlins**) a large fish of warm and tropical seas, with a long spear-like upper jaw. — Also called *spearfish*. [from MARLIN-SPIKE, because of its pointed snout]

marlinspike *or* **marlinespike** *noun Naut.* a pointed metal tool for separating the strands of rope to be spliced. [from Dutch *marlijn*, from *marren*, to tie + *lijn*, rope]

Marlowe, Christopher (1564–93) English dramatist, born in Canterbury, Kent. His *Tamburlaine the Great* (c.1587) shows his discovery of the strength and variety of blank verse, and this was followed by *The Jew of Malta* (c.1592), *The Tragical History of Dr Faustus* (c.1594), and *Edward II* (c.1592), which was partly written by others.

Marlowe, Philip the tough, world-weary private-eye in the novels (and stories) of Raymond Chandler, which include *The Big Sleep*, *The High Window*, and *The Long Goodbye*.

marly *adj.* **1** like marl. **2** containing marl.

Marmaduke a male first name. [probably derived from the Irish Gaelic name *Mael-Maedoc*, devotee of Maedoc]

marmalade *noun* jam made from any citrus fruit, especially oranges. [from Portuguese *marmelada*, from *marmelo*, quince, from which it was originally made]

Marmara *or* **Marmora, Sea of**, Turkish **Marmara Denizi**, ancient **Propontis** a sea in NW Turkey, between Europe in the N and Asia in the S. AREA 11 474sq km/4 429sq mi; length c.200km/125mi. It is connected in the E with the Black Sea through the Bosporus and in the W with the Aegean Sea through the Dardanelles. Istanbul lies on its NE shore; in the W part of the sea there is Marmara I (from which the sea gets its modern name), a source of marble, slate, and granite.

Marmion, in full *Marmion, A Tale of Flodden Field* a poem in six cantos by Sir Walter Scott (1808). It is set in 1513 and is centred around the deceitful life of the noble Lord Marmion. It contains the well-known poem 'Lochinvar'.

marmoreal *adj. formal* of or like marble. [from Latin *marmor*, marble]

marmoset *noun* any of various small S American monkeys with a long bushy tail and tufts of hair around the head and ears. [from Old French *marmouset*, grotesque figure]

marmot *noun* any of various stout, coarse-haired burrowing rodents of Europe, Asia, and N America. [from French *marmotte*]

Marne, Battle of the an early battle (1914) in World War I, in which the French armies under General Joffre and the British Expeditionary Force halted German forces that had crossed the R Marne and were approaching Paris. With hopes of a swift victory dashed, the German line withdrew across the R Aisne, dug in, and occupied much the same position until 1918.

Marne, River, ancient **Matrona** a river in central France, length 525km/326mi. Rising in the Langres Plateau, it flows NW and W across Champagne to meet the R Seine near Paris. Navigation is possible to St Dizier. Two major battles of World War I (1914, 1918) were fought on its banks.

Marner, Silas see SILAS MARNER.

maroon[1] — *adj.* having a dark brownish-red or purplish-red colour. — *noun* this colour. [from French *marron*, chestnut]

maroon[2] *verb* **1** to leave in isolation in a deserted place, especially on an island. **2** to leave helpless. [from Mexican Spanish *cimarrón*, wild]

Marot, Clément (c.1497–1544) French poet, born in Cahors. He entered the service of Margaret of Navarre but was forced into exile several times, on account of his Protestant inclinations. He produced a wide range of poetry, including elegies, epistles, ballads, and epigrams, and translated the Psalms into French.

Marple, Miss Jane the elderly spinster detective in *Murder at the Vicarage* and many other novels by Agatha Christie.

Marprelate Tracts seven pamphlets covertly published (1587–9) in London by a pseudonymous author 'Martin Marprelate', who satirized the Elizabethan Church and bishops, and favoured a Presbyterian system. The tracts led to statutes against dissenting sects and sedition (1593).

Marquand, J(ohn) P(hillips) (1893–1960) US writer, born in Wilmington, Delaware. He is known for his detective stories and social satires, some with an oriental background. These include *The Late George Apley* (1937, Pulitzer Prize).

marque *noun* a brand or make, especially of car. [from French *marque*]

marquee *noun* a very large tent used for circuses, parties, etc. [originally an army officer's tent, coined from MARQUISE, wrongly thought to be plural]

Marquesas Islands, French **Iles Marquises** POP (1988) 8 000, a mountainous, wooded volcanic island group of French Polynesia, situated 1 184km/736mi to the NE of Tahiti. AREA 1 189sq km/459 sq mi. It comprises Nuku Hiva (where Herman Melville lived), Ua Pu, Ua Huka, Hiva Oa (where Paul Gauguin painted), Tahuata, Fatu Hiva, and five smaller, uninhabited islands. The group was acquired by France in 1842. Taiohae (Hiva Oa) is the chief settlement. ECONOMY copra; cotton; vanilla.

marquess *noun* in the UK, a nobleman above an earl and below a duke in rank. [from Old French *marchis*, from Latin *marchensis*, prefect of the marches; see MARCH[2]]

marquetry *noun* the art or practice of making decorative arrangements of pieces of different woods, often set into the surface of wooden furniture. [from French *marqueterie*, from *marqueter*, to inlay]

◇ A popular technique in furniture decoration in 17c and 18c Europe, and widely used in England after the accession of William and Mary in 1688.

Some of the finest examples were by the French cabinet-makers of the reigns of Louis XIV, XV, and XVI, and patterns were usually of fruit, flowers, and foliage.

Márquez, Gabriel García see GARCIA MARQUEZ, GABRIEL.

marquis *noun* in European countries, a nobleman next in rank above a count. [variant of MARQUESS]

marquise *noun* in various countries, a marchioness. [from French *marquise*, related to MARQUESS]

Marrakesh *or* **Marrakech** POP (1990e) 1.5m, the second largest city in Morocco, founded in 1062. It is situated in Tensift province, in the centre of the country. The city lies in the N foothills of the Haut Atlas, 240km/150mi S of Casablanca. It is one of Morocco's four imperial cities. NOTABLE FEATURE Koutoubia Mosque (12c). The Medina is a World Heritage site.

marram *noun* a coarse grass that grows on sandy shores, often planted to stop sand erosion. [from Norse *marr*, sea + *halmr*, haulm or stem]

marriage *noun* **1** the state or relationship of being husband and wife. **2** the act of becoming husband and wife. **3** the ceremony within which this act is performed; a wedding. **4** a joining together; a union. [from Old French *mariage*]

marriageability *or* **marriageableness** *noun* suitability for marriage.

marriageable *adj.* suitable, especially at a legal age, for marriage.

Marriage à la Mode a painting by William Hogarth (1743–5, Tate Gallery, London).

marriage certificate an official piece of paper showing that two people are legally married.

Marriage Feast at Cana, The a painting by Paolo Veronese (1562–3, Louvre, Paris).

marriage guidance professional counselling given to couples with marital or personal problems.

marriage licence a paper giving official permission for a marriage to take place.

marriage of convenience a marriage entered into for the advantages it will bring, rather than for love.

Marriage of Figaro, The (Le Nozze di Figaro) a comic opera by Wolfgang Amadeus Mozart (1786), based on the character of Figaro in Beaumarchais's plays. Set in 18c Seville, it is a complicated story involving much misunderstanding and mistaken identity, and focusing on Count Almaviva's servants Susanna and Figaro who require his permission to get married.

married — *adj.* **1** having a husband or wife. **2** of or relating to marriage: *married life*. **3** fixed together; joined. — *noun* (**marrieds**) a married couple.

marrow *noun* **1** (*in full* **bone marrow**) the soft tissue that fills the internal cavities of bones. At birth it consists entirely of red marrow, which is the site of formation of red blood cells, platelets, and granular white blood cells. In later life the red marrow in the limb bones is replaced by fatty yellow marrow. **2** (*in full* **vegetable marrow**) an annual plant (*Cucurbita pepo*) with large prickly leaves, native to tropical America but cultivated worldwide for its large oblong edible fruit. **3** the fruit of this plant, which has a thick green or striped skin and soft white flesh, and is cooked as a vegetable. **4** the innermost, essential, or best part of anything.
— **to the marrow** right through.
[from Anglo-Saxon *mærg*]

marrowbone *noun* a bone containing edible marrow.

marrowfat *noun* a variety of large edible pea; the plant that bears it.

marry *verb* (**marries, married**) **1** to take someone as one's husband or wife. **2** to perform the ceremony of marriage between. **3** to give (a son or daughter) in marriage. **4** *intrans.* to become husband and wife. **5** (*also* **marry something up**) to assemble it, join it up, or match it correctly.
— **marry into something** to become involved in or associated with it by marriage: *married into money.*

marry someone off to find a husband or wife for (someone, especially a son or daughter). [from Latin *maritare*]

Marryat, Capt Frederick (1792–1848) English naval officer and novelist, born in London. He joined the navy (1806–30), and served in many parts of the world. He then became a man of letters and wrote a series of novels on sea life, notably *Peter Simple* (1833) and *Mr Midshipman Easy* (1834). After touring the USA, he retired (1843) to Langham, Norfolk, where he farmed and wrote stories for children, the best known of which is *The Children of the New Forest* (1847).

Mars in Roman mythology, the god of war, second only to Jupiter. He is identified with the Greek god Ares, though various annual ceremonies at Rome indicate that he was originally an agricultural deity who guarded the fields. The month of March is named after him.

Mars *Astron.* the fourth planet from the Sun, and the nearest planet to the Earth. Its orbit lies between those of the Earth and Jupiter.
◇ Mars is about 228 million km from the Sun, and has a diameter of 6794km. It is about half the size of the Earth, and takes 24h 37min to rotate once on its own axis, and 687days to orbit the Sun. Mars has polar ice caps which increase and decrease in size according to the seasons. It has a very thin atmosphere, composed mainly of carbon dioxide, and there may be water permanently frozen beneath the planet's surface (some features which resemble old water channels have been photographed).
The space probe *Viking 1* landed on Mars in 1976 and continued to send back information to Earth until 1982. It failed to establish whether there is any life on Mars, but it did verify that the temperature of the planet never exceeds 0°C, and at night can fall to –100°C. Photographs taken by *Viking 1* and *Viking 2* in 1976 showed a stony dusty reddish-brown landscape, covered with craters, volcanoes, and gorges. Its highest peak, Olympus Mons, rises 23km above the desert, and its largest valley, Valles Marineris, is 4 000km long (the width of the USA), 75km wide, and in places 7km deep. Mars has two irregularly shaped natural satellites, Phobos (which is 27km in length), and Deimos (which is even smaller). Phobos is only 6 000km above the surface of Mars, and is slowly spiralling inwards towards the planet.

Marsala *noun* a dark sweet sherry-like wine made in *Marsala*, Sicily.

Marseillaise, La the French National Anthem, originally a revolutionary song written and probably composed in 1792 by Claude Joseph Rouget De Lisle. Its original name was *Chant de guerre de l'armée du Rhin* (War Song of the Rhine Army), but it became known in Paris when it was sung by volunteers from Marseilles during the French Revolution, and was offically adopted in 1795.

Marseilles, French **Marseille**, ancient **Massilia** POP (1990) 1.1m, the capital of Provence-Alpes-Côte d'Azur region and of Bouches-du-Rhône department, S France. It is a principal commercial port situated on the NE shore of the Gulf of Lyons, 130km/81mi SW of Nice. Marseilles is France's second-largest city and the leading port of the Mediterranean Sea. It was founded in c.600 BC by Greeks, on a rocky peninsula N of the Vieux Port. The city is renowned for its bouillabaisse (fish soup). NOTABLE FEATURES the New Harbour (begun in 1844) has 25km/16mi of quays; the Basin de la Joliette is used by passenger ships; Church of St-

Victor (11c–14c); Basilica of Notre-Dame-de-la-Garde (19c); town hall (1663–83); Cathédrale de la Major (1852–93), Cathédrale St-Lazare (11c–12c); Musée des Beaux-Arts.

Marsh, Dame Ngaio (Edith) (1899–1982) New Zealand detective-story writer, born in Christchurch. She moved to England in 1928, and published her first novel, *A Man Lay Dead*, in 1934. It was followed by a series of novels and short stories featuring Superintendent Roderick Alleyn of Scotland Yard. These include *Vintage Murder* (1937), *Opening Night* (1951), and *Black as He's Painted* (1974).

marsh *noun* **1** a poorly drained low-lying area of land, commonly found at the mouths of rivers and alongside ponds and lakes, that is frequently flooded. It is dominated by grasses, sedges, rushes, and reeds, and its soil consists of silts, clays, and other mineral deposits. **2** (*in full* **salt marsh**) such an area of land that lies in the intertidal zone and is periodically flooded by seawater. [from Anglo-Saxon *mersc* or *merisc*]

marshal — *noun* **1** any of various high-ranking officers in the armed forces. **2** an official who organizes parades, etc, or controls crowds at large public events. **3** *North Amer., esp. US* a chief police or fire officer in some states. — *verb* (**marshalled, marshalling**) **1** to arrange (facts, etc) in order. **2** to direct, lead, or show the way to. [from Old French *mareschal*]

Marshall, George C(atlett) (1880–1959) US soldier and politician, born in Uniontown, Pennsylvania. He was appointed Chief-of-Staff (1939–45), and directed the US Army throughout World War II. After two years in China as special representative of President Truman, he became Secretary of State (1947–9) and initiated the Marshall Aid plan for the postwar reconstruction of Europe. He was awarded the Nobel Peace Prize in 1953.

Marshall, John (1755–1835) American jurist, born near Germantown, Virginia. In the 1790s he became a supporter of the nationalist measures of Washington and Hamilton, and was named Chief Justice by the outgoing President John Adams in 1801. From then until his death he dominated the Supreme Court, and established the US doctrine of the judicial review of federal and state legislation.

Marshall, Thurgood (1908–93) US lawyer and jurist, born in Baltimore, Maryland. He joined the legal staff of the National Association for the Advancement of Colored People, and argued many important civil rights cases. He served as a judge of the US Court of Appeals (1961–5) and Solicitor-General of the United States (1965–7), before he became the first black Justice of the US Supreme Court (1967–91).

marshalling-yard *noun* a place where railway wagons are arranged into trains.

Marshall Islands POP (1990e) 46 000, an independent republic forming an archipelago in the central Pacific Ocean. AREA c.180sq km/70sq mi. There are two parallel chains of coral atolls, Ratik in the E and Ralik in the W, which

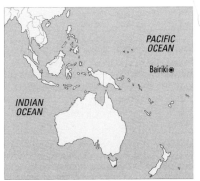

Marshall Islands

extend to a length of c.925km/800mi. The islands include Kwajalein and Jaluit. US nuclear weapon tests were held on the Bikini and Enewetak atolls from 1946 until 1962. The population is Micronesian; Christianity is the chief religion. LANGUAGES English and Marshallese. CURRENCY the US dollar. HISTORY explored by the Spanish in 1529; Trust Territory from 1947–78; became a self-governing republic in 1979; a compact of free association with the USA was signed in 1982; trusteeship ended in 1990; independence 1991. GOVERNMENT democratically governed by a President, elected by a 33-member parliament. ECONOMY farming; fishing; tropical agriculture.

Marshall Plan the popular name for the European Recovery Program, a scheme for large-scale, medium-term US aid to war-ravaged Europe, announced in 1947 by US Secretary of State George Marshall. 'Marshall Aid' was rejected by the USSR and the Eastern bloc, but it materially assisted W Europe's economic revival in 1948–50.

marsh gas methane.

marsh harrier a harrier hawk, found in marshy regions of Europe, that has an owl-like head, long wings, and long legs, and flies low over the ground, swooping down to kill its prey.

marshmallow *noun* a spongy pink or white sweet, originally made from the root of the marsh mallow.

marsh mallow a pink-flowered plant that grows wild in coastal marshes.

marsh marigold a marsh plant with flowers like large buttercups.

marshy *adj.* (**marshier, marshiest**) **1** of the nature of a marsh. **2** covered with marshes.

Marston, John (1576–1634) English dramatist, born in Wardington, Oxfordshire. Among his plays are *The Malcontent* (1604), and *Eastward Ho!* (1605), a satirical comedy written in conjunction with George Chapman and Ben Jonson. In 1607 he gave up playwriting and entered the Church.

Marston Moor, Battle of a major conflict (1644) near York in the English Civil Wars, in which a force of 27 000 Parliamentary and Scottish troops led by Oliver Cromwell defeated 18 000 Royalists led by Prince Rupert. The defeat led to the fall of the Royalist stronghold of York, and the virtual collapse of Charles I's cause in the north.

marsupial — *noun Zool.* any of a group of mammals in which the female lacks a placenta, and carries and suckles her young in a pouch (marsupium) that surrounds the mammary glands on her abdomen, eg kangaroo, wallaby, koala, wombat. — *adj.* of or like a marsupial. [from Latin *marsupium*, pouch]
◇ Young marsupials are tiny and very immature when born, and migrate to the mother's pouch where they remain until they are mature enough to survive independently. With the exception of the opossums of America, all marsupials are confined to Australasia.

Marsyas in Greek mythology, a satyr who challenged Apollo to a flute-contest. He was defeated and flayed alive by the god.

mart *noun* a trading place; a market. [from Dutch *markt*]

martello *noun* (PL. **martellos**) (*also* **martello tower**) a small circular fortified tower used for coastal defence. [named after Cape *Mortella*, Corsica, where such a tower was captured with difficulty by a British fleet in 1794]
◇ Many were erected on England's south and south-east coasts in the early 19c to provide observation posts and defence against a projected French invasion.

marten *noun* **1** any of various small tree-dwelling predatory mammals with a long thin body and a bushy tail. **2** their highly valued soft black or brown fur. [from Dutch *martren*, from Old French *martre*]

Martext, Sir Oliver the country vicar in Shakespeare's *As You Like It*.

Martha a female first name, borne by the sister of Lazarus and Mary of Bethany in the New Testament. [of Aramaic origin, = lady]

Martha's Vineyard an island in the Atlantic Ocean off the SE coast of Massachusetts, USA, part of Duke's County. AREA 280sq km/108sq mi. CHIEF TOWN Edgartown. Formerly a whaling and fishing centre, it is now a summer resort. Martha's Vineyard is so called because the first English settlers found an abundance of wild grapes growing there.

Martí, José (Julián) (1853–95) Cuban national hero, born in Havana, who devoted his life to the liberation of Cuba from Spain. As an adult he spent many years in exile, and he became famous for his journalism, plays, and poems. In 1892 he helped found the Cuban Revolutionary Party, which in 1895 mounted an armed rebellion in the island, during which he was killed.

Martial, properly **Marcus Valerius Martialis** (c.40–c.104 AD) Roman poet and epigrammatist, born in Spain. He went to Rome in 64 and became a client of the Spanish house of the Senecas. He is remembered for the first 12 books of his epigrams, which are mainly satirical comments on contemporary events and society.

martial *adj.* of, relating to, or suitable for war or the military. [from Latin *martialis*, of Mars, Roman god of war]

martial art any of various fighting sports or self-defence techniques of Far Eastern origin, eg karate or judo.

martial law law and order strictly enforced by the army when ordinary civil law has broken down, eg during a war or revolution.

Martian — *adj.* relating to or supposedly coming from the planet Mars. — *noun* a fictional inhabitant of Mars. [from Latin *Martius*]

Martin, Archer John Porter (1910–) English biochemist, born in London. Working at the Wool Industry Research Association in Leeds, he developed a technique known as partition chromatography to allow the separation and analysis of proteins; this technique revolutionized analytical biochemistry. He shared the 1952 Nobel Prize for Chemistry with Richard Synge.

Martin, John (1789–1854) English painter, born in Haydon Bridge, Northumberland. He began as a heraldic and enamel painter, and from 1811 onwards exhibited many works on a grand scale at the Royal Academy, London (eg *Joshua Commanding the Sun to Stand Still*, 1816). His major paintings, often on historical and Biblical themes, include *Belshazzar's Feast* (1821) and *The Deluge* (1826).

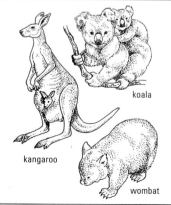

koala

kangaroo

wombat

marsupials

Martin, (Basil) Kingsley (1897–1969) English journalist, born in London. As editor of the *New Statesman and Nation* (1932–62), he transformed it into an internationally recognized weekly journal of socialist opinion through which he exerted socialist pressure on Labour under Clement Attlee. His books include *The Triumph of Lord Palmerston* (1924), *French Liberal Thought in the Eighteenth Century* (1929), *Critic's London Diary* (a selection from his *New Statesman* column of vigorous personal comment) and the autobiographical work *Editor* (1968).

Martin, Richard (1754–1834) Irish lawyer and humanitarian, born (probably) in Dublin. He became MP for Galway (1801–26), and in 1822 sponsored a bill to make illegal the cruel treatment of cattle, the first legislation of its kind. He was dubbed 'Humanity Martin' by George IV, and was one of the founders of the RSPCA (1824).

Martin a male first name. [a form of the Latin name *Marinus*, which is probably derived from *Mars*, the Roman god of war]

martin *noun* any of various small birds of the swallow family, with a square or slightly forked tail. [from the name *Martin*]

Martin Chuzzlewit a novel by Charles Dickens (1843–4). It describes the varying fortunes of the Chuzzlewit family, and in particular the reformation of young Martin.

Martin du Gard, Roger (1881–1958) French novelist, born in Neuilly. Also the author of several plays, he is best known for his eight-novel series *Les Thibault* (1922–40), which deals with family life during the first decades of the present century. He was awarded the Nobel Prize for Literature in 1937.

martinet *noun derog.* a person who maintains strict discipline. [from Martinet, one of Louis XIV's generals]

Martini, Simone (c.1284–1344) Italian painter, born in Siena. One of the major artists of the 14c Sienese School, his work is notable for its grace of line and use of colour. He worked in Assisi (1333–9), and then at the Papal court in Avignon until 1344. His works include the *Annunciation* (1333, Uffizi, Florence), and *Christ Reproved by his Parents* (1342, Walker Art Gallery, Liverpool).

Martini *noun trademark* **1** an Italian brand of vermouth. **2** a cocktail of gin and vermouth.

Martinique POP (1992e) 368 000, an Overseas Department of France formed by an island in the Windward group of the Lesser Antilles, E Caribbean Sea, between Dominica and St Lucia. AREA 1 079sq km/416sq mi. CAPITAL Fort-de-France. TIME ZONE GMT –4. The population is mainly of African or mixed descent; Roman Catholicism is the chief religion. OFFICIAL LANGUAGE French. CURRENCY the French franc. PHYSICAL DESCRIPTION the island is 61km/38mi long, 24km/15mi wide and rises steeply from the sea, particularly on the N coast; the highest point is Mt Pelée at 1 397m. CLIMATE tropical with high humidity; the average temperature at Fort-de-France is 21–29°C from Jan to Mar and 23–31°C from Jun to Oct; the wet season is Jul to Nov. HISTORY discovered by Columbus in 1502; became a French colony in 1635; its status changed to Overseas Department of France in 1946. GOVERNMENT administered by a Commissioner General and a 41-member Regional Council, both elected for up to six years. ECONOMY based largely on agriculture; sugar cane, bananas, rum, pineapples; construction; distilling; cement; oil refining; light industry; tourism.

Martin Luther King's Birthday 15 Jan, the birthday of the black US civil rights leader, commemorated in about half the states of the USA. The name and the date of the celebration varies from State to State.

Martinmas *noun* St Martin's day, 11 Nov.

martyr — *noun* **1** a person who is put to death for refusing to abandon religious or other beliefs. **2** (**a martyr to something**) a person who suffers greatly for any cause or reason: *is a martyr to arthritis*. — *verb* (**martyred, martyring**) to put to death as a martyr. [from Latin, from Greek *martus*, witness]

martyrdom *noun* the death or suffering of a martyr.

marvel — *noun* an astonishing or wonderful person or thing. — *verb intrans.* (**marvelled, marvelling**) (**marvel at something**) to be filled with astonishment or wonder by it. [from French *merveille*]

Marvell, Andrew (1621–78) English metaphysical poet, born in Winestead, Yorkshire. He travelled in Europe (1642–6), worked as a tutor, and became John Milton's assistant (1657). He is remembered for his pastoral and garden poems, notably 'To his Coy Mistress'. After becoming an MP (1659), his writing was devoted to pamphlets and satires attacking intolerance and arbitrary government (eg *The Rehearsal Transpos'd*, 1672).

marvellous *adj.* **1** so wonderful or astonishing as to be almost beyond belief. **2** *colloq.* excellent.

marvellously *adv.* in a marvellous way.

Marx, Karl (Heinrich) (1818–83) German founder of modern international communism, born in Trier. He studied law, but turned to history, Hegelian philosophy, and Ludwig Feuerbach's materialism. He edited a radical newspaper, but it was suppressed. In Brussels from 1845, with Friedrich Engels his closest collaborator and disciple, he reorganized the Communist League, which met in London in 1847. In 1848 his *Communist Manifesto* was finalized, which attacked the state as the instrument of oppression, and religion and culture as ideologies of the capitalist class. Expelled from Brussels, in 1849 he settled in London, where he studied economics, and wrote the first volume of his major work, *Das Kapital* (1867), which he left unfinished at his death.

Marx Brothers, The US family of film comedians, born in New York City, comprising Julius (1895–1977) or Groucho; Leonard (1891–1961), or Chico; Arthur (1893–1961), or Harpo; and Herbert (1901–79), or Zeppo. They began their stage career in vaudeville in a team called the Six Musical Mascots, which also included their mother and an aunt; another brother, Milton, known as Gummo, left the act early on. They later appeared as the Four Nightingales, and then as the Marx Brothers. Their main reputation was made in films such as *Animal Crackers* and *Monkey Business* (both 1932). Herbert retired from films in 1935, but the others had several further successes, such as *A Day at the Races* (1937), until they separated in 1949.

Marxism *noun* the theories of Karl Marx, German economist and political philosopher, stating that the struggle between different social classes is the main influence on political change, and that communism will eventually replace capitalism.

Marxism–Leninism a distinct variant of Marxism formulated by Lenin who, prior to the Bolshevik Revolution, argued for direct rule by the proletariat (ie workers and peasants), and in the circumstances of Russia after 1905 advocated direct democracy through the soviets (councils). In practice, the Bolshevik Revolution did not produce a democratic republic, but gave a 'leading and directing' role to the Communist Party, seen as the vanguard of a working class which had insufficient political consciousness to forge a revolution. Leninist principles of a revolutionary vanguard became the central tenet of nearly all communist parties. They were organized according to the idea of democratic centralism that afforded the leadership the right to dictate party policy, to select party officials from above, and to discipline dissenting party members. Lenin

developed a theory of imperialism which held that it was the last stage of a decaying capitalism. This was used to justify revolution in feudal Russia, because it was an imperial power, and later to justify communist intervention in underdeveloped countries as part of the struggle between socialism and imperialism. Serious doubts were cast upon Lenin's views by the many failures of the socialism to which they led, and eventually by the collapse of the USSR in 1991.

Marxist — *noun* a follower of Marxism. — *adj.* relating to or characteristic of Marxism or Marxists.

Marxist criticism a literary criticism derived from the writings of Karl Marx based on the premise that literature is conditioned by the material forces of society and history. Latterly, Marxist criticism has availed itself of the insights of psychoanalysis and structuralism in an attempt to form a new synthesis of conditions and codes. Marxist critics include Georg Lukács and, more recently, Terry Eagleton.

Mary I (1516–58) Queen of England and Ireland (1553–8), born in Greenwich, London, the daughter of Henry VIII by his first wife, Catherine of Aragon. A devout Catholic, during the reign of her half-brother Edward VI, she lived in retirement and refused to conform to the new religion. Despite Northumberland's conspiracy to prevent her succession on Edward's death, with the support of the country she entered London and ousted Lady Jane Grey. She then repealed anti-Catholic legislation and revived Catholic practices, intending to restore papal supremacy with the assistance of Cardinal Pole, and to cement a Catholic union with Philip II of Spain. These aspirations provoked Sir Thomas Wyatt's rebellion, followed by the execution of Jane Grey and the imprisonment of Mary's half-sister Elizabeth, on suspicion of complicity. Mary's unpopular marriage to Philip (1554) was followed by the persecution of some 300 Protestants, which earned her the name 'Bloody Mary'. Broken by childlessness, sickness, grief at her husband's departure from England, and the loss of Calais to the French, she died in London.

Mary, Queen of Scots (1542–87) Queen of Scotland virtually from birth, and queen-consort of Francis II of France (1559–60), daughter of James V of Scotland by his second wife, Mary of Guise, born in Linlithgow Palace, (now in West Lothian) Scotland. Her betrothal to Prince Edward of England was annulled by the Scottish parliament, an act that precipitated war with England. After the Scots' defeat at Pinkie (1547), she was sent to the French court and married the Dauphin in 1558 (later Francis II, 1559), but was widowed (1560) and returned to Scotland (1561). Her designs on the English throne led her to marry her cousin, Henry Stuart, Lord Darnley, a grandson of Margaret Tudor (1565), but his debauchery disgusted her and they were alienated. The vicious murder of Rizzio, her Italian secretary, by Darnley and a group of Protestant nobles (1566) confirmed her insecurity, and the birth of the future James VI failed to bring reconciliation. Soon after, Darnley was killed in a gunpowder explosion at Kirk o' Field in Edinburgh (1567); the chief suspect was the Earl of Bothwell, who underwent a mock trial and was acquitted. Mary's involvement is unclear, but she married Bothwell after he had 'abducted' her. The Protestant nobles under James Morton rose against her, and when she surrendered at Carberry Hill, she was imprisoned at Lochleven and compelled to abdicate, but she escaped, raised an army, and was defeated again by the confederate lords at Langside (1568). She placed herself under the protection of Queen Elizabeth, but was instead made a prisoner for life. Her presence in England gave rise to many plots to depose Elizabeth and restore Catholicism. Finally, after the Babington conspiracy (1586) she was brought to trial for treason, and executed in Fotheringay Castle, Northamptonshire.

Mary a female first name. [from Latin *stilla maris*, drop of the sea, which later became *stella maris*, star of the sea]

Mary (mother of Jesus), also entitled **Our Lady**, or **the Blessed Virgin Mary** (d.c.63 AD) the mother of Jesus Christ. The New Testament records the Annunciation, the conception of Jesus by the Holy Spirit (Matthew 1.18), her betrothal to Joseph, and the birth of Jesus. She only occasionally appears in Christ's ministry, but in John 19.25 she is at the Cross and is committed to the care of one of the disciples. She has become a subject of devotion in her own right, especially in Roman Catholic doctrine and worship. The belief that her body was taken up into heaven is celebrated in the festival of the Assumption, defined as Roman Catholic dogma in 1950. The Immaculate Conception has been a dogma since 1854. Belief in the apparitions of the Virgin in such places as Lourdes, Fatima, and Medjugorje attracts many thousands of pilgrims each year. In Roman Catholic and Orthodox Christianity, she holds a special place as an intermediary between God and humanity.

Mary (of Teck), formerly **Princess Victoria Mary Augusta Louise Olga Pauline Claudine Agnes**, known as **Princess May** (1867–1953) queen-consort of George V of Great Britain, born in London. She married Prince George, Duke of York, in 1893, and they had five sons and one daughter. After his accession (as George V) in 1910, she accompanied him to Delhi as Empress of India for the Coronation Durbar of Dec 1911. She helped to mould her husband into a 'people's king' and after the abdication of her eldest son, Edward VIII, she helped to strengthen the appeal of the monarchy throughout the reign of her second son, George VI, which included the organization of women's war work and many public and philanthropic activities.

Mary Magdalene a New Testament figure from whom Christ exorcized seven evil spirits (Luke 8.2). She was present with other women at the Crucifixion and later at the empty tomb, when the resurrected Christ appeared (Matthew 28.9). John 20 relates a private encounter with the resurrected Christ. [*Magdalene* possibly = of Magdala, in Galilee]

Maryland POP (1990) 4.9m, a state in E USA, divided into 23 counties and one city. AREA 27 090sq km/10 460sq mi. It is bounded E by Delaware and the Atlantic Ocean. PHYSICAL DESCRIPTION Chesapeake Bay stretches N through the state, almost splitting it in two; the Potomac R forms most of the S border; the Susquehanna and Patuxent rivers cross the state, emptying into Chesapeake Bay; the highest point is Mt Backbone (1 024m); to the N and W is the rolling Piedmont, rising up to the Blue Ridge and Pennsylvania Hills; to the S and E is Chesapeake Bay with indented shores, forming a popular resort area; the Eastern Shore with over 12 000sq km/4 500sq mi of forest is noted for its scenic beauty. HISTORY the first settlement (1634) was located at St Mary's (state capital until 1694); the seventh of the original 13 states to ratify the Constitution in 1788; gave up territory for the establishment of the District of Columbia; abolished slavery in 1864; Maryland is known as the 'Old Line State' or 'Free State'. CAPITAL Annapolis. CHIEF TOWN Baltimore (85% of the population live in this area). ECONOMY iron and steel; shipbuilding; electrical equipment; machinery; processed foods; chief agricultural products are poultry, dairy products, corn, soya beans, and tobacco.

Marylebone Cricket Club (ABBREV. MCC) a cricket club whose headquarters are at Lord's Cricket Ground, London, UK. It was founded in 1787 by a group of noblemen headed by the Earl of Winchilsea, Lord Charles Lennox, the Duke of York, and the Duke of Dorset. It retained responsibility for the making of cricket laws until 1969.

Mary Rose a warship built in 1511 for Henry VIII and rebuilt in 1536, which sank in action off Portsmouth in 1545. Its remains were salvaged in 1982 in a complex and much-publicized operation, and are now exhibited at Portsmouth.

marzipan *noun* a sweet paste of crushed almonds and sugar, used to decorate cakes, make sweets, etc. [from Italian *marzapane*]

Masada *or* **Mezada** a Roman hilltop fortress established 37–31 BC by the Palestinian ruler Herod in barren mountains W of the Dead Sea. It was seized by Zealots during the First Jewish Revolt in AD 66–70, and was taken by the Roman army in AD 73 after a lengthy siege which culminated in the mass suicide of all the defenders. It has become a symbol of Jewish solidarity and resistance, and is one of Israel's major tourist attractions.

Masai *or* **Maasai** a people of the Rift Valley area of Kenya and Tanzania, who speak a Nilotic language (present-day population is c.230 000). They are nomadic and semi-nomadic cattle herders, organized in a complex age-set system which provided warriors under control of ritual leaders. In some regions they are being encouraged to turn to sedentary farming.

Masaryk, Thomáš (Garrigue) (1850–1937) Czechoslovakian statesman, born in Hodonin, Moravia. An ardent Slovak, while in exile during World War I he organized the Czech independence movement. As the first President of the Czech Republic (1918–35), he was re-elected on three occasions.

masc. *abbrev.* masculine.

Mascagni, Pietro (1863–1945) Italian composer, born in Leghorn (Livorno). In 1890 he produced his highly successful one-act opera, *Cavalleria rusticana*. His many later operas failed to repeat this success, though arias and intermezzi from them are still performed (eg *L'Amico Fritz*, 1891 and *Le Maschere*, 1901).

mascara *noun* a cosmetic for darkening the eyelashes, applied with a brush. [from Italian *mascara*, mask]

Mascarene Islands, French **Archipel des Mascareignes** an island group in the Indian Ocean, 700–800km/450–500mi E of Madagascar. It includes Réunion, Mauritius, and Rodrigues. [named after the 16c Portuguese navigator, Mascarenhas.]

mascarpone *noun* a soft Italian cream cheese. [from Italian *mascarpone*]

mascot *noun* a person, animal, or thing thought to bring good luck. [from French *mascotte*, from Provençal *mascotto*, charm]

masculine — *adj.* **1** of, typical of, or suitable for men. **2** *said of a woman* mannish; unfeminine. **3** *Grammar* of or referring to one of the (usually two or three) classes into which nouns are divided in many languages, the class including males. — *noun Grammar* the masculine gender. [from Latin *masculinus*, from *masculus,* male]

masculinity *noun* **1** being masculine. **2** something that is masculine.

Masefield, John (1878–1967) English poet and novelist, born in Ledbury, Herefordshire. He served in the merchant navy, and returned to England in 1897 where he became a journalist. His sea poetry includes *Salt Water Ballads* (1902) and *Dauber* (1913), and his narrative poetry *Reynard the Fox* (1919). He also wrote novels (eg *Sard Harker*, 1924), and plays (eg *The Trial of Jesus*, 1925). He was made Poet Laureate in 1930.

maser *noun* a device for increasing the strength of microwaves, used in radar. [from the initial letters of *microwave amplification by stimulated emission of radiation*]

Maseru POP (1986) 109 000, the capital of Lesotho, founded in 1869. It is situated on the R Caledon, 130km/81mi E of Bloemfontein (South Africa); altitude 1 506m.

mash — *verb* **1** (*also* **mash something up**) to beat or crush it into a pulpy mass. **2** to mix (malt) with hot water. — *noun* **1** a boiled mixture of grain and water used to feed farm animals. **2** a mixture of crushed malt and hot water, used in brewing. **3** any soft mass. **4** *colloq.* mashed potatoes. [from Anglo-Saxon *masc*]

Mashhad *or* **Meshed** POP (1990e) 1.9m, the second-largest city in Iran and the capital of Mashhad district, Khorasan. It is situated in the NE of the country, near the Turkmenistan border, just S of the R Kashaf. NOTABLE FEATURE Shrine of Imam Ali Reza (9c).

mashie *or* **mashy** *noun* an old-fashioned iron golf club for playing lofting shots; the modern equivalent is the number five iron. [perhaps from French *massue*, club]

mask — *noun* **1** any covering for the face, worn for amusement, for protection, or as a disguise. **2** *literary* anything that disguises the truth, eg false behaviour: *a mask of light-heartedness.* — *verb* **1** to put a mask on. **2** to disguise or conceal. [from Arabic *maskharah*, clown]

masked *adj.* **1** wearing or as if wearing a mask. **2** disguised, concealed.

Maskell, Dan(iel) (1908–92) English tennis player and broadcaster. He was one of the leading professional tennis players of the 1930s, and a commentator from 1950.

masking *noun Photog.* the process of using a screen (or mask) to cover part of a light-sensitive surface, usually so that a second image may be superimposed subsequently.

masking tape sticky paper tape used in painting to cover the edge of a surface to be left unpainted.

masochism *noun* **1** the practice of deriving sexual pleasure from pain or humiliation inflicted by another person. **2** *colloq.* a tendency to take pleasure in one's own suffering. [from Leopold von Sacher Masoch (1836–95), the Austrian novelist who described it]

masochist *noun* a person who derives sexual pleasure from pain.

masochistic *adj.* relating to or typical of masochism or a masochist.

mason *noun* **1** same as STONEMASON. **2** (*often* **Mason**) a freemason. [from Old French *masson*]

Mason–Dixon Line the border between Maryland and Pennsylvania, drawn in 1763–7 by British astronomer Charles Mason (1730–87) and his colleague Jeremiah Dixon. It is regarded as the boundary of 'the South'.

masonic *adj.* (*often* **Masonic**) relating to freemasons.

masonry *noun* **1** the part of a building built by a mason; stonework and brickwork. **2** the craft of a mason. **3** (*often* **Masonry**) freemasonry.

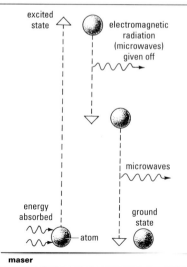

maser

Masoretes *or* **Massoretes** the Jewish scholars considered responsible for preserving traditions regarding the text of the Hebrew Bible, and for creating a system of vowel signs to reflect the pronunciation of the Hebrew consonantal text in their day. This vocalized text (c.9c–10c) was known as the Masoretic Text, the basis for the text normally used today. [Hebrew, = transmitters of tradition]

masque *noun* a kind of dramatic entertainment performed to music by masked actors in 16c–17c English royal courts. [from French *masque*, mask] ◇ Masques performed at the Tudor and (especially) Stuart courts in the period between 1600 and 1640 were extravagant spectacles in which a common theme or emblematic story was illustrated and acted through poetry, song, and dance, with elaborate costume and mechanical scenery. The most noteworthy were a result of the collaboration between the Court Poet, Ben Jonson (who was the first to use the French word for 'mask'), and the architect and scenic designer, Inigo Jones. Though masque was never revived after the Civil War, the techniques used in its production had a significant influence on the development of opera and ballet.

masquerade — *noun* **1** a pretence or show. **2** a formal dance at which the guests wear masks and costumes. — *verb intrans.* (*often* **masquerade as someone** *or* **something**) to disguise oneself; to pretend to be someone or something else: *was masquerading as a vicar / a squalid town masquerading as a city.* [from French *mascarade*]

Mass. *abbrev.* Massachusetts.

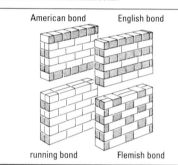

masonry: brickwork bonds

mass[1] — *noun* **1** *Physics* the amount of matter that an object contains, which is a measure of its inertia, ie the extent to which it resists acceleration if acted on by a force. **2** a large (usually shapeless) quantity gathered together; a lump. **3** *colloq.* (*also* **masses**) a large quantity or number. **4** majority; bulk. **5** *technical* a measure of the quantity of matter in a body. **6** (**the masses**) ordinary people. **7** an area of uniform colour or shading in art. — *adj.* involving a large number of people: *a mass meeting.* — *verb intrans., trans.* to gather or cause to gather in large numbers. [from French *masse*, from Latin *massa*, lump] ◇ Mass differs from weight in that it does not change according to the force of gravity. As an object moves away from Earth its weight gets smaller (because the force of gravity decreases), but its mass remains constant. The SI unit of mass is the kilogram.

mass[2] *noun* (*also* **Mass**) **1** *in the Roman Catholic and Orthodox Churches* the Eucharist, a celebration of Christ's last supper; the ceremony in which this occurs. **2** a part of the text of this ceremony set to music and sung by a choir or congregation. [from Anglo-Saxon *mæsse*] ◇ Bread and wine are consecrated by the priest and the elements (usually bread alone) distributed among the faithful. Masses perform different functions in the life of the Church, eg a Requiem Mass for the dead, a Nuptial Mass for a marriage, etc.

Massachusetts POP (1990) 6m, a New England state in NE USA, divided into 14 counties. AREA 21 455sq km/8 284sq mi. It is bounded E and S by the Atlantic Ocean and is the third most densely populated state in the USA. PHYSICAL DESCRIPTION rises from an indented coastline to a stony, upland interior and gentle, rolling hills to the W; the Connecticut R flows N–S across the W part of the state, the Housatonic R flows S near the W border, and the Merrimack R enters the Atlantic Ocean in the NE; in the SE is the Cape Cod peninsula; the Berkshire Hills rise between the Housatonic and Connecticut rivers; the highest point is Mt Greylock (1 049m). HISTORY the Pilgrim Fathers settled at Plymouth in 1620; the form of government by town meeting which developed is regarded as a foundation of American democracy; the first shots of the US War of Independence were fired at Lexington in 1775; it is one of the original states of the Union and the sixth to ratify the Constitution; Massachusetts is known as the 'Bay State' or 'Old Colony State'. CAPITAL Boston. CHIEF TOWNS Cambridge, Springfield, Worcester. ECONOMY electronics; printing and publishing; timber; nursery and greenhouse produce, vegetables, cranberries; tourism (many coastal resorts).

Massachusetts Bay Company a joint stock company established (1629) by royal charter in New England, America, to promote trade and colonization. In 1630 it transferred completely to Massachusetts, where its charter remained the legal basis of the colony until it was revoked in 1684.

Massachusetts Institute of Technology see MIT.

massacre — noun **1** a cruel killing of large numbers of people or animals. **2** colloq. an overwhelming defeat. — verb **1** to kill cruelly and in large numbers. **2** colloq. to defeat overwhelmingly. [from French massacre]

massage — noun a technique of easing pain or stiffness in the body, especially the muscles, by rubbing, kneading and tapping with the hands; a body treatment using this technique. — verb **1** to perform massage on. **2** to alter (eg statistics) to produce a more favourable result. [from French massage, from Greek massein, to knead]

Massawa or **Mitsiwa** POP (1984e) 15 000, a seaport in Eritrea, NE Africa. It is situated on the Red Sea coast, 65km/40mi NE of Asmara. HISTORY occupied by Italy from 1885 until 1941; capital of the Italian colony of Eritrea until 1897, largely rebuilt after an earthquake in 1921.

Masséna, André (1758–1817) French soldier, a leading general in the Revolutionary and Napoleonic Wars, born in Nice. He distinguished himself in Napoleon's Italian campaign (1796–7), when he defeated the Russians at Zürich (1799) and successfully defended Genoa (1800). Created Marshal of the Empire in 1804, he commanded the army in Italy, and was made Duke of Rivoli (1807). After the Austrian campaign (1809) he was made Prince of Essling. However, forced to retreat in the Iberian Peninsula by Wellington's forces, he was relieved of his command in 1810.

mass-energy equation Physics a relationship, expressed as $E=mc^2$ where E is energy, m is mass, and c is the velocity of light, according to which all energy has mass, as opposed to the view that mass and energy are interconvertible.

Massenet, Jules (Emile Frédéric) (1842–1912) French composer, born near St Etienne. He studied at the Paris Conservatoire and was professor there (1878–96) before he made his name with the comic opera Don César de Bazan (1872). Other operas include Manon (1884), Werther (1892), and Thaïs (1894), and he also wrote oratorios, orchestral suites, music for piano, and songs.

masseur noun a person trained to carry out massage. [from French masseur]

masseuse noun a woman trained to carry out massage. [from French masseuse]

mass extinction Biol. at certain times in the Earth's history, the dying out of many animal species at more or less the same time, eg the disappearance of the dinosaurs (and various marine invertebrates, including ammonites, about 65 million years ago.

massif noun Geol. a mountainous plateau that differs structurally and topographically from the surrounding lowland, the rocks of which it is composed usually being older and harder. [from French massif; see MASSIVE]

Massif Central an area of ancient rocks in SE central France, occupying about one sixth of the country, and generally lying over 300m above sea level. The highest peak is Puy de Sancy in the Monts Dore (1 885m). There are massive limestone beds with gorges, crags, and caves, as well as volcanic rocks such as the Monts Dômes. The Massif Central is the source of the Loire, Allier, Cher, and Creuse rivers. ECONOMY farming; several industrial centres; tourism (with winter sports at Le Mont Dore, Super Besse, and Super Lioran).

Massine, Léonide, originally **Leonid Fyodorovich Miassin** (1896–1979) Russian dancer and choreographer, born in Moscow. He was principal dancer and choreographer with Sergei Diaghilev (1914–21, 1925–8) and the Ballet Russe de Monte Carlo (1938–43), and produced and danced in many ballets in Europe and the USA. He also choreographed some controversial 'symphonic ballets', such as Choreartium (1933), which was danced to the fourth symphony of Brahms.

Massinger, Philip (1583–1640) English dramatist, born near Salisbury, Wiltshire. His early plays were written mainly in collaboration with others, particularly John Fletcher. His comedies include The City Madam (1632) and A New Way to Pay Old Debts (1633).

massive adj. **1** very big, solid, and heavy. **2** colloq. very large: a massive salary. [from French massif, from masse, mass]

massively adv. in a massive way; to a massive degree.

mass market Econ. a market for goods that have been mass-produced.

mass media those forms of communication that reach large numbers of people, eg television and newspapers.

mass number Chem. the total number of protons and neutrons in the nucleus of an atom. It has different values for different isotopes of the same element. — Also called nucleon number.

mass-produce verb to produce in a standard form in great quantities, especially using mechanization.

mass-produced adj. produced in a standardized form in large numbers.

mass-production noun the process or state of being mass-produced.

mass spectrograph a device in which beams of positively charged atoms, or ions, are passed through electric and magnetic fields to separate them according to their charge-to-mass ratios. It is used to give precise measurements of the atomic masses of different isotopes of an element.

mass spectrograph Chem. an instrument that is used to measure the relative atomic masses of isotopes of chemical elements, by passing beams of ions (charged atoms) through electric and magnetic fields so that they can be separated according to the ratio of their charge to their mass. The ions strike a photographic plate, which is then developed in order to show their distribution.

mass spectrometer Chem. a mass spectrograph that is used to measure the relative atomic masses of isotopes of chemical elements, and that uses an electrical detector, as opposed to a photographic plate, to determine the distribution of ions (charged atoms).

Massys or **Matsys, Quentin** (c.1466–c.1530) Flemish painter, born in Louvain, who worked in Antwerp from 1491. His pictures are mostly religious, treated with a reverent spirit, but with decided touches of realism. His many portraits include the notable Erasmus, and Le Prêteur et sa Femme (1514, The Banker and his Wife, Louvre, Paris).

mast[1] noun any upright wooden or metal supporting pole, especially one carrying the sails of a ship, or a radio or television aerial.
— **before the mast** Naut. serving as an apprentice seaman.
[from Anglo-Saxon mæst]

mast[2] noun the nuts of various forest trees, especially beech, oak, and chestnut, used as food for pigs. [from Anglo-Saxon mæst]

mastaba noun an ancient Egyptian tomb built of brick or stone with sloping sides and a flat roof. This superstructure contained an outer chamber or chapel in which offerings were made, connected to a secret inner chamber (the serdab) containing the image of the dead person. A shaft led to the underground burial chamber. [from Arabic mastabah, bench]

mastectomy noun (PL. **mastectomies**) the surgical removal of a woman's breast. [from Greek mastos, breast + -ECTOMY]

master — noun **1** a person, especially male, who commands or controls. **2** the owner, especially male, of a dog, slave, etc. **3** a person with outstanding skill in a particular activity. **4** the commanding officer on a merchant ship. **5** a fully qualified craftsman, allowed to train others. **6** old use a male teacher. **7** (**Master**) a title for the heads of certain university colleges. **8** (also **master copy**) an original from which copies are made. **9** (**Master**) a degree of the level above Bachelor, or a person who holds this degree: Master of Arts. **10** (**Master**) a title for a boy too young to be called Mr. — adj. **1** fully qualified; highly skilled; expert. **2** main; principal: master bedroom. **3** controlling: master switch. — verb **1** to overcome or defeat (eg feelings or an opponent). **2** to become skilled in. [from Latin magister, from magnus, great]

Master Antenna Television (ABBREV. **MATV**) in the UK, the use of a single antenna to serve a number of television receivers, either directly (eg in an apartment block) or from a central station by cable distribution.

master-at-arms noun (PL. **masters-at-arms**) a ship's officer responsible for maintaining discipline.

Master Builder, The (Bygmester Solness) a play by Henrik Ibsen (1892). Heavily reliant on symbolism, it is a treatment of ambition, guilt, and fantasy through the reactions of a leading architect when his views are challenged by a young woman.

masterful adj. showing the authority, skill, or power of a master.

masterfully adv. in a masterful way.

master key a key which opens a number of locks, each of which has its own different key.

masterliness noun being masterly.

masterly adj. showing the skill of a master.

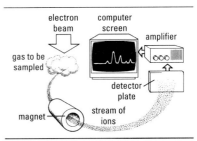

mass spectrometer

mastermind — *noun* **1** a person of great intellectual ability. **2** the person responsible for devising a complex scheme or plan. — *verb* to be the mastermind of (a scheme, etc).

master of ceremonies an announcer, especially of speakers at a formal dinner, or of performers in a stage entertainment.

Master of the Queen's Music *or* **Master of the King's Music** an office established (1626) by Charles I, first held by Nicholas Lanier (1588–1666), who directed the entire royal music personnel. Later, duties also included composing odes for special occasions. Since 1975 Malcolm Williamson has held the office; nowadays the title is an honour, and the Master's duties are nominal.

masterpiece *or* **masterwork** *noun* an extremely skilful piece of work, especially the greatest work of an artist or writer.

Masters, William Howell (1915–) US gynaecologist and sexologist, born in Cleveland, Ohio. He joined the faculty of the Washington University School of Medicine in St Louis (1947), where his studies in the psychology and physiology of sexual intercourse were carried out using volunteer subjects under laboratory conditions. Much of his research has been done in collaboration with his wife Virginia Johnson; they published *Human Sexual Response* (1966), an international best-seller, and *On Sex and Human Loving* (1986).

Masters the popular name for the US Masters invitational golf tournament, played every April over four rounds of the course in Augusta, Georgia. It was first held in 1934. The winner receives a coveted green jacket as part of the prize.

masterstroke *noun* a very clever or well-timed action.

mastery *noun* **1** (**mastery of something**) great skill or knowledge in it. **2** (**mastery over something** *or* **someone**) control over them.

masthead *noun* **1** the top of a ship's mast. **2** the title of a newspaper or periodical printed at the top of its front page.

mastic *noun* **1** a gum obtained from a Mediterranean evergreen tree, used in making varnish. **2** any of various waterproof putty-like pastes used as joint-sealers in the building trade. [from Greek *mastiche*]

masticate *verb trans., intrans. formal, technical* to chew (food). [from Latin *masticare*]

mastication *noun* chewing.

mastiff *noun* a large powerful short-haired breed of dog, formerly used in hunting. [from Old French *mastin*, from Latin *mansuetus*, tame]

mastitis *noun* inflammation of a woman's breast or an animal's udder, usually caused by bacterial infection. [from Greek *mastos*, breast + -ITIS]

mastodon *noun* any of several mammals, now extinct, that were widespread during the Tertiary Era, and from which elephants are thought to have evolved. The mastodon had two pairs of tusks, a long flexible trunk, and a hairy coat similar to that of the mammoth. [from Greek *mastos*, breast + *odontos*, tooth]

mastoid — *adj.* like a nipple or breast. — *noun* the raised area of bone behind the ear. [from Greek *mastoeides*, like a breast]

Mastroianni, Marcello (1923–) Italian film actor, born in Fontana Liri. His film career began in 1947, and leading roles in *Le Notti Bianche* (White Knights, 1957), *La Dolce Vita* (The Sweet Life, 1959) and *Otto e Mezzo* (8½, 1963) established him as an international star. He appeared several times with Sophia Loren, and in later years in *Blood Feud* (1981), *Oci Ciornie* (Black Eyes, 1987), and *Stanno Tutti Bene* (Everybody's Fine, 1990).

masturbate *verb intrans., trans.* to rub or stroke the genitals of (oneself or someone else) so as to produce sexual arousal, usually to the point of orgasm or ejaculation. [from Latin *masturbari*]

masturbation *noun* the act or practice of masturbating.

masturbatory *adj.* relating to or aiding masturbation.

mat¹ — *noun* **1** a flat piece of any of various materials in carpet-like form, used as a decorative or protective floor-covering, or for wiping shoes on to remove dirt. **2** a smaller piece of fabric, or a harder material, used under a plate, vase, etc to protect a surface from heat or scratches. **3** a carpet-like covering, eg of vegetation or hair. — *verb trans., intrans.* (**matted, matting**) to become or cause to become tangled into a dense untidy mass. [from Anglo-Saxon *matt* or *matte*]

mat² same as MATT.

Matabeleland POP (1982) 1.5m, a region in W and S Zimbabwe, between the Zambezi and Limpopo rivers. It is named after the Matabele Bantu, a Zulu tribe originally located in Natal and the Transvaal. The region was acquired by the British South Africa Company in 1889 and became part of Southern Rhodesia in 1923. CHIEF TOWN Bulawayo.

matador *noun* the principal toreador in a bullfight, the man who kills the bull. [from Spanish *matador*, from *matar*, to kill]

Mata-Utu POP (1983) 815, the capital of the French Overseas Territory of Wallis and Futuna, S central Pacific Ocean. It is situated on Uvea I in the Wallis Is.

match¹ *noun* **1** a short thin piece of wood or strip of card coated on the tip with a substance that ignites when rubbed against a rough surface, used to light fires, etc. **2** a slow-burning fuse used in cannons. [from Old French *mesche*]

match² — *noun* **1** a contest or game. **2** (**a match for someone** *or* **something**) a person or thing that is similar or identical to, or combines well with, another. **3** a person or thing able to equal, or surpass, another: *meet one's match*. **4** a partnership or pairing; a suitable partner, eg in marriage. — *verb* **1** *trans., intrans.* (*also* **match up** *or* **match something up**) to combine well; to be well suited or compatible; to put (matching people or things) together. **2** to set in competition; to hold up in comparison. **3** to be equal to; to make, produce, perform, etc an equivalent to: *cannot match let alone beat the offer.* [from Anglo-Saxon *gemœcca*, spouse]

matchbox *noun* a small cardboard box for holding matches.

matching *adj.* similar; compatible; part of the same set.

matchless *adj. literary* having no equal; superior to all.

matchmaker *noun* a person who tries to arrange romantic partnerships between people.

matchmaking *noun* the activity of a matchmaker.

match point the stage in a game at which only one more point is needed by a player to win; the winning point.

matchstick *noun* the stem of a wooden match.

matchwood *noun* **1** wood suitable for making matches. **2** splinters.

mate¹ — *noun* **1** an animal's breeding partner. **2** *colloq.* a person's sexual partner, especially a husband or wife. **3** *colloq.* a companion or friend, often used as a form of address, especially to a man. **4** (*in compounds*) a colleague; a person with whom one shares something: *workmate / flatmate*. **5** a tradesman's assistant. **6** one of a pair. **7** any officer below the rank of master on a merchant ship. — *verb* **1** *intrans. said of animals* to copulate. **2** to bring (animals) together for breeding. **3** *intrans., trans.* to marry. **4** to join as a pair. [related to Anglo-Saxon *gemetta*, guest at one's table]

mate² see CHECKMATE.

maté *or* **mate** *noun* **1** a S American species of holly tree. **2** a type of tea made from its dried leaves. [from Quechua *mati*, a gourd (in which the tea is made)]

mater *noun humorous, old colloq.* use a mother, also used as a form of address. [from Latin *mater*]

material — *noun* **1** any substance out of which something is, or may be, made. **2** cloth; fabric. **3** (**materials**) instruments or tools needed for a particular activity. **4** information providing the substance from which a book, television programme, etc is prepared. — *adj.* **1** relating to, or consisting of solid matter; not abstract or spiritual. **2** relating to physical, not emotional, well-being: *material comforts.* **3** (**material to something**) *technical* important; significant; relevant: *facts not material to the discussion.* [from Latin *materia*, matter]

materialism *noun* **1** *often derog.* excessive interest in material possessions and financial success. **2** *Philos.* the theory stating that only material things exist, especially denying the existence of a soul or spirit.

materialist — *noun* a follower of or believer in materialism.

materialistic *adj.* relating to or characteristic of materialism.

materialization *or* **materialisation** *noun* the act or process of materializing or being materialized.

materialize *or* **materialise** *verb intrans.* **1** to become real, visible, or tangible; to appear. **2** to become fact; to happen.

materially *adv.* **1** *formal* to an important or significant extent. **2** with regard to physical well-being.

maternal *adj.* **1** of, typical of, or like a mother. **2** related on the mother's side of the family. [from Latin *maternus*, from *mater*, mother]

maternally *adv.* in a maternal way.

maternity — *noun* the state of being or becoming a mother. — *adj.* relating to pregnancy or giving birth. [from Latin *maternus*]

matey *or* **maty** *adj.* (**matier, matiest**) *colloq.* friendly or familiar, often in an insincere way.

mathematical *adj.* **1** of, relating to, or using mathematics. **2** very exact or accurate.

mathematical linguistics, the study of language using mathematical concepts, particularly algebraic methods. It is especially important in the formalization of linguistic theory within generative grammar. See also STATISTICAL LINGUISTICS.

mathematically *adv.* by the use of mathematics.

mathematician *noun* a student of, or expert in, mathematics.

mathematics *sing. noun* the science dealing with measurements, numbers, quantities and shapes, usually expressed as symbols. [from Greek *mathematike*, relating to learning, from *manthanein*, to learn]

Mather, Cotton (1662–1728) American colonial minister, born in Boston, Massachusetts, who became the most prominent Puritan minister in New England during his time. A polymath, he reported on American botany, and was one of the earliest New England historians. However, his reputation was irrevocably harmed by his involvement in the Salem witchcraft trials of 1692.

Mathilda a female first name. [a Latin form of a Germanic name, composed of *maht* or *meht*, might + *hild*, battle]

maths *sing. noun colloq.* mathematics.

matily *adv.* with a matey manner.

matinée *or* **matinee** *noun* an afternoon performance of a play or showing of a film. [from French *matinée*, morning]

Mathematical Signs and Symbols

+	plus; positive; underestimate
−	minus; negative; overestimate
±	plus or minus; positive or negative; degree of accuracy
∓	minus or plus; negative or positive
×	multiplies (colloq. 'times') (6×4)
	multiplies (colloq. 'times') (6.4); scalar product of two vectors $(A \cdot B)$
÷	divided by $(6 \div 4)$
	divided by; ratio of (6/4)
—	divided by; ratio of ($\frac{6}{4}$)
=	equals
≠	not equal to
≡	identical with
≢	not identical with
	ratio of (6:4); scalar product of two tensors (Y:Z)
::	proportionately equals (1:2 :2:4)
≈	approximately equal to; equivalent to; similar to
>	greater than
≫	much greater than
≯	not greater than
<	less than
≪	much less than
≮	not less than
⩾, ≧, ≥	equal to or greater than
⩽, ≦, ≤	equal to or less than
∝	directly proportional to
( )	parentheses
[ ]	brackets
{ }	braces
—	vinculum; division (a−b); chord of circle or length of line (A̅B̅); arithmetic mean (X̅)
∞	infinity
→	approaches the limit
√	square root
³√, ⁴√	cube root, fourth root, etc.
!	factorial $(4! = 4 \times 3 \times 2 \times 1)$
%	percent
′	prime; minute(s) of arc; foot/feet
″	double prime; second(s) of arc; inch(es)
⌢	arc of circle
°	degree of arc
∠, ∠ˢ	angle(s)
⅄	equiangular
⊥	perpendicular
∥	parallel
○, Ⓢ	circle(s)
△, ⚠	triangle(s)
□	square
▭	rectangle
▱	parallelogram
≅	congruent to
∴	therefore
∵	because
m̲	measured by
△	increment
Σ	summation
∏	product
∫	integral sign
▽	del: differential operator
∪	union
∩	interaction

---

matinée jacket or **matinée coat** a baby's short jacket or coat.

matins *sing. or pl. noun* **1** *RC Church* the first of the seven canonical hours, periods during the day set aside for formal prayer. See also COMPLINE, LAUDS, NONE², SEXT, TERCE, VESPERS. **2** *Church of E.* the service of morning prayer. [from Latin *matutinus*, of the morning]

Matisse, Henri (Emile Benoît) (1869–1954) French artist, born in Le Cateau. He originally studied law, but turned to painting and from 1904 became the leader of the Fauves (Wild Beasts). Although he painted several pictures influenced by Cubism and Impressionism, his most characteristic paintings display a bold use of brilliant areas of primary colour, organized within a rhythmic two-dimensional design. His works include *Bonheur de vivre* (1906), *L'Escargot* (1953), and *La Liseuse* (1894, Woman Reading). He also produced works of sculpture, and his works in this field include the bronze *The Back I–IV* (1909–30).

Matlock POP (1981) 14 000, the county town of Derbyshire, central England, situated in West Derbyshire district. It lies 14km/9mi SW of Chesterfield and was formerly a spa town.

Mato Grosso, formerly **Matto Grosso** POP (1991) 2m, a state in Centro-Oeste region, central W Brazil, bordered to the SW by Bolivia. AREA 881 000sq km/340 000sq mi. PHYSICAL DESCRIPTION it is drained by tributaries of the R Amazon to the N, those of the R Paraguay to the S, and those of the R Araguaia to the E. Half the area is under forest; SW is the 611sq km/236sq mi Cará-Car Biological Reserve (1971) and NE is the Xingu National Park. CAPITAL Cuiabá. The states of Mato Grosso in the N and Mato Grosso do Sul (capital Campo Grande) in the S were separated in 1979. The name is also given to the whole plateau area in the S (the Planalto de Mato Grosso). ECONOMY timber; rubber; metallurgy.

Maṭraḥ POP (1981) 14 000, a commercial town and major port in Oman, on the Gulf of Oman. It lies on a peninsula backed by the E Hajar hill country. The town is the E terminus of the dual carriageway which runs parallel to the Gulf of Oman. NOTABLE FEATURES forts built by the Portuguese.

Matra Mountains a mountain range in N Hungary, which constitutes the S spur of the Carpathian Mts. The range rises to 1 014m at Mt Kékes, the highest peak in Hungary.

matri- *combining form* of a woman or a mother: *matricide*. [from Latin *mater*, mother]

matriarch *noun* the female head of a family, community, or tribe. [from MATRI-, PATRIARCH]

matriarchal *adj.* of, ruled by, or resembling a matriarch.

matriarchy *noun* (PL. **matriarchies**) a social system in which women are the heads of families or tribes, and property and power passes from mother to daughter.
◇ Matriarchy occurs in certain parts of central Africa (where it is often associated with polyandry), in the S Pacific, and in certain parts of India.

matric see MATRICULATION.

matrices see MATRIX.

matricidal *adj.* relating to or involving matricide.

matricide *noun* **1** the killing of a mother by her own child. **2** a person who kills his or her own mother.

matriculate *verb trans., intrans.* to admit or become eligible to be admitted as a member, especially of a university or college. [from Latin *matriculare*, to register]

matriculation *noun* **1** the process of matriculating. **2** *colloq.* **matric** formerly, a university or college entrance examination taken at school.

matrilineal *Anthropol.* denoting descent or kin-

ship reckoned through the mother, or through females alone.

matrimonial *adj.* relating to marriage.

matrimony *noun* (PL. **matrimonies**) **1** the state of being married. **2** the wedding ceremony. [from Latin *matrimonium*, wedlock]

matrix *noun* (PL. **matrices**, **matrixes**) **1** *Maths.* a square or rectangular arrangement of symbols or numbers, in rows or columns, usually enclosed by large parentheses, vertical lines, or square brackets. Matrices are used to summarize relationships between different quantities, and can be used to solve simultaneous equations. **2** *Biol.* in tissues such as bone and cartilage, the substance in which cells are embedded. **3** *Anat.* the tissue lying beneath the body and root of a fingernail or toenail, and from which it develops. **4** *Geol.* the rock in which a mineral or fossil is embedded. **5** *Printing* a mould, especially one from which printing type is produced. **6** *old use* the womb. [from Latin *matrix*, womb]

matron *noun* **1** the former title of the head of the nursing staff in a hospital (now usually called *senior nursing officer*). **2** a woman in charge of nursing and domestic arrangements in an institution, eg a school or old people's home. **3** any dignified or solemn middle-aged to elderly (especially married) woman. [from French *matrone*, from Latin *mater*, mother]

matronly *adj., said of a woman* **1** dignified; authoritative. **2** *euphemistic* plump because of middle-age.

matron of honour (PL. **matrons of honour**) a married woman who is a bride's chief attendant at a wedding. See also MAID OF HONOUR.

matt or **mat** *adj.* having a dull surface without gloss or shine. [from French *mat*, dull colour or unpolished surface]

matted *adj., often said of hair* tangled.

Matteotti, Giacomo (1885–1924) Italian politician, born in Fratta Polesine. A member of the Italian Chamber of Deputies, he began to organize the United Socialist Party in 1921 and became an outspoken opponent of Mussolini's fascists (1922–4). His protests against fascist election outrages in 1924 led to his murder in Rome, which provoked a crisis that almost ended the fascist regime.

matter — *noun* **1** the substance from which all physical things are made; material. **2** material of a particular kind: *vegetable matter*. **3** a subject or topic; a concern, affair, or question: *if it's a matter of money* / *matters of principle*. **4** content as distinct from style or form. **5** (**a matter of** ...) an approximate amount: *in a matter of minutes*. **6** pus. — *verb intrans.* to be important or significant.
— **as a matter of fact** in fact.
be the matter with someone or **something** to be the trouble, difficulty, or thing that is wrong.
for that matter as far as that is concerned.
no matter it is not important.
no matter ... regardless of: *no matter when she comes.*
[from Latin *materia*, subject or substance]

Matterhorn, French **Mont Cervin**, Italian **Monte Cervino** a mountain peak in Switzerland, situated in the Pennine Alps, on the Swiss–Italian border, SW of Zermatt. HEIGHT 4 478m.

matter-of-fact *adj.* calm and straightforward, not excited or emotional.

matter-of-factly *adv.* in a matter-of-fact way.

matter-of-factness *noun* being matter-of-fact.

matte shot a motion picture scene in which a mask, or matte, restricts the image exposed so that a second image can be superimposed subsequently.

Matthew, St (1c AD) one of the 12 Apostles of Jesus Christ. He was a tax collector before his conversion, and he is called Levi (his name may have been Matthew the Levite) in Mark 2.14 and

Luke 5.27. According to tradition, he was the author of the first Gospel, was a missionary to the Hebrews, and suffered martyrdom. His feast day is 21 Sep (W Church) or 16 Nov (E Church).

Matthew a male first name, borne by the Apostle and evangelist. [from Hebrew *Mattathia*, gift of God]

Matthew, Gospel according to the first work of the New Testament canon, one of the four canonical Gospels, attributed by 2c traditions to the Apostle and former tax-collector, Matthew. It is noteworthy for its story of the magi at the birth of Jesus Christ, its wealth of moral instruction (as in the Sermon on the Mount), and its emphasis on Christ as the fulfilment of the Old Testament expectations.

Matthew Paris (c.1200–59) English chronicler and Benedictine monk. Although he concentrated on the history of his own monastery, St Albans Abbey, he gave in his main work (*Chronica Majora*) the fullest available account of events in England between 1236 and 1259, as well as information on other European countries. He was noted for his maps and drawings.

Matthews, Drummond Hoyle (1931–) English geologist who worked in the Falkland Islands before becoming a researcher at Cambridge University. He predicted in 1963 the patterns of rock magnetization near mid-ocean ridges which would occur according to the 'sea-floor spreading' theory of Harry Hess. Once experimentally confirmed, this led to the widespread acceptance of the theory of continental drift.

Matthews, Sir Stanley (1915–) English footballer, born in Hanley, Staffordshire. He started his career with Stoke City in 1931, before a controversial transfer to Blackpool in 1947. In 1953 he played a significant role in the Football Association Cup Final, a game which has been called 'The Matthews Final'. He returned to Stoke in 1961, and continued to play First Division football until after the age of 50. He played for England 54 times, was twice the Footballer of the Year (1948, 1963), and was the inaugural winner of the European Footballer of the Year award in 1956. He later managed Port Vale, and became President of Stoke City Football Club in 1990.

matting *noun* material of rough woven fibres for making mats.

mattock *noun* a kind of pickaxe whose blade is flattened horizontally at one end, used for breaking up soil, etc. [from Anglo-Saxon *mattuc*]

mattress *noun* a large flat fabric-covered pad, now usually of foam rubber or springs, used for sleeping on, by itself or on a supporting frame. [from Old French *materas*, from Arabic *almatrah*, place where anything is thrown]

maturate *verb trans., intrans.* **1** to make or become mature. **2** *Medicine* to discharge or cause to discharge pus. [from Latin *maturare*]

maturation *noun* bringing or coming to maturity.

mature — *adj.* **1** fully grown or developed. **2** having or showing adult good sense. **3** *said of cheese, wine, etc* having a fully developed flavour. **4** *said of bonds, insurance policies, etc* paying out, or beginning to pay out, money to the holder. **5** *formal* carefully or thoroughly thought out. — *verb* **1** *trans., intrans.* to make or become fully developed, or adult in outlook. **2** *intrans. said of a life insurance policy, etc* to begin to produce a return. [from Latin *maturus*, ripe]

maturity *noun* ripeness, full development.

Matuyama, Motonori (1884–1958) Japanese geophysicist, born in Oita Prefecture. Professor at the Imperial University of Japan, from 1926 he studied the magnetism of rocks from Japan and Manchuria. These revealed how the Earth's magnetic field has changed over time,

sometimes reversing, allowing him to relate magnetic reversals to specific geological periods.

MATV *abbrev.* Master Antenna Television.

maty same as MATEY.

Mauchly, John William (1907–80) US physicist and inventor, born in Cincinnati. Working at the University of Pennsylvania, he collaborated in the development of some of the first modern computers. His team's conviction that computers had a commercial market played a large part in launching the computer revolution in the second half of the 20c.

Maud a poem by Alfred Lord Tennyson (1855) in which the melancholic narrator recounts the gloomy events of his life.

maudlin *adj.* foolishly sad or sentimental, especially when drunk. [from Anglo-Saxon *Maudelein*, Mary Magdalene, often portrayed weeping]

Maudling, Reginald (1917–79) English Conservative politician, born in London. Called to the Bar in 1940, he became an MP in 1950, and was Minister of Supply (1955–7), Paymaster-General (1957–9), President of the Board of Trade (1959–61), Colonial Secretary (1961–2), Chancellor of the Exchequer (1962–4), and Deputy Leader of the Opposition (1964). In 1970 he was Home Secretary in the government of Edward Heath, but resigned in 1972, when he became implicated in the bankruptcy proceedings of architect John Poulson.

Maudslay, Henry (1771–1831) English engineer, born in Woolwich, Kent. He was an apprentice to Joseph Bramah, set up on his own in 1797, and invented various types of machinery, including the metal lathe. With Joshua Field (1757–1863) he produced marine engines, and founded the firm of Maudslay, Sons and Field (1810).

Mauger, Ivan (Gerald) (1939–) New Zealand speedway rider, born in Christchurch. He rode for Wimbledon, Rye House, Eastbourne, Newcastle, Belle Vue, Exeter, and Hull between 1957 and 1982, and won the world individual title a record six times (1968–70, 1972, 1977, 1979). He also won two pairs world titles, four team titles, and the world long track title twice.

Maugham, W(illiam) Somerset (1874–1965) British writer, born in Paris. He qualified as a surgeon in London, and published his first novel *Liza of Lambeth* in 1897. After initial difficulty, he achieved success with his plays, four of which ran simultaneously in London in 1908. His later works include the novels *Of Human Bondage* (1915), *The Moon and Sixpence* (1919), *Cakes and Ale* (1930), and *The Razor's Edge* (1945). He is best known for his short stories, several of which were filmed, including *Quartet* (1949).

Maui POP (1988e) 84 000, the second-largest island in the US state of Hawaii, lying in the Pacific Ocean, NW of Hawaii I. It forms Maui County together with the islands of Lanai and Molokai. AREA 1 885sq km/728sq mi. CHIEF TOWN Wailuku. The town of Lahaina was once the capital of Hawaii; there is a resort at Kanapali. The island rises to 3 055m at Haleakala and has the only railway in the Pacific.

maul *verb* **1** to attack fiercely, usually tearing flesh. **2** to handle roughly or clumsily. **3** to subject to fierce criticism. — *noun Rugby* a quickly formed gathering of players from both teams around a player holding the ball. [from Latin *malleus*, hammer]

Mau Mau a secret society which led an anti-settler and anti-colonial revolt among the Kikuyu people of Kenya in the 1950s. It began (1952) with the murder of white settlers and Kikuyu 'loyalists' thought to be collaborating with colonial authorities, and the disruption it caused hastened the transition from colony to independent state.

Mauna Kea a dormant volcano in N central Hawaii I, USA, and the highest island mountain in the world. HEIGHT 4 201m. It has numerous cinder cones and is snow-capped in winter. On the summit at Mauna Kea Observatory there are several large telescopes.

Mauna Loa an active volcano in central Hawaii, USA, situated in Hawaii Volcanoes National Park. HEIGHT 4 169m. On its summit is Mokuaweoweo Crater which last erupted in 1984.

Maunder, Edward Walter (1851–1928) English astronomer, born in London. While working as an assistant at the Royal Greenwich Observatory, he kept daily records of the number of sunspots and established the pattern of latitude drift during the sunspot cycle, demonstrated in his 'butterfly diagram'. Studying historical records, he identified the period of very little sunspot activity in the 16c, the 'Maunder minimum'.

maunder *verb intrans.* (**maundered, maundering**) **1** (*also* **maunder on**) to talk in a rambling way. **2** to wander about, or behave, in an aimless way. [perhaps from obsolete *maunder*, to beg]

Maundy money *Brit.* silver money that is specially minted for the sovereign to distribute on Maundy Thursday.

Maundy Thursday the day before Good Friday. [from Old French *mande*, from Latin *mandatum*, command (from Christ's command in John 23.34)]

Maupassant, (Henry René Albert) Guy de (1850–93) French novelist and short-story writer, born near Dieppe. He served as a soldier and a government clerk, then took to writing and joined the Naturalist group led by Zola. His first success, *Boule de suif* (Ball of Fat, 1880), was followed by a decade in which he wrote c.300 short stories, as well as various novels including *Une Vie* (A Woman's Life, 1883) and *Bel-Ami* (1885). In 1892 he was committed to an asylum in Paris, where he died.

Mauretania a transatlantic Cunard passenger liner, launched in 1906. It made its maiden voyage in 1907, and held the Blue Riband Atlantic speed award until 1929. It was destroyed in 1935.

Mauriac, François (1885–1970) French novelist, born in Bordeaux. His works are set within Bordeaux provincial life, and deal with the Roman Catholic themes of temptation, sin, and redemption. His main works include the novels *Le Baiser au lépreux* (The Kiss to the Leper, 1922), *Thérèse Desqueyroux* (1927), and *Noeud de vipères* (Vipers' Tangle, 1932), and the play *Asmodée* (1938). He was awarded the Nobel Prize for Literature in 1952.

Maurice, Prins van Oranje, Graaf van Nassau (Prince of Orange, Count of Nassau) (1567–1625) son of William the Silent, born in Dilenburg. He became stadtholder of Holland and Zeeland (1587) and later (1589) of Utrecht, Overyssel, and Gelderland, and was also Captain-General of the armies of the United Provinces during their War of Independence from Spain. He checked the Spanish advance, and by his steady offensive (1590–1606) liberated the northern provinces of the Netherlands from Spain. During the renewed conflict with the Habsburgs, he commanded the new republic, and received help from England in the 1590s.

Maurice a male first name. [from the Latin name *Mauritius*, Moor]

Maurier, Dame Daphne du (1907–89) English novelist, born in London, the granddaughter of George du Maurier. She wrote several successful period romances and adventure stories, including *Jamaica Inn* (1936), *Rebecca* (1938), *My Cousin Rachel* (1951), and *The Flight of the Falcon* (1965). She also published plays, short stories, and literary reminiscences.

Maurier, George (Louis Palmella Busson) du (1834–96) British artist, illustrator, and writer, born in Paris. He studied chemistry but turned to art as a profession and from 1860 gained a reputation as a designer and book illustrator in London. He joined the staff of *Punch*, and became widely known as a gentle, graceful satirist of fashionable life. He also wrote and illustrated three novels, notably *Trilby* (1894).

Mauritania, French **Mauritanie**, Arabic **Muritaniyah**, official name **Islamic Republic of Mauritania**, French **République Islamique de Mauritanie** POP (1992e) 2.1m, a republic in NW Africa, divided into 12 regions and a capital district. AREA 1 029 920sq km/397 549sq mi. It is bounded SW by Senegal, S and E by Mali, NE by Algeria, N by Western Sahara, and W by the Atlantic Ocean. CAPITAL Nouakchott. CHIEF TOWNS Nouadhibou, Atar. TIME ZONE GMT. OFFICIAL LANGUAGES Arabic, French. CURRENCY the ouguija. PHYSICAL DESCRIPTION the Saharan zone in the N covers two thirds of the country with sand dunes, mountainous plateaux, and occasional oases; the coastal zone has minimal rainfall and little vegetation; savannah grasslands lie in the Sahelian zone; the Sénégal R zone is the chief agricultural region; the highest point is Kediat Idjill (915m) in the NW. CLIMATE dry and tropical with sparse rainfall; temperatures can rise to over 49°C in the Sahara. HISTORY discovered by the Portuguese in the 15c; became a French protectorate within French West Africa in 1903; became a French colony in 1920; gained independence in 1960; the Spanish withdrew from Western Sahara in 1976, and Mauritania occupied a large area in the S under the name of Tiris el Gharbia; they renounced all rights in 1979, after conflict with the Frenta Polisario guerrillas; there were military coups in 1978 and 1984; a new constitution in 1991 with the approval of multiparty elections; violent disturbances in 1989 on the border with Senegal resulted in the frontier being closed; it was re-opened and diplomatic relations with Senegal were restored in 1992. GOVERNMENT governed by an executive President (six-year term), who appoints a Prime Minister, National Assembly, and Senate. ECONOMY livestock, cereals, vegetables, dates; crop success is constantly under threat from drought; mining is based on vast iron ore reserves, also copper and gypsum; fish processing; gum arabic; textiles; cement, bricks; paints; industrial gas.

Mauritania

Mauritius POP (1992e) 1.1m, a small island nation in the Indian Ocean, c.800km/500mi E of Madagascar. AREA 1 865sq km/720sq mi; 61km/38mi long by 47km/29mi wide. It includes c.20 surrounding islets, and the dependencies of Rodrigues I, the Agalega Is, and the Cargados Carajos Is (St Brandon Is). The sovereignty of Tromelin I is in dispute between France and Mauritius. CAPITAL Port Louis. TIME ZONE GMT +4. More than two thirds of the population

are Indo-Mauritians; Hinduism (over 50%), Christianity (30%), and Islam (17%) are the chief religions. OFFICIAL LANGUAGE English; French is also spoken. CURRENCY the Mauritius rupee. PHYSICAL DESCRIPTION a volcanic island, with a central plateau reaching 550–730m in the S; it falls steeply to narrow coastlands in the S and SW; the highest peak is Piton de la Petite Rivière Noire (826m); dry lowland coast, with wooded savannah, mangrove swamp, and bamboo in the E; surrounded by coral reefs enclosing lagoons and sandy beaches. CLIMATE tropical-maritime with temperatures averaging between 22°C and 26°C; there is a wide variation in rainfall with most rain falling in the central plateau. HISTORY discovered by the Portuguese and Dutch in the 16c; settled by the French in 1722; ceded to Britain in 1814; governed jointly with the Seychelles as a single colony until 1903; became an independent sovereign state within the Commonwealth in 1968 and an independent republic in 1992. GOVERNMENT a Prime Minister is appointed from the National Assembly by a President, who is head of state. ECONOMY the sugar-cane industry employs over a quarter of the workforce; knitwear, clothing; diamond-cutting; watches; rum; fertilizer; tea; tobacco; potatoes; vegetables; fishing; tourism.

Mauritius

Mauritshuis an art gallery in The Hague, opened to the public in 1820. The collection includes Flemish and Dutch paintings from the 15c to the 17c.

Mauser rifle a model of rifle designed and first manufactured by the Mauser company in 1898, named after its German inventor, Paul von Mauser (1838–1914). It equipped the German and many other national armies throughout the first half of the 20c.

mausoleum *noun* (PL. **mausoleums**) a grand or monumental tomb. [from Latin *mausoleum*, named after the Tomb of Mausolus]
◇ Notable mausoleums include the Gur Amir (in present-day Uzbekistan), Lenin's Tomb in Moscow's Red Square, and the Taj Mahal in Agra, India.

Mausolus, Tomb of an ornate tomb built in c.350 BC in Halicarnassus in SW Asia Minor by Queen Artemisia, widow of King Mausolus of Caria. It was one of the seven wonders of the ancient world, and is the source of the word *mausoleum*.

mauve — *adj.* having a pale purple colour. — *noun* this colour. [from French *mauve*, from Latin *malva*, mallow]

maverick *noun* **1** *North Amer., esp. US* an unbranded stray animal, especially a calf. **2** a determinedly independent person; a nonconformist. [from Samuel Maverick (1803–70), Texas cattle-raiser]

maw *noun* **1** the jaws, throat, or stomach of a voracious animal. **2** *facetious* a greedy person's

stomach. **3** something that seems to swallow things up. [from Anglo-Saxon *maga*]

mawkish *adj.* weakly sentimental; sickly. [from Norse *mathkr*, maggot]

max. *abbrev.* maximum.

maxi- *combining form* forming words meaning 'extra long' or 'extra large': *maxi-coat*. [a shortening of MAXIMUM]

maxilla *noun* (PL. **maxillae**) *Biol.* **1** the upper jaw or jawbone in animals. **2** the chewing organ or organs of an insect, just behind the mouth. [from Latin *maxilla*]

maxillary *adj.* relating to or in the reigon of the maxilla.

Maxim, Sir Hiram Stevens (1840–1916) British inventor, born in Sangersville, Maine, USA. He became a coachbuilder, and from 1867 took out patents for gas apparatus, electric lamps, and other devices. He is best known for the invention of the first fully automatic machine-gun (1883).

maxim *noun* **1** a saying expressing a general truth. **2** a general rule or principle. [from Latin *maxima propositio* or *sententia*, greatest axiom or opinion]

maximal *adj.* of a maximum; of the greatest possible size, value, etc.

Maximilian I (1459–1519) Holy Roman Emperor (1493–1519), born Archduke of Austria at Weiner Neustadt, the eldest son of Emperor Frederick III and Eleanor of Portugal. Elected King of the Romans (1486), he inherited the Habsburg territories and assumed the Imperial title in 1493. His foreign policy was based on dynastic alliances and had far-reaching results for Habsburg power. His marriage to Mary of Burgundy brought his family the Burgundian inheritance, including the Netherlands, followed by union with the Spanish kingdoms of Castile and Aragon when the Spanish Crown passed to his grandson, Charles (1516). A double marriage treaty between the Habsburgs and the Jagiellons (1506) eventually brought about the union of Austria–Bohemia–Hungary (1526). He was involved in conflicts with the Flemish, the Swiss, the German princes, and especially with the Valois Kings of France. Financial difficulties weakened his campaigns, and he later had to cede Milan (1504) to Louis XII, and despite the League of Cambrai (1508), he was defeated by the Venetians. He died leaving his extended empire to his grandson Charles V.

Maximilian, Ferdinand Joseph (1832–67) Emperor of Mexico (1864–7) and an archduke of Austria, born in Vienna, the younger brother of Emperor Francis Joseph I. He accepted the offer of the Crown of Mexico in 1863, supported by France, but when Napoleon III withdrew his troops, he refused to abdicate, made a brave defence at Querétaro, and was betrayed and executed.

Maximilian a male first name. [from Latin *Maximus*, greatest + the name *Aemilianus*]

maximization *or* **maximisation** *noun* maximizing or being maximized.

maximize *or* **maximise** *verb* to make as high, great, etc as possible.

maximum — *adj.* greatest possible. — *noun* **1** the greatest possible number, quantity, degree, etc. **2** *Geom.* in coordinate geometry, the point at which the slope of a curve changes from positive to negative. A tangent to a curve at its maximum has a gradient of zero. [from Latin *maximus*, greatest]

Maxwell, James Clerk (1831–79) Scottish physicist, born in Edinburgh. He studied at Edinburgh and Cambridge, and became professor at Aberdeen, London, and Cambridge. During his brilliant career he studied gases and colour perception, and he demonstrated colour photography. His theory of electromagnetic radiation published in *Treatise on Electricity and Magnetism* (1873), which identified visible light as part of a spectrum of electromagnetic waves, established him as the leading theoretical physicist of the century, and paved the way for Einstein's work.

Maxwell, (Ian) Robert (1923–91) British publisher and politician, born in Czechoslovakia. Self-educated, he served in World War II, then founded the Pergamon Press. A former Labour MP (1964–70) whose many business interests included film production and television, he founded the Maxwell Communication Corporation, of which he became joint Managing Director in 1988, and the Maxwell Foundation. Also the Chairman of the Mirror group of newspapers, he was later revealed to have been involved in questionable transactions using money taken from the pension funds of some of his companies. He died in mysterious circumstances off the Canary Islands.

Maxwell a male first name, after the Scottish surname and place-name.

Maxwell Davies, Sir Peter (1934–) English composer, born in Manchester. He studied at Manchester, Rome, and Princeton, and was composer-in-residence at the University of Adelaide in 1966. Mainly written for chamber ensembles, often with a large percussion section, his works include operas (eg *Taverner*, 1972), *Eight Songs for a Mad King* (1969), symphonies, and concertos. Since 1970 he has worked mainly in Orkney, frequently making use of Orcadian or Scottish subject-matter, and in 1988 he received a commission of 10 concertos for the Scottish Chamber Orchestra.

May a female first name. [partly a short form of MARY, and partly after the month]

May *noun* 1 the fifth month of the year. 2 (**may** *or* **may tree**) any variety of hawthorn tree, or its blossom. [from *Maia*, in ancient Greek and Roman mythology the mother of the god Mercury]

may *verb aux.* (PAST TENSE **might** expressing:) 1 permission: *you may go now.* 2 possibility: *I may well leave.* 3 ability or competence: *may I help you?* 4 *formal* a wish: *may you prosper!* 5 *formal, old use* purpose: *listen, so that you may learn.* 6 *old affected use, facetious* a question: *who may you be?* 7 used to introduce the first of a pair of statements, with the sense of 'although': *you may be rich, but you're not happy.* [from Anglo-Saxon *mæg*, present tense of *magan*, to be able]

Maya a civilization of the classic period of Middle America (AD 250–900). The Maya rose to prominence (c.300) in present-day S Mexico, Guatemala, N Belize, and W Honduras. They inherited the inventions and ideas of earlier civilizations, such as the Olmec, and developed astronomy, calendrical systems, hieroglyphic writing, and ceremonial architecture, including pyramid temples. Most people farmed, while centres such as Tikal and Bonampak were largely ceremonial and political, with an élite of priests and nobles ruling over the countryside. Maya civilization started to decline, for reasons unknown, in c.900, although some peripheral centres still thrived, under the influence of Mexico. Today the Maya populate the same areas as their ancestors and maintain a traditional agricultural lifestyle. Most are nominally Roman Catholic, but the Christian religion overlays the native pagan one, which is still practised.

Mayaguez POP (1990) 100 000, a trading centre on the W coast of Puerto Rico, situated on Mona Passage, S of Arecibo. It was founded in 1760.

Mayakovsky, Vladimir (Vladimirovich) (1894–1930) Russian Futurist poet, born in Bagdadi, Georgia. He supported the Bolsheviks in the 1917 Revolution, and wrote the play *Mystery-Bouffe* (1918), and the long poem *150,000,000* (1919–20). Later works include the

poem *Vladimir Ilich Lenin* (1924), and the satirical plays *The Bedbug* (1929) and *The Bath-house* (1930). He committed suicide in Moscow.

maybe *adv.* it may be; it is possible; perhaps.

May Day the first day of May, a national holiday in many countries, traditionally a day of festivities.

mayday *noun* (*often* **Mayday**) the international radio distress signal sent out by ships and aircraft. [from French *m'aider*, help me]

Mayer, Louis B(urt), originally **Eliezer Mayer** (1885–1957) US film producer, born in Minsk, Russia. His family emigrated to the USA, where he became involved in cinema management. He set up a film production company in Los Angeles in 1919, and in 1924 became Vice-President of the newly merged group, Loew's Metro-Goldwyn-Mayer, where he was in charge of the studios for more than 25 years.

Mayfair a district in London where throughout the 17c a fair was held in May. It became a fashionable residential area in the late 19c and early 20c, but is now largely given over to offices. It lies between Piccadilly and Oxford St to the N and S, and between Hyde Park and Regent St to the E and W.

Mayflower a three-masted carrack in which the Pilgrim Fathers sailed from Plymouth to Massachusetts in 1620. The ship was 27.5m in length, and the voyage took 66 days.

Mayflower Compact an agreement (1620) to establish a 'civil body politic', signed aboard the ship *Mayflower* by members of the Pilgrim party (Pilgrim Fathers) about to settle in the Cape Cod region.

mayfly *noun* a short-lived insect with transparent wings, which appears briefly in spring.

mayhem *noun* 1 a state of great confusion and disorder; chaos. 2 *Legal* the crime of maiming someone. [from Old French *mahaignier*, to wound]

mayn't *contr.* may not.

Mayo, Charles Horace (1865–1939) US surgeon, born in Rochester, Minnesota. He made an important study of goitre, and helped his brother William James Mayo to organize the Mayo Clinic (1905) within what is now St Mary's Hospital, Rochester, founded by their father in 1899.

Mayo, Gaelic **Mhuigheo** POP (1991) 111 000, a county in Connacht province, W Irish Republic. AREA 5 398sq km/2 084sq mi. It is bounded N and W by the Atlantic Ocean. PHYSICAL DESCRIPTION drained by the R Moy (noted for its salmon fishing); Achill I lies off the W coast; Nephin Beg Range lies to the NW. CAPITAL Castlebar. ECONOMY sheep and cattle farming; potatoes; oats. NOTABLE FEATURES Knock, scene of the apparition of the Virgin Mary in 1879, now a major place of pilgrimage; Croagh Patrick, Ireland's holy mountain and scene of annual pilgrimage.

mayonnaise *noun* a cold creamy sauce made of egg yolk, oil, vinegar or lemon juice, and seasoning. [from French]

mayor *noun* the head of the local council in a city, town, or borough in England, Wales, and N Ireland, or of any of various communities in other countries. [from Latin *major*, comparative of *magnus*, great]

mayoral *adj.* relating to a mayor or the office of a mayor.

mayoralty *noun* (PL. **mayoralties**) the position, or period of office, of a mayor.

mayoress *noun* 1 a mayor's wife. 2 *old use* a female mayor.

Mayor of Casterbridge, The a novel by Thomas Hardy (1886). It describes the rise and tragic fall of the central character, Michael Henchard.

Mayotte, English **Mahore** POP (1991e) 85 000, a small island group of volcanic origin, E of the Comoros Is at the N end of the Mozambique Channel, W Indian Ocean. AREA 374sq km/144sq mi. The group is a French Territorial Collectivity, administered by France. The two main islands are Grande Terre, rising to 660m at Mt Benara, and La Petite Terre or Ilot de Pamandzi. CAPITAL Mamoudzou. OFFICIAL LANGUAGE French; Mahorian (a Swahili dialect) is also spoken. HISTORY a French colony between 1843 and 1914, it was attached with the Comoros Is to Madagascar; the Comoros were granted autonomy within the French Republic and became an Overseas Territory, but when the rest of the group voted to become independent in 1974, Mayotte voted to remain a French dependency. ECONOMY fishing; vanilla, coffee, copra, ylang-ylang.

maypole *noun* a tall pole set up for dancing round on May Day.

May queen a young woman, crowned with flowers, chosen to preside over May Day festivities.

Mayr, Ernst Walter (1904–) German-born US zoologist, born in Kempten. He studied at Berlin and emigrated to the USA in 1932, serving as Professor of Zoology at Harvard from 1953 to 1975. He is best known for his neo-Darwinian views on evolution, which produced a reconciling of the views of palaeontologists and geneticists.

Mays, Willie (Howard) (1931–) US baseball player, born in Westfield, Alabama. A former batter, fielder, and base runner with the San Francisco Giants and New York Mets (1951–73), he was the leading all-round player of the era, and the Most Valuable Player of the Year in the National League in 1954 and 1965. One of the few players to achieve more than 3 000 hits, he also hit 660 home runs.

Mazār-e-Sharīf POP (1988e) 131 000, the capital of Balkh province, N Afghanistan.

Mazarin, Jules, Cardinal (1602–61) Neapolitan cleric, diplomat, and statesman, born in Pescine. He was Papal Nuncio to the French court (1634–6), entered the service of Louis XIII in 1639, and rose to become cardinal through the influence of Richelieu, whom he succeeded as Chief Minister (1642). After Louis's death (1643), he retained his authority under the Queen Regent, Anne of Austria. Blamed by many for the civil disturbances of The Frondes, he twice fled the kingdom, and returned to Paris after the nobles' revolt had been suppressed (1653). His foreign policy was more fruitful: he concluded the Peace of Westphalia (1648), which increased French prestige, and negotiated the Treaty of the Pyrenees (1659), which ended the prolonged Franco-Spanish conflict.

Mazatlán POP (1990) 314 000, the largest Mexican port on the Pacific Ocean. Situated in Sinaloa state, S of the Gulf of California, it is the main industrial and commercial centre in W Mexico.

maze *noun* 1 a confusing network of paths, each bordered by high walls or hedges, designed to test orientation abilities. 2 any confusingly complicated system, procedure, etc. [related to AMAZE]

mazurka *noun* a lively Polish dance, or a piece of music for this. [from Polish *mazurka*, of Mazur, a Polish province]

MB *abbrev.* *Medicinae Baccalaureus* (Latin), Bachelor of Medicine.

MBA *abbrev.* Master of Business Administration.

Mbabane POP (1986) 38 000, the capital of Swaziland, 320km/200mi E of Johannesburg (South Africa) and 160km/100mi SW of Maputo (Mozambique). It became the capital in 1902 and is the administrative and commercial centre of the country.

MBE *abbrev.* Member of the Order of the British Empire.

MBO *abbrev.* management buyout.

MC *abbrev.* **1** master of ceremonies. **2** Military Cross.

McAdam, John Loudon (1756–1836) Scottish inventor and engineer, born in Ayr. He went to New York in 1770, where he made a fortune in his uncle's counting-house. On his return to Scotland he bought the estate of Sauchrie, Ayrshire, and in 1816 he was appointed surveyor to the Bristol Turnpike Trust. There he re-made the roads with crushed stone bound with gravel, raised to improve drainage — the 'macadamized' system. In 1827 he was made surveyor-general of metropolitan roads.

McAliskey, (Josephine) Bernadette, *née* **Devlin** (1947–) Northern Irish political activist. While at university in Belfast she became the youngest MP in the House of Commons since William Pitt the Younger: she was elected as an Independent Unity candidate in 1969. Her aggressive political style led to her arrest while leading Catholic rioters in the Bogside, and she was sentenced to nine months' imprisonment. In 1971 she lost Catholic support when she gave birth to an illegitimate child; she married two years later, and was defeated in the Feb 1974 general election. She was a founder member of the Irish Republican Socialist Party (1975).

McBride, Willie John (William James) (1940–) Irish rugby union player, born in Toomebridge, Co Antrim. A lock forward, he made a record 17 appearances for the British Lions, and played for Ireland 63 times. He toured with the Lions in 1966, 1968, 1971, and 1974, and was tour captain in 1974 (to South Africa) and manager in 1983 (to New Zealand). Most of his club rugby was played for Ballymena.

MCC *abbrev.* Marylebone Cricket Club.

McCarthy, Eugene J(oseph) (1916–) US politician, born in Watkins, Minnesota. A teacher of political science, he entered the House of Representatives as a Democrat (1949) and in 1958 was elected Senator from Minnesota. In 1968 he challenged President Johnson for the presidential nomination, on a policy of opposition to the Vietnam War. Although Johnson stood down, McCarthy did not gain the nomination and he left the Senate in 1970 to devote himself to teaching and writing, although he mounted an independent presidential campaign in 1976.

McCarthy, John (1957–) English journalist, born in Barnet. Having worked for Worldwide Television News since 1981, he went to Lebanon as acting bureau chief. After only 32 days there, on 17 Apr 1986 he was abducted by the revolutionary fundamentalist group Islamic Jihad. He was held as a hostage for 1943 days until his release on 8 Aug 1991. He wrote *Some Other Rainbow* (1993) with Jill Morrell about the experience.

McCarthy, Joseph R(aymond) (1909–57) US Republican politician and inquisitor, born in Grand Chute, Wisconsin. He became a circuit judge (1939), and after service in World War II was elected Senator (1945). He gained renown in the early 1950s for his unsubstantiated accusations that 205 communists had infiltrated the State Department. As Chairman of the powerful Permanent Subcommittee on Investigations from 1953, he used hectoring cross-examination and damaging innuendo to arraign many innocent citizens and officials, but overreached himself when he came into direct conflict with the army in 1954. He was formally condemned by the Senate, and lost his power after that.

McCarthy, Mary (Therese) (1912–89) US novelist and critic, born in Seattle, Washington. She worked as a publisher's editor, theatre critic, and teacher before she wrote her first novel *The Company She Keeps* in 1942. Other novels include *The Groves of Academe* (1952), *The Group* (1963), and *Cannibals and Missionaries* (1979). She has also published critical works, travel books, and the autobiographical *Memories of a Catholic Girlhood* (1957).

McCarthyism an anti-communist witchhunt which pervaded the USA at the height of the Cold War in the 1950s, named after Senator J R McCarthy of Wisconsin who made (unsubstantiated) claims that there were a large number of communists in the government, administration, and army. McCarthyism also includes the anti-communist measures taken during this period by Presidents Truman and Eisenhower, although they had nothing to do with McCarthy. The term 'McCarthyite' is often applied to political purges.

McCartney, (James) Paul (1942–) English songwriter, vocalist, and bass guitarist, born in Liverpool. One of the most distinctive lyricists in popular music, he saw fame as a member of the Beatles (until the group disbanded in 1970), then pursued a solo career. He made two albums before recruiting guitarist Denny Laine (1944–) to form Wings (1971–81). The political single 'Give Ireland Back to the Irish' (1972) was banned, but the albums *Band on the Run* (1973) and *Venus & Mars* (1975) were popular. His hit singles include 'Mull of Kintyre' (1977).

McClintock, Barbara (1902–92) US geneticist, born in Hartford, Connecticut. Working at the Cold Spring Harbor Laboratories, she demonstrated the existence of 'jumping genes', genes which control the activation and deactivation of other genes and which can move about on the chromosome to do this. She was awarded the 1983 Nobel Prize for Physiology or Medicine.

McCollum, Elmer Verner (1879–1967) US biochemist, born in Fort Scott, Kansas. Professor at Johns Hopkins University, he studied vitamins, showing that more than one vitamin is necessary for normal animal growth. He distinguished between vitamins A (fat-soluble) and B (water-soluble), and identified the 'rickets-preventative factor', vitamin D (1922).

McCormack, John (1884–1945) Irish-born US tenor, born in Athlone. He made his London début in 1905, sang at Covent Garden (1906–7), and also appeared in oratorio and as a lieder singer. As an Irish nationalist, during World War I he lost British support and remained in the USA; he then took US citizenship (1919), and turned to popular sentimental songs. He returned to England in 1924, and toured widely until he retired from the stage (1938), but during World War II he continued to sing on the radio.

McCormick, Cyrus H(all) (1809–84) US inventor of the reaper, born in Rockbridge Co, Virginia. He continued experiments begun by his father, and produced a successful model in 1831. Following his first sale (1840) he moved to Chicago (1847), where he manufactured more than six million harvesting machines.

McCoy *noun*
— **the real McCoy** *colloq.* the genuine article, not an imitation.

McCullers, Carson, *née* **Smith** (1917–67) US writer, born in Columbus, Georgia. She wrote realistic, tragic, and often symbolic novels, notably *The Heart is a Lonely Hunter* (1940) and *The Member of the Wedding* (1946, filmed 1952). Other works include the novella *The Ballad of the Sad Café* (1951). She also wrote various short stories and plays.

McEnroe, John (Patrick) (1959–) US lawn tennis player, born in Wiesbaden, Germany. He reached the semifinal at Wimbledon as a pre-qualifier in 1977, turned professional in 1978, and was runner-up to Björn Borg in the 1980 Wimbledon final. He won the Wimbledon title three times (1981, 1983–4), the US singles four times (1979–81, 1984), and eight Grand Slam doubles events, seven of them with Peter Fleming, and the most recent, at Wimbledon in 1992, with Michael Stich. He was Grand Prix winner in 1979 and 1984–5, and World Championship Tennis champion in 1979, 1981, and 1983–4. Throughout his professional career, his outbursts on court resulted in much adverse publicity.

McGonagall, William (1830–?) Scottish doggerel poet, the son of an Irish weaver. He went from Dundee to Edinburgh, where he gave readings in public houses and published broadsheets of topical verse. His *Poetic Gems*, characterized by their simplistic rhyme schemes and disregard for metre, originally appeared in 1890. His *Collected Works* were most recently published in 1992.

McGovern, George S(tanley) (1922–) US Democratic politician, born in Avon, South Dakota. He was Professor of History and Political Science at Dakota Wesleyan University (1949–53), a member of the House of Representatives (1956–61) and Senator for South Dakota (1963–81). He made a bid for the Democratic presidential nomination in 1968, and unsuccessfully opposed Nixon in the 1972 presidential election. He tried again for the presidential nomination in 1984, but withdrew.

McIndoe, Sir Archibald (1900–60) British plastic surgeon, born in Dunedin, New Zealand. Educated at Otago, the Mayo Clinic, and St Bartholomew's Hospital, he won fame in World War II as surgeon-in-charge at the Queen Victoria Hospital, East Grinstead, where the faces and limbs of injured airmen were remodelled with unsurpassed skill.

McKay, Heather (Pamela), *née* **Blundell** (1941–) Australian squash rackets player, born in Queanbeyan, New South Wales. She won the British Open in 16 successive years (1962–77), 14 Australian titles (1960–73), and was world champion in 1976 and 1979. Between 1962 and 1980 she was unbeaten in women's squash. She moved to Canada in 1975, and became Canadian racketball champion.

McKinley, William (1843–1901) US Republican statesman, the 24th President, born in Niles, Ohio. He served in the Civil War, became a lawyer, was elected to Congress (1877), and in 1891 was made Governor of Ohio, when his name was identified with the high protective tariff carried in the McKinley Bill of 1890. As President (1897–1901) he advocated a gold standard and high tariffs, and his first term was marked by the war with Spain (1898) and the conquest of Cuba and the Philippines. He was shot by an anarchist in Buffalo.

McKinley, Mount the highest peak in the USA and in N America. It is situated in S central Alaska, USA, in Denali National Park and Preserve. Covered almost completely by glaciers, it consists of two peaks (6 194m and 5 934m). Denali was the Native American name for the peak.

McLuhan, (Herbert) Marshall (1911–80) Canadian critic and cultural theorist, born in Edmonton, Alberta. He was founder-director of the University of Toronto's Centre for Culture and Technology (1963) and held controversial views claiming that it is the communication media *per se*, not the information and ideas which they broadcast, that influence society. His books include *The Gutenberg Galaxy* (1962) and *The Medium is the Message* (1967).

McNamara, Robert (Strange) (1916–) US Democratic politician and businessman, born in San Francisco. After service in the air force (1943–6), he worked his way up in the Ford Motor Company to be President (1960). In 1961 he joined the Kennedy administration as Secretary of Defense, and became particularly involved in the Vietnam War. He resigned to become President of the World Bank (1968–81). In the 1980s he emerged as a critic of the nuclear arms race.

MCP *abbrev.* male chauvinist pig.

McQueen, (Terence) Steve(n) (1930–80) US actor, born in Indianapolis. After a delinquent youth he took up acting on stage and television, and by 1955 was a film star with a reputation as a tough unconventional rebel, both on and off the screen. Typical of his successes were *The Magnificent Seven* (1960), *Bullitt* (1961), and *An Enemy of the People* (1977).

MD *abbrev.* **1** managing director. **2** Maryland. **3** *Medicinae Doctor* (Latin), Doctor of Medicine.

Md¹ *abbrev.* Maryland.

Md² *symbol Chem.* mendelevium.

ME *abbrev.* **1** Maine. **2** *Medicine* myalgic encephalomyelitis, severe muscle weakness and general fatigue, often the long-term effect of a viral infection.

Me *abbrev.* Maine.

me¹ *pron.* **1** the object form of I, used by a speaker or writer to refer to himself or herself. **2** used for *I* after the verb *be* or when standing alone: *it's only me.*
— **be me** *colloq.* to be suited to me: *this dress isn't really me.*
[from Anglo-Saxon *mē*]

me² same as MI.

mea culpa *literary, facetious* I am to blame. [from Latin *mea culpa*, my fault]

Mead, Margaret (1901–78) US anthropologist, born in Philadelphia. She carried out a number of field studies in the Pacific before World War II, and wrote both academic and popular books (eg *Coming of Age in Samoa*, 1928 and *New Lives for Old*, 1956). She held a position for many years at the American Museum of Natural History, and became particularly well known for her views on educational and social issues.

mead¹ *noun* an alcoholic drink made by fermenting honey and water, usually with spices added. [from Anglo-Saxon *meodu*]

mead² *noun old use, poetic* a meadow. [from Anglo-Saxon *mæd*]

Meade, James Edward (1907–) English economist, born in Swanage, Dorset. He was a member (latterly Director) of the economic section of the Cabinet Office (1940–6), then Professor of Commerce at the London School of Economics (1947–57) and of Political Economics at Cambridge (1957–74). A prolific writer, his principal contributions are in the area of international trade. He was jointly awarded the Nobel Prize for Economics in 1977 with Bertil Ohlin.

Meade, Richard (John Hannay) (1938–) British equestrian rider, born in Chepstow, Gwent, Wales. He won three Olympic gold medals — the Three Day Event team golds in 1968 and 1972, and the individual title in 1972 (on *Laurieston*). He has also won at Burghley (1964) and Badminton (1970, 1982), and has won world championship team gold medals (1970, 1982) and European championship team gold medals (1967, 1971, 1981).

meadow *noun* **1** a low-lying field of grass, used for grazing animals or making hay. **2** any moist grassy area near a river. [from Anglo-Saxon *mædwe*]

meadow pipit a ground-dwelling songbird, about the size of a sparrow, with brown streaky plumage and a slender bill.

meadow saffron same as AUTUMN CROCUS.

meadowsweet *noun* a European and Asian wild plant of the rose family, with fragrant cream-coloured flowers.

Meads, Colin (Earl), also called *Pinetree* (1936–) New Zealand rugby union player, born

in Cambridge, Waikato. A prop forward, he wore the All Black jersey in 133 representative matches, including a record 55 in Test Matches between 1957 and 1971.

meagre *adj.* **1** lacking in quality or quantity; inadequate; scanty. **2** *said of a person* thin, especially unhealthily so. [from Old French *maigre*, thin]

meal¹ *noun* **1** an occasion on which food is eaten. **2** an amount of food eaten on one occasion.
— **make a meal of something 1** to eat it as a meal. **2** *colloq.* to exaggerate the importance of, eg by taking unnecessary time or trouble.
[from Anglo-Saxon *mæl*, measure, portion of time]

meal² *noun* (*often in compounds*) **1** the edible parts of any grain, usually excluding wheat, ground to a coarse powder: *oatmeal*. **2** any other food substance in ground form: *bone meal*. [from Anglo-Saxon *melu* or *melo*]

mealie *noun South Afr.* an ear of maize. [from Afrikaans *mielie*, maize]

mealie meal *noun South Afr.* maize ground to a fine flour.

meals-on-wheels *pl. noun* a welfare service delivering cooked meals by car to the homes of old or sick people.

meal ticket 1 *North Amer., esp. US* a luncheon voucher. **2** *colloq.* a person or situation providing a source of income or other means of living.

mealy *adj.* (**mealier, mealiest**) containing meal; dry and powdery, like meal.

mealy-mouthed *adj. derog.* afraid to speak plainly or openly.

mean¹ *verb* (PAST AND PAST PARTICIPLE **meant**) **1** to express or intend to express, show, or indicate. **2** to intend; to have as a purpose: *didn't mean any harm.* **3** to be serious or sincere about: *he means what he says.* **4** to be important to (the stated degree); to represent: *your approval means a lot to me.* **5** to entail necessarily; to result in; to involve: *war means hardship.* **6** (**be meant for something**) to be destined to it: *she was meant for stardom.* **7** to foretell or portend: *cold cloudless evenings mean overnight frost.*
— **mean well** to have good intentions.
[from Anglo-Saxon *mænan*]

mean² *adj.* **1** not generous. **2** unkind; despicable. **3** poor; shabby; of inferior quality. **4** *colloq.* vicious; malicious. **5** *colloq.* good; skilful: *plays a mean guitar.*
— **no mean** ... *colloq.* **1** an excellent: *no mean singer.* **2** not an easy ...; a very difficult ...: *no mean feat.*
[from Anglo-Saxon *gemæne*]

mean³ — *noun* **1** a midway position, course, etc between two extremes. **2** *Maths.* a mathematical average, in particular: **a** (*in full* **arithmetic mean**) the average value of a set of *n* numbers, equal to the sum of the numbers divided by *n*. **b** (*in full* **weighted mean**) the average value of a set of *n* numbers, also taking into account their frequency. Each number is multiplied by the number of times it occurs, and the resulting values are summed and divided by *n*. **c** (*in full* **geometric mean**) the *n*th root of the product of *n* quantities or numbers, eg the geometric mean of 2 and 3 is the second (square) root of 6, ie √6. — *adj.* **1** midway; intermediate. **2** average. [from Old French *meien*, from Latin *medius*, middle]

meander — *verb intrans.* (**meandered, meandering**) *formal* **1** *said of a river* to bend and curve. **2** (*also* **meander about**) to wander randomly or aimlessly. — *noun* (*often* **meanders**) a bend; a winding course. [from Latin *Maeander*, winding river in Turkey (now *Menderes*)]

meanie *or* **meany** *noun* (PL. **meanies**) *colloq.* a selfish or ungenerous person.

meaning — *noun* **1** the sense in which a statement, action, word, etc is intended to be under-

stood. **2** significance, importance, or purpose, especially when hidden or special. — *adj.* intended to express special significance: *a meaning look.*

meaningful *adj.* **1** having meaning; significant. **2** *Logic* capable of interpretation.

meaningfully *adv.* in a meaningful or significant way.

meaningless *adj.* **1** without meaning or reason. **2** of no importance. **3** having no purpose; pointless.

meanly *adv.* in a mean way.

meanness *noun* being mean.

means *noun* **1** the instrument or method used to achieve some object. **2** wealth; resources.
— **by all means** yes, of course.
by any means using any available method.
by means of ... using ...
by no means *or* **not by any means** not at all; definitely not.
a means to an end something treated merely as a way of achieving a desired result, considered unimportant in every other respect.
[from MEAN³]

means test an official inquiry into a person's wealth or income to determine eligibility for financial benefit from the state.

means-test *verb* to carry out a means test on (someone).

meant see MEAN¹.

meantime — *noun* the time or period between. — *adv.* in the time between; meanwhile. [from MEAN³ + TIME]

meanwhile *adv.* during the time in between; at the same time. [from MEAN³ + WHILE]

meany see MEAN².

measles *sing. noun* a highly infectious viral disease, common in children, characterized by fever, a sore throat, and a blotchy red rash that initially appears on the skin of the face and neck, but eventually spreads to the rest of the body. An attack of measles usually confers lifelong immunity to the disease, as does vaccination. [from Middle English *maseles*]

measly *adj.* (**measlier, measliest**) **1** *derog. colloq., said of an amount or value* very small; miserable; paltry. **2** relating to, or suffering from, measles.

measurable *adj.* **1** able to be measured; of sufficient quantity to be measured. **2** noticeable; significant.

measure — *noun* **1** size, volume, etc determined by comparison with something of known size, etc, usually an instrument graded in standard units. **2** (*often in compounds*) such an instrument: *a tape-measure.* **3** a standard unit of size, etc; a system of such units; a standard amount: *metric measure / a measure of whisky.* **4** (*usually* **measures**) an action; a step: *drastic measures.* **5** a limited, or appropriate, amount or extent: *a measure of politeness / in some measure / had my measure of luck.* **6** *Mus.* time or rhythm; a bar. **7** *Poetry* rhythm. **8** (*usually* **measures**) a layer of rock containing a particular mineral, etc: *coal measures.* **9** *old use* a dance. — *verb* **1** *trans., intrans.* to determine the size, volume, etc of, usually with a specially made instrument. **2** *intrans.* to be a (stated) size. **3** (*also* **measure something off** *or* **out**) to mark or divide into units of known size, etc. **4** to set in competition with: *measure his strength against mine.*
— **beyond measure** *literary* exceptionally great; to an exceedingly great degree.
for good measure as something extra, or above the minimum necessary.
get the measure of someone to assess their character or abilities.
measure up to reach the required standard.
[from Latin *mensura*, measure]

Measures

Nautical

1 span = 9 inches = 23 centimetres
8 spans = 1 fathom = 6 feet
1 cable's length = 1/10 nautical mile
1 nautical mile (old) = 6 080 feet
1 nautical mile (international) = 6 076.1 feet =
　　1.151 statute miles (= 1 852 metres)
60 nautical miles = 1 degree
3 nautical miles = 1 league (nautical)
1 knot = 1 nautical mile per hour
1 ton (shipping) = 42 cubic feet
1 ton (displacement) = 35 cubic feet
1 ton (register) = 100 cubic feet

Crude oil (petroleum)

1 barrel = 35 imperial gallons
　　　　= 42 US gallons

Paper (writing)

25 sheets = 1 quire
20 quires = 1 ream = 500 sheets

Printing

1 point = 0.3515 millimetres
1 pica = 4.2175 millimetres = 12 points

Timber

1 000 millisteres = 1 stere = 1 cubic metre
1 board foot = 144 cubic inches (12 × 12 × 1 inch)
1 cord foot = 16 cubic feet
1 cord = 8 cord feet
1 hoppus foot = 4/π cubic feet (round timber)
1 Petrograd standard = 165 cubic feet

Cloth

1 ell = 45 inches
1 bolt = 120 feet = 32 ells

Brewing

4.5 gallons = 1 pin
2 pins = 9 gallons = 1 firkin
4 firkins = 1 barrel = 36 gallons
6 firkins = 1 hogshead = 54 gallons
4 hogsheads = 1 tun

Horses (height)

1 hand = 4 inches = 10 centimetres

---

measured *adj.* **1** slow and steady. **2** carefully chosen or considered: *a measured response.*

Measure for Measure a play by William Shakespeare (1604–5). Described as a 'problem' play, it is a dark comedy revolving around the hypocritical Angelo whose severe penalties for illegal sexual behaviour do not apply to his treatment of the virtuous Isabella, whose brother awaits execution.

measurement *noun* **1** (*often* **measurements**) a size, amount, etc determined by measuring. **2** (*often* **measurements**) the size of a part of the body. **3** the act of measuring. **4** a standard system of measuring.

meat *noun* **1** the flesh of any animal used as food. *Red meats* include beef and veal (from cattle), lamb and mutton (from sheep), and pork (from pigs). *White meat* is obtained from poultry, and *game* is the flesh of wild birds and animals, eg grouse, deer. Meat is a good source of protein, but it has a high cholesterol content. **2** the basic, most important part; the essence. **3** *old use* food in general; a meal.
— **meat and drink 1** a source of enjoyment. **2** one's basic means of support.
[from Anglo-Saxon *mete*]

meatball *noun* a small ball of minced meat mixed with breadcrumbs and herbs.

Meath, Gaelic **na Midhe** POP (1991) 105 000, a county in Leinster province, E Irish Republic. AREA 2 339sq km/903sq mi. To the E, it is bounded by the Irish Sea. It was formerly a kingdom. PHYSICAL DESCRIPTION drained by the Boyne and Blackwater rivers; crossed by the Royal Canal. CAPITAL Trim. ECONOMY sheep, cattle, potatoes, oats.

meatiness *noun* being meaty.

meatus *noun* (PL. **meatuses**) *Anat.* a passage between body parts, or an opening, eg the passage that leads from the external surface of the ear to the eardrum. [from Latin *meatus*, from *meare*, to go]

meaty *adj.* (**meatier**, **meatiest**) **1** full of, or containing, animal flesh. **2** resembling or tasting like meat, especially cooked meat. **3** full of interesting information or ideas: *a meaty article.*

Mecca, Arabic **Makkah**, ancient **Macoraba** POP (1980e) 550 000, an Islamic holy city in W central Saudi Arabia. It lies 64km/40mi E of its Red Sea port, Jeddah. The city is the birthplace of Muhammad and the site of the Kaba, the chief shrine of Muslim pilgrimage. Between 1.5 and 2 million pilgrims visit Mecca annually. The city is closed to non-Muslims. NOTABLE FEATURES Al-Harram Mosque with the Kaba and sacred Black Stone; large bazaars.

mecca *or* **Mecca** *noun* any place of outstanding importance or significance, especially one much visited: *St Andrews, the mecca of golf.* [after the city of Mecca]

mechanic *noun* a skilled worker who repairs or maintains machinery. [from Greek *mechane*, contrivance]

mechanical *adj.* **1** of or concerning machines. **2** worked by, or performed with, machinery. **3** done without or not requiring much thought.

mechanical advantage *Engineering* the ratio of the load (output force) to the effort (input force) for a simple machine.

mechanical engineering the branch of engineering concerned with the design, construction, and operation of machines of all types, and the design, operation, and testing of engines that produce power from steam, petrol, nuclear energy, etc.

mechanically *adv.* by means of or as regards mechanics.

mechanics *noun* **1** (*sing.*) the branch of physics that is concerned with the study of the motion of bodies and the forces that act on them. It includes dynamics (the study of forces that act on moving objects) and statics (the study of forces that do not produce motion). **2** (*sing.*) the art or science of machine construction. **3** (*pl.*) the system on which something works.

mechanism *noun* **1** a working part of a machine, or its system of working parts. **2** *Psychol.* an action serving some (often subconscious) purpose: *laughter is a common defence mechanism.*

mechanistic *adj.* **1** relating to mechanics. **2** relating to a mechanism.

mechanization *or* **mechanisation** *noun* the act or process of mechanizing.

mechanize *or* **mechanise** *verb* **1** to cause to operate with, or be operated by, machines rather than people. **2** to supply (troops) with motor vehicles rather than horses.

Mecklenburg Declaration of Independence resolutions adopted (1775) during the American Revolution in Mecklenburg County, North Carolina, that denied all British authority. They were ignored by the Continental Congress, which at the time was more interested in reconciliation with Britain than in independence from it.

MEd *abbrev.* Master of Education.

Med *noun* (**the Med**) *colloq.* the Mediterranean Sea.

med. *abbrev.* **1** medieval. **2** medical. **3** medicine. **4** medium.

medal *noun* a flat piece of metal decorated with a design or inscription and offered as an award for merit or bravery, or in celebration of a special

occasion. [from French *médaille*, from Latin *metallum*, metal]

medallion *noun* **1** a large medal-like piece of jewellery, usually worn on a chain. **2** an oval or circular decorative feature in architecture or on textiles. **3** a thin circular cut of meat. [from French *médaillon*; related to MEDAL]

medallist *noun* a person awarded a medal, especially for excellence in sport.

Medal of Honor (ABBREV. **MH**, **MOH**) in the USA, the highest decoration awarded for heroism, instituted in 1861. The ribbon is blue, with white stars.

Medawar, Sir Peter Brian (1915–87) British zoologist, born in Rio de Janeiro. Professor at Birmingham and London, and Director of the National Institute for Medical Research at Mill Hill from 1962, he carried out important research on the problems of tissue rejection following transplant operations. He demonstrated conclusively that tolerance to a certain substance can be artificially induced in an embryo and then retained after birth and at maturity. He shared the 1960 Nobel Prize for Physiology or Medicine with Macfarlane Burnet.

meddle *verb intrans.* **1** (**meddle in something**) to interfere in it. **2** (**meddle with something**) to tamper with it. [from Old French *medler*]

meddler *noun* a person who meddles.

meddlesome *adj. derog.* fond of meddling.

Medea in Greek mythology, an enchantress, the daughter of Aeetes, the King of Colchis. She assisted Jason in obtaining the Golden Fleece and on their return to Iolcos, she tricked the daughters of Pelias into destroying their father. In Corinth, she was deserted by Jason for Glauce, and she fled to Athens after killing Glauce, King Creon, and her own two children by Jason.

Medea a play by Euripides (431 BC). It is a tragedy revolving around the treacherous enchantress Medea whose desertion by Jason leads her to the vengeful murder of his new wife and father-in-law, and her own children.

Médée a play by Jean Anouilh (1946), based on the Greek myth of Medea.

Medellín POP (1992e) 1.6m, the second-largest city in Colombia, situated in the NW of the country, in Antioquia department. It is the commercial and industrial capital of Antioquia. The city is the headquarters of a drugs cartel and related violence is a major problem. NOTABLE FEATURES Cathedral of Villanueva in Parque Bolívar; Museo El Castillo, Museo Folklórico Tejicondor; zoo.

Medes an ancient people living in Media, SW of the Caspian Sea, often wrongly identified with the Persians. At their peak (7c–6c BC), they conquered Urartu and Assyria, extended their power as far west as central Turkey, and in the east ruled most of Iran. Their Empire passed to the Persians under Cyrus the Great in c.550 BC.

media see MEDIUM.

mediaeval see MEDIEVAL.

mediagenic *adj., said of a person* able to communicate well or present a good image in the media, especially on television. [from MEDIA + PHOTOGENIC]

medial *adj.* of or situated in the middle; intermediate. [from Latin *medialis*, from *medius*, middle]

medially *adv.* **1** in a medial way. **2** so as to be medial.

median — *noun* **1** a middle point or part. **2** *Geom.* a straight line between any vertex (angle) of a triangle and the centre of the opposite side. The point at which the three medians of a triangle intersect is the *centroid*. **3** *Statistics* the middle value in a set of numbers or measurements arranged in order from smallest to largest, eg the median of 1, 5, 11 is 5. If there is an even number of measurements, the median is the average of the middle two measurements. — *adj.* situated in or passing through the middle. [from Latin *medianus*, from *medius*, middle]

mediate — *verb* **1** *intrans.* to act as the agent seeking to reconcile the two sides in a disagreement. **2** to intervene in or settle (a dispute) in this way. **3** to convey or transmit (views, etc) as an agent or intermediary. — *adj.* **1** resulting from mediation. **2** indirectly related or connected, eg through some other person. [from Latin *mediare*, to be in the middle]

mediation *noun* the act of mediating.

mediator *noun* a person who mediates.

medic *noun colloq.* a doctor or medical student.

Medicaid *noun* a scheme in the USA which provides assistance with medical expenses for people with low incomes.

medical — *adj.* **1** of doctors or the science or practice of medicine. **2** concerned with medicine rather than surgery. — *noun* a medical examination, to discover a person's physical health. [from Latin *medicus*, physician, from *mederi*, to heal]

medical certificate a certificate, provided by a doctor, outlining a person's state of health, especially for employment purposes.

medically *adv.* by medical means or as regards medical practice.

medicament *noun formal* a medicine. [from Latin *medicamentum*, from *medicare*, to cure]

Medicare *noun* **1** a scheme in the USA which provides medical insurance for people aged 65 and over, and for certain categories of disabled people. **2** a system providing universal medical insurance in Australia.

medicate *verb* **1** to treat with medicine. **2** to add a healing or health-giving substance to: *medicated shampoo*. [from Latin *medicare*, to cure]

medication *noun* medicine, or treatment by medicine.

Medici, French **Médicis** a banking family which virtually ruled Florence (1434–94), without formally holding office. Overthrown at the start of the Italian Wars (1494), they were restored to power (1512) and became hereditary Dukes of Florence (1537) and Grand Dukes of Tuscany (from 1569). Their dynastic power base moved first to Rome when Giovanni (1475–1521) became Pope Leo X (1513), and then to France when Catherine, the niece of another Medici pope, Clement VII, was married to the heir to the throne (later Henry II).

medicinal *adj.* **1** having healing qualities; used as a medicine. **2** of or relating to healing.

medicinally *adv.* by medicinal means.

medicine *noun* **1** any substance used to treat or prevent disease or illness, especially taken internally. **2** the science or practice of treating or preventing illness, especially using prepared substances rather than surgery.
— **get a taste** *or* **dose of one's own medicine** to suffer the same unpleasant treatment one has used on others.
take one's medicine to accept an unpleasant but deserved punishment.
[from Latin *medicina*]

medicine ball a heavy, fabric-covered metal ball thrown from person to person as a form of exercise.

Medicine Hat POP (1991) 43 000, a town in SE Alberta, S Canada, on the S Saskatchewan R. HISTORY the railway arrived in 1873; deposits of natural gas were discovered in the same year; city status was achieved in 1906. NOTABLE FEATURE Dinosaur Provincial Park, a graveyard of dinosaur skeletons, is 104km/65mi W.

medicine man among certain peoples, a person believed to have magic powers, used for healing or sorcery.

medico *noun* (PL. **medicos**) *colloq.* a doctor or medical student.

medieval *or* **mediaeval** *adj.* relating to or characteristic of the Middle Ages. [from Latin *medius*, middle + *aevum*, age]

medievalist *or* **mediaevalist** *noun* a student of, or expert in, any area or aspect of study of the medieval period.

Medina, Arabic **Madinah, Al** POP (1980e) 290 000, an Islamic holy city in Medina province, Saudi Arabia, 336km/209mi N of Mecca. It is the second most important holy city of Islam (after Mecca), containing the tomb of Muhammad. After his flight from Mecca, Muhammad sought refuge here. The city has an important pilgrimage trade, served by the Red Sea port of Yanbu al-Bahr. It is closed to non-Muslims.

mediocre *adj. derog.* only ordinary or average; rather inferior. [from Latin *mediocris*, from *medius*, middle]

mediocrity *noun* (PL. **mediocrities**) *derog.* **1** the quality of being mediocre. **2** a mediocre person or thing.

meditate *verb* **1** *intrans.* to spend time in deep religious or spiritual thought, often with the mind in a practised state of emptiness. **2** (**meditate something** *or* **meditate on something**) to think deeply and carefully about it. [from Latin *meditari*, to reflect upon]

meditation *noun* **1** the act of meditating. **2** deep thought, contemplation.

meditative *adj.* inclined to meditate.

Mediterranean — *noun* (**the Mediterranean**) see MEDITERRANEAN SEA. — *adj.* **1** in or relating to the area of the Mediterranean. **2** characteristic of this area. [from Latin *mediterraneus*, from *medius*, middle + *terra*, earth]

Mediterranean climate *Meteorol.* a climate characterized by hot dry summers and mild rainy winters, typical of countries in the Mediterranean region, California, and other regions on the western side of continents, between latitudes of 30° and 60°.

Mediterranean Sea, ancient **Mediterraneum**, or **Mare Internum** the world's largest inland sea, lying between Africa, Asia, and Europe. AREA 2 510 000sq km/968 900sq mi; maximum depth 4 405m. This warm sea is connected to the Atlantic Ocean by the 15km–/9mi-wide Straits of Gibraltar, to the Black Sea by the Dardanelles, the Sea of Marmara, and the Bosporus, and to the Indian Ocean by the Suez Canal and Red Sea. It is subdivided into the Ligurian, Adriatic, Aegean, Ionian, and Tyrrhenian seas. Tides are weak and salt levels are higher than in the Atlantic Ocean. In ancient times, it formed a maritime highway between Europe and the E for the Phoenicians, Greeks, Venetians, and Crusaders but it was eclipsed in the 14c–16c because of Turkish dominance and new ocean highways, particularly around Africa. The Suez Canal (1869) restored much of its importance and its strategic significance was demonstrated during and after World War II. The seaboard is highly favoured as a holiday area.

medium — *noun* (PL. **mediums** except in sense 2, **media**) **1** something by or through which an effect is produced. **2** (*usually* **mass media**) means by which news, information, etc are communicated to the public, usually television, radio, and the press collectively. **3** a person through whom the spirits of dead people are said to communicate with the living. **4** *Biol.* a substance in which specimens are preserved, bacteria are grown, etc. **5** a middle position, condition, or course: *a happy medium*. **6** *Art* a particular category of materials seen as a means of expression, eg watercolours, photography, or clay. — *adj.* **1** intermediate; midway; average. **2** moderate. [from Latin *medius*, middle]

medium wave a radio wave with a wavelength between 200 and 1000 metres.

medium-wave *adj.* on the medium wave.

Medjugorje a village in Bosnia-Herzegovina, situated S of Mostar. Since 1981 it has been claimed to be the scene of regular appearances by the Virgin Mary to a group of local children. The village is now a major site of pilgrimage, having attracted over 10 million visitors in the 1980s.

medlar *noun* **1** a small brown apple-like fruit eaten only when already decaying. **2** the small Eurasian tree that bears it. [from Old French *medler*]

medley *noun* (PL. **medleys**) **1** a piece of music made up of pieces from other songs, tunes, etc. **2** a mixture or miscellany. **3** a race in stages, each stage a different length or, in swimming, swum using a different stroke. [from Old French *medler*, to mix]

Médoc a district in Gironde department, Aquitaine region, SW France. Bounded W by the Atlantic Ocean, it occupies a flat alluvial plain on the W bank of the estuary of the R Gironde, N of Bordeaux. The area is famous for its clarets, notably at Haut-Médoc. CHIEF TOWNS Lesparre, Pauillac.

medulla *noun* (PL. **medullae**, **medullas**) **1** *Anat.* the central part of an organ or tissue, when this differs in structure or function from the outer layer, eg pith of plant stem, adrenal medulla in animals. **2** *Anat.* the medulla oblongata. [from Latin *medulla*, marrow]

medulla oblongata *Anat.* in vertebrates, the part of the brain that arises from the spinal cord and forms the lower part of the brain stem. It contains centres that control breathing, heartbeat, and coordination of nerve impulses from special sense organs.

Medusa in Greek mythology, the name of one of the Gorgons, the only mortal one. Her snake-covered head was severed by Perseus, though it still had the power to turn those who looked at it into stone. Chrysaor and Pegasus, her children by Poseidon, emerged from her wounded neck.

medusa *noun* (PL. **medusae**) *Zool.* in the life cycle of a coelenterate (eg jellyfish), a member of the sexually reproducing generation, which produces gametes. The medusa is free-swimming, and typically has a disc-shaped or bell-shaped body with marginal tentacles and a centrally located mouth on the underside. [from Latin *Medusa*, from Greek *Medousa*, the Gorgon]

medusa

Medway Towns POP (1981) 217 000, an urban area in Kent, SE England. It includes Gillingham, Rochester, Chatham, and Strood on the R Medway.

Mee, Arthur (1875–1943) English journalist, editor, and writer, born near Nottingham. He is best known for his *Children's Encyclopaedia* (1908) and *Children's Newspaper*, and for a wide range of popular works on history, science, and geography.

Mee, Margaret Ursula (1909–88) English botanical artist and traveller. Trained at the Camberwell School of Art, she first visited the Amazon forests when she was 47, and later began collecting and painting many new Brazilian species. She was well known for her outspoken anger at the destruction of the Amazonia; the Margaret Mee Amazon Trust was set up in 1988 to draw attention to the area's ecological crisis.

meek *adj.* **1** having a mild and gentle temperament. **2** submissive. [from Norse *mjukr*]

meekly *adv.* in a meek way.

meekness *noun* being meek.

meerschaum *noun* **1** a fine whitish clay-like mineral. **2** a tobacco pipe with a bowl made of this. [from German *Meer*, sea + *Schaum*, foam]

meet[1] — *verb* (PAST TENSE AND PAST PARTICIPLE **met**) **1** *trans., intrans.* to come together with (someone) by chance or arrangement. **2** *trans., intrans.* to be introduced to (someone) for the first time. **3** to be present at the arrival of: *met the train.* **4** *trans., intrans.* (**meet something** *or* **meet with something**) to come into opposition against it. **5** *trans., intrans.* to join; to come into contact with: *where the path meets the road.* **6** to satisfy: *meet your requirements.* **7** to pay: *meet costs.* **8** to come into the view, experience, or presence of: *the sight that met my eyes.* **9** (*also* **meet with something**) to encounter or experience it: *met his death.* **10** (*also* **meet with something**) to receive it: *suggestions met with approval.* **11** to answer or oppose: *meet force with greater force.* — *noun* **1** a sporting event, especially a series of athletics competitions. **2** the assembly of hounds and huntsmen and -women before a fox-hunt.
— **more than meets the eye** more complicated, interesting, etc than it appears.
[from Anglo-Saxon *metan*, to meet]

meet[2] *adj. old use* proper, correct, or suitable. [from Anglo-Saxon *gemæte*]

meeting *noun* **1** an act of coming together. **2** an assembly or gathering. **3** a sporting event, especially in athletics or horse-racing.

meetly *adv.* correctly, suitably.

mega *adj. slang* excellent. [from MEGA-]

mega- *combining form* forming words meaning: **1** a million: *megawatt.* **2** (*also* **megalo-**) large or great. **3** *colloq.* great: *megastar.* [from Greek *megas megal-*, big]

megabyte *noun Comput.* a unit of storage capacity equal to 2^{20} or 1 048 576 bytes.

megalith *noun* a very large stone, especially one forming part of a prehistoric monument. [from MEGA- + Greek *lithos*, stone]
◊ In Europe, these prehistoric and mainly neolithic monuments are also known as *cromlechs.* Similar monuments are found in S India, Tibet, SE Asia, Japan, and Oceania.

megalithic *adj.* **1** *said of a period of prehistory* characterized by the use of megaliths. **2** made of megaliths.

megalomania *noun* **1** *Medicine* a mental illness characterized by an exaggerated sense of power and self-importance. **2** *colloq.* greed for power. [from MEGA- + MANIA]

megalomaniac — *noun* a person affected by megalomania. — *adj.* relating to or affected by megalomania.

megaphone *noun* a funnel-shaped device which, when spoken through, amplifies the voice. [from MEGA- + Greek *phone*, sound]

megastructure *noun Archit.* a structure of gigantic proportions. The term is applied in architecture to 20c fantasy designs for structures which contain all the requirements for human existence, eg the high-density 'Arcologies' designed by the archtect Paolo Soleri for up to six million people.

megaton *noun* **1** a unit of weight equal to one million tons. **2** a unit of explosive power equal to one million tons of TNT.

Megiddo an ancient town in N Palestine which controlled the main route from Egypt to Syria. It was under Israelite control from around 1000 BC, and was rebuilt by Solomon (c.970–933 BC) as a military and administrative centre.

Its remains include the 9c BC stables of the Israelite kings.

Mehemet Ali see MOHAMMED ALI.

Meidan Emam a public square built in Isfahan, central Iran, by Abbas I (1571–1629) in the late 16c. It is flanked by four notable buildings: the former Royal Mosque, the Sheikh Lotfollah Mosque, the Ali Qapu Palace, and the gateway to the Qeyssariyeh. It is a World Heritage site.

Meiji Restoration an important point in Japanese history, when the last Shogun was overthrown (1868) in a short civil war, and the position of the Meiji Emperor (Mutsuhito, who ruled 1867–1912) resumed symbolic importance. Also, powerful new leaders set about making Japan into an industrial state, the four hereditary classes of Tokugawa Japan were abolished, and new technology and technical experts were brought from the West.

Meiji Shrine a pilgrimage centre in Tokyo. The shrine was completed in 1920 and dedicated to Emperor Meiji. The present building is a reconstruction of the original which was destroyed in World War II.

Meiji Tenno, Mutsuhito (1852–1912) Emperor of Japan who came to symbolize the modernization of Japan. He is commemorated by the Meiji Shrine and the Meiji Memorial Picture Gallery in Tokyo, and a large mausoleum in Momoyama, near Kyoto.

meiosis *noun* (PL. **meioses**) **1** *Biol.* a type of cell division that results in the formation of male and female gametes (sperm and eggs). As a result of two successive divisions of the parent nucleus, four daughter nuclei are produced, each of which contains half the number of chromosomes of the parent nucleus. — Also called *reduction, division.* **2** *Grammar* understatement used for effect or as a figure of speech, as in *it's only a scratch* when referring to an injury. See also LITOTES. [from Greek *meion*, less]

Meir, Golda, *née* **Goldie Mabovich**, later **Goldie Myerson** (1898–1978) Israeli politician,

four chromosomes (two pairs) in nucleus

chromosomes come together in pairs

as the chromosomes align, crossing over may take place

chromosome pairs separate to opposite ends of the cell

chromatids of each chromosome separate

chromatids now represent single chromosomes

meiosis

born in Kiev. She emigrated with her family to Milwaukee, USA, at the age of eight, married in 1917, and settled in Palestine in 1921. She was Israeli Ambassador to the Soviet Union (1948–9), Minister of Labour (1949–56), Foreign Minister (1956–66), and Prime Minister (1969–74). Her efforts for peace in the Middle East were halted by the fourth Arab–Israeli War (1973).

Meissen porcelain porcelain made at a factory in Meissen, near Dresden, in Germany. It was the first factory in Europe to make true hard-paste porcelain. The technique of production was discovered in c.1710 by Johann Friedrich Böttger (1682–1719). The porcelain (also known as Dresden China) includes figures, table ware, chinoiseries, and other ornaments.

Meistersinger von Nürnberg, Die (The Mastersingers of Nuremberg) a comic opera by Richard Wagner (1868), based on historical fact. Set in 16c Nuremberg, it tells of a singing competition to find a husband for Eva, the daughter of one of the Mastersingers.

Meitner, Lise (1878–1968) Austrian physicist, born in Vienna. Professor at Berlin and a member of the Kaiser Wilhelm Institute for Chemistry, she discovered (with Otto Hahn) the radioactive element protactinium (1917). In 1938 she fled from Nazi Germany to Sweden, and with her nephew Otto Frisch, she correctly proposed the process of nuclear fission (the splitting of a nucleus) to explain some of Hahn's experimental results.

Mekele *or* **Makale** POP (1984e) 62 000, the capital of Tigray region, NE Ethiopia. It was a major refugee centre during the severe drought and famine which began in the mid-1980s.

Meknès POP (1982) 320 000, a city in Centre-Sud province, N Morocco. It is situated in the Moyen Atlas, 50km/30mi SW of Fez and is one of Morocco's four imperial cities. Founded in the 12c, it was formerly the capital. Palaces were built under Moulay Ismail (1672–1727) to rival Louis XIV's Versailles. NOTABLE FEATURES Musée des Arts Marocains; Bou Inania Médersa (14c, religious college); Grand Mosque; Moulay Ismail's Tomb; gardens of El Haboul.

Mekong River, Chinese **Langcang Jiang** a river in Indo-China, SE Asia. It measures c.4 000km/2 500mi long and is navigable for c.550km/340mi. It rises on the Tibet Plateau, China, as the Zi Qu and Za Qu, which join as the Langcang Jiang. It flows S and SW, forming the boundary between Laos and Burma, SE to form the Laos–Thailand boundary, then generally E and S into Cambodia and Vietnam, splitting into four major tributaries at its delta on the South China Sea. There is a link to the Tonlé Sap lake in central Cambodia, which acts as its flood reservoir during the wet season.

Melaka see MALACCA.

melamine *noun Chem.* a white crystalline organic compound that is condensed with aldehydes to form artificial resins that are resistant to heat, water, and many chemicals, and are widely used as laminated coatings. [from German *Melamin*]

melancholia *noun old use* mental depression. [see MELANCHOLY]

melancholic *adj.* relating to or suffering from melancholia or melancholy.

melancholy — *noun* **1** a tendency to be gloomy or depressed. **2** prolonged sadness. **3** a sad, pensive state of mind. — *adj.* sad; causing or expressing sadness. [from Greek *melas*, black + *chole*, bile]

melange *or* **mélange** *noun literary* a mixture, especially varied or confused. [from French *mélange*]

Melanie a female first name. [from Greek *melas melain-*, black]

melanin *noun* the black or dark brown pigment found to varying degrees in the skin, hair, and eyes of humans and animals. [from Greek *melas, melain-*, black]

melanoma *noun* (PL. **melanomas, melanomata**) *Medicine* a malignant (cancerous) tumour, usually of the skin, that is composed of melanocytes (cells that produce the dark pigment melanin), and may spread to other parts of the body, such as the lymph nodes. Melanomas are frequently associated with excessive exposure of the skin to sunlight. [from MELANIN + Greek *-oma*, suffix denoting the result of the action of a verb, used in English to denote a tumour]

melatonin *noun Physiol.* in vertebrates, a hormone secreted into the bloodstream by the pineal gland, higher levels being present in the blood during darkness than in the light. Melatonin is involved in the control of certain daily and seasonal changes (eg in reproductive behaviour), and changes in pigmentation. [from Greek *melas*, black]

Melba, Dame Nellie, originally **Helen Mitchell** (1861–1931) Australian prima donna, born near Melbourne. Taking her professional name from her home city, she appeared at Covent Garden in 1888, and the purity of her coloratura soprano voice won her worldwide fame. 'Peach Melba' and 'Melba toast' were named after her.

Melba toast very thin crisp toast. [named after the opera singer Dame Nellie Melba]

Melbourne, William Lamb, 2nd Viscount (1779–1848) English statesman, born in London. He became an MP in 1805, and was Chief Secretary for Ireland (1827–8) under George Canning, and Home Secretary (1830–4) under Charles Grey. As Whig Prime Minister (1834, 1835–41), he formed a benevolent relationship with the young Queen Victoria. Defeated in the election of 1841, he resigned and thereafter took little part in public affairs. His wife Lady Caroline Lamb (1785–1828) wrote novels, and was notorious for her nine months' devotion (1812–13) to Lord Byron.

Melbourne POP (1990e) 3.1m, the capital of the state of Victoria, SE Australia. Situated in Melbourne statistical division, on the Yarra R at the head of Port Phillip Bay, it is Australia's biggest cargo port. The city is a major financial and communications centre. HISTORY founded in 1835 and became state capital in 1851; capital of Australia from 1901 until 1927; the scene of the first Federal Parliament in 1901. NOTABLE FEATURES two cathedrals; Melbourne Cricket Ground; Flemington Racecourse (the Melbourne Cup horse race is held here). [named after the British Prime Minister, Lord Melbourne]

Melbourne Cup the principal horse race in Australia run over 3.2km/2mi at the Flemington Park racecourse in Victoria, first run in 1861. It is held on the first Tuesday in November, and is a social occasion similar to Royal Ascot.

Melchites a derisive term for the Christians who followed the Byzantine rite, and who belonged to the Patriarchates of Alexandria, Antioch, and Jerusalem. [from Syriac, = royalist]

Meleager in Greek mythology, the son of King Oeneus of Calydon. He led the hunt for, and killed, the Calydonian boar, sent by Artemis in revenge for Oeneus's failure to make a sacrifice to her.

melee *or* **mêlée** *noun literary* **1** a riotous brawl involving large numbers of people. **2** any confused or muddled collection. [from French *mêlée*, from *mêler*, to mix]

Melilla, ancient **Russadir** POP (1991) 57 000 (with Ceuta), a free port and modern commercial city on the N African coast of Morocco. It forms, with Ceuta, a region of Spain. HISTORY founded as a port by the Phoenicians; free port since 1863; re-occupied by Spain in 1926. NOTABLE FEATURES

old town; Church of the Purisima Concepción (16c).

Melissa a female first name. [from Greek *melissa*, bee]

mellifluous *or* **mellifluent** *adj. literary*, said of sounds, speech, etc having a smooth sweet flowing quality. [from Latin *mel*, honey + *fluere*, to flow]

mellifluously *adv.* in a mellifluous way.

mellifluousness *noun* being mellifluous.

Mellon, Andrew W(illiam) (1855–1937) US financier, philanthropist, and politician, born in Pittsburgh. He established himself as a banker and industrial magnate and entered politics. As Secretary of the Treasury (1921–32) he made controversial fiscal reforms, and in 1932–3 he was Ambassador to the UK. He endowed the National Gallery of Art in Washington, DC.

mellow — *adj.* **1** said of a person or character calm and relaxed with age or experience. **2** said of sound, colour, light, etc soft, rich, and pure. **3** said of wine, cheese, etc fully flavoured with age. **4** said of fruit sweet and ripe. **5** pleasantly relaxed or warm-hearted through being slightly drunk. — *verb trans., intrans.* to make or become mellow. [perhaps from Anglo-Saxon *mearu*, soft, tender]

melodic *adj.* **1** relating to melody. **2** pleasant-sounding; tuneful; melodious.

melodically *adv.* in a melodic way.

melodious *adj.* **1** pleasant to listen to. **2** having a recognizable melody.

melodiousness *noun* being melodious.

melodrama *noun* **1** drama featuring simplified characters, sensational events, and traditional justice, usually in the form of a happy ending. **2** a play or film of this kind. **3** *derog.* excessively dramatic behaviour. [from Greek *melos*, song + *drama*, action]

◊ The works of 18c and early 19c continental dramatists did much to popularize the genre, and it became one of the most fashionable forms of mass entertainment in Europe and the USA throughout the 19c. The earliest melodramas consisted of dialogue or mime accompanied by music, but the term was soon adopted to describe a style of drama (without music) with the emphasis on depiction of story, with sensational episodes and the creation of suspense, invariably ending in the triumph of virtue.

melodramatic *adj.* exaggerated or sensational in expressing emotion.

melodramatics *pl. noun* melodramatic behaviour.

melody *noun* (PL. **melodies**) **1** the sequence of single notes forming the core of a tune, as opposed to the harmony, the blend of other notes around it. **2** pleasantness of sound; tuneful music. **3** pleasant arrangement or combination of sounds, especially in poetry. [from Greek *melodia*, from *melos*, song + *aoidein*, to sing]

melon *noun* the large rounded edible fruit of any of various climbing plants, with a thick skin, sweet juicy flesh, and many seeds. [from Greek *melon*, apple]

Melos, Greek **Mílos** the most south-westerly island of the Cyclades, Greece, situated in the S Aegean Sea. AREA 151sq km/58sq mi. CHIEF TOWN Plaka. ECONOMY minerals; fruit; olives; cotton; tourism. The 'Venus de Milo' sculpture (now in the Louvre, Paris) was discovered here in 1820.

Melpomene in Greek mythology, one of the Muses, associated with tragedy and lyre playing.

melt *verb trans., intrans.* **1** to make or become soft or liquid, especially through the action of heat; to dissolve. **2** to combine or fuse, causing a loss of distinctness. **3** (*also* **melt away** *or* **melt something away**) to disappear or cause to disappear or disperse: *support for the scheme melted away*. **4** *colloq.* to make or become emotionally or romantically tender or submissive.

— **melt down** *technical, said of the core of a nuclear reactor* to overheat, causing radioactivity to escape.
[from Anglo-Saxon *meltan*]

meltdown *noun* **1** *technical* the overheating of the core of a nuclear reactor, causing radioactivity to escape. **2** *colloq.* a major disaster or failure.

melting point (ABBREV. **m.p.**) the temperature at which a particular substance changes from a solid to a liquid. It is the same as the freezing point, but is usually used to refer to substances that are solid at room temperature, eg most metals.

melting-pot *noun* a place or situation in which varying beliefs, ideas, cultures, etc are mixed.
— **in the melting-pot** in the process of changing and forming something new.

Melville, Herman (1819–91) US novelist, born in New York City. He became a bank clerk, then joined a whaling ship bound for the South Seas (1841). His journeys were the subject matter of his first novels *Typee* (1846) and *Omoo* (1847), and also of his most famous novel, *Moby Dick* (1851). After 1857 he wrote only poetry, apart from the manuscript for the novella *Billy Budd, Foretopman* (1924).

Melvin *or* **Melvyn** a male first name. [origin uncertain; perhaps from the surname, or from *Malvina*, a name in the poems of James Macpherson (1736–96)]

member *noun* **1** a person belonging to a group or organization; a plant or animal belonging to a class or group. **2** (*often* **Member**) an elected representative of a governing body, eg Parliament or a local council. **3** a part of a whole, especially a limb or a petal. [from Latin *membrum*, limb, part]

member of parliament (*also* **Member of Parliament**) a person elected to represent the people of a constituency in parliament.

membership *noun* **1** the state of being a member. **2** the members of an organization collectively; the number of members.

membrane *noun* **1** a thin sheet of tissue that lines a body cavity, surrounds a body part, or links adjacent structures, eg mucous membrane. **2** a thin layer of lipid and protein molecules that forms the boundary between a cell and its surroundings, and that usually allows only certain molecules to pass into or out of the cell. Such membranes also surround individual structures within the cell, such as the nucleus. — Also called *cell membrane, plasma membrane.* **3** any thin flexible covering or lining, eg plastic film. [from Latin *membrana*, skin of the body]

membranous *adj.* of the nature of or like a membrane.

memento *noun* (PL. **mementos, mementoes**) a thing that serves as a reminder of the past; a souvenir. [from Latin *memento*, from *meminisse*, to remember]

memento mori an object intended as a reminder of the inevitability of death. [Latin, = remember you are to die]

Memnon in Greek mythology, a prince from Ethiopia, the son of Eos and Tithonus, who was killed at Troy by Achilles. The Greeks thought that one of the gigantic statues at Thebes represented him; it gave out a musical sound at sunrise.

memo *noun* (PL. **memos**) a memorandum.

memoir *noun* **1** a written record of events in the past, especially based on personal experience. **2** (**memoirs**) a person's written account of his or her own life; an autobiography. **3** a learned essay on any subject. [from French *mémoire*, memory]

memorabilia *pl. noun* souvenirs of people or events. [from Latin *memorabilis*, things for remembering]

memorable *adj.* worth remembering; easily remembered. [from Latin *memorare*, to remember]

memorably *adv.* in a memorable way.

memorandum *noun* (PL. **memorandums**, **memoranda**) **1** a note of something to be remembered. **2** a written statement or record, especially one circulated for the attention of colleagues. [from Latin *memorandum*, thing to be remembered]

memorial — *noun* a thing that honours or commemorates a person or an event, eg a statue. — *adj.* serving to preserve the memory of a person or an event. [from Latin *memoriale*, reminder]

Memorial Day a national holiday in the USA, held on the last Monday in May in honour of American war dead. It was first instituted in 1868 (when it was known as *Decoration Day*) in honour of the soldiers who died in the American Civil War.

memorize *or* **memorise** *verb* to learn thoroughly, so as to be able to reproduce exactly from memory.

memory *noun* (PL. **memories**) **1** the ability of the mind to remember: *recite it from memory*. **2** the mind's store of remembered events, impressions, knowledge, and ideas. For a given piece of information, eg an event, memory is influenced by how long ago the event took place, and the importance that was attached to it at the time. **3** the mental processes of memorizing information, retaining it, and recalling it on demand. **4** any such impression reproduced in the mind. **5** the limit in the past beyond which one's store of mental impressions does not extend: *not in living memory*. (= the memory of any living person). **6** the act of remembering; commemoration: *in memory of*. **7** reputation after death. **8** the part of a computer that is used to store data and programs. [from Latin *memoria*]

Memphis POP (1990) 982 000, the seat of Shelby County, SW Tennessee, USA. It is a port on the Mississippi R and the largest city in the state. HISTORY a military fort was built here in 1797, and a city was established in 1819; captured by Union forces during the Civil War after the battle of Memphis in 1862; there were severe yellow-fever epidemics in the 1870s; Martin Luther King Jr was assassinated here in 1968. NOTABLE FEATURES Graceland, home of Elvis Presley; Beale Street, made famous by composer W C Handy and regarded as the birthplace of the blues; Mud Island Parko.

Memphis a town in ancient Egypt on the W bank of the Nile, S of the Delta. It was the capital of Lower Egypt under the pharaohs, but declined in importance under the Ptolemies, whose capital was at Alexandria. The remains of the town, its necropolis (Saqqarah), and its pyramid fields (eg Giza) form a World Heritage site.

memsahib *noun* formerly, in India, a European married woman; also used as a polite form of address. [from MA'AM + SAHIB]

men SEE MAN.

menace — *noun* **1** a source of threatening danger. **2** a threat; a show of hostility. — *verb* to threaten; to show an intention to cause damage or harm to. [from French *menace*, from Latin *minari*, to threaten]

Menaced Assassin, The a painting by René Magritte (1926, New York).

menacing *adj.* threatening.

ménage *noun literary* a group of people living together; a household. [from French *ménage*]

ménage à trois *literary* a household consisting of three people, especially a husband, a wife, and a lover of one of them. [French, = household of three]

menagerie *noun* **1** a collection of wild animals caged for exhibition; the place where they are kept. **2** a varied or confused mixture, especially of people. [from French *ménagerie*; related to MÉNAGE]

Menai Strait a channel separating Anglesey from the mainland of NW Wales, length 24km/15mi. It varies in width from 175m to 3.2km/2mi. The Menai Suspension Bridge, stretching across the channel, was built by Thomas Telford (1819–26). The channel is also crossed by the Britannia railway/road bridge (1980), rebuilt after fire seriously damaged the original tubular railway bridge of Robert Stephenson (1846–9).

Menander (c.343–291 BC) Greek comic dramatist and poet, born in Athens. Only a few fragments of his prolific works were known until 1906. In 1957 the complete text of his comedy *Dyskolos* (The Bad-Tempered Man) was found in Geneva.

Menchik-Stevenson, Vera (Francevna) (1906–44) Russian–British chess player, born in Moscow. She was the first women's world chess champion in 1927, a title she held until 1944, when she was killed during a London air-raid.

Mencius, properly **Mengzi,** or **Meng-tse** (c.372–c.289 BC) Chinese philosopher and sage, born in Shantung, who founded a school modelled on that of Confucius. For over 20 years he searched unsuccessfully for a ruler who would put into practice his system of social and political order, based on people's innate goodness. After his death his disciples collected his sayings and published them as the *Book of Meng-tse*.

Mencken, H(enry) L(ouis) (1880–1956) US philologist, editor, and satirist, born in Baltimore. He became a journalist and literary critic, and greatly influenced the US literary scene in the 1920s. His major work, *The American Language*, was first published in 1918. In 1924 he founded the *American Mercury*, which he edited until 1933.

mend — *verb* **1** to repair. **2** *intrans.* to improve, especially in health; to heal. **3** to improve or correct: *mend one's ways.* — *noun* a repaired part or place.
— **on the mend** getting better, especially in health.
[shortened from AMEND]

mendacious *adj.* lying or likely to lie.

mendacity *noun* (PL. **mendacities**) *formal* **1** untruthfulness; the tendency to lie. **2** a lie. [from Latin *mendax*, untruthful]

Mendel, Gregor Johann (1822–84) Austrian botanist, born near Udrau. Entering an Augustinian monastery in Brünn in 1843, he was ordained as a priest in 1847. After studying science at Vienna, he returned to the monastery and later became Abbot. His research into plant breeding eventually established 'laws' governing the nature of inheritance. Although not recognized in his lifetime, his concepts have become the basis of modern genetics.

mendelevium *noun* (SYMBOL **Md**, ATOMIC NUMBER **101**) an artificially produced radioactive metallic element. [named after D I Mendeleyev]

Mendeleyev, Dmitri Ivanovich (1834–1907) Russian chemist, born in Tobolsk, Siberia. Professor in St Petersburg, he arranged the chemical elements in a table according to their atomic weight, producing the earliest form of the modern periodic table; from it he predicted the existence of several elements which were subsequently discovered.

Mendelian *adj.* of or relating to the principles of heredity put forward by the Austrian monk and botanist Gregor Mendel.

Mendelssohn(-Bartholdy), (Jakob Ludwig) Felix (1809–47) German composer, the grandson of Moses Mendelssohn, born the son of a Hamburg banker who added the name Bartholdy. Among his early successes as a composer was the *Midsummer Night's Dream* overture (1826). He conducted his C minor symphony in London in 1829, and a tour of Scotland that summer inspired the *Hebrides Overture* and the *Scotch Symphony*. Other major works include his orato-

rios *St Paul* (1836) and *Elijah* (1846). He founded an Academy of Arts in Berlin (1841) and a music school in Leipzig (1843).

Menderes, Adnan (1899–1961) Turkish statesman, born near Aydin. Though educated for the law, he became a farmer, and entered politics in 1932, at first in opposition, then with the party in power under Atatürk. In 1945 he was one of the leaders of the new Democratic Party and became Prime Minister (1950–60) when it came to power. He was deposed in an army coup, put on trial, and hanged at Imrali.

Mendès-France, Pierre (1907–82) French politician, born in Paris. He entered parliament in 1932, and in 1941 escaped to join the Free French forces in England. He was Minister for National Economy under de Gaulle in 1945, and then opposed him as a prominent member of the Radical Party. As Prime Minister (1954–5), he ended the war in Indo-China, but his government was defeated on its N African policy and he lost his seat in the 1958 election.

mendicant — *noun* **1** *formal* a beggar. **2** a member of an order of monks that is not allowed to own property, and is therefore entirely dependent on charity. These include Dominicans, Franciscans, Augustinians, and Carmelites. — *adj.* **1** *formal* begging. **2** dependent on charity. [from Latin *mendicare*, to beg]

Mendip Hills a hill range in Somerset and Avon, SW England. The hills extend 37km/23mi NW–SE from Weston-super-Mare to near Shepton Mallet. Blackdown is the highest point (326m). NOTABLE FEATURES limestone caves of the Cheddar Gorge; traces of former Roman lead mines.

Mendoza 1 POP (1991) 122 000, the capital of Mendoza province, W Argentina. It lies at the foot of the Sierra de los Paramillos Range, on the R Tulumaya. HISTORY colonized by Chile in 1561; belonged to Chile until 1776; destroyed by fire and earthquake in 1861. The city is the trading and processing centre for a large, irrigated agricultural area, dealing mainly in wine. **2** a province in W Argentina with the city of Mendoza as its capital.

Menelaus in Greek legend, the King of Sparta and husband of Helen. He fought in the Trojan War under his elder brother Agamemnon, and after the fall of Troy he was reunited with Helen in Sparta.

menfolk *pl. noun* men collectively, especially the male members of a family or group.

Mengistu, Haile Mariam (1937–) Ethiopian soldier and politician, born in Addis Ababa. He trained at Guenet military academy, and took part in the coup that removed Emperor Haile Selassie (1960). He led another coup to oust the military regime in 1977, when he became Chairman of the Provisional Military Administrative Council (1977–87). Civilian rule was formally established in 1987, when he became Ethiopia's first President, but in 1991 he was overthrown by the Ethiopian People's Revolutionary Democratic Front (EPRDF), resigned, and fled to Zimbabwe. He modelled himself on Fidel Castro, and his goal was to create a socialist state in Ethiopia aligned with the communist bloc.

menhir *noun* a prehistoric monument in the form of a single standing stone. [from Breton *men*, stone + *hir*, long]

menial — *adj.*, *said of work* unskilled, uninteresting, and of low status. — *noun derog.* a domestic servant. [from Old French *meinie*, household]

Meninas, Las (Maids of Honour) a painting by Diego Velázquez (1655, Prado, Madrid).

meningitis *noun* inflammation of the meninges (the three membranes that cover the brain and spinal cord), usually caused by bacterial or viral infections.

◇ The main symptoms are severe headache, fever, stiffness of the neck, loss of appetite, and aversion to light. Bacterial meningitis is treated with antibiotics, which reduce the likelihood of complications such as brain damage or paralysis. Viral meningitis can only be treated with prolonged rest.

meninx *noun* (PL. **meninges**) any of the three membranes that envelop the brain and the spinal cord. [from Greek *meninx*, membrane]

meniscus *noun* (PL. **meniscuses**, **menisci**) **1** *Physics* the curved upper surface of a liquid in a partly filled narrow tube, caused by surface tension effects in which the liquid is either elevated or depressed in the tube. The meniscus may curve upward, as in mercury, or downward, as in water. **2** *Anat.* a crescent-shaped structure, such as the disc of cartilage that divides the cavity of the knee joint. **3** *Optics* a lens that is convex on one side and concave on the other. [from Greek *meniskos*, diminutive of *mene*, moon]

meniscus

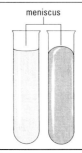

meniscus

Mennonites the Dutch and Swiss Anabaptists who later called themselves Mennonites after one of their Dutch leaders, Menno Simons (1496–1559). Mainly resident in the USA, they are pacifists who adhere to the Confession of Dordrecht (1632), baptise on confession of faith, refuse to hold civic office, and follow the teachings of the New Testament.

menopausal *adj.* **1** relating to or experiencing the menopause. **2** *colloq.* suffering from strange moods and behaviour in middle age.

menopause *noun* the period in a woman's life, typically between the ages of 45 and 55, when menstruation ceases and pregnancy is no longer possible. The hormonal changes involved sometimes cause undesirable symptoms such as hot flushes, vaginal dryness, and emotional disturbances, which can be relieved by hormone replacement therapy (HRT). [from Greek *men*, month + *pausis*, cessation]

menorah *noun* a candlestick with seven branches used in Jewish worship and regarded as a symbol of Judaism. [from Hebrew *menorah*, candlestick]

menorrhagia *noun Medicine* excessive and prolonged bleeding during menstruation. [from Greek *men*, month + *-rragia*, from *rhegnynai*, to break]

Menotti, Gian-Carlo (1911–) Italian-born US composer, born in Cadegliano. He settled in the USA aged 17, and achieved international fame with a series of operas that began with *Amelia goes to the Ball* (1937). *The Consul* (1950) and *The Saint of Bleecker Street* (1954) both won Pulitzer Prizes, and *Amahl and the Night Visitors* (1951) was a successful television opera. In 1958 he established the Festival of Two Worlds at Spoleto, Italy.

Mensa *noun Astron.* the Table, a faint constellation in the southern hemisphere that contains no particularly bright stars.

Mensa International an organization whose members are admitted only after they 'have established by some standard intelligence

test, that their intelligence is higher than that of 98 per cent of the population'. Founded in England in 1945, it has branches in over 60 countries.

menses *pl. noun Medicine* the fluids discharged from the womb during menstruation. [from Latin *mensis*, month]

menstrual *adj.* relating to or involving menstruation.

menstrual cycle *Biol.* in some primates including humans, a repeating cycle of reproductive changes that is regulated by sex hormones, and during which ovulation (the release of an egg from the ovary) occurs, about once in every 28 days in humans. At the end of the cycle, if the egg has not been fertilized, the lining of the womb is shed from the vagina in the process of menstruation.

menstruate *verb intrans.* to discharge blood and other fluids from the womb through the vagina. [from Latin *menstruare*, from *mensis*, month]

menstruation *noun* **1** in women of childbearing age, the periodic discharge through the vagina of blood and fragments of mucous membrane that takes place at approximately monthly intervals if fertilization of an ovum (egg cell) has not occurred. Its duration normally ranges from three to seven days. **2** the time or occurrence of menstruating.

mensuration *noun* **1** the application of geometric principles to the calculation of measurements such as length, volume, and area. **2** *formal* the process of measuring. [from Latin *mensurare*, to measure]

-ment *suffix* forming words denoting: **1** a process, action, or means: *repayment / treatment.* **2** a quality, state, or condition: *enjoyment / merriment.* [from Latin *-mentum*]

mental *adj.* **1** of, relating to, or done using the mind or intelligence: *a mental handicap / mental arithmetic.* **2** of, or suffering from, an illness or illnesses of the mind: *a mental patient.* **3** *colloq.* foolish; stupid. **4** *colloq.* ridiculous; unimaginable. [from Latin *mentalis*, from *mens*, the mind]

mental age *Psychol.* the age in years, etc at which an average child would have reached the same stage of mental development as the individual under consideration.

mental cruelty conduct, not involving physical cruelty or violence, that wounds feelings and personal dignity, especially such conduct by one of the partners in a marriage; formerly one of the grounds for separation or divorce in the UK.

mental disorder *Psychol.* any of various disorders with psychological or behavioural symptoms, excluding mental handicap, disorders of development, and normal reactions to distressing events. Common examples of mental disorders include dementia, eating disorders, and schizophrenia.

mental handicap a condition in which a person has impaired intellectual abilities, characteristically having an intelligence quotient (IQ) of less than 70, and also suffers from some form of social malfunction, eg inability to live independently.
◇ The cause of mental handicap is unknown in about 75% of cases, but known causes include genetic disorders (eg Down's syndrome), infectious diseases (eg infection of the mother with rubella during the early stages of pregnancy), and certain drugs (eg thalidomide). It can also be caused by injury during early childhood. Four categories of mental handicap are generally recognized, namely *mild* (IQ of 50 to 69), *moderate* (IQ of 35 to 49), *severe* (IQ of 20 to 34), and *profound* (IQ of less than 20).

mentality *noun* (PL. **mentalities**) **1** an outlook; a certain way of thinking. **2** intellectual ability.

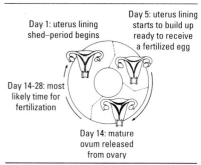

Day 1: uterus lining shed–period begins

Day 5: uterus lining starts to build up ready to receive a fertilized egg

Day 14-28: most likely time for fertilization

Day 14: mature ovum released from ovary

menstrual cycle

mentally *adv.* in the mind, relating to the mind.

menthol *noun* a sharp-smelling substance obtained from peppermint oil, used as a decongestant and a painkiller. [from Latin *mentha*, mint]

mentholated *adj.* containing menthol.

mention — *verb* (**mentioned**, **mentioning**) **1** to speak of or make reference to. **2** to remark on, usually briefly or indirectly. — *noun* **1** a remark, usually a brief reference: *made no mention of it.* **2** a reference made to an individual's merit in an official (especially military) report.
— **don't mention it** *colloq.* no thanks are needed.
not to mention ... without including (facts the speaker is nevertheless about to include, usually for emphasis).
[from Latin *mentio*, a calling to mind]

mentor *noun literary* a trusted teacher or adviser. [from *Mentor*, adviser to Telemachus in the Homeric poems]

menu *noun* **1** the range of dishes available in a restaurant, etc, or of the dishes to be served at a particular meal; also, a list of these: *the wedding menu.* **2** a list of optional computer functions displayed on a screen. [from French *menu*, small and detailed (list)]

Menuhin, Yehudi (1916–) US-born British violinist, born in New York City. He appeared at the age of seven as soloist with the San Francisco Symphony Orchestra, then all over the world as a prodigy. He won international renown as a virtuoso violinist, began to conduct in 1957, the year he set up the Gstaad Festival, and founded a school for musically talented children in 1962. He took British nationality in 1985. His sister Hephzibah (1920–81) was a gifted pianist.

MEP *abbrev.* Member of the European Parliament.

Mephistopheles the evil spirit through whom Faustus makes a contract with the Devil in Christopher Marlowe's *Dr Faustus.*

Mercalli scale *Geol.* a scale used to represent the intensity of an earthquake, ranging from 1 (not felt) to 12 (total devastation). It is an arbitrary scale because it is based on direct observation of the extent of destruction, which will vary depending on the type of buildings, the geology of the area, etc. [named after the Italian geologist Giuseppe Mercalli]

mercantile *adj. formal* of trade or traders; commercial. [from Italian, from *mercante*, merchant]

mercantilism *noun* the business of merchants; trade, commerce; also, advocacy of the *mercantile system*, an old economic strategy that was based on the theory that a nation's interests were best served by development of overseas trade and restriction of imports: the impetus of much 17c and 18c colonization by European powers.

Mercator, Gerhardus, originally **Gerhard Kremer**, or **Cremer** (1512–94) Flemish mathematician, geographer, and map-maker, born in Rupelmonde, Flanders, and a student at Louvain.

He introduced a map projection (Mercator's map projection) to aid navigators in 1569. In 1585 he published the first part of an 'Atlas' of Europe, said to be the first time that this word was used to describe a book of maps.

Mercator's map projection a cylindrical map projection devised in 1569 by Gerhardus Mercator, used for navigation purposes. It is based on parallels of latitude equal in length to that of the equator, intersected at right angles by equally spaced meridians. The distance between the lines of latitude increases away from the equator, which causes increasing distortion in the size of areas at high latitudes (eg Greenland appears as large as S America even though it is only c.10% of the latter's area).

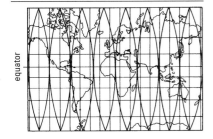

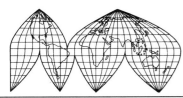

Mercator's cylindrical map projection

Mercedario, Cerro an Andean peak rising to 6 770m in San Juan province, W Argentina, near the Chilean border.

Mercedes POP (1990e) 34 000, the capital of Soriano department, SW Uruguay. It is situated on the S bank of the R Negro, 48km/30mi above its confluence with the R Uruguay. Mercedes is a yachting and fishing centre during the season. NOTABLE FEATURE the Eusebio Giménez Museum.

mercenary — *adj. derog.* excessively concerned with the desire for personal gain, especially money. — *noun* (PL. **mercenaries**) a soldier available for hire by a country or group. [from Latin *mercenarius*, from *merces*, reward, hire]

Mercer, David (1928–80) English dramatist, born in Wakefield, Yorkshire. His work, which often addresses the issues of personal alienation and the class struggle, includes the plays *Ride a Cock Horse* (1965), *After Haggerty* (1970), and *Cousin Vladimir* (1978). He also wrote screenplays (eg *Morgan*, 1965; *Family Life*, 1972) and many television plays.

mercerize *or* **mercerise** *verb* to treat (especially cotton) with a substance which strengthens it and gives it a silky appearance. [from John *Mercer* (1791–1866), English textile manufacturer]

mercerized *or* **mercerised** *adj.* strengthened by mercerizing.

merchandise — *noun* commercial goods. — *verb intrans., trans.* to trade; to buy and sell. [from French *marchandise*; related to MERCHANT]

Merchant, the a pompous, hypocritical member of the minor gentry in Chaucer's *The Canterbury Tales*, who tells the tale of January and May.

merchant — *noun* **1** a trader, especially wholesale. **2** *North Amer., esp. US, Scot.* a shopkeeper. **3** *slang* a person who indulges in a particular (especially undesirable) activity: *gossip mer-*

chant. — *adj.* used for trade; commercial: *merchant ship.* [from Latin *mercari*, to trade]

Merchant Adventurers a small company of local guilds that exported woollen cloth from 15c London, first to the Netherlands and later to Germany. Formed in 1407, they increasingly dominated trade, had headquarters in Antwerp from 1496, and were important in economy and finance until the mid-17c, because woollen cloth was England's leading export.

merchant bank a bank whose main activity is lending money to industry.

Merchant Navy the commercial ships of a nation, a term first used by King George V in a speech in 1922. The mercantile marine was classed as an armed service throughout World War II, and developed a highly efficient manning and recruiting service which was reconstituted for peace time. In 1939 there were over 9 000 ships in Britain's Merchant Navy. The number had dwindled to 154 in 1993.

Merchant of Venice, The a play by William Shakespeare (1596–8). Dealing with such themes as justice and religious discrimination, it is a comedy concerned with the outsmarting by Portia (disguised as a lawyer) of the miserly Jew Shylock, who has demanded a pound of flesh from Antonio for an unpaid loan.

Merchant Staplers, originally **Company of the Merchants of the Staple** a group of 26 English merchants (38 in the 15c) who from 1363 were granted exclusive royal authority to export wool to the continent via the staple port of Calais (where the wool market was concentrated), in return for which they lent money to English monarchs. The value of the monopoly declined with the rise of cloth exports, and the rising cost of maintaining the Calais garrison.

Mercia a kingdom of the Anglo-Saxon heptarchy, with main centres at Tamworth, Lichfield, and Repton. Mercian supremacy over the other Anglo-Saxon kingdoms reached its height under Offa, whom Charlemagne treated as an equal, but by the early 10c Mercia was under Wessex rule. [from Old English *Merce*, people of the marches (boundaries)]

merciful *adj.* showing mercy; forgiving.

mercifully *adv.* luckily; thankfully.

merciless *adj.* without mercy; cruel; pitiless.

mercilessly *adv.* in a merciless way.

Mercilla, Queen the virgin Queen in Spenser's *The Faerie Queene*, who represents Elizabeth I, dispensing mercy to all despite having many foes who wish to remove her from the throne.

Merckx, Eddy, also called **the Cannibal** (1945–) Belgian cyclist, born in Woluwe St Pierre, near Brussels. He won the Tour de France a record-equalling five times (1969–72, 1974), the Tour of Italy five times, and all the major classics, including the Milan–San Remo race seven times. He was the world professional road race champion three times. He won more races (445) and more classics than any other rider. He retired in 1978.

Mercouri, Melina, originally **Anna Amalia Mercouri** (1923–1994) Greek film actress, born in Athens. Her film career started in 1955, and she found fame in 1960 with *Never on Sunday*. Always politically involved, she was exiled from Greece (1967–74), so she played in British and US productions, such as *Topkapi* (1964) and *Gaily, Gaily* (1969). She returned to be elected to parliament in 1977, and was Minister of Culture and Sciences (1981–5) and of Culture, Youth, and Sports (1985–90).

mercurial *adj.* **1** of or containing mercury. **2** *said of a personality, mood, etc* lively or active; tending to change suddenly and unpredictably. [from the planet *Mercury*]

Mercury *or* **Mercurius** in Roman mythology, the god of merchants and trading, and of messages, who was identified with the Greek god Hermes.

Mercury *Astron.* the closest planet to the Sun. Its orbit lies within that of Venus.
◇ Mercury has a diameter of 4 878km, and a markedly elliptical orbit, unlike most of the other planets, whose orbits are almost circular. For this reason, its distance from the Sun ranges from 70 million km when it is furthest away to only 46 million km when it is closest. It takes 59 days to rotate once on its own axis, and 88 days to orbit around the Sun. The planet has no natural satellites.
Mercury has been visited by one spacecraft, *Mariner 10*, in 1974, which passed within 1 000km of the planet and showed it to have a strong magnetic field (produced by the planet's iron core), and no atmosphere (Mercury's gravity is too weak to hold on to any gases to form an atmosphere). Its surface is pitted with thousands of craters, similar to those on the Moon, produced by the impact of meteors. Unlike the Moon, Mercury has no dark dusty plains, and its surface has a wrinkled appearance. A huge body must have collided with it several thousand million years ago, forming a circular indentation 1 300km across, known as the Caloris Basin.
Mercury rotates very slowly, taking over 2 months to pass from sunrise to sunset. During this time the surface temperature increases to 450°C as a result of the Sun's constant heat, but during the long night the temperature falls to about -170°C.

mercury *noun* (SYMBOL **Hg**, ATOMIC NUMBER **80**) a dense silvery-white metallic element, and the only metal that is liquid at room temperature. If inhaled or ingested in more than trace amounts it can cause skin disorders, kidney and brain damage, and birth defects. [from Latin *Mercurius*, the Roman god Mercury]
◇ Mercury is mainly obtained from the bright red ore cinnabar (mercury sulphide). It can be alloyed with other metals to form non-toxic *amalgams*, which are widely used in dentistry to fill tooth cavities, and the metal is also used in thermometers, barometers, mercury-vapour lamps, batteries, and switches. Mercury compounds have been used in pigments, drugs, rat poisons, and insecticides, but are highly toxic. Mercury is a serious source of environmental pollution, and may enter the food chain as a result of its accumulation within food fish following the discharge of industrial waste into rivers, lakes, and seas.

Mercury programme *Astron.* the first US crewed space flight programme, and the precursor to the *Gemini* and *Apollo* programmes. The crew consisted of one astronaut, and the first manned orbital flight took place in February 1962.

Mercutio the mocking but close friend of Romeo who is killed by Tybalt in Shakespeare's *Romeo and Juliet*.

mercy *noun* (PL. **mercies**) **1** kindness or forgiveness shown when punishment is possible or justified. **2** an act or circumstance in which these qualities are displayed, especially by God. **3** a tendency to be forgiving. **4** a piece of good luck; a welcome happening: *grateful for small mercies*.
— **at the mercy of someone** *or* **something** wholly in their power; liable to be harmed by them.
[from Latin *merces*, reward, favour]

mercy flight a flight by an aeroplane or helicopter, eg taking a seriously ill or injured person to hospital or transporting human organs for transplantation, when other means of transport are impracticable or unavailable.

mercy killing *noun* an act of killing painlessly to relieve suffering; euthanasia.

mere[1] *adj.* nothing more than; no better, more important, or useful than. [from Latin *merus*, unmixed]

mere[2] *noun old use poetic, often in English place names* a lake or pool. [from Anglo-Saxon]

Meredith, George (1828–1909) English novelist, born in Portsmouth, Hampshire. He began to study law, then turned to journalism and letters. He achieved popularity with the novels *The Egoist* (1879) and *Diana of the Crossways* (1885). His main poetic work is *Modern Love* (1862), based partly on his first, unhappy, marriage.

Meredith a male and female first name. [from the Old Welsh name *Maredudd*, perhaps composed of Celtic elements meaning 'great' + 'chief lord']

merely *adv.* simply; only.

meretricious *adj.* **1** bright or attractive on the surface, but of no real value. **2** false and insincere. [from Latin *meretrix*, prostitute]

merganser *noun* any of various kinds of large diving duck of northern countries, with a long hooked serrated bill. [from Latin *mergus*, diving bird + *anser*, goose]

merge *verb* **1** *trans., intrans.* to blend, combine, or join with something else. **2** (**merge into something**) to become part of a larger whole, and therefore impossible to distinguish. [from Latin *mergere*, to plunge]

merger *noun* a joining together, especially of business firms.

meridian *noun* **1** *Geog.* an imaginary line on the Earth's surface passing through the poles at right angles to the equator; a line of longitude. **2** *literary* the peak, eg of success. **3** *Chinese Medicine* any of several lines or pathways through the body along which life energy flows. [from Latin *meridianus*, from *medius*, middle + *dies*, day]

meridional *adj.* **1** *technical* of, relating to, or along a meridian. **2** *literary* of the south, especially of Europe.

Mérimée, Prosper (1803–70) French novelist, born in Paris. He held posts in the ministries of the navy, commerce, and the interior, and became a senator in 1853. He wrote novels and short stories, archaeological and historical dissertations, and travel stories. His novels include *Colomba* (1841) and *Carmen* (1843), the source of Bizet's opera.

meringue *noun* a crisp cooked mixture of sugar and egg-whites, or a cake made from this. [from French]

merino *noun* (PL. **merinos**) **1** a type of sheep bred for its long fine wool. **2** fine yarn or fabric made from its wool. [from Spanish]

meristem *noun Bot.* in a plant, a region of actively dividing cells, mainly at the tips of shoots and roots. [from Greek *meristos*, divisible]

merit — *noun* **1** worth, excellence or praiseworthiness. **2** (*often* **merits**) a good point or quality. — *verb* (**merited, meriting**) to deserve; to be worthy of or entitled to. [from Latin *meritum*, reward]

meritocracy *noun* (PL. **meritocracies**) a social system based on leadership by people of great talent or intelligence, rather than of wealth or noble birth.

meritorious *adj.* deserving reward or praise.

Mer, La (The Sea) three symphonic pieces by Claude Debussy (1903–5): *De L'aube à midi sur la mer* (From Dawn to Noon on the Sea), *Jeux de vagues* (Play of the Waves), and *Dialogue du vent et de la mer* (Dialogue of the Wind and the Sea).

Merleau-Ponty, Maurice (1908–61) French phenomenological philosopher, born in Rochefort-sur-mer. With Jean-Paul Sartre and Simone de Beauvoir, he helped to found the journal *Les Temps modernes* (1945). He held posts at

Lyons (1948) and the Sorbonne (1949), and was appointed Professor of Philosophy at the Collège de France in 1952. His books include *La Structure du comportement* (The Structure of Behaviour, 1942) and *Phénoménologie de la perception* (The Phenomenology of Perception, 1945).

Merlin in Arthurian legend, the good wizard or sage whose magic was used to help King Arthur. He was the son of an incubus and a mortal woman, and therefore indestructible. However, he was finally entrapped by Vivien, the Lady of the Lake, and bound under a rock for ever.

merlin *noun* a species of small dark-coloured falcon with a black-striped tail. [from Old French *esmerillon*]

merlon *noun Fortification* the projecting part of the parapet between embrasures in a battlement. [from French *merlon*, from Italian *merlone*, battlements]

mermaid *noun* a mythical sea creature with a woman's head and upper body, and a fish's tail. [from Anglo-Saxon *mere*, lake, sea + MAID]
◇ Stories of mermaids are thought to originate from sailors' sightings of the dugong, a marine mammal whose head somewhat resembles a human, and whose habit of suckling its young by supporting it on its breast with one flipper is reminiscent of a woman with an infant.

merman *noun* the male equivalent of a mermaid.

Merovingian — *noun* a member of a Frankish dynasty (see MEROVINGIANS). — *adj.* relating to the Merovingians.

Merovingians a Frankish ruling dynasty, formerly chiefs of the Salians, named after the semi-legendary Merovech or Meroveus (the 'sea-fighter'). The first Merovingian king to control large parts of Gaul was Clovis I; the last to hold significant power was Dagobert I (d.638), although the royal dynasty survived until Childeric III's deposition (751).

Merrick a male first name. [a form of Welsh *Meurig*, a variant of MAURICE]

merrily *adv.* in a merry way.

merriment *noun* gaiety with laughter and noise, hilarity.

merry *adj.* (**merrier, merriest**) **1** cheerful and lively. **2** *colloq.* slightly drunk.
— **make merry** *old use* to have fun; to celebrate. [from Anglo-Saxon *myrige*]

merry-go-round *noun* a fairground amusement consisting of a revolving platform fitted with rising and falling seats in the form of horses or other figures.

merrymaker *noun* a person who is having fun, a reveller.

merrymaking *noun* cheerful celebration.

Merry Widow, The (Die Lustige Witwe) an operetta by Franz Lehár (1905). Danilo complies with the Pontevedrian ambassador's request to protect the wealthy widow Hanna from foreign suitors, to ensure her money stays in the impoverished Pontevedria. Though they have been in love since a previous liaison, Hanna is wary of men's desire for money, and Danilo prefers to be unattached, until he becomes jealous of her response to another's advances and can prove that love is his only motive for marrying her.

Merry Wives of Windsor, The a play by William Shakespeare (1597). Set in England, it is a comedy focusing on Falstaff's attempts to woo two women who are in charge of their husbands' money, but who conspire to bring him low.

Mersey, River a river in NW England, length 112km/70mi. Formed at the junction of the R Goyt and R Etherow, it flows past Warrington, Runcorn, Birkenhead, and Liverpool to form a wide estuary into the Irish Sea at Liverpool Bay. Tributaries include the R Weaver, the R Irwell, and the Manchester Ship Canal.

Merseyside POP (1992e) 1.5m, a metropolitan county area in NW England, comprising five districts. Controlled by a metropolitan county council until 1986, the area is now administered by metropolitan district councils. AREA 652sq km/252sq mi. It occupies both sides of the estuary of the R Mersey. CHIEF TOWN Liverpool. ECONOMY chemicals; vehicles; electrical equipment. NOTABLE FEATURES Prescot Museum; Croxteth Hall and Country Park; Speke Hall.

Meru, Mount in Hindu cosmology, a mythical golden mountain (popularly identified with one of the Himalayan peaks), considered the central axis of the universe and the paradisic abode of the gods. The subject of many myths (also in Buddhism), it is said to have Brahma's square city of gold at its summit and seven underworlds beneath.

Mervyn a male first name. [a form of Welsh *Myrddin*, thought to be from the place name Carmarthen (*Caerfyrddin* in Welsh), King Arthur's court magician being *Myrddin Emrys*, or 'Emrys of Carmarthen', Latinized as *Merlin Ambrosius*]

Merz School a form of Dada invented by German painter Kurt Schwitters (1887–1948). It is characterized by abstract collages with pieces of rubbish attached to them. The name 'Merz' derives from the word 'Kommerz', which appeared without its first three letters on a piece of torn paper in one of Schwitters's collages.

mesa *noun Geol.* an isolated flat-topped hill with at least one steep side or cliff, formed by the remnants of horizontal rocks resistant to erosion, which protect the softer rock lying underneath. [from Spanish *mesa*, from Latin *mensa*, table]

mésalliance *noun literary* a marriage to someone of lower social status. [from French, = misalliance]

Mesa Verde an area of precipitous canyons and wooded volcanic mesa in SW Colorado, USA, 55km/34mi W of Durango. It has been a National Park since 1906, and is renowned for its Anasazi cliff-dwellings — notably the four-storey Cliff Palace of the 13c, which has 220 rooms and 23 kivas (ceremonial chambers). It is a World Heritage site.

mescal *or* **peyote** *noun* a globe-shaped cactus of Mexico and the SW USA. Its sap is used to make the Mexican fermented drink, pulque, and the spirit, mescal. [from Aztec *mexcalli*]

mescalin *or* **mescaline** *noun* a hallucinogenic drug obtained from the button-like top of the mescal cactus. It is sometimes chewed, or can be made into tea or powder.

mesclun *noun* a mixed green salad of young leaves and shoots of rocket, chicory, fennel, etc. [from French, from Niçois *mesclumo*, mixture]

mesdames see MADAM, MADAME.

Meselson, Matthew Stanley (1930–) US molecular biologist, born in Denver, Colorado. In 1958, with Franklin Stahl, he demonstrated the way in which the double helix of the DNA molecule carries genetic information, with the two strands of one parent DNA molecule each forming new daughter DNA. He became professor at Harvard in 1964.

mesencephalon *noun Anat.* the mid-brain, which connects the forebrain to the hindbrain. [from Geek *mesos*, middle, + *encephalon*, brain]

mesentery *noun Anat.* in animals, the double layer of membrane on the inner surface of the body wall that serves to hold the stomach, small intestine, spleen, and other abdominal organs in place. [from Greek *mesos*, middle + *enteron*, intestine]

mesh — *noun* **1** netting, or a piece of netting made of (especially fine) wire or thread. **2** each of the openings between the threads of a net. **3** (*usually* **meshes**) a network. — *verb intrans.* **1** *technical, said of the teeth on gear wheels* to engage. **2** to fit or work together. **3** to become entangled. [perhaps from Old Dutch *maesche*]

Meshed see MASHHAD.

Mesmer, Franz Anton (1734–1815) Austrian physician and founder of 'mesmerism' (the early name for hypnosis), born near Constance. He studied medicine at Vienna, and around 1772 claimed that there exists a power, which he called 'magnetism', that could be used to cure diseases. He created a sensation in Paris, but in 1785 a commission reported unfavourably, and he retired into obscurity in Switzerland.

mesmerism *noun* 1 a former term for HYPNOTISM. 2 a former method of hypnosis based on the ideas of Franz Anton Mesmer (1734–1815), sometimes involving the use of magnets. [named after Franz Anton Mesmer, Austrian physician]

mesmerist *noun* a hypnotist.

mesmerize *or* **mesmerise** *verb* 1 *old use* to hypnotize. 2 to grip the attention of; to fascinate

mesmerizing *or* **mesmerising** *adj.* hypnotic.

Mesoamerican *adj.* relating to or originating from Central America, between N Mexico and Panama.

Mesoamerican ballgame a ritual athletic contest of notable brutality, widespread in Mexico from c.1000 BC to the Spanish Conquest in 1519. It was played with a large, solid rubber ball by two opposing teams on a purpose-built court; the ball represented the Sun, the court the cosmos. Ceremonies performed after the game included the sacrifice of the losers.

mesoderm *noun Zool.* in a multicellular animal that has two or more layers of body tissue, the layer of cells between the ectoderm and the endoderm, that develops into the circulatory system, muscles, and reproductive organs (and also the skeleton and excretory system in vertebrates). [from MESO- + Greek *derma*, skin]

mesolithic *adj.* (also **Mesolithic**) of the middle period of the Stone Age, from about 12 000 to 3 000 BC in Europe. [from Greek *mesos*, middle + *lithos*, stone]

meson *noun Physics* any of a group of unstable strongly interacting elementary particles, with a mass intermediate between that of an electron and a nucleon (a proton or neutron). Mesons are thought to have a role in holding nucleons together in the nucleus. [from Greek, from *mesos*, middle]

mesophyll *noun Bot.* the internal tissue that lies between the upper and lower epidermal surfaces of a plant leaf. It consists of parenchyma cells, many of which contain chloroplasts and carry out photosynthesis. [from Greek *mesos*, middle + *phyllon*, leaf]

Mesopotamia an ancient region lying between the Tigris and Euphrates, literally, 'the land between the rivers'. It was conventionally divided into two: Lower Mesopotamia, the home of the Sumerian and Babylonian civilizations, stretched from the alluvial plain at the head of the Persian Gulf to Baghdad (central Iraq); Upper Mesopotamia, the home of the Assyrians, extended from Baghdad to the foothills of E Turkey. Historically, the former is more important; it was here that the world's first urban civilization emerged during the fourth millennium BC.

mesosphere *noun* the layer of the atmosphere above the stratosphere and below the thermosphere, in which temperature rapidly decreases with height. [from Greek *mesos*, middle + SPHERE]

Mesozoic *adj.* 1 *Geol.* relating to the era of geological time extending from about 250 million to 65 million years ago, and subdivided into the Triassic, Jurassic, and Cretaceous periods. During the Mesozoic era dinosaurs flourished, becoming extinct at the end of the era, and small mammals first appeared. 2 relating to the rocks formed during this era. [from Greek *mesos*, middle + Greek *zoion*, animal]

mess — *noun* 1 an untidy or dirty state. 2 a state of disorder or confusion. 3 a badly damaged state. 4 something in a damaged or disordered state. 5 *colloq.* animal faeces. 6 a communal dining room, especially in the armed forces. 7 *old use* a portion of any pulpy food. — *verb* 1 *intrans. colloq.* (**mess with something**) to interfere or meddle in it. 2 (*also* **mess something up**) to put into an untidy, dirty, or damaged state. 3 *intrans. said of soldiers, etc* to eat, or live, together. 4 *intrans.* (**mess with someone**) *colloq.* to become involved in argument or conflict with them.
— **mess about** *or* **around** to behave in an annoyingly foolish way; to potter or tinker.
mess about *or* **around with someone** to treat them roughly or unfairly.
mess about *or* **around with something** to meddle or interfere in it.
no messing *colloq.* 1 without difficulty. 2 honestly; truthfully.
[from Old French *mes*, dish]

message *noun* 1 a spoken or written communication sent from one person to another. 2 the instructive principle contained within a story, religious teaching, etc. 3 (**messages**) *chiefly Scot.* an errand; household shopping.
— **get the message** *colloq.* to understand.
[from Latin *mittere*, to send]

messenger *noun* a person who carries communications between people.

messenger RNA (ABBREV. **mRNA**) *Biochem.* any of the single-stranded molecules of RNA that are responsible for transporting coded instructions for the manufacture of proteins from DNA in the nucleus to the ribosomes (which are the site of protein manufacture) in the cytoplasm.

Messenia an ancient region in Greece, the SW part of the Peloponnese. It was conquered by the Spartans (8c–7c BC) and its inhabitants were reduced to a state of serfdom called *helotry*. They regained their independence in 369 BC with the help of the Thebans.

Messerschmitt, Will (Wilhelm) (1898–1978) German aviation designer and production chief, born in Frankfurt-am-Main. In 1923 he established the Messerschmitt aircraft manufacturing works, and during World War II supplied the Luftwaffe with its foremost types of combat aircraft. From 1955 he worked in the aircraft and automobile industry.

Messiaen, Olivier (Eugène Prosper Charles) (1908–92) French composer and organist, born in Avignon. He studied at the Paris Conservatoire, where he later became Professor of Harmony, and taught at the Schola Cantorum. His music, which evolved new methods of pitch organization and intricate mathematical rhythmic systems, was inspired by religious mysticism and a keen interest in birdsong.

Messiah an oratorio by George Frideric Handel (1742), the text of which is based on the Bible and the Prayer Book Psalter.

Messiah *noun* (**the Messiah**) 1 in Christianity, Jesus Christ. 2 in Judaism, the king of the Jews still to be sent by God to free them. 3 a person who sets free a country or a people. [from Hebrew *mashiah*, anointed]

Messianic *adj.* 1 relating to or associated with a Messiah. 2 relating to any popular leader, especially a liberator.

Messianism *noun Relig.* belief in a Messiah, specifically Jewish movements expressing the hope for a new and perfected age.
◊ Jewish Orthodoxy adheres to traditional beliefs in the coming of a personal Messiah who will re-establish the Temple in Jerusalem and from there rule over a redeemed world. Reformed Judaism anticipates the world's perfection by the example of Judaism in human achievements, such as social reforms and justice, while preserving the identity of the Jewish race within existing states. Zionism places the emphasis on the physical restoration of the Jewish state in Palestine and the return of exiled Jews there.

messily *adv.* in a messy way.

Messina, Strait of, ancient **Fretum Siculum** a channel between Sicily and the Italian mainland, separating the Ionian and Tyrrhenian seas. It is 32km/20mi long, with a minimum width in the N of 3km/1.8mi. Chief ports are Messina (on Sicily) and Reggio di Calabria (on the mainland).

Messrs see MR.

messy *adj.* (**messier**, **messiest**) 1 involving or causing dirt or mess. 2 confused, untidy.

mestizo *or* **mestiza** *noun* (PL. **mestizos**, **mestizas**) a male (**-zo**) or female (**-za**) person of mixed Spanish-American and American Indian parentage. [from Spanish]

Met *noun* (**the Met**) *colloq.* the London Metropolitan Police Force.

met see MEET.

meta- *combining form* forming words denoting: 1 a change: *metabolism*. 2 an area of study related to another subject of study, but going beyond it in some way, eg by going beyond the normal limits of investigation in that subject or by the analysis of its theoretical concepts: *metalinguistics*. 3 a position behind or beyond: *metacarpal*. [from Greek *meta*, among, with, beside, after]

metabolic *adj.* 1 relating to an organism's metabolism. 2 exhibiting metamorphosis.

Metabolism a Japanese architectural concept and group originally founded in 1960 by Kiyonori Kitukake, Kisho Kurokawa, and Noburo Kawazoe. It is characterized by the use of forms reminiscent of science fiction, and by the synthesis of the public realm with private spaces.

metabolism *noun Biochem.* the sum of all the chemical reactions that occur within the cells of a living organism, including both formation (*anabolism*) and breakdown (*catabolism*) of complex organic compounds, eg proteins, fats, carbohydrates. The rates at which individual reactions occur are controlled by enzymes. [from Greek *metabole*, change]

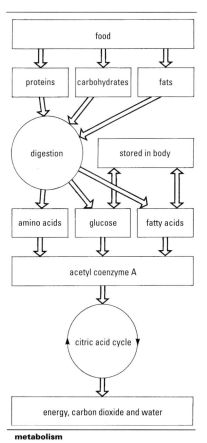

metabolism

metabolite *noun Biochem.* a molecule that participates in the biochemical reactions that take place in the cells of living organisms.

metabolize *or* **metabolise** *verb trans., intrans. Biochem.* within a living cell, to break down complex organic compounds into simpler molecules.

metacarpal *adj.* relating to or in the region of the metacarpus.

metacarpus *noun* (PL. **metacarpi**) the set of five bones in the hand between the wrist and the knuckles. [from META- + Greek *karpos*, wrist]

metal — *noun* 1 any of a class of chemical elements with certain characteristic properties. All metals except mercury are solid at room temperature, and most of them are shiny, malleable (able to be hammered into sheets and bent without fracture), and ductile (able to be drawn into thin wire). **2** road metal, small broken stones used to make and repair roads. **3** (**metals**) the rails of a railway. — *verb* (**metalled, metalling**) 1 to fit with metal. 2 to make or mend (a road) with small broken stones. [from Greek *metallon*, mine]
◇ Metals are generally good conductors of heat and electricity, due to the fact that their electrons can move around more freely than those of a non-metal. Most metals occur naturally as their oxides or sulphides in the form of mineral ores, although a few (eg gold, silver) are found uncombined and are known as *native metals*. Metals can be mixed to form *alloys*, and small quantities of certain metallic elements are essential requirements of plants and animals.

metallic *adj.* 1 made of metal. 2 characteristic of metal, eg in sound or appearance.

metallize *or* **metallise** *verb* 1 to give a metallic appearance to. 2 to apply a thin coating of metal to.

metalloid *noun Chem.* a chemical element that has both metallic and non-metallic properties, eg silicon, boron, germanium, arsenic. All metalloids are semiconductors, and are capable of combining with a metal to form an alloy.

metallurgist *noun* a person who studies or is expert in metallurgy.

metallurgy *noun* the scientific study of the nature and properties of metals and their extraction from the ground.

metalwork *noun* 1 the craft or practice of shaping metal. 2 articles made of metal.

metalworker *noun* a person who works with metal.

metamorphic *adj.* 1 relating to metamorphosis or metamorphism. 2 *Geol.* denoting any of a group of rocks that have been formed by the physical or chemical alteration of pre-existing rock as a result of the effects of intense heat or pressure, or both, beneath the Earth's surface, eg marble (formed from limestone). See also IGNEOUS, SEDIMENTARY.

metamorphism *noun Geol.* any changes in the structure or composition of a rock that take place in response to the effects of intense heat or pressure, or both, beneath the Earth's surface.

metamorphose *verb intrans., trans.* to undergo or cause to undergo metamorphosis.

Metamorphoses an epic Latin poem in fifteen books by Ovid (c.2c–8c). It is a collection of Classical and Near-Eastern legendary narratives.

metamorphosis *noun* (PL. **metamorphoses**) 1 a change of form, appearance, or character. 2 *Biol.* the change of physical form that occurs during the development into adulthood of some creatures, eg butterflies. [from META- + Greek *morphe*, form]

metaphase *noun Genetics* the second phase of mitosis and meiosis, during which the membrane surrounding the nucleus breaks down, and the chromosomes are lined up along the equatorial region of the cell between the two poles of the spindle.

metaphor *noun* 1 an expression in which the person, action or thing referred to is described as if it really were what it merely resembles, as when a rejection is referred to as 'a slap in the face'. 2 such expressions in general, or their use. [from Greek *metaphora*]

metaphorical *adj.* not actual or literal, only in a figure of speech.

metaphorically *adv.* in a metaphorical way; in terms of metaphor.

metaphysical *adj.* 1 relating to metaphysics. 2 (*also* **Metaphysical**) denoting any of a group of 17c poets who used elaborate images to express intense feelings and complex ideas.

metaphysically *adv.* 1 in a metaphysical way. 2 in a metaphysical sense.

metaphysical painting a modern art movement that flourished in Italy c.1911–18. The name *Pittura Metafisica* was used by Giorgio De Chirico to describe his paintings of mysterious empty landscapes inhabited by tailors' dummies and classical busts casting threatening shadows. It was an important precursor of surrealism.

metaphysical poetry a term applied by John Dryden and Dr Samuel Johnson (in a derogatory sense) to certain English poetry of the late 16c and early 17c, by, for example, John Donne, Thomas Carew, Andrew Marvell, and Abraham Cowley. Its chief characteristics are striking and unusual imagery, fanciful ideas, the use of paradox, flexible metre and rhythm, and intricate and ingenious word-play.

metaphysics *noun* 1 the branch of philosophy dealing with the nature of existence and the basic principles of truth and knowledge. 2 *colloq.* any type of abstract discussion, writing or thinking. [from Greek *ta meta ta physika*, the things after natural science, from the order of subjects dealt with in Aristotle's writings]

Metastasio, Pietro, originally **Pietro (Armando Domenico) Trapassi** (1698–1782) Italian poet, born in Rome. He made his reputation with his masque, *The Garden of Hesperides* (1722), and wrote the libretti for 27 operas, including Mozart's *Clemenza di Tito* (1734). He was made court poet at Vienna in 1729.

metastasis *noun* (PL. **metastases**) 1 *Medicine* the spread of a disease, especially a malignant (cancerous) tumour, from one part of the body to another via the bloodstream or lymphatic system, or across a body cavity. 2 a secondary tumour that has developed as a result of the spread of a malignant disease in this way. [from Greek *metastasis*, change of place]

metatarsal *adj.* relating to or in the region of the metatarsi.

metatarsus *noun* (PL. **metatarsi**) the set of five long bones in the foot, between the ankle and the toes. [from META- + Greek *tarsos*, instep]

metatheory *noun* broadly, any theory whose subject matter is another theory. In logic, it is the investigation of the various properties of a formal language, such as whether the language is consistent (ie no contradiction can be derived from its assumptions) and complete (ie every logical truth can be derived from its assumptions).

Metaxas, Ioannis (1870–1941) Greek soldier and politician, born in Ithaka. He fought against the Turks in 1897, studied military science in Germany, and in 1913 became Chief of the General Staff. On the fall of King Constantine I (1917) he fled to Italy, but returned with him in 1921, and later became Deputy Prime Minister (1935). As premier (1936–41), he established a fascist dictatorship and led the resistance to the Italian invasion of Greece in 1940.

Metazoa *pl. noun Zool.* in the classification of animals, a subkingdom consisting of all multicellular animals whose cells are organized into specialized tissues and organs, as opposed to the single-celled animals that belong to the subkingdom or phylum Protozoa. [from Greek *meta*, after + *zoion*, animal]

metazoan — *noun Zool.* any animal that belongs to the subkingdom Metazoa, which includes all multicellular animals, ie those with bodies composed of many cells organized into distinct tissues, including a nervous system. — *adj.* of or relating to the Metazoa. [from META- + Greek *zoion*, animal]

Metchnikoff *or* **Mechnikov, Elie**, originally **Ilya Ilich** (1845–1916) Russian biologist, born in Ivanovka, Ukraine. He became professor at Odessa (1870), and in 1888 joined Louis Pasteur in Paris. He shared the 1908 Nobel Prize for Physiology or Medicine with Paul Ehrlich for his work on immunology, in which he discovered the cells (phagocytes) which engulf infective organisms.

mete
— **mete something out** *verb* to give out or dispense (especially punishment). [from Anglo-Saxon *metan*, to measure]

meteor *noun* a dust particle that moves at high speed from space into the Earth's atmosphere, where it burns up as a result of friction, emitting a brief flash or streak of light. — Also called *shooting star.* [from Greek *ta meteora*, things on high]
◇ A *meteor shower* occurs when the Earth passes through a trail of dust left by a comet in interplanetary space. Tens of meteors per hour can then be seen emanating from the same part of the sky (the *radiant*).

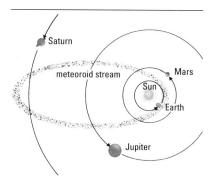

meteor showers

Meteora a group of rock formations (spikes, cones, and cliffs) in Trikala department, N Greece, which rise to 300m from the Pinios plain. It is the location of various monasteries, settled from the 10c, the highest and grandest of which is the Méga Metéoron at 550m.

meteoric *adj.* 1 of or relating to meteors. 2 *said of success, etc* very rapid; very short-lived.

meteorically *adv.* like a meteor; very rapidly or brilliantly.

meteorite *noun Astron.* a lump of rock or metallic material from outer space that is large enough to fall to the Earth's surface without burning up as it passes through the atmosphere.
◇ A falling meteorite leaves a brilliant trail in the sky, known as a *fireball. Stony meteorites* consist of rock, and *iron meteorites* are composed mainly of iron or iron-nickel alloy. Most meteorites are thought to be fragments from asteroids that broke up during collisions. Thousands of meteorites land on the Earth each year, the majority of which are not recorded because they fall in the sea or in remote areas. The largest known meteorite weighs about 60 tonnes and landed in Grootfontein, Namibia.

meteoroid *noun Astron.* in space, a small moving solid object or dust particle, known as a *meteorite* if it is large enough to pass through the

Earth's atmosphere and land on the ground, and known as a *meteor* if it enters the Earth's atmosphere as a dust particle which then burns up in a brief flash of light.

meteorological *adj.* of or relating to meteorology.

Meteorological Office see MET OFFICE.

meteorologist *noun* a person who studies or is expert in meteorology.

meteorology *noun* the scientific study of weather and climate over a relatively short period, as opposed to climatology, in which long-term weather patterns are studied. [from Greek *ta meteora*, things on high + -LOGY]

meter — *noun* **1** an instrument for measuring and recording, especially quantities of electricity, gas, water, etc used. **2** a parking-meter. — *verb* (**metered**, **metering**) to measure and record using a meter. [from Anglo-Saxon *metan*, to measure]

-meter *combining form* forming words denoting: **1** an instrument for measuring: *thermometer*. **2** a line of poetry with a specified number of units of stress, or feet: *pentameter*. [from Greek *metron*, measure]

methadone *noun* a drug similar to morphine, but less addictive, used as a painkiller and as a heroin substitute for drug-addicts. [from di*methyl*amino-*d*iphenyl-heptan*one*]

methanal *noun Chem.* same as FORMALDEHYDE.

methane *noun Chem.* (FORMULA CH_4) a colourless odourless flammable gas belonging to the alkane series of hydrocarbons. It is the main component of natural gas, and occurs naturally as marsh gas in swamps and marshes, where it is formed by decaying organic matter, and as firedamp, an explosive gas found in coal mines. It is used in the manufacture of organic chemicals and hydrogen, and as a cooking and heating fuel (in the form of natural gas). [from *methyl* as in METHYL ALCOHOL]

methanoic acid *Chem.* same as FORMIC ACID.

methanol *noun Chem.* (FORMULA CH_3OH) a colourless flammable toxic liquid, even small doses of which may cause blindness. It is used as a solvent and antifreeze, can be catalytically converted to petrol, and is added to ethanol (absolute alcohol) to make methylated spirits. — Also called *methyl alcohol*. [from METHANE + ALCOHOL]

methinks *verb* (PAST TENSE **methought**) *old use* it seems to me (that).

methionine *noun Biochem.* an essential amino acid found in proteins.

Method a style of acting and a system of actor-training derived from the teachings of Russian actor and director Stanislavsky. The style is characterized by improvisation, spontaneity, and an emphasis on psychological realism in the presentation of a role. It has been widely practised, especially in the USA (eg at the Actors Studio in New York City, under the tutelage of Lee Strasberg).

method *noun* **1** a way of doing something, especially an ordered set of procedures. **2** good planning; efficient organization. **3** (*often* **methods**) a technique used in a particular activity: *farming methods*. — **method in one's madness** reason or good sense underlying what seems an odd or chaotic situation or procedure. [from Greek *methodos*]

methodical *adj.* efficient and orderly; done in an orderly way.

methodically *adv.* in a methodical way.

Methodism a Christian denomination founded (1739) by John Wesley as an evangelical movement within the Church of England. It spread rapidly as Wesley travelled the country on horseback and sent other evangelical leaders to

the American colonies, where it flourished; the movement became a separate body in 1795. The principles and beliefs of the Church are laid down in Wesley's sermons, his notes on the New Testament, and his Articles of Religion.

Methodist — *noun* a member of the Methodist Church, founded on the principles of Methodism. — *adj.* relating to Methodism.

Methodius, St see CYRIL, ST.

methodological *adj.* relating to or according to methodology.

methodology *noun* (PL. **methodologies**) **1** the system of methods and principles used in a particular activity. **2** the study of method and procedure.

methought see METHINKS.

meths *sing. noun colloq.* methylated spirits.

Methuen, Sir Algernon (Methuen Marshall), originally **Algernon Stedman** (1856–1924) English publisher, born in London. He was a teacher of Classics and French (1880–95), and began publishing in 1889 to market his own textbooks. His first success was Rudyard Kipling's *Barrack-Room Ballads* (1892), and he published works by Hilaire Belloc, G K Chesterton, Joseph Conrad, John Masefield, R L Stevenson, and Oscar Wilde.

Methuselah the eighth of the Hebrew patriarchs, who lived before the Flood. His supposed 969 years make him the longest-lived man.

methyl alcohol see METHANOL.

methylated spirits *or* **methylated spirit** ethanol (absolute alcohol) that has been mixed with small quantities of methanol and pyridine to make it undrinkable, so that it can be sold without excise duty for use as a fuel and solvent. It often contains a blue or purple dye.

methylene blue *Chem.* a blue dye used as a pH indicator, as a stain in the preparation of slides of tissue specimens for examination under an optical microscope, and as a dye for textiles.

methyl group *Chem.* in organic chemical compounds, the CH_3 group, eg methyl alcohol (CH_3OH).

meticulous *adj.* paying, or showing, very careful attention to detail. [from Latin *meticulosus*, frightened]

meticulousness *noun* being meticulous.

Met Office *Brit. colloq.* the Meteorological Office, the government department that monitors national weather conditions and produces weather forecasts.

metonymy *noun* (PL. **metonymies**) the use of a word referring to an element or attribute of some related notion to mean the larger notion itself, eg *the bottle* for 'the drinking of alcohol' and *the Crown* for 'the sovereign'. [from META- + Greek *onoma*, name]

metope *noun Archit.* a slab or tablet of plain or sculpture marble located between the triglyphs in the frieze of a Doric entablature. [from Greek *metope*, from *meta*, beside + *ope*, an opening for the end of a beam]

metre¹ *noun* the principal unit of length in the metric system, equal to 39.37 inches. [from Greek *metron*, measure]

metre² *noun* **1** *Poetry* the arrangement of words and syllables in a rhythmic pattern according to their length and stress; a particular pattern. **2** tempo in music. [from Greek *metron*, measure]

metric¹ *adj.* of or based on the metre or the metric system.

metric² *or* **metrical** *adj. technical* of or in verse as distinct from prose.

-metric *combining form* forming words denoting scientific measurement: *thermometric*.

metrically *adv.* **1** in or with the metric system of measurement. **2** in terms of metre; in metre.

metricate *verb trans., intrans.* to convert to units of the metric system.

metrication *noun* conversion to metric measurement.

metric system a standard system of measurement, based on decimal units, in which each successive multiple of a unit is 10 times larger than the one preceding it. Metric units have a prefix that denotes what multiples or fractions of the basic unit they represent, eg kilo- (k) denotes 10^3.

metro *noun* (PL. **metros**) an urban railway system, usually mostly underground, especially (**Metro**) the system in Paris. [from French *métro*, abbrev. of *chemin de fer métropolitain*, metropolitan railway]

metronome *noun* a device that indicates musical tempo by means of a ticking pendulum that can be set to move at different speeds. [from Greek *metron*, measure + *nomos*, law]

Metric Conversion Factors

If measurements are in imperial, multiply by the conversion factors given below to find the metric equivalent; if they are in metric, divide by the conversion factors to find imperial.

1 acre = **0.4047** hectares
1 bushel (imperial) = **36.369** litres
1 centimetre = **0.3937** inch
1 chain = **20.1168** metres
1 cord = **3.62456** cubic metres
1 cubic centimetre = **0.0610** cubic inch
1 cubic decimetre = **61.024** cubic inches
1 cubic foot = **0.0283** cubic metre
1 cubic inch = **16.387** cubic centimetres
1 cubic metre = **35.3146** cubic feet = **1.3079** cubic yards
1 cubic yard = **0.7646** cubic metre
1 fathom = **1.8288** metres
1 fluid ounce (apothecary's) = **28.4131** millilitres
1 fluid ounce = **28.4** millilitres
1 foot = **0.3048** metre = **30.48** centimetres
1 foot per second = **0.6818** miles per hour = **1.097** kilometres per hour
1 gallon (imperial) = **4.5461** litres
1 gallon (US liquid) = **3.7854** litres
1 gill = **0.142** litre
1 gram = **0.0353** ounce = **0.002205** pound = **15.43** grains = **0.0321** ounce (Troy)
1 hectare = **2.4710** acres
1 hundredweight = **50.80** kilograms
1 inch = **2.54** centimetres
1 kilogram = **2.2046** pounds
1 kilometre = **0.6214** mile = 1 **093.6** yards
1 knot (international) = **0.5144** metres per second = **1.852** kilometres per hour
1 litre = **0.220** gallon (imperial) = **0.2642** gallon (US) = **1.7598** pints (imperial) = **0.8799** quarts
1 metre = **39.3701** inches = **3.2808** feet = **1.0936** yards
1 metric tonne = **0.9842** ton
1 mile (statute) = **1.6093** kilometres
1 mile (nautical) = **1.852** kilometres
1 millimetre = **0.03937** inch
1 ounce = **28.350** grams
1 peck (imperial) = **9.0922** litres
1 pennyweight = **1.555** grams
1 pica (printer's) = **4.2175** millimetres
1 pint (imperial) = **0.5683** litre
1 pound = **0.4536** kilogram
1 quart (imperial) = **1.1365** litres
1 square centimetre = **0.1550** square inch
1 square foot = **0.0929** square metre
1 square inch = **6.4516** square centimetres
1 square kilometre = **0.3860** square mile
1 square metre = **10.7639** square feet = **1.1960** square yards
1 square mile = **2.5900** square kilometres
1 square yard = **0.8361** square metre
1 ton = **1.0160** square metres
1 yard = **0.9144** metre

metroplex *noun* a large urban or metropolitan area, especially that formed by more than one city and the adjoining suburbs. [from METROPOLITAN + COMPLEX]

Metropolis a German film directed by Fritz Lang (1926). It is a vision of a 21c society where the technological luxury of the ruling class is maintained by an enslaved underclass who revolt and almost destroy the city.

metropolis *noun* (PL. **metropolises**) a large city, especially the capital city of a nation or region. [from Greek, from *meter*, mother + *polis*, city]

metropolitan — *adj.* **1** of, typical of, or situated in a large city. **2** of or referring to a country's mainland, as opposed to its overseas territories. — *noun* **1** in the Catholic and Orthodox Churches, a bishop (usually an archbishop) with authority over all the bishops in a province. **2** an inhabitant of a metropolis.

Metropolitan Museum of Art a US museum opened in New York City in 1872. It houses a large and comprehensive collection displaying the artistic achievements of many cultures, ancient and modern.

Metropolitan Opera, known as the **Met** an opera house and company in New York City, opened in 1883 with a production of Charles Gounod's *Faust*. Originally housed on Broadway, the company moved to the Lincoln Centre in 1966.

-metry *combining form* forming words denoting a science involving measurement: *geometry*. [from Greek *metron*, measure]

Metternich, Klemens (Wenzel Nepomuk Lothar), Fürst von (Prince of) (1773–1859) Austrian statesman, born in Coblenz. He became Austrian Minister at Dresden, Berlin, and Paris and as Foreign Minister from 1809, he negotiated the marriage between Napoleon and Marie Louise. He was prominent in the Congress of Vienna, and a powerful influence for conservatism in Europe in the years 1815 to 1848, contributing to the tension that produced the upheavals of 1848 and popular rebellions in many countries. After the fall of the Imperial government, he fled to England, and in 1851 retired to his castle of Johannesberg on the Rhine.

mettle *noun literary* **1** courage, determination and endurance. **2** character; personal qualities: *show one's mettle.*
— **on one's mettle** *literary* encouraged or forced to make one's best effort.
[variant of METAL]

mettlesome *adj. literary, said especially of horses* lively; high-spirited.

Metz, ancient **Divodurum Mediomatricum** POP (1990) 193 000, the capital of Moselle department, Lorraine region, NE France. It lies on the R Mosel near the German border, 285km/177mi NE of Paris. This fortified town has been a strategic focus of crossroads for over 2 000 years. HISTORY residence of the Merovingian kings in the 6c; later, part of Holy Roman Empire; taken by France in 1552; part of Germany from 1871 until after World War I; scene of a major German defence in the 1944 invasion by the Allies. NOTABLE FEATURES Gothic Cathedral of St-Etienne (1250–1380); Basilica of St-Pierre-aux-Nonnains (7c); Eglise Ste-Thérèse; town hall (18c); Porte des Allemands (13c); World War I cemetery nearby.

Meung, Jean de (c.1250–1305) French satirist. He translated many books into French, but his major work is the continuation (18 000 lines) of the *Roman de la Rose*, in which he replaced allegory by satirical pictures of actual life and an encyclopedic discussion of contemporary learning.

Meuse, River, Dutch **Maas**, ancient **Mosa** a river in NE France, Belgium, and the Netherlands, length 950km/590mi. It rises on the Langres Plateau, NE France and then flows N through the Ardennes into Belgium. From there, it flows into the Netherlands and west as the Maas to enter the North Sea through Hollandsch Diep in the Rhine Delta. It is navigable for 578km/359mi. Severe fighting took place in the Meuse valley during the German invasions of both World Wars.

mew[1] — *verb intrans.* to make the cry of a cat; to miaow. — *noun* a cat's cry. [imitative]

mew[2] *noun* a seagull. [from Anglo-Saxon *mæw*]

mews *noun* (PL. **mews**, **mewses**) a set of stables around a yard or square, especially converted into garages or accomodation; also used in streetnames. [from *mew*, cage for moulting hawks, originally the cages for royal hawks, later stables, at Charing Cross, London]

Mex. *abbrev.* **1** Mexican. **2** Mexico.

Mexican — *noun* a native or citizen of Mexico. — *adj.* of or pertaining to Mexico.

Mexican War a war (1846–8) between Mexico and the USA, declared by the US Congress after it received a message from President Polk calling for war over territory disputed between Texas (annexed by the USA but claimed by Mexico) and Mexico. US troops assaulted Mexico City (Sep 1847) and forced a capitulation in which Mexico ceded most of the present-day SW United States.

Mexican wave a rippling wave effect passing across the spectators in a stadium, as they stand up and raise their arms, then sit with lowered arms, in turn around the stadium. [so called because it was first publicized at the World Cup football competition in Mexico in 1986]

Mexico, Spanish **México**, official name **United Mexican States**, Spanish **Estados Unidos de México** POP (1992e) 89.5m, a federal republic in the S of North America, divided into 31 states and the federal district of Mexico City. AREA 1 978 800sq km/763 817sq mi. It is bounded by the USA in the N, the Gulf of California in the W, the Pacific Ocean in the W and SW, Guatemala and Belize in the S, and the Gulf of Mexico in the E. CAPITAL Mexico City. CHIEF TOWNS Guadalajara, Léon, Monterrey, Ciudad Juárez. TIME ZONES GMT −8 to −6. The population is mainly mestizo (S American Indian–Spanish) (60%) and S American Indian (30%). Roman Catholicism is the chief religion. OFFICIAL LANGUAGE Spanish; American Indian languages are also spoken. CURRENCY the peso. PHYSICAL DESCRIPTION bisected by the Tropic of Cancer; situated at the S end of the N American Western Cordillera; narrow coastal plains border the Pacific Ocean and the Gulf of Mexico; land rises steeply to a central plateau, reaching a height of c.2 400m around Mexico City; the plateau is bounded by the Sierra Madre Occidental in the W and Sierra Madre Oriental in the E; volcanic peaks lie to the S, notably Citlaltépetl (5 699m); limestone lowlands of the Yucatán peninsula stretch into the Gulf of Mexico in the SE; the country is subject to earthquakes which can be very severe. CLIMATE great climatic variation between the coastlands and mountains; desert or semi-desert conditions in the NW; typically tropical climate on the E coast; generally wetter on the S coast; extreme temperature variations in the N, very cold in winter, very warm in summer. HISTORY the centre of American Indian civilizations for over 2 500 years: Gulf Coast Olmecs based at La Venta, Zapotecs at Monte Albán near Oaxaca, Mixtecs at Mitla, Toltecs at Tula, Maya in the Yucatán, Aztecs at Tenochtitlán; the Spanish arrived in 1516; Cortés came ashore near Veracruz in 1519, destroying the powerful Aztec capital within two years and the Vice-royalty of New Spain was established; struggle for independence from 1810; became a federal republic in 1824; lost territory to the USA in 1836 and after the Mexican War (1846–8); civil war (1858–61); occupation of Mexico City by French forces in 1863, with Archduke Maximilian of Austria declared Emperor; withdrawal of French and execution of Maximilian in 1867; revolution (1910–17); financial difficulties in the 1980s; major earthquake in Mexico City (1985); Guadalajara gas explosion in 1992. GOVERNMENT the country is governed by a President, elected for six years, a Cabinet, and a bicameral Congress with a 64-member Senate elected for six years and a 500-member Chamber of Deputies elected for three years. ECONOMY wide range of mineral exports; major discoveries of oil and natural gas in the 1970s (now world's fourth largest producer); fluorite and graphite (world's leading producer); gold, silver, lead, zinc, arsenic, cadmium, phosphates, sulphur, copper, antimony, iron, salt; sugar, maize, coffee, tobacco, fruit; large petrochemical industry; iron, steel, aluminium, vehicles, cement, food processing, textiles, clothing, crafts, cotton, cattle, machinery, fishing, tourism.

Mexico, Gulf of a gulf on the SE coast of N America, forming a basin enclosed by the USA to the N and Mexico to the W, as far as the Yucatán Peninsula. AREA 1 507 600sq km/581 900sq mi. Sigsbee Deep (3 878m) is the deepest point. The gulf receives the Mississippi R and the Rio Grande del Norte. It has a low, sandy shoreline with many marshes, lagoons, and deltas. Oil and natural gas resources are on the continental shelves.

Mexico City, Spanish **Ciudad de México** POP (1990) 13.6m, the largest city in the world, the capital of Mexico, and a federal district. It is situated in the centre of the country, in a small, intermontane basin; AREA 50sq km/20sq mi, altitude 2 200m. It is the oldest capital in continental America and is built on the site of the Aztec capital, Tenochtitlán. HISTORY in 1521 the Aztec city was captured and destroyed by the Spaniards under Cortés and the new city built on the site was capital of the Vice-royalty of New Spain for 300 years until independence; a major industrial accident took place in 1984 when a liquefied gas tank exploded at the San Juan Ixhuatepec storage facility, killing over 450 people; there was a major earthquake in 1985, resulting in thousands of deaths. The city centre is a World Heritage site. NOTABLE FEATURES cathedral (16c–19c), National Palace (1692), Castle of Chapultepec (now the National Museum of History), National Museum of Anthropology; ruins of Teotihuacán, 40km/25mi NE.

Meyer, Adolf (1866–1950) Swiss-born US psychiatrist, born in Niederweingen. He emigrated to the USA in 1892, and worked at Johns Hopkins Medical School from 1910. Through his notion of 'psychobiology' he sought to integrate psychiatry and medicine, seeing mental disorder as the consequence of unsuccessful adjustment patterns. He also tried to improve the standards of patient record-keeping and long-term care in psychiatry.

Meyerbeer, Giacomo, originally **Jakob Liebmann Meyer Beer** (1791–1864) German operatic composer, born in Berlin. After studying in Italy, he produced operas in the new (Rossini's) style, which were at once well received. He then studied French opera and wrote the successful *Robert le Diable* (1831) and *Les Huguenots* (1836). In 1842 he was appointed kapellmeister at Berlin, but later returned to Paris.

Meyerhof, Otto Fritz (1884–1951) US biochemist, born in Hanover, Germany. Working in Kiel, Berlin, and Heidelberg, he studied the chemistry of muscle action, and determined the pathways whereby the energy-rich compounds used in muscle contraction are formed. He shared the 1922 Nobel Prize for Physiology or Medicine with Archibald Hill. In 1938 he left Nazi Germany, and worked in the USA from 1940.

Meyerhold, Vsevolod (Emilievich) (1874–1940) Russian actor and theatre director, born in Penza. When an actor at the Moscow Art

Mexico

Theatre, he was appointed by Stanislavsky as director of the new Studio on Povarskaya Street (1905). He later became director of the Theatre of the Revolution (1922–4) and of the Meyerhold Theatre (1923–38).

mezuzah *noun* (PL. **mezuzot**) a cylindrical box containing a parchment inscribed with religious texts from Deuteronomy, attached to the doorposts of Jewish houses as an act of faith. [Hebrew, = doorpost]

mezuzah

mezzanine *noun* a small floor built balcony-like between two other floors in a building, usually the ground and first floors. [from Italian *mezzanino*, from *mezzano*, middle]

mezzo *adv. Mus.* moderately, quite, rather, as in **mezzo-forte**, rather loud. [from Italian *mezzo*, half]

Mezzogiorno a geographical region comprising all the regions of S Italy, excluding Sardinia and the provinces of Latina, Frosinone, and Rieti in S Latium. It is largely an agricultural area, undergoing special development. The name, meaning 'midday', refers to the region's heat.

mezzo-soprano *noun* (PL. **mezzo-sopranos**) **1** a singing voice with a range between soprano and contralto. **2** a singer with this voice.

mezzotint *noun* a method of engraving a metal plate by polishing and scraping to produce areas of light and shade; a print from a plate engraved in this way. [from Italian *mezzotinto*, from *mezzo*, half + *tinto*, shade]
◊ The tonal rather than linear effects produced by the technique made it suitable for reproducing oil paintings. It was invented c.1640, but ren-

dered obsolete by photographic reproduction in the late 19c.

MG Morris Garages, which were W R Morris's original retail and repair business in Oxford, England. The first MG cars were assembled from normal Morris chassis by Cecil Kimber, the garages' manager, in 1924.

Mg *symbol Chem.* magnesium.

mg *abbrev.* milligram.

Mgr *abbrev.* **1** manager. **2** Monsignor.

MHz *abbrev.* megahertz.

MI *abbrev.* **1** Michigan. **2** Military Intelligence.

mi *noun* in tonic sol-fa, the third note of the major scale. [from the first syllable of the word *Mira* in a medieval Latin hymn, certain syllables of which were used in naming the notes of the scale]

Miami POP (1990) 1.9m, the seat of Dade County, SE Florida, USA. Situated on Biscayne Bay, the city is a port lying at the mouth of the Miami R. It is the processing and shipping hub of a large agricultural region. Miami, which was originally settled around a military post in the 1830s, has been one of the country's most famous and popular resorts since 1945; it has extensive recreational facilities catering for nearly 6m visitors each year. As the air gateway to Latin America, Miami receives large numbers of immigrants (nearly half of the metropolitan population is Hispanic). NOTABLE FEATURES Dade County Art Museum; Seaquarium; Villa Vizcaya; the Everglades; Biscayne Boulevard. EVENT Orange Bowl Festival (Dec).

Miami Beach POP (1990) 93 000, a town in Dade County, SE Florida, USA, situated on an island across Biscayne Bay from Miami. It is connected to Miami by four causeways. The area was developed in the 1920s and has become a popular year-round resort, famous for its 'gold coast' hotel strip.

miaow — *verb intrans.* to make the cry of a cat. — *noun* a cat's cry. [imitative]

Miao-Yao — *adj.* denoting a family of languages used in S China and parts of SE Asia. The two principal languages are Miao and Yao, both written in the Roman alphabet. — *noun* the languages forming this family.

miasma *noun* (PL. **miasmata**, **miasmas**) *literary* **1** a thick foul-smelling vapour, especially as given off by swamps, marshes, etc. **2** an evil

influence or atmosphere. [from Greek *miasma*, pollution]

miasmal *adj.* relating to or typical of miasma.

mica *noun Geol.* any of a group of transparent, black, or coloured silicate minerals that have a layered structure and are readily split into thin flexible sheets. Micas are poor conductors of heat and electricity, and are used as electrical insulators, and as dielectrics in capacitors. [from Latin *mica*, crumb]

Micah or Micheas, Book of one of the 12 so-called 'minor' prophetic writings of the Hebrew Bible and Old Testament, attributed to the prophet Micah of Moresheth-gath (in the hill country of Judah), a contemporary of Isaiah in Judah and active in the late 8c BC.

Micawber, Mr Wilkins the despairingly debt-ridden but ever-optimistic landlord in Dickens's *David Copperfield*. His wife is called Emma.

mice see MOUSE.

Mich. *abbrev.* **1** Michaelmas. **2** Michigan.

Michael (1921–) King of Romania (1927–30, 1940–7), born in Sinaia, the son of Carol II. He came to the throne on the death of his grandfather Ferdinand I, since his father Carol had renounced his own claims in 1925. In 1930 he was supplanted by Carol, but was again made king when the Germans gained control of Romania (1940). In 1944 he led a coup to overthrow the dictatorship of Antonescu, and declared war on Germany. Forced in 1945 to accept a communist-dominated government, he was later compelled to abdicate (1947) and leave Romania.

Michael 1 an archangel described in the Old Testament as the guardian of Israel (Daniel 10, 12). He appears as a great patron, intercessor, and warrior in later Jewish non-canonical works (eg 1 Enoch, the Ascension of Isaiah, the War Scroll at Qumran). In Jude 9, he disputes with the Devil over Moses' body, and in Revelation 12.7, fights against 'the dragon'. His feast day, Michaelmas Day, is 29 Sep. **2** a male first name. [from a Hebrew name meaning 'who is like the Lord?']

Michael VIII Palaeologus (c.1225–82) Eastern Roman Emperor (1259–82), born in Nicaea. He distinguished himself as a soldier, and was made regent for the heir to the throne, John Lascaris, whom he later deposed and banished. His army took Constantinople in 1261, thus re-establishing the Byzantine Empire.

Michaelis, Leonor (1875–1949) German-born US biochemist, born in Berlin. He became professor in Berlin and Japan before settling in the USA at the Johns Hopkins and Rockefeller institutes. He made important discoveries about the ways in which enzyme reactions take place, and formulated an equation relating the rate of reaction to the concentrations of the enzyme and the substance it acts on.

Michaelmas *noun* a Christian festival in honour of St Michael, held on 29 September. [from *Michael* + *mas*, from MASS²]

Michaelmas daisy any of various garden plants of the aster family, with purple, pink or white flowers that bloom in autumn.

Michelangelo, properly **Michelangelo di Lodovico Buonarroti Simoni** (1475–1564) Italian sculptor, painter, and poet, born in Caprese, Tuscany. His marble *Cupid* was bought by Cardinal San Giorgio, who summoned him to Rome (1496), where he stayed for four years and achieved fame with the statues the *Bacchus* (1496–7) and the *Pietà* (1499, St Peter's, Vatican City). He then returned to Florence, where he sculpted the marble *David* (1504, Accademia, Florence). From the same period are the two unfinished sculptures *Madonna and Child* (c.1503, Pitti Palace, Florence, and Royal Academy, London). In 1505 Julius II commissioned him to design his tomb in Rome, but instead he painted the Sistine Chapel with frescoes (1508–12). His last pictorial achievements include *The Last Judgement* (1536–41, Sistine Chapel), and the frescoes, the *Conversion of St Paul* and the *Crucifixion of St Peter* (1542–50, Pauline Chapel, Vatican). In 1546 he was appointed architect of St Peter's, to which he devoted himself until his death.

Michelangelo virus *Comput.* a virus set to destroy data on a computer's hard disk when the system date reads 6 Mar in any year. [named after Michelangelo Buonarroti, whose birthday was 6 Mar]

Michelin, André (1853–1931) French tyre manufacturer, born in Paris. He and his younger brother Edouard (1859–1940) established the Michelin tyre company in 1888, and were the first to use demountable pneumatic tyres on motor cars. They are also known for their road maps and Michelin guides. The guides were introduced by André Michelin to promote tourism by car and the first Red Guide, showing restaurant ratings, was published in 1900.

Michell, John (1724–93) English geologist and astronomer, born in Nottinghamshire. Professor at Cambridge and later Rector of Thornhill, Yorkshire, he studied artificial magnets and invented a torsion balance to measure the strength of small forces. He is best known as the founder of seismology, suggesting that earthquakes set up wave motions in the Earth and demonstrating methods of locating epicentres.

Michelson, Albert Abraham (1852–1931) German-born US physicist, born in Strelno (now Strzelno, Poland). Professor of Physics at Chicago from 1892, he invented an interferometer and made important studies of the spectrum, but is best remembered for the Michelson–Morley experiment which demonstrated that the 'ether', a hypothetical medium thought to pervade all space and to support the propagation of waves of light, did not exist; this result led Einstein to formulate the theory of relativity. He was awarded the 1907 Nobel Prize for Physics.

Michigan POP (1990) 9.4m, a state in N central USA, divided into 83 counties. AREA 151 579sq km/58 527sq mi. PHYSICAL DESCRIPTION split into two peninsulas by L Michigan and L Huron; the Montreal, Brule, and Menominee rivers mark the Wisconsin border; the border with Canada is formed by the St Clair R (between L Huron and L St Clair) and the Detroit R (between L St Clair and L Erie); within the state boundary lie 99 909sq km/38 565sq mi of the Great Lakes; the highest point is Mt Curwood (604m); the upper peninsula and the N part of the lower peninsula are mainly forested, containing several state parks; Michigan is known as the 'Great Lake State' or the 'Wolverine State'. HISTORY settled by the French in 1668; ceded to the British in 1763; handed over to the USA in 1783 and became part of Indiana Territory; the Territory of Michigan was established in 1805; its boundaries were greatly extended in 1818 and 1834; it was the 26th state to be admitted to the Union, in 1837. CAPITAL Lansing. CHIEF TOWNS Detroit, Grand Rapids, Warren, Flint. ECONOMY a major tourist area; the S part of the state is highly industrialized, producing motor vehicles and parts (though this industry was severely affected by recession in the early 1990s), machinery, cement, and iron and steel (second in the country for iron ore production); agriculture includes corn and dairy products.

Michigan, Lake the third-largest of the Great Lakes and the only one lying entirely within the USA. AREA 58 016sq km/22 394sq mi; length 494km/307mi; maximum width 190km/118mi; maximum depth 281m. The lake is linked in the NE with L Huron via the Strait of Mackinac, and to the Mississippi by canals and rivers. The large western arm of Green Bay indents the Wisconsin shore. Ports include Michigan City, Gary, Chicago, Evanston, Waukegan, Kenosha, Racine,

Milwaukee, Manitowoc, Escanaba, Muskegon, and Grand Haven.

mick *noun offensive slang* an Irishman. [from the name *Michael*]

mickey
— **take the mickey out of someone** *colloq.* to tease or make fun of them.
[origin uncertain]

Mickey Finn *slang* a drink, especially alcoholic, with a stupefying drug secretly added.

Mickey Mouse a cartoon film character created by Walt Disney in 1928, who became the symbol of Disney's cinema empire, and later of the Disney theme parks.

Mickey Mouse *adj. derog. colloq.* **1** of the nature of a cheap imitation. **2** ridiculously simple or unprofessional.

Mickiewicz, Adam (Bernard) (1798–1855) Polish poet, born near Novogrodek, Lithuania. He was exiled to Russia (1824–9) for political reasons, and taught at Lausanne and Paris (1840–3). His first collection (1822), contained the essay 'On Romantic Poetry', and after travelling in Europe, he wrote *Pan Tadeusz* (Thaddeus, 1834), an epic poem set in Lithuania. He was involved in the struggle for Polish nationalism, and is regarded as the national poet of Poland.

micro *noun* (PL. **micros**) *colloq.* a microcomputer, microprocessor, or microwave oven.

micro- *combining form* forming words meaning: **1** very small: *microchip*. **2** one millionth part: *micrometre*. [from Greek *mikros*, little]

microbe *noun* imprecise term for any microorganism, especially a bacterium that is capable of causing disease. [from Greek *mikros*, little + *bios*, life]

microbial *or* **microbic** *adj.* relating to or characteristic of microbes.

microbiological *adj.* relating to or involving microbiology.

microbiologist *noun* a person who studies or is expert in microbiology.

microbiology *noun* the branch of biology dealing with the study of micro-organisms.

microchip *noun* see SILICON CHIP.

microcircuit *noun* an electronic circuit with components formed in one microchip.

microclimate *noun Biol.* the local and rather uniform climate immediately surrounding a living organism (eg the climate surrounding the leaves of a tree) as opposed to the climate of the entire region in which the organism occurs (eg a forest).

microcomputer *noun* a small relatively inexpensive computer designed to be used by one person at a time, and containing an entire central processing unit on a single microchip. Microcomputers are widely used in small businesses, schools, and in the home, for word processing, accounting, database management, desktop publishing, computer games, etc. — Also called *personal computer*.

microcosm *noun* **1** any structure or system which contains, in miniature, all the features of the larger structure or system that it is part of. **2** *Philos.* man regarded as a model or epitome of the universe.
— **in microcosm** on a small scale; in miniature. [from MICRO- + Greek *kosmos*, world]

microcosmic *adj.* relating to or typical of a microcosm.

microdot *noun* a photograph, eg of secret documents, reduced to the size of a pinhead.

microeconomics *sing. noun* the branch of economics concerned with the financial circumstances of individual households, firms, industries, etc, and the way individual elements in an

economy behave (such as specific products, commodities, or consumers).

microelectronic *adj.* relating to or involving microelectronics.

microelectronics *sing. noun* the branch of electronics dealing with the design and use of small-scale electrical circuits.

microfiche *noun Photog.* a flat sheet of film bearing printed text that has been photographically reduced, formerly widely used as a means of storing bulky items such as library catalogues, but now largely superseded by databases and compact discs that allow much more sophisticated searches to be conducted. [from MICRO- + French *fiche*, sheet of paper]

microfilm *noun* thin film on which printed material is stored in miniaturised form.

microlight *noun* a very lightweight small-engined aircraft, like a powered hang-glider.

micrometer *noun* an instrument for accurately measuring very small distances, thicknesses, or angles.

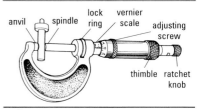

micrometer

micron *noun* (SYMBOL μ) former name for the micrometre, a unit of length equal to 10^{-6}m, which has now replaced the micron as the SI unit. [from Greek, from *mikros*, small]

Micronesia, Federated States of a republic consisting of a group of four states in the W Pacific Ocean. AREA 700sq km/270sq mi. The group, Yap, Chuuk, Pohnpei, and Kosrae, comprises all the Caroline Is except Palau. CAPITAL Palikir on Pohnpei. Most of the population are Micronesian; Christianity is the chief religion. OFFICIAL LANGUAGE English. CLIMATE tropical. HISTORY the states were established as a US Trust Territory of the Pacific Is in 1979 and achieved independence in 1991. GOVERNMENT an executive President and Vice-President and a one-chamber Legislature. ECONOMY fish; copra; tourism.

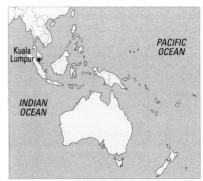

Micronesia

micronutrient *noun Biol.* any trace element, vitamin, or other essential nutrient required in minute quantities by a living organism, eg manganese, zinc.

micro-organism *noun* a general term for any living organism that can only be observed with the aid of a microscope. Micro-organisms include bacteria, viruses, protozoans, and single-celled algae, and the term is often taken to include microscopic fungi, eg yeasts.

microphone *noun Electron.* an electronic device that converts sound waves into electrical signals that can be amplified, recorded, or transmitted over long distances, used in radio and television broadcasting, telephone receiver mouthpieces, etc. [from MICRO- + Greek *phone*, voice]

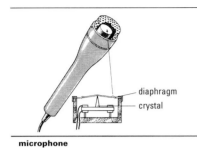

diaphragm
crystal

microphone

microphotography *noun* photography of normal-sized objects, especially documents, plans, and graphic material, as greatly reduced images of small area, which must be examined by magnification or enlarged projection.

microprocessor *noun Comput.* a single circuit performing most of the basic functions of a central processing unit.

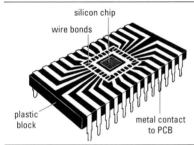

silicon chip
wire bonds
plastic block
metal contact to PCB

microprocessor

micropyle *noun Bot.* 1 in flowering plants, a small opening or pore at the tip of the ovule, through which the pollen tube normally enters during pollination. It normally persists as an opening through which water is absorbed prior to germination of the developing seed. 2 *Zool.* a tiny opening or pore in the protective layer surrounding an insect's egg, through which sperm enters during the process of fertilization. [from MICRO- + Greek *pyle*, gate]

microscope *noun* any of a range of different instruments consisting of a system of lenses that produce a magnified image of objects that are too small to be seen with the naked eye, eg light microscope, electron microscope. See also LIGHT MICROSCOPE, ELECTRON MICROSCOPE.

microscopic *adj.* 1 too small to be seen without the aid of a microscope. 2 extremely small. 3 of, or by means of, a microscope.

microscopically *adv.* 1 in a microscopic way; to a microscopic degree. 2 with the aid of a microscope.

microsecond *noun* a unit of time equal to one millionth part of a second.

microsurgery *noun Medicine* any intricate surgical procedure that is performed on very small body structures. It requires the use of a powerful microscope and small specialized instruments; it is typically used in eye or brain surgery, or during the reconnection of the nerves and blood vessels when reattaching an amputated finger or limb.

microteaching a technique used in the training of teachers, which involves the trainee practising a specific teaching skill (such as questioning or explaining) for a short time with a small group of children. The trainee's effectiveness is judged by a tutor, or by reviewing a videotape of the mini-lesson, and the specific skill is developed through a series of such lessons and appraisals.

microtome *noun Biol.* an instrument for cutting thin sections of objects for microscopic examination. [from MICRO- + Greek *tome*, a cut]

microtubule *noun Biol.* any of the microscopic hollow tubular filaments, composed of the protein tubulin, that are found in the cytoplasm of eukaryotic cells. Microtubules are constituents of cilia and flagella, and of the cytoskeleton that helps to maintain the shape of the cell, and they are also associated with cytoplasmic streaming, and with the formation of the spindle during mitosis and meiosis.

microwave — *noun* 1 (*in full* **microwave radiation**) a form of electromagnetic radiation with wavelengths in the range 1mm to 0.3m, ie intermediate .between those of infrared and radio waves, and overlapping with very high frequency radio waves. Microwaves are used in radar, communications, and cooking. 2 a microwave oven. — *verb* to cook in a microwave.

microwave oven an electrically operated oven that uses microwaves to cook food more rapidly than is possible in a conventional oven. Microwaves generate heat by causing water molecules within the food to vibrate.

micturate *verb intrans. formal* to urinate. [from Latin *micturire*]

micturition *noun* the act of urinating.

mid¹ *adj.* (*often in compounds*) being the part at or in the middle: *mid-March / in mid sentence*. [from Anglo-Saxon *midd*]

mid² *or* **'mid** *prep. poetic* amid.

mid-air *noun* any area or point above the ground.

Midas in Greek legend, a king of Phrygia who, as a reward for helping the satyr, Silenus, was granted a wish by Dionysus. He asked that everything he touched should turn to gold. However, this caused him to be unable to eat or drink, and he asked to be released; he was told to bathe in the River Pactolus, which thereafter had golden sands.

midday *noun* the middle of the day; twelve o'clock.

midden *noun* 1 *old use, dialect* a rubbish heap; a pile of dung. 2 *dialect* an untidy mess. [from Middle English, of Scandinavian origin]

middle — *adj.* 1 at, or being, a point or position between two others, usually two ends or extremes, and especially the same distance from each. 2 intermediate, not senior or chief: *middle management*. 3 moderate, not extreme; done, etc as a compromise: *a middle course*. 4 (**Middle**) *said especially of languages* belonging to a period coming after the Old period and before the Modern: *Middle English*. 5 the middle point, part, or position. 6 *colloq.* the waist. — *verb* 1 to place in the middle. 2 *Cricket* to hit (the ball) with the middle of the bat, therefore firmly and accurately.
— **be in the middle of something** to be busy with it, and likely to remain so.
in the middle of ... at a point during: *in the middle of the night*.
[from Anglo-Saxon *middel* (adjective)]

middle age the years between youth and old age, usually reckoned as between ages 40 and 60.

middle-aged *adj.* of middle age, between youth and old age.

Middle Ages the period of European history between the fall of the Roman Empire in the West and the Renaissance (c.500–1500), or more narrowly between 1100 and 1500.

middle-age spread *or* **middle-aged spread** fat around the waist, often regarded as a consequence of reaching middle age.

Middle America a geographical region encompassing Mexico, Central America, and the West Indies. It includes the Gulf of Mexico and the Caribbean Sea.

middlebrow *derog.* — *adj.* intended for, or appealing to, people with conventional tastes and average intelligence. — *noun* a middlebrow person.

middle class the social class between the working class and the upper class, traditionally containing educated people with professional or business careers.

middle-class *adj.* relating to or characteristic of the middle class.

middle ear an air-filled cavity lying between the eardrum and the inner ear in vertebrates. It contains three small bones (the malleus, incus, and stapes) which transmit sound waves from the outer ear to the inner ear.

Middle East a loosely defined geographical region encompassing the largely Arab states to the E of the Mediterranean Sea together with Cyprus and Turkey. It can also include the countries of N Africa.

Middle Eastern *adj.* relating to or characteristic of the Middle East.

middle lamella *Bot.* a thin layer, composed mainly of pectins, that cements together the walls of adjacent plant cells.

middleman *noun* 1 a dealer who buys goods from a producer or manufacturer and sells them to shopkeepers or to the public. 2 any intermediary.

middle management the junior managerial executives and senior supervisory personnel in a firm or institution.

Middlemarch, in full **Middlemarch, A Study of Provincial Life** a novel by George Eliot (1871–2). It is set in England a few years before the Great Reform Bill (1832), and describes the interweaving lives of various members of the community.

middle name 1 a name which comes between a first name and a surname. 2 a quality or feature for which a person is well known.

middle-of-the-road *adj. often derog.* not extreme; of widespread appeal; boringly average or familiar.

Middlesbrough POP (1992e) 146 000, a port town in Middlesbrough district, Cleveland, NE England, situated on the estuary of the R Tees. Part of the Teesside conurbation, it developed around the iron industry in the 19c. NOTABLE FEATURES town hall (1846); Custom House (1840); Captain Cook Museum.

middle school a school for children between the ages of 8 or 9 and 12 or 13.

Middleton, Thomas (c.1570–1627) English dramatist, born in London. He wrote *The Honest Whore* (1604, with Thomas Dekker), and was often employed to write the Lord Mayor's pageant. Other notable works include the satirical *A Game at Chess* (1624), and the posthumously published tragedies *Women Beware Women* and *The Changeling*.

Middleton POP (1981) 51 000, a town in Rochdale borough, Greater. Manchester, NW England. It is situated 6km/4mi N of Manchester. NOTABLE FEATURE St Leonard's Church (15c).

middleweight *noun* 1 a class for boxers, wrestlers, and weight-lifters of not more than a specified weight (73kg in professional boxing, 70kg for *light middleweight*, 77kg for *super-middleweight*; similar but·different weights in the other sports). 2 a boxer, etc of this weight.

middling *colloq.* — *adj.* average; moderate; mediocre. — *adv.* fairly good; moderately: *middling good*.
— **fair to middling** not bad; fairly good.
[from Scots, from MID¹ + -LING]

Midgard in Norse mythology, Middle Earth, the land in which human beings live.

midge *noun* any of various kinds of small insect that gather near water, especially the kinds that bite people. [from Anglo-Saxon *mycge*]

midget *noun* 1 an unusually small person whose limbs and features are of normal proportions. 2 any small thing of its kind. [related to MIDGE]

Mid Glamorgan POP (1992e) 543 000, a county in S Wales, divided into six districts. AREA 1 018sq km/393sq mi. It is bounded S by South Glamorgan, SW by the Bristol Channel, W by West Glamorgan, N by Powys, and E by Gwent. The Taff, Rhymney, and Ogmore rivers flow through the county. CHIEF TOWNS Aberdare, Merthyr Tydfil, Bridgend, Pontypridd; Cardiff in South Glamorgan is the administrative centre for South Glamorgan and Mid Glamorgan. ECONOMY farming and dairy products; engineering; coal; textiles; electrical goods; vehicle components. NOTABLE FEATURE castle at Caerphilly.

midi *combining form* of medium size or length: *midi-skirt.* — *noun colloq.* a midi-skirt or -coat. [from MID¹]

Midianites, also called **Ishmaelites** an ancient semi-nomadic people from the desert area of the Transjordan, who according to Genesis 25 were descended from the offspring (Midian) of one of Abraham's concubines (Keturah). Later they enticed the Israelites into idolatry, but were overcome by Gideon (Judges 6–8).

midiron *noun Golf* a heavy club used for long approach shots.

midi system *noun* a complete hi-fi system in the form of a single unit, compact but not portable.

midland *adj.* of the central inland part of a country.

Midland Canal see MITTELLAND CANAL.

Midlands, The the industrialized counties in central England of Derbyshire, Leicestershire, Northamptonshire, Nottinghamshire, Staffordshire, Warwickshire, and Worcestershire.

midmost *adj., adv. literary* in the middle.

midnight — *noun* twelve o'clock at night. — *adj.* of or at midnight.
— **burn the midnight oil** to work until very late into the night.

midnight sun *Astron.* a phenomenon that occurs during the summer in the Arctic and Antarctic regions, where the Sun remains visible for 24 hours a day (in winter there is a similar period during which the Sun never rises).

mid-on *or* **mid-off.** *noun Cricket* a fielder in a rough horizontal line with, but at some distance from, the non-striking batsman, on the on or off side.

midpoint *noun* a point at or near the middle in distance or time.

midrib *noun Bot.* the rib that runs along the centre of a leaf and forms an extension of the leaf stalk or petiole.

midriff *noun* the part of the body between the chest and the waist. [from MID¹ + Anglo-Saxon *hrif*, belly]

midshipman *noun* (PL. **midshipmen**) a trainee naval officer, stationed on land. [so called because originally housed in quarters that were *amidships*]

Midshipman Easy, Mr a novel by Capt Fredrick Marryat (1836). It describes the seafaring life of wealthy midshipman, Jack Easy.

midships see AMIDSHIPS.

midst
— **in the midst of something 1** among, or in the centre of it. **2** at the same time as something; during it.
in someone's midst among, or in the same place as them.
[from Anglo-Saxon *in middes*, amidst]

midstream *noun* the area of water in the middle of a river or stream, away from its banks.
— **in midstream** before a sentence, action, etc is finished.

midsummer *noun* the period of time near the summer solstice, around 21 June.

Midsummer Day *or* **Midsummer's Day** 24 June.

Midsummer's Night's Dream, A 1 a play by William Shakespeare (1595). It is a comedy combining reality and fantasy in a story about the love relationships within Oberon and Titania's fairy world and in the lives of various humans, who are susceptible to the fairies' love potion. **2** an overture by Felix Mendelssohn (Op 26, 1826).

midterm *noun* **1** the middle of an academic term, term of office, etc. **2** a holiday, examination, etc, in the middle of term. — *adj.* relating to, or occurring at or around, the middle of a term.

Midway, Battle of a US naval victory (1942), made possible by the breaking of Japanese naval codes to learn of their intentions. The first battle in which the use of aircraft enabled engagement beyond visual range, it helped to save Australia and Hawaii and halted the Japanese advance into the central Pacific.

midway *adj., adv.* halfway between two points in distance or time.

Midway Islands POP (1990) 2 000, a circular atoll enclosing two small islands in the central Pacific Ocean, lying 1 850km/1 150mi NW of Oahu, Hawaii. AREA 3sq km/1sq mi. The islands were annexed by the USA in 1867. They have been used as a submarine cable station since 1905, a commercial aircraft stopover since 1935, and a military airbase since 1941. The allied air victory in the Battle of Midway (1942) was a turning point in World War II.

midweek *noun* the period of time in the middle of the week, especially Wednesday.

Midwest *or* **Middle West** the region of the USA comprising the states between the Great Lakes and the upper Mississippi R valley. These are Illinois, Indiana, Iowa, Kansas, Minnesota, Missouri, Nebraska, Ohio, and Wisconsin. Much of this area is within the corn belt agricultural region.

Midwestern *adj.* relating to or typical of the US Midwest.

mid-wicket *noun Cricket* the area between the stumps on the on side, roughly midway between the wicket and the boundary.

midwife *noun* (PL. **midwives**) a nurse, especially female, trained to supervise childbirth and provide care and advice before and after. [from Anglo-Saxon *mid*, with + *wif*, woman]

midwifery *noun* the skills or practice of a midwife, obstetrics.

midwife toad a European frog that lives away from water, may dig burrows, and mates on dry land. The male wraps the eggs around its legs and carries them until they hatch, and then transports the tadpoles to water.

midwinter *noun* the period of time in the middle of winter, around 22 December.

mien *noun literary* an appearance, expression, or manner, especially reflecting a mood. [perhaps from obsolete *demean*, appearance]

Mies van der Rohe, Ludwig (1886–1969) German architect and designer, born in Aachen. He was Director of the Bauhaus at Dessau and Berlin (1930–3), and moved to the Illinois Institute of Technology, Chicago, in 1938. His designs include the German Pavilion for the Barcelona Exhibition (1929) and the Seagram Building, New York (1956–9).

miff *colloq.* — *verb* **1** to offend. **2** *intrans.* to be offended. — *noun* **1** a quarrel. **2** a fit of sulking; a huff. [from German *muffen*, to sulk]

miffed *adj. colloq.* offended, upset, annoyed.

miffy *adj.* (**miffier, miffiest**) *colloq.* easily offended; touchy.

might¹ *verb, aux.* **1** past tense of **may** : *he asked if he might be of assistance.* **2** used to express possibility: *he might win if he tries hard.* **3** used to request permission: *might I speak to you a moment?* **4** used in suggesting that a person is not doing what he or she ought: *you might carry these bags for me!* **5** *old affected use, facetious* used in asking a question: *and who might you be?* **6** used to introduce the first of a pair of statements, with the sense of 'although': *you might be the boss, but you're still an idiot!* [from Anglo-Saxon *miht*]

might² *noun* power or strength.
— **with might and main** *literary* with great strength; with all one's strength.
[from Anglo-Saxon *miht*]

mightily *adv.* **1** powerfully. **2** to a great extent.

mightiness *noun* being mighty.

mightn't *contr.* might not.

mighty — *adj.* (**mightier, mightiest**) **1** having great strength or power. **2** very large. — *adv. colloq. North Amer., esp. US* very: *mighty pretty.*

migmatite *noun Geol.* a complex rock with a characteristic banded or veined appearance, consisting of a mixture of igneous and metamorphic rocks. Migmatites often occur near large masses of granite. [from Greek *migma*, mixture]

migraine *noun* a severe and recurring throbbing headache, more common in women than in men, that usually affects one side of the head, and is often accompanied by nausea or vomiting, and sometimes preceded by visual disturbances, eg blurring of vision. It may be triggered by many factors, including certain foods (eg cheese, chocolate), alcohol, stress, fatigue, and loud or high-pitched noises. [from Greek *hemikrania*, half skull]

migrant — *noun* a person or animal that migrates. — *adj.* regularly moving from one place to another. [from Latin *migrare*, to migrate]

migrate *verb intrans.* **1** *said of animals, esp. birds* to travel from one region to another at certain times of the year. **2** to leave one place and settle in another, especially another country, often regularly. [from Latin *migrare*]

migration *noun Zool.* the movement of animals from one location to another, generally involving travel over very long distances by well-defined routes, in response to seasonal changes. It is usually associated with breeding or feeding.
◇ Migration generally involves a round-trip movement between two places, a particular migration pattern being characteristic of the members of a given species. Seasonal movements, eg between summer and winter feeding areas, are usually triggered by changes in daylength. The best-known migrations are those of birds, but many other animals migrate, eg caribou, antelope, whales, seals, salmon, eels, and certain butterflies and moths.
Many birds rear their young in north temperate regions, where food is plentiful during the summer, and then migrate south to warmer regions when food grows scarce in the autumn, eg swallows fly from N Europe to South Africa. The navigation methods used by migrating animals are still not clearly established, but birds appear to navigate largely by the Sun and stars, and the Earth's magnetic field.

migratory *adj.* **1** that migrate, or are accustomed to migrating. **2** wandering.

Mihailović, Dragoljub, also called **Drazha** (1893–1946) Serbian soldier, born in Ivanjica. Having risen to the rank of colonel in the Yugoslav army, he remained in Yugoslavia in

1941 after the German occupation and formed groups (*Chetniks*) to wage guerrilla warfare. He later allied himself with the Germans and then with the Italians to fight the communists, and was executed by the Tito government for collaboration.

mihrab *noun Relig.* a niche or slab in a mosque indicating the direction of Mecca. [from Arabic *mihrāb*]

M-II *trademark* a videotape recording system of broadcast standard introduced by Matsushita (1986).

Mikado, The, in full *The Mikado or the Town of Titipu* an operetta by W S Gilbert and Arthur Sullivan (1885). Set in Japan, it tells of Nanki-Poo's love for Yum-Yum (one of the 'Three Little Maids from school') and his attempts to escape impending marriage to a woman chosen by his father, the Mikado of Japan.

mikado *noun* (PL. **mikados**) (*often* **Mikado**) a title formerly given by foreigners to an emperor of Japan. [from Japanese *mikado*, exalted gate]

mike *noun colloq.* a microphone.

Mikonos *or* **Mykonos** POP (1982) 5 000, an island in the Cyclades, Greece, situated in the Aegean Sea. AREA 85sq km/33sq mi. It has several well-known resorts. NOTABLE FEATURES Agios Panteleimon Monastery; many churches built by sailors.

Mikoyan, Anastas Ivanovich (1895–1970) Soviet politician, born in Sanain, Armenia. A member of the Central Committee in 1922, he supported Stalin against Trotsky, and as Minister of Trade (from 1926) he helped improve Soviet standards of living and promoted many Western ideas. He was Vice-Chairman of the Council of Ministers (1955–64), and President of the Presidium of the Supreme Soviet (1964–5).

mil *noun* **1** a unit of length equal to one thousandth of an inch. **2** *colloq.* a millilitre or millimetre. [from Latin *mille*, a thousand]

milady *noun* (PL. **miladies**) a term formerly used to address or refer to a rich, especially aristocratic, English woman. [from French, from *my lady*]

Milan, Italian **Milano** POP (1990e) 1.4m, the capital of Lombardy region and of Milan province, N Italy. It lies on the R Olna, in a fertile plain near the S end of important passes through the Alps. The city is linked by shipping canals with the Ticino and Po rivers, and with L Maggiore and L Como. It is a leading financial and commercial centre. HISTORY a Gallic town, taken by the Romans in 222 BC; later it became the chief city of the Western Roman Empire; ruled from the 12c by the Dukes of Milan; the Duchy of Milan was held by Spain in the 16c; ceded to Austria in 1713; capital of the Kingdom of Italy from 1805 to 1814; held by Austria from 1815 to 1860. NOTABLE FEATURES Church of San Lorenzo (Early Christian period, with Renaissance dome); Church of Sant'Ambrogio (founded in AD 386); Church of Santa Maria delle Grazie (15c, with Leonardo da Vinci's *Last Supper* on the wall of the adjoining convent) is a World Heritage site; Gothic cathedral (14c); Palazzo dell'Ambrosiana (1603–9); Castello Sforzesco (1368); Teatro alla Scala (1776–9), world-famous opera house.

milch *adj., said of cattle* producing milk. [from Anglo-Saxon *milce*]

mild — *adj.* **1** gentle in temperament or behaviour. **2** not sharp or strong in flavour or effect. **3** not great or severe. **4** *said of climate, etc* not characterized by extremes; rather warm. — *noun* (*also* **mild ale**) dark beer less flavoured with hops than bitter beer. [from Anglo-Saxon *milde*]

mildew — *noun* **1** any of various parasitic fungi that produce a fine white powdery coating on the surface of infected plants, or white or grey patches on the surface of products made from

plant or animal material (eg paper, leather, fabrics) and subsequently exposed to moisture. A downy mildew (*Phytophthora infestans*) causes potato blight, the disease that was responsible for the Irish potato famine of the 1840s. **2** a white powdery coating that appears on the surface of a plant infected by certain parasitic fungi, or white or grey patches on the surface of products made from plant or animal material and subsequently exposed to moisture. — *verb trans., intrans.* to affect or become affected by mildew. [from Anglo-Saxon *mildeaw*]

mildewed *adj.* affected by mildew.

Mildred a female first name. [from the Anglo-Saxon name *Mildpryd*, composed of the elements *mild*, gentle + *pryd*, power]

mild steel *noun* steel that contains little carbon and is easily worked.

Mildura POP (1991) 23 000, a town in NW Victoria, SE Australia, situated on the Murray R. NOTABLE FEATURES Aboriginal Arts Centre.

mile *noun* **1** a unit of distance equal to 1 760yd (1.61km). **2** a race over this distance, especially on foot. **3** *colloq.* a great distance; a large margin: *miss by a mile.* [from Anglo-Saxon *mil*, from Latin *mille passuum*, a thousand paces]

mileage *noun* **1** the number of miles travelled or to be travelled. **2** the number of miles a motor vehicle will travel on a fixed amount of fuel. **3** *colloq.* use; benefit; advantage.

mileometer *or* **milometer** *noun* an instrument in a motor vehicle for recording the total number of miles travelled.

miler *noun* an athlete or horse that runs races of one mile.

Miles a male first name. [a Norman name of uncertain origin, perhaps connected with MICHAEL]

miles *adv.* **1** at a great distance: *miles away.* **2** *colloq.* very much: *miles better.*

milestone *noun* **1** a stone pillar at a roadside showing distances in miles to various places. **2** a very important event.

Miletus an ancient commercially-oriented Greek city-state in Ionia on the W coast of Asia Minor. It was the birthplace of Thales, one of the Seven Wise Men of Greece, and is commonly regarded as the cradle of Western philosophy.

Milhaud, Darius (1892–1974) French composer, born in Aix-en-Provence. He studied under D'Indy and for a time was a member of the group of young French composers known as 'Les Six'. In 1940 he went to the USA, where he was Professor of Music at Mills College, California (1940–7). One of the most prolific of modern composers, he wrote several operas, ballets, symphonies, and choral and chamber works.

milieu *noun* (PL. **milieux**, **milieus**) *literary* a social environment or set of surroundings. [from French *milieu*]

militancy *noun* being militant.

militant *adj.* **1** taking, or ready to take, strong or violent action; aggressively active. **2** *formal* engaged in warfare. [from Latin *militare*, to serve as a soldier]

Militant Tendency a British political group which came to prominence in the 1980s. Ostensibly, *Militant* is a newspaper published by Labour Party members espousing Marxist positions. Its opponents maintain that in practice, the newspaper is a front for a party within a party, a discrete organization of revolutionary Trotskyists who entered the Labour Party (by the process called *entryism*) to use its organizational base for its own political ends. In the 1980s, its supporters infiltrated a number of local Labour Parties and the Young Socialists (its youth wing). Fearing adverse electoral publicity, the Labour Party moved to expel members of Militant on the grounds that they belonged to a separate political

party. Since then, Militant's influence has declined.

militarily *adv.* in a military way; by military means.

militarism *noun often derog.* an aggressive readiness to engage in warfare; the vigorous pursuit of military aims and ideals.

militarist *noun* a supporter of militarism.

militaristic *adj.* relating to or characteristic of militarism.

militarization *or* **militarisation** *noun* the act or process of militarizing.

militarize *or* **militarise** *verb* **1** to provide with a military force. **2** to make military in nature or character.

military — *adj.* **1** of, by, or for the armed forces. **2** characteristic of members of the armed forces: *military bearing.* — *noun* (**the military**) the armed forces. [from Latin *militaris*, from *miles*, soldier]

military police a police force within an army, enforcing army rules.

military science the theoretical study of warfare and of the strategic, tactical, and logistic principles behind it. It concerns itself with objectives, concentration and economy of force, surprise, and manoeuvre. Notable theoreticians and writers on the subject include the Chinese general Sun Tzu (c.500 BC), the German general, Karl von Clausewitz (1780–1831), and the British writer, Basil Liddell Hart (1895–1972).

militate *verb intrans.* (**militate for** *or* **against** **something**) to act, or have a strong influence in favour of or against something. [from Latin *militare*, to serve as a soldier]

◆ Often confused with *mitigate*.

militia *noun* a civilian fighting force used to supplement a regular army in emergencies. [from Latin *militia*, military force]

militiaman *noun* a member of a militia.

milk — *noun* **1** a white or yellowish liquid that is secreted by the mammary glands of female mammals for the nourishment of their young. **2** any preparation that resembles this, eg milk of magnesia. — *verb* **1** to take milk from (an animal). **2** *colloq.* to obtain money, information, or other benefit from, cleverly or relentlessly.

— **cry over spilt milk** to waste time grieving over a mistake that cannot be undone.

milk and water weak or weakly sentimental speech or writing.

milk and honey comfort; luxury; plenty. [from Anglo-Saxon *milc*]

◇ Milk consists mainly of water, together with protein, fats, carbohydrates (especially lactose, also known as milk sugar), vitamins, and minerals (especially calcium). Skimmed milk is milk from which all the cream has been removed. In Western societies the milk of certain animals, especially cows, goats, and sheep, is widely consumed throughout adulthood.

milk chocolate chocolate containing milk.

Milk Cup, The in English association football, a former name (1982–6) of the present Coca-Cola Cup, originally known as the League Cup (1960–82).

milk float a vehicle, usually electrically-powered, used for delivering milk.

milkiness *noun* being milky.

milkmaid *noun* a woman who milks.

milkman *noun* a man who delivers milk to individual houses.

Milk Race, The in cycling, an annual road race formerly called (1951–7) the Tour of Britain.

milk round **1** a milkman's regular route from house to house. **2** the periodic recruitment of undergraduates by large companies.

milkshake *noun* a drink consisting of a mixture of milk, flavouring, and sometimes ice-cream, whipped until creamy.

milksop *noun old derog. use* a weak or ineffectual man or youth.

milk sugar *Biochem.* lactose.

milk tooth any of a baby's first set of teeth.

milky *adj.* (**milkier**, **milkiest**) **1** like milk. **2** of or containing milk.

Milky Way (the Milky Way) 1 strictly, a band of diffuse light that circles the night sky as seen from Earth, and represents the combined light of billions of stars, too faint to be seen individually, in the plane of our Galaxy. **2** commonly used to refer to the Galaxy to which our Sun belongs.

Mill, John Stuart (1806–73) English empiricist philosopher and utilitarian reformer, born in London. He was educated by his father, Scottish philosopher James Mill (1773–1836), under whom he began a career at the East India Company. He became an MP in 1865, and supported women's suffrage (*Subjection of Women*, 1869) and liberalism. His major writings include *System of Logic* (1843), *Principles of Political Economy* (1848), *On Liberty* (1859), and his most widely-known work, *Utilitarianism* (1863).

mill — *noun* **1** a large machine that grinds grain into flour, or a building containing this. **2** any of various smaller machines or devices for grinding: *a pepper mill.* **3** a large machine that presses, rolls, or otherwise shapes; a factory containing one or more of these; any factory: *a woollen mill.* — *verb* **1** to grind (grain, etc). **2** to shape (eg metal) in a mill. **3** to cut grooves into the edge of (a coin). **4** *intrans. colloq.* (**mill about** *or* **around**) to move in an aimless or confused manner.
— **go**, *or* **put someone**, **through the mill** to undergo or cause to undergo an unpleasant experience or difficult test.
[from Anglo-Saxon *myln*, from Latin *molere*, to grind]

Millais, Sir John Everett (1829–96) English painter, born in Southampton. He was a founder of the Pre-Raphaelite Brotherhood, and his works in this style include the controversial *Christ in the House of His Parents* (1850, Tate Gallery, London). His later work includes several portraits and landscapes, and he also became well known for his woodcut illustrations for magazines. Works include *The Boyhood of Raleigh* (1870) and *Bubbles* (1886).

Millay, Edna St Vincent (1892–1950) US poet, born in Rockland, Maine. Her works include *A Few Figs from Thistles* (1920), *The Harp-Weaver* (1922, Pulitzer Prize), *Conversation at Midnight* (1937) and *The Murder of Lidice* (1942). Her *Collected Poems* were published in 1956.

millenarian *noun* a person who believes that the coming of the millennium is a certainty.

millenarianism *noun* the beliefs of a millenarian.

millennial *adj.* of or relating to a or the millennium.

millennium *noun* (PL. **millennia**) **1** a period of a thousand years. **2** (**the millennium**) **a** a future period of a thousand years during which some Christians believe Christ will rule the world. **b** a future period of worldwide peace and happiness. [from Latin *mille*, a thousand + *annus*, year]

millepede same as MILLIPEDE.

Miller, Arthur (1915–) US dramatist, born in New York City. He began to write as a student and achieved recognition with *All My Sons* (1947), establishing his international reputation with *Death of a Salesman* (1949, Pulitzer Prize), *The Crucible* (1953), and *A View from the Bridge* (1955, Pulitzer Prize). In 1956 he gained considerable publicity from his marriage to Marilyn Monroe (divorced 1961), and an appearance before the Un American Activities Committee for alleged communist sympathies.

Miller, (Alton) Glenn (1904–44) US bandleader and trombonist, born in Clarinda, Iowa. From 1937 he led a succession of popular dance orchestras and became known for his 'sweet' ensemble sound, fox-trot rhythms, and slick showmanship. In 1939, his hit records included 'Moonlight Serenade' (his theme song), 'Sunrise Serenade', 'Little Brown Jug', and 'In the Mood'. He joined the US Army Air Force in 1942, and formed the Glenn Miller Army Air Force Band to entertain the troops. In Dec 1944 he joined a flight for France from England that disappeared without trace; years later it was revealed to have been inadvertently hit by bombs jettisoned over the English Channel by Allied bombers returning from a mission over Germany.

Miller, Henry (Valentine) (1891–1980) US writer, born in New York City. His early books, *Tropic of Cancer* (1934) and *Tropic of Capricorn* (1938), published in Paris, were originally banned in Britain and the USA for their sexual explicitness. Later work includes the series *Sexus* (1945), *Plexus* (1949), and *Nexus* (1960), and the Surrealist play *Just Wild About Harry* (1963).

Miller, Jacques Francis Albert Pierre (1931–) French–Australian immunologist, born in Nice. In the 1960s he demonstrated the previously unknown function of the thymus gland, showing it to be an important organ in development and in the control of the immunity system. He became head of the experimental pathology unit of the Walter and Eliza Hall Institute, Melbourne, in 1966.

Miller, Stanley Lloyd (1930–) US chemist, born in Oakland, California. After a period in Chicago, he taught at California University from 1960. In his best-known work he passed electric discharges (simulating thunderstorms) through mixtures of gases thought to be representative of the early Earth atmosphere and observed the production of organic molecules, showing this to be a plausible mechanism for the origin of complex organic molecules on Earth; the probable subsequent path from these chemicals to a living system is still not clear.

Miller, the the brawny, cheating drunkard in Chaucer's *The Canterbury Tales*, who plays the bagpipes at the head of the pilgrimage and tells a bawdy tale of deception.

miller *noun Hist.* a person who owns or operates a grain mill.

millesimal — *adj.* thousandth; consisting of thousandths. — *noun* a thousandth part. [from Latin *mille*, a thousand]

Millet, Jean François (1814–75) French painter, born in Grouchy. He went to Paris in 1837, and exhibited at the Salon in 1844. After the 1848 Revolution he settled in Barbizon and painted scenes from rustic French life. His works include *Sower* (1850), *The Gleaners* (1857, Louvre, Paris), and *The Angelus* (1859, Musée d'Orsay, Paris).

millet *noun* **1** the common name for several cereal grasses (especially *Panicum miliaceum* and *Sorghum bicolor*) that are tolerant of drought and poor soil, grow rapidly, and are cultivated as an important food crop in the drier regions of Africa and Asia, especially India and China. In other parts of the world millet is grown as fodder for animal livestock. **2** the small edible seeds (grain) of this plant, which in the case of certain species can be stored for several years, forming an important famine reserve. [from Latin *milium*]

milli- *combining form* forming words denoting a thousandth part: *millisecond*. [from Latin *mille*, a thousand]

milliard *noun old use* a thousand million. [from French, from Latin *mille*, a thousand]

millibar *noun* (SYMBOL **mbar**) a unit of atmospheric pressure equal to 10^{-3} (one thousandth) of a bar, or 100Pa, commonly used in meteorology.

Milligan, Spike (Terence Alan) (1918–) British comedian and writer, born in Ahmadnagar, India. A singer and trumpeter before serving in World War II, he made his radio début in *Opportunity Knocks* (1949) and, with Peter Sellers, Harry Secombe, and Michael Bentine, co-wrote and performed in *The Goon Show* (1951–9). A major influence on British humour in all the artistic media, he has published children's books, poetry, autobiography, and comic novels.

milligram *or* **milligramme** *noun* a unit of weight, equal to one thousandth of a gram.

Millikan, Robert Andrews (1868–1953) US physicist, born in Illinois. He worked at the University of Chicago and the California Institute of Technology. His oil drop experiment, carried out by observing drifting oil droplets in an electric field, demonstrated that electric charge always occurs in multiples of a fixed electron charge, which he measured very precisely. He was awarded the 1923 Nobel Prize for Physics.

millilitre *noun* a unit of volume, equal to one thousandth of a litre.

millimetre *noun* a unit of length, equal to one thousandth of a metre.

milliner *noun* a person who makes or sells women's hats. [originally from *Milaner*, a trader in the fancy goods for which *Milan* was once famous]

millinery *noun* the hats and trimmings made or sold by milliners; the craft of making them.

milling the grinding of cereal grain to produce flour for use in the making of bread and other foodstuffs.

million — *noun* (PL. **millions**, after a number **million**) **1** the number or quantity 10^6, a thousand thousands. **2** a numeral, figure or symbol representing this, eg 1 000 000. **3** *colloq.* a million pounds or dollars. **4** (*often* **millions**) *colloq.* a great number: *millions of books.* — *adj.* 1 000 000 in number.
— **in a million** very rare of its kind, and therefore very valuable.
[from Latin *millionis*, from *mille*, a thousand]

millionaire *noun* a person whose wealth amounts to a million pounds, dollars, etc or more.

millionairess *noun* a female millionaire.

millionth *noun, adj.* a thousand thousandth.

millipede *noun* a small worm-like creature with a many-jointed body and numerous pairs of legs. [from Latin *mille*, a thousand + *pedis*, foot]

Mill on the Floss, The a novel by George Eliot (1860). It is set in Dorlcote and centres on the lives of Maggie and Tom Tulliver, the children of a poor miller.

millpond *noun* a pond containing water which is, or used to be, used for driving a grain mill.

Mills, Barbara Jean Lyon (1940–) English lawyer, born in Chorley Wood, Hertfordshire. She was called to the Bar in 1963, made a Recorder of the Crown Court in 1982, and a QC in 1986. In 1990 she was made Director of the Serious Fraud Office, and in 1992 became the first woman to head the Department of Public Prosecutions.

Mills, Sir John (1908–) English actor, born in Felixstowe, Suffolk, into a theatrical family. He started in films in the 1930s, playing typically English roles, but also had outstanding character parts including *Great Expectations* (1946) and *The History of Mr Polly* (1949). His varied roles include *Ryan's Daughter* (1978), for which he was awarded an Oscar, *Gandhi* (1982), and *A Woman of Substance* (1986).

Mills of Gardanne, The a painting by Paul Cézanne (1885–6).

millstone *noun* **1** either of the large heavy stones between which grain is ground in a mill. **2** any heavy burden, eg a duty or responsibility.

millwheel *noun* a wheel, especially a waterwheel, driving a grain mill.

Milne, A(lan) A(lexander) (1882–1956) English writer, born in London. He joined the staff of *Punch*, and became well known for his light essays. In 1924 he achieved world fame with his book of children's verse, *When We Were Very Young*, written for his son, Christopher Robin. Other well-known works for children include *Winnie-the-Pooh* (1926) and *The House at Pooh Corner* (1928).

Milne, Edward Arthur (1896–1950) English astrophysicist, born in Hull. He worked at Cambridge, Manchester, and Oxford (from 1928), and from 1932 developed his theory of 'kinematic relativity', an unorthodox theory of cosmology. One outcome of this was the prediction that the universe is 10 000 million years old.

Milo *or* **Milon** (6c BC) Greek athlete, from the Greek colony of Crotona in S Italy. He was champion in wrestling twelve times at the Olympic and Pythian games, and is said to have carried a live ox on his shoulders through the stadium of Olympia. He commanded the army which defeated the Sybarites (511 BC). Tradition has it that in his old age he died attempting to split a tree, which closed upon his hands, and held him fast until he was devoured by wolves.

milometer see MILEOMETER.

milord *noun* a term formerly used on the continent to address or refer to a rich, especially aristocratic, English man. [from French, from *my lord*]

Milošević, Slobodan (1941–) Serb politician and President. He joined the Communist League (1959), entered government service (1966) as an economic adviser to the Mayor of Belgrade, and later held senior posts in the Yugoslav federal banks and gas industry (1969–83). Both a Serb nationalist and a hardline Communist Party leader, he became President of Serbia in 1988 and remained in power after the multi-party elections held in Serbia in 1990. In 1991, Milošević at first refused to accept a Croat, Stipe Mesić, as President of Yugoslavia, and it was revealed that he had appropriated Yugoslav federal reserves to buttress the Serb economy. Bitterly opposed to the break-up of Yugoslavia, after Slovenia and Croatia declared their independence (Jun 1991), he agitated for the Yugoslav federal army to be sent into Slovenia and Croatia and later (Apr 1992) into Bosnia-Herzegovina.

Miłosz, Czesław (1911–) Polish-born US poet, born in Szetejnie and brought up in Wilno. He worked for the Resistance during World War II, and was Professor of Slavic Languages and Literature at Berkeley in California (1961–78). His first two volumes were *Poem on Time Frozen* (1933) and *Three Winters* (1936). Later volumes include *Hymn of the Pearl* (1982), *The Unattainable Earth* (1986), and *Provinces* (1991), and his *Collected Poems* were published in 1988. He was awarded the Nobel Prize for Literature in 1980.

Milstein, Cesar (1927–) Argentinian-born British molecular biologist and immunologist, born in Bahía Blanca. Working in Cambridge, he devised a technique of producing large amounts of a single antibody (a *monoclonal antibody*), which has revolutionized biological research, and led to the production of new drugs and diagnostic tests. He shared the 1984 Nobel Prize for Physiology or Medicine with Georges Köhler and Niels Jerne.

milt *noun* the testis or sperm of a fish. [from Anglo-Saxon *milte*, spleen]

Miltiades (c.550–489 BC) Athenian general and statesman, the father of Cimon. He fought against the Persians under Darius I in the Ionian revolt (499 BC), then fled to Athens where, in 493 BC, he was appointed general. He was the chief strategist in the Greek victory over the Persians at Marathon (490 BC).

Milton, John (1608–74) English poet, born in London. While studying at his father's home in

Horton, he wrote *L'Allegro* and *Il Penseroso* (1632), *Comus* (1633), and *Lycidas* (1637). He became involved in the Civil War and wrote very little poetry for the next 20 years. Instead, he published a series of controversial pamphlets against episcopacy (1642), on divorce (1643), and in support of the regicides (1649), and became official apologist for the Commonwealth. Blind from 1652, he devoted himself wholly to poetry after the Restoration. His best-known work is the religious epic *Paradise Lost* (1667). It was followed by *Paradise Regained* and *Samson Agonistes* (both 1674).

Milton Keynes POP (1992e) 181 000, an industrial new town (since 1967) in Milton Keynes district, Buckinghamshire, S central England. It lies 80km/50mi NW of London and was designed on a grid pattern. The Open University has its headquarters in the town.

Milwaukee POP (1990) 1.4m, the seat of Milwaukee County, SE Wisconsin, USA, situated on the W shore of L Michigan. A major lake port and the largest city in Wisconsin, it was founded by German immigrants in the mid-19c. Milwaukee is famed for its beer-producing tradition. NOTABLE FEATURES Pabst Museum; brewery tours; Mitchell Park Horticultural Conservatory; Milwaukee Public Museum; Art Museum.

mime — *noun* **1** the theatrical art of acting using movements and gestures alone. **2** a play or dramatic sequence performed in this way. **3** (*also* **mime artist**) an actor who practises this art. — *verb trans., intrans.* **1** to act (feelings, etc) in this way. **2** to mouth the words to (a song) to match a recording, giving the illusion of singing. [from Greek *mimos*, imitator]

◇ In early classical drama, a mime was a short dramatic sketch with dialogue. In the modern sense, it is the art of conveying meaning without words through gesture, movement, and facial expression (used or learned by most professional actors and dancers), and is applied to the works of mime artists such as Etienne Decroux and Marcel Marceau.

mimeograph — *noun* a machine that produces copies of printed or handwritten material from a stencil; a copy produced in this way. — *verb* to make a copy of in this way. [from *Mimeograph*, originally a trademark]

mimesis *noun* in art or literature, imitative representation; mimicry. [from Greek *mimēsis*, imitation]

mimetic *adj.* **1** of or relating to imitation; imitative. **2** *Biol.* displaying mimicry. [from Greek *mimesis*, imitation]

mimic — *verb* (**mimicked, mimicking**) **1** to imitate, especially for comic effect. **2** to copy. **3** to simulate. **4** *Biol.* to resemble closely. — *noun* **1** a person skilled in (especially comic) imitations of others. **2** *Biol.* a plant or animal displaying mimicry. [from Greek *mimikos*, from *mimos*, imitator]

mimicry *noun* **1** the skill or practice of mimicking. **2** *Biol.* the close resemblance of one animal or plant species to another, or to a non-living feature of its natural environment, that serves to protect it from predators, or to deceive its prey. For example, a non-poisonous insect with the same warning coloration as a poisonous species will be avoided by its predators.

mimosa *noun* any of various tropical shrubs or trees with clusters of (especially yellow) flowers, and leaves that droop when touched. [from Greek *mimos*, imitator, from the leaf's imitation of a cowering animal]

Min. *abbrev.* **1** Minister. **2** Ministry.

min *noun colloq.* a minute.

min. *abbrev.* **1** minimum. **2** minute.

mina same as MYNA.

minaret *noun* a tower on a mosque, from which Muslims are called to prayer. [from Arabic *manarat*, lighthouse]

Minas Gerais POP (1991) 15.7m, a state in Sudeste region, SE Brazil, between the R Grande in the SW and the R São Francisco in the NE. AREA 587 172 sq km/226 648 sq mi. CAPITAL Belo Horizonte. ECONOMY coffee; iron ore; gold (the only two working mines in Brazil); diamonds; metal-working; timber; mineral waters; the wedge of land between Goiás in the N and São Paulo in the S is known as the Triângulo Mineiro (Mineral Triangle) because it accounts for half of Brazil's mineral production. NOTABLE FEATURES National Monument of Ouro Prêto; 400 caves and grottoes.

minatory *adj. formal* threatening. [from Latin *minari*, to threaten]

mince — *verb* **1** to cut or shred (especially meat) into very small pieces. **2** to soften the impact of (one's words). **3** *intrans. derog.* to walk or speak with affected delicateness. — *noun* minced meat, especially beef. [from Old French *mincier*]

mincemeat *noun* a spiced mixture of dried fruits, used as a filling for pies.

— **make mincemeat of something** *or* **someone** *colloq.* to defeat or destroy them thoroughly.

mince pie *noun* a pie filled with mincemeat or with minced meat.

mincing *adj. derog.* over-delicate and affected.

mincingly *adv.* in a mincing way.

MIND *abbrev.* National Association of Mental Health.

mind — *noun* **1** the power of thinking and understanding; the place where thoughts and feelings exist; the intelligence. **2** memory; recollection: *call something to mind.* **3** opinion; judgement: *to my mind.* **4** attention: *his mind wanders.* **5** wish; inclination: *have a mind to go / change one's mind.* **6** a very intelligent person. **7** right senses; sanity: *lose one's mind.* — *verb* **1** to look after, care for, or keep safe. **2** *trans., intrans.* to be upset, bothered or concerned (by). **3** to be careful or wary of: *mind the traffic.* **4** to take notice of, or pay attention to: *mind my advice / mind your own business.* **5** to take care to control: *mind one's language.* **6** *trans., intrans.* to take care to protect: *mind your jacket near this wet paint!* **7** *dialect* to remember. — *interj.* be careful; watch out!

— **bear something in mind** to remember it.

do you mind! an exclamation expressing disagreement or objection.

in one's mind's eye in one's imagination.

in two minds undecided.

know one's own mind to have firm opinions or intentions.

make up one's mind to decide.

never mind don't worry; it doesn't matter.

on one's mind being thought about, considered, worried about, etc.

a piece of one's mind a scolding or criticism.

put one in mind of something to remind one of it.

[from Anglo-Saxon *gemynd*, from *munan*, to think]

Mindanao POP (1990) 14.2m, an island in the S Philippines. AREA 99 040sq km/38 229sq mi. It is bounded by the Celebes Sea in the SW, the Sulu Sea in the W, and the Bohol Sea in the N. PHYSICAL DESCRIPTION it has an irregular shape with many bays and offshore islets; the terrain is mountainous, rising to 2 954m at Mt Apo. The island's major rivers include the Agusan and Mindanao. Laguna Lanao is the largest lake. CHIEF TOWNS Davao, Zamboanga. ECONOMY hemp, pineapples, maize; timber; gold.

mind-blowing *adj. colloq.* very surprising, shocking, or exciting.

mind-boggling *adj. colloq.* too difficult, large, strange, etc to imagine or understand.

minded *adj.* **1** having an intention or desire: *not minded to reply to your letter.* **2** (*in compounds*) having a certain kind of mind or attitude: *open-minded.*

Mindelo POP (1990) 47 000, a city and the chief port (Porto Grande) of Cape Verde, on the NW shore of São Vicente I. It is an important refuelling point for transatlantic ships.

minder *noun* **1** (*in compounds*) a person who takes care of or supervises: *childminder*. **2** *colloq.* a bodyguard.

mindful *adj.* (**mindful of something**) keeping it in mind; attentive to it.

mindfulness *noun* being mindful, awareness.

mindless *adj.* **1** *derog.* senseless; done without a reason. **2** *derog.* needing no effort of mind. **3** (**mindless of something**) taking no account: *mindless of his responsibilities*.

mindlessly *adv.* in a mindless way.

Mindoro POP (1980) 669 000, an island of the Philippines, SW of Luzon I. AREA 9 732sq km/ 3 756sq mi. It is bounded by the Sulu Sea in the S and the S China Sea in the W. The island rises to 2 585m at Mt Halcon. There are wide coastal plains to the E. CHIEF TOWN Calapan. ECONOMY timber; coal.

mind-reader *noun* a person claiming to know other people's thoughts.

mind-reading *noun* the process of apparently discovering the thoughts of another.

Mindszenty, Cardinal József (1892–1975) Hungarian Roman Catholic prelate, born in Mindszent, Vas. As Primate of Hungary (1945) and cardinal (1946), he became internationally known in 1948 when charged with treason by the communist government in Budapest, and sentenced to life imprisonment (1949). In 1956 he was granted asylum in the US legation in Budapest, where he remained as a voluntary prisoner until 1971, when he settled in a Hungarian religious community in Vienna.

mine¹ — *pron.* **1** something or someone belonging to, or connected with, me; those belonging to me. **2** my family or people. — *adj.* old use, poetic used for *my*, before a vowel sound or *h*: *mine eye / mine host*. — **of mine** belonging to, or connected with, me: *a cousin of mine*. [from Anglo-Saxon *min*]

mine² — *noun* **1** (*often in compounds*) an opening or excavation in the ground, used to remove minerals, metal ores, coal, etc, from the Earth's crust. **2** an explosive device that is placed in a fixed position just beneath the ground surface or in water, designed to destroy tanks, personnel, ships, etc, when detonated by contact. **3** a rich source: *a mine of information.* — *verb* **1** *trans., intrans.* to dig for (minerals, etc) in (an area). **2** to lay exploding mines in (land or water). **3** to destroy with exploding mines. [from French *miner*, to mine]

minefield *noun* **1** an area of land or water in which exploding mines have been laid. **2** a subject or situation presenting many (hidden) problems or dangers.

miner *noun* (*often in compounds*) a person who works in a mine, especially a coal mine.

mineral — *noun* **1** *Geol.* a naturally occurring substance that is inorganic (of non-biological origin), usually crystalline, and has characteristic physical and chemical properties by which it may be identified. Rocks consist of mixtures of minerals, eg quartz, mica, calcite, dolomite. **2** loose term for any substance obtained by mining, including fossil fuels (eg coal, natural gas, petroleum), which strictly speaking are not minerals because they are of organic origin. **3** (*usually* **minerals**) mineral water. — *adj.* of the nature of a mineral; containing minerals. [from French *minéral*, from *miner*, to mine]

mineralogical *adj.* relating to or involving mineralogy.

mineralogist *noun* a person who studies or is expert in mineralogy.

mineralogy *noun* the scientific study of minerals.

mineral oil *noun* any oil obtained from minerals, rather than from a plant or animal source.

mineral water **1** water containing small quantities of dissolved minerals, especially when occurring naturally in this state at a spring. **2** any fizzy non-alcoholic drink.

Minerva in Roman mythology, the goddess of handicrafts, identified with the Greek goddess Athena.

minestrone *noun* thick soup containing vegetables and pasta. [from Italian, from *minestrare*, to serve]

minesweeper *noun* a ship equipped to clear mines from an area.

minginess *noun* meanness.

mingle *verb* (*often* **mingle with something** *or* **someone**) **1** *intrans., trans.* to become or cause to become blended or mixed; to associate or have dealings (with). **2** *intrans.* to move from person to person at a social engagement, briefly talking to each. [from Anglo-Saxon *mengan*, to mix]

mingy *adj.* (**mingier, mingiest**) *derog. colloq.* ungenerous; mean; meagre. [perhaps a blend of MEAN² and STINGY]

Mini a car designed and developed by Alec Issigonis in 1959. Its revolutionary design — its front wheels were powered by a transverse engine — meant that it could easily seat 4 passengers despite its modest size (3m long). It became successful both in the domestic market — the 2 millionth Mini was delivered on 19 Jun 1969 — and the competition arena, winning saloon championships and international rallies including the prestigious Monte Carlo event.

mini *colloq.* — *noun* a small or short one of its kind, especially a miniskirt. — *adj.* small or short of its kind; miniature. [from MINI-]

mini- *prefix* forming words denoting something smaller or shorter than the standard: *miniskirt / mini-submarine*. [a shortening of MINIATURE or MINIMUM]

miniature — *noun* **1** a small copy or model of anything. **2** a very small painting, especially a portrait; the art of painting such pictures. — *adj.* of the nature of a miniature; small-scale. — **in miniature** on a small scale. [from Latin *miniatura*, from *miniare*, to paint red, to illustrate]

miniaturist *noun* an artist who paints miniatures.

miniaturize *or* **miniaturise** *verb* **1** to make very small. **2** to make something on a small scale.

minibus *noun* a small bus, usually with between 12 and 15 seats.

minicab *noun* a taxi ordered by telephone from a private company, not stopped in the street.

minicomputer *noun* a medium-sized computer, larger than a microcomputer but smaller than a mainframe computer.

minim *noun* **1** *Mus.* a note half the length of a semibreve. **2** a unit of liquid volume, equal to $\frac{1}{60}$ of a fluid drachm (0·06 ml). [from Latin *minimus*, smallest]

minimal *adj.* of the nature of a minimum; very small indeed; negligible. [from Latin *minimus*, smallest]

Minimal Art a modern art movement that has flourished since the 1950s, mainly in the USA. It is characterized by works of art with minimal art content. These include works such as the blank or monochrome canvases of US painter Ad Reinhardt (1913–67), and works which are exact or almost exact reproductions of everyday objects (eg the prefabricated firebricks of US sculptor Carl André, 1935–).

minimalism *noun* the policy of using the minimum means to achieve the desired result, especially in art or music.

minimalist — *noun* a follower of minimalism. — *adj.* characteristic of minimalism.

minimally *adv.* in a minimal way; to a minimal extent.

minimize *or* **minimise** *verb* **1** to reduce to a minimum. **2** to treat as being of little importance or significance. [from Latin *minimus*, smallest]

minimum — *noun* (PL. **minimums, minima**) the lowest possible number, value, quantity, or degree, or the lowest reached or allowed. — *adj.* of the nature of a minimum; lowest possible; lowest reached or allowed. [from Latin *minimus*, smallest]

minimum lending rate (ABBREV. **MLR**) *Econ.* formerly in the UK, the minimum rate of interest at which the Bank of England would lend to discount houses. Used as an instrument of government policy, it superseded the *bank rate* in 1973, and was itself superseded in 1981 by the *bank base rate*, on which all other interest rates are set.

minimum wage *noun* the lowest wage an employer is allowed to pay, by law or union agreement.

mining *noun* **1** the act or process of extracting minerals, etc from the ground. **2** the act or process of laying mines.

minion *noun* *derog.* **1** a subordinate. **2** an employee or follower, especially when fawning or subservient. [from French *mignon*, pretty, dainty]

miniscule see MINUSCULE.

mini-series a short series of related television programmes, usually dramas, broadcast usually over consecutive days or weeks.

miniskirt *noun* a very short skirt, with a hemline well above the knee.

minister — *noun* **1** the political head of, or a senior politician with responsibilities in, a government department. **2** a member of the clergy in certain branches of the Christian church. **3** a high-ranking diplomat, especially the next in rank below an ambassador. **4** *formal* a person acting as agent for another, especially in business. — *verb intrans.* (**ministered, ministering**) **1** *formal* (**minister to someone**) to provide help or a service for them. **2** to perform the duties of a religious minister. [from Latin *minister*, servant]

ministerial *adj.* relating to or typical of a minister or a ministry.

Minister of State *Brit.* an assistant to a Minister of the Crown in a large government department, with no place in the Cabinet.

Minister of the Crown *Brit.* the political head of a government department, with a place in the Cabinet.

minister without portfolio in the UK, a government minister without responsibility for a department.

ministration *noun formal* **1** the act of ministering. **2** (*usually* **ministrations**) help or service given.

ministry *noun* (PL. **ministries**) **1** a government department, or its premises. **2** (**the ministry**) the profession, duties, or period of service of a religious minister; religious ministers collectively.

Ministry of Agriculture, Fisheries, and Food see AGRICULTURE, FISHERIES, AND FOOD, MINISTRY OF.

Minitel *noun* a public videotext system in France providing banking and mail order services, electronic messaging, etc.

mink *noun* (PL. **mink**) **1** a semi-aquatic nocturnal mammal related to the weasel, found near water in Europe and N America, with a slender body, thick brown fur except for a white patch on the chin, and webbed feet. Mink are bred commercially on farms for the fur trade. **2** the highly valued fur of this animal. **3** a garment made of this, especially a coat. [perhaps from Swedish *mänk*]

mink

Minkowski, Hermann (1864–1909) Russian-born German mathematician, born near Kovno. Professor at Königsberg, Zurich, and Göttingen, he gave a precise mathematical description of the four-dimensional description of space and time as it appears in Einstein's relativity theory.

Minn. *abbrev.* Minnesota.

Minna von Barnhelm a play by Gotthold Lessing (1767), probably the first major German comedy. Set after the Seven Years War, it tells of a soldier's relationship with his fiancée following his unfair dismissal.

Minneapolis POP (1990) 2.5m, the seat of Hennepin County, SE Minnesota, USA, and the largest city in the state. It is a port on the Mississippi R, to the W of and adjacent to, its twin city, St Paul. An important processing and distribution centre for an enormous grain and cattle area, Minneapolis is also the financial capital of the upper Midwest, with a Federal Reserve Bank. HISTORY part of Fort Snelling military reservation in 1819; later developed as a centre of the timber and flour milling industries; achieved city status in 1867. NOTABLE FEATURES Institute of Arts; Guthrie Theatre; American Swedish Institute; Grain Exchange.

Minnehaha the beautiful wife of Hiawatha in Henry Wadsworth Longfellow's *The Song of Hiawatha*.

minneola *noun* an orange-like citrus fruit, a cross between a grapefruit and a tangerine. [perhaps from *Mineola*, in Texas, USA]

Minnesota POP (1990) 4.5m, a state in N USA, divided into 87 counties. It is known as the 'North Star State' or the 'Gopher State'. AREA 218 593sq km/84 377sq mi. It is bounded N by Canada and E by L Superior. PHYSICAL DESCRIPTION source of the Mississippi R in the N central region; the Minnesota and St Croix rivers empty into the Mississippi; over 15 000 lakes are scattered throughout the state; Lying within the state boundary are 5 729sq km/22 114sq mi of L Superior; the Sawtooth Mts rise in the extreme NE; the highest point is Mt Eagle (701m); the N region has a typical glaciated terrain, with boulder-strewn hills, marshland, and large areas of forest; in the E are mountains from which iron ore is mined, and in the S and W are prairies. HISTORY the land E of the Mississippi R was included in the Northwest Territory in 1787; the land to the W became part of the USA with the 1803 Louisiana Purchase; permanently settled after the establishment of Fort Snelling in 1820; Minnesota Territory was established in 1849; became a state in 1858, and was also the 32nd state to join the Union; in 1862 there was a Sioux rebellion in S Minnesota; settled by many Scandinavians in the 1880s. CAPITAL St Paul. CHIEF TOWNS Minneapolis, Duluth. ECONOMY a major tourist area; agriculture is the leading industry; the nation's second biggest producer of dairy products, hay, oats, rye, and turkeys; iron ore; granite; gravel; sand; chief manufactured products include processed foods, machinery, electrical equipment, and paper products. [from Siouan, = watery cloud]

minnow *noun* **1** any of several kinds of small freshwater fish of the carp family. **2** an insignificant person, group, etc. [probably from Anglo-Saxon *myne*]

Minoan — *adj.* relating to the Bronze Age civilization of Crete and other Aegean islands, approximately 3 000–1 100 BC. — *noun* an inhabitant of the Minoan world. [from *Minos*, mythological king of Crete]
◇ A picture of Minoan civilization has been built up through archaeological excavation in the 20c, most notably by the British archaeologist Arthur Evans (1851–1941), who uncovered the palace at Knossos between 1900 and 1936. Minoan art and architecture surpassed that of any other European culture of the period, and there is evidence of a complex centrally-controlled economy, a highly developed bureaucracy, and trading contacts far beyond the Aegean. The cause of the abrupt end of Minoan civilization c.1450 BC is unknown: an earthquake or volcanic eruption, and associated giant waves, and invading Mycenaeans, are all possible explanations.

minor — *adj.* **1** not as great in importance or size; fairly small or insignificant. **2** below the age of legal majority or adulthood. **3** *Mus.*, *said of a scale* having a semitone between the second and third, fifth and sixth, and seventh and eighth notes; based on such a scale. — *noun* **1** a person below the age of legal majority. **2** *Mus.* a minor key, chord, or scale. [from Latin *minor*, less]

Minorca, Spanish **Menorca**, ancient **Balearis Minor** POP (1990e) 98 000, the second largest of the Balearic Is of Spain, situated in the W Mediterranean Sea, NE of Majorca. AREA 700sq km/270sq mi; length 47km/29mi; width 10–19km/6–12mi. The island is low-lying, rising to 357m at Monte Toro. The British occupied Minorca for most of the 18c, until it was lost to the French. CAPITAL Mahón. ECONOMY lead; iron; copper; tourism.

minority *noun* (PL. **minorities**) **1** a small number; the smaller of two groups. **2** a group of people who are different, especially in terms of race or religion, from most of the people in a country, region, etc. **3** the state of being the smaller of two groups: *in a minority*. **4** the state of being below the age of legal majority. [from Latin *minoritas*; related to MINOR]

Minos in Greek mythology, the King of Crete, the son of Zeus and Europa. He demanded an annual (or nine-yearly) tribute from Athens of seven youths and seven maidens to feed the Minotaur. In the Underworld he became a judge of the dead.

Minotaur in Greek mythology, a creature which was half man and half bull, the son of Pasiphae (wife of Minos) and a bull from the sea. It was kept in a labyrinth made for King Minos by Daedalus, and fed Athenian youths and maidens, until killed by Theseus with the help of Ariadne. [from Greek *Minotaurus*, bull of Minos]

Minsk POP (1990e) 1.6m, the capital city of Belorussia, on the R Svisloch. HISTORY dates from the 11c; under Lithuanian and Polish rule; became part of Russia in 1793; badly damaged in World War II; a large Jewish population here was killed during the occupation by Nazi Germany; in 1989 the mass graves of people killed by state security police in the 1930s and 1940s were discovered in a forest outside the city. NOTABLE FEATURES Bernardine Convent (17c); Cathedral of the Holy Spirit (17c).

minster *noun* a large church or cathedral, especially one originally attached to a monastery. [from Anglo-Saxon *mynster*, from Latin *monasterium*, monastery]

minstrel *noun* **1** a travelling singer in the Middle Ages. **2** any of a group of white-skinned entertainers made up to look black, performing song and dance superficially of Negro origin. [from Old French *menestrel*]

minstrelsy *noun* the art or occupation of a medieval minstrel.

Minstrelsy of the Scottish Border, The a collection of Border ballads compiled by Sir Walter Scott (3 vols, 1802–3).

mint¹ *noun* **1** any of various aromatic plants of the genus *Mentha*, having square stems, paired opposite leaves, and small white or purple flowers, widely grown as a garden herb. Spearmint and peppermint are also used as a source of aromatic oils for food flavourings, perfumes, and medicines. **2** the pungent-smelling leaves of this plant, used fresh or dried as a flavouring for food. **3** a sweet flavoured with an extract of these leaves, or a synthetic substitute. [from Anglo-Saxon *minte*, from Latin *mentha*]

mint² — *noun* **1** a place where coins are produced under government authority. **2** *colloq.* a large sum of money. — *verb* **1** to manufacture (coins). **2** to invent or coin (a new word, phrase, etc).
— **in mint condition** brand new; never or hardly used.
[from Anglo-Saxon *mynet*, money]

Mintoff, Dom(inic) (1916–) Maltese Labour politician, born in Cospicua. Trained as a civil engineer, he joined the Malta Labour Party (1947), and in the first Labour government was Minister of Works and Deputy Prime Minister. As Prime Minister (1955–8), his demands for independence and the accompanying political agitation led to the suspension of Malta's constitution (1959). He resigned to lead the Malta Liberation Movement, became Opposition leader (1962), and was elected premier again (1971–84), when his policy was to move away from British influence.

Minton ceramics one of the principal British potteries of the 19c–20c, founded in 1796 by Thomas Minton (1765–1826). It produced pottery and porcelain, with large quantities of willow pattern, versions of maiolica, and finely-painted pieces in the Sèvres style.

minty *adj.* (**mintier, mintiest**) having the flavour of mint.

minuet *noun* a slow formal 17c–18c dance with short steps, or a piece of music for this. [from French *menuet*, from *menu*, small]

minus — *prep.* **1** made smaller by. **2** *colloq.* without. — *noun* (*also* **minus sign**) **1** a sign (–) indicating a negative quantity, or indicating that a following quantity is to be subtracted. **2** *colloq.* a negative point; a disadvantage. — *adj.* **1** negative or less than zero. **2** *colloq.* of the nature of a disadvantage. **3** *said of a student's grade* indicating a level slightly below that indicated by the letter: *got a B minus for my essay*. [from Latin, from *minor*, less]

minuscule — *adj.* **1** *said of a letter* lower-case, not upper-case or capital. **2** extremely small. — *noun* a lower-case letter. [from Latin *littera minuscula*, small letter]
◆ The spelling *miniscule*, influenced by the form *mini-*, is also found in the sense 'extremely small', and is reinforced by pronunciation, but it is generally regarded as incorrect.

minute¹ (with stress on *min-*) — *noun* **1** a unit of time equal to $\frac{1}{60}$ of an hour; 60 seconds. **2** *colloq.* a short while: *wait a minute*. **3** a particular point in time: *at that minute*. **4** the distance that can be travelled in a minute: *a house five minutes away*. **5** *Geom.* a unit of angular measurement equal to $\frac{1}{60}$ of a degree; 60 seconds. **6** (*usually* **minutes**) the official written record of what is said at a formal meeting. **7** a written note or statement sent to a colleague; a memorandum. — *verb* **1** to make an official written record of. **2** to send a memorandum to.
— **up to the minute** modern or recent.
[related to MINUTE², often in the sense 'minute (very small) part']

minute² *adj.* (with stress on -*nute*) **1** very small; tiny. **2** *formal* precise; detailed. **3** *formal* petty. [from Latin *minutus*, small]

minutely *adv.* in great detail.

Minuteman *noun Hist.* **1** each of a group of militiamen, particularly in New England, who were prepared to take up arms at very short notice. They were an important force in the first months of the US War of Independence, before the creation of a regular army under Washington. **2** a popular name in the 1950s and 1960s for a type of US three-stage intercontinental missile.

minute steak a thin steak that can be cooked quickly.

minutiae *pl. noun* small and often unimportant details. [from Latin *minutia*, smallness]

minx *noun old use* a cheeky, sly, or flirtatious young woman.

Miocene — *noun* the fourth epoch of the Tertiary period, lasting from about 25 million to 7 million years ago. During this time apes flourished in Africa, and herds of mammals grazed on the spreading grasslands. — *adj.* **1** relating to this epoch. **2** relating to rocks formed during this epoch. [from Greek *meion*, smaller + *kainos*, recent]

MIPS or **mips** *abbrev. Comput.* millions of instructions per second.

MIR *abbrev.* mortgage interest relief.

Mirabeau, Honoré Gabriel Riqueti, Comte de (Count of) (1749–91) French revolutionary politician and orator, born in Bignon. Elected to the Estates General by the Third Estate of Marseilles (1789), his political acumen gave him power in the National Assembly, while his audacity and eloquence endeared him to the people. He advocated a constitutional monarchy on the English model, but failed to convince Louis XVI, and as the popular movement progressed, his views were rejected by the revolutionaries as well.

Mirabel a female first name. [from Latin *mirablis*, wonderful]

miracle *noun* **1** an act or event breaking the laws of nature, and therefore thought to be the result of direct intervention by a supernatural force, especially God. **2** *colloq.* a fortunate happening; an amazing event. **3** *colloq.* an amazing example or achievement of something: *a miracle of modern technology.* [from Latin *miraculum*, from *mirari*, to wonder at]

miracle play see MYSTERY PLAY.

miraculous *adj.* **1** of the nature of a miracle. **2** *colloq.* wonderful; amazing; amazingly fortunate.

mirage *noun* **1** an optical illusion common in deserts and sometimes observed at sea, caused by the refraction (bending) of rays of light by a layer of very hot air near the ground, or a layer of very cold air near the surface of the sea. Desert mirages commonly resemble a pool of water reflecting light from the sky. **2** anything illusory or imaginary. [from French, from *mirer*, to reflect]

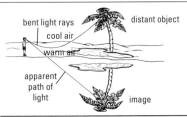

bent light rays
cool air
distant object
warm air
apparent path of light
image

mirage

Miranda 1 the innocent and beautiful daughter of Prospero in Shakespeare's *The Tempest*, who falls instantly in love with Ferdinand. **2** a female first name. [from the feminine form of Latin *mirandus*, to be admired, wonderful]

MIRAS *abbrev.* in the UK, mortgage interest relief at source, a system (used since 1 Apr 1983) by which the basic income tax relief on the interest paid on a mortgage loan is deducted by the lending bank or building society directly from the borrower's regular payment. The lender is later reimbursed by the Inland Revenue.

mire *literary* — *noun* **1** deep mud; a boggy area. **2** trouble; difficulty; anything unpleasant. — *verb* **1** *trans., intrans.* to sink or cause to sink in a mire. **2** to soil with mud. [from Norse *myrr*, bog]

mirin *noun* a sweet rice wine used in Japanese cookery. [from Japanese]

Mir Iskusstva, also called the **World of Art** an artistic avant-garde movement which began in Russia during the 1890s. The group published a periodical of the same name from 1898 to 1905, edited by Sergei Diaghilev. The broad aims of the group were to revive national interest in Russian culture, and to establish points of contact between Russian art and contemporary art movements in western Europe (eg Art Nouveau).

Miró, Joan (1893–1983) Spanish artist, born in Montroig. He exhibited in Paris with the Surrealists. Apart from a period in Spain (1940–4), he worked mainly in France. His paintings are predominantly abstract, and incorporate curvilinear, fantastical forms with a restricted range of pure colours and dancing shapes. His works include *Catalan Landscape* (1923–4, New York) and *Maternity* (1924). He also designed ballet sets, sculptures, murals, and tapestries.

Mirren, Helen, originally **Ilyena Mironoff** (1945–) English actress, born in Southend-on-Sea, Essex. She joined the Royal Shakespeare Company in 1967 as a fiery young performer. Her acclaimed performances (eg as Ophelia in *Hamlet*, 1970 and Lady Macbeth in *Macbeth*, 1974) led to success in films, such as *The Long Good Friday* (1980) and *Cal* (1984). Her other appearances include *The Cook, The Thief, His Wife and Her Lover* (1989), and the television dramas *Prime Suspect* (1991) and *Prime Suspect 2* (1992).

mirror — *noun* **1** any surface that reflects light. **2** specifically, a smooth highly polished surface coated with a thin layer of metal. Most mirrors are made from glass with a thin layer of silver on the back. **3** a faithful representation or reflection. — *verb* **1** to reflect as in a mirror. **2** to represent or depict faithfully. **3** to fit with a mirror or mirrors. [from Old French *mireor*, from Latin *mirari*, to wonder at]

◇ A *plane* (flat) mirror gives an undistorted image, whereas a *concave* mirror, which is curved inward like a saucer, can produce a magnified image (concave mirrors are used instead of lenses in reflecting telescopes). A *convex* mirror, which is curved outward like the back of a spoon, gives a 'wide-angle' image that is reduced in size (convex mirrors are used in shop security systems).

mirror image 1 a reflected image as produced by a mirror, ie with right and left sides reversed. **2** an object that matches another as if it were its image as seen in a mirror, ie with features reversed.

Mir space station *Astron.* a Soviet space station that was launched into orbit around the Earth in February 1986, and was developed from experience gained with the *Salyut* space station, having more solar panels and more docking ports than previous spacecraft.

mirth *noun* laughter; merriment. [from Anglo-Saxon *myrgth*, from *myrige*, merry]

mirthful *adj.* **1** full of mirth. **2** causing mirth.

mirthless *adj.* without humour.

MIRV *abbrev.* Multiple, Independently-targeted Re-entry Vehicle.

mis- *prefix* forming words meaning: **1** wrong or wrongly; bad or badly: *misconceive.* **2** a lack or

absence of something: *mistrust.* [from Anglo-Saxon; related to MISS¹]

misadventure *noun* **1** *formal* an unfortunate happening; bad luck. **2** *Legal* an accident, with total absence of intent to commit crime: *death by misadventure.* [from Old French *mésaventure*, from *mésavenir*, to turn out badly]

misalliance *noun formal* a relationship or alliance, especially a marriage, in which the parties are not suited to each other. [from French *mésalliance*]

Misanthrope, Le (The Miser) a play by Molière (1666). It is a comedy in which Alceste's dissatisfaction with genteel society blinds him to his own faults and makes him want to live as a recluse.

misanthrope or **misanthropist** *noun* a person who hates or distrusts all people. [from Greek *misanthropos*, from *miseein*, to hate + *anthropos*, man]

misanthropic *adj.* hating or distrusting all people.

misanthropy *noun* hatred or distrust of all people.

misapplication *noun* misapplying or being misapplied.

misapply *verb* (**misapplies**, **misapplied**) to use unwisely.

misapprehend *verb formal* to misunderstand.

misapprehension *noun* misunderstanding.

misappropriate *verb formal Legal* to take (something, especially money) dishonestly for oneself; to put to a wrong use.

misappropriation *noun* embezzlement, theft.

misbegotten *adj.* **1** *literary* illegally obtained. **2** *literary* foolishly planned or thought out. **3** *old use* illegitimate; bastard.

misbehave *verb intrans.* to behave badly.

misbehaviour *noun* bad behaviour.

miscalculate *verb trans., intrans.* to calculate or estimate wrongly.

miscalculation *noun* a mistake.

miscarriage *noun* **1** the expulsion of a fetus from the uterus (womb) before it is capable of independent survival, ie at any time up to about the 24th week of pregnancy. — Also called *spontaneous abortion*. **2** a failure of a plan, etc to reach a desired objective. **3** (*in full* **miscarriage of justice**) a failure of a judicial system to serve the ends of justice in a particular case.

miscarry *verb intrans.* (**miscarries**, **miscarried**) **1** *said of a woman* to have a miscarriage. **2** *formal* to fail.

miscast *verb* (PAST TENSE AND PAST PARTICIPLE **miscast**) to give an unsuitable part to (an actor) or put an unsuitable actor in (a part).

miscegenation *noun formal* marriage or breeding between people of different races, especially of different skin colours. [from Latin *miscere*, to mix + *genus*, race]

miscellaneous *adj.* made up of various kinds; mixed. [from Latin *miscellaneus*, from *miscere*, to mix]

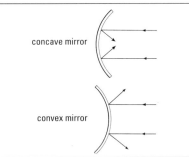

concave mirror

convex mirror

concave and convex mirrors

miscellany *noun* (PL. **miscellanies**) *formal* a mixture of various kinds, especially a collection of writings on different subjects, or by different authors. [from Latin *miscellanea*; as MISCELLANEOUS]

mischance *noun* bad luck, or an instance of this. [from Old French *meschance*]

mischief *noun* 1 behaviour that annoys or irritates but causes no serious harm: *make mischief*. 2 the desire to behave in this way: *full of mischief*. 3 *old use* a person with a tendency to behave in this way. 4 damage or harm; an injury: *do oneself a mischief*. [from Old French *meschief*, disaster]

mischievous *adj.* 1 tending to make mischief; playfully troublesome. 2 *old use* causing damage or harm.

mischievously *adv.* in a mischievous way.

mischievousness *noun* being mischievous.

miscibility *noun* being miscible.

miscible *adj. formal Chem.*, *said of a liquid or liquids* capable of dissolving in each other to form a single phase: *miscible with water*. [from Latin *miscere*, to mix]

misconceive *verb* 1 *trans.*, *intrans.* (**misconceive something** *or* **misconceive of something**) to have the wrong idea or impression about it; to misunderstand it. 2 to plan or think out badly.

misconception *noun* a wrong or misguided attitude, opinion, or view.

misconduct *noun* 1 improper or unethical behaviour. 2 bad management.

misconstruction *noun* an interpretation that is wrong.

misconstrue *verb* to interpret wrongly or mistakenly.

miscreant *noun literary, old use* a malicious person; a rogue or scoundrel. [from Old French *mescreant*, unbelieving, heretical]

misdate — *verb* to date wrongly. — *noun* a wrong date.

misdeal — *noun* a wrong deal, as at cards. — *verb trans.*, *intrans.* (PAST TENSE AND PAST PARTICIPLE **misdealt**) to deal or divide (especially playing cards) wrongly.

misdeed *noun literary* an example of bad or criminal behaviour; a wrongdoing. [from Anglo-Saxon *misdæd*]

misdemeanour *noun* 1 *formal* a wrongdoing; a misdeed. 2 *old use Legal* a crime less serious than a felony. [from obsolete *misdemean*, to misbehave]

misdirect *verb* 1 *formal* to give wrong directions to; to send to the wrong place. 2 *formal* to use (especially funds) for an unsuitable purpose. 3 *Legal, said of a judge* to provide incorrect legal information to (a jury).

misdirection *noun* 1 misdirecting or being misdirected. 2 the wrong directions or address.

Midsummer Marriage, The an opera by Michael Tippett (1955). The story begins on the midsummer wedding day of Mark and Jenifer, but the wedding is delayed, both by their decision to undertake separate journeys of self-discovery before committing themselves to, and, briefly, by the opposition of Jenifer's father King Fisher, who dies. Often compared with *The Marriage of Figaro*, the opera also tells of a parallel, uncomplicated love-affair between Jack and Bella, who are content with their surface harmony.

mise-en-scène *noun* 1 *Theatr.* the process of arranging, or the arrangement of, scenery and props. 2 *Cinema* the use of long scenes during which the position of the camera does not change. 3 *literary* the surroundings in which an event takes place. [French, = a putting-on-stage]

miser *noun* a person who lives in poor conditions in order to store up wealth; any ungenerous person. [from Latin *miser*, wretched]

miserable *adj.* 1 very unhappy; habitually bad-tempered. 2 marked by great unhappiness: *a miserable life*. 3 causing unhappiness or discomfort: *miserable weather*. 4 marked by poverty or squalor: *miserable living conditions*. 5 *dialect* ungenerous; mean. [from French *misérable*, from Latin *miser*, wretched]

Misérables, Les a novel by Victor Hugo (1862). It is set mainly in Paris and follows the life of the criminal Jean Valjean.

miserably *adv.* in a miserable way.

misère *noun Cards* an undertaking to take no tricks. [from French *misère*, misery]

misericord *noun* a ledge on the underside of a seat in the choir stalls of a church, used, when the seat is folded up, as a support for the standing person. [from Latin *misericordia*, compassion]

miserliness *noun* being miserly.

miserly *adj.* of or like a miser.

misery *noun* (PL. **miseries**) 1 great unhappiness, or a cause of unhappiness. 2 poverty or squalor. 3 *colloq.* a habitually sad or bad-tempered person. [from Latin *miseria*]

misfire — *verb intrans.* 1 *said of a gun* to fail to fire, or fail to fire properly. 2 *said of an engine* to fail to ignite the fuel at the right times. 3 to be unsuccessful; to produce the wrong effect. — *noun* an instance of misfiring.

misfit *noun* 1 a person not suited to a particular situation or environment. 2 something that fits badly or not at all.

misfortune *noun* bad luck; an unfortunate incident.

misgiving *noun* (*often* **misgivings**) a feeling of uneasiness, doubt, or suspicion.

misguided *adj.* acting from, or showing, mistaken ideas or bad judgement.

misguidedly *adv.* in a misguided way.

mishandle *verb* 1 to deal with carelessly or without skill. 2 to handle roughly; to mistreat.

mishap *noun* an unfortunate (especially minor) accident; bad luck. [from MIS- + old *hap*, luck, happening]

mishear *verb* (PAST TENSE AND PAST PARTICIPLE **misheard**) to hear incorrectly.

Mishima, Yukio, pseudonym of **Hiraoka Kimitake** (1925–70) Japanese novelist, poet and dramatist, born in Tokyo. His first major work was *Confessions of a Mask* (1949). His tetralogy, *Sea of Fertility* (1965–70), spanned Japanese life and events in the twentieth century. In 1968 he founded the Shield Society, dedicated to the revival of bushido, the Samurai knightly code of honour. He committed suicide in Tokyo.

mishit — *verb* (with stress on *-hit*) (**mishitting**; PAST TENSE AND PAST PARTICIPLE **mishit**) to fail to hit cleanly or accurately. — *noun* (with stress on *mis-*) an act of mishitting.

mishmash *noun colloq.* a disordered collection or mixture; a hotchpotch. [a reduplication of MASH]

Mishnah a written collection of rabbinic laws, which supplements the legislation in Jewish Scriptures, classified under six headings (*sedarim*): Seeds (agricultural tithes), Set Feasts, Women, Damages, Holiness (offerings), and Purities. Although the Mishnah's general arrangement can be traced to Rabbi Akiva (c.120 AD), its final editing was due to Rabbi Judah the Prince (c.200 AD). [Hebrew, = repetition, referring to the practice of learning by repetition]

misinform *verb* to give incorrect or misleading information to.

misinformation *noun* incorrect or misleading information.

misinterpret *verb* (**misinterpreted, misinterpreting**) to understand or explain incorrectly or misleadingly.

misinterpretation *noun* a wrong interpretation.

misjudge *verb* to judge wrongly; to have an unfairly low opinion of (someone).

misjudgement *or* **misjudgment** *noun* a wrong or unfair judgement.

miskey *verb* to key (data on a computer keyboard, etc) incorrectly.

Miskolc POP (1991e) 194 000, the capital of Borsod-Abaúj-Zemplén county, NE Hungary, lying on the R Sajo. It is Hungary's second largest city. NOTABLE FEATURES National Theatre; Castle of Diósgyör; 15c church on Avas Hill; Fazola Furnace.

mislay *verb* (PAST TENSE AND PAST PARTICIPLE **mislaid**) to lose (something), usually temporarily, especially by forgetting where it was put.

mislead *verb* (PAST TENSE AND PAST PARTICIPLE **misled**) to cause to take a wrong or undesirable course of action; to cause to have a false impression or belief.

misleading *adj.* likely to mislead; deceptive.

mismanage *verb* to manage or handle badly or carelessly.

mismanagement *noun* bad, wrong, or careless management or handling.

mismatch — *verb* (with stress on *-match*) to match unsuitably or incorrectly. — *noun* (with stress on *mis-*) an unsuitable or incorrect match.

misname *verb* 1 to give an unsuitable name to. 2 to call by the wrong name.

misnomer *noun* a wrong or unsuitable name; an act of using it. [from Old French *mesnommer*, to misname]

miso *noun* a soya bean paste that has been fermented in brine, used for flavouring. [from Japanese]

misogynist *noun* a person who hates women. [from Greek *miseein*, to hate + *gyne*, woman]

misogynous *adj.* hating women.

misogyny *noun* a hatred of women.

misplace *verb* 1 to lose (something), usually temporarily, especially by forgetting where it was put. 2 to give (trust, affection, etc) unwisely or inappropriately. 3 to put in the wrong place.

misprint — *noun* (with stress on *mis-*) a mistake in printing. — *verb* (with stress on *-print*) to print wrongly.

misprision *noun Legal* a failure to inform the authorities of a serious crime; deliberate concealment of one's knowledge of a serious crime. [from Old French *mesprision*, error]

mispronounce *verb* to pronounce (words, etc) incorrectly.

mispronunciation *noun* a wrong or careless pronunciation.

misquotation *noun* an inaccurate quotation.

misquote *verb* to quote inaccurately, often with the intention of deceiving.

misread *verb* (PAST TENSE AND PAST PARTICIPLE **misread**) 1 to read incorrectly. 2 to misunderstand or misinterpret.

misrepresent *verb* to give a false or misleading account or impression of, often intentionally.

misrepresentation *noun* 1 the act or process of misrepresenting. 2 an inaccurate or misleading representation.

◇ In law, misrepresentation is a false statement made by one prospective party to a contract to another, with the effect of inducing the other to enter into the contract. False statements about goods for sale are misrepresentations, and a customer may sue a seller under the

Misrepresentation Act (1967), even if the seller was acting innocently and unknowingly when the false statement was made.

misrule *formal* — *noun* **1** bad or unjust government. **2** civil disorder. — *verb* to govern in a disorderly or unjust way.

Miss. *abbrev.* Mississippi.

miss¹ — *verb* **1** *trans., intrans.* to fail to hit or catch (something). **2** to fail to arrive in time for. **3** to fail to take advantage of: *missed your chance.* **4** to regret the absence of. **5** to notice the absence of. **6** to fail to hear or see. **7** to refrain from going to (a place or an event): *I'll have to miss the next class.* **8** to avoid or escape: *just missed being run over.* **9** *intrans. said of an engine* to fail to burn fuel at the right times. — *noun* a failure to hit or catch something.
— **give something a miss** *colloq.* to avoid or refrain from it.
miss something out to fail to include it; to leave it out.
miss out on something to fail to benefit from it or participate in it.
[from Anglo-Saxon *missan*]

miss² *noun* **1** a girl or unmarried woman. **2** (**Miss**) a term used to address an unmarried woman. **3** (**Miss**) a term used to address a female school teacher, married or not. **4** (**Miss**) a title given to a beauty queen from a stated country, region, etc: *Miss France.* [an abbreviation of MISTRESS]

Missal the liturgical book of the Roman Catholic Church, which contains liturgies for the celebration of Mass throughout the year, and includes all the required prayers, biblical readings, chants, and instructions.

missal *noun RC Church* a book containing all the texts used in Mass in a year. [from Latin *missale*, from *missa*, mass]

missel-thrush same as MISTLE-THRUSH.

misshapen *adj.* badly shaped; deformed.

missile *noun* **1** a self-propelled flying bomb. **2** *formal* any weapon or object that is thrown or fired. [from Latin *missilis*, from *mittere*, to send]

Missile Experimental the code-name of a US third-generation land-based intercontinental ballistic missile. It was developed from the late 1960s, and was eventually deployed as the 'Peacekeeper' missile from 1987 onwards in land-based silos in the US Mid-West. This followed much political and strategic debate about the best way of basing these powerfully armed long-range missiles.

missing *adj.* **1** absent; lost; not able to be found. **2** not able to be located, but not known to be dead or destroyed.

missing link *noun* (**the missing link**) **1** any one thing needed to complete a series. **2** a hypothetical extinct creature at a supposed stage of evolutionary development between apes and humans.

mission *noun* **1** a purpose for which a person or group of people is sent. **2** a journey made for a scientific, military, or religious purpose; also, a group of people sent on such a journey. **3** a group of people sent to have (especially political) discussions. **4** one's supposed purpose or calling in life. **5** a group of missionaries, or the building occupied by them. [from Latin *missionis*, from *mittere*, to send]

missionary *noun* (PL. **missionaries**) a member of a religious organization seeking to carry out charitable works and religious teaching, often combined.

missis same as MISSUS.

Mississippi POP (1990) 2.6m, a state in S USA, divided into 82 counties. AREA 123 510sq km/ 47 689sq mi. It is known as the 'Magnolia State'. The Gulf of Mexico lies to the S. PHYSICAL

DESCRIPTION the main rivers are the Mississippi (forms the W border), Pearl (part of the S border), and Tennessee (follows the border in the NE); the highest point is Mt Woodall (246m); much of the S part of the state is covered in pine woods; the coastal plain is fertile; land rises in the NE. HISTORY held by France, Britain, and Spain in turn, becoming part of the USA in 1795; became a state in 1817 and was the 20th to join the Union; seceded in 1861 and was readmitted in 1870; Mississippi was a centre of the civil rights movement in the 1960s. CAPITAL Jackson. CHIEF TOWNS Biloxi, Meridian, Hattiesburg, Greenville, Gulfport. ECONOMY major cotton-producing area between the Mississippi and Yazoo rivers; agriculture includes soya beans, cattle, dairy products, poultry; fisheries are prominent along the Gulf coast; there are natural resources of petroleum and natural gas (over one third of the land is given over to oil and gas development); clothing, wood products, foods, and chemicals are manufactured; the state has the lowest per capita income in the USA. NOTABLE FEATURES Old Spanish Fort; Vicksburg National Military Park; historic Natchez.

Mississippi River a river in central USA. At 1 884km/1 171mi, it is the second-longest river in the USA, after its tributary the Missouri. The Missouri, however, is often considered part of the main stream, and from the Missouri's longest headstream, the Red Rock–Jefferson R, the length of the Mississippi is 6 019km/3 740mi. Rising in N Minnesota, the Mississippi flows S to form the border between the states of Minnesota, Iowa, Missouri, Arkansas, and Louisiana to the W and Wisconsin, Illinois, Tennessee, and Mississippi to the E. It enters the Gulf of Mexico in SE Louisiana, near New Orleans. Its major tributaries are the Minnesota, Des Moines, Missouri, Arkansas, and Red (to the W), and the Illinois and Ohio (on the E). The river drains an area of about 3.3m sq km/1.3m sq mi between the Appalachian and the Rocky Mts, including part of Alberta and Saskatchewan. Although several artificial levees on the banks of the lower river help to cope with flooding, severe floods can occur, resulting in loss of life and damage to crops and property. The delta consists of salt marsh, wooded swampland, and low-lying alluvial tracts, dissected by numerous distributaries (*bayous*). Practically no tide ascends the Mississippi, which is navigable as far as Minneapolis; it is a busy commercial waterway. Major ports are New Orleans, St Louis, Memphis, St Paul, Minneapolis, and Baton Rouge.

missive *noun literary Legal* a letter. [from Latin *missivus*, from *mittere*, to send]

Miss Julie (Fröken Julie) a play by August Strindberg (1888). It revolves around the developing sexual relationship between the aristocratic Miss Julie and a servant, symbolically providing an indictment of human nature through the battle between the sexes.

Missoni, Tai Otavio (1921–) Italian knitwear designer, born in Yugoslavia. He founded the Missoni company with his wife, Rosita, in Italy in 1953. At first they manufactured knitwear to be sold under other labels. Later they created, under their own label, innovative knitwear notable for its sophistication, and for its distinctive colours and patterns.

Missouri POP (1990) 5.2m, a state in central USA, divided into 115 counties. AREA 180 508sq km/69 697sq mi. It is known as the 'Show Me State'. PHYSICAL DESCRIPTION the E and W borders are largely defined by the Mississippi, Missouri, and Des Moines rivers; the Ozark Plateau lies in the SW; the highest point is Mt Taum Sauk (540m); split into two parts by the Missouri R; to the N there is open prairieland with corn and livestock, particularly hogs and cattle, and S of the river there are foothills and the Ozarks, much of which is forested. HISTORY

became part of the USA with the 1803 Louisiana Purchase; became a territory in 1812, but its application for admission as a state in 1817 was controversial, as it had introduced slavery; eventually admitted as the 24th state in 1821 under the Missouri Compromise; its position at the junction of the nation's two greatest rivers led to its development as a transport hub, and as the starting point for the pioneering advance W across the continent. CAPITAL Jefferson City. CHIEF TOWNS St Louis, Kansas City, Springfield, and Independence. ECONOMY Missouri has more farms than any other state except Texas; major agricultural products are cattle, hogs, soya beans, dairy produce; major industries are motor vehicles, aircraft and aerospace components, processed foods and chemicals, machinery, fabricated metals, and electrical equipment; Missouri mines yield over 90% of the nation's lead.

Missouri Compromise an agreement (1820) to admit Missouri, with slavery, and Maine (formerly part of Massachusetts), without it, to statehood simultaneously, in order to preserve a sectional balance in the US Senate. The compromise also forbade slavery in the rest of the Louisiana Purchase, north of 36°30', and was in effect until replaced by the Kansas–Nebraska Act (1854).

Missouri River the longest river in the USA, and the chief tributary of the Mississippi, length 3 725km/2 315mi (with its longest headstream, 4 135km/2 569mi). It is formed in SW Montana by the confluence of the Jefferson, Madison, and Gallatin rivers; flows through North and South Dakota, then forms the borders between Nebraska and Kansas in the W and Iowa and Missouri in the E; joins the Mississippi just N of St Louis. Navigation (possible as far as Fort Benton) is dangerous. Major tributaries are the Musselshell, Milk, Yellowstone, Little Missouri, Grand (of South Dakota), Moreau, Cheyenne, Bad, White, Niobrara, James, Platte, Kansas, Grand (of Iowa and Missouri), Gasconade, and Osage. Major dams include the Canyon Ferry, Hauser L, Holter L, Fort Peck L, Garrison, Oahe, and Fort Randall. The Missouri is used for irrigation, flood-control, and hydroelectricity.

misspell *verb* (PAST TENSE AND PAST PARTICIPLE **misspelt**, **misspelled**) to spell incorrectly.

misspend *verb* (PAST TENSE AND PAST PARTICIPLE **misspent**) to spend foolishly or wastefully.

missus *noun colloq.* **1** *humorous* a wife. **2** *old use* a term used to address an adult female stranger. [originally a spoken form of MISTRESS]

missy *noun old colloq. use* usu. *facetious*, *derog.* a term used to address a girl or young woman.

mist — *noun* **1** condensed water vapour in the air near the ground; thin fog or low cloud. **2** a mass of tiny droplets of liquid, eg forced under pressure from a container. **3** condensed water vapour on a surface. **4** *literary* a watery film: *a mist of tears.* **5** *literary* an obscuring influence: *the mists of time.* — *verb trans., intrans.* (also **mist up** or **over**) to cover or become covered with mist. [from Anglo-Saxon *mist*]

mistake — *verb* (PAST TENSE **mistook**; PAST PARTICIPLE **mistaken**) **1** (**mistake one person** *or* **thing for another**) to identify them incorrectly as someone or something else; to wrongly assume or understand them to be what they are not: *they might mistake us for intruders* / *she mistook my silence for disapproval.* **2** to misinterpret. **3** to make the wrong choice of: *he mistook his road in the fog.* — *noun* **1** an error. **2** a regrettable action. **3** an act of understanding or interpreting something wrongly. [from Norse *mistaka*, to take wrongly]

mistaken *adj.* **1** understood or identified wrongly. **2** guilty of, or displaying, a failure to understand or interpret correctly.

mistakenly *adv.* in a mistaken way.

mister *noun* **1** (**Mister**) the full form of the abbreviation *Mr.* **2** *colloq.* a term used to address an adult male stranger. **3** a man not belonging to the nobility; an untitled man. [originally a spoken form of MASTER]

mistily *adv.* in or through a mist; in a misty way.

mistime *verb* **1** to do or say at a wrong or unsuitable time. **2** *Sport* to misjudge the timing of (a stroke) in relation to the speed of an approaching ball.

mistiness *noun* being misty.

Mistinguett, stage name of **Jeanne Marie Bourgeois** (1874–1956) French dancer and actress, born in Pointe de Raquet. She made her début in 1895, and became the most popular French music hall artiste for the next 30 years, reaching the height of success partnering Maurice Chevalier at the Folies Bergère.

Misti, Volcán El *or* **El Misti** a dormant volcano in S Peru, in the Andean Cordillera Occidental. HEIGHT 5 843m. The last eruption was in 1600. Of religious significance to the Incas, the volcano is mentioned in poetry and legends. An observatory was established by Harvard University near its summit.

mistle-thrush *noun* a large European thrush fond of mistletoe berries. [from Anglo-Saxon *mistel*, mistletoe]

mistletoe *noun* a Eurasian evergreen shrub that grows as a parasite on trees and produces clusters of white berries in winter; a similar American plant. [from Anglo-Saxon *misteltan*]

mistook see MISTAKE.

Mistral, Frédéric (1830–1914) French poet, born in Maillane, near Avignon. He became a founder of the Provençal renaissance movement (the *Félibrige* school), and is best known for his long narrative poems, including *Miréio* (1859) and *Calendau* (1861), and for his Provençal–French dictionary (1878–86). He was awarded the Nobel Prize for Literature in 1904.

Mistral, Gabriela, pseudonym of **Lucila Godoy de Alcayaga** (1889–1957) Chilean poet, diplomat, and teacher, born in Vicuña. As a teacher she won a poetry prize with her *Sonetos de la muerte* (Sonnets of Death, 1914), and the cost of publication of her first book, *Desolación* (Desolation, 1922), was met by the teachers of New York. She was awarded the Nobel Prize for Literature in 1945.

mistral *noun* (**the mistral**) *Meteorol.* a cold gusty strong northerly wind that blows down the Rhône valley in S France. [from Provençal, from Latin *magistralis*, masterful]

mistreat *verb* to treat cruelly or without care.

mistreatment *noun* bad or cruel treatment.

mistress *noun* **1** a woman in a commanding or controlling position; a female head or owner. **2** a female teacher. **3** the female lover of a man married to another woman. **4** *old use* a term used to address any woman, especially one in authority. [from Old French *maistresse*]

mistrial *noun* *Legal* a trial not conducted properly according to the law, and declared invalid.

mistrust — *verb* to have no trust in; to be suspicious of. — *noun* lack of trust.

mistrustful *adj.* without trust, suspicious.

misty *adj.* (**mistier, mistiest**) **1** covered with, or obscured by, mist. **2** *literary* not clear; vague. **3** *said of the eyes* filled with tears.

misunderstand *verb trans., intrans.* (PAST TENSE AND PAST PARTICIPLE **misunderstood**) to fail to understand properly.

misunderstanding *noun* **1** a failure to understand properly. **2** *euphemistic* a disagreement.

misunderstood *adj., said of a person* not properly understood or appreciated as regards character, feelings, intentions, etc.

misuse — *noun* improper or inappropriate use: *the misuse of funds*. — *verb* **1** to put to improper or inappropriate use. **2** *formal* to treat badly.

MIT *abbrev.* the Massachusetts Institute of Technology, an institute of higher education which opened in Boston, Massachusetts, in 1865 and moved to Cambridge, Massachusetts, in 1916. The college is renowned for its science facilities and research work, although it also offers courses in the arts and humanities.

Mitchell, Margaret (1900–49) US novelist, born in Atlanta, Georgia. She studied for a medical career, turned to journalism, and in 1925 began the 10-year task of writing her only novel, *Gone with the Wind* (1936, Pulitzer Prize). It achieved an immediate popularity unprecedented in the USA, was translated into many languages, and filmed in 1939.

Mitchell, Peter Dennis (1920–92) English biochemist, born in Mitcham, Surrey. He set up his own research institute in Cornwall (1964), and proposed an entirely novel theory of the way energy is generated in biochemical cells at the molecular level. He was awarded the 1978 Nobel Prize for Chemistry.

Mitchell, R(eginald) J(oseph) (1895–1937) British aircraft designer. Trained as an engineer, he was led by his interest in aircraft to join an aviation firm (1916), where he soon became chief designer. He designed seaplanes for the Schneider trophy races (1922–31) and later the Spitfire, whose triumph he did not live to see.

mite[1] *noun* any of thousands of small, often microscopic, animals belonging to the same order (Acarina) as the ticks, with a simple rounded body and eight short legs. Many species are plant pests, eg red spider mite, while others transmit animal diseases, eg mange and scabies, or cause human allergies, eg dust mite. [from Anglo-Saxon]

mite[2] *noun* **1** any small person or animal, especially a child that is pitied. **2** a small amount of anything, especially money.
— **a mite** ... *colloq.* rather ...; somewhat: *a mite jealous*.
[from Old Dutch *mite*]

Mitford, Nancy (1904–73) English writer, born in London. She established a reputation with her novels which include *Pursuit of Love* (1945) and *Love in a Cold Climate* (1949). Her biographical works include *Madame de Pompadour* (1953) and *The Sun King* (1966). As editor and contributor to *Noblesse Oblige* (1956), she helped to originate the 'U' (upper-class) and 'non-U' classification of linguistic usage.

Mithra *or* **Mithras** in Indo-European mythology, a god worshipped in the early Roman Empire, of Persian origin, and identified with the Sun. The cult of Mithraism was predominantly military, restricted to males, and bore many resemblances to Christianity which eventually replaced it. The main story was of his fight with the cosmic bull, which he conquered and sacrificed.

Mithridates VI Eupator, also called **the Great** (d.63 BC) King of Pontus (c.120–63 BC), a Hellenized ruler of Iranian extraction. He expanded his empire into the Crimea and Colchis in the Black Sea area, and his attempts to expand further into Cappadocia and Bithynia led to a series of wars (the Mithridatic Wars) with Rome (88–66 BC). He was worsted by Sulla (c.86 BC) and Lucullus (72–71 BC), but was not finally defeated until Pompey took over the eastern command (66 BC). Mithridates avoided capture, but later took his own life when his son rebelled against him.

mitigate *verb* **1** *Legal* to partially excuse or make less serious: *mitigating circumstances*. **2** *formal* to make (pain, anger, etc) less severe. [from Latin *mitigare*, from *mitis*, mild + *agere*, to make]
◆ Often confused with *militate*.

Mitla an ancient city in central Oaxaca, S Mexico, in the Sierra Madre del Sur, 40km/25mi SE of the city of Oaxaca. It is the former centre of the Zapotec civilization. NOTABLE FEATURES well-preserved ruins include temples, subterranean tombs, and a building known as the 'hall of monoliths'.

mitochondrion (PL. **mitochondria**) *Biol.* a specialized oval structure, consisting of a central matrix surrounded by two membranes. It is found in large numbers in the cytoplasm of eukaryotic cells. [from Greek *mitos*, thread + *khondrion*, granule]
◇ The inner membrane of a mitochondrion is folded into finger-like projections called *cristae*, which are the site of the electron transport systems that produce energy in the form of the compound ATP (adenosine triphosphate) during aerobic respiration. The matrix is the site of the Krebs cycle, which is also involved in the release of energy during the breakdown of carbohydrate molecules. Mitochondria are most numerous in the cells of tissues that consume large amounts of energy, eg muscle tissue.

mitosis *noun Biol.* a type of cell division that results in the production of two daughter cells with identical nuclei, each of which contains the same genes and the same number of chromosomes as the parent nucleus, and is said to be *diploid*. Mitosis occurs in all cells except sex cells. See also MEIOSIS. [from Greek *mitos*, fibre]

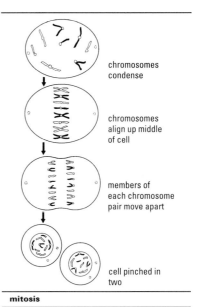

chromosomes condense

chromosomes align up middle of cell

members of each chromosome pair move apart

cell pinched in two

mitosis

mitre[1] *noun* the ceremonial headdress of a bishop or abbot, a tall pointed hat with front and back sections divided. [from French, from Greek *mitra*, fillet]

mitre[2] — *noun* (also **mitre joint**) a corner joint between two lengths of wood, etc made by fitting together two 45° sloping surfaces cut into their ends. — *verb* to join with a mitre. [perhaps the same word as MITRE[1]]

Mitsiwa see MASSAWA.

mitt *noun* **1** a mitten. **2** *colloq.* a hand. **3** a padded leather glove worn in baseball. [a shortening of MITTEN]

Mittelland Canal a system of German canals and rivers linking the Dortmund–Ems Canal with Magdeburg. The length of the system is 325km/202mi. The waterway, which together with side canals provides an important transportation network, was completed in the late 1930s.

mitten *noun* **1** a glove with one covering for the thumb and a large covering for all the other fingers together. **2** a glove covering the hand and wrist but not the whole length of the fingers. [from French *mitaine*]

Mitterrand, François (Maurice Marie) (1916–) French Socialist politician, born in Jarnac. After studying law at Paris, he served with the French Forces (1939–40), escaped from capture, and was active in the Resistance. A deputy in the French parliament almost continuously from 1946, he held various ministerial posts, and for many years was a stubborn opponent of de Gaulle, working for the unification of the French Left. He became Secretary of the Socialist Party (1971) and President of France (1981–), when he embarked on a programme of nationalization and job creation in an attempt to combat stagnation and unemployment.

Mitty, Walter see SECRET LIFE OF WALTER MITTY, THE.

mix — *verb* (*also in many senses* **mix up**) **1** (**mix one thing with another** *or* **things together**) to put them together or combine to form one mass. **2** to prepare or make by doing this: *mix a cake*. **3** *intrans.* to blend together to form one mass: *water and oil do not mix*. **4** *intrans.* to meet with people socially; to feel at ease in social situations. **5** to do at the same time; to combine: *mix business with pleasure*. **6** *technical* to adjust electronically (the sounds produced by individual musicians) to create an overall balance of sound. — *noun* **1** a collection of people or things mixed together. **2** a collection of (usually dried) ingredients from which something is prepared: *a cake mix*.
— **be mixed up** *colloq.* be upset or emotionally confused.
be mixed up in something *or* **with something** *or* **someone** *colloq.* be involved in or with them, especially in something illicit or suspect.
mix it *slang* to cause trouble, argument, a fight, etc.
mix something *or* **someone up 1** to confuse them: *I always mix him up with his brother*. **2** *colloq.* to upset or put into a state of confusion. [from Latin *miscere*, to mix]

mixed *adj.* **1** consisting of different and often opposite kinds: *mixed feelings*. **2** done, used, etc by people of both sexes.

mixed-ability *adj.* denoting the teaching of children of a wide range of ability in a single class, as opposed to *streaming*, where they are put into higher or lower groups according to their general ability. Children in mixed-ability groups progress at different rates, although it is maintained by some that the less able benefit from interaction with their more able classmates, and a higher general level of achievement may result.

mixed bag *colloq.* a collection of people or things of different kinds, standards, etc.

mixed blessing something which has both advantages and disadvantages.

mixed doubles a variety of tennis, table-tennis, or badminton played by two pairs, each consisting of a man and a woman.

mixed economy an economic system with some elements state-owned and others privately owned.

mixed farming farming of both crops and livestock.

mixed grill a dish of different kinds of grilled meat, and usually tomatoes and mushrooms.

mixed marriage a marriage between people of different races or religions.

mixed metaphor a combination of two or more metaphors which produces an inconsistent or incongruous mental image, and is often regarded as a stylistic flaw, as in *there are concrete steps in the pipeline*.

mixed-up *adj.* **1** mentally or emotionally confused. **2** socially badly adjusted.

mixer *noun* **1** a machine used for mixing. **2** a soft drink for mixing with alcoholic drinks. **3** col-

loq. a person considered in terms of his or her ability to mix socially: *a good mixer*.

mixture *noun* **1** a blend of ingredients prepared for a particular purpose: *cough mixture*. **2** a combination: *a mixture of sadness and relief*. **3** the act of mixing.

mix-up *noun* a confusion or misunderstanding; mistaking one person or thing for another.

mizzenmast *noun* on a ship with three or more masts, the third mast from the front of the ship. [from Italian *mezzano*, middle + MAST[1]]

Mjøsa, Lake *or* **Mjøsen** the largest lake in Norway, extending S–N from Eidsvall to Lillehammer. AREA 368sq km/142sq mi; length 100km/62mi; maximum depth 443m. The elongated lake, which is fed by the Lågen, is heavily stocked with trout. Chief towns on its banks are Lillehammer, Hamar, and Gjøvik.

Mk *abbrev.* mark (= a type of design, or model, especially of vehicles).

ml *abbrev.* **1** mile. **2** millilitre.

MLitt *abbrev. magister litterarum* (Latin), Master of Letters, or of Literature.

MLR *abbrev.* minimum lending rate.

MM *abbrev.* Military Medal.

mm *abbrev.* millimetre.

MMC *abbrev.* Monopolies and Mergers Commission.

Mme *abbrev.* (French) Madame.

MN *abbrev.* Minnesota.

Mn *symbol Chem.* manganese.

M'Naghten rules a set of legal principles which state that a defendant may not be convicted if insanity is proved. The rules were developed in England subsequent to the 19c murder trial of Daniel M'Naghten, a case in which insanity was proved. They serve as the legal standard for insanity in Britain, Canada, and many US jurisdictions, including federal law. In some US states, the standard for insanity is that set by the American Law Institute's Model Penal Code.

mnemonic — *noun* a device or form of words, often a short verse, used as an aid to memory. — *adj.* serving to help the memory. [from Greek *mneme*, memory]

mnemonically *adv.* in a mnemonic way.

Mnemosyne in Greek mythology, a Titaness, daughter of Earth and Heaven, and mother of all the Muses. She is the personification of memory.

MO *abbrev.* **1** Medical Officer, ie an army doctor. **2** Missouri. **3** modus operandi. **4** money order.

Mo[1] *abbrev.* Missouri.

Mo[2] *symbol Chem.* molybdenum.

mo *noun* (PL. **mos**) *colloq.* a short while; a moment. [a shortening of MOMENT]

moa *noun* an extinct flightless ostrich-like bird of New Zealand. [from Maori]

Moabites an ancient Semitic people who in Old Testament times inhabited the area to the SE of the Dead Sea. Like the Ammonites, they were believed to be descended from Lot.

Moabite Stone an inscribed basalt slab, discovered in 1868 and subsequently broken up, which describes the successful revolt of Mesha, King of Moab, against the Israelites during the reign of Ahab (7c BC), or possibly of his son Jehoram (2 Kings 1.1). It also sheds linguistic and historical light on the Hebrew biblical narratives.

moan — *noun* **1** a low prolonged sound expressing sadness, grief, or pain. **2** any similar sound, eg made by the wind or an engine. **3** *colloq.* a complaint; a person who complains a lot. — *verb intrans.* **1** to utter or produce a moan. **2** *colloq.* to complain, especially without good reason. [from Anglo-Saxon *mænan*, to grieve over]

moaner *noun* a person who moans.

moat *noun* a deep trench, often filled with water, dug round a castle or other fortified position, to provide extra defence. [from Old French *mote*, mound]

mob — *noun* **1** a large disorderly crowd. **2** *colloq.* any group or gang. **3** *colloq.* (**the mob**) ordinary people; the masses. **4** (**the mob**) an organized gang of criminals, especially the Mafia. — *verb* (**mobbed, mobbing**) **1** to attack as a mob. **2** to crowd round curiously or admiringly. [a shortening of Latin *mobile vulgus*, fickle masses]

Mobile POP (1990) 477 000, the seat of Mobile County, SW Alabama, USA. Situated on Mobile Bay, it is a major US port and the only seaport in Alabama. HISTORY settled by the French in 1711; ceded to the British in 1763; achieved city status in 1819; scene of a Federal victory at the naval battle of Mobile Bay in 1864.

mobile — *adj.* **1** able to be moved easily; not fixed. **2** set up inside a vehicle travelling from place to place: *a mobile shop*. **3** *said of a face* frequently changing expression. **4** able, or willing, to move house or change jobs. **5** moving, or able to move, from one social class to another: *upwardly mobile*. **6** *colloq.* provided with transport and able to travel. — *noun* a hanging decoration moved around by air currents. [from Latin *mobilis*, from *movere*, to move]
◇ The name was first applied in the artistic sense by Marcel Duchamp (1887–1968) to the hanging wire-and-metal sculptures of Alexander Calder (1898–1976). From c.1931 Calder perfected these popular and widely-imitated abstract constructions, sometimes adding a motor, sometimes relying on air currents to set them turning. Examples are his *Antennae with Red and Blue Dots* (1960) and *The Four Elements* (1962), an outdoor motorized mobile.

mobility *noun* **1** the ability to move. **2** a tendency to move.

mobility allowance money paid by the government to disabled people or the very ill to assist in meeting their travel costs. In the UK since 1992, mobility allowance became one of the two components of the benefit known as *disability living allowance*, designed to provide sufficient funds to meet both care and travel needs.

mobilization *or* **mobilisation** *noun* the act or process of mobilizing or being mobilized.

mobilize *or* **mobilise** *verb* **1** to organize or prepare for use. **2** *trans., intrans.* to assemble and make or become ready for war. [from MOBILE]

Möbius, August Ferdinand (1790–1868) German mathematician, born in Schulpforta. Professor at Leipzig, he worked on analytical geometry, topology, and theoretical astronomy, but is best known for the 'Möbius strip' (a one-sided surface formed by giving a rectangular strip a half-twist and then joining the ends together) and the 'Möbius net', an important concept in geometry.

mobster *noun slang* a member of an organized group of criminals, especially the Mafia.

Mobuto Sésé Seko, Lake, formerly **Lake Albert** a lake in E central Africa, in the W Rift Valley, on the frontier between Zaire and Uganda. AREA c.6 400sq km/2 500sq mi; length, c.160km/100mi; width, 40km/25mi. It receives the Victoria Nile in the NE and the Semliki R in the SW. The Albert Nile flows N from it.

Mobutu Seze Seko (1930–), formerly **Joseph Désiré Mobutu** Zairean soldier and politician. He became a commander in the Belgian army at the age of 30, and was a member of Patrice Lumumba's Congolese National Movement Party (MNC). Immediately after independence (1960) Mobutu took power for a short time, then took over permanently after the civil war (1963–5). He remained president, with a strong personal control, and a belief in the power of money rather than an organized social structure.

Moby Dick, in full *Moby Dick, or, The Whale* a novel by Herman Melville (1851). It is an intricate narrative which revolves around the hunt by Capt Ahab and the crew of the *Pequod* for the white sperm whale, Moby Dick.

moccasin *noun* **1** a deerskin shoe with a continuous sole and heel, as worn by Native Americans; any slipper or shoe resembling this. **2** (*also* **water moccasin**) a large poisonous snake of the swamps of the southern US. [from Native American languages]

mocha *noun* **1** dark brown coffee of fine quality. **2** a flavouring made from coffee and chocolate. [from *Mocha*, a port in the Yemen Arab Republic where the coffee was originally shipped from]

Moche an ancient Andean city near Trujillo, Peru, the capital c.200–550 AD of the Moche (or Mochica) state. It is particularly renowned for its twin pyramids of the Sun and Moon, made from adobe bricks.

mock — *verb* **1** *trans., intrans.* to speak or behave disparagingly or contemptuously (towards). **2** to mimic. **3** *literary* to cause to seem impossible or useless; to seem to defy or frustrate: *violent winds mocked my attempt to pitch the tent*. — *adj*. **1** false; sham: *mock sincerity*. **2** serving as practice for something similar coming later: *a mock examination*. — *noun colloq.* a mock examination. [from Old French *mocquer*]

mockers
— **put the mockers on someone** *or* **something** *colloq.* to end the chances of their success; to spoil them.
[perhaps from MOCK]

mockery *noun* (PL. **mockeries**) **1** ridicule; contempt; the subject of ridicule or contempt: *make a mockery of*. **2** an imitation, especially contemptible or insulting. **3** any ridiculously inadequate person, action, or thing.

mocking *adj*. that mocks.

mockingbird *noun* a grey American bird that copies the calls of other birds.

mock orange *noun* the philadelphus.

Mock Turtle, the a melancholy creature encountered by Alice in Lewis Carroll's *Alice's Adventures in Wonderland.*

mock turtle soup soup made in the style of turtle soup, but using a calf's head.

mock-up *noun* a full-size model or replica, built for experimental purposes.

MOD *or* **MoD** *abbrev.* Ministry of Defence.

Mod an annual musical and literary festival of Gaelic-speaking Scotland, first held in Oban in 1892, organized by An Comunn Gaidhealach (the Gaelic language society) on the model of the Welsh eisteddfod.

mod *colloq.* — *adj. old use* modern. — *noun* a follower of a British teenage culture originally of the 1960s, characterized by a liking for smart clothes and motor scooters. [a shortening of MODERN]

modal — *adj*. **1** relating to or concerning mode or a mode. **2** *said of music* using a particular mode. — *noun Grammar* (*also* **modal auxiliary** *or* **modal verb**) a verb used as the auxiliary of another verb to express grammatical mood such as condition, possibility, and obligation.
◊ In English the principal modals are *can, may, might, shall, should, will, would, must, ought to, used to, need, dare*. Of these, *need* and *dare* are often called semi-modals. Modals have features in common, such as lacking inflection and having the ability to take *not* to form a negative, as in *may not* and *dare not*.

modality *noun* **1** *Mus.* the quality or characteristic of music as determined by its mode. **2** *Grammar* the modal property of a verb or construction.

mod cons *colloq.* modern household conveniences, eg central heating.

Modder River, Battle of an engagement (1899) in the second Boer War whereby the British hoped to relieve the Siege of Kimberley. The Boers had command of a hilltop (a traditional Boer tactic), but as this made them vulnerable to modern artillery, they dug trenches by the river instead. The British failed to take the positions and were defeated two weeks later at Magersfontein, which delayed the relief of Kimberley by three months.

mode *noun* **1** *formal* a way of doing, living, operating, etc. **2** a fashion or style, eg in clothes or art. **3** *Mus.* any of several systems according to which notes are arranged. [from Latin *modus*, manner, measure]
◊ Specifically, either of two main scale systems (*major mode* and *minor mode*) in use since the 16c. In older musical theory, any of various scales of notes within an octave; the six modes recognized in Renaissance musical theory were the Dorian, Phrygian, Lydian, Mixolydian, Aeolian, and Ionian.

model — *noun* **1** a small-scale representation serving as a guide to construction. **2** a small-scale replica. **3** one of several types or designs of manufactured article. **4** a person who displays clothes to potential buyers by wearing them. **5** a (usually paid) human subject of the work of an artist, photographer, etc. **6** a thing from which something else is to be derived; a basis. **7** an excellent example; an example to be copied: *she's a model of loyalty / a model boss*. — *verb* (**modelled, modelling**) **1** *trans., intrans.* to display (clothes) by wearing them. **2** *intrans.* to work as a model for an artist, photographer, etc. **3** *trans., intrans.* to make models of. **4** to shape into a particular form: *to model clay*. **5** (**model one thing on another**) to plan, build, or create it according to a model. [from French *modelle*, from Latin *modulus*]

modelling *noun* **1** the act or activity of making a model or models. **2** the activity or occupation of a person who models clothes.

modello *noun* (PL. **modelli**) a small but complete and detailed painting or drawing made to present the artist's ideas for a full-size work. It was often made to impress a patron and obtain a commission. Oil modelli by Peter Paul Rubens and Giovanni Battista Tiepolo still exist. [from Italian *modello*, model]

modem *noun Comput.* an electronic device that transmits information from one computer to another along a telephone line, converting digital data into audio signals and back again. [from MODULATOR + DEMODULATOR]

moderate — *adj.* (pronounced *-rət*) **1** not extreme; not strong or violent. **2** average; middle rate: *moderate intelligence*. — *noun* (pronounced *-rət*) a person holding moderate (especially political) views. — *verb* (pronounced *-rate*) **1** to make or become less extreme or less violent. **2** *intrans.* to act as a moderator. [from Latin *moderatus*, from *modus*, measure]

moderately *adv.* in a moderate way; to a moderate degree.

moderation *noun* **1** the quality of being moderate. **2** an act of making or becoming less extreme. **3** lack of excess; self-control.
— **in moderation** to a moderate degree; in moderate amounts.

moderato *adv., adj. Mus.* to be played at a restrained and moderate tempo. [from Italian *moderato*]

moderator *noun* **1** a minister presiding over a court or assembly in any Presbyterian church. **2** a settler of disputes; a mediator. **3** a substance used for slowing down neutrons in nuclear reactors.

modern — *adj.* **1** belonging to the present or to recent times; not old or ancient. **2** *said of techniques, equipment, etc* involving, using, or being the very latest available: *modern transport*. **3** (*often*

Modern) *said of a language* in the most recent stage of development; as used at present: *Modern English*. — *noun* a person living in modern times, especially a follower of the latest trends. [from Latin *modernus*]

Modernism a generic term which refers to experimental methods in different art forms in the earlier part of the 20c. These experiments were stimulated by a sharpened sense of the arbitrariness of existing artistic conventions, and doubts about the human place and purpose in the world. Notable works include James Joyce's *Ulysses* (1922) and T S Eliot's *Waste Land* (1922); the Cubist paintings of Pablo Picasso and Georges Braque; the 12-tone music of Anton von Webern and Arnold Schoenberg.

Modernist *noun* a person who practises or advocates Modernism.

modernistic *adj.* relating to or typical of Modernism or modern ideas.

modernity *noun* **1** being modern. **2** something modern.

modernization *or* **modernisation** *noun* **1** the act or process of modernizing. **2** being modernized.

modernize *or* **modernise** *verb* **1** to bring up to modern standards. **2** *intrans.* to switch to more modern methods or techniques.

modest *adj.* **1** not having or showing pride; humble; not pretentious or showy. **2** not large; moderate: *a modest income*. **3** *old use, said especially of clothing* plain and restrained, not offending standards of decency: *a modest dress*. [from Latin *modestus*, from *modus*, a measure]

modestly *adv.* in a modest way.

modesty *noun* being modest.

modicum *noun formal, facetious* a small amount: *a modicum of decency*. [from Latin, from *modicus*, moderate]

modification *noun* modifying or being modified.

modifier *noun Grammar* a word or phrase that modifies or identifies the meaning of another word, eg *in the green hat* in the phrase *the man in the green hat*, and *vaguely* in the phrase *he was vaguely embarrassed*.

modify *verb* (**modifies, modified**) **1** to change the form or quality of, usually slightly. **2** *Grammar* to act as a modifier of. [from Latin *modificare*]

Modigliani, Amedeo (1884–1920) Italian painter and sculptor, born in Leghorn. His early work was influenced by the painters of the Italian Renaissance, and in 1906 he went to Paris, where he was further influenced by the Fauves. In 1909 he took to sculpture and produced a number of elongated stone heads in African style. He continued to use this style when he later resumed painting, with a series of richly-coloured, elongated portraits.

Modigliani, Franco (1918–) Italian-born US economist, born in Rome. He has been Professor at Illinois (1949–52), Carnegie–Mellon (1952–60), and Northwestern (1960–2) Universities, and at the Massachusetts Institute of Technology (1962–). He was awarded the Nobel Prize for Economics in 1985 for his work on personal saving and on corporate finance.

modish *adj. formal* stylish; fashionable. [from MODE]

modiste *noun old formal use* a fashion designer. [from French; related to MODE]

modular *adj.* consisting of modules; constructed like a module.

modular construction *Electron.* a method of constructing a hardware or software system using standard compatible units (with differing functions) which are quickly interchangeable or which may be built up in combinations to provide a wide range of configurations.

modulate *verb* **1** *technical* to alter the tone or volume of (a sound or one's voice). **2** *formal* to change or alter. **3** *Radio* to cause modulation of a carrier wave (signal-carrying wave). [from Latin *modulari*]

modulation *noun Radio* in radio transmission, the process whereby the frequency, amplitude, or some other property of a carrier wave (signal-carrying wave) is made to increase or decrease instantaneously in response to variations in the characteristics of the signal being transmitted. See also AMPLITUDE MODULATION, FREQUENCY MODULATION.

modulator *noun* a person or device that modulates.

module *noun* **1** a separate unit that combines with others to form a larger unit, structure, or system. **2** a separate self-contained part of a space vehicle used for a particular purpose: *lunar module*. [from Latin *modulus*, a small measure]

modulus *noun Maths.* the absolute value of a real number, regardless of whether it is positive or negative. The modulus of a vector quantity is equal to its length or magnitude, and does not take account of its direction. [from Latin *modulus*, a diminutive of *modus*, measure]

modus operandi (PL. ***modi operandi***) a way of working; the way something operates. [Latin, = way of working]

modus vivendi (PL. ***modi vivendi***) **1** an arrangement by which people or groups in conflict can work or exist together; a compromise. **2** *affected* a way of living. [Latin, = way of living]

Moerae *or* **Moirai** in Greek mythology, the Fates: a trio of goddesses, mentioned in Homer, who control human destiny and sometimes overrule the gods. In later writers, they are assigned names and functions: Lachesis, ('the distributor'), who allots the destinies of human beings; Clotho, ('the spinner'), who spins the thread of life; and Atropos, ('the inflexible'), who cuts it.

mog *or* **moggy** *noun* (PL. **moggies**) *slang* a cat.

Mogadishu, Somali **Muqdisho**, Italian **Mogadiscio** POP (1987e) 1m, the capital of Somalia, a seaport on the Indian Ocean coast. HISTORY founded in the 10c; bombarded by Vasco da Gama in 1499; captured by Tristão da Cunha in 1503; taken by the Sultan of Zanzibar in 1871; sold to Italy and became capital of Italian Somaliland in 1905; occupied by British forces in World War II; became the capital of the independent Somali Republic (Somalia) in 1960. Civil War in the country has led to destruction, starvation, and many casualties in Mogadishu in the 1990s. NOTABLE FEATURES fort; mosques (13c); cathedral (1928).

Mogao Caves a complex of 496 Buddhist cave temples on the edge of the Taklamakan desert, Gansu, China. Excavations of the caves (4c–14c) have uncovered notable wall paintings, particularly those executed during the 6c–9c. It is a World Heritage site.

Mogilev POP (1991e) 363 000, an industrial city in Belorussia, lying on the R Dnieper. It was founded in 1267. NOTABLE FEATURE Church of St Nicholas (begun in 1669).

Mogollon a prehistoric culture of the American SW (c.300–1350), which extended from S Arizona and New Mexico to the Chihuahuan and Sonoran deserts of Mexico. Its villages of pithouses were typically sited for defence on mountain-tops until c.600, when there was a movement towards river valleys to facilitate more intensive maize agriculture.

mogul — *noun* **1** an important, powerful, or influential person, especially in business or the film industry. **2** (**Mogul**) a Muslim ruler of India between the 16c and 19c centuries. — *adj.*

(**Mogul**) typical of or relating to the Moguls. [from Persian *Mughul*, Mongol]

MOH *abbrev.* Medical Officer of Health.

Mohács, Battle of a Turkish victory (1526) in Europe, when the army of the Ottoman sultan Sulaiman I, 'the Magnificent', annihilated a Hungarian force one fifth its size under King Louis II outside Buda. Louis was killed, Hungary was plunged into civil war, and a long period of Turkish and particularly Habsburg domination of the old Hungarian kingdom began. Since Louis had simultaneously been King of Bohemia and Moravia, the Habsburg Archduke Ferdinand occupied that throne, beginning a period of Austrian rule that lasted until 1918.

mohair *noun* the long soft hair of the angora goat; a yarn or fabric made of this, pure or mixed with wool. [from Arabic *mukhayyar*]

Mohammed see MUHAMMAD.

Mohammed II (1430–81) Ottoman Sultan (1451–81), born in Adrianople. He took Constantinople in 1453, and thereby extinguished the Byzantine Empire. Though checked by János Hunyadi at Belgrade, he nevertheless annexed most of Serbia, all of Greece, and most of the Aegean Is. Repelled from Rhodes by the Knights of St John (1479), he took Otranto in 1480, and died in a campaign against Persia.

Mohammed Ahmed (1844–85), known as **the Mahdi** (**divinely guided one**) Arab leader, born in Dongola, Sudan. He was for a time in the Egyptian civil service, then a slave trader, and finally a relentless and successful rebel who overthrew Egyptian rule in the E Sudan. He made El Obeid his capital (1883), defeated Hicks Pasha and an Egyptian army, and finally in 1885 Khartoum was taken and General Gordon killed. He died the same year at Omdurman.

Mohammed Ali *or* **Mehemet Ali** (c.1769–1849) Albanian soldier and Viceroy of Egypt (1805–48). He was sent to Egypt with a Turkish–Albanian force on the French invasion in 1798 and after the French left, he supported the Egyptian rulers in their struggles with the Mamluks. As the chief power in Egypt from 1805, he formed a regular army, improved irrigation, and introduced elements of European civilization. He extended Egyptian territory and routed the Ottoman army at Konya (1832), but the Quadruple Alliance of 1840 compelled him to limit his ambition to Egypt. He went insane and in 1848 was succeeded by his adopted son Ibrahim.

Mohawk an Iroquoian-speaking Native American group, living around L Champlain, New York state, USA. A member of the Iroquois League, they were defeated by US troops in 1777, and crossed into Canada, settling permanently in Ontario (present-day population c.6 000).

Mohenjo-daro a prehistoric walled city on the R Indus in Sind, Pakistan, one of the major cities of the Indus Valley Civilization. The site was first excavated in 1922 and its date of occupation is believed to be c.2300–1750 BC. The city covered 100ha and was laid out in a regular grid plan. It is a World Heritage site.

mohican *noun* a hairstyle popular amongst punks, in which the head is partially shaved, leaving a central front-to-back band of hair, usually coloured and formed into a spiky crest. [from *Mohicans*, Native American tribe on whose hairstyle this is based]

Mohism *or* **Moism** a Chinese philosophical tradition which originated with Mo Tzu (c.470–390 BC). Unlike Confucius, Mo Tzu claimed that one should not follow traditional practices for their own sake; one should love all people equally and adopt those practices that will most benefit people.

Mohorovičić, Andrija (1857–1936) Yugoslavian seismologist and meteorologist,

born in Volosko, Croatia. Professor in Zagreb, he deduced from studies of seismic waves that the Earth's crust must overlay a denser mantle and calculated the depth to the transition (the *Mohorovičić discontinuity* or *Moho*).

moiety *noun* (PL. **moieties**) *literary Legal* a half; one of two parts or divisions. [from Old French *moité*]

moire *noun* fabric, especially silk, with a pattern of glossy irregular waves. [from French]

moiré — *adj.*, *said of a fabric* having a pattern of glossy irregular waves. — *noun* this pattern.

Moissan, (Ferdinand Frédéric) Henri (1852–1907) French chemist, born in Paris, where he later became professor. He was the first to isolate fluorine (1886), and in 1892 invented the electric arc furnace, which he used to reduce and synthesize various chemical compounds; his furnace and chemical discoveries were soon shown to have many industrial applications. He was awarded the 1906 Nobel Prize for Chemistry.

moist *adj.* **1** damp; slightly wet. **2** *said of food, esp. cake* pleasantly soft and fresh, not dry. [from Old French *moiste*]

moisten *verb trans.*, *intrans.* to make or become moist.

moistness *noun* a moist quality or state.

moisture *noun* liquid in vapour or spray form, or condensed as droplets; moistness.

moisturize *or* **moisturise** *verb* to make less dry, especially to add moisture to (the skin) by rubbing in a cream.

moisturizer *or* **moisturiser** *noun* something which moisturizes.

Moivre, Abraham De see DE MOIVRE, ABRAHAM.

Mojave *or* **Mohave Desert** a desert in S California, USA, forming part of the Great Basin. AREA c.40 000sq km/15 400sq mi. The region consists of a series of flat basins with interior drainage, separated by low, bare ranges. Annual rainfall is slight and agriculture is possible only where artesian water occurs. The Mojave R, the desert's only stream, flows mainly underground into the Mojave Sink.

moke *noun* *slang* a donkey.

molar — *noun* any of the large back teeth in humans and other mammals, used for chewing and grinding. — *adj.*, *said of a tooth* serving to grind. [from Latin *mola*, millstone]

molarity *noun Chem.* the concentration of a solution, expressed as the number of moles of a dissolved substance present in a litre of solution. See also MOLE.

molasses *sing. noun* the thickest kind of treacle, left over at the very end of the process of refining raw sugar. [from Portuguese *melaço*]

Mold, Welsh **Yr Wyddgrug** POP (1981) 8 500, the county town of Clwyd, NE Wales, situated in Delyn district. It lies on the R Alyn, 18km/11mi SW of Chester.

Moldavia *or* **Moldova**, Russian **Moldavskaya** *or* **Moldaviya** POP (1992e) 4.4m, a republic in E Europe. AREA 33 700sq km/ 13 000sq mi. The republic is bounded W by Romania, and N, E, and S by the Ukraine. CAPITAL Kishinev. CHIEF TOWNS Tiraspol, Bendery, Beltsy. Most of the population are Moldavian (65%) with large Ukranian (14%) and Russian (13%) minorities; the majority are Orthodox. LANGUAGES Moldavian, Ukranian, and Russian. CURRENCY the leu. PHYSICAL DESCRIPTION the terrain consists of a hilly plain, reaching a height of 429m in the centre; chief rivers are the Dniester and Prut. HISTORY proclaimed a Soviet Socialist Republic in 1940; achieved independence as the Republic of Moldavia in 1991; a separatist movement of Ukranians and Russians within the country who objected to plans for unification with

Romania attempted to achieve independence in 1991; this was not recognized by the Government and war broke out; a ceasefire was agreed in 1992 but the issue has not been resolved. ECONOMY wine; tobacco; food-canning; machines; electrical engineering; instruments; knitwear; textiles; fruit.

Moldavia

Moldavia and Wallachia two independent Balkan principalities formed in the 14c. Moldavia lies in NE Romania, south-west of the R Dniester; Wallachia lies in S Romania, south of the Transylvanian Alps. In the 16c they were incorporated into the Ottoman Empire, but the Russo-Turkish wars in the 18c–19c weakened Turkish control of the Balkans, and by the Treaty of Adrianople (1829) the two states gained autonomy under a Russian protectorate. In 1862 Moldavia and Wallachia merged to form the unitary Principality of Romania, which achieved independence in 1878. In 1940 the part of historic Moldavia east of the R Prut became part of the USSR as the Moravian Soviet Socialist Republic.

Mole a shy but intrepid character in Kenneth Grahame's *The Wind in the Willows*.

mole[1] *noun* a raised dark permanent spot on the skin, caused by a concentration of melanin. [from Anglo-Saxon *mal*]

mole[2] *noun* **1** any of about 20 species of small insectivorous burrowing mammal belonging to the family Tapidae, which has velvety greyish-black fur, a naked muzzle, and very small eyes. **2** *colloq.* a spy working inside an organization and passing secret information to people outside it. [from Middle English *molle*]
◊ Moles live underground, and have strong front legs with very broad feet for digging tunnels. They also push loose soil up into characteristic 'molehills' on the ground surface while excavating underground. The European mole (*Talpa europea*) is found throughout Europe and much of Asia, and has a cylindrical body about 13cm long, and short legs. Like all moles, it has very weak eyesight and relies on its keen sense of smell and hearing to find food, which consists mainly of earthworms.

mole[3] *noun Chem.* (ABBREV. **mol**) the SI unit of amount of substance, equal to the amount of a substance (in grams) that contains as many atoms, molecules, etc, as there are atoms of carbon in 12 grams of the isotope carbon-12. One mole of a substance contains Avogadro's number (6.02×10^{23}) of atoms. [from German, from *Molekül*, molecule]

mole[4] *noun* a pier, causeway, or breakwater made of stone; a harbour protected by any of these. [from Latin *moles*, mass]

molecular *adj.* of or relating to molecules.

molecular biology the branch of biology that is concerned with the study of the structure, properties, and functions of the large organic molecules that are found in the cells of living organisms, especially proteins and the nucleic acids DNA and RNA. It includes the analysis of genes.

molecular weight *Chem.* relative molecular mass.

molecule *noun* the smallest particle of a chemical element or compound that can exist independently and participate in a chemical reaction. [from Latin *molecula*, from *moles*, mass]
◊ Molecules consist of two or more atoms bonded together, and carry no electrical charge, eg a molecule of water (H_2O) consists of two hydrogen atoms bonded to an oxygen atom. All gases and organic compounds, most liquids, and many solids consist of molecules, but metals and many compounds that form solutions (eg salts) consist of *ions* arranged in a crystalline structure.

molehill *noun* a little pile of earth thrown up by a burrowing mole.

moleskin *noun* **1** mole's fur. **2 a** a heavy twilled cotton fabric with a short nap. **b** (**moleskins**) trousers made of this.

molest *verb* **1** to attack or interfere with sexually. **2** *formal* to attack, causing physical harm. **3** *old use* to disturb or upset. [from Latin *molestare*]

molestation *noun* **1** the act of molesting. **2** being molested.

Molière, originally **Jean Baptiste Poquelin** (1622–73) French playwright and actor, born in Paris. He began a theatre company in 1643 and obtained the patronage of Philippe d'Orléans. His series of dramatic achievements included *Tartuffe* (1664), *Le Misanthrope* (The Misanthropist, 1666), *Le Bourgeois Gentilhomme* (1670) and *Le Malade Imaginaire* (The Imaginary Invalid, 1673).

moll *noun old slang use* **1** a gangster's girlfriend. **2** a prostitute. [from *Moll*, a woman's name]

Moll Flanders, in full ***Moll Flanders, The Fortunes and Misfortunes of the Famous*** a novel by Daniel Defoe (1722). It describes the fluctuating fortunes of the narrator Moll who is abandoned as a child when her mother is transported for theft.

mollification *noun* **1** the act of mollifying. **2** being mollified.

mollify *verb* (**mollifies, mollified**) **1** to make calmer or less angry. **2** to soothe or ease. [from Latin *mollis*, soft + *facere*, to make]

mollusc *noun Zool.* any invertebrate animal belonging to the phylum Mollusca and typically having a soft unsegmented body with a large flattened muscular foot on the underside, and a fold of skin (the mantle) covering the upper surface. Most molluscs are protected by a hard chalky shell secreted by the mantle. [from Latin *molluscus*]
◊ Molluscs breathe by means of gills, and most have a well-developed head with eyes and a tongue-like organ (radula) covered with horny teeth for rasping food. Molluscs include the classes Gastropoda (eg snails, slugs, winkles, whelks), Bivalvia (eg mussels, oyster, clams, cockles), and Cephalopoda (eg squids, octopuses, nautilus, cuttlefish). Most molluscs are aquatic, although some gastropods live in damp terrestrial habitats.

Mollusca *pl. noun Zool.* in the animal kingdom, a large phylum of invertebrates which have unsegmented bodies and in many cases a hard chalky shell, eg snails, slugs, mussels, squid. [from Latin *molluscus*, softish, from *mollis*, soft]

mollycoddle *verb colloq.* to treat with fussy care and protection. [from *Molly*, a woman's name + CODDLE]

Moloch in the Bible, a god of the Canaanites and other peoples, in whose cult children were sacrificed by fire. He is a rebel angel in John Milton's *Paradise Lost*.

Molokai POP (1988e) 7 000, an island in Maui County, Hawaii, USA. It lies in the Pacific Ocean, NW of Maui I. AREA 670sq km/260sq mi. Kalaupapa leper settlement was situated on the N coast. ECONOMY cattle.

Molotov, Vyacheslav Mikhailovich, originally **Vyacheslav Mikhailovich Skriabin**

(1890–1986) Russian politician and premier, born in Kukaida, Vyatka. From 1906 he organized the Bolshevik Party, and he later became chairman of the Council of People's Commissars (ie USSR Prime Minister, 1930–41). An international figure from 1939, when he also became Foreign Minister (1939–49, 1953–6), he was Stalin's chief adviser at the Allies' conferences in Teheran and Yalta, and was present at the founding of the United Nations (1945). After World War I, he emerged as the uncompromising champion of world Sovietism; his *nyet* ('no') at meetings of the UN became a byword, and fostered the Cold War. In 1956 he was demoted by Nikita Khrushchev, and in the 1960s retired to his home near Moscow.

Molotov cocktail a small crude bomb for throwing, consisting of a bottle filled with petrol, usually with a burning cloth as a fuse. [named after V M Molotov]

molten *adj.* in a melted state. [an old past participle of MELT]

Moltke, Helmuth (Karl Bernhard), Graf von (Count of) (1800–91) Prussian soldier, born in Parchim, Mecklenburg. He entered Prussian service in 1822, and became Chief of the General Staff in Berlin (1858–88). His reorganization of the Prussian army led to the successful wars with Denmark (1863–4), Austria (1866), and France (1870–1), and he was created field marshal in 1871.

molto *adv. Mus.* very. [from Italian *molto*]

Moluccas *or* **Spice Islands**, Indonesian **Maluku** POP (1990) 1.9m, an island group and a province of Indonesia, lying between Celebes (Sulawesi) in the W and New Guinea in the E. AREA 74 505sq km/28 759sq mi. It includes c.1 000 islands, notably Halmahera, Seram, and Buru. The islands are mostly volcanic and mountainous. CAPITAL Ambon. HISTORY discovered by the Portuguese in 1512; under Dutch rule in the early 17c; in the S Moluccas a secession movement began following Indonesian independence in 1949. ECONOMY copra, spices, sago, coconut oil, tuna.

molybdenum *noun Chem.* (SYMBOL **Mo**, ATOMIC NUMBER **42**) a hard silvery metal that is used as a hardening agent in various alloys, including alloy steels, and in resistors and X-ray tubes. Molybdenum disulphide is used as a lubricant. [from Greek *molybdaina*, lead-like substance]

Molyneux, Edward (1891–1974) English fashion designer, born in London. After World

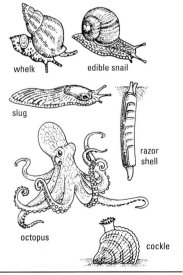

whelk edible snail slug razor shell octopus cockle

molluscs

War I, he opened his own house in Paris, with branches in London, Monte Carlo, Cannes, and Biarritz. He became famous for the elegant simplicity of his tailored suits with pleated skirts, and for his evening wear.

mom *or* **mommy** *noun* (PL. **mommies**) *North Amer. colloq.* mother.

Mombasa POP (1984e) 426 000, a seaport in Coast province, SE Kenya. It is Kenya's main port and second-largest city. Situated on Mombasa I, it is connected to the mainland by the Mukapa Causeway. HISTORY founded in the 11c; slave and ivory trading until the 16c; capital of British E Africa Protectorate from 1888 until 1907; Kilindini Harbour, one of Africa's best anchorages, was used as a British naval base in World War II. NOTABLE FEATURE Fort Jesus (1593), built by the Portuguese, is now a museum.

moment *noun* **1** a short while. **2** a particular point in time: *at that moment.* **3** *formal* importance; significance: *a literary work of great moment.* **4** *Physics* (*in full* **moment of force**) a measure of the turning effect or torque produced by a force which causes an object to rotate about an axis. It is equal to the force multiplied by the perpendicular distance of the axis from the line of action of the force. **5** *Physics* same as MOMENT OF INERTIA.
— **at the moment** at this particular time; now.
have one's *or* **its** *etc* **moments** *colloq.* to experience or provide occasional but irregular times of happiness, success, etc.
of the moment currently very popular, important, fashionable, etc.
[from Latin *momentum*, movement]

momentarily *adv.* **1** for a moment. **2** every moment.

momentary *adj.* lasting for only a moment.

moment of force *Physics* same as TORQUE.

moment of inertia *Physics* in mechanics, the notion that, for a rotating object, the turning force required to make the object turn faster depends on the way in which the object's mass is distributed about the axis of rotation, eg the force needed to spin a disc more rapidly about its centre will be greater if the mass of the disc is concentrated around its rim. For a uniform disc of mass *m* and radius *r* spinning horizontally about its centre, the moment of inertia is equal to $mr^2/2$.

moment of truth a very important or significant point in time, especially when a person or thing is put to the test.

momentous *adj.* of great importance or significance.

momentousness *noun* great significance.

momentum *noun* **1** *Physics* the product of the mass and the velocity of a moving object. See ALSO ANGULAR MOMENTUM, LINEAR MOMENTUM. **2** continuous speed of progress; impetus: *the campaign gained momentum.* [from Latin *momentum*, movement]

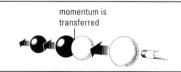

momentum is transferred

momentum

MOMI *abbrev.* Museum of the Moving Image.

Mommsen, Theodor (1817–1903) German historian, born in Garding, Schleswig-Holstein. He studied jurisprudence at Kiel (1838–43) and classical inscriptions in Italy (1844–7), and held posts at Leipzig (1848), Zürich (1852), Breslau (1854), and Berlin (1858). His greatest work is his *Romische Geschichte* (History of Rome, 3 vols, 1854–5), in which he applied the new method of critical examination of sources. He won the Nobel Prize for Literature in 1902.

mommy see MOM.

Mon an agricultural people of Burma (Myanma) and Thailand, thought to have come originally from W China. They established a kingdom in Burma in about the 9c, introduced Buddhism and Indian Pali writing into Burma, and were subjugated by the Burmese in the 18c. They speak an Austro-Asiatic language, also known as Tailang.

Mon *or* **Mon.** *abbrev.* Monday.

mon- see MONO-.

Mona a female first name. [from Irish Gaelic *muadh*, noble]

Monaco, official name **Principality of Monaco** POP (1990) 30 000, a small principality on the Mediterranean Riviera, close to the Italian frontier with France. AREA 1.9sq km/0.75sq mi. It is surrounded landward by the French department of Alpes-Maritimes. CAPITAL Monaco-Ville. CHIEF TOWN Monte Carlo. Around 58% of the population are French; Roman Catholicism is the main religion. TIME ZONE GMT +1. OFFICIAL LANGUAGE French. CURRENCY the French franc. CLIMATE warm, dry summers and mild winters. HISTORY the country has been under the protection of France since the 17c, apart from a period under Sardinia in 1815–61. GOVERNMENT executive power is held by the Prince and a Council of Government; legislative authority is held by the Prince and a unicameral National Council; Monaco has close political ties with France. ECONOMY chemicals; printing; textiles; precision instruments; plastics; postage stamps; tourism.

FRANCE

Monaco-Ville

Mediterranean Sea

Monaco

Monaco-Ville the capital and oldest part of the Principality of Monaco. It is situated on a rocky promontory of the Côte d'Azur on the S side of the Port de Monaco. NOTABLE FEATURES Palais du Prince (13c); Musée Océanographique which contains many marine specimens donated by Jacques Cousteau; stalactitic caves in the Jardin Exotique.

monad *noun* **1** *Philos.* any self-contained non-physical unit of being, eg a soul, God. **2** *Biol.* a single-celled organism. [from Greek, from *monas*, unit]

Monaghan, Gaelic **Mhuineachain** POP (1991) 51 000, a county in Ulster province, Irish Republic. AREA 1 290sq km/500sq mi. It is bounded N by Northern Ireland, and is watered by the R Finn. CAPITAL Monaghan. ECONOMY cattle; oats; potatoes.

Mona Lisa a portrait painting of a Florentine woman by Leonardo da Vinci (c.1504, Louvre, Paris).

monandrous *adj.* **1** *Sociol.* having or allowing only one husband or male sexual partner at a time. **2** *Bot.* having only one stamen in each flower. See also POLYANDROUS. [from Greek *monos*, single + *andros*, man]

monandry *noun* being monandrous.

monarch *noun* a king, queen, or other non-elected sovereign with a hereditary right to rule. [from Greek *monos*, single + *archein*, to rule]

monarchic *or* **monarchical** *adj.* relating to or of the nature of a monarchy.

monarchism *noun* **1** the principles of monarchic government. **2** support for monarchy.

monarchist *noun* a person in favour of rule by a monarch.

Monarch of the Glen a painting by Sir Edwin Landseer (1851).

monarchy *noun* (PL. **monarchies**) a form of government in which the head of state is a monarch; also, a country having this form of government.
◇ In European countries, the democratic revolutions of the 18c–20c ended this previously widespread form of government. In some countries (eg the UK), constitutional monarchies were established with the sovereign acting on the advice of government ministers who govern in his or her name.

monastery *noun* (PL. **monasteries**) the home of a community of monks, or sometimes nuns. [from Greek *monasterion*, from *monazein*, to live alone]

monastic *adj.* **1** of or relating to monasteries, monks, or nuns. **2** marked by simplicity and self-discipline, like life in a monastery. [from Greek *monastes*, monk]

monastically *adv.* in a monastic manner.

monasticism *noun* the monastic system or way of life.

Monck, George, 1st Duke of Albemarle (1608–70) English soldier, born in Great Potheridge, Devon. He fought in the Low Countries, and with the Royalists in Scotland, then joined the Commonwealth cause and served successfully in Ireland, Scotland, and in the first Dutch War (1652–4). He feared a return to Civil War during and after Richard Cromwell's regime (1658–9), and was instrumental (as commander of the army in Scotland) in bringing about the restoration of Charles II.

Mond, Ludwig (1839–1909) German-born British chemist and industrialist, born in Kassel. He settled in England in 1864, where he perfected a sulphur recovery process, founded an alkali works, and devised a process for the extraction of nickel. His son, Alfred Moritz Mond, 1st Baron Melchett (1868–1930), became Commissioner of Works (1916–21) and Minister of Health (1922), and helped to form Imperial Chemical Industries (ICI).

Mondale, Walter F(rederick) (1928–) US Democratic politician and lawyer, born in Ceylon, Minessota. He practised law privately, and became Minnesota Attorney-General (1960) and US Senator (1964). He served under President Carter as Vice-Presidet (1977–81), and was the Democratic nominee for president in 1984, when he lost to Ronald Reagan.

Monday *noun* the second day of the week. [from Anglo-Saxon *monandæg*, moon day]

Mondrian, Piet, originally **Pieter Cornelis Mondriaan** (1872–1944) Dutch artist, born in Amersfoort. With Theo van Doesburg (1883–1931) he founded the De Stijl movement in architecture and painting. He spent much of his working life in Paris, where his early work included a series of abstracts, *Trees*. His rectilinear 'Neoplastic' abstracts (grids of usually black horizontal and vertical lines enclosing white, grey, or primary-coloured rectangles) have had considerable influence. Later works include more colourful abstracts (eg *Broadway Boogie-Woogie*, 1942–3, New York).

Monet, Claude (1840–1926) French Impressionist painter, born in Paris. He exhibited at the first Impressionist exhibition in 1874; one of his works, *Impression: soleil levant* (Impression: Sunrise, 1872, Paris), gave the name to the movement. Other works include *A Field of Poppies* (1873) and several paintings of subjects under different aspects of light (eg *Haystacks*, 1890–1, Chicago, and *Rouen Cathedral*, 1892–4, Musée d'Orsay, Paris). During his last years he painted the series of *Water Lilies* (1899–26) in his garden at Giverny.

monetarism *noun* the theory or practice of basing an economy on control of the supply of money in circulation. [from Latin *moneta*, money] ◇ The essence of the theory is that if the money supply is allowed to rise too quickly, prices will rise, resulting in inflation. To curb these inflationary pressures, governments may need to reduce the supply of money and raise interest rates. Monetarism was a major influence on British and US economic policy in the 1980s.

monetarist — *noun* a person who advocates policies based on monetarism. — *adj.* relating to or typical of monetarism.

monetary *adj.* of, or consisting of, money. [from Latin *moneta*, money]

money *noun* **1** coins or banknotes used as a means of buying things. **2** wealth in general. **3** *colloq.* a rich person; rich people: *marry money*. **4** (**moneys** or **monies**) *Commerce, Legal* sums of money.
— **be in the money** *colloq.* to be wealthy.
for my, our, etc, **money** *colloq.* in my, our, etc opinion.
get one's money's worth to get full value for the money or other resources devoted to something.
[from Latin *moneta*]

moneybags *noun colloq.* a very rich person.

money-changer *noun* a person whose business is exchanging currencies.

moneyed *adj.* having much money; wealthy.

money-grubber *noun derog. colloq.* a person who greedily acquires as much money as possible.

money-grubbing — *noun* greed for money. — *adj.* greedy for money.

moneylender *noun* a person whose business is lending money at (often relatively high) interest.

moneymaker *noun colloq.* **1** *often derog.* a person whose main interest in life is acquiring money. **2** a project, company, etc that makes a large profit.

money-making — *noun* the earning of profit. — *adj.* profitable.

money markets the finance companies, banks, etc of a country that borrow and lend money for short periods.

money order a written order for the transfer of money from one person to another, through a post office or bank.

money-spinner *noun colloq.* an idea or project that brings in large sums of money.

money supply the amount of money in circulation in an economy at a given time. Control of the money supply is the method favoured by monetarists for controlling inflation.

Monge, Gaspard (1746–1818) French mathematician, physicist, and inventor of descriptive geometry, born in Beaune. Professor at Mézières and the Lycée in Paris, he published his treatise on the application of geometry to the arts of construction in 1795. He was made a Senator (1805), but lost his honours at the Restoration, and died in poverty in Paris.

-monger *combining form* **1** a trader or dealer: *fishmonger*. **2** a person who spreads or promotes something undesirable or evil: *scandalmonger*. [from Latin *mango*, dealer]

mongol *noun old use, now offensive* a person affected by Down's Syndrome. [from the supposed physical likeness of Down's Syndrome sufferers to members of the Mongol people of Asia]

Mongolia, in full **The State of Mongolia**, formerly **Outer Mongolia**, official name **Mongolian People's Republic**, Mongol **Bügd Nayramdakh Mongol Ard Uls** POP (1992e) 2.3m, a republic in E central Asia, divided into 18 counties (*aimag*). AREA 1 564 619sq km/604 099sq mi. It is bounded N by Russia and on other sides by China. CAPITAL Ulan Bator. CHIEF TOWNS Darhan, Erdenet. TIME ZONE GMT +7 in the W, +8 in the centre, +9 in the E. The majority of the population are Mongolian (90%); Tibetan Buddhism has traditionally been the chief religion although it is a communist state. OFFICIAL LANGUAGE Khalkha Mongol. CURRENCY the tugrik. PHYSICAL DESCRIPTION a landlocked, mountainous country with an average height of 1 580m; the highest point is Tavan-Bogdo-Uli at 4 373m; the high ground is mainly in the W, with folded mountains lying NW–SE to form the Mongolian Altai chain; the lower SE section runs into the Gobi Desert; the largest lakes are found in the NW; major rivers flow N and NE; the lowland plains are mainly arid grasslands. CLIMATE continental, with hard and long-lasting frosts in winter; the average temperature at Ulan Bator is −27° in Jan and 9–24°C in Jul; rainfall is generally low; arid desert conditions prevail in the S. HISTORY originally the homeland of nomadic tribes, which united under Ghengis Khan in the 13c to become part of the great Mongol Empire; assimilated into China, and divided into Inner and Outer Mongolia; Outer Mongolia declared itself an independent monarchy in 1911; the Mongolian People's Republic was formed in 1924, but was not recognized by China until 1946; a multiparty system was introduced in 1990 and the Government is introducing economic and political reform. GOVERNMENT a unicameral Great People's Hural (parliament) elects a Prime Minister, who appoints a Cabinet. ECONOMY traditionally a pastoral, nomadic economy; a series of five-year plans aims to create an agricultural–industrial economy; c.70% of agricultural production is derived from cattle raising; foodstuffs; animal products; wool; hides; fluorspar; copper, coal, gold, tungsten, uranium, lead.

Mongolia

Mongolian — *noun* **1** a native or citizen of Mongolia. **2** the main language of Mongolia. — *adj.* of or pertaining to Mongolia, its people, or the language.

mongolism *noun* Down's Syndrome.
◆ Now considered an offensive term.

Mongoloid any member of the mainly N, E, and SE Asian racial groups, featuring a flattish face, high cheekbones, a fold of the upper eyelid, straight black hair, and medium skin pigmentation. Mongoloid peoples include the Inuit of Arctic N America.

mongoloid *adj. offensive* bearing symptoms of Down's Syndrome.

Mongols the general name applied to the tribes of central Asia and S Siberia who effected the collapse of the Abbasid Empire before converting to Islam. They were united under Genghis Khan in 1206, and conquered China under his grandson Kublai, who ruled as first Emperor of the Yan dynasty (1271–1368). They now live in the Chinese autonomous region of Inner Mongolia, and in the People's Republic of Mongolia.

Mongo-Ma-Loba see CAMEROON, MOUNT.

mongoose *noun* (PL. **mongooses**) a small mammal related to the civet, found in SE Asia, Africa, and Madagascar, with a long slender body, pointed muzzle, and a bushy tail. It is best known for its ability to kill snakes, even large cobras, and it also feeds on eggs and rats. [from Marathi (a language of India) *mangus*]

mongoose

mongrel — *noun* **1** an animal, especially a dog, of mixed breeding. **2** *derog.* a person or thing of mixed origin or nature. — *adj.* of mixed origin or nature. [perhaps from Anglo-Saxon *mengan*, to mix]

Monica a female first name, and the name of St Augustine of Hippo's Carthaginian mother. [origin uncertain; associated with Greek *monos*, alone, or Latin *monere*, to warn]

monied, monies see MONEY.

monism *noun Philos.* the theory that reality exists in one form only, especially that there is no difference in substance between body and soul. [from Greek *monos*, single]

monist *noun* a follower of monism.

monistic *adj.* relating to or typical of monism.

monition *noun formal* a warning or telling-off. [from Latin *monere*, to warn or remind]

monitor — *noun* **1** any instrument designed to check, record, or control something on a regular basis. **2** a high-quality screen used in closed-circuit television systems. **3** the visual display unit of a computer, used to present information to the user. **4** a pupil who helps with specific tasks, or a senior pupil who helps to enforce discipline over other pupils. **5** (*in full* **monitor lizard**) any of various large carnivorous lizards of Africa, Asia, and Australia, so called because they are thought to give warnings of the presence of crocodiles. — *verb* to check, record, or control something on a regular basis; to observe. [from Latin *monere*, to warn or advise]

monitoring service an agency responsible for systematically checking foreign broadcasts. Such work entails watching and listening to broadcast material, and recording, translating, and deciphering it where necessary. When part of a country's intelligence operations, monitoring services are usually cloaked in secrecy. The central monitoring service in the UK is GCHQ.

monitory *adj. formal* serving as a warning or telling-off. [from Latin *monere*, to warn]

monk *noun* a member of a religious community of men living disciplined, austere lives devoted to worship. [from Greek *monachos*, from *monos*, alone]

monkey — *noun* (PL. **monkeys**) **1** any member of the primates other than humans, apes, chimpanzees, gibbons, orang utans, and lemurs. **2** *colloq.* a mischievous child. **3** *slang* £500 or $500. — *verb intrans. colloq.* (**monkey about** or **around**) to play, fool, interfere, etc.
— **make a monkey out of someone** *colloq.* to make them seem ridiculous; to make a fool of them.

not give a monkey's *slang* not to care at all. [perhaps from Old German dialect *moneke*]
◇ Monkeys usually live in trees, and have a hairy coat, nails instead of claws, and 32 teeth. They live in tropical and subtropical regions, and can be divided into two main groups, the Old World species of Africa and Asia, eg baboon, mandrill, and the New World species of America and the East Indies, eg spider monkey, marmoset, capuchin. With the exception of the Barbary ape of Gibraltar, they are not found in Europe. New World monkeys can be distinguished from their Old World relatives by their long prehensile (gripping) tails, and by their nostrils, which tend to be further apart. Old World monkeys are more intelligent and lively, and are more closely related to humans and apes.

monkey business *colloq.* mischief; illegal activities.

monkey nut a peanut.

monkey puzzle a S American conifer with close-set prickly leaves.

monkey wrench a spanner-like tool with movable jaws; an adjustable spanner.

monkfish *noun* a large cartilaginous fish, up to 1.8m in length, with a body shape intermediate between that of sharks and rays, a flattened head, lateral gill openings, broad pectoral fins, and a slender tail. It is a very popular food fish. — Also called *angel shark*.

monkish *adj.* **1** relating to or like a monk. **2** monastic.

monkshood see ACONITE.

Monmouth, James, Duke of (1649–85) illegitimate son of Charles II of England, born in Rotterdam, the Netherlands. He was created Duke of Monmouth in 1663, and became Capt-General in 1670. A Protestant, he had much popular support and became a focus of opposition to Charles II. After the discovery of the Rye House Plot (1683), he fled to the Low Countries, but in 1685 landed at Lyme Regis to assert his right to the Crown. He was defeated at the battle of Sedgemoor, captured, and beheaded.

Monmouth, Battle of an engagement (1778) in New Jersey between British and American troops during the US War of Independence. It was notable for Washington's suspension of General Charles Lee (1731–82) from command, and for the discipline of American troops under fire.

mono *colloq.* — *adj.* short for **monophonic**. — *noun* monophonic sound reproduction.

mono- or **mon-** *combining form* forming words meaning 'one, single': *monocle.* [from Greek *monos*, single]

Monoceros *Astron.* the Unicorn, a faint constellation in the Milky Way, next to Orion.

monochromatic *adj.* **1** *said of light* having only one wavelength. **2** monochrome.

monochrome *adj.* **1** *said of visual reproduction* done in one colour, or in black and white. **2** *said especially of painting* using shades of one colour only. [from MONO- + *chroma*, colour]

monocle *noun* a lens for correcting sight in one eye only, held in place between the bones of the cheek and brow. [from MONO- + Latin *oculus*, eye]

monoclonal antibody *Biol.* a highly specific antibody produced artificially by any of various identical cells, known as clones, derived from a single parent cell. Monoclonal antibodies are used in the identification of blood groups and the production of highly specific vaccines.

monocotyledon *noun Bot.* a flowering plant with an embryo that has one cotyledon (seed leaf), parallel leaf veins, vascular bundles scattered throughout the stem, and flower parts in multiples of three, eg lily, daffodil, cereals, and grasses, but only a few trees, eg palms. See also DICOTYLEDON.

monocular *adj.* having one eye only; for the use of one eye. [from MONO- + Latin *oculus*, eye]

monoculture *noun Agric.* the practice of growing the same crop each year on a given area of land, rather than growing different crops in rotation. It is a common practice among cereal growers in many parts of the world, but heavy use of chemical fertilizers may be necessary to maintain high yields.

Monod, Jacques Lucien (1910–76) French biochemist, born in Paris. He became head of the Cellular Biochemistry Department at the Pasteur Institute in Paris and professor at the Collège de France. For his work on the mechanisms governing the activity of genes, he shared the 1965 Nobel Prize for Physiology or Medicine with François Jacob and André Lwoff.

monodic *adj.* relating to or typical of monody.

monody *noun* (PL. **monodies**) **1** a mournful song or speech performed by a single actor, especially in Greek tragedy. **2** a song in which the melody is sung by one voice only, with other voices accompanying. [from MONO- + Greek *oide*, song]

monoecious *adj. Biol.* **1** having male and female reproductive parts in separate flowers on the same plant. **2** *said of an animal* having both male and female sexual organs; hermaphrodite. See also DIOECIOUS. [from MONO- + Greek *oikos*, house]

monogamous *adj.* having only one spouse.

monogamy *noun* the state or practice of having only one husband or wife at any one time. See also POLYGAMY. [from MONO- + Greek *gamos*, marriage]

monogram — *noun* a design made up of interwoven letters, usually a person's initials. — *verb* (**monogrammed**, **monogramming**) to mark with a monogram. [from MONO- + Greek *gramma*, letter]

monograph *noun formal* a book or essay dealing with one particular subject or aspect of it. [from MONO- + Greek *graphein*, to write]

monohybrid *noun Biol.* a living organism that carries one dominant allele and one recessive allele for a particular gene (for which it is said to be *heterozygous*), because it is the result of a cross between an individual with two dominant alleles and an individual with two recessive alleles for that gene.

monolingual *adj.* able to speak one language only; expressed in, or dealing with, a single language: *a monolingual dictionary.* [from MONO- + Latin *lingua*, language]

monolith *noun* **1** a single tall block of stone, often shaped into a column or pillar. **2** anything resembling this in uniformity, immovability or massiveness. [from MONO- + Greek *lithos*, stone]

monolithic *adj.* **1** relating to or like a monolith. *said of an organization, etc* large and unchanging.

monologue *noun* **1** a long speech by one actor in a film or play; a drama for one actor. **2** any long uninterrupted piece of speech preventing conversation. [from MONO- + Greek *logos*, speech]

monomania *noun* domination of the mind by a single subject or concern; an obsession. [from MONO- + Greek *mania*, madness]

monomaniac — *noun* a person affected by monomania. — *adj.* affected by monomania.

monomer *noun Chem.* a simple molecule that can be joined to many others to form a much larger molecule known as a *polymer*, eg amino acids are the monomers of which proteins are formed. [from MONO- + Greek *meros*, part]

mononucleosis *noun* glandular fever.

monophonic *adj.* recording or reproducing sound on one channel only, not splitting it into two, as with stereophonic systems. [from MONO- + Greek *phone*, sound]

monoplane *noun* an aeroplane with one set of wings.

Monoplane, Short-span, No. XI the plane in which the Frenchman Louis Blériot became the first person to cross the English Channel by air. He achieved the feat in 1909 by flying from Calais to Dover in 37 minutes. The *Daily Mail* awarded him £1000 for his accomplishment.

Monopolies Commission, in full **Monopolies and Mergers Commission** in the UK, a government body set up in 1948 as the *Monopolies and Restrictive Practices Commission*, renamed in 1973 under the Fair Trading Act. Its powers were extended by the Restrictive Trade Practices Act (1976), the Competition Act (1980), and the Broadcasting Act (1990). Its role is to investigate activities which may be against the public interest, particularly with respect to mergers, takeovers, and monopoly situations.

monopolist *noun* a person who monopolizes, who has a monopoly, or who favours monopoly.

monopolistic *adj.* related to or connected with a monopoly or system of monopolies.

monopolization or **monopolisation** *noun* monopolizing; exercise of a monopoly.

monopolize or **monopolise** *verb* **1** to have a monopoly or exclusive control of trade in (a commodity or service). **2** to dominate (eg a conversation), excluding all others.

Monopoly *trademark* a real-estate board game for two to six players, invented in the USA in c.1932. Players buy properties on particular squares, then charge rent to other players who land on those squares. Taxes, fines, etc are also charged to players who land on particular squares. The object is to gain the monopoly of the properties, thus earning the most money.

monopoly *noun* (PL. **monopolies**) (*often* **monopoly on** or **of something**) **1** the right to be, or the fact of being, the only supplier of a particular commodity or service. **2** a commodity or service controlled in this way. **3** exclusive possession or control of anything: *you don't have a monopoly on the truth!* [from MONO- + Greek *poleein*, to sell]
◇ Absolute monopoly is rare because there are few goods or services for which there is not some sort of substitute. In practice, it is most often applied to a firm that produces so large a proportion of the total output that it can raise price by restricting output, or where only one source of supply exists: so-called 'natural' monopolies, such as the supply of water.

monopsony *noun* a market structure where there is only one buyer of a product or service (a buyer's monopoly) or where there is only one major user of a factor of production. [from MONO- + Greek *opsonein*, to buy]

monorail *noun* a railway system in which the trains run on, or are suspended from, a single rail.

monosaccharide *noun Biochem.* a simple sugar that cannot be broken down into smaller units, eg glucose, fructose.

monosodium glutamate a white crystalline chemical substance used to enhance the flavour of many processed savoury foods without imparting its own taste. It may cause allergic reactions such as headaches, dizziness, and nausea, in some people.

monosyllabic *adj.* **1** having one syllable. **2** using short words, especially 'yes' and 'no': *a monosyllabic reply.*

monosyllable *noun* a word consisting of only one syllable.

monotheism *noun* the belief that there is only one God. [from MONO- + Greek *theos*, God]

monotheist *noun* a person who believes in only one God.

monotheistic *adj.* relating to monotheism.

monotone — *noun* **1** a single unvarying tone in speech or sound. **2** a sequence of sounds of the same tone. **3** sameness, especially in colour. — *adj.* lacking in variety; unchanging. [from MONO- + Greek *tonos*, tone]

monotonous *adj.* lacking in variety; tediously unchanging.

monotonously *adv.* in a monotonous way.

monotony *noun* **1** dullness. **2** sameness.

monotreme *noun Zool.* an egg-laying mammal belonging to the order Monotremata (the most primitive group of mammals) that lays soft-shelled eggs, suckles its young, and has no teeth as an adult, eg duck-billed platypus. [from MONO- + Greek *trema*, hole]

monotype *noun Art* a one-off print made by painting oil paint or ink on a sheet of glass or a metal plate, and pressing a sheet of paper against the wet surface to create a reverse image of the original. Monotype was used by Giovanni Benedetto Castiglione in the 17c, by William Blake in the 18c, and by Edgar Degas in the 19c (often combined with other media such as pastels).

monovalent *adj. Chem.* having a valency of one.

monoxide *noun* a chemical compound containing one oxygen atom in each molecule. [from MONO- + OXIDE]

Monroe, James (1758–1831) US statesman, the fifth President, born in Westmoreland Co, Virginia. After serving in the War of Independence, he entered politics and was a member of the Senate (1790–4), Minister to France (1794–6), Governor of Virginia (1799–1802), Minister in London and Madrid (1803–7), and Secretary of State (1811–17). His most popular acts as President (1817–25) were the recognition of the Spanish–American republics, and the promulgation of the Monroe Doctrine.

Monroe, Marilyn, originally **Norma Jean Mortenson** *or* **Baker** (1926–62) US film actress, born in Los Angeles. After a childhood spent largely in foster homes, she became a photographer's model. She began to make her name in films as a blonde sex symbol, and in 1953 made the successful *Gentlemen Prefer Blondes* but, wanting more serious roles, she studied at Lee Strasberg's Actors Studio. Following her success in *Bus Stop* (1956), she made *The Prince and the Showgirl* (1957) in London with Laurence Olivier, then returned to Hollywood to make *Some Like it Hot* (1959).

Monroe Doctrine a major statement of American foreign policy (1823), attributed to President James Monroe, but written by Secretary of State John Quincy Adams. It was issued after renewed interest in the Americas by European powers (eg Britain and Russia), following the Spanish–American revolutions for independence, and announced (1) the existence of a separate political system in the W hemisphere, (2) US hostility to further European colonization or attempts to extend European influence, and (3) non-interference with existing European colonies and dependencies or in European affairs.

Monrovia POP (1984) 421 000, the seaport capital of Liberia. It lies 362km/225mi SE of Freetown (Sierra Leone) on an area divided by lagoons into islands and peninsulas. The main port and industrial sector is on Bushrod I. HISTORY founded by the American Colonization Society in 1822 as a home for repatriated slaves from America; originally called Christopolis, it was renamed Monrovia after US President James Monroe (a member of the society).

Mons, Flemish **Bergen** POP (1992e) 92 000, the commercial and cultural capital of Hainaut province, S Belgium. It has an inland harbour, mostly handling coal from the Borinage, a major

mining region. HISTORY built on the site of one of Julius Caesar's camps; often a battlefield, notably in World War I (1914). NOTABLE FEATURES Gothic cathedral; town hall (15c).

Monsieur *noun* (ABBREV. **M**) a title equivalent to Mr, used especially of a French or French-speaking man. [from French, originally *mon*, my + *sieur*, lord]

Monsignor *noun* (PL. **Monsignors, Monsignori**) a title given to various high-ranking male members of the Roman Catholic church. [from Italian, from French *Monseigneur*, a title given to high-ranking clergy and nobility]

monsoon *noun* **1** in the area around the Indian Ocean and S Asia, and also around the coasts of W Africa and N Australia, a wind that blows from the north-east in winter and from the south-west in summer. The wind changes direction because of regional changes in air pressure associated with the changing seasons. **2** any strong relatively constant wind that blows in opposite directions at different times of year. **3** in India, the heavy rains accompanying the summer monsoon. **4** *colloq.* an extremely heavy fall of rain. [from Arabic *mawsim*, season]

rainfall Nov–April
winds in January
(winter)

rainfall Jun–Oct
winds in July
(summer)

monsoon

monster — *noun* **1** any large and frightening imaginary creature. **2** a cruel or evil person. **3** any unusually large thing. **4** *old use* a deformed person, animal or plant. — *adj.* huge; gigantic: *monster portions*. [from Latin *monstrum*, evil omen]

monstera *noun* a tall climbing plant (*Monstera deliciosa*), native to tropical America, which has stems with tough aerial roots, and large heart-shaped leaves that develop deep notches and sometimes holes as they mature. It is a popular house plant, but the flowers and edible fruit rarely appear when it is grown indoors. — Also called *Swiss cheese plant*. [a modern Latin form of *monster*]

monstrance *noun RC Church* a large gold or silver cup in which the host, bread representing

Christ's body, is displayed to the congregation during Mass. [from Latin *monstrare*, to show]

monstrosity *noun* (PL. **monstrosities**) **1** any ugly or outrageous thing. **2** the quality of being monstrous.

monstrous *adj.* **1** like a monster; huge. **2** outrageous; absurd. **3** extremely cruel; evil. **4** *old use* deformed.

monstrously *adv.* in a monstrous way.

Mont. *abbrev.* Montana.

montage *noun* **1** the process of creating a picture by piecing together elements from other pictures, photographs, etc; a picture made in this way. **2** the process of editing cinema film. **3** extensive use of changes in camera position to create an impression of movement or action in a filmed scene. See also MISE-EN-SCENE. **4** a film sequence made up of short clips, especially used to condense events taking place over a long period. [from French *montage*, from *monter*, to mount]

◇ In art, it is a technique whereby illustrations or photographs from various sources, such as newspapers or magazines, are arranged in new ways, and mounted. A development of collage, it was much used by in Dadaism and Surrealism.

Montagu, Lady Mary Wortley, *née* **Pierrepont** (1689–1762) English writer and socialite, born in London. The daughter of the Earl of Kingston, she married Edward Wortley Montagu in 1712, and lived primarily in London and Italy. While in Constantinople with her husband, she wrote her well-known *Letters* describing Eastern life. She also introduced inoculation for smallpox into England.

Montagu–Chelmsford Reforms after a report (Apr 1918) by the Secretary for State for India E S Montagu, and the Viceroy Lord Chelmsford, the British agreed the 1919 Government of India Act. It introduced partial provincial autonomy on matters such as education, ministerial responsibility in the provinces, and a central bicameral legislature comprising a Council of State and a Legislative Assembly.

Montague the supportive father of Romeo and archenemy of Capulet in Shakespeare's *Romeo and Juliet*, who is magnanimous in the final settling of their differences.

Montague a male first name, after the surname. [from *mons*, mountain + *actus*, pointed]

Montaigne, Michel (Eyquem) de (1533–92) French essayist, born in the Château de Montaigne, Périgord. He studied law, became a city counsellor, and in 1571 succeeded to the family estate, where he lived as a country gentleman. He is remembered for his *Essais* on the ideas and personalities of the time, which introduced a new literary genre, and provided a major contribution to literary history.

Montale, Eugenio (1896–1981) Italian poet, born in Genoa. A poet of the modern Italian 'Hermetic' school, his primary concern is with language and symbolic meaning. His works include *Ossi di Seppia* (Cuttlefish Bones, 1925) and *La bufera* (The Storm, 1956). He was awarded the Nobel Prize for Literature in 1975.

Montana, Joe (1956–) US football player, born in New Eagle, Pennsylvania. He joined the San Francisco 49ers in 1979, and played in their winning Super Bowl teams in 1982, 1985, 1989, and 1990. He won the Most Valuable Player award in 1982, 1985, and 1990. He joined the Kansas City Chiefs in 1993, after being unable to play for two years because of injury.

Montana POP (1990) 824 000, a state in NW USA, divided into 56 counties. AREA 380 834sq km/147 046sq mi. The fourth-largest US state, it is bounded N by the Canadian provinces of British Columbia, Alberta, and Saskatchewan. PHYSICAL DESCRIPTION crossed by the Missouri and Yellowstone rivers; the

Bitterroot Range, part of the Rocky Mts, lies along much of the W border; the highest point is Granite Peak (3 901m); the Great Plains to the E are largely occupied by vast wheat fields and livestock farms; the W is dominated by the Rocky Mts, covered in dense pine forests; part of Yellowstone National Park lies in the S; Glacier National Park is located in the W. HISTORY most of the state was acquired by the 1803 Louisiana Purchase; the border with Canada was settled by the Oregon Treaty in 1846; became the Territory of Montana in 1864; the gold rush followed discoveries in 1858; ranchers moved into the area in 1866, taking over Native American land; conflict with the Sioux resulted in the defeat of General Custer at the battle of the Little Bighorn in 1876 (there are now six Native American reservations in the state); became the 41st state to join the Union, in 1889; Montana is known as the 'Treasure State'. CAPITAL Helena. CHIEF TOWNS Billings, Great Falls. ECONOMY tourism is a major state industry; recreational attractions include hunting, fishing, skiing, hiking, and boating (on glacier lakes); the mountainous W has deposits of copper, silver, gold, zinc, lead, and manganese; E Montana produces petroleum and natural gas, and has large coal-mines; manufactures include timber, wood products, refined petroleum, and processed foods; chief agricultural products are cattle, wheat, hay, barley, and dairy products.

Mont Blanc 1 the highest peak in the Alps, in the Mont Blanc Massif, situated in France at the frontier with Italy. HEIGHT 4 807m. **2** the highest alpine massif of SE France, SW Switzerland, and NW Italy. The ridge includes 25 peaks of over 4 000m. At Mt Dolent (3 823m), the frontiers of France, Switzerland, and Italy meet. The 160km/100mi Sentier International de Tour du Mont Blanc is an important walking route. Chamonix is the chief resort in the area.

montbretia *noun* a perennial plant (*Crocosmia × crocosmiiflora*) that produces corms and spreads by means of stolons. It has sword-shaped leaves and yellow or orange trumpet-shaped flowers borne in spikes. It is a hybrid species, descended from South African plants. [named after the French botanist A F E Coquebert de Montbret (1780–1801)]

Monte Albán the ancient capital of the Zapotecs of S Mexico, strategically placed at an elevation of 400m above the Valley of Oaxaca. It was occupied from c.400 BC to c.800 AD, and at the peak of its development (c.200–700 AD) covered an area of 40sq km/15sq mi. Its artificially-levelled hilltop plaza contains platform pyramids and a ball court (used for religious festivals and games). It is a World Heritage site.

Monte Carlo a resort town in Monaco. It is situated on a rocky promontory of the Mediterranean Riviera, on the N side of the harbour opposite the town of Monaco. NOTABLE FEATURES famous casino, providing c.4% of the national revenue (1878); Palais des Congrès (Les Spélugues). EVENTS annual car rally; World Championship Grand Prix Motor Race.

Montefiore, Sir Moses (Haim) (1784–1885) Italian-born British philanthropist, born in Leghorn. He retired with a fortune from stockbroking in 1824, and from 1829 was prominent in the struggle for the rights of Jews, on whose behalf he made several journeys throughout Europe and to Palestine. In 1837 he was appointed Sheriff of London.

Montego Bay, locally **Mobay** POP (1991) 83 000, a port and the capital of St James parish, Cornwall county, on the NW coast of Jamaica. It is a free port and the principal tourist centre of the island. NOTABLE FEATURES Rose Hall Great House (1770); old British fort; church (18c).

Montenegro, Serbo-Croatian **Crna Gora** POP (1991) 616 000, a constituent republic of Yugoslavia. AREA 13 012sq km/5 331sq mi. It is a mountainous region bounded SW by the Adriatic

Sea, SE by Albania, and E and N by Bosnia-Herzegovina. Until 1918 it was an independent monarchy. CAPITAL Titograd. ECONOMY livestock, grain, tobacco.

Montespan, Françoise Athenaïs de Rochechouart, Marquise de (1641–1707) mistress of Louis XIV, born in Tonnay-Charente, the daughter of the Duc de Mortemart. She married the Marquis de Montespan (1663) and became lady-in-waiting to Queen Maria Theresa. From c.1667 she was the King's mistress, and after her marriage was annulled (1674) her position was given official recognition. She bore the King seven children, who were legitimized. Superseded first by Mlle de Fontanges and later by Mme de Maintenon, she left court in 1687 and retired to the convent of Saint-Joseph in Paris, where she became the Superior.

Montesquieu, Charles-Louis de Secondat, Baron de la Brède et de (1689–1755) French philosopher and jurist, born near Bordeaux. He became an advocate, but turned to scientific research and literary work. His best-known work is the comparative study of legal and political issues, *De l'esprit des lois* (The Spirit of Laws, 1748), which was a major influence on 18c Europe.

Montessori, Maria (1870–1952) Italian doctor and educationalist, born in Rome. The first woman in Italy to graduate in medicine, she opened her first 'children's house' in 1907, developing a system of education for children of three to six, based on freedom of movement, the provision of considerable choice for pupils, and the use of specially-designed activities and equipment. 'Montessori schools' were also later developed for older children.

Monteverdi, Claudio (1567–1643) Italian composer, born in Cremona. He became a violist, learnt the art of composition, became court musician to the Duke of Mantua (c.1590), and *maestro di cappella* (chapel music director) in 1601. In 1613 he took a similar post at St Mark's, Venice, where he remained until his death. His works include eight books of madrigals, operas, and the *Mass* and *Vespers* of the Virgin (1610), his greatest contribution to church music, which contain tone colours and harmonies well in advance of their time.

Montevideo POP (1990e) 1.2m, the federal and provincial capital of Uruguay, on the R Plate. HISTORY founded in 1726; became the capital in 1830; the German battleship *Graf Spee* was scuttled offshore during the battle of the River Plate in 1939. NOTABLE FEATURES cathedral (1790–1804); several museums and parks; sports stadium (Estadio Centenario); fort on Cerro hill.

Montezuma II (1466–1520) the last Aztec emperor to rule Mexico before the Spanish invasion, (1502–20), a distinguished warrior and legislator, who died at Tenochtitlán during the Spanish conquest. One of his descendants was Viceroy of Mexico (1697–1701).

Montfort, Simon de, Earl of Leicester (c.1208–65) English politician and soldier, born in Montfort, near Paris. In 1238 he married Henry III's youngest sister, Eleanor, and as the King's deputy in Gascony (1248), put down rebellion with a heavy hand. He returned to England in 1253, led the barons in opposition to the King, and defeated him at Lewes (1264). He called a parliament in 1265 and became virtual ruler of England, but the barons soon grew dissatisfied with him, and the King's army defeated him at Evesham.

Montgolfier, Joseph Michel (1740–1810) French aeronautical inventor, born in Annonay. In 1782, with his brother Jacques Étienne (1745–99), he constructed a balloon whose bag was lifted by lighting a cauldron of straw and wool beneath it, thus heating the air it contained. They achieved the world's first manned balloon flight of 12km/7.5mi, at an altitude of up to 1 000m, in 1783. Further experiments were frustrated by the outbreak of the French Revolution.

Montgomery (of Alamein), Bernard Law Montgomery, 1st Viscount (1887–1976) English soldier, born in London. A controversial and outspoken figure, he was nevertheless a 'soldier's general' and had a remarkable rapport with his troops. He commanded the 8th Army in N Africa, and defeated General Rommel at the battle of El Alamein (1942). He played a key role in the invasion of Sicily and Italy (1943), and was appointed field marshal and Commander-in-Chief, Ground Forces, for the Allied invasion of Normandy (1944). His military career was marred by only one defeat — the badly-planned airborne landings at Arnhem (Sep 1944). In 1945, German forces in NW Germany, Holland, and Denmark surrendered to him on Lüneberg Heath. He also served as Chief of the Imperial General Staff (1946–8) and Deputy Supreme Commander of NATO forces in Europe (1951–8).

Montgomery POP (1990) 293 000, the capital of the state of Alabama, USA. It lies on the Alabama R, in Montgomery County, central Alabama, and is an important market centre for farming produce. HISTORY became state capital in 1847; the Confederate States of America were formed here in 1861; occupied by Federal troops in 1865; scene of the 1955 bus boycott by black campaigners protesting against segregation, which contributed to the growth of the civil rights movement.

month *noun* **1** any of the 12 named divisions of the year, varying in length between 28 and 31 days. **2** a period of roughly four weeks or 30 days; the period between identical dates in consecutive months. [from Anglo-Saxon *monath*, from *mona*, moon]

Month in the Country, A a play by Ivan Turgenev (1850). Considered his finest theatre work, it is about several characters' relationships and inner motivations.

monthly — *adj.* happening, published, etc once a month; lasting one month. — *adv.* once a month. — *noun* (PL. **monthlies**) **1** a monthly periodical. **2** *colloq.* a menstrual period.

Monti, Eugenio (1928–) Italian bobsleigh driver. He won a record six Olympic bobsleighing medals, including golds in the two- and four-man events in 1968, silver in both events in 1964, and bronze in 1964. He was also a member of 11 Italian world championship winning teams between 1957 and 1968. After retiring in 1968, he was appointed manager to the Italian national team.

Monticello the home of Thomas Jefferson, begun in 1770, in Charlottesville, Virginia, USA. It is a domed mansion, filled with his many inventions, including a seven-day clock which uses cannonballs for counterweights. It is a World Heritage site.

montmorillonite *noun Geol.* any of a group of soft opaque clay minerals, composed of aluminium silicates, that expand when they absorb liquids, and can take up or lose positively charged ions. Montmorillonites are used for decolourizing solutions, and as a base for paper and cosmetics. — Also called *fuller's earth.* [named after Montmorillon in France]

Montpelier POP (1990) 8 000, the capital of the state of Vermont, USA. It lies on the Winooski R, in Washington County in the N of the state. Settled in 1780, it became state capital in 1805. There are notable skiing areas nearby at Pinnacle Mt, Judgement Ridge, Glen Ellen, Bolton Valley, Sugarbush Valley, and Mad River Glen.

Montpellier POP (1990) 237 000, the industrial and commercial capital of Languedoc-Roussillon region and of Hérault department, S France. Situated 123km/76mi NW of Marseilles, it was founded in the 8c around a Benedictine abbey. The philosopher Auguste Comte was born here in 1798. NOTABLE FEATURES Gothic Cathedral of St Pierre (1364); many 17c–18c houses where patricians and merchants lived, Doric triumphal arch (1691); Château d'Eau (aqueduct terminal,

1753–66); Jardin des Plantes, France's first botanical garden (1593); Musée Fabre; Atger Museum.

Montreal, French **Montréal** POP (1991e) 3.1m, a river-port city in S Quebec province, SE Canada. It is situated on Montreal I, on the St Lawrence R. Montreal is the largest city in Canada, and the second largest French-speaking city in the world. HISTORY first visited by Cartier in 1535; a fort was built here in 1611; developed as a fur-trading centre; surrendered to the British in 1760; capital of Canada from 1844 until 1849; the British garrison was withdrawn in 1870. NOTABLE FEATURES Notre Dame Church (1829), Christ Church Cathedral, St James Cathedral; Séminaire de Saint-Sulpice (1658); Maisonneuve

---

Month Equivalents

Gregorian equivalents to other calendars are given in parentheses; the figures refer to the number of solar days in each month.

Gregorian
(Basis: Sun)
January (31)
February (28 or 29)
March (31)
April (30)
May (31)
June (30)
July (31)
August (31)
September (30)
October (31)
November (30)
December (31)

Jewish
(Basis: Moon)
Tishri (Sep–Oct) (30)
Hesshvan (Oct–Nov) (29 or 30)
Kislev (Nov–Dec) (29 or 30)
Tevet (Dec–Jan) (29)
Shevat (Jan–Feb) (30)
Adar (Feb–Mar) (29 or 30)
Adar Sheni *leap years only*
Nisan (Mar–Apr) (30)
Iyar (Apr–May) (29)
Sivan (May–Jun) (30)
Tammuz (Jun–Jul) (29)
Av (Jul–Aug) (30)
Elul (Aug–Sep) (29)

Islamic
(Basis: Moon)
Muharram (Sep–Oct) (30)
Safar (Oct–Nov) (29)
Rabi I (Nov–Dec) (30)
Rabi II (Dec–Jan) (29)
Jumada I (Jan–Feb) (30)
Jumada II (Feb–Mar) (29)
Rajab (Mar–Apr) (30)
Shaban (Apr–May) (29)
Ramadan (May–Jun) (30)
Shawwal (Jun–Jul) (29)
Dhu al-Qadah (Jul–Aug) (30)
Dhu al-Hijjah (Aug–Sep) (29 or 30)

Hindu
(Basis: Moon)
Chaitra (Mar–Apr) (29 or 30)
Vaisakha (Apr–May) (29 or 30)
Jyaistha (May–Jun) (29 or 30)
Asadha (Jun–Jul) (29 or 30)
Dvitiya Asadha (*certain leap years*)
Sravana (Jul–Aug) (29 or 30)
Dvitiya Sravana (*certain leap years*)
Bhadrapada (Aug–Sep) (29 or 30)
Asvina (Sep–Oct) (29 or 30)
Karttika (Oct–Nov) (29 or 30)
Margasirsa (Nov–Dec) (29 or 30)
Pausa (Dec–Jan) (29 or 30)
Magha (Jan–Feb) (29 or 30)
Phalguna (Feb–Mar) (29 or 30)

Monument (1895); Château de Ramezay (now a museum).

Montreux POP (1990) 19 000, a winter sports centre and resort town in Vaud canton, SW Switzerland. It lies SE of Lausanne, at the E end of L Geneva. NOTABLE FEATURE 13c Château de Chillon nearby. EVENTS Golden Rose Television Festival (spring); International Jazz Festival (Jun–Jul); music festival (Sep).

Montrose, James Graham, 1st Marquis of (1612–50) Scottish soldier. He helped to draw up the Covenant in support of Presbyterianism, and served in the Covenanter army (1640), but transferred his allegiance to Charles I, and led the Royalist army to victory at Tippermuir (1644). After the Royalist defeat at Naseby (1645) and at Philiphaugh, he fled to Europe, but returned to Scotland to avenge Charles's death. However, much of his army had been shipwrecked, and the remnant met defeat at Invercharron (1650), following which he was hanged in Edinburgh.

Montrose POP (1981) 12 000, a port town in Angus district, Tayside, E Scotland. It lies 42km/26mi NE of Dundee. To the W of the town is Montrose Basin, a large tidal lagoon. NOTABLE FEATURES museum; William Lamb Memorial Studio.

Mont-Saint-Michel a rocky isle off the coast of Normandy, NW France, famous for its Gothic abbey. A Benedictine settlement was first established here in the 8c, and an abbey was built in 966; major parts of the surviving abbey date from the early 13c. It is a World Heritage site.

Montserrat *or* **Emerald Isle** POP (1992e) 11 000, a volcanic island in the Leeward Is, Lesser Antilles, E Caribbean Sea. AREA 106sq km/ 41sq mi. The island lies 43km/27mi SW of Antigua and is a British Colony. CAPITAL Plymouth. TIME ZONE GMT −4. The population is of mixed African and European descent; Christianity is the chief religion. OFFICIAL LANGUAGE English. CURRENCY the E Caribbean dollar. PHYSICAL DESCRIPTION the island, 18km/11mi long and 11km/7mi at its widest point, is mountainous and heavily forested; the highest point is Chance's Peak at 914m; there are seven active volcanoes. CLIMATE tropical, with low humidity; average annual rainfall is 1 500mm; hurricanes occur in Jun to Nov. HISTORY visited by Columbus in 1493; colonized by English and Irish settlers in 1632; plantation economy based on slave labour; became a British Crown Colony in 1871; joined the Federation of the West Indies in 1958–62. GOVERNMENT the British Sovereign is represented by a Governor; there is a seven-member Executive Council and a 12-member Legislative Council. ECONOMY tourism is the mainstay of the economy, accounting for 25% of national income; cotton; peppers; market gardening; livestock; electronic assembly; crafts; rum distilling; postage stamps; the island was severely damaged by Hurricane Hugo in 1989.

Monument a Doric column, surmounted by a representation of a flame-encircled globe, designed by Christopher Wren and erected (1671–7) in Fish Street Hill, to commemorate the Fire of London.

monument *noun* 1 something, eg a statue, built to preserve the memory of a person or event. 2 any ancient building or structure preserved for its historical value. 3 *formal* something serving as clear evidence; an excellent example: *the painting is a monument to her artistic skill.* 4 *formal* a tombstone. [from Latin *monumentum*, from *monere*, to remind]

monumental *adj.* 1 of or being a monument. 2 like a monument, especially huge and impressive. 3 *colloq.* very great; extreme: *monumental arrogance.* 4 *formal* of tombstones: *monumental sculptor.*

moo — *noun* the long low sound made by a cow. — *verb intrans.* to make this sound. [imitative]

---

mooch *verb colloq.* 1 *intrans.* (*usually* **mooch about** *or* **around**) to wander aimlessly. 2 *trans., intrans.* to get (things) for nothing by asking directly; to cadge. [perhaps from Old French *muchier*, to hide or lurk]

mood[1] *noun* 1 a state of mind at a particular time; a suitable or necessary state of mind: *not in the mood for dancing.* 2 a temporary grumpy state of mind. 3 an atmosphere: *the mood in the factory.* [from Anglo-Saxon *mod*, mind]

mood[2] *noun Grammar* each of several forms of a verb, indicating whether the verb is expressing a fact, a wish, possibility, or doubt, or a command: *the imperative mood.* [originally a variant of MODE]

moodily *adv.* in a moody way, sullenly.

moodiness *noun* being moody.

Moody, Dwight L(yman) (1837–99) US evangelist, born in Northfield, Massachusetts. A shoe salesman in Boston, in 1856 he went to Chicago, where he began missionary work. In 1870 he was joined by Ira David Sankey (1840–1908), who accompanied his preaching with singing and organ playing. They toured the USA as evangelists, visited Britain (1873 and 1883), published books of hymns, and founded the Moody Bible Institute in Chicago (1899).

moody *adj.* (**moodier, moodiest**) tending to change mood often; frequently bad-tempered.

moon — *noun* 1 (**Moon**) the Earth's natural satellite, illuminated to varying degrees by the Sun depending on its position, and often visible in the sky, especially at night. 2 the appearance of this body to an observer on Earth, in respect of its degree of illumination, eg full moon, half moon. 3 a natural satellite of any planet. 4 something impossible to obtain: *promised me the moon.* — *verb intrans.* 1 (**moon about** *or* **around**) to wander aimlessly; to spend time idly. 2 *slang* to make a show of one's bare buttocks in public. — **over the moon** *colloq.* thrilled, delighted. [from Anglo-Saxon *mona*]

◇ The Moon has a diameter of 3 476km, and it orbits the Earth at an average distance of 384 400km. It was formed at the same time as the Earth, about 4 550 million years ago, but since it is only a quarter of the Earth's diameter, it cooled down much more rapidly and its thick crust has now solidified, whereas the Earth's thin crust is still floating over the hot layer beneath it. The Moon's surface is pitted with craters, most of them produced by the impact of meteors, although some represent the sites of ancient volcanoes. The Moon has no atmosphere because its force of gravity is very weak, and so it cannot attract gas molecules. At one time it rotated rapidly, but the Earth's gravitational pull has slowed it down, and it now always keeps the same face towards the Earth. Half of the Moon is always in sunlight, and the different phases of the Moon (eg full moon, half moon) depend on how much of the illuminated half can be seen from the Earth. The month, based on a complete cycle of the Moon's phases from full moon to full moon, has been a unit of time since earliest recorded history, and the average time between full moons is 29.5 days. See illustrations p. 836. On 20 July 1969, *Apollo 11* astronauts Neil Armstrong and Edwin Aldrin became the first human beings to walk on the surface of the Moon.

moonbeam *noun* a ray of sunlight reflected from the moon.

Moonies, The see UNIFICATION CHURCH.

moonlight — *noun* 1 sunlight reflected by the moon. 2 (*attributive*) illuminated by moonlight: *a moonlight swim.* — *verb intrans.* (PAST TENSE AND PAST PARTICIPLE **moonlighted**) *colloq.* to work at a second job outside the working hours of the main job, often evading income tax on the extra earnings.

moonlighter *noun* a person who moonlights.

moonlighting *noun* the practice of working as a moonlighter.

Moonlight Sonata Beethoven's Piano Sonato No.14 in C sharp minor (Op 27, No.2, 1801), named because the reviewer Ludwig Rellstab (1799–1860) said it made him think him of moonlight on Lake Lucerne.

moonlit *adj.* illuminated by moonlight.

moonshine *noun colloq.* **1** foolish talk; nonsense. **2** smuggled or illegally distilled alcoholic spirit.

Moonstone, The a novel by Wilkie Collins (1868). It describes the investigation into the theft of a moonstone diamond.

moonstone *noun Geol.* a transparent or opalescent silvery or bluish form of feldspar, used as a semi-precious stone in jewellery, and so called because it was once thought that its appearance changed with the waxing and waning of the moon.

moonstruck *adj. colloq.* behaving in an unusually wild or excited way, as if affected by the moon.

moony *adj.* (**moonier, mooniest**) *colloq.* in a dreamy mood.

Moor *noun* a member of an Arab people of NW Africa. See also MOORS.

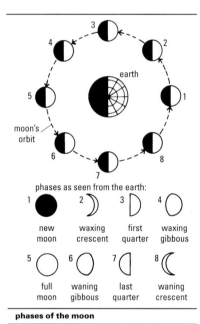

phases as seen from the earth:

| 1 new moon | 2 waxing crescent | 3 first quarter | 4 waxing gibbous |
| 5 full moon | 6 waning gibbous | 7 last quarter | 8 waning crescent |

phases of the moon

Bay of Rainbows — Humboldt's Seas
Sea of Showers — Sea of Serenity
Ocean of Storms — Sea of Crises
Copernicus — Sea of Tranquillity
Eratosthenes — Sea of Fertility
Sea of Clouds — Sea of Nectar
Sea of Moisture — Southern Sea

lunar seas

moor¹ *noun* a large area of open uncultivated upland dominated by heather, and having an acid peaty soil. [from Anglo-Saxon *mor*]

moor² *verb* **1** to fasten (a ship or boat) by a rope, cable, or anchor. **2** *intrans.* to be fastened in this way. [perhaps from Old Dutch *maren*]

Moore, Archie, properly **Archibald Lee Wright** (1913/1916–) US boxer, born in Benoit, Missouri. His actual date-of-birth is uncertain (by his own account), but he is still the oldest man to hold a world title. He was 39 (or 36) when he beat Joey Maxim (1922–) for the light-heavyweight title in 1952. He had 234 professional bouts and won 199, knocking out a record 145 opponents. He lost to Cassius Clay in 1962, and retired in 1965.

Moore, Bobby (1941–93) English footballer, born in Barking, Essex. During his career with West Ham United (1958–74) and later Fulham (1974–7), he played 1 000 matches at senior level, and won an FA Cup-winner's medal in 1964 and a European Cup-winner's medal in 1965. He was capped for England a record 108 times (107 in succession), 90 of them as captain. He captained the victorious England side in the 1966 World Cup, and also led the team in Mexico in the 1970 finals. From 1986 to 1990 he was Sports Editor for the *Sunday Sport.*

Moore, Brian (1921–) British novelist, born in Belfast, Northern Ireland. He emigrated to Canada in 1948, and has lived in California and New York. His first novel, *Judith Hearne* (1955) was filmed as *The Lonely Passion of Judith Hearne* in 1989. Later works include *The Doctor's Wife* (1976), *Black Robe* (1985, filmed 1991), and *Lies of Silence* (1990).

Moore, G(eorge) E(dward) (1873–1958) English empiricist philosopher, born in London. His major ethical work was *Principia Ethica* (1903), in which he analysed the moral concept of goodness and commended the value of friendship and aesthetic experience; the text was a major influence on the Bloomsbury group. At Cambridge he lectured in moral science and was Professor of Mental Philosophy and Logic (1925–39), and editor (1921–47) of the journal *Mind.*

Moore, Henry (Spencer) (1898–1986) English sculptor, born in Castleford, Yorkshire. He produced mainly figures and groups in a semi-abstract style based on the organic forms and rhythms found in landscape and natural rocks. His interest lay in the spatial quality of sculpture, an effect he achieved by the piercing of his figures. His major works include *Madonna and Child* (1943–4) in St Matthew's Church, Northampton, and the decorative frieze (1952) on the Time-Life building, London.

Moore, Sir John (1761–1809) Scottish soldier, born in Glasgow. From 1794 he served in many countries in Europe, and in the West Indies, but is remembered for his command of the English army in Spain (1808–9), where he was forced to retreat to Corunna. There he defeated a French attack, but was mortally wounded (as recounted in Charles Wolfe's poem, 'The Burial of Sir John Moore').

Moore, Patrick Alfred Calderwell (1923–) English author and broadcaster on popular astronomy. He served in the RAF (1940–5), and in 1957 began his continuing popular television series *The Sky at Night.* He has written more than 60 books, including *Atlas of the Universe* (1970, revised 1981), *Guide to the Planets* (1976), *Guide to the Moon* (1976), *TV Astronomer* (1987), and *A Passion for Astronomy* (1991).

Moore, Stanford (1913–82) US biochemist, born in Chicago. Working at the Rockefeller Institute in New York, his team invented a method to analyse and identify the number of amino acid molecules in proteins; by 1958 they had also developed an ingenious automated analyser to carry out all the steps of the analysis of structure of RNA on a small sample. He shared the 1972 Nobel Prize for Chemistry with William Stein and Christian Anfinsen.

Moore, Thomas (1779–1852) Irish poet and composer, born in Dublin. He became a lawyer, but found great success with his *Irish Melodies* (1807–34) and the oriental narrative poem, *Lalla Rookh* (1817). His other works include a novel, *The Epicurean* (1827), and a biography of his friend Byron (1830).

moorhen *noun* a small black water-bird with a red beak.

mooring *noun* **1** a place where a boat is moored. **2** (**moorings**) the ropes, anchors, etc used to moor a boat.

Moorish *adj.* relating to the Moors or their civilization.

moorland *noun* a moor.

Moors Muslims from N Africa who conquered the Iberian Peninsula in the 8c. The Hispanic Christian kingdoms (particularly Castile) fought wars of Reconquest, which by the mid-13c eliminated the Moors from all but the small S kingdom of Granada. Granada was conquered in 1492, and in 1502 all professed Muslims were expelled by order of Isabella I, 'the Catholic'. [from Latin *Maurus*]

moose *noun* (PL. **moose**) a large N American deer with flat rounded antlers, also found in Europe and Asia, where it is called an elk. [from Algonkian (a Native American language) *moos*]

moot — *verb* to suggest; to bring up for discussion. — *adj.* open to argument; debatable: *a moot point.* — *noun* a court or administrative assembly in Anglo-Saxon England. [from Anglo-Saxon *mot,* assembly]

mop — *noun* **1** a tool for washing or wiping floors, consisting of a large sponge or a set of thick threads on a long handle. **2** a similar smaller tool for washing dishes. **3** *colloq.* a thick mass of hair. — *verb* (**mopped, mopping**) **1** to wash or wipe with a mop. **2** to wipe or clean (eg a sweaty brow).
— **mop up** or **mop something up 1** to clean up with a mop. **2** *colloq.* to capture or kill (remaining enemy troops) after a victory; to deal with or get rid of (anything remaining).
[perhaps from Latin *mappa,* napkin]

mope — *verb intrans.* to behave in a depressed, sulky, or aimless way. — *noun* **1** a habitually sulky or depressed person. **2** (**the mopes**) low spirits; depression.

moped *noun* a small-engined motorcycle, especially one started using pedals. [a shortening of *motor-assisted pedal-cycle*]

moppet *noun* a term of affection used to a small child. [from obsolete *mop*, rag doll]

Mopti 1 POP (1987) 74 000, the capital of Mopti region, central Mali. Situated on three islands joined by a dyke, the 'Venice of Mali' lies at the confluence of the Niger and Bani rivers. **2** POP (1992e) 1.4m, a fertile region in central Mali. AREA 88 752sq km/34 258sq mi. CAPITAL Mopti.

moquette *noun* thick velvety material used to make carpets and upholstery. [from French]

Morag a female first name. [from the Scottish Gaelic name *Mor*, great]

moraine *noun* Geol. any jumbled accumulation of rock fragments of assorted sizes, ranging from sand to boulders, that has been carried from its place of origin and deposited by a glacier or ice sheet. [from French]

moral — *adj.* **1** of or relating to the principles of good and evil, or right and wrong. **2** conforming to what is considered by society to be good, right, or proper. **3** having a psychological effect: *moral support*. **4** considered in terms of psychological effect, rather than outward appearance: *a moral victory*. **5** capable of distinguishing between right and wrong. — *noun* **1** a principle to be learned from a story or event. **2** (**morals**) a sense of right and wrong, or a standard of behaviour based on this: *have no morals / loose morals*. [from Latin *moralis*, from *mores*, pl. of *mos*, custom]

moral certainty something about which there is hardly any doubt.

morale *noun* level of confidence or optimism; spirits. [from French]

moralist *noun* **1** a person who lives according to strict moral principles. **2** a person who tends to lecture others on their low moral standards.

moralistic *adj.* **1** pertaining to or typical of a moralist. **2** given to moralizing. **3** characterized by moralism.

morality *noun* (PL. **moralities**) **1** the quality of being right or wrong; behaviour in relation to accepted moral standards. **2** a particular system of moral standards.

morality play Hist. an allegorical drama, originating in the Middle Ages, in which the characters act out a conflict between good and evil.

moralize *or* **moralise** *verb* **1** intrans. to write or speak (especially critically) about moral standards. **2** trans. to explain in terms of morals.

moralizer *or* **moraliser** *noun* a person who moralizes.

Moral Majority a US pressure group founded in 1979 which campaigns for the election of morally conservative politicians and for changes to public policy in such areas as abortion, homosexuality, and school prayers. It is associated with Christian fundamentalists who in the 1980s played a prominent role in US politics.

Moral Rearmament (ABBREV. **MRA**) a movement founded (1938) in the USA by Frank Buchman to deepen the spirituality and morality of Christians. It succeeded the 'Oxford Group Movement' (founded 1921), and its individualistic and pietistic emphasis was expanded to include political and social concerns.

moral theology Relig. a theological discipline concerned with ethical questions considered from a specifically Christian perspective. Its sources include scripture, tradition, and philosophy. In Roman Catholic teaching, it deals traditionally with God as the goal of human life, and provides instruction on spirituality and the means of grace.

Morar, Loch the deepest loch in Britain, in W Highland region, W Scotland. Situated SE of Mallaig, on the W coast, it is 19km/12mi long and 310m deep. It drains into the Sound of Sleat via the R Morar.

morass *noun* **1** an area of marshy or swampy ground. **2** literary a dangerous or confused situation, especially one that entraps. [from Old French *maresc*]

moratorium *noun* (PL. **moratoriums**, **moratoria**) **1** an agreed temporary break in an activity. **2** a legally authorized postponement of payment of a debt. [from Latin, from *mora*, delay]

Moravia, Alberto, pseudonym of **Alberto Pincherle** (1907–90) Italian novelist and short-story writer, born in Rome. He became a journalist and travelled extensively. His first novel *Gli indifferenti* (The Time of Indifference, 1929), portrays in a fatalistic way the preoccupation with sex and money of bourgeois Roman society. Later works include *La disubbidienza* (Disobedience, 1948) and *Racconti romani* (Roman Tales, 1954).

Moravia, Czech **Morava**, German **Mähren** a historic province of central former Czechoslovakia, situated in the current Czech Republic and bounded N by Poland, S by Austria, W by the historic province of Bohemia, and E by Slovakia. PHYSICAL DESCRIPTION separated from Slovakia by the Little and White Carpathian Mts; a corridor (the Moravian Gate) provides an important communication link (N–S) between the SE Sudetes Mts and the W Carpathians; chief rivers include the Morava, Oder, Opava, and Dyje. HISTORY an early medieval kingdom (Great Moravia) in the 9c; became part of Bohemia in 1029; under Habsburg rule from the early 16c; became a province of Czechoslovakia in 1918; united with Silesia from 1927 to 1949. CHIEF TOWNS Brno, Ostrava, Olomouc. ECONOMY coal, iron ore, and other minerals.

Moravian Brethren a Protestant body descended from an association of Brethren formed in Bohemia in 1457, but driven out by persecution in 1722. They spread over parts of Europe, where they were influenced by Pietism (a 17c and 18c movement within Lutheranism which was a reaction against dogmatism, stressing good works, bible study, and holiness). In 1734 the Moravian Church was established in N America, where most members live today.

Moray, James Stuart, 1st Earl of (1531–70) Regent of Scotland (1567–70), illegitimate son of James V of Scotland, and half-brother of Mary, Queen of Scots. He acted as Mary's chief adviser (1560), but supported John Knox and opposed Mary's marriage to Darnley. After an attempted coup, he was outlawed and fled to England (1565). Pardoned the following year, he became regent for Mary's baby son when she abdicated (1567), and defeated her army at Langside (1568). His Protestant and pro-English policies alienated some Scots nobles, and he was killed at Linlithgow by one of Mary's supporters.

moray *noun* a sharp-toothed eel of warm coastal waters. [from Portuguese *moreia*]

morbid *adj.* **1** displaying an unhealthy interest in unpleasant things, especially death. **2** *Medicine* relating to, or indicating the presence of, disease. [from Latin *morbus*, disease]

morbidity *noun* being morbid; a morbid state.

mordant — *adj.* sharply sarcastic or critical; biting. — *noun* **1** *Chem.* a chemical compound, usually a metallic oxide or salt, that is used to fix colour on textiles that cannot be dyed directly. It is absorbed on to the fabric, and then combines with the dye to form an insoluble coloured complex that stains the fabric far more effectively than the dye alone. **2** a corrosive substance. [from Latin *mordere*, to bite]

Mordecai (c.5c BC) a biblical character, described in the Book of Esther as a Jew in exile in Persia, who cared for his orphaned cousin Esther and gained the favour of King Xerxes after uncovering a plot against him. He used his subsequent influence to protect Jews from an edict issued against them, an event commemorated by the annual Jewish feast of Purim.

More, Henry (1614–87) English philosopher and poet, known as the 'Cambridge Platonist', born in Grantham, Lincolnshire. He became a Fellow at Cambridge in 1639 and devoted his life to the study of philosophy, especially to Plato and the Neoplatonists. His works include the *Divine Dialogues* (1668).

More, James the renegade father of Catriona Drummond in Robert Louis Stevenson's *Catriona*.

More, Sir Thomas, also called **St Thomas More** (1478–1535) English statesman, born in London. He became a lawyer, then spent four years in a Carthusian monastery. He did not take holy orders, and under Henry VIII became Master of Requests (1514), Treasurer of the Exchequer (1521), and Chancellor of the Duchy of Lancaster (1525). On the fall of Wolsey (1529), he was appointed Lord Chancellor, but resigned in 1532 because he opposed Henry's break with Rome. His refusal to recognize Henry as head of the English Church led to his imprisonment and execution. A leading humanist scholar, his works include the Latin *Utopia* (1516), and he was canonized in 1935 (feast day 9 Jul).

more — *adj.* a greater or additional number or quantity of. — *adv.* **1** used to form the comparative of many adjectives and adverbs, especially those of two or more syllables. **2** to a greater degree; with a greater frequency. **3** again: *once more*. — *pron.* a greater, or additional, number or quantity of people or things.
— **more of** ... better described as ...; closer to being: *more of a painter than a writer*.
more or less 1 almost: *more or less finished*. **2** roughly: *more or less two hours*. [from Anglo-Saxon *mara*, greater]

Morecambe POP (1981) 42 000, a resort town in Lancaster district, Lancashire, NW England. It lies NW of Lancaster on the Irish Sea coast (Morecambe Bay). There is offshore oil and natural gas.

morel *noun* Bot. a highly prized edible fungus belonging to the genus *Morchella*. Its fruiting body consists of a pale stalk and a brownish egg-shaped head covered with a network of ridges. It appears in spring in woods and pastures and on bonfire sites. [from French *morille*]

morello *noun* (PL. **morellos**) a bitter-tasting dark-red cherry. [from Italian *morello*, blackish]

moreover *adv.* also; and what is more important.

mores *pl. noun formal* social customs reflecting the basic moral and social values of a particular society. [from Latin, from *mos*, custom]

Morgagni, Giovanni Battista (1682–1771) Italian physician, born in Forlì. Professor at Padua, he correlated the clinical aspects of illness during patients' lifetimes with the detailed results of their postmortems for over 600 cases, and is traditionally considered to be the 'father of morbid anatomy'.

Morgan, Charles (Langbridge) (1894–1958) English writer and critic, born in Bromley, Kent. He served in the navy, and was interned in Holland until 1917. He later became a journalist, and was principal dramatic critic of *The Times* (1926–39). His novels include *Portrait in a Mirror* (1929), *The Fountain* (1932), and *The Voyage* (1940), and he also wrote several plays and essays.

Morgan, Sir Henry (c.1635–88) Welsh buccaneer, born in Llanrhymney, Glamorgan. Kidnapped as a child and shipped to Barbados, he joined the buccaneers. His many raids against the Spanish and Dutch in the West Indies and Central America included the famous capture of Porto Bello and Panama (1671). Transported to London under arrest to placate the Spanish (1672), he was subsequently knighted (1674) on the renewal of hostilities, and died a wealthy planter and Deputy Governor of Jamaica.

Morgan, J(ohn) P(ierpont) (1837–1913) US financier and philanthropist, born in Hartford, Connecticut. In 1895 he founded the international banking firm of J P Morgan and Co, which provided US government finance, and developed interests in steel, railroads, and shipping. He bequeathed his art collection to the Metropolitan Museum of Art in New York.

Morgan, Thomas Hunt (1866–1945) US geneticist and biologist, born in Lexington, Kentucky. Professor at Columbia University and the California Institute of Technology, his early work was in embryology, but his fame rests on his work in genetics; he established a chromosome theory of heredity involving genes for specific tasks aligned on chromosomes. He was awarded the 1933 Nobel Prize for Physiology or Medicine.

Morgan a male and more recently also a female first name. [from Old Welsh *Morcant*, partly from Old Celtic *cant*, circle]

morganatic *adj. technical, said of marriage* between a person of high social rank and one of low rank, and allowing neither the lower-ranking person nor any child from the marriage to inherit the title or property of the higher-ranking person. [from Latin *matrimonium ad morganaticam*, marriage with a morning gift; the offering of the gift, after consummation, is the husband's only duty in such a marriage]

Morgan le Fay in Arthurian legend, an enchantress, 'Morgan the Fairy', the sister of King Arthur. She was generally hostile towards him and was one of the three queens who received him at his death.

morgue *noun* **1** a building where corpses are kept until buried or cremated. **2** any gloomy or depressing place. **3** a store of miscellaneous information for reference. [from French *morgue*]

MORI *abbrev.* Market and Opinion Research Institute.

Moriarty, Professor James the intelligent but villainous arch-enemy of Sherlock Holmes in Arthur Conan Doyle's *The Final Problem*.

moribund *adj.* **1** dying; near the end of existence. **2** lacking strength or vitality. [from Latin *mori*, to die]

Morison, Stanley (1889–1967) English typographer, born in Wanstead, Essex. Typographic adviser to Cambridge University Press and to the Monotype Corporation, he joined *The Times* in 1929, for which he designed the Times New Roman type. He also edited *The Times Literary Supplement* (1945–7), and wrote many works on typography and calligraphy.

Morley, Thomas (c.1557–1602) English composer and organist, born in Norwich. He studied under William Byrd, became organist at St Paul's, London, and from 1592 was a Gentleman of the Chapel Royal. He is best known for his *A Plaine and Easie Introduction to Practicall Musick* (1597), and for his volumes of madrigals and canzonets, which include such favourites as 'Now is the month of maying' and 'It was a lover and his lass'.

Morley–Minto Reforms the popular name given to the 1909 Indian Councils Act, which broadened the basis of Indian government, allowed Indians to sit on the Imperial Legislative Council, introduced direct elections for non-official seats in provincial legislative councils, and granted separate or communal electorates to minorities.

Mormon *noun* a member of the Church of Jesus Christ of Latter-Day Saints, established in the US in 1830, accepting as scripture both the Bible and the Book of Mormon (a book regarded as a record of certain ancient American prophets).

Mormonism *noun* the beliefs and practices of the Mormons.

Mormons the name given to religious sects that base their beliefs on the *Book of Mormon* (1830). The largest was founded by Joseph Smith as the Church of Jesus Christ of Latter-Day Saints in Fayette, New York (1830), based since 1847 in Salt Lake City, Utah, where it was taken by Brigham Young. Smith claimed to have been led to a hidden gospel written on golden plates and buried 1 000 years before on a hill near Palmyra, New York. Transcribed as the *Book of Mormon*, it tells of an ancient American people to whom Christ appeared after his ascension, and teaches Christ's future establishment of the New Jerusalem in America. Mormons take their doctrine also from the King James Version of the Bible, but they believe that humans can become gods, and that Jesus's Incarnation was unique only because it was the first.

morn *noun poetic* morning. [from Anglo-Saxon *morgen*]

Mornay, Philippe de, Seigneur du (Lord of) Plessay-Marly (1549–1623) French statesman, born in Buhy, Normandy. Converted to Protestantism in 1560, he was nicknamed the 'Pope of the Huguenots' for his role in the Wars of Religion (1562–98). As a Huguenot leader, he was counsellor to Henry of Navarre and undertook many embassies for the Protestant cause, but fell out of favour after Henry's conversion to Catholicism (1593).

mornay *adj.* served in a cheese sauce: *cod mornay*. [perhaps from Philippe de Mornay]

morning — *noun* **1** the part of the day from sunrise to midday, or from midnight to midday. **2** sunrise; dawn. — *adj.* taken, or taking place, in the morning: *morning coffee*.
— **the morning after** *colloq.* the morning after a celebration, as the time of a hangover. [from Middle English *morwening*]

morning-after pill *Medicine* a contraceptive drug, consisting of a combination of oestrogen and progestogen, taken within 72 hours of unprotected sexual intercourse.

morning coat a man's tailed black or grey jacket worn as part of morning dress.

morning dress men's formal dress for the daytime, consisting of morning coat, grey trousers, and usually a top hat.

morning glory a tropical climbing plant with blue, pink, or white trumpet-shaped flowers that close in the afternoon.

morning sickness nausea and vomiting often experienced during the early stages of pregnancy, especially in the morning.

morning star a planet, usually Venus, seen in the eastern sky just before sunrise.

Morocco, official name **The Kingdom of Morocco**, Arabic **Al-Mamlakah al-Maghribiyah** POP (1992e) 26.3m, a kingdom in N Africa, divided into seven provinces. AREA 409 200sq km/157 951sq mi. It is bounded SW by Western Sahara, SE and E by Algeria, NE by the Mediterranean Sea, and W by the Atlantic Ocean. CAPITAL Rabat. CHIEF TOWNS Casablanca, Fez, Marrakesh, Tangier, Meknès, Kenitra, Tétouan, Oujda, Agadir. TIME ZONE GMT. The population is almost all of Arab–Berber origin; Islam is the chief religion. OFFICIAL LANGUAGE Arabic; French is also spoken. CURRENCY the dirham. PHYSICAL DESCRIPTION dominated by a series of folded mountain ranges, rising in the Haut Atlas in the S to 4 165m at Mt Toubkal; the Atlas Mts descend SE to the NW edge of the Sahara Desert; the broad coastal plain is bounded W by the Atlantic Ocean. CLIMATE Mediterranean climate on the N coast; it is settled and hot in May–Sep; the average annual rainfall is 400–800mm, decreasing towards the Sahara, which is virtually rainless; Rabat, representative of the Atlantic coast, has average maximum daily temperatures of 17–28°C; heavy winter snowfall in the High Atlas; the desert region experiences

extreme heat in summer, with chilly winter nights. HISTORY from the 12c BC the N coast was occupied by Phoenicians, Carthaginians, and Romans; invasion by Arabs in the 7c AD; European interest in the region in the 19c; the Treaty of Fez in 1912 established Spanish Morocco (capital, Tétouan) and French Morocco (capital, Rabat); the international zone of Tangier was created in 1923; the protectorates gained independence in 1956; former Spanish Sahara (Western Sahara) came under the joint control of Spain, Morocco, and Mauritania in 1975; it became the responsibility of Morocco in 1979 but there is an independence movement in the region and Moroccan sovereignty is not recognized universally. GOVERNMENT a 'constitutional' monarchy, but the Monarch appoints and presides over a Cabinet, which is led by a Prime Minister; there is a unicameral 306-member Chamber of Representatives, of which 206 are elected every six years, and the remainder are chosen by an electoral college. ECONOMY over half the population is engaged in agriculture; cereals (wheat and barley), citrus fruits, olives, vegetables, sugar beet, cotton, sunflowers; the largest known reserves of phosphate; coal, barite, cobalt, copper, manganese, antimony, zinc, iron ore, fluorspar, lead, silver; fishing; textiles; cement; soap; tobacco; chemicals; paper; timber products; vehicle assembly; crafts; tourism is centred on the four imperial cities and the warm Atlantic resorts.

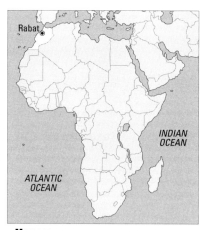

Morocco

morocco *noun* soft fine goatskin leather, originally brought from Morocco.

moron *noun* **1** *derog. colloq.* a very stupid person. **2** a term formerly used to describe a person with a mild degree of mental handicap, but now considered obsolete and offensive. [from Greek *moros*, foolish]

Moroni, Giovanni Battista (1525–78) Italian portrait and religious painter, born in Bondo. He specialized in portraits of Bergamo society, (eg *The Tailor*, National Gallery, London), and also painted several altarpieces.

Moroni POP (1988) 22 000, the capital of the Comoros, and the chief town on Grand Comore I. NOTABLE FEATURES several mosques; pilgrimage centre at Chiouanda.

moronic *adj.* **1** like or characteristic of a moron. **2** *colloq.* stupid, foolish.

morose *adj.* silently gloomy or bad-tempered. [from Latin *morosus*, peevish]

moroseness *noun* being morose.

Morpeth POP (1981) 15 000, the county town of Northumberland, NE England, lying on the R Wansbeck, 23km/14mi N of Newcastle upon Tyne. NOTABLE FEATURE remains of Morpeth Castle (14c).

morpheme *noun Grammar* any of the units of meaning contained in or forming a word, not divisible into smaller units, eg *out, go,* and *-ing,* contained in *outgoing.* See also MORPHOLOGY. [from Greek *morphe,* form]

Morpheus in Roman mythology, one of the sons of Somnus (the god of sleep) who sent images of people into the dreamer's mind. Later, as in Spenser, he was the god of sleep.

morphine *noun* a sedative narcotic drug obtained from opium and used mainly as an analgesic to relieve severe and persistent pain, and as a sedative to induce sleep. It produces feelings of euphoria and is highly addictive. Heroin and codeine (a non-addictive analgesic) are derivatives of morphine. [from *Morpheus,* Greek god of sleep]

morphing *noun* the use of computer graphics to blend one screen image into another in film-making, eg to transform or manipulate an actor's body. [from Greek *morphe,* form]

morphogenesis *noun Biol.* the development of form and structure in a living organism as a result of the growth and differentiation of its cells and tissues. [from Greek *morphe,* form + GENESIS]

morphological *adj.* relating to or involving morphology.

morphology *noun* **1** the study of morphemes and the rules by which they combine to form words. **2** the scientific study of the structure of plants and animals. **3** *formal* the structure of anything. [from Greek *morphe,* form + *logos,* discourse]

Morris, Desmond John (1928–) English ethologist and writer, born in Wiltshire. He was head of Granada Television and Film Unit at the Zoological Society of London (1956–9), and subsequently the society's curator of mammals; later he became Research Fellow at Oxford (1973–81). He is best known for his television programmes on animal and social behaviour, and has written several books which analyse human behaviour when viewed as an animal, such as *Manwatching* (1977) and *The Soccer Tribe* (1981).

Morris, Robert L(yle) (1942–) US psychologist, born in Canonsburg, Pennsylvania. In 1985 he was appointed the first Koestler Professor of Parapsychology at the University of Edinburgh.

Morris, William (1834–96) English craftsman and poet, born near London. He associated with the Pre-Raphaelite Brotherhood and became a major figure in the Arts and Crafts Movement, specializing in the revival of handicrafts and the art of house decoration and furnishing. He joined the Social Democratic Federation in 1883, and then organized the Socialist League. In 1890 he set up the Kelmscott Press which issued his own works and reprints of classics, such as the *Morte d'Arthur.*

morris dance a ceremonial form of traditional English dance, in which performers dressed in white, some wearing bells, stamp and hop, waving a stick, handkerchief, or garland, accompanied by an accordion or concertina with bass drum. [from Middle English *moreys,* Moorish]

morris dancer a person who performs morris dances.

morris dancing the practice of performing morris dances.

Morris Minor a car designed and developed at Morris Motors by Alec Issigionis in 1948. The first all-British car to exceed sales of one million, it remained in production until 1971.

Morrison, Toni, originally **Chloe Anthony Wofford** (1931–) US novelist, born in Lorain, Ohio. She moved to New York in 1965 and worked in publishing as an editor before becoming a full-time writer. Her novels portray the lives of black Americans and include *Sula* (1974), *Song of Solomon* (1977), *Tar Baby* (1981), *Beloved* (1987, Pulitzer Prize 1988), and *Jazz* (1992). She was awarded the Nobel Prize for Literature in 1993.

A	B	C	D	E	F	G	H	I	J	K	L	M
•—	—•••	—•—•	—••	•	••—•	——•	••••	••	•———	—•—	•—••	——

N	O	P	Q	R	S	T	U	V	W	X	Y	Z
—•	———	•——•	——•—	•—•	•••	—	••—	•••—	•——	—••—	—•——	——••

Morse code

Morrison (of Lambeth), Herbert Stanley Morrison, Baron (1888–1965) English Labour politician, born in London. Largely self-educated, he helped to found the London Labour Party and became its secretary in 1915. First elected an MP in 1923, he was Minister of Transport (1929–31), Minister of Supply (1940), and Home Secretary (1940–5). He served in the War Cabinet from 1942, and, a powerful postwar figure, became Deputy Prime Minister (1945–51), but was defeated by Hugh Gaitskell in the contest for the Party leadership in 1955.

Morrison, Mount *or* **Yu Shan** the highest peak in Taiwan, and the highest in NE Asia. HEIGHT 3 997m. It is situated in the central range of the island.

morrow *noun old use, poetic* (**the morrow**) **1** the following day; the time after an event. **2** the morning. [from Anglo-Saxon *morgen,* morning]

Morse code a code used for sending messages, each letter of a word being represented as a series of short or long radio signals or flashes of light. [from Samuel Morse (1791–1872), who invented it]

morsel *noun* a small piece, especially of food. [from Old French, from *mors,* bite]

mortal — *adj.* **1** certain to die at some future time. **2** of or causing death. **3** extreme: *mortal fear.* **4** characterized by intense hostility: *mortal enemies.* **5** used for emphasis; single: *every mortal thing.* — *noun* a mortal (especially human) being. [from Latin *mortalis,* from *mori,* to die]

mortality *noun* **1** the state of being mortal. **2** (*also* **mortality rate**) the number of deaths, eg in a war. **3** loss of life.

mortal sin *RC Church* a serious sin, for which there can be no forgiveness from God. See also VENIAL SIN.

mortar — *noun* **1** a mixture of sand, water, and cement or lime, used in building to bond bricks or stones. **2** the small dish into which substances are ground with a pestle. **3** a type of short-barrelled artillery gun for firing shells over short distances. — *verb* (**mortared;** MORTARING) **1** to fix (especially bricks) in place with mortar. **2** to bombard using a mortar. [from Latin *mortarium*]

mortarboard *noun* **1** a flat board used by bricklayers to carry mortar, held horizontally by a handle underneath. **2** a black cap with a hard square flat top, worn by academics at formal occasions.

Morte d'Arthur a poem by Alfred Lord Tennyson (1842). His first Arthurian poem, it describes the death of Arthur. It was later incorporated in the *Idylls of the King.*

Morte D'Arthur, Le a prose collection of the Arthurian legends by Sir Thomas Malory (21 books, 1485). It is divided into eight tales which are drawn largely from three French texts.

mortgage — *noun* **1** a legal agreement by which a financial institution grants a client a loan for the purpose of buying property, ownership of the property being held by the institution until the loan is repaid. **2** the money borrowed, or the regular amounts repaid. **3** any loan for which property is used as security. — *verb* to give ownership of (property) as security for a loan. [from French *mort,* dead + *gage,* pledge]

mortgage interest relief at source *see* MIRAS.

mortice same as MORTISE.

mortician *noun North Amer., esp. US* an undertaker. [from Latin *mortis,* death]

Mortier, Edouard Adolphe Casimir Joseph, Duc de Trevise (Duke of Treviso) (1768–1835) French soldier who fought in the Revolutionary and Napoleonic Wars, born in Cateau-Cambrésis. Promoted to general (1799) and Marshal of the Empire (1804), he campaigned in Germany, Russia, and Spain. He was Prime Minister and Minister of War (1834–5) under Louis Philippe, and was killed during an assassination attempt on the King.

mortification *noun* the act of mortifying or the state of being mortified.

mortify *verb* (**mortifies, mortified**) **1** to cause to feel humiliated or ashamed. **2** *Relig.* to control (physical desire) through self-discipline or self-inflicted hardship: *mortify the flesh.* **3** *intrans. said of a limb* to suffer from gangrene. [from Latin *mortificare,* to cause death to]

Mortimer, John (Clifford) (1923–) English playwright and novelist, born in London. He became a barrister, and came to prominence as a playwright with his one-act play *The Dock Brief* (1957), followed by *The Wrong Side of the Park* (1960) and *A Voyage Round My Father* (1970). He is best known for his series of televised novels about the disreputable barrister Horace Rumpole, which began with *Rumpole of the Bailey* (1978). Other novels include *Paradise Postponed* (1985) and *Summer's Lease* (1988).

mortise — *noun* a hole cut in a piece of wood, into which a tenon, or shaped end of a second piece, fits to form a mortise and tenon joint. — *verb* to cut a mortise in; to join with a mortise and tenon joint. [from Old French *mortoise*]

mortise lock a lock fitted into a hole cut in the side edge of a door, rather than on to the door's surface.

Morton, James Douglas, 4th Earl of (c.1525–81) Regent of Scotland (1572–8) for James VI. Although a Protestant, he was made Lord High Chancellor by Mary, Queen of Scots (1563). He led the Protestant nobles at Carberry Hill and Langside, and succeeded Moray as regent. His previous involvement in the murders of Rizzio (1566) and Darnley (1567), together with his high-handed treatment of the nobles and Presbyterian clergy, led ultimately to his execution.

Morton, Jelly Roll, originally **Ferdinand LaMenthe,** or **Lamothe** (1890–1941) US jazz composer, bandleader, and pianist, born in Gulfport, Louisiana. His genius as a jazz pioneer comes from his recordings (1923–7) while living in Chicago, and his unaccompanied piano solos made bestsellers of such tunes as 'King Porter Stomp', 'Wolverine Blues', and 'Jelly Roll Blues'. He formed the recording band the 'Red Hot Peppers' (1926), probably the first in jazz to combine arranged ensemble passages with collective improvisation and improvised solos.

Morton, John (c.1420–1500) English statesman and cardinal, born (probably) in Milborne St Andrew, Dorset. A trained lawyer, he was faithful to Henry VI until after the Lancastrian defeat at the battle of Tewkesbury (1471), when he made his peace with Edward IV, and became

Master of the Rolls (1473) and Bishop of Ely (1479). Richard III imprisoned him (1483), but he escaped, and after the accession of Henry VII was made Archbishop of Canterbury (1486), Chancellor (1487), and cardinal (1493).

Morton of Milnwood, Henry the moderate, sincere hero of Sir Walter Scott's *Old Mortality*, who reluctantly becomes involved with the Covenanters, jeopardising his chances with Edith Bellenden.

mortuary *noun* (PL. **mortuaries**) a building or room where corpses are kept until buried or cremated. [from Latin *mortuarius*, of the dead]

Mosaic *adj.* relating to Moses, or the laws attributed to him.

mosaic *noun* a design formed by fitting together small pieces of coloured stone or glass. [from French *mosaïque*]

Mosan school a style of illuminated Romanesque manuscript popular in France during the 11c–12c, especially in the Meuse River valley region. Leading artists included Godefroid de Claire and Nicholas of Verdun, and major works of Mosan art include the Stavelot Bible (British Museum, London).

Mosca Volpone's devious, flattering parasite in Ben Jonson's *Volpone*.

Moscow, Russian **Moskva** POP (1991e) 8.8m, the capital of Russia and of Moscow oblast, lying on the R Moskva. It is Russia's largest city and its political, cultural, industrial, and commercial centre. HISTORY became capital of the principality of Muscovy in the 13c; invaded by Napoleon in 1812; became capital of the Russian SFSR in 1918 and was capital of the USSR from 1922 until the dissolution of the Soviet Union in 1991; an attempt by German troops to capture the city in 1941 was stopped by Soviet forces. NOTABLE FEATURES Moscow Art Theatre; Bolshoi Theatre of Opera and Ballet; Moscow State Circus; Kremlin (1300); Spassky Tower (symbol of Moscow and the Soviet state); Cathedral of the Assumption (1475–9), Cathedral of the Archangel (1333, rebuilt 1505–9), Cathedral of the Annunciation; Great Palace (1838–49), Palace of Facets (1487–91); Armoury (1849–51); Palace of the Patriarchs (17c); Red Square; St Basil's Cathedral (16c, now a museum); numerous theatres, art galleries, museums, notably the Museum of the Revolution.

Moscow Art Theatre a prestigious Russian theatrical institution, which began as a company of student and amateur actors, founded in 1898 by Stanislavsky and Nemirovich-Danchenko, who advocated theatre as a serious and important art. Its fame rests also on its innovative productions of Chekhov and Gorki, and on its studios, which were established from 1913 onwards for training and experimental work.

Mosel, River *or* **Moselle**, ancient **Mosella** a river in Germany, Luxembourg, and NE France. It is 514km/319mi long and is navigable for 240km/150mi. Rising in the French Vosges, it flows N and NE to enter the R Rhine at Coblenz. The Mosel has been canalized since 1964, with a series of 10 dams to regulate its flow. It is a major wine-producing area.

Moseley, Harry (Henry Gwyn Jeffreys) (1887–1915) English physicist, born in Weymouth. Educated at Oxford, he joined Ernest Rutherford in Manchester before returning to the Oxford in 1913. He determined by means of X-ray spectra the atomic numbers of the elements, firmly establishing that the properties of the chemical elements are based on atomic number rather than atomic weight, and revealed gaps in the periodic table corresponding to elements not yet discovered. He was killed in action at Gallipoli.

moselle *noun* (*often* **Moselle**) a dry German white wine from the regions around the river *Mosel* or *Moselle*.

Moser-Pröll, Annemarie, *née* **Pröll** (1953–) Austrian alpine skier, born in Kleinarl. She won a women's record 62 World Cup races (1970–9), and was overall champion (1979), downhill champion (1978, 1979), Olympic downhill champion (1980), world combined champion (1972, 1978), and world downhill champion (1974, 1978, 1980). She temporarily retired in 1975–6, and finally retired after the 1980 Olympics.

Moses, Hebrew *Môsheh* (c.13c–15c BC) a biblical character, a prophet and lawgiver, who escaped the slaughter of all male Jewish babies by being found by one of Pharoah's daughters and brought up in the Egyptian court. He fled to Midian and was called by God to lead the enslaved Hebrews out of Egypt, which involved the miraculous crossing of Red Sea (Exodus 14). Moses was leader of the Israelites during their 40 years of wilderness wanderings, and received the revelation of the Ten Commandments on Mt Sinai (Exodus 20). He was traditionally considered the author of the five books of the Law, the Pentateuch of the Hebrew Bible.

Moses, Ed(win) (1955–) US track athlete, born in Dayton, Ohio. A 400m hurdler, between Aug 1977 and Jun 1987 he ran a record 122 races without defeat. He was the World Cup gold medal winner in 1977, 1979, and 1981, the world champion in 1983, and Olympic champion in 1976 and 1984. He won the bronze medal at the 1988 Olympics. Between 1976 and 1983 he broke the world record four times.

Moses a sculpture by Michelangelo (c.1513–15). It is one of the surviving pieces from the uncompleted tomb of Pope Julius II.

Moses and Aaron (Moses und Aron) an opera by Arnold Schoenberg (1954), based on the book of Exodus. The story is about Moses being appointed as prophet to receive God's word on the Mountain of Revelation (Sinai), whilst his more eloquent but less spiritual brother Aaron misguidedly provides a golden calf for the people to worship, much to Moses' dismay on his return. The last act is spoken, as the music was left incomplete.

Moses basket a portable cot for babies. [referring to the biblical story of Moses in the bulrushes]

mosey *verb intrans.* (**moseys**, **moseyed**, **moseying**) (*usually* **mosey along**) *colloq.* to walk in a leisurely way; to saunter or amble. [origin uncertain]

moshing *noun* a style of energtic and sinuous dancing done in a crowded space to heavy metal or thrash music. [perhaps a mixture of SQUASH and MASH]

Moslem see MUSLIM.

Mosley, Sir Oswald (Ernald), 6th Baronet (1896–1980) English politician, born in London. He was successively a Conservative, Independent, and Labour MP, and a member of the 1929 Labour government. He resigned from Labour, and founded the New Party (1931). Following a visit to Italy, he became the founding Leader of the British Union of Fascists (1932–40), and its successor, the Union Movement (from 1948), groups known for their violent anti-Semitic stance.

mosque *noun* a Muslim place of worship. [from Arabic *masjid*]

mosquito *noun* (PL. **mosquitos**, **mosquitoes**) any of about 2 500 species of small two-winged insects belonging to the family Culicidae, and having thin feathery antennae, long legs, and a slender body, distributed worldwide, although most species live in tropical regions. They transmit several serious diseases, including malaria and yellow fever. [from Spanish, a diminutive of *mosca*, fly]

◇ Female mosquitos suck the blood of birds and mammals, including humans, through their piercing needle-like mouthparts. At the same time, they secrete a substance that prevents the blood from clotting immediately, and this is responsible for the irritation produced by many mosquito bites. Male mosquitos do not have piercing mouthparts, and they feed on nectar. The females lay eggs, either singly or in raft-like masses, on the surface of water, and the larvae that hatch from the eggs develop into comma-shaped pupae which hang suspended from the water surface. The adult mosquitos can fly as soon as they break out of the pupal cases.

Mosquito Coast an undeveloped, lowland area in E Honduras and E Nicaragua, Central America. It follows the Caribbean coast in a 65km-/40mi-wide strip of tropical forest, lagoons, and swamp. Miskitos are native to the area. HISTORY a British protectorate from 1687 until 1860, with a succession of 'Mosquito kings' being appointed.

mosquito net a fine net designed to keep away mosquitos, especially hung over a bed at night.

Moss, Stirling (1929–) English racing driver, born in London. He won many major races in the 1950s, including the British Grand Prix (1955, 1957), the Mille Miglia, and the Targa Florio. Between 1951–61, he won 16 races from 66 starts. He retired in 1962 after a crash at Goodwood. He then became a journalist and broadcaster, and returned to saloon car racing in 1980.

moss *noun* **1** the common name for any plant belonging to the class Musci, which consists of about 10 000 species of small spore-bearing bryophytes without a vascular system, closely related to liverworts, and typically found growing in dense spreading clusters in moist shady habitats, such as damp ground, rocks, and tree trunks, although some species prefer dry conditions. **2** any of various unrelated plants which superficially resemble true moss, eg clubmoss (a vascular plant), Irish moss (an alga). **3** *dialect* an area of boggy ground. [from Anglo-Saxon *mos*, bog]

◇ Mosses, like all bryophytes, show *alternation of generations*. The visible plant is the *gametophyte* (which bears gametes), that develops from a filamentous structure (a *protonema*) resembling a green alga. The gametophyte has erect or prostrate stems, simple delicate leaves, and multicellular root-like structures or *rhizoids*. The *sporophyte* (which bears spores) arises from the stem of the gametophyte, and consists of a stalk bearing a capsule that contains numerous spores, which are released via pores or slits, or in some species explosively, and develop into new plants.

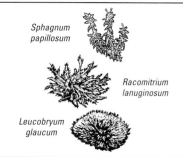

Sphagnum papillosum

Racomitrium lanuginosum

Leucobryum glaucum

mosses

MOSSAD *noun* the Israeli state intelligence service, formed in 1951. [from Hebrew *Mossad le Alujeh Beth*, Committee for Illegal Immigration, the original name of the organization, founded in 1937 to oversee illegal Jewish immigration into Palestine]

Mössbauer, Rudolf Ludwig (1929–) German physicist, born in Munich. While a student, he observed what is known as the 'Mössbauer effect' concerning the interaction of gamma radiation with crystals. He shared the 1961 Nobel Prize for Physics with Robert Hofstadter, and has since held professorships in Munich and at the California Institute of Technology.

Mossmorran an industrial location in Fife region, Scotland. Fractionation and ethylene plants, converting North Sea natural gas liquids into products for the chemical industry, are linked by pipeline to St Fergus in Grampian region and on to the Brent gas field in the North Sea.

mossy *adj.* (**mossier, mossiest**) **1** covered with moss. **2** like moss. **3** boggy.

most — *adj.* the greatest part, amount, or number (of): *most children enjoy parties / who can count the most sheep?* — *adv.* **1** (*also* **the most**) used to form the superlative of many adjectives and adverbs, especially those of more than two syllables. **2** (**the most**) to the greatest degree; with the greatest frequency. **3** extremely. — *pron.* the greatest number or quantity, or the majority of people or things: *most of them are here / who has the most?* — ... **at the most** certainly not more than ...: *three at the most.* **for the most part** mostly. **make the most of something** to take the greatest possible advantage of it. [from Anglo-Saxon *mast* or *mæst*]

-most *combining form* forming words meaning 'furthest in a particular direction': *southernmost.*

Mostaganem 1 POP (1987) 114 000, the seaport capital of Mostaganem department, NW Algeria. It is 72km/45mi NE of Oran. HISTORY founded in the 11c; occupied by France in 1833. The capital has expanded since the beginning of the 20c as a result of the development of port facilities. **2** a department in NW Algeria with the port of Mostaganem as its capital.

Mostar a town in S Bosnia-Herzegovina, situated on the R Neretva and regarded as the gateway to central Bosnia. The most fought-over area in Bosnia, in 1992–3 it suffered a relentless siege by Serbo-Croat forces who wanted to have the town as their new capital. Although two thirds of the 80 000 population had fled in early 1992, by the end of 1993 there were 55 000 Bosnian Muslims (including 30 000 refugees) trapped in E Mostar. During the heavy fighting the Stari Most, a spectacular bridge designed by the Turkish architect Hajrudin and built (1566) using mortar made from egg whites and goats' hair, was destroyed.

mostly *adv.* usually; mainly.

Mosul POP (1985e) 571 000, the capital of Neineva governorate, NW Iraq. It is situated on the W bank of the R Tigris, 352km/219mi NW of Baghdad. Mosul was the chief town of N Mesopotamia from the 8c until the 13c. NOTABLE FEATURE the ruins of ancient Nineveh are located nearby.

MOT *noun Brit.* an official annual test of roadworthiness, required by the Department (formerly Ministry) of Transport on all vehicles over three years old; the certificate supplied on successful completion of this.

mote *noun* a speck, especially of dust. [from Anglo-Saxon *mot*]

motel *noun* a hotel near a main road, intended for overnight stops by motorists, with extensive parking facilities. [from *motor hotel*]

motet *noun* a short piece of sacred music for several voices. [from Old French, diminutive of *mot*, word]

moth *noun* the common name for any of about 130 000 species of winged insect belonging to the same order (Lepidoptera) as butterflies, and, apart from a few species in which the female is wingless, having four broad wings covered with tiny overlapping scales.

◇ Moths usually have a feeding tube (known as a *proboscis*) for sucking nectar from flowers, although a number of moths have no proboscis and do not feed in the adult state. In some moths the proboscis is several centimetres long, and when not in use is coiled up like a watch spring under the head. Unlike butterflies, most moths do not have clubbed antennae, and when resting they fold their wings down. In general, they are duller in colour than butterflies, and fly by night rather than during the day, but there are exceptions. The life history of the moth consists of four stages (egg, caterpillar, chrysalis, and adult). [from Anglo-Saxon *moththe*]

mothball *noun* a small ball of camphor or naphthalene hung in wardrobes, etc to keep away clothes moths.

moth-eaten *adj.* **1** *said of cloth* damaged by clothes moths. **2** *colloq.* old and worn.

mother — *noun* **1** a female parent. **2** (**Mother** *or* **Mother Superior**) the head of a female religious (especially Christian) community. **3** the cause or origin: *necessity is the mother of invention.* — *adj.* like a mother in being protective, or being a source from which others spring: *Mother Church.* — *verb* **1** to give birth to; to give rise to. **2** to treat with (excessive) care and protection. [from Anglo-Saxon *modor*]

motherboard *noun* a printed circuit board that can be plugged into the back of a computer, and into which other boards can be slotted to allow the computer to operate various peripherals.

mother country 1 a person's native country. **2** the country that pilgrims leave to settle elsewhere.

Mother Courage and Her Children (Mutter Courage und ihre Kinder) a play by Bertolt Brecht (1939). Set during the Thirty Years War, it apparently focuses on a canteen-woman's actions, but is in fact a discussion of wartime responsibilities, comparing an individual's smallest act of support to a country's worst atrocities, and exposing war in all its cruelty.

motherese *noun* the speech used by adults to young children while they are learning to speak, typically consisting of shorter expressions than those normally used by adults, with clear pronunciation, often with exaggerated intonation patterns.

Mother Goose rhymes in the US, the name for nursery rhymes, taken from *Mother Goose's Melody*, a US rhyme-collection of 1780. The name derives ultimately from *Tales of Mother Goose*, the title of Charles Perrault's book of fairy tales (1697).

motherhood *noun* being a mother.

Mothering Sunday the fourth Sunday in Lent, traditionally a day on which children honour their mothers with gifts (see also MOTHER'S DAY).

mother-in-law *noun* (PL. **mothers-in-law**) the mother of one's husband or wife.

motherland *noun* a person's native country.

Mother Lode the gold-mining region in the W foothills of the Sierra Nevada, California, USA. It was the centre of the Californian gold rush, with peak production in 1852.

motherly *adj.* like or characteristic of a mother.

mother-of-pearl *noun* a hard shiny iridescent substance, consisting mainly of calcium carbonate, that forms the inner layer of the shell of certain bivalve molluscs, eg oysters. It is used to make buttons, beads, etc.

Mother's Day a day set apart in honour of mothers. In the USA, Canada, and Australia, it is the second Sunday in May; in the UK, it is Mothering Sunday.

mother tongue one's native language.

Motherwell POP (1981) 31 000, the capital of Motherwell district, Strathclyde, central Scotland. It lies 20km/12mi SE of Glasgow. In 1920 it united with Wishaw burgh. Pilgrimages are made to the Grotto of Our Lady of Lourdes at Carfin, 3km/2mi N.

mothproof *adj., said of cloth* treated with chemicals which resist attack by clothes moths. — *verb* to treat in this way.

motif *noun* **1** a shape repeated many times within a pattern; a single design or symbol, eg on clothing. **2** something often repeated throughout a work or works of art, eg a passage of music in a symphony, or a theme in a novel. [from French *motif*, motive]

motile *adj. Biol.* describing a living organism or a structure that is capable of spontaneous movement, eg spermatozoa. [from Latin *motus*, movement]

motion — *noun* **1** the act, state, or way of moving. **2** a single movement, especially of the body. **3** the ability to move a part of the body. **4** a proposal for formal discussion at a meeting. **5** *Medicine* an act of discharging faeces; (**motions**) faeces. — *verb trans., intrans.* (**motioned, motioning**) (**motion to someone**) to give them a signal or direction. — **go through the motions** to pretend; to perform a task mechanically or half-heartedly. **in motion** moving. [from Latin *motio*, from *movere*, to move]

motionless *adj.* without moving, completely still.

motion picture *North Amer., esp. US* a cinema film.

motivate *verb* **1** to be the motive of. **2** to cause or stimulate (a person) to act; to be the underlying cause of (action).

motivation *noun* motivating force, incentive.

motive — *noun* a reason for, or underlying cause of, action of a certain kind. — *adj.* **1** causing motion: *motive power.* **2** stimulating action: *motive force.* [from Latin *motivus*, from *movere*, to move]

motley — *adj.* **1** made up of many different kinds: *a motley crew.* **2** many-coloured. — *noun* a jester's multicoloured costume. [perhaps from Anglo-Saxon *mot*, speck]

motocross *noun* a form of motorcycle racing in which specially adapted motor cycles compete across rough terrain. Competitions are usually organized according to engine size. The first race was held at Camberley, Surrey in 1924.

motor — *noun* **1** *Electr.* a device that converts electrical energy into mechanical energy, using the forces that act on a current-carrying conductor, eg a coil, in the presence of a magnetic field. Motors are used in domestic appliances, eg vacuum cleaners, electric razors, and in large industrial motors for driving heavy machinery, electric trains, etc. **2** an engine, especially the internal combustion engine of a vehicle or machine. **3** *colloq.* a car. — *adj.* **1** of or relating to cars or other road vehicles: *a motor show.* **2** driven by a motor: *a motor boat.* **3** *Anat.* denoting a nerve that transmits impulses from the central nervous system (the brain and spinal cord) to a muscle or gland. **4** *Anat.* denoting a neurone (nerve cell) that forms part of such a nerve. — *verb intrans.* (**motored, motoring**) **1** to travel by motor vehicle, especially by private car. **2** *colloq.* to move, work, etc fast and effectively. [from Latin, from *movere*, to move]

motorbike *noun colloq.* a motorcycle.

motorcade *noun* a procession of cars carrying important (especially political) figures.

motor car a motor vehicle, usually four-wheeled, for carrying a small number of people. ◇ Karl Benz produced the first petrol-driven motor car in 1885. The first car produced by assembly-line methods was the Model T Ford, of which 15 million were made between 1908 and 1927. After World War II, the manufacture of small family saloon cars made car-ownership affordable for a greater number of people, and until the 1970s the world market was dominated by the large US and European manufacturers. The Japanese challenged these companies in their own countries, and this led to a series of amalgamations into larger multinationals, including the Japanese, in the 1980s. Modern car design emphasizes fuel efficiency and pollution control: research into non-fossil fuels, such as electricity, has produced several practical alternatives to the petrol-driven standard motor car, though none has yet been sufficiently adaptable to challenge it, except in specialist roles.

motorcycle *noun* any two-wheeled road vehicle powered by a petrol engine. See also MOTORCYCLE RACING.
◇ Motorcycles became a practical proposition when Gottlieb Daimler fitted a lightweight petrol engine to a bicycle frame in 1885. Commercial production began in the early 1900s (eg by Triumph in the UK and Harley Davidson in the USA): by the 1960s the market was dominated by the Japanese manufacturers (eg Honda and Yamaha). Motorcycles use either a two-stroke or four-stroke internal combustion engine, and larger machines may have up to six cylinders.

motorcycle racing the racing of motorcycles, first organized (1906) by the Automobile Club de France, from Paris to Nantes and back. The most famous races are the TT (Tourist Trophy) races; first held in 1907, they take place annually in Jun on the roads of the Isle of Man. A season-long grand prix world championship takes place each year, and a series of races is held for each of the following engine-size categories: 80cc, 250cc, 500cc, and sidecar. Other forms of motorcycle racing include speedway moto-cross (scrambling) and motorcycle trials riding.

motorcyclist *noun* a person who drives a motorcycle.

motoring *noun* travelling by car, especially for pleasure.

motorist *noun* a person who drives a car.

motorize *or* **motorise** *verb* 1 to fit a motor to. 2 to supply (eg soldiers) with motor vehicles.

motor neurone *Anat.* a nerve cell that carries impulses from the spinal cord or the brain to an effector organ such as a muscle or gland.

motor racing the racing of finely-tuned motor cars, either purpose-built or modified production vehicles. The most popular form of motor racing is Formula One grand prix racing for high-powered purpose-built cars which can average more than 240kph/150mph. A season-long world championship (Mar–Nov) involves usually 16 races at different venues worldwide. Other popular forms include formula 3000, formula three, rallying, sports car, Indy car racing in the USA, Formula Ford, hill climbing, and production car races.

motorway *noun* a major dual-carriageway road for fast-moving traffic, especially one with three lanes per carriageway.

Motown *noun* a style of music combining the styles of pop and rhythm and blues. [from *Motor Town*, a nickname for Detroit in the USA, where it originated in the early 1960s]

Mott, Lucretia (1793–1880) US abolitionist and feminist, born in Nantucket, Massachusetts. A Quaker, she became deeply involved in anti-slavery agitation in the 1830s by helping to organize the American Anti-Slavery Society (1833) and the Anti-Slavery Convention of American Women (1837). She was a driving force at the world's first women's rights convention, held at Seneca Falls, New York (1848).

Mott, Sir Nevill Francis (1905–) English physicist, born in Leeds. Professor at Bristol and

Cambridge, he shared the 1977 Nobel Prize for Physics with Philip Anderson and John van Vleck for his work on the electronic properties of materials.

motte and bailey an earth and timber fortification commonly built by the Normans and consisting of an artificial mound (*motte*) surrounded by a ditch, with a walled outer court (*bailey*) adjoining it to one side. Four examples are depicted on the Bayeux Tapestry, and it was widely used in England in the late 11c and 12c. [from Old French *mote*; see BAILEY]

mottled *adj.* with a pattern of different coloured blotches or streaks. [probably from MOTLEY]

motto *noun* (PL. **mottos**, **mottoes**) 1 a phrase adopted as a principle of behaviour. 2 a printed phrase or verse contained in a paper cracker. 3 a quotation at the beginning of a book or chapter, hinting at what is to follow. [from Italian, from Latin *muttum*, utterance]

mould¹ *noun* 1 any of various fungi that produce an abundant woolly network (or *mycelium*) of thread-like strands (or *hypae*), which may be white, grey-green, or black in colour. Many moulds can cause food spoilage, and release toxic substances known as *mycotoxins* into infected food, but some of them, eg *Penicillium* species, are used in the ripening of cheese and the production of antibiotics, eg penicillin. 2 a loose soft soil rich in decayed organic matter. [from Middle English *mowle*]

mould² — *noun* 1 a hollow shaped container into which a liquid substance is poured to take on the container's shape when it cools and sets. 2 food, eg a pudding, shaped in such a container. 3 nature, character or personality. 4 a framework on which certain manufactured objects are built up. — *verb* 1 to shape using a mould. 2 to shape (a substance) with the hands; to form by shaping a substance with the hands. 3 *intrans., trans.* to fit or cause to fit tightly. 4 to exercise a controlling influence over the development of. [from Latin *modulus*, measure]

mould³ *noun* loose soft earth, especially rich in decayed matter: *leaf mould.* [from Anglo-Saxon *molde*]

moulder *verb intrans.* (*also* **moulder away**) to become gradually rotten with age; to decay.

moulding *noun* 1 a shaped decorative strip, especially of wood or plaster. 2 a technique used to convert molten plastics, clay, glass, brick, and other materials into specific three-dimensional shapes by using hollow moulds and applying heat or pressure. The moulding of metals is known as casting.

mouldy *adj.* (**mouldier**, **mouldiest**) 1 covered with mould; old and stale. 2 *derog. colloq.* a general term of dislike: *I don't want your mouldy advice.*

Moulin Rouge a Parisian dance hall, opened in 1899. It became known as an early venue featuring the can-can, as well as for Mistinguett's management and Toulouse-Lautrec's advertisements.

moult — *verb intrans.*, said of an animal to shed feathers, hair, or skin to make way for a new growth. — *noun* the process of moulting, or the time taken to moult. [from Anglo-Saxon *mutian*, to exchange]

mound *noun* 1 any small hill, or bank of earth or rock, natural or man-made. 2 a heap or pile.

mount¹ — *verb* 1 *trans., intrans. formal* to go up: *mount stairs.* 2 *trans., intrans.* to get up on (eg a horse). 3 *intrans.* (*also* **mount up**) to increase in level or intensity. 4 to put in a frame or on a background for display; to hang or put up on a stand or support. 5 to organize or hold (a campaign, etc). 6 to carry out (eg an attack). — *noun* 1 a support or backing on which a thing is placed for display. 2 *formal* a horse that is ridden. [from Old French *monter*, to go up]

mount² *noun poetic* (*also* **Mount** *in place-names*) a mountain. [from Latin *montis*]

Mountain, The a group of Jacobin extremist Deputies in the French Convention, led by Robespierre, so-called because they sat on the highest tiers of seats in the chamber, where they overlooked their political opponents, the Girondins, and the uncommitted majority who were known collectively as 'the Plain'.

mountain *noun* 1 a very high steep hill, often of bare rock. 2 *colloq.* a great quantity; a heap or mass. 3 a huge surplus of some commodity.
— **make a mountain out of a molehill** to exaggerate the seriousness or importance of a trivial matter.
[from Latin *mons*]

Highest Mountains	
	Height m
Asia	
Everest (Himalaya-Nepal/Tibet)	8 848
K2 (Pakistan/India)	8 611
Kangchenjunga (Himalaya-Nepal/India)	8 586
Makalu (Himalaya-Nepal/Tibet)	8 475
Dhaulagiri (Himalaya-Nepal)	8 167
Nanga Parbat (Himalaya-India)	8 126
Annapurna (Himalaya-Nepal)	8 091
South America	
Aconcagua (Andes-Argentina)	6 960
North America	
McKinley (Alaska Range)	6 194
Africa	
Kilimanjaro (Tanzania)	5 895
Europe	
Elbruz (Caucasus)	5 642
Mont Blanc (Alps-France)	4 807
Antarctica	
Vinson Massif	5 140
Australasia	
Jaja (New Guinea)	5 029

mountain ash the rowan, a tree of the rose family, with feather-shaped leaves and red berries.

mountain beaver a squirrel-like rodent, native to the Pacific coast of N America, the most primitive living rodent, and not a true beaver. It has a stocky body with a minute hairy tail, and a white spot under each ear. It lives in burrows in cool moist regions (not necessarily mountains).

mountain bike a sturdy bicycle with thick, deep-tread tyres and straight handlebars.

mountain dew whisky, especially when made illicitly.

mountaineer — *noun* a person skilled in climbing mountains. — *verb intrans.* to climb mountains.

mountaineering *noun* the sport of climbing mountains, usually aided by ropes and other accessories, such as crampons. In the UK, the most popular form is rock climbing, with snow and ice climbing being practised mainly on the higher peaks of the world. Since all the highest peaks have now been conquered, modern mountaineers frequently aim to climb previously untried routes. Skilled rock climbers are increasingly attempting long and difficult ascents with the minimum of equipment, often carrying only powdered chalk to prevent their hands from becoming slippery.

mountain lion *noun* a puma.

mountainous *adj.* 1 containing many mountains. 2 huge.

mountain sickness feelings of nausea and light-headedness as a result of breathing low-oxygen mountain air.

Mount Athos, Greek **Agíon Óros** POP (1991) 2 000, an autonomous administration in Macedonia region, Greece. AREA 336sq km/130sq mi. Mt Athos, rising to 1 956m, is the 'Holy Mountain' of the Greek Church, and has been associated with the monastic order of St Basil since the 9c. The area was declared a theocratic republic in 1927.

Mountbatten (of Burma), Louis (Francis Albert Victor Nicholas) Mountbatten, 1st Earl (1900–79) English admiral of the fleet and statesman, born in Windsor, Berkshire, the younger son of Prince Louis of Battenberg (later Louis Mountbatten, Marquess of Milford Haven) and Princess Victoria of Hesse, the granddaughter of Queen Victoria. He joined the Royal Navy in 1916 and in World War II became chief of Combined Operations Command (1942). In 1943 he was appointed Supreme Commander, SE Asia, where he defeated the Japanese offensive into India (1944), and worked closely with Field Marshal Slim to reconquer Burma (1945). He received the Japanese surrender at Singapore, and in 1947 was sworn in as last Viceroy of India prior to independence. Created an earl in 1947, he returned to the Admiralty, and became First Sea Lord (1954) and Chief of the Defence Staff (1959). He retired in 1965 but remained in the public eye, and was assassinated by terrorists while fishing near his summer home at Mullaghmoor, in the Irish Republic.

mountebank *noun literary derog.* **1** originally, a person who sells quack medicines from a public platform. **2** any person who swindles or deceives. [from Italian *montimbanco*, a person who mounts a bench]

mounted *adj.* **1** on horseback. **2** hung on a wall, or placed in a frame or on a background.

Mountie *or* **Mounty** *noun* (PL. **Mounties**) *colloq.* a member of the Royal Canadian Mounted Police.

Mounties *or* **The Royal Canadian Mounted Police** the force was founded (1873) as the Royal North-West Mounted Police by Lt-Col George Arthur French, who recruited mainly from the British Army. They retained the red jackets and pillbox hats and, organized on strictly military lines, established tight control over the new territories. In the North-West, the Department of Northern Affairs took over most of their civic duties (1953), and in the other provinces the Mounties were amalgamated with the federal Dominion Police (1920) and became the Royal Canadian Mounted Police. In 1928 Saskatchewan contracted the RCMP to provide a police force, followed by Alberta and other provinces, but Ontario and Quebec have not followed their example.

Mount Vernon the family home of George Washington on the Potomac River in Virginia. The 18c building and its gardens have been restored and decorated as in Washington's time, and his tomb is in the grounds. It is one of the most visited historic sites in the USA.

mourn *verb trans., intrans.* (**mourn for** *or* **over someone** *or* **something**) to feel or show deep sorrow at the death or loss of a person or thing. [from Anglo-Saxon *murnan*]

Mourne Mountains a granitic mountain range in SE Co Down, SE Northern Ireland. It extends 24km/15mi from Carlingford Lough in the NE to Dundrum Bay, and rises to 852m at Slieve Donard. Most of Belfast's water supply comes from these mountains.

mourner *noun* **1** a person who mourns. **2** a person attending a funeral.

mournful *adj.* **1** feeling or expressing grief. **2** suggesting sadness or gloom.

mournfully *adv.* in a mournful way.

mourning *noun* **1** grief felt or shown over a death. **2** a symbol of grief, especially a black costume or armband; a period of time during which such symbols are worn.

Mourning Becomes Electra a trilogy in 13 acts by Eugene O'Neill (1921–31). Based on the *Oresteia* by Aeschylus, it is set in Puritan New England and depicts the incestuous and extra-marital relationships pursued by various characters.

mouse — *noun* (PL. **mice**) **1** any of various small rodents, especially members of the genus *Mus*, found worldwide, and having a grey or brown coat, a pointed muzzle and bright eyes, sharp teeth, and a long naked tail. **2** *colloq.* a very shy quiet person. **3** *Comput.* a computer input device which can be moved around on a flat surface, causing a cursor to move around the computer screen in response. It usually has at least one selection button, and can be used to choose one of a number of specified options displayed. — *verb intrans., said of an animal* to hunt mice. [from Anglo-Saxon *mus*]
◇ Mice feed mainly on plant material, and are often pests, eg of stored foodstuffs, and transmitters of disease. Despite the fact that they have many predators, including hawks, owls, weasels, foxes, and cats, their ability to produce large litters of young several times a year ensures that they remain numerous. The house mouse (*Mus musculus*) is found worldwide in association with humans, and albino strains of this species are widely used as laboratory animals in scientific research.

mouse deer see CHEVROTAIN.

mouse-milking *noun* the pursuit of a project requiring considerable time and money but yielding little profit. [referring to scientific efforts in the 1990s to produce human proteins in the milk of mice which had been injected with human genes]

mouser *noun* a cat used for catching mice.

mousetrap *noun* **1** a mechanical trap for catching and often killing mice. **2** *old colloq. use* poor quality cheese.

mousiness *noun* being mousy.

moussaka *noun* an oven-cooked dish of minced meat and vegetables covered with a cheese sauce, traditionally eaten in Greece. [from modern Greek *moussaka*]

mousse *noun* **1** a dessert made from a whipped mixture of cream, eggs and flavouring, eaten cold. **2** a similar meat or fish dish. **3** (*also* **styling mousse**) a frothy chemical preparation applied to hair to make styling easier. [from French *mousse*, froth]

moustache *noun* a line of unshaved hair above a man's upper lip. [from French, from Italian *mostaccio*]

mousy *or* **mousey** *adj.* (**mousier, mousiest**) **1** of or like a mouse: *mousy smells.* **2** *said of hair* of a dull light brown colour. **3** shy or quiet, especially tiresomely so.

mouth — *noun* **1** in humans, animals, etc, an opening in the head through which food is taken in and speech or sounds emitted; in other creatures, an opening with similar functions. **2** the lips; the outer visible parts of the mouth. **3** an opening, eg of a bottle. **4** the part of a river that widens to meet the sea. **5** a person considered as a consumer of food: *five mouths to feed.* **6** *derog. colloq.* boastful talk. **7** backchat or cheek: *don't want any of your mouth.* **8** *derog. colloq.* a person who talks too much, especially indiscreetly. — *verb* **1** to form (words) without actually speaking. **2** *trans., intrans. derog.* to speak (words) pompously or without sincerity.
— **down in the mouth** *colloq.* dejected; unhappy.
[from Anglo-Saxon *muth*]

-mouthed *combining form* forming words meaning: **1** using a certain kind of language: *foul-*

mouthed. **2** having a certain kind of mouth: *wide-mouthed.*

mouthfeel *noun* the sensory perception of a particular food while being chewed or tasted in the mouth.

mouthful *noun* (PL. **mouthfuls**) **1** as much as fills the mouth. **2** a small quantity, especially of food. **3** *colloq.* a word or phrase difficult to pronounce. **4** *colloq.* an outburst of forceful, often abusive language.

mouth organ a harmonica.

mouthpiece *noun* **1** the part of a musical instrument, telephone receiver, tobacco pipe, etc held in or against the mouth. **2** a person or publication expressing the views of a group.

mouth-to-mouth *adj.* denoting a method of resuscitation in which air is breathed directly into the mouth of the person to be revived.

mouthwash *noun* an antiseptic liquid gargled to freshen the mouth.

mouth-watering *adj.* **1** *said of food* having a delicious appearance or smell. **2** *colloq.* highly desirable.

movable *or* **moveable** *adj.* **1** not fixed in one place; portable. **2** *said of a religious festival* taking place on a different date each year: *Easter is a movable feast.*

move — *verb* **1** *trans., intrans.* to change or cause to change position or go from one place to another. **2** *intrans.* to make progress of any kind: *move towards a political solution.* **3** (**move on, out, away**, *etc, or* **move house**) to change (one's place of living, working, operating, etc). **4** to affect the feelings or emotions of. **5** (**move someone to do something**) to affect them so as to do it: *what moved him to say that?* **6** *trans., intrans.* to change the position of (a piece in a board game). **7** *intrans., trans. formal* (**move for something**) to propose or request it formally. **8** *intrans.* to spend time; to associate with people: *move in fashionable circles.* **9** *intrans. colloq.* to progress speedily. **10** *trans., intrans. colloq.* to sell or be sold. **11** *trans., intrans. said of the bowels* to be evacuated or cause them to be evacuated. — *noun* **1** an act of moving the body. **2** an act of moving a piece in a board game, or the rules governing how the pieces are moved; any of a series of actions taken as part of an overall strategy. **3** an act of changing homes.
— **get a move on** *or* **get moving** *colloq.* to hurry up.
make a move 1 to take a step; to begin to proceed. **2** *colloq.* to leave.
move heaven and earth to make strenuous efforts to achieve something.
move in to begin to occupy new premises.
move in on someone 1 to advance towards them, especially threateningly. **2** to take steps towards controlling them or usurping their position, etc.
on the move 1 moving from place to place. **2** advancing or making progress.
[from Latin *movere*]

Movement, The a group of writers of the 1950s in England, who shared a mistrust of rhetoric and the grand gesture, and advocated common sense and rationality. They included Kingsley Amis and Philip Larkin.

movement *noun* **1** a process or act of changing position or going from one point to another. **2** an organization or association, especially one promoting a particular cause. **3** a general tendency. **4** the theatrical art of moving the body gracefully or with expression. **5** (**movements**) a person's actions during a particular time. **6** the moving parts of a watch or clock. **7** *Medicine* an act of evacuating the bowels; the waste matter evacuated. **8** a section of a large-scale piece of music, especially a symphony.

mover *noun* a person or thing that moves.

movie *noun* a cinema film. [a shortening of *moving picture*]

Movietone the trade name for one of the first sound-on-film recording and reproducing systems, launched by Fox in 1927. It was used initially for newsreels, and subsequently for all their feature-film production.

moving *adj.* **1** having an effect on the emotions; touching; stirring. **2** in motion; not static: *a moving staircase.*

mow *verb* (PAST TENSE **mowed**; PAST PARTICIPLE **mown**) to cut (grass or a crop) by hand or with a machine.
— **mow someone** or **something down** *colloq.* to knock them down or kill them in large numbers.
[from Anglo-Saxon *mawan*]

mower *noun* a machine for cutting grass.

Mowgli the boy who is raised in the jungle by wolves in Rudyard Kipling's *The Jungle Book.*

moxa *noun* a pithy material, eg wormwood down, sunflower pith, or cotton wool, formed into a cone or stick and burned as a counter-irritant or for cauterization in oriental medicine. [from Japanese *mogusa*]

moxibustion *noun* the burning of moxa as a counter-irritant or for cauterization in oriental medicine. [from MOXA + COMBUSTION]

Mozambique, official name **People's Republic of Mozambique**, Portuguese **República Popular de Moçambique** POP (1992e) 14.9m, a republic in SE Africa, divided into 10 provinces. AREA 789 800sq km/ 304 863sq mi. It is bounded S by Swaziland, S and SW by South Africa, W by Zimbabwe, NW by Zambia and Malawi, N by Tanzania, and E by the Mozambique Channel and the Indian Ocean. CAPITAL Maputo. CHIEF TOWNS Nampula, Beira, Pemba. TIME ZONE GMT +2. The population consists mainly of the Makua-Lomwe (37%), Shona (10%), and Thonga (23%) groups; most people follow local beliefs, with the remainder being Christian or Muslim. OFFICIAL LANGUAGE Portuguese; Swahili is widely spoken. CURRENCY the metical. PHYSICAL DESCRIPTION the main rivers are the Zambezi and Limpopo, providing irrigation and hydroelectricity; S of the Zambezi, the coast is low-lying, with sandy beaches and mangroves; low hills of volcanic origin are found inland; the Zimbabwe Plateau lies further N; the coast N of the Zambezi is more rugged and is backed by a narrower coastal plain; a savannah plateau inland has an average elevation of 800–1 000m; the highest peak, Mt Binga, is 2 436m. CLIMATE tropical, with relatively low rainfall in the coastal lowlands; average annual rainfall at Beira, representative of the central coast zone, is 1 520mm with maximum daily temperatures of 25–32°C; in the drier areas of the interior lowlands, rainfall decreases to 500–750mm; Mozambique has one rainy season in Dec–Mar. HISTORY originally inhabited by Bantu peoples from the N in the 1c–4c; the coast was settled by Arab traders and discovered by Portuguese explorers by the late 15c; administered as part of Portuguese India since 1751, Mozambique acquired separate colonial status as Portuguese East Africa in the late 19c; became an overseas province of Portugal in 1951; an independence movement formed in 1962, the Frente de Libertação de Moçambique (FRELIMO), with armed resistance to colonial rule; gained independence in 1975; continuing Civil War, with the first peace talks in 1990; a ceasefire took effect in 1992 as the first stage of a peace agreement; the country suffered severe drought in 1992. GOVERNMENT a socialist one-party state from 1975 until 1990; a new constitution under a multiparty system was implemented in 1990; a President is Head of State and a Legislative Assembly has 200–250 members. ECONOMY badly affected by drought in 1981–4, internal strife, and a lack of foreign exchange; c.85% of the population is involved with agriculture; cashew nuts, tea, cotton, sugar cane, copra, sisal, groundnuts, fruit, maize, rice, cassava, tobacco; forestry, livestock; reserves of gemstones, diamonds, iron ore, copper, marble, alabaster, aluminium, fluorspar, coal, tin, gold.

Mozambique

Mozart, (Johann Chrysostom) Wolfgang Amadeus (1756–91) Austrian composer, born in Salzburg, the son of the violinist and composer Leopold Mozart (1719–87). A child prodigy, he made his first professional European tour (as a pianist) at the age of six. He was a prolific composer, and travelled widely, but failed to find a permanent position. After some years in Salzburg as konzertmeister to the Archbishop, he resigned (1781) and settled in Vienna, where his operas *The Marriage of Figaro* (1786) and *Don Giovanni* (1787) led to his appointment as court composer to Joseph II in 1787. He wrote over 600 compositions (indexed by Ludwig von Köchel, 1862), including 41 symphonies, and many concertos, string quartets, and sonatas. In writing a requiem mass commissioned for Count Walsegg, he felt he was writing his own requiem; he died before it was finished.

mozzarella *noun* a soft white Italian cheese, especially used as a topping for pizza. [from Italian *mozzarella*]

MP *abbrev.* **1** Member of Parliament. **2** military police; military police officer. **3** mounted police.

mpg *abbrev.* miles per gallon.

mph *abbrev.* miles per hour.

MPhil *abbrev.* Master of Philosophy.

Mr *noun* (PL. **Messrs**) the standard title given to a man, used before his surname; a title given to a man who holds an official position: *Mr Jones / Mr Chairman.* [an abbreviation of MISTER]

MRC *abbrev.* Medical Research Council.

MRCP *abbrev.* Member of the Royal College of Physicians.

Mrs *noun* the standard title given to a married woman, used before her family name. [an abbreviation of MISTRESS]

Mr Smith Goes to Washington a US film directed by Frank Capra (1939). It is the story of a gullible Scoutmaster (played by James Stewart) who attains a seat in the Senate through wheeler-dealers with a vested interest.

MS *abbrev.* **1** (PL. **MSS**) manuscript. **2** Mississippi. **3** multiple sclerosis.

Ms *noun* the standard title given to a woman, married or not, used before her family name: *Ms Brown.*

MSc *abbrev.* Master of Science.

MSDOS *abbrev.* trademark *Comput.* a widely used disk-operating system developed by the Microsoft Corporation. It is the standard operating system for all IBM-compatible computers. [from *Microsoft disk-operating system*]

MSG *abbrev.* monosodium glutamate.

Msgr *abbrev.* Monsignor.

MSS *abbrev.* manuscripts.

MT *abbrev.* Montana.

Mt *abbrev.* Mount.

Mubarak, (Mohammed) Hosni (Said) (1928–) Egyptian politician, born in al-Minufiyah. A former pilot and flying instructor, he became Commander of the Egyptian Air Force, and Vice-President under Sadat (1975). Becoming President after Sadat's assassination (1981), he continued the same domestic and international policies, including firm treatment of Muslim extremists, and the peace process with Israel.

much — *adj.*, *pron.* (**more**, **most**) a great amount or quantity (of something). — *adv.* **1** by a great deal: *much prettier.* **2** to a great degree: *don't like her much.*
— **a bit much** *colloq.* very unreasonable.
make much of something to treat as very important.
as much as ... although: *I cannot come, as much as I would like to.*
not much of ... *colloq.* not very good as: *not much of a singer.*
not up to much *colloq.* of a poor standard.
[from Middle English *muche*, from Anglo-Saxon *mycel*]

Mucha, Alphonse, originally **Alfons Maria Mucha** (1860–1939) Czech graphic artist, painter, and designer, born in Ivancise. He designed jewellery, wallpaper, and furniture, and gained instant fame in Paris with his posters for Sarah Bernhardt, which marked him as a master of Art Nouveau. He devoted himself mainly to painting from c.1903, and returned to Prague in 1914, where he painted a series of 20 monumental pictures, *The Slav Epic.*

Much Ado About Nothing a play by William Shakespeare (1598). It is a dark comedy revolving around disguise and deception in the relationships between Beatrice and Benedick, and Claudio and Hero, among others.

muchness
— **much of a muchness** *colloq.* very similar; more or less the same.

mucilage *noun* **1** *Bot.* any of a group of gum-like substances that become viscous and slimy when added to water, present in the cell walls of many aquatic plants, the seed coats of certain terrestrial species, and also secreted by plant roots. **2** a sticky substance used as an adhesive. [from Latin *mucilago*, mouldy juice]

mucilaginous *adj.* like or characteristic of mucilage.

muck — *noun* **1** *colloq.* dirt. **2** animal dung; manure. **3** *derog. colloq.* anything disgusting, or of very poor quality. — *verb* **1** *trans., intrans.* (usually **muck out** or **muck something out**) to clear dung from a farm building. **2** to treat (soil) with manure.
— **make a muck of something** *colloq.* to do it badly; to ruin or spoil it.
muck about or **around** *colloq.* to behave foolishly.
muck someone about or **around** to treat them without consideration; to try their patience.
muck in *colloq.* to take a share of work or responsibilities.
muck something up *colloq.* **1** to make it dirty. **2** to do it badly or wrongly; to ruin or spoil it.
[from Middle English *muk*]

muck-rake *verb intrans.* to seek out and expose scandal.

muck-raker *noun* a person who muck-rakes.

muck-raking *noun colloq.* the practice of searching for and exposing scandal, especially about famous people.

mucky *adj.* (**muckier**, **muckiest**) *colloq.* **1** very dirty; like muck. **2** featuring explicit sex; pornographic: *mucky films.*

mucous *adj.* of, like, or producing mucus.

mucous membrane *Zool.* in vertebrates, the moist mucus-secreting lining of various internal cavities of the body, eg nasal passages, gut.

mucus *noun* the thick slimy substance that serves to protect and lubricate the surface of mucous membranes (such as those lining the nasal and other body cavities) and to trap bacteria and dust particles. It contains water, the protein *mucin*, white blood cells, and various salts. [from Latin *mucus*, from *mungere*, to wipe away]

mud *noun* **1** soft wet earth. **2** any semi-solid mixture resembling this. **3** *colloq.* insults; slanderous attacks: *throw mud at.*
— **my, his, etc name is mud** *colloq.* I am, he is, *etc* disgraced or out of favour.
[probably from Old German *mudde*]

mudbath *noun* **1** a medical treatment in which the body is covered in (especially hot) mud rich in minerals. **2** *colloq.* any outdoor event taking place in muddy conditions.

muddiness *noun* being muddy.

muddle — *verb* (*also* **muddle something up**) **1** to put into a disordered or confused state. **2** to confuse the mind of; to confuse (different things) in the mind. — *noun* a state of disorder or mental confusion.
— **muddle along** *colloq.* to manage or make progress haphazardly.
muddle through *colloq.* to succeed by persevering in spite of difficulties.
[perhaps from Old Dutch *moddelen*, to make muddy]

muddled *adj.* confused.

muddle-headed *adj.* not capable of clear thinking; confused.

muddy — *adj.* (**muddier, muddiest**) **1** covered with or containing mud. **2** *said of a colour, a liquid, etc* dull or cloudy. **3** *said of thoughts, etc* not clear; vague. — *verb* (**muddies, muddied**) to make muddy, especially unclear or difficult to understand.

Mudéjares 1 a style of architecture and decoration, originally typical of Muslims within Christian Spain, and subsequently integrated within Spanish styles. **2** the Moors remaining, mostly as peasants or craftsmen, in regions of medieval Spain reconquered for Christianity. Many were expelled during the final stages of Reconquest (15c).

mudflat *noun* (*often* **mudflats**) a relatively flat area of land, especially situated near an estuary or sheltered bay, that consists of an accumulation of fine silt or mud that is brought in by the tide. Mudflats are covered by a shallow layer of water at high tide.

mudguard *noun* a curved metal guard over the upper half of the wheel of a bicycle or motorcycle to keep rain or mud from splashing up.

mudhopper *or* **mudskipper** *noun* a very distinct fish widespread in the Indo-Pacific, locally common on mudflats of estuaries and mangrove swamps, and living for much of the time out of the water. It is 15cm to 25cm in length, the eyes are raised on the top of the head, and the paired fins are used as props and for moving across the mud.

mudhopper

mudpack *noun* a thick paste applied to the face as a skin cleanser.

mudpuppy *noun* (PL. **mudpuppies**) a salamander from N America that spends its entire life in water, is brownish-grey with feathery gills, and has limbs with four toes, and a deep narrow tail. It feeds on invertebrates and fish.

mudskipper *see* MUDHOPPER.

mud-slinger *noun* a person who makes slanderous allegations to discredit another.

mud-slinging *noun* *colloq.* the making of slanderous personal attacks.

mudstone *noun* *Geol.* a fine-grained sedimentary rock that is a hardened consolidated form of mud, composed of approximately equal amounts of clay and silt. Mudstone is brittle, and disintegrates in water.

Mueller, Erwin Wilhelm (1911–77) German-born US physicist, born in Berlin. He worked for industrial laboratories in Berlin and at the Fritz Haber Institute until 1952, when he emigrated to the USA and joined Pennsylvania State University. He invented the field-emission microscope (1936) and the field-ion microscope (1951), which gave the first photographs affording a direct view of individual atoms and some heat-stable molecules.

muesli *noun* a mixture of crushed grain, nuts and dried fruit, eaten with milk, especially for breakfast. [from Swiss German]

muezzin *noun* the Muslim official who calls worshippers to prayer, usually from a minaret. [from Arabic *mu'adhdhin*]

muff[1] *noun* a wide fur tube, carried usually by women, inside which the hands are placed, one at each end, for warmth. [probably from Dutch *mof*]

muff[2] *colloq.* — *verb* **1** *Sport* to miss (a catch); to perform (a stroke) awkwardly or unsuccessfully. **2** to miss (an opportunity, etc). — *noun* a failure, especially to hold a catch.

muffin *noun* a small round flat bread-like cake, usually eaten hot with butter.

muffle *verb* **1** to make quieter; to suppress (sound). **2** to prevent from saying something.
— **be muffled up** to wear warm clothing, especially round the head, as a protection against the cold.
[from Old French *moufle*, thick glove]

muffler *noun* a thick scarf.

mufti *noun* *old use* civilian clothes when worn by people who usually wear a uniform. [from Arabic]

Mufulira POP (1990) 153 000, a mining city in Copperbelt province, S central Zambia. It is the fourth largest city in the country. The world's second largest underground copper mine is located nearby.

mug[1] *noun* **1** a drinking-cup with a handle, used without a saucer. **2** the amount a mug will hold.

mug[2] *verb* (**mugged, mugging**) to attack and rob violently or under threat of violence.

mug[3] *noun* *colloq.* a face or mouth.

mug[4] *noun* *colloq.* an easily fooled person.
— **a mug's game** a worthless or foolish activity.

mug[5] *verb trans., intrans.* (**mugged, mugging**)
— **mug something up** *or* **mug up on something** *colloq.* to study or revise a subject thoroughly, especially for an examination.

Mugabe, Robert (Gabriel) (1924–) Zimbabwean statesman, born in Kutama, Southern Rhodesia. After short periods in the National Democratic Party and Joshua Nkomo's Zimbabwe African People's Union (ZAPU) he was briefly detained, but escaped to co-found the Zimbabwe African National Union (ZANU) in 1963. After his 10-year detention in Rhodesia (1964–74), the ZAPU and ZANU formed the Popular Front (1976) to press for black majority rule. (In the early 1980s however, there was discord between Mugabe and Nkomo, which led to Nkomo's dismissal from the Cabinet). When Zimbabwe was granted independence (1980), Mugabe became the first Prime Minister (1980–7), and when in 1987 Parliament agreed to combine the roles of head of state and head of government, he was appointed President (from 1987).

mugful *noun* (PL. **mugfuls**) the amount a mug (see MUG[1]) will hold.

mugger *noun* a person who attacks and robs another.

Muggeridge, (Thomas) Malcolm (1903–90) English journalist, born in Croydon. He was a lecturer in Cairo before entering journalism in 1930, working mainly abroad until after World War II, when he was decorated. He was editor of *Punch* (1953–7) and also a television reporter and interviewer, contributing regularly to *Panorama* (1953–60). His own series include *Appointment With . . .* (1960–1) and *Let Me Speak* (1964–5), in which he quizzed the great figures of the day and challenged minorities to defend their beliefs. He became a Roman Catholic in 1982. Among his publications are *The Earnest Atheist* (1936), *Tread Softly for You Tread on My Jokes* (1966), *Chronicle of Wasted Time* (1982), and *Conversion: a spiritual journey* (1988).

mugginess *noun* being muggy.

mugging *noun* a beating up; assault and robbery.

muggins *noun* *colloq.* a foolish person, especially used of oneself when taken advantage of by others. [from MUG[4]]

muggy *adj.* (**muggier, muggiest**) *said of the weather* unpleasantly warm and damp; close. [perhaps from Norse *mugga*, mist]

Mughal Empire an important Indian Muslim state (1526–1857) founded by Babur. It temporarily declined under Humayun (1530–40), who lost control to the Afghan chieftain Sher Shah (1540–5). Humayun's son Akbar the Great defeated the Afghan challenge at Panipat (1556) and extended the empire to include territory between Afghanistan and Deccan. Akbar was succeeded by Jehangir (1605–27) and Shah Jehan (1627–58). The last great Mughal emperor was Aurangzeb (1658–1707), who extended the limits of the empire further south; however, religious bigotry alienated non-Muslim supporters and undermined the unity of the empire, and it disintegrated under Maratha and British pressure. By the mid-18c it ruled only a small area around Delhi, but its administrative forms and culture continued to have great influence. Its last emperor, Bahadur Shah II (1837–57) was exiled by the British to Rangoon after the 1857–8 Indian Uprising.

mugshot *noun* *colloq.* a photograph of a criminal's face, taken for police records.

Mughal Dynasty	
1526–30	Babur
1530–56	Humayun
1556–1605	Akbar the Great
1605–27	Jahangir
1627–58	Shah Jahan
1658–1707	Aurangzeb (Alamgir)
1707–12	Bahadur Shah I (Shah Alam I)
1712–13	Jahandar Shah
1713–19	Farrukh-siyar
1719	Rafi-ud-Darajat
1719	Rafi-ud-Daulat
1719	Neku-siyar
1719	Ibrahim
1719–48	Muhammad Shah
1748–54	Ahmad Shah
1754–9	Alamgir II
1759–1806	Shah Alam II
1806–37	Akbar II
1837–57	Bahadur Shah II

mugwump *noun* **1** someone who is politically aloof. **2** a great man; a boss. [from Algonkian *mugquomp*, a great chief]

Muhammad *or* **Mohammed** *or* **Mahomet** (c.570–c.632) Arab prophet and founder of Islam, born in Mecca. Orphaned at six, he was brought up by his grandfather and then his uncle, who trained him as a merchant. At 24 he entered the service of a rich widow, whom he later married. Increasingly drawn to religious contemplation, he was moved to teach a new faith, which would dispense with idolatry, narrow Judaism, and corrupt Christianity. After the year 600 he received revelations of the word of Allah (God) commanding him to preach the true religion. The basis of his teaching was the Koran, which was also revealed to him. He attacked superstition, and exhorted people to a pious, moral life, and belief in an all-powerful, all-just, and merciful God, who had chosen him as his prophet. God's mercy was principally to be obtained by prayer, fasting, and almsgiving. At first dismissing him as a poet, the Meccans finally rose against him and his followers. He sought refuge at Medina in 622 (the date of the Muhammadan Era, the Hegira), and assumed the position of highest judge and ruler of the city. He then engaged in war against the enemies of Islam. In 630 he took Mecca, where he was recognized as chief and prophet, and thus secured the new religion in Arabia. In 632 he undertook his last pilgrimage to Mecca, and there on Mt Arafat fixed the ceremonies of the pilgrimage (Hajj). He fell ill after his return, and died in the home of Ayeshah, the favourite of his nine wives, who was the daughter of an early follower, Abu Bekr.

Muharram *noun* **1** the first month of the Muslim year. **2** among Shiite Muslims, a period of mourning for Hasan and Husain, grandsons of Muhammad, during the first ten days of the month; with processions in which the faithful beat their breasts or whip themselves and a fast on the ninth day. [from Arabic *muharram*, sacred]

Muir, Edwin (1887–1959) Scottish poet, born in Deerness, Orkney. He married Willa Anderson in 1919 and migrated to Prague, where they produced translations of Kafka and other authors. He also worked in Rome and Scotland, and was Professor of Poetry at Harvard (1955–6). From 1925, his poems appeared in eight slim volumes, including *The Voyage* (1946) and *The Labyrinth* (1949), and his *Collected Poems 1921–1958* were published in 1960. He also wrote several critical works, including *Scott and Scotland* (1936).

Muir, Jean (1933–) English fashion designer, born in London. She was employed by Liberty from 1950, then by Jaeger from 1956, and started on her own as Jane & Jane in 1961. In 1966 she established her company, Jean Muir. Her clothes are noted for their classic shapes and for their softness and fluidity.

Muir, John (1838–1914) Scottish-born US naturalist, born in Dunbar. He emigrated with his family to the USA in 1849, and studied at the the University of Wisconsin. He was an ingenious inventor of mechanical devices but after an industrial accident in 1867, he devoted himself to natural history, exploring the American West and especially the Yosemite area in California. He campaigned vigorously to promote the idea of wildlife conservation, and was largely responsible for the creation of the Yosemite and Sequoia National Parks in 1890. The John Muir Trust to acquire wild land in Britain was established in 1984.

Muirfield a championship golf course in Gullane, near Edinburgh, Scotland, built in 1891. It is home to the Honourable Company of Edinburgh Golfers (founded in 1744).

Mujahadeen *or* **Majahidin** Muslim guerrillas who resisted the Soviet occupation of Afghanistan after the invasion (Dec 1979). Based in Iran and Pakistan, they formed various armed bands united by their common aim of defeating the invaders, and the conflict was proclaimed a *jihad* ('holy war'). The Russians withdrew from Afghanistan in 1989, and the Mujahadeen subsequently experienced much internal dissent over their role in the country's future. [from Arabic, = holy warriors]

Mukden see SHENYANG.

mulatto *noun* (PL. **mulattos, mulattoes**) *old use, now usually offensive* a person of mixed race, especially with one black and one white parent. [from Spanish *mulato*, young mule]

mulberry *noun* (PL. **mulberries**) **1** a deciduous tree of temperate regions, producing small purple edible berries. **2** such a berry. **3** a dark purple colour. [from Old German *mulberi*]

mulch — *noun* straw, compost, or any of various man-made substances laid on the soil around plants to retain moisture and prevent the growth of weeds. — *verb* to cover with mulch. [from obsolete *mulch*, soft]

mulct — *noun* a fine or penalty. — *verb* **1** to fine. **2** (**mulct someone of something**) to deprive them of it. **3** to swindle. [from Latin *mulcta*, fine]

Muldoon, Sir Robert (David) (1921–92) New Zealand politician, born in Auckland. He served in World War II, trained as an accountant, and became a National Party MP in 1960. After five years as Minister of Finance, he became Deputy Prime Minister (1972), Leader of the Party (1974), and Prime Minister (1975–84).

mule¹ *noun* **1** the offspring of a male donkey and a female horse, used as a working animal in many countries. **2** a stubborn person. [from Latin *mulus* or *mula*]

mule² *noun* a shoe or slipper with no back part covering the heel. [from French]

muleteer *noun* a person who drives mules.

Mulhouse, German **Mulhausen** POP (1990) 224 000, an industrial and commercial river port in Haut-Rhin department, Alsace region, NE France. It lies on the R Ill and the Rhine-Rhône Canal, 35km/22mi S of Colmar, and is the second largest town in Alsace. HISTORY an imperial free city from 1308; allied with the Swiss from 1515 to 1648; an independent republic until 1798, then voted to become French; under German rule in 1871, reverting to France in 1918. NOTABLE FEATURES Renaissance town hall (1552); Church of St-Etienne; Musée National de l'Automobile; French Railway Museum; 31-storey Tour de l'Europe.

mulish *adj.* stubborn; obstinate.

Mull an island in Argyll and Bute district, Strathclyde region, W Scotland. It is the second largest of the Inner Hebrides. AREA 925sq km/357sq mi. The island is separated from the mainland to the NE by a narrow channel, the Sound of Mull, and to the E and SE by the Firth of Lorne. Its mountainous terrain peaks at 3 169m at Ben More. CHIEF TOWN Tobermory. ECONOMY fishing; crofting; tourism. NOTABLE FEATURES ancient castles include Aros and Duart, seat of the clan Maclean.

mull¹ *verb* — **mull something over** to consider it carefully; to ponder on it. [perhaps from obsolete *mull*, grind to powder]

mull² *verb* to spice, sweeten, and warm (wine or beer).

mull³ *noun* Scot. a headland or promontory: *the Mull of Kintyre*. [from Gaelic *maol*]

mullah *noun* a Muslim scholar and adviser in Islamic religion and sacred law. [from Arabic *maula*]

mulled *adj., said of ale, wine, etc* sweetened and spiced.

Müller, Hermann Joseph (1890–1967) US geneticist, born in New York City. Professor at the University of Texas, he spent 1933–40 in Europe, and became professor at Indiana University in 1945. His major work was on the use of X-rays to cause genetic mutations, for which he was awarded the 1946 Nobel Prize for Physiology or Medicine.

Müller, Johannes Peter (1801–58) German physiologist, born in Coblenz. Professor at Berlin and Bonn, he was probably the most significant life scientist in Germany in the first half of the 19c; his wide-ranging studies investigated electrophysiology, the glandular system, vision, embryos, and the nervous system. His *Handbuch der Physiologie des Menschen* (Handbook of Human Physiology, 1833–40) was extremely influential.

mullet *noun* any of a family of thick-bodied edible marine fish. [from Latin *mullus*]

mulligatawny *noun* a thick curry-flavoured meat soup, originally made in E India. [from Tamil *milagu-tannir*, pepper-water]

Mulliken, Robert Sanderson (1896–1986) US chemical physicist, born in Newburyport, Massachusetts. Professor at the University of Chicago, he was awarded the 1966 Nobel Prize for Chemistry for his work on chemical bonds and on the electronic structure of molecules.

Mullingar, Gaelic **Muileann Cearr** POP (1991) 12 000, the capital of Westmeath county, Leinster province, E Irish Republic. It is a market town, situated on the Royal Canal, NW of Dublin. NOTABLE FEATURE cathedral.

mullion *noun* Archit. a vertical bar or post separating the panes or casements of a window. [from Old French *moinel*]

mullioned *adj.* having mullions.

Mulroney, (Martin) Brian (1939–) Canadian Conservative politician and Prime Minister. While practising as a lawyer in Montreal, he became increasingly active in the Progressive Conservative Party. In 1983 he replaced Joe Clark as Party Leader, and then became Prime Minister (1984), with a landslide victory over the Liberals. He initiated a number of radical measures, including the Meech Lake Accords (which recognized French-speaking Quebec as a 'distinct society') and the negotiation of a free-trade agreement with the USA. Decisively re-elected in 1988, he resigned abruptly in 1993.

Multan POP (1981) 730 000, a city in Punjab province, Pakistan. It is situated 314km/195mi SW of Lahore. HISTORY captured by Mahmud of Ghazni in 1005 and by Timur in 1398; ruled by the emperors of Delhi from 1526 until 1779, and by the Afghans until 1818, when the city was seized by the Sikhs; came under British rule in 1849. NOTABLE FEATURES 14c tombs of Muslim saints.

multi- *combining form* forming words meaning 'many': *multicoloured*. [from Latin *multus*, much]

multicellular *adj.* Biol. having or made up of many cells.

multicoloured *adj.* having many colours.

multicultural *adj.* relating to or involving the cultures of several peoples within a single community.

multicultural education the education together of more than one ethnic or cultural group, and accommodation of the various religious and cultural traditions of these groups in general education.

multifarious *adj. formal* of many different kinds; very varied. [from Latin *multifarius*, manifold]

multiform *adj. formal* having many different forms or shapes.

multilateral *adj.* **1** involving or affecting several people, groups or nations. **2** many-sided.

multilateralism *Econ.* support for an economic trading system where many countries are encouraged to trade with each other. It is the principal objective of GATT, which aims to increase world trade in a wide range of areas and among many countries.

multilingual *adj.* written or expressed in, or able to speak, several different languages.

multimedia *adj. Comput., said of a computer system* able to present and manipulate data in a variety of forms, eg text, graphics, and sound, often simultaneously.

multimillionaire *noun* a person whose wealth is valued at several million pounds, dollars, etc.

multinational — *adj.* operating in several different countries. — *noun* a multinational business or organization.

multinational corporation a large business company which has production and/or distribution operations in several countries, via subsidiaries, holding companies, etc.

multiparous *adj. Biol.* producing several young at one birth. [from Latin *multiparus*]

multiparty *adj., said of a state, etc* having a political system with more than one organized party.

multiple — *adj.* having, involving or affecting many parts, especially of the same kind; many, especially more than several. — *noun* a number or expression for which a given number or expression is a factor, eg 24 is a multiple of 12. [from Latin *multiplus*]

multiple-choice *adj., said of a test or exam* for which the correct answer must be chosen from several possible answers provided.

Multiple, Independently-targeted Re-entry Vehicle (ABBREV. **MIRV**) a nuclear-armed warhead, numbers of which may be incorporated in the front end of a large ballistic missile to be dispensed over a target area. A 'MIRVed' missile may therefore make attacks on several targets at once.

multiple sclerosis (ABBREV. **MS**) an incurable disease of the central nervous system caused by degeneration of the myelin sheath that encloses the neurones (nerve cells) in the brain and spinal cord.
◇ The main symptoms of multiple sclerosis are inability to coordinate movements, weakness of the muscles of the limbs, speech difficulties, blurring of vision, and an abnormal tingling sensation. These symptoms usually appear at intervals, separated by periods of remission which may be very long, and gradually become more severe, eventually causing severe disability. Multiple sclerosis mainly affects young and middle-aged adults, and the cause of the nerve damage is not known.

multiplex — *adj. formal* having very many parts; complex. — *noun* a large cinema building divided into several smaller cinemas. [from Latin, from *plicare*, to fold]

Multiplex Analogue Components (ABBREV. **MAC**) in the UK, a system of colour television transmission in which coded signals representing luminance, chrominance, and sound, along with synchronizing data, are sent in succession as separate components during each television line.

multiplicand *noun Maths.* a number to be multiplied by a second number, the *multiplier.* [from Latin *multiplicare*, to multiply]

multiplication *noun* **1** a mathematical operation in which one number is added to itself as many times as is indicated by a second number; the process of performing this operation. **2** the process of increasing in number.

multiplication sign the symbol ×, used between two numbers to indicate that they are to be multiplied.

multiplication table a table listing the products of multiplying pairs of numbers, especially all pairs from 1 to 12 inclusive.

multiplicity *noun* (PL. **multiplicities**) *formal* **1** a great number and variety. **2** the state of being many and various. [from Latin *multiplex*, of many kinds]

multiplier *noun Maths.* a number indicating by how many times another number, the *multiplicand*, to which it is attached by a multiplication sign is to be multiplied.

multiply *verb* (**multiplies, multiplied**) **1** (**multiply one number by another**) to add a number to itself a given number of times; to combine two numbers in multiplication. **2** *intrans.* to increase in number, especially by breeding. [from Latin *multiplicare*, from *multi*, much + *plicare*, to fold]

multiprogramming *noun Comput.* the execution of two or more programs by a single central processing unit, usually achieved by carrying out several instructions from one program, and then rapidly switching to the next one.

multipurpose *adj.* having many uses.

multiracial *adj.* of, for, or including people of many different races.

multistorey — *adj., said of a building* having many floors. — *noun* (PL. **multistoreys**) *colloq.* a multistorey car-park.

multitasking *noun Comput.* the action of running several processes or jobs simultaneously on a system.

multitude *noun* **1** a great number. **2** a huge crowd of people. **3** (**the multitude**) ordinary people. [from Latin *multitudo*]

multitudinous *adj.* very numerous.

multiuser *Comput. adj., said of a computer system* consisting of several terminals linked to a central computer, allowing access by several users at the same time.

multi-vision *Telecomm.* a technique of audio-visual presentation in which groups of slide projectors are programmed to show a complex sequence of images on a wide screen with accompanying sound from tape recording.

mum¹ *noun* a mother; a term used to address one's own mother. [a child's word, derived from a baby's babbling]

mum² *adj. colloq.* silent; not speaking.
— **mum's the word!** *colloq.* an exhortation to secrecy.
[a sound produced with closed lips]

mumble — *verb trans., intrans.* to speak unclearly, especially with the mouth partly closed. — *noun* the sound of unclear or hushed speech. [from Middle English *momelen*, from MUM²]

mumbo-jumbo *noun* (PL. **mumbo-jumbos**) *derog. colloq.* **1** foolish talk, especially of a religious or spiritual kind. **2** baffling jargon. **3** something, eg a statue, foolishly treated as an object of worship. [from Malinke (a W African language) *Mama Dyanbo*, a tribal god]

Mumford, Lewis (1895–1990) US sociologist and author, born in Flushing, New York. He became a literary critic and journal editor, and began to write on architecture and urbanization in such works as *The Story of Utopias* (1922) and *The City in History* (1961), which stressed the unhappy effects of technology on society.

mummer *noun* **1** *Hist.* an actor in a traditional mimed folk play, usually performed at Christmas. **2** a disguised child taking part in traditional merrymaking during religious festivals, especially Hallowe'en; a guiser. [from Old French *momer*, to mime]

◇ In medieval England, the mummers were masked actors who entered houses during winter festivals, distributed gifts, and danced. In the 18c, the mummers' Christmas play evolved, based on the legend of St George, with a duel between champions ending in the death of one of them and his revival by a doctor.

mummery *noun* (PL. **mummeries**) **1** a performance of mumming. **2** *derog.* ridiculous or pretentious ceremony.

mummification *noun* **1** the process of mummifying. **2** being mummified.

mummify *verb* (**mummifies, mummified**) to preserve (a corpse) as a mummy.

mumming *noun* the activity of a mummer.

mummy¹ *noun* (PL. **mummies**) a child's word for mother. [a variant of MUM¹]

mummy² *noun* (PL. **mummies**) a human or animal corpse preserved with spices and bandaged, especially in preparation for burial in ancient Egypt. [from Arabic and Persian *mumiya*, from Persian *mum*, wax]
◇ The ancient Egyptians routinely preserved the corpses, not only of humans, but also of cats. Before the body was wrapped, the internal organs were removed, and often stored separately.

mumps *noun* (also **the mumps**) an infectious viral disease, mainly affecting children, that causes fever, headache, and painful swelling of the salivary glands on one or both sides of the cheeks, and under the jaw. An attack of mumps during childhood usually confers lifelong immunity to the disease. [from archaic *mump*, to grimace]

Munch, Edvard (1863–1944) Norwegian painter, born in Löten. He travelled in Europe, was influenced by Paul Gauguin while in Paris, and settled in Norway in 1908. He was obsessed by subjects such as death and love, which he illustrated in an Expressionist Symbolic style, using bright colours and a tortuously curved design, as in *The Scream* (1893). Other works include many self-portraits (eg *Between the Clock and the Bed*, Oslo, 1940) and various woodcuts and engravings.

munch *verb trans., intrans.* to chew with a steady movement of the jaws, especially noisily. [probably imitative]

Münchhausen, (Karl Friedrich Hieronymus), Baron von (1720–97) German soldier, born in Bodenwerder, Hanover. He served in Russian campaigns against the Turks, and became notorious as the narrator of ridiculously exaggerated exploits. The best of the material attributed to him was published by Rudolf Erich Raspe (1737–94), who became Professor of Archaeology at Cassel.

munchies *pl. noun colloq.* **1** (**the munchies**) an alcohol- or drug-induced craving for food. **2** food to snack on; nibbles. [from MUNCH]

Muncie POP (1990) 120 000, the seat of Delaware County, E Indiana, USA. It lies on the W fork of the White R. Settled in 1824, it achieved city status in 1865. It was represented as the 'average American town' in the 1929 sociological study *Middletown* by R & H Lynd.

Munda an Austro-Asiatic-speaking people settled in hilly and forested regions of E and central India. Although physically indistinguishable from Indians, and culturally similar to other Indians, they have retained a separate identity and religion.

mundane *adj.* **1** ordinary; dull; everyday. **2** of this world, not some other spiritual world. [from Latin *mundus*, world]

mung bean **1** an E Asian plant producing an edible green or yellow bean, the source of beansprouts. **2** a bean from this plant. [from Hindi *mung*]

Mungo a Scottish male first name, a byname of St Kentigern, the 6c lowland apostle. [origin uncertain]

Munich, German **München** POP (1990e) 1.2m, the capital of Bavaria state, S Germany, on the R Isar. Munich is the third-largest city in Germany. HISTORY founded in 1158, it became capital of Bavaria in 1506; the Nazi movement was based here in the 1920s; the Munich Agreement was signed in 1938; the city was badly bombed in World War II. NOTABLE FEATURES Church of St Peter (1181); town hall (1470); cathedral (15c); art gallery. EVENT Oktoberfest (annual beer festival).

Munich Agreement an agreement signed (29 Sep 1938) at a conference in Munich by British Prime Minister Neville Chamberlain, French Prime Minister Edouard Daladier, and the fascist dictators of Italy and Germany, Mussolini and Hitler. In the absence of the Czech President Beneš (who resigned as a result) and Russia, they agreed that the Sudeten area of Czechoslovakia was to be ceded to Germany, and the rest of Czechoslovakia was to be guaranteed against unprovoked aggression.

Munich Putsch the abortive attempt (1923) by Hitler to overthrow the state government of Bavaria, as a prelude to the March on Berlin and the establishment of the Nazi regime in Germany. Though supported by General Ludendorff, it was badly planned and suppressed by Bavarian police action. Hitler was tried for treason, and sentenced to five years' imprisonment.

municipal adj. of, relating to, or controlled by the local government of a town or region. [from Latin municipium, free town]

municipality noun (PL. **municipalities**) a town or region having its own local government; the local government itself.

municipally adv. with regard to a municipality or municipal affairs.

munificence noun magnificent generosity.

munificent adj. formal extremely generous. [from Latin munus, gift + facere, to make]

muniments pl. noun Legal official papers proving ownership, especially title deeds to property. [from Latin munimentum, title deed]

munitions pl. noun military equipment, especially ammunition and weapons. [from Latin munire, to defend or fortify]

Munnings, Sir Alfred (1878–1959) English painter, born in Suffolk. He specialized in the painting of horses and sporting pictures and was President of the Royal Academy (1944–9). He was well known for his forthright criticism of modern art.

Munsell colour system a system for measuring and naming colours, devised by US painter Albert H Munsell (?–1918). The Munsell Book of Colour contains 1 200 samples grouped according to minimum discriminable intervals of hue, saturation, and brilliance.

Munster POP (1991) 1m, a province in the S Irish Republic. AREA 24 127sq km/9 313sq mi. It is bounded S and W by the Atlantic Ocean. A former kingdom, it comprises the counties of Clare, Cork, Kerry, Limerick, Tipperary (N and S Ridings), and Waterford.

Münster POP (1991e) 259 000, a city in North Rhine-Westphalia state, NW Germany. It lies on the R Aa and the Dortmund-Ems Canal, 125km/78mi NE of Cologne. HISTORY a member of the Hanseatic League; capital of the former province of Westphalia; the Treaty of Westphalia was signed here in 1648, ending the Thirty Years War. NOTABLE FEATURE cathedral (1225–65).

muntin or **munting** noun Archit. a vertical framing piece separating the panels of a door. [from French montant, from monter, to rise]

muntjac or **muntjak** noun a true deer, native to India and SE Asia, and having a face with a V-shaped ridge, the arms of the 'V' being continued as freely projecting bony columns, the ends of the columns in the male bearing short antlers. In both sexes there are projecting canine teeth. The animal's call resembles the bark of a dog. [from a Malay name]

Müntzer or **Münzer, Thomas** (c.1489–1525) German preacher and Anabaptist, born in Stolberg. In 1520 he began preaching (at first in Zwickau, then more widely), but his socialism and mystical doctrines led to conflict with the authorities. In 1525 he was elected pastor of the Anabaptists of Mülhausen, where his communistic ideas soon aroused the whole country. He joined the Peasants' Revolt of 1524–5, but was defeated at the battle of Frankenhausen, and executed.

muon noun Physics an elementary particle that behaves like a heavy electron, but decays to form an electron and neutrinos. [from Greek mu, the letter]

mural — noun a painting painted directly on to a wall. — adj. formal of or relating to a wall or walls. [from Latin murus, wall]

muralist noun a painter of murals.

Murasaki, Shikibu (978–c.1031) Japanese noblewoman and writer, born in Kyoto. She wrote the saga Genji Monagatari (The Tale of Genji), often considered by some critics to be the world's earliest novel.

Murat, Joachim (1767–1815) French soldier and King of Naples (1808–15), born in La Bastide-Fortunière. He enlisted in the cavalry on the eve of the French Revolution (1787), and was promoted to general of division in the Egyptian campaign (1799). He married Napoleon's sister, Caroline, after helping him become First Consul. He was proclaimed King of the Two Sicilies (1808), and took possession of Naples. After Napoleon's defeat at Leipzig (1813), he made a treaty with the Austrians in an attempt to keep his throne. On Napoleon's escape from Elba, Murat recommenced war against Austria, but was twice defeated and failed to recover Naples. He was captured and executed in Pizzo, Calabria.

Murcia 1 POP (1991) 319 000, a region and province in SE Spain. AREA 11 313sq km/4 367sq mi. It is thinly populated, except in the river valleys. Murcia was formerly capital of a Moorish kingdom. CAPITAL Murcia (on the R Segura). ECONOMY oranges, lemons, dates; coastal tourism; lead, zinc, iron. NOTABLE FEATURES cathedral (14c); Salzillo Museum. **2** a region in SE Spain with Murcia as its capital.

murder — noun **1** the act of unlawfully and intentionally killing a person. **2** colloq. something, or a situation, which causes hardship or difficulty: the traffic in town was murder. — verb (**murdered, murdering**) **1** trans., intrans. to kill unlawfully and intentionally. **2** colloq. to spoil or ruin (eg a piece of music, by performing it very badly). **3** colloq. to defeat easily and by a huge margin.

— **get away with murder** colloq. to behave very badly or dishonestly and not be caught or punished.

scream or **shout** or **cry blue murder** colloq. to protest loudly or angrily.

[from Anglo-Saxon morthor, from morth, death]

◇ In England and Wales, the crime of murder is the killing of a person where there has been malice aforethought, and the victim must have died within a year and a day of the commission of the crime. In Scotland, and in many US states, murder is homicide committed purposefully and knowingly. In the UK, the sentence for murder is life imprisonment.

murderer noun a person who has intentionally killed another unlawfully.

murderess noun old use a female murderer.

Murder in the Cathedral a religious verse play by T S Eliot (1935), based on the murder (1170) of Thomas Becket in Canterbury.

murderous adj. intending, intended for, or capable of murder.

Murders in the Rue Morgue, The a short story by Edgar Allan Poe (1841). It is a pioneering work of detective fiction and features the sleuth, C Auguste Dupin.

Murdo a male first name. [from Gaelic muir, sea]

Murdoch, Dame (Jean) Iris (1919–) Irish novelist and philosopher, born in Dublin of Anglo-Irish parents. A professional philosopher, she took up novel-writing as a hobby, and produced a series of books which explore human relationships with subtlety and humour. These include Under the Net (1954), The Bell (1958), A Severed Head (1961), The Black Prince (1973), The Sea, The Sea (1978, Booker Prize), and The Philosopher's Pupil (1983). She has also written plays and several philosophical and critical studies.

Murdoch, (Keith) Rupert (1931–) American media proprietor, born in Melbourne, Australia. After attending Oxford University, he worked for two years on the Daily Express in London, returning to Australia in 1952, where he inherited The News in Adelaide on the death of his father. He built a substantial newspaper and magazine publishing empire in Australia, the USA, Hong Kong, and the UK, including The Sun, the News of the World, and The Times (acquired in 1981) and its related publications in Britain. He moved into the US market in 1976 with the purchase of the New York Post. He also has major business interests in other media industries, especially television, films, and publishing, in three continents.

Murdockson, Meg a character in Sir Walter Scott's The Heart of Midlothian, who sells Effie's son. Her itinerant daughter Magdalen, known as 'Madge Wildfire', sings haunting lyrics, including the lament 'Proud Maisie in the Wood'.

Muriel a female first name. [from Celtic, perhaps meaning 'sea-bright']

Müritz, Lake, German **Müritz-See** a lake in NE Germany. AREA 117sq km/45sq mi.

murk noun literary darkness. [from Anglo-Saxon mirce]

murkiness noun being murky.

murky adj. (**murkier, murkiest**) **1** dark; gloomy. **2** said of water dark and dirty. **3** suspiciously vague or unknown; shady: her murky past.

Murmansk, formerly **Romanov-na-Murmane** (to 1917) POP (1991e) 473 000, the seaport capital of Murmansk oblast, NW Russia. It lies on the E coast of Kola Bay, 50km/31mi from the open sea. Founded in 1916, it developed into Russia's most important fishing port (ice-free all year round). It is the country's northernmost tourist centre.

murmur — noun **1** a quiet continuous sound, eg of running water or low voices. **2** anything said in a low, indistinct voice. **3** a complaint. **4** Medicine an abnormal rustling sound made by the heart, usually indicating the presence of disease. — verb (**murmured, murmuring**) **1** trans., intrans. to speak (words) softly and indistinctly. **2** intrans. to complain or grumble. [from Latin murmurare]

murmurous adj. making murmurs.

Murphy, Gardner (1895–1979) US psychologist, born in Ohio. He was Professor of Psychology at Columbia and City College of New York, and later Director of Research at the Menninger Foundation. He wrote widely on personality, social psychology, biofeedback, and parapsychology.

Murphy's Law same as SOD'S LAW.

murrain noun any infectious cattle disease, especially foot-and-mouth disease. [from Old French morine, pestilence]

Murray, (George) Gilbert (Aimé) (1866–1957) Australian-born British classical scholar and writer, born in Sydney. He was Professor of Greek at Glasgow (1889–99) and at Oxford (1908–36). His work as a classical historian and translator of Greek dramatists brought him acclaim as the leading Greek scholar of his time. He was also President of the League of Nations Union (1923–38).

Murray, Sir James (Augustus Henry) (1837–1915) Scottish philologist and lexicographer, born in Denholm, Roxburghshire. He was a grammar school teacher for 30 years (1855–85), during which time he established his scholarly reputation with a work on Scots dialects (1873). His major project, the editing of the Philological Society's *New* (later *Oxford*) *English Dictionary*, was begun at Mill Hill (1879). He edited about half the work himself, and created the organization and the inspiration for its completion (in 1928).

Murray (of Epping Forest), Len (Lionel) Murray, Baron (1922–) English trade union leader, born in Shropshire. As General Secretary of the Trades Union Congress (1973–84), he played a major role in the 'social contract' partnership between the TUC and the Labour governments of Harold Wilson and James Callaghan (1974–8). His main publication is *Trade Unions and the State* (1970).

Murray a male first name, after the surname *Murray* and the regional name *Moray* in NE Scotland.

Murrayfield a rugby stadium in Edinburgh, Scotland, the home of the Scottish national team since 1925. It is the headquarters of the Scottish Rugby Union.

Murray River the longest river in Australia, length 2 570km/1 600mi. It rises in the Australian Alps near Mt Kosciusko, and enters the Southern Ocean at Encounter Bay, SE of Adelaide. The river forms the border between New South Wales and Victoria for 1 930km/1 200mi and receives the R Darling 640km/400mi from its mouth. Extending into four states, the river system covers one seventh of the continent. Its waters are used extensively for irrigation and hydroelectric power. Navigation is now generally confined to tourist steamers. Major tributaries are the Darling, Murrumbidgee, Mitta Mitta, Goulburn, Campaspe, and Loddon.

Murrow, Edward (Egbert) R(oscoe) (1908–65) American broadcasting journalist, born in Greensboro, Carolina. He joined the CBS radio network in 1935 as director of talks and education, but made his name as a radio journalist during the Battle of Britain and the Blitz. He was appointed director of the US Information Agency in 1961.

Murrumbidgee River a river in New South Wales, Australia, length 1 759km/1 093mi. Rising in the Snowy Mts, it flows N through Australian Capital Territory, then W to join the Murray R on the Victoria border. The river's major tributary is the Lachlan R. At an altitude below 600m, the floodplain of the Murrumbidgee and the Molonglo rivers forms the major part of the low land of the Australian Capital Territory, irrigating a large agricultural basin.

Murry, John Middleton (1889–1957) English writer and critic, born in London. The husband of Katherine Mansfield, he introduced her work in *The Adelphi*, of which he was editor (1923–48). He became a pacifist, and was editor of *Peace News* (1940–6). His poetry, essays, and criticism were influential on the young intellectuals of the 1920s.

Mururoa POP (1985e) 3 000, a remote atoll in French Polynesia, S Pacific Ocean. It has been used by France as a nuclear testing site. Between 1966 and 1974 tests were carried out in the atmosphere. Since then, they have been held underground within an extinct volcano.

mus. *abbrev.* music.

Musala *or* **Mousalla** *or* **Rila Dagh** the highest peak in Bulgaria, situated in the Rila Mts in the W of the country. HEIGHT 2 925m. It was called Stalin Peak between the 1930s and 1960s.

MusB *or* **MusBac** *abbrev.* *Musicae Baccalaureus* (Latin), Bachelor of Music.

Musca *noun Astron.* the Fly, a small constellation in the southern hemisphere.

Muscadet *noun* a white wine from the Loire region of France; the grape variety from which it is produced.

Muscat, Arabic **Masqat** POP (1990e) 380 000, the seaport capital of Oman, on a peninsula in the Gulf of Oman. It was occupied by the Portuguese from 1508 until 1650. The town was once of great commercial importance, but has now lost much of its trade to the adjacent port of Matrah. Muscat is the residence of the Sultan. NOTABLE FEATURES two forts (16c).

muscat *noun* **1** a variety of white grape with a musky smell. **2** muscatel. [from Provençal]

muscatel *or* **muscat** *or* **muscadel** *noun* a sweet white wine made from muscat grapes.

muscle *noun* **1** an animal tissue composed of bundles of fibres that are capable of contracting (shortening) and so producing movement of different parts of the body. **2** a body structure composed of this tissue, eg biceps. **3** bodily strength. **4** power or influence of any kind: *financial muscle.*
— **muscle in on something** *colloq.* to force one's way into it; to grab a share of it. [from Latin *musculus*]
◇ Muscles consist of bundles of small fibres, each of which is in turn composed of many protein myofibrils, which lengthen or shorten as their filaments slide past each other. This movement, which occurs in response to a stimulus from the nervous system, or a hormonal signal, causes contraction of the whole muscle.
Voluntary muscle, which is under conscious control, produces voluntary movements by pulling against the bones of the skeleton, to which it is attached by means of tendons, so that contractions of such muscles cause the bones to move. Movement of a limb requires the combined action of a pair of muscles which can pull in opposite directions and are said to be *antagonistic*. For example, when the biceps muscle at the front of the upper arm contracts, and the triceps muscle at the back of the arm relaxes, the arm bends at the elbow. When the triceps contracts and the biceps relaxes, the arm is straightened again.
Involuntary muscle (also called smooth muscle) maintains the movements of the internal body systems, and forms part of many internal organs, such as the intestines and uterus. *Cardiac muscle*, found only in the heart, does not become

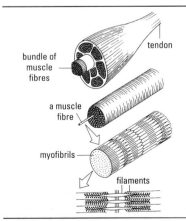

muscle fibres

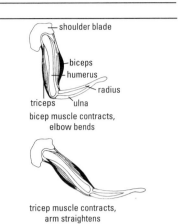

muscle contraction

fatigued, and continues to contract rhythmically even when it is disconnected from the nervous system.

muscle-bound *adj.* having over-enlarged muscles that are stiff and difficult to move.

muscleman *noun* a man with very big muscles, especially one employed to intimidate others.

Muscovite — *noun* a native or citizen of Moscow. — *adj.* relating to Moscow. [from *Muscovy*, an old name for Russia]

muscovite *noun Geol.* any of a group of colourless, silvery-grey, or pale brown mineral forms of potassium aluminosilicate, that are important members of the mica group of minerals, and commonly occur as flat sheets in sedimentary, igneous, and metamorphic rocks. Muscovite is used as an electrical and heat insulator, a filler in paint, wallpaper, and roofing materials, and (because of its transparency and heat resistance) is often used in the windows of furnaces.

Muscovy Company an English trading company granted a charter (1554) to monopolize trade between England and Russia. In 1568 Tsar Ivan IV, 'the Terrible' allowed the company to conduct trade with the Orient via the R Volga. Political intrigues led to the expulsion of the company's agents from Russia in 1649, after which it ceased to exist.

muscular *adj.* **1** of, relating to, or consisting of muscle. **2** having well-developed muscles; strong.

muscular dystrophy any of various forms of a hereditary disease in which there is progressive wasting of certain muscles, which are eventually replaced by fatty tissue. There is no cure for the disease, although physiotherapy can relieve the disability to some extent.

muscularity *noun* being muscular.

musculature *noun* the arrangement, or degree of development, of muscles in a body or organ.

MusD *or* **MusDoc** *abbrev.* *Musicae Doctor* (Latin), Doctor of Music.

Muse *noun* any of the nine mythical Greek goddesses of the arts, said to be a source of creative inspiration to all artists, especially poets. [from Greek *Mousa*]
◇ In Homer, they are the daughters of Zeus and Mnemosyne; in later writers they are located at Helicon and Parnassus, and are associated with fountains, such as the Pierian spring. They are: Calliope, muse of epic poetry; Clio, history; Erato, lyric poetry and hymns; Euterpe, flute; Melpomene, tragedy; Polyhymnia, acting, music, and dance; Terpsichore, lyric poetry and dance; Thalia, comedy; and Urania, astronomy.

muse *verb* **1** *intrans.* to reflect or ponder on something. **2** *trans.* to say in a reflective way. [from Old French *muser*]

museum *noun* a place where objects of artistic, scientific or historic interest are displayed to the public. [from Greek *mouseion*, temple of the Muses]

Museum of Modern Art a US museum in New York City founded by a group of philanthropists in 1929. Prior to 1939, when the present building was erected to house a permanent collection, the organization staged loan exhibitions of contemporary art in rented premises.

Museum of the Moving Image (ABBREV. **MOMI**) in the UK, a museum in London which depicts the history of television and cinema from its conception to the latest in modern technology.

museum-piece *noun* **1** any article displayed in a museum. **2** *humorous colloq.* any very old or old-fashioned person or thing.

Musgrave Ranges the mountain ranges in South Australia which lie close to the Northern Territory border. They extend 80km/50mi and rise to 1 440m at Mt Woodroffe, the highest point in the state.

mush¹ *noun* **1** a soft half-liquid mass of anything. **2** *derog. colloq.* sloppy sentimentality. [probably a variant of MASH]

mush² — *interj.*, used especially to a team of dogs go on!; go faster! — *verb intrans. North Amer., esp. US* to travel on a sledge pulled by dogs. [probably from French *marcher*, to walk]

mushroom — *noun* **1** any of various fungi that produce a fruiting body consisting of a pale fleshy umbrella-shaped cap, on the underside of which are numerous brown or pinkish spore-bearing gills, supported by a short white stem. The term is usually used to refer to edible species of such fungi, some of which are grown commercially as a food crop. See also TOADSTOOL. **2** anything resembling this in shape or in speed of growth or development. — *verb intrans.* to develop or increase with alarming speed. [from Old French *mousseron*, perhaps from *mousse*, moss]

mushroom-cloud *noun* a huge mushroom-shaped cloud of radioactive dust produced by a nuclear explosion.

mushy *adj.* (**mushier, mushiest**) **1** in a soft half-liquid state. **2** sentimental in a sickly way.

Musial, Stan (1920–) US baseball player, born in Donora, Pennsylvania. He spent his entire career with the St Louis Cardinals, for whom he made his début in 1941. He topped the National League's batting list seven times (1943–57) and was three times the Most Valuable Player of the Year. He retired in 1962 with a National League record of 3 630 hits to his credit.

music *noun* **1** the art of making sound in a rhythmically organized harmonious form, either sung or produced with instruments and usually communicating some idea or emotion. **2** such sound, especially produced by instruments rather than voices. **3** any written form in which such sound is expressed.
— **face the music** *colloq.* to confront one's critics; to deal with the consequences of one's actions.
music to one's ears anything one is glad to hear.
[from Greek *mousike*, of the Muses]

musical — *adj.* **1** of or producing music. **2** pleasant to hear; melodious. **3** having a talent for playing music. — *noun* a play or film featuring much singing and dancing.

musical chairs a game in which players walk round a number of chairs while music is playing and rush to sit on the chairs when the music stops, those unable to find an empty chair being eliminated and the number of chairs available

being reduced in each round until only one remains.

musical comedy a form of light entertainment derived from burlesque and light opera which became popular in the UK and the USA from the 1890s. Early examples include *In Town*, 1892; *The Shop-Girl*, 1894, and the American shows *Lady, Be Good!*, *No, No, Nanette*, and *Showboat*, all produced in London in the 1920s.

musicality *noun* a musical quality.

musically *adv.* in a musical way; as regards music.

music box *or* **musical box** a small box containing a device that plays music when the box is opened.

music centre a hi-fi unit incorporating an amplifier, radio, record-player, CD-player, and cassette recorder.

Music for the Royal Fireworks an instrumental work by George Frideric Handel (1749) to accompany the firework display at the celebration of the Peace of Aix-La-Chapelle. Originally written for wind ensemble, its string parts were added later for concert performance.

music hall **1** theatre entertainment including singers, dancers and comedians. **2** a theatre in which such entertainment can be seen.

musician *noun* a person skilled in performing or composing music.

musicianship *noun* skill in music.

musicologist *noun* an academic expert in music.

musicology *noun* the academic study of music in all its aspects.

music theatre a staged performance of a dramatic kind with music and (usually) singing, produced on a smaller scale than traditional opera. The term is usually applied to avant-garde works composed from the 1960s onwards, for example, by Alexander Goehr, Peter Maxwell Davies, and Hans Werner Henze. However, it may also be extended to include earlier works such as Igor Stravinsky's *The Soldier's Tale*, and the musical plays of Bertolt Brecht and Kurt Weill.

music therapy *Psychol.* the use of music in the treatment, education, etc, of people with physical or mental disabilities, also sometimes used as an aid to recovery from mental disorders.

musings *pl. noun literary* thoughts.

musique concrète a type of mid-20c music made up of recorded sounds (not necessarily musical) from various sources, which were mixed, distorted, and manipulated on tape by the composer. Both the term and the technique were originated in the 1940s by the French composer–engineer Pierre Schaeffer.

musk *noun* **1** a strong-smelling substance secreted by the glands of various animals, especially the male musk deer, much used in perfumes; any similar synthetic substance. **2** the smell of such substances. [from Latin *muscus*]

musk deer a small hornless central Asian mountain deer.

musket *noun* an early rifle-like gun loaded through the barrel and fired from the shoulder, used by soldiers between the 16th and 18th centuries. [from Old French *mousquet*]

musketeer *noun* a soldier armed with a musket.

musketry *noun* **1** muskets. **2** the use of or skill in using muskets etc. **3** a fusillade of muskets. **4** a body of troops armed with muskets.

muskiness *noun* being musky.

musk ox a long-haired ox of Canada and Greenland, whose breath has a musky smell.

muskrat *noun* **1** a large N American water rodent. **2** its highly prized thick brown fur, used to make clothes.

musk rose a Mediterranean rambling rose whose flowers have a musky scent.

musky *adj.* (**muskier, muskiest**) of, or like the smell of, musk.

Muslim *or* **Moslem** — *noun* a follower of the religion of Islam. — *adj.* relating to Muslims or to Islam. [from Arabic *muslim*, one who submits]

Muslim Brotherhood an Islamic movement, founded (1928) in Egypt by an Egyptian schoolteacher, Hasan al-Banna, which had as its original goal the reform of Islamic society by the elimination of Western influences. Subsequently, it became more radical, and its goal of a theocratic Islamic state found support in many other Sunni countries.

muslin *noun* a fine cotton cloth with a gauze-like appearance. [from French *mousseline*]

musquash *noun* same as MUSKRAT. [from Algonkian (a Native American language group)]

muss *verb chiefly North Amer. colloq.* (usually **muss something up**) to make (something, especially clothes or hair) untidy; to ruffle.

mussel *noun* any of various species of bivalve mollusc, especially the common or edible mussel, often found in dense beds several miles long on temperate and subtropical coasts. It has a bluish-black shell consisting of two hinged valves that can open and close, and it anchors itself to rocks, sea walls, etc, by a mass of tough threads called a *byssus*. Freshwater mussels are a source of mother-of-pearl. [from Latin *musculus*, diminutive of *mus*, mouse]

Musset, (Louis Charles) Alfred de (1810–57) French poet and dramatist, born in Paris. From 1830 he devoted himself to an 'armchair theatre', with plays intended for reading only (though several were later staged successfully). He had an affair with the novelist George Sand (1833–35), which is chronicled in his 4-volume series of *Nuits* (1835–1837). Other works include the autobiographical poem *La Confession d'un enfant du siècle* (1835, The Confession of a Child of his Time).

Mussolini, Benito (Amilcare Andrea), also called *Il Duce* (**the Leader**) (1883–1945) Italian politician, born in Predappio, Romagna. In 1919 he helped found the *Fasci di Combattimento* as a would-be revolutionary force. He became Prime Minister in 1922 and by 1925 had established himself as dictator. His rule saw the replacement of parliamentarism by a 'Corporate State' and an officially totalitarian system; the establishment of the Vatican state (1929); the annexation of Abyssinia (1935–6) and Albania (1939); and the formation of the Axis with Germany. His declaration of war on Britain and France exposed Italy's military unpreparedness, and was followed by a series of defeats in N and E Africa and in the Balkans. Following the Allied invasion of Sicily (Jun 1943) his supporters began to desert him, and he was overthrown and arrested (Jul 1943). Rescued from imprisonment by German paratroopers, he was placed in charge of the puppet Italian Social Republic, but in 1945 he was captured by the Italian Resistance and shot.

Mussorgsky *or* **Moussorgsky Modest (Petrovich)** (1839–81) Russian composer, born in Karevo. Educated for the army, he resigned through ill health, and studied music under Mily Alexeyevich Balakirev. A member of the Glinka-inspired nationalist group in St Petersburg (which included Nikolai Andreyevich Rimsky-Korsakov), he gained renown first for his songs and then for the opera *Boris Godunov* (1874). His piano suite *Pictures from an Exhibition* (1874) has remained a popular concert piece.

must¹ — *verb, aux.* expressing **1** need: *I must earn some extra money.* **2** duty or obligation: *you must help him.* **3** certainty: *you must be Charles.* **4** determination: *I must remember.* **5** probability:

she must be there by now. **6** inevitability: *we must all die some time.* — *noun* something essential: *fitness is a must in professional sport.* [from Anglo-Saxon *moste*]

must² *noun* the juice of grapes or other fruit before it is fermented to become wine. [from Latin *mustum vinum*, new wine]

mustachio *noun* an elaborately curly moustache. [from Italian *mostaccio*]

mustachioed *adj.* having a mustachio.

mustang *noun* a small wild horse native to the plains of the western US. [from Spanish *mestengo*]

mustard *noun* **1** any of several annual plants of the cabbage family, native to Europe and W Asia, that have bright yellow flowers, especially white mustard (*Sinapis alba*), which produces white seeds, and whose seedlings are eaten as a salad vegetable, and black mustard (*Sinapis nigra*), which produces black seeds. **2** a hot-tasting paste, used as a condiment or seasoning, prepared by grinding the seeds of black and/or white mustard to a powder, or crushing whole seeds, and mixing them with water or vinegar. **3** a light yellow or brown colour.
— **as keen as mustard** *colloq.* extremely keen or enthusiastic.
[from Old French *moustarde*]

mustard and cress a mixture of the seedlings of the mustard plant and cress, used as a salad vegetable.

mustard gas a highly poisonous gas that causes severe blistering of the skin, widely used as a chemical warfare agent in World War I.

muster — *verb* **1** *trans., intrans.* to gather (especially soldiers) together, for duty or inspection. **2** (*also* **muster something up**) to summon or gather (eg courage or energy). — *noun* any assembly or gathering, especially of troops for duty or inspection.
— **pass muster** to be accepted as satisfactory. [from Latin *monstrare*, to show]

mustiness *noun* being musty.

mustn't *contr.* must not.

musty *adj.* (**mustier, mustiest**) **1** mouldy or damp. **2** smelling or tasting stale. [perhaps from obsolete *moisty*, moist]

Mutabilitie the Titan goddess in Spenser's *The Faerie Queene*, who wields power over all mortal things, and perverts nature by breaking its laws of justice.

mutability *noun* the ability or tendency to change.

mutable *adj.* subject to change; variable. [see MUTATE]

mutagen *noun Biol.* a chemical or physical agent that induces or increases the frequency of mutations in living organisms, either by altering the DNA of the genes, or by damaging the chromosomes, eg X-rays, ultraviolet radiation, colchicine and various other chemicals.

mutant — *noun* a living organism or cell that carries a specific mutation (alteration) of a gene which usually causes it to differ from previous generations with regard to a particular characteristic, especially a visible one. — *adj.* denoting an organism or cell carrying a mutation. [from Latin *mutare*, to change]

mutate *verb trans., intrans.* **1** *Biol.* to undergo or cause to undergo mutation. **2** *formal* to change.

mutation *noun* **1** *Genetics* in a living organism, a sudden change in the structure of a single gene, the arrangement of genes on a chromosome, or the number of chromosomes. It may result in a change in the appearance (phenotype) or behaviour of the organism. **2** *formal* a change of any kind. **3** *Linguistics* a change in a speech sound,

especially a vowel, because of the nature of the sound next to it. [from Latin *mutatio*, from *mutare*, to change]
◇ A mutation can occur in any cell, but the most important mutations are those that affect the reproductive cells, because the new characteristics are passed on to the next generation. A mutation may involve deletion, breakage, or rearrangement of chromosomal material, or loss, duplication, or rearrangement of sections of DNA.
Mutations are sometimes lethal, but they can also produce advantageous changes that allow an organism to adapt to alterations in its environment. This is the basis of the theory of evolution. Natural mutations are relatively rare, but they can be induced artificially by exposing plants or animals to radiation or certain chemicals. Living organisms that display the effects of mutations are known as *mutants*.

mutatis mutandis allowing for respective differences of detail; with necessary adjustments made. [Latin, = having changed what needs to be changed]

mute — *adj.* **1** *said of a person* physically or psychologically unable to speak; dumb. **2** silent. **3** felt, but not expressed in words: *mute anger.* **4** *said of a letter in a word* not sounded. — *noun* **1** a person who is physically unable to speak, eg as a result of deafness since birth, or brain damage; also, a person who refuses to speak, eg as a result of psychological trauma. **2** any of various devices that soften or deaden the sound of a musical instrument. **3** an unsounded letter in a word. — *verb* to soften or deaden the sound of (a musical instrument). [from Latin *mutus*]

muted *adj.* **1** *said of sound or colour* not loud or harsh; soft. **2** *said of feelings, etc* mildly expressed; not outspoken: *muted criticism.*

mute swan the commonest European swan.

mutilate *verb* **1** to cause severe injury to, especially by removing a limb or organ. **2** to severely damage, especially to alter (a text) beyond recognition. [from Latin *mutilare*, to cut off]

mutilation *noun* **1** severe physical injury usually visible and permanent. **2** severe damage.

mutineer *noun* a person who mutinies.

mutinous *adj.* **1** having mutinied; likely to mutiny. **2** of or relating to mutiny.

mutiny — *noun* (PL. **mutinies**) rebellion, or an act of rebellion, against established authority, especially in the armed services. — *verb intrans.* (**mutinies, mutinied**) to engage in mutiny. [from Old French *mutin*, rebellious]

mutt *noun colloq.* **1** a dog, especially a mongrel. **2** a foolish person. [perhaps from MUTTONHEAD]

mutter — *verb* (**muttered, muttering**) **1** *trans., intrans.* to utter (words) in a quiet, barely audible voice. **2** *intrans.* to grumble or complain. — *noun* **1** a soft, barely audible tone of voice. **2** a complaint. [from Middle English *moteren*]

mutton *noun* the flesh of an adult sheep, used as food.
— **mutton dressed as lamb** *derog. colloq.* an older person, especially a woman, dressed (especially unbecomingly) in youthful clothes.
[from Old French *moton*, sheep]

muttonchops *pl. noun* men's long side whiskers, narrow at the ears and broad and rounded at the lower jaw.

muttonhead *noun derog. colloq.* a stupid person.

mutual *adj.* **1** felt by each of two or more people about the other or others; reciprocal: *mutual admiration.* **2** of, to or towards each other: *mutual supporters.* **3** *colloq.* shared by each of two or

more; common: *a mutual friend.* [from Latin *mutuus*, borrowed or reciprocal]

mutual fund an investment company that pools the funds of its shareholders, and invests in a diversified portfolio of stocks and shares. It grows continually by offering new shares from sale. A UK example is the unit trust company.

mutualism *noun Biol.* a relationship between two organisms of different species, that is beneficial to both of them.

mutuality *noun* being mutual.

mutually *adv.* **1** with mutual action or feeling, reciprocally. **2** jointly.

Muybridge, Eadweard James, originally Edward James Muggeridge (1830–1904) English-born US photographer, born in Kingston-upon-Thames, Greater London. He worked mainly in the USA, and was a pioneer in the study of animal movement by sequences of photographs. He recorded a galloping horse in 1877, and subsequently projected images from such records as moving pictures, thus encouraging the development of cinematography.

Muzak *noun trademark* light recorded music continuously played in restaurants, shops, lifts, etc; also, the system on which it is played.

muzzily *adv.* in a muzzy way.

muzziness *noun* being muzzy.

muzzle — *noun* **1** the projecting jaws and nose of an animal, eg a dog. **2** an arrangement of straps fitted round an animal's jaws to prevent it biting. **3** the open end of a gun barrel. — *verb* **1** to put a muzzle on (eg a dog). **2** to prevent from speaking; to silence or gag. [from Old French *musel*]

muzzy *adj.* (**muzzier, muzziest**) **1** not thinking clearly; confused. **2** blurred; hazy.

MW *abbrev.* **1** medium wave. **2** megawatt.

MX missile *abbrev.* Missile Experimental.

my — *adj.* **1** of or belonging to me. **2** used with nouns in various exclamations: *my goodness! / my foot!* — *interj.* expressing surprise: *my, how grown-up you look!* [from Anglo-Saxon *min*]

myalgia *noun Medicine* pain in the muscles. [from Greek *mys*, muscle + *algos*, pain]

myalgic encephalomyelitis (ABBREV. **ME**) a debilitating disorder characterized by extreme fatigue, muscular pain, lack of concentration, memory loss, and depression. The symptoms eventually subside, but recovery may take many months. The existence and causes of ME have been the subject of much controversy, but in a number of cases it has been associated with a previous long-term viral infection.

Myall Creek massacre in Australian history, the massacre of 28 Aborigines in NE New South Wales (1838) by a party of assigned convicts for an alleged attack on cattle. Seven of the men charged with the massacre were found guilty and hanged.

Mycale, Battle of a naval battle (479 BC) in coastal Ionia in which the Greeks defeated the Persians.

mycelium *noun* (PL. **mycelia**) *Biol.* in multicellular fungi, a mass or network of threadlike filaments (known as hyphae) that is formed as a result of the growth of the non-reproductive tissues. [from Greek *mykes*, mushroom]

Mycenae an ancient fortified city in the Argolid, associated in Greek tradition with Agamemnon, the conqueror of Troy. Its extensive Bronze Age remains indicate that Mycenae was the seat of a warrior chieftain in the 16c BC, although this is no longer thought to be that of Agamemnon himself. See illustration p. 852.

The Lion Gate, Mycenae

Mycenaean — *adj.* relating to the ancient Bronze Age civilization in Greece (1500–1100 BC), known from the Homeric poems and from remains at Mycenae and other sites in S Greece. — *noun* an inhabitant of the Mycenaean world.
◇ Mycenaean civilization reached its zenith in mainland Greece in the 13c BC. Archaeological evidence from sites such as Mycenae itself, Pylos, and Tiryns, indicates that there was a palace system of government similar to that which may be found earlier in Minoan Crete. There appears, however, to have been a warrior class, absent in Minoan civilization. The flourishing Mycenaean art and architecture were much influenced by the Minoans, and the Cretan syllabic script (Linear A) was developed into a writing system (Linear B). The Mycenaeans appear to have lost their expansionist drive c.1 200 BC and many palace sites were destroyed or abandoned.

mycology *noun Biol.* the study of fungi. [from Greek *mykes*, mushroom + -LOGY]

mycotoxin *noun Biol.* any poisonous substance produced by a fungus.

myelin *noun Zool.* a soft white substance that forms a thin insulating sheath around the axons (long threadlike outgrowths) of the nerve cells of vertebrates. [from Greek *mylos*, marrow]

myelitis *noun* 1 inflammation of the spinal cord, most commonly associated with multiple sclerosis, which results in paralysis of the body below the affected region. 2 inflammation of the bone marrow, characterized by severe pain and swelling, which if untreated may result in bone deformity. It is caused by infection, eg after a compound fracture, or during surgery when the marrow is exposed. — Also called *osteomyelitis*. [from Greek *myelos*, marrow]

myeloma *noun Medicine* a tumour of the bone marrow, caused by the proliferation of malignant plasma cells. [from Greek *myelos* marrow]

Myers, Frederic William Henry (1843–1901) English psychical researcher, poet, essayist, and (from 1872) school inspector, born in Keswick, Cumbria. In 1882 he helped found the Society for Psychical Research, and for the rest of his life was one of its busiest researchers.

Myfanwy a female first name. [from the Welsh name *Mabanwy*, child of water, or *my-manwy*, my fine one]

Myingyan POP (1973) 220 000, a town in Mandalay division, central Burma (Myanma). It is situated on the R Irrawaddy.

Mykonos see MIKONOS.

Mylae, Battle of a naval battle (260 BC) off Sicily in the First Punic War in which the Romans defeated the Carthaginian fleet. It was Rome's first victory with her newly built navy.

My Lai incident the massacre of several hundred unarmed inhabitants of the S Vietnamese village of My Lai by US troops in Mar 1968, an incident exposed by *Life* magazine photos in 1969. The officer responsible, Lieutenant Calley, was court-martialled in 1970–1.

mylonite *noun Geol.* a dark fine-grained hard metamorphic rock, often banded or streaked and having a glassy appearance, formed as a result of recrystallization of mineral fragments after crushing and grinding. [from Greek *mylon*, mill]

myna *or* **mynah** *noun* any of various large SE Asian birds of the starling family, some of which can be taught to imitate human speech. [from Hindi *maina*]

myocardiac *adj.* myocardial.

myocardial *adj.* relating to or in the region of the myocardium.

myocarditis *noun Medicine* inflammation of the heart muscle (the myocardium).

myocardium *noun* (PL. **myocardia**) *Anat.* the muscular tissue of the heart. [from Greek *myos*, muscle + *kardia*, heart]

myofibril *noun Zool.* any of the minute filaments which together make up a single muscle fibre. [from Greek *myos*, muscle + FIBRIL]

myoglobin *noun Biochem.* a protein that stores oxygen in the muscles of vertebrates. [from Greek *mys myos*, muscle]

myopia *noun Medicine* short-sightedness, in which parallel rays of light entering the eye are brought to a focus in front of the retina, so that distant objects appear blurred, usually because the distance between the lens and the retina is too great, or the lens is too convex. It is corrected by wearing contact lenses or spectacles with concave (diverging) lenses. [from Greek *myops*, short-sighted]

myopic *adj.* short-sighted.

Myra a female first name, devised by the Elizabethan poet Fulke Greville (1554–1628). [origin unknown; possibly an anagram of MARY]

Myrdal, (Karl) Gunnar (1898–1987) Swedish economist, politician, and international civil servant. He became Professor of Political Economy at Stockholm in 1933, and was also Executive Secretary of the UN Economic Commission for Europe (1947–57). He was jointly awarded the Nobel Prize for Economics in 1974, principally for his work on the critical application of economic theory to Third World countries.

myriad *noun, adj.* denoting an exceedingly great number: *a myriad of stars / her myriad admirers.* [from Greek *myrias*, ten thousand]

myrmidon *noun literary* 1 a hired thug; a henchman. 2 a follower. [named after the MYRMIDONS]

Myrmidons in Greek legend, a band of warriors from Thessaly who went to the Trojan War with Achilles.

Myron (5c BC) Greek sculptor, born in Eleutherae. A contemporary of Phidias, he lived in Athens. He worked in bronze, and is known for the celebrated *Discobolus* (Discus Thrower).

myrrh *noun* 1 any of various African and Asian trees and shrubs producing a brown aromatic resin, used medicinally and in perfumes. 2 the resin produced by these. [from Greek *myrra*]

Myrtle a female first name, after the name of the shrub.

myrtle *noun* a S European evergreen shrub with pink or white flowers and dark blue aromatic berries; any of various related shrubs. [from Greek *myrtos*]

myself *pron.* 1 the form of *me* used when the speaker or writer is the object of an action he or she performs. *I did myself a favour / I said to myself.* 2 used to emphasize I or me: *I myself prefer tea.*

3 my normal self: *am not myself today.* 4 (*also* **by myself**) alone; without help.

Mysore POP (1991) 480 000, a city in Karnataka state, SW India, situated 850km/528mi SE of Bombay. It is known as the 'garden city of India' because of its wide streets and numerous parks. HISTORY formerly the dynastic capital of Mysore state; founded in the 16c. NOTABLE FEATURES Maharaja's Palace, within an ancient fort (rebuilt in the 18c); statue of Nandi (sacred bull of Shiva) on Chamundi Hill in the SE, a place of pilgrimage.

mysterious *adj.* 1 difficult or impossible to understand or explain; deeply curious. 2 creating or suggesting mystery.

mysteriously *adv.* in a mysterious way.

mystery *noun* (PL. **mysteries**) 1 an event or phenomenon that cannot be, or has not been, explained. 2 the quality of being difficult or impossible to explain or understand, or of being odd or obscure and arousing curiosity. 3 a person about whom very little is known. 4 a story about a crime that is difficult to solve. 5 a religious rite, especially the Eucharist. [from Greek *mysterion*]

mystery play a medieval play based on the life of Christ, or of a saint.
◇ Originally called *miracle plays*, ie representations of the miracles performed by the saints, they later encompassed enactments of events throughout the Bible (though usually only up to the Ascension) and were an important type of early theatre.

mystery religion a religious cult of the Graeco-Roman world, admission to which was restricted to those who had undertaken secret initiation rites or mysteries. The best known are those of Demeter at Eleusis in Greece; the cults of Dionysus, Isis, and Mithras all had some element of secrecy.

mystery tour a round trip to a destination not revealed in advance.

mystic — *noun* a person whose life is devoted to meditation or prayer in an attempt to achieve direct communication with God, regarded as the ultimate reality. — *adj.* mystical. [from Greek *mystikos*, from *mystes*, an initiate]

mystical *adj.* 1 relating to or involving truths about the nature of God and reality revealed only to those people with a spiritually enlightened mind; esoteric. 2 mysterious. 3 wonderful or awe-inspiring.

mysticism *noun* the practice of gaining direct communication with God through prayer and meditation; the belief in the existence of such a state as a reality hidden from ordinary human understanding.
◇ Christian mysticism tends to focus on the person and sufferings of Christ, attempting to move beyond the image and word to the immediate presence of God. In contrast to other forms of mysticism, Christian mystics reject the idea of the absorption of the individual into the divine, and retain the distinction between the individual believer and God. Notable Christian mystics include St Augustine, St Francis of Assisi, and St Teresa of Avila.

mystification *noun* 1 the act of mystifying. 2 being mystified.

mystify *verb* (**mystifies, mystified**) 1 to puzzle or bewilder. 2 to make mysterious. [from French *mystifier*]

mystifying *adj.* that mystifies.

mystique *noun* a mysterious quality possessed by a person or thing. [from French]

myth *noun* 1 an ancient story dealing with gods and heroes, especially one explaining some natural phenomenon; such stories in general. 2 a commonly held false notion. **3** a non-existent person or thing. [from Greek *mythos*]

mythical *adj.* **1** relating to myth. **2** imaginary.

mythically *adv.* in a mythical way.

mythological *adj.* relating or belonging to mythology.

mythology *noun* (PL. **mythologies**) **1** myths in general. **2** a collection of myths.

myxomatosis *noun Biol.* an infectious viral disease of rabbits that is usually fatal and is transmitted by fleas. [Greek *myxa*, mucus + *-oma*, tumour]

M'Zab Valley an oasis in a fertile gorge along the Oued M'zab watercourse in the Saharan region of central Algeria. The area was settled in the 11c by the M'zabites, a nonconformist Islamic sect. It is renowned for its five ancient towns, its 4 000 wells, and its palm groves. It is a World Heritage site.

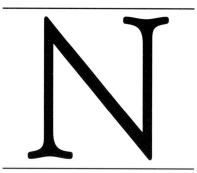

N¹ *or* **n** *noun* (PL. **Ns, N's, n's**) the fourteenth letter of the English alphabet.

N² *abbrev.* **1** National or Nationalist. **2** newton. **3** New. **4** North or Northern.

N³ *symbol* **1** *Chem.* nitrogen. **2** *Chess* knight. **3** *as an international vehicle mark* Norway.

n¹ — *noun* **1** *Maths.* an indefinite number. **2** *colloq.* a large number. — *adj.* of an indefinite or large number.

n² *abbrev.* **1** noun. **2** neuter. **3** note. **4** nano-. **5** neutron.

'n' *colloq. abbrev.* and.

NA *abbrev., as an international vehicle mark* Netherlands Antilles.

Na *symbol Chem.* sodium. [from Latin *natrium*]

NAACP *abbrev.* in the USA, the National Association for the Advancement of Colored People, a pressure group which aims to extend awareness among the country's black population of their political rights. It has successfully used the courts to remove certain legal barriers to the equal rights of blacks, despite political opposition.

NAAFI — *abbrev.* Navy, Army and Air Force Institutes. — *noun* a canteen or shop run by the NAAFI.

Naas, Gaelic **Nás na Riogh** POP (1991) 11 000, the capital of Kildare county, Leinster province, Irish Republic. It is a market town, lying on a branch of the Grand Canal, SW of Dublin. It was formerly the capital of the kings of Leinster. The area is noted for its horse-racing.

nab *verb trans.* (**nabbed, nabbing**) *colloq.* **1** to catch in the act of doing wrong. **2** to arrest. **3** to grab or take.

Nabis a small group of artists working in Paris (c.1890–c.1900) under the influence of Paul Gauguin. Its leading members included Maurice Denis, Pierre Bonnard, and Edouard Vuillard. [Hebrew, = prophet]

Nablus POP (1971e) 44 000, a city on the Israeli-occupied West Bank, NW Jordan. It is situated 48km/30mi N of Jerusalem. The town is the market centre for the surrounding agricultural region. NOTABLE FEATURES Great Mosque; Jacob's Well is nearby.

nabob *noun* **1** *colloq.* a wealthy and influential person. **2** *old use* a European returned from India with a vast fortune. **3** *Hist.* a Muslim governor under the Mogul empire in India; a nawab. [from Urdu *nawwab*]

Nabokov, Vladimir (Vladimirovich) (1899–1977) US writer, born in St Petersburg, Russia. He settled in the USA in 1940, and became Professor of Russian Literature at Cornell in 1948. A considerable Russian author, he established himself as a novelist in English, notably with his controversial novel *Lolita* (1955). His later work includes *Pale Fire* (1962) and *Ada* (1969), and he is also known for his short stories.

nacelle *noun Aeron.* **1** the streamlined outer casing of an aircraft engine. **2** the basket or gondola of a balloon or airship. [from French *nacelle*, from late Latin *navicella*, from Latin *navis* ship]

nachos *pl. noun* a Mexican dish of tortilla chips topped with chillis and melted cheese. [from Mexican Spanish *nacho*]

nacre *noun* mother-of-pearl obtained from the shell of certain molluscs. [from Arabic *naqqarah*, drum]

nacreous *adj.* like or made of nacre.

NACRO *abbrev.* National Association for the Care and Resettlement of Offenders.

Nadine a female first name. [a French form of Russian *Nadezda*, hope]

nadir *noun* **1** *Astron.* the point on the celestial sphere that is directly below an observer. It is diametrically opposite the zenith. See also ZENITH. **2** the absolute depth, eg of despair or degradation. [from Arabic *nazir-as-samt*, opposite the zenith]

naevus *noun* (PL. **naevi**) a birthmark or mole on the skin. [from Latin *naevus*]

naff *adj. slang* **1** stupid; foolish. **2** tasteless; vulgar. **3** rubbishy; of poor quality.

NAFTA *or* **Nafta** *abbrev.* **1** North American Free Trade Association. **2** North American Free Trade Agreement, an agreement between the USA, Mexico, and Canada ratified in 1993, allowing for the progressive lifting of tariffs and elimination of most import and export restrictions between the three counties.

Nafud a desert area in the N part of the Arabian Peninsula. It is c.290km/180mi long and 225km/140mi wide. Occasional violent windstorms have formed crescent-shaped dunes, which rise to heights of c.200m. Dates, vegetables, barley, and fruit are grown in oases, especially near the Hejaz Mts.

nag¹ *noun* **1** *derog.* a broken-down old horse. **2** a small horse for riding. [from Middle English *nagge*]

nag² — *verb* (**nagged, nagging**) **1** *trans., intrans.* (*also* **nag at someone**) to scold them constantly; to keep finding fault. **2** *trans.* (**nag someone into something**) to keep urging someone to do something. **3** *intrans.* (**nag at someone**) to cause them anxiety: *a nagging suspicion.* **4** *intrans. said of pain* to persist. — *noun* a person who nags. [from Norse *nagga*, to rub, grumble, or quarrel]

Nagaland POP (1991) 1.2m, a state in NE India, bounded to the E by Burma (Myanma). AREA 16 527sq km/6 379sq mi. The administrative centre is located at Kohima. HISTORY former territory of Assam; became a state in 1963; a strong movement for independence; talks with the Naga tribes underground movement resulted in the Shillong Peace Agreement in 1975. GOVERNMENT governed by a 60-member State Assembly. ECONOMY rice, sugar cane, pulses; forestry; weaving.

Nagasaki POP (1991e) 445 000, the capital of Nagasaki prefecture, W Kyushu, Japan. HISTORY discovered by the Portuguese in 1545; centre for Christian missionaries from the 16c; the target for the second atomic bomb of World War II, dropped on 9 Aug 1945, killing or wounding c.75 000 people, and destroying over one third of the city. NOTABLE FEATURES stone bridges across the R Nakajima, including Spectacles Bridge (1634); Sofukuji Pavilions; Peace Statue in Peace Park.

Nägeli, Karl Wilhelm von (1817–91) Swiss botanist, born in Kilchberg, near Zurich. Professor at Munich (from 1858), he was one of the early writers on evolution. He investigated the growth of cells and originated a theory describing the structure of starch grains, cell walls, and cell organelles.

nagger *noun* a person or problem that nags or annoys.

nagging *noun, said of a problem or anxiety* constantly worrying or causing concern.

Nag Hammadi texts a library of religious texts recorded in Coptic and discovered in 1945 near the town of Nag Hammadi, Egypt. It comprises some 12 books containing 52 tractates, the Scriptures of the Christian Gnostic movement in Egypt; some works, however, are neither openly 'Gnostic' or 'Christian', but philosophical or Jewish in character. It is valuable evidence for this early form of 'heretical' Christianity.

Nagorno Karabakh *or* **Nagorno Karabach** *or* **Nagorny Karabakh** POP (1990) 192 000, an autonomous region in Azerbaijan. AREA 4 400sq km/1 700sq mi. CAPITAL Stepanakert. PHYSICAL DESCRIPTION steppe on the lowland and dense forest on the lower slopes; peaks rise to 3 724m at Mt Gyamysh. The population is mainly Armenian (76%); Christianity (Armenians) and Shiite Muslim (Azeris) are the chief religions. HISTORY became an autonomous protectorate in 1917; annexed to Azerbaijan in 1923; a dispute between Armenia and Azerbaijan since 1989 over control of the region has resulted in armed conflict. ECONOMY barley; fruit; silk; cotton.

Nagoya POP (1991e) 2.2m, the port capital of Aichi prefecture, central Honshu, Japan. It lies on the NE shore of Ise-wan Bay. Originally founded as a castle in the 17c, it is now the fifth-largest city in Japan. The city was heavily bombed in World War II. NOTABLE FEATURES Nagoya Castle (rebuilt in 1959); Atsuta Shrine (c.1c); Tokugawa Art Museum.

Nagpur POP (1991) 1.7m, a city in Maharashtra, W central India. It is situated on the R Pench, 675km/419mi NE of Bombay. HISTORY founded in the 18c; the scene of the final British overthrow of the Mahrattas in 1817; former capital of Berar and Madhya Pradesh states.

Nagy, Imre (1895–1958) Hungarian politician, born in Kaposvar. He had a minor post in the Béla Kun revolutionary government in Hungary, but in 1929 fled to the USSR. He returned with the Red Army (1944) and became Minister of Agriculture, and as Prime Minister (1953–5) introduced milder political control. When Soviet forces began to suppress the 1956 revolution, he appealed to the world for help, but was displaced by the Soviet puppet János Kdr, and was executed in Budapest.

Nahanni a national park in the Northwest Territories of Canada. It is the habitat of the peregrine falcon, golden eagle, grey wolf, and grizzly bear, as well as many other species. It is accessible only by air or water as there are no roads. The park is a World Heritage site. AREA 4 770sq km/1 842sq mi.

NAHT *abbrev.* National Association of Head Teachers.

Nahuatl see AZTEC.

Nahum, Book of one of the 12 so-called 'minor' prophetic writings of the Hebrew Bible and Old Testament, attributed to a prophet called Nahum. The oracle vigorously announces the imminent downfall of Assyria and the destruction of Nineveh (612 BC). Interpreted as the Lord's judgement upon its wickedness and as good news for Judah, it was perhaps intended to encourage Judaean moves for independence from the occupying power.

naiad *noun* (PL. **naiads, naiades**) in Greek mythology, a nymph who inhabits springs, fountains, rivers, and lakes; also, the aquatic larva of a dragonfly, mayfly, stone-fly, or damselfly. [from Greek *naias, naiados*, from *naein*, to flow]

nail — *noun* **1** a horny plate covering the upper surface of the tip of a finger or toe. **2** a metal spike hammered into something eg to join two objects together or to serve as a hook. — *verb* **1** (*also* **nail something down** *or* **together**) to fasten it with, or as if with, a nail or nails. **2** *colloq.* to catch, trap, or corner. **3** to detect, identify, or expose (a lie, deception, etc).
— **hit the nail on the head** to pinpoint a problem exactly; to describe something in terms that sum it up precisely.
nail someone down *colloq.* to extract a definite decision or promise from them.
nail something down to define or identify it clearly.
on the nail *colloq., said of payment* made immediately.
[from Anglo-Saxon *nægl*]
◇ The nail is a specialized modification of the outer two layers of the epidermis in higher mammals, taking the place of the lower mammal's claw. It is partly surrounded by a fold of skin (the *nail wall*), and is firmly anchored to the underlying nail bed. Nails grow at a rate of about 1mm per week, and faster in summer than in winter.

Naipaul, V(idiadhar) S(urajprasad) (1932–) West Indian novelist, born in Chaguanas, Trinidad. He has lived in England since 1950, and his wide travelling experiences are recorded in such books as *The Middle Passage* (1962, on the West Indies) and *An Area of Darkness* (1964, on India). His early short stories are collected in *Miguel Street* (1959), and a sequence of comic novels set in Trinidad concludes with *A House for Mr Biswas* (1961). Later novels reveal a darker vision (eg *The Mimic Men*, 1967, and *A Bend in the River*, 1979). In 1993, he was the first recipient of the British Literature Prize.

Nairobi **1** (1990e) 1.5m, the capital of Kenya, on the central Kenya Plateau, 450km/280mi NW of Mombasa. The city is the largest in E Africa and home of the headquarters of the United Nations Environment Programme Secretariat. It

is a centre of communications and commerce. NOTABLE FEATURES cathedral (1963); Sikh Temple; National Museum (including largest collection of African butterflies in the world); Snake Park. **2** a province in SW Kenya with Nairobi as its capital.

naïve *or* **naive** *adj.* **1** simple, innocent or unsophisticated. **2** *derog.* too trusting; credulous; not worldly enough. [from French *naïve*, feminine of *naïf*, from Latin *nativus*, native]

naïvely *or* **naively** *adv.* in a naïve or innocent way.

naïvety *or* **naivety** *noun* excessive trust or innocence.

Nakasone, Yasuhiro (1917–) Japanese politician, born in Gumma Prefecture, E Japan. As Prime Minister (1982–7), he supported the renewal of the US–Japan Security Treaty, and maintained close relations with US President Reagan.

naked *adj.* **1** wearing no clothes. **2** without fur, feathers, or foliage. **3** barren; blank; empty. **4** undisguised; blatant or flagrant: *naked greed*. **5** *said of a light or flame* uncovered; exposed. **6** *said of the eye* unaided by a telescope or microscope. **7** *literary* vulnerable; defenceless. [from Anglo-Saxon *nacod*]

Naked and the Dead, The a novel by Norman Mailer (1948). His first, it is an account of soldiers on a Pacific Island in World War II.

nakedly *adv.* in a naked or undisguised way.

nakedness *noun* a naked state; being naked or undisguised.

naker *noun* a small high-pitched kettledrum of Arabic origin, played in pairs, and used throughout medieval Europe. [from Old French *nacre*, from Arabic *naqara*]

Nakhon Ratchasima POP (1989e) 207 000, an ancient walled city and trade centre in E central Thailand. It lies on the R Mun, on the edge of the NE plateau, 260km/161mi NE of Bangkok. NOTABLE FEATURES many temples.

NALGO *abbrev.* National and Local Government Officers' Associaton.

Namangan POP (1991e) 319 000, a city in Uzbekistan. It is situated on the R Syr Darya.

Namaqualand *or* **Namaland** an arid region in S Namibia and W South Africa. Little Namaqualand extends S from the Orange R on the Namibia–South Africa frontier. CHIEF TOWN Springbok. Great Namaqualand extends N from the Orange R into central Namibia. CHIEF TOWN Keetmanshoop. There has been a European presence in the region since 1665. The indigenous peoples are known as Namaquas or Nama. ECONOMY diamond mines.

Namath, Joe (Joseph William) (1943–) US footballer, born in Beaver Falls, Pennsylvania. He joined the New York Jets from the unbeaten University of Alabama team in 1964, and became one of the leading quarterbacks in the 1960s. His lifestyle outside football attracted a great deal of publicity, and since his retirement (1978) he has remained in the public eye with appearances in films and on television.

namby-pamby *adj. derog.* **1** feebly sentimental; soppy. **2** prim; over-demure. [from the scornful nickname of the 17c poet Ambrose Phillips]

name — *noun* **1** a word or words by which an individual person, place, or thing is identified and referred to. **2** reputation: *get a bad name / clear one's name*. **3** a famous or important person, firm, etc: *the big names in fashion*. — *verb trans.* **1** to give a name to. **2** to mention or identify by name: *name three French poets*. **3** to specify or decide on. **4** (**name as**) to choose or appoint.
— **call someone names** to insult or abuse them.
in all but name in practice, though not officially: *leader in all but name*.
in the name of ... **1** by the authority of ... **2** for the sake of; using as justification: *hundreds tortured in the name of religion*.

in name only officially, but not in practice: *ruler in name only*.
make a name for oneself to become famous.
name someone after someone else to call them by the same name as someone else, by way of commemoration, etc.
name the day to announce the date of one's wedding.
name someone for someone else *North Amer.* to call them by the same name as someone else.
name names to identify, eg culprits, by name.
the name of the game *colloq.* the predominant or essential aspect or aim of some activity.
to one's name belonging to one.
[from Anglo-Saxon *nama*]

name day the feast day of the saint after whom one is named.

name-drop *verb intrans.* (**name-dropped**, **name-dropping**) to indulge in name-dropping.

name-dropper *noun* a person who is given to name-dropping.

name-dropping *noun derog.* the practice of casually referring to well-known people as if they were friends, to impress one's hearers.

nameless *adj.* **1** having no name. **2** unidentified: *The culprit shall remain nameless*. **3** too awful to specify; unmentionable.

namely *adv.* used to introduce an expansion or explanation of what has just been mentioned: *her intention, namely to discredit the other candidates*.

Namen see NAMUR.

nameplate *noun* a plate on or beside a door, bearing the occupant's name, etc.

namesake *noun* a person with the same name as oneself.

Namib Desert a desert following almost the entire Atlantic Ocean seaboard of W Namibia. It is c.1 300km/800mi long and 50–160km/30–100mi wide. Some of the highest sand dunes in the world are found here.

Namibia, formerly **South-West Africa** (to 1968), earlier **German South-West Africa** POP (1992e) 1.5m, a republic in SW Africa, divided into 22 administrative districts. AREA 823 144sq km/317 734sq mi. It is bounded N by Angola, NE by Zambia, E by Botswana, S by South Africa, and W by the Atlantic Ocean. CAPITAL Windhoek. CHIEF TOWNS Lüderitz, Keetmanshoop, Grootfontein. TIME ZONE GMT –2. The population is mainly African (85%), chiefly Ovambo. OFFICIAL LANGUAGES Afrikaans, English. CURRENCY the Namibian dollar. PHYSICAL DESCRIPTION the Namib desert runs along the Atlantic Ocean coast; the inland plateau has a mean elevation of 1 500m; the highest point is Brandberg (2 606m); the Kalahari desert lies to the E and S; the Orange R forms the S frontier with South Africa. CLIMATE low rainfall on the coast, higher in the interior; the average annual rainfall at Windhoek, representative of the interior, is 360mm and the average maximum daily temperature range is 20–30°C. HISTORY British and Dutch missionaries arrived from the late 18c; German protectorate in 1884; mandated to South Africa by the League of Nations in 1920; the UN assumed direct responsibility in 1966, changing the name to Namibia in 1968, and recognizing the South-West Africa People's Organization (SWAPO) as representative of the Namibian people; South Africa continued to administer the area as South-West Africa; SWAPO commenced guerrilla activities in 1966; bases were established in S Angola, involving Cuban troops in the 1970s; an interim administration was installed by South Africa in 1985; gained full independence in 1990; agreement was reached with South Africa in 1993 that the Walvis Bay area would be governed by Namibia. GOVERNMENT governed within a multiparty system by an executive President, elected for a five-year term, assisted by a Cabinet headed by a Prime Minister; the legislative lower house of the bicameral parliament is an elected National Assembly, serving for up to five years; the National Council is the upper house representing regional leaders and serving for six years. ECONOMY agriculture employs c.60% of the population; livestock; subsistence farming in the N; major world producer of diamonds and uranium; copper, lead, zinc, arsenic, cadmium, salt, silver, tin, tungsten; fishing, food processing, brewing, plastics, furniture, textiles.

Namibia

Namier, Sir Lewis (Bernstein), originally **Ludwik Bernstein Niemirowski** (1888–1960) British historian, born near Warsaw, Poland. He came to England in 1906, studied at Oxford, took British nationality, and became Professor of Modern History at Manchester (1931–52). His school of history emphasized detailed analysis of institutions and events, particularly parliamentary elections, in order to discern the motivation of the individuals involved.

Namur, Flemish **Namen 1** POP (1992e) 104 000, the industrial capital of Namur province in Wallonia, S Belgium. It is situated at the confluence of the Sambre and Meuse rivers. HISTORY had military significance in the Roman era; with its outer forts, built in 1889–1902, Namur became a key strategic point of the Belgian defence line on the R Meuse; conquered by the Germans in 1914 and 1940. NOTABLE FEATURES cathedral (1751–67); citadel (17c). **2** a province in S Belgium with Namur as its capital.

nan noun a slightly leavened Indian bread, similar to pitta bread. [from Hindi *nan*]

Nana a novel by Emile Zola (1880). One of the *Rougon-Macquart* novels, it describes the corrupt lifestyle of a courtesan.

nana see NANNY.

Nanak, also called **Guru Nanak** (1469–1539) Indian religious leader and founder of Sikhism, born near Lahore, present-day Pakistan. Though originally a Hindu, his doctrine, set out later in the *Adi-Granth*, sought a fusion of Brahmanism and Islam on the grounds that both were monotheistic, although Nanak's own ideas leaned rather towards pantheism.

Nana Sahib, originally **Brahmin Dundhu Panth** (c.1820–59) Indian rebel, the adopted son of the ex-peshwa (head) of the Marathas. At the outbreak of the Indian Mutiny in 1857, he became leader of the Sepoys, and was held responsible for the massacres at Cawnpore (Kanpur). After the collapse of the rebellion he escaped into Nepal.

Nanchang or **Nan-ch'ang** POP (1990) 1.4m, the industrial capital of Jiangxi province, SE China. It is a distribution centre for kaolin pottery. HISTORY founded in 201 BC during the E Han Dynasty; scene of the Nanchang Uprising in 1927, when peasants defeated Nationalist forces.

NOTABLE FEATURES Jiangxi Provincial Museum; Bada Shanren Exhibition Hall.

Nancy POP (1990) 311 000, the manufacturing capital of Meurthe-et-Moselle department, Lorraine region, NE France. It lies on the R Meurthe and the Marne–Rhine Canal, 306km/190mi E of Paris, and is the former capital of Lorraine. It became part of France in 1766. NOTABLE FEATURES famed for its 18c Baroque architecture: Place Stanislas, Place de la Carrière, and Place d'Alliance comprise a World Heritage site; 17c town hall; 13c ducal palace; 15c Eglise des Cordeliers; 14c Porte de la Craffe; cathedral (1703–42).

Nancy 1 a member of Fagin's gang of pickpockets, and the mistress of Bill Sikes, in Charles Dickens's *Oliver Twist*. **2** a female first name. [originally a pet-form of CONSTANCE, now an independent name]

nancy noun (PL. **nancies**) (*also* **nancy boy**) derog. colloq. an effeminate young man.

Nanjing or **Nanking**, formerly **Chian-ning** POP (1990) 2.6m, the capital of Jiangsu province, SE China. It lies on the Yangtze R. HISTORY founded in 900 BC; capital of China in 220–589, 907–79, and 1928–49; centre of the Taiping Rebellion; grew in importance as a river port and trade centre; remained an open port after the Opium War in 1842. NOTABLE FEATURES many historical sites and relics; Nanjing Museum; Zhongshanling Mausoleum (in memory of Sun Yatsen); Mingxiaoling (Ming Emperor's Tomb); Zijin Mountain Observatory and Museum; Yuhuatai Park.

Nanking see NANJING.

Nanning or **Nan-ning** POP (1990) 1.3m, the capital of Guangxi autonomous region, S China. It is China's most southerly city. HISTORY founded during the Yuan Dynasty; served as a military supply town during the Vietnam War; closed to foreigners until 1977.

nanny — noun (PL. **nannies**) **1** a children's nurse. **2** colloq. (*also* **nana, nanna**) a child's name for a grandmother. — verb trans. (**nannies, nannied**) to over-protect or over-supervise. [from *Nanny*, a form of *Ann*]

nanny goat an adult female goat.

nano- combining form forming words denoting: **1** a thousand millionth: *nanometre / nanosecond.* **2** microscopic size: *nanoplankton.* [from Greek *nanos*, dwarf]

Nansen, Fridtjof (1861–1930) Norwegian explorer, scientist, and statesman, born near Oslo. In 1882 he travelled into the Arctic regions, and in 1888 made an E–W journey across Greenland. His major achievement was the partial accomplishment of his scheme to reach the North Pole by letting his specially-built ship, the *Fram*, get frozen into the ice N of Siberia and drift with a current setting towards Greenland. In this way, in 1895 he reached the highest latitude till then attained: 86° 14″N. He became Professor of Zoology (1897) and of Oceanography (1908) at Oslo, and was Norwegian Ambassador in London (1906–8). He was awarded the Nobel Peace Prize for Russian relief work in 1922.

Nantes, Breton **Naoned**, ancient **Condivincum**, later **Namnetes** POP (1990) 492 000, the capital of Pays de la Loire region and of Loire-Atlantique department, W France. Situated at the head of the estuary of the Loire, 171km/106mi W of Tours, it is a manufacturing and commercial seaport, and the seventh-largest city in France. HISTORY centre of the sugar and ebony trade between the 16c and the 18c; France's leading port by the end of the 18c; early 19c decline was halted by the construction of the harbour at St-Nazaire in 1856 and later river dredging; the writer Jules Verne was born in Nantes in 1828; major bomb damage in World War II. NOTABLE FEATURES Gothic Cathedral of St-Pierre-et-St-Paul; Museum of Fine Arts; Château

des Ducs (10c, rebuilt in 1466), where the Edict of Nantes was signed.

Nantes, Edict of a law declared (1598) by Henry IV of France to grant religious and civil liberties to his Huguenot subjects at the end of the Wars of Religion. As a threat to the integrity of the state, Cardinal Richelieu annulled its political clauses (1629), and Louis XIV was led by the same motive to order the revocation of the edict (1685).

Nantucket POP (1980) 5 000, a US island in the Atlantic Ocean lying off the NE coast. Together with the Muskeget and Tuckernuck Is it forms Nantucket County, Massachusetts. AREA 122sq km/47sq mi. The island is a summer resort.

Naomi 1 a biblical character (Book of Ruth), mother of Ruth and Orpah. **2** a female first name. [from Hebrew, = my delight]

nap[1] — noun a short sleep. — verb intrans. (**napped, napping**) to have a nap. — **catch someone napping** colloq. to find them unprepared or off guard. [from Anglo-Saxon *hnappian*, to sleep]

nap[2] noun the raised surface on cloth such as velvet, corduroy, etc. [from Middle English *noppe*]

napalm — noun Mil. a highly flammable material consisting of a mixture of petrol and a thickening agent, used in incendiary bombs and flame-throwers. — verb to attack or destroy with a bomb made of this material. [from *naphthenate palmitate*]

Napata an ancient city situated on the W bank of the Nile, in what is now the Sudan. It was the capital of the kingdom of Cush (c.750–590 BC). It remained the religious capital although political power passed to the city of Meroe.

nape noun the back of the neck. [from Middle English]

napery noun Scot. household linen, especially for the table. [from Old French *naperie*, from *nape*, tablecloth]

Naphtali, Tribe of one of the 12 tribes of ancient Israel, descended from Naphtali, Jacob's second son by Rachel's maid Bilhah. Its tribal territory was in N Palestine, immediately west of the Sea of Galilee and upper R Jordan.

naphtha noun Chem. a highly flammable mixture of hydrocarbons obtained from coal and petroleum, used as an ingredient of petrol and dry-cleaning fluids, and as an industrial solvent. [from Greek *naphtha*]

naphthalene noun Chem. (FORMULA $C_{10}H_8$) a white solid aromatic hydrocarbon obtained from crude oil and responsible for the strong smell of mothballs. It is used as a starting material for the manufacture of dyes, resins, plasticizers, polyesters, and certain drugs, and is the main ingredient of moth repellants.

Napier, John (1550–1617) Scottish mathematician, born at Merchiston Castle, Edinburgh. He matriculated at St Andrews University in 1563, travelled on the Continent, and settled down to a life of literary and scientific study. He is famous for the invention of logarithms to simplify computation, and he also devised a calculating machine using a set of rods, known as *Napier's bones*.

Napier (of Magdala), Robert (Cornelis) Napier, 1st Baron (1810–90) British soldier, born in Colombo, Ceylon. He joined the army in 1826 and gave distinguished service at the siege of Lucknow (1857). He carried out successful expeditions during the Chinese War (1860) and in Abyssinia (1868), and became Commander-in-Chief in India (1870), Governor of Gibraltar (1876–82), field marshal, and Constable of the Tower of London (1887).

Napier POP (1991) 53 000, a seaport in Hawke Bay on the E coast of North Island, New Zealand.

A modern seaside city was built largely on reclaimed land after the site was virtually destroyed by an earthquake in 1931. It is the centre of a rich farming area.

Napierian logarithm *Maths.* same as NATURAL LOGARITHM. [named after the Scottish mathematician John Napier]

napkin *noun* **1** (*also* **table napkin**) a piece of cloth or paper for wiping one's mouth and fingers at mealtimes. **2** a baby's nappy. [diminutive of Old French *nappe*, napkin, from Latin *mappa*]

Naples, Italian **Napoli**, Latin **Neapolis** POP (1990e) 1.2m, the seaport capital of Campania region and of Naples province, SW Italy. It lies on the Tyrrhenian Sea, 189km/117mi SE of Rome. HISTORY founded in c.600 BC by refugees from the Greek colony of Cumae; under Roman rule from the 4c BC; part of the Kingdom of the Two Sicilies in 1140; became capital of the Kingdom of Naples in 1282; capital of Napoleon's Parthenopean Republic in 1799 and of the Sicilian Kingdom in 1806; joined the Kingdom of Italy in 1860; severely damaged in World War II, and by earthquakes in 1980. Naples is struggling against bankruptcy and debt, and many areas of the city are economically deprived. NOTABLE FEATURES Cathedral of San Gennaro (13c–15c); Church of San Lorenzo Maggiore (1266–1324); Porta Capuana (15c–16c); Church of San Giovanni a Carbonara (14c); National Museum. [from Latin *neapolis*, new city]

Napoleon I, French **Napoléon Bonaparte**, Italian **Napoleone Buonaparte** (1769–1821) French soldier and Emperor (1804–15), born in Ajaccio, Corsica. Trained at military school in France, he helped defeat the supporters of the counter-rebellion and was appointed commander of the army in Italy (1796). In the same year he married Josephine, widow of the Vicomte de Beauharnais. His campaigns in Italy showed his military genius and at the Treaty of Campo Formio (1797) France gained Belgium, the Ionian Is, and Lombardy. The directory wanted him to invade England, but he sought to break British trade by conquering Egypt. He captured Malta (1798), entered Cairo, and defeated the Turks, but after the French fleet was destroyed by Lord Nelson at the battle of the Nile, he learned of French reverses in Europe and returned to France (1799). In the coup d'état of 18th Brumaire (9 Nov 1799), Napoleon assumed power as First Consul and instituted a military dictatorship. He then routed the Austrians at Marengo (1800), made further gains at the Treaty of Luneville (1801), and consolidated French domination by the Concordat with Rome (by which Pope Pius VII recognized the French Republic) and the Peace of Amiens with England (1802). Elected consul for life, he assumed the hereditary title of Emperor in 1804. His administrative, military, educational, and legal reforms (notably the *Code Napoléon*) made a lasting impact on French Society. War with England was renewed, and extended to Russia and Austria. England's naval supremacy at Trafalgar (1805) forced him to abandon his plans to invade, so he attacked the Austrians and Russians and gained victories at Ulm and Austerlitz (1805). Prussia was defeated at Jena and Auerstadt (1806), and Russia at Friedland (1807). After the Peace of Tilsit, by which Prussia lost half her territory, he became the arbiter of Europe. He then tried to cripple England with the Continental System, ordering the European states under his control to boycott British goods. He sent armies into Portugal and Spain, which resulted in the bitter Peninsular War (1808–14) which ended with victory for the British forces under the Duke of Wellington. Believing that Russia was planning an alliance with England, he invaded, defeated the Russians at Borodino, then entered Moscow, but he was forced to retreat, his army broken by hunger and the Russian winter. In 1813 his victories over the allied armies continued at Lützen, Bautzen, and Dresden, but he was routed at Leipzig, and

France was invaded. Forced to abdicate, he was given the sovereignty of Elba (1814). The unpopularity which followed the return of the Bourbons motivated him to return to France in 1815. He regained power for a period known as the Hundred Days, but was defeated by Wellington's and Gebbard Leberecht von Blücher's combined forces at Waterloo. He fled to Paris, abdicated, surrendered to the British, and was banished to St Helena, where he died. Napoleon's military and administrative talents allowed him to make France pre-eminent. His consolidation of power by putting relatives on European thrones, led in the end to the firmer establishment of the French Revolution. He had divorced the childless Josephine in order to marry Marie Louise, daughter of the Emperor of Austria, and by her had one son, briefly proclaimed Napoleon II in 1815.

Napoleon II, originally **François Charles Joseph Bonaparte** (1811–32) son of Napoleon I and the Empress Marie Louise, born in Paris. At birth he was named King of Rome, and after his father's abdication he was brought up in Austria. In 1818 he became Duke of Reichstadt, though was allowed no active political role.

Napoleon III, until 1852 **Louis-Napoleon**, in full **Charles Louis Napoleon Bonaparte** (1808–73) President of the Second French Republic (1848–52) and Emperor of the French (1852–70), born in Paris, the third son of Louis Bonaparte, King of Holland (the brother of Napoleon I) and Hortense Beauharnais. After the death of Napoleon II, Duke of Reichstadt (1832), he became head of the Napoleonic dynasty. He made two abortive attempts on the French throne (1836, 1840), for which he was imprisoned at Ham near Amiens, but he escaped to England (1846), then after the 1848 Revolution was elected to the presidency of the Second Republic (1848). Aided by the military, he engineered the dissolution of the constitution, assumed the title of Emperor, and in 1853 married Eugénie de Montijo de Guzman (1826–1920), a Spanish countess, who bore him a son, the Prince Imperial (1856). He encouraged economic expansion and the modernization of Paris, while the Second Empire was marked externally by the Crimean conflict (1854–6), the expeditions to China (1857–60), the annexation (1860) of Savoy and Nice, and the ill-starred intervention in Mexico (1861–7). Encouraged by the Empress Eugénie, he unwisely declared war on Prussia in 1870 and suffered defeat culminating in the battle of Sedan. Confined at Wilhelmshöle until 1871, the remainder of his life was spent in exile in England.

Napoleon the heartless pig, representing Joseph Stalin, in George Orwell's *Animal Farm*.

Napoleon a French film directed by Abel Gance (1927), based on the early life of Napoleon Bonaparte (played by Albert Dieudonne).

Napoleonic Wars the continuation (1800–15) of the Revolutionary Wars, fought to preserve French hegemony in Europe. They began with Napoleon I's destruction of the Second Coalition (1800). After a peaceful interlude (1802–3) Britain resumed hostilities, which prompted Napoleon to prepare for invasion and encouraged the formation of a Third Coalition (1805–7). While Britain retained naval superiority (1805), Napoleon established domination on land, which was sustained by economic warfare and resulted in the invasions of Spain (1808) and Russia (1812). Gradually the French were overwhelmed by the Fourth Coalition (1813–14), and were defeated at Waterloo (1815).

nappe *noun* **1** *Geol.* a large-scale arch-shaped geological fold structure consisting of a sheet-like body of solid rock that has been overturned (so that it is lying on its side) and then often transported several kilometres or more over the underlying rocks by compressional stresses. The Alps consist of several such nappes. **2** *Maths.* one

of the two parts of a conical surface defined by the vertex. [from French *nappe*, tablecloth, from Latin *mappa*]

nappy *noun* (PL. **nappies**) a piece of towelling, or other soft cloth, or a pad of paper, secured round a baby's bottom to absorb its urine and faeces. [diminutive of NAPKIN]

Nara POP (1991e) 352 000, the capital of Nara prefecture, S Honshu, Japan, 29km/18mi E of Osaka. The city was made the first capital of Japan in 710. It became a cultural and religious centre and the centre for Japanese Buddhism. NOTABLE FEATURES the Daibutsu-den (Great Buddha Hall) in Todaiji (East Great Temple, founded in 743), housing a bronze statue of Buddha which is 22m tall; Nara National Museum; the Shoso-in (8c), Kasuga-taisha Shrine; the buildings of Horyuji (6c) are nearby, the oldest temple complex in Japan, and the oldest wooden buildings in the world.

Narayanganj POP (1991) 269 000, a city in Narayanganj district, Dhaka region, Bangladesh. It is situated on the R Meghna, E of Dhaka. The city is the river-port for Dhaka, and one of the busiest trade centres. Narayanganj and Dhaka together make up the main industrial region of Bangladesh.

Narcissa the woman beloved by Roderick in Tobias Smollett's *Roderick Random*.

narcissism *noun* **1** *Psychol.* a condition of self-infatuation arising from difficulties at an early stage of psychological development. It may manifest itself as exhibitionism, arrogance, or sexual fantasy. In psychoanalytic theory, it is sexual self-interest regarded as a normal characteristic of a child's psychosexual development. **2** excessive admiration for oneself or one's appearance. [from NARCISSUS]

narcissistic *adj.* inclined to admire oneself excessively; characterized by narcissism.

Narcissus in Greek mythology, a beautiful youth who rejected the love of the nymph Echo and, as punishment, fell in love with his own reflection in a pool. He pined away and was changed into the flower named after him.

narcissus *noun* (PL. **narcissuses**, **narcissi**) a plant similar to the daffodil, which grows from a bulb and has white or yellow flowers. [from Greek *narkissos*, after NARCISSUS, later fancifully associated with *narke*, numbness, because of its narcotic properties]

narcissus

narcolepsy *noun Medicine* a disorder characterized by an uncontrollable tendency to fall asleep for brief periods, the onset of sleep often being accompanied by hallucinations. [from Greek *narke*, numbness + *lepsis*, seizure]

narcosis *noun* (PL. **narcoses**) a state of unconsciousness or arrested activity. It is most commonly produced by a narcotic drug such as opium, but may also be caused by toxins formed within the body, as in uraemia. [from Greek *narkosis*, a numbing, from *narke*, numbness]

narcoterrorism *noun* terrorism by or on behalf of an organization involved in narcotics or drug dealing.

narcotic — *noun* **1** a drug which, in low doses, reduces the brain's awareness of sensory impulses, particularly pain, and can produce a temporary sense of well-being. In large doses, it induces sleep or unconsciousness, and may cause coma or convulsions. **2** in general use, any addictive drug. — *adj.* relating to narcotics or to narcosis. [from Greek *narkotikos*, numbing]
◊ In common usage, the term has been adopted to include all addictive drugs. Narcotics such as morphine, heroin, and cocaine are used illegally for the euphoric sensations they induce, and are highly addictive.

nard *noun* **1** an aromatic oil — same as **spikenard**. **2** an Indian plant of the valerian family, from which this is obtained. [from Greek *nardos*]

nares *pl. noun Anat.* the paired openings of the nasal cavity. The external nares are the nostrils, and the internal nares open into the pharynx. [from Latin *nares*, nostrils]

nark — *noun slang* **1** a spy or informer working for the police. **2** a habitual grumbler. — *verb colloq.* **1** *trans.* to annoy. **2** *intrans.* to grumble. [perhaps from Romany *nak*, nose]

narky *adj.* (**narkier**, **narkiest**) *colloq.* irritable.

Narmada or **Narbada, River** a river in India, rising in the Maikala range of Madhya Pradesh. It forms the boundary of the traditional regions of Hindustan and Deccan. The river flows 1 245km/774mi generally SW across Gujarat state to meet the Gulf of Cambay. It is a sacred river to Hindus and there are many pilgrimage centres and bathing ghats along its course.

Narnia a mythical country, the scene of a sequence of novels by C S Lewis, beginning with *The Lion, The Witch, and The Wardrobe* (1950).

narrate *verb trans.* **1** to tell (a story); to relate. **2** to give a running commentary on (a film). [from Latin *narrare*, to relate]

narration *noun* a continuous story or account.

narrative — *noun* **1** an account of events. **2** those parts of a book, etc that recount events. — *adj.* **1** telling a story; recounting events: *narrative poetry*. **2** relating to the telling of stories: *narrative skills*. [from Latin *narrativus*, from *narrare*, to relate]

narrator *noun* a person who tells a story or narrative.

narrow — *adj.* **1** of little breadth, especially in comparison with length. **2** *said of interests or experience* restricted; limited. **3** *said of attitudes or ideas* illiberal or unenlightened; intolerant or bigoted. **4** *said of the use of a word* restricted to its precise or original meaning; strict. **5** close; only just achieved, etc: *a narrow victory*. — *noun* (**narrows**) a narrow part of a channel, river, etc. — *verb intrans., trans.* **1** to make or become narrow. **2** (*also* **narrow down**) *said eg of a range of possibilities* to reduce or be reduced or limited. [from Anglo-Saxon *nearu*]

narrow boat a canal barge.

narrowcasting *noun* the broadcasting of material to a limited number of users, eg cable television users. Also, the production and distribution of material on video tapes, cassettes, etc to special interest groups.

narrow-gauge *adj., said of a railway* less than the standard gauge: in the UK less than 4ft 8½in (1·4m) in width.

narrowly *adv.* **1** only just; barely. **2** with close attention: *eyed him narrowly*. **3** in a narrow or restricted way.

narrow-minded *adj. derog.* intolerant; prejudiced.

narrow-mindedness *noun* being narrow-minded or intolerant.

narrowness *noun* a narrow state; being narrow or restricted.

narthex *noun Archit.* **1** a transverse western portico or vestibule, inside or before the nave in an early Christian or Oriental church or basilica, to which women and catechumens were traditionally admitted. **2** any enclosed covered space before a main entrance. [from Greek *narthex*, casket]

Narvik POP (1991e) 19 000, a seaport in Nordland county, N Norway. It is situated at the W end of a peninsula in the Ofoten Fjord, opposite the Lofoten Is. As terminus of the Lappland railway from the Kiruna iron-ore mines in Sweden, and with an ice-free harbour, Narvik is of considerable economic importance. HISTORY occupied by Germany in 1940; the scene of World War II naval battles in which two British and nine German destroyers were lost.

narwhal *noun* an arctic whale, the male of which has a long spiral tusk. [from Danish *narhval*, from *hval*, whale]

NASA *abbrev.* National Aeronautics and Space Administration, a US government agency established in 1958, responsible for conducting non-military space research in areas such as launch vehicle development, manned and robotic spaceflight, artificial satellites, space probes, and aeronautics, and for developing operations that use such technology, eg the Apollo programme of Moon landings.

nasal *adj.* **1** relating to the nose. **2** *said of a sound, or letter such as m or n* pronounced through, or partly through, the nose. **3** *said of a voice, etc* abnormally or exceptionally full of nasal sounds. [from Latin *nasus*, nose]

nasalize or **nasalise** *verb trans., intrans.* to pronounce or speak nasally.

nasally *adv., said of sounds* through the nose.

nascent *adj.* in the process of coming into being; in the early stages of development. [from Latin *nasci*, to be born]

Naseby, Battle of a major conflict (14 Jun 1645) in Northamptonshire during the English Civil Wars. The Royalist forces of Charles I were outnumbered and defeated by Parliament's New Model Army led by Thomas Fairfax, with Oliver Cromwell commanding the cavalry. Royalist cavalry led by Prince Rupert left the main battle, which considerably weakened Charles's forces.

Nash, John (1752–1835) English architect and city planner, born in London. His country house designs brought him to the attention of the Prince of Wales, and he was engaged (1811–25) to plan the layout of the new Regent's Park. He recreated Buckingham Palace, designed the Marble Arch which originally stood in front of it, laid out Trafalgar Square and St James's Park, and rebuilt the Royal Pavilion, Brighton, in oriental style.

Nash, (Frederic) Ogden (1902–71) US humorous writer, born in Rye, New York. He worked in advertising, editing, and teaching before joining the *New Yorker* (1931), where his light, witty verse on the everyday life of middle-class America was first published. His collections include *Hard Lines* (1931) and *Marriage Lines* (1964).

Nash, Richard, known as **Beau Nash** (1674–1762) Welsh dandy, born in Swansea. After serving in the army and studying law, he made a shifty living by gambling. However, in 1705 he became master of ceremonies in Bath, where he conducted the public balls with a splendour never before witnessed, and where his reforms helped to create a fashionable holiday centre.

Nashe, Thomas (1567–1601) English dramatist and satirist, born in Lowestoft, Suffolk. He used his talent for abusive writing in the pamphlet *Pierce Penilesse* (1592), against the Puritans. Among his other works are the satirical masque *Summer's Last Will and Testament* (1592), the picaresque tale *The Unfortunate Traveller* (1594),

and *The Isle of Dogs* (1597), which caused his imprisonment.

Nashville POP (1990) 985 000, the port capital of the state of Tennessee, USA. It lies on the Cumberland R, in Nashville and Davidson County, N Tennessee. The city is famous for its music industry (country and western), and is also a centre for religious education. HISTORY settled as Nashborough in 1779, it was renamed Nashville in 1784; became state capital in 1843; scene of a Civil War battle in 1864 in which Union forces defeated Confederates; merged with Davidson in 1963. NOTABLE FEATURES the Capitol (with the tomb of US President James K Polk); Country Music Hall of Fame; Opryland USA (family entertainment complex).

Nasik POP (1991) 647 000, a city in Maharashtra state, W central India. It lies on a tributary of the Darna R, 145km/90mi NE of Bombay. The city is a holy place of Hindu pilgrimage. NOTABLE FEATURES many Vishnuite temples and shrines; Buddhist caves from the 2c.

Nasmyth, James (1808–90) Scottish engineer, son of painter Alexander Nasmyth, born in Edinburgh. In 1836 he established at Patricroft the Bridgewater Foundry. His steam hammer was devised in 1839 for forging an enormous wrought-iron paddle-shaft; this was adopted by the Admiralty in 1843. His other inventions included a steam pile-driver, a planing machine, and a hydraulic punching machine.

Nassau POP (1990) 172 000, the capital of the Bahamas, situated on the NE coast of New Providence I. It is a popular winter tourist resort. HISTORY frequented by pirates during the 18c; captured briefly by the Americans in 1776. NOTABLE FEATURES Fort Nassau (1697), Fort Charlotte (1787–94), and Fort Fincastle (1793) were built to protect the city from Spanish invasion.

Nassau a Burgundian noble family, who rose as servants of the Habsburgs, then rebelled against their authority in the Low Countries to be made stadtholders of Holland, Zeeland, and Friesland, Counts of Nassau, and Princes of Orange by Charles V. The heirs to the titles, William of Orange (1533–84), and his brother Louis (1538–74), Count of Nassau, supported and led the Dutch Revolt (1566–1648) against their former masters.

Nasser, Gamal Abd al- (1918–70) Egyptian statesman, born in Alexandria. An army officer, he became dissatisfied with the corruption of the Farouk regime, and was involved in the military coup of 1952. He assumed the office of Prime Minister (1954–6), and then President (1956–70) by deposing his fellow-officer General Mohammed Neguib. His nationalization of the Suez Canal led to Israel's invasion of Sinai and the intervention of Anglo-French forces. In order to build a N African Arab empire, in 1958 he created a federation with Syria called the United Arab Republic, but Syria withdrew in 1961. After the six-day Arab–Israeli War (1967), heavy losses on the Arab side led to his resignation, but he was persuaded to stay on, and died still in office, one year before the completion of one of his greatest projects, the Aswan High Dam.

Nasser, Lake, Arabic **Buheiret En Naser** a lake in S Egypt. AREA c.5 000sq km/1 930sq mi; length 500km/310mi. It was created as a result of the building of the Aswan High Dam which was completed in 1971. [named after the former Egyptian President, Gamal Abd al-Nasser]

nastic movement *Bot.* the non-directional movement of a plant organ in response to an external stimulus, eg the opening or closing of some flowers in response to changes in temperature. [from Greek *nastos*, close-pressed, from *nasso*, to press]

nastily *adv.* in a nasty or unpleasant way.

nastiness *noun* being nasty or unpleasant.

nasturtium *noun* a climbing garden plant with flat round leaves and red, orange, or yellow trumpet-like flowers. [from Latin *nasturtium*, cress, said to be from *nasus*, nose + *torquere*, to twist, from its pungency]

nasty — *adj.* (**nastier, nastiest**) **1** unpleasant; disgusting. **2** malicious; ill-natured. **3** worrying; serious: *a nasty wound / a nasty situation*. **4** *said of weather* wet or stormy. — *noun* (PL. **nasties**) **1** *Bot.* a nastic movement. **2** something unpleasant or disgusting: *video nasties*.

Nat. *abbrev.* **1** National. **2** Nationalist.

Natal POP (1991) 2.1m, the smallest province in South Africa. AREA 91 355sq km/35 263sq mi. It is bounded E by the Indian Ocean, N by Mozambique and Swaziland, and SW by Lesotho. The Drakensberg Mts follow the NW frontier. CAPITAL Pietermaritzburg. CHIEF TOWNS Durban, Ladysmith. HISTORY annexed to Cape Colony in 1844; became a separate colony in 1856; Zululand province was annexed in 1897; joined the Union of South Africa in 1910. ECONOMY sugar cane, citrus, grain, vegetables; chemicals; paper; food processing; iron and steel; oil refining; explosives; fertilizers; meat canning.

Natalia a female first name. [from Russian, from Latin *natalis*, birthday]

Nataraja one of the names of the Hindu deity, Shiva. As the Lord of the Dance he dances the creation of the universe.

Nataraja

Nathan 1 an Old Testament prophet. He rebuked King David for engineering the death of Uriah the Hittite so as to win his wife Bathsheba. **2** a male first name. [from Hebrew, = gift]

Nathaniel 1 one of the lesser-known apostles, perhaps the same as Bartholomew. **2** a male first name. [related to NATHAN]

Nathaniel, Sir the curate, and friend of Holofernes, in Shakespeare's *Love's Labour's Lost.*

nation *noun* **1** the people living in, belonging to, and together forming, a single state. **2** a race of people of common descent, history, language, culture, etc. **3** a Native American tribe, or federation of tribes. [from Latin *natio*, tribe]

national — *adj.* **1** belonging to a particular nation. **2** concerning or covering the whole nation. — *noun* a citizen of a particular nation. [from Latin *natio*, tribe]

National Academy of Sciences (ABBREV. **NAS**) a US non-governmental organization founded in 1863 to advance science and its applications, and to advise the government on scientific matters.

National American Woman Suffrage Association (ABBREV. **NAWSA**) a US feminist organization, founded in 1890. It united the National Woman Suffrage Association (for which the suffrage was just one cause amongst others) with the American Woman Suffrage Association

(for which the suffrage was the only cause). By 1912 the movement had become increasingly staid in contrast with the more militant National Women's Party, but nevertheless its intense lobbying was instrumental in achieving the passage of the 19th Amendment, which gave women the vote (ratified Jun 1919, effected Aug 1920).

national anthem a song or hymn adopted as a nation's official song and used to represent it on official occasions.
◇ The national anthem of the UK (in use from the 18c) is *God Save the Queen* (or *King*); of France (from 1795), *La Marseillaise*; and of the USA (from 1931), *The Star-Spangled Banner.*

National Audubon Society a US private conservation organization named after the US artist and naturalist John James Audubon. It manages more than 60 wildlife sanctuaries in the USA.

National Bureau of Standards (ABBREV. **NBS**) a US department established in 1901 to publicize standards of weights and measures in all branches of physical and industrial sciences.

National Curriculum in the UK, the curriculum prescribed by the government for use in schools. A National Curriculum was established for England and Wales by the Education Reform Act of 1988, with three core subjects (English, mathematics, science) and seven other (foundation) subjects (geography, history, technology, a foreign language, art, music, physical education). A separate curriculum (5–14) was established for Scotland.

national debt the money borrowed by the government of a country and not yet repaid.
◇ The national debt rises whenever the government's total revenues fail to finance total spending. Borrowing is generally done through the issue of interest-bearing securities promising to repay the amounts borrowed to their holder, at a specified date. The total interest payable on government borrowing is known as *debt servicing*.
In England, a permanent national debt was first established to finance the French wars of the 17c. It now stands at about £200 000m. Other countries with major national debts include the USA ($3.6m), Japan ($1.1m), Germany (DM0.5m), France (F1.8m), and Australia (A$89 000m).

National Economic Development Council (ABBREV. **NEDC**) also called **Neddy** in the UK, a forum set up in 1962 where government, industry, and unions could meet to discuss economic affairs. The Council is supported by a secretariat, the National Economic Development Office (NEDO).

National Film Theatre in the UK, a film theatre in London, opened in 1958. It is administered by the British Film Institute, shows almost 2 000 films a year, and houses the British Film Festival in November.

National Front (ABBREV. **NF**) in the UK, a strongly nationalist political party. Its policy focuses on opposition to immigration, and calls for the repatriation of ethnic minorities, including those born in Britain. The Party was created (1960) by the merger of the White Defence League and the National Labour Party, and in its early years was a small neo-Nazi grouping. It tried to develop a more respectable face and recruited some members from the right of the Conservative Party to widen its base beyond hardline neo-fascists. Its political appeal declined with the election of a Conservative government in 1979.

National Gallery an art gallery in London, opened in Pall Mall in 1824 and moved to Trafalgar Square in 1838. It houses the largest collection of paintings in Britain.

National Gallery of Art a US art gallery endowed by Andrew W Mellon and opened in Washington DC in 1941. It is a branch of the

National Anthems		
Country/Title	Composer	Adopted
Australia		
Advance Australia Fair*	Peter Dodds McCormick	1977
Canada		
O Canada	Calixa Lavallée	1980
France		
La Marseillaise	Claude-Joseph Rouget de Lisle	1795
Japan		
Kimigayo ('His Majesty's Reign')	Hayashi Hiromori	not officially adopted
Germany		
Deutschlandlied ('Song of Germany')	Haydn	1950
UK		
God Save the Queen/King	*not known*	18th-c
USA		
The Star-Spangled Banner	John Stafford Smith	1931
USSR		
Gimn Sovetskogo Soyuza ('Hymn of the Soviet Union')	*not known*	1944

*National tune. The official anthem is *God Save the Queen/King*, played when a regal or vice-regal personage is present.

Smithsonian Institution, but administered independently.

National Geographic Society in the USA, a scientific and educational organization, founded in 1890. The knowledge gained from the exploration and research it funds is published in its monthly journal *National Geographic.*

national grid *Brit.* **1** a national network of high-voltage electric power lines. **2** see NATIONAL GRID REFERENCE SYSTEM.

National Grid Reference System a unique grid reference for mapping purposes for any part of the UK, using letters and numbers. The country has been divided by the Ordnance Survey into a number of grid squares, 100 × 100km (62.14mi), each with its own identifying letters. Each square is further subdivided into numbered 1km (0.62mi) squares.

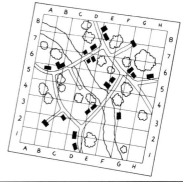

grid reference

National Health Service (ABBREV. **NHS**) in the UK, a comprehensive medical service established in 1948. It aims to provide free health care and is funded by national government and local taxation. However, charges have been in existence since 1951, and have since been extended to include many prescriptions, most dental treatments, and eye tests. Most hospitals are controlled by regional and district Health Boards. General Practitioners (GPs) are self-employed and are organized by local general medical practice committees. GPs receive capitation fees according to the number of patients registered, and often group together to form health centres which offer diagnostic clinics and other supportive services. In the late 1980s, NHS costs rose and private care increased. In 1991, government legislation gave NHS hospitals the option of becoming financially independent self-governing trusts, and GPs also have the choice of controlling their own budgets.

National Heritage, Department of in the UK, the government department established in 1992 to deal with government policy concerning heritage, tourism, broadcasting, the press, the arts, museums, galleries, libraries, sport, and recreation. It funds various organizations including the Arts Council of Great Britain, the British Library, and the British Film Institute.

National Heritage Memorial Fund a fund set up in 1980 by the National Heritage Memorial Act as a memorial to those who have died in service for the UK. It is the successor of the National Land Fund, and is administered by the Department of the Environment. The fund is used to help buy, maintain, and preserve land, buildings, and objects of outstanding scenic, historic, architectural, artistic, and scientific interest.

national insurance *Brit.* a system of state insurance contributed to by employers and employees, to provide for the sick, unemployed, and retired.

nationalism *noun* **1** extreme pride in the history, culture, successes, etc of one's nation; excessive patriotism. **2** a policy of, or movement aiming at, national unity or independence.

nationalist *noun* a person who supports nationalism.

nationalistic *adj.* characterized by nationalism or excessive patriotism.

nationalistically *adv.* in a way characterized by nationalism or excessive patriotism.

nationality *noun* (PL. **nationalities**) **1** the status of citizenship of a particular nation. **2** the racial or national group to which one belongs.

nationalization *or* **nationalisation** *noun* the process of bringing an industry under state ownership.
◇ In the 20c, nationalization has been widely implemented by communist and socialist governments as a means of achieving control of the state's means of production. In 1956, Egypt nationalized the Suez Canal Company, in order to gain access to the oil supplies of the Middle East.
In the UK, some industries were nationalized in the 1920s, including the Port of London, the Central Electricity Board, and the BBC. The Labour Government of 1945–50 implemented a major programme including the Bank of England, civil aviation, coal, gas, electricity, inland transport, and iron and steel. In the 1980s, Conservative governments under Margaret Thatcher passed a sweeping programme of denationalization.
see also PRIVATIZATION, SOCIALISM.

nationalize *or* **nationalise** *verb* to bring (eg an industry) under state ownership.

nationally *adv.* in terms of nations or of an entire nation: *the statistics are valid nationally*.

national park an area of countryside, usually important for its natural beauty, wildlife, etc, under the ownership and care of the nation.
◇ National Parks date back to 19c USA, where the first was established at Yellowstone, Montana, in 1872. The first parks in England and Wales were designated in 1951, and in 1992 there were 10. There are no national parks in Scotland or Northern Ireland.

National Party a political party whose policies claim to promote the interests of the whole nation rather than those of a particular class or group. National Parties, with differing policies, exist in many countries. In Australia, it is the third-largest political party; it is conservative in social matters, generally favours policies of free trade and low tariffs, and supports government public expenditure. In South Africa, the National Party came to power in 1948, and pursued a policy of apartheid until 1991. In Scotland, the National Party was formed in 1928, and in 1938 helped to form the Scottish National Party.

National Physical Laboratory a UK government research centre established in 1900 to develop industrial and scientific standards of measurement.

National Portrait Gallery a UK gallery of portraits of distinguished people in British history, opened in London in 1859. It moved to its present position adjoining the National Gallery in 1895.

National Radio Astronomy Observatory *Astron.* the principal radio astronomy observatory of the USA, with telescopes at Green Bank, West Virginia, and Socorro, New Mexico, and headquarters at Charlottesville, Virginia.

National Road a road built in the early 19c from Cumberland, Maryland, USA, to Vandalia, Illinois, and eventually to St Louis, Missouri. The building of the road played an important role in the expansion of the West.

National Security Adviser a member of staff who is responsible for advising the US President on security matters, a senior figure in the White House whose views may serve to balance or compete with those of the Secretary of State.

National Security Council (ABBREV. **NSC**) a body created by Congress in 1947 to advise the US President on the integration of domestic, foreign, and military policies relating to national security, designed to achieve effective co-ordination between the military services and other government agencies and departments. It comprises the President, Vice-President, Secretary of State, and Secretary of Defense. The Chairman of the Joint Chiefs of Staff and the Director of Central Intelligence are advisers.

national service a period of compulsory service in the armed forces.

National Socialism *Politics* the political doctrines of nationalism and racial superiority adopted by the German Nazi Party (see NAZI PARTY).

National Society for the Prevention of Cruelty to Children (ABBREV. **NSPCC**) a child welfare society, founded in 1884 as the London Society for the Prevention of Cruelty to Children. The NSPCC has over 200 inspectors in England, Wales, and Northern Ireland who investigate reports of cruelty to, and neglect of, children. In Scotland, the Royal Scottish Society for the Prevention of Cruelty to Children (also founded 1884) performs a similar function.

National Television Systems Commission (ABBREV. **NTSC**) it is responsible for the coding system for colour television that was introduced in the USA (1954) and has been generally adopted throughout the Americas and Japan for all 525-line 60Hz transmission.

National Theatre, properly **Royal National Theatre** a theatre complex situated on the South Bank, London, opened in 1976. It comprises the Olivier Theatre, the Lyttleton Theatre, and the Cottesloe Theatre, and has exhibitions and shops in the foyer. It is home of the National Theatre Company, directed by Richard Eyre from 1988. The history of the concept of a national theatre dates from c.1848, but the Shakespeare Memorial National Theatre Committee to bring it to fruition was not formed until 1907, and in 1944 Denis Lasdun was commissioned to design the complex. In the temporary home of the Old Vic Theatre, Sir Laurence Olivier became artistic director of the new National Theatre Company (1962), and was succeeded by Sir Peter Hall (1973); the company moved to the new complex in 1976.

national theatre a theatre endowed by the state, and usually situated in the national capital.
◇ The longest-established examples may be found in Europe (eg the National Theatre in Stockholm, opened in 1773), and today there are many state-endowed theatres found throughout the world. In Britain, a National Theatre was inaugurated in 1962 (see separate entry).

National Trust in the UK, a charity founded in 1895 with the full name The National Trust for Places of Historic Interest and Natural Beauty. The Trust owns historic houses, gardens, and sites of natural beauty, which it opens to the public. The National Trust for Scotland is a separate organization run on similar lines.

National Union of Mineworkers see NUM.

National Vocational Qualification see NVQ.

National Youth Dance a trust which organizes an annual festival for British youth dance companies to work with top professional choreographers and teachers. The National Youth Dance Theatre was founded in 1985.

nationwide *adj., adv.* (extending) throughout the whole nation.

native — *adj.* **1** being or belonging to the place of one's upbringing. **2** born a citizen of a particular place: *a native Italian*. **3** belonging naturally to one; inborn or innate: *native wit*. **4** having a particular language as one's first, or mother, tongue. **5** originating in a particular place: *native to China*. **6** belonging to the original inhabitants of a country: *native Balinese music*. — *noun* **1** a person born in a certain place. **2** a plant or animal originating in a particular place. **3** *often derog.* one of the original inhabitants of a place as distinct from later, especially European, settlers.
— **go native** *colloq., said of a visitor or immigrant* to adopt the customs, dress, routines, etc of the local people.
[from Latin *nativus*, natural, from *nasci*, to be born]

Native American an indigenous inhabitant of North America; an American Indian.

Native Americans		
Habitat	**People**	
North America		
Arctic	Aleut, Inuit	
Subarctic	Algonkin, Cree, Ottawa	
Woodlands	Cherokee, Choctaw, Creek, Hopewell, Huron, Iroquois, Mohican, Natchez, Seminole, Shawnee (Tecumseh)	
Great Plains	Blackfoot, Cheyenne, Comanche, Pawnee, Sioux	
Coast	Chinook, Tlingit, Tsimshian	
Desert	Apache, Hopi, Mojave, Navajo, Pueblo, Shawnee	
Central America		
	Aztec, Maya, Mexican, Toltec	
South America		
East	Carib, Xingu	
Centre	Guarani, Miskito	
West	Araucanian, Aymara, Chimú, Inca, Jivaro, Quechua	

nativity *noun* (PL. **nativities**) **1** birth, advent, or origin. **2** (**Nativity**) the birth of Christ. [from Latin *nativitas*, birth]

NATO *abbrev.* North Atlantic Treaty Organization, an organization established by a treaty signed in 1949 by Belgium, Canada, Denmark, France, Iceland, Italy, Luxembourg, the Netherlands, Norway, Portugal, the UK, and the USA; Greece and Turkey acceded in 1952, West Germany in 1955, and Spain in 1982. In 1966 France under Charles de Gaulle withdrew all its forces from NATO command, but it remains a member. NATO is a permanent military alliance established to defend W Europe against Soviet aggression. The treaty commits the members to consider an armed attack on one of them as an attack on all of them, and for all to assist the country attacked by such actions as are deemed necessary. The alliance forces are based on contributions from the member countries' armed services and operate under a multinational command. Its institutions include a Council, an International Secretariat, the Supreme Headquarters Allied Powers in Europe (SHAPE), and various committees to formulate common policies. In the 1970s and 1980s, the NATO policy of a first-strike nuclear attack to fend off a Soviet conventional attack became controversial in W Europe. After the 1989 changes in E Europe, a NATO summit in London (Jul 1990) began the process of redefining NATO's military and political goals.

natron *noun Geol.* a mineral form of hydrated sodium carbonate found in dried lake beds. [from Arabic *natrun*, from Greek *nitron*]

natter — *verb intrans.* (**nattered, nattering**) *colloq.* to chat busily. — *noun* an intensive chat. [imitative]

natterjack *noun* a European toad, and the rarer of the two UK species, with a greenish skin, a yellow stripe down its head and back, and very short legs. It runs rapidly instead of hopping after its prey, which includes insects, spiders, worms, and snails. When alarmed, adult natterjacks can inflate their bodies until they are almost spherical.

nattily *adv.* with a neat and smart manner: *he was nattily dressed.*

natty *adj.* (**nattier, nattiest**) *colloq.* 1 *said of clothes* flashily smart. 2 clever; ingenious. [related to NEAT]

Natufian *Archaeol.* — *noun* a Mesolithic culture of SW Syria, Lebanon, and Palestine (c.10 000–8 000 BC). Archaeological evidence has indicated that there was incipient agriculture (animal herding, harvesting of wild cereals) which led to increasingly permanent settlement, with open sites like Jericho being occupied, as well as caves and rock shelters. — *adj.* relating to this culture. [named after the Palestinian site of Wādi en-*Natūf*]

natural — *adj.* 1 normal; unsurprising. 2 instinctive; not learnt. 3 born in one; innate: *a natural talent / kindness was natural to her.* 4 being such because of inborn qualities: *a natural communicator.* 5 *said of manner, etc* simple, easy, and direct; not artificial. 6 *said of looks* not, or apparently not, improved artificially. 7 relating to nature, or to parts of the physical world not made or altered by man: *natural sciences / areas of natural beauty.* 8 following the normal course of nature: *died a natural death.* 9 *said of materials* derived from plants and animals as opposed to manmade: *natural fibres.* 10 wild; uncultivated or uncivilized. 11 related to one by blood: *one's natural parents.* 12 *euphemistic* born out of wedlock; illegitimate: *his natural son.* 13 *Mus.* not sharp or flat. — *noun* 1 *colloq.* a person with an inborn feel for something: *she's a natural when it comes to acting.* 2 *Mus.* (a sign (♮) indicating) a note that is not to be played sharp or flat. [from Latin *naturalis*, from *natura*, nature]

natural abundance *Chem.* the ratio of the number of atoms of a particular isotope of a chemical element to the total number of atoms of all the isotopes present. It is usually expressed as a percentage, and refers to a natural source of the element.

Natural Environment Research Council (ABBREV. **NERC**) a UK organization established in 1965 to undertake and fund research in the earth sciences, to advise on exploitation of natural resources and protection of the environment, and to support training of scientists in these fields.

natural frequency 1 *Physics* the frequency at which an object or system will vibrate freely, in the absence of external forces. For example, a pendulum moving with small swings under its own weight is displaying its natural frequency. 2 *Electr.* the lowest frequency at which resonance occurs in an electrical circuit.

natural gas *Geol.* a colourless highly flammable mixture of gaseous hydrocarbons, mainly methane, that occurs naturally in the Earth's crust, either alone or associated with petroleum (oil) deposits. It is an important fossil fuel, and is also used in the manufacture of some organic chemicals. The largest natural gas fields found to date are under the sea in the N hemisphere.

natural history the scientific study of plants, animals, and minerals. In technical use, it now denotes a purely descriptive treatment of the life sciences.

Natural History Museum the popular name for the British Museum (Natural History), housed since 1881 in S Kensington, London. The exhibition was originally built up in the 17c–18c around the collections of Sir Hans Sloane and Sir Joseph Banks.

Naturalism a term used in art criticism for the faithful copying of nature, with no attempt to improve or idealize the subject. It was used in this sense in 1672 by Giovanni Pietro Bellori to characterize the work of Caravaggio and his followers. It was later used to describe the incorporation of scientific method into art and literature, as in the late 19c novels of Emile Zola.

naturalism *noun* the view that rejects supernatural explanations of phenomena, maintaining that all must be attributable to natural causes.

naturalist *noun* 1 a person who studies animal and plant life. 2 a follower of naturalism.

naturalistic *adj.* characterized by naturalism, or the realistic treatment of subjects in art and literature.

naturalistically *adv.* in a naturalistic or realistic way.

naturalization *or* **naturalisation** *noun* the process of naturalizing, especially conferring citizenship.

naturalize *or* **naturalise** *verb trans.* 1 to confer citizenship on (a foreigner). 2 to admit (a word) into the language, or (a custom) among established traditions. 3 to cause (an introduced species of plant or animal) to adapt to the local environment.

natural logarithm *Maths.* a logarithm to the base *e* (where *e* is Euler's number, which may be represented to the sixth decimal place as 2.718 282), denoted by $\ln x$ or $\log_e x$. It has useful applications in differential calculus, and serves as a natural base for logarithms. — Also called *Napierian logarithm.*

naturally *adv.* 1 of course; not surprisingly. 2 in accordance with the normal course of things. 3 by nature; as a natural characteristic: *sympathy came naturally to her.* 4 by means of a natural process, as opposed to being produced by an artificial man-made process: *gold, silver, and other naturally-occurring elements.* 5 in a relaxed or normal manner.

naturalness *noun* a natural state or quality; being natural.

natural number *Maths.* any whole positive number, sometimes including zero.

natural philosophy physics.

natural resource, any material that occurs naturally in the environment, and which can be exploited commercially by humans, eg water, coal, forests. See also NON-RENEWABLE RESOURCE.

natural selection, the process whereby the survival and reproduction of certain members of a population of plants or animals that possess an advantageous hereditary characteristic is favoured, while other individuals lacking that characteristic do not survive and produce offspring. As a result, favoured genes become increasingly common in subsequent generations, eventually giving rise to organisms that differ so markedly from the original population that they can be regarded as new species. Natural selection is one of the central features of Charles Darwin's theory of evolution, propounded by him in *The Origin of Species* (1859). It is dependent on the random variation that exists between members of a population, as a result of mutations and of the new combinations of genes that are produced during sexual reproduction. See also DARWINISM.

natural wastage non-replacement of employees that leave or retire, as a means of reducing staffing levels.

nature *noun* 1 (*often* **Nature**) all living and non-living matter and energy that forms part of the physical world and is not made by man, eg plants, animals, mountains, rivers. 2 what something is, or consists of. 3 a fundamental tendency; essential character; attitude or outlook: *human nature / a person modest by nature.* 4 a kind, type, etc.
— **be second nature** to be instinctive.
one's better nature one's kinder or nobler side.
the call of nature *euphemistic colloq.* a need to urinate.
in the nature of... with the characteristics of ...; like ...
[from Latin *natura*]

Nature Conservancy Council a British government agency responsible for wildlife and nature conservation, originally established as the Nature Conservancy in 1949. The Council manages National Nature Reserves, selects and schedules Sites of Special Scientific Interest, and offers management agreements for these where needed. It also undertakes research on conservation issues.

nature reserve *Environ.* a protected area for the conservation and management of wildlife within a habitat. It often provides a sanctuary for a rare species.
◇ In the UK, nature reserves have been established by the Nature Conservancy Council, the National Trust, local authorities, and county naturalist trusts. By 1985 there were 200 National Nature Reserves, which represent the best-known examples of coastal, freshwater, marshland, bog, moorland, heathland, grassland, woodland, and alpine habitats.

nature study the study of plants and animals.

nature trail a path through countryside, with signposts and markers pointing out interesting features for study.

naturism *noun* 1 nudism, regarded as a natural instinct. 2 the worship of natural objects.

naturist *noun* a nudist.

naturopathy *noun Medicine* therapy based on the belief that illness can be cured by the natural self-healing processes of the body. Natural foods, light, warmth, massage, regular exercise, and the avoidance of medication are prescribed in order to restore optimum health.

naught *noun* 1 *old use* nothing. 2 *North Amer., esp. US* nought.
— **come to naught** to fail.
set at naught *old use* to despise.
[from Anglo-Saxon *nawiht*, from *na*, no + *wiht*, thing]

naughtily *adv.* in a naughty or mischievous way.

naughtiness *noun* **1** being naughty or mischievous. **2** mild indecency.

naughty *adj.* (**naughtier, naughtiest**) **1** mischievous; disobedient. **2** mildly shocking or indecent. [from NAUGHT, from its earlier meaning 'wickedness']

Naukratis an ancient Greek town in the Delta of Egypt, established by the Milesians (c.675 BC). It was the commercial and industrial centre of the Greeks in Egypt until the foundation of Alexandria by Alexander the Great (c.331 BC).

Nauru, official name **Republic of Nauru** POP (1992e) 10 000, an independent republic formed by a small, isolated island in the W central Pacific Ocean, 42km/26mi to the S of the Equator and 4 000km/2 500mi NE of Sydney, Australia. AREA 21sq km/8sq mi; circumference 20km/12mi. There is no capital as such but government offices are situated in Yaren District. The inhabitants live in several small, scattered settlements. TIME ZONE GMT +11.5. Half the population are Nauruans, the remainder are Australians, New Zealanders, Chinese, and other Pacific islanders; Protestantism and Roman Catholicism are the chief religions. OFFICIAL LANGUAGE Nauruan; English is also widely understood. CURRENCY the Australian dollar. PHYSICAL DESCRIPTION the ground rises from sandy beaches to form a fertile coastal belt, c.100–300m wide, the only cultivable soil; a central plateau inland, which reaches 65m at its highest point, is composed largely of phosphate-bearing rocks. CLIMATE tropical, with average daily temperatures of 24–34°C, and average humidity between 70 and 80 per cent; annual rainfall averages 1 524mm and falls mainly in the monsoon season from Nov to Feb, with marked yearly deviations. HISTORY under German administration from the 1880s until 1914; after 1919, a League of Nations mandate was administered by Australia; there was a movement for independence in the 1960s; achieved self-government in 1966; gained full independence in 1968. GOVERNMENT a unicameral parliament of 18 members, elected every three years; parliament elects the President, who appoints a Cabinet. ECONOMY based on phosphate mining, but reserves expected to run out by 2000, and over 60% of revenue from phosphate exports have been invested to provide future income; coconuts, some vegetables; tourism; tax haven.

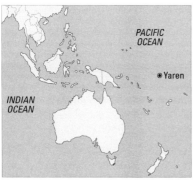

Nauru

nausea *noun* **1** an inclination to vomit. **2** disgust; revulsion. [from Latin *nausea*, from Greek *nausia*, seasickness, from *naus*, ship]

nauseate *verb trans.* **1** to cause to feel nausea. **2** to disgust. [from Latin *nauseare*, to be seasick]

nauseating *adj.* **1** offensively unpleasant. **2** causing nausea.

nauseatingly *adv.* to a nauseating degree, repulsively.

nauseous *adj.* **1** sickening; disgusting. **2** affected by nausea. [from Latin *nauseosus*, from Greek *nausia*, seasickness]

Nausicaa in Homer's *Odyssey*, the daughter of King Alcinous. When Odysseus was shipwrecked in Phaeacia, she was doing the laundry by the sea-shore and took him home to her father's palace.

nautical *adj.* relating to ships or sailors. [from Greek *nautikos*, from *nautes*, sailor]

nautically *adv.* as regards ships or sailors.

nautical mile *Naut.* a measure of distance used at sea, equal to 1.852km.

nautilus *noun* (PL. **nautiluses, nautili**) a sea creature related to the squid and octopus. It has a spiral chambered shell with a pearly interior. [from Greek *nautilos*, sailor]

Navajo *or* **Navaho** an Athapascan-speaking Native American people who migrated to the SW some time after AD 1000, and who are today the largest Native American group in the USA, numbering c.97 000 living eg in Arizona, New Mexico, and Utah. They carried out raids on Spanish settlers in the SW, but were themselves eventually defeated by US troops (1863–4), and settled in 1888 on a reservation in Arizona.

naval *adj.* relating to a navy or to ships generally. [from Latin *navalis*, from *navis*, ship]

Naval Conferences 1 a conference held in Washington DC (1921–2) to consider the reduction of naval armaments and problems in the Pacific. The UK, USA, Japan, France, and Italy limited their capital ships (most heavily armoured warships) and agreed not to construct any more for 10 years. A nine-power treaty was drawn up to ensure fair trading in China, and the Anglo-Japanese alliance of 1902 was replaced by a four-power pact between the UK, Japan, the USA, and France. **2** a conference held in London (1930), at which the USA, UK, and Japan agreed to limit their cruiser tonnage.

Navaratri *or* **Navaratra** *noun* a Hindu festival held in the autumn in honour of the goddess Durga, and also commemorating the victory of Rama over Ravana, the Demon King. [from Sanskrit *nava*, nine + *rātri* night]

Navarino Bay, Battle of a battle fought (1827) when the British and French (with the agreement of the Russians) destroyed the Turkish and Egyptian fleets off SW Greece. The outcome was an important factor in the achievement of Greek independence from the Ottoman Empire, formally recognized in 1828.

Navarre, Spanish **Navarra** POP (1989e) 524 000, an autonomous region and former kingdom of N Spain. AREA 10 421sq km/4 022sq mi. PHYSICAL DESCRIPTION its shape is determined by rivers flowing down from the Pyrenees; from the R Ebro Valley and the arid salt-steppe of Los Bardenas, the land rises towards the W Pyrenees and rainfall and forest cover increase with altitude. HISTORY the former kingdom had complete control over the Pyrenean passes and was an early centre of resistance to the Moors; united with Castile in 1515. CAPITAL Pamplona. ECONOMY cereals; vegetables; vines; food canning; cement; footwear; textiles; clothes; electrical equipment; iron and steel; furniture; metal products.

nave¹ *noun* the main central part of a church, where the congregation sits. [from Latin *navis*, ship, from its similarity to an inverted hull]

nave² *noun* the hub of a wheel. [from Anglo-Saxon *nafu*]

navel *noun* **1** in mammals, a scar on the abdomen marking the point of attachment of the umbilical cord to the body of the fetus. **2** the central point of something. [from Anglo-Saxon *nafela*, a diminutive of *nafu*, hub]

navel orange a seedless orange with a navel-like pit on top.

navigability *noun* **1** suitability for use by a ship or boat. **2** seaworthiness.

navigable *adj.* **1** *said of a river, channel, etc* able to be sailed along, through, etc. **2** *said of a ship* seaworthy. **3** *said of a balloon or other craft* steerable. [from Latin *navigabilis*, from *navigare*, to sail]

navigate *verb* **1** *intrans.* to direct the course of a ship, aircraft, or other vehicle. **2** *intrans.* to find one's way and hold one's course. **3** *trans.* to steer (a ship or aircraft). **4** *trans.* to manage to sail along or through (a river, channel, etc); generally, to find one's way through, along, over, across, etc. **5** *intrans.* as a vehicle passenger, to give the driver directions on the correct route. [from Latin *navigare*, from *navis*, ship]

navigation *noun* **1** the act, skill, or science of navigating. **2** the movement of ships and aircraft.

Navigation Acts legislation in Britain passed (1650–96) to increase England's share of overseas carrying trade by stating that all imports to England had to be in English ships or in those of the country of origin. Frequently contentious in the 18c, they added to the 13 American colonies' sense of grievance against the mother country, but were not repealed until 1849.

navigational *adj.* concerning or relating to navigation.

navigation satellite an artificial object placed in orbit around the Earth, which acts as an aid to navigation for ships and aeroplanes.

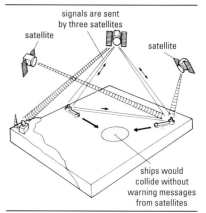

signals are sent by three satellites
satellite
satellite
satellite
ships would collide without warning messages from satellites

navigation satellite

navigator *noun* **1** a person who navigates, especially a ship or aircraft. **2** *old use* an explorer by sea.

Navratilova, Martina (1956–) Czech-born US lawn tennis player, born in Prague, Czech Republic. She has won a record nine singles titles at Wimbledon (1978–9, 1982–7, 1990) and is the most prolific winner in women's tennis. She won the Grand Slam in 1984, and by 1993 had won a total of 55 Grand Slam titles, including 18 singles. Other victories include the Virginia Slims championship (1981, 1983–6).

navvy *noun* (PL. **navvies**) a labourer, especially one employed in road-building. [from NAVIGATION, from its earlier meaning 'canal']

navy *noun* (PL. **navies**) **1** the warships of a state, usually considered together with the officers and other personnel manning them; the organization to which they belong, one of the three armed services. **2** a body or fleet of ships with their crews: *the merchant navy.* **3** (*also* **navy blue**) a dark blue colour, typically used for naval uniforms. [from Old French *navie*, from Latin *navis*, ship]

nawab *noun Hist.* a Muslim ruler or landowner in India. [from Urdu *nawwab*, from Arabic *nuwwab*, plural of *na'ib*, viceroy]

NAWSA *abbrev.* National American Woman Suffrage Association.

Naxos POP (1982) 4 000, the largest island of the Cyclades, Greece, in the S Aegean Sea. AREA 428sq km/165sq mi; length 35km/22mi; width 26km/16mi. The island rises to 1 002m. CHIEF TOWN Naxos. ECONOMY wine; emery; tourism.

nay — *interj. old use* **1** no. **2** rather; to put it more strongly: *a misfortune, nay, a tragedy*. — *noun* the word 'no'.
— **say someone nay** to contradict, or refuse something to, someone.
[from Norse *nei*]

Nazarene — *adj.* belonging to Nazareth. — *noun* **1** a person of Nazareth. **2** (**the Nazarene**) *Hist.* Jesus Christ. **3** *Hist.* a Christian. [from Greek *Nazarenos*]

Nazareth, Hebrew **Nazerat** POP (1988e) 25 000, the capital of Northern district, N Israel, situated above the Jezreel Plain. The town was the home of Christ for most of his life. The population is mainly Christian. NOTABLE FEATURES Church of the Annunciation, Church of St Joseph.

Nazca a pre-Columbian culture located along the S Peruvian coast. It flourished between c.200 BC and AD 500 and is noted for its distinctive style of pottery and large-scale 'lines' (best seen from the air) on the desert surface.

Naze, The, Norwegian **Lindesnes** or **Lindesnas** a cape on the S extremity of Norway, projecting into the North Sea at the entrance to the Skagerrak. The first beacon light in Norway was established here.

Naze, The a headland on the Essex coast, SE England, S of Harwich.

Nazi *noun* a member of the German Nazi Party.

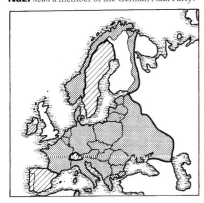

axis occupied areas   neutral areas
allied areas   — axis expansion

Nazi occupation

Nazi Party (ABBREV. **NSDAP**) a German political party which originated as the German Worker's Party, founded in 1919 to protest against the German surrender of 1918 and the Treaty of Versailles. Renamed the *Nationalsozialistische Deutsche Arbeiterpartei* (National Socialist German Worker's Party, or Nazi Party) in 1920 and led by Adolf Hitler from 1921, the Party's ideology was extremely nationalist, imperialist, and racist. Its ideas, written out in Hitler's *Mein Kampf* (1925), stemmed from the belief that the world had a hierarchy of races: Aryans, of whom Germans were the purest example, were the supreme culture-bearing race, while the Jews were considered the lowest, and were suspected of planning world conquest through infesting the Aryan race. Support came from people of all backgrounds, but was mainly from Protestants, the middle class, and the young; by 1932 the Nazi Party had become the largest party in the Reichstag. In 1933 Hitler was appointed Chancellor in a coalition government, a position from which he was able to build up a personal dictatorship, through legal measures,

terror, and propaganda. Once in power, the Nazis ruthlessly crushed opposition, indoctrinated the public with their ideas, engaged in extensive rearmament, and in the late 1930s invaded Austria, the Sudetenland, and the rest of Czechoslovakia, which according to the ideology was necessary for obtaining land for the 'master race'. During World War II, their actions included slave labour, plunder, and mass extermination. Nazism as a political ideology is now viewed as the expression of extreme inhumanity and fanatical nationalism.

Nazism *noun* the principles of the Nazis; the Nazi movement.

NB *abbrev.* **1** *nota bene* (Latin), note well. **2** Nebraska. **3** New Brunswick. **4** *Hist.* North Britain, ie Scotland.

Nb *symbol Chem.* niobium.

NBA *abbrev.* Net Book Agreement.

NBC *abbrev.* **1** National Broadcasting Company (in the USA). **2** *said of weapons* nuclear, biological, and chemical.

NBC suit a suit designed to protect the wearer against the physical effects of nuclear, biological, and chemical weapons.

NC *or* **N.C.** *abbrev.* North Carolina.

NCC *abbrev.* Nature Conservancy Council.

NCCL *abbrev.* National Council for Civil Liberties.

NCO *noun* (PL. **NCOs, NCO's**) non-commissioned officer.

ND *or* **N.D.** *abbrev.* North Dakota.

Nd *symbol Chem.* neodymium.

N. Dak. *abbrev.* North Dakota.

N'Djamena, formerly **Fort Lamy** (to 1973) POP (1992e) 688 000, the capital of Chad, and of Chari-Baguirmi prefecture, situated in the W of the country, close to the Cameroon border. It lies at the confluence of the R Chari and R Logone. HISTORY founded by the French in 1900; became a centre for the pacification of the kingdoms of central Sudan (1903–12); bombed by the Italians in 1942. NOTABLE FEATURE National Museum.

Ndola POP (1990) 376 000, the capital of Copperbelt province, central Zambia. It is situated 275km/171mi N of Lusaka. The city is the commercial centre of a major mining area.

NE *abbrev.* **1** north-east; north-eastern. **2** Nebraska.

Ne *symbol Chem.* neon.

Neagh, Lough the largest lake in the British Isles, situated in central Northern Ireland. AREA 396sq km/153sq mi; length 29km/18mi; width 18km/11mi. The lake has its outlet in the lower half of the R Bann, which flows N to the coast. It is well known for its eels. There is mining of the large deposits of lignite around the lake.

Neanderthal *adj.* denoting a primitive type of man of the early Stone Age in Europe, with a receding forehead and prominent brow ridges. [from *Neandertal*, a valley in Germany]

neap *or* **neaptide** *noun* a tidal pattern that occurs twice a month, when there is least difference in level between high and low tides. It occurs during the Moon's first and third quarters, when the gravitational effects of the Moon and Sun act at right angles to each other, so that the total tidal pull exerted on the Earth's oceans is decreased, making high tides lower and low tides higher. [from Anglo-Saxon *nepflod* (ie neap flood)]

near — *prep.* **1** at a short distance from. **2** close to (in amount, etc): *near tears / nearer 1 000 than 500*. — *adv.* **1** (**near to**) close: *came near to hitting her*. **2** *old use or colloq.* almost; nearly: *she damn near died / near-disastrous results / nowhere near enough*. — *adj.* **1** being a short distance away; close. **2** closer of two: *the near side*. **3** similar; comparable: *the nearest thing to a screwdriver*.

4 closely related to one: *a near relative*. **5** almost amounting to, or almost turning into: *a near tragedy*. **6** *old use* mean; miserly. — *verb trans., intrans.* to approach.
— **near at hand** conveniently close.
not go near someone *or* **something** to avoid them.
[from Anglo-Saxon *near*, comparative of *neah*, nigh]

nearby *adj., adv.* a short distance away; close at hand.

Near East an imprecise term formerly used to refer to an area including the Balkans and Turkey, and sometimes also to the countries west of Iran. The term is now synonymous with Middle East.

nearly *adv.* almost.
— **not nearly** very far from; nothing like.

near miss something not quite achieved or only just avoided.

nearness *noun* being near; closeness; proximity.

nearside — *noun* the side of a vehicle or horse nearer the kerb: in the UK the left side, and in most other countries the right side. — *adj.* denoting this side: *the nearside front tyre is flat*.

near-sighted *adj.* short-sighted.

near thing a narrow escape; a success only just achieved.

neat *adj.* **1** tidy; clean; orderly. **2** pleasingly small or regular. **3** elegantly or cleverly simple: *a neat explanation*. **4** skilful or efficient: *neat work!* **5** *North Amer.* excellent. **6** *said of an alcoholic drink* undiluted. [from French *net*, clean, tidy]

neaten *verb trans.* (**neatened**, **neatening**) to make neat.

neatly *adv.* with a neat or tidy manner.

neatness *noun* being neat or tidy; a neat quality.

Neb *or* **Nebr.** *abbrev.* Nebraska.

Neblina, Pico da the highest mountain in Brazil, situated in Amazonas state in the N of the country. HEIGHT 3 014m. Located in a national park, it lies in the Serra Imeri Range, on the frontier with Venezuela.

Nebraska POP (1990) 1.6m, a state in central USA. It is divided into 93 counties. AREA 200 342sq km/77 355sq mi. PHYSICAL DESCRIPTION the Platte R crosses the state to empty into the Missouri R, which forms the E border; Johnson Township (at 1 654m) is the highest point; the E part of the state is undulating fertile farmland, growing corn; further W, on the Great Plains, grass cover helps to stabilize eroded land; in the far W are the foothills of the Rocky Mts; Nebraska is known as the 'Cornhusker State'. HISTORY part of the 1803 Louisiana Purchase; Bellevue was the first permanent settlement; became a territory stretching to the Canadian border in 1854, but its area was reduced in 1863; in 1867 it became the 37th state to be admitted to the Union; in the same year, completion of the Union Pacific Railroad's transcontinental line resulted in a land boom. CAPITAL Lincoln. CHIEF TOWNS Omaha, Grand Island. ECONOMY agriculture is dominant; Nebraska is the nation's second-largest cattle producer; hogs; corn; wheat; grain sorghum; food processing; electrical machinery; chemicals.

Nebuchadnezzar II *or* **Nebuchadrezzar** (c.630–562 BC) King of Babylon (605–562 BC), the son of Nabopolassar, founder of the New Babylonian (Chaldean) Empire. He extended the Babylonian empire as far as the Mediterranean, defeating the Egyptians at Carchemish (605 BC) and gaining control of Syria. He captured Jerusalem, first in 597 BC and again in 586 BC, when he destroyed the city and deported the Jews into exile in Babylonia (the Babylonian exile).

nebula *noun* (PL. **nebulae**, **nebulas**) *Astron.* a region or cloud of interstellar dust or gas, forming a fuzzy luminous or dark patch that can be seen in the night sky with the aid of a telescope. *Astron.* formerly used to refer to galaxies too remote to be resolved into individual stars, and which therefore appeared as hazy smudges of light. [from Latin *nebula*, mist]

nebular *adj. Astron.* relating to a nebula or nebulae.

nebulous *adj.* vague; hazy; lacking distinct shape, form, or nature. [from Latin *nebulosus*, from *nebula*, mist]

nebulously *adv.* in a nebulous or vague way; hazily.

NEC *abbrev.* National Exhibition Centre.

necessarily *adv.* as a necessary or inevitable result.

necessary — *adj.* **1** needed; essential; indispensable; that must be done. **2** that must be; inevitable; inescapable: *a necessary evil.* **3** logically required or unavoidable. — *noun* (PL. **necessaries**) something that is necessary.
— **the necessary** *humorous colloq.* **1** money needed for a purpose. **2** action that must be taken.
[from Latin *necessarius*, from *necesse*, necessary]

necessitate *verb trans.* to make necessary or unavoidable. [from Latin *necessitare*, from *necessitas*, necessity]

necessity *noun* (PL. **necessities**) **1** something necessary or essential: *food and other necessities.* **2** circumstances that make something necessary, obligatory, or unavoidable: *from necessity rather than choice / must of necessity draw this conclusion.* **3** a pressing need: *no necessity to rush.* **4** poverty; want; need. [from Latin *necessitas*]

neck — *noun* **1** the part of the body between the head and the shoulders. **2** the part of a garment at or covering the neck. **3** a narrow part; a narrow connecting part: *joined to the mainland by a neck of land.* **4** *Racing* a head-and-neck's length; a small margin: *won by a neck.* **5** the meat from the neck of an animal. — *verb intrans., trans. slang* to hug and kiss amorously.
— **breathe down someone's neck** *colloq.* to supervise someone so closely as to inhibit them. **get it in the neck** *colloq.* to be severely rebuked or punished. **neck and neck** *said of competitors in a race, etc* exactly level. **risk one's neck** to risk one's life or do something dangerous. **save one's neck** to escape from danger, etc without loss or harm. **stick one's neck out** to put oneself at risk of being attacked, contradicted, etc. **up to one's neck in something** *colloq.* deeply involved in it; busy; preoccupied.
[from Anglo-Saxon *hnecca*]

neckband *noun* a band or strip of material sewn round the neck of a garment.

Necker, Jacques (1732–1804) French statesman and financier, born in Geneva, Switzerland. He founded a bank in Paris and became a wealthy speculator. By 1776–7 he was Director of the French Treasury and Director-General of Finances. His attempts to finance French involvement in the War of American Independence involved heavy borrowing, whilst he concealed the large state deficit. Dismissed in 1781, he was recalled (1788) to deal with the impending financial crisis. He summoned the Estates General, but his proposals for social and constitutional change aroused royal opposition, and he finally resigned in 1790.

neckerchief *noun* (PL. **neckerchiefs**, **neckerchieves**) a cloth for wearing round the neck. [from NECK + KERCHIEF]

necklace *noun* a string of beads or jewels, etc, or a chain, worn round the neck as jewellery. [from NECK + LACE in the sense 'cord', 'tie']

necklacing *noun* the practice of placing a petrol-soaked tyre over someone's head and setting it alight, used by some black South Africans as a punishment for those believed to be government sympathizers.

neckline *noun* the edge of a garment at the neck, or its shape.

neck of the woods *humorous* a neighbourhood or locality.

necktie *noun* a man's tie.

necromancer *noun* one who practises necromancy or divination; a magician.

necromancy *noun* divination or prophecy through communication with the dead; black magic; sorcery. [from Greek *nekros*, corpse + *mantis*, prophet]

necrophilia *noun* obsessive interest, especially of an erotic kind, in dead bodies. [from Greek *nekros*, corpse + -PHILIA]

necrophiliac *noun* a person with an obsessive interest in dead bodies.

necropolis *noun Archaeol.* a cemetery. [from Greek *nekros*, corpse + *polis*, city]

necrosis *noun* (PL. **necroses**) *Biol.* the death of cells in part of a tissue or organ as a result of disease, injury, or interruption of the blood supply. [from Greek *nekrosis*, from *nekros*, corpse]

necrotic *adj.* relating to or affected by necrosis.

nectar *noun* **1** *Bot.* the sticky concentrated sugar solution produced by the nectaries of flowers, which serves to attract insects and certain small birds which then pollinate the flowers as they retrieve the nectar. Bees use nectar to make honey. **2** *Greek Mythol.* the special drink of the gods. **3** any delicious drink. **4** anything delightfully welcome to the senses. [from Greek *nektar*]

nectarine *noun* a peach-like fruit with a shiny, downless skin. [from NECTAR]

nectary *noun* (PL. **nectaries**) *Bot.* in flowering plants, a specialized gland, usually situated at the base of the flower, that secretes nectar.

NEDC *abbrev.* National Economic Development Council.

née *adj.* born, used in giving a woman's maiden name: *Jane Day, née Osborn.* [from French *née*, feminine of *né*, born]

need — *verb* **1** *trans.* to have want of; to require. **2** *intrans.* **a** to be required or obliged to do something: *we need to find a replacement.* **b** (*in negative and interrogative without to and with third person singular need*) to be required or obliged to be or do something: *they needn't stay / need we tell them?* — *noun* **1** something one requires. **2** (**need of** or **for something**) a condition of lacking or requiring it; an urge or desire. **3** (**need for something**) necessity or justification.
— **if need** or **needs be** if necessary. **in need** needing help or financial support. See also NEEDS.
[from Anglo-Saxon *nead* or *nied*]

needful — *adj.* necessary. — *noun* (**the needful**) *humorous colloq.* **1** whatever action is necessary. **2** money needed for a purpose.

needle — *noun* **1** a slender pointed steel sewing instrument with a hole for the thread. **2** a longer, thicker implement of metal, wood, bone, plastic, etc without a hole, for knitting, crocheting, etc. **3** a hypodermic syringe, or its pointed end. **4** a gramophone stylus. **5** the moving pointer on a compass or other instrument. **6** the needle-shaped leaf of a tree such as the pine or fir. — *noun colloq.* provocation. — *verb trans. colloq.* to provoke or irritate, especially deliberately. [from Anglo-Saxon *nædl*]

needle bank a place where drug-users can exchange used hypodermic syringes for new ones free of charge, to help prevent the spread of disease or infection.

needlecord *noun* a finely ribbed corduroy.

needlepoint *noun* **1** embroidery on canvas. **2** lace made over a paper pattern, with needles rather than bobbins.

needless *adj.* unnecessary.

needlessly *adv.* without any need: *he needlessly locked the door.*

needlewoman *noun* a woman who sews; a seamstress.

needlework *noun* sewing and embroidery.

needn't *contr.* need not.

needs *adv. old use* of necessity; inevitably. [from Anglo-Saxon *niedes*, genitive of *nied*, need]

needy *adj.* (**needier**, **neediest**) in severe need; poverty-stricken; destitute.

Néel, Louis Eugène Félix (1904–) French physicist, born in Lyons. He was professor at Strasbourg University before moving to Grenoble in 1940. In research on magnetism he predicted that a special type of magnetic ordering known as 'antiferromagnetism' should exist, and this was experimentally confirmed in 1938. This led to the development of 'memories' in computers. He shared the 1970 Nobel Prize for Physics with Hannes Alfvén.

nefarious *adj.* wicked; evil. [from Latin *nefarius*, from *nefas*, wrong]

Nefertiti (14c BC) Queen of Egypt, the consort of King Akhenaton. She bore Akhenaton six daughters, and is believed to have followed the cult of the sun god Aten. A painted portrait bust of her was found in 1912, and is now in the Berlin Museum.

neg *abbrev.* negative.

negate *verb trans.* **1** to cancel or destroy the effect of. **2** to deny the existence of. [from Latin *negare*, to deny]

negation *noun* **1** the act of negating. **2** the absence or opposite of something. **3** the denial of the existence of something.

negative — *adj.* **1** meaning or saying 'no'; expressing denial, refusal, or prohibition. **2** *said of people, attitudes, etc* unenthusiastic, defeatist, or pessimistic. **3** *Maths.* less than zero. **4** contrary to, or cancelling the effect of, whatever is regarded as positive. **5** *Maths.* measured in the opposite direction to that chosen as positive. **6** *Electr.* having the kind of electric charge produced by an excess of electrons. **7** *Photog., said of film* having the light and shade of the actual image reversed, or complementary colours in place of actual ones. — *noun* **1** a word, statement, or grammatical form expressing denial: *replied in the negative.* **2** a photographic film with a negative image, from which prints are made. — *verb* **1** to reject; to veto. **2** to deny. **3** to neutralize or cancel out. **4** to disprove or prove the contrary of. [from Latin *negativus*, from *negare*, to deny]

negative equity a situation in which a property falls below the value of the mortgage held on it, usually caused by a drop in property values.

negative income tax a government payment to individuals whose income falls below a prescribed level, in order to bring them up to that level.

negatively *adv.* in a negative manner; so as to say 'no'.

Negeri Sembilan POP (1990) 724 000, a state in SW Peninsular Malaysia, bounded W by the Strait of Malacca. AREA 6 643sq km/2 564sq mi. CAPITAL Seremban. ECONOMY rubber; rice; tin. [from Malay *Negeri Sembilan*, nine states]

Negev a hilly desert region in S Israel, extending in a wedge from Beersheba in the N to Eilat on the Gulf of Aqaba. The N is irrigated by a conduit leading from L Tiberias. Kibbutz settlements are increasing in the region.

neglect — *verb trans.* **1** not to give proper care and attention to. **2** to leave (duties, etc) undone. **3** to fail or omit (to do something). — *noun* **1** lack of proper care. **2** a state of disuse or decay: *fell into neglect*. [from Latin *negligere*, to neglect]

neglectful *adj.* inattentive or negligent; undutiful or unconscientious.

négligé *or* **negligee** *noun* a woman's thin light dressing-gown. [from French *négligé*, carelessness, undress, from *négliger*, to neglect]

negligence *noun* lack of proper attention or care; carelessness. [from Latin *negligentia*]
◇ In law, negligence is a tort applicable in a wide range of situations. To prove negligence, the plaintiff must show that the defendant owed him or her a duty of care, that that duty was breached, and that the breach caused damage to the plaintiff.

negligent *adj.* **1** not giving proper care and attention. **2** careless or offhand.

negligible *adj.* small or unimportant enough to ignore. [from Latin *negligere*, to disregard]

negligibly *adv.* so as to be negligible or insignificant: *a negligibly small amount*.

Negoiul, Mount the highest mountain in Romania, situated in the Transylvanian Alps. HEIGHT 2 548m.

negotiable *adj.* **1** said of a cash order or other asset that can legally be negotiated, ie transferred to another person in exchange for its value in money. **2** open to discussion. **3** said of a hazard or obstacle able to be got past.

negotiate *verb* **1** (**negotiate with someone**) to confer with them to reach agreement on terms or arrangements affecting both parties. **2** to bring about (an agreement) or arrange (a treaty, price, etc) by conferring. **3** to pass safely (a hazard on one's way, etc). [from Latin *negotiari*, to trade, from *negotium*, business]

negotiation *noun* the process of negotiating; a round of negotiating.

negotiator *noun* a person who negotiates or is negotiating.

Negress *noun often offensive* a female Negro.

Negro, River a Patagonian river in S central Argentina. It is formed at the junction of the R Neuquén and R Limay and flows S and SE to the Atlantic, 32km/20mi SE of Viedma. The river is navigable for 400km/250mi upstream. It irrigates valleys of vineyards and is used for hydroelectric power.

Negro — *noun* (PL. **Negroes**) *often offensive* a person belonging to one of the black-skinned races originally from Africa. — *adj.* relating or belonging to these races. [from Spanish, from Latin *niger*, black]

Negroid — *adj.* having the physical characteristics of the Negro races, eg dark skin, a broad nose, and tightly curling hair. — *noun* a Negroid person.

Negro River an important N tributary of the R Amazon, N Brazil, length c.2 250km/1 400mi. The river rises in SE Colombia and flows generally SE through the Amazon tropical rainforest, joining the Amazon 18km/11mi below Manaus. Connected to the Orinoco R via the Casiquiare Canal, it is a major transport channel.

Neguib, Mohammed (1901–84) Egyptian leader. As general of an army division in 1952 he carried out a coup d'état in Cairo which banished King Farouk I and initiated the 'Egyptian Revolution'. He took the offices of Commander-in-Chief and Prime Minister, abolished the monarchy, and became President of the newly formed republic (1953). He was deposed in 1954 and succeeded by Col Gamal Abd al-Nasser.

Nehemiah, Book of a book of the Hebrew Bible and Old Testament, originally joined to the Book of Ezra, and probably also to 1 and 2 Chronicles, named after a Jewish official of the King of Persia, Nehemiah, who apparently led a return to Judea by Jewish exiles in Persia. He had two periods of governorship in Judea during the reign of Artaxerxes I (465–424 BC) or possibly Artaxerxes II (404–359 BC).

Nehru, Jawaharlal, known as **Pandit** ('teacher') (1889–1964) Indian statesman, born in Allahabad. After serving as a lawyer in the Allahabad High Court, he joined the Indian Congress Committee (1918), was influenced by Mahatma Gandhi, and was imprisoned several times by the British. He was elected President of the Indian National Congress (1929) and then became India's first Prime Minister (1947–64) and Minister of External Affairs. During the Cold War he followed a policy of neutrality, and he also embarked on industrialization, reorganized the states on a linguistic basis, and brought the dispute with Pakistan over Kashmir to a peaceful solution.

neigh — *noun* the characteristic cry of a horse. — *verb intrans.* to make this cry. [from Anglo-Saxon *hnægan*, to neigh]

neighbour *noun* **1** a person living near or next door to one. **2** an adjacent territory, person, etc. **3** *old use* any of one's fellow humans: *love your neighbour*. [from Anglo-Saxon *neah*, near + *gebur*, dweller]

neighbourhood *noun* **1** a district or locality. **2** the area near something or someone.
— **in the neighbourhood of** roughly: *it cost in the neighbourhood of £500.*

neighbourhood watch a scheme under which local residents agree to keep a general watch on each other's property and the surrounding streets to help prevent crime.

neighbouring *adj.* nearby.

neighbourliness *noun* being neighbourly or friendly.

neighbourly *adj.* friendly, especially to the people around one.

Neil, Andrew Ferguson (1949–) Scottish journalist, born in Paisley. He joined the *Economist* magazine (1973–83) and became UK editor. He was appointed editor of the *Sunday Times* in 1983 and altered the paper's soft-left bias, supporting most of the key policies of Margaret Thatcher's government. He identified himself publicly with the proprietor Rupert Murdoch's coup against the unions at Wapping in 1986, which led to the introduction of new labour practices in the newspaper industry.

Neil a male first name. [from the Gaelic name *Niall*, of uncertain origin; related to NIGEL]

Nei Mongol see INNER MONGOLIA.

neither — *adj., pron.* not the one nor the other (thing or person): *neither proposal is acceptable / neither of the proposals is acceptable.* — *conj.* (introducing the first of two or more alternatives; usually paired with *nor*) not: *I neither know nor care.* — *adv.* nor; also not: *if you won't, neither will I.*
— **neither here nor there** irrelevant; unimportant.
[from Anglo-Saxon *nawther* or *nahwæther*]
◆ *Neither* is normally followed by a singular verb, eg *neither of them is coming.* However, in more informal usage, the plural is common, eg *neither of them are coming.*

nekton *noun Zool.* the actively swimming organisms (eg fishes, whales) that inhabit seas, lakes, etc, as opposed to the passively floating or drifting organisms that form the plankton. [from Greek *nekton* (neuter), swimming]

nelly
— **not on your nelly** *old slang use* certainly not. [perhaps from the phrase 'not on your Nelly Duff', rhyming slang for 'puff', ie life]

Nelson, (John) Byron (1912–) US golfer, born in Fort Worth, Texas. He won a record 18 tournaments on the US Professional Golfers Association (PGA) tour in 1945, 11 of them successive, and also won the US Open (1939), the US PGA championship (1940, 1945), and the US Masters (1937, 1942) — a total of 54 US Tour events. He captained the 1965 US Ryder Cup team at Birkdale, and became a notable golf teacher and broadcaster after he retired from tournament play.

Nelson, Horatio Nelson, Viscount (1758–1805) English admiral, born in Burnham Thorpe, Norfolk. He joined the navy in 1770, and in 1784 was sent to the West Indies (where he was married to Frances Nisbet) to enforce the Navigation Act against the newly independent United States. At war with France from 1793, in 1794 he commanded the naval brigade at Bastia and Calvi, where he lost the sight of his right eye, and at Santa Cruz in 1796, where he lost his right arm. In 1798 he followed Napoleon and his French fleet to Egypt and destroyed the fleet in Aboukir Bay. On his return to Naples, he began a love affair with Emma, Lady Hamilton, which lasted until his death. In 1801 he was made rear-admiral, led the attack on Copenhagen, then became commander-in-chief. In 1805 he gained his greatest victory, against the combined French and Spanish fleet at Trafalgar, but during the battle he was mortally wounded on his flagship, HMS *Victory*.

nelson *noun* (*also* **full nelson**) a wrestling hold in which one passes one's arms under one's opponent's, from behind, and joins hands so that pressure can be applied against the back of the opponent's neck. [named after Horatio Nelson]

Nelson Lakes a national park, situated in the N of South I, New Zealand. AREA 961sq km/371sq mi. Located within it are the Rotoiti and Rotoroa lakes. They are surrounded by rugged, forest-clad mountains rising to over 1 800m. The park was established in 1956.

Neman, River, German **Memel** a river in Belorussia and Lithuania, length 955km/593mi. It rises 48km/30mi SW of Minsk, in central Belorussia, and flows W then N into Lithuania. Alexander I and Napoleon I had a meeting on a raft on the river which resulted in the signing of the Treaty of Tilsit (1807).

Nematoda *pl. noun Zool.* in the animal kingdom, a phylum of worms with unsegmented bodies, typically circular in cross-section, eg roundworms, pinworms. [from Greek *nema -atos*, thread + *eidos*, form]

nematode *noun Zool.* any invertebrate animal belonging to the phylum Nematoda, which includes both free-living and parasitic worms with long slender unsegmented bodies that taper at both ends, and a smooth skin. They include roundworms and pinworms, which live as parasites in humans, and eelworms, which attack the roots of plants. [from Greek *nema*, thread + *eidos*, form]

nem. con. *abbrev. nemine contradicente* (Latin), with no one disagreeing; unanimously.

Nemesis in Greek mythology, the goddess of retribution. She primarily represents the penalty the gods exact for human folly.

nemesis *noun* **1** retribution or just punishment. **2** something that brings this.

Nemirovich-Danchenko, Vladimir (Ivanovich) (1858–1943) Russian theatre director, dramatist, and teacher, born in Ozurgety. Co-founder with Stanislavsky of the Moscow Art Theatre, he became sole director in 1938. His notable productions included Dostoevsky's *The Brothers Karamazov* (1910) and *Nikolai Stavrogin* (1913), and Dmitry Shostakovich's opera *Katerina Izmailova* (Lady Macbeth of Mtsensk District, 1934).

Nemrut Dag the mountain site of the tomb-sanctuary of King Antiochus of Commagene (64–32 BC), S Anatolia, Turkey. The tomb is a conical tumulus 50m high and 150m in diameter at its base. It is a World Heritage site.

Nenets, originally **Samoyed** *or* **Yurak** a Uralic-speaking ethnic group living in N Russia. They are reindeer keepers, fishermen, and hunters (of wild reindeer). Formerly nomadic, they are now settled in villages.

Nennius (8c) Welsh writer, the reputed author of *Historia Britonum* (c.8c). The book gives the mythical account of the origins of the Britons, the Roman occupation, the settlement of the Saxons, and closes with King Arthur's 12 victories.

neo- *combining form* forming words meaning 'new, a new form, modern'. [from Greek *neos*, new]

neoclassical *adj., said of artistic or architectural style, especially in the late 18c and early 19c* imitating or adapting the styles of the ancient classical world.

Neoclassicism 1 a classical revival affecting all the visual arts, which flourished from c.1750 to the early 19c. See also CLASSICAL REVIVAL. **2** a 20c movement in music which sought to restore the ideals, and some of the style and vocabulary, of the 18c classical period.
◇ The movement arose partly as a reaction to Rococo and Baroque excesses in decoration, and partly from a renewed interest in the antique, especially 'the noble simplicity and calm grandeur' of Greek and Roman art. Centred in Rome, it later spread throughout W Europe and N America; its most important theoretician was the art historian Johann Winckelmann (1717–68). In painting, the classical themes and subjects were powerfully and dramatically represented in works by Jaques Louis David (for example, *The Oath of the Horatii*, 1784). The works of Antonio Canova typify the somewhat frigid and artificial of Neoclassical sculpture. In architecture, where Neoclassicism was perhaps most successfully applied, the style was characterized by pure geometric form and restrained decoration.
In music, Neoclassicism was mainly modelled on the style of J S Bach and was essentially anti-Romantic. It was associated particularly with Igor Stravinsky's middle-period works (c.1920–30), but also with such composers as Sergei Prokofiev and Paul Hindemith.

neo-Darwinism *Biol.* a later development of Darwinism, laying greater stress on natural selection and denying the inheritance of acquired characteristics.

neodymium *noun Chem.* (SYMBOL **Nd**, ATOMIC NUMBER **60**) a soft silvery metal, belonging to the lanthanide series, that is used to make special glass for lasers and astronomical lenses, and to give glass a violet colour. It is also used in electronic devices and certain alloys because it has a high electrical resistivity. [from NEO- + *didymium*, the name of a substance once thought to be an element]

Neoexpressionism a term sometimes used for all forms of abstract art which are regarded as conveying strong emotions, or which seem to have been produced by the artist in a heightened emotional state. Examples include Vasily Kandinsky's work after c.1920, or US Action Painting.

Neo-fascism *noun Politics* a term used to describe various post-war fascist ideas and movements reminiscent of, or modelled on, the policies and ideology of the inter-war fascist dictatorships. In W Europe, Neo-fascist movements have been, in particular, opposed to immigration from former colonial and Mediterranean countries. They have had some measure of success in regions or areas with large immigrant populations and/or high unemployment.

Neoimpressionism *noun Art* a movement lasting from c.1885 to c.1900. A group of French painters, including Georges Seurat and Paul

Signac, reacting against the romanticism of Impressionism, applied the scientific method of Divisionism, with its emphasis on the study of optical phenomena, to painting. The movement later spread to Belgium and Italy, and led directly to Fauvism.

neolithic *adj.* (*also* **Neolithic**) belonging or relating to the later Stone Age, in Europe lasting from about 40 000 to 2400 BC, characterized by the manufacture of polished stone tools. [from NEO- + Greek *lithos*, stone]

neologism *noun* **1** a new word or expression. **2** a new meaning acquired by an existing word or expression. [from NEO- + Greek *logos*, word]
◇ English neologisms of recent years include: new words such as *glitzy* and *yuppie*; and new usages such as *gay, green,* and *crucial*. In language pathology, the term refers to the coining of an obscure or meaningless word, characteristic of disorders such as aphasia and schizophrenia.

neon *noun Chem.* (SYMBOL **Ne**, ATOMIC NUMBER **10**) a colourless odourless inert gas that occurs in trace amounts in air. It is one of the rare or noble gases, and is used in fluorescent lighting, neon lamps (which give a red glow), and lasers. [from Greek *neon*, neuter form of *neos*, new]

neonatal *adj.* relating to newly born children. [from Latin *neonatus*, from Greek *neos*,new + Latin *natus*, born]

neonate *noun* a newly born child, especially one that is less than four weeks old.

neon lamp *or* **neon light 1** a neon-filled glass tube used for lighting. **2** *loosely* any similar tubular fluorescent light.

neophyte *noun* **1** a beginner. **2** a new convert to a religious faith. **3** a novice in a religious order. [from Greek *neophytos*, newly planted]

neoplasm *noun Medicine* a malignant or benign tumour consisting of a new and abnormal mass of tissue formed by the rapid and uncontrolled multiplication of cells.

Neo-Plasticism a term invented (c.1917) by Piet Mondrian to describe his own particularly severe form of abstract art. He permitted only primary colours, black, white, and grey, and restricted his shapes to squares or rectangles defined by vertical and horizontal lines.

Neoplatonism a school of philosophy founded by Plotinus (AD 205–270) and lasting into the 7c, which attempted to combine doctrines of Plato, Aristotle, and the Pythagoreans. Central to Plotinus's philosophy is The One, from which emanate Intelligence (which contains the Platonic ideas) and Soul (which includes individual souls).

Neoptolemus in Greek legend, the son of Achilles and Deidameia, sometimes called Pyrrhus. He went with Odysseus to Troy, and at the end of the war killed Priam and enslaved Andromache. Apollo prevented him from reaching his home, and he was killed in a dispute at Delphi.

Nepal, official name **Kingdom of Nepal**, Nepali **Sri Nepala Sarkar** POP (1992e) 20.6m, an independent kingdom lying along the S slopes of the Himalayas, central Asia. It is divided into 14 zones. AREA 145 391sq km/56 121sq mi; length E–W 880km/547mi; width 144–240km/90–150mi N–S. It is bounded N by the Tibet region of China, and E, S, and W by India. CAPITAL Kathmandu. CHIEF TOWNS Patan, Bhadgaon. TIME ZONE GMT +5.5. OFFICIAL LANGUAGE Nepali. The chief religion is Hinduism (90%); it is the only official Hindu kingdom in the world. CURRENCY the Nepalese rupee. PHYSICAL DESCRIPTION a landlocked country; it rises steeply from the Ganges Basin; high fertile valleys in the 'hill country' at 1 300m, such as the Vale of Kathmandu (a World Heritage site), are enclosed by ranges of folded mountains; the country is dominated by the glaciated peaks of the Himalayas, the highest of which is Mt

Everest at 8 848m. CLIMATE varies from subtropical lowland, with hot, humid summers and mild winters, to an alpine climate over 3 300m, where peaks are permanently snow-covered; temperatures at Kathmandu vary from 40°C in May to 2°C in Dec; the monsoon season occurs during summer (Jun–Sep); average annual rainfall decreases from 1 778mm in the E to 889mm in the W. HISTORY modern Nepal was formed from a group of independent hill states, united in the 18c; a parliamentary system was introduced in 1959, but was replaced in 1960 by a partyless system of *panchayats* (village councils). GOVERNMENT Nepal is a constitutional monarchy ruled by a hereditary King; a period of unrest in 1990 was followed by a reduction of the King's powers and the introduction of a new constitution with a multiparty parliamentary system; executive power is held by the King and a Council of Ministers and there is a bicameral legislature consisting of a House of Representatives and a National Council. ECONOMY one of the least developed countries in Asia; agriculture employs 90% of the people; rice, wheat, millet, maize, barley, sugar cane; few minerals are exploited commercially, although there are deposits of coal, copper, iron, mica, zinc, and cobalt; agricultural and forest-based goods, jute, handicrafts, carpets, medicinal herbs, ready-made garments, shoes, woollen goods; hydroelectric power is being developed; tourism has become increasingly important.

Nepal

nephew *noun* the son of one's brother or sister, or of one's brother- or sister-in-law. [from Old French *neveu*]

nephrectomy *noun Medicine* the surgical removal of a kidney. [from Greek *nephros*, kidney + -ECTOMY]

nephrite *noun Geol.* a hard glistening mineral, and one of the two minerals commonly known as jade (the other is jadeite). It occurs in a wide range of colours, including white and black. [from Greek *nephros*, kidney; so called because it was once thought to be effective in treating kidney disease]

nephritis *noun Medicine* inflammation of the kidneys. [from Greek *nephros*, kidney + -ITIS]

nephrology *noun Medicine* the branch of medicine concerned with the study of the structure, functions, and diseases of the kidney. [from Greek *nephros*, kidney + -LOGY]

nephron *noun Anat.* in the vertebrate kidney, one of over a million functional units responsible for the filtration of waste products from the blood to form urine. [from Greek *nephros*, kidney]

nepotism *noun* the practice of favouring one's relatives, especially in making official appointments. [from Latin *nepos*, grandson or nephew]

nepotistic *adj.* favouring one's relatives in giving favours or making appointments.

Neptune in Roman mythology, a water-god (the Romans originally had no sea gods). He was later identified with the Greek god Poseidon.

Neptune *noun Astron.* the eighth (or occasionally ninth) planet from the Sun. Its orbit normally lies between those of Uranus and Pluto, but once every 248 years, Pluto's orbit brings it closer to the Sun than Neptune for about 20 years. The two planets are now in such a period (lasting from 1979 to 1999).

◇ Neptune is on average about 4 497 million km from the Sun, and has a diameter of 48 600km at the equator. It takes 18 hours to rotate once on its own axis, and 164.8 years to orbit around the Sun. It cannot be seen from Earth without a telescope. Neptune has a faint ring system and eight natural satellites, the best-known being Triton (the largest) and Nereid. Triton is 2 700km in diameter, and is covered with icy mountains. It orbits the planet in the opposite direction to the other moons.

Neptune is thought to have a central rocky core, an outer mantle of ice, and a deep atmosphere consisting mainly of hydrogen, helium, methane, and ammonia. Methane in the outer atmosphere is responsible for the bluish colour of the planet. Photographs taken by the space probe *Voyager 2*, which passed Neptune in Aug 1989, revealed a long-lived oval rotating storm cloud as large as the Earth, and known as the Great Dark Spot, in the southern hemisphere. They also revealed a smaller dark cloud, and showed that Neptune has three faint rings. Winds were recorded blowing at up to 2 000kph through the bitterly cold atmosphere. The surface temperature of the planet appears to be about –210°C.

Neptune and Triton a sculpture by Gian Lorenzo Bernini (c.1620, Victoria and Albert Museum, London).

neptunium *noun Chem.* (SYMBOL **Np**, ATOMIC NUMBER **93**) a silvery-white radioactive metal that occurs naturally in trace amounts, but is usually obtained as a by-product of plutonium production. The isotope neptunium-237 is used to detect neutrons. [named after the planet Neptune]

NERC *abbrev.* Natural Environment Research Council.

nerd *noun derog. slang* a foolish or annoying person.

nereid *noun* in Greek mythology, a sea-nymph, a daughter of Nereus.

Nereus in Greek mythology, a sea god, the wise old man of the sea who always told the truth and was able to change his shape. Heracles had to wrestle with him to find the location of the Golden Apples.

Nergal in Mesopotamian religion, the god of the Underworld, who was at first a destructive solar deity. He forced Ereshkigal, the original goddess of the Underworld, to share her power with him.

nerine *noun Bot.* any of various species of S African plant with attractive brightly coloured pink, orange, red, or white flowers, belonging to the lily family. [from Latin *nerine*]

Nerissa the maid to Portia in Shakespeare's *The Merchant of Venice*, who marries Gratiano.

Nernst, Walther Hermann (1864–1941) German physical chemist, born in Briesen, W Prussia. Professor at Göttingen and Berlin, he formulated his 'heat theorem' (a statement of the third law of thermodynamics) in 1906. He later worked on quantum theory and chemical reactions involving light, and devised several inventions. He was awarded the 1920 Nobel Prize for Chemistry.

Nero, in full **Nero Claudius Caesar**, originally **Lucius Domitius Ahenobarbus** (AD 37–68) Roman emperor (54–68), the son of Gnaeus Domitius Ahenobarbus and Agrippina the Younger, and stepson and heir of the emperor Claudius, the fourth husband of his mother. He was advised well in his early reign by his mother, the philosopher Seneca, and the Praetorian Prefect Burrus. After the murder (at his command) first of Britannicus (son of Claudius), then of his mother (59) and his wife (62), Nero indulged himself in sex, singing, acting, and chariot-racing and neglected affairs of state. He was blamed for the Great Fire of Rome (64), and instead attempted to make scapegoats of the Christians. A major plot to overthrow him (the Conspiracy of Piso) was formed (65) but detected, and Rome had to endure three more years of tyranny before he was toppled from power by the army, and forced to commit suicide.

Neruda, Pablo (Neftali Reyes) (1904–73) Chilean poet and diplomat, born in Parral. He made his name with *Veinte poemas de amor ya una canción desesperada* (Twenty Love Poems and a Song of Despair, 1924). From 1927 he held diplomatic posts in various countries, and after returning to Chile in 1943 he joined the Communist Party. He travelled in Russia and China (1948–52), and was later the Chilean Ambassador in Paris (1970–2). His other works include *Residencia en la tierra* (Residence on Earth, 1925–31) and *Canto General* (General Song, 1950). He was awarded the Nobel Prize for Literature in 1971.

nerve — *noun* **1** a bundle of nerve fibres, linked to individual nerve cells, that carries nerve impulses between the central nervous system (the brain and spinal cord) and the rest of the body. **2** the vein of a leaf, consisting of a strand of vascular tissue that conducts water and nutrients. **3** *colloq.* cheek; impudence. **4** (**nerves**) *colloq.* nervousness; tension or stress: *calm one's nerves.* **5** *colloq.* one's capacity to cope with stress or excitement. — *verb* (**nerve oneself for something**) to prepare oneself for a challenge or ordeal.

— **get on someone's nerves** *colloq.* to annoy or irritate them.

lose one's nerve to lose one's courage or resolve.

strain every nerve to put every effort into an endeavour.

[from Latin *nervus*, sinew, tendon, nerve]

nerve cell a cell that transmits nerve impulses; a neurone.

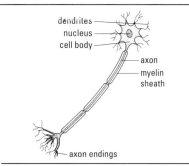

nerve cell

nerve centre **1** a cluster of nerve cells responsible for a particular bodily function. **2** the centre of control within an organization, etc.

nerve gas a poisonous gas that acts on the nerves, especially those of respiration, used as a weapon.

nerveless *adj.* **1** lacking feeling or strength; inert. **2** fearless.

nervelessly *adv.* without feeling or strength.

nerve-racking *adj.* causing one to feel tense and anxious.

Nervi, Pier Luigi (1891–1971) Italian architect, born in Sondrio. He set up as a building contractor, and achieved an international reputation with his designs for the Olympic Games in Rome (1960). He also designed the exhibition halls in Turin (1948–50), the Pirelli building (the first skyscraper in Italy, 1955), and San Francisco Cathedral (1970).

nervily *adv.* in a nervy or excitable manner.

nerviness *noun* a nervy or excitable manner.

nervous *adj.* **1** timid; easily agitated. **2** apprehensive; uneasy. **3** relating to the nerves: *nervous illnesses.* **4** consisting of nerves. [from Latin *nervosus*, sinewy, from *nervus*, sinew, nerve]

nervous breakdown a mental illness attributed loosely to stress, involving intense anxiety, low self-esteem, and loss of concentration.

nervously *adv.* with a nervous or apprehensive manner.

nervousness *noun* a nervous or apprehensive manner.

nervous system in multicellular animals, the highly organized network of cells and tissues that control the vital functions of the body, and enable the animal to be aware of and respond to the surrounding environment.

◇ In vertebrates, there is a *central nervous system*, consisting of the brain and spinal cord, and a *peripheral nervous system*, which comprises the rest of the nervous system. The central nervous system receives sensory information in the form of nerve impulses (electrical signals). These are carried along *sensory neurones* (sensory nerve cells) from sensory receptor cells and sense organs. The central nervous system then processes the information it has received, and relays a suitable response, again in the form of a nerve impulse, along *motor neurones* to muscles or glands (often referred to as *effectors*).

The *autonomic nervous system* controls vital body functions that are not under conscious control, such as breathing and heartbeat. Nerves of another category operate by means of *reflexes* (eg to produce rapid withdrawal of the hand from a hot object). These involve the transmission of sensory information only as far as the spinal cord, which then sends a response directly to the muscles, without the need for processing of information in the brain.

nervy *adj.* (**nervier, nerviest**) excitable.

Nesbit, E(dith), maiden and pen name of **Mrs Hubert Bland** (1858–1924) English writer, born in London. She began her literary career by writing poetry, but is best remembered for her children's stories. These include *The Story of the Treasure Seekers* (1899), *The Wouldbegoods* (1901), and *The Railway Children* (1906).

-ness *suffix* forming nouns indicating a state, condition, or degree: *slowness / darkness.*

Nessebar a town, formerly Menebria, situated on the E coast of Bulgaria. It has many ancient buildings and archaeological sites which testify to its 3 000-year history as a Thracian settlement, a Greek colony, and a Byzantine city. It is a World Heritage site.

Nesselrode, Karl (Robert Vasilyevich), Graf (Count) (1780–1862) Russian diplomat, born in Lisbon, Portugal. He represented Russia at the Congress of Vienna (1814–15), and was involved in the Holy Alliance (1815), a document delineating Christian principles that was drawn up by Tsar Alexander I and signed by Emperor Francis I, Frederick William III, and other European leaders. As Foreign Minister from 1822, he dominated Russian foreign policy for 30 years. His Balkan policy, which attempted to curb France's influence over the Ottoman Empire, contributed to the outbreak of the Crimean War (1853).

Ness, Loch a loch in Highland region, N Scotland. It extends NE from Fort Augustus along the Great Glen to 9km/6mi SW of Inverness. The loch measures 38km/24mi long, with an average width of 2km/1.3mi and a maximum depth of 230m (near Castle Urquhart). Part of the

Caledonian Canal, it is drained by the R Ness at the N end of the loch, which flows 11km/7mi NE to the Moray Firth. It is said to be inhabited by an unidentified creature known as 'the Loch Ness monster' or 'Nessie'; there have been several unconfirmed sightings, but scientific investigations have produced no clear results as to its existence. One famous photograph of the 'monster' was shown in 1994 to have been faked. NOTABLE FEATURE Loch Ness Monster Exhibition Centre at Drumnadrochit.

Nessus in Greek mythology, a centaur who attacked Heracles' wife, Deinira. Heracles shot him, and the dying centaur told Deinira that his blood would be a cure for infidelity. Later, through jealousy, she put the blood on Heracles' shirt which, instead of winning back his love, coated him with poison and killed him.

nest — *noun* **1** a structure built by birds or other creatures, eg rats, wasps, etc, in which to lay eggs or give birth to and look after young. **2** a cosy habitation or retreat. **3** a den or haunt (eg of thieves) or secret centre (of vice, crime, etc). **4** a set of things that fit together or one inside the other. — *verb* **1** *intrans.* to build and occupy a nest. **2** *trans., intrans.* to fit together compactly. **3** *intrans.* to go in search of birds' nests. [from Anglo-Saxon *nest*]

nest egg 1 a real or artificial egg left in a nest to encourage laying. **2** *colloq.* a sum of money saved up for the future; one's savings.

nestle *verb intrans.* (**nestle down** or **together**) to lie or settle snugly. [from Anglo-Saxon *nestlian*, to make a nest]

nestling *noun* a young bird still unable to fly. [from NEST + -LING]

Nestor in Greek legend, a King of Pylos and a senior Greek leader in the Trojan War. In the *Iliad*, Homer portrays him as a long-winded sage, whose advice is often not taken. In the *Odyssey*, he is still living at Pylos, where he welcomes Telemachus, the son of Odysseus.

Nestorians the members of a Christian sect that originated with the followers of Nestorius, Patriarch of Constantinople (AD 428–31). He taught that the divinity and humanity of Christ were not united in a single self-conscious personality, but his beliefs were condemned at the councils of Ephesus (AD 431) and Chalcedon (AD 451) and he was persecuted.

net¹ — *noun* **1** an openwork material made of thread, cord, etc knotted, twisted, or woven so as to form regularly shaped meshes. **2** a piece of this in any of various shapes or qualities appropriate to such uses as catching fish or insects, protecting fruit bushes, confining hair, etc. **3** a strip of net dividing a tennis or badminton court, etc. **4** the net-backed goal in hockey, football, etc. **5** a snare or trap. — *verb* (**netted, netting**) **1** *trans.* to catch in a net. **2** *trans.* to cover with a net. **3** *trans.* to hit, kick, etc (the ball) into the net or goal. **4** *intrans.* to construct net from thread, cord, etc. **5** *trans. Hist.* to make (a purse, etc) using a knotting and looping process.
— **slip the net** escape capture.
[from Anglo-Saxon *nett*]

net² — *adj.* (also **nett**) **1** *said of profit* remaining after all expenses, etc have been paid. **2** *said of weight* not including packaging or container. — *verb trans.* (**netted, netting**) to produce, or earn, as clear profit. [from French *net*, clear, neat]

netball *noun* a game played by women or girls on an outdoor court between teams of seven, the aim being to throw the ball the opponents' net hanging from a ring at the top of a pole.
◊ Invented in the USA in 1891 and derived from basketball, the game was introduced in England in 1895.

Net Book Agreement (ABBREV. **NBA**) an agreement within the book trade that net books may not be sold at less than the price fixed by the publisher.

nether *adj. old use* lower or under. [from Anglo-Saxon *nither*, down]

Netherlands, The, known as **Holland**, Dutch **Nederland**, official name **Kingdom of the Netherlands**, Dutch **Koninkrijk der Nederlanden** POP (1993e) 15.2m, a maritime kingdom in NW Europe, which is divided into 12 provinces. AREA 33 929sq km/13 097sq mi. Bounded W and N by the North Sea, E by Germany, and S by Belgium, the kingdom also includes Netherlands Antilles and Aruba in the Caribbean Sea. The European coastline of the Netherlands measures 451km/280mi long. The Netherlands is among the most densely populated countries in the world. CAPITAL Amsterdam. CHIEF TOWNS The Hague (seat of government), Rotterdam (largest city), Utrecht, Haarlem, Eindhoven, Arnhem, Groningen. TIME ZONE GMT +1. The population is mainly of Germanic descent; chief religions are Roman Catholicism, and the Dutch Reformed Church and other Protestant Churches. OFFICIAL LANGUAGE Dutch. CURRENCY the guilder. PHYSICAL DESCRIPTION generally low and flat, except in the SE where hills rise to 321m; much of the coastal area lies below sea level, protected by coastal dunes and artificial dykes; without these, two fifths of the country would be submerged; around 27% of the land area is below sea level, an area inhabited by c.60% of the population; the country is largely a delta comprising silt from the mouths of the Rhine, Waal, Maas, Ijssel, and Schelde rivers; the many canals connecting the rivers total 6 340km/3 940mi in length; land reclamation from the sea by polder dykes has been carried out for centuries; reclamation of the Zuiderzee (the remnant of which now forms the Ijsselmeer) began in 1920. CLIMATE cool, temperate, maritime; average temperatures are 1.7°C (Jan) and 17°C (Jul); annual rainfall, distributed fairly evenly throughout the year, exceeds 700mm. HISTORY part of the Roman Empire until the 4c AD; part of the Frankish Empire by the 8c before being incorporated into the Holy Roman Empire; in the 15c the Netherlands passed to the Dukes of Burgundy and then to Philip II, who succeeded to Spain and the Netherlands in 1555; attempts to stamp out Protestantism led to rebellion in 1572; the seven N provinces united against Spain in 1579; these United Provinces achieved independence in 1581, and so founded the modern Dutch state; between 1795 and 1813 it was overrun by the French, who established the Batavian Republic; thereafter, it was united with Belgium as the Kingdom of the United Netherlands but Belgium broke away to form a separate kingdom in 1830; neutral in World War I, but there was strong Dutch resistance to German occupation during World War II; joined with Belgium and Luxembourg to form the Benelux economic union in 1948; conflict over independence of Dutch colonies in SE Asia in the late 1940s. GOVERNMENT under a constitutional monarchy there is a parliamentary democracy; the government is led by a Prime Minister, and the States-General (*Staten-Generaal*) consists of a 75-member Chamber and a 150-member Chamber, both elected for four years. ECONOMY Rotterdam and the Europort are major European ports of transshipment, handling goods for EC member countries; Amsterdam is a world diamond centre; the Netherlands is the world's largest exporter of dairy produce; highly intensive agriculture includes animal husbandry, horticulture, potatoes, sugar beet, and grains; major industries include engineering, chemicals, oil products, foodstuffs, electrical and high technology goods, and natural gas; fishing and tourism are also important.

Netherlands, Revolt of the, also called **War of Independence**, **Eighty Years War**, and **Dutch Revolt** uprisings and wars (1566–1648) against Spanish Habsburg rule by 17 provinces in the Low Countries. The provinces were united by Emperor Charles V, but resistance to central-

ization and religious persecution (from the 1550s) led to wars that devastated the 10 southern provinces retained by the Spanish. The rebels, led by William of Orange and his Protestant naval force of 'sea beggars' (*Watergeuzen*), took refuge in seven northern provinces, chiefly Holland, which in 1606 was declared a republic with the Orange family as *stadtholder*. Independence was recognized by Spain in 1648.

Netherlands Antilles, Dutch **Nederlandse Antillen** POP (1992e) 175 000, a group of islands in the Caribbean Sea, forming a Self Governing Dependency of the Netherlands. It comprises the Southern group of Curaçao and Bonaire, lying with separate Aruba N of the Venezuelan coast, and the Northern group of St Maarten, St Eustatius, and Saba, lying E of Puerto Rico. AREA 800sq km/309sq mi. CAPITAL Willemstad. TIME ZONE GMT –4. About 85% of the population are of mixed African descent; Roman Catholicism is the chief religion. OFFICIAL LANGUAGE Dutch; English and Papiamento are also spoken. CURRENCY the Antillian guilder. PHYSICAL DESCRIPTION St Maarten, Bonaire, and Curaçao are composed of coralline limestone; there are no permanent rivers; Saba and St Eustatius are part of the volcanic inner arc of the Lesser Antilles; Saba is the highest island, rising to 870m at Mt Scenery. CLIMATE tropical maritime, with an average annual temperature of 28°C; average annual rainfall varies from 500mm in the S to 1 000mm in the N. HISTORY discovered by Christopher Columbus, initially claimed for Spain; occupied by Dutch settlers in the 17c. GOVERNMENT the Sovereign of the Netherlands is head of state, represented by a Governor, a Council of Ministers, and a unicameral Legislature (*Staten*) of 22 members, elected every four years. ECONOMY based on the refining of crude oil imported from Venezuela; salt; phosphate; attempts to encourage industrial diversification, and tourism; rum distilling; textiles; petrochemicals; beverages; ship repairing.

Netherlands East Indies a name applied to Indonesia from 1798 until independence in 1945.

nethermost *adj. old use* lowest.

nether world *noun* **nether regions** *pl. noun* the underworld; hell.

nett see NET².

netting *noun* any material with meshes, made by knotting or twisting thread, cord, wire, etc.

nettle — *noun* a plant covered with hairs that sting if touched. — *verb trans.* to offend or irritate.
— **grasp the nettle** to deal boldly with a difficult situation.
[from Anglo-Saxon *netele*]

nettle rash an allergic skin reaction with raised red or white itchy patches.

network — *noun* **1** any system resembling a mass of criss-crossing lines: *a network of streets.* **2** a system of interconnected telephone lines, electricity supply lines, etc, that allow information or resources to be passed from one location to another. **3** a group of radio or television stations

The Netherlands

that broadcast the same programmes at the same time. **4** *Comput.* a system of two or more computer terminals that are linked to each other, enabling users to share facilities such as printers, and to communicate and exchange data with other network users. Some networks support a very large number of users, eg a university or a national institution. **5** netting. — *verb* **1** to broadcast on a network. **2** *intrans. Comput.*, *said of computer users* to communicate and exchange data with other network users.

Neuchâtel, German **Neuenburg 1** POP (1990) 50 000, the capital of Neuchâtel canton in W Switzerland, lying on the W shore of L Neuchâtel, 40km/25mi W of Bern. Research for the Swiss watch industry is carried out here. NOTABLE FEATURES university church (13c); castle (mainly 16c). **2** a canton in W Switzerland with Neuchâtel as its capital.

Neuchâtel, Lake the largest lake to lie wholly within Switzerland, running SW–NE at the foot of the Jura Mts, W Switzerland. AREA 218sq km/84sq mi. Chief towns on the shore include Neuchâtel in the NW and Yverdon in the S. It is a major wine-growing area.

neur- see NEURO-.

neural *adj.* relating to the nerves or nervous system. [from Greek *neuron*, nerve]

neuralgia *noun* spasmodic pain along the course of a nerve. [from NEURO- + -ALGIA]

neuralgic *adj.* characterized or affected by neuralgia.

neural network *Comput.* an artificial network, consisting of many computer processing units connected in parallel, that attempts to imitate some of the structural and functional properties of the nerve cells (neurones) in the human nervous system. Neural networks are used in artificial intelligence, especially for recognition of patterns, eg human speech recognition.

neuritis *noun* inflammation of a nerve or nerves, in some cases with defective functioning of the affected part. [from NEURO- + -ITIS]

neuro- *or* **neur-** *combining form* forming words relating to the nerves: *neurosurgery*.

neurolinguistics *sing. noun* the study of the neurological basis of language development and use; in particular, the study of the areas of the brain thought to be involved in the processes of speech and comprehension.

neurology *noun Medicine* the branch of medicine concerned with the study of the structure, functions, and diseases and disorders of the central nervous system (the brain and spinal cord) and the peripheral nerves. [from NEURO- + -LOGY]

neurone *or* **neuron** *noun Anat.* any of a large number of specialized cells that transmit nerve impulses from one part of the body to another. — Also called *nerve cell.* [from Greek *neuron*, nerve]

◇ A typical neurone has a star-shaped *cell body* from which a number of cytoplasmic projections or *dendrites* radiate outward and receive incoming nerve impulses from other neurones. One much longer projection, known as the *axon*, carries nerve impulses outward away from the cell body. The regions where one neurone communicates with another are known as *synapses*.

neuropsychology *noun Psychol.* the application of knowledge about the structure and functioning of the brain and the rest of the nervous system to the study of human behaviour and mental activity.

neurosis *noun* (PL. **neuroses**) **1** any of various relatively mild disorders or conditions, in which disturbances of mental function may cause exaggerated or inappropriate behaviour or thinking. It differs from psychosis in that the person affected retains his or her insight (sense of reality), and so is distressed by the symptoms produced. Examples of neuroses include phobias, obses-

sions, anxiety, depression, hysteria and hypochondria. **2** a popular term for anxiety or obsession.

neurotic — *adj.* **1** relating to, or suffering from, a neurosis. **2** *colloq.* over-anxious, over-sensitive or obsessive. — *noun* a person suffering from a neurosis.

neurotransmitter *noun Physiol.* a chemical substance (eg acetylcholine, noradrenaline) that is released from nerve-cell endings in response to the arrival of a nerve impulse. Its role is to mediate transfer of the impulse across the narrow gap (*synapse*) between adjacent nerve cells, or between a nerve cell and a muscle cell.

neuter — *adj.* **1** *Grammar* denoting a gender of nouns that are neither masculine nor feminine. **2** *said of plants* lacking pistils or stamens. **3** *said of animals* sexually undeveloped or castrated. **4** *said of insects* sexually undeveloped. — *noun* **1** the neuter gender. **2** a neuter word. **3** a neuter plant, animal, or insect, eg a worker bee or ant. — *verb trans.* (**neutered, neutering**) to castrate (an animal). [from Latin *neuter*, from *ne*, not + *uter*, either]

neutral — *adj.* **1** not taking sides in a quarrel or war. **2** not belonging or relating to either side: *neutral ground.* **3** *said of colours, especially grey and fawn* indefinite enough to blend easily with brighter ones. **4** having no strong or noticeable qualities. **5** *Electr.* having no positive or negative electrical charge. **6** *Chem.* neither acidic nor alkaline. — *noun* **1** a person or nation taking no part in a war or quarrel. **2** the disengaged position of an engine's gears, with no power being transmitted to the moving parts. [from Latin *neutralis*, from *neuter*, neither]

neutrality *noun Politics* the fact or state of being neutral, especially in a war or dispute.

◇ Under international laws of neutrality, the neutral country may not permit the use of its territory as a base for military operations nor provide military assistance to the belligerents.

Neutrality Acts a series of US Acts passed in the 1930s to prevent the USA becoming involved in the escalating European conflict.

neutralization *or* **neutralisation** *noun* the process of neutralizing or making ineffective or harmless.

neutralize *or* **neutralise** *verb* **1** to cancel out the effect of; to make useless or harmless. **2** to declare (a country, etc) neutral.

neutrino *noun* (PL. **neutrinos**) *Physics* a stable subatomic particle that has no electric charge, virtually no mass, and travels at or near the speed of light. Neutrinos are produced in vast quantities by the nuclear reactions that take place in the Sun and other stars.

neutron *noun Physics* any of the uncharged subatomic particles that are found inside the nucleus at the centre of an atom, together with positively charged particles known as protons (hydrogen is exceptional in that it does not have any neutrons). Neutrons are slightly heavier than protons. Atoms with different numbers of neutrons but the same number of protons in their nuclei are known as isotopes. The mass of a neutron is 1.675×10^{-27} kg. Neutrons are used in nuclear fission reactions to produce nuclear energy. [from Latin *neuter*, neither]

neutron bomb *Mil.* a type of nuclear bomb that releases large amounts of intense radiation in the form of neutrons, and is designed to cause widespread death and disability of human beings, but relatively little structural damage to buildings, etc.

neutron star *Astron.* a star that has collapsed to such an extent under gravity that it consists almost entirely of neutrons (particles that are found only in the nucleus of atoms).

◇ Neutron stars are the smallest and densest types of star, eg Geninga, a star that is only 20 to 30km in diameter, but weighs more than our

Sun. Pulsars (sources of rapidly repeated radio signals) are believed to be rapidly rotating neutron stars.

Nev *or* **Nev.** *abbrev.* Nevada.

Neva, Battle of the a battle (1240) between Russian and Swedish forces on the R Neva. Russian troops led by Prince Alexander of Novgorod (later called Alexander Nevsky) attacked and defeated Swedish forces under cover of fog, and thus thwarted Sweden's attempts to control the northern mouth of the Baltic–Black Sea trade route.

Nevada POP (1990) 1.3m, a state in W USA, divided into 16 counties and one independent city. AREA 286 341sq km/110 528sq mi. PHYSICAL DESCRIPTION rivers include the Colorado (part of the Arizona border) and Humboldt; L Pyramid and L Winnemucca are in the W, and L Tahoe lies on the Californian border; the highest point is Boundary Peak (4 006m); Nevada lies mainly in the Great Basin, a large arid desert interspersed with barren mountain ranges; it is an area of internal drainage, with most of the rivers petering out in the desert or ending in alkali sinks; the S of the state includes part of the Mojave Desert; lying in the rain shadow of the Sierra Nevada Mts of California, it is the driest of all the states, mostly unpopulated and uncultivated, with a few oases of irrigation; the Hoover Dam creates L Mead. HISTORY Nevada was part of the region ceded by Mexico to the USA in the 1848 Treaty of Guadalupe Hidalgo; it was included in the Mormon-ruled Utah Territory in 1850; the settlement expanded after the Comstock Lode silver strike in 1859; became a separate territory in 1861; joined the Union in 1864 as the 36th state; Nevada is known as the 'Silver State', 'Battle Born State', or 'Sage Brush State'. CAPITAL Carson City. CHIEF TOWNS Las Vegas, Reno. ECONOMY a major gold supplier; mercury, barite, and other minerals are also mined; oil was discovered in 1954; agriculture is not highly developed; cattle, sheep; dairy products; hay; alfalfa; major industries are food processing, clay and glass products, chemicals, copper smelting, electrical machinery, and lumber; tourism focuses on the shores of L Tahoe, Death Valley National Monument (partly in Nevada), and the gambling resorts of Las Vegas and Reno; these resorts attract c.20 million visitors each year, and gaming taxes are a primary source of state revenue.

never *adv.* **1** not ever; at no time. **2** not: *I never realized that.* **3** emphatically not: *this will never do.* **4** surely not: *Those two are never twins!*
— **never ever** absolutely never.
well I never! an expression of astonishment. [from Anglo-Saxon *ne*, not + *æfre*, ever]

nevermore *adv.* never again.

Never Never Land an area in Northern Territory, Australia, lying SE of Darwin. CHIEF TOWN Katherine. Mrs Aeneas Gunn featured the area in her book *We of the Never Never.*

nevertheless *adv.* in spite of that.

Neville a male first name, after the surname and place-names in Normandy called *Néville* or *Neuvulle*, new settlement.

Nevinson, Henry Wood (1856–1941) English war correspondent and journalist, born in Leicester. His coverage of campaigns for various papers included the Boer War, the Balkans, and the Dardanelles, and his exposure in 1904 of the Portuguese slave trade in Angola. His publications include *Lines of Life* (verse, 1920), *Essays in Freedom and Rebellion* (1921), and an autobiographical series, *Changes and Chances* (1925–8).

new — *adj.* **1** recently made, bought, built, opened, etc. **2** recently discovered: *a new planet.* **3** never having existed before; just invented, etc: *new techniques.* **4** fresh; additional; supplementary: *a new consignment.* **5** recently arrived, installed, etc: *under new management.* **6** (**new to someone** *or* **something**) unfamiliar with it;

experienced or experiencing for the first time: *a sensation new to me / he's new to the work.* **7** changed physically, mentally, or morally for the better: *a new man since his operation.* **8** renewed: *gave us new hope.* **9** modern: *the new generation.* **10** used in naming a place just founded after an old-established one: *New York.* — *adv.* only just, or freshly: *a newborn babe / new-baked bread.* [from Anglo-Saxon *niwe*]

New Age a modern cultural trend concerned with the union of mind, body, and spirit and expressing itself in an interest in a variety of beliefs and disciplines such as mysticism, meditation, astrology, and holistic medicine.

New Amsterdam see NEW YORK CITY.

Newark, properly **Newark-on-Trent** POP (1981) 33 000, a town in Newark district, Nottinghamshire, central England. It is situated at the junction of a branch of the Trent and Devon rivers, 25km/15mi SW of Lincoln. King John died in Newark Castle, which was later repeatedly under siege in the Civil War.

Newark POP (1990) 1.8m, the seat of Essex County, NE New Jersey, USA, and the largest city in the state. Situated 14km/9mi W of New York, on the Passaic R and Newark Bay, this port is also an important road, rail, and air centre. Settled by Puritans from Connecticut in 1666, it became a city in 1836. NOTABLE FEATURES Trinity Cathedral; Newark Museum.

new blood new people with fresh ideas introduced into an organization, etc to revitalise it.

newborn *adj., said of a child* newly or recently born.

New Britain, formerly **Neu-Pommern** POP (1990) 312 000, the largest island of the Bismarck Archipelago in Papua New Guinea. AREA 37 799sq km/14 590sq mi. The island is 480km/298mi long and 80km/50mi wide. It is separated from New Ireland by St George's Channel. To the S is the Solomon Sea and to the N is the Bismarck Sea. CAPITAL Rabaul. ECONOMY oil palm, copra, cocoa, coconuts; timber; copper, gold, iron, coal.

new broom a new person in charge, bent on making sweeping improvements.

New Brunswick POP (1991) 724 000, a province in E Canada, bounded in the W by the USA, in the E by the Gulf of St Lawrence, and S by the Bay of Fundy. AREA 73 440sq km/28 350sq mi. PHYSICAL DESCRIPTION forested, rocky land, generally low-lying, rises in the NW; there are several rivers and lakes, the largest of which is Grand Lake (area 174sq km/67sq mi); in the E of the province is Fundy National Park. HISTORY known as Acadia, the area was first settled by French fur traders; ceded to Britain in the 1713 Treaty of Utrecht; in 1783 many United Empire Loyalist immigrants arrived; the area was then separated from Nova Scotia and was given the name New Brunswick; joined the Confederation in 1867. Over one third of the state's population is of French origin; some of these speak only French. GOVERNMENT governed by a Lieutenant-Governor and an elected 58-member Legislative Assembly. CAPITAL Fredericton. CHIEF TOWNS St John, Moncton. ECONOMY paper and wood products; potatoes; seafood; mining (zinc, lead, silver, potash, bismuth); food processing; dairy products; livestock; poultry; tourism.

Newbury POP (1981) 32 000, an industrial town in Newbury district, Berkshire, S England. It lies on the R Kennet and the Kennet and Avon Canal, 25km/15mi SW of Reading. HISTORY scene of two battles in the Civil War; as a centre of the cloth industry, Newbury was England's first industrial town. NOTABLE FEATURES Cloth Hall Museum; Church of St Swithin at Wickham (15km/9mi NW); racecourse.

New Caledonia, French **Nouvelle Calédonie** POP (1992e) 173 000, a French Overseas Territory in the SW Pacific Ocean, 1 100km/680mi E of Australia. It is made up of New Caledonia, the Loyalty Is, Isle des Pins, Isle Bélep, and the uninhabited Chesterfield I and Huon I. AREA 18 575sq km/7 170sq mi. CAPITAL Nouméa. TIME ZONE GMT +11. Most of the population are Melanesian (43%) and European (37%); Roman Catholicism is the chief religion. OFFICIAL LANGUAGE French; English is spoken widely. CURRENCY the French Pacific franc. PHYSICAL DESCRIPTION long, narrow main island, 400km/250mi in length rising to 1 639m at Mt Panie; the central mountain chain divides the island into two natural regions - the dry W coast, covered mostly by gum-tree savannah and the tropical E coast. CLIMATE mild, Mediterranean-type climate with average temperatures of 20°C in Jul and 26°C in Jan; warm and humid from Dec to Mar, cool and dry from Apr to Nov. HISTORY visited by Captain Cook in 1774; annexed by France as a penal settlement in 1853; became a French Overseas Territory in 1946; there were serious disturbances in the mid-1980s when indigenous Melanesians began their struggle for independence; as a result of a French referendum in 1988, New Caledonia will vote on self-determination in 1998. GOVERNMENT governed by a high commissioner and four Regional Councils, members of which serve on the national 46-member Territorial Council. ECONOMY beef, pork, poultry; coffee, maize, fruit, vegetables; copra; nickel (world's third-largest producer), chrome, iron; chlorine and oxygen plants; cement; soft drinks; clothing; foodstuffs; tourism.

Newcastle, properly **Newcastle upon Tyne**, Latin **Pons Aelii**, Anglo-Saxon **Monkchester** POP (1992e) 282 000, the county town of Tyne and Wear, NE England. Situated 440km/273mi N of London, it is an industrial port on the R Tyne (crossed by seven bridges). Newcastle forms part of the Tyneside urban area and is the cultural, commercial, and administrative centre for the NE of England. HISTORY originally a castle (11c), defending the English frontier against the Scots; a commercial centre developed from the 13c, trading in wool, then coal; George Stephenson's iron works were established here in the 1820s; achieved city status in 1882. NOTABLE FEATURES Cathedral of St Nicholas (15c); Roman Catholic cathedral (1844); castle keep (12c); art gallery; museums; Guildhall (1658).

Newcastle POP (1991) 428 000, a city in New South Wales, Australia. It is situated in Hunter statistical division, on the E coast 160km/100mi N of Sydney. It was founded as a penal settlement in 1804. In 1989 the city was the scene of Australia's biggest earthquake.

Newcastle under Lyme POP (1992e) 123 000, a town in the Potteries of Staffordshire, central England, situated 3km/2mi W of Stoke-on-Trent.

New Comedy Athenian comic theatre of the late 4c and early 3c BC, exemplified in the work of Menander and the Roman imitations of Plautus and Terence.

newcomer *noun* someone recently arrived.

Newcomes a novel by William Makepeace Thackeray (1853–5). It is narrated by Arthur Pendennis and describes the lives of the descendants of Thomas Newcome.

New Criticism a critical theory and method which concentrates on the text itself, the 'words on the page', to the exclusion of extrinsic biographical information. It was developed in the USA in the 1930s and 1940s by such critics as Cleanth Brooks (1906–) and John Crowe Ransom (1888–1974).

New Deal the administration and policies of US President Roosevelt, who pledged a 'new deal' for the country during the campaign of 1932. In a hectic 'first hundred days', he embarked on active state economic involvement to combat the Great Depression. Although some early legislation was invalidated by the Supreme Court, the New Deal left a lasting impact on US government, economy, and society, including the creation of the modern institution of the presidency. Major specific initiatives included the National Industrial Recovery Act (1933), the Tennessee Valley Authority (1933), the Agricultural Adjustment Act (1933), the National Youth Administration (1935), the National Labor Relations Act (1935), and the Social Security Act (1935). The 'first New Deal' (1933–4), aimed at restarting and stabilizing the economy, is sometimes distinguished from the 'second New Deal' (1935–9), aimed at social reform, but after 1940 Roosevelt's attention turned to foreign affairs.

New Delhi see DELHI.

newel *noun* **1** the central spindle round which a spiral stair winds. **2** (*also* **newel post**) a post at the top or bottom of a flight of stairs, supporting the handrail. [from Old French *nouel*, nut kernel]

New England Confederation an agreement (1643–84) by the American colonies of Massachusetts, Plymouth, Connecticut, and New Haven to establish a common government for the purposes of war and relations with the Native Americans. The Confederation declined in importance after 1664.

New English Art Club a British society founded in 1886 by a group of artists whose 'progressive work', largely inspired by recent French 'open air' painting, was rejected by the Royal Academy. Leading members included George Clauser (1852–1944), Wilson Steer (1860–1942), John Singer Sargent (1856–1925), John Lavery (1856–1941), and Walter Richard Sickert (1860–1942).

New English Bible an English translation of the Bible from the original languages (Hebrew, Aramaic, and Greek) undertaken by an interdenominational committee of scholars under the auspices of the University Presses of Cambridge and Oxford (from 1948). The New Testament was completed in 1961, and the first complete Bible was produced in 1970. The goal was to present the text in good English literary idiom, and to reflect the results of recent biblical scholarship. It was substantially revised in 1989 as the Revised English Bible.

newfangled *adj.* modern, especially objectionably so. [from Middle English *newefangel*, eager for novelty]

New Forest an area of heath, woodland, and marsh covering c.37 300ha in S Hampshire, England. The area was appropriated by William the Conqueror as his new 'forest' (royal hunting land) in 1079. It is known for its ponies, and is now administered by 10 Verderers, the head of which is appointed by the Crown.

Newfoundland POP (1991) 569 000, a province in E Canada, consisting of the island of Newfoundland and the coast of Labrador, which are separated by the Strait of Belle Isle. AREA 405 720sq km/156 648sq mi. Labrador is bounded to the E by the Labrador Sea and the Atlantic Ocean. PHYSICAL DESCRIPTION Labrador is drained by many rivers which flow from the interior to the coast; the island of Newfoundland is roughly triangular and has a deeply indented coastline; the Long Range Mts run the length of the Great Northern peninsula in the NW and the island rises to 814m in the extreme W; most of the island is a rolling plateau with low hills, and it has several peninsulas, lakes, and rivers; Gros Morne National Park lies on the W coast. HISTORY Vikings are thought to have visited Labrador in c.1000; Cabot rediscovered the island for England in 1497; British sovereignty was declared in 1583 (Britain's first colony); became a self-governing colony in 1855; placed under a Commission of Government appointed by Britain in 1934; voted to unite with Canada in 1949. GOVERNMENT governed by a Lieutenant-Governor and an elected 58-member House of Assembly. CAPITAL St

John's. ECONOMY food processing; pulp and paper; mining (iron ore); cod fishing (in the Grand Banks); oil; hydroelectric power; dairy products; poultry.

Newfoundland *noun* a breed of dog developed in Newfoundland, which has a large thick-set body, an enormous heavy head, a broad deep muzzle, and small ears and eyes. It has a thick black double-layered water resistant coat and webbed feet.

New France a name technically given to all the N American territories claimed by France between 1524 and 1803, but generally used for the north-eastern colonies. In 1534 a cross was planted on the shores of the Gaspée by Jacques Cartier, who thus claimed the territory for the King of France. Quebec became the centre of the French colony, and by 1663 it had become a royal province with a governor responsible for foreign relations and defence, an intendant to administer justice, and a bishop to impose spiritual discipline.

Newgate the City of London's main prison from the 13c to 1902, from which many convicted criminals were taken to be hanged at Tyburn.

New Grange a megalithic passage grave of c.3200 BC in the Boyne R valley, Ireland, 40km/25mi N of Dublin. The slab-roofed passage gives onto a cross-shaped burial chamber with a 6m high corbelled vault.

New Grub Street a novel by George Gissing (1891). It describes the lives of various characters in a corrupt literary world.

New Guinea an island situated in the SW Pacific Ocean. It lies to the N of the Australian mainland. AREA 790 000sq km/305 000sq mi. The island, which is one of the largest in the world, comprises Papua New Guinea on the E side and the Indonesian province of Irian Jaya on the W side.

New Hampshire POP (1990) 1.1m, a state in NE USA, divided into 10 counties, and bounded N by Canada. AREA 24 032sq km/9 279sq mi. PHYSICAL DESCRIPTION the W border is formed by the Connecticut R; Merrimack R flows S through the centre into Massachusetts; a low rolling coast is backed by hills and mountains which include the White Mts in the N; the highest point is Mt Washington (1 917m), the mountainous N is forested while the S is largely devoted to arable farming and grazing; New Hampshire is known as the 'Granite State'. HISTORY explored by Champlain and Pring in 1603–5; the first settlement was made at Little Harbor in 1623; it was the ninth of the original 13 states to ratify the Federal Constitution. CAPITAL Concord. CHIEF TOWNS Manchester, Nashua, Portsmouth. ECONOMY chief agricultural products are dairy and greenhouse products, maple syrup, hay, apples, and eggs; there are diverse manufacturing industries; tourism and forestry are also important.

New Haven, formerly **Quinnipiac** (to 1640) POP (1990) 130 000, a port town in New Haven County, S Connecticut, USA. It is situated on Long Island Sound, 58km/36mi SW of Hartford. HISTORY founded by Puritans in 1638; joint state capital with Hartford from 1701 to 1873. Inventions developed here include vulcanized rubber (Charles Goodyear) and the repeating revolver (Samuel Colt). NOTABLE FEATURE Yale University (1701).

Newhaven POP (1981) 11 000, a port town in Lewes district, East Sussex, SE England. It is situated at the mouth of the R Ouse, 14km/9mi E of Brighton. There are container and cross-Channel (to Dieppe) passenger terminals.

New Hebrides see VANUATU.

New Ireland, formerly **Neu-Mecklenburg** POP (1990) 87 000, the second-largest island in the Bismarck Archipelago, Papua New Guinea. AREA 8 647sq km/3 338sq mi. The island is 480km/

298mi long, with an average width of 24km/15mi. It is separated from New Britain in the SW by St George's Channel. CAPITAL Kavieng. ECONOMY tuna fishing; copra.

New Jersey (1990) 7.8m a state in E USA, which is divided into 21 counties. AREA 20 168sq km/7 787sq mi. It is bounded S by the Atlantic Ocean and Delaware Bay. PHYSICAL DESCRIPTION the Hudson R follows the NE border, and the Delaware R follows the W border; the Appalachian Highlands fall down through Piedmont Plateau to low coastal plains, broken by ridges of the Palisades; the highest peak is Mt High Point (550m); around 40% of the land is forested, mostly in the SE. New Jersey is known as the 'Garden State'. HISTORY colonized after the explorations of Giovanni da Verrazano (1524) and Henry Hudson (1609); one of the original states of the Union, and the third to ratify the Federal Constitution. CAPITAL Trenton. CHIEF TOWNS Newark, Jersey City, Paterson, Elizabeth. ECONOMY the NE is densely populated and highly industrialized: chemicals, pharmaceuticals, electronics, metals, machinery, textiles, and processed foods; the less populated areas are devoted mainly to arable farming and grazing (dairy products, hay, blueberries, cranberries, and soy beans); tourism is the second-largest industry, with 127 miles of beaches and a major gambling centre (Atlantic City).

New Jerusalem, Church of the a religious sect based on the teachings of the Swedish scientist and seer Emmanuel Swedenborg, who believed he had direct contact with the spiritual world through visionary experiences. He claimed that a first dispensation of the Christian Church had ended and a new one, the 'New Jerusalem', was beginning. His first Church was organized in London in 1783.

New Left a neo-Marxist movement which espoused a more libertarian form of socialism compared to orthodox Marxism. Partly inspired by the earlier essentially humanistic writings of Karl Marx, it also embraced the ideas of Italian politician Antonio Gramsci (1891–1937) regarding the importance of ideological hegemony, and drew on dialectical sociology and radical forms of existentialism. It had some influence during the 1960s in student politics and in opposition to the Vietnam War, but this declined in the 1980s as it gave way in part to the New Right.

newly *adv.* **1** only just; recently: *newly-mown grass.* **2** again; anew: *newly awakened desire.*

newly-weds *pl. noun* a recently married couple.

Newman, John Henry, Cardinal (1801–90) English theologian, born into a Calvinist family in London. A Fellow of Oriel College, Oxford, he was ordained (1824) and became a vigorous member of the Oxford Movement, for which he composed Tract 90, among others, arguing that the doctrine expressed in the Thirty-Nine Articles was Catholic in spirit. This led to the end of the Movement, and his own conversion to Catholicism (1845). He joined the Oratorians in Rome, then established his own community in Birmingham. A moderate in the Vatican Council controversies, he was made a cardinal in 1879. Among his publications of essays and sermons is his spiritual autobiography *Apologia pro Vita Sua* (1864).

Newman, Paul (Leonard) (1925–) US film actor, born in Cleveland, Ohio. He started in stage repertory and television, and moved to films in the mid-1950s. His continued success includes the films *Cat on a Hot Tin Roof* (1958), *Cool Hand Luke* (1967), *Butch Cassidy and the Sundance Kid* (1969), *The Sting* (1973), *The Verdict* (1982), and *The Color of Money* (1986), for which he won an Oscar. He also directs (eg *Rachel, Rachel,* 1968, and *The Glass Menagerie,* 1987), and has been active politically in the civil rights

movement. He was given an Honorary Academy Award in 1986 and another Oscar in 1994 for his philanthropical work: the donation of the profits from his food products to charity.

New Man a man who is prepared to show his feelings and who has adopted modern ideas on health, the environment, and sharing of family responsibilities.

Newmarket POP (1981) 16 000, a town in Forest Heath district, Suffolk, E England. Situated 20km/12mi E of Cambridge, it is a famous centre for training and racing horses.

new maths an approach to teaching mathematics that is more concerned with creating an early understanding of basic concepts than with drilling in arithmetic.

New Mexico POP (1990) 1.6m, a state in SW USA, which is divided into 32 counties. AREA 314 914sq km/121 593sq mi. Mexico forms part of the S boundary. Over one third of the population is Hispanic; there are several Native American mountain reservations. PHYSICAL DESCRIPTION rivers include the Pecos and the Rio Grande (forms part of the S border with Texas); the highest point is Wheeler Peak (4 011m); New Mexico is characterized by broad deserts, forested mountain wildernesses, and towering barren peaks; isolated mountain ranges, part of the Rocky Mts, flank the R Grande; forests lie mainly in the SW and N; most of the state is a semi-arid plain with little rainfall, but the well-irrigated valley of the R Grande permits farming; New Mexico with its warm, dry climate and striking scenery is known as the 'Land of Enchantment'. HISTORY explored by the Spanish in the early 16c; the first white settlement was made at Santa Fe in 1609; governed by Mexico from 1821; ceded to the USA in the 1848 Treaty of Guadalupe Hidalgo; in 1850 New Mexico was organized as a territory, including Arizona and part of Colorado; admitted to the Union as the 47th state in 1912; the first explosion of an atomic bomb, a test procedure, took place in 1945 at White Sands proving grounds. CAPITAL Santa Fe. CHIEF TOWNS Albuquerque, Las Cruces, Roswell. ECONOMY cattle, sheep; dairy products; hay, wheat, cotton; processed foods; chemicals; electrical equipment; lumbering; chief producer in the USA of uranium, potash, and perlite; there are also natural resources of oil, coal, and natural gas; tourism is important. NOTABLE FEATURES many Native American pueblos through the state, little changed since the 13c; the Carlsbad Caverns National Park; Aztec Ruins; White Sands; Chaco Canyon; Gila Cliff Dwellings; Gran Quivira; several military establishments; atomic energy centres include Los Alamos National Laboratory (1943).

New Model Army an English army established by Parliament (15 Feb 1645) to strengthen its forces in the civil war against Royalists. The county and regional armies of Essex, Manchester, and Waller were merged into a successful national force. The cavalry and artillery were augmented; the battle tactics of Gustav II Adolf were adopted; discipline and pay improved; and religious toleration was introduced.

newness *noun* being new; a new state or quality.

New Netherland a Dutch colony in the Hudson River valley. The first settlement of Fort Orange (1617, now Albany) was followed by Nieuw Amsterdam (1624, now New York City). Conquered by the English and named New York in 1664, the colony was restored by treaty to the English in 1674 after a second brief period of Dutch rule. Initially established on feudal social lines, it prospered through fur trading.

New Orleans POP (1990) 1.2m, a city in SE Louisiana, USA, situated between the Mississippi R and L Pontchartrain. Known as the 'Crescent City', it is located on a bend at the head of the Mississippi, and is one of the busiest ports in the

USA. HISTORY founded by the French in 1718; became capital of French Louisiana in 1722; ceded to Spain in 1763; passed to the USA in the 1803 Louisiana Purchase, but French influence is still evident today; prospered in the 19c as a market for slaves and cotton, gaining at the same time a lasting reputation for glamour and wild living; fell to Union troops during the Civil War; in the late 19c jazz music originated here among black musicians; there was industrial growth in the 20c after the discovery of vast oil and natural gas deposits. NOTABLE FEATURES the French Quarter; the Cabildo; St Louis Cathedral; Jazz Museum; Isaac Delgado Museum of Art. EVENTS Mardi Gras (Feb–Mar); Jazz and Heritage Festival (Apr).

Newport POP (1981) 20 000, the county town of the Isle of Wight, S England, situated in Medina district. It is a river port and market town on the R Medina, situated 8km/5mi from its mouth. NOTABLE FEATURES Parkhurst Prison nearby; Carisbrooke Castle (12c).

Newport, Welsh **Casnewydd** POP (1992e) 137 000, the industrial capital of Newport district, Gwent, SE Wales. It is situated on the R Usk, 32km/20mi NW of Bristol. In 1839, it was the scene of Chartist riots.

Newport POP (1990) 28 000, the seat of Newport County, SE Rhode Island, USA, lying at the mouth of Narragansett Bay (spanned by Newport Bridge, built 1969). HISTORY settled in 1639, it was a haven for religious refugees; became a city in 1853; Newport Jazz Festival was held here from 1954 to 1971 (now in New York City). The port has several US Navy establishments. NOTABLE FEATURES many palatial mansions (eg the Breakers, 1895); the sloop *Providence*; Tennis Hall of Fame. EVENTS music festival (Jul); yachting (host to the America's Cup and other races).

Newport News POP (1990) 170 000, a seaport and independent city in SE Virginia, USA, situated at the mouth of the James R. NOTABLE FEATURES Mariners' Museum; War Memorial Museum of Virginia.

new potatoes the first-dug potatoes of the new crop.

New Providence POP (1990) 172 000, an island in the N central Bahamas, on the Great Bahama Bank. AREA 207sq km/80sq mi; length 32km/20mi. CHIEF TOWN Nassau (national capital). More than half the total population of the Bahamas live on the island and it is a popular tourist resort.

Newquay POP (1981) 15 000, a town in Restormel district, Cornwall, SW England. Situated 17km/10mi N of Truro, it was formerly a fishing port and is now a resort town.

New Right a wide-ranging ideological movement associated with the revival of conservatism in the 1970s and 1980s, particularly in the UK and USA. Connected with the liberal economic theory of the 19c, it advocates state withdrawal from ownership, and the promotion of a free-enterprise system in the economy. There is also a strong moral conservatism — respect for authority, strong patriotism, and support for the family unit. The New Right was associated with the emergence of Christian fundamentalism (eg the Moral Majority) in the USA in the 1980s.

New Ross, Gaelic **Baila Nua** POP (1991) 6 000, a medieval town and river port in Wexford county, Leinster province, SE Irish Republic. It lies on the R Barrow, NE of Waterford. NOTABLE FEATURES a farmhouse in Dunganstown, 8km/5mi S, was the home of the Kennedy family; J F Kennedy Memorial Park is nearby.

news *sing. noun* **1** information about recent events, especially as reported in newspapers or on radio or television. **2** (**the news**) a radio or television broadcast report of news. **3** any fresh

interesting information. **4** a currently celebrated person, thing, or event: *he's big news in America.*
— **bad** *or* **good news** *slang* something or someone that is unwelcome (or welcome).
that's news to me *colloq.* I have not heard that before.

news agency an agency that collects news stories and supplies them to newspapers, etc.

newsagent *noun* a person selling newspapers, confectionery, etc.

newscast *noun* a radio or television broadcast of news items.

newscaster *noun* a person who reads out radio or television news items; a newsreader.

news conference a press conference.

newsdealer *noun* a newsagent.

newsflash *noun* a brief announcement of important news interrupting a radio or TV broadcast.

newshound *noun* *facetious* a newspaper reporter.

New Siberian Islands, Russian **Novosibirskiye Ostrova** an uninhabited Russian archipelago in the Arctic Ocean, which lies off the NE coast of Russia between the Laptev Sea to the W and the E Siberian Sea to the E. AREA 28 250sq km/10 900sq mi. The group is separated from the Lyakhov Is in the S by the Proliv Sannikova Strait. The chief islands are Kotelny, Faddeyevskiy, and New Siberia; the highest point is 374m. Mammoth fossils have been found on the islands.

newsletter *noun* a sheet containing news issued to members of a society or other organization.

newsman *noun* a male reporter for a newspaper or a broadcast news programme.

newsmonger *noun* a gossip.

Newsome, Chad the son of Mrs Newsome in Henry James's *The Ambassadors*, who refuses to return to America from Paris.

New South Wales POP (1992e) 6m, a state in SE Australia. AREA 801 428sq km/309 351sq mi. It is bordered in the E by the South Pacific Ocean and Tasman Sea. The state, which comprises 12 statistical divisions, is the most populous and heavily industrialized in Australia. PHYSICAL DESCRIPTION coastal lowlands give way to tablelands, formed by the Great Dividing Range; fertile irrigated plains further W comprise two thirds of the state; its main coastal rivers are the Hawkesbury, Hunter, Macleay, and Clarence, and its main inland rivers are the Darling, Murray, Murrumbidgee, Macquarie-Bogan, and Lachlan. HISTORY became the first British colony to be established in Australia; named by Captain Cook who landed at Botany Bay in 1770; the first settlement at Sydney was established in 1788. CAPITAL Sydney. CHIEF TOWNS Newcastle, Wollongong. ECONOMY beef cattle; dairy farming; wool; cereals; fishing; forestry; textiles; electrical machinery; chemicals; food processing; lead, zinc, and coal mining.

newspaper *noun* **1** a daily or weekly publication composed of folded sheets, containing news, advertisements, topical articles, correspondence, etc. **2** the printed paper which makes up such a publication: *chips wrapped in newspaper.*
◇ The modern newspaper can be traced back to the British publications, the *Corante* (1621) and *Weekly Newes* (1622). The first daily paper was the *Daily Courant* (1702), and the first true evening paper the *Courier* (1792). In the 19c, technical innovations, cheap paper, and the abolition of the Stamp Duty (1855) resulted in a great proliferation of publications. Recent developments have included the use of electronic databases, facilities for journalists to type copy straight into

the phototypesetter computer, make-up screens on which whole pages can be laid out and reviewed, and the inclusion of four-colour half-tone illustrations. The late 20c has seen tabloid circulation wars, price competition, and a reduction in the number of newspapers published.

newspeak *noun ironic* the ambiguous language, full of the latest distortions and euphemisms, used by politicians and other persuaders. [from *Newspeak*, a deliberately impoverished English used as an official language, in George Orwell's novel *1984*]

newsprint *noun* **1** the paper on which newspapers are printed. **2** the ink used to print newspapers.

newsreader *noun* a person who reads out radio or television news items.

newsreel *noun* a film of news events, once a regular cinema feature.

newsroom *noun* an office in a newspaper office or broadcasting station where news stories are received and edited for publication or broadcasting.

news stand a stall or kiosk selling newspapers, magazines, etc.

New Style, the present method of dating, using the Gregorian calendar. See also OLD STYLE.

news-vendor *noun* a person who sells newspapers.

newsworthy *adj.* interesting or important enough to be reported as news.

newsy *adj.* (**newsier, newsiest**) full of news.

newt *noun* any of various amphibians related to the salamanders, with long slender bodies and well-developed limbs, and differing from lizards in that the tail is flattened from side to side. Newts are found in Europe, Asia, N America, and N Africa, in or near ponds and lakes where they breed in the spring. They return to land to hibernate in winter. Their life cycle is similar to that of frogs and toads; the eggs hatch into tadpoles which breathe by means of gills. [from Anglo-Saxon *efeta* ; *an ewt* came to be understood as *a newt*]

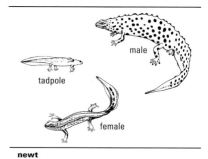

newt

New Territories a region of the British Crown Colony of Hong Kong. AREA 950sq km/367sq mi. It lies N of the Kowloon Peninsula and is bounded N by China. The region includes part of the mainland and over 200 islands. It is leased to Britain until 1997, when Hong Kong will be restored to China, under the Sino-British Agreement of 1984.

New Testament, the part of the Bible concerned with the teachings of Christ and his earliest followers. See also OLD TESTAMENT.
◇ It is so called because its writings are believed to represent a new covenant of God with his people, centred on the person, life, and work of Jesus Christ. The 27 writings were originally in Greek and were mainly composed in the 1c. These are usually grouped as the four gospels, the Acts of the Apostles, 13 letters attributed to Paul, the Letter to the Hebrews, seven general or 'Catholic' letters, and the Book of Revelation.

Newton, Sir Isaac (1642–1727) English scientist and mathematician, born in Woolsthorpe,

Lincolnshire. Educated at Cambridge, in 1665 he wrote on his discovery of 'fluxions' (an early form of calculus); and in 1665 or 1666 the fall of an apple in his garden suggested the train of thought that led to the law of gravitation. He studied the nature of light, concluding that white light is composed of all colours of the spectrum, separable by refraction, and devised the first reflecting telescope. He became Professor of Mathematics at Cambridge in 1669 and published his whole gravitation theory in *Philosophiae Naturalis Principia Mathematica* (Mathematical Principles of Natural Philosophy, 1687), describing his law of gravitation and his three laws of motion. He was appointed Warden (1696) and Master of the Mint (1699), and sat in parliament on two occasions.

Newton a statue of Isaac Newton by Louis François Roubiliac (1755, Cambridge).

newton *noun* (SYMBOL **N**) the SI unit of force, equal to the force required to give a mass of one kilogram an acceleration of one metre per second per second. [named after Isaac Newton]

Newtonian mechanics *Physics* a theory of mechanics, formulated by Sir Isaac Newton, which considers the relationships between force and motion for everyday objects, ie objects much larger than atoms and moving slowly relative to the speed of light.

Newton's laws of motion *Physics* the basic expression of Newtonian mechanics. The first law states that the velocity of an object does not change unless a force acts on it. The second law states that a force F applied to an object of mass m causes an acceleration a according to the equation $F=ma$. The third law states that every action has an equal and opposite reaction.

new town a town planned and built by the government as a unit, to relieve congestion in nearby cities, and encourage development.

new universities universities established to accommodate the expanding numbers entering higher education in Britain during the postwar period. They include Keele (1949); Sussex (1961); Essex (1961); York (1963); Lancaster (1964); East Anglia (1964); Kent (1965); Warwick (1965); Stirling (1967); and the Open University (1969) (see also RED-BRICK UNIVERSITIES).

New Wave see NOUVELLE VAGUE.

New World (**the New World**) the American continent. See also OLD WORLD.

New World, From the (Z nového světa) the subtitle to Dvořák's Symphony No.9 in E minor (Op 95, 1893), which contains melodies similar to American folk tunes and was written during a visit there.

New Year the first day of the year or the days immediately following or preceding it.

New Year's Day 1 Jan, the first day of a new year.

New Year's Eve 31 December.

New York POP (1990) 18.1m, a state in NE USA, which is divided into 62 counties. AREA 127 185sq km/49 108sq mi. It is bounded N by L Ontario and Canada, and S by the Atlantic Ocean. The state is the second most populous in the USA. PHYSICAL DESCRIPTION the Hudson R flows S through the E part of the state and forms the border with New Jersey; the St Lawrence R forms part of the N border, and the Delaware R part of the S border; the Niagara R with the Niagara falls forms the boundary with Ontario, between L Ontario and L Erie; the Adirondack Mts rise in the N, and the Catskill Mts in the S; the highest point is in the Adirondacks at Mt Marcy (1 629m); New York state contains 11 334sq km/4 375sq mi of the Great Lakes, as well as L Oneida and the Finger Lakes in the centre; there is extensive woodland and forest in the NE, and a mixture of cropland, pasture, and woodland elsewhere. HISTORY explored by Henry Hudson and Samuel de Champlain in 1609; the Dutch established posts near Albany in 1614 and settled Manhattan in 1626; New Netherlands was taken by the British in 1664; one of the original states of the Union, and the 11th to ratify the Federal Constitution; New York is known as the 'Empire State'. CAPITAL Albany. CHIEF TOWNS New York, Buffalo, Rochester, Yonkers, Syracuse. ECONOMY clothing; pharmaceuticals; publishing; electronics; automotive and aircraft components; dairy products, corn, beef.

New York City *or* **New York**, also called **the Big Apple** POP (1990) 8.5m, the largest city and port in the USA, and the county seat of New York County, SE New York State, situated at the mouth of the Hudson R. It is divided into five boroughs, each co-extensive with a county: Bronx (Bronx Co), Brooklyn (Kings Co), Manhattan (New York Co), Queens (Queens Co), and Staten Island (Richmond Co). HISTORY originally the site of a trading post established in 1609 by Henry Hudson; colonized by the Dutch and named New Amsterdam; captured by the British in 1664 and named New York after the King's brother, the Duke of York; scene of the reading of the Declaration of Independence (4 Jul 1776); held by the British throughout the War of Independence; George Washington was inaugurated here as the first US president; first capital of the nation (1789–90) and state capital until 1796; rapid commercial and industrial growth followed the opening of the Erie Canal in 1825; since World War II many middle-class residents have moved away from the city to the suburbs; emergency loans saved the city from bankruptcy in the mid-1970s. New York is a major world financial centre, with the Stock Exchange in Wall Street; it is also the focus of the fashion, arts, and entertainment worlds. Its many higher education institutions include Columbia University (1754). NOTABLE FEATURES Central Park; Brooklyn Bridge; Broadway; Chrysler Building; Empire State Building (448m); Greenwich Village; Statue of Liberty (off Manhattan on Liberty I); Fifth Avenue; Madison Avenue; Rockefeller Center; United Nations Headquarters; World Trade Center; Lincoln Center for the Performing Arts; Carnegie Hall; museums include the Metropolitan Museum of Art, Guggenheim Museum, and Museum of Modern Art.

New York Philharmonic a US orchestra, founded in 1842, and based at the Lincoln Centre. Uri Corelli Hill (1802–75) was its first conductor; others have included Wilhelm Furtwängler, Bruno Walter, and Leonard Bernstein.

New York School a term applied to a group of mainly abstract and Expressionist US painters who worked in New York during the 1940s and 1950s. They included Jackson Pollock (1912–56), Arshile Gorky (1904–48), Willem De Kooning (1904–), and Mark Rothko (1903–70).

New Zealand POP (1992e) 3.4m, an independent state, comprising a group of islands in the Pacific Ocean SW of Australia, divided into 13 statistical divisions. AREA 268 812sq km/103 761sq mi. It is bounded in the W by the Tasman Sea and in the E by the South Pacific Ocean. The Cook Is and Niue are New Zealand self-governing territories and Tokelau and the Ross Dependency are New Zealand non-self-governing territories. CAPITAL Wellington. CHIEF TOWNS Auckland, Christchurch, Dunedin, Hamilton. TIME ZONE GMT +12. The population is mostly of European (87%), and Maori (9%) origin; the chief religion is Christianity (81%). OFFICIAL LANGUAGE English. CURRENCY the New Zealand dollar. PHYSICAL DESCRIPTION the two principal islands, North and South, are separated by the Cook Strait, Stewart Island, and several minor islands; from the northernmost point to the southernmost point the total length of the country is 1 770km/1 100mi; North I is mountainous in the centre, with many hot springs; peaks rise to 2 797m at Mt Ruapehu; South I is mountainous for its whole length, rising in the Southern Alps to 3 764m at Mt Cook; there are many glaciers and mountain lakes; the largest area of level lowland is the Canterbury Plain on the E side of South I. CLIMATE highly changeable weather, with all months moderately wet; it is almost subtropical in the N and on the E coast, with mild winters and warm, humid summers; Auckland daily temperatures are 8–13°C (Jul), 16–23°C (Jan), average monthly rainfall 145mm (Jul), 79mm (Dec–Jan); the temperatures in South I are generally lower. HISTORY it was settled by the Maoris from SE Asia before 1350; the first European sighting was made by Abel Tasman in 1642, and he named it Staten Landt; it later became known as Nieuw Zeeland, after the Dutch province; Captain Cook sighted it in 1767; the first settlement was established in 1792; remained a dependency of New South Wales until 1841; outbreaks of war between immigrants and Maoris occurred in 1860–70; became the Dominion of New Zealand in 1907; gained independence within the Commonwealth in 1947. GOVERNMENT governed by a Prime Minister, Cabinet, and unicameral 95-member House of Representatives; elections take place every three years. ECONOMY based on farming, especially sheep and cattle; one of the world's major exporters of dairy produce; the third-largest exporter of wool; kiwi fruit; venison; mohair; textiles; timber; food processing; substantial coal

Prime Ministers of New Zealand	
1856	Henry Sewell
1856	William Fox
1856–61	Edward William Stafford
1861–2	William Fox
1862–3	Alfred Domett
1863–4	Frederick Whitaker
1864–5	Frederick Aloysius Weld
1865–9	Edward William Stafford
1869–72	William Fox
1872	Edward William Stafford
1873	William Fox
1873–5	Julius Vogel
1875–6	Daniel Pollen
1876	Julius Vogel
1876–7	Harry Albert Atkinson
1877–9	George Grey
1879–82	John Hall
1882–3	Frederick Whitaker
1883–4	Harry Albert Atkinson
1884	Robert Stout
1884	Harry Albert Atkinson
1884–7	Robert Stout
1887–91	Harry Albert Atkinson
1891–3	John Ballance
1893–1906	Richard John Seddon
1906	William Hall-Jones
1906–12	Joseph George Ward
1912	Thomas Mackenzie
1912–25	William Ferguson Massey
1925	Francis Henry Dillon Bell
1925–8	Joseph Gordon Coates
1928–30	Joseph George Ward
1930–5	George William Forbes
1935–40	Michael Joseph Savage
1940–9	Peter Fraser
1949–57	Sidney George Holland
1957	Keith Jacka Holyoake
1957–60	Walter Nash
1960–72	Keith Jacka Holyoake
1972	John Ross Marshall
1972–4	Norman Eric Kirk
1974–5	Wallace Edward Rowling
1975–84	Robert David Muldoon
1984–89	David Russell Lange
1989–90	Geoffrey Palmer
1990	Mike Moore
1990–	Jim Bolger

and natural gas reserves; 80% of the country's electricity is supplied by hydroelectric power; tourism is a growing sector.

New Zealand

next — *adj.* **1** following in time or order: *the next on the list / the next day.* **2** following this one: *next week.* **3** adjoining; neighbouring: *in the next compartment.* **4** first, counting from now: *the very next person I meet.* — *noun* someone or something that is next. — *adv.* **1** immediately after that or this: *what happened next?* **2** on the next occasion: *when I next saw her.* **3** following, in order of degree: *the next longest river after the Amazon.*
— **next to someone** *or* **something 1** beside or close by them. **2** after something in order of degree: *next to swimming I like dancing.* **3** almost: *wearing next to no clothes.*
[from Anglo-Saxon *nehst*, superlative of *neah*, near]

next door in or to the neighbouring house.

next-door *adj.* at or belonging to the neighbouring house.

next of kin one's closest relative.

nexus *noun* (PL. **nexus**, **nexuses**) **1** a connected series or group. **2** a bond or link. [from Latin *nectere*, to bind]

Ney, Michel, Duke of Elchingen (1769–1815) French soldier, born in Saarlouis. He fought in the Revolutionary Wars, became a general of division (1799), and a Marshal of the Empire. Created Duke of Elchingen (1805), he distinguished himself at Jena (1806), Eylau, and Friedland (1807). He commanded the third corps of the Grand Army in the Russian campaign (1813), for which he received the title of Prince of Moskowa. After Napoleon's abdication (1814) he accepted the Bourbon restoration, but instead of obeying orders to fight against Napoleon (1815), Ney deserted to his former master and led the centre of his army at Waterloo. On Louis XVIII's second restoration, he was condemned for high treason, and shot in Paris.

NF *or* **Nfd** *or* **Nld** *abbrev.* Newfoundland.

NFU *abbrev.* National Farmers' Union.

NFWI *abbrev.* National Federation of Women's Institutes (see WOMEN'S INSTITUTES, NATIONAL FEDERATION OF).

Ngorongoro Crater a crater in N Tanzania, in the Rift Valley. AREA c.260sq km/100sq mi. The rim, at an altitude of over 2 100m, is c.600m above the crater floor. The crater is the centre of a designated conservation area which enables the Masai to live and farm their cattle and also provides free range to wildlife, such as wildebeest, gazelle, and zebra.

Nguni a group of Bantu-speaking peoples of southern Africa, who originally occupied present-day Natal and Transkei. In the 19c they carried out a series of migrations. The main groups today include the Zulu, Swazi, and Xhosa of South Africa and Swaziland, the Ndebele of Zimbabwe, and the Ngoni of Zambia, Malawi, and Tanzania.

NH *or* **N.H.** *abbrev.* New Hampshire.

NHBRC *abbrev.* National House-Builders' Registration Council (or Certificate).

NHS *abbrev.* the National Health Service.

NI *abbrev.* **1** National Insurance. **2** Northern Ireland.

Ni *symbol Chem.* nickel.

niacin *noun* same as NICOTINIC ACID.

Niagara Falls the two waterfalls in W New York, USA and S Ontario, Canada, situated between L Erie and L Ontario on the international border. The American Falls are 55.5m high and 328m wide; the Canadian Falls, known as the Horseshoe Falls, are 54m high and 640m wide; they are separated by Goat I. Behind the American Falls is the Cave of the Wind; Rainbow Bridge (1941), lying below the falls, stretches between Canada and USA. Part of the flow above the Canadian Falls is diverted to supplement the shallower US Falls. The average daily flow over both falls before diversion is c.5 000m³. The Niagara Falls have been a world-famous tourist attraction since the early 19c following the arrival of the railway in 1836. There are twin resort towns named Niagara Falls in Ontario and New York. The falls have been the scene of many daredevil exploits, such as the tightrope crossing by Charles Blondin in 1859 and Annie Edson Taylor's 'shooting' of the Horseshoe Falls in a sealed barrel in 1901.

Niamey POP (1988) 398 000, the river-port capital of Niger. It is situated 800km/500mi NW of Lagos (Nigeria). NOTABLE FEATURES National Museum; zoo; Botanical Gardens.

Nias an island in the Indian Ocean, 125km/78mi off the W coast of Sumatra, Indonesia. It is 240km/150mi long by 80km/50mi wide. CHIEF TOWN Gunungsitoli. The island is populated by the Niah tribe. NOTABLE FEATURES prehistoric stone sculptures.

nib *noun* **1** the writing-point of a pen, especially a metal one with a divided tip. **2** (**nibs**) crushed coffee or cocoa beans. [perhaps a variant of *neb*, nose]

nibble — *verb* **1** *trans., intrans.* (*also* **nibble at something**) to take very small bites of it. **2** to bite gently. **3** *intrans. colloq.* to show cautious interest in a proposal, etc. — *noun* **1** an act of nibbling, or something nibbled. **2** *Comput.* a unit of storage capacity equal to half a byte, ie a series of four bits.

nibbler *noun* a person or animal that nibbles.

Nibelungen in medieval German legends, a race of dwarfs who lived in Norway and possessed a famous treasure. The *Nibelungenlied* recounts how the treasure was obtained by Siegfried and the later misfortunes which befell him. Wagner conflated this with other legends for his opera cycle, *The Ring of Nibelung.*

niblick *noun Golf* an old-fashioned club with a heavy head and a wide face, used to make lofting shots; the modern equivalent is a number eight or nine iron. [origin uncertain]

nibs *noun*
— **his** *or* **her nibs** *facetious* a derogatory mock title for an important or would-be important person.

nicad *noun* **1** nickel-cadmium, used to make batteries. **2** a battery made using nickel-cadmium.

Nicaea, Council of 1 the first ecumenical Council of the Church, called (AD 325) by Emperor Constantine to settle the doctrinal dispute between the Arians and the Orthodox on the person of Christ. **2** a Council of the Church called (AD 787) to deal with the question of the veneration of images.

NICAM *abbrev.* near-instantaneous companded audio multiplexing, a system by which digital stereo sound signals are transmitted along with the standard television signal, to allow the viewer to receive sound of CD quality.

Nicaragua, official name **Republic of Nicaragua**, Spanish **Replúblic de Nicaragua** POP (1992e) 4.1m, the largest of the Central American republics S of Mexico, divided into 16 departments. AREA 148 000sq km/57 128sq mi. It is bounded N by Honduras, E by the Caribbean Sea, S by Costa Rica, and W by the Pacific Ocean. CAPITAL Managua. CHIEF TOWNS León, Granada, Masaya, Chinandega, Matagalpa, Corinto. TIME ZONE GMT –6. The population is mainly of mixed S American Indian, Spanish, and African descent; Roman Catholicism is the chief religion. OFFICIAL LANGUAGE Spanish. CURRENCY the córdoba. PHYSICAL DESCRIPTION mountainous W half with volcanic ranges rising to over 2 000m in the NW; two large lakes, L Nicaragua and L Managua, lie in a broad structural depression extending NW–SE behind the coastal mountain range; rolling uplands and forested plains lie to the E; many short rivers flow into the Pacific Ocean and the lakes. CLIMATE tropical, with average annual temperatures ranging from 15–35°C according to altitude; there is a rainy season from May–Nov when humidity is high; the average annual rainfall at Managua is 1 140mm. HISTORY the Pacific coast was colonized by the Spaniards in the early 16c; gained independence from Spain in 1821 and left the Federation of Central America in 1838; the plains of E Nicaragua, the Mosquito Coast, remained largely undeveloped under British protection until 1860; a dictatorship under Anastasio Somoza in 1938; the Sandinista National Liberation Front seized power in 1979 and established a socialist junta of national reconstruction; under the 1987 constitution, a President and a 96-member national Constituent Assembly are elected for six-year terms; the former supporters of the Somoza government (the Contras), based in Honduras and supported by the USA, carried out guerrilla activities against the junta from 1979; a ceasefire and disarmament were agreed in 1990 but unrest continued; severe earthquake in 1992. GOVERNMENT a President with executive power and a unicameral National Assembly, both elected for a six-year period. ECONOMY agriculture accounts for over two thirds of total exports: cotton, coffee, sugar cane, rice, corn, beans, bananas, tobacco; livestock; shellfish; oil; natural gas; gold; silver; food processing; chemicals; metal products; textiles; beverages.

Nicaragua

Nicaragua, Lake *or* **Gran Lago** the largest lake in Central America and Nicaragua. AREA 8 026sq km/3 098sq mi; length 148km/92mi; width 55km/34mi. It is separated from the Atlantic Ocean in the W by a 15km–/9mi-wide isthmus. There are over 300 small islands in the lake, notably the Isla de Ometepe, with two volcanoes. The town of Granada lies on the NW shore.

Nice, Italian **Nizza**, ancient **Nicaea** POP (1990) 476 000, the capital of Alpes-Maritimes department, Provence-Alpes-Côte d'Azur region, SE France. Situated 157km/98mi NE of Marseilles and encircled by hills, it is a fashionable coastal resort on the Baie des Anges, a bay of the Mediterranean Sea. Nice is the fifth-largest city in France and the leading tourist centre of the French Riviera. NOTABLE FEATURES cathedral (1650); several 17c–18c Baroque churches; 17c Palais Lascaris; Palais de la Méditerranée; Palais des Expositions; Chagall Memorial; opera house

(19c); casinos; palm-lined Promenade des Anglais; flower market.

nice *adj.* **1** pleasant. **2** *often ironic* good; satisfactory. **3** *ironic* nasty: *a nice mess.* **4** fine; subtle: *nice distinctions.* **5** exacting; particular: *nice in matters of etiquette.*
— **nice and** ... *colloq.* satisfactorily; commendably: *nice and firm.*
[originally 'foolish', 'coy', 'exotic', from Latin *nescius*, ignorant, or unknown]

nicely *adv.* **1** in a nice or satisfactory way. **2** precisely; carefully: *judged it nicely.* **3** suitably; effectively: *that will do nicely.*

Nicene Creed an expanded formal statement of Christian belief, based on the creed of the first Council of Nicaea (AD 325), and still recited as part of the Eucharistic liturgies of the Orthodox and Roman Catholic Churches, and many Protestant Churches.

niceness *noun* a nice or satisfactory quality; precision.

nicety *noun* (PL. **niceties**) **1** precision. **2** a subtle point of detail.
— **to a nicety** exactly.

niche *noun* **1** a shallow recess in a wall, suitable for a lamp, ornament, statue, etc. **2** a position in life in which one feels fulfilled and/or at ease. **3** *Biol.* the unique position of a particular living organism in its environment, defined by the physical space it inhabits, the food it consumes, its tolerance of physical and chemical factors, its interaction with other organisms, etc. Two species that occupy identical niches cannot co-exist indefinitely, because competition for the same food supply will ensure that one species eventually becomes extinct. The characteristics of a particular habitat will determine the number of niches available; warm wet habitats such as tropical rainforests contain the largest number of niches and therefore the greatest number of species. [from French *niche*, from Latin *nidus*, nest]

niche marketing marketing of a product aimed at a relatively small and specialized group of consumers.

Nichiren Buddhism a sect founded by the Japanese Buddhist reformer Nichiren (1222–82), sometimes called the Lotus sect, because of his claim that the *Lotus Sutra* contained the ultimate truth. He attacked other forms of Buddhism, and called the nation to convert to true Buddhism.

Nicholas I (1796–1855) Emperor of Russia (1825–55), born near St Petersburg, the third son of Paul I. An absolute despot, he warred with Persia and Turkey, suppressed a rising in Poland, and attempted to make all the inhabitants of the empire adopt the Russian language and ways of life. He helped to quell the 1848 Hungarian insurrection, and tightened the alliance with Prussia. The re-establishment of the French Empire confirmed these alliances, but when he planned to absorb Turkey the opposition of Britain and France precipitated the Crimean War, during which he died.

Nicholas II (1868–1918) the last emperor of Russia (1894–1917), born near St Petersburg, the son of Alexander III. His reign was marked by an alliance with France (1894), an *entente* with Britain, a disastrous war with Japan (1904–5), and the establishment of the national assembly, or Duma (1906). He led the Russian armies against the Central Powers (Germany and Austria-Hungary) in 1915. Forced to abdicate at the Revolution, he was shot with his family by the Red Guards.

Nicholas, St (4c AD) Christian prelate and saint, widely associated with the feast of Christmas. Allegedly the Bishop of Myra in Lycia (now Turkey), he was imprisoned under Diocletian and released under Constantine. In legend he gave gifts of gold to three poor girls for their dowries, which gave rise to the custom of

giving gifts on his feast day, still followed in the Netherlands and Germany; elsewhere this has transferred to 25 Dec (Christmas Day). His identification with Father Christmas began in Europe and spread to America, where the name became *Santa Claus.* He is the patron saint of Greece and Russia, and his feast day is 6 Dec.

Nicholas a male first name. [from a late Greek name *Nikolaos*, from *nike*, victory + *laos*, people]

Nicholas Nickleby a novel by Charles Dickens (1838–9). It describes what happens to 19-year old Nicholas and his impoverished mother and sister following the death of his father.

Nicholson, Jack (1937–) US film actor, born in Neptune, New Jersey. His first major success was in *Easy Rider* (1969). Often playing the antihero, his other performances include *One Flew over the Cuckoo's Nest* (1975), for which he won an Oscar, *The Shining* (1980), *The Postman Always Rings Twice* (1981), *Terms of Endearment* (1984), *The Witches of Eastwick* (1986), and *Batman* (1989).

nick — *noun* **1** a small cut. **2** *colloq.* a prison or police station. — *verb trans.* **1** to make a small cut in; to cut slightly. **2** *slang* to arrest (a criminal). **3** *slang* to steal.
— **in good nick** *colloq.* in good condition.
in the nick of time at the last possible moment; just in time.

nickel *noun* **1** *Chem.* (SYMBOL **Ni**, ATOMIC NUMBER **28**) a silvery-white metal that is very resistant to corrosion and tarnishing. It is used as a catalyst, and for electroplating, and is a component of various alloys (eg stainless steel, nickel silver), as well as temperature-resistant alloys for watches and other scientific instruments, and magnetic alloys, eg for transformer cores. **2** in the US and Canada, a coin worth five cents. [from German *Küpfernickel*, copper devil, so called by miners mistaking it for copper]

nickel silver *Chem.* an alloy of nickel, copper, and zinc, so called because it resembles silver in appearance. It is used to make coinage, cutlery, drawing instruments, cheap jewellery, etc.

nicker *noun* (PL. **nicker**) *old slang use* a pound sterling.

Nicklaus, Jack (William), also called **the Golden Bear** (1940–) US golfer, born in Columbus. He won the US amateur title in 1959 and 1961, then turned professional. Runner-up to Arnold Palmer in the 1960 US Open, he went on to win all the world's major tournaments: the British Open (1966, 1970, 1978), the US Open (1962, 1967, 1972, 1980), the US Professional Golfers Association tournament a record-equalling five times (1963, 1971, 1973, 1975, 1980), and the US Masters a record six times (1963, 1965–6, 1972, 1975, 1986). His win in 1986 was at the age of 46 years 82 days, the oldest winner of the event. His 18 professional majors is a world record, and in 1988 he was voted 'Golfer of the Century'.

Nickleby, Kate, Mrs, and **Ralph** the sister, widowed mother, and miserly uncle of Nicholas in Charles Dickens's *Nicholas Nickleby.*

nick-nack *noun* same as KNICK-KNACK.

nickname — *noun* a name, usually additional to the real one, given to a person or place in fun, affection, or contempt. — *verb trans.* to give a nickname to. [from Middle English *eke*, addition, extra; *an ekename* came to be understood as *a nickname*]

Nicobar Islands see ANDAMAN AND NICOBAR ISLANDS.

Nicolai, (Carl) Otto (Ehrenfried) (1810–49) German composer and conductor, born in Königsberg. He became court conductor in Vienna (1841) and kapellmeister of the Royal Opera in Berlin (1847), where his opera *The Merry Wives of Windsor* was produced just before his death.

Nicolle, Charles Jules Henri (1866–1936) French physician and microbiologist, born in Rouen. Director of the Pasteur Institute in Tunis, he discovered that typhus fever is spread by lice (1909). He was awarded the 1928 Nobel Prize for Physiology or Medicine.

Nicomedia in antiquity, the capital first of the kingdom and then of the Roman province of Bithynia. It was the capital of the E half of the Roman Empire under Diocletian (AD 284–316).

Nicopolis, Battle of a battle beside the R Danube following a disastrous attack (1396) by Christians on the major fortress of the Turks, who in the early 14c had become the conquerors of much of E Europe. The Christian forces were led by King Sigismund of Hungary (later Holy Roman Emperor) and John the Fearless (1371–1419), Duke of Burgundy, who was captured by the Turks and ransomed for a huge sum.

Nicosia, Greek **Levkosia**, Turkish **Lefkosa**, ancient **Ledra 1** POP (1991e) 167 000, the capital of Cyprus and of Nicosia district, situated on the R Pedias, in the centre of the Mesaoria Plain. HISTORY capital since the 12c; ruled by the Turks in the 16c and by the British from 1878 to 1960. The 'Green Line' divides the city into northern (Turkish) and southern (Greek) sectors. NOTABLE FEATURES Cathedral of St John; the old city is surrounded by Venetian-built walls (late 16c). **2** a district in central Cyprus with the city of Nicosia as its capital.

nicotine *noun* a poisonous alkaloid compound, obtained from the tobacco plant, that is used as an insecticide. It is responsible for the addictive effects of cigarette smoke, as in small doses it acts as a mild stimulant and suppresses appetite. In the long term it is toxic and causes an increase in blood pressure and heartbeat rate, among other symptoms. [named after J Nicot (1530–1600), said to have introduced tobacco into France]

nicotinic acid *Biochem.* a member of the vitamin B complex, which is needed to make the coenzymes NAD and NADP, which act as hydrogen acceptors in many of the chemical reactions in living cells. It is manufactured by plants and animals, but is also required in the diet, and sources include liver, yeast extracts, cereals, peas, and beans. In human beings a deficiency of nicotinic acid causes pellagra. — Also called *niacin, vitamin B*.

nictitating membrane *Zool.* in many reptiles, amphibians, and birds, and some mammals, eg seals, a transparent membrane that forms a third eyelid which can be drawn across the eye for protection. [from Latin *nictitare*, to wink]

niece *noun* the daughter of one's sister or brother, or of one's sister- or brother-in-law. [from Latin *neptis*, granddaughter or niece]

niello *noun* (PL. **nielli**) a small decorative silver or gold plate with the design engraved into the metal, which is then filled with a black composition called niello. Metal-workers in the 15c tested the engraved design before filling it up by taking an impression on paper. This practice led to the development of line engraving in Italy. [from Italian *niello*, from Late Latin *nigellum*, a black enamel]

nielsbohrium *noun Chem.* the name formerly suggested by Soviet scientists for the chemical element unnilpentium. [named after the Danish physicist Niels Bohr]

Niemöller, (Friedrich Gustav Emil) Martin (1892–1984) German Lutheran pastor, born in Lippstadt, Westphalia. After serving as a leading submarine commander in World War I, he took orders (1924) and became pastor at Berlin-Dahlem (1931). He was summoned with other Protestant Church leaders before Hitler, publicly opposed the Nazi regime, and was arrested and placed in concentration camps until 1945. He was responsible for the 'Declaration of Guilt' (1945) by the German Churches for not opposing Hitler more strenuously, but he also condemned the abuses of the de-Nazification courts. He later became Church President of the Evangelical Church in Hesse and Nassau (1947–64), and President of the World Council of Churches (1961).

Niépce, Joseph Nicéphore (1765–1833) French scientist and very early pioneer in photography, born in Chalon-sur-Seine. In 1826 he succeeded in obtaining an image on a bitumen-coated pewter plate exposed for some hours in a camera obscura. From 1829 he collaborated with Louis Daguerre, and his son Isidore (1805–68) continued the association.

Nietzsche, Friedrich (Wilhelm) (1844–1900) German philosopher, writer, and critic, born in Röcken, Saxony, the son of a Lutheran pastor. He was appointed Professor of Classical Philology at Basle (1869–79) at the age of 24. He was influenced by Schopenhauer, and dedicated his first book, *Die Geburt der Tragödie* (The Birth of Tragedy, 1872) to his friend Richard Wagner, whose operas he regarded as the true successors to Greek tragedy. His major work, *Also sprach Zarathustra* (Thus Spake Zarathustra, 1883–5) develops the idea of the *Übermensch* or Superman. He detested democratic ideals and repudiated Christian and liberal ethics. Much of his esoteric doctrine appealed to the Nazis, and he was a major influence on existentialism. Dogged by psychosomatic illness from 1878, he died in Weimar after twelve years of insanity.

niff — *noun slang* a bad smell. — *verb intrans.* to smell bad.

niffy *adj.* (**niffier, niffiest**) smelly.

nifty *adj.* (**niftier, niftiest**) **1** clever; adroit; agile. **2** stylish.

Nigel a male first name. [a form of earlier *Nigellus*, from Latin *niger*, black]

Niger, official name **Republic of Niger**, French **République de Niger** POP (1992e) 8.3m, a republic in W Africa, divided into seven departments. AREA 1 186 408sq km/457 953sq mi. It is bounded NE by Libya, NW by Algeria, W by Mali, SW by Burkina, S by Benin and Nigeria, and E by Chad. CAPITAL Niamey. CHIEF TOWNS Agadès, Diffa, Dosso, Maradi, Tahoua, Zinder. TIME ZONE GMT +1. Most of the population are Hausa (54%); Islam is the chief religion. OFFICIAL LANGUAGE French; Hausa and Djerma are spoken widely. CURRENCY the franc CFA. PHYSICAL DESCRIPTION Niger lies on the S fringe of the Sahara Desert, on a high plateau; the Hamada Manguene Plateau lies in the far N; the Aïr Massif is in the centre; the Ténéré du Tafassasset desert is in the E; the W Talk desert occupies the centre and N; water in quantity is found only in the SW around the R Niger and in the SE around L Chad. CLIMATE one of the hottest countries in the world; marked rainy season in the S from Jun to Oct;

Niger

rainfall decreases in the N to almost negligible levels in desert areas; the annual rainfall at Niamey is 554mm; drought can occur. HISTORY occupied by the French from 1883 until 1899; became a territory within French West Africa in 1904; gained independence in 1960; there was a military coup in 1974. GOVERNMENT governed by a Higher Council for National Orientation led by a President who appoints a Council of Ministers; elected National Assembly in 1989; the constitution was suspended in 1991. ECONOMY dominated by agriculture and mining; groundnuts; cotton; cowpeas; gum arabic; livestock; production was badly affected by severe drought conditions in the 1970s; uranium, tin; phosphates; coal; salt; natron; building materials; textiles; food processing.

Niger, River a river in W Africa, the third-longest in the African continent. Its total length is c.4 100km/2 550mi and it is navigable seasonally in sections. The river rises 280km/175mi from the Atlantic coast and flows NE through Guinea and Mali. It is dammed at Markala and Sansanding in Mali and splits into several courses and a cluster of lakes in the Macina Depression. The river forms part of Niger's SW border with Benin and is dammed to form the Kainji Reservoir in Nigeria. It then flows SE and S, spreading into a delta c.320km/200mi across, before entering the Gulf of Guinea. It is known as the Upper Niger or Djoliba as far as Timbuktu, the Middle Niger from there to Jebba in W Nigeria, and the Lower Niger or Kovarra (Kawarra, Kwara) from Jebba to its delta. The river is frequently interrupted by rapids.

Nigeria, official name **Federal Republic of Nigeria** POP (1991) 88.5m, a republic in W Africa, divided into 19 states and a federal capital district. AREA 923 768sq km/356 574sq mi; maximum length, 1 000km/650mi, width 1 100km/700mi. It is bounded to the W by Benin, N by Niger, NE by Chad, E by Cameroon, and S by the Gulf of Guinea and the Bight of Benin. CAPITAL Abuja. CHIEF TOWNS Lagos, Ibadan, Ogbomosho, Kano, Oshogbo, Ilorin, Abeokuta, Port Harcourt. TIME ZONE GMT +1. There are over 250 tribal groups, notably the Hausa and Fulani in the N, Yoruba in the S, and Ibo in the E; Islam and Christianity are the chief religions. OFFICIAL LANGUAGE English; Hausa, Yoruba, Edo, and Ibo are also spoken. CURRENCY the naira. PHYSICAL DESCRIPTION the coastal strip has a long, sandy shoreline with mangrove swamp, dominated by the R Niger delta; an undulating area of tropical rainforest and oil palm bush lie N of the coastal strip; the relatively dry central plateau is characterized by open woodland and savannah; the far N of the country is on the edge of the Sahara Desert and is largely a gently undulating savannah with tall grasses; there are numerous rivers in Nigeria, notably the Niger and Benue; the Gotel Mts are on the SE frontier and the highest point is at Mt Vogel (2 024m). CLIMATE there are two rainy seasons in the coastal areas; the wettest part is the Niger delta and the mountainous SE frontier, with an annual rainfall above 2 500mm, decreasing towards the W; Ibadan in the SE has an average daily maximum temperature of 31°C and an average annual rainfall of 1 120mm; there is only one rainy season in the N; the dry season extends from Oct to Apr, when little rain falls. HISTORY the centre of the Nok culture in 500 BC–AD 200; several African kingdoms developed throughout the area in the Middle Ages (eg Hausa, Yoruba); Muslim immigrants arrived in the 15c–16c; European interests in gold and the slave trade; a British colony was established at Lagos in 1861; protectorates of N and S Nigeria were created in 1900; amalgamated as the Colony and Protectorate of Nigeria in 1914; became a federation in 1954; gained independence in 1960; declared a federal republic in 1963; a military coup took place in 1966; the E area formed the Republic of Biafra in 1967; civil war and the surrender of Biafra in 1970; military

coups in 1983 and 1985; military rule ended in 1993 with power being transferred to a Transitional Council but the military re-established control later in the year. ECONOMY based on agriculture until oil production began in the late 1950s; oil provides c.90% of exports; half the population is still engaged in agriculture; cocoa, rubber, palm oil, groundnuts, cotton, yams, cassava, rice, sugar cane, tobacco; livestock; fishing; forestry; natural gas, coal, tin, lead, zinc, lignite, iron ore, columbite (world's largest supplier), tantalite, limestone, marble; food; pulp and paper; textiles; rubber; sugar; beer; vehicles; pharmaceuticals.

Nigeria

Niger-Congo — *adj.* denoting the largest family of African languages, containing c.1 000 languages and several thousand varieties and dialects. Its use extends over the whole of Africa S of the Sahara and W of the Nile, and E Africa as far N as the Horn. — *noun* the languages forming this family.

niggard *noun* a stingy person.

niggardliness *noun* being niggardly or stingy.

niggardly *adj.* **1** stingy; miserly. **2** meagre: *niggardly praise*.

nigger *noun offensive* a person of black African origin or race. [from French *nègre*, from Spanish *negro*]

niggle — *verb* **1** *intrans.* to complain about unimportant details. **2** *trans.* to bother, especially slightly but continually. — *noun* **1** a slight nagging worry. **2** a small complaint or criticism.

niggler *noun* a person who complains or criticizes trivially.

niggling *adj.* trivially troublesome or worrying.

nigh *adv. old use, poetic* near.
— **nigh on** *or* **well nigh** nearly; almost. [from Anglo-Saxon *neah*]

night *noun* **1** the time of darkness between sunset and sunrise, during which most people sleep. **2** nightfall. **3** *poetic* darkness. **4** the evening: *stayed at home last night.* **5** an evening on which a particular activity or event takes place: *my aerobics night.*
— **make a night of it** *colloq.* to celebrate late into the night.
[from Anglo-Saxon *niht*]

night blindness abnormally reduced vision in dim light or darkness.

Night Café a painting by Vincent van Gogh (1888).

nightcap *noun* **1** a cap formerly worn in bed at night. **2** a drink, especially alcoholic, taken before going to bed.

nightclub *noun* a club open at night for drinking, dancing, entertainment, etc.

nightdress *noun* a loose garment worn in bed by women.

nightfall *noun* the beginning of night; dusk.

nightie *noun* (PL. **nighties**) *colloq.* a nightdress.

Nightingale, Florence, also known as **Lady of the Lamp** (1820–1910) British hospital reformer, born in Florence, Italy. She trained as a nurse at Kaiserswerth and Paris, and during the Crimean War led a party of 38 nurses to Scutari (1854), where she soon had 10 000 patients under her care. She later formed an institution for the training of nurses at St Thomas's Hospital, and spent several years on army sanitary reform, the improvement of nursing, and public health in India.

nightingale *noun* any of several species of small brown thrush, found in woodland undergrowth, scrub, and marshy areas of Europe and W Asia, although it overwinters in Africa. It is best known for the nocturnal song of the male common nightingale. [from Anglo-Saxon *nihtegale*]

nightingale

nightjar *noun* a nocturnal bird of the swift family with a harsh discordant cry. [from NIGHT + JAR²]

nightlife *noun* entertainment available in a city, etc late into the night.

night light a dim-shining lamp or slow-burning candle that can be left alight all night.

nightlong *adj., adv.* throughout the night.

nightly *adj., adv.* every night.

nightmare *noun* **1** a frightening dream. **2** an intensely distressing or frightful experience or situation. [from NIGHT + Anglo-Saxon *mare*, an incubus, or nightmare-producing monster]

nightmarish *adj.* like a nightmare; intensely distressing or frightful.

Night of the Long Knives the event which took place in Germany (30 Jun–1 Jul 1934) when the SS, on Hitler's orders, murdered Ernst Röhm and other leaders of the SA (*Sturmabteilung*, or Stormtroopers). The aim was to crush the SA's political power and to settle old political scores, and resulted in the murder of an estimated 150 of Hitler's political opponents and rivals, including the former Chancellor von Schleicher.

night owl a person who likes to stay up late at night.

nights *adv.* at night; most nights or every night: *chooses to work nights.*

night safe a safe built into the outer wall of a bank, in which to deposit money when the bank is closed.

night school an institution providing educational evening classes for people who are at work during the day.

nightshade *noun* any of several wild plants, some with poisonous berries, including the belladonna or deadly nightshade. [from Anglo-Saxon *nihtscada*]

night shift **1** a session of work or duty during the night. **2** the staff working during this period. See also BACK SHIFT, DAY SHIFT.

nightshirt *noun* a long shirt-like garment, formerly usually for men, worn in bed.

night soil *old use* human excrement collected at night for use as a soil fertiliser.

night spot a nightclub.

night stick *North Amer.* a police truncheon.

night-time *noun* the time of darkness between sunset and sunrise.

Night Watch, The a group portrait of a militia band by Rembrandt (1642, Rijksmuseum, Amsterdam).

nightwatchman *noun* **1** someone who looks after industrial, etc premises at night. **2** *Cricket* a batsman, not a high scorer, put in to defend a wicket till close of play.

nihilism *noun* **1** the rejection of moral and religious principles. **2** a 19c Russian movement aimed at overturning all social institutions. **3** the view that nothing has real existence; extreme scepticism. [from Latin *nihil*, nothing]

nihilist *noun* a supporter of nihilism.

nihilistic *adj.* characterized by nihilism or extreme scepticism.

Nihon the Japanese name for Japan. Considered more appropriate postwar than the 'imperialistic' form *Nippon*, the two characters for *Nihon* mean 'sun' and 'origin' or 'essence' — hence the 'Land of the Rising Sun'. The country's former name was *Yamato*, after the ancient capital district, as in *Yamato-damashii*, 'spirit of Japan'.

Niigata POP (1991e) 488 000, the port capital of Niigata prefecture, N Honshu, Japan. It is situated on the Sea of Japan at the mouth of the R Shinano.

Nijinska, Bronislava (1891–1972) Russian ballet-dancer and choreographer, born in Minsk, the sister of Vaslav Nijinsky. She became a soloist with the Maryinski company and danced with Diaghilev's Ballets Russes in Paris and London (1909–14) before returning to Russia during World War I. In 1921 she became principal choreographer for Diaghilev, from whom she created *Les Noces* (1923) and *Les Biches* (1924). After 1938 she lived and worked mainly in the USA, where she founded a ballet school.

Nijinsky, Vaslav (1890–1950) Russian dancer, born in Kiev. He first appeared in ballet at the Maryinski Theatre (later Kirov Ballet), then went to Paris with Sergei Diaghilev's Ballet Russes in 1909, and appeared as Petrushka in the first performance of the Fokine/Stravinsky ballet (1911). His choreography foreshadowed the development of modern ballet; in 1913 his *Le sacre du printemps* (The Rite of Spring) was regarded as outrageous. Interned in Hungary early in World War I, he rejoined Diaghilev for a world tour, but retired in 1917 when he was diagnosed a paranoid schizophrenic.

Nijmegen or **Nimeguen**, German **Nimwegen**, ancient **Noviomagus** POP (1992e) 146 000, a city in S Gelderland province, E Netherlands. It lies on the R Waal, 19km/12mi S of Arnhem. HISTORY founded as a hilltop Roman fort in AD 69; former residence of the Carlovingian kings; a member of the Hanseatic League in the Middle Ages. NOTABLE FEATURES town hall (16c); Groote Kerk (13c); remains of Charlemagne's Valkhof Palace (8c).

Nijo-jo Castle a stronghold built in 1603 in Kyoto, Japan, by Tokugawa Ieyasu. The complex includes the Ninomaru Palace and the famous Karamon gate (originally from Fushimi Castle).

-nik *suffix sometimes derog.* forming nouns denoting someone concerned or associated with a certain cause, activity, etc: *peacenik / refusenik*. [from Yiddish, from Slavic]

Nike in Greek mythology, the goddess of Victory, either in war or in an athletic contest. She is the frequent subject of sculpture, often shown as a winged figure, as in *Victory of Samothrace*. — Also called *Nike of Samothrace*. The Roman equivalent was Victoria.

Nikkei Index the indicator of the relative prices of stocks and shares on the Tokyo stock exchange. [from the title of the newspaper publishing it]

nil *noun* in games, etc, a score of nothing; zero. [from Latin *nil* (*nihil*), nothing]

Nile, River, Arabic **Nahr En Nil** the longest river in the world, situated in E and NE Africa. From its most remote headstream (Luvironza R), the length is 6 695km/4 160mi. The Luvironza rises in S central Burundi, and flows generally NE and N under various names, entering L Victoria in the W. The Victoria Nile flows N through L Kyoga into the NE end of L Albert. The Albert Nile flows N through NW Uganda, becoming known as the White Nile at the Sudanese frontier. It is joined by the Blue Nile, which rises in the mountains of Ethiopia, at Khartoum to become the Nile, c.3 000km/1 900mi from its delta on the Mediterranean Sea. Joining from the E at Atbara, the R Atbara is the Nile's only significant tributary. On entering Egypt, it flows into L Nasser, created by the Aswan High Dam. The river opens out into a broad delta N of Cairo, from Alexandria in the W to Port Said in the E, 250km/155mi E–W and 160km/100mi N–S. It flows through two mouths (Rosetta and Damietta), both c.240km/150mi long. Egypt's population and cultivated land is almost entirely along the floodplain.

Nilgiri Hills the hills linking the Eastern Ghats with the Western Ghats, S India.

Nilo-Saharan — *adj.* denoting a family of more than 100 African languages spoken by the peoples of the Upper Nile in Sudan, Egypt, Uganda, and Kenya, in the Sahara, and in the area of the River Chari in central Africa. They include Masai, Luo, Dinka, Kanuri, and Nugian (which has the longest written history dating from the 8c). — *noun* the languages forming this group.

Nilotes the peoples of NE Africa who originated in the Nile regions and moved south probably before the 16c. New ethnic groupings were created when these pastoralists mingled with agriculturalists. The Nilotic group inlcudes the Acholi and Alur of N Uganda, and the Luo who inhabit the eastern shores of L Victoria. It is thought that some Nilotic migrants, known as the Bito, became the aristocracies of some of the states of Uganda, eg Buganda, Bunyoro, and Toro.

Nilsson, (Märta) Birgit (1918–) Swedish soprano, born near Karup, Kristianstadslaen. She studied in Stockholm and made her début there in 1946. Her international reputation developed in the 1950s, particularly in Wagnerian roles, and she retired from the stage in 1982.

nimble *adj.* **1** quick and light in movement; agile. **2** *said of wits* sharp; alert. [from Anglo-Saxon *næmel*, receptive, and *numol*, quick to learn]

nimbleness *noun* being nimble; sharpness; alertness.

nimbly *adv.* with a nimble or alert manner or movement.

nimbus *noun* (PL. **nimbuses**, **nimbi**) **1** *Meteorol.* a general term used to refer to any cloud, usually dark grey in colour, that produces precipitation, especially rainfall; a rain cloud. **2** a luminous mist or halo surrounding a god or goddess. [from Latin *nimbus*]

NIMBY *abbrev.* not in my back yard.

Nîmes, ancient **Nismes** or, **Nemausus** POP (1990) 139 000, the ancient capital of Gard department, Languedoc-Roussillon region, S France, situated 102km/63mi NW of Marseilles. HISTORY principal city of Roman Gaul; Protestant stronghold in the 16c; the Pacification of Nîmes was signed here in 1629. It is a centre of the wine and fruit trade and of the silk industry. The type of cloth known as 'de Nîmes' was once made here; this name was later contracted to 'denim'. The writer Alphonse Daudet was born here in

1840. NOTABLE FEATURES Roman buildings and monuments include an amphitheatre (1c), Pont du Gard (aqueduct), Maison Carrée (Corinthian temple, now a museum), Tour Magne (tower remains on Mont Cavalier), and Temple of Diana; Cathedral of St Castor (11c).

Nimitz, Chester William (1885–1966) US admiral, born in Fredericksburg, Texas. Trained at the US Naval Academy, he served mainly in submarines, and by 1938 was Rear-Admiral. He was Chief of the Bureau of Navigation (1939–41) and then commanded the US Pacific Fleet, when his organization of naval operations was instrumental in the defeat of Japan. He was made Fleet Admiral (1944), Chief of Naval Operations (1945–7), and Special Assistant to the Navy Secretary (1947–9).

Nimrod a biblical character, the son of Cush and great-grandson of Noah (Genesis 10). A mighty hunter, he was one of the first to rule over a great empire after the Flood, and apparently became King of Babylon and S Mesopotamia as well as of Assyria, where he founded Nineveh. Some rabbinic traditions considered him the builder of the Tower of Babel (Genesis 11).

Nimrud an Upper Mesopotamian city which became the royal seat and military capital of the Assyrian Empire in the 9c BC.

nincompoop noun a fool; an idiot.

nine — noun **1** the number or figure 9; any symbol for this number. **2** the age of 9. **3** something, eg a garment or a person, whose size is denoted by the number 9. **4** 9 o'clock. **5** a set of 9 people or things. **6** a playing-card with 9 pips. **7** a score of 9 points. — adj. **1** 9 in number. **2** aged 9.
— **dressed up to the nines** colloq. wearing one's best clothes.
[from Anglo-Saxon nigon]

ninefold — adj. **1** equal to nine times as much or many. **2** divided into, or consisting of, nine parts. — adv. by nine times as much.

ninepins sing. noun a game similar to skittles, using a wooden ball and nine skittles arranged in a triangle.

nineteen — noun **1** the number or figure 19; any symbol for this number. **2** the age of 19. **3** something, eg a garment or a person, denoted by the number 19. **4** a set of 19 people or things. — adj. **1** 19 in number. **2** aged 19.
— **talk nineteen to the dozen** colloq. to chatter away animatedly.
[from Anglo-Saxon nigontiene]

Nineteen Counties an unsuccessful attempt by the government of New South Wales to limit the spread of settlement. The counties, which covered 9 million ha, were proclaimed by Governor Darling in 1829. The boundaries of the counties were ignored, and Pastoralists 'squatted' on the land outside them. In 1836 Governor Bourke permitted squatters to graze their sheep outside the counties for an annual licence fee. In 1847, the Nineteen Counties were absorbed into a new administrative division of the Colony.

Nineteen Eighty Four a novel by George Orwell (1949). It is a prophetic work which warns of a world ruled by three interlocking totalitarian dictatorships, where the very concept of the individual has been destroyed.

nineteenth noun, adj. the position in a series corresponding to 19 in a sequence of numbers.

nineties pl. noun **1** the period of time between one's 90th and 100th birthdays. **2** the range of temperatures between 90 and 100 degrees. **3** the period of time between the 90th and 100th years of a century.

ninetieth noun, adj. the position in a series corresponding to 90 in a sequence of numbers.

ninety — noun **nineties 1** the number or figure 90; any symbol for this number. **2** the age of 90.

3 a set of 90 people or things. — adj. **1** 90 in number. **2** aged 90. [from Anglo-Saxon nigontig]

ninety-five theses Relig. a series of points of academic debate with the pope, posted on the church door at Wittenburg in 1517 by Martin Luther. They challenged many practices of the Church, including indulgences and papal powers, and are generally regarded as initiating the Protestant Reformation.

Nineveh an ancient Assyrian city located E of the Tigris, the site of royal residences from c.11c BC. It was founded in prehistoric times, although some Biblical legends associate its origin with Nimrod. It was at its height in the 8c–7c BC under Sennacherib, but fell in 612 BC to the Medes and Persians. Its royal libraries contain thousands of clay tablets, and are a valuable source for Mesopotamian history.

Ningbo or **Ningpo** or **Yin-hsien** POP (1990) 1.1m, a port city in Zhejiang province, E China. It lies at the confluence of the Fenghua, Tong, and Yuyao rivers. For 800 years it was an outlet for silk and porcelain. The city has been designated a special economic zone. NOTABLE FEATURES Tianyi Ge Library (1561, the oldest in China); Tianfeng Ta Pagoda (1330).

Ningxia or **Ningxia-Hui** or **Ningsia Hui** POP (1990) 4.7m, an autonomous region in N China. AREA 170 000sq km/66 000sq mi. CAPITAL Yinchuan. ECONOMY grain; sheep raising; coal mining.

ninja noun (PL. **ninja**, **ninjas**) especially in medieval Japan one of a body of professional assassins trained in martial arts and stealth. [from Japanese nin-, endure + -ja, person]

ninjutsu or **ninjitsu** noun an armed Japanese martial art with a strong emphasis on stealth and camouflage. In the 1980s, it became a popular element in cinema, video games, and children's toys in the West. [from Japanese]

ninny noun (PL. **ninnies**) a foolish person.

Nintendo noun trademark a handheld device which allows video games to be viewed and played on a television screen.

ninth noun, adj. the position in a series corresponding to nine in a sequence of numbers.

ninthly adv. as ninth in a series.

Ninurta in Mesopotamian mythology, the Sumerian god of war, champion of the gods in the struggle for power. He also controlled thunderstorms and spring rainstorms.

Niobe in Greek mythology, the daughter of Tantalus and the wife of Amphion. She had many children and said she was better than her mother, including Leto. This provoked Leto's children, Apollo and Artemis, who killed all (or most of) the children, and turned the weeping Niobe into a weeping rock on Mt Sipylos.

niobium noun Chem. (SYMBOL **Nb**, ATOMIC NUMBER **41**) a relatively unreactive soft greyish-blue metal with a brilliant lustre. It is resistant to corrosion, and is used in stainless steels and other alloys with high melting points, superconductors, and nuclear reactors. Formerly known as columbium. [named after Niobe]

Niokolo-Koba a national park and game reserve in E Senegal, W Africa, established in 1953. AREA 9 130sq km/3 524sq mi. The park is a World Heritage site.

Nip noun offensive a Japanese person. [short for Nipponese, 'Japanese']

nip¹ — verb **1** trans. to pinch or squeeze sharply. **2** trans. to give a sharp little bite to. **3** trans., intrans. to sting; to cause smarting. **4** intrans. colloq. (**nip off**, **nip away**) to go quickly: nip round to the shop. **5** trans. to halt the growth or development of: nip it in the bud. — noun **1** a pinch or squeeze. **2** a sharp little bite. **3** a sharp biting coldness, or stinging quality. [from Norse hnippa, to poke]

nip² noun a small quantity of alcoholic spirits: a nip of brandy. [from Dutch nippen, to sip]

nipper noun **1** the claw of a crab, lobster, etc. **2** (**nippers**) pincers, tweezers, forceps, or other gripping or severing tool. **3** old colloq. use a small child.

nippiness noun being nippy or quick-moving.

nipple noun **1** the deep-coloured pointed projection on a breast, in the female the outlet of the ducts from which the young suck milk. **2** North Amer. the teat on a baby's feeding-bottle. **3** Mech. any small projection with a hole through which a flow is regulated or machine parts lubricated.

Nippur an ancient city in Sumer. It was the religious centre of the Sumerians where their kings were crowned and perhaps also buried, and the seat of the god Enlil, the head of the Sumerian pantheon.

nippy adj. (**nippier**, **nippiest**) colloq. **1** cold; chilly. **2** quick-moving; nimble.

nirvana noun (**also Nirvana**) **1** Buddhism, Hinduism the ultimate state of spiritual tranquillity attained through release from everyday concerns and extinction of individual passions. **2** colloq. a place or state of perfect bliss. [from Sanskrit nirvana, extinction]

Niš or **Nish**, ancient **Naisus** POP (1991) 248 000, an industrial town in Yugoslavia, situated in SE central Serbia, on the R Nišava. NOTABLE FEATURES open-air theatre; Tower of Skulls; Turkish citadel; Constantine's villa at Mediana.

nisi adj., said of a court order to take effect on the date stated, unless in the meantime a reason is given why it should not. See also DECREE NISI. [from Latin nisi, unless]

Nissan, in full **Nissan Motor Company Ltd** an automotive corporation founded in Japan in 1925 and given its present name in 1934. Its products, which are manufactured under the names Nissan® and Datsun®, include cars, buses, satellites, and industrial machinery.

Nissen hut a corrugated-iron hut in the shape of a semi-cylinder lying lengthwise. [from P N Nissen (1871–1930), its designer]

nit¹ noun the egg or young of a louse, found eg in hair. [from Anglo-Saxon hnitu]

nit² noun slang an idiot. [a shortening of NITWIT]

Niterói POP (1991) 416 000, a port in Rio de Janeiro state, SE Brazil, on the SE shore of Guanabara Bay, opposite Rio de Janeiro. It was founded in 1573 and is the former state capital. The city is connected to Rio by a 14km-/9mi-long bridge. NOTABLE FEATURES colonial forts of Santa Cruz (16c); Barão do Rio Branco (1633); Gragoatá, and Nossa Senhora da Boa Viagem; Church of Boa Viagem (1633); archaeological site and museum.

nit-picker noun a person who indulges in nit-picking or petty criticism.

nit-picking noun petty criticism or fault-finding.

nitrate — noun Chem. a salt or ester of nitric acid, that contains the NO_3^- ion. Nitrates are essential for plant growth, and are used as artificial fertilizers. In areas where large amounts of such fertilizers are used, contamination of water supplies with high levels of nitrates has become a serious environmental problem. Nitrates are also used in explosives. — verb **1** to treat with nitric acid or a nitrate. **2** trans., intrans. to convert into a nitrate.

nitration noun Chem. a chemical reaction in which a nitro ($-NO_2$) group is incorporated into the structure of a molecule. It is usually achieved by treating an organic compound with a nitrating mixture of concentrated nitric and sulphuric acids.

nitre noun Chem. a former name for potassium nitrate; saltpetre. [from Greek nitron, sodium carbonate]

nitric *adj. Chem.* of or containing nitrogen.

nitric acid *Chem.* a colourless or yellowish toxic corrosive acid manufactured by the catalytic oxidation of ammonia. It is a strong acid and oxidizing agent, and its salts are nitrates. It is used as a laboratory reagent, and in the manufacture of explosives, nitrate fertilizers, dyes, and plastics. Nitric acid is also used for etching and photoengraving.

nitric oxide *Chem.* same as NITROGEN MONOXIDE.

nitride *noun* a compound of nitrogen with another, metallic, element.

nitrification *noun Biochem.* **1** treatment with nitric acid. **2** in the nitrogen cycle, the conversion of ammonia first to nitrites and then to nitrates, which can be taken up by the roots of plants. Nitrification is carried out by certain bacteria, known as *nitrifying bacteria*.

nitrify *verb trans., intrans.* (**nitrifies, nitrified**) *Chem.* to undergo or cause to undergo the process of nitrification.

nitrite *noun Chem.* a salt or ester of nitrous acid, containing the NO_2^- ion, eg potassium nitrite (KNO_2).

nitro- *combining form Chem.* forming words meaning: **1** of, made with, or containing nitrogen, nitric acid, or nitre. **2** containing the group $-NO_2$.

nitrogen *noun* (SYMBOL **N**, ATOMIC NUMBER **7**) a gas that is colourless, odourless, and tasteless and represents about 78% of the Earth's atmosphere by volume. [from NITRE + -GEN]
◇ Pure nitrogen is relatively inert chemically, but it forms many important compounds, including ammonia, nitric acid, nitrates, and cyanide compounds. It is an important constituent of the amino acids and proteins in all living organisms, and also occurs in various minerals. Nitrogen is obtained commercially by fractional distillation of liquid air, and is used in the production of ammonia, and to provide an inert atmosphere in electrical devices and for welding. Liquid nitrogen is used as a refrigerant. Compounds of nitrogen, especially nitrates, are used in fertilizers and explosives.

nitrogen cycle *Biol.* the continuous circulation of nitrogen and its compounds between the atmosphere and the biosphere as a result of the activity of living organisms.
◇ Atmospheric nitrogen can be directly converted into organic nitrogen compounds, or 'fixed', by certain bacteria and blue-green algae that are found in the root nodules of leguminous plants (plants belonging to the pea family), eg peas, beans, clover. The majority of plants, which cannot fix nitrogen directly, absorb it in the form of nitrates from the soil. A certain amount of nitrogen is also fixed during thunderstorms, when lightning flashes result in the formation of oxides of nitrogen, which dissolve in rainwater to form nitrates, and then enter the soil. Nitrogen taken up by plants is incorporated into proteins, and when such plants are subsequently eaten by animals, it is incorporated into animal protein. The excreta of animals, together with the decomposing remains of dead plants and animals, are broken down by nitrifying bacteria to form ammonia, which is oxidized first to nitrites and then to nitrates in a process known as *nitrification*. The ammonia and nitrates may be used as plant nutrients, and nitrates are also converted to molecular nitrogen (which is released back to the atmosphere) by bacteria that live in waterlogged soils, in a process known as *denitrification*.

nitrogen dioxide *Chem.* (FORMULA **NO_2**) a reddish-brown gas that is used in the production of nitric acid.

nitrogen fixation *Biochem.* the conversion of nitrogen in the atmosphere to nitrogen-containing compounds, especially nitrates, which can be

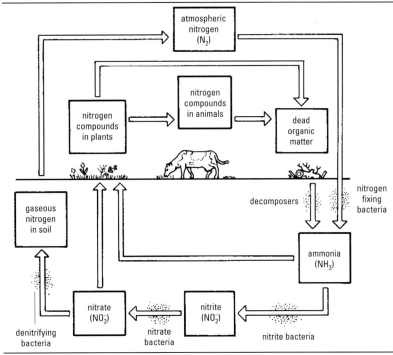

nitrogen cycle

utilized by plants. The process is carried out by nitrifying bacteria in the soil, and blue-green algae.

nitrogen monoxide *Chem.* (FORMULA **NO**) a colourless gas that reacts spontaneously with oxygen at room temperature to form nitrogen dioxide (NO_2). Nitrogen monoxide is an intermediate in the oxidation of ammonia to nitric acid. — Also called *nitric oxide*.

nitrogenous *adj. Chem.* containing nitrogen.

nitroglycerine *or* **nitroglycerin** *noun Chem.* an explosive toxic oily yellow liquid that is an ester of nitric acid. It is used as a rocket fuel, an explosive (eg in dynamite) and as a vasodilatory drug in medicine.

nitrous *adj. Chem.* of or containing nitrogen in a low valency.

nitrous acid *Chem.* (FORMULA **HNO_2**) a weak unstable acid that decomposes in water, and is formed when a nitrite salt reacts with an acid. It is used as a source of nitric oxide, and in the synthesis of organic compounds.

nitrous oxide *Chem.* nitrogen monoxide.

nitty-gritty *noun colloq.* (**the nitty-gritty**) the fundamental issue or essential part of any matter, situation, activity, etc. [originally US; perhaps rhyming compound of *grit*]

nitwit *noun* a stupid person. [from German dialect *nit*, variant of *nicht*, not + WIT[1]]

Niue POP (1992e) 2 000, a Self-Governing Territory of New Zealand, located in the S Pacific Ocean, 2 140km/1 330mi NE of New Zealand. AREA 263sq km/101sq mi. The main settlement on the island is Alofi. TIMEZONE GMT +12. Christianity is the chief religion. OFFICIAL LANGUAGE English; Niuean is also spoken widely. CURRENCY the New Zealand dollar. PHYSICAL DESCRIPTION mainly coral, with a flat, rolling interior and porous soils. CLIMATE subtropical and damp; hurricanes in the hot season (Dec–Mar); rainfall throughout the year. HISTORY the island was visited by Captain Cook in 1774; European missionaries arrived in the mid-19c; it became a British protectorate in 1900, and was annexed to New Zealand in 1901. GOVERNMENT since 1974, the island has had internal self-government in free association with New Zealand, which still maintains responsibility for defence and foreign affairs; the territory is governed by an elected 24-member Legislative Assembly, headed by a premier. ECONOMY mainly agricultural; passion-fruit; bananas; copra; crafts.

Niven, David, originally **James David Graham Nevins** (1910–83) English film actor, born in London. He had his first leading part in *Dodsworth* (1936) and became established in urbane English-style romantic roles. His later successes included *A Matter of Life and Death* (1946), *Around the World in 80 Days* (1956), *Separate Tables* (1958), for which he won an Oscar, and the adventure story *The Guns of Navarone* (1961).

nix — *noun slang* nothing. — *interj. North Amer.* no. [from German, a form of *nichts*, nothing]

Nixon, Richard M(ilhous) (1913–94) US Republican politician, the 37th President, born in Yorba Linda, California. He became a lawyer, served in the US Navy, was elected to the House of Representatives (1946), then became Senator (1950) and Vice-President (1952). He lost the 1960 presidential election to Kennedy, but won in 1968 and became President (1969–74). In 1974 he resigned under the threat of impeachment after several leading members of his government had been found guilty of involvement in the Watergate affair, but was given a full pardon by President Ford. As President, he sought to end the Vietnam War, but only after the US invasion of Cambodia and Laos. He had diplomatic successes with China and the USSR.

Nizhniy Novgorod, formerly **Gorky** (1932–1990) POP (1990e) 1.4m, the industrial capital of Nizhegorod oblast, NW Russia. It is a port lying at the confluence of the Volga and Oka rivers. HISTORY founded as a frontier post in 1221; from 1817 to 1930 it was famous for its annual trade fairs; birthplace of Maxim Gorky, after whom the city was renamed in 1932.

NJ *or* **N.J.** *abbrev.* New Jersey.

Nkomo, Joshua (Mqabuko Nyongolo) (1917–) Zimbabwean nationalist and politician, born in Semokwe, Matabeleland. He became a member of the African National Congress in 1952, and in 1961 President of the

Zimbabwe African People's Union (ZAPU). Following a long period during which he was under government restrictions, in 1976 he formed the Popular Front with Robert Mugabe and the Zimbabwe African People's Union (ZAPU) to press for black majority rule in an independent Zimbabwe, and was given a Cabinet post in the Mugabe government in 1980. Tension between his party and Mugabe's led to his dismissal in 1982, but they were reconciled and in 1988 their parties reunited to make Zimbabwe effectively a one-party state with Mugabe as President, and Nkomo as Vice-President from 1990.

Nkrumah, Kwame (1909–72) Ghanaian statesman, born in Nkroful, Gold Coast. After studying in the USA and UK, he returned to Ghana (1947), and in 1949 formed the nationalist Convention People's Party. In 1950 he was imprisoned, but elected to parliament while still in jail. Released in 1951, he became leader of business in the Assembly, Prime Minister (1957–60) and President (1960–6), when Ghana became a republic. Called the 'Gandhi of Africa', he was a leader both of the movement against white domination and of Pan-African feeling (promoting political unity in Africa), and championed the Charter of African States (1961). Economic reforms led to political opposition and several attempts on his life, interference with the judiciary, and the formation of a one-party state in 1964. His regime was overthrown in 1966 by a military coup during his absence in China, and he sought asylum in Guinea, where he was given the status of co-head of state.

NM *or* **N.M.** *or* **N.Mex.** *abbrev.* New Mexico.

NNE *abbrev.* north-north-east.

NNEB *abbrev.* Nursery Nurses' Examination Board.

NNW *abbrev.* north-north-west.

No¹ see NOH.

No² *symbol Chem.* nobelium.

No. or no. *abbrev.* (usually followed by a numeral) number: *No.3.*

no¹ — *interj.* used as **1** a negative reply, expressing denial, refusal, or disagreement: *it's a deal, no?* **2** *colloq.* a question tag expecting agreement: *it's a deal, no?* **3** an astonished rejoinder: *No! You don't say!* — *adv.* **1** (*with comparative*) not any: *no bigger than one's thumb.* **2** (*used to indicate a negative alternative*) not: *whether he's willing or no.* — *noun* (PL. **noes**) a negative reply or vote. [from Anglo-Saxon *na,* from *ne,* not + *a,* ever]

no² *adj.* **1** not any. **2** certainly not a; far from a: *he's no fool / no easy task.* **3** hardly any: *do it in no time.* **4** not allowed: *no smoking.*
— **no go** *colloq.* impossible; no good.
no way *colloq.* no; definitely not.
[from Middle English, a variant of NONE]

no. see NO.

Noah a biblical character, the son of Lamech. A righteous and blameless man, he was instructed by God to build an ark in which he, his immediate family, and a selection of animals were saved from a devastating flood (Genesis 6–9). In the Table of Nations (Genesis 10), Noah's sons (Japheth, Ham, and Shem) are depicted as the ancestors of all the nations on Earth.

nob *noun slang* a person of wealth or high social rank.

no-ball *noun Cricket, Baseball* a ball bowled in a manner disallowed by the rules.

nobble *verb trans. colloq.* **1** *Racing* to drug or otherwise interfere with (a horse) to stop it winning. **2** to persuade by bribes or threats. **3** to obtain dishonestly. **4** to catch (a criminal). **5** to swindle. [from *an hobbler,* a person who lames horses (later understood as *a nobbler*)]

Nobel, Alfred (1833–96) Swedish chemist and industrialist, born in Bernhard. He invented dynamite (a relatively safe and manageable explosive made from nitroglycerine) and gelignite, as well as several kinds of smokeless powder. His huge fortune was left to fund the rich Nobel prizes which have been awarded since 1901.

nobelium *noun Chem.* (SYMBOL **No**, ATOMIC NUMBER **102**) a synthetic radioactive metallic element produced by bombarding curium with carbon ions. [named after the Nobel Institute, Stockholm, where it was first produced]

Nobel prize any of the prizes, awarded annually for work in physics, chemistry, medicine, literature, and the promotion of peace, instituted by Alfred Nobel, Swedish inventor of dynamite.

nobility *noun* **1** the quality of being noble, in character, conduct, or rank. **2** (**the nobility**) the class of people of noble birth. [from Latin *nobilitas,* from *nobilis,* noble]

noble — *adj.* **1** honourable. **2** generous. **3** of high birth or rank. **4** grand, splendid, or imposing in appearance. — *noun* a person of noble rank. [from Latin *nobilis,* originally *gnobilis,* knowable, ie well-known]

noble gas *Chem.* any of the colourless odourless tasteless gases in group 0 of the periodic table of the elements, ie helium, neon, argon, krypton, xenon, and radon, in order of increasing atomic number. Most of the noble gases are chemically inert. — Also called *inert gas.*

nobleman *noun* a male member of the nobility.

noble metal *Chem.* any metal that is highly unreactive, such as gold or platinum, and is therefore resistant to oxidation, tarnishing, etc.

nobleness *noun* a noble state or quality.

noble rot *Bot.* on white grapes, a rot caused by the fungus *Botrytis cinerea.* Sweet white wines are made using the infected fruit.

noblesse oblige the maxim that it is the duty of those who are privileged to use their privilege to the benefit of the less fortunate. [French, = nobility obliges]

noblewoman *noun* a female member of the nobility.

nobly *adv.* with a noble or honourable manner: *behave nobly.*

nobody — *pron.* no person; no one. — *noun* (PL. **nobodies**) a person of no significance.

Nobunaga, Oda (1534–82) Japanese soldier, who became the first of the three great historical unifiers of Japan (followed by Hideyoshi and Tokugawa), born near Nagoya. He was made a general, and in 1568 occupied the old capital, Kyoto, where he destroyed the power of the Buddhist Church, and favoured Christianity as a counter-balance. He built Azuchi Castle, near Kyoto, as his headquarters.

no-claims bonus a reduction in the fee one pays for insurance if one has made no claim for payment over a particular period.

nocturnal *adj.* **1** *said of animals, etc* active at night. **2** happening at night. **3** of, belonging to, or relating to the night. [from Latin *nocturnus,* from *nox,* night]

nocturnally *adv.* at night.

nocturne *noun* **1** a dreamy piece of music, usually for the piano. **2** *Art* a night or moonlight scene. [from French *nocturne,* from Latin *nocturnus,* from *nox,* night]

nod *verb* (**nodded, nodding**) **1** *intrans., trans.* to make a brief bowing gesture with the head, in agreement, greeting, etc; to bow (the head) briefly. **2** *intrans.* to let the head droop with sleepiness; to become drowsy. **3** *intrans.* to make a mistake through momentary loss of concentration. **4** *trans.* to indicate or direct by nodding: *nodded her approval / was nodded through the*

Customs. **5** *intrans. said of flowers, plumes, etc* to sway or bob about.
— **have a nodding acquaintance with someone** to know them slightly.
the Land of Nod the imaginary country to which sleepers go.
nod off *intrans.* to fall asleep in a chair, etc.
on the nod *colloq., said of the passing of a proposal, etc* by general agreement, without the formality of a vote.

nodal *adj.* relating to or consisting of a node or nodes.

noddle *noun colloq.* the head or brain.

noddy *noun* (PL. **noddies**) **1** a tropical bird of the tern family, so unafraid as to seem stupid. **2** a simpleton. [perhaps from an obsolete word *noddy,* silly]

noddy suit *Mil. slang* an NBC suit.

node *noun* **1** *Anat.* a small lump or mass of tissue, eg lymph node, or a junction of a system or network, eg of muscle fibres in the pacemaker of the heart. **2** *Bot.* the point on a plant stem from which leaves and axillary buds arise. **3** *Geom.* the point at which two or more branches of a curve meet. **4** *Astron.* the point at which one orbit crosses another, especially one of two points at which the orbit of a celestial body crosses a reference plane, such as the ecliptic (apparent path of the sun). **5** *Physics* in a system of standing waves, a point, line, or surface where there is zero amplitude (minimum disturbance), eg near the closed end of a resonating pipe. [from Latin *nodus,* knot]

nodular *adj.* relating to or consisting of a nodule or nodules.

nodule *noun* **1** a small round lump. **2** *Bot.* any of a number of small round swellings on the roots of leguminous plants, eg peas, beans, clover, containing bacteria capable of converting atmospheric nitrogen into nitrogen compounds that can be used by the plant. [from Latin *nodulus,* a diminutive of *nodus,* knot]

Noel 1 *old use* Christmas. **2** a male first name. [from Old French *noel,* from Latin *natalis,* birthday]

Noel-Baker (of the City of Derby), Philip (John) Noel-Baker, Baron (1889–1982) English Labour politician, born in London. He was a brilliant athlete at Cambridge, and captained the British Olympic team in 1912. He served on the secretariat of the League of Nations (1919–22), became the Cassel Professor of International Relations at London (1924–9), and an MP (1929–31, 1936–70). He resigned from the Labour Party in 1969, and later joined the SDP (1981–3), then the Conservative Party (1984). Among his writings are *Disarmament* (1926) and *The Arms Race* (1958). He was awarded the Nobel Peace Prize in 1959.

no-fault principle *Legal* the principle that it should be possible to claim compensation for injury without proving fault against a defendant. The compensation scheme for personal injuries in New Zealand is a notable example of the principle in operation.

nog *noun* an alcoholic drink made with whipped eggs; an egg nog.

noggin *noun* **1** a small measure or quantity of alcoholic spirits. **2** a small mug or wooden cup. **3** *colloq.* one's head.

no-go area an area of a city to which access is controlled by one of the groups involved in an armed conflict or civil war, and is forbidden to others.

Noh *or* **No** classical Japanese theatre in which imitation, gesture, dance, mask-work, costume, song, and music are fused in a concise stage art. The philosophy and style, and much of the repertoire, was established by Kan'ami (1333–84) and his son Zeami (1363–1443). Five schools of Noh exist, and most of the plays they perform were written before 1600. [from Japanese *no,* ability]

Nobel Prizes 1983–93							
Year	Peace	Literature	Economic Science	Chemistry	Physics	Phisiology/Medicine	Year
1983	Lech Walesa	William Golding	Gerard Debreu	Henry Taube	Subrahmanyan Chandrasekhar William A Fowler	Barbara McClintock	1983
1984	Desmond Tutu	Jaroslav Seifert	Richard Stone	Robert B Merrifield	Carlo Rubbia Simon van der Meer	Niels K Jerne Georges J F Köhler César Milstein	1984
1985	International Physicians for the Prevention of Nuclear War	Claude Simon	Franco Modigliani	Herbert Hauptman Jerome Karle	Klaus von Klitzing	Joseph L Goldstein Michael S Brown	1985
1986	Elie Wiesel	Wole Soyinka	James M Buchanan	Dudley R Herschbach Yuan Tseh Lee John C Polanyi	Gerd Binnig Heinrich Rohrer Ernst Ruska	Stanley Cohen Rita Levi-Montalcini	1986
1987	Oscar Arias Sánchez	Joseph Brodsky	Robert M Solow	Charles Pedersen Donald Cram Jean-Marie Lehn	Georgi Bednorz Alex Müller	Susumu Tonegawa	1987
1988	UN Peacekeeping Forces	Naguib Mahfouz	Maurice Allais	Johann Deisenhofer Robert Huber Hartmut Michel	Leon Lederman Melvin Schwartz Jack Steinberger	James Black Gertrude Elion George Hitchings	1988
1989	Tenzin Ciyatso (Dalai Lama)	Camilo José Cela	Trygve Haavelmo	Sydney Altman Thomas Cech	Hans Dehmelt Woifgang Paul Norman Ramsay	J Michael Bishop Harold E Varmus	1989
1990	Mikhail Gorbachev	Octavio Paz	Harry M Markovitz Merton Miller William Sharpe	Elias James Corey	Jerome Friedman Henry Kendall Richard Taylor	Joseph E Murray E Donnall Thomas	1990
1991	Aung San Suu Kyi	Nadine Gordimer	Ronald Coase	Richard R Ernst	Pierre-Gilles de Gennes	Erwin Neher Bert Sakmann	1991
1992	Rigoberta Menchú	Derek Walcott	Gary S Becker	Rudolph A Marcus	George Charpak	Edmond H Fisher Edwin G Krebs	1992
1993	Nelson Mandela F W de Klerk	Toni Morrison	Robert Fugel Douglas North	Kary Banks Mullis Michael Smith	Russell Hulse Joseph Hooton Taylor Jr	Richard Roberts Phillip Allen Sharp	1993

nohow *noun dialect* in no way.

noise — *noun* **1** a sound, especially a harsh or disagreeable sound. **2** a series of unpleasant or confused sounds, causing a continuous din. **3** unwanted and often random interference that makes it hard to detect the content of an electrical signal, such as a particular radio frequency band. Sources of noise include radio waves, electrical equipment, electric cables, computers, lightning, etc. **4** *facetious* something one utters by way of conventional response, vague indication of inclinations, etc: *make polite noises.* — *verb* (**noise something abroad**) to make it generally known; to spread a rumour, etc. [from Old French, from Latin *nausea*, sea-sickness]

noiseless *adj.* lacking noise; silent.

noiselessly *adv.* without noise; silently.

noise pollution an excessive or annoying degree of noise in a particular area, eg from traffic or aircraft.

noisily *adv.* with much noise; loudly.

noisiness *noun* much noise; loudness.

noisome *adj.* **1** disgusting; offensive; stinking. **2** harmful; poisonous: *noisome fumes.* [from earlier *noy*, a variant of ANNOY]

noisy *adj.* (**noisier, noisiest**) **1** making a lot of noise: *noisy children.* **2** full of noise: *noisy streets.*

Nok a culture of N Nigeria that has been dated to the period 900 BC– AD 200, the artefacts of which were recovered from a village of that name during tin-mining operations in the 1930s. Its people produced terracotta figurines remarkable for their sophistication of style, smelted iron from at least 300 BC, and used the lost wax process for casting tin.

Nolan, Sir Sidney (Robert) (1917–92) Australian painter, born in Melbourne. He took up full-time painting in 1938 and made his name with a series of *Ned Kelly* paintings, begun in 1946. He followed these with an 'explorer' series based on the travels of Robert O'Hara Burke and William Wills. He was also a theatrical designer and book illustrator.

Nollekens, Joseph (1737–1823) English neoclassical sculptor, born in London. He spent 10 years in Rome and returned to London in 1770. He sculpted busts of most of his famous contemporaries, including Oliver Goldsmith, Samuel Johnson, Charles James Fox, and George III.

nom. *abbrev. Grammar* nominative.

nomad *noun* **1** a member of a people without permanent home, who travel from place to place seeking food and pasture. **2** a wanderer. [from Greek *nomas*, from *nomos*, pasture]

nomadic *adj., said of a people* wandering from place to place; not settled.

nomadism *noun* the way of life of nomads, characterized by frequent movement from place to place.

no-man's-land *noun* **1** unclaimed land; waste land. **2** neutral territory between opposing armies or between two countries with a common border. **3** a state or situation that is neither one thing nor another.

nom-de-plume *noun* (PL. **noms-de-plume**) a pseudonym used by a writer; a pen-name. [French, = pen-name]

nomenclature *noun* **1** a classified system of names, especially in scientific terminology, eg binomial nomenclature, in which each living organism is given a two-part scientific name, usually Latinized, denoting the genus and the species. **2** a list or set of names. [from Latin *nomenclatura*, from *nomen*, name + *calare*, to call]

nominal *adj.* **1** in name only; so called, but actually not: *a nominal head of state.* **2** very small in comparison to actual cost or value: *a nominal rent.* **3** *Grammar* of, being, or relating to a noun. [from Latin *nominalis*, from *nomen*, name]

nominalism *noun Philos.* the view that a general term such as 'book' is no more than a name, and does not refer to an actual entity.

nominally *adv.* in name only; theoretically rather than actually.

nominal value the stated or face value, on a bond, share certificate, etc.

nominate *verb* **1** (**nominate someone for something**) to propose them formally as a candidate for election, for a job, etc. **2** (**nominate someone to something**) to appoint them to a post or position. **3** to specify formally (eg a date). [from Latin *nominare*, to name]

nomination *noun* a formal proposal of a candidate for election or appointment.

nominative *Grammar* — *adj.* denoting the case used, in inflected languages such as Latin, for the subject of the verb. — *noun* **1** the nominative case. **2** a word in this case. [from Latin *nominativus*, from *nominare*, to name]

nominee *noun* a person who is nominated as a candidate, or for or to a job, etc. [from Latin *nominare*, to name]

non- *prefix* forming words meaning: **1** not; the opposite: *non-essential / non-existent.* **2** *ironic* not deserving the name: *a non-event.* **3** not belonging to the specified category: *non-fiction / non-metals.* **4** not having the skill or desire: *non-swimmers / non-smokers.* **5** rejection, avoidance, or omission: *non-aggression / non-payment.* **6** not liable to: *non-shrink / non-drip.* **7** not requiring a certain treatment: *non-iron.* [from Latin *non*, not]

Nona a female first name. [from Latin *nonus nona*, ninth, ie ninth-born child]

nonage *noun Legal* the condition of being under age; one's minority or period of immaturity. [from Old French, from *non*, non- + *age*, age]

nonagenarian *noun* someone between 90 and 99 years old. [from Latin *nonagenarius*, containing or consisting of 90]

nonagon *noun Geom.* a nine-sided figure. [from Latin *nonus*, ninth + Greek *gonia*, angle]

non-aligned *adj., said of a country* not allied to any of the major power blocs in world politics.

◇ The non-aligned movement is a grouping of states which do not take sides in the major division(s) within world politics, specifically the major power blocs headed by the USA and former USSR. Members of the non-aligned movement include a number of de-colonized countries who favour neutrality as a mark of their independence.

non-alignment *noun* being non-aligned; neutrality.

non-belligerent — *adj.* taking no part in a war. — *noun* a non-belligerent country.

nonce
— **for the nonce** for the time being; for the present.
[originally *for then ones*, *for the once* (*then once* coming to be understood as *the nonce*)]

nonce-word *noun* a word coined for one particular occasion.

nonchalance *noun* calm or indifferent lack of concern.

nonchalant *adj.* calmly or indifferently unconcerned. [from French *nonchaloir*, to lack warmth]

nonchalantly *adv.* with calm or indifferent lack of concern.

non-combatant *noun* a non-fighting member of the armed forces, eg a surgeon or chaplain.

non-commissioned officer an officer such as a corporal or sergeant, appointed from the lower ranks of the armed forces, not by being given a commission.

non-committal *adj.* avoiding expressing a definite opinion or decision.

non-committally *adv.* without expressing a definite opinion or decision.

non compos mentis not of sound mind. [Latin, = not in command of the mind]

non-conductor *noun* a substance that does not conduct heat, electricity or sound.

nonconformism *noun* refusal to conform to generally accepted practice.

nonconformist — *noun* **1** someone who refuses to conform to generally accepted practice. **2** (**Nonconformist**) in England, a member of a Protestant church separated from the Church of England. — *adj.* of or relating to nonconformists.

nonconformity *noun* **1** refusal to conform to established practice. **2** lack of correspondence or agreement between things.

non-contributory *adj.*, *said of a pension scheme* paid for by the employer, without contributions from the employee.

Non-Co-operation Movement an unsuccessful nationalist campaign (1919–22) led by M K Gandhi and Congress in protest against the Amritsar Massacre and the Montagu–Chelmsford Reforms, and to force the British to grant Indian independence. The Movement involved the boycott of government institutions and foreign goods, and was abandoned when the protest became violent.

non-custodial *adj.*, *said of a judicial sentence* not involving imprisonment.

non-denominational *adj.* not linked with any particular religious denomination; for the use or participation of members of all denominations.

nondescript *adj.* having no strongly noticeable characteristics or distinctive features. [from NON- + Latin *descriptus*, past participle of *describere*, to describe]

none[1] *pron.* **1** not any. **2** no one: *none were as kind as she.*
— **none but** only: *none but the finest ingredients.*
none of ... I won't put up with: *none of your cheek.*
none other than someone or something the very person or thing mentioned or thought of: *it was none other than Bill.*

none the ... (*followed by a comparative*) not any: *none the worse for his adventure.*
none too ... by no means: *none too clean.*
[from Anglo-Saxon *nan*, not one, no]
◆ When referring to a plural noun, *none* may be followed by either a singular or a plural verb, whichever is logically appropriate. If the emphasis is on the individuals in a group (and *none* is equivalent to *no one* or *not one*), the verb should be singular, eg *none of us has the answer*, but if the emphasis is on the group as a whole, the verb should be plural, eg *none of us speak French*.

none[2] *or* **nones**, the fifth of the canonical hours, originally said at the ninth hour (ie 3 pm). See also COMPLINE, LAUDS, MATINS, SEXT, TERCE, VESPERS. [from Latin *nona hora*, the ninth hour]

nonentity *noun* (PL. **nonentities**) a person of no significance, character, ability, etc.

nones[1] *pl. noun* in the Roman calendar, the seventh day of March, May, July, and October, the fifth day of other months. [from Latin *nonae*, from *nonus*, ninth: the nones were the ninth day before the Ides, counting inclusively]

nones[2] see NONE[2].

nonetheless nevertheless, in spite of that.

non-Euclidean geometry any system of geometry that is not based on the theories of the Greek mathematician Euclid.

non-event *noun* an event one has been greatly looking forward to that turns out to be a disappointment.

non-ferrous *adj.*, *said of metals* not iron or steel.

non-fiction *noun* literature other than fiction, including biography, reference books, and textbooks.

non-flammable *adj.* not liable to catch fire or burn easily.

nonintervention *noun* Politics a policy of systematic abstention from interference in the affairs of other nations.

non-metal *noun* Chem. any chemical element that does not have the properties of a metal or a metalloid, and that does not form positive ions. Non-metals are usually solids with low melting points (eg iodine, sulphur) or gases (eg hydrogen, chlorine).

no-no *noun* (PL. **no-nos**) colloq. something which must not be done, said, etc.

non-observance *noun* failure to observe a rule, etc.

no-nonsense *adj.* sensible; practical.

nonpareil — *adj.* having no equal. — *noun* an unequalled person or thing. [from French *nonpareil*, from *non*, non- + *pareil*, equal]

Nonpartisan League a quasi-socialist organization of farmers, founded in North Dakota (1915), which advocated public ownership of public utilities. It spread across the northern wheat belt but declined after 1920, partly because of opposition to involvement in World War I.

non-person *noun* a person, once prominent, who has slipped into obscurity.

nonplus *verb trans.* (**non-plussed**, **non-plussing**) to puzzle; to disconcert. [from Latin *non plus*, no further]

non-proliferation *noun* the policy of limiting the production and ownership of nuclear or chemical weapons.

Non-Proliferation Treaty (ABBREV. **NPT**) a treaty signed in 1968 by the USA, Soviet Union, UK, and an open-ended list of over 100 other countries. It sought to limit the spread of nuclear weapons by restricting their transfer by the signatories, and to encourage states without nuclear weapons to pursue only peaceful uses of nuclear energy.

non-renewable resource any naturally occurring substance that is economically valuable, but which forms over such a long time period (often millions of years) that for all practical purposes it cannot be replaced once it has been used, eg fossil fuels, mineral resources. The availability of such resources is thus fixed and limited, although in some cases they may be recycled.

nonsense — *noun* **1** words or ideas that do not make sense. **2** foolishness; silly behaviour. — *interj.* you're quite wrong.
— **make a nonsense of something** to destroy the effect of; to make pointless.

nonsense verse verse deliberately written to convey an absurd meaning, or with no obvious meaning at all. The most famous examples include the limericks, poems, and songs by Edward Lear (eg *The Jumblies* and *The Pobble Who Has No Toes*), and the verses in Lewis Carroll's two *Alice* books.

nonsensical *adj.* making no sense; absurd.

nonsensically *adv.* in a way that makes no sense.

non sequitur an illogical step in an argument; a conclusion that does not follow from the premises. [from Latin *non sequitur*, it does not follow]

non-standard *adj.*, *said of use of language* not generally accepted as correct.

non-starter *noun* a person, thing, idea, etc that has no chance of success.

non-stick *adj.*, *said of a pan, etc* having a coating to which food does not stick during cooking.

non-stop *adj.*, *adv.* without a stop.

non-U *adj. Brit. colloq.*, *said especially of language* not acceptable among the upper classes. [from U[2], = upper class]
◇ The terms U and non-U were coined by the English linguist Alan Ross (1907–), in an essay highlighting the class-based variation in British English, published in *Noblesse Oblige*. He classified vocabulary, and certain features of grammar and pronunciation, as being either upper-class (U), or non-upper-class (non-U). For example, the usages *have a bath*, *riding*, and *pudding* are all U; *take a bath*, *horse-riding*, and *sweet* are non-U.

non-union *adj.* **1** not belonging to a trade union. **2** employing, or produced by, workers not belonging to a trade union.

nonverbal communication (NVC) forms of communication between people that supplement the spoken or written word, including gesture and posture (body language), and facial expression. The messages communicated may be deliberate (eg winking or bowing), or may be beyond conscious control (eg blushing or shivering).

non-voting *adj.*, *said of shares* not giving the holder the right to vote on company decisions.

non-white — *adj.*, *said of a person* not belonging to one of the white-skinned races. — *noun* a non-white person.

noodle[1] *noun* (usually **noodles**) a thin strip of pasta, usually made with egg.

noodle[2] *noun colloq.* a simpleton.

nook *noun* **1** a secluded retreat. **2** a corner or recess.
— **every nook and cranny** absolutely everywhere.

noon *noun* midday; twelve o'clock. [from Latin *nona (hora)*, the ninth hour, originally 3 pm]

no one *or* **no-one** *noun* nobody; no person.

noose *noun* a loop made in the end of a rope, etc with a sliding knot, used eg for killing by hanging.
— **put one's head in a noose** to walk into danger.
[from Old French *nous*, from Latin *nodus*, knot]

NOP *abbrev.* National Opinion Poll.

nor — *conj.* **1** used to introduce alternatives after *neither*: *he neither knows nor cares / they eat neither fish nor meat nor eggs.* **2** and ... not: *it didn't look appetizing, nor was it.* — *adv.* not either: *if you* won't, nor shall I. [a contraction of Anglo-Saxon *nother*, from *ne*, not + *other*, either]

nor' combining form Naut. north: *a nor'-wester / nor'-nor'-east*.

Nora a female first name. [a short form of ELEANOR and other names in *-nor* and *-nora*]

noradrenaline noun Physiol. a hormone, closely related to adrenaline, produced in small amounts by the adrenal glands. It also serves as a neurotransmitter in the sympathetic nervous system and brain. It increases blood pressure by constricting small blood vessels, increases the rate and depth of breathing, and slows the heartbeat.

Nordic adj. **1** of or belonging to Scandinavia or its inhabitants. **2** Germanic or Scandinavian in appearance, typically tall, blond, and blue-eyed. **3** (**nordic**) denoting a type of competitive skiing with cross-country racing and ski-jumping. [from French *nordique*, from *nord*, north]

Nördliche Kalkalpen a mountain range of the E Alps in central Austria, rising to 2 995m at Hoher Dachstein.

Norf. abbrev. Norfolk.

Norfolk POP (1992e) 763 000, a flat, arable county in E England, divided into seven districts. AREA 5 368sq km/2 072sq mi. It is bounded N and E by the North Sea, S by Suffolk, SW by Cambridgeshire, and NW by Lincolnshire. PHYSICAL DESCRIPTION low-lying land, with fens in the W; the Norfolk Broads are in the E; drained by the Yare, Ouse, Waveney, and Bure rivers. CHIEF TOWNS Norwich (county town), King's Lynn, Great Yarmouth (major resort and fishing port). ECONOMY offshore natural gas; tourism; agriculture; turkeys; fishing. NOTABLE FEATURES Grime's Graves (Neolithic flint mines); Sandringham royal residence; Shrine of Our Lady of Walsingham; Halvergate Marshes wildlife preserve.

Norfolk POP (1990) 261 000, a seaport in SE Virginia, USA. Situated on the Elizabeth R, it is the largest city in the state. HISTORY settled in 1682; became a city in 1845; centre of fighting in the American Revolution and the Civil War. It is the headquarters of the US Atlantic Fleet, and the largest naval base in the world. NOTABLE FEATURES Chrysler Museum; Douglas MacArthur Memorial; Hampton Roads Naval Museum; Botanical Gardens.

Norfolk Island POP (1986) 2 000, an island external territory of Australia in the W Pacific Ocean, lying 1 488km/925mi NE of Sydney. AREA 35sq km/14sq mi; length 8km/5mi. The island is fertile and hilly. Both English and Tahitian are spoken widely. HISTORY a British penal settlement from 1788 until 1806 and from 1826 until 1855; many people from the Pitcairn Is transferred to Norfolk Island in 1856; it became an Australian external territory in 1913 and was formerly part of the colony of New South Wales. GOVERNMENT the island is governed by the Norfolk I Legislative Assembly, and is represented in Australia by an Administrator appointed by the Governor-General. ECONOMY postage stamps; tourism.

norm noun **1** (**the norm**) a typical pattern or situation. **2** an accepted way of behaving, etc: *social norms*. **3** a standard, eg for achievement in industry: *production norms*. [from Latin *norma*, carpenter's square, rule]

Norma a female first name, first appearing in Italian as the heroine of Bellini's opera. [perhaps from Latin *norma*, rule, precept]

Norma an opera by Vincenzo Bellini (1831), based on Alexandre Soumet's tragedy. Set in Roman-occupied Gaul (c.50 BC), it focuses on the high priestess Norma who has broken her vows and secretly become mother of two, the father of whom (the hated Roman Pollione) is caught by the Druids trying to run off with another priestess and brought before Norma to be judged.

normal — adj. **1** usual; typical; not extraordinary. **2** mentally or physically sound: *a normal baby*. **3** Geom. at right angles, perpendicular.

4 Chem. denoting a solution that contains 1 gram-equivalent of solute (dissolved substance) per litre of solution. — noun **1** what is average or usual. **2** Geom. a line that is drawn perpendicular to another line or surface. [from Latin *normalis*, regulated by a carpenter's square, from *norma*, carpenter's square]

normal distribution Maths. in statistics, a frequency distribution represented by a symmetrical bell-shaped curve. Such a curve would be obtained, for example, for variation in height within members of a population, where the peak represents the intermediate or 'normal' height of the majority of the population, while the number of people with heights above or below this value steadily decreases on either side of the peak of the curve.

normality or North Amer. **normalcy** noun being normal; a normal state or quality.

normalization or **normalisation** noun making or becoming normal or regular.

normalize or **normalise** verb trans., intrans. to make or become normal or regular.

normally adv. **1** in an ordinary or natural way. **2** usually.

Norman, Barry Leslie (1933–) English journalist and broadcaster, born in London, the son of film director Leslie Norman (1914–93). He worked for various newspapers before specializing in the world of show business and presenting radio programmes (eg *Today*, 1974–6 and *Going Places*, 1977–81). He made his name as an influential film critic through the television series that began with *Film '73* (1973–81, 1983–). His other documentary series include *The Hollywood Greats* (1977–9, 1984–5) and *Talking Pictures* (1988).

Norman a male first name. [of Germanic origin, = northman]

Norman — noun **1** a person from Normandy, especially one of the Scandinavian settlers of N France who conquered England in 1066 (see NORMANS). **2** Norman French. — adj. **1** relating to the Normans or their language or culture. **2** Archit. denoting a form of architecture prevalent in 11c and 12c England, corresponding to the European Romanesque (eg Durham Cathedral, 1093–1133). [from Old French *Normant*, from Norse *Northmathr*]

Norman Conquest the conquest of England by William of Normandy in 1066. It was a watershed in English political and social history, which saw a dynasty of Norman kings (1066–1154) start to rule, and Normans, Bretons, and Flemings, many of whom retained lands in N France, take the place of most of the Anglo-Saxon nobility. Between 1066 and 1144 England and Normandy were normally united under one king-duke, and the result was the formation of a single cross-Channel state. The Angevin conquest of Normandy (1144–5) and accession to the throne of England (1154) ensured that England's fortunes would continue to be linked with France, even after the French annexation of Normandy (1204).

Normandy, French **Normandie** a former duchy and province in NW France, along the littoral of the English Channel between Brittany and French Flanders. It now occupies the regions of Haute-Normandie and Basse-Normandie. HISTORY settled by the Normans in the 9c; a leading state in the Middle Ages; William, Duke of Normandy conquered England in 1066; focus of English–French dispute between the 12c and the 14c, until becoming part of France in 1449; scene of Allied invasion in 1944. CHIEF TOWNS Alençon, Rouen, Cherbourg, Dieppe, Caen, Le Havre. ECONOMY fertile agricultural area; sheep; dairy farming; flax; fruit.

Normandy Campaign (1944) a World War II campaign which began on D-Day (6 Jun 1944). Allied forces under the command of General Eisenhower began the liberation of W Europe from Germany by landing on the Normandy coast between the Orne River and St Marcouf

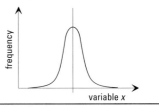

normal distribution

using artificial harbours. Three weeks' heavy fighting ensued before Allied troops captured Cherbourg (27 Jun). Then tanks broke through the German defences, Paris (25 Aug) and Brussels (2 Sep) were liberated, and the German frontier was crossed (12 Sep).

Norman French the dialect of Old French spoken by the Normans.

Normans a name applied, by the early 11c, to all the people inhabiting Normandy, a duchy (and later province) in N France; probably only a few were actually of Scandinavian descent. Their remarkable achievements during the later 11c and early 12c included the conquest and aristocratic colonization of England and most of Wales, the establishment of a kingdom in S Italy and Sicily, and the founding of the Norman principality of Antioch. They also fought against the Muslims in Spain and settled peacefully in Scotland. [from Northmen (ie Vikings)]

normative adj. establishing a guiding standard or rules: *normative grammar*. [from NORM]

Norn noun Scandinavian Mythol. any of three goddesses of destiny, the equivalent of the Fates, three sisters who sit under the tree Yggdrasil and spin the web of Destiny. Their names are Urd (who knows the past), Verdandi (the present), and Skuld (the future). [from Norse *Norn*]

Norris, Mrs a malicious character in Jane Austen's *Mansfield Park*.

Norse — adj. **1** of or belonging to ancient or medieval Scandinavia. **2** Norwegian. — noun **1** (pl.) esp. Hist. the Scandinavians, especially the Norwegians. **2 a** the Germanic language group of Scandinavia. **b** (also **Old Norse**) the language of this group used in medieval Norway and its colonies. [perhaps from Old Dutch *noorsch*]. See panel p. 004.

North, Frederick, 8th Lord North (1732–92) English statesman, born in London. He was a Lord of the Treasury (1759) and Chancellor of the Exchequer (1767), and as Prime Minister (1770–82) brought George III a period of political stability. Criticized both for failing to avert the Declaration of Independence by the N American colonies (1776) and for failing to defeat them in the subsequent war (1776–83), he resigned in 1782. He formed a coalition with his former Whig opponent, Charles James Fox (1783), but it did not survive the King's hostility and he was dismissed (1783). North remained an opposition politician until his death.

North, Sir Thomas (c.1535–c.1601) English translator, born in London. A lawyer, diplomat, and soldier, he is known for his translation of Plutarch's *Lives of the noble Grecians and Romans* (1579), which Shakespeare used in many of his plays.

north — noun (also **the north** or **the North**) the direction to one's left when one faces the rising sun, or any part of the earth, a country, town, etc lying in that direction. — adj. **1** in the north; on the side that is on or nearest the north. **2** coming from the direction of the north: *a north wind*. — adv. towards the north. [from Anglo-Saxon]

North African Campaign a campaign fought (1940–3) during World War II. After an initial Italian invasion of Egypt, Italian forces were driven back deep into Libya, and General

Rommel was sent to N Africa with Germany's specially trained Afrika Corps to stem a further Italian retreat. Though driven back to the Egyptian border, the British defended Tobruk (in Libya) and counter-attacked late in 1941. Fighting continued into 1942, when Rommel once more gained the initiative, but British troops under Montgomery defeated him at the battle of El Alamein (Oct 1942). In February 1943, the Germans attacked US troops in Tunisia, were driven back, and finally 250 000 Axis troops, half of them German, were caught in a pincer movement by Allied forces advancing from east and west.

North America the third largest continent, bounded by the Beaufort Sea in the NW, the Arctic Ocean in the N, Baffin Bay and Davis Strait in the NE, the Atlantic Ocean in the E, and the Pacific Ocean in the W. It is separated from Asia by the Bering Strait. AREA c.24m sq km/9.3m sq mi. It comprises Canada, USA, Mexico, and numerous islands including Baffin I, Newfoundland, and the West Indies. PHYSICAL DESCRIPTION ranges include the Rocky Mts, Alaska Range (including Mt McKinley, the highest point in the continent), and Appalachian Mts; the Great Lakes form a major lake system; important rivers include the Mississippi, Missouri, R Grande, and St Lawrence.

North American Free Trade Agreement (ABBREV. **NAFTA**) a trade agreement linking the USA, Canada, and Mexico, which came into effect on 1 Jan 1994. Over the next two decades NAFTA will bring into effect the elimination of tariffs between the USA,

---

Norse Gods

Aegir God of the sea
Aesir Race of warlike gods, including Odin, Thor, Tyr
Alcis Twin gods of the sky
Balder Son of Odin and favourite of the gods
Bor Father of Odin
Bragi God of poetry
Fafnir Dragon god
Fjorgynn Mother of Thor
Freyja Goddess of libido
Frey God of fertility
Frigg Goddess of fertility; wife of Odin
Gefion Goddess who received virgins after death
Heimdall Guardian of the bridge Bifrost
Hel Goddess of death; Queen of Niflheim, the land of mists
Hermod Son of Odin
Hoenir Companion to Odin and Loki
Hoder Blind god who killed Baldur
Idunn Guardian goddess of the golden apples of youth; wife of Bragi
Kvasir God of wise utterances
Logi Fire god
Loki God of mischief
Mimir God of wisdom
Nanna Goddess wife of Balder
Nehallenia Goddess of plenty
Nerthus Goddess of earth
Njord God of ships and the sea
Norns Goddesses of destiny
Odin (Woden, Wotan) Chief of the Aesir family of gods, the 'father' god; the god of battle, death, inspiration
Otr Otter god
Ran Goddess of the sea
Sif Goddess wife of Thor
Sigyn Goddess wife of Loki
Thor (Donar) God of thunder and sky; good crops
Tyr God of battle
Ull Stepson of Thor, an enchanter
Valkyries Female helpers of the gods of war
Vanir Race of benevolent gods, including Njord, Frey, Freyja
Vidar Slayer of the wolf, Fenvir
Weland (Volundr, Weiland, Wayland) Craftsman god

Canada, and Mexico; the reduction of Mexican car market tariffs from 20 to 10 per cent; the elimination of Mexico's restrictions on foreign investment so that US firms can extract profits; and access for US and Canadian companies to the petroleum, electricity, and energy services of Mexico. NAFTA creates the largest trade bloc in the world, and is the first agreement of its kind between a rich and a poor country.

Northampton POP (1992e) 186 000, the county town of Northampton district, Northamptonshire, central England. It lies on the R Nene, SE of Coventry and 97km/60mi NW of London. HISTORY originally a Saxon town; Thomas Becket was tried here in 1164; in was destroyed by fire in 1675; in 1968 it was designated a 'new town'. NOTABLE FEATURES 12c Church of the Holy Sepulchre, one of four round churches in England; All Saints' Church; Church of St Peter.

Northamptonshire POP (1992e) 590 000, an agricultural county in central England, divided into seven districts. AREA 2 367sq km/914sq mi. It is drained by the Welland and Nene rivers. CHIEF TOWNS Northampton (county town), Kettering, Daventry. ECONOMY cereals; livestock; sugar beet; potatoes; iron mining; shoemaking; printing; engineering.

North and South a novel by Mrs Gaskell (1854–5). It contrasts, through the education of the central character Margaret Hale, the values and lifestyles of rural Hampshire with the industrial mill-towns of N England.

Northanger Abbey a novel by Jane Austen (1818). It is a parody of Gothic fiction, realized through the overly romantic nature of the central character, Catherine Morland.

Northants. *abbrev.* Northamptonshire.

North Atlantic Treaty Organization see NATO.

northbound *adj.* going or leading towards the north.

North Cape, Norwegian **Nordkapp** a cape on N Magerøy I, N Norway, 96km/60mi NE of Hammerfest. It is considered to be the most northerly point in Europe.

North Carolina POP (1990) 6.8m, a state in SE USA, divided into 100 counties. AREA 136 407sq km/52 669sq mi. It is bounded E by the Atlantic Ocean. North Carolina is known as 'Tar Heel State' of 'Old North State'. PHYSICAL DESCRIPTION crossed by the Roanoke and Yadkin (becomes the Pee Dee) rivers; highest point is Mt Mitchell (2 037m); off the coast lies a chain of coastal islands with constantly shifting sand dunes, enclosing several lagoons; sandy beaches attract many tourists; the mainland coastal strip is flat and swampy; inland, this low land gives way to the rolling hills of the Piedmont, the fast-flowing rivers of which provide hydroelectric power for manufacturing industries; in the W lie the Blue Ridge and Great Smoky Mts; there are four national forests. HISTORY unsuccessful settlement made on Roanoke I in the 1580s; formed part of the Carolina grant given by Charles II in 1663; named North Carolina in 1691; became a royal province in 1729; twelfth of the original 13 states to ratify the Constitution in 1789; withdrew from the Union in 1861 following the Mecklenburg Declaration of Independence; slavery was abolished in 1865; readmission to the Union in 1868. CAPITAL Raleigh. CHIEF TOWNS Charlotte, Greensboro, Winston-Salem, Durham, Asheville. ECONOMY grows 40% of all US tobacco; cotton; silk goods, synthetic fibres; furniture; electrical machinery; chemicals; feldspar, mica, and lithium are mined; corn, soya beans, peanuts; hogs; poultry.

Northcliffe, 1st Viscount see HARMSWORTH, ALFRED.

North Dakota POP (1990) 638 000, a sparsely-populated state in N central USA, divided into 53

---

counties. AREA 183 111sq km/70 702sq mi. It is known as the 'Sioux State' or 'Flickertail State'. PHYSICAL DESCRIPTION crossed by the Missouri R; the Red R follows the E state border; the highest point is White Butte (1 069m); the Badlands area of fossil deposits is in the SW; conditions generally in the W are semi-arid; cultivation here is possible only in the river valleys, the remainder being covered in short prairie grasses on which cattle graze; the E region is a flat, fertile plain covered almost entirely by crops; there are several Native American reservations. HISTORY first explored by the French in the 18c; became part of the USA in the 1803 Louisiana Purchase; included in Dakota Territory in 1861; separated from South Dakota to become the 39th state admitted to the Union in 1889. CAPITAL Bismarck. CHIEF TOWNS Fargo, Grand Forks, Minot. ECONOMY spring wheat, barley, sunflowers, flaxseed (nation's leading producer of all these crops); also a major cattle state; oil in the NW and lignite coal in the W; food processing; machinery.

North Downs Way a long-distance footpath in S England, length 227km/141mi. It follows the crest of the North Downs from Farnham to Dover.

north-east — *noun* the direction midway between north and east or any part of the earth, a country, etc lying in that direction. — *adj.* **1** in the north-east. **2** from the direction of the north-east: *a north-east wind.*

northeaster *noun* a wind blowing from the north-east.

north-easterly *adj., adv.* from the north-east.

north-eastern *adj.* to the north-east.

Northeast Passage a shipping route through the S Arctic Ocean along the N coast of Europe and Asia, connecting the Atlantic and Pacific Oceans. Its crossing was first attempted in 1550, but it was not travelled successfully until 1878–9.

northerly — *adj.* **1** *said of a wind, etc* coming from the north. **2** looking, lying etc towards the north. — *adv.* to or towards the north. — *noun* (PL. **northerlies**) a northerly wind.

northern *adj.* **1** of or in the north. **2** facing or directed towards the north.

Northern Donets *or* **Severskiy Donets** *or* **Donets** the chief tributary of the R Don, Ukraine and Russia. The river is 1 010km/628mi long.

northerner *noun* a person who lives in or comes from the north, especially the northern part of England or of the USA.

Northern Ireland *or* **Ulster** POP (1992e) 1.6m, a constituent division of the United Kingdom of Great Britain and Northern Ireland, traditionally divided into six counties. For the purposes of local government it comprises 26 districts. AREA 14 120sq km/5 450sq mi (including 663sq km/256sq mi of inland water). CAPITAL Belfast. CHIEF TOWNS Londonderry, Lisburn, Ballymena, Armagh. TIME ZONE GMT. The chief religions are Roman Catholicism (28%), Presbyterianism (23%), and the Protestant Church of Ireland (19%). OFFICIAL LANGUAGE English. CURRENCY the pound sterling. PHYSICAL DESCRIPTION Northern Ireland occupies the NE part of Ireland, and is centred on Lough Neagh; to the N and E are the Antrim Mts; the Mourne Mts are in the SE. CLIMATE a temperate and maritime climate, wetter in the W; average January temperature is 2°C; July temperatures often rise to 18°C. HISTORY AND GOVERNMENT a separate parliament to the rest of Ireland was established in 1920, with a House of Commons and a Senate; there is a Protestant majority in the population, generally supporting political union with Great Britain; many of the Roman Catholic minority look for union with the Republic of Ireland; violent conflict between the communities broke out in 1969, leading to the establishment of a British army peace-keeping force; sectarian murders and bombings continued both within and outside the province; as a result of the disturbances, parliament was abolished in 1973; powers are now vested in the UK Secretary of State for Northern Ireland; formation of a 78-member Assembly in 1973; replaced by a Constitutional Convention in 1975; Assembly reformed in 1982, but Nationalist members did not take their seats; under the 1985 Anglo-Irish agreement, the Republic of Ireland was given a consultative role in the government of Northern Ireland; all Northern Ireland MPs in the British Parliament resigned in protest in 1986; the agreement continued to attract controversy in the late 1980s; direct negotiations between the political parties took place in Belfast in 1991 and 1992; Downing St Declaration by UK and Irish governments in 1993. ECONOMY agriculture; linen; shipbuilding; textiles; engineering; chemicals; service industries; the economy has been affected by the sectarian troubles since 1969. NOTABLE FEATURE Giant's Causeway.

Northern Ireland Office a government department established in London in 1972 by the Northern Ireland (Temporary Provisions) Act. This allows direct rule of Northern Ireland by the UK parliament in Westminster. It is headed by the Secretary of State for Northern Ireland.

northern lights (the northern lights) the aurora borealis.

northernmost *adj.* situated furthest north.

Northern Territory POP (1991e) 168 000, an Australian mainland territory covering about a sixth of the continent. AREA 1 346 200 sq km/ 520 000 sq mi. It is bordered N by the Arafura Sea and the Gulf of Carpentaria. PHYSICAL DESCRIPTION most of the territory lies within the tropics; from Arnhem Land in the N the land rises S to the Macdonnell Ranges, reaching 1 524m at Mt Liebig; there is good pasture land in the N and NE but the S is largely flat and arid; the major rivers in the N are the Victoria, Daly, South Alligator, East Alligator, McArthur, and Roper; rivers in the interior flow only after heavy rain; there are many Aboriginal settlements and Aboriginal art can be found throughout the area. HISTORY became part of New South Wales in 1824; annexed by South Australia in 1863; transferred to Federal Government control in 1911; achieved self-government in 1978. MAIN ISLANDS Groote Eylandt, Melville, Bathurst. CAPITAL Darwin, the chief port. CHIEF TOWNS Alice Springs, Katherine, Nhulunbuy. ECONOMY prawns; beef cattle; bauxite, gold, copper, uranium. NOTABLE FEATURE Ayers Rock in the Uluru National Park.

North German Confederation the state system and constitutional arrangement created in 1866 by Prussian Minister-President Bismarck, following the Prussian defeat of Austria and the dissolution of the German Confederation. Utterly dominated by Prussia, the new Confederation was itself dissolved with the creation of the German Empire (1871).

North Island POP (1991) 2.6m, the smaller but more densely populated of the two major islands of New Zealand, separated from South I by the Cook Strait. AREA 114 834sq km/44 326sq mi. PHYSICAL DESCRIPTION irregularly shaped with a long peninsula projecting NW, the island has several mountain ranges; the highest volcanic mountain is Ruapehu (2 797m) and L Taupo, the largest of New Zealand's lakes, lies in a crater to the N of Ruapehu; there are many hot springs in the N central area, and fertile plains in the coastal areas. Most of New Zealand's native Maori population live on North I; 15 000sq km/5 800sq mi of Maori land is under protection, either farmed as corporate enterprises or planted in forest. CHIEF TOWNS Wellington (capital of New Zealand), Auckland, Napier, Hastings, New Plymouth, Palmerston North. ECONOMY citrus and subtropi-

cal fruit; wine; farming; horse breeding; coal; natural gas (in the centre); mineral spas and health resorts; most industry is in the S.

North Korea, official name **Democratic People's Republic of Korea**, Korean **Choson Minjujuui In'min Konghwaguk** POP (1992e) 22.6m, a socialist state in E Asia, in the N half of the Korean Peninsula. AREA 122 098sq km/ 47 130sq mi. It is divided into nine provinces and is bordered N by China, NE by Russia, W by Korea Bay and the Yellow Sea, and E by the Sea of Japan. It is separated from South Korea to the S by a demilitarized zone of 1 262sq km/487sq mi. CAPITAL Pyongyang. CHIEF TOWNS Chongjin, Sinuiju, Wonsan, Kaesong. TIME ZONE GMT +9. OFFICIAL LANGUAGE Korean. The traditional religions are Buddhism and Confucianism, but religious activities are now minimal. CURRENCY the won. PHYSICAL DESCRIPTION lies on a high plateau occupying the N part of a mountainous peninsula which projects SE from China; many areas rise to over 2 000m; the plateau falls NW to the Yalu R Valley; lower mountains and foothills in the S descend to narrow coastal plains in the E and wider coastal plains in the W. CLIMATE temperate, with warm summers and severely cold winters; rivers freeze for 3–4 months, and ice blocks harbours; daily temperatures at Pyongyang in the W range from –3°C to –13°C in Jan, and from 20°C to 29°C in Jul–Aug; average rainfall in Pyongyang ranges between a minumum of 11mm in Feb and a maximum of 237mm in Jul. HISTORY the Korean Peninsula was conquered by the Chinese in 1392; formally annexed by Japan in 1895; with the downfall of the Japanese in 1945, Korea was occupied by Soviet troops from the N and US troops from the S, both meeting along latitude 38°N; the Korean War took place from 1950 until 1953; a demilitarized zone was established in 1953; reunification talks in 1980 were broken off by North Korea; summit talks with South Korea in 1990; Western nations were concerned in the early 1990s by North Korea's secret development of nuclear weapons. GOVERNMENT governed by a Supreme People's Assembly of 655 members, elected every four years; power lies in the hands of the Korean Workers' (Communist) Party,

North Korea

which elects a Central Committee, and whose leader is the President. ECONOMY traditionally agricultural on low coastal zones in the E and W; extensive destruction during the Korean War, but rapid recovery with Soviet and Chinese aid; Western technology and increased military spending in the 1970s resulted in considerable overseas debts; machine building; chemicals; mining; metallurgy; textiles; food processing; coal, phosphates, iron, magnesium, tungsten, copper, lead, zinc; c.48% of the workforce is employed in agriculture, generally on large-scale collective farms; rice, maize, vegetables, wheat, barley, rape, sugar, millet, sorghum, beans, tobacco; livestock; timber; fishing.

North Land *or* **Nicholas II Land**, Russian **Severnaya Zemlya**, formerly **Zemlya**

Imperatora an uninhabited archipelago in the Arctic Ocean, lying N of the Taymyr Peninsula, N Siberia, Russia. AREA 37 001sq km/ 14 282sq mi. It separates the Laptev Sea in the E from the Kara Sea in the W. There are glaciers on the larger islands.

north-north-east a direction midway between north and north-east.

north-north-west a direction midway between north and north-west.

North Pole (the North Pole) the northernmost point of the Earth's axis of rotation, at 90°N, longitude 0°, lying beneath the Arctic Ocean.

Northrop, John Howard (1891–1987) US biochemist, born in Yonkers, New York. He discovered the fermentation process for the manufacture of acetone, and for his investigations of methods for producing purified enzymes and virus products, he shared the 1946 Nobel Prize for Chemistry with Wendell Stanley and James Sumner. He became professor at the University of California at Berkeley in 1949.

North Sea the arm of the Atlantic Ocean between the continent of Europe and the UK, stretching S from the Shetland Is to the Straits of Dover. The sea is bounded by the UK, Norway, Denmark, the Netherlands, Germany, Belgium, and France. AREA 520 000sq km/201 000sq mi; length c.950km/600mi; maximum width 650km/400mi. Lying on a wide continental shelf, it is generally shallow as a result of banks running across from the Yorkshire coast (eg Dogger Bank) and the seafloor is irregular. It reaches a maximum depth of 660m near the Norwegian coast. High tides sometimes cause flooding in E England and the Netherlands. Important fishing grounds have been the subject of territorial disputes between Iceland and the UK and these led to the Cod Wars of the 1960s and 1970s. There is extensive offshore oil and gas exploitation.

Northumb. *abbrev.* Northumberland.

Northumberland POP (1992e) 307 000, a county in NE England, divided into six districts. AREA 5 032sq km/1 942sq mi. It is bounded N by Scotland, E by the North Sea, SE by Tyne and Wear, and W by Cumbria. PHYSICAL DESCRIPTION the Pennines lie in the W; the Cheviots form part of the NW border; Northumberland rises in the N to 755m at The Cheviot; drained by the Tweed, Tyne, Blyth, Wansbeck, Coquet, Aln, and Till rivers; Holy I and the Farne Is lie off the coast; Kielder Water is an artificial lake, created in 1982. CHIEF TOWNS Newcastle upon Tyne (administrative centre), Morpeth, Berwick-upon-Tweed, Hexham, Blyth, Alnwick. ECONOMY sheep; barley, oats; fishing; forestry; coal. NOTABLE FEATURES many Roman remains, the most famous of which is Hadrian's Wall; castles at Alnwick and Bamburgh.

Northumberland National Park a national park in NE England, established in 1956. It is bounded S by Hadrian's Wall and N by the Cheviot Hills. AREA 1 031sq km/398sq mi.

Northumbria the largest kingdom of the Anglo-Saxon heptarchy, which in the 7c was pre-eminent in Britain both N and S of the Humber, and in the 8c contained monasteries with a European-wide reputation for sanctity and learning. The kingdom came to an end in 876, and by the 12c Northumbria was equivalent to the earldom or county of Northumberland.

northward *or* **northwards** *adv.*, *adj.* towards the north.

north-west — *noun* the direction midway between north and west or any part of the earth, a country, etc lying in that direction. — *adj.* **1** in the north-west. **2** from the direction of the north-west: *a north-west wind.*

northwester *noun* a wind blowing from the north-west.

north-westerly *adj., adv.* from the north-west.

north-western *adj.* to the north-west.

Northwest Frontier POP (1985e) 12.3m, a federal province of Pakistan. AREA 74 521sq km/ 28 765sq mi. It is bounded W and S by Afghanistan, and N by India. The R Indus crosses the province, which is linked to Afghanistan by the strategically-important Khyber Pass. HISTORY a province of British India (1901–47); in the 1980s many refugees fled here from Afghanistan. The population is mainly made up of Pathans. CAPITAL Peshawar. ECONOMY livestock; grains, tobacco, fruit.

Northwest Ordinance of 1787 an Act of the American Continental Congress to establish procedures by which newly-settled Western territories entering the American union could have political equality with the original states. It was one of several Northwest Ordinances passed in 1784–7.

Northwest Passage a route through the S Arctic Ocean, Arctic Archipelago, N Canada, and along the N coast of Alaska. From the 16c attempts were made to find this Atlantic–Pacific sea route, but it was not traversed until 1903–6, by Roald Amundsen. The first commercial ship, an ice-breaking tanker, completed the route in 1969. Canadian sovereignty is disputed by the USA and other countries, who view the route as an international waterway.

Northwest Territories POP (1991) 58 000, a Canadian territory extending over the N of Canada, consisting of the Arctic islands, the islands in Hudson and Ungava Bays, and the land between Hudson Bay and the Yukon Territory. Two thirds of the sparsely-populated territory are nomadic Native Americans and Inuit. AREA 3 426 320sq km/1 322 902sq mi. PHYSICAL DESCRIPTION lakes include the Great Slave and Great Bear; the Mackenzie R runs NW through the territory; much of the W is treeless. HISTORY the land held by the Hudson's Bay Company (Rupert's Land and North West Territory) was changed to the present name on entering the Canadian Federation in 1870; a 1992 referendum approved the creation of the Inuit autonomous homeland of Nunavut. GOVERNMENT governed by a Commissioner and an elected 24-member Legislative Assembly. CAPITAL Yellowknife. ECONOMY mining (lead, zinc, gold); handicrafts; fur products; fishing; oil; tourism. Two thirds of the sparsely-populated territory are nomadic Native Americans and Inuit.

North Yemen see YEMEN.

North York Moors a national park in North Yorkshire and Cleveland, England, established in 1952. It follows the coast N of Scarborough to Hambleton Hills in the W; the coast is characterized by headlands and sandy beaches. The interior consists of open moorland and wooded valleys. NOTABLE FEATURES Mount Grace Priory; Rievaulx Abbey; Byland Abbey. AREA 1 432sq km/553sq mi.

North Yorkshire see YORKSHIRE, NORTH.

Norway, Norwegian **Norge**, official name **Kingdom of Norway**, Norwegian **Kongeriket Norge** POP (1992e) 4.3m, a kingdom in NW Europe, occupying the W part of the Scandinavian peninsula, divided into 19 counties (*fylker*). AREA 323 895sq km/125 023sq mi. It is bounded N by the Arctic Ocean, E by Sweden, Finland, and Russia, W by the North Sea and Norwegian Sea, and S by the Skagerrak. The Norwegian kingdom includes the dependencies of Svalbard and Jan Mayen (Arctic) and Bouvet I, Peter I Island, and Queen Maud Land (Antarctic). CAPITAL Oslo. CHIEF TOWNS Bergen, Trondheim, Stavanger, Kristiansand. TIME ZONE GMT +1. Most of the population is of Nordic descent, and there is a Lapp minority in the far N; the chief religion is Evangelical-Lutheran. OFFICIAL LANGUAGE Norwegian, in the varieties of Bokmål and Nynorsk. CURRENCY the krone. PHYSICAL DESCRIPTION a mountainous country, with the Kjölen Mts forming the N part of the boundary with Sweden, the Jotunheimen range in S central Norway, and extensive plateau regions, especially in the SW and centre; much of the interior rises above 1 500m; there are numerous lakes, the largest of which is L Mjøsa (368sq km/ 142sq mi); major rivers include the Glåma, Dramselv, and Lågen; the coastline is irregular with many small islands and long deep fjords; the two largest island groups, off the NW coast, are Lofoten and Vesterålen. CLIMATE an Arctic winter climate in the interior highlands, with snow, strong winds, and severe frosts; comparatively mild winter conditions exist on the coast; rainfall is heavy on the W coast; average annual rainfall at Bergen is 1 958mm; there are colder winters and warmer, drier summers in the S lowlands. HISTORY a royal race from Sweden settled itself in S Norway in the 7c; the establishment of Norway as a united kingdom was achieved in the 11c by St Olaf, whose successor, Cnut, brought Norway under Danish rule; united with Sweden and Denmark in 1389; Sweden was allowed to annex Norway in 1814 as a reward for its assistance against Napoleon; growing nationalism resulted in independence in 1905; declared neutrality in both World Wars, but was occupied by Germany in 1940–4; in 1992 an international ban on whaling was disregarded and the industry continued. GOVERNMENT a hereditary monarchy with limited powers; government is led by a Prime Minister; Parliament (*Storting*) comprises an Upper House (*Lagting*) and a Lower House (*Odelsting*); members are elected every four years. ECONOMY based on the extraction and processing of raw materials (oil, natural gas), using plentiful hydroelectric power; major export manufactures are paper and paper products, industrial chemicals, and basic metals; industries include shipbuilding, engineering, food processing, fishing, and tourism; less than 3% of the land is under cultivation, producing barley, hay, and oats; forest covers c.25% of the land. [from Old Norse *nordweg*, the northern way]

Norway

Norwegian — *adj.* of or belonging to Norway, its inhabitants, or their language. — *noun* **1** a native of Norway. **2** the language of Norway. [from Latin *Norvegia*, from Norse *northr*, north + *vegr*, way]

Norwegian Sea a North Atlantic sea bounded by the NW coast of Norway and the E coast of Iceland. Depths in the Norwegian Basin reach 1 240m, and in the Jan Mayen Fracture Zone, close to the continental shelf, 2 740m. It is generally ice-free because of the influence of the warm North Atlantic Drift. The sea provides rich fishing grounds.

Norwich POP (1992e) 128 000, the county town of Norwich district, Norfolk, E England. It lies near the confluence of the Yare and Wensum rivers, 160km/99mi NE of London. It was a major textile-producing town in the 16c–17c, and is today the provincial centre of the largely agricultural region of East Anglia. The North Sea is reached via the R Yare and Great Yarmouth (32km/20mi E). NOTABLE FEATURES Norman cathe-dral (1096); Church of St Peter Mancroft (1430–55); Guildhall (15c).

Nos. *or* **nos.** *abbrev.* numbers.

nose — *noun* **1** in humans and many other vertebrates, the organ above the mouth that acts as an air passage and is responsible for the sense of smell (olfaction). **2** the sense of smell. **3** (**a nose for something**) a faculty for detecting or recognizing something. **4** a scent or aroma, especially a wine's bouquet. **5** the front or projecting part of anything, eg a motor vehicle. **6** the nose as a symbol of inquisitiveness or interference: *poke one's nose into something / keep one's nose out of it.* — *verb trans., intrans. said of a vehicle or its driver* to move carefully and slowly forward: *nosed the car out of the drive / nosed slowly forward.*
— **blow one's nose** to clear one's nose of mucus by breathing sharply through it.
by a nose by a narrow margin.
cut off one's nose to spite one's face to act from resentment in a way that can only cause injury to oneself.
follow one's nose *colloq.* to go straight forward.
get up someone's nose *colloq.* to annoy or irritate them.
keep one's nose clean *colloq.* to avoid doing anything that might get one into trouble.
lead someone by the nose to dominate them completely.
look down *or* **turn up one's nose at someone** *or* **something** *colloq.* to show disdain for them.
nose about *or* **around** *colloq.* to pry.
nose something out 1 to discover it by prying; to track it down. **2** to detect it by smell. **3** *said of an animal* to sniff at or nuzzle it.
nose to tail *said of motor vehicles* moving slowly and close together in heavy traffic.
pay through the nose *colloq.* to pay an exorbitant price.
powder one's nose *euphemistic, said of a woman* to go to the lavatory.
put someone's nose out of joint *colloq.* to affront them by neglecting or frustrating them.
rub someone's nose in it *colloq.* to humiliate them by reminding them of a failure.
under one's very nose *said of something sought* prominently in front of one.
◇ The nose contains two openings, the nostrils, which are lined with mucous membrane and fine hairs that filter inhaled air, which is then moistened in the nasal cavity at the back of the nose before it passes to the lungs. Specialized sensory cells at the top of the nasal cavity react with airborne chemicals and relay impulses to the brain where the smell is identified. The nose also influences the tone of the voice.

nosebag *noun* a food bag for a horse, hung over its head.

nose band the part of a bridle that goes over the horse's nose.

nosebleed *noun* a flow of blood from the nose.

nose cone the cone-shaped cap on the front of a rocket, etc.

nosedive — *noun* **1** a steep and rapid plunge by an aircraft, with the nose pointed down. **2** a sharp plunge or fall. **3** a sudden drop, eg in prices. — *verb intrans.* to plunge or fall suddenly.

nosegay *noun* a posy of flowers. [from NOSE + GAY in the obsolete sense 'ornament']

nosey see NOSY.

Nosferatu (Nosferatu, Eine Symphonie Des Grauens) a German film directed by F W Murnau (1922). A version of the vampire myth, it is about real-estate clerk Hutter conducting business with the 'undead' Graf Orlok (played by Max Schreck) whose liking for Hutter's wife proves fatal.

nosh *slang* — *noun* food. — *verb intrans.* to eat. [from Yiddish]

nosh-up *noun slang* a hearty feed.

nostalgia *noun* **1** a yearning for the past. **2** homesickness. [from Greek *nostos*, homecoming + *algos*, pain]

nostalgic *adj.* yearning for the past.

nostalgically *adv.* with a yearning for the past.

Nostradamus, also called **Michel de Notredame** (1503–66) French astrologer, born in St Remy, Provence. He became a doctor of medicine in 1529, and after practising in several cities, set himself up as a prophet c.1547. He established a great reputation with his *Centuries* of predictions in rhymed quatrains (1555–8), expressed generally in obscure and enigmatical terms.

nostril *noun* either of the two openings in the nose, through which one breathes, smells, etc. [from Anglo-Saxon *nosthyrl*, from *nosu*, nose + *thyrel*, hole]

Nostromo a novel by Joseph Conrad (1904). It describes the smuggling of silver from a South American mine and how this affects the various characters, especially Nostromo, an Italian sailor.

nostrum *noun* **1** a patent medicine; a panacea or cure-all. **2** a pet solution or remedy, eg for political ills. [from Latin *nostrum*, our own (make, brand, etc)]

nosy *or* **nosey** *adj.* (**nosier, nosiest**) *derog.* inquisitive about the affairs, property etc of other people. [from NOSE]

nosy parker *derog. colloq.* a nosy person; a busybody.

not *adv.* (*with auxiliary and modal verbs, often shortened to* -*n't* *and joined to the verb*) **1** used to make a negative statement, etc: *that is not fair / those aren't right / why didn't they come?* **2** used with verbs of opinion, intention, etc to make the clause or infinitive following the verb negative: *I don't think he's right* (= I think he is not right). **3** used in place of a negative clause or predicate: *might be late, but I hope not.* **4** (indicating surprise, an expectation of agreement, etc) surely it is the case that: *haven't you heard? / lovely, isn't it?* **5** used to contrast the untrue with the true: *it's a cloud, not a mountain.* **6** barely: *with his face not two inches from mine.* **7** (**not a**) absolutely no: *not a sound.* **8** by no means: *not nearly enough / not everyone would agree.* **9** used with *only, just,* etc to introduce what is usually the lesser of two points, etc: *not just his family, but his wider public.*
— **not at all** don't mention it; it's a pleasure.
not that ... though it is not the case that: *not that I care.*
[a Middle English variant of NOUGHT]

notability *noun* being notable; a notable person or thing.

notable *adj.* **1** worth noting; significant. **2** distinguished. **3** (**notable for something**) famous on account of it: *Dundee is notable for its cake.* [from Latin *notabilis*, from *notare*, to note or observe]

notably *adv.* as something or someone notable, especially in a list or group: *several people, notably my father.*

notarial *adj.* **1** relating to notaries or their work. **2** *said of a document* drawn up by a notary.

notary *noun* (PL. **notaries**) (*also* **notary public**) a public officer with the legal power to draw up and witness official documents. [from Latin *notarius*, secretary, clerk]

notation *noun* **1** the representation of quantities, numbers, musical sounds, movements, etc by symbols. **2** any set of such symbols. [from Latin *notatio*, marking]

notch — *noun* a small V-shaped cut. — *verb trans.* to cut a notch in.
— **notch something up** to record it as a score; to achieve it.
[from Old French *oche* (*an oche* coming to be understood as *a notch*)]

note — *noun* **1** (*often* **notes**) a brief record made for later reference: *lecture notes / took a note of the number.* **2** a short informal letter. **3** a brief comment explaining a textual point, etc: *a footnote.* **4** a short account or essay. **5** a banknote. **6** a formal, especially diplomatic, communication. **7** attention; notice: *buildings worthy of note / take note of the warning.* **8** distinction; eminence: *women of note.* **9** a written symbol indicating the pitch and length of a musical sound; the sound itself. **10** *poetic* the call or cry of a bird or animal. **11** an impression conveyed; feeling; mood: *with a note of panic in his voice / end on an optimistic note.* — *verb* **1** (*also* **note something down**) to write it down. **2** to notice; to be aware of: *note this.*
— **compare notes** to exchange ideas and opinions.
strike the right note to act or speak appropriately.
[from Latin *nota*, mark, sign]

notebook *noun* **1** a small book in which to write notes. **2** *Comput.* a laptop computer small enough to fit into a briefcase.

notecase *noun* a case for banknotes; a wallet.

noted *adj.* well known: *noted for their generosity.*

notelet *noun* a folded piece of notepaper, often decorated, for short letters.

notepad *noun* a block of writing-paper for notes.

notepaper *noun* paper for writing letters.

noteworthiness *noun* a noteworthy or remarkable quality.

noteworthy *adj.* worthy of notice; remarkable.

nothing — *noun* **1** no thing; not anything. **2** very little; something of no importance or not very impressive. **3** the number 0. **4** absence of anything: *a shriek and then nothing.* — *adv.* not at all: *nothing daunted.*
— **be nothing to** ... to be much less than ...; to be trivial compared with ...: *that's nothing to what I saw.*
be nothing to do with someone or something 1 to be unconnected with them. **2** to be of no concern to them.
come to nothing to fail.
for nothing 1 free; without payment or personal effort. **2** for no good reason; in vain: *all that work for nothing.*
have nothing on someone or something *colloq.* to be not nearly as good, beautiful, etc as them.
have nothing to do with someone *or* **something 1** to avoid them. **2** to be unconnected with them. **3** to be of no concern to them.
like nothing on earth *colloq.* **1** grotesque. **2** frightful.
make nothing of someone *or* **something** not to understand.
mean nothing to someone 1 to be incomprehensible to them. **2** to be unimportant to them.
nothing but ... *usually said of something unwelcome* only ...; merely ...: *nothing but trouble.*
nothing doing *colloq.* **1** an expression of refusal. **2** no hope of success.
nothing for it but to ... no alternative except to ...: *nothing for it but to own up.*
nothing if not ... primarily ...; above all ...; very ...: *nothing if not keen.*
nothing like ... by no means: *nothing like good enough.*
nothing like someone or something not at all like them.
nothing much very little.
nothing short of *or* **or less than** ... **1** downright ...; absolute ...: *they were nothing less than criminals.* **2** only: *will accept nothing less than an apology.*
nothing to it *or* **in it** straightforward; easy.
think nothing of something to regard it as normal or straightforward.
think nothing of it it doesn't matter; there is no need for thanks.

to say nothing of ... as well as ...; not to mention...

nothingness *noun* the state of being nothing or of not existing; emptiness.

notice — *noun* **1** an announcement displayed or delivered publicly. **2** one's attention: *something has come to my notice / it escaped their notice.* **3** a warning or notification given, or before leaving, or dismissing someone from, a job: *give in one's notice / give notice of one's intentions / will continue until further notice.* **4** a review of a performance, book, etc. — *verb trans.* **1** to observe. **2** to remark on.
— **at short notice** with little warning, time for preparation, etc.
take notice to take interest in one's surroundings, etc.
take notice of someone *or* **something** to pay attention to them; to heed them.
[from Old French, from Latin *notitia*, from *notus*, known]

noticeable *adj.* easily seen; clearly apparent.

noticeably *adv.* in a noticeable way; to a noticeable degree: *it has grown noticeably.*

notice-board *noun* a board on which notices are displayed.

notifiable *adj.* denoting any disease that, if diagnosed or even suspected, is required by law to be reported to public health authorities so that appropriate action can be taken to prevent its spread. Examples of notifiable diseases in the UK include AIDS, cholera, diphtheria, smallpox, and tetanus.

notification *noun* **1** an announcement or warning. **2** the act of giving this.

notify *verb trans.* (**notifies, notified**) (**notify someone of something**) to inform or warn them about it. [from Latin *notus*, known + *facere*, to make]

notion *noun* **1** an impression, conception, or understanding. **2** a belief or principle. **3** an inclination, whim or fancy. **4** (**notions**) *North Amer., esp. US* pins, needles, and other small items used in sewing. [from Latin *notio*, idea, notion]

notional *adj.* existing in imagination only; theoretical; hypothetical.

notochord *noun* *Zool.* a flexible rod-like structure, which strengthens and supports the body in the embryos and adults of more primitive animals belonging to the phylum Chordata, but in vertebrates is replaced by a spinal column before birth. [from Greek *notos*, back + *chorde*, string]

notoriety *noun* fame or reputation, usually for something disreputable.

notorious *adj.* famous, usually for something disreputable. [from Latin *notorius*, well known]

notoriously *adv.* famously, usually for something disreputable.

Notre Dame (de Paris) an early Gothic cathedral on the Ile de la Cité in Paris. It was commissioned by Maurice de Sully, Bishop of Paris, in 1159 and constructed over a period of two centuries (1163–1345). By the 19c it was derelict, and it was restored by Viollet-Le-Duc.

Nottingham, Anglo-Saxon **Snotingaham** *or* **Notingeham** POP (1981) 272 000; urban area 599 000, the industrial county town of Nottinghamshire, central England, situated in Nottingham district. It lies on the R Trent, 200km/124mi NW of London, and is connected to both the Irish and North Seas by canal. HISTORY founded by the Danes; developed an important lace and hosiery industry; became a city in 1897; the Civil War started here in 1642. NOTABLE FEATURES Nottingham Castle (17c); St Mary's Church (15c); Theatre Royal; Playhouse; nearby are Newstead Abbey (home of Byron) and Eastwood (home of D H Lawrence). [from Anglo-Saxon, village or home of the sons of Snot the Wise]

Nottinghamshire POP (1992e) 1m, a county in the R Trent basin of central England, divided into eight districts. AREA 2 164sq km/835sq mi. It is bounded N by South Yorkshire and Humberside, E by Lincolnshire, S by Leicestershire, and W by Derbyshire. PHYSICAL DESCRIPTION the Pennines are in the W; the remains of Sherwood Forest can be found in the SW; the county is drained by the R Trent. CHIEF TOWNS Nottingham (county town), Worksop, Newark, Mansfield. ECONOMY arable and dairy farming; coal; gypsum; limestone; textiles; chemicals. NOTABLE FEATURE the Dukeries.

Notts. abbrev. Nottinghamshire.

notwithstanding — prep. in spite of. — adv. in spite of that.

Nouadhibou, French **Port Etienne** POP (1988e) 59 000, the capital of Dakhlet-Nouadhibou region, Mauritania. It is situated at the N end of the Bay of Levrier and is the main seaport in Mauritania.

Nouakchott POP (1988) 393 000, the capital of Mauritania. It is situated near the Atlantic coast and was founded in 1960 on an important caravan route. A harbour is located 7km/4mi SW.

nougat noun a chewy sweet containing nuts, etc. [from French nougat, from Latin nux, nut]

nought noun 1 the figure 0; zero. 2 old use nothing; naught. [from Anglo-Saxon noht, from nowiht, from ne, not + owiht, aught]

noughts and crosses a game for two players with alternate turns, the aim being to complete a row of three noughts (for one player) or three crosses (for the other) within a square framework of nine squares.

Nouméa, formerly **Port de France** POP (1989e) 65 000, the seaport capital of New Caledonia. HISTORY became the capital in 1854 and was a US air base in World War II. NOTABLE FEATURE cathedral.

noun noun Grammar a word used as the name of a person, animal, thing, place, or quality. [from Latin nomen, name]
◇ Nouns that are names of people, places, days of the week, months, trade names, etc, are known as proper nouns. All other nouns are common nouns. These may be divided into groups: abstract nouns, words that refer to concepts, eg beauty, integrity; concrete nouns, words which refer to real things, eg father, dog, desk, beach; and collective nouns, words which refer to groups of people or animals, eg crowd, gang, herd, gaggle. Nouns which have a singular and plural form are known as countable nouns, eg boy/boys, man/men, beach/beaches. Nouns which have no plural form are known as uncountable nouns, eg furniture, happiness. Some nouns are both countable and uncountable, eg housing/housings, space/spaces, time/times. Mass nouns refer to substances which may be divided but which cannot be counted, eg meat, earth, water. Partitive nouns refer to parts of mass or uncountable nouns, eg a piece of meat, an item of furniture.

nourish verb trans. 1 to supply with food needed for survival and growth. 2 to encourage the growth of; to foster (an idea, etc). [from Old French norir]

nourishing adj., said of food affording nourishment.

nourishment noun something that nourishes; food.

nous noun 1 colloq. common sense. 2 Philos. the intellect. [from Greek nous, mind]

nouveau riche (PL. nouveaux riches) derog. a person who has recently acquired wealth but lacks the upper-class breeding to go with it. [French, = new rich]

nouvelle cuisine a simple style of cookery characterized by much use of fresh produce and elegant presentation. [French, = new cookery]

Nouvelle Vague, also known as **New Wave** a group of young French film directors of the late 1950s and 1960s, who wished to discard many of the conventional formulae of the cinema of their time.

Nov or **Nov.** abbrev. November.

nova noun (PL. **novae**) a faint star that suddenly becomes several thousand times brighter than normal, and remains so for a few days or weeks before fading again. Novae are believed to be formed by nuclear explosions involving binary stars that contain a white dwarf and a giant star. A nova explosion, unlike a supernova, does not destroy the star, and the phenomenon can recur. [from Latin nova stella, new star]

Novalis, pseudonym of **Friedrich Leopold von Hardenberg, Baron** (1772–1801) German Romantic poet, born in Oberwiederstedt, Saxony. He studied law, and became a government auditor in Weissenfels. Known as the 'prophet of Romanticism', he is best known for his Geistliche Lieder (1799, Sacred Songs) and Hymnen an die Nacht (1800, Hymns to the Night).

Nova Scotia POP (1991) 900 000, a province in SE Canada, bounded by the Atlantic Ocean (in the E, S, and W), the Bay of Fundy in the W, the Northumberland Strait in the N, and the Gulf of St Lawrence in the NE. AREA 55 490sq km/21 424sq mi. It includes Cape Breton I to the NE, separated by the Strait of Canso, 3km/1.8mi wide; the mainland and island are connected by a causeway. PHYSICAL DESCRIPTION Nova Scotia is a peninsula connected with the Canadian mainland by the isthmus of Chignecto; the coastline is deeply indented, with numerous bays and inlets; there are low hill ranges, and many lakes and small rivers; the Atlantic coast is generally rocky, while the E coast consists of fertile plains and river valleys. CHIEF TOWNS Halifax, Dartmouth, Sydney, Glace Bay, Truro, New Glasgow. HISTORY probably first visited by Vikings and European fishermen; settled by the French as Acadia in 1604–5; the mainland of the province was assigned to Britain in the Treaty of Utrecht (1713), Cape Breton I remaining French until 1763; British domination was established in 1749 by the foundation of Halifax as a military and naval base; in 1755 the original Acadian settlers were expelled; many United Empire Loyalists settled here after the American Revolution; Cape Breton I was a separate province from 1784, but was reincorporated into Nova Scotia in 1820; joined the Canadian federation in 1867. GOVERNMENT governed by a Lieutenant-Governor and an elected 52-member House of Assembly. ECONOMY dairy farming; fruit; fishing (especially lobster); timber; coal, gypsum, tin; tourism.

Novaya Zemlya a Russian archipelago in the Arctic Ocean, situated off the NW coast of Russia, between the Barents Sea to the W and the Kara Sea to the E. AREA 81 279sq km/31 374sq mi; length 960km/596mi. It consists of two large islands separated by a narrow strait, and numerous offshore islands. PHYSICAL DESCRIPTION glaciated land in the N gives way to tundra lowland in the S; the archipelago is an extension of the Ural Mts, rising to heights above 1 000m. The heavily indented W coast has allowed some settlement. There are copper, lead, zinc, and asphaltite deposits; the islands have also been used for thermonuclear testing.

novel[1] noun a book-length fictional story usually involving relationships between characters and events concerning them. [from Italian novella, short story, from Latin novellus, new]

novel[2] adj. new; original; unheard-of previously. [from Latin novellus, new]

novelette noun derog. a short, especially trite or sentimental novel.

novelist noun the writer of a novel.

novella noun a short story or short novel. [from Italian novella]

Novello, Ivor, originally **David Ivor Davies** (1893–1951) Welsh actor, composer, songwriter, and dramatist, born in Cardiff. He was a chorister at school, and his song 'Keep the Home Fires Burning' was one of the most notable of World War I. He appeared on the stage in London from 1921, and enjoyed great popularity. His most successful works were the 'Ruritanian' musical plays such as The Dancing Years (1939) and King's Rhapsody (1949).

novelty noun (PL. **novelties**) 1 the quality of being new and intriguing. 2 something new and strange. 3 a small cheap toy or souvenir. [from Old French novelete, from Latin novellitas, newness]

November noun the eleventh month of the year. [from Latin, = the ninth month, from novem, nine]

Novembergruppe a group of German Expressionist artists formed in Berlin in Nov 1918. Their aim was to bring art into contact with the workers, and they established the Workers' Council for Art in 1919. Artists associated with the group included the architect Walter Gropius, who went on to establish the Bauhaus.

novena noun (PL. **novenas**) RC Church a series of special prayers and services held over a period of nine days. [from Latin noveni, nine each, from novem, nine]

Novgorod POP (1991e) 234 000, **1** the capital of Novgorod oblast, NW Russia, lying on the R Volkhov, 6km/4mi from L Ilmen. The city, now the centre of an important agricultural area, was first known in the 9c as the capital of the Russian state. It was badly damaged during World War II. Since 1945 there have been major excavations of deep, waterlogged deposits; these revealed two-storied log cabin houses of the medieval town, arranged along timber roadways. NOTABLE FEATURES St Sophia's Cathedral (1045–50); Dukhov Monastery (12c). **2** an oblast in NW Russia with Novgorod as its capital.

novice noun 1 a beginner. 2 a person who has recently joined a religious community but not yet taken vows; a probationary member. [from Latin novicius, from novus, new]

noviciate or **novitiate** noun 1 the period of being a novice in a religious community. 2 the novices' quarters in such a community.

Novi Sad, German **Neusatz** POP (1991) 265 000, the commercial and industrial capital of the province of Vojvodina, Yugoslavia, lying on the R Danube. It was formerly an important stronghold against the Turks. NOTABLE FEATURES Niška Banja health resort nearby; Bishop's Palace; Petrovaradin Castle; cathedral.

Novosibirsk, formerly **Novonikolaevsk 1** POP (1990e) 1.4m, the river-port capital of Novosibirsk oblast, S Siberia, Russia, lying on the R Ob. Founded in 1893, it is the leading economic centre of Siberia, with the Kuznetsk Basin coal and iron deposits nearby. There are also many educational and cultural institutions in Novosibirsk; important scientific research is carried out in the satellite town of Akademgorodok. **2** an oblast in S Siberia, Russia, with the city of Novosibirsk as its capital.

now — adv. **1** at the present time or moment. **2** immediately. **3** in narrative then: he now turned from journalism to fiction. **4** in these circumstances; as things are: I planned to go, but now I can't. **5** up to the present: has now been teaching 13 years. **6** used conversationally to accompany explanations, warnings, commands, rebukes, words of comfort, etc: now, this is what happened / careful, now! — noun the present time. — conj. (**now that**) because at last; because at this time: now we're all here, we'll begin.

— **any day** or **moment** or **time now** at any time soon.

as of now from this time onward.
for now until later; for the time being.

just now 1 a moment ago. **2** at this very moment.

now and then *or* **now and again** sometimes; occasionally.

now for ... used in anticipation, or in turning from one thing to another: *now for some fun! / now for your second point.*

now ... now ... one moment ... the next: *now crying, now laughing.*
[from Anglo-Saxon *nu*]

nowadays *adv.* in these present times. [from NOW + *a*, on + Anglo-Saxon *dæges*, of a day]

Nowell *noun* same as NOEL.

nowhere *adv.* in or to no place; not anywhere.
— **from** *or* **out of nowhere** suddenly and inexplicably: *they appeared from nowhere.*
get nowhere to make no progress.
in the middle of nowhere *colloq.* isolated; remote from towns or cities, etc.
nowhere near ... *colloq.* not nearly ...; by no means ...: *nowhere near fast enough.*

nowt *noun colloq., dialect* nothing. [Anglo-Saxon, as for NAUGHT]

noxious *adj.* harmful; poisonous. [from Latin *noxius*, harmful]

noxiously *adv.* in a noxious or poisonous way.

nozzle *noun* a fitting attached as an outlet to the end of a hose, etc. [a diminutive of NOSE]

Np *symbol Chem.* neptunium.

NPL *abbrev.* National Physical Laboratory.

nr *abbrev.* near.

NRA *abbrev.* National Rifle Association.

NSPCC *abbrev.* National Society for the Prevention of Cruelty to Children.

NSW *abbrev.* New South Wales.

NT *abbrev.* National Trust.

-n't *contr.* forming negatives of auxiliary and modal verbs: *haven't / daren't.*

nth *adj.* **1** denoting an indefinite position in a sequence: *to the nth degree.* **2** denoting an item or occurrence that is at many removes from the first in a sequence: *I'm telling you for the nth time.*

NTP *Physics* normal temperature and pressure, the former name for *standard temperature and pressure.*

NTS *abbrev.* National Trust for Scotland.

NTSC *abbrev.* National Television Systems Commission. a body responsible for the coding system of colour television introduced in the USA in 1954, and since widely used in the Americas and Japan for all 525/60 Hz transmission. See also PAL, SECAM.

Nu, U (1907–) Burmese politician, born in Wakema. At first a teacher, in 1934 he came to prominence through student political movements. Imprisoned by the British for sedition (1940), he was released by the Japanese and served in Ba Maw's puppet administration. In 1946 he became President of the Burmese Constituent Assembly, and was the first Prime Minister of the independent Burmese Republic (1948–56, 1957–8, 1960–2). He was overthrown by a military coup and imprisoned, but following his release (1966) he lived abroad and organized resistance to the military regime. In 1980 he returned to Burma (Myanma) to become a Buddhist monk.

NUAAW *abbrev.* National Union of Agricultural and Allied Workers.

nuance *noun* a subtle variation in colour, meaning, expression, etc. [from French *nuance*, shade, hue]

nub *noun* the central, most important issue; the crux. [from Old German *knubbe*, knob]

Nubian Desert a desert in NE Sudan. AREA c.400 000sq km/155 000sq mi. It lies between the Red Sea and the R Nile on a sandstone plateau. The ancient state of Nubia occupied the area from the First Cataract of the Nile to Khartoum.

Nubian monuments a group of monuments around L Nasser in Egypt, many of which were rescued from flooding during the construction of the Aswan High Dam. They include the 13c BC temples of Ramses II at Abu Simbel; Philae, the island of sanctuaries, sacred to Isis from the 4c BC; Amada, with its temples from the 15c and 13c BC; Kalabsha, built during the reign of Augustus; the 11c monastery of St Simeon; and 11c–12c Islamic cemeteries. The complex is a World Heritage site.

nubile *adj., said of a young woman* **1** physically mature and ready for marriage. **2** sexually attractive. [from Latin *nubilis*, from *nubere*, to veil oneself, marry]

nucellus *noun* (PL. **nucelli**) in seed-bearing plants, the tissue of which most of the ovule is composed, consisting of a mass of thin-walled cells. [a diminutive of Latin *nux*, nut]

nuclear *adj.* **1** having the nature of a nucleus: *the nuclear family.* **2** of or relating to atoms or their nuclei: *nuclear physics / nuclear fission.* **3** relating to or produced by the fission or fusion of atomic nuclei: *nuclear energy / nuclear weapons.*

nuclear accident an accident that occurs during the operation of a nuclear reactor or the production of nuclear weapons, or during the disposal of nuclear waste arising from either of these processes, eg the explosive leak of radioactivity from the nuclear reactor in Chernobyl, Ukraine, in Apr 1986.

nuclear disarmament a country's act of giving up its nuclear weapons.

nuclear energy, the energy that exists within the nuclei of atoms and is released during nuclear fission or nuclear fusion. It is used in nuclear reactors to generate electricity, and in nuclear weapons to cause widespread destruction. – Also called *atomic energy.*
◇ Nuclear energy can be produced in large amounts from a very small amount of fuel, and does not produce gases that contribute to the greenhouse effect. The main disadvantage of this form of energy is that it is difficult to store and dispose of the nuclear waste produced, and extremely costly to make an old nuclear reactor safe. There is also an associated but small risk that a nuclear accident may occur.

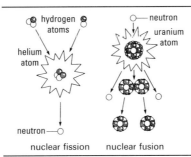

nuclear energy

nuclear family, the family consisting of mother, father, and children only. See also EXTENDED FAMILY.

nuclear fission a nuclear reaction in which a heavy nucleus of a radioactive element such as uranium or plutonium splits into two lighter nuclei (fission products), with the simultaneous release of large amounts of energy, and the emission of two or three neutrons that strike other nuclei and cause them to split in turn. The resulting chain reaction can be used as an energy source which is either harnessed in a controlled manner by absorbing excess neutrons, as in nuclear reactors for generation of electricity, or uncontrolled, as in the nuclear explosion of an atomic bomb.

nuclear-free *adj.* where nuclear weapons and nuclear energy are banned: *nuclear-free zones.*

nuclear fuel a naturally occurring or artificially manufactured material, usually an isotope of uranium or plutonium, that is used as the main source of nuclear energy in a nuclear reactor.

nuclear fusion a nuclear reaction in which two light atomic nuclei combine to form a heavier nucleus, with the release of large amounts of energy. This process provides a continuous source of energy in the Sun and other stars, and in hydrogen bombs, but has not yet been successfully harnessed for commercial power production. The possibility that nuclear fusion can take place at room temperature (*cold fusion*) is under investigation.

nuclear medicine *Medicine* the branch of medicine concerned with the use of radioactive isotopes to study, diagnose, and treat diseases.

nuclear power power, especially electricity, that is obtained from nuclear fission or nuclear fusion reactions, especially a controlled reaction that takes place within a nuclear reactor.

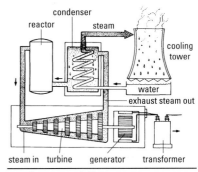

nuclear power station

nuclear reaction any reaction involving a change in an atomic nucleus, such as its spontaneous radioactive decay, nuclear fusion, or artificial bombardment with high-energy particles, as in nuclear fission. Nuclear reactions often result in the release of large amounts of energy and the emission of one or more particles, and they are distinct from *chemical reactions*, which only affect the electrons surrounding the nucleus.

nuclear reactor a device that produces nuclear energy by allowing nuclear fission to take place in the form of a controlled chain reaction, using the radioactive isotopes uranium-235, uranium-233, or plutonium-239 as fuel.
◇ In a *thermal reactor*, the splitting of uranium atoms results in the release of neutrons. In the centre or *core* of the reactor the *fuel rods* are surrounded by a *moderator* such as graphite which slows down the neutrons produced, thereby increasing the probability that they will collide with and split other uranium atoms, so releasing more neutrons and heat energy. The speed of the reaction is regulated by *control rods*, which absorb excess neutrons when lowered into the core of the reactor. The core of the reactor is enclosed in a pressure vessel, and heat generated by the fission of uranium fuel converts water into steam that drives a turbine linked to electricity generators.

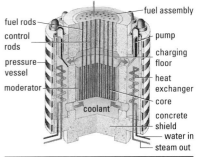

thermal nuclear reactor

Nuclear Test-Ban Treaty a 1963 treaty prohibiting the testing of nuclear weapons on or above the surface of the Earth, put forward by the USA, USSR, and UK as an indirect means of slowing down the proliferation of countries with nuclear weapons. Though it was quickly signed by more than 100 governments, it has been boycotted by two nuclear nations, France and China.

nuclear waste the radioactive waste material that is produced during the operation of a nuclear reactor (eg at a nuclear power station), the manufacture of nuclear weapons, or the mining and extraction of nuclear fuels such as uranium.

◇ Fast-breeder reactors produce large amounts of radioactive by-products with long half-lives, some taking thousands of years to decay into non-radioactive substances. During this time such material is extremely harmful to all living organisms with which it comes into contact. Nuclear waste that has been *reprocessed* in order to extract usable material is stored in strong metal canisters and buried deep within the Earth's crust, either below the seabed, or in deep disused mines or stable rock formations such as granite. All forms of disposal are a potential source of environmental pollution, eg in the event of an earthquake.

nuclear weapon *Mil.* a bomb, missile, or other weapon that derives its destructive force from the energy released during nuclear fission or nuclear fusion.

nuclear winter *Environ.* the environmental conditions that some scientists have suggested might follow a nuclear war, in which the large quantities of smoke and dust particles produced would prevent sunlight from reaching the Earth for several years, resulting in global darkness and extremely low temperatures, with catastrophic effects on plant and animal life.

nuclease *noun Biochem.* any enzyme that catalyses the splitting of the chains of molecules of nucleic acids such as DNA.

nucleate — *verb trans., intrans.* to form, or form into, a nucleus. — *adj.* having a nucleus.

nucleic acid either of the acids DNA or RNA, found in all living cells. [from NUCLEUS]

nucleolus *noun Biol.* a small spherical body, composed mainly of protein, together with DNA and RNA, found within the nucleus of most plant and animal cells. It produces a special type of RNA, known as *ribosomal RNA*, that is used in the manufacture of ribosomes (the main sites of protein synthesis) in the cytoplasm of the cell.

nucleon *noun Physics* a proton or neutron. [from NUCLEUS]

nucleonics *sing. noun* the study of the uses of radioactivity and nuclear energy.

nucleon number *Chem.* same as MASS NUMBER.

nucleotide *noun Biochem.* an organic compound consisting of a purine or pyrimidine base, a sugar molecule, and a phosphate group bonded together. DNA and RNA are composed of long chains of nucleotides.

nucleus *noun* (PL. **nuclei**) **1** *Physics* the tiny central core of an atom, which is extremely dense and accounts for almost the entire mass of the atom. It contains protons (positively charged particles) and, except in the case of hydrogen, neutrons (uncharged particles). The nucleus is surrounded by negatively charged electrons. **2** *Biol.* a large spherical or oval structure, surrounded by a double membrane (known as the nuclear envelope), in the cytoplasm of virtually all animal and plant cells. It contains the genetic material of the cell in the form of DNA, which becomes organized into chromosomes when the cell is ready to divide, but at other times consists of loose threads. The chromosomes carry the genes, and when the cell divides the nucleus splits into two parts, one for each of the two new daughter cells. Mammalian red blood cells and certain plant cells

do not have a nucleus. **3** a core round which things accumulate. [from Latin *nucleus*, kernel]

nuclide *noun Physics* one of two or more atoms that contain the same number of protons and the same number of neutrons in their nuclei, and so have the same atomic number and mass number.

NUCPS *abbrev.* National Union of Civil and Public Servants.

nude — *adj.* wearing no clothes; naked. — *noun* **1** a representation of a naked figure in painting, sculpture, etc. **2** someone naked. **3** the state of nakedness: *in the nude.* [from Latin *nudus*, naked]

nudge — *verb trans.* **1** to poke or push gently, especially with the elbow, to get attention, etc. **2** to push slightly or little by little. — *noun* a gentle prod.

nudism *noun* the practice of not wearing clothes, as a matter of principle.

nudist *noun* someone who wears no clothes, as a matter of principle.

nudity *noun* the state or practice of being nude or naked.

nuée ardente *Geol.* a turbulent incandescent cloud of hot gas and volcanic ash erupted from a volcano and travelling at great speed down its sides. [French, = burning cloud]

Nueva Esparta POP (1990) 281 000, a Venezuelan state consisting of Caribbean islands lying off the coast. AREA 1 149sq km/444sq mi. It consists of Margarita I, Coche, and several smaller islands. CAPITAL La Asunción. ECONOMY fishing; pearling; tourism.

Nuffield, William Richard Morris, 1st Viscount (1877–1963) English motor magnate and philanthropist, born in Worcestershire. He started in the cycle business in Cowley, Oxford, and became the first British manufacturer to develop the mass production of affordable (Morris) cars. In 1937 he founded Nuffield College, Oxford, and in 1943 established the Nuffield Foundation for medical, scientific, and social research.

Nuffield Radio Astronomy Laboratories *Astron.* the radio astronomy department of the University of Manchester, located at Jodrell Bank, Cheshire, UK. Its largest radio telescope is a 76-m fully steerable dish, now called the Lovell Telescope. It is also responsible for the MERLIN array telescope, with antennae throughout England, as well as an educational centre and a public planetarium.

nugatory *adj. formal* **1** worthless; trifling; valueless. **2** ineffective; futile. **3** invalid. [from Latin *nugae*, trifles]

nugget *noun* **1** a lump, especially of gold. **2** a small piece of something precious: *nuggets of wisdom.*

NUGMW *abbrev.* National Union of General and Municipal Workers.

nuisance *noun* **1** an annoying or troublesome person, thing, or circumstance. **2** *Legal* something obnoxious to the community or an individual, that is disallowed by law.

— **make a nuisance of oneself** to behave annoyingly.
[from Old French, from *nuire*, to injure]

NUJ *abbrev.* National Union of Journalists.

nuke — *verb trans. slang* to attack with nuclear weapons. — *noun* a nuclear weapon.

Nuku'alofa the port capital of Tonga. It is situated on Tongatapu I, 690km/430mi SE of Suva, Fiji. NOTABLE FEATURE Royal Palace (1867).

null *adj.* **1** legally invalid: *declared null and void.* **2** *Maths., said of a set* having no members; empty. [from Latin *nullus*, none]

Nullarbor Plain a vast plateau in South Australia and Western Australia, between the Great Victoria Desert and the Great Australian

Bight. It extends 480km/300mi W from Ooldea, South Australia to Kalgoorlie, Western Australia, and its maximum height is 305m. The plateau consists of sand dunes and sparse vegetation. Nullarbor National Park is on the coast.

null hypothesis *Maths.* a hypothesis consisting of a statement, which may be true or false, against which results can be tested, usually in order to disprove it.

nullification *noun* the act or process of nullifying or declaring invalid.

nullify *verb trans.* (**nullifies**, **nullified**) **1** to cause or declare to be legally invalid. **2** to make ineffective; to cancel out. [from Latin *nullus*, of no account + *facere*, to make]

nullity *noun* the status of being null and void.

NUM *abbrev.* in the UK, the National Union of Mineworkers, a union formed in 1945 when 41 mineworkers' organizations joined together, though each branch still controls its own funds. Arthur Scargill, who had introduced 'flying pickets' during the 1972 six-week strike and had helped to organize the 1973 national overtime ban which forced Edward Heath to impose a three-day working week and call a general election in 1974, succeeded Joe Gormley as NUM President in 1982. Determined to safeguard miners' jobs and prevent the closure of uneconomic pits planned by National Coal Board President Ian MacGregor, Scargill led a year-long national strike in 1984–5, which involved much violence and hardship and resulted in the mineworkers' unity nationwide being destroyed. NUM membership, which was 800 000 in 1945, had decreased to 33 000 by 1993.

numb *adj.* **1** deprived completely, or to some degree, of sensation. **2** too stunned to feel emotion; stupefied: *numb with shock.* [from Middle English *nomen*, seized (ie with paralysis)]

number — *noun* **1** the means or system by which groups, sets, etc of individual things, etc are counted; a quantity calculated in units. **2** *Maths.* an arithmetical symbol, one or more of which can be used to represent a quantity or amount during such procedures as counting, measuring, and the performance of calculations. **3** a numeral or set of numerals identifying something or someone within a series: *telephone numbers.* **4** (followed by a numeral) the person, animal, vehicle, etc identified by the numeral: *number 21 is pulling ahead.* **5** a single issue of a magazine, etc. **6** a quantity of individuals. **7** an act or turn in a programme. **8** a piece of popular music or jazz. **9** *colloq.* an article or person considered appreciatively: *drives a white sports number.* **10** a group or set: *isn't one of our number.* **11** (**numbers**) numerical superiority: *by sheer weight of numbers.* **12** *Grammar* the property of expressing, or classification of word forms into, singular and plural. — *verb* (**numbered**, **numbering**) **1** to give a number to; to mark with a number. **2** to include: *I number her among my closest friends.* **3** to amount to: *a crowd / numbering about 500.*

— **any number of** ... many ...

one's days are numbered one is soon to suffer or die.

have someone's number *colloq.* to have a grasp of their real character or intentions.

one's number is up *colloq.* one is due for some unpleasant fate, especially death.

safety in numbers security or comfort afforded in difficult circumstances by the support of others.

without number more than can be counted; countless.
[from French *nombre*, from Latin *numerus*]

◇ *Natural* or *cardinal numbers*, ie 1, 2, 3, 4,..., are used for counting, and are always whole numbers. *Integers* include all the natural numbers (positive integers), zero, and the corresponding negative numbers, ie -1, -2, -3,.... The *rational numbers* are all the numbers that can be expressed in the form of a fraction m/n, where m and n are positive or negative integers. They include *proper fractions* (in which the numerator is less than the denominator, eg $\frac{3}{8}$) and *improper fractions* (in which the numerator is greater than the denominator, eg $\frac{8}{3}$). *Mixed numbers* are the sum of an integer and a proper fraction, eg $2\frac{1}{2}$. In *decimal fractions*, eg 0.345, the denominator is a power of 10. *Irrational numbers* are all real numbers that cannot be expressed as fractions, eg $\sqrt{2}$, π, and can never be given an exact value. *Real numbers* are all numbers that do not contain an *imaginary number* (a square root of a negative number).

number-crunching *noun colloq.* the performing of vast and complex mathematical calculations on a computer.

numberless *adj.* too many to count; innumerable.

number one — *colloq., ironic* oneself. — first; of primary importance: *give it number-one priority.*

number plate one of the two plates at the front and rear of a motor vehicle, bearing its registration number.

Numbers, Book of a book of the Hebrew Bible and Old Testament, the fourth book of the Pentateuch, entitled in the Hebrew text 'In the Wilderness' or 'And He Spoke', but called 'Numbers' in Greek tradition because of the census of the tribes recorded in the first chapters. It describes the wilderness wanderings of Israel after the Exodus, starting with the preparations for leaving Sinai, and including the journeys to Kadesh-barnea and to Transjordan prior to the entry into Canaan. The narrative has Moses as its dominant character, and also contains much information on ritual and law.

Number Ten *Brit. colloq.* 10 Downing Street, the official home of the Prime Minister.

number theory *Maths.* the branch of mathematics that is concerned with the abstract study of the relationships between and properties of positive whole numbers.

numbly *adv.* in a numb or paralysing manner.

numbness *noun* a numb or stupefied state.

numbskull see NUMSKULL.

numeracy *noun* being numerate; ability with numbers.

numeral *noun* an arithmetical symbol used to express a number; a figure. [from Latin *numerus*, number]

numerate *adj.* **1** able to perform arithmetical operations. **2** having some understanding of mathematics and science. [from Latin *numerus*, number, in imitation of LITERATE]

numeration *noun* **1** the process of counting or numbering. **2** a system of numbering. [from Latin *numerare*, to count]

numerator *noun* the number above the line in a fraction. See also DENOMINATOR. [from Latin, numberer, from *numerare*, to count]

numerical *adj.* relating to, using, or consisting of, numbers: *numerical superiority.* [from Latin *numerus*, number]

numerical control *Engineering* the automatic control of a machine tool by means of a computer (formerly by data stored on punched cards).

numerically *adv.* as regards number; by means of numbers.

numerology *noun* the study of numbers as an influence on human affairs. [from Latin *numerus*, number]

numerous *adj.* **1** many. **2** *said of an assembly, body, etc* containing a large number of people. [from Latin *numerosus*, from *numerus*, number]

numerously *adv.* to a numerous extent; in great numbers.

Numidia the Roman name for the region in N Africa to the W and S of Carthage, which roughly corresponds to modern Algeria.

numinous *adj.* **1** mysterious; awe-inspiring. **2** characterized by the sense of a deity's presence. [from Latin *numen*, deity]

numismatic *adj.* relating to numismatics or the study of coins and medals.

numismatics *sing. noun* the study or collecting of coins and medals. [from Greek *nomisma*, coin]

numismatist *noun* a person who collects or studies coins and medals.

numskull *or* **numbskull** *noun colloq.* a stupid person. [from NUMB + SKULL]

nun *noun* a member of a female religious order living, in obedience to certain vows, in a community. [from Latin *nonna*]

nuncio *noun* (PL. **nuncios**) an ambassador from the pope. [from Latin *nuntius*, messenger]

Nuneaton POP (1981) 61 000; urban area 82 000, a town in Nuneaton and Bedworth district, Warwickshire, central England. It is situated on the R Anker, 13km/8mi NE of Coventry. NOTABLE FEATURE ruins of a Benedictine Nunnery (12c).

Nunn, Trevor (Robert) (1940–) English stage director, born in Ipswich. In 1968 he succeeded Peter Hall as artistic director for the Royal Shakespeare Company, for whom he directed many outstanding productions. During his directorship (1968–87) the RSC opened two new theatres in Stratford: The Other Place (1974) and The Swan (1986). Among Nunn's productions are the Lloyd Webber musicals *Cats, Starlight Express* (1984), *Chess* (1986) and *Aspects of Love* (1989), and he has also directed operas at Glyndebourne.

nunnery *noun* (PL. **nunneries**) a house in which a group of nuns live.

NUPE *abbrev.* National Union of Public Employees.

nuptial — *adj.* relating to marriage, or *Zool.* to mating. — *noun* (*usually* **nuptials**) a marriage ceremony. [from Latin *nuptialis*, from *nuptiae*, marriage]

nuptiality *noun* the marriage rate in a society.

NUR *abbrev.* National Union of Railwaymen.

Nuremberg, German **Nürnberg** POP (1991e) 491 000, a commercial and manufacturing city in Mittelfranken district, Bavaria, Germany. It lies on the R Pegnitz and the Rhine-Main-Danube Canal, 147km/91mi NW of Munich, and is the second largest city in Bavaria. HISTORY scene of Mastersingers' contests during the Renaissance; renowned as a centre of learning, declining only in the late 17c; annual meeting place of the Nazi Party after 1933; badly bombed in World War II; scene of German war criminal trials (1945–6). The painter Albrecht Dürer and the poet Hans Sachs were born here in 1471 and 1494 respectively. NOTABLE FEATURES Lawrence's Church (13c–15c); Imperial Castle; Academy of Arts, the oldest in Germany (1662).

Nuremberg Laws two racial laws promulgated (1935) in Nuremberg at a Reichstag meeting held during a Nazi Party Congress, the first formal steps in the process of separating off Jews and other 'non-Aryans' in Nazi Germany. By the first, those not of 'German or related blood' were deprived of German citizenship, and by the second, marriage and extra-marital relations between Germans and Jews were made illegal.

Nuremberg Trials proceedings held by the Allies in Nuremberg after World War II to try Nazi war criminals. An International Military Tribunal was set up (Aug 1945), and from November 1945 to October 1946, 21 Nazis were tried in person, including Goering and Ribbentrop (who were sentenced to death), and Hess (who was given life imprisonment).

Nureyev, Rudolf (Hametovich) (1938–93) Russian ballet-dancer, born in Irkutsk, Siberia. He became principal dancer with the Kirov Ballet in St Petersburg, but while on tour in 1961 he defected and obtained political asylum in Paris. In 1962 he made his début at Covent Garden, London, with Margot Fonteyn, whose regular partner he became. His emotional expressiveness made him one of the greatest male dancers of his time, in both classical and modern ballets, and he choreographed and danced for many European companies. He also appeared in films, including *Swan Lake* (1966) and *Valentino* (1977). He was artistic director of the Paris Opera (1983–9).

Nurmi, Paavo (Johannes) (1897–1973) Finnish track athlete, born in Turku. He won nine gold medals at three Olympic Games (1920–8), and set 22 world records at distances ranging from 1 500–20 000m. His first world record was in 1921, when he clocked 30 min 40.2 seconds for the 10 000m. He retired from racing in 1933. His statue stands outside the Helsinki Olympic Stadium.

Nürnberg see NUREMBERG.

Nurse the garrulous nurse-maid of Juliet in Shakespeare's *Romeo and Juliet*, who mediates between the young lovers.

nurse — *noun* **1** a person who looks after sick or injured people, especially in hospital. **2** a person, especially a woman, who looks after small children in a household. — *verb* **1** *trans.* to look after (sick or injured people) especially in a hospital. **2** *intrans.* to follow the career of a nurse. **3** *trans., intrans.* to feed (a baby) at the breast, or (of a baby) to feed at the breast. **4** *trans.* to hold with care: *gave him the bag of meringues to nurse.* **5** *trans.* to tend with concern: *was at home nursing a cold.* **6** *trans.* to encourage (a feeling) in oneself. [from Old French *norrice*, from Latin *nutrire*, to nourish]

nursemaid *noun* a children's nurse in a household.

nursery *noun* (PL. **nunneries**) **1** a place where children are looked after while their parents are at work, etc. **2** *old use* a room in a house reserved for young children and their nurse. **3** a place where plants are grown for sale. [from NURSE]

nurseryman *noun* a person who grows plants for sale.

nursery rhyme a short simple traditional rhyme for children.

◇ Most date from no earlier than the 18c; some celebrate contemporary personalities or events; some are 'counting-out' rhymes, chanted while selecting a 'victim' from a group. The earliest printed collections appeared in 1740 and 1780 and included 'Little Tommy Tucker', 'Ba, Ba, Black Sheep', 'Sing a Song of Sixpence', 'Who Killed Cock Robin', and 'Hush-a-bye Baby'.

nursery school a school for children aged between three and five.

nursery slopes *skiing* the lower gentle slopes used for practice by beginners.

nursing *noun* the branch of medicine which provides care for the sick and injured, the very young, and the very old, and assumes responsibility for the physical, social, and emotional needs of patients with the aim of restoring, maintaining, or promoting health.

◇ Nurses represent the largest single group of health workers. They do not have the authority to prescribe specific treatments or drugs, but carry out routine medical and surgical procedures under the supervision of a physician, either in a hospital, clinic, health centre or similar institution, or in the patient's home. They are also responsible for monitoring the effects of treatment. Many nurses specialize in particular subdisciplines, including midwifery, health visiting, intensive care, paediatric, psychiatric, geriatric, and dental nursing, as well as community health and social welfare.

nursing home a small private hospital or home, eg for old people.

nursing officer *Brit.* any of several grades of nurses having administrative duties.

nurture — *noun* care, nourishment, and encouragement given to a growing child, animal or plant. — *verb trans.* **1** to nourish and tend (a growing child, animal, or plant). **2** *trans.* to encourage the development of (a project, idea, feeling, etc). [from Old French *norriture*, from Latin *nutrire*, to nourish]

NUS *abbrev.* National Union of Seamen, National Union of Students.

NUT *abbrev.* National Union of Teachers.

nut *noun* **1** *Bot.* a dry fruit containing a single seed enclosed by a hard woody shell (the *pericarp*) that does not split open on ripening to release the seed, but is shed intact from the plant, eg acorn, hazelnut. Many nuts have edible kernels that are rich in fat and protein, and are cultivated as food crops. **2** popular name for any hard fruit that resembles this structure, eg coconut, walnut, almond. **3** a small usually hexagonal piece of metal with a hole through it, for screwing on the end of a bolt. **4** *colloq.* a person's head. **5** *colloq.* a crazy person. **6** a small lump: *a nut of butter.*
— **do one's nut** *colloq.* to be extremely angry or anxious.
for nuts *colloq.* (*after a negative*) at all: *can't sing for nuts.*
a hard *or* **tough nut to crack** *colloq.* a difficult problem to solve or an awkward person to deal with.
off one's nut *colloq.* mad, crazy.
[from Anglo-Saxon *hnutu*]

nutation *noun* **1** the act of nodding. **2** *Astron.* the irregular nodding or 'side-to-side' movement of the Earth's axis of rotation, caused by small changes in the gravitational pull of the Sun and Moon on the Earth. **3** *Bot.* the spiral growth pattern of the parts of some plants, eg climbing plants, especially the tips of the stems. **4** the periodic oscillation of a spinning top or gyroscope. [from Latin *nutare*, to nod]

nutcase *noun colloq.* a crazy person.

nutcracker *noun* **1** (*usually* **nutcrackers**) a utensil for cracking nuts. **2** a bird of the crow family that feeds on nuts and pine seeds.

Nutcracker, The (Shchelkunchik) ballet by Piotr Ilyich Tchaikovsky (1892), based on a version of E T A Hoffman's story *Der Nussknacker und der Maüsekönig* (The Nutcracker and the King of the Mice), and from which he arranged an orchestral suite (1892).

nuthatch *noun* a small bird that inhabits rocks and woodland in the northern hemisphere, and has a short tail and a sharp straight bill. It feeds on insects, and sometimes nuts, and hunts by walking 'head first' down tree trunks or rock faces.

nuthouse *noun colloq., offensive* a mental hospital.

nutmeg *noun* the hard aromatic seed of the fruit of an E Indian tree, used ground or grated as a spice. [from Middle English *notemugge*]

nutrient — *noun* any substance taken in by a living organism that acts as a source of energy and materials for growth, maintenance, and repair of tissues. — *adj.* nourishing. [from Latin *nutrire*, to nourish]

nutriment *noun* nourishment; food. [from Latin *nutrimentum*, from *nutrire*, to nourish]

nutrition *noun* **1** the process of nourishment. **2** the study of the body's dietary needs. **3** food. [from Latin *nutrire*, to nourish]

nutritional *adj.* relating to nutrition or nourishment.

nutritious *adj.* nourishing; providing nutrition.

nutritive *adj.* **1** nourishing. **2** relating to nutrition.

nuts *adj. colloq.* **1** insane; crazy. **2** (**nuts about** *or* **on someone** *or* **something**) infatuated with or extremely fond of them.

nuts and bolts essential or practical details.

nutshell *noun* the case containing the kernel of a nut.
— **in a nutshell** concisely or very briefly expressed.

nutter *noun colloq.* a crazy person.

nuttiness *noun* **1** a taste of nuts. **2** *colloq.* a crazy state or quality.

nutty *adj.* (**nuttier, nuttiest**) **1** full of, or tasting of, nuts. **2** *colloq.* crazy.

Nuuk *or* **Nûk**, Danish **Godthåb** *or* **Godthaab** POP (1990) 12 000, the capital and largest town of Greenland, situated on the SW coast. The Davis Strait lies to the W. Nuuk was founded in 1721. NOTABLE FEATURES radio and scientific installations; ruins of a 10c Norse settlement nearby.

nux vomica the seed of an E Indian tree, containing strychnine. [Latin, = vomiting nut]

Nuzi an ancient town in Upper Mesopotamia, E of the Tigris. It was a flourishing Hurrian community in the second millennium BC, with strong commercial interests.

nuzzle *verb trans., intrans.* (**nuzzle up to** *or* **against someone**) *usually said of animals* to push or rub them with the nose. [related to NOSE]

NV *abbrev.* Nevada.

NVQ *abbrev.* (in the UK) the National Vocational Qualification, a certificate of attainment of up to five grades by which employees can prove their level of competence. The National Council of Vocational Qualifications (NCVQ) was established in 1986 by the government to work with existing examining bodies and employers and create a national framework for the many different vocational qualifications available. In Sep 1992 General NVQs were introduced into schools and colleges.

NW *abbrev.* north-west; north-western.

NWT *abbrev.* Northwest Territories.

NY *or* **N.Y.** *abbrev.* New York.

Nyasa *or* **Malawi, Lake**, in Mozambique **Niassa** the third largest lake in Africa, lying in the S section of the Great Rift Valley, within Malawi and Mozambique and bordering Tanzania. AREA 28 500sq km/11 000sq mi. Navigation is possible over the whole lake. A World Heritage site, it is sometimes known as the 'Calendar Lake' because it is 365 miles long and 52 miles across at its widest point.

NYC *abbrev.* New York City.

Nyerere, Julius (Kambarage) (1922–) Tanzanian nationalist leader and politician, born in Butiama, L Victoria. After becoming a teacher at Makerere, and studying at Edinburgh, he returned and organized the nationalists into the Tanganyika African National Union (1954), of which he became President, and Chief Minister (1960). He became Prime Minister when Tanganyika was granted internal self-government (1961), and President on independence (1962–85). In 1964 he negotiated the union of Tanganyika and Zanzibar, as Tanzania. He tried to establish policies of socialism and self-reliance, but these failed and he retired.

nylon — *noun* **1** *Chem.* any of various strong elastic thermoplastics that are resistant to wear and chemicals, used to make textile fibres for durable fabrics, coatings, ropes, brushes, etc. **2** (**nylons**) *old use* a woman's nylon stockings. — *adj.* relating to such a material. [originally a trademark]

Nym an incorrigible rogue and thief, and associate of Falstaff, in Shakespeare's *The Merry Wives of Windsor*, who becomes a reluctant soldier in *Henry V.*

nymph *noun* **1** *Mythol.* a goddess inhabiting eg water or trees. **2** *poetic* a beautiful young woman. **3** *Zool.* the larval stage in the life cycle of certain insects, eg dragonfly, grasshopper, resembling a miniature version of the adult, but lacking wings and mature reproductive organs. The nymph develops directly into an adult without forming a pupa. [from Greek *nymphe*, nymph, bride]

Nymphenburg porcelain porcelain made at the Nymphenburg factory near Munich, which from 1753 produced fine table wares and figures. Its most celebrated modeller was Franz Anton Bustelli (1723–63), who made elegant Rococo miniature sculptures of stylized humans in contemporary dress.

nymphet *noun facetious* a sexually attractive and precocious girl in early adolescence. [from Old French *nymphette*, from Greek *nymphe*, nymph + feminine diminutive *-ette*]

nympho *noun* (PL. **nymphos**) *colloq.* a nymphomaniac.

nymphomania *noun* excessive sexual desire in women. [from Greek *nympho-* relating to brides]

nymphomaniac — *noun* a woman with excessive sexual desire. — *adj.* relating to or affected by nymphomania.

Nymphs in Greek mythology, beautiful young women who were associated with different aspects of nature. They were secondary divinities with limited powers who, although not immortal, could live for several centuries. They included water nymphs (Nereids, Naiads, and Oceanids), mountain nymphs (Oreads), and wood nymphs (Dryads).

NYO *abbrev.* National Youth Orchestra.

nystatin *noun Medicine* an antibiotic, produced by the bacterium *Streptomyces noursei*, that is used to treat fungal infections. [from *New York State* (where it originated) + *-in*]

Nyx *or* **Nox** *or* **Nux** in Greek mythology, a very ancient deity ('Night'), born of Chaos, and mother of various powers including Death, Sleep, the Hesperides, and the Moerae. In the Orphic religion, Night was the original first principle; she laid an egg from which sprang other gods.

NZ *abbrev.* New Zealand.

Nzambi *noun Relig.* a name for God in wide use throughout West Central Africa.

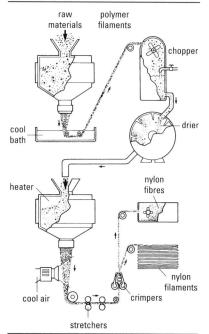

nylon production

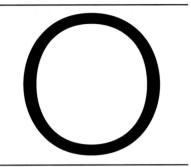

O¹ *or* **o** *noun* (PL. **Os, O's, o's**) **1** the fifteenth letter of the English alphabet. **2** zero; nought.

O² *or* **oh** *interj.* **1** (*usually* **oh**) used to express surprise, admiration, pleasure, anger, fear, etc. **2** used in addressing a person or thing, or in expressing a wish: *O God! / Oh for a bit of peace!*

O³ *abbrev.* **1** Ocean. **2** Old. **3** (*also* **o**) octavo.

O⁴ *symbol Chem.* oxygen.

O. *abbrev.* Ohio.

o' *prep.* **1** of. See also O'CLOCK. **2** on.

oaf *noun* a stupid or awkward person. [from Norse *alfr*, elf]

oafish *adj.* loutish, clumsy, idiotic.

oafishly *adv.* in an oafish way.

oafishness *noun* being oafish, oafish behaviour.

Oahu POP (1988e) 839 000, the third largest island in the US state of Hawaii. It lies in the Pacific Ocean, SE of Kauai, and forms part of Honolulu County. AREA 1 526sq km/589sq mi. It rises to 1 233m at Kaala. CHIEF TOWN Honolulu. ECONOMY sugar; fruit; tourism. There is a naval base at Pearl Harbor.

Oak, Gabriel the loyal shepherd in Thomas Hardy's *Far from the Madding Crowd*, who devotedly loves Bathsheba Everdene.

oak *noun* **1** any tree or shrub of the genus *Quercus*, found mainly in north temperate regions, including both deciduous species with lobed leaves, and evergreen species, usually with unlobed leaves. It produces fruit in the form of a round thin-shelled nut in a cup-shaped outer case, known as an acorn. **2** the hard durable wood of this tree, which is attractively grained, and widely used in building construction, furniture, and flooring. It was formerly used for shipbuilding. **3** (**the Oaks**) a race for three-year-old fillies run annually at Epsom. [from Anglo-Saxon *ac*]

oak-apple *noun* (*also* **oak-gall, oak-nut**) a ball-like growth on an oak caused especially by the eggs of certain insects.

oaken *adj. old use* made of oak.

Oakland POP (1990) 2.1m, the port capital of Alameda County, W California, USA, on the E shore of San Francisco Bay. It is linked to San Francisco by the San Francisco–Oakland Bay Bridge (1936). The city was founded in 1850. NOTABLE FEATURES observatory; art gallery; museums.

Oakley, Annie, originally **Phoebe Anne Oakley Moses** (1860–1926) American sharpshooter and Wild West performer, born near Woodland, Ohio. She married a sharpshooter and toured with him, later winning fame in Buffalo Bill's Wild West Show.

Oak Ridge POP (1990) 27 000, a town in Anderson County, E Tennessee, USA, on the R Clinch. It was founded by the US Government in 1942 to house workers developing the uranium-235 and plutonium-239 isotopes for the atomic bomb; the community was kept secret until after the first bombs were dropped in 1945. The town is a centre of atomic energy and nuclear physics research. NOTABLE FEATURE American Museum of Atomic Energy.

Oaks see CLASSICS.

oakum *noun* pieces of old rope untwisted and pulled apart, used to fill small holes and cracks in wooden boats and ships. [from Anglo-Saxon *acumba*, from *a-* away + *cemban*, to comb]

OAP *abbrev. Brit.* old age pensioner.

oar *noun* **1** a long pole with a broad, flat blade used for rowing a boat. **2** a rower.
— **put** *or* **stick one's oar in** *colloq.* to interfere or meddle, especially by offering one's own opinion when it is not wanted.
[from Anglo-Saxon *ar*]

oarfish *noun* a long ribbon-shaped fish widespread in tropical and warm temperate seas, up to 7m in length, and having an extremely slender body, a dorsal fin that extends the full length of the body, and no tail fin.

oarsman *or* **oarswoman** *noun* a man or woman who rows.

oarsmanship *noun* skill in rowing.

OAS *abbrev.* **1** Organisation de l'Armée Secrète (in Algeria). **2** Organization of American States.

oasis *noun* (PL. **oases**) **1** a fertile area in a desert where water is found and plants grow. **2** any place of rest or pleasure in the middle of hard work, problems, or trouble. [from Greek *oasis*, from Egyptian]

oast *noun* a kiln for drying hops. [from Anglo-Saxon *ast*, kiln]

oast-house *noun* a building with a cone-shaped roof containing several such kilns.

oat *noun* **1** (*also* **oats**) a cereal (*Avena sativa*) belonging to the grass family (Gramineae), thought to be native to the Mediterranean region, and now cultivated mainly in cool moist north temperate regions as a food crop. It tolerates a wide range of climates, and can grow where other cereals are unable to survive. The crushed or rolled grains are used as a feedstuff for animal livestock, and a relatively small proportion of the crop is now used as human food. Porridge oats and oatmeal (used in oatcakes, biscuits, etc) are produced from oat grains. The stalks of the plant are used as straw. **2** (**oats**) the seeds of this plant, used as a feedstuff for animal livestock, and also as human food.
— **off one's oats** *colloq.* having no appetite.
sow one's oats *or* **one's wild oats** *colloq.* to indulge in adventures, excessive drinking, promiscuity, etc during youth.
[from Anglo-Saxon *ate*]

oatcake *noun* a thin, hard, dry biscuit made from oatmeal.

oaten *adj.* made of oats.

Oates, Lawrence (Edward Grace) (1880–1912) English explorer, born in London. He joined the army and served in South Africa. In 1910 he joined Scott's Antarctic Expedition and was one of the party of five to reach the South Pole in 1912. On the return journey the explorers became weatherbound and Oates was lamed by severe frostbite. Convinced that his condition would fatally handicap his companions' prospect of survival, he walked out into the blizzard and sacrificed his life.

Oates, Titus (1649–1705) English conspirator and perjurer, born in Oakham, Rutland. He took Anglican orders, but was dismissed from his curacy for misconduct. In 1677 he fabricated the 'Popish Plot', allegedly to murder Charles II and establish Roman Catholicism in England. He feigned conversion to Catholicism, and for a while attended the Jesuit seminaries of Valladolid and St Omer. When the plot was made public (1678) he was considered a hero, but two years later he was found guilty of perjury, flogged, and imprisoned until the Revolution of 1688 set him free.

oath *noun* **1** a solemn promise to tell the truth, be loyal, etc, usually naming God as a witness. **2** the form of words used to take an oath. **3** a swear-word, obscenity, or blasphemy.
— **on** *or* **under oath** having sworn to tell the truth, eg in a court of law.
[from Anglo-Saxon *ath*]
◇ The traditional wording of an oath taken in a court of law is, 'I swear by Almighty God that the evidence which I shall give shall be the truth, the whole truth, and nothing but the truth'. As an alternative, it is possible to solemnly promise to tell the truth, and other traditional or religious practices may be recognized either in the wording of the oath taken, or in some associated ritual.

oatmeal *noun* oats ground into meal.

OAU *abbrev.* Organization of African Unity.

Ob, River the chief river in the W Siberian Lowlands, Russia. It is 3 650km/2 268mi long; with its chief tributary, the Irtysh, the length of the Ob increases to 5 570km/3 461mi, making it the world's fourth longest river. It is formed in the N foothills of the Altai Mts by the union of the Biya and Katun rivers. It flows generally NW and W to the mouth of the R Irtysh at Khanty-Mansiysk, turns N and divides into numerous channels to enter Ob Bay, an inlet of the Kara Sea. Although frozen for 5–6 months of the year, the Ob is an important transport route, with vast oil reserves within its basin.

ob. *abbrev. obiit* (Latin), he or she died.

Obad. *or* **Obad** *abbrev. Biblical* Obadiah.

Obadiah the uncontrollable servant of the Shandy family in Laurence Sterne's *Tristram Shandy*.

Obadiah, Book of, also called **Book of Abdias** one of the 12 so-called 'minor' prophetic writings of the Hebrew Bible and Old Testament, and the shortest book of the Hebrew Bible. Named after a prophet whose name means 'Servant of God', the work may have originated soon after the fall of Jerusalem (587/6 BC).

Oban POP (1981) 8 100, a port town in Argyll and Bute district, Strathclyde, W Scotland. It lies 97km/60mi NW of Glasgow. NOTABLE FEATURE McCaig's Tower (1897–1900).

obbligato — *noun* (PL. **obbligatos, obbligati**) a musical accompaniment forming an essential part of a piece of music, especially that played by a single instrument accompanying a voice. — *adj.* to be played with an obbligato. [from Italian *obbligato*, obligatory]

obduracy *noun* being obdurate, obstinacy.

obdurate *adj.* 1 hard-hearted. 2 hard to influence or change, especially morally. [from Latin *ob*, against + *durus*, hard]

obdurately *adv.* in a hard-hearted way.

OBE *abbrev. Brit.* Order of the British Empire, an award given to honour personal or professional excellence or services to the country.

obedience *noun* 1 the act or practice of obeying. 2 willingness to obey orders. [from Latin *obedientia*]

obedient *adj.* obeying, ready to obey.

obediently *adv.* in an obedient way.

obeisance *noun* a bow, act or other expression of obedience or respect. [from Old French *obeissance*]

obeli see OBELUS.

obelisk *noun* 1 a tapering, needle-like, usually four-sided, stone pillar. 2 *Printing* a dagger-shaped mark used especially for referring to footnotes. [from Greek *obeliskos*, small spit]
◊ Obelisks were frequently placed in and around temples and other public buildings in ancient Egypt, for religious or commemorative purposes. The most famous examples of Egyptian obelisks are Cleopatra's Needles (c.1475 BC), two massive granite pillars now located on the Victoria Embankment, London, and Central Park, New York.

belus *noun* (PL. **obeli**) 1 *Printing* a dagger-shaped mark used especially for referring to footnotes. 2 a sign used in ancient texts to mark passages which may not be by the original author of the text. [from Greek *obelos*, spit]

Oberon the fairy king, and husband of Titania, in Shakespeare's *A Midsummer Night's Dream*.

Oberpfälzer Wald the low NW section of the Bohemian Forest, between the Fichtelgebirge and the Bavarian Forest.

obese *adj.* very fat. [from Latin *obesus*, plump]

obesity *noun* the condition of someone who is overweight as a result of the accumulation of excess fat in the body.
◊ Obesity occurs when a person's energy intake as food exceeds his or her energy expenditure over a long period, and is often defined as a body weight of more than 20% above that recommended for a person of a specified height, sex, and build. It is usually treated by restricting energy intake (as calories) by strictly controlled dieting, and if untreated may cause cardiovascular disease, diabetes mellitus, hypertension, gallstones, or other serious disorders. It is the commonest nutritional disorder in developed countries.

obey *verb* (**obeys, obeyed**) 1 to do what one is told to do by (someone). 2 to carry out (a command). 3 *intrans.* to do what one is told. 4 to be

controlled by (a force, impulse, etc). [from Latin *obedire*, from *ob*, towards + *audire*, to hear]

obfuscate *verb* to confuse or make difficult to understand; to bewilder. [from Latin *ob*, completely + *fuscus*, dark]

obfuscation *noun* 1 obfuscating. 2 being obfuscated. 3 something that obfuscates.

obfuscatory *adj.* tending to obscure or confuse.

obiter dictum *noun* (PL. **OBITER DICTA**) a remark that is in some way related to, but not essential to, the main argument. [Latin, = thing said by the way]

obituary *noun* (PL. **obituaries**) a notice or announcement of a person's death, often with a short account of his or her life. [from Latin *obitus*, death]

object[1] *noun* (with stress on *ob*-) 1 a thing that can be seen or touched. 2 an aim or purpose. 3 the person or thing to which action, feelings, or thought are directed. 4 *Grammar* the noun, noun phrase, or pronoun affected by the action of the verb, or a preposition. See also SUBJECT, DIRECT OBJECT, INDIRECT OBJECT. 5 *Philos.* a thing which is outside of, and can be perceived by, the mind.
— **be no object** not to be a difficulty or obstacle. [from Latin *objectus*, a throwing before]

object[2] *verb* (with stress on *-ject*) 1 *intrans.* (**object to** or **against something**) to feel or express dislike or disapproval for it. 2 *trans.* to state as a ground for disapproval or objection: *objected that they had not been consulted.* [from Latin *ob*, in the way of + *jacere*, to throw]

object glass the lens in a camera, telescope, etc which is nearest to the object being viewed.

objection *noun* 1 an expression of disapproval. 2 (**objection against** or **to something**) a reason for disapproving.

objectionable *adj.* unpleasant; likely to cause offence.

objectionably *adv.* in an objectionable way.

objectival *adj.* relating to or of the nature of an objective.

objective — *adj.* 1 not depending on, or influenced by, personal opinions or prejudices. 2 *Philos.* having existence outside the mind; based on fact or reality. See also SUBJECTIVE. 3 *Grammar, said of a case or word* indicating the object; in the relation of object to a verb or preposition. — *noun* 1 a thing aimed at or wished for; a goal. 2 *Grammar* the object case. 3 an object glass. [from Latin *objectivus*, from *ob*, in the way of + *jacere*, to throw]

objectively *adv.* in an objective way.

objectivism *noun* a tendency to emphasize what is objective.

objectivity *noun* being objective.

objectless *adj.* without an object.

object lesson an experience, event, etc, which gives a practical example of especially a principle or ideal.

objector *noun* a person who objects.

objet d'art *noun* (PL. **objets d'art**) a small object of artistic value. [French, = object of art]

objet trouvé same as FOUND OBJECT.

oblast an administrative district in some republics of the former Soviet Union.

oblate *adj. Geom., said of something approximately spherical* flattened at the poles, like the Earth. [from Latin *oblatus*, lengthened]

oblation *noun* 1 a sacrifice or religious offering. 2 the offering of the bread and wine to God at a Eucharist. [from Latin *oblatio*]

obligate *verb* to bind by contract, duty, or moral obligation. [from Latin *ob*, down + *ligare*, to bind]

obligation *noun* 1 a moral or legal duty or tie. 2 the binding power of such a duty or tie. 3 a debt of gratitude for a service: *be under obligation to her.*

obligatorily *adv.* in an obligatory way.

obligatoriness *noun* being obligatory.

obligatory *adj.* legally or morally binding; compulsory.

oblige *verb* 1 to bind morally or legally; to compel. 2 to bind by a service or favour. 3 to please or do a favour for: *please oblige me by leaving at once.* 4 *intrans.* to do something stated as a favour or contribution: *obliged us with a song.*
— **much obliged** an expression of gratitude. [from Latin *ob*, down + *ligare*, to bind]

obliging *adj.* willing to help others; courteously helpful.

obligingly *adv.* in an obliging way.

oblique — *adj.* 1 sloping; not vertical or horizontal. 2 not straight or direct; roundabout; underhand. 3 *Geom., said of lines, etc* not at a right angle. 4 *Grammar* being, or in, any case other than the nominative or vocative. — *noun* 1 an oblique line (/). 2 anything that is oblique. [from Latin *ob*, completely + *liquis*, slanting]

obliquely *adv.* in an oblique way.

obliqueness or **obliquity** *noun* 1 being oblique. 2 a slanting direction. 3 crookedness.

obliterate *verb* 1 to destroy completely. 2 to cover and prevent from being seen. [from Latin *obliterare*, to blot out]

obliteration *noun* being obliterated, extinction.

oblivion *noun* 1 the state of having forgotten or being unconscious. 2 the state of being forgotten. [from Latin *oblivio*, forgetfulness]

oblivious *adj.* (**oblivious of** or **to something**) unaware or forgetful of it.

obliviously *adv.* in a state of oblivion, unconsciously.

obliviousness *noun* being oblivious.

oblong — *adj., said of a figure* rectangular with adjacent sides unequal; having a greater breadth than height. — *noun* (not in technical use) a rectangular figure. [from Latin *ob*, over + *longus*, long]

obloquy *noun* (PL. **obloquies**) 1 abuse, blame or censure. 2 loss of honour, good name, or reputation. [from Latin *ob*, against + *loqui*, to speak]

obnoxious *adj.* offensive; objectionable. [from Latin *ob*, exposed to + *noxa*, harm]

obnoxiously *adv.* in an obnoxious way.

obnoxiousness *noun* 1 being obnoxious. 2 obnoxious behaviour.

oboe *noun* a wind instrument with a double reed, treble pitch, and a penetrating tone. [from Italian *oboe*, from French *hautbois*, from *haut*, high + *bois*, wood]

oboist *noun* a person who plays an oboe.

O'Brien, Edna (1932–) Irish novelist, born in Tomgraney, Co Clare. Her novels, which include *The Country Girls* (1960), *Girls in their Married Bliss* (1963), and *The Girl with Green Eyes* (1965), are characterized by their frank depiction of female sexuality and their lyrical powers of natural description.

O'Brien, Flann, pseudonym of **Brian O'Nuallain** (1911–66) Irish writer, born in Strabane, Co Tyrone. As 'Myles na Gopaleen' he made regular satirical contributions to the *Irish Times*. His first novel, *At Swim-Two-Birds* (1939), combines satire with wild fantasy and farce. His later works display a darker comic vision and include the Gaelic novel *An Beal Bocht* (1941, The Poor Mouth, 1973), *The Hard Life* (1960) and *The Dalkey Archive* (1964).

obscene *adj.* **1** offensive to accepted standards of behaviour or morality, especially sexual morality. **2** *colloq.* indecent; disgusting. **3** *Brit. Legal, said of a publication* tending to deprave or corrupt. [from Latin *obscenus*, foul, indecent]

obscenely *adv.* in an obscene way.

obscenity *noun* (PL. **obscenities**) **1** the state or quality of being obscene. **2** an obscene act or word.

obscurantism *noun* opposition to inquiry or the spreading or use of new knowledge, up-to-date scientific research, etc. [from Latin *obscurare*, to obscure]

obscurantist — *noun* a person who tries to prevent enlightenment or reform. — *adj.* relating to or characteristic of obscurantism.

obscure — *adj.* **1** dark; dim. **2** not clear; hidden; difficult to see. **3** not well known. **4** difficult to understand. — *verb* to hide; to make dark, or difficult to see or understand. [from Latin *obscurus*, dark]

obscurely *adv.* in an obscure way.

obscurity *noun* (PL. **obscurities**) **1** the state of being obscure. **2** something that is obscure.

obsequies *pl. noun* funeral rites. [from Latin *obsequiae*]

obsequious *adj.* submissively obedient; fawning. [from Latin *obsequiosus*, compliant]

obsequiously *adv.* with an obsequious manner.

obsequiousness *noun* being obsequious.

observable *adj.* discernible, perceptible. **1** notable, worthy of note. **2** to be observed.

observably *adv.* so as to be observable.

observance *noun* **1** the act of obeying rules, keeping customs, etc. **2** a custom or religious rite observed. [from Latin *observantia*, from *observare*, to observe]

observant *adj.* **1** quick to notice. **2** carefully attentive.

observantly *adv.* in an observant way.

observation *noun* **1** the act of noticing or watching; the state of being observed or watched. **2** the ability to observe; perception: *test her powers of observation.* **3** a remark or comment. **4** the noting of behaviour, symptoms, phenomena, etc as they occur, especially before analysis or diagnosis: *keep the patient under observation.* **5** the result of such observing.
— **take an observation** to observe the position of the sun or stars in order to calculate one's geographical position.
[from Latin *observatio*]

observational *adj.* **1** relating to or consisting of observing or noticing. **2** based on observation of behaviour, phenomena, etc as opposed to experiments.

observation car *noun* a railway carriage with large windows to allow passengers to view the scenery.

observatory *noun* (PL. **observatories**) a room, building, or site specially equipped for making systematic observations of natural phenomena, especially of the stars and other celestial objects visible in the night sky. Observatories are also carried on some aircraft, satellites, and space vehicles, including the Space Shuttle. [from Latin *observatorium*]

observe *verb* **1** to notice or become conscious of. **2** to watch carefully. **3** *trans., intrans.* to examine and note (behaviour, symptoms, phenomena, etc). **4** to obey, follow, or keep (a law, custom, religious rite, etc). **5** *trans., intrans.* to make a remark or comment: *observed that he was late again.* [from Latin *ob*, towards + *servare*, to keep]

observer *noun* **1** a person who observes. **2** a person who goes to meetings, etc to watch and listen but not take part.

obsess *verb* to occupy, grip, or haunt the mind of completely, persistently, or constantly: *be obsessed with winning.* [from Latin *obsidere*, to besiege]

obsession *noun* **1** a persistent or dominating idea. **2** *Psychol.* a recurring thought, feeling, or impulse, generally of an unpleasant nature, that preoccupies a person and is a source of constant anxiety that cannot be suppressed, eg the desire to wash the hands repeatedly because of fear of contamination. The person dominated by the obsession is aware that it has no rational basis, and often struggles to overcome it. Obsessions are a form of neurosis, and can be treated by psychotherapy.

obsessional *adj.* in the nature of an obsession.

obsessive *adj.* **1** relating to or resulting from an obsession or obsessions. **2** *said of a person* affected by an obsession.

obsessive-compulsive disorder *Psychol.* a form of neurosis in which a person becomes preoccupied with a recurring thought, feeling, or impulse, which is a source of constant anxiety. See also OBSESSION.

obsessively *adv.* in an obsessive way.

obsessiveness *noun* being obsessive.

obsidian *noun Geol.* the commonest type of volcanic glass, usually black, but sometimes red or brown in colour, and formed by the rapid cooling and solidification of granite magma. [from Latin *obsidianus*]

obsolescence *noun* being obsolescent.

obsolescent *adj.* going out of use; becoming out of date. [from Latin *obsolescere*, to become obsolete]

obsolete *adj.* no longer in use; out of date. [from Latin *obsoletus*]

obstacle *noun* a person or thing that stands in a person's way or prevents progress. [from Latin *obstaculum*, from *ob*, before + *stare*, to stand]

obstacle race a race in which runners have to climb over, crawl through, etc various obstacles.

obstetric *adj.* relating to obstetrics.

obstetrician *noun* a doctor specially qualified in obstetrics.

obstetrics *sing. noun* the branch of medicine and surgery which deals with pregnancy, childbirth and the care of the mother. [from Latin *obstetrix*, a midwife, from *ob*, before + *stare*, to stand]

obstinacy *noun* **1** being obstinate. **2** obstinate behaviour; an obstinate act.

obstinate *adj.* **1** refusing to change one's opinion or course of action; stubborn; inflexible. **2** difficult to defeat, remove, or treat; unyielding. [from Latin *obstinatus*, from *ob*, in the way of + *stare*, to stand]

obstinately *adv.* in an obstinate way.

obstreperous *adj.* noisy and hard to control; unruly. [from Latin *ob*, before + *strepere*, to make a noise]

obstreperously *adv.* in an obstreperous way.

obstreperousness *noun* being obstreperous.

obstruct *verb* **1** to block or close. **2** to prevent or hinder the movement or progress of. [from Latin *ob*, in the way of + *struere*, to pile up]

obstruction *noun* **1** a thing that obstructs or blocks. **2** the act of obstructing. **3** an act of hindering or unfairly getting in the way, eg in sport.

obstructionism *noun* the practice of obstructing parliamentary or legal action.

obstructionist *noun* a person, especially a politician, who practises obstruction.

obstructive *adj.* causing or designed to cause an obstruction.

obstructively *adv.* in an obstructive way; so as to obstruct.

obstructiveness *noun* **1** being obstructive. **2** obstructive behaviour.

obtain *verb* **1** to get; to become the owner, or come into possession of, often by effort or planning. **2** *intrans.* to be established, exist or hold good. [from Latin *obtinere*, to lay hold of]

obtainable *adj.* capable of being obtained.

obtrude *verb* **1** *intrans.* to be or become unpleasantly noticeable or prominent. **2** (**obtrude something on** *or* **upon someone**) to push oneself, one's opinions, etc forward, especially when they are unwelcome. [from Latin *ob*, against + *trudere*, to thrust]

obtruder *noun* a person who obtrudes.

obtrusion *noun* **1** an act of obtruding. **2** that which obtrudes.

obtrusive *adj.* **1** unpleasantly noticeable or prominent: *an obtrusive new housing scheme on the edge of town.* **2** sticking out; protruding.

obtrusively *adv.* in an obtrusive way.

obtrusiveness *noun* being obtrusive.

obtuse *adj.* **1** blunt; not pointed or sharp. **2** *colloq.* stupid and slow to understand. **3** *Geom.* denoting an angle that is greater than 90° and less than 180°. [from Latin *obtusus*, dull]

obtusely *adv.* in an obtuse way.

obtuseness *noun* being obtuse.

obverse *noun* **1** the side of a coin with the head or main design on it. See also REVERSE. **2** the face, side, etc of anything which is normally on view. **3** an opposite or counterpart, eg of a fact or truth. [from Latin *obversus*, turned against]

obviate *verb* to prevent or remove (a potential difficulty, problem, etc) in advance. [from Latin *obviare*, to go to meet]

obvious *adj.* easily seen or understood; evident. [from Latin *obvius*, from *ob*, in the way of + *via*, way]

obviously *adv.* in an obvious way; as is obvious, clearly.

obviousness *noun* being obvious.

ocarina *noun* a small simple wind instrument with an egg-shaped body and projecting mouthpiece. [from Italian *ocarina*, from *oca*, goose, so-called because of its shape]

O'Casey, Sean, originally **John Casey** (1884–1964) Irish playwright, born in Dublin. His notable early plays, dealing with life in the tenements of Dublin, are *The Shadow of a Gunman* (1923), *Juno and the Paycock* (1924), and *The Plough and the Stars* (1926) and his more experimental and impressionistic later work includes *Cock-a-doodle Dandy* (1949) and *The Bishop's Bonfire* (1955).

occasion — *noun* **1** a particular event or happening or the time at which it occurs. **2** a special event or celebration. **3** a suitable opportunity. **4** a reason; grounds: *have no occasion to be angry.* **5** an event which determines the time at which something happens, but which is not the actual cause of it. — *verb* to cause.
— **on occasion** from time to time.
rise to the occasion to produce the extra energy or ability needed by unusual circumstances.
[from Latin *occasio*, from *ob*, in the way of + *cadere*, to fall]

occasional *adj.* **1** happening irregularly and infrequently. **2** produced on or for a special occasion.

occasionally *adv.* on occasions; now and then.

occasional table a small, usually decorated table with no regular use.

Occident *noun* **1** (**the Occident**) the countries in the west, especially those in Europe and America regarded as culturally distinct from eastern countries (the *Orient*). **2** that part of the sky where the sun sets. [from Latin *occidens*, from *occidere*, to go down]

occidental — *adj.* from or relating to the Occident; western. — *noun* (**Occidental**) a person born in the Occident; a westerner.

occipital *adj.* relating to or in the region of the back of the head.

occiput *noun Anat.* the back of the head. [from Latin, from *ob*, over + *caput*, head]

occlude *verb* **1** to block up or cover (eg a pore or some other opening). **2** *Chem.*, *said of a solid* to absorb a gas so that atoms or molecules of the latter occupy the spaces within the lattice structure of the solid. **3** *Medicine* to close an opening, eg to obstruct a blood vessel. **4** *Medicine* to close the surfaces of the upper teeth on those of the lower teeth. **5** to shut in or out. [from Latin *occludere*, to shut up]

occluded front *Meteorol.* the final stage in an atmospheric depression, when a cold front catches up with and overtakes a warm front, lifting the warm air mass off the ground.

occlusion *noun* **1** the closing of an orifice, etc. **2** the act of occluding or absorbing.

occult — *adj.* **1** involving, using, or dealing with that which is magical, mystical or supernatural. **2** beyond ordinary understanding. **3** secret, hidden, or esoteric. — *noun* (**the occult**) the knowledge and study of that which is magical, mystical, or supernatural. [from Latin *occultus*, hidden]

occultation *noun Astron.* a phenomenon that is observed when one celestial body (eg a planet or moon) passes directly in front of another (eg a star), so obscuring it. [from Latin *occulere*, to hide]

occultism *noun Relig.* the doctrine or study of the supernatural, and practices purporting to achieve communication with things hidden and mysterious, including magic, divination, certain types of spritiualism, and witchcraft.

occultist *noun* a person who believes in occult things.

occult sciences astrology, palmistry, tarot, etc.

occupancy *noun* (PL. **occupancies**) **1** the act of occupying (a house, etc). **2** a period of time during which a house, etc is occupied. [from Latin *occupare*, to seize]

occupant *noun* a person who occupies, has, or takes possession of something, not always the owner.

occupation *noun* **1** a person's job or profession. **2** an activity that occupies a person's attention, free time, etc. **3** the act of occupying or state of being occupied. **4** the period of time during which a town, house, etc is occupied. **5** the act of taking and keeping control of a foreign country, using military power. [from Latin *occupatio*, seizing]

occupational *adj.* of, connected with, or caused by a person's job: *occupational disease*.

occupational hazard a risk or danger caused by the working conditions of a particular job.

occupationally *adv.* in an occupational way; as regards occupation.

occupational psychology *Psychol.* the branch of psychology that is concerned with the scientific study of human behaviour in the workplace, including the study of work skills and the working environment, vocational guidance, personnel selection, all forms of training, and principles of management.

occupational therapist a person who provides occupational therapy.

occupational therapy a form of rehabilitation in which patients with physical or mental illnesses are encouraged to participate in selected activities that will equip them to function independently in everyday life, such as household management, social skills, industrial work, educational programmes, woodwork, metalwork, art and crafts, pottery, printing, and gardening.

occupier *noun* a person who lives in a building, as either a tenant or owner.

occupy *verb* (**occupies**, **occupied**) **1** to have possession of or live in (a house, etc). **2** to be in or fill (time, space, etc). **3** to take possession of (a building, a foreign country, etc) by force. **4** to keep (oneself, a person, one's mind, etc) busy; to fill in (time). **5** to hold (a post or office). [from Latin *occupare*, to seize]

occur *verb intrans.* (**occurred**, **occurring**) **1** to happen or take place. **2** (**occur to someone**) to come into the mind, especially unexpectedly or by chance: *it occurred to her that the train might be late / an idea has occurred to me*. **3** to be found or exist. [from Latin *occurrere*, to run towards]

occurrence *noun* **1** anything which occurs; an event, especially an unexpected one. **2** the act of occurring.

ocean *noun* **1** the continuous expanse of salt water that covers about 70% of the Earth's surface, and surrounds the continental land masses. **2** any one of its five main divisions, the Atlantic, Indian, Pacific, Arctic, and Southern. **3** the sea. **4** (*often* **oceans**) a very large number or expanse: *oceans of people*. [from Greek *Okeanos*, the stream supposed by the ancients to run round the earth]

oceanarium *noun* (PL. **oceanariums**) a large aquarium supplied with salt water, or an enclosed part of the sea, in which sea creatures are kept for research purposes or for display to the public. See also OCEAN, AQUARIUM.

ocean-going *adj.*, *said of a ship* built to sail in the sea rather than in rivers, etc.

Oceania *or* **Oceanica** a general name applied to the isles of the Pacific Ocean including Polynesia, Melanesia, Micronesia, Australasia, and sometimes the Malaysian islands.

oceanic *adj.* **1** relating to the ocean. **2** found or formed in the ocean.

oceanic ridge any undersea mountain range. They are the sites of numerous shallow earthquakes. The Mid-Atlantic Ridge is the best-known ridge system, and consists of a high fractured plateau, rift mountains, and a rift valley.

Oceanides in Greek mythology, the innumerable nymphs who inhabit the ocean and other watery places. They are the daughters of Oceanus and Tethys.

oceanographer *noun* an expert on oceanography.

oceanographic *adj.* relating to or involving oceanography.

oceanography *noun* the scientific study of the oceans, including the structure and origin of the ocean floor, the chemical properties of sea water, the physical processes that take place in the oceans, eg currents, waves, and tides, and the ecology of the marine organisms that inhabit the oceans.

Oceanus in Greek mythology, a river which surrounded the earth. In Hesiod, it was personified as a Titan, the son of Uranus and Gaea.

ocelot *noun* a medium-sized wild cat, found in the forests of Central and S America, which has dark yellow fur marked with spots and stripes. [from Aztec *ocelotl*, jaguar]

och *interj. Scot., Irish* an expression of surprise, impatience, disagreement, annoyance, regret, etc. [a Gaelic word]

ochone *or* **ohone** *interj.* used in the Scottish Highlands and Ireland to express lamentation. [from Gaelic *ochoin*]

ochre *noun* **1** a kind of fine earth or clay, used as a yellow, red, or brown dye. **2** a pale brownish-yellow. [from Greek *ochros*, pale]

ochreous *adj.* **1** of the nature of, containing, or full of ochre. **2** of the colour of ochre, yellowish.

Ockham *or* **Occam William of** (c.1285–c.1349) English scholastic philosopher, born in the village of Ockham, Surrey. He entered the Franciscan order, and in 1324 was summoned to Avignon to respond to charges of heresy, where he became involved in a dispute between the Franciscans and Pope John XXII over apostolic poverty. He fled to Bavaria in 1328, where he remained until 1347, writing treatises on papal v. civil authority.

Ockham's razor, also called the **Principle of Parsimony** a philosophical principle attributed

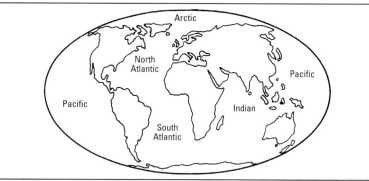

the oceans

	Oceans					
Name	Area			Average depth		
	sq km	sq mi	%*	m	Greatest depth	m
Arctic	9 485 000	3 661 000	3%	1 330	Eurasia Basin	5 122
Atlantic	86 557 000	33 411 000	24%	3 700	Puerto Rico Trench	8 684
Indian	73 427 000	28 343 000	20%	3 900	Java Trench	7 125
Pacific	166 241 000	64 169 000	46%	4 300	Mariana Trench	10 195

* Proportion of world's water coverage

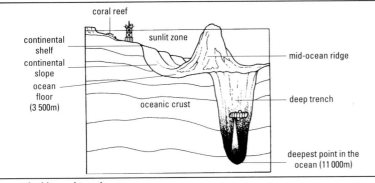

oceanic ridge and trench

to William of Ockham. Its essence is 'do not multiply entities beyond necessity', ie a theory should not propose the existence of anything more than is needed for its explanations.

o'clock *adv.* used after a number in specifying the time. [from the phrase *of the clock*]

O'Connell, Daniel, known as **the Liberator** (1775–1847) Irish Catholic political leader, born near Cahirciveen, Co Kerry. As a lawyer, he formed the Catholic Association in 1823, which successfully fought elections against the landlords. When he was elected MP for Co Clare, Wellington's government had eventually to grant Catholic Emancipation (1829), which enabled O'Connell to take his seat in the Commons. In 1840 he founded the Repeal Association, which increased agitation to end the union with Britain (1801). In 1844 he was imprisoned for 14 weeks on a charge of sedition. In conflict with the Young Ireland movement (1846), and failing in health, he left Ireland for Italy in 1847.

O'Connor, Feargus Edward (1794–1855) Irish Chartist leader, born in Connorville, Co Cork. He entered parliament in 1832 but became estranged from Daniel O'Connell and devoted himself to the cause of the working classes in England. His Leeds *Northern Star* (1837) became the most influential Chartist newspaper. He attempted to unify the Chartist movement via the National Charter Association (1842), and presented himself as leader of the Chartist cause.

O'Connor, Sandra Day (1930–) US lawyer and jurist, born in El Paso, Texas. After practising law she entered Arizona politics as a Republican, and became majority leader in the State Senate before moving to the state bench. In 1981 President Reagan named her as the first woman justice of the US Supreme Court.

OCR *abbrev. Comput.* optical character recognition, or reader.

Oct *or* **Oct.** *abbrev.* October.

oct-, octa- *see* OCTO-.

octad *noun* a group, series, set, etc of eight things. [from Greek *okto*, eight]

octagon *noun* a flat figure with eight straight sides and eight angles. [from Greek *okto*, eight + *gonia*, angle]

octagonal *adj.* having eight sides and angles.

octahedral *adj.* 1 shaped like an octahedron. 2 having eight plane surfaces.

octahedron *noun* (PL. **octahedra**, **octahedrons**) a solid figure with eight plane faces. [from Greek *okto*, eight + *hedra*, seat]

octane *noun Chem.* (FORMULA C_8H_{18}) a colourless liquid belonging to the alkane series of hydrocarbons, present in petroleum, and used in petrol, as a solvent, and in the manufacture of organic chemicals. [from Greek *okto*, eight + *-ane* as in METHANE]

octane number *or* **octane rating** a numerical system for classifying motor fuels according to their resistance to knocking. The higher the octane number, the better the quality of the petrol, and the lower the likelihood of knocking.

Octans *noun Astron.* the Octant, an inconspicuous constellation in the southern hemisphere. [from Latin *octans*, an eighth part]

octant *noun Maths.* 1 one eighth of the circumference of a circle. 2 a section, formed by drawing two straight lines from the centre to the circumference, of one eighth of a circle. [from Latin *octans*, an eighth]

octave *noun* 1 *Mus.* the range of sound, or the series of notes, between the first note and the eighth note on a major or minor scale, eg from C to the C above. 2 a musical note that is an eighth above or below another. 3 *Poetry* a verse or stanza with eight lines. 4 the first eight lines of a sonnet. [from Latin *octavus*, eighth]

Octavian *see* AUGUSTUS.

octavo *noun* (PL. **octavos**) 1 a size of book or page produced by folding a standard-sized sheet of paper three times to give eight leaves. 2 a book of this size. [from Latin *octavus*, eighth]

octet *noun* 1 a group of eight, eg musicians, lines in a poem, etc. 2 a piece of music written for eight musicians or singers. 3 the first eight lines in a sonnet. [from Latin *octo*, eight + DUET]

octo- *or* **oct-** *or* **octa-** *combining form* forming words meaning eight. [from Greek *okto*, eight]

October *noun* the 10th month of the year. [from Latin, from *octo*, eight, so called because it was the eighth month in the Roman calendar]

October Revolution the overthrow (1917) of the Russian provisional government by Bolshevik-led armed workers (Red Guards), soldiers, and sailors (25–6 Oct 1917 old style; 7–8 Nov new style), organized by the Military Revolutionary Committee of the Petrograd Soviet but based on Lenin's tactical exploitation of the lack of effective leadership in a rapidly escalating crisis. The Soviet of People's Commissars (*Sovnarkom*) chaired by Lenin became the first Soviet government.

Octobrist *noun* a member of a Russian political party which supported the political changes proposed by Tsar Nicholas II in October 1905.

octogenarian — *adj.* between 80 and 89 years old. — *noun* a person of this age. [from Latin *octogenarius*, of eighty]

octopus *noun* (PL. **octopuses**) any of about 150 species of marine mollusc, found mainly in tropical regions, with a soft rounded body, no external shell, and eight arms, each of which bears two rows of suckers. Many species live at the bottom of the sea, but the common octopus lives among rocks in shallow water, feeding on small fish and crustaceans which it seizes with its long arms and then paralyses with poison. When threatened by a predator the octopus emits clouds of dark ink from a special sac. [from Greek *okto*, eight + *pous*, foot]

octopush *noun* an underwater game resembling hockey. It is played in a swimming pool by two teams of six players, who attempt to score goals by pushing a lead puck (a *squid*) along the bottom and hitting it against the opposing team's end of the pool. [from OCTOPUS + PUSH]

octoroon *or* **octaroon** *noun* a person having one black African or Caribbean great-grandparent. [from Latin *octo*, eight]

octosyllabic *adj.* consisting of eight syllables or composed of lines of eight syllables.

octosyllable *noun* 1 a word with eight syllables. 2 a line of verse containing eight syllables. [from Latin *octo*, eight + *syllaba*, syllable]

octuple *adj.* eight times as large; eightfold. [from Latin *octuplus*]

ocular *adj.* of or related to the eyes or vision. [from Latin *oculus*, eye]

oculist *noun* an optician or ophthalmologist. [from Latin *oculus*, eye]

oculus *noun* (PL. **oculi**) *Archit.* a round window. [from Latin *oculus*, eye]

OD *slang* — *noun* (PL. **ODs**, **OD's**) an overdose of drugs. — *verb* (**OD'd**, **OD'ing**) *intrans.* to take a drug overdose. [abbreviation]

odalisque *or* **odalisk** *noun Hist.* a female slave or concubine in a harem, especially that belonging to the Turkish Sultan. [from Turkish *odalik*, from *oda*, room]

odd *adj.* 1 left over when others are put into groups or pairs. 2 not matching: *odd socks*. 3 not one of a complete set. 4 *Maths.* not exactly divisible by two. 5 unusual; strange. 6 occasional; not regular: *odd jobs*. 7 (*in compounds with a number*) a little more than the number stated: *twenty-odd replies*. 8 *said of pages, etc* numbered consecutively having an odd number: *put pictures on the odd pages*. 9 out of the way; standing apart. — **odd man out** 1 a person or thing that is different from, and often unwilling to be like, others. 2 a person or thing left over when teams, sets, etc have been formed. [from Norse *oddi*, odd number]

oddball *noun colloq.* a strange or eccentric person.

oddity *noun* (PL. **oddities**) 1 a strange person or thing. 2 the state of being strange or unusual.

oddly *adv.* in an odd way; as an odd circumstance: *oddly, he refused to stay.*

oddments *pl. noun* pieces left over from something much larger.

oddness *noun* 1 being odd. 2 an odd act. 3 odd behaviour.

odds *pl. noun* (*sometimes treated as sing.*) 1 the chance or probability, expressed as a ratio, that something will or will not happen: *the odds are 10–1 against.* 2 the difference between the amount placed as a bet and the money which might be won, expressed as a ratio: *offer odds of 2 to 1.* 3 an advantage that is thought to exist: *the odds are in her favour / it makes no odds how we go.* 4 likelihood: *the odds are he'll be late again.* — **against all the odds** in spite of great difficulty or disadvantage. — **at odds** in disagreement or dispute: *at odds with the management.* — **odds and ends** *colloq.* small objects, of different kinds, and usually of little value or importance. — **over the odds** more than is required or expected. — **what's the odds?** *colloq.* what difference does it make?; what does it matter?

odds-on *adj., said of a chance* better than even.

ode *noun* a usually long lyric poem, with lines of different lengths, addressed to a particular person or thing. [from Greek *oide*, from *aeidein*, to sing]

Odense POP (1992e) 180 000, the chief town on Fyn I, Denmark. It is the third largest city in Denmark. The author Hans Andersen was born here in 1805. NOTABLE FEATURES St Knud's Church (reconstructed in the 13c); palace (18c).

Ode on a Grecian Urn a poem by John Keats (1820). It is a reflection on art and life and contains the well-known line 'Beauty is truth, truth beauty'.

Oder, River, Czech, Polish **Odra**, ancient **Viadua** a river in central Europe, length 854km/531mi. Rising in the E Sudetes Mts, in the Czech Republic, it flows N through Poland, eventually following the German frontier to meet the Baltic Sea near Szczecin. Its chief tributary is the Neisse. It is navigable for 711km/442mi, and provides canal links to W and E Europe.

Odes 1 Greek Epinician ('victory') poems by Pindar. They celebrate the victories in the Olympian, Pythian, Nemean, and Isthmian games. **2** Latin poems in four books by Horace (c.23–c.13 BC). They are lyric poems in the style of Pindar and other Greek poets.

Odessa POP (1990e) 1.1m, a seaport in the Ukraine, on the NW shore of the Black Sea. It is the leading Black Sea port, a naval base, and the home port for a fishing fleet. Icebreakers ensure that the port is ice-free throughout the year. HISTORY founded in 1795 by Catherine II; scene of the mutiny on the battleship, *Potemkin* during the 1905 Revolution; suffered heavy damage in World War II. NOTABLE FEATURES Uspensky Cathedral (1855–69); large health resorts nearby.

Ode to a Nightingale a poem by John Keats (1820). It contrasts the unending beauty of the nightingale's song with the mortality of the narrator.

Ode to Autumn a poem by John Keats (1820). Also known simply as 'To Autumn', it is an elegiac acceptance of the transience of life.

Ode to the West Wind a poem by Percy Bysse Shelley (1820). It is an impassioned appeal to the all-encompassing spirit of the West Wind.

Odets, Clifford (1903–63) American playwright and actor, born in Philadelphia. His works, marked by a strong social conscience formed out of the conditions of the Great Depression of the 1930s, include *Waiting for Lefty* (1935) and *Golden Boy* (1937).

Odin, also called **Woden**, or **Wotan** in Norse mythology, the principal god, possessed of magical powers. He was the god of poetry, war, and the dead; slain warriors were brought to him in Valhalla. He gave one eye to the Giant Mimir in exchange for wisdom.

odious *adj.* hateful, extremely unpleasant or offensive. [from Latin *odiosus*, from *odi*, to hate]

odiously *adv.* in an odious way.

odiousness *noun* being odious.

odium *noun* hatred, strong dislike, or disapproval of a person or thing, especially when widespread. [from Latin *odium*, hatred]

Odoacer *or* **Odovacer** (c.433–93 AD) Germanic warrior who destroyed the W Roman Empire, and became the first barbarian king of Italy (476–93). He was challenged and overthrown by the Ostrogothic king Theoderic (489–93), at the instigation of the E Roman emperor, Zeno.

odometer *noun North Amer. Engineering* an instrument for measuring and displaying the distance travelled by a motor vehicle or a person, eg the milometer incorporated in the speedometer of a car. It consists of a wheel of known circumference, the number of revolutions made being used to calculate the distance travelled. [from Greek *hodos*, way + -METER]

Odo of Bayeux (c.1036–1097) Anglo-Norman prelate, who was Bishop of Bayeux (1049–97) and half-brother of William the Conqueror. He fought at the battle of Hastings (1066) and acted as regent during William's absences, but left England after rebelling against

William II Rufus. He rebuilt Bayeux cathedral and may have commissioned the Bayeux tapestry.

odoriferous *adj.* having or giving off a sweet or pleasant smell. [from Latin *odorifer*, from *odor*, smell]

odorous *adj.* giving off an odour, especially a sweet or pleasant one.

odour *noun* **1** a distinctive smell. **2** reputation; standing; relationship: *in bad odour with someone.* **3** a characteristic or quality. [from Latin *odor*]

odourless *adj.* without odour.

Odysseus, Latin **Ulixes**, English **Ulysses** in Greek legend, a King of Ithaca, known for his cunning. He took part in the Trojan War and took ten years to return from Troy, having many adventures (eg an encounter with the Cyclops, Polyphemus) which are described in Homer's *Odyssey*. Eventually he returned to Ithaca, and with the help of his son Telemachus, slaughtered the suitors who were besieging his wife Penelope.

Odyssey, The an epic poem by Homer (c.8c BC). The sequel to the *Iliad*, it tells the story of the 10-year journey of the Greek general Odysseus back to Ithaca after the fall of Troy.

odyssey *noun* (PL. **odysseys**) a long and adventurous journey. [after the Greek *Odysseia*; see ODYSSEY]

OECD *abbrev.* Organization for Economic Cooperation and Development.

OED *abbrev.* Oxford English Dictionary.

oedema *noun* (PL. **oedemata**, **oedemas**) an abnormal build-up of fluid in the tissues in the body, causing swelling. [from Greek *oidema*, swelling]

oedematous *adj.* relating to or affected by oedema.

Oedipal *adj.* relating to or characterized by the Oedipus complex.

Oedipus in Greek legend, a Theban hero of whom it was foretold that he would kill his father and marry his mother. He was brought up in Corinth by King Polybus, but he fled from his adoptive parents when an oracle revealed his destiny. On the way to Thebes he killed his natural father Laius by chance, and, having guessed the riddle of the sphinx, was made the new ruler of the city and married its queen, Jocasta (his mother). Later, when the truth was revealed, he blinded himself and went into exile, and Jocasta committed suicide.

Oedipus at Colonus a play by Sophocles (c.401 BC). The sequel to *Oedipus Rex*, it is a tragedy depicting the final years of the exiled and self-blinded Oedipus and his ultimate redemption through suffering.

Oedipus complex *Psychol.* **1** in psychoanalysis, the repressed sexual desire of a son for his mother, and the subsequent rivalry with his father. Freud considered that the Oedipus complex represented a normal stage of child development. **2** the corresponding sexual desire of a daughter for her father, and the subsequent rivalry with her mother, also known as *Elektra complex*. [from Greek Oidipous, a king of Thebes, who unwittingly killed his father and married his mother]

Oedipus Rex a neoclassical opera-oratorio by Igor Stravinsky (1927), with a text by Jean Cocteau based on Sophocles' play.

Oedipus Rex (Oedipus Tyrannus) a play by Sophocles (c.429 BC). It is a tragedy based on the Greek myth of the incestuous Oedipus, who unwittingly kills his father and marries his mother.

OEEC *abbrev.* Organization for European Economic Cooperation.

Oehlenschlager, Adam (Gottlob) (1779–1850) Danish poet, born in Vesterbro. The

leader of the Danish Romantic movement, his fame rests mainly on his 24 tragedies, beginning with *Hakon Jarl* (1807). In 1810 he was made Professor of Aesthetics at Copenhagen, and in 1849 was publicly proclaimed as the national poet of Denmark.

o'er *prep., adv. poetic, old use* over. [shortened form]

Oersted, Hans Christian (1777–1851) Danish physicist, born in Rudkøbing, Langeland. Professor at Copenhagen University, he discovered in 1820 the magnetic effect produced by an electric current. He also made an extremely accurate measurement of the compressibility of water, and succeeded in isolating aluminium for the first time (1825).

Oesling see ÖSLING.

oesophageal *adj.* relating to or in the region of the oesophagus.

oesophagus *noun* (PL. **oesophagi**) the tube by which food passes from the mouth to the stomach. [from Greek *oisophagos*]

oestradiol *or* **estradiol** *noun Physiol.* the most important female sex hormone, a steroid that is produced by the ovary and controls the development of the female secondary sexual characteristics and the functioning of the reproductive organs.

oestrogen *noun Biochem.* any of a group of steroid hormones, produced mainly by the ovaries, that control the growth and functioning of the female sex organs and the appearance of female secondary sexual characteristics, eg breast development, and that regulate the menstrual cycle. High levels of oestrogen are secreted during ovulation, to stimulate the body to prepare for pregnancy. [from OESTRUS + Greek *genes*, born, produced]

oestrus *noun* a regularly recurring period of fertility and sexual preparedness in many female mammals, when pregnancy is possible; heat. [from Greek *oistros*, a gadfly noted for its frenzy]

of *prep.* **1** used to show origin, cause, or authorship: *people of Glasgow / die of hunger / poems of Keats.* **2** belonging to; connected with. **3** used to specify a component, ingredient, characteristic, etc: *built of bricks / an area of marsh / a heart of gold.* **4** at a given distance or amount of time from: *two miles out of the city / within a minute of arriving.* **5** about; concerning: *tales of Rome / think of the children.* **6** belonging to or forming a part: *most of the story.* **7** existing, happening, etc at, on, in, or during: *battle of Hastings / he works of a night.* **8** used with words denoting loss, removal, separation, etc: *cured of cancer / cheated of the money.* **9** used to show the connection between a verbal noun and the person who is performing, or who is the object of, the action stated: *the running of the deer / the eating of healthy food.* **10** North Amer., esp. US to; before a stated hour: *a quarter of one.* [from Anglo-Saxon]

off — *adv.* **1** away; at or to a distance. **2** in or into a position which is not attached; loose; separate: *the handle came off / take your coat off.* **3** ahead in time: *Easter is a week off.* **4** in or into a state of no longer working or operating: *turn the radio off.* **5** in or into a state of being stopped or cancelled: *the match was rained off.* **6** in or into a state of sleep: *doze off.* **7** to the end, so as to be completely finished: *finish the work off.* **8** away from work or one's duties: *take an hour off.* **9** away from a course; aside: *turn off into a side street.* **10** not available as a choice, especially on a menu: *peas are off.* **11** in or into a state of decay: *the milk has gone off.* **12** situated as regards money: *well off.* **13** in or into a state of being completely mesmerized: *have the speech off pat.* — *adj.* **1** most distant; furthest away. **2** *said of the side of a vehicle, etc* nearest the centre of the road, on the right in Britain. **3** not good; not up to standard: *an off day.* **4** *Cricket* on the side of the field towards which the batsman's feet are pointing,

usually the bowler's left. See also ON 6. — *prep.* **1** from; away from. **2** removed from; no longer attached to. **3** opening out of; leading from: *a side street off the main road*. **4** not wanting; no longer attracted by: *go off him / off one's food*. **5** no longer using: *be off the tablets*. **6** not up to the usual standard: *off one's game*. **7** out to sea from: *off the coast of Spain*. — *noun* **1** the start, eg of a race or journey: *ready for the off*. **2** *Cricket* the side of a field towards which the batsman's feet are pointing, usually the bowler's left. See also ON.
— **a bit off** *colloq.*, said of behaviour unacceptable or unfair.
off and on now and then; occasionally.
[from Anglo-Saxon *of*, away]

Offa (d.796) King of Mercia (757–96). Anglo-Saxon ruler. He styled himself 'King of the English', and asserted his authority over all the kingdoms south of the Humber, treating their rulers as subordinate provincial governors and earning Charlemagne's respect. He constructed Offa's Dyke, and established a new currency based on the silver penny. His was an important but flawed attempt to unify England, and the Mercian supremacy collapsed soon after his death.

offal *noun* **1** the heart, brains, liver, kidneys, etc of an animal, used as food. **2** rubbish, waste or refuse. [from Middle English, from *of*, off + *fal*, fall]

Offaly, Gaelic **Ua bhFailghe** POP (1991) 59 000, a county in Leinster province, central Irish Republic. AREA 1 997sq km/771sq mi. PHYSICAL DESCRIPTION bounded W by the R Shannon; other rivers include the Brosna, Clodagh, and Broughill; the Slieve Bloom Mts rise in the SW. CAPITAL Tullamore. ECONOMY cattle; grain; large tracts of peat are used as fuel for power stations.

Offa's Dyke An interrupted linear earthwork linking the R Dee near Prestatyn, N Wales, with the Severn estuary at Chepstow. It was erected in the late 8c by Offa, King of Mercia, to define the W boundary between his kingdom and Wales. Offa's Dyke Path, opened in 1971, follows most of its course.

offbeat *adj. colloq.* unusual; not conventional; eccentric.

off-Broadway *adj.* a collective term used since the 1950s to designate theatres and plays operating outside the commercial US theatre centred on Broadway. In general, productions are more experimental with less emphasis on achieving a commercial success.

off chance see CHANCE.

off-colour *adj.* **1** *Brit.* unwell; not in good health. **2** *said of humour* rude; smutty.

offcut *noun* a small piece left over from a larger piece of eg wood, cloth, or meat.

Offenbach, Jacques, originally **Jakob Eberst** (1819–80) German-Jewish composer, born in Cologne. He composed many light, lively operettas, but is best known as inventor of modern *opera bouffe* (funny or farcical opera), represented by *Orphée aux enfers* (Orpheus in the Underworld, 1858). His one grand opera *Les Contes d'Hoffmann* (The Tales of Hoffmann) was produced posthumously in 1881.

offence *noun* **1** the breaking of a rule; a crime. **2** any cause of anger, annoyance, or displeasure. **3** displeasure, annoyance or resentment: *mean no offence*. **4** an attack or assault.
— **give offence** to cause displeasure or annoyance.
take offence at something to be offended by it. [from Latin *offendere*, to strike against]

offend *verb* **1** to cause (someone) to feel hurt or angry; to insult. **2** to be unpleasant or annoying to (someone). **3** *intrans.* (**offend against someone** *or* **something**) to commit a sin or crime; to act in a way that is not in accordance with custom, etc. [from Latin *offendere*, to strike against]

offended *adj.* insulted, having taken offence.

offender *noun* a person who has committed an offence.

offending *adj.* that offends, offensive.

offensive — *adj.* **1** giving or likely to give offence; insulting. **2** unpleasant, disgusting, repulsive, especially to the senses. **3** used for attacking. — *noun* **1** an aggressive action or attitude: *go on the offensive*. **2** an attack. **3** a great or aggressive effort to achieve something: *a peace offensive*. [from Latin *offendere*, to strike against]

offensively *adv.* in an offensive way.

offensiveness *noun* being offensive.

offer — *verb* (**offered**, **offering**) **1** to put forward (a gift, payment, suggestion, etc) to be accepted, refused, or considered. **2** to provide: *a hill offering the best view*. **3** *intrans.* to state one's willingness (to do something). **4** to present for sale. **5** *said of a thing* to present for consideration, acceptance or refusal; to provide an opportunity for: *a job offering rapid promotion*. **6** *intrans.* to present itself; to occur: *if opportunity offers*. **7** *trans., intrans.* to propose (a sum) as payment (to someone): *offer him £250 for the car*. **8** (*also* **offer something up**) to present (a prayer or sacrifice) to God. **9** to show (resistance, etc). — *noun* **1** an act of offering. **2** that which is offered, especially an amount of money offered to buy something. **3** a proposal, especially of marriage.
— **on offer** for sale, especially at a reduced price.
under offer *said of a house for sale* with a possible buyer who has made an offer, but still waiting for the contracts to be signed.
[from Latin *offerre*, from *ob*, towards + *ferre*, to bring]

offering *noun* **1** anything offered, especially a gift. **2** a gift of money given to a church, usually during a religious service, used for charity, etc. **3** a sacrifice made to God.

offertory *noun* (PL. **offertories**) *Christianity* **1** the offering of bread and wine to God during a Eucharist. **2** an anthem or hymn sung while this is happening. **3** money collected during a church service. [from Latin *offerre*, to offer]

offhand *or* **offhanded** *adj.* casual or careless, often with the result of being rude.

offhandedly *adv.* with an offhand manner.

offhandedness *noun* being offhanded.

Offiah, Martin (1966–) English Rugby League player, born in London. He started out as a rugby union player with Rosslyn Park. He made the move to Rugby League in 1987 when he signed for Widnes, and by early 1988 had played for Great Britain. He has since made regular international appearances. He joined Wigan in 1992.

office *noun* **1** the room, set of rooms or building in which the business of a firm is done. **2** a room or building used for a particular kind of business. **3** a local centre or department of a large business. **4** a position of authority, especially in the government or in public service: *run for office*. **5** *said of a political party* forming the government: *out of office*. **6** (**Office**) a government department: *the Home Office*. **7** the group of people working in an office. **8** a function or duty. **9** (*usually* **offices**) an act of kindness or service: *through her good offices*. **10** an authorized form of Christian worship or service, especially one for the dead (see also DIVINE OFFICE). [from Latin *officium*, favour, duty, service]

office-bearer *or* **office-holder** *noun* a person with an official duty in a society, church organization, etc.

office-block *noun* a large, multistorey building divided into offices.

Office of Management and Budget see MANAGEMENT AND BUDGET, OFFICE OF.

officer *noun* **1** a person in a position of authority and responsibility in the armed forces. **2** a person with an official position in an organization, society, or government department. **3** a policeman or policewoman. **4** a person in authority on a non-naval ship.

official — *adj.* **1** of or relating to an office or position of authority. **2** given or authorized by a person in authority: *an official report*. **3** formal; suitable for or characteristic of a person holding office: *official dinners*. — *noun* a person who holds office or who is in a position of authority. [from Latin *officialis*]

officialdom *noun* officials and bureaucrats as a group.

officialese *noun* the language of the government, civil service, etc, which is unclear, wordy and pompous.

officially *adv.* in an official way; in an official capacity.

official receiver a government officer appointed to deal with the affairs of a company, etc which has gone bankrupt.

officiate *verb intrans.* **1** to act in an official capacity; to perform official duties, especially at a particular function. **2** to conduct a religious service. [from Latin *officiare*, to serve]

officious *adj.* **1** offering help, advice, etc when this is not wanted; interfering. **2** *said of a diplomatic agreement* informal; unofficial. [from Latin *officiosus*, obliging]

officiously *adv.* with an officious manner.

officiousness *noun* being officious.

offing *noun* the more distant part of the sea that is visible from the shore.
— **in the offing** not far off; likely to happen soon.

off-key *adj., adv.* **1** out of tune. **2** not quite suitable.

off-licence *noun Brit.* a shop licensed to sell alcohol to be drunk elsewhere.

off-limits *adj.* not to be entered.

off-line *adj. Comput.*, said of a peripheral device, eg a printer not connected to a computer, and therefore not controlled by it. Most peripheral devices have a switch so that they can be turned off-line if required. See also ON-LINE.

offload *verb* to get rid of (especially something unpleasant) by giving it to someone else.

off-peak *adj., said of services* used at a time when there is little demand, and therefore usually cheaper.

offprint *noun* a copy of an article forming part of a larger magazine or periodical.

off-putting *adj. colloq.* disturbing; unpleasant.

off-season *noun* the less popular and less busy period.

offset — *noun* **1** a side-shoot on a plant, used for developing new plants. **2** a printing process in which an image is inked on to a rubber roller which then transfers it to paper, etc. **3** anything which compensates or is a counterbalance for something else. — *verb* (**offsetting**; PAST AND PAST PARTICIPLE **offset**) **1** to counterbalance or compensate for (something): *price rises offset by tax cuts*. **2** to print (something) using an offset process.

offset lithography *or* **offset litho** a method of printing, developed at the beginning of the 20c, by which an image created by photographic means on a printing plate is transferred to a rubber 'blanket' cylinder and then to the paper (or other material such as metal or plastic).

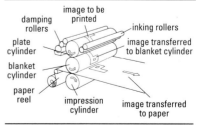

offset lithography

offshoot noun **1** a shoot growing from a plant's main stem. **2** anything which is a branch of, or has developed from, something else.

offshore adv., adj. **1** situated in, at, or on the sea, not far from the coast: offshore industries. **2** said of the wind blowing away from the coast, out to sea.

offside — adj., adv. Football, Rugby in an illegal position between the ball and the opponents' goal. — noun the side of a vehicle or horse nearest the centre of the road, in the UK the right side.

offspring noun (PL. **offspring**) **1** a person's child. **2** the young of an animal. **3** a result or outcome.

off-stage adj., adv. not on the stage, so unable to be seen by the audience.

off-street adj., said of parking not on a road.

off-the-peg adj., said of clothing ready to wear; ready-made.

off-white — adj. yellowish or greyish white. — noun this colour, or anything which is this colour, eg paint.

OFT abbrev. Office of Fair Trading.

oft adv. old use, poetic often. [from Anglo-Saxon]

often adv. **1** many times; frequently. **2** in many cases.
— **as often as not** quite often; in about half the cases.
every so often sometimes; now and then.
more often than not usually; in most of the cases.
[from Middle English, from OFT]

Ogaden a geographical area in SE Ethiopia. It is a dry plateau intermittently watered by the Fafen Shet and Jerer rivers and largely inhabited by Somali-speaking nomads. HISTORY part of Abyssinia in 1890; part of Italian East Africa from 1936 until 1941; area claimed by Somalia in the 1960s; the Somali invasion in 1977 was repulsed by Ethiopian forces; fighting continued throughout the 1980s.

Ogam or **Ogham** noun an ancient alphabet used from the 4c BC in Celtic and Pictish inscriptions, especially on stone monuments found in Ireland and Wales. It consists of 20 characters composed of sets of parallel lines (numbering one to five) meeting or crossing a base line, usually the corner of a stone monument.

Ogbomosho POP (1992e) 661 000, the third largest city in Oyo state, W Nigeria. It lies 88km/55mi NE of Ibadan.

Ogden, C(harles) K(ay) (1889–1957) English linguistic reformer, born in Fleetwood, Lancashire. He founded the Cambridge Magazine (1912–22), and the Orthological Institute (1917). In the 1920s he conceived the idea of Basic English, a simplified form of English with only 850 words, to provide a practical means of international communication. He developed the approach with the help of I A Richards (1893–1979), and though by the 1940s it was attracting considerable interest, its popularity soon declined.

Ogdon, John (Andrew Howard) (1937–89) English pianist, born in Mansfield Woodhouse, Nottinghamshire. In 1962 he was joint winner (with Ashkenazy) of the Moscow Tchaikovsky Competition. He had a powerful technique, a remarkable memory, and a huge repertoire in the virtuoso pianist-composer tradition (eg Liszt, Busoni, Stevenson, and Sorabji). His own compositions included a piano concerto.

ogee noun an S-shaped curve, line or moulding. [from Old French ogive, a diagonal rib in a vault]

ogle verb trans., intrans. to look or stare at (a person) expressing sexual desire with the eyes. [perhaps from Dutch oogen, to make eyes at]

Oglethorpe, James Edward (1696–1785) English soldier and colonial settler, born in

London. He joined the army (1712), and entered parliament (1722), where he became involved in prison reform. He had the idea of establishing a colony in America for debtors from English jails and persecuted Protestants, received a grant of land (later called Georgia), and in 1732 led out the first group of settlers. After war with Spain was declared in 1739, he invaded Florida, and in 1742 repulsed a Spanish invasion, before he returned to England the following year.

O-grade or **Ordinary grade** noun formerly in Scotland, an examination in a subject usually taken at the end of the fourth year in secondary schools; replaced by Standard Grade.

ogre or **ogress** noun **1** in fairy stories, a frightening, cruel, ugly, man-eating male or female giant. **2** a cruel or frightening person. [from French ogre]

ogrish or **ogreish** adj. characteristic of or like an ogre.

OH abbrev. Ohio.

oh see O².

O'Hara, John (Henry) (1905–70) US novelist and short-story writer, born in Pottsville, Pennsylvania. He worked as a journalist and wrote his first novel Appointment in Samarra in 1934. His writing is characterized by its documentary realism which led to several novels being made into successful films, including Butterfield 8 (1935, filmed, 1960) and Ten North Frederik (1955, filmed 1958). Pal Joey (1940) was adapted by the author and others into a successful musical comedy.

O'Hara, Kimball see KIM.

O'Hara, Scarlett the wilful, vivacious Southern belle at the centre of Margaret Mitchell's Gone with the Wind.

Ohio POP (1990) 11m, a state in E USA, divided into 88 counties. AREA 107 041sq km/ 41 330sq mi. It is known as the 'Buckeye State'. PHYSICAL DESCRIPTION part of the Allegheny Plateau, the state is drained by the Muskingum, Scioto, and Great Miami rivers, which flow to meet the Ohio R and L Erie. HISTORY visited by La Salle in 1669, claimed for France, and settled by fur traders from 1685; taken by the British in 1754; the 17th state to join the Union, in 1803. CAPITAL Columbus. CHIEF TOWNS Cleveland, Cincinnati, Toledo, Akron, Dayton. ECONOMY agriculture based on wheat, soya beans, vegetables, dairy cattle, and livestock; natural resources include coal (the E and SE Appalachian coalfield), natural gas, salt, lime, stone, sand, and gravel; a major industrial centre, producing steel, metal products, vehicles, paper, chemicals, rubber, clothing, electrical goods, and foodstuffs.

Ohio River a river in E central USA, length 2 101km/1 306mi (including the Allegheny). The second longest tributary of the Mississippi R (after the Missouri), it is formed at Pittsburgh by the union of the Monongahela and Allegheny rivers. Flowing generally SW for 1 578km/980mi, it joins the Mississippi at Cairo, Illinois, and separates the states of Ohio, Indiana, and Illinois in the N from West Virginia and Kentucky in the S. Its chief tributaries are the Kanawha, Licking, Kentucky, Tennessee (to the left); Scioto, Miami, and Wabash (to the right). The river is navigable for all its length, with the help of a canal at Louisville.

Ohm, Georg Simon (1787–1854) German physicist, born in Erlangen, Bavaria. Professor at Nuremberg and Munich, he published 'Ohm's law', relating voltage, current, and resistance in an electrical circuit in 1827. The SI unit of electrical resistance is named after him.

ohm noun (SYMBOL Ω) the SI unit of electrical resistance, equal to the resistance of a circuit in which a potential difference of one volt is required to maintain a current of one ampere. [named after Georg Simon Ohm]

OHMS abbrev. Brit. On Her (or His) Majesty's Service, often written on mail from government departments.

Ohm's law Physics a law which states that the direct current flowing in an electrical circuit is directly proportional to the potential difference (voltage) applied to the circuit, and inversely proportional to the resistance of the circuit, ie $V = IR$, where V is voltage, I is current, and R is resistance. [named after Georg Simon Ohm]

oho interj. old use an expression of surprise or triumphant satisfaction.

-oholic see -AHOLIC.

Ohrid POP (1989e) 69 000, a town in SW Macedonia, lying on the shores of L Ohrid. NOTABLE FEATURES Cathedral of St Sophia, St Clement's Church (13c); castle; the old town is a World Heritage site.

Ohrid, Lake, Serbo-Croatian **Ohridsko Jezero** a lake situated on the frontier between Albania and Macedonia, to the E of Elbasan. AREA 350sq km/135sq mi. Two thirds of it lie in Macedonia.

-oid suffix forming nouns and adjectives meaning 'having the form of': humanoid / rhomboid. [from Greek eidos, shape]

-oidal suffix forming adjectives corresponding to nouns in -oid.

oik noun Brit. a person thought of as inferior, especially because of being rude, ignorant, badly educated, or lower class.

oil — noun **1** any greasy, viscous, and usually flammable substance that is liquid at room temperature (20°C) and insoluble in water, used as a fuel, lubricant, or food. Oils may be derived from animals, plants, or mineral deposits, or may be manufactured artificially. **2** petroleum. **3** (often **oils**) oil-paint. **4** a picture painted with oil-paints. — verb to apply oil to, lubricate, or treat with oil.
— **oil the wheels** to do something in order to make things go more smoothly or successfully.
pour oil on troubled waters to soothe or calm a person or situation.
[from Latin oleum, from Greek elaia, olive tree]
◇ Naturally occurring plant and animal oils usually consist of triglycerides (three fatty acid chains linked to a glycerol molecule). Together with fats, they belong to a large class of organic compounds called lipids. Animal oils are mainly formed by heating animal fats. Common vegetable oils are extracted from maize (corn), soya beans, olives, and some nuts, and are used in cooking. Linseed oil (obtained from flax seeds) is used to make paints and varnishes. Essential oils (eg peppermint oil, rose oil) which evaporate rapidly and consist of volatile mixtures of terpenes (unsaturated hydrocarbons) and esters, are used in perfumes and flavourings, and in aromatherapy.

oil-cake noun a cattle-food made from linseed which has had its oil removed.

oilcloth noun canvas coated with oil to make it waterproof, used especially formerly as a covering for tables, etc.

oil-colour noun an oil-paint.

oiled adj. **1** smeared, treated, lubricated, or impregnated with oil. **2** preserved in oil. **3** colloq. drunk.

oilfield noun an area with reserves of mineral oil under the ground.

oil-fired adj. using oil as a fuel.

oilily adv. in an oily way, with an oily manner.

oiliness noun being oily.

oil-paint noun a paint made by mixing ground pigment with oil.

oil-painting noun **1** a picture painted with oil-paints. **2** the activity or art of painting in oils.
— **no oil-painting** colloq. not very beautiful.

oil-rig *noun* a structure, plus all the equipment, machinery, etc that it supports, used for drilling oil.

oilseed rape an annual plant (*Brassica napus*) growing up to 1m high, and belonging to the cabbage family (Cruciferae). It has bluish-green leaves and yellow cross-shaped flowers, and tolerates a wide range of climatic conditions. The leaves can be grazed by animal livestock, and the seeds of the plant contain large amounts of an edible oil, known as rapeseed oil, that is now increasingly used in margarine, cooking oils, and some lubricating oils. The residual 'cake' that remains after the oil has been extracted from the crushed seeds is used as an animal feedstuff.

oil shale *Geol.* a fine-grained sedimentary rock containing high levels of organic matter, from which an oily substance can be distilled by heating the shale in the absence of air.

oilskin *noun* **1** a cloth treated with oil to make it waterproof. **2** (*often* **oilskins**) a garment made of this.

oil slick a patch of oil forming a film on the surface of water, eg as a result of damage to or discharge from an oil tanker.

oil-tanker *noun* a large ship for carrying oil in bulk.

oil well a well bored in the ground or sea-bed to obtain petroleum.

oily *adj.* (**oilier, oiliest**) **1** of, containing, or like oil. **2** covered with oil. **3** *derog., said of a person, behaviour, etc* unpleasantly friendly or polite; servile and flattering.

oink — *noun* the characteristic noise of a pig. — *verb intrans.* to make this noise. [imitative]

ointment *noun* any greasy substance rubbed on the skin to heal injuries or as a cosmetic. — **a fly in the ointment** a minor nuisance or irritation which disturbs one's enjoyment. [from Latin *unguentum*, unguent]

Oireachtas an annual Irish gathering organized by the Gaelic League, on the lines of the Welsh Eisteddfod. It was first held in 1898.

Ojibwa, also called **Chippewa** an Algonkian-speaking Native American group originally concentrated around L Superior and L Huron (the Great Lakes region), USA. They were traditionally hunters, who were impoverished following the decline of the fur trade. The present-day population is c.42 000 in areas of Canada, North Dakota, and Montana.

Ojos del Salado, Cerro an Andean peak rising to 6 908m on the Argentina–Chile border. It is the second highest peak in the W hemisphere, after Aconcagua.

OK¹ *abbrev.* Oklahoma.

OK² *or* **okay** *colloq.* — *adj.* all right; satisfactory. — *adv.* well; satisfactorily. — *interj.* yes; I agree. — *noun* (PL. **OKs, OK's, okays**) approval, sanction, or agreement. — *verb* (**OK'ed, okayed, OK'ing, okaying**) to approve or pass as satisfactory. [from an abbreviation of American English *oll korrect*, a facetious spelling of *all correct*]

okapi *noun* (PL. **okapis, okapi**) an animal from Central Africa, related to the giraffe but with a shorter neck, and with a reddish-brown coat, white stripes on the legs and small horns. [a Central African word]

okapi

Okavango, River the third largest river in southern Africa, flowing through Angola, Namibia, and Botswana. The river is c.1 600km/1 000mi long. It rises in central Angola, and flows SE then S to enter the sea in a wide delta (c.15 000sq km/6 000sq mi), containing forest, swamp, marsh, and lagoon. The delta is a major wildlife area. Flooding fills nearby rivers and sometimes L Ngami.

Okayama POP (1991e) 597 000, the port capital of Okayama prefecture, SW Honshu, Japan, 112km/70mi W of Osaka. NOTABLE FEATURES 'Castle of the Crow' (16c); Koraku-en Gardens (17c).

Okeechobee, Lake the largest lake in S USA, lying in S central Florida. AREA 815sq km/315sq mi; maximum depth 4.6m. It is linked to the Atlantic Ocean by the St Lucie and Miami canals; rivers drain S through the Everglades.

O'Keefe, Georgia (1887–1986) US painter, born in Wisconsin. She was one of the pioneers of abstract art in America (eg *Blue and Green Music*, 1919, Art Institute of Chicago). She later moved towards a more figurative style, painting architectural subjects and close-ups of parts of flowers and plants, frequently with a Surrealist flavour. Her works include *Black Iris* (New York, 1949).

Okefenokee Swamp an area of swampland in SE Georgia and NE Florida, USA. Drained SW by the Suwannee R, it is an important wildlife refuge and tourist centre. [from Muskogean, = water-shaking]

okey-dokey *adv., adj., interj. slang* OK.

Oki Archipelago, Japanese **Oki Retto** an island group in Chugoku region, Japan. AREA 375sq km/145sq mi. It is situated in the Sea of Japan, 56km/35mi N of SW Honshu and includes Dogo, the largest island, and Dozen, a group of three islands. The islands are generally mountainous and forested. Dogo rises to 608m. The chief town and port is Saigo on Dogo. ECONOMY timber; fishing.

Okinawa POP (1984e) 6 000, a town in Santa Cruz department, central Bolivia. It was established by Japanese settlers in 1954 and over one quarter of its population today is Japanese.

Okinawa a region of Japan comprising the S part of the Ryukyu group. AREA 2 246sq km/867sq mi. The island of Okinawa is the largest of the group. It was taken by the USA in World War II and was returned to Japan in 1972.

Okla. *abbrev.* Oklahoma.

Oklahoma POP (1990) 3.2m, a state in SW USA, divided into 77 counties. AREA 181 083sq km/69 919sq mi. It is known as the 'Sooner State'. PHYSICAL DESCRIPTION rivers include the Red (forms the S border), Arkansas, Canadian, and Cimarron; the Ouachita Mts lie in the SE, and the Wichita Mts in the SW; the highest point is Black Mesa (1 516m); high prairies in the W are part of the Great Plains. HISTORY mostly acquired by the USA in the 1803 Louisiana Purchase; Native Americans were forced to move here in the 1830s, and Allem Wright, a Choctaw chief, coined the name Indian Territory to describe the land held by his people; for taking the Confederate side during the Civil War, the Native Americans were forced to forfeit the W part of their territory to whites (called Oklahoma Territory from 1890); the merged territories were admitted into the Union as the 46th state in 1907; part of the Dust Bowl of the 1930s. CAPITAL Oklahoma City. CHIEF TOWNS Tulsa, Lawton. ECONOMY major agricultural products are livestock and wheat, also cotton, dairy products, and peanuts; large oil reserves and associated petroleum industry; manufactures include machinery, fabricated metals, and aircraft. [from Muskogean, = red people]

Oklahoma! a musical by Richard Rodgers and Oscar Hammerstein II (1943), telling the story of the cowboy Curly and labourer Jud who are both determined to win Laurie's affections.

Oklahoma City POP (1990) 959 000, the industrial capital and largest city in the state of Oklahoma, USA. It lies on the North Canadian R, Oklahoma County. HISTORY settled around a railway station in 1889, it became state capital in 1910; developed rapidly after the discovery of oil in 1928. NOTABLE FEATURES National Cowboy Hall of Fame; Western Heritage Centre; State Historical Museum.

okra *noun* a tropical plant which produces long, green, edible pods used as a vegetable. [a W African word]

Öland POP (1984) 24 000, an elongated island, the largest in Sweden. It is situated in the Baltic Sea off the SE coast of the mainland, separated from it by Kalmar Sound. AREA 1 344sq km/519sq mi; length 136km/84mi. CHIEF TOWN Borgholm. ECONOMY potatoes; sugar beet; cattle; sugar refining; quarrying. NOTABLE FEATURE Borgholm Castle (12c–13c).

Olav V (1903–91) King of Norway (1957–91), born near Sandringham, Norfolk, the only child of Haakon VII and Maud, daughter of Edward VII. Appointed head of the Norwegian Armed Forces in 1944, he escaped with his father to England on the Nazi occupation, but returned in 1945. In 1929 he married Princess Martha (1901–54) of Sweden, and had two daughters and a son, Harald (1937–), who succeeded to the Norwegian throne as Harald V.

Olbers, Heinrich Wilhelm Matthäus (1758–1840) German astronomer, born in Ardbergen, near Bremen. While practising medicine at Bremen, he devised a method for calculating the orbits of comets (1779), discovered the minor planets Pallas (1802) and Vesta (1807), and the comet named after him (1815). He is also remembered for highlighting 'Olbers' paradox'.

Olbers' paradox a paradox expressed by Heinrich Olbers in 1826: why is the sky dark at night? In an infinitely large, unchanging universe uniformly populated with stars and galaxies, the sky would be dazzlingly bright. The paradox is resolved by modern cosmological theories of the expanding universe.

old — *adj.* **1** advanced in age; having existed for a long time. **2** having a stated age: *five years old*. **3** of or relating to the end period of a long life or existence: *old age*. **4** worn out or shabby through long use: *old shoes*. **5** no longer in use; out of date; old-fashioned. **6** belonging to the past. **7** former or earlier; earliest of two or more things: *their old house had no garden*. **8** of long standing or long existence: *an old member of the society*. **9** familiar, practised, or skilled through long experience: *an old hand / the same old excuses*. **10** having the characteristics (eg experience, maturity, or appearance) of age: *be old beyond one's years*. **11** *colloq.* used in expressions of affection or contempt: *good old Bill / silly old fool*. **12** *said of a language* being the earliest form known: *Old English*. **13** *colloq.* used for emphasis: *come round any old time*. — *noun* **1** an earlier time: *men of old*. **2** (**the old**) old people. — **as old as the hills** *colloq.* very old. **of old** formerly; a long time ago. [from Anglo-Saxon *eald*]

old age the later part of life.

old age pension a state pension paid to people who have retired from work.

old age pensioner a person in receipt of such a pension.

Old Bailey a street in the City of London, and, by association, the Central Criminal Court located there. The first court-house was erected in 1539, and the present building dates from 1907.

Old Believers *Relig.* Russian Orthodox traditionalists who rejected the reforms instituted in 1666. Although persecuted, they survived, established their own hierarchy in 1848, and were recognized by the state in 1881.

old boy 1 *Brit.* a former male pupil of a school. **2** *colloq.* an elderly man. **3** *colloq.* an affectionate or familiar form of address.

old boy network *Brit.* the system by which former members of the same public school secure advantages for each other in later life.

Oldcastle, Sir John (c.1378–1417) English Lollard leader and knight. After serving in the Scottish and Welsh wars, and becoming an intimate of the Prince of Wales (the future Henry V), he was convicted on charges of heresy in 1413. He escaped from the Tower, and conspired with other Lollards to capture Henry V and take control of London, but the rising was abortive, and Oldcastle was eventually hanged and burned. The Shakespearean character Falstaff is based partly on him.

Old Church Slavonic see SLAVIC LANGUAGES.

Old Comedy Athenian comic theatre of the 5c BC. Its unique structure includes an *agon* (a contest) and a *parabasis* (a choral address to the audience on a contemporary social issue). The only complete plays extant are by Aristophanes.

old country the country of origin of immigrants.

Old Curiosity Shop, The a novel by Charles Dickens (1841). It centres around the life of Little Nell Trent and her impoverished shop-owning grandfather.

old dear *slang, often derog.* **1** an old woman. **2** one's mother.

olden *adj.* old use former; past: *in olden days.*

Old English see ENGLISH.

Old English sheepdog a breed of dog developed in the UK in the 18c to protect cattle, having a large body, with the hindquarters higher than the shoulders, and a long untidy coat, often hiding the ears and eyes, and usually white with large dark patches.

old-fashioned *adj.* **1** belonging to, or in a style common, some time ago; out of date. **2** in favour of or living and acting according to the habits and moral views of the past.

Oldfield, Bruce (1950–) English fashion designer, born in London. He taught art, then studied fashion in Kent and in London, after which he became a freelance designer. He designed for Bendel's store in New York City, sold sketches to Yves St Laurent, and showed his first collection in London in 1975. His designs include evening dresses for royalty and screen stars, and ready-to-wear clothes.

old flame *colloq.* a person with whom one used to be in love.

old girl 1 *Brit.* a former female pupil of a school. **2** *colloq.* an elderly woman. **3** *colloq.* an affectionate or familiar form of address.

old guard the original or most conservative members of a society, group, or organization.

Oldham, Richard Dixon (1858–1936) Irish geologist and seismologist, born in Dublin. A member of the Geological Survey of India (1878–1903), he distinguished for the first time between primary and secondary seismic waves (1897), and characterized many other phenomena of earthquake activity. In 1906 he established from seismographical records the existence of the Earth's core.

Oldham POP (1992e) 220 000, an industrial town in Oldham borough, Greater Manchester, NW England. It lies 12km/7mi NE of Manchester. NOTABLE FEATURE town hall.

old hat *colloq.* something tediously familiar or well known.

Old High German, the oldest form of official and literary German with written records dating from the 8c AD. See also GERMANIC LANGUAGES, HIGH GERMAN.

oldie *noun colloq.* an old person, song, story or thing.

old lady *slang* a person's wife or mother.

old lag *Brit. slang* a habitual criminal.

old maid *derog. colloq.* **1** a woman who is not married and is thought of as being unlikely ever to marry. **2** a woman or man who is prim and fussy.

old-maidish *adj.* characteristic of or like an old maid.

old man 1 *slang* a person's husband or father. **2** an affectionate form of address for a man or boy.

old man's beard a wild plant with fluffy white hairs around the seeds.

old master any great painter or painting from the period stretching from the Renaissance to about 1800.

old moon the moon in its last quarter, before the new moon.

Old Mortality a novel by Sir Walter Scott (1816). It is set at the time of the Covenanters and revolves around the life of Henry Morton of Milnwood.

Old Nick *colloq.* the devil.

Old Persian, the old form of Persian spoken in the area of present-day Iran from around 1000 BC, and with surviving written records from c.6c BC. See also FARSI, IRANIAN LANGUAGES.

old school people with traditional or old-fashioned ways of thinking, ideas, beliefs, etc.

old school tie 1 a tie with a characteristic pattern or colour worn by former members of a public school. **2** *Brit.* the system by which former members of the same public school do favours for each other in later life. See also OLD BOY NETWORK.

oldster *noun colloq.* an old person.

old story something which one has heard before or which has happened before, especially frequently.

Old Style, a method of dating using the Julian calendar. See also NEW STYLE.

Old Testament, the first part of the Christian Bible, containing the Hebrew scriptures. See also NEW TESTAMENT.
◇ The sacred Jewish scriptures of the Hebrew Bible became known as the Old Testament among Christians to distinguish it from the New Testament. In the traditional Jewish canon the writings are arranged into three parts: the Law (the five books of the Pentateuch); the Prophets (Joshua, Judges, Samuel, Kings, Isaiah, Jeremiah, Ezekiel, and the Book of the Twelve Prophets); and the Writings (containing all the remaining works). All the books of the Hebrew Bible appear in the version of the Old Testament used by Protestant Churches today, but divided so as to number 39; Roman Catholic version accept 46 works, with the additions taken from Greek versions and the Vulgate, and known collectively as the Apocrypha by Protestants.

old-time *adj.* belonging to or typical of the past.

old-timer *noun* **1** a person who has been in a job, position, profession, etc for a long time; a veteran. **2** *North Amer. colloq., especially as a form of address* an old person.

Old Trafford 1 a cricket ground in Manchester, England, the home of Lancashire CCC and a regular Test venue. It was opened in 1857. **2** A football ground in Manchester, England, the home of Manchester United FC, opened on 19 Feb 1910. It is adjacent to the cricket ground.

Olduvai Gorge a gorge within the Ngorongoro conservation area of the Rift Valley,

N Tanzania. It is of great archaeological importance as the source of some of the oldest known 'human' remains, notably the Leakeys' 1959 discovery of the skull of *Zinjanthropus boisei* ('nut-cracker man'), and remains of *Australopithecus*, *Homo habilis*, and *Homo erectus*.

Old Vic Theatre a theatre built in 1816–18 near Waterloo Bridge, London, originally called the Royal Coburg and renamed the Royal Victoria in 1833. In 1912 Lilian Baylis began to transform what was a working-class temperance music hall into a leading centre for Shakespearean plays. The Vic–Wells Ballet Company was formed there by Ninette de Valois in 1931, but it later moved to the Sadler's Wells Theatre (1933). From 1963 to 1976 it was the home of the National Theatre Company under Peter Hall.

old wives' tale an ancient belief or theory considered foolish and unscientific.

Old Wives' Tale, The a novel by Arnold Bennett (1908). It focuses on the lives of sisters Constance and Sophia Baines.

old woman *slang* **1** a person's wife or mother. **2** a person, especially a man, who is timid or fussy.

Old Woman Cooking Eggs, The a painting by Diego Velázquez (1618, Edinburgh).

old-womanish *adj.* characteristic of or like an old woman.

Old World 1 the E hemisphere, comprising Europe, Asia, and Africa, which forms that part of the world known before the discovery of the Americas. **2** (*attributive*) **a** (**old-world**) belonging to earlier times, especially in being considered quaint or charming; not modern. **b** (**Old-World**) of the Old World.

oleaginous *adj.* of, like or producing oil. [from Latin *oleaginus*, from *oleum*, oil]

oleander *noun* a poisonous Mediterranean shrub with leathery evergreen leaves and clusters of white, pink, or purple flowers. [from Latin *oleander*]

olefin *noun Chem.* alkene. [from Latin *oleum*, oil]

oleograph *noun* a lithograph printed in oil colours to imitate an oil painting. [from Latin *oleum*, oil + Greek *graph(e bar)*, writing]

Oléron, Ile d', ancient **Uliarus** a wooded fertile island in the E Bay of Biscay, W France. It is France's second largest off-shore island (after Corsica), lying 3km/2mi from the mainland, to which it is linked by a modern toll-bridge. AREA 175sq km/68sq mi; length 30km/19mi. CHIEF TOWNS Le Château d'Oléron, St-Pierre d'Oléron. ECONOMY oysters; farming; tourism.

O-Level, in full **General Certificate of Education (GCE) Ordinary-level** formerly, in England, Wales, and Northern Ireland, an examination taken by (usually) secondary school pupils at around the age of 16. In 1988, it was replaced, along with the Certificate of Secondary Education (CSE), by the General Certificate of Secondary Education (GCSE).

olfactory *adj.* relating to the sense of smell. [from Latin *olfacere*, to smell]

Olga a female first name. [a Russian name, of Scandinavian origin, = holy]

oligarch *noun* a member of an oligarchy.

oligarchic or **oligarchical** *adj.* relating to or characteristic of an oligarchy.

oligarchy *noun* (PL. **oligarchies**) **1** government by a small group of people. **2** a state or organization governed by a small group of people. **3** a small group of people which forms a government. [from Greek *oligarchia*, from *oligos*, little, few + *archos*, leader]

oligo- *combining form* forming words denoting few in number. [from Greek *oligos*, little, few]

Oligocene — *noun Geol.* the third epoch of the Tertiary period, lasting from about 38 million to 25 million years ago. During this time the first apes appeared, many modern mammals began to evolve, and flowering plants became more abundant. — *adj.* **1** relating to this epoch. **2** relating to rocks formed during this epoch. [from Greek *oligos*, few + *kainos*, recent]

oligopoly *noun* an economic situation in which there are few sellers of a particular product or service, and a small number of competitive firms control the market. [from Greek *oligos*, little, few + *poleein*, to sell]

Olive a female first name, after the plant.

olive — *noun* **1** a small evergreen tree (*Olea europea*) with a twisted gnarled trunk and narrow leathery silvery-green leaves, cultivated mainly in the Mediterranean region for its edible fruit. **2** the small oval edible fruit of this tree, which has a hard stone and bitter oily flesh, and is harvested either when green and unripe or when purplish-black and ripe. Olives may be eaten fresh, and are also pickled in brine. Olive oil is obtained by pressing black olives. **3** the wood of this tree, used to make furniture. **4** (*in full* **olive green**) the dull yellowish-green colour of unripe olives. — *adj.* **1** dull yellowish-green in colour. **2** *said of a complexion* sallow. [from Latin *oliva*]

olive branch a sign of a wish for peace or a gesture towards peace or reconciliation.

olive drab the dull grey-green colour of American army uniforms.

olive oil the pale yellow oil obtained by pressing ripe olives, used as a cooking and salad oil, and in soaps, ointments, and lubricants.

Oliver, King (Joe) (1885–1938) US cornettist, composer, and bandleader, born in Abend, Louisiana, and raised in New Orleans. In 1922 he formed his 'Hot' Creole Jazz Band, in which he performed with Louis Armstrong. Some of his compositions, eg 'Dippermouth Blues' and 'Dr Jazz', are part of the standard jazz repertoire.

Oliver (de Bois) the cruel elder brother of Orlando in Shakespeare's *As You Like It*, who mends his ways and marries Celia.

Oliver! a musical (1960) by Lionel Bart, based on the novel *Oliver Twist* by Charles Dickens.

Oliver Twist a novel by Charles Dickens (1837–9). It describes the life of a child in a workhouse and in the criminal underworld of London.

Olives, Mount of or **Mount Olivet** a rocky outcrop overlooking the Old City of Jerusalem across the Kidron Valley, a site of sanctuaries during the reigns of David and Solomon, and a traditional Jewish burial ground. Known as the place where Jesus taught about the coming of the end of the age (Mark 13), it is near the Garden of Gethsemane where he was arrested, and is the supposed location of the ascension of the risen Christ (Acts 1.6–12).

Olivetti, Adriano (1901–60) Italian manufacturer, born in Ivrea. He spent time in the USA assimilating the methods of mass-production. On his return to Italy he transformed the manufacturing methods of the typewriter firm founded by his father Camillo Olivetti (1868–1943). He also established a strong design policy which embraced products, graphics, and the architecture of the company's buildings. His strong social concerns led him to provide housing of a high standard for his employees. The company also manufactures computers and information systems.

Olivia **1** the rich countess in Shakespeare's *Twelfth Night*, who is pursued by Orsino, falls in love with 'Cesario', and marries Sebastian. **2** a female first name, after Shakespeare's character.

Olivier (of Brighton), Laurence (Kerr) Olivier, Baron (1907–89) English actor, producer, and director, born in Dorking, Surrey. With the Old Vic company in London from 1937 (co-director 1944), he played many Shakespearean roles, but proved his versatility as Archie Rice in *The Entertainer* (1957). The films he acted in and directed include *Henry V*, *Hamlet*, and *Richard III*. He was married to actresses Vivien Leigh (1940–60) and Joan Plowright (from 1961). In 1962 he became Director of the Chichester Festival Theatre and (1962–73) the National Theatre. After 1974 he appeared chiefly in films and television (eg *Brideshead Revisited*, 1982).

olivine *noun Geol.* any of a group of hard glassy rock-forming silicate minerals, typically olive green in colour, but sometimes yellowish or brown, commonly found in gabbros and basalts. One of the green crystalline forms is classed as a gem, known as *peridot*.

Olmecs members of a highly-elaborate Middle American Indian culture on the Mexican Gulf Coast, prominent 1200–600BC. They probably had the first large planned religious and ceremonial centres (characterized by monumental sculptures and massive altars), at San Lorenzo, La Venta, and Tres Zapotecs. They were probably also the first people in the area to devise glyph writing and the 260-day Mesoamerican calendar.

-ology see -LOGY.

Olwen a female first name. [of Welsh origin, from *ol*, track + *(g)wen*, white]

Olympia a village and national sanctuary in Ilia department, S Greece, on the N bank of R Alfios. It was established as the chief sanctuary of Zeus from c.1000 BC. From 776 BC it was the site of the Panhellenic religious festival held every four years, the ancestor of the modern Olympic Games. Major excavations from the 19c have uncovered the Temple of Zeus (5c BC), the Temple of Hera, and a stadium.

Olympia POP (1990) 161 000, the seaport capital of the state of Washington, USA, and of Thurston County in the W of the state. It lies at the S end of Puget Sound, at the mouth of the Deschutes R. HISTORY founded at the end of the Oregon Trail in 1850, it became capital of Washington Territory in 1853.

Olympia a painting by Edouard Manet (1865, Musée d'Orsay, Paris). Its depiction of a reclining nude attended by her black maid caused a scandal when it was first exhibited at the Salon.

Olympiad *noun* **1** a celebration of the modern Olympic Games. **2** a period of four years between Olympic Games, used by the ancient Greeks as a way of reckoning time. **3** an international contest in especially chess or bridge. [from Greek *Olympias*, of Olympus]

Olympian — *noun* **1** *Greek Mythol.* any of the twelve ancient Greek gods thought to live on Mount Olympus in N Greece. **2** a person who competes in the Olympic Games. — *adj.* **1** *Greek Mythol.* of or relating to Mount Olympus or the ancient Greek gods thought to live there. **2** god-like, especially in being superior or condescending in behaviour or manners. [from Greek *Olympios*, from Greek *Olympos*, Olympus]

Olympic — *adj.* **1** of the Olympic Games. **2** of ancient Olympia. — *noun* (**Olympics**) the Olympic Games. [from Greek *Olympikos*]

Olympic Games **1** *Hist.* games celebrated every four years in Olympia in ancient Greece, including athletic, musical, and literary competitions. **2** a modern international sports competition held every four years. See panel p. 904.
◇ The modern games were inaugurated at Athens in 1896. They are held at a different venue every four years, and today more than 6 000 competitors from around 100 countries compete in more than 20 sports. Since 1924, a separate Winter Olympic Games has been staged, and is held in the same year as the Summer Games. The governing body of the Olympic movement is the International Olympic Committee (IOC). See panel p. 904.

Olympic National Park a national park in the Olympic Mountains, Washington, USA, established in 1938. A World Heritage area, it is noted as a refuge for the rare Roosevelt elk; the park has varied scenery, including glaciers and a stretch of the Pacific coastline. AREA 3 678sq km/ 1 420sq mi.

Olympus, Greek **Ôlimbos** a range of mountains between Macedonia and Thessaly regions, N Greece. Its highest point is Mitikas (2 917m). Olympus is traditionally regarded as the home of the dynasty of gods in Greek mythology headed by Zeus.

Olympus, Mount the highest peak on the island of Cyprus, situated in the Troödos range, central Cyprus. HEIGHT 1 951m.

OM *abbrev. Brit.* Order of Merit.

Om in Hinduism, a mystical and sacred monosyllable. Believed to have a divine power, it is used at the beginning and end of prayers, and as a mantra for meditation. It is discussed in some of the Upanishads.

the sacred symbol Om

Omagh, Gaelic **An Omaigh** POP (1991) 17 000, the county town of Co Tyrone, W central Northern Ireland, in Omagh district. It lies on the R Strule. NOTABLE FEATURE inside the 19c Catholic parish church is the 9c Black Bell of Drumragh.

Omaha POP (1990) 618 000, the seat of Douglas County, E Nebraska, USA, lying on the Missouri R. The port is the largest city in the state, serving as a major livestock market and meat-processing

The Principal Greek Gods

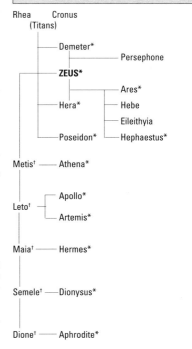

† = a consort of Zeus
* = one of the 12 Olympians in the 'central group' of gods on the Parthenon frieze

Olympic Venues

Summer Games

1896	Athens, Greece	1932	Los Angeles, USA	1972	Munich, West Germany
1900	Paris, France	1936	Berlin, Germany	1976	Montreal, Canada
1904	St Louis, USA	1948	London, UK	1980	Moscow, USSR
1908	London, UK	1952	Helsinki, Finland	1984	Los Angeles, USA
1912	Stockholm, Sweden	1956	Melbourne, Australia	1988	Seoul, South Korea
1920	Antwerp, Belgium	1960	Rome, Italy	1992	Barcelona, Spain
1924	Paris, France	1964	Tokyo, Japan	1996	Atlanta, USA
1928	Amsterdam, Holland	1968	Mexico City, Mexico	2000	Sydney, Australia

Winter Games

1924	Chamonix, France	1956	Cortina, Italy	1980	Lake Placid, New York, USA
1928	St Moritz, Switzerland	1960	Squaw Valley, California, USA	1984	Sarajevo, Yugoslavia
1932	Lake Placid, New York, USA	1964	Innsbruck, Austria	1988	Calgary, Canada
1936	Garmisch-Partenkirchen, Germany	1968	Grenoble, France	1992	Albertville, France
		1972	Sapporo, Japan	1994	Lillehammer, Norway
1948	St Moritz, Switzerland	1976	Innsbruck, Austria	1998	Nugano, Japan
1952	Oslo, Norway				

Olympic games were also held in 1906 to commemorate the 10th anniversary of the birth of the Modern Games. The 1956 equestrian events were held at Stockholm, Sweden, due to quarantine laws in Australia.

---

centre. HISTORY a fur-trading post was established here in 1812; achieved city status in 1867. NOTABLE FEATURES Joslyn Art Museum; Aerospace Museum; Boys Town.

Omaha a Siouan-speaking Native American Plains people, originally from the Atlantic seaboard, who migrated to Minnesota but in the late 17c were pushed into Nebraska by Dakotas, where they farmed and hunted buffalo. In 1854 they sold most of their land to white settlers, but were granted some land by the government in 1882. The present-day population is c.1 500 on reservations in Nebraska.

Omai (c.1753–84) a Polynesian from Ra'iatea (Society Islands) who joined Capt Cook's second expedition as an interpreter in 1773. In 1774 he was the first Pacific Islander to visit England, where he was welcomed into high society and made the object of much interest and literary discussion before being returned home during Cook's third voyage (1777).

Oman, formerly **Muscat and Oman**, official name **Sultanate of Oman** POP (1992e) 1.6m, an independent state in the extreme SE corner of the Arabian peninsula. AREA 300 000sq km/ 115 800sq mi. The State is bounded NW by the United Arab Emirates, N and W by Saudi Arabia, SW by Yemen, NE by the Gulf of Oman, and SE and E by the Arabian Sea. CAPITAL Muscat. CHIEF TOWNS Matrah, Nizwa, Salalah. TIME ZONE GMT +4. The population is mainly Arabic; Ibadhi Muslim is the chief religion. OFFICIAL LANGUAGE Arabic. CURRENCY the Omani rial. PHYSICAL DESCRIPTION the tip of the Musandam peninsula in the Strait of Hormuz is separated from the rest of the country by an 80km/50mi strip belonging to the United Arab Emirates; the Hajar range runs NW–SE parallel to the coast; several peaks in the Jabal Akhdar are over 3 000m; the alluvial plain of the Batinah lies E and N of the Hajar; a vast sand desert is to the NE. CLIMATE a desert climate with much regional variation; hot and humid coast from Apr to Oct with a maximum temperature of 47°C; hot and dry interior during this summer period; relatively temperate in mountains; light monsoon rains in the S from Jun to Sep. HISTORY dominant maritime power of the W Indian Ocean in the 16c; internal dissension in 1913–20 between supporters of the Sultanate and members of the Ibadhi sect who wanted to be ruled exclusively by their religious leader; a separatist tribal revolt in 1964 led to a police coup that installed a new Sultan from the ruling family in 1970. GOVERNMENT an independent state ruled by a Sultan who is both head of state and Premier. ECONOMY oil discovered in 1964 now provides over 90% of government revenue; natural gas is an important source of industrial power;

attempts made to diversify the economy; copper smelting, date processing, banana packing, electric wire and cables, paper bags; c.70% of the population relies on agriculture; alfalfa, wheat, tobacco, fruit, vegetables, fishing.

Oman

Oman, Gulf of the NW arm of the Indian Ocean, lying between Oman and Iran. It is linked to the Arabian Gulf by the Strait of Hormuz and, SE, to the Arabian Sea. The gulf is a vital waterway for ocean traffic to and from the Gulf states. It is 480km/300mi long.

Omar or **'Umar** (c.581–64) the second caliph (634–44), and the father of one of Muhammad's wives. He succeeded Abu-Bekr and built up an empire comprising Persia, Syria, and all N Africa. He was assassinated in Medina by a slave.

Omar a male first name, occurring in the Bible and also with an Arabic origin, as borne eg by the actor Omar Sharif.

Omar Khayyám (c.1050–c.1123) Persian astronomer-poet, born in Nishapur. He reformed the Muslim calendar, and was known to the Western world as a mathematician, until in 1859 Edward FitzGerald published a translation of his *Rubáiyt* ('Quatrains'). The work is now regarded as an anthology of which little or nothing may be by Omar.

ombudsman *noun* (PL. **ombudsmen**) an official appointed to investigate complaints against public authorities, government departments, or the people who work for them. [from Swedish *ombudsman*, legal representative]

◇ Most ombudsmen do not investigate issues that can be considered by courts or tribunals. Their findings do not have the force of law, and

are put in the form of reports from which it is hoped remedial action will result.

Omdurman POP (1983) 526 000, a major suburb of Khartoum, central Sudan. It is connected to the main city by a tramline bridge over the White Nile. HISTORY the military headquarters of Muhammad Ahmed in 1884; captured by the British in 1898. NOTABLE FEATURE ruins of the Mahdi's tomb.

Omdurman, Battle of an engagement (1898) outside Khartoum, across the Nile, which confirmed the British reconquest of the Sudan. The British campaign under Kitchener had been authorized in 1895, and instituted with powerful Anglo-Egyptian forces in 1896. The overwhelming defeat of the massed forces of the Khalifa (the successor of the Mahdi) illustrated the power of modern weapons.

omega *noun* **1** the last letter of the Greek alphabet (Ω, ω). **2** the last of a series; a conclusion. [from Greek *o mega*, great O]

omelette or *North Amer., esp. US* **omelet** *noun* a dish of beaten eggs fried in a pan, often folded round a savoury or sweet filling such as cheese or jam. [from Old French *alemette*, from *lemelle*, knife-blade]

omen *noun* **1** a sign of a future event, either good or evil. **2** threatening or prophetic character: *bird of ill omen*. [from Latin *omen*]

ominous *adj.* threatening; containing a warning of something evil or bad that will happen. [from Latin *ominosus*, from *omen*, omen]

ominously *adv.* in an ominous way; as an ominous circumstance.

ominousness *noun* being ominous.

omission *noun* **1** something that has been left out or neglected. **2** the act of leaving something out or neglecting it. [from Latin *omissio*, from *omittere*, to omit]

omit *verb* (**omitted**, **omitting**) **1** to leave out, either by mistake or on purpose. **2** to fail (to do something). [from Latin *omittere*, from *ob*, in front + *mittere*, to send]

omni- *combining form* forming words meaning 'all', 'every'. [from Latin *omnis*, all]

omnibus — *noun* (PL. **omnibuses**) **1** *old use, formal* a bus. **2** a book containing a number of novels or stories by a single author. **3** a television or radio broadcast which brings together a number of programmes originally broadcast separately. — *adj.* **1** made up of or bringing together several different items or parts. **2** serving several different purposes at the same time. [from Latin *omnibus*, for all]

OMNIMAX or **Omnimax** *adj. trademark, said of a film* designed to be viewed on a special domed screen, producing a near-hemispherical image to the audience.

omnipotence *noun* unlimited power.

omnipotent *adj.* having very great or absolute power. [from Latin *omnis*, all + *potens*, powerful]

omnipotently *adv.* in an omnipotent way.

omnipresence *noun* being present everywhere at the same time.

omnipresent *adj., said especially of a god* present everywhere at the same time. [from Latin *omnis*, all + *praesens*, present]

omniscience *noun* knowledge of all things.

omniscient *adj.* knowing everything. [from Latin *omnis*, all + *scire*, to know]

omnisciently *adv.* in an omniscient way.

Omnium, Duke of the English politician, formerly known as Plantagenet Palliser, who eventually becomes Prime Minister in the 'Palliser' novels of Anthony Trollope. His wife, the Duchess of Omnium, was formerly known as Lady Glencora.

omnivore *noun* an animal or plant that eats any type of food.

omnivorous *adj.* **1** eating any type of food, especially both meat and vegetable matter. **2** taking in, reading, using, etc everything. [from Latin *omnis*, all + *vorare*, to devour]

omnivorously *adv.* in an omnivorous way.

omnivorousness *noun* being omnivorous.

Omo a national park in S Ethiopia. The lower valley is a World Heritage site. AREA 4 015sq km/1 550sq mi.

Omsk 1 POP (1990e) 1.2m, the industrial riverport capital of Omsk oblast, W Siberia, Russia. It lies at the confluence of the Irtysh and Om rivers. Founded as a fortress in 1716, it is the greenest city in Siberia with 25sq km/10sq mi of boulevards and gardens. **2** an oblast in W Siberia, Russia, with the city of Omsk as its capital.

on — *prep.* **1** touching, supported by, attached to, covering, or enclosing: *a chair on the floor / a dog on a lead / a sheet on a bed.* **2** in or into (a vehicle, etc). **3** carried with: *I've got no money on me.* **4** very near to or along the side of: *a house on the shore.* **5** at or during (a certain day, time, etc). **6** immediately after, at, or before: *he found the letter on his return.* **7** within the (given) limits of: *a picture on page nine.* **8** about: *a book on Jane Austen.* **9** towards: *march on the town.* **10** through contact with; as a result of: *cut oneself on the broken bottle.* **11** in the state or process of: *on fire / on a journey.* **12** using as a means of transport. **13** using as a means or medium: *talk on the telephone / a tune on the piano.* **14** on the occasion of: *shoot on sight.* **15** having as a basis or source: *on good authority / arrested on suspicion.* **16** working for or being a member of: *on the committee / work on the case.* **17** at the expense of; to the disadvantage of: *treatment on the National Health / the joke's on him.* **18** supported by: *live on bread and cheese.* **19** regularly taking or using: *on tranquillizers.* **20** in a specified manner: *on the cheap.* **21** staked as a bet: *put money on a horse.* **22** following: *disappointment on disappointment.* — *adv.* **1** said especially of clothes covering; in contact with: *have no clothes on.* **2** ahead, forwards, or towards in space or time: *go on home / later on.* **3** continuously; without interruption: *keep on about something.* **4** in or into operation or activity: *put the radio on.* — *adj.* **1** working, broadcasting, or performing: *you're on in two minutes.* **2** taking place: *which films are on this week?* **3** *colloq.* possible, practicable, or acceptable: *that just isn't on.* **4** *colloq.* talking continuously, especially to complain or nag: *always on at him to try harder.* **5** in favour of a win: *odds of 3 to 4 on.* **6** *Cricket* on the side of the field towards which the bat is facing, usually the batsman's left and the bowler's right. See also OFF 4.

— **be on to someone** *or* **something** *colloq.* **1** realize their importance or intentions. **2** be in touch with them: *we'll be on to you about the party on Saturday.*

get on to someone *colloq.* get in touch with them.

just on ... almost exactly: *have collected just on £50.*

on and off now and then; occasionally.

on and on continually; at length.

on time promptly; at the right time.

on to ... to a position on or in ...
[from Anglo-Saxon]

onager *noun* a wild ass found in central Asia. [from Greek *onagros*]

onanism *noun* **1** sexual intercourse in which the penis is withdrawn from the vagina before ejaculation. **2** masturbation. [from *Onan*, a character in the Bible (Gen 38.9)]

Onassis, Aristotle (Socrates) (1906–75) Greek millionaire shipowner, born in Smyrna, Turkey. He bought his first ships in 1932–3, built up one of the world's largest independent fleets, and became a pioneer in the construction of supertankers. He was divorced in 1960, and after a long relationship with Maria Callas, in 1968 he married Jacqueline Bouvier Kennedy, the widow of US President John F Kennedy.

ONC *abbrev.* Ordinary National Certificate, a qualification in a technical subject, more or less equivalent to an A-level.

once — *adv.* **1** a single time; on one occasion. **2** at some time in the past. **3** ever; at any time: *if once you are late.* **4** by one degree of relationship: *a cousin once removed.* — *conj.* as soon as. — *noun* one time or occasion.

— **all at once 1** suddenly. **2** all at the same time.

at once immediately; without any delay.

just for once on this one occasion only; as an exception.

once again *or* **once more** one more time, as before.

once and for all *or* **once for all** for the last time; now and never again.

once in a way *or* **while** occasionally; rarely.

once or twice a few times.

once upon a time *used to begin fairy-tales* at a certain time in the past.
[from Anglo-Saxon *ænes*]

Once and Future King, The a series of four novels on the legend of King Arthur by T H White (1958). It includes *The Sword in the Stone* (1937), *The Queen of Air and Darkness* (originally published as *The Witch in the Wood*, 1940), *The Ill-Made Knight* (1941), and *The Candle in the Wind* (1958).

once-over *noun colloq.* a quick, often casual examination: *give the car the once-over.*

oncogene *noun Genetics* a gene that causes a normal cell to develop into a cancerous cell, or to multiply in an uncontrolled manner. Its effects are often the result of rearrangement of the chromosomal material, so that the gene appears at a new location on the chromosome, where it is no longer subject to the control mechanisms previously present. [from Greek *onkos* bulk, mass, tumour]

oncologist *noun* a doctor who specializes in studying and treating tumours.

oncology *noun* the study of tumours, especially those which are cancerous. [from Greek *onkos*, mass, tumour + -LOGY]

oncoming — *adj.* approaching; advancing. — *noun* an approach.

oncovirus *noun Medicine* any virus that causes cancer.

OND *abbrev.* Ordinary National Diploma, a qualification in a technical subject reached after a two-year full-time or sandwich course, recognized by many professional institutions.

ondes Martenot *or* **ondes musicales** an electronic musical instrument patented in 1922 by Maurice Martenot. An early type of synthesizer, it consisted of a keyboard capable of producing a vibrato, with controls for timbre and dynamics, and loudspeakers. Several (especially French) composers have written music for the instrument, eg Olivier Messiaen, Pierre Boulez, and Darius Milhaud.

one — *adj.* **1** being a single unit, number, or thing. **2** being a particular person or thing, especially as distinct from another or others of the same kind: *lift one leg and then the other.* **3** being a particular but unspecified instance or example: *visit him one day soon.* **4** being the only such: *the one woman who can beat her.* **5** same; identical: *of one mind.* **6** undivided; forming a single whole: *a choir singing with one voice.* **7** first: *page one.* **8** *colloq.* an exceptional example or instance of: *one hell of an argument.* **9** aged 1. — *noun* **1** the number or figure 1; any symbol for this number. **2** the age of 1. **3** a unity or unit. **4** something, especially a garment or a person whose size is denoted by the number 1. **5** 1 o'clock. **6** *colloq.* a story or joke: *heard the one about the singing policeman?* **7** *colloq.* (**one for**) an enthusiast: *she's quite a one for chess.* **8** *colloq.* a drink, especially an alcoholic one: *drop in for a quick one.* **9** *colloq.* a daring, remarkable, or cheeky person: *you are a one!* **10** a score of 1 point. — *pron.* **1** (often referring to a noun already mentioned or implied) an individual person, thing, or instance: *buy the blue one.* **2** anybody: *one can't do better than that.* **3** I; me: *one doesn't like to pry.*

— **all one** just the same; of no consequence.

at one with someone in complete agreement with them.

be one up on someone *colloq.* to have an advantage over them.

for one as one person: *I for one don't agree.*

all in one 1 together; combined; as one unit, object etc. **2** in one go or attempt.

just one of those things an unfortunate event or situation that must be accepted.

one and all everyone.

one and only *used for emphasis* only.

one another used as the object of a verb or preposition when an action takes place between two (or more than two) people, etc: *love one another / refuse to speak to one another.* See also EACH OTHER.

one by one one after the other; individually.

one or two *colloq.* a few.
[from Anglo-Saxon *an*]

one-armed bandit *noun* a fruit machine with a long handle at the side which is pulled down hard to make the machine work.

One Day in the Life of Ivan Denisovich a novel by Alexander Solzhenitsyn (1962). It gives a meticulous description of life in a Russian prison camp.

***One Flew Over the Cuckoo's Nest* 1** a novel by US author Ken Kesey, published in 1963, based on his experiences as a ward attendant in a mental hospital. **2** a US film, based on the novel directed by Milos Forman (1975), and starring Jack Nicholson, which won five Oscars.

Onega, Lake, Russian **Ozero Onezhskoye** the second largest lake in Europe, situated in NW Russia, close to the Finnish border. It lies between L Ladoga in the S and the White Sea in the NE. AREA 9 720sq km/3 752sq mi; length 250km/155mi; maximum depth 120m. In the N of the lake there are numerous islands, and narrow bays which extend up to 112km/70mi inland. Chief ports include Petrozavodsk, Voznesenye, and Povenets. The lake is connected by canal to the R Volga and the White Sea and is frozen over from Nov until May.

one-horse *adj.* **1** using a single horse. **2** *colloq.* small, poor, and of little importance.

100 Soup Cans a painting by Andy Warhol (1962). It shows repeated, exact reproductions of a tin of soup.

One Hundred Years of Solitude (Cien años de soledad) a novel by Gabriel García Márquez (1967). It is an apocalyptic vision focusing on the disintegration of a Spanish town, as seen through the eyes of various generations of one family.

Oneida an Iroquian-speaking Native American agricultural group, the smallest tribe of the Iroquois League, originally based in central New York state. They supported the colonists during the American Revolution and were attacked by pro-British Iroquois. They later divided into factions and settled in Ontario, Wisconsin, and New York. The present-day population is c.5 700.

O'Neill, Eugene (Gladstone) (1888–1953) US dramatist, the first to win the Nobel Prize for Literature (1936), born in New York City. He joined the Provincetown Players in 1915, for whom *Beyond the Horizon* (1920, Pulitzer Prize) was written. His best-known works are *Mourning Becomes Electra* (1921–31), *Desire Under the Elms* (1924), *Long Day's Journey into Night* (1941, Pulitzer Prize), and *The Iceman Cometh* (1946).

O'Neill (of the Maine), Terence (Marne) O'Neill, Baron (1914–90) Northern Irish politician and Prime Minister, born in Co Antrim. He was a member of the Northern Ireland parliament (1946–70), and became Minister for Home Affairs (1956), Finance (1956–63), and then Prime Minister (1963–9). A supporter of closer cross-border links with the Republic, he angered many Unionists, and his acceptance in 1969 of civil rights for the Roman Catholic minority forced his resignation.

one-liner *noun colloq.* a short, amusing remark or joke made in a single sentence.

one-man *or* **one-woman** *adj.* done by one person.

oneness *noun* **1** the state or quality of being one; singleness. **2** agreement. **3** the state of being the same. **4** the state of being unique.

one-night stand 1 a performance given only once in any place, the next performance taking place elsewhere. **2** *colloq.* a brief or opportunistic sexual encounter.

one-off *colloq.* — *adj. chiefly Brit.* made or happening on one occasion only. — *noun* something that is one-off.

one-parent family *noun* a family consisting of a child or children and one parent, the other parent being dead or estranged.

one-piece *adj.* made in a single piece as opposed to separate parts.

onerous *adj.* heavy; hard to bear or do; demanding a lot of effort. [from Latin *onerosus*, from *onus*, burden]

onerously *adv.* in an onerous way.

onerousness *noun* being onerous.

oneself *pron.* **1** the reflexive of *one* : *not able to help oneself.* **2** used for emphasis. **3** one's normal self: *one can hardly be feeling oneself after an operation.*

one-sided *adj.* **1** *said of a competition* with one person or side having a great advantage over the other. **2** seeing, accepting, representing, or favouring only one side of a subject; unfair; partial.

one-sidedly *adv.* in a one-sided way.

one-sidedness *noun* being one-sided.

One Thousand Guineas see CLASSICS.

one-time *adj.* former.

one-to-one *adj.* **1** with one person or thing exactly corresponding to or matching another. **2** in which a person is involved with only one other person: *one-to-one teaching.*

one-track mind *colloq.* an obsession with one idea.

one-up *adj.* having a particular advantage.

one-upmanship *noun* the art of gaining pyschological, social, or professional advantages over other people.

one-way *adj.* **1** *said of a road or street* in which traffic can move in one direction only. **2** *said of a feeling or relationship* not returned or reciprocated. **3** *North Amer., esp. US, said of a ticket* valid for travel in one direction only, not back again.

one-woman see ONE-MAN.

ongoing *adj.* continuing; in progress.

onion *noun* **1** any of numerous varieties of a biennial plant (*Allium cepa*) belonging to the lily family, native to SW Asia but widely cultivated for its edible bulb, which consists of white fleshy scales rich in sugar and a pungent oil, surrounded by a brown papery outer layer. **2** the bulb of this plant, which may be eaten raw, cooked, or pickled. **3** the long tubular leaves of a young onion plant (spring onion), eaten as a salad vegetable. — **know one's onions** *colloq.* to know one's subject or one's job well.
[from Latin *unio*, unity, large pearl, onion]

onion dome *Archit.* a bulb-shaped dome topped with a sharply tapering point, characteris-

tic of Eastern Orthodox, especially Russian, church architecture.

oniony *adj.* containing or like onion.

on-line *adj. Comput., said of a peripheral device, eg a printer* connected to and controlled by a computer. See also OFF-LINE.

onlooker *noun* a person who watches and does not take part; an observer.

only — *adj.* **1** without any others of the same type. **2** *said of a child* having no brothers or sisters. **3** *colloq.* best: *flying is the only way to travel.* — *adv.* **1** not more than; just. **2** alone; solely. **3** not longer ago than; not until: *only a minute ago.* **4** merely; with no other result than: *I arrived only to find he had already left.* — *conj.* **1** but; however: *come if you want to, only don't complain if you're bored.* **2** if it were not for the fact that: *I'd come with you on the boat only I know I'll be sick if I do.* — **if only** ... I wish: *if only you could be on time for once.*

only too ... very ...; extremely ...
[from Anglo-Saxon *anlic*]

o.n.o. *abbrev. Brit.* or near offer; or nearest offer.

on-off *adj., said of a switch* able to be set to either the 'on' position or the 'off' position.

onomasticon *noun Linguistics* a dictionary or collection of proper names. [from Greek *onomastikos, -on*, from *onoma*, a name]

onomastics *sing. noun Linguistics* the study of the history, development, and geographical distribution of proper names. All categories of names are included: personal first names and surnames, place names, home names, and the names of boats, trains, and pets.

onomatopoeia *noun* the formation or use of a word which imitates the sound or action represented, such as *boo, hiss, squelch.* [from Greek *onoma*, name + *poieein*, to make]

onomatopoeic *adj.* relating to or characterized by onomatopoeia.

onrush *noun* a sudden and strong movement forward.

onscreen *adj., adv.* relating to information that is displayed on a television or computer screen.

onset *noun* **1** a beginning, especially of something unpleasant. **2** an attack.

onshore *adj., adv.* **1** *said of the wind* blowing or moving towards the shore. **2** on, on to, or near the shore.

onside *adj., adv. Football, Rugby* in a position where the ball may legally be played.

onslaught *noun* a fierce attack. [from Old Dutch *aenslag*]

on-stage *adj., adv.* on the stage and able to be seen by the audience.

on-stream *adj. adv., said of an industrial plant, process, etc* in operation or ready to go into operation.

Ontario POP (1991) 10.1m, the second largest province in Canada, situated in the SE of the country. It is the most populated province in Canada. AREA 1 068 580sq km/412 578sq mi. Ontario is bounded in the N by Hudson Bay, in the NE by James Bay, and in the S by the USA and the Great Lakes. PHYSICAL DESCRIPTION the N of the province lies in the rocky Canadian Shield, but contains a clay belt suitable for farming; several rivers flow into Hudson Bay, James Bay, the St Lawrence, and the Great Lakes; there are numerous lakes in the province besides the Great Lakes; the N area is sparsely populated and densely wooded. HISTORY widely explored by French fur traders and missionaries in the 17c; became a British territory in 1763; many United Empire Loyalist immigrants came after the American War of Independence; constituted as Upper Canada in 1791; invaded by American forces in the War of 1812; a separatist rebellion took place in 1837–8; Upper joined Lower

Canada in 1840; the modern province of Ontario was established in 1867 at the time of the Canadian confederation. GOVERNMENT governed by a Lieutenant-Governor and a 125-member Legislature. CAPITAL Toronto. CHIEF TOWNS Ottawa, Thunder Bay, Hamilton. ECONOMY the wealthiest province in Canada; tobacco; corn; livestock; poultry; dairy products; fur; vehicles and parts; food processing; iron and steel; machinery; mining (nickel, copper, uranium, zinc, gold, and iron); hydroelectricity.

Ontario, Lake the smallest of the N American Great Lakes, situated on the US–Canadian border. AREA 19 011sq km/7 338sq mi; length 311km/193mi; breadth 85km/53mi; maximum depth 244m. Just over half of the lake is in Canada. It is connected in the SW with L Erie via the Niagara R and the Welland Ship Canal; its outlet is the St Lawrence R in the NE. Canals link with the Hudson R, L Huron, and Ottawa. Ports include Kingston, Hamilton, Toronto, Rochester, and Oswego. Lake Ontario is never ice-bound.

On the Road a novel by Jack Kerouac (1957). It is a semi-autobiographical account of the hedonistic travelling experiences of a group of friends in the USA.

On the Threshold of Liberty a painting by René Magritte (1930).

On The Town a US film directed by Gene Kelly and Stanley Donen (1949). Marking the beginning of the modern musical, it is the story of how three sailors (played by Gene Kelly, Frank Sinatra, and Jules Munshin) spend a day's leave in New York.

On The Waterfront a US film directed by Elia Kazan (1954). A classic realist drama, it features Marlon Brando as a redemptive figure who informs on his murderous gang.

onto on to.
◆ Although in common use, *onto* is not as widely accepted as *into* is. Note that *onto* should not be used when *on* and *to* need to retain their separate meanings: *let's walk on to the pier* means 'in the direction of the pier' (ie *let's walk on* and *let's walk to the pier*), whereas *let's walk onto the pier* means 'into contact with the pier itself' with *on* and *to* having a combined meaning.

ontogeny *noun Biol.* the history of the development of a living organism, from fertilization of the ovum (egg cell) to sexual maturity. [from Greek *on ontos*, being]

ontological *adj.* relating to or involving ontology.

ontologically *adv.* as regards ontology.

ontology *noun Philos.* the science dealing with the nature of being. [from Greek *on*, being + -LOGY]

onus *noun* (PL. **onuses**) a responsibility or burden. [from Latin *onus*, burden]

onward — *adj.* moving forward in place or time. — *adv.* (*also* **onwards**) **1** towards or at a place or time which is advanced or in front. **2** forward. **3** continuing to move forwards or progress.

onyx *noun Geol.* a very hard variety of agate with straight alternating bands of one or more colours, the form with black and white bands being widely used to make jewellery and ornaments. [from Greek *onyx*, nail]

oocyte *noun Biol.* an early stage in the development of an ovum (egg cell). *Primary oocytes* are diploid, and undergo cell division by meiosis to give *secondary oocytes*, which are haploid. An ovum is produced by meiosis of a secondary oocyte. In human females, primary oocytes are present in the ovaries at birth. [from Greek *oion*, egg]

oodles *pl. noun colloq.* lots.

oogamy *noun Biol.* a form of sexual reproduction in which a large non-motile female gamete (the ovum or egg cell) is fertilized by a small motile male gamete.

oogenesis *noun Biol.* the production and development of an ovum (egg cell) in the ovary of an animal.

ooh *interj.* an expression of pleasure, surprise, excitement, or pain.

oölite *or* **oolite** *noun Geol.* a sedimentary rock, usually a form of limestone, consisting of masses of small round particles of calcium carbonate (*oöliths*) that resemble fish eggs. [from Greek *oion*, egg + *lithos*, stone]

oompah *noun colloq.* a common way of representing the deep sound made by a large, brass musical instrument. [imitative]

oomph *noun colloq.* **1** energy; enthusiasm. **2** personal attractiveness, especially sex appeal.

oops *interj. colloq.* an exclamation of surprise or apology made when a person makes a mistake, drops something, etc.

oops-a-daisy *interj. colloq.* an expression used typically when helping up or encouraging a child who has had a slight accident, fallen over, etc.

Oort, Jan Hendrik (1900–92) Dutch astronomer, born in Franeker. Working mainly at the Leiden Observatory, he proved through observations that our galaxy is rotating, and calculated the distance of the Sun from the centre of the galaxy and its period of revolution. In 1932 he made the first measurement that indicated that there is 'dark matter' in the galaxy. He later proposed that there is a huge circular reservoir of comets surrounding the solar system; this 'Oort cloud' was the suggested source of long-period comets which only rarely come close to the Sun.

oospore *noun Biol.* **1** a fertilized ovum (egg cell). **2** in certain algae and fungi, the zygote that is produced as a result of fertilization of a large non-motile female gamete by a smaller motile male gamete. It has a thick protective outer wall, and contains food reserves.

Oostende see OSTEND.

ooze¹ — *verb* **1** *intrans.* to flow or leak out gently or slowly. **2** *intrans. said of a substance* to give out moisture. **3** to give out (a liquid, etc) slowly: *a wound oozing blood.* **4** to overflow with (a quality or feeling): *ooze charm.* — *noun* **1** anything which oozes. **2** a slow gentle leaking or oozing. **3** an infusion of bark and other vegetable matter used for tanning leather. [from Anglo-Saxon *wos*, sap, juice]

ooze² *noun* **1** *Geol.* on the ocean floor, a deposit of fine organic sediments, shells of diatoms, etc, that accumulates very slowly over millions of years. **2** soft, boggy ground. [from Anglo-Saxon *wase*, marsh, mire]

oozy *adj.* (**oozier**, **ooziest**) like ooze; slimy, oozing.

op¹ *abbrev.* opus.

op² *noun colloq.* a surgical or military operation. [abbreviation]

opacity *noun* **1** opaqueness. **2** the state of having an obscure meaning and being difficult to understand. [from Latin *opacitas*, from *opacus*, opaque]

opal *noun Geol.* a milky white, black, or coloured form of silica, combined with variable amounts of water, usually with a characteristic internal 'play' of red, blue, green, or yellow flashes caused by light reflected from different layers within the stone. Opals can be cut and polished, and are used as gemstones in jewellery and ornaments. [probably Sanskrit *upala*, precious stone]

opalescence *noun* being opalescent.

opalescent *adj.* reflecting different colours as the surrounding light changes, like an opal.

opaque *adj.* **1** not allowing light to pass through, ie not transparent or translucent. **2** difficult to understand. See also OPACITY. [from Latin *opacus*]

opaquely *adv.* without transmitting light; obscurely.

opaqueness *noun* being opaque, lack of transparency.

Oparin, Alexandr Ivanovich (1894–1980) Russian biochemist, born in Uglich, near Moscow. He worked at Moscow University and the Bakh Institute of Biochemistry of the USSR Academy of Sciences. Intrigued by the origins of life on Earth, he suggested a possible scenario for the biochemical steps by which life may have come into being.

Op Art *or* **Optical Art** a modern art movement which exploits the illusions created by abstract compositions of spirals, grids, undulating lines, stripes, spots, etc to produce sensations of movement, space, and volume. Leading exponents are the Hungarian-born French artist Victor Vasarely (1908–), and the British painter Bridget Riley (1931–).

op. cit. *abbrev. opere citato* (Latin), in the work already quoted.

OPEC see ORGANIZATION OF ARAB PETROLEUM EXPORTING COUNTRIES.

open — *adj.* **1** allowing things or people to go in or out; not blocked, closed, or locked. **2** *said of a container* not sealed; with the inside visible. **3** not enclosed, confined, or restricted: *the open sea / an open view.* **4** not covered, guarded, or protected: *an open wound.* **5** spread out or unfolded: *an open book.* **6** *said of a shop, etc* receiving customers; ready for business. **7** generally known; public: *an open secret.* **8** able to be attacked or questioned: *leave oneself open to abuse.* **9** not restricted, allowing anyone to compete or take part, especially both amateurs and professionals. **10** free from restraint or restrictions of any kind: *the open fishing season.* **11** not decided; still being discussed: *an open question.* **12** ready to consider new ideas; unprejudiced: *an open mind.* **13** ready and willing to talk honestly; candid. **14** *combining form* eagerly attentive, surprised, or alarmed: *open-mouthed disbelief / open-eyed.* **15** *said of cloth, etc* having a lot of small openings or gaps. **16** *Phonetics, said of a vowel* produced with the tongue low in the mouth. **17** *Phonetics, said of a syllable* ending in a vowel. **18** *Mus., said of a string* not stopped by a finger. **19** *Mus., said of a note* played on an open string, or without holes being covered by fingers. **20** *said of a cheque* to be paid in cash to the person named on it, not crossed. — *verb* (**opened**, **opening**) **1** *trans., intrans.* to make or become open or more open. **2** *trans., intrans.* to unfasten or become unfastened to allow access. **3** *trans., intrans.* (also **open out** or **open something out**) to spread out or be spread out or unfolded, especially so as to see or be seen. **4** *trans., intrans.* to start or begin working: *the shops open at nine.* **5** to declare open with an official ceremony: *open the new hospital.* **6** *trans., intrans.* to begin or start speaking, writing, etc: *opened with a joke about the weather.* **7** *intrans.* (**open into** or **on to something**) to provide access to it: *a gate opening into a field.* **8** to arrange (a bank account), usually by making an initial deposit. **9** *trans., intrans. Cricket* to begin (the batting) for one's team. **10** *intrans. said of legal counsel* to make a preliminary statement about a case before beginning to call witnesses. — *noun* **1** (**the open**) an area of open country; an area not obstructed by buildings, etc. **2** (**the open**) public notice or attention: *bring the issue out into the open.* **3** (**Open**) a sports contest which both amateurs and professionals may enter. — **open and above board** thoroughly honest or legal.

open out *or* **up** to begin to reveal one's feelings and thoughts or to behave with less restraint.

open up 1 to open the door. **2** to start firing. **3** *said of a game, etc* to become more interesting as it develops.

open something up 1 to make it more accessible or available: *roads opening up the more remote areas.* **2** to increase the speed of an engine, vehi-

cle, etc. (**open up one's thoughts**, **mind**, *etc* to **someone**) to reveal them. [from Anglo-Saxon]

open air unenclosed space outdoors.

open-air *adj.* in the open air; outside.

open-and-shut *adj.* easily proved, decided, or solved.

open book a person who keeps no secrets and is easily understood.

opencast *adj. Geol., said of mining* using a method in which the substance to be mined, eg coal or copper, is exposed by removing the overlying layers of material, without the need for shafts or tunnels.

open cluster *Astron.* a cluster of several hundred to several thousand relatively young stars that are usually loosely distributed, in contrast to the densely packed groups of stars that form globular clusters.

open day a day when members of the public are allowed to visit a place which is usually closed to them.

open-ended *adj.* with no limits or restrictions, eg of time, set in advance.

opener *noun* **1** *combining form* a device for opening something: *bottle-opener.* **2** the first item on a programme. **3** *Cricket* either of the two batsmen who begin the batting for their team. — **for openers** *colloq.* to start with.

open fire a fireplace in a house where coal, coke, or wood may be burnt.

open-handed *adj.* generous.

open-handedly *adv.* in an open-handed way.

open-handedness *noun* being open-handed, generosity.

open-hearted *adj.* **1** honest, direct, and hiding nothing; candid. **2** kind; generous.

open-heartedly *adv.* in an open-hearted way.

open-heartedness *noun* **1** honesty, frankness. **2** generosity.

open-hearth process *Chem.* a traditional steel-making process in which the molten pig iron from which the steel is to be made is not in direct contact with the fuel providing the heat, but only with the hot flames which play on a shallow open hearth containing pig iron, malleable scrap iron, and a flux, in a furnace with a low roof. The steel can be withdrawn continuously.

open-heart surgery surgery performed on a heart that has been stopped and opened up while the blood circulation is maintained by a heart-lung machine.

open house the state of being willing to welcome and entertain visitors at any time: *keep open house.*

opening — *noun* **1** a hole, gap. **2** the act of making or becoming open. **3** a beginning. **4** the first performance of a play, opera, etc. **5** *Chess* a recognized sequence of moves played at the beginning of a game. **6** an opportunity or chance. **7** a preliminary statement about a legal case made by counsel before witnesses are called. — *adj.* of, relating to or forming an opening; first: *opening night at the opera.*

opening time the time at which a public house, bar, hotel etc can begin to sell alcoholic drinks.

open letter a letter, especially one of protest, addressed to a person or organization, etc but intended also for publication in a newspaper or magazine.

openly *adv.* without trying to hide anything; in a direct and honest manner.

open market a market in which buyers and sellers are allowed to compete without restriction.

open-minded *adj.* willing to consider or receive new ideas; unprejudiced.

open-mindedly *adv.* in an open-minded way.

open-mindedness *noun* being open-minded.

openness *noun* being open, frankness.

open-plan *adj.* having few internal walls and large, undivided rooms.

open prison a prison which allows prisoners who are neither dangerous nor violent considerably more freedom of movement than in normal prisons.

open sandwich a sandwich without a top slice of bread.

open season a period of the year in which particular animals, birds, fish, etc may be legally killed for sport.

open sesame a means of gaining access to something which is otherwise out of one's reach.

open shop, a firm, business, etc which does not oblige its employees to belong to a trade union. See also CLOSED SHOP.

open stage a stage in a theatre building which is in the same space as the auditorium, with no separation between them. Usually it is a raised platform built against one wall of the auditorium, with the audience on three sides.

Open University an institution of higher education which enables students to study for a degree without attendance. The teaching is carried out through correspondence units and broadcast or taped supporting programmes, though often with some personal tutoring at local study centres. Entry qualifications are often more permissively framed than in conventional universities, and in many cases no formal qualifications are required.

open verdict a verdict given by the coroner's jury at the end of an inquest that death has occurred, but without giving details of whether it was suicide, accidental, murder, etc.

open work work in cloth, metal, wood, etc, so constructed to have gaps or holes in it, used especially for decoration.

Opéra see PARIS OPÉRA.

opera[1] *noun* **1** a dramatic work set to music, in which the singers are usually accompanied by an orchestra. **2** operas as an art-form. **3** a theatre where operas are performed. **4** a company which performs operas. [from Italian *opera*, from Latin, work]
◇ The genre originated in Florence c.1600: it was well-established throughout Italy by the end of the 17c, and had spread throughout W Europe by the middle of the 18c. The history of opera has largely been one of reforms introduced to correct an imbalance between the demands of music and those of drama. Richard Wagner's music dramas aimed to unite the arts of music, poetry, gesture, and painting, but the course of opera since his time has been dictated as much by financial as by artistic considerations.

opera[2] see OPUS.

operability *noun* being operable.

operable *adj.* **1** *said of a disease, injury, etc* that can be treated by surgery. **2** that can be operated. [from Latin *operabilis*, from *opus*, work]

opera buffa comic opera in the form that developed in Italy in the 18c. [Italian, = comic opera]
◇ The music was less formal and elaborate than that of *opera seria*, and the subject matter was light with plots and characters drawn from normal life. The libretto was in Italian, and it was sung throughout (unlike French *opéra-comique* which had passages of spoken dialogue). Mozart's *Cosí fan tutte* and *The Marriage of Figaro* are notable examples of the form.

opéra-comique a tradition of French opera with some spoken dialogue. In the 19c, the term was applied to any French opera with spoken dialogue alternating with songs, whether the subject matter was comic or tragic. Thus the original version of Bizet's *Carmen* (which included spoken dialogue) is designated an *opéra-comique*. [French, = comic opera]

opera-glass *noun* small binoculars used at the theatre or opera.

opera-hat *noun* a man's collapsible top hat.

opera-house *noun* a theatre specially built for the performance of operas.

Opera North an English opera company formed (1975) in Leeds by David Lloyd-Jones (1934–), its first musical director (1977–90). It opened as English National Opera North with *Samson et Dalila* in 1978, and took its present name when it became independent in 1981.

opera seria 'serious' opera: the most common form of opera in the late 17c and throughout most of the 18c. It was characterized by its use of noble, often classical, subjects; the libretto was in Italian; and there was a rigid separation of the elaborate arias (and occasional ensemble) and recitative, with a general sense of formality. Handel, Gluck, and Mozart were among the leading exponents, though the genre had declined in popularity by the time Mozart composed his best known examples, *Idomeneo*, (1781) and *La clemenza di Tito* (1791). [Italian, = serious opera]

operate *verb* **1** *trans., intrans.* to function or cause to function or work. **2** *intrans.* to produce an effect or have an influence. **3** to manage, control, or direct (a business, etc). **4** *intrans.* (**operate on someone**) to treat them with surgery. **5** *intrans.* to perform military, naval, police, etc operations. [from Latin *operari*, to work]

operatic *adj.* of or like an opera, especially in being dramatic.

operatically *adv.* in an operatic way.

operating system (ABBREV. **OS**) *Comput.* a group of programs that control all the main activities of a computer. It loads programs to be run, opens and closes files, recognizes input from the keyboard, sends output to the visual display unit or printer, controls the disk drive, keeps a record of files and directories on the disk, and controls the running of all other programs.

operating table a special table on which surgery is performed.

operating theatre *or* **operating room** the specially equipped room in a hospital where surgery is performed.

operation *noun* **1** an act, method, or process of working or operating. **2** the state of working or being active: *the factory is not yet in operation*. **3** an activity; something done. **4** an action or series of actions which have a particular effect. **5** any surgical procedure that is performed in order to treat a damaged or diseased part of the body. **6** (*often* **operations**) one of a series of military, naval, police, etc actions performed as part of a much larger plan. **7** *Maths.* a specific procedure, such as addition or multiplication, whereby one numerical value is derived from another value or values. **8** *Comput.* a series of actions that are specified by a single computer instruction. **9** a financial transaction. [from Latin *operatio*]

operational *adj.* **1** of or relating to an operation. **2** able or ready to work.

operationally *adv.* in an operational way.

operational research *or* **operations research** the analysis of problems in business and industry in order to bring about more efficient work practices.

operative — *adj.* **1** working; in action; having an effect. **2** *said of a word* especially important or significant: *'must' is the operative word*. **3** of or relating to a surgical operation. — *noun* **1** a worker, especially one with special skills. **2** *North*

Amer., esp. US a private detective. [from Latin *operativus*, from *opus*, work]

operator *noun* **1** a person who operates a machine or apparatus. **2** a person who operates a telephone switchboard, connecting calls, etc. **3** a person who runs a business. **4** *Maths.* any symbol used to indicate that a particular mathematical operation is to be carried out, eg × which shows that two numbers are to be multiplied. **5** *colloq.* a calculating, shrewd, and manipulative person.

operculum *noun* (PL. **opercula**) **1** *Zool.* a plate that covers the opening of the shell in some gastropods. **2** in bony fishes, a flap that protects the gills. [from Latin *operculum*, from *operire*, to cover]

operetta *noun* a short light opera, with spoken dialogue and often dancing. The form is exemplified in the stage works of Jacques Offenbach (eg *Orpheus in the Underworld*), Johann Strauss (eg *Die Fledermaus*), and Arthur Sullivan (eg *The Mikado* and *The Pirates of Penzance*). [from Italian *operetta*, a diminutive of *opera*]

operon *noun Genetics* a group of closely linked genes that occur next to each other on a chromosome, and may be switched on and off as an integrated unit. Operons are more common in bacteria than in higher organisms, and most of them contain genes which code for enzymes catalysing different reactions in the same biochemical pathway.

Ophelia 1 the obedient daughter of Polonius in Shakespeare's *Hamlet*, whose love for Hamlet drives her to insanity and suicide. **2** a female first name, after Shakespeare's character. [from the Greek name *Ophelos*, = help]

Ophir a land mentioned in the Bible as famous for its resources of gold; 1 Kings 9.28, 10.11, and 22.48 state that it was reached from Palestine by ship, so it is variously placed in Arabia, India, or E Africa. The 'gold of Ophir' is known also from archaeological inscriptions.

ophthalmia *noun* inflammation of the eye, especially of the conjunctiva. [from Greek *ophthalmos*, eye]

ophthalmic *adj.* of or relating to the eye. [from Greek *ophthalmos*, eye]

ophthalmic optician an optician qualified to test people's eyes and prescibe, make, and sell glasses or contact lenses.

ophthalmologist *noun* an expert in ophthalmology.

ophthalmology *noun* the scientific study of the eye. [from Greek *ophthalmos*, eye + -LOGY]

ophthalmoscope *noun* an instrument that is used to examine the interior of the eye, by directing a reflected beam of light through the pupil. [from Greek *ophthalmos*, eye + -SCOPE]

Ophuls *or* **Opüls Max**, orignally **Max Oppenheimer** (1902–57) Franco-German film director, born in Saarbrücken, who chose French nationality in the plebiscite of 1934. He worked in films from 1930, in Germany, France, and the USA. These included *Liebelei* (1932), *The Exile* (1947), *The Reckless Moment* (1949), *La Ronde* (The Round, 1950), and *Lola Montes* (1955).

opiate *noun* **1** any of a group of drugs containing or derived from opium, eg morphine, heroine, codeine. Opiates depress the central nervous system, and are mainly used medicinally to relieve severe pain. The narcotic drugs morphine and heroin are highly addictive, and their use is strictly controlled. **2** anything that dulls physical or mental sensation.

opine *verb* to suppose or express as an opinion. [from Latin *opinari*, to think]

opinion *noun* **1** a belief or judgement which seems likely to be true, but which is not based on proof. **2** (**opinion on** *or* **about something**) what one thinks about something. **3** a professional judgement given by an expert: *medical opin-*

ion. **4** estimation or appreciation: *have a low opinion of his abilities.*

— **a matter of opinion** a matter about which people have different opinions.

be of the opinion that ... to think or believe that ...

[from Latin *opinio*, belief]

opinionated *adj.* having very strong opinions which one refuses to change; stubborn.

opinion poll *Politics* a test of public opinion made by questioning a representative sample of the population. It is used to determine the voting intentions of the electorate, their view of political leaders, and wider political attitudes. Polls originated in the USA in the 1930s, and today are commonplace both at and between elections.

Opitz (von Boberfeld), Martin (1597–1639) German poet, born in Bunzlau, Silesia. He served several German princes, and became historiographer to Wladyslaw IV of Poland. In 1617 he wrote the Latin *Aristarchus*, advocating the poetic value of the German language. His writings and translations were influential in the development of German poetry.

opium *noun* **1** an addictive drug made from juice from the seeds of a variety of poppy, used in medicine to cause sleep and relieve pain. **2** anything which has a soothing, calming, or dulling effect on people's minds. [from Greek *opion*, poppy-juice]

opium poppy an annual plant (*Papaver somniferum*), native to Europe and Asia, and having oblong, shallowly lobed leaves, flowers with four petals, and a pepperpot-shaped capsule with a ring of pores around its rim. In the garden form (subspecies *hortense*), the flowers are mauve with a dark centre, and in the drug-producing form (subspecies *somniferum*) the flowers are white.

Oporto, Portuguese **Porto 1** POP (1991) 1.2m, the capital of Oporto district, N Portugal, and the country's second largest city. It is situated 318km/198mi N of Lisbon on the N bank of the R Douro, near its mouth. Port wine is the city's major export; the suburb of Vila Nova de Gaia on the S bank of the R Douro is famous for its port wine lodges. NOTABLE FEATURES cathedral (13c); Stock Exchange Palace; Clerigos Tower. **2** a district in N Portugal with the city of Oporto as its capital.

opossum *noun* any of several small, tree-dwelling, American or Australian marsupials with thick fur and a strong tail for gripping. [from an American Indian language]

opp. *abbrev.* opposite.

Oppenheimer, (Julius) Robert (1904–67) US nuclear physicist, born in New York City. He established schools of theoretical physics at Berkeley and the California Institute of Technology, and during World War II pioneered theoretical studies on the atomic bomb, leading to his selection as leader of the atomic bomb development project. After the War he became Director of the Institute for Advanced Studies at Princeton and continued to play an important role in US atomic energy policy. Opposed to the development of the hydrogen bomb, he was suspended from secret nuclear research in 1953.

opponent *noun* a person who belongs to the opposing side in an argument, contest, or battle. [from Latin *opponere*, to set before or against]

opportune *adj.* **1** *said of an action* happening at a time which is suitable, proper, or correct. **2** *said of a time* suitable; proper. [from Latin *opportunus*, from *ob*, before + *portus*, harbour, used originally of a wind blowing towards a harbour]

opportunely *adv.* at an opportune time, in an oppportune way.

opportuneness *noun* being opportune.

opportunism *noun* the practice of regulating actions by favourable opportunities rather than by consistent principles.

opportunist *noun* a person whose actions are governed by opportunism.

opportunistic *adj.* **1** characterized or determined by opportunism. **2** *Medicine*, said of an *infection* not affecting healthy people but attacking those whose immune system is weakened by drugs or disease.

opportunity *noun* (PL. **opportunities**) **1** an occasion offering a possibility; a chance. **2** favourable or advantageous conditions. [from Latin *opportunitas*, from *opportunus*, opportune]

opportunity cost *Econ.* the real cost of acquiring any item, which is the alternative to be foregone in order to do so. For example, the opportunity cost of holding money is the amount of income that is sacrificed by holding assets in the form of money rather than investing them in interest-earning or dividend-paying securities.

oppose *verb* **1** to resist or fight against by force or argument. **2** *intrans.* to object. **3** *intrans.* to compete in a game, contest, etc against another person or team. **4** to place opposite or in contrast to so as to counterbalance.

— **as opposed to** ... in contrast to ...; as distinct from ...

[from Latin *opponere*, to set before or against + French *poser*, to place]

opposer *noun* a person who opposes.

opposing *adj.* that opposes.

opposite — *adj.* **1** being on the other side of, or at the other end of, a real or imaginary line or space. **2** facing in a directly different direction: *opposite sides of the coin.* **3** completely or diametrically different. **4** being the other of a matching or contrasting pair: *the opposite sex.* **5** *Bot.*, said of *leaves or other organs* arranged in pairs on a stem, so that the two members of a pair are exactly opposite each other. — *noun* an opposite person or thing. — *adv.* in or into an opposite position: *live opposite.* — *prep.* **1** across from and facing: *a house opposite the station.* **2** *said of an actor* in a role which complements that taken by another actor; co-starring with: *played opposite Olivier.* [from Latin *oppositus*, from *ob*, against + *ponere*, to place]

opposite number a person with an equivalent position or job in another company, country, etc.

opposition *noun* **1** the act of resisting or fighting against (someone or something) by force or argument. **2** the state of being hostile or in conflict. **3** a person or group of people who are opposed to something. **4** (**Opposition**) a political party which opposes the party in power. **5** an act of opposing or being placed opposite. **6** *Astron.*, *Astrol.* the position of a planet or star when it is directly opposite another, especially the sun, as seen from the earth. [from Latin *oppositio*]

oppress *verb* **1** to govern with cruelty and injustice. **2** to worry, trouble, or make anxious; to weigh heavily upon. [from Latin *oppressare*, from *ob*, against + *premere*, to press]

oppression *noun* **1** the state of suffering cruelty and injustice. **2** worry or mental distress.

oppressive *adj.* **1** cruel, tyrannical, and unjust. **2** causing worry or mental distress; weighing heavily on the mind. **3** *said of the weather* hot and sultry.

oppressively *adv.* in an oppressive way.

oppressiveness *noun* being oppressive.

oppressor *noun* a person who oppresses.

opprobrious *adj.* insulting, abusive, or severely critical. [from Latin *opprobriosus*]

opprobriously *adv.* in an opprobrious way.

opprobrium *noun* public shame, disgrace, or loss of favour. [from Latin, from *ob*, against + *probrum*, reproach, disgrace]

oppugn *verb* to call into question; to dispute. [from Latin *ob*, against + *pugnare*, to fight]

Ops in Roman mythology, the goddess of plenty, the consort of Saturn, identified with the Greek goddess, Rhea.

ops *pl. noun* Mil. operations.

opt *verb intrans.* (**opt for something**) to decide between several possibilities.

— **opt out of something 1** to choose not to take part in something. **2** *said of a school or hospital* to leave local authority control.
[from Latin *optare*, to choose]

optic *adj.* of or concerning the eye or vision. [from Greek *optikos*]

optical *adj.* **1** of or concerning sight or what one sees. **2** of or concerning light or optics. **3** *said of a lens* designed to help sight.

optical activity *Chem.* the ability of certain chemical compounds, when placed in the path of a beam of polarized light, to rotate the plane of polarization of the light to the left or to the right. Optical activity can be used to identify and measure the concentrations of transparent solutions such as sugar solution.

optical character recognition *Comput.* the scanning, identification, and recording of printed characters by a photoelectric device attached to a computer.

optical fibre *Telecomm.* a thin flexible strand of glass or plastic that transmits light with little leakage through the walls of the fibre, which are covered with a material of lower refractive index. This covering acts as a mirror, so that light is continually reflected back into the core of the fibre. Bundles of optical fibres are used in endoscopes (long flexible instruments for viewing internal body organs), and for transmitting computer data, telephone messages, television signals, etc, over long distances in the form of modulated light signals. They can carry much more information than conventional cables, with very little loss of intensity.

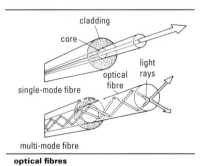

optical fibres

optical illusion a thing which has an appearance which deceives the eye; misunderstanding caused by a deceptive appearance.

optically *adv.* as regards light or optics.

optical sensing the process of detecting light and converting it into electrical signals. In the human eye, the light stimulation from an image results in electrical impulses to the brain, which are then interpreted. Optical sensing by artificial means includes the use of photoelectric cells and photographic light meters.

optician *noun* **1** a person who fits and sells spectacles and contact lenses. — Also called *dispensing optician*. **2** a person qualified both to examine the eyes and vision and to prescribe and dispense spectacles and contact lenses for the improvement of vision. — Also called *ophthalmic optician, optometrist*. [from French *opticien*; as OPTIC]

optic nerve *Anat.* the second cranial nerve in vertebrates, responsible for the sense of vision. It transmits information from the retina of the eye to the visual cortex of the brain.

optics *sing. noun* the branch of physics that is concerned with the study of light (especially visible light, but also including ultraviolet and infra-red light), including the phenomena associated with its generation, propagation, and detection, and its practical applications in a range of devices and systems.

optimal *adj.* the best or most favourable. [from Latin *optimus*, best]

optimism *noun* **1** a tendency to take a bright, hopeful view of things and expect the best possible outcome. **2** *Philos.* the belief that we live in the best of all possible worlds. **3** the theory that good will ultimately triumph over evil. [from Latin *optimus*, best]

optimist *noun* **1** a person who has a hopeful, cheerful nature. **2** a person who follows the doctrine of optimism.

optimistic *adj.* relating to or characterized by optimism.

optimistically *adv.* in an optimistic way.

optimize *or* **optimise** *verb* to make the most or best of; to make the most efficient use of. [from Latin *optimus*, best]

optimum — *noun* (PL. **optimums**, **optima**) the most favourable condition or situation. — *adj.* the best or most favourable. [from Latin *optimus*, best]

option *noun* **1** an act of choosing. **2** that which is or which may be chosen. **3** the power or right to choose: *you have no option.* **4** the exclusive right to buy or sell something, eg stocks, at a fixed price and within a specified time-limit.
— **keep** *or* **leave one's options open** to avoid making a choice or committing oneself to a particular course of action.
[from Latin *optio*, from *optare*, to choose]

optional *adj.* a matter of choice; not compulsory.

optionally *adv.* in an optional way, as an option.

optometrist *noun Optics* a person qualified both to examine the eyes and vision and to prescribe and dispense spectacles and contact lenses for the improvement of vision. [from Greek *optikos*, optic]

opulence *noun* conspicuous wealth, luxury.

opulent *adj.* **1** rich; wealthy. **2** luxurious. **3** abundant. [from Latin *opulentus*]

opulently *adv.* in an opulent way.

opus *noun* (PL. **opuses**, **opera**) an artistic work, especially a musical composition, often used with a number to show the order in which a composer's works were written or catalogued: *Beethoven, opus 18.* [from Latin *opus*, work]

OR *abbrev.* Oregon.

or[1] *conj.* used to introduce: **1** alternatives: *red or pink or blue.* **2** a synonym or explanation: *a puppy or young dog.* **3** an afterthought: *she's laughing — or is she crying?* **4** the second part of an indirect question: *ask her whether she thinks he'll come or not.* **5** because if not; or else: *run or you'll be late.* **6** and not: *never joins in or helps.*
— **or else** **1** otherwise. **2** *colloq.* expressing a threat or warning: *give it to me or else!*
or rather or to be more accurate: *he went too, or rather I heard he did.*
or so about; roughly: *been there two hours or so.* [from Middle English *other*]

or[2] *noun Heraldry* a gold colour. [from French, from Latin *aurum*, gold]

-or *suffix* forming words denoting a person or thing that performs an action or function: *actor / elevator.* [from Middle English, from Old French]

Oracle *noun trademark* a former teletext service run by the Independent Broadcasting Authority.

oracle *noun* **1** a holy place in ancient Greece or Rome where a god was believed to give advice and prophecy. **2** a priest or priestess at an oracle, through whom the god was believed to speak.

3 the usually mysterious or ambiguous advice or prophecy given at an oracle. **4** a person who is believed to have great wisdom or be capable of prophesying the future. **5** a statement made by such a person. [from Latin *oraculum*]

oracular *adj.* **1** of or like an oracle. **2** difficult to interpret; mysterious and ambiguous. **3** prophetic.

oracy *noun* the ability to express oneself coherently and to communicate freely with others by word of mouth. The development of these skills is seen as an important goal of childhood education, together with literacy and numeracy. [from Latin *os, oris*, mouth]

oral — *adj.* **1** spoken or verbal; not written. **2** of or used in the mouth. **3** *said especially of a medicine* taken in through the mouth. **4** *Psychol.* of a supposed stage of infant development, when satisfaction is obtained through sucking. — *noun* a spoken test or examination. [from Latin *os*, mouth]
♦ Often confused with *aural*, which refers to the ear and hearing.

orally *adv.* with the mouth; in words.

Oran 1 POP (1987) 629 000, a seaport in Oran department, N Algeria. It lies 355km/220mi W of Algiers. HISTORY founded in the 8c; first ruled by Arabs, then Spaniards from 1509 to 1708, Turks from 1708 to 1732, and the French from 1831 to 1962; landing point for Allied forces in World War II. A former French naval base is situated nearby at Mers el Kabir. NOTABLE FEATURES Santa Cruz fortress (16c); Municipal Museum. **2** a department in N Algeria with Oran as its capital.

Orange a town in the Vaucluze department, SE France. It developed around a group of Roman monuments, which include a well-preserved theatre with a 4m statue of Augustus, and an 18m high triumphal arch, commemorating Julius Caesar's victories over local Gauls. It is a World Heritage site.

orange — *noun* **1** a round citrus fruit with a tough reddish-yellow outer rind or peel enclosing membranous segments filled with sweet or sharp-tasting juicy flesh that is rich in vitamin C. The sweet orange is eaten raw or squeezed for its juice, and the bitter (Seville) orange is used to make marmalade. **2** the evergreen tree of the genus *Citrus* that bears this fruit, cultivated in most subtropical regions. Its fragrant white flowers are used as a source of essential oils for perfumery. **3** the reddish-yellow colour of the skin of this fruit. **4** an orange-flavoured drink. — *adj.* orange-coloured or orange-flavoured. [from Sanskrit *naranga*]

orangeade *noun* a usually fizzy orange-flavoured drink.

Orange Bowl in US college football, a post-season challenge match between the Big Eight Conference champion and an invited opposition.

Orange Free State POP (1991) 1.9m, a province in E central South Africa. AREA 127 993sq km/49 405sq mi. It is bounded S by the Orange R, NW by the Vaal R, and SE by Lesotho. CAPITAL Bloemfontein. CHIEF TOWNS Springfontein, Kroonstad, Bethlehem, Harrismith, Koffiefontein. HISTORY many settlements date from the Great Trek of 1831; claimed by the British as the Orange River Sovereignty in 1848; gained independence in 1854; joined the Union of South Africa as Orange Free State in 1910. ECONOMY a largely rural province; grain, livestock; oil; agricultural equipment; fertilizers; wool; clothing; cement; pharmaceuticals; pottery.

Orangeman *noun* (PL. **Orangemen**) a member of a society founded in 1795 to support Protestantism in Ireland. [from William of *Orange*, later William III of Great Britain and Ireland]

Orange Order an association that developed from the Orange Society, which had been

formed (1795) to counteract growing Catholic influence in Ireland and 'to maintain the laws and peace of the country and the Protestant constitution'. The name was taken from the Protestant Dutch dynasty represented by William III. Organized in 'Lodges', it provided the backbone of resistance to Home Rule proposals from the mid-1880s, and has operated as organized Protestantism in Northern Ireland since partition (1921).

Orange River, Afrikaans **Oranjerivier** a river in Lesotho, South Africa, and Namibia. It is 2 090km/1 300mi long. Rising in the Drakensberg Mts in NE Lesotho, it flows S into South Africa, then generally W and NW, following the border between South Africa and Namibia, to enter the Atlantic Ocean at Alexander Bay. The river is dammed in several places as part of the Orange River Project (begun 1963) to provide irrigation and power.

orangery *noun* (PL. **orangeries**) a greenhouse or building which allows orange trees to be grown in cool climates.

orangey *adj.* somewhat orange in colour or flavour, etc.

orang utan *or* **orang outang** the only tree-dwelling great ape, found in tropical forests in Borneo and Sumatra. Its arms are considerably longer than its legs, and it has a characteristic high forehead and coarse grey skin sparsely covered with long reddish hair. The male grows a moustache and beard, but the rest of the face is hairless. The orang utan has become an endangered species as a result of deforestation and hunting. [from Malay *orang*, man + *hutan*, forest]

Oranjestad POP (1986e) 20 000, the port capital of Aruba I, S Netherlands Antilles, E Caribbean Sea. It lies on the W coast of the island, 32km/20mi N of the Venezuelan coast.

oration *noun* a formal or ceremonial public speech in dignified language. [from Latin *oratio*]

orator *noun* **1** a person who is skilled in persuading, moving, or exciting people through public speech. **2** a person who gives an oration. [from Latin, from *orare*, to pray]

oratorial *adj.* of an orator, an oratory, or an oratorio.

oratorical *adj.* **1** of an orator. **2** like oratory, especially in using rhetoric.

oratorically *adv.* in an oratoric way.

oratorio *noun* (PL. **oratorios**) a theme or story, usually on a Biblical or religious topic, set to music and sung by soloists and a chorus accompanied by an orchestra, but without scenery, costumes, or acting. [from Italian *oratorio*, from Latin *oratorium*, oratory, so called because it developed out of singing in religious services held in oratories]
◇ The oratorio has come to be regarded more as a religious than a dramatic work, although Handel wrote more than 20 which were originally performed in theatres, eg *Israel in Egypt* (1739) and *Messiah* (1742). Notable composers after Handel include: Haydn (*The Creation*, 1798); Mendelssohn (*Elijah*, 1846); and Elgar (*The Dream of Gerontius*, 1900).

oratory *noun* (PL. **oratories**) **1** the art of speaking well in public, especially using elegant rhetorical devices. **2** a small place or chapel for private prayer.

orb *noun* **1** a globe decorated with jewels and with a cross on top, carried by the monarch during important ceremonies. **2** anything in the shape of a globe. **3** *poetic* a star, the sun, or a planet. **4** *poetic* the eyeball. [from Latin *orbis*, circle]

orbit — *noun* **1** *Astron.* in space, the path of one celestial body around another, eg the Earth's orbit around the Sun, or the path of an artificial satellite around a celestial body. Most orbits are elliptical in shape. **2** *Physics* the path of an electron around the nucleus of an atom. **3** a sphere of influence or action. **4** *Anat.* in the skull of vertebrates, one of the two bony hollows in which the eyeball is situated. — *verb* (**orbited, orbiting**) **1** *intrans., trans.* to follow an orbital path around an object. **2** to put (a spacecraft, etc) into orbit. [from Latin *orbitus*, from *orbis*, circle]

orbital — *noun Chem.* any region of space outside the nucleus of an atom or molecule where there is a high probability of finding an electron. Up to two electrons are associated with each orbital. — *adj.* **1** of or going round in an orbit. **2** *said of a road* forming a complete circle or loop round a city.

Orcadian — *adj.* of the Orkney Islands. — *noun* a person who lives or was born in the Orkney Islands. [from Greek *Orkades*, Orkney]

orchard *noun* a garden or piece of land where fruit trees are grown. [from Anglo-Saxon *ortgeard*]

orchestra *noun* **1** a usually large group of musicians who play a variety of different instruments as an ensemble, led by a conductor. **2** (*also* **orchestra pit**) that part of a theatre or opera-house where the orchestra sits, usually in front of or under the stage. **3** in the ancient Greek theatre, a semicircular area in front of the stage where the chorus danced. [from Greek, from *orcheisthai*, to dance]
◇ The orchestra as it is known today developed from the groups of instruments used in 17c opera houses and at the courts of London, Paris, and Vienna. Division into the four standard groups of strings, woodwind, brass, and percussion took place in the classical period and the symphony orchestra was further expanded in the 19c. A modern symphony orchestra is normally made up of around 100 players including sixty or more stringed instruments, triple or quadruple woodwind, brass including tuba, and at least three trombones, harp, and a wide array of percussion.

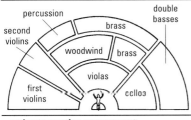

orchestra seating arrangement

orchestral *adj.* of, for, or played by an orchestra.

orchestrate *verb* **1** to arrange or compose (a piece of music) for an orchestra. **2** to organize or arrange (something) so as to get the desired or best result.

orchestration *noun* **1** the process or technique of orchestrating music. **2** music which has been orchestrated.

orchestrator *noun* a person who orchestrates music.

orchid *noun* a perennial plant belonging to the family Orchidaceae, one of the largest and most advanced families of flowering plants, containing about 30 000 species. Orchids are best known for their complex and exotic flowers, and for their highly sophisticated pollination mechanisms. [from Greek *orchis*, testicle, so called because of the shape of its root-tubers]
◇ Orchids are classified as monocotyledons, ie they have a single cotyledon or seed leaf. They are found in virtually all parts of the world except Antarctica, but are especially abundant in tropical and subtropical forests. Almost all tropical species are epiphytes (ie they grow on other plants, but are not parasites), and those that grow in temperate regions are found in damp habitats such as woods and meadows. Orchids com-

monly possess *pseudobulbs*, cylindrical or bulb-like swellings of the stems just above soil level, which store nutrients and water, and from which the leaves and flowers arise. The fleshy leaves are often spotted or blotched, and the flowers typically have two similar petals, with a third petal forming a lower lip or *labellum* which differs from the others in form and colour. It may be enlarged, lobed, frilled, or divided, and is usually strikingly marked. Insects, bats, and even frogs may act as pollinators, and many of them are species specific, although orchids do interbreed with great facility, and a large number of hybrids are known in the wild as well as in cultivation.

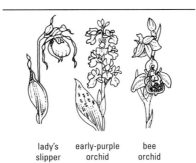

| lady's slipper | early-purple orchid | bee orchid |

orchids

Orczy, Emmuska, Baroness (1865–1947) British writer, born in Tarnaörs, Hungary. She is best known for *The Scarlet Pimpernel* (1905), which was the most successful of her many popular adventure romances.

ordain *verb* **1** to make (someone) a priest, vicar, etc. **2** to order or command formally. **3** to destine in mathematics, which shows that two numbers are to be multiplied. See also ORDINATION. [from Latin *ordinare*, from *ordo*, order]

ordained *adj.* appointed, consecrated, decreed, ordered.

ordainment *noun* ordaining.

ordeal *noun* **1** a difficult, painful, or testing experience. **2** *Hist.* a method of trial in which the accused person was subjected to physical danger from fire, water, etc, survival of which was taken as a sign from God of that person's innocence. [from Anglo-Saxon *ordal*]

order — *noun* **1** a state in which everything is in its proper place; tidiness. **2** an arrangement of objects according to importance, value, position, etc. **3** a command, instruction, or direction. **4** a state of peace and harmony in society, characterized by the absence of crime and the general obeying of laws. **5** the condition of being able to function properly: *out of order.* **6** a social class or rank making up a distinct social group: *the lower orders.* **7** a kind or sort. **8** an instruction to a manufacturer, supplier, waiter, etc to provide something. **9** the goods, food, etc supplied. **10** an established system of society: *a new world order.* **11** *Biol.* a category in the classification of animals and plants which is below a class and above a family. **12** *Commerce* a written instruction to pay money. **13** the usual procedure followed at especially official meetings and during debates: *a point of order.* **14** (**Order** *or* **Religious Order**) a religious community living according to a particular rule and bound by vows. **15** any of the different grades of the Christian ministry. **16** (**orders**) same as HOLY ORDERS. **17** the specified form of a religious service: *order of marriage.* **18** (**Order**) a group of people to which new members are admitted as a mark of honour or reward for services to the sovereign or country: *the Order of the Garter.* **19** any of the five classical styles of architecture characterized by the way a column and entablature are moulded and decorated. — *verb* (**ordered, ordering**) **1** to give a command to. **2** to command (someone) to go to a specified place: *order the regiment to Germany.* **3** to instruct a

manufacturer, supplier, waiter to supply or provide (something). **4** to arrange or regulate: *order one's affairs.* **5** *intrans.* to give a command, request, or order, especially to a waiter for food. — *interj.* (**Order! Order!**) a call for quiet, calm, proper behaviour to be restored, especially during a debate.
— **call to order 1** to request calm or attention. **2** to declare a formal meeting open.
in order 1 in accordance with the rules; properly arranged. **2** suitable or appropriate: *such behaviour just isn't in order.* **3** in the correct sequence.
in the order of ... approximately (the number stated).
in order that ... so that ...
in order to ... so as to be able to ...
on order *said of goods* having been ordered but not yet supplied.
order someone about *or* **around** to give them orders continually and officiously.
order someone off *Sport* to order a player to leave the field because of bad or illegal behaviour.
out of order not correct, proper, or suitable: *your behaviour is out of order.*
a tall order *colloq.* a difficult or demanding job or task.
to order according to a customer's particular or personal requirements.
under orders having been commanded or instructed (to do something).
[from Latin *ordo*]

ordered *adj.* **1** placed in order. **2** well organized or arranged.

Order in Council in British government, legislation made by the monarch on the advice of the Privy Council, which does not need to be ratified by parliament. It is the main means through which the powers of the royal prerogative are exercised (eg the declaration of war or peace). In practice, the decisions are taken by government ministers, not by the monarch, and most orders of council concern legislation approved by parliament.

orderliness *noun* being orderly.

orderly — *adj.* **1** in good order; well-arranged. **2** well-behaved; quiet. — *noun* (PL. **orderlies**) **1** an attendant, usually without medical training, who does various jobs in a hospital, such as moving patients. **2** *Mil.* a soldier who carries an officer's orders and messages.

order of battle the positions adopted by soldiers or ships before a battle.

Order of Merit (ABBREV. **OM**) in the UK, an order instituted in 1902 by Edward VII, comprising a military and a civil class. Limited to 24 members, it is awarded to distinguished men and women for whom a knighthood might not be appropriate. The ribbon is blue and scarlet.

Order of the British Empire see OBE.

order of the day 1 an agenda, eg for a meeting or for business in parliament. **2** that which is necessary, normal, or fashionable at a given time.

order paper a programme showing the order of business, especially in Parliament.

Orders see AUSTRALIA, BATH, BRITISH EMPIRE, CANADA, COMPANIONS OF HONOUR, GARTER, ROYAL VICTORIAN ORDER, ST MICHAEL AND ST GEORGE, THISTLE.

Orders, Holy the grades of ministry in Orthodox, Roman Catholic, and Anglican Churches. Major Orders consist of ordained ministers, bishops, priests, and deacons (and, in the Western Church, subdeacons); these constitute the hierarchy of the Church, to be distinguished from the laity. Minor Orders include, in the Western Church, lectors, porters, exorcists, acolytes; in the Eastern Church, subdeacons.

ordinal — *noun* **1** a Roman Catholic service book, or a service book containing the services for the ordination of ministers. **2** same as ORDINAL NUMBER. — *adj.* denoting an ordinal or to a position in a sequence. [from Latin *ordinalis*, from *ordo*, order]

ordinal number, a number which shows a position in a sequence, eg *first, second, third,* etc. See also CARDINAL NUMBER.

ordinance *noun* **1** a law, order, or ruling. **2** an authorized religious ceremony. [from Latin *ordinare*, from *ordo*, order]

ordinand *noun* a person who is training to become a minister of the church. [from Latin *ordinare*, from *ordo*, order]

ordinarily *adv.* usually, normally.

ordinariness *noun* being ordinary.

ordinary — *adj.* usual; normal; unexceptional; familiar. — *noun* (PL. **ordinaries**) (**Ordinary**) those parts of the Mass which do not vary from day to day.
— **in the ordinary way** if things are as normal; usually.
out of the ordinary unusual; strange.
[from Latin *ordinarius*, from *ordo*, order]

Ordinary grade see O-GRADE.

Ordinary level see O-LEVEL.

ordinary seaman a sailor of the lowest rank in the Royal Navy.

ordinate *noun Maths.* in coordinate geometry, the second of a pair of numbers (x,y), known as the y coordinate. It specifies the distance of a point from the horizontal or x-axis. See also ABSCISSA. [from Latin *ordinatus*, ordained, from *ordo*, order]

ordination *noun* the act or ceremony of ordaining a priest or minister of the church. [from Latin *ordinatio*, from *ordo*, order]

ordnance *noun* **1** heavy guns and military supplies. **2** the government department responsible for military supplies. [see ORDINANCE]

Ordnance Datum (ABBREV. **OD**) the mean sea level in the UK, used as a fixed reference from which the elevations of all points in the country are surveyed. It was determined by hourly measurements of sea level made between 1915 and 1921 at Newlyn, Cornwall. The equivalent in the USA is the Sea Level Datum, calculated from the mean sea level for the whole US coastal area.

Ordnance Survey the survey and mapping agency of Great Britain, established by the 1841 Ordnance Survey Act, although founded initially in 1791 as the Trigonometrical Survey. Maps were originally produced at a scale of 1:63 360 (1in:mi), the metric equivalent of which is 1:50 000 (where 1 represents 1cm). Other basic scales include 1:1 250 (c.50in:mi), 1:2 500 (c.25in:mi) and 1:10 000 (c.6in:mi). These are produced by ground fieldwork, topographical survey, and aerial photography, kept up-to-date by a system of continuous revision. The survey also produces archaeological and historical maps.

Ordovician *adj. Geol.* denoting the second period of the Palaeozoic era, lasting from about 505 million to 440 million years ago. During this period the first vertebrates (jawless fishes) appeared, graptolites and trilobites were abundant, and echinoderms (eg starfish and sea urchins) became more widespread. [from Latin *Ordovices*, a British tribe]

ordure *noun* waste matter from the bowels; excrement. [from Old French *ord*, foul]

Ore *or* **Oreg.** *abbrev.* Oregon.

ore *noun Geol.* a solid naturally occurring mineral deposit from which one or more economically valuable substances, especially metals, can be extracted, and for which it is mined. [from Anglo-Saxon *ora*, unwrought metal combined with Anglo-Saxon *ar*, brass]

Örebro 1 POP (1992e) 122 000, the capital of Örebro county, S central Sweden. It lies 160km/100mi W of Stockholm at the mouth of the R Svärtan, by the W end of L Hjälmaren.

NOTABLE FEATURES St Nicholas's Church (18c); castle (16c, restored in the 18c); town hall (1856–62). **2** a county in S central Sweden.

oregano *noun* a sweet-smelling Mediterranean herb used as a flavouring in cooking. [from Greek *origanon*]

Oregon POP (1990) 3m, a state in NW USA, divided into 36 counties. AREA 251 409sq km/ 97 044sq mi. Oregon is sometimes known as the 'Beaver State'. It is bounded W by the Pacific Ocean. PHYSICAL DESCRIPTION split by the Cascade Range in which lies the state's highest peak, Mt Hood (3 424m); rivers include the Columbia, Snake, and Willamette; the fertile Willamette R Valley lies in the W, with the Coast Ranges beyond; the High Desert is in the E, a semi-arid plateau used for ranching and wheat-growing; in the NE are the Blue Mts and Wallowa Mts; the Fremont Mts and Steens Mts lie in the S; several small lakes lie to the S, including Upper Klamath L and L Albert; the Crater Lake National Park is in the SW; about half the state is forested. HISTORY established as a fur-trading post in 1811 on the site of the present town of Astoria; occupied by both Britain and the USA from 1818 to 1846, when the international boundary was settled on the 49th parallel; became a territory in 1848; joined the Union as the 33rd state in 1859; the population grew after 1842 with settlers following the Oregon Trail, and again in the late 19c after the completion of the transcontinental railway. CAPITAL Salem. CHIEF TOWNS Albany, Eugene, Springfield. ECONOMY produces over one quarter of the USA's softwood and plywood; electronics; food processing; paper; fishing; livestock; wheat, hay; dairy produce; fruit; vegetables; river fishing, especially salmon; a major tourist region.

Oresteia a trilogy of plays by Aeschylus (458 BC), comprising *The Agamemnon* (perhaps the greatest Greek play that has survived), *The Choëphoroe*, and *The Eumenides.* Founded on the history of Agamemnon, the first is set in Argos after the fall of Troy and ends at Agamemnon's murder by his wife Clytemnestra; the second focuses on Orestes who returns from exile to avenge his father; and the third sees the return of Orestes, his pursuit by the Furies, and acquittal at court.

Orestes in Greek legend, the son of Agamemnon and Clytemnestra. He went into exile after his father's murder, but returned to kill his mother and her lover, Aegisthus, for which he was pursued by the Erinyes.

Orff, Carl (1895–1982) German composer, born in Munich, where he studied under Kaminski and in 1925 helped to found the Günther music school. The influence of Igor Stravinsky is apparent in his compositions, which include his operatic setting of a 13c poem, *Carmina Burana* (1937); later works include *Oedipus* (1959), and *Prometheus* (1968).

organ *noun* **1** a part of a body or plant which has a special function, eg a kidney or leaf. **2** a usually large musical instrument with a keyboard and pedals, in which sound is produced by air being forced through pipes of different lengths. **3** any similar instrument without pipes, such as one producing sound electronically or with reeds. **4** a means of spreading information, such as a newspaper. **5** *euphemistic, humorous* the penis. [from Greek *organon*, tool]
◇ Modern church pipe organs usually have at least two manual keyboards (larger instruments may have up to five), and an array of pedals operated by the player's feet. The pipes are brought into action by means of stops, and the player can select a *registration* (or combination of stops) appropriate to the music. The cinema organ was developed in the USA in the early 20c to accompany silent films, and in modern electronic organs the pipes have been replaced with other means of tone production, such as electromagnets and oscillators.

organdie *noun* a very fine, thin cotton fabric which has been stiffened. [from French *organdi*]

organelle *noun Biol.* in the cell of a living organism, any of various different types of membrane-bound structure, each of which has a specialized function, eg mitochondria (which produce energy by breaking down carbohydrate molecules), ribosomes (which manufacture proteins), and chloroplasts (which are the site of photosynthesis in green plants).

organ-grinder *noun* a musician who plays a barrel organ in the streets for money.

organic *adj.* **1** *Medicine* relating to an organ of the body, eg organic disease. **2** *Biol.* relating to living organisms. **3** *Agric.* relating to farming practices that avoid the use of fertilizers, pesticides, etc, or to crops, especially fruit and vegetables, produced in this way. **4** being an inherent or natural part. **5** systematically organized. **6** *Chem.* relating to that branch of chemistry that is concerned with compounds that contain carbon atoms arranged in chains or rings, or relating to such compounds.

organically *adv.* in an organic way.

organic architecture architecture which appears to grow out of, or be closely linked with, the surrounding landscape. The concept was first promoted by the US architect, Frank Lloyd Wright, who believed that architects should be inspired by the special spirit of a place, and that buildings should achieve a harmony with nature. These ideas are best illustrated in his designs for private houses in the early 20c, such as the Kaufmann House (1936), which is built over a waterfall. The principles of organic architecture have been adopted by modern architects in many countries, particularly in the USA, Sweden, Denmark, and Japan.

organic chemistry, the branch of chemistry concerned with the study of compounds that contain chains or rings of carbon atoms, eg alcohols, aldehydes, plastics. Many organic compounds occur naturally in living organisms, eg proteins. See also INORGANIC CHEMISTRY.

organic compound *Chem.* a chemical compound that contains carbon atoms arranged in chains or rings, together with smaller amounts of other elements, mainly hydrogen and oxygen, but also often including nitrogen, sulphur, and halogens such as chlorine.

organic farming a system of farming that avoids the use of industrially manufactured chemical fertilizers and pesticides.
◇ In organic farming, composts or animal manures are used as fertilizers, weeds are controlled by cultivation or by hand-weeding, and pests are controlled by the introduction of natural predators (eg insects that feed on them), or by the

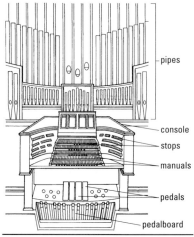

organ

use of permitted insecticides derived from plants, eg pyrethrum. The rotation of crops, whereby two or more different crops are grown one after the other on the same piece of land, is encouraged, as it helps to maintain the fertility of the soil, especially if the rotation includes nitrogen-fixing plants such as clover. It also limits the damage caused by weeds, pests, and diseases. Mixed farms, which combine arable and animal farming, are preferred to those that specialize in either plant crops or the rearing of animal livestock. In some countries there is a premium market for certified organic produce, including animal products (eg meat) obtained from livestock which are guaranteed to have been fed exclusively on organically grown feedstuffs.

organic fertilizer a fertilizer that consists of natural animal or plant products, eg manure, compost, bonemeal. Organic fertilizers are much less harmful to the environment than inorganic ones.

Organisation de l'Armée Secrète (Secret Army Organization) (ABBREV. **OAS**) a clandestine organization of French Algerians, led by rebel army generals Jouhaud and Salan, active (1960–2) in resisting Algerian independence. It caused considerable violence in Algeria and metropolitan France until thrown into rapid decline by the Franco-Algerian cease-fire (Mar 1962), Salan's capture (Apr 1962), and Algerian independence (Jul 1962).

organism *noun* **1** any living structure, such as a plant, animal, fungus, or bacterium, capable of growth and reproduction. **2** any establishment, system, or whole made up of parts that depend on each other. [from French *organisme*, from Latin *organizare*]

organist *noun* a person who plays the organ.

organization *or* **organisation** *noun* **1** a group of people formed into a society, union, or especially business. **2** the act of organizing. **3** the state of being organized.

organizational *or* **organisational** *adj.* relating to organization or an organization.

organizationally *or* **organisationally** *adv.* as regards organization.

Organization for Economic Co-operation and Development (ABBREV. **OECD**) an international organization set up in 1961 to assist member states to develop economic and social policies aimed at high sustained economic growth with financial stability. Its 24 members are Australia, Austria, Belgium, Canada, Denmark, Finland, France, Germany, Greece, Iceland, Ireland, Italy, Japan, Luxembourg, The Netherlands, New Zealand, Norway, Portugal, Spain, Sweden, Switzerland, Turkey, the UK, and the USA. It is located in Paris.

Organization for European Economic Co-operation (ABBREV. **OEEC**) an organization established (1948–61) by 16 W European countries and by the occupying forces on behalf of West Germany to promote trade, stability, and expansion. It also provided a framework for handling aid from the USA.

Organization of African Unity (ABBREV. **OAU**) an organization founded (1963) by representatives of 32 African governments meeting in Addis Ababa, which reflected the views of the moderate leaders, such as Nyerere, rather than radicals such as Nkrumah. It provided the main forum for the African continent to express its political views and, through its Liberation Committee in Dar es Salaam, assisted the decolonization of southern Africa.

Organization of American States (ABBREV. **OAS**) a regional agency established in 1948 to co-ordinate the work of a variety of inter-American agencies, recognized within the terms of the United Nations Charter. The organization was formed to promote peace, economic co-operation, and social advancement in the W

hemisphere. Its central organ, the General Secretariat, is housed in Washington, DC, and consists of one representative from each member country, of which there are 31 within the Americas.

Organization of Arab Petroleum Exporting Countries (ABBREV. **OAPEC**) an organization formed (1968) under the umbrella of the Organization of Petroleum Exporting Countries (OPEC) by Saudi Arabia, Kuwait, and Libya, with its headquarters in Kuwait, and which all the Arab oil producers had joined by 1972.

Organization of Central American States an agency established in 1951 by Costa Rica, El Salvador, Guatemala, Honduras, and Nicaragua (Panama refused to join) to promote economic, social, and cultural co-operation, extended in 1965 to include political and educational co-operation. It has also been involved in legal reform.

organize *or* **organise** *verb* **1** to give an orderly structure to: *organized the books into a neat pile.* **2** to arrange, provide, or prepare: *will organize a meal.* **3** to form or enrol (people or a person) into a society or organization, especially a trade union. **4** *intrans.* to form a society or organization, especially a trade union. [from Latin *organizare*]

organizer *or* **organiser** *noun* **1** someone or something that organizes. **2** a small bag or wallet which has (often removable) sections in which personal notes and information may be kept; a similar electronic device.

organza *noun* a very fine, thin dress material made of silk or synthetic fibres.

orgasm — *noun* **1** the highest point of sexual excitement. **2** violent excitement. — *verb intrans.* to experience an orgasm. [from Greek *orgasmos*, swelling]

orgasmic *adj.* relating to or associated with an orgasm.

orgiastic *adj.* relating to or characteristic of orgies.

orgy *noun* (PL. **orgies**) **1** a wild party or celebration involving excessive drinking and sexual activity. **2** any act of excessive or frenzied indulgence: *an orgy of shopping.* [from Greek *orgia*, secret rites]

Orhon Gol, River a river in Mongolia. It flows for 1 117km/694mi from the NE edge of the Gobi Desert to the W of Altanbulag, where it joins the Selenge R.

oriel-window *noun* (*also* **oriel**) a window which projects from the wall of a house, usually at an upper storey, and which is held in place by brackets. [from Old French *oriol*, gallery]

orient — *noun* **1** (**the Orient**) the countries in the east, especially those of E Asia regarded as culturally distinct from western countries (the *Occident*). **2** that part of the sky where the sun rises. — *verb* **1** to place in a definite position in relation to the points of the compass or some other fixed or known point. **2** to acquaint (oneself or someone) with the position relative to points known, or with details of a situation. **3** to position so as to face east. **4** to build a church so that it runs from east to west. [from Latin *oriens*, from *oriri*, to rise]

oriental — *adj.* from or relating to the Orient; eastern. — *noun* (**Oriental**) a person born in the Orient; an Asiatic.

Orientalist *noun* a person who studies, or is expert in, oriental culture, languages, etc.

orientate *verb* **1** to orient. **2** *intrans.* to face east; to be oriented.

orientated *adj.* oriented.

orientation *noun* **1** the act or an instance of orienting or being oriented. **2** a position relative to a fixed point. **3** a person's position or attitude

relative to his or her situation or circumstances. **4** a meeting giving information or training needed for a new situation; a briefing.

oriented *adj.* **1** directed towards something. **2** interested in something.

orienteering *noun* a sport in which contestants race over an unfamiliar cross-country course, finding their way to official check points using a map and compass. [from Swedish *orientering*]

Orient-Express a luxury express train which ran (1883–1977) from Paris to Constantinople (Istanbul). The first transcontinental train in Europe, it was developed by Georges Nagelmackers, a Belgian businessman, and featured luxurious carriages which included smoking compartments and ladies' drawing rooms. Its service, which was interrupted during both World Wars, finally came to an end in 1977. The allure of the train is celebrated in the work of various writers (eg Agatha Christie's *Murder on the Orient Express*, 1974).

orifice *noun* an opening or hole, especially in the body. [from Latin *os*, mouth + *facere*, to make]

origami *noun* the originally Japanese art of folding paper into shapes and figures. [from Japanese *ori* folding + *kami*, paper]
◇ Originating in 10c Japan, it is now popular in many countries. It is particularly useful as an educational aid for young children, developing manipulative skills and helping in the appreciation of the relationships between shapes.

Origen (c.185–c.254 AD) Christian scholar, theologian, and an early Greek Father of the Church, born probably in Alexandria. He was head of the catechical school in Alexandria (c.211–232), and was ordained in Palestine (c.230), but was denied the office of presbyter by an Alexandrian synod, returned to Palestine and established a new school in Caesarea. He was imprisoned and tortured during the persecution under Decius in 250. His writings were prolific, but his views on the unity of God and speculations about the salvation of the Devil were condemned by Church Councils in the 5c–6c.

origin *noun* **1** a beginning or starting-point; a source. **2** (**origins**) a person's family background or ancestors. **3** *Anat.* the point of attachment of a muscle. **4** *Maths.* in coordinate geometry, the point where the horizontal x-axis and the vertical y-axis cross each other. It has a value of zero on both axes. [from Latin *origo*]

original — *adj.* **1** existing from the beginning; earliest; first. **2** *said of an idea* not thought of before; fresh or new. **3** *said of a person* creative or inventive. **4** being the first form from which copies, reproductions, or translations are made. — *noun* **1** the first example of something which is copied, reproduced, or translated to produce others. **2** a model from which a painting, etc is made. **3** an odd or eccentric person.

originality *noun* **1** the quality of being original. **2** being creative or innovative. **3** an original act, idea, saying, etc.

originally *adv.* **1** in the first place, at the beginning. **2** in an original way.

original sin *Christianity* the supposed sinfulness of the human race as a result of Adam's disobedience to God.
◇ In traditional Christian doctrine, every human being inherits a 'flawed' or 'tainted' nature in need of regeneration, and has a disposition to sinful conduct.

originate *verb trans., intrans.* to bring or come into being; to start.

origination *noun* **1** originating. **2** a source.

originator *noun* an author, inventor, or creator.

Orinoco, River a river in Venezuela, rising in the Serra Parima. It flows in a wide curve W, N, and E until it empties into the Atlantic Ocean through a wide delta which begins c.240km/150mi from the coast. In S Venezuela the river forks, the S branch (Casiquiare) flowing 228km/142mi to the Rio Negro, the other forming a section of the Columbia–Venezuela boundary. The river passes over the cataracts of Maipures and Atures and curves round, through the Venezuelan *llanos*, crossing the width of the country. There are many tributaries of the river.

oriole *noun* any of several song-birds, the common European species of which has bright yellow and black plumage. [from Latin *aureolus*, from *aurum*, gold]

Orion 1 in Greek mythology, a gigantic hunter, beloved by Eos and killed by Artemis. He was changed into a constellation, and this generated further astronomical stories — for example, that he pursues the Pleiades. 2 *Astron.* the Hunter, a large bright constellation that lies on the celestial equator, so is visible in both hemispheres, and is perhaps the best known and most conspicuous of all constellations. It contains the bright stars Rigel and Betelgeuse, and is a dominant sight in the mid-winter sky in the N hemisphere. Three of its bright stars form *Orion's belt*.

Orissa POP (1991) 31.7m, a state in E India, bounded E by the Bay of Bengal. AREA 155 782sq km/60 132sq mi. HISTORY ceded to the Mahrattas in 1751; taken by the British in 1803; subdivision of Bengal until 1912, when the provinces of Bihar and Orissa were created; became a separate province in 1936 and a state in 1950. CAPITAL Bhubaneswar. CHIEF TOWN Cuttack. GOVERNMENT governed by a 147-member Legislative Assembly. The R Mahanadi is dammed to form the Hirakaud Reservoir. It was completed in 1957 and is the largest earth dam in the world. ECONOMY rice, wheat, oilseed, sugar cane; jute, forestry; fishing; chromite, dolomite, graphite, iron ore, limestone; cement; fertilizer; sugar; glass; machinery; textiles; crafts; tourism in the Golden Triangle (Konark, Puri, Bhubaneswar).

Orkney Islands POP (1992e) 20 000, a group of islands lying off NE Scotland, separated from the mainland to the S by the Pentland Firth. AREA 976sq km/377sq mi. There are 15 main islands (notably Mainland, South Ronaldsay, Sanday, Westray, and Hoy), and many smaller islands; c.20 of the islands are inhabited. PHYSICAL DESCRIPTION generally low-lying and treeless. CAPITAL Kirkwall (on Mainland). HISTORY the Orkney and Shetland Is were a Norse dependency from the 9c; annexed by Scotland from Norway and Denmark in 1472; Scapa Flow, a sea area within the islands, was used in World Wars I and II as a major naval anchorage; the German Fleet surrendered there in 1918, but in 1919 was scuppered by its skeleton crews. ECONOMY fishing; farming; weaving; wind power (generator at Burgar Hill); North Sea oil terminal on Flotta; oil service bases on Mainland and Hoy. NOTABLE FEATURES several prehistoric remains, notably Standing Stones at Stenness (W Mainland), dating to c.3000 BC, and the Neolithic village at Skara Brae (W Mainland); NW of Hoy is the Old Man of Hoy, an isolated stack 137m high.

Orlando the strong and courteous lover of Rosalind in Shakespeare's *As You Like It*, who becomes a figure of fun in the Forest of Arden.

Orlando POP (1990) 1.1m, the seat of Orange County, central Florida, USA. Founded in c.1844, it is a popular tourist centre. NOTABLE FEATURES Walt Disney World; Epcot Center.

Orlando a novel by Virginia Woolf (1928). It describes the fantastic life of the aristocratic poet Orlando as he travels through four centuries, changing sex on the way.

Orlando Furioso a poem by Ariosto (1516, 1532). One of the definitive texts of the Italian Renaissance, it is a Roland epic which forms a continuation of Boiardo's *Orlando Innamorato*.

Orléans, Charles, Duc d' (1391–1465) French poet, born in Paris. In 1406 he married his cousin Isabella, widow of Richard II of England. He commanded at Agincourt (1415) and was captured and taken to England where he lived for 25 years, composing courtly poetry in French and English. Ransomed in 1440, he then maintained a kind of literary court at Blois. His son became Louis XII.

Orléans, Louis Philippe Joseph, Duc d' (Duke of), also called **Philippe Egalité (equality)** (1747–93) French Bourbon prince, born in Saint-Cloud, the cousin of King Louis XVI and father of Louis Philippe. During the Revolution he proved a strong supporter of the Third Estate against the privileged orders, and in 1792 renounced his title of nobility for his popular name. At the Convention he voted for the King's death but was himself arrested after the defection of his eldest son to the Austrians (1793), and guillotined.

Orleans, French **Orléans,** ancient **Aurelianum** POP (1990) 243 000, the capital of Centre region and of Loiret department, central France. It lies on the right bank of the R Loire, 92km/57mi SW of Paris. HISTORY associated with Joan of Arc, 'The Maid of Orleans', who raised the English siege here in 1429; formerly the ancient capital of the province of Orléannais. NOTABLE FEATURES cathedral (13c–16c); town hall (16c); Episcopal Palace; Museum of Fine Art.

Orléans, House of the junior branch of the Valois and Bourbon dynasties in France, the title of which fell to four individual lines: Philippe de Valois, created Duke in 1344 but died without issue; Louis I de Valois (1372–1407) whose descendants held the title until 1544; Gaston (1608–60), the Bourbon third son of Henry IV, made Duke in 1626; and Louis XIV's younger brother Philippe (1640–1701), from whom descended the Regent Orléans (1674–1723), Louis Philippe Joseph, Duke of Orléns, Philippe 'Egalité' (1747–93), who died in the French Revolution, and Louis-Philippe (1773–1850), 'King of the French', whose son was the last to hold the ducal title.

Orléans, Siege of the English blockade (Oct 1428–May 1429) during the Hundred Years War of the main stronghold still loyal to Charles VII of France, which was relieved by troops inspired by Joan of Arc. Anglo-Burgundian forces, who already controlled most of N France, were prevented from pressing south, but the event was less of a turning-point in the war than the Franco-Burgundian rapprochement of 1435.

orlop *noun* the lowest deck in a ship with four or more decks, forming a covering for the hold. [from Dutch *overloop*, covering]

ormolu *noun* a gold-coloured alloy, eg copper, zinc and sometimes tin, which is used to decorate furniture, make ornaments, etc. [from French *or*, gold + *moulu*, ground]

ornament — *noun* 1 anything that decorates or adds grace or beauty to a person or thing. 2 a small, usually decorative object. 3 a person whose talents add honour to the group, company, etc to which he or she belongs. 4 (*usually* **ornaments**) *Mus.* a note which embellishes or decorates the melody or harmony but does not belong to it. — *verb* to decorate or be an ornament to. [from Latin *ornare*, to adorn]

ornamental *adj.* used for decoration.

ornamentally *adv.* in an ornamental way.

ornamentation *noun* ornamenting.

ornate *adj.* 1 highly or excessively decorated. 2 *said of language* not plain and simple; using many elaborate literary words or expressions. [from Latin *ornare*, to adorn]

ornately *adv.* in an ornate way.

ornateness *noun* being ornate.

ornithine *Biochem.* an amino acid that is found in proteins. [from Greek *ornis ornith-*, bird]

ornithological *adj.* relating to or involving ornithology.

ornithologically *adv.* as regards ornithology.

ornithologist *noun* a person who studies ornithology.

ornithology *noun* the scientific study of birds and their behaviour. [from Greek *ornis*, bird + -LOGY]

orogeny *or* **orogenesis** *noun* 1 *Geol.* a period of mountain-building, often lasting for hundreds of millions of years, involving such processes as deformation and the subsequent uplift of rocks, folding, and usually the intrusion of igneous rocks. 2 the process of mountain-building. [from Greek *oros* mountain + GENESIS]

orographic *or* **oreographic** *adj. Geol.* denoting effects that are related to the presence of mountains or high ground, eg rainfall. [from Greek *oros, oreos* mountain + -GRAPHY]

orotund *adj.* 1 *said of the voice* full, loud, and grand. 2 *said of speaking* boastful or self-important; pompous. [from Latin *os*, mouth + *rotundus*, round]

orotundity *noun* being orotund.

Orozco, José Clemente (1883–1949) Mexican painter, born in Zapotlán, Jalisco. He decorated public buildings in Mexico (eg in Guadalajara) and the USA and is generally regarded as one of the foremost mural painters of the 20c. His powerful realistic style, verging on caricature, acted as a vehicle for his revolutionary socialist ideas.

orphan — *noun* a child who has lost both parents, or, more rarely, one parent. — *verb* (**orphaned**, **orphaning**) to cause to be an orphan. [from Greek *orphanos*]

orphanage *noun* a home for orphans.

Orpheus in Greek legend, a poet from Thrace, able to enchant gods, men, animals, and inanimate objects with the music of his lyre. In this way he obtained the release of his wife Eurydice from Hades, but he lost her because he turned round to look at her before she had completely emerged from the Underworld. He was killed by the Maenads of Dionysus, and his head, still singing, floated to Lesbos.

Orpheus and Eurydice (Orfeo ed Euridice) an opera by Christoph Gluck (1762). Based on the Classical legend, it is the story of Orpheus's journey to Hades to reclaim his deceased wife Eurydice. It tells of how he uses his music to charm Pluto, the Furies, and Cerberus (the three-headed dog) to reach her, but forgets he must not look back while leading her home.

Orphism 1 *Relig.* a set of unorthodox religious ideas that appeared in Greece in the 6c BC, taking its name from poems ascribed to the mythical singer Orpheus. The fate of the soul after death was the central concern, and the self was seen as a stranger in exile within the body. Orphic poetry seems to have described a primal crime through which all humankind became guilty, thus requiring purification through ritual. 2 *Art* a modern art movement that developed out of Cubism between 1910 and 1914. The principal artists were Robert Delauney (1885–1941), and Frantisek Kupka (1871–1957), who experimented with pure colour within the Cubist framework, in an effort to achieve harmony of colour and form. The term was applied to the movement by Guillaume Apollinaire.

orrery *noun* (PL. **orreries**) a clockwork model of the Sun and the planets which revolve around it. [from Charles Boyle, Earl of Orrery (1676–1731), for whom one was made]

orris *noun* an iris, especially the Florentine iris. [a form of IRIS]

orris-root *noun* the dried, sweet-smelling root of this plant, used in perfumes and formerly in medicines.

Orsini a powerful Roman noble family which periodically dominated papal politics and appointments (including the papacy itself) from the 11c. In the 1400s, 'by custom', one Orsini, along with a French and a Venetian cardinal, was entitled to sit in the College of Cardinals. In the same period the family inter-married with the Medici of Florence.

Orsino the love-obsessed Duke of Illyria in Shakespeare's *Twelfth Night*, who pursues Olivia but is quite happy to marry Viola when he realises that she is in love with him.

Ortelius, originally **Abraham Ortel** (1527–98) Flemish cartographer and engraver, born in Antwerp. He was trained as an engraver, and in c.1560 became interested in map-making. His *Theatrum Orbis Terrarum* (1570, Epitome of the Theatre of the World) was the first major atlas.

ortho- *combining form* forming words meaning 'correct, straight, upright'. [from Greek *orthos*, straight]

orthodontic *adj.* relating to orthodontics.

orthodontics *sing. noun Dentistry* the branch of dentistry concerned with the correction of irregularities in the alignment of the teeth, eg by fitting dental braces, usually performed during childhood. [from ORTHO- + Greek *odous odont-*, tooth]

orthodontist *noun* a dentist who specializes in preventing or correcting irregularities of teeth.

orthodox *adj.* **1** believing in, living according to or conforming with established or generally accepted opinions, especially in religion or morals; conventional. **2** (**Orthodox**) of the Orthodox Church. **3** (**Orthodox**) of the branch of Judaism which keeps to strict, traditional interpretations of doctrine and scripture. [from Greek *orthos*, straight + *doxa*, opinion]

Orthodox Church or **Eastern Orthodox Church** a communion of self-governing churches that recognize the honorary primacy of the Patriarch of Constantinople and confess the doctrine of the seven Ecumenical Councils (from Nicaea I, 327, to Nicaea II, 787). It includes the patriarchates of Alexandria, Antioch, Constantinople, and Jerusalem, and the Churches of Russia, Bulgaria, Cyprus, Serbia, Georgia, Romania, Greece, Poland, Albania, and Czechoslovakia. It developed historically from the Eastern Roman or Byzantine Empire.

orthodoxy *noun* (PL. **orthodoxies**) **1** the state of being orthodox or of having orthodox beliefs. **2** an orthodox belief or practice.

orthogonal *adj. Maths.* right-angled; perpendicular. [from ORTHO- + Greek *gonia*, angle]

orthographic or **orthographical** *adj.* relating to spelling.

orthographically *adv.* in an orthographic way, using spelling.

orthography *noun* (PL. **orthographies**) **1** correct or standard spelling. **2** the study of spelling.

orthopaedic *adj.* relating to orthopaedics.

orthopaedics *sing. noun Medicine* the branch of medicine concerned with the correction by surgery, manipulation, etc, of deformities arising from injury or disease of the bones and joints, eg broken bones, dislocated joints, arthritis. [from ORTHO- + Greek *pais*, child]

orthopaedist *noun* a specialist in orthopaedics.

orthoptics *sing. noun* the science or practice of correcting weak eyesight, especially through exercising the eye muscles. [from ORTHO- + Greek *optikos*, of sight]

ortolan *noun* a small European song-bird, eaten as a delicacy. [from Latin *hortulus*, small garden]

Orton, Joe, originally **John Kingsley** (1933–67) English dramatist, born in Leicester. His first stage play, *Entertaining Mr Sloane* (1964), was in the style of absurdist drama, but this was quickly followed by more extreme, erotic, and anarchic farces, among them *Loot* (1965) and *What the Butler Saw* (first performed 1969). He was murdered by his lover, Kenneth Halliwell.

Orust a Swedish island in the Kattegat, separated from the SW coast of the mainland by a narrow channel 1.6–5km/1–3mi wide. AREA 346sq km/134sq mi; length 22km/14mi; width 16km/10mi. Orust is the second largest island in Sweden.

Orwell, George, pseudonym of **Eric Arthur Blair** (1903–50) British novelist and essayist, born in Motihari, Bengal. He served in Burma in the Indian Imperial Police (1922–7), was wounded in the Spanish Civil War, and served as a war correspondent during World War II. He developed his own brand of socialism in *The Road to Wigan Pier* (1937) and other essays, and also wrote four novels in the 1930s, notably *Coming up for Air* (1939). He is best known for his satire of totalitarian ideology in *Animal Farm* (1945), and the prophetic novel, *Nineteen Eighty-Four* (1949).

Ory, Kid (1886–1973) US trombonist and bandleader, born in Louisiana. One of the first polyinstrumentalists, singers, and composers in jazz, he formed Kid Ory's Sunshine Orchestra in 1922, played with Louis Armstrong's Hot Five and Jelly Roll Morton's Red Hot Peppers, and took part in the New Orleans Revival from 1942. His compositions include 'Muskrat Ramble'.

-ory¹ *suffix* forming nouns denoting a place for a specified activity: *dormitory / laboratory*. [from Latin *-orium*]

-ory² *suffix* forming adjectives and occasionally nouns with the sense of relating to or involving the action of the verb: *depository / signatory*. [from Latin *-orius*]

oryx *noun* a grazing antelope with very long slender horns and a pale coat, with striking white and dark markings on the face and underparts. [from Greek *oryx*]

OS *abbrev.* **1** *Comput.* operating system. **2** ordinary seaman. **3** Ordnance Survey. **4** outsize.

Os *symbol Chem.* osmium.

Osaka, formerly **Naniwa** POP (1991e) 2.6m, the port capital of Osaka prefecture, S Honshu, Japan. It lies on the NE shore of Osaka-wan Bay and is the third largest city in Japan. It developed around a castle built in the 16c. The city was almost completely destroyed in World War II. NOTABLE FEATURES famous puppet theatre; Osaka Castle; Municipal Museum, Electric Science Museum, Fujita Museum; Shintennoji Temple (6c); Sumiyoshi Shrine, present buildings built in 1808.

Osbaldistone, Francis the romantically inclined, moderate hero of Sir Walter Scott's *Rob Roy*. His name is shared by his dissipated uncle, Sir Hildebrand, and his scheming Jacobite cousin, Rashleigh.

Osborne, George the shallow, unfaithful husband of Amelia Sedley in William Makepeace Thackeray's *Vanity Fair*. His father is Mr Osborne, and his sisters are Maria and Jane.

Osborne, John (James) (1929–) English playwright and actor, born in London. He became established as a leading exponent of British social drama with his play *Look Back in Anger* (1956), whose 'hero', Jimmy Porter, became the prototype 'Angry Young Man', and then *The Entertainer* (1957). Other works include *Luther* (1961), *Inadmissible Evidence* (1964), and *A Patriot for Me* (1965).

Oscar a male first name, borne in recent times most famously by Oscar Wilde. [of Irish Gaelic origin, from *os*, deer + *cara*, friend]

Oscar *noun* each of a number of statuettes awarded annually by the American Academy of Motion Picture Arts and Sciences for outstanding acting, directing, etc in films during the previous year. — Also called *Academy Award*. [from the name *Oscar*; of uncertain origin]

oscillate *verb* **1** *trans., intrans.* to swing or cause to swing backwards and forwards like a pendulum. **2** *intrans.* to vary between opinions, choices, courses of action, etc. **3** *intrans. said of an electrical current* to vary regularly in strength or direction between certain limits. [from Latin *oscillare*, to swing]

oscillation *noun* **1** oscillating. **2** a regular movement or change, such as the movement of a pendulum. **3** one such move from one position to another.

oscillator *noun* **1** an electronic device that produces an alternating current of a particular frequency. Oscillators are used to produce high-frequency radio waves for television and radio, and to make electronic musical instruments. **2** a person or thing that oscillates.

oscillograph *noun* an apparatus for recording (electrical) oscillations.

oscilloscope *noun* an apparatus with which electrical oscillations, appearing as waves, are shown on the screen of a cathode-ray tube.

osier *noun* **1** a willow tree whose branches and twigs are used for making baskets. **2** a flexible branch or twig from this tree. [from Old French]

Osiris in Egyptian religion, the god of fertility and the dead, and the husband of Isis. Originally he was the king of Egypt, and was murdered by his brother Seth, who scattered the pieces of his body over the earth. These were collected by Isis; Osiris, given renewed life, was made the king of the Underworld. In the cult of the dead, he came to represent the personification after death of all the pharoahs and, later, of all men.

-osis *suffix* (PL. **-oses**) forming nouns denoting: **1** a condition or process: *hypnosis / metamorphosis*. **2** a diseased or disordered state: *neurosis*. [from Greek *-osis*]

Osler, Sir William (1849–1919) Canadian–US–British physician, born in Bond Head, Ontario. Professor at McGill University, the University of Pennsylvania, Johns Hopkins, and Oxford, he wrote widely on clinical medicine and medical history, and his textbook *The Principles and Practice of Medicine* (1892) became a standard work.

Ösling or **Oesling** a geographical region in the Ardennes, N Luxembourg. AREA 828sq km/320sq mi (32% of Luxembourg). It is wooded and less fertile than the Gutland ('good land') to the S, but is largely agricultural.

Oslo, formerly **Christiania** or **Kristiania** POP (1992e) 467 000, the capital of Norway and the country's largest port, situated at the head of Oslo Fjord, SE Norway. HISTORY founded in the 11c; under the influence of the Hanseatic League in the 14c; destroyed by fire in 1624; rebuilt by Christian IV of Denmark and Norway and renamed Christiania; a cultural revival began in the 19c, with notable writers such as Ibsen and Bjørnson; became capital in 1905; renamed Oslo in 1925. The port is the base of a large merchant shipping fleet. NOTABLE FEATURES cathedral (17c); Royal Palace (1825–48); Akershus Castle (13c); Norwegian Folk Museum; National Gallery; National Theatre.

osmiridium *noun Chem.* a hard white naturally occurring alloy of osmium and iridium, in which the iridium content is less than 35 per cent. It is used to make the tips of pen nibs.

osmium *noun Chem.* (SYMBOL **Os**, ATOMIC NUMBER **76**) a very hard dense bluish-white metal used as a catalyst, and as a hardening agent in alloys with platinum and iridium, eg in pen nibs. Osmium tetroxide is used in fingerprint detection, and as a biological stain and fixative in microscopy. [from Greek *osme*, smell, from the unpleasant smell of one of its forms]

osmoregulation *noun Biol.* the process whereby the water content and concentration of salts within a living organism are maintained at a constant level. In many animals the kidneys are responsible for osmoregulation. [from Greek *osmos*, impulse]

osmosis *noun* **1** *Chem.* the spontaneous movement of a solvent, eg water, across a semi-permeable membrane from a more dilute solution to a more concentrated one. The process continues until the concentrations of the two solutions are equal, or until an external pressure is applied to the more concentrated solution. The minimum pressure required to stop the movement of solvent is known as the osmotic pressure. Osmosis is largely responsible for the movement of water molecules into and out of cells of living organisms. **2** a gradual process of absorption. [from Greek *osmos*, impulse]

osmotic *adj.* relating to or caused by osmosis.

osmotically *adv.* by osmosis.

osmotic pressure **1** *Chem.* the minimum pressure that must be applied to prevent the spontaneous movement by osmosis of a solvent across a semi-permeable membrane from a more dilute solution to a more concentrated one. **2** the minimum pressure that must be applied to prevent the spontaneous movement by osmosis of a solvent across a semi-permeable membrane separating the pure solvent from a solution. See also OSMOSIS.

Osnabrück POP (1991e) 163 000, a manufacturing city in SW Lower Saxony state, Germany. It lies in the Haase Valley, 48km/30mi NE of Münster. The city was badly bombed in World War II. NOTABLE FEATURES cathedral (13c); Episcopal Palace (17c).

osprey *noun* (PL. **ospreys**) **1** a large bird of prey found near water in most parts of the world, with a dark brown body, white head and legs, and a characteristic dark line on the side of the head. It feeds almost entirely on fish, and for a while was extinct in the UK, but careful guarding of nesting sites has led to its gradual return in recent years. **2** a feather used for trimming women's hats. [from Latin *ossifraga*, bone-breaker]

Ossa, Mount the highest mountain in Tasmania. HEIGHT 1 617m. It is situated within the Cradle Mountain–L St Clair National Park.

osseous *adj.* of, like, containing or formed from bone. [from Latin *os*, bone]

Ossian *or* **Oisín** Legendary Irish poet and warrior, the son of the 3c hero Fingal or Fionn MacCumhail. The Scottish poet James Macpherson (1736–96) professed to have collected and translated his works, though it was later shown that the poems, (eg the epic *Fingal*), were largely of his own devising.

ossification *noun Zool.* the process by which bone is formed, usually from cartilage. [from Latin *os ossis*, bone]

ossified *adj.* **1** made into bone. **2** like bone, hardened.

ossify *verb* (**ossifies**, **ossified**) **1** *intrans., trans.* to turn into or cause to turn into bone. **2** *intrans. said of one's opinions, etc* to become rigid, fixed, or inflexible. [from Latin *os*, bone + *facere*, to make]

Ossory an ancient Irish kingdom, co-extensive with the diocese of Ossory, conquered by Anglo-Norman invaders in the late 12c. The most powerful families in the area were the Marshals, Earls of Pembroke, Wales, and Lords of Leinster (1199–1245), and the Butlers, created Earls of Ormond (1328) and Ossory (1528).

Ostend, Flemish **Oostende**, French **Ostende** POP (1992e) 69 000, an important seaport and large seaside resort in West Flanders province, W Belgium, on the North Sea coast. It is the principal ferry port for England (Dover and Folkestone) and the headquarters of the Belgian fishing fleet. NOTABLE FEATURES promenade; casino; racecourse; Chalet Royal.

Ostend Manifesto a statement (1854) presented by the US ambassadors to Great Britain, France, and Spain, effectively asserting US claims over the then Spanish colony of Cuba, saying that if Spain refused to sell Cuba, then the USA was justified in taking it by force. Although repudiated by the US government, the manifesto gave notice of future US interest in Cuba and the Caribbean.

ostensibility *noun* being ostensible.

ostensible *adj.*, *said of reasons, etc* stated or claimed, but not necessarily true; apparent. [from Latin *ostendere*, to show]

ostensibly *adv.* in an ostensible way; to outward appearance.

ostensive *adj.* directly showing.

ostentation *noun* pretentious display of wealth, knowledge, etc, especially to attract attention or admiration. [from Latin *ostendere*, to show]

ostentatious *adj.* characterized by ostentation; pretentious, showy.

ostentatiously *adv.* in an ostentatious way.

ostentatiousness *noun* beng ostentatious.

osteoarthritis *noun Medicine* the commonest form of arthritis, found mainly in the elderly, in which degeneration of the cartilage overlying the bones at a joint (especially the hip, knee, or thumb joint) leads to deformity of the bone surface. It causes stiffness, swelling, and eventually deformity of the affected joint. [from Greek *osteon*, bone + ARTHRITIS]

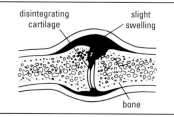

osteoarthritis

osteomalacia *noun Medicine* a disorder characterized by softening of the bones due to a reduction in the availability of calcium salts, caused by a deficiency of vitamin D, which is required for the uptake of calcium from food. [from Greek *osteon*, bone + *malakos*, soft]

osteopath *noun* a person who practises osteopathy.

osteopathic *adj.* relating to or involving osteopathy.

osteopathy *noun Medicine* a system of healing or treatment, mainly involving manipulation of the bones and joints and massage of the muscles, that provides relief for many bone and joint disorders. [from Greek *osteon*, bone + *patheia*, suffering]

osteoporosis *noun Medicine* a disease in which the bones become porous, brittle and liable to fracture, owing to the loss of calcium from the bone substance. It is a common feature of ageing. [from Greek *osteon* bone, + *poros*, passage]
◇ For hormonal reasons osteoporosis affects more women than men. After the menopause women lose 1% of their bone each year, owing to the fact that their ovaries are no longer producing oestrogen, which helps to maintain bone mass. Osteoporosis can also be caused by infection and injury, removal of the ovaries, long-term treatment with corticosteroids, certain hormonal disorders, and a diet deficient in calcium. Contributing factors may include lack of exercise, heavy drinking, smoking, hereditary factors and childlessness. Hormone replacment therapy (HRT) has proved to be a very effective treatment for osteoporosis in post-menopausal women. The disorder can also be treated with calcium and vitamin D supplements.

Ostia an ancient Roman town situated at the mouth of the Tiber in W Italy. It was Rome's main naval base during the Punic Wars (3c–2c BC), and the main port under the Roman Empire.

ostler *noun Hist.* a person who attends to horses at an inn. [from Old French *hostelier*]

Ostmark *noun Hist.* the standard unit of currency in the former German Democratic Republic (East Germany).

Ostpolitik the policy initiated in West Germany in the 1960s as part of the process of détente to normalize relations with communist countries which recognized the German Democratic Republic (GDR), and with the GDR itself. Largely masterminded by Willy Brandt, the policy sought to prevent the schism deepening between the Federal Republic and GDR, and had the broader aim of improving West–East relations generally. It culminated in German reunification in 1990.

ostracism *noun* **1** in ancient Athens, a process by which a citizen could be banished for up to ten years (without loss of property or citizenship) by popular vote. **2** social exclusion. [from Greek *ostrakismos*, from *ostrakon*, potsherd, used as a means of voting in ancient Greece]

ostracize *or* **ostracise** *verb* **1** to exclude (someone) from a group, society, etc; to refuse to associate with (someone). **2** in Athens and other ancient Greek cities, to banish (a person) for a fixed period by popular vote.

Ostrava POP (1991) 328 000, a city in the Czech Republic. Lying near the junction of the Oder and Ostravice rivers, it held an important strategic position in medieval times.

ostrich *noun* **1** the largest living bird, up to 2.5m in height and incapable of flight, found on dry plains in E Africa, and having an extremely long neck and legs. The plumage of the male ostrich is black, with white plumes on the wings. **2** a person who refuses to face or accept unpleasant facts. [from Latin *avis*, bird + *struthio*, ostrich]
◇ Although ostriches cannot fly, they are capable of running at speeds of up to 60km per hour, and unlike most birds, they have only two toes on each foot, instead of four. They feed mainly on fruits, seeds, and leaves, sometimes swallowing stones and other hard objects to aid digestion of food. They can live for up to 70 years, and contrary to popular belief, the ostrich does not bury its head in the sand in order to 'hide' from danger, but if threatened it often defends itself by kicking with its powerful legs. At one time demand for ostrich feathers or 'plumes' caused a great reduction in numbers, but ostrich populations have now increased again, and it is not an endangered species.

ostrich

Ostrogoths a Germanic tribe who by the beginning of the 4c had migrated from the Baltic to S Russia but were conquered by the Huns in AD 375. After Attila's death, they freed themselves, and under their leader Theodoric the Great, they conquered Italy and established a powerful and highly civilized kingdom. After Theodoric's death, the kingdom disintegrated under pressure from the eastern empire.

Ostwald, (Friedrich) Wilhelm (1853–1932) German chemist, born in Riga. He taught in his home town and later became professor at Leipzig (1887–1906), where he was a pioneer of physical chemistry. He worked on catalysis, discovered the dilution law which bears his name, and was awarded the 1909 Nobel Prize for Chemistry.

Oswald, St (c.605–642) Anglo-Saxon King of Northumbria (633–41), the son of Ethelfrith of Benicia. He was converted at Iona, then established Christianity in Northumbria with the help of the Celtic monk St Aidan. He fell in battle with the pagan King Penda. His feast day is 5 Aug.

Oswald, Lee Harvey (1939–63) US alleged killer of President John F Kennedy, born in New Orleans. A Marxist and former US Marine who had lived for a while in the USSR (1959–62), he worked in the Texas School Book Depository, from the sixth floor of which he allegedly shot Kennedy as he passed in his motor cavalcade. Two days after the assassination Oswald was killed at point-blank range during a jail transfer in Dallas by nightclub owner Jack Ruby (1911–67), before he could stand trial.

Oswald a male first name. [of Germanic origin, from *os*, god + *weald*, rich]

Oswestry POP (1992e) 34 000, a town in Oswestry district, Shropshire, W central England. It lies 26km/16mi NW of Shrewsbury. NOTABLE FEATURES castle; grammar school (15c). [named after St Oswald, who was killed here in 642.]

OT abbrev. Old Testament.

OTC abbrev. Brit. Officers' Training Corps.

Otello (Othello) an opera by Giuseppe Verdi (1887), based on Shakespeare's play.

Othello, The Moor of Venice a play by William Shakespeare (1604). It is a tragedy culminating in the downfall of the admirable soldier Othello, which is brought about by the skilful scheming of the resentful Iago playing on Othello's violent jealousy for his wife Desdemona.

other — adj. **1** remaining from a group of two or more when one or some have been specified already: *close the other eye / the other children.* **2** different from the one or ones already mentioned, understood or implied: *other people.* **3** additional; further: *need to buy one other thing.* **4** far or opposite: *the other side of the garden.* — pron. another person or thing. — adv. colloq. otherwise; differently: *couldn't do other than hurry home.*
— **every other** each alternate.
other than … **1** except …; apart from … **2** different from …
the other day, **week**, etc a few days, weeks, etc, ago.
[from Anglo-Saxon]

other ranks chiefly Brit. members of the armed services not having the rank of officer.

otherwise — conj. or else; if not. — adv. **1** in other respects: *he is good at languages but otherwise not very bright.* **2** in a different way: *couldn't act otherwise than as she did.* **3** under different circumstances: *might otherwise have been late.* — adj. different: *the truth is otherwise.*
— **or otherwise** or the opposite; or not: *check all cars, fast or otherwise.*

otherworldliness noun being otherworldly.

otherworldly adj. concerned with spiritual or intellectual matters to the complete exclusion of practical matters.

otic adj. of or relating to the ear. [from Greek *ous*, ear]

otiose adj. serving no purpose; unnecessary; useless. [from Latin *otiosus*, from *otium*, leisure]

otitis noun Medicine inflammation of the ear. [from Latin *ous, otos* ear + -ITIS]

Otley POP (1981) 14 000, a market town in Leeds borough, West Yorkshire, N England. It lies on the R Wharfe, 15km/9mi NW of Leeds. The town's market regulations date back to 1222. Thomas Chippendale, the cabinet-maker who gave his name to a style of furniture, was born here in 1718. NOTABLE FEATURE All Saints' Church (7c).

O'Toole, Peter (Seamus) (1932–) Irish film actor, born in Connemara. His title role in *Lawrence of Arabia* (1962) brought him the first of his seven Academy Award nominations. Among the others were *Goodbye Mr Chips* (1969), *The Ruling Class* (1972), and *The Stunt Man* (1980). He also appeared in the television film *Rebecca's Daughters* (1992).

OTT abbrev. slang over the top.

ottava rima Prosody an Italian stanza of eight lines, rhyming *abababcc*. [Italian, = eighth rhyme]

Ottawa POP (1991e) 921 000, the capital of Canada, in SE Ontario, standing on the Ottawa R at its junction with the Rideau R. HISTORY founded as Bytown in 1826, it received its present name in 1854; became capital of the United Provinces in 1858, then national capital in 1867. LANGUAGE two thirds of the population are English-speaking, one third French. NOTABLE FEATURES Peace Tower in the parliament buildings; Eternal Flame on Parliament Hill, lit in 1967; National War Memorial; several important museums; National Library; National Gallery of Canada.

Ottawa Agreements a series of agreements concluded (1932) in Canada at an economic conference held between Britain and its dominions at the height of the world depression. The conference decided in favour of a limited amount of imperial preference (the favouring of trade within the British Empire by discriminating tariffs) after a new protective tariff had been adopted by the British government earlier that year.

Ottawa River, French **Rivière des Outaouais** a river in Canada, the largest tributary of the St Lawrence, length 1 271km/790mi. It rises in the Canadian Shield, and flows W, then S and SE to the St Lawrence SW of Montreal. For most of its course it forms the Ontario–Quebec border; the Rideau Canal connects the river to L Ontario. The lower river has numerous rapids which are used to generate hydroelectric power. The Ottawa River Valley was an important route for explorers, fur traders, and missionaries.

otter noun any of about 20 species of solitary and rather elusive aquatic mammals belonging to the same family (Mustelidae) as badgers and weasels, found in all parts of the world except Australasia and Antarctica, and having a long body, a broad flat head, short legs, and a stout tail which is thick at the base and tapers towards the tip. [from Anglo-Saxon *otor*]
◇ Otters make burrows in the banks of rivers and lakes, and spend much of their time in the water. The animal's sleek coat consists of a fawn-coloured waterproof underlayer of fur, and an outer layer of stiff guard hairs, which are grey at the base and dark brown at the tip. It has small front feet and large webbed hind feet, and it is a strong swimmer, noted for its speed and manoeuvrability in the water (it can also move very quickly on land). It feeds on fish, crayfish, frogs, birds, and small mammals, eg rabbits, and is a very playful animal, sometimes seen sliding down slippery banks into the water. The giant otter, found in S America, has been hunted for its valuable fur to such an extent that it is now the most endangered Amazonian mammal.

Otto I, known as **the Great** (912–73) King of the Germans (from 936) and Holy Roman Emperor (from 962). He subdued many turbulent tribes, maintained almost supreme power in Italy, and encouraged Christian missions to Scandinavian and Slavonic lands.

Otto, Nikolaus August (1832–91) German engineer, born in Holzhausen, Nassau. He invented in 1876 the four-stroke internal combustion engine; its sequence of operations is known as the *Otto cycle*.

Otto, Rudolf (1869–1937) German Protestant theologian and philosopher, born in Peine, Hanover. He became Professor of Systematic Theology at Göttingen (1904), and later held chairs at Breslau (1914) and Marburg (1917). His best-known work, *Das Heilige* (The Idea of the Holy, 1917), explores the non-rational aspect of religion, termed 'the numinous' (the deity or awareness of it).

Otto a male first name. [of Germanic origin, = rich]

Ottoman — adj. relating to the Ottomans or the Ottoman Empire, which lasted from the 13c until the end of World War I. It was centred in what is now Turkey, and at different times reached into Europe and the Near East. — noun (PL. **Ottomans**) **1** an inhabitant of the Ottoman Empire; a Turk. **2** (**ottoman**) a long low seat, usually without a back or arms, and often in the form of a padded and upholstered box. [from Arabic *uthman*, Othman (1259–1326), the founder of the Ottoman Empire]

Ottoman Empire a Muslim empire founded c.1300 by Sultan Osman I (1259–1326) in Asia Minor. Ottoman forces entered Europe (1345), conquered Constantinople (1453), and by 1520 controlled most of SE Europe, including part of Hungary, the Middle East, and N Africa. Following the 'golden age' of Sulaiman the Magnificent, the Empire began its slow decline. During the 19c and early 20c, Ottoman power was eroded by the SE European ambitions of Russia and Austria, the N African ambitions of France, Britain, and Italy, the emergence of the Balkan nations, and internal loss of authority. It joined the Central Powers in 1914, and collapsed with their defeat in 1918.

Otway, Thomas (1652–85) English dramatist, born in Trotton, Sussex. He translated Jean Racine and Molière, and wrote Restoration comedies, but his best-known works are tragedies, including *Venice Preserved, or a Plot Discovered* (1682).

Ötztal Alps, German **Ötztaler Alpen** a mountain range in Tirol state, W Austria. It rises to 3 774m at Wildspitze, Austria's second highest peak.

OU abbrev. **1** Open University. **2** Oxford University.

Ouagadougou POP (1985) 442 000, the capital of Burkina. HISTORY part of the Ivory Coast until 1947; capital of the Mossi Empire from the 15c; captured by the French in 1896. NOTABLE FEATURES cathedral; Palace of Moro Naba (Mossi Emperor).

oubliette noun Hist. a secret dungeon with a single often concealed opening at the top. [from French, from *oublier*, to forget]

ouch interj. an expression of sudden sharp pain. [imitative]

Oudenaarde, French **Audenarde** POP (1991e) 27 000, a town in East Flanders province, W Belgium. It lies on the R Scheldt. The town is a traditional centre for carpet-weaving and tapestries. Nearby is the site of the defeat of the French by the Grand Alliance under Marlborough and Prince Eugene (1708) in the War of the Spanish Succession. NOTABLE FEATURES town hall (1526–37); Church of Onze Lieve Vrouw Pamele (begun in 1235).

Oudenaarde, Battle of a Grand Alliance victory (1708) in Flanders during the War of the Spanish Succession. While laying siege to Oudenarde, the French under the Duke of Vendôme and Burgundy were surprised and defeated by Allied troops led by Prince Eugene of Savoy and the Duke of Marlborough, and later (1709) withdrew to their frontier.

ought *verb aux.* used to express: **1** duty or obligation: *you ought to help if you can.* **2** advisability: *you ought to see a doctor.* **3** probability or expectation: *she ought to be here soon.* **4** shortcoming or failure: *he ought to have been here hours ago.* **5** enthusiastic desire on the part of the speaker: *you really ought to read this book.* **6** logical consequence: *the answer ought to be 'four'.*
— **ought not to** ... used to express moral disapproval: *you ought not to speak to him like that.* [from Anglo-Saxon *ahte*]

Ouija *noun* (in full **Ouija board**) *trademark* a board with the letters of the alphabet printed round the edge, used at séances with a glass, pointer, or other object to spell out messages supposed to be from spirits. [from French *oui*, yes + German *ja*, yes]

Oujda POP (1982) 260 000, the capital of Oriental province, NE Morocco. It lies close to the Algerian frontier.

Oulu, Swedish **Uleaborg** **1** POP (1992e) 102 000, the industrial seaport capital of Oulu province, W Finland. It is situated on the Gulf of Bothnia, at the mouth of the R Oulu. It was established in 1605 and destroyed by fire in 1822. **2** a province in N central Finland with the city of Oulu as its capital.

ounce¹ *noun* **1** a unit of weight equal to one sixteenth of a pound (28.35g). **2** a fluid ounce. **3** a small amount. [from Latin *uncia*, twelfth part]

ounce² *noun* a big cat native to Asia, with leopard-like markings on a thick, soft, cream-coloured coat. [from Old French *once*, from Greek *lynx*, lynx]

our *adj.* **1** of, belonging to, associated with or done by us: *our children.* **2** *formal* used by a sovereign to mean 'my': *our royal will.* [from Anglo-Saxon *ure*]

Ouranus see URANUS.

Our Father same as LORD'S PRAYER.

Our Lady the Virgin Mary.

Our Mutual Friend a novel by Charles Dickens (1864–5). His last complete novel, it depicts the evils of greed and materialism.

Ouro Prêto, formerly **Vila Rica** a city founded in 1711 in Minas Gerais, the mining area of NE Brazil. It was the centre of gold and diamond trading during the colonial era. Much of its religious architecture is the work of sculptor Antonio Francisco Lisboa (1738–1814). It is a World Heritage site.

ours *pron.* the one or ones belonging to us.
— **of ours** of or belonging to us.

ourselves *pron.* **1** used as the reflexive form of we: *we helped ourselves to cakes.* **2** used for emphasis: *we ourselves know nothing about that.* **3** our normal self: *we can relax and be ourselves.* **4** (also **by ourselves**) alone; without anyone else's help.

Our Town a play by Thornton Wilder (1938, Pulitzer Prize). An Expressionist drama, it evokes without scenery or costumes a universal flavour of provincial life in an American town during the years 1901–13.

-ous *suffix* forming adjectives meaning: **1** having a particular character, quality, or nature: *marvellous / venomous.* **2** *Chem.* formed with an element in its lower valency. [from Latin *-osus*]

ousel same as OUZEL.

Ouse, River **1** a river in East Sussex, S England, length 48km/30mi. It rises 10km/6mi SW of Crawley and flows E and S to meet the English Channel at Newhaven. **2** a river in Yorkshire, NE England, length 96km/60mi. Formed at the junction of the Ure and Swale rivers near Boroughbridge, it flows SE to meet the R Trent where it becomes the estuary of the R Humber. **3** a river rising in Northamptonshire, central England, length 256km/159mi. It flows from its source NW of Brackley past Buckingham and Bedford and through the S fenland to meet the Wash NW of King's Lynn. It is also known as the Great Ouse. **4** a tributary of the Great Ouse R, E England, length 38km/24mi. It flows W along part of the Norfolk–Suffolk border to meet the Great Ouse at Brandon Creek. It is also known as the Little Ouse.

oust *verb* to force (someone) out of a position and take their place. [from Old French *ouster*]

out — *adv., adj.* **1** away from the inside; not in or at a place: *go out into the garden.* **2** not in one's home or place of work: *I called but you were out.* **3** to or at an end; to or into a state of being completely finished, exhausted, extinct, etc: *the milk has run out / before the day is out / put the candle out.* **4** aloud: *cry out.* **5** with, or taking, care: *listen out for the baby / watch out.* **6** in all directions from a central point: *share out the sweets.* **7** to the fullest extent or amount: *spread the blanket out.* **8** to public attention or notice; revealed: *the secret is out.* **9** *Sport,* said of a person batting no longer able to bat, eg because of having the ball caught by an opponent: *bowled out.* **10** in or into a state of being removed, omitted or forgotten: *miss him out / rub out the mistake.* **11** not to be considered; rejected: *that idea's out.* **12** removed; dislocated: *have a tooth out.* **13** not in authority; not having political power: *vote them out of office.* **14** into unconsciousness: *pass out in the heat.* **15** in error: *your total is out by three.* **16** *colloq.* existing: *the best car out.* **17** said of a flower in bloom. **18** said of a book published. **19** visible: *the moon's out.* **20** no longer in fashion. **21** said of workers on strike: *call the men out.* **22** said of a jury considering its verdict. **23** *old use,* said of a young woman introduced into fashionable society. **24** said of a tide at or to the lowest level of water. — *adj.* **1** external. **2** directing or showing direction outwards: *the out tray.* — *prep. North Amer., esp. US* out of. — *interj.* expressing: **1** *Sport* that the batsman is dismissed. **2** that a radio transmission has finished: *over and out.* — *noun* a way out, a way of escape; an excuse. — *verb* **1** *intrans.* to become publicly known: *murder will out.* **2** *trans.* to make public the homosexuality of (a famous person who has been attempting to keep his or her homosexuality secret).
— **be out for something** *colloq.* be determined to achieve it: *out for revenge.*

out and about active outside the house, especially after an illness.

out and away by far; much.

out of something 1 from inside it: *drive out of the garage.* **2** not in or within it: *be out of the house.* **3** having exhausted a supply of it: *be out of butter.* **4** from among several: *two out of three cats.* **5** from a material: *made out of wood.* **6** because of it: *out of anger.* **7** beyond the range, scope, or bounds of it: *out of reach / out of the ordinary.* **8** excluded from it: *leave him out of the team.* **9** no longer in a stated condition: *out of practice.* **10** at a stated distance from a place: *a mile out of town.* **11** without or so as to be without something: *cheat him out of his money.*

out of date old-fashioned and no longer of use; obsolete.

out of doors in or into the open.

out of it 1 *colloq.* not part of, or wanted in, a group, activity, etc. **2** *slang* unable to behave normally or control oneself, usually because of drink or drugs.

out of pocket having spent more money than one can afford.

out of the way 1 difficult to reach or arrive at. **2** unusual; uncommon.

out to lunch *slang, said of a person* slightly crazy; in a dream world.

out with it! an exhortation to speak openly. [from Anglo-Saxon *ut*]

out- *combining form* forming words meaning; **1** external; separate; from outside: *outpatient / outhouse.* **2** away from the inside, especially as a result: *output / outpouring.* **3** going away or out of; outward: *outdoor / outboard.* **4** so as to excel or surpass: *outrun / outmanoeuvre.*

outage *noun* a period of time during which a power supply fails to operate.

out-and-out *adj.* complete; thorough: *an out-and-out liar.*

outback *noun* isolated, remote areas of a country, especially Australia.

outbalance *verb* to weigh more than or be more important than.

outbid *verb* (**outbidding**; PAST TENSE AND PAST PARTICIPLE **outbid**) to offer a higher price than (someone else), especially at an auction.

outboard — *adj.* **1** *said of a motor or engine* portable and designed to be attached to the outside of a boat's stern. **2** *said of a boat* having such a motor or engine. — *adv., adj.* of, nearer, or towards the outside of a ship or aircraft. — *noun* **1** an outboard motor or engine. **2** a boat with an outboard motor or engine. See also INBOARD.

outbound *adj., said of a vehicle or passenger* going away from home, a station, etc; departing.

outbreak *noun* a sudden, usually violent beginning or occurrence, usually of something unpleasant.

outbreeding *noun Genetics* mating between distantly related or unrelated members of a species. It results in the production of greater genetic variation among the offspring than inbreeding.

outbuilding *noun* a building such as a barn, stable or garage, that is separate from the main house but within the grounds surrounding it.

outburst *noun* **1** a sudden, violent expression of strong emotion, especially anger. **2** a sudden period of great activity.

outcast *noun* a person who has been rejected by his or her friends or society.

outcaste *noun* **1** a Hindu who has lost his or her caste. **2** a person who has no caste.

outclass *verb* to be much better than.

outcome *noun* a result or consequence.

outcrop *noun* **1** a rock or group of rocks which sticks out above the surface of the ground. **2** an appearance or occurrence.

outcry *noun* (PL. **outcries**) a widespread and public show of anger or disapproval.

outdated *adj.* no longer useful or in fashion.

outdistance *verb* to leave (a competitor) far behind.

outdo *verb* (**outdoes**; PAST TENSE **outdid**; PAST PARTICIPLE **outdone**) to do much better than.

outdoor *adj.* **1** done, taking place, situated, for use, etc in the open air. **2** preferring to be in the open air: *an outdoor person.*

outdoors — *adv.* in or into the open air; outside a building. — *sing. noun* the open air; the world outside buildings.

outer — *adj.* **1** external; belonging to or for the outside. **2** further from the centre or middle. — *noun Archery* **1** the outermost ring on a target. **2** a shot which hits this.

outer ear *Anat.* the part of the ear that transmits sound waves from outside the ear to the eardrum in vertebrates.

outermost *adj.* nearest the edge, furthest from the centre.

outer space space beyond the earth's atmosphere.

outface *verb* **1** to stare at (someone) until he or she looks away. **2** to fight or deal with (someone) bravely.

outfall *noun* the mouth of a river, sewer, etc where it flows into the sea.

outfield *noun* **1** *Cricket* the area of the pitch far from the part where the stumps, etc are laid out. **2** *Baseball* the area of the field beyond the diamond-shaped pitch where the bases are laid out. **3** *Cricket, Baseball* the players who have positions in this area. See also INFIELD.

outfielder *noun Cricket, Baseball* a fielder in the outfield.

outfight *verb* (PAST TENSE AND PAST PARTICIPLE **outfought**) to fight better than; to defeat.

outfit — *noun* **1** a set of clothes worn together, especially for a particular occasion. **2** a set of articles, tools, equipment, etc for a particular task. **3** *colloq.* a group of people working as a single unit or team. — *verb* (**outfitted**, **outfitting**) to provide with an outfit, especially clothes.

outfitter *noun* a person who provides outfits, especially one who sells men's clothes.

outflank *verb* **1** to go round the side or sides of an enemy's position and attack from behind. **2** to get the better of, especially by a surprise action.

outflow *noun* **1** a flowing out. **2** anything that flows out. **3** the amount that flows out.

outfox *verb* to get the better of (someone) by being more cunning than; to outwit.

outgoing — *adj.* **1** friendly and sociable. **2** leaving: *the outgoing president / the outgoing flight.* — *noun* (**outgoings**) money spent.

outgrow *verb* (PAST TENSE **outgrew**; PAST PARTICIPLE **outgrown**) **1** to grow too large for (one's clothes). **2** to become too old for (childish amusements, children's games, etc). **3** to grow larger or faster than.

outgrowth *noun* **1** a natural product. **2** anything which grows out of something else; a by-product.

outhouse *noun* a usually small building such as a shed, etc built close to a house.

outing *noun* a short pleasure trip.

outlandish *adj.*, *said of appearance, manner, habit, etc* very strange; odd; queer.

outlandishly *adv.* in an outlandish way.

outlandishness *noun* being outlandish.

outlast *verb* to last or live longer than.

outlaw — *noun* a criminal who is a fugitive from, or deprived of the protection of, the law. — *verb* **1** to make (someone) an outlaw. **2** to forbid officially. [from Anglo-Saxon *utlaga*]

outlawry *noun* the state of being or act of making someone an outlaw.

outlay *noun* money, or occasionally time, spent on something.

outlet *noun* **1** a way or passage out, especially for water or steam. **2** a way of releasing or using energy, talents, strong feeling, etc: *an outlet for her frustrations.* **3** a market for, or a shop that sells, the goods produced by a particular manufacturer: *an outlet for free-range eggs.* **4** *North Amer., esp. US* an electrical power point.

outline — *noun* **1** a line forming or marking the outer edge of an object. **2** a drawing with only the outer lines and no shading. **3** the main points, etc without the details. **4** (*usually* **outlines**) the most important features of something. **5** a line representing a word in shorthand. — *verb* **1** to draw the outline of. **2** to give a brief description of the main features of.

outlive *verb* **1** to live or survive longer than. **2** to survive the effects of (a disease, etc).

outlook *noun* **1** a view from a particular place. **2** a person's mental attitude or point of view. **3** a prospect for the future.

outlying *adj.* distant; away from (a city or central area).

outmanoeuvre *verb* to gain an advantage over or defeat by more skilful manoeuvring.

outmoded *adj.* no longer in fashion; out of date.

outnumber *verb* (**outnumbered**, **outnumbering**) to be more in number than.

outpace *verb* to walk faster than; to outstrip.

outpatient *noun* a patient who visits a hospital for treatment but does not stay there overnight.

outplay *verb* to defeat or play better than in a game or contest.

outpost *noun* **1** a group of soldiers stationed at a distance from the main body, especially to protect it from a surprise attack. **2** a distant or remote settlement or branch.

outpouring *noun* **1** (*usually* **outpourings**) a powerful or violent show of emotion. **2** the amount that pours out.

output — *noun* **1** the quantity or amount produced. **2** *Comput.* the data that is transferred from the main memory of a computer to a disk, tape, or output device such as a visual display unit or printer. **3** the power or energy produced by an electrical component or apparatus. — *verb* (**outputting**; PAST TENSE AND PAST PARTICIPLE **output**) **1** to produce (information, power, etc) as output. **2** *Comput.* to transfer data from the main memory of a computer to a disk or tape, or to an output device such as a visual display unit or printer.

output device *Comput.* a device that displays computer-processed data to the user in an intelligible form, eg a visual-display unit (VDU), printer, or plotter.

outrage — *noun* **1** an act of great cruelty or violence. **2** an act which breaks accepted standards of morality, honour and decency. **3** great anger or resentment. — *verb* **1** to insult, shock or anger greatly. **2** to do physical violence to, especially *euphemistic* to rape. [from Old French *outrer*, to exceed]

outrageous *adj.* **1** not moderate in behaviour; extravagant. **2** greatly offensive to accepted standards of morality, honour, and decency. **3** *colloq.* terrible; shocking.

outrageously *adv.* in an outrageous way; to an outrageous degree: *outrageously expensive.*

outrageousness *noun* being outrageous.

outrank *verb* to have a higher rank than.

outré *adj.* not conventional; eccentric; shocking. [from French, from *outrer*, to exceed]

outride *verb* (PAST TENSE **outrode**; PAST PARTICIPLE **outridden**) **1** to ride faster than. **2** *said especially of a ship* to come safely through (a storm).

outrider *noun* an attendant or guard who rides a horse or motorcycle at the side or ahead of a carriage or car conveying an important person.

outrigger *noun* **1** a beam or framework sticking out from the side of a boat to help balance the vessel and prevent it capsizing. **2** a boat that is fitted with this sort of structure.

outright — *adv.* **1** completely: *be proved outright.* **2** immediately; at once: *killed outright.* **3** openly; honestly: *ask outright.* — *adj.* **1** complete: *an outright fool.* **2** clear: *the outright winner.* **3** open; honest: *outright disapproval.*

outrun *verb* (**outrunning**; PAST TENSE **outran**; PAST PARTICIPLE **outrun**) **1** to run faster or further than. **2** to do better than or exceed.

outsell *verb* (PAST TENSE AND PAST PARTICIPLE **outsold**) to sell or be sold more quickly or in greater quantities than.

outset *noun* a beginning or start.

outshine *verb* (PAST TENSE AND PAST PARTICIPLE **outshone**) **1** to shine brighter than. **2** to be very much better than.

outside — *noun* **1** the outer surface; the external parts. **2** everything that is not inside or within the bounds or scope of something: *view the problem from the outside.* **3** the farthest limit. **4** the side of a pavement next to the road. — *adj.* **1** of, on, or near the outside. **2** not forming part of a group, organization, one's regular job, etc: *outside interests.* **3** unlikely; remote. **4** *said of a guess, etc* stating the highest possible amount. — *adv.* **1** on or to the outside; outdoors. **2** *slang* not in prison. — *prep.* **1** on or to the outside of. **2** beyond the limits of. **3** except; apart from.
— **at the outside** at the most.
get outside of something *slang* to eat or drink it.
outside in inside out (see INSIDE).

outside broadcast a radio or television programme that is recorded or filmed somewhere other than in a studio.

outside left *Brit. Football* the position at the extreme left of the middle of the field, or a player in this position.

outside line a connection by telephone from a building to another place.

outsider *noun* **1** a person who is not part of a group, etc or who refuses to accept the general values of society. **2** *in a race, contest, etc* a competitor who is not expected to win.

outside right *Brit. Football* the position at the extreme right of the middle of the field, or a player in this position.

Outsider, The (L'Étranger) a novel by Albert Camus (1942). It describes how the mundane existence of the central character is brought to an end when he almost involuntarily commits a murder.

outsize — *adj.* (*also* **outsized**) over normal or standard size. — *noun* anything which is larger than standard, especially a garment.

outskirts *pl. noun* the outer parts or area, especially of a town or city.

outsmart *verb colloq.* to get the better of by being more cunning or cleverer than; to outwit.

outspoken *adj.* saying exactly what one thinks; frank.

outspokenly *adv.* in an outspoken way.

outspokenness *noun* being outspoken.

outspread *adj.*, *said of the arms, etc* stretched or spread out widely or fully.

outstanding *adj.* **1** excellent; superior; remarkable. **2** not yet paid, done, etc: *outstanding debts.*

outstandingly *adv.* in an outstanding way.

outstare *verb* to outdo in staring; to discomfort by staring.

outstation *noun* a position, post, or station in a remote or lonely area far from towns.

outstay *verb* **1** to stay longer than the length of (one's invitation, etc): *outstay one's welcome.* **2** to stay longer than (other people).

outstretch *verb* to stretch or spread out.

outstretched *adj.* extended, proffered.

outstrip *verb* (**outstripped**, **outstripping**) **1** to go faster than. **2** to leave behind; to surpass.

outtake *noun Cinema* a sequence of film removed from the final edited version of a motion picture or video. These include any takes which have had to be repeated during filming because of errors or technical problems, and any sequences that are discarded.

out-tray *noun* a shallow basket used in offices for letters, etc that are ready to be sent out.

outvote *verb* to defeat by a majority of votes.

outward — *adj.* **1** on or towards the outside. **2** *said of a journey* away from a place. **3** apparent or seeming: *outward appearances.* — *adv.* (*also*

outwards) towards the outside; in an outward direction.

outwardly *adv.* in appearance; on the outside.

outweigh *verb* to be greater than in weight, value or importance.

outwit *verb* (**outwitted**, **outwitting**) to get the better of or defeat by being cleverer than.

outwith *prep. Scot.* outside; beyond.

outwork *noun* 1 (*usually* **outworks**) a defence work that is outside the main line of fortifications. 2 work done for a company, factory or shop by employees who work at home.

outworker *noun* a person who is commissioned to do outwork.

outworn *adj.* no longer useful or in fashion; out of date.

ouzel *noun* 1 (*also* **ring ouzel**) a thrush with a broad white band across its throat. 2 (*also* **water ouzel**) a small aquatic songbird; a dipper.

ouzo *noun* (PL. **ouzos**) a Greek alcoholic drink, flavoured with aniseed and usually diluted with water. [from Modern Greek *ouzon*]

ova see OVUM.

Oval, the, a cricket ground in Kennington, S London, England. It is owned by the Duchy of Cornwall, and is the headquarters of Surrey County Cricket Club.

oval — *adj.* shaped like an egg. — *noun* any egg-shaped figure or object. [from Latin *ovum*, egg]

oval window *Anat.* the upper of two membrane-covered openings between the middle ear and the inner ear in vertebrates. — Also called *fenestra ovalis*.

Ovamboland a region in N Namibia. It extends W along the Namibia–Angola frontier from the Okavango R; in the S lies the Etosha National Park. The chief indigenous peoples are the Ovambo. The region has been an area of conflict since the 1970s between SWAPO guerrilla forces based in S Angola and South African forces.

ovarian *adj.* relating to or in the region of an ovary or ovaries.

ovarian follicle *Anat.* see GRAAFIAN FOLLICLE.

ovary *noun* (PL. **ovaries**) 1 in a female animal, the reproductive organ in which the ova (eggs) are produced. In vertebrates there are two ovaries, and they also produce the sex hormones. In mammals the ovaries release their eggs down oviducts or Fallopian tubes. 2 in plants, the enlarged hollow base of the carpel of a flower, which contains one or more ovules. After fertilization the wall of the ovary develops into a fruit which contains one or more seeds. [from Latin *ovum*, egg]

ovation *noun* cheering or applause, etc to express approval, welcome, etc. [from Latin *ovare*, to exult]

oven *noun* an enclosed compartment which may be heated for baking or roasting food, or drying clay, etc. [from Anglo-Saxon *ofen*]

ovenproof *adj., said of dishes, plates, etc* that will not crack at a high temperature.

oven-ready *adj., said of food* prepared and only needing to be cooked.

ovenware *noun* heat-resistant dishes for use in ovens.

over — *adv.* 1 above and across. 2 outwards and downwards: *knock him over / the kettle boiled over.* 3 across a space; to or on the other side: *fly over from Australia.* 4 from one person, side, or condition to another: *win them over / turn the card over.* 5 through, from beginning to end, usually with concentration: *read the letter over / think it over thoroughly.* 6 again; in repetition: *do it twice over.* 7 at an end. 8 so as to cover completely: *paper the*

cracks over. 9 beyond a limit; in excess. 10 remaining: *left over.* 11 until a later time: *hold payment over until February.* — *prep.* 1 in or to a position which is above or higher in place, importance, authority, value, number, etc. 2 above and from one side to another: *fly over the sea.* 3 so as to cover: *hair flopping over his eyes.* 4 out and down from: *fall over the edge.* 5 throughout the extent of: *read over that page again.* 6 during: *visit him sometime over the weekend.* 7 until after: *stay over Monday night.* 8 more than: *over a year ago.* 9 concerning; about: *argue over who would pay.* 10 while occupied with: *chat about it over coffee.* 11 occupying time with: *spend a day over the preparations.* 12 recovered from the effects of: *be over the accident.* 13 by means of: *hear about it over the radio.* 14 divided by. — *adj.* 1 upper; higher. 2 outer. 3 excessive. See also OVER-. — *interj.* used during two-way radio conversations to show that one has finished speaking and expects a reply. — *noun Cricket* 1 a series of six or eight balls bowled by the same bowler from the same end of the pitch. 2 play during such a series of balls.

— **be all over someone** to make a great fuss of them, often ingratiatingly.
over again once more.
over against something opposite it; in contrast with it.
over and above something in addition to it.
over and over again repeatedly.
over head and ears completely submerged.
over the top *colloq.* excessive.
[from Anglo-Saxon *ofer*]

over- *combining form* forming words meaning: 1 excessively: *overconfident.* 2 above; in a higher position or authority: *overlord.* 3 across the surface; covering: *overcoat.* 4 down; away from an upright position: *overturn / overhang.* 5 completely: *overwhelm.*

overact *verb intrans., trans.* to act (a part) with too much expression or emotion.

over-age *adj.* 1 beyond a specified age limit. 2 too old.

overall — *noun* 1 *Brit.* a loose-fitting, coat-like garment worn over ordinary clothes to protect them. 2 (**overalls**) a one-pieced garment with trousers to cover the legs and either a dungaree-type top, or top with sleeves, worn to protect clothes. — *adj.* 1 including everything: *the overall total.* 2 from end to end: *the overall length.* — *adv.* as a whole; in general.

over-anxious *adj.* excessively solicitous or eager (especially to please).

overarm *adj., adv.* bowled or thrown with the hand and arm raised over and moving round the shoulder.

overawe *verb* to make silent by filling with awe, fear, or astonishment.

overbalance *verb intrans., trans.* to lose or cause to lose one's balance and fall.

overbearing *adj.* 1 domineering; too powerful and proud. 2 of particularly great importance.

overbearingly *adv.* in an overbearing way.

overblown *adj.* 1 self-important and pretentious. 2 *said of flowers* past their best; beginning to die.

overboard *adv.* over the side of a ship or boat into the water.
— **go overboard** *colloq.* to be very or too enthusiastic.
throw something *or* **someone overboard** to abandon or get rid of.

overbook *verb trans., intrans.* to make or allow more reservations (for an aircraft, restaurant, etc) than there are seats available.

overburden *verb* (**overburdened**, **overburdening**) to give (someone) too much to do, carry, or think about.

overburdened *adj.* having too great a burden; overworked.

overcast *adj., said of the sky* cloudy.

overcharge *verb* 1 *trans., intrans.* to charge too much. 2 to fill or load with too much.

overcloud *verb* 1 *trans., intrans.* to cover, or become covered, with clouds. 2 to make sad or worried.

overcoat *noun* a warm, heavy coat worn in winter.

overcome *verb* (PAST TENSE **overcame**; PAST PARTICIPLE **overcome**) 1 to defeat; to succeed in a struggle against; to deal successfully with. 2 *intrans.* to be victorious. 3 to affect strongly; to overwhelm: *overcome with sleep.* [from Anglo-Saxon *ofercuman*]

over-confident *adj.* excessively confident in one's abilities or personal attributes.

overcrowd *verb* to cause too many people or things to be in (a place).

overcrowded *adj.* too full of people or things.

overcrowding *noun* 1 being overcrowded. 2 filling with too many people, etc.

overdo *verb* (**overdoes**; PAST TENSE **overdid**; PAST PARTICIPLE **overdone**) 1 to do too much; to exaggerate. 2 to cook for too long. 3 to use too much of.
— **overdo it** to work too hard.

overdose — *noun* an excessive dose of a drug, etc. — *verb intrans.* to take an overdose.

overdraft *noun* 1 a state in which one has taken more money out of one's bank account than was in it. 2 the excess of money taken from one's account over the sum that was in it.

overdraw *verb* (PAST TENSE **overdrew**; PAST PARTICIPLE **overdrawn**) 1 *trans., intrans.* to draw more money from (one's bank account) than one has in it. 2 to exaggerate in describing.

overdrawn *adj.* having an overdraft at a bank.

overdress *verb trans., intrans.* to dress or be dressed in clothes that are too formal, smart, or expensive for the occasion.

overdressed *adj.* wearing clothes which are too formal for the occasion.

overdrive *noun* an additional very high gear in a motor vehicle's gear box, which reduces wear on the engine and saves fuel when travelling at high speeds.

overdue *adj., said of bills, work, etc* not yet paid, done, delivered, etc although the date for doing this has passed.

over-emotional *adj.* given to displays of excessive or inappropriate emotion.

overestimate — *verb* (pronounced *-mate*) estimate, judge, etc too highly. — *noun* (pronounced *-mət*) too high an estimate.

overestimation *noun* 1 overestimating. 2 an overestimate.

overexert *verb* to force (oneself) to work too hard.

overexertion *noun* excessive work or effort.

overexpose *verb* 1 to expose to too much publicity. 2 to expose (photographic film) to too much light.

overexposure *noun* excessive exposure, especially to publicity.

overfishing the removal of so many fish from a sea, river, etc, that the numbers of fish can no longer be maintained by breeding, and populations of particular species become much reduced or even rare. The cod and haddock populations in the N Atlantic Ocean are now severely depleted as a result of overfishing.

overflow — *verb* (with stress on *-flow*) (**overflowed**, **overflowing**) 1 to flow over (a brim) or go beyond (the limits or edge of). 2 *intrans.* to be filled so full that the contents spill over or out. 3 *intrans.* (**overflow with something**) to be full of it: *was overflowing with gratitude.* — *noun* (with stress on *over*-) **1** that which overflows. **2** the act of flowing over. **3** a pipe or outlet for spare water. [from Anglo-Saxon *oferflowan*]

overgrown *adj.* **1** *said of a garden, etc* dense with plants that have grown too large and thick. **2** grown too large.

overhand *adj., adv.* thrown, done, etc with the hand brought down from above the shoulder.

overhang — *verb* (with stress on *-hang*) (PAST TENSE AND PAST PARTICIPLE **overhung**) **1** *trans., intrans.* to project or hang out over. **2** to threaten. — *noun* (with stress on *over*-) **1** a piece of rock, part of a roof, etc that overhangs. **2** the amount by which something overhangs.

overhaul — *verb* **1** to examine carefully and repair. **2** to catch up with and pass. — *noun* a thorough examination and repair.

overhead — *adv., adj.* above; over one's head. — *noun* (**overheads**) the regular costs of a business, such as rent, wages and electricity.

overhead projector a projector which sits on the speaker's desk and projects images on a screen behind it.

overhear *verb trans., intrans.* (PAST TENSE AND PAST PARTICIPLE **overheard**) to hear (someone or something) without the speaker knowing, either by accident or on purpose.

overheat *verb* to make or become too hot.

overheated *adj., said of an argument, discussion, etc* angry and excited; passionate.

overjoyed *adj.* very glad; elated.

overkill *noun* **1** action, behaviour, treatment, etc which is far in excess of what is required. **2** the capability to destroy an enemy using a larger force than is actually needed to win a victory.

overladen *adj.* overloaded.

overland *adv. adj., said of a journey, etc* across land.

Overland Telegraph in Australia, a telegraph line linking Australia with the outside world, opened in 1872. The line crossed the centre of Australia, and covered 3 175km/ 1 972mi between Port Augusta (South Australia) and Darwin (Northern Territory), where it joined an undersea cable to Java.

overlap — *verb* (with stress on *-lap*) (**overlapped, overlapping**) **1** *said of part of an object* to partly cover (another object). **2** *intrans. said of two parts* to have one part partly covering the other. **3** *said of two things* to have something in common; to partly coincide. — *noun* (with stress on *over*-) an overlapping part.

overlay — *verb* (PAST TENSE AND PAST PARTICIPLE **overlaid**) (**overlay one thing with another**) to cover it with a usually thin layer of something else, especially for decoration. — *noun* something that is laid over something else, especially for decoration.

overleaf *adv.* on the other side of the page.

overlie *verb* (**overlying**; PAST TENSE **overlay**; PAST PARTICIPLE **overlain**) **1** to lie on. **2** to smother and kill (a baby or small animal) by lying on it.

overload — *verb* (with stress on *-load*) **1** to load too heavily. **2** to put too great an electric current through (a circuit). — *noun* (with stress on *over*-) too great an electric current flowing through a circuit.

overlook *verb* **1** to give a view of from a higher position. **2** to fail to see or notice. **3** to allow (a mistake, crime, etc) to go unpunished. **4** to supervise.

overlord *noun* a lord or ruler with supreme power.

overly *adv. formal* too much; excessively.

overmuch *adv., adj.* too much.

overnice *adj.* fussy, critical, and hard to please.

overnight — *adv.* **1** during the night. **2** for the duration of the night. **3** suddenly. — *adj.* **1** done or occurring in the night. **2** sudden: *an overnight success.* **3** for use overnight: *an overnight case.*

overnight bag a small grip or case for carrying the clothes, toilet articles, etc, needed for an overnight stay.

overpass *noun North Amer., esp. US* same as FLYOVER.

overplay *verb* to exaggerate or overemphasize. — **overplay one's hand** to overestimate or overtax one's talents, assets, etc.

overpower *verb trans.* (**overpowered, overpowering**) **1** to defeat by greater strength. **2** to weaken or reduce to helplessness.

overpowering *adj.* very great; overwhelming.

overpoweringly *adv.* in an overpowering way.

overprint — *verb* to print over (something already printed, eg a stamp). — *noun* extra material printed on top of something printed, eg a stamp.

overrate *verb* to think too highly of.

overreach *verb* **1** to defeat (oneself) by trying to do too much, be too clever, etc. **2** *intrans. said of a horse* to strike the hind foot against the forefoot.

overreact *verb intrans.* (**overreact to something**) to react too strongly to it.

overreaction *noun* a too strong reaction.

override — *verb* (with stress on *-ride*) (PAST TENSE **overrode**; PAST PARTICIPLE **overridden**) **1** to annul or set aside, especially to cancel the functioning of (eg an automatic control). **2** to be of more importance than. — *noun* (with stress on *over*-) the process or a means of overriding.

overriding *adj.* dominant; most important: *overriding considerations.*

overrule *verb* **1** to rule against or cancel (especially a previous decision or judgement) by higher authority. **2** to impose a decision on (a person) by higher authority.

overrun *verb* (**overrunning**; PAST TENSE **overran**; PAST PARTICIPLE **overrun**) **1** to spread over or through (something); to infest. **2** to invade and take possession of (another country) quickly and by force. **3** *trans., intrans.* to go beyond (a fixed limit): *overrun the budget for the job.* [from Anglo-Saxon *oferyrnan*]

overseas — *adv.* abroad. — *adj.* (*also* **oversea**) across or from beyond the sea; foreign.

oversee *verb* (PAST TENSE **oversaw**; PAST PARTICIPLE **overseen**) to supervise.

overseer *noun* a person who oversees workers, a supervisor.

oversell *verb* (PAST TENSE AND PAST PARTICIPLE **oversold**) **1** *trans., intrans.* to sell at too high a price or in greater quantities than can be supplied. **2** to praise too highly.

oversew *verb* (PAST TENSE **oversewed**; PAST PARTICIPLE **oversewn, oversewed**) to sew (two edges) with close stitches that pass over both edges.

oversexed *adj.* having unusually strong sexual urges.

overshadow *verb* **1** to seem much more important than. **2** to cast a shadow over; to make seem more gloomy. [from Anglo-Saxon *ofersceadian*]

overshoe *noun* a shoe, usually made of rubber or plastic, worn over normal shoes to protect them in wet weather.

overshoot *verb* (PAST TENSE AND PAST PARTICIPLE **overshot**) to go farther than (a target aimed at).

— **overshoot the mark** to make a mistake as a result of misjudging a situation.

oversight *noun* a mistake made through a failure to notice something.

oversimplification *noun* oversimplifying, or an instance of this.

oversimplify *verb trans., intrans.* (**oversimplifies, oversimplified**) to simplify (something) so much as to cause a mistake or distortion.

oversleep *verb intrans.* (PAST TENSE AND PAST PARTICIPLE **overslept**) to sleep longer than one intended.

overspend — *verb intrans.* (with stress on *-spend*) (PAST TENSE AND PAST PARTICIPLE **overspent**) to spend too much money. — *noun* (with stress on *over*-) an amount overspent.

overspill *noun Brit.* the people leaving an overcrowded or derelict town area to live elsewhere.

overstate *verb* to state too strongly or with unnecessary emphasis.

overstatement *noun* exaggeration, or an instance of this.

overstay *verb* to stay longer than the length of (one's invitation, etc): *overstay one's welcome.*

oversteer *verb intrans., said of a vehicle* to turn more sharply than the driver intends.

overstep *verb* (**overstepped, overstepping**) — **overstep the mark** to go beyond what is prudent or reasonable.

overstretched *adj.* stretched too far; extended to the limit.

overstrung *adj.* too sensitive and nervous; tense.

oversubscribe *verb* to apply for or try to purchase in larger quantities than are available.

oversubscribed *adj.* having too few shares, places, etc to meet demand.

overt *adj.* not hidden or secret; open; public. [from Old French *ovrir*, to open]

overtake *verb* (PAST TENSE **overtook**; PAST PARTICIPLE **overtaken**) **1** *trans., intrans. chiefly Brit.* to catch up with and go past (a car, a person, etc) moving in the same direction. **2** to draw level with and begin to do better than. **3** to come upon (someone) suddenly or without warning: *overtaken by the bad weather.*

overtax *verb* **1** to put too great a strain on (someone or oneself). **2** to demand too much tax from.

overthrow — *verb* (with stress on *-throw*) (PAST TENSE **overthrew**; PAST PARTICIPLE **overthrown**) **1** to defeat completely. **2** to upset or overturn. — *noun* (with stress on *over*-) **1** a defeat or downfall. **2** *Cricket* an inaccurate return of the ball by a fielder which often allows the batsman to score extra runs.

overtime — *noun* **1** time spent working at one's job beyond one's regular hours. **2** the money paid for this extra time. — *adv.* in addition to one's regular hours.

overtly *adv.* in an overt way.

overtone *noun* **1** (*usually* **overtones**) a subtle hint, quality, or meaning: *political overtones.* **2** *Mus.* a tone that contributes towards the musical sound and adds to its quality. [from German *Oberton*]

overture *noun* **1** an orchestral introduction to an opera, oratorio or ballet. **2** (*usually* **overtures**) a proposal or offer intended to open a discussion. [from Old French, = opening]

overturn *verb* **1** *trans., intrans.* to turn or be turned over or upside down. **2** to bring down or destroy (a government). **3** to overrule or cancel (a previous legal decision).

overview *noun* a brief general account or description.

overweening *adj.* **1** *said of a person* arrogant. **2** *said of pride* inflated and excessive.

overweight *adj.* above the desired, required, or usual weight.

overwhelm *verb* **1** to crush mentally; to overpower (a person's) emotions, thoughts, etc. **2** to defeat by superior force or numbers. **3** to supply or offer something in great amounts to: *overwhelmed with offers of help.*

overwhelming *adj.* physically or mentally crushing; intensely powerful.

overwhelmingly *adv.* in an overwhelming way; so as to overwhelm.

overwork — *verb* **1** *intrans.* to work too hard. **2** to make (someone) work too hard. **3** to make too much use of. — *noun* the act of working too hard.

overworked *adj.* having too much work to do.

overwrite *verb* (PAST TENSE **overwrote**; PAST PARTICIPLE **overwritten**) **1** *Comput.* to write new information over (existing data), thereby destroying it. **2** to write excessively.

overwrought *adj.* very nervous or excited; over-emotional.

Ovid, in full **Publius Ovidius Naso** (43 BC–AD 17) Roman poet, born at Sulmo, in the Abruzzi. He trained as a lawyer, but subsequently devoted himself to poetry. His first success was the tragedy *Medea*, followed by *Heroides*, love letters from legendary heroines to their lords. His major poems are the three-book *Ars Amatoria* (Art of Love) and the 15-book *Metamorphoses*. In AD 8 he was banished by Augustus to Tomi on the Black Sea.

oviduct *noun* the tube which carries the egg from the ovary. [from Latin *ovum*, egg + *ducere*, to lead]

Oviedo POP (1991) 195 000, the capital of Asturias region and of Oviedo province, NW Spain. It lies 450km/280mi NW of Madrid. In the 10c it became capital of the kingdom of Asturias. NOTABLE FEATURE cathedral (14c).

oviform *adj.* egg-shaped. [from Latin *ovum*, egg + -FORM]

ovine *adj.* of or like sheep. [from Latin *ovis*, sheep]

oviparity *noun Zool.* the laying of fertilized eggs which hatch outside the body of a female animal. [from Latin *ovum*, egg + *parere*, to bring forth]

oviparous *adj.*, *said of birds, fish, etc* producing eggs which hatch outside the mother's body. See also VIVIPAROUS. [from Latin *ovum*, egg + *parere*, to produce]

ovipositor *noun Zool.* in female insects, the egg-laying organ, which is often long and tube-like, at the rear end of the abdomen. [from Latin *ovum*, egg + *positor*, from *ponere*, to place]

ovoid — *adj.* egg-shaped. — *noun* an egg-shaped form or object. [from Latin *ovum*, egg + -OID]

ovoviviparous *adj. Zool.* describing certain fish and reptiles, and many insects, in which the fertilized eggs hatch within the body of the female. The developing embryo is retained within the body of the mother, and derives nutrients from a yolk store instead of a placenta. [from Latin *ovum*, egg + VIVIPAROUS]

ovulate *verb intrans.* to produce eggs from the ovary. [from Latin *ovulum*, diminutive of *ovum*, egg]

ovulation *noun* **1** the production and release of eggs in an ovary. **2** an instance of this.

ovule *noun Bot.* in flowering and cone-bearing plants, the structure that develops into a seed after fertilization. It consists of a mass of tissue (the *nucellus*) containing the embryo sac, surrounded by one or two protective layers (*integuments*), which develop into the seed coat. [from Latin *ovulum*, diminutive of *ovum*, egg]

ovum *noun* (PL. **ova**) *Biol.* an unfertilized egg or egg cell produced by the ovary of an animal; a female gamete. [from Latin *ovum*, egg]

ow *interj.* used to express sudden, usually mild, pain.

owe *verb* **1** *trans., intrans.* to be under an obligation to pay (money) to (someone). **2** to feel required by duty or gratitude to do or give: *owe you an explanation.* **3** to have or enjoy as a result of: *owe her promotion to her hard work.* [from Anglo-Saxon *agan*, to own]

Owen, David (Anthony Llewellyn) Owen, Baron (1938–) English politician, born in Plymouth. He trained in medicine, then became a Labour MP (1966), and was Under-Secretary to the Navy (1968), Secretary for Health (1974–6), and Foreign Secretary (1977–9). One of the so-called 'Gang of Four' who formed the Social Democratic Party (SDP) in 1981, he succeeded Roy Jenkins as its leader in 1983. When the Liberal leader David Steel wanted to merge the two parties after the 1987 general election, Owen resigned the leadership and led a minority of members in a reconstituted SDP, but the party was dissolved in 1990. In 1991 he was appointed Co-Chairman of the International Peace Conference on the former Yugoslavia.

Owen, Robert (1771–1858) Welsh social reformer, born in Newtown, Montgomeryshire. In 1800 he became manager of the New Lanark cotton mills, Lanarkshire, where he set up a social welfare programme and established a model community with improved housing and working conditions. His socialistic theories were tested (without success) in other experimental co-operative 'Owenite' communities, such as in Orbiston, near Glasgow, and New Harmony, Indiana, USA.

Owen, Wilfred (1893–1918) English poet of World War I, born in Oswestry, Shropshire. His poems, expressing a horror of the cruelty and waste of war, were first edited by his friend Siegfried Sassoon in 1920. Several of them were set to music by Benjamin Britten in his *War Requiem* (1962), and *The Collected Poems* appeared in 1963. He was killed in action on the Western Front a week before the Armistice was signed.

Owen a male first name. [from Welsh and Irish Gaelic, perhaps = youth]

Owen Falls Dam a major gravity dam on the Victoria Nile River in Uganda, completed in 1954. It is 30m high and 830m long, and has the capacity to generate 120 megawatts of hydro-electricity.

Owens, Jesse, properly James Cleveland Owens (1913–80) US track and field athlete, born in Danville, Alabama. He set several world records within 45 min on 25 May 1935 at Ann Arbor, Michigan (100yd, long jump, 220yd, 220yd hurdles). His long jump record stood for 25 years. In 1936 he won four gold medals at the Berlin Olympics, a feat which confounded Adolf Hitler's desire for a display of Aryan superiority. It was equalled only in 1984, by Carl Lewis.

owing *adj.* still to be paid; due.
— **owing to something** because of it; on account of it: *trains will be delayed owing to bad weather.*
◆ Often used instead of *due to* when there is no noun antecedent, as in the above example; cf *the lateness of the trains is due to bad weather* (with the antecedent *lateness*).

owl *noun* any nocturnal bird of prey belonging to the order Strigiformes, found in all parts of the world except Antarctica, and having a large broad head, a flat face, large forward-facing eyes, and a short hooked beak. It is noted for its hooting call. [from Anglo-Saxon *ule*]

◇ Most owls are woodland birds, and some live close to humans, nesting in church towers and old buildings. Owls fly almost noiselessly because the long flight feathers of their wings are tipped with down, which deadens the sound of the wing beats, so that they are able to surprise their prey. They feed mainly on small mammals (particularly rodents, such as mice, voles, and rats) and insects, although some species eat fish. The owl seizes its prey with its powerful talons, tears it into chunks and swallows them whole. Fur, feathers, and bones which the owl cannot digest are later regurgitated in the form of small pellets. Owls have very keen eyesight, their forward-facing eyes giving them excellent binocular vision, and their sense of hearing is also well developed. Flaps of skin that form the 'outer ears' are hidden beneath the feathers, and the 'ear tufts' on the heads of many owls are in fact feathers.

owlet *noun* a young owl.

owlish *adj.* **1** like an owl. **2** solemn or wise.

owlishly *adv.* in an owlish way.

owlishness *noun* being owlish.

own — *adj.*, often used for emphasis belonging to or for oneself or itself: *my own sister.* — *pron.* one or something belonging to oneself or itself: *have a room of one's own.* — *verb* **1** to have as a possession or property. **2** (**own something** or **own to something**) to admit or confess it: *one should own one's faults / owned to many weaknesses.*
— **get one's own back on someone** *colloq.* to get even with them; to have one's revenge.
on one's own 1 alone. **2** without help.
own up to something to admit a wrongdoing, etc.
[from Anglo-Saxon *agen*]

owner *noun* a person who owns something.

owner-occupier *noun* a person who owns the property he or she is living in.

ownership *noun* **1** the status of owner. **2** legal right or possession.

own goal 1 a goal scored by mistake for the opposing side. **2** *colloq.* a move that turns out to be to the disadvantage of the person who took it.

ox *noun* (PL. **oxen**) **1** any common domestic cattle, both bulls and cows, used for pulling loads, or supplying meat and milk. **2** a castrated bull. [from Anglo-Saxon *oxa*]

oxalic acid *Chem.* (FORMULA **COOH**$_2$) A highly poisonous white crystalline solid that occurs in the leaves of rhubarb, wood sorrel, and certain other plants, and is also excreted in the form of crystals by many fungi. It is used as a rust and stain remover, a cleaner for car radiators, and in tanning and bleaching. — Also called *ethane-dioic acid.* [from Greek *oxalis*, wood sorrel]

oxbow lake *Geol.* a shallow curved lake found on a flat floodplain alongside a meandering river, and formed when one of the meanders has been cut off from the river as a result of the formation of a stream across the neck of the bend, which shortens the course of the river.

Oxbridge *noun Brit.* the universities of Oxford and Cambridge considered together and usually in contrast to other universities.

oxen see OX.

Oxenstjerna or **Oxenstern Axel, Greve (Count)** (1583–1654) Swedish statesman, born near Uppsala. From 1612 he served as Chancellor, and negotiated peace with Denmark, Russia, and Poland. Despite his attempts to prevent Gustavus Adolphus from entering the Thirty Years War, he supported the war effort, even after the King's death (1632). During most of Queen Christina's minority he was effective ruler of the country (1636–44), and confirmed his policies by the terms of the Peace of Westphalia (1648).

oxeye daisy a daisy with long white petals and a dark yellow centre.

OXFAM in the UK, a charity based in Oxford, England, founded as the Oxford Committee for Famine Relief (1942). It is dedicated to alleviating poverty and distress throughout the world, mainly through long-term development aid in Third World countries.

Oxford, Latin **Oxonia** POP (1992e) 132 000, a university city and the county town of Oxfordshire, S central England, situated in Oxford district. It lies on the Thames and Cherwell rivers, 80km/50mi NW of London. HISTORY the famous 12c university was granted its first official privileges in 1214; Oxford was the Royalist headquarters in the Civil War. NOTABLE FEATURES cathedral (12c); university colleges; Bodleian Library (1488); Sheldonian Theatre (1664–8); Ashmolean Museum; Radcliffe Camera.

Oxford, Provisions of a baronial programme (1258) imposing constitutional limitations on the English Crown, by which Henry III of England had to share power with a permanent council of barons, parliaments meeting three times a year, and independent executive officers (chancellor, justiciar, treasurer). However the pope absolved Henry from his oath to observe the Provisions (1261).

Oxford English Dictionary (ABBREV. **OED**) a dictionary originally published in 125 parts between 1884 and 1928, more than half of which was edited by Dr James Murray. Its original name was 'A New English Dictionary on Historical Principles' (NED). The present name first appeared in 1933.

Oxford Movement, also known as **Tractarianism** a movement within the Church of England, which was initiated (1833) in Oxford by 'tracts' written by John Keble, Cardinal Newman, and E B Pusey. Its aim was the revival of high doctrine and ceremonial, in opposition to liberal tendencies in the Church. It led to Anglo-Catholicism and Ritualism, and has remained influential in certain quarters of Anglicanism.

Oxfordshire POP (1992e) 587 000, a county in S central England, divided into five districts. AREA 2 608sq km/1 007sq mi. It is bounded S by the R Thames and Berkshire, W by Wiltshire and Gloucestershire, NW by Warwickshire, NE by Northamptonshire, and E by Buckinghamshire. PHYSICAL DESCRIPTION the Cotswold Hills lie to the NW, the Chiltern Hills to the SW; drained by the R Thames and its tributaries. CAPITAL Oxford. CHIEF TOWNS Abingdon, Banbury, Henley-on-Thames. ECONOMY agriculture; vehicles; paper; textiles. NOTABLE FEATURES Vale of the White Horse (chalk hill figure over 100m long); Atomic Energy Authority laboratories at Culham.

Oxford University the oldest university in Britain, having its origins in informal groups of masters and students gathered in Oxford in the 12c. The closure of the University of Paris to Englishmen in 1167 accelerated Oxford's development into a *universitas*. The university institutions include the Bodleian Library, the Ashmolean Museum, and the Oxford University Press (founded in 1585).

oxidant *noun* **1** *Chem.* an oxidizing agent. **2** *Engineering* a chemical compound, usually containing oxygen, that is mixed with fuel and burned in the combustion chamber of a rocket.

oxidase *noun Biochem.* any of a group of enzymes that catalyse oxidation in plant and animal cells.

oxidation *noun Chem.* a chemical reaction that involves the addition of oxygen to or the removal of hydrogen from a substance, which loses electrons. It is always accompanied by *reduction*. Both combustion and corrosion, such as rusting, are examples of processes involving oxidation. See also REDUCTION.

oxide *noun Chem.* a compound of oxygen and another element. [from French, from *oxygène*, oxygen]

oxidization *or* **oxidisation** *noun* the process of oxidizing.

oxidize *or* **oxidise** *verb trans., intrans. Chem.* **1** to combine with oxygen. **2** to make or become rusty.

oxidizing agent *Chem.* any substance that oxidizes another substance in a chemical reaction, and is itself reduced in the process, by accepting electrons.

oxlip *noun* **1** a naturally occurring hybrid of the common primrose (*Primula vulgaris*) and the cowslip (*Primula veris*), with deep yellow flowers that are not borne in a one-sided cluster. — Also called *false oxlip*. **2** the true oxlip (*Primula elatior*), which is a separate species to the primrose and cowslip, and has pale yellow flowers borne in a one-sided cluster.

Oxon *abbrev.* **1** Oxfordshire. **2** *especially in degree titles* Oxford University. [from Latin *Oxoniensis*, of Oxford]

Oxonian — *noun* **1** an inhabitant of Oxford. **2** a student or graduate of Oxford University. — *adj.* of Oxford or Oxford University. [from Latin *Oxonia*, Oxford]

oxtail *noun* the tail of an ox, used especially in soups and stews.

Oxus, River see AMUDARYA, RIVER.

oxyacetylene *noun* a mixture of oxygen and acetylene, which burns at a very high temperature, and is used for cutting and welding metals. [from OXYGEN + ACETYLENE]

oxygen *noun* (SYMBOL **O**, ATOMIC NUMBER **8**) a colourless odourless tasteless gas, produced by

Oxford Colleges	
College	Founded
University	1249
Balliol	1263
Merton	1264
St Edmund Hall	1278
Exeter	1314
Oriel	1326
Queen's	1340
New College	1379
Lincoln	1427
All Souls	1438
Magdalen	1458
Brasenose	1509
Corpus Christi	1517
Christ Church	1546
Trinity	1554
St John's	1555
Jesus	1571
Wadham	1612
Pembroke	1624
Worcester	1714
Regent's Park	1810
Keble	1868
Hertford	1874
Lady Margaret Hall	1878
Somerville[1]	1879
Mansfield	1886
St Hugh's	1886
St Hilda's[1]	1893
Campion Hall	1896
St Benet's Hall	1897
Greyfriars	1910
St Peter's	1929
Nuffield	1937
St Antony's	1950
St Anne's	1952
Linacre	1962
St Catherine's	1962
St Cross	1965
Wolfson	1966
Green	1979
Rewley House	1990
Manchester	1990

[1]Women's colleges

photosynthesis, and an essential requirement of most forms of plant and animal life. It is the most abundant element in the Earth's crust, and constitutes about 21% (by volume) of the Earth's atmosphere. [from Greek *oxys*, sharp + *gennaein*, to generate, from the old belief that all acids contained oxygen]

◇ Oxygen forms oxides with all the elements except the noble gases, and is essential for combustion (burning). It exists both as O_2 and, particularly in the upper atmosphere, as O_3 or ozone, which shields the Earth from harmful ultraviolet radiation. Oxygen is present in combined form in water, carbon dioxide, and many other compounds, as well as being a constituent of most rocks and minerals. Pure oxygen, obtained by fractional distillation of liquid air, is used for oxyacetylene welding, metal-cutting, and steelmaking, as an explosive, in rocket fuel, and as a respiratory aid in hospitals and during high-altitude flight.

oxygenate *verb* **1** to supply (eg the blood) with oxygen. **2** to treat with oxygen.

oxygenation *noun* **1** *Physiol.* the recharging of the blood with oxygen from air inhaled into the lungs. **2** *Chem.* treatment with or combination with oxygen.

oxygenator *noun* an apparatus that oxygenates the blood, especially while a patient is being operated on.

oxygen debt a temporary loss of oxygen from the body during very active exercise.

oxygen mask a mask through which oxygen is supplied from a tank.

oxygen tent a tent-like apparatus erected over a patient's bed, into which oxygen can be pumped to help his or her breathing.

oxyhaemoglobin *noun Biochem.* the red compound formed in blood by the combination of oxygen and the pigment haemoglobin as a result of respiration.

oxymoron *noun* a figure of speech in which contradictory terms are used together: *holy cruel.* [from Greek *oxymoros*, from *oxys*, sharp + *moros*, foolish]

oxytocin *noun Medicine* a hormone, released by the pituitary gland, that induces contractions of the smooth muscle of the uterus during labour, and stimulates the flow of milk from the breasts during suckling. A synthetic form of the hormone is used to accelerate labour by inducing uterine contractions. [from Greek *oxys*, sharp + *tokos*, birth]

oyez *or* **oyes** *interj. Hist.* a cry for silence and attention, usually shouted three times by an official before a public announcement or in a court of law. [from Old French *oir*, to hear]

oyster *noun* **1** the common name for a marine bivalve mollusc belonging to the family Ostreidae, and having a soft fleshy body enclosed by a hinged shell. The fleshy part is a popular sea food. **2** the pale greyish beige or pink colour of an oyster.

— **the world is one's oyster** one has everything one needs or wants within one's grasp. [from Greek *ostreon*]

◇ The oysters used for food do produce pearls, but belong to a different family from the most important pearl-producing species, pearl oysters being more similar to mussels. The right-hand side, or valve, of a true oyster shell is flat, and the left-hand valve is rounded. Oysters anchor themselves to the sea bed by means of the rounded half of the shell, in which the body of the oyster rests, with the flat valve serving as a lid, and they filter food particles from water which they draw in at a rate of up to 11 litres an hour.

oyster bed a place where oysters breed or are bred.

oystercatcher *noun* a black and white wading bird with a long orange-red beak, that feeds on mussels and limpets (but not oysters).

Oz *noun slang* Australia.

oz *abbrev.* ounce. [from Italian *onza*, ounce]

Ozark Mountains a highland area in S central USA, lying between the Arkansas and Missouri rivers. AREA c.129 500sq km/ 50 000sq mi. The area lies at an altitude generally of 300–360m with the highest point at 747m. Hydroelectricity is generated from Bagnell Dam on the Lake of the Ozarks. ECONOMY mining; forestry; tourism.

Ozbeck, Rifat (1954–) Turkish fashion designer, born in Istanbul. He studied architecture at Liverpool University but, without completing the course, moved to St Martin's School of Art in London. He presented his first collection in 1984, and now has a multi-million pound business. He was named Designer of the Year in 1989 and 1992. His vivid collections embrace myriad styles and display cross-cultural references.

ozone *noun* **1** *Chem.* (FORMULA O_3) a pungent unstable bluish gas that is an allotrope of oxygen, and contains three oxygen atoms in its molecule. **2** *colloq.* fresh, bracing sea air. [from Greek *ozein*, to smell]
◇ Ozone is formed by the action of ultraviolet light on oxygen in the upper atmosphere, where it forms a protective layer that shields the Earth's surface from harmful ultraviolet radiation. Ozone is a very strong oxidizing agent, and is used in the purification of drinking water, and as a disinfectant and bleach.

ozone-friendly *adj.* denoting a product that does not contain chemicals that deplete the ozone layer, eg chlorofluorocarbons.

ozone layer a layer of the upper atmosphere, between 15 and 30km above the Earth's surface, where ozone is formed. It filters harmful ultraviolet radiation from the Sun and prevents it from reaching the Earth.
◇ Ozone is formed in the atmosphere when ultraviolet radiation from the Sun is absorbed by oxygen, which then splits into separate oxygen atoms and reforms as ozone. Concern was caused in the 1980s by the discovery of a 'hole' in the ozone layer over the South Pole. It is thought that the damage has been caused by gases known as chlorofluorocarbons (CFCs), because chlorine from CFCs reacts with the ozone layer to form chlorine oxide, and ozone is used up during the reaction. Conservationists fear that CFCs may destroy the ozone layer altogether, and many countries have signed international agreements to ban the use of these substances, which have until very recently been widely used in aerosol sprays and refrigeration systems.

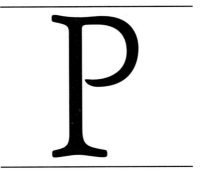

P¹ *or* **p** *noun* (PL. **Ps, P's, p's**) the sixteenth letter of the English alphabet.
— **mind one's ps and qs** *colloq.* to behave well and carefully.

P² *abbrev.* **1** *as a street sign* parking. **2** *Chess* pawn. **3** *Knitting* purl.

P³ *symbol Chem.* phosphorus.

p *or* **p.** *abbrev.* **1** page. **2** penny or pence.

PA *abbrev.* **1** (*also* **Pa**) Pennsylvania. **2** personal assistant. **3** public-address (system).

Pa *symbol Chem.* protactinium.

p.a. *abbrev. per annum* (Latin), yearly; per year.

Paardeberg, Battle of the first major British victory (1900) of the second Boer War, following the relief of the Siege of Kimberley. The Boers abandoned the position they had held at Magersfontein, and moved east to defend Bloemfontein. Their defeat at Paardeberg facilitated the full-scale attack on the Orange Free State and the Transvaal, and the taking of the Boer cities.

Pabst, G(eorg) W(ilhelm) (1895–1967) German film director, born in Raudnitz (now in Czechoslovakia). He began directing in 1923, and developed a darkly realistic, almost documentary style in *Die Liebe der Jeanne Ney* (The Love of Jeanne Ney, 1927). Other works, all examples of the New Realism, include *Westfront 1918* (1930), *Kameradschaft* (Comradeship, 1931), and he recreated the last days of Hitler in *Der Letzte Akt* (The Last Act, 1955).

pace¹ — *noun* **1** a single step. **2** the distance covered by one step. **3** rate of movement or progress: *can't stand the pace / at one's own pace*. **4** a manner of walking or running. **5** any of the gaits used by a horse. — *verb* **1** *intrans., trans.* (*often* **pace about** *or* **around**) to keep walking about: *was pacing about all morning / began to pace the floor.* **2** *intrans.* to walk steadily. **3** *trans.* to set the pace for (others) in a race, etc. **4** (**pace something out**) to measure out a distance in paces.
— **go through** *or* **show one's paces** to demonstrate one's skills at something.
keep pace with someone to go as fast as them.
put someone through their paces to test them in some activity.
set the pace to be ahead of, and so set the rate for, others.
[from French *pas*, step]

pace² *prep.* with the permission of; with due respect to (someone with whom one is disagreeing). [from Latin *pace*, ablative of *pax*, peace, pardon]

pacemaker *noun* **1** *Physiol.* the sinoatrial node, a small mass of specialized muscle cells in the heart which control the rate and the rhythm of the heartbeat. **2** *Medicine* an electronic device that stimulates the heart muscle to contract at a specific and regular rate, used to correct weak or irregular heart rhythms. **3** a pacesetter.

pacesetter *noun* a person who sets the pace; a leader.

Pachelbel, Johann (c.1653–1706) German composer and organist, born in Nuremberg. He held a variety of organist's posts before returning in 1695 to Nuremberg as organist of St Sebalds' Church. His works, which include organ fugues and six suites for two violins, profoundly influenced J S Bach.

pachisi *noun* an Indian board game resembling backgammon or ludo. [form Hindi *pacīsī*, of 25, referring to the highest throw in the game]

pachyderm *noun* a large thick-skinned animal, especially a rhinoceros, elephant, or hippopotamus. [from Greek *pachys*, thick + *derma*, skin]

Pacific — *noun* (**the Pacific**) see PACIFIC OCEAN. — *adj.* in or relating to the area of the Pacific. [from PACIFIC, because the ocean was notably calm when discovered by Ferdinand Magellan]

Pacific, War of the a war fought (1879–83) by Chile with Peru and Bolivia (in alliance since 1873), which arose out of Chilean grievances in the then Bolivian-held Atacama desert. Chile won command of the sea in the early months of the war, and sent large expeditions to Peru to occupy Lima, the capital (Jan 1881). Peace treaties with Peru (1883) and Bolivia (1904) gave Chile large territorial gains.

pacific *adj.* tending to make peace or keep the peace; peaceful; peaceable. [from Latin *pacificus*]

pacification *noun* the policy or process of pacifying.

Pacific Islands see UNITED STATES TRUST TERRITORY OF THE PACIFIC ISLANDS.

Pacific Ocean the largest ocean on Earth, extending from the Arctic to the Antarctic. On its E side are N and S America and on its W side are Asia and Oceania. AREA c.166 241 000sq km/64 169 000sq mi; average depth 4 300m; the greatest known depth is the Challenger Deep in the Mariana Trench at 10 915m. The ocean covers a third of the Earth and almost half the total water surface area. The S part is sometimes known as the South Sea. Principal arms are the Bering, Ross, Okhotsk, Yellow, E China, S China, Philippine, Coral, Tasman, Arafura, Celebes, and Japan seas, and the Gulf of California. Narrow continental shelves lie on the E shores, and wider shelves on the W; there are deep, open trenches and the E Pacific Ridge (Albatross Cordillera) is a major ridge system; a rim of volcanoes around the ocean is known as the 'Pacific Ring of Fire'. The Pacific and the N American plates are converging at the rate of 5.2–5.6cm per year, and the sea floor is contracting; at the Nazca Plate, there is divergent plate motion and the sea floor is spreading by 17.2cm per year. The ocean has many volcanic and coral islands. Spain, Portugal, Great Britain, and the Netherlands held colonies from the 17c, France and Russia in the 18c, and USA, Germany, and Japan in the 19c. The Pacific's commercial importance has increased since the opening of the Panama Canal in 1920.

pacifier *noun North Amer.* a baby's dummy.

pacifism *noun Politics* the beliefs and practices of pacifists.
◇ Pacifism has long been associated with certain Christian religions, and in the 20c is also practised by many who oppose war from secular moral standpoints. A more limited form is nuclear pacifism, which is opposed to nuclear war but not to conventional war.

pacifist *noun* someone who believes that violence is unjustified and who refuses to take part in making war.

pacify *verb* (**pacifies, pacified**) **1** to calm, soothe, or appease. **2** to restore to a peaceful condition. **3** *euphemistic* to subdue. [from Latin *pax*, peace + *facere*, to make]

Pacino, Al(fred James) (1940–) US film actor, born in East Harlem, New York. He studied under Charles Laughton and entered film in 1969. Among his successful roles are Michael Corleone in *The Godfather* (1972) and its sequels, Sonny in *Dog Day Afternoon* (1975), Big Boy Caprice in *Dick Tracy* (1990), and Johnny in *Frankie and Johnny* (1991).

pack¹ — *noun* **1** things tied into a bundle for carrying. **2** a rucksack; a backpack. **3** a complete set of playing-cards. **4** a troop of animals hunting together, eg dogs or wolves. **5** a compact package, eg of equipment for a purpose: *a first-aid pack.* **6** *derog.* a collection or bunch: *a pack of idiots / a pack of lies.* **7** a troop of Brownie Guides or Cub Scouts. **8** *Rugby* the forwards in a team. **9** a medicinal or cosmetic skin preparation: *a face pack.* **10** pack ice. — *verb* **1** to stow (goods, clothes, etc) compactly in cases, boxes, etc for transport or travel. **2** *intrans.* to put one's belongings into a travelling-bag, etc, ready for a journey. **3 a** (*also* **pack something out**) to fill it tightly. **b** (*also* **pack something in**) to cram it in. **4** to be capable of giving (a punch) of some force. **5** *North Amer. colloq.* to make a habit of carrying (a gun). **6** *intrans. said of animals* to form a pack.
— **pack it in** *colloq.* to give up or stop what one is doing.
pack someone off to send them off hastily or abruptly: *packed the children off to their friend's house.*
pack up 1 to stop work, etc. **2** *colloq., said of machinery, etc* to break down.
pack something up to put it in containers and store it.
send someone packing *colloq.* to dismiss them unceremoniously.
[origin unknown]

pack² *verb* to fill (a jury, meeting, etc) illicitly with people one can rely on to support one.

package — *noun* **1** something wrapped and secured with string, adhesive tape, etc; a parcel. **2** a package deal. **3** *Comput.* a group of related computer programs designed to perform a particular function and therefore meeting the requirements of a large number of users, eg Microsoft's Wordstar®. Packages are usually written and marketed by a software company rather than a computer manufacturer. — *verb* to wrap up in a parcel.

package deal a deal covering a number of related proposals that must be accepted as a whole or not at all.

package holiday *or* **package tour** a holiday or tour for which one pays a fixed price that includes travel, accommodation, meals, etc.

packaging *noun* the wrappers or containers in which goods are packed.

Packer, Kerry (Francis Bullmore) (1937–) Australian media proprietor, born in Sydney. He took over as Chairman of the Australian Consolidated Press (ACP) group from his father, Sir Frank Packer (1906–74). In 1977 he was responsible for the creation of World Series Cricket, a knock-out series of one-day matches and 'Super-Tests', played in colourful costume.

packet *noun* **1** a paper, cardboard, or plastic bag, wrapper, or container, with its contents. **2** a small pack or package. **3** (*also* **packet boat**) a mail boat also carrying cargo and passengers, plying a fixed route. **4** *colloq.* a large sum of money: *cost a packet.* [from Old French *pacquet*]

packet switching *Telecomm.* a method of directing digitally-encoded data communications over a network from source to receiver. The message is broken down into small 'packets' comprising address, control, and data signals, and these are sent over the network to be reconstituted into the full message at the destination. Network resources are used only when data is actually being sent, and the circuit can be shared.

packhorse *noun Hist.* a horse used to carry luggage or goods for sale.

pack ice pieces of floating ice driven together into a mass by wind and currents.

packing *noun* materials used for padding or wrapping goods for transport, etc.

packing-case *noun* a wooden crate in which to pack goods for transport or storage.

pact *noun* an agreement reached between two or more especially opposing parties, states, etc. [from Latin *pactum*]

pad¹ — *noun* a wad of material used to cushion, protect, shape, or clean. **1** a leg-guard for a cricketer, etc. **2** a quantity of sheets of paper fixed together into a block. **3** a rocket-launching platform. **4** the fleshy underside of an animal's paw. **5** a compactly laid out set of keys pressed to dial a telephone number, operate a television set, etc: *a key pad.* **6** *North Amer., esp. US* a large water-lily leaf. **7** *slang* one's living quarters. — *verb* (**padded**, **padding**) **1** to cover, fill, stuff, cushion, or shape with layers of soft material. **2** (*also* **pad something out**) to include unnecessary or irrelevant material in a piece of writing, speech, etc for the sake of length.

pad² *verb* (**padded**, **padding**) **1** *intrans.* to walk softly or with a muffled tread. **2** *trans., intrans.* to tramp along (a road); to travel on foot. [from Old Dutch *pad*, path]

Padang POP (1980) 481 000, the third-largest city in Sumatra and the capital of Sumatra Barat province, Indonesia. It is the main seaport on the W coast of Sumatra. An outlet for exports of rubber, copra, tea, and coffee is located at Telukbajur, 6km/4mi S.

padding *noun* **1** material for cushioning, shaping, or filling. **2** irrelevant or unnecessary matter in a speech or piece of writing.

paddle¹ — *verb* **1** *intrans.* to walk about barefoot in shallow water. **2** *trans.* to trail or dabble (fingers, etc) in water. — *noun* a spell of paddling.

paddle² — *noun* **1** a short light oar with a blade at one or both ends, used to propel and steer a canoe, etc. **2** one of the slats fitted round the edge of a paddle wheel or mill wheel. — *verb trans., intrans.* **1** to propel (a canoe, etc) with paddles. **2** *intrans.* (*also* **paddle along**) to move through water using, or as if using, a paddle or paddles.

paddle steamer a steamer driven by paddle wheels.

paddle wheel a large engine-driven wheel at the side or back of a ship which propels the ship through the water as it turns.

paddock *noun* **1** a small enclosed field for keeping a horse in. **2** *Racing* an enclosure beside a race track where horses are saddled and walked round before a race. [from Anglo-Saxon *pearroc*, fence, enclosure]

paddy¹ *noun* (PL. **paddies**) **1** (*also* **paddy field**) a field filled with water in which rice is grown. **2** rice as a growing crop; harvested rice grains that have not been processed in any way. [from Malay *padi*]

paddy² *noun* (PL. **paddies**) *colloq.* a fit of rage. [from *Paddy*, colloquial name for an Irishman]

Paderewski, Ignacy (Jan) (1860–1941) Polish pianist, composer, and patriot, born in Kuryłowka, Podolia. He became professor in the Warsaw Conservatory (1878) and a virtuoso pianist, and appeared throughout Europe and the USA. In 1919 he became one of the first premiers of Poland, but soon retired from politics, lived in Switzerland, and resumed concert work. He was elected President of Poland's provisional parliament in Paris in 1940.

padlock — *noun* a detachable lock with a U-shaped bar that pivots at one side so that it can be passed through a ring or chain and locked in position. — *verb* to fasten with a padlock.

padre *noun* a chaplain in any of the armed services. [from Portuguese, Spanish, and Italian *padre*, father (as a form of address to a priest)]

padsaw *noun* a small saw-blade with a detachable handle, used for cutting curves and awkward angles. [from PAD¹]

Padua, Italian **Padova**, ancient **Patavium** POP (1991e) 218 000, the capital of Padua province, Veneto region, NE Italy. Situated on the R Bacchiglione, 30km/19mi W of Venice, it was the birthplace of the historian Livy (c.59 BC) and the painter Andrea Mantegna (1431). The 16c university is associated with Galileo, Dante, and Petrarch. NOTABLE FEATURES Church of Sant'Antonio (1232–1307), with the tomb of St Antony of Padua, is a pilgrimage site; cathedral (16c); Donatello's equestrian statue of Gattamelata (1447); Church of the Eremitani (13c); oldest botanical garden in Europe (1545).

paean *noun* a song of triumph, praise, or thanksgiving. [from Greek *Paian*, healer, used in hymns as a title of Apollo]

paed- see PAEDO-.

paederast *or* **paederasty** see PEDERAST.

paediatric *adj.* relating to or involving paediatrics.

paediatrician *noun* a doctor specializing in studying and treating children's illnesses.

paediatrics *sing. noun Medicine* the branch of medicine concerned with the care of children, and with the diagnosis and treatment of children's diseases. [from Greek *pais*, child + *iatrikos*, medical]

paedo- *or* **paed-** *combining form* forming words associated with a child or children: *paedophile / paediatrics.* [from Greek *pais*, child]

paedophile *noun* an adult who is sexually attracted to or engages in sexual activity with children.

paedophilia *noun* sexual attraction to children.

paella *noun* a Spanish dish of rice, fish, or chicken, vegetables, and saffron. [from Catalan *paella*, from Latin *patella*, pan]

Paestum an ancient Greek town in SW Italy in the region of Naples, founded in c.600 BC by colonists from Sybaris, and conquered by Rome in 273 BC. It was renowned in antiquity for its Doric temples (eg the Temple of Ceres), the remains of which still survive.

pagan — *adj.* **1** not a Christian, Jew, or Muslim; of or following a religion in which a number of gods are worshipped. **2** without religious belief. — *noun* a pagan person. [from Latin *paganus*, rustic, peasant, civilian (ie not a soldier of Christ)]

Paganini, Niccolò (1782–1840) Italian violin virtuoso, born in Genoa. He gave his first concert in 1793, began professional tours in 1797, and later visited Austria, Germany, Paris, and London (1828–31). His dexterity and technical brilliance acquired an almost legendary reputation, and in revolutionizing violin technique he introduced stopped harmonics. Among his compositions for violin are six concertos.

paganism *noun* pagan beliefs and practices.

Page, Sir Frederick Handley (1885–1962) British pioneer aircraft designer and engineer, born in Cheltenham, Gloucestershire. In 1909 he founded the firm of aeronautical engineers which bears his name. His twin-engined 0/400 (1918) was one of the earliest heavy bombers, and his Hampden and Halifax bombers were used in World War II. His civil aircraft included the Hannibal, Hermes, and Herald transports.

Page, Mistress one of the two 'merry wives' who receives a love-letter from Falstaff in Shakespeare's *The Merry Wives of Windsor*. She has a trusting husband, George.

page¹ — *noun* **1** one side of a leaf in a book, etc. **2** a leaf of a book, etc. **3** *literary* an episode or incident in history, one's life, etc. — *verb* to paginate (a text). [from French *page*, from Latin *pagina*]

page² — *noun* **1** a boy who carries messages or luggage, etc. **2** *Hist.* a boy attendant serving a knight, and training for knighthood. **3** a boy attending the bride at a wedding. — *verb* to summon through a public-address system or pager. [from Old French *page*, from Old Italian *paggio*]

pageant *noun* **1** a series of tableaux or dramatic scenes, usually depicting historical events. **2** any colourful and varied spectacle. [from Latin *pagina*, page, scene, stage]

pageantry *noun* splendid display, pomp.

pageboy — *noun* a page. — *adj.* denoting a smooth jaw-length hairstyle with the ends curling under.

page description language (ABBREV. **PDL**) *Comput.* a programming language used to describe the composition of a printed page, which can be interpreted by a compatible printer.

pager *noun Radio* a small individually worn radio receiver and transmitter that enables its user to receive a signal, typically a 'beep', or to send a signal to alert another person. Pagers are widely used by hospital personnel.

Paget, Sir James (1814–99) English physician and pathologist, born in Yarmouth. One of the founders of modern pathology, he studied at St Bartholomew's Hospital, London, where he became full surgeon in 1861. He discovered the cause of trichinosis, a disease in which the intestine and muscles become infested with parasites from undercooked pork, and described Paget's disease, a chronic disorder of the skeleton.

paginate *verb* to give numbers to the pages of (a text) as part of the printing process. [from Latin *pagina*, page]

pagination *noun* **1** a system or process of paginating. **2** the figures and symbols used to mark pages.

Pagliacci, I (The Clowns), also known as ***The Strolling Players*** a one-act opera by Ruggiero Leoncavallo (1892). Canio, a travelling player, threatens fatal reprisals if his wife Nedda is unfaithful to him. His discovery that she has a lover is followed by the staging of a play which is so realistic that Canio becomes confused and carries out his threat. *Pagliacci* is usually performed as part of a double bill with Pietro Mascagni's *Cavalleria rusticana* (1890), hence the tag 'Cav and Pag'.

pagoda *noun* an oriental temple, especially in the form of a tall tower, each storey having its own projecting roof with upturned eaves. [from Portuguese *pagode*, from Persian *butkada*, from *but*, idol + *kada*, temple]

Pago Pago POP (1990) 4 000, the capital of American Samoa. It lies on the E coast of Tutuila I, in the S Pacific Ocean.

Pahang POP (1990) 1.1m, a state in E Peninsular Malaysia. AREA 35 965sq km/13 882sq mi. It is bounded E by the S China Sea and is watered by the R Pahang. The state was formerly part of the kingdom of Malacca. CAPITAL Kuantan. CHIEF TOWNS Bentong, Raub, Mentakab. ECONOMY timber; rubber; tin; rice; tourism.

Pahang, River the longest river in Peninsular Malaysia. It flows 456km/283mi E into the South China Sea, S of Kuantan.

Paharpur Vihara the ruins of a Buddhist monastery (*vihara*) at Paharpur, NW Bangladesh. It is said to have been founded by King Dharma Aal in 700, and is the largest Buddhist building S of the Himalayas. It is a World Heritage site.

Pahlavi, Mohammad Reza (1919–80) Shah of Iran. He succeeded on the abdication of his father Reza Shah (1941), and his long reign was marked by social reforms. However, opposition to his Western-style 'decadence' grew among the religious fundamentalists in the late 1970s and he was forced to leave Iran (1979). He was admitted to the USA for medical treatment, and then lived in Egypt.

Pahsien see CHONGQING.

paid see PAY.

paid-up *adj., said of a society member, etc* having paid a membership fee.

Päijänne, Lake the largest single lake in Finland. AREA 1 090sq km/420sq mi. Situated in the S central area of the country, it is drained southwards to the Gulf of Finland by the R Kymi.

pail *noun* **1** a bucket. **2** the amount contained in a bucket. [from Anglo-Saxon *pægel*, gill (liquid measure), associated with Old French *paielle*, pan]

pailful *noun* (PL. **pailfuls**) the amount a pail will hold.

pain — *noun* **1** an uncomfortable, distressing, or agonizing sensation that is usually relatively localized, and is caused by the stimulation of specialized nerve endings by a strong stimulus, eg heat, cold, pressure, or tissue damage. **2** emotional suffering. **3** (*also* **pain in the neck**) *derog. colloq.* an irritating or troublesome person. **4** (**pains**) trouble taken or efforts made in doing something. — *verb* to cause distress to.
— **be at pains to do something** to be anxious to do it with due care and thoroughness.
for one's pains *ironic* as a (usually poor) reward for the trouble one has taken.
on pain of something at the risk of incurring it as a punishment.
take pains to be careful to do something properly; to be thorough over a task, etc.
[from Latin *poena*, punishment]

Paine, Thomas (1737–1809) English radical political writer, born in Thetford, Norfolk. In 1774 he sailed for Philadelphia, where his pamphlet *Common Sense* (1776) argued for complete independence. In 1787 he returned to England, where he wrote *The Rights of Man* (1791–2), in support of the French Revolution. Arraigned for treason, he fled to Paris, where he was elected a deputy to the National Convention, but imprisoned (until 1796) for his proposal to offer the King asylum in the USA. At this time he wrote *The Age of Reason*, in favour of deism.

pained *adj.* expressing distress or disapproval: *a pained look*.

painful *adj.* **1** causing pain: *a painful injury*. **2** affected by something which causes pain: *a painful finger*. **3** causing distress: *a painful duty*. **4** laborious: *painful progress*.

painfully *adv.* in a painful way; so as to cause pain.

painkiller *noun* a drug that reduces or gets rid of pain.

painless *adj.* without pain.

painlessly *adv.* in a painless way.

painstaking *adj.* conscientious and thorough.

paint — *noun* **1** colouring matter in the form of a liquid, for applying to a surface; a dried coating of this. **2** a tube or tablet of colouring matter for creating pictures. **3** *old use* face make-up; cosmetics. — *verb* **1** to apply a coat of paint to (walls, woodwork, etc). **2** to turn (something) a certain colour by this means: *paint the door yellow*. **3** *trans., intrans.* to make (pictures) using paint. **4** to depict (a person, place or thing) in paint. **5** *trans., intrans. old use* to put make-up on (one's face). [from Old French *peint*, past participle of *peindre*]

paintball *noun* a game in which participants stalk each other and fight battles with paint fired from compressed-air guns.

paintbox *noun* a case of paints in a variety of colours, for painting pictures.

paintbrush *noun* a brush used for applying paint.

painter[1] *noun* **1** a person who decorates houses internally or externally with paint. **2** an artist who paints pictures.

painter[2] *noun Naut.* a rope for fastening a boat. [perhaps related to Old French *pentoir*, rope]

painting *noun* **1** the art or process of applying paint to walls, etc. **2** the art of creating pictures in paint. **3** a painted picture.

pair — *noun* **1** a set of two identical or corresponding things, eg shoes, gloves, etc, intended for use together. **2** something consisting of two joined and corresponding parts: *a pair of pants / a pair of scissors*. **3** one of a matching pair: *where's its pair?* **4** two people associated in a relationship. **5** two mating animals, birds, fishes, etc. **6** two horses harnessed together: *a coach and pair*. — *verb* **1** *trans., intrans.* (*also* **pair off**) to divide into pairs. **2** (**pair up with someone**) to join with them for some purpose.
— **in pairs** in twos.
[from Old French *paire*]

pair-royal *noun Cards* a set of three cards of the same denomination. — Also called *prial*.

Paisley, Bob (Robert) (1919–) English football manager, born in Hetton-le-Hole, Durham. He joined Liverpool in 1939, and spent nearly 50 years at the club. Under his management (1974–83), Liverpool became the most successful club side in England. He was Manager of the Year on six occasions, and in 1992 was made Life Vice-President of the club.

Paisley, Rev Ian (Richard Kyle) (1926–) Northern Irish Protestant clergyman and politician, born in Armagh. Ordained in 1946, he formed his own Church (the Free Presbyterian Church of Ulster) in 1951, and from the 1960s became deeply involved in Ulster politics. He founded the Protestant Unionist Party and stood as its MP for four years until 1974, when he became the Democratic Unionist MP for North Antrim. A member of the European Parliament since 1979, he is a rousing orator, strongly pro-British, and fiercely opposed to the IRA and the unification of Ireland.

Paisley POP (1981) 85 000, the capital of Renfrew district, Strathclyde, W Scotland, situated 11km/7mi W of Glasgow. It is known for its production of textiles in the Paisley pattern. NOTABLE FEATURES observatory; museum and art gallery; Paisley Abbey (1163, restored in the 20c).

Paiute, also (disparagingly) called **Diggers** two separate Numic-speaking Native American groups, traditionally hunter-gatherers, divided into the S Paiute (Utah, Arizona, Nevada, California) and the N Paiute (California, Nevada, Oregon). The S Paiute, who had relatively peaceful relations with whites, were put into reservations in the 19c. The N group fought intermittently with white prospectors and farmers until 1874, when the US government appropriated their land. The present-day population is c.5 000, in or near reservations.

pajamas see PYJAMAS.

Pakistan, official name **Islamic Republic of Pakistan** POP (1992e) 115.5m, an Asian state, divided into four provinces, a federal capital territory, and federally administered tribal areas. AREA 803 943sq km/310 322sq mi. It is bounded S by India, W by Afghanistan and Iran, and N by China. The state is situated between the Hindu Kush mountain range in the N and the Arabian Sea in the S. The disputed area of Jammu and Kashmir lies to the N. CAPITAL Islamabad. CHIEF TOWNS Karachi, Lahore, Faisalabad, Rawalpindi. TIME ZONE GMT +5. The population includes nearly 5m refugees from Afghanistan. Chief ethnic groups are Punjabi, Sindhi, Pathan, and Baluchi; Islam is the main religion. OFFICIAL LANGUAGES Urdu and English; several local languages are also spoken. CURRENCY the Pakistan rupee. PHYSICAL DESCRIPTION largely centred on the alluvial floodplain of the R Indus; bounded N and W by mountains rising to 8 611m at K2; mostly flat plateau, low-lying plains, and arid desert to the S of the Karakoram range. CLIMATE dominated by the Asiatic monsoon; in the mountains and foothills of the N and W the climate is cool with summer rain and winter snow; in the upland plateaus, summers are hot and winters are cool, with the possibility of some winter rain; in summer the Indus Valley is extremely hot and is fanned by dry winds, often carrying sand; throughout the country, the hottest season lasts from Mar to Jun, with the highest temperatures occurring in the S; the rainy season lasts from late Jun to early Oct and coincides with the SW monsoon; HISTORY walled cities at Mohenjo-Daro, Harappa, and Kalibangan are evidence of civilization in the Indus valley over 4 000 years ago; Muslim rule under the Mughal Empire from 1526 to 1761; British rule over most areas in the 1840s; separated from India to form a state for the Muslim minority in 1947, consisting of West Pakistan (Baluchistan, North-West Frontier, West Punjab, Sind) and East Pakistan (East Bengal), physically separated by 1 600km/1 000mi; Pakistan occupied Jammu and Kashmir in 1949 (disputed territory with India, and the cause of wars in 1965 and 1971); proclaimed an Islamic republic in 1956; differences between E and W Pakistan developed into civil war in 1971, resulting in E Pakistan becoming an independent state (Bangladesh); military coup by General Zia ul-Haq in 1977, with the execution of former Prime Minister Bhutto in 1979, despite international appeals for clemency; in 1991 there was increased violence within the country, particularly in Sind; several changes of government amid allegations of corruption in the early 1990s. GOVERNMENT governed by an elected President and a bicameral federal Parliament. ECONOMY agriculture employs 55% of the labour force;

concentrated on the floodplains of the five major rivers of Pakistan, and supported by an extensive irrigation network; wheat, maize, sugar cane, rice, cotton; cotton production is important, supporting major spinning, weaving, and processing industries; textiles; food processing; tobacco; engineering; cement; fertilizers; chemicals; natural gas; limestone; gypsum; iron ore; rock salt; uranium.

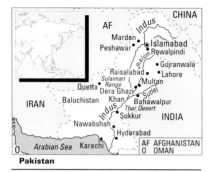

Pakistan

pakora *noun* an Indian dish of chopped spiced vegetables formed into balls, coated in batter, and deep-fried. [from Hindi]

PAL *abbrev.* Phase Alternating Line: the coding system for colour television developed in Germany and the UK from 1965 and widely adopted in Europe and many other parts of the world for 625 line/50 Hz transmission (see also NTSC, SECAM).

pal *colloq.* — *noun* a friend. — *verb intrans.* (**palled**, **palling**) (*usually* **pal up with someone**) to make friends with them. [from Romany *pal*, brother]

palace *noun* **1** the official residence of a sovereign, bishop, archbishop, or president. **2** a spacious and magnificent residence or other building. [from Old French *paleis*, from Latin *Palatium*, the Roman emperors' residence on the Palatine Hill]

Palach, Jan (1948–69) Czech philosophy student, who, as a protest against the invasion of Czechoslovakia Warsaw Pact forces (Aug 1968), burnt himself to death in Wenceslas Square, Prague (Jan 1969). A hero and symbol of hope, he was mourned by thousands, and in 1989 there were huge popular demonstrations in Prague to mark the 20th anniversary of his death.

pala d'altare the type of altarpiece that first appeared in Florence c.1430, consisting of a single large picture or panel (instead of several small ones). Raphael's *Sistine Madonna* (c.1512) is an example of the type. [from Italian *pala d'altare*, altarpiece]

Palade, George Emil (1912–) Romanian cell biologist, born in Iassy. He moved to the USA in 1946, and worked at the Rockefeller Institute, New York, and Yale Medical School before becoming professor at the University of California. His work on the fine structure of cells as revealed by electron microscopy led him in 1956 to discover the small organelles within cells, called ribosomes, in which proteins are manufactured. He shared the 1974 Nobel Prize for Physiology or Medicine with Albert Claude and Christian de Duve.

paladin *noun Hist.* **1** any of the 12 peers of Charlemagne's court. **2** a knight errant; a champion of a sovereign. [from Italian *paladino*, from Latin *palatinus*, belonging to the palace]

palaeo- *or* **palae-** *combining form* forming words meaning 'old, ancient, former'. [from Greek *palaios*, old]

palaeobotany *or* **paleobotany** *noun Geol.* the scientific study of fossil plants.

Palaeocene *adj. Geol.* the earliest epoch of the Tertiary period, lasting from about 65 to 54 mil-

lion years ago. During this time many reptiles became extinct and mammals became the dominant vertebrates, primates and rodents having appeared by the end of the epoch. [from PALAEO- + Greek *kainos*, new]

palaeoecology *or* **paleoecology** *noun Geol.* the scientific study of the ecology of fossil animals and plants.

palaeographer *noun* a person who studies ancient manuscripts.

palaeography *noun* the study of ancient writing and manuscripts.

palaeolithic *or* **Palaeolithic** *adj.* relating to or belonging to the early part of the Stone Age, during which chipped stones served as primitive tools. [from PALAEO- + Greek *lithos*, stone] ◇ Palaeolithic art, developed c.30 000 years ago, is the oldest known. It includes cave paintings and small sculptures, notably the 'Venus of Willendorf', a stylized stone carving of a pregnant woman. The Palaeolithic period included the Neanderthal and Cromagnon peoples.

Palaeologus a Byzantine family prominent from the 11c. Michael VIII, emperor in Nicaea (1259–61) and restorer of the Byzantine Empire (1261–82), founded the imperial dynasty of Palaeologi. The dynasty ruled until the last Byzantine emperor, Constantine XI, was killed when the Ottoman Turks stormed Constantinople in 1453.

palaeontologist *adj.* an expert in palaeontology.

palaeontology *noun Geol.* the scientific study of the structure, distribution, environment, and evolution of extinct life forms by interpretation of the fossil remains of animals and plants. [from PALAEO- + Greek *onta*, neuter pl. present participle of *einai*, to be + -LOGY]

Palaeosiberian — *adj.* denoting a family of languages used in NE Siberia, using the Cyrillic alphabet. — *noun* the languages forming this family.

Palaeozoic *adj. Geol.* relating to the era of geological time extending from about 580 million to 250 million years ago, and subdivided into the Cambrian, Ordovician, Silurian, Devonian, Carboniferous, and Permian periods. During this era the first vertebrates appeared, including jawless fish, bony and cartilaginous fish, amphibians, and reptiles. [from PALAEO- + Greek *zoion*, animal]

Palamon and Arcite the two young knights who, despite being friends, fight each other for the love of Emelye in 'The Knight's Tale', in Chaucer's *The Canterbury Tales*.

palanquin *or* **palankeen** *noun Hist.* a light portable bed used in the Orient, suspended from poles carried on the shoulders of four bearers. [from Portuguese *palanquim*]

palatable *adj.* **1** having a pleasant taste; appetizing. **2** acceptable; agreeable. [from PALATE]

palate *noun* **1** the roof of the mouth. **2** the sense of taste; an ability to discriminate between wines, etc. [from Latin *palatum*]

palatial *adj.* like a palace in magnificence, spaciousness, etc. [from Latin *palatium*, palace]

Palatinate, The a German Rhenish principality, with Heidelburg as its capital. Acquired by the Wittelsbach family (1214), it was elevated to an imperial electorate by the Golden Bull of 1356, and became increasingly wealthy and important in the 13c–15c. Frederick III (reigned 1559–76) introduced Calvinism and thereafter it was the leading Protestant German state and head of the Protestant Union (1608), before its division and systematic devastation in the Thirty Years War (1618–48) and later by France (1685). In the 18c it lost significance and it was finally absorbed into the German Reich (1871).

Palau *or* **Pelau** *or* **Belau**, official name **Republic of Palau** POP (1990) 15 000, a group of

c.350 small islands and islets, W Pacific Ocean. AREA 494sq km/191sq mi. It is the smallest of the four political units to emerge out of the US Trust Territory of the Pacific Islands. The group lies c.960km/600mi E of the Philippines and is the most westerly group of the Caroline Is. The largest island is Babeldoab (AREA 367sq km/142sq mi). TIME ZONE GMT +10. OFFICIAL LANGUAGES Palauan, English. CLIMATE warm all year, with high humidity; the average annual temperature is 27°C and the average annual rainfall is 3 810mm; typhoons are common. HISTORY held by Germany between 1899 and 1914; mandated to Japan by the League of Nations in 1920; invaded by USA in 1944. GOVERNMENT the government combines elements of a modern democratic system and a system of hereditary chiefs. ECONOMY taro, pineapple, breadfruit, bananas, yams, citrus fruit, coconuts, pepper; fishing; tourism.

palaver *noun* **1** *colloq.* unnecessary fuss. **2** *Hist.* an act of conferring between European traders, settlers, etc and native inhabitants. [from Portuguese *palavra*, from Latin *parabola*, speech]

Palawan, formerly **Paragua** (1902–5) POP (1980) 312 000, an island of the W Philippines. AREA 11 780sq km/4 547sq mi. It is bounded by the Sulu Sea in the E and the S China Sea in the W. Mindoro I to the NE is separated by Mindoro Strait. PHYSICAL DESCRIPTION Palawan is long and narrow, with a mountain chain running almost the whole length; it rises in the S to 2 054m at Mt Mantalingajan. CHIEF TOWN Puerto Princesa. ECONOMY timber; chromite; fishing.

Pale the 'land of peace' under English rule in late medieval Ireland. Pale diminished during this time as the Anglo-Irish nobles (the earls of Desmond, Kildare, and Ormond) increased in importance, until its reconquest under Henry VIII of England. Though defined as the counties of Dublin, Kildare, Louth, and Meath in 1464, the Act of 1495 under Poynings' Law showed a smaller area.

pale¹ — *adj.* **1** *said of a person, face, etc* having less colour than normal, eg from illness, fear, shock, etc. **2** *said of a colour* closer to white than black; light: *pale green*. **3** lacking brightness or vividness; subdued: *pale sunlight*. — *verb intrans.* **1** to become pale. **2** to fade by comparison: *pale into insignificance*. [from Old French *palle*, from Latin *pallidus*]

pale² *noun* **1** a post used for making fences. **2** a fence made of these; a boundary fence. — **beyond the pale** outside the limits of acceptable behaviour. [from Latin *palus*, stake]

paleface *noun* the term supposed to have been used by Native Americans for the white settlers.

palely *adv.* in a pale way, faintly.

Palembang POP (1980) 787 000, the river-port capital of Sumatra Selatan province, Indonesia. It lies on the R Musi, to the S of Sumatra I. The city was capital of the Sriwijaya Empire from the 7c until the 12c.

paleness *noun* a pale quality or colour.

Palenque a Mayan city dating from 600–800 excavated from the jungle on the slopes of the Chiapas Mts, S Mexico, celebrated for its beauty and distinctive architecture. Its monuments include a labyrinthine palace complex, temple pyramids of the Sun, Cross, and Foliate Cross, and the Temple of Inscriptions, which was built to house the tomb of Pacal, ruler of Palenque (615–84). It is a World Heritage site.

paleo- same as PALAEO-.

Palermo POP (1991e) 734 000, the seaport capital of Sicily and of Palermo province, Italy. It is situated on the N coast of the island and was founded in the 8c BC by the Phoenicians. NOTABLE FEATURES cathedral (12c), Church of San Cataldo, ruined Church of San Giovanni degli Eremiti (1132), Church of La Mortorana (1143); Teatro Massimo (1875–97).

Palestine a region bordering the E Mediterranean, occupied by the Philistines (12c BC), then the Israelites. It was a territory under the mandate of the UK (granted by the League of Nations) from 1920 to 1948. See also JORDAN.

Palestine Liberation Organization see PLO.

Palestinian — *noun* **1** a native of ancient or modern Palestine. **2** an Arab who is a native or a descendant of a native of the area formerly called Palestine. — *adj.* relating to ancient or modern Palestine.

Palestrina, Giovanni Pierluigi da (c.1525–1594) Italian composer, born in Palestrina. He learned composition and organ playing in Rome, and in 1544 became organist and *maestro di canto* at the cathedral of St Agapit, Palestrina. In 1551 he became master of the Julian choir at St Peter's, the first of several appointments in Rome. The most distinguished composer of the Renaissance, his works include over 100 masses, motets, hymns, and other church pieces, and in 1577 he began a revision of the Gradual (a book containing the sung parts of the Mass), which he later abandoned.

palette *noun* **1** a hand-held board with a thumb hole, on which an artist mixes colours. **2** the assortment or range of colours used by a particular artist, in a particular picture, etc. [from French, from Italian *paletta*, diminutive of *pala*, spade]

palette knife **1** an artist's knife for mixing and applying paint. **2** a flexible-bladed, round-ended knife used for spreading butter, mixing ingredients, etc.

Palgrave, Francis Turner (1824–97) English poet and critic, born in Great Yarmouth, Norfolk. Professor of Poetry at Oxford (1886–95), he is best known as the editor of the *Golden Treasury of Lyrical Poetry* (1875), which influenced poetic taste for many years.

Palikir POP (1980e) 6 000, the capital of the Federated States of Micronesia. It lies within Pohnpei state.

palimpsest *noun* **1** a parchment or other writing surface re-used after the original content has been erased. **2** a monumental brass that has been turned over and inscribed on the reverse. [from Greek *palin* again + *psaein*, to rub]

palindrome *noun* a word or phrase that reads the same backwards and forwards, eg *eye*, *radar*, and *sums are not set as a test on Erasmus*. [from Greek *palin*, back + *dromein*, run]

palindromic *adj.* in the nature of a palindrome; having the same spelling backwards and forwards.

paling *noun* any of a row of wooden posts fixed edge to edge to form a solid fence; a fence of this kind. [from Latin *palus*, stake]

palisade *noun* a tall fence of pointed wooden stakes fixed edge to edge, for defence or protection. [from Provençal *palissada*, from Latin *palus*, stake]

pall¹ *noun* **1** the cloth that covers a coffin at a funeral; the coffin itself. **2** anything spreading or hanging over: *a pall of smoke*. [from Anglo-Saxon *pæll*, robe, covering]

pall² *verb intrans.* to begin to bore or seem tedious. [a variant of APPAL]

Palladianism an architectural style of the 17c and 18c derived from the Renaissance buildings and writing of Andrea Palladio, and characterized by the use of symmetrical planning and the application of Roman architectural forms. It was first used in England by Inigo Jones in the Banqueting House, London (1619–22). The style is also found in Italy, Germany, Holland, and the USA.

Palladio, Andrea, originally **Andrea di Pietro della Gondola** (1508–80) Italian architect, born in Vicenza. He was a major figure in the development of modern Italian architecture. The 'Palladian' style, modelled on the ancient Roman, can be seen in many palaces, villas, and churches in the Vicenza region, notably the Villa Rotonda (1550–1) and the Church of San Giorgio Maggiore, Venice (begun 1556). *I quattro libri dell' architetura* (The Four Books of Architecture, 1570) greatly influenced his successors.

Palladium in Greek legend, an image of Pallas Athene which fell from heaven and became 'the luck of Troy'. Odysseus and Diomedes stole it, and made the capture of Troy possible. The Romans believed that it was brought to Rome by Aeneas.

palladium *noun* *Chem.* (SYMBOL **Pd**, ATOMIC NUMBER **46**) a soft silvery-white metal used as a catalyst, and in gold dental alloys, jewellery, electrical components, and catalytic converters for car exhausts. It is also combined with gold to form the alloy white gold. [named after the asteroid *Pallas*, discovered in 1802]

pall-bearer *noun* one of those carrying the coffin or walking beside it at a funeral.

pallet¹ *noun* **1** a small wooden platform on which goods can be stacked for lifting and transporting by fork-lift truck. **2** a flat-bladed wooden tool used for shaping pottery. [see PALETTE]

pallet² *noun* **1** a straw mattress. **2** a small makeshift bed. [from Old French *paillette*, from *paille*, straw]

palliasse *noun* a straw mattress. [from French *paillasse*, from *paille*, straw]

palliate *verb* **1** to ease the symptoms of (a disease) without curing it. **2** to serve to lessen the gravity of (an offence, etc); to excuse to some extent. **3** to reduce the effect of (anything disagreeable). [from Latin *pallium*, cloak]

palliative — *noun* anything used to reduce pain or anxiety. — *adj.* having the effect of palliating or reducing pain.

pallid *adj.* **1** pale, especially unhealthily so. **2** lacking vigour or conviction. [from Latin *pallidus*, pale]

palliness *noun* chumminess, friendliness.

Palliser novels, The a sequence of political novels by Anthony Trollope, including *Can You Forgive Her?* (1964–5), *Phineas Finn* (1869), *The Eustace Diamonds* (1873), *Phineas Redux* (1874), *The Prime Minister* (1876), and *The Duke's Children* (1880).

pallium *or* **pall** *noun* *Relig.* a white woollen vestment shaped like a double Y embroidered with six purple crosses signifying episcopal power, and union with the Holy See (of Rome). It is worn by the pope, and conferred by him on archbishops. [from Latin *pallium*, a cloak]

pallor *noun* paleness, especially of complexion. [from Latin *pallor*]

pally *adj.* (**pallier**, **palliest**) *colloq.* friendly.

palm¹ — *noun* **1** the inner surface of the hand between the wrist and the fingers. **2** the part of a glove covering this. — *verb* to conceal in the palm of the hand.
— **palm something off on someone**, *or* **someone off with something** *colloq.* to give them something unwanted or unwelcome, especially by trickery.
[from Latin *palma*]

palm² *noun* **1** a large tropical plant belonging to the family Palmae, found in tropical and subtropical regions worldwide, with a few species reaching warm temperate regions (and even cool temperate regions in special situations, eg areas influenced by the Gulf Stream). Palms are typical of and prominent on oceanic islands. **2** a leaf of this carried as a symbol of triumph or victory; the supreme prize. [from Latin *palma*, originally palm of the hand]
◇ Palms are monocotyledons, ie they have a single cotyledon or seed leaf. Some species are climbers, but most are trees. The woody unbranched trunk is covered with old leaf sheaths, or their scars, and bears a crown of large evergreen leaves, which are usually fan-shaped or feather-shaped. The huge flower-heads can contain 250 000 flowers, and in some species they are produced only once, after which the plant dies. Such a massive burst of flowering requires considerable energy reserves, and in these species the trunk often contains large quantities of starch or sugar. The fruits are dry, fleshy, or fibrous one-seeded berries, often brightly coloured, and vary greatly in size.
Palms are of great economic importance, especially in the tropics, where they provide a range of basic products, including vegetables, starch, fruits and nuts, timber, fibre, sugar, alcohol, and wax. Palm oil obtained from the flesh of the fruit of certain types of palm, eg coconut palm, is widely used for the manufacture of margarines, as well as in soap, candles, lubricants, etc.

dwarf fan palm
date palm
coconut palm
Washington palm

palms

Palma (de Mallorca) POP (1991) 297 000, the seaport capital of the Balearic Is, Spain, situated on Majorca I. NOTABLE FEATURES Bellver Castle (14c); Church of St Francis; cathedral (13c–16c); Spanish Pueblo Open-Air Museum.

palmate *adj.* **1** *Bot., said of a leaf* divided into lobes that radiate from a central point, resembling an open hand. **2** *Zool., said of an animal* having webbed toes, as in many aquatic birds. [from Latin *palmatus*, from *palma*, palm of the hand]

Palmer, Arnold (Daniel) (1929–) US golfer, born in Latrobe, Pennsylvania. US Amateur champion in 1954, he won the Canadian Open (1955), the British Open (1961–2), the US Open (1960), and the US Masters (1958, 1960, 1962, 1964). The first golfer (1968) to win $1m in his career, he has since been involved in various business enterprises.

Palmer, Samuel (1805–81) English landscape painter and etcher, born in London. He produced mainly watercolours in a mystical and imaginative style derived from his friend, William Blake. His work was outmoded during his lifetime by the Victorian demand for realistic sentimentality.

Palmerston see DARWIN.

Palmerston (of Palmerston), Henry John Temple, 3rd Viscount (1784–1865) English statesman, born in Broadlands, Hampshire. He became a Tory MP in 1807, served as Secretary of War (1809–28), joined the Whigs (1830), and was three times Foreign Secretary (1830–4, 1835–41, 1846–51). His assertive manner and robust defences of what he considered to be British interests abroad secured him the name of 'Firebrand Palmerston'. Home Secretary in Aberdeen's coalition (1852), he became Liberal Prime Minister (1855–8, 1859–65) and vigorously opposed the Crimean War with Russia.

Palmerston North POP (1990) 71 000, a city on the SW coast of North I, New Zealand, situated NE of Wellington. NOTABLE FEATURE Manawatu Rugby Museum.

palmetto noun (PL. **palmettos**) a small palm tree with fan-like leaves. [from Spanish palmito, diminutive of palma, palm]

palmistry noun the art or practice of telling a person's fortune by the lines on their palm.

palmitic acid Chem. (FORMULA $C_{15}H_{31}COOH$) a fatty acid, obtained from many animal and plant oils and fats, including palm oil and spermaceti, that is insoluble in water, and is used in the manufacture of soaps, lubricating oils, and waterproofing agents.

palm oil the red oil obtained from the outer pulp of the fruit of the oil palm, used in cooking fats and margarines.

Palm Springs POP (1990) 40 000, a resort city in Riverside County, S California, USA, lying in the N Coachella Valley. Founded in 1876, it developed as a luxurious desert resort in the early 1930s. NOTABLE FEATURES nearby Palm Canyon (an ancient grove of native palms); Tahquitz Bowl (a natural amphitheatre); hot springs; golf courses.

Palm Sunday in the Christian Church, the Sunday before Easter, commemorating Christ's triumphal entry into Jerusalem, when the crowd spread palm branches before him.

palmtop noun a portable computer small enough to be held in the hand.

palmy adj. (**palmier, palmiest**) humorous colloq. characterized by effortless success and prosperity: one's palmy days. [from PALM², as a symbol of triumph]

Palmyra an uninhabited atoll enclosing 50 small islets in the Pacific Ocean, situated 1 600km/1 000mi S of Honolulu. It has been a site for nuclear waste disposal since 1986. HISTORY annexed by the USA in 1912; important air transport base in World War II; since 1962 it has been under the jurisdiction of the US Department of the Interior.

Palmyra, also called **Tadmor** an ancient Syrian town on the E fringe of the Roman Empire, whose wealth came from controlling the desert trade routes between N Syria and Babylonia. At the height of its power in the 3c AD, it briefly ruled the E half of the Empire, before being destroyed by the Romans in AD 273.

palomino noun (PL. **palominos**) a golden or cream horse with a white tail and mane. [from Spanish palomino, dove-like]

palpable adj. **1** easily detected; obvious. **2** Medicine able to be felt. [from Latin palpare, to touch]

palpably adv. in a palpable way, obviously.

palpate verb Medicine to examine (the body or a part of it) by touching or pressing, especially in order to diagnose medical disorders or diseases. [from Latin palpare, to touch]

palpitate verb intrans. **1** Medicine, said of the heart to beat abnormally rapidly, eg as a result of physical exertion, fear, emotion, or heart disease. **2** to tremble or throb. [from Latin palpitare, to throb]

palpitation noun (often **palpitations**) **1** palpitating. **2** a trembling.

palsy — noun paralysis, or loss of control or feeling in a part of the body. — verb (**palsies, palsied**) to affect with palsy; to paralyse. [from Old French paralisie, from Latin and Greek paralysis]

paltriness noun inadequacy, insignificance.

paltry adj. (**paltrier, paltriest**) worthless; trivial; meagre; insignificant; insultingly inadequate. [from German dialect paltrig, ragged]

palynolgy noun the analysis of spores and pollen grains, principally those preserved in ancient sediments and soils, in order to reconstruct variations in vegetation over time. This information can provide evidence of the impact made by prehistoric peoples and early agriculture on the natural environment, or give some indication of the prevailing climatic conditions at a given period in the Earth's history. [from Greek palynein, to sprinkle + -LOGY]

Pamela a female first name, devised (with stress on the second syllable) by the Elizabethan poet Sir Philip Sidney.

Pamela, in full **Pamela, or, Virtue Rewarded** an epistolary novel by Samuel Richardson (1740–1). It focuses on the fortunes of the impoverished heroine, Pamela Andrews.

pampas or **pampa** the extensive grassland (prairie) region of Argentina and Uruguay around the estuary of the R Plate. It is a major centre for cattle ranching.

pampas grass a large perennial grass (Cortaderia selloana), native to S America, that forms dense tufts of arching bluish leaves and has tall erect stems, 3m high, bearing silvery-white, sometimes pink, plume-like panicles. It is widely grown as an ornamental.

pamper verb (**pampered, pampering**) to treat over-indulgently and over-protectively; to cosset or spoil. [from Middle English, originally Germanic]

pamphlet noun a booklet or leaflet providing information or dealing with a current topic. [from Old French pamphilet, from the title of the medieval Latin love poem, Pamphilus, seu de Amore]

Pamplona, Latin **Pampeluna**, or **Pompaelo** POP (1991) 179 000, the capital of Navarre region, N Spain. It lies on the R Arga, 407km/253mi N of Madrid. In the 10c it was capital of the Kingdom of Navarre. NOTABLE FEATURES cathedral (14c–15c); museum. The Fiesta of San Fermin (Jul) involves bull-running in the streets.

Pamporovo an international ski resort in Smolyan province, S Bulgaria. It lies 15km/9mi N of Smolyan in the Rhodopi Mts, at an altitude of 1 650m.

Pan in Greek mythology, the god of flocks and herds, originally a rural goat-god from Arcadia, depicted with goat-like ears, horns, and legs. His pan-pipe was made of reeds, and he was believed to be the cause of uncontrollable fear ('panic') which could seize groups of travellers.

Pan, Peter see PETER PAN.

pan¹ — noun a usually metal pot used for cooking. **1** (often in compounds) any of various usually shallow vessels, with domestic, industrial or other uses: a dustpan / bedpan etc. **2** the bowl of a lavatory. **3** either dish on a pair of scales. **4** a shallow hollow in the ground: a salt pan. **5** Hist. the hollow part of an old gun lock, holding the priming. — verb (**panned, panning**) **1** intrans., trans. to wash (river gravel) in a shallow metal vessel in search of gold. **2** colloq. to criticize or review harshly.

pan² — verb trans., intrans. (**panned, panning**) said of a film camera, etc to swing round so as to follow a moving object or show a panoramic view. — noun a panning movement or shot. [a shortening of PANORAMA]

pan- combining form forming words meaning 'all, entire': Pan-African. [from Greek pas pantos, all]

panacea noun a universal remedy; a cure-all for any ill, problem, etc. [from PAN- + Greek akos, remedy]

panache noun flamboyant self-assurance. [from French panache, plume]

Pan-Africanism an ideal and a movement that draws its ideas from black American and West Indian writers and activists, reflecting a pride in the African continent and culture, and commitment to self-rule. Although great desire for continental unity is expressed, Pan-Africanism has failed to provide an ideology strong enough to transcend local self-interest and rivalries, nor has the Organization of African Unity managed to provide an acceptable institutional framework.

Panama, Spanish **Panamá**, official name **Republic of Panama**, Spanish **República de Panamá** POP (1992e) 2.5m, a republic occupying the SE end of the isthmus of Central America, divided into nine provinces and one American Indian territory. AREA 77 082sq km/29 753sq mi. It is bounded N by the Caribbean Sea, S by the Pacific Ocean, W by Costa Rica, and E by Colombia. CAPITAL Panama City. CHIEF TOWNS David, Colón, Santiago. TIME ZONE GMT –5. The chief ethnic groups are 70% mestizo (mixed race) and 14% West Indian; Roman Catholicism is the chief religion. OFFICIAL LANGUAGE Spanish. CURRENCY the balboa. PHYSICAL DESCRIPTION mostly mountainous; the Serranía de Tabasará in the W rises to over 2 000m; the Azuero peninsula lies to the S; lake-studded lowland cuts across the isthmus; dense tropical forests lie on the Caribbean coast. CLIMATE tropical, with a mean annual temperature of 32°C; the average annual rainfall at Colón, on the Caribbean coast, is 3 280mm, while in Panama City it is 1 780mm. HISTORY discovered by Columbus in 1502; under Spanish colonial rule from 1538 until 1821; joined the Republic of Greater Colombia; separation from Colombia after a US-inspired revolution in 1903; assumed sovereignty of the Panama Canal Zone, previously administered by the USA, in 1979; US military intervention in 1989 ousted the illegally appointed military President; the armed forces were abolished in 1991. GOVERNMENT governed by a President, elected for five years, and a Cabinet, with a 67-member Legislative Assembly. ECONOMY centred mainly on the Panama Canal and the ports of Colón and Panama; Canal revenue accounts for four fifths of the country's wealth; great increase in the banking sector since 1970; attempts to diversify include oil refining, cigarettes, clothing, beverages, construction materials, paper products, shrimps, tourism; copper, gold, silver deposits; bananas, coffee, cacao, sugar cane.

Panama

panama noun (also **panama hat**) a lightweight brimmed hat for men made from the plaited leaves of a palm-like Central American tree. [from Panama in Central America]

Panama Canal a canal bisecting the Isthmus of Panama and linking the Atlantic and Pacific Oceans. It is 82km/51mi long, and 150m wide in most places. The canal was built by the US Corps of Engineers between 1904 and 1914. In 1979, US control of the Panama Canal Zone (8km/5mi of land flanking the canal on either side) was passed to the Republic of Panama; Panama has guaranteed the neutrality of the waterway itself when it takes over operational control of the canal in 2000.

Panama City, Spanish **Panamá** POP (1990) 585 000, the capital of Panama, on the N shore of the Gulf of Panama, near the Pacific Ocean end of the Panama Canal. It was founded in 1673 and is, today, the industrial and transportation centre of the country. NOTABLE FEATURE Church of San José.

Panama Congress (1826) a meeting that has come to symbolize (1826) the quest for Latin American unity, attended by delegates from Mexico, Peru, Grancolombia, and the Central American Federation at the invitation of Simón Bolívar (who did not himself attend), and at which the treaty of Spanish–American confederation (of no practical effect) was agreed.

Pan-American Games a multi-sports competition held every four years for athletes from N, S, and Central American nations. They were first held in Buenos Aires, Argentina, in 1951.

Pan-American Highway a network of designated roads extending 27 000km/17 000mi across the Americas from Alaska to Chile. The proposal, which was put to the Fifth International Conference of American States in 1923, was originally for a single route, but it grew to include several alternative designated routes.

Pan-American Union an organization founded as the International Bureau for American Republics (1890) to foster political and economic co-operation among American states, and to draw N and S America closer together. Until World War II it concluded many agreements covering trade, migration, and neutrality zones around their coasts, despite fears of domination by the USA. In 1948 it became part of the Organization of American States, and now forms its permanent administrative and advisory machinery.

panatella *noun* a long slim cigar. [from American Spanish *panatella*, long thin biscuit]

Panathenaea an ancient religious festival held annually in Athens in honour of Athene, the patron goddess of the city. It consisted of a procession from the town to the Acropolis, the sacrifice at the great altar there of a hekatomb (100 cattle), and then athletic contests.

pancake *noun* a round of thin batter cooked on both sides in a frying-pan or on a griddle.

Pancake Day Shrove Tuesday, when pancakes are traditionally eaten.

pancake landing an aircraft landing made in an emergency, with the wheels up and landing flat on the belly of the aircraft.

Panchen Lama a spiritual leader and teacher in Tibetan Buddhism, second in importance to the Dalai Lama, and said to be the reincarnation of the Buddha Amitabha. The late Panchen Lama (1938–89), the tenth reincarnation, became the ward of the Chinese in his childhood, and some Tibetans disputed his status.

panchromatic *adj. Photog.*, said of a film sensitive to all colours.

pancreas *noun* in vertebrates, a large carrot-shaped gland lying between the duodenum and the spleen, that has hormonal and digestive functions. [from PAN- + Greek *kreas*, flesh] ◇ The pancreas secretes pancreatic juice, which contains a mixture of digestive enzymes (amylase, trypsin, and lipase), directly into the duodenum via a short duct known as the pancreatic duct. Pancreatic juice is strongly alkaline, in order to counteract the acidity of food that has just passed to the duodenum from the stomach. The pancreas also contains small groups of specialized cells, known as the *islets of Langerhans*, that produce and secrete the hormones insulin and glucagon into the bloodstream. Insulin lowers blood sugar levels by promoting the storage of glucose in the liver in the form of glycogen, and glucagon raises blood sugar levels by converting glycogen back to glucose. If energy is needed, the pancreas releases glucagon, but if blood sugar levels become too high, it releases insulin.

panda *noun* **1** see GIANT PANDA. **2** (*also* **red panda**) a tree-dwelling mammal (*Ailurus fulgens*) related to the giant panda, found in mountain forests of Nepal, Sikkim, Bhutan, and China. About the same size as a large cat, it has thick chestnut fur with white patches on its face and dark rings on its bushy tail. It is nocturnal and feeds mainly on leaves and fruit. [from Nepalese]

panda car in the UK, a small police patrol car, formerly white with black markings.

Pandarus 1 in Greek legend, a Trojan prince. In the *Iliad*, he is killed by Diomedes. **2** the uncle and guardian of Criseyde in Chaucer's *Troilus and Criseyde*, who acts as a go-between for the young lovers.

pandemic *adj. Medicine* describing a widespread epidemic of a disease, eg one that affects a whole country or the whole world. [from Greek *pandemios*, from *demos*, people]

pandemonium *noun* noise, chaos, and confusion. [from John Milton's name for the capital of Hell in *Paradise Lost*, from PAN- + Greek *daimon*, demon]

pander — *verb intrans.* (**pandered, pandering**) (**pander to someone**) to indulge or gratify them or their wishes or tastes. — *noun* a person who obtains a sexual partner for another. [from *Pandarus* in Chaucer and Shakespeare, the go-between who procures Cressida for Troilus]

Pandit, Vijaya Lakshmi, *née* **Swarup Kumari Nehru** (1900–) Indian politician and diplomat, born in Allahabad, the sister of Nehru. Leader of the Indian United Nations delegation (1946–8, 1952–3), she also held several ambassadorial posts (1947–51). In 1953, she became the first woman President of the UN General Assembly, and Indian High Commissioner in London (1954–61).

Pandora in Greek mythology, the first woman, made by Hephaestus, and adorned by the gods with special qualities; she was sent to be the wife of Epimetheus. Zeus gave her a box (or she found a storage-jar) from which all the evils which plague mankind escaped; only Hope was left in the bottom of the box. [from PAN- + Greek *doron*, gift]

Pandora's box a potential source of unlimited evils.

pane *noun* a sheet of glass, especially one fitted into a window or door. [from Old French *pan*, strip of cloth]

panegyric *noun* a speech or piece of writing in praise of someone or something; a eulogy. [from Greek *panegyrikos*, fit for a national festival]

panel — *noun* **1** a rectangular wooden board forming a section, especially ornamentally sunken or raised, of a wall or door. **2** one of several strips of fabric making up a garment. **3** any of the metal sections forming the bodywork of a vehicle. **4** a board bearing the instruments and dials for controlling an aircraft, etc. **5** a team of people selected to judge a contest, or participate in a discussion, quiz, or other game before an audience. **6** a list of jurors; the people serving on a jury. — *verb* (**panelled, panelling**) to fit (a wall or door) with wooden panels. [from Old French, diminutive of *pan*, a strip of cloth, etc]

panel-beater *noun* a person whose job is panel-beating.

panel-beating *noun* the removal of dents from metal, especially from the bodywork of a vehicle, using a soft-headed hammer.

panel game one played by a panel of people.

panelling *noun* panels in walls or doors, or material for making these.

panellist *noun* a member of a panel or team of people, especially in broadcasting.

panel pin a small slender nail with a very small head.

pang *noun* a painfully acute feeling of hunger, remorse, etc.

Pangaea *or* **Pangea** *noun Geol.* the name given to the hypothetical 'supercontinent' that is thought to have represented the entire land mass of the Earth about 200 million years ago, before it drifted apart to form Laurasia and Gondwanaland. [from PAN- + Greek *ge*, earth]

pangolin *noun* a mammal native to Africa and S and SE Asia, which has a pointed head with small eyes, a long broad tail, a long tongue, and no teeth. It is covered with large overlapping horny plates, and can curl into an armoured ball when threatened by a predator. Pangolins feed on ants and termites. [from Malay *peng-goling*, roller]

pangram *noun* a sentence containing all the letters of the alphabet, such as *the quick brown fox jumps over the lazy dog*. [from PAN- + Greek *gramma*, letter]

Pan Gu in Chinese mythology, the first being of the creation myth. He is said to have emerged from a primal egg, and to have used his knowledge of yin and yang to make the earth. His body became the mountains, his hair the stars, and his eyes the Sun and Moon.

Panhandle 1 any territory which comprises a narrow strip of land running out from a large area in the shape of a pan handle. **2** a term applied in the USA to areas in (1) NW Texas (the Texas Panhandle), (2) NW Oklahoma, (3) N Idaho, (4) NE West Virginia (Eastern Panhandle), (5) N West Virginia, (6) SE Alaska, (7) Nebraska, and (8) an extension of the Golden Gate Park in San Francisco.

panic — *noun* a sudden overpowering fear, especially one that grips a crowd or population. — *verb trans., intrans.* (**panicked, panicking**) to feel or cause to feel panic. [from Greek *panikon*, baseless terror, caused by *Pan*, god of flocks and pastures]

panic attack *Psychol.* an attack of intense terror and anxiety, lasting from several minutes to several hours.

panic-buy *verb* to buy (a commodity) in large quantities, in expectation of a shortage.

panicky *adj.* panicking or likely to panic.

panicle *noun Bot.* a branched inflorescence (flower-head), common in grasses, in which the youngest flowers are at the tip of the flower stalk, and the oldest ones are near its base. [from Latin *panicula*, tuft]

panic-stricken *adj.* terrified.

Panjabi same as PUNJABI.

panjandrum *noun humorous* a pompous official. [from a string of nonsense composed by Samuel Foote (1720–77)]

Pankhurst, Emmeline, *née* **Goulden** (1858–1928) English suffragette, born in Manchester. In 1903 (with her daughter Christabel Harriette, 1880–1958) she organized the Women's Social and Political Union. A militant campaigner for women's suffrage, she was frequently imprisoned and also undertook hunger strikes. After the outbreak of World War I, she turned her attention to the industrial mobilization of women.

pannier *noun* **1** one of a pair of baskets carried over the back of a donkey or other beast of burden; one of a pair of bags carried on either side of the rear wheel of a bicycle, etc. **2** *Hist.* a tucked-up arrangement of fabric on either side of a woman's skirt. [from French *panier*, from Latin *panarium*, bread basket]

panoply *noun* (PL. **panoplies**) **1** the full splendid assemblage got together for a ceremony, etc: *the full panoply of a society wedding.* **2** *Hist.* a full set of armour and weapons. [from Greek *panoplia*, from *pan-*, all + *hopla*, weapons]

panorama *noun* **1** an open and extensive or all-round view, eg of a landscape. **2** a view of something in all its range and variety: *the panorama of history.* [from PAN- + Greek *horama*, view]

panoramic *adj., said of a view or prospect* like a panorama; open and extensive.

panoramically *adv.* in a panoramic way.

panpipes *pl. noun* a musical instrument consisting of pipes of graded lengths bound together, played by blowing along their open ends. [from *Pan*, Greek god of forests and pastures]
◊ Of great antiquity, panpipes are still widely used in certain folk cultures, such as those of S America and Romania.

pansy *noun* (PL. **pansies**) **1** a small garden plant of the violet family with multi-coloured broad-petalled flowers. **2** *offensive slang* an effeminate man or boy; a male homosexual. [from Old French *pensée*, thought]

pant — *verb* **1** *intrans.* to breathe in gasps as a result of exertion. **2** *trans.* to say breathlessly. **3** (**be panting for something**) to be longing for it: *panting for a drink.* — *noun* a gasping breath. [from Old French *pantaisier*, from Greek *phantasioun*, to hallucinate]

pantaloons *pl. noun* **1** baggy trousers gathered at the ankle. **2** tight-fitting trousers for men worn at the turn of the 19c. [from *Pantalone*, a figure from Italian comedy, a skinny old man in tight hose]

pantechnicon *noun* a large furniture-removal van. [from the name of the premises of a London art-dealer (later a furniture warehouse), from PAN- + Greek *techne*, art]

pantheism *noun* **1** the belief that equates all the matter and forces in the universe with God. **2** readiness to believe in any god. [from PAN- + Greek *theos*, god]

pantheist *noun* a person who upholds the doctrine of pantheism.

pantheistic *adj.* relating to pantheism or pantheists.

pantheon *noun* **1** all the gods of a particular people: *the ancient Greek pantheon.* **2** a temple sacred to all the gods. **3** a building in which the glorious dead of a nation have memorials or are buried. [from Greek *pantheios*, of all the gods]
◊ The term is often used to refer specifically to the Pantheon at Rome, built (c.119–125 AD) by Hadrian, and regarded as one of the greatest surviving classical buildings. It was conceived entirely as an interior, dedicated to the seven Roman planetary gods. Its coffered hemispherical dome is 43.2m in diameter; the interior is lighted by a single central opening; and there is a Corinthian portico supported by 16 granite columns. It is now converted to the church of Santa Maria Rotonda.

panther *noun* **1** common name for a black leopard. **2** *North Amer.* a puma. [from Greek *panther*, leopard]

panties *pl. noun* thin light knickers for women.

pantihose see PANTY HOSE.

pantile *noun* a roofing-tile with an S-shaped cross-section, laid so that the upward curve of one tile fits under the downward curve of the next. [from PAN[1] + TILE]

panto *noun* (PL. **pantos**) *colloq.* pantomime.

panto- or pant- *combining form* forming words meaning 'all, entire'. [from Greek *pas pantos*, all]

pantograph *noun* **1** a device consisting of jointed rods forming an adjustable parallelogram, for copying maps, plans, etc to any scale. **2** a similarly shaped metal framework on the roof of an electric train, transmitting current from an overhead wire.

pantomime *noun* **1** a Christmas entertainment usually based on a popular fairy tale, with songs, dancing, comedy acts, etc. **2** communication by gesture and facial expression; dumbshow. [from Greek *pantomimos*, mime actor, literally 'imitator of all']
◊ Pantomime is derived from the harlequinade, first brought to London in the early 18c. As it developed in the 19c, elements from burlesque, and variety acts from the music halls were incorporated, so that modern pantomime is a conglomeration of romance, slapstick, comedy, song, dance, acrobatics, male and female impersonation, specialized solo acts, and elaborate costume.

pantothenic acid *Biochem.* a member of the vitamin B complex that is found in many foods, especially cereal grains, egg yolk, liver, yeast, and peas. It is required for the oxidation (breakdown) of fats and carbohydrates, and deficiency of vitamin is rare. [from Greek *pantothen*, from every side, because of its wide occurrence]

pantry *noun* (PL. **pantries**) a room or cupboard for storing food. [from Old French *paneterie*, from Latin *panis*, bread]

pants *pl. noun* **1** *Brit.* an undergarment worn over the buttocks and genital area. **2** *North Amer.* trousers.
— **caught with one's pants down** *colloq.* caught embarrassingly unprepared.
wear the pants *colloq.* to be the member of a household who makes the decisions.
[a shortening of PANTALOONS]

pant suit or **pants suit** *North Amer.* a trouser suit.

panty hose or **pantihose** *North Amer.* women's tights.

Panzer a term used in the German armed forces, applied to warships (*Panzerschiffe*, 'armoured ship') but more particularly to armoured fighting vehicles. The Panzer divisions (essentially tank forces) were the most important component of the German army's fighting strength during World War II. [from German *Panzer*, armour]

pap[1] *noun* **1** soft semi-liquid food for babies and invalids. **2** *derog.* trivial or worthless reading matter or entertainment.

pap[2] *noun* **1** *old use* a nipple or teat. **2** *Scot.* in place-names, a rounded hill.

papa *noun old use* a child's word for father. [from French *papa* and Greek *pappas*, father]

papacy *noun* (PL. **papacies**) **1** the position, power, or period of office of a pope. **2** government by popes. [from Latin *papatia*, from *papa*, pope]

papal *adj.* of, or relating to, the pope or the papacy. [from Latin *papalis*, from *papa*, pope]

Papal States the 'States of the Church' in rural central Italy, which comprised territories received by treaties and donations during the Middle Ages. The papal government was often ineffective, and relied upon local lords (Malatesta of Rimini, Montefeltro of Urbino) appointed as 'vicars in temporal matters'. Annexed in 1870, the papacy recognized their loss only by the Lateran Treaty (1929), which established the Vatican papal state.

paparazzo *noun* (PL. **paparazzi**) a newspaper photographer who follows famous people about in the hope of photographing them in unguarded moments. [from the name of the photographer in the film *La Dolce Vita* (1959)]

papaya *noun* **1** a small evergreen tree with a crown of large segmented leaves and yellow flowers, widely cultivated in the tropics for its edible fruit. **2** the large yellow or orange fruit of this tree, which has sweet orange flesh and may be eaten raw, squeezed for its juice, or canned. — Also called *pawpaw*. [from Spanish *papaya*]

Papeete POP (1988) 79 000, the capital and chief port of French Polynesia. It lies on the NW coast of Tahiti.

paper *noun* **1** a material manufactured in thin sheets from wood, rags, etc, used for writing on, printing on, wrapping things, etc. **2** a loose piece of paper, eg a wrapper or printed sheet. **3** wallpaper. **4** a newspaper. **5** a set of questions on a certain subject for a written examination. **6** a written article dealing with a certain subject, especially for reading to an audience. **7** (**papers**) personal documents establishing one's identity, nationality, etc. **8** (**papers**) a person's accumulated correspondence, diaries, etc. — *verb* (**papered**, **papering**) to decorate with wallpaper: *paper the hall.*
— **on paper 1** in theory as distinct from practice: *plans that look good on paper.* **2** captured in written form: *get one's ideas down on paper.*
paper over something to conceal or avoid an awkward fact, mistake, etc.
[from Old French *papier*, from Greek *papyros*, papyrus]
◊ Paper was probably invented by the Chinese in the 2c. It was introduced to medieval Europe by the Moors, eventually superseding parchment as the standard material for written and printed documents. Early paper was handmade in single sheets; from the 19c wood pulp and cellulose were the principal materials used in its manufacture, and plant fibres and rags continue to be used to make high quality papers. The first machines for making continuous rolls (or webs) of paper were introduced in France in the late 18c; and the recycling of waste paper is now increasingly practised on ecological grounds.

International Paper Sizes		
A series	**mm**	**in**
A0	841 × 1 189	33.11 × 46.81
A1	594 × 841	23.39 × 33.1
A2	420 × 594	16.54 × 23.39
A3	297 × 420	11.69 × 16.54
A4	210 × 297	8.27 × 11.69
A5	148 × 210	5.83 × 8.27
A6	105 × 148	4.13 × 5.83
A7	74 × 105	2.91 × 4.13
A8	52 × 74	2.05 × 2.91
A9	37 × 52	1.46 × 2.05
A10	26 × 37	1.02 × 1.46
B series	**mm**	**in**
B0	1 000 × 1 414	39.37 × 55.67
B1	707 × 1 000	27.83 × 39.37
B2	500 × 707	19.68 × 27.83
B3	353 × 500	13.90 × 19.68
B4	250 × 353	9.84 × 13.90
B5	176 × 250	6.93 × 9.84
B6	125 × 176	4.92 × 6.93
B7	88 × 125	3.46 × 4.92
B8	62 × 88	2.44 × 3.46
B9	44 × 62	1.73 × 2.44
B10	31 × 44	1.22 × 1.73
C series	**mm**	**in**
C0	917 × 1 297	36.00 × 51.20
C1	648 × 917	25.60 × 36.00
C2	458 × 648	18.00 × 25.60
C3	324 × 458	12.80 × 18.00
C4	229 × 324	9.00 × 12.80
C5	162 × 229	6.40 × 9.00
C6	114 × 162	4.50 × 6.40
C7	81 × 114	3.20 × 4.50
DL	110 × 220	4.33 × 8.66
C7/6	81 × 162	3.19 × 6.38

All sizes in these series have sides in the proportion of 1:√2.
A series is used for writing paper, books, and magazines.
B series for posters.
C series for envelopes.

paperback *noun* a book with a paper binding.

paperboy or **papergirl** *noun* a boy or girl who delivers or sells newspapers.

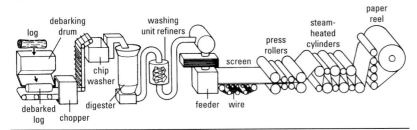

paper-making machine

paper chase a cross-country race in which runners follow a trail of dropped shreds of paper.

paper chromatography *Chem.* a form of chromatography used to analyse complex mixtures of chemical compounds that are applied to one end of a sheet of a special grade of filter paper, which is then suspended vertically in a solvent. The compounds dissolve in the solvent, which moves down the paper by capillary action, different compounds moving at different rates and so becoming physically separated from each other. The distance moved by the various compounds within a certain time can be used to identify them.

paper clip 1 a metal clip formed from bent wire, for holding papers together. 2 a round-headed brass device with two flexible legs that can be pushed through papers, then separated and folded back to secure them.

paper fastener same as PAPER CLIP 2.

paper hanger a person who puts up wallpaper.

paper knife a knife for slitting open envelopes, etc.

paper mâché same as PAPIER-MACHÉ.

paper money bank notes.

paper tiger something or someone more apparently threatening than actually dangerous.

paperweight *noun* a heavy usually ornamental object for holding papers down.

paperwork *noun* routine written work, eg keeping files, writing letters and reports, etc.

papery *adj.* like paper in texture.

Paphos POP (1991e) 31 000, the capital of Paphos district, SW Cyprus, situated on the Mediterranean Sea. During Roman times it was the capital of Cyprus; it is now a holiday resort. NOTABLE FEATURES the old city, probably founded in the Mycenaean period, is a World Heritage site; remains of a Roman villa (House of Dionysus); Byzantine castle (7c); 3c BC 'Tombs of the Kings'; Saranda Kolones (remains of a Byzantine castle); Chrysopolitissa Basilica (early Christian basilica).

papier-mâché *noun* a light material consisting of pulped paper mixed with glue and sometimes other substances, moulded into shape while wet. [from French *papier mâché*, chewed paper]

papilla *noun* Anat. (PL. **papillae**) *Biol.* a small nipple-like projection from the surface of a structure, eg any of the protuberances on the tongue that are associated with the taste buds.

papilloma *noun* Medicine a benign tumour on the surface of the skin or an organ lined with mucous membrane (eg the vagina), such as a wart. [from Latin *papilloma*]

papillon *noun* a breed of toy dog developed in France, which has a small body and a long fine coat that is thickest on the neck, chest, and upper legs. The ears have fringes of hair resembling a butterfly's wings. [from French *papillon*, butterfly]

papist *noun offensive* a Roman Catholic. [from Latin *papa*, pope]

papoose *noun* a Native American baby or young child. [from Narragansett (native American language) *papoos*]

Pappus of Alexandria (4c AD) Greek mathematician. He wrote a mathematical *Collection* covering a wide range of geometrical problems, some of which inspired Descartes and contributed to the development of projective geometry in modern times. It has been of great importance for the understanding of Greek mathematics.

paprika *noun* a powdered seasoning for food, made from red peppers. [from Hungarian *paprika*]

Papua New Guinea, official name **Independent State of Papua New Guinea** POP (1992e) 4.1m, an independent island group in the SW Pacific Ocean, situated 160km/100mi NE of Australia. AREA 462 840sq km/178 656sq mi. It comprises the E half of the island of New Guinea, the Bismarck and Louisiade Archipelagos, the Trobriand and D'Entrecasteaux Is, and other offlying groups. It is divided into 19 provinces and a national capital district. CAPITAL Port Moresby. CHIEF TOWNS Lae, Madang, Rabaul. TIME ZONE GMT +10. Most of the population are of Melanesian origin; Christianity and magico-religious beliefs are followed. OFFICIAL LANGUAGE pidgin English; approximately 750 other languages are spoken. PHYSICAL DESCRIPTION complex system of mountains, with snow-covered peaks rising above 4 000m; the highest point is Mt Wilhelm (4 509m); large rivers flow to the S, N, and E; mainly covered with tropical rainforest; vast mangrove swamps lie along the coast; the archipelago islands are mountainous, mostly volcanic, and fringed with coral reefs. CLIMATE typically monsoonal, with temperatures and humidity constantly high; the average temperature range is 22–33°C; high rainfall, which averages 2 000–2 500mm. HISTORY the British proclaimed a protectorate in SE New Guinea in 1884; some of the islands came under a German protectorate in 1884; German New Guinea was established in the NE in 1899; German colony annexed by Australia in World War I; Australia was mandated to govern both German and British areas in 1920; combined in 1949 as the United Nations Trust Territory of Papua and New Guinea; gained independence within the Commonwealth in 1975; since 1989 there has been fighting between separatists and government forces on the island of Bougainville. GOVERNMENT a Governor-General represents the British Crown; governed by a Prime Minister and Cabinet, with a unicameral 109-member national Parliament elected for five years. ECONOMY over two thirds of the workforce are engaged in farming, fishing, and forestry; yams, sago, cassava, bananas, vegetables, copra, coffee, cocoa, timber, palm oil, rubber, tea, sugar, peanuts; copper, gold; hydro-electric power, natural gas; food processing; brewing; tourism.

papyrus *noun* (PL. **papyri**, **papyruses**) 1 a tall plant (*Cyperus papyrus*) of the sedge family, common in ancient Egypt. The pith from the flowering stems was cut into thin strips, which were then soaked, pressed together into thin sheets, and dried to form a writing material similar to

paper. 2 the writing material prepared from this plant, used by the ancient Egyptians, Greeks, and Romans. 3 an ancient manuscript written on this material. [from Greek *papyros*]

par *noun* 1 a normal level or standard. 2 *Golf* the standard number of strokes that a good golfer would take for a certain course or hole. 3 *Commerce* (also **par of exchange**) the established value of the unit of one national currency against that of another.
— **below** or **not up to par** *colloq.* 1 not up to the usual or required standard. 2 unwell.
on a par with something or **someone** equal to them; the equivalent of them.
par for the course *colloq.* only to be expected; predictable; typical.
[from Latin *par*, equal]

par. or **para.** *abbrev.* paragraph.

par- see PARA-¹.

para *noun colloq.* a paratrooper.

para-¹ or **par-** *combining form* forming words meaning 1 alongside: *parathyroid*. 2 beyond: *parapsychology*. 3 resembling: *paramilitary*. 4 auxiliary: *paramedical*. 5 abnormal: *paraesthesia*. [from Greek *para*]

para-² *combining form* forming words denoting protection: *paratrooper*. [from Latin *parare*, defend]

parable *noun* a story whose purpose is to convey a moral or religious lesson; an allegorical tale. [from Greek *parabole*, analogy]

parabola

parabola *noun* Geom. a conic section produced when a plane intersects a cone parallel to its sloping side. [from Greek *parabole*, placing alongside]
◇ A parabola can also be defined as the locus (path) of a point that moves so that its distance from a fixed point (the *focus*) is equal to its distance from a fixed straight line (the *directrix*). A projectile moving within the Earth's gravitational field follows the path of a parabola. If a source of light or other radiation is placed at the focus of a parabola, it produces a parallel beam (a property that is used in the parabolic reflectors of torches and headlights, and in radio telescopes and radar aerials).

parabolic *adj.* 1 like or expressed in a parable. 2 like or in the form of a parabola.

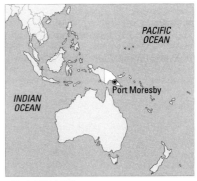

Papua New Guinea

Paracelsus, originally **Theophrastus Bombastus von Hohenheim** (1493–1541) German alchemist, physician, and self-styled seer, born in Einsieden, Switzerland. Thought to have studied in Vienna and Ferrara, he travelled widely in Europe and the Middle East. In 1526 he was appointed town physician in Basle, where he aroused significant antagonism; he was soon forced to leave and finally settled in Salzburg in 1541. As well as mystical tracts, he wrote works on medicine, chemistry, and alchemy. As a physician he had enormous influence, particularly through the emphasis he laid on observation and experiment and the need to assist, rather than hinder, natural processes.

paracetamol *noun* a mild pain-relieving and fever-reducing drug. [from the medical name *para-acetylaminophenol*]

parachute — *noun* an apparatus consisting of a loose umbrella of light fabric, with a harness for attaching to, and slowing the fall of, a person or package dropped from an aircraft. — *verb intrans., trans.* to drop by parachute. [from PARA-[2] + French *chute*, fall]

parachuting the act of jumping out of an aircraft and eventually landing with the aid of a parachute. As a sport, the competitor free-falls for several hundred metres before opening the chute, normally at c.750m. In competition, the object is to land within a predetermined target area. French aeronaut André-Jacques Garnerin (1769–1823) made the first recorded descent over Paris in Oct 1797, when he was released from a balloon.

parachutist *noun* a person who parachutes.

Parade a '*ballet réaliste*' (1917) by the French composer Erik Satie (1866–1925) to a libretto by Jean Cocteau. Among the unusual additions to the orchestra are a revolver and a typewriter. It was first performed by Sergei Diaghilev's Ballets Russes, with set design by Pablo Picasso.

parade — *noun* **1** a ceremonial procession of people, vehicles, etc. **2** *said of soldiers, etc* the state of being drawn up in rank for formal marching or inspection; a body of soldiers, etc drawn up in this way: *be on parade.* **3** a self-advertising display: *make a parade of one's generosity.* **4** used as a name for a promenade, shopping street, etc. — *verb* **1** *intrans., trans.* to walk or cause to walk or march in procession. **2** to display ostentatiously; to flaunt. [from French, from Spanish *parada*, halt, stopping-place]

parade ground the square or yard where soldiers assemble for inspection, marching practice, etc.

paradigm *noun* **1** an example, model, or pattern. **2** *Grammar* a table of the inflected forms of a word serving as a pattern for words of the same declension or conjugation; the words showing a particular pattern. [from Greek *paradeigma*, pattern]

paradigmatic *adj.* serving as a paradigm or example.

paradise *noun* **1** heaven. **2** a place of utter bliss or delight. **3** the Garden of Eden. [from Greek *paradeisos*, park]

Paradise Lost an epic poem in 12 books by John Milton (1667). It is a religious work based on the biblical Fall of Man.

Paradise Regained an epic poem in four books by John Milton (1671). It is a sequel to *Paradise Lost* and focuses on the temptation of Christ in the wilderness.

paradox *noun* **1** a statement that seems to contradict itself, as *more haste, less speed.* **2** a situation involving apparently contradictory elements. **3** *Logic* a proposition that is essentially absurd or leads to an absurd conclusion. [from Greek *paradoxos*, incredible, from *para*, against + *doxa*, opinion]

◇ The form has been used in literary expression from classical times to the present day. It was a

common device of the metaphysical poets and writers of the Restoration period, eg William Congreve; more recent writers who favoured the paradox include George Bernard Shaw, and G K Chesterton. The following example is from George Orwell's *Nineteen Eighty-Four*: War is Peace, Freedom is Slavery, Ignorance is Strength.

paradoxical *adj.* **1** of the nature of a paradox. **2** showing or using paradox. **3** showing contradictions.

paradoxically *adv.* in a paradoxical way.

paradoxical sleep a phase of sleep in which there is increased electrical activity in the brain, and, in humans, dreaming and rapid eye movement.

paraesthesia *noun Medicine* an abnormal tingling sensation, sometimes described as 'pins and needles', and often caused by pressure on a nerve. [from PARA-[1] + Greek *aisthesis*, sensation]

paraffin *noun* **1** a fuel oil obtained from petroleum or coal and used in aircraft, domestic heaters, etc. **2** any of a range of unreactive, saturated hydrocarbons. [from Latin *parum*, little + *affinis*, having an affinity, with reference to its unreactiveness]

paraffin oil **1** *Chem.* a viscous yellow oil made from petroleum and used as a lubricant and a laxative. **2** kerosene.

paraffin wax *Chem.* a white tasteless odourless translucent solid, insoluble in water, consisting of a mixture of solid hydrocarbons obtained from petroleum, and used to make candles, lubricants, polishes, wax crayons, and cosmetics, and for coating paper. — Also called *petroleum wax.*

paraglider *noun Aeron.* a glider with inflatable wings.

paragliding *noun* a sport in which the participant is towed through the air by a light aircraft while wearing a modified type of parachute, then released to drift to the ground.

paragon *noun* someone who is a model of excellence or perfection. [from Old Italian *paragone*, comparison]

paragraph — *noun* **1** a section of a piece of writing, starting on a fresh, often indented, line, and dealing with a distinct point or idea. **2** a short report in a newspaper. **3** (*also* **paragraph mark**) *Printing* a sign (§), indicating the start of a new paragraph. — *verb* to divide (text) into paragraphs. [from Greek *paragraphe*, marked passage, from *para*, beside + *graphein*, to write]

Paraguay, official name **Republic of Paraguay**, Spanish **República del Paraguay** POP (1992) 4.1m, a landlocked country in central S America, divided into two regions and split into 19 departments and the national capital. AREA 406 750sq km/157 000sq mi. It is bounded NW by Bolivia, N and E by Brazil, and SW by Argentina. CAPITAL Asunción. time zone GMT –3. The population is mainly mixed Spanish–Guaraní (95%); Roman Catholicism is the chief religion. OFFICIAL LANGUAGE Spanish; Guaraní is also spoken. CURRENCY the guaraní. PHYSICAL DESCRIPTION divided into two regions by the R Paraguay, lying mostly at altitudes below 450m; bordered S and E by the R Paraná; the Gran Chaco in the W is mostly cattle country or scrub forest; more fertile land lies in the E; the Paraná Plateau at 300–600m is mainly wet, treeless savannah. CLIMATE tropical NW, with hot summers, warm winters, and rainfall up to 1 250mm; temperate SE, with rainfall up to 1 750mm; the temperature at Asunción ranges from 12°C in winter to 35°C in summer. history originally inhabited by Guaranís; arrival of the Spanish in 1537; arrival of Jesuit missionaries in 1609; gained independence from Spain in 1811; War of the Triple Alliance against Brazil, Argentina, and Uruguay between 1864 and 1870, when Paraguay lost over half of its population; regained disputed territory in 1935 after the three-year Chaco War with Bolivia; civil war in 1947; General Alfredo Stroessner seized power in

1954, and was appointed President, being forced to stand down following a coup in 1989. GOVERNMENT a President elected for five years and a bicameral National Congress consisting of a Chamber of Deputies and a Senate; no one having held the office of President may be re-elected. ECONOMY agriculture employs 40% of the labour force; oilseed, cotton, wheat, manioc, sweet potato, tobacco, corn, rice, sugar cane; livestock rearing; meat packing; pulp; timber; textiles; fertilizers; cement; kaolin; glass.

Paraguay

Paraguay, River, Portuguese **Rio Paraguai** a river in central S America and a chief tributary of the R Paraná. It is 2 300km/1 450mi long. The river rises in Brazil (Mato Grosso) and flows S, forming part of the Brazil–Bolivia, Brazil–Paraguay, and Paraguay–Argentina borders, flowing into the Paraná above Corrientes, Argentina. It is used widely by local river traffic.

parakeet *noun* any of various small, long-tailed parrots. [from Old French *paroquet*, parrot]

paralanguage *noun* those elements of communication other than words, ie tone of voice, gesture, or body language, facial expression, etc.

paraldehyde *noun Chem.* (FORMULA $C_6H_{12}O_3$) a colourless flammable toxic liquid that is a polymer of acetaldehyde, and is used as a solvent and sleep-inducing drug.

parallax *noun* **1** *Physics* the apparent change in the position of an object, relative to a distant background, when it is viewed from two different positions. **2** *Astron.* the angle between two straight lines joining two different observation points to a celestial body. Parallax is used to measure the distance of stars from the Earth. [from Greek *parallaxis*, change]

parallel — *adj.* (*often* **parallel to something**) **1** *said of lines or planes* being at every point the same distance apart. **2** similar; exactly equivalent; corresponding. — *adv.* (*often* **parallel to something**) alongside and at an unvarying distance from. — *noun* **1** *Geom.* a line or plane parallel to another. **2** a corresponding or equivalent instance. **3** (*also* **parallel of latitude**) any of the lines of latitude circling the earth parallel to the equator and representing the angular degrees of distance from it. **4** (**parallels**) *Printing* the sign (‖) used as a reference mark. — *verb* (**paralleled**, **paralleling**) **1** to equal. **2** to correspond to or be equivalent to.

— **in parallel** *said of electrical appliances* so co-ordinated that terminals of the same polarity are connected.

on a parallel with something corresponding to it.

without parallel unequalled; unprecedented. [from Greek *parallelos*, side by side]

parallel bars two parallel shoulder-height rails fixed to upright posts, used by men for gymnastic exercises.

parallel circuit *Physics* an electrical circuit in which only a fraction of the total current flows through each of the circuit components, because they are arranged in such a way that the current is split between two or more parallel paths.

parallelism *noun* **1** being parallel. **2** resemblance in corresponding details.

parallelogram *noun Geom.* a four-sided plane (two-dimensional) figure in which opposite sides are parallel and equal in length, and opposite angles are equal. A parallelogram in which all four sides are of equal length is known as a *rhombus*.

parallelogram of vectors *Maths.* a figure that is constructed in order to add two vectors, by drawing them to scale so that they form two adjacent sides of the parallelogram, and then completing the remaining two sides of the figure. The diagonal of the parallelogram, from the angle between the two added vectors, is equal to their sum.

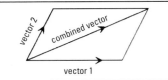

parallelogram of vectors

paralympics *noun* an Olympic competition for people with physical disabilities, held at the same time as the traditional Olympic games. [from PARALLEL + OLYMPICS]

paralyse *verb* **1** to affect (a person or bodily part) with paralysis. **2** *said of fear, etc* to have an immobilizing effect. **3** to disrupt or bring to a standstill. [from Greek *paralyein*, to enfeeble]

paralysis *noun* **1** a temporary or permanent loss of muscular function or sensation in any part of the body, the most commonly affected muscles being those that are normally under voluntary control. It is usually caused by damage to the motor nerves or central nervous system (the brain and spinal cord), eg as a result of disease or injury. **2** a state of immobility; a standstill.

paralytic — *adj.* **1** relating to, caused by, or suffering from paralysis. **2** *colloq.* helplessly drunk. — *noun* a person affected by paralysis.

paralytically *adv.* so as to be paralytic.

Paramaribo POP (1990e) 200 000, the federal capital of Surinam. It is the chief port and the only large town in the country, on the R Suriname. HISTORY founded by the French in 1540; became the capital of the country, then under British rule, in 1650; came under Dutch rule in 1816. NOTABLE FEATURES People's Palace

(former governor's mansion); Fort Zeelandia; cathedral (19c).

Paramecium *noun* a single-celled protozoan, common in aquatic habitats, ovoid in shape, and up to 0.33mm in length. Its cell contains two types of nucleus (a macronucleus and a micronucleus), and it feeds by ingestion of bacteria. Its surface is uniformly covered with hair-like processes known as cilia. [from Greek *paramekes*, long-shaped]

paramedic *noun* a person, such as a technician or member of an ambulance crew, who helps medical staff or whose work supplements medical work.

paramedical *adj. Medicine* denoting personnel or services that are supplementary to and support the work of the medical profession, eg nursing staff, physiotherapists, and ambulance crews.

parameter *noun* **1** *Maths.* a constant or variable that, when altered, affects the form of a mathematical expression in which it appears. **2** *Physics* a quantity which under a particular set of conditions remains constant, but may be altered if the conditions change. **3** (*often* **parameters**) a limiting factor that serves to define the scope of a task, project, discussion, etc. [from modern Latin *parametrum*, from PARA-¹ + Greek *metron*, measure]

paramilitary *adj.* organized on the same basis as a military force, and usually reinforcing it.

paramount *adj.* foremost; supreme; of supreme importance. [from Old French *par*, by + *amont*, above, upwards]

Paraná, River, in Brazil **Alto Parana** a major river in S America. It forms, with its tributaries (notably the Paraguay) and the R Uruguay, S America's second-largest drainage system. The river rises in E central Brazil and flows generally S along Paraguay's E and S border into Argentina. There it joins the Uruguay after 3 300km/2 000mi to form the estuary of the R Plate on the Atlantic. The river is dammed at various points for hydroelectricity, with a major scheme at Itaipu in Brazil.

paranoia *noun* **1** *Psychol.* a rare mental disorder, characterized by delusions of persecution by others, especially if this is attributed to one's own importance or unique gifts. It is not usually accompanied by other symptoms of mental illness. **2** a strong feeling that one is being persecuted by others, resulting in a tendency to be suspicious and distrustful, and to become increasingly isolated. [from Greek *paranoia*, from *para*, beside, beyond + *nous*, mind]

paranoiac *or* **paranoid** — *adj.* relating to or affected by paranoia. — *noun* a person affected by paranoia.

paranoiacally *adv.* in a paranoiac way.

paranormal — *adj.*, *said of occurrences* beyond the normal scope of scientific explanation. — *noun* (**the paranormal**) paranormal occurrences.

parapet *noun* **1** a low wall along the edge of a bridge, balcony, etc. **2** an embankment of earth

or sandbags protecting the soldiers in a military trench. [from Italian *parapetto*, from *parare*, to defend + *petto*, chest]

paraphernalia *pl. noun* **1** the equipment and accessories associated with an activity, etc. **2** personal belongings. [from Greek *parapherna*, a bride's personal effects, ie not part of her dowry, from *para*, beside + *pherne*, dowry]

paraphrase — *noun* a restatement of something giving its meaning in other words; a rewording or re-phrasing. — *verb* to express in other words. [from PARA-¹ + Greek *phrazein*, to speak]

paraplegia *noun Medicine* paralysis of the lower half of the body, including both legs, usually caused by injury or disease of the spinal cord. [from Greek *paraplegia*, a one-sided stroke, from *para*, beside + *plege*, blow]

paraplegic — *adj.* **1** affected with paraplegia. **2** marked by or typical of paraplegia. — *noun* a person affected with paraplegia.

parapsychological *adj.* relating to or involving parapsychology.

parapsychologist *noun* a person who studies parapsychology.

parapsychology *noun* the study of those mental phenomena, eg telepathy and clairvoyance, that imply an acquisition of knowledge otherwise than through the known senses.

Paraquat *noun trademark* a weedkiller highly poisonous to humans. [from part of the technical description of the chemical]

parasailing *noun* a sport similar to paragliding in which the participant is towed into the air by a motorboat, wearing water-skis and a modified type of parachute. [from PARA-² + SAIL]

parasite *noun* **1** a plant or animal that for all or part of its life obtains food and physical protection from a living organism of another species (the *host*), which is usually damaged by the presence of the parasite, and never benefits from the association. An *obligate* parasite can only survive in partnership with a host, whereas a *facultative* parasite is capable of independent existence. Many parasites cause important diseases, eg rust fungi are serious pests of crops. Human parasites include fleas, tapeworms, etc. **2** *derog.* a person who lives at the expense of others. [from PARA-¹ + Greek *sitos*, food]

parasitic *or* **parasitical** *adj.* **1** *said of an animal or plant* living on another. **2** *said of a person* depending on others.

parasitically *adv.* in a parasitic way; as a parasite.

parasitism *noun* a close association between two living organisms in which one (the parasite) obtains food and physical protection from the other (the host).

parasitology *noun Zool.* the scientific study of parasites, especially protozoans, worms, and arthropods (eg mosquitoes, lice) that cause or transmit diseases to humans and animals.

parasol *noun* a light umbrella used as a protection against the sun; a sunshade. [from French, from Italian *parasole*, from *parare*, to ward off + *sole*, sun]

Parasurama in Hindu mythology, a Brahman warrior, the son of Jamadagni. He fought 21 battles to free the world from the oppressive Kshatriya warriors, and poured the blood of his victims into five holes in the earth.

parasympathetic nervous system *Zool.* in vertebrates, a subdivision of the autonomic nervous system. The activity of the parasympathetic nervous system tends to slow down the heart rate, promote digestion, dilate blood vessels, and generally conserve energy by decreasing the activity of the glands and smooth muscles. It has the opposite effects to the sympathetic

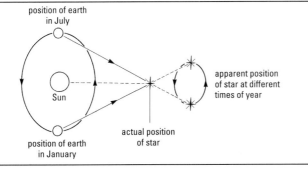

parallax

nervous system. See also SYMPATHETIC NERVOUS SYSTEM.

parathormone *noun Physiol.* parathyroid hormone.

parathyroid *noun Physiol.* in mammals, any of four small glands near or within the thyroid, producing parathyroid hormone.

parathyroid hormone *Medicine* a hormone, released by the parathyroid glands in response to low blood calcium levels, that raises blood calcium levels by stimulating the removal of calcium from bone, and inhibiting its excretion by the kidneys. — Also called *parathormone*.

paratrooper *noun* a member of the paratroops.

paratroops *pl. noun* troops trained to parachute into enemy territory or a battle zone.

paratyphoid *noun Medicine* an infectious disease, similar to but milder than typhoid fever, caused by the bacterium *Salmonella paratyphi*, and characterized by a pink rash, fever, abdominal pain, and diarrhoea. Outbreaks of the disease are linked to poor sanitation and the consumption of contaminated food.

parboil *verb* to boil until partially cooked. [from Old French *parboillir*, from Latin *perbullire*, to boil thoroughly; meaning altered by confusion of *par-* with PART]

Parcae in Roman mythology, the three Fates, who were originally birth-goddesses. They were later identified with the Greek Moerae, the goddesses who allot the destiny of human beings.

Parc des Princes a sports stadium in Paris, S of the Bois de Boulogne. It is the traditional home of the French football and rugby union teams.

parcel — *noun* 1 something wrapped in paper, etc and secured with string or sticky tape. 2 a portion, eg of land. 3 a group of people, etc. 4 a lot or portion of goods for sale; a deal or transaction. — *verb* (**parcelled**, **parcelling**) 1 (*also* **parcel something up**) to wrap it up in a parcel. 2 (*also* **parcel something out**) to divide into portions and share out. [from Old French *parcelle*, from Latin *particula*, diminutive of *pars*, part]

parch *verb* 1 to dry up; to deprive (soil, plants, etc) of water. 2 to make thirsty. 3 to roast (peas) slightly. [from Middle English *perchen*]

parchment *noun* 1 a material formerly used for bookbinding and for writing on, made from goatskin, calfskin, or sheepskin; a piece of this, or a manuscript written on it. 2 stiff off-white writing-paper resembling this. [from Old French *parchemin* from Latin *Pergamena charta*, paper of Pergamum, influenced by Old French *parche*, leather]

pardon — *verb* (**pardoned**, **pardoning**) 1 to forgive or excuse (someone) for (a fault or offence). 2 to cancel the punishment of. — *noun* 1 forgiveness. 2 the cancellation of a punishment. — **I beg your pardon** *or* **pardon me** a formula of apology, or (*often shortened to* **pardon**) a request to repeat something said. [from French *pardonner*, from Latin *perdonare*, to overlook]

pardonable *adj.* that may be pardoned; excusable.

pardonably *adv.* in a pardonable way.

Pardoner, the the foppish cleric in Chaucer's *The Canterbury Tales*, whose tale reflects his own standing as a confidence trickster.

pardoner *noun* in the Middle Ages, a person licensed to sell pardons from the pope, freeing people from punishment for their sins.

pare *verb* 1 (*also* **pare something away**) to trim off (skin, etc) in layers. 2 to cut (fingernails or toenails). 3 to peel (fruit). 4 (*also* **pare something down**) to reduce expenses, funding, etc

gradually, in order to economize. [from French *parer*, from Latin *parare*, to prepare]

parechyma *noun* 1 *Bot.* in plants, a tissue composed of thin-walled relatively unspecialized cells, that serves mainly as a packing tissue. 2 *Zool.* the loosely packed cells that form much of the body tissue of simple animals such as flatworms. [from PARA-[1] + Greek *enchyma*, infusion]

parent — *noun* 1 a father or mother. 2 the adopter or guardian of a child. 3 an animal or plant that has produced offspring. 4 that from which anything is derived; a source or origin. — *verb intrans., trans.* to be or act as a parent; to care for as a parent. [from Latin *parens*, from *parere*, to bring forth]

parentage *noun* family or ancestry.

parental *adj.* related to or concerning parents.

parentally *adv.* in a parental way; by parents.

parent company a business company owning other, usually smaller companies.

parenthesis *noun* (PL. **parentheses**) 1 a word or phrase inserted into a sentence as a comment, usually marked off by brackets or dashes. 2 (**parentheses**) a pair of round brackets ( ) used to enclose such a comment. [from PARA-[1] + Greek *en*, in + *thesis*, placing]

parenthetic *or* **parenthetical** *adj.* 1 of the nature of a parenthesis. 2 using parenthesis.

parenthetically *adv.* in a parenthetic way; in parenthesis.

parenthood *noun* 1 being a parent. 2 the responsibilities of a parent.

parenting *noun* the activities and duties of a parent.

Parent–Teacher Association (ABBREV. **PTA**) an organization within a school for bringing parents and teachers together to discuss education and matters affecting the general running of the school, eg fund-raising.

par excellence in the highest degree; in the truest sense of the word; beyond compare. [French, = as an example of excellence]

pariah *noun* 1 someone scorned and avoided by others; a social outcast. 2 in S India and Burma, a person of no, or low, caste. [from Tamil *paraiyan*, drummer]

Paricutín an active volcano in W Michoacán, W central Mexico. HEIGHT 2 774m. An eruption in 1943 buried the town of San Juan and church spires are now all that can be seen.

parietal *adj.* relating to, or forming, the wall of a bodily cavity, eg the skull: *the parietal bones*. [from Latin *paries*, wall]

Paris, also called **Alexander** in Greek legend, a prince of Troy, the son of Priam and Hecuba. He was abandoned by his family on Mt Ida because of a prophecy, and was brought up as a shepherd. He chose Aphrodite as the fairest of three goddesses ('the judgement of Paris') because she offered him the most beautiful woman in the world. His subsequent abduction of Helen caused the Trojan War, during which he killed Achilles and was himself killed by the archer Philoctetes.

Paris, Count the wealthy nobleman in Shakespeare's *Romeo and Juliet*, who offers to marry Juliet and is killed by Romeo.

Paris, Matthew see MATTHEW PARIS.

Pa`ris, ancient **Lutetia** POP (1990) 9.1m, the capital of France, of Ile-de-France region, and of Ville de Paris department, lying on the R Seine. The Seine is spanned here by 30 bridges, the oldest being the Pont Neuf (1578–1604). The city is bounded by the Bois de Boulogne in the W and the Bois de Vincennes in the E. It is divided into 20 arrondissements, but is often more simply divided between the 'Left Bank' (formerly associated with the aristocracy) and the 'Right Bank' (formerly associated with the middle class). Paris is one of the world's main tourist destinations

with famous hotels, night clubs, theatres, restaurants, and shops. It is also one of the world's most densely-populated capitals. It serves as the headquarters of many international organizations, notably UNESCO. Renowned for its luxury goods such as perfume and jewellery, it is a world centre of haute couture. Montparnasse and the Latin Quarter are traditionally associated with artists and writers. HISTORY originally a Roman settlement, it was capital of the Frankish kingdom in the 6c; it was established as the capital of France in 987. NOTABLE FEATURES Arc de Triomphe (at the focal point of 12 avenues); Champs Elysées; Place de la Concorde; Centre Pompidou (1977); Louvre; Church of La Madeleine (1861–75); Tuileries Gardens; Eiffel Tower (1889); Hôtel des Invalides (with the tomb of Napoleon); Jardins des Plantes (1626); Luxembourg Palace; Notre-Dame Cathedral (1163); many art galleries and museums, notably the Musée d'Orsay; Sorbonne University (12c); horse racing takes place at Longchamp, Vincennes, and Auteuil. [named after the Parisii, a Celtic tribe]

Paris, School of a term in art history which applies to Paris in the 13c as the European centre for illuminated manuscripts and, in the 20c, as the focus of most of the modern art movements (c.1900–50).

Paris, Siege of a siege on Paris carried out (1870–1) by the Prussian Army, during which food shortages forced the Government of National Defence to ask for an armistice. The hysterical atmosphere of the siege, and the existence of the National Guard, which was not disarmed by the terms of the armistice, were important causes of the insurrection of 18 Mar, leading to the Paris Commune.

Paris, Treaties of successive peace settlements (1814–15) involving France and the victorious coalition of Britain, Austria, Prussia, Russia, Sweden, and Portugal, restoring the Bourbon monarchy to France in place of the Napoleonic Empire, before and after the Hundred Days (1815). In 1815 a large indemnity and army of occupation replaced the generous terms of 1814.

Paris, Treaty of 1 (1763) the peace settlement that ended the Seven Years War (1756–63), signed by Britain, France, and Spain. Spain surrendered Florida to the British, but received the Louisiana Territory and New Orleans from France, and Havana and Manila from Britain. France ceded Canada, America east of the Mississippi, Cape Breton and the St Lawrence islands, Dominica, Tobago, the Grenadines, and Senegal to Britain. 2 (30 Mar 1856) the treaty that ended the Crimean War and enshrined the defeat of Russia by Britain and France. Russia was made to cede S Bessarabia to Moldavia, give up its virtual protectorate over Moldavia and Wallachia, and accept the neutrality of the Black Sea, including the dismantling of its own coastal fortresses. The Ottoman Empire was admitted to the so-called Concert of European Powers, but did not keep its promise to respect the rights of its subjects. Russia was driven back in on itself and under Alexander II embarked upon its first serious programme of domestic reform. 3 (10 Feb 1947) the treaty that exacted indemnities from nations allied with Germany during World War II, and by which Italy was obliged to surrender the Dodecanese Islands to Greece.

Paris, University of a university founded (c.1170) on the Left Bank of the R Seine in Paris. Thomas Aquinas, Bonaventure, and Alexander of Hales were among those who taught there during the 13c, and in 1253 the college of Sorbonne was founded as part of the University by Robert de Sorbon (1201–74). As a result of student demands for educational reform in May 1968, the University was re-organized into 13 independent faculties, known as *Universités de Paris I à XIII*.

Paris Commune an uprising (18 Mar–28 May 1871) that followed France's humiliating defeat in the Franco-Prussian War. An attempt to disarm the National Guard resulted in an insurrection and the election of a municipal council or Commune. The government, headed by the veteran Orléanist Adolphe Thiers, retreated to Versailles, where the monarchist National Assembly refused all compromise. Forces were gathered and Paris recaptured after heavy loss of life, leaving an unprecedented legacy of bitterness.

parish *noun* **1** a district or area served by its own church and priest or minister. **2** (*also* **civil parish**) especially in England, the smallest unit of local government. **3** the inhabitants of a parish. [from Old French *paroisse*, from Greek *paroikia*, from *paroikos*, neighbour]

parish clerk an official performing various duties connected with a parish church.

parish council the administrative body of a civil parish.

parish councillor a member of a parish council.

parishioner *noun* a member or inhabitant of a parish.

parish register a book in which the christenings, marriages, and deaths in a parish are recorded.

Paris Opéra, properly **Théâtre National de l'Opéra** a French opera company, formed from the Académie de Musique in 1672. In the 19c it was noted for its productions of grand opera.

Paris Pacts a series (1954) of amendments and protocols to the Treaty of Brussels and the Brussels Treaty Organization. Italy and the Federal Republic of Germany became members of what was later known as the Western European Union. Germany agreed not to manufacture atomic, bacteriological, or chemical weapons, which cleared the way for its rearmament and membership of NATO.

Paris Peace Conference 1 a meeting (1919–20) of 32 'allied and associated powers' who met in Paris to draw up a peace settlement after World War I. Five treaties were concluded: with Germany (Treaty of Versailles, 1919), Austria (Treaty of St Germain, 1919), Hungary (Treaty of Trianon, 1920), Bulgaria (Treaty of Neuilly, 1919), and Turkey (Treaties of Sèvres, 1920, and Lausanne, 1923). **2** the meetings (1946–7) of the five members of the Council of Foreign Ministers — the main World War II Allies (USA, Russia, UK, France, and China) — and delegates from 16 other nations involved against the Axis powers, which resulted in peace treaties with Bulgaria, Finland, Hungary, Romania, and Italy.

parity *noun* (PL. **parities**) **1** equality, eg in pay. **2** precise equivalence; exact correspondence. **3** *Commerce* an established equivalence between a unit of national currency and an amount in another national currency. [from Latin *paritas*, from *par*, equal]

Park, Mungo (1771–1806) Scottish explorer of Africa, born in Fowlshiels, Selkirk. He became a surgeon in Edinburgh, and in 1792 served on an expedition to Sumatra. In 1795–6 he made a journey along the Niger River, recounted in *Travels in the Interior of Africa* (1799). He settled as a surgeon in Peebles, then in 1805 undertook another journey to the Niger. His expedition reached Bussa, where he was drowned following an attack by natives.

park — *noun* **1** an area in a town with grass and trees, reserved for public recreation. **2** an area of land kept as a nature reserve, etc: *a wildlife park*. **3** the woodland and pasture forming the estate of a large country house. **4** (**Park**) used in street names. **5** *chiefly North Amer.* a sports field or stadium. **6** (**the park**) *colloq.* the pitch in use in a football game. **7** a place where vehicles can be

left temporarily. — *verb* **1** *trans., intrans.* to leave (a vehicle) temporarily at the side of the road or in a car park; to manoeuvre (a vehicle) into this position. **2** *colloq.* to lay, place, or leave (something) somewhere temporarily. **3** *colloq.* to install or sit (oneself). [from Old French *parc*]

parka *noun* **1** a hooded jacket made of skins, worn by the Inuit and Aleut people of the Arctic. **2** a windproof jacket, especially quilted with a fur-trimmed hood; an anorak. [from Aleut *parka*, skin, coat, from Russian *parka*, pelt, skin jacket]

park-and-ride *noun* a system of travel to an urban centre by means of bus and train links from large car parks on the outskirts.

Parker, Charlie (Charles Christopher, Jr), also called **Bird**, or **Yardbird** (1920–55) US jazz saxophonist, bandleader, and composer, born in Kansas City, Kansas. A very influential performer in post-1940s modern jazz, he worked with Jay McShann's orchestra, then joined such musicians as Dizzy Gillespie and Thelonious Monk to develop the new jazz idiom 'bebop'. Despite his heroin addiction, he continued into the 1950s leading the style-setting small groups of modern jazz, which included the trumpeter Miles Davis. Many of his compositions (eg 'Now's the Time' and 'Ornithology') have become standard jazz works. In 1988 Clint Eastwood's film *Bird* presented an entertaining but sanitized version of his life.

Parker, Dorothy, *née* **Rothschild** (1893–1967) US writer, born in West End, New Jersey. She worked as a drama critic for *Vanity Fair* and the *New Yorker*, then became a freelance writer. She was noted for her satirical humour, as shown in her verse collections which include *Enough Rope* (1926), and her short stories which include *Here Lies* (1939).

Parker, Matthew (1504–75) English prelate, the second Protestant Archbishop of Canterbury, born in Norwich, Norfolk. He became chaplain to Anne Boleyn (1535) and later Dean of Lincoln, was deprived of his preferments by Mary I, but made Archbishop of Canterbury by Elizabeth I (1559). He adopted a middle road between Catholic and Puritan extremes, and revised the Thirty-Nine Articles of Anglican doctrine (1562).

parkin *noun* a moist ginger-flavoured oatmeal cake made with treacle.

parking-lot *noun North Amer.* a car park.

parking-meter *noun* a coin-operated meter in the street beside which a car may be parked for a limited period.

parking-ticket *noun* an official notice of a fine served on a motorist for illegal parking.

Parkinson, C(yril) Northcote (1909–93) English writer, historian, and political scientist, born in Barnard Castle, Durham. He was Professor of History at Malaya (1950–8) and visiting Professor at Harvard (1958), and Illinois and California (1959–60). He wrote many works on historical, political, and economic subjects, but achieved wider renown by his serio-comic tilt at bureaucratic malpractices in *Parkinson's Law: the Pursuit of Progress* (1957). 'Parkinson's Law' — that work expands to fill the time available for its completion, and subordinates multiply at a fixed rate, regardless of the amount of work produced — has passed into the language.

Parkinson, James (1755–1824) English physician and amateur palaeontologist. In 1817 he gave the first description of paralysis agitans, or Parkinson's disease. He had already described appendicitis and perforation (1812), and was the first to recognize the latter condition as a cause of death.

parkinsonism *noun Medicine* the symptoms of Parkinson's disease, which have developed as a complication of another disease, such as encephalitis, or as a side-effect of certain drugs. [named after James Parkinson]

Parkinson's disease *Medicine* a slowly progressive disorder of the central nervous system that usually occurs later in life. The main symptoms are trembling of the muscles of the hands and limbs, a mask-like facial expression, slowing of voluntary movements, muscular weakness, a flat voice, and a slow shuffling gait and stooping posture. [named after James Parkinson]
◇ Parkinson's disease is caused by degeneration of the neurones of the basal ganglia (masses of nerve cell bodies) in the brain. These neurones secrete the neurotransmitter *dopamine*, lack of which impairs the control of muscle movement and tone. There is no cure for the disease, but it may respond to various drugs, including *levodopa*, which is a precursor of dopamine.

Parkinson's law the maxim that work expands to fill the time available for its completion. [from C Northcote Parkinson]

parkland *noun* pasture and woodland forming part of a country estate.

parkway *noun* a broad thoroughfare incorporating grassy areas and lined with trees, often connecting the parks of a town.

parky *adj.* (**parkier, parkiest**) *Brit. colloq.*, *said of the weather* somewhat cold; chilly.

parlance *noun* a particular style of using words: *in legal parlance*. [from Old French, from *parler*, to talk]

parley — *verb intrans.* (**parleys, parleyed**) to discuss peace terms, etc with an enemy. — *noun* (PL. **parleys**) a meeting with an enemy to discuss peace terms, etc. [from Old French *parler*, to talk]

parliament *noun* the highest law-making assembly of a nation; (**Parliament**) in Britain, the House of Commons and House of Lords. [from Old French *parlement*, from *parler*, to talk]

parliamentarian *noun* **1** an expert in parliamentary procedure. **2** an experienced parliamentary debater. **3** *Hist.* a supporter of the Parliamentary party in the 17c English Civil War.

parliamentary *adj.* **1** relating to, or issued by, a parliament. **2** *said of conduct or procedure* in keeping with the rules of parliament. **3** *said of language* admissible in parliament.

Parliamentary Commissioner for Administration the British ombudsman for central administration, established in 1967. A servant of parliament, the Commissioner examines complaints of maladministration (which have to be channelled through MPs), and works closely with a House of Commons select committee.

parlour *noun* **1** a sitting-room for receiving visitors. **2** a shop or commercial premises providing particular goods or services: *an ice-cream parlour / beauty parlour / funeral parlour* etc. [from Old French *parlur*, from *parler*, to talk]

parlour game a game such as charades, suitable for playing in the sitting-room.

parlous *adj.* precarious; perilous; dire. [a variant of PERILOUS]

Parma POP (1991e) 174 000, the capital of Parma province, Emilia-Romagna region, N Italy. It lies on the R Parma, 126km/78mi SE of Milan and was a major cultural centre during the Middle Ages. Parmesan cheese is produced here, as well as the famed Parma ham. NOTABLE FEATURES baptistery (12c–13c); cathedral (12c); Palazzo della Pilotta (begun in 1583); Church of the Madonna della Steccata (1521–39), modelled on St Peter's in Rome.

Parmenides (c.515–c.445 BC) Greek Presocratic philosopher from the settlement of Elea in S Italy, the founder of the Eleatic school. He was the first philosopher to insist on a distinction between the world of appearances and reality, and in *On Nature*, he advocated the view that everything was permanently in a state of 'being' — non-existence was simply an illusory state.

Parmesan *noun* a hard dry Italian cheese, especially served grated with pasta dishes. [from Italian *Parmegiano*, from Parma]

Parmigiano *or* **Parmigianino**, pseudonym of **Girolamo Francesco Maria Mazzola** (1503–40) Italian painter of the Lombard School, born in Parma. He began to paint in Parma, moved to Rome in 1523, but was forced to flee to Bologna when the city was sacked in 1527. In Bologna he painted a Madonna altarpiece for the nuns of St Margaret before returning to Parma in 1531. His work there includes *Madonna of the Long Neck* (c.1535, Uffizi, Florence).

Parnassians a group of 19c French poets associated with the journal *Le Parnasse Contemporain* (1866–76), who advocated a move away from Romanticism to a more austere and objective poetry They included Charles Leconte de Lisle (1818–94), José Heredia (1842–1905), and Sully-Prudhomme (1839–1907).

Parnell, Charles Stewart (1846–91) Irish politician, born in Avondale, Co Wicklow. He became an MP in 1875, supported Home Rule, and gained popularity in Ireland by his audacious use of obstructive parliamentary tactics. In 1878 he was elected President of the Irish National Land League, and in 1886 allied with the Liberals in support of Gladstone's Home Rule bill. He remained an influential figure until 1890, when he was cited as co-respondent in a divorce case, and was forced to retire as leader of the Irish Nationalists.

parochial *adj.* **1** *derog.* concerned only with local affairs; narrow, limited, or provincial in outlook. **2** of, or relating to, a parish. [from Latin *parochialis*, from *parochia*, parish]

parochialism *noun* **1** narrowness of view, provincialism. **2** a system of local government based on the parish as a unit.

parochially *adv.* in a parochial way.

parodist *noun* the author of a parody.

parody — *noun* (PL. **parodies**) **1** a comic or satirical imitation of a work, or the style, of a particular writer, composer, etc. **2** a poor attempt at something; a mockery or travesty. — *verb* (**parodies**, **parodied**) to ridicule through parody; to mimic satirically. [from PARA-[1] + Greek *oide*, song] ◇ Literary examples include Cervantes' *Don Quixote* (a parody of medieval romances), Shakespeare's *Hamlet* and *Love's Labour Lost*, Max Beerbohm's *A Christmas Garland* (1912), and Stella Gibbons's *Cold Comfort Farm* (1932).

parole — *noun* **1** the release of a prisoner before the end of his or her sentence, on promise of good behaviour: *released on parole.* **2** the promise of a prisoner so released to behave well. — *verb* to release or place (a prisoner) on parole. [from French *parole d'honneur*, word of honour]

Parolles the boasting, cowardly companion of Bertram in Shakespeare's *All's Well that Ends Well.*

Paros POP (1982) 3 000, the third-largest island of the Cyclades, Greece, in the S Aegean Sea, W of Naxos. AREA 195sq km/75sq mi. Parikia is the chief town.

parousia *noun* *Relig.* the second coming of Christ. In Christian thought, it will be marked by a heavenly appearance, God's judgement of all humanity, and the resurrection of the dead. [from Greek *parousia*, prescence, arrival]

paroxysm *noun* **1** a sudden emotional outburst, eg of rage or laughter. **2** a spasm, convulsion, or seizure, eg of coughing or acute pain. **3** a sudden reappearance of or increase in the severity of the symptoms of a disease or disorder. [from Greek *paroxysmos*, a fit]

paroxysmal *adj.* relating to or of the nature of a paroxysm; marked by paroxysms.

parquet *noun* flooring composed of small inlaid blocks of wood arranged in a geometric pattern. [from Old French, diminutive of *parc*, enclosure]

parquetry *noun* inlaid work in wood used for flooring.

Parr, Catherine (1512–48) queen-consort of Henry VIII as his sixth wife, the daughter of Sir Thomas Parr of Kendal. She married first Edward Borough, then Lord Latimer, before she became Queen of England (1643). A learned and tactful woman, she persuaded Henry to restore the succession to his daughters and showed her stepchildren much kindness. Shortly after Henry's death (1547) she married a former suitor, Lord Thomas Seymour of Sudeley, and died in childbirth the following year.

parr *noun* (PL. **parr**, **parrs**) a young salmon aged up to two years.

parricidal *adj.* relating to or involving parricide.

parricide *noun* the killing of, or a person who kills, a parent or near relative. [from Latin *parricidium* (the killing), *parricida* (the killer), probably from *pater*, father + *caedere*, to kill]

parrot — *noun* **1** any of about 317 species of bird, including the cockatoos, lories, macaws, parakeets, budgerigars, and lovebirds, found in forests in most of the warmer regions of the world. All parrots have large heads, short necks, strong hooked bills, short stout legs, and two of the four toes pointing backwards, enabling them to grip branches firmly and to hold food with one foot. They usually have brightly coloured plumage, and their long lifespan, agility, and ability to mimic human speech make them popular cage birds. Owing to destruction of tropical forests and trade in exotic species, parrots are among the most endangered bird species. **2** a person who merely imitates or mimics others. — *verb* (**parroted**, **parroting**) to repeat or mimic (another's words, etc) unthinkingly. [from Old French *paroquet*, perhaps diminutive of *Pierre*]

parrot-fashion *adv.* by mindless repetition.

parrotfish *noun* a colourful fish, so called because the jaw teeth are fused into a parrot-like beak that is used for scraping algal and coral growth from reefs.

Parry, Sir (Charles) Hubert (Hastings) (1848–1918) English composer, born in Bournemouth, Hampshire. He was a professor at the Royal College of Music (1883), Professor of Music at Oxford (1900), and wrote three oratorios, an opera, five symphonies, and many other works. His best-known work is his unison chorus 'Jerusalem' (1916), sung as an unofficial anthem at the end of each season of Promenade Concerts in London.

Parry, Joseph (1841–1903) Welsh musician, born in Merthyr Tydfil, Glamorgan. He was professor at University College, Cardiff, and composed oratorios, operas, and songs. One of the leading hymn-writers in the Welsh tradition, his best-known hymn tune is *Aberystwyth*.

parry — *verb* (**parries**, **parried**) **1** to fend off (a blow). **2** to sidestep (a question) adroitly. — *noun* (PL. **parries**) an act of parrying. [from French *parer*, to ward off]

parse *verb trans., intrans.* **1** *Grammar* to analyse (a sentence) grammatically; to give the part of speech and explain the grammatical role of (a word). **2** *Comput.* to analyse (a string of input symbols) in terms of the computing language being used. [from Latin *pars orationis*, part of speech]

parsec *noun* *Astron.* a unit of distance in space equal to 3.26 light years or 3.09×10^{13}km, used for distances that extend beyond the Solar System. [from PARALLAX + SECOND]

Parsee *noun* one of the descendants of the ancient Zoroastrians, who fled from Persia to settle in the Bombay area of India in the 8c AD. [from Persian *Parsee*, Persian]

Parseeism the religion of the Parsees, based on a rule of life that conforms to the purity of Ahura Mazda.

parser *noun* *Comput.* a program which analyses and structures text or other input data.

Parsifal see PERCEVAL, SIR.

Parsifal a 'sacred festival drama' by Richard Wagner (1882). The young Parsifal meets the order of the Knights of the Holy Grail, and sees Amfortas's dreadful wound, which can be cured only by the holy power of the Sacred Spear. This spear was lost when Amfortas was seduced by Kundry, and can be recovered only by a 'poor fool made wise by pity'. The magician responsible instructs Kundry to seduce Parsifal too, but he is wise to her temptations and procures the spear, though his return to the knights is delayed for three years due to her curse.

parsimonious *adj.* too careful in spending money; stingy. [from Latin *parsimonia*, thrift]

parsimoniously *adv.* in a parsimonious way.

parsimony *noun* **1** reluctance or extreme care in spending money. **2** praiseworthy economy. **3** avoiding excess. **4** meanness.

parsley *noun* a plant with curled feathery leaves used as a garnish and flavouring. [from Greek *petroselinon*, from *petra*, rock + *selinon*, parsley]

parsnip *noun* a pungent-tasting root vegetable that looks like a thick white carrot. [from Latin *pastinacum* (from *pastinum*, dibble) + Middle English *nepe*, turnip]

parson *noun* **1** a parish priest in the Church of England. **2** any clergyman. [from Latin *persona*, parish priest, person, personage, mask]

parsonage *noun* the residence of a parson.

Parsons, Sir Charles Algernon (1854–1931) Irish engineer, born in London, son of the 3rd Earl of Rosse. He became an engineering apprentice, and in 1884 developed the high-speed steam turbine. He also built the first turbine-driven steamship, the *Turbinia*, in 1897.

parson's nose *colloq.* a piece of fatty flesh at the rump of a plucked fowl, especially a turkey or chicken.

part — *noun* **1** a portion, piece, or bit; some but not all. **2** one of a set of equal divisions or amounts that compose a whole: *in the proportion of five parts cement to two of sand.* **3** an essential piece; a component: *vehicle spare parts.* **4** a section of a book; any of the episodes of a story, etc issued or broadcast as a serial. **5** a performer's role in a play, opera, etc; the words, actions, etc belonging to the role. **6** the melody, etc given to a particular instrument or voice in a musical work. **7** one's share, responsibility or duty in something: *do one's part / want no part in/of it.* **8** (*usually* **parts**) a region: *foreign parts.* **9** (**parts**) talents; abilities: *a woman of parts.* — *verb* **1** to separate (eg curtains, combatants, etc). **2** *intrans.* (**part from** *or* **with someone**) to leave them or separate from them. **3** *intrans. said of more than one person* to leave one another; to separate or diverge. **4** (**part with something** *or* **be parted from it**) to give it up or hand it over: *they were reluctant to part with/be parted from their money.* **5** to put a parting in (hair).

— **the better** *or* **best** *or* **greater part of something** most of it.

for the most part 1 usually. **2** mostly or mainly.

for my part as far as I am concerned.

in great *or* **large part** mostly.

in part partly.

on the part of someone 1 as done by them. **2** so far as they are concerned.

part and parcel of something an essential part of it.

part company with someone to separate from them.

play a part to be involved.

take something in good part to take no offence at a criticism, joke, etc.

take part in something to participate in it; to share in it.

take someone's part to support someone; to take someone's side.
[from Latin *pars*, part]

partake *verb intrans.* (PAST TENSE **partook**; PAST PARTICIPLE **partaken**) (*usually* **partake in** *or* **of** **something**) **1** to participate in something. **2** to eat or drink. **3** *literary* to have a certain quality, etc to a degree. [formed from *partaking*, from Middle English *part-taking*]

parterre *noun* **1** a formal, ornamental flower-garden laid out with lawns and paths. **2** the pit of a theatre. [from French *par terre*, on the ground]

part exchange a purchase or sale made by exchanging used goods for part of the value of new goods.

parthenogenesis *noun Biol.* in some insects and plants, reproduction without fertilization by the male. [from Greek *parthenos*, maiden + -GENESIS]

Parthenon the principal building of the Acropolis in Athens, dedicated to Athena Parthenos. A Doric temple of Pentelic marble, it was built (447–433 BC) to the plans of Ictinus and Callicrates under the supervision of Phidias, the sculptor responsible for its 9m-high gold and ivory cult statue of Athena. A low-relief Ionic frieze, depicting the Panathenaea (a procession held annually in honour of Athena), can be seen on the outer walls of the roof structure. The building was later converted into a church, then a mosque, before it was reduced by explosion to a shell in 1687 during the Turkish–Venetian war. It is a World Heritage site.

Parthian — *noun* a member of an ancient people (see PARTHIANS). — *adj.* relating to the Parthians.

Parthians an ancient people who inherited the eastern territories of the Seleucids. From the 3c BC, they ruled an empire that stretched from the Euphrates to the Indus. They resisted conquest by Rome during the 1c BC, but failed in their turn to take over her eastern provinces. The Parthian Empire was finally conquered in AD 224 by the Sassanids of Persia.

Parthian shot, a final hostile remark made on departing. See also PARTING SHOT. [from the practice of the horsemen of ancient Parthia of turning to shoot arrows at following enemies as they rode off]

partial *adj.* **1** incomplete; in part only. **2** (**partial to something**) having a liking for it. **3** favouring one side or person unfairly; biased. [from Latin *partialis*, from *pars*, part]

partial fraction *Maths.* one of a number of fractions into which another fraction can be separated, eg $\frac{1}{2}$ and $\frac{1}{4}$ are partial fractions of $\frac{3}{4}$.

partiality *noun* **1** being partial. **2** favourable bias or prejudice. **3** fondness.

partially *adv.* not completely or wholly; not yet to the point of completion.
◆ See note at *partly*.

participant *or* **participator** *noun* a person or group that takes part.

participate *verb intrans.* (**participate in** **something**) to take part or be involved in it. [from Latin *pars*, part + *capere*, to take]

participation *noun* participating; involvement.

participatory *adj.* capable of being participated in or shared.

participial *adj. Grammar* having the role of an participle.

participially *adv.* as a participle.

participle *noun* a word formed from a verb and used as an adjective or to form tenses. In English the present participle is formed with -*ing* (as in *going* and *hitting*), and the *past participle* generally with -*ed*, -*t*, -*en*, or -*n* (as in *asked*, *burned* or *burnt*, *taken*, and *shown*). The adjectival use is illustrated by *a going concern* and *a burnt cake*, and the formation of tenses by *are going*, *were hitting*, and *have shown*. [from Latin *participium*, a sharing, participle, from *pars*, part + *capere*, to take (from its sharing features of both a verb and an adjective)]

particle *noun* **1** *Physics* a tiny unit of matter such as a molecule, atom, or electron. **2** a tiny piece. **3** the least bit: *not a particle of sympathy*. **4** *Grammar* an uninflected word, eg a preposition, conjunction, or interjection. **5** *Grammar* an affix, such as *un-* and -*ly*. [from Latin *particula*, diminutive of *pars*, part]

particle accelerator *Physics* a device that is used to accelerate charged subatomic particles, especially electrons or protons, to a high velocity.

particle beam weapons weapons in which high-energy sub-atomic particles, generated in nuclear accelerators, are turned into a directable beam. The development of such weapons, especially those which could shoot down missiles in space, has been one of the goals of late-20c military research, especially in the USA and former USSR.

particle physics the branch of physics concerned with the study of the elementary particles that are the fundamental components of matter, and the forces between them. Many experiments in particle physics involve the use of particle accelerators, needed to force particles close enough together to produce interactions.

particoloured *adj.* partly one colour, partly another; variegated. [from Old French *parti*, variegated]

particular — *adj.* **1** specific; single; individually known or referred to. **2** especial: *took particular care*. **3** difficult to satisfy; fastidious; exacting. **4** exact; detailed. — *noun* **1** a detail. **2** (**particulars**) personal details: *took down her particulars*.
— **in particular** especially; specifically.
[from Latin *particularis*, from *particula*, diminutive of *pars*, part]

particularization *or* **particularisation** *noun* particularizing, detailing.

particularize *or* **particularise** *verb* **1** to specify individually. **2** to give specific examples of. **3** *intrans.* to go into detail.

particularly *adv.* more than usually: *particularly good*. specifically; especially: *particularly hates board games*.

parting *noun* **1** the act of taking leave. **2** a divergence or separation: *a parting of the ways*. **3** a line of exposed scalp dividing hair brushed in opposite directions.

parting shot a last hostile remark made on leaving. See also PARTHIAN SHOT.

partisan — *noun* **1** an enthusiastic supporter of a party, person, cause, etc. **2** a member of a resistance group in a country occupied by an enemy. — *adj.* strongly loyal to one side, especially blindly so; biased. [from French *partisan*]

partisanship *noun* the quality of being partisan.

partita *noun Mus.* **1** (PL. **partite**) in the 17c, one of a set of instrumental variations. **2** (PL. **partitas**) especially in the 18c, a suite of instrumental dances, as in J S Bach's three partitas for solo violin and six partitas for harpsichord. [from Italian *partita*, division]

partition — *noun* **1** a screen or thin wall dividing a room. **2** the dividing of a country into two or more independent states. — *verb* (**partitioned**, **partitioning**) **1** to divide (a country) into independent states. **2** (*also* **partition** **something off**) to separate it off with a partition. [from Latin *partitio*, division]

partitive *Grammar* — *adj.*, *said of a word, form, etc* denoting a part of a whole. — *noun* a partitive word or form, eg *some*, *any*, *most*. [from Latin *partire*, to divide]

partitively *adv.* in a partitive way.

partly *adv.* in part, or in some parts; to a certain extent; not wholly.
◆ Note the difference between *partly* and *partially*. *Partly* means 'in part', eg *the house is built partly of stone and partly of wood*. *Partially* means 'not yet to the point of completion', eg *the house is only partially built*.

partner — *noun* **1** one of two or more people jointly owning or running a business or other enterprise on an equal footing. **2** a person one dances with. **3** a person who is on the same side as oneself in a game of eg bridge, tennis, etc. **4** a person with whom one has an especially long-term sexual relationship, eg one's husband or wife. — *verb* (**partnered**, **partnering**) to act as a partner to. [from Middle English *partener*, from *parcener*, joint inheritor, influenced by PART]

partnership *noun* **1** a relationship in which two or more people or groups operate together as partners. **2** the status of a partner: *offered her a partnership*. **3** a business or other enterprise jointly owned or run by two or more people, etc.

part of speech *Grammar* any of the grammatical classes of words, eg noun, adjective, verb, preposition, etc.

partook see PARTAKE.

Partridge, Eric (Honeywood) (1894–1979) British lexicographer, born near Gisborne, New Zealand. He served in World War I, and lectured at Manchester and London. After serving in the RAF in World War II, he became a freelance author and lexicographer. He specialized in studies of style, slang, and colloquial language, notably *A Dictionary of Slang and Unconventional English* (1937) and *Usage and Abusage* (1947). He also wrote a detailed study of punctuation, *You Have a Point There* (1957).

partridge *noun* a plump-bodied, grey-and-brown game bird. [from Old French *perdriz*, from Latin and Greek *perdix*]

partridge

part song a song for singing in harmonized parts.

part-time *adj.*, *adv.* during only part of the full working day.

part-timer *noun* a person who works, serves, etc on a part-time basis.

parturient *adj. Medicine* giving birth. [from Latin *parturire*, to give birth]

parturition *noun Medicine* the process of giving birth; childbirth.

party *noun* (PL. **parties**) **1** a social gathering, especially of invited guests, for enjoyment or celebration. **2** a group of people involved in a certain activity together. **3** an especially national organization of people united by a common, especially political, aim. **4** *Legal* each of the individuals or groups concerned in a contract, agreement, lawsuit, etc: *third-party insurance*. **5** *old facetious use* a person: *an elderly party*.
— **be a party to something** to be involved in or partly responsible for an agreement, decision, action, etc.
[from Old French *partie*, past participle of *partir*, to divide]

party line 1 a telephone line shared by two or more people. **2** the official opinion of a political party on any particular issue.

party piece an act or turn that one can be called on to perform to entertain others, eg at a party.

party wall a wall that divides two houses, etc, being the joint responsibility of both owners.

par value the value shown on a share certificate at time of issue; face value.

parvenu *or* **parvenue** *noun derog.* respectively a man or woman who has recently acquired substantial wealth but lacks the social refinement to go with it. [from French, past participle of *parvenir*, to arrive]

pas *noun* (PL. **pas**) *Ballet* a step. [from French *pas*]

Pasadena POP (1990) 132 000, a resort city in Los Angeles County, SW California, USA, lying in the San Gabriel foothills. It was founded in 1874. NOTABLE FEATURES Pasadena Art Museum; Civic Centre.

Pasargadae an ancient site in Persia chosen by Cyrus the Great in 546 BC to be the capital of the new Achaemenid empire. It was also the site of Cyrus's tomb.

Pascal, Blaise (1623–62) French mathematician, physicist, and theologian, born in Clermont-Ferrand. A mathematical genius as a child, he later invented the barometer, the hydraulic press, and the syringe. In 1647 he patented a calculating machine, and during the 1650s he laid the foundations of probability theory. Following his experience of a religious revelation in 1654, he joined his sister at the Jansenist retreat at Port-Royal (1655), and concentrated on theological works.

Pascal a male first name. [from late Latin *paschalis*, relating to Easter]

PASCAL *noun Comput.* a high-level computer programming language, designed in the 1960s as an aid to the teaching of structured programming, and still widely used for general programming purposes, especially in universities. [named after Blaise Pascal]

pascal *noun* (ABBREV. **Pa**) the SI unit of pressure, equal to a force of one newton per square metre.

Pascal's triangle *Maths.* a triangular pattern of numbers in which, except for the number 1, each digit is the sum of the two digits above it. [named after Blaise Pascal]

paschal *adj.* 1 relating to the Jewish festival of Passover. 2 relating to Easter. [from Latin *paschalis*, from Greek *pascha*, from Hebrew *pesah*, Passover]

Pascua, Isla de see EASTER ISLAND.

pas de deux (PL. **pas de deux**) a dance for two performers.

pasha *noun Hist.* a high-ranking Turkish official; placed after the name in titles. [from Turkish *pasha*]

Pashtun a group of Pashto-speaking agricultural and herding people of NW Pakistan and SE Afghanistan. Traditionally warriors, many are employed in the national armies. Numbering 6.2m, they are the most numerous and dominant group in Afghanistan; 6.7m live in Pakistan.

Pašić, Nikola (c.1846–1926) Serbian statesman, born in Zaječar. Though condemned to death in 1883 for his part in the plot against King Milan, he survived on the accession of King Peter and was Prime Minister of Serbia (five times, from 1891) and later of Yugoslavia (1921–4, 1924–6), which he helped to found.

Pasiphae in Greek mythology, the daughter of Helios, and wife of Minos, King of Crete. She loved a bull sent by Poseidon, and became the mother of the Minotaur.

Pasolini, Pier Paulo (1922–75) Italian film director, born in Bologna. He became a Marxist following World War II, moved to Rome, wrote novels and also worked as a film scriptwriter and actor. Directing from 1961, his films include *Il Vangelo secondo Matteo* (The Gospel According to St Matthew, 1964), *Il Decamerone* (The Decameron, 1971), and *The Canterbury Tales* (1973).

pasqueflower *noun* a purple-flowered anemone that blooms at Easter. [from Old French *passefleur* (from *passer*, to surpass + *fleur*, flower), influenced by *pasques*, Easter]

pass *verb* 1 *trans., intrans.* to come alongside and progress beyond: *passed her on the stairs.* 2 *intrans.* to run, flow, progress, etc: *the blood passing through our veins.* 3 *trans., intrans.* (also **pass** *or* **pass something through**, **into**, *etc*) to go or cause it to go, penetrate, etc: *pass through a filter.* 4 *trans., intrans.* to move lightly across, over, etc: *pass a hand over the furniture.* 5 *intrans.* to move from one state or stage to another: *pass from the larval to the pupal stage.* 6 to exceed or surpass: *pass the target.* 7 *trans., intrans. said of a vehicle* to overtake. 8 *trans., intrans.* to achieve the required standard in (a test, etc); to award (a student, etc) the marks required for success in a test, etc. 9 *intrans.* to take place: *what passed between them.* 10 *intrans., trans. said of time* to go by; to use up (time) in some activity, etc. 11 *trans., intrans.* (**pass** *or* **be passed round**, **on**, *etc*) to hand or transfer; to be transferred; to circulate. 12 *trans., intrans.* (**pass down** *or* **pass something down**) to be inherited; to hand it down. 13 *trans., intrans. Sport* to throw or kick (the ball, etc) to another player in one's team. 14 *trans., intrans.* to agree to (a proposal or resolution) or be agreed to; to vote (a law) into effect. 15 *said of a judge or law court* to pronounce (judgement). 16 *intrans.* to go away after a while: *her nausea passed.* 17 *intrans.* to be accepted, tolerated, or ignored: *let it pass.* 18 (**pass as** *or* **for something** *or* **someone**) to be accepted as or mistaken for something or someone: *insults that pass as wit / a child that would pass for an adult.* 19 *intrans.* to choose not to answer in a quiz, etc or bid in a card game. 20 to make (a comment, etc). 21 to discharge (urine or faeces). — *noun* 1 a route through a gap in a mountain range. 2 an official card or document permitting one to enter somewhere, be absent from duty, etc. 3 a successful result in an examination, but usually without distinction or honours. 4 *Sport* a throw, kick, hit, etc to another player in one's team. 5 a state of affairs: *reach a sorry/pretty pass.* 6 a decision not to answer in a quiz, etc, or not to bid in a card game.
— **come** *or* **be brought to pass** to happen.
in passing while dealing with something else; casually; by allusion rather than directly.
make a pass at someone make a casual sexual advance towards them: *made a pass at the girl in the flower shop.*
pass away *or* **on** *euphemistic* to die.
pass by to go past.
pass by something *or* **someone** to go past them.
pass something *or* **someone by** to overlook or ignore them.
pass off 1 *said of a sickness or feeling, etc* to go away; to diminish. 2 *said of an arranged event* to take place with the result specified: *the party passed off very well.*
pass oneself off as someone *or* **something** to represent oneself in that way: *tried to pass themselves off as students.*
pass out 1 to faint. 2 to leave a military or police college having successfully completed one's training.
pass over something to overlook it; to ignore it.
pass something up *colloq.* to neglect or sacrifice an opportunity.
[from Latin *passus*, step, pace]

passable *adj.* 1 barely adequate or *colloq.* fairly good. 2 *said of a road, etc* able to be travelled along, crossed, etc.

passably *adv.* in a passable way, reasonably well.

passacaglia *noun Mus.* a slow stately old Spanish dance in triple time; also, the music for it. The form was introduced into keyboard music in the 17c, and was usually a set of uninterrupted variations on a continuously repeated bass line or harmonic progression. Examples include passacaglias for organ by Diderik Buxtehude and J S

Bach. See also CHACONNE. [Italian, probably from Spanish *passacalle*, street song]

passage *noun* 1 a route through; a corridor, narrow street, or channel. 2 a tubular vessel in the body. 3 a piece of a text or musical composition. 4 the process of passing: *the passage of time.* 5 a journey by boat; also, the cost of a journey. 6 permission or freedom to pass through a territory, etc. 7 the voting of a law, etc into effect. [from Old French, from *passer*, to pass]

passage grave *Archaeol.* an underground burial chamber connected to the surface by a passage.

passage rites *Anthropol.* rituals that involve the public declaration of a change of status of an individual. Their number and significance vary widely from culture to culture, but they usually follow a similar pattern: a phase marking removal of an individual from their old social status (*separation rites*); an intermediate stage (*transition rites*); and finally, a phase marking acceptance of the new status (*aggregation rites*). The principal passage rites include birth, baptism, confirmation or initiation, marriage, and death.

Passage to India, A 1 a novel by E M Forster (1924). It is set in India at the time of the British Raj and focuses on the cultural tensions between the two civilizations. 2 a British film (1984) directed by David Lean, and starring Peggy Ashcroft, Judy Davis, Alec Guinness, and Victor Banerjee.

passageway *noun* a narrow passage or way, usually with walls on each side.

passata *noun* an Italian sauce of puréed and sieved tomatoes. [from Italian *passata*, passed (ie through a sieve)]

passbook *noun* a book in which the amounts of money put into and taken out of a bank account, etc are recorded.

Passchendaele, Battle of (1917) the third battle (31 Jul–10 Nov 1917) of Ypres during World War I. It was a British offensive that continued even after the original objective (a breakthrough to the Belgian ports) was recognized as futile. Notable for the appallingly muddy conditions, minimal gains, and British casualties of at least 300 000, the outcome was the capture by Canadians of the village of Passchendaele, 10km/6mi NE of Ypres.

passé *adj.* outmoded; old-fashioned; having faded out of popularity. [French, = passed]

passenger *noun* 1 a traveller in a vehicle, boat, aeroplane, etc driven, sailed, or piloted by someone else. 2 *derog.* someone not doing his or her share of the work in a joint project, etc. [from Old French *passagier*, from *passage*, with inserted *n* as in *messenger*]

passer-by *noun* (PL. **passers-by**) a person walking past.

passerine *Zool.* — *adj.*, *said of a bird* belonging to the order of perching birds, including all British songbirds. — *noun* a passerine bird. [from Latin *passer*, sparrow]

passim *adv.*, *said of a word, etc* occurring frequently throughout the literary or academic work in question. [Latin, = here and there]

passing *adj.* 1 lasting only briefly. 2 casual: *a passing glance, reference etc.*

passion *noun* 1 a violent emotion, eg hate, anger, or envy. 2 a fit of anger. 3 sexual love or desire. 4 an enthusiasm; something for which one has great enthusiasm. 5 (**the Passion**) the suffering and death of Christ; an account of this from one of the Gospels; a musical setting of one of these accounts. [from Old French, from Latin *passio*, from *pati*, to suffer]

passionate *adj.* 1 easily moved to passion; strongly emotional. 2 keen; enthusiastic.

passionately *adv.* in a passionate way, with passion.

passion flower any of several tropical climbing plants of the genus *Passiflora*, so called because the different parts of the large distinctive flowers were once thought to resemble the crown of thorns, nails, and other emblems of Christ's Passion. Some species are widely cultivated for their round edible fruit (known as a passion fruit or granadilla), and some are also grown as ornamental plants.

passion flower

passion fruit the edible fruit of the passion flower, egg-shaped, with a yellow or purple hard skin. Also called *granadilla*.

Passionists, properly the **Congregation of the Barefooted Clerics of the Most Holy Cross and Passion of our Lord Jesus Christ** a religious order, founded (1720) in Italy by St Paul of the Cross. It has houses in Europe and the USA, and its declared objective is to maintain the memory of Christ's sufferings and death.

Passion music music to which words describing the sufferings and death of Christ are set. One of the most renowned is the oratorio the *St Matthew Passion* (1727/9), by J S Bach.

passion play a religious drama representing the suffering and death of Christ.

passive *adj.* **1** lacking positive or assertive qualities; submissive. **2** lethargic; inert. **3** *Grammar* denoting the form of the verb used when the subject undergoes, rather than performs, the action of the verb. See also ACTIVE.

passively *adv.* in a passive way.

passiveness *or* **passivity** *noun* being passive.

passive resistance the use of non-violent means, eg fasting, to resist authority.

passive smoking the involuntary breathing in of others' tobacco smoke.

passkey *noun* a key designed to open a varied set of locks; a master key.

pass law formerly in South Africa, a law restricting the movement of non-whites, requiring them to carry identification at all times.

Passover *noun* an annual Jewish festival held in March or April. It commemorates the deliverance of the Israelites from bondage in Egypt, and is so called because the angel of death passed over the houses of the Israelites when he killed the first-born of the Egyptians (Exodus 13).

passport *noun* **1** an official document issued by the government, giving proof of the holder's identity and nationality, and permission to travel abroad with its protection. **2** an asset that guarantees one something: *a degree is your passport to a good job*.

password *noun* **1** a secret word allowing entry to a high-security area or past a checkpoint, etc. **2** *Comput.* a set of characters which a user inputs to gain access to a computer or network.

past — *adj.* **1** of an earlier time; of long ago; bygone. **2** recently ended; just gone by: *the past year.* **3** over; finished. **4** former; previous: *past presidents.* **5** *Grammar, said of the tense of a verb* indicating a past action or condition. — *prep.* **1** up to and beyond: *went past me.* **2** after in time or age. **3** beyond; farther away than. **4** having advanced too far for: *she's past playing with dolls.* **5** beyond the reach of: *past help / past belief.* — *adv.* **1** so as to pass by: *go past.* **2** ago: *two months past.* — *noun* **1** the time before the present; events, etc belonging to this. **2** one's earlier life or career. **3** a

disreputable episode earlier in one's life: *who hasn't a past?* **4** *Grammar* the past tense.
— **not put it past someone** *colloq.* to believe them quite liable or disposed to do a certain thing.

past it *colloq.* having lost the vigour of one's youth or prime.
[an obsolete past participle of PASS]

pasta *noun* **1** a dough made with flour, water, and eggs shaped in a variety of forms such as spaghetti, macaroni, lasagne, etc. **2** a cooked dish of this, usually with a sauce. [from Italian, from Latin *pasta*, paste, dough, from Greek *pasta*, barley porridge]

paste — *noun* **1** a stiff moist mixture usually of powder and water, eg a mixture of flour and water used as an adhesive. **2** a spread for sandwiches, etc made from ground meat or fish. **3** any fine dough-like mixture: *almond paste.* **4** a hard brilliant glass used in making imitation gems. — *verb* **1** to stick with paste. **2** *colloq.* to thrash or beat soundly. **3** (*also* **paste something up**) *Printing* to mount (text, illustrations, etc) on a backing for photographing, etc. [from Old French, from Latin *pasta*, paste, dough, from Greek *pasta*, barley porridge]

pasteboard *noun* stiff board built up from thin sheets of paper pasted together.

pastel — *noun* **1** a chalk-like crayon made from ground pigment. **2** a picture drawn with pastels. — *adj., said of colours* delicately pale. [from French, from Italian *pastello*, from Latin *pastillus*, a ball or cake of something]

pastern *noun* part of a horse's foot between the hoof and the fetlock. [from Old French *pasturon*, from *pasture*, pasture, tether]

Pasternak, Boris (Leonidovich) (1890–1960) Russian lyric poet and novelist, born in Moscow. During the Stalin years he became the official translator into Russian of several major authors, including Shakespeare, Paul Verlaine, and Goethe. His major work, *Dr Zhivago*, caused a political furore and was banned in the USSR, but was an international success after its publication in Italy in 1957. Expelled by the Soviet Writers' Union, he was compelled to refuse the Nobel Prize for Literature in 1958.

paste-up *noun* a set of text, illustrations, etc, mounted on a board, prepared for copying or photographing.

Pasteur, Louis (1822–95) French chemist, the father of modern bacteriology, born in Dôle. He held academic posts at Strasbourg, Lille, and Paris, where in 1867 he became Professor of Chemistry at the Sorbonne. He showed that fermentation and putrefaction are essentially due to micro-organisms, not spontaneous generation, and introduced the technique of pasteurization, a mild and short heat treatment to destroy pathogenic bacteria. In a famous experiment in 1881, he demonstrated that sheep and cows vaccinated

with attenuated bacilli of anthrax were protected from the disease. The Pasteur Institute, of which he became first director, was founded in 1888 for his research.

pasteurization *or* **pasteurisation** *noun* the partial sterilization of a food, especially milk, by heating it to a specific temperature for a short period before rapidly cooling it. This kills or inactivates harmful bacteria, and delays the development of others. Pasteurization prolongs the storage life of milk, but reduces its nutritive value. [named after Louis Pasteur]

pasteurize *or* **pasteurise** *verb* to submit (food, especially milk) to the process of pasteurization.

pastiche *noun* a musical, artistic, or literary work in someone else's style, or in a mixture of styles. [from French, from Italian *pasticcio*, pie, bungle, pastiche]

pastille *noun* **1** a small fruit-flavoured, especially medicinal, sweet. **2** a cone of fragrant paste for scenting a room. [from French, from Latin *pastillus*, a ball or cake of something]

pastime *noun* a spare-time pursuit; a hobby. [from PASS + TIME]

pastiness *noun* being pasty.

pasting *noun colloq.* a thrashing.

past master an expert.

Paston Letters an invaluable collection of over 500 letters written by a 15c family from Norfolk, England. Depicting family life, estate management, local feuds, and national politics during the Wars of the Roses (1455–87), they are particularly valuable because the Pastons were of middling rank and so were more typical of landed society than the dominating lords.

pastor *noun* a member of the clergy, especially in Churches other than Anglican and Catholic, with responsibility for a congregation. [from Latin *pastor*, shepherd]

pastoral — *adj.* **1** relating to, or (of a poem, painting, musical work, etc) depicting the countryside or country life. **2** relating to a member of the clergy and his or her work. **3** relating to a shepherd and his or her work. **4** *said of land* used for pasture. — *noun* **1** a pastoral poem or painting. **2** *Mus.* same as PASTORALE. **3** a letter from a bishop to the clergy and people of the diocese. [from Latin *pastor*, shepherd]
◇ The conventions of the pastoral mode, as exemplified in classical examples by Theocritus and Virgil, have been much imitated and adapted in poetry, prose, and drama. Essentially, the pastoral poem, novel, or drama displays nostalgia for the past and a longing for the simple innocence of an idealized rural existence.

pastoral care help, advice, and moral guidance offered by a clergyman or other spiritual advisor to a group, such as the children in a school, members of the armed forces, a church congregation, etc.

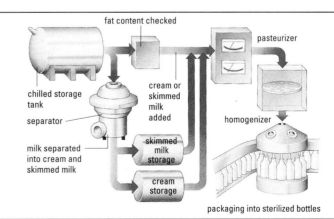

pasteurization of milk

pastorale *noun* (PL. **pastorales**) a musical work evoking the countryside. [from Italian *pastorale*, pastoral]

pastoralism *noun* a way of life characterized by keeping herds of animals, such as cattle, sheep, camels, reindeer, goats, and llamas. It is common in dry, mountainous, or severely cold climates not suitable for agriculture, although some groups, such as the Nilotic peoples of S Sudan, combine pastoralism with agriculture.

Pastoral Letters *or* **Pastoral Epistles** three New Testament writings (Letters 1 and 2 to Timothy and the Letter to Titus) which purport to convey Paul's advice to his colleagues Timothy and Titus about Church leadership. So-named in the 18c, their direct authorship by Paul is now widely doubted on grounds of vocabulary, theology, and setting.

Pastoral Symphony Beethoven's Symphony No.6 in F (Op 68, 1808), which, among other things, evokes bird-song and storm.

pastorate *noun* **1** the office, authority, or residence of a pastor. **2** a body of pastors.

past participle see PARTICIPLE.

pastrami *noun* strongly spiced smoked beef. [from Yiddish *pastrami*]

pastry *noun* (PL. **pastries**) **1** dough made with flour, fat, and water, used for piecrusts. **2** a sweet baked article made with this; a pie, tart, etc. [from PASTE]

pasturage *noun* an area of land where livestock is allowed to graze.

pasture — *noun* (*also* **pasture-land**) an area of grassland suitable or used for the grazing of livestock, in contrast to a meadow which is cut to produce hay or silage. — *verb* **1** to put (animals) in pasture to graze. **2** *intrans. said of animals* to graze. [from Old French, from Latin *pastura*, from *pascere*, to feed]

pasty[1] *adj.* (**pastier, pastiest**) *said of the complexion* unhealthily pale. [from PASTE]

pasty[2] *noun* (PL. **pasties**) a pie consisting of pastry folded round a savoury or sweet filling. [from Old French *pastée*]

Pat. *abbrev.* patent.

pat — *verb* (**patted, patting**) **1** to strike lightly or affectionately with the palm of one's hand. **2** to shape by striking lightly with the palm or a flat instrument: *pat it into shape*. — *noun* **1** a light, especially affectionate, blow with the palm of the hand. **2** a round flat mass. — *adv., especially of things said* immediately and fluently, as if memorized: *their answers came too pat*. — *adj., said of answers, etc* quickly and easily supplied.

— **have** *or* **know something off pat** to have memorized and know it perfectly.

a pat on the back an approving word or gesture.

pat someone on the back to congratulate them approvingly.

stand pat *North Amer.* to stand firmly by one's opinion, decision, etc.
[imitative]

Patagonia POP (1991) 1.1m, a region in S Argentina. AREA 489 541sq km/188 963sq mi. It comprises the provinces of Chubut, Rio Negro, Santa Cruz, and the territory of Tierra del Fuego. CHIEF TOWNS Rawson, Ushuaia, Comodoro Rivadavia, Rio Gallegos, and the resort town of Bariloche. PHYSICAL DESCRIPTION a semi-arid tableland rising in terraces from the Atlantic coast to the base of the Andes; several rivers. The name is sometimes applied to the whole of the S part of S America, including Chilean territory. In 1520, Ferdinand Magellan sailed along the Patagonian coast, passing through the strait that now bears his name. ECONOMY oil, iron ore, coal, copper, uranium, manganese; sheep; irrigated crops.

Patan, also **Lalitpur** POP (1981) 80 000, a city in central Nepal. It lies 5km/3mi SE of Kathmandu, in the Kathmandu Valley. HISTORY founded in the 7c; built in a circular plan with Buddhist stupas on the four points of the compass; became capital of the Nepali kingdom in the 17c; captured by the Gurkhas in 1768. It is the centre of the Banra sect of goldsmiths and silversmiths and is known as the 'city of artists'. NOTABLE FEATURES Palace of the Malla Kings (16c); Temple of Lord Krishna; Royal Bath (*Tushahity*).

patch — *noun* **1** a piece of material sewn on or applied so as to cover a hole or reinforce a worn patch. **2** a plot of earth: *a vegetable patch*. **3** a pad or cover worn as protection over an injured eye. **4** a small expanse contrasting with its surroundings: *patches of ice*. **5** *Hist.* a tiny piece of black silk worn on the face in imitation of a mole or beauty spot, to enhance the whiteness of the complexion. **6** a scrap or shred. **7** *colloq.* a phase or period: *go through a bad patch*. **8** *slang* the area patrolled by a policeman or covered by a particular police station. **9** *Comput.* a set of instructions added to a program to correct an error. — *verb* **1** to mend (a hole or garment) by sewing patches on. **2** (*also* **patch something up**) to repair it hastily and temporarily. **3** (*also* **patch something together**) to assemble it hastily. **4** *Comput.* to make a temporary correction in (a program).

— **not a patch on someone** *or* **something** *colloq.* not nearly as good as them.

patch something up *colloq.* to settle a quarrel, etc, especially hurriedly or temporarily. [from Middle English *pacche*]

patchily *adv.* in a patchy way.

patchiness *noun* being patchy.

patchouli *noun* a shrubby aromatic perennial plant (*Pogostemon cablin*) that grows to a height of 1m or more, native to the tropics and subtropics of SE Asia. It has square stems, oval toothed leaves, and whorls of white tubular flowers, and yields an aromatic essential oil that is used in perfumery. [from Tamil *pacculi*]

patch pocket a pocket made by sewing a piece of fabric on the outside of a garment.

patch test an allergy test in which substances are applied to areas of skin which are later examined for signs of irritation.

patchwork *noun* **1** needlework done by sewing together pieces of contrastingly patterned fabric. **2** a variegated expanse: *a patchwork of fields*.

patchy *adj.* (**patchier, patchiest**) **1** forming, or occurring in, patches. **2** uneven or variable in quality.

pate *noun old use, facetious* the head or skull.

pâté *noun* a spread made from ground or chopped meat or fish blended with herbs, spices, etc. [from French *pâté*, pasty]

pâté de foie gras pâté made from the livers of specially fattened geese.

patella *noun* (PL. **patellae, patellas**) the triangular plate of bone covering the front of the knee joint; the knee-cap. [from Latin, diminutive of *patina*, dish]

paten *noun Relig.* a circular metal plate, often of silver or gold, on which the bread is placed at the celebration of the Eucharist. [from Latin *patena, patina*, a plate]

patent — *noun* **1** an official licence from the government granting a person or business the sole right, for a certain period, to make and sell a particular article. **2** the right so granted. **3** the invention so protected. — *verb* to obtain a patent for (an invention, design, etc). — *adj.* **1** very evident. **2** concerned with the granting of, or protection by, patents. **3** *said of a product* made or protected under patent. **4** *colloq.* ingenious; infallible; original. **5** open for inspection: *letters patent*. [from Latin *patere*, to lie open]

◇ Patents are normally granted for 20 years in European countries; in the USA, it is 17 years.

patentee *noun* the person obtaining or holding a patent.

patent leather leather made glossy by varnishing.

patently *adv.* obviously; clearly.

patent medicine 1 *technical* a patented medicine which is available without prescription. **2** *colloq.* any proprietary medicine, especially one claimed as an infallible cure.

Patent Office the government department that issues patents.

patent theatres the theatres which between 1660 and 1843 were granted Letters Patent by Charles II and thus held a monopoly on legitimate theatre in England. Permission was granted to Thomas Killigrew at Drury Lane and William Davenant at Lincoln's Inn Fields (eventually at Covent Garden) to re-establish companies in the theatres that had been closed by the Puritans. Gradually other 'theatres royal' opened and by 1843 the rules had been relaxed, although Covent Garden and Drury Lane still operate under the terms of their original charter.

Pater, Walter (Horatio) (1839–94) English critic and essayist, born in London. He became known with his *Studies in the History of the Renaissance* (1873), a series of essays on Renaissance art. His philosophic romance *Marius the Epicurean* (1885) appealed to a wider audience, dealing with the spread of Christianity in the days of the catacombs. He developed a highly polished prose style, and exercised considerable influence on the aesthetic movements of his time (eg the pre-Raphaelites).

pater *noun old slang use* father. [from Latin *pater*]

paterfamilias *noun* (PL. **patresfamilias**) the father as head of the household. [from Latin *pater*, father + *familias*, a form of *familia*, family]

paternal *adj.* **1** of, relating to, or appropriate to, a father. **2** *said of a relation or ancestor* related on one's father's side. [from Latin *paternalis*, from *pater*, father]

paternalism *noun* governmental or managerial benevolence taken to the extreme of over-protectiveness and authoritarianism.

paternalistic *noun* characterized by or involving paternalism.

paternally *adv.* in a paternal way.

paternity *noun* **1** fatherhood. **2** the identity of a child's father. **3** the authorship, source, or origin of something. [from Latin *paternitas*, from *pater*, father]

paternity leave leave of absence from work granted to a husband or father so that he can be with his wife or partner and assist her during and after childbirth. Where formal agreements exist, the period of paternity leave is usually around one to two weeks.

paternity suit a lawsuit brought by the mother of a child to establish that a certain man is the father of her child and therefore liable for its financial support.

paternoster *noun* the Lord's Prayer, especially in Latin. [from Latin *Pater noster*, Our Father]

Paterson, A(ndrew) B(arton), also called **Banjo** (1864–1941) Australian journalist and poet, born in Narrambia, New South Wales. A World War I correspondent and the author of several books of light verse, including *The Animals Noah Forgot* (1933), he is best known as the author of 'Waltzing Matilda', which became Australia's national song.

Paterson, William (1658–1719) Scottish financier and founder of the Bank of England, born in Tinwald, Dumfriesshire. He worked in the West Indies, and then promoted a scheme for a colony in Darien, Central America. In 1964 he founded the Bank of England, and was one of its first directors. He sailed with the expedition to Darien (1698), and after its failure returned to England (1699). In 1715 the government awarded him an indemnity for his Darien losses.

Paterson's curse a herb (*Echium lycopsis*) introduced into Australia in c.1869, named after a landowner in Victoria thought to have been responsible for its spread. A noxious weed in agricultural areas, it is also known as 'Salvation Jane' and 'Lady Campbell Weed'.

path *noun* **1** a track trodden by, or specially surfaced for, walking. **2** the line along which something is travelling: *the path of Jupiter.* **3** a course of action: *the path to ruin.* **4** *Comput.* the location of a file in terms of a computer's disk drives and directory structure.
— **beat a path to someone's door** *colloq.* to compete for their services or attention.
cross someone's path to encounter them, especially by chance.
[from Anglo-Saxon *pæth*]

path- see PATHO-.

-path *combining form* forming words denoting: **1** a sufferer from a disorder: *psychopath.* **2** a practitioner of a therapy: *homoeopath / osteopath.*

Pathan see PASHTUN.

Pathé, Charles (1863–1957) French film pioneer, born in Paris. In 1896 he founded Société Pathé Frères with his three brothers. By 1912 it had become one of the world's largest film production organizations, also including a hand-colouring stencil process, Pathécolor. They introduced the newsreel in France (1909), and then in the USA and Britain.

Pather Panchali (Song of the Little Road) an Indian film directed by Satyajit Ray (1955). It gives a simple portrait of 1920s village life from the point of view of two children.

pathetic *adj.* **1** moving one to pity; touching, heart-rending, poignant, or pitiful. **2** *derog. colloq.* hopelessly inadequate.

pathetically *adv.* in a pathetic way.

pathetic fallacy especially in literature, the transference of human qualities to inanimate things, as in *a frowning landscape.*

Pathétique Sonata Beethoven's Piano Sonata No.8 in C minor (Op 13, 1798), called by the composer 'Grande sonate pathétique'.

pathfinder *noun* **1** an explorer who finds routes through unexplored territory. **2** someone who devises new methods of doing things.

-pathic *combining form* forming adjectives corresponding to nouns in *-pathy.*

patho- or **path-** *combining form* forming words denoting disease: *pathology.* [from Greek *pathos*, experience, suffering]

pathogen *noun Pathol.* any micro-organism, eg a bacterium or virus, that causes disease in a living organism.

pathogenic *adj.* producing disease.

pathogenicity *noun* the capacity to produce disease.

pathological *adj.* **1** relating to pathology. **2** caused by, or relating to, illness: *a pathological fear of dirt.* **3** *colloq.* compulsive; habitual: *a pathological liar.*

pathologically *adv.* in a pathological way.

pathologist *noun* a person skilled in pathology.

pathology *noun* the branch of medicine concerned with the study of the nature and causes of diseases.

pathos *noun* a quality in a situation, etc that moves one to pity. [from Greek *pathos*, feeling, suffering]

Paths of Glory a US film directed by Stanley Kubrick (1957). Set in France in World War I, it is a powerful anti-war statement comparing the military fanaticism of General Mireau (George Macready) with the quiet dignity of Col Dax (Kirk Douglas).

-pathy *combining form* forming words denoting **1** feeling: *telepathy.* **2** disease or disorder: *psy-*

chopathy. **3** a method of treating disease: *homoeopathy.* [from Greek *pathos*, suffering]

patience *noun* **1** the ability to endure delay, trouble, pain, or hardship calmly. **2** tolerance and forbearance. **3** perseverance. **4** *Cards* a solo game in which the player, in turning each card over, has to fit it into a certain scheme. [from Latin *patientia*]

patient — *adj.* having or showing patience. — *noun* a person who is being treated by, or is registered with, a doctor, dentist, etc.

patiently *adv.* in a patient way; with patience.

patina *noun* **1** a coating formed on a metal surface through oxidation, especially the greenish coating of verdigris on bronze or copper. **2** a mature shine on wood resulting from continual polishing and handling. **3** any fine finish acquired with age. **4** *Archaeol.* a surface appearance that develops with prolonged exposure or burial. [from Italian *patina*, coating, from Latin *patina*, dish]

patio *noun* (PL. **patios**) **1** an open paved area beside a house. **2** an inner courtyard in a Spanish or Spanish-American house. [from Spanish *patio*]

patisserie *noun* a shop selling fancy cakes, sweet pastries, etc. [from French *pâtisserie*, from Latin *pasta*, dough]

Patmore, Coventry (Kersey Dighton) (1823–96) English poet, born in Woodford, Essex. He was a library assistant at the British Museum, and was associated with the Pre-Raphaelite Brotherhood. He is best known for *The Angel in the House* (1854–62), a poetic treatment of married love. He converted to Catholicism after the death of his wife in 1862, and subsequently wrote mainly on mystical or religious themes, as in *The Unknown Eros* (1877).

Patmos POP (1982) 3 000, an island in the Dodecanese, Greece, in the Aegean Sea, off the W coast of Turkey. AREA 34sq km/13sq mi. CAPITAL Hora. St John the Apostle (son of Zebedee) lived here for two years. NOTABLE FEATURES Monastery of St John (11c); resort beaches.

Patna POP (1991) 1.1m, the winter capital of Bihar, E India. It is situated on the S bank of the R Ganges, at the centre of a major rice-growing region, 467km/290mi NW of Calcutta. The ancient city of Pataliputra, capital of the 6c Magadha Kingdom, is buried beneath the present city. In 1732 a French trading post was established here, the rights of which were renounced in 1947. The city is noted for its handicrafts (brassware, furniture, carpets). NOTABLE FEATURES Sikh temple; Mosque of Sher Shah.

patois *noun* (PL. **patois**) **1** the local dialect of a region, used usually in informal everyday situations, as opposed to the language used in literature, education, etc. **2** jargon. [from French *patois*]

Paton, Alan (Stewart) (1903–88) South African writer and educator, born in Pietermaritzburg. In 1935 he became principal of the Diepkloof Reformatory, where he became known for the success of his enlightened methods, and from 1953 to 1968 he was President of the Liberal Association of South Africa. His deep concern with the racial problem in South Africa prompted several novels, notably *Cry the Beloved Country* (1948) and *Too Late the Phalarope* (1953).

Patou, Jean (1880–1936) French fashion designer, born in Normandy. In 1912 he opened Maison Parry in Paris, and in 1913 sold his collection outright to an American buyer. After war service he successfully opened again as a couturier in 1919. He was noted for his designs for sports stars, actresses, and society women, and for his perfume 'Joy'.

patrial *noun formerly* a person who, being a citizen of the UK, a British colony, or the British Commonwealth, or the child or grandchild of someone born in the UK, has a legal right to live in the UK. [from Latin *patria*, fatherland]

patriality *noun* the condition of being a patrial.

patriarch *noun* **1** the male head of a family or tribe. **2** in the Eastern Orthodox Church, a high-ranking bishop. **3** in the Roman Catholic Church, the pope. **4** in the Old Testament, any of the ancestors of the human race or of the tribes of Israel, eg Adam, Abraham, or Jacob. **5** a venerable old man, especially the senior member of a community or group. [from Greek *patriarches*, senior bishop, father of a family]

patriarchal *adj.* **1** of the nature of a patriarch. **2** like a patriarch. **3** belonging to or subject to a patriarch.

patriarchal society a society governed by a patriarch or patriarchs. Many tribal societies, eg in Africa, are ruled by elders, who are venerated for their wisdom.

patriarchate *noun* the office, authority, or residence of a church patriarch.

patriarchy *noun* (PL. **patriarchies**) a social system in which a male is head of the family and descent is traced through the male line; also, a society based on this system.

Patricia a female first name. [a feminine form of PATRICK]

patrician — *noun* **1** a member of the ancient Roman nobility; a descendant of one of the founding families of Rome. **2** an aristocrat. **3** a person of taste, culture, and refinement. — *adj.* **1** relating to the ancient Roman nobility. **2** aristocratic; noble; of refined tastes. [from Latin *patricius*, patrician, noble]

patricidal *adj.* relating to or involving patricide.

patricide *noun* **1** the act of killing one's father. **2** a person who commits this act. [variant of earlier PARRICIDE, influenced by Latin *pater*, father]

Patrick, St (c.385–c.461 AD) apostle and patron saint of Ireland, born (perhaps) in S Wales. At 16 he was carried to Ireland by pirates, and sold to an Antrim chief. Six years later he escaped, and became a monk in France. Ordained a bishop at 45, he then became a missionary to Ireland (432) and travelled widely among the clan chiefs, until in 454 he fixed his see at Armagh (454). His feast day is 17 Mar.

Patrick a male first name. [in Latin *Patricius*, patrician, nobleman; perhaps ultimately of Celtic origin]

patrilineal *Anthropol.* denoting descent or kinship reckoned through the father, or through males alone.

patrimonial *adj.* being or involving patrimony.

patrimony *noun* (PL. **patrimonies**) **1** property inherited from one's father or ancestors. **2** something inherited; a heritage. **3** a church estate or revenue. [from Latin *patrimonium*, from *pater*, father]

patriot *noun* someone who loves and serves his or her fatherland devotedly. [from Greek *patriotes*, fellow-countryman]

patriotic *adj.* **1** loyal or devoted to one's country. **2** like a patriot.

patriotically *adv.* in a patriotic way.

Patriotic Front (ABBREV. **PF**) a Zimbabwean movement formed by the merging of ZANU and ZAPU in 1976, aimed at uniting the exiled nationalist movements in concerted opposition, both political and military, to the white minority regime of Ian Smith. However, the rivalry between the two organizations proved too strong and PF's two wings competed against each other in the first independence elections.

patriotism *noun* loyalty to and devotion to one's country.

Patroclus in Greek legend, the son of Menoetius, the faithful follower of Achilles at Troy. He went into battle wearing Achilles' armour, but was cut down by Hector. His death made Achilles return to the battle.

patrol — *verb* (**patrolled**, **patrolling**) to make a regular systematic tour of (an area) to maintain security or surveillance. — *noun* **1** a person or group of people performing this duty. **2** the act of patrolling: *on patrol.* **3** any of the units of six or so into which a troop of Scouts or Guides is divided. [from French *patrouiller*]

patrol car a police car equipped with a radio telephone, used to patrol streets and motorways.

patrolman *noun* **1** *North Amer.* the lowest-ranking police officer; a police officer on the beat. **2** a person employed by a motoring organization to patrol a certain area and help motorists in difficulty.

patron *noun* **1** a person who gives financial support and encouragement eg to an artist, the arts, a movement, or charity. **2** a regular customer of a shop, attender at a theatre, etc. [from Latin *patronus*, protector]

patronage *noun* **1** the support given by a patron. **2** regular custom given to a shop, theatre, etc. **3** the power of bestowing, or recommending people for, offices.

patronize *or* **patronise** *verb* **1** to treat condescendingly, or with benevolent superiority, especially inappropriately. **2** to give especially regular custom to (a shop, theatre, restaurant, etc).

patronizing *or* **patronising** *adj.* treating condescendingly.

patronizingly *or* **patronisingly** *adv.* in a patronizing way.

patron saint the guardian saint of a country, profession, craft, etc.

patronymic *noun* a name derived from one's father's or other male ancestor's name, usually with a suffix or prefix, as in *Donaldson Macdonald.* [from Greek *pater*, father + *onyma*, name]

Pattadakal an old town in Karnataka, SW India, which was at its peak in the 7c–8c, when most of its temples were built. The most notable is the Lokeshwari or Virupaksha temple, with sculptures that narrate episodes from Hindu epics. The various temples form a World Heritage site.

Pattaya POP (1993e) 50 000, a beach resort in E Thailand. It lies on the NE shore of the Gulf of Thailand S of Bang Phra. Pattaya is regarded as the 'Riviera' of Thailand, with resort facilities.

patten *noun Hist.* an overshoe with a wooden or metal mount, for raising the wearer above mud or water. [from Old French *patin*, clog]

patter[1] — *verb intrans.* (**pattered**, **pattering**) **1** *said of rain, footsteps, etc* to make a light rapid tapping noise. **2** to move with light rapid footsteps. — *noun* the light rapid tapping of footsteps or rain. [from PAT]

patter[2] — *noun* **1** the fast persuasive talk of a salesman, or the quick speech of a comedian. **2** the jargon or speech of a particular group or area: *Glasgow patter.* — *verb intrans., trans.* (**pattered**, **pattering**) to say or speak rapidly or glibly. [from Latin *pater noster*, Our Father, from the fast mumbling of the prayer]

pattern — *noun* **1** a model, guide, or set of instructions for making something. **2** a decorative design eg on wallpaper or fabric. **3** a piece, eg of fabric, as a sample. **4** any excellent example suitable for imitation. **5** a coherent series of occurrences or set of features: *a pattern of events.* — *verb* (**pattern one thing on another**) to model it on another type, design, etc. [from Old French, from Latin *patronus*, example, defender]

patterned *adj.*, *said of a fabric, etc* having a decorative design; not plain.

Patron Saints of Occupations	
Accountants	Matthew
Actors	Genesius, Vitus
Advertisers	Bernardino of Siena
Architects	Thomas (Apostle)
Artists	Luke, Angelico
Astronauts	Joseph (Cupertino)
Astronomers	Dominic
Athletes	Sebastian
Authors	Francis de Sales
Aviators	Our Lady of Loreto
Bakers	Honoratus
Bankers	Bernardino (Feltre)
Barbers	Cosmas and Damian
Blacksmiths	Eligius
Bookkeepers	Matthew
Book trade	John of God
Brewers	Amand, Wenceslaus
Builders	Barbara, Thomas (Apostle)
Butchers	Luke
Carpenters	Joseph
Chemists	Cosmas and Damian
Comedians	Vitus
Cooks	Lawrence, Martha
Dancers	Vitus
Dentists	Apollonia
Doctors	Cosmas and Damian, Luke
Editors	Francis de Sales
Farmers	Isidore
Firemen	Florian
Fishermen	Andrew, Peter
Florists	Dorothy, Thérèse of Lisieux
Gardeners	Adam, Fiacre
Glassworkers	Luke, Lucy
Gravediggers	Joseph Arimathea
Grocers	Michael
Hotelkeepers	Amand, Julian the Hospitaler
Housewives	Martha
Jewellers	Eligius
Journalists	Francis de Sales
Labourers	James, John Bosco
Lawyers	Ivo, Thomas More
Librarians	Jerome, Catherine of Alexandria
Merchants	Francis of Assisi
Messengers	Gabriel
Metalworkers	Eligius
Midwives	Raymond Nonnatus
Miners	Anne, Barbara
Motorists	Christopher
Musicians	Cecilia, Gregory the Great
Nurses	Camillus de Lellis, John of God
Philosophers	Thomas Aquinas, Catherine of Alexandria
Poets	Cecilia, David
Police	Michael
Postal workers	Gabriel
Priests	Jean-Baptiste Vianney
Printers	John of God
Prisoners	Leonard
Radio workers	Gabriel
Sailors	Christopher, Erasmus, Francis of Paola
Scholars	Thomas Aquinas
Scientists	Albert the Great
Sculptors	Luke, Louis
Secretaries	Genesius
Servants	Martha, Zita
Shoemakers	Crispin, Crispinian
Singers	Cecilia, Gregory
Soldiers	George, Joan of Arc, Martin of Tours, Sebastian
Students	Thomas Aquinas
Surgeons	Luke, Cosmas and Damian
Tailors	Homobonus
Tax collectors	Matthew
Taxi drivers	Fiacre
Teachers	Gregory the Great, John Baptist de la Salle
Theologians	Augustine, Alphonsus Liguori, Thomas Aquinas
Television workers	Gabriel
Undertakers	Dismas, Joseph of Arimathea
Waiters	Martha
Writers	Lucy

Patton, George (Smith), also called **Old Blood and Guts** (1885–1945) US soldier, born at San Gabriel, California. He became one of the most daring and flamboyant US combat commanders in World War II. He played a key role in the Allied invasion of French N Africa (1942), led the US 7th Army in its assault on Sicily (1943), commanded the 3rd Army in the invasion of France, contained the German counter-offensive in the Ardennes (1944), and was appointed general (1945) before he was killed in a road accident in Germany.

patty *noun* (PL. **patties**) **1** *North Amer.* a flat round cake of minced meat, vegetables, etc. **2** a small meat pie. [from French *pâté*, from Latin *pasta*, dough, paste]

Pau POP (1990) 135 000, the capital and economic centre of Pyrénées-Atlantiques department, Aquitaine region, SW France. It lies on the right bank of the R Gave de Pau, 174km/108mi S of Bordeaux and is a health resort and winter sports centre. Its administrative importance has increased since the discovery of natural gas nearby. HISTORY became the capital of the former province of Béarn in 1464; Henry IV of France and Charles XIV of Sweden were born here. NOTABLE FEATURES castle (12c–15c); Boulevard des Pyrénées; Musée des Beaux-Arts, Musée Bernadotte.

paucity *noun* smallness of quantity; fewness; a scarcity or lack. [from Latin *pauci*, few]

Paul I (of Greece) (1901–64) King of Greece (1947–64), born in Athens. In 1922 he served with the Greek navy against the Turks, but when a Republic was proclaimed (1924) he went into exile. Following his return to Greece as Crown Prince in 1935, he served with the Greek general staff in the Albanian campaign in World War II, and was a member of the Greek government in exile in London (1941–6). His reign was marked by the Greek Civil War (1946–9) and its difficult aftermath, and during the early 1960s his personal role and that of his wife Queen Frederika became sources of bitter political controversy.

Paul III, originally **Alessandro Farnese** (1468–1549) Italian pope (1534–49), born in Canino, Papal States. The first of the popes of the Counter-Reformation, in 1538 he issued the bull of excommunication and deposition against Henry VIII of England, and also the bull instituting the Order of the Jesuits in 1540.

Paul VI, originally **Giovanni Battista Montini** (1897–1978) Italian pope, born in Concesio. Ordained in 1920, he worked in the Vatican diplomatic service until 1944. As Archbishop of Milan (1954) he became known for his liberal views and support of social reform. Made cardinal (1958) and then pope (1963), he travelled more widely than any previous pope, and initiated important advances in the move towards Christian unity.

Paul, St, also known as **Saul of Tarsus** (d.c.62/65AD) a New Testament figure, born of Jewish parents in Tarsus, Cilicia. A trained rabbi, he became a fervent Pharisee and persecutor of Christians. However, a vision of Christ converted him to Christianity during a journey to Damascus (c.34–5 AD), and he became a passionate evangelist and missionary in Cyprus, Antioch of Pisidia, Iconium, Lystra, and Derbe. He also went, with Silvanus (Silas), to Asia Minor and through Galatia and Phrygia to Macedonia and Achaia, where he was especially influential in Corinth, and later to Ephesus. On his return to Jerusalem, he was imprisoned for two years, following disturbances caused by the Jews' opposition to him. He was transferred to Caesarea and to Rome after appealing to Caesar, and two years later was executed by Nero (although some traditions suggest that he was released and went to Spain). Thirteen New Testament letters and some extracanonical works are traditionally attributed to him.

Paul a male first name, the name in English of the early Church founder. [from the Latin name *Paulus*, small]

Paula a female first name. [a feminine form of PAUL]

Pauli, Wolfgang (1900–58) Austrian–Swiss theoretical physicist, born in Vienna. Professor at Hamburg and Zürich, he introduced the concept of the electron quantum property 'spin' (the electron's angular momentum) and formulated the Pauli exclusion principle (1924), which states that no two electrons in an atom can exist in exactly the same state, with the same quantum numbers. He also predicted the existence of the fundamental particle known as the neutrino, later confirmed experimentally, and was awarded the 1945 Nobel Prize for Physics.

Paulina the wife of Antigonus in Shakespeare's *The Winter's Tale*, who strongly protests Hermione's innocence to Leontes and gives him false information about her death.

Pauline Letters or **Pauline Epistles** a set of (usually 13) New Testament writings attributed to the apostle Paul. Modern scholars are confident about Paul's authorship of Romans, 1 and 2 Corinthians, Galatians, Philippians, 1 Thessalonians, and Philemon, but debate the authenticity of 2 Thessalonians, Colossians, Ephesians, and the Pastoral Letters. The accepted writings were actual letters to specific Churches and situations in areas where Paul had a pastoral or missionary interest.

Pauling, Linus Carl (1901–) US chemist, born in Portland, Oregon. Professor at the California Institute of Technology, he made important discoveries concerning chemical bonding and complex molecular structures; this interest led him into work on the chemistry of biological molecules and the chemical basis of hereditary disease. He was awarded the 1954 Nobel Prize for Chemistry. An active member of the peace movement, he also won the 1962 Nobel Peace Prize.

paunch *noun* a protruding belly, especially in a man.

paunchiness *noun* having a paunch.

paunchy *adj.* (**paunchier, paunchiest**) having a large paunch.

pauper *noun* **1** a poverty-stricken person. **2** *Hist.* someone living on public charity. [from Latin *pauper*, poor]

pauperism *noun* **1** poverty. **2** being a pauper.

pause — *noun* **1** a relatively short break in some activity, etc. **2** *Mus.* the prolonging of a note or rest beyond its normal duration, or a sign indicating this. — *verb intrans.* **1** to have a break; to stop briefly. **2** to hesitate.
— **give someone pause** to cause them to hesitate before acting.
[from Latin *pausa*]

pavan or **pavane** *noun* a stately 16c and 17c dance, or a piece of music for this. [from Spanish or Italian *pavana*, from Spanish *pavo*, peacock, or Italian *Padovana*, (dance) of Padua]

Pavarotti, Luciano (1935–) Italian tenor, born in Modena. He won the international competition at the Teatro Reggio Emilia in 1961, and made his operatic début there in *La Bohème* the same year. He performed with the La Scala tour of Europe in 1963–4, and made his US début in 1968. Internationally known as a concert performer, he has made many recordings and television appearances.

pave *verb* to surface (a street, path, etc) with stone slabs, cobbles, etc.
— **pave the way for something** or **someone** to prepare for the introduction or development of something, or for the arrival of someone.
[from Latin *pavire*, to ram or tread down]

pavement *noun* **1** a raised paved footpath edging a road, etc. **2** a paved road or expanse: *a mosaic pavement*. **3** a road surface; road-surfacing material. [from Latin *pavimentum*, hard floor]

pavement artist 1 an artist who draws sketches and coloured pictures on a pavement, especially in order to receive money from passers-by. **2** an artist who sells pictures displayed on a pavement.

Pavia, ancient **Ticinum** POP (1990e) 80 000, the capital of Pavia province, Lombardy, N Italy, lying on the R Ticino. NOTABLE FEATURES cathedral (begun in 1487), Church of San Michele (1155), Church of San Pietro in Ciel d'Oro (1132, restored in the 19c).

Pavia, Battle of a Habsburg victory (1525) over French forces which, commanded by Francis I, were besieging Pavia during the Italian Wars. Francis was taken prisoner after an abortive French cavalry attack on the garrison, and the defeat temporarily checked the French threat in Italy, which had led to the taking of Milan in 1524.

pavilion *noun* **1** a building in a sports ground in which players change their clothes and store equipment. **2** a light temporary building in which to display exhibits at a trade fair, etc. **3** a summerhouse or ornamental shelter. **4** a large ornamental building for public pleasure and entertainment. **5** a large and elaborate tent. [from French *pavillon*, from Latin *papilio*, butterfly, tent]

paving *noun* **1** stones or slabs used to pave a surface. **2** a paved surface.

paving-stone *noun* a large flat regular-shaped stone used for paving.

Pavlov, Ivan Petrovich (1849–1936) Russian physiologist, born near Ryazan. Professor in St Petersburg, he studied the circulatory system, the digestive system, and higher nervous activity including the brain, and was awarded the 1904 Nobel Prize for Physiology or Medicine. He is most famous for his work which showed that if a bell is sounded whenever food is presented to a dog, it will eventually begin to salivate when the bell is sounded without food being presented. This he termed a 'conditioned' or acquired reflex.

Pavlova, Anna (1881–1931) Russian ballerina, born in St Petersburg. After training there at Imperial Ballet School, she travelled to Paris with Sergei Diaghilev's Ballets Russes in 1909, and then worldwide, dancing reduced versions of the classics with her own company. *Le Cygne* (The Dying Swan, 1907) was choreographed for her by Fokine, and she also choreographed her own works, eg *Autumn Leaves* (1919).

pavlova *noun* a dessert consisting of meringue topped with fruit and whipped cream. [named after Anna Pavlova]

Pavo *noun Astron.* the Peacock, a small constellation in the S hemisphere, consisting of a few bright stars.

paw — *noun* **1** the foot of a four-legged mammal. **2** *colloq.* a hand. — *verb* **1** (**paw something** or **paw at something**) *said of an animal* to scrape or strike it with a paw. **2** to finger or handle clumsily; to touch or caress (someone) with unwelcome familiarity. [from Old French *poue*]

pawkily *adv.* in a pawky way.

pawkiness *noun* being pawky.

pawky *adj.* (**pawkier, pawkiest**) drily witty. [from Scot. *pawk*, a trick]

pawl *noun* a catch that engages with the teeth of a ratchet wheel to limit its movement to one direction only.

pawn¹ — *verb* **1** to deposit (an article of value) with a pawnbroker as a pledge for a sum of money borrowed. **2** to pledge or stake. — *noun* **1** the condition of being deposited as a pledge: *in pawn*. **2** an article so pledged. [from Old French *pan*, pledge, surety]

pawn² *noun* **1** a chess piece of lowest value. **2** a person used and manipulated by others. [from Old French *poun*, from Latin *pedones*, infantry]

pawnbroker *noun* a person who lends money in exchange for pawned articles.

pawnbroking *noun* the business of a pawnbroker.

pawnshop *noun* a pawnbroker's place of business.

pawpaw see PAPAYA.

pay — *verb* (PAST TENSE AND PAST PARTICIPLE **paid**) **1** *trans., intrans.* to give (money) to (someone) in exchange for goods, services, etc: *I paid him £10 for the books.* **2** *trans., intrans.* to settle (a bill, debt, etc). **3** *trans., intrans.* to give (wages or salary) to an employee. **4** *trans., intrans.* to make a profit, or make as profit: *businesses that don't pay / an investment that pays £500 per annum.* **5** *intrans., trans.* to benefit; to be worthwhile: *it pays one to be polite / dishonesty doesn't pay.* **6** *trans., intrans.* (also **pay for something**) to suffer a penalty on account of it; to be punished for it: *pay dearly for one's crimes / paid with his life.* **7** to do (someone) the honour of (a visit or call); to offer (someone) (a compliment or one's respects). **8** to give (heed or attention). — *noun* money given or received for work, etc; wages; salary.
— **in the pay of someone** employed by them, especially for a secret or dishonest purpose.
pay someone back to revenge oneself on them.
pay something back to return money owed.
pay something in to put money, etc into a bank account.
pay off to have profitable results.
pay people off to make them redundant with a final payment.
pay something off to finish paying a debt, etc.
pay something out 1 to spend or give (money), eg to pay bills, debts, etc. **2** to release or slacken (a rope, etc) especially by passing it little by little through one's hands.
pay up *colloq.* to pay what is due, especially reluctantly.
pay one's way to pay one's own debts and living expenses.
put paid to something or **someone** *colloq.* to put an end to them; to deal effectively or finally with them.
[from Latin *pacare*, to pacify, settle (a debt)]

payable *adj.* that can or must be paid: *make cheques payable to me / payable by 1 July.*

Payachata, Nevados de an Andean massif on the Chile–Bolivia border. It lies 129km/80mi NW of Arica and includes two snow-capped peaks, Cerro de Pomarepe (6 240m) and Cerro de Parinacota (6 342m).

pay-as-you-earn *noun* a method of collecting income tax from employees by deducting it from the wages or salary due to be paid to them.

pay-bed *noun* a bed in a National Health Service hospital reserved for patients paying for their own treatment.

pay day the day when wages or salaries are paid.

PAYE *abbrev.* pay-as-you-earn.

payee *noun* a person to whom money is paid or a cheque made out.

payer *noun* a person who pays.

paying guest a lodger.

payload *noun* **1** the revenue-earning part of a vehicle's load. **2** the operating equipment carried by a spaceship or satellite. **3** the quantity and strength of the explosive carried by a missile. **4** the quantity of goods, passengers, etc carried by an aircraft.

paymaster *noun* an official in charge of the payment of wages and salaries.

payment *noun* **1** a sum of money paid. **2** the act of paying or process of being paid. **3** a reward or punishment.

pay-off *noun colloq.* **1** a fruitful result. **2** a bribe. **3** a final settling of accounts. **4** a climax, outcome, or final resolution.

payola *noun* **1** a bribe for promoting a product, given to someone, eg a disc jockey, in a position to do this. **2** the practice of giving or receiving such bribes. [from PAY + suffix -*ola*, of no precise meaning]

pay packet *said of the container or its contents* an envelope or packet containing an employee's weekly wages.

payphone *noun* a telephone operated by coins or a phonecard.

payroll *noun* **1** a register of employees listing the wage or salary due to each. **2** the total amount of money required for employees' wages or salaries.

pay slip a note of pay, showing deductions for tax or national insurance, supplied weekly or monthly to employees.

Payton, Walter (1954–) US footballer, born in Columbia, Mississippi. In his career with the Chicago Bears (1975–88), he rushed for 16 726 yards, a National Football League record. In one game (1977) he rushed for a record 275 yards. He scored 125 touchdowns between 1975 and 1987.

pay TV *colloq.* non-broadcast video entertainment distributed to an audience of subscribers who pay for the programmes viewed. Programmes are received either through a cable network or by a scrambled microwave or satellite transmission requiring a rented decoder.

Paz, Octavio (1914–) Mexican poet, born in Mexico City. A diplomat, he served as the Mexican ambassador to India (1962–8), and taught at Texas, Harvard, and Cambridge Universities. His many collections of poetry include *Collected Poems* (1957–87), in Spanish and English, which were published in 1987. He has also written important prose works, notably *Tiempo Nublado* (One Earth, Four or Five Worlds, 1984). He was awarded the Nobel Prize for Literature in 1990.

Paz Estenssoro, Víctor (1907–) Bolivian revolutionary and politician, born in Tarija, founder of the National Revolutionary Movement (1941). Following the 1952 Revolution he served as President from 1952 to 1956 and from 1960 to 1964 (when he was ousted by a military coup), and from 1985 to 1990.

Pazyryk an ancient Scythian burial site in the Altai Mts, central Siberia. It consists of a group of frozen tombs of prehistoric nomad chieftains perfectly preserved since their deposition in timber-lined burial chambers in the 4c BC. The contents included various artefacts and clothing, as well as a number of embalmed, tattooed bodies.

Pb *symbol Chem.* lead.

PC *abbrev.* **1** personal computer. **2** Police Constable. **3 a** political correctness. **b** politically correct. **4** Privy Councillor.

pc *abbrev.* **1** per cent. **2** *colloq.* postcard.

PCB *abbrev. Comput.* printed circuit board.

pcm *abbrev.* per calendar month.

Pd *symbol Chem.* palladium.

pd *abbrev.* paid.

pd *or* **PD** *abbrev. Physics* potential difference.

Pde *abbrev.* Parade, as a street name.

PDL *abbrev. Comput.* page description language.

PDSA *abbrev.* People's Dispensary for Sick Animals.

PE *abbrev.* physical education.

pea *noun* **1** an annual climbing plant (*Pisum sativum*) of the pulse family (Leguminosae), cultivated in cool temperate regions for its edible seeds, which are produced in long dehiscent pods and harvested while green and unripe. — Also called *garden pea*. **2** the round seed of this plant, which has a very high protein content. It is either eaten fresh, or preserved by freezing, canning, or drying. [a singular form of *pease*, which was mistaken for a plural; see PEASE PUDDING]

peace *noun* **1** freedom from war. **2** a treaty or agreement ending a war. **3** freedom from noise, disturbance, or disorder; quietness or calm. **4** freedom from mental agitation; serenity: *peace of mind*. — **at peace 1** not at war; not fighting. **2** in harmony or friendship. **3** in a calm or serene state. **4** freed from earthly worries; dead. **hold one's peace** to remain silent. **keep the peace 1** *Legal* to preserve law and order. **2** to prevent, or refrain from, fighting or quarrelling. **make peace** to end a war, quarrel, etc. **make one's peace with someone** to be reconciled with them. [from Old French *pais*, from Latin *pax*]

peaceable *adj.* peace-loving; mild; placid.

peaceably *adv.* in a peaceable way.

Peace Corps a US government agency of volunteers, established in 1961 and aimed at providing assistance (in the form of skilled workers) in development projects in other countries. By 1966 there were more than 15 000 volunteers in 52 countries, but in the 1980s the budget was reduced, and volunteers also had to leave some countries hostile to US policies. There are similar agencies in France, Germany, and the UK.

peace dividend money left over from a government's defence budget as a result of negotiated arms reduction policies, available for non-military use.

peaceful *adj.* **1** calm and quiet. **2** unworried; serene. **3** free from war, violence, disturbance, or disorder.

peacefully *adv.* in a peaceful way.

peacefulness *noun* being peaceful.

peacemaker *noun* a person who makes or brings about peace.

Peace Memorial Museum a museum in the Heiwa Koen ('Peace Park'), Hiroshima, Japan, housing information and exhibits chronicling the effects of the atomic bomb which destroyed the city in 1945.

peace offering something offered to end a quarrel or as an apology.

peace pipe (**pipe of peace**) a long ornate pipe smoked by Native Americans as a token of peace.

Peace River a river in W Canada. Rising in the Omineca Mts, British Columbia, as the Finlay R, it flows SE to Finlay Forks where it becomes the Peace R. It then flows E and N to enter the Slave R near its outflow from L Athabasca. The length to the head of the Finlay R is 1 923km/1 195mi. The river is used for hydroelectricity.

peace studies educational courses designed to explore the role of the military in society, international strategic relationships, and those conditions that most promote peace and human welfare in society.

peacetime *noun* periods that are free of war.

peach¹ *noun* **1** any of numerous varieties of a small deciduous tree (*Prunus persica*) of the rose family, widely cultivated in warm temperate regions for its edible fruit. Some varieties are grown for their ornamental pink or white double flowers, or for their purple foliage. **2** the large round fruit of this tree, which contains a hard stone surrounded by sweet juicy yellow flesh and a yellowish-pink velvety skin (nectarines are a smooth-skinned variety of peach). Peaches may be eaten raw, dried, or canned. **3** the yellowish-pink colour of this fruit. **4** *colloq.* something delightful: *a peach of a day*. **5** *colloq.* a lovely young woman. [from Old French *peche*, from Latin *persicum malum*, Persian apple]

peach² *verb intrans.* (**peach on someone**) *colloq.* to betray or inform on someone, especially an accomplice. [from Middle English *peche* from *apeche*, to hinder]

peach Melba a dessert consisting of peaches, ice-cream and raspberry sauce.

Peachum, Thomas the corrupt lawyer in John Gay's *The Beggar's Opera*. His daughter Polly falls in love with and marries Capt MacHeath.

peachy *adj.* (**peachier, peachiest**) **1** coloured like or tasting like a peach. **2** *colloq.* very good.

Peacock, Thomas Love (1785–1866) English novelist, born in Weymouth, Dorset. He entered the service of the East India Company (1819–56) after producing three satirical romances, *Headlong Hall* (1816), *Melincourt* (1817), and *Nightmare Abbey* (1818). He later produced four other works along similar lines.

peacock *noun* (PL. **peacock**, **peacocks**) **1** (*also* **peafowl**) any of three species of large bird belonging to the pheasant family. The male of the common peacock, native to India and Sri Lanka, but domesticated worldwide, is best known for the train of green and gold eye-spot feathers which it fans during courtship. **2** the male peafowl, the female being known as the peahen. **3** *derog.* a vain person. [from Anglo-Saxon *pea*, from Latin *pavo*, peacock + COCK]

peacock blue the rich greenish blue in a peacock's plumage.

peacock butterfly a medium-sized butterfly with a prominent eyespot on each reddish-brown wing. The caterpillars feed on stinging nettles.

pea green bright green or yellowish green.

pea-green *adj.* having a colour of pea green.

peahen *noun* a female peacock.

peak — *noun* **1** a pointed summit; a pointed mountain or hill. **2** a maximum, eg in consumer use: *electricity consumed at peak periods*. **3** a time of maximum achievement, etc. **4** the front projecting part of a cap. — *verb intrans.* **1** to reach a maximum. **2** to reach the height of one's powers or popularity. [perhaps related to PICK]

Peak District a national park in N central England, which was established in 1951. AREA 1 404sq km/542sq mi. It is situated mainly in Derbyshire, with parts in adjacent counties. In the S and E there are limestone uplands and woodlands; the limestone caves, notably at Peak Cavern near Castleton, are a major tourist attraction. Moorlands and crags in the N provide a good walking and climbing area. The highest point is at Kinder Scout (636m).

Peake, Mervyn (1911–68) British writer and artist, born in Kuling, S China. He became a painter, and taught at the Westminster School of Art. He is best known for the novel *Mr Pye* (1953), and the Gothic fantasy trilogy of novels which includes *Titus Groan* (1946), *Gormenghast* (1950), and *Titus Alone* (1959). He also published books of verse, and illustrated several classics and children's books.

peakiness *noun* being peaky.

peaky *adj.* (**peakier, peakiest**) ill-looking; pallid.

peal — *noun* **1** the ringing of a bell or set of bells. **2** a set of bells, each with a different note. **3** a burst of noise: *peals of laughter/thunder*. — *verb* **1** *intrans.* to ring or resound. **2** *trans.* to sound or signal (eg a welcome) by ringing. [from Middle English *pele*]

Peano, Giuseppe (1858–1932) Italian mathematician, born in Cuneo. Professor at the

University of Turin, he did important work on differential equations and studied mathematical logic, advocating an entirely formal mathematical language. He also promoted the universal language Interlingua.

peanut *noun* **1** a low-growing annual plant (*Arachis hypogaea*) of the pulse family (Leguminosae). It is native to S America, but widely cultivated as an important food crop for its edible seeds, which are produced in wrinkled yellowish underground pods. **2** the seed of this plant, consisting of white flesh rich in protein, surrounded by a reddish-brown papery skin. When the pod has been removed, peanuts can be eaten raw or roasted, ground to make peanut butter, or used as a source of oil for cooking oil, margarine, and soap. They are a staple food in many tropical regions. — Also called *groundnut, monkey nut*.

peanut butter a spread made from ground roasted peanuts.

pear *noun* **1** a deciduous tree belonging to the genus *Pyrus* of the rose family, especially varieties of *P. communis*, widely cultivated in temperate regions for its edible fruit and its ornamental flowers. **2** the cone-shaped fruit of this tree, which consists of a core of small seeds surrounded by sweet juicy white pulp and a yellowish-green skin. It can be eaten raw, dried, or canned. [from Anglo-Saxon *peru*, from Latin *pirum*]

Pearl a female first name, after the stone.

pearl — *noun* **1** a bead of smooth hard lustrous material found inside the shell of certain molluscs, eg oysters. It is formed by the deposition of layers of nacre (mother-of-pearl) around a minute grain of sand or other foreign particle that has entered the shell. **2** an artificial imitation of this. **3** (**pearls**) a necklace of pearls. **4** mother-of-pearl. **5** something resembling a pearl. **6** something valued or precious: *pearls of wisdom*. — *adj.* **1** like a pearl in colour or shape. **2** made of or set with pearls or mother-of-pearl. — *verb* **1** to set with, or as if with, pearls. **2** to grind down (barley) into small pearl-like grains. **3** *intrans.* to form pearl-like beads or drops. [from Middle English *perle*, from a diminutive of Latin *perna*, sea mussel]

pearl barley seeds of barley ground into round polished grains, used in soups and stews.

Pearl Fishers, The (Les pêcheurs de perles) an opera by Georges Bizet (1863, revised 1889). The story concerns two fishermen friends, Zurga and Nadir, who once quarrelled over love for the same woman, Leila, who arrives in their village as a veiled priestess. Her affair with Nadir is rekindled and they are both sentenced to death for sacrilege, but are saved by Zurga when he recognizes her as the girl who once saved his life.

Pearl Harbor an inlet occupied by a US naval base on the island of Oahu in the US state of Hawaii. A treaty of 1887 granted the USA rights as a coaling and repair base, and the naval base was established in 1908. On 7 Dec 1941, the base was bombed by the Japanese, with 19 ships and 120 aircraft either sunk or disabled. This action brought the USA into World War II.

pearlies *pl. noun* the traditional costume of costermongers, sewn with pearl buttons.

Pearl Islands, Spanish **Archipiélago de las Perlas** POP (1980) 3 000, a Panamanian island group in the Gulf of Panama, Central America. It consists of over 180 islands, the largest being Isla del Rey. CHIEF TOWN San Miguel.

Pearl River *or* **Chu-kiang** *or* **Zhu Jiang** a river in S China formed by the confluence of the Xi Jiang, Bei Jiang, and Dong Jiang rivers. The length of the Pearl R is taken as 2 197km/1 365mi and it is navigable as far as Wuzhou for large vessels. It forms a wide estuary between Hong Kong and Macao, S of Guangzhou (Canton), flowing

into the S China Sea. The river valley is densely populated and fertile.

pearl spar *Geol.* a crystalline carbonate mineral that has a pearly lustre.

pearly *adj.* (**pearlier, pearliest**) **1** like pearl. **2** covered in pearl.

pearly gates *colloq.* the gates of Heaven.

pearly king and queen the London costermonger couple whose pearl-button-covered costumes are judged the most splendid.

Pears, Sir Peter (Neville Luard) (1910–86) English tenor, born in Farnham, Surrey. He was organ scholar at Oxford, then studied singing (1933–4) in London. He toured the USA and Europe with Benjamin Britten, and in 1943 joined Sadler's Wells. After the success of *Peter Grimes* (1945) he joined Britten in the English Opera Group, and was co-founder with him of the Aldeburgh Festival (1948).

Pearse, Patrick (Pádraic) Henry (1879–1916) Irish writer, educationist, and nationalist, born in Dublin. A barrister, he was a leader of the Gaelic League, and editor of its journal. He commanded the insurgents in the Easter Rising of 1916, and was proclaimed President of the provisional government, but after the revolt had been quelled, he was court-martialled and shot, along with his brother William.

Pearson, Sir Cyril Arthur (1866–1921) English newspaper and periodical proprietor, born in Wookey, Somerset. He founded various periodicals before becoming associated with newspapers, founding the *Daily Express*, and amalgamating the *St James Gazette* with the *Evening Standard*. After he lost his sight, he founded the St Dunstan's home for blinded soldiers and became President of the National Institution for the Blind.

Pearson, Karl (1857–1936) English mathematician and scientist, born in London. Professor of Applied Mathematics at University College London, he was a founder of modern statistical theory, introducing an important test of statistical significance and the concept of standard deviation. Also interested in evolution and heredity, he later became Professor of Eugenics.

Peary, Robert Edwin (1856–1920) US admiral and explorer, born in Cresson Springs, Pennsylvania. He made eight Arctic voyages to the Greenland coast, arriving on the east coast in 1891–2 by crossing the ice. In 1909 he led the first expedition to the North Pole, though his achievement was disputed by his fellow-explorer Frederick Cook, who claimed to have reached the Pole in 1908 — a claim generally discredited.

Peary Land a region in N Greenland on the Arctic Ocean, forming a mountainous peninsula. Its N cape, Kap Morris Jesup, is the most northerly point of land in the Arctic. Unlike most of Greenland it is not covered by ice. It was explored by Robert Edwin Peary in 1892 and 1900.

peasant *noun* **1** in poor agricultural societies, a farm worker or small farmer. **2** *derog.* a rough, unmannerly or culturally ignorant person. [from Old French *paisant*, from Latin *pagus*, country district]

Peasant Dance a painting by Pieter Breughel (c.1568, Vienna).

peasantry *noun* the peasant class.

Peasants' Revolt an English popular rising (Jun 1381) among townsmen and peasants, based in Essex, Kent, and London, which was quickly suppressed. Precipitated by the three oppressive poll taxes of 1377–81, its main underlying causes were misgovernment and the desire for personal freedom.

Peasants' War probably the largest peasant uprising (1524–5) in European history, which raged through Germany from the Rhineland to

Pomerania. It sought to defend traditional agrarian rights against lords and princes, and appealed to notions of divine law fostered by the Lutheran Reformation, but was denounced by Martin Luther and brutally suppressed by the princes.

Peasant Wedding Dance a painting by Pieter Breughel (1566, Detroit).

pease pudding a purée made from split peas soaked and then boiled. [from Anglo-Saxon *pise*, pea, from Latin *pisa*]

pea-shooter *noun* a short tube through which to fire dried peas by blowing.

pea soup thick soup made from dried peas.

pea-souper *noun colloq.* a thick yellowish fog.

peat *noun* **1** a mass of dark brown or black fibrous plant material produced by the compression of partially decomposed vegetation in a waterlogged environment where the temperatures are relatively low. It is an early stage in the development of coal, used in compost and manure to improve the quality of soil, and in dried form as a fuel in parts of N Europe. **2** a cut block of this material.

peaty *adj.* (**peatier, peatiest**) **1** like or consisting of peat. **2** having a smoky taste or smell reminiscent of peat.

pebble *noun* **1** a small fragment of rock, with a diameter of 4 to 64mm, often worn round and smooth by water or wind action. **2** a colourless rock crystal; also, a lens made from this. [from Anglo-Saxon *papol*]

pebbledash *noun* cement or plaster with small stones embedded in it, used as a coating for exterior walls.

pebbly *adj.* (**pebblier, pebbliest**) full of or covered with pebbles.

pecan *noun* **1** an oval brown smooth-shelled oily nut. **2** the hickory tree of the southern USA, which bears this nut. [from Illinois (Native American language) *pakani*]

peccadillo *noun* (PL. **peccadillos, peccadilloes**) a minor misdeed. [from Spanish *pecadillo*, diminutive of *pecado*, sin]

peccary *noun* (PL. **peccaries**) a small wild pig of tropical America. [from Carib (S American Indian language) *pakira*]

Pechora a river in N Russia, length 1 790km/1 112mi. It rises on the W slopes of the Ural Mts and flows generally N through forest and tundra regions, then W from Trosh, and then N again from Ust'tsil'ma. It finally flows through NE Archangel oblast to discharge into the Barents Sea at Pechora Bay. The river has a drainage basin area of 327 000sq km/126 000sq mi. The Pechora coal basin extends E from the middle course of the river.

peck¹ — *verb* **1** (**peck something** *or* **peck at something**) *said of a bird* to strike, nip, or pick it with the beak. **2** to poke (a hole) with the beak. **3** (**peck at something**) to eat food desultorily and without relish. **4** to kiss perfunctorily: *pecked her on the cheek*. — *noun* **1** a tap or nip with the beak. **2** a perfunctory kiss. [related to PICK]

peck² *noun* an old measure of capacity of dry goods, especially grain, equal to two gallons (9.1 litres) or a quarter of a bushel. [from Old French *pek*]

pecker *noun* **1** that which pecks; a beak. **2** *colloq.* spirits: *keep one's pecker up*. **3** *North Amer. coarse slang* the penis.

pecking order a scale of ascendancy noticeably operating in a flock of poultry, such that any bird may peck one of lesser importance but must submit to being pecked by those of greater importance; any social hierarchy in animals or humans or system of ranks and associated privileges.

Peckinpah, Sam (1925–84) US film director, born in Fresno, California. He started work on television westerns, and directed his first feature film, *The Deadly Companions*, in 1961. He portrayed a harshly realistic view of the lawless and violent US West, as in *Major Dundee* (1965) and *The Wild Bunch* (1969).

peckish *adj. colloq.* somewhat hungry.

Pecksniff, Seth the hypocritical widowed architect at the centre of Charles Dickens's *Martin Chuzzlewit*. He has two daughters, Charity and Mercy.

Pecos River a river in southern USA, length 1 490km/925mi. Rising in New Mexico in the Sangre de Cristo Mts, it flows S through Texas to join the R Grande NW of Del Rio. It is used for irrigation.

Pécs, German **Fünfkirchen**, Latin **Sopianae** POP (1991e) 170 000, the industrial capital of Baranya county, S Hungary, situated at the foot of the Mecsek Mts. HISTORY capital of E Pannonia under Roman rule; surrounded by city walls during the Middle Ages. It is the centre of a noted wine-producing and coalmining area.

pectic acid *Biochem.* an acid that is obtained from the pectin found within ripening fruits.

pectin *noun Biochem.* a complex polysaccharide carbohydrate that functions as a cement-like material within plant cell walls and also between adjacent cell walls, and is particularly abundant in ripening fruit, eg apples. Pectin forms a gel at low temperatures, and for this reason is widely used in jam-making. [from Greek *pektos*, congealed]

pectoral — *adj.* **1** of or relating to the breast or chest. **2** worn on the breast. — *noun* **1** a pectoral muscle or pectoral fin. **2** a neck ornament worn covering the chest. [from Latin *pectoralis*, from *pectus*, chest]

pectoral fin in fishes, one of a pair of fins situated just behind the gills and corresponding to the forelimbs of terrestrial vertebrates. The pectoral fins are used to control the angle of ascent or descent in the water, and for braking.

peculiar *adj.* **1** strange; odd. **2** (**peculiar to** someone *or* something) exclusively or typically belonging to or associated with them: *habits peculiar to cats*. **3** special; individual: *their own peculiar methods*. **4** especial; particular: *of peculiar interest*. [from Latin *peculium*, private property]

peculiarity *noun* (PL. **peculiarities**) **1** the quality of being strange or odd. **2** a distinctive feature, characteristic or trait. **3** an eccentricity or idiosyncrasy.

peculiarly *adv.* in a peculiar way.

pecuniary *adj.* of, concerning or consisting of money. [from Latin *pecunia*, money, from *pecus*, flock]

ped- see PEDI-.

-ped *or* **-pede** *combining form* forming words meaning 'foot': *quadruped* / *millipede*. [from Latin *pes*, foot]

pedagogic *or* **pedagogical** *adj.* relating to or characteristic of a pedagogue.

pedagogically *adv.* in a pedagogic way.

pedagogue *noun old derog. use* a teacher, especially a strict or pedantic one. [from Greek *paidagogos*, a child's tutor]

pedagogy *noun* the science, principles, or work of teaching. [from Greek *paidagogia*, tutorship, from *pais*, child + *agein*, to lead]

pedal — *noun* a lever operated by the foot on a machine, vehicle, or musical instrument. — *verb trans., intrans.* (**pedalled, pedalling**) to move or operate by means of a pedal or pedals. [from Latin *pedalis*, of the foot]

pedalo *noun* (PL. **pedalos**) a small pedal-operated pleasure boat.

pedant *noun derog.* someone over-concerned with correctness of detail, especially in academic matters. [from Italian *pedante*, teacher]

pedantic *adj.* over-concerned with correctness.

pedantically *adv.* in a pedantic way.

pedantry *noun* **1** excessive concern with correctness. **2** a pedantic expression. **3** unnecessary formality.

peddle *verb* **1** *trans., intrans.* to go from place to place selling (small goods); to be a pedlar. **2** *colloq.* to deal illegally in (narcotic drugs). **3** *colloq.* to publicize and try to win acceptance for (ideas, theories, etc). [from PEDLAR]

peddler *noun* **1** *North Amer., esp. US* a pedlar. **2** someone dealing illegally in narcotics: *a dope peddler*.

-pede see -PED.

pederast *or* **paederast** *noun* a man who is sexually attracted to or has sexual relations with boys. [from Greek *pais*, child + *erastes*, lover]

pederasty *or* **paederasty** *noun* sexual relations between a man and a boy.

pedestal *noun* the base on which a statue or column is mounted.
— **put someone on a pedestal** to admire or revere them extremely; to idolize them. [from Italian *piedistallo*, foot of stall]

pedestrian — *noun* a person travelling on foot, especially in a street; a walker. — *adj.* **1** of or for pedestrians. **2** dull; unimaginative: *a pedestrian rendering by the orchestra*. [from Latin *pedester*, on foot]

pedestrian crossing a specially marked crossing-place for pedestrians, where they have priority over traffic.

pedestrianization *or* **pedestrianisation** *noun* pedestrianizing or being pedestrianized.

pedestrianize *or* **pedestrianise** *verb* to convert (a street, etc) into an area for pedestrians only.

pedestrian precinct a shopping street or area from which traffic is excluded.

pedi- *or* **ped-** *combining form* forming words meaning 'foot': *pedicure*. [from Latin *pes*, foot]

pediatrics another spelling of **paediatrics**.

pedicure *noun* a medical or cosmetic treatment of the feet and toenails. [from PEDI- + Latin *curare*, to look after]

pedigree — *noun* **1** a person or animal's line of descent, especially if long and distinguished, or proof of pure breeding. **2** a genealogical table showing this; a family tree. — *adj., said of an animal* pure-bred; descended from a long line of known ancestors of the same breed. [from Old French *pie de grue*, crane's foot, from its similarity to a branching family tree]

pediment *noun* **1** *Archit.* a wide triangular gable set over a classical portico or the face of a building. **2** *Geol.* a gently sloping surface, usually consisting of bare rock covered by a thin layer of sediment, formed by the erosion of cliffs or steep slopes. [earlier *periment*, thought to be a corruption of PYRAMID]

pedlar *noun* a person who goes from place to place peddling small articles. [from Middle English *ped*, basket]

pedo- same as PAEDO-.

pedology *noun Geol.* the scientific study of the origin, properties, and uses of soil. *Medicine* the scientific study of physiological and psychological aspects of childhood. [from Greek *pedon*, ground + *logos*, discourse]

pedometer *noun* a device that measures distance walked by recording the number of steps taken.

Pedro, Don the childishly good-humoured Prince of Aragon in Shakespeare's *Much Ado About Nothing*, who woos Hero on behalf of Claudio.

peduncle *noun* **1** *Bot.* a short stalk, eg one carrying a single flower head. **2** *Anat., Pathol.* any stalk-like structure. [from Latin *pedunculus*, diminutive of *pes*, foot]

pee *colloq.* — *verb intrans.* to urinate. — *noun* **1** an act of urinating. **2** urine. [from the first letter of PISS]

Peebles POP (1981) 6 700, the capital of Tweeddale district, Borders Region, SE central Scotland. It lies on the R Tweed, 33km/20mi S of Edinburgh. NOTABLE FEATURES Tweeddale Museum; medieval Neidpath Castle nearby; Traquair House, the oldest inhabited house in Scotland, is 13km/8mi SE.

peek — *verb intrans.* to glance briefly and surreptitiously; to peep. — *noun* a brief furtive glance. [from Middle English *piken*, to peek]

Peel, Sir Robert (1788–1850) English statesman, born near Bury, Lancashire. A Tory MP from 1809, as Secretary for Ireland (1812–18) he displayed a strong anti-Catholic spirit and was fiercely attacked by Daniel O'Connell, earning the nickname 'Orange Peel'. As Home Secretary (1822–7, 1828–30), he carried through the Catholic Emancipation Act (1829) and reorganized the London police force ('Peelers' or 'Bobbies'). As Prime Minister (1834–5, 1841–6), his second ministry concentrated on economic reforms, but his decision to phase out agricultural protection by repealing the Corn Laws (1846) split his party, and precipitated his resignation, though he remained in parliament as leader of the 'Peelites'.

peel — *verb* **1** to strip the skin or rind off (a fruit or vegetable). **2** *intrans.* to be able to be peeled: *peel easily.* **3** (*also* **peel something away** *or* **off**) to strip off (an outer layer). **4** *intrans. said of a wall or other surface* to shed its outer coating in flaky strips. **5** *intrans. said of skin, paint, or other coverings* to flake off in patches. **6** *intrans. said of a person or part of the body* to shed skin in flaky layers after sunburn. — *noun* the skin or rind of vegetables or fruit, especially citrus fruit.
— **peel off 1** *said of an aircraft or vehicle* to veer away from the main group. **2** *colloq.* to undress. [from Anglo-Saxon, from Latin *pilare*, to deprive of hair]

peeler *noun* a small knife or device for peeling fruit and vegetables.

peelings *pl. noun* strips of peel removed from a fruit or vegetable.

peep¹ — *verb intrans.* **1** to look quickly or covertly, eg through a narrow opening or from a place of concealment; to peek. **2** to emerge briefly or partially. — *noun* **1** a quick covert look. **2** a first faint glimmering: *at peep of day.* [a variant of PEEK]

peep² — *noun* **1** the faint high-pitched cry of a baby bird, etc; a cheep. **2** the least utterance: *not another peep out of you!* — *verb intrans.* **1** *said of a young bird, etc* to utter a high-pitched cry; to cheep. **2** *colloq.* to sound or cause to sound: *peep the horn.* [imitative]

peepers *pl. noun old colloq. use* eyes.

peephole *noun* **1** a hole, crack, etc through which to peep. **2** a tiny aperture in a front door, fitted with a convex lens, through which one can check on callers before opening the door.

peeping Tom a voyeur.

peepshow *noun* a box with a peephole through which a series of moving pictures can be watched.

peer¹ *noun* **1** a member of the nobility, ie, in Britain, a duke, marquess, earl, viscount, or baron. **2** someone who is one's equal in age, rank, etc; a contemporary, companion, or fellow. [from Old French *per*, from Latin *par*, equal]

peer² *verb intrans.* **1** (**peer at something** *or* **someone**) to look hard at them, especially through narrowed eyes, as if having difficulty in seeing. **2** to peep out or emerge briefly or partially.

peerage *noun* **1** the title or rank of a peer: *granted a peerage / raised to the peerage*. **2** (*sing., pl.*) the members of the nobility as a group. **3** a book containing a list of peers with details of their families and descent.
◇ In the UK, the nobility is made up of holders of the title of duke, marquis, earl, viscount, and baron or baroness (whether hereditary or for life). Their traditional privileges have been steadily reduced over the centuries, the principal two remaining being their right to sit in the House of Lords, and their exemption from jury service.

peeress *noun* **1** the wife or widow of a peer. **2** a female peer in her own right.

peer group one's peers or companions as a group, especially as an influence on one's attitude and aspirations.

Peer Gynt **1** a play by Henrik Ibsen (1867). Using many sources from folklore, it is an existentialist and poetic examination of the Norwegian character. **2** incidental music by Edvard Grieg for Ibsen's play. Some of it was later arranged for concert performance as two orchestral suites.

peerless *adj.* without equal; excelling all; matchless.

peerlessly *adv.* without equal.

peerlessness *noun* being without equal.

peer of the realm a member of the nobility with the right to sit in the House of Lords.

peeve — *verb colloq.* to irritate, annoy, or offend. — *noun* a cause of vexation or irritation. [a back-formation from PEEVISH]

peeved *adj.* annoyed, irritated, offended.

peevish *adj.* irritable; cantankerous; inclined to whine or complain.

peevishly *adv.* in a peevish way.

peevishness *noun* being peevish.

peewit *noun* a lapwing. [imitative of its cry]

peg — *noun* **1** a little shaft of wood, metal, or plastic shaped for any of various fixing, fastening, or marking uses. **2** a coat hook fixed to a wall, etc. **3** a wooden or plastic clip for fastening washed clothes to a line to dry; a clothes peg. **4** any of several wooden pins on a stringed instrument, turned to tune it. **5** a point of reference on which to base an argument, etc. **6** *old colloq. use* a drink of spirits. — *verb* (**pegged, pegging**) **1** to insert a peg into. **2** to fasten with a peg or pegs. **3** to freeze (prices, incomes, etc) at a certain level.
— **off the peg** *said of clothes* ready to wear; ready-made.
peg away at something *colloq.* to work steadily at it.
peg out *colloq.* to die.
peg something out to mark out (ground) with pegs.
a square peg in a round hole a person who does not fit in well in his or her environment, job, etc.
take someone down a peg or two *colloq.* to humble them.
[from Old Dutch *pegge*]

Pegasus **1** in Greek mythology, a winged horse, which sprang from the body of Medusa after her death. Bellerophon caught it with Athene's assistance, but later fell off and was killed while trying to fly to heaven. It became a constellation and the servant of Zeus. **2** *Astron.* a large but dim constellation in the northern hemisphere.

peg board a board with holes for receiving pegs that are used for scoring in games, or for attaching matter for display.

Peggotty, Clara the adored nursemaid and loyal friend to David in Charles Dickens's *David*

Copperfield. Other family members include her brother Daniel Peggotty and his nephew Ham.

peg leg *colloq.* an artificial leg, or a person with an artifical leg.

pegmatite *noun Geol.* any of various very coarse-grained igneous rocks, many of which are important sources of economically important minerals such as mica, feldspar, tourmaline, topaz, beryl, and garnet. The commonest type is granite pegmatite. [from Greek *pegma*, bond, framework]

Pegu **1** POP (1983) 255 000, the capital of Pegu division, SE central Burma (Myanma). NOTABLE FEATURE Shwemawdaw Pagoda. **2** POP (1983) 3.8m, a division of S Burma (Myanma). It is bordered in the SE by the Gulf of Martaban and the R Irrawaddy forms part of the W border. CAPITAL Pegu.

PEI *abbrev.* Prince Edward Island.

Peierls, Sir Rudolf Ernst (1907–) German–British theoretical physicist, born in Berlin. Professor at the Universities of Birmingham and Oxford, his study of uranium fission during World War II indicated the feasibility of the atomic bomb. Supported by the British government, he led a group developing ways of separating uranium isotopes. The work was moved to the USA as part of the Manhattan Project in 1943.

peignoir *noun* a woman's light dressing-gown. [from French *peignoir*, from *peigner*, to comb]

pejorative — *adj., said of a word or expression* disapproving, derogatory, disparaging, or uncomplimentary. — *noun* a word or affix with derogatory force. [from Latin *peiorare*, to make worse]

pejoratively *adv.* in a pejorative way.

peke *noun colloq.* a Pekinese.

Pekinese *or* **Pekingese** *noun* (PL. **Pekinese**) a small dog with a flat face and a silky coat, originally a Chinese breed. [from *Peking* (Beijing) in China]

Peking see BEIJING.

Peking Man the fossils of *Homo erectus* found before World War II in a cave near Beijing (Peking), and originally named *Sinanthropus pekinensis*. Their likely age is c.350 000 years.

Peking Opera a form of Chinese theatre which has its roots in Yuan drama and a variety of ancient entertainments. Highly disciplined in style, it combines acting, dancing, singing, juggling, and acrobatics, and has an orchestral accompaniment. Its precise stage language comprises ideographic sleeve movements, hand and pheasant-feather movements, conventions of painted-face (indicating character-types), symbolic costumes, and traditional stage-properties.

pekoe *noun* a high-quality black China tea. [from Chinese dialect *pek-ho*]

pelagic *adj.* **1** *technical* relating to, or carried out on, the deep open sea. **2** denoting plankton that float and fish and other organisms that swim freely (nekton) in the surface waters, as opposed to *benthic* organisms that live on the bottom of a sea or lake. [from Greek *pelagos*, sea]

Pelagius (c.360–c.420 AD) British monk and heretic, of British or Irish origin. He settled in Rome c.400, where he disputed with Augustine on the nature of grace and original sin. His view that salvation could be achieved by the exercise of one's basically good moral nature (Pelagianism) was condemned as heretical by the Councils in 416 and 418, and he was excommunicated and banished from Rome.

pelargonium *noun* any of a genus of plants of the geranium family, with red, pink, or white flowers and strong-smelling leaves, often grown as house and garden plants under the name of geranium. [from Greek *pelargos*, stork]

Pelasgians the name given by the ancient Greeks to the indigenous peoples who inhabited Greece before the 12c BC.

Pelé, properly **Edson Arantes do Nascimento** (1940–) Brazilian footballer, born in Três Corações. He made his international début at age 16, and appeared in four World Cup championships (1958–70). He scored two goals for Brazil in their 4–2 victory over Sweden in the 1958 World Cup final, and again led them to victory in the 1962 and 1970 finals. His first-class career was spent at Santos (1955–74) and with the New York Cosmos (1975–7). He appeared in 1 363 first-class games (1955–77) and scored 1 281 goals. He is a national hero in Brazil.

Pelée, Mount an active volcano on Martinique I, E Caribbean Sea. HEIGHT 1 397m. It erupted in 1902 killing over 26 000 people in the town of St Pierre.

Peleus in Greek mythology, the King of Phythia in Thessaly, husband of Thetis (a sea nymph), and father of Achilles.

Pelham, Thomas, Baron, properly **Thomas Pelham-Holles, 1st Duke of Newcastle-under-Lyme** (1693–1768) English statesman. A Whig and a supporter of Walpole, in 1724 he became Secretary of State for 30 years. He succeeded his brother Henry Pelham (c.1695–1754) as Prime Minister (1754–6, 1757–62), and was very influential during the reigns of George I and George II. In 1757 he was in coalition with William Pitt ('the elder') during the Seven Years War, but resigned in 1762 due to hostility from the new king, George III.

pelican *noun* (PL. **pelican, pelicans**) an aquatic bird related to the cormorants, found on coasts and inland waters in most warm regions of the world. It has a large light body, a long neck, short legs, and mainly white plumage except for dark primary (wing-tip) feathers. It also has an enormous beak with a pouch below that is used to scoop up fish. [from Greek *pelekan*]

pelican crossing a pedestrian crossing with pedestrian-controlled traffic lights. [from *pedestrian light-controlled crossing*]

pellagra *noun Medicine* a disease caused by a dietary deficiency of nicotinic acid (a member of the vitamin B complex) or the amino acid tryptophan, from which it is made. It is characterized by scaly discoloration of the skin, diarrhoea, vomiting, and psychological disturbances such as depression. [from Italian *pellagra*, from Latin *pellis*, skin + Greek *agra*, seizure]

Pelléas et Mélisande **1** a play by Maurice Maeterlinck (1892). A tragedy based on legendary sources and using minimalist effects, it provided the inspiration for Debussy's opera (1902). **2** an opera by Claude Debussy (1902), based on Maeterlinck's tragedy. It tells of the widower Golaud who marries a woman (Mélisande) after discovering her weeping in the forest. On hearing through his half-brother Pelléas that his grandfather (King Arkel) approves the new marriage, the couple go to his castle, where Pelléas begins an affair with the mysterious Mélisande that makes Golaud unbearably jealous.

pellet *noun* **1** a small rounded mass of compressed material, eg paper. **2** a piece of small shot for an airgun, etc. **3** a ball of undigested material regurgitated by an owl or hawk. [from Old French *pelote*, from Latin *pila*, ball]

Pelletier, Pierre Joseph (1788–1842) French chemist, born in Paris. Working in his home town, he investigated the green pigment of leaves, naming it chlorophyll, and isolated many alkaloids, plant-derived compounds which are important to medicine and industry, including strychnine, quinine, and caffeine. He later studied alkaloid structures, and in 1838 discovered toluene.

pell-mell *adv.* headlong; in confused haste; helter-skelter. [from Old French *pesle-mesle*, rhyming compound from *mesler*, to mix]

pellucid *adj.* **1** transparent. **2** absolutely clear in expression and meaning. [from Latin *per*, utterly + *lucidus*, clear]

pelmet *noun* a strip of fabric or a narrow board fitted along the top of a window to conceal the curtain rail.

Peloponnese, Greek **Peloponnisos** POP (1991) 1.1m, a peninsular region of Greece, comprising the most southerly part of the Greek mainland, to which it is linked by the narrow Isthmus of Corinth. AREA 21 379sq km/ 8 252sq mi. There is a range of hills in the N; the highest peak is Killini (2 376m). CHIEF TOWNS Argos, Corinth, Patras, Pirgos, Sparta, Calamata. It is a popular holiday region. [from Greek, = the island of Pelops]

Peloponnesian War a war (431–404 BC) fought throughout the ancient Greek world on land and sea between Athens and Sparta and their respective allies. The underlying cause was the fear, especially on the part of Corinth and Sparta, of Athenian naval expansion; Sparta began hostilities by invading Attica in 431 BC. The first phase of the war ended in 421 BC with the Peace of Nicias. The second phase began when Athens invaded Sicily in 415 BC, and ended when the Spartan navy under Lysander, aided by the Persians, destroyed the Athenian navy and invaded Athens. The Athenian empire was dismantled and a Spartan-backed puppet regime, the so-called Thirty Tyrants, was installed in Athens.

Pelops in Greek mythology, the son of Tantalus. In order to marry Hippodameia, he bribed Myrtilus, the charioteer of her father Oenomaus, to put a wax linch-pin in his chariot-wheel. After Oenomaus's death he also killed Myrtilus, and this brought a curse upon his sons, Atreus and Thyestes.

pelota *noun* a Spanish and Latin American court game, in which the players use a basket strapped to their wrists to hit a ball against a specially marked wall. [from Spanish *pelota*, ball]

peloton *noun* the leading group of cyclists in a race. [from French *peloton*, small ball, cluster]

pelt¹ — *verb* **1** to bombard with missiles: *was pelted with stones*. **2** (*also* **pelt down**) *said of rain, hail, etc* to fall fast and heavily. **3** *intrans.* to rush along at top speed. — *noun* an act or spell of pelting.
— **at full pelt** as fast as possible.

pelt² *noun* **1** the skin of a dead animal, especially with the fur still on it. **2** the coat of a living animal. **3** a hide stripped of hair for tanning. [from Old French *pelleterie*, animal skins, from Latin *pellis*, skin]

pelvic *adj.* relating to or in the region of the pelvis.

pelvic inflammatory disease *Medicine* any pelvic infection of the upper reproductive tract in women, usually affecting the uterus, Fallopian tubes, and ovaries, and generally caused by the spread of infection from an infected organ nearby, eg the vagina or the appendix. It can cause blockage of the Fallopian tubes.

pelvis *noun Anat.* **1** the basin-shaped cavity formed by the bones of the pelvic girdle. **2** the pelvic girdle itself, which articulates with the spine and the bones of the legs or hindlimbs. **3** in the mammalian kidney, the expanded upper end of the ureter, into which the urine drains. [from Latin *pelvis*, basin]

Pemba POP (1987e) 52 000, an island region of Tanzania. It is situated in the Indian Ocean, N of Zanzibar and E of Tanga. AREA 981sq km/ 379sq mi. CAPITAL Chake Chake. ECONOMY cloves (world's largest producer); copra.

Pembrokeshire Coast a national park in SW Wales, established in 1952. It is characterized by long stretches of coastline alternating between cliffs and sandy beaches, and includes Milford Haven Harbour, St David's Cathedral, and several Norman castles. AREA 579sq km/ 223sq mi.

pemmican *noun* **1** a Native American food of dried meat beaten to a paste and mixed with fat. **2** a similarly condensed and nutritious mixture of dried ingredients used as emergency rations. [from Cree (Native American language) *pimekan*]

PEN *abbrev.* Poets, Playwrights, Editors, Essayists, and Novelists, an international association of writers founded by C A Dawson Scott in 1921. It promotes friendship and understanding between writers, and defends freedom of expression within and between all nations.

pen¹ — *noun* **1** a small enclosure for animals. **2** (*often in compounds*) any small enclosure or area of confinement: *a playpen*. **3** a bomb-proof dock for submarines. — *verb* (**penned, penning**) (**pen someone** *or* **something in** *or* **up**) to enclose or confine them in a pen, or as if in a pen. [from Anglo-Saxon *penn*]

pen² — *noun* **1** a writing instrument that uses ink, formerly a quill, now any of various implements fitted with a nib, rotating ball, or felt or nylon point. **2** this as a symbol of the writing profession. — *verb* (**penned, penning**) to compose and write (a letter, poem, etc) with a pen. [from Latin *penna*, feather]

pen³ *noun North Amer. colloq.* a penitentiary.

pen⁴ *noun* a female swan.

penal *adj.* relating to punishment, especially by law. [from Latin *poenalis*, from *poena*, penalty]

penal code a system of laws concerning the punishment of crime.

penalization *or* **penalisation** *noun* penalizing or being penalized.

penalize *or* **penalise** *verb* **1** to impose a penalty on, for wrongdoing, cheating, breaking a rule, committing a foul, etc. **2** to disadvantage: *income groups that are penalized by the new tax laws*.

Penal Laws collectively, statutes passed in the 16c–17c against the practice of Roman Catholicism in Britain and Ireland, when Catholic nations were perceived as a threat. Catholics were prevented from voting and holding public office, and fined or imprisoned for participating in Catholic services; officiating priests could be executed. The laws were repealed in stages, from the late 18c to 1926.

penally *adv.* as punishment.

penal servitude *Hist.* imprisonment with hard labour.

penalty *noun* (PL. **penalties**) **1** a punishment for wrongdoing, breaking a contract or rule, etc. **2** a punishment that one brings on oneself through ill-advised action: *pay the penalty for my error*. **3** *Sport* a handicap imposed on a competitor or team for a foul or other infringement of the rules, in team games taking the form of an advantage awarded to the opposing side. [from Latin *poenalitas*, from *poena*, punishment]

penalty area *or* **penalty box** *Football* an area in front of either goal within which a foul by any player in the defending team is punished by a penalty awarded to the attacking team.

penalty kick **1** *Rugby* a free kick. **2** *Football* a free kick at goal from a distance of 11m (12yd), awarded to the attacking team for a foul committed in the penalty area by the defending team.

penance *noun* **1** repentance or atonement for an offence or wrongdoing, or an act of repentance: *do penance*. **2** *RC Church* a sacrament involving confession, repentance, forgiveness, and the performance of a penance suggested by one's confessor. [from Old French *penance*, from Latin *paenitentia*, penitence]

Penang, also **Pulau Pinang** POP (1990) 1.1m, a state in NW Malaysia. AREA 1 044sq km/ 403sq mi. It consists of a coastal strip on the NW coast of the Malay Peninsula and the island of Penang in the Strait of Malacca. CAPITAL George Town. ECONOMY rice; rubber; tin.

Penates in Roman religion, the guardians of the storeroom; 'Lares and Penates' were the household gods. The *penates publici* were the 'luck' of the Roman state, originally brought by Aeneas from Troy and kept at Lavinium.

pence see PENNY.

-pence *combining form* denoting a number of pennies (as a value): *threepence*.

penchant *noun* a taste, liking, inclination, or tendency: *a penchant for childish pranks*. [from French *penchant*, present participle of *pencher*, to lean]

pencil — *noun* **1** a writing and drawing instrument consisting of a wooden shaft containing a stick of graphite or other material, sharpened for use and making more or less erasable marks. **2** such material, especially with regard to the alterability of marks made with it: *written in pencil*. **3** something with a similar function or shape: *an eyebrow pencil / a pencil of light*. — *verb* (**pencilled, pencilling**) to write, draw, or mark with a pencil.
— **pencil something in** to note down a provisional commitment in one's diary, for later confirmation.
[from Latin *penicillus*, painter's brush, diminutive of *peniculus*, little tail]

Penda (c.575–655) King of Mercia (c.632–55), who mastered the English Midlands, and frequently warred with the kings of Northumbria. His forces defeated and killed Edwin at Hatfield in Yorkshire (633), and also Edwin's successor, Oswald, when he invaded Penda's territories (642). Penda was slain in battle near Leeds while campaigning against Oswald's successor, Oswiu.

pendant *noun* **1** an ornament suspended from a neck chain, necklace, bracelet, etc; a necklace with a pendant hanging from it. **2** any of several hanging articles, eg an earring, ceiling light, etc. **3** a companion piece, eg a painting or poem. [from Latin *pendere*, to hang]

pendent *adj.* **1** hanging; suspended; dangling. **2** projecting; jutting; overhanging. **3** undetermined or undecided; pending. [from Latin *pendere*, to hang]

pending — *adj.* **1** waiting to be decided or dealt with. **2** *said of a patent* about to come into effect. — *prep.* until; awaiting; during: *held in prison pending trial*. [from Latin *pendere*, to hang]

pendulous *adj.* hanging down loosely; drooping; swinging freely. [from Latin *pendulus*, hanging]

pendulously *adv.* in a pendulous way.

pendulum *noun* **1** *Physics* a weight that is suspended from a fixed point and swings back and forth through a small angle with *simple harmonic motion*. **2** a swinging lever used to regulate the movement of a clock. [from Latin *pendulum*, neuter of *pendulus*, hanging]

Penelope **1** in Greek legend, the wife of Odysseus, who faithfully waited 20 years for his return from Troy. She tricked her insistent suitors by weaving a web (a shroud for Odysseus's father, Laertes, which had to be finished before she could marry), and undoing her work every night. **2** a female first name. [from Greek, a name perhaps associated with weaving]

penetrability *noun* the quality of being penetrable.

penetrable *adj.* capable of being penetrated.

penetrate *verb* **1** (**penetrate something** *or* **into something**) to find a way in; to enter, especially with difficulty. **2** to infiltrate (an organization, etc). **3** to find a way through; to pierce or permeate: *penetrate enemy lines / penetrated the silence*. **4** *intrans.* to be understood: *the news didn't penetrate at first*. **5** to see through (a disguise). **6** to fathom, solve, or understand (a mystery). **7** *said of a man* to insert his penis into the vagina of (a woman). [from Latin *penetrare*, to penetrate]

penetrating *adj.* **1** *said of a voice, etc* all too loud and clear; strident; carrying. **2** *said of a person's mind* acute; discerning. **3** *said of the eyes or a look* piercing; probing.

penetration *noun* **1** the process of penetrating or being penetrated. **2** mental acuteness; perspicacity; insight.

penfriend *or* **penpal** *noun* a person, especially foreign and otherwise unknown to one, with whom one regularly corresponds.

Penghu *or* **P'eng-hu Qindao**, Spanish, Portuguese **Pescadores** POP (1982e) 104 000, an island archipelago and county of Taiwan. AREA 127sq km/49sq mi. It is situated in the Taiwan Strait astride the Tropic of Cancer and consists of 64 islands, one third of which are uninhabitable. Most of the population (85%) live on the largest island, Penghu. Penghu Bay Bridge is the largest inter-island bridge in the Far East (5 541m long). ECONOMY fishing; vegetables; coral. NOTABLE FEATURES many temples (the oldest was built in 1593 in honour of Matsu, the Goddess of the Sea).

penguin *noun* any of 17 species of a flightless sea bird belonging to the family Spheniscidae, found in the S hemisphere, especially the Antarctic region. The penguin has a stout body, small almost featherless wings modified to form powerful flippers, short legs set far back on the body, and bluish-grey or black waterproof plumage, with a white belly.
◇ The penguin's powerful flippers propel it forward through the water, and it is an excellent swimmer and diver, catching fish and squid in its strong bill. On land, it has a characteristic upright waddling walk. Penguins nest in colonies on land, and usually a single egg is laid by the female. The largest species is the emperor penguin, which stands about 1.2m high, and has a bright yellow or orange collar. In this species, the male is left to incubate the egg, which he balances on his feet for two months. During this time he does not eat, and the female returns soon after the egg is hatched.

penicillin *noun* any of a group of antibiotics derived from the mould *Penicillium notatum*, or produced synthetically, that prevent the growth of a wide range of bacteria by inhibiting manufacture of the bacterial cell wall. Penicillin is widely used medically to treat bacterial infections. [from Latin *penicillus*, hairy tuft, from the appearance of the mould]

penile *adj.* relating to or resembling the penis.

peninsula *noun* a piece of land almost surrounded by water or projecting into water from a larger land mass. [from Latin *paene*, almost + *insula*, island]

peninsular *adj.* relating to or of the nature of a peninsula.

Peninsular Campaign an attempt (1862) during the American Civil War by the Union army led by General McClellan to take Richmond, Virginia (the Southern capital), by moving up the peninsula between the James and York rivers. Although his troops won most of the battles, McClellan failed to take the offensive and instead slowly moved away from the capital.

Peninsular Malaysia *or* **Malay Peninsula** a peninsula in S Asia separating the Andaman Sea and the Strait of Malacca in the E from the Gulf of Thailand and the S China Sea in the W. S Thailand occupies the N part of the peninsula; 11 states and a federal territory of Malaysia lie to the S. The island of Singapore is situated at the S tip.

Peninsular War the prolonged struggle (1808–14) for the Iberian peninsula between the occupying French and a British army under the Duke of Wellington, supported by Portuguese forces. Known in Spain as the 'War of Independence' and to Napoleonic France as the 'Spanish ulcer', it began as a revolt against Napoleon's brother Joseph Bonaparte becoming King of Spain, but developed into a bitter conflict as British troops repulsed Masséna's Lisbon offensive (1810–11) and advanced from their base behind the Torres Vedras to liberate Spain. Following Napoleon's Moscow campaign (1812), French resources were over-extended, which enabled Wellington's army to invade SW France (1813–14).

penis *noun* in higher vertebrates, the male organ of copulation, which is used to transfer sperm to the female reproductive tract. In mammals it is made erect by the swelling of vessels that fill with blood. It also contains the urethra through which urine is passed. [from Latin *penis*, originally = tail]

penitence *noun* being penitent and wishing to improve.

penitent — *adj.* regretful for wrong one has done; repentant. — *noun* a repentant person, especially one doing penance on the instruction of a confessor. [from Latin *paenitens*, repentant]

penitential *adj.* relating to penitence or penance.

penitential psalms *Relig.* a set of seven Old Testament psalms which have been used in Christian liturgy since at least the early Middle Ages, when they were regularly recited on Fridays during Lent. They are mainly laments, although not all are directly concerned with the repentance of sin. They comprise Psalms 6, 32, 38, 51 (Miserere), 102, 130 (De Profundis), and 143.

penitentiary — *noun* (PL. **penitentiaries**) *North Amer.* a federal or state prison. — *adj.* of or relating to punishment or penance. [from Latin *paenitens*, repentant]

penitently *adv.* in a penitent way.

penknife *noun* a pocket knife with blades that fold into the handle. [originally used for cutting quills]

penmanship *noun* skill with the pen, whether calligraphic or literary.

Penn, William (1644–1710) English Quaker leader and founder of Pennsylvania, USA, born in London. Sent down from Oxford for his opposition to Anglicanism, he joined the Quakers in 1666, and while imprisoned for his writings (1668) he wrote the most popular of his books, *No Cross, No Crown*. In 1681 he obtained a grant of land in N America, named it Pennsylvania in honour of his father, and governed the colony (1682–4). After his return to England, he supported James II, and worked for religious tolerance.

Penn. *abbrev.* Pennsylvania.

pen name a pseudonym used by a writer.

pennant *noun* a small narrow triangular flag, used on vessels for identification or for signalling. [probably from PENNON + PENDANT]

Penney, William George Penney, Baron (1909–91) British physicist, born in Sheerness. Professor of Mathematics in London, he worked at Los Alamos on the atom bomb project during World War II, and later became Director of the Atomic Weapons Research Establishment at Aldermaston (1953–9), Chairman of the UK Atomic Energy Authority (1964–7), and Rector of Imperial College (1967–73). He was the key figure in the UK's success in producing its own atomic (1952) and hydrogen (1957) bombs.

penniless *adj.* poverty-stricken.

Pennines *or* **Pennine Chain**, also called **the backbone of England** a mountain range in N England, extending S from Northumberland to Derbyshire. It consists of a fold of carboniferous limestone and overlying millstone grit, worn into high moorland and fell. The range is separated from the Cheviot Hills to the N by the Tyne Gap, and is dissected in the S by the Yorkshire Dales. Rising to 893m at Cross Fell, the Pennines form the main watershed for the rivers of N England. The Pennine Way footpath extends 402km/250mi from Derbyshire to the Scottish Borders.

pennon *noun* **1** *Hist.* a long narrow flag with a tapering divided tip, eg borne on his lance by a knight. **2** a pennant. [from Latin *penna*, feather]

Pennsylvania POP (1990) 12m, a state in NE USA, which is divided into 67 counties. AREA 117 343sq km/45 308sq mi. It is known as the 'Keystone State'. PHYSICAL DESCRIPTION the Delaware R forms the E border; other rivers include the Susquehanna, Allegheny, and Monongahela, the latter two forming the Ohio R at Pittsburgh; the Allegheny Mts lie in the SW of the state. HISTORY first settled by the Swedish in 1643; taken by the Dutch, and then by the British in 1664; region given by King Charles II to William Penn in 1681; farming areas of SE were settled by persecuted German religious sects (Pennsylvania Dutch); scene of many battles in the American Revolution and Civil War; one of the original states of the Union, and the second to ratify the Federal Constitution. CAPITAL Harrisburg. CHIEF TOWNS Philadelphia, Pittsburgh, Erie. ECONOMY a major industrial state, with coal mining and oil drilling; manufactures include steel and other metals, machinery, and electrical equipment; agricultural produce centres on dairy products, cereals, vegetables, apples, hay, tobacco, and grapes.

Pennsylvania, University of a university in Philadelphia, founded as a school in 1940, opened as an academy in 1753, and (with the help of Benjamin Franklin) chartered as a college in 1755. With the foundation of its medical school in 1765 (the first in N America) it became a university, though it was not renamed as such until 1779.

penny *noun* (PL. **pence**, **pennies**) **1** in the UK, a hundredth part of £1, or a bronze coin having this value. **2** in the UK before decimalization in 1971, $\frac{1}{12}$ of a shilling or $\frac{1}{240}$ of £1, or a bronze coin having this value. **3** the least quantity of money: *won't cost a penny*. **4** *North Amer.* one cent, or a coin having this value. **5** a coin of low value in certain other countries.
— **in for a penny, in for a pound** (*often shortened to* **in for a penny**) once involved, one may as well be totally committed.
in penny numbers *colloq.* in small quantities.
the penny dropped *colloq.* understanding came.
a pretty penny *ironic* a huge sum.
spend a penny *euphemistic colloq.* to urinate.
turn an honest penny *colloq.* to earn one's living honestly.
two *or* **ten a penny** very common.
[from Anglo-Saxon *pening*]

-penny *combining form* denoting a number of pennies (as a value): *a five-penny piece*.

penny dreadful *colloq.* a cheap trivial novel or thriller.

penny farthing *Brit.* an early type of bicycle with a large front wheel and small back wheel.

penny-halfpenny *noun* formerly in the UK, one and a half pre-decimal pence.

penny-in-the-slot *adj., said of a machine* coin-operated.

penny-pincher *noun* a person who is too careful with money, a miser.

penny-pinching *adj. derog.* too careful with one's money; miserly; stingy.

pennyworth *noun old use* an amount that can be bought for one penny.

penological *adj.* relating to or involving penology.

penologist *noun* a person who studies and is expert in penology.

penology *noun* the study of crime and punishment.

pen-pusher *noun* a clerk or minor official whose job includes much tedious paperwork.

pen-pushing *noun* doing tedious paperwork.

Penrith POP (1981) 12 000, a town in Eden district, Cumbria, NW England, situated 30km/19mi S of Carlisle. NOTABLE FEATURES castle (14c–15c); St Andrew's Church.

Penrose, Roger (1931–) British mathematical astronomer, born in Colchester. Professor at Oxford, he showed with Stephen Hawking that once the collapse of a very massive star at the end of its life has started, the formation of a black hole is inevitable. Penrose also put forward the hypothesis of 'cosmic censorship', proposing that there must be an 'event horizon' around a black hole, isolating its physically unlawful behaviour from the rest of the universe.

pension — *noun* a government allowance to a retired, disabled, or widowed person; a regular payment by an employer to a retired employee. — *verb* (**pensioned, pensioning**) to grant a pension to. — **pension someone off** to put them into retirement on a pension. [from Old French, from Latin *pensio*, payment]

pensionable *adj.* entitling one to a pension.

pensioner *noun* a person in receipt of a pension.

pensive *adj.* preoccupied with one's thoughts; thoughtful. [from Old French *pensif*, from *penser*, to think]

pensively *adv.* in a pensive way.

pent
— **pent up** *said of feelings, energy, etc* repressed or stifled; bursting to be released. [an old past participle of PEN[1]]

penta- *or* **pent-** *combining form* forming words meaning 'five': *pentatonic.* [from Greek *pente*, five]

Pentagon the central offices of the US military forces and the Defense Department, in Arlington, Virginia. The complex was built in 1941–3, covers 14ha, and is composed of five five-storey, concentric, pentagonal buildings.

pentagon *noun* a two-dimensional figure with five sides and five angles. [from Greek *pente*, five + *gonia*, angle]

pentagonal *adj.* having five sides and angles.

pentagram *noun* a five-pointed star, especially used as a magic symbol. [from Greek *pente*, five + *gramma*, character, letter]

pentameter *noun* a line of verse with five metrical feet. [from Greek *pente*, five + *metron*, measure]

Pentateuch, also called (by Jews) **the Torah** the five Books of Moses in the Hebrew Bible and Old Testament: Genesis, Exodus, Leviticus, Numbers, and Deuteronomy. Although attributed to Moses since ancient times, the works as a whole are believed by modern scholars to be composed of several discrete strands of traditions from various periods. They trace Israel's origins from the earliest times, through the patriarchs, to the Exodus and Sinai periods prior to the entry to Canaan. They also contain much cultic and legal instruction.

Pentateuchal *adj.* of the Pentateuch.

pentathlon *noun* any of several athletic competitions composed of five events in all of which contestants must compete, the **modern pentathlon** comprising swimming, cross-country riding and running, fencing, and pistol-shooting. [from Greek, *pente*, five + *athlon*, contest]

pentatonic *adj. Mus., said of a musical scale* having five notes to the octave, most commonly equivalent to the first, second, third, fifth, and sixth degrees of the major scale. Five-note scales are common in traditional music (eg in China, Japan, and Africa), in some Scottish and Irish folk music, and in Black American gospel music. [from Greek *pente*, five + *tonos*, tone]

pentavalent *adj. Chem.* having a valency of five.

Pentecost *noun* **1** *Christianity* a festival on Whit Sunday, the seventh Sunday after Easter, commemorating the descent of the Holy Spirit on the Apostles. **2** *Judaism* Shabuoth or the Feast of Weeks. [from Greek *pentecoste hemera*, fiftieth day]

Pentecostal *adj.* **1** denoting any of several fundamentalist Christian groups that put emphasis on God's gifts through the Holy Spirit. **2** relating to Pentecost.

Pentecostalism *noun Relig.* a modern Christian renewal movement begun in 1901 at Topeka, Kansas, USA, and becoming organized in 1905 at Los Angeles, which was inspired by the descent of the Holy Spirit experienced by the Apostles at the first Christian Pentecost. Pentecostal Churches have spread throughout the world and are characterized by literal interpretation of the Bible and informal worship with enthusiasm and spontaneous exclamations of praise and thanksgiving. Pentecostalism has appeared within the established Protestant, Roman Catholic, and Greek Orthodox Churches where it is commonly called 'charismatic renewal'.

Pentheus in Greek mythology, a king of Thebes who did not welcome Dionysus. He disguised himself as a woman and tried to spy on the orgiastic rites of the Maenads who, encouraged by his mother, tore him to pieces.

penthouse *noun* an apartment, especially luxuriously appointed, built on to the roof of a tall building. [earlier *pentice*, from Old French *appentis*, from Latin *appendicium*, appendage]

pent-up SEE PENT.

penultimate *adj.* the last but one. [from Latin *paene*, almost + *ultimus*, last]

penumbra *noun* (PL. **penumbrae, penumbras**) **1** a rim of lighter shadow round the shadow proper of a body, eg the sun or moon during an eclipse; an area where dark and light blend. **2** a lighter border round the edge of a sunspot. [from Latin *paene*, almost + *umbra*, shadow]

penumbral *adj.* relating to or characterized by a penumbra.

penurious *adj.* **1** mean with money; miserly. **2** poor; impoverished.

penuriously *adv.* in a penurious way.

penury *noun* **1** extreme poverty. **2** lack; scarcity. [from Latin *penuria*]

Penutian languages a group of about 20 Native American languages spoken by small numbers in SW Canada and W USA. In some classifications, a further 40 languages of Mexico and Central and S America are included in the group: the most widely spoken of these include Maya (or Yucatan), Kekchi, and Quiché.

Penzance POP (1981) 20 000, a town in Kerrier district, Cornwall, SW England. Situated 40km/25mi SW of Truro, it is the chief resort town of 'the Cornish Riviera', overlooking Mounts Bay. NOTABLE FEATURE Chysauster Iron Age Village (to the N).

Penzias, Arno Allan (1933–) US astrophysicist, born in Munich, Germany. He joined the Bell Telephone Laboratories in 1961, and while investigating the radio noise that was interfering with satellite communications, he discovered 'microwave background radiation'. The

existence of this residual relic of the intense heat that was associated with the formation of the universe following the Big Bang had been predicted in 1948. He shared the 1978 Nobel Prize for Physics with Robert Wilson and Peter Kapitza.

peon *noun* **1** in India and Ceylon, an office messenger; an attendant. **2** in Latin America, a farm labourer. [from Spanish *peón*, from Latin *pedo*, foot soldier]

peony *noun* (PL. **peonies**) a garden plant or small shrub with large globular red, pink, yellow, or white flowers. [from Greek *paionia*, from *Paion*, the healer of the gods, from the plant's medicinal use]

people — *noun* (usually *pl.*) **1** persons. **2** men and women in general. **3** (**the people**) ordinary citizens without special rank; the populace. **4** (**the people**) the voters as a body. **5** subjects or supporters of a monarch, etc. **6** (*sing.*) a nation or race: *a warlike people.* **7** *colloq.* one's parents, or the wider circle of one's relations. — *verb* **1** to fill or supply (a region) with people; to populate. **2** to inhabit.
— **of all people** especially; more than anyone else.
[from Old French *poeple*]

PEP *abbrev.* personal equity plan.

pep — *noun colloq.* energy; vitality; go. — *verb* (**pepped, pepping**) (*often* **pep someone** *or* **something up**) to enliven or invigorate them. [a shortening of PEPPER]

Pepin III, known as **the Short** (c.715–68) King of the Franks (751–68), the founder of the Frankish dynasty of the Carolingians, the father of Charlemagne. He was chosen king after the deposition of Childeric, the last of the Merovingians. He led an army into Italy (754), and defeated the Lombards. The rest of his life was spent in wars against the Saxons and Saracens.

Peploe, Samuel John (1871–1935) Scottish painter, born in Edinburgh. He became a leading member of the Scottish Colourists in the 1930s. He spent much of his time in S France and painted still-life and figure subjects.

peplum *noun* a short skirt-like section attached to the waistline of a dress, blouse, or jacket. [from Greek *peplos*, an outer robe or overskirt worn by women in ancient Greece]

pepper — *noun* **1** a perennial climbing shrub (*Piper nigrum*), widely cultivated for its pea-sized red berries which are dried to form peppercorns. **2** a pungent seasoning prepared from the dried berries of this plant. Black pepper, which may be marketed whole as peppercorns or ground to a powder, is prepared by drying unripe peppercorns until the red outer skin turns black. White pepper, which has a milder flavour, is produced by removing the outer skin from ripe berries before they are dried and crushed to a powder. **3** any of various tropical shrubs of the genus *Capsicum*, unrelated to true pepper, cultivated for their large red, green, or yellow edible fruits. It includes varieties with a hot spicy flavour such as chilli pepper, the fruit of which is dried and ground to a powder (cayenne pepper) that is used as a spice. **4** the fruit of this plant, which has a hollow seedy interior. It is eaten raw in salads when green and unripe, or cooked as a vegetable. — Also called *capsicum.* — *verb* (**peppered, peppering**) **1** to bombard (with missiles). **2** to sprinkle liberally: *a text peppered with errors.* **3** to season with pepper. [from Anglo-Saxon *pipor*, from Latin *piper*]

peppercorn *noun* the dried berry of the pepper plant.

peppermill *noun* a device for grinding peppercorns.

peppermint *noun* **1** a species of mint (*Mentha piperita*) with dark green leaves and spikes of small purple flowers, widely cultivated in

Europe, America, and N Africa for its aromatic oil, which is used in confectionery, as a food flavouring, and as a treatment for indigestion. **2** this flavouring. **3** a sweet flavoured with peppermint.

peppery *adj.* **1** well seasoned with pepper; tasting of pepper; hot-tasting or pungent. **2** short-tempered; irascible.

pep pill a pill containing a stimulant drug.

pepsin *noun Biochem.* a digestive enzyme produced by the gastric glands in the stomach of vertebrates, which under acid conditions brings about the partial breakdown of dietary protein to polypeptides (chains of amino acids). [from Greek *pepsis*, digestion]

pep talk a brief talk intended to raise morale.

peptic *adj.* **1** relating to, or promoting, digestion. **2** relating to pepsin or the digestive juices. [from Greek *peptikos*]

peptic ulcer *Medicine* an ulcer, usually of the stomach or duodenum, that is caused by digestion of part of the lining of the digestive tract by gastric juices containing pepsin and acid. It is often associated with anxiety or other forms of stress.

peptide *noun Biochem.* a molecule that consists of a relatively short chain of amino acids, and is obtained by the partial hydrolysis of proteins. [from Greek *pepsis*, digestion]

Pepys, Samuel (1633–1703) English naval administrator and diarist, born in London. After the Restoration he rose rapidly in the naval service, and became Secretary to the Admiralty in 1672. His Diary runs from 1 Jan 1660 to 31 May 1669: it gives a detailed personal record and a vivid picture of contemporary life, particularly of the great plague, the burning of London, and the arrival of the Dutch fleet (1665–7). It was written in cipher, and not decoded until 1825.

per *prep.* **1** out of every: *two per thousand*. **2** for every: *£5 per head*. **3** in every: *60 miles per hour / 100 accidents per week*. **4** through; by means of: *per post*.
— **as per** ... according to ...: *proceed as per instructions*.
as per usual *colloq.* as always.
[from Latin *per*, for, each, by]

per- *prefix* forming words denoting: **1** *Chem.* the highest degree of combination with oxygen or other element or radical. **2** *in words derived from Latin* through, beyond, thoroughly, utterly. [from Latin *per-*, prefix]

peradventure *adv.* perhaps; by chance. [from Old French *par aventure*, by chance]

Perak POP (1990) 2.2m, a state in W Peninsular Malaysia. AREA 21 005sq km/8 108sq mi. It is bounded W by the Strait of Malacca and watered by the R Perak. Since the discovery of tin in the 1840s it has been one of the wealthiest states in Malaysia. Kinta Valley is the leading tin-mining area. CAPITAL Ipoh. CHIEF TOWNS Taiping, Teluk Intan, Kampar, Sungai Siput, Kuala Kangsar. ECONOMY rubber, coconuts, rice, timber.

perambulate *verb formal* **1** to walk about (a place). **2** *intrans.* to stroll around. [from Latin *per*, through + *ambulare*, to walk]

perambulation *noun* perambulating.

perambulator *noun* a pram.

per annum for each year; by the year. [from Latin *per annum*]

per capita for each person: *income per capita*. [from Latin *per capita*, by heads]

perceivable *adj.* capable of being perceived.

perceive *verb* **1** to observe, notice, or discern: *perceived a change*. **2** to understand, interpret, or view: *how one perceives one's role*. [from Old French *percever*, from Latin *percipere*]

per cent (SYMBOL **%**) — *adv.* **1** in or for every 100. **2** on a scale of 1 to 100: *90 per cent certain*. —

noun (*usually* **percent**) **1** a percentage or proportion. **2** (*usually* **percents**) a security yielding a certain rate of interest: *invest in four-percents*. **3** one part on every 100: *half a percent*. [from Latin *per centum*, for every 100]

percentage *noun* **1** an amount, number, or rate stated as a proportion of one hundred. **2** a proportion: *a large percentage of students fail*.

percentile *noun Statistics* one of the points or values that divide a range of statistical data, such as numerical scores or measurements, arranged in order, into 100 equal parts, eg the 90th percentile is the value below which 90 per cent of the scores lie. The *median* is the 50th percentile.

perceptibility *noun* being perceptible.

perceptible *adj.* able to be perceived; noticeable; detectable.

perceptibly *adv.* in a perceptible way.

perception *noun* **1** *Psychol.* the process whereby information about one's environment, received by the senses, is organized and interpreted so that it becomes meaningful. **2** one's powers of observation; discernment; insight. **3** one's view or interpretation of something. [from Latin *percipere*, to perceive]

perceptive *adj.* quick to notice or discern; astute.

perceptively *adv.* with perception.

Perceval, Spencer (1762–1812) English statesman, born in London. An MP from 1796, he was Solicitor-General (1801), Attorney-General (1802), and Chancellor of the Exchequer (1807), before he became Prime Minister (1809–12). An efficient administrator, he had established his Tory government well by the time he was shot dead by a bankrupt Liverpool broker, John Bellingham.

Perceval, Sir, also called **Parsifal** in Arthurian legend, a knight who went in quest of the Holy Grail. In the German version (*Parzival*) his bashfulness prevented him from asking the right questions of the warden of the Grail castle, and as a result the Fisher King was not healed.

perch[1] — *noun* **1** a branch or other narrow support above ground for a bird to rest on. **2** any place selected, especially temporarily, as a seat. **3** a high position or vantage point. **4** an old measure of length equal to 5.03m or 5.5yd (also called ROD, POLE). — *verb* **1** *intrans.* said of a bird to alight and rest on a perch. **2** *intrans.* to sit, especially insecurely or temporarily. **3** *intrans., trans.* to sit or place high up. [from Old French *perche*, from Latin *pertica*, rod]

perch[2] *noun* (PL. **perch**, **perches**) any of several edible, spiny-finned fish. [from Greek *perke*]

perchance *adv. old use* **1** by chance. **2** perhaps. [from Old French *par chance*, by chance]

percipient *adj.* perceptive; acutely observant; discerning. [from Latin *percipere*, to perceive]

Percival a male first name. [from Old French, from *perce(r)*, to pierce + *val*, valley]

percolate *verb* **1** *intrans., trans.* to pass through a porous material; to ooze, trickle, or filter. **2** *intrans. colloq.*, said of news or information to trickle or spread slowly. **3** *trans., intrans.* said of coffee to make it or be made in a percolator. [from Latin *percolare*, to filter through]

percolation *noun* percolating.

percolator *noun* a pot for making coffee, in which boiling water is kept circulating up through a tube and down through ground coffee beans.

percussion *noun* **1** the striking of one hard object against another. **2** musical instruments played by striking, eg drums, cymbals, xylophone, etc; these as a section of an orchestra. **3** *Medicine* a technique whereby part of the body is examined by tapping it with the fingers and using the sound or vibrations produced to deter-

mine the size, location, and condition of internal structures, or to detect the presence of fluid. [from Latin *percussio*, striking]

percussion cap a metal case containing a material that explodes when struck, formerly used for firing rifles.

percussionist *noun* a person who plays percussion instruments.

percussive *adj.* relating to or involving percussion.

Percy a noble N England family, whose founder, William de Percy (c.1030–96) went to England with William I, the Conqueror. The most famous member was Henry (1364–1403), 'Hotspur', who fell fighting against Henry IV at Shrewsbury His father, the fourth Lord Percy and Earl of Northumberland, who had helped Henry of Lancaster to the throne, was dissatisfied with the King's gratitude, and with his son plotted the insurrection. See also HOTSPUR.

Perdita **1** the daughter of Hermione and Leontes in Shakespeare's *The Winter's Tale*. After being abandoned as a baby, she grows up as a shepherdess in Bohemia and falls in love with Florizel. **2** a female first name, after Shakespeare's character. [from Latin *perdita* (feminine), lost]

perdition *noun* everlasting punishment after death; damnation; hell. [from Latin *perditio*, from *perdere*, to lose utterly]

peregrinate *verb intrans.* to travel, voyage, or roam; to wander abroad. [from Latin *peregrinari*, to roam, from *per*, through + *ager*, field]

peregrination *noun* (*usually* **peregrinations**) a journey or travel.

peregrine *noun* (*also* **peregrine falcon**) a small falcon with a dark back and streaked underparts, notable for its acrobatic flight. [from Latin *peregrinus*, wandering abroad, the birds being captured during flight]

Peregrine Pickle, The Adventures of a novel by Tobias Smollett (1751). It is a picaresque depiction of the wandering life of roguish young Peregrine.

peremptorily *adv.* in a peremptory way.

peremptory *adj.* **1** *said of an order* made in expectation of immediate compliance: *a peremptory summons*. **2** *said of a tone or manner* arrogantly impatient. **3** *said of a statement, conclusion, etc* allowing no denial or discussion; dogmatic. [from Latin *peremptorius*, deadly]

perennial — *adj.* **1** *Bot.* a plant that lives for several to many years, either growing continuously, as in the case of woody trees and shrubs, or having stems that die back each autumn and are replaced by new growth the following spring, as in the case of herbaceous perennials. See also ANNUAL, BIENNIAL. **2** lasting throughout the year. **3** constant; continual. — *noun* a perennial plant. [from Latin *perennis*, from *per*, through + *annus*, year]

perennially *adv.* every year; year by year; everlastingly.

perestroika *noun* a restructuring or reorganization, specifically that of the economic and political system of the former USSR begun in the 1980s. [from Russian *perestroika*, reconstruction]

Pérez de Cuéllar, Javier (1920–) Peruvian diplomat, born in Lima. After a period as Peru's first Ambassador to the USSR, he became a representative to the United Nations (1971). His time as UN Secretary-General (1982–91) was marked by his efforts to secure peaceful solutions to the Falklands Crisis (1982), the Iran–Iraq War (1980–88), and the Gulf War (1991).

perfect — *adj.* (with stress on *per-*) **1** complete in all essential elements. **2** faultless; flawless. **3** excellent; absolutely, or quite, satisfactory. **4** exact: *a perfect circle*. **5** *colloq.* absolute; utter:

perfect nonsense. **6** *Grammar*, said of the tense of a verb denoting completed action. — *noun* (with stress on *per-*) *Grammar* the perfect tense, in English formed with the auxiliary verb *have* and the past participle. — *verb* (with stress on *-fect*) **1** to improve to one's satisfaction: *perfect one's German*. **2** to finalize or complete. **3** to develop (a technique, etc) to a reliable standard. [from Latin *perficere*, to complete]

perfectibility *noun* capability of becoming perfect.

perfectible *adj.* capable of becoming perfect.

perfection *noun* **1** the state of being perfect. **2** the process of making or being made perfect, complete, etc. **3** flawlessness. **4** *colloq.* an instance of absolute excellence: *the meal was perfection*.

— **to perfection** perfectly.

perfectionism *noun* **1** the doctrine that perfection is attainable. **2** an expectation of the very highest standard.

perfectionist *noun* a person inclined to be dissatisfied with standards of achievement, especially his or her own, if they are not absolutely perfect.

perfectly *adv.* **1** in a perfect way. **2** completely, quite: *a perfectly reasonable reaction*.

perfect number *Maths.* a number that is equal to the sum of all its factors (except itself), eg the number 6, because the sum of its factors (1+2+3) is equal to 6.

perfect pitch *or* **absolute pitch** the ability to recognize a note from its pitch, or spontaneously sing any note with correct pitch.

perfidious *adj.* treacherous, double-dealing, or disloyal. [from Latin *perfidus*]

perfidiously *adv.* in a perfidious way.

perfidy *noun* (PL. **perfidies**) perfidious behaviour, or an instance of this.

perforate *verb* **1** to make a hole or holes in; to pierce. **2** to make a row of holes in, for ease of tearing. **3** *intrans.* said of an ulcer, diseased appendix, etc to develop a hole; to burst. [from Latin *perforare*, to pierce]

perforation *noun* **1** a hole made in something. **2** a row of small holes made in paper, a sheet of stamps, etc for ease of tearing. **3** the process of perforating or being perforated.

perforce *adv.* necessarily; inevitably or unavoidably. [from Old French *par force*]

perform *verb* **1** to carry out (a task, job, action, etc); to do or accomplish. **2** to fulfil (a function) or provide (a service, etc). **3** *trans., intrans.* to act, sing, play, dance, etc to entertain an audience. **4** *intrans.* said eg of an engine to function. **5** *intrans.* to conduct oneself, especially when presenting oneself for assessment: *performs well in interviews*. **6** *intrans.* said of commercial products, shares, currencies, etc to fare in competition. [from Old French *parfournir*]

performance *noun* **1** the performing of a play, part, dance, piece of music, etc before an audience; a dramatic or artistic presentation or entertainment. **2** the act or process of performing a task, etc. **3** a level of achievement, success, or, in commerce, profitability. **4** manner or efficiency of functioning. **5** *derog.* an instance of outrageous behaviour, especially in public.

performer *noun* **1** a person who performs, especially music. **2** a person who accomplishes what is expected of them. **3** an entertainer.

performing arts (**the performing arts**) the forms of art that require performance to be appreciated, especially music, drama, and dance.

perfume — *noun* **1** a sweet smell; a scent or fragrance. **2** a fragrant liquid prepared from the extracts of flowers, etc, for applying to the skin or clothes; scent. — *verb* to give a sweet smell to; to apply perfume to. [from Old French *parfum*, from Latin *per* through + *fumare*, to impregnate with smoke]

perfumer *noun* a maker of or dealer in perfumes.

perfumery *noun* (PL. **perfumeries**) **1** perfumes. **2** making perfumes. **3** a place where perfumes are made or sold.

perfunctorily *adv.* in a perfunctory way.

perfunctory *adj.* done merely as a duty or routine, without genuine care or feeling. [from Latin *perfunctorius*, slapdash]

perfusion *noun* **1** *Biol.* the movement of a fluid through a tissue or organ. **2** the deliberate introduction of a fluid into a tissue or organ, usually by injection into a nearby blood vessel. [from Latin *perfusus* poured over]

Pergamene school a style of Hellenistic sculpture associated with the city of Pergamum in Asia Minor from the 3c BC. It is particularly associated with the Attalid kings and is characterized by a realistic intensity of expression. Works include several versions of the *Dying Gaul* (examples in the Capitoline Museum, Rome, and the Louvre, Paris).

Pergamum *or* **Pergamon** an ancient city in NW Asia Minor (modern Turkey), which in the 3c and 2c BC was the capital of the Attalid kings. Under their patronage it became a major centre of art and learning; its school of sculpture was internationally renowned, and its library came second only to that of Alexandria. The kingdom was bequeathed to Rome in 133 BC, and it was formed into the province of Asia.

Pergamum Museum a branch of the Staatliche (state) museum in Berlin, Germany. A reconstruction of the Great Altar from Pergamum (2c BC) is housed in it.

pergola *noun* a framework constructed from slender branches, for plants to climb up; a trellis. [from Italian, from Latin *pergula*, shed]

Pergolesi, Giovanni Battista (1710–36) Italian composer, born in Jesi. He attended the Conservatorio dei Poveri di Gesù Cristo in Naples, became a violinist, and in 1732 was appointed *maestro di cappella* to the Prince at Naples. His comic intermezzo *La serva padrona* (1733) was very popular, and influenced the development of opera buffa. He wrote much church music, and later left Naples for a Capuchin monastery in Pozzuoli, where he composed his *Stabat Mater* (1736).

perhaps *adv.* possibly; maybe. [earlier *perhappes*, from Old French *par*, by + Norse *happ*, fortune]

peri- *prefix* forming words meaning: **1** around: *periscope* / *pericardium*. **2** near: *perinatal* / *perigee*. [from Greek *peri*, round]

perianth *noun Bot.* the outer part of a flower, usually consisting of a circle of petals (the *corolla*) within a circle of sepals (the *calyx*), that surrounds the stamens and carpels. [from PERI- + Greek *anthos*, flower]

pericardium *noun* (PL. **pericardia**) the sac enclosing the heart. [from PERI- + Greek *kardia*, heart]

pericarp *noun Bot.* in plants, the wall of a fruit, which develops from the ovary wall after fertilization. [from PERI- + Greek *karpos*, fruit]

Pericles (c.495–429 BC) Athenian general and statesman from the Alcmaeonid family, who presided over the 'Golden Age' of Athens, and was virtually its uncrowned king (443–429 BC). He helped push through the constitutional reforms that brought about full Athenian democracy (462–461 BC), and himself became leader of the democratic party in 461 BC, when his rival Cimon was forced into exile. Associated with the leading philosophers and artists of the time, he was responsible for the construction of the Parthenon and other great buildings on the Acropolis (begun 447 BC). Despite the Thirty Years' Peace he was opposed to Sparta, and his hostility contributed towards the outbreak of the

Periodic Table

The elements, listed with their symbols and atomic numbers, lie horizontally in order of their atomic numbers. Those with chemically similar

1 Hydrogen H								
3 Lithium Li	4 Beryllium Be							
11 Sodium Na	12 Magnesium Mg							
19 Potassium K	20 Calcium Ca	21 Scandium Sc	22 Titanium Ti	23 Vanadium V	24 Chromium Cr	25 Manganese Mn	26 Iron Fe	27 Cobalt Co
37 Rubidium Rb	38 Strontium Sr	39 Yttrium Y	40 Zirconium Zr	41 Niobium Nb	42 Molybdenum Mo	43 Technetium Tc	44 Ruthenium Ru	45 Rhodium Rh
55 Caesium Cs	56 Barium Ba	57–71 Lanthanide series	72 Hafnium Hf	73 Tantalum Ta	74 Wolfram W	75 Rhenium Re	76 Osmium Os	77 Iridium Ir
87 Francium Fr	88 Radium Ra	89–103 Actinide series	104 Rutherfordium Rf					

57 Lanthanum La	58 Cerium Ce	59 Praseodymium Pr	60 Neodymium Nd	61 Prometheum Pm	62 Samarium Sm	63 Europium Eu
89 Actinium Ac	90 Thorium Th	91 Protactinium Pa	92 Uranium U	93 Neptunium Np	94 Plutonium Pu	95 Americium Am

of Elements

properties fall under one another in the columns. Elements with atomic numbers of 93 and over are man-made.

								2 Helium He
			5 Boron B	6 Carbon C	7 Nitrogen N	8 Oxygen O	9 Fluorine F	10 Neon Ne
			13 Aluminium Al	14 Silicon Si	15 Phosphorus P	16 Sulphur S	17 Chlorine C	18 Argon Ar
28 Nickel Ni	29 Copper Cu	30 Zinc Zn	31 Gallium Ga	32 Germanium Ge	33 Arsenic As	34 Selenium Se	35 Bromine Br	36 Krypton Kr
46 Palladium Pd	47 Silver Ag	48 Cadmium Cd	49 Indium In	50 Tin Sn	51 Antimony Sb	52 Tellurium Te	53 Iodine I	54 Xenon Xe
78 Platinum Pt	79 Gold Au	80 Mercury Hg	81 Thallium Tl	82 Lead Pb	83 Bismuth Bi	84 Polonium Po	85 Astatine At	86 Radon Rn
64 Gadolinium Gd	65 Terbium Tb	66 Dysprosium Dy	67 Holmium Ho	68 Erbium Er	69 Thulium Tm	70 Ytterbium Yb	71 Lutecium Lu	
96 Curium Cm	97 Berkelium Bk	98 Californium Cf	99 Einsteinium Es	100 Fermium Fm	101 Mendelevium Md	102 Nobelium No	103 Lawrencium Lr	

Peloponnesian War (431–404 BC). He died of the plague that afflicted Athens in the early years of that war.

peridotite noun Geol. a coarse-grained igneous rock, composed mainly of olivine, with smaller amounts of pyroxene or other minerals. It is thought to be a constituent of the Earth's upper mantle. [from French péridot]

perigee noun Astron. the point in the orbit of the Moon or an artificial satellite around the Earth when it is closest to the Earth. See also APOGEE. [from French perigée, from Greek perigeion, from peri, near + ge, earth]

Périgord a part of the former province of Guyenne, SW France, now mostly in the department of Dordogne. It is an extensively forested, chalky area, known for truffles. CHIEF TOWN Périgueux. NOTABLE FEATURES Palaeolithic (Perigordian) caves near Montignac, Rouffignac, and Le Bugue.

perihelion noun (PL. **perihelia**) the point in a planet's orbit round the Sun when it is closest to the Sun. See also APHELION. [from PERI- + Greek helios, sun]

peril noun 1 grave danger. 2 a hazard. — at one's peril at the risk of one's life. [from Old French, from Latin periculum, danger]

perilous adj. dangerous.

perilously adv. dangerously.

perimeter noun 1 the boundary of an enclosed area. 2 Geom. the enclosing line or circumference of a two-dimensional figure; its length. [from Greek perimetros, from peri, round + metros, measure]

perinatal adj. Medicine denoting the period extending from the 28th week of pregnancy to about one month after childbirth.

period — noun 1 a portion of time. 2 a phase or stage in history, development, etc. 3 Geol. a unit of geological time that is a subdivision of an era, and is itself divided into epochs. It represents the time interval during which a particular sys-

tem of rocks was formed, eg the Cretaceous period. **b** any long interval of geological time, eg glacial period. 4 any of the sessions of equal length into which the school day is divided, and to which particular subjects or activities are assigned. 5 a punctuation mark (.), used at the end of a sentence and to mark an abbreviation; a full stop. 6 colloq. added to a statement to emphasize its finality: you may not go, period. 7 the periodic discharge of blood during a woman's menstrual cycle. 8 Chem. in the periodic table, any of the seven horizontal rows of chemical elements, which show a steady progression from alkali metals on the left-hand side to non-metals on the right-hand side, each period ending with a noble gas. 9 Physics the time interval after which a cyclical phenomenon, eg a wave motion, or the orbit of a planet around the Sun, repeats itself. — adj. dating from, or designed in the style of, the historical period in question: period costume / period furniture. [from Greek periodos, from peri, round + hodos, way]

periodic adj. happening at especially regular intervals; occasional.

periodical — adj. periodic. — noun a magazine published weekly, monthly, quarterly, etc.

periodically adv. from time to time, occasionally.

periodic function Maths. one whose values recur in a cycle as the variable increases.

periodicity noun the fact of recurring, or tendency to recur, at intervals.

periodic law Chem. the law that the properties of elements are periodic functions of their atomic numbers.

periodic table Chem. a table of all the chemical elements arranged in order of increasing atomic number.
◇ The properties of chemical elements in the periodic table tend to change with increasing atomic number in a periodic (regularly recurring) manner. This is because the electrons in atoms are arranged in shells, and each shell can only

hold a certain number of electrons. The periodic table consists of horizontal rows or periods, and vertical columns or groups. Going across a period, the number of electrons in the outermost shell steadily increases, and the elements change from metals on the left-hand side of the period, to metalloids, to non-metals on the right-hand side. Going down a group, all elements show very similar chemical properties because their atoms contain the same number of electrons in the outermost shell. Elements with an atomic number greater than that of uranium (92), known as transuranic elements, are all highly unstable and radioactive.

periodontitis noun Medicine inflammation of the tissues surrounding a tooth. [from PERI- + odous, odontos tooth]

period piece 1 a piece of furniture, etc dating from, and in the distinctive style of, a certain historical period. 2 facetious something quaintly old-fashioned.

peripatetic — adj. 1 travelling about from place to place. 2 said of a teacher employed by several schools and so obliged to travel between them. 3 (also **Peripatetic**) denoting the school of philosophers founded by Aristotle, given to promenading while lecturing. — noun a peripatetic teacher or philosopher. [from Greek peri, round + pateein, to tread]

peripatetically adv. in a peripatetic way.

peripheral — adj. 1 relating to, or belonging to, the outer edge or outer surface: peripheral nerves. 2 (**peripheral to something**) not central to the issue in hand; marginal. 3 Comput. supplementary; auxiliary. 4 relating to the outer edge of the field of vision. — noun Comput. (also **peripheral device**) a device concerned with the input, output, or backing storage of data, eg a printer, mouse, or disk drive. Peripheral devices are connected to a computer system and controlled by it, but are not part of the central processing unit or main memory.

periphery noun (PL. **peripheries**) 1 the edge or boundary of something. 2 the external surface of something. [from Greek periphereia, circumference, surface]

periphrasis noun (PL. **periphrases**) a roundabout way of saying something; a circumlocution. [from Greek peri, round + phrasis, speech]

periphrastic adj. using periphrasis.

periphrastically adv. in a periphrastic way.

periscope noun Optics a system of reflecting prisms or angled mirrors that enables the user to view objects that are above eye level, or which are positioned so that they are obscured by a closer object. Periscopes are used in submerged submarines (often in conjunction with telescopes) for scanning the horizon, and in military tanks. [from Greek periskopeein, to look around]

periscopic adj., said of a lens giving a wide field of vision.

perish verb 1 intrans. to die; to be destroyed or ruined. 2 trans., intrans. said of materials to decay or cause to decay or rot. [from Old French perir]

perishability noun being perishable.

perishable adj., said of commodities, especially food liable to rot or go bad quickly.

perished adj. colloq. feeling the cold severely.

perisher noun old colloq. use a mischievous child or other troublesome person.

perishing adj. 1 colloq. very cold. 2 old colloq. use damned, infernal, or confounded.

perishingly adv. so as to perish; intensely: is perishingly cold.

peristalsis noun Physiol. in hollow tubular organs, especially the intestines and oesophagus, the involuntary muscle contractions that force the contents of the tube, eg food, further forward. [from Greek *peristellein*, to contract round]

peristaltic *adj.*, *said of the alimentary canal* forcing onward by waves of contraction.

peristyle *noun Archit.* a colonnade round a courtyard or building. [from Greek *peri*, round + *stylos*, column]

peritoneal *adj.* relating to or in the region of the peritoneum.

peritoneum *noun* (PL. **peritonea**, **peritoneums**) the membrane that lines the abdominal cavity. [from Greek *peritonaion*, from *periteinein*, to stretch all round]

peritonitis *noun* inflammation of the peritoneum.

periwig *noun* a man's wig of the 17c and 18c. [a variant of PERUKE]

periwinkle[1] *noun* any of several evergreen plants with trailing stems and blue or white flowers. [from Anglo-Saxon *perwince*, from Latin *pervinca*]

periwinkle[2] *noun* any one of several edible marine snails; its shell. [from Anglo-Saxon *pinewincle*]

perjure *verb* to forswear (oneself) in a court of law, ie lie while under oath to tell the truth. [from Latin *perjurare*]

perjurer *noun* a person who commits perjury.

perjury *noun* (PL. **perjuries**) the crime of lying while under oath in a court of law.

perk[1] *verb intrans.*, *trans.* (also **perk up** or **perk someone up**) **1** to become or make more lively and cheerful. **2** *said of an animal's ears* to prick up. [from Middle English *perken*]

perk[2] *noun colloq.* a benefit, additional to income, derived from employment, such as the use of a company car. [a shortening of PERQUISITE]

perk[3] *verb intrans.*, *trans. colloq.* to percolate.

perkily *adv.* in a perky way.

perkiness *noun* being perky.

perky *adj.* (**perkier**, **perkiest**) lively and cheerful.

Perlis POP (1990) 188 000, the smallest state in Malaysia, situated in NW Peninsular Malaysia. AREA 818sq km/316sq mi. It is bounded N by Thailand and SW by the Strait of Malacca. The Langkawi Is lie off shore. CAPITAL Kangar. ECONOMY rice, rubber, coconuts; tin.

Perm, formerly **Molotov 1** POP (1990e) 1.1m, the industrial capital of Perm oblast, NW Russia, situated on the R Kama. HISTORY dates from 1723 when a copper foundry was built; rapid industrial development in the 19c. **2** an oblast in NW Russia with Perm as its capital.

perm[1] — *noun* a hair treatment using chemicals that give a long-lasting wave or curl. — *verb* to curl or wave (hair) with a perm. [a shortening of PERMANENT WAVE]

perm[2] *colloq.* — *noun* a permutation (see PERMUTATION 2). — *verb* to make a permutation of.

permafrost *noun Geol.* an area of subsoil or rock that has remained below freezing point (0°C) for at least a year, although it does not necessarily contain ice. Permafrost is found in arctic, subarctic, and alpine regions, or on high mountains which have been glaciated. [from *permanent frost*]

permanence or **permanency** *noun* being permanent.

permanent *adj.* **1** lasting, or intended to last, indefinitely; not temporary. **2** *said of a condition, etc* unlikely to alter. [from Latin *permanere*, to remain]

permanently *adv.* so as to be permanent; everlastingly.

permanent magnet *Physics* a magnet that retains its magnetic properties after the force which magnetized it has been removed.

permanent tooth *Anat.* each of the set of teeth that develops in most mammals for use in adult life, after the milk or deciduous teeth have been shed.

permanent wave a perm.

permanent way a railway track, including the rails, sleepers, and stones.

permanganate *noun* any of the salts of *permanganic acid*, especially *potassium permanganate*, used as an oxidizing and bleaching agent and disinfectant. [from PER- + MANGANESE]

permeability *noun* being permeable.

permeable *adj.* able to be permeated by liquids, gases, etc. [from Latin *permeabilis*]

permeate *verb* **1** (**permeate something** or **through something**) *said of a liquid* to pass or seep through a fine or porous material, a membrane, etc. **2** *trans.*, *intrans. said of a smell, gas, etc* to spread through a room or other space; to fill or impregnate. [from Latin *permeare*, to penetrate]

permeation *noun* permeating or being permeating.

Permian *adj.* **1** *Geol.* relating to the last period of the Palaeozoic era, lasting from about 290 million to 250 million years ago. During this period reptiles became more abundant, amphibians became less so, and primitive conifers and ginkgoes appeared. **2** relating to the rocks formed during this period. [from *Perm* in Russia]

permissibility *noun* being permissible.

permissible *adj.* allowable; permitted.

permission *noun* consent, agreement, or authorization. [from Latin *permissio*]

permissive *adj.* allowing usually excessive freedom, especially in sexual matters; tolerant; liberal.

permissively *adv.* in a permissive way.

permissiveness *noun* being permissive.

permit — *verb* (with stress on *-mit*) (**permitted**, **permitting**) **1** to consent to or give permission for. **2** to give (someone) leave or authorization. **3** to allow (someone something): *permitted him access to his children*. **4** (**permit something** or **permit of something**) to enable it to happen or take effect; to give scope or opportunity for it: *an outrage that permits of no excuses*. — *noun* (with stress on *per-*) a document authorizing something. [from Latin *permittere*, to allow]

permittivity (*in full* **absolute permittivity**) *Physics* (SYMBOL ε) the ratio of the electric displacement (the electric charge per unit area that would be displaced across a layer of conductor placed across an electric field) in a medium to the intensity of the electric field that is producing it. It is measured in farads per metre.

permutability *noun* being permutable.

permutable *adj.* interchangeable.

permutation *noun* **1** *Maths.* **a** any of a number of different ways in which a set of objects or numbers can be arranged. **b** any of the resulting combinations. **2** a fixed combination in football pools for selecting the results of matches. [from Latin *permutare*, to change completely]

permute or **permutate** *verb* to rearrange (a set of things) in different orders, especially in every possible order in succession. [from Latin *permutare*, to interchange]

pernicious *adj.* harmful; destructive; deadly. [from Latin *perniciosus*, from *pernicies*, ruin, bane]

pernicious anaemia *Medicine* a form of anaemia caused by a dietary deficiency of vitamin B_{12}, or by failure of the body to absorb the vitamin, leading to a reduction in red blood cells, sometimes accompanied by degeneration of the spinal cord.

perniciously *adv.* in a pernicious way.

pernickety *adj.* **1** over-particular about small details; fussy. **2** *said of a task* tricky; intricate.

Perón, (Maria) Eva (Duarte de), also called **Evita** (1919–52) the second wife of Argentine President Juan Perón, born in Los Toldos. A radio and screen actress before her marriage in 1945, she became a powerful political influence and a mainstay of the Perón government. She was idolized by the poor, and after her death her husband's popularity waned. Her body was stolen, taken to Europe, and hidden until 1976. The musical *Evita* (1979) is based on her life.

Perón, Isabelita, originally **Maria Estela Martínez de Perón** (1931–) Argentinian dancer and politician, born in La Rioja province. The third wife of Juan Perón from 1961, she lived with him in Spain until his return to Argentina as President in 1973, when she was made Vice-President. On his death in 1974 she took over the presidency, but her inadequacy led to a military coup (1976) and a five-year imprisonment, following which she settled in Madrid.

Perón, Juan (Domingo) (1895–1974) Argentine soldier and politician, born in Lobos. Instrumental in the army coup of 1943, he gained widespread support through his social reforms, and became President (1946–55). He was deposed and exiled in 1955, having antagonized the Church, the armed forces, and many of his former Labour supporters. He returned in triumph in 1973, and won an overwhelming electoral victory, but died the following year.

peroration *noun* **1** the concluding section of a speech, in which the points made are summed up. **2** *colloq.* a long formal speech. [from Latin *peroratio*]

peroxide — *noun* **1** *Chem.* any chemical compound that contains the O_2^{2-} ion, and releases hydrogen peroxide when treated with acid. Peroxides are strong oxidizing agents, and are used in rocket fuels, antiseptics, disinfectants, and bleaches. **2** a solution of hydrogen peroxide (H_2O_2), used as a bleach for hair and textiles. — *verb* to bleach (hair) with hydrogen peroxide. [from PER- 1 + OXIDE]

perpendicular — *adj.* **1** vertical; upright. **2** at right angles. **3** *said of a cliff, etc* precipitous; steep. **4** (*usually* **Perpendicular**) *Archit.* see PERPENDICULAR STYLE. — *noun* a perpendicular line, position, or direction. [from Latin *perpendicularis*, from *perpendiculum*, a plumbline]

perpendicularity *noun* being perpendicular; a perpendicular direction or position.

perpendicularly *adv.* so as to be perpendicular; vertically.

Perpendicular style the form of English Gothic architecture from the late 14c to the 16c, developed from the Decorated style, and characterized by the used of slender vertical lines, vaulting (especially fan-vaulting), and large areas of windows decorated with simple tracery and stained glass. King's College Chapel, Cambridge (1446–1515), with its delicate fan-vaulting, is a good example of the style.

perpetrate *verb* to commit, or be guilty of (a crime, misdeed, error, etc). [from Latin *perpetrare*, to bring about, commit]

perpetration *noun* **1** perpetrating. **2** something that is perpetrated.

perpetrator *noun* a person who perpetrates; the one who is guilty.

perpetual *adj.* everlasting; eternal; continuous; permanent: *in perpetual bliss*. continual: *perpetual quarrels*. [from Latin *perpetualis*, from *perpetuus*, uninterrupted]

perpetual calendar 1 a calendar for ascertaining on which day of the week any date falls. **2** a calendar that is usable for any year or for several years.

perpetual motion the motion of a hypothetical machine that keeps going indefinitely without any external source of energy.

perpetuate *verb* **1** to cause to last or continue: *perpetuate a feud / perpetuate a species.* **2** to preserve the memory of (a name, etc). **3** to repeat and pass on (an error, etc). [from Latin *perpetuare*, to make perpetual]

perpetuation *noun* perpetuating, continuation.

perpetuity *noun* (PL. **perpetuities**) **1** the state of being perpetual. **2** eternity. **3** duration for an indefinite period. **4** something perpetual, eg an allowance to be paid indefinitely.
— **in perpetuity** for ever.
[from Latin *perpetuitas*, from *perpetuus*, perpetual]

Perpignan POP (1990) 139 000, the resort capital of the Pyrénées-Orientales department in Languedoc-Roussillon region, S France. It is a market town lying near the Spanish border, 154km/96mi S of Toulouse. HISTORY settled in Roman times; capital of the former province of Roussillon; chartered in 1197; scene of the Church Council in 1408; united with France in 1659. NOTABLE FEATURES citadel (17c–18c); château (14c, now a museum); town hall (13c–17c); Cathedral of St-Jean (14c–17c); Church of St-Jacques (14c–18c), Church of Notre-Dame-la-Réal (14c).

perplex *verb* **1** to puzzle, confuse, or baffle. **2** to complicate. [from Latin *per-*, thoroughly + *plexus*, entangled]

perplexedly *adv.* in a perplexed way.

perplexing *adj.* that perplexes; puzzling.

perplexity *noun* (PL. **perplexities**) **1** the state of being perplexed. **2** something baffling or confusing.

per pro. *abbrev. per procurationem* (Latin), by the agency of.

perquisite *noun* **1** a benefit, additional to income, derived from employment, such as the use of a company car. **2** a tip expected on some occasions. **3** something regarded as due to one by right. [from Latin *perquisitum*, something acquired]

Perrin, Jean Baptiste (1870–1942) French physicist, born in Lille. Professor at the University of Paris, he escaped to the USA in 1940 following the invasion of France. His work on cathode rays helped to establish their nature as negatively charged particles. He is best remembered for his demonstration that the suspended particles which show Brownian motion in colloidal solutions essentially obey the gas laws, and he used such systems to determine a value for the Avogadro number. He was awarded the 1926 Nobel Prize for Physics.

Perry, Fred(erick John) (1909–   ) English-born US lawn tennis and table tennis player, born in Stockport, Cheshire. He won the world table tennis title in 1929. Between 1933 and the end of 1936, he won the men's lawn tennis singles title at Wimbledon three times (1934–6), the US singles (three times), and the French and Australian championships. He was the first man to win all four major titles.

perry *noun* (PL. **perries**) an alcoholic drink made from fermented pear juice. [from Old French *peré*, from Latin *pirum*, pear]

pers. *abbrev.* person or personal.

per se in itself; intrinsically: *not valuable per se.* [Latin, = through itself]

persecute *verb* **1** to ill-treat, oppress, or torment, especially on the grounds of religious or political beliefs. **2** to harass, pester, or bother continually. [from Latin *persequi*, to pursue, ill-treat]

persecution *noun* persecuting or being persecuted.

persecutor *noun* a person who persecutes.

Persephone, Latin **Proserpine** in Greek mythology, the goddess of the Underworld, the daughter of Demeter and Zeus. She was gathering flowers when Hades abducted her and made her queen of the Underworld. Zeus commanded that she be released, but she had eaten the seeds of the pomegranate, which meant (in fairy lore) that she was bound to stay. A compromise was arranged so that she returned for half of every year (an allegory of the return of Spring).

Persepolis an ancient Persian city in Fars province, SW Iran. Its construction was begun by Darius I, and further developed by his successors Xerxes and Artaxerxes until it was sacked by Alexander the Great in 330 BC. The palaces and graves of the Achaemenid rulers of Persia are located here. It is a World Heritage site.

Perseus **1** in Greek mythology, the son of Zeus and Danae. He and his mother were shut in a chest and thrown into the sea by Danae's father Acrisius, who feared for his life after receiving a prophecy that he would be killed by his grandson. Perseus grew up on the island of Seriphos. Later, he killed the Gorgon, Medusa, and used its head to rescue Andromeda (whom he married), and save his mother. He later accidentally killed his grandfather, thus fulfilling the prophecy. **2** *Astron.* a large constellation in the northern hemisphere, lying in the Milky Way, and containing a conspicuous pair of open clusters, known as the Double Cluster, visible to the naked eye.

Perseus with the Head of Medusa a sculpture in bronze by Benvenuto Cellini (1545–54).

perseverance *noun* persevering; continued effort despite setbacks.

persevere *verb intrans.* (**persevere in** *or* **with something**) to keep on striving for it; to persist steadily with an endeavour. [from Old French *perseverer*]

Pershing, John J(oseph), known as **Black Jack** (1860–1948) US soldier, born in Laclede, Missouri. He served in several Indian Wars, the Cuban War (1898), the Russo–Japanese War (1904–5), and in Mexico (1916). In World War I he commanded the American Expeditionary Force in Europe (1917), and afterwards became Chief of Staff (1921–4).

Pershing missile a medium-range land-based missile with a nuclear warhead, deployed by the US Army in West Germany from 1983 onwards as part of NATO's theatre nuclear force modernization programme. [named after John J Pershing]

Persia, old name for Iran. See also PERSIAN EMPIRE.

Persian — *adj.* relating to Persia (modern Iran), or its people or language. — *noun* **1** a native or citizen of Persia. **2** the language of Persia or Iran.

Persian carpet a distinctively patterned hand-woven woollen or silk carpet made in Persia or elsewhere in the Near East.

Persian cat a breed of cat with long silky fur.

Persian Empire an empire created by the Achaemenids in the second half of the 6c BC through their conquests of the Medes, Babylonians, Lydians, and Egyptians. It extended from NW India to the E Mediterranean and although it was overthrown by Alexander the Great (333–330 BC), its administrative structure, the satrapal system, survived.

Persian Gulf see ARABIAN GULF.

Persian lamb the black curly fur of the karakul lamb, used for coats and trimmings.

Persian Wars, also called **Greek-Persian Wars** the name given to the two expeditions launched by the Persian kings, Darius I and Xerxes, against Greece in 490 BC and 480–479 BC.

The first was in retaliation for Greek intervention in the Ionian revolt of 499 BC, and was directed only at Athens and Eretria. It ended with the defeat of the Persians at Marathon in 490 BC. The second was in response to Marathon and it ended in the twin defeats for the Persians on land and at sea, at Plataea and Mycale.

persiflage *noun* banter, teasing, flippancy, or frivolous talk. [from French *persiflage*]

persimmon *noun* a tropical plum-like fruit of America and Asia, or the tree that bears it. [from an Algonkian (Native American) language]

persist *verb* **1** *intrans.* (**persist in** *or* **with something**) to continue in it in spite of resistance, discouragement, etc. **2** *said of rain, etc* to continue steadily. **3** *said eg of a mistaken idea* to remain current. [from Latin *persistere*, to stand firm]

persistence *noun* **1** persisting. **2** being persistent.

Persistence of Memory, The, also called ***Limp Watches*** a painting by Salvador Dali (1931, New York).

persistence of vision *Physiol.* the persistence of a visual image on the retina for a short period after removal of the visual stimulus. This phenomenon plays an important role in the viewing of films or television.

persistent *adj.* **1** continuing with determination in spite of discouragement; dogged. **2** constant; unrelenting: *persistent questions.*

persistently *adv.* in a persistent way.

person *noun* **1** (PL. **persons, people**) an individual human being. **2** (PL. **persons**) one's body: *drugs concealed on his person.* **3** (PL. **persons**) *Grammar* each of the three classes to which pronouns and verb forms fall, *first person* denoting the speaker (or the speaker and others), *second person* the person addressed (with or without others) and *third person* the person(s) or thing(s) spoken of. **4** (**Person**) *Relig.* in Christian doctrine, any of the three forms or manifestations of God (Father, Son, and Holy Spirit) that together form the Trinity.
— **be no respecter of persons** to make no allowances for rank or status.
in person 1 actually present oneself: *was there in person.* **2** doing something oneself, not asking or allowing others to do it for one.
[from Latin *persona*, actor's mask]

-person *combining form* used instead of *-man*, *-woman*, *-lady*, etc, to denote a specified activity or office: *chairperson.*

persona *noun* (PL. **personae, personas**) one's character as one presents it to other people. See also PERSONA NON GRATA. [from Latin *persona*, actor's mask]

personable *adj.* good-looking or likeable.

personably *adv.* in a personable way.

personage *noun* a well-known, important, or distinguished person. [from Latin *personagium*, from *persona*, person]

personal *adj.* **1** coming from someone as an individual, not from a group or organization: *my personal opinion.* **2** done, attended to, etc by the individual person in question, not by a substitute: *give it my personal attention.* **3** relating to oneself in particular: *a personal triumph.* **4** relating to one's private concerns: *details of her personal life.* **5** *said of remarks* referring, often disparagingly, to an individual's physical or other characteristics. **6** relating to the body: *personal hygiene.* [from Latin *personalis*, from *persona*, person]

personal assistant a secretary, especially of a senior executive, manager, etc.

personal column a newspaper column or section in which members of the public may place advertisements, enquiries, etc.

personal computer a microcomputer that is designed for use by one person, especially for applications involving word-processing, or database or spreadsheet programs.

personal effects a person's belongings, especially those regularly carried about.

personality *noun* (PL. **personalities**) **1** a person's nature or disposition; the qualities that give one's character individuality. **2** strength or distinctiveness of character: *lots of personality*. **3** a well-known person; a celebrity. **4** (**personalities**) offensive personal remarks. [from Latin *personalitas*, from *persona*, person]

personalize *or* **personalise** *verb* **1** to mark distinctively as the property of a particular person. **2** to focus (a discussion) etc on personalities instead of the matter in hand. **3** to personify.

personally *adv.* **1** as far as one is concerned: *personally, I disapprove*. **2** in person. **3** as a person. **4** as directed against one: *take a remark personally*.

personal pronoun *Grammar* any of the pronouns representing a person or thing, eg *I, you, he, him, she, it, they, us*.

personal property, everything one owns other than land or buildings. See also REAL[1] *noun* 5.

personal stereo a small audio cassette player with earphones, that can be worn on one's person.

persona non grata (PL. *personae non gratae*) a person who is not wanted or welcome within a particular group. [Latin, = person not welcome]

personification *noun* **1** giving human qualities to things or ideas. **2** in art or literature, representing an idea or quality as a person. **3** a person or thing which personifies. **4** a person or thing that is seen as embodying a quality: *the personification of patience*.

personify *verb* (**personifies, personified**) **1** in literature, etc, to represent (an abstract quality, etc) as a human or as having human qualities. **2** *said of a figure in art, etc* to represent or symbolize (a quality, etc). **3** to embody in human form; to be the perfect example of: *she's patience personified*.

personnel *noun* **1** (*pl.*) the people employed in a business company, an armed service, or other organization. **2** a department within such an organization dealing with matters concerning employees. [from French *personnel*, personal]

perspective *noun* **1** the observer's view of objects in relation to one another, especially with regard to the way they seem smaller the more distant they are. **2** the representation of this phenomenon in drawing and painting. **3** the balanced or objective view of a situation, in which all its elements assume their due importance: *get things into/out of perspective*. **4** an individual way of regarding a situation, eg one influenced by personal experience or considerations. [from Latin *ars perspectiva*, optical science]

Perspex *noun trademark* the trade name for polymethylmethacrylate, a tough transparent lightweight plastic used to make windshields, visors, domestic baths, advertising signs, etc.

perspicacious *adj.* shrewd, astute, perceptive, or discerning. [from Latin *perspicax*]

perspicaciously *adv.* in a perspicacious way.

perspicacity *noun* being perspicacious.

perspicuity *noun* clarity of expression.

perspicuous *adj., said of speech or writing* clearly expressed and easily understood. [from Latin *perspicuus*, transparent, manifest]

perspicuously *adv.* in a perspicuous way.

perspiration *noun* the salty moisture produced by the sweat glands of the skin.

perspire *verb intrans.* to sweat. [from Latin *perspirare*, to breathe through, sweat]

persuadable *or* **persuasible** *adj.* capable of being persuaded.

persuade *verb* **1** to urge successfully; to prevail on or induce. **2** (**persuade someone of something**, *or* **to do something**) to convince them that it is true, valid, advisable, etc. [from Latin *persuadere*]

persuader *noun* a person or thing that persuades.

Persuasion a novel by Jane Austen (1818). Her last, it focuses primarily on the lives of the Elliots and the Musgroves, and describes the rekindling of a love affair.

persuasion *noun* **1** the act of urging, coaxing, or persuading. **2** a creed, conviction, or set of beliefs, especially that of a political group or religious sect.

persuasive *adj.* having the power to persuade; convincing or plausible.

persuasively *adv.* in a persuasive way.

persuasiveness *noun* being persuasive.

pert *adj.* **1** impudent; cheeky. **2** *said of clothing or style* jaunty; saucy. [from Old French *apert*, open]

pertain *verb intrans.* (*often* **pertain to someone** *or* **something**) **1** to concern or relate to; to have to do with. **2** to belong to: *skills pertaining to the job*. **3** to be appropriate; to apply. [from Old French *partenir*]

Pertelote the commonsensical hen who is wife to Chauntecleer in 'The Nun's Priest's Tale', in Chaucer's *The Canterbury Tales*. She also features in the 12c French poem *Le Roman de Renart* (Reynard the Fox).

Perth POP (1981) 43 000, the capital of Perth and Kinross district, Tayside, E Scotland. It lies on the R Tay, 50km/31mi N of Edinburgh. HISTORY capital of Scotland until the mid-15c; James I was assassinated here in 1437. NOTABLE FEATURES Balhousie Castle; art gallery and museum; St John's Kirk (15c).

Perth POP (1990e) 1.2m, the state capital of Western Australia. It is situated near the mouth of the Swan R and is an important commercial, cultural, and transportation centre on the W coast. The city is the fifth-largest in Australia and is the most isolated of Australia's state capitals (Adelaide is 2 250km/1 400mi away). HISTORY founded in 1829; achieved city status in 1856; rapid development followed after the discovery of gold and the opening of Fremantle Harbour in 1897. NOTABLE FEATURES Western Australian Museum; Old Court House.

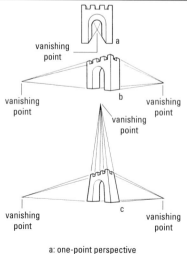

a: one-point perspective
b: two-point perspective
c: three-point perspective

perspective

pertinacious *adj.* determined in one's purpose; dogged; tenacious. [from Latin *pertinax*]

pertinaciously *adv.* in a pertinacious way.

pertinacity *noun* being pertinacious or resolute; obstinacy.

pertinence *or* **pertinency** *noun* being pertinent; relevance.

pertinent *adj.* (**pertinent to someone** *or* **something**) relating to or concerned with them; relevant. [from Latin *pertinere*, to relate]

pertly *adv.* in a pert way.

pertness *noun* being pert; impudence.

perturb *verb* to make anxious or agitated. [from Latin *perturbare*, to throw into confusion]

perturbation *noun* perturbing or being perturbed.

perturbed *adj.* disturbed, worried.

pertussis *noun Medicine* whooping cough. [from PER- 2 + Latin *tussis*, cough]

Peru, official name **Republic of Peru**, Spanish **República de Peru** POP (1992e) 22.5m, a republic on the W coast of S America. It is divided into one province and 24 departments. AREA 1 284 640sq km/495 871sq mi. It is bounded by Ecuador in the N, Colombia in the NE, Brazil and Bolivia in the E, and Chile in the S. CAPITAL Lima. TIME ZONE GMT –5. The population consists mainly of S American Indian (45%) and mixed S American Indian and European (37%); Roman Catholicism is the chief religion. OFFICIAL LANGUAGES Spanish and Quechua. CURRENCY the new sol. PHYSICAL DESCRIPTION arid plains and foothills on the coast, with areas of desert and fertile river valleys; the central sierra, with an average altitude of 3 000m, contains 50% of the population; rivers cut through the plateau, forming deep canyons; the forested Andes and Amazon basin lie to the E; the major rivers flow to the Amazon. CLIMATE mild temperatures all year on the coast; dry, arid desert in the S; in the N, the coastal region has bursts of torrential rain every 10 years or so with rising sea temperatures and the cold current retreats S: this phenomenon is known as El Niño. Andean temperatures never rise above 23°C with a large daily temperature range and night frost in the dry season; in the Peruvian portion of the Amazon basin to the E, the climate is typically wet and tropical. HISTORY AND GOVERNMENT highly developed Inca civilization; arrival of the Spanish in 1531; the Vice-royalty of Peru was established; gold and silver mines made Peru the principal source of Spanish power in S America; independence was declared in 1821; frequent border disputes in the 19c (eg the War of the Pacific in 1879–83); clashes between Ecuador and Peru continued in recent decades; several military coups; drug-related violence and terrorist activities resulted in large areas being declared under a state of emergency; the constitution was suspended in 1992 to allow the President absolute power to implement reform and deal with terrorism; the constitution was reinstated in 1993 with plans to hold a referendum on a new constitution. ECONOMY one of the world's leading producers of silver, zinc, lead, copper, gold, iron ore; 80% of Peru's oil is extracted from the Amazon forest; cotton, potatoes, sugar, rice, grapes, fruit, olives; sheep, cattle, steel, iron; vehicles; tyres; cement; wool; fishmeal, fish canning; fishing was severely affected by the adverse weather conditions of 1982–3 and by continuous overfishing; tourism, especially to ancient sites.

Perugia POP (1991e) 151 000, the capital of Umbria region and of Perugia province, central Italy. It lies on a hill c.300m above the Tiber Valley, 141km/88mi N of Rome. HISTORY founded by the Etruscans; taken by the Romans in 310 BC. NOTABLE FEATURES Cathedral of San Lorenzo (15c); town hall (13c); Arco d'Augusto (Etruscan town gate); Church of San Pietro dei Cassiensi.

peruke *noun* a 17c to 18c style of wig, with side curls and a tail at the back. [from Old French *perruque*, head of hair]

perusal *noun* perusing; careful study, reading.

peruse *verb* 1 to read through carefully. 2 to browse through casually. 3 to examine or study attentively. [from PER- 2 + USE¹]

Perutz, Max Ferdinand (1914–) Austrian-born British biochemist, born in Vienna. Working at Cambridge, he elucidated the structure of haemoglobin, and for this work shared the 1962 Nobel Prize for Chemistry with John Kendrew.

pervade *verb* to spread or extend throughout; to affect throughout. [from Latin *pervadere*]

pervasive *adj.* tending to spread everywhere.

perverse *adj.* deliberately departing from what is normal and reasonable; unreasonable, awkward, stubborn, or wilful. [from Latin *perversus*, from *pervertere*, to overturn]

perversely *adv.* in a perverse way.

perversion *noun* 1 the process of perverting or condition of being perverted. 2 a distortion. 3 an abnormal sexual activity. [from Latin *pervertere*, to corrupt]

perversity *noun* (PL. **perversities**) being perverse.

pervert — *verb* (with stress on -*vert*) 1 to divert illicitly from what is normal or right. 2 to lead into evil or unnatural behaviour; to corrupt. 3 to distort or misinterpret (words, etc). — *noun* (with stress on *perv*-) someone who is morally or sexually perverted. [from Latin *pervertere*, to corrupt]

Pesach *or* **Pesah** *noun* the Hebrew name for the Jewish festival of Passover.

peseta *noun* the standard unit of currency in Spain. [from Spanish *peseta*, diminutive of *pesa*, weight]

Peshawar POP (1981) 566 000, the capital of North-West Frontier province, Pakistan. It lies 172km/107mi W of Islamabad and 16km/10mi E of the Khyber Pass. It is a city of the Pathan people and a major trade centre on the Afghan frontier. HISTORY under Sikh rule in the early 19c; occupied by the British in 1849. NOTABLE FEATURES Balahisar Fort; Mosque of Mahabat; Qissa Khawani Bazaar.

peskily *adv.* so as to be annoying; infuriating.

pesky *adj.* (**peskier, peskiest**) *North Amer. colloq.* troublesome or infuriating. [probably from PEST]

Peru

peso *noun* (PL. **pesos**) the standard unit of currency in many Central and S American countries and the Philippines. [from Spanish *peso*, weight]

pessary *noun* (PL. **pessaries**) 1 a medicated dissolving tablet inserted into the vagina to treat an infection, etc; a vaginal suppository. 2 a device worn in the vagina as a contraceptive, or as a support for the womb. [from Latin *pessarium*, from Greek *pessos*, pebble, plug]

pessimism *noun* 1 the tendency to emphasize the gloomiest aspects of anything, and to expect the worst to happen. 2 the belief that this is the worst of all possible worlds, and that evil is triumphing over good. [from Latin *pessimus*, worst]

pessimist *noun* 1 a person who has a sombre, gloomy nature. 2 a person who follows the doctrine of pessimism.

pessimistic *adj.* relating to or characterized by pessimism.

pessimistically *adv.* in a pessimistic way.

pest *noun* 1 a living organism, such as an insect, fungus, or weed, that has a damaging effect on animal livestock, crop plants, or stored produce. 2 a person or thing that is a constant nuisance. [from Latin *pestis*, plague]

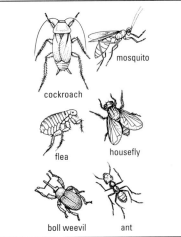

mosquito

cockroach

flea

housefly

boll weevil

ant

pests

Pestalozzi, Johann Heinrich (1746–1827) Swiss educationalist, a pioneer of mass education for poor children, born in Zürich. After several failed attempts, he managed to open a school at Berthoud (Burgdorf), where he wrote *Wie Gertrud ihre Kinder lehrt* (How Gertrude Educates her Children, 1801), the recognized exposition of the Pestalozzian method, in which the process of education is seen as a gradual unfolding, prompted by observation, of the child's innate faculties. Pestalozzi International Children's Villages were established at Trogen, Switzerland (1946) and Sedlescombe, Surrey, UK (1958).

pester *verb* (**pestered, pestering**) 1 to annoy constantly. 2 to harass or hound with requests. [from Old French *empestrer*, to entangle, influenced by PEST]

pesticide *noun* any chemical compound that is used to kill pests, ie living organisms that are considered to be harmful to plants, animals, humans, or stored foodstuffs.
◇ There are many different types of pesticides, including *insecticides*, which kill insects, *herbicides*, which kill weeds, and *fungicides*, which kill fungi. Most pesticides are manufactured artificially but some insecticides, eg pyrethrum, are obtained from plants, and these are believed to be the safest type. There is much concern about the fact that pesticides enter the food chain and have a detrimental effect on wildlife (eg birds and small mammals) and possibly humans. Fish may also

be harmed by pesticides that are washed off the land into rivers, streams, and lakes. The use of highly toxic herbicides such as DDT is now strictly controlled by law in many countries. In general, the levels of pesticide residues in food in the UK are very low. Various methods of biological control are being developed in an attempt to reduce the use of pesticides, or replace them altogether.

pestilence *noun* a deadly epidemic disease such as bubonic plague. [from Latin *pestilentia*, from *pestis*, plague]

pestilent *adj.* 1 deadly, harmful, or destructive. 2 infuriating; troublesome. [from Latin *pestilens*, from *pestis*, plague]

pestilential *adj.* infuriating; troublesome.

pestilently *adv.* in a pestilent way.

pestle *noun* a club-like utensil for pounding substances in a mortar. [from Old French *pestel*]

pesto *noun* an Italian sauce originating in Liguria and made from fresh basil leaves, pine kernels, olive oil, garlic, and Parmesan cheese. [from Italian *pesto*, from *pestare*, to crush, pound]

pet¹ — *noun* 1 a tame animal or bird kept as a companion. 2 someone's favourite. 3 a darling or love. — *adj.* 1 kept as a pet. 2 of or for pets. 3 favourite; own special. — *verb* (**petted, petting**) 1 to pat or stroke (an animal, etc). 2 to treat indulgently; to make a fuss of. 3 *trans., intrans.* to fondle and caress for erotic pleasure.

pet² *noun* a fit of bad temper or sulks.

Pétain, (Henri) Philippe (1856–1951) French soldier and politician, born in Cauchy-à-la-Tour. During World War I his defence of Verdun (1916) made him a national hero, and he became Commander-in-Chief (1917) and Marshal of France (1918). When France collapsed in 1940, he negotiated the armistice with Germany and Italy, became chief of state, and established his government at Vichy. He then collaborated with Germany in an attempt to unite France under the slogan 'Work, Family and Country', and keep it out of the war. After the liberation he was tried in the French courts, but his death sentence for treason was commuted to life imprisonment. His role in the war remains controversial; he is regarded by some as a patriot, by others as a traitor.

petal *noun Bot.* in a flower, one of the modified leaves, often scented and brightly coloured, that together form the *corolla*, and in insect-pollinated plants serve to attract passing insects. In wind-pollinated plants the petals are usually much reduced or absent. [from Greek *petalon*, leaf]

Petaling Jaya POP (1980) 208 000, an industrial satellite in Selangor state, W Peninsular Malaysia. Situated 6km/4mi W of Kuala Lumpur, it was built in the 1950s as a squatter resettlement city.

petard *noun Hist.* a small bomb for blasting a hole in a wall, door, etc.
— **hoist with one's own petard** blown up by one's own bomb, ie the victim of one's own trick or cunning.
[from Old French, from *peter*, to crack or explode, from Latin *pedere*, to break wind]

Peter I, known as **the Great** (1672–1725) Tsar of Russia (1682–1721) and Emperor (1721–5), born in Moscow, the son of Tsar Alexey and his second wife Natalia Naryshkin. On the death of Ivan (1696), his mentally retarded half-brother with whom he had been joint Tsar under the regency of his half-sister Sophia, he embarked on a series of sweeping military, fiscal, administrative, educational, cultural, and ecclesiastical reforms, many of them based on W European models. All classes of society suffered from the impact of the reforms, which were harshly implemented — his own son Alexey died under torture (1718), suspected of conspiring against his father. Peter fought major wars with the

Ottoman Empire, Persia, and in particular Sweden, which Russia defeated in the Great Northern War. This victory established Russia as a major European power, and gained a maritime exit on the Baltic coast, where Peter founded St Petersburg. He was succeeded by his wife, Catherine.

Peter, St, originally **Simeon**, or **Simon bar Jona** (**son of Jonah**) (1c AD) one of the 12 Apostles of Jesus Christ, originally a fisherman living in Capernaum, renamed by Christ as Cephas or Peter ('rock'). Often the spokesman for the other Apostles, he was a member of the inner group which accompanied Christ at the Transfiguration and Gethsemane. After Christ's resurrection and ascension, Peter became the leader of the Christian community in Jerusalem; later he may have engaged in missionary work outside Palestine (eg in Antioch), but little is known of these activities. Tradition says he was executed with his head downward in Rome, and he is regarded by the Roman Catholic Church as the first Bishop of Rome. Two New Testament letters are attributed to him, as are some apocryphal writings, such as the Acts of Peter and the Apocalypse of Peter.

Peter a male first name. [from Greek *petros*, rock]

Peter, Letters of two New Testament writings attributed to the Apostle Peter (although now widely thought to be pseudonymous). The first letter claims to be written from 'Babylon' (possibly a cipher for Rome) to Christians in Asia Minor; it encourages them to withstand persecution, and reminds them of their Christian commitment. The second letter appears to oppose teachers who deny the second coming of Christ and espouse gnostic-tending doctrines.

peter *verb intrans.* (**petered, petering**) (**peter out**) to dwindle away to nothing. [originally US mining slang]

Peter and Paul Fortress a stronghold founded in 1703 by Peter the Great on a small island in the Neva R delta, around which the city of St Petersburg sprang up. The fortress, which was notorious throughout the 19c for its political prison, has been a museum since 1922.

Peter and the Wolf (Petya i volk) a symphonic fairy-tale for narrator and orchestra by Sergei Prokofiev (Op 67, 1936), in which each instrument represents a different character.

Peterborough, ancient **Medeshamstede** POP (1992e) 156 000, an industrial city in Peterborough district, Cambridgeshire, E central England. Situated on the R Nene, 117km/73mi N of London, it originally developed around a Benedictine monastery. It was designated a 'new town' in 1967. NOTABLE FEATURES 12c cathedral (tomb of Catherine of Aragon); Burghley House (24km/15mi NW).

Peterhead POP (1981) 17 000, a port town in Banff and Buchan district, Grampian region, NE Scotland, situated 44km/27mi N of Aberdeen. The most easterly town on the Scottish mainland, it is a leading fishing port and an oilfield supply base. NOTABLE FEATURE Arbuthnot Museum.

Peterkin, in full **Peterkin Gay** the youngest and most vulnerable of the three shipwrecked boys in R M Ballantyne's *The Coral Island*.

Peterloo Massacre the name given to the forcible break-up (1819) of a mass meeting about parliamentary reform held at St Peter's Fields, Manchester, which ultimately strengthened the reform campaign. When the Manchester Yeomanry charged into the crowd, 11 people were killed; this gave rise to the sardonic reference (in 'Peterloo') to the Waterloo victory of 1815.

Peter Pan, in full **Peter Pan, or, The Boy Who Would Not Grow Up** a play by Sir J M Barrie

(1904, in *Peter and Wendy*, 1911). It describes the adventures of the Darling children when they fly into Never Land in the company of Peter, the boy who never grew up.

Petersburg POP (1990) 38 000, an independent city in E Virginia, USA, lying on the Appomattox R, 37km/23mi S of Richmond. It was besieged by Union forces in the Civil War (1864–5) until the Confederate army retreated to surrender at Appomattox. NOTABLE FEATURES Centre Hill Mansion; Old Blandford Church; Siege Museum; Petersburg National Battlefield Site.

petersham *noun* a stiff ribbed silk ribbon used for reinforcing waistbands, etc. [from Lord Petersham, 19c English army officer]

Peters' map projection an equal area map projection, produced in 1973 by German cartographer and mathematician, Arno Peters (1916–). It shows continents and oceans in proportion to their relative sizes The Peters' projection avoids the Eurocentric view of the world, and shows the densely populated equatorial regions in correct proportion to each other. See also MERCATOR'S MAP PROJECTION.

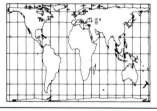

Peters' map projection

pethidine *noun* a synthetic pain-relieving drug widely used in childbirth.

petiole *noun Bot.* the stalk that attaches a leaf to the stem of a plant. [from Latin *petiolus*, little foot]

Petipa, Marius (1818–1910) French dancer, ballet master, and choreographer, born in Marseilles. After touring France, Spain, and the USA as a dancer, he went to St Petersburg to join the Imperial Ballet (1847). As ballet master from 1869 until his retirement in 1903, he created 46 original ballets, the most famous of which are Tchaikovsky's *The Sleeping Beauty* (1890) and *Swan Lake* (1895).

petit bourgeois (PL. **petits bourgeois**) a member of the lower middle class. [French]

petite *adj.*, *said of a woman or girl* having a small and dainty build. [from French *petite*, feminine of *petit*, small]

petite bourgeoisie the lower middle class. [French]

petit four (PL. **petits fours**) a small sweet biscuit, usually decorated with icing. [from French *petit four*, little oven]

petition — *noun* 1 a formal written request to an authority to take some action, signed by a large number of people. 2 any appeal to a higher authority. 3 *Legal* an application to a court for some procedure to be set in motion. — *verb trans.*, *intrans.* (**petitioned, petitioning**) (**petition** or **petition someone for** or **against something**) to address a petition to them for some cause; to make an appeal or request. [from Latin *petitio*, from *petere*, to seek]

petitioner *noun* 1 a person who petitions. 2 a person who applies for a divorce.

petition of right in the UK, before the Crown Proceedings Act of 1947, a personal petition by which someone could take certain proceedings against the Crown, such as in cases of breach of contract. The 1947 Act permitted action in tort against servants of the Crown,

though the monarch remains personally immune from civil or criminal liability.

petit mal *Medicine* a mild form of epilepsy without convulsions, characterized by short periods of loss of consciousness or 'absences'.

petit point 1 a small diagonal stitch used for fine work in needlepoint. 2 needlework using this stitch. [from French *petit point*, small point]

Petit Prince, Le (The Little Prince) a tale by Antoine de Saint-Exupéry (1943). It is ostensibly a story for children which addresses the adult themes of grief and mortality.

pet name a special name used as an endearment.

Petra an ancient rock-cut city in Maan governorate, East Bank, SW Jordan, the capital of the Nabataean Arabs until their conquest by Rome in the early 2c. It was a wealthy commercial city for several centuries, and controlled the international spice trade. Approachable only via a series of narrow ravines, it is renowned for its numerous temples, tombs, houses, shrines, altars, and a theatre carved out of red sandstone cliffs. It is a World Heritage site.

Petrarch, properly **Francesco Petrarca** (1304–74) Italian poet and scholar, born in Arezzo. In 1327 at Avignon he first saw the woman called Laura who inspired the love poetry for which he is best known, notably the *Canzoniere* in the lyric collection, *Rime Sparse*. He wrote widely on the classics, and was crowned Poet Laureate in Rome in 1341.

petrel *noun* any of several seabirds that live far from land, especially the storm petrel. [altered from earlier *pitteral*, perhaps by association with St Peter's walking on the water, as some species of storm petrel walk across the surface of the sea while feeding]

Petri-dish *noun Biol.* a shallow circular glass or plastic plate with a flat base and a loosely fitting lid, used mainly for culturing bacteria and other micro-organisms. [named after the German bacteriologist Julius R Petri (1852–1921)]

Petrie, Sir (William Matthew) Flinders (1853–1942) English archaeologist and Egyptologist, born in Charlton, Kent. He surveyed Stonehenge (1874–7), and from 1881 turned entirely to Egyptology, beginning by surveying the pyramids and temples of Giza, and excavating the mounds of Tanis and Naucratis. He was Professor of Archaeology at London (1892–1933), wrote more than 100 books, and continued excavations in Egypt and Palestine until well into his 80s.

petrifaction or **petrification** *noun Geol.* the process whereby the hard parts of an organism (eg wood, shell, bone) are turned into stone as the original tissue is gradually replaced by minerals, the shape and minute structural detail being preserved.

petrify *verb* (**petrifies, petrified**) 1 to terrify; to paralyse with fright. 2 *trans.*, *intrans.* said of organic material to turn into stone by the process of petrifaction. 3 *trans.*, *intrans.* to fix or become fixed in an inflexible mould. [from Greek *petra*, stone]

petro- *combining form* forming words meaning: 1 relating to petroleum and its products: *petrochemical*. 2 relating to stone or rocks: *petrology*.

petrochemical *noun* any chemical, eg ethyl alcohol or acetone, obtained from petroleum or natural gas.

petrochemically *adv.* using petrochemicals.

petrochemistry *noun* 1 the chemistry of petroleum and its derivatives. 2 the chemistry of rocks.

petrocurrency *noun* currency, usually in the form of US dollars (*petrodollars*), pounds sterling, or Deutschmarks, available in oil-producing countries on their balance of payments, and which is surplus to their own requirements. The currency is available for investment elsewhere, mainly in the USA and W Europe.

petrodollar *noun* the US dollar as representative of the foreign currency earned on a vast scale by oil-exporting countries.

petrol *noun* a volatile flammable liquid fuel, used in most internal combustion engines, consisting of a mixture of hydrocarbons obtained by purification of petroleum. — Also called *gasoline*. [from Old French *petrole*, from Latin *petroleum*]

petrolatum *noun* petroleum jelly. [from modern Latin *petrolatum*]

petrol bomb a crude bomb consisting of a petrol-filled bottle stopped with rags that are set alight just as the bottle is thrown.

petrol engine a type of internal combustion engine in which a mixture of petrol and air is burned inside a cylinder fitted with a piston. It is the type of engine most widely used in motor vehicles.

petroleum *noun* a naturally occurring oil consisting of a thick black, brown, or greenish liquid mixture of hydrocarbons. The largest petroleum reserves are in the Middle East, the USA, the former Soviet Union, and beneath the North Sea. [from Latin *petroleum*, from Greek *petra*, rock + Latin *oleum*, oil]
◇ Petroleum is a fossil fuel, believed to have been formed millions of years ago from the decayed remains of microscopic marine plants and animals. It is extracted from the Earth's crust by drilling wells, and the crude oil is processed in oil refineries to give a mixture of liquid and gas fuels, including methane, ethane, propane, butane, kerosene, petrol, diesel oil, and fuel oils. Asphalt (bitumen), paraffin wax, petroleum jelly, and lubricating oils are obtained from the residue of the refining process. The *petrochemical industries* use the products of petroleum refining as raw materials for the manufacture of plastics, synthetic rubber, solvents, drugs, artificial fibres (eg nylon), detergents, fertilizers, cosmetics, insecticides, antiseptics, etc.

petroleum jelly a greasy jelly-like substance obtained from petroleum, used in ointments and as a lubricant.

petrological *adj.* relating to or involving petrology.

petrologist *noun* a person who studies and is expert in petrology.

petrology *noun Geol.* the scientific study of the structure, origin, distribution, and history of rocks.

petrol station a filling-station.

Petrov affair the defection by Soviet embassy third secretary, Vladimir M Petrov, and his wife in Canberra in Apr 1954; he was granted political asylum by the Australian government. Later the Petrovs revealed they had been spying in Australia, and in one of their documents they implicated two members of the staff of Dr H V Evatt, the Federal Leader of the Labor opposition. The affair helped to split the Labor Party and

kept it from winning national government for nearly 20 years.

Petruchio the fortune-seeking Verona gentleman in Shakespeare's *The Taming of the Shrew*, who marries and tames Katharina.

Petrushka a ballet by Igor Stravinsky (1911), from which various orchestral suites have been written, and which was commissioned by Sergei Diaghilev's Ballets Russes. The story tells of the coming to life of a Russian puppet.

petticoat — *noun* **1** a woman's underskirt. **2** (**petticoats**) *Hist.* skirts in general, those worn by boys in early childhood in particular. **3** (*attributive*) *said eg of organization, tactics, etc* of or by women; feminine or female. [from PETTY + COAT]

pettifog *verb* (**pettifogged**, **pettifogging**) to act as a pettifogger.

pettifogger *noun* **1** a lawyer dealing with unimportant cases, especially somewhat deceitfully or quibblingly. **2** *derog.* someone who argues over trivial details; a quibbler. [from PETTY + German dialect *voger*, arranger]

pettifogging — *noun* trivial or petty behaviour. — *adj.* trivial or petty.

pettish *adj.* peevish, sulky.

pettishly *adv.* with a bad-tempered manner; sulkily.

pettishness *noun* being pettish.

petty *adj.* (**pettier**, **pettiest**) **1** of minor importance; trivial. **2** small-minded or childishly spiteful. **3** of low or subordinate rank. [from Old French *petit*, small]

petty cash money kept for small everyday expenses in an office, etc.

petty officer a non-commissioned officer in the navy.

petulance *noun* being petulant, peevish.

petulant *adj.* ill-tempered; peevish. [from Latin *petulans*, from *petere*, to seek]

petulantly *adv.* in a petulant way.

petunia *noun* a plant native to tropical America, with white, pink, or purple funnel-shaped flowers. [from French *petun*, tobacco plant (from its similarity), from Guaraní (S American Indian language) *pety'*]

Peugeot a French automobile company founded in 1890 by Armand Peugeot (1849–1915). It merged with Citroën in 1976. It also produces bicycles and motorcyles.

Pevsner, Antoine (1886–1962) Russian-born French sculptor, born in Oryol, Russia. In Moscow he helped to form the Suprematist group, but in 1920 broke away to issue the *Realist Manifesto* with his brother, Naum Gabo (1890–1977). He settled in Paris, and became known for his completely nonfigurative constructions (mainly in copper and bronze), several

of which are in the Museum of Modern Art, New York.

Pevsner, Sir Nikolaus (Bernhard Leon) (1902–83) German-born British art historian, born in Leipzig. He lost his lecturer's post at Göttingen on the advent of Hitler and went to Britain, where he became an authority on (especially English) architecture. He was Professor of Fine Art at Cambridge (1949–55). His best-known works are *An Outline of European Architecture* (1942), and the 50-volume series *The Buildings of England* (1951–74).

pew *noun* **1** one of the long benches with backs used as seating in a church. **2** *humorous colloq.* a seat: *take a pew.* [from Old French *puie*, from Latin *podium*, part of a choir stall]

pewter *noun* **1** a silvery alloy with a bluish tinge, consisting of tin and small amounts of lead, used to make tableware (eg tankards), jewellery, and other decorative objects. **2** articles made of pewter. [from Old French *peutre*]

peyote *noun* the Mexican cactus mescal, or the intoxicant got from it. [from Aztec *peyotl*]

Pfeiffer, Michelle (1958–) US film actress, born in Santa Ana, California. Following television series and commercials, her first feature film was *Falling in Love Again* (1980). Later appearances include *The Witches of Eastwick* (1987), *Dangerous Liaisons* (1988), *Frankie and Johnny* (1991), *Batman Returns* (1992), and *The Age of Innocence* (1994).

pfennig *noun* a German unit of currency worth a hundredth of a mark. [from German *pfennig*, related to PENNY]

PG *abbrev.* **1** *colloq.* paying guest. **2** *as a film classification* parental guidance, ie containing scenes possibly unsuitable for children.

PGA *abbrev.* Professional Golfers' Association.

pH *noun* (also **pH value**) *Chem.* a measure of the relative acidity or alkalinity of a solution.
◇ The pH of a solution is equal to the logarithm of the reciprocal of the hydrogen ion concentration, and it is measured using a glass electrode or coloured indicators, eg litmus. Neutral solutions have a pH of 7, the pH values of acidic solutions range from 0 to nearly 7, and those of alkaline solutions range from just above 7 to 14.
[a shortening of German *Potenz*, power, exponent + *H*, the symbol for hydrogen]

Phaedra in Greek mythology, the daughter of Minos and the second wife of Theseus. While he was away she fell in love with her step-son Hippolytus. He rejected her so she hung herself, but left a note accusing him of trying to rape her. Theseus called on Poseidon to punish Hippolytus with death.

Phaedrus or Phaeder (1c AD) The translator of Aesop's fables into Latin verse, born a slave in Macedonia. He went to Italy, where he became the freedman of Emperor Augustus, and published five books of fables, many his own invention, which were still widely read in medieval Europe.

Phaethon in Greek mythology, the son of Helios the Sun-god and Clymene. Challenged to prove his ancestry to his friends, he found his way to his father's palace and asked to drive the chariot of the Sun for one day. He was unable to control the horses, scorched the earth, and was destroyed by a thunderbolt sent by Zeus.

phagocyte *noun* a cell, especially a white blood cell, that engulfs and absorbs microorganisms such as bacteria. [from Greek *phagein*, to eat + -CYTE]

phagocytosis *noun Biol.* the process whereby specialized cells, such as phagocytes and macrophages, engulf and digest bacteria, cell debris, or other solid material that is outside the cell. Various single-celled organisms, especially protozoans, engulf food particles by phagocytosis.

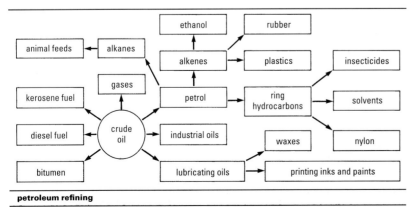

petroleum refining

phalange 1 *Anat.* same as PHALANX 3. 2 (**Phalange**) a right-wing activist Maronite faction in Lebanon. [from French *phalange*, = PHALANX]

phalanger *noun* a tree-dwelling, thick-furred Australasian marsupial with webbed hind toes and a long prehensile tail. [from Greek *phalangion*, spider's web, from its webbed toes]

phalanges *noun pl.* (SING. **phalanx**) *Anat.* the bones of the digits (fingers and toes) in vertebrates. The first digit (thumb or big toe) has two phalanges, and the other digits have three phalanges each. [from Greek *phalanx -angos*, roller]

phalanx *noun* 1 *Hist.* in ancient Greece, a body of infantry in close-packed formation. 2 a solid body of people, especially representing united support or opposition. 3 any of the bones of the finger or toe. [from Greek *phalanx*, line of soldiers drawn up for battle]

phalarope *noun* a wading bird of the sandpiper family, native to northern parts but wintering in the southern tropics. [from Greek *phalaris*, coot + *pous*, foot]

phallic *adj.* relating to or resembling a phallus.

phallus *noun* (PL. **phalluses**, **phalli**) a representation or image of an erect penis, especially as a symbol of male reproductive power. [from Greek *phallos*]

Phanerozoic *adj. Geol.* relating to the eon that consists of the Palaeozoic, Mesozoic, and Cenozoic eras, extending from about 570 million years ago until the present time. Most fossils are associated with the Phanerozoic eon. [from Greek *phaneros*, visible + *zoion*, animal]

phantasm *noun* 1 an illusion or fantasy. 2 a ghost or phantom. [from Greek *phantasma*, apparition]

phantasmagoria *noun* a fantastic succession of real or illusory images seen as if in a dream. [from Greek *phantasma*, apparition + (perhaps) *agora*, assembly]

phantasmagoric *or* **phantasmagorical** *adj.* relating to or like a phantasmagoria.

phantasmal *adj.* of the nature of a phantasm; spectral, unreal.

phantasy *noun* (PL. **phantasies**) an old spelling of **fantasy**.

phantom — *noun* 1 a ghost or spectre. 2 an illusory image or vision. — *adj.* of the nature of a phantom; spectral, imaginary; fancied; not real. [from Old French *fantosme*, from Greek *phantasma*, apparition]

Phantom of the Opera a musical by Andrew Lloyd Webber (1986), based on Gaston Leroux's story about the Paris Opéra being haunted by a mad composer.

pharaoh *noun* the title of the kings of ancient Eygpt. [from Greek *pharao*, from Hebrew *par'oh*, from Egyptian *pr-'o*, great house]
◊ Specifically, the god-kings of the New Kingdom (c.1500 BC) onwards. Best known of the New Kingdom pharaohs are Tutankhamun (c.1352 BC), Rameses II (the pharaoh of the Exodus), and Rameses III (the conqueror of the Sea Peoples). Pharaohs were mediators between their mortal subjects and the gods, and after death were believed to become gods themselves.

Pharisaic *adj.* 1 relating to or characteristic of the Pharisees or their faith. 2 (*often* **pharisaic**) self-righteous, hypocritical.

Pharisee *noun* 1 a member of the Pharisees. 2 a self-righteous or hypocritical person. [from Greek *pharisaios*, from Hebrew *parush*, separated]

Pharisees an influential minority group, mainly of laymen, within Palestinian Judaism before AD 70. They lived apart from the common people, rigorously observed the laws regarding ritual purity, cleansings, and food, and even took on priests' obligations. In the New Testament

Gospels, they are often portrayed as the opponents of Christ. After the fall of Jerusalem (AD 70), it was from Pharisaic circles that the rabbinic movement arose.

Phar Lap a New Zealand chestnut gelding which became Australia's most famous racing horse in the late 1920s and early 1930s. His most renowned win was the 1930 Melbourne Cup. He was taken to N America, where he won a major race in Mexico but died several weeks later in San Francisco. The autopsy showed his heart was twice normal size.

pharmaceutical *adj.* of or relating to the preparation of drugs and medicines. [from Greek *pharmakeutikos*, from *pharmakon*, drug]

pharmaceutics *sing. noun* the preparation and dispensing of drugs and medicine.

pharmacist *noun* a person trained to prepare and dispense drugs and medicines.

pharmacological *adj.* relating to or involving pharmacology.

pharmacologist *noun* an expert in pharmacology.

pharmacology *noun* the scientific study of medicines and drugs and their effects and uses. [from Greek *pharmakon*, drug + -LOGY]

pharmacopoeia *noun Medicine* an authoritative book containing a list of drugs, together with details of their properties, uses, side-effects, methods of preparation, and recommended dosages. [from Greek *pharmakopoiia*, preparation of drugs]

pharmacy *noun* (PL. **pharmacies**) 1 the mixing and dispensing of drugs and medicines. 2 a dispensary in a hospital, etc. 3 a pharmacist's or chemist's shop. [from Greek *pharmakeia*, use of drugs]

Pharos of Alexandria a marble watchtower and lighthouse on the island of Pharos in the harbour of Alexandria, built (285–246 BC) for Ptolemy II. It was one of the seven wonders of the ancient world.

Pharsalus, Battle of a battle (48 BC) in Thessaly, N Greece, in which Julius Caesar defeated his main rival, Pompey.

pharyngeal *adj.* relating to or in the region of the pharynx.

pharyngitis *noun Medicine* inflammation of the mucous membrane of the pharynx, characterized by a sore throat, fever, and difficulty in swallowing, and often associated with tonsillitis.

pharynx *noun* (PL. **pharynxes**, **pharynges**) 1 *Anat.* in mammals, the part of the alimentary canal that links the mouth and nasal passages with the oesophagus (gullet) and trachea (windpipe). 2 the throat. [from Greek *pharynx*, throat]

phase — *noun* 1 a stage or period in growth or development. 2 *Astron.* any of the different shapes assumed by the illuminated surface of a celestial body, eg the Moon, resulting from changes in its position relative to the Sun and the Earth. 3 *Physics* the stage that a periodically varying waveform has reached at any particular moment, usually in relation to another waveform of the same frequency. 4 *Chem.* a homogeneous part of a chemical system that is separated from other such parts of the system by distinct boundaries, eg ice and water form a two-phase mixture. — *verb* to organize or carry out in stages.
— **in** *or* **out of phase** coinciding, or failing to coincide, phase by phase throughout a series of changes.

phase something in *or* **out** to introduce it, or get rid of it, in stages.
[from Greek *phasis*, appearance]

phase difference *Physics* the amount by which one wave is behind or ahead of another wave of the same frequency (see WAVE 2).

phatic communion *Linguistics* spoken language used for social reasons rather than to com-

municate ideas or facts. Its main purpose is to maintain a rapport between people, and it includes many conventional greetings such as *hello*, and statements or observations about the weather such as *isn't it a nice day*. [from Greek *phasis*, utterance]

PhD *abbrev. philosophiae doctor* (Latin), Doctor of Philosophy. See also DPHIL.

pheasant *noun* (PL. **pheasant**, **pheasants**) 1 any of various species of ground-dwelling bird, mainly of E Asia, including the junglefowl, partridge, peafowl, and true pheasant. The males are usually brightly coloured and have long pointed tails. 2 the common or ringed pheasant, introduced to many parts of the world as a gamebird. The male has coppery plumage, with a dark green head and neck, and red wattles (flaps of skin) around the eyes. [from Old French *fesan*, from Greek *phasianos ornis*, bird of the Phasis river in Asia Minor]

Phèdre a play by Jean Racine (1677), based on Euripides's *Hippolytus*. It is a tragedy about the love Phèdre feels for her husband's son Hippolyte, concluding with his death and her suicide.

Phelps, Samuel (1804–78) English actor-manager, born in Devonport, Devon. He was well known as an actor by 1837, especially in the role of Shylock. He became manager of Sadler's Wells after the monopoly of patent theatres ended, and for 18 years successfully produced all but four of Shakespeare's plays, often appearing himself in both comic and tragic roles.

phenobarbitone *or chiefly North Amer.* **phenobarbital** *noun* a hypnotic and sedative drug used to treat epilepsy and insomnia.

phenocryst *noun Geol.* in an igneous rock, a conspicuous crystal that is larger than the others. Rocks characterized by the presence of such crystals are described as *porphyritic*. [from Greek *phainein*, to show + CRYSTAL]

phenol *noun Chem.* 1 (FORMULA C_6H_5OH) a colourless crystalline toxic solid, soluble in water and alcohol, that turns pink on exposure to air and light. It is used in the manufacture of phenolic and epoxy resins, nylon, solvents, explosives, drugs, dyes, and perfumes. — Also called *carbolic acid*. 2 any member of a group of organic chemical compounds that contain one or more hydroxyl groups attached to a benzene ring, and are weakly acidic. Many phenols are used as antiseptics, eg trichlorophenol (TCP). [from *phene*, an old name for benzene]

phenolphthalein *noun Chem.* a dye, consisting of pale yellow crystals soluble in alcohol, that is used as a pH indicator, as it is colourless in acidic solutions and turns carmine red in alkaline solutions. It is also used as a laxative.

phenomenal *adj.* 1 remarkable; extraordinary; abnormal. 2 of the nature of a phenomenon. 3 relating to phenomena.

phenomenalism *noun Philos.* a theory that human knowledge is confined to collections of sense-data (phenomena) and that we know nothing that is not given to us by sense experience.

phenomenally *adv.* in a remarkable way or to a remarkable degree: *phenomenally rich*.

phenomenon *noun* (PL. **phenomena**) 1 a happening perceived through the senses, especially if something unusual or scientifically explainable. 2 an extraordinary or abnormal person or thing; a prodigy. 3 a feature of life, social existence, etc: *stress as a work-related phenomenon*. [from Greek *phainomenon*, neuter present participle of *phainesthai*, to appear]
♦ Note that *phenomena* is a plural form; *a phenomena* is incorrect, though often heard.

phenotype *noun Genetics* the observable characteristics of an organism, determined by the interaction between its genetic make-up (*genotype*) and environmental factors.

phenylalanine *or* **phenylalanin** *noun Biochem.* an essential amino acid present in most proteins.

phenylketonuria *noun Medicine* in infants, an inherited metabolic disorder in which the amino acid phenylalanine accumulates in the body, damages the nervous system, and may cause mental retardation. It can be detected in infancy by a screening test, and is treated by prescribing a phenylalanine-free diet.

pheromone *noun Zool.* any chemical substance secreted in minute amounts by an animal, especially an insect or mammal, which has a specific effect on the behaviour of other members of the same species. Pheromones play a role in the attraction of mates, trail marking, and other forms of social behaviour. [from Greek *pherein*, to bear + HORMONE]

phew *interj.* used to express relief, astonishment, or exhaustion. [imitative of a whistle]

phial *noun* a little medicine bottle. [from Greek *phiale*, shallow dish]

Phidias (5c BC) Greek sculptor, born in Athens. He received from Pericles a commission to execute the chief statues for the city, and became superintendent of all public works. He constructed the Propylaea and the Parthenon, where he carved the gold and ivory *Athena*, and also sculpted the *Zeus* at Olympia.

Phil. *abbrev.* 1 Philadelphia. 2 philosophy or (Latin) *philosophiae*, of philosophy.

phil- *or* **philo-** *combining form* forming words denoting fondness or liking. [from Greek *philos*, loving]

-phil see -PHILE.

Philadelphia POP (1990) 4.9m, the seat of Philadelphia County, SE Pennsylvania, USA, lying at the confluence of the Schuylkill and Delaware rivers. It is co-extensive with Philadelphia County. The fourth-largest city in the USA and a major deep-water port, it is a noted centre for culture, education, and medical research. HISTORY first settled by Swedes in the 1640s; British settlement was organized by William Penn in 1681, and the town was laid out in 1682; many Scottish and Irish immigrants settled in the 18c; birthplace of the nation, where the Declaration of Independence was signed in 1776; Constitutional Convention met here and adopted the Constitution of the United States in 1787; US capital from 1790 to 1800; heavily involved in the anti-slavery movement and the Civil War; site of the 1876 Centennial Exposition. NOTABLE FEATURES Liberty Bell (Independence Hall); Pennsylvania Academy of the Fine Arts (oldest art museum in the USA); Museum of Art; Franklin Institute Science Museum and Planetarium; Independence National Historical Park; symphony orchestra.

Philadelphia Story, The a US film directed by George Cukor (1940). Two tycoon socialites (played by Cary Grant and Katharine Hepburn) and a journalist (James Stewart) are the focus of this high-society comedy involving marriage plans and scandal magazines.

philadelphus *noun* any of a genus of tall deciduous shrubs with highly perfumed showy flowers, especially the mock orange. [from Greek *philadelphon*, loving one's brother]

philander *verb intrans.* (**philandered, philandering**) to flirt, or have casual love affairs, with women. [from Greek *philandros*, loving men, used in Greek literature as a proper name for a lover]

philanderer *noun* a womanizer.

philanthropic *adj.* benevolent.

philanthropist *noun* a philanthropic or benevolent person.

philanthropy *noun* a charitable regard for one's fellow human beings, especially in the form of benevolence to those in need. [from Greek *philanthropia*, from phil-, loving + *anthropos*, man]

philatelic *adj.* relating to or concerned with philately.

philatelist *noun* a stamp-collector.

philately *noun* the study and collecting of postage stamps. [from PHIL- + Greek *ateles*, untaxed (mail being delivered 'free' if prepaid by a stamp)]

Philby, Kim (Harold Adrian Russell) (1912–88) British double agent, born in Ambala, India. Together with Guy Burgess, Donald Maclean, and Anthony Blunt, he became a communist at Cambridge, and was recruited as a Soviet agent. He was employed by the British Secret Intelligence Service (MI6), and was head of anti-communist counter-espionage (1944–6). As first secretary of the British embassy in Washington (where Guy Burgess, who shared his house, was second secretary), he worked in liaison with the CIA (1949–51), but was eventually asked to resign because of his earlier communist sympathies. From 1956 he worked in Beirut as a journalist, then in 1963 he admitted his espionage and defected to Russia, where he was granted citizenship.

-phile *or* **-phil** *combining form* forming words denoting fondness or attraction: *bibliophile / paedophile*. [from Greek *philos*, loving]

Philemon, Letter of Paul to the shortest of Paul's letters, written to a Christian named Philemon, whose runaway slave Onesimus had been converted by Paul in prison. Philemon is asked to forgive and receive Onesimus as a fellow Christian, and not to seek punishment under Roman law.

Philemon and Baucis in Greek mythology, an old couple, man and wife, who were the only ones to entertain the Greek gods Zeus and Hermes when they visited the Earth to test people's hospitality. In return they were saved from a flood, made priest and priestess, and allowed to die at the same time, when they were changed into trees.

philharmonic *adj.*, *used in names of choirs and orchestras* dedicated to music. [from PHIL- + Greek *harmonia*, harmony]

-philia *combining form* forming words denoting: 1 a tendency: *haemophilia*. 2 an unnatural liking: *necrophilia*.

-philiac *combining form* forming nouns and adjectives corresponding to nouns in -*philia*: *haemophiliac*.

Philip II, also called **Philip of Macedon** (382–336 BC) King of Macedonia (359–336 BC), the father of Alexander the Great. He created the unified state of Macedonia (359–353 BC), established its military and economic power, and defeated the Greeks at Chaeronea (338 BC), effectively ending the political independence of the Greek city-states. The planned Macedonian conquest of Persia, aborted by his assassination in 336 BC, was eventually carried out by his son.

Philip II (of France) (1165–1223) King of France (1179–1223), born in Paris, the son of Louis VII. His reign was important to the development of the medieval kingdom of France, for although he embarked on the Third Crusade in 1190, he returned the following year to concentrate on attacking the continental lands belonging to the Angevin kings of England. By the time he died most of France was under Capetian control.

Philip II (of Spain) (1527–98) King of Spain (1556–98) and Portugal (as Philip I, 1580–98), born in Valladolid, the only son of Emperor Charles V and Isabella of Portugal. After his first wife Maria of Portugal died during the birth of their son Don Carlos (1545), he married Mary I (1554) and became joint sovereign of England. By the time of Mary's death (1558), he had inherited the Habsburg possessions in Italy, the Netherlands, Spain, and the New World. To seal the end of Valois-Habsburg conflict, he married Elizabeth of France (1559), who bore him two daughters. His brief fourth marriage to his cousin, Anna of Austria (1570) produced another son, the future Philip III. He championed the Counter-Reformation, tried to destroy infidels and heretics, and sought to crush Protestantism, first in the Low Countries (from 1568), then in England and France. His reign was marked by the destruction of the Armada (1588), the continuing revolt of the Netherlands, domestic economic problems, and internal unrest, but there were political achievements in the reduction of Ottoman seapower after the battle of Lepanto (1571) and the conquest of Portugal (1580).

Philip V (1683–1746) the first Bourbon King of Spain (1700–46), born in Versailles, the grandson of Louis XIV and Maria Theresa, and great-grandson of Philip IV of Spain. After a long struggle with the Habsburg rival for the Spanish succession, he gained the throne at the Peace of Utrecht (1713), but lost the Spanish Netherlands and Italian lands. The influence of his second wife Elizabeth Farnese of Parma, who desired to secure Italian possessions for her sons, brought Spain into conflict with Austria, Great Britain, France, and the United Provinces.

Philip VI (1293–1350) the first Valois King of France (1328–50), nephew of Philip IV. He became king on the death of Charles IV, but his right was denied by Edward III of England, son of Philip IV's daughter, who declared that females, though excluded by the Salic law, could transmit their rights to their children. Thus began the Hundred Years' War with England (1337), and in 1346 Edward III landed in Normandy and defeated Philip at Crécy, just as the Black Death was about to spread through France.

Philip, Prince see EDINBURGH, DUKE OF.

Philip, St (1c AD) one of the 12 Apostles of Jesus Christ, from Bethsaida in Galilee. He is listed in Mark 3.14 and Acts 1, and John's Gospel relates that he led Nathanael to Christ (1.43), was there at the feeding of the 5 000 (6.1), brought some Greeks to meet Christ (12.21), and asked 'Lord, show us the Father' (14.8). Traditionally martyred by crucifixion, his feast day is 1 May. He is not to be confused with Philip 'the Evangelist' (Acts 6.5 and Acts 8).

Philip the Good (1396–1467) Duke of Burgundy (1419–67), born in Dijon, the grandson of Philip the Bold. He at first recognized Henry V of England as heir to the French crown, but then concluded a separate peace with the French in 1435 and created one of the most powerful states in later medieval Europe. A committed crusader, he maintained a fleet for operations against the Ottoman Turks.

Philip a male first name, the name in English of one of the Apostles and of several other saints in the Christian Church. [from Greek, from *philos*, loving + *hippos*, horse]

Philippa a female first name. [a feminine form of PHILIP]

Philippi, Battle of a battle (42 BC) in N Greece in which Mark Antony and Octavian (later the emperor Augustus) defeated Brutus and Cassius, and thus avenged the murder of Julius Caesar.

Philippians, Letter of Paul to the a New Testament writing, accepted as being from the apostle Paul to a Christian community that he had founded earlier at Philippi in Macedonia. Writing while imprisoned, Paul thanks them for a gift sent to him, tells them of his difficulties, warns them of sectarian teaching, but conveys a warm regard for their commitment.

philippic *noun* a speech making a bitter attack on someone or something. [from the orations of the Athenian Demosthenes against Philip of Macedon]

Philippines, official name **Republic of the Philippines**, Spanish **Republica de Filipinas** POP (1992e) 64.3m, a republic consisting of an archipelago of more than 7 100 islands and islets, NE of Borneo and S of Taiwan. It is divided into 72 provinces. AREA 299 679sq km/115 676sq mi. It is separated from Borneo by the Sulu Sea, bounded E by the Philippine Sea and W by the S China and Luzon seas. MAIN ISLANDS Luzon, Mindanao, Samar, Palawan, Mindoro, Panay, Negros, Cebu, Leyte, Masbate, Bohol. CAPITAL Manila (on Luzon I). CHIEF TOWNS Quezon City, Basilan, Cebu, Bacolod, Davao, Iloilo. TIME ZONE GMT +8. Most of the population are Filipino, with several minorities; Roman Catholicism is the chief religion. OFFICIAL LANGUAGE Pilipino; English and many local languages are also spoken. CURRENCY the peso. PHYSICAL DESCRIPTION largely mountainous, with N–S ridges rising to over 2 500m; there are narrow coastal margins and broad interior plateaux; forests cover half the land area; some islands are ringed by coral reefs. CLIMATE the lowlands have a warm and humid tropical climate throughout the year, with an average temperature of 27°C; average rainfall at Manila is 2 080mm; lying astride the typhoon belt, the Philippines are affected by c.15 cyclonic storms annually. HISTORY claimed for Spain by Magellan in 1521 but ceded to the USA after the Spanish–American War of 1898; became a self-governing Commonwealth in 1935; occupied by the Japanese during World War II; achieved independence in 1946; during the period 1945–53 the communist-dominated Huk rebellion was suppressed; Muslim separatist movement in the S; martial law from 1972 to 1981 followed political unrest; the exiled political leader Benigno Aquino was assassinated on returning to Manila in 1983; a coup in 1985 ended the 20-year rule of President Ferdinand Marcos; a new constitution was formed in 1987; several attempted coups followed and political unrest continued; the eruption of Mt Pinatubo in 1991 resulted in many deaths. GOVERNMENT the republic is governed by a President and a bicameral legislature, the Congress, comprising a Senate of 24 members elected for five years, and a House of Representatives with up to 250 members serving for three years. ECONOMY lumber, veneer, plywood; oil, copper, lead, iron, nickel, chromite, gold; rubber; textiles; oil products; food processing; electronics; vehicles; fishing; tourism; nearly half the workforce is employed in farming.

Philippines

philistine — adj. having no interest in or appreciation of art, literature, music, etc, and tending rather towards materialism. — noun a philistine person. [named after the Philistines]

Philistines an ancient Aegean warlike people who inhabited the SE coast of Palestine in the 12c BC. They were constantly in conflict with the Israelites of the hinterland — a struggle epitomized by the Biblical stories of Samson and of David and Goliath.

philistinism noun being a philistine; the beliefs and practices of a philistine.

Phillips' curve in economics, the shape of a curve in a diagram which shows the relationship between inflation and levels of unemployment. It derives from the work of British economist A W Phillips (1914–75) in the early 1960s.

philo- see PHIL-.

Philoctetes in Greek legend, the son of Poeas, who inherited the bow of Heracles and its poisoned arrows. On the way to Troy he was bitten by a snake, and left behind on the island of Lemnos. It was prophesied that only with the arrows of Heracles could Troy be taken, so Diomedes and Odysseus returned to find Philoctetes. His wound was healed and he entered the battle and killed Paris.

Philo Judaeus (c.20 BC–c.40 AD) Hellenistic Jewish philosopher, born in Alexandria. His work brought together Greek philosophy and the Hebrew scriptures. His commentaries on the Pentateuch interpret it according to the philosophical ideas of Plato and Aristotle; their doctrines in turn were modified by him in the light of scripture. In his old age, he formed part of a deputation to Emperor Caligula in support of Jewish rights.

philological adj. relating to or involving philology.

philologically adv. as regards philology.

philologist noun a person who studies or is expert in philology.

philology noun 1 the study of language, its history and development; the comparative study of related languages; linguistics. 2 the study of especially older literary and non-literary texts. [from Greek philologia, love of argument, literature or learning, from philo-, loving + logos, reason, word]

Philomela and Procne or **Philomel and Progne** in Greek mythology, the daughters of Pandion, King of Athens. Procne married Tereus, King of Thrace, who raped Philomela and removed her tongue; she was able to tell Procne by a message in her embroidery. In revenge, Procne served up her son Itys, or Itylos, in a meal to his father. While pursuing the sisters, the gods changed Tereus into the hoopoe, Philomela into the swallow, and Procne into the nightingale.

philosopher noun a person who studies philosophy, especially one who develops a particular set of doctrines or theories.

philosopher's stone Hist. a hypothetical substance able to turn any metal into gold, long sought by alchemists.

philosophical adj. 1 of or relating to philosophy or philosophers. 2 calm and dispassionate in the face of adversity; resigned, stoical, or patient.

philosophically adv. in a philosophical way.

philosophize or **philosophise** verb intrans. to form philosophical theories; to reason or speculate in the manner of a philosopher.

philosophizer or **philosophiser** noun a person who philosophizes.

philosophy noun (PL. **philosophies**) 1 the search for truth and knowledge concerning the universe, human existence, perception, and behaviour, pursued by means of reflection, reasoning, and argument. 2 any particular system or set of beliefs established as a result of this. 3 a set of principles serving as a basis for making judgements and decisions: one's philosophy of life. [from Greek philosophia, love of wisdom, from philo-, loving + sophia, wisdom]
◊ Philosophy differs from science, in that its questions cannot be answered empirically or by experiment; and from religion, in that its purposes are entirely intellectual, and allows no role for faith or revelation. The main branches of philosophy are metaphysics, epistemology, ethics, and logic. Western philosophy began in the 6c BC in the Greek-speaking region around the Aegean and S Italy.

philtre noun a magic potion for arousing sexual desire. [from Greek philtron, love charm]

Phipps, Sir William (1651–95) American colonial governor, born in Pemmaquid, Maine. He was successively shepherd, carpenter, and trader, and in 1687 recovered treasure from a wrecked Spanish ship off the Bahamas, which gained him a knighthood and the appointment of Provost-Marshal of New England. In 1692 he became Governor of Massachusetts and, also in that year, when his wife was accused of witchcraft, the force behind the Salem witchcraft trials finally diminished.

phlebitis noun Medicine inflammation of the wall of a vein, often resulting in the formation of a thrombus (blood clot) at the affected site. It most often occurs as a complication of varicose veins in the legs. [from Greek phleps phlebos, vein + -ITIS]

phlebotomy noun Medicine the removal of blood by puncturing or making a surgical incision in a vein. [from Greek phleps phlebos, a vein]

phlegm noun 1 a thick, yellowish substance produced by the mucous membrane lining the nose, throat, and lungs, brought up by coughing. 2 calmness or impassiveness; stolidity or sluggishness of temperament. [from Greek phlegma, flame, heat, phlegm (thought to be the result of heat), inflammation]

phlegmatic adj. 1 said of a person calm, not easily excited. 2 producing or having phlegm.

phlegmatically adv. in a phlegmatic way.

phloem noun Bot. the plant tissue that is responsible for transport of sugars (mainly sucrose) and other nutrients from the leaves, where they are manufactured by photosynthesis, to all other parts of the plant. Phloem tissue consists of vertical chains of living cells joined end to end to form long hollow sieve tubes. See also XYLEM. [from Greek phloios, bark]

phlogiston a substance believed in the 18c to separate from a material during combustion; the theory was discredited as it was clear that the products of combustion weigh more than the material before burning.

phlox noun a plant with clusters of variegated flowers in purple, red, and white. [from Greek phlox, flame, wallflower]

Phnom Penh POP (1990e) 1m, the river port capital of Cambodia. It is situated at the confluence of the Mekong R and Tonlé Sap (lake). HISTORY founded by the Khmers in 1371; became the capital in 1434; abandoned as capital several times, but became the permanent capital in 1867; under Japanese occupation during World War II; after the communist victory of 1975, the population was removed to work in the fields. NOTABLE FEATURES Royal Palace; several museums and pagodas.

-phobe combining form denoting a person affected by a particular form of phobia.

phobia noun an obsessive and persistent fear of a specific object or situation (eg spiders, open spaces, flying), known as a simple phobia, or of one's behaviour in front of others, known as a social phobia. The object or situation that provokes anxiety does not arouse similar fears in the average person, and is not specifically dangerous. The most common response is avoidance of the object or situation, even if this causes considerable inconvenience. Phobias are a form of neurosis, and are often treated by psychotherapy, or by desensitization (in which the feared object or situation is very gradually introduced to the patient, either in fantasy or in reality). [an absolute use of the element -PHOBIA]

-phobia combining form forming nouns denoting obsessive and persistent fears: claustrophobia. [from Greek phobos, fear]

phobic adj. 1 relating to or involving a phobia. 2 affected by a phobia.

-phobic combining form forming adjectives corresponding to nouns in -phobia: claustrophobic.

Phobos Astron. the larger of the two natural satellites of Mars, irregularly shaped and 27km in length.

Some Common Phobias				
Phobia	Meaning	Origin of name		
acrophobia	fear of heights and high places	Greek	akron	peak
aerophobia	fear of air or draughts	Greek	aer	air
agoraphobia	fear of open spaces	Greek	agora	market place
aichmophobia	fear of knives	Greek	aichmē	point of a spear
ailurophobia	fear of cats	Greek	ailouros	cat
algophobia	fear of pain	Greek	algos	pain
androphobia	fear of men	Greek	anēr andros	man
anemophobia	fear of wind	Greek	anemos	wind
anthropophobia	fear of people	Greek	anthrōpos	person
arachnophobia	fear of spiders	Greek	arachnē	spider
astraphobia	fear of thunder and lightning	Greek	astrapē	lightning
aviophobia	fear of flying	Latin	avis	bird
bathophobia	fear of depths and deep places	Greek	bathos	depth
belonephobia	fear of needles	Greek	belonē	needle
bibliophobia	fear of books	Greek	biblion	book
claustrophobia	fear of confined spaces	Latin	claustrum	an enclosed space
cynophobia	fear of dogs or rabies	Greek	kyōn kynos	dog
dromophobia	fear of crossing a street	Greek	dromos	road
erotophobia	fear of sexual activity		see	EROTIC
erythrophobia	fear of the colour red, or of blushing	Greek	erythros	red
gephyrophobia	fear of crossing a bridge or river	Greek	gephyra	bridge
gerontophobia	fear of old age	Greek	gerōn gerontos	old man
graphophobia	fear of writing		see	GRAPH
gynophobia	fear of women	Greek	gynē	woman
haemophobia	fear of blood	Greek	haima	blood
hierophobia	fear of sacred objects or rituals	Greek	hieros	sacred
hodophobia	fear of travel	Greek	hodos	road, way
homophobia	fear of or hostility to homosexuals		see	HOMOSEXUAL
hydrophobia	fear of water	Greek	hydōr	water
kenophobia	fear of empty spaces	Greek	kenos	empty
monophobia	fear of being alone	Greek	monos	alone
mysophobia	fear of contamination or dirt	Greek	mysos	contamination
necrophobia	fear of corpses or death	Greek	nekros	dead body
neophobia	fear of new situations, places, or objects	Greek	neos	new
nosophobia	fear of disease	Greek	nosos	disease
nyctophobia	fear of the night or darkness	Greek	nyx, nyktos	night
ochlophobia	fear of crowds	Greek	ochlos	crowd
oikophobia	fear of one's surroundings	Greek	oikos	house
ornithophobia	fear of birds	Greek	ornis	bird
ophidiophobia	fear of snakes	Greek	ophidion	snake
pantophobia	fear of everything	Greek	pas pantos	everything
phagophobia	fear of food or eating	Greek	phagein	to eat
phengophobia	fear of daylight	Greek	phengos	light, brightness
phobophobia	fear of fearing	Greek	phobos	fear
phonophobia	fear of sounds or of speaking aloud	Greek	phonos	sound
photophobia	fear of light	Greek	phōs phōtos	light
ponophobia	fear of work	Greek	ponos	work, toil
pteronophobia	fear of feathers	Greek	pteron	wing, feathers
pyrophobia	fear of fire	Greek	pyr	fire
scopophobia	fear of being looked at	Greek	skopein	to view
scotophobia	fear of the dark	Greek	skotos	dark
sitophobia	fear of food or eating	Greek	sitos	food
spectrophobia	fear of mirrors	Latin	spectrum	image
taphephobia	fear of being buried alive	Greek	taphos	tomb
theophobia	fear of God	Greek	theos	god
toxiphobia	fear of poisoning		see	TOXIC
triskaidekaphobia	fear of the number thirteen	Greek	treiskaideka	thirteen
xenophobia	fear of or hostility to foreigners	Greek	xenos	stranger
zoophobia	fear of animals	Greek	zōion	animal

Phocis a region in central ancient Greece to the W of Boeotia, in which Delphi and the Delphic oracle were situated.

Phoebe 1 in Greek mythology, a Titaness, identified with the Moon and associated with Artemis. **2** a female first name. [from Greek *phoibos*, bright]

Phoenicia a narrow strip in the E Mediterranean between the mountains of Lebanon and the sea, where the ancient cities of Arad, Byblos, Sidon, and Tyre were located. It derived its name from the Phoenicians (descendants of the Canaanites) who were the dominant people of the area from the end of the second millennium BC, and was their base for trading all over the Mediterranean. From the 8c BC, they established trading posts and colonies in the W

Mediterranean (eg Leptis Magna and Carthage in N Africa). The Phoenician alphabet is the ancestor of modern western alphabets.

Phoenician — *adj.* relating to ancient Phoenicia or its people or culture. — *noun* **1** a member of the Phoenician people. **2** their Semitic language.

Phoenix POP (1990) 2.1m, the capital of the state of Arizona, USA, in Maricopa County, S central Arizona, lying on the Salt R. Settled in 1870, it became state capital in 1889. It is the largest city in the state, the hub of the rich Salt River Valley, and an important centre for data-processing and electronics research. With its dry sunny climate, Phoenix is a popular winter and health resort. NOTABLE FEATURES Heard Museum of Anthropology and Primitive Arts; Pueblo

Grande Museum; Desert Botanical Garden; Pioneer Arizona Museum.

Phoenix *noun Astron.* a relatively inconspicuous constellation in the S hemisphere.

phoenix *noun* in Arabian legend, a bird which every 500 years sets itself on fire and is reborn from its ashes to live a further 500 years. [from Greek *phoinix*]

Phoenix Islands POP (1990) 45 (all on Kanton I), a coral island group of Kiribati. It lies c.1 300km/800mi SE of the Gilbert Is. The group was formerly an important source of guano. Most of the inhabitants were resettled in the Solomon Is in 1978.

Phoenix Park Murders the murder in Dublin on 6 May 1882 of the Chief Secretary for Ireland Lord Frederick Cavendish (b.1836) and his Under-Secretary, Thomas Henry Burke (b.1829), by a nationalist group called 'The Invincibles'. More murders followed that summer, to which the British government responded with a Prevention of Crimes Act (which for three years suspended trial by jury and gave extra powers of arrest to the police) and the execution of five of the murderers.

phone — *noun* a telephone. — *verb trans., intrans.* to telephone.
— **phone in** to take part in a broadcast phone-in. [a shortening of TELEPHONE]

-phone *combining form* forming nouns and adjectives denoting: **1** an instrument transmitting or reproducing sound: *telephone / microphone*. **2** a musical instrument: *saxophone*. **3** a speech sound: *homophone*. **4** speaking, or a speaker of, a language: *Francophone*. [from Greek *phone*, sound, voice]

phonecard *noun* a card obtainable from post offices, etc and usable in place of cash to pay for calls from cardphones.

phone-in *noun* a radio or television programme in which telephoned contributions from listeners or viewers are invited and discussed live by an expert or panel in the studio.

phoneme *noun* the smallest unit of sound in a language that has significance in distinguishing one word from another. [from Greek *phonema*, a sound uttered]

phonemic *adj.* relating to a phoneme or phonemics.

phonemically *adv.* by means of phonemes.

phonemics *sing. noun* **1** the study and analysis of phonemes. **2** the system or pattern of phonemes in a language.

phonetic *adj.* **1** of or relating to the sounds of a spoken language. **2** *said eg of a spelling* intended to represent the pronunciation. **3** denoting a pronunciation scheme using symbols that each represent one sound only. [from Greek *phonetikos*, from *phoneein*, to speak]

phonetically *adv.* as regards phonetics; by means of phonetic characters.

phonetics *sing. noun* the branch of linguistics dealing with speech sounds, how they are produced and perceived.

phoney — *adj.* (**phonier, phoniest**) not genuine; fake, sham, bogus, or insincere. — *noun* (PL. **phoneys**) someone or something bogus; a fake or humbug.

phoneyness *noun* being phoney.

phonic *adj.* **1** relating to especially vocal sound. **2** denoting a method of learning to read by pronouncing each word letter by letter. [from Greek *phonikos*, from *phone*, sound, voice]

-phonic *combining form* forming adjectives corresponding to nouns ending in *-phone*.

phonically *adv.* in terms of or by means of sound.

phonics or phonic method, a method used in the teaching of reading, based on recognition of the relationships between individual letters and sounds. Pronunciation of new words may be built up by saying them sound by sound, beginning with simple one-to-one correspondences and gradually introducing more complex constructions. See also LOOK AND SAY.

phoniness *noun chiefly North Amer.* same as PHONEYNESS.

phono- *or* **phon-** *combining form* forming words denoting sound or voice: *phonology / phonograph*. [from Greek *phone*, sound, voice]

phonograph *noun North Amer. old use* a record-player.

phonological *adj.* relating to or involving phonology.

phonologically *adv.* in terms of phonology.

phonologist *noun* a person who studies and is expert in phonology.

phonology *noun* (PL. **phonologies**) **1** the study of speech sounds, or of those in any particular language. **2** any particular system of speech sounds.

phony (PL. **phonies**) *chiefly North Amer.* same as PHONEY.

phooey *interj. colloq.* an exclamation of scorn, contempt, disbelief, etc.

phosphate *noun Chem.* a salt or ester of phosphoric acid (H_3PO_4) that contains the PO_4^{3-} ion.
◇ Phosphates occur naturally in living organisms (eg in bone, and in the compound ATP, which is involved in energy production in cells) and in many minerals. They are used in fertilizers, detergents, and water softeners, which can be harmful to the environment if they are discharged into rivers, lakes, and streams. [see PHOSPHORUS]

phosphor *noun Chem.* any substance that is capable of phosphorescence. Phosphors are used to coat the inner surface of television screens and fluorescent light tubes, and as brighteners in detergents. [from Greek *phosphoros*; see PHOSPHORUS]

phosphoresce *verb intrans.* to be phosphorescent; to shine in the dark.

phosphorescence *noun* **1** the emission of light from a substance after it has absorbed energy from a source such as ultraviolet radiation, X-rays, etc. It differs from fluorescence in that light is emitted for a considerable time after the energy source has been removed. **2** a general term for the emission of light by a substance in the absence of a significant rise in temperature, eg the glow of white phosphorus in the dark.

phosphorescent *adj.* **1** phosphorescing. **2** having the property of phosphorescing.

phosphoric acid *Chem.* (FORMULA H_3PO_4) a transparent crystalline compound that is soluble in water. It is used in soft drinks, rust removers, and for forming a corrosion-resistant layer on iron and steel. Its salts, known as phosphates, are used in fertilizers and detergents. — Also called *orthophosphoric acid*.

phosphorus *noun Chem.* (SYMBOL **P**, ATOMIC NUMBER **15**) a non-metallic element that exists in several different allotropes, and is mainly obtained from the mineral apatite.
◇ White (yellow) phosphorus is a soft waxy poisonous solid that ignites spontaneously in air, and is stored under water. Red phosphorus is a relatively stable dark red powder formed by heating white phosphorus, and black phosphorus is also stable and has a structure similar to graphite. Phosphorus compounds are used as fertilizers, detergents, insecticides, rat poisons, drying agents, pharmaceutical products, incendiaries, fireworks, and in match heads. Phosphorus is required by all living organisms, and calcium phosphate is an important constituent of bones and teeth.
[from Greek *phosphoros*, bringer of light]

Photius (c.820–891) Byzantine prelate and patriarch of Constantinople, where he was born. When Ignatius was deposed from the patriarchate, Photius was hurried through holy orders and installed (858), but in 862 Pope Nicholas I called a Council at Rome to declare Photius's election invalid and reinstate Ignatius. Supported by the emperor, Photius assembled a Council at Constantinople (867) which condemned many points of doctrine of the Western Church and excommunicated Nicholas. Photius was then deposed and reinstated on several occasions, erased the *Filioque* clause from the Creed (879), and was exiled to Armenia (886). His feast day is 6 Feb (E).

photo *noun* (PL. **photos**) *colloq.* a photograph.

photo- *combining form* forming words meaning: **1** relating to photography: *photomontage*. **2** (*also* **phot-**) relating to light: *photoelectric*. [from Greek *phos*, light]

photocell *noun* same as PHOTOELECTRIC CELL.

photochemistry *noun Chem.* the branch of chemistry concerned with the study of chemical reactions that will only take place in the presence of visible light or ultraviolet radiation, as well as chemical reactions in which light is produced. Everyday examples of photochemical reactions include photography, photosynthesis by plants in the presence of sunlight, and the bleaching of dyes by sunlight.

photocopier *noun* a machine that makes copies of printed documents or illustrations by any of various photographic techniques, especially xerography. Many modern photocopiers are also capable of reducing or enlarging copied material, collating multiple copies of documents, and copying in colour and on both sides of the paper.

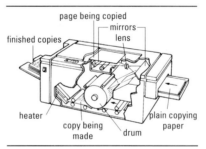

photocopier

photocopy — *noun* (PL. **photocopies**) a photographic copy of a document, drawing, etc. — *verb trans.* (**photocopies**, **photocopied**) to make a photographic copy of.

photodegradable *adj.* able to be broken down by the action of light, and so decay naturally. See also BIODEGRADABLE. [from PHOTO- + DEGRADE]

photoelectric *adj.* relating to electrical or electronic activity triggered by light or other electromagnetic radiation.

photoelectric cell a device activated by photoelectricity, used eg in burglar alarms.

photoelectric effect *Physics* the emission of electrons from the surface of some semi-metallic materials as a result of irradiation with light. It is exploited in photoelectric cells, which convert light energy into an electric current and are used in light meters (eg in photography), light detectors (eg in burglar alarms), etc.

photoelectricity *noun* electrical or electronic activity triggered by light or other electromagnetic radiation.

photoengraving *noun* techniques for producing metal printing plates on cylinders carrying the image of continuous-tone and half-tone text and illustrations, for both letterpress and gravure

printing. The image is photographed and the film exposed on to the metal plate which is first coated with light-sensitive emulsion. The resulting image will be in relief (on a letterpress plate) or etched into the surface (on a gravure cylinder).

photo finish a race finish in which the runners are so close that the result must be decided by photograph.

Photofit *noun trademark* **1** a system used by the police for building up a likeness of someone to fit a witness's description, similar to Identikit but using photographs rather than drawings of individual features. **2** a likeness so produced.

photogenic *adj.* **1** having the quality of photographing well; looking attractive in photographs. **2** producing, or produced by, light.

photogrammetry *noun* the use of photographic records for precise measurements of distances or dimensions, for example aerial photographs used in surveying and map-making. The technique is also used for medical, forensic, and architectural purposes.

photograph — *noun* a permanent record of an image that has been produced on photosensitive film or paper by the process of photography. — *verb trans., intrans.* to take a photograph of (a person, thing, etc).

photographer *noun* a person who takes photographs, especially professionally.

photographic *adj.* **1** relating to or similar to photographs or photography. **2** *said of memory* retaining images in exact detail.

photographically *adv.* **1** in a photographic way. **2** by means of photography or photographs.

photography *noun* the process of making a permanent record of an image on light-sensitive film or some other sensitized material using visible light, X-rays, or some other form of radiant energy. Photography is a popular leisure pursuit, and is widely used in journalism, advertising, art, fashion, medical diagnosis, etc.
◇ In black-and-white photography, light-sensitive film is coated with an emulsion containing silver salts (silver halides). When the film is exposed to a focused image of an object, particles of the silver salts that are exposed to light break down into silver atoms. These areas are then made visible by *developing* the film in a reducing agent, resulting in the production of a negative image formed by grains of dark metallic silver. The image is made permanent by *fixing* in a solution of ammonium or sodium thiosulphate, which removes the unaffected silver salts (those that were not exposed to light). At this stage the film is no longer sensitive to light. Prints are prepared by shining light through the negative film on to light-sensitive paper which is also coated with an emulsion of silver halides.

photogravure *noun* **1** a method of engraving in which the design is photographed on to a metal plate, and then etched in. **2** a picture so produced. [from PHOTO- + French *gravure*, engraving]

photolithography *noun* a process of lithographic printing from a photographically produced plate.

photolysis *noun Chem.* a chemical reaction in which the breaking of a chemical bond within a molecule of a substance is brought about by exposure to light or ultraviolet radiation.

photometry *noun Physics* the measurement of visible light and its rate of flow. Photometry takes account of the varying sensitivity of the eye to light of different frequencies, and has important applications in photography and lighting design.

photomicrograph *noun Physics* a photograph of an object observed through a microscope.

photomicrography *noun* photography of objects or details through the lens of a microscope. Optical microscopes can provide magnifications of up to ×2 000; with an electron microscope, magnifications up to ×10[6] (and more) are possible.
◆ Not to be confused with *microphotography*.

photomontage *noun* the assembling of selected photographic images, either by mounting cut-out portions of prints on a backing, or by combining several separate negatives in succession during printing. The technique is widely used in advertising display material, and is sometimes used in artistic creations. See also MONTAGE. [from PHOTO- + French *montage*, mounting]

photomultiplier *noun Physics* a device for the electronic detection of very low intensities of light. It consists of a photoelectric cell, and incoming light causes the emission of electrons via the photoelectric effect. The number of electrons emitted is multiplied by a series of electrodes until a detectable current is obtained.

photon *noun Physics* a particle of electromagnetic radiation that travels at the speed of light. It can be regarded as a unit of energy equal to *hv*, where *h* is Planck's constant (a fundamental constant) and *v* is the frequency of the electromagnetic radiation. This means that the energy of the photon is proportional to the frequency of the radiation. Photons are used to explain phenomena that require light to behave as particles rather than waves. [from Greek *phos photon*, light]

photo opportunity an event organized or attended by a public figure intended to draw press photographers or television cameras to record it.

photoperiodism *noun Biol.* the physiological and behavioural responses of living organisms to changes in daylength, eg flowering of plants or migration of animals.

photophobia *noun Medicine* **1** a fear of or aversion to light. **2** an abnormal intolerance of and avoidance of light, which may be a symptom of various disorders, eg migraine, measles, meningitis. [from Greek *phos photos*, light + -PHOBIA]

Photorealism, also called **Hyperrealism**, or **Superrealism** a style of modern painting in which pictures are meticulously painted in a style of extreme naturalism like a sharply-focused coloured photograph. Photorealism has flourished since the 1960s, especially in the USA.

photoreceptor *noun Zool.* a cell or group of cells that is sensitive to and responds to light stimuli.

photosensitive *adj.* reacting to light or other electromagnetic radiation.

photosensitivity *noun* being photosensitive.

photosphere *noun* **1** *Astron.* the visible surface of the Sun, consisting of a layer of gas about 500km thick, and having an average temperature of about 6 000°C. It is the zone where the Sun's layers progress from being completely opaque to radiation to being transparent, and hence it is the zone from which the light is emitted. **2** the visible surface of any other star.

Photostat — *noun trademark* **1** a photographic apparatus for copying documents, drawings, etc. **2** a copy made by this. — *verb* (**photostat**) (**photostatted, photostatting**) to make a Photostat of.

photosynthesis *noun* **1** *Bot.* the process whereby green plants manufacture carbohydrates from carbon dioxide and water, using the light energy from sunlight trapped by the pigment chlorophyll. Photosynthesis takes place in chloroplasts, specialized structures that are present in the cells of green plants, especially in the leaves. **2** a similar process that occurs in certain bacteria, whereby carbohydrates are manufac-

tured using a hydrogen source other than water, and byproducts other than oxygen are produced.
◇ Photosynthesis takes place in two main stages. During the *light reactions*, energy from sunlight is converted into chemical energy by using it to split water into oxygen, protons (hydrogen ions), and electrons, with the simultaneous release of oxygen. The protons and electrons are then used to convert carbon dioxide into simple carbohydrates by a series of steps known as the *dark reactions* (because they can occur in the absence of sunlight). Not only does photosynthesis provide plants with all the organic compounds they require for normal growth and functioning, but it is essential for the survival of virtually all other living organisms, since all animals are directly or indirectly dependent on plants for food, eg carnivorous animals eat herbivores that feed on plants. Oxygen released as a by-product of photosynthesis is the main source of atmospheric oxygen.

photosynthesize *or* **photosynthesise** *verb intrans., trans.* to practise or undergo photosynthesis.

photosynthetic *adj.* relating to or affected by photosynthesis.

phototaxis *noun Biol.* the movement of a cell (eg a gamete) or a motile organism in response to a directional light stimulus.

phototropism *noun Bot.* the growth of the roots or shoots of plants in response to light. Shoots show positive phototropism, ie they grow in the direction of light, whereas roots show negative phototropism, ie they grow away from light.

phototypesetter *noun* a machine for composing type (and certain illustrations) and creating an image of the composed type on film or on paper, ready for exposure to a plate for printing.

phrasal *adj.* relating to phrases; consisting of, or of the nature of, a phrase.

phrasally *adv.* by means of phrases.

phrasal verb a phrase consisting of a verb plus adverb or preposition, or a combination of these, frequently, as with *let on* and *come up with*, with a meaning or meanings that cannot be determined from the meanings of the individual words.

phrase — *noun* **1** a set of words expressing a single idea, forming part of a sentence though not constituting a clause. **2** an idiomatic expression. **3** *Mus.* a run of notes making up an individually distinct part of a melody. — *verb* **1** to express; to word: *a carefully phrased reply*. **2** *Mus.* to bring out the phrases in (music) as one plays. [from Greek *phrasis*, expression, from *phrazein*, to tell]

phrase book a book listing words and phrases in a foreign language, especially for the use of visitors.

phraseological *adj.* relating to or involving phraseology.

phraseology *noun* **1** one's choice of words and way of combining them, in expressing oneself. **2** the language belonging to a particular subject, group, etc: *legal phraseology*.

phreaking *or* **phone phreaking** *colloq.* the practice of tampering electronically with a telephone to enable the user to make free calls. [a variant of FREAK]

phrenological *adj.* relating to or involving phrenology.

phrenologist *noun* a person skilled in phrenology.

phrenology *noun* the practice, popular in the 19c but now discredited, of assessing a person's character and aptitudes by examining the shape of the skull. [from Greek *phren*, mind + -LOGY]

Phrygia an ancient kingdom in central and W Asia Minor with which the legendary king Midas is associated. It was dominated by the Phryges (a

Thracian people) from the collapse of the Hittite Empire in the 12c BC to its conquest by Lydia in the 7c BC.

phthisis *noun* (PL. **phthises**) any wasting disease, especially tuberculosis. [from Greek *phthisis*, emaciation, consumption]

Phuket, formerly **Salang**, or **Junkseylon** POP (1993e) 50 000, the largest island of Thailand. It lies in the Andaman Sea, 900km/560mi S of Bangkok. The island is a resort area with notable limestone caves and columns at Phang Nga Bay. It is also a marine biological centre. The port of Phuket is a major outlet to the Indian Ocean.

phut *colloq. noun* the noise of a small explosion.
— **go phut 1** to break down or cease to function. **2** to go wrong.
[imitative, or connected with Hindi and Urdu *phatna*, to burst]

phycology *noun Bot.* the scientific study of algae. [from Greek *phykos* seaweed + -LOGY]

phylactery *noun* (PL. **phylacteries**) **1** either of two small boxes containing religious texts worn on the arm and forehead by Jewish men during prayers. **2** a charm or amulet. [from Greek *phylakterion*, from *phylassein*, to guard]

Phyllis 1 *Greek Mythol.* a nymph who died of love and was turned into an almond tree. **2** a female first name. [from Greek *phyllis*, leafy shoot]

phyllite *noun Geol.* any of various fine-grained metamorphic rocks intermediate between slate and schist. Phyllites have a silky sheen, with light and dark minerals arranged in bands, and they are derived from sedimentary rocks. [from Greek *phyllon*, a leaf]

phyllotaxis *or* **phyllotaxy** *noun Bot.* the arrangement of leaves on a plant stem. [from Greek *phyllon*, a leaf + *taxis*, arrangement]

phylogeny *noun Biol.* the sequence of changes that has occurred during the evolution of a particular species of living organism, or a group of related organisms. [from Greek *phylon*, race + GENESIS]

phylum *noun* (PL. **phyla**) *Biol.* each of the major groups into which the animal kingdom is divided, eg Arthropoda (insects, crustaceans, and spiders), Mollusca (molluscs). Each phylum is in turn subdivided into one or more classes. [from Greek *phylon*, race]

physic *old use* — *noun* **1** the skill or art of healing. **2** a medicine. **3** anything with a curative or reinvigorating effect. — *verb* (**physicked, physicking**) to dose with medicine. [from Greek *physike episteme*, knowledge of nature]

physical *adj.* **1** of the body rather than the mind; bodily: *physical strength. fitness exercise*, etc. **2** relating to objects that can be seen or felt; material: *the physical world*. **3** relating to nature or to the laws of nature: *physical features / a physical impossibility*. **4** relating to physics. **5** involving bodily contact: *physical force*. [from Greek *physikos*, of nature, from *physis*, nature]

physical anthropology the study of local biological adaptions in man and man's evolutionary history.

physical chemistry the branch of chemistry concerned with the relationship between the chemical structure of compounds and their physical properties.

physical education *or* **physical training** instruction in sport and gymnastics as part of a school or college curriculum.

physical geography the study of the earth's natural features, eg mountain ranges, ocean currents, etc.

physicality *noun* **1** a physical quality. **2** preoccupation with bodily matters.

physical jerks *colloq.* bodily exercises, especially done regularly to keep fit.

physically *adv.* in terms of the material world.

physical science any of the sciences dealing with non-living matter, eg astronomy, physics, chemistry, and geology.

physician *noun* **1** in the UK, a registered medical practitioner who specializes in medical as opposed to surgical treatment of diseases and disorders. **2** in other parts of the world, any person who is legally qualified to practise medicine.

physicist *noun* a student of or expert in physics.

physics *sing. noun* the scientific study of the properties and interrelationships of matter and energy. Classical physics includes mechanics, thermodynamics, electricity, magnetism, optics, and acoustics, and important recent developments include quantum mechanics and relativity theory. [from Greek *ta physika*, natural things]

physio *noun* (PL. **physios**) *colloq.* a physiotherapist.

physio- *or* **physi-** *combining form* forming words meaning 'physical or physiological'. [from Greek *physis*, nature, make-up]

physiognomy *noun* (PL. **physiognomies**) **1** the face or features, especially as a key to personality. **2** the general appearance of something, eg the countryside. [from Greek *physis*, nature, *gnomon*, interpreter]

physiological *adj.* relating to or involving physiology.

physiologist *noun* a person skilled in physiology.

physiology *noun* *Biol.* the branch of biology that is concerned with the internal processes and functions of living organisms, such as respiration, nutrition, and reproduction, as opposed to anatomy, which is concerned with their structure. [from Greek *physis*, nature + -LOGY]

physiotherapist *noun* a person skilled in treatment by physiotherapy.

physiotherapy *noun* *Medicine* the treatment of injury and disease by external physical methods, such as remedial exercises, manipulation, heat, or massage, as opposed to drugs or surgery.

physique *noun* the structure of the body with regard to size, shape, proportions, and muscular development. [from French *physique*, originally = physical, from Greek *physikos*, of nature]

phytomenadione *noun* vitamin K. [from the names of related chemicals]

phytopathology *noun* *Bot.* the scientific study of plant diseases. [from Greek *phyton*, plant]

phytoplankton *noun* *Bot.* the part of the plankton that is composed of microscopic plants.

pi *noun* **1** the sixteenth letter of the Greek alphabet (π). **2** *Maths.* this as a symbol representing the ratio of the circumference of a circle to its diameter, in numerical terms 3·14159.

Piacenza, ancient **Placentia** POP (1991e) 104 000, the capital of Piacenza province, Emilia-Romagna region, N Italy. It lies on the R Po, 61km/38mi SW of Milan, and dates from 218 BC. NOTABLE FEATURES Palazzo Gotico (begun in 1281); cathedral (begun 12c–13c); Church of Sant'Antonino (11c–12c); Church of Santa Maria di Campagna (1522–8); well-preserved circuit of 16c walls.

Piaf, Edith, originally **Edith Giovanna Gassion** (1915–63) French singer, born in Paris. She began singing in music hall and cabaret, where she became known as *Piaf* (Parisian argot 'little sparrow'). She appeared in stage-plays and films, but is mainly remembered for her songs, with their undercurrent of sadness and nostalgia, such as 'La vie en rose' and 'Non, je ne regrette rien'.

Piaget, Jean (1896–1980) Swiss psychologist, born in Neuchâtel. Professor at Geneva, he is best known for his research on the development of cognitive functions in children, in such pioneering studies as *La Naissance de l'intelligence chez l'enfant* (The Origins of Intelligence in Children, 1948).

pia mater *noun* (PL. **piae matres**) *noun Anat.* the delicate innermost membrane enclosing the brain and spinal cord. [from Latin *pia mater*, tender mother]

pianissimo *adj., adv. Mus.* played very softly. [from Italian *pianissimo*, superlative of *piano*, quiet]

pianist *noun* a person who plays the piano.

piano¹ *noun* (PL. **pianos**) a large musical instrument with a keyboard, the keys being pressed down to operate a set of hammers that strike tautened wires to produce the sound. [from PIANOFORTE]
◇ The mechanism of the instrument was originated in 1710 by Bartlomeo Cristofiori in Florence. The earliest instruments had strings extending away from the keyboard (as in the modern grand piano), or at right angles to the keys (as in the clavichord). The upright model, with strings set perpendicularly, was not developed until the 19c. A succession of famous 19c instrument makers developed the piano's volume and sustaining power, extended its compass, and refined its action: they included Sébastian Érard (1752–1831), Heinrich Steinway (1797–1871), and Karl Bechstein (1826–1900).

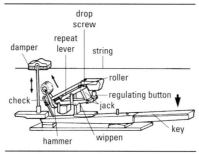

piano key

piano² *adj., adv. Mus.* played softly. [from Italian *piano*]

piano accordion an accordion with a keyboard like that of a piano.

pianoforte *noun* the full formal term for a piano. [from Italian *piano e forte*, soft and loud]

Pianola *noun trademark* a mechanical piano operated by means of interchanging paper rolls bearing coded music in the form of perforations.

Piatra *or* **Piatra-Neamț** POP (1992) 123 000, the industrial capital of Neamț county, NE Romania, lying on the R Bistrița. NOTABLE FEATURE Bistrița Monastery (1402).

piazza *noun* a public square in an Italian town. [from Italian *piazza*, from Latin *platea* and Greek *plateia*, street]

Piazzi, Giuseppe (1746–1826) Italian astronomer, born in Ponte, N Italy. He became a Theatine monk (1764), was appointed professor at Palermo (1780), and founded observatories at Naples and at Palermo. He published a monumental catalogue of 7 646 stars (1813), and discovered the first minor planet (or asteroid) which he named Ceres (1801).

pibroch *noun* a series of variations on a martial theme or lament, played on the Scottish bagpipes. [from Gaelic *piobaireachd*]

pic *noun* (PL. **pics, pix**) *colloq.* a photograph or picture.

pica *noun Printing* an old type size, giving about six lines to the inch. [from Latin *pica*, magpie]

picador *noun Bullfighting* a horseman who weakens the bull by wounding it with a lance. [from Spanish *picador*, from *pica*, lance]

Picard, (Charles) Émile (1856–1941) French mathematician, born in Paris. Professor at the Sorbonne, he was specially noted for his work in complex analysis, and integral and differential equations. He introduced the method of 'successive approximations', a powerful technique for determining whether solutions to differential equations exist.

Picardy, French **Picardie** POP (1991e) 1.8m, a region and former province of N France, comprising the departments of Aisne, Oise, and Somme. AREA 19 399sq km/7 488sq mi. It is bounded on the NW by the English Channel. The landscape is flat and crossed by several rivers (eg Somme and Oise) and canals. CHIEF TOWNS Abbeville, Amiens, St-Quentin, Laon, Beauvais, Compiègne. HISTORY seized by Philippe-Auguste in 1185 and annexed to the crown in 1477; Picardy was the scene of heavy fighting during World War I. ECONOMY chemicals; metalworking.

picaresque *adj., said of a novel, etc* telling of the adventures of a usually likeable rogue in separate, only loosely connected, episodes. [from Spanish *picaro*, rogue]

Picasso, Pablo (Ruiz y) (1881–1973) Spanish artist, born in Málaga. In 1901 he set up a studio in Montmartre, Paris, and entered his 'blue period' (1902–4), a series of melancholy studies of the poor (eg *Child Holding a Dove*, Courtauld College, London). This gave way to the life-affirming 'pink period' (1904–6), full of harlequins, acrobats, and the incidents of circus life. His break with tradition came with his *Les Demoiselles d'Avignon* (1906–7, Museum of Modern Art, New York), which heralded the start of Cubism (an attempt to render the three-dimensional on the flat picture surface without resorting to perspective), a movement which he developed with Georges Braque from 1909 to 1914. From 1917 he became associated with Sergei Diaghilev's Russian Ballet, designing costumes and sets. Other works include the painting *Guernica* (1937, Prado, Madrid), which expresses his horror at the bombing of the Basque town of Guernica during the Civil War, and *The Charnel House* (1945, Museum of Modern Art, New York). He also illustrated classical texts and experimented in sculpture, ceramics, and lithography.

piccalilli *noun* a pickle consisting of mixed vegetables in a mustard sauce.

piccaninny *or North Amer., esp. US* **pickaninny** *noun* (PL. **piccaninnies**) *now offensive* a Negro or Aboriginal child. [perhaps from Portuguese *pequenino*, diminutive of *pequeno*, little]

piccolo *noun* (PL. **piccolos**) a small transverse flute pitched one octave higher than the standard instrument, and with a range of about three octaves. It did not become a regular orchestral instrument until the middle of the 19c. [a shortening of Italian *flauto piccolo*, little flute]

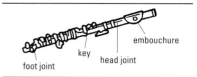

piccolo

Pichincha 1 an Andean volcano in Pichincha province, N central Ecuador. It lies 10km/6mi NW of Quito. HEIGHT 4 794m. The last eruption was in 1881 and it still emits gases. It was the site of a decisive battle in 1822 in the fight for independence from Spain. **2** a province in N central Ecuador with Quito as its capital.

Pichincha, Battle of a decisive battle (1822) during the Spanish–American Wars of Independence, fought on the slopes of Mt Pichincha overlooking the city of Quito. It secured the liberation of Quito (now Ecuador) from Spanish rule.

pick¹ — *verb* **1** *trans., intrans.* to choose or select. **2** to detach and gather (flowers from a plant, fruit from a tree, etc). **3** (**pick something up, off, out,** *etc*) to lift, remove, detach, or extract it: *picked a crumb off the carpet.* **4** to open (a lock) with a device other than a key. **5** to get, take, or extract whatever is of use or value from: *pick a bone clean / pick someone's brains.* **6** to steal money or valuables from (someone's pocket). **7** to undo; to unpick: *pick a dress to pieces.* **8** to make (a hole) by unpicking. **9** to remove pieces of matter from (one's nose, teeth, a scab, etc) with one's fingernails, etc. **10** to provoke (a fight, quarrel, etc) with someone. — *noun* **1** the best of a group: *the pick of the bunch.* **2** one's own preferred selection. — **have** *or* **take one's pick** to keep selecting and rejecting until one is satisfied.
pick and choose be over-fussy in one's choice.
pick at something 1 to eat only small quantities of one's food. **2** to keep pulling at a scab, etc with one's fingernails.
pick holes in something to find fault with it.
pick people *or* **things off 1** to shoot them. **2** to deal with opposition bit by bit.
pick on someone 1 to blame them unfairly. **2** to bully them. **3** to choose them for an unpleasant job.
pick on something to choose it; to light on it.
pick someone out 1 to select them from a group. **2** to recognize or distinguish them among a group or crowd.
pick something out 1 to play a tune uncertainly, especially by ear. **2** to mark so as to distinguish from its surroundings: *beige walls with the picture rail picked out in brown.*
pick something over to examine one by one and reject whatever is unwanted.
pick someone *or* **something to pieces** to criticize them severely.
pick up *said of a person, a person's health, or a situation* to recover or improve: *she picked up after seeing me / sales have picked up now.*
pick up *or* **pick something up** to resume: *pick up where one left off / pick up the threads of a relationship / pick up the trail.*
pick someone up 1 to arrest or seize them: *was picked up by the police.* **2** *colloq.* to approach someone, especially with a view to sexual relations.
pick oneself up to restore oneself to an upright position after a fall.
pick something up 1 to lift or raise it from a surface, from the ground, etc. **2** to learn or acquire (a habit, skill, language, etc) over a time. **3** to notice or become aware of something: *picked up a faint odour.* **4** to obtain or acquire casually, by chance, etc: *pick up a bargain / pick up an infection.* **5** to go and fetch someone or something waiting to be collected. **6** *Telecomm.* to receive a signal, programme, etc. **7** to refer back in conversation or discourse to a point previously made, in order to deal with it further. **8** *colloq.* to agree to pay a bill.
pick someone *or* **something up** to stop one's vehicle for, and give a lift to or take someone or something where required.
pick someone up on something to point out their error.
pick up the pieces to have to restore things to normality or make things better after some trouble or disaster.
pick up speed to increase speed gradually.
pick one's way to go carefully so as to avoid hazards.
[from Middle English *piken*]

pick² *noun* **1** a tool with a long metal head pointed at one or both ends, for breaking ground, rock, ice, etc. **2** a poking or cleaning tool: *a toothpick.* **3** a plectrum. [from Middle English *pikke*]

pickaback see PIGGYBACK.

pickaxe *noun* a large pick, especially with a point at one end of its head and a cutting edge at the other. [from Old French *picois*]

picker *noun* **1** a person who picks or gathers. **2** a tool or machine for picking.

picket — *noun* **1** a person or group stationed outside a place of work to persuade other employees not to go in during a strike. **2** a body of soldiers on patrol or sentry duty. **3** a stake fixed in the ground, eg as part of a fence. — *verb* (**picketed, picketing**) **1** to station pickets, or act as a picket, at (a factory, etc). **2** to guard or patrol with, or as, a military picket. [from French *piquet*, diminutive of *pic,* pick]

picket line a line of people acting as pickets in an industrial dispute.

Pickford, Mary, originally **Gladys Mary Smith** (1893–1979) US actress, born in Toronto. Known as 'America's sweetheart', she began as a film extra for D W Griffith, and then played the innocent heroine in many silent films, including *Rebecca of Sunnybrook Farm* (1917) and *Little Lord Fauntleroy* (1921). She won a Best Actress Oscar for her sound début, *Coquette* (1929). She was also a co-founder of United Artists Corporation (1919).

pickings *pl. noun colloq.* profits made easily or casually from something.

Pickle, Gamaliel the listless father of Peregrine in Tobias Smollett's *Peregrine Pickle.*

pickle — *noun* **1** a preserve of vegetables, eg onions, cucumber, or cauliflower, in vinegar, salt water, or a tart sauce. **2** a vegetable so preserved. **3** the liquid used for this preserve. **4** *colloq.* a mess; a quandary: *get oneself in a pickle.* — *verb* to preserve in vinegar, salt water, etc. [from Old German *pekel*]

pickled *adj.* **1** preserved in pickle. **2** *colloq.* drunk.

pick-me-up *noun* **1** a stimulating drink. **2** anything that revives and invigorates.

pickpocket *noun* a thief who steals from people's pockets.

pick-up *noun* **1** the stylus on a record-player. **2** a small lorry, truck, or van. **3** *colloq.* an acquaintance made casually, especially with a view to sexual relations; the making of such an acquaintance. **4** a halt to load goods or passengers; the goods or passengers so loaded.

Pickwick, Samuel the eccentric, affable Chairman of the Pickwick Club in Charles Dickens's *The Pickwick Papers.*

Pickwick Papers, The, in full *The Posthumous Papers of the Pickwick Club* a novel by Charles Dickens (1836–7). His first, it describes the disparate adventures of Samuel Pickwick and various members of the Club.

picky *adj.* (**pickier, pickiest**) *colloq.* choosy; difficult to please.

picnic — *noun* **1** an outing on which one takes food for eating in the open; the food so taken or eaten. **2** (*usually* **no picnic**) *colloq.* an agreeable job or situation: *minding young children is no picnic.* — *verb intrans.* (**picnicked, picnicking**) to have a picnic. [from French *pique-nique*]

Picnic at Hanging Rock an Australian film directed by Peter Weir (1975). It is an atmospheric account of the unexplained disappearance of a schoolteacher and three of her pupils.

picnicker *noun* a person having a picnic.

pico- *combining form* denoting a millionth of a millionth part, or 10^{-12}. [from Spanish *pico,* a small quantity]

Pico de Orizaba see CITLALTÉPETL.

Pict *noun* a member of an ancient British people (see PICTS). [from Latin *picti,* painted men]

Pictish *adj.* belonging or relating to the Picts.

pictograph *or* **pictogram** *noun* **1** a picture or symbol representing a word, as in Chinese writing. **2** a pictorial or diagrammatic representation of values, statistics, etc. [from Latin *pictus,* painted + -GRAPH, -GRAM]

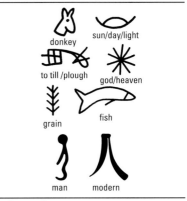

donkey
sun/day/light
to till /plough
god/heaven
grain
fish
man
modern

pictographs

pictorial — *adj.* relating to, or consisting of, pictures. — *noun* a periodical with a high proportion of pictures. [from Latin *pictor,* painter]

pictorially *adv.* by means of pictures.

Picts a general term coined by the Romans in the 3c for their barbarian enemies in Britain north of the Antonine Wall, and then used for the subjects of kings who ruled north and south of the E Grampians. They disappeared from history soon after being united with the Scots under Kenneth I (d.858), but traces of their language and art (eg the enigmatic Pictish symbol stones) still survive. [from Latin *picti,* painted people]

picture — *noun* **1** a representation of someone or something on a flat surface; a drawing, painting, or photograph. **2** someone's portrait. **3** a view; a mental image: *a clear picture of the battle.* **4** a situation or outlook: *a gloomy financial picture.* **5** a person or thing strikingly like another: *she is the picture of her mother.* **6** a visible embodiment: *was the picture of happiness.* **7** an image of beauty: *looks a picture.* **8** the image received on a television screen. **9** a film; a motion picture. **10** *colloq.* (**the pictures**) the cinema. — *verb* **1** to imagine or visualise. **2** to describe vividly; to depict. **3** to represent or show in a picture or photograph. — **in the picture** informed of all the relevant facts. [from Latin *pictura*]

Picture of Dorian Gray, The a novel by Oscar Wilde (1890). It is a Gothic tale about a young man who sells his soul in order to become immortal.

picture postcard a postcard with a picture on the front.

picture rail a narrow moulding running round the walls of a room just below the ceiling, from which to hang pictures.

Pictures at an Exhibition (Kartinka s vystavki) a solo piano suite by Modest Mussorgsky (1874), comprising a musical description of 10 pictures by the Russian artist Victor Hartmann. Among the orchestral versions are those written by Maurice Ravel and Henry Wood.

picturesque *adj.* **1** *said of places or buildings* charming to look at, especially if rather quaint. **2** *said of language* colourful, expressive, or graphic; *facetious* vivid or strong to the point of offensiveness. [from French *pittoresque,* influenced by PICTURE]

picturesquely *adv.* in a picturesque way.

picture window a large window with a plate-glass pane, usually affording an extensive view.

piddle — *verb intrans. colloq.* **1** to urinate. **2** (**piddle about** *or* **around**) to mess about or waste time. — *noun* urine or the act of urinating.

piddling *adj.* trivial; trifling.

pidgin *noun* **1** a type of simplified language used especially for trading purposes between speakers of different languages, consisting of a combination and often simplification of the vocabulary, grammar, and pronunciation systems of the languages concerned. See also CREOLE. **2** *colloq.* (*also* **pigeon**) one's own affair, business, or concern. [said to be a Chinese pronunciation of *business*]
◇ Pidgins, based on English, French, Spanish, and Portuguese, were common in the colonial era in the East and West Indies, Africa, and the Americas. Some pidgins have developed into more general systems of communication, eg Tok Pisin in Papua New Guinea, which is used in the press and on radio.

pidgin English a pidgin in which one element is English, especially that formerly spoken between the Chinese and Europeans.

Pidurutalagala, sometimes called **Pedrotalagala** the highest peak in Sri Lanka at 2 524m. It is situated 95km/59mi E of Colombo, to the NE of Nuwara-Eliya.

pie *noun* a savoury or sweet dish, usually cooked in a container, consisting of a quantity of food with a covering and/or base of pastry.
— **easy as pie** very easy.
pie in the sky some hoped-for but unguaranteed future prospect.

piebald — *adj.* having contrasting patches of colour, especially black and white. — *noun* a piebald horse. [from *pie*, magpie + BALD]

piece — *noun* **1** a portion of some material; a bit. **2** any of the sections into which something (eg a cake) is divided; a portion taken from a whole. **3** a component part: *a jigsaw piece.* **4** an item in a set: *an 18-piece teaset.* **5** an individual member of a class of things represented by a collective noun: *a piece of fruit / a piece of clothing.* **6** a specimen: *a fine piece of Chippendale.* **7** an instance: *a piece of nonsense.* **8** a musical, artistic, literary, or dramatic work. **9** an article in a newspaper, etc. **10** a coin: *a 50-penny piece.* **11** *Chess* one of the tokens or men used in a board game. **12** a cannon or firearm. **13** *offensive colloq.* a woman. — *verb* **1** (**piece something** *or* **things together**) to join them together to form a whole. **2** (**piece something up**) to patch or insert pieces into a garment.
— **all of a piece** forming an indivisible whole.
go to pieces *colloq.* to lose emotional control; to panic.
all in one piece undamaged, unhurt, intact.
in pieces 1 separated into a number of component parts. **2** broken; shattered.
of a piece with something consistent or uniform with it.
say one's piece to make one's contribution to a discussion.
to pieces 1 into its component parts: *take to pieces.* **2** into fragments, shreds, tatters, etc. [from Old French *piece*]

pièce de résistance (PL. **pièces de résistance**) the best or most impressive item. [French]

piecemeal *adv.* a bit at a time.

piece of eight (PL. **pieces of eight**) an old Spanish gold coin worth eight reals.

piece rate a fixed rate of pay for a particular amount of work done.

piecework *noun* work paid for according to the amount done, not the time taken to do it.

pie chart a diagram consisting of a circle divided into sectors, used to display statistical data. Each sector contains one category of information, and its size is calculated as a percentage of the total.

pied *adj.*, *said of a bird* having variegated plumage, especially of black and white. [from *pie*, magpie]

pied-à-terre *noun* (PL. **pieds-à-terre**) a house or apartment, eg in a city, that one keeps as a lodging for one's occasional visits there. [from French *pied-à-terre*, literally 'foot on the ground']

Piedmont, Italian **Piemonte** POP (1991) 4.3m, a region in N Italy, bounded N by Switzerland and W by France. AREA 25 400sq km/9 804sq mi. PHYSICAL DESCRIPTION the region is encircled by the Appenines in the S and the Alps in the N and W; it is drained by the R Po and its tributaries. HISTORY in the 19c it was the centre for the movement towards Italian unification. CAPITAL Turin. CHIEF TOWNS Cuneo, Saluzzo, Asti, Alessandria. ECONOMY industries (metalworking, machinery, cars, textiles, leather, foodstuffs) centred around Turin, Ivrea, Biella; fruit-growing, arable farming; cattle; tourism in hill regions.

Pied Piper of Hamelin in German legend, a 13c piper who charmed the rats of Hamelin out of the city with his pipe-music. He was refused his fee, and in revenge lured all the children away from the city. Goethe and Robert Browning tell the tale, which may have its roots in the Children's Crusade of 1212.

Piedras, Las POP (1985) 58 000, a town in Canelones department, Uruguay.

pie-eyed *adj. colloq.* drunk.

pier *noun* **1** a structure built of stone, wood, or iron, projecting into water for use as a landing-stage or breakwater. **2** a pillar supporting a bridge or arch. **3** the masonry between two openings in the wall of a building. [from Middle English *per*, from Latin *pera*]

pierce *verb* (**pierce something** *or* **pierce through something**) **1** *said of a sharp object, or a person using one* to make a hole in or through; to puncture; to make (a hole) with something sharp. **2** to penetrate or force a way through or into: *the wind pierced through her thin clothing.* **3** *said of light or sound* to burst through (darkness or silence). **4** to affect or touch (someone's heart, soul, etc) keenly or painfully. [from Old French *percer*]

Pierced Form a sculpture by Dame Barbara Hepworth (1931). It was destroyed during World War II.

piercing *adj.* that pierces; penetrating, acute, keen, sharp.

Piero della Francesca (c.1420–92) Italian painter, born in Borgo San Sepolcro. He is known especially for his series of frescoes, *The Legend of the Holy Cross* (c.1452–c.1466) in the Church of San Francesco in Arezzo. Other works include the *Flagellation* (c.1456–7) at Urbino. He also wrote a treatise on geometry and a manual on perspective.

Piero di Cosimo, originally **Piero de Lorenzo** (c.1462–c.1521) Italian painter, born in Florence. He was influenced by Luca Signorelli and Leonardo da Vinci, and is best known for his mythological scenes, notably *Death of Procris* (c.1500, National Gallery, London), *Perseus and Andromeda* (c.1515, Uffizi, Florence), and *The Battle of the Lapiths and Centaurs* (1486, National Gallery, London).

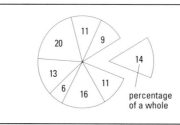

pie chart

Pierre POP (1990) 13 000, the capital of the state of South Dakota, USA, situated in Hughes County on the Missouri R. Founded as a railway terminus in 1880, it became state capital in 1889. It is the centre of a grain and dairy farming region. NOTABLE FEATURES L Oahe and the Oahe Dam nearby.

Pierrot a traditional male character from French pantomime, with a whitened face, white frilled outfit, and pointed hat. [from French name *Pierrot*, diminutive of *Pierre*, Peter]
◇ The character originated from Pedrolino, a servant role in the commedia dell' arte. A dumb and solitary character, Pierrot gained his white face and white floppy costume on the French stage, and his childlike manner was the creation of the 19c pantomimist Deburau.

Piers a male first name. [a Middle English form of PETER]

Piers Plowman a medieval poem in alliterative verse by William Langland (late 14c). It survives in three versions known as the A-, B-, and C-texts. It is an allegorical dream-vision narrated by 'Will', in which the ploughman Piers progresses to a state of Christ-like serenity.

Pietà **1** a painting of the pietà by an unknown artist (c.1460, Louvre, Paris), generally considered to be the major work of the Avignon School. **2** a sculpture of the pietà by Michelangelo (1499, St Peter's, Vatican City, Rome). **3** a painting by Titian (1573–6, Accademia, Venice). It was unfinished at his death and completed by Palma Giovane.

pietà *noun* in painting and sculpture, the representation of the dead Christ mourned by angels, apostles, or holy women. [Italian, from Latin *pieta*, pity]

Pietermaritzburg *or* **Maritzburg** POP (1985e) 134 000, the capital of Natal province, E South Africa. It lies 73km/45mi NW of Durban at the centre of a rich farming area. The city was founded by the Boers from Cape Colony in 1838. NOTABLE FEATURES Voortrekker Museum, Macrorie House Museum.

Pieterse, Zola, *née* **Budd** (1966–) South African track athlete, born in Bloemfontein, South Africa. She caused a controversy by obtaining British citizenship in 1984 and then being selected for the British Olympic squad. There was further controversy at the 1984 Games when she was involved in an incident with US athlete Mary Decker during the 3 000m. She was the UK 1 500m champion in 1984, the European Cup gold medallist at 3 000m in 1985, and world amateur champion at 3 000m in 1985 and at 1 500m in 1986. She set the 5 000m world record in 1984 and 1985, and was world cross-country champion in 1985 and 1986. A hip injury and continuing controversy caused her to retire in 1988, and return to South Africa. She resumed competitive running under her married name, and ran for South Africa in the 3 000m at the 1992 Olympics.

pietism *noun* pious feeling, or an exaggerated show of piety.

pietist *noun* a person marked by strong devotional feeling.

pietistic *adj.* relating to pietists.

piety *noun* the quality of being pious, dutiful, or religiously devout. [from Latin *pietas*]

piezoelectric *adj.* relating to or using piezoelectricity.

piezoelectric effect **1** *Physics* the generation of an electrical potential across certain crystals, eg quartz, when they are stretched or compressed. This effect is exploited in the crystal pick-ups of record players, and in certain types of microphone. **2** the reverse effect, in which an electrical potential can produce slight physical distortion in such crystals. For example, in a quartz watch or clock the piezoelectric effect causes the crystal to vibrate at a particular frequency by expanding and contracting rhythmically, so that the instrument keeps almost perfect time.

piezoelectricity *noun* electricity produced by the piezoelectric effect. [from Greek *piezo*, to press + ELECTRICITY]

piffle *noun* nonsense; rubbish.

piffling *adj.* trivial, trifling, or petty.

pig — *noun* **1** an ungulate (hoofed mammal) belonging to the family Suidae, kept worldwide for its meat. It has a stout heavy body covered with coarse bristly hairs, relatively short legs, and a protruding flattened snout. **2** an abusive term for a person, especially someone greedy, dirty, selfish, or brutal. **3** *slang* an unpleasant job or situation. **4** *offensive slang* a policeman. **5** a quantity of metal cast into an oblong mass. — *verb* (**pigged, pigging**) **1** *said of a pig* to produce young. **2** *said of a person* to eat greedily. — **make a pig of oneself** *colloq.* to eat greedily. **make a pig's ear of something** *colloq.* to make a mess of it; to botch it.
a pig in a poke *colloq.* a purchase made without preliminary investigation as to suitability.
pig it *colloq.* **1** to eat greedily. **2** to live squalidly.
pigs might fly *colloq.* an expression of scepticism.
[from Middle English *pigge*]
◇ Pigs are omnivorous, ie they feed on a wide variety of plant and animal material. Their canine teeth form large tusks, which often protrude from the mouth and are used for defence, and for digging up tubers and other underground food. The domesticated pig (*Sus scrofa*) is descended from the wild boar, and there are many distinct breeds. Careful selection and breeding has led to the development of animals in which the weight is concentrated around the hindquarters, where the best meat is produced. The fat, skin, and hair of pigs are used to make products such as lard, leather, and brushes.

pigeon¹ *noun* **1** any of many species of medium-sized bird belonging to the same family (Columbidae) as doves, and having a plump body, rounded tail, and dense soft grey, brown, or pink plumage. **2** *slang* a dupe or simpleton. [from Old French *pijon*, from Latin *pipio*, from *pipare*, to cheep]
◇ Pigeons are found in woodland in most parts of the world, and they feed mainly on nuts, seeds, buds, and leaves, often causing serious damage to crops. Large numbers of pigeons have moved into towns and cities, and the bird has also been domesticated for carrying messages and for racing. There is no real difference between a pigeon and a dove, but smaller members of the family with more pointed tails are often called doves.

pigeon² same as PIDGIN 2.

pigeonhole — *noun* **1** any of a set of compartments, eg in a desk, for filing letters or papers. **2** a compartment of the mind or memory. — *verb* **1** to put into a pigeonhole. **2** to put mentally into a category, especially too readily. **3** to set aside for future consideration.

pigeon-toed *adj., said of a person* standing and walking with the toes turned in.

piggery *noun* (PL. **piggeries**) **1** a place where pigs are bred. **2** *colloq.* greediness or otherwise disgusting behaviour.

piggish *adj. derog.* greedy, dirty, selfish, mean, or ill-mannered.

piggishness *noun* **1** being piggish. **2** piggish behaviour.

Piggott, Lester (Keith) (1935–) English jockey, born in Wantage, Berkshire. He rode his first winner in 1948, and his first Epsom Derby winner, *Never Say Die*, in 1954. He subsequently rode a record nine Derby winners, and a record 29 English Classic winners between 1954 and 1985. During his career (1948–85) he rode 4 349

winners in Britain, a figure bettered only by Gordon Richards, and was champion jockey 11 times. He retired in 1985 and took up training at Newmarket. He was imprisoned for tax offences (1987–8), returned to riding in 1990, and won the 2 000 Guineas (his 30th Classic victory) at Newmarket in 1992.

piggy — *noun* (PL. **piggies**) a child's diminutive for a pig; a little pig. — *adj.* (**piggier, piggiest**) **1** pig-like. **2** *said of the eyes* small and mean-looking.

piggyback *or* **pickaback** — *noun* a ride on someone's back, with the legs supported by the bearer's arms. — *adv.* on the back of someone else.

piggy bank a child's pig-shaped china container for saving money.

pigheaded *adj.* stupidly obstinate.

pigheadedly *adv.* in a pigheaded way.

pigheadedness *noun* being pigheaded.

pig-in-the-middle *noun* **1** a game in which one person stands between two others and tries to intercept the ball they are throwing to each other. **2** any person helplessly caught between two contending parties.

pig iron *Metall.* an impure form of iron containing about 4% carbon, produced by smelting iron in a blast furnace, and so called because it is cast into blocks called *pigs*. Most pig iron is processed to make steel.

Piglet the abiding friend of Pooh in A A Milne's *The House at Pooh Corner* and other works.

piglet *noun* a young pig.

pigment — *noun* **1** any insoluble colouring matter that is used in suspension in water, oil, or other liquids to give colour to paint, paper, etc. **2** a coloured substance that occurs naturally in plant and animal tissues, eg the red blood pigment haemoglobin, chlorophyll in the leaves of green plants. — *verb* to colour with pigment; to dye or stain. [from Latin *pigmentum*]

pigmentation *noun* coloration or discoloration caused by pigments in the tissues.

pigmy another spelling of **pygmy**.

pigskin *noun* **1** leather made from the skin of a pig. **2** *North Amer. colloq.* a football.

pigsty *noun* (PL. **pigsties**) **1** a pen on a farm, etc for pigs; a sty. **2** a place of filth and disorder.

pigswill *noun* kitchen or brewery waste fed to pigs.

pigtail *noun* a plaited length of hair, especially one of a pair, worn hanging at the sides or back of the head.

pika *noun* a mammal, native to Asia and N America, that resembles a small rabbit and has short legs, short rounded ears, and a minute tail. It inhabits rocky areas or open country. — Also called *cony*. [from a N American name]

pike¹ *noun* (PL. **pike, pikes**) a fierce freshwater fish with a long pointed snout. [from Anglo-Saxon *pic*, point, pick]

pike² *noun Hist.* a weapon like a spear, consisting of a metal point mounted on a long shaft. [from Anglo-Saxon *pic*, point]

pikestaff *noun* the shaft of a pike.
— **plain as a pikestaff** all too obvious.

pilaff *or* **pilaf** *or* **pilau** *noun* an oriental dish of spiced rice with chicken, fish, etc. [from Turkish *pilaw*]

pilaster *noun* a rectangular column standing out in relief from the façade of a building, as a decorative feature. [from French *pilastre*, from Latin *pila*, pillar]

Pilate, Pontius, properly **Pontius Pilatus** (1c AD) Roman prefect of Judea (AD 26–36), who is infamous for presiding over the trial of Jesus of Nazareth and giving the order for his crucifixion.

pilau see PILAFF.

pilchard *noun* an edible sea fish of the herring family, but smaller, thicker, and rounder.

pile¹ — *noun* **1** a number of things lying on top of each other; a quantity of something in a heap or mound. **2** (**a pile** *or* **piles**) *colloq.* a large quantity. **3** a fortune: *made a/her pile on the horses.* **4** a massive or imposing building. **5** (*also* **funeral pile**) a pyre. **6** (*also* **atomic pile**) a nuclear reactor. **7** *Electr.* a vertical series of plates of two different metals arranged alternately to produce an electric current. — *verb* **1** (*usually* **pile up** *or* **pile something up**) to accumulate into a pile. **2** (**pile in, into something, off, out,** *etc*) to move in a crowd or confused bunch.
— **pile it on** *colloq.* to exaggerate.
[from Latin *pila*, stone pier]

pile² *noun* the raised cropped threads that give a soft thick surface to carpeting, velvet, etc; a nap. [from Latin *pilus*, hair]

pile³ *noun* a heavy wooden shaft, stone, or concrete pillar, etc driven into the ground as a support for a building, bridge, etc. [from Latin *pilum*, javelin]

pile⁴ *noun* (*usually* **piles**) a haemorrhoid. [from Latin *pila*, ball]

pile-driver *noun* a machine for driving piles into the ground.

pile-up *noun* a multi-vehicle collision.

pilfer *verb trans., intrans.* (**pilfered, pilfering**) to steal in small quantities. [from Old French *pelfre*, booty]

pilferer *noun* a person who pilfers.

pilgrim *noun* **1** a person who makes a journey to a holy place as an act of reverence and religious faith. **2** a traveller. [from Latin *peregrinus*, foreigner, stranger]

pilgrimage *noun* a journey to a shrine or other holy place, or to a place celebrated or made special by its associations.
◇ Among Christians, pilgrimages became common and were highly organized in the Middle Ages. These included (and still include) pilgrimages to the Holy Land, Rome, the tomb of St James at Compostella in Spain, Canterbury (the shrine of St Thomas à Becket), and various shrines associated with Mary (eg Lourdes in France) and other Saints. Places of pilgrimage for other major religions are: for Jews, Jerusalem; for Muslims, Mecca; for Hindus, Benares and the River Ganges; and for Buddhists, various sites associated with the life of Buddha.

Pilgrimage of Grace a major Tudor rebellion (Oct 1536–Jan 1537) in England. Consisting of a series of armed demonstrations in six northern counties, it was directed against the policies and ministers of Henry VIII, and combined upper-class and popular discontent over religious and secular issues (eg the Dissolution of the Monasteries). It was led by Lord Thomas Darcy and Robert Aske (who were executed for treason) and 'pilgrims' carrying banners of the Five Wounds of Christ.

Pilgrim Fathers the English religious dissenters who established Plymouth Colony in America in 1620, after crossing the Atlantic on the *Mayflower*. The 102 men, women, and children who sailed (one was born at sea), included separatists and non-separatists; before disembarking the adult males signed the Mayflower Compact.

Pilgrim's Progress, The, in full *The Pilgrim's Progress, from this World to that which is to come* a religious allegory by John Bunyan (Part I, 1678, Part II, 1684). It tells of the journey of Christian (Part I) and his wife Christiana (Part II) from the City of Destruction to the Celestial City.

Pilgrim's Way a long-distance footpath in Surrey and Kent, S England, opened in 1972. The path is pre-Roman; its name derives from the popular belief that it was used by medieval pilgrims travelling from Winchester to Canterbury.

Pilipino — *noun* the national language of the Philippines, a standardized version of Tagalog. — *adj.* relating to or spoken or written in Pilipino.

Pilkington, Sir Alastair, originally **Sir Lionel Alexander Bethune Pilkington** (1920–) English inventor. He joined the family firm of glass-makers (of which he became President in 1985) and in 1952 conceived the idea of float glass as a method of manufacturing plate glass without having to grind it to achieve a satisfactory finish. He led the team which successfully introduced the new technique of pouring glass straight from the furnace on to the surface of a bath of molten tin. It floats while cooling, the mirror-perfect surface of the tin giving to the glass a similarly perfect finish allied to a uniform thickness and an absence of defects.

pill *noun* 1 a small ball or tablet of medicine, for swallowing. 2 something unpleasant that one must accept. 3 (**the pill**) any of various oral contraceptives.
— **sugar** or **sweeten the pill** to make something unpleasant easier to accept or cope with. [from Latin *pila*, ball]

pillage — *verb trans., intrans.* to plunder or loot. — *noun* 1 the act of pillaging. 2 loot, plunder, or booty. [from Old French *piller*, to pillage]

pillager *noun* a person who pillages.

pillar *noun* 1 a vertical post of wood, stone, metal, or concrete serving as a support; a column. 2 any slender vertical mass, eg of smoke, rock, etc. 3 a strong and reliable supporter of a cause or organization.
— **from pillar to post** from one place to another, especially in desperation, frustration, etc.
[from Old French *piler*, from Latin *pila*, pillar]

pillar box a free-standing cylindrical public letter box.

Pillars of Hercules the ancient mythological name for the promontories flanking the Strait of Gibraltar (the Rock of Gibraltar and Cueta, N Africa), which guard the entrance to the Mediterranean Sea.

pillbox *noun* 1 a small round container for pills. 2 *Mil.* a small usually circular concrete shelter for use as a lookout post and gun emplacement. 3 a small round flat-topped hat.

pillion — *noun* a seat for a passenger on a motorcycle or horse, behind the rider. — *adv.* on a pillion. [from Gaelic *pillinn* or Irish *pillín*, diminutive of *peall*, skin or blanket]

pillory — *noun* (PL. **pillories**) *Hist.* a wooden frame with holes for the hands and head into which wrongdoers were locked as a punishment, and publicly ridiculed. — *verb* (**pillories, pilloried**) 1 to hold up to public ridicule. 2 to put in a pillory. [from Old French *pilori*]

pillow — *noun* a cushion for the head, especially a large rectangular one on a bed. — *verb* 1 to rest (one's head) as though on a pillow: *pillowed her head on her arms.* 2 to serve as pillow for. [from Anglo-Saxon *pylwe*, from Latin *pulvinus*, cushion]

pillowcase or **pillowslip** *noun* a washable cover for a pillow.

pillow lace lace worked over a cushion-like support, using bobbins.

pilot — *noun* 1 a person who flies an aircraft. 2 a person employed to conduct or steer ships into and out of harbour. 3 a guide. 4 *Mech.* a device that guides a tool or machine part. 5 (*attributive*) *said of a scheme* serving as a preliminary test; experimental. — *verb* (**piloted, piloting**) 1 to act as pilot to. 2 to direct, guide, or steer (a project, etc). [from Old French *pillote*, from Old Italian *pilota*, earlier *pedota*, from Greek *pedon*, oar]

pilot light 1 a small permanent gas flame, eg on a gas cooker, that ignites the main burners when they are turned on. 2 an indicator light on an electrical apparatus, showing when it is switched on.

pilot officer the lowest-ranking officer in the Royal Air Force.

Pilsen see PLZEŇ

Piltdown Man a supposed early fossil man found in 1912 near Piltdown, Sussex, England, named *Eoanthropus* ('Dawn Man'). Later study proved the find a forgery, with a modern human cranium and the jawbone of an orang-utan.

pimento *noun* (PL. **pimentos**) 1 the dried unripe fruit of a West Indian tree of the myrtle family; allspice. 2 the pimiento. [altered from Spanish *pimiento*; see PIMIENTO]

pimiento *noun* (PL. **pimientos**) 1 the red mild-tasting fruit of the sweet pepper, used as a relish, a stuffing for olives, etc. 2 the pimento or allspice. [from Spanish *pimiento*, from Latin *pigmenta*, spiced drink, spice, pepper]

pimp — *noun* a man who finds customers for a prostitute or a brothel, and lives off the earnings. — *verb intrans.* to act as a pimp.

pimpernel *noun* a sprawling plant with small five-petalled flowers on long slender stems. [from Old French *pimprenelle*]

pimple *noun* a small raised pus-containing swelling on the skin; a spot. [from Anglo-Saxon *pyplian*, to break out in pimples]

pimply *adj.* (**pimplier, pimpliest**) having pimples.

PIN *noun, abbrev.* personal identification number, a multi-digit number used to authorize electronic transactions, such as cash withdrawal from a dispenser at a bank, etc.

pin — *noun* 1 a short slender usually stainless steel implement with a sharp point and small round head, for fastening, attaching, etc, used especially in dressmaking. 2 (*in compounds*) any of several fastening devices consisting of or incorporating a slender metal or wire shaft: *hatpin / safety pin.* 3 a narrow brooch. 4 (*in compounds*) any of several cylindrical wooden or metal objects with various functions: *a rolling-pin.* 5 a peg of any of various kinds. 6 any or either of the cylindrical or square-sectioned legs on an electric plug. 7 *Bowling* a club-shaped object set upright for toppling with a ball. 8 the clip on a grenade, removed before throwing. 9 *Golf* the metal shaft of the flag marking a hole. 10 (**pins**) *colloq.* one's legs. 11 *old use* the least bit: *doesn't care a pin.* — *verb* (**pinned, pinning**) 1 (**pin something together, back, up,** *etc*) to secure it with a pin. 2 (**pin something on someone**) *colloq.* to put the blame for a crime or offence on someone.
— **for two pins** *colloq., said of a wish, inclination, etc* expressed as likely to be realized with minimum persuasion (although not normally realized): *for two pins, I'd come with you.*
pin one's hopes on something or **someone** to rely on them entirely.
pin someone down to force a commitment or definite expression of opinion from.
pin something down to identify or define precisely. (**pin something** or **someone down**) to hold them fast or trap them: *was pinned to the ground by a fallen tree.*
[from Anglo-Saxon *pinn*, from Latin *pinna*, point]

pinafore *noun* 1 an apron, especially one with a bib. 2 (*also* **pinafore dress**) a sleeveless dress for wearing over a blouse, sweater, etc. [from PIN + AFORE because it was formerly 'pinned afore', ie pinned to the front of a dress]

Pinakothek a museum founded in 1836 in Munich, Germany. It houses a major collection of German, Dutch, Flemish, and Spanish paintings from the 14c to the 18c. The adjacent Neue Pinakothek was established in 1853, and houses 19c and 20c paintings and sculptures.

pinball *noun* a game played on a slot machine in which a small metal ball is propelled round a course, the score depending on what hazards it avoids and targets it hits; a form of bagatelle.

pince-nez *pl. noun* spectacles that are held in position by gripping the nose instead of being supported over the ears. [from French *pince-nez*, pinch-nose]

pincer movement *Mil.* an advance that closes in on a target from both sides simultaneously.

pincers *pl. noun* 1 a hinged tool with claw-like jaws for gripping things. 2 the hinged end of a crab's or lobster's claw, adapted for gripping. [from Old French *pincer*, to pinch]

pinch — *verb* 1 to squeeze or nip the flesh of, between thumb and finger. 2 to compress or squeeze painfully. 3 *trans., intrans. said of tight shoes* to hurt or chafe. 4 *trans., intrans. colloq.* to steal. 5 *intrans. said of controls, restrictions, shortages, etc* to cause hardship. 6 (**pinch something off, out, back,** *etc*) to prune a plant by removing the tips of shoots. 7 *intrans.* to economize: *pinch and scrape.* 8 *colloq.* to arrest. — *noun* 1 an act of pinching; a nip or squeeze. 2 a quantity of eg salt that can be held between thumb and finger; a small amount.
— **at a pinch** if absolutely necessary.
[from Old French *pincier*, to pinch]

pinchbeck — *noun* a copper alloy with the appearance of gold, used in cheap jewellery. — *adj.* cheap, artificial, sham, counterfeit, or imitation.

pinched *adj. said of a person's appearance* pale and haggard from tiredness, cold, or other discomfort.

Pincus, Gregory Goodwin (1903–67) US physiologist, born in Woodbine, New Jersey. He worked at Harvard and Clark University before establishing the Worcester Foundation for Experimental Research (1944), which became internationally renowned for work on steroid hormones and mammalian reproduction. He is best known for developing the contraceptive pill, which has been widely used since his successful trials of new synthetic hormones in 1954.

pincushion *noun* a pad into which to stick dressmaking pins for convenient storage.

Pindar (c.522–c.440 BC) Greek lyric poet, born near Thebes. He became famous as a composer of diverse odes, although the only works to survive in their entirety are the four books of the *Epinikia* (Triumphal Odes), which celebrate the victories in the Olympian, Pythian, Nemean, and Isthmian games.

Pindus Mountains, Greek **Píndhos Óros** a mountain range in W central and NW Greece. It extends c.500km/310mi from the Albanian frontier to near the Gulf of Corinth. The range forms a watershed between rivers flowing to the Aegean Sea and to the Ionian Sea. Its highest peak is Smolikas (2 633m).

Pine, Courtney (1964–) British saxophonist, born in London of Jamaican parents. Acclaimed as the leading light of the 'British jazz boom' and influenced by John Coltrane, Pine moved away from reggae, soul, and funk and towards jazz. He gained success with his début album *Journey to the Urge Within* (1986). His later albums, some of which feature a mystical tone, include *Destiny's Dance (& the Image of Pursuance)* (1988), *The Vision's Tale* (1989), and *Closer to Home* (1992).

pine[1] *noun* 1 any of about 200 species of evergreen coniferous tree belonging to the genus *Pinus* of the family Pinaceae, and having narrow needle-like leaves, widespread in cool north temperate regions. Pines reproduce by means of woody cones which contain winged seeds, and are planted on a vast scale for their timber, which is resistant to decay because of its very high resin content. Some species are tapped for their resin, which yields turpentine and rosin, and is the source of the distinctive scent of pine foliage. **2** the pale durable wood of this tree, which is used to make furniture, telegraph poles, etc, and paper pulp, and is widely used in construction work. [from Latin *pinus*]

pine² *verb intrans.* **1** to long or yearn. **2** (*also* **pine away**) to waste away from grief or longing. [from Anglo-Saxon *pinian*, to torment]

pineal gland *or* **pineal body** *Physiol.* in vertebrates, a small outgrowth from the roof of the forebrain. It produces the hormone melatonin, and may be involved in the control of biological rhythms related to seasonal changes in daylength, eg breeding. — Also called *epiphysis*. [from Latin *pinea*, pine cone, from its shape]

pineapple *noun* **1** a tropical plant (*Ananas comosus*) with spiky sword-shaped leaves, native to S America but widely cultivated in tropical regions for its large edible fruit, which develops from a mass of 100 to 200 flowers borne on a swollen stem. **2** the fruit of this plant, which has sweet juicy yellow flesh covered by a yellowish-brown spiny skin, and is crowned by a rosette of pointed green leaves. It is eaten raw, squeezed for its juice, or canned. [from Middle English *pinappel*, pine cone, the name passing in the 17c to the tropical fruit]

Pineapple Poll a ballet by Arthur Sullivan (1951) to a story by John Cranko based on W S Gilbert's *The Bumboat Woman's Story*. A concert suite has been written based on the score.

pine cone *Bot.* the fruit of the pine. There are separate male and female cones.

pine marten an animal found especially in coniferous forests, which is related to the weasel and has dark brown fur with yellowish underparts.

Pinero, Sir Arthur Wing (1855–1934) English playwright and actor, born in London. He wrote several farces, but is best known for his social dramas, notably *The Second Mrs Tanqueray* (1893), which made him the most successful playwright of his day.

ping — *noun* a sharp ringing sound like that made by plucking a taut wire, lightly striking glass or metal, etc. — *verb intrans., trans.* to make or cause to make this sound. [imitative]

ping-pong *noun* table tennis. [imitative of the sound of the ball]

pinhead *noun* the little rounded or flattened head of a pin, proverbial for smallness.

pinion¹ — *verb* (**pinioned, pinioning**) **1** to immobilize by holding or binding the arms of; to hold or bind (someone's arms). **2** to hold fast or bind: *pinioned against a wall*. — *noun* **1** the extreme tip of a bird's wing. **2** a bird's flight feather. [from Old French *pignon*, wing]

pinion² *noun* a small cogwheel that engages with a larger wheel or rack. [from Old French *pignon*, cogwheel]

pink¹ — *noun* **1** a colour between red and white. **2** a genus of plants with fragrant red, pink, or variegated flowers, including the carnation and sweet william. **3** a scarlet hunting-coat or its colour. **4** the highest point; the acme: *in the pink of condition*. **5** a person of mildly left-wing views. — *adj.* **1** of the colour pink. **2** slightly left-wing or communist. — **in the pink** *colloq.* in the best of health.

pink² *verb* to cut (cloth) with a notched or serrated edge that frays less readily than a straight edge. [from Anglo-Saxon *pyngan*, to prick]

pink³ *verb intrans., said of a vehicle engine* to make a metallic knocking noise due to faulty combustion timing. [imitative]

Pinkerton, Allan (1819–84) Scottish-born US detective, born in Glasgow. He was a Chartist who in 1842 settled in Dundee, Illinois, and became a detective and deputy-sheriff. He was

the founder of the Pinkerton National Detective Agency (1850) that successfully foiled the 'Baltimore Plot' to assassinate Abraham Lincoln on his way to inauguration in Washington (1861). After he headed a Federal intelligence network during the Civil War, his agency later took a leading part in breaking up the Molly Maguires (a secret miners' organization) and in policing other labour disputes.

pink eye an inflamed condition of the membrane covering the eye; conjunctivitis.

pink gin gin flavoured with and stained pink by angostura bitters.

Pinkie, Battle of a battle fought (10 Sep 1547) between the English and the Scots near Musselburgh, east of Edinburgh. It resulted in victory for the English forces under Protector Somerset, but failure in their aim of 'rough wooing' (to secure Mary, Queen of Scots as a bride for Edward VI) — Mary and Scotland formed an alliance with the French, and England was forced to leave by the Treaty of Boulogne (1550).

pinkie *or* **pinky** *noun* (PL. **pinkies**) *Scot., North Amer., esp. US* the little finger. [from Dutch *pinkje*]

pinking shears scissors for cutting a notched or serrated edge in cloth (see PINK²).

pinkish *adj.* somewhat pink.

pinko *noun* (PL. **pinkos**) *colloq.* a mild or half-hearted socialist.

pink pound the combined purchasing power of homosexuals considered as a consumer group.

pinky *adj.* (**pinkier, pinkiest**) slightly pink.

pin money extra cash earned for spending on oneself, on luxury items, etc.

pinna *noun* (PL. **pinnae**) **1** *Anat.* in mammals, the part of the outer ear that projects from the head, and that in certain mammals (eg dogs) can be moved independently in order to detect the direction of sounds. It consists of a thin layer of cartilage covered with skin. **2** in a compound leaf, one of the leaflets on either side of the midrib. **3** in birds, a feather or wing. **4** in fish, a fin. [from Latin *pinna*, feather]

pinnace *noun* a small boat carried on a larger ship; a ship's boat. [from Old French *pinace*, from Old Spanish *pinaza*, something of pine]

pinnacle *noun* **1** a slender spire crowning a buttress, gable, roof, or tower. **2** a rocky peak. **3** a high point of achievement. [from Latin *pinnaculum*, diminutive of *pinna*, feather]

pinnate *adj. Bot.* denoting a compound leaf that consists of pairs of leaflets, the members of each pair being arranged opposite each other on either side of a central axis or midrib. [from Latin *pinnatus*, feathered]

pinny *noun* (PL. **pinnies**) *colloq.* a pinafore.

Pinochet (Ugarte), Augusto (1915–) Chilean soldier and dictator, born in Valparaíso. A career army officer, he led the coup that overthrew the government of Salvador Allende (1973) and established himself at the head of the ensuing military regime. In 1980 he enacted a constitution giving himself an eight-year presidential term (1981–9), but a plebiscite held in 1988 rejected his candidacy as President beyond 1990.

pinochle *noun* a card game derived from bézique, especially popular in the USA. The standard game is played with two packs of 24 cards shuffled together, with all cards of a lower value than nine discarded. The object is to win tricks, as in whist, and to score points according to the value of the cards won. [origin unknown]

pinole *noun* a fine flour made from parched Indian corn or other seeds, sweetened with sugar and eaten with milk in Mexico and SW states of the USA. [from Spanish *pinole*, from Nahuatl *pinolli*]

pinpoint *verb* to place, define, or identify precisely.

pinprick *noun* **1** a tiny hole made by, or as if by, a pin. **2** a slight irritation or annoyance.

pins and needles a prickling sensation in a limb, etc, felt as the flow of blood returns to it after being temporarily obstructed.

pinstripe *noun* a narrow stripe in cloth.

pint *noun* **1** a unit of liquid measure, ⅛ of a gallon. **2** *colloq.* a drink of beer of this quantity. [from Old French *pinte*]

pinta *noun colloq.* a pint of milk. [a contraction of *pint of*]

pintail *noun* a type of duck with a pointed tail.

Pinter, Harold (1930–) English playwright, born in London. His major plays include *The Birthday Party* (1958), *The Caretaker* (1960), and *The Homecoming* (1965). He wrote some short plays, often with radical political themes, and television and film scripts, before *Moonlight* (1993), his first full-length play for 15 years.

pint-size *or* **pint-sized** *adj. humorous, said of a person* small.

pin tuck a narrow decorative tuck in a garment.

pin-up *noun* **1** a picture of a glamorous or otherwise admirable person that one pins on one's wall. **2** the person in such a picture.

pinwheel *noun* **1** a whirling firework; Catherine wheel. **2** *North Amer., esp. US* a toy windmill.

Pinyin *noun* a system for writing Chinese with letters of the Roman alphabet. [from Chinese *Pinyin*, phonetic spelling]

pioneer — *noun* **1** an explorer of, or settler in, hitherto unknown or wild country. **2** someone who breaks new ground in anything; an innovator or initiator. — *verb* **1** *intrans.* to be a pioneer; to be innovative. **2** to explore and open up (a route, etc). **3** to try out, originate, or develop (a new technique, etc). [from Old French *peonier*, from Latin *pedo*, foot soldier]

Pioneer programme *Astron.* a series of space probes launched by the USA between 1958 and 1978.
◇ *Pioneers 1* to 3 were unsuccessful lunar flights. *Pioneers 4* to 9 were placed in orbit around the Sun, at about the same distance from it as Earth, in order to study the Sun's activity, solar winds, etc. *Pioneers 10* and *11*, launched in 1972 and 1973, respectively, were the first probes to reach Jupiter (*Pioneers 10* and *11*) and Saturn (*Pioneer 11*). Two *Pioneer* Venus probes were launched in 1978. One orbited Venus, and the other successfully explored the atmosphere of the planet. *Pioneers 10* and *11* are still sending information about the light intensity of stars to Earth.

pious *adj.* **1** religiously devout. **2** dutiful. **3** *derog.* ostentatiously virtuous; sanctimonious. [from Latin *pius*, dutiful]

piously *adv.* in a pious way.

piousness *noun* being pious.

Pip, in full **Philip Pirrip** the narrator and central character who learns humility in Charles Dickens's *Great Expectations*.

pip¹ *noun* the small seed of a fruit such as an apple, pear, orange, or grape. [shortening of PIPPIN]

pip² *noun* (*usually* **pips**) one of a series of short high-pitched signals on the radio, telephone, etc. [imitative]

pip³ *verb* (**pipped, pipping**) to defeat narrowly. — **pipped at the post** *colloq.* overtaken narrowly in the closing stages of a contest, etc.

pip⁴ *noun* **1** one of the emblems or spots on playing-cards, dice, or dominoes. **2** *Mil.* in the British army, a star on a uniform indicating rank.

pip⁵ *noun* a disease of poultry and other fowl. — **give someone the pip** *colloq.* to irritate them. [from Middle English *pippe*]

pipe — *noun* **1** a tubular conveyance for water, gas, oil, etc. **2** a little bowl with a hollow stem for smoking tobacco, etc; a quantity of tobacco so smoked. **3** a wind instrument consisting of a simple wooden or metal tube. **4** (**pipes**) the bagpipes. **5** any of the vertical metal tubes through which sound is produced on an organ. **6** *old use* esp. *combining form* any of the air passages in an animal body: *the windpipe*. — *verb* **1** to convey (gas, water, oil, etc) through pipes. **2** *trans., intrans.* to play on a pipe or the pipes. **3** to welcome or convoy with music from the bagpipes. **4** *intrans., trans. said of a child* to speak or say in a small shrill voice. **5** using a bag with a nozzle, to force (icing or cream) into long strings for decorating a cake or dessert; to make (designs, etc) on a cake, etc by this means. **6** *Comput.* to direct (the output of one program) into (another program) as its input.
— **pipe down** *colloq.* to stop talking; to be quiet.
pipe up to speak unexpectedly, breaking a silence, etc.
put that in your pipe and smoke it *colloq.* a dismissive conclusion to a frank censure, disagreement, instruction, etc.
[from Anglo-Saxon *pipe*, from Latin *pipare*, to chirp or play a pipe]

pipeclay *noun* fine white clay for making tobacco pipes and delicate crockery.

pipe-cleaner *noun* a piece of wire with a woolly tufted covering, for cleaning a tobacco pipe.

piped music recorded music played through loudspeakers, especially in public places.

pipe dream a delightful fantasy of the kind indulged in while smoking a pipe, originally one filled with opium.

pipeline *noun* a series of connected pipes laid underground to carry oil, natural gas, water, etc, across large distances in cases where alternative forms of transport would be more costly.
— **in the pipeline** *colloq.* under consideration; forthcoming or in preparation.

pipe of peace see PEACE PIPE.

Piper, John (Egerton Christmas) (1903–92) English painter, born in Epsom, Surrey. He was an abstract artist in the 1930s, but later developed a representational style, as seen in his pictures of war damage and in his topographical pictures (eg the watercolours of *Windsor Castle* commissioned by the Queen in 1941–2). He is also known for his theatre sets, as well as the stained glass design in Coventry Cathedral.

Piper, Leonora E (1857–1950) US medium, discovered in 1885 by William James. Her trance speech and writing were studied extensively (1885–1911) by James and other members of the American and British Societies for Psychical Research. She became for William James his 'white crow', and he was convinced of the paranormal origin of some of her trance utterances.

piper *noun* a player of a pipe or the bagpipes.

pipette *noun* a narrow glass tube into which liquid can be sucked for transferring or measuring. [from French *pipette*, diminutive of *pipe*, pipe]

piping — *noun* **1** the art of playing a pipe or the bagpipes. **2** a length of pipe, or system, or series of pipes conveying water, oil, etc. **3** covered cord forming a decorative edging on upholstery or clothing. **4** strings and knots of icing or cream decorating a cake or dessert. — *adj., said of a child's voice* small and shrill.
— **piping hot** *said of food* satisfyingly hot.

pipistrelle *noun* a reddish-brown bat, the smallest in Britain. [from French *pipistrelle*, from Italian *pipistrello*, from Latin *vespertilio*, bat, from *vesper*, evening]

pipit *noun* any of several lark-like songbirds related to the wagtail. [imitative of its call]

Piłsudski, Józef (1867–1935) Polish soldier and politician, born near Vilna. Often imprisoned

in the cause of Polish independence, he was Leader of the Polish Socialist Party (1892) and gathered together troops which fought on the side of Austria during World War I. In 1918 he declared Poland's independence, and became President (1918–22) and the first Marshal of Poland (1920). He returned to power by means of a military coup in 1926, and established a dictatorship.

pippin *noun* any of several sweet apples, usually rosy-skinned. [from Old French *pepin*]

pipsqueak *noun derog. colloq.* someone or something insignificant or contemptible. [perhaps from PEEP[2]]

piquancy *noun* being piquant.

piquant *adj.* **1** having a pleasantly spicy taste or tang. **2** amusing, intriguing, provocative, or stimulating. [from French *piquer*, to prick]

pique — *noun* resentment; hurt pride. — *verb* **1** to hurt the pride of; to offend or nettle. **2** to arouse (curiosity or interest). **3** to pride (oneself) on: *piqued himself on his good taste*. [from French *piquer*, to prick]

piqué *noun* a stiff corded fabric, especially of cotton. [from French *piquer*, to prick]

Piquet, Nelson, properly **Nelson Souto Maior** (1952–) Brazilian motor racing driver, born in Rio de Janeiro. He changed his name so that his parents would not find out about his racing exploits. He was British Formula Three champion in 1978, and world champion in 1981, 1983 (both Brabham), and 1987 (Williams). He won 20 races from 157 starts between 1978 and 1988.

piquet *noun* a card game for two, played with 32 cards. [from French *piquet*, from *pic*, the score of 30 points in this game, literally 'prick']

piracy *noun* **1** the activity of pirates. **2** unauthorized publication or reproduction of copyright material.

Piraeus, Greek **Piraiéus** POP (1991) 170 000, a major port in Attica department, Greece, situated on a hilly peninsula 8km/5mi SW of Athens. It has been the port of Athens since the 5c BC and is now the largest Greek port. The main harbour is Kantharos, and two ancient harbours to the E are still used.

Pirandello, Luigi (1867–1936) Italian dramatist and novelist, born in Girgenti, Sicily. After writing several realistic novels and short stories, he became a leading exponent of the 'grotesque' school of contemporary drama. Among his plays are *Six Characters in Search of an Author* (Sei personaggi in cerca d'autore, 1921) and *Enrico IV* (1922). In 1934 he was awarded the Nobel Prize for Literature.

Piranesi, Giovanni Battista, or **Giambattista** (1720–78) Italian architect and copper-engraver of Roman antiquities, born in Venice. He settled in Rome in 1745, where he developed original techniques of etching and produced c.2 000 plates of the city, both in ancient times and in his own day.

piranha *noun* a small fierce carnivorous S American freshwater fish. [from Portuguese *piranha*, from Tupí (S American Indian language) *piranya*]

pirate — *noun* **1** someone who attacks and robs ships at sea. **2** the ship used by pirates. **3** someone who publishes material without permission from the copyright-holder, or otherwise uses someone else's work illegally. **4** someone who runs a radio station without a licence. — *verb* to publish, reproduce, or use (someone else's literary or artistic work, or ideas) without legal permission. [from Greek *peirates*, from *peiraein*, to try one's fortune]

Pirates of Penzance an operetta by W S Gilbert and Arthur Sullivan (1879). Focusing on the 21-year-old former pirate apprentice Frederic, it tells of his dilemma about whether to bring his colleagues to justice, a failed attempt by the

police force to subdue them, his love for the Major-General's daughter Mabel, and the revelation that the pirates are in fact of noble birth and therefore eligible suitors for Mabel's many sisters.

piratical *adj.* **1** relating to pirates. **2** practising piracy.

Pire, Dominique (Georges) (1910–69) Belgian Dominican priest, born in Dinant. He lectured at Louvain (1937–47), and worked in the resistance during World War II. He was awarded the 1958 Nobel Peace Prize for his scheme of 'European villages' for elderly refugees and destitute children.

pirouette — *noun* a spin or twirl executed on tiptoe in dancing. — *verb intrans.* to execute a pirouette or a series of them. [from French *pirouette*, originally a spinning top]

Pisa POP (1991e) 102 000, the capital of Pisa province, Tuscany, W Italy. It is situated on both banks of the R Arno, 10km/6mi from the Ligurian Sea. Formerly a major port, it is now distanced from the sea through river silting. Its university dates from 1343. The scientist Galileo was born here in 1564. NOTABLE FEATURES cathedral (11c–12c); baptistery (12c–14c); Campo Santo Cemetery; the 'Leaning Tower', a 55m-high campanile now in danger of collapse (1173–1350); Piazza del Duomo, the location of the cathedral, baptistery, and tower, is a World Heritage site.

Pisanello, properly **Antonio Pisano** (c.1395–c.1455) Italian painter and medallist, born in Pisa. He travelled widely and painted frescoes (all since destroyed) in the Doge's Palace at Venice (1415–20) and in the Lateran Basilica in Rome (1431–2). His surviving frescoes include the *Annunciation* (1423–4, Saint Fermo, Verona), and *St George and the Princess of Trebizond* (c.1437–8, San Anastasia, Verona). Other surviving works include numerous precise drawings of costumes, birds, and animals. He is also known as a portrait medallist.

Pisano, Andrea, also called **Andrea da Pontedera** (c.1270–1349) Italian sculptor, born in Pontedera. He became famous as a worker in bronze and marble, and settled in Florence, where he completed the earliest bronze doors of the baptistery (1336). In 1347 he produced reliefs and statues for the cathedral at Orvieto.

Pisano, Giovanni (c.1250–c.1320) Italian sculptor and architect, the son of Nicola Pisano. He worked with his father on the pulpit in Siena and on the fountain in Perugia, and then between 1284 and 1286 on the façade of Siena Cathedral. He also sculpted figures for the entrance to the Baptistery at Pisa (now in the Museo Nazionale), and made a number of free-standing Madonnas, the most famous of which is in the Arena Chapel, Padua.

Pisano, Nicola (c.1225–c.78) Italian sculptor. His major works include the pulpit of the Baptistery in Pisa (1260), the shrine of St Dominic for a church at Bologna (1267), and the pulpit of Siena cathedral (1268). His son Giovanni was also a sculptor.

Piscator, Erwin (Friedrich Max) (1893–1966) German theatre director, born in Ulm. A major exponent of German political theatre, he developed a style of agitprop which underlies the later epic theatre. He also worked in the USA (1938–51), where his adaptation of *War and Peace* was first produced (1942), and from 1962 was director of the Freie Volksbuhne in Berlin.

piscatorial *adj. formal* relating to fish or fishing. [from Latin *piscatorius*, fisherman]

Piscean — *noun* a person born under the sign Pisces. — *adj.* relating to this sign.

Pisces *noun* **1** *Astron.* the Fishes, a large but faint northern constellation of the zodiac, most clearly seen in the autumn, and lying between

Aquarius and Aries. **2** the twelfth sign of the zodiac, the Fishes. **3** a person born between 20 Feb and 20 Mar, under this sign. **4** *Zool.* in the animal kingdom, the superclass of fishes, consisting of the classes Agnatha (jawless fish, ie hagfish and lampreys), Elasmobranchii (cartilaginous fish, eg sharks, rays) and Osteichthyes (bony fish). [from Latin *pisces*, fishes]

pisciculture *noun* the rearing of fish by artificial methods or under controlled conditions. [from Latin *piscis*, fish + CULTURE]

piscina *noun* a basin with a drain, found in older churches, in which to empty water used for rinsing the sacred vessels. [from Latin *piscina*, basin, originally fish pond]

Piscis Austrinus *Astron.* the Southern Fish, a small constellation in the southern hemisphere. Its brightest star is Fomalhaut.

Pisistratus (c.600–527 BC) tyrant of Athens (c.561 BC, c.556 BC, 546–527 BC). He improved the lot of the small farmer in Attica, and promoted Athenian trade abroad, especially in the Black Sea area. A patron of the arts, he tried to foster a sense of national unity by instituting or expanding religious and cultural festivals. He was succeeded by his sons Hippias and Hipparchus, the so-called *Pisistratidae*, but the dynasty was overthrown in 510 BC.

piss *coarse slang* — *verb* **1** *intrans.* to urinate. **2** to discharge (eg blood) in the urine. **3** to wet with one's urine: *piss the bed.* **4** *intrans.* (*also* **piss down**) to rain hard. — *noun* **1** urine. **2** an act of urinating.
— **piss about** *or* **around** to mess about; to waste time.
piss off to go away.
piss someone off to irritate or bore them.
take the piss out of someone *or* **something** to ridicule them.
[from French *pisser*, from a colloquial Latin word; imitative]

Pissarro, Camille (1830–1903) French Impressionist painter, born in St Thomas, West Indies. He went to Paris in 1855, where he was much influenced by Corot's landscapes. Most of his works were painted in or around Paris (eg *Boulevard Montmartre*, 1897, National Gallery, London). He was one of the original Impressionists, and the only one to exhibit at all eight of the Group exhibitions in Paris (1074–06). He had considerable influence on Cézanne and Gauguin.

pissed *adj. coarse slang* drunk.

Pissis, Monte an Andean peak on the border between Catamarca and La Rioja provinces, Argentina.

pistachio *noun* (PL. **pistachios**) the edible nut of a Eurasian tree, of the cashew family, with a green kernel. [from Italian *pistacchio*]

piste *noun* a ski slope or track of smooth compacted snow. [from French *piste*, race track]

pistil *noun Bot.* the female reproductive structure in a flowering plant, which may be a single carpel consisting of a stigma, style, and ovary, or a group of carpels that are fused to form a single structure. [from Latin *pistillum*, pestle]

Pistoia POP (1990e) 90 000, the capital of Pistoia province, Tuscany, Italy, 32km/20mi NW of Florence. The pistol was reputedly invented here. NOTABLE FEATURES cathedral (12c); Church of the Madonna dell'Umiltà (1494–1509); octagonal baptistery (14c).

Pistol the short-tempered, boastful companion of Falstaff, who is fond of an inflated turn of phrase, in Shakespeare's *Henry IV Part II*, *Henry V*, and *The Merry Wives of Windsor*.

pistol *noun* a small gun held in one hand when fired. [from Old French *pistole*, from Czech]

piston *noun* **1** *Engineering* a cylindrical device, usually closed at one end, that moves up and

down in the cylinder of a petrol, diesel, or steam engine, and is driven by the pressure of hot gases or the expansion of steam. The motion of the piston is converted into the rotating motion of the driving wheels by the crankshaft. **2** a sliding valve on a brass wind instrument. [from French, from Italian *pistone*, from *pestare*, to pound]

piston ring a split metal ring fitting into a groove round a piston and forming an airtight seal between it and its containing cylinder.

piston rod in a vehicle engine, a rod attached to the piston, that transfers its motion by means of a crankshaft to the wheels.

pit¹ — *noun* **1** a big deep hole in the ground. **2** a coalmine. **3** a cavity sunk into the ground from which to inspect vehicle engines, etc. **4** *Motor Racing* any of a set of compartments beside a racetrack, where vehicles can refuel, etc. **5** an enclosure in which fighting animals or birds are put. **6** the floor of the auditorium in a theatre, or the people sitting there. **7** (*also* **orchestra pit**) a sunken area in front of a stage, in which an orchestra is positioned. **8** *Anat.* a hollow, indentation, or depression, eg (**pit of the stomach**) the small hollow below the breastbone. **9** a scar left by a smallpox or acne pustule. **10** *old use* (**the pit**) hell. **11** (**the pits**) *slang* an awful or intolerable situation. — *verb* (**pitted**, **pitting**) **1** to set or match in competition or opposition. **2** marked by scars and holes: *pitted with craters.* **3** to put in a pit. [from Anglo-Saxon *pytt*, from Latin *puteus*, well]

pit² — *noun North Amer., esp. US* the stone in a peach, apricot, plum, etc. — *verb* (**pitted**, **pitting**) to remove the stone from. [from Dutch *pit*, kernel]

pit-a-pat — *noun* a noise of pattering. — *adv.* with this noise. [imitative]

pit bull terrier a large breed of bull terrier originally developed for dogfighting.

Pitcairn Islands POP (1992e) 71, an island group in the SE Pacific Ocean, E of French Polynesia. AREA 27sq km/10sq mi. They comprise Pitcairn I and the uninhabited islands of Ducie, Henderson, and Oeno. The chief settlement is Adamstown. TIME ZONE GMT −8.5. Seventh Day Adventism is the main religion. OFFICIAL LANGUAGE English. CURRENCY the New Zealand dollar. PHYSICAL DESCRIPTION volcanic islands, with high lava cliffs and rugged hills; Pitcairn I rises to 335m. CLIMATE equable; average annual rainfall, 2 000mm; average monthly temperatures, 24°C (Jan), 19°C (Jul). HISTORY visited by the British in 1767; occupied by nine mutineers from HMS *Bounty* in 1790; overpopulation led to emigration to Norfolk I in 1856 but some returned in 1864; control of the island was transferred to the Governor of Fiji in 1952; it is now a British Colony, governed by the High Commissioner in New Zealand. GOVERNMENT an island Magistrate presides over a 10-member Council. ECONOMY postage stamps; tropical and subtropical crops; crafts; forestry.

pitch¹ — *verb* **1** to set up (a tent or camp). **2** to throw or fling. **3** *trans., intrans.* to fall or cause to fall heavily forward. **4** *intrans. said of a ship* to plunge and lift alternately at bow and stern. **5** *trans., intrans. said of a roof* to slope: *pitched at a steep angle.* **6** to give a particular musical pitch to (a note) in singing or playing, or to set (a song, etc) at a higher or lower level within a possible range: *pitched too high for me.* **7** to choose a level, eg of difficulty, sophistication, etc at which to present (a talk, etc). **8 a** *Cricket* to bowl (the ball) so that it lands where the batsman can hit it. **b** *Golf* to hit (the ball) high and gently, so that it stays where it is on landing. **c** *trans., intrans. Baseball, said of the pitcher* to throw to the batter overarm or underarm. — *noun* **1** the field or area of play in any of several sports. **2** an act or style of pitching or throwing. **3** a degree of intensity; a level: *reached such a pitch.* **4** the angle of steepness of a slope. **5** *Mus.* the degree of highness or low-

ness of a note that results from the frequency of the vibrations producing it. **6** a street trader's station. **7** a line in sales talk, especially one often made use of. **8** the distance between points on a saw, or between threads on a screw. **9** the plunging and rising motion of a ship.
— **pitch in** *colloq.* **1** to begin enthusiastically. **2** to join in; to make a contribution.
pitch into someone *colloq.* to rebuke or blame them angrily.
[from Middle English *picchen*, throw, put up]

pitch² — *noun* **1** a thick black sticky substance obtained from tar, used for filling ships' seams, etc. **2** any of various bituminous or resinous substances. **3** resin from certain pine trees. — *verb* to coat or treat with pitch. [from Anglo-Saxon *pic*]

pitch-black *or* **pitch-dark** *adj.* utterly, intensely, or unrelievedly black or dark.

pitchblende *noun Geol.* a radioactive glossy brown or black form of uraninite, a mineral variety of uranium(IV) oxide. It is the main ore of uranium and radium. [from German *Pechblende*]

pitched battle **1** a battle between armies that are prepared and drawn up in readiness. **2** a fierce dispute.

pitched roof a sloping roof as distinct from a flat one.

pitcher¹ *noun* a large earthenware jug with one or two handles. [from Old French *pichier*, from Latin *bicarium*, beaker]

pitcher² *noun Baseball* the player who throws the ball to the batter to hit.

pitcher plant any of various insectivorous plants belonging to the genera *Nepenthes* or *Sarracenia*, so called because it has modified leaves resembling pitchers that collect rainwater, in which insects attracted to the plant by its colouring and nectar are trapped and drowned. The plant then secretes digestive enzymes that enable it to absorb nutrients from the dead insect.

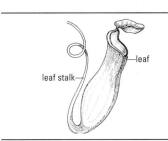

leaf

leaf stalk

pitcher plant

pitchfork *noun* a long-handled fork with two or three sharp prongs, for tossing hay.

piteous *adj.* rousing one's pity; moving, poignant, heart-rending or pathetic.

Piteşti POP (1992) 180 000, the industrial capital of Argeş county, Romania.

pitfall *noun* a hidden danger, unsuspected hazard, or unforeseen difficulty.

pith *noun* **1** *Bot.* the soft white tissue lying beneath the rind of many citrus fruits, eg orange. **2** *Bot.* in the stem of many plants, a central cylinder of generally soft tissue, composed of parenchyma cells, that is surrounded by vascular (conducting) tissue in dicotyledonous species. **3** the most important part of an argument, etc. **4** substance, forcefulness, or vigour as a quality in writing, etc. [from Anglo-Saxon *pitha*]

pithead *noun* the entrance to a mineshaft and the machinery round it.

pith helmet a large light rigid hat made from the pith of the sola plant, worn especially formerly in the tropics to protect the head from the sun.

pithy *adj.* (**pithier**, **pithiest**) *said of a saying, comment, etc* brief, forceful, and to the point.

pitiable *adj.* **1** arousing pity. **2** miserably inadequate; contemptible.

pitiful *adj.* **1** arousing pity; wretched or pathetic. **2** sadly inadequate or ineffective.

pitifully *adv.* in a pitiful way.

pitiless *adj.* showing no pity; merciless, cruel or relentless.

Pitman, Sir Isaac (1813–97) English inventor of a shorthand system, born in Trowbridge, Wiltshire. He became a clerk, then a teacher, but was dismissed for joining the New (Swedenborgian) Church. After 1843 he specialized in the development of shorthand, and spelling reform. In 1842 he brought out the *Phonetic Journal*, and in 1845 opened premises in London.

piton *noun Mountaineering* a metal peg or spike with an eye for passing a rope through, hammered into a rockface as an aid to climbers. [from French *piton*, ringbolt]

pitstop *noun* a pause made at a refuelling pit by a racing driver.

Pitt, William, 1st Earl of Chatham, known as **the Elder** (1708–78) English statesman and orator, born in London. He joined the army (1731) and then entered parliament for the family borough, Old Sarum (1735). He led the young 'Patriot' Whigs, and in 1756 became nominally Secretary of State, but virtually Prime Minister. He had to resign in 1757 due to King George II's hostility, but he was recalled by public demand. Again compelled to resign when his Cabinet refused to declare war with Spain (1761), he later criticized the Treaty of Paris (1763) for being too generous to France. He formed a new ministry in 1766, but resigned due to ill health (1768). His eldest son, John, 2nd Earl of Chatham (1756–1835), commanded the luckless Walcheren Expedition (1809). His second son, William, was twice Prime Minister, known as 'Pitt the Younger'.

Pitt, William, known as **the Younger** (1759–1806) English statesman, born in Hayes, Kent, the second son of the Earl of Chatham (William Pitt, the Elder). He became an MP in 1781 and was Chancellor of the Exchequer under Shelburne (1782), First Lord of the Treasury (1783), and Prime Minister (1783–1801, 1804–6). His first ministry was marked by important reforms, and a policy influenced by the political economy of Adam Smith. He negotiated coalitions against France (1793, 1798), but these had little success. After the Irish rebellion of 1798, he proposed a legislative union which would be followed by Catholic emancipation. The union was effected in 1800, but Pitt resigned office in 1801 rather than contest George III's hostility to emancipation. He resumed office in 1804, but was a heavy drinker and died early.

pitta *noun* **a** a Middle-Eastern slightly leavened bread, usually baked in hollow ovals that can be filled with other foods; **b** one such oval. [from Modern Greek *pitta*, cake, pie]

pittance *noun* a meagre allowance or wage. [from Old French *pietance*, ration]

pitter-patter — *noun* the sound of pattering. — *adv.* with this sound. [imitative]

Pitti Palace a palace in Florence, Italy, designed by Brunelleschi in the 15c. It was originally the residence of the Grand Dukes of Tuscany and (1866–70) of Victor Emanuel II. The palace now houses museums of silverware and of modern art, and the Palatine Gallery, an art collection principally of Italian masters.

Pittsburgh POP (1990) 2.1m, the county seat of Allegheny County, W Pennsylvania, USA, and the nation's largest inland port. It lies at the confluence of the Allegheny and Monongahela rivers where they form the Ohio R. The city is noted for recent urban redevelopment and a dramatic reduction in air and water pollution. HISTORY Fort

Duquesne built here by the French; taken by the British and renamed Fort Pitt in 1758; achieved city status in 1816. NOTABLE FEATURES Carnegie Institute (library and concert hall); Frick Art Museum; Point State Park; Heinz Hall, Phipps Conservatory; Pittsburgh Symphony Orchestra.

pituitary — *noun* (PL. **pituitaries**) (*in full* **pituitary gland**) *Physiol.* in vertebrates, a gland at the base of the brain that is responsible for the production of a number of important hormones, many of which control the activity of other glands. It therefore has a central role in the control of growth, sexual development, reproduction, water balance, adrenaline production, and general metabolism. — *adj.* relating to this gland. [from Latin *pituita*, phlegm, rheum]

pit viper a viper of the subfamily Crotalinae, sometimes treated as a separate family (Crotalidae), the remaining vipers being called true vipers. It is absent from Africa, and there is a small heat-sensitive pit on each side of the front of the head, used for sensing the prey's body heat while hunting and attacking in complete darkness.

pit viper

pity — *noun* **1** a feeling of sorrow for the troubles and sufferings of others; compassion. **2** a cause of sorrow or regret. — *verb* (**pities, pitied**) to feel or show pity for.

— **for pity's sake** an expression of earnest entreaty or of exasperation.

have *or* **take pity on someone** to feel or show pity for them, especially in some practical way.

more's the pity *colloq.* a formula of regret: unfortunately; I'm sorry to say. [from Old French *pite*, from Latin *pietas*, piety, dutifulness]

pitying *adj.* compassionate.

pityingly *adv.* with pity, compassionately.

Pius V, originally **Michele Ghislieri** (1504–72) Italian pope, born near Alessandria. He became a bishop in 1556, and a cardinal in 1557. As pope (1566–72), he implemented the decrees of the Council of Trent (1545–63), excommunicated Elizabeth I (1570), and organized the expedition against the Turks, which resulted in the naval engagement of Lepanto (1571). He was canonized in 1712 and his feast day is 30 Apr.

Pius VI, originally **Giovanni Angelo Braschi** (1717–99) Italian pope, born in Cesena, Papal States. Ordained in 1758, he became a cardinal (1773), then pope (1775–99). To him Rome owes the drainage of the Pontine Marsh, and the completion of St Peter's. When Napoleon invaded the Papal States (1796), Rome was occupied (1798), and a group of Italian patriots declared a republic. Pius was expelled and died in prison.

Pius VII, originally **Barnaba Gregorio Chiaramonti** (1742–1823) Italian pope, born in Cesena, Papal States. He became a cardinal in 1785, then pope (1800–23). He arranged a concordat with Napoleon (1801), and in 1804 was compelled to consecrate him as Emperor. In 1809 the French annexed the Papal States; Pius was taken prisoner until the fall of Napoleon (1814) allowed his return to Rome, and papal territory was restored by the Congress of Vienna.

Pius IX, originally **Giovanni Maria Mastai-Ferretti**, also called **Pio Nono** (1792–1878)

Italian pope, born in Senigallia, Papal States. He became Archbishop of Spoleto in 1827, cardinal in 1840, and as pope (1846–78), he introduced several reforms. Forced to flee from Rome during the 1848 revolutions, he then became progressively more conservative. He decreed the dogma of the Immaculate Conception in 1854, and called the Vatican Council (1869–79), which proclaimed papal infallibility. He refused to recognize the new unified state of Italy (1870), and spent his remaining years as a voluntary 'prisoner' within the Vatican. His pontificate is the longest in papal history.

Pius XI, originally **Ambrogio Damiano Achille Ratti** (1857–1939) Italian pope, born in Desio, near Milan. Ordained in 1879, he was a great linguist and scholar, and librarian of the Ambrosian (Milan) and Vatican libraries. He became Cardinal Archbishop of Milan in 1921, and as pope (1922–39), he signed the Lateran Treaty (1929), which brought into existence the Vatican state, and made concordats with many countries.

Pius XII, originally **Eugenio Maria Giuseppe Giovanni Pacelli** (1876–1958) Italian pope, born in Rome. Ordained in 1899, he became a papal diplomat, cardinal (1929), and Secretary of State to the Holy See. As pope (1939–58), he led the Vatican in much humanitarian work during World War II, notably for prisoners of war and refugees. In the postwar years he was particularly concerned with the plight of persecuted churchmen in communist countries.

pivot — *noun* **1** a central pin, spindle, or shaft round which something turns, swivels, or revolves. **2** someone or something crucial, on which everyone or everything else depends. — *verb intrans.* (**pivoted, pivoting**) (*often* **pivot on something**) **1** to turn, swivel, or revolve: *pivot on one's heel.* **2** to depend. [from French *pivot*]

pivotal *adj.* **1** constructed as or acting like a pivot. **2** crucially important; critical.

pix see PIC.

pixel *noun Electron.* the smallest element of the image displayed on a computer or television screen, consisting of a single dot which may be illuminated (on) or dark (off). The resolution of the screen is determined by the number of pixels available. [a contraction of *picture element*]

pixie *or* **pixy** *noun* (PL. **pixies**) a kind of fairy, traditionally with mischievous tendencies. [originally dialect]

Pizarro, Francisco (c.1478–1541) Spanish conquistador, born in Trujillo. He took part in the expedition that discovered the Pacific (1513), and in 1526 he and Almagro sailed for Peru to begin the conquest of the Incas (1531). After killing the Inca king, Atahualpa, he worked to consolidate the new empire. He founded Lima (1535) and other cities, but dissensions between Pizarro and Almagro led to the latter's execution and to Pizarro's assassination by Almagro's vengeful followers.

pizza *noun* a circle of dough spread with cheese, tomatoes, etc and baked, made originally in Italy. [from Italian *pizza*]

pizzazz *or* **pizazz** *or* **pzazz** *noun colloq.* a quality that is a combination of boldness, vigour, dash and flamboyance. [thought to have been coined in the 1930s by Diana Vreeland, US fashion editor]

pizzeria *noun* a restaurant specializing in pizzas. [from Italian *pizzeria*, from *pizza*]

pizzicato *adj. adv.*, *said of music for stringed instruments* played using the fingers to pluck the strings. [from Italian *pizzicato*, twitched]

Pk *abbrev.*, *used in street names* Park.

Pl *abbrev.*, *used in street names* Place.

pl *or* **pl.** *abbrev.* plural.

placard — *noun* a board or stiff card bearing a notice, advertisement, slogan, message of protest, etc, carried or displayed in public. — *verb* **1** to put placards on (a wall, etc). **2** to announce (a forthcoming event, etc) by placard. [from Old French *placard*]

placate *verb* to pacify or appease (an angry person, etc). [from Latin *placere*, to appease]

placation *noun* placating.

placatory *adj.* that placates.

place — *noun* **1** an area, region, district, locality, etc; a country, city, town, village, building, room, etc. **2** *colloq.* one's home or lodging. **3** (*often in compounds*) somewhere with a certain association or function: *one's birthplace / a hiding-place.* **4** a seat or space, eg at table: *lay three places.* **5** an area on the surface of something, eg the body: *point to the sore place.* **6** something or someone's customary position: *put it back in its place.* **7** a point reached, eg in a conversation, narrative, series of developments, etc: *a good place to stop.* **8** a point in a book, etc, where one stopped reading: *made me lose my place.* **9** a position within an order eg of competitors in a contest, a set of priorities, etc: *finished in third place / lost his place in the queue / lets her family take second place.* **10** social or political rank: *know/keep one's place / corruption in high places.* **11** a vacancy at an institution, on a committee, in a firm, etc: *gain a university place.* **12** one's role, function, duty, etc: *not my place to tell him.* **13** a useful role: *there's a place for judicious lying.* **14** *often used in street names* an open square, or row of houses: *the market place.* **15** *Maths.* the position of a number in a series, especially of decimals after the point. — *verb* **1** to put. **2** to submit: *place an order / place an advertisement.* **3** to find a place, home, job, publisher, etc for. **4** to assign final positions to (contestants, etc): *was placed fourth.* **5** to identify or categorize: *a familiar voice that I couldn't quite place.* — **all over the place** in disorder or confusion. **be placed 1** *Racing, Athletics* to finish as one of the first three. **2** to be in a position to do something: *was well placed to influence the decision.* **fall into place** to become clear; to make sense. **give place to someone** *or* **something** to make way for them or yield to them. **go places** *colloq.* **1** to travel. **2** to be successful. **in the first place** in any event; anyway: *I never liked it in the first place.* **in the first, second,** *etc* **place** used to introduce successive points. **in place** in the correct position. **in place of** ... instead of ... **in places** here and there. **in your,** *etc* **place** if I were you, etc. **out of place 1** not in the correct position. **2** inappropriate. **put someone in his** *or* **her place** to humble them as they deserve. **take place** to happen, occur, be held, etc. **take the place of someone** *or* **something** to replace or supersede them. [from Anglo-Saxon *plæce* and Old French *place*, open place or street]

placebo *noun* (PL. **placebos**) *Medicine* a substance that is administered as a drug but has no medicinal content, either given to a patient for its reassuring and therefore beneficial effect (the *placebo effect*), or used in a clinical trial of a real drug, in which participants who have been given a placebo (without their knowledge) serve as untreated control subjects for comparison with those given the drug. [from Latin *placebo*, I shall please]

place card a small card at someone's place at table, bearing his or her name.

place kick *Rugby* a kick made with the ball placed ready on the ground.

placeman *noun* (PL. **placemen**) *colloq.* someone appointed by a government, etc to a committee or organization, and expected to represent the appointer's opinion.

place mat a table mat for use in a place setting.

placement *noun* **1** the act or process of placing or positioning. **2** the finding of a job or home for someone. **3** a temporary job providing work experience, especially for someone on a training course.

place-name *noun* the name of a town, village, hill, lake, etc.

placenta *noun* (PL. **placentae, placentas**) **1** *Anat.* in mammals, a disc-shaped organ attached to the lining of the uterus (womb) during pregnancy, and to which the fetus is linked by the umbilical cord. It provides the embryo with nutrients and oxygen, secretes hormones that maintain the pregnancy, and removes waste products. After birth the placenta is expelled from the womb as the afterbirth. **2** *Bot.* in seed-bearing plants, that part of the ovary to which the ovules are attached. [from Latin *placenta*, flat cake]

place of work same as WORKPLACE.

place setting see SETTING.

Placid, Lake see LAKE PLACID.

placid *adj.* calm; tranquil. [from Latin *placidus*, from *placere*, to please]

placidity *noun* being placid.

placidly *adv.* in a placid way.

plagiarism *noun* plagiarizing.

plagiarist *noun* a person who plagiarizes.

plagiarize *or* **plagiarise** *verb trans., intrans.* to copy (ideas, passages of text, etc) from someone else's work, and use them as if they were one's own. [from Latin *plagiarius*, kidnapper]

plague — *noun* **1** *Medicine* any of several epidemic diseases with a high mortality rate; specifically, an infectious epidemic disease of rats and other rodents, caused by the bacterium *Yersinia pestis*, and transmitted to humans by flea bites. The commonest form of the disease, *bubonic plague*, is characterized by *buboes* (painful swellings of the lymph glands), fever, headache, and delirium, known in the Middle Ages as the Black Death. It can now be successfully treated with antibiotics. **2** an overwhelming intrusion by something unwelcome: *a plague of tourists.* **3** *colloq.* a nuisance. — *verb* **1** to afflict: *plagued by headaches.* **2** to pester; to annoy continually. [from Middle English *plage*, from Latin *plaga*, blow, disaster, pestilence]

plaice *noun* (PL. **plaice**) a flatfish related to the dab, flounder, and sole, found in shallow coastal waters of the northern oceans, and one of the most important food fish. The brown upper surface of its body is covered with bright orange spots, and the lower surface is colourless. [from Old French *plais*, from Latin *platessa*, flatfish]

plaid *noun* **1** tartan cloth. **2** *Hist.* a long piece of this worn over the shoulder with a kilt. [from Gaelic *plaide*, blanket]

Plaid Cymru the Welsh National Party, founded in 1925. Its goal is independence for Wales, and its electoral support comes mainly from the north of the country. Its success has been moderate; four MPs were returned in 1992.

plain — *adj.* **1** all of one colour; unpatterned; undecorated. **2** simple; unsophisticated; without improvement: *plain food / not Dr or Professor, just plain Mr.* **3** obvious; clear. **4** straightforward; direct: *plain language / plain dealing.* **5** frank; open. **6** *said of a person* lacking beauty. **7** sheer: *plain selfishness.* — *noun* **1** a large area of relatively smooth flat land without significant hills or valleys. **2** *Knitting* the simpler of two basic stitches, with the wool passed round the front of the needle. See also PURL. — *adv.* utterly; quite: *plain ridiculous.* [from Old French, from Latin *planus*, level]

plain chocolate dark chocolate made without milk.

plain clothes ordinary clothes worn by police detectives on duty, as distinct from a uniform.

plain-clothes *or* **plain-clothed** *adj.* wearing ordinary clothes, not uniformed.

plain flour flour containing no raising agent.

plainly *adv.* **1** in a plain way. **2** clearly.

plainness *noun* being plain.

plain sailing 1 easy, unimpeded progress. **2** *Naut.* sailing in unobstructed waters.

Plains Indians a name given to various Native American groups who lived on the Great Plains between the Mississippi R and the Rocky Mts in the USA and Canada. Most were nomadic or semi-nomadic buffalo hunters living together in small bands. Their lives were changed by the introduction of horses by the Spanish, which led to intensified warring between groups, and hunting over much greater expanses. Eventually the buffalo was exterminated, and white settlers finally destroyed their power, placing the surviving people in reservations.

plainsong *or* **plainchant** *noun* in the medieval Church, music for unaccompanied voices, sung in unison.

plain-spoken *adj.* frank to the point of bluntness.

plaint *noun* **1** *poetic* an expression of woe; a lamentation. **2** *Legal* a written statement of grievance against someone, submitted to a court of law. [from Old French, from Latin *planctus*, a blow]

plaintiff *noun* a person who brings a case against someone else in a court of law. See also DEFENDANT. [from Old French *plaintif*, complaining]

plaintive *adj.* mournful-sounding; sad; wistful. [from Old French *plaintif*]

plaintively *adv.* in a plaintive way.

plait — *verb* to arrange (especially hair) by interweaving three or more lengths. — *noun* a length of hair or other material so interwoven. [from Old French *pleit*, from Latin *plicare*, to fold]

plan — *noun* **1** a thought-out arrangement or method for doing something. **2** (*usually* **plans**) intentions. **3** a sketch, outline, scheme, or set of guidelines. **4** a drawing or diagram of a floor of a house, the streets of a town, etc done as though from above. — *verb* (**planned, planning**) **1** to devise a scheme for. **2** *intrans.* to prepare; to make plans: *plan ahead.* **3** (**plan something** *or* **plan for something**) to make preparations or arrangements for it. **4** (**plan something** *or* **plan on something**) to intend it. **5** (**not plan on** *or* **for something**) not to reckon on or allow for it; to be surprised or embarrassed by it: *had not planned on all of them coming.* **6** to draw up plans for; to design. [from French *plan*, ground plan, from Latin *planus*, flat]

Planck, Max Karl Ernst Ludwig (1858–1947) German physicist, born in Kiel. Professor at Kiel from 1885 and at Berlin from 1888, his work on the second law of thermodynamics and black-body radiation led him to abandon classical Newtonian principles and develop the quantum theory; for this work he was awarded the 1918 Nobel Prize for Physics. In 1930 he was elected President of the Kaiser Wilhelm Institute; he resigned in 1937 in protest against the Nazi regime, but was later reappointed President of the renamed Max Planck Institute.

Planck's constant *Physics* (SYMBOL *h*) a fundamental constant, equal to 6.626×10^{-34} joule seconds, that relates the energy E of a quantum of light to its frequency v by the equation $E = hv$. [named after Max Planck]

plane¹ *noun* an aeroplane. [a shortening of AEROPLANE]

plane² — *noun* **1** *Maths.* a flat surface, either real or imaginary, such that a straight line joining any two points lies entirely on it. **2** a level surface. **3** a level or standard: *on a higher intellectual plane.* — *adj.* **1** flat; level. **2** *Maths.* lying in one plane: *a plane figure / plane geometry.* — *verb intrans.* **1** *said of a boat* to skim over the surface of the water. **2** *said of a bird* to wheel or soar with wings motionless. [from Latin *planum*, level surface]

plane³ — *noun* a carpenter's tool for smoothing wood by shaving away unevennesses. — *verb* **1** (*also* **plane something down**) to smooth a surface, especially wood, with a plane. **2** (**plane something off** *or* **away**) to remove it from a surface with a plane. [from French *plane*, from Latin *planare*, to smooth]

plane⁴ *noun* **1** a tree with large lobed leaves and flaking bark. **2** *Scot.* the sycamore tree. [from French *plane*, from Greek *platanos*]

plane angle *Geom.* the two-dimensional angle formed by two lines in a plane figure, such as a polygon.

planet *noun* **1** a celestial body, in orbit around the Sun or another star, which has too small a mass to become a star itself, and is not luminous but shines by reflecting light from the star around which it revolves. Planets may be solid rocky or metallic objects, or mainly gaseous with a solid core. **2** one of nine such bodies (Mercury, Venus, Earth, Mars, Jupiter, Saturn, Uranus, Neptune, and Pluto) that revolve around the Sun in the Solar System. [from French *planète*, from Greek *planetes*, wanderer]

planetarium *noun* (PL. **planetaria, planetariums**) **1** a special projector by means of which the positions and movements of stars and planets can be projected on to a hemispherical domed ceiling in order to simulate the appearance of the night sky to an audience seated below. **2** the building that houses such a projector. [from Latin *planetarius*, planetary]

planetary *adj.* **1** relating to planets. **2** consisting of or produced by planets. **3** *Astrol.* under the influence of a planet. **4** erratic. **5** revolving in an orbit.

planetology *noun* *Geol.* the scientific study of the planets, their natural satellites, and the interplanetary material of the solar system, including the asteroids and meteors.

Planets, The a seven-movement orchestral suite by Gustav Holst (Op 32, 1914–16), comprising *Mars, the Bringer of War; Venus, the Bringer of Peace; Mercury, the Winged Messenger; Jupiter, the Bringer of Jollity; Saturn, the Bringer of Old Age; Uranus, the Magician; Neptune, the Mystic.*

plangency *noun* being plangent.

plangent *adj.*, *said of a sound* deep, ringing, and mournful. [from Latin *plangere*, to beat]

plangently *adv.* in a plangent way.

planimeter *noun* a mathematical instrument for measuring the area of a plane figure, eg an indicator diagram. A tracing point on an arm is moved round the closed curve, whose area is then given to scale by the revolutions of a small wheel supporting the arm. [from Latin *planus*, level]

plank — *noun* **1** a long flat piece of timber. **2** any of the policies forming the platform or programme of a political party. — *verb* **1** to fit or cover with planks. **2** (**plank something down**) *colloq.* to put down roughly or noisily.
— **walk the plank** to be made to walk blindfold along a plank projecting over a ship's side until one falls into the sea and drowns.
[from Latin *planca*, board]

planking *noun* planks, or a surface, etc constructed of them.

plankton *pl. noun* (SING. **plankter**) *Biol.* microscopic animals (*zooplankton*) and plants (*phytoplankton*) that float or drift with the current in the surface waters of seas and lakes. Plankton are an important food source for invertebrates, fish, and even whales, and form the basis of all marine food chains. Much of the Earth's oxygen is produced as a result of photosynthesis by the phytoplankton. [from Greek *planktos*, wandering]

planner *noun* **1** someone who draws up plans or designs: *a town planner.* **2** a wall calendar showing the whole year, on which holidays, etc can be marked.

planning *noun* control exercised by a local authority over the erection and alteration of buildings and use of land.

planning permission *Brit.* permission required from a local authority to erect or convert a building or to change the use to which a building or piece of land is put.

planographic printing 'flat surface' printing using lithography; it is the simplest method by which an artist may create an image that will print. The image is drawn on a litho-stone or flexible metal plate of zinc or aluminium, from which a positive image is reproduced.

plant — *noun* **1** any living organism (extant or extinct) belonging to the kingdom Plantae, and characterized by its ability to manufacture carbohydrates by the process of photosynthesis. Unlike animals, plants typically possess cell walls that contain cellulose, are unable to move spontaneously, and lack a nervous system or sensory organs. **2** a relatively small organism of this type, eg a herb or shrub as opposed to a tree. **3** the buildings, equipment, and machinery used in manufacturing or production industries, eg a factory or nuclear power station. **4** *colloq.* something deliberately placed for others to find and be misled by. — *verb* **1** to put (seeds or plants) into the ground to grow. **2** to put plants or seeds into (ground, a garden, bed, etc). **3** to introduce (an idea, doubt, etc) into someone's mind. **4** to place

firmly. **5** (**plant something on someone**) to give them a kiss or blow. **6** to post (someone) as a spy, in an office, factory, etc. **7** *colloq.* to place (something) deliberately so as to mislead the finder, eg as a means of incriminating an innocent person. **8** to establish (a colony, etc). [from Latin *planta*, shoot, sprig]
◇ In most modern classifications, plants include the bryophytes, ie mosses and liverworts, and vascular plants, ie ferns, horsetails, clubmosses, gymnosperms (conifers, cycads, etc), and angiosperms (flowering plants). Traditionally, fungi, algae, and blue-green algae have also been classified as plants, but they are now usually placed in separate kingdoms. With the exception of a few parasitic species, plants differ from animals in that they can manufacture simple carbohydrates (mainly sugars) from carbon dioxide and water in the presence of sunlight, using the pigment chlorophyll which is present in specialized structures known as chloroplasts. They also show a relatively open growth pattern, unlike animals.
Plants play an important ecological role in removing carbon dioxide from the atmosphere and generating oxygen, and they are the primary producers in all food chains, eg the microscopic plants present in plankton manufacture their own food by photosynthesis, and are eaten by animals in the plankton, which then serve as food for larger animals, such as fish. Plants protect the land from erosion by wind and water, they provide shelter for wildlife, and many of them are important sources of food, timber, and other materials for humans, although there is mounting concern over the long-term ecological effects of the present rate of destruction of tropical rainforests.

The Main Groups of the Plant Kingdom

Some of the smaller groups have been omitted

Division	Representative classes	Examples
Bacillariophyta	Bacillariophyceae	diatoms
Chlorophyta	Chlorophyceae	green algae
Phaeophyta	Phaeophyceae	brown algae
Rhodophyta	Rhodophyceae	red algae
Bryophyta	Hepaticae	liverworts
	Musci	mosses
Pteridophyta	Pteropsida	ferns
	Lycopsida	clubmosses
	Sphenopsida	horsetails
Spermatophyta *subdivision*		
Gymnospermae (cone-bearing plants)	Coniferopsida	conifers
	Cycadopsida	cycads
subdivision		
Angiospermae (flowering plants)	Dicotyledonae	rose, oak, sunflower
	Monocotyledonae	lily, palms, grasses

Plantagenet Dynasty the name given by historians to the royal dynasty in England from Henry II to Richard II (1154–1399), then continued until 1485 by the two rival houses of Lancaster and York. The dynasty was allegedly named after the sprig of broom (Old French, *plante genêt*) that Henry II's father Geoffrey, Count of Anjou, sported in his cap.

plantain¹ *noun* a tropical green-skinned fruit like a large banana. [from Spanish *plátano*]

plantain² *noun* a plant that presses its leaves close to the ground, having a flower on a tall slender stem. [from Latin *plantago*, from *planta*, sole of the foot]

plantation *noun* **1** an estate, especially in the tropics, that specializes in the large-scale production of a single cash crop, eg tea, coffee, cotton, or rubber. **2** an area of land planted with a certain kind of tree for commercial purposes, eg conifer

Planetary Data

Planet	Distance from sun (million km)		Planet year	Planet day (equatorial)	Diameter (equatorial) km
	Maximum	Minimum			
Mercury	69.4	46.8	88 d	59 d	4 878
Venus	109.0	107.6	224.7 d	243 d	12 104
Earth	152.6	147.4	365.26[1]	23 h 56 m	12 756
Mars	249.2	207.3	687 d	24 h 37 m	6 794
Jupiter	817.4	741.6	11.9 y	9 h 50 m	142 700
Saturn	1 512	1 346	29.5 y	10 h 14 m	120 000
Uranus	3 011	2 740	84 y	16–28 h[2]	52 000
Neptune	4 543	4 466	164.8 y	18–20 h[2]	48 600
Pluto	7 364	4 461	248.5 y	6 d 9 h	2 300

[1] 365 d 5 h 48 m 46 s
[2] Different latitudes rotate at different speeds.
y: earth years d: earth days h: hours m: minutes

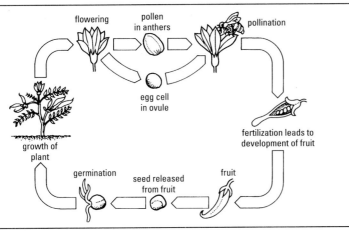

plant life cycle

plantation. **3** *Hist.* a colony. [from Latin *plantatio*, a planting]

Plantation of Ireland the colonization and conquest of Ireland from 1556 to 1660, at first mainly by the English, but also by Scottish settlers who came to Ulster in 1608–11. The settlement policy led to rebellions by the native Irish and Anglo-Irish aristocracy (1563–9, 1580–3, 1598–1603, 1641) and the eventual conquest of Ireland under Cromwell, in which possibly two thirds of the Irish died.

planter *noun* **1** the owner or manager of a plantation. **2** a device for planting bulbs, etc. **3** a container for house plants.

plantigrade *adj. Zool.* denoting animals that walk with the entire lower surface of the foot in contact with the ground, including humans, bears, and many other mammals. [from Latin *planta*, sole + *gradi*, to walk]

plant pot a pot for growing a plant.

plaque *noun* **1** a commemorative inscribed tablet fixed to or set into a wall. **2** a wall ornament made of pottery, etc. **3** *Dentistry* a thin layer of food debris, bacteria, and calcium salts that forms on the surface of teeth. It may cause gingivitis (inflammation of the gums) or dental caries (tooth decay). **4** *Medicine* a raised area of scar tissue on a body part or surface. [from French *plaque*]

plasma *noun* **1** the colourless liquid component of blood or lymph, in which the blood cells are suspended. **2** *Physics* a gas that has been heated to a very high temperature so that most of its atoms or molecules are broken down into approximately equal numbers of free electrons and positive ions. Plasmas occur in discharge tubes, thermonuclear reactors, and in the atmosphere of stars such as the Sun. [from Greek *plasma*, something moulded]

plasma membrane *Biol.* a thin membrane, composed mainly of lipid and protein, that surrounds the cytoplasm of all living cells, as well as the organelles (eg the nucleus) within cells. It acts as a filter, only allowing certain substances to pass across it in either direction. — Also called *cell membrane*.

plasmid *noun Biol.* a small circular loop of DNA that moves from one bacterium to another, transferring genetic information and often endowing its host with useful characteristics, eg resistance to antibiotics. Plasmids have proved to be a very useful tool for genetic engineering.

Plasmodium *noun* any of various species of parasitic protozoan that carry the microorganisms which cause malaria in humans. Its life cycle is complex, involving stages in an intermediate host (the mosquito) and stages in the blood or other organs of a final vertebrate host. [related to PLASMA]

Plassey, Battle of a decisive British victory (1757) under Robert Clive over Siraj ud-Daula, Nawab of Bengal, India, also an important step in the British acquisition of Bengal. Clive's success was aided by the treachery of the Nawab's general, Mir Jafar, whom the British subsequently placed on the throne.

plaster — *noun* **1** a material consisting of lime, sand, and water, that is applied to walls when soft and dries to form a hard smooth surface. **2** plaster of Paris. **3** (*also* **sticking-plaster**) a piece of sticky tape, usually with a dressing attached, for protecting a wound. — *verb* (**plastered, plastering**) **1** to apply plaster to (walls). **2** *colloq.* to coat or spread thickly: *plaster gel on one's hair / plaster one's hair with gel*. **3** to fix with some wet or sticky substance: *hair plastered to his skull*. **4** to cover liberally: *walls plastered with photos*. [from Latin *plastrum*, from Greek *emplastron*, salve]

plasterboard *noun* board consisting of a layer of plaster between two layers of fibreboard, used for making partitions, ceilings, etc.

plastered *adj. colloq.* drunk.

plasterer *noun* a person who applies plaster to walls, ceilings, etc.

plaster of Paris powdered gypsum, mixed with water to make a material that dries hard, used for sculpting and for making casts for broken limbs.

plastic — *noun* **1** any of a large number of synthetic materials that can be moulded by heat and/or pressure into a rigid or semi-rigid shape that is retained when the heat and pressure are removed. **2** *colloq.* a credit card, or credit cards collectively: *do you have any plastic?* — *adj.* **1** made of plastic. **2** easily moulded or shaped; pliant. **3** easily influenced. **4** *derog.* artificial; lacking genuine substance. **5** *said of money* in the form of, or funded by, a credit card. **6** relating to sculpture and modelling. [from Greek *plastikos*, moulded, from *plassein*, to mould]
◇ There are two main types of plastic. *Thermoplastics*, eg Perspex, polythene, and polyvinyl chloride (PVC) can be repeatedly softened and hardened by heating and cooling, without any appreciable change in their properties. *Thermosetting materials*, eg polyurethane and epoxy resins, are initially soft but set hard after heating, and cannot be softened again by further heating. The main source of raw materials for the manufacture of plastics is petroleum, and the accumulation of large amounts of plastic waste has led to environmental problems, because plastic does not decay, and in most cases emits toxic fumes when burned. Several biodegradable plastics have been developed, but they are expensive to produce.
Plastics are widely used to make bottles, bowls, buckets, and other containers, fibres, film, rope,

packaging, paints, adhesives, varnishes, records, toys, contact lenses, artificial body parts, insulation for electric wires and cables, floor tiles, motor vehicle parts, and construction materials.

plastic arts (the plastic arts) the sculptural arts.

plastic bomb a bomb made with plastic explosive.

plastic bullet a small solid plastic cylinder fired by the police to disperse riots.

plastic explosive an explosive substance resembling putty that can be moulded by hand, eg Semtex, which is favoured by terrorist groups because it has no detectable smell, and can only be ignited by a detonator.

Plasticine *noun trademark* a non-hardening modelling material, used especially by children.

plasticity *noun* being plastic.

plasticizer *or* **plasticiser** *noun Chem.* any substance that is added to a rigid synthetic resin or plastic in order to make it flexible and so more easily workable.

plastic surgeon a surgeon who specializes in plastic surgery.

plastic surgery *Medicine* the branch of surgery concerned with the repair, restoration, or reconstruction of deformed or damaged tissue or body parts, or the replacement of missing parts. It mainly involves the treatment of burns and other injuries, and the correction of congenital deformities, eg cleft palate, but also includes cosmetic surgery, eg facelifts.

plastid *noun Bot.* any of various highly specialized membrane-bound structures found within the cytoplasm of plant cells, eg chloroplasts (which are the site of photosynthesis), and amyloplasts (which store starch). [from Greek *plastis*, *-idos*]

Plataea an ancient Greek city-state in Boeotia, whose inhabitants helped the Athenians defeat the Persians at Marathon in 490 BC. It was also the site of a Greek victory over the Persians in 479 BC. During the Peloponnesian War it was attacked and sacked by Sparta (429–427 BC). It was restored and destroyed by the Thebans (373 BC), then rebuilt by Philip of Macedon after 338 BC.

plate — *noun* **1** a shallow dish, especially of earthenware or porcelain, for serving food on. **2** the amount held by this; a plateful. **3** a shallow vessel in which to take the collection in church. **4** a sheet of metal, glass or other rigid material. **5** a flat piece of metal, plastic, etc inscribed with a name, etc. **6** gold and silver vessels or cutlery; a gold or silver cup as the prize in a horse race, etc. **7** a thin coating of gold, silver, or tin applied to a base metal. **8** an illustration on glossy paper in a book. **9** *Photog.* a sheet of glass prepared with a light-sensitive coating for receiving an image. **10** a sheet of metal with an image engraved on it, or a print taken from it. **11** any of various surfaces set up with type ready for printing. **12** a moulded plastic fitting for the mouth with false teeth attached; a denture. **13** any of the rigid sections that make up the earth's crust. **14** *Anat.* a thin flat piece of bone or horn. — *verb* **1** to coat (a base metal) with a thin layer of a precious one. **2** to cover with metal plates.
— **have a lot** *or* **much on one's plate** *colloq.* have a great deal of work, commitments, etc.
on a plate *colloq.* presented to one without one's having to make the least effort.
[from Old French *plate*, something flat]

plateau *noun* (PL. **plateaux, plateaus**) **1** an extensive area of relatively flat high land, usually bounded by steep sides, common in limestone areas. **2** a stable, unvarying condition of prices, etc after a rise. [from French, from Old French *platel*, something flat]

Plateau Indians a name given to various Native American groups who lived on the plateau between the Rocky Mts and the Cascade Range. Most groups lived in camps during the summer, hunting and fishing; during the winters, they sheltered in earth lodges in permanent villages located along the rivers. This way of life was radically affected by fur traders and trappers arriving from the east. During the 19c European settlers and prospectors fought with the native population over land, and in the ensuing wars, most groups were decimated, and the survivors forced into reservations.

plateful noun (PL. **platefuls**) **1** the amount a plate will hold. **2** (usually **platefuls**) colloq. a great deal; a lot.

plate glass glass made in tough sheets for shop windows, mirrors, etc.

platelayer noun a person who lays and repairs railway lines.

platelet noun Anat. in mammalian blood, any of the small disc-shaped cell fragments, without nuclei, that are responsible for starting the formation of a blood clot when bleeding occurs. [a diminutive of PLATE]

platen noun **1** a plate in some printing-presses that pushes the paper against the type. **2** the roller of a typewriter. [from Old French platine]

Plate, River, Spanish **Río de la Plata** a wide, shallow estuary of the Paraná and Uruguay rivers. area 35 000sq km/13 510sq mi; length 320km/200mi; width 220km/140mi at its mouth and 45km/28mi at Buenos Aires. It is situated on the E coast of S America, between Argentina on the S and W shore and Uruguay on the N shore. HISTORY the river was discovered by Juan Diaz de Solís in 1516; it was the scene of a naval engagement in Dec 1939 (Battle of the River Plate) between three out-gunned British cruisers and the formidable German pocket-battleship Graf Spee; the Graf Spee inexplicably disengaged and was trapped in the neutral port of Montevideo, to be scuttled a few days later.

plate tectonics Geol. a geological theory, developed in the late 1960s, according to which the Earth's crust is composed of a small number of large plates of solid rock, whose movements in relation to each other are responsible for continental drift.

◇ According to the theory of plate tectonics, the plates of the Earth's crust are floating on the moving molten rock of the mantle which lies beneath the crust. It is believed that the plates move as a result of convection currents which occur deep within the mantle. New crust is formed at the edges of plates where rising convection currents bring up new material from the mantle. Some plates may be 'sliding' in relation to one another along margins where there are huge fault systems, eg the San Andreas fault system off the coast of California. It is thought that mountain ranges are formed when one crustal plate pushes into another, forcing the land upward under great pressure.

platform noun **1** a raised floor for speakers, performers, etc. **2** the raised walkway alongside the track at a railway station, giving access to trains. **3** a floating installation moored to the sea bed, for oil-drilling, marine research, etc. **4** an open step at the back of some, especially older, buses, for passengers getting on or off. **5** a thick rigid sole for a shoe. **6** the publicly declared principles and intentions of a political party, forming the basis of its policies. **7** any situation giving one access to an audience, that one can exploit to promote one's views. [from Old French platte forme, flat figure]

Plath, Sylvia (1932–63) US poet, born in Boston. She married the poet Ted Hughes in 1956, and they lived in Spain and the USA, then returned to England in 1959. Her first collection The Colossus appeared in 1960, and a novel The Bell Jar in 1963, shortly before she committed suicide in London. Ariel was published posthumously in 1965, and it contains many of the poems for which she is best known. Her Collected Poems, edited by Ted Hughes, appeared in 1981.

plating noun same as PLATE noun 7.

platinum noun Chem. (SYMBOL **Pt**, ATOMIC NUMBER 78) a silvery-white precious metal that does not tarnish or corrode, used as the free metal and in alloys to make jewellery, coins, electrical contacts and resistance wires, electrodes, thermocouples, and surgical instruments. It is also used in the form of a finely divided black powder as a catalyst.

platinum-blond adj., said of hair of a silvery fairness.

platinum blonde a woman with silvery fair hair.

platitude noun an empty, unoriginal, or redundant comment, especially made as though it were important. [from French platitude, flatness]

platitudinous adj. **1** characterized by or of the nature of a platitude. **2** using platitudes. **3** full of platitudes.

Plato (c.427–347 BC) Athenian philosopher, born of an aristocratic family and one of the most important philosophers of all time. He became a disciple of Socrates, then travelled widely, before founding his Academy in Athens (where Aristotle was his pupil). He remained for the rest of his life, apart from visits to Syracuse where he tried (unsuccessfully) to train Dionysus II as a philosopher-statesman. His work consists of 30 dialogues and a series of Letters. The dialogues can be grouped as follows: the early dialogues, in which the main interlocutor is Socrates, and the main interest is the definition of moral concepts (eg piety in Euthyphron, courage in Laches); the middle dialogues, in which Plato increasingly outlines his own doctrines (eg on learning and metaphysics, and the theory of forms in the Republic); the later dialogues, which express his rigorous self-criticism (eg the Parmenides and the Sophist). The Republic, one of the most influential works in the history of philosophy, describes Plato's political utopia, ruled by philosopher-kings. Plato is particularly known for his theory of ideas, or forms, in which the world of transient, finite, ever-changing objects of sense experience is to be distinguished from that of the timeless, unchanging, universal forms, which are the true objects of knowledge.

Platonic adj. **1** relating to the Greek philosopher Plato. **2** (usually **platonic**) said of human love not involving sexual relations. **3** restricted to theorizing; not involving action.

platonically adv. in a platonic way.

Platonic solid Maths. any solid whose faces are congruent regular polygons. There are five such solids: the tetrahedron (four faces, each an equilateral triangle); the cube (six faces, each a square); the octahedron (eight faces, each a pentagon); the dodecahedron (12 faces, each a hexagon); and the icosahedron (20 faces, each an equilateral triangle). All five were described by Plato, who showed how to construct models of the solids.

Platonism any philosophical position which includes many of the central features of Plato's philosophy. These include a belief in a transcendent realm of abstract, perfect entities; the inferiority of the physical world; the power of reason to know these perfect entities; bodily separability and the immortality of the soul.

platoon noun **1** Mil. a subdivision of a company. **2** a squad of people acting in co-operation. [from French peloton, diminutive of pelote, ball]

platter noun **1** a large flat dish. **2** North Amer. colloq. a gramophone record. [from Old French plater, from plat, plate]

platypus noun (PL. **platypuses**) (in full **duck-billed platypus**) an egg-laying amphibious mammal with dense brown fur, a long flattened toothless snout, webbed feet, and a broad flat tail, found in Tasmania and E Australia. It feeds on worms, shellfish, and aquatic insects, and lives and lays its eggs in burrows along river banks. [from Greek platys, wide + pous, foot]

duck-billed platypus

plaudit noun (usually **plaudits**) a commendation; an expression of praise. [from Latin plaudite, imperative of plaudere, to praise]

plausibility noun a plausible quality.

plausible adj. **1** said of an explanation, etc credible, reasonable, or likely. **2** said of a person having a pleasant and persuasive manner; smooth-tongued or glib. [from Latin plausibilis, deserving applause]

plausibly adv. in a plausible way.

Plautus, Titus Maccius (c.250–184 BC) Roman comic dramatist, born in Sarsina, Umbria. About 130 plays have been attributed to him, but many are thought to be revisions of other dramatists' work. His own have been limited to 21 influential comedies, which are full of robust life and vigorous dialogue.

play — verb **1** intrans. said especially of children to spend time in recreation. **2** (**play about** or **around with something** or **someone**) to fiddle or meddle with it; to behave irresponsibly towards someone, someone's affections, etc. **3** (**play something** or **play at something**) to take part in a recreative pursuit, game, sport, match, round, etc. **4** (**play someone** or **play against someone**) to compete against in a game or sport. **5** intrans. colloq. to co-operate: he refuses to play. **6** to include as a team member: playing McGuire in goal. **7** to hit or kick (the ball), deliver (a shot), etc in a sport. **8** Cards to use (a card) in the course of a game. **9** to speculate or gamble on (the Stock Exchange, etc). **10** (**play something on someone**) to perpetrate a trick or joke against them. **11** trans., intrans. to act or behave in a certain way: play it cool / not playing fair. **12** to act (a role) in a play, etc. **13** trans., intrans. to perform a role in a play. **14** trans., intrans. to perform in (a place). **15** said of a film, play, etc being shown or performed publicly: playing all next week. **16** trans., intrans. to pretend to be: play the dumb blonde. **17** to act as: play host to the delegates. **18** to perform (music) on an instrument; to perform on (an instrument). **19** to turn on (a radio, tape-recording, etc). **20** intrans. **a** said of recorded music, etc to be heard from a radio, etc. **b** said of a radio, etc to produce sound. **21** (**play over** or **across something**) said eg of light, facial expression, etc to flicker over, across, etc. **22** intrans. said of a fountain to be in operation. **23** to direct (a hose, etc). **24** to allow (a fish) to tire itself by its struggles to get away. — noun **1** recreation; playing games: children at play. **2** the playing of a game, performance in a sport, etc: rain stopped play. **3** colloq. behaviour; conduct: fair/foul play. **4** a dramatic piece for the stage, or a performance of it. **5** fun; jest: said in play. **6** range; scope: give full play to the imagination. **7** freedom of movement; looseness: too much play in the brake. **8** action or interaction: play of sunlight on water / play of emotions. **9** use: bring all one's cunning into play.
— **in** or **out of play** Sport, said of a ball in (or not in) a position where it may be played.
make great play of something to emphasize it or stress its importance.
make a play for something to try to get (eg someone's attention).
make play with something to make effective or over-obvious use of it.

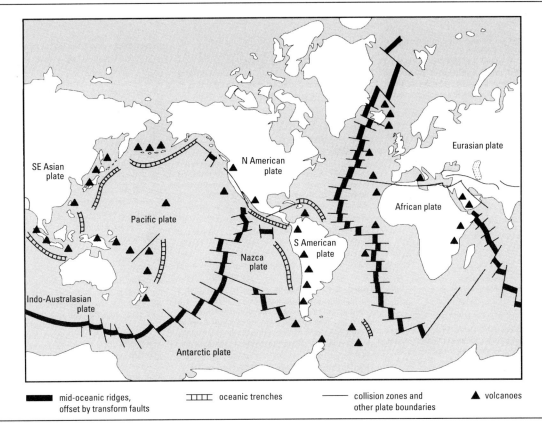

mid-oceanic ridges, offset by transform faults   ⊔⊔⊔⊔ oceanic trenches   ——— collision zones and other plate boundaries   ▲ volcanoes

Continental plates

---

play about *or* **around with something** to behave ineffectively or irresponsibly.

play along with someone to co-operate for the time being; to humour them.

play at something 1 to make a pretence of it, especially in play: *play at being cowboys.* **2** to indulge in it trivially or flippantly: *play at politics.* **3** *ironic* to try to achieve: *what are they playing at?*

play something back to play a film or sound recording through immediately after making it.

play something down to represent it as unimportant; to minimize, make light of, or discount it.

play off to replay a match, etc after a draw.

play one person against another to set them in rivalry, especially for one's own advantage.

play on something 1 to exploit someone's fears, feelings, sympathies, etc for one's own benefit. **2** to make a pun on it: *played on the two meanings of 'batter'.*

play something out 1 to act out in real life a part, scene, etc that is so predictable that it could have come from a play. **2** (*usually* **be played out**) *colloq.* to be exhausted or over-used.

play up 1 *colloq.* to behave unco-operatively. **2** *colloq.* to cause one pain or discomfort. **3** *colloq.* to function faultily. **4** to try one's hardest in a game, match, etc.

play something up to highlight it or give prominence to it.

play up to someone to flatter them ; to ingratiate oneself with them.

play with something to contemplate it: *played with the idea of becoming a writer.* [from Anglo-Saxon *plegan*]

playable *adj.* **1** *said of a pitch, ground, etc* fit to be played on. **2** *said of a ball* lying where it can be played.

play-act *verb intrans.* to behave in an insincere fashion, disguising one's true feelings or intentions.

play-acting *noun* insincere or misleading behaviour.

playback *noun* a playing back of a sound recording or film.

playbill *noun* a poster advertising a play or show.

playboy *noun* a man of wealth, leisure, and frivolous lifestyle.

Playboy of the Western World, The a play by J M Synge (1907). It is a comedy using the rhetoric of ordinary Irish people in a story about a man on the run who impresses by pretending that he has killed his father.

played out exhausted; lacking energy.

Player, Gary (Jim) (1935–) South African golfer, born in Johannesburg, the only golfer to win a major tournament in each of four decades (1950s–1980s). His first major success was the 1959 British Open, a title he also won in 1968 and 1974. He was the first non-American for 45 years to win the US Open (1965), and the first to win the US Professional Golfers Association title (1962, regained 1972) and the US Masters (1961, regained 1974, 1978). He won the South African Open 13 times, the Australian Open seven times, and the world match-play title a record five times. He now breeds horses in South Africa, and plays golf on the US Seniors tour.

player *noun* **1** a participant in a game or sport. **2** a performer on a musical instrument. **3** *old use* an actor.

player piano a piano fitted with a machinery enabling it to be played automatically.

playfellow *noun* a playmate.

playful *adj.* **1** full of fun; frisky. **2** *said of a remark, etc* humorous.

playfully *adv.* in a playful way.

playfulness *noun* being playful.

playground *noun* **1** an area for children's recreation, especially as part of a school's grounds. **2** a resort for people who take frivolous recreation seriously.

playgroup *noun* a number of children organized into a group for regular supervised play together.

playhouse *noun old use* a theatre.

playing-card *noun* each of a pack of usually 52 cards used in card games.
◇ The pack, as standardized in the 15c, is divided into four suits: hearts, clubs, diamonds, and spades. Each suit has 13 cards numbered as follows: ace, 2-10, and the court (or picture) cards, jack (or knave), queen, and king. Most packs also include two cards known as jokers, which can be given any value. The earliest playing-cards were used in China in the 10c, and first appeared in Europe in the 14c.

playing-field *noun* a grassy expanse prepared and marked out for playing games.

playmate *noun* one's companion in play.

play-off *noun* a match or game played to resolve a draw or other undecided contest.

play on words a pun or punning.

playpen *noun* a collapsible frame that when erected forms an enclosure inside which a baby may safely play.

playschool *noun* a playgroup, or a school for children between two and five.

plaything *noun* a toy.

playtime *noun* a period for recreation, especially as part of a school timetable.

playwright *noun* an author of plays.

plaza *noun* **1** a large public square or market place especially in a Spanish town. **2** *North Amer.* a shopping centre or complex. [from Spanish *plaza*, a square or market place]

PLC *or* **plc** *abbrev.* public limited company.

plea *noun* **1** an earnest appeal. **2** a statement made in a court of law by or on behalf of the defendant. **3** an excuse: *refused the invitation on the plea of a headache.* [from Old French *plaid*]

plead *verb* (PAST TENSE AND PAST PARTICIPLE **pleaded**) *Scot., North Amer., esp. US* (**pled**) **1** (*usually* **plead with someone for something**) to appeal earnestly. **2** *intrans.* *said of an accused person* to state in a court of law that one is guilty or not guilty. **3** (**plead for something**) to argue in defence of it: *plead someone's case.* **4** to give as an excuse: *plead ignorance.* [from Old French *plaidier*]

pleading *adj.* appealing earnestly.

pleadingly *adv.* in a pleading way, with pleading.

pleadings *pl. noun* the formal statements submitted by defendant and plaintiff in a lawsuit.

pleasant *adj.* **1** giving pleasure; enjoyable; agreeable. **2** *said of a person* friendly; affable. [from Old French *plaisant*, from *plaisir*, to please]

pleasantly *adv.* with a pleasant manner.

pleasantness *noun* being pleasant.

pleasantry *noun* (PL. **pleasantries**) **1** (*usually* **pleasantries**) a remark made for the sake of politeness or friendliness. **2** humour; teasing.

please — *verb* **1** *trans., intrans.* to give satisfaction, pleasure, or enjoyment; to be agreeable to. **2** (with *it* as subject) to be the inclination of: *if it should please you to join us.* **3** *trans., intrans.* to choose; to like: *do what/as you please.* — *adv.* used politely to accompany a request, order, acceptance of an offer, protest, a call for attention, etc. — **if you please 1** *old use* please. **2** *ironic* of all things: *is engaged to a baronet, if you please.* **please oneself** to do as one likes. [from Old French *plaisir*]

pleased *adj.* **1** (**pleased about** *or* **with someone** *or* **something**) happy; satisfied. **2** glad; delighted. — **pleased with oneself** *derog.* self-satisfied; conceited.

pleasing *adj.* causing pleasure or satisfaction.

pleasingly *adv.* in a pleasing way.

pleasurable *adj.* enjoyable; pleasant.

pleasurably *adv.* in a pleasurable way.

pleasure — *noun* **1** a feeling of enjoyment or satisfaction: *take pleasure in one's surroundings.* **2** a source of such a feeling: *have the pleasure of your company.* **3** one's will, desire, wish, preference, or inclination. **4** recreation: *combine business with pleasure.* **5** gratification of a sensual kind: *pleasure and pain.* — *verb old use* to give (especially sexual) pleasure to. — *adj.* used for or done for pleasure: *a pleasure boat / a pleasure trip.* — **a** *or* **my pleasure** a formula of courtesy: not at all; it's no trouble. **at pleasure** when or as one likes. **with pleasure** a formula of courtesy: gladly; willingly; of course. [from Old French *plaisir*, originally infinitive]

pleat — *noun* a fold sewn or pressed into cloth, etc. — *verb* to make pleats in. [a variant of PLAIT]

pleated *adj.* having pleats.

pleb *noun derog.* a person of coarse or vulgar tastes, manners, or habits. [a shortening of PLEBEIAN]

plebeian — *noun* **1** a member of the common people, especially of ancient Rome. **2** *derog.* a person lacking refinement or culture. — *adj.* **1** of or belonging to the common people. **2** *derog.* coarse; vulgar; unrefined. [from Latin *plebeius*, from *plebs*, the people]

plebiscite *noun* a vote of all the electors, taken to decide a matter of public importance; a referendum. [from Latin *plebiscitum*, decree of the plebs]

plectrum *noun* a small flat implement of metal, plastic, horn, etc, used for plucking the strings of a guitar. [from Latin, from Greek *plectron*, from *plessein*, to strike]

pled see PLEAD.

pledge — *noun* **1** a solemn promise. **2** something left as security with someone to whom one owes money, etc. **3** something put into pawn. **4** a token or symbol: *a ring as a pledge of love.* **5** a toast drunk as proof of friendship, etc. — *verb* **1** to promise (money, loyalty, etc) to someone. **2** to bind or commit (oneself, etc). **3** to offer or give as a pledge or guarantee. **4** *old use* to drink the health of. — **take** *or* **sign the pledge** *old facetious use* to undertake to drink no alcohol. [from Old French *plege*]

Pléiade, La a group of 16c French poets who sought to emancipate the French language (and literature) from medievalism by introducing Greek and Latin models. The best known were Ronsard (1524–85) and du Bellay (1522–60), whose *Défense et illustration de la langue française* (1549) served as a manifesto.

Pleiades in Greek mythology, the seven daughters of Atlas and Pleione: Maia, Taygete, Elektra, Alkyone, Asterope, Kelaino, and Merope. They were changed into the star-cluster of the same name, after being pursued by Orion.

plein air a term used in art history, and applied to pictures, especially landscapes, which give a vivid sense of the light and atmosphere of the open air. Also applied to pictures painted out of doors, instead of in the studio; the Impressionists worked largely plein air. [from French *plein air*, open air]

Pleiocene another spelling of PLIOCENE.

Pleistocene *adj. Geol.* denoting the first of the two epochs of the Quaternary period, lasting from about two million to 10 000 years ago. ◇ During the Pleistocene epoch modern man (*Homo sapiens*) evolved, and many mammals, including the mammoth and mastodon, became extinct. It is often called the Ice Age because there were a number of major advances of ice (glaciations) in the northern hemisphere, separated by interglacial periods when the ice retreated. [from Greek *pleisto-*, most + *kainos*, recent]

Plekhanov, Giorgiy Valentinovich, known as the **Father of Russian Marxism** (1856–1918) Russian Marxist philosopher, historian, and journalist, born in Gundalovka. He left Russia in 1880, and in 1883 founded the first Russian Marxist group, the Liberation of Labour Group, in Geneva, where he remained until 1917. He was a major intellectual influence on the young Lenin, but sided with the Mensheviks against Lenin's Bolsheviks, and denounced the October Revolution.

plenary *adj.* **1** full; complete: *plenary powers.* **2** *said of a meeting* attended by all members. [from Latin *plenarius*, from *plenus*, full]

plenipotentiary — *adj.* entrusted with, or conveying, full authority to act on behalf of one's government or other organization. — *noun* (PL. **plenipotentiaries**) someone, eg an ambassador, invested with such authority. [from Latin *plenus*, full + *potentia*, power]

plenitude *noun* **1** abundance; profusion. **2** completeness; fullness. [from Latin *plenitudo*, from *plenus*, full]

plenteous *adj.* plentiful; abundant. [from Middle English *plentivous*, from Old French *plentif*, from *plente*, plenty]

plenteously *adv.* plentifully; abundantly.

plenteousness *noun* being plenteous.

plentiful *adj.* in good supply; abundant. [from PLENTY]

plentifully *adv.* in a plentiful way.

plenty — *pron.* **1** enough, or more than enough. **2** a lot: *plenty of folk would agree.* — *noun* wealth or sufficiency: *in times of plenty.* — *adv. colloq.* fully: *plenty wide enough.* — **in plenty** in abundant quantities.

[from Old French *plente*, from Latin *plenitas*, abundance]

pleonasm *noun* **1** the use of more words than are needed to express something. **2** a superfluous word or words. [from Greek *pleonasmos*, superfluity]

pleonastic *adj.* characterized by pleonasm; using more words than are needed.

pleonastically *adv.* by means of pleonasm.

plethora *noun* a large or excessive amount. [from Greek *plethora*, fullness]

pleura *noun Anat.* in mammals, the double membrane that covers the lungs and lines the chest cavity. [from Greek *pleura*, side, rib]

pleurisy *noun* inflammation of the pleura. [from Old French *pleurisie*]

Pleven 1 POP (1991e) 138 000, the agricultural and industrial capital of Pleven province, N Bulgaria. It is situated 178km/111mi NE of Sofia, near the R Vit. **2** POP (1990e) 357 000, a province in N Bulgaria. AREA 4 364sq km/1 684sq mi. CAPITAL Pleven. The province is crossed by the Vit and and Osum rivers with the R Danube on its N boundary and the R Iskur to the W.

plexus *noun Anat.* a network of nerves or blood vessels, such as the *solar plexus* behind the stomach. [from Latin *plexus*, a weaving]

pliability *noun* being pliable.

pliable *adj.* **1** easily bent; flexible. **2** adaptable or alterable. **3** easily persuaded or influenced. [from French *plier*, to fold]

pliably *adv.* in a pliable way.

pliancy *noun* being pliant.

Pliant, Dame the foolish but wealthy young widow who marries Lovewit in Ben Jonson's *The Alchemist.*

pliant *adj.* **1** bending easily; pliable, flexible, or supple. **2** easily influenced. [from Old French, from *plier*, to fold]

pliers *pl. noun* a hinged tool with jaws for gripping, bending, or cutting wire, etc. [from *ply*, to bend or fold]

plight¹ *noun* a danger, difficulty, or situation of hardship that one finds oneself in; a predicament. [from Middle English *plit*, fold, condition, influenced by the spelling of PLIGHT²]

plight² *verb old use* to promise solemnly; to pledge. — **plight one's troth** to pledge oneself in marriage. [from Anglo-Saxon *pliht*, peril, risk]

plimsoll *noun old use* a light rubber-soled canvas shoe worn for gymnastics, etc; a gymshoe. [from the resemblance of the line of the sole to the Plimsoll line] See illustration p. 1153.

Plimsoll line a line painted round a ship's hull showing how far down into the water it may safely sit when loaded. [named after Samuel Plimsoll (1824–98), who put forward the Merchant Shipping Act of 1876]

plinth *noun* **1** *Archit.* a square block serving as the base of a column, pillar, etc. **2** a base or pedestal for a statue or other sculpture, or a vase. [from Greek *plinthos*, brick, stone block]

Pliny (the Elder), in full **Gaius Plinius Secundus** (AD 23–79) Roman scholar, born in Novum Comum (Como), Gaul. He served in the army in Germany, and later settled in Como, where he devoted himself to study and writing. Nero appointed him procurator in Spain, and through his brother-in-law's death (71) he became guardian of his nephew, Pliny (the Younger), whom he adopted. He continued his studies, and wrote a 37-volume encyclopedia, the *Historia Naturalis* (77, Natural History), his only surviving work. In 79 he was in command of the Roman fleet, and was killed when he landed at Stabiae to view the eruption of Vesuvius.

Pliny (the Younger), in full **Gaius Plinius Caecilius Secundus** (c.62–114 AD) Roman writer and administrator, born in Novum Comum (Como), Gaul. The nephew and adopted son of Pliny the Elder, he became a lawyer and a successful orator. He served as a military tribune in Syria, and progressed to be quaestor, praetor, and (in 100) consul, and held several posts throughout the empire. His many letters provide an insight into the life of the upper class in the 1c.

Pliocene *adj. Geol.* the last epoch of the Tertiary period, lasting from about seven million to two million years ago. During this time the climate became cooler, many mammals became extinct, and primates appeared that walked upright and had teeth similar to those of modern man. [from Greek *pleion*, more + *kainos*, recent]

Plitvice Lakes National Park a national park, founded in 1949, in W Croatia. It is a World Heritage site.

PLO *abbrev.* the Palestine Liberation Organization, an organization that consists of several of the Palestinian groups opposed to Israel, led by Yasser Arafat. Founded in 1964, its charter denied the right of Israel to exist and called for Palestine to be liberated by armed conflict. In 1974 the Arab Summit in Rabat, Morocco, recognized the PLO as the sole legitimate representative of the Palestinian people, but this further marginalized the role of Jordan, a potential ruler of the Palestinian groups in the occupied West Bank and Gaza Strip. However, some Palestinian groups remained independent, notably the Popular Front for the Liberation of Palestine. The PLO has been responsible for several terrorist actions of recent years. In 1982 its forces were expelled from Lebanon. Secret talks in 1991–3 between the Israeli Prime Minister Yitzhak Rabin and the PLO in Norway led to the agreement signed in Washington (13 Sep 1993) by Rabin and Arafat on mutual recognition and limited self-rule in the Gaza Strip and West Bank town of Jericho.

plod *verb intrans.* (**plodded, plodding**) 1 to walk slowly with a heavy tread. 2 to work slowly, methodically, and thoroughly, if without inspiration. [imitative]

plodder *noun* 1 a person who plods on. 2 a dull uninteresting person. 3 a person who progresses by toil rather than by inspiration.

ploidy *noun Biol.* the number of chromosome sets that are present in the nucleus of a cell.

Ploieşti POP (1992) 252 000, the capital of Prahova county, S central Romania. It is a major centre for the petroleum industry, with pipelines to Giurgiu, Bucharest, and Constanţa.

plonk[1] *colloq.* — *noun* the resounding thud made by a heavy object falling. — *verb* 1 to put or place with a thud or with finality: *plonked himself in the best chair.* 2 *intrans.* to place oneself, fall, etc with a plonk. — *adv.* with a thud: *landed plonk beside her.* [imitative]

plonk[2] *noun colloq.* cheap, undistinguished wine. [said to be from French *vin blanc*, white wine]

plop — *noun* the sound of a small object dropping into water. — *verb intrans., trans.* (**plopped, plopping**) to fall or drop with this sound. — *adv.* with a plop. [imitative]

plosive — *adj., said of a sound* made by the sudden release of breath after stoppage. — *noun* a plosive consonant or sound. [a shortening of EXPLOSIVE]

plot[1] — *noun* 1 a secret plan, especially laid jointly with others, for contriving something illegal or evil; a conspiracy. 2 the story of a play, film, novel, etc. — *verb* (**plotted, plotting**) 1 *trans., intrans.* to plan (something, especially illegal or evil), usually with others. 2 to make a plan of; to mark the course or progress of. 3 *Maths.* to mark a series of individual points on

a graph, or to draw a curve through them. [from PLOT[2], influenced by French *complot*, conspiracy]

plot[2] *noun* a piece of ground for any of various uses. [from Anglo-Saxon *plot*]

Plotinus (AD 205–70) Greek philosopher, the founder of Neoplatonism, born possibly in Lycopolis in Egypt. He settled in Rome in 244, where he became a popular lecturer, advocating asceticism and the contemplative life. In his old age, he made an unsuccessful attempt to found a platonic 'Republic' in Campania. His 54 works, which established the foundations of Neoplatonism as a philosophical system, were edited by his pupil, Porphyry, who arranged them in six groups of nine books, or *Enneads*.

plotter *noun Comput.* in a computer system, an output device which draws graphs, diagrams, contour maps, plans, overhead slides, etc, on paper or film using an automatically controlled pen.

plough — *noun* 1 a bladed farm implement used to turn over the surface of the soil, forming ridges and furrows, and burying stubble, weeds, or other surface vegetation in preparation for the cultivation of a crop. 2 any similar implement, especially one for shovelling snow off roads. 3 *Astron.* (**the Plough**) the seven brightest stars in the constellation Ursa Major, whose configuration resembles the shape of a plough. Two of them, Merak and Dubhe, form a line that effectively points to Polaris, the Pole Star. — Also called *Big Dipper.* — *verb* 1 (*also* **plough something up**) to till or turn over soil, land, etc with a plough. 2 to make a furrow or to turn over the surface of the soil with a plough. 3 (*usually* **plough through something**) to move through it with a ploughing action. 4 (*usually* **plough through** *or* **on**) *colloq.* to make steady but laborious progress. 5 (*usually* **plough into something**) *colloq., said of a vehicle or its driver* to crash into something at speed. 6 *Brit. old colloq.* use **a** to fail (a candidate in an examination). **b** *intrans. said of a candidate* to fail an examination.

— **plough something back** to re-invest profits in a business.

plough something in to mix the remains of a crop with the soil by means of a plough after harvesting. [from Anglo-Saxon *plog, ploh*]

Plough and the Stars, The a play by Sean O'Casey (1926). Set in the Dublin slums during the 1916 Easter Rising, it depicts the grim effects of the struggle, and it provoked nationalist rioting at its first performance.

ploughman *noun* a person who steers a plough.

ploughman's lunch a cold meal of bread, cheese, pickle, and (sometimes) meat, often served in pubs.

Plough Monday the Monday following the Epiphany, so called because it was the day when traditionally ploughmen and others resumed their daily work after the Christmas holidays.

ploughshare *noun* a blade of a plough.

Plovdiv, formerly **Philippopoli**, Latin **Evmolpia Trimontium** POP (1991e) 379 000, the industrial capital of Plovdiv province, central Bulgaria, situated on the R Maritsa, 156km/97mi SE of Sofia. It is the country's second largest city. NOTABLE FEATURES Roman amphitheatre; Old Plovdiv has many buildings from the Middle Ages and the National Revival Period.

plover *noun* any of various, especially seashore, birds, most with long wings and a short straight beak. [from Old French *plovier*, rain bird]

plow *noun* the US spelling of **plough**.

ploy *noun* a stratagem, dodge, or manoeuvre to gain an advantage. [possibly from Latin *plicare*, to bend]

PLP *abbrev.* Parliamentary Labour Party.

PLR *abbrev.* public lending right.

pluck — *verb* 1 to pull the feathers off (a bird) before cooking. 2 to pick (flowers or fruit) from a plant or tree. 3 (*also* **pluck something out**) to remove it by pulling: *plucked out his grey hairs.* 4 to shape by removing hairs from (eyebrows). 5 (**pluck** *or* **pluck at something**) to pull or tug it. 6 to sound (the strings of a violin, etc) using the fingers or a plectrum. 7 to grab or save at the last minute: *plucked from the jaws of death.* — *noun* 1 courage; guts. 2 a little tug. 3 the heart, liver, and lungs of an animal.

— **pluck up courage** to strengthen one's resolve for a difficult undertaking, etc. [from Anglo-Saxon *pluccian*, to pluck or tear]

pluckily *adv.* in a plucky way.

pluckiness *noun* being plucky.

plucky *adj.* (**pluckier, pluckiest**) *colloq.* courageous; spirited.

plug — *noun* 1 a piece of rubber, plastic, etc shaped to fit a hole as a stopper, eg in a bath or sink. 2 (*often in compounds*) any device or piece of material for a similar purpose: *earplugs.* 3 the plastic or rubber device with metal pins, fitted to the end of the flex of an electrical apparatus, that is pushed into a socket to connect with the power supply; also *colloq.* the socket. 4 *colloq.* a piece of favourable publicity given to a product, programme, etc, eg on television. 5 a spark plug. 6 a lump of tobacco for chewing. — *verb* (**plugged, plugging**) 1 (*also* **plug something up**) to stop or block up a hole, etc with something. 2 *colloq.* to give favourable publicity to (a product, programme, etc), especially repeatedly. 3 *slang* to shoot with a gun. 4 (**plug away** *or* **along**) *colloq.* to work or progress steadily.

— **plug something in** to connect an electrical appliance to the power supply by means of an electrical plug. [from Dutch *plug*, bung, peg]

plughole *noun* the hole in a bath or sink through which water flows into the wastepipe.

plum *noun* 1 any of a number of varieties of shrub or small tree belonging to the genus *Prunus*, cultivated in temperate regions for its edible fruit, or for its ornamental pink or white flowers and deep red or purple foliage. 2 the smooth-skinned red, purple, green, or yellow fruit of this tree, which has a hard central stone surrounded by sweet juicy flesh, eg damson, greengage. It may be eaten raw or cooked, and certain varieties are dried artificially or on the tree in order to produce prunes. 3 a raisin used in cakes, etc: *plum pudding.* 4 (*also attributive*) *colloq.* something especially valued or sought: *a plum job.* [from Anglo-Saxon *plume*, from Greek *proumnon*]

plumage *noun* a bird's feathers, especially with regard to colour. [from Old French, from *plume*, feather]

plumb[1] — *noun* a lead weight hanging on the end of a line, used for measuring water depth or for testing a wall, etc for perpendicularity. — *adj., adv.* straight, vertical, or perpendicular. — *adv.* 1 *colloq.* exactly: *plumb in the middle.* 2 *North Amer., esp. US colloq.* utterly: *plumb crazy.* — *verb* 1 to measure the depth of (water), test (a structure) for verticality, or adjust to the vertical, using a plumb. 2 to penetrate, probe, or understand (a mystery, etc).

— **out of plumb** not vertical.

plumb the depths of something to experience the worst extreme of a bad feeling, etc: *plumb the depths of misery.* [from Latin *plumbum*, lead]

plumb[2] *verb* (**plumb something in**) to connect a water-using appliance to the water supply or waste pipe. [from Latin *plumbum*, lead, used for making pipes]

plumbago *noun Chem.* graphite. [from Latin *plumbago*, Pliny's translation of the Greek name *molybdaina*, lead, lead ore]

plumber *noun* a person who fits and repairs water pipes, and water- or gas-using appliances.

plumbing *noun* **1** the system of water and gas pipes in a building, etc. **2** the work of a plumber. **3** *facetious* the lavatory.

plumbline *noun* a line with a plumb on it for measuring depth or testing for verticality.

plume — *noun* **1** an imposing feather. **2** such a feather, or a tuft or bunch of feathers, worn as an ornament or crest, represented in a coat of arms, etc. **3** a curling column (of smoke etc). — *verb* **1** *said of a bird* to clean or preen (itself or its feathers). **2** to decorate with plumes. **3** (**plume oneself on something**) to pride or congratulate oneself on something, usually trivial. [from Old French, from Latin *pluma*, soft feather]

plummet — *verb intrans.* (**plummeted, plummeting**) to fall or drop rapidly; to plunge or hurtle downwards. — *noun* the weight on a plumbline or fishing-line. [from Old French *plommet*, diminutive of *plomb*, lead]

plummy *adj.* (**plummier, plummiest**) **1** *colloq.*, *said of a job, etc* desirable; worth having; choice. **2** *derog.*, *said of a voice* affectedly or excessively rich and deep.

plump¹ — *adj.* full, rounded, fleshy, chubby, or not unattractively fat. — *verb* (*also* **plump something up**) to shake cushions or pillows to give them their full soft bulk. [from Old Dutch *plomp*, blunt]

plump² — *verb trans., intrans.* (*also* **plump down** *or* **plump something down**) to put down, drop, fall, or sit heavily. — *noun* a sudden heavy fall, or the sound of it. — *adv.* with a plump.
— **plump for something** *or* **someone** to decide on or choose them.
[imitative]

plumply *adv.* in a plump way.

plumpness *noun* being plump.

plumule *noun* **1** *Bot.* the embryonic shoot of a germinating seedling. **2** *Zool.* one of the down feathers of a bird. [from Latin *plumula*, diminutive of *pluma*, feather]

plumy *adj.* (**plumier, plumiest**) **1** covered or adorned with down or plumes. **2** like a plume.

plunder — *verb trans., intrans.* (**plundered, plundering**) to steal (valuable goods), or loot (a place), especially with open force during a war; to rob or ransack. — *noun* the goods plundered; loot; booty. [from Dutch *plunderen*]

plunderer *noun* a person who plunders.

plunge — *verb* (*usually* **plunge in** *or* **into something**) **1** *intrans.* to dive, throw oneself, fall or rush headlong. **2** *intrans.* to involve oneself rapidly and enthusiastically. **3** to thrust or push. **4** to put into a particular state or condition. **5** to dip briefly into water or other liquid. **6** *intrans.* to dip steeply: *plunging necklines / the ship plunged and rose.* — *noun* **1** an act of plunging; a dive. **2** *colloq.* a dip or swim.
— **take the plunge** *colloq.* to commit oneself finally after hesitation; to take an irreversible decision.
[from Old French *plungier*, from Latin *plumbum*, lead]

plunger *noun* **1** a rubber cup at the end of a long handle, used with thrusting action to clear blocked drains, etc. **2** a part of a mechanism that moves up and down like a piston.

pluperfect *Grammar* — *adj.* denoting a tense, formed in English by *had* and a past participle, referring to action already accomplished at the time of the past action being related, as in *they had often gone there before, but this time they lost their way.* — *noun* the pluperfect tense, or a word in the pluperfect tense. [from Latin *plus quam perfectum tempus*, more than perfect time]

plural — *noun Grammar* the form of a noun, pronoun, adjective, or verb used for two or more people, things, etc. See also SINGULAR. — *adj.* **1** *Grammar* denoting or in the plural. **2** consisting

of more than one, or of different kinds. [from Latin *plus*, more]

pluralism *noun* **1** the existence within a society of a variety of ethnic, cultural and religious groups. **2** the holding of more than one post, especially in the Church.

pluralist *noun* **1** a person who holds more than one office at once. **2** a believer in pluralism.

pluralistic *adj.* relating to or characterized by pluralism.

plurality *noun* (PL. **pluralities**) **1** the fact of being plural or more than one. **2** a large number or variety. **3** a majority that is not absolute, ie a winning number of votes that represents less than half of the votes cast; any majority.

plural society a society in which pluralism is found, ie one in which everybody has a say in the ruling of the society. According to some political scientists, the term describes the power structure of many liberal Western societies, such as the UK, USA, Sweden, France, and Germany, in which a number of pressure groups promote the interests of their members on an equal footing.

plus — *prep.* **1** *Maths.* with the addition of: *2 plus 5.* **2** in combination with; with the added factor of: *bad luck, plus his own obstinacy.* **3** (*after an amount*) with something more besides: *earns £20 000 plus.* — *adj.* **1** denoting the symbol '+': *the plus sign.* **2** mathematically positive; above zero: *plus 3°.* **3** advantageous: *a plus factor.* **4** *in grades* denoting a slightly higher mark than the letter alone: *B plus.* **5** *Physics, Electr.* electrically positive. — *noun* (PL. **pluses**) **1** (*also* **plus sign**) the symbol +, denoting addition or positive value. **2** *colloq.* something positive or good; a bonus, advantage, surplus, or extra. — *conj. colloq.* in addition to the fact that. [from Latin *plus*, more]

plus fours loose breeches gathered below the knee, once popular as golfing wear. [from *plus 4* inches of fabric extending below the knee]

plush — *noun* cotton, silk, etc fabric with a long velvety pile. — *adj.* **1** made of plush. **2** *colloq.* plushy. [from French *pluche*, earlier *peluche*, from Latin *pilus*, hair]

plushy *adj.* (**plushier, plushiest**) *colloq.* luxurious, opulent, stylish, or costly.

Plutarch *or* **Ploutarchos** (c.46–c.120 AD) Greek historian, biographer, and philosopher, born in Chaeronea, Boeotia. His extant writings comprise *Opera Moralia*, a series of essays on ethical, political, religious, and other topics, and several historical works, notably *Bioi paralleloi* (Parallel Lives), a gallery of 46 portraits of the great characters of preceding ages. Sir Thomas North's translation of this work into English (1579) was the source of Shakespeare's Roman plays.

Pluto **1** in Greek mythology, originally the god of wealth, Plutos. Hades was also called Pluton, 'the Rich One', and the name later became a synonym for Hades. **2** *Astron.* the ninth planet (or occasionally eighth) from the Sun, and the smallest planet in the solar system. Pluto's orbit normally lies outside that of Neptune, but once every 248 years its orbit brings it closer to the Sun than Neptune for about 20 years. The two planets are now in such a period (lasting from 1979 to 1999).
◊ Pluto is on average about 5.8 billion km from the Sun, and has a diameter of about 2 300km. It takes six days nine hours to rotate once on its own axis, and about 248.5 years to orbit around the Sun. Pluto is even smaller than our Moon, and its one known satellite, Charon, is about half the diameter of Pluto. It has a more elliptical orbit than any of the other planets, and in 1989 it was at its *perihelion*, ie the point when it is closest to the Sun.
Pluto is the only planet in the solar system which has not been visited by a spacecraft, and very little is known about it. It is thought to be com-

posed of rock and ice, with frozen methane on its surface, and astronomers have recently detected a very thin atmosphere of methane gas, but it is possible that this only forms when the planet is nearer the Sun, and that the gas freezes back on the surface again when Pluto is at the furthest reaches of its orbit.

plutocracy *noun* (PL. **plutocracies**) **1** government or domination by the wealthy. **2** a state governed by the wealthy. **3** an influential group whose power is backed by their wealth. [from Greek *ploutos*, wealth + -CRACY]

plutocrat *noun* **1** a member of a plutocracy. **2** *colloq.* a wealthy person.

plutocratic *adj.* relating to or characteristic of a plutocracy.

plutonic *adj. Geol.* relating to coarse-grained igneous rocks that are formed by the slow crystallization of magma deep within the Earth's crust, eg granites, gabbros.

plutonium *noun Chem.* (SYMBOL **Pu**, ATOMIC NUMBER **94**) a dense highly poisonous silvery-grey radioactive metal that is prepared in quantity from uranium-238 in breeder reactors. The isotope plutonium-239 is used as an energy source for nuclear weapons and some nuclear reactors. [named after the planet *Pluto*]

ply¹ *noun* (PL. **plies**) **1** thickness of yarn, rope, or wood, measured by the number of strands or layers that compose it: *three-ply wool.* **2** a strand or layer. [from Old French *pli*, fold]

ply² *verb* (**plies, plied**) **1** (**ply someone with something**) to keep supplying or importuning them: *plied them with drinks / plied them with questions.* **2** *trans., intrans.* (**ply between one place and another**) to travel a route regularly; to go regularly to and fro between destinations. **3** *old use* to work at (a trade). **4** *old use* to use (a tool, etc): *ply one's needle.* [from APPLY]

Plymouth POP (1992e) 258 000, a seaport in Plymouth district, Devon, SW England. It lies on Plymouth Sound, at the confluence of the Tamar and Plym rivers, 340km/211mi SW of London. Plymouth is a major base for the Royal Navy. HISTORY the home port of Sir Francis Drake; the Pilgrim Fathers set out from here in the *Mayflower* in 1620; there was much rebuilding after severe bombing in World War II. NOTABLE FEATURES Plymouth Hoe, where Drake is said to have finished his game of bowls before leaving to fight the Spanish Armada; Eddystone Lighthouse at the harbour entrance.

Plymouth POP (1980) 36 000, the seat of Plymouth County, SE Massachusetts, USA, situated on Plymouth Bay, 29km/18mi SE of Brockton. It was the first permanent European settlement in New England, founded by the Pilgrim Fathers in 1620. NOTABLE FEATURES Plymouth Rock; replica *Mayflower II*; 'living history' community at Plimoth Plantation.

Plymouth POP (1985e) 4 000, the port capital of Montserrat, Lesser Antilles, E Caribbean Sea. It is situated on the SW tip of the island.

Plymouth Brethren a religious movement founded (1827) by John Nelson Darby (1800–82) and a group of Christian evangelicals in Dublin, Ireland. It spread to England, where meetings began (1831) in Plymouth, and then throughout the English-speaking world and Europe. Millenarian in outlook, the movement is characterized by a simplicity of belief, practice, and style of life based on the New Testament. By 1848 they had split into the 'Open' and the 'Exclusive' Brethren.

Plymouth Colony the American colony established (1620) by the *Mayflower* Pilgrims (Pilgrim Fathers), comprising the south-east corner of modern Massachusetts. A separate entity until 1686, it was then absorbed into the Dominion of New England, and became part of Massachusetts in 1691.

Plynlimon Fawr a mountain on the Dyfed–Powys border, central Wales, 23km/14mi NE of Aberystwyth. HEIGHT 752m.

plywood *noun* wood made up of thin layers glued together.

Plzeň, German **Pilsen** POP (1991) 173 000, the modern industrial capital of Západočeský region, Czech Republic. It lies at the junction of the Uhlava, Uslava, Radbuza, and Mze rivers.

PM *abbrev.* **1** Paymaster. **2** Postmaster. **3** post mortem. **4** Prime Minister.

Pm *symbol Chem.* promethium.

p.m. or **pm** *abbrev. post meridiem* (Latin), after midday; in the afternoon.

PMG *abbrev.* Paymaster-General.

PMS *abbrev.* premenstrual syndrome.

PMT *abbrev.* premenstrual tension.

pneumatic *adj.* **1** relating to air or gases. **2** containing or inflated with air, eg pneumatic tyres, which are inflated by increasing the air pressure within them by means of a pump. **3** denoting a tool or piece of machinery that is operated or driven by compressed air, eg pneumatic drill. [from Greek *pneuma*, wind, breath]

pneumatically *adv.* by pneumatic means.

pneumonia *noun* inflammation of one or more lobes of the lungs, usually as a result of infection by bacteria or viruses. The *alveoli* (clustered air sacs) at the ends of the air passages become congested with fluid so that oxygen and carbon dioxide can no longer be exchanged, and the affected areas of the lung become solid. [from Greek *pneumon*, lung]
◇ The main symptoms of pneumonia are chest pain, fever, coughing, and breathlessness. Pneumonia was formerly a major cause of death, but can now be treated with antibiotics, and is much less common than previously. It is still a major risk to people whose immune sytems are suppressed, eg AIDS patients.

PNG *abbrev.* Papua New Guinea.

PO *abbrev.* **1** Petty Officer. **2** Pilot Officer. **3** Post Office.

Po, River, ancient **Padus**, German **Eridanos** the longest river in Italy, length 652km/405mi. Rising in the Cottian Alps near the French frontier, NW Italy, it flows generally E to enter the Adriatic Sea 56km/35mi S of Venice. The river has an irregular flow, tending to silt up and alter its course; there have been artificial embankments below Piacenza since ancient times. The Po Valley is the most fertile agricultural region in the country.

Po *symbol Chem.* polonium.

po[1] *noun* (PL. **pos**) *colloq.* a chamberpot.

po[2] *abbrev.* postal order.

poa *Bot.* any of various species of grass belonging to the genus *Poa*. The annual meadow grass (*P.annua*) has green hairless often wrinkled leaves, and is found mainly on waste land and as a weed. The rough meadow grass (*P.trivialis*) has rough stems, deep green sharply pointed leaves, often with a purplish tinge, and is abundant in meadows and pastures, and as a weed of cultivation. [from Greek grass]

poach[1] *verb* **1** to cook (an egg without its shell) in or over boiling water. **2** to simmer (fish) in milk or other liquid. [from Old French *pocher*, to pocket (the egg yolk inside the white), from *poche*, pocket]

poach[2] *verb* **1** *trans., intrans.* to catch (game or fish) illegally on someone else's property. **2** *intrans.* (**poach on something**) to intrude on another's territory or area of responsibility. **3** to steal (ideas, etc). **4** to lure away personnel at a rival business, etc to work for one's own. [from Old French *pocher*, to gouge]

poacher *noun* **1** a container in which to poach eggs. **2** a person who poaches game, work, customers, etc.

poaching *noun* **1** cooking by gentle simmering. **2** the activity of a poacher, stealing.

Pobedy, Peak the highest peak in the Tien Shan Range, situated on the China-Kirghizia frontier. HEIGHT 7 439m.

PO box a numbered box, pigeonhole, etc at a post office, to which mail may be sent for collection by a recipient without a permanent address.

Pocahontas, Powhatan name **Matoaka** (1595–1617) Native American princess, the daughter of the inter-tribal chief Powhatan. According to Capt John Smith, leader of a group of colonists who settled in Chesapeake Bay in 1607, she twice saved his life when he was at the mercy of her tribe. Held captive and lured by the English to Jamestown in 1612, she embraced Christianity, was baptised Rebecca, married an Englishman, John Rolfe (1585–1622), and went to England with him in 1616 to be received at court as a symbol of potentially harmonious Anglo–Indian relations. She died of smallpox off Gravesend on her way back to Virginia. She left one son, and several Virginia families claim descent from her.

pochade *noun Art* a quick sketch in colour, usually oils, made in the open air. Many landscape painters make studies of this type as a preliminary stage in the planning of a full-size picture. [from French *pochade*]

pochard any of various diving ducks found in Europe and N America. The common pochard (*Aythya ferina*) breeds in freshwater ponds and lakes, and spends the winter on brackish water, eg in coastal marshes. It has a short neck, a steep sloping forehead, and a large bill, and reveals a pale grey wing bar in flight.

pock *noun* **1** a small inflamed area on the skin, containing pus, especially one caused by smallpox. **2** a pockmark. [from Anglo-Saxon *poc*]

pocket — *noun* **1** an extra piece sewn into or on to a garment to form an enclosed section for carrying things in. **2** any container similarly fitted or attached. **3** one's financial resources: *well beyond my pocket*. **4** a rock cavity filled with ore. **5** in conditions of air turbulence, a place in the atmosphere where the air pressure drops or rises abruptly. **6** an isolated patch or area of something: *pockets of unemployment*. **7** *Billiards, etc* any of the nets or pouches hanging from the side of the table, into which balls are played. — *adj.* designed, or small enough, to be carried in a pocket; smaller than standard. — *verb* (**pocketed, pocketing**) **1** to put in one's pocket. **2** *colloq.* to take dishonestly; to steal. **3** *Billiards, etc* to drive (a ball) into a pocket. **4** to swallow or suppress (one's pride), eg to make a humble request.
— **in one another's pocket** *said of two people* in close intimacy with, or dependence on, one another.
in one's pocket in one's power.
in or **out of pocket** having gained (or lost) money on a transaction.
out-of-pocket expenses those incurred on behalf of an employer.
line one's pocket to make money, especially dishonestly or immorally, from something.
put one's hand in one's pocket to be willing to contribute money.
[from Old French *poquet*, diminutive of *poque*, from Old Dutch *poke*, pocket]

pocketbook *noun* **1** *North Amer., esp. US* a wallet for money and papers. **2** *North Amer., esp. US* a woman's strapless handbag or purse. **3** a notebook.

pocket borough *Hist.* in the UK before the 1832 Reform Act, an electoral constituency under the control of one person or family.

pocketful *noun* (PL. **pocketfuls**) the amount a pocket will hold.

pocket knife a knife with folding blades; a penknife.

pockmark *noun* a small pit or hollow in the skin left by a pock, especially in chicken-pox or smallpox.

pockmarked *adj.* pitted, scarred.

pod — *noun* **1** *Bot.* the long dry fruit produced by plants belonging to the Leguminosae family, eg peas and beans, which splits down both sides to release its seeds. **2** *Aeron.* in an aeroplane or space vehicle, a detachable container or housing, eg for an engine. — *verb* (**podded, podding**) **1** to extract (peas, beans, etc) from their pods. **2** *intrans. said of a plant* to produce pods.

Podgorniy, Nikolay Victorovich (1903–) Soviet politician, born in Karlovka, Ukraine. He joined the Communist Party (1930), and after World War II took a leading role in the economic reconstruction of the liberated Ukraine. He held various senior posts (1950–65), and after the dismissal of Khrushchev (1964) became Chairman of the Presidium of the Supreme Soviet from 1965 until 1977, when he was replaced by Brezhnev.

podgy *adj.* (**podgier, podgiest**) *derog.* plump or chubby; short and squat. [from *podge*, a short fat person]

podiatrist *noun* a chiropodist.

podiatry *noun North Amer.* chiropody. [from Greek *pod-* foot + *iatros*, doctor]

podium *noun* (PL. **podiums, podia**) **1** a small platform for a public speaker, orchestra conductor, etc. **2** *Archit.* a projecting base for a colonnade, wall, etc. [from Latin *podium*, platform, from Greek *pous*, foot]

podsol *or* **podzol** *noun Geol.* any of a group of soils characterized by a bleached upper layer, from which aluminium and iron compounds have leached, and a lower layer where they have accumulated to from a *hardpan* or iron band. Podsols are found under heathland and coniferous forests in cold temperate regions. [from Russian, from *pod*, under + *zola*, ash]

Poe, Edgar Allan (1809–49) US poet and story writer, born in Boston, Massachusetts. Orphaned at three, he was adopted and brought up partly in England. He began to write poetry, became a journalist in Richmond, then settled in Philadelphia, where he worked for literary magazines. His publications include *Tales of the Grotesque and Arabesque* (1840), and several short stories, notably 'The Murders in the Rue Morgue' (1841), the first detective story. In 1844 he moved to New York, where his poem 'The Raven' (1845) won him immediate fame.

poem *noun* **1** a composition in verse, often of elevated and imaginatively expressed content. **2** an object, scene, or creation of inspiring beauty. [from Greek *poiema*, creation, poem, from *poiein*, to make]

poesy *noun old use* poetry. [from *poiein*, to make]

poet *noun* a writer of poems. [from Greek *poietes*, from *poiein*, to make]

poetess *noun* a female poet.

poetic *adj.* **1** of, relating, or suitable to poets or poetry. **2** having grace, beauty, or inspiration suggestive of poetry.

poetical *adj.* **1** poetic. **2** written in verse: *the complete poetical works*.

poetically *adv.* **1** in a poetic way. **2** in or by means of poetry.

poetic justice a situation in which evil is punished or good rewarded in a strikingly fitting way.

poetic licence a poet's or writer's departure from strict fact or correct grammar, for the sake of effect.

Poetics, The a philosophical treatise on poetry by Aristotle (4c BC). A very influential work, it established many poetic and dramatic conventions, particularly in Classical drama.

poet laureate (PL. **poets laureate, poet laureates**) in the UK, an officially appointed court poet, commissioned to produce poems for state occasions.

Poets Laureate	
1619–37	Ben Jonson*
1638–68	Sir William Davenant*
1668–88	John Dryden
1689–92	Thomas Shadwell
1692–1715	Nahum Tate
1715–18	Nicholas Rowe
1718–30	Laurence Eusden
1730–57	Colley Cibber
1757–85	William Whitehead
1785–90	Thomas Warton
1790–1813	Henry James Pye
1813–43	Robert Southey
1843–50	William Wordsworth
1850–92	Lord Tennyson
1896–1913	Alfred Austin
1913–30	Robert Bridges
1930–67	John Masefield
1968–72	Cecil Day Lewis
1972–84	Sir John Betjeman
1984–	Ted Hughes

* The post was not officially established until 1668.

poetry *noun* **1** the art of composing poems. **2** poems collectively. **3** poetic quality, feeling, beauty, or grace. [from Latin *poetria*, from *poeta*, poet]
◊ Poetry is a comprehensive term for any literary composition which is an imaginative expression of thought, emotion, or narrative, often using figurative language, and usually (but not always) in metrical form. Blurring of the traditional distinction between poetry and prose arises when forms such as the prose poem and poetic novel are considered; and poetry is usually judged to be a more elevated form than simple verse. Broadly, two categories of poetry may be identified: lyric forms, such as the ode, sonnet, and elegy; and narrative forms, such as the epic, lay, and ballad.

po-faced *adj. derog. colloq.* wearing a disapproving expression.

pogo stick a spring-mounted pole with a handlebar and foot rests, on which to bounce, or progress by bounces.

pogrom *noun* an organized massacre, originally of Jews in 19c Russia. [from Russian *pogrom*, destruction]

poignancy *noun* a poignant quality.

poignant *adj.* **1** painful to the feelings: *a poignant reminder*. **2** deeply moving; full of pathos. [from Old French, present participle of *poindre*, to sting]

poignantly *adv.* in a poignant way.

poikilothermic *adj. Zool.* describing an animal that has no mechanism for maintaining its internal body temperature at a constant level, as a result of which its body temperature fluctuates with changes in environmental temperature. Although poikilothermic animals are often described as cold-blooded, their body temperatures may in fact reach a high level as a result of activity or basking in the sun. — Also called *cold-blooded*. [from Greek *poikilos*, variegated]

Poincaré, Jules Henri (1854–1912) French mathematician, born in Nancy. Professor in Paris from 1881, he was eminent in physics, mechanics, and astronomy, and contributed to many fields of mathematics, especially the theory of

functions. He was well known for his popular expositions of science.

Poincaré, Raymond (Nicolas Landry) (1860–1934) French statesman, Prime Minister (1912–13, 1922–24, 1926–9), and President (1913–20), born in Bar-le-Duc. He became a deputy (1887) and senator (1903), and held ministerial posts in Public Instruction, Foreign Affairs, and Finance, before being elected three times premier, and President of the Third Republic during World War I. He ordered French occupation of the Ruhr in 1923 when Germany delayed in reparation payments, and his National Union ministry averted economic ruin in 1926.

poinsettia *noun* a Central American shrub, popular because of its scarlet leaves. [from J R Poinsett (1779–1851), American Minister to Mexico]

point — *noun* **1** a sharp or tapering end or tip. **2** a dot, eg that inserted before a decimal fraction, as in *2.1* or *2·1 = two point one*. **3** a punctuation mark, especially a full stop. **4** *Geom.* a position found by means of coordinates. **5** a position, place or location: *a look-out point*. **6** a moment: *lost his temper at that point*. **7** a stage in a process, etc. **8** a stage, temperature, etc: *boiling-point*. **9** the right moment for doing something: *lost courage when it came to the point*. **10** a feature or characteristic: *her good points*. **11** a detail or particular. **12** aim or intention: *the point of this procedure*. **13** use or value: *no point in trying*. **14** the significance (of a remark, story, joke, etc). **15** a unit or mark in scoring. **16** any of the 32 directions marked on, or indicated by, a compass. **17** (*usually* **points**) an adjustable tapering rail by means of which a train changes lines. **18** *Electr.* a socket or power point. **19** (*usually* **points**) in an internal combustion engine, either of the two electrical contacts completing the circuit in the distributor. **20** *Printing* a unit of type measurement, equal to $\frac{1}{12}$ of a pica. **21** *Cricket* an off-side fielding position at right angles to the batsman. **22** (*usually* **points**) *Ballet* the tip of the toe, or a block inserted into the toe of a ballet shoe. **23** a headland or promontory. **24** (*usually* **points**) any of an animal's extremities, eg ears, tail, and feet. **25** the tip of a deer's horn or antler. — *verb* **1** to aim: *pointed a gun at her*. **2** *trans., intrans.* **a** to extend one's finger or a pointed object towards someone or something, so as to direct attention there. **b** *said of a sign, etc* to indicate a certain direction. **3** *intrans.* to extend or face in a certain direction: *lay with toes pointing upward*. **4** *intrans. said of a gun dog* to stand with the nose turned to where the dead game lies. **5** *often facetious* to direct (someone): *point me towards a pub*. **6** (**point to something** or **someone**) to indicate or suggest them: *it points to one solution*. **7** to extend (the toes) to form a point, as in dancing. **8** to fill gaps or cracks in (stonework or brickwork) with cement or mortar.
— **beside the point** irrelevant.
carry or **gain one's point** to persuade others of the validity of one's opinion.
come or **get to the point** to cut out the irrelevancies and say what one wants to say.
in point of fact actually; in truth.
make a point of doing something to be sure of doing it or take care to do it.
make one's point to state one's opinion forcefully.
on the point of doing something about to do it.
point something out to indicate or draw attention to it.
point something up to highlight or emphasize it.
score points off someone to argue cleverly and successfully against them, usually on trivial or detailed grounds.
to the point relevant.
to the point of … to a degree that could be fairly described as: *brave to the point of recklessness*.
up to a point to a limited degree.
[from Old French, from Latin *pungere*, to pierce]

point-blank — *adj.* **1** *said of a shot* fired at very close range. **2** *said of a question, refusal, etc* bluntly worded and direct. — *adv.* **1** at close range. **2** in a blunt, direct manner. [from POINT *verb* + BLANK, the white centre of a target, from French *blanc*, white]

point duty the task or station of a policeman or woman who is directing traffic.

Pointe-à-Pitre POP (1988e) 25 000, the seaport capital of Guadeloupe. It is situated on the SW coast of the island of Grande-Terre and is the largest town in Guadeloupe. Pointe-á-Pitre is a commercial, agricultural trade, and tourist centre.

pointed *adj.* **1** having, or ending in, a point. **2** *said of a remark, etc* intended for, though not directly addressed to, a particular person; intended to convey a particular meaning or message although not directly expressing it.

pointedly *adv.* in a pointed way.

pointedness *noun* being pointed.

Pointe-Noire POP (1992e) 576 000, a seaport in Kouilou province, SW Congo, W Africa. It is situated on the Atlantic coast 385km/239mi SW of Brazzaville. Harbour facilities, begun in 1934, were completed after 1945. The city is the centre of Congo's oil industry.

pointer *noun* **1** a rod used by a speaker for indicating positions on a wall map, chart, etc. **2** the indicating finger or needle on a measuring instrument. **3** *colloq.* a suggestion or hint. **4** a breed of gun dog trained to point its muzzle in the direction where the dead game lies.

Pointillism *noun Art* a method of painting by which shapes and colour tones are suggested by means of small dabs of pure colour painted side by side. It was used by certain Impressionists, and developed by Seurat and Signac into a systematic approach to the use of colour. See also DIVISIONISM. [from French *pointillisme*, from *pointillé*, stippled]

Pointillist *noun* a painter using Pointillism.

pointing *noun* the cement or mortar filling the gaps between the bricks or stones of a wall.

pointless *adj.* lacking purpose or meaning.

pointlessly *adv.* to no purpose; without a point or objective.

point of no return a stage reached in a process, etc after which there is no possibility of stopping or going back.

point of order (PL. **points of order**) a question raised in an assembly as to whether the business is being done according to the rules.

point of sale (PL. **points of sale**) the place in a shop, etc where goods are paid for; a pay desk or checkout.

point-of-sale *adj., said of a payment or computer terminal, etc* made or installed at the point of sale.

point of view (PL. **points of view**) one's own way of seeing something, influenced by personal considerations and experience; one's standpoint or viewpoint.

point-to-point *noun* (PL. **point-to-points**) a horse race across open country, from landmark to landmark.

Poirot, Hercule the small, moustached Belgian detective in *The Mysterious Affair at Styles* and many other novels by Agatha Christie.

poise — *noun* **1** self-confidence, calm, or composure. **2** grace of posture or carriage. **3** a state of equilibrium, balance, or stability eg between extremes. — *verb* **1** to balance or suspend. **2** (*often* **be poised for something** or **to do something**) to hold in a state of readiness. [from Old French *pois*, weight]

poised *adj., said of behaviour, etc* calm and dignified.

poison — *noun* **1** any substance that damages tissues or causes death when absorbed or swallowed by living organisms, especially a substance that is harmful in relatively small amounts, eg arsenic, cyanide. **2** any destructive or corrupting influence: *a poison spreading through society*. — *verb* (**poisoned, poisoning**) **1** to harm or kill with poison. **2** to put poison into (food, etc). **3** to contaminate or pollute: *rivers poisoned by effluents*. **4** to corrupt or pervert (someone's mind). **5** (**poison one person against another**) to influence them to be hostile. **6** to harm or spoil in an unpleasant or malicious way: *poison a relationship*. **7** *colloq.* to infect: *a poisoned toe*. [from Old French *puisun*, from Latin *potio*, drink, potion]

poison-arrow frog see ARROW-POISON FROG.

poisoner *noun* a person who poisons.

poison gas any of several gases used in chemical warfare, that cause injury or death through contact or inhalation.

poison ivy an American climbing plant whose leaves produce a juice that causes intense skin irritation.

poisonous *adj.* **1** liable to cause injury or death if swallowed or absorbed. **2** producing, or able to inject, a poison: *poisonous snakes*. **3** *colloq.*, *said of a person, remark, etc* malicious.

poisonously *adv.* in a poisonous way.

poison-pen letter a malicious anonymous letter.

Poisson, Siméon Denis (1781–1840) French mathematical physicist, born in Pithiviers. Professor of Mechanics at the Sorbonne, he achieved a leading position in the French scientific establishment. He published extensively on mathematical physics, discovering the important probability distribution which bears his name, although his work was often criticized for lack of originality by many of his contemporaries.

Poitiers POP (1990) 105 000, the capital of Poitou-Charentes region and of Vienne department, W France. It is a market town, situated 160km/99mi SE of Nantes. HISTORY a Roman settlement; once the capital of the ancient province of Poitou; site of a French defeat by the English in 1356. NOTABLE FEATURES 4c Baptistery (France's oldest Christian building); Cathedral of St-Pierre (12c–13c); Church of Notre-Dame-de-la-Grande (11c–12c); town hall (1869–76), containing the Musée des Beaux-Arts; Romanesque Church of St-Hilaire-le-Grand (11c–12c).

Poitou a former province of W France, now occupying the departments of Vendée, Deux-Sèvres, and Vienne. CHIEF TOWN Poitiers. The area was held by England until 1369.

poke¹ *verb* **1** to thrust (something pointed): *poke a stick into the hole*. **2** to prod or jab: *poke the fire / poked her in the ribs with his elbow*. **3** to make (a hole) by prodding. **4** *trans., intrans.* to project or cause to project: *poked his head out of the door / her big toe poked through a hole in her sock*. **5** to make (a fire) burn more brightly by stirring it with a poker. — **poke about** or **around** to search; to pry or snoop. **poke one's nose into something** *colloq.* to pry into or interfere in it. [from Middle English *poke*, from a Germanic source]

poke² *noun* Scot. a paper bag. [from Middle English *poke*, from Old Dutch]

poker¹ *noun* a metal rod for stirring a fire to make it burn better.

poker² *noun* a card game in which players bet on the hands they hold, relying on bluff to outwit their opponents.
◇ Hands are ranked, with the best being a Royal Flush, ie 10-Jack-Queen-King-Ace all of the same suit. There are many variants, the most popular being five-card draw, five-card stud, and seven-card stud. The game was invented in the USA in the 19c and was particularly popular in the gambling saloons on the Mississippi steamboats.

poker face the expressionless countenance of an experienced poker-player, or of anyone who gives nothing away.

poker-faced *adj.* having a poker-face.

pokeweed or **pokeberry** *noun Bot.* a hardy American plant of the genus *Phytolacca*, with pale yellow flowers and purple berries.

Pokhara Valley a valley in Nepal, central Asia, 203km/126mi NW of Kathmandu. The small town of Pokhara, at an altitude of 913m, is dominated by the summit of Machhapuchhre at 7 993m. The valley is accessible from Kathmandu by road and air. Pokhara is situated at the centre of one of Nepal's Development Regions.

pokiness *noun* being poky; a cramped condition.

poky *adj.* (**pokier, pokiest**) *colloq., said of a room, house, etc* small and confined or cramped. [from POKE¹]

Poland, Polish **Polska**, official name **The Republic of Poland** POP (1992e) 38.4m, a republic in central Europe, divided into 49 voivodships (provinces). AREA 312 612sq km/120 668sq mi. It is bounded N by Russia and the Baltic Sea, W by Germany, SW by the Czech Republic, S by Slovakia, SE by the Ukraine, and NE by Belorussia and Lithuania. CAPITAL Warsaw. CHIEF TOWNS Łódź, Kraków, Wrocław, Poznań, Gdańsk, Katowice, Lublin. TIME ZONE GMT +1. The population is mainly Polish, of W Slavic descent, with Ukrainian, Belorussian, and Jewish minorities; Roman Catholicism is the chief religion. OFFICIAL LANGUAGE Polish. CURRENCY the złoty. PHYSICAL DESCRIPTION mostly part of the great European plain, with the Carpathian and Sudetes Mts in the S rising in the High Tatra to 2 499m at Mt Rysy; the Polish plateau in the N of the Tatra is cut by the Bug, San, and Vistula rivers; Europe's richest coal basin lies in the W (Silesia); N of the plateau there are lowlands with many lakes; the Baltic coastal area is flat, with sandy heathland and numerous lagoons (coastline length is 491km/305mi); the main Polish rivers are the Vistula and Oder; rivers are often frozen in winter, and liable to flood; forests cover one fifth of the land. CLIMATE continental climate, with severe winters and hot summers; rain falls chiefly in summer and seldom exceeds 650mm annually. HISTORY the Poles emerged as the most powerful of a number of Slavic groups in 1025; united with Lithuania in 1569; weakened by attacks from Russia, Brandenburg, Turkey, and Sweden; eventually in 1772, 1793, and 1795 Poland was divided between Prussia, Russia, and Austria; became a semi-independent state following the 1815 Congress of Vienna, and was incorporated into the Russian Empire; the independent Polish state emerged after World War I; Germany invaded Poland in 1939; partition of Poland between Germany and the USSR in the same year; there was a major resistance movement, and a government in exile during World War II; a People's Democracy was established under Soviet influence in 1944 and by 1947 Communists controlled the Government; rise of an independent trade union, Solidarity, in the late 1970s; from 1981 to 1983 Solidarity leaders were detained, and a state of martial law was imposed; worsening economic situation, with continuing unrest in the 1980s; there was loss of support for the Communist government and major success for Solidarity in the 1989 elections; the transition to a market economy was accompanied by popular discontent and political difficulties. GOVERNMENT the constitution was amended in 1989 to provide for a two-chamber legislature, comprising a 460-member Lower Assembly (the *Seym*) and a 100-member Senate. ECONOMY nearly 50% of the land is under cultivation, growing rye, wheat, barley, oats, potatoes, and sugar beet; bacon, eggs, geese, turkeys, pork; major producer of coal; other deposits include lead, zinc, sulphur, potash, and copper; major industries are ship-

building, vehicles, machinery, electrical equipment, food processing, and textiles.

Poland

Poland, Partitions of agreements between Russia, Austria, and Prussia to partition a weakening Poland in the late 18c. The first, second, and third partitions (1772, 1793, 1795) deprived Poland of its independent statehood and gave Russia the lion's share of its territories. Throughout the 19c and early 20c the Poles struggled for national liberation, which they eventually won at the end of World War I (1918).

Polanski, Roman (1933–) Franco-Polish film director, scriptwriter, and actor, born in Paris. Brought up in Poland, he started film work there as an actor, then writer and director, his first feature *Nóz w Wodzie* (The Knife in the Water, 1962), finding international recognition. His films explored the nature of evil and personal corruption, as in his first Hollywood film, *Rosemary's Baby* (1968). Later productions include *Chinatown* (1974), controversial interpretations of *Macbeth* (1971) in England and *Tess* (1979) in France, *Frantic* (1988), and *Bitter Moon* (1992).

Polanyi, Michael (1891–1976) Hungarian physical chemist and social philosopher, born in Budapest. He lectured at Berlin, but after Hitler's rise to power, emigrated to Britain, and became Professor of Physical Chemistry (1933–48) and of Social Studies (1948–58) at Manchester. He did notable work on reaction kinetics and crystal structure, and wrote much on the freedom of scientific thought, philosophy of science, and social science.

polar *adj.* **1** relating to the earth's North or South Pole or the regions round them. **2** relating to, or having, electric or magnetic poles. **3** as different as possible: *polar opposites*. [from Latin *polaris*, from *polus*, from Greek *polos*, pivot, axis, pole]

polar bear a large white bear (*Thalarctos maritimus*) belonging to the same family (Ursidae) as the brown bear, but found only in the Arctic region, and having thick creamy-white fur, and a smaller more pointed head and longer neck than most other bears.
◇ The polar bear grows to a length of up to 2.7m, and weighs up to 790kg. It survives the cold because its thick coat consists of a layer of dense fur lying beneath the long visible guard hairs, and a thick layer of fat beneath the skin provides further insulation. The undersides of its broad feet are hairy, enabling it to walk on the ice without slipping. Polar bears are strong swimmers, and prey mainly on seals, but they also eat fish, sea birds and, in spring and early summer, grass, lichen, seaweed, and berries. Formerly hunted for their skins, they are now protected by international agreement.

Polar Circle see ARCTIC CIRCLE.

polarimetry *noun Physics* the measurement of the optical activity of any of various chemical compounds which, when placed in the path of a beam of polarized light, rotate the plane of polarization of light to the left or to the right. The optical activity can be used to identify and measure concentrations of transparent solutions such as sugar solutions.

Polaris *noun* **1** *Astron.* the Pole Star, the brightest star in the constellation Ursa Minor, currently lying within one degree of the north celestial pole. It was formerly much used for navigation. **2** a guide or director. [from Greek *polos*, pivot, axis, firmament]

Polaris missile a first-generation US submarine-launched ballistic missile under development from the mid-1950s. The US Navy's first Polaris deterrent patrol was made in 1960, and the system was operational with the Royal Navy in 1968. It is no longer operational with the US Navy; a modified version with three separate warheads and advanced penetration aids was maintained by the Royal Navy's four Polaris-equipped submarines, but is currently (since 1993) being replaced by the Trident system.

polarity *noun* (PL. **polarities**) **1** the state of having two opposite poles: *magnetic polarity.* **2** the status, i.e. whether positive or negative, of an electrode, etc: *negative polarity.* **3** the tendency to develop, or be drawn, in opposite directions; oppositeness or an opposite: *the political polarities of left and right.*

polarization *or* **polarisation** *noun* **1** *Chem.* the separation of the positive and negative charges of an atom or molecule, especially by an electric field. **2** *Physics* the process whereby waves of electromagnetic radiation, eg light, which would normally vibrate in all directions, are restricted to vibration in one direction only. Lasers produce polarized light, and some sunglasses reduce glare by blocking polarized reflected light.

polarize *or* **polarise** *verb* **1** to give magnetic or electrical polarity to. **2** to restrict the vibrations of electromagnetic waves, eg light, to one direction only by the process of polarization. **3** *trans., intrans.* said of people or opinions to split according to opposing views.

polarizing filter *Telecomm.* a filter which allows the passage of light which is polarized in one direction only. It is used in general photography for the control of surface reflections, eg from glass or water, and to darken blue skies. Other applications include definition of mineral structures in photomicrography.

Polaroid *noun trademark* a plastic material able to polarize light, used in sunglasses, etc to reduce glare.

Polaroid camera a camera with an internal developing and printing process, which produces a print within seconds of exposure.

polder *noun* an area of land lying below sea level, from which the sea has been drained; a piece of reclaimed land. [from Old Dutch *polre*]

Pole, Reginald (1500–58) English Roman Catholic churchman, born in Stourton Castle, Staffordshire. He received several Church posts, and gained Henry VIII's favour, but lost it after opposing the King on divorce and left for Italy, where he was made a cardinal by the pope (1536). In 1554, during the reign of the Catholic Queen Mary, he returned to England as papal legate, became one of her most powerful advisers, returned the country to Rome, and became Archbishop of Canterbury.

Pole *noun* a native or citizen of Poland.

pole¹ *noun* **1** either of two points representing the north and south ends of the axis about which the Earth rotates, and known as the North Pole and South Pole, respectively. **2** *Astron.* either of two corresponding points on the celestial sphere, towards which the north and south ends of the Earth's axis point, and about which the stars appear to rotate daily. **3** same as magnetic pole. **4** either of the two terminals of a battery. **5** either

of two opposite positions in argument, opinion, etc.
— **poles apart** *colloq.* widely different or apart. [from Latin *polus*, from Greek *polos*, axis, pivot]
◊ The North Pole is covered by the Arctic Ocean, and the South Pole by the land mass of Antarctica. The magnetic poles are the positions towards which the needle of a magnetic compass will point. They differ from the geographical poles by an angle known as the *declination* or *magnetic variation*, which itself varies at different points of the Earth's surface and at different times.
The Norwegian explorer, Amundsen, first reached the South Pole on 14 Dec 1911, a month before the British team, led by Scott, which arrived on 17 Jan 1912. The North Pole was first reached by US explorer Robert E Peary in Apr 1909.

pole² *noun* **1** a rod, especially cylindrical in section and fixed in the ground as a support. **2** an old measure of length equal to 5½yd; a perch or rod.
— **up the pole** *colloq.* mad; crazy.
[from Anglo-Saxon *pal*, from Latin *palus*, stake]

poleaxe — *noun* **1** a short-handled axe with a spike or hammer opposite the blade, used, especially formerly, for slaughtering cattle. **2** *Hist.* a long-handled battleaxe. — *verb* to strike, fell, or floor with or as if with a poleaxe. [from Middle English *pollax*, head axe, from POLL, head]

polecat *noun* **1** a dark-brown animal of the weasel family, that emits a foul smell. **2** *North Amer., esp. US* a skunk. [from Middle English *polcat*]

polemic — *noun* a piece of writing or a speech fiercely attacking or defending an idea, opinion, etc; writing or oratory of this sort. — *adj.* (also **polemical**) relating to or involving polemic or polemics. [from Greek *polemikos*, from *polemos*, war]

polemically *adv.* in a polemic way, controversially.

polemicist *noun* someone who writes polemics or engages in controversy.

polemics *sing. or pl. noun* the art of verbal wrangling; the cut and thrust of fierce disputation.

polenta *noun* an Italian dish of cooked ground maize. [from Italian, from Latin *polenta*, hulled and crushed grain]

pole position the position at the inside of the front row of cars at the start of a race; an advantageous position at the start of any contest.

Pole Star a popular name for the star *Polaris.*

pole vault an athletic event consisting of a jump over a high horizontal bar with the help of a long flexible pole to haul one's body into the air.

pole-vaulter *noun* an athlete who takes part in a pole-vault.

police — *pl. noun* **1** the body of men and women employed by the government of a country to keep order, enforce the law, prevent crime, etc. **2** members of this body: *over 200 police were on duty.* — *verb* **1** to keep law and order in (an area) using the police, army, etc. **2** to supervise (an operation, etc) to ensure that it is fairly or properly run. [from French *police*, from Greek *politeia*, political constitution]

police constable a police officer of the lowest rank.

police dog a dog trained to work with policemen.

policeman *noun* a police officer.

police officer a member of a police force.

police state a state with a repressive government that operates through secret police to eliminate opposition to it.

police station the office of a local police force.

policewoman *noun* a female police officer.

policy¹ *noun* (PL. **policies**) **1** a plan of action, usually based on certain principles, decided on by a body or individual. **2** a principle or set of principles on which to base decisions: *it is not our policy to charge for service.* **3** a course of conduct for following: *your best policy is to keep quiet.* [from Old French *policie*, from Greek *politeia*, political constitution]

policy² *noun* (PL. **policies**) (also **insurance policy**) an insurance agreement, or the document confirming it. [from Old French *police*, from Latin *apodixis*, receipt, from Greek *apodeixis*, proof]

policy-holder *noun* a person who holds a contract of insurance.

policy unit *Politics* a group of officials in a government department or other public agency, whose role is to supply information, advice, and analysis to policy makers.

Polignac, Auguste Jules Armand Marie, Prince de (1780–1847) French statesman, born in Versailles. He was arrested for conspiring against Napoleon (1804), became a peer at the Bourbon Restoration, and received the title of prince from the pope in 1820 for being a committed exponent of papal and royal authority. English Ambassador in 1823, in 1829 he became head of the last Bourbon ministry, which decreed the St Cloud Ordinances that cost Charles X his throne (1830). Imprisoned until 1836, he then lived in exile in England, and returned to Paris in 1845.

polio *noun colloq.* poliomyelitis.

poliomyelitis *noun* a viral disease of the brain and spinal cord, in some cases resulting in permanent paralysis. [from Greek *polios*, grey + *myelos*, marrow + -ITIS]

Polish — *adj.* of or relating to Poland, its language, culture, or people. — *noun* the language of Poland.
◊ Polish is a Slavic language of the Indo-European family, with some 35–40 million speakers in Poland and surrounding areas, and the USA.

polish — *verb* **1** *trans., intrans.* to make or become smooth and glossy by rubbing. **2** to improve or perfect. **3** to make cultivated, refined, or elegant: *polished manners.* — *noun* **1** a substance used for polishing surfaces. **2** a smooth shiny finish; a gloss. **3** an act of polishing. **4** refinement or elegance.
— **polish something off** *colloq.* to complete work, etc or consume food, especially speedily.
polish something up 1 to work up a shine on it by polishing. **2** to improve a skill, etc by working at it.
[from Old French *polir*, from Latin *polire*]

polisher *noun* a person, device, or machine that polishes.

politburo *noun* (PL. **politburos**) (also **Politburo**) the policy-forming committee of a Communist state. [from Russian *politburo*]

polite *adj.* **1** well-mannered; considerate towards others; courteous. **2** well-bred, cultivated, or refined: *polite society.* [from Latin *politus*, from *polire*, to polish]

politely *adv.* in a polite way.

politeness *noun* being polite, courtesy.

politic — *adj.* **1** *said of a course of action* prudent; wise; shrewd. **2** *said of a person* cunning; crafty. **3** *old use* political: *the body politic* (= the people of a state considered as a political group). — *verb intrans.* (**politicked, politicking**) *derog.* to indulge in politics. [from Old French *politique*, from Greek *politikos*, civic]

political *adj.* **1** of or relating to government or public affairs. **2** relating to politics. **3** interested or involved in politics. **4** *said of a course of action* made in the interests of gaining or keeping power. **5** *said of a map* showing political and social structure rather than physical features.

political asylum protection given by a country to political refugees from a foreign country.

political correctness the avoidance of expressions or actions that may be understood to exclude or denigrate people on the grounds of race, gender, or sexual orientation.

politically *adv.* in a political way; in terms of politics.

political prisoner a person imprisoned for dissenting from the government.

political science the study of politics and government.

politician *noun* **1** someone engaged in politics, especially as a member of parliament. **2** *derog.* someone who goes in for power-seeking manoeuvres. [from Greek *politikos*, civic]

politicization *or* **politicisation** *noun* politicizing or being politicized.

politicize *or* **politicise** *verb* **1** *intrans.* to go in for political activities or discussion. **2** to give a political nature to: *the politicizing of sport.* **3** to make (someone) aware of or informed about politics.

politico *noun* (PL. **politicos**, **politicoes**) *derog.* a politician or someone keen on politics. [from Italian or Spanish *politico*]

politico- *combining form* forming words meaning 'political': *politico-philosophical writings.*

politics *noun* (*usually sing.*) **1** the science or business of government. **2** political science. **3** a political life as a career. **4** (*sing., pl.*) political activities, wrangling, etc. **5** (*pl.*) moves and manoeuvres concerned with the acquisition of power or getting one's way, eg in business. **6** (*pl.*) one's political sympathies or principles: *what are your politics?*

polity *noun* (PL. **polities**) **1** a politically organized body such as a state, church, or association. **2** any form of political institution or government. [from Greek *politeia*, political constitution]

Polixenes the king of Bohemia, and father of Florizel, in Shakespeare's *The Winter's Tale*, who is accused by his friend Leontes of having an affair with his wife Hermione.

Polk, James K(nox) (1795–1849) US statesman, the 11th President, born in Mecklenburg Co, North Carolina. Admitted to the Bar in 1820, he entered Congress as a Democrat (1825), and became Governor of Tennessee (1839). During his presidency (1845–9) Texas was admitted to the Union (1845), after the Mexican War (1846–7) the USA acquired California and New Mexico, and the Oregon boundary was settled by a compromise with England. His policies included condemnation of the antislavery agitation, and commitment to state rights, a revenue tariff, and an independent treasury.

polka — *noun* a lively dance performed usually with a partner, with a pattern of three steps followed by a hop; also, a piece of music for this. — *verb intrans.* (**polkaed**, **polkaing**) to dance a polka. [from Czech *pulka*, half-step, or *Polka*, polish woman]

polka dot any of numerous regularly spaced dots forming a pattern on fabric, etc.

poll — *noun* **1** (**polls**) a political election: *victory at the polls.* **2** the voting, or votes cast, at an election: *a heavy poll.* **3** (*also* **opinion poll**) a survey of public opinion carried out by directly questioning a representative sample of the populace. **4** *old use* the head; this as a unit in numbering. — *verb* **1** to win (a number of votes) in an election. **2** to register the votes of (a population). **3** *trans., intrans.* to cast (one's vote). **4** to conduct an opinion poll among. **5** to cut off the horns of (cattle). **6** to cut the top off (a tree); to make a pollard of. [from Middle English *polle*, (the hair of) the head]

pollack *noun* (PL. **pollack**, **pollacks**) an edible fish of northern waters, related to the cod.

pollard — *noun* **1** *Bot.* a tree whose branches have been cut back, usually to a height of about 2m above the ground, in order to produce a crown of shoots at the top of the trunk, out of reach of farm livestock and deer. Wood is then periodically harvested for firewood, fencing, etc. **2** *Zool.* an animal whose horns have been removed. — *verb* to make a pollard of (a tree or animal). [from POLL + suffix -*ard* denoting a person, animal, etc of a certain type]

pollen *noun* the fine dust-like powder, usually yellow in colour, that is produced by the anthers of the stamens of angiosperms (flowering plants), and by the male cones of gymnosperms (cone-bearing plants).
See POLLINATION.
◇ Pollen consists of a mass of tiny grains (known as *microspores*), each containing a developing male gamete (reproductive cell). The pollen grains of wind-pollinated plants are usually smooth and light, whereas those of insect-pollinated plants are usually larger, with rough, sticky, or spiny walls that adhere to the hairs of bees and other insects.

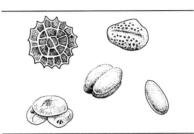

pollen grain shapes

pollen count a measure of the amount of pollen in the air at any particular time, published for the benefit of those who have a pollen allergy.

pollen sac *Bot.* in flowering plants, one of the four cavities in the anther of a stamen in which the pollen is produced and stored.

pollen tube *Bot.* a slender tube that grows out from the wall of a pollen grain after pollination. In flowering plants it grows down through the stigma and style, and into the ovule, and carries within it two male gametes, one of which fertilizes the egg cell after the pollen tube has entered the ovule.

pollinate *verb Bot.* in flowering and cone-bearing plants, to transfer pollen by the process of pollination in order to achieve fertilization and subsequent development of seed. [from Latin *pollen*, flour]

pollination *noun Bot.* in flowering plants, the transfer of pollen from the anther of a stamen to the stigma of the same flower (*self-pollination*) or another flower of the same species (*cross-pollination*). In cone-bearing plants it involves the transfer of pollen from the male cone to the female cone. Pollination can be achieved by any of a number of different agents, eg insects, wind, water, birds, or humans.

polling-booth *noun* an enclosed compartment at a polling-station in which to mark one's ballot paper in private.

polling-station *noun* the centre one attends to cast one's vote.

Pollitt, Big Daddy the rich, vulgar Mississippi cotton planter in Tennessee Williams' *Cat on a Hot Tin Roof.* The play also features his strident, loquacious wife, Big Mama, his favourite son Brick, who is an introverted alcoholic, and his elder son Gooper, who is grasping and hypocritical.

Pollock, (Paul) Jackson (1912–56) US artist, born in Cody, Wyoming. He is best known for his 'drip' paintings (the paint is poured or dripped onto the canvas, rather than painted with a brush) which first appeared in 1947. This technique of painting resulted in him being identified as one of the leading exponents of 'action painting' in the USA. His works include *One* and the black and white *Echo and Blue Poles.*

pollster *noun* a person who organizes opinion polls.

poll tax 1 *Hist.* a fixed tax levied on each member of a population. **2** the community charge.
◇ A poll tax was first levied on each adult or 'head' in 1377, and periodically reimposed (eg in 1513, 1641, and in the reign of Charles II). The idea that each member of the adult population should make a contribution to the cost of local government was the main principle behind the *community charge* introduced by the Conservative government, but, as with previous poll taxes, it soon proved to be unworkable.

pollutant — *noun* something that pollutes. — *adj.* polluting.

pollute *verb* **1** to contaminate with harmful substances; to make impure. **2** to corrupt (someone's mind, etc). [from Latin *polluere*, to soil, defile]

pollution *noun* the adverse effect on the natural environment, including human, animal, or plant life, of a harmful substance that does not occur naturally (eg industrial and radioactive waste, pesticides), or the concentration to harmful levels of a naturally occurring substance (eg nitrates). It also includes the damaging effects of noise and changes in temperature.
◇ *Air pollution* occurs when poisonous gases are released into the atmosphere, eg carbon monoxide from vehicle exhaust emissions, smoke from factory chimneys, nitrogen oxide and sulphur dioxide from burning fossil fuels. Acid rain, which damages vegetation, kills aquatic life, and erodes buildings, is a form of air pollution. *Water pollution* is caused by the discharge of harmful materials, such as heavy metals, industrial waste, chemical fertilizers, or pesticides, into rivers, streams, or lakes. *Thermal pollution* (heat pollution) occurs, for example, when hot but otherwise pure water that has been used for industrial cooling is released into rivers, as the rise in water temperature may be harmful to aquatic wildlife. *Noise pollution* can be caused by excessive noise from aircraft, traffic, etc. *Land pollution* is caused by the dumping of rubbish, eg on landfill sites, and *marine pollution* occurs when the sea is contaminated by sewage, oil spills, or the dumping of highly toxic materials.

Polo, Marco (1254–1324) Venetian merchant and traveller, born in Venice. He accompanied his father and uncle on their second journey (1271–5) to the court of Kublai Khan in China (the first had been made in 1260–9). Marco

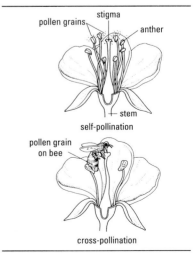

types of pollination

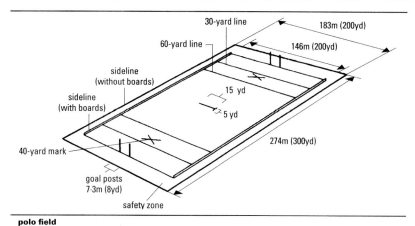

polo field

became an envoy in Kublai's service, and served as Governor of Yang Chow. He left China in 1292, and after returning to Venice (1295), fought against the Genoese, but was captured. During his imprisonment, he compiled an account of his travels: *Il milione* (The Million, translated as The Travels of Marco Polo), which became widely read.

polo *noun* a stick-and-ball game played on horseback by teams of four using long-handled hammers to propel the ball along the ground. [from Tibetan dialect *polo*, ball]
◇ When the side lines of the ground are boarded, the playing area measures 274m by 146m, making it the largest of all ball games. The object is to strike the ball with a hand-held mallet into the opposing goal, which measures 7.3m wide by 3m high. Each game is divided into seven-minute periods known as *chukkas*. The number of chukkas varies according to each competition. Polo was first played in central Asia c.500 BC.

polonaise *noun* a stately Polish promenading dance, or a piece of music for this. [from French *polonaise*, feminine of *polonais*, Polish]

polo neck 1 a high close-fitting neck band on a sweater or shirt, worn folded over. **2** a sweater or shirt with such a neck.

polo-neck *adj.* having a polo neck.

polonium *noun Chem.* (SYMBOL **Po**, ATOMIC NUMBER **84**) a rare radioactive metal that emits alpha particles, occurs naturally in uranium ores, and is prepared artificially by bombarding bismuth with neutrons. It is used in portable radiation sources, as an energy source in satellites, and for dissipating static electricity. [from Latin *Polonia*, Poland, the discoverer's native country]

Polonius the Lord Chamberlain, and father to Laertes and Ophelia in Shakespeare's *Hamlet*, whose pompous meddling eventually costs him his life.

Polonnaruwa POP (1981) 12 000, the capital of Polonnaruwa district, North Central province, Sri Lanka. It lies on the N shore of L Parakrama Samudra. The city has many fine buildings dating from the 11c–14c, when it was the island's capital. It was formerly fortified by three concentric walls. Today the town is a World Heritage site. NOTABLE FEATURES King Parakrama Bahu's Palace, Kumara Pokuna.

polony *noun* (PL. **polonies**) a dry sausage made of partly cooked meat. [probably from *Bologna*, Italy]

Pol Pot (1928–) Cambodian politician, born in Kompong Thom Province. He was active in the anti-French resistance under Ho Chi Minh, and in 1946 joined the pro-Chinese Communist Party. As leader of the Khmer Rouge guerrillas, he defeated Lon Nol's military government (1976) and became Prime Minister. He set up a

totalitarian regime which caused the death, imprisonment, or exile of millions, but was overthrown in 1979, when the Vietnamese invaded Cambodia. He withdrew to the mountains to lead the Khmer Rouge forces in guerilla warfare. In 1991 he signed the Paris Peace Accords and returned the Khmer Rouge to Phnom Penh, but despite the peace settlement and his official 'retirement' from the Khmer Rouge (1985), he apparently led a later brutal campaign against Cambodia's ethnic Vietnamese people (1993).

Poltava POP (1991e) 320 000, the industrial capital of Poltava region, Ukraine, lying on the R Vorskla. HISTORY one of the oldest settlements in the Ukraine, known since the 7c; site of a Swedish defeat by Peter the Great in 1709; the first Marxist circles arose here in the 1890s. NOTABLE FEATURE Cathedral of the Krestovozdvizhenskii Monastery (1689–1709).

poltergeist *noun* a type of household ghost responsible for otherwise unaccountable noises, given also to shifting objects about. [from German *poltern*, to make a racket + *Geist*, spirit, ghost]

poltroon *noun* a despicable coward. [from Italian *poltrone*, lazybones]

poly *noun* (PL. **polys**) *noun colloq.* a polytechnic.

poly- *combining form* forming words meaning: **1** many or much. **2** *Chem.* polymerized. [from Greek *poly*, many, much]

polyamide *noun Chem.* a polymer formed by the linking of the amino group of one molecule with the carboxyl group of the next, eg nylon.

polyandrous *adj.* **1** having more than one husband at the same time. **2** *Bot.* having many stamens. See also MONANDROUS. [from POLY- + Greek *aner*, man, husband]

polyandry *noun* the custom or practice of having more than one husband at the same time.

polyanthus *noun* (PL. **polyanthuses**) a cultivated hybrid plant related to the primrose, with several brightly coloured flowers to each stem. [from POLY- + Greek *anthos*, flower]

polyarchy *noun Politics* government by the many: a characteristic of modern, Western, liberal democracies. The main features are opposition, and the absence of strictly hierarchical organizations (these tend to be segmented with people participating in political processes of direct interest to them).

polycarbonate *noun Chem.* a strong rigid thermoplastic material, formed by the polymerization of monomers that are linked to each other by means of carbonate groups, and used to make safety helmets, protective windows, soft drink bottles, and electrical terminals.

Polycarp, St (c.69–c.155 AD) Greek Christian martyr and one of the Apostolic Fathers. He was Bishop of Smyrna during the little-known period

between the Apostle John, who was his teacher in Ephesus, and his own disciple Irenaeus. The author of the *Epistle to the Philippians*, he visited Rome to discuss the timing of Easter, and was martyred on his return to Smyrna. His feast day is 23 Feb.

polycentrism *noun Politics* the condition of having, or the tendency to have, many centres. In politics, the term has been applied to the growing independence of European communist parties from the Soviet Union after the Stalinist era. This trend was begun by the Yugoslavian Communist Party under Tito, and was adopted to varying degrees by other national parties as a means of taking account of local conditions.

polychromatic *adj.* **1** multicoloured. **2** *said of radiation* having more than one wavelength. [from POLY- + Greek *chroma*, colour]

polychromy *noun* **1** *Art* the practice of colouring sculpture, especially common in ancient Egypt and Greece, and in medieval times, but largely abandoned from c.1500 in favour of monochrome sculpture. It has been revived in the 20c. **2** *Archit.* the use of coloured marbles, bricks, flint, stone, etc on buildings for decorative effect.

Polyclitus (5c BC) Greek sculptor from Samos. He was a contemporary of Phidias, and was known for his statues of athletes, which were often copied. His best-known work is the bronze statue *Doryphorus* (Spear Bearer).

Polycrates (6c BC) tyrant of Samos (540–522 BC), who established Samos as a major naval power in the E Aegean. He allied Samos with Egypt but later supported Cambyses of Persia in his invasion of Egypt. He was lured to the mainland by a Persian satrap, Oroetes, and crucified.

polyester *noun* a synthetic resin made from certain alcohols and acids, and used to form artificial fibres, eg Terylene®, that are strong, durable, resistant to creasing, and quick drying. These are widely used in textiles to make clothing, often in blends with natural fibres. [from POLY- + ESTER]

polyethylene *noun* polythene.

polygamist *noun* a person who has more than one husband or wife at the same time.

polygamous *adj.* having more than one husband or wife at the same time.

polygamously *adv.* in a polygamous way.

polygamy *noun* the custom or practice of having more than one husband/wife at the same time. [from POLY- + *gamos*, marriage]
◇ Polygamy is permitted in Islam (where a man may have up to four wives) and is still common in African tribal societies. Certain Christian sects, such as the Mormons, have practised polygamy.

polyglot — *adj.* speaking, using, or written in, many languages. — *noun* a person who speaks many languages. [from POLY- + *glotta*, tongue, language]

polygon *noun Geom.* a plane (two-dimensional) figure with a number of straight sides, usually more than three, eg pentagon, hexagon, octagon. In a *regular polygon* all the sides are of the same length, and all the internal angles are equal. The greater the number of sides, the larger the sum of the internal angles, and the more closely the polygon resembles a circle. [from Greek *poly-*, many + *gonia*, angle]

polygonal *adj.* having the form of a polygon, many-sided.

polygraph *noun Medicine* a device that monitors several body functions simultaneously, eg pulse, blood pressure, and conductivity of the skin (to detect perspiration). Such devices have sometimes been used as lie-detectors, although the scientific accuracy of the data obtained is debatable, and cannot generally be used as legal evidence. [from POLY- + *graphein*, to write]

polygyny *noun* the condition or custom of having more than one wife at the same time. [from POLY- + Greek *gyne*, woman, wife]

polyhedral *adj.* having the form of a polyhedron, many-sided.

polyhedron *noun* (PL. **polyhedrons**, **polyhedra**) *Geom.* a solid (three-dimensional) figure with four or more faces, all of which are polygons, eg tetrahedron (four triangular faces). In a *regular polyhedron* all the faces are regular polygons, eg cube (six square faces), and the greater the number of faces, the more closely the polyhedron resembles a sphere. [from Greek *poly-*, many + *hedra*, seat, base, face]

Polyhymnia in Greek mythology, one of the Muses, associated with dancing or mime.

polymath *noun* a person who is learned in a large variety of subjects. [from POLY- + *manthanein*, to learn]

polymer *noun Chem.* a very large molecule consisting of a long chain of much smaller molecules (*monomers*) linked end to end to form a series of repeating units.
◇ Polymers may occur naturally, eg proteins, DNA, starch, cellulose, natural rubber, or they may be manufactured artificially, eg plastics such as polythene and polystyrene, and artificial fibres such as nylon and polyester. Many polymers contain thousands of monomers.
[from Greek *poly-*, many + *meros*, part]

polymeric *adj.* related to or of the nature of a polymer.

polymerization *or* **polymerisation** *noun Chem.* a chemical reaction in which two or more small molecules or *monomers* are joined together in a chain to form a large molecule or *polymer*.

polymerize *or* **polymerise** *verb trans., intrans. Chem.* to undergo or cause to undergo polymerization.

polymorphism *noun* **1** *Biol.* the occurrence of a living organism in two or more different structural forms at different stages of its life cycle. **2** *Genetics* the occurrence of several genetically determined and distinct forms within a single population, eg the different blood groups in humans. **3** *Chem.* the occurrence of a chemical substance in two or more different crystalline forms, eg diamond and graphite are different crystalline forms of carbon.

polymorphous *or* **polymorphic** *adj. Biol.* **1** denoting a living organism that occurs in different structural forms at different stages of its life cycle. **2** denoting a species or population in which several distinct forms exist, eg worker, drone, and queen bees. [from POLY- + Greek *morphe*, shape]

Polynices *or* **Polyneices** in Greek legend, the second son of Oedipus, who led the Seven against Thebes. He killed, and was killed by, his brother Eteocles. Creon's refusal to bury him led eventually to the death of Antigone.

polyp *noun* **1** *Zool.* a tiny tube-shaped sea creature with a ring of tentacles round its mouth. **2** *Pathol.* a small growth with a stalk-like base, projecting from the mucous membrane, eg inside the nose. [from Greek *polypous*, many-footed, from *poly-*, many + *pous*, foot]

Polyphemus in Greek mythology, one of the Cyclopes, who imprisoned Odysseus and some of his companions in his cave. They blinded his one eye, and escaped by hanging onto the undersides of the sheep when they were let out of the cave to graze.

polyphonic *adj.* **1** having many voices. **2** relating to polyphony.

polyphony *noun* a style of musical composition in which each part or voice has an independent melodic value (as distinct from *homophony*, in which only one part or voice carries the melody, with simple choral accompaniment).

True polyphony first appeared in the 11c, and its most important forms are the motet, the rota or round, the canon, polyphonic masses, madrigals, and (in the 18c) the fugue. The term generally denotes contrapuntal music. [from Greek *poly*, much, many + *phōne*, a voice, sound]

polyploidy *noun Genetics* the condition in which three or more sets of chromosomes are present within a cell nucleus. It arises spontaneously and is common in many crop plants, including wheat, but rarely occurs in animals (and would result in sterility).

polypous *adj.* of the nature of a polyp.

polypropene *noun Chem.* a white translucent thermoplastic, formed by the polymerization of propene (propylene), that is tough, and resistant to water, solvents, oil, and high temperatures. It is used to make fibres, film, rope, and moulded articles, eg toys.

polypropylene *noun* same as POLYPROPENE.

polyptych *noun* an altarpiece consisting of several panels with a separate picture in each, surrounded by an elaborate, usually gilded, frame. Common in the Middle Ages, the form was partly superseded in the Renaissance by the unified *pala d'altare*. [from POLY- + Greek *ptychos*, a fold]

polysaccharide *noun Biochem.* a large carbohydrate molecule consisting of a large number of monosaccharides (simple sugars) linked together to form long chains which may or may not be branched, eg starch, cellulose.

polystyrene *noun Chem.* a tough transparent thermoplastic, formed by the polymerization of styrene (phenylethene), that is a good thermal and electrical insulator, with a high resistance to impact. It is widely used in packaging, insulation, ceiling tiles, etc, and can also be expanded to form polystyrene foam.

polysyllabic *adj., said of a word* having three or more syllables.

polysyllable *noun* a word of three or more syllables.

polysynthetic language a language type using long and complex words made up of many smaller words, parts of words, and inflected forms. Examples include certain Native American languages such as Mohawk and Eskimo, and the Australian aboriginal languages.

polytechnic — *noun* a college of higher education in which courses in a large range of subjects, especially of a technical or vocational kind, are available. — *adj.* relating to technical training. [from POLY- + Greek *techne*, art]
◇ In the UK, many former polytechnics offer degree courses and have been redesignated universities. Their main emphasis remains in the technical and vocational areas and many have close links with industry.

polytheism *noun* belief in, or worship of, more than one god. [from POLY- + Greek *theos*, god]

polytheist *noun* a believer in the doctrine of polytheism.

polytheistic *adj.* relating to or characterized by polytheism.

polythene *noun* a waxy translucent thermoplastic, formed by the polymerization of ethene (ethylene), that is a good insulator, easily moulded, and resistant to chemicals such as acids. It is used in the form of film or sheeting to package food products, clothing, etc, and to make pipes, moulded articles, and electrical insulators. — Also called *polyethylene*.

polyunsaturated *adj. Chem.* denoting a compound, especially a fat or oil, that contains two or more double bonds per molecule, eg polyunsaturated margarine. It has been suggested that such compounds are less likely to cause cardiovascular

disease, but it has not yet been established whether they also have adverse effects.

polyurethane *noun Chem.* any of various polymers that contain the urethane group, and are used in protective coatings, adhesives, paints, varnishes, plastics, rubbers, and foams. [from POLY- + *urethane*, an ester]

polyvinyl chloride *Chem.* (ABBREV. **PVC**) a tough white thermoplastic, formed by the polymerization of vinyl chloride, that is resistant to fire, chemicals, moisture, and weathering, is easily dyed, and can be softened by mixing with a plasticizer. It is used in pipes and other moulded products, gramophone records, food packaging, waterproof clothing, and insulation for electric wires and cables.

pom *noun colloq. Austral., New Zealand* a pommy.

pomace *noun* **1** crushed apples for cider-making; the residue of these or of any similar fruit after pressing. **2** anything crushed or ground to a pulp. [from Latin *pomum*, fruit, apple]

pomade *noun Hist.* a perfumed ointment for the hair and scalp. [from French *pomade*, from Italian *pomata*, from Latin *pomum*, apple, a one-time ingredient]

pomander *noun* **1** a perfumed ball composed of various substances, used to scent wardrobes, originally carried to ward off infection. **2** a perforated container for this or, now more commonly, a mixture of scented flower-petals, etc. [from Old French *pomme d'ambre*, apple of amber]

Pombal, Sebastião (José) de Carvalho (e Mello), Marquês de (Marquis of) (1699–1782) Portuguese statesman, born near Coimbra. He became Ambassador to London (1739) and Vienna (1745), and Secretary for Foreign Affairs (1750). He showed great resourcefulness in replanning the city of Lisbon after the disastrous earthquake of 1755, and was made Prime Minister (1756–77). He opposed church influence, reorganized the army, and improved agriculture, commerce, and finance. His power ended with the accession of Maria I.

pome *noun Bot.* a type of fruit in which a fleshy outer layer, which develops from the receptacle of the flower, surrounds a central core that develops from the fused carpels, and contains a number of seeds, eg apple, pear. [from Latin *pomum*, apple]

pomegranate *noun* **1** a small deciduous tree or shrub of the genus *Punica*, native to Asia but widely cultivated in warm temperate regions both for its edible fruit and for its attractive white, orange, or red flowers. **2** the fruit of this plant, similar in size to an apple, which has tough red or brown skin surrounding a mass of seeds, each of which is enclosed by red juicy edible flesh. It is eaten raw, squeezed for its juice, or used to make grenadine syrup. [from Latin *pomum granatum*, seedy apple]

pomelo *noun* (PL. **pomelos**) a yellow citrus fruit similar to a grapefruit, native to SE Asia. [from Dutch *pompelmoes*, shaddock, grapefruit]

Pomerania, German **Pommern**, Polish **Pomorzr** a region in N central Europe, extending along the Baltic Sea from Stralsund in Germany to the R Vistula in Poland. HISTORY a disputed territory in the 17c–18c; divided among Germany, Poland, and the free city of Danzig from 1919 to 1939; most of the area became Polish in 1945. The region has many lakes; its chief towns include Gdańsk, Szczecin, and Koszalin.

Pomeranian *noun* a small breed of dog with a sharp-pointed face and thick long silky coat.

pomfret *noun* (also **pomfret cake**) a disc-shaped liquorice sweet traditionally made in *Pontefract*, Yorkshire. [from Old French *Pomfret*, Pontefract, from Latin *pons*, bridge + *fractus*, broken]

pommel — noun **1** the raised forepart of a saddle. **2** a rounded knob forming the end of a sword hilt. — verb (**pommelled, pommelling**) to pummel. [from Old French *pomel*, knob]

pommy noun (PL. **pommies**) Austral., New Zealand derog. colloq. a British, or especially English, person.

Pomona in Roman mythology, the goddess of fruit-trees and their fruit, especially apples and pear.

pomp noun **1** ceremonial grandeur. **2** vain ostentation. [from Latin *pompa*, procession]

Pompadour, Jeanne Antoinette Poisson, Marquise de, also called **Madame de Pompadour** (1721–64) mistress of Louis XV, born in Paris. A woman of great beauty, wit, and fashion, she attracted the attention of the King at a ball. Installed at Versailles (1745), and ennobled as Marquise de Pompadour, she assumed control of all public affairs, and for 20 years swayed state policy and appointed her own favourites, often leading France down disastrous paths. She founded the royal porcelain factory at Sèvres, and was a lavish patroness of architecture, the arts, and literature.

Pomp and Circumstance five marches for orchestra by Edward Elgar (Op 39, 1901–30). The melody later used for 'Land of Hope and Glory' features in No.1.

Pompeii a ruined ancient city near Naples, SW Italy, at the S foot of Vesuvius. The eruption of Vesuvius in AD 79 covered the whole city with a layer of ashes and pumice-stone 6–7m deep. Excavations since the 18c have revealed a city roughly elliptical in shape, 3km/1.8mi in circumference, with eight gates, and many buildings well-preserved by the volcanic ash. Part of the city still remains buried; the modern town lies to the east, with the pilgrimage Church of Santuario della Madonna del Rosario.

Pompey, known as **the Great**, originally **Gnaeus Pompeius Magnus** (106–48 BC) Roman politician and general of the late Republic. His victories over the Marians (83–82 BC), Sertorius (77 BC), Spartacus (71 BC), the pirates (67 BC), and Mithridates VI of Pontus (66 BC), put him at the forefront of Roman politics. His organization of the eastern provinces after the Mithridatic Wars (63 BC) established the pattern of Roman administration there for over a century. He joined with Julius Caesar and Crassus to form the 'First Triumvirate' (60 BC), but was consistently outmanoeuvred by Caesar in the 50s BC. He supported the Senate's call for Caesar to surrender his command, was finally defeated by him in the battle of Pharsalus (48 BC), and was assassinated in Egypt shortly after.

Pompidou, Georges (Jean Raymond) (1911–74) French statesman, born in Montboudif. He trained as an administrator, joined de Gaulle's staff in 1944, and held various government posts from 1946. He helped to draft the constitution for the Fifth Republic (1959), negotiated a settlement in Algeria (1961) and in the student-worker revolt of 1968, and was Prime Minister (1962–8) and President (1969–74).

Pompidou Centre see CENTRE BEAUBOURG.

pompom or **pompon** noun a ball of cut wool or other yarn, used as a trimming on clothes. [from French *pompon*]

pom-pom noun an automatic quick-firing gun; a machine gun; a multi-barrelled anti-aircraft gun. [imitative]

pomposity noun a pompous quality or manner.

pompous adj. **1** solemnly self-important. **2** said of language inappropriately grand and flowery; pretentious. [from Latin *pomposus*, from *pompa*, procession]

pompously adv. in a pompous way.

Ponape POP (1990) 33 000, a member state of the Federated States of Micronesia. AREA 345sq km/133sq mi. It comprises the island of Ponape and eight outlying atolls. CAPITAL Kolonia. ECONOMY copra, tropical fruit; tourism.

Ponce POP (1990) 188 000, the second largest city in Puerto Rico, situated on the Caribbean coast in the S of the country. NOTABLE FEATURES colonial mansions; Ponce fort (1760).

ponce — noun offensive slang **1** an effeminate man. **2** a pimp. — verb intrans. (**ponce about** or **around**) **1** to move about in an effeminate manner. **2** to mess around.

Ponce de León, Juan (1460–1521) Spanish explorer, born in San Servas. A page at the Aragonese court, he was a member of Columbus's second expedition (1493–6), served against the Moors, and explored and governed Puerto Rico (1510–12). In 1512 he discovered Florida and, while Acting Governor, occupied Trinidad, but failed to conquer his new subjects, the Carib Indians. He eventually retired to Cuba, where he died from a poisoned arrow wound.

Poncelet, Jean Victor (1788–1867) French engineer and geometrician, born in Metz. A military engineer during Napoleon's Russian campaign, he was taken prisoner by the Russians on the retreat from Moscow; he later became professor at Metz and Paris. His book on geometry, *Traité des propriétés projectives des figures* (Treatise on the Projective Properties of Figures, 1822), made his name and revived interest in the development of projective geometry. He sought to found geometry on basic principles as general as those of algebra.

poncho noun (PL. **ponchos**) an originally S American outer garment made of, or like, a blanket with a hole for the head to go through. [from Spanish *poncho*]

pond noun a small body of water, whether natural or artificial. [from Middle English *ponde*, enclosure]

ponder verb trans., intrans. (**pondered, pondering**) (**ponder something** or **on something**) to consider or contemplate it. [from Latin *ponderare*, to weigh]

ponderous adj. **1** said of speech, humour, etc heavy-handed, laborious, over-solemn, or pompous. **2** heavy or cumbersome; lumbering in movement. **3** weighty; important. [from Latin *ponderosus*, from *ponderare*, to weigh]

ponderously adv. in a ponderous way.

ponderousness noun being ponderous.

Pondicherry POP (1991) 808 000, a union territory in S India. AREA 492sq km/190sq mi. HISTORY founded in 1674, it was once the chief French settlement in India; administration was transferred from France to India in 1954; became a union territory in 1962. CAPITAL Pondicherry. GOVERNMENT governed by a Council of Ministers responsible to a Legislative Assembly. ECONOMY rice, millet, groundnuts, sugar cane, cotton; textiles, paper, brewing.

pong colloq. — noun a stink; a bad smell. — verb intrans. to smell badly.

pongy adj. (**pongier, pongiest**) colloq. stinking, smelly.

poniard noun a slim-bladed dagger. [from French *poignard*, from *poing*, fist]

pons noun (PL. **pontes**) Anat. in the brain of mammals, the mass of nerve fibres that connects the medulla oblongata to the thalamus, and is responsible for relaying nerve impulses between different parts of the brain. [from Latin *pons*, bridge]

Ponta Delgada POP (1991) 63 000, the largest town in the Azores, Portugal, on the S coast of São Miguel I. It is a tourist and commercial centre. NOTABLE FEATURES Churches of São Sebastião and Pedro; Convent of Santo Andre.

Pontefract POP (1981) 29 000, a town in Wakefield borough, West Yorkshire, N England, situated 20km/12mi SE of Leeds. A coal-mining town, it is also known for its liquorice confectionery. NOTABLE FEATURES 11c castle, where Richard II died; racecourse.

Ponte Vecchio a bridge across the R Arno in Florence, Italy, completed in 1345. The lower walkway is lined with jewellers' shops, and the upper corridor links the Pitti Palace with the Uffizi.

Pontiac's Conspiracy an attempt (1763) by Native Americans of the Ohio and Great Lakes country to drive whites out of the area, led by Pontiac (c.1720–69), Chief of the Ottawa tribe, in retaliation against the English treatment of the Native Americans and the threat of expanding white settlements. The movement reached its peak with an unsuccessful siege of Detroit, and a final peace was signed in 1766.

pontiff noun a title for the Pope, formerly applied to any Roman Catholic bishop. [from Latin *pontifex*, high priest]

pontifical adj. **1** belonging or relating to a pontiff. **2** derog. pompously opinionated; dogmatic. [from Latin *pontificalis*, from *pontifex*, high priest]

pontificals pl. noun the ceremonial dress of a bishop or pope.

pontificate — verb intrans. (pronounced -kate) to pronounce one's opinion pompously and arrogantly. — noun (pronounced -kət) the office of a pope. [from Latin *pontificatus*, high-priesthood, from *pontifex*, priest]

pontoon¹ noun any of a number of flat-bottomed craft, punts, barges, etc, anchored side by side across a river, to support a temporary bridge. [from French *ponton*, from Latin *ponto*, punt]

pontoon² noun Cards a game in which the object is to collect sets of cards that add up to 21 and no more. [alteration of French *vingt-et-un*, twenty-one]
◇ Also known formerly as *vingt-et-un* or *twenty-one*, pontoon is similar to the popular casino game, blackjack, and is usually played for small stakes in homes and public houses. Suits are irrelevant, with only the numerical value of the cards counting; court or picture cards count as 10 and the ace may be 1 or 11 at the player's discretion.

pontoon bridge a bridge supported on pontoons.

Pontus an ancient region in NE Asia Minor lying E of Bithynia and S of the Black Sea. It was established as a kingdom from the 4c BC, and in the early 1c BC, it became the centre of the empire of Mithridates VI. He was defeated by Pompey in 64 BC, and Pontus became a Roman province.

pony noun (PL. **ponies**) any of several small breeds of horse, usually less than 14.2 hands (1.5m) in height when fully grown, and noted for their intelligence, hardiness, and endurance. [from Scot. *powney*, from French *poulenet*, diminutive of *poulain*, colt]

Pony Club a world-wide organization established in 1929 with the aim of establishing good horsemanship among children. It holds championships and rallies throughout the year.

ponytail noun a person's hair drawn back and tied at the back of the head, so that it hangs free like a pony's tail.

pony-trekking noun the recreational activity of cross-country pony-riding in groups.

poodle noun a breed of dog whose curly coat is traditionally clipped in an elaborate style. [from German *Pudel*, from *pudeln*, to splash]

poof noun offensive slang a male homosexual. [from French *pouffe*, puff]

Pooh see WINNIE-THE-POOH.

pooh *interj. colloq.* an exclamation of scorn or of disgust, eg at a smell. [imitative]

pooh-pooh *verb colloq.* to express scorn for (a suggestion, etc).

pool¹ *noun* **1** a small area of still water: *a rock pool*. **2** a puddle; a patch of spilt liquid: *pools of blood*. **3** a swimming-pool. **4** a deep part of a stream or river. [from Anglo-Saxon *pol*]

pool² — *noun* **1** a reserve of money, personnel, vehicles, etc used as a communal resource: *a typing pool*. **2** the combined stakes of those betting on something; a jackpot. **3** *Commerce* a group of businesses with a common arrangement to maintain high prices, so eliminating competition and preserving profits. **4** a game like billiards played with a white cue ball and usually 15 numbered coloured balls, the aim being to shoot specified balls into specified pockets using the cue ball. **5** (*also* **football pool** *or* **pools**) a competition involving betting by post on the results of a number of football matches. — *verb* to put (money or other resources) into a common supply for general use. [from French *poule*, hen, stakes]

Poole, Grace the mysterious servant in Charlotte Brontë's *Jane Eyre*.

Poole POP (1992e) 136 000, a port town in Poole district, Dorset, S England. It is situated in Poole Harbour 6km/4mi W of Bournemouth.

Poona see PUNE.

poop¹ *noun* the raised, enclosed part at the stern of old sailing ships. [from Latin *puppis*]

poop² *colloq. verb* **1** (*usually* **be pooped**) to exhaust. **2** *intrans.* to become exhausted. — **poop out** to give up from exhaustion.

poop deck a ship's deck surmounting the poop.

Poopó, Lake the second-largest lake in Bolivia. AREA 2 512sq km/970sq mi; length 97km/60mi; width 32–48km/20–30mi; c.2.5m deep. It is situated 56km/35mi S of Oruro, in the W part of the country.

poop scoop *or* **pooper scooper** *colloq.* a small scoop used to lift and remove dog faeces from pavements, etc.

poor *adj.* **1** not having sufficient money or means to live comfortably. **2** (**poor in something**) not well supplied with it: *a country poor in minerals*. **3** not good; weak; unsatisfactory. **4** unsatisfactorily small or sparse: *a poor attendance*. **5** used in expressing pity or sympathy: *poor fellow!* — **poor man's** *derog.* denoting a substitute of lower quality or price: *a flower called 'poor man's orchid'*. [from Old French *povre*, from Latin *pauper*, poor]

poorhouse *noun Hist.* an institution maintained at public expense, for sheltering the poor; a workhouse.

poor law *Hist.* a law or set of laws concerned with the public support of the poor.

Poor Laws legislation in Britain (originally formulated 1598 and 1601), whereby relief of poverty was the responsibility of individual parishes, with funds provided by local property rates. As the population grew and rates rose at the end of the 18c, the poor laws were increasingly criticized; the 1834 Poor Law Amendment Act radically changed the system by making application for poor relief less attractive and instituting a centralized poor law commission.

poorly — *adv.* not well; badly. — *adj. old colloq. use, dialect* ill.

poorness *noun* being poor.

poor white *derog.* a member of an impoverished and deprived class of white people living amongst blacks in the southern USA or South Africa.

pop¹ — *noun* **1** a sharp explosive noise, like that of a cork coming out of a bottle. **2** *colloq.* sweet non-alcoholic fizzy drinks. — *verb* (**popped, popping**) **1** *trans., intrans.* to make or cause to make a pop. **2** *trans., intrans.* to burst with a pop. **3** (*also* **pop out**) to spring out; to protrude. **4** *intrans. colloq.* to go quickly in a direction specified: *pop next door*. **5** *colloq.* to put quickly or briefly: *just pop it in the oven*. — *adv.* with a pop. — **pop off** *colloq.* to die.

pop the question *humorous colloq.* to propose marriage.

pop up *intrans.* to appear or occur, especially unexpectedly. [imitative]

pop² — *noun* (*also* **pop music**) modern music popular especially among young people, usually with a strong beat, often played with electronic equipment (guitars, keyboards, etc). — *adj.* **1** performing or featuring pop music. **2** popular: *pop culture*. [a shortening of POPULAR]
◇ The popular commercial music inaugurated in the 1950s by rock and roll has since developed to include diverse styles such as soul, reggae, country and western, and various folk and ethnic influences. It is generally played, presented, and marketed for a teenage audience, with success measured in terms of various pop charts.

pop³ *noun North Amer. colloq., often as a form of address* one's father or an elderly man. [see PAPA]

pop. *abbrev.* population.

Pop Art a modern art form based on the commonplace and ephemeral aspects of 20c urban life, such as soup cans, comics, movies, and advertising. Pioneer British Pop Artists in the mid-1950s included Eduardo Paolozzi (1924–) and Richard Hamilton (1922–), and leading US contributors in the 1960s included Jasper Johns (1930–), Andy Warhol (1926–87), and Roy Lichtenstein (1923–).

Popayán POP (1992e) 204 000, a historic city and the capital of Cauca department, SW Colombia. It was founded in 1536. In 1983 it suffered a serious earthquake.

popcorn *noun* maize grains heated till they puff up and burst open.

Pope, Alexander (1688–1744) English poet, born in London. He suffered from poor health, and his growth was stunted by a tubercular infection of the spine when he was twelve. He became well-known as a satirical poet, and for his use of the heroic couplet, notably in *The Rape of the Lock* (1712). Other works include a translation of the *Iliad* (1715–20), which established his reputation firmly and made him financially secure, and the mock-heroic satire *The Dunciad* (1728, continued 1742). He also wrote the *Epistle to Doctor Arbuthnot* (1735) and *Martinus Scriblerus peri Bathous:or The Art of Sinking in Poetry*, another attack on his fellow poets which fuelled a long-running literary feud, and the philosophical *Essay on Man* (1733–4).

Pope, Giant a character in John Bunyan's *The Pilgrim's Progress*.

pope *noun* **1** (*often* **Pope**) the Bishop of Rome, the head of the Roman Catholic Church. **2** a priest in the Eastern Orthodox Church. [from Greek *pappas*, papa, in the early Church used respectfully to bishops]

Popes of the 20c	
1878–1903	Leo XIII
1903–14	Pius X
1914–22	Benedict XV
1922–39	Pius XI
1939–58	Pius XII
1958–63	John XXIII
1963–78	Paul VI
1978	John Paul I
1978–	John Paul II

popery *noun offensive* Roman Catholicism.

pop-eyed *adj. colloq.* with eyes protruding, especially in amazement.

popgun *noun* a toy gun that fires a cork or pellet with a pop.

popinjay *noun old derog. use* someone vain or conceited; a dandy or fop. [from Old French *papegai*, parrot]

popish *adj. offensive* Roman Catholic; of Roman Catholicism.

Popish Plot an apocryphal Jesuit conspiracy (1678) to assassinate Charles II of England, burn London, slaughter Protestants, and place James, Duke of York (later James VII and II), on the throne. Invented by opportunist rogues, Titus Oates (1649–1705) and Israel Tonge (1621–80), it resulted in 35 executions, bills in three parliaments for the exclusion of James from the succession, and the fall of the Danby government.

poplar *noun* **1** a tall slender deciduous tree of the genus *Populus*, found in north temperate regions, with broad simple leaves, which often tremble in a slight breeze, and and flowers produced in catkins. Poplars grow fast and are often planted as ornamental trees or to give shelter. **2** the soft fine-grained yellowish wood of this tree, which is used to make plywood, matches, boxes, and paper pulp. [from Latin *populus*]

poplin *noun* a strong cotton cloth with a finely ribbed finish. [from French *popeline*, from Italian *papalina*, papal cloth, because it was made in the *papal* city of Avignon]

Popocatepetl a dormant volcano in central Mexico. It is situated 72km/45mi SE of Mexico City, in the Ixtaccihuatl-Popocatépetl National Park. HEIGHT 5 452m. It is the second highest peak in Mexico, and has a snow-capped symmetrical cone. The crater is c.1km in circumference and 402m deep. The last eruption was in 1802.

poppadum *or* **poppadom** *noun* a paperthin pancake grilled till crisp for serving with Indian dishes. [from Tamil *poppadum*]

popper *noun* a press stud.

poppet *noun* **1** a term of endearment for someone lovable. **2** in vehicle engines, a valve that rises and falls in its housing. [an earlier form of PUPPET]

popping-crease *noun Cricket* the line behind which the batsman must stand, parallel to, and four feet in front of, the wicket.

pop poetry a term used from the 1970s for a type of verse which is written primarily for public performance rather than private reading. It is often topical, satirical, and may be accompanied by music.

poppy *noun* (PL. **poppies**) **1** a cornfield plant with large scarlet flowers and a hairy, wiry stem; any of several related plants, eg one from which opium is obtained. **2** an artificial red poppy, worn for Poppy Day, symbolising the poppies that grew on the battlefields of Flanders after World War I. [from Anglo-Saxon *popig*]

poppycock *noun colloq.* nonsense. [from Dutch dialect *pappekak*, soft dung]

Poppy Day another name for REMEMBRANCE DAY.

Popski's Private Army British fighting unit in World War II. It was raised in Oct 1942 by Lt-Col Vladimir Peniakoff, also called 'Popski' (1897–1951), a Belgian of Russian parentage. It had a maximum strength of 195 men, and engaged in intelligence-gathering and hit-and-run attacks behind enemy lines in N Africa and Italy.

popsy *noun* (PL. **popsies**) *old use, derog. colloq.* a girlfriend.

populace *noun* the body of ordinary citizens; the common people. [from French *populace*, from Italian *popolaccio*, from Latin *populus*, people]

popular *adj.* **1** liked or enjoyed by most people: *a pastime still popular with the young.* **2** *said of beliefs, etc* accepted by many people. **3** catering for the tastes and abilities of ordinary people as distinct from specialists, etc: *a popular history of science.* **4** *said of a person* generally liked and admired. **5** involving the will or preferences of the public in general: *by popular demand.* [from Latin *popularis*, from *populus*, people]

popular front a left-wing group or faction, eg any of those set up from the 1930s onwards to oppose fascism.

popularity *noun* being popular.

popularization *or* **popularisation** *noun* popularizing or being popularized.

popularize *or* **popularise** *verb* **1** to make popular: *popularize a fashion.* **2** to present in a simple, easily understood way, so as to have general appeal.

popularly *adv.* in a popular way; in terms of most people: *is popularly believed to be a hero.*

populate *verb* **1** *said of people, animals, or plants* to inhabit or live in (a certain area). **2** to supply (uninhabited places) with inhabitants; to people. [from Latin *populare*, from *populus*, people]

World Population Estimates			
Date (AD)	Millions	Date (AD)	Millions
1	200	1940	2 295
1000	275	1950	2 500
1250	375	1960	3 050
1500	420	1970	3 700
1700	615	1980	4 450
1800	900	1985	4 845
1900	1 625	1990	5 246
1920	1 860	2000	6 100
1930	2 070	2050	11 000

Estimates for 2000 and 2050 are United Nations 'medium' estimates. They should be compared with the 'low' estimates for these years of 5 400 and 8 500, and 'high' estimates of 7 000 and 13 500, respectively

population *noun* **1** all the people living in a particular country, area, etc. **2** the number of people living in a particular area, etc: *a population of two million.* **3** a group of animals or plants of the same species living in a certain area; the total number of these: *the declining elephant population.* **4** the process of populating an area. **5** *Statistics* a group consisting of all the possible quantities or values relevant to a statistical study, from which representative samples are taken in order to determine the characteristics of the entire population.

populism *noun* political activity or notions that are thought to reflect the opinions and interests of ordinary people. [from Latin *populus*, people]

populist *noun* **1** a person who believes in the right and ability of the common people to play a major part in government. **2** a person who studies, supports, or attracts the support of the common people.

populous *adj.* thickly populated. [from Latin *populosus*, from *populus*, people]

pop-up *adj.*, *said of a picture book* having cut-out parts designed to stand upright as the page is opened.

porbeagle *noun* mackerel shark. [a Cornish dialect word]

porcelain *noun* **1** a fine white translucent earthenware, originally made in China. **2** objects made of this. [from Old French *porcelaine*, from Italian *porcellana*, cowrie shell]
◇ Chinese porcelain was first manufactured in the Sung dynasty (960–1279), and was introduced into Europe c.1300. It was so prized as a semi-precious material that it was often mounted

in gold and silver. Attempts were made to produce porcelain at the Medici factory in Florence in the 1570s, but the technique was not perfected in Europe until the early 18c (at Meissen).

porch *noun* **1** a structure forming a covered entrance to the doorway of a building. **2** *North Amer.* a verandah. [from Old French *porche*]

porcine *adj.* of or like a pig. [from Latin *porcus*, pig]

porcupine *noun* any of various large nocturnal rodents belonging to either of two families, namely Hystricidae (Old World species) and Erethizontidae (New World species), and noted for the long sharp black and white spikes, known as quills, borne on the back and sides of the body. These serve as defence and are also rattled to warn off predators. [from Old French *porc d'espine*, literally 'spiny pig']
◇ Old World or terrestrial porcupines, found in forests and savannas of S Europe, S Asia, Africa, and the East Indies, spend the daytime in burrows or rock crevices, emerging at night to feed on bulbs, roots, fruits, and berries. New World or arboreal (tree-dwelling) porcupines are found in N and S America, and are generally smaller than the Old World species. They climb trees in order to obtain food, and spend the daytime in hollow trees or nests of leaves.

pore¹ *noun* **1** a small usually round opening in the surface of a living organism, eg in the skin, or the undersurface of plant leaves, through which fluids, gases, and other substances can pass, eg during sweating in mammals. **2** any tiny cavity or gap, eg in soil or rock. [from Latin *porus*, from Greek *poros*, passage, duct]

pore² *verb intrans.* (**pore over something**) to study books, etc with intense concentration. [from Middle English *pouren*]

Porgy and Bess the first notable US opera, by George Gershwin (1935), incorporating American folk-song and jazz. Set in a 1920s black tenement (Catfish Row) in Charleston, the story concerns the relationships between Bess, her boyfriend Crown, who has to leave the town after killing a man, and her new lover the crippled Porgy, who tries to protect her against the temptations of the drug-dealer Sportin' Life, and the return of Crown.

pork *noun* the flesh of a pig used as food. [from Old French *porc*, from Latin *porcus*, pig]

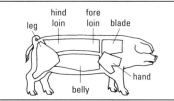

pork cuts

porker *noun* a pig that shows fast growth and reaches maturity at a relatively light weight, reared for fresh meat as opposed to processed meats such as bacon.

porky *adj.* (**porkier**, **porkiest**) **1** of or like pork. **2** *colloq.* plump.

porn *noun colloq.* pornography.

porno *colloq.* — *noun* pornography. — *adj.* pornographic.

pornographer *noun* a person who makes or sells pornography.

pornographic *adj.* relating to or of the nature of pornography.

pornographically *adv.* in a pornographic way.

pornography *noun* books, pictures, films etc designed to be sexually arousing, often offensive owing to their explicit nature. [from Greek

pornographos, writing about prostitutes, from *porne*, prostitute + *graphein*, to write]
◇ In most Western societies, a distinction is made between 'soft' and illegal 'hard core' pornography. Soft pornography in magazines, videos, etc is freely available to adults through retailers or specialist shops and mail-order companies. It is nonetheless the subject of vigorous opposition by groups, such as feminists, who consider it degrading to women (and men), and by moral campaigners.

porosity *noun* **1** being porous. **2** *Geol.* the ratio of the volume of pores to the total volume of a rock, etc.

porous *adj.* **1** having pores or cavities. **2** that liquids can pass through. [from Latin *porosus*, from *porus*, pore]

porphyritic *adj.* **1** like or of the nature of porphyry. **2** having large crystals scattered among small.

Porphyry (c.233–304 AD) Neoplatonist philosopher, born in Tyre or Batanea. He went to Rome (c.263), where he studied under Plotinus, and became his disciple and biographer. He wrote a treatise against the Christians, of which only fragments remain. His most influential work was the *Isagoge*, a commentary on Aristotle's *Categories*, widely used in the Middle Ages.

porphyry *noun* **1** *Geol.* a loose term for any igneous rock that contains large crystals surrounded by much smaller crystals. **2** a very hard purple and white rock used in sculpture. [from Greek *porphyrites*, purplish]

porpoise *noun* **1** a small beakless whale, smaller than a dolphin and with a blunt snout, found in northern coastal waters and around the coasts of S America and SE Asia. Porpoises feed on fish, and often swim in the bow waves of fast-moving ships. **2** a loose term for a dolphin. [from Latin *porcus*, pig + *piscis*, fish]

porridge *noun* **1** a dish of oatmeal boiled in water, or of some other cereal boiled in water or milk. **2** *slang* time served by a criminal in prison. [a variant of POTTAGE]

porringer *noun* a bowl for soup or porridge, with a handle. [from Middle English *potinger*, variation of *potager*, soup bowl]

Porsche, Ferdinand (1875–1951) German automobile designer, born in Hafersdorf, Bohemia. He designed cars for Daimler and Auto Union, then set up his own studio, and in 1934 produced the plans for a revolutionary type of cheap car with engine in the rear, to which the Nazis gave the name 'Volkswagen' ('people's car'). The Porsche sports car was introduced in 1950.

port¹ *noun* **1** harbour. **2** a town with a harbour. [from Latin *portus*]

port² *noun* the left side of a ship or aircraft.

port³ *noun* **1** an opening in a ship's side for loading, etc. **2** a porthole. **3** *Comput.* a socket on a computer through which electronic information can pass to and from peripheral units. **4** *old Scot. use* a town gate. [from Latin *porta*, gate]

port⁴ *noun* a dark-red or tawny fortified wine of Portugal. [from *Oporto*, originally the place from which it was exported]

port⁵ *verb Mil.* to hold (a rifle, etc) across the body with both hands, the barrel close to the left shoulder. [from French *porter*, to carry]

portability *noun* the quality of being portable.

portable — *adj.* **1** easily carried or moved, and usually designed to be so. **2** *Comput.*, *said of a program* adaptable for use in a variety of systems. — *noun* a portable radio, television, typewriter, etc. [see PORT⁵]

portage — *noun* **1** the carrying of ships, equipment, etc overland from one waterway to another. **2** the route used for this. — *verb* to transport (ships, etc) overland. [from French *portage*, from *porter*, to carry]

portal *noun* an entrance, gateway, or doorway, especially an imposing or awesome one. [from Old French, from Latin *portale*, from *porta*, gate]

portal vein *Anat.* any vein that connects two networks of capillaries, eg the hepatic portal vein which connects the capillaries of the intestine to those of the liver.

Port Augusta POP (1991) 15 000, a town in Northern statistical division, SE South Australia, at the head of the Spencer Gulf. It is a starting point for the 'Ghan' train to Alice Springs and the Indian Pacific train to Perth. The town is a base for the flying doctor service.

Port-au-Prince POP (1992e) 1.3m, the seaport capital of Haiti. It is situated on the Gulf of Gonâve, on the W coast of Hispaniola I. There is a commercial and processing centre at the west end of the fertile Plaine du Cul-de-Sac. NOTABLE FEATURE cathedral (18c).

portcullis *noun Hist.* a vertical iron or wooden grating fitted into a town gateway or castle entrance, lowered to bar intruders. [from Old French *porte coleice*, sliding gate]

Port Elizabeth POP (1985e) 273 000, a seaport in Cape province, South Africa. It is situated on Algoa Bay, Indian Ocean, 725km/450mi E of Cape Town. HISTORY Fort Frederick was built here by British forces in 1799; founded in 1820. NOTABLE FEATURE the Addo Elephant National Park is nearby.

portend *verb* to warn of; to signify or foreshadow; to be an omen of. [from Latin *portendere*]

portent *noun* 1 a prophetic sign; an omen. 2 fateful significance: *an event of grim portent.* 3 a marvel or prodigy. [from Latin *portentum*]

portentous *adj.* 1 ominous or fateful; of or relating to portents. 2 weighty, solemn, or pompous.

Porter the hungover and talkative doorman in Shakespeare's *Macbeth*, who lets Macduff and Lennox into Macbeth's castle after being woken by their knocking on the morning following the murder of Duncan.

Porter, Cole (1892–1964) US songwriter, born in Peru, Indiana. Although his success as composer and lyricist came late (it began with 'What Is This Thing Called Love?' in 1930), he ultimately ranked high in the golden period of American popular song, with such pieces as 'Night and Day' (1932), 'Begin the Beguine' (1935), and 'Don't Fence Me In' (1944), and such musical comedies as *Kiss Me Kate* (1948) and *Can-Can* (1953).

Porter, Katherine Anne (1890–1980) US novelist and short-story writer, born in Indian Creek, Texas. Her short stories were published in *Collected Short Stories* (1965, Pulitzer Prize). She is also known for a long allegorical novel, *The Ship of Fools* (1962), about a journey from Mexico to Germany on the eve of Hitler's rise to power.

Porter, Peter (Neville Frederick) (1929–) Australian poet, born in Brisbane. He worked as a journalist, moved to England in 1951, and became a full-time poet in 1968. His collections include satirical treatments of Britain in the 1960s (eg *Once Bitten, Twice Bitten*, 1961 and *Poems Ancient and Modern*, 1970) and the more reflective and elegiac *The Cost of Seriousness* (1978) and *The Automatic Oracle* (1987, Whitbread Award). His *Collected Poems* appeared in 1983. More recent works include *The Chair of Babel* (1992).

Porter, Rodney Robert (1917–85) English biochemist, born in Newton le Willows, Lancashire. He worked at the National Institute for Medical Research and St Mary's Hospital Medical School in London before becoming professor at Oxford in 1967. He proposed an overall molecular structure for antibodies, which later results have confirmed and refined, and shared

the 1972 Nobel Prize for Physiology or Medicine with Gerald Edelman.

porter[1] *noun* a doorman, caretaker, or janitor at a college, office, or factory. [from Latin *portarius*, gatekeeper]

porter[2] *noun* 1 a person employed to carry luggage or parcels, eg at a railway station. 2 a heavy, dark-brown beer formerly reputed to be popular with porters. 3 *North Amer.* a sleeping-car attendant. [from Old French *porteour*, from Latin *portator*, from *portare*, to carry]

porterhouse *noun* a choice cut of beefsteak from the back of the sirloin. [originally a public house or chop-house]

Porter (of Luddenham), George Porter, Baron (1920–) English physical chemist, born in Stainforth, Yorkshire. Professor at Sheffield University and later at the Royal Institution, he developed a technique which became important in the study of very rapid gas reactions. He shared the 1967 Nobel Prize for Chemistry with Ronald Norrish and Manfred Eigen.

portfolio *noun* (PL. **portfolios**) 1 a case for carrying papers, drawings, photographs, etc; the contents of such a case. 2 the post of a government minister with responsibility for a specific department. 3 a list of one's investments. [from Italian *portafoglio*, from *portare*, to carry + *foglio*, leaf]

Port Harcourt POP (1992e) 371 000, the seaport capital of Rivers state, S Nigeria. The city lies on the R Bonny, 65km/40mi from the sea. It is Nigeria's second largest port, established in 1912.

porthole *noun* a usually round opening in a ship's side to admit light and air. [from PORT[3] + HOLE]

Porthos the second, strong, and swaggering Musketeer in Alexandre Dumas's *The Three Musketeers.*

Portia 1 the rich heroine of Shakespeare's *The Merchant of Venice*, who marries Bassanio and disguises herself as an advocate to save Antonio. 2 The devoted, stoical wife of Brutus in Shakespeare's *Julius Caesar.*

portico *noun* (PL. **porticos**, **porticoes**) *Archit.* a colonnade forming a porch or covered way alongside a building. [from Italian *portico*, from Latin *porticus*, porch]

portion — *noun* 1 a piece or part of a whole: *divide into 12 equal portions.* 2 a share; a part allotted to one. 3 an individual helping. 4 one's destiny or fate. 5 *Legal* a woman's dowry. — *verb* (**portioned**, **portioning**) (*also* **portion something out**) to distribute it portion by portion. [from Latin *portio*]

Portishead POP (1981) 14 000, a port town in Bristol district, Avon, SW England. Lying on the estuary of the R Severn, it is a major port serving Bristol.

Portland POP (1990) 1.2m, the capital of Multnomah County, NW Oregon, USA. It is the largest city in the state and a freshwater port, lying on the Willamette R near its confluence with the Columbia R. The city was laid out in 1845; it served as a supply point in the 1850s during the California gold rush, and from 1897 until 1900 during the Alaska gold rush.

Portland POP (1990) 215 000, the business capital and chief port of Maine, USA, and the seat of Cumberland County. It lies on the coast of Casco Bay, SE of Sebago L. HISTORY established in 1632; became state capital in 1820, until 1832; it achieved city status in 1832. The poet H W Longfellow was born here in 1807.

Portland, Isle of a rocky peninsula on the Dorset coast, S England. It extends into the English Channel and is connected to the mainland by a shingle ridge (Chesil Beach). AREA 12sq km/5sq mi. Limestone (Portland Stone) is still quarried and used in many London buildings.

NOTABLE FEATURES Portland Castle, built by Henry VIII (1520); naval base at Portland Harbour.

Portlaoighise or **Port Laoise**, formerly **Maryborough** POP (1991) 8 000, the capital of Laoighis county, Leinster, Irish Republic, situated SW of Dublin. It is the site of a top-security prison.

Port Louis POP (1991e) 143 000, the seaport capital of Mauritius, established in 1735. Trade developed until the building of the Suez Canal. Port Louis handles almost all trade in Mauritius. NOTABLE FEATURES two cathedrals.

portly *adj.* (**portlier**, **portliest**) *said especially of a man* somewhat stout. [from Old word *port*, deportment]

portmanteau *noun* (PL. **portmanteaus**, **portmanteaux**) a leather travelling-bag that opens flat in two halves. [from French *portemanteau*, from *porter*, to carry + *manteau*, coat, cloak]

portmanteau word an invented word composed of parts of two words and conveying the sense of both, eg *motel* from *motor* and *hotel.*

Port Moresby POP (1990) 193 000, the seaport capital of Papua New Guinea. It lies on the S coast of New Guinea. Port Moresby was an allied base in World War II. It is a base for overseas telecommunications and national broadcasting.

Port Natal see DURBAN.

port of call (PL. **ports of call**) a place called at during a journey.

Port of Spain POP (1990) 51 000, the seaport capital of Trinidad and Tobago. It is situated on the NW coast of Trinidad and became the capital of Trinidad in 1783. It is the principal commercial centre in the E Caribbean. NOTABLE FEATURES Botanical Gardens; two cathedrals; San Andres Fort (1785).

Porton Down a research centre established by the Ministry of Defence in Wiltshire, S England, for the investigation of biological and chemical warfare.

Porto Novo POP (1982e) 208 000, the seaport capital of Benin. It lies on a lagoon in Ouémé province. Porto Novo was settled by the Portuguese who made it their headquarters for slave and tobacco trading with Brazil. Although it is the official capital, there is little political and economic activity, this taking place in Cotonou. NOTABLE FEATURES Palace of King Toffa; museum.

portrait *noun* 1 a drawing, painting, or photograph of a person, especially of the face only. 2 a written description, film depiction, etc of someone or something: *a portrait of country life.* [from Old French *portrait*, past participle of *portraire*, to portray]

Portrait of a Lady, The a novel by Henry James (1881). It centres around the unhappy life in Europe of a young American woman, Isabel Archer.

Portrait of the Artist as a Young Man, A an autobiographical novel by James Joyce (1914–15, one volume, 1916). It describes the life of Stephen Dedalus as he grows to maturity in Ireland.

portraiture *noun* the art of making portraits, or of depiction in writing, film, etc.

portray *verb* 1 to make a portrait of. 2 to describe or depict. 3 to act the part of (a character) in a play, film, etc. [from Old French *portraire*, to portray]

portrayal *noun* 1 representation in a picture or pictures. 2 portraying.

Portree POP (1981) 1 500, the port capital of the island of Skye, and of Skye and Lochalsh district, Highland region, NW Scotland. It lies by Loch Portree on the E coast and is the largest town on the island.

Portrush, Gaelic **Port Rois** POP (1991) 6 000, a town in Coleraine district, Co Antrim, NE

Northern Ireland, lying on the N coast. It is the tourist centre for the Giant's Causeway, 11km/7mi NE.

Port Said, Arabic **Bur Said 1** POP (1990e) 461 000, the seaport capital of Port Said governorate, NE Egypt. It lies on the Mediterranean coast at the N end of Suez Canal, 169km/105mi NE of Cairo. The city was founded in 1859 at the beginning of the Canal construction. **2** a governorate in NE Egypt with Port Said as its capital.

Port San Carlos a settlement on the W coast of East Falkland, Falkland Is. The British Task Force landed near here in 1982, during the Falklands War.

Portsmouth POP (1992e) 190 000, a city and seaport in Portsmouth district, Hampshire, S England. It is a major naval base, situated on Portsea I, 133km/83mi SW of London. The novelist Charles Dickens was born here in 1812. NOTABLE FEATURES Nelson's flagship HMS *Victory*; Tudor warship *Mary Rose*; Royal Navy Museum; Royal Marines Museum; Southsea Castle including Round Tower and Point Battery; Fort Widney (Portsdown Hill).

Portsmouth POP (1990) 26 000, a seaport and summer resort town in Rockingham County, SE New Hampshire, USA. It lies on the Atlantic coast at the head of the Piscataqua R, 70km/43mi NE of Manchester. HISTORY established in 1624; achieved city status in 1849; the treaty ending the Russo–Japanese War was signed here in 1905. The naval base on Seavy's I specializes in submarine construction. NOTABLE FEATURES John Paul Jones House (1758); Strawberry Banke.

Portsmouth POP (1990) 104 000, a port and independent city in SE Virginia, USA, lying on the Elizabeth R. HISTORY founded in 1752; a base for British and then Revolutionary troops during the War of Independence; evacuated and burned by Union troops during the Civil War in 1861, then retaken in 1862. It is part of a US naval complex, and the ships *Chesapeake* and *Merrimack* were built here.

Port Sudan POP (1983) 207 000, the seaport capital of Eastern region, Sudan, on the Red Sea coast. It is the main port in Sudan and handles most of the country's trade. The port was founded in 1906.

Portugal, official name **Republic of Portugal**, Portuguese **República Portuguesa**, ancient **Lusitania** POP (1992e) 9.9m, a country in SW Europe on the W side of the Iberian peninsula, divided into 18 districts and two autonomous regions (Azores and Madeira Is). It is also traditionally divided into 11 mainland provinces. Macao is an Overseas Territory. AREA 88 500sq km/34 200sq mi; greatest length is 560km/348mi (N–S); greatest width is 220km/137mi. It is bounded N and E by Spain, and S and W by the Atlantic Ocean. CAPITAL Lisbon. CHIEF TOWNS Oporto, Setúbal, Coimbra. TIME ZONE GMT. The chief religion is Roman Catholicism. OFFICIAL LANGUAGE Portuguese. CURRENCY the escudo. PHYSICAL DESCRIPTION there are several mountain ranges formed by the W spurs of the Spanish mountain system; the chief range

Portugal

is the Serra da Estrêla in the N, rising to 1 991m; the four main rivers (the Douro, Minho, Tagus, and Guadiana) are the lower courses of rivers beginning in Spain. CLIMATE basically a maritime climate, with increased variation between summer and winter temperatures inland; the W coast is relatively cool in summer; there is most rainfall in winter. HISTORY became a kingdom under Alphonso I in 1139; the 15c was a major period of world exploration and the beginning of the Portuguese Empire; under Spanish domination from 1580 to 1640; invaded by the French in 1807; monarchy overthrown and republic established in 1910; dictatorship of Dr Salazar from 1932 to 1968; a military coup in 1974 was followed by 10 years of political unrest under 15 governments; Portugal joined the EC in 1985. GOVERNMENT governed by a President, elected for five years, a Prime Minister and Council of Ministers, and a 250-member unicameral Assembly of the Republic, elected every four years. ECONOMY there are several labour-intensive areas in the economy, such as textiles, leather, wood products, cork, and ceramics; other exports include timber, wine, fish, chemicals, and electrical machinery; steelworks, shipbuilding; mineral deposits (copper, wolfram, tin, iron ore, pyrites, zinc, lead, barium, titanium, uranium, sodium, and calcium); agricultural products include wheat, maize, rice, rye, beans, potatoes, fruit, olive oil, meat, and dairy produce; large forests of pine, oak, cork-oak, eucalyptus, and chestnut cover about 20% of the country; tourism, especially in the S.

Monarchs of Portugal	
1095–1112	Henry of Burgundy
1112—85	Alfonso I
1185–1211	Sancho I
1211–23	Alfonso II
1223–45	Sancho II
1245–79	Alfonso III
1279–1325	Diniz
1325–57	Alfonso IV
1357–67	Peter I
1367–83	Ferdinand
1385–1433	John I of Aviz
1433–8	Edward
1438–81	Alfonso V
1481–95	John II
1495–1521	Manuel I
1521–57	John III
1557–78	Sebastian
1578–80	Henry
1580–98	Philip I (II of Spain)
1598–1621	Philip II (III of Spain)
1621–40	Philip III (IV of Spain)
1640–56	John IV of Braganza
1656–83	Alfonso VI
1683–1706	Peter II
1706–50	John V
1750–77	Joseph
1777–1816	Maria I
1777–86	Peter III (King Consort)
1816–26	John VI
1826	Peter IV (I of Brazil)
1826–8	Maria II
1828–34	Miguel
1834–53	Maria II
1853–61	Peter V
1861–89	Luis
1889–1908	Charles
1908–10	Manuel II

Portuguese — *noun* **1** a native or citizen of Portugal. **2** (**the Portuguese**) the people of Portugal. **3** the language of Portugal. — *adj.* relating to Portugal, or its inhabitants or language.
◇ Portuguese is a Romance language of the Indo-European family. It is spoken by c.120–150m people and is the official language of Portugal, Brazil, Angola, Mozambique, Guinea-Bissau, and Sao Tomé and Principe.

Portuguese man-of-war a jellyfish with an inflated sail-like crest, whose sting is highly poisonous.

Portuguese man-of-war

Port-Vila *or* **Vila** POP (1989) 19 000, the port capital of Vanuatu. It lies on the SW coast of Éfaté I.

Porvoo, Swedish **Borgå** POP (1990) 20 000, a picturesque town in Uudenmaa province, SE Finland, lying near the mouth of the R Porvoonjoki. Established in 1346, it is the second oldest town in Finland. In the 19c it was the home of the national poet, Johan Runeberg. NOTABLE FEATURE cathedral (15c).

POS *abbrev.* point of sale.

pose — *noun* **1** a position or attitude of the body: *adopt a relaxed pose*. **2** an artificial way of behaving, adopted for effect: *his punk style is just a pose*. — *verb* **1** *intrans., trans.* to take up a position oneself, or position (someone else), for a photograph, portrait, etc. **2** *intrans. derog.* to behave in an exaggerated or artificial way so as to draw attention to oneself. **3** *intrans.* (**pose as someone** *or* **something**) to pretend to be someone or something. **4** to ask or put forward (a question). **5** to cause (a problem, etc) or present (a threat, etc).
— **strike a pose** to adopt a position or attitude, especially a commanding or impressive one.
[from Old French *poser*, to place, from Latin *pausare*, to cease, pause, but influenced by Latin *ponere*, to place]

Poseidon in Greek mythology, the brother of Zeus, god of water and the sea, depicted with a trident in his hand. He was a violent god, responsible for earthquakes and similar destructive forces. He was also connected with horse-taming. He was later associated with the Roman god Neptune.

poser *noun* **1** *derog.* someone who tries to impress others by putting on an act; a poseur. **2** *colloq.* a difficult problem; a puzzle.

poseur *noun derog.* a person who behaves affectedly or insincerely. [from French *poseur*]

posh *colloq.* — *adj.* **1** high-quality, expensive, smart or stylish. **2** upper-class. — *adv.* in a posh manner: *talk posh*. — *verb* (*also* **posh something up**) to smarten it. [perhaps related to *posh*, a dandy]

Posidonius (c.135–c.51 BC) Greek philosopher, scientist, and polymath, born in Apamea, Syria. He studied at Athens, spent many years on travel and scientific research in Europe and Africa, then settled in Rhodes and later Rome. He wrote on an enormous range of subjects, including geometry, geography, astronomy, meteorology, history, and philosophy, although only fragments of his works survive.

posit *verb* (**posited**, **positing**) to lay down, or assume, as a basis for discussion; to postulate. [from Latin *ponere*, to place]

position — *noun* **1** a place where something or someone is: *a fine position overlooking the bay.* **2** the right or proper place: *in/out of position.* **3** the relationship of things to one another in space; arrangement. **4** a way of sitting, standing, lying, facing, being held or placed, etc: *an upright position.* **5** *Mil.* a place occupied for strategic purposes. **6** one's opinion or viewpoint. **7** a job or post: *a senior position at the bank.* **8** rank; status; importance in society: *wealth and position.* **9** the place of a competitor in the finishing order, or at an earlier stage in a contest: *lying in fourth position.* **10** *Games* one's allotted place on the pitch, as a team member: *the centre-forward position.* **11** the set of circumstances in which one is placed: *not in a position to help.* — *verb* (**positioned, positioning**) to place; to put in position. — **be in no position to do something** to have no right to complain, criticize, etc. [from Latin *positio*, from *ponere*, to place]

positional *adj.* relating to or determined by position.

positive — *adj.* **1** sure; certain; convinced. **2** definite; allowing no doubt: *positive proof of her guilt.* **3** expressing agreement or approval: *a positive response.* **4** optimistic: *feeling more positive.* **5** forceful or determined; not tentative. **6** constructive; contributing to progress or improvement; helpful. **7** clear and explicit: *positive directions.* **8** *colloq.* downright: *a positive scandal.* **9** denoting a chemical test result that confirms the existence of the suspected condition. **10** *Maths.* denoting a number or quantity greater than zero. **11** *Physics, Electr.* having a deficiency of electrons, and so being able to attract them, ie attracted by a negative charge; describing one of two terminals having the higher electrical potential. **12** *Photog.* having light and shade, or colours, as in the actual image, not reversed, etc. **13** *Grammar* expressing quality in the simple form, as distinct from the comparative or superlative forms. — *noun* **1** *Photog.* a print in which light, shade, and colour correspond to those of the actual image. **2** *Grammar* a positive adjective or adverb; the positive form or degree in comparison. **3** a positive thing, especially a positive quantity or a positive electrical terminal. [from Latin *positivus*, from *ponere*, to place]

positive discrimination the creation of special employment opportunities, etc for those previously disadvantaged or discriminated against.

positive feedback *Engineering, Biol.* a form of feedback in which the output of a system is used to increase the input.

positively *adv.* **1** in a positive way. **2** definitely.

positiveness *noun* being positive.

positive vetting investigation of the connections and sympathies of a person being considered for a position of trust, eg in the senior civil service.

positivism *noun* **1** a school of philosophy maintaining that knowledge can come only from observable phenomena and positive facts. **2** (*also* **logical positivism**) a 20c development of this, concerned with the significance and verifiability of statements.

positivist — *noun* a believer in positivism. *adj.* characteristic of positivism.

positron *noun Physics* a particle that has the same mass as an electron, and an equal but opposite charge. [a contraction of *positive electron*]

poss — *adj. colloq.* possible. — *abbrev.* (*usually* **poss.**) **1** possible or possibly. **2** *Grammar* possessive.

posse *noun North Amer. Hist.* a mounted troop of men at the service of a local sheriff. [from Latin *posse*, to be able]

possess *verb* **1** to own. **2** to have as a feature or quality: *possesses a quick mind.* **3** said of an emo-

tion, evil spirit, etc to take hold of (someone): *what possessed you to behave like that?* [from Old French *possesser*, from Latin *possessio*, possession]

possessed *adj.* **1** *formal* (**possessed of something**) owning it; having it: *possessed of great wealth.* **2** controlled or driven by demons, etc.

possession *noun* **1** the condition of possessing something; ownership: *take possession of / come into one's possession.* **2** the crime of possessing something illegally: *charged with possession of firearms.* **3** occupancy of property: *take possession of the house.* **4** *Football* control of the ball by one or other team in a match. **5** something owned. **6** (**possessions**) one's property or belongings. **7** (**possessions**) a country's dominions abroad: *foreign possessions.* — **be in possession of something** to hold or possess it.

possessive — *adj.* **1** relating to possession. **2** unwilling to share, or allow others use of, things one owns: *possessive about my car.* **3** inclined to dominate, monopolise, and allow no independence to, eg one's wife, husband, child, etc: *a possessive husband.* **4** *Grammar* denoting the form of a noun, pronoun, or adjective that shows possession, eg *Jack's, its, her.* — *noun Grammar* **1** the possessive form of a word. **2** a word in the possessive.

possessively *adv.* in a possessive way.

possessiveness *noun* being possessive.

possessor *noun* a person who possesses something.

possibility *noun* (PL. **possibilities**) **1** something that is possible. **2** the state of being possible. **3** a candidate for selection, etc. **4** (**possibilities**) promise or potential: *an idea with possibilities.*

possible — *adj.* **1** achievable; able to be done. **2** that may happen: *the possible outcome.* **3** imaginable; conceivable: *a possible explanation / it's possible that he's dead.* — *noun* a person or thing potentially selectable; a possibility. [from Latin *possibilis*, from *posse*, to be able]

possibly *adv.* **1** perhaps; maybe. **2** within the limits of possibility: *doing all we possibly can.* **3** used for emphasis: *how could you possibly think that?*

possum *noun colloq.* an opossum. — **play possum** to pretend to be unconscious, asleep, or unaware of what is happening.

post[1] — *noun* **1** a shaft or rod fixed upright in the ground, as a support, marker, etc. **2** (*often in compounds*) a vertical timber supporting a horizontal one: *a doorpost.* **3** an upright pole marking the beginning or end of a race track. — *verb* **1** (*also* **post something up**) to put up (a notice, etc) for public viewing. **2** to announce the name of (someone) among others in a published list: *posted missing.* [from Latin *postis*] ◇ Private post, at rates related to distance, was first delivered in 1635. National postal services have existed since the early 19c, and a standardized rate for delivery (based on weight) was introduced by Rowland Hill in 1840. In some countries, private operators now provide competition for the former state monopoly suppliers of postal services.

post[2] *noun* **1** a job: *a teaching post.* **2** a position to which one is assigned for military duty: *never left his post.* **3** a settlement or establishment, especially in a remote area: *trading-post / military post.* **4** *Mil.* a bugle call summoning soldiers to their quarters at night, or (**last post**) sounded at funerals. — *verb* to station (someone) somewhere on duty; to transfer (personnel) to a new location: *posted abroad.* [from Italian *posto*, from Latin *positum*, from *ponere*, to place]

post[3] — *noun* **1** the official system for the delivery of mail. **2** letters and parcels delivered by this system; mail. **3** a collection of mail, eg from a postbox: *catch the next post.* **4** a delivery of mail: *came by the second post.* **5** a place for mail collec-

tion; a postbox or post office: *took it to the post.* **6** used as a newspaper title: *the Washington Post.* — *verb* **1** to put (mail) into a postbox; to send by post. **2** *Commerce* **a** to enter (an item) in a ledger. **b** (*usually* **post up**) to update (a ledger). **3** to supply with the latest news: *keep us posted.* [from Italian *posta*, from Latin *posita*, from *ponere*, to place]

post- *combining form* forming words meaning 'after': *postwar.* [from Latin *post*, after, behind]

postage *noun* the charge for sending a letter, etc through the post.

postage stamp a small printed label stuck on a letter, etc showing that the appropriate postage has been paid. ◇ Prepayment of postage charges by means of stamps began in Britain in 1840 with the 'Penny Post', one old penny being charged for each half ounce of a letter's weight, regardless of its destination.

postal *adj.* **1** of or relating to the post office or delivery of mail. **2** sent by post: *a postal vote.*

postal code same as POSTCODE.

postal order a money order available from, and payable by, a post office.

postbag *noun* **1** a mailbag. **2** the letters received by eg a radio or television programme, magazine, or celebrated person.

postbox *noun* a public box in which to post letters; a letter box.

postcard *noun* a card for writing messages on, often with a picture on one side, designed for sending through the post without an envelope.

post chaise a fast usually four-wheeled coach carrying up to four passengers, and mail, drawn by posthorses. [see POST[3]]

postcode *noun* a code used to identify a postal address, often a combination of letters and numerals.

post-consumer waste newspapers and other household waste, as opposed to industrial; waste used for recycling.

postdate *verb* **1** to put a future date on (a cheque, etc). **2** to assign a later date than that previously accepted to (an event, etc). **3** to occur at a later date than.

poster *noun* **1** a large notice or advertisement for public display. **2** a large printed picture. [from POST[1]]

poster art posters as an art form from the late 19c, when there were improvements in printing techniques, especially in colour lithography. Many major artists worked in the field: Toulouse-Lautrec is especially renowned for his striking commercial posters; Aubrey Beardsley's illustrations were influenced by his study of Japanese prints; and posters by the Czech artist Alphonse Mucha have enjoyed a wide revival.

poste restante a facility at a post office for holding mail until collected by the recipient, eg when a private address is not available. [from French *poste restante*, post remaining]

posterior — *noun facetious* one's buttocks. — *adj. Anat., Archit.* placed behind or after. [from Latin *posterior*, comparative of *posterus*, coming after]

posterity *noun* **1** future generations. **2** one's descendants. [from Latin *posteritas*, from *posterus*, coming after]

postern *noun Hist.* a back door, back gate, or private entrance. [from Old French *posterne*]

poster paint *or* **poster colour** a water-based paint in a bright opaque colour.

post-free *adj.* **1** with postage prepaid. **2** without charge for postage.

postgraduate — *noun* a person studying for an advanced degree or qualification after obtaining a first degree. — *adj.* relating to such a person or degree.

posthaste *adv.* with all speed. [from *post*, a courier + HASTE]

posthouse *noun Hist.* an inn where horses were kept for conveying the mail and for the use of travellers wishing to change horses, etc.

posthumous *adj.* **1** published after the death of the author, composer, etc. **2** *said of a child* born after its father's death. **3** awarded or coming after death: *posthumous decoration/acclaim*. [from Latin *postumus*, superlative of *posterus*, coming after; *h* inserted by mistaken association with *humus*, earth, ie burial]

posthumously *adv.* after death.

Posthumus Leonatus the worthy hero of Shakespeare's *Cymbeline*, and husband of Imogen, who is driven to distraction by misguided jealousy.

postilion *or* **postillion** *noun Hist.* a rider on the nearside horse of one of the pairs of posthorses drawing a carriage, who, in the absence of a coachman, guides the team. [from Italian *postiglione*, from *posta*, *post*[5]]

Postimpressionism *noun* an imprecise term associated with the art critic Roger Fry, used to describe the more progressive forms of French painting since c.1880. Painters included in the designation were Van Gogh, Gauguin, Cézanne, and Matisse, who all developed the Impressionist style far beyond the merely representational.

post-industrial society a term coined in 1973 by the US sociologist Daniel Bell (1919–) to describe an economically and technologically advanced society no longer dependent for its productivity on large-scale, labour intensive industrial manufacture.

postman *or* **postwoman** *noun* a man or woman whose job is to deliver mail.

postmark *noun* a mark stamped on mail by the post office, cancelling the stamp and showing the date and place of posting.

postmaster *or* **postmistress** *noun* a man or woman in charge of a local post office.

Postmaster General (PL. **Postmasters General**) a government minister in charge of the country's postal services.

postmeridian *adj.* **1** occurring after noon. **2** relating to the afternoon.

post meridiem after noon. [from Latin *post meridiem*]

Post-Modernism a term used in architecture to describe a style or concept that supersedes 20c modernism and the International Style in particular. It is generally applied to buildings which draw upon an eclectic range of stylistic precedents (eg the A T & T building, New York, 1978–83, by Johnson and Burgee). The term has been increasingly used to identify a basic rejection of previously widely-held architectural beliefs.

post-mortem *noun* **1** a medical examination of a dead person to establish the cause of death. **2** *facetious* an after-the-event discussion. [from Latin *post mortem*, after death]

postnatal *adj.* belonging to, or occurring in, the period immediately after birth, or after giving birth.

postnatal depression *Psychol.* a relatively common form of depression that occurs shortly after giving birth.

post office 1 a local office handling postal business, issuing various types of licence, etc. **2** (**Post Office**) the government department in charge of postal services.

post-operative *adj.* belonging to, or occurring in, the period immediately following a surgical operation: *post-operative discomfort*.

post-paid *adj.* with postage prepaid.

postpartum *adj. Medicine* after childbirth.

postpone *verb* to defer or put off till later. [from Latin *postponere*, to place after]

postponement *noun* postponing.

postprandial *adj. facetious* following a meal: *a postprandial doze*. [from POST- + Latin *prandium*, breakfast, lunch]

post-production *noun* the stages in the making of a film or video after shooting and before the first public showing. Processes include recording and adding music and sound track, and final editing.

postscript *noun* **1** a message added to a letter as an afterthought, after one's signature. **2** anything serving as an addition or follow-up to something. [from Latin *postscribere*, to write after]

post-traumatic stress disorder *or* **post-traumatic stress syndrome** *Psychol.* a psychological disorder associated with an extremely traumatic event, such as military combat, rape, torture, natural disasters (eg earthquake), or serious physical injury. Symptoms, which may not appear until many months after the event, include nightmares, flashback experiences, feelings of numbness, isolation, or guilt, and disturbed sleep and concentration.

postulancy *noun* the state or time of being a postulant.

postulant *noun* a candidate for holy orders or for admission to a religious community. [from Latin *postulare*, to ask]

postulate — *verb* to assume or suggest as the basis for discussion; to take for granted. — *noun* something postulated. [from Latin *postulare*, to demand]

postulation *noun* **1** postulating. **2** a request, claim, or assumption.

postural *adj.* relating to posture.

posture — *noun* **1** the way one holds one's body in standing, sitting, or walking. **2** a particular position or attitude of the body. **3** an attitude adopted towards a particular issue, etc. **4** a pose adopted for effect. — *verb intrans. derog.* to pose, strike attitudes, etc so as to draw attention to oneself. [from Latin *positura*, from *ponere*, to place]

posturer *noun* a person who poses or assumes attitudes for effect.

postviral syndrome a condition following viral infection, characterized by fatigue, poor concentration, depression and dizziness.

postwar *adj.* relating or belonging to the period following a war.

posy *noun* (PL. **posies**) a small bunch of flowers. [a variant of POESY]

pot[1] — *noun* **1** any of various usually deep and round domestic containers used as cooking or serving utensils or for storage. **2** the amount held by such a container: *a pot of tea*. **3** *Pottery* any handmade vessel. **4** the pool of accumulated bets in any gambling game. **5** *Billiards* a shot that pockets a ball. **6** a casual shot: *take a pot at something*. **7** a chamberpot. **8** a flowerpot or plant pot. **9** (**pots**) *colloq.* a great deal, especially of money. **10** *colloq.* a trophy, especially a cup. **11** a potbelly. — *verb* (**potted, potting**) **1** to plant in a plant pot. **2** to preserve (a type of food) in a pot. **3** to summarize, especially in a popular style: *a potted history*. **4** *Billiards* to shoot (a ball) into a pocket. **5** (**pot** *or* **pot at someone** *or* **something**) *colloq.* to shoot at them, especially indiscriminately or wildly. — **go to pot** *colloq.* to degenerate badly. **keep the pot boiling** *colloq.* to sustain public interest in something. [from Anglo-Saxon *pott*]

pot[2] *noun colloq.* marijuana. [from Mexican Spanish *potiguaya*]

potable *adj.* fit for drinking; drinkable. [from Latin *potabilis*]

Potala Palace a 13-storey stronghold constructed on a rocky outcrop near Lhasa, Tibet, in the 17c. The complex, which was once the religious and political centre of Tibet, includes the Red Palace (the former seat of the Dalai Lamas) as well as many halls, chapels, and prisons.

potash *noun* any of various compounds of potassium, especially the fertilizer potassium carbonate or (*also* **caustic potash**) potassium hydroxide.

potassium *noun Chem.* (SYMBOL **K**, ATOMIC NUMBER **19**) a soft silvery-white metal that occurs as various compounds in the Earth's crust and in seawater. The pure metal reacts violently with water and is generally stored under paraffin. Its compounds are used in fertilizers, explosives, laboratory reagents, soaps, and some types of glass. It is an essential element for plants and animals, and plays a central role in the transmission of nerve impulses. [from POTASH]

potassium bicarbonate *Chem.* same as potassium hydrogencarbonate.

potassium hydrogencarbonate *Chem.* (FORMULA $KHCO_3$) a white crystalline powder, soluble in water, that is used in baking powder, some detergents, carbonated soft drinks, carbon-dioxide fire extinguishers, and as an antacid to treat indigestion.

potassium hydrogentartrate *Chem.* (FORMULA $KHC_4H_4O_6$) a white crystalline powder, soluble in water, found in vegetables and fruit juices, and used in baking powders and carbonated drinks. – Also called *cream of tartar*.

potassium hydroxide *Chem.* (FORMULA **KOH**) a highly corrosive white crystalline solid that readily absorbs moisture from the atmosphere, and dissolves in water to form a strong alkaline solution. It is used in the manufacture of soft soap, and as an electrolyte in batteries and an intermediate in the manufacture of other chemicals. – Also called *caustic potash*.

potassium nitrate *Chem.* (FORMULA KNO_3) a white or transparent crystalline solid, soluble in water, that is highly explosive and a very strong oxidizing agent. It is used in the manufacture of fireworks, matches, gunpowder, fertilizers, and some types of glass, and as a food preservative, especially for curing meats. – Also called *nitre*, *saltpetre*.

potassium permanganate *Chem.* (FORMULA $KMnO_4$) a dark purple crystalline solid that is soluble in water, and an extremely powerful oxidizing agent. It is used in disinfectants, fungicides, dyes, and bleaches, and in chemical analysis. – Also called *permanganate of potash*, *potassium manganate(VII)*.

potation *noun facetious* **1** the act of drinking. **2** an especially alcoholic drink. [from Latin *potatio*]

potato *noun* (PL. **potatoes**) **1** any of thousands of varieties of a perennial plant (*Solanum tuberosum*) that produces edible tubers (swollen underground stems) and is a staple crop of temperate regions worldwide. It has compound leaves, consisting of two rows of leaflets, and bears clusters of drooping white or purple flowers, each having five yellow stamens forming a prominent cone. The tubers, which are produced in abundance at the ends of stolons, vary greatly in size, shape, colour, and flavour, but are often round or oval in shape with a brown or reddish skin. The 'eyes' of a potato are dormant buds, which under favourable conditions give rise to new stems. The potato was originally cultivated by the Indians of S America, and was introduced to Europe by the Spanish conquerors in the 16c. **2** the tuber of this plant, which is rich in starch, vitamin C, and protein, and can be cooked and eaten as a vegetable, or processed to form crisps or chips. [from Spanish *batata*, from a S American language]

potato blight *Bot.* a widespread disease of potato and related plants, in which the entire plant is affected and rapidly dies, caused by the fungus *Phytophthora infestans*, especially in wet weather. A severe outbreak of the disease in Ireland in the 1840s caused the great Irish potato famine.

potato crisp same as CRISP NOUN.

Potato Eaters, The a dark painting by Vincent van Gogh (1885, Amsterdam), his first masterpiece.

pot-bellied *adj.* having a pot-belly.

pot-belly *noun* (PL. **pot-bellies**) *derog. colloq.* a large overhanging belly.

potboiler *noun derog.* an inferior work of literature or art produced by a writer or artist capable of better work, simply to make money and stay in the public view.

potbound *adj., said of a plant* with its roots cramped by too small a pot.

poteen *noun Irish* illicitly distilled Irish whiskey. [from Irish *poitín*]

Potemkin, Grigoriy Aleksandrovich (1739–91) Russian soldier, born near Smolensk. He entered the Russian army, attracted the notice of Catherine II, and as her intimate favourite (possibly her secret husband), heavily influenced Russian foreign policy. He was created field marshal (1784), and distinguished himself in the Russo-Turkish Wars (1768–74, 1787–92), during which Russia gained the Crimea and the north coast of the Black Sea. The cities he founded include Nikolaev.

potency *noun* (PL. **potencies**) **1** being potent, power. **2** the capacity for development.

potent *adj.* **1** strong; effective; powerful. **2** *said of an argument, etc* persuasive; convincing. **3** *said of a drug or poison* powerful and swift in effect. **4** *said of a male* capable of sexual intercourse. [from Latin *potens*, present participle of *posse*, to be able]

potentate *noun literary* a powerful ruler; a monarch. [from Latin *potentatus*, from *potens*, powerful]

potential — *adj.* possible or likely, though as yet not tested or actual. — *noun* **1** the range of capabilities that a person or thing has; powers or resources not yet developed or made use of: *fulfil one's potential.* **2** *Physics* the energy required to move a unit of mass, electric charge, etc, from an infinite distance to the point in a gravitational or electric field where it is to be measured. **3** potential difference. [from Latin *potentialis*, from *potentia*, power]

potential difference (pd) *Physics* the difference in electric potential between two points in an electric field or circuit, usually expressed in volts. It is equal to the work done in moving a unit charge from one point to the other. Potential difference is the driving force for flow of electric currents, because electric charges tend to flow to the point where their energy value is lowest. – Also called *voltage, electromotive force.*

potential energy *Physics* the energy stored by an object by virtue of its position. For example, if an object is raised above the Earth's surface, then it acquires potential energy equal to the work done against the force of gravity in lifting it. Work done in compressing a spring is stored as elastic potential energy in the spring.

potentially *adv.* in terms of potential; possibly: *a potentially difficult problem.*

potentilla *noun Bot.* any plant of the genus *Potentilla* of the rose family.

potentiometer *noun Physics* an instrument that is used to measure electric potential. Potentiometers are used in electronic circuits, especially as volume controls in transistor radios.

potherb *noun* a plant whose leaves or stems are used in cooking to season or garnish food.

pothole *noun* **1** a roughly circular hole worn in the bedrock of a river as pebbles are swirled around by water eddies. **2** a vertical cave system or deep hole eroded in limestone. **3** a hole worn in a road surface. [from POT[1]]

potholer *noun* a person who takes part in potholing.

potholing *noun* the sport of exploring deep caves and potholes.

pothook *noun* **1** a hook on which to hang a pot over a fire. **2** a hooked stroke in handwriting.

potion *noun* a draught of medicine, poison, or some magic elixir. [from Latin *potio*, from *potare*, to drink]

pot luck whatever is available.

Potomac River a river in West Virginia, Virginia, and Maryland, USA, length 459km/285mi. Formed at the junction of two branches (the N and the S Potomac), it rises in the Allegheny Mts, and flows into Chesapeake Bay. It is navigable for large craft as far as Washington. The main tributary of the Potomac is the Shenandoah. The Great Falls lie 24km/15mi above Washington.

Potosí 1 POP (1989e) 111 000, the capital of Potosí department, SW Bolivia. At an altitude of 4 060m, it is the highest city of its size in the world. It is Bolivia's chief industrial centre. HISTORY founded by the Spanish in 1545; major silver-mining town in the 17c–18c, becoming the most important city in S America at the time. NOTABLE FEATURES Convent of Santa Teresa (art collection); Las Cajas Reales (Cabildo and Royal Treasury); cathedral; thermal baths at the Laguna de Tarapaya; nearby mint (Casa Real de Moneda), founded in 1542, rebuilt in 1759, now a museum and World Heritage site. **2** a department in SW Bolivia with Potosí as its capital.

potpourri *noun* **1** a fragrant mixture of dried flowers, leaves, etc placed in containers and used to scent rooms. **2** a medley or mixture: *a potpourri of old tunes.* [from French *potpourri*, literally 'rotten pot']

pot roast a cut of meat braised with a little water in a covered pot.

Potsdam POP (1991e) 140 000, the capital of the state of Brandenburg, NE Germany. It lies on the R Havel, W of Berlin. HISTORY former residence of German emperors and Prussian kings; badly bombed in World War II; scene of the 1945 Potsdam Conference; capital of Potsdam county as part of East Germany. NOTABLE FEATURES Sans Souci Palace and Park (1745–7); Garrison Church (18c).

Potsdam Conference a conference (17 Jul–2 Aug 1945) to discuss the post-World War II settlement in Europe, attended by Churchill (and later Attlee), Stalin, and Truman. Soviet power in E Europe was recognized, Poland's western frontier was set to run along the Oder–Neisse line, and Germany was to be divided into four occupation zones. Political differences between the USA and USSR marked the start of the Cold War.

potsherd *noun* a fragment of pottery.

pot-shot *noun* **1** an easy shot at close range. **2** a shot made without taking careful aim.

Potter, (Helen) Beatrix (1866–1943) English writer, born in London. She is remembered as the author and illustrator of the popular children's books which feature characters such as Peter Rabbit (1900), Squirrel Nutkin (1903), and Benjamin Bunny (1904).

Potter, Stephen (1900–69) English writer and radio producer. He joined the BBC in 1938, and is best known in radio as co-author with Joyce Grenfell of the *How* series. In his writing, he is remembered for his humorous studies of the art of demoralizing the opposition, including

Gamesmanship (1947), *Lifemanship* (1950), and *One-Upmanship* (1952).

potter[1] *noun* a person who makes pottery.

potter[2] *verb intrans.* (**pottered, pottering**) **1** (*usually* **potter about**) to busy oneself in a mild way with trifling tasks. **2** (*usually* **potter about** *or* **along**) to progress in an unhurried manner; to dawdle. [from Anglo-Saxon *potian*, to thrust]

Potteries, the POP (1981) 377 000, an urban area in the upper Trent Valley of Staffordshire, central England. It extends c.14km/9mi (NW–SE) by 5km/3mi (W–E), and includes Stoke-on-Trent. Since the 18c, the Potteries area has been the heart of the English china and earthenware industry, based on local clay and coal.

potter's wheel an apparatus with a heavy rotating stone platter, on which clay pots can be shaped by hand before firing.

pottery *noun* **1** vessels or other objects of baked clay. **2** the art of making such objects. **3** a factory where such objects are produced commercially.

pottiness *noun* being potty.

potting-shed *noun* a shed in which to keep garden tools, put plants into pots, etc.

potty[1] *adj.* (**pottier, pottiest**) *colloq.* **1** mad; crazy. **2** (**potty about someone** *or* **something**) intensely interested in or keen on them.

potty[2] *noun* (PL. **potties**) *colloq.* a child's chamberpot. [a diminutive of POT[1]]

pouch *noun* **1** *old use* a purse or small bag. **2** in marsupials such as the kangaroo, a pocket of skin on the belly, in which the young are carried till weaned. **3** a fleshy fold in the cheek of hamsters and other rodents, for storing undigested food. **4** a puffy bulge under the eyes. [from Old French *poche*, pocket]

pouffe *noun* a firmly stuffed drum-shaped or cube-shaped cushion for use as a low seat. [from French *pouffe*]

Poulenc, Francis (1899–1963) French composer, born in Paris. He became a member of *Les Six*, and was prominent in the reaction against 'Debussyesque' Impressionism. His works include much chamber music and the ballet *Les Biches*, produced by Sergei Diaghilev in 1924, but he is best known for his considerable output of songs, such as *Fêtes Galantes* (1943).

poulterer *noun* a dealer in poultry and game. [from *poult*, a chicken]

poultice *noun* a hot, semi-liquid mixture spread on a bandage and applied to the skin to reduce inflammation, formerly used as a treatment for boils. [from Latin *pultes*, plural of *puls*, porridge]

poultry *noun* **1** a collective term for domesticated birds that are kept for their eggs or meat, or both, eg chickens, which are the most common poultry birds. Ducks, geese, and turkeys are also classified as poultry, and are farmed mainly for their meat. **2** the meat of such birds. [from *poult*, chicken, from Old French *poulet*, chicken]

pounce — *verb* (*often* **pounce on something** *or* **someone**) **1** *intrans.* to leap on a victim or prey. **2** *intrans.* to seize on; to grab eagerly. — *noun* an act of pouncing.

Pound, Ezra (Loomis) (1885–1972) US poet, born in Hailey, Idaho. He travelled widely in Europe, working as a journalist and editor, and lived in London, Paris, and Italy. An experimental poet, and a leader of the Imagist school, his early publications include *Personae* (1909), *Homage to Sextus Propertius* (1919), and *Hugh Selwyn Mauberley* (1920). During World War II, he made pro-fascist broadcasts on Italian radio, and in 1945 he was escorted back to the USA and indicted for treason, but was judged insane and placed in an asylum until 1958. His main work is the poetic series *The Cantos*, which were published over many decades, beginning in 1917.

pound[1] *noun* **1** (*in full* **pound sterling**) (SYMBOL **£**) the principal currency unit of the United Kingdom, divided into 100 pence. **2** the English name for the principal currency unit in several other countries, eg Malta, Cyprus, and Egypt. **3** (ABBREV. **lb**) a measure of weight equal to 16 ounces (453 grams) avoirdupois, or 12 ounces (373 grams) troy. [from Anglo-Saxon *pund*]

pound[2] *noun* an enclosure where stray animals or illegally parked cars that have been taken into police charge are kept for collection. [from Anglo-Saxon *pund-*, enclosure]

pound[3] *verb* **1** *trans., intrans.* (**pound something** *or* **on** *or* **at something**) to beat or bang it vigorously. **2** (*also* **pound something out**) to produce it by pounding: *pounding out articles on her typewriter.* **3** *intrans.* to walk or run with heavy thudding steps. **4** to crush or grind to a powder. [from Anglo-Saxon *punian*]

poundage *noun* a fee or commission charged per pound in weight or money.

-pounder *combining form* forming words meaning: **1** something weighing a certain number of pounds: *a three-pounder trout.* **2** a field gun designed to fire shot weighing a certain number of pounds: *a twenty-four-pounder.*

pound force *Physics* a unit of force equal to the gravitational force experienced by a pound mass when the acceleration due to gravity has a value of $9.8 \mathrm{m \ s^{-2}}$.

pound of flesh the strict exacting of one's due in the fulfilment of a bargain, to the extent of causing unreasonable suffering to the other party. [used in allusion to Shakespeare, *The Merchant of Venice* IV.I, in which a pound of flesh is stipulated as a penalty in a bargain]

pour *verb* **1** *trans., intrans.* to flow or cause to flow in a downward stream. **2** *intrans., trans.* said of a jug, etc to discharge (liquid) in a certain way: *doesn't pour very well.* **3** (*also* **pour something out**) to serve a drink, etc by pouring. **4** *intrans.* to rain heavily. **5** *intrans.* (**pour in** *or* **out**) to come or go in large numbers: *people were pouring out of the cinema.* **6** *intrans.* (**pour in** *or* **out**, *etc*) to flow or issue plentifully: *donations poured in / words poured from her pen.* **7** (**pour something out**) to reveal it without inhibition: *pour out one's feelings.* **8** to invest (money, energy, etc) liberally in something: *poured all his savings into the company.* — **pour cold water on something** to be discouraging or depreciatory about an idea, scheme, etc.

pour scorn on something to be contemptuous about it. [origin unknown]

pourboire *noun* a tip or gratuity. [from French *pourboire*]

pourer *noun* a person or thing that pours: *the jug is not a good pourer.*

Poussin, Nicolas (1594–1665) French painter, born near Les Andelys. He went to Rome in 1624 and spent the rest of his life there, apart from a short visit (1640–2) to Paris. He was influenced by Raphael and was a major figure in the development of French Classical painting. His works include *The Adoration of the Golden Calf* (c.1635, National Gallery, London), two sets of the *Seven Sacraments*, and *The Four Seasons* (1660–4, Louvre, Paris).

pout — *verb* **1** *intrans., trans.* to push the lower lip or both lips forward as an indication of sulkiness or seductiveness. **2** *intrans.* said of the lips to stick out in this way. — *noun* an act of pouting or a pouting expression.

pouter *noun* a variety of pigeon that can puff out its crop.

poverty *noun* **1** the condition of being poor; want. **2** poor quality: *poverty of the soil.* **3** inadequacy; deficiency: *poverty of imagination.* [from Old French *poverte*]

poverty line the minimum income needed to purchase the basic needs of life.

poverty-stricken *adj.* suffering from poverty.

poverty trap the inescapable poverty of someone who, in achieving an improvement in income, has his or her state benefits cut.

POW *abbrev.* prisoner of war.

powder — *noun* **1** any substance in the form of fine dust-like particles. **2** (*also* **face powder**) a cosmetic patted on to the skin to give it a soft smooth appearance. **3** gunpowder. **4** a dose of medicine in powder form. — *verb* (**powdered, powdering**) **1** to apply powder to; to sprinkle or cover with powder. **2** to reduce to a powder by crushing; to pulverise. [from Old French *poudre*]

powder metallurgy *Chem.* a method of shaping heat-resistant metals or alloys, by reducing them to powder form, pressing them into moulds and heating them to very high temperatures. First used to make tungsten lamp filaments, the process is now used to make tungsten carbide cutting tools, self-lubricating bearings, etc.

powder puff a pad of velvety or fluffy material for patting powder on to the skin.

powder room a women's toilet in a restaurant, hotel, etc.

powdery *adj.* **1** of the consistency or nature of powder. **2** covered with or full of powder. **3** dusty. **4** friable.

Powell, Anthony (Dymoke) (1905–) English novelist, born in London. He worked in publishing and journalism, and served in World War II. His best-known work is a major series of satirical social novels, *A Dance to the Music of Time* (1951–75) — 12 volumes covering 50 years of British upper-middle-class life and attitudes. Other works include four volumes of memoirs under the general title *To Keep the Ball Rolling* (1976–82).

Powell, Cecil Frank (1903–69) English physicist, born in Tonbridge, Kent. Professor at the University of Bristol and Director of the Wills Physics Laboratory there, he developed new photographic emulsions for the detection of nuclear particles; these were used in cosmic-ray detectors carried by balloon to high altitudes. Such experiments revealed the existence of an elementary particle known as the 'charged pion'. He was awarded the 1950 Nobel Prize for Physics.

Powell, (John) Enoch (1912–) English Conservative politician, born in Birmingham. After being Professor of Greek in Sydney (1937–9), he became an MP (1950) and was Minister of Health (1960–3). His outspoken opinions on non-white immigration and racial integration came to national attention in 1968, and so he was dismissed from the shadow Cabinet. Opposing the Common Market, he did not stand for election in Feb 1974, but returned to parliament in Oct 1974 as an Ulster Unionist MP, until defeated in the 1987 general election.

Powell, Michael (1905–90) English film director, scriptwriter, and producer, born near Canterbury. He worked as a director on minor productions in the 1930s, and co-directed on *The Thief of Baghdad* (1940) for Alexander Korda, who introduced him to the Hungarian scriptwriter, Emeric Pressburger (1902–88). Powell and Pressburger formed The Archers company in 1942, and made some unusual and colourful features, such as *Black Narcissus* (1947) and *The Tales of Hoffman* (1951). After the partnership broke up, Powell's productions included the controversial *Peeping Tom* (1960) and *The Boy Who Turned Yellow* (1972).

power — *noun* **1** control and influence exercised over others. **2** strength, vigour, force, or effectiveness. **3** military strength: *sea power.* **4** the physical ability, skill, opportunity, or authority, to do something: *if it is within my power.* **5** an individual faculty or skill: *the power of speech / at the height of one's powers.* **6** a right, privilege, or responsibility: *the power of arrest / power of attorney.* **7** political control: *assume power.* **8** a state that has an influential role in international affairs. **9** a person or group exercising control or influence: *the real power behind the prime minister.* **10** *colloq.* a great deal: *did her a power of good.* **11** any form of energy, especially when used as the driving force for a machine, eg nuclear power. **12** *Maths.* an exponent or index, denoted by a small numeral placed above and to the right of a numerical quantity, which indicates the number of times that quantity is multiplied by itself, eg 12 to the power of 4, or 12^4, is equal to $12 \times 12 \times 12 \times 12$. A quantity raised to the power of 2 is said to be squared, and a quantity raised to the power of 3 is said to be cubed. **13** *Physics* the rate of doing work or converting energy from one form into another. The SI unit of power is the watt (W), which is equivalent to one joule per second. **14** mechanical or electrical energy, as distinct from manual effort: *power-assisted steering.* **15** *Optics* a measure of the extent to which a lens, optical instrument, or curved mirror can deviate light rays and so magnify an image of an object. For a simple lens the unit of power is the dioptre. — *adj.* using mechanical or electrical power; motor-driven: *power tools.* — *verb* (**powered, powering**) to supply with power: *nuclear-powered warships.*
— **the powers that be** those in authority.
[from Old French *poer*, originally an infinitive, related to Latin *posse*, to be able]

Power and the Glory, The a novel by Graham Greene (1940). It is set in Mexico during a time of religious persecution and centres around the last days of a lapsed priest.

powerboat racing the racing of boats fitted with high-powered and finely-tuned inboard or outboard engines, fuelled by petrol or diesel. The first boat to be fitted with a petrol engine was introduced on the Seine in 1865 by the Frenchman Jean Joseph Lenoir (1822–1900). The first race of note took place in 1903 from Calais to Dover. Nowadays, races are held offshore and inshore.

power cut a break in an electricity supply.

power dressing the wearing by businesswomen of tailored suits and dresses, intended to convey professionalism and assertiveness.

powerful *adj.* having great power, strength, vigour, authority, influence, force, or effectiveness.

powerfully *adv.* in a powerful way.

powerhouse *noun* **1** a power station. **2** *colloq.* a forceful or vigorous person.

powerless *adj.* deprived of power or authority.

power lunch a high-level business discussion held over lunch.

power pack a device for adjusting an electric current to the voltages required by a piece of electronic equipment.

power plant 1 a power station. **2** the engine and parts making up the unit that supplies the propelling power in a vehicle.

power point a socket for connecting an electrical device to the mains.

power station a building where electricity is generated on a large scale from another form of energy, eg coal, nuclear fuel, moving water. The main power stations in the UK are connected by the *national grid*, a network that allows the exchange of power between areas with differing demands for electricity.

power steering *or* **power-assisted steering** in a motor vehicle, a system in which a hydraulic ram connects to the steering linkage and assists the steering effort. The ram is powered by a hydraulic pump driven off the engine and is controlled by a valve which responds to movements of the steering wheel.

Powhatan Confederacy a group of Algonkin-speaking Native N American tribes who inhabited the Tidewater region of Virginia at the time of the first white contact. Named after Chief Powhatan, the group was initially receptive to the settlers, but grew suspicious and twice launched massive (but fruitless) attacks on them (1622 and 1644). Scattered descendants of these tribes were still found in Virginia in the mid-20c.

powwow — *noun* **1** *colloq.* a meeting for discussion. **2** *Hist.* a meeting of N American Indians. — *verb intrans.* to hold a powwow. [from Narragansett (N American Indian language) *powwaw*, priest]

Powys, John Cowper (1872–1964) English writer and critic, born in Shirley, Derbyshire. He worked as a teacher and lecturer and spent much of his time in the USA. He wrote poetry and essays, but is best known for his long novels on West Country and historical themes, including *A Glastonbury Romance* (1932) and *Owen Glendower* (1940).

Powys POP (1992e) 119 000, a mountainous county in E Wales, divided into three districts. AREA 5 077sq km/1 960sq mi. It is bounded E by Shropshire and Hereford and Worcester, S by Gwent, Mid Glamorgan, and West Glamorgan, W by Dyfed, NW by Gwynedd, and N by Clwyd. PHYSICAL DESCRIPTION the Black Mts lie in the SE; drained by the Usk, Wye, Taff, and Tawe rivers; Lake Vyrnwy (a reservoir) is the water source for Liverpool and Birmingham. CAPITAL Llandrindod Wells. ECONOMY agriculture; forestry; tourism. NOTABLE FEATURE Brecon Beacons National Park.

pox *noun* *combining form Medicine* any of various infectious viral diseases that cause a skin rash consisting of pimples that contain pus, eg chickenpox, smallpox. **2** former name for syphilis. [a variant of *pocks*]

Poyang Hu a lake in N Jiangxi province, SE China. AREA 3 583sq km/1 383sq mi. It has been much reduced from its earlier size by silt deposits and land reclamation but it is China's largest freshwater lake. It merges with the Yangtze R in the N.

Poynings' Law statutes enacted (1494) by the Irish parliament at the direction of English Lord Deputy Sir Edward Poynings (1459–1521), which removed its right to meet or pass laws without the agreement of the English government. The immediate aim was to suppress Yorkist support, but it ultimately helped English claims to sovereignty. It was effectively repealed in 1782.

Poynting, John Henry (1852–1914) English physicist, born in Monton, Lancashire. He became Professor of Physics at Birmingham (1880). He investigated electrical phenomena and radiation pressure, and determined the constant of gravitation by a torsion experiment (1891). In 1884 he introduced the 'Poynting vector', giving a simple expression for the rate of flow of electromagnetic energy.

Poznań, German **Posen** POP (1992e) 590 000, the industrial capital of Poznań voivodship, W Poland, lying on the R Warta. HISTORY founded in the 10c; capital of Poland until the 13c; part of Prussia from 1793 until returned to Poland in 1919. NOTABLE FEATURES cathedral (18c, largely rebuilt); Franciscan church (17c–18c); castle (13c) with museum of crafts; remains of old Prussian forts on the Citadel Hill; National Museum; Great Poland Army Museum.

Pozzo a character in Samuel Beckett's *Waiting for Godot*.

pp *abbrev.* **1** pages. **2** *per procurationem* (Latin), by the agency of. **3** *Mus.* pianissimo.

PPARC *abbrev.* Particle Physics and Astronomy Research Council.

PPE *abbrev.* Philosophy, Politics, and Economics.

ppm *abbrev.* parts per million.

PPS *abbrev.* **1** Parliamentary Private Secretary. **2** *post postscriptum* (Latin), after the postscript, ie an additional postscript.

PR *abbrev.* **1** proportional representation. **2** public relations.

Pr *symbol Chem.* praseodymium.

practicability *noun* being practicable.

practicable *adj.* **1** capable of being done, used, or successfully carried out; feasible. **2** *said eg of a road* fit for use. [from Latin *practicare*, to practise]

practicably *adv.* in a practicable way.

practical — *adj.* **1** concerned with action with some purpose or result in contrast to theory: *put one's knowledge to practical use.* **2** effective, or capable of being effective, in actual use: *practical ideas / a practical knowledge of German.* **3** *said eg of clothes* designed for tough or everyday use; sensibly plain. **4** *said of a person* sensible and efficient in deciding and acting; good at doing manual jobs. **5** in effect; virtual: *a practical walkover.* — *noun* a practical lesson or examination, eg in a scientific subject. [from obsolete *practic*, practical, from Greek *praktikos*]

practicality *noun* (PL. **practicalities**) **1** being practical. **2** a practical matter. **3** a practical aspect or feature.

practical joke a trick played on someone, as distinct from a joke told.

practically *adv.* **1** almost. **2** in a practical manner.

practice *noun* **1** the process of carrying something out: *easier in theory than in practice / put one's ideas into practice.* **2** a habit, activity, procedure, or custom: *don't make a practice of it.* **3** repeated exercise to improve one's technique in an art, sport, etc. **4** a doctor's or lawyer's business or clientele. — **be in** *or* **out of practice** to have maintained, or failed to maintain, one's skill in an art, sport, etc. [from PRACTISE]

practise *verb* **1** *trans., intrans.* to do exercises repeatedly in (an art, sport, etc) so as to improve one's performance. **2** to make a habit of: *practise self-control.* **3** to go in for as a custom: *tribes that practise bigamy.* **4** to work at, or follow (an art or profession, especially medicine or law). **5** to perform (a wrongful act) against someone: *had practised a cruel deception on them.* [from Latin *practicare*, from Greek *praktikos*, practical]

practised *adj.* skilled; experienced; expert.

practitioner *noun* someone practising an art or profession, especially medicine. [altered from earlier *practician*]

Prado the Spanish national museum in Madrid, founded in 1818 by Ferdinand VII of Spain, and opened to the public in 1819. It houses many important Spanish art works, as well as numerous exhibits from other major European schools. The collection evolved from the private collections of the Spanish royal house.

praetor *noun* in ancient Rome, one of the chief law officers of the state, elected annually, second to the consul in importance. The office could not be held before the age of 33.

Praetorian Guard an élite corps in imperial Rome, officially established in 27 BC by Augustus. They acted as bodyguard to the emperor and had most political influence from the 20s AD, when they were concentrated in a single barracks in Rome itself, and put under the control of a single commander.

Praetorius, Michael (1571–1621) German composer, born in Creuzburg, Thuringia. He was

court organist and (from 1604) kapellmeister at the court of Wolfenbüttel. As well as being one of the most prolific composers of his time (especially church music), he wrote an important treatise, *Syntagma musicum* (1614–20).

pragmatic *adj.* concerned with what is practicable, expedient, and convenient, rather than with theories and ideals; matter-of-fact; realistic. [from Greek *pragma*, deed]

Pragmatic Sanction a Habsburg family law devised (1713) by Emperor Charles VI to establish an order of succession to the Habsburg lands. It decreed that the empire should not be divided; that on the failure of male heirs, the succession should pass to Charles's daughters; and that on the extinction of his line, the lands should pass to the daughters of his deceased brother Joseph I and their heirs. On his death (1740) however, the Sanction was contested by two powers that had agreed to it (Charles Albert of Bavaria and Frederick II, 'the Great', of Prussia), which led to the War of the Austrian Succession.

pragmatism *noun* **1** a practical, matter-of-fact approach to dealing with problems, etc. **2** *Philos.* a school of thought that assesses concepts' truth in terms of their practical implications.

pragmatist *noun* a pragmatic person.

Prague, Czech **Praha** POP (1991) 1.2m, the industrial and commercial capital of the Czech Republic, lying on the R Vltava. HISTORY an important trading centre since the 10c; capital of the newly-created Czechoslovakia in 1918; occupied by Warsaw Pact troops in 1968. NOTABLE FEATURES Hradčany Castle; Cathedral of St Vitus; Royal Palace (Královsky Palc); St Nicholas Cathedral; Wallenstein Palace; St George Church (10c, Romanesque); National Gallery; the historic centre of Prague is a World Heritage site.

Prague Spring the period of political liberalization and reform in Czechoslovakia in early 1968, ended by Soviet intervention in the summer of the same year.

Praia POP (1990) 62 000, the port capital of the Republic of Cape Verde. It is situated on the S shore of São Tiago I.

prairie *noun* in N America, a treeless, grass-covered plain. [from French *prairie*, meadow]

prairie dog a N American rodent similar to a marmot, that lives in labyrinthine burrows and barks like a dog.

prairie dog

prairie schooner a type of long covered wagon used by emigrants making the journey W across the USA in the 19c. Also called *Conestoga wagon*, from the place in Pennsylvania where they were originally manufactured.

praise — *verb* **1** to express admiration or approval of. **2** to worship or glorify (God) with hymns, thanksgiving, etc. — *noun* **1** the expression of admiration or approval; commendation. **2** worship of God.
— **sing the praises of someone** to commend them enthusiastically.
[from Old French *preisier*, from Latin *pretiare*, to value]

praiseworthily *adv.* in a praiseworthy way.

praiseworthiness *noun* being praiseworthy.

praiseworthy *adj.* deserving praise; commendable.

praline *noun* a sweet consisting of nuts in caramelized sugar. [from Marshal Duplessis-Praslin (1598–1675), French soldier whose cook invented it]

pram *noun* a wheeled carriage for a baby, pushed by someone on foot. [a shortening of PERAMBULATOR]

Prambanan Temples a compound of temples (built 9c–10c) in the village of Prambanan, Yogyakarta, Indonesia. It contains three large Hindu temples, and there were originally 244 minor ones, arranged in four rows. It is a World Heritage site.

prance *verb intrans.* **1** *said especially of a horse* to walk with lively springing steps. **2** to frisk or skip about. **3** to parade about in a swaggering manner. [from Middle English *praunce*]

prang *colloq.* — *verb* to crash (a vehicle). — *noun* a vehicle crash. [imitative]

prank *noun* a trick; a practical joke.

prankster *noun* a person who plays pranks, a practical joker.

Prasad, Rajendra (1884–1963) Indian politician, born in Zeradei, Bihar. He left legal practice to become a supporter of Mahatma Gandhi, and was President of the Indian National Congress on several occasions between 1934 and 1948. He became Minister for Food and Agriculture (1946), and India's first President (1950–62).

praseodymium *noun Chem.* (SYMBOL **Pr**, ATOMIC NUMBER **59**) a soft silvery metallic element that is used in the alloy mischmetal, eg to make lighter flints. [from Greek *prasios*, leek-green]

Praslin POP (1985) 5 000, a granite island in the Seychelles, Indian Ocean. AREA 38sq km/15sq mi. The main island of Mahé lies to the SW. Praslin is the home of the coco-de-mer palm and three rare bird species: the Seychelles bulbul, the fruit pigeon, and the black parrot. There are tourist facilities and an airfield for light aircraft.

prat *slang* **1** *offensive* someone stupid. **2** the buttocks.

prate *verb intrans., trans.* to talk or utter foolishly. [from Old Dutch *praeten*]

Pratt, J(oseph) G(aither) (1910–79) US parapsychologist, born in Winston-Salem, North Carolina. He conducted research in parapsychology for over 40 years at Duke, Columbia, and the University of Virginia. His numerous publications include *Extrasensory Perception After Sixty Years* (with J B Rhine, 1940) and *Parapsychology: An Insider's View* (1977).

prattle — *verb intrans., trans.* to chatter or utter childishly or foolishly. — *noun* childish or foolish chatter. [from Old German *pratelen*, to chatter]

prattler *noun* a person who prattles.

prawn *noun* an edible shellfish like a large shrimp. [from Middle English *prane*]

Praxiteles (4c BC) Greek sculptor, a citizen of Athens. His works have almost all perished, though his *Hermes Carrying the Infant Dionysus* was found at Olympia in 1877. Several of his statues are known from Roman copies.

pray — *verb* **1** *intrans.* to address one's god, making earnest requests or giving thanks. **2** *old use* to entreat or implore. **3** to hope desperately. — *interj.* meaning 'please', or 'may I ask', uttered with quaint politeness or cold irony: *pray come in / who asked you, pray?* [from Old French *preier*, from Latin *precari*, to pray]

prayer *noun* **1** an address to one's god, making a request or giving thanks: *say one's prayers.* **2** the activity of praying. **3** an earnest hope, desire, or entreaty.

prayer book a book of set prayers appropriate for various occasions and types of church service.

prayer rug *or* **prayer mat** a small carpet on which a Muslim kneels when praying.

prayer wheel *Buddhism* a drum that turns on a spindle, inscribed with prayers that are regarded as uttered as the drum is rotated.

praying mantis, any of about 1 800 species of predatory insect, usually green or brown in colour, found mainly in tropical regions, and so called because the spiky front legs are held up in front of the head as if in an attitude of prayer while the insect is waiting for its prey, which includes grasshoppers, flies, moths, and butterflies. – Also called *mantis, mantid.*

praying mantis

Pré, Jacqueline du (1945–87) English cellist, born in Oxford. She studied under Tortelier, Casals, and Rostropovich, and made her concert début aged 16. In 1967 she married the pianist Daniel Barenboim, with whom she gave many recitals. After 1973, when she developed multiple sclerosis, she stopped playing and pursued a teaching career.

pre- *prefix* forming words meaning 'before': **1** in time: *pre-war.* **2** in position: *premolar.* **3** in importance: *pre-eminent.* [from Latin *prae-*]

preach *verb* **1** *intrans., trans.* to deliver (a sermon) as part of a religious service. **2** (**preach at someone**) to give them advice in a tedious or obtrusive manner. **3** to advise; to advocate: *preach caution.* [from Latin *praedicare*, to give advice, command]

preamble *noun* an introduction or preface, eg to a speech or document; an opening statement. [from Latin *praeambulare*, to walk before]

prearrange *verb* to arrange in advance: *a prearranged signal.*

prearrangement *noun* an arrangement made previously.

prebend *noun* an allowance paid out of the revenues of a cathedral or collegiate church to its canons or chapter members. [from Latin *praebenda*, allowance]

prebendal *adj.* relating to a prebend or prebendary.

prebendary *noun* (PL. **prebendaries**) a clergyman in receipt of a prebend.

Precambrian *adj.* **1** *Geol.* relating to the earliest geological era, extending from the formation of the Earth about 4 550 million years ago, to the beginning of the Palaeozoic era, about 580 million years ago. During this era life appeared on Earth, probably about 3 500 million years ago, the oldest known fossils being found in rocks of that age. Precambrian fossils are relatively rare, probably because most primitive animals were soft-bodied. **2** relating to the rocks formed during this period.

precancerous *adj.* denoting a condition that could become cancerous if untreated.

precarious *adj.* **1** unsafe; insecure; dangerous. **2** uncertain; chancy. [from Latin *precarius*, obtained by prayer, uncertain, from *prex*, prayer]

precariously *adv.* in a precarious state or way.

precariousness *noun* being precarious.

precast *adj., said of concrete, etc* made into blocks, etc ready for use in building.

precaution *noun* a measure taken to ensure a satisfactory outcome, or to avoid a risk or danger. [from Latin *praecautio*]

precautionary *adj.* **1** suggesting precaution. **2** of the nature of precaution.

precede *verb trans., intrans.* **1** to go or be before, in time, order, position, rank, or importance. **2** to preface or introduce: *preceded her lecture with a word of explanation.* [from Latin *praecedere*, to go before]

precedence *noun* **1** priority: *safety takes precedence over all else.* **2** the fact of preceding, in order, rank, importance, etc; the right to precede others: *were introduced in order of precedence.*

precedent *noun* a previous incident, legal case, etc that is parallel to one under consideration; the measures taken or judgement given in that case, serving as a basis for a decision in the present one.

precentor *noun* a person who leads the singing of a church congregation, or leads the prayers in a synagogue. [from Latin *praecentor*, from *prae-*, before + *canere*, to sing]

precept *noun* a rule or principle, especially of a moral kind, that guides one's behaviour. [from Latin *praeceptum*]

precession *noun* **1** *Physics* the gradual change in direction of the axis of rotation of a spinning body. For example, the axis of a spinning top gradually moves in a circle because of precession. As the top slows down, the circle of precession gets larger and larger until the top wobbles and finally falls over. The Earth's axis undergoes precession caused by the gravitational pull of the Moon, Sun, and planets. **2** *Astron.* (in full **precession of the equinoxes**) the progressively earlier occurrence of the equinoxes, resulting from the gradual change in direction of the Earth's axis of rotation, which over thousands of years produces an apparent change in the position of the stars as seen from Earth. **3** the act of preceding. [from Latin *praecessio*, from *praecedere*, to precede]

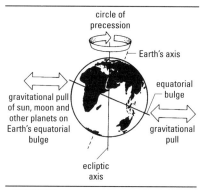

circle of precession
Earth's axis
equatorial bulge
gravitational pull of sun, moon and other planets on Earth's equatorial bulge
gravitational pull
ecliptic axis

precession

precessional *adj.* relating to or involving precession.

precinct *noun* **1** (also **precincts**) the enclosed grounds of a large building, etc: *the cathedral precinct / within the university precincts.* **2** (also **precincts**) the neighbourhood or environs of a place. **3** a traffic-free zone in a town, etc: *a pedestrian precinct.* **4** *North Amer., esp. US* any of the districts into which a city is divided for administrative or policing purposes. [from Latin *praecinctum*, from *praecingere*, to surround]

preciosity *noun* affectedness or exaggerated refinement in speech or manner. [from Latin *pretiositas*, from *pretiosus*, valuable]

precious *adj.* **1** valuable. **2** dear; beloved; treasured: *memories still precious to her.* **3** *derog., said of speech or manner* affected or over-precise. **4** *ironic* confounded: *him and his precious goldfish!* — **precious few** *or* **little** almost none. [from Latin *pretiosus*, valuable]

preciously *adv.* in a precious way.

precious metal gold, silver, or platinum.

preciousness *noun* being precious.

precious stone a mineral valued for its beauty and rarity; a gem.

precipice *noun* a sheer cliff. [from Latin *praecipitium*, from *praecipitare*, to fall headlong]

precipitate — *verb* **1** to cause, or hasten the advent of: *precipitate a war.* **2** to throw or plunge: *precipitated himself into the controversy.* **3** *Chem.* to (cause to) form a suspension of small solid particles in a solution as a result of certain chemical reactions. — *adj.*, *said of actions or decisions* recklessly hasty or ill-considered. — *noun* **1** *Chem.* a suspension of small solid particles that are formed in a solution as a result of certain chemical reactions. **2** moisture deposited as rain, snow, etc. [from Latin *praecipitare*, to fall or throw headlong]

precipitately *adv.* in a precipitate way.

precipitation *noun* **1** rash haste. **2** frozen or liquid water that falls from clouds in the atmosphere to the Earth's surface in the form of rain, snow, sleet, hail, etc. **3** the act of precipitating or process of being precipitated. **4** *Chem.* the formation of a precipitate.

precipitous *adj.* **1** dangerously steep. **2** *said of actions or decisions* precipitate. [from French *précipiteux*]

précis — *noun* (PL. **précis**) a summary of a piece of writing. — *verb* (**précised**, **précising**) to make a précis of. [from French *précis*, cut short]

precise *adj.* **1** exact; very: *at this precise moment.* **2** clear; detailed: *precise instructions.* **3** accurate: *precise timing.* **4** *said of a person* careful over details. [from Latin *praecisus*, shortened]

precisely *adv.* **1** exactly. **2** in a precise manner. **3** *said as a rejoinder* you are quite right.

preciseness *noun* being precise.

precision — *noun* accuracy. — *adj.*, *said of tools, etc* designed to operate with minute accuracy.

precision-approach radar (ABBREV. **PAR**) *Aeron.* a radar system that shows the exact position of an approaching aircraft, and allows an air traffic controller to issue detailed landing instructions to the pilot.

preclude *verb* **1** to rule out, eliminate, or make impossible. **2** (**preclude someone from something**) to prevent their involvement in it: *precluded from attending the meeting.* [from Latin *praecludere*, to impede]

preclusion *noun* **1** precluding. **2** prevention.

precocious *adj.* **1** *said eg of a child* unusually advanced in mental development, speech, behaviour, etc. **2** *said of behaviour, achievements, etc* indicating advanced development. [from Latin *praecox*, ripening early, precocious]

precociously *adv.* with a precocious manner.

precocity *noun* being precocious.

precognition *noun* the supposed ability to foresee events; foreknowledge. [from Latin *praecognitio*]

precognitive *adj.* characterized by precognition.

precolumbian *adj.* denoting the period of American history before the discovery of America by Christopher Columbus.

preconceive *verb* (usually **preconceived**) to form (an idea) of something before having direct experience of it.

preconception *noun* an assumption about something not yet experienced; a preconceived idea.

precondition *noun* a condition to be satisfied in advance.

precursor *noun* **1** something that precedes, and is a sign of, an approaching event. **2** *Chem.* any chemical compound from which another

compound, such as a hormone or enzyme, is directly produced by some form of chemical modification. [from Latin *praecursor*, forerunner, advance guard]

predacious *adj.* predatory. [altered from PREDATORY]

pre-date *verb* **1** to write a bygone date on (a document, etc). **2** to occur at an earlier date than.

predator *noun* **1** any living organism that obtains food by catching, usually killing, and eating other organisms (the prey). **2** *derog.* a predatory person. [from Latin *praedator*, plunderer, hunter]

predatoriness *noun* being predatory.

predatory *adj.* **1** *said of an animal* killing and feeding on others. **2** *said of people* cruelly exploiting the weakness or good will of others for personal gain.

predecease *verb* to die before (someone).

predecessor *noun* **1** the person who preceded one in one's job or position. **2** the previous version, model, etc of a particular thing or product. **3** an ancestor. [from Latin *praedecessor*, from *prae-*, before + *decedere*, to withdraw, give place]

predella *noun* **1** a small painting or panel enclosed in a compartment attached to the lower edge of an altarpiece. An altarpiece often has several such panels illustrating scenes from the life of the saint represented in the main panel. **2** the platform or uppermost step on which an altar stands. **3** a retable. [from Italian *predella*, altar-step]

predestination *noun* **1** the act of predestining or fact of being predestined. **2** *Relig.* the doctrine that whatever is to happen has been unalterably fixed by God from the beginning of time, especially with regard to which souls are to be saved and which damned.

◊ In Christian theology, it was first fully articulated by Augustine during his controversy with the Pelagians, who upheld the doctrine of free will. Protestant reformers Luther and Calvin defended the doctrine, though in varying degrees. Jacobus Arminius rejected the Calvinist view of predestination, and argued that the divine sovereignty was compatible with human free will. In Islam, the concept takes the form of believing that the outcome of human actions is predetermined, although individual acts themselves are not, and that the time of a person's death is preordained.

predestine *verb* (usually **be predestined**) **1** to destine or doom: *were predestined to meet.* **2** to ordain or decree by fate: *it happened as if predestined.* [from Latin *praedestinare*, to determine in advance]

predetermination *noun* predetermining or being predetermined.

predetermine *verb* **1** to decide, settle, or fix in advance. **2** to influence, shape, or cause to tend a certain way.

predicament *noun* a difficulty that one finds oneself in; a plight or dilemma. [from Latin *praedicamentum*, something asserted]

predicate — *noun* (pronounced -kət) **1** *Grammar* the word or words in a sentence that make a statement about the subject. It usually consists of a verb and its complement, eg *knew what to do* in *the people in charge knew what to do.* **2** *Logic* what is stated as a property of the subject of a proposition. — *verb* (pronounced -kate) **1** to assert. **2** to imply; to entail the existence of. **3** *Logic* to state as a property of the subject of a proposition. **4** (**predicate one thing on another**) to make the viability of an idea, etc depend on something else being true. [from Latin *praedicare*, to assert]

predication *noun* **1** predicating or asserting, or an instance of this. **2** *Logic* an assertion made of or about a subject.

predicative *adj.* **1** *Grammar*, *said of an adjective* forming part of a predicate, as *asleep* in *they were asleep.* See also ATTRIBUTIVE. **2** relating to predicates.

predicatively *adv.* *Grammar* with a predicative function.

predict *verb* to prophesy, foretell, or forecast. [from Latin *praedicare*, to foretell]

predictability *noun* being predictable.

predictable *adj.* **1** able to be predicted; easily foreseen. **2** *derog.* boringly consistent in one's behaviour or reactions, etc; unoriginal.

predictably *adv.* in a predictable way.

prediction *noun* **1** the act or art of predicting. **2** something foretold.

predilection *noun* a special liking or preference for something. [from Latin *praediligere*, to prefer]

predispose *verb* **1** to incline (someone) to react in a particular way: *clear handwriting will predispose the examiners in your favour.* **2** to make susceptible to (especially illness).

predisposition *noun* **1** the condition of being predisposed. **2** *Medicine* a likelihood of being affected by certain diseases or conditions.

predominance *noun* being predominant.

predominant *adj.* more numerous, prominent, or powerful.

predominantly *adv.* in a predominant way.

predominate *verb intrans.* **1** to be more numerous: *girls predominate over boys in this class.* **2** to be more noticeable or prominent. **3** to have more influence: *the 'green' lobby is beginning to predominate.* [from Latin *prae-*, above others + *dominari*, to have mastery]

pre-eminence *noun* a pre-eminent quality.

pre-eminent *adj.* outstanding; excelling all others. [from Latin *praeeminere*, to be prominent]

pre-eminently *adv.* in a pre-eminent way.

pre-empt *verb* **1** to forestall and so make pointless (an action planned by someone else). **2** to obtain in advance for oneself.

pre-emption *noun* **1** the buying of, or right to buy, property, before others get the chance. **2** the act of pre-empting. [from Latin *praeemere*, to buy before]

pre-emptive *adj.* **1** having the effect of pre-empting. **2** *Mil.*, *said of an attack or strike* effectively destroying the enemy's weapons before they can be used.

pre-emptive strike *Mil.* an attack which has the effect of destroying the enemy's weapons before they can be used.

preen *verb* **1** *trans., intrans. said of a bird* to clean and smooth (its feathers) with its beak. **2** to groom (oneself), especially in a vain manner. **3** (**preen oneself on something**) to pride or congratulate oneself on account of it. [from Middle English *prene*]

prefab *noun* a prefabricated building, especially a dwelling.

prefabricate *verb* to manufacture standard sections of (a building) for later quick assembly.

prefabrication *noun* prefabricating or being prefabricated.

preface — *noun* **1** an explanatory statement at the beginning of a book. **2** anything of an introductory or preliminary character. — *verb* **1** to provide (a book, etc) with a preface. **2** to introduce or precede with some preliminary matter. [from Latin *praefatio*, from *praefari*, to say beforehand]

prefatory *adj.* **1** relating to a preface. **2** serving as a preface or introduction. **3** introductory.

prefect *noun* **1** a senior pupil with minor disciplinary powers in a school. **2** in some countries, the senior official of an administrative district. [from Latin *praefectus*, an official in charge, overseer, director, etc]

prefecture *noun* the office of, or the district presided over by, a prefect.

prefer *verb* (**preferred, preferring**) **1** (**prefer one thing to another**) to like it better: *prefer tea to coffee*. **2** *Legal* to submit (a charge, accusation, etc) to a court of law for consideration. **3** to promote (a person) over his or her colleagues. [from Latin *praeferre*, to place before, especially in esteem]

preferable *adj.* more desirable, suitable, or advisable; better. [from French *préférable*]

preferably *adv.* **1** by preference; from choice. **2** as is better or more desirable.

preference *noun* **1** the preferring of one thing, etc to another: *chose pink in preference to purple*. **2** one's choice of, or liking for, someone or something particular: *have no special preferences*. **3** favourable consideration: *give preference to experienced applicants*.

preference shares shares on which the dividend must be paid before that on ordinary shares.

preferential *adj.* bestowing special favours or advantages: *preferential treatment*.

preferment *noun* promotion to a more responsible position.

prefiguration *noun* prefiguring or representation beforehand, or an instance of this.

prefigure *verb* to be an advance sign or representation of something that is to come; to foreshadow. [from Latin *praefigurare*]

prefix — *noun* **1** *Grammar* an element such as *un-, re-, non-,* and *de-* added to the beginning of a word to create a new word. **2** a title such as *Mr, Dr,* and *Ms,* used before a person's name. — *verb* **1** to add as an introduction. **2** to attach as a prefix to a word. **3** to add a prefix to. [from Latin *praefixum*]

prefrontal lobotomy *Medicine* a surgical procedure, formerly used in the treatment of some severe mental disorders, in which the nerve fibres connecting the frontal lobes to the rest of the brain are severed. The operation had serious side-effects and often caused marked personality changes.

pregnancy (PL. **pregnancies**) *noun* in female mammals, including humans, the period during which a developing embryo is carried in the womb. In humans it usually lasts for up to 40 weeks (280 days), from conception until birth. – Also called *gestation*.
◇ Human pregnancy can be confirmed by various tests, based on the presence of the hormone gonadotrophin in the urine, and by detection of the fetal heart beat. About one in five pregnancies fail, usually at a very early stage, so the only sign of this may be a late menstrual period. During pregnancy several changes are brought about by the hormone progesterone, which is produced initially by the ovary and later by the placenta. Menstruation ceases, morning sickness may occur, the breasts enlarge in preparation for lactation, and the area around the nipples darkens. There may be an increase in appetite and an urge to urinate more frequently. Enlargement of the uterus can be felt towards the end of the third month, after which time the abdomen enlarges progressively. In the later stages of pregnancy the baby may be felt moving around. Certain infections (eg German measles), alcohol consumption, and smoking during pregnancy constitute a risk to the fetus.

pregnant *adj.* **1** carrying an unborn child or young in the womb. **2** *said of a remark, pause, etc* loaded with a significance only too obvious to those present. [from Latin *praegnans*]

preheat *verb* to heat (an oven, furnace, etc) before use.

prehensile *adj.* denoting a part of an animal that is adapted for grasping, eg the tail of certain vertebrates which enables them to hang from tree branches. [from Latin *prehendere*, to grasp]

prehistoric *adj.* belonging or relating to the period before historical records.

prehistorically *adv.* in prehistoric times.

prehistory *noun* the period before historical records. Prehistory is classified (according to the types of tools and weapons used by early humans) as part of the Stone Age, Bronze Age, and Iron Age.

prejudge *verb* **1** to form an opinion on (an issue, etc) without having all the relevant facts. **2** to condemn (someone) unheard.

prejudgement *noun* prejudging; a conclusion reached before examining the facts.

prejudice — *noun* **1** a biased opinion, based on insufficient knowledge. **2** unthinking hostility, eg towards a particular racial or religious group. **3** *Legal* harm; detriment: *without prejudice to your parental rights*. — *verb* **1** (*often* **be prejudiced**) to cause (someone) to feel prejudice; to bias. **2** to harm or endanger: *a poor interview will prejudice your chances of success*. [from Latin *praejudicium*, harm]

prejudicial *adj.* **1** causing prejudice. **2** harmful.

prelacy *noun* (PL. **prelacies**) **1** the office of a prelate. **2** the entire body of prelates. **3** administration of the church by prelates.

prelate *noun* a bishop, abbot, or other high-ranking ecclesiastic. [from Latin *praelatus*, from *praeferre*, to prefer]

preliminary — *adj.* occurring at the beginning; introductory or preparatory. — *noun* (PL. **preliminaries**) **1** (*usually* **preliminaries**) something done or said by way of introduction or preparation. **2** a preliminary round in a competition. [from Latin *prae-*, before + *limen*, threshold]

Length of Pregnancy in some Mammals	
Animal	Gestation Period*
camel	406
cat	62
cow	280
chimpanzee	237
dog	62
dolphin	276
elephant, African	640
ferret	42
fox	52
giraffe	395–425
goat	151
guinea pig	68
hamster	16
hedgehog	35–40
horse	337
human	266
hyena	110
kangaroo	40
lion	108
mink	50
monkey, rhesus	164
mouse	21
opossum	13
orang-utan	246–275
pig	113
rabbit	32
rat	21
reindeer	215–245
seal, northern fur	350
sheep	148
skunk	62
squirrel, grey	44
tiger	105–109
whale	365
*average number of days	

prelims *pl. noun colloq.* **1** a set of preliminary examinations; the first public examinations in certain universities. **2** *Printing* the title page, contents page, and other matter preceding the main text of a book.

Prelude, The, in full **The Prelude, or, Growth of a Poet's Mind** an autobiographical poem in blank verse by William Wordsworth (1850). It is primarily a reflection on the growth of the poetic imagination.

prelude *noun* **1** *Mus.* an introductory passage or first movement, eg of a fugue or suite. **2** a name sometimes given to a short musical piece, a poetical composition, etc. **3** some event that precedes, and prepares the ground for, one of greater significance: *talks that are being seen as a prelude to peace*. [from Latin *praeludium*, from *prae-*, before + *ludere*, to play]

Prélude à l'après-midi d'un faune a 10-minute orchestral tone-poem by Claude Debussy (1894) to illustrate Mallarmé's poem.

premarital *adj.* belonging to, or occurring in, the period before marriage.

premature *adj.* **1** *Medicine*, said of human birth occurring before the expected time, ie less than 37 weeks after conception, or involving a birth weight of less than 2 500g (5.5lb). **2** occurring before the usual or expected time: *premature senility*. **3** *said of a decision, etc* over-hasty. [from Latin *praematurus*]

prematurely *adv.* so as to be premature, too early.

premed *noun colloq.* premedication.

premedication *noun* the drugs given to a surgical patient in preparation for a general anaesthetic.

premeditate *verb* to plan; to think out beforehand: *premeditated murder*. [from Latin *praemeditari*]

premenstrual *adj.* belonging to the time just before a menstrual period.

premenstrual tension *or* **premenstrual syndrome** (ABBREV. **PMT, PMS**) *Medicine* a group of symptoms associated with hormonal changes and experienced by some women for up to 10 days before the onset of menstruation. The symptoms include bloating (as a result of retention of fluid in the tissues), tenderness of the breasts, headache, food cravings, depression, and irritability.

premier — *adj.* first in rank; most important; leading. — *noun* a prime minister. [from Old French *premier*, first, of first rank]

première — *noun* the first public performance of a play or showing of a film. — *verb* (**premièred, premièring**) to present a première of. [from French *première*, feminine of *premier*, first]

premiership *noun* the office of prime minister.

Preminger, Otto (1906–86) Austrian film director and producer, born in Vienna. He made his first film in Vienna in 1932, then emigrated to the USA (1935). After directing on Broadway, he made *Laura* (1944), a *film noir*. Later films included *Carmen Jones* (1954), *Bonjour Tristesse* (1959), *Porgy and Bess* (1959), *Exodus* (1960), and *The Human Factor* (1979).

premise *noun* **1** something assumed to be true as a basis for stating something further, especially in logic either of the propositions introducing a syllogism. **2** (**premises**) *Legal* the preliminary matter in a document, etc; matters explained, or property referred to, earlier in the document. **3** (**premises**) a building and its grounds. [from Latin *praemissa*, things preceding, premise]

premiss *noun* same as PREMISE 1.

premium *noun* **1** an amount paid usually annually on an insurance agreement. **2** an extra sum added to wages or to interest.

— **be at a premium** to be scarce and greatly in demand.

put a premium on something to attach special importance to it: *put a premium on punctuality.* [from Latin *praemium*, prize]

Premium Bond *or* **Premium Savings Bond** in the UK, a government bond yielding no interest, but eligible for a draw for cash prizes.

premolar *noun* any of the four teeth between the canines and first molars.

premonition *noun* a feeling that something is about to happen, before it actually does; an intuition or presentiment. [from Latin *praemonitio*, forewarning]

Premonstratensians, also known as the **Norbertines**, or **White Canons** a religious order founded (1120) by St Norbert in Prémontré, France. It is noted for parish education and mission work, and continues chiefly in Belgium. [from Latin *pratum monstratum*, the meadow pointed out, the source of the name *Prémontré*]

prenatal *adj.* belonging to the period before childbirth.

preoccupation *noun* **1** being preoccupied. **2** something that preoccupies.

preoccupied *adj.* (**preoccupied by** *or* **with something**) **1** lost in thought. **2** having one's attention completely taken up, engrossed. **3** already occupied.

preoccupy *verb* (**preoccupies, preoccupied**) to occupy the attention of wholly; to engross or obsess. [from Latin *praeoccupare*, to occupy beforehand]

preordain *verb* to decree or determine in advance. [from Latin *praeordinare*, to ordain in advance]

prep *noun colloq.* homework; preparation.

prep. *abbrev. Grammar* preposition.

prepack *verb* to pack (eg food) before offering it for sale.

preparation *noun* **1** the process of preparing or being prepared. **2** (*usually* **preparations**) something done by way of preparing or getting ready. **3** preparatory work done by students; homework. **4** a medicine, cosmetic, or other such prepared substance.

preparatory *adj.* **1** serving to prepare for something; introductory; preliminary. **2** (**preparatory to something**) before it; in preparation for it: *checked the windows preparatory to leaving.*

preparatory school 1 in Britain, a private school for children aged between seven and thirteen, usually preparing them for public school. **2** in the US, a private secondary school, preparing pupils for college.

prepare *verb* **1** *trans., intrans.* to make or get ready. **2** to make (a meal). **3** to clean or chop (vegetables or fruit). **4** to get (someone or oneself) into a fit state to receive a shock, etc: *we must be prepared for bad news.* **5** *intrans.* to brace oneself (to do something): *prepare to jump.* [from Latin *praeparare*, to prepare]

prepared *adj.* willing: *not prepared to lend any more.*

prepay *verb* (PAST TENSE AND PAST PARTICIPLE **prepaid**) **1** to pay for in advance. **2** to pay the postage on in advance.

prepayment *noun* payment in advance.

preponderance *noun* **1** the circumstance of being more numerous. **2** a superior number; a majority. [from Latin *praeponderare*, to outweigh]

preponderant *adj.* greater in force, influence, or weight, etc.

preponderate *verb intrans.* to be more numerous; to predominate.

preposition *noun Grammar* a word such as *to, from, into, against*, that deals with the position,

movement, etc of things or people in relation to one another, and is followed by an object. [from Latin *praepositio*, from *praeponere*, to put before]

◇ In English, a preposition may be a single word, or it may consist of two or more words, as in *due to, on top of,* and *out of.* Where a preposition combines with a verb to create a new meaning, this is a (type of) phrasal verb, as in *stand for.* Many prepositions may also be classed as adverbs, depending on how they are used, eg *across, beneath, over,* and *under.*

prepositional *adj. Grammar* having the role of a preposition.

prepossess *verb* **1** to charm: *I was not prepossessed by his manners.* **2** to win over; to incline or bias: *was prepossessed in her favour.*

prepossessing *adj.* attractive; winning.

preposterous *adj.* ridiculous, absurd, or outrageous. [from Latin *praeposterus*, literally 'back to front']

preposterously *adv.* in a preposterous way; to a preposterous degree.

prep school a preparatory school.

prepuce *noun Anat.* the loose skin that covers the top of the penis. – Also called *foreskin.* [from Latin *praeputium*]

prequel *noun* a book or film produced after one that has been a popular success, based on the same leading characters but with the story beginning prior to the start of the original story. [from PRE- + SEQUEL]

Pre-Raphaelite — *noun* a member of the Pre-Raphaelite Brotherhood. — *adj.* relating to or characteristic of the Pre-Raphaelites.

Pre-Raphaelite Brotherhood (ABBREV. **PRB**) a group of artists formed in London in 1848 with the aim of revolutionizing early Victorian art; the name comes from their preference for the styles of the 15c (ie pre-Raphael). Leading members were Sir John Everett Millais, William Holman Hunt, and Dante Gabriel Rossetti. They rejected the sentimental medievalism and academic formulae of the time, and sought instead a new direct approach to nature, often inspired by Romantic poetry (eg of Keats and Tennyson). PRB pictures (the initials appear on some early pictures) are recognizable by their bright colours, hard-edged forms, shallow picture-space, and meticulous attention to detail.

prerecord *verb* to record (a programme for radio or television) in advance of its scheduled broadcasting time.

prerequisite — *noun* a preliminary requirement that must be satisfied. — *adj., said of a condition, etc* that must be satisfied beforehand.

prerogative *noun* an exclusive right or privilege arising from one's rank or position. [from Latin *praerogativa*, privilege]

Pres. *abbrev.* President.

presage — *verb* to be a warning sign of; to foreshadow, forebode, or portend. — *noun* a portent, warning, or omen. [from Latin *praesagire*, to forebode]

presbyopia *noun* difficulty in focusing the eye, a defect common in old age. [from Greek *presbys*, old + *-opia*, condition of the eyes]

presbyter *noun* **1** in the early church, an administrative official with some teaching and priestly duties. **2** in episcopal churches, another word for a priest. **3** in presbyterian churches, an elder. [from Greek *presbyteros*, elder]

presbyterian — *adj.* **1** denoting Church administration by presbyters or elders. **2** (**Presbyterian**) designating a church governed by elders. — *noun* (**Presbyterian**) a member of a Presbyterian church.

Presbyterianism the form of Church government of the Reformed Churches, which derived from the 16c Reformation led by John

Calvin in Geneva and John Knox in Scotland. It operates through courts at local congregational (eg kirk session), regional (presbytery), and national (General Assembly) levels. Both elders (laymen and women elected by the kirk session and ordained for life) and ministers play a leading part in all courts. Through emigration and missionary activity from Scotland, Ireland, and England, Presbyterianism has spread worldwide. The World Presbyterian Alliance (formed 1878) was succeeded in 1970 by the World Alliance of Reformed Churches.

presbytery *noun* (PL. **presbyteries**) **1** in a presbyterian church, an area of local administration. **2** a body of elders or presbyters, especially one sitting as a local church court. **3** the eastern section of a church, beyond the choir. **4** the residence of a Roman Catholic priest.

pre-school *adj.* denoting or relating to children before they are old enough to attend school: *pre-school playgroups.*

preschool education the education of children who have not yet reached the statutory school age. This may be provided in nursery or kindergarten, where there are usually trained personnel; or in playgroups, where parent volunteers work with playgroup leaders. In some countries, the provision of state preschool education is widespread, but in others it is almost nonexistent, or is provided mainly by the private sector.

prescience *noun* foreknowledge, foresight.

prescient *adj.* having or showing an understanding of what the future will bring. [from Latin *praescientia*, from *praescire*, to know beforehand]

prescribe *verb* **1** *said especially of a doctor* to advise (a medicine) as a remedy, especially by completing a prescription for it. **2** to recommend officially (eg a text for academic study). **3** to lay down or establish officially (a duty, penalty, etc). [from Latin *praescribere*, to write down beforehand]

prescript *noun* a law, rule, principle, etc that has been laid down. [from Latin *praescriptum*, from *praescribere*, to write down beforehand]

prescription *noun* **1** a set of instructions from a doctor for preparing and taking a medicine, etc. **2** the medicine, etc so prescribed by a doctor. **3** the act of prescribing.

— **on prescription** *said of medicines* available only on the presentation to the pharmacist of a prescription from a doctor.

[from Latin *praescriptio*, order]

prescriptive *adj.* **1** having an authoritative role or purpose; laying down rules. **2** *said of a right, etc* established by custom. [from Latin *praescribere*, to write down beforehand]

prescriptivism *noun* the practice of laying down rules, especially on the correct or incorrect use of language. Examples of these rules as applied to the English language include: the use of *'I shall'*, not *'I will'*, to express future time; and the rule that a sentence should never end with a preposition (eg *to whom do I owe the money?* and not *who do I owe the money to?*). Many of these rules bear little correspondence to everyday usages in English speech, and nowadays are often considered to be unnecessarily formal. However, they have been associated with educated speech and writing since the 19c.

presence *noun* **1** the state, or circumstance, of being present. **2** one's attendance at an event, etc: *your presence is requested.* **3** someone's company or nearness: *said so in my presence.* **4** one's physical bearing, especially if commanding or authoritative: *people with presence.* **5** a being felt to be present, especially in a supernatural way. **6** a situation or activity demonstrating influence or power in a place: *maintain a military presence in the area.* [from Latin *praesentia*, from *praesens*, present]

presence of mind calmness and the ability to act sensibly, especially in an emergency.

present[1] (with stress on *pres-*) — *adj.* **1** being at the place or occasion in question. **2** existing, detectable, or able to be found: *gases present in the atmosphere*. **3** existing now: *the present situation*. **4** now being considered: *the present subject*. **5** *Grammar*, said of the tense of a verb denoting action now, or action that is continuing or habitual. — *noun* **1** the present time. **2** *Grammar* the present tense, or a verb in the present tense. **3** (**presents**) *old use Legal* (**present these**) the present document; this statement, these words, etc.
— **at present** now.
for the present for the time being.
[from Latin *praesens*]

present[2] *verb* (with stress on *-sent*) **1** (**present someone with something**) to give it to them, especially formally or ceremonially: *presented them with gold medals*. **2** (**present one person to another**) to introduce them, especially formally. **3** to introduce or compère (a television or radio show). **4** to stage (a play), show (a film), etc. **5** to offer for consideration: *presented proposals*. **6** to pose; to set: *shouldn't present any problem / presented us with a few problems*. **7** said of an idea to suggest (itself). **8** to hand over (a cheque) for acceptance or (a bill) for payment. **9** to set out: *presents her work neatly*. **10** to depict; to represent: *her biographer presents her in an over-sympathetic light*. **11** to put on (eg a cheerful face) in public. **12** to offer (one's compliments) formally. **13** to hold (a weapon) in aiming position. **14** *intrans. Medicine* to report to a doctor with certain symptoms or signs. **15** *intrans. Medicine*, said of a baby's head or buttocks in childbirth to be in a position to emerge first.
— **present arms** to hold a rifle or other weapon vertically in front of one as a salute.
present oneself to appear in person.
[from Latin *praesentare*, to present]

present[3] *noun* (with stress on *pres-*) something given; a gift. [related to PRESENT[2]]

presentability *noun* a presentable quality.

presentable *adj.* **1** fit to be seen, appear in company, etc. **2** passable; satisfactory.

presentably *adv.* in a presentable way; so as to be presentable.

presentation *noun* **1** the act of presenting. **2** the manner in which something is presented, laid out, explained, or advertised. **3** something performed for an audience; a play, show, or other entertainment. **4** *Medicine* the position of a baby in the womb just before birth, i.e. whether head or buttocks downward.

present-day *adj.* modern; of nowadays.

presenter *noun Broadcasting* a person who introduces a programme and provides a linking commentary between items.

presentiment *noun* a feeling that something, especially bad, is about to happen, just before it does. [from French *presentiment*, earlier spelling of *pressentiment*, foreboding]

presently *adv.* **1** soon; shortly. **2** *North Amer., esp. US* at the present time; now.

preservation *noun* preserving or being preserved.

preservative — *adj.* having the effect of preserving. — *noun* a chemical substance that when added to food or other perishable material slows down or prevents its decay by bacteria and fungi, eg salt, sugar, sulphur dioxide, essential oils.

preserve — *verb* **1** to save from loss, damage, decay, or deterioration. **2** to treat (food), eg by freezing, smoking, drying, pickling, or boiling in sugar, so that it will last. **3** to maintain (eg peace, the status quo, standards, etc). **4** to keep safe from danger or death. — *noun* **1** an area of work or activity restricted to certain people: *politics was once a male preserve*. **2** an area of land or water

where creatures are protected for private hunting, shooting, or fishing: *a game preserve*. **3** a jam, pickle, or other form in which fruit or vegetables are preserved by cooking in sugar, salt, vinegar, etc. [from Latin *praeservare*, to guard]

preserver *noun* a person or thing that preserves or keeps safe.

preset — *verb* (with stress on *-set*) (**presetting**; PAST TENSE AND PAST PARTICIPLE **preset**) to adjust (a piece of electronic equipment, etc) so that it will operate at the required time. — *noun* (with stress on *pre-*) a device or facility for presetting.

Prešov POP (1990) 89 000, a town in Východoslovenský region, E Slovakia. It lies on the R Torysa and was founded in the 12c.

preside *verb intrans.* **1** (**preside at** or **over something**) to take the lead at an event, the chair at a meeting, etc; to be in charge. **2** to dominate; to be a dominating presence in: *his statue presided over the park*. [from Latin *praesidere*, to command, preside]

presidency *noun* (PL. **presidencies**) the rank or office of a president.

president *noun* **1** (*often* **President**) the elected head of state in a republic. **2** the chief office-bearer in a society or club. **3** the head of a business organization. **4** the head of a college or other higher-education institution. [from Latin *praesidens*, present participle of *praesidere*, to preside]
◇ Certain presidents perform a largely formal and ceremonial role, ensuring that a government is formed (as in the Irish Republic); others share in governing with the prime minister, cabinet, and legislature (as in France); and yet others effectively act as head of the government (as in the USA).

presidential *adj.* **1** relating to a president or the office of president. **2** of the nature of a president.

presidium *noun* (PL. **presidiums**, **presidia**) a standing executive committee in a Communist state. [from Latin *presidium*, guard, garrison]

Presley, Elvis (Aaron) (1935–77) US rock singer, born in Tupelo, Mississippi. He began singing in his church choir and taught himself to play the guitar. Discovered in 1953 by the President of Sun Records in Memphis, Tennesseee, by 1956 his ability to combine White country and western with Black rhythm and blues had made him the most popular performer in the USA. His performances, featuring his overtly sexual style, incited hysteria in teenagers and outrage in their parents. He made 45 records that sold in the millions, including 'Heartbreak Hotel', 'Blue Suede Shoes', 'Hound Dog', and 'Love Me Tender'. His early Hollywood films included the box-office hits *Loving You* (1957), *King Creole* (1958), and *GI Blues* (1960), but these were followed by more mediocre fare. During the 1970s he became a nightclub performer in Las Vegas, and most of his records (still successful) were lachrymose ballads.

Presocratics *pl. noun* the earliest Western philosophers who preceded Socrates, and were active in Greece, Asia Minor, and Italy in the 5c BC and 6c BC. They include Thales, Pythagoras, Xenophanes, Parmenides, Zeno, Empedocles, Anaxagoras, and Democritus. Aristotle described the Pre-Socratics as 'investigators of nature'; they all attempted to define the nature of reality and the constitution of the world as a whole.

press[1] — *verb* **1** to push steadily, especially with the finger: *press the bell*. **2** to hold firmly against something; to flatten: *press one's nose against the glass*. **3** (**press against** or **on** or **down on something**) to push it; to apply pressure to it: *press down on the accelerator*. **4** to compress or squash. **5** to squeeze (eg someone's hand) affectionately. **6** to preserve (plants) by flattening and drying, eg between the pages of a book. **7** to

squeeze (fruit) to extract juice; to extract (juice) from fruit by squeezing. **8** to iron (clothes, etc). **9** to urge or compel; to ask insistently. **10** to insist on; to urge recognition or discussion of: *press one's claim / press the point*. **11** (**press for something**) to demand it: *press for a pay rise*. **12** (**press something on someone**) to insist on giving it to them. **13** *Legal* to bring (charges) officially against someone. **14** (**press round something**) to crowd round it. **15** (**press on** or **ahead** or **forward**) to hurry on. **16** to produce (eg a gramophone record) from a mould by a compressing process. — *noun* **1** an act of pressing. **2** any apparatus for pressing, flattening, squeezing, etc. **3** a printing-press. **4** the process or art of printing. **5** a printing-house. **6** newspapers or journalists in general. **7** newspaper publicity or reviews received by a show, book, etc: *got a poor press*. **8** a crowd: *the press of onlookers*. **9** *old use Scot.* a cupboard.
— **go to press** to be sent for printing.
[from Old French *presser*]

press[2] *verb* **1** to force (men) into the army or navy. **2** to put to especially emergency use: *press something or someone into service*. [from older *prest*, to recruit, originally 'enlistment money']

press agent a person who arranges newspaper advertising or publicity for a performer or other celebrity, etc.

Pressburg see BRATISLAVA.

Pressburg, Treaty of **1** an agreement concluded (1491) by the Habsburgs that secured their rights to the Hungarian succession on King Vladislav II's death without heirs. **2** a treaty (1805) that followed Napoleon I's victories at Ulm and Austerlitz. It imposed harsh terms on Austria, effectively ended the Holy Roman Empire, and established a ring of French client states.

press conference an interview granted to reporters by a politician or other person in the news, for the purpose of announcing something, answering questions, etc.

press cutting a paragraph or article cut from a newspaper, etc.

pressed *adj.* under pressure; in a hurry.
— **be hard pressed** to be in difficulties: *will be hard pressed to find a replacement*.
be pressed for something *colloq.* to be short of it, especially time or money.

press gallery in the UK, the gallery reserved for journalists in parliament or the law courts.

pressgang — *noun* a gang employed to seize men and force them into the army or navy. — *verb* **1** to force into the army or navy. **2** *facetious* to force into service: *pressganged into helping with the party*.
◇ In the British Navy in the 18c, the Impress Service recruited sailors both from the civilian population and from merchant ships. The Service and its agents often used armed parties to effectively kidnap men from taverns, etc, and so-called *pressed men* often formed up to half a ship's crew. The method was abandoned by the Royal Navy in the 1830s.

pressing — *adj.* urgent: *pressing engagements*. — *noun* a number of gramophone records produced from a single mould.

pressman *or* **presswoman** *noun* a journalist or reporter.

press officer a person employed by an organization to give information about it to journalists.

press release an official statement given to the press by an organization, etc.

press stud a type of button-like fastener, one part of which is pressed into the other.

press-up *noun* an exercise performed face down, raising and lowering the body on the arms while keeping the trunk and legs rigid.

pressure — *noun* **1** the force exerted on a surface divided by the area of the surface to which it is applied. The SI unit of pressure is the pascal (Pa), which is equal to a force of one newton per square metre of surface. Other units of pressure include bars and millibars (used in meteorology), millimetres of mercury (used in barometers), and atmospheres. **2** the act of pressing or process of being pressed. **3** force or coercion; forceful persuasion: *bring pressure to bear.* **4** the need to perform a great deal at speed: *work under pressure.* **5** tension or stress: *the pressures of family life.* — *verb* to try to persuade; to coerce, force, or pressurise. [from Latin *pressura*]

pressure cooker a thick-walled pan with an airtight lid, in which food is cooked at speed by steam under high pressure.

pressure gauge *Physics* a gauge which measures the pressure of fluids (liquids or gases) in enclosed vessels and containers, such as boilers and pipes.

pressure group a number of people who join together to influence public opinion and government policy on some issue.

pressurize *or* **pressurise** *verb* **1** to adjust the pressure within (an enclosed compartment such as an aircraft cabin) so that nearly normal atmospheric pressure is constantly maintained. **2** to put pressure on; to force or coerce: *was pressurized into resigning.*

pressurized water reactor a nuclear reactor in which the coolant is water under such pressure that it reaches a high temperature without evaporation and can be used to heat boiler water through a heat exchanger.

Prester John a mythical Christian priest-king of an empire in central Asia. Reports of his existence, wealth, and military might, substantiated by a famous letter purporting to have come from him in 1165, raised the morale of Christian Europe as it faced the Muslim threat. The story almost certainly related to the Christian kingdom of Ethiopia, which had been cut off by the Islamic conquest of Egypt.

prestidigitation *noun* sleight of hand.

prestidigitator *noun* someone expert at sleight of hand; a conjurer. [from French *prestidigitateur*, conjurer, a 19c coinage from *preste*, adroit + Latin *digitus*, finger]

prestige *noun* **1** fame, distinction, or reputation due to rank or success. **2** standing and influence: *a job with prestige.* **3** (*attributive*) *said of a job, etc* considered to give prestige. [from Latin *praestigiae*, sleight of hand, magic]

prestigious *adj.* having prestige; esteemed, influential, impressive.

presto *Mus.* — *adj., adv.* very fast. — *noun* (PL. **prestos**) a passage to be played very fast. [from Italian *presto*]

Preston POP (1992e) 132 000, the industrial county town of Lancashire, NW England, in Preston district. It lies on the R Ribble, 45km/28mi NW of Manchester, and forms part of Central Lancashire New Town. HISTORY Cromwell defeated the Royalists here during the Civil War in 1648; it was the centre of the cotton industry in the 18c. The inventor Richard Arkwright was born here in 1732. NOTABLE FEATURE Harris Museum.

Prestonpans POP (1981) 7 600, a town in East Lothian district, Lothian Region, E Scotland. It lies on the S shore of the Firth of Forth, 5km/3mi NE of Musselburgh. Prestonpans was the site of a Scottish victory over the English in 1745.

pre-stressed *adj., said of concrete* having stretched wires or rods embedded in it in order to increase its tensile strength.

Prestwick POP (1981) 14 000, a town in Kyle and Carrick district, Strathclyde, SW Scotland. It is situated on the W coast, 5 km/3mi N of Ayr and has an important international airport.

presumably *adv.* I suppose.

presume *verb* **1** to suppose (something to be the case) though one has no proof; to take for granted: *presumed he was dead.* **2** to be so bold as (to do something) without the proper right or knowledge; to venture: *wouldn't presume to advise the experts.* **3** (**presume on** *or* **upon something**) to count on someone's goodwill, especially without justification; to take unfair advantage of someone's good nature, etc. [from Latin *praesumere*, to take in advance, suppose]

presumption *noun* **1** the act of presuming. **2** something presumed: *she remarried on the presumption that her first husband was dead.* **3** grounds or justification for presuming something. **4** *derog.* unsuitable boldness in one's behaviour towards others; insolence or arrogance. [from Latin *praesumptio*]

presumptive *adj.* presumed rather than absolutely certain. See also under HEIR.

presumptuous *adj. derog.* over-bold in one's behaviour towards others; insolent or arrogant. [from Latin *praesumptuosus*]

presumptuously *adv.* in a presumptuous way.

presuppose *verb* **1** to take for granted; to assume as true. **2** to require as a necessary condition; to imply the existence of: *forgiveness presupposes offence.*

presupposition *noun* **1** assuming or presupposing. **2** something taken for granted. **3** an assumption.

pretence *noun* **1** the act of pretending. **2** make-believe. **3** an act one puts on deliberately to mislead: *his anger was mere pretence.* **4** a claim, especially an unjustified one: *make no pretence to expert knowledge.* **5** show, affectation or ostentation; pretentiousness. **6** (*usually* **pretences**) a misleading declaration of intention: *won their support under false pretences.* **7** show or semblance: *abandoned all pretence of fair play.* [from Old French *pretensse*, from Latin *praetendere*, to pretend]

pretend — *verb* **1** *trans., intrans.* to make believe; to act as if, or give the impression that, something is the case when it is not: *pretend it's winter / pretend to be asleep.* **2** *trans., intrans.* to imply or claim falsely: *pretended not to know.* **3** (**pretend to something**) to claim to have a skill, etc, especially falsely; to lay especially doubtful claim to (eg the throne). **4** to claim to feel; to profess falsely: *pretend friendship towards someone.* — *adj. colloq., especially used by or to children* imaginary: *a pretend cave.* [from Latin *praetendere*, to give as an excuse, pretend]

pretender *noun* someone who lays especially dubious claim to something, especially the throne.

pretension *noun* **1** foolish vanity, self-importance or affectation; pretentiousness. **2** a claim or aspiration: *a house with no pretensions to elegance.* [from Latin *praetensio*]

pretentious *adj.* **1** pompous, self-important, or foolishly grandiose. **2** phoney or affected. **3** showy; ostentatious. [formerly *pretensious*, from Latin *praetensio*, pretension]

pretentiously *adv.* in a pretentious way.

pretentiousness *noun* being pretentious.

preterite — *noun Grammar* **1** a verb tense that expresses past action, eg *hit, moved, ran.* **2** a verb in this tense. — *adj.* denoting this tense. [from Latin *praeteritum tempus*, past time]

preternatural *adj.* **1** exceeding the normal; uncanny; extraordinary. **2** supernatural. [from Latin *praeternaturalis*, from *praeter naturam*, beyond nature]

preternaturally *adv.* in a preternatural way.

Prêteur et sa Femme, Le (The Banker and his Wife) a painting by Quentin Massys (1514, Louvre, Paris).

pretext *noun* a false reason given for doing something, to disguise the real one; an excuse. [from Latin *praetextum*, from *praetexere*, to fringe, adorn, give as an excuse]

Pretoria POP (1985e) 823 000, the administrative capital of South Africa, and the capital of Transvaal province. It is situated 48km/30mi NE of Johannesburg. HISTORY founded in 1855; became capital of the South African Republic in 1881. NOTABLE FEATURES Voortrekker Memorial, Paul Kruger Memorial; Transvaal Museum.

Pretorius, Andries (Wilhelmus Jacobus) (1799–1853) Afrikaner leader, born in Graaff-Reinet, Cape Colony. A prosperous farmer, he joined the Great Trek of 1835 into Natal, where he became Commandant-General. He later accepted British rule, but disagreements with the Governor led him to trek again, this time across the Vaal. Eventually the British recognized the Transvaal Republic, later the South African Republic, the new capital of which was named Pretoria after him.

prettification *noun* prettifying or being prettified.

prettify *verb* (**prettifies, prettified**) to attempt to make prettier by superficial ornamentation.

prettily *adv.* in a pretty way, pleasingly.

prettiness *noun* being pretty.

pretty — *adj.* (**prettier, prettiest**) **1** *usually said of a woman or girl* facially attractive, especially in a feminine way. **2** charming to look at; decorative. **3** *said of music, sound, etc* delicately melodious. **4** neat, elegant, or skilful: *a pretty solution.* **5** *ironic* grand; fine: *a pretty mess.* — *adv.* fairly; satisfactorily; rather; decidedly. — **pretty much** *colloq.* more or less. **pretty nearly** almost. **pretty well** *colloq.* almost; more or less. **sitting pretty** *colloq.* happily unaffected by problems besetting others; in an advantageous position. [from Anglo-Saxon *prættig*, astute]

pretty pass *colloq.* a deplorable state of affairs.

pretty-pretty *adj. derog. colloq.* pretty in an over-sweet way.

pretzel *noun* a salted and glazed biscuit in the shape of a knot. [from German *pretzel*]

prevail *verb intrans.* **1** (**prevail over** *or* **against someone** *or* **something**) to be victorious; to win through. **2** to be common, usual, or generally accepted: *the prevailing opinion / custom.* etc. **3** to be predominant: *the prevailing mood.* **4** (**prevail on** *or* **upon someone**) to persuade them: *prevailed on us to stay.* [from Latin *praevalere*, to prove superior]

prevailing wind the wind most commonly blowing in a region: *the prevailing south-west wind.*

prevalence *noun* being prevalent; common practice or acceptance.

prevalent *adj.* common; widespread. [from Latin *praevalere*, to prevail]

prevalently *adv.* in a prevalent way.

prevaricate *verb intrans.* to avoid stating the truth or coming directly to the point; to behave or speak evasively. [from Latin *praevaricari*, to walk with splayed legs, behave dishonestly] ◆ Often confused with *procrastinate.*

prevarication *noun* prevaricating.

prevaricator *noun* a person who prevaricates.

prevent *verb* **1** to stop (someone from doing something, or something from happening); to hinder. **2** to stop the occurrence of; to make impossible; to avert. [from Latin *praevenire*, to anticipate, prevent]

preventable *or* **preventible** *adj.* capable of being prevented.

prevention *noun* preventing.

preventive *or* **preventative** — *adj.* tending, or intended, to prevent something, eg illness. — *noun* **1** a preventive drug. **2** a precautionary measure taken against something.

preventive detention a term of imprisonment for a habitual or dangerous criminal.

preventive medicine the branch of medicine concerned with the prevention of disease, as opposed to its treatment and cure.
◊ Methods of preventing disease include environmental control measures (eg clean air legislation), the provision of uncontaminated food and a clean water supply, and mass immunization programmes to protect against infectious diseases such as smallpox, diphtheria, and whooping cough. Other important areas of preventive medicine include health education (advice on hygiene, nutrition, alcohol and drug abuse, smoking, AIDS, and other health hazards), health-screening programmes to prevent diseases that might otherwise go undetected (eg breast and cervical cancer), and the elimination of important vectors of disease (eg malaria-carrying mosquitoes).

preview — *noun* an advance showing of a film, play, exhibition, etc, before presentation to the general public. — *verb* to show or view in advance to a select audience.

Previn, André (George) (1929–) German-born US conductor and composer, born in Berlin. His family fled to the USA in 1938, and he spent some years as a jazz pianist before he became musical director of symphony orchestras in Houston (1967–9), London (1968–79), and Pittsburgh (1976–86). He has composed musicals, film scores, and orchestral works, including a cello concerto (1967) and a guitar concerto (1971). Both on television and in the concert hall he achieved popular success by bringing classical music to the attention of a wide public.

previous *adj.* **1** earlier: *a previous occasion.* **2** former: *the previous chairman.* **3** prior: *a previous engagement.* **4** *facetious* premature; over-prompt or over-hasty. **5** (**previous to something**) before an event, etc. [from Latin *praevius*, leading the way]

previously *adv.* before, earlier.

Prévost (Antoine François), l'Abbé (1697–1763) French novelist, born in Hesdin, Artois. He served in the army, became a Benedictine monk, lived in exile in England and Holland, and returned to France by 1735, where he was appointed honorary chaplain to the Prince de Conti. He wrote many novels and translations, but is best known for *Manon Lescaut* (1731), originally published as the final part of a seven-volume novel.

pre-war *adj.* belonging to the period before a war, especially World War II.

prey — *noun* **1** a creature, or the creatures, that a predatory beast hunts and kills as food: *in search of prey.* **2** a victim or victims: *easy prey for muggers.* **3** (**a prey to something**) liable to suffer from an illness, a bad feeling, etc. — *verb intrans.* **1** (**prey on something**) *said of an animal* to attack it as prey. **2** (**prey on someone**) **a** to bully, exploit, or terrorize them as victims. **b** to afflict them: *preyed on by anxieties.* [from Old French *preie*, from Latin *praeda*, booty]

prial *noun Cards* a set of three cards of the same denomination. [a contraction of PAIR-ROYAL]

Priam in Greek legend, the last King of Troy, the son of Laomedon, husband of Hecuba, and father of many children including Hector and Paris. He is presented in the *Iliad* as an old man. When Hector was killed in the Trojan War, he went secretly to Achilles to beg his son's body for burial. At the sack of Troy, he was killed by Neoptolemus, the son of Achilles.

priapism *noun Medicine* persistent abnormal erection of the penis, which may be a symptom of spinal injury, or of various diseases and disorders. [from Greek *Priapos*, a phallic deity]

Priapus in Greek mythology, a minor fertility god, introduced in Hellenistic times. He was portrayed as a little man with a huge phallus, and his statue stood in gardens, acting as a kind of scarecrow.

Pribilof Islands POP (1990) 901, a group of four islands in the Bering Sea, Alaska, USA. AREA 168sq km/65sq mi. Two of the islands, St Paul and St George, are inhabited.

Price, Fanny the impoverished but high-principled heroine of Jane Austen's *Mansfield Park*.

price — *noun* **1** the amount, usually in money, for which a thing is sold or offered. **2** what one must give up or suffer in gaining something: *loss of freedom is the price of celebrity.* **3** the sum by which one may be bribed. **4** *Betting* odds. — *verb* **1** to fix a price for, or mark a price on. **2** to find out the price of.
— **a price on someone's head** a reward offered for capturing or killing someone.
at a price at great expense.
beyond *or* **without price** priceless; invaluable. [from Old French *pris*, from Latin *pretium*]

price control a maximum or, rarely, minimum limit set on prices by the government.

price-fixing *noun* the fixing of a price by agreement between suppliers.

priceless *adj.* **1** too valuable to have a price; inestimably precious. **2** *colloq.* hilariously funny.

price tag **1** a label showing a price. **2** the cost of something, eg a proposed building, etc.

pricey *or* **pricy** *adj.* (**pricier, priciest**) *colloq.* expensive.

prick — *verb* **1** to pierce slightly with a fine point. **2** to make (a hole) by this means. **3** *trans., intrans.* to hurt by this means. **4** *intrans., trans.* to smart or cause to smart: *feel one's eyes pricking.* **5** *trans., intrans.* (*also* **prick up**) *said of a dog or its ears* to stick them upright in response to sound. **6** to mark out (a pattern) in punctured holes. — *noun* **1** an act of pricking or feeling of being pricked; the pain of this. **2** a puncture made by pricking. **3** *coarse slang* a penis. **4** *coarse slang* an abusive term for a man, especially a self-important fool.
— **kick against the pricks** to react against discipline or authority.
prick up one's ears *colloq.* to start listening attentively.
[from Anglo-Saxon *prica*, point]

prickle — *noun* **1** a sharp point or thorn-like growth on a plant or creature, eg a hedgehog. **2** a pricking sensation: *a prickle of fear.* — *verb intrans., trans.* to cause, affect with, or be affected with, a pricking sensation. [from Anglo-Saxon *pricel*]

prickliness *noun* being prickly.

prickly *adj.* (**pricklier, prickliest**) **1** having prickles. **2** causing prickling. **3** *colloq., said of a person* irritable; over-sensitive. **4** *said of a topic* liable to cause controversy.

prickly heat an itchy skin condition, with inflammation around the sweat glands, occurring in intensely hot weather.

prickly pear a prickly reddish pear-shaped fruit; the cactus on which it grows.

Pride, Sir Thomas (d.1658) English Parliamentarian during the Civil War. He commanded a regiment at Naseby (1645), and served in Scotland. When some members in the House of Commons intimated making a settlement with Charles I, he was appointed by the army (1648) to expel its Presbyterian Royalist members, and by 'Pride's Purge' about 100 were excluded. He sat among the King's judges, signed the death warrant, and was knighted by Cromwell (1656).

pride — *noun* **1** a feeling of pleasure and satisfaction at one's own or another's accomplishments, one's possessions, etc. **2** whatever inspires this feeling: *it's my pride and joy.* **3** self-respect; personal dignity. **4** an unjustified assumption of superiority; arrogance. **5** *poetic* the finest state; prime or bloom. **6** the finest item: *the pride of the collection.* **7** a number of lions keeping together as a group. — *verb* (**pride oneself on something**) to congratulate oneself on account of it: *prided himself on his youthful figure.*
— **swallow one's pride** to be forced to humble oneself.
take a pride in something *or* **someone 1** to be proud of them. **2** to be conscientious about maintaining high standards in one's work, etc. [from Anglo-Saxon *pryde*]

Pride and Prejudice a novel by Jane Austen (1813). It describes the relationships of the various members of the Bennett family, and focuses on the development of the relationship between Elizabeth Bennett and Fitzwilliam Darcy.

pride of place special prominence; the position of chief importance.

priest *noun* **1** in the Roman Catholic and Orthodox churches, an ordained minister; in the Anglican church a minister ranking between deacon and bishop. **2** in non-Christian religions, an official who performs sacrifices and other religious rites. [from Anglo-Saxon *preost*, from Latin *presbyter*, elder]

priestess *noun* in non-Christian religions, a female priest.

priesthood *noun* **1** the office of a priest. **2** the role or character of a priest. **3** priests collectively: *members of the priesthood.*

Priestley, J(ohn) B(oynton) (1894–1984) English writer, born in Bradford, Yorkshire. He made a reputation with his critical writings, and gained wide popularity with his novel *The Good Companions* (1929). It was followed by other humorous novels, including *Angel Pavement* (1930), and he made his name as a dramatist with *Dangerous Corner* (1932), *Time and the Conways* (1937), and other plays on space-time themes, as well as popular comedies, including *Laburnum Grove* (1933).

Priestley, Joseph (1733–1804) English clergyman and chemist, born in Fieldhead, Yorkshire. In 1755 he became a Presbyterian minister, and while working in Leeds, he took up the study of chemistry. He is best known for his research into the chemistry of gases, in particular for identifying a new gas later named oxygen by Lavoisier. A supporter of the French Revolution, his controversial views on politics and religion forced him to emigrate to the USA (1794), where he settled in Pennsylvania.

priestly *adj.* relating to or characteristic of a priest or priests.

prig *noun* a person who is self-righteously moralistic. [originally a coxcomb]

priggish *adj.* self-righteously moralistic.

priggishly *adv.* in a priggish or self-righteous way.

priggishness *noun* being priggish.

Prigogine, Ilya, Vicomte (1917–) Belgian theoretical chemist, born in Moscow. Professor in Brussels and director of a research centre at the University of Texas, he studied the development of the thermodynamics of irreversible processes, and discovered how to treat systems far from equilibrium. For this work he was awarded the 1977 Nobel Prize for Chemistry.

prim *adj.* **1** stiffly formal, over-modest, or over-proper. **2** prudishly disapproving. [from 17c slang]

prima ballerina the leading female dancer in a ballet company. [from Italian *prima ballerina*, first ballerina]

primacy *noun* (PL. **primacies**) **1** the condition of being first in rank, importance, or order. **2** the rank, office, or area of jurisdiction of a primate of the Church. [from Latin *primatia*, from *primus*, first]

prima donna 1 a leading female opera singer. **2** someone difficult to please, especially if given to melodramatic tantrums when displeased. [from Italian *prima donna*, first lady]

primaeval see PRIMEVAL.

prima facie — *adv.* at first sight; on the evidence available; on the face of it. — *adj.* apparent; based on first impressions: *prima facie evidence.* [from Latin *prima facie*]

primal *adj.* **1** relating to the beginnings of life; original: *man's primal innocence.* **2** basic; fundamental. [from Latin *primus*, first]

primarily *adv.* **1** chiefly; mainly. **2** in the first place; initially.

primary — *adj.* **1** first or most important; principal: *our primary concern.* **2** earliest in order or development: *the primary stage.* **3** (**Primary**) *Geol.* Palaeozoic. **4** basic; fundamental: *primary causes.* **5** of the elementary stage or level. **6** *said of education* for children aged between 5 and 11: *primary schools.* See also SECONDARY, TERTIARY. **7** *said of a bird's wing feather* outermost and longest. **8** first-hand; direct: *primary sources of information.* **9** *said of a product or industry* being or concerned with produce in its raw natural state. **10** *Electr.* **a** *said of a battery or cell* producing electricity by an irreversible chemical reaction. **b** *said of a circuit or current* inducing a current in a neighbouring circuit. — *noun* (PL. **primaries**) **1** something that is first in order, importance, etc. **2** a primary school. **3** (*also* **primary election**) in the US, a preliminary election at state level in which voters choose candidates for political office. **4** a bird's primary feather. [from Latin *primarius*, principal]

primary cell *or* **primary battery** *Physics* a cell or battery that produces an electric current by chemical reactions that are not readily reversible, so that the cell cannot be recharged by applying an electric current.

primary colour 1 when mixing lights, any of the three colours red, green, and blue-violet, which together give white light. They can also be combined in various proportions to give all the other colours of the spectrum. **2** when mixing pigments, any of the three colours red, yellow, and blue, which together give black. They can also be combined in various proportions to give all the other colours of the spectrum.

primary sexual characteristics *Zool.* sexual features that are present from birth, ie the testes in males and the ovaries in females, as opposed to the secondary sexual characteristics that develop after the onset of puberty.

primary stress *Linguistics* the main stress on a word in which there is more than one stress, as in *fundamentalism*, in which the primary stress is on the syllable *-ment-*.

primate *noun* **1** an archbishop. **2** *Zool.* any mammalian vertebrate belonging to the order Primates, which includes humans, apes, gibbons, monkeys, lemurs, bushbabies, lorises, tarsiers, and tree shrews. [from Latin *primas*, from *primus*, first]
◇ Primates characteristically have a large brain (in relation to body size) with well-developed cerebral hemispheres, forward-facing eyes (often with binocular vision), nails instead of claws, and hands and (usually) feet with grasping thumbs facing the other digits, adapted for grasping and climbing. Their limbs are modified for walking, swinging, climbing, or leaping. Primates display complex social behaviour patterns, and take a relatively long time to reach maturity, during which period they are cared for by their parents.

Primavera (Spring) a mythological painting by Sandro Botticelli (c.1478, Uffizi, Florence).

prime — *adj.* **1** chief; fundamental. **2** of best quality: *prime beef.* **3** excellent: *in prime condition.* **4**

supremely typical: *a prime example.* **5** having the greatest potential for attracting interest or custom: *prime viewing time / prime sites on the high street.* — *noun* the best, most productive or active stage in the life of a person or thing: *vehicles past their prime / cut off in her prime / in the prime of life.* — *verb* **1** to prepare (something), eg (wood for painting) by applying a sealing coat of size, etc, (a gun or explosive device for firing or detonating) by inserting the igniting material, or (a pump for use) by filling it with water, etc. **2** to supply (someone) with the necessary facts in advance; to brief. **3** *facetious* to supply (someone) with drink and food by way of relaxing, emboldening, or bribing him or her. [from Latin *primus*, first]

prime lending rate the lowest rate of interest charged by a bank at any time to creditworthy customers.

prime meridian the 0° line of longitude, passing through Greenwich.

prime minister the chief minister of a government.
◇ In general, a prime minister has to work through collective decision-making in a cabinet, although they can enjoy certain separate powers. In electoral systems, a prime minister is invariably leader of the largest party or coalition in parliament; unlike a president, their power base is more that of the party than that of personality.

prime mover the force that is most effective in setting something in motion.

prime number a whole number that can only be divided by itself and 1, eg 3, 5, 7, 11.

Prime of Miss Jean Brodie, The a novel by Muriel Spark (1961). It is set in Edinburgh during the 1930s and describes the life and loves of an unconventional and egocentric schoolmistress.

primer[1] *noun* a first or introductory book of instruction. [from Latin *primarium*, from *primarius*, primary]

primer[2] *noun* **1** a substance for sealing wood, before painting. **2** an igniting or detonating device for firing the main charge in a gun or mine.

prime rate the US bank base lending rate, at which the bank will lend to its best ('prime') customers. The rate applies to only 50 or so large US corporations, all others paying higher rates. An increase in the prime rate triggers increases in all other interest rates.

primeval *or* **primaeval** *adj.* **1** belonging to earth's beginnings. **2** primitive. **3** instinctive. [from Latin *primaevus*, young, from *primus*, first + *aevum*, age]

primigravida *noun Medicine* a woman who is pregnant for the first time. [from *primus*, first + *gravida*, pregnant]

primitive — *adj.* **1** belonging to earliest times, or the earliest stages of development: *primitive stone tools.* **2** simple, rough, crude, or rudimentary: *living in primitive conditions.* **3** *Art* an artist working in a simple, naïve, or unsophisticated style; also, a work by such an artist. — *noun* a work by an artist in naïve style; also, the artist. [from Latin *primitivus*]

primitively *adv.* in a primitive way.

primitiveness *noun* being primitive.

primitivism *noun Art* the deliberate rejection of Western techniques and skills in pursuit of stronger effects found, for example, in African tribal or Oceanic art. In this sense, it has been applied to Gauguin, and to Picasso's work from c.1906. The term is also synonymous with naïve art, ie works by contemporary untrained artists whose appeal is in their freshness of vision, for example, Henri Rousseau, the American artist Edward Hicks (1780–1840), and the English 'primitive' Alfred Wallis (1855–1942).

primly *adv.* in a prim way.

primness *noun* being prim.

Primo de Rivera (y Orbaneja), Miguel (1870–1930) Spanish soldier, born in Jerez de la Frontera. He served in Cuba, the Philippines, and Morocco, and led a military coup in Spain that inaugurated a dictatorship (1923–30). In 1928–9 he lost the support of the army, the ruling class, and King Alfonso XIII, and in 1930 gave up power. His son José Antonio (1903–36) founded the Spanish Fascist Party *Falange Española* (1933), and was executed by the Republicans.

primogeniture *noun* **1** the circumstance of being the first-born child. **2** the right or principle of succession or inheritance of an eldest son. [from Latin *primogenitura*, first birth]

primordial *adj.* existing from the beginning, especially of the world; formed earliest: *primordial matter.* [from Latin *primordialis*, from *primus*, first + *ordiri*, to begin]

primordially *adv.* in a primordial way.

primp *verb trans., intrans.* to groom, preen, or titivate (oneself). [perhaps related to PRIM]

Primrose a female first name, after the flower.

primrose *noun* **1** a small, low-growing wild plant with pale yellow flowers that appear in spring. **2** the pale yellow colour of these flowers. [from Latin *prima rosa*, first rose]

primrose path an untroubled pleasurable way of life.

primula *noun* (PL. **primulae**, **primulas**) any of a genus of plants that includes the primrose and cowslip, especially a low-growing cultivated variety with white, pink, or purple five-petalled flowers. [from Latin *primula veris*, first little one of the spring]

Primus *noun* (PL. **Primuses**) (*also* **Primus stove**) *trademark* a portable camping stove fuelled by vaporized oil.

prince *noun* **1** the son of a sovereign. **2** a non-reigning male member of a royal or imperial family. **3** a sovereign of a small territory. **4** a ruler or sovereign generally. **5** a nobleman in certain countries. **6** someone or something celebrated or outstanding within a type or class: *the prince of highwaymen.* See also PRINCIPALITY. [from Latin *princeps*, leader, ruler]

Prince Charming the prince in the tale of Cinderella, as representing the ideal handsome husband.

prince consort the title given to a reigning queen's husband, who is himself a prince.

princedom *noun* a principality; the estate, jurisdiction, sovereignty, or rank of a prince.

Prince Edward Island POP (1991) 130 000, an island province in E Canada, situated in the Gulf of St Lawrence and separated from the mainland to the S by the Northumberland Strait. AREA 5 660sq km/2 185sq mi. PHYSICAL DESCRIPTION an irregular coastline with large bays and deep inlets; none of its inland waters are navigable; the province rises to 142m. HISTORY visited by Jacques Cartier in 1534; claimed by the French as Ile St Jean; first settled by Acadians, it was occupied by the British in 1758; annexed to Nova Scotia in 1763 but became a separate province in 1769; in 1798 it received its modern name, after Queen Victoria's father; joined Canada in 1873. GOVERNMENT governed by a Lieutenant-Governor and a 32-member elected Legislative Assembly. CAPITAL Charlottetown. CHIEF TOWNS Summerside, Tignish, Souris. ECONOMY potatoes; tobacco; vegetables; grains; dairy products; fishing; food processing; tourism.

princely *adj.* **1** of, or suitable to, a prince. **2** *often ironic* lavish; generous: *the princely sum of five pence.*

Prince of Wales in the UK, the title conferred by custom on the sovereign's eldest son. Tradition holds that after the death in battle (1282) of Llewelyn ap Gruffudd (the first independent ruler of Wales to be acknowledged by an

English king) and the execution of his brother, Edward I presented his own infant son to the Welsh people at Caernarvon Castle as their prince.

prince regent a prince ruling on behalf of a sovereign who is too ill, young, etc to rule.

princess *noun* **1** the wife or daughter of a prince. **2** the daughter of a sovereign, or a non-reigning female member of a royal or imperial family.

Princess Royal in the UK, a title sometimes bestowed on the eldest, or only, daughter of a sovereign. George V's daughter Mary was Princess Royal until her death in 1965; the title was conferred by Elizabeth II on Princess Anne in 1987.

Princeton POP (1980) 12 000, a borough in Mercer County, W central New Jersey, USA, lying on the Millstone R. HISTORY founded by Quakers in 1696; the scene of a British defeat by George Washington in 1777. Einstein made his home here after emigrating to the USA. Princeton is a noted centre for education and research; its university, dating from 1746, is a member of the Ivy League.

Princeton University in the USA, a university in Princeton, New Jersey, founded in 1746 as the College of New Jersey in Elizabeth, New Jersey. It moved to Princeton in 1756, and was renamed in 1896. It has been co-educational since 1969.

principal — *adj.* first in rank or importance, chief; main. — *noun* **1** the head of an educational institution. **2** a leading actor, singer or dancer in a theatrical production. **3** *Legal* the person on behalf of whom an agent is acting. **4** *Legal* a person ultimately responsible for fulfilling an obligation. **5** a person who commits or participates in a crime. **6** *Commerce* the sum of money on which interest is paid. [from Latin *principalis*, chief, principal]

principal boy the part of the young male hero in a pantomime, usually played by a woman.

principal clause a main clause.

principality *noun* (PL. **principalities**) **1** a territory ruled by a prince, or one that he derives his title from. **2** (**the Principality**) Wales. [from Latin *principalitas*]

principally *adv.* mainly, mostly.

principal parts *Grammar* the main forms of a verb from which all other forms can be deduced, eg in English the infinitive, the past tense, and the past participle.

principle *noun* **1** a general truth or assumption from which to argue. **2** a scientific law, especially as explaining a natural phenomenon or the way a machine works. **3** a general rule of morality that guides one's conduct; the having of or holding to such rules: *a woman of principle*. **4** a norm of procedure: *the principle of primogeniture*. **5** a fundamental element or source: *the vital principle*. **6** *Chem.* a constituent of a substance that gives it its distinctive characteristics.

— **in principle** *said of a decision or action* as far as a principle or rule is concerned, although not necessarily in a particular case: *they have agreed to make a donation in principle.*

on principle on the grounds of a particular principle of morality or wisdom.

[from Latin *principium*, beginning, source]

principled *adj.* having, or proceeding from, especially high moral principles.

Pringsheim, Ernst (1859–1917) German physicist, born in Breslau (now Wrocław, Poland), where he later became professor. He studied the radiation emitted by hot bodies, and highlighted inconsistencies which arose from the black-body radiation formulae previously derived; this led Max Planck to return to the problem and to formulate his quantum theory.

Pringsheim, Nathaniel (1823–94) German botanist, born in Wziesko, Silesia (now in Poland). Noted for his research on the fertilization of plants, he was professor at Jena for a short time, but mainly worked privately in Berlin. He was the first scientist to observe and demonstrate sexual reproduction in algae.

prink *verb trans., intrans.* to dress (oneself) up; to smarten (oneself) up. [perhaps related to older *prank*, to dress up]

print — *verb* **1** to reproduce (text or pictures) on paper with ink, using a printing-press or other mechanical means. **2** to publish (a book, article, etc). **3** *trans., intrans.* to write in separate, as opposed to joined-up, letters, in the style of mechanically printed text. **4** to make (a positive photograph) from a negative. **5** to mark designs on (fabric). **6** to fix (a scene) indelibly (on the memory, etc). — *noun* **1** (*often in compounds*) a mark made on a surface by the pressure of something in contact with it: *footprints / fingerprints*. **2** a fingerprint. **3** hand-done lettering with each letter written separately. **4** mechanically printed text, especially produced on a printing-press: *small print*. **5** a printed publication. **6** a design printed from an engraved wood block or metal plate. **7** a positive photograph made from a negative. **8** a fabric with a printed or stamped design.

— **be in** or **out of print** *said of a publication* to be currently available, or no longer available, from a publisher.

print something out to produce a printed version of it, eg computer data.

[from Middle English *prenten*, from Old French *priente*, a print]

printable *adj.* **1** capable of being printed. **2** fit to be published.

printed circuit **1** *Electron.* an electronic circuit that contains no loose wiring, but is formed by printing or etching thin strips of a conductor such as copper on to the surface of a thin board of insulating material, allowing automatic assembly of large numbers of circuits without wiring errors. Circuit components are then attached to the board by inserting their connecting wires into pre-drilled holes. **2** the board of such a circuit.

printed circuit board (ABBREV. **PCB**) *Electron.* a piece of insulating material mounted with interconnected chips, which is added to a computer to enhance its memory or provide new features.

printer *noun* **1** a person or business engaged in printing books, newspapers, etc. **2** a machine that prints, eg photographs. **3** *Comput.* a computer output device that produces printed copies of text or graphics. There are many different types, and the optimum choice depends on the acceptable cost, print quality, and printing speed. ◇ The laser and ink-jet printers are the most widely used *non-impact printers*. Laser printers provide high speed and quality, but are expensive to operate, while ink-jet printers, which spray ink on to the paper via tiny nozzles, produce almost as high a print quality. Among *impact printers*, the daisywheel gives the best print quality, although the dot-matrix printer, which uses patterns of dots to create characters and images, has the advantage of low cost and greater versatility.

printing *noun* **1** the art or business of producing books, etc in print. **2** the run of books, etc printed all at one time; an impression. **3** the form of handwriting in which the letters are separately written. ◇ Moveable type was introduced into Europe in the 15c; William Caxton brought printing to England; and the wooden handpress was superseded by the first all-metal press, the Stanhope, in 1795. The commonest method for printing text until the late 19c was letterpress, in which raised type is inked and pressed on to paper. Later developments included the mechanized planographic or 'flat surface' methods, in particular,

lithography; and intaglio or recess printing, in which the printing plate is etched or engraved to form the image. Recently, typesetting by computer programs has been developed.

printing-press *noun* a machine for printing books, newspapers, etc, operating in any of various ways.

printout *noun Comput.* output in printed form.

print run the number of copies of a book, newspaper, etc printed at a time.

Prior, Matthew (1664–1721) English poet and diplomat, born in Wimborne, Dorset. He became an MP (1700), and carried out diplomatic work in Holland, where he was instrumental in concluding the Treaty of Utrecht (1713). He wrote several political and philosophical poems, but is best known for his light occasional verse, collected as *Poems on Several Occasions* (1709).

prior¹ *adj.* **1** *said of an engagement* already arranged for the time in question; previous. **2** more urgent or pressing: *a prior claim.*

— **prior to something** before an event: *prior to departure.*

[from Latin *prior*, previous]

prior² *noun* **1** the head of a community of certain orders of monks and friars. **2** in an abbey, the deputy of the abbot. [from Latin *prior*, head]

Prioress, the, also called **Madame Eglantine** the pretentious, shallow woman in Chaucer's *The Canterbury Tales*, whose tale of sentimental piety is marred by rampant anti-semitism.

prioress *noun* a female prior.

prioritize or **prioritise** *verb* to schedule for immediate, or earliest, attention.

priority *noun* (PL. **priorities**) **1** the right to be or go first; precedence or preference. **2** something that must be attended to before anything else. **3** the fact or condition of being earlier. [from Latin *prioritas*, from *prior*, previous]

priory *noun* (PL. **priories**) a religious house under the supervision of a prior or prioress.

Priscilla **1** a woman with whom St Paul stayed at Corinth (Acts 18.3). **2** a female first name. [from the Roman family name *Priscus*]

prise *verb* to lever (something) open, off, out, etc: *prised open the lid / prised the shell off the rock.* [from Old French *prise*, something captured]

Priština POP (1989e) 258 000, the capital of Kosovo autonomous province, S Serbia, S Yugoslavia. It was formerly the capital of Serbia. NOTABLE FEATURES many Turkish buildings, including the Sultan Murad Mosque; nearby marble cave of Donje and Monastery of Gračanica.

prism *noun* **1** *Geom.* a solid figure in which the two ends are matching parallel polygons (eg triangles, squares) and all other surfaces are rectangles or parallelograms. A cross-section at any point along the length of a prism remains the same. **2** *Optics* a transparent block, usually of glass and with triangular ends and rectangular sides, that disperses (separates) a beam of white light into the colours of the visible spectrum. [from Greek *prisma*, something sawn]

prismatic *adj.* **1** of, like, or using a prism: *a prismatic compass.* **2** *said of colour or light* produced or separated by, or as if by, a prism; bright and clear.

prison *noun* **1** a public building for the confinement of convicted criminals and accused persons waiting to be tried. **2** any place of confinement or situation of intolerable restriction. **3** custody; imprisonment: *no alternative to prison.* [from Old French *prisun*, from Latin *prehensio*, right of arrest]

prison camp an enclosed guarded camp where prisoners of war or political prisoners are kept.

prisoner *noun* **1** a person who is under arrest or confined in prison. **2** a captive, especially in war.

— **take someone prisoner** to capture and hold them as a prisoner.

prisoner of conscience a person imprisoned for his or her political beliefs.

prisoner of war (PL. **prisoners of war**) (ABBREV. **POW**) someone taken prisoner during a war, especially a member of the armed forces.
◇ The treatment of prisoners of war was first codified by International Treaty at the Hague Conference of 1899. This stated that they must be humanely treated, and not obliged to divulge military information other than name, rank, and number.

prissily adv. in a prissy way.

prissiness noun being prissy.

prissy adj. (**prissier, prissiest**) insipidly prim and prudish. [probably from PRIM + SISSY]

pristine adj. **1** former: restore to its pristine glory. **2** original; unchanged or unspoilt: still in its pristine state. **3** fresh, clean, unused, or untouched. [from Latin pristinus, former, early]

privacy noun **1** freedom from intrusion by the public, especially as a right: respect her privacy. **2** seclusion: in the privacy of one's own home.

private — adj. **1** not open to, or available for the use of, the general public: a private bathroom. **2** not holding public office: private individuals. **3** kept secret from others; confidential: private discussions. **4** relating to one's personal, as distinct from one's professional, life: a private engagement. **5** said of thoughts or opinions personal and usually kept to oneself. **6** quiet and reserved by nature. **7** said of a place secluded. **8** not coming under the state system of education, health care, social welfare, etc.; paid for, or paying, individually by fee, etc. **9** said of an industry, etc owned and run by private individuals, not by the state. **10** said of a soldier not an officer or NCO. **11** said of a member of parliament not holding government office. — noun **1** a private soldier. **2** (**privates**) colloq. the private parts.
— **in private** not in public; in secret; confidentially.
[from Latin privare, to withdraw or separate from public life]

private detective or **private investigator** someone who is not a member of the police force, engaged by a private individual to do detective work.

private enterprise the management and financing of industry, etc by private individuals or companies, not the state.

privateer noun Hist. **1** a privately owned ship engaged by a government to seize and plunder an enemy's ships in wartime. **2** the commander, or a crew member, of such a ship.

Private Lives a play by Noël Coward (1930). It is a comedy about two recently remarried couples who spend their (disastrous) second honeymoons in the same hotel.

privately adv. in a private way.

private means or **private income** income from investments, etc, not from one's employment.

private parts euphemistic the external genitals and excretory organs.

private sector that part of a country's economy consisting of privately owned and operated businesses, etc.

privation noun the condition of not having, or being deprived of, life's comforts or necessities; a lack of something particular. [from Latin privatio, deprivation]

privatization noun the sale of state-owned industries into private ownership.
◇ In the UK, Conservative governments since 1979 have undertaken a steady programme of privatization, in most instances returning nationalized industries to private ownership. In this way, the government was able to raise considerable sums of money through the sale of shares, helping to reduce its borrowing requirements and to cut tax rates.

privatize or **privatise** verb to transfer (a nationally owned business) to private ownership.

privet noun a type of bush of which hedges are commonly composed.

privilege noun **1** a right granted to an individual or a select few, bestowing an advantage not enjoyed by others. **2** advantages and power enjoyed by people of wealth and high social class. **3** an opportunity to do something that brings one delight; a pleasure or honour: have the privilege of meeting you. [from Latin privilegium, prerogative]

privileged adj. **1** enjoying the advantages of wealth and class. **2** favoured with the opportunity to do something.

privily adv. old use secretly.

privy — adj. **1** (**privy to something**) allowed to share in secret discussions, etc or be in the know about secret plans, happenings, etc. **2** old use secret; hidden. — noun (PL. **privies**) old use a lavatory. [from Old French privé, private, a private place or close friend]

Privy Council a private advisory council appointed by the sovereign, consisting chiefly of current and former members of the Cabinet, whose functions are mainly formal.
◇ Formerly, and particularly in the Tudor period, it was a highly influential group, and might be regarded as the precursor of the Cabinet. Today its membership is over 300, but the quorum is three.

Privy Councillor a member of the Privy Council.

Privy Purse an allowance granted to the sovereign by Parliament, for his or her private expenses.

Prix de l'Arc de Triomphe a horse race, held annually at the end of the season over 2.4km/1.5mi at Longchamp near Paris on the first Sunday in October. It was first run in 1920, and is the leading race for inter-age horses in Europe.

Prix de Rome an art scholarship which was provided by the French Academy in Rome (founded in 1666). It enabled the best young painters, sculptors, and architects from France to spend time working in Rome. It was especially coveted by artists during the 18c–19c.

Prix Goncourt (in France) a literary prize founded in 1903 from the legacy of Edmond de Goncourt. It is presented annually to the best prose work (usually a novel) in French published during the preceding year.

prize¹ — noun **1** something won in a competition, lottery, etc. **2** a reward given in recognition of excellence. **3** something striven for, or worth striving for. **4** something captured or taken by force, especially a ship in war; a trophy. **5** (attributive) **a** deserving, or having won, a prize: a prize bull. **b** valued highly by a person: her prize possession. **c** ironic perfect; great: a prize fool. — verb to value highly.

prize² same as PRISE.

prize fight a boxing-match fought for a money prize. [partly Old French pris, price, partly Old French prise, something captured]

prize-fighter noun a professional boxer.

prize-fighting noun professional boxing.

Prizren POP (1989e) 166 000, a town in Kosovo autonomous province, SW Serbia, S Yugoslavia. It lies on the R Prizrenska Bistrica, near the Albanian frontier. The old town is picturesque, with several mosques. HISTORY built on the site of a Roman town (Theranda); an important medieval trade centre; it was part of Albania from 1941 to 1944.

PRO abbrev. Public Relations Officer.

pro¹ — adv. in favour. — prep. in favour of. — noun (PL. **pros**) a reason, argument, or choice in favour of something.

pro² noun (PL. **pros**) colloq. **1** a professional. **2** a prostitute.

pro- prefix forming words meaning: **1** in favour of; admiring or supporting: pro-French. **2** serving in place of; acting for: procathedral / proconsul. [from Latin pro]

proa or **prahu** or **prau** noun a Malay sailing-boat or rowing-boat, especially a fast sailing-vessel with a large triangular, usually lateen, sail, an outrigger kept to leeward, and both ends (ie prow and stern) alike. [from Malay prāū]

proactive adj. **1** actively instigating changes in anticipation of future developments, as opposed to merely reacting to events as they occur. **2** ready to take the initiative; acting without being prompted by others. **3** Psychol., said of a prior mental experience tending to affect, interfere with, or inhibit a subsequent process, especially a learning process.

pro-am adj. Golf denoting a competition involving both professionals and amateurs.

probability noun (PL. **probabilities**) **1** the state of being probable; likelihood. **2** something that is probable. **3** Statistics a mathematical expression of the likelihood or chance of a particular event occurring, usually expressed as a fraction or numeral: a probability of one in four.
— **in all probability** most probably.
◇ The probability of a given event is defined using a scale ranging from 0 (an impossibility) to 1 (a certainty). All probabilities are expressed as a ratio of the number of times a possible event could occur to the total number of possible outcomes, eg the probability of obtaining an odd number on one roll of a dice is $\frac{3}{6}$, ie 1 in 2. To determine the probability of two independent events occurring, their probabilities are multiplied, eg the probability of obtaining two sixes is $\frac{1}{6} \times \frac{1}{6}$, ie 1 in 36. To determine the probability of one of two alternative outcomes occurring, their probabilities are added, eg the probability of obtaining a three or a six on one roll of a dice is $\frac{1}{6} + \frac{1}{6}$, ie 1 in 3. Probability theory has important applications in statistics, quantum theory, and the development of suitable schemes by insurance companies.

probability theory Maths. see PROBABILITY.

probable — adj. **1** likely to happen: the probable outcome. **2** likely to be the case; likely to have happened: probable that she's left. **3** said of an explanation, etc likely to be correct. — noun a person or thing likely to be selected. [from Latin probabilis, from probare, to prove]

probably adv. almost certainly; in all likelihood.

proband noun Genetics a person who is regarded as the starting point for an investigation of the inheritance of a particular disease or disorder within a family. [from Latin probandus, gerundive of probare, to test]

probate noun **1** Legal the process of establishing that a will is valid. **2** an official copy of a will, with the document certifying its validity. [from Latin probare, to prove]

probation noun **1** the system whereby (especially young or first) offenders are allowed their freedom under supervision, on condition of good behaviour: was put on probation for six months. **2** in certain types of employment, a period during which a new employee is observed on the job, to confirm whether or not he or she can do it satisfactorily. [from Latin probatio, trial, test]

probationary adj. **1** relating to or serving as probation. **2** on probation. **3** that is a probationer or is made up of probationers.

probationer noun a person on probation.

probation officer a person with responsibility as supervisor for an offender on probation.

probe — *noun* **1** a long slender usually metal instrument used by doctors to examine a wound, locate a bullet, etc. **2** an investigation: *a police probe into drug-dealing.* **3** (*also* **space probe**) an unmanned spacecraft that records and transmits back to earth data about the environment it is passing through. **4** an act of probing; a poke or prod. — *verb trans., intrans.* (**probe** or **probe into something**) **1** to investigate it closely. **2** to examine it with a probe. **3** to poke or prod it. [from Latin *probare*, to test, prove]

probity *noun* integrity; honesty. [from Latin *probitas*]

problem *noun* **1** a situation or matter that is difficult to understand or deal with. **2** a person or thing that is difficult to deal with. **3** a puzzle or mathematical question set for solving. **4** (*attributive*) **a** *said of a child, etc* difficult to deal with, especially in being disruptive or anti-social. **b** *said of a play, etc* dealing with a moral or social problem. — **no problem** *colloq.* **1** *said in response to a request, or to thanks* it's a pleasure, no trouble, etc. **2** easily: *found our way, no problem.* [from Greek *problema*, question for solving]

problematic or **problematical** *adj.* **1** causing problems. **2** uncertain.

problematically *adv.* in a problematic way.

proboscis *noun* **1** a flexible, elongated nose or snout, eg the trunk of an elephant. **2** the elongated mouth part of certain insects. **3** *facetious* the human nose. [from Greek *proboskis*, from *pro*, in front + *boskein*, to nourish]

proboscis monkey an Old World monkey native to Borneo, and having a pale coat with a darker 'cap' on its head, and a dark back. It has a long tail and a protruding nose, which in adult males becomes bulbous and pendulous. It is an excellent swimmer, inhabits forest near fresh water, and feeds on leaves.

procedural *adj.* relating to or concerning (correct) procedure.

procedurally *adv.* as regards (correct) procedure.

procedure *noun* **1** the method and order followed in doing something. **2** an established routine for conducting business at a meeting or in a law case. **3** a course of action; a step or measure taken. [from French *procédure*, from Latin *procedere*, to advance, proceed]

proceed *verb intrans.* **1** to make one's way: *proceeding along the road.* **2** (**proceed with something**) to go on with it; to continue after stopping: *proceed with one's work / please proceed.* **3** to set about a task, etc: *instructions on how to proceed.* **4** *colloq.* to begin: *proceeded to question her.* **5** (**proceed from something**) to arise from it: *fear proceeds from ignorance.* **6** (**proceed against someone**) *Legal* to take legal action against them. [from Latin *procedere*, to advance, proceed]

proceeding *noun* **1** an action; a piece of behaviour. **2** (**proceedings**) a published record of the business done or papers read at a meeting of a society, etc. **3** (**proceedings**) legal action: *begin divorce proceedings.*

proceeds *pl. noun* money made by an event, sale, etc.

process — *noun* **1** a series of operations performed on something during manufacture, etc. **2** a series of stages passed through, resulting in development or transformation. **3** an operation or procedure: *a slow process.* **4** *Anat.* a projection or prominence, eg on a bone: *the mastoid process.* — *verb* **1** to put through the required process; to deal with appropriately: *process a film / process an application.* **2** to prepare (agricultural produce) for marketing, eg by canning, bottling, or treating chemically. **3** to analyse (data) by computer. — **in the process of** ... in the course of ... [from Latin *processus*, progression]

procession *noun* **1** a file of people or vehicles proceeding ceremonially in orderly formation. **2** this kind of succession or sequence: *moving in procession.* [from Latin *processio*, an advance]

processor *noun* **1** a machine or person that processes something: *a word processor.* **2** *Comput.* a central processing unit.

pro-choice *adj.* supporting the right of a woman to have an abortion.

proclaim *verb* **1** to announce publicly. **2** to declare (someone) to be (something): *proclaimed a traitor.* **3** to attest or prove all too clearly: *cigarette smoke proclaimed his presence.* [from Latin *proclamare*, to cry out]

proclamation *noun* **1** an official public announcement of something nationally important. **2** the act of proclaiming. [from Latin *proclamatio*]

proclivity *noun* (PL. **proclivities**) a tendency or liking: *has a proclivity for gourmet meals.* [from Latin *proclivitas*, from *proclivis*, sloping]

Proclus (c.412–85 AD) Greek Neoplatonist philosopher, born in Constantinople. He became the last head of Plato's Academy, and his approach, based on Plotinus, combined the Roman, Syrian, and Alexandrian schools of thought in Greek philosophy into one theological metaphysic. His works were translated into Arabic and Latin, and were influential in the Middle Ages.

Procopius (c.499–c.565 AD) Byzantine historian, born in Caesarea, Palestine. He studied law, and accompanied Belisarius on his campaigns against the Persians, the Vandals in Africa, and the Ostrogoths in Italy. Highly honoured by Justinian, he seems to have been appointed prefect of Constantinople in 562. His principal works are histories of the above wars, and of the court of Justinian.

procrastinate *verb intrans.* to keep putting off doing something that should be done straight away. [from Latin *procrastinare*, to delay or defer, from *cras*, tomorrow]
◆ Often confused with *prevaricate*.

procrastination *noun* procrastinating, dilatoriness.

procrastinator *noun* a person who procrastinates.

procreate *verb trans., intrans.* to produce (offspring); to reproduce. [from Latin *procreare*, to beget]

procreation *noun* **1** procreating. **2** being generated or begotten.

Procrustes in Greek legend, a robber, living in Attica. He made travellers lie on his bed, and either cut or stretched them to make them fit it; his name means 'the stretcher'. He was killed by Theseus, who gave him the same treatment.

proctor *noun* an official in some English universities whose functions include enforcement of discipline. [a contraction of PROCURATOR]

procurator *noun* **1** in the Roman empire, a financial agent or administrator in a province. **2** an agent with power of attorney in a law court. [from Latin *procurator*, agent, manager]

procurator fiscal in Scotland, a district official who combines the roles of coroner and public prosecutor.

procuratorship or **procuracy** *noun* (PL. **procuracies**) the office of a procurator.

procure *verb* **1** to manage to obtain or bring about. **2** *trans., intrans.* to provide (prostitutes) for clients. [from Latin *procurare*, from *pro*, on behalf of + *curare*, to attend to]

procurement *noun* procuring.

procurer or **procuress** *noun* a man or woman who provides prostitutes for clients.

prod — *verb* (**prodded, prodding**) **1** (**prod** or **prod at something**) to poke or jab it. **2** to

nudge, prompt, or spur into action. — *noun* **1** a poke, jab, or nudge. **2** a reminder. **3** a goad or similar pointed instrument.

prodigal — *adj.* **1** heedlessly extravagant or wasteful. **2** (**prodigal of something**) lavish in bestowing it; generous: *be prodigal of praise.* — *noun* **1** a squanderer, wastrel, or spendthrift. **2** (*also* **prodigal son**) a repentant ne'er-do-well or a returned wanderer. [from Latin *prodigus*, wasteful]

prodigality *noun* **1** being prodigal or extravagant. **2** profusion. **3** great liberality.

prodigally *adv.* in a prodigal way; to a prodigal degree.

prodigious *adj.* **1** extraordinary or marvellous. **2** enormous; vast: *prodigious wealth.* [from Latin *prodigiosus*, from *prodigium*, wonder]

prodigiously *adv.* in a prodigious way.

prodigy *noun* (PL. **prodigies**) **1** something that causes astonishment; a wonder; an extraordinary phenomenon. **2** a person, especially a child, of extraordinary brilliance or talent. [from Latin *prodigium*, portent, wonder]

produce — *verb* (with stress on *-duce*) **1** to bring out or present to view. **2** to bear (children, young, leaves, etc). **3** to yield (crops, fruit, etc). **4** to secrete (a substance), give off (a smell), etc. **5** to make or manufacture. **6** to give rise to or prompt (a reaction) from people: *produced a subdued response.* **7** to direct (a play), arrange (a radio or television programme) for presentation, or finance and schedule the making of (a film). **8** *Geom.* to extend (a line). — *noun* (with stress on *prod-*) foodstuffs derived from crops or animal livestock, eg fruit, vegetables, eggs, and dairy products: *farm produce.* [from Latin *producere*, to bring forth]

producer *noun* a person, organization, or thing that produces.

producible *adj.* capable of being produced.

product *noun* **1** something produced, eg through manufacture or agriculture. **2** a result: *the product of hours of thought.* **3** *Maths.* the value obtained by multiplying two or more numbers: *the product of 2 and 4 is 8.* **4** *Chem.* a substance formed during a chemical reaction. [from Latin *producere*, to produce]

production *noun* **1** the act of producing; the process of producing or being produced: *goes into production next year.* **2** the quantity produced or rate of producing it. **3** something created; a literary or artistic work. **4** a particular presentation of a play, opera, ballet, etc. [from Latin *productio*, from *producere*, to produce]

productive *adj.* **1** yielding a lot; fertile; fruitful. **2** useful; profitable: *a productive meeting.* **3** (**productive of something**) giving rise to it; resulting in it: *productive of ideas.*

productively *adv.* in a productive way.

productivity *noun* rate and efficiency of work in industrial production, etc.

proem *noun* an introduction, prelude, or preface. [from Greek *prooimion*, from *pro*, before + *oime*, song]

prof *noun colloq.* a professor .

profanation *noun* profaning, violation, pollution.

profane — *adj.* **1** showing disrespect for sacred things; irreverent. **2** not sacred or spiritual; temporal or worldly. — *verb* **1** to treat (something sacred) irreverently. **2** to violate or defile (what should be respected). [from Latin *profanus*, not holy]

profanely *adv.* in a profane way.

profanity *noun* (PL. **profanities**) **1** lack of respect for sacred things. **2** blasphemous language; a blasphemy, swear word, oath, etc.

profess *verb* **1** to make an open declaration of (beliefs, etc). **2** to declare one's adherence to: *profess Christianity.* **3** to claim or pretend: *profess igno-*

rance / profess to be an expert. [from Latin *profiteri*, to declare]

professed *adj.* **1** self-acknowledged; self-confessed: *a professed agnostic.* **2** claimed by oneself; pretended: *a professed indifference to money.*

professedly *adv.* avowedly, ostensibly.

profession *noun* **1** an occupation, especially one that requires specialist academic and practical training, eg medicine, law, teaching, engineering. **2** the body of people engaged in a particular one of these: *the medical profession.* **3** an act of professing; a declaration: *a profession of loyalty.*

professional — *adj.* **1** earning one's living in the performance, practice, or teaching of something that is a pastime for others. **2** belonging to a trained profession: *professional skills.* **3** having the competence, expertise, or conscientiousness of someone with professional training: *a professional performance, attitude,* etc. — *noun* someone who is professional.

professionalism *noun* **1** a professional status. **2** professional expertise or competence.

professionally *adv.* in a professional way; in terms of one's profession: *professionally qualified.*

professor *noun* **1** a teacher of the highest rank in a university; the head of a university department. **2** *North Amer., esp. US* a university teacher. [from Latin *professor*, public teacher]

professorial *adj.* relating to or having the status of a professor.

professorship *noun* the office of a professor.

proffer *verb* (**proffered, proffering**) to offer. [from Old French *proffrir*]

proficiency *noun* **1** being proficient. **2** degree of expertise.

proficient *adj.* fully trained and competent; expert. [from Latin *proficere*, to make progress]

proficiently *adv.* in a proficient way.

profile *noun* **1** a side view of something, especially a face or head; a side face. **2** a brief outline, sketch, or assessment, especially of a person. **3** the extent to which one advertises one's presence or involvement: *keep a low profile.* [from Italian *profilo*, from *profilare*, to outline]

profit — *noun* **1** money gained from selling something for more than one paid for it. **2** an excess of income over expenses. **3** advantage or benefit. — *verb intrans.* (**profited, profiting**) (**profit from** *or* **by something**) to benefit from it.

profitability *noun* the capacity for being profitable.

profitable *adj.* **1** *said of a business, etc* making a profit. **2** useful; fruitful.

profitably *adv.* in a profitable way.

profiteer — *noun* a person who takes advantage of a shortage or other emergency to make exorbitant profits. — *verb intrans.* to make excessive profits in such a way.

profiterole *noun* a small sweet or savoury confection of choux pastry. [from French, said to be a diminutive from *profiter*, to profit]

profit margin the difference between the buying or production price and the selling price.

profit-sharing *noun* an agreement whereby employees receive a proportion, fixed in advance, of a company's profits.

profligacy *noun* being profligate.

profligate — *adj.* **1** immoral and irresponsible; licentious or dissolute. **2** scandalously extravagant. — *noun* a profligate person. [from Latin *profligare*, to strike down]

profligately *adv.* in a profligate way.

pro forma (*also* **pro-forma invoice**) an invoice sent in advance of the goods ordered. [from Latin *pro forma*, for the sake of form]

profound *adj.* **1** radical, extensive, far-reaching: *profound changes.* **2** *said of a feeling* deeply felt or rooted. **3** *said of comments, etc* showing understanding or penetration. **4** intense; impenetrable: *profound deafness / profound silence.* **5** *said of sleep* deep; sound. [from Latin *profundus*, deep, profound]

profoundly *adv.* in a profound way; deeply, intensely: *profoundly sorry.*

Profumo, John (Dennis) (1915–) English Conservative politician. He became an MP in 1940, and Secretary of State for War in 1960. He resigned in 1963 during the 'Profumo Affair', when he admitted that he had deceived the House of Commons over the nature of his relationship with Miss Christine Keeler, who was at the time also involved with a Russian diplomat. He turned to charitable service, for which he was awarded the CBE in 1975.

profundity *noun* (PL. **profundities**) **1** being profound. **2** depth. **3** something which is profound.

profuse *adj.* **1** overflowing; exaggerated; excessive: *offered profuse apologies.* **2** copious: *profuse bleeding.* [from Latin *profusus*, lavish]

profusely *adv.* in a profuse way; to a profuse or copious degree.

profusion *noun* **1** being profuse. **2** extravagance.

progenitor *noun* **1** an ancestor, forebear, or forefather. **2** the begetter or originator of a movement, etc. [from Latin, from *progignere*, to beget]

progeny *pl. noun* **1** children; offspring; descendants. **2** what results from or is generated by something; derivatives and offshoots. [from Latin *progenies*, offspring]

progesterone *noun* Biochem. a steroid sex hormone that is produced mainly by the corpus luteum of the ovary. It prepares the lining of the uterus (womb) for implantation of a fertilized egg, and if pregnancy occurs progesterone is secreted in large amounts by the placenta to maintain the pregnancy, stimulate growth of the mammary glands, and prevent the release of further eggs from the ovary. [from PRO- + GESTATION + STEROL]

prognosis *noun* (PL. **prognoses**) **1** an informed forecast of developments in any situation. **2** a doctor's prediction on the course of a patient's illness and his or her chances of recovery. [from Greek *prognosis*, knowing before]

prognosticate *verb* to foretell, to indicate in advance; to be a sign of. [from Latin *prognosticare*, to foretell, from Greek *prognostikon*, sign of the future]

prognostication *noun* **1** prognosticating. **2** a prophecy. **3** a foreboding.

prognosticator *noun* a person or thing that prognosticates.

programmable *adj.* capable of being programmed to perform a task automatically.

programme *or North Amer.* **program** — *noun* **1** the schedule of proceedings for, and list of participants in, a theatre performance, entertainment, ceremony, etc; also, a leaflet or booklet describing these. **2** an agenda, plan, or schedule. **3** a series of planned projects to be undertaken: *the building programme for 1995.* **4** a scheduled radio or television presentation. **5** (*usually* **program**) a set of coded instructions to a computer for the performance of a series of operations. — *verb* (**programmed, programming**) **1** to include in a programme; to schedule. **2** to draw up a programme for. **3** to set (a computer) by program to perform a set of operations. **4** to set so as to operate at the required time: *heating programmed to come on at 7.00pm.* [from Greek *programma*, the order of the day, schedule]

programmed learning a form of learning developed in the 1960s, and based on the

behaviourist learning theories of US psychologist B F Skinner. The learner is given short frames of information which he or she must follow with some active response, and correct answers are immediately reinforced. Principles of programmed learning have been influential in the development of microcomputer software and the interactive video disc.

programme music instrumental music which aims to depict a story or scene.

◇ Examples of programme music include the Italian caccias of the 14c, which depict hunting scenes, Vivaldi's *The Four Seasons* (1725), Berlioz's *Symphonie fantastique* (1830), and a number of pieces by Liszt, Smetana, and Richard Strauss.

programmer *noun* a person who writes computer programs.

progress — *noun* (with stress on *pro*-) **1** movement while travelling in any direction. **2** course: *watched her erratic progress / followed the progress of the trial.* **3** movement towards a destination, goal, or state of completion: *make slow progress.* **4** advances or development: *make progress in the treatment of cancer.* **5** *old use* a journey made in state by a sovereign, etc. — *verb* (with stress on -*gress*) **1** *intrans.* to move forwards or onwards; to proceed towards a goal. **2** *intrans.* to advance or develop. **3** *intrans.* to improve. **4** to put (something planned) into operation; to expedite.
— **in progress** taking place; in the course of being done.
[from Latin *progressus*, from *progredi*, to move forward]

progression *noun* **1** the process of moving forwards or advancing in stages. **2** *Mus.* a succession of chords, the advance from one to the next being determined on a fixed pattern. **3** *Maths.* a sequence of numbers, each of which bears a specific relationship to the preceding term. The numbers in an *arithmetic progression* increase or decrease by a constant amount, eg 2, 4, 6, 8, 10 ... In a *geometric progression* the ratio of each number to its predecessor is constant, eg 1, 2, 4, 8, 16, ...

progressive — *adj.* **1** advanced in outlook; using, or favouring, new methods. **2** moving forward or advancing continuously or by stages: *progressive loss of memory.* **3** *said of a disease* continuously increasing in severity or complication. **4** *said of a dance or game* involving changes of partner at intervals. **5** *said of taxation* increasing as the sum taxed increases. **6** *Grammar* denoting the forms of a verb that express continuing action, in English formed with the present participle, as in *I am doing it* and *they will be going.* — *noun* **1** a person with progressive ideas. **2** *Grammar* a verb in a progressive form.

progressive education a term used for an educational system which places greater emphasis on the needs and capacities of the individual child than traditional forms of teaching. It usually involves greater freedom of choice, activity, and movement, and stresses social as well as academic development. Progressive education was pioneered in schools such as Summerhill and Dartington Hall in the UK, but its influences have spread to other schools, particularly in the primary sector.

progressively *adv.* in a progressive way; gradually and steadily.

prohibit *verb* (**prohibited, prohibiting**) **1** to forbid, especially by law; to ban. **2** to prevent or hinder. [from Latin *prohibere*, to hinder, forbid]

Prohibition an attempt (1920–33) to forbid the manufacture and sale of all alcoholic drinks in the USA, authorized by the 18th Amendment to the US Constitution (1919). Issuing from 19c temperence movements and Anti-Saloon League lobbying, it was passed as a wartime emergency measure and enforced by the Volstead Act, which gave rise to much political controversy and led to various 'bootlegging' operations. It was repealed in 1933 by the 21st Amendment (1933).

prohibition *noun* **1** the act of prohibiting or state of being prohibited. **2** a law or decree prohibiting something. **3** a ban by law on the manufacture and sale of alcoholic drinks.

prohibitionist *noun* a person who supports prohibition.

prohibitive *adj.* **1** banning; prohibiting. **2** tending to prevent or discourage. **3** *said of prices, etc* unaffordably high.

prohibitory *adj.* prohibiting; restraining.

project — *noun* (with stress on *proj-*) **1** a plan, scheme, or proposal. **2** a research or study assignment. — *verb* (with stress on *-ject*) **1** *intrans.* to jut out; to protrude. **2** to throw forwards; to propel. **3** to throw (a shadow or image) on to a surface. **4** to propose or plan. **5** to forecast from present trends and other known data; to extrapolate. **6** to imagine (oneself) in another situation, especially a future one. **7** to ascribe (feelings of one's own) to other people. **8** to cause (one's voice) to be heard clearly at some distance. **9** *intrans. colloq.* to make good contact with an audience through the strength of one's personality. [from Latin *projicere*, to throw forward]

projectile — *noun* an object designed to be propelled with force, especially a missile such as a bullet or rocket. — *adj.* hurling, or (designed to be) hurled, forwards. [from Modern Latin *projectilis*, from *projicere*, to throw forward]

projection *noun* **1** the act of projecting or process of being projected. **2** something that protrudes from a surface. **3** the showing of a film or transparencies on a screen. **4** a forecast based on present trends and other known data. **5** *Maths.* maps the representation of a solid object, especially part of the Earth's sphere, on a flat surface. **6** *Psychol.* a mental process by which a subjective mental image is perceived as belonging to the external world.

projectionist *noun* a person who operates a projector, especially in a cinema.

projector *noun* an instrument containing a system of lenses that projects an enlarged version of an illuminated image on to a screen. The image may be still (as in a slide projector) or moving (as in a film projector).

prokaryote *or* **procaryote** *Biol.* an organism in which the cells lack a distinct nucleus containing chromosomes, and the genetic material consists of a single double-stranded DNA molecule coiled in a loop. See also EUKARYOTE. [from PRO- + Greek *karyon*, kernel]
◊ Prokaryotes, which are usually single-celled, include only the bacteria and cyanobacteria (blue-green algae), and they are usually placed in a separate kingdom, Monera. The cells of prokaryotes do not divide by mitosis or meiosis, but always reproduce asexually, usually by binary fission (simple cleavage of a cell into two parts). They have a cell wall, but do not contain organelles (specialized structures with a specific function) such as mitochondria and ribosomes, and chlorophyll, if present, is not confined within chloroplasts.

Prokofiev, Sergei Sergeyevitch (1891–1953) Russian composer, born in Sontsovka, Ukraine. He began to compose at the age of five, studied at the St Petersburg Conservatory, and gained a reputation as a virtuoso pianist. He wrote many occasional works for official celebrations, as well as popular pieces such as *Peter and the Wolf* (1936) and film music. His vast range of works includes seven symphonies, nine concertos, ballets, operas, suites, cantatas, sonatas, and songs.

Prokop (the Bald) *or* **Procop(ius)** (c.1380–1434) Bohemian Hussite leader, a follower of Žiška, and on his death, the leader of the Taborites. He carried out raids into Silesia, Saxony, and Franconia, and repeatedly defeated German armies. With his colleague Prokop (the Younger), he fell in battle at Lipany, Hungary.

prolactin *noun Physiol.* a hormone, secreted by the pituitary gland, which initiates lactation (secretion of milk) in mammals, and stimulates the production of another hormone, progesterone, by the corpus luteum.

prolapse *noun Medicine* the slipping out of place or falling down of an organ or other body part, especially the slipping of the uterus (womb) into the vagina. [from Latin *prolabi prolapsus* to slip forward]

prole *noun, adj. derog. colloq.* proletarian.

proletarian — *adj.* relating to the proletariat. — *noun* a member of the proletariat. [from Latin *proletarius*, a citizen who has nothing to offer society but his offspring, from *proles*, offspring]

proletariat *noun* the working class, especially unskilled labourers and industrial workers.

pro-life *adj.* opposing abortion, euthanasia, and experimentation on human embryos.

proliferate *verb* **1** *intrans. said of a plant or animal species* to reproduce rapidly. **2** *intrans.* to increase in numbers; to multiply. **3** to reproduce (cells, etc rapidly). [from Latin *prolifer*, bearing offspring]

proliferation *noun* **1** a great and rapid increase in numbers. **2** *Biol.* in living organisms, the multiplication of cells, tissues, or structures. **3** the spread of nuclear weapons to countries not already possessing them.

prolific *adj.* **1** abundant in growth; producing plentiful fruit or offspring. **2** *said of a writer, artist, etc* constantly productive of new work. **3** (**prolific of** *or* **in something**) productive of it; abounding in it. [from Latin *prolificus*, fertile]

prolifically *adv.* in a prolific way; to a prolific degree.

proline *noun Biochem.* an amino acid that is found in proteins. [from German *Prolin*]

prolix *adj., said of speech or writing* tediously long-winded; wordy; verbose. [from Latin *prolixus*, stretched out]

prolixity *noun* (PL. **prolixities**) being prolix.

PROLOG *noun Comput.* a high-level programming language, often used in artificial intelligence research. [contraction of *programming in logic*]

prologue *noun* **1** a speech addressed to the audience at the beginning of a play; the actor delivering it. **2** a preface to a literary work. **3** an event serving as an introduction or prelude. [from Greek *prologos*, from *pro-*, before + *logos*, discourse]

prolong *verb* to make longer; to extend or protract. [from Latin *prolongare*]

prolongation *noun* a continuation or lengthening; a piece added in continuation.

PROM *abbrev. Comput.* programmable read-only memory, a type of read-only memory which can be programmed, usually only once, after manufacture, and thereafter fixed.

prom *noun colloq.* **1** a walk or promenade. **2** a promenade concert.

promenade — *noun* **1** a broad paved walk, especially along a sea front. **2** *facetious* a stately stroll. — *verb* **1** *intrans.* to stroll in a stately fashion. **2** to walk (the streets, etc). **3** to take for an airing; to parade: *promenaded her children through the park.* [from French, from *promener*, to lead about]

promenade concert a concert at which part of the audience is accommodated in a standing area and can move about.

Promenade Concerts in the UK, a series of summer concerts held since 1941 in the Royal Albert Hall, London, begun in 1895 by Sir Henry Wood.

promenade deck an upper deck on board a ship, along which passengers can promenade.

promenader *noun* an especially regular attender at promenade concerts.

Prometheus in Greek mythology, a Titan, son of Iapetus and brother of Epimetheus, originally a trickster who outwits Zeus; his name means 'the foreseeing'. He made human beings out of clay, and taught them the arts of civilization. He also stole fire from heaven to help mankind, whom Zeus wished to destroy, and was punished by being chained to a rock in the Caucasus; every day an eagle fed on his liver, which grew again in the night. He was finally set free by Heracles.

Prometheus Unbound a lyrical drama in four acts by Percy Bysshe Shelley (1820). It is a rewriting of the Greek myth of Prometheus, the champion of humankind, whose characterization here is also inspired by John Milton's Satan.

promethium *noun Chem.* (SYMBOL **Pm**, ATOMIC NUMBER 61) a radioactive metallic element, produced by the fission of uranium, thorium, or plutonium, that occurs naturally in minute amounts as a result of the fission of uranium in pitchblende and other uranium ores, and is also found in nuclear waste material. It is manufactured artificially by bombarding neodymium with neutrons, and is used as an X-ray source, and in phosphorescent paints. [named after the Greek Titan Prometheus]

prominence *noun* **1** being prominent. **2** a prominent point or thing. **3** a projection.

prominent *adj.* **1** jutting out; projecting; protruding; bulging: *a prominent chin / prominent eyes.* **2** noticeable; conspicuous: *a prominent landmark.* **3** leading; notable: *a prominent politician. role, etc.* [from Latin *prominere*, to jut out]

prominently *adv.* in a prominent way.

promiscuity *noun* **1** being promiscuous. **2** mixture without order or distinction. **3** promiscuous sexual activity.

promiscuous *adj.* **1** *derog.* indulging in casual or indiscriminate sexual relations. **2** haphazardly mixed. [from Latin *promiscuus*, mixed up]

promiscuously *adv.* in a promiscuous way.

promise — *verb* **1** to give an undertaking (to do or not do something). **2** to undertake to give (someone something). **3** to show signs of bringing: *clouds that promise rain.* **4** to look likely (to do something): *promises to have a great future.* **5** to assure or warn: *will be heavy going, I promise you.* — *noun* **1** an undertaking to give, do, or not do, something. **2** a sign: *a promise of spring in the air.* **3** signs of future excellence: *shows promise.* — **promise well** *or* **badly** to give grounds for hope, or despondency. [from Latin *promissum*, from *promittere*, to send forth, promise]

promised land 1 *Biblical* the fertile land promised by God to the Israelites. **2** any longed-for place of contentment and prosperity.

promising *adj.* **1** showing promise; talented; apt. **2** seeming to bode well for the future.

promisingly *adv.* in a promising way.

promissory *adj.* expressing a promise, especially in **promissory note**, a signed promise to pay a stated sum of money. [from Latin *promissorius*, from *promissum*, promise]

promontory *noun* (PL. **promontories**) a usually hilly part of a coastline that projects into the sea; a headland. [from Latin *promontorium*, mountain ridge, promontory]

promote *verb* **1** to raise to a more senior position: *was promoted to lieutenant.* **2** to contribute to: *exercise promotes health.* **3** to work for the cause of: *promote peace.* **4** to publicize; to try to boost the sales of (a product) by advertising. **5** to be the organizer or financer of (an undertaking). [from Latin *promovere*, to cause to advance]

promoter *noun* the organizer or financer of a sporting event or other undertaking.

promotion *noun* **1** promoting. **2** advancement in rank or honour. **3** encouragement. **4** preferment. **5** a venture or undertaking, especially in show business. **6** advertising, or an effort to publicize and increase sales of a particular brand.

promotional *adj.* relating to or involving promotion.

prompt — *adj.* **1** immediate; quick; punctual. **2** instantly willing; ready; unhesitating: *prompt with offers of help.* — *adv.* punctually: *at 2.15 prompt.* — *noun* **1** something serving as a reminder. **2** words supplied by a prompter to an actor. **3** a prompter. — *verb* **1** to cause, lead, or remind (someone to do something). **2** to produce or elicit (a reaction or response): *what prompted that remark?* **3** *trans., intrans.* to help (an actor) to remember his or her next words by supplying the first few. [from Latin *promptus*, ready, quick, and *promptare*, to incite]

prompter *noun* a person positioned offstage to prompt actors when they forget their lines.

promptitude *noun* being prompt.

promptly *adv.* **1** without delay. **2** punctually.

promptness *noun* being prompt.

promulgate *verb* **1** to make (a decree, etc) effective by means of an official public announcement. **2** to publicize or promote (an idea, theory, etc) widely. [from Latin *promulgare*, to make known]

promulgation *noun* promulgating or being promulgated.

promulgator *noun* a person who promulgates.

pron. *abbrev.* pronoun.

prone *adj.* **1** lying flat, especially face downwards. **2** (**prone to something**) predisposed to it, or liable to suffer from it: *is prone to bronchitis / accident-prone.* **3** inclined or liable to do something: *prone to make mistakes.* [from Latin *pronus*, bent forwards]

proneness *noun* being prone.

prong *noun* a point or spike, especially one of those making up the head of a fork. [from Middle English *pronge*, pang]

pronged *adj.* having a certain number of prongs or directions: *a three-pronged attack* (ie one made by forces attacking from three directions).

pronghorn *or* **prongbuck** *noun* a N American mammal, often referred to as the pronghorn antelope, but not in fact a true antelope. It has a pale brown coat and prominent eyes. The female has short horns, and the male has horns with a frontal 'prong' and backward curving tips. The animal will approach moving objects (including predators), and it inhabits grasslands.

pronking *noun* *Zool.* behaviour exhibited by the springbok and several other ungulates, in which the back is arched and the legs held stiffly downwards as the animal leaps off the ground and then lands on all four legs simultaneously, repeating the action several times as if on springs. [from Afrikaans *pronk*, to show off, strut, prance]

pronominal *adj.* of, or being, a pronoun; relating to pronouns. [from Latin *pronominalis*, from *pronomen*, pronoun]

pronominally *adv.* *Grammar* as a pronoun.

pronoun *noun* a word such as *she, him, they,* and *it* used in place of, and to refer to, a noun or noun phrase. [from Latin *pronomen*, from *pro-*, on behalf of + *nomen*, noun]

pronounce *verb* **1** to say or utter (words, sounds, letters, etc); to articulate or enunciate. **2** to declare officially, formally, or authoritatively: *pronounced her innocent.* **3** to pass or deliver (judgement). **4** (**pronounce on something**) to give one's opinion or verdict on it. See also PRO-NUNCIATION. [from Latin *pronuntiare*, to declaim, pronounce]

pronounceable *adj.* capable of being pronounced.

pronounced *adj.* noticeable; distinct: *a pronounced limp.*

pronouncedly *adv.* in a pronounced way.

pronouncement *noun* **1** a formal announcement. **2** a declaration of opinion; a verdict.

pronto *adv. colloq.* immediately. [from Spanish *pronto*, quick]

pronunciation *noun* the act, or a manner, or the usual way, of pronouncing words, sounds, letters, etc. [from Latin *pronuntiatio*, expression, delivery]

proof — *noun* **1** evidence, especially conclusive, that something is true or a fact. **2** *Legal* the accumulated evidence on which a verdict is based. **3** the activity or process of testing or proving: *capable of proof.* **4** a test, trial, or demonstration: *as a proof of her love.* **5** *Maths.* a step-by-step verification of a proposed mathematical statement. **6** *Printing* a trial copy of a sheet of printed text for examination or correction. **7** a trial print from a photographic negative. **8** a trial impression from an engraved plate. **9** a measure of the alcohol content of a distilled liquid, especially an alcoholic beverage. It is expressed in degrees of proof as the percentage of proof spirit (which contains about 57% alcohol by volume) present. — *adj.* (*often in compounds*) able or designed to withstand, deter, or be free from: *proof against storms / leakproof.* — *verb* **1** (*also in compounds*) to make resistant to, or proof against, something; to waterproof. **2** to take a proof of (printed material). [from French *preuve*, from Latin *proba*, test, proof]

proof-read *verb trans., intrans.* to read and mark for correction the proofs of (a text, etc).

proof-reader *noun* a person who reads and corrects proofs.

proof spirit a mixture of alcohol and water in which the alcohol content is 49·28% of the weight or 57·1% of the volume.

prop¹ — *noun* **1** a rigid, especially vertical, support of any of various kinds. **2** a person or thing that one depends on for help or emotional support. **3** *Rugby* (*also* **prop forward**) a forward at either end of the front row of the scrum. — *verb* (**propped, propping**) **1** (*also* **prop something up**) to support or hold it upright with, or as if with, a prop. **2** (**prop one thing against another**) to lean or put it against something: *propped her bike against the wall.* **3** to serve as a prop to. [from Middle English *proppe*]

prop² *noun colloq.* **1** a propeller. **2** *Theatr.* a stage property.

propaganda *noun* the organized circulation by a political group, etc of information, misinformation, rumour or opinion, presented so as to influence public feeling; also, the material circulated in this way. [from the Roman Catholic *Congregatio de propaganda fide* 'congregation for propagating the faith', responsible for foreign missions and training missionaries]

propagandist *noun* a person who prepares or circulates propaganda.

propagandize *or* **propagandise** *verb* **1** *trans.* to subject to propaganda. **2** *intrans.* to circulate propaganda.

propagate *verb* **1** *intrans., trans. Bot.*, *said of a plant* to multiply. **2** *Bot.* to grow (new plants), either by natural means or artificially. **3** to spread or popularize (ideas, etc). **4** *Physics* to transmit energy, eg sound, electromagnetism, over a distance in wave form. [from Latin *propagare*, to grow plants by grafting, etc]

propagation *noun* **1** *Bot.* the multiplication of plants, especially in horticulture, either by nat-ural means, eg from seed, or by artificial methods which allow the mass production of plants with desirable traits that might be lost if they were bred from seed, eg grafting, taking cuttings, growing new plants from stolons, tubers, or runners, tissue culture. **2** *Physics* the transmission of energy (eg sound, electromagnetism) from one point to another in the form of waves in a direction perpendicular to the wavefront.

propagator *noun* **1** a person or thing that propagates. **2** a heated box with a cover in which plants may be grown from cuttings or seeds.

propane *noun Chem.* (FORMULA C_3H_8) a colourless odourless flammable gas obtained from petroleum and belonging to the alkane series of hydrocarbons. It readily liquefies under pressure, and is used as a fuel supply for portable stoves, etc, and as a solvent and refrigerant. [from *propionic acid*, a fatty acid]

propel *verb* (**propelled, propelling**) **1** to drive or push forward. **2** to steer or send in a certain direction. [from Latin *propellere*, to drive forward]

propellant *noun* **1** something that propels. **2** *Chem.* a compressed inert gas in an aerosol that is used to release the liquid contents as a fine spray when the pressure is released. **3** *Engineering* the fuel and oxidizer that are burned in a rocket in order to provide thrust. **4** an explosive charge that is used to propel a projectile, eg a bullet or shell.

propellent *adj.* driving; propelling.

propeller *noun* a device consisting of a shaft with radiating blades that rotate to propel a ship or an aircraft.

propelling-pencil *noun* a type of pencil in which the lead is held in a casing and can be propelled forward as it is worn down.

propensity *noun* (PL. **propensities**) a tendency or inclination. [from Latin *propendere*, to be inclined]

proper *adj.* **1** real; genuine; that can rightly be described as: *have a proper holiday.* **2** right; correct: *learn the proper grip.* **3** appropriate: *at the proper time.* **4** own particular; correct: *everything in its proper place.* **5** socially accepted; respectable: *the proper way to behave.* **6** *derog.* morally strict; prim: *is a bit proper.* **7** (**proper to something**) belonging or appropriate to it; suitable: *the form of address proper to her rank.* **8** (*used after a noun*) strictly so called; itself: *we are now entering the city proper.* **9** *colloq.* utter: *felt a proper fool.* [from Old French *propre*, own]

proper fraction *Maths.* a fraction such as $\frac{1}{2}$ and $\frac{3}{4}$ in which the number above the line is smaller than the one below.

properly *adv.* **1** suitably; appropriately; correctly. **2** with strict accuracy: *spiders can't properly be called insects.* **3** fully; thoroughly; completely. **4** *colloq.* utterly.

proper noun *or* **proper name** *Grammar* the name of a particular person, place, or thing. See also COMMON NOUN.

propertied *adj.* owning property, especially land.

Propertius, Sextus (c.48–c.15 BC) Roman elegiac poet, born (probably) at Asisium (Assisi), Italy. He was educated in Rome, where he became a poet and won the favour of Maecenas and Augustus. The central figure of his inspiration was his mistress, to whom he devoted the first of his four surviving books, *Cynthia.*

property *noun* (PL. **properties**) **1** something one owns: *that book is my property.* **2** one's possessions collectively. **3** the concept of ownership. **4** land or real estate, or an item of this. **5** a quality or attribute: *the properties of copper sulphate.* **6** *Theatr.* an object or piece of furniture used on stage during a performance. [from Middle English *proprete*, from Latin *proprietas*, attribute, ownership]

property man or **property mistress** *Theatr.* a person in charge of stage properties.

propfan *noun* a propeller fan: an aircraft propeller consisting of a rotor carrying several blades working in a cylindrical casing, sometimes provided with fixed blades, and usually driven by a direct-coupled motor. The swept back or 'skew' blades allow quieter operation for the rotational speeds involved.

prophase *noun Biol.* the first stage of cell division in mitosis and meiosis, during which the chromosomes coil and thicken, and divide longitudinally to form chromatids, and the membrane surrounding the nucleus disintegrates.

prophecy *noun* (PL. **prophecies**) 1 the interpretation of divine will or the foretelling of the future; a gift or aptitude for this. 2 a prophetic utterance; something foretold; a prediction. [from Old French *prophecie*, from Greek *propheteia*]

prophesy *verb* (**prophesies**, **prophesied**) 1 *trans., intrans.* to foretell (future happenings); to predict. 2 *intrans.* to utter prophecies; to interpret divine will. [a variant of PROPHECY]

prophet *noun* 1 a person inspired to express the divine will or reveal the future. 2 *Biblical* any of the writers of prophecy in the Old Testament, or the books attributed to them. 3 (**the Prophet**) Muhammad. 4 someone claiming to be able to tell what will happen in the future: *prophets of mass destruction.* 5 a leading advocate of, or spokesperson for, a movement or cause: *a prophet of the green revolution.* [from Greek *prophetes*, an expounder of divine will]

prophetess *noun* a female prophet.

prophetic *adj.* 1 foretelling the future: *prophetic remarks.* 2 of or relating to prophets or prophecy.

prophetically *adv.* in a prophetic way.

prophylactic — *adj.* guarding against, or preventing, disease or other mishap. — *noun* a prophylactic drug or device; a precautionary measure. [from Greek *prophylassein*, to take precautions against]

prophylaxis *noun* action or treatment to prevent something unwanted; precautionary measures.

propinquity *noun* 1 nearness in place or time; proximity. 2 closeness of kinship. [from Latin *propinquitas*, from *propinquus*, near]

propitiable *adj.* capable of being propitiated or made propitious.

propitiate *verb* to appease or placate (an angry person or god). [from Latin *propitiare*, to appease]

propitiation *noun* propitiating, atonement.

propitiator *noun* a person who propitiates.

propitiatory *adj.* propitiating, making up for a wrong.

propitious *adj.* 1 favourable; auspicious; advantageous: *a propitious moment to sell.* 2 (**propitious for** or **to something**) likely to favour or encourage it: *circumstances propitious to development.* [from Latin *propitius*, favourable]

propitiously *adv.* in a propitious way; so as to be propitious.

proponent *noun* a supporter or advocate: *a proponent of recycling.* [from Latin *proponere*, to propose]

proportion — *noun* 1 a part of a total: *a large proportion of the population.* 2 the size of one element or group in relation to the whole or total: *only a small proportion of lawyers are women.* 3 the size of one group or component in relation to another: *mixed in a proportion of two parts to one.* 4 the correct balance between parts or elements: *the hands are out of proportion with the head / put things into proportion.* 5 (**proportions**) size; dimensions: *a task of huge proportions.* 6 *Maths.* correspondence between the ratios of two pairs of quantities, as expressed in *2 is to 8 as 3 is to 12.* — *verb* (**proportioned, proportioning**) 1 to adjust the proportions, or balance the parts, of: *a well-proportioned room.* 2 (**proportion one thing to another**) to adjust their proportions. — **in proportion to something** 1 in relation to it; in comparison with it. 2 in parallel with it; in correspondence with it; at the same rate. [from Latin *proportio*, proportion, symmetry]

proportional *adj.* (**proportional to something**) 1 corresponding or matching in size, rate, etc. 2 in correct proportion; proportionate.

proportionally *adv.* in a proportional way; in proportion.

proportional representation an electoral system in which each political party is represented in parliament in proportion to the votes it receives.

proportionate *adj.* (**proportionate to something**) being in correct proportion: *a reward proportionate to the work done.*

proportionately *adv.* in a proportionate way.

proposal *noun* 1 the act of proposing something. 2 something proposed or suggested; a plan. 3 an offer of marriage.

propose *verb* 1 to offer (a plan, etc) for consideration; to suggest. 2 to suggest or nominate (someone for a position, task, etc). 3 *trans., intrans.* to be the proposer of (the motion in a debate). 4 to intend: *don't propose to sell.* 5 to announce the drinking of (a toast) or of (someone's health). 6 *intrans.* (**propose to someone**) to make them an offer of marriage. [from Latin *proponere*, to propose]

proposer *noun* 1 someone who proposes or advocates something. 2 the leading speaker in favour of the motion in a debate.

proposition — *noun* 1 a proposal or suggestion. 2 something to be dealt with or undertaken: *an awkward proposition.* 3 *euphemistic colloq.* an invitation to have sexual intercourse. 4 *Logic* a form of statement affirming or denying something, that can be true or false; a premise. 5 *Maths.* a statement of a problem or theorem, especially incorporating its solution or proof. — *verb* (**propositioned, propositioning**) *euphemistic colloq.* to propose sexual intercourse to. [from Latin *propositio*, a setting forth, premise, proposition]

propound *verb* to put forward (an idea, theory, etc) for consideration or discussion. [from Latin *proponere*, to propose]

propranolol *noun Medicine* a beta-blocker drug used especially in the treatment of abnormal heart rhythms, angina, and high blood pressure. It can also prevent migraine attacks and relieve symptoms of anxiety. [from PROPYL + PROPANOL]

proprietary *adj.* 1 *said eg of rights* belonging to an owner or proprietor. 2 suggestive or indicative of ownership: *had a proprietary attitude towards his wife.* 3 *said of medicines, etc* marketed under a tradename. 4 privately owned and managed. [from Latin *proprietarius*, from *proprietas*, ownership]

proprietary name a tradename.

proprietor *noun* an owner, especially of a shop, hotel, business, etc. [from Latin *proprietarius*, from *proprietas*, ownership]

proprietorial *adj.* 1 having the position of proprietor. 2 characteristic of a proprietor.

proprietress *noun* a female proprietor.

propriety *noun* (PL. **proprieties**) 1 socially acceptable behaviour, especially between the sexes; modesty or decorum. 2 rightness; moral acceptability: *the dubious propriety of getting children to report on their teachers.* 3 (**proprieties**) the details of correct behaviour; accepted standards of conduct: *observe the proprieties.* [from Middle English *propriete*, one's own nature, from Old French, from Latin *proprietas*, ownership]

proprioceptor *noun Zool.* a cell or group of cells that is sensitive to movement, pressure, or stretching within the body. Proprioceptors play an important role in the maintenance of balance and posture, and the coordination of muscular activity. [from Latin *proprius*, own]

props *noun Theatr.* a property man or property mistress.

propulsion *noun* the process of driving, or of being driven, forward; a force that propels: *jet propulsion.* [from Latin *propulsio*]

propulsive *adj.* having a tendency to propel or the quality of propelling; driving forward.

propylaeum or **propylon** *noun* (PL. **propylaea, propyla**) *Archit.* in classical architecture, a monumental entrance gateway or vestibule, usually in front of a temple. A famous example is the Propylaea at the W of the Acropolis, Athens, built 437–432 BC. [from Greek *propylaion*, and *propylon*, from *pro*, before + *pyle*, a gate]

pro rata in proportion; in accordance with a certain rate. [from Latin *pro rata*]

prorogation *noun* proroguing.

prorogue *verb* 1 to discontinue the meetings of (a legislative assembly) for a time, without dissolving it. 2 *intrans. said of a legislative assembly* to suspend a session. [from Latin *prorogare*, to prorogue, continue, defer]

prosaic *adj.* 1 unpoetic; unimaginative. 2 dull, ordinary and uninteresting. [from Latin *prosaicus*, from *prosa*, prose]

prosaically *adv.* in a prosaic way.

pros and cons advantages and disadvantages. [from Latin *pro*, in favour of, and *contra*, against]

proscenium *noun* (PL. **prosceniums, proscenia**) *Theatr.* 1 the part of a stage in front of the curtain. 2 (*also* **proscenium arch**) the arch framing the stage and separating it from the auditorium. [from Greek *proskenion*, from *pro-*, in front + *skene*, stage]

prosciutto *noun* finely cured uncooked ham, often smoked. [Italian, = pre-dried]

proscribe *verb* 1 to prohibit or condemn (something, eg a practice). 2 *Hist.* to outlaw or exile (someone). [from Latin *proscribere*, to outlaw]

proscription *noun* proscribing or being proscribed.

proscriptive *adj.* characterized by proscribing; tending to proscribe.

prose *noun* 1 ordinary written or spoken language as distinct from verse or poetry. 2 a passage of prose set for translation into a foreign language. [from Latin *prosa oratio*, straightforward speech]

prosecute *verb* 1 *trans., intrans.* to bring a criminal action against (someone). 2 *formal* to carry on or carry out: *prosecuting her enquiries.* [from Latin *prosequi*, to pursue]

prosecution *noun* 1 the act of prosecuting or process of being prosecuted. 2 the bringing of a criminal action against someone. 3 (*sing., pl.*) the prosecuting party in a criminal case, or the lawyers involved in this. 4 *formal* the process of carrying something out: *in the prosecution of my duties.*

prosecutor *noun* a person who brings or conducts a criminal action against someone.

proselyte *noun* a convert, especially to Judaism. [from Greek *proselytos*, new arrival, convert to Judaism]

proselytism *noun* 1 the process of becoming a convert; conversion. 2 the practice of making converts.

proselytize *or* **proselytise** *verb trans., intrans.* to try to convert; to make converts.

prose poem a work or passage printed continuously as prose but having many of the elements found in poetry (eg striking imagery, rhythm, internal rhyme). The form was established by Aloysius Bertrand's *Gaspard de la nuit* (Gaspard of the Night, 1842), and Baudelaire's *Petits poemes en prose* (Little Prose Poems, 1869): other writers of prose poems include Oscar Wilde and T S Eliot.

Proserpine see PERSEPHONE.

prosodic *adj.* relating to or characterized by prosody.

prosodics *sing. noun* same as PROSODY 2.

prosodist *noun* a person skilled in prosody.

prosody *noun* **1** the study of verse-composition, especially poetic metre. **2** the study of rhythm, stress, and intonation in speech. [from Greek *prosoidia*, from *pros*, to + *oide*, song]

prospect — *noun* (with stress on *pros-*) **1** a visualization of something due or likely to happen: *the prospect of losing her job.* **2** an outlook for the future. **3** (**prospects**) chances of success, improvement, recovery, etc. **4** (**prospects**) opportunities for advancement: *a job with prospects.* **5** a potentially selectable candidate, team member, etc: *is a doubtful prospect for Saturday's match.* **6** a potential client or customer. **7** a broad view: *a prospect of the bay.* **8** *Gold-mining* an area with potential as a mine. — *verb* (with stress on *-spect*) *intrans.* (**prospect for**) **1** to search for (gold, etc). **2** to hunt for or look out for (eg a job).
— **in prospect** expected soon.
[from Latin *prospectus*, view]

prospective *adj.* likely or expected; future: *a prospective buyer.*

prospector *noun* a person prospecting for oil, gold, etc.

prospectus *noun* (**prospectuses**) **1** a booklet giving information about a school or other institution; a brochure. **2** a document outlining a proposal for something, eg a literary work, or an issue of shares. [from Latin *prospectus*, prospect]

prosper *verb intrans.* (**prospered, prospering**) to do well, especially financially; to thrive or flourish. [from Latin *prosperari*, to prosper]

prosperity *noun* the state of being prosperous; success; wealth.

Prospero the usurped island-bound Duke of Milan in Shakespeare's *The Tempest*, who develops his magical powers in order to control his enemies.

Prospero and Ariel a relief sculpture by Eric Gill (1931) above the entrance to Broadcasting House, London.

prosperous *adj.* wealthy and successful.

prosperously *adv.* in a prosperous way.

Prost, Alain (1955–) French motor racing driver, born in St Chamond, the first Frenchman to win the world title. He won the world championship for McLaren in 1985–6 and 1989. In 1987 he surpassed Jackie Stewart's record of 27 wins. He was with Ferrari from 1990 to 1992, and in 1993 he again won the world championship, this time for the Williams team. He retired in Nov 1993, after a record 51 Grand Prix wins.

prostaglandin *noun Physiol.* any of a group of hormones that are secreted by many of the body tissues and have a wide range of specific effects (eg the regulation of kidney function and the contraction or relaxation of smooth muscle). Prostaglandins are sometimes used therapeutically to induce contractions of the uterus, either to accelerate labour or to induce abortion.

prostate *noun* (*in full* **prostate gland**) *Anat.* in male mammals, a muscular gland around the base of the bladder, controlled by sex hormones, which produces an alkaline fluid that activates sperm during ejaculation. In humans it sometimes enlarges and requires surgical removal. [from Greek *prostates*, literally 'one that stands in front']

prosthesis *noun* (PL. **prostheses**) **1** *Medicine* an artificial substitute for a part of the body that is missing (as a result of surgery or injury) or nonfunctional, eg an artificial eye, hand, limb, breast, or pacemaker. **2** the fitting of such a part to the body. [from Greek, from *pros*, to + *tithenai*, to put]

prostitute — *noun* a person, especially a woman or homosexual man, who accepts money in return for sexual intercourse or sexual acts. — *verb* **1** to put (eg one's talents) to an unworthy use. **2** to offer (oneself or someone else) as a prostitute. [from Latin *prostituere*, to offer for sale]

prostitution *noun* the act or practice of prostituting.

prostrate — *adj.* (with stress on *pros-*) **1** lying face downwards in an attitude of abject submission, humility or adoration. **2** lying flat. **3** exhausted by illness, grief, etc. — *verb* (with stress on *-strate*) **1** to throw (oneself) face down in submission or adoration. **2** to exhaust physically or emotionally. [from Latin *prosternere*, to throw forwards]

prostration *noun* the act of prostrating.

prosy *adj.* (**prosier, prosiest**) *said of speech or writing* dull and tedious.

prot- see PROTO-.

protactinium *noun* (SYMBOL **Pa**, ATOMIC NUMBER **91**) a radioactive metallic element that occurs in all uranium ores. [from PROTO- + ACTINIUM]

protagonist *noun* **1** the main character in a play or story. **2** the person, or any of the people, at the centre of a story or event. **3** a leader or champion of a movement, cause, etc. [from Greek *protagonistes*, from *protos*, first + *agonistes*, combatant]

Protagoras (c.490–421 BC) Greek Sophist, born in Abdera. He taught mainly in Athens, presenting a system of practical wisdom fitted to train men for citizens' duties, and based on the doctrine that 'man is the measure of all things'. His doctrine that all beliefs are true was examined in great detail and rejected by Plato. All his works are lost except a fragment of his treatise *On the Gods*.

protea *noun Bot.* any plant of the S African genus *Protea* of shrubs and small trees.

protean *adj.* **1** readily able to change shape or appearance; variable; changeable. **2** versatile; diverse. [from *Proteus*, a Greek sea god able to assume different shapes]

protease *noun Biochem.* any enzyme that breaks down proteins. [from Greek *proteios* primary]

protect *verb* **1** to shield from danger; to guard against injury, destruction, etc; to keep safe. **2** to cover against loss, etc by insurance. **3** to shield (home industries) from foreign competition by taxing imports. [from Latin *protegere*, to cover in front, protect]

protection *noun* **1** the action of protecting or condition of being protected; shelter, refuge, cover, safety, or care. **2** something that protects: *grow a hedge as a protection against the wind.* **3** the system of protecting home industries against foreign competition by taxing imports. **4** the criminal practice of extorting money from shop-owners, etc in return for leaving their premises unharmed; (*also* **protection money**) the money so extorted. **5** insurance cover.

protectionism *noun* the policy of protecting home industry from foreign competition.

protectionist *noun* a person who favours protectionism.

protective *adj.* **1** giving, or designed to give, protection. **2** inclined or tending to protect: *feel protective towards one's children.*

protective custody the detention of someone in prison, officially for his or her own safety.

protectively *adv.* in a protective way.

protectiveness *noun* being protective.

protector *noun* **1** a person or thing that protects. **2** a patron or benefactor. **3** a person ruling a country during the childhood of the sovereign, or in the absence of a sovereign; a regent.

Protectorate a regime established (1653) by the *Instrument of Government*, England's only written constitution. The Lord Protectors, Oliver Cromwell (ruled 1653–8) and his son Richard (ruled 1658–9), issued ordinances and controlled the armed forces, subject to the advice of a Council of State and with Parliament as legislative partner. It failed to win support, and its collapse led to the Restoration.

protectorate *noun* **1** the office, or period of rule, of a protector. **2** protectorship of a weak or backward country assumed by a more powerful one; the status of a territory that is so protected without actual annexation.

protectress *noun* a female protector.

protégé *or* **protégée** *noun* a man or woman under the guidance, protection, and patronage of a more important or wiser person. [from French *protéger*, to protect]

protein *noun Biochem.* any of a group of thousands of different organic compounds that are present in all living organisms and have large molecules consisting of long chains of amino acids. [from Greek *proteios*, primary]
◇ Proteins play a central role in the structure and functioning of all living cells, eg all enzymes are proteins, as are many structural tissues, such as muscle. Different proteins consist of a wide variety of combinations of 20 different amino acids linked to each other by peptide bonds to form *polypeptide chains*. Proteins are manufactured on specialized structures called *ribosomes* within the cytoplasm of cells, each polypeptide chain being generated by the linking of amino acids in an order that is specified by the genetic material of the cell (DNA and RNA). The completed chain then folds up into a specific three-dimensional shape that gives each protein its unique properties. Foods rich in protein include meat, fish, cheese, eggs, and pulses (eg peas, beans, and lentils).

pro tem *colloq.* short for *pro tempore* (Latin), for the time being.

Proterozoic *adj. Geol.* denoting the eon of geological time between the Archaean and Phanerozoic eons, lasting from about 2 500 million years ago until the beginning of the Cambrian period about 580 million years ago. It is usually regarded as representing the second of the two major subdivisions of the Precambrian, but is sometimes used to refer to the entire Precambrian. [from Greek *proteros*, earlier = *zoe*, life]

protest — *verb* **1** *intrans.* to express an objection, disapproval, opposition or disagreement. **2** *North Amer., esp.* US to challenge or object to (eg a decision or measure). **3** to declare solemnly, eg in response to an accusation: *protest one's innocence.* **4** *Legal* to obtain or write a protest with reference to (a bill). — *noun* **1** a declaration of disapproval or dissent; an objection. **2** an organized public demonstration of disapproval. **3** *Legal* a written statement that a bill has been presented and payment refused.
— **under protest** reluctantly; unwillingly.
[from Latin *protestari*, to declare, testify]

Protestant — *noun* a member of any of the Christian Churches which in the 16c embraced the principles of the Reformation and, rejecting the authority of the pope, separated from the Roman Catholic Church; a member of any body descended from these. — *adj.* relating or belonging to Protestants. [originally applied to those princes and others who in 1529 protested against an edict denouncing the Reformation]

Protestantism *noun* the beliefs and practices of Protestants.

◇ One of the major divisions of the Christian Church, which grew out of challenges to Roman Catholicism (by Luther, Calvin, and Zwingli, amongst others) at the Reformation, prompted by a desire to return to the precepts of the early Church. There are many separate forms; the common characteristics of the various groupings include emphasis on the authority of Scripture, justification by faith alone, and the priesthood of all believers, in which each believer may hear the confession of sin, this no longer being the domain only of the clergy. The principal branches are the Anglican Communion, Lutherans, Methodists, Presbyterians, Baptists, Unitarians, and the Pentecostal Movement.

protestation *noun* 1 a protest or objection. 2 a solemn declaration or avowal.

protester *or* **protestor** *noun* a person who protests.

Proteus 1 in Greek mythology, a prophetic sea god, and shepherd of Poseidon's seals. He was able to change his shape, and would give answers to questions only after a wrestling match. 2 one of the two idealistic 'gentlemen' in Shakespeare's *The Two Gentlemen of Verona*, whose fickle nature leads him to betray both his friend, Valentine, and his lover, Julia.

Proteus Bluebird the vehicle in which Donald Campbell (1921–67) broke the land speed record on 17 Jul 1964. He recorded a speed of 649kph/403.1mph at Lake Eyre, Australia.

prothrombin *noun Biochem.* one of the clotting factors in blood, which is manufactured in the liver and converted to the enzyme thrombin, which catalyses the conversion of the soluble protein fibrinogen to the insoluble protein fibrin.

Protista *pl. noun Biol.* in the classification of animals and plants, the kingdom that includes algae, bacteria, fungi, and protozoans. [from Greek *protistos* very first, from *protos* first]

proto- *or* **prot-** *combining form* forming words meaning 'first, earliest': *prototype*. [from Greek *protos*, first]

protocol *noun* 1 correct formal or diplomatic etiquette or procedure. 2 a first draft of a diplomatic document, eg setting out the terms of a treaty. 3 *North Amer., esp.* US a plan of a scientific experiment or other procedure. [from Greek *protokollon*, a note of the contents of a document, glued to the front sheet, from *protos*, first + *kolla*, glue]

Protocols of the Elders of Zion a fraudulent document, originally printed in Russia (1903) and much translated, ostensibly reporting discussions among Jewish elders of plans to subvert Christian civilization and erect a world Zionist state. Exposed as forgeries in *The Times* (1921), the 'Protocols' are nevertheless a staple of right-wing, anti-semitic propaganda.

Proto-Indo-European — *noun* the parent language from which all Indo-European languages are descended, thought to have been spoken throughout Europe and S Asia before 3 000 BC. There are no written texts of the language, and its vocabulary has been reconstructed from the common features found in extant Indo-European languages using the linguistic process known as internal reconstruction. — *adj.* relating to this parent language.

proton *noun Physics* any of the positively charged subatomic particles that are found inside the nucleus at the centre of an atom, together with uncharged particles known as neutrons.

Protons are slightly lighter than neutrons but about 1 850 times heavier than electrons. The number of protons in the nucleus is known as the *atomic number*. The mass of a proton is 1.672×10^{27}kg, and it carries a charge of 1.602×10^{19} coulombs. [from Greek *protos*, first]

protoplasm *noun* the translucent, colourless, semi-liquid substance of which living cells are chiefly composed. [from PROTO- + *plasma*, form]

prototype *noun* 1 an original model from which later forms are copied, developed or derived. 2 a first working version, eg of a vehicle, aircraft, etc. 3 a person or thing that exemplifies a type. 4 a primitive or ancestral form of something. [from Greek *prototypos*, primitive, original]

Protozoa *pl. noun Zool.* in the animal kingdom, a phylum or subkingdom of single-celled organisms that include both plant-like and animal-like forms, commonly known as protozoans, eg amoeba.

protozoan — *noun* a single-celled organism belonging to the phylum Protozoa, eg amoeba, paramecium. Many protozoans are parasitic, and some cause important diseases, eg *Plasmodium*, the malaria parasite. — *adj.* relating to the Protozoa. [from PROTO- + Greek *zoion*, animal]

protozoon *noun* same as PROTOZOAN.

protract *verb* to prolong; to cause to last a long time. [from Latin *protrahere*, to drag forth, prolong]

protracted *adj.* lasting longer than usual or longer than expected.

protractor *noun Geom.* an instrument, usually a transparent plastic semicircle marked in degrees, for drawing and measuring angles. [from Latin, from *protrahere*, to draw forth]

protrude *verb* 1 *intrans.* to project; to stick out. 2 *trans.* to push out or forward. [from Latin *protrudere*, to thrust forward]

protrusion *noun* 1 protruding. 2 something which protrudes.

protrusive *adj.* thrusting forward, protruding.

protuberance *noun* a bulging out, a swelling.

protuberant *adj.* projecting; bulging; swelling out. [from Latin *protuberare*, to swell out]

proud *adj.* 1 (*often* **proud of someone** *or* **something**) feeling pride at one's own or another's accomplishments, one's possessions, etc. 2 being a cause or occasion for pride: *a proud day / her proudest possession.* 3 arrogant; conceited: *too proud to talk to us.* 4 concerned for one's dignity and self-respect: *too proud to accept help.* 5 honoured; gratified; delighted: *proud to be invited.* 6 splendid; imposing: *a proud sight.* 7 *poetic* lofty; high: *trees waving their proud tops.* 8 projecting slightly from the surrounding surface. 9 *said of flesh* forming a protuberant mass round a healing wound.

— **do someone proud** to entertain or treat them grandly.

do oneself proud to succeed gloriously. [from Anglo-Saxon *prud*]

Proudhon, Pierre Joseph (1809–65) French socialist and political theorist, born in Besançon, whose writings became the basis of French radicalism. His first important book was *Qu'est-ce que la propriété?* (What is Property?, 1840), which affirms the bold paradox 'property is theft', because it involves the exploitation of others' labour. Then came his greatest work, the *Système des contradictions économiques* (System of Economic Contradictions, 1846). During the 1848 Revolution, the violence of his utterances brought him three years' imprisonment. In 1858 his three-volume *De la justice dans la Révolution et dans l'eglise* (On Justice in the Revolution and the Church) was seized, and he fled to Belgium until 1862.

Proudie, Dr the weak, incompetent bishop of Barchester in Anthony Trollope's *Barchester Towers* and other titles in the 'Barsetshire' novels. Mrs Proudie is his supercilious, evangelical wife.

proudly *adv.* in a proud way.

Proust, Joseph Louis (1754–1826) French analytical chemist, born in Angers. Director of the Royal Laboratories in Madrid from 1789, he returned to France in 1808 after the fall of his patron Charles IV. He developed the use of hydrogen sulphide as a reagent, and discovered the 'law of definite proportions' (1794), observing that the proportions of the constituents in any chemical compound are always the same regardless of the method used to prepare it.

Proust, Marcel (1871–1922) French novelist, born in Auteuil. He was a semi-invalid on account of his asthma, and after the death of his mother in 1905, he withdrew from society and lived in a sound-proofed flat. He then devoted himself to writing, and in 1912 produced the first part of his major 13-volume work, *A la recherche du temps perdu* (Remembrance of·Things Past). The second volume of this work, delayed by the war, won the Prix Goncourt in 1919. The next volumes brought him an international reputation, and he was able to complete the last six volumes (but not revise them) before his death.

provable *or* **proveable** *adj.* capable of being proved.

prove *verb* (PAST PARTICIPLE **proved, proven**) 1 to show to be true, correct or a fact. 2 to show to be: *was proved innocent / drugs of proven effectiveness.* 3 *intrans.* to be found to be, when tried; to turn out to be: *her advice proved sound.* 4 to show (oneself) to be: *has proved himself reliable.* 5 to show (oneself) capable or daring. 6 *Legal* to establish the validity of (a will). 7 *said of dough* to rise or cause it to rise.

— **not proven** *Scot. Legal* a verdict resorted to where there is insufficient evidence to prove guilt.

[from Latin *probare*, to test, prove]

provenance *noun* the place of origin, or source, of eg a work of art, archaeological find, etc. [from French *provenance*, from Latin *provenire*, to come forth]

Provençal — *adj.* of or relating to Provence in the south of France, its inhabitants, culture, or language. — *noun* 1 a language spoken in Provence, related to French and Spanish. 2 a native of Provence.

Provence, Latin **Provincia** a former province in SE France on the Mediterranean coast, now occupying the departments of Bouches-du-Rhône, Var, Alpes-de-Haute-Provence, and parts of Alpes-Maritimes and Vaucluse. It was formerly part of the kingdom of Arles, and became a part of France in 1481. The area has the distinctive Romance dialect of Provençal. ECONOMY coal, bauxite, lead, zinc; salt; market-gardening, grapes, olives; perfumes; tourism (especially on the Riviera).

provender *noun* 1 dry food for livestock, eg corn and hay. 2 *facetious* food. [from Old French *provendre*, from Latin *praebenda*, payment]

proverb *noun* any of a body of well-known, neatly expressed sayings that give advice or express a supposed truth. [from Latin *proverbium*]

proverbial *adj.* 1 of, like or being a proverb. 2 referred to in a proverb; traditionally quoted; well known: *a cat's proverbial nine lives.*

proverbially *adv.* in a proverbial way; by tradition or reputation.

Proverbs, Book of a book of the Hebrew Bible and Old Testament, attributed to Solomon, but probably a collection of wisdom traditions from several centuries. Chapters 1 to 9 include poems about personified Wisdom, and moral admonitions of a father to his son; chapters 10 to 29 present sets of individual sayings on virtues and vices with little thematic arrangement, similar to Egyptian wisdom instructions; chapters 30

Proverbs

1 The date is the first known occurrence in print in English in a recognizable form. In many cases related sentiments are attested earlier, often in Greek and Latin. A number of other proverbs are derived from medieval French sources.
2 Some of the uses are not in the precise form given here. Proverbs often appear in many forms.

Proverb/Date/Notable Uses

absence makes the heart grow fonder   19c
actions speak louder than words   17c
all's well that ends well   14c
an *apple* a day keeps the doctor away   19c
don't throw out the *baby* with the bathwater   19c   *Thomas Carlyle*
beauty is in the eye of the beholder   18c   *Hume*
beauty is only skin deep   17c
beggars can't be choosers   16c
the early *bird* catches the worm   17c
a *bird* in the hand is worth two in the bush   15c
birds of a feather flock together   16c   *Bible: Ecclesiasticus xxvii*
once *bitten*, twice shy   19c
when the *blind* lead the blind, both shall fall into the ditch   9c
   Bible: Matthew xv
you can't get *blood* from a stone   17c
blood is thicker than water   19c
brevity is the soul of wit   17c   *Shakespeare, Hamlet*
you can't make *bricks* without straw   17c   *Bible: Exodus v*
don't cross your *bridges* until you come to them   19c
a new *broom* sweeps clean   16c
you can't have your *cake* and eat it   16c
if the *cap* fits, wear it   18c
when the *cat's* away the mice will play   17c
a *change* is as good as a rest   19c   *Conan Doyle*
charity begins at home   14c   *John Wycliffe*
don't count your *chickens* before they are hatched   16c
clothes make the man   15c
every *cloud* has a silver lining   19c
cut your *coat* according to your cloth   16c
too many *cooks* spoil the broth   16c
curiosity killed the cat   19c
there's none so *deaf* as those that will not hear   16c
needs must when the *devil* drives   15c   *Shakespeare, All's Well that Ends Well* the
devil finds work for idle hands to do   14c   *Chaucer*
the *devil* looks after his own   17c
better the *devil* you know than the devil you don't   16c
discretion is the better part of valour   16c   *Shakespeare, Henry IV Pt. 1*
give a *dog* a bad name and hang him   18c
you can't teach an old *dog* new tricks   16c
let sleeping *dogs* lie   14c   *Chaucer*
barking *dogs* seldom bite   16c
to *err* is human, to forgive divine   17c
the *exception* proves the rule   17c
familiarity breeds contempt   14c
there are as good *fish* in the sea as ever came out of it   16c
a *fool* and his money are soon parted   16c
there's no *fool* like an old fool   16c
fools rush in where angels fear to tread   18c   *Pope*
forewarned is forearmed   15c
a *friend* in need is a friend indeed   11c
those who live in *glass* houses shouldn't throw stones   17c   *Chaucer*
all that glitters is not *gold*   13c   *Shakespeare, Merchant of Venice*,
   as 'all that glisters...'
don't teach your *grandmother* to suck eggs   18c
the *grass* is always greener on the other side of the fence   20c
old *habits* die hard   18c   *Benjamin Franklin*
many *hands* make light work   14c
first catch your *hare*   19c   *Thackeray*
more *haste* less speed   14c
he who *hesitates* is lost   18c
there is *honour* among thieves   17c
never look a gift *horse* in the mouth   16c
you make take a *horse* to water but you can't make him drink   12c
hunger is the best sauce   16c
where *ignorance* is bliss, 'tis folly to be wise   18c   *Thomas Gray*
strike while the *iron* is hot   14c   *Chaucer*
a little *knowledge* is a dangerous thing   18c   *Pope*
better *late* than never   14c
he who *laughs* last, laughs longest   20c

Proverb/Date/Notable Uses

least said, soonest mended   15c
a *leopard* doesn't change its spots   16c   *Bible: Jeremiah 13.23*
many a *little* makes a mickle   13c
half a *loaf* is better than no bread   16c
look before you leap   14c
one man's *meat* is another man's poison   16c
it's no use crying over spilt *milk*   17c
a *miss* is as good as a mile   17c
if the *mountain* won't come to Mahomet, Mahomet must go to the mountain
   17c   *Bacon*
necessity is the mother of invention   16c
no news is good *news*   17c   *James I*
don't cut off your *nose* to spite your face   16c
nothing venture, nothing gain   17c
great *oaks* from little acorns grow   14c   *Chaucer*
you can't make an *omelette* without breaking eggs   19c
out of sight, out of mind   13c
the *pen* is mightier than the sword   16c
take care of the *pence* and the pounds will take care of themselves   18c
in for a *penny*, in for a pound   17c
he that pays the *piper* calls the tune   19c
little *pitchers* have large ears   16c
there's no *place* like home   16c
a watched *pot* never boils   19c   *Mrs Gaskell*
practice makes perfect   16c
prevention is better than cure   17c
pride goes before a fall   14c
procrastination is the thief of time   18c   *Bible: Proverbs xvi*
the *proof* of the pudding is in the eating   14c
you can't make a silk *purse* out of a sow's ear   16c
it never *rains* but it pours   18c
the *road* to hell is paved with good intentions   16c
spare the *rod* and spoil the child   11c   *Bible: Proverbs xiii*
Rome was not built in a day   16c
when in *Rome*, do as the Romans do   15c
better *safe* than sorry   19c
there is *safety* in numbers   17c   *Bible: Proverbs xi, and John Bunyan*
what's *sauce* for the goose is sauce for the gander   17c
as well be hanged for a *sheep* as a lamb   17c
there's no *smoke* without fire   14c
speech is silver, but silence is golden   19c   *Thomas Carlyle*
it's no use shutting the *stable* door after the horse has bolted   14c
a *stitch* in time saves nine   18c
a rolling *stone* gathers no moss   14c
it's the last *straw* that breaks the camel's back   17c
little *strokes* fell great oaks   15c
one *swallow* doesn't make a summer   16c
what you lose on the *swings* you gain on the roundabouts   20c
you can have too much of a good *thing*   15c
little *things* please little minds   16c
time and tide wait for no man   14c   *Chaucer, in Latin*
don't put off till *tomorrow* what you can do today   14c   *Chaucer*
it's better to *travel* hopefully than to arrive   19c   *R L Stevenson*
the *tree* is known by its fruit   16c   *Bible: Matthew xii*
trouble shared is trouble halved   20c   *Dorothy L Sayers*
there's many a good *tune* played on an old fiddle   20c   *Samuel Butler*
one good *turn* deserves another   15c
variety is the spice of life   18c
all things come to those who *wait*   16c
waste not, want not   18c
still *waters* run deep   15c
where there's a *will* there's a way   17c
it's an ill *wind* that blows nobody any good   16c   *Shakespeare, Henry VI, Pt 3*
it's easy to be *wise* after the event   17c   *Ben Jonson*
the *wish* is father to the thought   16c   *Shakespeare*
fine *words* butter no parsnips   17c
all *work* and no play makes Jack a dull boy   17c
a bad *workman* blames his tools   17c

to 31 comprise two appendices, and end with a poem about the virtuous wife.

provide *verb* **1** to supply. **2** *said eg of a circumstance, situation, etc* to offer: *provide enjoyment / provide an opportunity.* **3** (**provide for** or **against something**) to be prepared for an unexpected contingency, an emergency, etc. **4** (**provide for someone**) to support or keep a dependant. **5** *chiefly Legal* to stipulate or require (that something should be done, etc). **6** (**provide for something**) *chiefly Legal* to specify it as a requirement, or enable it to be done. [from Latin *providere*, to see ahead, provide for]

provided or **providing (that)** *conj.* **1** on the condition or understanding that. **2** if and only if.

Providence POP (1990) 655 000, the port capital of the state of Rhode Island, USA, situated at the head of Providence R, in Providence County. Its excellent harbour makes it a popular sailing resort, as well as a major port for oil tankers. HISTORY established in 1636; an early haven for religious dissenters; achieved city status in 1832. NOTABLE FEATURES first Baptist and Unitarian churches; State Capitol; Museum of Art; Brown University, established in 1764.

providence *noun* **1** a mysterious power or force that operates to keep one from harm, etc; the benevolent foresight of God. **2** (**Providence**) God or Nature regarded as an all-seeing protector of the world. **3** the quality of being provident; prudent foresight or thrifty planning. [from Latin *providentia*, foresight]

Providencia see SAN ANDRÉS-PROVIDENCIA.

provident *adj.* careful and thrifty in planning ahead.

providential *adj.* due to providence; fortunate; lucky; opportune.

providentially *adv.* in a providential way.

providently *adv.* in a provident way.

provider *noun* a person who provides, a supplier.

province *noun* **1** an administrative division of a country. **2** *Roman Hist.* a territory outside Italy, governed by Rome as part of its empire. **3** one's allotted range of duties, or one's field of knowledge or experience: *a task outside my province.* **4** (**the provinces**) the parts of a country away from the capital, typically thought of as culturally backward. [from Latin *provincia*, official charge, province]

provincial *adj.* **1** of, belonging to, or relating to a province. **2** relating to the parts of a country away from the capital: *a provincial accent.* **3** supposedly typical of provinces in being culturally backward, unsophisticated, or narrow in outlook. [from Latin *provincialis*, from *provincia*, province]

provincialism *noun* **1** being provincial. **2** the attitude, behaviour, or speech peculiar to a province or country district. **3** a local expression. **4** ignorance and narrowness of interests.

provincially *adv.* in a provincial way or capacity.

proving-ground *noun* a place used for scientific testing; a place where something is tried out for the first time.

provision — *noun* **1** the act of providing. **2** something provided or made available; facilities: *provision for disabled pupils.* **3** preparations; measures taken in advance: *make provision for the future.* **4** (**provisions**) food and other necessaries. **5** *Legal* a condition or requirement; a clause stipulating or enabling something. — *verb* (**provisioned, provisioning**) to supply with food. [from Latin *provisio*, forethought, precaution]

provisional *adj.* temporary; conditional; for the time being, or immediate purposes, only; liable to be altered.

provisionally *adv.* for the time being, temporarily.

proviso *noun* (PL. **provisos**) **1** a condition: *agreed, with one proviso.* **2** *Legal* a clause stating a condition. [from Latin *proviso quod*, it being provided that]

provisory *adj.* **1** containing a proviso or condition, conditional. **2** making provision for the time being.

provocateur see AGENT PROVOCATEUR.

provocation *noun* **1** the act of provoking or state of being provoked; incitement. **2** a cause of anger, irritation, or indignation. [from Latin *provocatio*, calling forth, challenge]

provocative *adj.* **1** tending, or intended, to cause anger; deliberately infuriating. **2** sexually arousing or stimulating, especially by design: *provocative clothes / provocative behaviour.*

provocatively *adv.* in a provocative way.

provoke *verb* **1** to annoy or infuriate, especially deliberately. **2** to incite or goad. **3** to rouse (someone's anger, etc). **4** to cause, stir up or bring about: *provoked a storm of protest.* [from Latin *provocare*, to call forth, challenge, stimulate]

provoking *adj.* annoying.

provost *noun* **1** the head of some university colleges. **2** in Scotland, the chief magistrate of a burgh. [from Old French, from Latin *propositus*, placed at the head]

provost marshal an officer in charge of military police.

prow *noun* the projecting front part of a ship; the bow. [from French *proue*]

prowess *noun* **1** skill; ability; expertise. **2** valour; dauntlessness. [from Old French *proesse*]

prowl — *verb intrans.* **1** to go about stealthily, eg in search of prey. **2** to pace restlessly. — *noun* an act of prowling.
— **on the prowl** prowling about menacingly. [from Middle English *prollen*]

prowler *noun* a person who prowls.

proxemics *sing. noun* the study of how people use physical space as an aspect of non-verbal communication. It is concerned with the intimate, personal, social, and public distances that individuals, classes, and cultures maintain in their interactions with each other. Several research studies have looked at how closely people sit together, how much they touch each other while talking, how they vary in their practices in eg greeting each other or handshaking, and significant cultural and personal differences have been demonstrated. [from PROXIMITY]

Proxima Centauri *Astron.* the closest star to the Sun, and a faint companion to the double star Alpha Centauri in the constellation Centaurus.

proximal *noun Biol.* pertaining to or situated at the inner end, nearest to the point of attachment. [from Latin *proximus*, next]

proximate *adj.* nearest; immediately before or after in time, place, or order of occurrence. [from Latin *proximare*, to approach]

proximity *noun* nearness; closeness in space or time: *lives in close proximity to the station.* [from Latin *proximitas*, from *proximus*, next]

proxy *noun* (PL. **proxies**) **1** a person authorized to act or vote on another's behalf; the agency of such a person. **2** the authority to act or vote for someone else, or a document granting this. [a contraction of PROCURACY]

PRS *abbrev.* Performing Rights Society.

prude *noun* a person who is or affects to be shocked by improper behaviour, mention of sexual matters, etc; a prim or priggish person. [from French *prude femme*, respectable woman]

Prudence a female first name. [from Latin *prudentia*, providence]

prudence *noun* **1** being prudent. **2** caution, discretion. **3** taking care of one's resources or one's own interests.

prudent *adj.* **1** wise or careful in conduct. **2** shrewd or thrifty in planning ahead. **3** wary; discreet: *a prudent withdrawal.* [from Latin *prudens*, contracted from *providens*, from *providere*, to see ahead]

prudential *adj. old use* characterized by, or exercising, careful forethought. [from Latin *prudentialis*, from *prudentia*, prudence]

prudently *adv.* in a prudent way.

prudery *noun* **1** being prudish. **2** prudish opinions or behaviour.

Prudhoe Bay a bay on the N coast of Alaska, USA, on the Beaufort Sea. A pipeline links the Arctic oil fields with Valdez on the Gulf of Alaska.

prudish *adj.* having the character of or being like a prude.

prudishly *adv.* in a prudish way.

prudishness *noun* being prudish, prudish behaviour.

prune¹ — *verb* **1** to cut off (unneeded branches, etc) from (a tree or shrub) to improve its growth. **2** to cut out (superfluous matter) from (a piece of writing, etc); to trim or edit. — *noun* an act of pruning. [from Old French *proognier*, to prune (vines)]

prune² *noun* a dried plum. [from Latin *prunum*, plum]

pruning-hook *noun* a garden tool with a curved blade, for pruning.

prurience *noun* marked or excessive interest in sexual matters.

prurient *adj.* **1** unhealthily or excessively interested in sexual matters. **2** tending to arouse such unhealthy interest. [from Latin *prurire*, to itch, lust after]

pruriently *adv.* in a prurient way.

pruritis *noun Medicine* itching. [from Latin *prurire*, to itch]

Prussia a N European state, originally centred in the E Baltic region as a duchy created by the 13c Teutonic Knights but later owing suzerainty to Poland. Inherited by the German House of Brandenburg in the early 17c, Brandenburg–Prussia was consolidated and expanded, and Polish sovereignty thrown off, by Frederick William, the 'Great Elector'. The Kingdom of Prussia was founded in 1701; under Frederick William I (1713–40) and Frederick II, 'the Great', it acquired W Prussia and Silesia, and gained considerable territory in W Germany at the Congress of Vienna (1814–15). During the 19c it emerged as the most powerful German state, and was the focus of German unification. Within the federated German Empire (1871–1918) and the Weimar Republic (1919–33), it retained considerable autonomy and influence. As a legal entity, Prussia ceased to exist with the post-1945 division of Germany and the establishment of a revised E German–Polish frontier.

Prussian — *adj.* relating to Prussia. — *noun* a native or inhabitant of Prussia.

Prussian blue a deep blue pigment first made in Berlin; its colour.

prussic acid a deadly poison first obtained from Prussian blue; a solution of hydrogen cyanide in water.

pry¹ *verb intrans.* (**pries, pried**) **1** (*also* **pry into something**) to investigate matters that do not concern one, especially the personal affairs of others; to nose or snoop. **2** to peer or peep inquisitively. [from Middle English *prien*]

pry² *verb* (**pries, pried**) *North Amer., esp. US* to prise. [from PRISE, regarded as *pries*, which suggested a notional form *pry*]

PS *abbrev.* postscript.

PSA *abbrev.* Property Services Agency.

psalm *noun* a sacred song, especially one from the Book of Psalms in the Old Testament, traditionally attributed to King David. [from Greek *psalmos*, song sung to a harp]

psalmist *noun* a composer of psalms.

psalmody *noun* **1** the art of singing psalms. **2** a collected body of psalms. [from Greek *oide*, song]

Psalms, Book of, also known as the **Psalter** a book of the Hebrew Bible and Old Testament, named from the Greek translation and also designated *tehillim* (Hebrew 'songs'). There are 150 hymns or poems, including songs of thanksgiving, individual and community laments, wisdom poetry, and royal and enthronement songs. Many have individual titles and attributions, and the collection represents material from several centuries, brought together probably in the post-exilic period. The Psalter is regularly used in Jewish and Christian worship. It was also the most important type of medieval illustrated book.

psalter *noun* **1** (**Psalter**) the Book of Psalms. **2** a book containing the Biblical psalms. [from Greek *psalterion*, stringed instrument]

psaltery *noun* (PL. **psalteries**) *Hist.* a zither-like stringed instrument played by plucking. [from Greek *psalterion*, stringed instrument, harp]

PSBR *abbrev.* public-sector borrowing requirement, the money needed by the public sector to finance services, etc not covered by revenue.

psephological *adj.* relating to or involving psephology.

psephologist *noun* a person who studies or is expert in psephology.

psephology *noun* the study of elections and voting patterns. [from Greek *psephos*, pebble, vote + -LOGY]
◇ It is popularly associated with the analysis of voting figures and the forecasting of outcomes, but also covers all aspects of elections including legal frameworks, candidate selection, sociological and geographical analysis of voting patterns, and electoral systems.

pseud *colloq.* — *noun* a pretentious person; a bogus intellectual; a phoney. — *adj.* bogus, sham or phoney. [see PSEUDO-]

Pseudepigrapha an ancient Jewish body of literature which is not part of the Jewish Scriptures or of major Christian versions of the Old Testament or of the Apocrypha, but which are ascribed to Old Testament characters. [from Greek *pseudepigraphos*, falsely inscribed or ascribed]
◇ The writings span the period from 200 BC–AD 200, and include apocalypses (eg Book of Enoch), testaments (eg Testaments of the Twelve Patriarchs), wisdom, literature, prayers and psalms (eg Prayer of Manasseh, Psalms of Solomon), and additions to Old Testament stories (eg Life of Adam and Eve).

pseudo *adj. colloq.* false; sham; phoney.

pseudo- *or* **pseud-** *combining form* forming words meaning: **1** false. **2** pretending to be: *pseudo-intellectuals.* **3** deceptively resembling: *pseudo-scientific jargon.* [from Greek *pseudes*, false]

pseudocarp *noun Bot.* false fruit.

pseudonym *noun* a false name used by an author; a pen name or nom de plume. [from Greek *pseudes*, false + *onyma*, name]

pseudonymous *adj.* **1** assuming a false name, especially as an author. **2** written under a pseudonym.

pseudopodium *noun* (PL. **pseudopodia**) *Zool.* any of a number of temporary lobe-like protrusions from the cell of a protozoan (eg amoeba), produced by the streaming of cytoplasm into a projection that gradually increases in length, and is used as a means of locomotion, as well as for engulfing food particles. [from PSEUDO- + Greek *pous podos*, foot]

psi *abbrev.* pounds per square inch, a unit of pressure measurement.

psittacosis *noun* a disease of parrots that can be transmitted to human beings. [from Greek *psittakos*, parrot + -OSIS]

Pskov School a group of Russian icon and mural painters active (c.1200–c.1500) in the city of Pskov and influenced by Byzantine art.

psoriasis *noun Medicine* a common non-contagious skin disease characterized by red patches covered with white scales, mainly on the elbows, knees, scalp, and trunk. The cause of the disease is unknown, although attacks may be triggered by stress, injury, or drugs. It is usually hereditary. [from Greek, from *psora*, itch]

PSV *abbrev.* public service vehicle.

psych *verb colloq.* **1** (**be psyched up**) to prepare or steel oneself for a challenge, etc. **2** (**psych someone out**) to undermine the confidence of an opponent, etc; to intimidate or demoralize them. **3** to psychoanalyse. [a shortening of PSYCHOLOGICAL and related words]

psych- see PSYCHO-.

Psyche in Greek mythology, 'the soul', usually represented as a butterfly in folklore. In Apuleius's allegorical story in *The Golden Ass*, she was beloved by Cupid, who hid her in an enchanted palace and visited her at night, forbidding her to look at him. She eventually lit a lamp to look at him, was separated from him, and given impossible tasks by Venus, who impeded her search for him. She was finally made immortal and reunited with him in heaven.

psyche *noun* one's mind, especially with regard to the deep feelings and attitudes that account for one's opinions and behaviour. [from Greek *psyche*]

psychedelic *adj.* **1** denoting a state of mind with heightened perceptions and increased mental powers. **2** *said of a drug* inducing such a state. **3** *said of perceived phenomena, eg colour* startlingly clear and vivid. [from PSYCHE + Greek *delos*, clear]

psychedelic art an art style of the late 1960s, influenced by the prevalence of hallucinatory drugs, especially LSD. Typical designs feature abstract swirls of intense colour with curvilinear calligraphy reminiscent of Art Nouveau.

psychiatric *adj.* relating to or involving psychiatry.

psychiatrist *noun* an expert in or practitioner of psychiatry.

psychiatry *noun* the branch of medicine concerned with the study, diagnosis, treatment, and prevention of mental and emotional disorders, including psychoses, neuroses, depression, eating disorders, childhood behavioural problems, drug and alcohol dependence, schizophrenia, and mental handicap. The main forms of psychiatric treatment are psychotherapy, and the use of certain drugs to relieve symptoms. There is a considerable overlap between psychiatry and clinical psychology. [from PSYCHO- + Greek *iatros*, doctor]

psychic *adj.* **1** (*also* **psychical**) relating to mental processes or experiences that are not scientifically explainable, eg telepathy. **2** *said of a person* sensitive to influences producing such experiences; having mental powers that are not scientifically explainable. [from Greek *psychikos*, relating to the psyche]

Psycho a US film directed by Alfred Hitchcock (1960). A masterpiece of suspense and terror, it is the story of a woman who absconds with money to the Bates Motel where she is terrorized by the proprietor (played by Anthony Perkins), who is a murderous schizophrenic.

psycho — *noun* (PL. **psychos**) *colloq.* a psychopath. — *adj.* psychopathic.

psycho- *or* **psych-** *combining form* forming words denoting the mind and its workings: *psychodrama / psychology.*

psychoanalyse *or* **psychoanalyze** *verb* to examine or treat by psychoanalysis.

psychoanalysis *noun Psychol.* a theory and method of treatment for mental disorders, pioneered by Sigmund Freud, which emphasizes the effects of unconscious motivation and conflict on a person's behaviour.
◇ Psychoanalysis includes the analysis of dreams, and *free association* (in which the patient gives an immediate verbal response to words suggested by the psychoanalyst), which is said to bring back repressed fears and memories to the conscious mind, where they can be interpreted and dealt with. It is typically a prolonged and expensive form of treatment, and its effectiveness has been the subject of considerable controversy.

psychoanalyst *noun* a person who practises psychoanalysis.

psychoanalytic *or* **psychoanalytical** *adj.* relating to or involving psychoanalysis.

psychoanalytic criticism an approach to literary criticism using the analytic techniques and insights of psychoanalysis as described by Sigmund Freud, and applied by Freud himself to his reading of *Hamlet*, in terms of the Oedipus complex. It makes the assumption that the writer's unconscious desires may shape the text or that it is possible to analyse the characters by exposing their repressed emotions.

psychobabble *noun colloq.* language made impenetrable by the overuse of popular psychological jargon.

psychodrama *noun Psychol.* a technique involving a combination of behavioural and psychoanalytic psychotherapy in which, by acting out real-life situations, a patient learns new ways of dealing with both emotional and interpersonal problems.

psychological *adj.* relating to the mind or to psychology.

psychologically *adv.* in a psychological way; as regards psychology.

psychological moment the moment at which one is most likely to succeed in influencing someone to react as one wants.

psychological warfare propaganda and other methods used in wartime to influence enemy opinion and sap enemy morale.

psychologist *noun* an expert in psychology.

psychology *noun* **1** the scientific study of the mind and behaviour of humans and animals. **2** the mental attitudes and associated behaviour characteristic of a certain individual or group: *mob psychology.* **3** the ability to understand how people's minds work, useful when trying to influence them: *good/bad psychology.*
◇ Psychology includes a number of subdisciplines, such as *developmental psychology* (the study of mental development from birth to maturity), *clinical psychology* (the study of mental disorders, including their diagnosis, treatment and prevention), *occupational psychology* (the study of human behaviour in the workplace, eg personnel selection and management), and *social psychology* (the study of the social interactions between people). *Experimental psychology* uses rigorous scientific methods to study mental phenomena.

psychometrics *noun Psychol.* the branch of psychology concerned with the measurement of psychological characteristics, especially intelligence, personality, and mood states.

psychopath *noun* **1** *technical* a person with a personality disorder characterized by extreme callousness, who is liable to behave antisocially or violently in getting his or her own way. **2** *colloq.* a person who is dangerously unstable mentally or emotionally. [from PSYCHO- + -PATH]

psychopathic *adj.* relating to or characteristic of a psychopath.

psychopathically *adv.* in a psychopathic way.

psychopathology *noun Medicine* **1** the scientific study of mental disorders, as opposed to the treatment of such disorders. **2** the symptoms of a mental disorder.

psychopathy *noun Psychol.* a personality disorder characterized by an inability to form close relationships with other people, lack of social responsibility, and rejection of authority and discipline, with little or no guilt for antisocial behaviour such as violence and vandalism.

psychosis *noun* (PL. **psychoses**) *Psychol.* any of various severe mental disorders in which there is a loss of contact with reality, in the form of delusions (false beliefs) or hallucinations. [from Greek *psykhosis*, animation; in modern use, condition of the psyche]
◇ The two main types of psychosis are *organic psychoses*, caused by diseases which affect the brain, and *functional psychoses* (eg schizophrenia, manic-depressive illness), which have no known physical cause. Hospitalization or special care arrangements are often necessary in both cases.

psychosomatic *adj. Medicine*, said of physical symptoms or disorders strongly associated with psychological factors, especially mental stress. Common psychosomatic disorders include peptic ulcers, eczema, and asthma. [from PSYCHO- + Greek *soma*, body]

psychosomatically *adv.* in a psychosomatic way.

psychosurgery *noun Psychol.* brain surgery that is performed with the aim of treating a mental disorder.

psychotherapist *noun* an expert in psychotherapy.

psychotherapy *noun Psychol.* the treatment of mental disorders and emotional and behavioural problems by psychological means, rather than by drugs or surgery.
◇ Different approaches to psychotherapy include behaviour therapy (which aims to modify undesirable behaviour patterns), cognitive therapy (which aims to correct distorted thinking patterns), psychoanalysis, and Gestalt therapy. Group therapy involves the joint participation of several people (under the guidance of a trained therapist) who discuss their problems and possible ways of overcoming them or changing undesirable mental states or behaviour, eg alcoholism, depression. Family therapy aims to resolve longstanding problems in communication within a family by discussing these difficulties with all family members present.

psychotic — *adj.* relating to or involving a psychosis. — *noun* a person suffering from a psychosis.

psychotically *adv.* in a psychotic way.

PT *abbrev.* physical training.

Pt¹ *abbrev.* Port.

Pt² *symbol Chem.* platinum.

pt *abbrev.* **1** part. **2** pint. **3** point.

PTA *abbrev.* Parent–Teacher Association.

Ptah in ancient Egyptian religion, a god associated with Memphis, and represented as a mummified figure. He was originally the creator of the world, and later the god of craftsmanship, associated with Hephaestus. The bull Apis was his sacred animal and believed to be his reincarnation.

ptarmigan *noun* a mountain-dwelling grouse with white winter plumage. [from Gaelic *tàrmachan* ; the *p* wrongly added under the influence of Greek words beginning with *pt-*]

Pte *abbrev. Mil.* Private, the title for an ordinary soldier.

pteridophyte *Bot.* any plant belonging to the division Pteridophyta (according to some classifi-

cations of the plant kingdom), which includes the ferns, clubmosses, and horsetails. [from Greek *pteris*, fern + *phyton*, plant]
◇ Pteridophytes, unlike flowering and conebearing plants, do not produce seeds, but they do have a vascular system. They show marked alternation of generations, in which the dominant generation is a free-living spore-bearing *sporophyte* that has true leaves or fronds, stems, and roots, and alternates with a free-living *gametophyte* (which bears gametes). The pteridophytes include many extinct forms that flourished during the Carboniferous period. Present-day forms are widely distributed, but are most widely represented in the tropics.

pterodactyl *noun* same as PTEROSAUR. [from Greek *pteron*, wing + *daktylos*, finger]

pterosaur *noun* an extinct flying reptile that lived during the Jurassic and Cretaceous periods (at the same time as the dinosaurs), and was similar in size to a present-day bird, with a fur-covered body and leathery wings. Formerly called PTERODACTYL. [from Greek *pteron*, wing, after DINOSAUR]

PTO *abbrev.* please turn over.

Ptolemy I Soter (c.366–c.283 BC) Macedonian general in the army of Alexander the Great, who became ruler of Egypt after Alexander's death (323 BC). He secured control over Palestine, Cyprus, and parts of Asia Minor, and in 304 BC he adopted the royal title. He received the title Soter (Saviour) from the Rhodians, whom he defended against Antigonus (304 BC). His capital, Alexandria, became the centre of commerce and Greek culture, and he founded the museum and library there.

Ptolemy II Philadelphus (308–246 BC) King of Egypt (283–246 BC), the son and successor of Ptolemy I Soter. He increased the power of Egypt, and extended the Museum and Library of Alexandria, purchasing many valuable manuscripts of Greek literature. The Egyptian history of Manetho was dedicated to him.

Ptolemy III Euergetes I (d.222 BC) King of Egypt (246–222 BC), the son and successor of Ptolemy II Philadelphus. He conquered Syria and Cilicia, and was an ally of the Spartans against the Achaean League.

Ptolemy IV Philopator (d.204 BC) King of Egypt (222–204 BC), the son and successor of Ptolemy III Euergetes I. He began his reign by murdering his mother, Berenice. A hostile tradition portrays him as indolent and ascribes to him the decline of Ptolemaic power at home and abroad.

Ptolemy V Epiphanes (c.210–180 BC) King of Egypt (203–180 BC), who succeeded his father, Ptolemy IV Philopator, while still a boy. It was during his reign that internal conflicts in the court began, which were to affect the dynasty for the remainder of the Ptolemaic period. A trilingual inscription (in Greek, demotic, and hieroglyphic)

on the Rosetta stone record the ceremonies connected to his coronation, along with steps to secure the allegiance of the priesthood. This inscription provided the key to understanding the ancient scripts of Egypt.

Ptolemy VI Philometor (d.145 BC) King of Egypt, the son and successor of Ptolemy V Epiphanes. He acceded to the throne as a child and his mother, Cleopatra, governed the country during his minority. On her death (176 BC), power devolved on courtiers, who went to war with the Seleucid King, Antiochus IV of Syria. As a result, Egypt was invaded in 170 BC; Memphis was attacked and the young Ptolemy was captured, but reinstated as king. However, his brother (later Ptolemy VIII Euergetes II) had assumed the title of king in Alexandria. The Seleucids attacked Egypt again in 168 BC but were forced to withdraw by the Romans. In 164 BC Euergetes II expelled Philometer, who went to Rome and was restored by the Romans to his kingdom, while Euergetes obtained Cyrene as a separate realm. From this time onward, Egypt was under the protection of Rome.

Ptolemy VIII Euergetes II (d.116 BC) King of Egypt (170–63 BC and 145–116 BC). He was nicknamed Physcon ('Pot-belly') on account of his corpulence, and his cruelty and luxurious habits were notorious. He ruled jointly with his brother, Ptolemy VI Philometor, and in 164 BC expelled him from Egypt. The intervention of Rome restored Ptolemy VI, and Euergetes II was established as ruler of Cyrene. He married his sister, Cleopatra II, the widow of Ptolemy VI, and executed his nephew, Ptolemy Eupator, to have sole right to the throne. His reign was characterized by intrigue and ruthless elimination of rivals. In 130 BC, Cleopatra II was declared Queen in Egypt after he was forced to flee to Cyprus because of a revolt in Alexandria. As a result he had Memphitis (his son by Cleopatra) murdered.

Ptolemy XII Neos Dionysos, also called **Auletes** ('Flute-Player') (c.112–51 BC) King of Egypt (80–51 BC), who was proclaimed as king by the Alexandrians. He achieved the Roman senate's support for his title to the throne of Egypt through his bribery of Julius Caesar, who was consul in 59 BC. His over-taxed subjects forced him into exile in Rome (58–55 BC), where he endeavoured to get the senate to restore him to his kingdom. He arranged the assassination of members of a delegation sent by his opponents in Alexandria, and by further bribes was again placed on the throne through the agency of the pro-consul of Syria. On his return, he executed his eldest daughter, Berenice IV, who had ruled Egypt during his exile.

Ptolemy, Latin **Claudius Ptolemaeus** (c.90–168 AD) Egyptian astronomer and geographer who flourished in Alexandria. Considered the greatest astronomer of late antiquity, his book which later became known as the *Almagest* (The Greatest) was one of the most important compendiums of astronomy produced before the 16c. His Earth-centred view of the universe dominated cosmological thought until swept aside by Copernicus.

ptomaine *noun Biochem.* any of a group of organic compounds containing nitrogen, some of which are poisonous, produced during the bacterial decomposition of dead animal and plant matter, eg putrescine, cadaverine. [from Italian *ptomaina*, from Greek *ptoma*, corpse]

pty *abbrev.* proprietary.

ptyalin *noun Biochem.* in mammals, an enzyme present in the saliva that is responsible for the initial stages of breakdown of starch. [from Greek *ptyalon*, spittle]

Pu *symbol Chem.* plutonium.

pub *noun* a public house, a place where alcoholic drinks may be bought for consumption on the premises.

Ptah

puberty *noun* the onset of sexual maturity in humans and other primates, when the secondary sexual characteristics appear and the reproductive organs become functional. It includes breast development and the start of menstruation in females, and deepening of the voice and sperm production in males. [from Latin *pubertas*]

pubes *noun* (PL. **pubes**) **1** *Anat.* the pubic region of the lower abdomen; the groin. **2** the hair that grows on this part from puberty onward. [from Latin *pubes*]

pubescence *noun* **1** the onset of puberty. **2** a soft downy covering on plants. [from Latin *pubescere*, to reach puberty, become downy]

pubescent *adj.* reaching or having reached puberty.

pubic *adj.* relating to the pubis or pubes.

pubis *noun* (PL. **pubes**) *Anat.* in most vertebrates, one of the two bones forming the lower front part of each side of the pelvis. They meet at the *pubic symphysis*. [from Latin *os pubis*, bone of the pubes]

public — *adj.* **1** of, or concerning, all the people of a country or community: *public health / public opinion.* **2** relating to the organization and administration of a community: *the public prosecutor.* **3** provided for the use of the community: *public parks.* **4** well known through exposure in the media: *public figures.* **5** made, done, held, etc openly, for all to see, hear or participate in: *a public announcement / a public inquiry.* **6** known to all: *when the facts became public / is public knowledge / make one's views public.* **7** watched or attended by an audience, spectators, etc: *her last public appearance.* **8** open to view; not private or secluded: *it's too public here.* — *sing. or pl. noun* **1** the people or community. **2** a particular class of people: *the concert-going public.* **3** an author's, performer's, etc audience or group of devotees: *mustn't disappoint my public.*
— **go public** to become a public company.
in public in the presence of other people.
in the public eye *said of a person, etc* well known through media exposure.
[from Latin *publicus*, from *populus*, people]

public-address system (ABBREV. **PA**) a system of microphones, amplifiers, and loudspeakers, by means of which public announcements, etc can be communicated over a large area.

publican *noun* **1** *Brit.* the keeper of a public house. **2** *Biblical* a tax-collector. [from Latin *publicanus*, tax-farmer]

publication *noun* **1** the act of publishing a printed work; the process of publishing or of being published. **2** a book, magazine, newspaper, or other printed and published work. **3** the act of making something known to the public.

public bar a bar less well furnished and serving drinks more cheaply than a lounge bar.

public company a company whose shares are available for purchase by the public.

public convenience a public toilet.

public enemy someone whose behaviour threatens the community, especially a criminal.

public holiday a day kept as an official holiday, on which businesses, etc are closed.

public house an establishment where alcoholic drinks are sold for consumption on the premises; a pub.

publicity *noun* **1** advertising or other activity designed to rouse public interest in something. **2** public interest so attracted. **3** the condition of being the object of public attention.

publicize *or* **publicise** *verb* **1** to make generally or widely known. **2** to advertise.

Public Lending Right (ABBREV. **PLR**) in the UK, the right of authors (established by the Public Lending Right Act, 1979) to receive payments when their books are borrowed from public libraries. The annual payments, which vary according to the estimated frequency of public borrowing, are made from public funds; in 1993, the maximum sum any one author could receive was £6 000. The scheme was implemented in 1983.

public nuisance an illegal act causing trouble or danger to the general public.

public prosecutor a public official whose function is to prosecute those charged with criminal offences.

Public Record Office (ABBREV. **PRO**) the British national depository of government papers, selected archives, and legal documents to be permanently preserved. It was established by an Act of Parliament in 1838. The museum is now housed in a neoclassical building in Chancery Lane, London.

public relations (ABBREV. **PR**) **1** (*pl., sing.*) the relationship of an organization, etc with the public, especially with regard to its reputation and its communication of information about itself. **2** (*sing.*) the department of an organization responsible for this.

Public Safety, Committee of a French Revolutionary political body, set up in the war crisis (Apr 1793) to organize defence against internal and external enemies. Elected by the National Convention, its members exercised dictatorial powers during the Reign of Terror, particularly under Robespierre's leadership, but after his downfall (Jul 1794) they were strictly limited.

public school 1 in the UK, a secondary school run independently of the state, financed by endowments and by pupils' fees. **2** in the US, a school run by a public authority.
◊ In England, public schools for boys usually take pupils from the age of 13; for girls, it is more often from the age of 11. Famous examples include Charterhouse, Eton, Harrow, Radley, Roedean, Rugby, and Westminster.

public sector that part of a country's economy consisting of nationalized industries and of institutions and services run by the state or local authorities.

public servant an elected or appointed holder of public office; a government employee.

public spending spending by a government or local authority, financed either by tax revenues or by borrowing. In the UK, public spending levels by various government departments (and by local government) are broadly determined by negotiation between the departments and the Treasury.

public-spirited *adj.* acting from, or showing, concern for the general good of all.

public utility a supply eg of gas, water or electricity, or other service, provided for a community.

public works buildings, roads, etc built by the state for public use.

publish *verb trans., intrans.* **1** to prepare, produce, and distribute (printed material, computer software, etc) for sale to the public. **2** *intrans., trans. said of an author* to have (one's work) published. **3** to publish the work of (an author). **4** to announce publicly: *published their engagement.* **5** *Legal* to circulate (a libel). [from Old French *publier*, from Latin *publicare*, to make public]

publisher *noun* **1** a person or company engaged in the business of publishing books, newspapers, music, software, etc. **2** *North Amer.* a newspaper proprietor.

publishing *noun* the activity or trade of a publisher, or of publishers collectively. It includes the selection or commissioning of material for publication; production of books, magazines, newspapers, audio-visual material, and computer-based information; and marketing.

Pucci, Emilio, Marchese (Marquess) di Barsento (1914–92) Italian fashion designer, born in Naples. He studied in Italy and the USA, gaining a doctorate in political science in 1941. A member of the Italian ski team in 1934, in 1947 he was photographed wearing ski clothes he had designed. He then began to create and sell clothes for women, opened his couture house in 1950, and became famed for his use of bold patterns and brilliant colour. He became a member of the Italian parliament in 1965.

Puccini, Giacomo (Antonio Domenico Michele Secondo Maria) (1858–1924) Italian operatic composer, born in Lucca. An organist and choirmaster, his first compositions were for the church. His first great success was *Manon Lescaut* (1893), but this was eclipsed by *La Bohème* (1896), *Tosca* (1900), and *Madama Butterfly* (1904). His last opera, *Turandot*, was left unfinished.

puce *noun* a colour anywhere in the range between deep purplish pink and purplish brown. [from French *couleur de puce*, flea colour]

Puck, also called **Robin Goodfellow** the naughty, spell-casting sprite in Shakespeare's *A Midsummer Night's Dream*.

puck *noun* a thick disc of hard rubber used in ice-hockey in place of a ball. [perhaps connected with POKE[1]]

pucker — *verb trans., intrans.* (**puckered, puckering**) to gather into creases, folds or wrinkles; to wrinkle. — *noun* a wrinkle, fold or crease. [perhaps connected with POKE[2]]

puckish *adj.* mischievous; impish. [from Anglo Saxon *puca*, from Old Norse *puki*, a mischievous demon]

pudding *noun* **1** any of several sweet or savoury foods usually made with flour and eggs and cooked by steaming, boiling, or baking. **2** any sweet food served as dessert; the dessert course. **3** a type of sausage made with minced meat, spices, blood, oatmeal, etc: *black pudding.* [from Middle English *poding*]

puddle — *noun* **1** a small pool, especially of rainwater on the road. **2** (*in full* **puddle clay**) a non-porous watertight material consisting of thoroughly mixed clay, sand, and water. — *verb* **1** to make watertight by means of puddle. **2** to knead clay, sand, and water to make puddle. **3** *Metall.* to produce (wrought iron) from molten pig iron by the now obsolete process of puddling. [probably a diminutive of Anglo-Saxon *pudd*, ditch]

puddling the original process for converting pig iron into wrought iron by melting it in a furnace in the presence of iron oxide. Carbon is removed as a result of oxidation by air, and other impurities are removed as slag. When the process is complete, the iron melt is removed from the furnace in large lumps, which are then hammered and rolled.

pudenda *noun* the external sexual organs, especially of a woman. [plural of Latin *pudendum*, something to be ashamed of; the singular is also occasionally used]

pudgy *adj.* (**pudgier, pudgiest**) same as PODGY.

Pudovkin, Vsevolod (Ilarionovich) (1893–1953) Russian film director and writer, born in Penza. He joined the State Institute for Cinematography in Moscow and in his first feature, *Mat* (Mother, 1926), applied his techniques of cross-cutting and montage to depict visually the characters' emotions. There followed the silent classics, *Konets Sankt-Peterburga* (The End of St Petersburg, 1927) and *Potomok Chingis-Khan* (Storm Over Asia, 1928), and such sound films as *Dezertir* (Deserter, 1933).

Puebla *or* **Puebla de Zaragoza 1** POP (1990) 1.1m, the capital of Puebla state, S central Mexico. It lies 190km/120mi SE of Mexico City at an of altitude 2 150m. The city was damaged by an earthquake in 1973. Glazed tiles, for which Puebla is known, cover the domes of many of its 60 churches. NOTABLE FEATURES cathedral (17c);

Church of Santo Domingo (1659); Archbishop's Palace (16c); Teatro Principal (1790). The historic centre is a World Heritage site. **2** a state in S central Mexico with Puebla as its capital.

Pueblo the Native American peoples of SW USA, who live in settlements called *pueblos* in multi-storied, permanent houses made of clay. Culturally and linguistically diverse, they are divided into E and W Pueblo, the latter including the Hopi and Zuni. They are famed for their weaving, basketry, sand paintings, and pottery.

Pueblo, USS a US spy ship shelled and boarded by N Koreans in 1968. Its crew were detained for nearly a year. The US government was forced to sign a public apology to obtain the crew's release.

pueblo *noun* (PL. **pueblos**) a town or settlement in Spanish-speaking countries. [from Spanish *pueblo*, town, from Latin *populus*, a people]

puerile *adj.* childish; silly; immature. [from Latin *puerilis*, from *puer*, boy]

puerility *noun* a puerile state or quality.

puerperal *adj.* connected with childbirth. [from Latin *puerpera*, woman in labour]

puerperal fever fever accompanying blood-poisoning caused by infection of the uterus during childbirth.

puerperium *noun Medicine* the period between childbirth and the return of the womb to its normal state, usually about six weeks. [from Latin *puerpera*, a woman in labour]

Puerto Cortes POP (1988e) 43 000, a port town in Cortés department, NW Honduras. It lies at the mouth of the R Ulúa, on the Caribbean Sea and is the principal port of Honduras.

Puerto Presidente Stroessner or **Ciudad Presidente Stroessner** POP (1990) 111 000, the capital of Alto Paraná department, N Paraguay. The city lies on the R Paraná. It is the fastest-growing city in the country, and the centre for the construction of the Itaipú Dam, the largest hydroelectric project in the world. A bridge links the city with Brazil and the town of Foz do Iguaçu. [named after the former President of Paraguay]

Puerto Rico, formerly **Porto Rico** (to 1932), official name **Commonwealth of Puerto Rico** POP (1992e) 3.6m, the easternmost island of the Greater Antilles, situated between the Dominican Republic in the W and the US Virgin Is in the E, c.1 600km/1 000mi SE of Miami. AREA 8 897sq km/3 434sq mi. CAPITAL San Juan. CHIEF TOWNS Ponce, Bayamón, Mayaguez. TIME ZONE GMT −4. The population is mainly of European descent; Roman Catholicism is the chief religion. OFFICIAL LANGUAGE Spanish; English is also widely spoken. CURRENCY the US dollar. PHYSICAL DESCRIPTION almost rectangular in shape; length 153km/95mi; width 58km/36mi; crossed W–E by mountains, rising to 1 338m at Cerro de Punta; the islands of Vieques and Culebra also belong to Puerto Rico. CLIMATE the average annual temperature is 25°C and humidity is high. HISTORY originally occupied by Carib and Arawaks; discovered by Columbus in 1493; remained a Spanish colony until it was ceded to the USA in 1898; high levels of emigration to the USA in the 1940s–50s; became a semi-autonomous Commonwealth in association with the USA in 1952; US investment and trade important. GOVERNMENT executive power is exercised by a Governor, elected for a four-year term; a bicameral Legislative Assembly consists of a 27-member Senate and 51-member House of Representatives, also elected every four years; a Resident Commissioner, who is a member of the US House of Representatives, is elected for four years. ECONOMY manufacturing is the most important sector of the economy; textiles; clothing; electrical and electronic equipment; food processing; petrochemicals; dairying, livestock;

sugar, tobacco, coffee, pineapples, coconuts; tourism.

puff — *noun* **1** a small rush, gust or blast of air, wind, etc; the sound made by it. **2** a small cloud of smoke, dust, or steam emitted from something. **3** *colloq.* breath: *quite out of puff.* **4** an act of inhaling and exhaling smoke from a pipe or cigarette; a drag or draw. **5** a light pastry: *jam puffs.* **6** a powder puff. **7** an item of publicity intended, or serving, as an advertisement. — *verb trans., intrans.* **1** to blow or breathe in small blasts. **2** *intrans. said of smoke, steam, etc* to emerge in small gusts or blasts. **3** to inhale and exhale smoke from, or draw at (a cigarette, etc). **4** *intrans.* (**puff along**) *said of a train, boat, etc* to go along emitting puffs of steam. **5** *intrans.* to pant, or go along panting: *puffing up the hill.* **6** (**be puffed** or **puffed out**) to be breathless after exertion. **7** *trans., intrans.* (*also* **puff out** *or* **up**) to swell or cause to swell: *puffed out its feathers / a puffed-up eye.* **8** to praise extravagantly by way of advertisement.
— **be puffed up** show great self-importance. [from Anglo-Saxon *pyffan*; imitative]

puff adder a large African viper that inflates the upper part of its body when startled.

puffball *noun* the fruiting body (spore-bearing structure) of fungi of the genus *Lycoperdon*, consisting of a hollow ball of white or beige fleshy tissue. When it is mature, a hole develops at the top, through which clouds of spores are released as puffs of fine dust.

puffer *noun Scot. Hist.* a small steam-boat used to carry cargo around the west coast and western isles of Scotland.

puffer fish *Zool.* any of several fish, found mainly near tropical reefs, that are able to inflate their spine-covered bodies to become almost spherical, in response to attacks by predators. The internal organs of many species are highly poisonous, but when correctly prepared the fish is regarded as a delicacy in Japan.

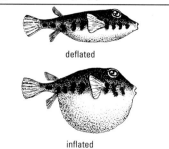

deflated

inflated

puffer fish

puffin *noun* a short stout black and white seabird of the auk family, found on the N Atlantic, N Pacific, and Arctic coasts, and best known for its large triangular bill with red, yellow, and blue stripes. It swims underwater using its wings while searching for food, and is able to hold many small fishes in its beak at once.

puffiness *noun* a puffy quality or condition.

puff pastry light flaky pastry made with a high proportion of fat.

puffy *adj.* (**puffier**, **puffiest**) swollen as a result of injury or ill health.

pug *noun* a small dog with a flattened snout and curly tail.

Pugachev, Emelyan (c.1742–75) Russian Cossack soldier and pretender to the Russian throne. He proclaimed himself to be Peter III, the murdered husband of Catherine II, and promised to restore ancient freedoms. He led a ferocious mass rebellion against Catherine (1773–5), but was defeated at Tsaritsyn and executed. His name later became a byword for the spirit of peasant revolution in Russia.

pugilism *noun old use* the sport of boxing or prize-fighting. [from Latin *pugil*, boxer]

pugilist *noun* a boxer.

Pugin, Augustus (Welby Northmore) (1812–52) English architect, born in London. He worked with Charles Barry and designed a large part of the decorations and sculpture for the new Houses of Parliament (1836–7). At the forefront of the Gothic revival in England, he became a Catholic (c.1833), and most of his plans were made for churches within that faith, including Birmingham Cathedral (1839–41).

pugnacious *adj.* given to fighting; quarrelsome, belligerent, or combative. [from Latin *pugnax*, from *pugnare*, to fight]

pugnaciously *adv.* in a pugnacious way.

pugnacity *noun* a tendency or inclination to quarrel or fight.

pug nose a short upturned nose.

pug-nosed *adj.* having a pug nose.

Pugwash Conference a series of conferences which brought together scientists concerned about the impact on humanity of nuclear weapons, especially arms control. The first was held in Pugwash, Nova Scotia, in 1957, and owed much to the initiative of Bertrand Russell.

puissance *noun Showjumping* a competition testing the horse's ability to jump high fences. [from Old French *puissance*, power]

puissant *adj. old use, poetic* strong, mighty or powerful. [from Old French, from Latin *posse*, to be able]

puke *colloq.* — *verb trans., intrans.* to vomit. — *noun* **1** vomit. **2** an act of vomiting. [possibly imitative]

pukka *adj. colloq.* **1** superior; high-quality. **2** upper-class; well-bred. **3** genuine. [from Hindi *pakka*, cooked, firm, ripe]

Pula, Italian **Pola**, Latin **Pietas Iulia** POP (1991) 62 000, a seaport and resort town in W Croatia, on the Adriatic coast. It was built on the site of a former Roman colony and was controlled by Venice for over 400 years. NOTABLE FEATURES Roman amphitheatre; Temple of Augustus; cathedral; castle (17c).

pulchritude *noun literary* beauty of face and form. [from Latin *pulchritudo*, beauty]

Pulci, Luigi (1432–84) Italian Renaissance poet, born in Florence. He is best known for his epic poem *Morgante Maggiore* (Morgante the Giant, 1481), a burlesque with Roland for hero.

Pulitzer, Joseph (1847–1911) US newspaper proprietor, born in Makó, Hungary. He was discharged from the US Army in 1865, and became a reporter in St Louis. He then began to acquire and revitalize old newspapers, including the *New York World* (1883); he founded the *Evening World* in 1887. In his will he established annual Pulitzer Prizes for literature, drama, music, and journalism, which were first awarded in 1917.

Pulitzer Prize in the US, a prize founded in 1917 from the legacy of publisher Joseph Pulitzer.

pull — *verb* **1** *trans., intrans.* (**pull** or **pull at something**) to grip it strongly and draw or force it towards oneself; to tug or drag it. **2** to remove or extract a cork, tooth, weeds, etc with this action. **3** to operate (a trigger, lever, or switch) with this action. **4** to draw (a trailer, etc). **5** to open or close (curtains or a blind). **6** to tear or take apart with a tugging action: *pulled it to pieces.* **7** (**pull something on someone**) to produce a weapon as a threat to them: *pulled a gun on us.* **8 a** to row (a boat). **b** (*often* **pull away, off, etc**) *said of a boat* to be rowed or caused to move in a particular direction. **c** *intrans.* (**pull at an oar**) to execute strokes with it. **9** to draw (beer, etc) from a cask by operating a lever. **10** *intrans. said of a driver or vehicle* to steer or move in a particular direction: *pulled right.* **11** *Golf, Cricket* to hit (a ball) so that it veers off its intended course, especially to the left or the leg side. **12** *intrans. said of an engine or vehicle* to produce the required propelling power. **13** (**pull at something**) to inhale and exhale smoke from a cigarette, etc; to draw or suck at it. **14** to attract (a crowd, votes, etc). **15** to strain (a muscle or tendon). **16** to practise or execute (especially a trick) successfully: *pull a fast one.* **17** *Printing* to print (a proof). — *noun* **1** an act of pulling. **2** attraction; attracting force: *magnetic pull / the pull of one's homeland.* **3** useful influence: *has some pull with the education department.* **4** a drag at a pipe; a swallow of liquor, etc. **5** a tab, etc for pulling. **6** a stroke made with an oar. **7** *Printing* a proof.

— **pull ahead of** *or* **away from someone** *or* **something** to get in front of them; to gain a lead. **pull something apart 1** to rip or tear it; to reduce it to pieces. **2** to criticize it severely. **pull back** *or* **pull something back** to withdraw or cause it to withdraw or retreat. **pull something down** to demolish a building, etc. **pull in 1** *said of a train* to arrive and halt at a station. **2** *said of a vehicle* to move off, or to the side of, the road. **pull someone in** *colloq.* to arrest them. **pull something in** *slang* to make money, especially a large amount. **pull something off** *colloq.* to arrange or accomplish it suscessfully: *pull off a deal.* **pull something on** to put on clothes hastily. **pull out** *or* **pull someone out** to withdraw from combat, from a competition, project, etc. **pull something out 1** to extract or remove it. **2** *intrans. said of a driver or vehicle* to move away from the kerb, or into the centre of the road to overtake. **pull over** to move off, or to the side of, the road and stop. **pull round** *or* **pull someone round** to recover or help them to recover from an illness. **pull together** to work together towards a common aim; to co-operate. **pull oneself together** to regain self-control. **pull through** *or* **pull someone through** to recover or help them to recover from an illness. **pull up** *said of a driver or vehicle* to stop. **pull someone up** to reprimand them: *was pulled up for being late.* **pull something up** to uproot a plant. **pull up on** *or* **with someone** *or* **something** to catch up with them. **pull someone up short 1** to check someone, often oneself. **2** to take them aback. [from Anglo-Saxon *pullian*, to pluck, draw, pull]

pullet *noun* a young female hen in its first laying year. [from Old French *poulet*, chicken]

pulley *noun* (PL. **pulleys**) **1** a device for lifting and lowering weights, consisting of a wheel with a grooved rim over which a rope or belt runs. **2** a clothes-drying frame suspended by ropes from the ceiling, lowered and raised by means of such a device. [from Old French *polie*]

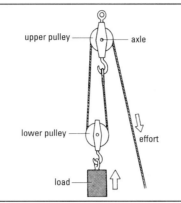

double 'block and tackle' pulley

pull-out *noun* **1** a self-contained detachable section of a magazine designed to be kept for reference. **2** a withdrawal from combat, etc.

pullover *noun* a knitted garment pulled on over one's head; a sweater or jumper.

pullulate *verb* **1** *literary* to teem or abound. **2** *Biol.* to reproduce by pullulation. [from Latin *pullulare*, from *pullulus*, chick]

pullulation *noun Biol.* **1** reproduction by vegetative budding, as in yeast cells. **2** germination of a seed.

pulmonary *adj.* **1** of, relating to, or affecting the lungs. **2** having the function of a lung. [from Latin *pulmonarius*, from *pulmo*, lung]

pulp — *noun* **1** the flesh of a fruit or vegetable. **2** a soft wet mass of mashed food or other material: *wood pulp.* **3** *derog.* worthless literature, novels, magazines, etc, printed on poor paper. — *verb trans., intrans.* to reduce, or be reduced, to a pulp. [from Latin *pulpa*, flesh, pulp]

pulpit *noun* **1** a small enclosed platform in a church, from which the preacher delivers the sermon. **2** church preachers in general: *the message from the pulpit.* [from Latin *pulpitum*, platform]

pulpy *adj.* (**pulpier, pulpiest**) consisting of or like pulp.

pulsar *noun Astron.* in space, a source of electromagnetic radiation emitted in brief regular pulses, mainly at radio frequency. Pulsars are believed to be rapidly revolving neutron stars that emit a pulse of radiation each time they rotate. [from *pulsating star*]

pulsate *verb intrans.* **1** to beat or throb. **2** to contract and expand rhythmically. **3** to vibrate. **4** *Physics* to vary in force or intensity in a regularly recurring pattern. [from Latin *pulsare*, to beat]

pulsating star *Astron.* a variable star whose brightness changes in a regular manner as it alternately expands and contracts.

pulsation *noun* **1** a beating or throbbing. **2** a motion of a heart or pulse.

pulse¹ — *noun* **1** the rhythmic beat that can be detected in an artery, eg the radial artery, corresponding to the regular contraction of the left ventricle of the heart as it pumps blood around the body and so generates a series of pressure waves. **2** the rate of this beat, often measured as an indicator of a person's state of health. The average resting pulse rate is 60 to 80 beats per minute, but it is increased by physical exertion, illness, injury, fear, and other emotions: *feel/take someone's pulse.* **3** a regular throbbing beat in music. **4** *Physics* a signal, eg of light or electric

current, of very short duration. **5** the hum or bustle of a busy place. **6** a thrill of excitement, etc. **7** the attitude or feelings of a group or community at any one time: *check the pulse of the electorate.* — *verb intrans.* to throb or pulsate. [from Latin *pulsus*, a beating]

pulse² **1** the dried seed of a legume (a plant belonging to the pea family), used as food, eg pea, bean, lentil. **2** any plant that bears this seed. [from Latin *puls*, meal porridge or bean pottage]

pulverization *or* **pulverisation** *noun* pulverizing; reducing to powder or dust.

pulverize *or* **pulverise** *verb* **1** *trans., intrans.* to crush or crumble to dust or powder. **2** *facetious* to defeat utterly; to annihilate. [from Latin *pulverizare*, from *pulvis*, dust]

puma *noun* one of the large cats of America, with short yellowish-brown or reddish fur, found in mountain regions, forests, plains, and deserts. Pumas feed mainly on deer and other small mammals, and in the USA, where they are regarded as pests, they have been hunted almost to extinction. – Also called *cougar, mountain lion, panther.* [from Spanish, from Quechua (a S American Indian language)]

pumice *noun* (*in full* **pumice stone**) *Geol.* a very light porous white or grey form of solidified lava, full of cavities formed by the sudden release of dissolved gases at the time when the lava solidified. It is used as an abrasive and polishing agent. [from Latin *pumex*]

pummel *verb* (**pummelled, pummelling**) to beat repeatedly with the fists. [a variant of POMMEL]

pump¹ — *noun* **1** any of various piston-operated or other devices for forcing or driving liquids or gases into or out of something, etc. **2** a standing device with a handle that is worked up and down for raising water from beneath the ground, especially one serving as the water supply to a community. **3** a device for forcing air into a tyre. **4** (*also* **petrol pump**) a device for raising petrol from an underground storage tank to fill a vehicle's petrol tank. — *verb* **1** *trans., intrans.* to raise, force or drive (liquids or gases) out of or into something with a pump. **2** (*also* **pump something up**) to inflate a tyre, etc with a pump. **3** to force in large gushes or flowing amounts: *pumping waste into the sea.* **4** to pour (money or other resources) into a project, etc. **5** to force out the contents of (someone's stomach) to rid it of a poison, etc. **6** to try to extract information from (someone) by persistent questioning. **7** to work (something) vigorously up and down, as though operating a pump handle: *pumped my hand in greeting.* **8** to fire (bullets); to fire bullets into: *pumped bullets into her / pumped her full of bullets.* — **pump iron** *colloq.* to exercise with weights; to go in for weight-training. [from Old Dutch *pumpe*, pipe]

pump² *noun* **1** a rubber-soled canvas sports shoe; a gymshoe or plimsoll. **2** a light dancing shoe for men. **3** *North Amer., esp. US* a plain, low-cut shoe for women; a court shoe.

pumpernickel *noun* a dark heavy coarse rye bread, eaten especially in Germany. [from German *pumpernickel*, lout, perhaps literally 'stink-devil' or 'fart-devil']

pumpkin *noun* **1** a perennial trailing or climbing plant (*Cucurbita maxima* or *C. pepo*) which produces yellow flowers and large round orange fruits at ground level. **2** the fruit of this plant, which contains pulpy flesh and many seeds, enclosed by a hard leathery orange rind. It is used to make pumpkin pie (traditionally eaten on Thanksgiving Day in the USA), and whole fruits are carved into lanterns at Hallowe'en. [from Old French *pompon*, from Greek *pepon*, melon]

pun — *noun* a form of joke consisting of a play on words, especially one where an association is created between words of similar sound but different meaning, eg *A pun is a punishable offence.* — *verb intrans.* (**punned**, **punning**) to make a pun.

Punch *noun* a humpbacked puppet character in the traditional show called *Punch and Judy.*
— **pleased as Punch** highly gratified.
[from Italian *Pulcinella*, a commedia dell'arte character]

punch¹ — *verb trans., intrans.* to hit with one's fist. — *noun* **1** a blow with the fist. **2** vigour and effectiveness in speech or writing: *lacks punch.*
— **pack a punch** *colloq.* to be capable of delivering a powerful blow; to be forceful or effective.
pull one's punches to be deliberately less hardhitting than one might be.
[from Middle English *punchen*, variant of POUNCE]

punch² — *noun* **1** a tool for cutting holes or notches, or stamping designs, in leather, paper, metal, etc. **2** a tool for driving nail heads well down into a surface. — *verb* **1** to pierce, notch or stamp with a punch: *punched our tickets / punch a hole.* **2** *Comput.* to use a key punch to record (data) on (a card or tape).
— **punch in** *or* **out** *North Amer.* to clock in (or out).
[from Middle English *puncheon*, piercing tool]

punch³ *noun* a drink made originally from five ingredients (spirits, water, lemon juice, sugar, and spice) but now also from a variety of others. [said to be from Hindi *panch*, five]

Punch and Judy a glove-puppet show, named after the man and wife who are its central characters, which developed in Britain from the marionette plays based on Pulcinella, the impudent hunchback of the commedia dell'arte. The Victorian era was the heyday of the itinerant puppeteer, but the major features of the tradition have remained constant: Punch, operated by the right hand, is constantly 'on stage', while the left hand introduces various characters to be defeated by Punch's anarchic vigour.

punch-bag *noun* a heavy stuffed leather bag hanging from the ceiling on a rope, used for boxing practice.

punch-ball *noun* a leather ball mounted on a flexible stand, used for boxing practice.

punch bowl 1 a large bowl for mixing and serving punch. **2** a bowl-shaped hollow in mountains.

punch-drunk *adj.* **1** *said of a boxer* brain-damaged from repeated blows to the head, with resultant unsteadiness and confusion. **2** dazed from over-intensive work or other shattering experience.

punched card *or* **punch card** *Comput.* a card bearing coded data or instructions in the form of punched holes.

punchline *noun* the words that conclude a funny story and contain its point.

punch-up *noun colloq.* a fight.

punchy *adj.* (**punchier**, **punchiest**) *said of speech or writing* vigorous and effective; forcefully expressed.

punctilio *noun* (PL. **punctilios**) **1** strictness in observing the finer details of etiquette, ceremony, or correct formal behaviour. **2** a fine detail of this kind. [from Italian *puntiglio*, from Spanish diminutive of *punto*, point]

punctilious *adj.* carefully attentive to details of correct, polite or considerate behaviour; making a point of observing a rule or custom: *always punctilious about remembering birthdays.*

punctiliously *adv.* in a punctilious way.

punctual *adj.* **1** arriving or happening at the arranged time; not late. **2** *said of a person* making a habit of arriving on time. [from Latin *punctualis*, from *punctus*, point]

punctuality *noun* being punctual.

punctually *adv.* on time.

punctuate *verb* **1** *trans., intrans.* to put punctuation marks into (a piece of writing). **2** to interrupt repeatedly: *a speech punctuated by bursts of applause.* **3** to give emphasis to: *punctuating her comments with taps on the desk.* [from Latin *punctuare*, to prick, point, from *punctus*, point]

punctuation *noun* **1** a system of marks used in a text to clarify its meaning for the reader. **2** the use of such marks, or the process of inserting them.

punctuation mark any of the set of marks such as the full stop, comma, question mark, colon, etc that in written matter indicate the pauses and intonations that would be used in speech, and make the meaning clear to the reader.

puncture — *noun* **1** a small hole pierced in something with a sharp point. **2** a perforation in an inflated object, especially a pneumatic tyre; the resulting flat tyre. — *verb* **1** *trans., intrans.* to make a puncture in, or be punctured. **2** to deflate (someone's pride, self-importance, etc). [from Latin *punctura*, pricking]

pundit *noun* **1** an authority or supposed authority on a particular subject, especially one regularly consulted. **2** a Hindu learned in Hindu culture, philosophy, and law. [from Hindi *pandit*]

Pune *or* **Poona** POP (1991) 2.5m, a city in Maharashtra state, W India. It is situated 120km/75mi SE of Bombay. HISTORY former capital of the Mahrattas; it came under British rule in 1818 and was an important colonial military and administrative centre. NOTABLE FEATURES 17c–18c palaces and temples.

pungency *noun* **1** having a pungent flavour or smell. **2** such a flavour or smell.

pungent *adj.* **1** *said of a taste or smell* sharp and strong. **2** *said of remarks, wit, etc* cleverly caustic or biting. [from Latin *pungere*, to prick]

pungently *adv.* in a pungent way.

Punic Wars the three wars fought and won in the 3c BC and 2c BC by Rome against her only remaining rival for supreme power in the W Mediterranean, the Phoenician (Punic) city, Carthage. The first (264–241 BC) resulted in Rome's acquisition of her first overseas province, Sicily, hitherto a Carthaginian territory. The second war (218–201 BC) saw Carthage under Hannibal and Hasdrubal surrender to Rome all her remaining overseas possessions, and become a dependent, tribute-paying ally. The third (149–146 BC) ended in the capture and total destruction of Carthage itself.

punish *verb* **1** to cause (an offender) to suffer for an offence. **2** to impose a penalty for (an offence). **3** *colloq.* to treat roughly: *really punishes that car of hers.* **4** to beat or defeat (an opponent, etc) soundly. [from French *punir*, from Latin *punire*]

punishable *adj.*, *said of an offence* liable to be punished, especially by law.

punishing *adj.* harsh; severe: *punishing conditions.*

punishment *noun* **1** the act of punishing or process of being punished. **2** any method of punishing; a type of penalty. **3** *colloq.* rough treatment, suffering, or hardship.

punitive *adj.* **1** relating to, inflicting, or intended to inflict, punishment: *punitive measures.* **2** severe; inflicting hardship: *punitive taxation.* [from Latin *punitivus*, from *punire*, to punish]

punitively *adv.* in a punitive way.

Punjab POP (1985e) 53.8m, a province in E Pakistan. AREA 205 334sq km/79 259sq mi. It is bounded E and S by India and the Thar Desert and N by Baltistan. The province is crossed by the Sutlej, Chenab, Jhelum, Ravi, and Indus rivers. It has a chiefly Muslim population. CAPITAL Lahore. ECONOMY cereals, cotton, sugar cane, fruit, vegetables; textiles; foodstuffs; metal goods; bicycles; machinery.

Punjab POP (1991) 20.3m, a state in NW India. AREA 50 362sq km/19 440sq mi. It is bounded W and NW by Pakistan. CAPITAL (jointly with Haryana) Chandigarh. CHIEF TOWNS Amritsar, Jalandhar, Faridkot, Ludhiana. The population is c.60% Sikh. HISTORY part of the Mughal Empire until the end of the 18c; annexed by the British after the Sikh Wars of 1846 and 1849; became an autonomous province in 1937; partitioned between India and Pakistan into East and West Punjab on the basis of religion in 1947; the Indian state was renamed Punjab in 1956 and reformed as a Punjabi-speaking state in 1956 and 1966; the Alkai Dai Party campaigns for Sikh autonomy. GOVERNMENT governed by a 117-member Legislative Assembly. ECONOMY wheat, maize, rice, sugar cane, cotton; textiles; sewing machines; sugar; fertilizers; bicycles; electrical goods; machine tools; scientific instruments.

Punjabi *or* **Panjabi** — *noun* an Indo-Aryan language spoken by c.15 million people in the state of Punjab, India, and in Pakistan. See also INDO-ARYAN LANGUAGES, INDO-IRANIAN LANGUAGES. — *adj.* relating to or spoken or written in Panjabi.

punk — *noun* **1** an anti-establishment movement among the youth of the 1970s and 1980s, manifesting itself in aggressive music and weirdness of dress and hairstyle, and the wearing of cheap utility articles, eg safety pins, as ornament. **2** a follower of punk styles or punk rock. **3** punk rock. **4** *North Amer.* a worthless or stupid person. — *adj.* **1** relating to, or characteristic of, punk as a movement. **2** *North Amer.* worthless; inferior. [perhaps a combination of older *punk*, prostitute + *punk*, fire-lighting tinder]

punk rock a type of loud, aggressive rock music popular in the late 1970s and early 1980s, with violent and often crude lyrics.

punnet *noun* a small basket or container, usually of cardboard or plastic, for soft fruit.

punster *noun* a person who makes puns, especially habitually.

Punt, Land of an ancient Egyptian name for the land to the S of Egypt near the mouth of the Red Sea. From the third millennium BC, it was the source for the Egyptians of incense, myrrh, gold and ivory.

punt¹ — *noun* a long flat-bottomed open boat with square ends, propelled by a pole pushed against the bed of the river, etc. — *verb* **1** *intrans.* to travel by, or operate, a punt. **2** to propel (a punt, etc) with a pole. **3** to convey (passengers) in a punt. [from Latin *ponto*, punt, pontoon]

punt² — *noun Rugby* a kick given with the toe of the boot to a ball dropped directly from the hands. — *verb trans., intrans.* to kick in this way.

punt³ *verb intrans.* **1** *colloq.* to bet on horses. **2** *Cards* to bet against the bank. [from French *ponter*, to bet]

punt⁴ *noun* the chief currency unit of the Republic of Ireland. [from Irish Gaelic *punt*, pound]

Punta Arenas POP (1991e) 125 000, the port capital of Magallanes-La Antártica Chilena region, Chile. It is the most southerly city in Chile, on the Straits of Magellan. NOTABLE FEATURES museum at Colegio Salesiano, Museo del Recuerdo; Patagonian Institute.

punter *noun colloq.* **1** someone who bets on horses; a gambler. **2** the average consumer, customer, or member of the public.

puny *adj.* (**punier**, **puniest**) **1** small, weak, or undersized. **2** feeble or ineffective. [from Old French *puisne*, born later]

pup — *noun* **1** a young dog. **2** the young of other animals, eg the seal, wolf and rat. — *verb intrans.* (**pupped**, **pupping**) to give birth to pups.
— **be sold a pup** *colloq.* to be swindled.
in pup *said of a bitch* pregnant.
[a shortening of PUPPY]

pupa *noun* (PL. **pupae**, **pupas**) in the life cycle of insects that undergo metamorphosis, eg butterflies and moths, the inactive stage during which a larva is transformed into a sexually mature adult, by undergoing extensive changes in body structure while enclosed in a protective case. [from Latin *pupa*, doll]

pupal *adj.* relating to or having the form of a pupa.

pupil¹ *noun* **1** someone who is being taught; a schoolchild or student. **2** someone studying under a particular master, etc: *a pupil of Beethoven's*. **3** *Legal* a ward. [from Old French *pupille*, from Latin *pupillus*, *pupilla*, diminutives of *pupus*, boy, *pupa*, girl]

pupil² *noun Anat.* in the eye of vertebrates, the circular opening in the centre of the iris through which light passes to the retina. Its size can be altered, according to the amount of light available, by tiny muscles in the iris. [from Latin *pupilla*, diminutive of *pupa*, girl, doll]

puppet *noun* **1** a doll that can be made to move in a lifelike way, of any of several types, eg operated by strings or sticks attached to its limbs, or designed to fit over the hand and operated by the fingers and thumb. **2** a person who is being controlled or manipulated by someone else. [a variant of POPPET from Latin *pupa*, doll]

puppeteer *noun* a person skilled in manipulating puppets and giving puppet shows.

puppetry *noun* the art of making and manipulating puppets.

puppet show an entertainment with puppets as performers.

puppet state an apparently independent country actually under the control of another.

puppy *noun* (PL. **puppies**) **1** a young dog. **2** a conceited young man. [related to French *poupée*, doll]

puppy fat a temporary plumpness in children, usually at the pre-adolescent stage.

puppy love the romantic love of an adolescent for an older person of the opposite sex; calf love.

Puranas in Indian tradition, an important set of sacred compositions dating from the Gupta period (c.4c AD onwards) which deal with the mythology of Hinduism.

purblind *adj.* **1** nearly blind; dim-sighted. **2** dull-witted; obtuse. [originally = completely blind, from PURE + BLIND]

Purcell, Edward Mills (1912–) US physicist, born in Taylorville, Illinois. Professor at Harvard, he developed the technique of 'nuclear magnetic resonance', which has since revolutionized methods of determining chemical structures and provided new means of medical diagnosis; for this work he shared the 1952 Nobel Prize for Physics with Felix Bloch.

Purcell, Henry (1659–95) English composer, born in London. A Chapel Royal chorister, he held posts as organist there and at Westminster Abbey, and was keeper of the king's instruments (1683). Although his harpsichord pieces and his trio-sonatas for violins and continuo have retained their popularity, he is best known for his vocal and choral works. He also wrote a great deal of incidental stage music, and an opera, *Dido and Aeneas* (1689).

purchase — *verb* **1** to obtain in return for payment; to buy. **2** to get or achieve through labour, effort, sacrifice, or risk. — *noun* **1** something that has been bought. **2** the act of buying. **3** firmness in holding or gripping; a sure grasp or foothold. **4** *Mech.* the advantage given by a device such as a pulley or lever. [from Old French *pourchacier*, to seek to obtain]

purchaser *noun* a buyer.

purchase tax a tax levied on goods, at a higher rate on those considered non-essential.

purdah *noun* the seclusion or veiling of women from public view in some Muslim and Hindu societies. [from Hindi and Urdu *pardah*, curtain]

pure *adj.* **1** consisting of itself only; unmixed with anything else: *pure gold / pure white.* **2** unpolluted; uncontaminated; wholesome: *pure water / pure air.* **3** virtuous; chaste; free from sin or guilt: *pure thoughts.* **4** utter; nothing but: *pure lunacy; pure coincidence.* **5** *said of mathematics or science* dealing with theory and abstractions rather than practical applications. **6** of unmixed blood or descent: *of pure Manx stock.* **7** *said of sound, eg a sung note* clear, unwavering and exactly in tune. **8** absolutely true to type or style: *pure Art Deco.* **9** *said of speech or language* free of imported, intrusive or debased elements. **10** *said of a vowel* simple in sound quality, like the *o* in *box*, as distinct from a diphthong like the *oy* in *boy*.
— **pure and simple** and nothing else: *jealousy pure and simple.*
[from Latin *purus*]

pure-bred *adj.* denoting an animal or plant that is the offspring of parents of the same breed or variety.

purée — *noun* a quantity of fruit or vegetables reduced to a pulp by liquidising or rubbing through a sieve. — *verb* (**purées**, **puréed**) to reduce to a purée. [from French *purer*, to strain]

Pure Land Buddhism a school of Buddhism allegedly founded by the Chinese monk Hui Yuan (AD 334–417) and characterized by devotion to the Bodhisattva Amitabha, who rules over a 'pure land'. The goal of those devoted to Amitabha and the pure land is to be reborn there, and attain enlightenment.

purely *adv.* **1** in a pure way. **2** wholly; entirely: *won purely on her merits.* **3** merely: *purely a formality.*

pure mathematics *Maths.* the branch of mathematics concerned with the study of abstract mathematical theory without application to observed phenomena in everyday life.

pureness *noun* a pure state or quality.

purgative — *noun* a medicine that causes the bowels to empty. — *adj., said of a medicine, etc* having this effect. [from Latin *purgativus*, from *purgare*, to clean out]

purgatory *noun* **1** (**Purgatory**) *chiefly RC Church* a place or state into which the soul passes after death to be cleansed of pardonable sins before going to heaven. **2** *humorous colloq.* any state of discomfort or suffering; an excruciating experience. [from Latin *purgatorium*, from *purgare*, to cleanse]

purge — *verb* **1** to rid (eg the soul or body) of unwholesome thoughts or substances; to get rid of (impure elements) from (anything). **2** to rid (a political party, community, etc) of (undesirable members). **3** *trans., intrans. old use* to take or give a purgative to empty (the bowels), or the bowels of (a person). **4** *Legal* to rid (oneself) of guilt by atoning for one's offence. **5** *Legal* to clear (oneself or someone else) of an accusation. — *noun* **1** an act of purging. **2** the process of purging a party or community of undesirable members. **3** the process of purging the bowels. **4** a medicine to empty the bowels. [from Latin *purgare*, to cleanse, purify]

puri *noun* a small cake of unleavened Indian bread, deep-fried and served hot. [from Hindi *puri*]

purification *noun* purifying, cleansing.

purifier *noun* a person, apparatus, or thing that purifies.

purify *verb* (**purifies**, **purified**) **1** to make pure. **2** to cleanse of contaminating or harmful substances. **3** to rid of intrusive elements. **4** *Relig.* to free from sin or guilt. [from Latin *purus*, pure + *facere*, to make]

Purin *noun* the Jewish Festival of Lots held about 1 March, commemorating the deliverance of the Jews from the plot of Haman to have them massacred, as related in the Book of Esther. [from Hebrew *pūrîm* (singular *pūr*), lots]

purine *or* **purin** *noun Biochem.* a nitrogenous base with a double ring structure. The most important derivatives of purine are adenine and guanine, which are major constituents of nucleotides and the nucleic acids DNA and RNA. [contracted from Latin *purum uricum acidum*, pure uric acid]

Purism a modern art movement founded in 1918 by French artist Amédée Ozenfant (1886–1966) and the architect Le Corbusier (1887–1965). They rejected Cubism, and sought an art of pure and impersonal forms based, however, on the observation of real things.

purism *noun* insistence on purity, especially of language.

purist *noun* a person who insists on correctness of word usage, grammar, etc or authenticity of detail in design, etc.

puritan *noun* **1** (**Puritan**) *Hist.* a supporter of the 16c to 17c Protestant movement in England and America that sought to rid church worship of ritual. **2** a person of strict, especially over-strict, moral principles; someone who disapproves generally of luxuries and amusements. [from Latin *puritas*, purity]

puritanical *adj.* realting to or characteristic of puritans; having the qualities or characteristics of a puritan or puritans.

Puritanism a movement based on the belief that further reformation was required in the Church of England under Elizabeth I and the Stuarts, which arose in the 1560s out of disapproval of the 'popery' (eg surplices) retained by the Elizabethan religious settlement. Comprising a diverse body of opinions which occasionally came together, it included the anti-episcopal Presbyterian movement of John Field (1545–88) and Thomas Cartwright (1535–1603) in the 1570s and 1580s; the separatist churches that left England for Holland and America (1590–1640); the 'presbyterian', 'independent', and more radical groups which emerged during the English Civil Wars and interregnum; and the nonconformist sects persecuted by the Cavalier Parliament's 'Clarendon Code' under Charles II.

purity *noun* **1** the state of being pure or unmixed. **2** freedom from contamination, pollution or unwholesome or intrusive elements. **3** chasteness or innocence. [from Latin *puritas*, from *purus*, pure]

Purkinje, Jan Evangelista, also **Purkyne** (1787–1869) Czech physiologist, born in Libochowitz. Professor at Breslau and later in Prague, he was an early user of the improved compound microscope, discovering a number of new and important microscopic anatomical structures, some of which are named after him. He was also an early user of the microtome for cutting sections.

purl¹ — *noun* **1** *Knitting* the more complex of two basic stitches, with the wool passed behind the needle. See also PLAIN. **2** cord made from gold or silver wire. **3** a decorative looped edging on lace, braid, etc. — *verb* to knit in purl. [from Middle English *pirl*, to twist, *purl*, to embroider]

purl² *verb intrans.* **1** to flow with a murmuring sound. **2** to eddy or swirl. [related to Norwegian *purla*, to babble]

purlieus *pl. noun* the surroundings, or immediate neighbourhood, of a place. [from Old French *puralé*, a going through]

purlin *or* **purline** *noun* a roof timber stretching across the principal rafters or between the tops of walls, and supporting the common or subsidiary rafters or the sheets of roof-covering material. [origin unknown]

purloin *verb* to steal, filch, or pilfer. [from Old French *purloigner*, to remove to a distance]

purple — *noun* **1** a colour that is a mixture of blue and red. **2** *Hist.* a crimson dye got from various shellfish. **3** crimson cloth, or a robe made from it worn by eg emperors and cardinals, sym-

bolic of their authority. — *adj.* **1** of either of these colours. **2** *said of writing* self-consciously fine in style; over-elaborate; flowery.
— **born in the purple** born into a royal or noble family.
[from Greek *porphyra*, dye-yielding shellfish]

Purple Heart (ABBREV. **PH**) in the USA, a decoration instituted in 1782 as an award for gallantry. Since its revival in 1932, it has been awarded for wounds received in action. The ribbon is purple edged in white.

purple heart *colloq.* a heart-shaped violet pill containing a stimulant drug.

purple patch a passage of purple prose.

purport — *noun* (with stress on *pur-*) meaning, significance, point, or gist. — *verb intrans.* (with stress on *-port*) to present itself so as to seem or claim: *a work purporting to have been written by Charles I.* [from Old French *purporter*, to convey]

purpose — *noun* **1** one's object or aim in doing something. **2** the function for which something is intended: *a multi-purpose gadget.* **3** one's intentions, aspirations, aim, or goal: *one's purpose in life / a sense of purpose.* **4** determination; resolve: *a woman of purpose.* — *verb* to intend (to do something).
— **on purpose** intentionally; deliberately.
to little *or* **no purpose** with few (or no) useful results.
to the purpose relevant; to the point.
[from Old French *pourpos*, from Latin *proponere*, to intend]

purpose-built *adj.* designed to meet specific requirements: *a purpose-built medical centre.*

purposeful *adj.* determined; intent; resolute; showing a sense of purpose.

purposefully *adv.* in a purposeful way.

purposeless *adj.* without purpose, aimless.

purposely *adv.* intentionally; on purpose.

purposive *adj.* **1** having a clear purpose. **2** purposeful.

purr — *verb* **1** *intrans. said of a cat* to make a soft, low, vibrating sound associated with contentment. **2** *intrans. said of a vehicle or machine* to make a sound similar to this, suggestive of good running order. **3** *intrans., trans.* to express pleasure, or say, in a tone vibrating with satisfaction. — *noun* a purring sound. [imitative]

purse — *noun* **1** a small container carried in the pocket or handbag, for keeping one's cash, etc in. **2** *North Amer.* a woman's handbag. **3** the funds available to one for spending: *beyond my purse.* — *verb* to draw (the lips) together in disapproval or deep thought.
— **hold the purse strings** to be the person in control of spending, eg in a family or organization.
[from Anglo-Saxon *purs*]

purser *noun* the ship's officer responsible for keeping the accounts and, on a passenger ship, seeing to the welfare of passengers.

pursuance *noun* the process of pursuing: *in pursuance of his duties.*

pursue *verb* **1** *trans., intrans.* to follow in order to overtake, capture, attack, etc; to chase. **2** to proceed along (a course or route). **3** to put one's efforts into achieving (a goal or aim). **4** to occupy oneself with (one's career, etc). **5** to continue with, or follow up (investigations, enquiries, etc). [from Old French *pursuer*]

pursuer *noun* **1** someone pursuing one: *escaped their pursuers.* **2** *Scot. Legal* a plaintiff or prosecutor.

pursuit *noun* **1** the act of pursuing or chasing: *the pursuit of happiness / followed in hot pursuit.* **2** an occupation or hobby. [from Old French *pursuete*]

pursuivant *noun Heraldry* an officer of the College of Arms ranking below a herald. [from French *poursuivre*, to follow]

purulence *noun* **1** being purulent. **2** the formation of secretion of pus. **3** pus.

purulent *adj.* full of, or discharging, pus. [from Latin *purulentus*, from *pus*, pus]

purvey *verb trans., intrans.* (**purveys, purveyed**) *technical, said of a trader* to supply (food, provisions, etc). [from Old French *purveier*, from Latin *providere*, to provide for]

purveyance *noun* purveying.

purveyor *noun* a person whose business is to provide food or meals.

purview *noun* **1** scope of responsibility or concern, eg of a court of law. **2** the range of one's knowledge, experience, or activities. [from Old French *purveu*, provided]

pus *noun* the thick, yellowish liquid that forms in abscesses or infected wounds, composed of dead white blood cells, serum, bacteria and tissue debris. [from Latin *pus*]

Pusan *or* **Busan** POP (1990) 3.8m, a seaport and special city in SE South Korea, on the Korea Strait. NOTABLE FEATURES municipal museum; UN Memorial Cemetery from the Korean War; Yongdu San park; Pusan Tower; T'aejongdae Park; Tongnae Hot Springs nearby; Pomosa Buddhist temple nearby (founded in 678).

Pusey, E(dward) B(ouverie) (1800–82) English theologian, born in Pusey, Berkshire. An ascetic, deeply religious man, he was Professor of Hebrew at Oxford from 1828 until his death, and his main aim was to prevent the spread of Rationalism in England. He joined Cardinal Newman and John Keble in the Oxford Movement (1833), and contributed important tracts on Baptism and the Eucharist.

push — *verb* **1** (**push something** *or* **push against, at,** *or* **on something**) to exert pressure to force it away from one; to press, thrust, or shove it. **2** to touch or grasp and move forward in front of one: *push a wheelchair.* **3** *intrans., trans.* (**push** *or* **push one's way through, in, past,** *etc*) to force one's way, thrusting aside people or obstacles. **4** *intrans.* to progress especially laboriously: *pushing forward through the unknown.* **5** (*often* **push something down, up,** *etc*) to force in a particular direction: *push up prices.* **6** (**push someone into something**) to coax, urge, persuade, or goad them to do it: *pushed them into agreeing.* **7** to pressurize them into working harder, achieving more, etc: *pushes himself too hard.* **8** (**push something** *or* **push for something**) to recommend it strongly; to campaign or press for it. **9** to promote products or urge acceptance of ideas. **10** to sell drugs illegally. — *noun* **1** an act of pushing; a thrust or shove. **2** a burst of effort towards achieving something. **3** determination, aggression, or drive.
— **at a push** if forced; at a pinch.
be pushed for something *colloq.* to be short of (eg time or money).
be pushing *colloq.* to be nearly (a specified age).
get the push *colloq.* to be dismissed from a job, etc; to be rejected by someone.
give someone the push to dismiss or reject them.
push along *colloq.* to leave; to make one's departure.
push someone around *or* **about** *colloq.* **1** to bully them; to treat them roughly. **2** to dictate to them; to order them about.
push off *colloq.* to make one's departure; to go away.
push on to continue on one's way, etc.
push someone *or* **something over** to knock them down.
push something through to force acceptance of a proposal, bill, etc by a legislative body, etc. [from Old French *pousser*]

pushbike *noun colloq.* a bicycle propelled by pedals alone.

push button a button pressed to operate a machine, etc.

push-button *adj.* operated by pushing a button.

push-chair *noun* a small folding perambulator for a toddler.

pusher *noun colloq.* a person who sells illegal drugs.

Pushkin, Alexander Sergeyevich (1799–1837) Russian poet, born in Moscow. In 1817 he entered government service, but was exiled to South Russia (1820) on account of his revolutionary writings, until after the accession of Nicholas I (1826). Hailed in Russia as its greatest poet, his works include the romantic poem, *Ruslan and Lyudmila* (1820), the verse novel *Eugene Onegin* (1828) and the historical tragedy, *Boris Godunov* (1831). He also wrote many lyrical poems, tales, and essays, and was appointed Russian historiographer. He died in a duel over his wife, Natalia Goncharova.

pushover *noun colloq.* **1** someone who is easily defeated or outwitted. **2** a task easily accomplished.

pushy *adj.* (**pushier, pushiest**) *colloq.* aggressively self-assertive or ambitious.

pusillanimity *noun* being pusillanimous; cowardliness, timidity.

pusillanimous *adj.* timid, cowardly, weak-spirited or faint-hearted. [from Latin *pusillus*, diffident + *animus*, spirit]

pusillanimously *adv.* in a pusillanimous way.

puss¹ *noun colloq.* a cat. [related to Dutch *poes*]

puss² *noun slang* the face. [from Irish *pus*, mouth]

pussy *noun* (PL. **pussies**) **1** *colloq.* a cat. **2** *coarse slang* the female genitals; the vulva.

pussyfoot *verb intrans.* **1** to behave indecisively; to avoid committing oneself. **2** to pad about stealthily.

pussy willow a willow tree with silky grey catkins.

pustular *adj.* **1** relating to or of the nature of pustules. **2** characterized by pustules.

pustule *noun* a small inflammation on the skin, containing pus; a pimple. [from Latin *pustula*]

put *verb* (**putting**; PAST TENSE AND PAST PARTICIPLE **put**) **1** to place in, or convey to, a position or situation that is specified. **2** to fit: *put a new lock on the door.* **3** to cause to be: *put someone in a good mood.* **4** to apply: *put pressure on them / put paint on the brush.* **5** to set or impose: *put a tax on luxuries / put an end to free lunches.* **6** to lay (blame, reliance, emphasis, etc) on something. **7** to set (someone) to work, etc or apply (something) to a good purpose, etc. **8** to translate: *put this into French.* **9** to invest or pour (energy, money or other resources) into something. **10** to classify, categorize or put in order: *would put accuracy before speed.* **11** to estimate: *put the costs at £10 000.* **12** to submit (questions for answering, ideas for considering) to someone; to suggest: *put it to her that she was lying.* **13** to express: *don't know how to put it / a disaster, to put it mildly.* **14** to write: *don't know what to put.* **15** *intrans. Naut.* to sail in a certain direction: *put out to sea.* **16** *Athletics* to throw (the shot).
— **put about** *Naut.* to turn round; to change course.
put something about to spread reports or rumours.
put something across to communicate ideas, etc to others.
put something aside 1 to save money, especially regularly, for future use. **2** to discount or deliberately disregard problems, differences of opinion, etc for the sake of convenience, peace, etc.
put someone away *colloq.* to imprison them, or confine them in a mental institution.
put something away 1 to replace it tidily. **2** to save it for future use. **3** *colloq.* to consume food or drink, especially in large amounts. **4** *old use* to reject, discard, or renounce.
put something back 1 to replace it. **2** to postpone it: *put the meeting back a month.* **3** to adjust a clock, etc to an earlier time.
put something by to save it for the future.
put down *said of an aircraft* to land.
put someone down to humiliate or snub them.
put something down 1 to put it on a surface after holding it, etc. **2** to crush a revolt, etc. **3** to

kill an animal painlessly, especially one near death. **4** to write it down: *put down suggestions.* **5** to pay money as a deposit on an intended purchase.

put someone down for something 1 to sum them up or dismiss them as specified: *had put him down for a playboy.* **2** to include them in a list of participants, subscribers, etc: *put me down for the trip / put them down for ten pounds.*

put something down to something else to regard it as caused by something specified: *the errors were put down to inexperience.*

put something forward 1 to offer a proposal or suggestion. **2** to propose someone's name for a post, etc; to nominate them. **3** to advance the time or date of an event or occasion: *will have to put the wedding forward a month.* **4** to adjust a clock, etc to a later time.

put in *Naut.* to enter a port or harbour.

put something in 1 to fit or install it. **2** to spend time working at something: *puts in four hours' violin practice daily.* **3** to submit a claim, etc. **4** to interrupt with a comment, etc.

put in for something to apply for it.

put someone off 1 to cancel or postpone an engagement with them: *have to put the Smiths off.* **2** to cause to lose concentration; to distract. **3** to cause them to lose enthusiasm, or to feel disgust, for something: *her accident put me off climbing / he was put off the cheese by its smell.*

put something off 1 to switch off a light, etc. **2** to postpone an event or arrangement.

put something on 1 to switch on an electrical device, etc. **2** to dress oneself in it. **3** to gain weight or speed. **4** to present a play, show, etc. **5** to provide transport, etc. **6** to assume an accent, manner, etc for effect or to deceive. **7** to bet money on a horse, etc.

put someone on to something *or* **someone 1** to recommend them to try it: *a friend put me on to these biscuits.* **2** to give them an indication of someone's whereabouts or involvement: *what put the police on to her?*

put one over on someone *colloq.* to trick or fool them.

put someone out 1 to inconvenience them. **2** to offend or annoy them. **3** *Cricket* to dismiss a player or team from the field.

put something out 1 to extinguish a light or fire. **2** to issue eg a distress call. **3** to publish eg a leaflet. **4** to strain or dislocate a part of the body.

put something over to communicate ideas, etc to someone else.

put something right to mend or make it better.

put someone through to connect them by telephone: *was put through to the manager.*

put something through 1 to arrange a deal, agreement, etc. **2** to make a telephone call: *will you put through a call to Zurich?*

put something together to join up the parts of it; to assemble it.

put up to stay for the night: *we'd better put up at the local hotel.*

put someone up to give them a bed for the night.

put something up 1 to build it; to erect it. **2** to raise prices. **3** to present a plan, etc. **4** to offer one's house, etc for sale. **5** to provide funds for a project, etc. **6** to show resistance; to offer a fight.

put up *or* **put someone up for something** to offer oneself, or nominate someone, as a candidate: *we are putting you up for chairman.*

put someone up to something *colloq.* to coerce or manipulate them into doing something devious or illicit: *someone put them up to forging lottery tickets.*

put up with someone *or* **something** to bear or tolerate them.

put upon someone to presume on their good will; to take unfair advantage of them. [from Anglo-Saxon *putian*]

putative *adj.* supposed; assumed: *the putative father of the child.* [from Latin *putativus*, from *putare*, to think]

put-down *noun colloq.* a snub or humiliation.

put-on — *adj., said of an accent, manner, etc* assumed; pretended. — *noun colloq.* a trick or deception.

putrefaction *noun* becoming bad or putrid; festering.

putrefy *verb intrans.* (**putrefies, putrefied**) to go bad, rot or decay, especially with a foul smell. [from Latin *putrefacere*, to rot]

putrescent *adj.* decaying; rotting; putrefying. [from Latin *putrescere*, to rot]

putrid *adj.* **1** decayed; rotten. **2** stinking; foul; disgusting. **3** *colloq.* repellent; worthless. [from Latin *putridus*, rotten]

putsch *noun* a secretly planned, sudden attempt to remove a government from power. [from Swiss German *putsch*]

putt — *verb trans., intrans. Golf, Putting* to send (the ball) gently forward along the ground towards the hole. — *noun* a putting stroke. [originally a form of PUT]

putter *noun* **1** a golf club used for putting. **2** a person who putts.

putting *noun* **1** the act of putting a ball towards a hole. **2** a game somewhat similar to golf, played on a putting-green using only putting strokes.

putting-green *noun* **1** on a golf course, a smoothly mown patch of grass surrounding a hole. **2** an area of mown turf laid out like a tiny golf course, on which to play putting.

putty *noun* (PL. **putties**) a paste of ground chalk and linseed oil, used for fixing glass in window frames, filling holes in wood, etc. [from French *potée*, potful]

put-up job something dishonestly prearranged to give a false impression.

put-upon *adj., said of a person* taken advantage of, especially unfairly.

Pu Yi *or* **P'u-i**, personal name of **Hsuan T'ung** (1906–67) the last Emperor of China (1908–12) and the first of Manchukuo (1934–5), born in Beijing (Peking). Emperor at the age of two, after the 1912 revolution he was given a pension and a summer palace. Known in the West as Henry Puyi, in 1932 he was called from private life by the Japanese to be provincial dictator of Manchukuo, under the name of Kang Teh. Taken prisoner by the Russians in 1945, he was tried in China as a war criminal (1950), pardoned (1959), and became a private citizen. The story of his life was made into a film in 1988 (*The Last Emperor*, directed by Bernardo Bertolucci).

puzzle — *verb* **1** to perplex, mystify, bewilder or baffle. **2** *intrans.* (**puzzle about** *or* **over something**) to brood, ponder, wonder, or worry about it. **3** (*usually* **puzzle something out**) to solve it after prolonged thought. — *noun* **1** a baffling problem. **2** a game or toy taking the form of something for solving, designed to test one's knowledge, memory, powers of reasoning or observation, manipulative skill, etc.
— **puzzle one's brains** *or* **head** to think hard about a problem.

puzzlement *noun* a puzzled state.

puzzler *noun* **1** a challenging problem or question; a poser. **2** a person who enjoys solving puzzles.

puzzling *adj.* that puzzles.

PVC *abbrev.* polyvinyl chloride.

PW *abbrev.* policewoman.

Pwyll in Celtic mythology, the King of the land of Dyfed, whose adventures are recounted in the *Mabinogion*. He was taught courtesy by Arawn, the King of Annwn (the underworld), and married the goddess Rhiannon, who bore him a son, Pryderi. Pryderi was abducted by Gwawl (a rival of Pwyll), but was later restored, and became ruler in both Dyfed and Annwn.

pyaemia *or* **pyemia** *noun Medicine* a form of blood poisoning caused by the release of pus-forming micro-organisms, especially bacteria, into the bloodstream from an abscess or wound, and resulting in the formation of multiple abscesses in different parts of the body. [from Greek *pyon*, pus + *haima*, blood]

pye-dog *or* **pie-dog** *noun* a stray mongrel in Oriental regions; a pariah dog. [from Hindi *pahi*, outsider]

Pygmalion a play by George Bernard Shaw (1913). It is an anti-romantic comedy focusing on a young flower-seller, Eliza Doolittle, whose Cockney speech and mannerisms are transformed by the teaching of Henry Higgins. It was adapted as the successful musical play, *My Fair Lady* (1956, filmed 1964).

Pygmalion in Greek mythology, a king of Cyprus, who made a statue of a beautiful woman. He prayed to Aphrodite, and the sculptured figure came to life.

pygmy *or* **pigmy** — *noun* (PL. **pygmies**) **1** (**Pygmy**) a member of one of the unusually short peoples of equatorial Africa. **2** an undersized person; a dwarf. **3** *derog.* someone of no significance: *an intellectual pygmy.* — *adj.* of a small-sized breed: *pygmy hippopotamuses.* [from Greek *pygmaios*, literally 'measuring a *pygme* (= the distance from knuckle to elbow)']
◇ The best known pygmy tribes are the forest-dwelling Mbuti of Zaire and the Twa of the Great Lakes savannah. Traditionally hunter-gatherers, most pygmies live in close relationship with, and speak the Bantu languages of, their non-Pygmy neighbours. Collectively they number c.200 000.

pygmy shrew a small shrew, the most widespread in Europe, 3.9 to 6.4cm long (not including the tail) with a brown coat and pale underparts. It is rarely visible, although its shrill squeaking can often be heard in hedge bottoms.

pyjamas or *North Amer.* **pajamas** *pl. noun* a sleeping-suit consisting of a loose jacket or top, and trousers. [from Persian and Hindi *payjamah*, leg-clothing]

pylon *noun* **1** a tall steel structure for supporting electric power cables. **2** a post or tower to guide a pilot at an airfield. **3** an external structure on an aircraft for supporting an engine, etc. **4** *Archaeol.* a gate tower or ornamental gateway. [from Greek *pylon*, from *pyle*, gate]
◇ Pylons were a characteristic feature of Egyptian temples of the New Kingdom (c.1560–1085 BC); there are notable examples at Karnak.

Pylos, also called **Navarino** a town on the W coast of the Peloponnese, associated in Greek tradition with Nestor, a Greek chief at the time of the Trojan War. Excavations have revealed a large, unfortified Mycenaean palace, and many clay tablets inscribed with Linear B script.

Pym, Barbara (Mary Crampton) (1913–80) English novelist, born in Oswestry, Shropshire. For most of her adult life she worked at the International African Institute in London. She is best known for her series of satirical novels on English middle-class society, including *Excellent Women* (1952) and *Quartet in Autumn* (1977).

Pym, John (1584–1643) English politician, born in Brymore, Somerset. An MP from 1614, in 1641 he took a leading part in the impeachment of Strafford, helped to draw up the Grand Remonstrance, and was one of the five members whose attempted seizure by Charles I (1642) precipitated the Civil War.

Pynchon, Thomas (1937–) US novelist, born in Glen Cove, New York. His novels include *V* (1963), *The Crying of Lot 49* (1966), *Gravity's Rainbow* (1973), and *Vineland* (1989). Other works include the short story collection, *Slow Learner* (1984).

Pyongyang, Japanese **Heijo** POP (1990e) 2.2m, the capital of North Korea, overlooking the R Taedong. It is North Korea's oldest city, allegedly founded in 1122 BC. HISTORY capital of the Choson Kingdom from 300 BC until 200 BC; became a colony of China in 108 BC; taken and destroyed by Japan in the 1590s; rebuilt after the Korean War. NOTABLE FEATURES 1c tombs.

pyorrhoea *or* **pyorrhea** *noun* a discharge of pus, especially from the gums or tooth sockets. [from Greek *pyon*, pus + *rheein*, to flow]

pyramid *noun* **1** any of the huge ancient Egyptian royal tombs built on a square base, with four sloping triangular sides meeting in a common apex. **2** *Geom.* a solid of this shape, with a square or triangular base. **3** any structure, pile, etc of similar shape. [from Greek *pyramis*]
◇ Specifically, the Fourth Dynasty pyramids of the Giza plateau on the SW outskirts of modern Cairo. The Great Pyramid of Cheops is 146m high and made up of 2.5 million limestone blocks each weighing approximately 2.5 tonnes.

pyramidal *adj.* having the form of a pyramid.

Pyramids, Battle of the a battle fought (1798) between French forces under Napoleon I and the Mamluk rulers of Egypt, which enabled Napoleon to take Cairo and establish control of Egypt. The Egyptian campaign was aimed at constricting British lines of communication with India.

pyramid selling the sale of goods in bulk to a distributor who divides them and sells them to sub-distributors at a profit, and so on.

Pyramus and Thisbe in a story told by Ovid, two lovers who were kept apart by their parents. They agreed to meet at Ninus's tomb outside the city of Babylon but Thisbe was frightened by a lion and fled, dropping her cloak, which the lion tore apart. Pyramus found it, thought she had been killed by a lion, and committed suicide. When she found him, Thisbe killed herself on his sword. The story is incorporated into Shakespeare's *A Midsummer Night's Dream*.

pyre *noun* a pile of wood on which a dead body is ceremonially cremated. [from Greek *pyra*, from *pyr*, fire]

Pyrenean mountain dog a breed of dog developed in the Pyrenees several centuries ago to protect sheep. It has a large powerful body with a heavy head, and a thick coat, usually pale in colour.

Pyrenees, French **Pyrénées**, Spanish **Pirineos** a major mountain range in SW Europe. It extends W–E from the Bay of Biscay to the Mediterranean Sea, separating the Iberian Peninsula from the rest of Europe; it stretches 450km/280mi along the French–Spanish frontier and includes Andorra. The highest point is Aneto Peak (3 404m). Hannibal made a famous crossing in 218 BC on his way to Italy. NOTABLE FEATURES Gouffre de la Pierre St Martin, one of the deepest caves in the world; Grotte Casteret, the highest ice cave in Europe; observatory at Pic du Midi de Bigorre.

Pyrenees, Treaty of the a treaty (7 Nov 1659) between France and Spain that ended the Thirty Years War. King Louis XIV of France gained the Spanish Netherlands but withdrew from most of Italy; his marriage to Maria Theresa, daughter of Philip IV of Spain, was arranged; and war in the S Netherlands (now Belgium), as well as Spanish military and political dominance in W Europe, was brought to a close.

pyrethrum *noun* **1** a flower of the chrysanthemum family. **2** an insecticide prepared from its flower-heads. [from Greek *pyrethron*, a plant of the nettle family]

pyretic *adj. Medicine* relating to, or accompanied by, fever. [from Greek *pyretos*, fever]

Pyrex *noun trademark* a type of heat-resistant glass used especially for ovenware.

pyrexia *noun Medicine* fever. [from Greek *pyrexis*, from *pyressein*, to be feverish]

pyridine *noun Chem.* (SYMBOL C_5H_5N) a carcinogenic flammable colourless liquid with a strong unpleasant smell, present in coal tar, that is used in the manufacture of other organic chemicals, in paints and textile dyes, and as a solvent. [from Greek *pyr*, fire]

pyridoxine *noun* vitamin B_6. [from *pyridine* + OXYGEN]

pyrimidine *noun Biochem.* a nitrogenous base with a single ring structure. The most important derivatives of pyrimidine are cytosine, thymine, and uracil, which are major components of nucleotides and the nucleic acids DNA (which contains cytosine and thymine) and RNA (which contains cytosine and uracil).

pyrite *noun Geol.* the commonest sulphide mineral, used as a source of sulphur, and in the production of sulphuric acid. It is often called fool's gold because of its yellowish-gold colour and metallic lustre, although it is harder and more brittle than gold. — Also called *iron pyrites*.

pyro- *combining form* forming words denoting fire: *pyromania / pyrotechnics*. [from Greek *pyr*, fire]

Pyrochles the brother of Cymochles in Edmund Spenser's *The Faerie Queene*, who represents rage and is renowned for his fiery disposition and cruelty.

pyroclast *noun Geol.* an individual fragment of lava, of any size, that has been ejected into the atmosphere during a volcanic eruption. [from Greek *pyr*, fire + *klastos*, broken]

pyrolusite *noun Geol.* (SYMBOL MnO_2) a soft black mineral that is the most important ore of manganese.

pyrolysis *noun Chem.* the chemical decomposition of a substance (eg heavy oil, rubber) that occurs when it is heated to a high temperature in the absence of air.

pyromania *noun Psychol.* an obsessive urge to set fire to things. [from PYRO- + -MANIA]

pyrometer *noun Physics* a type of thermometer that is used to measure high temperatures.

pyrotechnics *noun* **1** (*sing.*) the art of making fireworks. **2** (*pl.*) a fireworks display. **3** (*pl.*) a display of fiery brilliance in speech, music, etc.

pyroxene *noun Geol.* any of a group of important rock-forming silicate minerals that are found both in igneous and in metamorphic rocks, and may be white, yellow, green, greenish-black, or brown in colour. They include jadeite (the most highly prized form of jade). [from PYRO- + Greek *xenos*, stranger, because it was thought that pyroxene crystals in lava had been caught up accidentally]

Pyrrhic victory a victory won at so great a cost in lives, etc that it can hardly be regarded as a triumph at all. [named after *Pyrrhus*, king of Epirus in Greece, who won such victories against the Romans in the 3c BC]

Pyrrho Greek philosopher, born in Elis. His opinions are known from the writings of his pupil, Timon. He taught that we can know nothing of the nature of things, but that the best attitude of mind is suspense of judgement, which brings with it calmness of mind. Pyrrhonism is often regarded as the foundation of Scepticism.

Pyrrhus (c.318–272 BC) King of Epirus (modern Albania) (307–303 BC, 297–272 BC). He came into conflict with Rome when he supported Tarentum (a Greek colony in southern Italy) against the Romans. Though he won two battles against Rome at Tarentum and Asculum (280–279 BC), his losses were so heavy that they gave rise to the phrase 'Pyrrhic victory'.

pyruvic acid *Biochem.* an organic acid that is the end-product of the breakdown of carbohydrates by glycolysis, and if oxygen is available is then oxidized to carbon dioxide and water by the Krebs cycle, a sequence of reactions that release large amounts of energy. [from Greek *pyr*, fire + Latin *uva*, grape]

Pythagoras (6c BC) Greek philosopher and mathematician, born in Samos. He founded a moral and religious school in Crotona, Magna Graecia. He eventually fled from there because of persecution and settled at Metapontum in Lucania. Pythagoreanism was first a way of life, of moral abstinence and purification, not solely a philosophy; its teaching included the doctrine of the transmigration of souls between successive bodies. The school is best known for its studies of the relations between numbers. Pythagorean thought exerted considerable influence on Plato's doctrines.

Pythagoras's theorem *Maths.* a theorem which states that, in a right-angled triangle, the square of the length of the hypotenuse (the longest side) is equal to the sum of the squares of the other two sides. It can be used to calculate the length of any side of such a triangle if the lengths of the other two sides are known. [named after the Greek philosopher and mathematician Pythagoras]

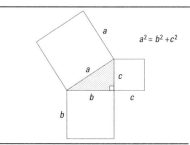

$$a^2 = b^2 + c^2$$

Pythagoras' theorem

Pythagoreanism a philosophical school founded by Pythagoras in the 6c BC which held that the soul is immortal and superior to the body, and transmigrates upon death to another body. One's goal should be to escape transmigration by assimilating one's soul to the cosmos, which requires understanding the mathematical nature of the cosmos.

Pytheas *or* **Pytheas** (4c BC) Greek mariner, born in Massalia (Marseilles), Gaul. In c.330 BC he sailed past Spain, Gaul, and the E coast of Britain, and reached the island of 'Thule', six days' sail from N Britain (Iceland possibly). His account of the voyage is lost, but referred to by several later writers.

Pythian Games in ancient Greece, one of the main Pan-Hellenic festivals, held every four years in the sanctuary of Apollo Pythios in Delphi. 'Pythios' or 'python slayer' was the name under which Apollo was worshipped there.

Python in Greek mythology, a monster which lived at Delphi, killed by Apollo when he took over the shrine. The name Pythia continued in use, and the Pythian games were celebrated there.

python *noun* any non-venomous constricting egg-laying snake of the boa family, found in most tropical regions except for N and S America and Madagascar. It coils its body around its prey, which includes hares, rats, and antelopes, and squeezes it until it suffocates. [named after *Python*, a monster killed by the Greek god Apollo]

pyx *noun* **1** *Christianity* a container in which the consecrated Communion bread is kept. **2** a box at the Royal Mint in which sample coins for testing are kept. [from Greek *pyxis*, a box of boxwood]

pzazz see PIZZAZZ.

Q

Q¹ *or* **q** *noun* (PL. **Qs**, **Q's**, **q's**) the seventeenth letter of the English alphabet.

Q² *abbrev.* **1** Queen or Queen's. **2** *Chess* queen. **3** question.

Qaddafi, Muammar see GADDAFI, MUAMMAR.

Qantas *abbrev.* Queensland and Northern Territory Aerial Service Limited, founded in 1922 and the national airline of Australia since 1947. In 1967 it became Qantas Airways Ltd.

Qat *or* **Ambat** in Melanesian mythology, a heroic spirit born from a rock who organized both life and death. He created men and women by carving them from a tree, burying their bodies in the ground for three days, and then giving them life by exposing them to the light and beating a drum for three days. His friendly rival Marawa tried to do the same but on digging the bodies up after six days found they had completely decomposed, thus inventing death.

Qatar, official name **State of Qatar**, Arabic **Dawlat al-Qatar** POP (1992e) 453 000, a low-lying state on the E coast of the Arabian Peninsula, comprising the Qatar Peninsula and numerous small offshore islands. AREA 11 437sq km/4 415sq mi. It is bounded S by Saudi Arabia and the United Arab Emirates, elsewhere by the Arabian Gulf. CAPITAL Doha. TIME ZONE GMT +3. The population is 40% Arab, 18% Pakistani, and 18% Indian; Islam is the chief religion. OFFICIAL LANGUAGE Arabic. CURRENCY the riyal. PHYSICAL DESCRIPTION the peninsula, 160km/100mi long and 55–80km/34–50mi wide, slopes gently from the Dukhan Heights (98m) to the E shore; barren terrain, mainly sand and gravel; coral reefs offshore. CLIMATE desert climate with average temperatures of 23°C in the winter and 35°C in the summer; high humidity; sparse annual rainfall not exceeding 75mm per annum. HISTORY British protectorate after the Turkish withdrawal in 1916; declared its independence in 1971. GOVERNMENT a hereditary monarchy, with an Emir who is both head of state and Prime Minister; a Council of Ministers is assisted by a 30-member nominated Consultative Council. ECONOMY based on oil; offshore gas reserves are thought to constitute an eighth of known world reserves; oil refineries, petrochemicals, liquefied natural gas; fertilizers; steel; cement; ship repairing; engineering; food processing; fishing; aubergines, lucerne, squash, hay, tomatoes.

QC *abbrev.* Queen's Counsel.

QC *abbrev.* quality control.

QE2 *abbrev.* Queen Elizabeth 2.

QED *abbrev. quod erat demonstrandum* (Latin), which was what had to be proved.

qi *or* **chi** *noun Chinese Medicine* an individual person's life force, the free flow of which within the body is believed to ensure physical and spiritual health. [from Chinese *qi*, breath, energy]

qi gong a system of meditational exercises combined with deep breathing designed to promote physical and spiritual health. [from Chinese *qi*, breath, energy]

Qingdao *or* **Tsingtao** *or* **Ching-tao** POP (1990) 2m, a resort city and seaport on the Yellow Sea, situated in Shandong province, E China. HISTORY a small fishing village until after 1898, when it was developed by Germans into a modern city; occupied by Japan in World War I.

Qinghai Hu a salt lake in NE Qinghai province, W central China. AREA 4 583sq km/1 769sq mi. It lies at an altitude of 3 196m and is the largest salt lake in China. The island in the centre of the lake is a nature protection zone, well known for its water birds.

Qinghai–Tibet Plateau see TIBET PLATEAU.

Qinhuangdao POP (1990) 365 000, a port in Hebei province, N China, lying on the NW coast of the Bohai Gulf. The city was designated a special economic zone in 1985. Just N of the town is Shan Haiguan, the E end of the Great Wall.

Qin Shihuangdi Mausoleum the tomb of Emperor Qin Shihuangdi (259–210 BC), discovered in 1974 at Mount Li, near Lintong, Shaanxi province, China. Excavation, which is still in progress, has revealed an army of over 6 000 life-size painted terracotta warriors and horses arranged as if for battle. Many other items (eg weapons, chariots, silk and linen articles) have been discovered on the site, where a museum has been erected in which to exhibit them. It is a World Heritage site.

QM *abbrev.* quartermaster.

Qom POP (1986) 543 000, an industrial city in Qom district, Markazi, Iran. It lies on the R Anarbar 120km/75mi SW of Tehran and is a pilgrimage centre for Shiite Muslims. NOTABLE FEATURE Shrine of Fatima.

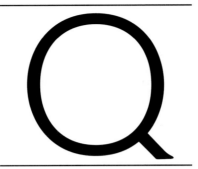

Qatar

qq.v. *or* **qqv.** *abbrev. quae vide* (Latin), which see; see these words (used when referring to more than one item).

qr *abbrev.* quarter.

qt *abbrev.* quart.

q.t.
— **on the q.t.** *colloq.* on the quiet; secretly.

qua *prep.* considered as; as being: *the cartoonist's art / qua art.* [from Latin *qua*, feminine ablative singular of *qui*, who]

quack¹ — *noun* the cry of a duck. — *verb intrans.* **1** *said of a duck* to make this cry. **2** to talk in a loud silly voice. [imitative]

quack² *noun* **1** a medically unqualified person who claims a doctor's knowledge and skill. **2** *colloq., often derog.* a doctor. [from Old Dutch *quacksalver*]

quackery *noun* the activities or methods of a quack.

quad¹ *noun colloq.* a quadruplet.

quad² *noun colloq.* a quadrangle.

quad³ *colloq.* — *adj.* quadraphonic. — *noun* quadraphonics.

quadr- *or* **quadri-** *combining form* forming words meaning 'four'. [from Latin, from *quattuor*, four]

Quadragesima *noun* in the Christian calendar, the first Sunday in Lent. [from Latin *quadragesima dies*, fortieth day]

quadrangle *noun* **1** *Geom.* a square, rectangle, or other four-sided two-dimensional figure. **2** an open rectangular court within the buildings of a college, school, etc. [from Latin *quadrangulum*, from *quadr-*, four + *angulus*, angle]

quadrant *noun* **1** *Geom.* a quarter of the circumference of a circle. **2** *Geom.* a quarter of a circle, ie an area bounded by two radii meeting at right angles. **3** *Geom.* a quarter of a sphere, ie a section cut by two planes intersecting at right angles at the centre. **4** any device or mechanical part in the shape of a 90° arc. **5** *Naut., Astron.* an instrument incorporating a graduated 90° arc, used for measuring altitude, eg of the stars.

quadraphonic *adj., said of sound reproduction* using four loudspeakers fed by four separate channels. [from QUADR- + STEREOPHONIC]

quadraphonics *sing. noun* a sound system employing at least four loudspeakers fed by four separate amplified signals.

quadraphony *noun* a quadraphonic sound system.

quadrat *noun Biol.* a random sample area of ground enclosed within a frame, often one metre square, which is studied in order to determine the plant and animal species it supports.

Permanent quadrats can be examined at intervals in order to assess changes in species composition over time. [from Latin *quadratus*, squared]

quadrate — *noun Anat.* in the upper jaw of bony fish, amphibians, birds, and reptiles, one of a pair of bones that articulates with the lower jaw. In mammals it is represented by the *incus*, a small bone in the middle ear. — *adj. Bot.* square or almost square in cross-section or face view. [from Latin *quadrare*, to make square]

quadratic equation *Maths.* an algebraic equation that involves the square, but no higher power, of an unknown quantity or variable. It has the general formula $ax^2 + bx + c = 0$, where x is the unknown variable. In coordinate geometry, a quadratic equation represents a parabola.

quadrennial *adj.* **1** lasting four years. **2** occurring every four years. [from Latin *quadriennium*, four-year period, from *quadri-*, four + *annus*, year]

quadrennially *adv.* every four years.

quadrilateral — *noun Geom.* a four-sided two-dimensional figure. — *adj.* four-sided. [from Latin *quadrilaterus*, from *quadri-*, four + *latus*, side]

quadrille¹ *noun* a square dance for four couples, in five or six movements; music for this. [from Spanish *cuadrilla*, troop]

quadrille² *noun Cards* a game for four players using 40 cards. [from Spanish *cuartillo*]

quadriplegia *noun* paralysis affecting the arms and legs. [from QUADR- + Greek *plege*, blow, stroke]

quadriplegic *adj.* paralysed in all four limbs.

quadruped *noun* a four-footed animal, especially a mammal. [from Latin *quadrupes*, from *quadru-*, four + *pes*, foot]

quadruple — *verb trans., intrans.* to multiply by four or increase fourfold. — *adj.* **1** four times as many or much. **2** composed of four parts. **3** *Mus.*, said of time having four beats to the bar. — *noun* a quadruple number or amount. [from Latin *quadruplus*, fourfold]

Quadruple Alliance a treaty signed (2 Aug 1718) when the Dutch joined the triple alliance of Britain, France, and the Habsburg emperor Charles VI, to maintain the Treaty of Utrecht (1713). It provided for mutual guarantees of titles, possessions, and rights of succession, despite Spain's hostility to Italian territorial provisions, and secured peace for a generation (1718–33).

quadruplet *noun* each of four children or animals born at one birth.

quadruplicate — *verb* (pronounced *-kate*) to make quadruple or fourfold. — *adj.* (pronounced *-kət*) fourfold; copied four times. — **in quadruplicate** copied four times. [from Latin *quadruplicare*, to multiply by four]

quadruply *adv.* in a fourfold way.

quaff *verb trans., intrans. literary, facetious* to drink eagerly or deeply.

quagga *noun* an extinct Southern African wild ass, related to the zebra but striped on head and shoulders only. [perhaps from Hottentot *quacha*]

quagmire *noun* an area of soft marshy ground; a bog. [from *quag*, bog + MIRE]

quaich *noun Scot.* a two-handled drinking-cup usually of silver or pewter. [from Gaelic *cuach*, cup]

Quai d'Orsay the embankment on the Left Bank of the R Seine in Paris, and by association the French Foreign Ministry located there.

quail¹ *verb intrans.* to lose courage or feel fear; to flinch.

quail² *noun* a small bird of the partridge family. [from French *quaille*]

quaint *adj.* charmingly or pleasingly odd or old-fashioned. [from Old French *cointe*, from Latin *cognitus*, known]

quake¹ — *verb intrans.* **1** *said of people* to shake or tremble with fear, etc. **2** *said of a building, etc* to rock or shudder. — *noun* a shudder or tremor, of fear, etc. [from Anglo-Saxon *cwacian*]

quake² *noun colloq.* an earthquake.

Quaker *noun* a member of a Christian movement, the Society of Friends, founded by George Fox in the 17c (see FRIENDS).

qualification *noun* **1** an official record that one has completed a training, performed satisfactorily in an examination, etc. **2** a skill or ability that fits one for some job, etc. **3** the act, process, or fact of qualifying. **4** an addition to a statement, etc that narrows or restricts it; a condition, limitation, or modification.

qualifier *noun* a person or thing that qualifies.

qualify *verb* (**qualifies, qualified**) **1** *intrans.* to complete a training, pass an examination, etc, that gives one professional status: *has qualified as a nurse.* **2** to make suitable for a task, job, etc: *is hardly qualified to judge.* **3** *intrans.* (**qualify for something**) to fulfil requirements that give one a right to an award, privilege, etc: *doesn't qualify for a grant.* **4** *intrans.* to be seen as having the right characteristics to be: *what qualifies as news these days?* **5** to add something to (a statement, etc) that restricts or limits it. **6** to modify, tone down, or restrict: *qualified approval.* **7** *Grammar, said of an adjective* to define or describe (a noun). **8** *intrans. Sport* to reach a standard in a preliminary round that entitles one to participate in subsequent rounds. [from Latin *qualis*, of what kind + *facere*, to make]

qualitative *adj.* relating to, investigating, or affecting the qualities or standard of something.

quality *noun* (PL. **qualities**) **1** standard of goodness. **2** excellence; high standard: *novels of quality.* **3** (*attributive*) of a high quality or standard: *quality newspapers.* **4** a characteristic or attribute: *has a silky quality.* **5** the character given to a voice or other sound by attributes other than pitch or loudness. **6** *old use* high social status. [from Latin *qualitas*, from *qualis*, of what kind]

quality control the regular sampling of the output of an industrial process in order to detect any variations in quality.

quality time a concentrated amount of time spent with a companion or child without interruptions or distractions.

qualm *noun* **1** a sudden feeling of nervousness or apprehension. **2** a feeling of uneasiness about whether what one is doing is right; a scruple, misgiving, or pang of conscience. **3** a feeling of faintness or nausea. [from Anglo-Saxon *cwealm*, death, murder, slaughter, plague]

quandary *noun* (PL. **quandaries**) a situation in which one is at a loss what to do; a dilemma or predicament.

quango *noun* (PL. **quangos**) a government-funded body responsible for some area of public concern. Its senior appointments are made by the government. [from quasi- autonomous non-governmental organization]

Quant, Mary (1934–) English designer, born in London. She began fashion design when she opened a shop in Chelsea in 1955. Her clothes were particularly fashionable in the 1960s, when the geometric simplicity of her designs, especially the miniskirt, and the originality of her colours became a feature of the 'swinging Britain' era. In the 1970s she extended into cosmetics and textile design.

quantify *verb* (**quantifies, quantified**) to find out the quantity of; to express as a quantity. [from Latin *quantus*, how much + *facere*, to make]

quantitative *adj.* **1** relating to quantity. **2** estimated, or measurable, in terms of quantity.

quantity *noun* (PL. **quantities**) **1** the property things have that makes them measurable or countable; size or amount. **2** an amount that can be counted or measured; a specified amount: *a tiny quantity.* **3** largeness of amount; bulk: *buy in quantity / quality, not quantity, is what counts.* **4** (**quantities**) a large amount: *quantities of food.* **5** *Maths.* a value that may be expressed as a number, or the symbol or figure representing it. **6** *Prosody* the length or duration of a vowel sound or syllable.

— **an unknown quantity** a person or thing whose importance or influence cannot be foreseen.

[from Latin *quantitas*, from *quantus*, how much]

quantity surveyor a person who estimates the quantities of materials needed to build something, and their probable cost.

quantize *or* **quantise** *verb Physics* to form into quanta (see QUANTUM).

quantum *noun* (PL. **quanta**) **1** an amount or quantity. **2** *Physics* a tiny indivisible packet of energy, representing the form in which atoms give off electromagnetic radiation, eg light, according to quantum theory (a quantum of electromagnetic radiation is known as a *photon*). In classical physics it was originally assumed that light is sent out in a continuous wave flow, but quantum mechanics suggests that it consists of a stream of quanta that behave both as waves and as particles. [from Latin *quantus*, how much]

quantum leap *or* **quantum jump** a sudden transition; a spectacular advance.

quantum theory *Physics* a theory which states that electromagnetic radiation, such as light, is emitted in separate packets of energy called *quanta* or *photons*. Electrons move in fixed orbits around the nucleus of an atom, and when that atom absorbs energy (eg as a result of being heated), one of its electrons may be raised to a higher energy level or orbit. When the electron returns to its original orbit, it emits the same 'packet' of energy as a photon of radiation.

quarantine — *noun* the isolation of people or animals to prevent the spread of any infectious disease that they could be developing; the duration of such isolation. — *verb* to impose such isolation on; to put into quarantine. [from Italian *quarantina*, period of 40 days]

quark *noun Physics* any of a group of subatomic particles of which all hadrons (subatomic particles such as protons and neutrons) are composed. It is thought that there are six types or 'flavours' of quark (up, down, top, bottom, strange, and charm), and each type of quark is believed to have an antiparticle known as an antiquark. [coined by the writer James Joyce in *Finnegans Wake*; adopted for scientific use by the American physicist Murray Gell-Mann]

Quarles, Francis (1592–1644) English religious poet, born near Romford, Essex. He was cup-bearer to the Princess Elizabeth (1613), secretary to Archbishop Ussher (c.1629), and chronologer to the City of London (1639). His best-known work is the emblem book (a series of symbolic pictures with verse commentary), *Emblems* (1635), and a prose book of aphorisms, *Enchyridion* (1640).

quarrel — *noun* **1** an angry disagreement or argument. **2** a cause of such disagreement; a complaint: *I've no quarrel with the management.* **3** a break in a friendship; a breach or rupture. — *verb intrans.* (**quarrelled, quarrelling**) **1** to argue or dispute angrily. **2** to disagree and remain on bad terms: *I think they must have quarrelled.* **3** to find fault: *I can't quarrel with her reasoning.* [from Latin *querela*, complaint]

quarrelsome *adj.* inclined to quarrel or dispute.

quarry¹ — *noun* (PL. **quarries**) **1** an open excavation for the purpose of extracting stone or slate for building. **2** any source from which a supply of information or other material is obtained. — *verb* (**quarries, quarried**) **1** to extract (stone, etc) from a quarry. **2** to excavate a quarry in (land).

3 to get a supply of (material or information) from a source. [from Latin *quadrare*, to square]

quarry² *noun* (PL. **quarries**) **1** a hunted animal or bird; a prey. **2** someone or something that is the object of pursuit. [from Old French *cuiree*, from *cuir*, hide]

quarry tile an unglazed floor tile.

quart *noun* a liquid measure equivalent to quarter of a gallon or two pints (1·136 litres). [from Latin *quartus*, fourth]

quarter — *noun* **1** one of four equal parts into which an object or quantity may be divided; the fraction ¼, one divided by four. **2** any of the three-month divisions of the year, especially beginning or ending on a quarter day. **3** a unit of weight equal to a quarter of a hundredweight or 28 lbs. **4** *colloq.* 4 ozs, or a quarter of a pound. **5** a unit of measure for grain, equal to eight bushels. **6** *North Amer.* 25 cents, or a coin of this value. **7** a period of 15 minutes; a point of time 15 minutes after or before any hour. **8** a fourth part of the moon's cycle; either of the visible shapes (phases) of the moon when half its surface is lit, at the point between the first and second, and the third and fourth, quarters of its cycle. **9** any of the four compass directions; any direction. **10** a district of a city, etc, eg identified by the predominant nationality of its population: *living in the Spanish quarter*. **11** (*often* **quarters**) a section of the public; certain people or a certain person: *disapproval in certain quarters / no sympathy from that quarter*. **12** (**quarters**) lodgings or accommodation, eg for soldiers and their families: *married quarters*. **13** *old use* mercy shown to someone in one's power, eg a defeated enemy: *give no quarter*. **14** *Heraldry* any of the four parts into which a shield is divided by intersecting horizontal and vertical lines. **15** any limb of a four-limbed animal: *hindquarters*. **16** *Sport* any of four equal parts into which a match in some sports is divided. — *verb* (**quartered, quartering**) **1** to divide into quarters. **2** to accommodate or billet in lodgings. **3** *Hist.* to divide (the body of a hanged traitor, etc) into four parts. **4** *Heraldry* to fill each quarter of (a shield) with bearings. **5** *said of hounds* to cross and recross (an area) searching for game. — *adj.* being one of four equal parts: *a quarter hour*. [from Old French *quartier*, from Latin *quartarius*, fourth part]

quarterback *noun Amer. Football* a player between the forwards and halfbacks, who directs his team's attacking play.

quarter day any of the four days beginning or ending one of the year's quarters, on which rent or interest are paid.

quarterdeck *noun* the stern part of a ship's upper deck, usually reserved for officers.

quarter final (*also* **quarter finals**) the round of a competition involving four participants or teams, preceding the semi-final.

quarter-finalist *noun* a person who qualifies to take part in a quarter final.

quartering *noun Heraldry* (*usually* **quarterings**) the coats of arms displayed on a shield to indicate family alliances.

quarterlight *noun* a small window in either front door of a car, that pivots open for ventilation.

quarterly — *adj.* done, occurring, or published once every quarter of a year. — *adv.* once every quarter. — *noun* (PL. **quarterlies**) a quarterly publication.

quartermaster *noun* **1** an army officer responsible for soldiers' accommodation, food, and clothing. **2** *Naut.* a petty officer responsible for navigation and signals.

quarter note *North Amer.* a crotchet.

quarter sessions *Hist.* a local court of law presided over by a justice of the peace, formerly held quarterly.

quarterstaff *noun Hist.* a 6ft (1.83m) pole used as a weapon.

quartet *or* **quartette** *noun* **1** an ensemble of four singers or instrumental players. **2** a piece of music for four such performers. **3** any group or set of four. [from Italian *quartetto*, from Latin *quartus*, fourth]

quarto *noun* (PL. **quartos**) *Printing* a size of paper produced by folding a sheet into four leaves or eight pages. [from Latin *in quarto*, in one fourth]

quartz *noun Geol.* one of the commonest minerals, consisting of pure silica. [from German *Quarz*]

◇ Quartz is a major component of beach deposits, eg sand particles, and of sandstone and many other sedimentary, igneous, and metamorphic rocks, eg granite, gneisses, schists. Pure colourless crystalline quartz is known as rock crystal, and several of the coloured varieties, eg amethyst, are used as gemstones. Quartz crystals exhibit the piezoelectric effect, and are used to make quartz clocks, watches, crystal pick-ups for record players, etc. Quartz is also used as an abrasive, and in optical instruments, glass, mortar, and cement.

quartz clock a clock whose moving mechanism is controlled by the vibrations of a piezoelectric crystal of quartz, which oscillates at a fixed frequency over a long period of time when a suitable electrical signal is applied to it. Such a system is also used in quartz watches.

quartz crystal **1** a transparent colourless form of quartz, either naturally occurring or manufactured synthetically, used in optics and electronics. **2** a piezoelectric crystal of quartz that vibrates at a fixed frequency when a suitable electrical signal is applied to it, used to control the moving mechanism of quartz clocks and watches.

quartzite *noun* **1** *Geol.* any of various pale or white highly durable metamorphic rocks, composed largely or entirely of quartz, and formed by the recrystallization of sandstone under increasing temperature and pressure. Quartzites are used as a construction material in the building industry. **2** a non-metamorphic sandstone consisting of grains of quartz cemented together by silica.

quasar *noun* a highly luminous star-like point source of radiation (including radio waves) outside our galaxy. Quasars are thought to be the most distant and luminous bodies so far discovered in the universe. [from *quasi-stellar object*]

◇ Quasars were first observed by radio astronomers, who measured such powerful signals that they thought the objects emitting them were in the Milky Way. However, when their redshift was measured, it was found to be very high, indicating that these objects were much further away than any normal galaxy could be detected, and millions of times brighter than normal galaxies.

quash *verb* **1** to reject (a verdict, etc) as invalid. **2** to annul (a law, etc). **3** to subdue, crush, or suppress (a rebellion, etc). [from Latin *quassare*, to shake]

quasi- *prefix* forming words meaning: **1** to some extent; virtually: *a quasi-official role*. **2** in many respects similar to; virtual: *a quasi-deity*. **3** seeming or seemingly, but not actually so: *quasi-technical jargon / quasi-experts*. [from Latin *quasi*, as if]

Quasimodo, Salvatore (1901–68) Italian poet, born in Syracuse, Sicily. A professor of literature at the Conservatory of Music in Milan, his early work is Symbolist in character, as in *Ed è subito sera* (And Suddenly it's Evening, 1942). He became a leader of the 'hermetic' poets, and his later poetry shows a concern with social issues and the fate of Italy, as in *La Vita non e sogno* (Life is not a Dream, 1949). He was awarded the Nobel Prize for literature in 1959.

quassia *noun* **1** a S American tree whose bitter wood and bark are used as a tonic. **2** a West Indian tree of the same family. [from Graman Quassi, an 18c Negro slave in Surinam who discovered its medicinal properties]

quaternary — *adj.* **1** having four parts. **2** (**Quaternary**) *Geol.* belonging or relating to the second period of the Cenozoic era, which began about two million years ago at the end of the Tertiary. It is the most recent period of geological time, and includes the Pleistocene and Holocene epochs. Modern man (*Homo sapiens*) evolved during this period. — *noun Geol.* this period. [from Latin *quaterni*, four each]

quatrain *noun Poetry* a verse or poem of four lines, usually rhyming alternately. [from French, from *quatre*, four]

quatrefoil *noun* **1** *Bot.* **a** a flower with four petals. **b** a leaf composed of four lobes or leaflets. **2** *Archit.* a four-lobed design used especially in open stonework. [from Old French *quatre*, four + *foil*, leaf]

quattrocento *noun* the 15c, usually with reference to Italian Renaissance art. [from Italian *quattrocento*, four (for fourteen) hundred]

quaver — *verb* (**quavered, quavering**) **1** *intrans. said of someone's voice* to be unsteady; to shake or tremble. **2** *trans.* to say or sing in a trembling voice. — *noun* **1** *Mus.* a note that lasts half as long as a crotchet. **2** a tremble in the voice. [perhaps imitative]

quavery *adj.* likely to quaver, quavering.

quay *noun* a wharf for the loading and unloading of ships. [from Old French *kay*]

Quayle, J(ames) Danforth, also called **Dan Quayle** (1947–) US politician, born in Indianapolis. He worked as a lawyer, journalist, and public official, before he was a member of Congress (1977–81) and the Senate (1981–8). He served as Vice-President under George Bush (1988–92).

queasily *adv.* in a queasy way.

queasiness *noun* a queasy state or feeling.

queasy *adj.* (**queasier, queasiest**) **1** feeling slightly sick. **2** *said of the stomach or digestion* easily upset. **3** *said of food* causing feelings of nausea. **4** *said of the conscience* readily made uneasy.

Quebec, French **Québec** POP (1991c) 645 000, the capital of Quebec province, SE Canada, lying on the St Lawrence R where it meets the St Charles R. It was built on Cape Diamond, a cliff rising 100m above the St Lawrence. Most of the city's population are French-speaking (92%). HISTORY visited by Jacques Cartier (1491–1557) in 1535; a French colony was founded in 1608; taken by the English in 1629 but returned to France in 1632; became capital of New France in 1663; captured by the British under James Wolfe (1727–59) in 1759, and ceded to Britain in 1763; became capital of Lower Canada in 1791. NOTABLE FEATURES Château Frontenac (the setting for the World War II meetings between the USA and the UK); N America's oldest lift (linking the Upper and Lower Towns); Musée du Fort; Citadel Fortress (c.105m above the St Lawrence, and a World Heritage site); Battlefield Park (including the Provincial Museum and the Plains of Abraham); Quebec Museum.

Quebec, French **Québec** POP (1991) 6.9m, the largest province in Canada. Its boundaries include James and Hudson bays in the W, Hudson Strait and Ungava Bay to the NE, the Gulf of St Lawrence in the E, and the USA in the S. AREA 1 540 680sq km/594 703sq mi. PHYSICAL DESCRIPTION four fifths of the province lie in the Canadian Shield, a rolling plateau dotted with lakes; there is tundra in the extreme N, and the Notre Dame Mts in the S; several rivers flow into James and Hudson bays and into the St Lawrence, in which there are several islands. The S part is intensely cultivated and most of the population is in the St Lawrence Valley. HISTORY claimed for France by Jacques Cartier in 1534; a province of New France from 1608; captured by the British in 1629, it was restored to France in 1632; transferred to Britain by the 1763 Treaty of Paris; constituted as Lower Canada in 1791; it became the province of Quebec in 1867; a strong separatist movement emerged in the 1960s, but a 1980 referendum decided against secession; a further referendum in 1992 resulted in a vote against measures to give the province greater autonomy. GOVERNMENT governed by a lieutenant-governor and a 122-member elected Legislative Assembly. CAPITAL Quebec. CHIEF TOWNS Montreal, Laval, Sherbrooke, Verdun, Hull, Trois Rivières. OFFICIAL LANGUAGES English, French. ECONOMY agriculture; timber; paper; hydroelectric power; aluminium, bauxite, iron ore, copper, gold, zinc, asbestos; textiles; high-technology industries; tourism.

Quebec Railroad Bridge a cantilever railway bridge built (1918) over the St Lawrence River, Canada. Its span of 549m is the largest of its kind in the world.

Quechua — *noun* a S American language of the Andean–Equatorial group. It is the official language of the Incas, and has a written history dating from the 7c AD. It is spoken by more than six million people from Colombia to Chile, and is widely used as a lingua franca. — *adj.* relating to or spoken or written in Quechua.

Queen, Ellery, pseudonym of **Frederic Dannay** (1905–82) and his cousin **Manfred B Lee** (1905–71) two US writers of crime fiction, both born in New York City. As business men they won a detective-story competition with *The Roman Hat Mystery* (1929), and then wrote many popular books in this genre, using 'Ellery Queen' both as their pseudonym and as the name of their detective. They also used the pseudonym Barnaby Ross as the author of their other detective, Drury Lane. They began *Ellery Queen's Mystery Magazine* (1941) and co-founded Mystery Writers of America.

queen — *noun* **1** a woman who rules a country, having inherited her position by birth. **2** the wife of a king. **3** a woman supreme in her field; a place or thing considered supreme in some way. **4** a large female ant, bee, or wasp that lays eggs. **5** the most powerful chess piece, able to move forwards, backwards, sideways, or diagonally. **6** a playing-card bearing the picture of a queen. **7** *offensive slang* an effeminate male homosexual. — *verb trans., intrans. Chess* to make (a pawn) into a queen; (of a pawn) to be converted into a queen. — **queen it** *colloq., said of a woman* to behave overbearingly.

Queen Anne's lace cow parsley.

Queen Anne style an English style of architecture, furniture, and silver designed during the reign of Queen Anne (1702–14), notable for carefully calculated proportions and a lack of applied ornament. Chairs and cabinets were characterized by robust carved legs (*cabriole*) and Baroque shapes. The style was revived in English architecture in the second half of the 19c, characterized by compositions of mullioned windows, handsome brickwork, and imposingly grouped chimneys.

Queen Anne's War the second (1702–13) of the four intercolonial wars waged by Britain and France for control of colonial N America, known in Europe as the War of the Spanish Succession. Both sides made considerable use of Native American allies. Settled by the Treaty of Utrecht (1713), its result was British control of Newfoundland, Acadia, and Hudson's Bay, and acquisition of the Assiento, which allowed trade with Spanish America.

Queen Charlotte Islands POP (1981) 6 000, an archipelago of c.150 islands in British Columbia, W Canada. It lies off the W coast of the province. AREA 9 790sq km/3 779sq mi. ECONOMY timber; fishing.

Queen Christina a US film directed by Rouben Mamoulian (1933). It is the story of how a 17c Swedish queen (played by Greta Garbo) disguises herself in order to discover the true nature of the Spanish ambassador she loves.

queen consort the wife of a reigning king.

Queen Elizabeth a British passenger liner, launched in 1938, which carried troops and was equipped as a battleship during World War II. It served on the transatlantic Cunard Line from 1946 to 1968. It sank in 1972 after going on fire during refurbishment.

Queen Elizabeth 2 (ABBREV. **QE2**) a British passenger liner, launched in 1967, the successor to the *Queen Elizabeth*. Its maiden voyage was made in 1969.

Queen Elizabeth II two portraits by Pietro Annigoni (1955, 1970; the latter is in the National Portrait Gallery, London).

Queen Elizabeth Islands the northernmost islands in the Canadian Arctic Archipelago. AREA 390 000sq km/150 000sq mi. They include Ellesmere, Devon, Prince Patrick, the Cornwallis Is, and the Sverdrup and Parry groups. The area was named in 1953.

queenly *adj.* characteristic of or suitable for a queen.

Queen Mab a poem in nine cantos by Percy Bysshe Shelley (1813). It is a visionary, polemical poem which attacks the whole conventional framework of society and advocates such things as free love, atheism, and vegetarianism.

Queen Mary a British ocean liner built at Clydebank and launched in 1934. It was the first British liner to exceed 1 000ft (305m).

Queen Maud Land, Norwegian **Dronning Maud Land** the main part of the Norwegian Antarctic Territory. Lying between 20°W and 45°W and S of 60°S, it extends to the South Pole. It was claimed by Norway in 1939. Scientific bases are located at Sanae (South Africa) and Novo Lazarevskaya (Russia).

queen mother the widow of a king who is also the mother of a reigning king or queen.

queen post *Archit.* one of two upright posts in a trussed roof, supporting the principal rafter.

Queens POP (1990) 2m, a borough of New York City, USA, co-extensive with Queens County. AREA 283sq km/109sq mi. Lying at the W end of Long Island, it is connected to the mainland by the Hell Gate Bridge, and with Manhattan by the Queensboro Bridge. It has been a borough since 1898, and is the location of the two New York airports.

Queen's Award in the UK, an award given annually on the Queen's birthday (21 Apr) since 1965. There are now two separate awards: one for export achievement, and one for technological achievement.

Queen's Bench *or* **King's Bench** in the UK, a division of the High Court of Justice.

Queensberry, Sir John Sholto Douglas, 8th Marquis of (1844–1900) British aristocrat, a keen patron of boxing, who supervised the formulation in 1867 of new rules to govern that sport, known since as the Queensberry Rules. In 1895 he was tried and acquitted for publishing a defamatory libel on Oscar Wilde — an event which led to Wilde's trial and imprisonment.

Queensberry Rules the code of rules used in boxing, drawn up in 1867 for the Marquess of Queensberry.

Queen's Counsel *or* **King's Counsel** (ABBREV. **QC, KC**) a senior member of the English or Scottish Bar. A practising barrister of 10 years' standing may apply to become a Queen's Counsel (or 'take silk' — a reference to the gowns worn by such counsel). Application is made to

the Lord Chancellor; a list of those selected each year is published on Maundy Thursday.

Queen's English *or* **King's English** standard written or spoken English, generally regarded as the most correct or acceptable form.

Queen's evidence *or* **King's evidence** evidence for the prosecution given by a participant in a crime. — **turn Queen's** *or* **King's evidence** *said of a criminal* to give such evidence.

Queen's Guide *or* **King's Guide** a Guide who has reached the highest level of proficiency.

Queen's highway *or* **King's highway** a public road, regarded as being under royal control.

Queensland POP (1992e) 3m, the second-largest state in Australia. AREA 1 727 200sq km/666 700sq mi. The state is divided into 11 statistical divisions and is bordered in the N by the Gulf of Carpentaria, the Torres Strait, and the Coral Sea, and in the E by the S Pacific Ocean. Most of the population lives in the SE of the state. PHYSICAL DESCRIPTION the Cape York Peninsula is in the N and the Great Dividing Range runs N–S, separating a fertile coastal strip to the E from dry plains to the W; on the border with New South Wales lies the Scenic Rim Mountain Range; the Great Barrier Reef runs parallel to the Pacific coast; the state has a coastline measuring 5 200km/3 200mi, including the 'sunshine coast' and the 'gold coast', on which there are many major resort areas with fine surfing beaches. HISTORY established as a penal colony in 1824; open to free settlers in 1842; part of New South Wales until 1859. CAPITAL Brisbane. CHIEF TOWNS Gold Coast, Townsville, Cairns, Ipswich, Toowoomba, Rockhampton. ECONOMY provides 22% of Australia's agricultural production, with sugar the main export crop; wheat, sorghum, tomatoes, citrus and tropical fruit; bauxite, coal, copper, zinc, lead, phosphate, nickel; oil, gas; machinery; chemicals; textiles; food processing; furniture; plastics; rubber products; forest products; paper; motor vehicles.

Queen's Scout *or* **King's Scout** a Scout who has reached the highest level of proficiency.

Queequeg a lofty Polynesian prince, and Starbuck's harpooner, in Herman Melville's *Moby Dick*.

queer *adj.* **1** odd, strange, or unusual. **2** *colloq.* slightly mad. **3** faint or ill: *feeling queer.* **4** *colloq.* suspicious; shady: *queer doings.* **5** *offensive slang, said of a man* homosexual. — **in queer street** *colloq.* in debt or financial difficulties.

queer someone's pitch *colloq.* to spoil their plans; to thwart them.

queerly *adv.* in a queer way; oddly.

queerness *noun* a queer state or feeling.

Queiros, José Mari Eca de (1845–1900) Portuguese novelist, born in Povoado do Varzim. He served as a diplomat in Cuba (1872–74), London (1874–88), and Paris (1888–1900), and wrote most of his work while in England. This includes *O Crimo do Padre Amaro* (The Sin of Father Amaro, 1875) and *O Primo Basilio* (Cousin Basilio, 1878). His best-known work is the social satire *Os Maias* (The Maias, 1888).

quell *verb* **1** to crush or subdue (riots, disturbances, opposition, etc). **2** to suppress or overcome (unwanted feelings, etc). [from Anglo-Saxon *cwellan,* to kill]

Queluz POP (1991) 61 000, a market town in Lisbon district, central Portugal, situated 15km/9mi NW of Lisbon. NOTABLE FEATURE Roco Palace, former summer residence of the Braganza kings.

quench *verb* **1** to get rid of (one's thirst) by drinking. **2** to extinguish (a fire). **3** to damp or crush (ardour, enthusiasm, desire, etc). **4** to cool a metal rapidly by plunging it in a liquid or gas, eg water, oil, or air, in order to alter its properties, especially to harden steel or to soften copper. [from Anglo-Saxon *acwencan*]

quenelle *noun* a dumpling of fish, chicken, veal, etc. [from French *quenelle*]

Querétaro 1 POP (1990) 454 000, the capital of Querétaro state, central Mexico. It is situated 200km/124mi NW of Mexico City and stands at an altitude of 1 865m. HISTORY important in the 1810 independence rising; scene of the surrender and execution of Emperor Maximilian in 1867. NOTABLE FEATURES Church of Santa Cruz; Convent of San Francisco; Federal Palace. 2 a state in central Mexico with Querétaro as its capital.

quern *noun* Hist., Archaeol. a stone implement of any of several kinds for grinding grain by hand. [from Anglo-Saxon *cweorn*]

querulous *adj.* 1 inclined to complain. 2 *said of a voice, tone, etc* complaining, grumbling, or whining. [from Latin *querulus*, from *queri*, to complain]

query — *noun* (PL. **queries**) 1 a question, especially one that raises a doubt. 2 a request for information; an inquiry. 3 a question mark. — *verb* (**queries, queried**) 1 to raise a doubt about: *query a bill.* 2 to ask: *'How much' she queried.* [from Latin *quaere*, imperative of *quaerere*, to ask]

quest — *noun* 1 a search or hunt. 2 the object of one's search; one's goal. — *verb intrans. (often* **quest about for something**) 1 to search about; to roam around in search of something. 2 *said of a dog* to search for game. — **in quest of something** looking for it. [from Latin *quaerere*, to seek]

question — *noun* 1 an utterance which requests information or other answer; the interrogative sentence or other form of words in which this is expressed. 2 a doubt or query: *raises questions about their loyalty.* 3 an uncertainty: *no question about the cause.* 4 a problem or difficulty: *the Northern Ireland question.* 5 a problem set for discussion or solution in an examination paper, etc. 6 an investigation or search for information: *still pursuing the question.* 7 a matter or issue: *when it's a question of safety.* 8 an issue on which something is dependent: *a question of time rather than money.* — *verb* (**questioned, questioning**) 1 to ask (someone) questions; to interrogate. 2 to raise doubts about; to query: *would question her motives / question whether it's possible.* — **beyond question** not in doubt; beyond doubt. **bring something into question** to focus attention on it. **call something in** or **into question** to suggest reasons for doubting. **in question** 1 presently under discussion or being referred to: *has an alibi for the time in question.* 2 in doubt: *her ability is not in question.* **no question of** ... no possibility or intention of ... **out of the question** impossible and so not worth considering. **without question** unhesitatingly. [from Latin *quaestio*, from *quaerere*, to ask]

questionable *adj.* 1 doubtful; dubious; suspect: *questionable motives.* 2 of dubious value or benefit: *questionable schemes.*

questioner *noun* a person who questions.

question mark 1 the punctuation mark (?) placed after a question. 2 a doubt: *still a question mark over funds.*

question master the person who asks the questions in a quiz, etc.

questionnaire *noun* a set of questions, usually in the form of a printed leaflet, for distribution to a number of people, as a means of collecting information, surveying opinions, etc. [from French *questionnaire*]

question time in parliament, a daily period set aside for members' questions to government ministers.

Quetta POP (1981) 286 000, the capital of Baluchistan province, W Pakistan. It lies in the central Brahui Range, 590km/367mi N of Karachi, in the centre of a fruit-growing area. For centuries it was a strategic location on the trade route between Afghanistan and the Lower Indus Valley. From its position, control of the Bolan Pass and the Khojak Pass is possible. HISTORY acquired by the British in 1876; badly damaged by an earthquake in 1935.

Quetzalcoatl in pre-Columbian Aztec and Mayan cultures of central America, the feathered serpent god of wind, master of life, and inventor of metallurgy. He was associated with the invention of the calendar and the recreation of human life. He provoked the anger of another god, Tetzcatlipoca, and fled in a boat made of serpent skin, promising to return to reclaim his throne — a promise used to advantage by the invader Hernando Cortés in 1519–21.

Quetzalcoatl

queue — *noun* 1 a line or file of people or vehicles waiting for something. 2 *Comput.* a list of items, eg programs or data, held in a computer system in the order in which they are to be processed. The items that arrive earliest are processed first, and subsequent ones are placed at the end of the list. — *verb intrans.* 1 (*also* **queue up**) to form a queue or wait in a queue. 2 *Comput.* to line up tasks for a computer to process. [from French *queue*, tail]

Quezaltenango 1 POP (1989e) 246 000, the capital of Quezaltenango department, SW Guatemala. It is surrounded by volcanic peaks. Quezalenango is the second industrial and trading centre in Guatemala. Much of the town is modern, having been rebuilt since the earthquakes of 1818 and 1902. 2 a department in SW Guatemala with Quezaltenango as its capital.

Quezon City POP (1990) 1.6m, a residential city in Capital province, Philippines. It is situated on Luzon I, NE of Manila. HISTORY laid out in 1940; former capital from 1948 to 1976.

quibble — *verb intrans.* to argue over trifles; to make petty objections. — *noun* 1 a trifling objection. 2 *old use* a pun.

quiche *noun* a tart with a savoury filling usually made with eggs. [from French *quiche*, from German *Kuchen*, cake]

quick — *adj.* 1 taking little time; speedy. 2 lasting briefly: *a quick glance.* 3 not delayed; immediate: *a quick response.* 4 intelligent; alert; sharp: *quick-witted.* 5 (of the temper) easily roused: *quick-tempered.* 6 nimble, deft, or brisk. 7 not reluctant or slow (to do something); apt or ready: *quick to take offence.* — *adv.* rapidly: *came as quick as we could / a quick-acting drug.* — *noun* 1 an area of sensitive flesh, especially at the base of the finger- or toenail. 2 (**the quick**) *old use* those who are alive: *the quick and the dead.* [from Anglo-Saxon *cwic*, living]

quicken *verb* (**quickened, quickening**) 1 *intrans., trans.* to make or become quicker. 2 to stimulate or stir (someone's interest, imagina-

tion, etc). 3 *intrans.* a *said of a baby in the womb* to begin to move perceptibly. b *said of a pregnant woman* to begin to feel her baby's movements.

quick-freeze *verb* (PAST TENSE **quick-froze**; PAST PARTICIPLE **quick-frozen**) to freeze (food) rapidly by exposing it to moving air at a very low temperature, so that only small ice crystals form, and the internal structure of the food, eg soft fruit such as strawberries, is not damaged.

quickie *noun colloq.* something quickly dealt with or done, eg an easy question.

quicklime *noun* calcium oxide.

Quickly, Mistress the stout landlady of the Boar's Head Tavern, prone to unwitting double entendres and malapropisms, in Shakespeare's *Henry IV Part I, Henry IV Part II, The Merry Wives of Windsor*, and *Henry V.* She eventually marries Pistol after having been betrothed to both Falstaff and Nym.

quickly *adv.* rapidly, speedily.

quickness *noun* 1 a quick understanding. 2 speed.

quick one *colloq.* a quickly consumed alcoholic drink.

quicksand *noun* loose, wet sand that sucks down people or heavy objects standing on it.

quickset — *adj., said of cuttings, etc* planted so as to grow into a hedge. — *noun* a hedge so formed.

quicksilver *noun old use* mercury.

quickstep *noun* a ballroom dance with fast steps; a piece of music for this.

quid[1] *noun* (PL. **quid**) *slang* a pound (sterling). — **quids in** in a profitable or advantageous position.

quid[2] *noun* a bit of tobacco for chewing. [from dialect *quid*, cud]

quiddity *noun* 1 the essence of anything. 2 a quibble; a trifling detail or point. [from Latin *quidditas*, essence]

quid pro quo (PL. **QUID PRO QUOS**) something given or taken in recompense or retaliation for something. [Latin, = something for something]

quiescence *noun* a quiescent state.

quiescent *adj.* 1 quiet; silent; at rest; in an inactive state, especially one unlikely to last. 2 *Biol.* denoting an organism or structure which, because of unfavourable environmental conditions, eg low temperature, has temporarily stopped growing or functioning. [from Latin *quiescere*, to rest]

quiet — *adj.* 1 making little or no noise; soft. 2 *said of a place, etc* peaceful; tranquil; without noise or bustle. 3 silent; saying nothing: *kept quiet about it.* 4 *said of a person* reserved; unassertive. 5 *said of the weather* calm. 6 not disturbed by trouble or excitement: *a quiet life.* 7 without fuss or publicity: *a quiet wedding.* 8 *said of business or trade* poor; not flourishing. 9 secret; private: *had a quiet word with her.* 10 undeclared: *quiet satisfaction.* 11 *said of humour* subtle; not overdone. 12 enjoyed in peace: *a quiet read.* 13 *said of the mind or conscience* untroubled by anxiety, guilt, etc. — *noun* absence of, or freedom from, noise, commotion, etc; calm, tranquillity, or repose: *longing for peace and quiet.* — *verb trans., intrans.* (**quieted, quieting**) to make or become quiet or calm. — **on the quiet** secretly; discreetly. [from Latin *quietus*, quiet]

quieten *verb* (**quietened, quietening**) 1 *trans., intrans.* to make or become quiet. 2 to calm (doubts, fears, etc).

quietism *noun* calm, passive acceptance of events.

quietist *noun* a person characterized by quietism.

quietly *adv.* in a quiet way; with little or no sound.

quietness *noun* being quiet.

quietude *noun* quietness; tranquillity.

quietus *noun* **1** release from life; death. **2** release or discharge from debts or duties. [from Latin *quietus est*, he is at peace]

quiff *noun* a lock of hair brushed up into a point over the forehead.

quill *noun* **1** a large stiff feather from a bird's wing or tail; the hollow base part of this. **2** a pen made from a bird's feather. **3** one of the long spines on a porcupine. [related to German dialect *quiele*]

Quiller-Couch, Sir Arthur (1863–1944) British man of letters, born in Bodmin, Cornwall. He lectured in classics at Oxford (1886–7), and was Professor of English Literature at Cambridge (1912–44). He edited the *Oxford Book of English Verse* (1900) and other anthologies, and published several volumes of essays and criticism. He also wrote poems, short stories, and (under the pseudonym of 'Q') several humorous novels about Cornwall and the sea.

quilt — *noun* **1** a bedcover containing padding or a filling of feathers, etc, kept in place by intersecting seams. **2** a duvet; a continental quilt. — *verb trans., intrans.* to sew (material, garments, etc) in two layers with a filling, especially with decorative seaming. [from Old French *cuilte*, from Latin *culcita*, mattress, cushion]

quilted *adj.* padded.

Quimper *or* **Quimper Corentin** POP (1990) 63 000, the manufacturing and commercial capital of Finistère department, Brittany, NW France. It lies on the estuary of the R Odet, 179km/111mi W of Rennes. It was capital of the old countship of Carnouailles. Since the 16c it has produced the pottery known as Quimper or Brittany ware. NOTABLE FEATURES Gothic Cathedral of St Corentin (13c); former bishop's palace (early 16c), now a museum.

Quin, James (1693–1766) English actor, born in London. He became established as a leading tragic actor at Lincoln's Inn Fields Theatre (1718–32) and then both at Covent Garden and Drury Lane. His last years were spent in vain rivalry with David Garrick, whose more 'natural' style superseded the declamatory tradition mastered by Quin.

quin *noun colloq.* a quintuplet.

quince *noun* the round or pear-shaped acid fruit of an Asian tree, used to make jams, jellies, etc. [originally pl. of Middle English *quyne*, quince, from Greek *melon Kydonion*, apple of Cydonia, in Crete]

quincentenary *noun* (PL. **quincentenaries**) a 500th anniversary. [from Latin *quinque*, five + CENTENARY]

quincunx *noun* **1** an arrangement of five things at the corners and centre of a square. **2** a repeating pattern based on this arrangement, eg in tree-planting. [from Latin *quincunx*, five twelfths]

quinine *noun Medicine* a bitter-tasting alkaloid drug, obtained from cinchona bark, that has antipyretic (fever-reducing) and analgesic properties, and was formerly widely used to treat malaria. It has now been largely superseded by less toxic drugs. [from Spanish *quina*, cinchona bark]

Quinnipiac see NEW HAVEN.

quinoa *noun* **1** a S American plant with edible seeds and leaves. **2** a rice-like grain consisting of the seeds of this plant. [from Spanish *quínoa*, from Quechua *kinua*]

quinoline *noun Chem.* an aromatic nitrogen compound, formerly obtained from quinine, consisting of an oily colourless liquid that is soluble in water and used in the manufacture of dyes and drugs.

Quinquagesima *noun* in the Christian calendar, the Sunday before Lent. [from Latin *quinquagesima*, fiftieth (day before Easter Day)]

quinquennial *adj.* **1** lasting five years. **2** occurring every five years. [from Latin *quinque*, five + *annus*, year]

quinquennially *adv.* every five years.

quinquereme *noun colloq.* a galley of the ancient world with five oarsmen to each oar, or five banks of oars. [from Latin *quinque*, five + *remus*, oar]

quinsy *noun* inflammation of the throat with an abscess on the tonsils. [from Latin *quinancia*, from Greek *kynanche*, 'throttle-dog', from *kyon*, dog + *anchein*, to strangle]

quintal *noun* **1** a metric unit of weight equal to 100kg. **2** formerly a hundredweight, 112 lbs. [from Arabic *qintar*, from Latin *centum*, 100]

quintessence *noun* **1** the central, essential nature of something. **2** a perfect example or embodiment of something. **3** old use the purest, most concentrated extract of a substance. [from Latin *quinta essentia*, fifth essence]

quintessential *adj.* central, essential.

quintessentially *adv.* centrally, essentially.

quintet *or* **quintette** *noun* **1** an ensemble of five singers or instrumental players. **2** a piece of music for five such performers. **3** any group or set of five. [from Italian *quintetto*, from Latin *quintus*, five]

Quintin a male first name. [from the Roman name *Quintus*, fifth]

quintuple — *verb trans., intrans.* to multiply by five or increase fivefold. — *adj.* **1** five times as many or much. **2** composed of five parts. — *noun* a quintuple number or amount. [from Latin *quintuplus*, fivefold]

quintuplet *noun* one of five children born to a mother at one birth.

quip — *noun* a witty remark. — *verb* (**quipped**, **quipping**) **1** *intrans.* to make a quip or quips. **2** *trans.* to say in jest. [perhaps from Latin *quippe*, to be sure]

quipu *noun* a device consisting of a complex system of knotted cords of various lengths, shapes, and colours, used by the Peruvian Incas as an accounting system for keeping detailed records, such as census information, and for sending messages. [from Quechua *quipu*, knot]

quire *noun* **1** a paper measure, 25 (formerly 24) sheets. **2** old use a set of folded sheets fitting inside one another for binding into book form. [from Old French *quaier*, from Latin *quattuor*, four]

Quirigua the ruins of a Maya city, dating from 600–900, in a 30ha forest preserve in E Guatemala. The ruins are notable for their sandstone stelae (one is 11m tall), altars, and animal carvings. It is a World Heritage site.

Quirk, Sir (Charles) Randolph (1920–) British grammarian and writer on the English language, born on the Isle of Man. He was Professor of English Language at University College (1960–81), where he also directed the Survey of English Usage. Major grammars in which he was involved are *A Grammar of Contemporary English* (1972) and *A Comprehensive Grammar of the English Language* (1985). He was Vice-Chancellor of London University (1981–5) and President of the British Academy (1985–9).

quirk *noun* **1** an odd habit, mannerism, or aspect of personality that someone has. **2** an odd twist in affairs or turn of events; a strange coincidence: *quirks of fate*.

quirky *adj.* (**quirkier**, **quirkiest**) odd, tricky.

Quisling, Vidkun (Abraham Lauritz Jonsson) (1887–1945) Norwegian diplomat and fascist leader, born in Fyresdal. He was Defence Minister in Norway (1931–2), founded the *Nasjonal Samling* (National Unity) in imitation of the German National Socialist Party (1933), and became a puppet Prime Minister in occupied Norway. In May 1945 he gave himself up and was executed.

quisling *noun* a traitor or collaborator. [named after Vidkun Quisling]

quit — *verb* (**quitting**; PAST TENSE AND PAST PARTICIPLE **quitted**, **quit**) **1** to leave (a place, etc). **2** *trans., intrans.* to leave, give up or resign (a job). **3** *colloq. esp. North Amer., esp. US* to cease (something, or doing something): *quit that racket.* **4** *trans., intrans. said of a tenant* to move out of (rented premises). — *adj.* (**quit of something**) free of it; rid of it. [from Old French *quiter*, from Latin *quietare*, to pay]

quitch *noun* couch grass. [from Anglo-Saxon *cwice*]

quite *adv.* **1** completely; entirely: *don't quite understand / not quite clear.* **2** to a high degree: *quite exceptional.* **3** rather; fairly; to some, or a limited, degree: *quite promising / quite a nice day / quite enjoyed it.* **4** used in reply I agree, see your point, etc.
— **quite a .. or some ...** a striking, impressive, daunting, challenging: *that's quite a task / some task you have there.*

quite so I agree; you're right.

quite something something impressive. [variant of QUIT]

Quit India Movement a campaign launched (Aug 1942) by the Indian National Congress that called for immediate independence from Britain and threatened mass non-violent struggle if its demands were not met. Mahatma Gandhi and other Congress leaders were arrested, and the movement quickly suppressed.

Quito POP (1990) 1.4m, the capital of Ecuador. The city is situated in the Andean Sierra in the N central part of the country, at the E foot of Pichincha Volcano. It stands at an altitude of 2 850m, giving it a temperate climate. HISTORY former Inca capital; captured by the Spanish in 1533. NOTABLE FEATURES the old city, designated a World Heritage Site; cathedral; Archbishop's Palace; Government Palace; Parque Alameda (with observatory); School of Fine Arts; Church and Monastery of San Francisco (1535); Church and Monastery of La Merced (with twin clock to London's Big Ben, 1817).

quits *adj. colloq.* even with one another; on an equal footing.
— **call it quits** to agree to stop a quarrel or dispute, acknowledging that the outcome is even.

quittance *noun* a person's release from debt or other obligation, or a document acknowledging this.

quitter *noun colloq.* **1** someone who gives up too easily. **2** a shirker.

quiver[1] — *verb intrans.* (**quivered**, **quivering**) to shake or tremble slightly; to shiver. — *noun* a tremble or shiver. [perhaps from older meaning *quiver*, nimble]

quiver[2] *noun* a long narrow case for carrying arrows in. [from Old French *cuivre*]

quixotic *adj.* **1** absurdly generous or chivalrous. **2** unrealistically romantic or idealistic. [from Don Quixote, hero of a romance by the Spanish writer Cervantes]

quiz — *noun* (PL. **quizzes**) **1** an entertainment, eg on radio or television, in which the knowledge of a panel of contestants is tested. **2** any series of questions as a test of general or specialized knowledge. **3** an interrogation. — *verb* (**quizzed**, **quizzing**) to question; to interrogate.

quizmaster *noun* the question master in a television quiz, etc.

quizzical *adj., said of a look, expression, etc* mocking; questioning; amused.

quizzically *adv.* in a quizzical way.

Qumran, Community of an exclusive Jewish sect (c.2c BC–1c AD) located near the NW corner of the Dead Sea, apparently closely related to the Essene sect mentioned by Josephus. They opposed the Hasmonean high priesthood of the 2c BC, and considered themselves (kept pure by strict legal observance and community discipline) to be the true Israel awaiting God's new kingdom. They were destroyed during the Jewish revolt of AD 66–70, but many of their writings were discovered in 1947 as part of the Dead Sea Scrolls.

quod *noun slang* jail; prison.

quoin *noun* **1** the angle of a building. **2** a cornerstone. **3** a wedge, eg *Printing* for locking type into a frame. [variant of *coin*]

quoit *noun* **1** a ring of metal, rubber, or rope used in the game of quoits. **2** (**quoits**) a game in which such rings are thrown at pegs, with the aim of encircling them.

quondam *adj.* former: *his quondam secretary.* [from Latin *quondam*, formerly]

quorate *said of a meeting, etc* attended by enough people to amount to a quorum.

Quorn *noun trademark* a fibrous vegetable protein made from microscopic plant filaments, used as a low-calorie and cholesterol-free meat substitute in cooking.

quorum *noun* (PL. **quorums**) the minimum number of members who must be present at a meeting for its business to be valid. [from Latin *quorum*, of whom]

quota *noun* **1** a total number or quantity that is permitted or required. **2** someone's allocated share, eg of work. [from Latin *quotus*, of what number]

quotable *adj.* worth quoting.

quotation *noun* **1** something quoted. **2** the act of quoting. **3** an estimated price for a job submitted by a contractor to a client.

quotation mark each of a pair of punctuation marks (" " or ' ') used to show the beginning and end of a quotation, or on either side of a word or phrase on which attention is focused for some reason.

quote — *verb* **1** *trans., intrans.* to repeat the exact words of: *quote Milton, a poem, from a speech, etc.* **2** to refer to (a law, etc) as authority or support. **3** *trans., intrans.* (**quote for something**) *said of a contractor* to submit (a price) for a particular job. — *noun* **1** a quotation. **2** a price quoted. **3** (**quotes**) quotation marks. — *interj. colloq.* used in speech to indicate that one is quoting: *her quote 'reluctance' unquote.* [from Latin *quotare*, to mark passages with numbers]

quoth *verb old use* said: *quoth she, he, I.* [from Anglo-Saxon *cwæth*]

quotidian *adj.* everyday; commonplace. **1** daily. **2** *said of a fever* recurring daily. [from Latin *quotidianus*, daily]

quotient *noun* the number of times one number is contained in another, found by dividing the latter by the former. [from Latin *quotiens*, how often?]

Qur'an *or* **Quran** same as KORAN.

Qusayr Amra *or* **Quseir Amra** an Arab palace in Jordan, built in c.715. A hemispherical fresco, showing stars and constellations, is painted in a dome in the palace. It is a World Heritage site.

Qutb Minar *or* **Kutab Minar** a city landmark in Delhi, India. It was built in 1199 as a Muslim tower of victory, and is 72.5m high.

q.v. *or* **qv**. *abbrev. quod vide* (Latin), which see, see this word (used to refer a reader from a word used in a dictionary or encyclopedia text, etc to the entry dealing with it).

QwaQwa POP (1991) 314 000, a national state or non-independent black homeland in South Africa. It achieved self-governing status in 1974.

qwerty *noun* the standard arrangement of keys on a typewriter or keyboard designed for English-language users, with the letters q w e r t y, in that order, at the top left of the letters section of the keyboard.

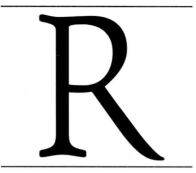

R¹ *or* **r** *noun* (PL. **Rs**, **R's**, **r's**) the eighteenth letter of the English alphabet.
— **the three Rs** reading, writing, and arithmetic, regarded as the three most important skills to be taught in primary school.

R² *abbrev.* **1** *Regina* (Latin), Queen. **2** *Rex* (Latin), King. **3** River. **4** *Chess* rook.

r *abbrev.* **1** radius. **2** recto. **3** right.

RA *abbrev.* **1** *Brit.* Royal Academy or Academician. **2** Rear Admiral.

Ra *symbol Chem.* radium.

RAAF *abbrev.* Royal Australian Air Force.

Rab, ancient **Arba** POP (1989e) 9 000, an island in the Adriatic Sea, off the coast of W Croatia. It became a leading resort island in the 1950s and is noted for its fruit and wine.

Rabat POP (1990e) 1.5m, the capital of Morocco, 90km/56mi NE of Casablanca. It is situated at the mouth of the Bou Regreg. Rabat is one of Morocco's four imperial cities. HISTORY originally a fortified monastery; the city was founded in the 12c; French colonialists established a Residency-General in 1912. NOTABLE FEATURES Mausoleum of Muhammad V; Hassan Tower; Chella Fortress (14c); Arts Museum; Archaeological Museum.

rabbet — *noun* a groove cut along the edge of a piece of wood, etc, usually to join with a tongue or projection in a matching piece. — *verb* (**rabbeted**, **rabbeting**) **1** to cut a rabbet in. **2** to join by a rabbet. [from Old French *rabattre*, to beat down]

rabbi *noun* **1** a Jewish religious leader. **2** a Jewish scholar or teacher of the law. [from Hebrew *rabbi*, my master]

rabbinical *adj.* relating to the rabbis, or their teachings and writings.

rabbit — *noun* **1** any of various herbivorous mammals belonging to the same family (Leporidae) as the hare, native to SW Europe and NW Africa, but now distributed worldwide. Rabbits are smaller than hares, and have greyish-brown fur, long ears, prominent eyes, and a very short tail, upturned at the tip and white below. **2** *Brit. colloq.* a poor performer in any sport or game. — *verb intrans.* (**rabbited**, **rabbiting**) **1** to hunt rabbits. **2** (**rabbit on**, **away**, *etc*) *colloq.* to talk at great length; to chatter idly. [from Middle English *rabet*]
◇ Rabbits, which are noted for their prolific breeding habits, are found mainly in grassland or open woodland, and differ from hares in that they live together in large numbers in extensive underground burrows, emerging at dawn and dusk to feed on grass and other plants. In areas where they are not disturbed they also feed during the daytime. The wild rabbit has become a pest in many parts of the world, destroying cereal crops, roots, and young trees. During the 1950s

the disease myxomatosis greatly reduced the rabbit populations of Europe, but their numbers have now increased again, despite recurring localized strains of the disease. Domesticated rabbits, which are popular pets, are descended from wild rabbits, and vary widely in size, shape, and fur colour.

rabbit punch a sharp blow on the back of the neck.

rabbit warren a system of burrows in which wild rabbits live.

rabble *noun* **1** a noisy disorderly crowd. **2** (**the rabble**) the lowest class of people. [from Middle English]

rabble-rouser *noun* a person who makes speeches, especially calling for social or political change, which are meant to arouse feelings of anger and violence in those listening.

rabble-rousing — *adj.* characteristic of a rabble-rouser. — *noun* the language and tactics of a rabble-rouser.

Rabelais, François (c.1494–c.1553) French satirist, physician, and humanist, born near Chinon. After a period with a Franciscan order, he studied medicine at Montpellier, and became a physician in Lyons. He then wrote the series of books for which he is best known, beginning with the comic and satirical *Pantagruel* (1532) and *Gargantua* (1534), published under his pseudonym. Both were successful, though condemned by the Church for their unorthodox ideas and mockery of religious practices. In 1546 he published his *Tiers Livre* (Third Book, 1546) under his own name, which was also condemned, and he fled to Metz. He later published a *Quart Livre* (Fourth Book, 1552), and there is also a *Cinquième Livre* (Fifth Book, 1564), published after his death, whose authorship is uncertain.

Rabelaisian *adj.* relating to or characteristic of the works of François Rabelais, especially in being satirical and coarsely humorous.

Rabi, Isidor Isaac (1898–1988) Austrian–US physicist, born in Rymanow. Professor at Columbia University, he developed a method for accurately determining the magnetic moments of fundamental particles, and was awarded the 1944 Nobel Prize for Physics. His work in defining the properties of atoms and nuclei led to the inventions of the laser and atomic clock.

rabid *adj.* **1** *said of dogs, etc* suffering from rabies. **2** fanatical; unreasoning. [from Latin *rabidus*]

rabidity *noun* being rabid.

rabidly *adv.* as if rabid, madly.

rabidness *noun* being rabid.

rabies *noun* a disease of the nervous system that causes madness and usually death, and which is transmitted by the bite of an infected animal. [from Latin *rabere*, to rave]

RAC *abbrev. Brit.* Royal Automobile Club, a British organization which helps drivers with breakdowns or technical problems, gives travel information, etc. See also AA.

raccoon *or* **racoon** *noun* any of seven species of solitary nocturnal mammal, about the size of a cat, found in N and Central America, with dense greyish fur, characteristic black patches around the eyes, and black rings on the tail. It feeds on earthworms, insects, frogs, crayfish, shellfish, nuts, and seeds, and will also raid dustbins. Its coat is highly prized by the fur trade. [a Native American name]

race¹ — *noun* **1** a contest of speed between runners, horses, cars, etc. **2** (**races**) a series of such contests over a fixed course, especially for horses or dogs. **3** any contest or rivalry, especially to be the first to do or get something. **4** a strong or rapid current of water in the sea or a river. **5** a channel conveying water to and from a mill wheel. **6** a groove in which something, eg a ball-bearing, moves or slides. — *verb intrans.* **1** to take part in a race. **2** to have a race with (someone). **3** to enter (a horse, car, etc) in a race. **4** (**race about** *or* **along** *or* **around**) to run or move quickly and energetically. **5** *trans., intrans.* to move or cause to move more quickly than usual. **6** *intrans.* to own racehorses, or watch horse-racing as a hobby. [from Norse *ras*]

race² *noun* **1** a major division of mankind having a particular set of physical characteristics, such as size, hair type, or skin colour. **2** a tribe, nation, or other group of people thought of as distinct from others. **3** human beings as a group: *the human race.* **4** a group of animals or plants within a species, which have characteristics which make them distinct from other members of that species. See also RACIAL. [from Italian *razza*]

racecard *noun* a list of all the competitors and races at a race meeting.

racecourse *or* **racetrack** *noun* a course or track used for racing horses, cars, bicycles, runners, etc.

racehorse *noun* a horse bred and used for racing.

raceme *noun Bot.* a flower-head consisting of individual flowers attached to a long stem by means of short stalks, the youngest flowers being at the tip of the stem and the oldest ones near its base, eg bluebell, lupin. [from Latin *racemus*, bunch of grapes]

race meeting a series of horse races taking place over the same course and on the same day.

racer *noun colloq.* a bicycle or horse used for racing.

race relations social relations between people of different races in the same community or country.

race riot a riot caused by hostility between people of different races or alleged discrimination against people of a particular race.

Rachel 1 a biblical character, daughter of Laban and wife of Jacob. Jacob worked seven years to earn Rachel as his wife, but was tricked into taking her elder sister Leah, and had to work another seven for Rachel (Genesis 29). At first Rachel was barren, but God gave her a child, Joseph (Genesis 30.24); she died giving birth to Benjamin (Genesis 35.19). 2 a female first name. [from Hebrew, = ewe]

rachis *or* **rhachis** *noun* 1 *Bot.* the main axis of a compound leaf or a flower-head. 2 *Zool.* the main axis or shaft of a feather. [from Greek *rhachis*, spine]

Rachmaninov *or* **Rakhmaninov, Sergei Vasilyevich** (1873–1943) Russian composer and pianist, born in Nijni-Novgorod. He won the gold medal for composition in Moscow, travelled all over Europe on concert tours, then fled from the Russian Revolution and settled in the USA (1918). He wrote operas, orchestral works, and songs, but is best known for his piano music, which includes four concertos, the popular *Prelude in C Sharp Minor*, and his last major work, the *Rhapsody on a Theme of Paganini* (1934) for piano and orchestra.

racial *adj.* 1 relating to a particular race. 2 based on race.

racialism *or* **racism** *noun* 1 a belief that a particular race is inherently superior to others. 2 abusive, oppressive behaviour, discrimination, and prejudice caused by such a belief.

racially *adv.* in a racial way.

racily *adv.* in a racy way.

Racine, Jean (Baptiste) (1639–99) French dramatic poet, born at La Ferté-Milon, A master of tragic pathos, his major verse tragedies include *Andromaque* (1667) and *Phèdre* (1677), and he later wrote religious plays on Old Testament subjects (eg *Esther*, 1689).

raciness *noun* being racy.

racing *noun* the sport or practice of using animals (such as horses or dogs) or vehicles in contests of speed.

racist *or* **racialist** — *noun* a person who practises or supports racism. — *adj.* relating to or characteristic of racism.

rack¹ — *noun* 1 a framework with rails, shelves, hooks, etc for holding or storing things. 2 a framework for holding hay, etc from which livestock can feed. 3 a bar with teeth which connect with teeth on a cogwheel or pinion to change the position of something, or to convert linear motion into rotary motion or vice versa. 4 *Hist.* an instrument for torturing people by stretching their bodies. — *verb* 1 to cause pain or suffering to: *be racked with guilt.* 2 to put in a rack. 3 *Hist.* to torture on a rack. — **rack one's brains** to think as hard as one can. [from Middle English *rakke*]

rack² — **go to rack and ruin** to get into a state of neglect and decay. [from Anglo-Saxon *wræc*, misery]

rack³ *verb* to draw off (wine or beer) from its sediment. [from Provençal *raca*, dregs]

rack⁴ *noun* a joint of meat, especially of lamb, including the neck and front ribs.

racket¹ *or* **racquet** *noun* a wooden or metal oval frame with catgut or nylon strings stretched across it, used for playing tennis, badminton, squash, etc. [from French *raquette*]

racket² *noun* 1 a loud confused noise or disturbance; din. 2 a fraudulent or illegal means of making money. 3 *slang* a job or occupation.

racketeer — *noun* a person who makes money in some illegal way, often by threats of violence. — *verb intrans.* to make money as a racketeer.

racketeering *noun* operating a racket.

rackets *sing. noun* a ball game for two or four players played using rackets in a court with four walls.

Rackham, Arthur (1867–1939) English artist, born in London. A water-colourist and book illustrator, he was well known for his typically Romantic and grotesque pictures in books of fairy tales, including *Peter Pan* (1906) and his own *The Arthur Rackham Fairy Book* (1933).

rack railway a mountain railway with a toothed rack which engages with the cogged wheels of the locomotive.

rack rent an excessive or unreasonably high rent.

raconteur *noun* a person who tells anecdotes in an amusing or entertaining way. [from French *raconteur*]

racoon see RACCOON.

racquet see RACKET¹.

racy *adj.* (**racier**, **raciest**) 1 lively or spirited. 2 slightly indecent; risqué.

rad *noun Physics* the unit formerly used to measure the amount of ionizing radiation absorbed, equal to 0.01 joules per kilogram of absorbing material. It has now been replaced by the gray in SI units.

RADA *abbrev.* Royal Academy of Dramatic Art.

radar *noun* 1 *Radio* a system for detecting the presence, position, speed, and direction of movement of distant objects by transmitting short pulses of high-frequency radio waves from a rotating aerial, and detecting the signals reflected back from the surface of any object in their path, which produce 'blips' of light on a screen. Radar is widely used in air and sea navigation (especially under conditions of poor visibility, eg darkness or fog), for air traffic control at airports, weather forecasting, and in warfare to detect enemy aircraft. 2 the equipment for sending out and receiving such radio waves. [from *radio detection and ranging*]

radar astronomy *Astron.* the use of pulsed radio signals to measure the distances and map the surfaces of objects in the solar system, and to determine their speed of rotation.

radar trap a device using radar which allows the police to detect vehicles travelling faster than the speed limit.

Radcliffe, Ann, *née* Ward (1764–1823) English novelist, born in London. She lived a retired life, and became well known for her Gothic novels, notably *The Romance of the Forest* (1791), *The Mysteries of Udolpho* (1794), and *The Italian* (1797). Her contemporary reputation was considerable, and she influenced Byron, Percy Bysshe Shelley, and others, many of whom imitated her 'gothick romances'.

Radcliffe-Brown, A(lfred) R(eginald) (1881–1955) English anthropologist, born in Birmingham. He was Professor of Social Anthropology at Cape Town (1920), Sydney (1925), Chicago (1931), and Oxford (1937). He did field studies in the Andaman Islands and in Australia, and published the influential monographs *The Andaman Islanders* (1922) and *The Social Organization of Australian Tribes* (1930). His influence was based mainly on his development of Emile Durkheim's theories and the foundation of 'structural-functionalism'.

raddled *adj.* worn out and haggard-looking through debauchery. [from *raddle*, red ochre]

Radek, Karl Bernhardovich, originally **Sobelsohn** (1885–c.1939) Soviet revolutionary and politician, born in Lvov. He became a journalist, organized the German communists during their revolution (1918), and was imprisoned

(1919). On his return to the Soviet Union, he became a leading member of the Communist International, but his growing distrust of extremist tactics caused respect for him to wane. He was charged as a Trotsky supporter and expelled from the Party (1927–30). In 1937 he fell victim to one of Stalin's show trials for treason — he was sentenced to 10 years' imprisonment in a labour camp, where he died.

radial — *adj.* 1 *said of lines* spreading out from the centre of a circle, like rays. 2 of or relating to rays, a radius, or radii. 3 along or in the direction of a radius or radii. 4 *Anat.* of the radius. — *noun* 1 (*in full* **radial-ply tyre**) a tyre which has fabric cords laid at a right angle to the centre of the tread, allowing the walls to be flexible. See also CROSS-PLY. 2 *Anat.* a radial artery or nerve. [from Latin *radius*, spoke, ray]

radially *adv.* in the manner of radii or rays; outward from the centre.

radial symmetry the arrangement of parts in an object or living organism such that a line drawn through its centre in any direction produces two halves that are mirror images of each other, eg the arrangement of parts in a jellyfish, or the stems and roots of plants.

radian *noun Maths.* (ABBREV. **rad**) the SI unit of plane angular measurement, defined as the angle that is made at the centre of a circle by an arc (a segment of the circumference) whose length is equal to the radius of the circle. One radian is approximately 57°, and there are 2π radians in a circle. [from Latin *radius*, spoke, ray]

radiance *noun* 1 being radiant. 2 a measure of the amount of electromagnetic radiation being transmitted from or to a point on a surface.

radiant — *adj.* 1 emitting electromagnetic radiation, eg rays of light or heat. 2 glowing or shining. 3 beaming with abundant joy, love, hope, or health. 4 transmitted by or as radiation. — *noun* 1 a point or object which emits electromagnetic radiation, eg light or heat. 2 *Astron.* the point in the sky from which meteors appear to radiate outward during a meteor shower. [from Latin *radiare*, to radiate]

radiant energy energy given out as electromagnetic radiation.

radiant heat heat transmitted by electromagnetic radiation.

radiantly *adv.* in a radiant way.

radiate — *verb* 1 *trans., intrans.* to send out rays of (light, heat, electromagnetic radiation, etc). 2 *intrans. said of light, heat, radiation, etc* to be emitted in rays. 3 to show a lot of (happiness, good health, etc) clearly: *radiate vitality.* 4 *trans., intrans.* to spread or cause to spread out from a central point as radii. — *adj.* having rays, radii, or a radial structure. [from Latin *radiare*, to shine]

radiation *noun* 1 energy that is emitted from a source and travels in the form of waves or particles (photons) through a medium, eg air or a vacuum. The term usually refers to electromagnetic radiation, eg radio waves, microwaves, infrared, visible light, ultraviolet, X-rays. See also ELECTROMAGNETIC RADIATION. 2 a stream of particles, eg alpha particles, beta particles, electrons, neutrons, etc, emitted by a radioactive substance. 3 the act of radiating.

radiation sickness an illness caused by exposure to high levels of radiation, eg nuclear fallout, or to relatively low levels over a long period.
◇ Symptoms of radiation sickness may include diarrhoea, vomiting, loss of hair, internal bleeding, bone-marrow damage, a reduction in fertility, and a significantly increased risk of cancer, leukaemia, and birth defects. High doses irreversibly damage the central nervous system, causing death within hours.

radiator *noun* 1 an apparatus for heating, consisting of a series of pipes through which hot water (or hot oil) is circulated. **2** an apparatus for heating in which wires are made hot by electricity. **3** an apparatus for cooling an internal combustion engine, eg in a car, consisting of a series of tubes which water passes through, and a fan.

radical — *adj.* **1** concerning or relating to the basic nature of something; fundamental. **2** far-reaching; thoroughgoing: *radical changes*. **3** in favour of or tending to produce thoroughgoing or extreme political and social reforms. **4** of a political group or party in favour of extreme reforms. **5** *Bot.* of or relating to the root of a plant. **6** *Maths.* relating to the root of a number. **7** *Linguistics* relating to the roots of words. — *noun* **1** a person who is a member of a radical political group, or who holds radical political views. **2** *Chem.* within a molecule, a group of atoms which remains unchanged during a series of chemical reactions, but is normally incapable of independent existence. **3** *Maths.* the root of a number, usually denoted by the radical sign $\sqrt{}$. **4** *Linguistics* the root of a word. [from Latin *radix*, root]

radicalism *noun* **1** the beliefs and opinions of radicals, especially a set of ideas which advocates more substantial social and political change than is supported by the political mainstream. **2** extreme thoroughness.

radically *adv.* in a radical way.

radicalness *noun* being radical.

radical sign the sign $\sqrt{}$, showing a square root.

radicchio *noun* (PL. **radicchios**) a purple-leaved variety of chicory, used raw in salads. [from Italian *radicchio*]

radicle *noun* **1** *Bot.* the part of a plant embryo which develops into the root. **2** *Anat.* the root-like origin of a vein or nerve. [from Latin *radicula*, small root]

radii see RADIUS.

radio — *noun* (PL. **radios**) **1** the use of radio waves (a form of electromagetic radiation) to transmit and receive information such as television or radio programmes, telecommunications, and computer data, without connecting wires. **2** a wireless device that receives, and may also transmit, information in this manner. **3** a message or broadcast that is transmitted in this manner. — *adj.* **1** of or for transmitting or transmitted by radio. **2** controlled by radio. — *verb* (**radios**, **radioed**) **1** to send (a message) to (someone) by radio. **2** *intrans.* to broadcast or communicate by radio. [from Latin *radius*, spoke, ray]

◇ In a *radio transmitter*, sound waves are converted into electrical signals by means of a microphone. The signal is then amplified and made to modulate (vary) a *carrier wave* of high frequency produced by an oscillator. In amplitude modulation (AM), used for long- and medium-wave broadcasts, the signal modulates the amplitude of the carrier wave. In frequency modulation (FM), used for VHF broadcasts, the signal modulates the frequency of the carrier wave. Each radio station has its own specific carrier-wave frequency, and the modulated carrier wave is broadcast from a *transmitter aerial* into the atmosphere or into space.

In a *radio receiver*, modulated radio waves are picked up by a receiving aerial or *antenna*, which forms part of a circuit that can be tuned to select a particular frequency of carrier wave (corresponding to a particular radio station). The electrical signal is then separated from the carrier wave by a *demodulator*, and amplified and fed to a loudspeaker, which produces an almost exact replica of the original sound.

Radio waves with very short wavelengths, eg VHF waves used for television broadcasting, pass through the atmosphere into space, and such broadcasts can only be transmitted over long distances by reflecting them back to Earth by means of artificial satellites. Radio waves of longer wavelength are reflected back to Earth by the ionosphere, and can be transmitted around the world by bouncing them off this layer of the atmosphere.

radio- *combining form* forming words denoting: **1** radio or broadcasting. **2** radioactivity. **3** rays or radiation.

radioactive *adj.* relating to or affected by radioactivity.

radioactive decay *Physics* the spontaneous decay of the nucleus of an atom, which results in the emission of alpha particles, beta particles, or gamma rays.

radioactive tracer *Biochem.* a radioactive isotope of a chemical element that is deliberately substituted for one of the atoms in a chemical compound in order to 'tag' it. In this way the path of a particular atom through a whole series of reactions can be followed. Radioactive tracers are widely used in scientific and medical research.

radioactive waste. See NUCLEAR WASTE.

radioactivity *noun* **1** the spontaneous disintegration of the nuclei of certain atoms, accompanied by the emission of alpha particles, beta particles, or gamma rays. Radioactivity is measured in units called becquerels. **2** the subatomic particles or radiation emitted during this process.

Radioactivity Units			
Name	Definition	Unit	Old unit
activity	rate of disintegrations	Bq	Ci (curie)
absorbed dose	energy deposited in object, divided by mass of object	Gy	rad
dose equivalent	absorbed dose × RBE	Sv	rem

RBE	Radiation
20	alpha
10	neutron
1	beta, gamma, X-ray

radio astronomy the exploration of the Universe by studying the radio waves emitted or reflected by stars (especially the Sun), planets (especially Jupiter), pulsars, quasars, interstellar gas, radio galaxies, etc, as well as the cosmic background radiation of the Universe itself.

radiobiology *noun Biol.* the branch of biology concerned with the study of the effect of radiation and radioactive materials on living matter.

radiocarbon *noun* a radioactive isotope of carbon, especially carbon-14.

radiocarbon dating same as CARBON DATING.

radiochemistry *noun Chem.* the branch of chemistry concerned with the study of radioactive elements and their compounds, including their preparation, properties, and practical uses.

radio frequency a frequency of electromagnetic waves used for radio and television broadcasting.

radio galaxy *Astron.* a galaxy that is an intense source of cosmic radio waves, about one galaxy in a million. Investigation of radio galaxies led directly to the discovery of quasars.

radiogram *noun* **1** same as RADIOGRAPH. **2** *old use* an apparatus consisting of a radio and record-player.

radiograph *noun* a photograph taken using a form of radiation other than light, such as X-rays or gamma rays, especially of the inside of the body.

radiographer *noun* a technician involved in radiology, eg in taking radiographs or giving radiotherapy.

radiography *noun Medicine* the technique of examining the interior of the body by means of recorded images, known as *radiographs*, produced by X-rays on photographic film. It is widely used in medicine and dentistry, eg to detect tumours, broken bones, kidney stones, and dental caries (tooth decay).

radioisotope *noun Physics* a naturally occurring or synthetic radioactive isotope of a chemical element, eg tritium. Radioisotopes are used in radiotherapy to treat cancer, as radioactive tracers in scientific research, and as long-term power sources in spacecraft and satellites.

radiological *adj.* **1** relating to or involving radiology. **2** involving radioactive materials.

radiologist *noun* a specialist in the use of X-rays and in methods of imaging the internal structure of the body for diagnosis and treatment of disease.

radiology *noun* the branch of medicine concerned with the use of radiation (eg X-rays) and radioactive isotopes to diagnose and treat diseases.

radio-pager *noun* a very small radio receiver which emits a bleeping sound in response to a signal, used for paging people.

radio-paging *noun* paging by means of a radio-pager.

radiophonic *adj.* relating to sound produced electronically. [from RADIO- + Greek *phone*, sound]

radioscopic *adj.* relating to or involving radioscopy.

radioscopy *noun* the examination of the inside of the body, or of opaque objects, using X-rays.

radio telephone a telephone which works by radio waves, used especially in cars and other vehicles.

radio telescope a large usually dish-shaped aerial, together with amplifiers and recording equipment, that is used to study distant stars, galaxies, etc, by detecting the radio waves they emit. Many celestial bodies are so faint or distant that they can only be detected by radio telescope. ◇ Most radio telescopes consist of a large hollow metal or mesh-covered parabolic dish that reflects weak radio signals from space on to a receiver or *antenna* in the centre of the dish, which then sends the signals to an amplifier. Usually the dish can be pointed in any direction, and the largest 'steerable' dish, at Effelsberg, Germany, is 100m in diameter. The largest radio telescope in the world has a dish 305m in diameter, formed by hanging a wire-mesh reflector over a natural hollow in Arecibo, Puerto Rico. Several radio telescopes can be used together, forming an *array*.

radiotherapy *noun* the treatment of disease, especially cancer, by X-rays and other forms of radiation.

radio wave *Physics* an electromagnetic wave that has a low frequency and a long wavelength (in the range of about 1mm to 10^4m), widely used for communication.

radish *noun* a plant of the mustard family, with pungent-tasting, red-skinned white roots, which are eaten raw in salads. [from Anglo-Saxon *rædic*, from Latin *radix*, root]

radium *noun Chem.* (SYMBOL **Ra**, ATOMIC NUMBER **88**) a silvery-white highly toxic radioactive metal obtained from uranium ores, especially pitchblende. The radioactive isotope radium-226 is used in radiotherapy to treat cancer, and as a neutron source. Radium compounds are used in luminous paints. [from Latin *radius*, ray]

radius *noun* (PL. **radii**, **radiuses**) **1** a straight line running from the centre of a circle to a point on its circumference. **2** the length of such a line. **3** a usually specified distance from a central point, thought of as limiting an area: *all the houses within a radius of 10km.* **4** *Anat.* the shorter of the two bones in the human forearm, on the thumb side. **5** anything placed like a radius, such as a spoke in a wheel. [from Latin *radius* spoke, ray]

radon *noun Chem.* (SYMBOL **Rn**, ATOMIC NUMBER **86**) a highly toxic colourless radioactive gas that emits alpha particles and is formed by the decay of radium. It is one of the rare or noble gases, forms very few compounds, and is used in radiotherapy to treat cancer, and as a tracer to detect leakages of radioactivity. It occurs naturally in certain areas of granite rock, which are a recognized health hazard. [from RADIUM]

Raeburn, Sir Henry (1756–1823) Scottish portrait painter, born near Edinburgh. He first produced watercolour miniatures, then worked in oils. He studied in Rome (1785–7), then settled in Edinburgh, where he painted the leading members of Edinburgh society (eg Sir Walter Scott) in a typically bold, strongly-shadowed style. Other works include *The Reverend Robert Walker Skating* (1784, National Gallery, Edinburgh).

RAEC *abbrev.* Royal Army Educational Corps.

RAF *abbrev.* Royal Air Force.

raffia *noun* ribbon-like fibre obtained from the leaves of certain palm trees, used for weaving mats, baskets, etc. [a native word from Madagascar]

raffish *adj.* slightly shady or disreputable; rakish. [related to RIFF-RAFF]

raffishly *adv.* in a raffish way.

raffishness *noun* being raffish.

raffle — *noun* a lottery, often to raise money for charity, in which certain numbered tickets win prizes. — *verb* to offer as a prize in a raffle. [from Middle English *rafle*, dice game]

Raffles, Sir (Thomas) Stamford (1781–1826) British colonial administrator, born at sea, off Port Morant, Jamaica. He became Lt-Governor of Java (1811–16), where he completely reformed the administration, but had to return home to England due to ill health. As Lieutenant-Governor of Benkoelen (1818–23), he established a settlement at Singapore.

statue of Raffles, Singapore

Rafsanjani, Ali Akbar Hashemi (1934–) Iranian politician, born in Rafsanjan. He supported Ayatollah Khomeini after the latter's exile in 1963, and became a wealthy property speculator in the 1970s. After the 1979 revolution, he helped to found the ruling Islamic Republican Party, and in 1980 was chosen as Speaker of the

Majlis (Lower House), representing the moderates who favoured improved relations with the West. A very influential figure in Iran during the 1980s, he succeeded Khomeini as President in 1989 and thereafter held more radical policies.

raft — *noun* **1** a flat structure of logs, timber, etc fastened together so as to float on water, used for transport or as a platform. **2** a flat, floating mass of ice, vegetation, etc. — *verb* **1** to transport by raft. **2** *intrans.* to travel by raft. [from Norse *raptr*, rafter]

rafter *noun* any of several sloping beams supporting a roof. [from Anglo-Saxon *ræfter*]

Raft of Medusa, The a painting by Théodore Géricault (1819, Louvre, Paris). It is a powerful depiction of the survivors of a shipwreck which had caused a political scandal in France.

rag¹ *noun* **1** a scrap of cloth, especially a piece which has been worn, or torn off old clothes. **2** (*usually* **rags**) a piece of clothing, especially when old and tattered. **3** *derog. colloq.* a newspaper.
— **lose one's rag** *slang* to lose one's temper. [from Anglo-Saxon *raggig*, shaggy]

rag² — *verb* (**ragged**, **ragging**) **1** *trans., intrans. esp. Brit.* to tease; to play rough tricks on (someone). **2** to scold. — *noun Brit.* a series of stunts and events put on by university or college students to raise money for charity: *rag week.*

rag³ *noun* a piece of ragtime music.

raga *noun* **1** a traditional pattern of notes in Hindu classical music, around which melodies can be improvised. **2** a piece of music composed around such a pattern. [from Sanskrit *raga* colour, musical tone]

ragamuffin *noun* a ragged, disreputable child. [from Middle English *Ragamoffyn*, the name of a demon in the poem *Piers Plowman* by William Langland]

rag-and-bone man *noun* a person who collects and deals in old clothes and furniture, etc.

rag-bag *noun* **1** *colloq.* a scruffy, untidy person. **2** a bag for storing rags and scraps of material.

rage — *noun* **1** violent anger, or a fit of anger. **2** violent, stormy action, eg of the wind, sea, or a battle. **3** an intense desire or passion for something. **4** a widespread, usually temporary fashion or craze. — *verb intrans.* **1** to be violently angry. **2** to speak wildly with anger or passion; to rave. **3** *said of the wind, sea, a battle, etc* to be stormy and unchecked.
— **all the rage** *colloq.* very much in fashion. [from Latin *rabies*, madness]

ragga *noun* a style of rap music influenced by dance rhythms. [from RAGAMUFFIN]

ragged *adj.* **1** *said of clothes* old, worn, and tattered. **2** dressed in old, worn, tattered clothing. **3** with a rough and irregular edge; jagged. **4** untidy; straggly.

raggedly *adv.* in a ragged way.

raggedness *noun* being ragged.

ragged Robin a wild flower with pink, ragged-edged petals.

raging *adj.* **1** that rages. **2** very angry.

Raging Bull a US film directed by Martin Scorsese (1980). The irrepressible brutality, ambition, and jealousy of a boxer, Jake La Motta (played by Robert De Niro), provides the focus for a study of the masculine ethos.

raglan *adj.* **1** *said of a sleeve* attached to a garment by two seams running diagonally from the neck to the armpit. **2** *said of a garment* having such sleeves. [named after Lord Raglan]

Raglan (of Raglan), Fitzroy James Henry Somerset, 1st Baron (1788–1855) English soldier, born in Badminton, Gloucestershire. He joined the army in 1804, fought at Waterloo (1815), in 1854 led an ill-prepared force

against the Russians in the Crimea, and saw victory at Alma. His ambiguous order led to the Charge of the Light Brigade (1854) at Balaclava. His name was given to the raglan sleeve, which dates from the 1850s.

Ragnarok in Norse mythology, the final battle between the gods and the monstrous evil forces hostile to them. Though gods and monsters die, a new world will arise, populated by the offspring of Lif and Lifthrasir, the sole survivors of the battle.

ragout *noun* a highly seasoned stew of meat and vegetables. [from French *ragoût*]

ragtime *noun* a type of jazz piano music with a highly syncopated rhythm, originated by black American musicians in the 1890s. [a contraction of *ragged time*]
◊ Ragtime was popularized by the pianist–composer Scott Joplin and his contemporaries from c.1890 up to the early years of the jazz age. While most rags were composed for piano, other famous examples include Irving Berlin's song 'Alexander's Ragtime Band', and Igor Stravinsky's *Ragtime* (1918) for 11 instruments.

rag trade the business of designing, making, and selling clothes.

ragwort *noun* a common plant with yellow flowers with ragged petals.

Rahman, Sheikh Mujibur (1920–75) Bangladeshi politician, born in Tongipara, E Bengal (now Bangladesh). He studied law and helped found the Awami League (1949). Elected to the East Pakistan Provincial Assembly in 1954, he took an oppositional role during the 1960s, and in 1966 was arrested and imprisoned for two years for provoking separatism. After he won an overall majority in the Pakistani elections of 1970, but was denied office, he launched a non-co-operation campaign which escalated into civil war and the creation of Bangladesh. He became its first Prime Minister (1972–5) and President in 1975, when he was overthrown and killed in a coup in Dacca.

Rahner, Karl (1904–84) German theologian, born in Freiburg im Breisgau. Ordained in 1932, he played a major role as consultant at the Second Vatican Council (1962–6), and was probably the most influential Roman Catholic theologian of the 20c. His lectures and prolific writings (eg *Theological Investigations*, 1961–81) maintained a dialogue between traditional dogma and contemporary existential questions, based on the principle that grace is already present in human nature.

rai *noun* a style of popular music from Algeria, blending traditional Arabic, Spanish flamenco, and Western disco rhythms. [from Arabic *ra'y*, opinion, view]

raid — *noun* **1** a sudden unexpected attack. **2** a sudden unexpected visit by the police searching for suspected criminals or illicit goods. **3** the selling of shares by a group of speculators in an attempt to lower share prices. — *verb* **1** to make a raid on. **2** *intrans.* to go on a raid. [from Anglo-Saxon *rad*, road]

raider *noun* a person that raids.

Raikes, Robert (1735–1811) English philanthropist and pioneer of the Sunday-School movement, born in Gloucester, where he succeeded his father as proprietor of the *Gloucester Journal* (1757). The misery and ignorance of many children in his native city led him in 1780 to start a Sunday School, where they might learn to read and repeat the Catechism; similar schools soon spread over England.

rail¹ — *noun* **1** a usually horizontal bar supported by vertical posts, forming a fence or barrier. **2** a horizontal bar used to hang things on. **3** either of a pair of lengths of steel forming a track for the wheels of a train. **4** the railway. — *verb* (**rail something off**) to enclose a space within a rail or rails.

— off the rails not functioning or behaving normally or properly.
[from Old French *reille*]

rail² *verb intrans.* (**rail at** *or* **against something** *or* **someone**) to complain or criticize abusively or bitterly. [from Old French *railler*, to deride]

rail³ *noun* any of various species of birds, usually living near water, with a short neck and wings and long legs, such as the corncrake and coot. [from Old French *rasle*]

railcar *noun North Amer.* **1** a railway carriage. **2** a self-propelled railway carriage.

railcard *noun* a special card, eg for students, the elderly, etc, giving the holder the right to reduced train fares.

railhead *noun* **1** a railway terminal. **2** the furthest point reached by a railway under construction.

railing *noun* **1** (*usually* **railings**) a fence or barrier. **2** material for building fences.

raillery *noun* good-humoured teasing, or an instance of this. [related to RAIL²]

railroad — *noun North Amer., esp. US* a railway. — *verb colloq.* (**railroad someone into something**) to rush them unfairly into doing something.

railway *noun* **1** a track or set of tracks formed by two parallel steel rails fixed to sleepers, for trains to run on. **2** a system of such tracks, plus all the trains, buildings, and people required for it to function. **3** a company responsible for operating such a system. **4** a similar set of tracks for a different type of vehicle: *funicular railway.*
◇ The world's first railway, linking the English towns of Stockton and Darlington, opened in 1825 and mainly transported coal and other goods. The first passenger-carrying railway became operational in 1830 between Manchester and Liverpool. From that time, railways spread rapidly across Europe and the USA, and, through colonial and trade expansion, into most other areas of the world. Most modern national railway systems are state-owned and subsidized. In an effort to counter competition from road and rail transport, new fast trains have been developed, notably in Japan and France.

raiment *noun old use, poetic* clothing. [from Old French *areer*, to array]

rain — *noun* **1** a form of precipitation consisting of water droplets that fall from the clouds. **2** (*also* **rains**) the season of heavy rainfall in tropical countries. **3** a heavy fall of something. — *verb* **1** *intrans. said of rain* to fall. **2** *intrans., trans.* to fall or cause to fall like rain: *bullets raining down on them / rain down compliments on her head.*
— be rained off *Brit., said of a sporting or other event* to be cancelled because of rain.
come rain or shine whatever the weather or circumstances.
rain cats and dogs *colloq.* to rain very hard.
right as rain *colloq.* perfectly all right or in order.
[from Anglo-Saxon *regn*]

Rainbow, The a novel by D H Lawrence (1915). It chronicles the relationships of three generations of the Brangwen family from Nottinghamshire.

rainbow *noun* **1** an arch of all the colours of the spectrum, ie red, orange, yellow, green, blue, indigo, and violet, that can be seen in the sky when falling raindrops reflect and refract sunlight that is shining from behind the observer. **2** a collection or array of bright colours.

rainbow coalition a political alliance between minority groups or parties of varying opinions.

Rainbow Snake, also called **Julunggul** in Australian aboriginal religion, the great fertility spirit, both male and female, creator and destroyer. It is associated with streams and waterholes, from which it emerges in the cre-

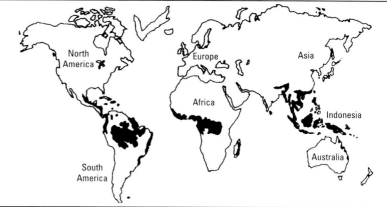
the distribution of rainforests worldwide

ation story and leaves special markings on the ground.

rainbow trout a freshwater N American and European trout.

raincoat *noun* a light waterproof coat worn to keep out the rain.

rainfall *noun* **1** the amount of rain, hail, and snow that falls in a certain place over a certain period. **2** a shower of rain.

rainforest *noun* a type of dense forest, generally dominated by tall broad-leaved evergreen trees, that usually occurs in hot humid equatorial regions (tropical rainforest), but is also found in some temperate regions with high rainfall (temperate rainforest).
◇ Temperate rainforests are found on the eastern coasts of certain continents and islands, eg Korea and Japan, whereas tropical rainforests, to which the term rainforest most commonly refers, are largely confined to Central and S America, Africa, and SE Asia.
Tropical rainforests are characterized by a great diversity of plant and animal species, and a closed canopy layer which allows little light to reach the forest floor. Some of these forests have flourished for more than 40 million years. Rainforest trees include such commercially valuable trees as mahogany and teak. Deforestation to obtain timber and to clear large areas of land for agriculture (eg cattle ranching) and industry (eg mining) is threatening the continued existence of many plant and animal species that normally inhabit rainforest. It is suggested that it may be contributing to the greenhouse effect, and could disrupt global weather patterns, which are to some extent stabilized by rainforests. Furthermore, the felling of rainforest trees leads to severe soil erosion, as the shallow and relatively infertile soils exposed by deforestation are rapidly washed away by running water.

Rainier III, properly **Rainier Louis Henri Maxence Bertrand de Grimaldi** (1923–) Prince of Monaco (1949–), born in Monaco. In 1956 he married the US film actress Grace Kelly,

whose successful career included *High Noon* (1952), *Rear Window* (1954), and *High Society* (1956). There are two daughters, Princess Caroline Louise Marguerite (1957–) and Princess Stephanie Marie Elisabeth (1965–), and a son, Prince Albert Alexandre Louis Pierre (1958–). Princess Grace died after a car accident in 1982.

Rainier, Mount a dormant volcano and the highest point in the Cascade Range, W central Washington, USA. HEIGHT 4 395m. It has the largest single-peak glacier system in the USA; there are 26 glaciers, notably Emmons (c.8km/5mi long) and Nisqually (c.6km/4mi long). It is situated in Mt Rainier National Park.

rain shadow *Meteorol.* a region on the lee side of mountains or hills that receives significantly less rainfall than land on the windward side, because prevailing winds are forced to rise, cool, and thereby lose most of their moisture by precipitation while moving across the high ground.

Rain, Steam and Speed a painting by J M W Turner (1844, National Gallery, London).

Rainwater, (**Leo**) **James** (1917–) US physicist, born in Council, Idaho. During World War II he contributed to the development of the atomic bomb. He later became professor at Columbia University, and his work led to an improved model of the nucleus, which explained for the first time the observations that some nuclei are deformed. He shared the 1975 Nobel Prize for Physics with Aage Bohr and Ben Mottelson.

rainy *adj.* (**rainier, rainiest**) **1** *said of the weather, etc* having many rain showers. **2** *said of clouds, etc* threatening rain.

rainy day a notional time of particular need in the future: *saving it for a rainy day.*

raise — *verb* **1** to move or lift to a high position or level. **2** to put in an upright or standing position. **3** to build. **4** to increase the value, amount, or strength of: *raise prices / raise one's voice.* **5** to put forward for consideration or discussion: *raise an objection.* **6** to collect, levy, or gather together. **7** to stir up or incite: *raise a protest.* **8** to bring into being; to provoke: *raise a laugh / raise the alarm.* **9** to promote to a higher rank. **10** to awaken or arouse from sleep or death. **11** to grow (vegetables, a crop, etc). **12** to bring up or rear: *raise a family.* **13** to bring to an end or remove: *raise the siege.* **14** to cause (bread or dough) to rise with yeast. **15** to establish radio contact with. **16** *Maths.* to increase (a quantity) to a given power: *3 raised to the power of 4 is 81.* **17** *Cards* to bet more than (another player). **18** *Naut.* to cause (land) to come into sight by approaching. **19** to produce a nap on (cloth) by brushing. **20** to cause (a lump, blister, etc) to form or swell. — *noun* **1** an act of raising or lifting. **2** *colloq. esp. North Amer.* an increase in salary.
— raise hell *or* **the devil** *colloq.* to make a lot of trouble.

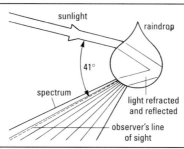
rainbow formation

raise someone's hopes to give them reason to be hopeful.

raise someone's spirits to make them more cheerful or optimistic.
[from Norse *reisa*]

raisin *noun* a dried grape. [from Old French *raisin*, grape]

raison d'être (PL. **raisons d'être**) a purpose or reason that justifies a thing's or person's existence. [French, = reason for being]

raita *noun* an Indian dish of chopped vegetables, especially cucumber, in yoghurt. [from Hindi]

Raj *noun Hist.* the British rule in India, 1858–1947. [from Sanskrit *rajan*, king]

rajah *or* **raja** *noun Hist.* an Indian king or prince.

Rajasthan POP (1991) 44m, a state in NW India. AREA 342 214sq km/132 095sq mi. It is bounded W by Pakistan. PHYSICAL DESCRIPTION crossed by numerous rivers; the Thar Desert is situated in the W; the Anavalli Range lies to the S. CAPITAL Jaipur. GOVERNMENT governed by a 200-member Legislative Assembly. ECONOMY pulses, sugar cane, oilseed, cotton; textiles; cement; glass; phosphate; silver; asbestos; copper; feldspar; limestone; salt.

rake[1] — *noun* **1** a long-handled tool with a comb-like part at one end, used for smoothing or breaking up earth, gathering leaves together, etc. **2** any tool with a similar shape or use, eg a croupier's tool for gathering money together. — *verb* **1** (**rake things up** *or* **together**) to collect, gather, or remove with, or as if with, a rake. **2** (**rake something over**) to make it smooth with a rake. **3** *intrans.* to work with a rake. **4** *trans., intrans.* (**rake through** *or* **among something**) to search it carefully. **5** to sweep gradually along the length of, especially with gunfire or one's eyes. **6** to scratch or scrape.
— **rake something in** *colloq.* to earn or acquire it in large amounts.
rake something up *colloq.* **1** to revive or uncover (something forgotten or lost): *rake up old memories.* **2** to find it, especially with difficulty. [from Anglo-Saxon *raca*]

rake[2] *noun old use* a fashionable man who lives a dissolute and immoral life. [a shortening of obsolete *rakehell*]

rake[3] *noun* **1** a sloping position, especially of a ship's funnel or mast backwards towards the stern, of a ship's bow or stern in relation to the keel, or a theatre stage. **2** the amount by which something slopes. — *verb* **1** *trans., intrans.* to set or be set at a sloping angle. **2** *intrans. said of a ship's mast or funnel* to slope backwards towards the stern. **3** *intrans. said of a ship's bow or stern* to project out beyond the keel.

rake-off *noun slang* a share of the profits, especially when dishonest or illegal.

Rake's Progress, A a series of eight paintings by William Hogarth (1733–5, Soane Museum, London).

Rake's Progress, The an opera by Igor Stravinsky (1951) with text by W H Auden. It tells of the country lad Tom Rakewell who squanders his fortune in the city, aided by his 'servant' Shadow (the Devil in disguise). Misfortunes accumulate and culminate in a contest for Tom's soul, which Tom wins by thinking of his former sweetheart Anne Trulove.

rakish *adj.* **1** *said of a ship* having a smart sleek appearance. **2** confident, adventurous, and jaunty.

rakishly *adv.* with a rakish manner.

rakishness *noun* a rakish style or manner.

Rakoczi a princely family of Hungary and Transylvania which became extinct in 1780. The most important member was Francis II (1676–1735), who in 1703 led a Hungarian revolt against Austria. He had little success but was

hailed as a patriot and a hero. His later years were spent as a Carmelite monk.

raku *noun* a type of coarse-grained, lead-glazed pottery fired at low temperature, traditionally used in Japan to make tea bowls. [from Japanese, = pleasure, enjoyment]

Raleigh *or* **Ralegh, Sir Walter** (1552–1618) English courtier, navigator, and author, born in Hayes Barton, Devon. He became prime favourite of Queen Elizabeth and was knighted in 1584, the year he sent the first of three expeditions to America, one of which brought back tobacco and potatoes. Superseded by the Earl of Essex at court, he went to Ireland, but returned and was committed to the Tower (1592) on Elizabeth's discovery of his secret affair with Bessy Throckmorton, one of her maids-of-honour. On his release, he married Bessy, led an expedition to explore the coasts of Trinidad and the Orinoco, and took part in the sack of Cadiz. His enemies turned James I against him, and he was imprisoned again in the Tower (1603), where he wrote his *History of the World* (1614), and several other works. Released in 1616, he made an unsuccessful expedition to the Orinoco in search of a gold mine. His suspended death sentence was eventually invoked by the Spanish minister in London following his attack on a Spanish town, and he was executed.

Raleigh POP (1990) 208 000, the capital of the state of North Carolina, USA, in Wake County, E central North Carolina. It was established in 1788 and named after Sir Walter Raleigh. President Andrew Johnson was born here in 1808.

rallentando — *adj., adv. Mus.* becoming gradually slower. — *noun* (PL. **rallentandos, rallentandi**) a passage to be played in this way. [from Italian *rallentando*]

rally — *verb* (**rallies, rallied**) **1** *trans., intrans.* to come or bring together again after being dispersed. **2** *trans., intrans.* to come or bring together for some common cause or action. **3** to revive (one's spirits, strength, abilities, etc) by making an effort. **4** *intrans.* to recover one's lost health, fitness, strength, etc, especially after an illness. **5** *intrans. said of share prices* to increase again after a fall. — *noun* (PL. **rallies**) **1** a reassembling of forces to make a new effort. **2** a mass meeting of people with a common cause or interest. **3** a recovering of lost health, fitness, strength, especially after an illness. **4** *Tennis* a usually long series of strokes between players before one of them finally wins the point. **5** a competition to test skill in driving, usually held on public roads.
— **rally round someone** to come together to support or help them.
[from Old French *rallier*, to rejoin]

rallycross *noun* motor racing over a course made up of both proper roads and rough ground.

Ralph, in full **Ralph Rover** the resourceful companion to Jack in R M Ballantyne's *The Coral Island*.

Ralph a male first name. [from Germanic, from *rad*, counsel + *wulf*, wolf]

RAM *abbrev.* **1** *Comput.* random access memory, a temporary memory available to the user which allows programs to be loaded and run, and data to be changed. **2** Royal Academy of Music.

ram — *noun* **1** an uncastrated male sheep or goat. **2** (**the Ram**) the constellation Aries. **3** a battering-ram. **4** a pointed device on a warship's prow, for making holes in enemy ships. **5** the falling weight of a pile-driver. **6** a piston or plunger operated by hydraulic or other power. — *verb* (**rammed, ramming**) **1** to force down or into position by pushing hard. **2** *trans., intrans.* to strike or crash against violently: *ram the car into the wall.*
— **ram something down someone's throat** *colloq.* to force them to believe, accept, or listen to (a statement, idea, etc) by talking about it or repeating it constantly.

ram something home to emphasize it forcefully.
[from Anglo-Saxon *ramm*]

Rama in Hindu mythology, the incarnation of the god Vishnu on earth, and the hero of the epic *Ramayana*. In that poem, he is a hero who defeats the demon Ravana and wins back his abducted wife Sita. He becomes deified and is regarded as a king and upholder of ethical duty (dharma).

Ramadan *or* **Ramadhan** *noun* **1** the ninth month of the Muslim year, during which Muslims fast between sunrise and sunset. **2** the fast itself. [from Arabic]
◇ The fast is one of the five 'pillars' or basic duties of Islam, and ends with *Id-ul-Fitr*, the Feast of breaking the Fast.

Ramakrishna, also called **Gadadhar Chattopadhyaya** (1836–86) Hindu religious teacher, born in Hooghly, Bengal, the son of a poor Brahmin family with little formal education. He formed a religious order which bore his name, and established its headquarters in Calcutta. His most noteworthy disciple was Swami Vivekananda.

Raman, Sir Chandrasekhara Venkata (1888–1970) Indian physicist, born in Trichinopoly. Professor at Calcutta, and later Director of the Indian Institute of Science in Bangalore, he showed that the interaction of vibrating molecules with photons of light altered the spectrum of the scattered light, and was awarded the 1930 Nobel Prize for Physics. This 'Raman effect' became an important spectroscopic technique used throughout the world.

Ramaphosa, (Matamela) Cyril (1952–) South African trade unionist and politician. He became Chairman of the all-black South African Students' Organization in 1974 and after 11 months' detention (1974–5) became an articled clerk in Johannesburg and was active in the BPC (Black People's Convention). He later became General-Secretary of the National Union of Mineworkers (1982) and led the first legal strike by black mineworkers (Sep 1984). He brought the NUM into COSATU (Congress of South African Trade Unions) and was elected Secretary-General of the ANC (Jul 1991).

Ramayana an epic Hindu poem written in Sanskrit and ascribed to the poet Valmiki. It is approximately one quarter of the length of the *Mahabharata* and tells the story of Rama, his wife Sita, and the evil forces ranged against them.

Rambert, Dame Marie, originally **Cyvia Rambam** (1888–1982) Polish-born British ballet-dancer and teacher, born in Warsaw. Though sent to study medicine in Paris, she became involved in artistic circles and took up dancing. She worked on Igor Stravinsky's *Rite of Spring* with Sergei Diaghilev's Ballets Russes (1913), then went to London and took British citizenship (1918). From 1926 she formed small companies to present classical and new ballets, and encouraged collaboration between painters, musicians, and choreographers. In 1935 she formed the Ballet Rambert, and remained closely associated with it as it changed to become a modern dance company in the 1960s.

Rambert Dance Company an English dance company, formerly Ballet Rambert, founded by Marie Rambert (1926). Noted for generating new choreography and for encouraging collaboration between visual artists and musicians, it developed from a major classical company into a streamlined modern dance company. When Richard Alston became director in 1986, he introduced a style derived from the US choreographer Merce Cunningham, and renamed the company (1987).

ramble — *verb intrans.* **1** to go for a long walk or walks, especially in the countryside, for pleasure. **2** (*also* **ramble on**) to speak or write in an aimless or confused way. **3** to grow or extend in a straggling, trailing way. — *noun* a walk, especially in the countryside, for pleasure.

rambler *noun* **1** a climbing plant, especially a rose. **2** a person who goes walking in the country for pleasure.

Ramblers' Association a British federation of local rambling clubs, established in 1935. It campaigns for access to open countryside, defends outstanding landscape and rights of way, and is one of the main advocates of long-distance footpaths (eg the Pennine Way).

rambling — *noun* walking for pleasure, usually in the countryside. — *adj.* that rambles; wandering, straggling. *said of speech* disconnected.

ramblingly *adv.* in a rambling way.

rambutan *noun* **1** a tree (*Nephelium lappaceum*) of the same family as the lychee, found throughout SE Asia. **2** the fruit of this tree, which has edible translucent flesh and a thick red shell covered with hooked hairs. [from Malay, from *rambut*, hair]

RAMC *abbrev. Brit.* Royal Army Medical Corps.

Rameau, Jean Philippe (1683–1764) French composer, born in Dijon. He became an organist, and in 1722 settled in Paris, where he published his *Traité de l'harmonie* (Treatise on Harmony, 1722), a work of fundamental importance in the history of musical style. He wrote many operas, notably *Hippolyte et Aricie* (1733) and *Castor et Pollux* (1737), as well as ballets, harpsichord pieces, and vocal music.

ramekin *noun* **1** a small baking dish for a single serving of food. **2** an individual serving of food, especially of a savoury dish containing cheese and eggs, served in a ramekin. [from French *ramequin*]

Ramesses II *or* **Rameses II**, also called **Ramesses the Great** (13c BC) King of Egypt (1304–1237 BC) of the 19th dynasty. He had an indecisive victory over the Hittites at Kadesh in N Syria (1299 BC), made peace with them (1283 BC), and married a Hittite princess (1270 BC). He enjoyed a long and prosperous reign and built on an enormous scale. Outstanding examples are the hypostyle hall of the Temple of Amun at Karnak and the rock-cut temples at Abu Jimbel.

Ramesses III *or* **Rameses III** (12c BC) King of Egypt (1186–1154 BC), of the 20th dynasty. He is well known for his victories over the Sea Peoples, invaders from Asia Minor and the Aegean Islands. Tradition identifies him with the Pharaoh who oppressed the Hebrews of the Exodus.

ramification *noun* **1** an arrangement of branches; a branched structure. **2** a single part or section of a complex subject, plot, etc. **3** a consequence, especially a serious or complicated one. [from Latin *ramus*, branch]

ramify *verb trans., intrans.* (**ramifies, ramified**) to separate or cause to separate into branches or sections.

Ramillies, Battle of a spectacular victory (1706) in the War of the Spanish Succession, won by the Duke of Marlborough over Louis XIV of France's army commanded by Marshal Villeroi (1644–1730).

ramjet *noun Aeron.* **1** a type of jet engine that consists of a tube with two open ends. Air enters at one end and is compressed by the forward movement of the vehicle. Fuel is then injected into the compressed air, and the mixture is continuously burned. The hot gases produced during combustion are ejected backwards in the form of a jet, which produces the forward thrust. Ramjets cannot operate when the vehicle is stationary. **2** an aircraft or missile that is propelled by such an engine.

Rammelsberg, Mines of see GOSLAR.

Ram Mohan Roy, Raja (1774–1833) Indian religious reformer, born in Burdwan, Bengal, of high Brahman ancestry, which he rejected. He studied Buddhism, published various works aimed at uprooting idolatry, and helped to abolish suttee. His *The Precepts of Jesus* (1820) accepted the morality preached by Christ, but rejected his deity and miracles. He began the Brahmo Samaj association (1828) and received the title of Raja (1830).

Ramón y Cajal, Santiago (1852–1934) Spanish physician and histologist, born in Petilla de Aragon. Professor at Valencia, Barcelona, and Madrid, his major work was on the microstructure of the nervous system, revealing how nerve impulses are transmitted to the brain. He shared the 1906 Nobel Prize for Physiology or Medicine with Camillo Golgi.

ramp — *noun* **1** a sloping surface between two different levels, especially one which can be used instead of steps. **2** a set of movable stairs for entering and leaving an aircraft. **3** *Brit.* a low hump lying across a road, designed to slow traffic down. **4** *Brit.* a place where the level of the road surface changes or is uneven due to roadworks. — *verb* **1** to provide with a ramp. **2** *intrans.* to slope from one level to another. **3** *intrans.* to dash about in a wild, violent, and threatening way. [from Old French *ramper*, to creep]

rampage *verb intrans.* to rush about wildly, angrily, violently, or excitedly.
— **on the rampage** rampaging, often destructively.
[related to RAMP]

rampant *adj.* **1** uncontrolled; unrestrained: *rampant violence.* **2** *Heraldry* in profile and standing erect on the left hind leg with the other legs raised. [related to RAMP]

rampantly *adv.* in a rampant way.

rampart *noun* a broad mound or wall for defence, usually with a wall or parapet on top. [from Old French *remparer*, to defend]

ramping *noun* the practice of causing large false increases in the prices of shares, etc by dishonest means.

ram-raid *noun* a robbery done by ram-raiding.

ram-raiding *noun* the practice of smashing through the front window of a shop or store with a heavy vehicle and looting the goods inside.

ramrod *noun* **1** a rod for ramming charge down into, or for cleaning, the barrel of a gun. **2** a person who is strict, stern, and inflexible, both physically and morally.

Ramsay, Allan (c.1685–1758) Scottish poet, born in Leadhills, Lanarkshire. He worked as a wigmaker, became a full-time writer and bookseller, and later (1725) began a circulating library, apparently the first in Britain. His works include the pastoral comedy, *The Gentle Shepherd* (1725), an edited collection of Scots poetry, *The Evergreen* (1724), and *Thirty Fables* (1730).

Ramsay, Allan (1713–84) Scottish portrait painter, the eldest son of the poet Allan Ramsay. He became well known for his portraits, especially those of women, including his wife. He settled in London in 1762 and was appointed portrait painter to George III in 1767.

Ramsay, Sir William (1852–1916) Scottish chemist, born in Glasgow. Professor in Bristol and at University College London, he discovered argon in conjunction with Lord Rayleigh (1894), and later obtained helium, krypton, neon, and xenon. He was awarded the 1904 Nobel Prize for Chemistry.

Ramsgate POP (1981) 37 000, a port town in Thanet district, Kent, SE England. It lies S of Margate, on the English Channel, and is a resort made popular by George IV. NOTABLE FEATURES St Augustine's Abbey and Church; model village; Celtic cross, marking the spot where St Augustine is supposed to have landed in 597.

ramshackle *adj., said especially of buildings* badly made and likely to fall down; rickety. [from obsolete *ranshackle*, to ransack]

Ram Singh (1816–85) Sikh philosopher and reformer, born in Bhaini, Punjab. As a boy, he was a member of the Namdhari movement, of which he later became leader. He entered the army of Ranjit Singh, formed a sect to rejuvenate Sikhism, built up a *khalsa* (private army), and prophesied that British rule would be broken. Following attacks on Muslims in 1872, he was exiled to Rangoon as a state prisoner.

ramsons *noun* a perennial plant (*Allium ursinum*), native to woodland of Europe and Asia, that forms large carpets of long-stalked, spear-shaped shiny leaves which smell strongly of garlic. Its slender upright stems bear flat-topped clusters of white star-shaped flowers. The presence of this plant is a good indicator of ancient woodland. [from Anglo-Saxon *hramsa*]

ran see RUN.

Rancagua POP (1991e) 200 000, the capital of Cachapoal province, central Chile. It is situated S of Santiago. The city was the scene of a royalist victory in 1814 during the Spanish–American Wars of Independence. El Teniente, the world's largest underground copper mine, is located nearby and the thermal springs of Cauquenes lie to the S. NOTABLE FEATURES Merced Church (national monument); museum.

ranch — *noun* **1** an extensive grassland farm, especially in N America, S America, or Australia, where sheep, cattle, or horses are raised. **2** in N America, a farm that specializes in the production of a particular crop or animal. — *verb intrans.* to raise large numbers of sheep, cattle, or horses on a ranch. [from Spanish *rancho*, mess-room]

rancher *noun* a person who ranches.

rancid *adj., said of butter, oil, etc* tasting or smelling sour. [from Latin *rancidus*, stinking]

rancidity *or* **rancidness** *noun* a rancid state or quality.

rancorous *adj.* resentful, bitter.

rancorously *adv.* in a rancorous way.

rancour *noun* a long-lasting feeling of bitterness, dislike, or hatred. [from Latin *rancor*, from *rancere*, to be rancid]

Rand see WITWATERSRAND.

rand *noun* (PL. **rand**, **rands**) the standard monetary unit used in South Africa and some neighbouring countries. [from Witwatersrand, a large gold-mining area near Johannesburg]

Randal a male first name, and a medieval form of *Randolph*. [from Germanic, from *rand*, rim of a shield, + *wulf*, wolf]

R & B *abbrev.* rhythm and blues.

R & D *abbrev.* research and development.

Randers POP (1992e) 61 000, a seaport in Arhus county, E Jutland, Denmark. It is situated on the R Gudenå where it enters Randers Fjord, 24km/15mi from the Kattegat. NOTABLE FEATURES church (15c); town hall (18c).

randily *adv.* in a randy way.

randiness *noun* being randy.

Random, Roderick see RODERICK RANDOM, THE ADVENTURES OF.

random *adj.* lacking a definite plan, system, or order; irregular; haphazard.
— **at random** without any particular plan, system or purpose.
[from Old French *randon*, gallop]

random access a method of access that enables a particular item of data stored on a disk or in the memory of a computer to be located without the need to read any other data stored on the same device, ie it can be read out of sequence.

random access memory see RAM.

randomly *adv.* in a random way.

randomness *noun* being random.

Random Sketches see MANGA.

Randstad an urban conurbation of settlements in NW Netherlands, forming a horseshoe shape around a central agricultural zone. Most of the Dutch population live within this conurbation. Administrative functions are not concentrated in one centre but are distributed over a number of cities; the chief cities are Amsterdam, Rotterdam, Utrecht, and The Hague.

randy *adj.* (**randier, randiest**) *colloq.* sexually excited; lustful. [perhaps related to RANT]

ranee see RANI.

rang see RING².

range — *noun* 1 an area between limits within which things may move, function, etc; the limits forming this area. 2 a number of items, products, etc forming a distinct series. 3 the distance between the lowest and highest notes which may be produced by a musical instrument or a singing voice. 4 the distance to which a gun may be fired or an object thrown. 5 the distance between a weapon and its target. 6 the distance that can be covered by a vehicle without it needing to refuel. 7 an area where shooting may be practised and rockets tested. 8 a group of mountains forming a distinct series or row. 9 *North Amer.* a large area of open land for grazing livestock. 10 the region over which a plant or animal is distributed. 11 *Maths.* the set of values that a function or dependent variable may take. 12 an enclosed kitchen fireplace fitted with a large cooking stove with one or more ovens and a flat top surface for heating pans. — *verb* 1 to put in a row or rows. 2 to put (someone, oneself, etc) into a specified category or group: *he ranged himself among her enemies.* 3 *intrans.* to vary or change between specified limits. 4 (**range over** *or* **through something**) to roam freely in it. 5 *intrans.* to stretch or extend in a specified direction or over a specified area. [from Old French *range,* row, rank]

rangefinder *noun* an instrument which can estimate the distance of an object, especially a target to be shot or photographed.

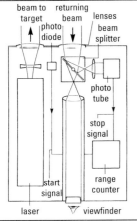

laser rangefinder

ranger *noun* 1 a person who looks after a royal or national forest or park. 2 *North Amer., esp. US* a soldier who has been specially trained for raiding and combat; a commando. 3 *North Amer., esp. US* a member of a group of armed men who patrol and police a region. 4 (**Ranger** *or* **Ranger Guide**) *Brit.* a member of the senior branch of the Guide Association.

Rangoon (Yangon) 1 POP (1990e) 3.3m, the capital and chief port of Burma (Myanma), situated in Rangoon division, in the S part of the country, on the R Rangoon. There is a large Indian and Chinese population. HISTORY settlement around Dagon Pagoda in the 6c; became capital in 1886. NOTABLE FEATURES Sule Pagoda

and Botataung Pagoda (both over 2 000 years old), Shwedagon Pagoda (height 99.4m), reclining Buddha Image of Chauk-Htat-Gyi Pagoda, seated Buddha Image of Koe-Htat-Gyi Pagoda, Kaba Aye (World Peace Pagoda); National Museum, Natural History Museum. 2 a division in S Burma (Myanma) with the city of Rangoon (Yangon) as its capital.

rangy *adj.* (**rangier, rangiest**) *said of a person* having long thin limbs and a slender body.

rani *or* **ranee** *noun Hist.* the wife or widow of a rajah. [from Sanskrit *rajni,* queen]

Ranjit Singh, known as **Lion of the Punjab** (1780–1839) Sikh ruler, born in Budrukhan. He succeeded his father, a Sikh chief, as ruler of Lahore (now in Pakistan), fought to unite all the Sikh provinces, and with the help of a modernized army trained by Western soldiers, became the most powerful ruler in India. In 1813 he procured the Koh-i-noor diamond from an Afghan prince, as the price of assistance in war.

rank¹ — *noun* 1 a line or row of people or things. 2 a line of soldiers standing side by side. 3 a position of seniority within an organization, society, the armed forces, etc. 4 a distinct class or group, eg according to ability. 5 high social position or status. 6 (**the ranks**) ordinary soldiers (eg privates and corporals) as opposed to officers. 7 *Brit.* a place where taxis wait for passengers. 8 a row of squares along the player's side of a chessboard. — *verb* 1 to arrange (people or things) in a row or line. 2 *trans., intrans.* to give or have a particular grade, position, or status in relation to others. 3 to have a higher position, status, etc than (someone); to outrank (someone).

— **close ranks** *said of a group of people* to keep their solidarity.

pull rank to use one's higher rank or status to get what one wants.

the rank and file 1 the ordinary members of an organization or society as opposed to the leaders or principal members. 2 the ordinary soldiers as opposed to the officers.
[from Old French *renc*]

rank² *adj.* 1 coarsely overgrown and untidy. 2 offensively strong in smell or taste. 3 bold, open, and shocking: *rank disobedience.* 4 complete: *a rank beginner.* [from Anglo-Saxon *ranc,* proud, overbearing]

ranker *noun* a soldier who serves or has served in the ranks, especially an officer who has been promoted up through the ranks.

Rankine, William John Macquorn (1820–72) Scottish natural philosopher and engineer, born in Edinburgh. Professor at the University of Glasgow, he researched the steam engine, machinery, shipbuilding, and applied mechanics. He was one of the architects of the new science of thermodynamics, particularly in its practical dimension, and introduced the terms actual (kinetic) and potential energy.

rankle *verb intrans.* to continue to cause feelings of annoyance or bitterness: *his refusal still rankles.* [from Old French *draoncle,* festering sore]

rankly *adv.* in a rank way.

rankness *noun* being rank.

Rank (of Sutton Scotney), J(oseph) Arthur Rank, 1st Baron (1888–1972) English film magnate, born in Hull. He became chairman of many film companies, including Gaumont-British and Cinema-Television, and did much to promote the British film industry. An active supporter of the Methodist Church, he was keenly interested in social problems.

Rannoch a loch in Perth and Kinross district, Tayside, Scotland. It is situated W of Loch Tummel and Pitlochry, and forms part of Rannoch Moor Nature Reserve. Remnants of the old Caledonian pine forest lie to the S.

ransack *verb* 1 to search thoroughly and often roughly. 2 to rob or plunder. [from Norse *rannsaka,* from *rann,* house + *sœkja,* to seek]

ransom — *noun* 1 money paid in return for the release of a kidnapped person. 2 the releasing of a kidnapped person in return for this. — *verb* (**ransomed, ransoming**) 1 to pay a ransom for (someone's) release. 2 to demand a ransom before releasing (someone).

— **hold someone to ransom** 1 to keep them prisoner until a ransom is paid. 2 to blackmail them into agreeing to one's demands.

a king's ransom a vast amount of money.
[from Latin *redemptio,* redemption]

Ransome, Arthur (Mitchell) (1884–1967) English writer, born in Leeds. He worked for a publisher, and was a war correspondent in World War I. He wrote critical and travel books before making his name with books for young readers, notably *Swallows and Amazons* (1931).

ransomer *noun* a person who ransoms.

rant — *verb* 1 *intrans.* to talk in a loud, angry, pompous way. 2 *trans.* to declaim in a loud, pompous, self-important way. — *noun* loud, pompous, empty speech. [from Dutch *ranten,* to rave]

ranter *noun* a person who rants.

ranting — *noun* 1 a rant. 2 raving, scolding. — *adj.* that rants.

Rao, P(amulaparti) V(enkata) Narasimha (1921–) Indian politician and Prime Minister. A follower of Indira Gandhi, he joined the Congress Party when it was new, and was Minister of the State of Andhra Pradesh (1969–73) and Minister for Foreign Affairs (1980–4) before he became Prime Minster (1991). He survived a no-confidence vote in Jul 1993. His administration has been marked by continuing opposition from the growing Hindu nationalist movement, secessionists fighting against Indian rule in Kashmir, bribery scandals, and a pact with China (Sep 1993) to reduce the armed troops along the 3 915km/2 433mi border (an attempt to bring peace to the Himalayas).

RAOC *abbrev. Brit.* Royal Army Ordnance Corps.

Raoult, François Marie (1830–1901) French physical chemist, born in Fournes, near Lille. Professor at the University of Grenoble, he discovered the law (named after him) that the vapour pressure of solvent above a solution is proportional to the relative number of molecules of solvent in the solution.

rap¹ — *noun* 1 a quick sharp tap or blow, or the sound made by this. 2 *slang* blame or punishment: *take the rap.* 3 a fast rhythmic monologue recited over a musical backing with a pronounced beat. 4 (*in full* **rap music**) a style of rock music based on rhythmic monologues. 5 *colloq.* a conversation. — *verb* (**rapped, rapping**) 1 to strike sharply. 2 *intrans.* to make a sharp tapping sound. 3 (*usually* **rap something out**) to utter (eg a command) sharply and quickly. 4 to criticize sharply. 5 to communicate (a message) by raps or knocks. 6 *intrans. colloq.* to talk or have a discussion. 7 *intrans. colloq.* to perform a fast rhythmic monologue to music with a pronounced beat.

— **beat the rap** *North Amer. slang* to escape punishment for a crime (whether guilty or not).
[from Middle English *rappen*]

rap² *noun* the least bit: *not care a rap.* [a former Irish counterfeit halfpenny]

rapacious *adj.* 1 greedy and grasping, especially for money. 2 *said of an animal or bird* living by catching prey. [from Latin *rapere,* to seize and carry off]

rapaciously *adv.* in a rapacious way.

rapaciousness *or* **rapacity** *noun* 1 being rapacious. 2 rapacious behaviour.

rape¹ — *noun* 1 the crime of forcing a woman to have sexual intercourse against her will. 2 the crime of sodomising a person against his or her will. 3 violation, despoiling, or abuse. — *verb* to commit rape on. [from Latin *rapere*, to seize and carry off]

rape² *noun* same as OILSEED RAPE. [from Latin *rapum*, turnip]

Rape of Europa 1 a painting by Titian (1573–6). 2 a painting by Rembrandt (c.1632).

Rape of Lucrece, The a narrative poem by William Shakespeare, originally titled *Lucrece* (1594). It is based on the Roman story of the rape by Tarquinius of Lucretia.

Rape of the Lock, The a mock-heroic poem by Alexander Pope (two cantos, 1712, five cantos, 1714). It describes the events which follow the unlawful cutting of a lock of hair from the heroine Belinda's head.

Raphael, properly **Raffaello Sanzio** (1483–1520) Italian painter, born in Urbino. He studied at Perugia under Perugino, whose style is reflected in his earliest paintings (eg the *Crucifixion*, c.1503, National Gallery, London). In c.1504 he went to Florence, where he was influenced by Leonardo da Vinci and Michelangelo. He completed several Madonnas (eg *Madonna del Prato*, c.1505, *Madonna of the Goldfinch*, c.1505, Uffizi, Florence), as well as such works as the *Holy Family* (Madrid) and *The Entombment* (Borghese). In 1508 he went to Rome where he produced his greatest works, including the frescoes in the papal apartments of the Vatican (eg *The School of Athens*, 1509–11), the cartoons for the tapestries of the Sistine Chapel, and the *Sistine Madonna* (c.1512–13, Dresden Gallery). In 1514 he succeeded Donato Bramante as architect of St Peter's. His last work was the unfinished *Transfiguration* (Vatican Gallery).

rapid — *adj.* moving, acting, or happening quickly; fast. — *noun* (**rapids**) a part of a river where the water flows quickly, usually over dangerous, sharply descending rocks. [from Latin *rapidus*]

rapid eye movement (ABBREV. **REM**) *Physiol.* a stage of relatively shallow sleep during which the eyes move rapidly from side to side behind the closed eyelids, generally accompanying a period of dreaming.

rapidity *or* **rapidness** *noun* being rapid, speed.

rapidly *adv.* quickly.

rapier *noun* a long, thin, two-edged sword for thrusting. [from French *rapière*]

rapine *noun* plundering; robbery. [from Latin *rapere*, to seize and carry off]

rapist *noun* a person who commits rape.

rapper *noun* 1 a person that raps something, eg a knocker. 2 a performer of rap music.

rapport *noun* a feeling of sympathy and understanding; a close emotional bond. [from French *rapport*]

rapprochement *noun* the establishment or renewal of a close, friendly relationship, especially between states. [from French *rapprochement*]

rapscallion *noun* old use a rascal or scamp. [perhaps related to RASCAL]

rapt *adj.* 1 enraptured; enchanted. 2 completely absorbed. [from Latin *rapere*, to seize and carry off]

raptor *noun* any bird of prey, eg an owl or falcon. [from Latin *raptor*, plunderer]

raptorial *adj.* 1 predatory. 2 adapted to predatory life.

rapture *noun* 1 great delight; ecstasy. 2 (**raptures**) great enthusiasm for or pleasure in something. [related to RAPT]

rapturous *adj.* experiencing or demonstrating rapture.

rare¹ *adj.* 1 not done, found, or occurring very often. 2 *said of the atmosphere at high altitudes* thin;

rarefied. 3 excellent; unusually good: *rare abilities*. 4 *colloq.* extreme; severe: *a rare old fright*. [from Latin *rarus*, sparse]

rare² *adj.*, *said of meat* cooked on the outside but still raw on the inside. [from Anglo-Saxon *hrere*, lightly boiled]

rarebit see WELSH RABBIT.

rare earth *Chem.* an oxide of a rare earth element, an element of the lanthanide series.

rarefied *adj.* 1 *said of the air, atmosphere, etc* thin; with a very low oxygen content. 2 select; exclusive: *move in rarefied circles*. 3 esoteric, mysterious, spiritual.

rarefy *verb* (**rarefies**, **rarefied**) 1 *trans., intrans.* to make or become less dense or solid. 2 to refine or purify. [from Latin *rarus*, rare + *facere*, to make]

rare gas same as NOBLE GAS.

rarely *adv.* 1 not often. 2 extremely well.

raring *adj.* keen and enthusiastic: *raring to go*. [related to REAR²]

rarity *noun* (PL. **rarities**) 1 the state of being rare. 2 something valued because it is rare.

Ras al Khaimah POP (1985) 117 000, the northernmost of the United Arab Emirates. AREA 1 690sq km/652sq mi. It is bounded W by the Arabian Gulf. CAPITAL Ras al Khaimah. ECONOMY offshore oil production began in 1984; industrial development is largely concentrated at Khor Khuwair.

rascal *noun* 1 a dishonest person; a rogue. 2 *humorous* a cheeky or mischievous child. [from Old French *rascaille*, rabble]

rascally *adj.* dishonest.

Ras Dashan a mountain in the Simien Range, NE Gonder region, NW Ethiopia. HEIGHT 4 620m. It is the highest point in Ethiopia.

rase same as RAZE.

rash¹ *adj.* acting, or done, with little caution or thought; hasty. [from Middle English]

rash² *noun* 1 a temporary outbreak of red spots or patches on the skin, often accompanied by itching, and usually either a symptom of an infectious disease such as measles or chickenpox, or of a skin allergy. 2 a large number of instances of a thing happening at the same time: *a rash of burglaries*. [from Latin *radere*, to scratch]

rasher *noun* a thin slice of bacon or ham.

rashly *adv.* in a rash way.

rashness *noun* 1 being rash. 2 rash behaviour.

Rashomon a Japanese film directed by Akira Kurosawa (1951). A narrative in many layers, it begins as a woodcutter's tale about three people caught up in an incident involving murder and rape and becomes an inquiry into the nature of truth.

Rasmussen, Knud (Johan Victor) (1879–1933) Danish explorer and ethnologist, born in Jacobshavn, Greenland. From 1902 he directed several expeditions to Greenland in support of the theory that the Inuit and the Native American peoples were both descended from migratory tribes from Asia. In 1910 he established Thule base on Cape York, and in 1921–4 crossed by dog-sledge from Greenland to the Bering Strait.

rasp — *noun* 1 a coarse, rough file. 2 a harsh, rough, grating sound. — *verb* 1 to scrape roughly, especially with a rasp. 2 to grate upon or irritate (eg someone's nerves). 3 *intrans., trans.* to speak or utter in a harsh, grating voice. [from Old French *raspe*]

raspberry *noun* (PL. **raspberries**) 1 a deciduous shrub of the genus *Rubus* that produces upright thorny canes, and is cultivated in Europe and N America for its edible fruit. 2 the cone-shaped fruit of this plant, consisting of red, black, or pale yellow drupelets (small spherical struc-

tures) each of which contains a single seed. It may be eaten raw, preserved by canning or freezing, or used to make jam. 3 *slang* a sound made by sticking the tongue out and blowing through the lips, usually to express disapproval. [from earlier *raspis*, of unknown origin]

rasper *noun* a person or thing that rasps.

rasping *adj.* grating, harsh.

raspingly *adv.* with a grating sound.

Rasputin, Grigoriy (c.1871–1916) Russian peasant and self-styled religious 'elder' (*starets*), born in Pokrovskoye, Siberia. A member of the schismatic sect of Khlysty (flagellants), he gained the confidence of the emperor (Nicholas II) and empress by his ability to hypnotize and thereby control the bleeding of the haemophiliac heir to the throne, Tsarevich Alexey. He was notorious also for his sexual and alcoholic excesses, and his political influence in securing the appointment of government ministers. He was murdered by a clique of aristocrats, led by Prince Felix Yusupov, a distant relative of the Tsar.

raspy *adj.* (**raspier**, **raspiest**) rough.

Rasselas, in full **The History of Rasselas, Prince of Abyssinia** a moral romance by Samuel Johnson (1759). It describes what happens when Rasselas, the son of the emperor of Abyssinia, decides to discover life outside his insulated environment. Its wide theme is the 'choice of life'.

Ras Shamra texts about 350 texts, inscribed on tablets, found between 1928 and 1960 on the site of ancient Ugarit in NW Syria. Written in a previously unknown cuneiform script now described as 'Ugaritic', or in Babylonian, the texts date from c.1400 BC and include stories about the Canaanite gods El, Baal, Astarte, and Asherah.

Rasta *noun, adj. colloq.* Rastafarian.

Rastafarian — *noun* a follower of an originally West Indian sect, which regards blacks as the chosen people and reveres Haile Selassie, the former Emperor of Ethiopia, as God. — *adj.* relating to or characteristic of Rastafarians. [from *Ras Tafari*, the name and title of Haile Selassie]

rat — *noun* 1 any of various small rodents belonging to the family Muridae, found worldwide in huge numbers, usually blackish-brown in colour with a long scaly tail. They are notorious pests and transmitters of disease. 2 any of various unrelated rodents that resemble this animal, eg kangaroo rat. 3 *colloq.* a person who is disloyal towards his or her friends, party, etc. 4 *colloq.* a strike-breaker; a blackleg. — *verb intrans.* (**ratted**, **ratting**) 1 to hunt rats. 2 (**rat on someone**) *colloq.* to betray or desert them. 3 *colloq.* to work as a blackleg.
— **smell a rat** *colloq.* to sense that something is not as it should be.
[from Anglo-Saxon *ræt*]
◇ The two commonest European rats are the black ship rat (*Rattus rattus*) and the brown rat (*Rattus norvegicus*), which is the commoner species. Both are in fact brownish-black in colour, but the black rat, often found on ships and in docks and warehouses, is smaller and more slimly built. The bubonic plague which swept through Europe in the 14c was transmitted by fleas carried by the black rat. Rats are scavengers, and they are serious pests of stored foodstuffs, eg cereal grains, which they contaminate with their droppings. The prolific breeding habits of the rat have led to its widespread use as a laboratory animal for scientific research.

ratable same as RATEABLE.

ratafia *noun* 1 a flavouring essence made with the essential oil of almonds. 2 a cordial or liqueur flavoured with fruit kernels and almonds. 3 an almond-flavoured biscuit or small cake. [from French *ratafia*, probably from Creole or *tafia*, a type of rum]

ratan same as RATTAN.

rat-a-tat-tat *noun* a sound of knocking on a door. [imitative]

ratatouille *noun* a southern French stew made with tomatoes, peppers, courgettes, aubergines, onions, and garlic. [from French *ratatouille*]

ratbag *noun slang* a mean, despicable person.

ratchet *noun* **1** a bar which fits into the notches of a toothed wheel so as to cause the wheel to turn in one direction only. **2** (*also* **rachet-wheel**) a wheel with a toothed rim. **3** the mechanism including the bar and toothed wheel together. [from French *rochet*]

rate[1] — *noun* **1** the number of times something happens, etc within a given period of time; the amount of something considered in relation to, or measured according to, another amount: *a high yearly suicide rate / at the rate of 40kph.* **2** a price or charge, often measured per unit: *the rate of pay for the job.* **3** a price or charge fixed according to a standard scale: *rate of exchange.* **4** class or rank: *second-rate.* **5** the speed of movement or change: *rate of progress.* **6** (**rates**) in the UK until 1990, a tax collected by a local authority, the amount of each person's contribution being based on the value of their property, used to pay for public services, such as libraries, rubbish collection, etc. See also COMMUNITY CHARGE. — *verb* **1** to give a value to: *be rated an excellent teacher / rate him number two in the world.* **2** to be worthy of; to deserve: *an answer not rating full marks.* **3** *intrans.* to be placed in a certain class or rank: *rates as the best book on the subject for years.* **4** in the UK until 1990, to determine the value of (property) for the purposes of assessing the rates payable on it.
— **at any rate** in any case; anyway.
at this *or* **that rate** if this or that is or continues to be the case.
[from Latin *rata*, from *reri*, to reckon]

rate[2] *verb* to scold severely. [from Middle English *raten*]

rateable *adj.* **1** able to have its value estimated for the purposes of rates. **2** in the UK until 1990, having to pay rates.

rateable value in the UK until 1990, the fixed value of a piece of property used to calculate the rates to be paid on it.

rate-cap *verb* (**rate-capped**, **rate-capping**) *said of a government* to impose rate-capping on (a local authority).

rate-capping *noun* the setting by central government of an upper limit on the rate that can be levied by a local authority.

rate of reaction *Chem.* the speed of a chemical reaction, usually expressed as the rate at which the products are formed or the rate at which the reactants disappear, and influenced by temperature, the concentration of the reactants, and the presence of a catalyst. In living cells the rates of chemical reactions depend on the activity of enzymes.

ratepayer *noun Brit. Hist.* a person or institution that pays local rates.

brown
rat

muskrat

kangaroo rat

types of rat

Rathenau, Walther (1867–1922) German industrialist and statesman, born in Berlin. He organized German war industries during World War I, and as Minister of Reconstruction (1921) and Foreign Minister (from Feb 1922), dealt with reparations. His attempts to negotiate a reparations agreement with the victorious Allies, and the fact that he was Jewish, made him extremely unpopular in nationalist circles, and he was murdered by extremists in the summer of 1922.

rather — *adv.* **1** more readily; from preference. **2** more truly or properly: *my parents, or rather my mother and stepfather.* **3** to a certain extent; somewhat. **4** on the contrary: *she said she'd help me; rather, she just sat around watching.* — *interj.* yes indeed; very much. [from Anglo-Saxon *hrathor*]

Rathlin Island an island in Moyle district, N Co Antrim, Northern Ireland. It is situated off the N coast, 5km/3mi NW of Fair Head. AREA 14sq km/6sq mi; 8km/5mi long; up to 5km/3mi wide; it rises to 137m. St Columba founded a church here in the 6c. On the island are the ruins of a castle where it is reputed that Robert Bruce took refuge in 1306 and the incident with the spider and the web took place (although other traditions place this event at other sites).

ratification *noun* **1** ratifying or being ratified. **2** confirmation, sanction.

ratify *verb* (**ratifies**, **ratified**) to give formal consent to (eg a treaty, agreement, etc), especially by signature. [from Latin *ratificare*]

rating *noun* **1** a classification according to order, rank or value. **2** *Brit.* an ordinary seaman. **3** an estimated value of a person's position, especially as regards credit. **4** the proportion of viewers or listeners forming the estimated audience of a television or radio programme, used as a measure of that programme's popularity.

ratio *noun* (PL. **ratios**) **1** the number or degree of one class of things in relation to another, or between one thing and another, expressed as a proportion: *the ratio of dogs to cats is 5 to 3.* **2** the number of times one mathematical quantity can be divided by another. [from Latin *ratio*, reckoning]

ration — *noun* **1** a fixed allowance of food, clothing, petrol, etc during a time of shortage. **2** (**rations**) one's daily allowance of food, especially in the army. — *verb* (**rationed**, **rationing**) **1** (**ration something out**) to distribute or share out something (especially in short supply), usually in fixed amounts. **2** to restrict the supply of provisions to (someone). [from Latin *ratio*, reckoning]

rational *adj.* **1** of or based on reason or logic. **2** able to think, form opinions, make judgements, etc. **3** sensible; reasonable. **4** sane. [from Latin *rationalis*]

rationale *noun* the underlying principles or reasons on which a decision, belief, action, etc is based. [from Latin *rationalis*]

rationalism *noun* the theory that an individual's actions and beliefs should be based on reason rather than on intuition or the teachings of others.
◇ The philosophical tradition of rationalism maintains that knowledge is independent of sense experience, and is usually contrasted with empiricism. Versions of it flourished with Descartes, Spinoza, and Leibnitz.
In architecture, rationalism is a 20c conception which aims to find the most logical possible solution to every aspect of building. It is particularly associated with the Bauhaus and with International-style architects of the 1920s and 1930s.

rationalist *noun* a person who forms opinions by reasoning.

rationalistic *adj.* **1** characterized by rationalism. **2** inclined to rationalism.

rationality *noun* **1** being rational. **2** the possession or due exercise of reason. **3** reasonableness.

rationalization *or* **rationalisation** *noun* rationalizing or being rationalized.

rationalize *or* **rationalise** *verb* **1** to attribute (one's behaviour or attitude) to sensible, well-thought-out reasons or motives, especially after the event. **2** *intrans.* to explain one's behaviour, etc in this way. **3** to make logical or rational. **4** to make (an industry or organization) more efficient and profitable by reorganizing it to get rid of unnecessary costs and labour.

rationally *adv.* in a rational way.

rational number *Maths.* a number which can be expressed in the form of a fraction, eg $\frac{4}{5}$, where *a* and *b* are whole numbers, and *b* is not zero, eg $\frac{4}{5}$.

ration book *or* **ration card** a book or card containing coupons which can be exchanged for rationed goods.

rationing *noun* supplying rations; dividing into rations.

ratpack *noun slang* **1** a rowdy gang of young people. **2** a group of photographers, especially from tabloid newspapers, who follow and photograph famous people.

rat race *colloq.* the fierce, unending competition for success, wealth, etc in business, society, etc.

rattan *noun* a climbing palm with very long, thin, tough stems which are used to make walking sticks and wickerwork. [from Malay *rotan*]

ratter *noun* a dog or other animal that catches and kills rats.

Rattigan, Sir Terence (Mervyn) (1911–77) English dramatist, born in London. His first major success was a comedy, *French Without Tears* (1936), and his other internationally acclaimed works include *The Winslow Boy* (1946), *The Browning Version* (1948), and *Separate Tables* (1954).

Rattle, Simon (1955–) English conductor, born in Liverpool. He won the Bournemouth International Conducting Competition at the age of 17, and made his London début at both the Royal Albert and Royal Festival Halls in 1976. He was assistant conductor of the BBC Scottish Symphony Orchestra from 1977 to 1980, when he became principal conductor of the City of Birmingham Symphony Orchestra. In 1980 he married the US soprano Elise Ross.

rattle — *verb* **1** *intrans.* to make a series of short, sharp, hard sounds in quick succession. **2** to cause (eg crockery) to make such a noise. **3** *intrans.* to move along rapidly, often with a rattling noise. **4** *intrans.* (*usually* **rattle on**) to chatter thoughtlessly or idly. **5** (**rattle something off** *or* **rattle through something**) to say or recite it rapidly and unthinkingly. **6** *colloq.* to make anxious or nervous; to upset. — *noun* **1** a series of short sharp sounds made in quick succession, having the effect of a continuous sound. **2** a baby's toy consisting of a container filled with small pellets which rattle when the container is shaken. **3** a device for making a whirring sound, used especially at football matches. **4** the loose horny structures at the end of a rattlesnake's tail, which produce a rattling sound when vibrated. **5** lively, empty chatter. **6** the rough harsh breathing sound caused by air passing through mucus in the back of the throat. [from Middle English *ratelen*]

rattler *noun colloq.* a rattlesnake.

rattlesnake *noun* any of 29 species of poisonous American snake of the pit viper family, that prey on small mammals and give birth to live young. If threatened, the snake vibrates a series of dry horny structures at the end of its tail, producing a loud rattling sound. See illustration p. 1048.

rattlesnake

rattletrap *noun colloq.* a broken-down, rickety old vehicle, especially a car.

rattling *adj., adv. old use* **1** smart or smartly. **2** brisk or briskly. **3** *as a general intensifying word* good or well; very: *told us a rattling good yarn*.

rattly *adj.* (**rattlier, rattliest**) making a rattling noise; often rattling.

Ratty a country-loving gastronome in Kenneth Grahame's *The Wind in the Willows*.

ratty *adj.* (**rattier, rattiest**) **1** of or like a rat. **2** *colloq.* irritable.

raucous *adj.* hoarse, harsh. [from Latin *raucus*]

raucously *adv.* in a raucous way.

raucousness *noun* being raucous.

Rauma, Swedish **Raumo** a seaport on the W coast of Turku-Pori province, SW Finland. It was established in 1442, and is noted for its Rauma lace. The old part of the city is a World Heritage site.

raunchily *adv.* in a raunchy way.

raunchy *adj.* (**raunchier, raunchiest**) *slang* coarsely or openly sexual.

ravage — *verb trans., intrans.* to cause extensive damage to a place; to destroy. — *noun* (*usually* **ravages**) damage or destruction: *the ravages of time*. [from Old French *ravir*, to ravish]

rave — *verb* **1** *intrans.* to talk wildly as if mad or delirious. **2** *intrans.* (**rave about** or **over something**) to talk enthusiastically or passionately about it. — *noun colloq.* **1** extravagant praise. **2** a rave-up. **3** an acid-house party. — *adj. colloq.* extremely enthusiastic: *rave reviews*. [from Middle English *raven*]

Ravel, Maurice (1875–1937) French composer, born in Ciboure. He studied under Gabriel Fauré at the Paris Conservatoire, and won recognition with *Pavane pour une infante défunte* (Pavane for a Dead Princess, 1899). He wrote several successful piano pieces, *Rapsodie espagnole* (1908), and the music for Sergei Diaghilev's ballet *Daphnis et Chloé* (first performed 1912). His later works (after active service in World War I) included the 'choreographic poem' *La Valse* (1920), the opera *L'Enfant et les sortilèges* (The Child and the Enchantments, 1925), and *Boléro* (1928), intended as a miniature ballet.

ravel — *verb* (**ravelled, ravelling**) **1** *trans., intrans.* to tangle or become tangled up. **2** (**ravel something out**) to untangle, unravel, or untwist it. **3** *intrans.* to fray. — *noun* **1** a tangle or knot. **2** a complication. **3** a loose or broken thread. [from Dutch *rafelen*]

raven — *noun* a large blue-black bird of the crow family. — *adj.* glossy blue-black in colour: *raven-haired*. [from Anglo-Saxon *hræfn*]

ravening *adj., said especially of meat-eating animals* hungrily seeking food. [from *raven*, to devour, hunt for food]

Ravenna POP (1991e) 137 000, the capital of Ravenna province, Emilia-Romagna region, NE Italy. It lies 8km/5mi from the Adriatic Sea, to which it is connected by canal. It was capital of the W Roman Empire in AD 402, and of the later Ostrogothic and Byzantine rulers. NOTABLE FEATURES Church of San Vitale (begun in 526), with famous mosaics; cathedral (18c); octagonal baptistery (5c) in the Church of Sant' Apollinare Nuovo; tomb of Empress Galla Placidia (5c); tomb of Theodoric (c.520).

ravenous *adj.* **1** extremely hungry or greedy. **2** *said of hunger, a desire, etc* intensely strong. **3** *said of an animal, etc* living on prey; predatory.

ravenously *adv.* in a ravenous way.

ravenousness *noun* being ravenous.

raver *noun colloq.* a person who leads a full, lively, uninhibited social life.

rave-up *noun colloq.* a lively party or celebration.

Ravi, ancient **Hydraotes** a river in NW India and Pakistan. It is 765km/475mi long and is one of the five rivers of the Punjab. The river rises in the SE Pir Panjal Range and flows generally SW across the Pakistan Punjab, past Lahore, to join the R Chenab 53km/33mi NE of Multan. The Ravi forms part of the border between Pakistan and India.

ravine *noun* a deep, narrow, steep-sided gorge. [from Old French *ravine*, violent rushing]

raving — *adj., adv.* **1** frenzied; delirious. **2** *colloq.* great; extreme: *a raving beauty.* — *noun* (*usually* **ravings**) wild, frenzied, or delirious talk.

ravioli *sing. or pl. noun* small, square pasta cases with a savoury filling of meat, cheese, etc. [from Italian *ravioli*]

ravish *verb* **1** to cause to be overcome with joy, delight, etc; to enrapture. **2** to rape. [from Latin *rapere*, to seize and carry off]

ravishing *adj.* delightful; lovely.

ravishingly *adv.* in a ravishing way.

raw — *adj.* **1** not cooked. **2** not processed, purified or refined. **3** *said of alcoholic spirit* undiluted. **4** *said of statistics, data, etc* not analysed. **5** *said of a person* not trained or experienced. **6** *said of a wound, etc* with a sore, inflamed surface. **7** *said of the weather* cold and damp. — *noun* a sore, inflamed, or sensitive place. — **in the raw 1** in a natural or crude state. **2** naked. [from Anglo-Saxon *hreaw*]

Rawalpindi POP (1990e) 1.1m, a city in Punjab province, Pakistan. It lies 258km/160mi NW of Lahore and has a strategically important location, controlling routes to Kashmir. The city is also an important military and commercial centre. HISTORY occupied by the British in 1849; interim capital from 1959 until 1969.

rawboned *adj.* lean and gaunt.

raw deal *colloq.* harsh, unfair treatment.

rawhide *noun* **1** untanned leather. **2** a whip made from this.

Rawlings, Jerry (John) (1947–) Ghanaian leader, born in Accra. He led a peaceful coup by the Armed Forces Revolutionary Council in 1979, but handed the power over to a civilian government after a few months. Despite being forcibly retired from the armed forces and discredited by the government, his popularity remained high and he again established himself as Chairman of the Provisional National Defence Council of Ghana at the end of 1981, and has been effective head of state since 1982.

raw material 1 any material, in its natural unprocessed state, that serves as the starting point for a production or manufacturing process. **2** material out of which something is or can be made, or may develop.

rawness *noun* being raw.

raw umber untreated umber.

Ray, John (1627–1705) English naturalist, born in Black Notley, Essex. Educated at Cambridge, he subsequently held a post there which he lost at the Restoration for religious reasons. Accompanied by naturalist Francis Willoughby, he toured extensively in Europe and developed a classification of plants, with emphasis on the species as the basic unit; this was the foundation of modern taxonomy. He also developed the most natural pre-Linnaean classification of the animal kingdom.

Ray, Man, pseudonym of **Emanuel Rabinovitch** (1890–1976) US painter, sculptor, photographer and film-maker, born in Philadelphia, Pennsylvania. He was a major figure in the development of Modernism, and co-founded the New York Dadaist movement. He experimented with new techniques in painting and photography, then moved to Paris (1921), where he became interested in films. During the 1930s he produced many photographs and 'rayographs' (photographic montages).

Ray, Satyajit (1921–92) Indian film director, born in Calcutta. His first film, *Pather Panchali* (On the Road, 1954) was undertaken in his spare time with very limited finance. Its international success at the Cannes Film Festival allowed him to complete the trilogy with *Aparajito* (The Unvanquished, 1956) and *Apur Sansar* (The World of Apu, 1959). Later features include *The Kingdom of Diamonds* (1980), *Pickoo* (1982), and *The Home and The World* (1984).

ray[1] *noun* **1** a narrow beam of light or radioactive particles. **2** any of a set of lines fanning out from a central point. **3** a small amount of the beginnings of (especially hope or understanding). **4** any of the set of spines which support a fish's fin. [from Latin *radius*, rod]

ray[2] *noun* any of numerous cartilaginous fish, related to the sharks, with a flattened body, large pectoral fins extending from the head to the base of the tail, and both eyes on the upper surface, eg stingray, manta ray, sawfish. Most of the marine species live on the sea bed, where they feed on shellfish. [from Latin *raia*]

ray

ray[3] same as RE[1].

Ray-Bans *pl. noun trademark* a type of sunglasses with dark green lenses and gold frames.

ray-gun *noun* especially in science fiction, a gun that fires destructive rays, used as a weapon.

Rayleigh, John William Strutt, 3rd Baron (1842–1919) English physicist, born near Maldon, Essex. Professor at Cambridge and the Royal Institution, he discovered argon in conjunction with William Ramsay (1894), and for this and his work on gas densities, he was awarded the 1904 Nobel Prize for Physics. He also studied radiation, his research leading to a formula which accurately predicts the long-wavelength radiation emitted by hot bodies.

Raymond a male first name. [from Germanic, from *ragin*, advice, decision + *mund*, protector]

Raynaud's disease *Medicine* a disorder in which the fingers, toes, ears, and nose turn white or develop a bluish tinge as a result of spasm of the arteries supplying the affected parts. It usually occurs in response to exposure to cold or emotional stress. [named after the French physician Maurice Raynaud (1834–81)]

rayon *noun* a strong durable easily dyed artificial fibre consisting of regenerated cellulose that has been spun into filaments, used to make textiles for clothing, conveyer belts, hoses, etc. [probably from RAY[1]]

raze *verb* to destroy or demolish (buildings, a town, etc) completely. [from Latin *radere*, to scrape]

Razin, Stepan Timofeyevich, also called **Stenka** (c.1630–71) Russian Cossack and leader of a Cossack and peasant revolt (1670–1), which was directed against the boyars and landowning nobility. In Apr 1671 he was captured and publicly executed. He became a folk hero celebrated in legend as the embodiment of popular rebellion against authority.

razor noun a sharp-edged instrument used for shaving. [from Old French rasour]

razorbill noun a type of seabird with a sharp-edged bill.

razor edge 1 a very fine, sharp edge. **2** a critical, delicately balanced situation.

razor shell a burrowing marine bivalve with two similar elongated shell valves, the two halves of the shell being closed by two muscles. It burrows actively in the sand using a muscular foot.

razor wire thick wire with sharp pieces of metal attached, used like barbed wire for fences, etc.

razzle noun slang a lively spree, outing or party, especially involving a lot of drinking: on the razzle. [related to DAZZLE]

razzle-dazzle noun slang **1** excitement, confusion, dazzling show, etc. **2** a lively spree.

razzmatazz noun **1** razzle-dazzle. **2** humbug.

Rb symbol Chem. rubidium.

RC abbrev. **1** Red Cross. **2** Roman Catholic.

RCA abbrev. Radio Corporation of America.

RCAF abbrev. Royal Canadian Air Force.

RCM abbrev. Royal College of Music.

RCMP abbrev. Royal Canadian Mounted Police.

RCN abbrev. Royal Canadian Navy.

Rd abbrev. road.

RDA abbrev. recommended daily (or dietary) allowance: the amount of essential nutrient (vitamins, protein, etc) needed to meet a normal healthy person's nutritional requirements. Judged by a national or international committee, RDAs have several uses, including dietary planning, the assessment of food aid, and food labelling.

Re or **Ra** in Egyptian religion, the Sun-god of Heliopolis. He emerged from the primeval waters at the beginning of time and created the universe. He was depicted as a falcon with the Sun's disc on his head; at night he appeared as a ram-headed god who sailed through the Underworld.

Re symbol Chem. rhenium.

RE abbrev. religious education.

re¹ noun Mus. the second note in the sol-fa scale. [from the first syllable of the word resonare in a medieval Latin hymn, certain syllables of which were used to name the notes]

re² prep. with regard to; concerning. [from Latin res, thing]

re- prefix forming words denoting a repetition or reversal of the action of the root word: reread / rewrite / replacement. [from Latin re-]

reach — verb **1** to arrive at; to get as far as. **2** trans., intrans. to be able to touch or get hold of. **3** trans., intrans. to project or extend to a point. **4** intrans. (**reach across, out, up**, etc) to stretch out one's arm to try to touch or get hold of something. **5** colloq. to hand or pass. **6** to make contact or communicate with, especially by telephone. — noun **1** the distance one can stretch one's arm, hand, etc: out of reach / within reach. **2** the distance that can be travelled easily: within reach of London. **3** an act of reaching out. **4** range of influence, power, understanding, or abilities. **5** (usually **reaches**) a section within clear limits, eg part of a river or canal between two bends or locks. **6** (usually **reaches**) level or rank: the upper reaches of government. [from Anglo-Saxon ræcan]

reachable adj. capable of being reached or achieved.

reach-me-down noun a second-hand or ready-made item of clothing.

react verb **1** (**react to something** or **someone**) to respond to in a certain way to something said or done. **2** (**react against something**) to respond to it in a way which shows dislike or disapproval. **3** intrans., trans. to undergo or cause to undergo a chemical reaction. [from Latin reagere]

reactance noun Electr. in an electric circuit carrying alternating current, the property of an inductor or capacitor that causes it to oppose the flow of current. Like resistance, it is measured in ohms, and together with resistance it represents the impedance of the circuit.

reaction noun **1** a reacting or response to something. **2** opposition to change, especially political change, and a desire to return to a former system. **3** a complete change of opinions, feelings, etc to the opposite of what they were: the idea was popular at first but then a reaction set in. **4** a bodily response (eg to a drug). **5** Chem. a chemical reaction in which one or more elements or compounds (reactants) react to form one or more new compounds (products). Only the electrons surrounding the nucleus are involved in such reactions. **6** Physics a nuclear reaction involving a change in an atomic nucleus, eg radioactive decay, nuclear fission, nuclear fusion. **7** Physics the force offered by a body that is equal in magnitude but opposite in direction to a force applied to that body.

reactionary — adj., said of a person or policies opposed to change or progress and in favour of a return to a former system. — noun (PL. **reactionaries**) a reactionary person.

reactivate verb to make active again.

reactivation noun reactivating or being reactivated.

reactive adj. showing a reaction; liable to react; sensitive to stimuli.

reactor same as NUCLEAR REACTOR.

Read, Sir Herbert (1893–1968) English poet and art critic, born near Kirby Moorside, Yorkshire. He was an assistant keeper at the Victoria and Albert Museum, London, editor of the Burlington Magazine (1933–39), and held several academic posts, including that of Professor of Fine Art at Edinburgh (1931–3). His works on art and design include The Meaning of Art (1931), and Art and Industry (1936). His poetic works include Naked Warriors (1919) and Collected Poems (1966).

read — verb (PAST TENSE AND PAST PARTICIPLE **read**) **1** trans., intrans. to look at and understand (printed or written words). **2** trans., intrans. to speak (words which are printed or written). **3** trans., intrans. to learn or gain knowledge of by reading: read the election results in the newspaper. **4** trans., intrans. to pass one's leisure time reading (books): I have little time for reading. **5** to look at or be able to see (something) and get information from it: cannot read the clock without my glasses. **6** to interpret or understand the meaning of: read a map. **7** to interpret or understand (signs, marks, etc) without using one's eyes: read Braille. **8** to know (a language) well enough to be able to understand something written in it: speaks Chinese but cannot read it. **9** intrans. to have a certain wording: the letter reads as follows. **10** trans., intrans. to think that (a statement, etc) has a particular meaning: read it as criticism. **11** intrans. said of writing to be, or not to be, coherent, fluent, and logical: an essay which reads well. **12** said of a dial, instrument, etc to show a particular measurement: the barometer reads 'fair'. **13** to replace (a word, phrase, etc) to be replaced by another: for 'three' read 'four'. **14** to put into a specified condition by reading: she read the child to sleep. **15** to study (a subject) at university. **16** to hear and understand, especially when using two-way radio. **17** (**read something in** or **out**) Comput. to transfer data

from a disk or other storage device into the main memory of a computer. — noun **1** a period or act of reading. **2** a book, etc thought of as being interesting, etc: a good read.

— **read between the lines** to understand a meaning which is implied but not stated.

read into something to find (in a person's writing, words, etc) a meaning which is not stated clearly and which may not have been intended.

read something out to read it aloud.

read something up to learn a subject by reading books about it.

take something as read to accept or assume it.

well or **widely read** educated, especially in literature, through reading.

[from Anglo-Saxon rædan]

readability or **readableness** noun the capacity to be readable.

readable adj. **1** legible; able to be read. **2** pleasant or quite interesting to read.

Reade, Charles (1814–84) English writer, born in Ipsden, Oxfordshire. He became a lawyer in 1843, and began writing in 1850. He wrote a succession of plays after 1852, which lost him money, and successful novels on social injustice and cruelty, notably the long historical novel set in the 15c, The Cloister and the Hearth (1861).

reader noun **1** a person who reads. **2** Brit. a university lecturer ranking between professor and senior lecturer. **3** a person who reads prayers in a church. **4** a book containing usually short texts, especially one used for learning a foreign language. **5** a person who reads and reports on manuscripts for a publisher. **6** a person who reads and corrects proofs. **7** a machine which produces a magnified image from a microfilm so that it can be read.

readership noun **1** the total number of people who read a newspaper, the novels of a particular author, etc. **2** Brit. the post of reader in a university.

readily adv. **1** promptly, willingly. **2** quickly.

readiness noun **1** promptness, willingness. **2** quickness.

Reading POP (1992e) 137 000, the county town of Berkshire, S England. It lies at the junction of the Kennet and Thames rivers, 63km/39mi W of London. In medieval times it was a centre of the textile industry. NOTABLE FEATURES 12c Benedictine abbey, the burial place of Henry I; Hexagon (theatre); Museum of English Rural Life; Museum of Greek Archaeology.

reading — noun **1** the action of a person who reads. **2** the ability to read: his reading is poor. **3** books, material, etc for reading. **4** an event at which a play, poetry, etc is read to an audience. **5** any one of three stages in the passage of a bill through parliament. **6** the actual word or words that can be read in a text, especially where more than one version is possible: one of many disputed readings in the Bible. **7** information, figures, etc shown by an instrument or meter. **8** an understanding or interpretation: one's reading of the situation. — adj. of, for, or fond of reading.

read-only memory see ROM.

read-out noun Comput. **1** the act of copying data from the main memory of a computer into an external storage device, eg a disk or tape, or a display device, eg a visual display unit or plotter. **2** data that has been copied in this way.

read-write head Comput. a head in a disc drive which allows data to be written on to, or retrieved from, the disc.

read-write memory a computer memory which allows data to be both read and changed.

ready — adj. (**readier, readiest**) **1** prepared and available for action or use. **2** willing: always ready to help. **3** prompt; quick: be too ready to find fault. **4** likely or about to do: a plant just ready to flower. — noun (PL. **readies**) colloq. (also **ready money**) cash, especially bank notes, for immediate use. — adv. prepared or made beforehand: *ready cooked meals.* — verb to make ready.

— **at the ready 1** *said of a gun* aimed and ready to be fired. **2** ready for immediate action. [from Anglo-Saxon *ræde*]

ready-made adj. **1** *said of clothes* made to a standard size, not made-to-measure. **2** convenient; useful: *a ready-made excuse.*

ready money *colloq.* money available for immediate use.

ready reckoner a book listing standard or useful calculations.

Ready-to-Halt, Mr a pilgrim on crutches in John Bunyan's *The Pilgrim's Progress.*

ready-to-wear adj., *said of clothes* same as READY-MADE.

reafforest verb *Bot.* to replant trees in a cleared area of land that was formerly forested.

reafforestation noun *Bot.* replanting or being replanted with trees.

Reagan, Ronald (Wilson) (1911–) US Republican politician, the 40th President, born in Tampico, Illinois. Educated at Eureka College, Illinois, he became a radio sports announcer, went to Hollywood (1937), and appeared in more than 50 films, beginning with *Love Is On the Air* (1937). Although originally a Democrat and supporter of liberal causes, he became increasingly anti-communist, and in 1962 joined the Republican Party as an extreme right-winger. He became Governor of California (1966), stood unsuccessfully for the Republican presidential nomination twice (1968, 1976), but won it in 1980 and defeated Jimmy Carter to become President (1981–9). He introduced a major programme of economic changes aimed at reducing government spending and inflation, took a strong anti-communist stand, especially in the Middle East and Central America, and introduced the Strategic Defence Initiative ('Star Wars'). In 1981 he was wounded in an assassination attempt. He defeated Walter Mondale in 1984 to win a second term, during which he formed a less confrontational attitude towards the USSR and achieved a major arms-reduction accord with Soviet leader Mikhail Gorbachev. His domestic popularity remained high throughout his presidency, despite charges of corruption against his aides, and his inability to get much of his programme through Congress, which resulted in record budget and trade deficit problems for his successor George Bush. The reputation of his administration was tarnished in the last two years by the Iran-Contra affair.

Reaganomics *sing.* noun the economic practice of cutting taxes to stimulate production, as advocated by Ronald Reagan.

reagent noun *Chem.* **1** any chemical compound that participates in a chemical reaction. **2** a common laboratory chemical that is used in chemical analysis and experiments, eg hydrochloric acid, sodium hydroxide. [from Latin *reagere*, to react]

real¹ — adj. **1** which actually exists; not imaginary. **2** not imitation; genuine. **3** actual; true: *the real reason.* **4** great, important, or serious: *a real problem.* **5** *Legal* consisting of or relating to property which cannot be moved, such as land and houses. **6** *said of income, etc* measured in terms of what it will buy rather than its nominal value. **7** *Maths.* involving or containing real numbers. — adv. *North Amer., Scot.* really; very: *real nice.*

— **for real** *slang* in reality; seriously. [from Latin *realis*, from *res*, thing]

real² noun *Hist.* a small silver Spanish or Spanish-American coin. [from Spanish, from Latin *regalis*, royal]

real estate *North Amer.* property in the form of houses or land.

realign verb **1** to group in a new or different way. **2** to bring back into line or alignment.

realignment noun realigning or being realigned.

Realism a term in art criticism referring to the deliberate choice of ugly or unidealized subject-matter, sometimes to make a social or political point. More generally, in literature and art, the term refers to the advocacy of verisimilitude (the quality of appearing to be real or true), as in the Realist movement of mid-19c France, which flourished as Naturalism.

realism noun **1** an acceptance of things or a willingness to deal with things as they really are. **2** realistic or lifelike representation in writing and the arts (see also REALISM). **3** *Philos.* the theory that physical objects exist even when they are not perceived by the mind (see also IDEALISM).

realist noun **1** a person who is aware of and accepts reality. **2** a writer or artist who represents matters in a realistic way.

realistic adj. **1** representing things as they really are; lifelike. **2** relating to realism or realists.

realistically adv. in a realistic way.

reality noun (PL. **realities**) **1** the state or fact of being real. **2** the real nature of something; the truth. **3** that which is real and not imaginary.

— **in reality** as a fact, often as distinct from a thought or idea.

realizable or **realisable** adj. capable of being realized.

realization or **realisation** noun realizing or being realized.

realize or **realise** verb **1** *trans., intrans.* to begin to know or understand. **2** to make real; to make come true. **3** to cause to seem real; to act out: *realize the story on film.* **4** to convert (property or goods) into actual money: *realize one's assets.* **5** to gain (money): *realized £45 000 on the sale of the house.* [from Old French *realiser*]

really — adv. **1** actually; in fact. **2** very; genuinely: *a really lovely day.* — *interj.* an expression of surprise, doubt, or mild protest.

realm noun **1** a kingdom. **2** a field of interest, study, or activity. [from Old French *realme*]

real number *Maths.* any rational or irrational number.

realpolitik noun politics based on the practical needs of life rather than on moral or ethical ideas. [German, = politics of realism]

real property *Brit. Legal* land or buildings. See also PERSONAL PROPERTY, REAL ESTATE.

real tennis, an early form of tennis played on a walled, indoor court. See also LAWN TENNIS.

◇ Also known as *royal* or *court tennis*, the game is similar to rackets but with specifically designed hazards. It developed from the French game, *jeu de paume*, and the racket was introduced in the 16c. It was very popular in the 17c, but today has become a minority sport, eclipsed by lawn tennis and other derivatives. The oldest British court still used for the game is at Falkland Palace in Fife, built by James V of Scotland in 1539.

real-time adj. *Comput.* of or relating to a system in which data is processed as it is generated.

realtor noun *North Amer.* (also **Realtor**) an estate agent, especially one who is a member of the National Association of Realtors.

realty same as REAL ESTATE.

ream noun **1** a number of sheets of paper equivalent to 20 quires, formerly 480, now usually 500 or 516. **2** (**reams**) *colloq.* a large amount, especially of paper or writing: *wrote reams.* [from Old French *reame*, from Arabic *rizmah*, bale]

reap verb *trans., intrans.* **1** to cut or gather (grain, etc). **2** to clear (a field) by cutting a crop. **3** to receive as a consequence of one's actions. [from Anglo-Saxon *ripan*]

reaper noun **1** a person or machine that reaps. **2** (**the reaper** or **grim reaper**) death.

reapply verb *trans., intrans.* to apply again or afresh.

rear¹ — noun **1** the back part; the area at the back. **2** that part of an army which is farthest away from the enemy. **3** *euphemistic colloq.* the buttocks. — adj. at the back: *rear window.*

rear² verb **1** to feed, care for, and educate: *rear three children.* **2** to breed (animals) or grow (crops). **3** (also **rear up**) *said especially of a horse* to rise up on the hind legs. **4** to raise (the head, etc) upright. **5** *intrans.* to reach a great height, especially in relation to surroundings. [from Anglo-Saxon *ræran*]

rear admiral a naval officer with the rank below vice-admiral.

Reardon, Ray(mond) (1932–) Welsh snooker player, born in Tredegar, Monmouthshire. He was Welsh amateur champion six times (1950–5), and turned professional in 1968, after careers as a miner and policeman. He was world professional champion six times (1970, 1973–6, 1978), and until 1982 was top of the snooker ratings.

rearguard noun a group of soldiers who protect the rear of an army, especially in retreats.

rearguard action 1 military action undertaken by the rearguard. **2** an effort to prevent or delay defeat, eg in an argument.

rearm verb *trans., intrans.* to arm or become armed again with new or improved weapons.

rearmament noun the process of rearming.

rearmost adj. last of all.

rear-view mirror a mirror fixed to a car's windscreen, or attached to a motorbicycle's handles, which allows the driver to see vehicles, etc behind.

rearward — adj. at or to the rear. — adv. (also **rearwards**) towards the rear.

reason — noun **1** a justification or motive for an action, belief, etc. **2** an underlying explanation or cause. **3** the power of the mind to think, form opinions and judgements, reach conclusions, etc. **4** sanity. — verb (**reasoned**, **reasoning**) **1** *intrans.* to use one's mind and reason to form opinions and judgements, reach conclusions, etc. **2** (**reason with someone**) to try to persuade them by means of argument. **3** (**reason someone into** or **out of something**) to persuade or influence them with argument. **4** (also **reason something out**) to think or set it out logically.

— **by reason of** ... because of ...; as a consequence of ...

it stands to reason it is obvious or logical.

within reason within the bounds of what is sensible or possible. [from Old French *reison*]

reasonable adj. **1** sensible; showing reason or good judgement. **2** willing to listen to reason or argument. **3** in accordance with reason; fair; not extreme or excessive. **4** satisfactory or equal to what one might expect.

reasonableness noun being reasonable.

reasonably adv. in a reasonable way.

reasoning noun **1** the forming of judgements or opinions using reason or careful argument. **2** the opinions or judgements formed in this way.

reassurance noun reassuring.

reassure verb to relieve (someone) of anxiety and so give confidence to.

reassuring adj. that reassures.

reassuringly adv. in a reassuring way.

Réaumur, René Antoine Ferchault de (1683–1757) French natural philosopher, born in La Rochelle. In 1703 he moved to Paris, where he was put in charge of a project to assemble information on all the arts, industries, and professions in France. He developed methods for producing iron, steel, and porcelain, and became a leading naturalist. His alcohol and water thermometer (1731) introduced the Réaumur temperature scale, with 80 degrees between the freezing and boiling points of water.

rebate — *noun* **1** a return of part of a sum of money paid. **2** a discount. [from Old French *rabattre*, to beat back]

Rebecca **1** a biblical character, the wife of Isaac and the mother of Jacob and Esau. **2** a female first name. [from Hebrew *Rebekah*, = noose]

Rebecca **1** a novel by Daphne Du Maurier (1938). It is a suspenseful romantic mystery set in the West Country. **2** a British film directed by Alfred Hitchcock (1940), based on the novel. It won two Academy Awards.

rebel — *noun* **1** a person who opposes or fights against people in authority or oppressive conditions. **2** a person who does not accept the rules of normal behaviour, dress, etc. — *adj.* rebelling. — *verb intrans.* (**rebelled, rebelling**) **1** to resist authority or oppressive conditions openly and with force. **2** to reject the accepted rules of behaviour, dress, etc. **3** to feel aversion or dislike. [from Latin *rebellis*, from *bellum*, war]

rebellion *noun* an act of rebelling; a revolt.

rebellious *adj.* rebelling or likely to rebel.

rebelliously *adv.* in a rebellious way.

rebelliousness *noun* being rebellious.

Rebel Without a Cause a US film directed by Nicholas Ray (1955). A moody adolescent (played by James Dean) embodies the rebelliousness of the 1950s teenager in a story of rival gangs and emotional struggle.

Reber, Grote (1911–) US radio engineer, born in Wheaton, Illinois. Following the discovery of astronomical radio sources, he built the first radio telescope in his own back yard (1937), and for several years was the only radio astronomer in the world. He confirmed that the centre of our galaxy emits radio waves, and also found other sources, including the Andromeda galaxy and the Sun.

rebirth *noun* a revival, renaissance, or renewal, often a spiritual one.

rebirthing *noun* a type of psychotherapy involving reliving the experience of being born in order to release anxieties believed to result from the original experience.

reboot *Comput. verb trans., intrans.* to restart (a computer), either by switching off at the power source or pressing a reset button, etc.

rebore — *verb* (with stress on *-bore*) to renew or widen the bore of (a cylinder) in an internal combustion engine. — *noun* (with stress on *re-*) the process or result of this.

reborn *adj.* born again, especially in the sense of having received new spiritual life.

rebound — *verb intrans.* (with stress on *-bound*) **1** to bounce or spring back. **2** (**rebound on** *or* **upon someone**) *said of an action* to have a bad effect on the person performing the action. — *noun* (with stress on *re-*) an instance of rebounding; a recoil. — **on the rebound 1** while still recovering from an emotional shock, especially the ending of a love affair or attachment. **2** while bouncing. [from Old French *rebonder*]

rebuff — *noun* an unkind or unfriendly refusal to help someone or a rejection of help, advice, etc from someone. — *verb* to reject or refuse (an offer of or plea for help, a request, etc) unkindly. [from Old French *rebuffe*]

rebuild *verb* (PAST TENSE AND PAST PARTICIPLE **rebuilt**) to build again or anew.

rebuke — *verb* to speak severely to (someone) because he or she has done wrong. — *noun* the

act of speaking severely to someone, or being spoken severely to. [from Old French *rebuker*]

rebus *noun* (PL. **rebuses**) a puzzle in which pictures and symbols are used to represent words and parts of words to form a message or phrase. [from Latin *rebus*, by things]

◇ As a form of visual pun, rebuses are often used to puzzle or amuse, such as a drawing of a ray-gun (= Reagan), or the letters CU (= see you); some have become part of everyday writing, such as IOU (= I owe you).

rebut *verb* (**rebutted, rebutting**) **1** to disprove (a charge or claim) especially by offering opposing evidence. **2** to force to turn back. [from Old French *rebouter*]

♦ See note at *refute*.

rebuttal *noun* a rejection or contradiction.

recalcitrance *noun* **1** being recalcitrant. **2** recalcitrant behaviour.

recalcitrant *adj.* not willing to accept authority or discipline. [from Latin *recalcitare*, to kick back]

recall — *verb* (with stress on *-call*) **1** to order to return. **2** to remember. **3** to cancel or revoke. — *noun* (with stress on *re-*) **1** an act of recalling. **2** the ability to remember accurately and in detail: *total recall*. — **beyond recall** unable to be stopped or cancelled.

recant *verb* **1** *intrans.* to reject one's (usually religious or political) beliefs, especially publicly. **2** *trans., intrans.* to withdraw (a statement). [from Latin *recantare*, to revoke]

recantation *noun* recanting.

recap *colloq.* — *verb trans., intrans.* (**recapped, recapping**) to recapitulate. — *noun* recapitulation.

recapitulate *verb trans., intrans.* to go over the chief points of (an argument, statement, etc) again. [from Latin *recapitulare*]

recapitulation *noun* **1** an act or instance of recapitulating or summing up. **2** *Mus.* the final repetition of themes, after development, in a movement written in sonata form.

recapture — *verb* **1** to capture again. **2** to convey, produce, or experience (images or feelings from the past): *recapture the atmosphere of Victorian London.* — *noun* the act of recapturing or being recaptured.

recce *colloq.* — *noun* a reconnaissance. — *verb trans., intrans.* (**recced** *or* **recceed, recceing**) to reconnoitre.

recede *verb intrans.* **1** to go or move back or backwards. **2** to become more distant. **3** to grow less. **4** to bend or slope backwards. [from Latin *recedere*]

receding *adj.* that recedes.

receipt *noun* **1** a written note saying that money or goods have been received. **2** the act of receiving or being received: *acknowledge receipt of the money.* **3** (*usually* **receipts**) money received during a given period of time, especially by a shop or business. [from Latin *recipere*, to receive]

receive *verb* **1** to get, be given, or accept. **2** to experience or suffer: *receive injuries.* **3** to give attention to or consider: *receive a petition.* **4** to react in a specified way in response to: *receive the news well.* **5** to be awarded (an honour). **6** *trans., intrans.* to welcome or greet (guests), especially formally. **7** to permit to become part of: *be received into the priesthood.* **8** *trans., intrans.* Tennis to be the player who returns (the opposing player's service). **9** *trans., intrans.* Brit. to accept and often sell (goods one knows are stolen). **10** *trans., intrans.* to change (radio or television signals) into sounds or pictures. [from Latin *recipere*]

received *adj.* generally accepted.

Received Pronunciation the particular pronunciation of British English which is

regarded by many as being least regionally limited, most socially acceptable, and most 'standard'.

receiver *noun* **1** a person or thing that receives. **2** (*in full* **official receiver**) a person who is appointed by a court to take control of the business of someone who has gone bankrupt or who is certified as insane. **3** the part of a telephone which is held to the ear. **4** the equipment in a telephone, radio, or television that changes signals into sounds or pictures. **5** a person who receives stolen goods.

receivership *noun* the status of a business that is under the control of an official receiver, the office of receiver.

recent *adj.* happening, done, having appeared, etc not long ago. [from Latin *recens*, fresh]

recently *adv.* a short time ago.

receptacle *noun* **1** a container. **2** *Bot.* the top of a flower stalk, from which the different flower parts (sepals, petals, stamens, and carpels) arise. **3** *Bot.* in certain algae, any of a number of swollen regions that contain the reproductive structures. [from Latin *receptaculum*, reservoir]

reception *noun* **1** the act of receiving or being received. **2** a response, reaction, or welcome: *a hostile reception.* **3** a formal party or social gathering to welcome guests, especially after a wedding. **4** the quality of radio or television signals received: *poor reception because of the weather.* **5** an office or desk where visitors or clients are welcomed on arrival, eg in a hotel or factory. [from Latin *receptio*]

receptionist *noun* a person employed in a hotel, office, surgery, etc to deal with visitors and guests, accept telephone bookings, etc.

receptive *adj.* able, willing, and quick to understand and accept new ideas.

receptively *adv.* in a receptive way.

receptiveness *or* **receptivity** *noun* being able or willing to receive or take in.

receptor *noun Biol.* **1** an element of the nervous system adapted for reception of stimuli, eg a sense organ or sensory nerve-ending. **2** an area on the surface of a cell to which a specific antigen may attach itself. **3** a site in or on a cell to which a drug or hormone can become attached, stimulating a reaction inside the cell. [from Latin *recipere, receptum* to receive]

recess — *noun* **1** an open space or alcove set in a wall. **2** (*often* **recesses**) a hidden, inner, or secret place: *the dark recesses of her mind.* **3** a temporary break from work, especially of a law-court, or of Parliament during a vacation. **4** *North Amer.* a short break between school classes. — *verb* **1** to put in a recess. **2** to make a recess in. **3** *intrans.* to take a break or adjourn. [from Latin *recessus*, retreat]

recession *noun* **1** a temporary decline in economic activity, trade, and prosperity. **2** the act of receding or state of being set back.

◇ In economic terms, recession is usually defined as a situation where gross domestic product declines for two successive quarters (three-month periods). A recession is not as severe as a *depression* or *slump*, but is nonetheless characterized by sluggish demand, stagnant output, business failures, and increases in unemployment.

recessional *noun* a hymn sung during the departure of the clergy and choir after a service.

recessive *adj.* **1** tending to recede. **2** *Biol.* denoting a gene, or the characteristic determined by it, whose phenotype is only expressed in an individual if its allele is also recessive, ie two recessive genes must be present if their effect is to be apparent. If a dominant gene is present it will mask the effect of the recessive gene. **3** describing a characteristic determined by such a gene. See also DOMINANT.

recheck *verb trans., intrans.* to check again. — *noun* a second or further check.

recherché *adj.* **1** rare, exotic, or particularly choice. **2** obscure and affected. [from French *recherché*]

rechipping *noun* the practice of changing the electronic identity of stolen mobile telephones in order to resell them.

recidivism *noun* the habit of relapsing into crime. [from Latin *recidivus*, falling back]

recidivist *noun* a person who relapses, especially one who habitually returns to a life of crime.

Recife POP (1991) 2.9m, the port capital of Pernambuco state, Nordeste region, NE Brazil. It lies at the mouth of the R Capibaribe and consists of Recife proper (on a peninsula), Boa Vista (on the mainland), and Santo Antônio (on an island between the two). The three districts are connected by bridges. It is the most important commercial and industrial city in the NE. The first Brazilian printing house was installed here in 1706. NOTABLE FEATURES São Francisco de Assisi Church (1612), Church of Conceição dos Militares (1708), Church of Nossa Senhora das Prazeres; Fort Brum (1629), Conco Pontas (fort, 1677); Casa da Cultura (old prison); Museu do Açúcar (Sugar Museum).

recipe *noun* **1** a list of ingredients for and set of instructions on how to prepare and cook a particular kind of meal, cake, etc. **2** (**a recipe for something**) a way of achieving something (usually desired): *a recipe for success*. [from Latin *recipere*, to take]

recipient *noun* a person or thing that receives. [from Latin *recipere*, to receive]

reciprocal — *adj.* **1** given to and received from in return; mutual. **2** *Grammar, said of a pronoun* expressing a relationship between two people or things, or mutual action, eg *one another* in *John and Mary love one another*. — *noun Maths.* the value obtained when 1 is divided by the number concerned, eg the reciprocal of 4 is ¼. There is no reciprocal of zero.

reciprocally *adv.* in a reciprocal way.

reciprocate *verb* **1** to return (affection, love, etc). **2** (**reciprocate with something**) to give it in return: *reciprocate with an offer of money*. **3** *intrans. said of part of a machine* to move backwards and forwards. [from Latin *reciprocus*]

reciprocation *noun* reciprocating.

reciprocity *noun* **1** reciprocal action. **2** a mutual exchange of privileges or advantages between countries, trade organizations, businesses, etc.

recital *noun* **1** a public performance of music or songs usually by one person or a small number of people. **2** a detailed statement about or list of: *a recital of his grievances*. **3** an act of reciting.

recitalist *noun* a person who gives recitals.

recitation *noun* **1** something which is recited from memory. **2** an act of reciting.

recitative *noun* **1** a style of singing akin to speech, used for narrative sequences in opera or oratorio. It may be accompanied or unaccompanied, and its main purpose is to progress the action. **2** a passage sung in this way. [from Italian *recitativo*]

recite *verb trans., intrans.* **1** to repeat aloud from memory. **2** to make a detailed statement about or list: *recite one's grievances*. [from Latin *recitare*]

reckless *adj.* very careless; acting or done without any thought of the consequences. [from Anglo-Saxon *receleas*]

recklessly *adv.* in a reckless way.

recklessness *noun* **1** being reckless. **2** reckless behaviour or an instance of this.

reckon *verb* (**reckoned, reckoning**) **1** to calculate, compute, or estimate. **2** to think of as part of or belonging to: *reckon him among my friends*. **3** to consider or think of in a specified way: *be reck-*

oned a world authority. **4** *intrans. colloq.* to think or suppose. **5** *intrans.* (**reckon on someone** or **something**) to rely on or expect them: *we reckoned on their support*. **6** *slang* to esteem or admire highly.
— **reckon something up** to count or calculate it: *reckon up the cost*.
reckon with *or* **without something** to expect, or not expect, trouble or difficulties.
someone *or* **something to be reckoned with** a person or thing that is not to be ignored.
[from Anglo-Saxon *recenian*, to explain]

reckoning *noun* **1** calculation; counting: *by my reckoning, we must be about eight miles from the town.* **2** a settling of accounts, debts, grievances, etc.
— **day of reckoning** a time when one has to account for one's actions; a time of judgement.

reclaim *verb* **1** to seek to regain possession of; to claim back. **2** to make available for agricultural or commercial purposes marshland (especially by draining), land that has never been cultivated, or land that is derelict or has already been developed. **3** to recover useful materials from industrial or domestic waste. **4** *old use* to reform (someone). [from Latin *reclamare*, to cry out against]

reclaimable *adj.* capable of being reclaimed.

reclamation *noun* reclaiming or being reclaimed.

recline *verb* **1** *intrans.* to lean or lie on one's back or side. **2** *trans.* to lean or lay (eg one's head) in a resting position. [from Latin *reclinare*]

recliner *noun* someone or something that reclines, especially a comfortable chair with a back which can slope at different angles.

recluse *noun* a person who lives alone and in seclusion; a hermit. [from Latin *reclusus*, from *claudere*, to shut]

recognition *noun* the act or state of recognizing or being recognized.

recognizable *or* **recognisable** *adj.* capable of being recognized.

recognizably *or* **recognisably** *adv.* in a recognizable way.

recognizance *or* **recognisance** *noun* **1** a legally binding promise made to a magistrate or court to do or not do something specified. **2** money pledged as a guarantee of such a promise being kept.

recognize *or* **recognise** *verb* **1** to identify (a person or thing known or experienced before). **2** to admit or be aware of: *recognize one's mistakes.* **3** to show approval of and gratitude for: *recognize her courage by giving her a medal.* **4** to acknowledge the status or legality of (especially a government or state). **5** to accept as valid: *recognize the authority of the court.* [from Latin *recognoscere*]

recoil — *verb intrans.* (with variable stress) **1** (**recoil at** *or* **from something**) to move or jump back or away quickly or suddenly, usually in horror or fear. **2** to spring back or rebound. **3** *said of a gun* to spring powerfully backwards under the force of being fired. — *noun* (with stress on *re*-) the act of recoiling, especially the backwards movement of a gun when fired. [from Old French *reculer*]

recollect *verb* to remember, especially with an effort. [from Latin *recolligere*, to gather up]

recollection *noun* **1** the act or power of recollecting. **2** a memory or reminiscence. **3** something remembered.

recombinant DNA *Biol.* genetic material produced by the combining of DNA molecules from different organisms.

recombination *noun Genetics* the process whereby the genetic material is rearranged or 'shuffled' during the formation of gametes (specialized reproductive cells), so that the offspring possess different combinations of characteristics to either of the parents.

recommend *verb* **1** to advise. **2** to suggest as being suitable to be accepted, chosen, etc; to commend. **3** to make acceptable, desirable or pleasing: *an applicant with very little to recommend him*. [from Latin *commendare*, to commend]

recommendable *adj.* capable of being recommended.

recommendation *noun* **1** recommending. **2** something that recommends; a testimonial. **3** something that is recommended.

recommended daily (or dietary) allowance see RDA.

recompense — *verb* to pay or give (someone) compensation for injury or hardship suffered or reward for services, work done, etc. — *noun* money, etc given in compensation for injury or hardship suffered or as a reward for work done, etc. [from Latin *compensare*]

reconcile *verb* **1 a** (**reconcile one person with another**) to put them on friendly terms again, especially after a quarrel. **b** (**be reconciled**) *said of two or more people* be on friendly terms again. **2** (**reconcile one thing with another**) to bring two or more different aims, points of view, etc into agreement; to harmonize them. **3** (**be reconciled to** *or* **reconcile oneself to something**) to agree to accept an unwelcome fact or situation patiently. [from Latin *reconciliare*]

reconciliation *noun* the act of reconciling or being reconciled.

reconciliatory *adj.* that reconciles.

recondite *adj.* **1** *said of a subject or knowledge* little known. **2** dealing with profound, abstruse, or obscure knowledge. [from Latin *reconditus*, hidden]

recondition *verb* (**reconditioned, reconditioning**) to repair or restore to original or good working condition, eg by cleaning or replacing broken parts.

reconditioned *adj.* repaired, restored.

reconnaissance *noun* **1** a survey of land, enemy troops, etc to obtain information about the enemy. **2** a preliminary survey. [from French *reconnaissance*]

Reconnaissance Satellite (ABBREV. RECONSAT) a military space system placed into Earth orbit. It is equipped with cameras and other sensors capable of recording objects (eg military units) and activities on the ground, and relaying that information to Earth stations for analysis by intelligence experts.

reconnoitre *verb trans., intrans.* to make a reconnaissance of (land, enemy troops, etc). [from Old French *reconnoître*, to examine, recognize]

RECONSAT *abbrev.* Reconnaissance Satellite.

reconsider *verb trans., intrans.* (**reconsidered, reconsidering**) to consider (something) again and possibly change one's opinion or decision.

reconsideration *noun* reconsidering or being reconsidered.

reconstitute *verb* **1** to put or change back to the original form, eg by adding water. **2** to form or make up in a different way.

reconstitution *noun* **1** reconstituting. **2** restoration to an original condition.

reconstruct *verb* **1** to create a description or idea (of eg a crime) from the evidence available. **2** to rebuild.

Reconstruction the period after the American Civil War when the South was occupied by Northern troops. The major changes that took place included the destruction of slavery and the attempted integration of the freed black people. Reconstruction resulted in various new laws and amendments to the US Constitution; once scorned by historians as a 'tragic era' of corruption, it is now seen as a period of necessary but incomplete social change. Resistance to it among white southerners resulted in the founding of the Ku Klux Klan (1866), which gained in power until the Compromise of 1877, when a bargain among politicians gave a disputed presidential election to the Republicans in return for 'home' (ie white) rule in the South, following which a policy of racial segregation evolved to keep black people firmly subordinate.

reconstruction *noun* **1** a period or process of reconstructing or being reconstructed. **2** something that is reconstructed.

record *noun* (with stress on *rec*-) **1** a formal written report or statement of facts, events, or information. **2** (*often* **records**) information, facts, etc, collected over a usually long period of time. **3** the state or fact of being recorded. **4** a thin plastic disc used as a recording medium for reproducing music or other sound. **5** *especially in sports* a performance which is officially recorded as the best of a particular kind or in a particular class. **6** a description of the history and achievements of a person, institution, company, etc. **7** a list of the crimes of which a person has been convicted. **8** *Comput.* in database systems, a subdivision of a file, consisting of a collection of fields, each of which contains a particular item of information, eg a name or address. A record can be treated as a single unit of stored information. **9** anything that recalls or commemorates past events. — *verb* (with stress on -*cord*) **1** to set down in writing or some other permanent form, especially for use in the future. **2** *trans., intrans.* to register (sound, music, speech, etc) on a record or tape so that it can be listened to in the future. **3** *said of a dial, instrument, person's face, etc* to show or register (a particular figure, feeling, etc).
— **go on record** to make a public statement.
off the record *said of information, statements, etc* not intended to be repeated or made public.
on record officially recorded; publicly known.
set the record straight to correct a mistake or false impression.
[from Latin *recordari*, to remember]

recorded delivery a Post Office service in which the sending and receiving of a letter or parcel are recorded.

recorder *noun* **1** a wooden or plastic wind instrument with a tapering mouthpiece and holes which are covered by the player's fingers. **2** a solicitor or barrister who sits as a part-time judge in a court. **3** a person who records something. **4** a tape-recorder.
◇ The recorder was used from medieval times until the 18c: it has been revived in the 20c as a school instrument, and for playing early music. It is made in various sizes, the most common being the descant and the treble.

recording *noun* **1** the process of registering sounds or images on a record, tape, etc. **2** sound or images which have been recorded.

record-player *noun* an apparatus which reproduces the sounds recorded on records.

recount *verb* (with stress on -*count*) to tell (a story, etc) in detail. [from Old French *reconter*, from *conter*, to tell]

re-count — *verb* (with stress on -*count*) to count again. — *noun* (with stress on *re*-) a process of re-counting, especially of votes in an election.

recoup *verb* **1** to recover or get back (something lost, eg money). **2** to compensate (eg for something lost). [from French *recouper*, to cut back]

recoupment *noun* recouping or being recouped.

recourse *noun* **1** a source of help or protection. **2** the right to demand payment.
— **have recourse to someone or something** to turn to them for help, especially in an emergency or in a case of extreme need.
[from Latin *recursus*, return]

recover *verb* (**recovered, recovering**) **1** to get or find again. **2** *intrans.* to regain one's good health, spirits, or composure. **3** *intrans.* to regain a former and usually better condition. **4** to regain control of (one's emotions, actions, etc): *recover one's senses.* **5** to gain (compensation or damages) by legal action. **6** to get money to make up for (expenses, loss, etc). **7** to obtain (a valuable or usable substance) from a waste product or by-product. [from Latin *recuperare*]

recoverability *noun* being recoverable.

recoverable *adj.* capable of being recovered.

recovery *noun* (PL. **recoveries**) an act, instance, or process of recovering, or state of having recovered.

recreant — *noun* a cowardly or disloyal person. — *adj.* cowardly or disloyal. [from Middle English]

recreate *verb* to create again; to reproduce.

recreation *noun* a pleasant, enjoyable, and often refreshing activity done in one's spare time.

recreational *adj.* relating to or of the nature of recreation.

recreation ground an area of land for playing sports, games, etc on.

recrimination *noun* an accusation made by an accused person against his or her accuser. [from Latin *criminari*, to accuse]

recriminatory *adj.* of the nature of or involving recrimination.

recrudesce *verb intrans. technical, said especially of a disease* to become active again, especially after a dormant period. [from Latin *recrudescere*]

recrudescence *noun* the act of breaking out again.

recrudescent *adj.* breaking out again.

recruit — *noun* **1** a newly enlisted member of the army, air force, navy, etc. **2** a new member of a society, group, organization, etc. — *verb trans., intrans.* to enlist (people) as recruits. [from French *recrue*, new growth]

recruitment *noun* recruiting.

recrystallization *or* **recrystallisation** *noun* **1** *Chem.* the purification of a substance by repeated crystallization from fresh solvent. **2** a change in crystalline structure that is not accompanied by a chemical change.

recta see RECTUM.

rectal *adj.* of the rectum.

rectangle *noun* a four-sided figure with opposite sides which are equal and four right angles. [from Latin *rectus*, straight + *angulus*, angle]

rectangular *adj.* **1** of or like a rectangle. **2** placed at right angles.

rectifiable *adj.* capable of being rectified.

rectification *noun* rectifying or being rectified.

rectifier *noun Electr.* an electrical device, usually a semiconductor diode, that is used to convert an alternating current into a direct current. Rectifiers are used in power supplies, and to detect radio and television signals.

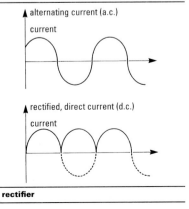

rectifier

rectify *verb* (**rectifies, rectified**) **1** to put right or correct (a mistake, etc). **2** to purify (eg alcohol) by repeated distillation. **3** to change (an alternating current) into a direct current. **4** to determine the length of (a curve). [from Latin *rectus*, straight + *facere*, to make]

rectilinear *adj.* **1** in or forming a straight line. **2** bounded by straight lines. [from Latin *rectus*, straight + *linea*, line]

rectitude *noun* honesty; correctness of behaviour or judgement; moral integrity. [from Latin *rectus*, straight]

recto *noun* (PL. **rectos**) the right-hand page of an open book. See also VERSO. [from Latin *recto*, on the right]

rector *noun* **1** in the Church of England, a clergyman in charge of a parish where the tithes would formerly all have gone to him. **2** in the Roman Catholic Church, a priest in charge of a congregation or a religious house, especially a Jesuit seminary. **3** the headmaster of some schools and colleges, especially in Scotland. **4** *Scot.* a senior university official elected by and representing the students; occasionally in other countries, the head of a university or college. [from Latin *rector*, from *regere*, to rule]

rectorial *adj.* of a rector.

rectorship *noun* the office of a rector.

rectory *noun* (PL. **rectories**) the house of a rector.

rectum *noun* (PL. **recta, rectums**) the lower part of the alimentary canal, ending at the anus. [from Latin *rectus*, straight]

recumbent *adj.* lying down; reclining. [from Latin *recumbere*, to recline]

recuperable *adj.* recoverable.

recuperate *verb* **1** *intrans.* to recover, especially from illness. **2** *trans.* to recover (something lost, one's health, etc). [from Latin *recuperare*]

recuperation *noun* recovery.

recuperative *adj.* **1** capable of restoring to health. **2** relating to or involving a recovery.

recur *verb intrans.* (**recurred, recurring**) **1** to happen or come round again or at intervals. **2** *said of a thought, etc* to come back into one's mind. [from Latin *recurrere*, to run back]

recurrence *noun* **1** the process of recurring. **2** something that recurs.

recurrent *adj.* **1** happening often or regularly. **2** *said of a nerve, vein, etc* turning back to run in the opposite direction.

recurrently *adv.* in a recurrent way.

recurring decimal a decimal fraction in which a figure or group of figures is repeated to infinity, eg 1 divided by 3 gives the recurring decimal 0·3333...

recusancy *noun* **1** *Hist.* refusal of Roman Catholics to attend services of the Church of England. **2** refusal to obey a command or authority.

recusant — *noun* **1** *Hist.* a person (especially a Roman Catholic) who refused to attend Church of England services when these were obligatory (between c.1570 and c.1790). **2** a person who refuses to submit to authority. — *adj.* of or like recusants. [from Latin *recusare*, to object]

recyclable *adj.* capable of being recycled.

recycle *verb* to pass through a series of changes so as to return to a former state, especially to process waste material so that it can be used again.

recycling the processing of industrial and domestic waste material (eg paper, glass, scrap metal, some plastics) so that it can be used again, so minimizing wastage and reducing the problems of environmental pollution associated with the disposal of large amounts of non-biodegradable refuse (eg many plastics).

◇ Recycling is advocated by many conservationists because it allows the use of smaller amounts of non-renewable resources, ie resources that do not renew themselves naturally. It also reduces production costs, as fewer raw materials are needed. Some governments and organizations now arrange the collection of waste paper so that it can treated and recycled (many newspapers use between 25 and 50 per cent recycled paper, and in the packaging industry nearly 80 per cent of all cardboard boxes are recycled). Central collection points, such as 'bottle banks' for the disposal of glass bottles and jars, are also becoming more widely available. The most commonly recycled metal is aluminium, from soft-drink cans and beer cans, nearly half of which are recycled. Incentives for recycling can be provided by government subsidies or by a deposit tax on containers.

red — *adj.* (**redder, reddest**) **1** of the colour of blood. **2** *said of hair or fur* of a colour which varies between a golden brown and a deep reddish-brown. **3** *said of the eyes* bloodshot or with red rims. **4** having a red or flushed face, especially from shame or anger. **5** *said of wine* made with black grapes whose skins colour the wine. **6** *derog. colloq.* communist. **7** (**Red**) relating to the former USSR; Soviet: *the Red Army.* — *noun* **1** the colour of blood, or a similar shade. **2** red dye or paint. **3** red material or clothes. **4** the red traffic light, a sign that cars should stop. **5** anything that is red. **6** the debit side of an account; the state of being in debt eg to a bank. **7** *derog. colloq.* (*often* **Red**) a communist or socialist. — **paint the town red** *colloq.* to go out to enjoy oneself in a lively, noisy, and often drunken way. **see red** *colloq.* to become angry. [from Anglo-Saxon *read*]

red admiral a common N American and European butterfly which has broad red bands on its wings.

red alga *Bot.* any alga belonging to the class Rhodophyceae, typically having a pink or reddish colour due to the presence of the pigment phycoerythrin, which masks the green colour of chlorophyll.

Red Army, in full **Red Army of Workers and Peasants**, Russian *Rabochekrest'yanshi Krasny* (ABBREV. **RKKA**) the official name of the army of the Soviet Union (1918–45). It was the most important land force engaged in the defeat of Nazi Germany (1941–5).

red blood cell *or* **red corpuscle**, a doughnut-shaped blood cell, produced in the bone marrow, that contains the pigment haemoglobin, which gives the cell its red colour. Red blood cells take up oxygen in the lungs and release it in the body tissues. — Also called *erythrocyte.*

red-blooded *adj.* active; manly; virile.

red-bloodedness *noun* being red-blooded.

redbreast *noun* a robin.

redbrick *adj., said of a British university* founded in the late 19c or early 20c.
◇ These included Manchester, Liverpool, Leeds, Birmingham, Sheffield, Bristol, Reading, Southampton, and Leicester.

Red Brigades, Italian *Brigate Rosse* (ABBREV. **BR**) an Italian left-wing terrorist organization, founded in 1970. At its most active in 1976–80, the BR undertook the kidnapping and killing of Italian judges, politicians (eg Aldo Moro 1916–78), businessmen, and journalists. Lack of public sympathy and a more efficiently co-ordinated anti-terrorist campaign (using former BR members as informers) led to widespread arrests and a virtual end to its activities by the early 1980s.

Redcar POP (1981) 35 000, a resort town in Langbaurgh district, Cleveland, NE England. It lies on the North Sea, 12km/7mi NE of Middlesbrough. NOTABLE FEATURE racecourse.

red card *Football* a piece of red card or plastic shown by the referee to a player who is being sent off. See also YELLOW CARD.

red carpet a strip of carpet put out for an important person to walk on; special treatment given to an important person or guest.

redcoat *noun* **1** *Hist.* a British soldier. **2** an attendant at a Butlin's holiday camp.

red corpuscle see RED BLOOD CELL.

Red Crescent an organization equivalent to the Red Cross in Muslim countries.

Red Cross, in full **International Movement of the Red Cross and Red Crescent** an international agency, formerly the International Red Cross (until 1986), which arose from the work of Henri Dunant and was founded by the Geneva Convention (1864) to assist those wounded or captured in war. Its activities in peacetime include worldwide relief duties, first aid, blood banks, maintenance of clinics, and training of nurses' and mothers' assistants. There are national branches (eg the British Red Cross) in most countries; most use the symbol of the red cross on white, but Muslim branches use a red crescent, and Iran uses a red lion and sun.

Redcrosse Knight, The the Knight of Holiness in Book I of Edmund Spenser's *The Faerie Queene*, who represents St George and is the partner of Una.

redcurrant *noun* a small edible red berry which grows on a widely cultivated European shrub.

red deer a species of deer, similar to but smaller than the elk, with a reddish-brown summer coat and brownish-grey winter coat, found in dense forest and on moorland in Europe, W Asia, and NW Africa, and introduced to various other parts of the world.

redden *verb* (**reddened, reddening**) **1** *trans., intrans.* to make or become red or redder. **2** *intrans.* to blush.

reddish *adj.* somewhat red.

Redditch POP (1992e) 79 000, a town in Redditch district, Hereford and Worcester, W central England. It lies 20km/12mi SW of Birmingham and was designated a 'new town' in 1964.

red dwarf *Astron.* a cool faint star of about one-tenth the mass and diameter of the Sun, eg Proxima Centauri, Barnard's Star.

redeem *verb* **1** to buy back. **2** to recover (eg something that has been pawned or mortgaged) by payment or service. **3** to fulfil (a promise). **4** to set (a person) free or save (a person's life) by paying a ransom. **5** to free (someone, oneself) from blame or debt. **6** *Christianity, said of Christ* to free (humanity) from sin by his death on the cross. **7** to make up or compensate for (something bad or wrong). **8** to exchange (tokens, vouchers, etc) for goods. **9** to exchange (bonds, shares, etc) for cash. [from Latin *redimere*, to buy back]

redeemable *adj.* capable of being redeemed.

redeemer *noun* **1** a person who redeems. **2** (**the Redeemer**) a name for Jesus Christ.

redeeming *adj.* that redeems.

redemption *noun* **1** the act of redeeming or state of being redeemed, especially the freeing of humanity from sin by Christ. **2** anything which redeems. — **beyond** *or* **past redemption** too bad to be redeemed, improved, or saved. [from Latin *redemptio*, buying back]

redemptive *adj.* redeeming, tending to redeem.

Red Ensign see ENSIGN.

redeploy *verb trans., intrans.* to move (soldiers, workers, etc) to another place or job.

redeployment *noun* redeploying or being redeployed.

redevelop *verb* (**redeveloped, redeveloping**) to build new buildings, etc in a run-down urban area.

redeveloper *noun* a person or organization that redevelops, especially land.

redevelopment *noun* redeveloping, especially of land.

red flag 1 a red banner used as a symbol of socialism or of revolution. **2** a flag used to warn of danger.

Redford, (Charles) Robert (1937–) US actor and director, born in Santa Barbara, California. Good performances on Broadway and on television led him to Hollywood, but his first great success was not until the film version of his stage role in *Barefoot in the Park* (1967). His other major film roles include *Butch Cassidy and the Sundance Kid* (1969), *The Sting* (1973), *All the President's Men* (1976), *Out of Africa* (1985), and *Indecent Proposal* (1993). As a director he was awarded an Oscar for *Ordinary People* (1980).

red fox a fox native to Europe, temperate Asia, N Africa, and N America, which has a reddish-brown coat with white underparts.

red giant *Astron.* a large cool red star, 10 to 100 times the diameter of the Sun but of similar mass. It appears very bright because of its size, eg Betelgeuse, a red supergiant in the constellation Orion. Red giants represent a late stage in stellar evolution, when a star has exhausted the nuclear fuel in its central core, and its outer layers have expanded greatly in size.

Redgrave, Sir Michael (Scudamore) (1908–85) English stage and film actor, born in Bristol, Avon. His distinguished career included performances on stage as Richard II (1951), Prospero (1952), Antony (1953), and Uncle Vanya (1962), and in Alfred Hitchcock's film *The Lady Vanishes* (1938).

Redgrave, Vanessa (1937–) English actress, born in London, daughter of the actor Sir Michael Redgrave. She joined the Royal Shakespeare Company in the 1960s, and took the lead in several feature films, including *Morgan, a Suitable Case for Treatment* (1966) and *Julia* (1977), for which she won an Oscar. Her later film appearances include *The Bostonians* (1984), *Prick Up Your Ears* (1987), and *Howard's End* (1992). She is well known for her active support of left-wing causes.

red-handed *adj.* in the act of committing a crime or immediately after having committed it: *caught red-handed.*

red hat a cardinal's hat; a symbol of a cardinal's office.

redhead *noun* a person, especially a woman, with red hair.

redheaded *adj.* **1** *said of a person* having red hair. **2** *said of an animal, etc* having a red head.

red herring 1 a herring which has been cured and smoked to a dark reddish colour. **2** a subject, idea, clue, etc introduced into a discussion, investigation, etc to divert attention from the real issue or to mislead someone (from the fact that a red herring drawn across a track can put a dog off the scent).

red-hot *adj.* **1** *said of metal, etc* heated until it glows red. **2** feeling or showing passionate or intense emotion or excitement: *red-hot anger.* **3** *colloq.* feeling or showing great enthusiasm: *a red-hot favourite.* **4** *said of news, information, etc* completely new and up to date.

red-hot poker a garden plant with long spikes of usually red or orange flowers.

redial *verb trans., intrans.* to dial (a telephone number) again.

Red Indian *often offensive* — *noun* a Native American. — *adj.* of a Native American.

red lead a bright red poisonous oxide of lead, used in making paints.

red-letter day a day which will always be remembered because something particularly pleasant or important happened on it (from the custom of marking saints' days in red on ecclesiastical calendars).

red light 1 a red warning light, especially one which warns vehicles to stop. 2 a refusal or rejection.

red-light district *colloq.* a district where prostitutes work.

red-lining *noun* the practice of refusing credit to those living in an area with a bad record of repayment.

Redmond, John (Edward) (1856–1918) Irish politician, born in Ballytrent, Co Wexford. He entered parliament in 1881, and was called to the Bar in 1886. A champion of Home Rule, he was Chairman of the Nationalist Party in 1900. He declined a seat in H H Asquith's coalition ministry (1915), but supported World War I, deplored the Irish rebellion, and opposed Sinn Féin.

redness *noun* a red quality.

redo *verb* (**redoes**; PAST TENSE **redid**; PAST PARTICIPLE **redone**) 1 to do again or differently. 2 to redecorate.

redolence *noun* sweet smell, perfume.

redolent *adj.* (**redolent of** *or* **with something**) 1 smelling strongly of it. 2 suggesting it strongly: *a street redolent of Victorian England.* [from Latin *redolere*, to give off a smell]

redolently *adv.* so as to be redolent.

redouble *verb trans., intrans.* 1 to make or become greater or more intense. 2 *Bridge* to double (a bid that an opponent has already doubled).

redoubt *noun* 1 a fortification, especially a temporary one defending a pass or hilltop. 2 a stronghold. [from Latin *reductus*, refuge]

redoubtable *adj.* 1 causing fear or respect. 2 brave; valiant. [from Old French *redouter*, to fear greatly]

redoubtably *adv.* in a redoubtable way.

redound *verb intrans.* 1 (**redound to someone**) to have a direct, usually advantageous effect on them. 2 (**redound on someone**) to come back to them as a consequence. [from Latin *redundare*, to surge]

redox reaction *Chem.* a chemical reaction in which one of the reacting substances (reactants) is reduced, while the other is simultaneously oxidized. [from REDUCTION + OXIDATION]

red panda see PANDA.

red pepper 1 cayenne pepper. 2 a red capsicum or sweet pepper, eaten as a vegetable. See also GREEN PEPPER.

red rag anything which is likely to provoke someone or make him or her very angry.

redress — *verb* 1 to set right or compensate for (something wrong). 2 to make even or equal again: *redress the balance.* — *noun* 1 the act of redressing or being redressed. 2 money, etc paid as compensation for loss or wrong done. [from Old French *redrecier*, to straighten]

Red River a river in S USA, and the southernmost tributary of the Mississippi R, length 1 966km/1 222mi. Rising in N Texas in the Llano Estacado, it flows SE and E, forming the Texas–Oklahoma and Texas–Arkansas borders. It then flows SE across Arkansas to a point NW of Baton Rouge, where it enters two distributaries; the Atchafalaya R which flows S to the Gulf of Mexico, and the Old R which joins the Mississippi. The major tributaries of the Red R are the Pease, Wichita, Washita, Little, and Black. The river is used for flood-control, irrigation, and hydroelectricity; it is navigable to Shreveport.

Red River, Chinese **Yuan Jiang**, Vietnamese **Song Hong** a river rising in central Yunnan province, China, SW of Kunming. It is c.800km/500mi long. The river flows SE into Vietnam to meet the Gulf of Tongking in a large delta, 32km/20mi E of Haiphong.

redshank *noun* a wading bird with a scarlet bill and legs, a white rump, and a broad white wing bar that can be clearly seen during flight. It is commonly found on coasts in winter.

redshift *noun Astron.* an increase in the wavelength of light or other electromagnetic radiation emitted by certain galaxies or quasars, so called because an increase in wavelength moves light towards the *red* end of the visible spectrum. It is generally interpreted as a *Doppler effect* resulting from the movement of the source of radiation away from the Earth, and is regarded as evidence that the Universe is expanding.

Red Shoes, The a British film directed by Michael Powell and Emeric Pressburger (1948). It is film about a ballet-dancer (played by Moira Shearer), and incorporates love, intrigue, and a mysteriously alluring pair of red shoes.

redskin *noun derog. colloq.* a Native American.

red spider mite a pest that infests the underside of the leaves of garden and houseplants, and weaves sheet webs between the leaves and the main stem. Large numbers of mites live within the webs and feed on plant sap which they suck with their specialized mouthparts.

Red Spot *Astron.* a large oval feature, varying in colour from pale pink to orange-red, in the atmosphere of the planet Jupiter, S of the equator. Space probes have shown that it rotates like a giant anticyclone, but the reason for its existence has not been established.

Red Square the central square of Moscow, Russia. Its Russian name (*krasnaya ploshchad*) derives from the Old Slavonic *krasny* ('beautiful' or 'red').

red squirrel a native British squirrel with reddish-brown fur.

redstart *noun* 1 a European bird having a conspicuous chestnut-coloured tail. 2 an American warbler that is superficially similar.

red tape *derog.* unnecessary rules and regulations which result in delay.

reduce *verb* 1 *trans., intrans.* to make or become less, smaller, etc. 2 to change into a usually worse or undesirable state or form: *reduced her to tears.* 3 to lower the rank, status, or grade of. 4 to bring into a state of obedience; to subdue. 5 to make weaker or poorer: *reduced circumstances.* 6 to lower the price of. 7 *intrans.* to lose weight by dieting. 8 to convert (a substance) into a simpler form: *reduce chalk to a powder.* 9 to simplify or make more easily understood by considering only the essential elements: *reduce the plan to four main points.* 10 to thicken (a sauce) by boiling off excess liquid. 11 *Chem.* to cause a substance to undergo a chemical reaction whereby it gains hydrogen or loses oxygen. 12 *Maths.* to convert (a fraction) to a form with numerator and denominator as low in value as possible, eg $\frac{3}{8}$ to $\frac{1}{3}$. 13 to convert (ore, etc) into metal. [from Latin *reducere*, to lead back]

reducer *noun* 1 a person who reduces. 2 a means of reducing.

reducibility *noun* being reducible.

reducible *adj.* capable of being reduced.

reducing agent *Chem.* any substance that brings about chemical reduction of an atom, molecule, or ion of another substance, by donating electrons, usually by adding hydrogen or removing oxygen, eg hydrogen, carbon monoxide.

reductase *noun Biochem.* an enzyme which brings about the reduction of organic compounds.

reductio ad absurdum *noun* 1 a way of proving that a premise is wrong by showing that its logical consequence is absurd. 2 the applying of a principle or rule so strictly that it is carried to absurd lengths. [Latin, = reduction to the absurd]

reduction *noun* 1 an act or instance of reducing; the state of being reduced. 2 the amount by which something is reduced. 3 a reduced copy of a picture, document, etc. 4 *Chem.* a chemical reaction that involves the addition of hydrogen to or the removal of oxygen from a substance, which in both cases gains electrons. It is always accompanied by *oxidation.* See also OXIDATION. [from Latin *reductio*]

redundancy *noun* (PL. **redundancies**) 1 being redundant, or an instance of this. 2 a dismissal or a person dismissed because of redundancy.

redundant *adj.* 1 *said of an employee* no longer needed and therefore dismissed. 2 not needed; superfluous. 3 *said of a word or phrase* expressing an idea which is already conveyed by another word or phrase, eg *little* in *little midget* is redundant because *midget* already conveys the sense of smallness. [from Latin *redundare*, to overflow]

reduplicate *verb* 1 to repeat, copy, or double. 2 *Grammar* to repeat (a word or syllable), often with some minor change, to form a new word, as in *hubble-bubble, riff-raff.* [from Latin *reduplicare*]

reduplication *noun* a folding or doubling.

Redwood a national park in N California, USA, lying on the Pacific coast. AREA 228sq km/88sq mi. It protects the Coast redwood trees (*Sequoia sempervirens*) which are among the tallest in the world.

redwood *noun* 1 either of two extremely tall coniferous trees, native to California. Both species, the giant sequoia (*Sequoiadendron giganteum*) and the coast redwood (*Sequoia sempervirens*), are very long-lived, and the coast redwood is probably the world's tallest tree,

Red Square

reaching heights of 120m. **2** the soft fine-grained reddish-brown wood of these trees.

Reed, Sir Carol (1906–76) English film director, born in London. He joined the cinema as an actor and director in 1930 and produced or directed several major films, such as *The Fallen Idol* (1948), Graham Greene's *The Third Man* (1949), for which he is best known, and *Oliver!* (1968), for which he won an Oscar.

Reed, Walter (1851–1902) US army surgeon, born in Belroi, Virginia. He joined the Army Medical Corps in 1875, and was later appointed Professor of Bacteriology at the Army Medical College, Washington (1893). His research on the cause and transmission of yellow fever proved that it is transmitted by the mosquito, and led to the eradication of the disease from this region.

reed *noun* **1** *Bot.* any of a group of grasses, most of which are species of the genus *Phragmites*, that grow in shallow water by the margins of streams, lakes, and ponds. The common reed is used to make thatched roofs, furniture, and fencing. **2** a thin piece of cane or metal in certain musical instruments which vibrates and makes a sound when air passes over it. **3** a wind instrument or organ pipe with reeds. **4** a comb-like device on a loom for spacing the threads of the warp evenly and putting the weft into position. [from Anglo-Saxon *hreod*]

reedily *adv.* in a reedy way, with a reedy sound.

reediness *noun* being reedy.

reedmace *noun* *Bot.* a reed-like plant of the genus *Typha*.

reed warbler a warbler that frequents marshy places and builds its nest on reeds.

reedy *adj.* (**reedier, reediest**) **1** full of reeds. **2** having a tone like a reed instrument, especially in being thin and piping. **3** thin and weak.

reef¹ *noun* **1** in shallow coastal water, a mass of rock that either projects above the surface at low tide, or is permanently covered by a shallow layer of water. **2** a coral reef. [from Dutch *rif*]

reef² — *noun* a part of a sail which may be folded in in rough weather or let out in calm weather, so as to alter the area exposed to the wind. — *verb* to reduce the area of (a sail) exposed to the wind. [from Middle English *refe*]

reefer *noun* **1** (*also* **reefer-jacket**) a thick woollen double-breasted jacket. **2** *slang* a cigarette containing marijuana.

reefing-jacket *noun* same as REEFER 1.

reef knot a knot made by passing one end of the rope over and under the other end, and then back over and under it again.

reek — *noun* **1** a strong, unpleasant, and often offensive smell. **2** *Scot., dialect* smoke. — *verb intrans.* **1** to give off a strong, usually unpleasant smell. **2** (**reek of something**) to suggest or hint at something unpleasant: *this scheme reeks of racism*. **3** *Scot. dialect* to give off smoke. [from Anglo-Saxon *reocan*]

reel — *noun* **1** a round wheel-shaped or cylindrical object of plastic, metal, etc on which thread, film, fishing-lines, etc can be wound. **2** the quantity of film, thread, etc wound on one of these. **3** a device for winding and unwinding a fishing-line. **4** a lively Scottish or Irish dance, or the music for it. — *verb* **1** to wind on a reel. **2** (*usually* **reel something in** *or* **up**) to pull it in or up using a reel: *reel in a fish*. **3** *intrans.* to stagger or sway; to move unsteadily. **4** *intrans.* to whirl or appear to move: *the room began to reel and then she fainted*. **5** *intrans.* (*also* **reel back**) to be shaken physically or mentally: *reel back in horror*. **6** *intrans.* to dance a reel.

— **reel something off** to say, repeat, or write it rapidly and often unthinkingly. [from Anglo-Saxon *hreol*]

re-entry *noun* (PL. **re-entries**) *Astron.* the return of a spacecraft to the Earth's atmosphere.

Rees-Mogg, William Rees-Mogg, Baron (1928–) English journalist, born in Bristol. He joined the *Financial Times* in 1952 and moved to the *Sunday Times* in 1960, becoming Deputy Editor in 1964. He held this post until 1967 when he assumed the editorship of *The Times*, which he held for 14 years. In 1988 he was appointed to head the new Broadcasting Standards Council.

Reeve, the foreman and former carpenter in Chaucer's *The Canterbury Tales*, who retaliates against the Miller's Tale with the story of a dishonest miller who is cheated and cuckolded by two students.

reeve¹ *noun Hist.* **1** the chief magistrate of a town or district. **2** an official who supervises a lord's manor or estate. [from Anglo-Saxon *refa*]

reeve² *verb* (PAST TENSE **rove, reeved**) to pass (a rope, etc) through a hole, opening, or ring. [from Dutch *reven*, to reef]

reeve³ *noun* a female ruff. See RUFF³.

ref *noun colloq.* a referee in a game.

refectory *noun* (PL. **refectories**) a dining-hall in a monastery or college. [from Latin *reficere*, to refreshen]

refer *verb* (**referred, referring**) (*usually* **refer to something** *or* **someone**) **1** *intrans.* to talk or write about them; to mention them. **2** *intrans.* to relate, concern, or apply to them: *does this refer to me?* **3** *intrans.* to look for information in a specified place: *I must refer to my notes*. **4** to direct (a person, etc) to some authority for discussion, information, a decision, treatment, etc. **5** to explain (something) as being caused by. **6** to consider as belonging to a specified place, time, or category. [from Latin *referre*, to carry back]

referable *or* **referrable** *adj.* capable of being referred or assigned.

referee — *noun* **1** an umpire or judge, eg of a game or in a dispute. **2** a person who is willing to testify to a person's character, talents, and abilities. — *verb trans., intrans.* to act as a referee in a game or dispute.

reference *noun* **1** (*usually* **reference to something**) a mention of it; an allusion to it. **2** a direction in a book to another passage or book where information can be found. **3** a book or passage referred to. **4** the act of referring to a book or passage for information. **5** a written report on a person's character, talents, and abilities, especially of his or her aptitude for a particular job or position. **6** a person referred to for such a report. **7** the providing of facts and information: *a reference library*. **8** the directing of a person, question, etc to some authority for information, a decision, etc. **9** a relation, correspondence, or connection: *with reference to your last letter*. **10** a standard for measuring or judging: *a point of reference*.

reference book any book, such as an encyclopedia or dictionary, that is consulted occasionally for information and which is not usually read through as, for example, a novel or biography is.

referendum *noun* (PL. **referendums, referenda**) the act or principle of giving the people of a country the chance to state their opinion on a matter by voting for or against it. [from Latin *referre*, to carry back]

◇ Referendums are most commonly held on constitutional changes, rather than on government policy. Recent examples include those held in some countries of the European Community on the Maastricht Treaty on European Union. In Britain, the last referendum was held in 1979 on the subject of a separate parliament for Scotland.

referential *adj.* **1** containing a reference. **2** having reference to something. **3** used for reference.

referral *noun* the act of referring someone to an expert, especially the sending of a patient by a GP to a specialist for treatment.

referred *adj. Medicine, said of pain* felt in a part of the body other than its actual source.

refill — *noun* (with stress on *re-*) a new filling for something which becomes empty through use, or a container for this. — *verb* (with stress on *-fill*) to fill again.

refillable *adj.* capable of being refilled.

refine *verb* **1** to make pure by removing dirt, waste substances, etc. **2** *trans., intrans.* to make or become more elegant, polished, or subtle.

refined *adj.* **1** very polite; well-mannered; elegant. **2** having had all the dirt, waste substances, etc removed. **3** improved; polished.

refinement *noun* **1** the act or process of refining. **2** good manners or good taste; polite speech; elegance. **3** an improvement or perfection. **4** a subtle distinction.

refinery *noun* (PL. **refineries**) a factory where raw materials such as sugar and oil are refined.

refining *noun* any process whereby a substance is purified by the removal of impurities, eg the separation of petroleum (crude oil) into its various components, such as hydrocarbon fuels, or the removal of impurities from a metal after it has been extracted from its ore.

refit — *verb* (with stress on *-fit*) (**refitted, refitting**) **1** to repair or fit new parts to (especially a ship). **2** *intrans. said of a ship* to be repaired or have new parts fitted. — *noun* (with stress on *re-*) the process of refitting or being refitted.

reflag *verb* (**reflagged, reflagging**) to change the country of registration of (a merchant ship) usually for some commercial advantage; also, to replace the national flag of (a ship) with that of a more powerful nation, so that it sails under that nation's protection.

reflate *verb* to cause reflation of (an economy).

reflation *noun* an increase in the amount of money and credit available and in economic activity, designed to increase industrial production after a period of deflation. See also DEFLATION, INFLATION.

reflationary *adj.* characterized by or involving inflation.

reflect *verb* **1** *trans., intrans. said of a surface* to send back (light, heat, sound, etc). **2** *trans., intrans. said of a mirror, etc* to give an image of. **3** *intrans. said of a sound, image, etc* to be reflected back. **4** to have as a cause or a consequence of: *price increases reflect greater demand for the goods*. **5** to show or give an idea of: *a poem which reflects one's mood*. **6** (**reflect on** *or* **upon something**) to consider it carefully. **7** (**reflect on** *or* **upon someone**) *said of an action, etc* to bring praise, or blame, to them: *her behaviour reflects on* (= reflects badly on) *her mother / your behaviour reflects well on you*. [from Latin *reflectere*, to bend back]

reflectance *noun Physics* the ratio of the intensity of the radiation that is reflected by a surface to the intensity of radiation that is incident (falling) on that surface.

reflecting telescope a telescope in which light rays are collected and focused by means of a concave mirror. The largest astronomical telescopes are of this type.

reflection *or* **reflexion** *noun* **1** the change in direction of a particle or wave, eg the turning back of a ray of light, either when it strikes a smooth surface that it does not penetrate, such as a mirror or polished metal, or when it reaches the boundary between two media. See also REFRACTION. **2** the act of reflecting. **3** a reflected image. **4** careful and thoughtful consideration; contemplation. **5** blame, discredit or censure.

reflective *adj.* **1** thoughtful; meditative. **2** *said of a surface* able to reflect images, light, sound, etc. **3** reflected: *reflective glare of the sun on the water*.

reflectively *adv.* in a reflective way.

reflector *noun* **1** a polished surface which reflects light, heat, etc, especially a piece of red plastic or glass on the back of a bicycle which glows when light shines on it. **2** a reflecting telescope.

reflex — *noun* **1** a series of nerve impulses that produce a rapid involuntary response to an external stimulus, eg withdrawal of the finger from a pin-prick, or an internal stimulus, eg control of blood pressure or walking movements. The rapidity of a reflex response is due to the fact that the brain is not directly involved. **2** the ability to respond rapidly to a stimulus. **3** reflected light, sound, heat, etc, or a reflected image. **4** a sign or expression of something. **5** a word formed or element of speech which has developed from a corresponding earlier form. — *adj.* **1** occurring as an automatic response without being thought about. **2** bent or turned backwards. **3** directed back on the source; reflected. **4** *said of a thought* introspective. **5** *Maths.* denoting an angle that is greater than 180° but less than 360°. [from Latin *reflexus*, bent back]

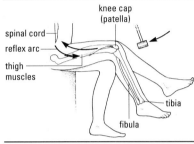

reflex action

reflex action a rapid involuntary movement produced by a reflex.

reflex camera a camera in which the image transmitted through the lens is directed by a mirror to the viewfinder for more accurate composition and focusing.

reflexion see REFLECTION.

reflexive *adj. Grammar* **1** *said of a pronoun* showing that the object of a verb is the same as the subject, eg in *he cut himself*, *himself* is a reflexive pronoun. **2** *said of a verb* used with a reflexive pronoun as object.

reflexively *adv.* in a reflexive way.

reflexologist *noun* a therapist who specializes in reflexology.

reflexology *noun* therapy for particular health problems and illnesses in which the soles of the feet are massaged, based on the belief that different parts of the soles relate to different parts of the body and different organs.

reflux *noun Chem.* the boiling of a liquid for long periods in a vessel attached to a condenser (known as a *reflux condenser*), so that the vapour produced condenses and continuously flows back into the vessel. It is widely used in the synthesis of organic chemical compounds. [from RE- + Latin *fluxus*, flow]

reform — *verb* **1** to improve or remove faults from (a person, behaviour, etc). **2** *intrans.* to give up bad habits, improve one's behaviour, etc. **3** to stop or abolish (misconduct, an abuse, etc). —

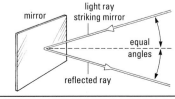

reflection of light

noun **1** a correction or improvement, especially in some social or political system. **2** improvement in one's behaviour or morals. [from Latin *reformare*]

reformable *adj.* capable of reform.

Reform Acts legislation in Britain which altered parliamentary constituencies and increased the size of the electorate. The main Acts were: 1832 (the subject of furious controversy and preceded by widespread radical agitation), which gave the vote to almost all male members of the middle classes, and introduced a uniform £10 franchise in the boroughs (ie all householders paying a minimum annual rental of £10 could vote); 1867, which gave the vote to all male settled tenants in the boroughs, thus creating a substantial working-class franchise for the first time; 1884, which extended a similar franchise to rural and mining areas; 1885, which aimed to create parliamentary constituencies of roughly equal size; 1918, which created a universal male suffrage and gave the vote to women of 30 years and over; 1928, which gave the vote to all adult women; and 1969, which lowered the minimum voting age from 21 years to 18.

Reformation the Protestant reform movements in the Christian Church, inspired by and derived from Martin Luther, John Calvin, and others in 16c Europe. Various factors are common to all reforms: a biblical revival and translation of the Word of God into the vernacular; an improvement in the intellectual and moral standards of the clergy; emphasis on the sovereignty of God; and insistence that faith and scripture are at the centre of the Christian message. Non-religious factors aiding the spread of the Reformation included the invention of the printing press; the political, social, and economic uncertainties of the age; and a general feeling of revival caused by the Renaissance. The doctrine of the priesthood of all believers and the importance placed on preaching the Word of God led to an educated clergy, and decentralized church communities were better able to prevent abuse of ecclesiastical privilege. In England, Henry VIII declared that the king was the supreme head of the English Church; in 1549 the Book of Common Prayer, embodying Reformation doctrine, was published. In Scotland, under the leadership of John Knox, the Presbyterian Church of Scotland was established in 1560; it remains the national Church. The Reformation also took root as Lutheran and Reformed Churches in France, Scandinavia, Czechoslovakia, Hungary, Romania, and Poland.

Reformation, Catholic a 16c reform movement in the Roman Catholic Church, which developed both as a reaction to the Protestant Reformation, and from a desire for internal reform. The Council of Trent affirmed papal authority and rejected conciliation with Protestants.

reformation *noun* the act or process of reforming or being reformed; improvement.

reformative *adj.* reforming.

reformatory *noun* (PL. **reformatories**) *old use esp. North Amer., esp. US* a school for reforming the behaviour of young people who break the law.

Reformed Churches the Churches that derived from Calvin's Reformation in 16c Geneva, and adopted a conciliar or presbyterian form of Church government. Now worldwide in extent, most of them are members of the World Alliance of Reformed Churches.

reformer *noun* a person who reforms or who advocates reform.

reformism *noun Politics* any doctrine or movement that advocates social and political change in a gradual manner within a democratic framework, rather than revolutionary change.

Reform Judaism a movement that began in early 19c Germany for the reform of Jewish worship, ritual, and beliefs in the light of modern scholarship. Greater emphasis is placed on the ethical teachings of the prophets than on ritual law, and belief is assessed primarily through reason and experience.

refract *verb, said of a medium, eg water, glass* to cause the direction of (a wave of light, sound, etc) to change when it crosses the boundary between one medium and another through which it travels at a different speed, eg air and glass. [from Latin *refringere*, to break up]

refracting telescope *or* **refractor** a telescope in which light rays are collected by means of a lens of long focal length (the *objective*) and magnified by means of a lens of short focal length (the *eyepiece*).

refraction *noun Physics* a change in the direction of a wave when it passes from one medium to another in which its speed is different, eg a light wave passing from air to glass. Mirages, and the distortion of all partially submerged objects, are caused by the refraction of light.

refractive *adj.* **1** relating to or involving refraction. **2** capable of causing refraction.

refractive index *Physics* (SYMBOL ***n***) the ratio of the speed of light (or other electromagnetic radiation) in air or a vacuum to its speed in another medium. For example, the refractive index between air and glass is approximately 1.6, ie light travels 1.6 times faster through air than through glass.

refractoriness *noun* being refractory.

refractory — *adj.* **1** *said of a material* having a high melting point and therefore able to withstand high temperatures without crumbling or softening, eg silica, fireclay, and metal oxides, which are used to line furnaces, etc. **2** difficult to control; stubborn; unmanageable. **3** *said of a disease* not responding to treatment. — *noun* (PL. **refractories**) *Chem.* a refractory material. [from Latin *refractarius*, stubborn]

refrain¹ *noun* a phrase or group of lines, or the music for them, repeated at the end of each stanza or verse in a poem or song. [from Old French *refrain*, from Latin *frangere*, to break]

refrain² *verb intrans.* (**refrain from something**) to keep oneself from acting in some way; to avoid it. [from Latin *refrenare*, from *frenum*, bridle]

refrangibility *noun* being refrangible.

refrangible *adj.* able to be refracted. [from Latin *refringere*, from *frangere*, to break]

refresh *verb* **1** *said of food, rest, etc* to give renewed strength, energy, and enthusiasm to. **2** to revive (someone, oneself, etc) with food, rest, etc. **3** to provide a new supply of; to replenish. **4** to make cool. **5** to make (one's memory) clearer and stronger by reading or listening to the source of information again. [from Old French *refreschir*]

refresher *noun* **1** anything, eg a cold drink, that refreshes. **2** *Legal* an extra fee paid to counsel during a long case or an adjournment.

refresher course a course of study or training intended to increase or update a person's previous knowledge or skill.

refreshing *adj.* **1** giving new strength, energy, and enthusiasm; cooling. **2** particularly pleasing because different, unexpected, or new.

refreshingly *adv.* in a refreshing way.

refreshment *noun* **1** the act of refreshing or state of being refreshed. **2** anything which refreshes. **3** (**refreshments**) food and drink.

refrigerant — *noun* a liquid used in the cooling mechanism of a refrigerator. — *adj.* cooling.

refrigerate *verb* to make or keep (food) cold or frozen to prevent it from going bad. [from Latin *refrigerare*, from *frigus*, cold]

refrigeration *noun* the process whereby a cabinet or room and its contents are kept at a temperature significantly lower than that of the surrounding environment, especially in order to slow down the rate of decay of food or other perishable materials. It occurs as a result of a continuous cycle in which a volatile liquid *refrigerant* evaporates, absorbing heat as it does so, and is then compressed back to a liquid by means of a compressor pump outside the cabinet or room.

refrigerator *noun* an insulated cabinet or room maintained at a temperature above 0°C and below 5°C in order to slow down the rate of decay of food or other perishable materials stored within it.

refuel *verb* (**refuelled**, **refuelling**) 1 to supply (an aircraft, etc) with more fuel. 2 *intrans. said of an aircraft, etc* to take on more fuel.

refuge *noun* 1 shelter or protection from danger or trouble. 2 any place, person, or thing offering such shelter. [from Latin *refugium*]

refugee *noun* a person who seeks refuge, especially from religious or political persecution, in another country.
◇ The United Nations' refugee organizations provide international assistance to displaced peoples, aiding their transport and resettlement. Many countries, including Britain, make a distinction between so-called 'economic' refugees and those who have been the subject of persecution, rejecting the first category and largely discouraging the second.

refulgence *noun* 1 being refulgent. 2 brightness.

refulgent *adj. literary* shining brightly; radiant; beaming. [from Latin *refulgere*, to shine brightly]

refund — *verb* (with stress on *-fund*) to pay (money, etc) back to (someone). — *noun* (with stress on *re-*) 1 the paying back of money, etc. 2 the money, etc paid back. [from Latin *refundere*, to pour back]

refundable *adj., said of a deposit, etc* that may be refunded.

refurbish *verb* to renovate and redecorate.

refurbishment *noun* refurbishing or being refurbished.

refusal *noun* an act of refusing.
— also **first refusal** the opportunity to buy, accept or refuse something before it is offered, given, sold, etc to anyone else.

refuse[1] *verb* (with stress on *-fuse*) 1 *trans., intrans.* to declare oneself unwilling to do what one has been asked or told to do, etc; to say 'no'. 2 not to accept (something): *refuse the offer of help.* 3 not to allow (access, etc) or give (permission). 4 *trans., intrans.* to show or express unwillingness: *the car refused to start.* 5 *trans., intrans. said of a horse* to stop at (a fence), and not jump over it. [from Old French *refuser*, to pour back]

refuse[2] *noun* (with stress on *ref-*) rubbish; anything thrown away; waste. [from Old French *refus*, rejection]

refuse-derived fuel 1 refuse which has had any metal or mineral content removed so that it can be fed into a suitably-designed furnace. 2 the product of small-scale fermentation of domestic and animal waste to produce gas (methane) for domestic use. The process has been promoted in certain Third World countries as a cheaper alternative to the burning of wood or fossil fuels.

refusenik *noun* a person, especially a Jew, living in the countries of the former Soviet Union who was refused permission to emigrate (usually to Israel).

refutable *adj.* capable of being refuted.

refutation *noun* 1 refuting. 2 an argument, etc that refutes.

refute *verb* 1 to prove that (a person, statement, theory, etc) is wrong. 2 *colloq.* to deny. [from Latin *refutare*, to drive back]

◆ Note that *refute* denotes the expounding of argument or proof. If simple rejection is meant, the word to use is *rebut* or *reject* or *repudiate*.

regain *verb* 1 to get back again or recover. 2 to get back to (a place).

regal *adj.* of, like, or suitable for a king or queen. [from Latin *regalis*, royal]

regale *verb* 1 (**regale someone with something**) to amuse them with stories or other entertainment. 2 to entertain (someone) lavishly. [from French *régaler*]

regalia *pl. noun* 1 objects such as the crown and sceptre which are a sign of royalty, used at coronations, etc. 2 any ornaments, ceremonial clothes, etc worn as a sign of a person's importance or authority, eg by a mayor. [from Latin *regalia*, things worthy of a king]

regality *noun* 1 being regal. 2 royalty. 3 sovereignty.

regally *adv.* in a regal way.

Regan the cruel second daughter of Lear in Shakespeare's *King Lear*, who blinds Gloucester with the aid of her husband, Cornwall.

regard — *verb* 1 to consider (someone or something) in a specified way: *regarded him as a friend.* 2 to pay attention to; to take notice of. 3 to look at attentively or steadily. 4 to have a connection with or relate to. — *noun* 1 thought or attention. 2 care or consideration; sympathy. 3 respect and affection: *be held in high regard.* 4 a gaze or look. 5 (**regards**) greetings; good wishes. — **as regards** ... concerning ...; as far as ... is concerned.
with regard to ... about ...; concerning ... [from Middle English]

regardful *adj.* (**regardful of something**) paying attention to it; taking notice of it.

regarding *prep.* about; concerning.

regardless — *adv.* not thinking or caring about costs, problems, dangers, etc; in spite of everything: *carry on regardless.* — *adj.* (**regardless of something**) taking no notice of it: *regardless of the consequences.*

regardlessly *adv.* heedlessly, inconsiderately.

regatta *noun* a meeting for yacht or boat races. [from Italian *regata*]

Regency the period in Britain when the Prince of Wales ruled as regent, 1811–20. 2 the period in France when Philip of Orleans ruled as regent, 1715–23. 3 (*in full* **Regency Style**) a florid neoclassical decorative style of architecture, furniture, dress, etc current in England in the early 19c. Like the Empire Style in France, it made bold use of Greek motifs (eg key-pattern), and also displayed Egyptian and Oriental characteristics.

regency — *noun* (PL. **regencies**) 1 the position of a regent. 2 government, or the period of government, by a regent. [from Latin *regens*, from *regere*, to rule]

regenerate — *verb* 1 *trans., intrans.* to make or become morally or spiritually improved. 2 *trans., intrans.* to develop or give new life or energy; to be brought back or bring back to life or original strength again. 3 to grow new tissue to replace (a damaged part of the body). 4 *intrans. said of a damaged part of the body* to be replaced by new tissue. — *adj.* having been regenerated, especially in having improved morally, spiritually, or physically. [from Latin *regenerare*, to bring forth again]

regeneration *noun* 1 regenerating or being regenerated. 2 the regrowth of parts that have been destroyed.

regenerative *adj.* characterized by regeneration; likely to regenerate.

regenerator *noun* a person or thing that regenerates.

Regensburg, French **Ratisbon**, ancient **Castra Regina** POP (1991e) 122 000, a commercial city in Bavaria, S Germany. It lies at the confluence of R Regen and R Danube, 104km/65mi NE of Munich. Imperial Diets were held here between 1663 and 1806. The medieval city is well-preserved. NOTABLE FEATURES Gothic cathedral (13c–16c), old town hall, Benedictine Monastery of St Emmeram (7c).

regent — *noun* a person who governs a country during a monarch's childhood or illness. — *adj.* acting as regent; ruling.

Regents of the Old Men's Alms House a group portrait of old men by Frans Hals (1664, Haarlem, Netherlands). He also painted *Regentesses of the Old Men's Alms House* (1664, Haarlem, Netherlands), a group portrait of old women.

reggae *noun* popular West Indian music which has a strong syncopated beat. [from Jamaican English]
◇ Reggae usually has four beats to the bar with a characteristic, strongly-accented upbeat; it draws on the Afro-Caribbean musical tradition with strong rock music influences. From its origins in Jamaica, it has been popularized in Europe and the USA, especially by artists such as Bob Marley (1945–81) and the Wailers.

Reggio di Calabria POP (1991e) 179 000, the seaport capital of Reggio di Calabria province, Calabria region, S Italy. It lies on the E side of the Strait of Messina, and was founded by Greek colonists in the 8c BC. The town is a major producer of oil of bergamot.

Reggio nell'Emilia POP (1991e) 132 000, the capital of Reggio nell'Emilia province, Emilia-Romagna region, N Italy. It was founded by the Romans. NOTABLE FEATURES cathedral (13c); Church of the Madonna della Chiaira (1597–1619).

regicide *noun* 1 the killing of a king. 2 a person who kills a king. [from Latin *rex*, king + -CIDE]

regime *or* **régime** *noun* 1 a system of government or a particular government. 2 a regimen. [from French *régime*]

regimen *noun* a course of treatment, especially of diet and exercise, which is necessary for one's good health. [from Latin *regimen*, from *regere*, to rule]

regiment — *noun* 1 a permanent army unit consisting of several companies, etc and commanded by a colonel. 2 a large number. — *verb* 1 to organize or control strictly, usually too strictly. 2 to form into a regiment or regiments. [from Latin *regimentum*, from *regere*, to rule]

regimental — *adj.* of a regiment. — *noun* (**regimentals**) a military uniform, especially of a particular regiment.

regimentation *noun* regimenting.

regimented *adj.* 1 strictly organized. 2 formed into a regiment or regiments.

Regina POP (1991) 179 000, the capital of Saskatchewan province, S central Canada. It lies on Moosejaw Creek, in S Saskatchewan. HISTORY founded in 1882 as capital of Northwest Territories; named in honour of Queen Victoria; it was made capital of Saskatchewan when the province was created in 1905. It is the centre of a grain, potash, and oil region. NOTABLE FEATURES Royal Canadian Mounted Police Museum; Wascana Park; Diefenbaker Homestead; Saskatchewan Centre of Arts; Museum of Natural History. EVENTS Buffalo Days (pioneer celebration, July); Canadian Western Agribition (autumn).

Regina *noun* the reigning queen, now used mainly on coins and in official documents. [from Latin *regina*, queen]

Reginald a male first name. [of Norman origin, from Latin *Reginaldus*, from *Regina*, queen]

region *noun* 1 an area of the world or a country with particular geographical, social, etc characteristics. 2 an administrative area, especially in

Scotland. **3** an area of the body round or near a specific part, organ, etc: *the abdominal region.* **4** any of the different layers which the atmosphere and sea are divided into according to height or depth. **5** an area of activity or interest. — **in the region of** ... approximately ...; nearly: *it cost in the region of a hundred pounds.* [from Latin *regio,* from *regere,* to rule]

regional *adj.* **1** of a region. **2** *said of pain* affecting a particular area of the body.

regionally *adv.* in a regional way; by regions.

register — *noun* **1** a written list or record of names, events, etc, or a book containing this. **2** a machine or device which records and lists information, especially (**cash register**) one in a shop which lists sales and in which money is kept. **3** the range of tones produced by the human voice or a musical instrument. **4** the set of pipes controlled by an organ stop. **5** a style of speech or language suitable for and used in a particular situation. — *verb* (**registered, registering**) **1** to enter (an event, name, etc) in an official register. **2** *intrans.* to enter one's name and address in a hotel register on arrival. **3** *trans., intrans.* (**register for something**) to enrol formally for it. **4** to insure (a letter or parcel) against getting lost in the post. **5** *said of a device* to record and usually show (speed, information, etc) automatically. **6** *said of a person's face, etc* to show (a particular feeling). **7** *intrans.* to make an impression on someone, eg being understood, remembered, etc: *the name didn't register.* **8** to obtain, achieve, or win: *register one's first success.* [from Latin *regesta,* things recorded]

◇ A speech or language register can be identified by a range of features which distinguish it from other registers in the language. Religion, law, science, advertising, journalism, and conversation may have distinctive vocabulary or usages: for example, traditional religious language in English makes use of the archaic forms *goeth, knowest,* and *seeketh.*

registered *adj.* recorded, entered (in a list, etc), enrolled.

Registered General Nurse, a nurse who has passed the examination of the General Nursing Council for Scotland. See also STATE REGISTERED NURSE.

register office *Brit.* an office where records of births, deaths, and marriages are kept and where marriages may be performed.

registrar *noun* **1** a person who keeps an official register, especially of births, deaths, and marriages. **2** a senior administrator in a university responsible for student records, enrolment, etc. **3** *Brit.* a middle-ranking hospital doctor who is training to become a specialist, and who works under a consultant. [related to REGISTER]

registration *noun* **1** registering. **2** something registered. **3** the art or act of combining stops in organ-playing.

registration number the sequence of letters and numbers by which a vehicle is registered, displayed on its number plate.

registry *noun* (PL. **registries**) **1** an office or place where registers are kept. **2** registration.

registry office same as REGISTER OFFICE.

Regius professor *Brit.* a professor holding a chair which was founded by a king or queen. [from Latin *regius,* royal]

Règle du Jeu, La (The Rules of the Game) a French film directed by Jean Renoir (1939). It is a tragi-comic portrait of a decadent society gradually destroying itself, depicted through the events of a country weekend.

Regnault, Henri Victor (1810–78) French chemist and physicist, born in Aix-la-Chapelle (Aachen, now in Germany). Professor at the Ecole Polytechnique and the Collège de France, and director of the porcelain factory at Sèvres, he discovered vinyl chloride and other industrially

important materials, improved the techniques for determining specific heats, and showed how real gases deviate from the ideal gas laws.

regrade *verb* to assign or award a different grade to (something).

regress — *verb intrans.* to return to a former less perfect, less desirable, less advanced, etc state or condition. — *noun* a return to a former less perfect, less advanced, etc state or condition. [from Latin *regressus,* return]

regression *noun* **1** an act of regressing. **2** *Psychol.* a return to an earlier level of functioning, eg a return to infantile or adolescent behaviour by an adult. It may accompany mental illness such as schizophrenia. **3** *Medicine* the stage of a disease in which symptoms disappear. **4** *Statistics* a measure of the relationship between the value of a particular variable and the values of one or more possibly related variables.

regressive *adj.* going back, reverting, returning.

regressively *adv.* in a regressive way.

regret — *verb* (**regretted, regretting**) to feel sorry, repentant, distressed, disappointed, etc about. — *noun* **1** a feeling of sorrow, repentance, distress, disappointment, etc. **2** (**regrets**) a polite expression of disappointment, etc used especially when declining an invitation. [from Old French *regreter*]

regretful *adj.* feeling or showing regret.

regretfully *adv.* with regret.

regrettable *adj.* that should be regretted; unwelcome; unfortunate.

regrettably *adv.* in a regrettable way, unfortunately.

regroup *verb trans., intrans.* **1** to form into a new or different group. **2** *Mil.* to organize (soldiers) into a new fighting formation.

regt *abbrev.* regiment.

regular — *adj.* **1** usual; normal; customary. **2** arranged, occurring, acting, etc in a fixed pattern of predictable or equal intervals of space or time: *visit one's parents at regular intervals.* **3** agreeing with some rule, custom, or normal practice, etc and accepted as correct. **4** symmetrical or even; having all the faces, sides, or angles, etc the same. **5** having bowel movements or menstrual periods with normal frequency. **6** of ordinary size: *a regular portion of chips.* **7** *colloq.* complete; absolute: *that child is a regular little monster.* **8** *Grammar, said of a noun, verb, etc* following one of the usual patterns of formation. **9** *said of troops, the army, etc* of or forming a permanent professional body. **10** officially qualified or recognized; professional. **11** belonging to a religious order and subject to the rule of that order. **12** *North Amer. colloq.* behaving in an acceptable, likeable way: *a regular guy.* — *noun* **1** a soldier in a professional regular army. **2** *colloq.* a frequent customer. **3** a member of a religious order. [from Latin *regula,* rule]

regularity *noun* being regular.

regularization *or* **regularisation** *noun* regularizing.

regularize *or* **regularise** *verb* to make regular.

regularly *adv.* **1** in a regular way. **2** at a regular time.

regulate *verb* **1** to control or adjust (a piece of machinery, the heat or sound available, etc) as required. **2** to control or direct (a person, thing, etc) according to rules. [from Latin *regula,* rule]

regulation — *noun* **1** a rule or instruction. **2** the act of regulating or state of being regulated. — *adj.* conforming to or governed by rules or by stated standards.

regulator *noun* a thing that regulates eg a piece of machinery.

Regulator Movements rural insurgencies in South Carolina (mid-1760s) and North Carolina (militarily defeated 1771) shortly before independence. In both disputes the slave-holding seacoast was pitched against small farmers of the interior, and the ensuing bitterness fed into the American Revolution, but the causes and outcomes of each were different. The term 'regulator' was also used elsewhere in early America to describe popular insurrectionary movements.

regulo *noun* each of several numbers in a series which indicate the temperature of a gas oven: *bake at regulo five.* [from *Regulo,* originally a trademark for a thermostatic control system for gas ovens]

regurgitate *verb* **1** to bring back (food) into the mouth after it has been swallowed. **2** *derog.* to repeat exactly (something already said). **3** *intrans.* to gush back up again. [from Latin *regurgitare*]

regurgitation *noun* regurgitating.

rehabilitate *verb* **1** to help (usually a prisoner or someone who has been ill) re-adapt to normal life, especially by providing vocational training. **2** to restore to a former state or rank, or to restore former rights or privileges. [from Latin *rehabilitare*]

rehabilitation *noun* rehabilitating or being rehabilitated.

rehash *colloq.* — *verb* (with stress on *-hash*) to use or present (subject matter which has been used before) in a slightly different from but with no improvements. — *noun* (with stress on *re-*) a speech, book, etc which re-uses existing subject matter with little or no change.

rehearsal *noun* **1** the act of rehearsing. **2** a performance of a play, etc for practice.

rehearse *verb* **1** *trans., intrans.* to practise (a play, piece of music, etc) before performing it in front of an audience. **2** to train (a person) for performing in front of an audience. **3** to give a list of or describe: *rehearse one's grievances.* **4** to repeat or say over again. [from Old French *rehercier,* to harrow again]

reheat — *verb* (with stress on *-heat*) to heat again. — *noun* (with stress on *re-*) a device for injecting fuel into the hot exhaust gases of a turbojet in order to obtain increased thrust; also the use of such a device.

rehouse *verb* to provide with new and usually better quality accommodation.

Reich the term formerly used to describe the German Empire and the German national state between 1918 and 1945. The Holy Roman Empire was regarded as the First Reich, and unified Germany after 1870 was referred to as the Second Reich (*Kaiserreich*). After 1933, the enlarged Germany planned by Hitler was known as the Third Reich. [from German *Reich,* kingdom]

Reichenbach, Hans (1891–1953) German-born US philosopher of science, born in Hamburg. He was Professor of Philosophy at Berlin (1926–33), Istanbul (1933–8), and California (from 1938). An early associate of the logical positivists, he was best known for his *Warscheinlichkeitslehre* (Theory of Probability, 1935) and *Philosophie der Raum-Zeit-Lehre* (Philosophy of Space and Time, 1978).

Reichstag Fire the deliberate burning down of Germany's parliament building (27 Feb 1933) shortly after the Nazi accession to power. A deranged Dutch ex-communist, Marinus van der Lubbe, was accused of arson and executed. The new Nazi government, who insisted that the act was evidence of a wider communist conspiracy (though it was not), used the situation to ban and suppress the German Communist Party. Though the fire seemed rather convenient to the Nazi regime, it is now agreed that Van der Lubbe acted alone.

Reigate POP (1981) 49 000, a residential town linked with Redhill, in Reigate and Banstead district, Surrey, SE England. It lies below the N Downs, 15km/9mi N of Crawley. NOTABLE FEATURE Church of St Mary Magdalene (burial place of Lord Howard of Effingham).

reign — noun 1 the time during which a king or queen rules. 2 the time during which something rules or is in control: *reign of terror.* — verb intrans. 1 to be a monarch. 2 to be present, exist, or dominate: *silence reigns.* [from Latin *regnum*]

reigning adj., *said of a winner, champion, etc* holding the title of champion, etc.

reiki noun a Japanese natural therapy, developed in the 19c, using the laying on of hands to channel healing energy into the body and so activate natural healing processes. [from Japanese, = universal energy]

reimburse verb to pay (a person) money to cover (expenses, losses, etc). [from RE- + Latin *imbursare*, from *bursa*, purse]

reimbursement noun 1 reimbursing. 2 repayment.

Reims see RHEIMS.

rein — noun 1 (*usually* **reins**) each of two straps attached to a bridle for guiding a horse. 2 (**reins**) a set of similar straps for guiding a young child. 3 a means of control or government: *take the reins.* — verb (*usually* **rein someone** or **something in**) to stop or restrain them with or as if with reins.
— **give a free rein to someone** to allow them freedom to act as they think fit.
keep a tight rein on something or **someone** to keep strict control of them.
[from Old French *resne*]

reincarnate — verb to cause (a person or soul) to be born again after death in a different body. — adj. reborn. [from Latin *incarnare*, to make flesh]

reincarnation noun 1 in some beliefs, the rebirth of the soul in another body after death. 2 a person who has been reincarnated. 3 an idea or principle presented in a different form.

reindeer noun (PL. **reindeer**, **reindeers**) a species of deer found in arctic and subarctic regions of Europe and Asia, closely related to the N American caribou. It is the only deer in which the female bears antlers, and it has been domesticated in Scandinavia and S Siberia for centuries for its meat, milk, hide, and hair, and for pulling sledges, etc. The Chernobyl accident in 1986 caused serious pollution of reindeer herds that had eaten contaminated plants. [from Norse *hreindyri*]

reinforce verb 1 to make stronger or give additional support to. 2 to make (an army, force, etc) stronger by providing more soldiers and weapons, etc. [from earlier *renforce*, from French *renforcer*]

reinforced concrete *Engineering* concrete in which steel bars or wires have been embedded in order to increase its tensile strength.

reinforcement noun 1 the act of reinforcing. 2 anything which reinforces. 3 (**reinforcements**) soldiers, etc added to an army, force, etc to make it stronger.

Reinhardt, Django (Jean Baptiste) (1910–53) Belgian jazz guitarist, born into a gypsy family of entertainers in Liverchies. Despite losing the use of two fingers in a fire, he devised a new chording method for his guitar and developed an outstanding technique. He played in the Quintet of the Hot Club of France with Stephane Grappelli, developing a distinctive French jazz style and becoming a powerful influence among swing-style guitarists in Europe and the USA.

Reinhardt, Max, originally **Max Goldmann** (1873–1943) Austrian theatre manager, born in Baden, Germany. An innovator in theatre art and technique, often involving large-scale productions (eg in *The Miracle*, London 1911, which used over 2 000 actors), he was also a co-founder of the Salzburg Festival (1920) and opened a theatre workshop in Hollywood.

reinstate verb to restore to a former, more powerful, position, status, or rank. [from RE- + *instate*, to install]

reinstatement noun 1 reinstating. 2 re-establishment.

reissue verb to issue again. — noun a magazine, etc that is issued again.

reiterate verb to repeat, especially several times. [from Latin *reiterare*]

reiteration noun reiterating.

Reith (of Stonehaven), John (Charles Walsham) Reith, 1st Baron (1889–1971) Scottish politician and engineer, born in Stonehaven, Kincardineshire. Trained in engineering, he entered the field of radio communication, and became the first general manager of the BBC in 1922, and was its director general from 1927 to 1938. He developed public service broadcasting in the UK, and so the BBC inaugurated the Reith Lectures in 1948 in honour of his influence.

reject — verb (with stress on -ject) 1 to refuse to accept, agree to, admit, believe, etc. 2 to throw away or discard. 3 *said of the body* to fail to accept (new tissue or an organ from another body). — noun (with stress on re-) a person or thing which is rejected. [from Latin *rejicere*, from *jacere*, to throw]
◆ See note at *refute*.

rejection noun 1 rejecting or being rejected. 2 something that is rejected.

rejig verb (**rejigged**, **rejigging**) 1 to re-equip. 2 to rearrange, often in a way which is considered dishonest or unethical.

rejoice verb 1 intrans. to feel or show great happiness. 2 trans. to give joy to; to make glad. [from Old French *rejouir*]

rejoicer noun 1 a person who rejoices. 2 a person or thing that causes rejoicing.

rejoicing noun 1 being joyful. 2 an expression, subject, or experience of joy. 3 festivities, celebrations, merrymaking.

rejoin[1] verb 1 to say in reply, especially abruptly or wittily. 2 intrans. *Legal* to reply to a charge or pleading. [from Old French *rejoindre*]

rejoin[2] verb intrans., trans. to join again.

rejoinder noun 1 an answer or remark, especially one made abruptly or wittily in reply. 2 *Legal* a defendant's answer to a plaintiff.

rejuvenate verb trans. to make (a person) feel, look, etc young again. [from Latin *juvenis*, young]

rejuvenation noun rejuvenating.

relapse — verb intrans. to return to a former bad or undesirable state or condition such as ill health or bad habits. — noun the act or process of relapsing, especially a return to ill health after a partial recovery. [from Latin *relabi*, from *labi*, to slide]

relate verb 1 to tell or narrate (a story). 2 (**relate one thing to** or **with another**) to show or form a connection or relationship between facts, events, etc: *related his unhappiness to a deprived childhood.* 3 (**relate to** or **with something**) to have or form a connection or relationship: *crime relates to poverty.* 4 (**relate to something**) to be about or concerned with: *I have information relating to/that relates to their activities.* 5 (**relate to someone**) *colloq.* to get on well with them; to react favourably to them. [from Latin *relatus*, brought back]

related adj. 1 belonging to the same family. 2 connected.

relation noun 1 a connection or relationship between one person or thing and another. 2 a person who belongs to the same family through birth or marriage; a relative. 3 kinship. 4 reference; respect: *in relation to.* 5 a telling or narrating. 6 (**relations**) **a** social, political, or personal contact between people, countries, etc. **b** sexual intercourse.

relationship noun 1 the state of being related. 2 the state of being related by birth or marriage. 3 the friendship, contact, communications, etc which exist between people, countries, etc. 4 an emotional or sexual affair.

relative — noun a person who is related to someone else by birth or marriage. — adj. 1 compared with something else; comparative: *the relative speeds of a car and train.* 2 existing only in relation to something else: *'hot' and 'cold' are relative terms.* 3 (**relative to something**) in proportion to it: *salary relative to experience.* 4 which relates to; relevant: *information relative to the problem.* 5 *Grammar* **a** *said of a pronoun* referring to something real or implied which has already been stated and attaching a subordinate clause to it, as *who* in *the children who are leaving.* **b** *said of a clause* attached to a preceding word, phrase, etc by a relative word such as *which* and *who.* 6 *Mus.*, *said of major and minor keys* having the same key signature. [from Latin *relativus*]

relative atomic mass *Chem.* the average mass of one atom of all the naturally occurring isotopes of a particular chemical element, expressed in atomic mass units. — Also called *atomic weight.*

relative density *Physics* the ratio of the density of a particular substance to that of some standard, usually water at 20°C; formerly known as specific gravity.

relative humidity *Physics* the ratio of the amount of water vapour present in the air to the amount that would be present if the air was saturated (at the same temperature and pressure). It is usually expressed as a percentage.

relatively adv. in a relative way, comparatively.

relativism noun a philosophical position that maintains that there are truths and values, but denies that they are absolute. It asserts that what may be true or rational in one situation may not be true or rational in another.

relativity noun 1 the condition of being relative to and therefore affected by something else. 2 (*in full* **general theory of relativity**, **special theory of relativity**) two theories of motion developed by Albert Einstein, which recognize the dependence of space, time, and other physical measurements on the position and motion of the observer who is making the measurements.

relax verb 1 trans., intrans. to make or become less tense, nervous, or worried. 2 trans., intrans. to give or take rest completely from work or effort. 3 trans., intrans. to make or become less strict or severe: *relax the rules.* 4 to lessen the force, strength, or intensity of: *relax one's vigilance.* 5 intrans. to become weak or loose. [from Latin *relaxare*]

relaxant noun *Medicine* a drug that can make a person feel less tense and help him or her relax.

relaxation noun 1 the act of relaxing or state of being relaxed. 2 rest after work or effort. 3 a relaxing activity.

relaxation therapy *Medicine* a form of therapy that involves learning to relax certain muscle groups, with the aim of eventually being able to relax the entire body, especially in stressful situations.

relaxed adj. 1 loosened, not tense, at ease. 2 informal, tolerant, not strict.

relaxing adj. that relaxes.

relay — noun (with stress on re-) 1 a set of people, supply of materials, etc that replace others doing or being used for some task, etc. **2** *old use* a supply of horses which relieve others on a journey. **3** a relay race. **4** *Electr.* an electrical switching device that, in response to a change in an electric circuit, eg a small change in current, opens or closes one or more contacts in the same or another circuit. Relays have been largely superseded by transistors and other solid-state devices. **5** *Telecomm.* a device fitted at regular intervals along TV broadcasting networks, underwater telecommunications cables, etc to amplify weak signals and pass them on from one communication link to the next. **6** something, especially a signal or broadcast, which is relayed. — *verb* (with variable stress) (**relayed**) **1** to receive and pass on (news, a message, a television programme, etc). **2** *Radio* to rebroadcast (a programme received from another station or source). [from Old French *relaier*, to leave behind]

relay race a race between teams of runners, swimmers, etc in which each member of the team runs, swims, etc part of the total distance to be covered.

release — *verb* **1** to free (a prisoner, etc) from captivity. **2** to relieve (someone) suffering from something unpleasant, a duty, burden, etc. **3** to loosen one's grip and stop holding. **4** to make (news, information, etc) known publicly. **5** to offer (a film, record, book, etc) for sale, performance, etc. **6** to move (a catch, brake, etc) so that it no longer prevents something from moving, operating, etc. **7** to give off or emit (heat, gas, etc). — *noun* **1** the act of releasing or state of being released, from captivity, duty, oppression, etc. **2** the act of making available for sale, performance, publication, etc. **3** something made available for sale, performance, etc, especially a new record or film. **4** an item of news which is made public, or a document containing this. **5** an order or document allowing a prisoner, etc to be released. **6** a handle or catch which holds and releases part of a mechanism. [from Old French *relaissier*]

relegate *verb* **1** to move (someone, a sports team, etc) down to a lower grade, position, status, division, etc. **2** to refer (a decision, etc) to (someone or something) for action to be taken. [from Latin *relegare*, to send away]

relegation *noun* relegating or being relegated.

relent *verb intrans.* **1** to become less severe or unkind. **2** to give way and agree to something one initially would not accept. [from Latin *re-*, back + *lentus*, flexible]

relentless *adj.* **1** without pity; harsh. **2** never stopping; unrelenting: *a relentless fight against crime.*

relentlessly *adv.* in a relentless way.

relentlessness *noun* being relentless.

relet *verb* to let (property, land, etc) again.

relevance *or* **relevancy** *noun* being relevant.

relevant *adj.* directly connected with the matter in hand, being discussed, etc. [from Latin *relevare*, to raise up, relieve]

reliability *noun* being reliable.

reliable *adj.* able to be trusted or relied on.

reliably *adv.* in a reliable way.

reliance *noun* the act or state of relying or depending upon, or trusting in, a person or thing.

reliant *adj.* relying on or having confidence in, trusting.

relic *noun* **1** (*often* **relics**) a part or fragment of an object left after the rest has decayed. **2** any object valued as being a memorial or souvenir of the past. **3** something left from a past time, especially a custom, belief or practice, etc. **4** part of the body of a saint or martyr or of some object connected with him or her, preserved as holy. **5** (**relics**) the remains of a dead person; a corpse. [from Latin *reliquiae*, remains]

◇ In many religions, including the Roman Catholic and Orthodox Churches, these are objects of veneration, and the churches in which they are housed places of pilgrimage.

relict *noun Biol.* a species occurring in circumstances different from those in which it originated. [from Latin *relictus*, left]

relief *noun* **1** the lessening or removal of pain, worry, oppression, or distress. **2** the calmness, relaxation, happiness, etc which follows the lessening or removal of pain, worry, etc. **3** anything which lessens pain, worry, boredom or monotony. **4** help, often in the form of money, food, clothing, and medicine, given to people in need. **5** a person who takes over a job or task from another person, usually after a given period of time. **6** a bus, train, etc which supplements public transport at particularly busy times. **7** the freeing of a besieged or endangered town, fortress, or military post. **8** a method of sculpture in which figures project from a flat surface. **9** a clear, sharp outline caused by contrast. **10** the variations in height above sea level of an area of land. [from Old French *relief*, from Latin *relevare*, to reduce the load]

relief map a map which shows the variations in the height of the land, either by shading, or by being a three-dimensional model.

relieve *verb* **1** to lessen or stop (a person's pain, worry, boredom, etc). **2** (**relieve someone of something**) **a** to take a physical or mental burden from them: *relieved her of many responsibilities.* **b** *facetious* to take or steal it from them: *the thief relieved him of his wallet.* **3** to give help or assistance to (someone in need). **4** to make less monotonous or tedious, especially by providing a contrast. **5** to free or dismiss from a duty or restriction. **6** to take over a job or task from (someone). **7** to come to the help of (a besieged town, fortress, military post, etc).
— **relieve oneself** to urinate or defecate. [from Latin *relevare*, to reduce the load]

relieved *adj.* freed from anxiety or concern, usually about a particular matter.

Religion, Wars of a series (1562–98) of religious and political conflicts in France, caused by the growth of Calvinism, noble factionalism, and weak royal government (eg the Valois kings after 1559). Civil wars were encouraged by Philip II of Spain's support of the Catholic Guise faction and by Elizabeth I of England's aid to the Huguenots. They ended when Henry of Navarre (Henry IV) returned to Catholicism and crushed the Guise Catholic League (1589–98).

religion *noun* **1** a belief in, or the worship of, a god or gods. **2** a particular system of belief or worship, such as Christianity or Judaism. **3** anything to which one is totally devoted and which rules one's life: *mountaineering is his religion.* **4** the monastic way of life. [from Latin *religio*]
◇ Religion is generally taken to mean belief in, recognition of, or an awakening sense of a higher unseen controlling power or powers with the emotion and morality concerned with such; a code of practice or belief which is maintained independently of reason, ie by faith. A religion may have one God (eg Judaism, Christianity, Islam), many gods (eg many ancient religions, Hinduism, and primitive religions), or no gods at all (eg Buddhism). The term may also be applied to certain philosophical systems such as Confucianism and Marxism.

religious — *adj.* **1** of or relating to religion. **2** following the rules or forms of worship of a particular religion very closely; pious; devout. **3** taking great care to do something properly; conscientious. **4** of or relating to the monastic way of life. — *noun* (PL. **religious**) a person bound by monastic vows, eg a monk or nun.

religiously *adv.* **1** in a religious way. **2** conscientiously.

religiousness *noun* being religious.

religious order see ORDER.

relinquish *verb* **1** to give up or abandon. **2** to release one's hold of. **3** to renounce possession or control of (a claim, right, etc). [from Latin *relinquere*, to leave behind]

relinquishment *noun* relinquishing.

reliquary *noun* (PL. **reliquaries**) a container for holy relics. [from Latin *reliquiae*, remains]

relish — *verb* **1** to enjoy greatly or with discrimination. **2** to look forward to with great pleasure. — *noun* **1** pleasure; enjoyment. **2** a spicy appetizing flavour, or a sauce or pickle which adds this to food. **3** zest, charm, liveliness, or gusto. [from Old French *reles*, remainder]

relive *verb* to experience again, especially in the imagination.

reload *verb trans., intrans.* **1** to load (a gun, etc) with fresh ammunition, etc. **2** to load (data) into a computer again.

relocate *verb trans., intrans.* to move (a business, one's home, etc) from one place, town, etc to another.

relocation *noun* relocating or being relocated.

reluctance *noun* **1** unwillingness; lack of enthusiasm. **2** *Physics* (SYMBOL **R**) a measure of the opposition to magnetic flux in a magnetic circuit, analogous to resistance in an electric circuit. [from Latin *reluctari*, to resist]

reluctant *adj.* unwilling; not wanting.

reluctantly *adv.* with reluctance, in a reluctant way.

rely *verb* (**relies**, **relied**) (**rely on** *or* **upon someone** *or* **something**) **1** to depend on or need them. **2** to trust someone to do something; to be certain of something happening. [from Old French *relier*, to bind together]

REM *abbrev.* rapid eye movement.

remain *verb intrans.* **1** to be left when something else, another part, etc has been lost, taken away, used up, etc. **2** to stay in the same place; to not leave. **3** to be still (the same); to continue to be. **4** to still need (to be done, shown, dealt with, etc): *that remains to be decided.* [from Latin *remanere*, to stay behind]

remainder — *noun* **1** the number or part that is left after the rest has gone, been taken away, used up, etc. **2** *Maths.* the amount left over when one number cannot be divided exactly by another number: *7 divided by 2 gives 3 with a remainder of 1.* **3** *Maths.* the amount left when one number is subtracted from another. **4** a copy of a book which is sold at a reduced price when demand for that book comes to an end. **5** *Legal* an interest in an estate which comes into effect only if another interest established at the same time comes to an end. — *verb* (**remaindered**, **remaindering**) to sell (a book) at a reduced price because demand for it has come to an end.

remains *pl. noun* **1** what is left after part has been taken away, eaten, destroyed, etc. **2** a dead body.

Remak, Robert (1815–65) German physician and pioneer in electrotherapy, born in Poznań. He studied the structure of nerves, discovering the 'fibres of Remak' (1830) and the nerve cells in the heart known as Remak's ganglia (1844). Also a pioneer embryologist, he was one of the first to describe cell division, and to suggest that all animal cells arise from pre-existing cells.

remake — *verb* (with stress on *-make*) (PAST TENSE AND PAST PARTICIPLE **remade**) to make again, especially in a new way. — *noun* (with stress on *re-*) something which is made again, especially a new version of a cinema film.

remand — *verb* to send (a person accused of a crime) back into custody until more evidence can be collected and the case can be tried. — *noun* the act of remanding.

— on remand having been remanded in prison or on bail.
[from Latin *remandare*, to send back word, to repeat a command]

remand centre *Brit.* a place of detention for those on remand or awaiting trial.

remand home *Brit. old use* a place to which a judge may send a child or young person who has broken the law, either on remand or as punishment.

remark — *verb* **1** *trans., intrans.* (**remark something** *or* **remark on something**) to notice and comment on it. **2** to make a comment. — *noun* a comment; an observation. [from Old French *remarque*]

remarkable *adj.* worth mentioning or commenting on; unusual; extraordinary.

remarkably *adv.* in a remarkable way.

Remarque, Erich (Maria) (1898–1970) German novelist, born in Osnabrück. He joined the German army at 18, and was wounded in World War I. After the war, he became a journalist and wrote his first war novel, *Im Westen nichts Neues* (All Quiet on the Western Front, 1929, filmed 1930). He left Germany in 1933, and his books were banned by the Nazis.

remarry *verb trans., intrans.* (**remarries, remarried**) to marry again, especially after a separation.

Rembrandt, properly **Harmenszoon van Rijn** (1606–69) Dutch painter, born in Leyden. His early works include religious and historical scenes, unusual in Protestant Holland. He settled in Amsterdam (1631), where he ran a large studio. *The Anatomy Lesson of Dr Tulp* (1632, Mauritshuis, The Hague) assured his reputation as a portrait painter. In 1642 he produced his best-known picture, *The Night Watch* (Rijksmuseum, Amsterdam). His preserved works number over 650 oil paintings, 2 000 drawings and studies, and 300 etchings. They include the *Blinding of Samson* (1636, Frankfurt), *The Syndics of the Drapers Guild* (1662, Rijksmuseum, Amsterdam), and *The Return of the Prodigal Son* (unfinished, 1669).

REME *abbrev.* Royal Electrical and Mechanical Engineers.

remediable *adj.* capable of being remedied.

remedial *adj.* **1** serving as a remedy; able to or intended to correct or put right. **2** *said of teaching* intended to help those pupils with learning difficulties.

remedially *adv.* as a remedy.

remedy — *noun* (PL. **remedies**) **1** any drug or treatment which cures or controls a disease. **2** anything which solves a problem or gets rid of something undesirable: *a remedy for the country's economic problems.* — *verb* (**remedies, remedied**) to put right or correct; to be a remedy for. [from Latin *remedium*]

remember *verb* (**remembered, remembering**) **1** *trans., intrans.* to bring to mind (something or someone) that had been forgotten. **2** to keep (a fact, idea, etc) in one's mind. **3** to reward or make a present to, eg in one's will. **4** to pass (a person's) good wishes and greetings to: *remember me to your parents.* **5** to commemorate. [from Latin *rememorari*]

remembrance *noun* **1** the act of remembering or being remembered. **2** something which reminds a person of something or someone; a souvenir. **3** a memory or recollection: *a dim remembrance of the night's events.*

Remembrance Day *or* **Remembrance Sunday** in the UK, the Sunday nearest to 11 Nov, on which services are held to commemorate servicemen and servicewomen who have died in war.

Remembrance of Things Past see À LA RECHERCHE DU TEMPS PERDU.

remind *verb* (**remind someone of something**) **1** to cause them to remember it. **2** to make them think about someone or something else, especially because of a similarity: *she reminds me of her sister.*

reminder *noun* something that makes a person remember something or someone.

reminisce *verb intrans.* to think, talk, or write about things remembered from the past. [from Latin *reminisci*, to remember]

reminiscence *noun* **1** the act of thinking, talking, or writing about the past. **2** an experience remembered from the past.

reminiscent *adj.* **1** (**reminiscent of something** *or* **someone**) similar, so as to remind one of them: *a painting reminiscent of Turner.* **2** *said of a person* thinking often about the past; given to reminiscing.

remiss *adj.* careless; failing to pay attention; negligent. [from Latin *remittere*, to loosen]

remission *noun* **1** a lessening in force or effect, especially in the symptoms of a disease. **2** a reduction of a prison sentence. **3** pardon; forgiveness from sin. **4** an act of remitting. [from Latin *remissio*, from *remittere*, to loosen]

remissly *adj.* carelessly, negligently.

remissness *noun* being remiss.

remit — *verb* (with stress on *-mit*) (**remitted, remitting**) **1** to cancel or refrain from demanding (a debt, punishment, etc). **2** *trans., intrans.* to make or become loose, slack, or relaxed. **3** to send (money) in payment. **4** to refer (a matter for decision, etc) to some other authority. **5** to refer (a case) to a lower court. **6** *intrans. said of a disease, pain, rain, etc* to become less severe for a period of time. **7** to send or put back into a previous state. **8** *said of God* to forgive (sins). — *noun* (usually with stress on *re-*) the authority or terms of reference given to an official, committee, etc in dealing with a matter. [from Latin *remittere*, to loosen]

remittance *noun* **1** the sending of money in payment. **2** the money sent.

remittent *adj., said of a disease* becoming less severe at times.

remix — *verb* (with stress on *-mix*) to mix again in a different way, especially to mix (a record) again, changing the balance of the different parts, etc. — *noun* (with stress on *re-*) a remixed recording.

remnant *noun* **1** a small piece or amount of something larger, or a small number of a large quantity of things left unsold, especially a piece of material from the end of a roll. **2** a surviving trace or vestige. [from Old French *remenoir*, to remain]

remonstrance *noun* **1** an act of remonstrating. **2** a strong, usually formal, protest. [from Latin *remonstrare*, to demonstrate]

Remonstrants, also known as **Arminians** the Christians who adhered to the Calvinistic doctrine of Jacobus Arminius (in 17c Holland). Named after the 'Remonstrance' (a statement of Arminian teaching dating from 1610), they were not many, but were nevertheless influential among Baptists, and in Methodism and Calvinism.

remonstrate *verb trans., intrans.* **1** (**remonstrate with someone**) to protest to them. **2** to protest forcefully: *remonstrated that they knew nothing about it.* [from Latin *remonstrare*, to demonstrate]

remonstration *noun* **1** remonstrating. **2** an instance of this.

remorse *noun* a deep feeling of guilt, regret, and bitterness for something wrong or bad which one has done. [from Latin *remorsus*]

remorseful *adj.* full of remorse, sorrowful.

remorsefully *adv.* in a remorseful way, sorrowfully.

remorseless *adj.* cruel; without pity.

remorselessly *adv.* in a remorseless way.

remote *adj.* **1** far away or distant in time or place. **2** out of the way; away from civilization. **3** operated or controlled from a distance. **4** distantly related. **5** very small or slight: *a remote chance.* **6** *said of a person's manner* not friendly or interested; aloof. [from Latin *remotus*, removed]

remote control *Electron.* the control of machinery or electrical devices from a distance, by the making or breaking of an electric circuit, or by means of radio waves, eg remote control television.

remote-controlled *adj.* operated by remote control.

remotely *adv.* in a remote way or degree: *not remotely the same.*

remoteness *noun* being remote.

remould — *verb* (with stress on *-mould*) to bond new tread on to (an old or worn tyre). — *noun* (with stress on *re-*) a worn tyre which has had new tread bonded on to it.

remount — *verb trans., intrans.* (with stress on *-mount*) to mount again, especially on a fresh horse. — *noun* (with stress on *re-*) a fresh horse.

removable *adj.* capable of being removed.

removal *noun* **1** the act of removing or state of being removed. **2** the moving of furniture, etc to a new home.

remove — *verb* **1** to move (a person, thing, etc) to a different place. **2** to take off (a piece of clothing). **3** to get rid of. **4** to dismiss (from a job, position, etc). **5** *intrans.* to change one's position, place, location, etc, especially to move to a new house. — *noun* **1** a removal. **2** the degree of difference separating two things: *a form of government which is at only one remove from tyranny.* **3** *Brit.* an intermediate form or class in some schools. [from Latin *removere*]

removed *adj.* **1** separated or distant. **2** *said of cousins* separated by a usually specified number of generations.
◇ A person's first cousin once removed is either the child of his or her first cousin or the first cousin of one of his or her parents.

remover *noun* a person or thing that removes, especially who moves furniture, etc from one house to another.

remunerate *verb* **1** to pay for services done. **2** to recompense. [from Latin *remunerari*, from *munus*, gift]

remuneration *noun* **1** remunerating or being remunerated. **2** recompense, reward, pay.

remunerative *adj.* bringing a good profit or having a good salary.

Remus, Uncle see UNCLE REMUS.

Renaissance the revival of arts, literature, and classical scholarship, and the beginnings of modern science, in Europe in the 14c to 16c. The Renaissance began in Italy in the 14c with the work of Dante, Boccaccio, and Petrarch. The period was characterized by the study and imitation of Greek and Latin literature and art, the critical study of Christian texts (eg by Erasmus), a belief in the individual and the power of education, and a general desire to enlarge the boundaries of learning. Major figures of the Renaissance include Machiavelli, Leonardo da Vinci, Michelangelo, and Raphael. The period 1490-1520 in Italy is often referred to as the High Renaissance.

renaissance *noun* a rebirth or revival, especially of learning, culture, and the arts. [from Latin *renasci*, to be born again]

renal *adj.* of, relating to, or in the area of the kidneys. [from Latin *renes*, kidneys]

rename *verb* to give a new name to.

renascence *noun* being born again.

renascent *adj.* becoming active or lively again. [from Latin *renasci*, to be born again]

rend *verb* (PAST TENSE AND PAST PARTICIPLE **rent**) *old use* **1** to tear, especially using force or violence. **2** *intrans.* to become torn, especially violently. [from Anglo-Saxon *rendan*]

Rendell, Ruth (1932–) English detective-story writer, born in London. She worked as a journalist and managing director of a local newspaper before the publication of her first novel, *From Doon with Death* (1964). She has written various detective stories featuring Chief Inspector Wexford (eg *Shake Hands Forever*, 1975), and mystery thrillers (eg *A Judgement in Stone*, 1977). Since 1986, she has also written under the pen name of Barbara Vine. Several of her works have been filmed or televised.

render *verb* (**rendered, rendering**) **1** to cause to become. **2** to give or provide (help, a service, etc). **3** to pay (money) or perform (a duty), especially in return for something: *render thanks to God.* **4** (*also* **render something up**) to give up, release, or yield: *the grave will never render up its dead.* **5** to translate. **6** to perform (the role of a character in a play, a piece of music, etc). **7** to portray or reproduce, especially in painting or music. **8** to present or submit for payment, approval, consideration, etc. **9** to cover (brick or stone) with a coat of plaster. **10** (**render something down**) to melt down fat, especially to clarify it; to remove fat by melting. [from Old French *rendre*]

rendering *noun* **1** a coat of plaster. **2** a performance.

rendezvous — *noun* **1** an appointment to meet, or the meeting itself, at a specified time and in a specified place. **2** the place where such a meeting is to be; a place where people meet. — *verb intrans.* (**rendezvous, rendezvoused**) to meet at an appointed place. [from French *rendezvous*, present yourselves]

rendition *noun* **1** a performance or interpretation (of a piece of music or a dramatic role, etc). **2** an act of rendering, especially of translating. [from Old French]

rendzina *noun Geol.* any of a group of dark fertile soils, rich in humus and calcium carbonate, that have developed over limestone bedrock. Large areas of such soils are found in humid or semi-arid grassland and limestone regions. [from Russian *rendzina*, from Polish *redzina*]

Rene a male first name. [French, from Latin *Renatus*, = born again]

renegade *noun* a person who deserts the religious, political, etc group to which he or she belongs to join an enemy or rival group. [from Spanish *renegado*]

renege *verb* **1** *intrans.* (**renege on something**) to go back on a promise, agreement, one's word, etc. **2** to renounce (a promise, etc) or desert (a person, faith, etc). **3** *Cards* to revoke. [from Latin *renegare*, from *negare*, to deny]

reneger *noun* a person who reneges.

renew *verb* **1** to make fresh or like new again; to restore to the original condition. **2** to begin or begin to do again; to repeat. **3** to begin (some activity) again after a break. **4** *trans., intrans.* to make (a licence, lease, loan, etc) valid for a further period of time. **5** to replenish or replace: *renew the water in the vases.* **6** to recover (youth, strength, etc).

renewable *adj.* capable of renewal.

renewable resource, any energy source that is naturally occurring and that cannot in theory be exhausted, eg solar energy, hydroelectric power, tidal, wind, or wave power, geothermal energy. See also NON-RENEWABLE RESOURCE.

renewal *noun* **1** renewing or being renewed. **2** something that is renewed.

renewer *noun* a person who renews something.

renin *noun Physiol.* a hormone, produced by the kidneys, that is secreted into the bloodstream, where it constricts the arteries and thereby raises the blood pressure. [from Latin *renes*, the kidneys]

Renner, Karl (1870–1950) Austrian politician, born in Unter-Tannowitz, Bohemia. He trained as a lawyer, joined the Austrian Social Democratic Party, and became the first Chancellor of the Austrian Republic (1918–20). Imprisoned as a socialist leader following the brief civil war (Feb 1934), he was Chancellor again in 1945, and then first President of the new Republic (1945–50).

Rennes, Breton **Roazon**, ancient **Condate** POP (1990) 245 000, the capital of Ille-et-Vilaine department, Brittany, NW France. It lies at the confluence of the canalized Ille and Vilaine rivers, 309km/192mi SW of Paris and is the industrial, economic, and cultural centre of Brittany. HISTORY capital of Brittany in the 10c; largely rebuilt after a major fire in 1720; badly bombed during World War II. NOTABLE FEATURES Baroque town hall (1734); Palais de Justice; former abbey church of Notre-Dame (11c–13c), cathedral (largely rebuilt in the 19c); La Porte Mordelaise; Thabor Gardens; university (founded at Nantes in 1461, transferred to Rennes in 1735).

rennet *noun* an extract obtained from the stomachs of calves that contains the enzyme rennin, which curdles milk. It is used to make junket and certain cheeses. [from Middle English]

Rennie, John (1761–1821) Scottish civil engineer, born in East Lothian. Educated at Edinburgh, in 1791 he set up in London as an engineer, and soon became famous as a bridge-builder, constructing several bridges over the Thames (none now remaining). He also built canals, drained fens, designed London and other docks, and improved harbours and dockyards, including the breakwater at Plymouth.

rennin *noun Biochem.* an enzyme, found in gastric juice, that causes milk to curdle. [from RENNET]

Reno POP (1990) 255 000, the seat of Washoe County, W Nevada, USA, on the Truckee R. Settled in 1859, it developed with the arrival of the railway in 1868. Couples seeking a quick divorce travel across the Californian border to Reno. The town is noted for its casinos.

Renoir, Jean (1894–1979) French film director, born in Paris, the son of Pierre Auguste Renoir. He turned from scriptwriting to film-making and his major works include his anti-war masterpiece, *La Grande Illusion* (Grand Illusion, 1937) and *La Règle du jeu* (The Rules of the Game, 1939). Later he worked in the USA, India, and Europe on films such as *French Can-Can* (1955).

Renoir, Pierre Auguste (1841–1919) French Impressionist artist, born in Limoges. He first painted porcelain and fans, then began to paint in the open air (c.1864) and from 1870 he obtained several commissions for portraits. He exhibited with the Impressionists, and his picture of sunlight filtering through leaves *Moulin de la Galette* (1876, Louvre, Paris) epitomizes his colourful, happy art. His visit to Italy in 1880 was followed by a series of *Bathers* (1884–7) in a more cold and classical style. He then returned to reds, orange, and gold to portray nudes in sunlight, a style which he continued to develop until his death. His works include *The Umbrellas* (c.1883, National Gallery, London) and *The Judgement of Paris* (c.1914).

renounce *verb* **1** to give up (a claim, title, right, etc), especially formally and publicly. **2** to refuse to recognize or associate with. **3** to give up (a bad habit). **4** *intrans. Cards* to fail to follow suit. [from Latin *renuntiare*]

renouncement *noun* **1** renouncing. **2** a renunciation.

renouncer *noun* a person who renounces.

renovate *verb* to restore (especially a building) to a former and better condition. [from Latin *renovare*, from *novus*, new]

renovation *noun* **1** renovating or being renovated. **2** a renewal.

renovator *noun* a person who renovates.

renown *noun* fame. [from Old French *renom*]

renowned *adj.* famous; celebrated.

Renshaw, Willie (William Charles) (1861–1904) English lawn tennis player, born in Cheltenham, Gloucestershire. He started playing at Cheltenham School with his twin brother Ernest (1861–99), who also became a champion. Willie was Wimbledon singles champion seven times (1881–6, 1899), and also won the Wimbledon doubles title seven times with Ernest (1880–1, 1884–6, 1888–9).

rent¹ — *noun* money paid to the owner of a property by a tenant in return for the use or occupation of that property. — *verb* **1** to pay rent for (a building, etc). **2** (**rent something** *or* **rent something out**) to allow the use of (one's property) in return for payment of rent. **3** *intrans.* to be hired out for rent. [from Old French *rente*]

rent² *noun old use* an opening or split made by tearing, often violently. [a form of REND]

rental *noun* **1** money paid as rent. **2** the act of renting.

rent boy a young male homosexual prostitute.

renunciation *noun* **1** an act of renouncing. **2** a formal declaration of renouncing something. **3** self-denial. [from Latin *renuntiatio*]

reopen *verb* (**reopened, reopening**) **1** *trans., intrans.* to open again. **2** to begin to discuss (a subject which has already been discussed) again.

reorder *verb* **1** to order again; to place a repeat order for (a product, etc). **2** to place or arrange in a different order.

rep *noun* **1** a representative. **2** a repertory company or theatre.

repaint — *verb* (with stress on -*paint*) to paint over or again. — *noun* (with stress on *re*-) a repainted golf ball.

repair¹ — *verb* **1** to restore (something damaged or broken) to good, working condition. **2** to put right, heal, or make up for (something wrong that has been done). — *noun* **1** an act of repairing. **2** a condition or state: *in good repair.* **3** a part or place that has been mended or repaired. [from Latin *reparare*]

repair² *verb intrans.* (**repair to a place**) *old use* to go there; to take oneself off to it. [from Latin *repatriare*, to return to one's homeland]

repairable *adj.* capable of being repaired.

reparable *adj.* able to be put right. [from Latin *reparabilis*, able to be repaired]

reparation *noun* **1** the act of making up for (something wrong that has been done). **2** money paid or something done for this purpose. **3** (*usually* **reparations**) compensation paid after a war by a defeated nation for the damage caused. [from Latin *reparatio*]

repartee *noun* **1** the practice or skill of making spontaneous witty replies. **2** conversation having many such replies. [from French *repartie*]

repast *noun formal, old use* a meal. [from Old French *repaistre*, to eat a meal]

repatriate *verb* to send (someone) back to their country of origin. [from Latin *repatriare*]

repatriation *noun* repatriating or being repatriated.

repay *verb* (PAST TENSE AND PAST PARTICIPLE **repaid**) **1** to pay back (money). **2** to do or give something to (someone) in return for (something done or given to oneself): *repay his kindness.*

repayable *adj.* that may or must be repaid.

repayment *noun* repaying.

repeal — *verb* to make (a law, etc) no longer valid. — *noun* the act of repealing (a law, etc). [from Old French *repeler*]

repealable *adj.* capable of being repealed.

repeat — *verb* **1** to say, do, etc again. **2** to tell (something one has heard) to someone else, especially when one ought not to. **3** to say (something) from memory. **4** *intrans. said of food* to be tasted again after being swallowed. **5** *intrans.* to occur again; to recur. **6** *intrans. said of a gun* to fire several times without being reloaded. **7** *intrans. said of a clock or watch* to strike the last hour or quarter hour when a spring is pressed. — *noun* **1** an act of repeating. **2** something which is repeated, especially a television programme which has been broadcast before. **3** *Mus.* a musical passage which is to be repeated, or a sign which marks this. — *adj.* repeated: *a repeat showing*.
— **repeat itself** to happen in exactly the same way more than once.
repeat oneself to say the same thing more than once.
[from Latin *repetere*, to attack again]

repeatable *adj.* **1** fit to be told to others. **2** able to be repeated.

repeated *adj.* **1** done again. **2** reiterated.

repeatedly *adv.* again and again, frequently.

repeater *noun* **1** a clock or watch which strikes the last hour or quarter hour if a spring is pressed. **2** a gun which can be fired several times without having to be reloaded. **3** *Maths.* a figure or sequence of figures in a decimal fraction which would recur infinitely.

repel *verb* (**repelled**, **repelling**) **1** to force or drive back or away. **2** to cause a feeling of disgust or loathing. **3** *trans., intrans.* to fail to mix with, absorb, or be attracted by (something else): *oil repels water*. **4** to reject: *repel his advances*. [from Latin *repellere*, to drive back]

repellent — *noun* something that repels, especially insects. — *adj.* repelling, esp causing a feeling of disgust or loathing.

repellently *adv.* in a repellent way.

repent *verb* **1** *trans., intrans.* (**repent something** *or* **repent of something**) to feel great sorrow or regret for something one has done; to wish an action, etc undone. **2** *intrans.* to be sorry for all the evil or bad things one has done and decide to live a better life. [from Old French *repentir*]

repentance *noun* **1** repenting. **2** being penitent.

repentant *adj.* experiencing or expressing repentance.

repercussion *noun* **1** (*often* **repercussions**) a usually bad unforeseen or indirect result or consequence of some action or event. **2** an echo or reverberation. [from Latin *repercussio*]

repercussive *adj.* reverberating, echoing, repeated.

repertoire *noun* **1** the list of songs, plays, operas, etc that a performer, singer, group of actors, etc is able or ready to perform. **2** a range or stock of skills, techniques, talents, etc that someone or something has, eg the total list of commands and codes that a computer can execute. [from French *répertoire*]

repertory *noun* (PL. **repertories**) **1** the complete list of plays that a theatre company is able and ready to perform. **2** (*also* **repertory company**) a group of actors who perform a series of plays from their repertoire in the course of a season at one theatre. **3** (*also* **repertory theatre**) a theatre where a repertory company performs its plays. **4** repertory theatres in general: *worked in repertory for a few years*. [from Latin *repertorium*, inventory]

repetition *noun* **1** the act of repeating or being repeated. **2** a thing that is repeated. **3** a copy or replica. **4** something, eg a piece of music, which is played or recited from memory. [from Latin *repetere*, to attack again]

repetitious *or* **repetitive** *adj.* having too much repetition.

repetitiously *or* **repetitively** *adv.* in a repetitious or repetitive way.

repetitiousness *or* **repetitiveness** *noun* being repetitious.

repetitive strain injury (ABBREV. **RSI**) inflammation of the tendons and joints of the hands and lower arms, caused by repeated performance of identical manual operations.

repine *verb intrans.* to fret or feel discontented. [from PINE[2]]

replace *verb* **1** to put (something) back in a previous or proper position. **2** to take the place of or be a substitute for. **3** (**replace one person** *or* **thing by** *or* **with another**) to use or substitute another person or thing in place of an existing one: *was replaced by a man twenty years younger / we want to replace it with a new one*.

replaceable *adj.* capable of being replaced.

replacement *noun* **1** the act of replacing something. **2** a person or thing that replaces another.

replant *verb trans., intrans.* to plant again or anew, to replace surgically (a severed limb, digit, etc).

replay — *noun* (with stress on *re-*) **1** the playing of a tape or recording again. **2** the playing of a football, etc match again, usually because neither team won the previous match. — *verb* (with stress on *-play*) to play (a tape, recording, football match, etc) again.

replenish *verb* to fill up again or stock, especially a supply of something which has been used up. [from Old French *replenir*, from Latin *plenus*, full]

replenishment *noun* **1** replenishing. **2** that which replenishes. **3** a fresh supply.

replete *adj.* **1** (**replete with something**) completely or well supplied with it. **2** *formal* having eaten enough or more than enough. [from Latin *replere*, to refill]

repleteness *or* **repletion** *noun* being replete.

replica *noun* **1** an exact copy, especially of a work of art, sometimes by the original artist, and often on a smaller scale. **2** a facsimile. [from Latin *replicare*, to repeat]

replicable *adj.* capable of being replicated.

replicate *verb* **1** to make a replica of. **2** to repeat (an experiment). **3** *intrans. said of a molecule, virus, etc* to make a replica of itself. [from Latin *replicare*, to fold back]

reply — *verb* (**replies**, **replied**) **1** *intrans.* to respond in words, writing, or action. **2** to say or do (something) in response. **3** *intrans.* to make a speech of thanks in answer to a speech of welcome. **4** *intrans. Legal* to answer a defendant's plea. — *noun* (PL. **replies**) something said, written, or done in answer or response. [from Latin *replicare*, to fold back]

repoint *verb* to repair (stone or brickwork) by renewing the mortar between the joints.

report — *noun* **1** a detailed statement, description, or account, especially after investigation. **2** a detailed and usually formal account of the discussions and decisions of a committee, inquiry, or other group of people. **3** *Brit.* a statement of a pupil's work and behaviour at school given to the parents, usually at the end of each school year or each term. **4** rumour; general talk. **5** character or reputation. **6** a loud, explosive noise, eg of a gun firing. — *verb* **1** to bring back as an answer, news, or account. **2** *trans., intrans.* to give a formal or official account or description of, especially after an investigation. **3** to make a complaint about (someone), especially to a person in authority. **4** to make (something) known to a person in authority. **5** *intrans.* (**report for something** *or* **to someone**) to present oneself at an appointed place or time, for a particular purpose: *please report to reception on arrival*. **6** (**report to someone**) to be responsible to them or under their authority. **7** *intrans.* to account for oneself in a particular way: *report sick*. **8** *intrans.* to act as a news reporter. [from Latin *reportare*, to carry back]

reportedly *adv.* according to report.

reported speech *Grammar* indirect speech.

reporter *noun* a person who writes articles and reports for a newspaper, or for broadcast on television or radio.

repose[1] — *noun* a state of rest, calm, or peacefulness. — *verb* **1** *intrans.* to lie resting. **2** to lay (oneself, one's head, etc) to rest. **3** *intrans.* to lie dead. [from Latin *repausare*]

repose[2] *verb* **1** to place (confidence, trust, etc) in a person or thing. **2** *intrans.* to be placed (in a person or thing). [from Latin *reponere*, to replace]

repository *noun* (PL. **repositories**) **1** a place or container where things may be stored, especially a museum or warehouse. **2** a person or thing thought of as a store of information, knowledge, etc. **3** a trusted person to whom one can confide secrets. [from Latin *reponere*, to replace]

repossess *verb, said of a creditor* to regain possession of (property or goods), especially because the debtor has defaulted on payment.

repossession *noun* repossessing or being repossessed.

reprehend *verb* to find fault with; to blame or reprove. [from Latin *reprehendere*, to seize, blame]

reprehensible *adj.* deserving blame or criticism. [from Latin *reprehensibilis*]

reprehensibly *adv.* in a reprehensible way.

represent *verb* **1** to serve as a symbol or sign for; to stand for or correspond to: *letters represent sounds / a thesis represents years of hard work*. **2** to speak or act on behalf of. **3** to be a good example of; to typify: *what he said represents the feelings of many people*. **4** to present an image of or portray, especially through painting or sculpture. **5** to bring clearly to mind: *a film representing all the horrors of war*. **6** to describe in a specified way; to attribute a specified character or quality to: *represented themselves as experts*. **7** to show, state, or explain: *represent the difficulties forcibly to the committee*. **8** to be an elected member of Parliament for. **9** to act out or play the part of on stage. [from Latin *repraesentare*]

representation *noun* **1** the act of representing or state of being represented. **2** a person or thing (especially a painting) which represents someone or something else. **3** a body of representatives. **4** (*often* **representations**) a strong statement made to present facts, opinions, complaints, or demands.

representational *adj., said especially of art* depicting objects in a realistic rather than an abstract form.

representative — *adj.* **1** representing. **2** being a good example (of something); typical. **3** standing or acting as a deputy for someone. **4** *said of government* carried on by elected people. — *noun* **1** a person who represents someone or something else, especially a person who represents, or sells the goods of, a business or company, or a person who represents a constituency in Parliament. **2** a typical example.

representatively *adv.* in a representative way.

representativeness *noun* being representative.

repress *verb* **1** to keep (an impulse, a desire to do something, etc) under control. **2** to put down, especially using force: *repress the insurrection.* **3** to exclude (an unpleasant thought) from one's conscious mind. [from Latin *reprimere*, to keep back]

repression *noun Psychol.* in psychoanalysis, the defence mechanism whereby an unpleasant or unacceptable thought, memory, or wish is deliberately excluded from conscious thought. Such repressed material still controls behaviour, and may later give rise to symptoms of neurosis.

repressive *adj.* severe; harsh.

repressiveness *noun* being repressive.

repressor *noun* a person or thing that represses.

reprieve — *verb* **1** to delay or cancel the punishment of (a prisoner condemned to death). **2** to give temporary relief from trouble, difficulty, pain, etc. — *noun* **1** the act of delaying or cancelling a death sentence. **2** temporary relief from trouble, difficulty, pain, etc. [from Old French *repris*, taken back]

reprimand — *verb* to criticize or rebuke angrily or severely, especially formally. — *noun* angry or severe and usually formal criticism or rebuke. [from Latin *reprimere*, to keep back]

reprint — *noun* (with stress on *re-*) **1** a copy of a book made by reprinting the original without any changes. **2** an occasion of reprinting. **3** the number of copies of a book which is reprinted. — *verb* (with stress on *-print*) **1** to print more copies of (a book). **2** *intrans. said of a book* to have more copies printed.

reprisal *noun* **1** an act of taking revenge or retaliating. **2** the usually forcible taking of foreign land in retaliation. [from Old French *reprisaille*]

reprise — *noun* a repeated passage or theme in music. — *verb* to repeat (an earlier passage or theme) in music. [from Old French *reprise*, a taking back]

reproach — *verb* to express disapproval of or disappointment with (a person) for a fault or some wrong done. — *noun* **1** an act of reproaching. **2** (*often* **reproaches**) a rebuke or expression of disappointment. **3** a cause of disgrace or shame.
— **above** *or* **beyond reproach** too good to be criticized; excellent; perfect.
[from Old French *reprochier*]

reproachful *adj.* expressing or full of reproach.

reproachfully *adv.* in a reproachful way.

reprobate — *noun* a person of immoral habits with no principles. — *adj.* immoral and unprincipled. [from Latin *reprobatus*, disapproved of]

reproduce **1** to make or produce a copy or imitation of; to duplicate. **2** to make or produce again or anew. **3** *intrans.* to turn out (well, badly, etc) when copied. **4** *intrans., trans.* to produce (new individuals) either sexually or asexually, so perpetuating a species.

reproducible *adj.* capable of being reproduced.

reproduction — *noun* **1** the act or process of reproducing offspring. **2** a copy or imitation, especially of a work of art. — *adj., said of furniture, etc* made in imitation of an earlier style.

reproductive *adj.* of or for reproduction.

reproductively *adv.* in a reproductive way.

reproof *noun* blame or criticism; a rebuke. [related to REPROVE]

reprove *verb* to blame or condemn (someone) for a fault or some wrong done. [from Old French *reprover*, from Latin *reprobare*, to disapprove of]

reproving *adj.* disapproving, condemnatory.

reprovingly *adv.* with a reproving manner.

reptile *noun* **1** *Zool.* any cold-blooded vertebrate animal belonging to the class Reptilia, eg lizards, snakes, tortoises, turtles, crocodiles, alligators, and many extinct species, including dinosaurs and pterodactyls. **2** a mean or despicable person. [from Latin *reptilis*, creeping]
◇ Reptiles typically have a dry waterproof skin covered with horny scales or plates, and they breathe by means of lungs. Young reptiles usually hatch from eggs with porous leathery shells laid on land, although some ovoviviparous species produce eggs that hatch within the body. Reptiles evolved from amphibians, and although a few of them are aquatic, most live entirely on land.

reptilian *adj.* of or like reptiles.

Repton, Humphrey (1752–1818) English landscape designer, the successor to Lancelot 'Capability' Brown, born in Bury St Edmunds, Suffolk. He completed the change from the formal gardens of the early 18c to the 'picturesque' types favoured later, and coined the phrase 'landscape gardening'. His work can still be seen at Sheringham Hall, Norfolk, and elsewhere.

Republic, The a dialogue in 10 books by Plato (c.4c BC). It is a philosophical presentation, expressed as conversations between Socrates and his pupils, of how an ideal society could be achieved.

republic *noun* **1** a form of government in which there is no monarch, and in which supreme power is held by the people or their elected representatives, especially one in which the head of state is an elected or nominated president. **2** a country, state, or unit within a state (eg in the former Soviet Union) having such a form of government. [from Latin *respublica*, from *res*, concern, affair + *publicus*, public]

republican — *adj.* **1** of or like a republic. **2** in favour of or supporting a republican system of government. **3** (**Republican**) of the Republican Party in the US. — *noun* **1** a person who favours a republican system of government. **2** (**Republican**) a member or supporter of the US Republican Party.

republicanism *noun* **1** the principles and theory of a republican system of government. **2** support for republican government, or a particular example of this.

Republican Party a US political party, formed (1854) by Northern anti-slavery factions

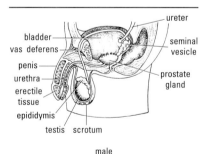

bladder
vas deferens
penis
urethra
erectile tissue
epididymis
testis   scrotum

ureter
seminal vesicle
prostate gland

male

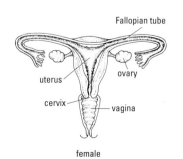

Fallopian tube
uterus
cervix
ovary
vagina

female

male and female reproductive organs

of the existing Whig and Democratic Parties who opposed the Fugitive Slave Act (1850) and the Kansas–Nebraska Act (1854). The Party's presidential candidate Abraham Lincoln won the 1860 election. With the exception of four terms, the Republicans continued to hold the presidency until the Great Depression, when the election of Franklin Delano Roosevelt (1932) ushered in 20 years of Democratic presidents. The Republicans won the 1952 presidential election with the popular war hero Dwight D Eisenhower. The next 40 years saw a series of split governments on the national level, when the Republicans often won the presidency while the Democrats held majorities in Congress. The Watergate scandal, which led to the first resignation of an American president (Richard M Nixon) was a black mark for the Party, but it regained the presidency with the election of Ronald Reagan in 1980 and held it for the next 12 years through George Bush's one-term administration. The Party has traditionally been identified with big business rather than with labour, and favoured states' rights, limited government regulation, free market economic policies, and (in the Cold War period that followed World War II) a strong military and firm anticommunistic stance. It has generally had the support of voters of high socioeconomic status and of white Anglo-Saxons rather than of ethnic minorities.

repudiate *verb* **1** to deny or reject: *repudiate the suggestion.* **2** to refuse to recognize or have anything to do with; to disown. **3** to refuse to acknowledge or pay (a debt, obligation, etc). [from Latin *repudiare*]
◆ See note at *refute.*

repudiation *noun* repudiating.

repugnance *noun* aversion.

repugnant *adj.* **1** (**repugnant to someone**) causing them a feeling of disgust or loathing. **2** (**repugnant with something**) inconsistent or incompatible with it. [from Latin *repugnare*, to fight against]

repugnantly *adv.* in a repugnant way.

repulse — *verb* **1** to drive or force back (an enemy). **2** to reject (a person's offer of help, kindness, etc) with coldness and discourtesy. **3** to cause a feeling of disgust, horror, or loathing in. — *noun* **1** an act of repulsing or state of being repulsed. **2** a cold, discourteous rejection. [from Latin *repulsus*, driven back]

repulsion *noun* **1** a feeling of disgust, horror, or loathing. **2** a forcing back or being forced back. **3** *Physics* a force that tends to push two objects further apart, such as that between like electric charges or like magnetic poles. See also ATTRACTION. [from Latin *repulsus*, driven back]

repulsive *adj.* causing a feeling of disgust, horror, or loathing.

repulsively *adv.* in a repulsive way.

repulsiveness *noun* being repulsive.

reputable *adj.* respectable; well thought of; trustworthy. [from Latin *reputabilis*]

reputably *adv.* in a reputable way.

reputation *noun* **1** a generally held opinion about a person with regard to his or her abilities, moral character, etc. **2** a high opinion generally held about a person or thing; a good name. [from Latin *reputatio*]

repute — *verb* (**be reputed**) to be generally considered: *she is reputed to be a fine tennis player.* — *noun* reputation.
— **by repute** reputedly.
a person of repute a person who is generally well thought of and respected.
[from Latin *reputare*, to reckon]

reputedly *adv.* as is generally believed; by reputation.

request — *noun* **1** the act of asking for something. **2** something asked for. **3** the state of being

asked for or sought after: *be in request.* — *verb* to ask (someone) for (something), especially politely or as a favour.
— **on request** if or when requested.
[from Latin *requirere*, to seek for]

request stop a bus stop that a bus will only stop at if signalled to do so.

requiem *noun* 1 (*also* **Requiem**) in the Roman Catholic Church, a mass for the souls of the dead. 2 a piece of music written to accompany this service. [from Latin *requiem*, rest, the first word of the Latin version of this mass]

require *verb* 1 to need; to wish to have. 2 to have as a necessary or essential condition for success, fulfilment, etc. 3 to demand, exact or command by authority. [from Latin *requirere*, to search for]

requirement *noun* something that is needed, asked for, essential, ordered, etc.

requisite — *adj.* required; necessary; indispensable. — *noun* something which is required, necessary, or indispensable for some purpose: *toilet requisites.* [from Latin *requisitus*, sought for]

requisition — *noun* 1 a (usually written) formal and authoritative demand or request, especially for supplies or the use of something, and especially by the army. 2 the act of formally demanding, requesting or taking something. — *verb* (**requisitioned**, **requisitioning**) to demand, take or order (supplies, the use of something, etc) by official requisition. [from Latin *requisitio*, a searching for]

requital *noun* 1 requiting. 2 recompense, reward.

requite *verb formal* 1 to make a suitable return to or repay (a person) for some act. 2 (**requite one thing for** *or* **with another**) to repay (eg good with good or evil with evil). [from Middle English *quitten*, to pay]

reredos *noun* a usually ornamental stone or wooden screen or partition wall behind an altar. [from Old French *areredos*, from *arere*, behind + *dos*, back]

reroute *verb* (**rerouteing**) to direct (traffic, aircraft, etc) along an alternative route.

rerun — *verb* (with stress on -*run*) (**rerunning**; PAST TENSE **reran**; PAST PARTICIPLE **rerun**) 1 to run (a race) again. 2 to broadcast (a series of television or radio programmes) for a second or further time. — *noun* (with stress on *re*-) 1 a race that is run again. 2 a series of television or radio programmes which are broadcast for a second or further time.

resale price maintenance a device, now illegal in the UK, used by sellers acting together to prevent price-cutting by retailers. All agree to maintain their prices at a certain level, in effect forming a cartel. Except for a few special cases, manufacturers cannot now print 'the price' of the product on their goods; they may only show a 'recommended retail price'.

rescind *verb* to cancel, annul or revoke (an order, law, custom, etc). [from Latin *rescindere*, to cut off]

rescindment *or* **rescission** *noun* rescinding.

rescue — *verb* to free (a person or thing) from danger, evil, trouble, captivity, etc. — *noun* the act of rescuing or being rescued. [from Old French *rescourre*]

rescuer *noun* a person who rescues.

research — *noun* (with stress on -*search*, or on *re*-) a detailed and careful investigation into some area of study to (try to) discover and apply (new) facts or information. — *verb trans., intrans.* (with stress on -*search*) (**research into something**) to carry out such an investigation. [from Old French *recercher*, to seek]

◆ Stress on *re*- in the noun is increasingly common, and is established in the USA.

researcher *noun* a person who carries out research.

resemblance *noun* 1 likeness. 2 appearance. 3 an image.

resemble *verb* to be or look like or similar to. [from Old French *resembler*]

resent *verb* to feel anger, bitterness, or ill-will towards. [from Old French *ressentir*]

resentful *adj.* full of or caused by resentment.

resentfully *adv.* in a resentful way, with resentment.

resentfulness *or* **resentment** *noun* being resentful.

reservation *noun* 1 the act of reserving something for future use. 2 a booking; something (eg a hotel room, a table in a restaurant) which has been reserved. 3 (*usually* **reservations**) a doubt or objection which prevents one being able to accept or approve something wholeheartedly. 4 a limiting condition or proviso. 5 an area of land set aside for a particular purpose, especially in the US and Canada for the original inhabitants. 6 *Brit.* a strip of land between the two carriageways of a dual carriageway or motorway. 7 in some Christian churches, the practice of keeping back part of the consecrated bread and wine for some particular purpose after the service, eg for taking to the sick. 8 the right of the pope to nominate someone to a vacant benefice.

reserve — *verb* 1 to obtain or order in advance. 2 to keep back or set aside for the use of a particular person or for a particular purpose. 3 to delay or postpone (a legal judgement, taking a decision, etc). — *noun* 1 something which is kept back or set aside for later use or possible need. 2 the state or condition of being reserved or an act of reserving. 3 an area of land set aside for a particular purpose, especially for the protection of animals, for hunting or fishing, or (especially in Australia) for the original native inhabitants. 4 shy, cool, cautious, and distant manner. 5 (*also* **reserves**) one of those members of a nation's armed forces who are not part of the regular services, but who are called up when needed. 6 an extra player or participant who can take the place of another if needed. 7 (*also* **reserves**) a company's money or assets, or a country's gold and foreign currency, held at a bank to meet liabilities. [from Latin *reservare*, to keep back]

reserved *adj.* 1 booked. 2 shy, cool, cautious and distant; not open and friendly.

reserve price the lowest price that the owner of something which is being sold by auction is prepared to accept.

reservist *noun* a member of a nation's reserve forces.

reservoir *noun* 1 a place, usually a man-made lake, where water is collected and stored for use by the community. 2 a part of a machine, etc where liquid is stored. 3 a large store or supply of something. [from French]

reshuffle — *verb* (with stress on -*shuffle*) 1 to shuffle (cards) again or differently. 2 to reorganize or redistribute (eg government posts). — *noun* (with stress on *re*-) an act of reshuffling.

reside *verb intrans.* 1 *formal* to live or have one's home (in), especially permanently. 2 (**reside in someone** *or* **something**) *said of power, authority, a quality, etc* to be present in or attributable to them. [from Latin *residere*, to settle down]

residence *noun* 1 a house or dwelling, especially a large, impressive and imposing one. 2 the act of living in a place. 3 the period of time one lives in a place.
— **in residence** 1 living in a particular place, especially officially. 2 *said especially of a creative artist* working in a particular place for a period of time: *the university has an artist in residence.* [from Latin *residere*, to settle down]

residency *noun* (PL. **residencies**) 1 a residence, especially the official dwelling of a governor, etc in a colony, etc. 2 a period of advanced, specialised medical training in hospitals for doctors.

resident — *noun* 1 a person who lives in a place. 2 a bird or animal that does not migrate. 3 a guest staying in a hotel. 4 a doctor undergoing advanced or specialized training in a hospital. — *adj.* 1 living or dwelling (in). 2 living or required to live in the place where one works. 3 *said of birds and animals* not migrating.

residential *adj.* 1 containing houses rather than factories and businesses, etc. 2 requiring residence in the same place as one works or studies: *a residential course.* 3 used as a residence: *a residential home for the elderly.* 4 relating to or connected with residence or residences: *residential qualifications.*

residual — *adj.* remaining; left over. — *noun* something which remains or is left over.

residue *noun* 1 what remains or is left over when a part has been taken away. 2 *Legal* what is left of a dead person's estate after all of the debts and legacies have been paid. 3 *Chem.* a substance which remains after evaporation, combustion, or distillation. [from Latin *residuus*, remaining]

resign *verb* 1 *intrans.* to give up one's employment or official position. 2 to give up or relinquish (a right, claim, etc). 3 (**resign oneself to something**) to come to accept something (especially unwelcome) with patience. [from Latin *resignare*, to unseal]

resignation *noun* 1 the act of resigning. 2 a formal letter or notice of one's intention to resign. 3 the state or quality of having or showing patient and calm acceptance.

resigned *adj.* having or showing patient and calm acceptance of something thought of as inevitable.

resignedly *adv.* with resignation.

resilience *or* **resiliency** *noun* being resilient.

resilient *adj.* 1 *said of a person* able to deal readily with or recover quickly from differing circumstances, unexpected difficulties, etc. 2 *said of an object* quickly returning to its original shape after being bent, twisted, stretched, etc. [from Latin *resilire*, to leap back]

resin *noun Chem.* any of several natural or synthetic organic compounds, mostly polymers, usually in the form of a brittle translucent solid or viscous liquid. Natural resins are produced by various trees, especially conifers, and synthetic resins are used to make plastics, and as components of paints, varnishes, textiles, etc. [from Latin *resina*]

resinous *adj.* like or containing resin.

resist *verb* 1 *trans., intrans.* to fight against (someone or something); to refuse to give in or comply. 2 to remain undamaged by or withstand: *a metal which resists corrosion.* 3 to be unaffected by in spite of temptation or attraction: *he just can't resist chocolate.* [from Latin *resistere*, to oppose, resist]

resistance *noun* 1 the act of resisting. 2 a measure of the extent to which a living organism can limit the effects of an infection. 3 *Physics* in damped harmonic motion, the ratio of the frictional forces to the speed. 4 *Electr.* a measure of the extent to which a material or an electrical device opposes the flow of an electric current through it. It is equal to the ratio of the voltage across the device to the current passing through it. The SI unit of resistance is the ohm. 5 a measure of the extent to which a material opposes the flow of heat through it. 6 a resistor. 7 (*often* **Resistance**) an underground organization which fights for the freedom of a country which has been conquered by a foreign power.

resistant — *adj.* able to resist or remain unaffected or undamaged by something. — *noun* a person or thing that resists.

Resistencia POP (1991) 218 000, the agricultural, commercial, and industrial capital of Chaco province, N Argentina. It lies on the R Barranqueras and was founded as a Jesuit mission in the mid-18c.

resistible *adj.* capable of being resisted.

resistivity *noun Physics* (SYMBOL ρ) a measure of the ability of a cubic metre of material to oppose the flow of an electric current. It is measured in ohm metres, and the reciprocal of resistivity is conductivity.

resistor *noun* a device which introduces a known value of resistance into a circuit, etc.

Reşiţa POP (1983) 105 000, the capital of Caraş-Severin county, W Romania. It is situated in the W foothills of the Transylvanian Alps.

Resnais, Alain (1922–) French film director, born in Vannes. He began by making a series of prize-winning short documentaries, such as *Van Gogh* (1948), which won an Oscar, and *Guernica* (1950). His first feature film was *Hiroshima mon amour* (Hiroshima my Love, 1959), which was followed by the controversial *L'Année dernière à Marienbad* (Last Year at Marienbad, 1961). His later films include *Mon Oncle d'Amérique* (My American Uncle, 1980), *La Vie est un roman* (Life is a Bed of Roses, 1983), *L'Amour à mort* (Love Until Death, 1984), and *Mélo* (1986).

resocialization *noun* the process of altering the behaviour of criminals and other deviants so that they learn to conform to the norms in a society. Resocialization may take place within the penal system, in institutions, or in the community.

resoluble *adj.* able to be resolved or analysed. [from Latin *resolvere*, to loose]

resolute *adj.* having a fixed purpose or belief, and determined and firm in pursuing it. [from Latin *resolutus*]

resolutely *adv.* in a resolute way.

resoluteness *noun* being resolute.

resolution *noun* **1** the act of making a firm decision. **2** a firm decision. **3** a formal expression of opinion, will, etc by a group of people, eg at a public meeting. **4** determination or resoluteness. **5** the act of solving or finding the answer to (a problem, question, etc). **6** the ability of a television screen, photographic film, etc to reproduce an image in very fine detail. **7** *Mus.* the passing of a chord from discord to concord. **8** the ability of a microscope, telescope, etc to distinguish between objects which are very close together. **9** the act of separating something (eg a chemical compound) into its constituent parts. [from Latin *resolutio*]

resolve — *verb* **1** (**resolve on something** *or* **to do something**) to take a firm decision about it. **2** to pass (a resolution), especially formally by vote. **3** to find an answer to (a problem, question, etc). **4** to take away or bring an end to (a doubt, fear, etc). **5** *trans., intrans.* to break up or cause to break up into separate or constituent parts. **6** *said of a television screen, photographic film, etc* to produce an image of fine detail. **7** *Mus.* to make (a chord) pass from discord into concord. **8** *said of a microscope, telescope, etc* to distinguish clearly between (objects which are very close together). — *noun* **1** determination or firm intention. **2** a firm decision; a resolution. [from Latin *resolvere*, to loose]

resolved *adj.* determined; fixed in purpose.

resolving power same as RESOLUTION 8.

resonance *noun* **1** the quality or state of being resonant. **2** *Physics* a phenomenon that occurs when an object or system is made to vibrate at its natural frequency. A large vibration can be set up if a force is applied that vibrates at the same natural frequency. **3** *Chem.* the movement of electrons from one atom of a molecule to another atom of the same molecule to form a stable structure called a *resonance hybrid*. Resonance occurs in aromatic compounds such as benzene. **4** the ringing quality of the human voice when produced in such a way that the vibration of the vocal cords is accompanied by sympathetic vibration of air in areas in the head, chest and throat. [from Latin *resonare*, to resound]

◇ Electrical resonance is used in radio and television receivers. A radio is tuned by adjusting the natural frequency of the receiver circuit until it is the same as the frequency of the radio waves that fall on the receiving aerial.

resonant *adj.* **1** *said of sounds* echoing; continuing to sound; resounding. **2** producing echoing sounds: *resonant walls*. **3** full of or made stronger by a ringing quality: *a resonant voice*.

resonantly *adv.* in a resonant way.

resonate *verb trans., intrans.* to resound or cause to resound or echo.

resonator *noun* a resonating body or device.

resort — *verb intrans.* (**resort to something**) **1** to turn to it as a means of solving a problem, etc. **2** to go to a place, especially frequently or in great numbers. — *noun* **1** a place visited by many people, especially one providing accommodation and recreation for holidaymakers. **2** someone or something looked to for help.
— **in the last resort** when all other methods, etc have failed.
[from Old French *resortir*, to rebound]

resound *verb* **1** *intrans. said of sounds* to ring or echo. **2** *intrans.* (**resound with** *or* **to something**) to be filled with echoing or ringing sounds: *the hall resounded to their cheers*. **3** *intrans.* to be widely known: *her fame resounded throughout the country*. **4** *said of a place* to cause (a sound) to echo or ring. **5** to repeat or spread (the praises of a person or thing). [from Latin *resonare*]

resounding *adj.* **1** echoing and ringing; reverberating. **2** thorough, clear and decisive: *a resounding victory*.

resoundingly *adv.* in a resounding way.

resource *noun* **1** a person or thing which gives help, support, etc when needed. **2** a means of solving difficulties, problems, etc. **3** skill at finding ways of solving difficulties, problems, etc. **4** a supply of energy, natural materials, or minerals, which may or may not be renewable. **5** (*usually* **resources**) a means of support, eg money and property. **6** (*usually* **resources**) the principal source of wealth or income of a country or institution: *natural resources*. **7** a means of occupying one's spare time or amusing oneself. [from Latin *resurgere*, to rise again]

resourceful *adj.* good at finding ways of solving difficulties, problems, etc.

resourcefully *adv.* in a resourceful way.

resourcefulness *noun* being resourceful.

respect — *noun* **1** admiration; good opinion: *be held in great respect*. **2** the state of being admired or well thought of. **3** (**respect for something** *or* **someone**) consideration of or attention to them: *show no respect for the law*. **4** (**respects**) a greeting or expression of admiration, esteem, and honour. **5** a particular detail, feature, or characteristic. **6** reference or connection: *in what respect are they different?* — *verb* **1** to show or feel admiration for or high regard for. **2** to show consideration, attention or thoughtfulness to: *respect other people's feelings*.
— **in respect of** ... *or* **with respect to** ... with reference to ...; in connection with ...
pay one's respects to someone to visit them as a sign of respect or out of politeness.
[from Latin *respicere*, to look back]

respectability *noun* being respectable.

respectable *adj.* **1** deserving respect. **2** having a good reputation or character, especially as regards morals. **3** *said of behaviour* correct, acceptable. **4** presentable, decent. **5** fairly or relatively good or large.

respectably *adv.* in a respectable way.

respectful *adj.* having or showing respect.

respectfully *adv.* in a respectful way.

respectfulness *noun* being respectful.

respecting *prep.* about; concerning.

respective *adj.* belonging to or relating to each person or thing mentioned; particular; separate: *our respective homes*.

respectively *adv.* referring to each person or thing separately and in turn.

respell *verb* to spell anew or in a different way.

Respighi, Ottorino (1879–1936) Italian composer, born in Bologna. He studied under Max Bruch and Rimsky-Korsakov, and in 1913 became Professor of Composition at the St Cecilia Academy in Rome. His works include nine operas, the symphonic poems, *Fontane di Roma* (Fountains of Rome, 1916) and *Pini di Roma* (Pines of Rome, 1924), and the ballet *La Boutique fantasque*, produced by Sergei Diaghilev in 1919.

respiration *noun* **1** the act of breathing. **2** *Physiol.* the exchange of gases between an organism and its environment, consisting of the uptake of oxygen from and the release of carbon dioxide to the environment. It takes place in the lungs of terrestrial vertebrates, and in the gills of fishes and many other aquatic animals. In plants it occurs via specialized pores called stomata, which are found mainly on the lower surface of leaves. **3** (*in full* **tissue respiration**) *Biochem.* a biochemical process that takes place in the cells of all living organisms, and involves the release of energy as a result of the breakdown of carbohydrates or other foodstuffs.

◇ Energy is released during tissue respiration either by the complete oxidation (breakdown) of carbohydrates in the presence of oxygen to form carbon dioxide and water (*aerobic respiration*), or by the partial breakdown (fermentation) of carbohydrates in the absence of oxygen to form ethanol (alcohol) or lactic acid (*anaerobic respiration*). Aerobic respiration yields much more energy than anaerobic respiration, but in both cases the energy released is trapped and stored in molecules of ATP (adenosine triphosphate), a compound that serves as a source of chemical energy for the many different processes that occur within living cells.

respirator *noun* **1** a mask worn over the mouth and nose to prevent poisonous gas, dust, etc being breathed in. **2** apparatus used to help very ill or injured people breathe when they are unable to do so naturally.

respiratory *adj.* relating to breathing or respiration.

respire *verb* **1** *intrans., trans.* to breathe. **2** *intrans.* to release energy as a result of the breakdown of organic compounds such as fats or carbohydrates. [from Latin *respirare*]

respite — *noun* **1** a pause; a period of rest or relief from, or a temporary stopping of, something unpleasant, difficult, etc. **2** a temporary delay; a reprieve. — *verb* **1** to grant a respite to. **2** to delay (eg the execution of a sentence). [from Old French *respit*]

resplendence *noun* brilliance.

resplendent *adj.* brilliant or splendid in appearance. [from Latin *resplendere*, to shine brightly]

resplendently *adv.* in a resplendent way.

respond *verb* **1** *intrans., trans.* to answer or reply; to say in reply. **2** *intrans.* to act or behave in reply or response: *I smiled at her, but she didn't respond*. **3** *intrans.* to react favourably or well: *respond to treatment*. [from Latin *respondere*, to return like for like]

respondent — *noun* **1** a person who answers or makes replies. **2** *Legal* a defendant, especially in a divorce suit. — *adj.* answering; making a reply or response.

response *noun* **1** an act of responding, replying, or reacting. **2** a reply or answer. **3** a reaction: *meet with little response.* **4** an answer or reply, especially in the form of a short verse which is either sung or spoken, made by the congregation or the choir to something said by the priest or minister during a service. [from Old French *respons*]

responsibility *noun* (PL. **responsibilities**) **1** something or someone for which one is responsible. **2** the state of being responsible or having important duties for which one is responsible.

responsible *adj.* **1** (**responsible for someone** *or* **something**) having charge or control over them and being accountable for them: *was responsible for a class of 20 children / is responsible for ordering the stationery.* **2** (**responsible to someone**) having to account for one's actions to them. **3** *said of a job, position, etc* having many important duties, especially the taking of important decisions; involving much responsibility. **4** (**responsible for something**) being the cause of it: *who is responsible for this?* **5** *said of a person* **a** able to be trusted. **b** able to answer for one's own conduct; capable of rational and socially acceptable behaviour. [from Latin *respondere*, to respond]

responsibly *adv.* in a responsible way.

responsive *adj.* **1** *said of a person* quick to react or respond. **2** reacting well or favourably: *a disease responsive to drugs.* **3** made as or forming a response: *a responsive smile.* [from Latin *responsivus*]

responsively *adv.* in a responsive way.

responsiveness *noun* being responsive.

respray — *verb* (with stress on *-spray*) to spray (especially the bodywork of a vehicle) with new paintwork. — *noun* (with stress on *re-*) the act or an instance of respraying.

rest[1] — *noun* **1** a period of relaxation or freedom from work, activity, worry, etc. **2** sleep; repose. **3** calm; tranquillity. **4** a state of not moving or working. **5** death thought of as repose: *lay someone to rest* (= to bury a corpse). **6** (*often in compounds*) something which holds or supports (something): *a headrest on a car seat.* **7** a pause in reading, speaking, etc. **8** an interval of silence in a piece of music, or a mark showing this. **9** a place for resting, especially a lodging for sailors. — *verb* **1** *trans., intrans.* to stop or cause to stop working or moving. **2** *intrans.* to relax, especially by sleeping. **3** *trans., intrans.* to set, place, or lie on or against something for support. **4** *intrans.* to be calm and free from worry. **5** *trans., intrans.* to give or have as a basis or support: *rested her arm on the chair / will rest my argument on practicalities.* **6** *trans., intrans.* to depend or cause to depend or be based on or in. **7** *trans., intrans. said of the eyes* to remain or cause them to remain looking in a certain direction. **8** *intrans.* to be left without further attention, discussion, or action: *let the matter rest there.* **9** *intrans.* to lie dead or buried. **10** *intrans. said of farmland* to lie without a crop in order to regain its fertility. — **at rest 1** not moving. **2** free from pain, worry, etc: *set his mind at rest.* **3** dead. **rest one's case** to conclude the calling of witnesses and presentation of arguments in a law case. [from Anglo-Saxon]

rest[2] — **the rest 1** what is left when part of something is taken away, finished, etc, the remainder. **2** the others. — *verb intrans.* to continue to be: *rest assured.* [from Latin *restare*, to remain]

restaurant *noun* a place where meals may be bought and eaten. [from French]

restaurant car a carriage on a train in which meals are served to travellers.

restaurateur *noun* the owner or manager of a restaurant. [from French]

restful *adj.* **1** bringing rest or causing a person to feel calm, peaceful, and rested. **2** relaxed; at rest.

restfully *adv.* in a restful way.

restfulness *noun* being restful.

resting potential *Physiol.* the potential difference between the inner and outer surfaces of a nerve that is not conducting a nerve impulse. It has a negative value, in contrast to the positive value of the *action potential* which occurs during the passage of a nerve impulse. See also ACTION POTENTIAL.

restitution *noun* **1** the act of giving back to the rightful owner something lost or stolen. **2** the paying of compensation for loss or injury. [from Latin *restituere*, to put up again]

restive *adj.* **1** unwilling to accept control or authority. **2** restless; nervous. **3** *said of a horse* unwilling to move forwards. [from Old French *restif*, inert]

restively *adv.* in a restive way, nervously.

restiveness *noun* being restive.

restless *adj.* **1** constantly moving or fidgeting; unable to stay still or quiet. **2** giving no rest: *a restless night.* **3** worried, nervous and uneasy.

restlessly *adv.* in a restless way.

restlessness *noun* being restless.

restorable *adj.* capable of being restored.

Restoration the return of Charles II to England (May 1660) at the request of the Convention Parliament following the collapse of the Protectorate regime, although many royal prerogative powers and institutions were not restored. The bishops and the Church of England returned, but it was Parliament that passed the Clarendon Code (1661–5) to make dissent from the Book of Common Prayer illegal (1662).

restoration *noun* **1** the act or process of restoring. **2** the act of giving back something lost or stolen. **3** something restored or given back. **4** a model or reconstruction (eg of a ruin, extinct animal, etc). **5** the act of returning to a former and higher status, rank, etc. [from Latin *restauratio*, from *restaurare*, to restore]

restorative — *adj.* tending or helping to restore or improve health, strength, spirits, etc. — *noun* a restorative food or medicine.

restore *verb* **1** to return (a building, painting, etc) to a former condition by repairing or cleaning it, etc. **2** to bring (someone or something) back to a normal or proper state: *be restored to health.* **3** to bring back (a normal or proper state): *restore discipline.* **4** to return (something) lost or stolen to the rightful owner. **5** to bring or put back to a former and higher status, rank, etc. **6** to reconstruct or make a model or representation of (a ruin, extinct animal, etc). [from Latin *restaurare*]

restorer *noun* a person who restores.

restrain *verb* **1** to prevent (someone, oneself, etc) from doing something. **2** to keep (one's temper, ambition, etc) under control. **3** to take away (a person's) freedom, especially by arresting them. [from Latin *restringere*, to draw back tightly]

restrained *adj.* **1** controlling, or able to control, one's emotions. **2** showing restraint; without excess.

restraint *noun* **1** the act of restraining or state of being restrained. **2** a limit or restriction. **3** the avoidance of exaggeration or excess; the ability to remain calm and reasonable.

restrict *verb* **1** to keep (someone or something) within certain limits. **2** to limit or regulate the use of, especially to withhold from general use. [from Latin *restrictus*, drawn back]

restricted *adj.* **1** limited in space; narrow; confined. **2** not for general use, circulation, etc. **3** *said of an area, place, etc* which only certain people, especially military personnel, may enter.

restricted area an area in which a special speed limit is in force, or to which access is limited.

restriction *noun* **1** an act or instance of restricting. **2** something which restricts. **3** a regulation or rule which restricts or limits.

restriction enzyme *Biochem.* any of a large group of enzymes that can be used to break molecules of DNA at specific points. Restriction enzymes are used extensively in genetic engineering to analyse the structure of chromosomes.

restrictive *adj.* restricting or intended to restrict, especially excessively.

restrictive covenant *Legal* a deed, most commonly found in title deeds for land or property, which restricts the purchaser's use of it in some way.

restrictively *adv.* in a restrictive way.

restrictive practice (*often* **restrictive practices**) **1** an agreement between manufacturers, companies, etc to keep production of goods down or limit the supply of goods on the market to keep prices high. **2** a practice by a trade union which limits and restricts the activities of members of other trade unions.

rest room *North Amer.* a room with lavatories, wash basins, and sometimes a seating area, in a shop, theatre, factory, etc, for the use of the staff or public.

result — *noun* **1** an outcome or consequence of something. **2** (*often* **results**) a positive or favourable outcome or consequence. **3** a number or quantity obtained by calculation, etc. **4** (**results**) a list of final scores (in a series of football matches, etc). **5** *colloq.* a win in a game. **6** (**results**) a list of marks a student has obtained in an examination or series of examinations. — *verb intrans.* **1** (**result from something**) to be a consequence or outcome of some action, event, etc. **2** (**result in something**) to end in a specified way: *carelessness results in mistakes.* [from Latin *resultare*, to leap back]

resultant — *adj.* resulting. — *noun Maths., Physics* a single force which is the equivalent of two or more forces acting on an object.

resume *verb* **1** *trans., intrans.* to return to or begin again after an interruption. **2** to take back or go to (a former position, etc): *resume one's seat.* [from Latin *resumere*]

résumé *noun* **1** a summary. **2** *North Amer.* a curriculum vitae. [from French]

resumption *noun* the act of resuming. [from Latin *resumptio*]

resurgence *noun* the act of returning to life, to a state of activity, importance, influence, etc after a period of decline. [from Latin *resurgere*, to rise again]

resurgent *adj.* capable of rising again; that rises again.

resurrect *verb* **1** to bring back to life from the dead. **2** to bring back into general use, view, activity, etc.

resurrection *noun* **1** the act of resurrecting or bringing (something) back into use. **2** the act of coming back to life after death. **3** (**Resurrection**) *Christianity* **a** Christ's coming back to life three days after his death on the cross. **b** the coming back to life of all the dead at the Last Judgement. [from Latin *resurgere*, to rise again]

Resurrection: Cookham, The a painting by Sir Stanley Spencer (1922–7, Tate, London).

Resurrection: Port Glasgow, The a painting by Sir Stanley Spencer (1950, Tate, London).

resuscitate — *verb trans., intrans.* to bring or come back to consciousness; to revive. [from Latin *resuscitare*, to raise again]

resuscitation — *noun* resuscitating or being resuscitated.

retail — *noun* the sale of goods either individually or in small quantities to customers who will not resell them. — *adj.* relating to or concerned with such sale of goods. — *adv.* by retail; at a retail price. — *verb* **1** *trans., intrans.* to sell (goods) in small quantities to customers; (of goods) to be sold in this way. **2** to tell or recount (a story, gossip, etc) in great detail. [from Old French *retailler*, to cut off]

retailer *noun* a retail oulet.

retail price index a monthly index of the retail prices of certain household goods, taken as indicative of the cost of living for that month, and as a way of monitoring changes in the cost of living over a period of time.

retain *verb* **1** to continue to have, contain, hold, use, etc. **2** *said of a person* to be able to remember. **3** to hold back or keep in place. **4** to secure the services of (a person, especially a lawyer) by paying a preliminary fee, often before the actual work begins. [from Latin *retinere*, to hold back]

retainer *noun* **1** a fee paid to secure a person's professional services, especially those of a lawyer or barrister. **2** a domestic servant who has been with a family for a long time. **3** a reduced rent paid for property while it is not occupied.

retaining wall a wall built to support and hold back a mass of earth, rock, or water.

retake — *verb* (with stress on *-take*) (PAST TENSE **retook**; PAST PARTICIPLE **retaken**) **1** to capture again. **2** to take (eg an examination) again. **3** to photograph (eg a scene in a film) again. — *noun* (with stress on *re-*) a second taking of a photograph, filming of a scene, or sitting of an exam.

retaliate *verb intrans.* to repay an injury, wrong, etc in kind; to get revenge. [from Latin *retaliare*]

retaliation *noun* an act of retaliating; revenge.

retaliatory *adj.* relating to or involving retaliation.

retard *verb* **1** to make slow or delay. **2** to keep back the progress, development, etc (eg a person's mental abilities). [from Latin *retardare*, from *tardus*, slow]

retardant *adj.* making something slower or delayed.

retardation *noun* retarding or being retarded.

retarded *adj.* not having made the expected physical or especially mental development.

retch — *verb intrans.* to strain to vomit or almost vomit, but not actually do so. — *noun* an act of retching. [from Anglo-Saxon *hræcan*]

retention *noun* **1** the act of retaining or state of being retained. **2** the ability to remember experiences and things learnt. **3** the failure to get rid of fluid from the body. [from Latin *retentio*]

retentive *adj.* able to retain or keep, especially fluid, memories, or information.

retentively *adv.* in a retentive way.

retentiveness *noun* being retentive.

retexture *verb* to treat (a blanket, garment, etc) with chemicals which restore the original texture of the material.

rethink — *verb* (with stress on *-think*) (PAST TENSE AND PAST PARTICIPLE **rethought**) to think about or consider (a plan, etc) again, usually with a view to changing one's mind. — *noun* (with stress on *re-*) an act of rethinking.

reticence *noun* being reticent.

reticent *adj.* not saying very much; not willing to communicate; not communicating everything that one knows. [from Latin *reticere*, to be silent]

reticulate — *adj.* (pronounced *-lət*) like a net, especially in having lines, veins, etc crossing. — *verb trans., intrans.* (pronounced *-late*) to form or be formed into a network; to mark or be marked with a network of lines, etc. [from Latin *reticulatus*, like a net]

reticule *noun Hist.* a woman's small, often netted or beaded pouch-like bag which fastens with a drawstring. [from Latin *reticulum*, little net]

retina *noun* (PL. **retinas**) *Anat.* the light-sensitive tissue that lines the back of the vertebrate eye. In humans it consists of an outer pigmented layer, and an inner layer containing two types of light-sensitive cell, the rods and cones. Nerve impulses generated in these cells are relayed to the brain, where they are interpreted as vision. [from Latin, from *rete*, net]

retinal *adj.* relating to or in the region of the retina.

retinol *noun* vitamin A. [from Greek *rhetine*, resin]

retinue *noun* the servants, officials, aides, etc who travel with and attend to an important person. [from Old French *retenue*]

retiral *noun* an act of retiring (eg from work) or going away from (a place).

retire *verb* **1** *trans., intrans.* to stop or cause to stop working permanently, usually on reaching an age at which a pension can be received. **2** *intrans.* to go away to rest, especially to go to bed. **3** *intrans.* to go away from or to; to leave: *retire to the drawing room.* **4** *trans., intrans.* to withdraw or cause to withdraw from a sporting contest, especially because of injury. **5** *trans., intrans. said of a military force, etc* to move or be moved back away from a dangerous position. [from French *retirer*]

retired *adj.* **1** having permanently stopped working because of age. **2** secluded.

retirement *noun* **1** the act of retiring or state of being retired from work. **2** seclusion and privacy.

retirement pension *Brit.* a weekly payment by the state to people who have retired from work.

retirement pregnancy artificially induced pregnancy in an elderly or postmenopausal woman.

retiring *adj.* shy and reserved; not liking to be noticed.

retiringly *adv.* in a retiring way.

retort — *verb* **1** *intrans.* to make a quick and clever or angry reply. **2** to turn (an argument, criticism, blame, etc) back on the person who first used that argument, criticism, blame, etc. **3** to heat and purify (metal). — *noun* **1** a quick and clever or angry reply. **2** an argument, criticism, blame, etc which is turned back upon the originator. **3** a glass vessel with a long neck which curves downwards, used in distilling. **4** a vessel for heating metals such as iron and carbon to make steel, or for heating coal to produce gas. [from Latin *retorquere*, to twist back]

retouch *verb* to improve or repair (a photograph, negative, painting, etc) by adding extra touches.

retrace *verb* **1** to go back over (one's route, path, etc). **2** to go over (recent events, etc) again in one's memory. **3** to trace back: *retrace one's roots.*

retract *verb trans., intrans.* **1** to withdraw (a statement, claim, charge, etc) as wrong, offensive, or unjustified. **2** to refuse to acknowledge (a promise, agreement, etc that one has made). **3** to draw in or back or be drawn in or back. [from Latin *retrahere*, to draw back]

retractable *adj.* able to be drawn up, in, or back.

retractile *adj. technical, said eg of a cat's claws* able to be drawn up, in, or back.

retraction *noun* a retracting, especially of something one has said, agreed or promised.

retrain *verb* **1** to teach (someone) new skills, eg those necessary to qualify them for alternative employment. **2** *intrans.* to learn new skills.

retread — *verb* (with stress on *-tread*) (PAST TENSE **retrod**; PAST PARTICIPLE **retrodden**, **retreaded**) to bond new tread on to (an old or worn tyre). — *noun* (with stress on *re-*) an old or worn tyre which has had new tread bonded on to it.

retreat — *verb* **1** *intrans., trans. said of a military force* to move back or away from, or be caused to move back or away from, a position or battle. **2** *intrans.* to slope backwards; to recede. — *noun* **1** the act of retreating, especially from battle, a military position, danger, etc. **2** a signal, especially one given on a bugle, to retreat. **3** a place of privacy, safety and seclusion. **4** a period of retirement from the world, especially for prayer, meditation and study. [from Latin *retrahere*, to draw back]

retrench *verb trans., intrans.* to reduce or cut down (expenses, money spent, etc); to economize. [from Old French *retrenchier*, to cut off or back]

retrenchment *noun* **1** cutting down, limitation, reduction. **2** economizing.

retrial *noun* a further judicial trial.

retribution *noun* deserved punishment, especially for sin or wrongdoing. [from Latin *retribuere*, to give back]

retributive *adj.* being or forming a punishment which is deserved or suitable.

retrievable *adj.* capable of being retrieved.

retrieval *noun* the act or possibility of retrieving or getting back.

retrieve *verb* **1** to get or bring back again; to recover. **2** to rescue or save: *retrieve the situation.* **3** to recover (information) from storage in a computer memory. **4** to remember or recall to mind. **5** *trans., intrans. said of a dog* to search for and bring back (game which has been shot by a hunter, or a ball, stick, etc which has been thrown). [from Old French *retrouver*, to find again]

retriever *noun* a breed of dog with a short golden or black water-resistant coat, trained to retrieve game.

retro- *prefix* forming words meaning: **1** back or backwards in time or space. **2** behind. [from Latin *retro*, backwards]

retroactive *adj.* applying to or affecting things from a date in the past: *retroactive legislation.* [from Latin *retroagere*, to drive back]

retroactively *adv.* in a retroactive way.

retroactivity *noun* being retroactive.

retrograde — *adj.* **1** being, tending towards or causing a worse, less advanced or less desirable state. **2** moving or bending backwards. **3** in a reversed or opposite order. **4** *Astron., said of a planet, etc* seeming to move in the opposite or contrary direction to other planets, etc. **5** *Astron., said of a planet, etc* seeming to move from east to west. — *verb intrans.* **1** to move backwards. **2** to deteriorate or decline. **3** *Astron., said of a planet* to show retrograde movement. [from Latin *retrogradus*, going backwards]

retrogress *verb intrans.* to go back to an earlier, worse, or less advanced condition or state; to deteriorate. [from Latin *retrogressus*, a movement backwards]

retrogression *noun* **1** a going backward or reversion. **2** a decline in quality or merit. **3** *Astron.* retrograde movement.

retrogressive *adj.* involving retrogression.

retro-rocket *noun Astron.* a small rocket motor that is fired in the opposite direction to that in which a spacecraft, artificial satellite, etc is moving, in order to slow it down.

retrospect
— **in retrospect** when considering or looking back on what has happened in the past. [from Latin *retrospicere*, to look back]

retrospection *noun* **1** an act of looking back at the past. **2** a tendency to look back on one's past life.

retrospective — *adj.* **1** *said of a law, etc* applying to the past as well as to the present and to the future. **2** looking back on past events. — *noun* an exhibition which shows how an artist's work has developed over the years.

retrospectively *adv.* in a retrospective way.

retroussé *adj.*, *said especially of the nose* turned up at the end. [from French *retroussé*, tucked up]

retrovirus *noun* any of a group of viruses with genetic material consisting of RNA rather than DNA, including many carcinogenic (cancer-causing) viruses, as well as the HIV virus which causes AIDS. [from *reverse transcriptase* (the active enzyme in these viruses) + VIRUS]

retry *verb* (**retries**, **retried**) **1** to submit to a further judicial trial. **2** to make a further attempt.

retsina *noun* a Greek white resin-flavoured wine. [from modern Greek]

return — *verb* **1** *intrans.* to come or go back again to a former place, state, or owner. **2** to give, send, put back, etc in a former position. **3** *intrans.* to come back to in thought or speech: *return to the topic later.* **4** to repay with something of the same value: *return the compliment.* **5** *trans.*, *intrans.* to answer or reply. **6** to report or state officially or formally. **7** to earn or produce (profit, interest, etc). **8** to elect as a Member of Parliament. **9** *said of a jury* to give (a verdict). **10** *Tennis, Badminton* to hit (a ball, etc) served by one's opponent. — *noun* **1** an act of coming back from a place, state, etc. **2** an act of returning something, especially to a former place, state, ownership, etc. **3** something returned, especially unsold newspapers and magazines returned to the publisher or a theatre ticket returned to the theatre for resale. **4** profit from work, a business, or investment. **5** (*often* **returns**) a statement of a person's income and allowances, used for calculating the tax which must be paid. **6** (*usually* **returns**) a statement of the votes polled in an election. **7** *Brit.* a return ticket. **8** an answer or reply. **9** a ball, etc hit back after one's opponent's service in tennis, etc. — *adj.* forming, causing, or relating to a return. — **by return of post** by the next post in the return direction.
in return in exchange; in reply; as compensation.
many happy returns of the day an expression of good wishes on a person's birthday. [from Old French *retorner*]

returnable *adj.* that may or must be returned.

Returned Services League in Australia, an organization recruited from men and women with military service overseas. Its functions are social (eg welfare care and clubs) and political (it is a major pressure group, and has direct access to the Cabinet). Its motto is: 'The price of liberty is eternal vigilance'.

returning officer *Brit.* an official in charge of running an election in a constituency, counting the votes, and declaring the result.

return match a second match played between the same players or teams, usually at the home ground of the side previously playing away.

Return of the Native, The a novel by Thomas Hardy (1878). It is set on Egdon Heath and chronicles the tragic relationships of Damon Wildeve, Eustacia Vye, and Thomasin Wildeve.

Return of the Prodigal Son, The a painting by Rembrandt (unfinished, 1669).

return ticket a ticket which allows a person to travel to a place and back again.

Retz *or* **Rais** *or* **Raiz, Gilles de Laval, Baron** (1404–40) Breton nobleman. He fought beside Joan of Arc at Orleans and became Marshal of France at 25. He allegedly thereafter indulged in satanism and orgies, and was hanged and burned at Nantes, after being tried and condemned for heresy.

Reuben **1** a biblical character, a son of Jacob who gave his name to one of the twelve tribes of Israel. **2** a male first name. [from Hebrew, = behold a son, renewer]

Reuben, Tribe of one of the 12 tribes of ancient Israel, descended from Jacob's first son by Leah. Its territory included the region east of the Dead Sea and south of Gad.

Réunion, formerly **Bourbon** POP (1992e) 624 000, an island in the Indian Ocean, to the E of Africa, forming an Overseas Department of France. CAPITAL St Denis. TIME ZONE GMT +4. PHYSICAL DESCRIPTION there are several volcanoes on this forested island, one of which is active; the highest point is Le Piton des Neiges at 3 071m. HISTORY established as a French penal colony in 1638; became an Overseas Department in 1946. GOVERNMENT governed by a Commissioner, a 36-member General Council, and a 45-member Regional Council; both councils are elected for six-year terms; Réunion administers several uninhabited small islands nearby. ECONOMY sugar, maize, potatoes, tobacco, vanilla; rum; tourism.

reunion *noun* **1** a meeting of people (eg relatives or friends) who have not met for some time. **2** the act of reuniting or state of being reunited.

reunite *verb trans.*, *intrans.* to bring or come together after being separated.

Reuter, Paul Julius, Baron von, originally **Israel Beer Josaphat** (1816–99) British founder of the first news agency, born in Kassel, Germany. He developed the idea of a telegraphic news service, and in 1851 moved his headquarters to London. His news service extended worldwide with the development of international cables.

Rev. *or* **Revd** *abbrev.* Reverend.

rev *colloq.* — *noun* (*usually* **revs**) a revolution in an internal combustion engine, the number of revolutions often being used as an indication of engine speed. — *verb* (**revved**, **revving**) *colloq.* (*also* **rev up**) **1** to increase the speed of a car engine, etc. **2** *intrans.* *said of an engine or vehicle* to run faster. [a shortening of REVOLUTION]

revalue *or* **revaluate** *verb* **1** to make a new valuation of. **2** to adjust the exchange rate of (a currency).

revamp *verb* to revise, renovate, or patch up, usually with the aim of improving.

Revd see REV.

reveal *verb* **1** to make known (a secret, etc). **2** to show; to allow to be seen. **3** *said of a deity* to make known through divine inspiration or supernatural means. [from Latin *revelare*, to unveil]

revealing *adj.* that reveals; indicative, significant.

reveille *noun* a bugle or drum call at daybreak to waken soldiers, etc. [from French *réveillez!*, wake up!]

revel — *verb intrans.* (**revelled**, **revelling**) **1** (**revel in something**) to take great delight in it. **2** to enjoy oneself in a noisy, lively way. — *noun* (*usually* **revels**) noisy, lively enjoyment, festivities or merrymaking. [from Old French *reveler*, to riot]

revelation *noun* **1** the act of revealing (secrets, information, etc). **2** that which is made known or seen. **3** something revealed to man by God through divine inspiration or supernatural means. **4** (**Revelation** *or* **Revelations**) the last book of the New Testament; See REVELATION OF JOHN. [from Latin *revelatio*, from *revelare*, to unveil]

Revelation of John, The *or* **The Apocalypse of St John** the last book of the New Testament, whose author is named as John, an exile on the island of Patmos (1.9). Chapters 1 to 3 are letters of exhortation to seven churches in Asia Minor, and chapters 4 to 22 consist of symbolic visions about future tribulations and judgements that will mark the End Times and the return of Christ.

revelatory *adj.* revealing.

reveller *noun* a merrymaker, a partygoer.

revelry *noun* (PL. **revelries**) noisy lively enjoyment, festivities, or merrymaking.

revenge — *noun* **1** malicious injury, harm, or wrong done in return for injury, harm, or wrong received. **2** something done as a means of returning injury, harm, etc for injury, harm, etc received. **3** the desire to do such injury, harm, etc. — *verb* **1** to do injury, harm, etc in return for (injury, harm, etc) received. **2** to take revenge on someone on behalf of (oneself or someone else). [from Old French *revenger*]

revengeful *adj.* ready to seek revenge.

revenue *noun* **1** money which comes to a person, etc from any source (eg property, shares), especially the money raised by the government from taxes, etc. **2** (*often* **Revenue**) a government department responsible for collecting this money. [from Old French, from *revenir*, to return]

reverberate *verb* **1** *intrans.* *said of a sound, light, heat, etc* to be echoed, repeated or reflected repeatedly. **2** to echo, repeat or reflect (a sound, light, etc) repeatedly. **3** *intrans.* *said of a story, scandal, etc* to be repeated continually. [from Latin *reverberare*, to beat back]

reverberation *noun* reverberating.

reverberatory furnace a furnace in which the material (eg steel, ceramics, or glass) is not heated directly by the burning fuel, but by flame directed at a low roof which radiates heat downwards on to the material.

Revere, Paul (1735–1818) American patriot, born in Boston, Massachusetts. He served as a lieutenant of artillery (1756), then was a goldsmith and copperplate printer by trade. One of the raiders in the Boston Tea Party (1773), he was also at the head of a secret society formed to watch the British. On 18 Apr 1775, the night before the battle of Lexington and Concord, he rode from Charleston to Lexington and Lincoln, rousing the minutemen (militiamen in the War of Independence) as he went, an action immortalized in Longfellow's poem 'The Midnight Ride of Paul Revere'.

revere *verb* to feel or show great affection and respect for. [from Latin *revereri*, to stand in awe of]

reverence *noun* **1** great respect, especially that shown to something sacred or holy. **2** (**His** *or* **Your Reverence**) a title used to address or refer to some members of the clergy.

reverend — *adj.* worthy of being revered or respected. (**Reverend**) used before proper names as a title for members of the clergy. — *noun colloq.* a member of the clergy.

reverent *adj.* showing or feeling great respect.

reverential *adj.* showing great respect or reverence.

reverentially *adv.* in a reverential way.

reverently *adv.* with reverence.

reverie *noun* **1** a state of pleasantly dreamy and absented-minded thought. **2** a day-dream or absent-minded idea or thought. [from Old French *reverie*, from *rever*, to speak wildly]

revers *noun* (PL. **revers**) any part of a garment that is turned back, especially a lapel. [from French *revers*, reverse]

reversal *noun* **1** the act of reversing or state of being reversed. **2** a change in fortune, especially for the worse.

reverse — *verb* **1** *trans., intrans.* to move or cause to move in an opposite or backwards direction. **2** to put into an opposite or contrary position, state, order, etc. **3** to change (a policy, decision, etc) to the exact opposite or contrary. **4** to set aside or overthrow (a legal decision or judgement). — *noun* **1** the opposite or contrary of something. **2** an act of changing to an opposite or contrary position, direction, state, etc or of being changed in this way. **3** the back or rear side of something, especially the back cover of a book. **4** the side of a coin, medal, note, etc with a secondary design on. See also OBVERSE. **5** a piece of bad luck; a defeat; a reversal. **6** a mechanism, eg a car gear, which makes a machine, vehicle, etc move in a backwards direction. — *adj.* opposite, contrary or turned round in order, position, direction, etc.
— **in reverse** in an opposite or backwards direction.
reverse the charges to make a telephone call to be paid for by the person called instead of by the caller.
[from Latin *reversare*, to turn round]

reversed *adj.* **1** turned the other way about, backwards, or upside down. **2** overturned, annulled.

reversible *adj.* **1** able to be reversed. **2** *said of clothes* able to be worn with either side out.

reversible reaction 1 *Chem.* a chemical reaction that occurs in both directions simultaneously, so that products are being converted back to reactants at the same time that reactants are being converted to products. **2** a chemical reaction that can be made to proceed in one direction or the other by changing the conditions.

reversing light a usually white light on the rear of a vehicle which warns the drivers and pedestrians behind that the vehicle is going to move backwards.

reversion *noun* **1** a return to an earlier state, belief, etc. **2** the legal right (eg of an original owner or that owner's heirs) to possess a property when the present owner dies. **3** property to which a person has such a right. **4** insurance which is paid on a person's death. **5** *Biol.* a return to an earlier, ancestral, and usually less advanced, type. [from Latin *reversio*]

revert *verb usually intrans.* **1** to return to a topic in thought or conversation. **2** to return to a former and usually worse state, practice, etc. **3** *Biol.* to return to an earlier, ancestral, and usually simpler type. **4** *said especially of property* to return to an original owner or his or her heirs after belonging temporarily to someone else. **5** *trans.* to turn (something) back. [from Latin *revertere*, to turn back]

review — *noun* **1** an act of examining, reviewing, or revising, or the state of being examined, reviewed, or revised. **2** a general survey. **3** a survey of the past and past events: *the newspaper's annual review of the year.* **4** a critical report on a book, play, film, etc. **5** a magazine or newspaper, or a section of one, which contains mainly reviews of books, etc and other feature articles. **6** a second or additional study or consideration of facts, events, etc. **7** a formal or official inspection of troops, ships, etc. **8** *Legal* a re-examination of a case. — *verb* **1** to examine or go over, especially critically or formally. **2** to look back on and examine (events in the past). **3** to inspect (troops, ships, etc), especially formally or officially. **4** to write a critical report on (a book, play, film, etc). **5** *intrans.* to write reviews. **6** *Legal* to re-examine (a case). [from Old French *revue*, from *revoir*, to see again]

reviewer *noun* a person who writes critical reviews of books, plays, etc.

revile *verb* **1** to abuse or criticize (someone or something) bitterly or scornfully. **2** *intrans.* to speak scornfully or use abusive language. [from Old French *reviler*, from Latin *vilis*, worthless]

revilement *noun* **1** reviling. **2** a speech that reviles.

reviler *noun* a person who reviles.

revise *verb* **1** to examine again in order to identify and correct faults, take new circumstances into account, or otherwise improve. **2** to correct faults in, make improvements in and bring up to date (a previously printed book) usually to prepare a new edition. **3** *trans., intrans.* to study (a subject or one's notes on it) again, to prepare for an examination. **4** to change or amend (an opinion, etc). [from Latin *revisere*, to look back]

reviser *noun* a person who revises.

revision *noun* **1** the act of revising or process of being revised. **2** a revised book, edition, article, etc.

revisionism *noun* **1** a policy of revising a doctrine. **2** a form of Communism which favours evolution rather than revolution as a way of achieving socialism.

revisionist *noun* an advocate of revision.

revitalize *or* **revitalise** *verb* to give new life and energy to.

revival *noun* **1** the act of reviving or state of being revived. **2** a renewed interest, especially in old customs and fashions. **3** a new production or performance, eg of an old and almost forgotten play. **4** a period of renewed religious faith and spirituality. **5** a series of evangelistic and often emotional meetings to encourage renewed religious faith.

revivalism *noun* the promotion of renewed religious faith and spirituality through evangelistic meetings.

revivalist *noun* a person who promotes revival or revivalism.

revive *verb trans., intrans.* **1** to come or bring back to consciousness, strength, health, vitality, etc. **2** to come or bring back to use, to an active state, to notice, etc: *revive an old play.* [from Latin *revivere*, to live again]

revivification *noun* revival.

revivify *verb* (**revivifies, revivified**) to put new life into.

revocable *adj.* capable of being revoked or recalled.

revocation *noun* revoking.

revoke — *verb* **1** to cancel or make (a will, agreement, etc) no longer valid. **2** *intrans.* to fail to follow suit in cards when able to do so. — *noun* an act of revoking at cards. [from Latin *revocare*, to call back]

revolt — *verb* **1** *intrans.* to rebel against a government, authority, etc. **2** *trans., intrans.* to feel or cause to feel disgust, loathing, or revulsion. — *noun* an act of rebelling; a rebellion against authority. [from Latin *revolvere*, to roll back]

revolted *adj.* disgusted, horrified.

revolting *adj.* causing a feeling of disgust, loathing, etc; nauseating.

revoltingly *adv.* in a revolting way.

revolution *noun* **1** the usually violent overthrow of a government or political system by the governed. **2** in Marxism, the class struggle which will end in the working class becoming the ruling class and the establishment of Communism. **3** a complete, drastic and usually far-reaching change in ideas, ways of doing things, etc: *the Industrial Revolution.* **4** a complete circle or turn round an axis. **5** an act of turning or moving round an axis. **6** a planet's orbit, or the time taken to go round it once. **7** a cycle of events, or the time taken to go through all of them and return to the beginning. [from Latin *revolutio*]
◇ Although revolution is normally viewed as involving violent overthrow and the use of force,

this is not a necessary condition. It is any change of regime characterized by a major reconstitution of the political, social, and economic order.

revolutionary — *adj.* **1** of or like a revolution. **2** in favour of and supporting revolution. **3** completely new or different; involving radical change. — *noun* (PL. **revolutionaries**) a person who takes part in or is in favour of revolution in general or a particular revolution.

revolutionize *or* **revolutionise** *verb* to cause great, radical or fundamental changes in.

Revolution of 1905 1 a series of nationwide strikes, demonstrations, and mutinies in Russia, sparked off by the massacre by soldiers of workers demonstrating peacefully in St Petersburg on 'Bloody Sunday' (9 Jan 1905 new style). Faced with continuing popular unrest, Tsar Nicholas II was forced to make some marginal concessions, including the legalization of most political parties, and elections to form a national assembly — the State Duma.

Revolutions of 1848 1 a succession of popular uprisings in some central and W European countries in 1848–9. Fuelled by political and economic grievances against established governments, some were inspired by liberal and socialist ideas, others by demands for national independence from foreign rule (as in the Italian states, Bohemia, and Hungary). In France the abdication of Louis Philippe was followed by the Second Republic and the socialist experiment of National Workshops; liberal constitutions were granted in Austria and in many German states; Britain experienced Chartism.

revolvable *adj.* capable of being revolved.

revolve *verb* **1** *trans., intrans.* to move or turn, or cause to move or turn in a circle around a central point; to rotate. **2** *intrans.* (**revolve around** *or* **about something**) to have it as a centre, focus, or main point. **3** *intrans.* to occur in cycles or regularly. **4** *trans., intrans.* to consider or be considered in turn; to ponder: *revolve the ideas in her head.* [from Latin *revolvere*, to roll back]

revolver *noun* a pistol with a revolving cylinder which holds several bullets, and which can be fired several times without needing to be reloaded.

revolving — *noun* turning, rotation. — *adj.* that revolves.

Rev Robert Walker Skating, The a painting by Henry Raeburn (1784, National Gallery, Edinburgh).

revue *noun* an amusing and varied show, with songs, sketches, etc which are often satirical, and which usually feature popular performers. [from French *revue*, review]

revulsion *noun* **1** a feeling of complete disgust, distaste, or repugnance. **2** a sudden and often violent change of feeling, especially from love to hate. [from Latin *revulsio*]

reward — *noun* **1** something given or received in return for work done, a service rendered, good behaviour, etc. **2** something given or received in return for good or evil. **3** a sum of money offered usually for finding or helping to find a criminal, stolen or lost property, etc. — *verb* to give a reward of some form to (someone) for work done, services rendered, help, good behaviour, etc. [from Old French *reguarder*]

rewarding *adj.* giving personal pleasure or satisfaction.

rewind *verb* to wind (tape, film, etc) back to the beginning.

rewire *verb* to fit (a house, etc) with a new system of electrical wiring.

reword *verb* to express in different words.

rewrite — *verb* (with stress on *-write*) **1** to write again or anew. **2** *Comput.* to retain (data) in an area of store by recording it in the location from which it has been read. — *noun* (with stress on *re-*) the process or result of rewriting.

Rex a male first name. [from Latin *rex*, king]

Rex *noun* the reigning king, now used mainly on coins and in official documents. [from Latin *rex*, king]

Reykjavík POP (1991e) 100 000, the capital and commercial centre of Iceland, lying on Faxa Bay, SW Iceland. It is the country's chief port and is the most northerly capital in the world. HISTORY founded in 874; chartered in 1786; made a seat of Danish administration in 1801; seat of the Icelandic parliament since the 1880s; capital of Iceland since 1918; the meeting-place of US and Soviet leaders in 1986 to discuss arms control. The city's heating system uses nearby hot springs. NOTABLE FEATURES National Museum; Arb'jarsafn Open-air Museum.

Reynolds, Albert (1932–) Irish politician, born in Rooskey, Roscommon county. He became Fianna Fáil MP for Longford-West Meath (1977) and was Minister for Industry and Commerce (1987–8) and Finance (1988–91). Dismissed after an unsuccessful challenge to Charles Haughey (1991), he nevertheless won the party leadership by a large majority after Haughey's resignation (Feb 1992), and became Prime Minister. During 1993 he entered into talks concerning the future of Northern Ireland with British Prime Minister John Major.

Reynolds, Sir Joshua (1723–92) English portrait painter, born in Plympton, Devon. He established himself in London, and by 1760 was at the height of his fame as a portrait painter. He became the first President of the Royal Academy in 1768. His works include *Commodore Keppel* (1753, National Maritime Museum, London), *Dr Samuel Johnson* (c.1756, National Portrait Gallery, London), and *Sarah Siddons as the Tragic Muse* (1784, San Marino, California). He died in London, leaving well over 2 000 works, from which 700 engravings have been executed.

Reynolds, Osborne (1842–1912) English engineer, born in Belfast. Professor at Manchester, he investigated a wide range of engineering and physical problems, and made improvements to the centrifugal pump. The 'Reynolds number', characterizing the dynamic state of a fluid, takes its name from him.

RFC *abbrev.* **1** Royal Flying Corps. **2** *Hist.* Rugby Football Club.

RGN *abbrev.* Registered General Nurse.

RGV *abbrev.* Remote Guidance Vehicle.

Rh *symbol* **1** rhesus. **2** *Chem.* rhodium.

Rhadamanthus *or* **Rhadamanthys** in Greek mythology, a Cretan, son of Zeus and Europa, who did not die but was taken to the paradise of Elysium, where he became the just judge of the dead.

Rhaetian — *noun* a generic name for the various Romance dialects spoken in Switzerland and N Italy. They are: Romansch, spoken in Switzerland (Grisons) and N Italy; Ladin, spoken in Italy (S Tyrol); and Friulian, spoken in N Italy. — *adj.* relating to these dialects. [from *Rhaetia*, a province of the Roman Empire]

rhapsodic *or* **rhapsodical** *adj.* relating to or characteristic of rhapsodies.

rhapsodically *adv.* in a rhapsodic way.

rhapsodize *or* **rhapsodise** *verb trans., intrans.* to speak or write with great enthusiasm or emotion.

rhapsody *noun* (PL. **rhapsodies**) **1** an enthusiastic and highly emotional speech, piece of writing, etc. **2** an emotional piece of music usually written to suggest a free form or improvisation. [from Greek *rhapsoidia*, an epic]

Rhapsody in Blue a concert piece for piano and orchestra by George Gershwin (1924), one of the first to incorporate jazz into a work for a symphony orchestra.

Rhätikon a mountain range of the Eastern or Rhaetian Alps on the frontier between Austria, Switzerland, and Liechtenstein. It rises to 2 965m at Schesaplana, and is a major skiing area.

Rhea *or* **Rheia** in Greek mythology, a Titan, sister and wife of Cronus, and mother of Zeus and other Olympian gods. When Cronus consumed his children, Rhea gave him a stone to eat instead of Zeus, who was saved and later rebelled against his father.

rhea *noun* a S American flightless bird resembling, but smaller than, the ostrich. [from Greek *Rhea*, the mother of Zeus in Greek mythology]

Rhee, Syngman (1875–1965) Korean politician, born near Kaesong. Imprisoned (1897–1904) for his part in an independence campaign, he later went to the USA, but returned to Japanese-annexed Korea in 1910. After the unsuccessful rising of 1919, he became President of the exiled Korean provisional government. On Japan's surrender (1945) he returned to become the first elected President of South Korea (1948). Re-elected for a fourth term (1960), he was obliged to resign after a month following major riots and the resignation of his cabinet, and went into exile.

Rheims, French **Reims**, ancient **Durocortorum**, later **Remi** POP (1990) 206 000, a historic town situated in Marne department, Champagne-Ardenne region, NE France. It lies on the right bank of R Vesle, 133km/83mi NE of Paris. HISTORY a bishopric since the 4c, and now an archbishopric; the former coronation site of French kings; suffered extensive damage in World War I; scene of German surrender in 1945. The textile industry is the city's oldest industry; Rheims is also a major wine-producing centre (especially champagne), with an extensive network of storage caves. NOTABLE FEATURES 13c Gothic cathedral (badly damaged in World War I, now restored), Church of St Rémi (11c); Musée St Denis; Roman remains which include the Porte de Mars (2c).

Rheingold, Das (The Rhinegold) a music drama by Richard Wagner (1853, first performed 1869), the prologue to the cycle of *Der Ring des Nibelungen*.

Rhenish Slate Mountains, German **Rheinisches Schiefergebirge** an extensive plateau in Germany, lying between the Belgian border in the W, the Lahn R in the E, Bingen in the S, and Bonn in the N. It is dissected by the Rhine and its tributaries. The highest peak in the area is the Grosser Feldberg (879m), in the Taunus Range.

rhenium *noun Chem.* (SYMBOL **Re**, ATOMIC NUMBER **75**) a rare silvery-white metal with a very high melting point, used to make alloys that act as superconductors or that are resistant to high temperatures, eg for use in thermocouples, electrical components and filaments, and photographic flash lamps. [from Latin *Rhenus*, the Rhine]

rheology *noun Physics* the scientific study of the deformation and flow of materials subjected to force. It includes the viscosity of fluids (liquids and gases), strain and shear due to stresses in solids, and plastic deformation in metals. [from Greek *rheos*, flow + -LOGY]

rheostat *noun* a variable resistor that enables the resistance of an electric circuit to be increased or decreased, thereby varying the current without interrupting the current flow. [from Greek *rheos*, flow + *statos*, stationary]

rhesus *noun* (*also* **rhesus monkey**) a small N Indian monkey. [from Greek *Rhesos*, a mythical king of Thrace]

rhesus factor *or* **Rh factor** *Medicine* an antigen that is present in the red blood cells of about 84% of the human population, who are said to be rhesus-positive, and absent in the remaining 16%, who are said to be rhesus-negative.

◇ If the rhesus (Rh) antigen enters the bloodstream of an Rh-negative person, eg if an Rh-negative mother is carrying an Rh-positive fetus, or an Rh-negative person is given a transfusion of Rh-positive blood, antibodies may be produced that destroy the Rh-positive blood cells. The rhesus blood group is always carefully checked so that appropriate transfusions or an anti-Rh globulin can be given in such cases.

rhetoric *noun* **1** the art of speaking and writing well, elegantly and effectively, especially when used to persuade or influence others. **2** language which is full of unnecessarily long, formal or literary words and phrases, and which is also often insincere or meaningless. [from Greek *rhetorike techne*, rhetorical art]

rhetorical *adj.* **1** relating to or using rhetoric. **2** over-elaborate or insincere in style.

rhetorical question a question which is asked to produce an effect and not because the speaker wants an answer.

rheum *noun* a watery discharge from the nose or eyes. [from Greek *rheuma*, flow]

rheumatic — *noun* **1** a person suffering from rheumatism. **2** (**rheumatics**) *colloq.* rheumatism, or pain caused by it. — *adj.* relating to or caused by rheumatism.

rheumatic fever *Medicine* a disease caused by infection with streptococci (a type of bacterium), mainly affecting children and young adults, and characterized by fever, arthritis that spreads from one joint to another, skin disorders, and inflammation of the heart which may cause permanent damage or lead to heart failure.

rheumatism *noun* a disease marked by painful swelling of the joints (eg one's hips, knees, fingers, etc) and which causes stiffness and pain when moving them. [from Greek *rheumatismos*, from *rheuma*, flow]

rheumatoid *adj.* of or like rheumatism or rheumatoid arthritis.

rheumatoid arthritis *Medicine* a form of arthritis, particularly common in women, that causes pain, swelling, stiffness, and deformity of the joints, especially of the fingers, wrists, ankles, feet, or hips.

Rhiannon a female first name. [a Welsh name, from the Celtic goddess *Rigantona*, = great queen]

Rhine, J(oseph) B(anks) (1895–1980) US psychologist, a pioneer of parapsychology, born in Waterloo, Pennsylvania. He was Professor of Psychology at Duke University (1927–65). His laboratory-devised experiments involving packs of specially designed cards established the phenomenon of extrasensory perception on a statistical basis. His books include *Extra-Sensory Perception* (1934) and *Parapsychology* (with J G Pratt, 1957).

Rhine, River, German **Rhein**, Dutch **Rijn**, French **Rhin**, ancient **Rhenus** a river in central and W Europe, length 1 320km/820mi, the main waterway of W Europe. It rises in SE Switzerland, in the Rheinwaldhorn Glacier, then flows N to L Constance, W to Basle, then generally N, forming part of the Germany–France border; divides into two major branches in the Netherlands, the Lek and the Waal, before entering the North Sea. It flows through major industrial areas and is widely connected by canals to other rivers. The Rhine Valley is a popular tourist area.

rhinestone *noun* an imitation diamond usually made from glass or plastic. [from *Rhine*, a river in Germany + STONE]

rhinitis *noun Medicine* inflammation of the mucous membrane of the nasal passages, accompanied by the discharge of mucus, eg as a symptom of the common cold, or of certain allergies. [from Greek *rhis rhinos*, nose + -ITIS]

rhino *noun* (PL. **rhinos**) a rhinoceros.

rhinoceros *noun* (PL. **rhinoceroses, rhinoceros**) any of five species of a large herbivorous mammal, including three Asian species (genus *Rhinoceros*) and two African species (genus *Diceros*), with a huge body, very thick skin that is usually almost hairless, and either one or two horns on its snout. [from Greek *rhinokeros*, from *rhis*, nose + *keros*, horn]

◇ The rhinoceros is one of the heaviest of all land animals, and a large male may weigh up to 3.5 tonnes. The weight of each leg is borne on the central toe, and the horns are made of fibres cemented together, and contain no bone. Asian species have a short horn (or horns) and long tusk-like lower canine teeth, and their skin is folded, resembling armour plating. The African species (the black rhino and white rhino) have two long horns, lack front teeth, and have much smoother skin. Both black and white rhinos are in fact grey. All five species have been hunted almost to extinction for their horns, which in some parts of the world are believed to have magical powers.

rhinovirus *noun Biol.* a virus belonging to a subgroup thought to be responsible for the common cold and other respiratory diseases. [from Greek *rhis rhinos*, nose]

rhizoid *noun Bot.* a small often colourless hair-like outgrowth that functions as a root in certain algae, and in mosses, liverworts, and some ferns, absorbing water and mineral salts, and providing anchorage.

rhizome *noun* a thick, horizontal, underground stem which produces roots and leafy shoots. [from Greek *rhiza*, root]

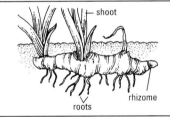

rhizome

Rhoda 1 a character in the New Testament, a servant of John's mother. 2 a female first name. [from the Greek name *Rhodon*, rose]

Rhode Island POP (1990) 1m, a New England state in NE USA, divided into five counties. Known as 'Little Rhody' or the 'Ocean State', it is the smallest US state but the second most densely populated. AREA 3 139sq km/1 212sq mi. PHYSICAL DESCRIPTION rises from the Narragansett Basin in the E to flat and rolling uplands in the W; the highest point is Jerimoth Hill (247m). HISTORY one of the original states, and the 13th to ratify the Federal Constitution; gave protection to Quakers in 1657 and to Jews who came from the Netherlands in 1658. CAPITAL Providence. CHIEF TOWNS Warwick, Cranston, Pawtucket, Newport. ECONOMY textiles; electronics; silverware; jewellery; potatoes, apples, corn; summer tourism.

Rhodes, Cecil (John) (1853–1902) South African statesman, born in Bishop's Stortford, Hertfordshire, UK. He entered the Cape House of Assembly, where he secured Bechuanaland as a protectorate (1884) and the charter for the British South Africa Company (1889), whose territory was later to be named after him, as Rhodesia. In 1890 he became Prime Minister of Cape Colony, but was forced to resign in 1896 because of complications arising from the Jameson raid (when in Jan 1896 the Boers defeated Dr Jameson's attempt to reach Johannesburg). He was a con-

spicuous figure during the Boer War of 1899–1902, when he organized the defences of Kimberley. He died in Muizenberg and in his will founded scholarships at Oxford for Americans, Germans, and colonials ('Rhodes scholars').

Rhodes, Wilfred (1877–1973) English cricketer, born in Kirkheaton, Yorkshire. He played for Yorkshire and England, and during his career (1898–1930) took a world record 4 187 wickets and scored 39 722 runs. He took 100 wickets in a season 23 times, and performed the 'double' of 1 000 runs and 100 wickets 16 times — first-class cricket records. The oldest man to play Test cricket, he was 52 years and 165 days old when he played for England against the West Indies at Kingston in Apr 1930.

Rhodes, Zandra (1940–) English fashion designer, born in Chatham, Kent. She studied textile printing and lithography at Medway College of Art, then won a scholarship to the Royal College of Art. She designed and printed textiles and, with others, opened the Fulham Road Clothes Shop in 1967, afterwards setting up on her own. She showed her first collection in 1969, and is noted for her distinctive, exotic designs in floating chiffons and silks. She was British Designer of the Year in 1972, and in 1984 won an Emmy for her costumes for the televised *Romeo and Juliet on Ice*.

Rhodes, Greek **Ródhos**, Italian **Rodi** POP (1988e) 60 000, the largest island of the Dodecanese, Greece, in the SE Aegean Sea, off the SW coast of Turkey. It is the fourth largest island in Greece. AREA 1 398sq km/540sq mi; length 72km/45mi; maximum width 35km/22mi. A long ridge of hills, rising to 1 215m, crosses the island. HISTORY originally settled by Mycenean Greeks in 1400 BC; the statue of the Sun-god Chares was one of the Seven Wonders of the World; Knights of the Order of St John settled here between 1309 and 1522; held by Italy from 1912 to 1947. CAPITAL Rhodes. ECONOMY wine, cereals, fruit, tobacco; tourism. NOTABLE FEATURES acropolis; Temple of Aphrodite (3c BC); Hospital of the Knights (1440–89), now an archaeological museum.

Rhodes, Knights of see HOSPITALLERS.

rhodium *noun Chem.* (SYMBOL **Rh**, ATOMIC NUMBER **45**) a silvery-white metal, resistant to tarnishing and chemicals, that is used to make temperature-resistant platinum alloys for thermocouples and electrical components, to plate jewellery, and to coat reflectors on optical instruments. It is also used as a catalyst to control car exhaust emissions. [from Greek *rhodon*, rose, from its rose-coloured salts]

rhododendron *noun* a flowering shrub with thick evergreen leaves and large, showy, colourful flowers. [from Greek *rhodon*, rose + *dendron*, tree]

Rhodope Mountains, Bulgarian **Rhodopi Planina Despoto Planina**, Greek **Rodopi** a range of mountains stretching 290km/180mi NW–SE in SW Bulgaria and NE Greece. It rises to 2 925m at Musala in Bulgaria. The range is a major climatic divide between central Bulgaria and the Aegean.

rhodopsin *noun Biochem.* the light-sensitive pigment found in rod cells in the retina of the vertebrate eye. On exposure to light, rhodopsin is chemically converted to its components, opsin and retinal, and this stimulates the production of a nerve impulse. — Also called *visual purple*. [from Greek *rhodos*, rose, red + *opsis*, sight]

rhomboid — *noun* a four-sided shape with opposite sides and angles equal, two angles being greater and two smaller than a right angle, and two sides being longer than the other two. — *adj.* (*also* **rhomboidal**) shaped like a rhomboid or a rhombus. [from Greek *rhomboeides*, from *rhombos*, rhombus]

rhombus *noun* (PL. **rhombuses, rhombi**) a four-sided shape with all four sides equal, two

opposite angles being greater than a right angle and two smaller; a diamond shape. [from Greek *rhombos*, anything which may be spun round]

Rhona a female first name. [of Welsh origin, = ardour]

Rhondda, Welsh **Ystradyfodwg** POP (1992e) 79 000, a district in Mid Glamorgan, S Wales. It extends along the Rhondda Fawr and Rhondda Fach valleys. Until 1990 the Rhondda Valley was an important coal mining area.

Rhône, River a river in central and SW Europe, length 812km/504mi. Rising in the Rhône Glacier in S Switzerland, it flows through L Geneva, then W and S between the Jura and the Alps to its delta on the Mediterranean Sea. It is joined at Lyons by its largest tributary, the Saône. From Lyons, it flows S to Arles where it splits into the Grand Rhône and the Petit Rhône (E and W respectively); the two deltas water the Camargue area. The Rhône Valley forms an important routeway and is renowned for its scenery. The river is a source of hydroelectricity and irrigation. Its strong current allows little navigation until well below Lyons; between Lyons and the coast there is a canal system.

rhubarb *noun* 1 a perennial plant of the genus *Rheum*, cultivated in north temperate regions, that has very large leaves with long fleshy edible stalks. The leaves are poisonous. 2 the reddish fleshy leafstalks of this plant which can be sweetened with sugar, cooked, and eaten. 3 the roots of a type of rhubarb found in China and Tibet, dried and taken as a laxative. 4 *colloq.* the sound of continuous murmured background conversation made by a group of actors, especially by repeating the word *rhubarb*. 5 *colloq.* nonsense; rubbish. [from Old French *reubarbe*, from Greek *rheon barbaron*, foreign rhubarb]

Rhyl POP (1981) 23 000, a seaside resort town in Rhuddlan district, Clwyd, NE Wales. It is part of the Abergele-Rhyl-Prestatyn urban area, situated at the mouth of Clwyd R. NOTABLE FEATURES funfair; promenade; Floral Hall.

rhyme — *noun* 1 a pattern of words which have the same final sounds at the ends of lines in a poem. 2 the use of such patterns in poetry, etc. 3 a word which has the same sound as another: '*beef*' is a rhyme for '*leaf*'. 4 a short poem, verse, or jingle written in rhyme. — *verb* 1 *intrans. said of words* to have the same final sounds and so form rhymes. 2 to use (a word) as a rhyme for another. 3 *intrans.* to write using rhymes. 4 to put (a story, etc) into rhyme.

— **without rhyme or reason** without sense, reason, or any discernible system. [from Greek *rhythmos*, rhythm]

rhyming slang slang in which the word meant is replaced by a phrase in which the last word rhymes with the word meant, the phrase then often being shortened to the first word, eg '*butcher's hook*' is rhyming slang for '*look*', normally shortened to '*butcher's*', as in '*have a butcher's*'.

rhyolite *noun Geol.* any of a group of light-coloured igneous rocks that often contain larger crystals (phenocrysts) of potassium feldspar embedded within a fine-grained glassy matrix. Rhyolite is the volcanic equivalent of granite. [from Greek *rhyax*, lava stream + *lithos*, stone]

Rhys, Jean (1894–1979) British novelist, born in Roseau, Dominica. She went to England in 1910, and joined a touring theatre company. After World War I she lived in Paris, where she wrote short stories and several novels on the theme of female vulnerability. She returned to Cornwall where she lived in retirement for nearly 30 years, and in 1966 published her best-known novel, *Wide Sargasso Sea* (a 'prequel' to Charlotte Bronte's *Jane Eyre*).

rhythm *noun* 1 a regular repeated pattern, movement, beat, or sequence of events. 2 the regular arrangement of stress, notes of different lengths and pauses in a piece of music. **3** a particular pattern of stress, notes, etc in music: *tango rhythm*. **4** a regular arrangement of sounds and stressed and unstressed syllables in poetry or other writing, suggesting movement; metre. **5** an ability to sing, speak, move, etc rhythmically. **6** (*in full* **rhythm section**) a group of instruments (eg drums, guitar and bass) in a dance or jazz band which supply the rhythm for the music. **7** *in painting, sculpture, architecture, etc* a regular and harmonious pattern of shapes, colours, areas of shade and light, empty spaces, etc. [from Greek *rhythmos*, from *rheein*, to flow]

rhythm and blues (**R & B**) a style of popular music of the 1950s and 1960s, almost exclusively played by US black artists. It combined certain features of the blues with lively rhythms which came to be more widely associated with rock music, played on guitars, drums, and keyboard. It has since been superseded by soul music.

rhythmic *or* **rhythmical** *adj.* of or with rhythm.

rhythmically *adv.* in a rhythmic way; as regards rhythm.

RI *abbrev.* **1** religious instruction. **2** Rhode Island.

ria *noun Geol.* a long narrow coastal inlet, differing from a fjord in that it gradually decreases in depth and width from its mouth inland. Most rias are surrounded by hills, and they are formed by the flooding of river valleys. [from Spanish *ría* rivermouth]

Rialto Bridge a bridge spanning the Grand Canal in Venice, built (1587–92) by the Italian architect-engineer Antonio da Ponte (1512–c.1595).

Rialto Bridge

rib¹ — *noun* **1** any one of the slightly flexible bones which curve round and forward from the spine, forming the chest wall and protecting the heart and lungs. **2** a cut of meat including one or more ribs. **3** a rod-like bar which supports and strengthens a layer of fabric, membrane, etc, eg in an umbrella, insect's wing or aircraft wing. **4** one of the pieces of wood which curve round and upward from a ship's keel to form the framework of the hull. **5** a raised ridge in knitted or woven material. — *verb* (**ribbed, ribbing**) **1** to provide or enclose with ribs. **2** to knit ribs in by alternating plain and purl stitches. [from Anglo-Saxon *ribbe*]

rib² *verb* (**ribbed, ribbing**) *colloq.* to tease. [perhaps from the phrase *rib tickle*, to make someone laugh]

RIBA *abbrev.* Royal Institute of British Architects.

ribald *adj., said of language, a speaker, humour, etc* humorous in a rude, vulgar, indecent and disrespectful way. [from Old French *ribauld*]

ribaldry *noun* ribald talk or behaviour.

riband *or* **ribband** *noun* a ribbon, especially one awarded as a prize. [from Old French *reubon*]

ribbed *adj.* having ribs; ridged.

Ribbentrop, Joachim von (1893–1946) German politician, born in Wesel. He became a member of the National Socialist Party in 1932, and as Hitler's adviser in foreign affairs, was responsible in 1935 for the Anglo-German naval pact. He became Ambassador to Britain (1936)

and Foreign Minister (1938–45), but was captured by the British in 1945 and condemned and executed at Nuremberg.

ribbing *noun* a pattern or arrangement of ribs, especially in knitting.

Ribble, River a river in North Yorkshire, N England, length 120km/75mi. Rising in the Pennine Hills, it flows S and SW past Preston to meet the Irish Sea in a broad estuary.

ribbon *noun* **1** a long narrow strip of usually coloured material used for decorating clothes, tying hair and parcels, etc. **2** any ribbon-like strip. **3** a small piece of coloured cloth worn to show membership of a team, or as a sign of having won an award. **4** a narrow strip of inked cloth used to produce print in a typewriter. **5** (**ribbons**) strips or tatters of torn material: *hanging in ribbons*. [from Old French *reubon*]

ribbon development the extensive building of houses, etc along the side of a main road leading out of a town.

rib cage the chest wall formed by the ribs which protects the heart and lungs.

riboflavin *noun Biochem.* a member of the vitamin B complex that is found in yeast, liver, milk, and green vegetables. It is required for the metabolism of all major nutrients, and deficiency of the vitamin causes retarded growth, mouth sores, and inflammation of the tongue and lips. — Also called *vitamin B₂*. [from *ribose* (a sugar) + Latin *flavus*, yellow]

ribonucleic acid *Biochem.* (ABBREV. **RNA**) the nucleic acid, containing the sugar ribose, that participates in the copying of the genetic code from DNA (another nucleic acid) and the manufacture of proteins from a long chain of amino acids, the order of which is specified by the genetic code. [from *ribose* (a sugar) + NUCLEIC ACID]

◇ One type of RNA, known as *messenger RNA*, is produced when certain compounds in the cell, known as *bases*, line up along a single strand of a DNA molecule (which serves as a template), creating a strand of RNA that matches the DNA in a manner similar to a key fitting into a lock. In this way coded genetic information is transferred from DNA to messenger RNA, which now contains the instructions for manufacturing one of the thousands of proteins present in living cells. Two other types of RNA, known as *ribosomal RNA* and *transfer RNA*, then participate in the manufacture of proteins on specialized structures within the cell known as *ribosomes*. A long-chain protein molecule is gradually assembled as amino acids, brought to the ribosome by *transfer RNA*, are lined up along the messenger RNA in the order specified by the genetic code of the latter.

ribose *noun Biochem.* (FORMULA $C_5H_{10}O_5$) a monosaccharide sugar that is an important component of RNA (ribonucleic acid). One of its derivatives, deoxyribose, is an important component of DNA (deoxyribonucleic acid).

ribosome *Biol.* in the cytoplasm of a living cell, any of many small particles that are the site of protein manufacture. Each consists of two subunits of different sizes, and is composed of RNA (ribonucleic acid) and protein.

Ricardo, David (1772–1823) English political economist, born in London. He set up in business as a young man, and in 1817 produced the work on which his reputation chiefly rests, *Principles of Political Economy and Taxation*. In 1819 he became an MP, where he was influential in the free-trade movement.

Ricci, Matteo (1552–1610) Italian founder of the Jesuit missions in China, born in Macerata, Papal States. He studied in Rome, was ordained in India (1580), and then went on to China (1582). He so mastered Chinese as to write works which received much commendation from the Chinese literati, and was a successful missionary.

rice *noun* **1** an important cereal plant (*Oryza sativa*) of the grass family (Gramineae), native to SE Asia, and having branched flower-heads bearing numerous starchy grain-like seeds. It is the main food crop of Asia, and the staple food for over half the world's population. *Lowland rice,* the commonest type, is cultivated in flooded paddy fields, and produces higher yields per acre than any other grain. *Upland rice,* which is cultivated on dry land, is low-yielding, but can be grown in cooler drier regions. Rice can also be classified according to the shape of its seeds. *Long-grain rice,* which does not clump together when cooked, is grown in tropical climates, eg India, whereas *short-grain rice,* which is more sticky when cooked and has a waxy translucent appearance, is grown in colder climates, eg Japan. **2** the edible starchy seeds, resembling grains, produced by this plant. The seeds are covered with a fibrous husk which is removed by milling, leaving brown rice. The bran is then removed by polishing to produce white rice. During this last process most of the vitamins are removed, and prolonged use of white rice as a staple food is associated with deficiency diseases, especially beriberi. [from Greek *oryza*]

rice paper very thin paper made from the bark of an oriental tree, used in cookery and for painting on.

rich *adj.* **1** having a lot of money, property, or possessions. **2** costly and elaborate: *rich clothes.* **3** high in value or quality: *a rich harvest.* **4** (**rich in something**) well supplied with it; having in great abundance. **5** *said of soil, a region, etc* productive, fertile. **6** *said of colours* vivid and deep. **7** *said of a drink, especially alcoholic* with a full, mellow, well-matured flavour. **8** *said of food* heavily seasoned, or containing much fat, oil, or dried fruit. **9** *said of an odour* pungent and spicy. **10** *said of a voice* full, mellow, and deep. **11** *said of a remark or suggestion* unacceptable; outrageous; ridiculous: *that's a bit rich!* **12** *said of the mixture in an internal combustion engine* having a high proportion of fuel to air. [from Anglo-Saxon *rice*, strong, powerful]

Richard I, also called **Coeur de Lion**, or **the Lionheart** (1157–99) King of England (1189–99), the third son of Henry II and Eleanor of Aquitaine. For most of his 10-year reign he was crusading and defending the Angevin lands against Philip II of France, spending only five months in England, where the government was controlled by the justiciar, Hubert Walter. Known as an outstanding soldier, he took Messina (1190), Cyprus, and Acre (1191) during the Third Crusade, and advanced to within sight of Jerusalem, but on the return journey he was arrested at Vienna (1192), and remained a prisoner of the German emperor Henry VI until he agreed to be ransomed (1194).

Richard II (1367–1400) King of England (1377–99), born in Bordeaux, the younger son of Edward the Black Prince. He succeeded his grandfather, Edward III, and displayed great bravery in confronting the rebels in London during the Peasants' Revolt (1381). He quarrelled with Parliament, notably his uncle, John of Gaunt, and his main supporters were found guilty of treason in the 'Merciless Parliament' of 1388. After his minority ended (1389), he built up a stronger following, and in 1397–8 took his revenge by having the Earl of Arundel executed, the Duke of Gloucester murdered, and several lords banished, including Gaunt's son, Henry Bolingbroke (later Henry IV), ending his acts of oppression with the confiscation of the Lancastrian estates after Gaunt's death (1399). Throughout Richard's reign the magnates had tried to curb his power, and since they had failed by constitutional means, Bolingbroke invaded England unopposed and took his throne (Sep 1399).

Richard II a play by William Shakespeare (1595). It is a historical tragedy that begins with King Richard exiling Henry Bolingbroke for 10 years, but events following the latter's return culminate in Richard's imprisonment and downfall.

Richard III (1452–85) King of England (1483–5), born in Fotheringay Castle in Northamptonshire, the youngest son of Richard, Duke of York. He was created Duke of Gloucester by his brother, Edward IV, in 1461, accompanied him into exile (1470), and played a key role in his restoration (1471). Rewarded with part of the Neville inheritance, he exercised viceregal powers in N England, and in 1482 recaptured Berwick-upon-Tweed from the Scots. When Edward died (1483) and was succeeded by his under-age son, Edward V, Richard acted first as protector, but before long he had overthrown the Woodvilles (relations of Edward IV's queen), seen to the execution of Lord Hastings, and had crowned himself king. Young Edward and his brother were probably murdered in the Tower on Richard's orders. He died in battle at Bosworth Field, fighting his rival, Henry Tudor (later Henry VII).

Richard III a play by William Shakespeare (1592–3). It is a historical tragedy about the deformed but brilliant Richard of Gloucester, whose defiant and murderous accession to the throne returns to haunt him and eventually leads to his death in battle by the Earl of Richmond, who becomes the first Tudor king, Henry VII.

Richard a male first name, borne by three kings of England. [of Norman origin, from *ric*, rule + *hard*, hardy]

Richards, Sir Gordon (1904–86) English jockey and trainer, born in Oakengates, Shropshire. Between 1921 and 1954 he rode a record 4 870 winners in Britain, and was champion jockey a record 26 times between 1925 and 1953. On 12 occasions he rode 200 winners in a season, and his 269 winners in 1947 remains a record. He won 14 English Classics between 1930 and 1953, and in 1933 rode 12 consecutive winners, including all six at Chepstow. He won his only Epsom Derby in 1953 on *Pinza*. He took up training in 1954 after retirement.

Richards, I(vor) A(rmstrong) (1893–1979) English literary critic and scholar, born in Sandbach, Cheshire. He pioneered the detailed critical study of literary texts in the 20c, and with C K Ogden he wrote *The Meaning of Meaning* (1923), followed by the influential *Principles of Literary Criticism* (1924) and *Practical Criticism* (1929). During the 1930s he helped to develop Basic English, worked in China (1929–30, 1936–38), and was Professor of English at Harvard (1944–63).

Richards, Theodore William (1868–1928) US chemist, born in Germantown, Pennsylvania. Professor at Harvard, he made important advances in determining the atomic weights of the elements, and his investigations of the variation of the atomic weight of lead with source proved the existence of isotopes (1914). He was awarded the 1914 Nobel Prize for Chemistry.

Richardson, Sir Ralph (David) (1902–83) English actor, born in Cheltenham, Gloucestershire. He gained an early reputation with the Birmingham Repertory Theatre from 1926, then moved to the Old Vic company (1930), playing many major roles and later leading its postwar revival. His films include *Anna Karenina* and *Oh, What a Lovely War*.

Richardson, Samuel (1689–1761) English novelist, born in Mackworth, Derbyshire. He was apprenticed to a printer, married his master's daughter, and set up in business in London. *Pamela* (1740), his first epistolary novel, is 'a series of familiar letters now first published in order to cultivate the Principles of Virtue and Religion'. Other works in the same vein include *Clarissa* (1748), published in seven volumes, and *Sir Charles Grandison* (1754).

Richelieu, Armand Jean du Plessis, Cardinal and Duc de (Duke of) (1585–1642) French statesman, born in Richelieu, near Chinon. A protégé of the Queen Mother, Marie de' Medici, he became Minister of State (1624), and as Chief Minister to Louis XIV (1624–42) he was the effective ruler of France. He aims included securing universal obedience to the Bourbon monarchy and enhancing France's international prestige, which were achieved despite the opposition of some groups in French society. He also managed to check Habsburg power, ultimately by sending forces into the Spanish Netherlands, Alsace, Lorraine, and Roussillon.

riches *pl. noun* wealth. [from Old French *richesse*]

Richler, Mordecai (1931–) Canadian writer, born in Montreal. He was brought up in Montreal's Jewish ghetto, attended university in Montreal, then lived in Paris (1951–2). His novels include *The Apprenticeship of Duddy Kravitz* (1959), which was later filmed, *St Urbain's Horseman* (1971), and *Solomon Gursky Was Here* (1990). He has also written essays, and scripts for cinema, radio, and television.

richly *adv.* **1** in a rich or elaborate way. **2** fully and suitably: *richly deserved*.

Richmond, John (1960–) English fashion designer, brought up in Rochdale. He made his mark in the fashion world in the 1980s, in partnership with Maria Cornejo; his hallmark was the combination of traditional British materials — flannel, gaberdine, pinstripes — with bikers' leather jackets. The partnership dissolved in 1986, after which he concentrated on his own label and his shop in Soho. In 1993 he showed in Paris for the first time, combining leather and traditional fabrics in new ways.

Richmond, properly **Richmond-upon-Thames** POP (1987e) 163 000, a borough in SW Greater London, England, on the R Thames. It includes the suburbs of Twickenham, Richmond, and Barnes. NOTABLE FEATURES Hampton Court Palace; Royal Botanic Gardens (Kew Gardens); Ham House.

Richmond POP (1990) 203 000, the port capital of the state of Virginia, USA. It lies on the James R, in E Virginia, 155km/96mi S of Washington. HISTORY settled as a trading post (Fort Charles) in 1645; became state capital in 1779; scene of Virginia Convention (1788) for the ratification of the Federal Constitution; Confederate capital during the Civil War; captured by Union forces in 1865. NOTABLE FEATURES Virginia Museum of Fine Arts, Museum of the Confederacy; National Battlefield Park.

richness *noun* the state of being rich; wealth, abundance.

Richter, Burton (1931–) US particle physicist, born in New York City. Professor at Stanford University, he shared the 1976 Nobel Prize for Physics with Samuel Ting for the discovery of an elementary particle known as the 'J/ψ hadron'.

Richter, Charles Francis (1900–85) US seismologist, born near Hamilton, Ohio. While working at the Carnegie Institute of Washington, he introduced the original instrumental scale (ranging from 1 to 9) for determining the energy released by an earthquake; his name has been popularly ascribed to all the subsequent magnitude scales devised and that in use today. He later became a professor at the California Institute of Technology.

Richter, Hans (1843–1916) Hungarian conductor, born in Raab. After conducting in Munich, Budapest, and Vienna, he gave a series of annual concerts in London (1879–97). In 1893 he became first court kapellmeister at Vienna, and then conducted the Hallé orchestra (1897–1911). He was an authority on the music of Richard Wagner, with whom he was closely associated in the Bayreuth festival.

Richter, Sviatoslav (Theofilovich) (1915–) Russian pianist, born in Zhitomir. He studied at the Moscow Conservatory (1937–42), and won the Stalin Prize in 1949. He has made extensive concert tours, with a repertoire ranging from Bach to 20c composers, and has been associated with the music festivals at Aldeburgh and Spoleto.

Richter scale *Meteorol.* a logarithmic scale, ranging from 0 to 10, used to measure the magnitude of an earthquake. A value of 2 corresponds to a barely perceptible tremor, and values of more than 6 result in structural damage. The highest value recorded is 8.9. [named after Charles Richter]

Mercalli and Richter Scales		
Mercalli		Richter
1	detected only by seismographs	<3
2	**feeble**	3–3.4
	just noticeable by some people	
3	**slight**	3.5–4
	similar to passing of heavy lorries	
4	**moderate**	4–4.4
	rocking of loose objects	
5	**quite strong**	4.5–4.8
	felt by most people even when sleeping	
6	**strong**	4.9–5.4
	trees rock and some structural damage is caused	
7	**very strong**	5.5–6
	walls crack	
8	**destructive**	6.1–6.5
	weak buildings collapse	
9	**ruinous**	6.6–7
	houses collapse and ground pipes crack	
10	**disastrous**	7.1–7.3
	landslides occur, ground cracks and buildings collapse	
11	**very disastrous**	7.4–8.1
	few buildings remain standing	
12	**catastrophic**	>8.1
	ground rises and falls in waves	

rick¹ *noun* a stack or heap, especially of hay or corn and usually thatched. [from Anglo-Saxon *hreac*]

rick² — *verb* to sprain or wrench (one's neck, ankle, etc). — *noun* a sprain or wrench. [a form of WRICK]

rickets *sing. or pl. noun Medicine* a disease of children in which the bones fail to harden and so become deformed. It is caused by deficiency of vitamin D, which is needed for the deposition of calcium salts within the bones to make them rigid, and may be due either to a dietary deficiency or lack of sunlight. [origin uncertain; perhaps from Greek *rachitis*]

rickety *adj.* **1** having or affected by rickets. **2** unsteady and likely to collapse.

rick-rack *noun* a zigzag braid for decorating or trimming clothes, soft furnishings, etc. [related to RACK¹]

rickshaw *or* **ricksha** *noun* a small, two-wheeled, hooded carriage drawn either by a person on foot, or attached to a bicycle or motorcycle. [from Japanese *jinrikisha*, from *jin*, man + *riki*, power + *sha*, carriage]

ricochet — *noun* the action, especially of a bullet or other missile, of hitting a surface and then rebounding. — *verb intrans.* (**ricocheted, ricocheting** *or* **ricochetted, ricochetting**) *said of a bullet, etc* to hit a surface and rebound. [from French]

RICS *abbrev.* Royal Institute of Chartered Surveyors.

rid *verb* (**ridding**; PAST TENSE AND PAST PARTICIPLE **rid**) (**rid someone of something**) to free or clear them from something undesirable or unwanted.

— **get rid of something** *or* **someone** to free or relieve oneself of something or someone unwanted.

[from Norse *rythja*, to clear]

riddance *noun* the act of freeing oneself from something undesirable or unwanted.

— **good riddance** a welcome relief from an undesirable or unwanted person or thing.

ridden see RIDE.

riddle[1] — *noun* **1** a short usually humorous puzzle, often in the form of a question, which describes an object, person, etc in a mysterious or misleading way, and which can only be solved using ingenuity. **2** a person, thing or fact which is puzzling or difficult to understand. — *verb* **1** *intrans.* to speak in riddles. **2** *trans.* to solve (a riddle). [from Anglo-Saxon *rædels*]

riddle[2] — *noun* a large coarse sieve used eg for sifting gravel or grain. — *verb* **1** to pass (gravel, grain, etc) through a riddle. **2** to fill with holes, especially with gunshot: *riddled with bullets*. **3** to spread through; to fill: *a government department riddled with corruption*. [from Anglo-Saxon *hriddel*]

ride — *verb* (PAST TENSE **rode**; PAST PARTICIPLE **ridden**) **1** to sit on and control (a bicycle, horse, etc). **2** *intrans.* to travel or be carried in a car, train, etc or on a bicycle, horse, etc. **3** *chiefly North Amer.* to travel on (a vehicle). **4** *intrans.* to go out on horseback, especially regularly. **5** to ride a horse in (a race). **6** to move or float on: *a ship riding the waves*. **7** *intrans. said of a ship* to float at anchor. **8** *intrans. said especially of the moon* to appear to float. **9** to travel over or across by car, horse, etc. **10** *intrans.* to rest on or be supported while moving: *a kite riding on the wind*. **11** (**be ridden**) to be dominated or oppressed by a feeling: *ridden with guilt*. **12** *intrans.* to remain undisturbed or unchanged: *let matters ride*. **13** (**ride on something**) to depend on it. **14** to bend before (a blow, punch, etc) to reduce its impact. **15** *coarse slang* to have sexual intercourse with. — *noun* **1** a journey on horseback or by vehicle. **2** a lift: *gave him a ride to the shop*. **3** the type of movement felt in a vehicle: *a smooth ride*. **4** a path, especially one through a wood, for horseback riding. **5** a fairground entertainment, such as a roller-coaster or big wheel.

— **ride something out** to survive or get through it safely: *ride out the storm*.

ride up *said of an item of clothing* to move gradually up the body out of position.

riding high successful, confident, and elated.

take someone for a ride *colloq.* to trick, cheat, or deceive them.

[from Anglo-Saxon *ridan*]

rider *noun* **1** a person who rides, especially a horse. **2** an addition to what has already been said or written, especially an extra clause added to a document; a qualification or amendment.

ridge — *noun* **1** a strip of ground raised either side of a ploughed furrow. **2** any long, narrow raised area on an otherwise flat surface. **3** the top edge of something where two upward sloping surfaces meet, eg on a roof. **4** a long narrow strip of relatively high ground with steep slopes on either side. Ridges are often found between valleys. **5** *Meteorol.* a long narrow area of high atmospheric pressure, often associated with fine weather and strong breezes. — *verb trans., intrans.* to form or make into ridges. [from Anglo-Saxon *hrycg*]

ridged *adj.* having ridges.

ridgepole *noun* **1** (*also* **ridgepiece**) the beam along the ridge of a roof to which the upper ends of the rafters are attached. **2** the horizontal pole at the top of a tent.

Ridgeway a long-distance route in England running 137km/85mi from Beacon Hill, Buckinghamshire, to Overton Hill, Wiltshire. The modern path follows the Great Ridgeway, a prehistoric trading route (used by drovers in the 18c); it also follows the old Icknield Way for a stretch.

ridicule — *noun* language, laughter, behaviour, etc which makes someone or something appear foolish or humiliated; derision; mockery: *held him up to ridicule*. — *verb* to laugh at, make fun of, or mock. [from Latin *ridere*, to laugh]

ridiculous *adj.* very silly or absurd; deserving to be laughed at.

ridiculously *adv.* in a ridiculous way; to a ridiculous degree.

ridiculousness *noun* being ridiculous.

riding[1] *noun* the art and practice of riding horses.

riding[2] *noun* (*often* **Riding**) any of the three former administrative divisions of Yorkshire, the *East Riding*, the *North Riding*, and the *West Riding*. [from Norse *thridjungr*, third part]

riding the marches the traditional ceremony of riding round the boundaries of a town, or a border district (especially in S Scotland).

Ridley, Nicholas (c.1500–55) English Protestant churchman and martyr, born near Haltwhistle, Northumberland. His various posts included chaplain to Cranmer and Henry VIII, Bishop of Rochester (1547), and Bishop of London (1550). An ardent reformer, he helped Cranmer prepare the Thirty-Nine Articles. On the death of Edward VI he denounced Mary I and Elizabeth I as illegitimate, and espoused the cause of Lady Jane Grey, but was imprisoned and executed.

Riefenstahl, Leni, in full **Helene Berta Amalie Riefenstahl** (1902–) German filmmaker, born in Berlin. After acting in several films, she formed her own company, and made *Triumph des Willens* (Triumph of the Will, 1935) and *Olympia* (1938), an epic documentary of the Berlin Olympic Games. Her films were thought to glorify the Nazi regime and she was unable to find work as a director after World War II.

Riemann, (Georg Friedrich) Bernhard (1826–66) German mathematician, born in Breselenz. Professor at Göttingen from 1859, he was forced to retire by illness in 1862 and died of tuberculosis in Italy. His early work was on the theory of functions, but he is best known for developing the idea of non-Euclidean geometry, describing space of more than three dimensions. His ideas played a vital role in Einstein's formulation of the general theory of relativity.

Rienzi *or* **Rienzo, Cola di** (1313–54) Italian patriot, born in Rome. In 1347 he incited the citizens against the rule of the nobles, and when the senators were driven out, he was made tribune. Papal authority then turned against him, and he fled from Rome. He returned in 1354, and tried to re-establish his position, but was killed in a rising against him. Wagner wrote the opera *Rienzi* on his story (1840).

Riesling *noun* a dry white wine produced in Germany and Austria from a grape of the same name.

Rif *or* **Riff** various Berber agricultural and herding groups of NE Morocco. They were famed as warriors, and in the 1920s they defeated the Spanish, but were eventually conquered by combined French and Spanish forces in 1926. They later served in the French and Spanish regiments in Morocco.

rife *adj.* **1** *usually said of something unfavourable* very common; extensive. **2** (**rife with something**) having a large amount or number of something bad or undesirable. [from Anglo-Saxon *ryfe*]

riff *noun Jazz* a short passage of music played repeatedly. [perhaps a shortening of REFRAIN[1]]

riffle — *verb* **1** *trans., intrans.* (**riffle something** *or* **riffle through something**) to flick or leaf through (the pages of a book, a pile of papers, etc) rapidly, especially in a casual search for something. **2** to shuffle (playing cards) by dividing the

pack into two equal piles, bending the cards back slightly, and controlling the fall of the corners of the cards with the thumbs, so that cards from each pile fall alternately. — *noun* **1** the action of riffling (eg cards), or the sound made by this. **2** *North Amer.* a section of a stream or river where shallow water flows swiftly over a rough rocky surface. **3** *North Amer.* a ripple or patch of ripples on the surface of water. [a combination of RIPPLE and RUFFLE]

riff-raff *noun* worthless, disreputable or undesirable people. [from Old French *rif et raf*]

rifle[1] — *noun* **1** a large gun fired from the shoulder, with a long barrel with a spiral groove on the inside which gives the gun greater accuracy over a long distance. **2** (*usually* **rifles**) a body of soldiers armed with rifles. — *verb* to cut spiral grooves in (a gun or its barrel). [from Old German *rifeln*, to groove]

rifle[2] *verb* **1** *trans., intrans.* to search through (a house, safe, etc) thoroughly in order to steal something from it. **2** to steal (something). [from Old French *rifler*, to plunder]

rift — *noun* **1** a split or crack, especially one in the ground. **2** a breaking of friendly relations between previously friendly people. — *verb* to tear apart or split. [from Norse *ript*, breaking of an agreement]

Rift Valley *or* **Great Rift Valley** a major geological feature running from the Middle East S to SE Africa. It extends from Syria to Mozambique and covers a sixth of the Earth's circumference. For much of its length the Rift Valley takes the form of a depression interrupted by plateaux and mountains. Parts are filled by seas and lakes. In the Middle East it contains the Sea of Galilee, Dead Sea, Gulf of Aqaba, and Red Sea. In N Africa it runs between the Ethiopian Highlands and the Somali Plains. It branches in Kenya, S of L Turkana; the E branch lakes include the Baringo Nakuru, Naivasha, and Magadi; the W branch (also known as the Albertine Rift), along the edge of the Congo Basin, includes Lakes Albert, Edward, Kivu, and Tanganyika. Once rejoined, the rift holds L Nyasa, follows the valley of the R Zambezi, and ends on the Mozambique coastal lowlands.

rift valley *Geol.* a long steep-sided valley with a flat floor, formed when part of the Earth's crust subsided between two faults.

rig — *verb* (**rigged, rigging**) **1** to fit (a ship) with ropes, sails, and rigging. **2** to control or manipulate for dishonest purposes, for personal profit or advantage. — *noun* **1** the arrangement of sails, ropes, and masts on a ship. **2** an oil-rig. **3** gear or equipment, especially that used for a specific task. **4** clothing or a uniform worn for a particular occasion or task.

— **rig someone out 1** to dress them in clothes of a stated or special kind. **2** to provide them with special equipment.

rig something up to build or prepare it, especially quickly and with whatever material is available.

[probably Scandinavian]

Riga POP (1991e) 910 000, the seaport capital of Latvia, lying on the R Daugava, near its mouth on the Gulf of Riga. The city is an industrial, scientific, and cultural centre. HISTORY founded as a trading station in 1201; member of the Hanseatic League in 1282; capital of independent Latvia from 1918 to 1940; occupied by Germany during World War II. NOTABLE FEATURES Riga Castle (1330); Lutheran cathedral (13c, rebuilt in the 16c).

rigging *noun* **1** the system of ropes, wires, etc which support and control a ship's masts and sails. **2** the ropes and wires, etc which support the structure of an airship or the wings of a biplane.

right — *adj.* **1** of or on the side of someone or something which is towards the east when the

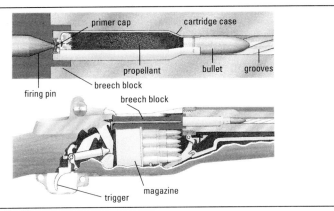

primer cap   cartridge case

propellant   bullet   grooves

breech block

firing pin   breech block

magazine

trigger

semi-automatic rifle

front is facing north. **2** on or close to a spectator's right side: *stage right*. **3** *said of a river bank* on the right hand of a person going downstream. **4** correct; true. **5** morally or legally correct or good. **6** suitable; appropriate. **7** in a correct, proper, satisfactory, or healthy condition: *not in one's right mind / put things right*. **8** of or on the side of fabric, a garment, etc which is intended to be seen: *turn the right side of the dress out*. **9** with an axis perpendicular to the base: *a right angle*. **10** relating to the political right. **11** socially acceptable: *know all the right people*. **12** *Brit. colloq.* complete; utter; real: *a right mess.* — *adv.* **1** exactly or precisely. **2** immediately; without delay: *he'll be right over*. **3** completely; all the way: *right round the field*. **4** straight; directly: *right to the top*. **5** to or on the right side. **6** correctly; properly; satisfactorily. **7** *old use, dialect* very; to the full: *be right glad to see her.* — *noun* **1** (*often* **rights**) a power, privilege, etc that a person may claim legally or morally. **2** (*often* **rights**) a just or legal claim to something: *mineral rights*. **3** that which is correct, good, or just: *the rights and wrongs of the case*. **4** fairness, truth, and justice. **5** the right side, part, or direction. **6** the members of any political party holding the most conservative views. **7** (**the Right**) the political party, group of people within a party, etc which has the most conservative views (from the practice of European parliaments in which members holding the most conservative views sat on the president's right). **8** *Boxing* the right hand, or a punch with this. **9** (**rights**) *Commerce* the privilege given to a company's existing shareholders to buy new shares, usually for less than the market value. **10** (**rights**) the legal permission to print, publish, film, etc a book, usually sold to a company by the author or by another company. — *verb* **1** *trans., intrans.* to put or come back to the correct, especially upright, position. **2** to avenge or compensate for (something wrong done). **3** to correct; to put in order. — *interj.* an expression of agreement, assent or readiness.
— **by rights** rightfully.
in one's own right because of one's own qualifications, abilities, work, possessions, etc.
in the right right; with justice on one's side.
keep on the right side of someone to maintain their goodwill.
put *or* **set something** *or* **someone to rights** to put them in a proper order, place, or state.
right away *or* **right now** immediately; at once.
serve someone right to be what they deserve, especially as a consequence of ill-advised or malicious action.
[from Anglo-Saxon *riht*]

right angle an angle of 90°, formed by two lines which are perpendicular to each other.
— **at right angles** perpendicular.

right-angled *adj.* having a right angle.

right ascension *Astron.* a coordinate on the celestial sphere that is analogous to longitude on Earth. It is measured in hours, minutes, and sec-

onds eastward along the celestial equator from the vernal equinox.

righteous *adj.* **1** *said of a person* virtuous, free from sin or guilt. **2** *said of an action* morally good. **3** caused by justifiable anger: *righteous indignation*. [from Anglo-Saxon *rihtwis*, from *riht*, right + *wise*, manner]

righteously *adv.* in a righteous way.

righteousness *noun* being righteous.

rightful *adj.* **1** having a legally just claim. **2** *said of property, a privilege, etc* held by just right. **3** fair; just; equitable.

rightfully *adv.* fairly, justly, legally.

rightfulness *noun* being rightful.

right-hand *adj.* **1** at, on or towards the right. **2** done with the right hand.

right-handed *adj.* **1** using the right hand more easily than the left. **2** *said of a tool, etc* designed to be used by the right hand. **3** *said of a blow, etc* done with the right hand. **4** *said of a screw* needing to be turned clockwise to be screwed in.

right-handedness *noun* being right-handed.

right-hander *noun* **1** a right-handed person. **2** a blow with the right hand.

right-hand man *or* **right-hand woman** a valuable, indispensable, and trusted assistant.

right-hand rule **1** *Physics* a rule that is used to demonstrate the relative directions of the induced current, magnetic field, and movement in an electric generator. The right hand is held with the thumb (representing the direction of movement), the first finger (representing the direction of the magnetic field), and the second finger (representing the direction of the induced current) at right angles to each other. **2** a rule that is used to demonstrate the direction of a concentric magnetic field around a current-carrying conductor. The right hand is held with the thumb (representing the direction of the current) pointing upwards, and the fingers (representing the direction of the magnetic field) curled around the base of the thumb joint.

Right Honourable a title given to British peers below the rank of marquis, privy councillors, present and past cabinet ministers, and to some Lord Mayors and Lord Provosts.

rightism *noun* the political opinions of conservatives or the right; also, support for and promotion of this.

rightist — *noun* a supporter of the political right, a conservative. — *adj.* relating to or characteristic of the political right.

rightly *adv.* **1** correctly. **2** justly. **3** fairly; properly. **4** with good reason; justifiably. **5** with certainty.

right-minded *adj.* thinking, judging, and acting according to principles which are just, honest, and sensible.

right of way (PL. **rights of way**) **1** the right of the public to use a path that crosses private property. **2** a path used by this right. **3** the right of one vehicle to proceed before other vehicles coming from different directions at junctions, roundabouts, etc.

Right Reverend a title of a bishop.

rightward *or* **rightwards** *adj., adv.* on or towards the right.

right whale a baleen whale with a large head that represents up to 40 per cent of the total body length.

right wing **1** the more conservative members of a political party. **2** the right-hand side of a football pitch, etc, or the player in this position.
◇ Originally identified with those who supported the institutions of the monarchy in the French Revolution, in the 19c it came to be applied to those who supported authority, the state, tradition, property, patriotism, and institutions, such as the Church and family, and were strongly opposed to socialism. In the 20c, the right wing has, in addition, developed a radical, non-conservative side: on the one hand associated with extreme nationalism (fascism), and, on the other, with attempts to reverse what are perceived as socialist developments.

right-wing *adj.* politically conservative.

right-winger *noun* a member of a political right wing.

rigid *adj.* **1** completely stiff and inflexible. **2** not able to be moved. **3** *said of a person* strictly and inflexibly adhering to one's ideas, opinions and rules. **4** *said of rules, etc* strictly maintained and not relaxed. [from Latin *rigidus*]

rigidity *or* **rigidness** *noun* a rigid state or quality.

rigidly *adv.* in a rigid state; stiffly, without yielding.

rigmarole *noun* **1** an unnecessarily or absurdly long, complicated series of actions, instructions or procedures. **2** a long rambling or confused statement or speech. [from *ragman rolls*, a series of documents in which the Scottish nobles promised allegiance to Edward I of England in 1291–2 and 1296]

Rigoletto an opera by Giuseppe Verdi (1851). It is a dark melodrama of seduction and vengeance, focusing on the sharp-tongued hunchback jester Rigoletto and his rapacious master the Duke of Mantua, who seduces all the women he can, including Rigoletto's daughter.

rigor mortis the temporary stiffening of the body after death. [from Latin *rigor mortis*, stiffness of death]

rigorous *adj.* **1** showing or having rigour; strict; harsh; severe. **2** *said of the weather or climate* cold, harsh, and unpleasant. **3** strictly accurate.

rigorously *adv.* in a rigorous way.

rigorousness *noun* being rigorous.

rigour *noun* **1** stiffness; hardness. **2** strictness or severity of temper, behaviour, or judgement. **3** strict enforcement of rules or the law. **4** (*usually* **rigours**) a harsh or severe condition, especially of weather or climate. **5** harshness or severity of life; austerity. **6** strict precision or exactitude, eg of thought. [from Latin *rigor*, stiffness]

rig-out *noun colloq.* a person's full set of clothes.

Rijeka, Italian **Fiume** POP (1991) 206 000, a seaport town in W Croatia, lying on the R Rečina where it meets Rijeka Bay on the Adriatic coast. HISTORY once a Roman base (Tarsatica), it was occupied from the 7c by the Slavs; Rijeka was the naval base of the Austro-Hungarian Empire until 1918; it was ceded to Italy in 1924 and to Yugoslavia in 1947. NOTABLE FEATURES Trsat

Castle; Jadran Palace; cathedral; National Museum.

Rijksmuseum a Dutch word generally used to indicate the national art gallery in Amsterdam, the Netherlands. The collection, which includes many works by Dutch masters, derives from that of the National Art Gallery, opened in The Hague in 1800. It was moved to the Trippenhuis in 1815 and opened as the Rijksmuseum in 1817. The present building was designed by Petrus Cuypers and erected between 1877 and 1885. [Dutch, = state museum]

Rikki-Tikki-Tavi the heroic, cobra-fighting mongoose in Rudyard Kipling's *The Jungle Book.*

Rila Monastery a monastery in the Rila Mts, Bulgaria, founded by Ivan Rilski (876–946). It became a major spiritual centre and in the 14c an extended monastery was erected — most of which was destroyed by fire in 1833. The present complex (built 1834–60), is a World Heritage site.

Rila Mountains, Bulgarian **Rila Planina** a range of mountains in W Bulgaria on the border with Yugoslavia, forming the NW part of the Rhodope Mts. It is the highest range in the Balkan Peninsula, rising to 2 925m at Musala. Forestry and livestock grazing are important.

rile *verb* to anger or annoy. [a variant of *roil*, to make (water) muddy or turbid]

Riley, Bridget (Louise) (1931–) English artist, born in London. She is a leading practitioner of Op Art (the use of repeated shapes or undulating lines to dazzle the beholder and (often) create an illusion of movement). She became well-known following her one-woman shows in London in 1962 and 1963. Her works include *Fall* (Tate Gallery, 1963).

Rilke, Rainer Maria (1875–1926) Austrian lyric poet, born in Prague. His three-part poem cycle, *Das Stundenbuch* (1905, The Book of Hours), written after visiting Russia, shows the influence of Russian Pietism. He married Klara Westhoff, a pupil of Rodin, and moved to Paris to become Rodin's secretary. Later works include *Neue Gedichte* (1907–8, New Poems), *Duineser Elegien* (Duino Elegies) and *Die Sonnette an Orpheus* (Sonnets to Orpheus). His poetry has been translated into many languages.

rill *noun* a small stream or brook. [from German *Rille*, channel]

rille *or* **rill** *noun* a long broad winding valley on the surface of the Moon. — Also called *rima*. [from German *Rille*, channel]

rim — *noun* 1 a raised and often curved edge or border. 2 the outer circular edge of a wheel to which the tyre is attached. — *verb* (**rimmed**, **rimming**) to form or provide an edge or rim to. [from Anglo-Saxon *rima*]

Rimbaud, (Jean Nicolas) Arthur (1854–91) French poet, born in Charleville. He published his first book of poems in 1870, following this with his best-known work, *Le Bateau ivre* (The Drunken Boat, 1871). He had a turbulent relationship with Paul Verlaine (1871–73), who shot and wounded him when he tried to end the friendship. During this time however he wrote many of the poems in *Les Illuminations* (published 1886), where the use of images show him as a precursor of Symbolism. The poor reception of *Une Saison en enfer* (A Season in Hell, 1873) prompted him to give up writing and lead an itinerant lifestyle in Europe and Africa.

rime[1] — *noun* thick white frost formed especially from frozen water droplets from cloud or fog. — *verb* to cover with rime. [from Anglo-Saxon *hrim*]

rime[2] same as RHYME.

Rime of the Ancient Mariner, The a poem by Samuel Taylor Coleridge (in *Lyrical Ballads*, 1798). It is a supernatural ballad detailing the ghostly experiences of an old sailor.

rimless *adj.* without a rim.

rimmed *adj.* having a rim.

Rimsky-Korsakov, Nikolai (Andreyevich) (1844–1908) Russian composer, born in Tikhvin, Novgorod. His interest in music was kindled chiefly after meeting Balakirev (1861), after which he wrote his first symphony (1865). In 1871 he became professor at the St Petersburg Conservatoire, where he could develop his technique. In 1887–8 he produced his three great orchestral masterpieces (*Capriccio Espagnol, Easter Festival* and *Sheherazade*), and his main works thereafter were operas, such as *The Golden Cockerel* (1907). Conscious of his previous technical shortcomings, he rewrote almost all his early work.

rimy *adj.* (**rimier**, **rimiest**) frosty, covered with rime.

rind — *noun* 1 a thick, hard outer layer or covering as on cheese or bacon, or the peel of fruit. 2 the bark of a tree or plant. — *verb* to strip bark from. [from Anglo-Saxon *rinde*]

ring[1] — *noun* 1 a small circle of gold, silver, or some other metal or material, worn on the finger. 2 a circle of metal, wood, plastic, etc for holding, keeping in place, connecting, hanging, etc. 3 any object, mark, or figure which is circular in shape. 4 a circular course. 5 a group of people or things arranged in a circle. 6 an enclosed and usually circular area for competitions or exhibitions, especially at a circus. 7 a square area marked off by ropes on a platform, where boxers or wrestlers fight. 8 (**the ring**) boxing as a profession. 9 a group of people who act together to control an antiques or drugs market, betting, etc for their own profit. 10 a circular electric element or gas burner on top of a cooker. 11 *Chem.* a closed chain of atoms in a molecule. 12 a thin band of particles orbiting some planets, such as Saturn and Uranus. — *verb* 1 to make, form, draw, etc a ring round. 2 to put a ring on the leg of (a bird) as a means of identifying it. 3 to fit a ring in the nose of (a bull) to make it easy to lead.

— **run rings round someone** *colloq.* to beat them or be much better than them.

throw one's hat into the ring *colloq.* to offer oneself as a candidate or contestant. [from Anglo-Saxon *hring*]

ring[2] — *verb* (PAST TENSE **rang**; PAST PARTICIPLE **rung**) 1 *trans., intrans.* to make or cause to make a sound, especially a ringing, bell-like sound. 2 *trans., intrans.* (**ring someone up**) *Brit.* to call them by telephone. 3 (**ring for someone**) to ring a bell as a summons to them. 4 *intrans. said of a place or building* to be filled with sound: *the office rang with the news.* 5 *intrans.* to sound repeatedly; to resound: *criticisms rang in his ears.* 6 *intrans. said of the ears* to be filled with a buzzing, humming or ringing sensation or sound. 7 *intrans. said of words, etc* to give a stated impression: *his promises rang false.* — *noun* 1 the act or sound of ringing. 2 the act of ringing a bell. 3 the clear, resonant sound of a bell, or a similarly resonant sound. 4 *Brit.* a telephone call. 5 a suggestion or impression of a particular feeling or quality: *a story with a ring of truth about it.* 6 a set of bells, especially in a church.

— **ring someone back** 1 to telephone someone again. 2 to telephone someone who telephoned earlier.

ring the changes 1 to vary the way something is done, used, said, etc. 2 to go through all the various orders possible when ringing a peel of church bells.

ring down *or* **up the curtain** 1 to give the signal for lowering, or raising, the curtain in a theatre. 2 to put an end to, or begin, a project or undertaking.

ring someone in *or* **out** to announce their arrival or departure with, or as if with, bell-ringing: *ring out the old year.*

ring off to end a telephone call.

ring out to make a sudden clear loud sound: *shots rang out.*

ring someone up to call them by telephone.

ring something up to record the price of an item sold on a cash register. [from Anglo-Saxon *hringan*]

ring binder a loose-leaf binder with metal rings which can be opened to add more pages or take them out.

ringbolt *noun* a bolt with a ring attached.

Ring des Nibelungen, Der (The Nibelungen's Ring), also called **the *Ring* Cycle** a music drama in a prologue and three parts by Richard Wagner (1869–76), comprising the introductory *Das Rheingold* (The Rhinegold, 1853, first performed 1869), *Die Walküre* (The Valkyrie, 1856, performed 1870), *Siegfried* (1857, performed 1876), and *Götterdämmerung* (The Twilight of the Gods, 1848, performed 1876). The first complete performance took place in Bayreuth over four evenings (1876). It relates an allegorical power-struggle between the Giants, the Gods and the Nibelung Dwarfs.

ring dove a wood pigeon.

ringed *adj.* 1 surrounded by, marked with, bearing, or wearing a ring or rings. 2 ring-shaped. 3 made up of rings.

ringer *noun* 1 a person or thing that rings. 2 (*also* **dead ringer**) *colloq.* a person or thing that is almost identical to some other person or thing. 3 *North Amer., esp. US* a horse or athlete entered into a race or competition under a false name or other false pretences. 4 *North Amer., esp. US* an impostor or fake.

ring finger the third finger, especially on the left hand, on which a wedding ring is worn.

ringleader *noun* the leader of a group of people who are doing something wrong or making trouble.

ringlet *noun* a long spiral curl of hair.

ring main a domestic electrical supply system in which power points are connected to the mains in a closed circuit.

ringmaster *noun* a person who is in charge of performances in a circus ring.

ring ouzel see OUZEL.

ring-pull *noun* a tongue of metal with a ring attached to it, which when pulled breaks a seal and opens a can or similar container.

ring road *Brit.* a road that goes round a town or through its suburbs to keep its centre relatively free of traffic.

ringside *noun* 1 the seating area immediately by a boxing, circus, etc ring. 2 any place that gives a good clear view.

ringway *noun* same as RING ROAD.

ringworm *noun Medicine* a highly contagious fungal infection characterized by the formation of small red itchy circular patches on soft areas of skin such as the scalp or groin. One of the commonest forms is *athlete's foot*, which affects the skin between the toes. — Also called *tinea*.

rink *noun* 1 an area of ice prepared for skating, curling, or ice-hockey, or a building containing this. 2 an area of smooth floor for roller skating, or a building containing this. 3 a strip of grass or ice allotted to a team or set of players in bowling and curling. [from Old French *renc*, rank, row]

rinse — *verb* 1 to wash (soap, detergent, etc) out of (clothes, hair, dishes, etc) with clean water. 2 to remove traces of dirt by washing lightly in clean water, usually without soap. 3 (*also* **rinse something out**) to clean (a cup, one's mouth, etc) by filling it with water, swirling the water round and throwing or spitting it out. 4 (*also* **rinse something away**) to remove (soap, detergent, dirt, etc) from a place using clean water. — *noun* 1 an act of rinsing. 2 liquid used for rinsing. 3 a solution used in hairdressing to give a temporary tint to the hair. [from Old French *recincier*]

rinser *noun* a board or rack for rinsing washed dishes.

Rio de Janeiro, byname **Rio** 1 POP (1991) 9.6m, the port capital of Rio de Janeiro state, SE Brazil. It lies on the Bahía de Guanabara and covers an area of 20km/12mi along a narrow strip of land between mountains and sea. Pão de Açúcar (Sugar Loaf Mountain) rises to 396m and forms a background to the city. HISTORY discovered in 1502; first settled by the French in 1555; taken by the Portuguese in 1567; seat of the Viceroy in 1763; capital of Brazil from 1834 to 1960. The city is a major international tourist centre, with famous beaches at Copacabana, Ipanema, and Leblon. NOTABLE FEATURES the suburb of Santa Teresa contains many colonial and 19c buildings; figure of Christ on the highest peak, Corcovado (690m); Monastery of São Bento (1633), Convent of Carmo (17c), Church of Nossa Senhora da Glória do Outeiro; Municipal Theatre, replica of the Paris Opera House; National Museum. EVENT world-famous Carnival, on the days preceding Lent, with parades, competitions, and fancy-dress balls. 2 a state in SE Brazil with Rio de Janeiro as its capital.

Rio Grande, in Mexico **Río Bravo**, or **Río Bravo del Norte** a river in SW USA and forming the border with N Mexico, length 3 033km/1 885mi. Rising in the Rocky Mts, SW Colorado, it flows SE through New Mexico, then along the Texas–Mexico border. It enters the Gulf of Mexico E of Brownsville, Texas. The river is used for irrigation and flood-control. Its major tributaries are the Pecos and Conchos. Navigation beyond Brownsville is forbidden by international agreement.

Rioja, La POP (1989e) 265 000, a region in N Spain co-extensive with the modern province of Logroño. AREA 5 034sq km/1 943sq mi. It is watered by the R Ebro and its tributaries. La Rioja is the best-known wine-producing area in Spain. CAPITAL Logroño.

Río Muni the mainland territory of Equatorial Guinea. AREA 26 016sq km/10 042sq mi. It is bounded W by the Gulf of Guinea, E and S by Gabon, and N by Cameroon. CHIEF TOWN Bata. The R Mbini flows from the mountains to the coast.

riot — *noun* 1 a noisy public disturbance or disorder by a usually large group of people, or *Legal* by three or more people. 2 uncontrolled or wild revelry and feasting. 3 a striking display (especially of colour). 4 a very amusing person or thing. — *verb intrans.* (**rioted**, **rioting**) to take part in a riot.
— **read the riot act** to give an angry warning that bad behaviour must stop.
run riot to act, speak, grow, etc in a wild and uncontrolled way.
[from Old French *riote*, debate, quarrel]

Riot Act legislation (1714) in Britain aimed at preserving public order. When 12 or more people were assembled unlawfully and refused to disperse, they were, after the reading of a section of this Act by a person in authority, immediately considered to have committed a crime.

rioter *noun* a person who takes part in a riot or uprising.

riotous *adj.* 1 participating in, likely to start, or like, a riot. 2 very active, noisy, cheerful, and wild. 3 filled with wild revelry, parties, etc: *riotous living.*

riotously *adv.* in a riotous way.

riotousness *noun* being riotous.

RIP *abbrev.* requiescat in pace (Latin), may he or she rest in peace.

rip — *verb* (**ripped**, **ripping**) 1 *trans., intrans.* to tear or come apart violently or roughly. 2 (**rip something off, out, etc**) to remove it quickly and violently. 3 *intrans. colloq.* to rush along or move quickly without restraint. 4 to saw (wood

or timber) along the grain. — *noun* 1 a violent or rough tear or split. 2 an act of ripping.
— **rip someone off** *colloq.* 1 to cheat or steal from them. 2 to overcharge them.

riparian *adj. formal* of, occurring on, or living on a riverbank. [from Latin *ripa*, riverbank]

ripcord *noun* a cord which releases a parachute from its pack when pulled.

ripe *adj.* 1 *said of fruit, grain, etc* fully matured and ready to be picked and eaten. 2 *said of cheese* having been allowed to age to develop its full flavour. 3 resembling ripe fruit, especially in being plump and pink. 4 mature in mind and body; fully developed. 5 (**ripe for something**) suitable or appropriate to it. 6 (**ripe for something**) eager or ready for it. 7 *said of language, etc* slightly indecent; smutty.
— **ripe old age** a very old age.
[from Anglo-Saxon *ripe*]

ripen *verb trans., intrans.* (**ripened**, **ripening**) to make or become ripe or riper.

ripeness *noun* being ripe.

ripieno *Mus.* — *noun* (PL. **ripieni**, **ripienos**) 1 the full body (or full section) of the orchestra. The term is most often applied in the concerto grosso of the Baroque period to distinguish those passages to be played by the full orchestra from those to be played by the soloist or solo group. 2 a supplementary instrument or performer. — *adj.* supplementary, full. [from Italian *ripieno*, full]

rip-off *noun colloq.* 1 an act or instance of stealing from, cheating, or defrauding someone. 2 an item which is outrageously overpriced.

Ripon POP (1981) 13 000, a city and market town in Harrogate district, North Yorkshire, N England. It is considered to be England's second oldest city. NOTABLE FEATURES Cathedral of St Peter and St Wilfrid; Wakeman's House (13c); Fountains Abbey ruins nearby; racecourse.

riposte — *noun* 1 a quick, sharp reply; a retort. 2 a fencer's quick return thrust. — *verb intrans.* to answer with a riposte. [from French, from Italian *risposta*, reply]

ripper *noun* 1 a person who rips. 2 a tool for ripping.

ripple — *noun* 1 a slight wave or series of slight waves on the surface of water. 2 a sound that rises and falls quickly and gently like that of rippling water, especially of laughter or applause. 3 a wavy appearance, eg of material. — *verb* 1 *intrans., trans.* to form or cause to form or flow with ripples or a rippling motion. 2 *intrans.* to make a rippling sound.

ripple tank *Physics* a shallow tank of water, used to demonstrate the behaviour of waves, especially properties such as reflection, refraction, diffraction, and interference.

rippling *or* **ripply** *adj.* (**ripplier**, **rippliest**) having ripples.

rip-roaring *adj.* wild, noisy, and exciting.

ripsaw *noun* a saw for cutting along the grain of timber.

Rip Van Winkle a tale by Washington Irving (in *The Sketch Book*, 1820). It describes how Rip falls asleep on a mountain for 20 years and wakens as an old man to find everything has changed.

RISC *abbrev. Comput.* reduced instruction set computer, a computer with a central processor which has a very small instruction set to enable faster processing.

rise — *verb intrans.* (PAST TENSE **rose**; PAST PARTICIPLE **risen**) 1 to get or stand up, especially from a sitting, kneeling, or lying position. 2 to get up from bed, especially after a night's sleep. 3 to move upwards; to ascend. 4 to increase in size, amount, volume, degree, intensity, etc. 5 *said of the sun, moon, planets, etc* to appear above

the horizon. 6 to stretch or slope upwards: *ground which rises gently.* 7 (**rise up** *or* **rise against someone**) to rebel. 8 to move from a lower position, rank, level, etc to a higher one. 9 to begin or originate: *a river that rises in the mountains.* 10 *said especially of a person's spirits* to become more cheerful. 11 *said especially of an animal's fur, a person's hair, etc* to become straight and stiff, eg because of fear or anger. 12 *said of a committee, court, parliament, etc* to finish a session; to adjourn. 13 to come back to life. 14 to come to the surface of water: *wait for the fish to rise.* 15 *said of dough* to swell up. 16 to be built: *new office blocks rising all over town.* 17 (**rise to something**) to respond to something (eg provocation or criticism). — *noun* 1 an act of rising. 2 an increase in size, amount, volume, strength, status, rank, etc. 3 *Brit.* an increase in salary. 4 a piece of rising ground; a slope or hill. 5 a beginning or origin. 6 the vertical height of a step or flight of stairs.
— **get** *or* **take a rise out of someone** *colloq.* to make them angry or upset, especially through teasing or provocation.
give rise to something to cause it.
rise above something to remain unaffected by teasing, provocation, criticism, etc.
rise to the bait to do what someone else suggests by means of suggestions, hints, etc that one should do.
[from Anglo-Saxon *risan*]

riser *noun* 1 a person who gets out of bed: *an early riser.* 2 any of the vertical parts between the horizontal steps of a set of stairs.

risibility *noun* 1 laughter. 2 inclination to laugh.

risible *adj.* 1 causing laughter; ludicrous; ridiculous. 2 inclined to laughter. [from Latin *risibilis*]

rising — *noun* 1 the act of rising. 2 a rebellion. — *adj.* 1 moving or sloping upwards; getting higher. 2 approaching greater age, maturity, status, reputation, or importance. 3 approaching a stated age: *the rising sevens.*

rising damp wetness which rises up through the bricks of a wall.

risk — *noun* 1 the chance or possibility of suffering loss, injury, damage, or failure. 2 a person or thing likely to cause loss, injury, damage, etc. 3 a person or thing thought of as likely (a *bad risk*) or unlikely (a *good risk*) to suffer loss, injury, damage, etc. — *verb* 1 to expose to danger or risk. 2 to take the chance of (risk, danger, etc occurring): *not risk being late.*
— **at one's own risk** accepting personal responsibility for any loss, injury, etc which might occur.
at risk in danger; in a position which might lead to loss, injury, etc.
at the risk of something with the possibility of loss, injury, or some other unfortunate consequence.
run the risk of something to risk it: *run the risk of being late.*
run *or* **take a risk** to act in a certain way despite the risk involved.
[from French *risque*]

risk analysis a methodical investigation undertaken to assess the financial and physical risks which may affect a business venture. In insurance, risk is calculated by actuaries for the purpose of determining premium levels.

riskily *adv.* in a risky way.

risky *adj.* (**riskier**, **riskiest**) dangerous, liable to accident or mishap.

Risorgimento the 19c movement by which Italy achieved unity and nationhood. Although its origins lay in the 18c Enlightenment and the Napoleonic period, it is usually held to have started properly in the decades after the Congress of Vienna (1814–15). After the failure of the popular revolts of 1848–9, the Risorgimento reached fruition with the wars of unification (1859–70) and the creation of a single state under Victor

Emmanuel II. [from Italian *risorgimento*, resurgence]

risotto *noun* (PL. **risottos**) an Italian dish of rice cooked in a meat or seafood stock with onions, tomatoes, cheese, etc. [from Italian *riso*, rice]

risqué *adj.*, *said of a story, joke, etc* bordering on the rude or indecent. [from French *risqué*, risky]

rissole *noun* a small fried cake or ball of chopped meat coated in breadcrumbs. [from Old French *roissole*]

ritardando *adj.*, *adv.*, *noun* (PL. **ritardandos**, **ritardandi**) *Mus.* same as RALLENTANDO. [from Italian]

rite *noun* **1** a religious ceremony or observance. **2** the required words or actions for such a ceremony. **3** a body of such acts or ceremonies which are characteristic of a particular church: *the Latin rite of the Roman Catholic church*. [from Latin *ritus*]

Rite of Spring, The (Vesna svyash-chennaya), French *Le sacre du printemps* a ballet by Igor Stravinsky (1913), commissioned by Sergei Diaghilev's Ballets Russes. The score was later adapted for a four-hand piano piece.

ritual — *noun* **1** the set order or words used in a religious ceremony. **2** a body of such rituals, especially of a particular church. **3** the use of rituals in a religious ceremony. **4** an often repeated series of actions or procedure. — *adj.* relating to or like rites or ritual. [from Latin *ritualis*]

ritualism *noun* excessive belief in the importance of, or excessive practice of, ritual.

ritualist *noun* a person skilled in or devoted to a ritual.

ritualistic *adj.* **1** relating to or characteristic of ritualism. **2** fond of or devoted to ritual.

ritualistically *adv.* in a ritualistic way.

ritually *adv.* according to ritual.

ritzy *adj.* (**ritzier**, **ritziest**) *colloq.* very smart and elegant. [from *Ritz*, a name often used for luxury hotels]

rival — *noun* **1** a person or group of people that tries to compete with another for the same goal or in the same field. **2** a person or thing which equals another in quality, ability, etc: *be without equal*. — *adj.* being a rival; in competition for the same goal or in the same field. — *verb* (**rivalled**, **rivalling**) **1** to try to gain the same goal as (someone else); to be in competition with. **2** to try to equal or be better than. **3** to be able to be compared with as being equal or nearly so. [from Latin *rivalis*, one who uses the same stream as another]

rivalry *noun* (PL. **rivalries**) **1** the state of being a rival or rivals. **2** an act of rivalling.

Rivals, The a play by Richard Brinsley Sheridan (1775). Set in Bath, it is a comedy about a rich young officer who assumes the guise of a poorer man to woo the romantic Lydia Languish, whose aunt and guardian, Mrs Malaprop (of word-confusion fame), does not approve the match.

riven *adj.* having been violently torn or split apart. [from Norse *rifa*]

river *noun* **1** *Geol.* a permanent natural flow of water, larger than a stream, along a fixed course. **2** an abundant or plentiful stream or flow. [from Old French *riviere*, from Latin *ripa*, riverbank]

Rivera, Diego (1886–1957) Mexican painter, born in Guanajuato. In 1921 he began a series of murals in public buildings depicting the life and history of the Mexican people. He also executed frescoes in the USA (1930–4), mainly of industrial life. His art is a blend of folk art and revolutionary propaganda, with overtones of Byzantine and Aztec symbolism. He was married to the painter Frida Kahlo.

river basin *Geol.* the area of land drained by a river and its tributaries. — Also called *drainage basin*.

river dolphin any of various species of a small toothed whale with a long narrow beak, found in rivers and brackish water in S Asia and S America.

riverine *adj.* of, on, or near a river.

Riverside POP (1990) 227 000, a city in Riverside County, S California, USA. It lies on the Santa Ana R, 80km/50mi E of Los Angeles, and was established in 1870. The navel orange was introduced into California here in 1873. NOTABLE FEATURES Citrus Experiment Station (1913); International Raceway.

rivet — *noun* *Engineering* a metal pin or bolt, with a head at one end, that is passed through a hole in each of two or more pieces of metal that are to be joined. The protruding end is then hammered flat. — *verb* (**riveted**, **riveting**) **1** to fasten two or more pieces of metal with such a device. **2** to flatten or beat down (the head of a nail, etc). **3** to fix securely. **4** to attract and hold firmly, to engross (eg a person's attention). **5** to cause (a person) to be fixed, especially with horror or fear: *be riveted to the spot*. [from Old French *river*, to attach]

riveter *noun* a person or tool that rivets.

riveting *adj.* **1** the joining of two or more pieces of metal by passing a metal rivet through a hole in each piece and then hammering the protruding end of the rivet flat. Formerly widely used in the building of ships, bridges, etc, riveting has now been largely superseded by welding. **2** fascinating; enthralling.

riviera *noun* **1** a coastal area with a warm climate. **2** (**Riviera**) the Mediterranean coast between Toulon, France, and La Spezia, Italy. It is a narrow coastal strip bordered by the Alps to the N, and includes many holiday resorts. [from Italian *riviera*, coast]

rivulet *noun* a small stream or river. [from Latin *rivulus*]

Riyadh, Arabic **Ar Riyad 1** POP (1991e) 1.5m, the capital of Saudi Arabia. It was a walled city until the 1550s when the walls were demolished to allow for expansion. The city is the political and communications centre of Saudi Arabia and is situated in a fertile dry river valley where fruit and date palms are grown and grain is cultivated. NOTABLE FEATURES over 1 000 mosques; Royal Palace. The 'Solar Village' to the N is a prototype project for the use of solar power. **2** a province in Saudi Arabia with Riyadh as its capital.

Rizzio or **Riccio, David** (c.1533–1566) Italian courtier and musician, born in Pancalieri, near Turin. He went to Scotland with the Duke of Savoy's embassy, entered the service of Mary,

Queen of Scots (1561), became her favourite, and was made her French secretary (1564). He negotiated her marriage with Darnley (1565), who became jealous of his influence and with a group of nobles (eg Morton and Ruthven) arranged his murder at the Palace of Holyroodhouse.

RM *abbrev.* **1** Resident Magistrate. **2** Royal Mail. **3** Royal Marines.

rm *abbrev.* room.

RMA *abbrev.* Royal Military Academy, Sandhurst.

RN *abbrev.* Royal Navy.

Rn *symbol Chem.* radon.

RNA *abbrev.* ribonucleic acid.

RNAS *abbrev.* Royal Navy Air Service(s).

RNIB *abbrev.* Royal National Institute for the Blind.

RNID *abbrev.* Royal National Institute for the Deaf.

RNLI *abbrev.* Royal National Lifeboat Institution.

RNR *abbrev.* Royal Naval Reserve.

RNVR *abbrev.* Royal Naval Volunteer Reserve.

RNZAF *abbrev.* Royal New Zealand Air Force.

RNZN *abbrev.* Royal New Zealand Navy.

Roach, Hal, originally **Harald Eugene Roach** (1892–1992) US film producer, born in Elmira, New York. In 1915 he formed a production company to make short silent comedies, whose players included Harold Lloyd and Will Hays. After 1928 he continued with sound and made the comedy features *Topper* (1937) and *Topper Returns* (1941). In 1984 he received a Special Academy Award.

roach[1] *noun* a silvery freshwater fish of the carp family. [from Old French *roche*]

roach[2] *noun North Amer.* **1** a cockroach. **2** *slang* the butt of a marijuana cigarette.

road *noun* **1** an open, usually specially surfaced or paved way, for people, vehicles, or animals to travel on from one place to another. **2** a route or way: *the road to ruin*. **3** (*usually* **roads**) a relatively sheltered area of water near the shore where ships may be anchored.
— **get out of someone's road** *colloq. chiefly Scot.* to get out of their way.
one for the road a final, usually alcoholic, drink before leaving.
on the road travelling from place to place, especially as a commercial traveller or tramp. [from Anglo-Saxon *rad*]

roadbed *noun* **1** the foundation of a railway track on which the sleepers are laid. **2** the material laid down to form a road, and which forms a foundation for the road surface.

Longest Rivers			
Name	Outflow	Length[1]	
		km	mi
Nile-Kagera-Ruvuvu-Ruvusu-Luvironza	Mediterranean Sea (Egypt)	6 695	4 160
Amazon-Ucayali-Tambo-Ene-Apurimac	Atlantic Ocean (Brazil)	6 449	4 007
Yangtze	E China Sea (China)	6 300	3 900
Mississippi-Missouri-Jefferson-Beaverhead-Red Rock	Gulf of Mexico (USA)	6 019	3 740
Yenisei-Angara-Selenga-Ider	Kara Sea (Russia)	5 870	3 650
Amur-Argun-Kerulen	Tartar Strait (Russia)	5 780	3 590
Ob-Irtysh	Gulf of Ob, Kara Sea (Russia)	5 410	3 360
Plata-Parana-Grande	Atlantic Ocean (Argentina/Uruguay)	4 880	3 030
Yellow	Yellow Sea (China)	4 840	3 010
Zaire	Atlantic Ocean (Angola-Zaire)	4 630	2 880
Lena	Laptev Sea (Russia)	4 400	2 700
Mackenzie-Slave-Peace-Finlay	Beaufort Sea (Canada)	4 240	2 630
Mekong	S China Sea (Vietnam)	4 000	2 500
Niger	Gulf of Guinea (Nigeria)	4 100	2 550

[1]Lengths include the river plus tributaries comprising the longest watercourse.

roadblock *noun* a barrier put across a road (eg by the police or army) to stop and check vehicles and drivers.

road-hog *noun colloq.* an aggressive and selfish driver, especially one who tries to intimidate other drivers.

roadholding *noun* the extent to which a vehicle remains stable when turning corners at high speed, in wet conditions, etc.

roadhouse *noun* a public house or inn on the side of a major road.

roadie *noun colloq.* a person who helps move the instruments and equipment which belong to especially a rock or pop group.

road metal broken stone or rock used for building or mending roads.

roadside *noun* a strip of ground or land beside or along a road.

road sign a sign beside or over a road, motorway, etc, giving information on routes, speed limits, hazards, traffic systems, etc.

roadstead same as ROAD 3.

roadster *noun* **1** an open sports car for two people. **2** a strong bicycle. **3** a horse for riding or pulling carriages on roads.

Road Town POP (1991e) 6 000, the capital of the British Virgin Is, Greater Antilles, in the E Caribbean Sea. It is a seaport situated on the E coast of Tortola I.

roadway *noun* the part of a road or street used by cars.

roadwork *noun* **1** (**roadworks**) the building or repairing of a road. **2** training, eg for marathons, boxing matches, etc in the form of long runs on roads.

roadworthiness *noun* a roadworthy state.

roadworthy *adj.* in a suitable condition and safe to be used on the road.

roam — *verb trans., intrans.* to ramble or wander about. — *noun* the act of roaming; a ramble. [from Middle English *romen*]

roamer *noun* a person who roams, a wanderer.

roan — *adj., usually said of horses or cattle* having a reddish-brown or bay coat thickly flecked with grey or white hairs. — *noun* an animal, especially a horse, with a coat of this type. [from Old Spanish *roano*]

Roanoke POP (1990) 224 000, an independent industrial city in SW Virginia, USA. It lies on the Roanoke R, 240km/149mi W of Richmond. Settled in 1740, it is the gateway to the Shenandoah Valley.

roar — *verb* **1** *intrans.* to give a loud growling cry. **2** *intrans.* to laugh loudly, deeply, and wildly. **3** *intrans.* to make a deep loud reverberating sound, as of cannons, busy traffic, wind, and waves in a storm, or a fiercely burning fire. **4** to say (something) with a deep, loud cry, especially as in anger. **5** (**roar about**, **away**, **past**, *etc*) to go fast and noisily, usually in a motor vehicle. **6** (**roar someone on**) to shout encouragement to them. **7** *intrans. said of a horse* to breathe with a loud noise as a sign of disease. — *noun* **1** a loud, deep, prolonged cry, as of lions, a cheering crowd, a person in pain or anger, etc. **2** a loud, deep, prolonged sound, as of cannons, busy traffic, an engine made to roar, the wind or waves in a storm, or a fiercely burning fire.
— **do a roaring trade** to do very brisk and profitable business.
[from Anglo-Saxon *rarian*]

roaring *adj.* **1** uttering or emitting roars. **2** riotous. **3** proceeding with great activity or success.

roaring drunk *colloq.* very drunk.

roaring forties *Meteorol.* a belt of strong westerly winds, lying between 40° and 50° S of the Equator, that are not interrupted by landmasses and often blow at gale force.

roast — *verb* **1** *trans., intrans.* to cook (meat or other food) by exposure to dry heat, especially in an oven. **2** to dry and make brown (coffee beans, nuts, etc) by exposure to dry heat. **3** *intrans. said of meat, coffee beans, nuts, etc* to be cooked or dried and made brown by being exposed to dry heat. **4** *trans., intrans. colloq.* to make or become extremely or excessively hot. **5** *colloq.* to criticize severely. — *noun* **1** a piece of meat which has been roasted or is suitable for roasting. **2** *North Amer.* a party in the open air at which food is roasted and eaten. — *adj.* roasted: *roast potatoes.* [from Old French *rostir*]

roaster *noun* **1** an oven or dish for roasting food. **2** a vegetable, fowl, etc suitable for roasting.

roasting *colloq.* — *adj.* very hot. — *noun* a dose of severe criticism.

rob *verb* (**robbed**, **robbing**) **1** to steal something from (a person or place), especially by force or threats. **2** to deprive (someone) of something expected as a right or due. **3** *intrans.* to commit robbery. [from Old French *robber*]

Robbe-Grillet, Alain (1922–) French novelist, born in Brest. He worked as an agronomist, then in a publishing house, and in 1953 published his first novel *Les Gommes* (The Erasers). He emerged as the leader of the *nouveau roman* group, with novels such as *Le Voyeur* (The Voyeur, 1955) and *La Jalousie* (Jealousy, 1959), and the theoretical work *Pour un nouveau roman* (Towards the New Novel, 1963). He has also written essays and film scenarios, notably *L'Année dernière à Marienbad* (Last Year at Marienbad, 1961).

robber *noun* a person who robs; a thief.

robbery *noun* (PL. **robberies**) the act of robbing, especially theft with threats, force, or violence.

Robbins (of Clare Market), L(ionel Charles) Robbins, Baron (1898–1984) English economist and educationalist, born in Sipson, Middlesex. He was Professor of Economics at the London School of Economics (1929–61), directed the economic section of the War Cabinet, then became Chairman of the *Financial Times* (until 1970). He also chaired the 'Robbins Committee' on the expansion of higher education in the UK (1961–4), which was followed by the founding of new universities and polytechnics. His best-known work is *An Essay on the Nature and Significance of Economic Science* (1932).

robe — *noun* **1** (*often* **robes**) a long, loose, flowing garment, especially one worn for special ceremonies by peers, judges, mayors, academics, etc. **2** *North Amer.* a dressing-gown or bathrobe. — *verb trans., intrans.* to clothe (oneself or someone) in a robe or robes. [from Old French *robe*, booty]

Robert II (1316–90) King of Scots (1371–90), the son of Walter. He acted as sole regent during the exile and captivity of David II. On David's death, he became king in right of his descent from his maternal grandfather, Robert Bruce, and founded the Stuart royal dynasty.

Robert a male first name, borne by three kings of Scotland. [of Norman origin, from *hrod*, fame + *berht*, bright]

Roberts (of Kandahar, Pretoria and Waterford), Frederick Sleigh Roberts, 1st Earl (1832–1914) British soldier, born at Cawnpore, India. He took an active part in the Indian Mutiny, and won the VC in 1858. Commander-in-Chief in India (1885–93), he served as Supreme Commander in South Africa during the Boer War, and relieved Kimberley (1900). He died while visiting troops in the field in France.

Robeson, Paul (Bustill) (1898–1976) American black singer and actor, born in Princeton, New Jersey. He appeared in works ranging from *Show Boat* to *Othello*, gave song recitals, notably of Negro spirituals, and appeared in numerous films. In the 1950s, his left-wing views caused him to leave the USA for Europe (1958–63).

Robespierre, (Maximilien François Marie Isidore de) (1758–94) French revolutionary leader, born in Arras. Elected to the Estates General (1789) and a member of the Jacobin Club, he emerged in the National Assembly as a popular radical, known as 'the Incorruptible'. In 1791 he was public accuser, and in 1792 presented a petition to the Legislative Assembly for a Revolutionary Tribunal. Elected first deputy for Paris in the National Convention, he emerged as leader of the Mountain, strongly opposed to the Girondins, whom he helped to destroy. In 1793 he joined the Committee of Public Safety and for three months dominated the country, and introduced the Reign of Terror and the cult of the Supreme Being. He wielded his power ruthlessly however, and his popularity decreased. He was attacked in the Convention, arrested, and guillotined on the orders of the Revolutionary Tribunal.

Robey, Sir George (1869–1954) English comedian, born in Herne Hill, Kent. He made his name in musical shows such as *The Bing Boys* (1916), and later emerged as a Shakespearean actor in the part of Falstaff. Dubbed the 'Prime Minister of Mirth', he was famous for his bowler hat, black coat, hooked stick, and thickly painted eyebrows.

Robin, Fanny the unfortunate mistress of Troy in Thomas Hardy's *Far from the Madding Crowd*.

robin *noun* **1** (*also* **robin redbreast**) a small brown European thrush with a red breast. **2** a N American thrush with an orange-red breast, larger than the European robin. [a diminutive of *Robert*]

Robin Goodfellow, also called **Puck**, or **Hobgoblin** in English 16c–17c superstition, a mischievous fairy who would do housework if duly rewarded. His name held sufficient terror for nurses to use it as a threat to naughty children. His characteristic activities are listed in *A Midsummer Night's Dream* (2.i).

Robin Hood in English folklore, a 13c outlaw who lived in Sherwood Forest in the English N Midlands, celebrated in ballads dating from the 14c. He protected the poor, and outwitted, robbed, or killed the wealthy and unscrupulous officials of Church and State. The legend may have had its origins in the popular discontent that led to the Peasants' Revolt of 1381.

Robinson, Edward G, originally **Emanuel Goldenberg** (1893–1973) US film actor, born in Bucharest, Romania, of Jewish parents who emigrated to the USA in 1903. He began in silent films, but became famous as the gangster Rico in *Little Caesar* (1930). His support of democratic causes harmed his career at the time of the McCarthy witch-hunts, but he had later successes including *The Cincinatti Kid* (1965). He received a Special Academy Award in 1972.

Robinson, Edwin Arlington (1869–1935) US poet, born in Head Tide, Maine. He was brought up in the town of Gardiner, Maine, which is the prototype of the 'Tilbury Town' of his poems. He won Pulitzer Prizes for his *Collected Poems* (1922), *The Man Who Died Twice* (1925), and *Tristram* (1928), one of his several modern renderings of Arthurian legends.

Robinson, Joan V(iolet) (1903–83) English economist, born in Camberley, Surrey. She taught economics at Cambridge (1931–71), succeeding her husband as Professor in 1965. She was an influential economic theorist, and a leader of the Cambridge School, which developed macro-economic theories of growth and distribution, based on the work of Keynes.

Robinson, Mary (1944–) Irish Labour politician and President, born in Ballina, Co Mayo. In 1969 she became Professor of Law at Trinity College, Dublin. As a member of the Irish Senate (1969–89), she participated in numerous legal associations in the EC, and campaigned for women's and single-parents' rights and the decriminalization of homosexuality. Nominated by the Labour Party, from which she had resigned in 1985 over the Anglo-Irish Agreement, she unexpectedly defeated the Fine Fáil candidate Brian Lenihan in the presidential elections of Nov 1990, since when she has gained the support and confidence of most of the Irish people. In Jun 1993 she went on a mission of reconciliation to Belfast where she met the Sinn Féin leader Gerry Adams.

Robinson, Sir Robert (1886–1975) English chemist, born in Chesterfield. He was professor at Sydney, Liverpool, St Andrews, Manchester, London, and Oxford, and is particularly noted for his work on plant pigments, alkaloids, and other natural products, and in the development of penicillin. He was awarded the 1947 Nobel Prize for Chemistry.

Robinson Crusoe, in full **The Life and strange and surprising Adventures of Robinson Crusoe,** a prose romance by Daniel Defoe (1719). It describes how a man survives for almost 30 years after being shipwrecked on a desert island. It is based on events in the life of Alexander Selkirk, a Scottish sailor.

robot *noun* **1** especially in science fiction stories, etc, a machine which looks and functions like a human. **2** an automatic machine that can be programmed to perform specific tasks. **3** a person who works efficiently but who lacks human warmth or sensitivity. [from Czech *robota*, work]

robotic *adj.* relating to or characteristic of robots.

robotics *sing. noun* **1** the branch of engineering concerned with the design, construction, operation, and use of industrial robots. It incorporates many of the concepts that are used in artificial intelligence. **2** a form of dancing in which dancers imitate the stiff, jerky, and sharp movements of robots.

Rob Roy, Gaelic for **Red Robert**, originally **Robert MacGregor** (1671–1734) Scottish outlaw, born in Buchanan, Stirlingshire. After his lands were seized by the Duke of Montrose, he gathered his clansmen and became a brigand. His career gave rise to many stories about his allegedly brave exploits and generosity to the poor. Captured and imprisoned in London, he was sentenced to transportation, but pardoned in 1727.

Rob Roy a novel by Sir Walter Scott (1817). It is set against the background of the 1715 Jacobite Rebellion and features the real-life outlaw.

Robson, Dame Flora (McKenzie) (1902–84) English actress, born in South Shields, Tyne and Wear. She first appeared in 1921, and became famous for her historical roles in plays and films, such as Queen Elizabeth in *Fire over England* (1931).

robust *adj.* **1** strong and healthy; with a strong constitution. **2** strongly built or constructed. **3** *said of exercise, etc* requiring strength and energy. **4** rough, earthy, and slightly rude. **5** *said of wine* with a full, rich quality. [from Latin *robustus*, from *robur*, oak, strength]

robustly *adv.* in a robust way.

robustness *noun* being robust.

ROC *abbrev.* Royal Observer Corps.

roc *noun* an enormous bird in Arabian legends, strong enough to carry off an elephant. [from Persian *rukh*]

Roca–Runciman Pact a commercial treaty (May 1933) between Britain and Argentina that guaranteed Argentina a share of the British meat market in return for various economic concessions. It was negotiated by Vice-President Julio A Roca (Argentina) and Walter Runciman (Britain).

Rochdale POP (1992e) 206 000, a town in Rochdale borough, Greater Manchester, NW England. It lies on the R Roch, 16km/10mi NE of Manchester. The Cooperative Society was founded here in 1844.

Rochester, Edward Fairfax the capricious hero of Charlotte Brontë's *Jane Eyre*.

Rochester, John Wilmot, 2nd Earl of (1647–80) English courtier and poet, born in Ditchley, Oxfordshire. A prominent figure at the court of Charles II, he led a life of debauchery, and produced a varied output of bacchanalian and amatory songs, verses, satires, and letters. These works include *Verses Upon Nothing* and 'A Satyr against Mankind'.

Rochester POP (1990) 1m, the seat of Monroe County, W New York State, NE USA. It is a port on the Genesee R, 10km/6mi from L Ontario. First settled in 1811, it achieved city status in 1834. Important manufactures include optical and photographic instruments. NOTABLE FEATURES International Museum of Photography; Rochester Museum; Memorial Art Gallery.

Rochester POP (1990) 106 000, the seat of Olmsted County, SE Minnesota, USA. It lies on the Zumbro R. The Mayo Clinic, a world-famous medical centre established in 1889, is situated here.

Rochester upon Medway, ancient **Durobrivae** POP (1981) 24 000, a town in Rochester upon Medway district, Kent, SE England. It lies W of Chatham and is part of the Medway Towns urban area. It was an important early settlement at a ford over the R Medway. NOTABLE FEATURES cathedral (12c); castle (11c); Dickens Centre; Gad's Hill nearby, the home of Charles Dickens.

rochet *noun Relig.* a full-length white linen robe worn by bishops, especially of the Anglican Communion, on ceremonial occasions. [from Old French; of Germanic origin]

rock¹ *noun* **1** *Geol.* a loose or consolidated mass of one or more minerals that forms part of the Earth's crust, eg granite, limestone. Rocks are classified as igneous, metamorphic, or sedimentary, according to the way in which they were formed, and may be hard or soft. **2** a large natural mass of this material forming a reef, tor, etc. **3** a large stone or boulder. **4** *North Amer.* a stone or pebble. **5** someone or something which provides a firm foundation or support and can be depended upon. **6** (*usually* **rocks**) a cause or source of difficulty, danger or disaster. **7** *Brit.* a hard sweet usually made in the form of long, cylindrical sticks, which is brightly coloured and flavoured with peppermint, etc. **8** *slang* a precious stone, especially a diamond.
— **on the rocks** *colloq.* **1** *said of a marriage* broken down; failed. **2** *said of an alcoholic drink* served with ice cubes. **3** *said of a business firm* in a state of great financial difficulty. [from Old French *rocque*]

rock² — *verb* **1** *trans., intrans.* to sway or cause to sway gently backwards and forwards or from side to side: *rock the baby to sleep.* **2** *trans., intrans.* to move or cause to move or shake violently. **3** to disturb, upset, or shock. **4** *intrans.* to dance to or play rock music. — *noun* **1** a rocking movement. **2** (*also* **rock music**) a form of popular music with a very strong beat, usually played on electronic instruments and derived from rock and roll. **3** rock and roll. — *adj.* relating to rock music. [from Anglo-Saxon *roccian*]
◇ The terms *rock* and *rock and roll* were originally applied to music of the 1950s which blended the styles of rhythm and blues and country and western. Major artists of this period included Bill Haley (1925–81), Elvis Presley (1935–77), and Chuck Berry (1926–). During the 1960s, the format was expanded considerably by such artists as Bob Dylan (1941–) and Jimi Hendrix (1942–70), and by bands such as the Beatles and the Rolling Stones. A series of subgenres, from 'hard rock' to 'punk rock' have developed, most of which are characterized by both musical differences and associated features in dress, lifestyle, etc.

rockabilly *noun* a style of music which combines elements from both rock and roll and hillbilly.

rock and roll *or* **rock 'n' roll** — *noun* a form of popular music with a lively jive beat and simple melodies. — *verb intrans.* to dance to or play rock and roll music.

rock bottom the lowest level possible.

rock-bottom *adj., said of prices, etc* having reached the lowest possible level.

rock cake a small round cake with a rough surface, made with fruit and spices.

rock crystal a transparent colourless quartz.

Rockefeller, John D(avison) (1839–1937) US industrialist and philanthropist, born in Richford, New York. In 1875, with his brother William (1841–1922), he founded the Standard Oil Company, securing control of the US oil trade. He withdrew from active business in 1897, and devoted the rest of his life to philanthropy. He gave over 500m dollars to medical research, universities, and churches, and in 1913 established the Rockefeller Foundation 'to promote the wellbeing of mankind'. His grandson, Nelson A(ldrich) (1908–79), became Republican Governor of New York State (1958–73), and was Vice-President (1974–7) under President Ford.

Rockefeller, John D(avison) II (1874–1960) US businessman and philanthropist, son of John D Rockefeller. He was chairman of the Rockefeller Institute of Medical Research, built the Rockefeller Center in New York City, and was responsible for the restoration of colonial Williamsburg in Virginia.

Rockefeller Center a complex of 14 skyscrapers commissioned by John D Rockefeller II and built (1931–40) in Manhattan, New York

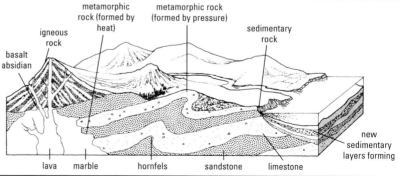

rock formation

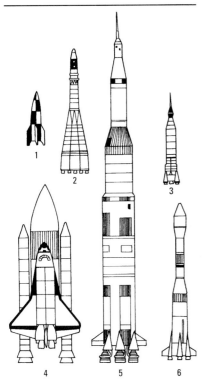

1: V2, Germany 1944   4: US shuttle, 1981
2: Vostok, USSR 1961   5: Apollo-Saturn V, USA 1968
3: Mercury-Atlas, USA 1962   6: Ariane, Europe 1981

rocket types

City. The centre now consists of offices, restaurants, shops, cinemas, broadcasting stations, and the Radio City Music Hall.

Rockefeller Foundation in the USA, a philanthropic organization for distributing private wealth for public benefit (eg education, international activities, health, the arts, social welfare, and religious groups), founded by the US industrialist and philanthropist John D Rockefeller (1839–1937) in 1913.

rocker *noun* **1** one of usually two curved supports on which a chair, cradle, etc rocks. **2** something that rocks on such supports, especially a rocking chair. **3** a person or thing that rocks. **4** a device which is operated with a movement from side to side, backwards and forwards, or up and down, especially a switch between the 'on' and 'off' positions. **5** *Brit.* (**Rocker**) in the 1960s, a member of a sometimes violent teenage gang, typically wearing leather jackets and riding motorcycles. See also MOD. **6** an object with a part which is curved like a rocker, especially a skate with a curved blade.
— **off one's rocker** *colloq.* mad; crazy.

rockery *noun* (PL. **rockeries**) a garden made with both rocks and earth, and where rock plants are grown.

rocket — *noun* **1** a cylinder containing inflammable material, which when ignited is projected through the air for signalling, carrying a line to a ship in distress, or as part of a firework display. **2** a projectile or vehicle, especially a space vehicle, that obtains its thrust from a backward jet of hot gases produced by the burning of a mixture of fuel and oxygen that is carried within the projectile or vehicle. **3** *Brit. colloq.* a severe reprimand. — *verb* (**rocketed**, **rocketing**) **1** *intrans.* to move (especially upwards) extremely quickly, as if with the speed of a rocket. **2** to attack with rockets. [from Italian *rochetta*]
◇ Rockets do not require oxygen from the air, so can be used to propel vehicles in space. In a space rocket, a fuel and an oxidizer (a chemical that contains oxygen) are mixed and burned in a combustion chamber. The burning fuel expands, and is forced out of the engine as a jet of gas through a bell-shaped nozzle, propelling the rocket in the opposite direction. A typical *liquid fuel rocket* has separate tanks containing liquid oxygen and a propellant, such as kerosene or liquid hydrogen. Another tank holds nitrogen, which is used to drive pumps for the oxygen and propellant, which mix and burn in the combustion chamber, producing a high-speed exhaust of very hot gases that give the rocket thrust. In World War II long-range liquid fuel rockets were developed, but since then rockets have been used mainly for space exploration and launching satellites.

Rockford POP (1990) 284 000, the seat of Winnebago County, N Illinois, USA. It lies on the R Rock, 128km/80mi NW of Chicago, and is an agricultural centre. NOTABLE FEATURE Burpee Art Gallery.

rock garden a rockery, or a garden containing rockeries.

Rockhampton POP (1991) 56 000, a city in Fitzroy statistical division, Queensland, Australia. It is situated on the Fitzroy R. The city is the centre of Australia's largest beef-producing area. To the W lies an area rich in gemstones.

rockily *adv.* in a rocky way.

rockiness *noun* being rocky.

rocking chair a chair which rocks backwards and forwards on two curved supports.

Rockingham, Charles Watson Wentworth, 2nd Marquess of (1730–82) English statesman. After serving as gentleman of the bedchamber to kings George II and George III, he became leader of a prominent Whig opposition group, and Prime Minister (1765–6, 1782). He repealed the Stamp Act, which affected the American colonies, then had to resign due to court intrigues. He opposed Britain's war against the colonists and headed the most consistent opposition Whig group to George III's government in the 1760s and 1770s, attracting leading spokesmen such as Charles James Fox and Edmund Burke. He died soon after taking office a second time.

rocking horse a toy horse mounted on two curved supports on which a child can sit and rock backwards and forwards.

rock plant any small alpine plant which grows among rocks and needs very little soil.

rockrose *noun* a small evergreen shrub of the genus *Helianthemum*, native to the Mediterranean region and parts of Asia. It has lance-shaped or oblong leaves, and white, yellow, or red flowers with five petals. Some species are grown as ornamentals in gardens.

rock salmon the dogfish or other fish, especially when sold as food.

rock salt common salt occurring as a mass of solid mineral.

rocky[1] *adj.* (**rockier, rockiest**) **1** full of rocks; made of or like rock. **2** full of problems and obstacles.

rocky[2] *adj.* (**rockier, rockiest**) shaky; unsteady.

Rocky Mountains *or* **Rockies** a major mountain system in W North America. It extends from central New Mexico generally NW through the USA, into W Canada and N Alaska and reaches the Bering Strait N of the Arctic Circle. The system is 4 800km/3 000mi long, and forms the continental divide which separates the Pacific drainage from the Atlantic and Arctic drainage. The continental divide is a vast complex of separate ranges, interrupted by wide gaps of lofty, rolling plateaux. Mt Elbert (4 399m) in the USA is the highest point in the range; in Canada the highest point is Mt Robson (3 954m). The principal pass is the South Pass (in Wyoming), followed by the Oregon Trail. The Rocky Mts are divided into the Southern, Middle, Northern, and Arctic sections, and are an important source of mineral wealth. There are several national parks, including Rocky Mountain, Grand Teton, Yellowstone, Glacier (Montana), Banff, Jasper, Yoho, Kootenay, Glacier (British Columbia), Northern Yukon, and Gates of the Arctic.

Rocky Mountain School the name applied to a group of 19c US artists who produced large paintings of the Rocky Mountains.

Rococo in art history, the period following the late Baroque in European art and design. It flourished especially in France and S Germany (c.1700–50), until superseded by the neoclassical taste spreading from Rome. It was characterized by elaborate ornamental details and asymmetrical patterns, and was most successful as a style of interior decoration. [from French *rocaille*, rockwork]

rococo — *noun* an ornamental style, characteristic of 18c Rococo. — *adj.* **1** of or in this style. **2** florid and elaborate. [from French *rocaille*, rockwork]

rod *noun* **1** a long slender stick or bar of wood, metal, etc. **2** a stick or bundle of twigs used to beat people as a punishment. **3** a stick, wand, or sceptre carried as a symbol of office or authority. **4** a fishing-rod. **5** in surveying, a unit of length equivalent to 5.5yd (5.03m). **6** *Anat.* in the retina of the vertebrate eye, one of over 100 million rod-shaped cells containing the light-sensitive pigment rhodopsin, and concerned with the perception of light intensity. Rods are essential for vision in dim light. **7** *coarse slang* a penis. **8** *North Amer. slang* a pistol. [from Anglo-Saxon *rodd*]

Rodchenko, Alexander Mikhailovich (1891–1956) Russian painter, designer, and photographer born in St Petersburg. He trained at the Kazan Art School (1910–14), and became a member of the young Russian avant-garde. He taught at the Moscow Proletkult School from 1918 to 1926. His works include abstract spatial constructions and documentary photographs of the new communist society. His painting of a black square (*Black on Black*, 1918) owed much to the suprematism of Kasimir Malevich's *White on White* (see also SUPREMATISM).

Roddick, Anita Lucia (1942–) English retail entrepreneur, born in Brighton. In 1976 with her husband she founded the Body Shop International plc to sell cosmetics 'stripped of the hype' and made from natural materials. The company has over 750 stores worldwide (many of them franchised). A proponent of 'caring capitalism', she pioneered childcare in her company. She also lectures on green issues and conducts campaigns with Friends of the Earth. In 1989 she won the UN environmental award.

rode see RIDE.

rodent *noun* an animal belonging to the order Rodentia, a large group of mostly nocturnal mammals with chisel-like incisor teeth that grow continuously and are adapted for gnawing, eg rats, mice, squirrels, beavers. [from Latin *rodere*, to gnaw]

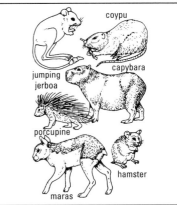

rodents

rodeo *noun* (PL. **rodeos**) a show or contest of cowboy skills, including riding, lassoing, and animal-handling. [from Spanish, from *rodear*, to go round]

Roderick a male first name. [of Germanic origin, from *hrod*, fame + *ric*, rule]

Roderick Random, The Adventures of a novel by Tobias Smollett (1748). His first, it is a picaresque depiction of the life on land and at sea of young Roderick.

Rodgers, Richard (1902–79) US librettist, born in New York City. After collaborating with lyricist Lorenz Hart (1895–1943) in such musical comdies as *On Your Toes* (1936) and *The Boys from Syracuse* (1938), he began a successful partnership with Oscar Hammerstein II. Their spectacular series of musicals includes *Oklahoma!* (1943), *South Pacific* (1949), *The King and I* (1951), and *The Sound of Music* (1959).

Rodin, (René François) Auguste (1840–1917) French sculptor, born in Paris. His first major work was *The Age of Bronze* (1877, Paris Salon). *The Gates of Hell* was commissioned for the Musée des Arts Décoratifs in 1880, and during the next 30 years he was mainly engaged on the 186 figures for these bronze doors. Other works include *The Kiss* (1898), *Balzac* (1898, erected 1939), *The Thinker* (1904), and *The Burghers of Calais* (1886, erected 1895). A major collection of his works can be found at the Musée Rodin in Paris (the Hôtel Biron, his home and workplace at the end of his life).

Rodney a male first name, after the surname.

Rodnina, Irina (1949–) Soviet figure skater, born in Moscow. She won the pairs title at three Olympics — 1972 (with Alexei Ulanov), 1976, and 1980 (both with Alexandr Zaitsev) — and won four world titles with Ulanov (1969–72) and six with Zaitsev (1973–8). During the same years she won the corresponding European titles. She married Zaitsev in 1975, retired in 1980, and trained to be an astronaut.

rodomontade — *noun* **1** boastful or bragging words or behaviour. **2** a boastful or bragging speech. — *verb intrans.* to talk boastfully; to brag. [from Italian *Rodomonte*, the boastful king of Algiers in Ariosto's *Orlando Furioso* (1516)]

Rodrigues Island POP (1991e) 38 000, an island in the Indian Ocean, E of Mauritius. It forms part of the Mascarene Is and is a dependency of Mauritius. The island rises to 396m at Mt Limon. CHIEF TOWN Port Mathurin.

roe[1] *noun* **1** (*in full* **hard roe**) the mass of eggs in the body cavity of a female fish. **2** (*in full* **soft roe**) the sperm of a male fish. [from Middle English *rowe*]

roe[2] *noun* (*also* **roe deer**) a small deer found in Europe and Asia. [from Anglo-Saxon *ra*]

Roebling, John Augustus (1806–69) US civil engineer, born in Muhlhausen, Prussia. After graduating in Berlin, he went to the USA (1831), where he built a wire-rope factory. In 1845 he built a suspension aqueduct across the Allegheny River; others followed, and he later built (1851–5) a road and rail suspension bridge at Niagara Falls. The success of this established the wire rope in bridge building.

Roemer, Olaus (1644–1710) Danish astronomer, born in Aarhuus. He discovered the finite velocity of light, which he measured by observing the time variations in the eclipse of Jupiter's satellites. He also invented the transit instrument, increasing accuracy in the determination of time and positions of astronomical objects. In 1681 he became professor at Copenhagen.

roentgen same as RÖNTGEN.

Rogation Day any of the three days before Ascension Day. [from Latin *rogatio*, from *rogare*, to ask]

Roger a male first name. [of Germanic origin, from *hrod*, fame + *ger*, spear]

roger — *interj.*, *in radio communications and signalling* message received and understood. — *verb* (**rogered, rogering**) *coarse slang, said of a man* to have sexual intercourse with. [from the name ROGER]

Rogers, John (c.1500–55) English Protestant reformer and martyr, born near Birmingham. He was a London rector who was converted to Protestantism in Antwerp, and helped to prepare the new translation called 'Matthew's Bible' (1537). He returned to England in 1548, preached an anti-Catholic sermon at St Paul's Cross in 1553, just after the accession of Mary I, and was burned as a heretic.

Roget, Peter Mark (1779–1869) English scholar and physician, born in London. He worked as a physician in Manchester and London, and was Professor of Physiology at the Royal Institution (1833–6). He is best known for his *Thesaurus of English Words and Phrases* (1852), which reached a 28th edition in his lifetime.

rogue — *noun* **1** a dishonest person. **2** a person, especially a child, who is playfully mischievous. **3** someone or something, especially a plant, which is not true to its type and is inferior. **4** a vicious wild animal which lives apart from or has been driven from its herd. — *adj.* of or like a rogue. [a cant word]

roguery *noun* (PL. **rogueries**) the behaviour or an action which is typical of a rogue.

rogues gallery a police collection of photographs of known criminals, used to identify suspects.

roguish *adj.* characteristic of a rogue; mischievous, dishonest.

roguishly *adv.* in a roguish way.

roguishness *noun* being roguish.

Rogun Dam one of the highest earth-fill dams in the world, situated on the R Vakhsh, Tajikistan, completed in the late 1980s. It is 335m high and 660m long, and has the capacity to generate 3 600 megawatts of hydroelectricity.

Röhm *or* **Roehm, Ernst** (1887–1934) German soldier, politician, and Nazi leader, born in Munich. He was an early supporter of Hitler, and the organizer and commander of the stormtroopers ('Brownshirts'), but his plans to increase the power of this force led to his execution on Hitler's orders.

Rohrer, Heinrich (1933–) Swiss physicist, born in Buchs. Working at the IBM Research Laboratory in Zürich, he developed the 'scanning tunnelling microscope' which now has widespread use, especially in the development of small solid-state electronic devices. He shared the 1986 Nobel Prize for Physics with Gerd Binnig.

roister *verb intrans.* (**roistered, roistering**) to enjoy oneself noisily. [from Old French *rustre*, ruffian]

roisterer *noun* a noisy reveller, a swaggering fellow.

Rokeby Venus, The a painting of a nude by Diego Velázquez (c.1651, National Gallery, London).

Roland (de la Platière), Jean Mari (1734–93) French politician, born near Villefranche-sur-Saône. A leader of the Girondins, in Mar 1792 Roland became Minister of the Interior. He was very unpopular with the Jacobins because he protested against the September Massacres (1792), in which demagogues had incited the Paris mob to invade the prisons, murdering innocent victims. He took part in the last struggle of the Girondins. On 31 May 1793 he was arrested, but escaped and fled to Rouen, where he attempted to organize insurrection. Later that year, following his wife's execution, he committed suicide.

Roland a male first name. [of Germanic origin, from *hrod*, fame + *land*, land]

role *or* **rôle** *noun* **1** an actor's part in a play, film, etc. **2** a part played in life, business, etc; a person's function. [from French *rôle*]

role model a person whose life and behaviour is taken as an example to follow by someone else.

Rolf a male first name. [from Germanic, from *rhod*, fame + *wulf*, wolf]

Rolfing *noun* a therapeutic technique for correcting postural faults and improving physical wellbeing through manipulation of the muscles and joints, so that the body is realigned symmetrically and the best used of gravity made in maintaining balance. [named after the originator of the technique, Ida Rolf]

roll — *noun* **1** anything flat (such as paper, fabric, etc) which is rolled up to form a cylinder or tube. **2** a small portion of bread for one person, often with a specified filling. **3** a folded piece of pastry or cake with a specified filling: *a sausage roll*. **4** a rolled mass of something: *rolls of fat*. **5** an official list of names, eg of school pupils, members of a club, or people eligible to vote. **6** an act of rolling. **7** a swaying or rolling movement, eg in walking or dancing, or of a ship. **8** a long, low, prolonged sound. **9** a series of quick beats on a drum. **10** a complete rotation around its longitudinal axis by an aircraft. **11** a roller or cylinder used to press, shape, or apply something. — *verb* **1** *trans., intrans.* to move or cause to move by turning over and over, as if on an axis, and often in a specified direction. **2** *trans., intrans.* to move or cause to move on wheels, rollers, etc, or in a vehicle with wheels. **3** (*also* **roll over**) *said of a person or animal, etc. lying down* to turn with a rolling movement to face in another direction. **4** *trans., intrans.* to move or cause to move or flow gently and steadily. **5** *intrans.* to seem to move like or in waves: *a garden rolling down to the river.* **6** *intrans.* *said eg of a ship* to sway or rock gently from side to side. **7** *intrans.* to walk with a swaying movement. **8** *intrans., trans.* to begin to operate or work: *the cameras rolled.* **9** *trans., intrans.* to move or cause (one's eyes) to move in a circle, especially in disbelief, despair, or amazement. **10** *trans., intrans.* to form or cause to form a tube or cylinder by winding or being wound round and round. **11** (*also* **roll up** *or* **roll something up**) to wrap it or be wrapped by rolling. **12** (*also* **roll out** *or* **roll something out**) to spread it out or make it flat or flatter, especially by pressing and smoothing with something heavy. **13** to make a series of long low rumbling sounds. **14** to pronounce (especially an 'r' sound) with a trill. **15** *intrans.* to move in the same direction as something so as to reduce its strength or impact: *roll with the punches.*

— **be rolling in something** *colloq.* to have large amounts of something (especially money).

roll by *or* **on** *said especially of time* to pass or follow steadily: *the weeks rolled by.*

roll in to come or arrive in large quantities.

roll on *interj.* may a particular or specified time come soon.

roll up 1 *colloq.* to arrive. **2** to come in large numbers.

roll up *or* **roll something up** to form or cause it to form into a roll. [from Old French *rolle*]

Rolland, Romain (1866–1944) French writer, born in Clamecy. In 1910 he became Professor of the History of Music at the Sorbonne. He resigned in 1912 to devote himself to writing, and published several biographies and a 10-volume novel, *Jean-Christophe* (1904–12). He was awarded the Nobel Prize for Literature in 1915.

roll-call *noun* the calling out of names from a list at an assembly, meeting, etc to check who is present.

rolled gold metal covered with a thin coating of gold.

roller *noun* **1** any of a number of cylindrical objects or machines used for flattening, crushing, spreading, printing, applying paint, etc. **2** a rod for rolling cloth, etc round. **3** a small cylinder on which hair is rolled for curling. **4** a solid wheel or cylinder attached to heavy machinery, etc, which makes it easier to move. **5** a long heavy sea wave. **6** a bird of a family related to the kingfishers, with a rolling manner of flight.

Rollerblades *pl. noun trademark* a set of roller skates with wheels set in a line along the centre of the shoe.

rollercoaster *noun* a raised railway with sharp curves and steep inclines, ridden on for pleasure and excitement, and usually found at funfairs.

roller skate a series of wheels attached to a framework which can be fitted over one's shoe, or a shoe with wheels attached to the sole.

roller-skate *verb intrans.* to move, dance, etc on roller skates.

roller-skater *noun* a person who roller-skates.

roller-skating *noun* the practice or skill of using roller skates.

roller towel a usually long towel with the ends sewn together, hung on a roller.

rollicking *adj.* boisterous, noisy, and carefree. [perhaps from ROMP + FROLIC]

rolling *adj.* **1** *said of land, countryside, etc* with low, gentle hills and valleys, and without steep slopes and crags. **2** *said of a contract* subject to review at regular intervals.

rolling mill 1 a machine for rolling metal ingots (slabs) into sheets, bars, or other shapes between pairs of rollers revolving in opposite directions. It is often used to improve the mechanical properties of a metal, or to give it a bright finish. **2** a factory containing such machines.

rolling-pin *noun* a wooden, pottery, etc cylinder for flattening out pastry.

rolling stock the engines, wagons, coaches, etc used on a railway.

rolling stone a person who leads a restless or unsettled life.

Rolling Stones English rock group, formed in 1961, consisting of members Mick Jagger (1944–) vocals, Keith Richard (1944–) guitar, Charlie Watts (1942–) drums, Ron Wood (1947–) guitar, and former members Brian Jones (1944–69) guitar and Bill Wyman (1941–) bass. One of the longest-running and most successful popular music groups to emerge in the 1960s, they began performing together in 1962. Although their uninhibited life styles and overtly sexual lyrics often hit the headlines, it was the excellence of their compositions (usually by Jagger and Richard) that ensured their continuing success.

rollmop *noun* a fillet of herring rolled up usually round a slice of onion, and pickled in spiced vinegar. [from German *Rollmops*, from *rollen*, to roll + *Mops*, pug-dog]

rollneck *adj., said of a piece of clothing* having a high neck which is turned down over itself.

Rollo (c.860–c.932) Viking leader who in 911 secured from Charles III of France a large district on the condition that Rollo be baptized and became Charles's vassal. This grant was the nucleus of the duchy of Normandy.

roll-on *noun* **1** a woman's light elastic corset. **2** a liquid deodorant or antiperspirant in a small container with a rotating ball at the top.

roll-on roll-off *adj., said of a passenger ferry, etc* with entrances at both the front and back of the ship, so that vehicles can be driven on through one entrance and off through the other.

Rolls, C(harles) S(tewart) (1877–1910) British motorist and aeronaut, born in London.

Educated at Cambridge, from 1895 he experimented with the earliest motor cars, and collaborated with Henry Royce for their production. In 1906 he crossed the English Channel by balloon, and in 1910 he made a double crossing by aeroplane. He died in a flying accident at Bournemouth, Dorset.

Rolls-Royce a British firm of car engine and aero-engine manufacturers, founded in 1904 by C S Rolls and Henry Royce. It produced the Silver Ghost in 1906, which became known as the 'best car in the world'. In the 1970s it was split into two separate companies, following financial problems caused by the high cost of aero-engine research and development. The aero-engine side of the business passed into British government ownership, whilst Rolls-Royce (Cars) remained a separate commercial enterprise. In 1987 the aero-engine business became a commercial company after being privatised by the government.

roll-top desk a desk with a flexible cover of slats that may be rolled down when the desk is not being used.

roll-up *noun Brit. colloq.* a cigarette which one makes oneself by rolling paper round loose tobacco.

roly-poly — *adj.* round and podgy. — *noun* (PL. **roly-polies**) a strip of suet pastry filled with jam and rolled up, then baked or steamed. [probably from ROLL]

ROM *abbrev. Comput.* read-only memory, a memory which holds data permanently and allows it to be read and used but not changed.

Roman — *adj.* **1** of or related to modern or ancient Rome and the Roman Empire, its history, culture, or inhabitants. **2** of the Roman Catholic Church. **3** (**roman**) (of printing type) written in ordinary upright letters (as opposed to italics). — *noun* **1** an inhabitant of modern or ancient Rome. **2** a Roman Catholic. **3** (**roman**) roman letters or type. [from Latin *Romanus*, from *Roma*, Rome]

roman-à-clef *noun* a novel with characters based on real people under disguised names. [French, = novel with a key]

Roman alphabet the alphabet developed by the ancient Romans for writing Latin, and now used for most writing in W European languages including English.

Roman Catholic — *adj.* of the Christian church which recognizes the pope as its head. — *noun* a member of this church.

Roman Catholicism the doctrine, worship, and life of the Roman Catholic Church, directly descended from the earliest Christian communities, and centred on the city of Rome, where St Peter (claimed as the first bishop of Rome) was martyred and St Paul witnessed. The Church survived the fall of Rome (5c) and became the only effective agency of civilization in Europe; after the 11c schism with the Byzantine or Eastern Church, it was the dominant force in the Western world, the Holy Roman Empire. The Protestant Reformation of the 16c inspired revival, and the need to restate doctrine and to purge the Church and clergy of abuses and corruption was recognized. The most dramatic reforms were enacted by the two Vatican Councils of the 19c and 20c, the second of which signalled a new era in the Church marked by a pervasive ecumenical spirit, although the doctrines of the faith remained largely untouched. With emphasis being placed on the Church as the 'people of God', the laity could take a more active part in liturgy (eg the Mass was said in the vernacular instead of Latin). Roman Catholic doctrine is declared by the pope, or by a General Council with the approval of the pope, and is summarized in the Nicene Creed. Scripture is authoritative, and authoritatively interpreted by the *magisterium* or teaching office of the Church. The tradition of the Church is accepted as

authoritative, and special importance is attributed to the early church fathers and to the medieval scholastics, notably St Thomas Aquinas. Principal doctrines are similar to those of mainstream Protestant and Orthdox Churches (ie God as Trinity, creation, redemption, the person and work of Jesus Christ and the place of the Holy Spirit); the chief doctrinal differences are the role of the Church in salvation, and its sacramental theology. Ancient traditional practices such as the veneration of the Virgin Mary and the Saints, and the Stations of the Cross, are still regarded as valuable aids to devotion. The hierarchy of the Church includes cardinals, bishops, priests, and several minor orders. The vast and complex organization of the Church is controlled by the Vatican, an independent state in Rome which, under the direction of the pope, implements Church policy, and administers property and finance. In predominantly Catholic countries, the Church maintains a degree of political influence, and extends canon law into the realm of civil law, notably on moral issues (eg birth control).

romance — *noun* **1** a love affair. **2** sentimentalized or idealized love, valued especially for its beauty, purity, and the mutual devotion of the lovers. **3** an atmosphere, the feelings or behaviour associated with romantic love. **4** a sentimental account, especially in writing or on film, of a love affair. **5** such writing, films, etc as a group or genre. **6** a fictitious story which deals with imaginary, adventurous, and mysterious events, characters, places, etc. **7** a medieval verse narrative dealing with chivalry, highly idealized love, and fantastic adventures. **8** an exaggeration or absurd account or lie. **9** (**Romance**) the group of languages, including French, Spanish, and Italian, which have developed from Latin. **10** a short, informal, ballad-like piece of music. — *adj.* (**Romance**) of or relating to the languages which have developed from Latin, such as French, Spanish, and Italian. — *verb* **1** to try to win the love of. **2** *intrans.* to talk or write extravagantly, romantically, or fantastically. **3** *intrans.* to lie. [from Old French *romanz*]
◊ Romance languages developed from vulgar or spoken Latin. The major Romance languages, French, Spanish, Italian, and Portuguese, have been dispersed throughout the world through trade and colonialism. The other languages in the group are Catalan and Galician (Spain), Provençal or Occitan (S France), Romanian, and Rhaetian (N Italy and Switzerland).

Roman Curia an organization in the Vatican which administers the affairs of the Roman Catholic Church under the authority of the pope. It comprises congregations (administrative), tribunals (judicial), and offices (ministerial), all as defined in canon law. [from Latin *curia*, court]

Roman de la Rose a medieval French poem by Guillaume de Lorris and Jean de Meung (c.13c). It is an influential allegorical dream-vision describing a lover's pursuit of the rose which symbolizes his lady's love. Also, *The Romaunt of the Rose*, a Middle English translation of 7 700 lines of the French text, usually partially attributed to Chaucer.

Roman Empire (31 BC–AD 476 in the W, 1453 in the E) the government structure of Rome following the end of the Republic. Augustus created a system of government known as a principate, with himself as 'princeps', or first citizen. The Senate still existed but Augustus and his successors were in fact absolute monarchs; the 'princeps' became emperor or 'dominus' (master), and the Empire became 'the Dominate'. Under Augustus, the expansionism of Republican days was abandoned. The Empire's frontiers were clearly defined as the Rhine and Danube in Europe and the Euphrates in Asia, and the only significant later additions to it were Britain (AD 43), and Dacia and Arabia (both annexed by Trajan in AD 106). From the outset, the Rhine–Danube frontier was the hardest to hold.

Roman Emperors

Dates overlap where there are periods of joint rule (eg Marcus Aurelius and Lucius Verus (161–9), and where the government of the empire divides between East and West.

Dates	Name	Dates	Name	Dates	Name	Dates	Name
27BC–AD14	Augustus (Caesar Augustus)	211–17	Caracalla	276	Florian	365–6	Procopius – (East)
14–37	Tiberius	211–12	Geta	276–82	Probus	375–83	Gratian – (West)
37–41	Caligula (Gaius Caesar)	217–18	Macrinus	282–3	Carus	375–92	Valentinian II – (West)
41–54	Claudius	218–22	Elagabalus	283–5	Carinus	379–95	Theodosius I, 'the Great'
54–68	Nero	222–35	Alexander Severus	283–4	Numerian	395–408	Arcadius – (East)
68–9	Galba	235–8	Maximin	284–305	Diocletian – (East)	395–423	Honorius – (West)
69	Otho	238	Gordian I	286–305	Maximian – (West)	408–50	Theodosius II – (East)
69	Vitellius	238	Gordian II	305–11	Galerius – (East)	421–3	Constantius III – (West)
69–79	Vespasian	238	Maximus	305–6	Constantius I, 'Chlorus' – (West)	425–55	Valentinian III – (West)
79–81	Titus	238	Balbinus			450–7	Marcian – (East)
81–96	Domitian	238–44	Gordian III	306–7	Severus – (West)	455	Petronius Maximus – (West)
96–8	Nerva	244–9	Philip	306–12	Maxentius – (West)	455–6	Avitus – (West)
98–117	Trajan	249–51	Decius	306–37	Constantine I, 'the Great'	457–74	Leo I – (East)
117–38	Hadrian	251	Hostilian	308–24	Licinius – (East)	457–61	Majorian – (West)
138–61	Antoninus Pius	251–3	Gallus	337–40	Constantine II	461–7	Libius Severus – (West)
161–80	Marcus Aurelius	253	Aemilian	337–50	Constans	467–72	Anthemius – (West)
161–9	Lucius Verus	253–60	Valerian	337–61	Constantius II	472–3	Olybrius – (West)
180–92	Commodus	253–68	Gallienus	350–3	Magnentius	474–5	Julius Nepos – (West)
193	Pertinax	268–70	Claudius II Gothicus	361–3	Julian	474	Leo II – (East)
193	Didius Julianus	269–70	Quintillus	363–4	Jovian	474–91	Zeno – (East)
193–211	Septimius Severus	270–5	Aurelian	364–75	Valentinian I – (West)	475–6	Romulus Augustulus – (West)
		275–6	Tacitus	364–78	Valens – (East)		

A new imperial capital (Nicomedia) was founded nearer this frontier in the 3c but in the early 5c the frontier was breached by various tribesmen (eg Huns, Vandals, Visigoths, Ostrogoths) and the city of Rome was sacked by the Visigoths in AD 410. The W half of the Empire was finally destroyed in AD 476 with the deposition of the last emperor, Romulus Augustulus. The E (Byzantine) Empire survived until the capital Constantinople fell to the Ottoman Turks in 1453.

Romanesque — *noun* the style of architecture found in W and S Europe from the 9c to the 12c, characterized by the use of a round arch, clear plans and elevations and, typically, a two-tower facade. — *adj.* in or relating to this style of architecture. [from French]

roman fleuve a series of novels, each of which exists as a separate novel in its own right, but which are linked, usually because some or all of the characters appear in each successive work. Examples include Emile Zola's 20-volume series *Les Rougon-Macquart* (1871–93), the seven parts of Proust's *A la recherche du temps perdu* (1913–27), John Galsworthy's *Forsyte Saga* (1906–28), C P Snow's *Strangers and Brothers* (1940–70), and Anthony Powell's 12-volume *Dance to the Music of Time* (1951–76). [French, literally = river novel]

Romania *or* **Roumania** *or* **Rumania**, official name **Socialist Republic of Romania**, Romanian **Republica Socialistă România** POP (1992) 22.8m, a republic in SE Europe, on the Balkan Peninsula and the lower Danube, divided into 41 counties (*judet*). AREA 237 500sq km/ 91 675sq mi. It is bounded S by Bulgaria, W by Yugoslavia and Hungary, and E by Moldavia and the Black Sea; the Ukraine borders it to the N and E. CAPITAL Bucharest. CHIEF TOWNS Braşov, Constanţa, Iaşi, Timişoara, Cluj-Napoca. TIME ZONE GMT +2. The population is mainly of Romanian origin, with Hungarian and Romany minorities; Orthodox Christianity is the chief religion. OFFICIAL LANGUAGE Romanian. CURRENCY the leu. PHYSICAL DESCRIPTION the Carpathian Mts separate Old Romania from Transylvania, and form the heart of the country; the E Carpathians, between the N frontier and the Prahova Valley, constitute an area of extensive forest cut by many passes; the higher S Carpathians are situated between the Prahova Valley and the Timiş-Cerna gorges; the W Carpathians lie between the R Danube and the R Someş; the highest peak is Negoiul (2 548m); the Romanian Plain in the S includes the Bărăgan Plain (to the E), the richest arable area, and the Oltenian Plain (to the W),

crossed by many rivers; there are c.3 500 glacial ponds, lakes, and coastal lagoons; over one quarter of the land is forested. CLIMATE continental, with cold, snowy winters and warm summers; the mildest area in winter is along the Black Sea coast; the plains of the N and E can suffer from drought; average annual rainfall is 1 000mm (in the mountains) and 400mm (in the Danube delta). HISTORY formed in 1862 after the unification of Wallachia and Moldavia; a monarchy was created in 1866; Romania joined the Allies in World War I, and united with Transylvania, Bessarabia, and Bucovina in 1918; support was given to Germany in World War II and Soviet forces occupied the country in 1944; territories were lost to Russia, Hungary, and Bulgaria after World War II; the monarchy was abolished and a People's Republic declared in 1947; in 1965 it became a Socialist Republic; it became increasingly independent of the USSR from the 1960s; relationships were formed with China, and several Western countries; the leading political force was the Romanian Communist Party, led by dictator Nicolae Ceauşescu; in 1989, violent repression of protest, resulting in the deaths of thousands of demonstrators, sparked a popular uprising and the overthrow of the Ceauşescu regime; a provisional government led by previously imprisoned dissidents promised free elections in 1990, but unrest and demonstrations continued; in 1991 the country became a multi-party democracy. GOVERNMENT a President is head of state and appoints a Prime Minister and Cabinet; there is a Senate and an Assembly of Deputies. ECONOMY since World War II there has been a gradual change from an agricultural to industrial economy; the state owned c.37% of the farmland, mainly organized as collectives and state farms; products included wheat, maize, sugar beet, fruit, potatoes, vines, and meat from livestock; there are natural resources of oil, natural gas, salt, iron ore, copper; industries include iron and steel, metallurgy, engineering, chemicals, textiles, foodstuffs, electrical goods, electronics, machinery, rubber, timber, and tourism; there were mounting economic difficulties in the 1980s and early 1990s.

Romanian — *noun* **1** the official language of Romania. **2** an inhabitant of or person from Romania. — *adj.* of or relating to the Romanian people, their country, language, history, or culture

◇ Romanian is a Romance language of the Indo-European family. It is spoken by c.20–25 million people in Romania, Macedonia, Albania, and parts of Greece. The Cyrillic alphabet was used

until the 19c, and the language has been strongly influenced by Slavic languages.

Romanist the name given by art historians to those Dutch and Flemish artists who, in the 16c, travelled to Italy to see the works of the great Renaissance masters. They included Jan Gossaert (Mabuse), who went to Italy in 1508.

Romanization the process in antiquity by which the subject peoples of W Europe adopted the language and customs of the Romans. Roman-style towns were built in the less developed provinces, and the provincial aristocracy were encouraged to learn Latin and participate in local government. Incentives included the award of Roman citizenship and later even enrollment into the Roman Senate itself.

romanization *or* **romanisation** *noun* the adoption of the Roman alphabet to transcribe a language that uses a different writing system, for example Arabic, Chinese, Greek, Hindi, and Russian. Since there are variations in the principles of romanization, romanized names from these languages can have several variants.

Roman Law the law of ancient Rome, from the founding of Rome in 753 BC to the four-part codification of Justinian in c.530 AD. The first codification was the Twelve Tables in 450 BC, and in the centuries that followed, the changes in the law reflected the changes in the size and governmental status of Rome. Under the Empire (from 31 BC), the emperor himself gradually became the sole source of law. His pronouncements (*edicta*), written opinions on legal points

Romania

(*rescripta*), and even instructions to his officials (*mandata*) were all legally binding. The collective name for these enactments is 'constitutions'. Older forms of law-making withered away, as the bodies formerly responsible (eg the people's assemblies (*comitia*) and the Senate) became obsolete or were radically altered.

Roman nose a nose with a high bridge.

Roman numeral any of the figures used to represent numbers in the system developed by the ancient Romans, eg I (= 1), V (= 5), X (= 10), etc. See also ARABIC NUMERALS.

Romanov Dynasty the second (and last) Russian royal dynasty (1613–1917). The first Romanov tsar, Mikhail, was elected in 1613 after the Time of Troubles. The Romanovs ruled as absolute autocrats, allowing no constitutional or legal checks on their political power. The dynasty ended with the abdication of Nicholas II (Feb 1917), and his execution by Bolshevik guards (Jul 1918).

Roman Republic (509–31 BC) the Republican system of government in Rome, brought into being with the overthrow of the monarchy. Executive power was entrusted to two annually elected officials (consuls); they were advised by the Senate, an influential ex-officio body of magistrates. The system brought stability, and Rome grew rapidly from a small city-state into an empire. The Punic Wars brought the W Mediterranean under her control, while the campaigns against the rulers of the Hellenistic world added Macedonia, Greece, Asia Minor, and the Levant. After decades of civil war in which warlords such as Caesar, Pompey, Antony, and Octavian fought for supreme power, the Republic was finally destroyed at Actium in 31 BC with the defeat of Antony by Octavius, who was subsequently crowned the first emperor of Rome.

Roman roads a network of roads radiating from ancient Rome. Main routes were usually very straight, constructed on an earth footing with a layer of small stones in mortar above, on top of which was a hard filling surfaced with stone slabs. Examples include the Appian Way (the first great Roman road), built in the 3c BC between Rome and present-day Capua; the Aurelian Way, between Rome and present-day Pisa; and the Flaminian Way, the main northern route.

Romans, Letter of Paul to the a New Testament book, written by the apostle Paul (perhaps c.55–8 AD. Although he did not establish the Church in Rome, he wrote to explain the availability of salvation for both Gentiles and Jews, and to warn against libertine and legalistic interpretations of the Christian message.

romantic — *adj.* **1** characterized by or inclined towards sentimental and idealized love. **2** dealing with or suggesting adventure, mystery, and sentimentalized love: *romantic fiction*. **3** highly impractical or imaginative, and often also foolish. **4** (*often* **Romantic**) *said of literature, art, music, etc* relating to or in the style of romanticism. — *noun* **1** a person with a romantic, idealized, and sentimental idea of love. **2** a person who writes, paints, etc in the style of romanticism. [from Old French *romanz*, romance]

romantically *adv.* in a romantic way; with romantic feeling.

Romanticism a late 18c and early 19c movement in art, literature, and music, characterized by an emphasis on feelings and emotions, often using imagery taken from nature, and creating forms which are relatively free from rules and set orders.
◊ Romanticism in art was a concept that regarded the emotions as the basis of composition rather than beauty of form or structure. In pictorial art, its development from the late 18c can best be seen in French painting, in both the

choice and treatment of subjects, as in David's *The Death of Marat* (1793), Géricault's *The Raft of the Medusa* (1819), and Delacroix's *Sardanapalus* (1827). Leading Romantic painters in Britain were Turner and Constable; in Germany, Caspar David Friedrich (1774–1840); and, in Spain, Goya.
Romanticism in literature is represented by Wordsworth, Coleridge, Blake, Keats, Shelley, and Byron; in France by Rousseau and Hugo; and in Germany by Goethe and Schiller.
Romanticism in music coincided with the romantic movements in art and literature at the beginning of the 19c. From c.1810 to c.1920, there was a move away from the objective detachment of the classical age and a greater emphasis on the lyrical and poetic, with content taking precedence over form. The rapid development of chromatic harmony, and expansion of the symphony orchestra together with technical developments in orchestral instruments, increased the composer's capacity for dramatic and poetic expression. New musical forms which developed in the 19c included German Lieder, the poetic piano-piece, the symphonic poem, and the concert overture.

Romanticist *noun* a person whose art or writing, etc is characterized by Romanticism.

romanticize *or* **romanticise** *verb* **1** to make seem romantic. **2** *trans., intrans.* to describe or think of in a romantic, idealized, unrealistic, and sometimes misleading way. **3** *intrans.* to hold romantic ideas or act in a romantic way.

Romany — *noun* (PL. **Romanies**) **1** a Gypsy. **2** the language spoken by Gypsies, belonging to the Indic branch of Indo-European. — *adj.* of the Romanies, their language, and culture. [from Romany *rom*, man]
◊ The Romany language is spoken by c.450 000–900 000 people, mainly in the Near East and Europe. Many of the words in the language demonstrate links with languages of S Asia, especially Hindustani. It includes many loan words from Greek and the Slavic languages, and from the languages of other countries through which the Gypsy people travelled.

Rome, Italian **Roma** POP (1990e) 3.8m, the capital of Italy, and of Lazio region, W central Italy, situated in Rome province. It lies on the R Tiber, 20km/12mi from the Tyrrhenian Sea to the E. On the river's left bank are the Seven Hills of Rome — the Capitoline (50m), Quirinal (52m), Viminal (56m), Esquiline (53m), Palatine (51m), Aventine (46m), and Caelian (50m) — on which the ancient city was built during the 8c BC. The city is an important centre of fashion and film, and the headquarters of many cultural and research institutions. It is a major tourist destination. HISTORY the centre of the Roman Empire, sacked in the 5c by Germanic tribes; since the 6c it has been an ecclesiastical centre (the Vatican City lies on the W bank of the R Tiber); it became capital of unified Italy in 1871. NOTABLE FEATURES Palazzo Venezia (15c); Forum Romanum, with relics of ancient Rome (Arch of Titus, Via Sacra, Curia, and Arch of Septimius Severus); Trajan's Column (27m high); Colosseum (AD 75); Baths of Caracalla (AD 216), Arch of Constantine (AD 312); Pantheon (27 BC); Trevi Fountain (1762); Galleria Borghese; several Renaissance palaces; numerous churches, notably St Peter's (in the Vatican), St John Lateran (Rome's cathedral), San Lorenzo and San Paolo outside the Walls, and Santa Maria Maggiore; university (1303); the centre of the city is a World Heritage site.

Romeo 1 the love-struck hero of Shakespeare's *Romeo and Juliet*. **2** (PL. **Romeos**) an ardent young male lover.

Romeo and Juliet 1 a play by William Shakespeare (1595–6). It is a romantic tragedy about two young lovers whose families are long-standing bitter enemies. **2** a ballet by Sergei Prokofiev (*Romeo i Dzulyetta*, 1938), after which

he also arranged three symphonic suites (Op 64b, 1936; Op 64c, 1937; Op 101, 1946).

Romish *adj. derog.* Roman Catholic.

Rommel, Erwin (Johannes Eugen), known as **the Desert Fox** (1891–1944) German soldier, born in Heidenheim. He fought in World War I, taught at Dresden Military Academy, and became an early Nazi sympathizer. He commanded Hitler's headquarters guard during the early occupations, and led a Panzer division during the 1940 invasion of France. He then achieved major successes commanding the Afrika Corps, but was eventually defeated by Montgomery at El Alamein (1942). He condoned the plot against Hitler's life, and after its discovery committed suicide.

romp — *verb intrans.* **1** to play in a lively, boisterous way. **2** (**romp in**, **home**, **through**, *etc*) to succeed in a race, competition, task, etc quickly and easily. — *noun* **1** an act of romping; boisterous play. **2** a swift pace. **3** a young person, especially a girl, who romps. [perhaps a variant of RAMP]

rompers *pl. noun* (*also* **romper suit**) a suit for a baby, with short-legged trousers and either a short-sleeved top or a bib top.

Romulus and Remus in Roman legend, the founders of Rome, the twin sons of Mars and the Vestal Virgin Rhea Silvia. They were thrown into the Tiber, which carried them to the Palatine, where they were suckled by a she-wolf. Later, they built the city wall at the place where they had been found, and Remus was killed by Romulus or one of his followers. Romulus named the city after himself and became the first king.

Ronda POP (1987e) 33 000, a picturesque town in Málaga province, Andalusia, S Spain, lying on the R Guadalevin. Situated in the Sierra de Ronda, it lies close to the Tajo de Ronda Ravine. The town is famous for its school of bullfighters.

rondeau *noun* (PL. **rondeaux**) a poem of 10 or 13 lines with only two rhymes, and with the first line used as a refrain after the eighth, and thirteenth lines. [from Old French *rondel*, from *rond*, round]

rondo *noun* (PL. **rondos**) a piece of music, especially one forming the last movement of a sonata or a concerto, with a principal theme which recurs or is repeated as a refrain. [from Italian]

Ronsard, Pierre de (1524–85) French Renaissance poet, born in La Possonière. He trained as a page, but when he became deaf he took up writing and became a leader of the Pléiade group. His early works include *Odes* (1550) and *Amours* (1552), and he later wrote reflections on the state of the country.

Röntgen, Wilhelm Konrad von (1845–1923) German physicist, born in Lennep, Prussia. He became professor at Giessen, Würzburg, and Munich. While investigating the properties of cathode rays, he discovered the electromagnetic rays which he called X-rays (1895), because of their unknown properties. He was awarded the first Nobel Prize for Physics (1901).

röntgen *noun* a unit used for measuring the dose of X-rays. [named after Wilhelm Konrad von Röntgen]

rood *noun* **1** a cross or crucifix, especially a large one at the entrance to a church. **2** *literary* the cross on which Christ was crucified. [from Anglo-Saxon *rod*]

rood screen an ornamental wooden or stone screen separating the choir from the nave.

roof — *noun* (PL. **roofs**) **1** the top, usually rigid covering of a building or vehicle. **2** the top inner surface of an oven, refrigerator, the mouth, etc. **3** a dwelling or home: *two families sharing a single roof*. **4** a high, or the highest, level: *the roof of the* world. — verb **1** to cover with a roof. **2** to serve as a roof or shelter for.

— **go through** or **hit the roof** colloq. to become very angry.

raise the roof colloq. to be very noisy.

[from Anglo-Saxon hrof]

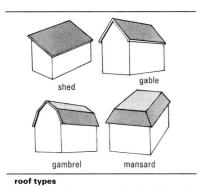

roof types

roof garden a garden on a building's flat roof.

roofing noun materials for building a roof.

roof rack a frame for attaching to the roof of a car to carry luggage.

rooftop noun the outside of a roof of a building.

rook¹ — noun a large, crow-like bird which nests in colonies in the tops of trees, found in Europe and Asia. — verb colloq. to cheat or defraud, especially at cards. [from Anglo-Saxon hroc]

rook² Chess see CASTLE. [from Persian rukh]

rookery noun (PL. **rookeries**) **1** a colony of rooks. **2** a colony of penguins, other sea birds, or seals.

rookie noun colloq. a new or raw recruit. [a corruption of RECRUIT]

room — noun **1** a part of a building which is separated from the rest of the building by having a ceiling, floor, and walls. **2** a space or area which is occupied by or is available to someone or something. **3** all of the people present in a room: the room suddenly became silent. **4** opportunity, scope, or possibility: room for improvement. **5** (**rooms**) rented lodgings. — verb intrans. chiefly North Amer. to lodge or share a room. [from Anglo-Saxon rum]

Room at the Top a British film directed by Jack Clayton (1959). An ambitious social climber (played by Laurence Harvey) strives to marry for material incentive and pays the price when his true lover (played by Simone Signoret) kills herself.

roomful noun (PL. **roomfuls**) as many or as much as a room will hold.

roominess noun being roomy.

roommate noun a person who shares a room with another person, especially in a students' hostel.

room service the serving of food, drinks, etc to a hotel guest in his or her bedroom or suite.

roomy adj. (**roomier, roomiest**) having plenty of room; spacious.

Roon, Albrecht (Theodor Emil), Graf von (Count of) (1803–79) Prussian soldier, born in Pleushagen. He became War Minister (1859–73), and with Bismarck's support effectively reorganized the army, which helped make possible Prussian victories in the Danish, Austrian, and Franco-Prussian Wars of the 1860s and 1870s.

Roosevelt, (Anna) Eleanor (1884–1962) US humanitarian and diplomat, the niece of Theodore Roosevelt and wife of Franklin D Roosevelt. She became active in politics during her husband's illness from polio and proved herself invaluable to him as an adviser on social issues when he became president. In 1941 she became Assistant Director of the Office of Civilian Defence and after her husband's death (1945) extended the scope of her activities to become a US delegate to the UN Assembly (1945–53, 1961), Chairman of the UN Human Rights Commission (1946–51), and US representative to the General Assembly (1946–52).

Roosevelt, Franklin D(elano), also called **FDR** (1882–1945) US Democratic statesman, the 32nd President, born in Hyde Park, New York. He was a lawyer (1907), New York state senator (1910–13), Assistant Secretary of the Navy (1913–20), Democratic candidate for the vice-presidency in 1920, and Governor of New York (1928–32), when he had been stricken with polio in 1921. As President (1933–45) he met the economic crisis with his 'New Deal' for national recovery (1933), and was unique in being re-elected three times. He strove in vain to ward off war, modified the USA's neutrality to favour the Allies, and was brought in to World War II by Japan's action at Pearl Harbor (1941). He met with Winston Churchill and Stalin at Teheran (1943) and Yalta (1945), but died three weeks before the German surrender.

Roosevelt, Theodore, also called **Teddy** (1858–1919) US Republican statesman, the 26th President, born in New York City. He became leader of the New York legislature (1884), raised a volunteer cavalry ('Roosevelt's Roughriders') in the Cuban War (1898), and returned to be Governor of New York state (1898–1900). Elected Vice-President in 1900, he became President (1901–9) on the assassination of McKinley, and was re-elected in 1904. An 'expansionist', he insisted on a strong navy, the regulation of trusts and monopolies, and introduced a 'Square Deal' policy for social reform. As Progressive candidate for the presidency in 1912, he was defeated by Woodrow Wilson.

roost — noun **1** a branch, perch, etc on which birds, especially domestic fowl, rest at night. **2** a group of birds, especially domestic fowl, resting together on the same branch or perch. **3** a place offering temporary sleeping accommodation. — verb intrans., said especially of birds to settle on a roost, especially for sleep.

— **come home to roost** said of a scheme, etc to have unpleasant consequences for or a bad effect on the originator.

rule the roost to be dominant.

[from Anglo-Saxon hrost]

rooster noun North Amer. a farmyard cock.

root¹ — noun **1** Bot. in vascular plants, the descending structure, lacking leaves and chlorophyll, that usually grows beneath the soil surface, and whose function is to anchor the plant in the soil, and to absorb water and mineral nutrients. **2** the part by which anything is attached to or embedded in something larger. **3** Anat. the embedded part of a tooth, hair, nail, or similar structure. **4** the basic cause, source, or origin of something. **5** (**roots**) one's ancestry or family origins. **6** (**roots**) one's feeling of belonging to a community or in a place. **7** the basic element in a word which remains after all the affixes have been removed, and which may form the basis of a number of related words, eg love is the root of lovable, lovely, lover, and unloved. **8** Maths. a factor of a quantity that when multiplied by itself a specified number of times produces that quantity again, eg 2 is the square root of 4 and the cube root of 8. **9** Maths. in an algebraic equation, the value or values of an unknown quantity or variable that represent the solution to that equation. **10** Mus. the fundamental note on which a chord is built. — verb **1** intrans. to grow roots; to become firmly established. **2** (also **root something up**) to dig it up by the roots. **3** to fix with or as if with roots. **4** to provide with roots.

— **root something out** to remove or destroy it completely.

take root 1 to grow roots. **2** to become firmly established.

[from Anglo-Saxon rot]

root² verb **1** intrans. said especially of pigs to dig up the ground with the snout in search of food. **2** intrans. (usually **root around** or **about**) to poke about in looking for something; to rummage. **3** (usually **root something out** or **up**) to find or extract it rummaging, etc. [from Anglo-Saxon wrotan, from wrot, snout]

root³ verb intrans. (**root for someone**) chiefly North Amer. colloq. to support them with loud cheering and encouragement.

root beer North Amer., esp. US a fizzy drink made from the roots of certain plants, eg dandelions, and flavoured with herbs.

root crop any plant that is grown mainly for its edible root, tuber, or corm, eg carrot, swede, turnip, potato, sugar beet, yam. The foliage of many root crops serves as valuable fodder for animal livestock.

rooted adj. fixed by or as if by roots; firmly established.

root hair Bot. any of many fine tubular outgrowths from the surface cells of plant roots. The root hairs greatly increase the surface area of the root that is available to absorb water from the soil.

rootless adj. **1** having no roots. **2** having no home; wandering.

Roots a play by Arnold Wesker (1959). An eloquent manifesto of Wesker's socialism, it is the second in a family trilogy (begun with Chicken Soup with Barley, 1958, and followed by I'm Talking about Jerusalem, 1960), which echoes the march of events, pre- and post-World War II, in the aspirations and disappointments of the members of the left-wing Kahn family.

roots music popular music of a style showing the influence of folk music and having a certain ethnic identity.

rootstock noun Bot. an underground plant stem that bears buds; a rhizome.

ropable or **ropeable** adj. Austral. colloq. **1** said of cattle or horses wild and unmanageable. **2** said of a person extremely or uncontrollably angry.

rope — noun **1** strong thick cord made by twisting fibres together; also, a length of this. **2** a number of objects, especially pearls or onions, strung together. **3** a hangman's noose. **4** a long thin sticky strand. — verb **1** to tie, fasten, or bind with a rope. **2** (**rope something off**) to enclose, separate, or divide it with a rope. **3** (also **rope up** or **rope someone up**) to attach climbers or be attached to a rope for safety. **4** chiefly North Amer. to catch with a rope; to lasso.

— **know the ropes** to have a thorough knowledge and experience of what needs to be done in a particular circumstance or for a particular job.

rope someone in to persuade them to take part. [from Anglo-Saxon rap]

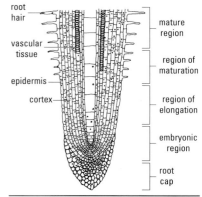

longitudinal section through a root

rope walk a long narrow shed or covered alley where ropes are made.

ropeway *noun* a means of transmission by ropes.

ropy *or* **ropey** *adj.* (**ropier**, **ropiest**) **1** *colloq.* poor in quality. **2** forming sticky strands.

Roquefort *noun* a strong, soft, blue-veined cheese made from ewes' milk. [from the village in S France where it was originally made]

Roraima, Mount a peak at the junction of the Brazil, Guyana, and Venezuela borders, S America. It lies 442km/275mi SE of Ciudad Bolivar (Venezuela) in the Serra de Pakaraima. Roraima Mt (2 875m) is the highest peak in the Guiana Highlands. It is a giant table mountain with a total area of 67sq km/26sq mi.

ro-ro *adj., said of a passenger ferry, etc* same as ROLL-ON ROLL-OFF.

Røros a mining town on the Glomma R in Norway, founded in 1644 after the discovery of large deposits of copper in the region. It is a World Heritage site.

rorqual (*in full* **common rorqual**) a baleen whale, found worldwide, having a throat with 10 to a hundred longitudinal furrows, allowing it to expand when feeding. There is a small dorsal fin near the tail. — Also called *fin whale*. [from Norwegian *røyrkval*]

Rorschach, Hermann (1884–1922) Swiss psychiatrist and neurologist, born in Zürich. He devised a diagnostic procedure for mental disorders based upon the patients' interpretation of a series of standardized ink blots (the *Rorschach test*). His work received little attention until after his death.

Rorschach test *Psychol.* a test designed to show intelligence, type of personality, mental state, etc in which the subject is asked to describe the pictures formed by a number of inkblots. [named after Hermann Rorschach]

Rory a male first name. [from the Irish Gaelic name *Ruaidhri* or the Scottish Gaelic name *Ruairidh* or *Ruaraidh*, red]

rosaceous *adj.* **1** *Bot.* denoting a plant that belongs to the family Rosaceae, eg rose, apple, strawberry, cherry, almond. **2** *Bot.* resembling a rose. [from Latin *rosa*, rose]

Rosalind **1** the daughter of the banished Duke and heroine of Shakespeare's *As You Like It* (1599) who, disguised as Ganymede, effects Orlando's wooing of her in the Forest of Arden. **2** a female first name. [of Germanic origin, from *hros*, horse + *lind*, weak]

Rosaline one of the witty ladies attending the Princess of France in Shakespeare's *Love's Labour's Lost*, who is sought after by Berowne.

Rosamund a female first name. [of Germanic origin, from *hros*, horse + *mund*, protection]

Rosario POP (1991) 1.1m, the third-largest city in Argentina and the chief city in Santa Fe province. It lies on the R Paraná, NW of Buenos Aires. Rosario is Argentina's biggest inland port, founded in 1725. NOTABLE FEATURES museums; cathedral; Municipal Palace (1896); Monument of the Flag (1957).

rosary *noun* (PL. **rosaries**) *RC Church* **1** a string of beads used to count prayers as they are recited. **2** a series of prayers with a set form and order counted on a string of beads. [from Latin *rosarium*, rose garden]

Rosas, Juan Manuel de (1793–1877) Argentine dictator, born in Buenos Aires. An enterprising rancher and exporter of salted beef, he rose to prominence as a Federalist leader and acted as Governor of Buenos Aires. As effective ruler of Argentina (1829–32, 1835–52), he operated a personal and at times repressive regime, was ousted in 1852, and died in exile in England.

Roscius, in full **Quintus Roscius Gallus** (c.134–62 BC) Roman comic actor. Born into slavery, he became the greatest comic actor in Rome, and was freed by the dictator, Sulla. He gave Cicero lessons in elocution, and was defended by him in a lawsuit.

Roscoe, Sir Henry Enfield (1833–1915) English chemist, born in London. Professor at Owens College, Manchester, he also served as a Liberal MP. He studied the way photochemical reactions depend on the properties of the light source used, and isolated vanadium from copper ores (1865); he went on to show that this element belongs to the same family as phosphorus and arsenic.

Roscommon, Gaelic **Ros Comáin** POP (1991) 52 000, a county in Connacht province, W central Irish Republic. AREA 2 463sq km/951sq mi. PHYSICAL DESCRIPTION it is bounded E by the R Shannon and watered by the R Suck; there are numerous lakes. CAPITAL Roscommon, formerly a wool town. NOTABLE FEATURES 13c abbey and castle. ECONOMY agriculture; cattle.

Rose, Pete, properly **Peter (Edward)** (1942–) US baseball player, born in Cincinatti. He surpassed Ty Cobb's 57-year-old record of 4 191 base hits in 1985, and was the Most Valuable Player of the Year in 1973. In his career (1963–86), spent mainly with the Cincinatti Reds, he had a record 4 256 base hits. He was banned from baseball in 1989 after an investigation into alleged gambling offences.

Rose a female first name, after the flower.

rose[1] — *noun* **1** an erect or climbing thorny shrub of the genus *Rosa*, that produces large and often fragrant flowers which may be red, pink, yellow, orange, white, or some combination of these colours, followed by brightly coloured fleshy fruits known as hips. The rose is cultivated worldwide as an ornamental garden plant, and it is a very popular cut flower. Its petals are used in perfumery, and rose-hip syrup is a rich source of vitamin C. **2** the flower produced by this plant. **3** this flower as the national emblem of England. **4** any flowering plant that superficially resembles a rose, eg Christmas rose. **5** a darkish pink colour. **6** (**roses**) a light pink, glowing complexion: *put the roses back in one's cheeks.* **7** a nozzle with holes, usually attached to the end of a hose, watering can, shower, etc to make the water come out in a spray. **8** a circular fitting in a ceiling through which an electric light flex hangs. **9** a rose-like design, eg round the sound hole of a guitar or lute, or on a compass card. **10** a cut diamond with a flat base and many small triangular facets forming a rounded shape which rises to a point. **11** a rose window. **12** a rosette. — *adj.* of or like roses, especially in colour or scent. [from Anglo-Saxon, from Latin *rosa*]

rose[2] see RISE.

rosé *noun* a light pink wine made by removing the skins of red grapes after fermentation has begun. [from French *rosé*, pink]

roseate *adj.* **1** like a rose, especially in colour. **2** unrealistically hopeful or cheerful.

Roseau, formerly **Charlotte Town** POP (1991) 21 000, the capital of Dominica. It is situated on the SW coast of the island. The town was badly damaged by a hurricane in 1979. NOTABLE FEATURES cathedral (1841); thermal springs nearby; Victoria Memorial Museum.

rosebay willowherb a common wild plant that has spikes of dark pink flowers and produces many fluffy seeds.

Rosebery, Archibald Philip Primrose, 5th Earl of (1847–1929) English statesman, born in London. After holding various educational and political posts, he became Foreign Secretary (1886, 1892–4) under Gladstone, whom he succeeded as Prime Minister for a brief period in 1894 before the Liberals lost the elec-

tion of 1895. He was noted for his racehorse stables, and as a biographer of British statesmen.

Rose Bowl in US college football, a post-season challenge match held annually in Pasadena, California, between (since 1947) the Big Ten Conference champion and the Pacific Eight (later the Pacific Ten) Conference champion. The Rose Bowl, which was first held in 1902, is traditionally preceded by a parade known as the Tournament of Roses parade.

rose-coloured *or* **rose-tinted** *adj.* pink. — **see through rose-coloured glasses** to have an unrealistically hopeful or cheerful view of circumstances.

rosehip *noun* the red, berry-like fruit of the rose.

Rosemary a female first name, after the herb.

rosemary *noun* an evergreen fragrant shrub with stiff needle-like leaves used in cookery and perfumery. [from Latin *rosmarinus*, from *ros*, dew + *marinus*, sea]

Rosenberg, Julius (1918–53) US spy, born in New York City. He and his wife Ethel (1915–53) joined the Communist Party and became part of a transatlantic spy ring uncovered after the trial of Klaus Fuchs. Aided by Ethel's brother, who worked at the nuclear research station at Los Alamos, they passed on atomic secrets through an intermediary to the Soviet consul. They were the first US civilians to be executed for espionage.

Rosencrantz and Guildenstern the King's undergraduate courtiers in Shakespeare's *Hamlet*, whose transparent attempts to spy on Hamlet ensure their downfall.

Rosencrantz and Guildenstern are Dead a play by Tom Stoppard (1967). Revolving around the two 'attendant lords' in Shakespeare's *Hamlet*, it hilariously examines the meaninglessness of life and questions the possibility of free will.

Rosenkavalier, Der (The Knight of the Rose) an opera by Richard Strauss (1911). Set in 18c Vienna, the story is about Octavian, the kindly Marschallin's young lover, who falls in love with Sophie, the chosen bride for the Marschellin's uncouth country cousin Baron Ochs, when he is sent to deliver a silver rose to Sophie on the Baron's behalf.

Roses, Wars of the a series (1455–85) of civil wars involving small armies and intermittent warfare in England, which started during the weak monarchy of Henry VI. Named from the emblems of the two rival branches of the House of Plantagenet — York (white rose) and Lancaster (red rose) — the wars began when Richard, Duke of York, claimed the protectorship of the Crown after the King's mental breakdown (1453–4), and ended with Henry Tudor's defeat of Richard III at Bosworth (1485).

Rosetta Stone a black basalt slab with a trilingual inscription in Greek and Egyptian hieroglyphic and demotic, found in 1799 at Rosetta (Raschid), near Alexandria. The work of Thomas Young and, particularly, Jean François Champollion allowed hieroglyphs to be deciphered for the first time, and provided the key to the Ancient Egyptian language. It is now in the British Museum.

rosette *noun* **1** a badge or decoration made in coloured ribbon to resemble the shape and form of a rose, often awarded as a prize or worn as a sign of affiliation. **2** *Bot.* a circular cluster of leaves arising from a central point. [from French *rosette*, little rose]

rose water water distilled from rose petals.

rose window a circular window with ornamental tracery coming out in a symmetrical pattern from the centre. See illustration p. 1090.

rose window

rosewood *noun* a valuable dark red or purplish wood used in making furniture of the highest quality.

Rosh Hashanah *noun* the Jewish festival of New Year, which falls in September or October. During the New Year's service, a ram's horn is blown as a call to repentance and spiritual renewal. [from Hebrew, literally head of the year]

Rosicrucianism an esoteric movement which spread across Europe in the early 17c. In 1614–15 two pamphlets inviting men of learning to join the Order of the Rosy Cross appeared in Germany and were attributed to Christian Rosenkreutz (1378–1484), who claimed to possess occult powers based on scientific and alchemical knowledge he had brought from the East. No trace of the Order remains, but many occult organizations claim Rosicrucian origins.

rosily *adv.* like a rose, in a rosy way.

rosin — *noun* a clear hard resin produced by distilling turpentine prepared from dead pine wood, rubbed on the bows of stringed musical instruments. — *verb* (**rosined, rosining**) to rub rosin on (a violin bow, etc). [a variant of RESIN]

rosiness *noun* being rosy.

Roskilde POP (1990e) 40 000, a port and ancient town at the S end of Roskilde Fjord, Zealand, Denmark. HISTORY capital of Denmark from the 10c to 1443; by the Peace of Roskilde (1658), Denmark lost land E of The Sound to Sweden. NOTABLE FEATURES triple-towered cathedral (12c); Viking Ships Museum.

Ross, Sir James Clark (1800–62) Scottish polar explorer, born in London, the nephew of Arctic explorer Sir John Ross (1777–1856). He discovered the north magnetic pole in 1831, when on an expedition led by his uncle, then commanded an expedition to the Antarctic seas (1839–43), where Ross Barrier, the Ross Sea, and Ross Island are named after him.

Ross, Sir Ronald (1857–1932) British physician, born in Almara, Nepal. He joined the Indian Medical Service in 1881, returned to England in 1899 to lecture at the Liverpool School of Tropical Medicine, and moved to London in 1912. For his discovery of the malaria parasite and studies of its life cycle, he was awarded the 1902 Nobel Prize for Physiology or Medicine.

Ross a male first name, after the surname and place-name. [from Scottish Gaelic *ros*, headland]

Rossby, Carl-Gustaf Arvid (1898–1957) Swedish-born US meteorologist, born in Stockholm. Professor at the Massachusetts Institute of Technology, Chicago University, and Stockholm, he studied the large-scale wave-like motions or 'Rossby waves' in the upper atmosphere, found to be of considerable value in weather forecasting; his work did much to create modern weather-prediction methods.

Ross Dependency an antarctic territory administered by New Zealand since 1923. AREA (land) 413 540sq km/159 626sq mi; (permanent shelf ice) 336 770sq km/129 993sq mi. There are no permanent inhabitants. Scientific stations are located near L Vanda and at Scott Base on Ross I.

Rossellini, Roberto (1901–77) Italian film director, born in Rome. His first independent film was *Roma, città aperta* (Rome, Open City, 1945), one of the first in the neorealist style, and followed by *Paisà* (Paisan, 1946) and *Germania, anno zero* (Germany, Year Zero, 1947). He also made films with spiritual themes, and the wartime story *Il generale della Rovere* (General della Rovere, 1959).

Rossetti, Christina (Georgina) (1830–94) English poet, born in London, the sister of Dante Gabriel Rossetti. A devout Anglican, influenced by the Oxford Movement and the Pre-Raphaelite artistic movement, she wrote mainly religious poetry, such as *Goblin Market and Other Poems* (1862).

Rossetti, Dante Gabriel (1828–82) English poet and painter, born in London. He co-founded the Pre-Raphaelite Brotherhood, which aimed to return to pre-Renaissance art forms involving vivid colour and detail. His early work was on religious themes (eg *The Annunciation*, 1850, Tate, London); his later manner became more secular, and more ornate in style. Other works include the paintings *The Girlhood of Mary Virgin* (1849) and *Arthur's Tomb*, and the book *Ballads and Sonnets* (1881). He became a recluse after the death of his wife in 1862, whom he painted as *Beata Beatrix* (1863, Tate Gallery, London).

Rossi, Bruno (1905–) Italian–US physicist, born in Venice. Professor at Padua, in 1939 he moved to Manchester and then to the USA, where he worked at Chicago, Cornell, and the Massachusetts Institute of Technology. He showed that cosmic rays consist mainly of positively charged particles, which may collide with atoms in the atmosphere causing nuclear reactions and generating cascades of secondary particles, now called 'showers'.

Rossini, Gioacchino (Antonio) (1792–1868) Italian composer, born in Pesaro. Tiring of strict music study, he turned to writing comic operas. Among his early successes were *Tancredi* (1813) and *L'Italiana in Algeri* (The Italian Girl in Algiers, 1813), and in 1816 he produced his masterpiece, *Il barbiere di Siviglia* (The Barber of Seville). As director of the Italian Theatre in Paris (1823), he adapted several of his works to French taste, and wrote *Guillaume Tell* (William Tell, 1829). In 1836 took charge of the Liceo in Bologna, which he raised to a high position in the world of music.

Rosslare, Gaelic **Ros Láir** POP (1991) 847, a port town in Wexford county, Leinster province, SE Irish Republic. It lies on St George's Channel, 8km/5mi SE of Wexford.

Ross Sea the extension of the Pacific Ocean between Marie Byrd Land and Victoria Land in New Zealand's territory of Antarctica. Its S arm is covered by the Ross Ice Shelf. McMurdo Sound in the W is generally ice-free in late summer and is an important base point for exploration. The main islands are Roosevelt in the E and Ross in the W. The active volcano, Mt Erebus, is on Ross.

Rostand, Edmond (1868–1918) French poet and dramatist, born in Marseilles. He achieved international fame with *Cyrano de Bergerac* (1897), which was followed by several other verse plays, such as *L'Aiglon* (The Eaglet, 1900) and *Chantecler* (1910).

roster — *noun* a list of people showing the order in which they are to do various duties, go on leave, etc. — *verb* (**rostered, rostering**) to put (a name) on a roster. [from Dutch *rooster*, list]

Rostock *or* **Rostock-Warnemünde** POP (1991e) 248 000, an industrial port lying in Mecklenburg-West Pomerania state, N Germany. It lies at the mouth of the R Warnow, on the Baltic Sea. HISTORY founded in the 12c; a former Hanseatic League port; badly bombed in World War II, and rebuilt in the 1950s; the chief cargo port of former East Germany. NOTABLE FEATURES Navigation Museum; town hall (15c).

Rostov-on-Don, Russian **Rostov-na-Donu** POP (1990e) 1m, the port capital of Rostov oblast, SW Russia. It lies on the R Don, 46km/29mi from the river's entrance into the Sea of Azov. It was a major grain-exporting centre in the 19c.

rostral *adj.* of or like a rostrum.

Rostropovich, Mstislav (Leopoldovich) (1927–) Russian cellist and conductor, born in Baku. Awarded the Lenin prize in 1964, he left the USSR in 1974 with his wife, soprano Galina Vishnevskaya (1926–). In 1977 he became musical director of the National Symphony Orchestra, Washington, and joint artistic director of the Aldeburgh Festival in England, and in 1978 was deprived of Soviet citizenship (restored 1990). Benjamin Britten was a close friend and wrote several cello works for him.

rostrum *noun* (PL. **rostrums, rostra**) **1** a platform on which a public speaker stands. **2** a raised platform, eg that one which a conductor stands before the orchestra, or for a carrying a camera. **3** *Zool.* the beak of a bird, or a structure similar to a beak in other animals. [from Latin *rostrum*, beak]

rosy *adj.* (**rosier, rosiest**) **1** rose-coloured; pink. **2** hopeful; optimistic; cheerful.

rot — *verb* (**rotted, rotting**) **1** *trans., intrans.* (*also* **rot down**) to decay or cause to decay or become putrefied as a result of the activity of bacteria and/or fungi. **2** *intrans.* to become corrupt. **3** *intrans.* to become physically weak. — *noun* **1** decay; something which has rotted or decomposed. **2** *colloq.* nonsense; rubbish. **3** (*in compounds*) any of several plant or animal diseases caused by fungi or bacteria, eg foot rot, the name given to a bacterial disease of sheep and a fungal disease of peas. See also ROTTEN. [from Anglo-Saxon *rotian*]

Rota POP (1980) 1 000, a major island in the Northern Mariana Is, W Pacific. AREA 85sq km/33sq mi. It lies 51km/32mi NE of Guam and is 18km/11mi in length. ECONOMY sugar cane, sugar refining. NOTABLE FEATURE site of ancient stone columns.

rota *noun Brit.* a list of duties that are to be done and the names and order of the people who are to take turns in doing them. [from Latin *rota*, wheel]

Rotarian *noun* a member of Rotary International.

rotary — *adj.* turning on an axis like a wheel. — *noun* (PL. **rotaries**) **1** a rotary machine. **2** *North Amer.* a traffic roundabout. [from Latin *rota*, wheel]

Rotary Club a local branch of Rotary International.

Rotary International the first service club, formed in 1905 by US lawyer Paul Harris (1868–1947) in Chicago, Illinois, for men to perform volunteer community service. The members originally took turns to host the meetings (hence the name *Rotary*) in their offices. The organization admitted women members for the first time in 1987. Its motto is 'Service above Self'.

rotate *verb* **1** *trans., intrans.* to turn or cause to turn on an axis like a wheel. **2** to arrange in an ordered sequence. **3** *intrans.* to take turns according to an ordered sequence. [from Latin *rota*, wheel]

rotation *noun* **1** an act of rotating or state of being rotated. **2** one complete turn around an axis. **3** a regular and recurring sequence. **4** (*also* **crop rotation**) the growing of different crops on a field, usually in an ordered sequence, to help keep the land fertile.

rote *noun* the mechanical use of the memory without necessarily understanding what is memorized.

— **by rote** by memory; by heart.
[from Middle English]

rotgut *noun slang* cheap, poor-quality alcoholic drink, especially spirits.

Roth, Philip (1933–) US novelist and short story writer, born in Newark, New Jersey. He has taught at various US universities, and published his first collection of short stories, *Goodbye, Columbus*, in 1959. His first novel, *Letting Go* (1962), focuses on young Jewish intellectuals in various American locations. Other works include the comic novel *Portnoy's Complaint* (1969), and a novel trilogy recording the history of a central character, Nathan Zuckerman, beginning with *My Life as a Man* (1974).

Rotherham POP (1981) 123 000, a town in Rotherham borough, South Yorkshire, N England. It lies on the R Don, 9km/5mi NE of Sheffield. NOTABLE FEATURES late Gothic All Saints Church; Chantry Chapel of Our Lady (1383).

Rothermere, 1st Viscount see HARMSWORTH, HAROLD.

Rothschild, Meyer Amschel (1743–1812) German financier, named from the 'Red Shield' signboard of his father's house, born in Frankfurt. He began as a moneylender, and became the financial adviser of the Landgrave of Hesse. The house transmitted money from the English government to Wellington in Spain, paid the British subsidies to Continental princes, and negotiated loans for Denmark (1804–12). His five sons continued the firm, establishing branches in other countries, and negotiated many of the government loans of the 19c.

roti *noun* (PL. **rotis**) **1** a cake of unleavened bread, traditionally made in parts of India and the Caribbean. **2** a kind of sandwich made of this wrapped around curried vegetables, seafood, or chicken. [from Hindi, = bread]

rotifer *noun Zool.* a microscopic aquatic invertebrate animal, belonging to the phylum Rotifera, that has an unsegmented body. Rotifers swim by means of a ring of beating hair-like structures (cilia) that resembles a spinning wheel. [from Latin *rota*, wheel + *ferre*, to carry]

rotisserie *noun* **1** a cooking apparatus with a spit on which meat, poultry, etc may be cooked by direct heat. **2** a shop or restaurant which sells or serves meat cooked in this way. [from French *rôtisserie*, from *rôtir*, to roast]

rotor *noun* **1** a rotating part of a machine, especially in an internal combustion engine. **2** a system of blades projecting from a cylinder which rotate at high speed to provide the force to lift and propel a helicopter.

Rotorua POP (1991) 54 000, a health resort on North I, New Zealand. It is located in a region of thermal springs, geysers, and boiling mud. NOTABLE FEATURES Whakarewarewa (Maori village); Maori Arts and Crafts Centre.

Rotovator *or* **Rotavator** *noun trademark* a machine with a rotating blade for breaking up the soil. [a contraction of *rotary cultivator*]

rotten *adj.* **1** having gone bad, decayed, rotted, or fallen to pieces. **2** morally corrupt. **3** *colloq.* miserably unwell. **4** *colloq.* unsatisfactory: *a rotten plan.* **5** *colloq.* unpleasant; disagreeable: *rotten weather.* [from Norse *rotinn*]

rotten borough *Hist.* before 1832, a borough that could elect an MP even though it had few or no inhabitants.

rottenness *noun* being rotten.

rotter *noun old slang use* a worthless, despicable, or depraved person.

Rotterdam POP (1992e) 590 000, an industrial city and the chief port of the Netherlands, in South Holland province, W Netherlands. It lies at the junction of the R Rotte with the Nieuwe Maas, 24km/15mi from the North Sea, and is one of the world's foremost cargo ports. With the

largest shipyard in Europe, Rotterdam's major industry is shipbuilding; it also has the largest petrochemical plant on the European continent. HISTORY a major commercial centre of NW Europe since the 14c; the philosopher Erasmus was born here in 1466; the city centre was almost completely destroyed by German bombing in 1940; the Europoort harbour area was inaugurated in 1966, and the approach channel was deepened in 1984. NOTABLE FEATURES restored Groote Kerk; several museums; philharmonic orchestra.

Rottweiler *noun* a large powerfully built black and tan dog, originally from Germany. [from *Rottweil* in SW Germany]

rotund *adj.* **1** round. **2** plump. **3** impressive or grandiloquent. [from Latin *rotundus*, from *rota*, wheel]

rotunda *noun* a round, usually domed, building or hall. [from Italian *rotonda camera*, round room]

rotunda

rotundity *or* **rotundness** *noun* **1** roundness. **2** a round mass.

rotundly *adv.* in a rotund way.

Roubaix POP (1990) 98 000, an industrial and commercial town in Nord department, Nord-Pas-de-Calais region, NW France. It lies on the Belgian border, 11km/7mi NE of Lille. It was chartered in 1469 and is the centre of the textile industry in N France. NOTABLE FEATURE Gothic Church of St-Martin (15c).

Roubiliac *or* **Roubillac, Louis François** (1702 or 1705–62) French sculptor, born in Lyons. He settled in London (c.1730), where he became known through his statue of Handel for Vauxhall Gardens (1738). Other statues include that of Sir Isaac Newton in Cambridge (1755) and of Shakespeare (1758) now in the British Museum.

rouble *or* **ruble** *noun* the standard unit of currency in the countries of the former Soviet Union, equal to 100 kopecks. [from Russian *rubl*]

roué *noun old use* a disreputable man; a rake. [from French *roué*, a man deserving to be broken on a wheel. This was a former method of torture or capital punishment in which victims were stretched out on a wheel and their arms and legs were broken with an iron bar]

Rouen, ancient **Rotomagus** POP (1990) 308 000, the river-port capital of Haute-Normandie region and of Seine-Maritime department, NW France. The fifth-largest port in France, it lies on the right bank of the R Seine, 86km/53mi NW of Paris. HISTORY formerly capital of Upper Normandy; scene of the trial and burning of Joan of Arc in 1431; birthplace of the novelist, Gustave Flaubert, in 1821; badly damaged in World War II but reconstructed largely as a Ville Musée (museum town). NOTABLE FEATURES restored 13c–16c Gothic Cathedral of Notre-Dame; Abbey Church of St-Ouen (14c); late Gothic Palais de Justice; Gros Horloge (clock tower), on a Renaissance arch.

Rouen Cathedral a series of paintings by Claude Monet (1892–4). Each painting is done under different aspects of light.

rouge — *noun* a pink or red powder or cream used to colour the cheeks. — *verb* **1** *intrans.* to use

rouge. **2** to apply rouge to. [from French *rouge*, red]

Rouge et le Noir, Le (The Red and the Black) a novel by Stendhal (1830). It describes the ill-fated life of young Julian Sorel in Restoration France. In very general terms, *le rouge* represents the armies of Napoleon, while *le noir* represents the Church.

Rouget de Lisle, Claude Joseph (1760–1836) French soldier and composer, born in Lons-le-Saunier. He wrote and composed the *Marseillaise* (French National Anthem) when stationed as captain of engineers at Strasbourg in 1792.

rough — *adj.* **1** *said of a surface* not smooth, even, or regular. **2** *said of ground* covered with stones, tall grass, bushes and/or scrub. **3** covered with shaggy or coarse hair. **4** harsh or grating: *a rough voice.* **5** *said of a person's character, behaviour, etc* noisy, coarse, or violent. **6** stormy. **7** requiring hard work or considerable physical effort, or involving great difficulty, tension, etc: *a rough day at work.* **8** (**rough on**) unpleasant and hard to bear: *a decision which is rough on the employees.* **9** *said of a guess, calculation, etc* approximate. **10** not polished or refined: *a rough draft.* **11** *colloq.* slightly unwell and tired, especially because of heavy drinking or lack of sleep. — *noun* **1** rough ground, especially the uncut grass at the side of a golf fairway. **2** the unpleasant or disagreeable side of something: *take the rough with the smooth.* **3** a rough or crude state. **4** a crude preliminary sketch. **5** a thug or hooligan.
— **rough it** *colloq.* to live primitively, without the usual comforts of life.
rough something out to do a preliminary sketch of it or give a preliminary explanation of it.
rough someone up *colloq.* to beat them up.
sleep rough to sleep in the open without proper shelter.
[from Anglo-Saxon *ruh*]

roughage *noun* dietary fibre.

rough-and-ready *adj.* **1** quickly prepared and not polished or perfect but good enough. **2** *said or a person* friendly and pleasant but not polite or refined.

rough-and-tumble *noun* a bout of disorderly but usually friendly fighting or scuffling.

roughcast — *noun* a mixture of plaster and small stones used to cover outside walls. — *verb* (PAST TENSE AND PAST PARTICIPLE **roughcast**) to cover with roughcast.

rough diamond 1 an uncut and unpolished diamond. **2** a good-natured person with rough, unrefined manners.

roughen *verb trans., intrans.* (**roughened, roughening**) to make or become rough.

rough-hew *verb* to shape crudely and without refining.

rough-hewn *adj.* crude, unpolished, unrefined.

roughhouse *noun colloq.* a disturbance or brawl.

roughly *adv.* **1** in a rough way. **2** approximately.

roughneck *noun* **1** a worker on an oil rig. **2** a rough and rowdy person.

roughness *noun* a rough quality.

Rough Riders the nickname for the First US Volunteer Cavalry Regiment, commanded during the Spanish–American War (1898) by Col Leonard Wood (1860–1927) and Lt-Col Theodore Roosevelt. The Rough Riders' fabled 'charge' up San Juan Hill in Cuba (1 Jul 1898) was actually carried out on foot.

roughshod *adj., said of a horse* having horseshoes with projecting nails which prevent the horse from slipping in wet weather.

— **ride roughshod over someone** to treat them arrogantly and without regard for their feelings.

roulette *noun* **1** a gambling game in which a ball is dropped into a spinning wheel divided up into many small, numbered compartments coloured black and red alternately, with the players betting on which compartment the ball will come to rest in. **2** a small tool with a toothed wheel, used for making a line of dots and perforating paper. [from French]

round — *adj.* **1** shaped like, or approximately, a circle or a ball. **2** not angular; curved and plump. **3** moving in or forming a circle. **4** *said of numbers* complete and exact: *a round dozen.* **5** *said of a number* without a fraction. **6** *said of a number* approximate, without taking minor amounts into account. **7** *said of a sum of money* considerable; substantial. **8** plain-spoken; candid. — *adv.* **1** in or to the opposite direction, position or opinion: *win someone round.* **2** in a circular direction or with a circular or revolving movement. **3** in, by, or along a circuitous or indirect route. **4** on all sides so as to surround: *gather round.* **5** from one person to another: *pass it round.* **6** in rotation, so as to return to the starting point: *wait until spring comes round.* **7** from place to place: *drive round for a while.* **8** in circumference: *measures six feet round.* **9** to a particular place, especially a person's home: *come round for supper.* — *prep.* **1** on all sides of so as to surround or enclose. **2** so as to move or revolve around a centre or axis and return to the starting point: *run round the field.* **3** *colloq.* having as a central point or basis: *a story built round her experiences.* **4** from place to place in: *we went round the town shopping.* **5** in all or various directions from; close to (a place). **6** so as to pass, or having passed, in a curved course: *drive round the corner.* — *noun* **1** something round (and often flat) in shape. **2** a complete revolution round a circuit or path. **3** a single complete slice of bread. **4** a sandwich, or set of sandwiches, made from two complete slices of bread. **5** the playing of all 18 holes on a golf course in a single session. **6** one of a recurring series of events, actions, etc: *a round of talks.* **7** a series of regular activities: *one's daily round.* **8** a regular route followed, especially for the delivery of something: *a milk round.* **9** (*usually* **rounds**) a sequence of visits made by a doctor to patients, in a hospital or in their homes. **10** a stage in a competition. **11** a single period of play, competition, etc in a group of several, eg in boxing. **12** a burst of applause or cheering. **13** a single bullet or charge of ammunition. **14** a set of drinks bought at the same time for all the members of a group. **15** an unaccompanied song in which different people all sing the same part continuously but start (and therefore end) at different times. — *verb* **1** *trans., intrans.* to make or become round. **2** to go round: *the car rounded the corner.*

— **go the rounds** *said of news, information, etc* to be passed round from person to person.

in the round 1 with all details shown or considered. **2** *Theatr.* with the audience seated on at least three, and often four, sides of the stage.

round about 1 on all sides; in a ring surrounding. **2** approximately.

round the clock all day and all night; for twenty-four hours.

round on someone to turn on them in anger, usually in speech.

round something down to lower a number so that it can be expressed as a round number: *round 15.47 down to 15.*

round something off 1 to make corners, angles, etc smooth. **2** to complete something successfully and pleasantly: *round off the meal with a glass of brandy.*

round something up 1 to raise a number so that it can be expressed as a round number: *round 15.89 up to 16.* **2** to collect (people, or things such as livestock or facts) together. [from Latin *rotundus*]

roundabout — *noun* **1** *Brit.* a revolving platform, usually with seats, on which one can ride for pleasure; a merry-go-round. **2** *Brit.* a circular road junction, usually with an island in the middle, where several roads meet, and round which traffic must travel in the same direction. — *adj.* not direct; circuitous.

rounded *adj.* curved.

roundel *noun* **1** a small circular window or design. **2** a coloured round identification disc on the wing of a military aircraft. [from Old French *rondel*, little circle]

roundelay *noun* a simple song with a refrain. [from Old French *rondelet*, from *rondel*, little circle]

rounders *noun* a team game similar to baseball, in which each team sends players in to bat in turn while the other team bowls and fields, with the batter scoring a run if he or she successfully runs round a square course in one go.

Roundhead *noun Hist.* a supporter of the parliamentary party against Charles I in the English Civil War (1642–9).

roundly *adv.* plainly and often rudely; bluntly; thoroughly.

roundness *noun* a round quality.

round robin 1 a petition or protest, especially one in which the names are written in a circle to conceal the ringleader. **2** a tournament in which each competitor plays each of the others in turn.

round-shouldered *adj.* with stooping shoulders and a back which bends forward slightly at the top.

round table 1 (**Round Table**) the table at which King Arthur and his knights sat, round in shape so that no individual knight should have precedence. **2** a meeting or conference at which the participants meet on equal terms.

Round the World Yacht Race a yacht race, sponsored by Whitbread, which takes place every four years and is open to several classes of yacht. The race is held over four stages.

round trip a trip to a place and back again, usually by a different route.

round-up *noun* **1** a rounding up of people or things. **2** a summary or résumé.

round window *Anat.* the lower of the two membrane-covered openings between the middle ear and the inner ear in vertebrates. — Also called *fenestra rotunda.*

roundworm *noun Zool.* an invertebrate animal with a long slender unsegmented body, belonging to the phylum Nematoda. Some species live as parasites within the bodies (usually the intestines) of humans and animals. Roundworms include hookworms and threadworms, and can cause various diseases.

Rous, (Francis) Peyton (1879–1970) US pathologist, born in Baltimore. He spent his career at the Rockefeller Institute for Medical Research in New York, and demonstrated that a sarcoma in chickens is caused by a virus; this was the first time a virus was implicated in cancer, and stimulated much further research. He shared the 1966 Nobel Prize for Physiology or Medicine with Charles Huggins.

rouse *verb trans., intrans.* **1** to arouse (someone or oneself) or become aroused from sleep, listlessness or lethargy. **2** to excite or provoke, or be excited or provoked.

rousing *adj.* stirring; exciting.

Rousseau, Henri, also called **Le Douanier** (**The Customs Officer**) (1844–1910) French Primitive painter, born in Laval. He worked for many years as a minor customs official, hence his byname. He retired in 1885 and spent his time painting and copying at the Louvre, and exhibited for several years at the Salon des Indépendants. His work includes portraits, exotic imaginary landscapes, dream scenes, and military and sporting scenes (eg *Sleeping Gypsy*, 1897, New York, *The Dream*, 1910, New York, *The Football Players*, 1908, New York).

Rousseau, Jean Jacques (1712–78) French political philosopher, educationist, and essayist, born in Geneva, Switzerland. Largely self-taught, he had various menial occupations until he moved to Paris (1741), where he met Denis Diderot and the Encyclopedists. In 1754 he wrote *Discours sur l'origine de l'inégalité parmi les hommes* (Discourse on the Origin and Foundations of Inequality Amongst Men, 1755), which emphasizes the natural goodness of humans, and the corrupting influences of institutionalized life. In Luxembourg from 1757, he wrote his masterpiece, *Du contrat social* (The Social Contract, 1762), a great influence on French revolutionary thought; it introduced the slogan 'Liberty, Equality, Fraternity'. In 1762 he also published his major work on education, *Emile*, in novel form, but its views on monarchy and governmental institutions forced him to flee to Swizerland, and then England, at the invitation of David Hume. There he wrote most of his *Confessions* (published posthumously, 1782). He returned to Paris (1767), where he continued to write, but gradually became insane.

Rousseau, (Pierre Etienne) Théodore (1812–67) French landscape painter, born in Paris. He began painting directly from nature in the Forest of Fontainebleau in the 1930s. During the 1840s he settled in Barbizon, where he worked with a group of painters who collectively became known as the Barbizon School.

roustabout *noun* an unskilled labourer, eg on an oil-rig or a farm.

rout[1] — *verb* to defeat completely and cause to flee in confusion. — *noun* **1** a complete and overwhelming defeat. **2** a confused and disorderly retreat. **3** *Legal* a group of three or more people gathered together to commit a crime or some unlawful act. **4** a disorderly and noisy group of people. [from Old French *route*, from Latin *rumpere*, to break]

rout[2] *verb* **1** *trans., intrans.* to dig up, especially with the snout. **2** (**rout someone out** *or* **up**) to find or fetch them by searching. [a variant of ROOT[1]]

route — *noun* **1** the way travelled on a regular journey. **2** a particular group of roads followed to get to a place. — *verb* (**routed**, **routeing**) to arrange a route for; to send by a selected route. [from Latin *rupta via*, broken road]

route march a long and tiring march, especially one for soldiers in training.

routine — *noun* **1** a regular or fixed way of doing things. **2** a set series of movements in a dance, performance, etc. **3** a part of a computer program which performs a specific function. — *adj.* unvarying; regular; ordinary; done as part of a routine. [related to ROUTE]

routinely *adv.* in a routine way; at routine intervals.

Routledge, George (1812–88) English publisher, born in Brampton, Cumberland. He went to London in 1833, and started up as a bookseller (1836) and publisher (1843), later taking his two brothers-in-law, W H and Frederick Warne, into partnership.

Roux, (Pierre Paul) Emile (1853–1933) French bacteriologist, born in Confolens, Charente. He became an assistant to Louis Pasteur, and in 1904 succeeded him as Director of the Pasteur Institute. In 1894 he helped to discover diphtheria antitoxin, and he also worked on rabies and anthrax.

roux *noun* (PL. **roux**) a cooked mixture of flour and fat, used to thicken sauces. [from French *beurre roux*, brown butter]

Rovaniemi POP (1991e) 34 000, the capital of Lappi province, Finland. It lies 160km/99mi N of Oulu, just S of the Arctic Circle, and was established in 1929. With its river access to the Baltic, it became an important centre for the exploitation of timber in Lapland. It was largely destroyed by fire in 1944–5, and rebuilt by Alvar Aalto, who laid out the main streets in the design of a reindeer's antlers.

rove *verb* **1** *trans., intrans.* to wander or roam over aimlessly. **2** *intrans. said of the eyes* to keep looking in different directions.

rover *noun* a wanderer, especially a wandering pirate or robber.

roving *adj.* wandering; likely to ramble or stray.

Rovno, Polish **Rowne**, German **Rowno** POP (1991e) 239 000, a city in the Ukraine. It lies on the R Uste and was formerly in Poland. NOTABLE FEATURE wooden Church of the Assumption (1756).

row¹ *noun* (pronounced like *so*) **1** a number of people or things, such as theatre seats, numbers, vegetables, etc arranged in a line. **2** a street with a line of houses on one or both sides.
— **a hard row to hoe** a difficult job or destiny.
in a row in an unbroken sequence; in succession. [from Anglo-Saxon *raw*]

row² (pronounced like *so*) — *verb* **1** *trans., intrans.* to move (a boat) through the water using oars. **2** to carry (people, goods, etc) in a rowing boat. **3** *intrans.* to race in rowing boats for sport. **4** to compete in (a race) in a rowing boat. See ROWING. — *noun* **1** an act of rowing a boat. **2** a trip in a rowing boat. [from Anglo-Saxon *rowan*]

row³ (pronounced like *now*) — *noun* **1** a noisy quarrel. **2** a loud unpleasant noise or disturbance. **3** a severe reprimand. — *verb intrans.* to quarrel noisily.

rowan *noun* **1** a European tree with clusters of white flowers and bright red berries. — Also called *mountain ash*. **2** a small red berry from this tree. [from Scandinavian]

rowboat *noun* North Amer. a rowing boat.

rowdily *adv.* in a rowdy way.

rowdiness *noun* **1** being rowdy. **2** rowdy behaviour.

rowdy — *adj.* (**rowdier, rowdiest**) noisy and rough. — *noun colloq.* a noisy, rough person. [perhaps from ROW³]

rowdyism *noun* rowdy behaviour.

Rowe, Nicholas (1674–1718) English poet and dramatist, born in Little Barford in Bedfordshire. He became a lawyer, but from 1692 devoted himself to literature. His most successful plays were *Tamerlane* (1702), *The Fair Penitent* (1703), and *Jane Shore* (1714). He was the first to publish a critical edition of Shakespeare (1709–10), and he was made Poet Laureate in 1715.

rowel *noun* a small spiked wheel on a spur. [from Old French *roel*, small wheel]

Rowena a female first name. [12c in the history of Geoffrey of Monmouth; possibly of Germanic origin, from *hrod*, fame + *wynn*, joy, or a misunderstanding of Welsh *Rhonwen*, white skirt]

rower *noun* a person who rows.

rowing a sport or pastime in which a boat is propelled by oars as opposed to mechanical means. If there is only one rower with two oars it is known as *sculling*. Rowing involves two or more people, each rower having one oar. It dates from ancient times, but as an organized sport it can be traced to 1715, when the first Doggetts Coat and Badge race took place on the R Thames. Famous races include the Oxford–Cambridge Boat Race, and the Diamond Sculls and Grand Challenge Cup, both contested annually at Henley Royal Regatta.

rowing boat *Brit.* a small boat which is moved by oars.

Rowlandson, Thomas (1756–1827) English caricaturist, born in London. He travelled widely in Britain, and became a specialist in humorous watercolours commenting on the social scene.

His works include his illustrations to the *Dr Syntax* series (1812–21), *The English Dance of Death* (1815–16), and *Cobbler's Cure for a Scolding Wife*.

rowlock *noun* a device for holding an oar in place and serving as a pivot for it to turn on. [a variant of *oarlock*, from Anglo-Saxon *arloc*]

Rowntree, Joseph (1836–1925) English Quaker industrialist and reformer, born in York, the son of a grocer. With his brother Henry Isaac (d.1883) he became a partner in a cocoa manufacturer in York in 1869, and built up welfare organizations for his employees.

Roy a male first name. [from the Scottish Gaelic nickname *Ruadh*, red]

royal — *adj.* **1** of or suitable for a king or queen. **2** under the patronage or in the service of the king or queen: *Royal Geographical Society*. **3** belonging to the king or queen. **4** being a member of the king's or queen's family. **5** regal; magnificent. **6** larger and more splendid than usual. — *noun* **1** *colloq.* a member of the royal family. **2** a sail immediately above the topgallant sail. **3** a stag with antlers of 12 or more points. **4** a size of paper, either 19 by 24in (483 by 610mm) of writing paper or 20 by 25in (508 by 635mm) of printing paper. [from Old French *roial*, from Latin *regalis*]

Royal Academy of Arts a British academy founded in 1768 under royal patronage. Its aim was to hold annual exhibitions (still held) to raise the status of artists, and to foster the development of a national school of painting to rival the schools of the continent. The Academy's first President was Sir Joshua Reynolds. Its premises were initially in Pall Mall, London, but since 1867 they have been at Burlington House.

Royal Academy of Dramatic Art (ABBREV. **RADA**) in the UK, a stage school founded in 1904 by Sir Herbert Beerbohm Tree.

Royal Academy of Music a London conservatory founded in 1822, opened in 1823, and granted its royal charter in 1830. It moved to its present location in Marylebone in 1912.

Royal Air Force (ABBREV. **RAF**) the British air force, established in Apr 1918 from the combined forces of the Royal Flying Corps and the Royal Naval Air Service. It played a vital role in both World Wars, and today it comprises two Commands: Strike and Support. RAF Germany (formerly a third Command) became Number 2 Group of Strike Command in Apr 1993. Responsibility for operating Britain's nuclear deterrent was transferred from the RAF's bomber squadrons to the Royal Navy's Polaris submarine force in 1969. The Women's Royal Air Force (WRAF) was founded in 1918, disbanded in 1920, reformed in 1949 and officially combined with the RAF in 1994.

Royal Albert Hall a large round, domed hall in London, England, built in 1871 on the site of the Great Exhibition as a memorial to Prince Albert. It seats c.6 000 and is used as a venue for music, sport, and exhibitions.

Royal and Ancient Golf Club of St Andrews (ABBREV. **R & A**) a ruling golf organization, founded in St Andrews on 14 May 1754 when 22 noblemen formed themselves into the Society of St Andrews golfers. It adopted its present name in 1834.

royal assent in the UK, formal permission given by the sovereign for a parliamentary act to become law.

Royal Ballet a British ballet company, founded as the Vic–Wells ballet (1931) under Ninette de Valois and Lilian Baylis, from a ballet school founded by de Valois in 1926. Known from the late 1930s as the Sadler's Wells Ballet, it received a royal charter in 1956 and became the Royal Ballet. Among its famous dancers are Margot Fonteyn, Alicia Markova, and Anthony Dowell (director of the company from 1986), and

its choreographers have included Kenneth MacMillan and George Balanchine.

royal blue a rich, bright, deep-coloured blue.

Royal British Legion an organization formed in 1921 as the British Legion under Douglas Haig, to promote the welfare and perpetuate the memory of all ex-servicemen and women, serving members of HM Forces, and their dependents. It became the Royal British Legion in 1971. It supplies the poppies for the Remembrance Appeal each November from its factory in Edinburgh.

Royal College of Music a London conservatory founded by royal charter and opened in 1883. It moved to its present location in Prince Consort Road in 1894.

Royal College of Organists a British music institution, founded in 1864. Originally aimed at organ and choir training, it now hosts some recitals and acts mainly as an examining body.

royal commission in the UK, a group of people appointed by the crown at the request of the government to inquire into and report on some matter.

Royal Court Theatre a small theatre in Sloane Square, London, opened in 1888, on the site of a Chelsea theatre which was demolished. It established a reputation for avant-garde productions, beginning with many of George Bernard Shaw's plays, and became the home of the English Stage Company.

Royal Festival Hall a concert hall at the South Bank Centre arts complex in London, England, a venue for orchestral and choral performances. Built in 1949–51 for the Festival of Britain, its design is a successful example of early acoustic science.

Royal Geographical Society (ABBREV. **RGS**) in the UK, an organization founded in 1830 as the Geographical Society of London to help intending explorers and to accumulate a library of books, maps, and charts. It received a royal charter in 1859.

Royal Greenwich Observatory In the UK, an observatory founded by Charles II at Greenwich in 1675. The prime meridian of longitude runs through this site. The observatory moved to Herstmonceux in 1948 and to Cambridge in 1990. Since 1994 it has been part of the Royal Observatories.

Royal Horticultural Society in the UK, an organization founded in 1804 'for the improvement of horticulture'. It maintains an experimental garden at Wisley, Surrey, and hosts annual shows such as the Chelsea Flower Show in London. It received a royal charter in 1809.

Royal Hunt of the Sun, The a play by Peter Shaffer (1964). It is about the destruction of Peru's Inca civilization by the Spanish conquistadores and examines the differences in their cultures.

Royal Institution, The in the UK, a learned scientific society founded in 1799 by the physicist Benjamin Thompson Rumford. Its laboratories became Britain's first research centre, and were used in the 19c by Sir Humphrey Davy and Michael Faraday. Its headquarters in Albemarle Street, London, are the venue for lectures, notably for young people at Christmas time.

royalism *noun* belief in or support of the institution of monarchy.

royalist — *noun* **1** a supporter of the monarchy. **2** (**Royalist**) *Hist.* a supporter of Charles I during the English Civil War (1642–9). — *adj.* relating to royalists.

royal jelly *noun* a rich protein substance secreted by worker bees and fed by them to certain female larvae that are destined to develop into queen bees instead of sterile workers. Royal jelly is used in face creams and as a health food supplement.

royally *adv.* in a royal way, with a royal manner.

Royal Marines (ABBREV. **RM**) the British Marine force, which can trace its origin to the Lord High Admiral's Regiment first raised in 1664. The title *Royal Marines* was conferred in 1800. The first RM Commando units were raised in 1942.

Royal Mint the British government department responsible for manufacturing metal coins. The mint was probably founded in London in c.825, and since the mid-16c it has enjoyed a legal monopoly of coinage. It is now situated in Llantrisant, S Wales.

Royal National Lifeboat Institution (ABBREV. **RNLI**) in the UK, a rescue organization manned by volunteers and financed by voluntary contributions, founded in 1824 by Sir William Hillery (1771–1847) as the Royal National Institution for the Preservation of Life from Shipwreck. The modern RNLI operates over 210 lifeboat stations and maintains 400 vessels.

Royal Navy (ABBREV. **RN**) the naval branch of the British armed forces. A national English Navy existed in Saxon times, but the Royal Navy as such originated in the time of Henry VIII, when a Navy Board and the title of Lord High Admiral were established. The primary instrument of British imperial expansion in the 18c and 19c, it reached the peak of its global power at the end of World War II, when it had more than 500 warships. A fraction of that size today, the RN has been responsible for the operation of Britain's nuclear deterrent since 1969.

Royal Northern College of Music a British conservatory which began as the Northern College of Music in 1972 (renamed in 1973) by the amalgamation of the Royal Manchester College of Music (1893) and the Northern School of Music (1942, founded as the Matthay School of Music in 1920).

Royal Observatories in the UK, astronomical institutions administered by the Particle Physics and Astronomy Research Council, comprising the former Royal Greenwich Observatory and the former Royal Observatory, Edinburgh, together with their island sites in La Palma, Canary Islands, and Hawaii.

Royal Observatory, Edinburgh an observatory founded in Edinburgh by the Astronomical Institution of Edinburgh and granted royal status by George IV in 1822. First sited on Calton Hill, it moved to Blackford Hill in 1894. Since 1994 it has been part of the Royal Observatories.

Royal Opera House the home of the Royal Ballet and the Royal Opera in Bow Street, London. The site has been occupied by three successive buildings since the Theatre Royal opened there (1732). The present building, by Edward Middleton Barry (1830–80), opened in 1858.

Royal Pavilion a palace in Brighton, designed by John Nash and built (1815–22) for the Prince of Wales (later George IV). It is an elaborate blend of Indian and Chinese styles, with a large domed rotunda (originally the Marine Pavilion, designed by Henry Holland, 1787, enlarged 1801–4), minarets, and sumptuous oriental interior decorations. It now houses a museum and art gallery.

royal prerogative the rights of the monarch, in theory not restricted in any way, but in practice laid down by custom.

Royal Shakespeare Company (ABBREV. **RSC**) an English theatre company based in Stratford-upon-Avon and London. Developed out of the Shakespeare Memorial Theatre by Peter Hall between 1960 and 1968, its primary objective is the regular production of Shakespeare's plays, although it also commissions and produces works from the UK's leading living playwrights. Trevor Nunn took over as director (1968–87), succeeded by Terry Hands (1987–91), and Adrian Noble.

Royal Society, in full **Royal Society of London for the Promotion of Natural Knowledge** the oldest and most prestigious scientific institution in the UK, it originated in 1645 and was chartered in 1660. It members have included Christopher Wren, and Isaac Newton, who was President (1703–27).

Royal Society for Nature Conservation a British conservation society which co-ordinates the work of county naturalist trusts and urban wildlife groups. It was founded in 1912 as the Society for the Promotion of Nature Reserves.

Royal Society for the Protection of Birds (ABBREV. **RSPB**) a UK organization founded in 1889 to promote the conservation of birds and their habitats by maintaining nature reserves, to prevent the loss of rare species such as the osprey, and to popularize bird-watching. Now one of the major conservation bodies, it owns over 115 bird reserves.

royalty *noun* (PL. **royalties**) **1** the character, state, office or power of a king or queen. **2** members of the royal family, either individually or collectively. **3** a percentage of the profits from each copy of a book, piece of music, invention, etc sold, performed or used, which is paid to the author, composer, inventor, etc. **4** a payment made by companies who mine minerals, oil or gas to the person who owns the land or owns the mineral rights to the land that the company is mining. **5** a right (especially to minerals) granted by a king or queen to an individual or company.

Royal Victorian Order (ABBREV. **RVO**) an order of knighthood instituted in 1896 by Queen Victoria to reward personal service to the sovereign. There are five classes: Knights and Dames Grand Cross (GCVO), Knights and Dames Commanders (KCVO/DCVO), Commanders (CVO), Lieutenants (LVO), and Members (MVO). The motto is 'Victoria', and the ribbon is blue, edged with red and white.

royal warrant an official authorization to a tradesman to supply goods to a royal household.

Royce, Sir (Frederick) Henry (1863–1933) British engineer, born in Alwalton, Huntingdonshire. He began as a railway apprentice, but became interested in electricity and motor engineering, founding in Manchester the firm of Royce, Ltd (1884). He made his first car in 1904, and his meeting with C S Rolls in that year led to the formation (1906) of Rolls–Royce, Ltd.

Rozeanu, Angelica, *née* **Adelstein** (1921–) Romanian table tennis player. She won 12 world titles between 1950 and 1956, including the singles title a record six times (1950–5), and was a member of the Romanian Corbillon Cup winning team (1950–1, 1953, 1955–6). She was made a Master of Sport, and appointed to the Romanian Olympic Commission. She retired in 1960, and emigrated to Israel.

rozzer *noun Brit. old slang use* a policeman.

RP *abbrev.* Received Pronunciation.

RPI *abbrev. Brit.* retail price index, a list of the prices of selected consumer goods which is compiled regularly to show how prices are changing and how the cost of living is rising.

RPM *abbrev.* retail price maintenance.

rpm *abbrev.* revolutions per minute.

RR *abbrev.* Right Reverend.

RS *abbrev.* Royal Society.

RSA *abbrev.* **1** Republic of South Africa. **2** *Brit.* Royal Scottish Academy, or Academician. **3** *Brit.* Royal Society of Arts.

RSC *abbrev.* Royal Shakespeare Company.

RSI *Medicine abbrev.* repetitive strain injury.

RSM *abbrev.* regimental sergeant-major.

RSNO *abbrev.* Royal Scottish National Orchestra.

RSPB *abbrev.* the Royal Society for the Protection of Birds.

RSPCA *abbrev.* in the UK, the Royal Society for the Prevention of Cruelty to Animals, the main animal welfare society, founded in 1824, funded by voluntary contributions.

RSSPCC *abbrev.* Royal Scottish Society for the Prevention of Cruelty to Children.

RSV *abbrev.* Revised Standard Version (of the Bible).

RSVP *abbrev. répondez s'il vous plaît* (French), please reply.

RTE *abbrev. Radio Telfís Eireann* (Ir Gaelic) Irish Radio and Television.

Rt Hon *abbrev.* Right Honourable.

Rt Rev *abbrev.* Right Reverend.

Ru *symbol Chem.* ruthenium.

Ruapehu, Mount an active volcano and the highest peak on North I, New Zealand. It rises to 2 797m in Tongariro National Park.

rub — *verb* (**rubbed, rubbing**) **1** to move one's hand, an object, etc back and forwards over the surface of (something) with pressure and friction. **2** to move (one's hand, an object, etc) backwards and forwards over a surface with pressure and friction. **3** (**rub against** *or* **on something**) to move backwards and forwards over a surface with pressure and friction. **4** (**rub something in** *or* **on**) to apply ointment, lotion, polish, etc. **5** to clean, polish, dry, smooth, etc. **6** *trans., intrans.* (**rub** *or* **rub something away**, **off**, **out**, *etc*) to remove or be removed by pressure and friction. **7** *trans., intrans.* to make (something) sore by pressure and friction. **8** *trans., intrans.* to fray by pressure and friction. — *noun* **1** an act of rubbing. **2** an obstacle or difficulty.

— **rub along** *colloq.* to manage to get along, make progress, etc without any particular difficulties.

rub along with someone to be on more or less friendly terms with them.

rub something down 1 to rub one's body, a horse, etc briskly from head to foot, eg to dry it. **2** to prepare a surface to receive new paint or varnish by rubbing the old paint or varnish off.

rub something in 1 to apply ointment, etc by rubbing. **2** *colloq.* to insist on talking about or emphasizing an embarrassing fact or circumstance.

rub off on someone to have an effect on or be passed to someone else by close association: *some of his bad habits have rubbed off on you.*

rub someone out *North Amer. slang* to murder them.

rub something out to remove it by rubbing.

rub something up 1 to polish it. **2** to refresh one's memory or knowledge of it.

rub someone up the wrong way to annoy or irritate them.

[from Middle English *rubben*]

Rubáiyt of Omar Khayym, The a translation by Edward Fitzgerald of the poetic quatrains of Persian poet Omar Khayyám (1859). They date from the 12c and contain many frequently-quoted sayings, including 'A jug of wine, a loaf of bread, and thou'.

rubato *Mus.* — *noun* (PL. **rubati, rubatos**) a modified or distorted tempo in which notes may be deprived of part of their length (with a slight quickening of tempo) or may have their length increased (by a slight slowing of tempo) without the overall flow of the music being impaired. — *adj., adv.* with such freedom of tempo. [from Italian *rubato*, robbed]

rubber¹ — *noun* **1** a strong elastic substance obtained from the latex of various trees or plants or produced synthetically. **2** *Brit.* a small piece of rubber or plastic used for rubbing out pencil or ink marks on paper; an eraser. **3** *North Amer. slang* a condom. **4** (*usually* **rubbers**) *North Amer.* waterproof rubber overshoes; galoshes. **5** any person, device or machine part that rubs. — *adj.* of or producing rubber.

rubber² *noun* a match, especially in bridge or whist, consisting of either three or five games.

rubber band same as ELASTIC BAND.

rubberize *or* **rubberise** *verb* to coat or impregnate (a substance, especially a textile) with rubber. Rubberized fabric is used to make conveyer belts, pneumatic tyres, inflatable dinghies, etc.

rubberneck — *noun North Amer. slang* a person who stares or gapes inquisitively or stupidly, especially a tourist on a guided tour. — *verb intrans.* to behave in this way.

rubber plant 1 a house plant with large, shiny, dark green leaves. **2** (*also* **rubber tree**) any of several tropical trees grown for their latex, a valuable source of rubber.

rubber stamp 1 an instrument made of rubber with figures, letters, names, etc on it, used to stamp a name, date, etc on books or papers. **2** an automatic, unthinking or routine agreement or authorization. **3** a person or group of people required to approve or authorize another person's or group's decisions and actions without having the power, courage, etc to withhold this approval or authorization.

rubber-stamp *verb* to give automatic, unthinking, or routine approval of or authorization for.

rubber tree any of various trees which produce a milky white liquid (latex) that is used to make rubber, especially *Hevea brasiliensis*, a large tree native to S America, and extensively cultivated in plantations in SE Asia, especially Malaya. It is the source of about 90 per cent of the natural rubber produced worldwide.

rubbery *adj.* like rubber; flexible.

rubbing *noun* an impression or copy made by placing paper over a raised surface and rubbing the paper with crayon, wax, chalk, etc.

rubbish — *noun* **1** waste material; things that have been or are to be thrown away. **2** worthless or useless material or objects. **3** nonsense. — *verb colloq.* to criticize or dismiss as worthless. [from Middle English *rubbes*]

rubbishy *adj.* worthless, trashy.

rubble *noun* **1** broken stones, bricks, plaster, etc from ruined or demolished buildings. **2** small, rough stones used in building, especially as a filling between walls. [from Middle English *rubel*]

Rubbra, Edmund (1901–86) English composer and music critic, born in Northampton. His teachers included Gustav Holst, Ralph Vaughan Williams, and R O Morris, and he developed an interest in the polyphonic music of the 16c to 17c which is reflected in his 11 symphonies, chamber, choral and orchestral music, songs, and solo instrumental works.

rub-down *noun* an act of rubbing down, especially to clean or prepare a surface.

rubella *noun Medicine* a highly contagious viral disease characterized by a reddish-pink rash, similar to measles but milder, and swelling of the lymph glands. If the disease is contracted during the early stages of pregnancy it can cause abnormalities of the fetus, and most girls are now immunized against rubella before puberty. — Also called *German measles*. [from Latin *rubeus*, red]

Rubénisme a movement in French painting in the late 17c, which arose from a quarrel in the French Academy about the comparative impor-

tance of colour and design. The design party appealed to the example of Poussin (and were called Poussinistes); the colourists (who won) referred to Rubens (and were called Rubénistes).

Rubens, Sir (Peter Paul) (1577–1640) Flemish painter, born in Siegen, Westphalia. He went to Italy and entered the service of the Duke of Mantua. In 1605 he was sent to Spain as a diplomat, where he produced many portraits and works on historical subjects. He then travelled in Italy, producing work much influenced by the Italian Renaissance, and in 1608 settled in Antwerp where he became court painter to the Archduke Albert of Austria. His early works include the triptych *Descent from the Cross* (1611–14, Antwerp Cathedral). He became a prolific and renowned painter, and in 1622 was invited to France by Marie de' Medici, for whom he painted 21 large subjects on her life and regency (Louvre, Paris). His baroque style was bold and theatrical, with rich and glowing colours. In 1628 he was sent on a diplomatic mission to Philip IV of Spain, and there executed some 40 works. The following year he became envoy to Charles I of England, where his paintings included *Peace and War* (National Gallery, London). In 1630 he retired to Steen, where he engaged in landscape painting.

Rubicon *noun* a boundary which, once crossed, commits the person crossing it to an irrevocable course of action.
— **cross the Rubicon** to take an irrevocable decision.
[from Latin *Rubico*, a stream in N Italy separating Italy and the province of Cisalpine Gaul where Caesar was serving. Caesar's crossing of the stream with his army in 49 BC was tantamount to a declaration of war on the Roman republic, and began a civil war]

rubicund *adj., said especially of the face or complexion* red or rosy; ruddy. [from Latin *rubicundus*]

rubidium *noun Chem.* (SYMBOL **Rb**, ATOMIC NUMBER **37**) a silvery-white highly reactive metal, used in photoelectric cells. The naturally occurring radioactive isotope rubidium-87 is used to determine the age of rocks more than 10m years old. [from Latin *rubidus*, red, so called because of the two red lines in its spectrum]

Rubik's cube a cube-shaped puzzle consisting of 26 small cubes with faces coloured in any of six colours, fixed to a central spindle that allows them to be rotated on three axes, the solved puzzle presenting a uniform colour on each face. Millions of incorrect combinations are possible. [named after the Hungarian designer Ernö Rubik (1940–)]

Rubinstein, Anton (Grigoryevich) (1829–94) Russian pianist and composer, born in Vykhvatinets, Moldavia. He studied in Berlin and Vienna, and in 1848 settled in St Petersburg, where he taught music and helped to found the Conservatory. His compositions include operas, oratorios, piano concertos, and songs.

Rubinstein, Artur (1887–1982) US pianist, born in Łódź, Poland. At the age of 12 he appeared in Berlin, and after studying with Paderewski he began his career as a virtuoso, appearing in Paris, London, and the USA (1905–6). After World War II he lived in the USA and made frequent extensive concert tours.

ruble see ROUBLE.

rubric *noun* **1** a heading in a book or manuscript, especially one written or underlined in red. **2** an authoritative rule, especially one for the conduct of divine service added in red to the liturgy. [from Latin *rubrica*, red ochre]

Ruby a female first name, after the gemstone.

ruby — *noun* (PL. **rubies**) **1** *Geol.* a transparent red impure variety of the mineral corundum, containing traces of chromium. It is a valuable gemstone, and synthetic rubies are used in lasers, and as bearings in watches and other precision

intruments. **2** the rich, deep red colour characteristic of this colour. — *adj.* of this colour. [from Latin *rubinus lapis*, red stone]

ruby wedding a fortieth wedding anniversary.

RUC *abbrev.* Royal Ulster Constabulary.

ruche *noun* a pleated or gathered frill of lace, ribbon, etc used as a trimming. [from French *ruche*, beehive]

ruched *adj.* trimmed with ruches.

ruck¹ *noun* **1** a heap or mass of indistinguishable people or things. **2** *Rugby* a loose scrum that forms around a ball on the ground. [from Middle English *ruke*]

ruck² — *noun* a wrinkle or crease. — *verb trans., intrans.* (also **ruck up**) to wrinkle or crease. [from Norse *hrukka*]

rucksack *noun* a bag carried on the back by means of straps over the shoulders, used especially by climbers and walkers. [from German *Rücken*, back + *Sack*, bag]

ruction *noun* **1** a noisy disturbance; uproar. **2** (**ructions**) a noisy and usually unpleasant or violent argument.

rudd *noun* a freshwater fish, widespread in European rivers and lakes, greenish-brown in colour on the back, with yellow sides and reddish fins. It feeds on invertebrates and some plant material, and is a popular fish with anglers. [probably from Anglo-Saxon *rudu*, redness]

rudder *noun* **1** a flat piece of wood, metal, etc fixed vertically to a ship's stern for steering. **2** a movable aerofoil attached to the fin of an aircraft which helps control its movement along a horizontal plane. [from Anglo-Saxon *rothor*]

rudderless *adj.* **1** without a rudder. **2** aimless.

ruddy *adj.* (**ruddier, ruddiest**) **1** *said of the face, complexion, etc* having a healthy, glowing, rosy or pink colour. **2** red; reddish. [from Anglo-Saxon *rudig*]

rude *adj.* **1** impolite; showing bad manners; discourteous. **2** roughly made; lacking refinement or polish: *build a rude shelter*. **3** ignorant, uneducated or primitive: *rude chaos*. **4** sudden and unpleasant: *a rude awakening*. **5** vigorous; robust: *rude health*. **6** vulgar; indecent. [from Latin *rudis*, unwrought, rough]

rudely *adv.* in a rude way.

rudeness *noun* **1** being rude. **2** rude language or behaviour.

rudiment *noun* **1** (*usually* **rudiments**) a first or fundamental fact, rule or skill: *the rudiments of cooking*. **2** (*usually* **rudiments**) anything in an early and incomplete stage of development. **3** *Biol.* an organ or part which does not develop fully, usually because it no longer has a function, such as the breast in male mammals. [from Latin *rudimentum*]

rudimentary *adj.* **1** basic; fundamental. **2** primitive or undeveloped; only partially developed because now useless.

Rudolf a male first name. [of Germanic origin, from *hrod*, fame + *wulf*, wolf]

Rudolf I (1218–91) German King (1273–91), the founder of the Habsburg sovereign and imperial dynasty, born in Schloss Limburg, Breisgau. He increased his possessions by inheritance and marriage until he was the most powerful prince in Swabia. Chosen king by the electors, he was recognized by the pope in 1274.

Rudolf II (1552–1612) Holy Roman Emperor (1576–1612), born in Vienna, the eldest son of Maximilian II. He became King of Hungary (1572), and King of Bohemia and King of the Romans (or German King) in 1575. A mentally unstable and incompetent ruler, he was faced with revolts, and Hungary, Bohemia, Austria, and Moravia were taken from him by his brother, Matthias.

Rudolf, Lake see TURKANA, LAKE.

rue¹ *verb* (**rued, ruing, rueing**) to regret; to wish that (something) had not happened. [from Anglo-Saxon *hreowan*]

rue² *noun* a strongly scented evergreen plant with bitter leaves which were formerly used in medicine, taken as a symbol of repentance. [from Greek *rhyte*; the symbol of repentance is in allusion to RUE¹]

rueful *adj.* regretful or sorrowful, either genuinely so or not.

ruefully *adv.* with a rueful manner.

ruefulness *noun* being rueful.

ruff¹ *noun* **1** a circular pleated or frilled linen collar worn round the neck in the late 16c and early 17c, or in modern times by some choirs. **2** a fringe or frill of feathers or hair growing on a bird's or animal's neck. [perhaps from RUFFLE]

ruff² — *verb trans., intrans.* to trump at cards. — *noun* an act of trumping at cards. [from the name of a card game, French *roufle*]

ruff³ *noun* **1** a bird of the sandpiper family, the male of which grows a large ruff of feathers during the breeding season. **2** the male of this species; the female is called a *reeve*. [perhaps from RUFF¹]

ruffian *noun* a violent, brutal and lawless person. [from Old French *ruffian*]

ruffianly *adj.* **1** having the appearance, character, or manner of a ruffian. **2** characteristic or typical of a ruffian.

ruffle — *verb* **1** to make wrinkled or uneven; to spoil the smoothness of. **2** *trans., intrans.* to make or become irritated, annoyed or discomposed. **3** *said of a bird* to erect (its feathers), usually in anger or display. **4** to gather lace, linen, etc into a ruff or ruffle. — *noun* **1** a frill of lace, linen, etc worn either round one's neck or round one's wrists. **2** any ruffling or disturbance of the evenness and smoothness of a surface or of the peace, a person's temper, etc. **3** the feathers round a bird's neck which are ruffled in anger or display. [from Middle English *ruffelen*]

rufous *adj., said especially of a bird or animal* reddish or brownish-red in colour. [from Latin *rufus*, red, reddish]

Rufus a male first name. [from Latin *rufus*, red-haired]

rug *noun* **1** a thick heavy mat or small carpet for covering a floor. **2** a thick blanket or wrap, especially used when travelling or for horses. **3** *North Amer. slang* a toupee or hairpiece.
— **pull the rug from under someone** to leave them without defence, support, etc, especially by some sudden discovery, action, or argument. [from Norse *rogg*, wool]

Rugby POP (1992e) 87 000, a town in Rugby district, Warwickshire, central England. It lies on the R Avon, 17km/10mi E of Coventry. It is known for its famous boys' public school (1567) where, by tradition, the game of rugby football originated.

Rugby POP (1980) 3 000, a city in Pierce County, North Dakota, USA. It is the geographical centre of N America.

Rugby *noun* (*also* **rugby**; *in full* **Rugby** *or* **rugby football**) a form of football played with an oval ball which players may pick up and run with and may pass from hand to hand. [from *Rugby*, the public school in Warwickshire where the game was first played]
◇ The object of the game is to place the ball on the ground in the scoring area behind the opposing team's goal line. The ball cannot be passed forwards during play. The Rugby Football Union was formed in 1871, and a number of northern teams formed the breakaway Northern Union in 1895, which came to be known as the Rugby League. Today, Union is regarded as the amateur game, and League as the professional game. There are few differences between the two

codes, but Union has 15 players per side, League has 13 players per side, and there are variations in the numbers of points scored for penalties and dropped goals.

Rugby League (*also* **rugby league**) a partly professional form of Rugby, played with teams of 13 players.

Rugby Union (*also* **rugby union**) an amateur form of Rugby, played with teams of 15 players.

Rugby World Cup the major international competition in rugby union, held between 16 invited countries. It was first held in 1987, when it was won by New Zealand.

rugged *adj.* **1** *said of hills, ground, etc* having a rough, uneven surface; steep and rocky. **2** *said of the face* having features that are strongly marked, irregular and furrowed and which suggest physical strength. **3** *said especially of a person's character* stern, austere, and unbending. **4** involving physical hardships: *a rugged life.* **5** *said of machinery, equipment, etc* strongly or sturdily built to withstand vigorous use. [from Middle English]

ruggedly *adv.* in a rugged way.

ruggedness *noun* being rugged.

rugger *noun Brit. colloq.* Rugby (Union).

Ruhr, River a river in Germany, length 213km/132mi. Rising N of Winterberg in W central Germany, it flows W to the R Rhine at Duisburg. The Ruhr Valley is an important mining and industrial area; it includes the cities of Essen, Bochum, Duisburg, Gelsenkirchen, and Dortmund. The navigable length of the Ruhr is 41km/25mi.

ruin — *noun* **1** a broken, destroyed, decayed, or collapsed state. **2** something which has been broken, destroyed, or caused to decay or collapse, especially (**ruins**) a building. **3** a complete loss of wealth, social position, power, etc. **4** a person, company, etc that has lost all of his, her, or its wealth, social position, power, etc. **5** a cause of a complete loss of wealth, social position, etc, or of physical destruction, decay, etc. — *verb* (**ruined, ruining**) **1** to cause ruin to; to destroy. **2** to spoil (eg a child by treating him or her too indulgently).
— **in ruins** *said of buildings, or schemes, plans, etc* in a ruined state; completely wrecked or destroyed. [from Latin *ruina*, from *ruere*, to tumble down]

ruination *noun* the act of ruining or state of being ruined.

ruinous *adj.* **1** likely to cause ruin: *ruinous prices.* **2** ruined; decayed; destroyed.

ruinously *adv.* in a ruinous way; to a ruinous degree.

Ruisdael *or* **Ruysdael, Jacob van** (c.1628–82) Dutch landscape painter, born in Haarlem. He became a member of the Haarlem

painters' guild in 1648, moved to Amsterdam (c.1657), then travelled in Holland and Germany. He painted country landscapes and seascapes, notable for their cloud effects. His works include *The Jewish Cemetery* and *The Windmill at Wijk* (c.1665, Rijksmuseum, Amsterdam).

Ruiz, Nevado del an active Andean volcanic peak in W central Colombia. HEIGHT 5 399m. It is situated in the Cordillera Central, 32km/20mi SE of Manizales. Thermal springs are located at the NW foot. The volcano erupted in 1985, causing a flood and mudslide, resulting in the loss of many lives.

rule — *noun* **1** a principle, regulation, order or direction which governs or controls some action, function, form, use, etc. **2** government or control, or the period during which government or control is exercised. **3** a general principle, standard, guideline or custom: *make it a rule always to be punctual.* **4** the laws and customs which form the basis of a monastic or religious order and are followed by all members of that order: *the Benedictine rule.* **5** a strip of wood, metal or plastic with a straight edge marked off in units, used for measuring. **6** *Printing* a thin straight line or dash. **7** an order made by a court and judge which applies to a particular case only. — *verb* **1** *trans., intrans.* to govern; to exercise authority (over). **2** to keep control of or restrain. **3** to make an authoritative and usually official or judicial decision. **4** *intrans.* to be common or prevalent: *anarchy ruled after the war.* **5** to draw (a straight line). **6** to draw a straight line or a series of parallel lines on (eg paper).
— **as a rule** usually.

rule something off to draw a line in order to separate.

rule something out 1 to leave it out or not consider it. **2** to make it no longer possible; to preclude it.
[from Latin *regula*, straight stick]

rule of thumb a method of doing something, based on experience rather than theory or careful calculation.

ruler *noun* **1** a person, eg a sovereign, who rules or governs. **2** a strip of wood, metal or plastic with straight edges which is marked off in units (usually inches or centimetres), and is used for drawing straight lines and measuring.

ruling — *noun* an official or authoritative decision. — *adj.* **1** governing; controlling. **2** most important or strongest; predominant.

rum¹ *noun* a spirit distilled from sugar cane.

rum² *adj.* (**rummer, rummest**) *Brit. colloq.* strange; odd; queer; bizarre.

Rumanian same as ROMANIAN.

rumba *noun* **1** an originally Cuban dance, popular as a ballroom dance, with pronounced hip movements produced by transferring the weight

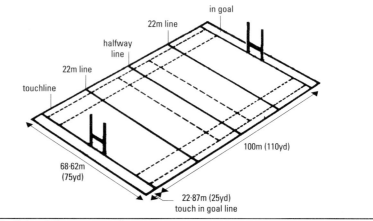

Rugby Union pitch

from one foot to the other. **2** music for the dance, with a stressed second beat. [from American Spanish *rumba*]

rum baba see BABA.

rumble — *verb* **1** *intrans.* to make a deep, low, grumbling sound. **2** *intrans.* (*usually* **rumble along**, **by**, **past**, *etc*) to move making a rumbling noise. **3** to say or utter with a rumbling voice or sound. **4** *Brit. slang* to find out about (someone or something). — *noun* **1** a deep low grumbling sound. **2** *North Amer. slang* a street fight, especially one between gangs. [from Middle English *romblen*]

rumbling *adj.* making a rumble.

rumbustious *adj. Brit. colloq.* noisy and cheerful; boisterous. [probably from ROBUST]

rumen *noun* (PL. **rumina**) *Zool.* the first chamber of the complex stomach of a ruminant animal, such as a cow or sheep, in which food is temporarily stored before being regurgitated. See also RUMINANT. [from Latin *rumen*, gullet]

Rumford, Benjamin Thompson, Count (1753–1814) English–US administrator and scientist, born in Woburn, Massachusetts. He joined the army, but fled to England in 1776, possibly due to political suspicion. In 1784 he entered the service of Bavaria, where he carried out military, social, and economic reforms. Always an enthusiastic amateur scientist, he first showed the relation between heat and work, a concept fundamental to modern physics. In 1799 he returned to London and founded the Royal Institution; he spent the last years of his life in France.

ruminant — *noun* a herbivorous mammal that chews the cud and has a complex stomach with four chambers, eg cattle, sheep, goats. The first chamber is the *rumen*, where food is temporarily stored while bacteria break down the cellulose in plant material. The partially digested food is then regurgitated and chewed in the mouth before finally being swallowed and digested. — *adj.* **1** of or belonging to this group of mammals. **2** meditating or contemplating. [from Latin *ruminari*, to chew the cud]

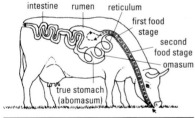

intestine   rumen   reticulum
first food stage
second food stage
omasum
true stomach (abomasum)

ruminant

ruminate *verb intrans.* **1** *said of a ruminant* to chew the cud. **2** to think deeply about something. [from Latin *ruminari*, to chew the cud]

rumination *noun* in ruminant animals, the act of regurgitating partially digested food from the rumen (first stomach chamber) to the mouth, where it is chewed to a pulp and then swallowed.

ruminative *adj.* meditative, contemplative.

rummage — *verb* **1** *intrans.* to search for something by turning things out or over untidily. **2** to search thoroughly or turn things over untidily in: *rummage one's drawers.* — *noun* **1** a thorough search. **2** things found by rummaging, especially *North Amer.* jumble. [from Old French *arrumage*, stowing of cargo on a ship]

rummy *noun* a card game in which each player tries to collect sets or sequences of three or more cards.

rumour — *noun* **1** an item of news or information which is passed from person to person and

which may or may not be true. **2** general talk or gossip; hearsay. — *verb* (*usually* **be rumoured**) to report or spread by rumour: *it is rumoured that she is going to have a baby.* [from Latin *rumor*, noise]

rump *noun* **1** the rear part of an animal's or bird's body; a person's buttocks. **2** (*in full* **rump steak**) a cut of beef from the rump. **3** *usually derog.* a small or inferior remnant. [from Middle English *rumpe*]

rumple — *verb trans.*, *intrans.* to make or become untidy, creased or wrinkled. — *noun* a wrinkle or crease. [from Dutch *rompel*, wrinkle]

rumpled *adj.* **1** crumpled. **2** dishevelled.

Rump Parliament the members of the British Long Parliament who were left after Pride's Purge of 96 conservative and moderate Presbyterian members (Dec 1648). It numbered about 60, and had grown to 125 by 1652. It abolished the monarchy and the House of Lords, but after a quarrel with the army, Oliver Cromwell dismissed it (Apr 1653). Recalled in 1659 with the fall of the Protectorate, it dissolved itself in 1660.

rumpus *noun* a noisy disturbance, brawl or uproar.

rumpy-pumpy *noun slang* sexual intercourse.

Rum Rebellion an uprising in Sydney which deposed the governor of New South Wales, Capt William Bligh, in 1808. It was provoked by Bligh's attempt to end the use of rum as a currency.

run — *verb* (**running**; PAST TENSE **ran**; PAST PARTICIPLE **run**) **1** *intrans. said of a person or animal* to move on foot in such a way that both or all feet are off the ground together for an instant during each step. **2** to cover or perform by, or as if by, running: *run a mile / run errands.* **3** *intrans.* to move quickly and easily on, or as if on, wheels. **4** *intrans.* to flee. **5** *trans.*, *intrans.* to move or cause to move in a specified way or direction or with a specified result: *run the car up the ramp / let the dog run free / run him out of town.* **6** *intrans. said of water, etc* to flow: *rivers running to the sea.* **7** to cause or allow (liquid) to flow: *run cold water into the bath.* **8** *trans.*, *intrans. said of a tap, container, etc* to give out or cause it to give out liquid: *run the tap / leave the tap running.* **9** to fill (a bath) with water: *run a hot bath.* **10** *intrans.* to come into a specified condition by, or as if by, flowing or running: *run dry / run short of time / her blood ran cold.* **11** to be full of or flow with. **12** *trans.*, *intrans.* to operate or work. **13** to organize or manage. **14** *intrans.* (**run over**, **round**, **up**, *etc*) to make a brief or casual visit: *run up to town for the afternoon.* **15** *intrans.*, *trans.* to travel or cause to travel on a regular route: *a train running between Paris and Nice / run an extra train.* **16** *intrans.*, *trans.* to continue or cause to continue or extend in a specified direction, for a specified time or distance, or over a specified range: *a road running south / colours running from pink to deep red / the play ran for ten years.* **17** *intrans.* to continue to have legal force: *a lease with a year still to run.* **18** to drive (someone) in a vehicle, usually to a specified place. **19** (**run** *or* **run something along**, **over**, **through**, *etc*) to move or cause it to move or pass quickly, lightly, or freely: *run your eyes over the report / excitement ran through the audience.* **20** *intrans.* to race or finish a race in a specified position. **21** *intrans. chiefly North Amer.* to stand as a candidate: *is running for governor.* **22** to enter (a contestant) in a race or as a candidate for office. **23** *intrans.* to spread, dissolve, or circulate quickly: *the colour in his shirt ran / the rumour ran through the office.* **24** *intrans.* to be worded: *the report runs as follows.* **25** to be affected by or subjected to, or likely to be affected by: *run a high temperature / run risks.* **26** *intrans.* to develop relatively quickly in a specified direction; to tend (towards): *run to fat.* **27** *intrans.* to have as or be an inherent or recurring part of: *blue eyes run in the family.* **28** to own, drive, and maintain (a car). **29** to publish: *run the story in the magazine.* **30** *trans.*, *intrans.* to accumulate or allow to accumulate: *run up debts at the bank.* **31** *intrans. said of*

stitches to become undone or (of a garment, eg hosiery) to have stitches come undone and form a ladder. **32** to graze (cattle): *run cattle in the valley.* **33** to hunt or track down. **34** to get past or through: *run a blockade.* **35** to smuggle: *run guns.* **36** *intrans. said of fish* to migrate upstream, especially to spawn. **37** to score (a run) by, or as if by, running. — *noun* **1** an act of running. **2** the distance covered or time taken up by an act of running. **3** a rapid running movement: *break into a run.* **4** a trip in a vehicle, especially one taken for pleasure. **5** a continuous and unbroken period or series of something: *a run of bad luck / the play had a run of six weeks.* **6** freedom to move about or come and go as one pleases: *have the run of the house.* **7** a high or urgent demand (for a currency, money, etc). **8** a route which is regularly travelled: *a coach on the London to Glasgow run.* **9** a row of unravelled stitches, especially in hosiery; a ladder. **10** the average type or class: *the usual run of new students.* **11** (**the runs**) *colloq.* diarrhoea. **12** a number produced in a single period of production: *a print run.* **13** three or more playing cards for a series or sequence. **14** an inclined course, especially one covered with snow used for skiing. **15** a point scored in cricket either by a batter running from one wicket to the other or in any of certain other ways. **16** a unit of scoring in baseball made by the batter successfully completing a circuit of four bases. **17** (*often in compounds*) an enclosure or pen for domestic fowls or animals: *a chicken-run.* **18** a shoal of migrating fish. **19** a track used regularly by wild animals.

— **on the run** fleeing, especially from the police.

run across someone to meet them unexpectedly.

run after someone *or* **something** to chase them.

run along *colloq.* (*usually as an exclamation*) to go away.

run away to escape or flee.

run away with someone 1 to elope with them. **2** *said of a horse* to gallop off uncontrollably with someone on its back.

run away with something 1 to steal it. **2** *said of a person* to be over-enthusiastic about or carried away by an idea, etc. **3** to win a competition, etc comfortably. **4** to use it up rapidly.

run down *said of a clock, battery, etc* to cease to work because of a gradual loss of power.

run someone down *said of a vehicle or its driver* to knock someone to the ground.

run something down to allow something (eg an operation or business) to be gradually reduced or closed.

run someone *or* **something down 1** to speak badly of them, usually without good reason. **2** to chase or search for them until they are found or captured.

be run down *said of a person* to be weak and exhausted, usually through overwork or a lack of proper food.

run for it *colloq.* to try to escape.

run high *said of feelings* to be very strong.

run something in to run a new car or engine gently to prevent damage to the engine.

run someone in *colloq.* **1** to arrest them. **2** to give them a lift in a car, etc for a short distance, especially to a regular destination.

run into someone *colloq.* to meet them unexpectedly.

run into someone *or* **something** to collide with them.

run into something 1 to suffer from or be beset by a problem, difficulty, etc: *our plans quickly ran into problems.* **2** to reach as far as; to extend into: *his debts run into hundreds.*

run off 1 to leave quickly; to run away. **2** *said of a liquid* to be drained.

run something off 1 to produce it (especially printed material) quickly or promptly. **2** to drain a liquid. **3** to decide a tied contest with a further round.

run off with something 1 to steal it. **2** to win a competition, etc comfortably.

run off with someone to elope with them.

run on 1 to talk at length or incessantly. **2** *Printing* to continue or be continued in the same line without starting a new paragraph.

run out *said of a supply* to come to an end; to be used up.

run out of something to use up a supply of it: *run out of money.*

run someone out 1 *Cricket* to put out a batter running towards a wicket by hitting that wicket with the ball. **2** *chiefly North Amer. colloq.* to force them to leave: *run them out of town.*

run out on someone *colloq.* to abandon or desert them.

run over 1 to overflow; to go beyond a limit. **2** to make a quick brief visit.

run over *or* **through something 1** to repeat or glance over quickly, especially for practice. **2** to read or perform it quickly, especially for practice or as a rehearsal.

run someone over *said of a vehicle or driver* to knock them down and injure or kill them.

run through something to use up money, resources, etc quickly and recklessly.

run someone through to pierce them with a sword or similar weapon.

run to something 1 to have enough money for it: *we can't run to a holiday this year.* **2** *said of money, resources, etc* to be sufficient for particular needs.

run something up 1 to make a piece of clothing quickly or promptly. **2** to amass or accumulate bills, debts, etc. **3** to hoist a flag.

run up against someone *or* **something** to be faced with a challenging opponent or difficulty. [from Anglo-Saxon *rinnan*]

runabout *noun* a small light car, boat, or aircraft.

runaway — *noun* a person or animal that has run away or fled. — *adj.* **1** that is running away or out of control. **2** *said of a race, victory, etc* easily and convincingly won. **3** done or managed as a result of running away.

Runcie, Robert (Alexander Kennedy) Runcie, Baron (1921–) English Anglican prelate and Archbishop of Canterbury. He served in the Scots Guards during World War II, was ordained in 1951, and was Bishop of St Albans for 10 years before being consecrated Archbishop (1980–91). His career was marked by a papal visit to Canterbury, the war with Argentina when he stressed reconciliation rather than triumphalism in victory, the ongoing controversies over homosexuality and women in the Church, and his envoy Terry Waite's captivity in Beirut (1987–91).

Runcorn POP (1981) 64 000, an industrial town in Halton district, Cheshire, NW central England. It lies on the S bank of the R Mersey and the Manchester Ship Canal, 3km/2mi S of Widnes. In 1964 it was designated a 'new town'.

run-down — *adj.* **1** *said of a person* tired or exhausted; in weakened health. **2** *said of a building* shabby; dilapidated. — *noun* **1** a gradual reduction in numbers, size, etc. **2** a brief statement of the main points or items; a summary.

rune *noun* any of the letters of an early alphabet used by the Germanic peoples between about AD 200 and AD 600, used especially in carvings. **2** a mystical symbol or inscription. [from Norse *run*, secret]
◇ The runic alphabet, known as the *futhark*, was made up of 24 basic symbols, although there was considerable regional variation in the overall number of symbols and symbol shapes used. Around 4 000 runic inscriptions and a few manuscripts survive, principally made by the early Scandinavians and Anglo-Saxons.

rung¹ *noun* **1** a step on a ladder. **2** a crosspiece on a chair. [from Anglo-Saxon *hrung*]

rung² see RING².

runic *adj.* **1** written in or inscribed with runes. **2** in the style of ancient interlaced ornamentation.

run-in *noun colloq.* a quarrel or argument.

runnel *noun* a small stream. [from Anglo-Saxon *rynel*]

runner *noun* **1** a person or thing that runs. **2** a messenger. **3** a groove or strip along which a drawer, sliding door, etc slides. **4** either of the strips of metal or wood running the length of a sledge, on which it moves. **5** a blade on an ice skate. **6** *Bot.* in certain plants, eg strawberry, creeping buttercup, a long stem that grows horizontally along the surface of the ground, putting down roots from nodes along its length, or from a terminal bud at the end of the stem. At each of these sites a new plant develops and eventually becomes detached from the parent plant. **7** a long narrow strip of cloth or carpet used to decorate or cover a table, dresser, floor, etc. **8** a runner bean. **9** a smuggler.
— **do a runner** *slang* to leave a place hastily; to escape.

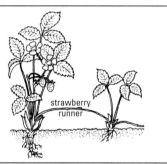
strawberry runner

runner bean a climbing plant which produces bright red flowers and long, green, edible beans.

runner-up *noun* (PL. **runners-up**) a competitor who finishes in second place.

running — *noun* **1** the act of moving quickly. **2** the act of managing, organizing or operating. — *adj.* **1** of or for running. **2** done or performed while running, working, etc: *running repairs / a running jump.* **3** continuous. **4** consecutive: *two days running.* **5** flowing. **6** giving out pus.
— **in** *or* **out of the running** having, or not having, a chance of success.

running-board *noun* a footboard along the side of a vehicle.

running head a title occurring at the top of every page in a book.

running knot a knot that changes the size of a noose as it is pulled.

running mate *North Amer.* a candidate standing for election to a post of secondary importance when considered as the partner of the candidate for a more important post; especially the candidate for the post of vice-president of the USA.

runny *adj.* (**runnier, runniest**) **1** tending to run or flow with liquid. **2** liquid; watery.

Runnymede a meadow on the S bank of the R Thames, Surrey, SE England. It lies 7km/4mi SE of Windsor, near Egham. Here, or on Magna Carta I in the river, King John signed the Magna Carta in 1215. Runnymede has been owned by

ᚠ	f	ᚷ	g	ᛁ	ï	ᛗ	e
ᚢ	u	ᚹ	w	ᛈ	p	ᛗ	m
ᚦ	þ	ᚻ	h	ᛉ	x	ᛚ	l
ᚩ	o	ᚾ	n	ᛋ	s	ᛝ	ng
ᚱ	r	ᛁ	i	ᛏ	t	ᛟ	œ
ᚲ	k	ᛃ	j	ᛒ	b	ᛞ	d

runic alphabet

the National Trust since 1931. NOTABLE FEATURES Commonwealth Air Forces War Memorial (1953); Kennedy Memorial.

run-off *noun* **1** rainwater that moves over the ground and flows into surface streams and rivers under conditions of heavy rainfall, when the ground is saturated with water. **2** an extra race, contest, etc, between two people or teams who have tied, to decide the winner.

run-of-the-mill *adj.* ordinary; not special.

runt *noun* **1** the smallest animal in a litter. **2** an undersized and weak person.

run-through *noun* **1** a practice or rehearsal. **2** a summary.

run time the time needed to run a computer program completely.

run-up *noun* an approach or period of preparation (eg for some event).

runway *noun* a wide, hard surface from which aircraft take off and on which they land.

Runyon, (Alfred) Damon (1884–1946) US writer, born in Manhattan, Kansas. After service in the Spanish–American War (1898), he became a journalist, then turned to writing poetry. He is best known for his short stories about underworld New York life, including the collection *Guys and Dolls* (1932), which was adapted for a stage musical (1950).

rupee *noun* the standard unit of currency in India, Pakistan, Bhutan, Nepal, Sri Lanka, Mauritius, and the Seychelles. [from Sanskrit *rupya*, wrought silver]

Rupert, Prince, also called **Rupert of the Rhine** (1619–82) English soldier, born in Prague, the third son of the Elector Palatine Frederick V and Elizabeth, daughter of James I of England. A cavalry officer, he was a Royalist commander in the English Civil War and won several victories, but was defeated at Marston Moor (1644), and after his surrender of Bristol, was dismissed by Charles I. Banished by Parliament, he led the small Royalist fleet until it was routed by Robert Blake (1650). He escaped to the West Indies, but returned to Europe in 1653, and lived there until the Restoration.

Rupert a male first name. [a variant of ROBERT]

rupture — *noun* **1** the act of breaking or bursting or state of being broken or burst. **2** a breach of harmony or friendly relations. **3** a hernia. — *verb trans., intrans.* **1** to break, tear, or burst. **2** to suffer or cause to suffer a breach of harmony or friendly relations. **3** to cause (someone or oneself) to suffer, or to be affected by, a hernia. [from Latin *rumpere*, to break]

rural *adj.* of the countryside; pastoral or agricultural. [from Latin *ruralis*, from *rus*, country]

rural dean in the Church of England, a clergyman with responsibility over a group of parishes.

Rural Rides an anthology of essays by William Cobbett (1830). They present his eye-witness accounts, made while travelling on horseback, of the rural conditions in England.

Ruse *or* **Rousse 1** POP (1991e) 192 000, the capital of Ruse province, N Bulgaria. It lies on the R Danube, 327km/203mi NE of Sofia, and is a major commercial and manufacturing centre. **2** POP (1992e) 837 000, a province in N Bulgaria. AREA 2 595sq km/1 002sq mi. CAPITAL Ruse. It is a vine-growing and horticultural area.

ruse *noun* a clever trick or plan intended to deceive or trick. [from Old French *ruser*, to retreat]

rush¹ — **1** *trans., intrans.* to hurry or cause to hurry or go quickly. **2** to perform or deal with too quickly or hurriedly. **3** to attack suddenly. **4** (**rush something** *or* **rush at something**) to

approach it or carry it out hastily and impetuously: *rush at one's work*. **5** to force (someone) to act more quickly than he or she wants to. — *noun* **1** a sudden quick movement, especially forwards. **2** a sudden general movement, usually towards a single goal: *a gold rush*. **3** haste; hurry: *be in a dreadful rush*. **4** a period of great activity. **5** a sudden demand (for something). **6** *slang* a feeling of euphoria after taking a drug. — *adj.* done, or needing to be done, quickly.
— **rush one's fences** to act too hastily. [from Old French *ruser*, from Latin *recusare*, to push back]

rush² *noun Bot.* a densely tufted annual or evergreen perennial plant belonging to the genus *Luzula* or the genus *Juncus*, typically found in cold wet regions of the northern hemisphere, usually on moors or marshy ground. Its leaves may be flat and narrow or cylindrical and pointed, and it bears dense heads of brownish flowers, which are sometimes below the tip of the stem. Rushes are used in mats, chair seats, and basketwork. [from Anglo-Saxon *risc*]

Rush–Bagot Convention an agreement (1817) between the USA and Britain to demilitarize the Great Lakes by limiting the number, tonnage, and armament of ships on each side, negotiated by acting US Secretary of State Robert Rush, and British Minister to the USA Charles Bagot. The convention ended the threat of a Great Lakes arms race, but complete disarmament on the US/Canada border did not follow until decades later.

rush candle *or* **rush light** a candle or night-light with a wick of rush.

Rushdie, (Ahmad) Salman (1947–) Indian writer, born in Bombay of Muslim parents. He became widely known after the publication of his second novel, *Midnight's Children* (1981, Booker Prize; 1993, Booker of Bookers). *The Satanic Verses* (1988) caused worldwide controversy because of its treatment of Islam from a secular point of view, and in Feb 1989 he was forced to go into hiding because of the *fatwa* (death sentence) passed on him by Ayatollah Khomeini of Iran. He has continued to write, and more recent publications include *Haroun and the Sea of Stories* (1990).

rush hour a period at the beginning or end of the day when traffic is at its busiest because people are travelling to or from work.

Rushmore, Mount *or* **Mount Rushmore National Memorial** a mountain in W South Dakota, USA, situated in the Black Hills, SW of Rapid City. HEIGHT 1 943m. A national memorial, it is famous for the gigantic sculptures of four past US presidents (Washington, Jefferson, Roosevelt, and Lincoln). Each head is 18m high. The memorial was constructed between 1927 and 1941 under the direction of Gutzon Borglum.

rushy *adj.* full of rushes.

Rusk, (David) Dean (1909–) US politician, born in Cherokee Co, Georgia. He was Professor of Government at Mills College, California (1934), and after service in World War II held several government posts. As Secretary of State under Kennedy and Johnson (1961–9), he played a major role in the Cuban crisis of 1962.

rusk *noun* a slice of bread which has been rebaked, or a hard dry biscuit resembling this, given as a food to babies. [from Spanish or Portuguese *rosca*, twist of bread]

Ruska, Ernst August Friedrich (1906–88) German electrical engineer, born in Heidelberg. He worked in Munich and Berlin, and following the discovery that electron beams can behave like waves, he developed the world's first electron microscope (1931). This allowed magnification of an unprecedented one million times.

He shared the 1986 Nobel Prize for Physics with Gerd Binnig and Heinrich Rohrer.

Ruskin, John (1819–1900) English writer and art critic, born in London. He championed Turner's painting in his first critical work, *Modern Painters* (1843–60). This book, along with *The Seven Lamps of Architecture* (1848) and *The Stones of Venice* (1851–3), established him as the major art and social critic of his day. He became the first Slade Professor of Fine Art at Oxford in 1870, and founded several educational institutions.

Russell, Bertrand (Arthur William), 3rd Earl (1872–1970) Welsh philosopher and mathematician, born in Trelleck, Monmouthshire. He became a lecturer at Cambridge in 1895, and published his *Principles of Mathematics* (1903), and collaborated with A N Whitehead in *Principia Mathematica* (1910–13). Ludwig Wittgenstein was his student in 1912 and 1913. In 1916 his outspoken pacifism lost him his lectureship, and in 1918 he was jailed for six months; he renounced his pacifism after the rise of Fascism and his fellowship at Trinity was restored in 1944. From the 1920s he lived by lecturing and journalism, and in 1927 started a progressive school with his second wife, Dora Black, near Petersfield. He visited the Soviet Union, and taught in China and the USA. His works include *The Problems of Philosophy* (1912, his first popular work), *On Education* (1926), *An Enquiry into Meaning and Truth* (1940), *History of Western Philosophy* (1945), and *Human Knowledge* (1948). He published many popular and provocative works on social, moral, and religious questions, some of his essays being collected in *Why I am not a Christian* (1927). After 1949 he became a champion of nuclear disarmament, and engaged in unprecedented correspondence with several world leaders. He was awarded the Nobel Prize for Literature in 1950. His last major publications were his three volumes of *Autobiography* (1967–9).

Russell, Henry Norris (1877–1957) US astronomer, born in Pyster Bay, New York. Professor at Princeton and director of the university observatory there, he is best known for formulating the Hertzsprung–Russell diagram (1913), correlating the types of spectrum of stars with their luminosity, which became of fundamental importance for the theory of stellar evolution.

Russell, Jack (John) (1795–1883) British 'sporting parson', born in Dartmouth, Devon. He was curate of Swymbridge near Barnstaple (1832–80), and master of foxhounds. A breed of terrier found in the West Country was named after him.

Russell, Ken, in full **Henry Kenneth Alfred Russell** (1927–) English film director, born in Southampton. In 1955 he made some documentary shorts which earned him a freelance assignment with BBC Television, for whom he produced some musical biographies. He turned to feature films with *Women in Love* (1969), but continued with musically inspired themes in *The Music Lovers* (1971) and *Mahler* (1974). Other productions include *The Devils* (1971), *Savage Messiah* (1972), *Crimes of Passion* (1984), and *The Rainbow* (1989).

Russell, Lord William (1639–83) English Whig politician. He travelled in Europe, and at the Restoration became an MP. A supporter of Shaftesbury, and a leading member of the movement to exclude James II from the succession, he was arrested with others for participation in the Rye House Plot (1683), and beheaded in London.

Russell a male first name, after the surname. [from Old French *Rousel*, little red one]

Russell (of Kingston Russell), John Russell, 1st Earl (1792–1878) English Whig–Liberal statesman, born in London. He became an MP in 1813, and was Home Secretary (1835–9) and Secretary for War (1839–41), and became Prime Minister after the Conservative

Party split over the repeal of the Corn Laws (1846–52). In Lord Aberdeen's coalition of 1852 he was Foreign Secretary and leader in the Commons. Alleged incompetence during the Crimean War caused him to lose popularity and retire (1855), but he became Foreign Secretary again in Lord Palmerston's second administration (1859). On Palmerston's death (1865) he again became Prime Minister, but he resigned in 1866.

russet — *noun* **1** a reddish-brown colour. **2** a variety of apple with a reddish-brown skin. — *adj.* reddish-brown in colour. [from Latin *russus*, red]

Russia *or* **The Russian Federation**, Russian **Rossiiskaya Federatsiya** POP (1993e) 148.7m, a republic occupying much of E Europe and N Asia, and divided into 89 regions and republics. AREA 17 075 400sq km/6 591 104sq mi. It is bounded N by the Arctic Ocean; NW by Norway, Finland, Estonia, Latvia, Belorussia, and the Ukraine; W by the Black Sea, Georgia, and Azerbaijan; SW by the Caspian Sea and Kazakhstan; SE by China, Mongolia, and North Korea; E by the Sea of Okhotsk and the Bering Sea. CAPITAL Moscow. CHIEF TOWNS St Petersburg, Nizhniy Novgorod, Rostov-on-Don, Volgograd, Yekaterinburg, Novosibirsk, Chelyabinsk, Kazan, Samara, and Omsk. TIME ZONE GMT +2 to +12. The population is largely of Russian origin, with some Tatar and Ukrainian minorities; Christianity is the chief religion and there are large Muslim populations. OFFICIAL LANGUAGE Russian. CURRENCY the rouble. PHYSICAL DESCRIPTION vast plains dominate the W half; the Ural Mts separate the E European Plain in the W from the W Siberian Lowlands in the E; the Central Siberian Plateau lies E of the R Yenisei; further E lies the N Siberian Plain; the Caucasus, Tien Shan, and Pamir ranges lie along the S frontier; the Lena, Ob, Severnaya Dvina, Pechora, Yenisey, Indigirka, and Kolyma rivers flow to the Arctic Ocean; the Amur, Amgun, and rivers of the Kamchatka Peninsula flow to the Pacific Ocean; the Caspian Sea basin includes the Volga and Ural rivers; there are over 20 000 lakes, the largest being the Caspian Sea, L Taymyr, and L Baikal. CLIMATE there are several different climate regions; variable weather in the N and the centre, and winter temperatures are increasingly severe in the E and N; average temperature in Moscow is –9°C in Jan, and 18°C in Jul; average annual rainfall is 630mm; Siberia has a continental climate, with very cold and prolonged winters, and short, often warm summers. HISTORY Russia has been settled by many ethnic groups, initially by the nomadic Slavs, Turks, and Bulgars in the 3c–7c AD; the Byzantine Christian Church had been established by the end of the 10c; Moscow was established as a centre of political power in the N during the 14c; the Tatars were expelled under Russia's first Tsar, Ivan IV (the Terrible); internal disorder amongst a feudal nobility and constant warfare with border countries (eg Poland and Sweden) prevented Russian development until Tsar Peter I (the Great); under Catherine II (the Great) Russia became a great power, extending territory into S and E Asia; defeat in the Russo–Japanese War of 1904–05 precipitated a revolution which, although unsuccessful, brought Russia's first constitution and parliament; the 1917 Revolution ended the monarchy; within the communist Union of Soviet Republics (formed in 1920), Russia was the dominating political force, covering 75% of the Soviet area with 50% of its population; with the disbandment of the Union in 1991, Russia became an independent republic; assumed the Soviet Union's permanent seat on the UN Security Council; relations with some other former Soviet republics deteriorated in the early 1990s; process of transition to a market economy caused severe economic crisis; in 1993 followed by a referendum and increased Presidential powers. ECONOMY oil, natural gas, coal, peat, gold, copper, platinum, zinc, tin, lead; wheat, fruit, vegetables, tobacco, cotton,

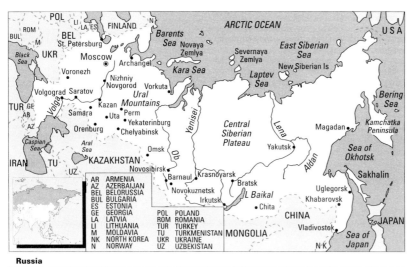

Russia

sugar beet; metallurgy; machines; ships; vehicles; chemicals; textiles; timber.

Russian — *noun* **1** a person born in or living in Russia or *loosely* the other former Soviet republics. **2** the Slavonic language spoken in Russia and the main official language of the former Soviet Union. — *adj.* of Russia or *loosely* the other former Soviet republics, their people, culture, or language.
◇ Russian is spoken by c.130–150 million people as a mother tongue in Russia and parts of the former USSR; and by a further 120–150 million people as a second language, and as the standard medium of communication in the former USSR. It is written in the Cyrillic alphabet.

Russian Civil War a war in Russia which followed the October 1917 Revolution. Anti-Bolshevik forces (whites) led by tsarist generals mounted a series of campaigns against the new Soviet regime, supported by Allied troops and the governments of Britain, France, the USA, and Japan. They were opposed by the Soviet Red Army, created by Trotsky, which successfully fought back between 1918 and 1922. There were five main theatres of war: the Caucasus and S Russia; the Ukraine; the Baltic provinces; the Far North; and Siberia. After the end of World War I the military justification for Allied intervention disappeared and the Allied governments eventually lost heart. The Red Army gradually defeated the counter-revolutionary forces on all fronts, and established Soviet military and political power throughout the whole of Russia and its borderlands, with the exception of Poland, Finland, and the Baltic states, which received their independence.

Russian Federation see RUSSIA.

Russian Orthodox Church a Church that originated from the missionary activity of the see of Constantinople of the Orthodox Church, with a community in Kiev in the 9c. In 988, Christianity was declared (by Vladimir I) the official faith of Russia; in the 14c, Moscow became the see of the metropolitan; and in the 15c, the Church declared itself autonomous. It existed in a state of tension with the emperor, and after the Revolution of 1917, was separated from the state and persecuted; however, it regained support from the authorities under Stalin (from 1943) and began to grow again.

Russian Revolution the revolution (1917) which overthrew the Russian imperialist regime and brought to power the first Communist government. Mass demonstrations of Revolutionary workers and soldiers in Petrograd led to the abdication of Nicholas II (Feb 1917). A period of 'dual power' followed, shared between a liberal-minded provisional government and the more

socialist Petrograd Soviet. Lenin's Bolsheviks refused to collaborate, and in October led an insurgency of armed workers, soldiers, and sailors, seized political power, and established the first Soviet government.

Russian roulette an act of daring, especially that in which one spins the cylinder of a revolver which is loaded with one bullet only, points the revolver at one's own head, and pulls the trigger.

Russian tea tea served with lemon instead of milk.

Russo- *combining form* of Russia or *loosely* the former Soviet republics: *a Russo-American treaty.*

Russo–Finnish War, also called the **Winter War** the war between the USSR and Finland during the winter of 1939–40. Soviet forces invaded Finland in order to secure Finnish territory from which to defend Leningrad against German attack. In spite of courageous resistance (though unsupported by eg Britain and France) and early Russian bungling, Finland capitulated (Mar 1940) and was forced to cede territory to the USSR.

Russo–Japanese War a war (1904–5) between an expanding Russian Empire and a modernizing Japan over rival territorial claims and imperial ambitions in N China. A series of military and naval disasters for Russia, it had little popular support and was marked by ineffectual command and political confusion. The war ended in Japanese victory with the Treaty of Portsmouth (1905).

Russo–Turkish Wars a series of wars (17c–19c) between an expanding Russian Empire and a decaying Ottoman Empire, principally for domination of the Black Sea and access to the Mediterranean. From the mid-18c they also involved national liberation struggles of the non-Turkish, Orthodox Christian peoples of the Balkans from Turkish, Islamic rule. The wars resulted in independence for many (eg Balkan) areas, and the absorption of others (eg N Black Sea coast and Caucasus) into the Russian Empire.

rust — *noun* **1** a reddish-brown coating that forms on the surface of iron or steel that has been exposed to air and moisture. It is caused by the oxidation of the metal by oxygen from the air to form hydrated iron oxides, and is a form of corrosion. **2** a similar coating which forms on other metals. **3** the colour of rust, usually a reddish-brown. **4** a parasitic fungus that causes a serious disease of cereals and other crops, characterized by the appearance of reddish-brown patches on the leaves and other surfaces of infected plants. It commonly refers to *Puccinia graminis*, which attacks wheat. **5** the disease caused by such a fungus, which may incur serious economic losses as it affects important cereal crops, such as

wheat. **6** a weakening or injurious influence or consequence, especially mental or physical laziness or inactivity. — *verb* **1** *trans., intrans.* to become or cause to become coated with rust. **2** *intrans.* to become weaker and inefficient, usually through lack of use. [from Anglo-Saxon]

rust belt an area with a concentration of declining heavy industries, such as steel production, especially that in the Midwestern and NE USA.

rustic — *adj.* **1** of or living in the country. **2** having the characteristics of country life or country people, especially in being simple and unsophisticated, or awkward and uncouth. **3** made of rough, untrimmed branches: *rustic furniture.* — *noun* a person from or living in the country, especially one who is thought of as being simple and unsophisticated. [from Latin *rusticus,* from *rus,* country]

rustically *adv.* in a rustic way.

rusticate *verb* **1** *trans., intrans.* to live, go to live or send to live in the country. **2** to suspend (a student) from college or university temporarily because of some wrongdoing. **3** to make rustic or rural. [from Latin *rusticari,* to live in the country]

rusticity *noun* being rustic.

rustily *adv.* in a rusty way or state.

rustiness *noun* a rusty state.

rustle — *verb* **1** *trans., intrans.* to make or cause to make a soft whispering sound as of dry leaves. **2** *intrans.* to move with such a sound. **3** *trans., intrans. esp. North Amer.* to steal (cattle or horses). — *noun* a quick succession of soft, dry, crisp, whisper-like sounds.
— **rustle something up** to arrange, gather together, or prepare quickly.
[from Middle English *rustlen*]

rustler *noun North Amer., esp. US* a person who steals cattle or horses.

rustproof *adj.* that will not rust or will prevent rust from forming.

rusty *adj.* (**rustier, rustiest**) **1** covered with or affected by rust. **2** *said of a skill, knowledge of a subject, etc* not as good as it used to be through lack of practice. **3** rust-coloured. **4** *said especially of black clothes* discoloured, often with a brownish sheen, through age.

rut¹ *noun* **1** a deep track or furrow in soft ground made by wheels. **2** an established and usually boring or dreary routine.

rut² — *noun* **1** in many male mammals, eg deer, a period of sexual excitement that occurs one or more times a year when they fight competitively for females and defend their territory prior to mating. **2** (*also* **rutting season**) the time of year when this occurs. — *verb intrans.* (**rutted, rutting**) *said of male animals* to be in a period of sexual excitement. [from Old French *rut,* roar]

Ruth, Babe, properly **George Herman Ruth** (1895–1948) US baseball star, born in Baltimore. He started his career as a pitcher with the Boston Red Sox in 1914, joined the New York Yankees in 1920, and hit a record 54 home runs in the season. He bettered the record to 60 in 1927, a figure which stood until 1961. In the 1926 World Series he became the first man to score three home runs in one game. When he retired in 1935 he had scored 714 home runs, a figure not bettered until 1974. The Yankee Stadium is affectionately known as 'The House Babe Ruth built' because of the increased income he brought to the club during his career.

Ruth **1** the wife of Boaz in the Book of Ruth. **2** a female first name. [origin obscure; it is often associated with English *ruth,* pity (see RUTHLESS), but this is not the origin]

Ruth, Book of a book of the Hebrew Bible and Old Testament, named after its central character, usually dated c.5c–4c BC. It tells of the marriage arranged by Ruth's mother, Naomi, of Ruth to Boaz, the rich kinsman of Naomi's deceased husband. It is a story significant for its liberal attitudes to non-Israelites and mixed marriages, since Ruth was a Moabite. She became the mother of Obed, grandfather of David.

ruthenium *noun Chem.* (SYMBOL **Ru**, ATOMIC NUMBER **44**) a silvery-white brittle metallic element that occurs in small amounts in some platinum ores. It has a high melting point, and is used to increase the hardness of platinum alloys. [from Latin *Ruthenia*, Russia, so called because it was discovered in ore from the Urals]

Rutherford, Dame Margaret (1892–1972) English theatre and film actress, born in London. She made her stage début in 1925 at the Old Vic theatre, and gained fame as a character actress and comedienne. Her gallery of eccentrics included 'Miss Prism' in *The Importance of Being Earnest* (stage 1939, film 1952), 'Miss Whitchurch' in *The Happiest Days of Your Life* (stage 1948, film 1950), and Agatha Christie's 'Miss Marple' in a series of films from 1962. She won an Oscar for her role in *The VIPs* (1964).

rutherfordium *noun Chem.* (SYMBOL **Rf**, ATOMIC NUMBER **104**) the name proposed in the USA for an unstable radioactive metal that is manufactured artificially by bombarding an actinide with carbon, oxygen, or neon atoms. [named after Ernest Rutherford]

Rutherford (of Nelson), Ernest Rutherford, 1st Baron (1871–1937) New Zealand-born British physicist, born near Nelson. Professor in Montreal, Manchester, and Cambridge, he discovered the three types of uranium radiations (alpha, beta, and gamma rays), and proposed with Frederick Soddy that radioactivity results from the disintegration of atoms (1903). He went on to develop a model of the atom and also predicted the existence of the as-yet-undiscovered neutron (1920). He was awarded the 1908 Nobel Prize for Chemistry.

ruthless *adj.* without pity. [from Middle English *ruthe*, pity + -LESS]

ruthlessly *adv.* in a ruthless way.

ruthlessness *noun* being ruthless.

Ruthwell Cross a runic stone cross at Ruthwell, near Dumfries, Scotland, dating from the 7c and standing 5m high. It is carved with scenes from the New Testament, and verses in the runic alphabet from the the Anglo-Saxon poem *The Dream of the Rood.*

rutile *noun Geol.* a reddish-brown or black lustrous mineral form of titanium oxide (TiO_2), commonly found in igneous and metamorphic rocks, and in beach sand. It is an important ore of titanium, and is also used as a brilliant white pigment in paper, paint, and plastics. [from Latin *rutilus*, reddish]

Rutland a former county in the UK, the smallest in England. It was incorporated into Leicestershire in 1974.

rutted *adj.* marked with ruts.

Ruysdael, Jacob van see RUISDAEL, JACOB VAN.

Ruyter, Michiel Adriaanzoon de (1607–76) Dutch admiral, born in Vlissingen. He gave distinguished service in the three Anglo-Dutch Wars (1652–4, 1665–7, 1672–8), which included victories in the Four Days' battle off Dunkirk (1666) and a daring raid up the Rivers Medway and Thames (1667), when much of the English fleet was destroyed. In the third war, his victories prevented a seaborne invasion of the United Provinces, but he was mortally wounded in a battle against the French off Sicily.

RV *abbrev.* Revised Version (of the Bible).

Rwanda, official name **Republic of Rwanda** POP (1992e) 7.5m, a landlocked republic in central Africa. AREA 26 338sq km/10 166sq mi. It is bounded N by Uganda, E by Tanzania, S by Burundi, and W by Zaire and L Kivu. CAPITAL Kigali. CHIEF TOWNS Butare, Ruhengeri. TIME ZONE GMT +2. The population is mainly Hutu (84%) and Tutsi (14%); Roman Catholicism and local beliefs are the chief religions. OFFICIAL LANGUAGES French and Kinyarwanda; Kiswahili is widely used in commerce. CURRENCY the Rwanda franc. PHYSICAL DESCRIPTION the country is situated at a relatively high altitude, the highest point being Karisimbi (4 507m) in the Virunga range; the W third of the country drains into L Kivu and then the R Congo, the remainder drains towards the R Nile; there are many lakes. CLIMATE a highland tropical climate; the two wet seasons run from Oct to Dec and Mar to May, with the highest rainfall in the W, decreasing in the central uplands and to the N and E; the average annual rainfall at Kigali is 1 000mm. HISTORY in the 16c the Tutsi tribe moved into the country and took over from the Hutu, forming a monarchy; became a German protectorate in 1899; mandated with Burundi to Belgium as the Territory of Ruanda-Urundi in 1919; became a United Nations Trust Territory administered by Belgium after World War II; unrest in 1959 led to a Hutu revolt and the overthrow of Tutsi rule; gained independence in 1962; military coup in 1973; return to civilian rule in 1980; further fighting in 1990; a peace accord in 1993; following the death of the Hutu President in 1994 in an air crash, fighting between rival tribes (Hutu and Tutsi) resulted in many thousands of deaths, and the flight of hundreds of thousands of refugees to Burundi and Tanzania. GOVERNMENT National Development Council, a President, and a Council of Ministers. ECONOMY largely agricultural; coffee, tea, pyrethrum, maize, beans; livestock; cassiterite; wolfram; columbo-tantalite; beryl; amblygonite; reserves of methane; agricultural processing; beer; soft drinks; soap; furniture; plastic goods; textiles; cigarettes.

Rwanda

Ryan, Elizabeth (1892–1979) US lawn tennis player, born in Anaheim, California. She won 19 Wimbledon titles (12 doubles and seven mixed doubles), a record which stood from 1934 until 1979, when it was surpassed by Billie Jean King. Six of her women's doubles titles were with Suzanne Lenglen (1899–1938).

Ryan, Nolan (1947–) US baseball player, born in Refugio, Texas. He is regarded as one of the fastest pitchers in major league baseball. He started his career with the New York Mets in 1966, then played for the California Angels, Houston Astros, and Texas Rangers. He has claimed more strikeouts (4 373) than any player in baseball history. His score of 383 strikeouts in 1973 is an all-time record.

Ryan a male first name, after the Irish surname.

Ryazan 1 POP (1991e) 527 000, the capital of Ryazan oblast, W Russia. It lies on the R Oka, 192km/119mi SE of Moscow. Founded in 1095, the city was formerly capital of a principality. **2** an oblast in W Russia with the city of Ryazan as its capital.

Rydberg, Johannes Robert (1854–1919) Swedish physicist, born in Halmstad. Professor at the University of Lund, he developed an empirical formula relating the frequencies of spectral lines of atoms, incorporating the constant known by his name, that was later derived by Niels Bohr using his quantum theory.

Ryde POP (1981) 20 000, a resort town in Medina district, I of Wight, S England. It lies on the NE coast of the island, 11km/7mi SW of Portsmouth. NOTABLE FEATURE Quarr Abbey (1132).

Ryder Cup an international golf tournament played every two years between male teams from the USA and Europe. It was first played in Worcester, Massachusetts, in 1927, between the USA and Great Britain. From 1973–7 the British team was extended to include players from Ireland, and from 1979 the team became a European team.

rye *noun* **1** a cereal (*Secale cereale*), belonging to the grass family (Gramineae), that resembles barley but has longer narrower ears. It can withstand low temperatures and poor soils, and is cultivated mainly in central Europe, and in the former USSR. Rye flour is used to make black bread, rye bread (which also contains wheat flour), and crispbreads, and rye is also used in the distillation of whisky, gin, vodka, and kvass. **2** (*in full* **rye whisky**) whisky distilled from fermented rye. [from Anglo-Saxon *ryge*]

Rye House Plot an alleged plot by Whigs (Apr 1683) to murder Charles II of England and James, Duke of York, at Rye House near Hoddesdon, Hertfordshire. A counterpart to the alleged Popish Plot of 1678, it was foiled by the early departure of the royal pair from Newmarket. The conspirators were betrayed and captured, including Algernon Sidney and William, Lord Russell, who were executed.

Rykov, Alexey Ivanovich (1881–1935) Russian revolutionary, and government official. He helped organize the October Revolution in Petrograd and was appointed People's Commissar for Internal Affairs in the first Soviet government. He held a number of senior government and Communist Party posts (1919–37), and became a member of the Politburo (1919–29). In 1928, together with N I Bukharin and M P Tomsky, he led the 'right opposition' against Stalin's economic policies. In 1937 he was arrested and shot for alleged anti-Party activities.

Ryle, Gilbert (1900–76) English philosopher, born in Brighton, Sussex. He served in World War II, then became Waynflete Professor of Metaphysical Philosophy at Oxford (1945–68) and editor of the journal *Mind* (1947–71). He was an influential defender of linguistic or 'ordinary language' philosophy, and is best-known for his book *The Concept of Mind* (1949) which argued against the mind/body dualism ('the ghost in the machine') proposed by Descartes.

S

S¹ *or* **s** *noun* (PL. **Ss, S's, s's**) **1** the nineteenth letter of the English alphabet. **2** something shaped like an S.

S² *abbrev.* **1** Society. **2** soprano. **3** South.

S³ *symbol Chem.* sulphur.

s *abbrev.* **1** second(s) of time. **2** *formerly* in the UK, shilling(s). [from Latin *solidus*]

's¹ *suffix* **1** used to form the possessive, as in: *John's / the children's*. **2** used to form the plural of numbers and symbols, as in *3's X's*.

's² **1** the shortened form of **is**, as in *he's not here*. **2** the shortened form of **has**, as in *she's taken it*. **3** the shortened form of **us**, as in *let's go*.

-s¹ *or* **-es** *suffix* forming the plural of nouns: *dogs / churches*.

-s² *or* **-es** *suffix* forming the third person singular of the present tense of verbs: *walks / misses*.

SA *abbrev.* **1** Salvation Army. **2** South Africa. **3** South America. **4** South Australia.

Saar, River, French **Sarre** a river in France and Germany, length 240km/150mi. Rising in the Vosges, it flows N through NE France, then NW across the German border to the R Mosel just above Treves. Its valley is a noted wine area. The river is navigable for 120km/75mi.

Saarbrücken, French **Sarrebruck** POP (1991e) 192 000, the capital of Saarland state, SW Germany. Situated 62km/39mi SE of Treves, Saarbrücken lies on the R Saar where the river follows the France–Germany border. It is the economic and cultural centre of Saarland and is noted for its trade fairs. NOTABLE FEATURE Collegiate Church of St Arnual (13c–14c).

Saarinen, Eero (1910–61) Finnish-born US architect, born in Kirkkonummi. He went to the USA in 1923 with his architect father Eliel Saarinen (1873–1950), studied sculpture in Paris (1929–30), and architecture at Yale (1930–4). His designs for Expressionist modern buildings include the Jefferson Memorial Arch, St Louis (1948–64) and the Trans-World Airlines Kennedy Terminal, New York (1956–62).

Sabadell POP (1991) 185 000, an industrial town in Barcelona province, Catalonia region, NE Spain. It lies on the R Ripoll, 15km/9mi N of Barcelona.

Sabah, formerly **North Borneo** POP (1990) 1.5m, a state in E Malaysia, on the N tip of Borneo. AREA 73 711sq km/28 452sq mi. It is bounded SW by Brunei, W by the S China Sea, E by the Sulu Sea, and S by Kalimantan (Indonesia). The highest peak is Mt Kinabalu at 4 094m. It is watered by the R Kinabatangan. HISTORY a British protectorate in 1882; became a member of the Federation of Malaysia in 1963. CAPITAL Kota Kinabalu. ECONOMY copper; oil; timber; copra; rice; rubber.

Sabbath *noun* (*usually* **the Sabbath**) a day of the week set aside for religious worship and rest, Saturday among Jews and Sunday among most Christians. [from Hebrew *shabbath*, rest]

sabbatical — *adj.* **1** of or being a period of leave given especially to teachers in higher education, especially for study. **2** relating to or typical of the Sabbath. — *noun* a period of sabbatical leave. [see SABBATH]

Sabin, Albert Bruce (1906–93) Polish–US microbiologist, born in Bialystok, Russia (now in Poland). Professor at the University of Cincinnati, he is best known for his research on the use of a live virus as a polio vaccine, which works by causing a harmless infection of the intestinal tract, stimulating immunity to natural infection without causing disease. This replaced Jonas Salk's vaccine as it gives longer-lasting immunity and can be taken orally.

Sabine, Wallace Clement Ware (1868–1919) US physicist, born in Richwood, Ohio. Working at Harvard, he made quantitative studies of the science of 'architectural acoustics', helping to prescribe the ideal construction of concert halls and theatres with the best sound characteristics. The unit of sound absorbing power was named after him.

Sabines a people of ancient Italy, who inhabited the mountainous country NE of Rome. They were often at war with the Romans, and were ultimately conquered by them. They were granted Roman citizenship in 268 BC.

sable¹ *noun* **1** a small flesh-eating mammal of N Europe and Asia, related to the marten. **2** its shiny dark-brown fur. **3** an artist's paintbrush made of this. [from Old French *sable*]

sable² *adj.* **1** *poetic* dark. **2** *Heraldry* black.

sable antelope a large southern African antelope, the male of which is mostly black.

sabot *noun* a wooden clog, or a shoe with a wooden sole. [from French *sabot*]

sabotage — *noun* **1** deliberate damage or destruction, especially carried out for military or political reasons. **2** action designed to disrupt any plan or scheme. — *verb* to destroy, damage, or disrupt deliberately. [from French *saboter*, to ruin through carelessness]

saboteur *noun* a person carrying out sabotage.

Sabra a Palestinian refugee camp on the outskirts of Beirut, Lebanon. It was created when Palestinians were evacuated from the city after an Israeli attack in 1982. Sabra was the scene of a massacre of Palestinians by Christian Phalangists in 1983.

Sabratha a Phoenician colony founded in the 8c BC on the NW coast of present-day Libya. The city was incorporated in Roman Africa in the 2c BC. The ruins, which include an ampitheatre and a reconstructed theatre facing the sea, are a World Heritage site.

sabre *noun* **1** a curved single-edged cavalry sword. **2** a lightweight fencing sword with a tapering blade. [from French *sabre*]

sabre-rattling *noun* aggressive talk or action, especially from politicians or military leaders, intended as a show of power.

sabretooth *noun Zool.* an extinct member of the cat family that lived during the late Tertiary era. It is often referred to as *sabre-toothed tiger*, but is not in fact closely related to the tiger. Its extremely long upper canine teeth were adapted for stabbing prey.

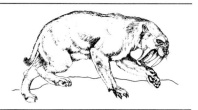

sabretooth

sac *noun Biol.* any bag-like part in a plant or animal, especially filled with fluid. [from Latin *saccus*, bag]

saccade *noun* the sharp lateral movement of the eye as it switches from one point to another, in contrast with its slow drifting movement. Saccades may be voluntary (as in reading) or involuntary, and their study can provide important information about the nature of the reading process and other visual activities. [from French *saccade*, a jerk]

saccharide *noun Chem.* any of a group of water-soluble carbohydrates composed of one or more simple sugars (monosaccharides), and typically having a sweet taste, eg glucose, fructose, sucrose (which consists of a glucose molecule and a fructose molecule linked together). [from Latin *saccharum*, sugar]

saccharin *or* **saccharine** — *noun* a white crystalline substance, about 550 times sweeter than sugar and with no energy value (calorie content), used as an artificial sweetener by diabetics and dieters. There is some evidence to suggest that it may be potentially carcinogenic in very large doses. — *adj.* over-sentimental or over-sweet; cloying. [from Greek *sakcharon*, sugar]

Saccharomyces *noun Biol.* the yeast genus of ascomycete fungi.

sacerdotal *adj.* **1** of or relating to priests. **2** resembling a priest; priestly. [from Latin *sacerdos*, priest]

Sacha a male and female first name. [a French spelling of the Russian name *sasha*, a diminutive of ALEXANDER]

sachet *noun* **1** a small sealed packet containing a liquid or powder. **2** a small bag containing a scented substance, used to perfume wardrobes, drawers, etc. [from French, diminutive of *sac*, bag]

Sachs, Hans (1494–1576) German poet and dramatist, born in Nuremberg. A trained shoe-maker, he wrote over 6 300 works (including verse, songs, tales, and plays), some celebrating the Reformation, others dealing with common life and manners. He headed the Meistersingers ('master singers') of Nuremberg in 1554, and in that role was idealized in Wagner's opera, *Die Meistersinger von Nürnberg*.

Sachs, Julius von (1832–97) German botanist, born in Breslau (now Wrocław, Poland). From 1868 he was Professor of Botany at Würzburg, where he carried out important experiments on the influence of light and heat upon plants, and the organic activities of veg-etable growth. His *Lehrbuch der Botanik* (1868) and its English translation *Textbook of Botany* (1875) had widespread influence.

Sachs, Nelly (Leonie) (1891–1970) Swedish poet and dramatist, born in Berlin. Of Jewish descent, she fled from Germany in 1940, settled in Stockholm, and took Swedish national-ity. Her best-known play is *Eli: Ein Mysterienspiel vom Leiden Israels* (Eli: A Mystery Play of the Sufferings of Israel, 1951). She shared the Nobel Prize for Literature in 1966 with the Israeli novel-ist Shmuel Yosef Agnon.

sack[1] — *noun* **1** a large bag, especially of coarse cloth or paper. **2** the amount a sack will hold. **3** *colloq.* (**the sack**) dismissal from employment: *give someone the sack / get the sack.* **4** (**the sack**) *slang* bed. — *verb* **1** *colloq.* to dismiss from employment. **2** to put into a sack or sacks. — **hit the sack** *slang* to go to bed. [from Latin *saccus*, bag]

sack[2] — *verb* to plunder and destroy (a town). — *noun* the act of sacking a town. [from French *mettre à sac*, to put (plunder) into a bag]

sack[3] *noun Hist.* a dry white wine from Spain, Portugal, and the Canary Islands. [from French *sec*, dry]

sackbut *noun* an early trombone-like wind instrument. [from French *saquebute*]

sackcloth *noun* **1** coarse cloth used to make sacks; sacking. **2** a garment made from this, for-merly worn in mourning or as a self-punishment for sin. — **sackcloth and ashes** a display of sorrow or remorse.

sackful *noun* (PL. **sackfuls**) the amount a sack will hold.

sacking *noun* **1** coarse cloth used to make sacks. **2** *colloq.* dismissal from, or the act of dis-missing from, employment.

Sackville, Thomas, 1st Earl of Dorset (1536–1608) English poet and statesman, born in Buckhurst, Sussex. He became a lawyer and entered parliament (1558), then collaborated with Thomas Norton (1532–84) in the tragedy *Gorboduc* (1561), the first English play in blank verse.

Sackville-West, V(ictoria Mary), also called **Vita** (1892–1962) English poet and novel-ist, born in Knole, Kent. Her book *Passenger to Teheran* (1926) records her years in Persia with her husband Harold Nicolson, and she herself was the inspiration for Virginia Woolf's novel, *Orlando* (1928). Her work expresses her closeness to the countryside where she lived, notably in the long poem, *The Land* (1926). Other works include the novels *The Edwardians* (1930) and *All Passion Spent* (1931), and *Collected Poems* (1933). She was also a passionate gardener (she wrote a gardening column for the *Observer* for many years) and created an elegant garden at her home, Sissinghurst in Kent, which is now owned by the National Trust.

sacra see SACRUM.

sacral[1] *adj.* relating to sacred rites.

sacral[2] *adj.* relating to or in the region of the sacrum.

sacrament *noun* **1** *Christianity* any of various symbolic ceremonies, eg marriage or baptism. **2** *Christianity cap* the service of the Eucharist or Holy Communion; the consecrated bread and wine consumed. **3** a sign, token, or pledge. [from Latin *sacrare*, to consecrate]
◇ Orthodox and Roman Catholic Churches rec-ognize seven sacraments: baptism, confirmation, the Eucharist (Mass), penance, extreme unction, holy orders (ordination), and matrimony. Protestant Churches recognize only baptism and the Eucharist (Communion).

sacramental *adj.* relating to or having the nature of a sacrament.

Sacramento POP (1990) 1.5m, the capital of the state of California, USA, in Sacramento County, central California. It lies on the E bank of the Sacramento R, 121km/75mi NE of San Francisco. HISTORY settled in 1839, it expanded rapidly after gold was discovered nearby in 1848; it became state capital in 1854. NOTABLE FEATURES Roman Corinthian State Capitol (1860) in Capitol Park; Crocker Art Gallery; Sutter's Fort (1840, now restored) contains a museum of Native American and pioneer relics.

Sacramento River the longest river in California, USA, length 615km/382mi. It rises in the Klamath Mts and flows S to Suisin Bay, the E arm of San Francisco Bay. Just before entering Suisin Bay, the river joins with the San Joaquin to form the basis of the immense Central Valley Project undertaken for purposes of flood-control, irrigation, and hydroelectricity. There are several dams and reservoirs. Sacramento is the principal port on the river; major tributaries include the Pit, Feather, and American.

sacred *adj.* **1** devoted to a deity and therefore regarded with deep and solemn respect. **2** con-nected with religion or worship: *sacred music.* **3 a** traditional and greatly respected. **b** *said of rules, etc* not to be challenged or broken in any cir-cumstances. **4** dedicated or appropriate to a saint, deity, etc: *a church sacred to the Trinity.* [from Latin *sacer*, holy]

Sacred and Profane Love an early alle-gorical painting by Titian (c.1515).

sacred baboon see HAMADRYAS BABOON.

sacred cow a thing, especially a custom or institution, regarded as above criticism.

sacred ibis an ibis native to Africa south of the Sahara, S Arabia, and Aldabra (formerly also Egypt). It has white plumage with a dark head and neck, and soft dark plumes on its tail. It feeds on fish and insects, and nests in trees or on the ground.

sacrifice — *noun* **1** the slaughter of a person or animal as an offering to God or a god; the per-son or animal slaughtered. **2** any offering made to a deity. **3** a thing of value given up or given away for the sake of another thing or person. — *verb* **1** to offer as a sacrifice to a deity. **2** to give up or give away for the sake of some other per-son or thing. [from Latin *sacer*, sacred + *facere*, to make]

sacrificial *adj.* relating to or having the nature of a sacrifice.

sacrilege *noun* wilful damage to or disrespect for something holy or something regarded with great respect by others. [from Latin *sacrilegus*, stealer of sacred things]

sacrilegious *adj.* committing or involving sacrilege.

sacristan *or* **sacrist** *noun* **1** a person respon-sible for the safety of the contents of a church. **2** a person who looks after the church buildings and churchyard; a sexton. [from Latin *sacer*, holy]

sacristy *noun* (PL. **sacristies**) a room in a church where sacred utensils and garments are kept. [from Latin *sacristia*, vestry]

sacrosanct *adj.* supremely holy or sacred; not to be violated. [from Latin *sacer*, holy + *sanctus*, hallowed]

sacrosanctity *noun* sacredness.

sacrum *noun* (PL. **sacra**) a large triangular bone in the lower back, forming part of the pelvis. [from Latin *os sacrum*, holy bone, from its use in sacrifices]

SAD *abbrev. Psychol.* seasonal affective disorder.

sad *adj.* (**sadder, saddest**) **1** feeling unhappy. **2** causing unhappiness: *sad news.* **3** expressing or suggesting unhappiness: *sad music.* **4** very bad; deplorable: *a sad state.* [from Anglo-Saxon *sæd*, weary]

Sadat, (Mohammed) Anwar Al- (1918–81) Egyptian statesman, born in the Tala district. He trained for the army in Cairo, and in 1952 was a member of the coup that deposed King Farouk. After becoming President (1970–81), he tem-porarily assumed the post of Prime Minister (1973–4). Seeking settlement of the conflict with Israel, he had meetings with the Israeli Prime Minister Menachem Begin in Jerusalem (1977) and at Camp David, USA (1978), following which he was jointly awarded the Nobel Peace Prize with Begin (1978). Criticized afterwards by other Arab statesmen and hardline Muslims, he was assassinated in Cairo by extremists.

sadden *verb trans., intrans.* (**saddened, sad-dening**) to make or become sad.

saddle — *noun* **1** a horse-rider's leather seat, which fits on the horse's back and is secured under its belly. **2** a fixed seat on a bicycle or motorcycle. **3** a cut of meat consisting of the two loins with a section of the backbone. **4** a moun-tain ridge connecting two peaks. — *verb* **1** to put a saddle on (a horse). **2** to burden (someone) with a problem, duty, etc: *did not wish to be sad-dled with the responsibility.* — **in the saddle 1** on horseback. **2** in a position of power or control. [from Anglo-Saxon *sadol*]

saddleback *noun* **1** an animal or bird with a saddle-shaped marking on its back. **2** a roof or mountain peak that dips in the middle.

saddlebacked *adj.* having a saddleback.

saddler *noun* a maker of saddles and harness for horses.

saddlery *noun* (PL. **saddleries**) **1** the occupa-tion of a saddler. **2** a saddler's shop or stock-in-trade. **3** a saddle-room at a stables, etc.

saddle soap soft soap for cleaning and pre-serving leather.

Sadducees a major party within Judaism (c.2c BC–AD 70), probably named from the priest Zadok, whose descendants held priestly office from the time of Solomon. Mainly aristo-crats, they were associated with the Jerusalem priesthood and influential in Israel's political and economic life.

Sade, Marquis de, pseudonym of **Donatien Alphonse François, Comte de (Count of) Sade** (1740–1814) French writer, born in Paris. He served in the army, and was condemned to death in 1772 at Aix for his cruelty and sexual practices. He escaped, but was later imprisoned at Vincennes (1777) and in the Bastille (1784), where he wrote *Les 120 Journées de Sodome* (The 120 Days of Sodom, c.1784). After his release (1790), he wrote licentious novels including *Justine* (1791) and *La Philosophie dans le boudoir* (Philosophy in the Bedroom, 1793). He died in a mental asylum in Charenton. The word 'sadism' is derived from his name.

sadhu *noun* a wandering Hindu holy man, liv-ing on charity. [from Sanskrit *sadhu*, pious]

sadism *noun* **1** the practice of gaining sexual pleasure from inflicting pain on others. **2** *loosely* the inflicting of suffering on others for one's own satisfaction. [named after Comte (called Marquis) de Sade, French novelist]

sadist *noun* a person who indulges in sadism, or enjoys inflicting pain on another.

sadistic *adj.* relating to or involving sadism.

Sadler's Wells Theatre a theatre in N London, built (1927–31) by Lilian Baylis to replace an 18c theatre, which in turn replaced 17c pleasure gardens (containing a medicinal spa) built by a Thomas Sadler. It is the former home of the Sadler's Wells Opera (now the English National Opera) and Sadler's Wells Ballet (now the Royal Ballet).

sadly *adv.* with sadness, in a sad way.

sadness *noun* being sad, unhappiness.

Sado an island in Chubu region, Japan. AREA 854sq km/330sq mi. It is located in the Sea of Japan, 48km/30mi W of Niigata, off N Honshu. The island is 56km/35mi long and 19km/12mi wide. PHYSICAL DESCRIPTION mountainous, with a central plain; rises to 1 173m in the N. CHIEF TOWN Ryotsu. ECONOMY farming; fishing; timber.

sado-masochism *noun* the practice of deriving sexual pleasure from inflicting pain on oneself and others.

sado-masochist *noun* a person who enjoys sado-masochism.

sado-masochistic *adj.* relating to or involving sado-masochism.

SAE *or* **sae** *abbrev.* stamped addressed envelope.

safari *noun* an expedition or tour to hunt or observe wild animals, especially in Africa: *on safari*. [from Swahili *safari*, journey]

safari jacket a long, square-cut jacket with four pleated pockets.

safari park a large enclosed area in which wild animals roam freely and can be observed by the public from vehicles driven through.

Safavids a dynasty, possibly of Kurdish origin, which provided the shahs of Persia (1501–1722) and laid the foundations of the modern Iranian state. They made Shiism the official religion, promoted the arts, and were overthrown by the Afghans in 1722.

safe — *adj.* **1** free from danger. **2** unharmed. **3** giving protection from harm; secure: *a safe place*. **4** not dangerous: *is it safe to go out?* **5** involving no risk of loss; assured: *a safe bet*. **6** cautious: *better safe than sorry.* — *noun* a sturdily constructed metal cabinet in which valuables can be locked away.
— **be** *or* **err on the safe side** to be doubly cautious; to choose the safer alternative.
[from Latin *salvus*]

safe-conduct *noun* official permission to pass or travel without arrest or interference, especially in wartime; also, a document authorizing this.

safe-deposit *or* **safety-deposit** *noun* a vault, eg in a bank, in which valuables can be locked away.

safeguard — *noun* a device or arrangement giving protection against danger or harm. — *verb* to protect; to ensure the safety of.

safekeeping *noun* care and protection.

safe light a light used in a photographic darkroom, etc, which emits light of an intensity and colour which will not damage the materials being processed.

safely *adv.* in a safe way.

safe sex sexual activity in which the transmission of disease, especially Aids, is guarded against, eg by the use of a condom or the avoidance of penetration.

safety *noun* the quality or condition of being safe.

safety belt any strap for securing a person and preventing accidents, especially a seat belt in a vehicle.

safety curtain a fireproof curtain above a theatre stage, lowered to control the spread of fire.

safety-deposit see SAFE-DEPOSIT.

safety-lamp *noun* a miner's oil lamp designed not to ignite any flammable gases encountered in the mine.

safety match a match that ignites only when struck on a specially prepared surface.

safety net 1 a large net positioned to catch a trapeze artist, etc, accidentally falling. **2** any measure protecting against loss or failure.

safety pin a U-shaped pin with an attached guard fitting over the point.

safety razor a shaving razor with a guard over the blade to prevent deep cuts.

safety valve 1 a device in a boiler or pipe system that opens when the pressure exceeds a certain preset level, and closes again when the pressure falls. **2** a way of harmlessly releasing emotion, eg anger or frustration.

safflower *noun* a Eurasian plant with large orange-yellow flowers, yielding a dye and an oil used in cooking. [from Old French *saffleur*]

saffron *noun* **1** a species of crocus with purple or white flowers whose pollen-receiving parts, or stigmas, are bright orange. **2** the dried stigmas, used to colour and flavour food. **3** a bright orange-yellow colour. [from Arabic *zafaran*]

sag — *verb intrans.* (**sagged**, **sagging**) **1** to sink or bend, especially in the middle, under or as if under weight. **2** to hang loosely or bulge downwards through lack of firmness. — *noun* a sagging state or position. [from Norse *sag*]

saga *noun* **1** a medieval Scandinavian tale of legendary heroes and events. **2** any long and detailed artistic work, especially a piece of modern fiction, often serialized, depicting successive generations of the same family. **3** *colloq.* a long series of events. [from Norse *saga*]

sagacious *adj. formal* having or showing intelligence and good judgement; wise. [from Latin *sagax*]

sagacity *noun* discernment, good judgement.

Sagan, Carl Edward (1934–) US astronomer, born in New York City. Professor at Cornell University since 1970, he has researched the physics and chemistry of planetary atmospheres and surfaces. He has also investigated the origin of life on Earth and the possibility of extraterrestrial life. Through books and a television programme, *Cosmos*, Sagan has done much to interest the general public in these aspects of science.

Sagan, Françoise, pseudonym of **Françoise Quoirez** (1935–) French novelist, born in Paris. Her works include the best-selling *Bonjour tristesse* (Good Morning, Sadness, 1954), and *Aimez-vous Brahms?* (Do You Like Brahms?, 1959). Her later novels and plays have had a mixed critical reception.

Sagarmatha a national park in Nepal. It encompasses the peak of Mt Everest and six other mountains over 7 000m. The park was established to protect the flora and fauna of the area, and the culture of the Sherpas who inhabit the region. It is a World Heritage site.

sage[1] *noun* a Mediterranean plant with aromatic grey-green leaves; the leaves used as a flavouring in cooking. [from Latin *salvia*, healing plant]

sage[2] — *noun* a man of great wisdom, especially an ancient philosopher. — *adj.* wise; prudent. [from Latin *sapere*, to be wise]

sagebrush *noun* a white-flowered aromatic shrub growing in clumps in the deserts of the USA.

saggar *or* **sagger** *noun* a large clay box in which pottery is packed for firing in a kiln.

saggy *adj.* (**saggier**, **saggiest**) tending to sag.

Sagitta *Astron.* the Arrow, a small constellation in the Milky Way. It contains a notable star cluster, M71.

Sagittarian — *noun* a person born under the sign Sagittarius. — *adj.* relating to this sign.

Sagittarius *noun* **1** *Astron.* the Archer, a large southern zodiacal constellation with many bright stars, lying partly in the Milky Way, and containing star clusters and gaseous nebulae. **2** the ninth sign of the zodiac, the Archer. **3** a person born between 22 Nov and 20 Dec, under this sign. [from Latin, from *sagitta*, arrow]

sago *noun* **1** a starchy grain or powder obtained from the soft pith inside the trunk of the sago palm. It is a staple food in Papua New Guinea, and is marketed in Europe for use in desserts. **2** any of various species of palm that yield this substance. [from Malay *sagu*]

sago palm a small tree of the genus *Metroxylon*, native to SE Asia and the Pacific region, characterized by large feathery leaves. The trunk contains abundant starch reserves which fuel a single burst of flowering by the mature tree, after which it dies. Sago, an important source of carbohydrate in the tropics, is obtained from the pith of trunks cut when the first flowers appear.

Sagrada Familia, La the unfinished Church of the Holy Family in Barcelona, Spain, on which Antonio Gaudí worked from 1884 until his death in 1926. It is the most extravagant example of his sinuous and undulating stonework.

Sagunto, Arabic **Murviedro** (to 1877), ancient **Saguntum** POP (1987e) 56 000, a town in Valencia province, Valencia region, E Spain. It stands on the R Palancia, 25km/16mi N of the town of Valencia. To the N lies the Costa del Azahar or 'Orange-Blossom Coast' resort region. NOTABLE FEATURES Roman theatre; fortress; Gothic Church of St Mary.

Saha, Meghnad (1894–1956) Indian astrophysicist, born in Dacca (now in Bangladesh). Professor of Physics at Calcutta, he worked on the thermal ionization that occurs in the extremely hot atmospheres of stars, and in 1920 demonstrated that elements in stars are ionized in proportion to their temperature (*Saha's equation*).

Sahara Desert a desert in N Africa, the largest in the world. AREA c.7.7m sq km/3m sq mi; average width, 1 440km/895mi across N Africa from the Atlantic Ocean to the Libyan Desert. It continues unbroken to the Nile, and beyond that in the Nubian Desert to the Red Sea. Wind erosion is intense, with only small amounts of unpredictable rain — usually brief, heavy thunderstorms. Scattered outlets of surface water are found at oases, the only places where agriculture is possible. There are areas of stunted scrub but the desert is generally void of vegetation. Oil exploration is carried out near the Algeria–Libya frontier and phosphates are mined in Morocco and Western Sahara. [from Arabic, meaning 'wilderness']

sahib *noun* in India, a term equivalent to 'Mr' or 'Sir', used after a man's surname, or (especially formerly) on its own to address or refer to a European man. [from Arabic *sahib*, lord or friend]

said past tense and past participle of SAY. — *adj.* (**the said ...**) *often formal* the previously mentioned or named ...

Saigon see HO CHI MINH CITY.

sail — *noun* **1** a sheet of canvas spread to catch the wind as a means of propelling a ship. **2** a trip

in a boat or ship (with or without sails); also, a voyage of a specified distance travelled by boat or ship. **3** (PL. usually **sail** especially after a number) *Naut.* a ship with sails: *thirty sail.* **4** any of a windmill's revolving arms. — *verb* **1** *trans., intrans.* to travel by boat or ship: *sail the Pacific.* **2** to control (a boat or ship). **3** *intrans.* to depart by boat or ship: *we sail at two-thirty.* **4** (*usually* **sail along** *or* **past**) to move smoothly and swiftly.
— **sail close to the wind 1** *Naut.* to arrange a ship's sails to catch as much wind as is safely possible. **2** to come dangerously close to overstepping a limit, eg of good taste or decency.
sail through something *colloq.* to succeed in it effortlessly: *she sailed through all her exams.*
set sail to begin a journey by boat or ship. [from Anglo-Saxon *segel*]

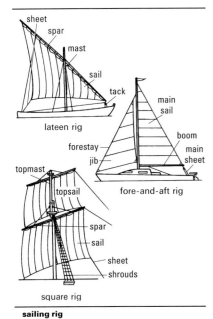

sailing rig

sailboard *noun* a windsurfing board, like a surfboard with a sail attached.

sailboarding *noun* windsurfing.

sailcloth *noun* **1** strong cloth, eg canvas, used to make sails. **2** heavy cotton cloth used for garments.

Sailer, Toni (Anton) (1935–) Austrian alpine skier, born in Kitzbühel. In 1956 he became the first man to win all three Olympic skiing titles (downhill, slalom, giant slalom). He was the world combined champion in 1956 and 1958, and the world downhill and giant slalom champion in 1958.

sailfish *noun* a large agile fish widely distributed in open ocean surface waters, up to 3.5m in length, bluish-grey in colour above and silver underneath, and easily recognized by its tall dorsal fin. It feeds on fish and squid, and is highly prized as an excellent sport fish, and is also fished commercially in some areas.

sailing a sport or pastime which involves travelling over water in a suitable craft. Small single- or double-sailed dinghies are used in sailing as a pastime; they are often fitted with an outboard motor or auxiliary engine for propulsion when there is no wind. Large ocean-going yachts may be 25m (82ft) or more in length. See also ADMIRAL'S CUP, AMERICA'S CUP, ROUND THE WORLD YACHT RACE.

sailor *noun* **1** any member of a ship's crew, especially one who is not an officer. **2** a person considered in terms of ability to travel on water without becoming seasick: *a good sailor.*

Saimaa a lake system extending over the Finnish Lake Plateau, SE Finland. It is the fifth-largest lake system in Europe. Its total area is 4 400sq km/1 700sq mi, of which L Saimaa comprises 1 300sq km/500sq mi; maximum depth is 100m. The lake system links to an inlet of the Gulf of Finland by the Saimaa Canal. Rivers, channels, and locks connect with about 120 lakes, the shores of which are mostly covered with coniferous forest. The lakes are important for timber floating.

sainfoin *noun* a flowering Eurasian plant of the pea family, grown as animal fodder. [from French *sain foin*, healthy hay]

Sainsbury, Alan John Sainsbury, Baron (1902–) English retailer, born in Hornsey, Middlesex. He joined the family grocery business (founded by his grandparents) in 1921. He was Chairman from 1956 to 1967, and since 1967 has been joint Honorary President of J Sainsbury plc with his younger brother Sir Robert (1906–). His elder son Sir John Davan (1927–) has been Chairman of the company since 1969.

saint *noun* **1** a person whose profound holiness is formally recognized after death by a Christian Church, and who is declared worthy of everlasting praise. **2** *colloq.* a very good and kind person. [from Latin *sanctus*, holy]
◇ In the New Testament, all Christian believers are referred to as saints; in the 2c AD, veneration of saints (often martyrs) began, and individual saints were eventually looked to for intercession and devotion. The practice of veneration was forbidden by 16c Reformers, but continued in the Orthodox and Roman Catholic Churches. In Buddhism, a saint is anyone who has lived a pure and holy life. In Islam, there are three levels of saints, and symbolically saints and their names (found in various parts of the Muslim world) are considered to be a bridge between heaven and earth.

St Albans, Latin **Verulamium** POP (1992e) 127 000, a city in St Albans district, Hertfordshire, England. It lies on the R Ver, 40km/25mi NW of London. St Albans received its royal charter in 1553 and achieved city status in 1887. The Magna Carta was drafted here. NOTABLE FEATURES cathedral (1115, founded as a Benedictine abbey in 793); Roman theatre; museum with Iron Age and Roman exhibits. [named after the first Christian martyr to be executed in Britain]

St Bartholomew's Day Massacre the slaughter (24 Aug 1572) of French Huguenots in Paris, ordered by King Charles IX and contrived by the Queen Mother, Catherine de' Medici, to coincide with celebrations for the marriage of Marguerite de Valois and Henry IV (18 Aug). An attempt (22 Aug) to assassinate the Huguenot leader Admiral Coligny failed, but mass butchery of Huguenots followed.

St Basil's Cathedral part of the Historical Museum in Moscow. It was built (1555–61) as the Cathedral of the Intercession of the Virgin, and the present title was adopted after 1588, when a chapel was added to house the remains of the ascetic Basil the Blessed.

Saint Bernard a very large dog with a thick brown and white coat, originally kept by monks to rescue snowbound travellers in the St Bernard Passes in the Alps.

St Bernard Passes two transalpine frontier passes in central Europe. The Great Saint Bernard crosses the Pennine Alps between Martigny in Switzerland and Aosta in Italy, and the Little Saint Bernard crosses the Graian Alps between Aosta and Bourg St Maurice in France. St Bernard of Menthon founded hospices in both passes in the 10c.

St Catharines POP (1991) 129 000, a town in SE Ontario, SE Canada. It lies S of Toronto, at the entrance to the Welland Ship Canal. Founded in 1784, it is the heart of Canada's major wine-growing region and fruit belt.

St Christopher-Nevis or **St Kitts-Nevis**, official name **Federation of St Christopher and Nevis** POP (1990e) 42 000, an independent state in the N Leeward Is, E Caribbean Sea. AREA 269sq km/104sq mi. It is situated c.360km/225mi SE of Puerto Rico. The state is divided into 14 parishes and comprises the islands of St Christopher (St Kitts), Nevis, and Sombrero. CAPITAL Basseterre. TIME ZONE GMT −4. The population is mainly of African descent; Protestantism is the chief religion. OFFICIAL LANGUAGE English. CURRENCY the E Caribbean dollar. PHYSICAL DESCRIPTION St Christopher is 37km/23mi long and has an area of 168sq km/65sq mi; a mountain range rises to 1 156m at Mt Misery; Nevis, 3km/2mi SE, has an area of 93sq km/36sq mi and is dominated by a central peak rising to 985m. CLIMATE warm, with an average annual temperature of 26°C and an average annual rainfall of 1 375mm; low humidity. HISTORY St Christopher was the first British colony in the West Indies, in 1623; control was disputed between France and Britain in the 17c–18c; ceded to Britain in 1783; St Christopher and Nevis were united in 1882, along with Anguilla; became a state in association with the UK in 1967; separation of Anguilla in 1980; gained independence in 1983. GOVERNMENT the British Monarch is represented by a Governor-General; governed by a Prime Minister and two legislative chambers, a 14-member National Assembly and an eight-member Nevis I Assembly. ECONOMY sugar and its products supply 60% of total exports; copra; cotton; electrical appliances; footwear; garments; tourism.

St Christopher - Nevis

St Cyr, Ecole de a French military academy founded by Napoleon in Fontainebleau in 1803 and transferred to St Cyr in 1808. The school was moved to Coetquidan in Brittany after World War II, but retained the name of its former home.

St David's, Welsh **Tyddewi** POP (1981) 1 800, a village in Preseli district, Dyfed, SW Wales. It lies 25km/16mi NW of Milford Haven on St Bride's Bay. A medieval place of pilgrimage, St David's is the smallest cathedral seat in the UK. The 12c cathedral honours the 6c Welsh patron saint, David (Dewi).

Saint-Denis, Michel (Jacques Duchesne) (1897–1971) French theatre director, actor, and teacher, born in Beauvais. In 1931 he founded the influential Compagnie des Quinze, later settling in England as co-founder of the London Theatre Studio (1936, with George Devine and others). His influence on British theatre continued at the Old Vic (1947–52) and later at the Royal Shakespeare Company (director, 1962).

St-Denis POP (1990) 101 000, a modern industrial town and railway centre in Seine-Saint-Denis department, Ile-de-France region, N central France. It is a N suburb of Paris, 10km/6mi N of its city centre. NOTABLE FEATURE 12c Gothic Basilica of St-Denis, containing the tombs of several French monarchs.

St Denis POP (1990) 101 000, the capital of Réunion, on the N coast. It is the commercial and administrative centre of the island.

sainted *adj.* **1** formally declared a saint. **2** greatly respected; hallowed.

St Elias, Mount a mountain in the St Elias Mts, on the Yukon–Alaska border, USA. It is the second-highest peak in the USA. HEIGHT 5 489m.

St Elmo's fire a blue-green coloured electrical discharge which occurs during thunderstorm weather around the masts of ships, weather vanes, and aircraft wing tips. It is especially common in the Doldrums.

St-Etienne POP (1990) 313 000, a manufacturing town and the capital of Loire department, Rhône-Alps region, SW France. It is situated on the Central Plateau, 51km/32mi SW of Lyons. Since the 16c it has been a centre of the metallurgical industry.

Saint-Exupéry, Antoine (Marie Roger) de (1900–44) French airman and writer, born in Lyons. A commercial and wartime pilot, his philosophy of 'heroic action' is found in such novels as *Vol de nuit* (Night Flight, 1931). He is also known for his popular children's fable for adults, *Le Petit prince* (The Little Prince, 1943). He was declared missing after a flight to N Africa during World War II.

St Gallen, French **St Gall**, German **Sankt Gallen 1** POP (1990) 83 000, an ancient abbey town and the capital of St Gallen canton, NE Switzerland. It lies in a high valley in the Pre-Alps, 62km/39mi E of Zürich, and is prominent as Switzerland's major textile centre. The town, now a World Heritage site, developed around the abbey founded by St Gall in the 7c. NOTABLE FEATURE cathedral (18c). **2** a canton in NE Switzerland with St Gallen as its capital.

St George and the Dragon a painting by Paolo Uccello (c.1460, National Gallery, London).

St George and the Princess of Trebizond a fresco by Antonio Pisanello (c.1437–8, San Anastasia, Verona).

St George's POP (1991e) 4 000, the port capital of Grenada, on the SW coast. It was founded as a French settlement in 1650.

St George's Channel a stretch of sea between the SE of Ireland in the W and Wales in the E, connecting the Atlantic Ocean with the Irish Sea. It is at its narrowest between Carnsore Point (Ireland) and St David's Head (Wales), where it measures 74km/46mi across.

St Gotthard Pass a mountain pass between Andermatt and Airolo, extending over the St Gotthard Massif in the Lepontine Alps, S central Switzerland. HEIGHT 2 108m. It is a bare, flat depression with a number of small lakes. The route, which was made passable in the Middle Ages, is open from Jun to Oct. NOTABLE FEATURE St Gotthard Hospice (14c).

St Helena POP (1992e) 6 000, a volcanic island in the S Atlantic Ocean. AREA 122sq km/47sq mi. It is a Colony, lying 1 920km/1 200mi from the SW coast of Africa. The highest point is Diana's Peak (823m). HISTORY discovered by the Portuguese on St Helena's feast day in 1502; annexed by the Dutch in 1633; annexed by the East India Company in 1659; Napoleon was exiled here from 1815 until 1821; Ascension I and Tristan da Cunha were made dependencies in 1922. CAPITAL Jamestown. ECONOMY fish (mostly tuna); coffee; postage stamps. The economy is heavily subsidized by the UK.

St Helens POP (1992e) 181 000, an industrial town in St Helens borough, Merseyside, NW England. It lies 18km/11mi E of Liverpool.

St Helens, Mount a volcano in SW Washington, USA, in the Cascade Range, rising to 2 549m. It erupted in 1980, causing damage amounting to $2.5 billion; 100 people were killed, 276 homes were destroyed, and volcanic ash affected a large area in the W states.

St Helier POP (1991) 28 000, the resort capital of the Channel Islands. It is situated on the S coast of the island of Jersey, at the E end of St Aubin's Bay. The town was the home of Victor Hugo in 1851–5. NOTABLE FEATURE nearby is the Hermitage, an ancient beehive chapel, cell of St Helier, the patron saint of Jersey.

sainthood *noun* the position or status of a saint.

St Ives POP (1981) 10 000, a resort town in Kerrier district, Cornwall, SW England. It lies 12km/7mi NE of Penzance.

St Ives Painters a group of painters who were based in St Ives, Cornwall in the mid-20c.

They included Barbara Hepworth, Ben Nicholson, and Peter Lanyon.

St James's Palace one of the principal royal palaces in London until the mid-19c. Only parts of the original Tudor palace built for Henry VIII remain (notably the gatehouse and the chapel royal), and much of the building dates from the 18c.

Saint Joan a play by George Bernard Shaw (1923). It is based on the martyrdom of Joan of Arc, exemplifying Shaw's genius for characterization (above all of saintly yet very human women), and his powers of dramatic argument, here concerning nationalism, the aristocracy, and religion.

St John POP (1991) 75 000, a seaport in S New Brunswick, SE Canada. It lies on the Bay of Fundy at the mouth of the St John R. HISTORY a French fort from 1631 until 1635; involved in the Anglo-French struggle for Acadia, finally being taken by an Anglo-American force in 1758 and becoming a British possession; received many United Empire Loyalist immigrants after the American Revolution; largely destroyed by fire in 1877. NOTABLE FEATURES Old Courthouse (1830); Trinity Church (rebuilt in 1877); Chubb's Corner (1878); New Brunswick Museum; Martello Tower (1812); Fort Howe (1778); Reversing Falls (where water falls in opposite directions over a rocky ledge according to the tide).

St John of Jerusalem, Order of the Hospital of, also called **Knights of St John of Jerusalem** see HOSPITALLERS.

Saint-John Perse, pseudonym of **Marie René Auguste Aléxis Saint-Léger Léger** (1887–1975) French poet and diplomat, born in St Léger des Feuilles, near Guadeloupe. He entered the French Diplomatic Service in 1914 but was dismissed in 1940 and fled to the USA, where he became an adviser to Franklin D Roosevelt on French affairs. His best-known works include *Anabase* (Anabasis, 1924), *Exile* (1942), and *Amers* (Seamarks, 1957). He was awarded the Nobel Prize for Literature in 1960.

St John's POP (1991) 96 000, the capital of Newfoundland province, E Canada. It is in the SE part of the island, on the NE coast of the Avalon Peninsula. HISTORY Genoese navigator John Cabot landed here in 1497; became a British possession in 1583; developed into a fishing settlement; held by the French, it was taken by the British in 1762. NOTABLE FEATURES two cathedrals; Signal Hill (where the first wireless message was received by Guglielmo Marconi in 1901); Colonial Building (1850).

St John's POP (1986e) 36 000, the port capital of Antigua and Barbuda, Lesser Antilles, E Caribbean Sea. It is situated on a sheltered bay in NW Antigua I. NOTABLE FEATURES cathedral; old fortifications.

St John the Baptist a painting by Leonardo da Vinci (c.1515, Louvre, Paris).

Saint-Just, Louis (Antoine Léon Florelle) de (1767–94) French revolutionary, born in Decize. He studied law, and while in Paris began to write poetry and essays, notably *L'Esprit de la révolution* (Spirit of the Revolution, 1791). He was elected to the National Convention (1792), attracted notice by his fierce tirades against Louis XVI, and as a devoted follower of Robespierre was sent on diplomatic and military missions. He joined the Committee of Public Safety (1793), and helped to destroy Danton and Hébert. As President of the Convention (1794), he sponsored the radical Ventôse Laws, redistributing property to the poor. He was guillotined with Robespierre during the Thermidorian Reaction, when, in the summer period known as the Thermidor, the Convention managed to end the Jacobin dictatorship.

St Kilda a group of small volcanic islands in the Atlantic Ocean, c.160km/100mi W of the Scottish mainland. They were abandoned in 1930, having been inhabited for 2 000 years. The cliffs (over 400m high) are colonized by over 1m sea birds. It is a World Heritage area.

St Kitts-Nevis see ST CHRISTOPHER-NEVIS.

Saint Laurent, Yves (Henri Donat Mathieu) (1936–) French fashion designer, born in Oran, Algeria. He was employed by Christian Dior in 1955 after winning an International Wool Secretariat design competition. On Dior's death in 1957, he took over the fashion house. In 1962 he opened his own house, and launched the first of his 160 Rive Gauche boutiques in 1966, selling ready-to-wear clothes, a trend which many other designers were to follow. His designs include costumes for ballets and films.

St Lawrence River, French **St Laurent** a principal river of N America, situated in E Canada. It is the chief outlet for the Great Lakes. It issues from the NE end of L Ontario and flows NE to the Gulf of St Lawrence, N of the Gaspé Peninsula; forms part of the border between Canada and the USA. The total length is 1 197km/744mi. The river widens into several lakes along its course and a major tourist area surrounds it. The Thousand Islands Rapids in Ontario are used for hydroelectric power. Principal cities on the banks include Kingston, Montreal, Trois-Rivières, and Quebec. The river is tidal below Quebec, and increases gradually in width to c.145km/90mi. It was formerly navigable for ocean-going vessels only as far as Montreal; the St Lawrence Seaway (1955–9) between L Ontario and Montreal now allows passage to the Great Lakes; in winter months the river is often unnavigable in parts.

St Lawrence Seaway a system of canals, locks, and dredged waterways providing a navigable channel from the Gulf of St Lawrence to the head of L Superior. From 1954 until 1959 the Canadian and US governments co-operated on a project to establish a shipping lane 8m deep along the St Lawrence R. The Welland Ship Canal is generally considered to be part of the present-day seaway.

St Leger, Barry (1737–89) British army colonel. He fought in the American Revolution, and in 1776 founded his horse-racing stables in Doncaster. The St Leger race was named after him in 1778.

St Leger see CLASSICS.

saintliness *noun* a saintly state.

St-Lô, ancient **Briovera**, later **Laudus** POP (1990) 23 000, the capital of Manche department, Basse-Normandie region, NW France. It is a market town, 54km/34mi W of Caen. The town was fortified by Charlemagne. It was almost completely destroyed in World War II, but the medieval part of the town is largely preserved. NOTABLE FEATURES 14c–15c Church of Notre-Dame (restored), Romanesque Church of Ste-Croix (restored); the St-Lô Stud breeds thoroughbred stallions.

St Louis POP (1990) 2.4m, a city and port in E Missouri, USA, lying on the Mississippi R. A major land transport hub and the largest city in Missouri, St Louis is also the busiest inland port on the Mississippi R. HISTORY settled by the French in 1764; under Spanish control from 1770 to 1800; ceded to the USA in 1804; achieved city status in 1822. NOTABLE FEATURES Gateway Arch (a giant steel arch on the river bank, 192m high, symbolizing St Louis as the gateway to the West); Art Museum; Science Centre; Missouri Botanical Garden; Goldenrod Showboat; Sports Hall of Fame.

St Louis POP (1992e) 126 000, the seaport capital of Saint Louis region, Senegal. It is situated on a small island at the mouth of the R Sénégal, 177km/110mi NE of Dakar, and is the transportation point for the surrounding area. HISTORY built in 1658 on Sor I as a French trading company fort, and prospered with the slave trade; capital of French W Africa from 1895 to 1902.

St Lucia POP (1991e) 153 000, an independent constitutional monarchy and the second-largest of the Windward Is, situated in the E Caribbean Sea. AREA 616sq km/238sq mi. It lies 32km/20mi N of St Vincent and the Grenadines and is divided into 16 parishes. CAPITAL Castries. CHIEF TOWNS Vieux Fort, Soufrière. TIME ZONE GMT −4. The population is mainly of African descent (90%); Roman Catholicism is the chief religion. OFFICIAL LANGUAGE English; French patois is also spoken. CURRENCY the E Caribbean dollar. PHYSICAL DESCRIPTION the island is 43km/27mi long and 23km/14mi wide; mountainous centre, rising to 950m at Mt Gimie; the twin volcanic peaks of Gros and Petit Piton rise steeply from the sea on the SW coast of the island. CLIMATE tropical; annual temperatures range from 18°C to 34°C; the wet season is Jun–Dec; average annual rainfall is 1 500mm on the N coast and 4 000mm in the interior. HISTORY reputedly discovered by Christopher Columbus in 1502; settled by the French; disputed ownership between Britain and France began in 1659; became a British Crown Colony in 1814; gained independence within the Commonwealth in 1979. GOVERNMENT the British monarch is represented by a Governor-General; there is a 17-member House of Assembly, elected every five years, and an 11-member Senate. ECONOMY tourism is the fastest-growing sector of the economy; bananas, cocoa, copra, citrus fruits, coconut oil; garments, textiles; electronic components; beverages; corrugated boxes; paper products; oil refining; transshipment.

St Lucia

saintly *adj.* **1** of or relating to a saint. **2** very good or holy.

St-Malo POP (1990) 49 000, an old port and resort in Ille-et-Vilaine department, Brittany, W France. It lies at the mouth of R France. The writer François Auguste René Chateaubriand was born in St-Malo in 1768. The town was badly damaged in World War II.

St Mark's Cathedral a church in Venice constructed in 1063–71 on the site of a 9c shrine which housed the relics of St Mark. It became a cathedral in 1807.

St Matthew Passion, Latin *Passio secundum Mattheum*, German *Matthäuspassion*, properly the *Passion According to St Matthew* a work for soloists, chorus, and orchestra by J S Bach (first performed Good Friday 1727 or 1729), based on the narrative of Christ's Passion in the Gospel according to St Matthew.

St Michael and St George, The Most Distinguished Order of in the UK, an order of knighthood founded in 1818 by the Prince Regent (later George IV) for those who have held high office or rendered distinguished service abroad (usually in the diplomatic service). There are three classes: Knights and Dames Grand Cross (GCMG), Knights and Dames Commanders (KCMG/DCMG), and Companions (CMG). The Latin motto is *Auspicium melioris aevi* ('a pledge of better times'), and the ribbon is equal blue and scarlet stripes.

St Michael and the Devil a sculpture in bronze by Sir Jacob Epstein (1958–9).

St Moritz, Romansch **San Murezzan** POP (1990) 6 000, a resort town in Graubünden canton, SE Switzerland. It lies in the Upper Engadine Valley, at an altitude of 1 853m. It is a winter sports resort. Facilities include a high ski-jump and the Cresta Run (bobsledding). NOTABLE FEA-

TURE Schiefer Turm (all that remains of the Romanesque Church of St Maurice).

St-Nazaire POP (1990) 132 000, a seaport and industrial town in Loire-Atlantique department, Pays de la Loire region, W France. Situated 53km/33mi NW of Nantes, it lies at the mouth of the R Loire, on its right bank. HISTORY it is thought to occupy the Roman site of Carbilo; developed as a deep-water port for Nantes in the 19c; a major debarkation port for the American Expeditionary Force in World War I; it was a German submarine base in World War II, during which the town was largely destroyed.

St Paul POP (1990) 272 000, the river-port capital of the state of Minnesota, USA, in Ramsey County, SE Minnesota. Lying on the Mississippi R, to the E of its twin city Minneapolis, St Paul is the major industrial and commercial centre for a vast agricultural region. HISTORY founded in 1838, it became capital of Minnesota Territory in 1849 and achieved city status in 1854; it has been state capital since 1858. NOTABLE FEATURE State Capitol, modelled on St Peter's in Rome, which has the largest unsupported marble dome in the world.

St Paul's Cathedral a Baroque cathedral on Ludgate Hill, London, built (1675–c.1710) by Christopher Wren to replace the medieval cathedral destroyed by the Fire of London in 1666. It has a double dome, and the Whispering Gallery runs round the inside of it. Words whispered close to the wall of it on one side may be heard clearly on the other side of the gallery.

St Peter's Basilica the largest Christian church, begun in 1506 in Rome on the site of the 4c basilica built by Emperor Constantine. The present building was originally designed by Donato Bramante on a Greek cross plan, modified in part by his successors, who included Raphael and Michelangelo, and changed into a Latin cross design by Carlo Maderna when he added a nave (1606–26).

St Petersburg, formerly **Petrograd** (1914–24), and **Leningrad** (1924–91) the capital of Leningrad oblast, NW Russia, lying on the R Neva at the head of the Gulf of Finland. It is the second largest Russian city and an important port (frozen from Jan to Apr). HISTORY founded by Peter the Great in 1703; former capital of the Russian Empire (1712–1918); the centre of the 1917 October Revolution, which began here; scene of a major siege by Germany in World War II (1941–4), in which nearly 1m people died. NOTABLE FEATURES Winter Palace (1754–62, rebuilt in 1839); St Isaac Cathedral (19c); Kazan Cathedral (1801–11); Fortress of Peter and Paul (1703); St Nicholas Navy Cathedral (1753–62); Academy of Sciences (1726); over 60 museums.

St Petersburg POP (1990) 239 000, a port town in Pinellas County, W Florida, USA. It lies on the tip of Pinellas Peninsula, between Tampa Bay and the Gulf of Mexico. St Petersburg was settled in 1876 and became a city in 1903. It is a major all-year tourist resort with a large yacht basin.

St Pierre et Miquelon POP (1990) 6 000, the two islands comprising a French Territorial Collectivity in the N Atlantic Ocean, S of Newfoundland. AREA 240sq km/93sq mi. CHIEF TOWN St Pierre. HISTORY settled by Breton and Basque fishermen in the 16c–17c; land-based fishing and drying rights were a source of dispute between the UK and France in the 19c; confirmed as a French Territory in 1946; in the 1970s and 1980s fishing zones were disputed by France and Canada. ECONOMY fishing; tourism.

St-Quentin POP (1990) 62 000, an industrial town in Aisne department, Picardy region, N France. It lies on the R Somme and there is a canal link to Belgium and N Germany. During the Middle Ages St-Quentin was a centre of the woollen industry. It was surrounded by battlefields throughout World War I. NOTABLE FEATURES basilica (12c–15c); late-Gothic town hall; Museum of Entomology.

Saint-Saëns, (Charles) Camille (1835–1921) French composer and music critic, born in Paris. He began to compose at five and wrote his first symphony in 1853. A distinguished pianist and organist, in 1871 he helped to found the Société Nationale de Musique. He wrote four further symphonies; 13 operas, including his best-known, *Samson et Dalila* (1877); symphonic poems; piano, violin, and cello concertos; the popular *Carnaval des animaux* (Carnaval of the Animals, 1886); church music, including his *Messe solennelle* (1855); chamber music; and songs.

St-Savin sur Gartempe, Church of an abbey church in St-Savin, W France. The original building was founded in 811 by Charlemagne over the tomb of the hermit St Savinus, but was soon destroyed. The present building dates from the 11c, and is noted for its life-size murals depicting biblical scenes. It is a World Heritage site.

saint's day a date in the Church calendar on which a particular saint is honoured.

St-Simon, Claude Henri de Rouvroy, Comte de (Count of) (1760–1825) French social reformer, the founder of French socialism, born in Paris. During the French Revolution he was imprisoned as an aristocrat. His writing was a reaction against the savagery of the revolutionary period, and proclaimed a brotherhood of man in which science and technology would become a new spiritual authority, as in *Du système industriel* (On the Industrial System, 1821) and *Nouveau christianisme* (New Christianity, 1825).

St Swithin's Day 15 Jul, the feast day of Saint Swithin, a 9c bishop of Winchester. According to a traditional rhyme, if it rains on this day, it will rain for 40 days; it it is dry on this day, it will remain dry for 40 days.

St-Tropez a fashionable resort on the Mediterranean coast, SE France, lying SW of Cannes. This former small fishing port is now frequented by yachtsmen, artists, and tourists.

St Valentine's Day 14 Feb, the feast day of two Christian martyrs of that name, on which special greetings cards are sent to sweethearts or people to whom one is attracted (see also VALENTINE).

St Vincent, Cape, Portuguese **Cabo de São Vicente** a rocky headland 60m above sea level on the Atlantic coast, Portugal. It is the SW extremity of Portugal and of continental Europe. In the 12c a ship bearing the body of St Vincent came ashore here. It was the scene of a British naval victory over the Spanish fleet in 1797.

Saint Vincent and the Grenadines or **St Vincent** POP (1991) 108 000, an island group of the Windward Is, situated in the E Caribbean Sea. AREA 390sq km/150sq mi (land). It lies 160km/100mi W of the Barbados and is divided into five parishes. CAPITAL Kingstown. TIME ZONE GMT −4. The population is mainly of African descent; Protestantism is the chief religion. OFFICIAL LANGUAGE English. CURRENCY the E Caribbean dollar. PHYSICAL DESCRIPTION comprises the island of St Vincent (length 29km/18mi; width 16km/10mi) and the N Grenadine Is; St Vincent is volcanic in origin; the highest peak is Soufrière, an active volcano rising to a height of 1 234m; the most recent eruption was in 1979. CLIMATE tropical, with an average annual temperature of 25°C, and an average annual rainfall of 1 500mm on the coast, 3 800mm in the interior. HISTORY visited by Christopher Columbus in 1498; first European settlement (by British) 1762; conflict with native Caribs and French; most Caribs deported 1797; black Africans imported as slave labour; part of the Windward Islands Colony (1880–1958); part of the West Indies Federation in 1958–62; gained independence in 1979. GOVERNMENT the British sovereign is represented by a Governor-General; a Prime Minister leads a 21-member House of Assembly, 15 of whom are elected. ECONOMY based on agriculture; bananas, arrowroot (world's largest producer), coconuts, nutmeg, mace, cocoa, sugar cane; food processing; cigarettes; textiles; beverages; furniture; tourism.

St Vincent and the Grenadines

Saint Vitus's dance chorea.

Saipan POP (1990) 39 000, the largest of the N Mariana Is, situated in the W Pacific Ocean. It lies 240km/150mi NE of Guam and is 23km/14mi long. AREA 122sq km/47sq mi. A barrier reef protects a wide lagoon off the W coast. ECONOMY tourism; copra, tropical fruit.

saith old use says.

Sakai POP (1991e) 808 000, a city in Osaka prefecture, S central Honshu, Japan. It lies on the E shore of Osaka-wan Bay. The city was formerly an important port, but the harbour has now silted up.

sake[1] noun benefit; behalf; account: for my sake.
— **for God's** or **heaven's** etc **sake** expressions used in annoyance or when begging, eg for forgiveness.
for the sake of ... for the purpose of ...; in order to ...
[from Anglo-Saxon sacu, lawsuit]

sake[2] or **saki** noun a Japanese alcoholic drink made from rice. [from Japanese sake]

Sakhalin, Japanese **Karafuto** an island in the Sea of Okhotsk, E Russia, separated from the Russian mainland to the W by the Tatar Strait, and from Japan to the S by La Pérouse Strait. AREA 74 066sq km/28 589sq mi; length, 942km/585mi; maximum width, 160km/100mi. HISTORY first discovered by Russians in 1644; colonized by the Japanese in the 18c; ceded to Russia in exchange for the Kuril Is in 1875; Japan gained control of the S area in 1905; ceded to the USSR in 1945. PHYSICAL DESCRIPTION two parallel mountain ranges run N–S; the coastline is marshy in the NW; the highest point of the island is 1 609m; the area is largely forested but agriculture is possible in the centre and the S. CLIMATE severe, with an annual average temperature of near freezing point. ECONOMY oil, coal; timber; paper; dairy farming.

Sakharov, Andrei Dimitrievich (1921–89) Soviet physicist and dissident, born in Moscow. He worked on nuclear fusion and cosmology in Leningrad, and was mainly responsible for the development of the Soviet hydrogen bomb. In 1975 he was awarded the Nobel Peace Prize following his peace and civil rights campaigns, but in 1980 was sent into internal exile in the 'closed city' of Gorky, where he undertook a series of hunger strikes in an attempt to secure permission for his wife, Yelena Bonner, to receive medical treatment overseas. He was released in 1986.

Sakhmet or **Sekmet** in ancient Egyptian religion, the goddess of Memphis, usually depicted with the head of a lioness. She is associated with savage cruelty, in particular towards the enemies of the Pharaoh.

salaam — noun **1** a word used as a greeting in Eastern countries, especially by Muslims. **2** a low bow with the palm of the right hand on the forehead, a Muslim greeting or show of respect. **3** (**salaams**) greetings; compliments. — verb

trans., intrans. to perform a salaam to someone. [from Arabic salam, peace]

salable same as SALEABLE.

salacious adj. **1** seeking to arouse sexual desire, especially crudely or obscenely. **2** unnaturally preoccupied with sex; lecherous. [from Latin salax, fond of leaping]

salaciousness noun being salacious.

salad noun a cold dish of usually raw vegetables, usually served with a dressing, often accompanying other foods.

salad days literary years of youthful inexperience and carefree innocence.

salad dressing any sauce served with a salad, eg mayonnaise or a mixture of oil and vinegar.

Saladin, in full **Salah-ed-din Yussuf ibn Ayub** (1137–93) Sultan of Egypt and Syria, born in Tekrit, Mesopotamia. He entered the service of Nur-eddin, Emir of Syria, on whose death (1174) he proclaimed himself sultan, reduced Mesopotamia, and received the homage of the Seljuk princes of Asia Minor. He then led the Muslims against the Christian crusaders in Palestine, whom he defeated near Tiberias in 1187, recapturing almost all their fortified places in Syria. A further crusade, headed by the kings of France and England, captured Acre in 1191 and defeated Saladin.

Salado, River a river forming part of a central Argentine system, total length 1 200km/750mi. It rises as the Bermejo in W La Rioja province, flowing S then SE to join the R Colorado 240km/150mi W of Bahía Blanca. Its lower course is sometimes called the Curacó. This river must be distinguished from the R Salado del Norte, N central Argentina, which rises in the Andes, and flows 2 000km/1 250mi SE to the Paraná at Santa Fe.

Salala POP (1982e) 10 000, a seaport on the Arabian Sea, Sultanate of Oman, S Arabian Peninsula. It is situated on a coastal plain backed by mountains. Excavations are being carried out at Al Balid, an 11c Islamic town.

Salam, Abdus (1926–   ) Pakistani theoretical physicist, born in Jhang. Professor at Imperial College of Science and Technology in London from 1957, he founded the International Centre of Theoretical Physics in Trieste in 1964. For producing a single unifying theory of both the weak and electromagnetic interactions between elementary particles, he shared the 1979 Nobel Prize for Physics with Steven Weinberg and Sheldon Glashow.

Salamanca, ancient **Helmantica Salmantica** POP (1991) 163 000, the capital of Salamanca province, Castilla-León, W Spain. It lies on R Tormes, 212km/132mi W of Madrid. The British defeated the French here in the Peninsular War (1812). NOTABLE FEATURES House of Shells (15c); San Stefano Monastery; old and new cathedrals; Plaza Mayor.

salamander noun **1** any of about 300 species of small amphibian belonging to the order Caudata, found in damp regions or in water, with a long body and tail similar to those of a lizard, but having a rounded head, moist skin without scales, and toes without claws. **2** a mythical reptile or spirit living in fire. [from Greek salamandra]
◇ Most salamanders have short delicate limbs and slither in a snake-like manner through wet vegetation. They breathe with a regular gulping movement, and also breathe through their skin. Some species lack lungs and breathe entirely through their skin, which is kept moist by special glands. Other glands produce poisons that discourage attack by predators. Aquatic salamanders live entirely in water, and terrestrial species return to water to breed. They rely largely on their keen eyesight and sense of smell when hunting for food, and terrestrial species eat only

moving prey, such as worms and slugs. Most salamanders lay eggs that hatch into larvae with gills, and some, such as the axolotl and mudpuppy, retain their gills throughout life.

salami noun (PL. **salamis**) a highly seasoned type of sausage, usually served sliced. [from Italian salami]

Salamis or **Koulouri** POP (1982) 20 000, a town in Attica department, Greece. It lies on the W coast of Salamis I (W of Piraeus). In 480 BC the Greeks decisively defeated the Persians in a naval battle to the E.

Salamis the principal city of prehistoric and classical Cyprus, on the E coast 8km/5mi N of Famagusta, its medieval and modern successor. It was founded in c.1075 BC, and flourished particularly during the 8c–4c BC. It was destroyed by an earthquake in AD 332–42, rebuilt as the Christian city of Constantia, but permanently abandoned after Arab raids in 647.

Salamis, Battle of a naval victory (480 BC) by the Greek, mainly Athenian, fleet over the Persian forces of Xerxes, which took place off the west coast of Attica. Xerxes retreated from Greece with part of his army; however, the bulk of the Persian infantry remained in Greece until defeated at Plateau the following year.

salami tactics the business practice of cutting staff or parts of an organization one by one.

sal ammoniac Chem. former name for ammonium chloride (NH_4Cl), a white or colourless crystalline mineral.

Salang a tunnel and pass in the Hindu Kush, E Afghanistan. It lies along the main supply route from Tajikistan to Kabul. The pass and tunnel were the focus of resistance activity by Mujahadeen guerrillas against Soviet troops and the Afghan Army during the occupation of Afghanistan in 1979–89.

salaried adj. **1** having or receiving a salary. **2** said of employment paid by a salary.

salary noun (PL. **salaries**) a fixed regular payment for (especially non-manual) work, usually made monthly. [from Latin salarium, soldier's allowance to buy salt]

Salazar, António de Oliveira (1889–1970) Portuguese dictator (1932–68), born near Coimbra. He taught economics and then gained extensive powers as Minister of Finance (1928). As premier, in 1932 he introduced a new, authoritarian regime called the Estado Novo (New State). He was also Minister of War (1936–44) and of Foreign Affairs (1936–47) during the delicate period of the Spanish Civil War.

Salcantay, Nevado an Andean peak in S central Peru. HEIGHT 6 271m. It lies 72km/45mi NW of Cuzco and is the highest point in the Cordillera Vilcabamba. The Inca city of Machu Picchu lies to the N.

Salchow, (Karl Emil Julius) Ulrich (1877–1949) Swedish figure skater. The first man to win an Olympic gold medal for this sport (1908), he was a record 10 times world champion (1901–11) and nine times European title holder between 1898 and 1913.

Sale POP (1981) 58 000, a town in Trafford borough, Greater Manchester, NW England. It lies 8km/5mi SW of Manchester.

Sale POP (1986) 14 000, a city in East Gippsland statistical division, SE Victoria, Australia. It is the supply centre for the Bass Strait oilfields. NOTABLE FEATURES Omega Navigation Tower (427m), the highest building in Australia; an oil and natural gas display; regional arts centre.

sale — noun **1** the act or practice of selling. **2** the selling of an item. **3** an item sold. **4** (usually **sales**) the value of the items sold. **5** a period during which goods are offered at reduced prices. **6** any event at which goods can be bought: a book sale. **7** (**sales**) the operations associated with, or the staff responsible for, selling. — *adj.* intended for selling, especially at reduced prices or by auction.

— **for** or **on sale** available for buying.

[from Anglo-Saxon *sala*]

saleable or **salable** *adj.* **1** fit to be sold. **2** for which there is a demand.

Salem POP (1990) 38 000, a seat of Essex County, NE Massachusetts, USA. It is a residential suburb of Boston on Massachusetts Bay. HISTORY settled in 1626, it developed as a port serving East Indies trade; in 1692, 20 people were executed as witches here; Salem is the birthplace of the novelist Nathaniel Hawthorne (1804). NOTABLE FEATURES Witch Museum; Salem Maritime National Historic Site; Pioneer Village.

Salem POP (1990) 278 000, the capital of the state of Oregon, USA, in Marion County, NW Oregon. It lies on the Willamette R. Founded by Methodist missionaries in 1841, it became capital of Oregon Territory in 1851 and then state capital in 1859.

Salem Witch Trials a series of incidents (1692) in colonial Massachusetts in which accusations were made that witchcraft was being practised. The town authorities were unable to control the situation, arrests were made on unsupported testimonies, and 19 people were executed. Judge Samuel Sewall later publicly confessed that the trials had been in error and that he believed no witchcraft had been practised.

sale of work a sale of items made in the community, to raise money for a charity or other organization.

Salerno POP (1991e) 151 000, the industrial capital of Salerno province, Campania, Italy. It lies on a bay of the Tyrrhenian Sea, 50km/31mi SE of Naples. HISTORY founded by the Romans in 197BC; one of the earliest universities in Europe with a notable school of medicine opened in the 11c and closed 1812; scene of major World War II fighting after an Allied landing in 1943. NOTABLE FEATURES cathedral (11c); Paestum ruins nearby.

saleroom *noun* a room in which public auctions are held, or goods to be auctioned displayed.

salesman or **saleswoman** or **salesperson** *noun* a person who sells goods to customers, especially in a shop.

salesmanship *noun* the techniques involved in persuading people to buy things.

sales talk persuasive talk used by salespeople.

Salford POP (1981) 98 000, a city in Salford borough, Greater Manchester, NW England. It lies on the R Irwell and Manchester Ship Canal, W of Manchester, for which it provides docks. Salford was chartered in 1230 and designated a city in 1926. NOTABLE FEATURES cathedral (1848); Peel Park Museum; art gallery.

Salic Law in normal usage, a rule of succession to the throne that bars all women and men whose royal descent is only through females. The principle was established in France from 1316, partly by invoking the law-code of the Salian Franks, issued c.511 and given definitive form c.798 — Salic Law in its original sense. [from Latin *Lex Salica*, the code of the Salian Franks]

salicylic acid *Chem.* a white crystalline solid that occurs naturally in certain plants, eg in willow bark and oil of wintergreen. It is used in the manufacture of aspirin, antiseptic ointments, dyes, food preservatives, and perfumes. [from Latin *salyx*, willow, from the bark of which it was originally prepared]

salient — *adj.* **1** striking; outstanding. **2** *Archit.* jutting out or up. — *noun* a projecting part or section, eg of a fortification or a defensive line of troops. [from Latin *salire*, to leap]

Salieri, Antonio (1750–1825) Italian composer, born in Verona. He arrived in Vienna at 16

and worked there for the rest of his life. A teacher of Beethoven and Schubert, he became court composer (1774) and hofkapellmeister (1788), wrote over 40 operas, an oratorio, and masses. He was also famous as a rival of Mozart.

saline — *adj.*, *said of a substance* containing sodium chloride; salty. — *noun* (also **saline solution**) a solution of sodium chloride (common salt) in water, having the same pH and concentration as body fluids. It is used to dilute drugs, and in intravenous drips, eg to treat shock. [from Latin *sal*, salt]

Salinger, J(erome) D(avid) (1919–) US writer, born in New York City. He served in World War II, then devoted himself to writing, much of which appeared in the *New Yorker* magazine. His fame rests on the novel *Catcher in the Rye* (1951), written from the viewpoint of a New York 16-year-old who has run away from school. Other books include *For Esmé, with Love and Squalor* (1953) and *Franny and Zooey* (1961).

salinity *noun* being saline.

Salisbury, sometimes called **New Sarum** POP (1981) 38 000, a city in Salisbury district, Wiltshire, S England. It lies at the junction of the Avon, Nadder, Bourne, and Wylye rivers, 34km/21mi NW of Southampton. HISTORY Old Sarum (3km/2mi to the N), an Iron Age hill fort, became the centre of settlement but was abandoned when New Sarum was founded in 1220; in 1483 the Duke of Buckingham was beheaded at Salisbury, at the time when it was the headquarters of Richard III. NOTABLE FEATURES the 13c cathedral, with the highest spire in Britain, contains one of the four copies of the Magna Carta; churches of St Thomas (15c), St Martin (13c–15c), and St Edmund (1407).

Salisbury see HARARE.

Salisbury Cathedral a painting by John Constable (1823, Victoria and Albert Museum, London).

Salisbury Plain a vast chalk plateau of open downs in Wiltshire, S England, rising to an average of 137m and covering c.777sq km/300sq mi. Much of the area is now either under cultivation or used for army training, but it remains remarkable for a number of prehistoric sites, particularly Stonehenge.

saliva *noun* the clear alkaline liquid produced by the salivary glands and mucous membranes of the mouth, that softens and moistens food and begins the process of digestion. It consists mainly of water, mucus, and the enzyme ptyalin (amylase), which breaks down starch. [from Latin *saliva*]

salivary *adj.* relating to, secreting, or conveying saliva.

salivate *verb intrans.* **1** to have (especially excessive amounts of) saliva in the mouth, as at the thought or sight of food. **2** to drool.

salivation *noun* the flow of saliva, especially in excess, and in the expectation of food.

Salk, Jonas Edward (1914–) US virologist, born in New York City. Professor at Pittsburgh and later Director of the Institute for Biological Studies in San Diego, he developed the first polio vaccine in 1954. It was found to be 80–90 per cent effective, but was superseded by Albert Sabin's vaccine.

sallow — *adj.*, *said of a person's complexion* yellowish-brown, often through poor health. — *verb trans.*, *intrans.* to make or become sallow. [from Anglo-Saxon *salo* or *salu*]

sally — *noun* (PL. **sallies**) **1** a sudden attack by troops rushing forward. **2** an excursion. — *verb intrans.* (**sallies, sallied**) **1** *said of troops* to carry out a sally. **2** *humorous* (also **sally forth**) to rush out or surge forward; to set off. [from Latin *salire*, to leap]

salmon *noun* (PL. **salmon, salmons**) **1** any of various medium-sized to large fish, belonging to

the family Salmonidae, that are native to the N Atlantic and N Pacific Oceans, but migrate to freshwater rivers and streams of Europe and N America in order to spawn. **2** the edible reddish-orange flesh of this fish, highly prized as a food. **3** (also **salmon pink**) an orange-pink colour. [from Latin *salmo*, from *salire*, to leap]

◇ The Atlantic salmon (*Salmo salar*) is a silvery streamlined fish up to 1.5m long, closely related to the European trout. The young fish hatches in freshwater rivers or streams, and makes its way downstream to the Atlantic Ocean, where it develops into a mature adult. It remains there for about three years before migrating back upstream to its birthplace in order to spawn. This upstream migration can involve journeys of up to 5 000km, and spectacular leaping up rocks and small waterfalls. Fishermen generally catch salmon when the fish are journeying back to their spawning grounds, and severe overfishing and pollution have caused the Atlantic salmon to become rare or absent in many rivers.

salmonella *noun* (PL. **salmonellae**) **1** (Salmonella) any member of a large genus of rod-shaped bacteria that are found in the intestines of humans and animals, and include many bacteria associated with food poisoning, gastroenteritis, and diseases such as typhoid and paratyphoid fever. **2** food poisoning caused by such bacteria, the main symptoms of which are violent diarrhoea and abdominal pain. [named after the US veterinary surgeon Daniel E Salmon (1850–1914)]

salmon ladder a series of steps built in a river to help salmon swim upstream to lay eggs.

Salome (1c AD) a New Testament character, the daughter of Herod Antipas's wife Herodias. Mark 6.17–28 relates how she was asked to choose a reward for dancing before Herod Antipas. At her mother's instigation, she requested the head of John the Baptist.

Salome an opera by Richard Strauss (1905), based on Oscar Wilde's play and biblical sources. Set in Herod's palace, c.30 AD , it depicts Herod's loathsome decadence and the murderous nature of his wife Herodias and step-daughter Salome through the biblical story of Salome's request for John the Baptist's head as a reward for entertaining Herod's dinner guests.

Salon in France, an exhibition of art sponsored by the French government, named after the *Salon d'Apollon* of the Louvre Palace, Paris, the first venue chosen by Louis XIV in 1667. Held annually and open to all artists since the late 18c, in the 19c the selection jury refused many of the Impressionist and post-Impressionist painters, whose work was then shown in the *Salon des Refusés* (1863). The *Salon des Indépendants* is an annual art exhibition of the Société des Artistes Indépendants, first held in Paris in 1884. The term has come to be applied to other kinds of exhibition, such as the book fair, *Salon du Livre*.

salon *noun* **1** a shop or other establishment where clients are beautified in some way: *a hairdressing salon*. **2** a drawing-room, especially in a large continental house. **3** a gathering of arts celebrities in a fashionable (especially 17c or 18c Parisian) household. **4** an art exhibition. [from French *salon*]

Salon d'Automne an annual art exhibition held in Paris since 1903, founded by the Fauves (eg Henri Matisse). Exhibitions have included a Paul Gauguin memorial (1903), and a Paul Cézanne memorial (1907).

Salon des Indépendants an annual art exhibition held in Paris by the Société des Artistes Indépendants since 1884. The Society was established in reaction to the rigours of the official Salon, with the aim of allowing any artist to exhibit his or her work without being subject to a selection committee.

Salon des Refusés an art exhibition held in Paris in 1863 on the command of Napoleon III. It included all the works which had been refused in that year by the official Salon (eg Edouard Manet's *Le Déjeuner sur l'herbe* and *Olympia*). It caused great controversy and was not repeated.

Salonga a national park in Zaire, established in 1970. AREA 36 560sq km/14 112sq mi. Its main rivers include the Salonga, Lomela, and Luilaka. The park is a World Heritage site.

Salonica *or* **Salonika**, Greek **Thessaloníki** POP (1991) 740 000, a seaport and the capital of Salonica department, Macedonia region, Greece. It is the country's second-largest city. HISTORY founded in 315 BC; became capital of Roman Macedonia in 148 BC; held by Turkey from 1430 to 1912; a base for Allied operations in World War I. NOTABLE FEATURES Arch of Galerius (AD297); Basilica of Ayia Paraskevi (5c), Basilica of Ayios Dimitrios (9c).

saloon *noun* **1** a large public room, eg for functions or some other specified purpose: *a billiard saloon.* **2** a large public room on a passenger ship. **3** *old use* a lounge bar. **4** *North Amer., esp. US* any bar where alcohol is sold. **5** *colloq.* (*in full* **saloon car**) any motor car not an estate, coupé, convertible, or sports model. [see SALON]

Salop *noun* a form used as an abbreviation of Shropshire. [from Old French *Salopescira*, Shropshire]

salopettes *pl. noun* skiing trousers reaching to the chest, held up by shoulder-straps. [from French *salopettes*]

Salote (1900–65) Queen of Tonga, who succeeded her father, George Tupou II, in 1918. She is remembered in Britain for her colourful and engaging presence during her visit for the Coronation of Elizabeth II (1953).

salpingectomy *noun Medicine* the surgical removal of a Fallopian tube. [from Greek *salpinx - ingos*, trumpet + -ECTOMY]

salsa *noun* **1** rhythmic dance music of S American origin, mixing jazz with rock. **2** a dance performed to such music. **3** a spicy sauce of Mexican origin, made with tomatoes, onions, chillies, and oil. [from Spanish *salsa*, sauce]

salsify *noun* (PL. **salsifies**) a purple-flowered Mediterranean plant with a long cylindrical edible root; the root. [from Italian *sassefrica*]

SALT *abbrev.* Strategic Arms Limitation Talks.

Salt POP (1989e) 48 000, the capital of Al Balqā governorate, East Bank, NW Jordan. It is 21km/13mi W of Amman.

salt — *noun* **1** (**common salt**) sodium chloride, a white crystalline compound that occurs as a mineral and in solution in seawater. It has been used since ancient times to season and preserve food. **2** a chemical compound that is formed when an acid reacts with a base, so that one or more hydrogen atoms of the acid are replaced by metal ions or other positive ions, eg the ammonium ion. Most salts are crystalline compounds that dissolve completely in water. **3** (**salts**) any substance resembling salt in appearance or taste, especially a medicine: *Epsom salts.* **4** liveliness; interest; wit. **5** (*also* **old salt**) an experienced sailor. — *verb* **1** to season or preserve (food) with salt. **2** to cover (an icy road) with a scattering of salt to melt the ice. — *adj.* **1** preserved with salt: *salt pork.* **2** containing salt: *salt water.* **3** tasting of salt; not bitter, sweet or sour.
— **rub salt in someone's wounds** to add to their discomfort.
salt something away to store it up for future use; to hoard it.
the salt of the earth a consistently reliable or dependable person.
take something with a pinch of salt to treat a statement or proposition sceptically or with suspicion.
worth one's salt competent; worthy of respect. [from Anglo-Saxon *salt*]

Salta 1 POP (1991) 374 000, the capital of Salta province, NW Argentina. It lies on the R Arias, in the Lerma Valley, at an altitude of 1 190m. The city is the commercial and trade centre for an extensive farming, timber, stock-raising, and mining area. HISTORY founded in 1582; site of a battle in which Spanish royalists were defeated in 1813. The cathedral contains venerated Christian images sent from Spain in 1592; these are thought to have caused a miracle in 1692 when an earthquake ceased on their being carried through the streets. A large parade is held each Sep in celebration of this event. **2** a province in NW Argentina with Salta as its capital.

salt cellar a container holding salt for use at the dinner table.

salted *adj.* **1** cured or preserved in salt. **2** containing salt.

Saltillo POP (1990) 441 000, the resort capital of Coahuila state, N Mexico. It lies 85km/53mi SW of Monterrey at an altitude of 1 609m. The city was founded in 1575. NOTABLE FEATURE cathedral (18c).

saltiness *noun* a salty quality.

Salt Lake City POP (1990) 160 000, the capital of the state of Utah, USA, in Salt Lake County, N Utah. It lies on the Jordan R, near the S end of the Great Salt Lake. Settled by Mormons in 1849, it expanded as a centre on the route to the California gold mines. The Mormon Church has its headquarters here, and 60% of the city's population are Mormons. NOTABLE FEATURES Temple Square; Trolley Square; Salt Lake Art Centre; Utah Museum of Fine Arts; Pioneer Memorial Museum; Hansen Planetarium; Utah Museum of Natural History.

saltpetre *noun* potassium nitrate. [from Latin *salpetra*, salt of rock]

salty *adj.* (**saltier**, **saltiest**) **1** containing salt. **2** tasting strongly or excessively of salt. **3** *said of humour* sharp.

salubrious *adj.* **1** *formal* health-giving; promoting well-being: *a salubrious climate.* **2** respectable; pleasant: *not a very salubrious neighbourhood.* [from Latin *salus*, health]

saluki *noun* (PL. **salukis**) a tall slender silkyhaired dog of Arabian origin, with a tufty tail and ears. [from Arabic *seluqi*]

salutarily *adv.* in a salutary way.

salutary *adj.* **1** beneficial, or intended to be beneficial: *a salutary warning.* **2** healthy; wholesome. [from Latin *salus*, health]

salutation *noun* an act, gesture, or phrase of greeting.

salutatory *adj.* relating to or of the nature of a salutation.

salute — *verb* **1** *trans., intrans. Mil.* to pay formal respect to (someone) with a set gesture, especially with the right arm or a weapon. **2** to pay tribute to: *we salute your bravery.* **3** to greet with a show of friendship or respect. — *noun* **1** a military gesture of respect. **2** a greeting. [from Latin *salutare*, to greet]

Salut, Iles du an island archipelago lying c.13km/8mi off the coast of French Guiana, NE South America. It includes Ile St Joseph, and Ile du Diable (Devil's I). The islands housed notorious French penal colonies from 1898 until the 1940s; political prisoners on Devil's I included Alfred Dreyfus. The hotel on Ile Royale is the warders' former mess hall.

Salvador, also known as **Bahia** POP (1991) 2.5m, the port capital of Bahia state, NE Brazil. It lies on the Atlantic coast, SE of Recife. HISTORY founded in 1549; capital of Brazil until 1763. NOTABLE FEATURES most of the city's 135 churches and fortifications date from the 17c–18c; older parts of the upper city are a national monument and World Heritage site; Government Palace; city

library (1811); Fort of Santo Antônio da Barra (1589).

salvage — *verb* **1** to rescue (eg property or a vessel) from potential damage or loss, eg in a fire or shipwreck, or from disposal as waste. **2** to recover (a sunken ship). **3** to manage to retain (eg one's pride) in adverse circumstances. — *noun* **1** the act of salvaging property, a vessel, etc. **2** property salvaged. **3** payment made as a reward for saving a ship from destruction or loss. [from Latin *salvare*, to save]

salvageable *adj.* capable of being salvaged.

salvation *noun* **1** the act of saving a person or thing from harm. **2** a person or thing that saves another from harm. **3** *Relig.* liberation from the influence of sin, or its consequences for the human soul. [from Latin *salvare*, to save]

Salvation Army a Christian organization, with a semi-military structure of ranks, aiming to help the poor and spread Christianity.

salve — *noun* **1** ointment to heal or soothe. **2** anything that comforts or consoles. — *verb* to ease or comfort: *salve one's conscience.* [from Anglo-Saxon *sealf*]

salver *noun* a small ornamented tray, usually of silver. [from French *salve*, tray for presenting the king's food for tasting]

salvia *noun Bot.* any plant of the genus *Salvia*, including sage. [from Latin *salvia*, sage]

salvo *noun* (PL. **salvos**, **salvoes**) **1** a burst of gunfire from several guns firing at the same time. **2** a sudden round of applause. **3** a ferocious outburst of criticism or insults. [from Italian *salva*, salute]

sal volatile an old name for ammonium carbonate, especially in a solution that slowly gives off ammonia gas, and is used as smelling salts. [from Latin *sal volatile*, volatile salt]

Salween, River, Burmese **Nu Jiang** a river in SE Asia, rising in SW China, length 2 815km/1 750mi. It flows generally S through Burma (Myanma), forms part of the border with Thailand, and enters the Gulf of Martaban, an inlet of the Andaman Sea. It is navigable only to Kamamaung (120km/75mi from its mouth).

Salyut *Astron.* any of a series of manned Earthorbiting Soviet space stations, the first of which was launched in 1971. It has demonstrated that astronauts can remain in orbit for periods of six months or more.

Salzburg 1 POP (1991) 144 000, the capital of Salzburg state, central Austria. It lies on the R Salzach. The Old Town lies between the left bank of the river and the Mönchsberg Ridge. Salzburg is a focal point for international tourism. The composer Wolfgang Amadeus Mozart was born here in 1756. NOTABLE FEATURES cathedral (1614–28); St Peter's Church (1130–43); Franciscan Church; Kollegienkirche (1694–1707); town hall (originally 1407); Mozartium (musical academy); the Fortress of Hohensalzburg (1077) dominates the town. EVENTS Mozart Festival (Jan), Salzburg Festival (Jul–Aug). **2** a state in central Austria with Salzburg as its capital.

Salzburg Alps a division of the E Alps which extends along the Austria–Germany border S of Salzburg. The highest peaks are the Hochkönig (2 938m) in Austria, and the Watzmann (2 713m) in Germany.

Salzkammergut an E Alpine region in central Austria. It is a popular tourist area with many lakes. Mountains in the region include Dachstein and Totes Gebirge; towns include Gmunden, Hallstatt, and Bad Aussee. The name originally applied to a salt-mining area around Bad Ischl.

Samantha a female first name. [origin uncertain; perhaps from Hebrew]

Samara, formerly **Kuybyshev** (1935–91) POP (1990e) 1.3m, the river-port capital of Kuybyshev oblast, SW Russia, lying on the R Volga where it meets the R Samara. HISTORY founded as a fortress in 1586; the Soviet government transferred here during World War II (1941–3).

Samaria, also called **Sebaste**, modern **Sebastiyah** the site in central Palestine of the ancient capital of the N kingdom of the Hebrews, Israel. It was destroyed by the Assyrians in c.722 BC, and rebuilt and enlarged by Herod the Great in the 20s BC. It remained a flourishing Greek-style city throughout the Roman period.

Samaritan — *noun* **1** (*also* **good Samaritan**) a kind or helpful person. **2** a worker with the Samaritans. **3** *Biblical* an inhabitant of ancient Samaria (see SAMARITANS). — *adj.* relating to Samaria or the Samaritans.

Samaritans 1 a sect of Jewish origin that lived in Samaria, the northern territory of Israel, who apparently were not deported in the Assyrian conquest of c.721 BC. They were in tension with the Jews of Judea during the rebuilding of Jerusalem after the return from exile, criticized for their mixed ancestry, their building of a rival temple on Mt Gerizim, and their schism from true Judaism. A small remnant survives today. **2** a group named after the Good Samaritan in Christ's parable, founded (1953) in London by an Anglican priest, Chad Varah. Operated by volunteers, it provides a 24-hour telephone counselling service in many cities in the UK to support those who are in emotional distress.

samarium *noun Chem.* (SYMBOL **Sm**, ATOMIC NUMBER **62**) a soft silvery metal that is used in magnetic alloys with cobalt to make very strong permanent magnets. It is also a neutron absorber, and some of its alloys are used in components of nuclear reactors. [named after Col Samarski, a 19c Russian mines inspector]

Samarkand 1 POP (1991e) 371 000, the capital of Samarkand region, Uzbekistan. It is a major industrial, scientific, and cultural centre situated in the fertile Zeravshan Valley. HISTORY the Abbasid family dynasty made it capital in the 9c–10c; known as the city of Timur from 1333 to 1405, after the Tatar conqueror; ruled by the Uzbeks from the 16c until the 19c. NOTABLE FEATURE Gur Amir Mausoleum. **2** a region in Uzbekistan with Samarkand as its capital.

samba *noun* **1** a lively Brazilian dance, or a short-stepping ballroom dance developed from it. **2** a piece of music for either. [from Portuguese *samba*]

same — *adj.* **1** exactly alike or very similar. **2** not different. **3** unchanged or unchanging. **4** previously mentioned; the actual one in question: *this same man.* — *pron.* (**the same**) the same person or thing, or the one previously mentioned: *she drank whisky, and I drank the same.* — *adv.* (**the same**) **1** similarly; likewise: *I feel the same.* **2** *colloq.* equally: *we love each of you the same.* — **all** *or* **just the same** nevertheless. **at the same time** however; on the other hand. **be all the same to someone** to make no difference to them. **same here!** *colloq.* an exclamation of agreement or involvement. [from Norse *samr*]

sameness *noun* **1** being the same. **2** tedious monotony.

samey *adj. colloq.* boringly similar or unchanging.

samizdat *noun* in the former Soviet Union, the secret printing and distribution of writings banned by the government; the writings themselves. [from Russian *samizdat*, self-published]

Samos POP (1991) 42 000, a wooded Greek island in the E Aegean Sea. AREA 476sq km/ 184sq mi. The island is separated from the W coast of Turkey by a strait only 2km/1mi wide and rises to 1 440m in the W. It is the site of the Heraion, a sanctuary to the goddess Hera and a cultural centre of the ancient world. The philoso-

pher Pythagoras was born here in the 6c BC. Samos is also famous for its wines.

samosa *noun* a small deep-fried triangular spicy meat or vegetable pasty of Indian origin. [from Hindi *samosa*]

Samothrace, Greek **Samothráki** POP (1982) 3 000, a Greek island in the NE Aegean Sea, 40km/25mi from the mainland. AREA 178sq km/69sq mi. The island is noted for its sanctuary of the Great Gods, the home of a mystery cult, and for the *Victory of Samothrace* sculpture (now held in the Louvre, Paris).

samovar *noun* a Russian urn for boiling water for tea, often elaborately decorated, traditionally heated by a central charcoal-filled pipe. [from Russian *samovar*]

Samoyed *noun* **1** see NENETS. **2** a sturdy dog of Siberian origin, with a thick cream or white coat and an upward-curling tail. [from Russian *Samoed*]

sampan *noun* any small flat-bottomed oriental boat propelled by oars rather than sails. [from Chinese *san*, three + *pan*, plank]

sampan

samphire *noun* a flowering cliff plant whose fleshy leaves are used in pickles. [from French *herbe de Saint Pierre*, herb of St Peter]

sample — *noun* a unit or part taken, displayed, or considered as representative of others or of a whole. — *verb* **1** to take or try as a sample. **2** to get experience of: *sampled life abroad.* [from Old French *essample*, from Latin *exemplum*, example]

sampler *noun* a piece of embroidery produced as a show or test of skill.

sampling *noun* the mixing of short extracts from previous sound recordings into a new backing track.

Samson (c.11c BC) a biblical hero, the last of Israel's tribal leaders ('judges') prior to Samuel and the establishment of the monarchy under Saul. He was a Nazirite consecrated to God from birth, and Judges 13–16 tells of his great strength (the secret of which was his uncut hair), his battles against the Philistines, his 20-year rule, and his fatal infatuation with a Philistine woman, Delilah, who discovered his secret and had his head shaved. The Philistines blinded him and put him in prison until his hair grew back and he pulled down their temple upon them.

Samudragupta (d.c.380 AD) N Indian emperor, with a reputation as a warrior, poet, and musician. He epitomized the ideal king of the golden age of Hindu history.

Samuel 1 (11c BC) a biblical character, the last of Israel's tribal leaders or judges and the first of the prophets, son of Elkanah and his wife Hannah. An Ephraimite who was dedicated to the priesthood as a child by a Nazirite vow, after the defeat of Israel and loss of the Ark of the Covenant to the Philistines, Samuel moved in a circuit among Israel's shrines and tried to keep the tribal confederation together. He reluctantly presided over the election of King Saul, but criticized him for assuming priestly prerogatives and disobeying divine instructions. Finally, he anointed David as Saul's successor, rather than Saul's own son, Jonathan. **2** a male first name. [from Hebrew, = asked of the Lord]

Samuel, Books of two books of the Old Testament, which were one in the Hebrew Bible and probably were also once combined with Kings; also called 1 and 2 Kings, in some Catholic versions. They comprise a narrative of Israel's history from the time of the prophet Samuel and

Israel's first king Saul (1 Samuel) to that of David's accession and reign (2 Samuel).

samurai *noun* (PL. **samurai**) **1** a member of an aristocratic class of Japanese warriors between the 11c and 19c; also, this class collectively. **2** *loosely* a samurai's sword, a two-handed sword with a curved blade. [from Japanese *samurai*]

San a river in SE Poland. It rises in the Carpathian Mts in the S and flows 443km/275mi NW, E and NW to meet the R Vistula NE of Stalowa Wola.

San'a POP (1990e) 500 000, the capital and commercial centre of Yemen. It is situated on a high plateau of the Arabian Peninsula, at an altitude of 2 170m, c.65km/40mi inland from Hodeida. Its port is on the Red Sea. NOTABLE FEATURES the walled city is a World Heritage site; Great Mosque; Museum of S Arabian Antiquities.

San Andreas Fault a fracture in the Earth's crust in California. It is the major fault in a network of faults which extends from NW California to the Gulf of California. It lies on the boundary of the N American plate and the Pacific plate, and extends at least 30km vertically into the Earth. Movement along the fault causes earthquakes.

San Andrés-Providencia POP (1992e) 42 000, an administrative area of Colombia, comprising two small islands and seven groups of coral reefs and cays in the Caribbean Sea. AREA 44sq km/17sq mi. They are situated 480km/300mi N of Colombia. The largest island is San Andrés. Providencia (also called Old Providence) lies 80km/50mi NE of San Andrés. The islands were the headquarters of pirate Henry Morgan in the 17c. Today they are a duty-free zone and San Andrés is an important international airline stop-over. ECONOMY coconuts; vegetable oil; tourism.

San Antonio POP (1990) 1.3m, the seat of Bexar County, S central Texas, USA. It lies on the San Antonio R, 120km/75mi SW of Austin. HISTORY settled by the Spanish in 1718; captured by the Texans in the Texas Revolution of 1835; the Mexican attack on the mission known as the Alamo was made here in 1836; five different flags have been flown during the city's history (Spain, Mexico, Republic of Texas, Confederate States of America, and the USA). An important industrial, financial, and cultural city, San Antonio is also a military aviation centre. NOTABLE FEATURES the Alamo; Paseo del Rio (the Spanish Governor's Palace); Museum of Art; Institute of Texan Cultures; Tower of the Americas (229m high).

sanatorium *noun* (PL. **sanatoriums, sanatoria**) **1** a hospital for the chronically ill, or for patients recovering from illnesses treated elsewhere. **2** a sickroom in a school, etc. [from Latin, from *sanare*, to heal]

San Bernardino POP (1990) 164 000, the seat of San Bernardino County, California, USA. It lies in the San Bernardino Valley, c.88km/55mi E of Los Angeles and was founded by Mormons in 1851. The Norton Air Force Base is nearby. NOTABLE FEATURE museum.

Sanchi a site in Madhya Pradesh state, India, the location of a group of Buddhist monuments, including the Great Stupa. It is a World Heritage site.

sanctification *noun* sanctifying, consecrating.

sanctify *verb* (**sanctifies, sanctified**) **1** to make sacred. **2** to free from sin. **3** to declare legitimate or binding in the eyes of the Church: *sanctify a marriage.* [from Latin *sanctus*, holy + *facere*, to make]

sanctimonious *adj.* displaying exaggerated holiness or virtuousness, especially hypocritically. [from Latin *sanctimonia*, sanctity]

sanctimoniousness *noun* being sanctimonious.

sanction — *noun* **1** official permission or authority. **2** an economic or military measure taken by one nation to persuade another to adopt a particular policy, eg restricting trade. **3** a means of encouraging adherence to a social custom, eg a penalty or reward. **4** any penalty attached to an offence. — *verb* (**sanctioned**, **sanctioning**) **1** to authorize or confirm formally. **2** to allow or agree to. **3** to encourage. [from Latin *sancire*, to decree]

sanctity *noun* **1** the quality of being holy or sacred. **2** the quality of deserving to be respected, and not violated or flouted. [from Latin *sanctitas*]

Sanctorius, Italian **Santorio Santorio** (1561–1636) Italian physician, born in Justinopolis, Venetian Republic. Professor at Padua, he invented a number of instruments, but is best known for his investigations into the fluctuation in the body's weight under different conditions due to 'insensible perspiration'. A friend of Galileo, his work illustrates the quantifying spirit in the medicine of his time.

sanctuary *noun* (PL. **sanctuaries**) **1** a holy or sacred place, eg a church or temple. **2** the most sacred area within such a place, eg around an altar. **3** a place, historically a church, giving immunity from arrest or other interference. **4** freedom from disturbance: *the sanctuary of the garden*. **5** a nature reserve in which the animals or plants are protected by law. [from Latin *sanctuarium*, from *sanctus*, holy]

sanctum *noun* (PL. **sanctums**, **sancta**) **1** a sacred place. **2** a place providing total privacy. [from Latin *sanctum*, holy]

Sand, George, pseudonym of **Amandine Aurore Lucile Dudevant**, née **Dupin** (1804–76) French novelist, born in Paris. She left her husband (Baron Dudevant) and family in 1831, and returned to Paris to take up literature. After 1848 she settled at Nohant, where she spent the rest of her life in literary activity, interspersed with travel. Her first novel, *Indiana* (1832), was followed by over 100 books, the most successful of which are those describing rustic life (eg *François le Champi*, 1848). She also wrote plays, autobiographical works, and letters.

sand — *noun* **1** *Geol.* particles of rock, especially quartz, with diameters ranging from 0.06 to 2mm, produced as a result of weathering and erosion by wind, water, and ice. It is commonly found in deserts and on seashores, and is used to make glass, mortar, and cement. **2** (**sands**) an area covered with this substance, especially a seashore or desert. — *verb* to smooth or polish with sandpaper or a sander. [from Anglo-Saxon *sand*]

Sandage, Allan Rex (1926–) US astronomer, born in Iowa City. Working at the Hale Observatories, he discovered a faint optical astronomical object with a very unusual spectrum at the same position as a compact radio source (1960); this was later shown to be the first optical identification of a quasar.

sandal *noun* a light shoe with little or no upper and straps attached for holding it on the foot. [from Greek *sandalon*]

sandalwood *noun* **1** a light-coloured fragrant wood from the heart of a SE Asian tree. It is used for carving, and yields an oil used in perfumes. **2** the tree. [from Sanskrit *candana*]

sandbag — *noun* a sand-filled sack used with others to form a barrier against gunfire or flood, or as ballast. — *verb* to barricade or weigh down with sandbags.

sandbank *noun* a bank of sand in a river or sea, formed by currents, often exposed at low tides.

sandblast — *noun* a jet of sand forced from a tube by air or steam pressure. — *verb* to clean (eg stonework) with a sandblast.

sandboy
— **as happy as a sandboy** extremely happy.

Sandburg, Carl (1878–1967) US poet, born in Galesburg, Illinois. He became a journalist in Chicago, and his volumes of poetry include *Chicago Poems* (1915), *Cornhuskers* (1918) and *Good Morning, America* (1928). He also published a collection of folksongs, *The American Songbag* (1927), and a *Life of Abraham Lincoln* (6 vols, 1926–39, Pulitzer Prize). He was awarded a Pulitzer Prize for his *Complete Poems* (1950).

sandcastle *noun* a pile of sand moulded for fun into a (perhaps only approximate) castle shape.

sander *noun* a power-driven tool to which sandpaper or an abrasive disc can be fitted for speedy sanding of wood, etc.

Sanderson, Tessa (Theresa Ione) (1956–) English field athlete and television presenter, born in Wolverhampton. She first threw the javelin for Great Britain in 1974. In a career latterly dogged by injury she won three Commonwealth gold medals (1978, 1986, 1990), and one Olympic gold (1984). In 1989 she became a sports newsreader for Sky TV.

sandhopper *noun* a semiterrestrial crustacean, with a flattened body, capable of vigorous jumping, often abundant along the seashore, feeding on detritus.

San Diego POP (1990) 2.5m, the seaport seat of San Diego County, SW California, USA. It lies on the E shore of San Diego Bay, just N of the Mexico border. The first permanent white settlement in California, it is today a cultural, research, and tourist centre, and host to many conventions. It is also a naval and military base. There are early 19c adobe buildings in the Old Town district. NOTABLE FEATURES San Diego de Alcalá Mission (established in 1769, now restored); first mission in California; Serra Museum; Cabrillo National Monument; aquatic park; zoo.

Sandino, Augusto César (1895–1934) Nicaraguan revolutionary, born in Niquinohomo (or La Victoria). He led guerrilla resistance to US occupation forces after 1926, and was later murdered, on Somoza's orders. The Nicaraguan revolutionaries of 1979 (later known as 'Sandinistas') regarded him as their principal hero.

sand lizard a lizard native to Europe and W Asia, brown or green in colour with small dark rings and two pale lines along its back. It inhabits heathland and sandy areas, and feeds mainly on insects.

sandman *noun* (**the sandman**) a man in folklore who supposedly sprinkles sand on children's eyes to make them sleepy.

sand martin a small European bird of the martin family that nests in tunnels hollowed out of sandy banks.

Sandown POP (1981) 16 000 (with Shanklin), a town in South Wight district, I of Wight, S England. It lies on Sandown Bay, S of Ryde and N of Shanklin. The poet Algernon Charles Swinburne lived here.

sandpaper — *noun* abrasive paper with a coating originally of sand, now usually of crushed glass, for smoothing and polishing wood. — *verb* to smooth or polish with sandpaper.

sandpiper *noun* any of various wading birds of northern shores, with a high-pitched piping call.

sandpit *noun* a shallow pit filled with sand for children to play in.

sandstone *noun* *Geol.* a sedimentary rock consisting of compacted sand cemented together with clay, calcium carbonate, iron oxide, or silica. It may be hard or soft, and there are many varieties of colour, widely used in the construction of buildings.

sandstorm *noun* a strong wind sweeping along clouds of sand.

Sandwich, John Montagu, 4th Earl of (1718–92) English politician, remembered as the inventor of sandwiches, which he is said to have devised in order to eat while playing round the clock at a gaming-table. He was First Lord of the Admiralty under both Henry Pelham and Lord North (1748–51, 1771–82), and was often attacked for corruption.

sandwich — *noun* a snack consisting of two slices of bread or a roll with a filling of cheese, meat, etc. — *verb* to place, especially with little or no gaps, between two other things. [named after the 4th Earl of Sandwich]

sandwich board either of two boards carried against a person's chest and back by means of shoulder straps, for the purpose of displaying advertisements.

sandwich course an educational course involving alternate periods of study and work experience.

Sandwich Island see ÉFATÉ.

sandy *adj.* (**sandier**, **sandiest**) **1** containing sand. **2** of the colour of sand, a pale yellowish-brown, or (of hair) reddish-brown.

sane *adj.* **1** sound in mind; not mad. **2** sensible. See also SANITY. [from Latin *sanus*, healthy]

sanely *adv.* in a sane way.

San Francisco POP (1990) 1.6m, a city co-extensive with San Francisco County, W California, USA. It is bounded W by the Pacific Ocean, N by the Golden Gate Bridge, and E by San Francisco Bay. Built on a series of hills, San Francisco is connected to Marin County in the N by the Golden Gate Bridge (one of the longest suspension bridges in the world) and to Oakland in the E by the Transbay Bridge. San Francisco is the financial capital of the W coast, and a major cultural, tourist, and convention centre. It has the largest Chinatown in the USA. HISTORY a mission and a small community were founded by the Spanish in 1776 (named Yerba Buena); the settlement came under Mexican control in 1821; taken by the US Navy in 1846, and renamed San Francisco in 1848, it grew rapidly after the discovery of gold nearby; developed as a commercial and fishing port from the 1860s and was the terminus of the first transcontinental railway (1869); earthquake and fire devastated the city in 1906; several areas were again seriously damaged by an earthquake in 1989. NOTABLE FEATURES Mission Dolores (1782); Cow Palace (shows, exhibitions, conventions, circuses); Museum of Art; Civic Centre complex at City Hall; Fisherman's Wharf; Nob Hill Mansions; Alcatraz I, in San Francisco Bay, is the site of the first lighthouse on the California coast and of a notorious prison (1934–63).

sang see SING.

Sangay an active Andean volcano in E central Ecuador. HEIGHT 5 230m. The Sangay National Park, established in 1975, is a World Heritage site.

Sanger, Frederick (1918–) English biochemist, born in Rendcombe, Gloucestershire. Working in Cambridge, he deduced the sequence of the 51 amino acids in the chains of the protein hormone insulin; for this work he was awarded the 1958 Nobel Prize for Chemistry. His subsequent work on nucleic acids led to new information on their structures, and he shared the 1980 Nobel Prize for Chemistry with Walter Gilbert and Paul Berg.

sangfroid *noun* cool-headedness; calmness; composure. [from French *sang froid*, cold blood]

sangria *noun* a Spanish drink of red wine, fruit juice, and sugar. [from Spanish *sangría*, bleeding]

sanguinary *adj.* **1** bloody; involving much bloodshed. **2** bloodthirsty. [see SANGUINE]

sanguine *adj.* **1** cheerful and full of hope. **2** *said of a complexion* ruddy. [from Latin *sanguis*, blood]

Sanhedrin, also called (by Josephus) the **gerousia** a Jewish council of elders that met in

Jerusalem (until AD 70), which during the Graeco-Roman period acquired internal administrative and judicial functions over Palestinian Jews, despite foreign domination. Convened by the high priest, its membership numbered 71, although local courts with this designation outside Jerusalem had fewer members and more limited jurisdiction. [from Greek *synedrion*, council; also Greek *gerousia*, senate]

San Ignacio POP (1990e) 8 000, a town in Cayo district, W Belize, 20km/12mi E of the frontier with Guatemala. It is linked to the town of Santa Elena on the E side of the R Belize by the Hawkesworth Bridge. NOTABLE FEATURE Maya ruins at Xunantunich.

sanitary *adj.* **1** promoting good health and the prevention of disease; hygienic. **2** relating to health, especially waste and sewage disposal. [from Latin *sanitas*, health]

sanitary towel an absorbent pad worn next to the vagina to catch menstrual fluids.

sanitation *noun* **1** standards of public hygiene. **2** measures taken to preserve public health, especially waste and sewage disposal. [see SANITARY]

sanitization *or* **sanitisation** *noun* sanitizing or being sanitized.

sanitize *or* **sanitise** *verb* **1** to make hygienic. **2** to make less controversial by removing potentially offensive elements. [see SANITARY]

sanity *noun* **1** soundness of mind. **2** good sense. [from Latin *sanitas*, health]

San Joaquin River a river in central California, USA, in the S part of the Central Valley, length is 510km/317mi. Rising in the Sierra Nevada, it joins the Sacramento R just above Suisin Bay. The San Joaquin is connected with the Sacramento in the Central Valley Project to increase irrigation, flood-control, and hydro-electricity. Major tributaries include the Fresno, Merced, and Mariposa.

San Jorge, Golfo, English **Gulf of St George** a broad inlet of the Atlantic Ocean in S Argentina. It extends 135km/84mi N–S between Cabo Dos Bahías in the N, where there is a penguin rookery, and Cabo Tres Puntas in the S. It measures 160km/100mi W–E. The port of Comodoro Rivadavia lies on its W shore.

San José **1** POP (1991e) 300 000, the capital of Costa Rica. It stands on the Pan-American Highway, in a broad, fertile valley of the Meseta Central; altitude 1 150m. The city was founded in 1737 and was laid out in a regular grid pattern. It became a capital in 1823. NOTABLE FEATURES cathedral; National Theatre; National Museum. **2** a province in Costa Rica with San José as its capital.

San José POP (1990) 1.5m, the capital of Santa Clara County, W California, USA. It lies in the fertile Santa Clara Valley, at the head of San Francisco Bay. San José was the state's first city in 1777 and was its capital from 1849 to 1851.

San Juan POP (1990e) 1.4m, the seaport capital of Puerto Rico, E Caribbean Sea. It is situated on an island which is linked to the N coast of the mainland by a bridge. The city was founded in 1510. NOTABLE FEATURES El Morro (1591, old Spanish fortress); cathedral (16c); Church of San José (16c); La Fortaleza (1533–40); Castillo de San Cristóbal (old fortress). La Fortaleza and the historic part of the town form a World Heritage site.

sank see SINK.

Sankara (c.700–c.750) Hindu philosopher and theologian, born in Kerala. The most famous exponent of Advaita (the Vedanta school of Hindu philosophy), he is the source of the main currents of modern Hindu thought.

San Lorenzo an early Olmec ceremonial centre in Veracruz province, Mexico. It was occupied from c.1500 BC, and flourished c.1200–900 BC until succeeded by La Venta. The

site is notable for its sculpture, which includes basalt heads up to 2.3m high and 20 tonnes in weight.

San Luis Potosí **1** POP (1990) 526 000, the capital of San Luis Potosí state, N central Mexico. It lies NW of Mexico City at an altitude of 1 877m. HISTORY founded as a Franciscan mission, San Luis Potosí became a important centre following the opening of the San Pedro silver mine in the 16c; seat of the Juárez government in 1863. NOTABLE FEATURES cathedral; Casa de la Cultura; Palacio de Gobierno (1770); Church of San Francisco. **2** a state in N central Mexico with San Luis Potosí as its capital.

San Marino POP (1991e) 23 000, the capital of the republic of San Marino. It lies on Mt Titano, accessible only by road, and is surrounded by three enclosures of walls, including many gateways, towers, and ramparts. NOTABLE FEATURES basilica; St Francis's Church; Governor's Palace.

San Marino

San Marino POP (1991e) 23 000, a small landlocked republic completely surrounded by central Italy, lying 20km/12mi from the Adriatic Sea. It is divided into nine districts (castles). AREA 61sq km/24sq mi. Its land boundaries measure 34km/21mi. CAPITAL San Marino. CHIEF TOWN Serravalle. TIME ZONE GMT +1. The chief religion is Roman Catholicism. OFFICIAL LANGUAGE Italian. CURRENCY the Italian lira and the San Marino lira. PHYSICAL DESCRIPTION ruggedly mountainous, centred on the limestone ridges of Mt Titano and the valley of the R Ausa. CLIMATE temperate climate, with cool winters and warm summers (20–30°C); rainfall is moderate, with an annual average of 880mm. HISTORY founded by a 4c Christian saint as a refuge against religious persecution; independence recognized by the pope 1631; in 1862 the treaty of friendship with the Kingdom of Italy preserved San Marino's independence. GOVERNMENT governed by an elected 60-member unicameral parliament (the Great and General Council) and an 11-member Congress of State. ECONOMY mainly farming, livestock raising, light industry, and tourism; manufacturing products include cotton, brick, and pottery; the largest share of government revenue is from the sale of postage stamps.

San Martín, José de (1778–1850) S American patriot, born in Yapeyú, Argentina. He played a major role in winning independence from Spain for Argentina, Chile, and Peru. In 1817 he led an army across the Andes into Chile, and defeated the Spanish at Chacubuco (1817) and Maipó (1818). After capturing Lima, he became Protector of Peru (1821), but resigned the following year after failing to reach an agreement with Simón Bolívar, and died in exile in France.

San Miguel **1** POP (1992) 183 000, the capital of San Miguel department, eastern El Salvador. It is situated 142km/88mi SE of San Salvador, at the foot of the volcanoes of San Miguel and Chinameca. The city was founded in 1530. NOTABLE FEATURE cathedral (18c). **2** POP (1987e) 502 000, a department in eastern El Salvador with San Miguel as its capital.

San Miguel de Tucumán *or* **Tucumán** POP (1991) 473 000, the capital of Tucumán province, NW Argentina. It lies on the R Salí and is the busiest city in N Argentina. history founded in 1565; the site of the defeat of Spanish royalists in 1812. Many colonial buildings remain. NOTABLE FEATURE cathedral.

San Pedro Sula POP (1989) 300 000, the industrial and commercial capital of Cortés department, NW Honduras. It is the second-largest city in the country and one of the fastest-growing cities in Latin America.

sanpro *noun colloq.* sanitary towels and tampons, etc collectively. [from SANITARY + PROTECTION]

San Salvador **1** POP (1992) 1.5m, the capital of El Salvador and of San Salvador department, on the R Acelhuate. It stands at an altitude of 680m. HISTORY founded in 1525; became capital in 1839; destroyed by an earthquake in 1854; present city built with a modern layout and buildings constructed to resist seismic shocks. NOTABLE FEATURE cathedral. **2** a department in El Salvador with the city of San Salvador as its capital.

San Salvador de Jujuy *or* **Jujuy** POP (1991) 125 000, the resort capital of Jujuy province, N Argentina. It lies on the R Grande de Jujuy. The city was founded in 1565 and again in 1575, after destruction by Native Americans. NOTABLE FEATURES cathedral (18c); Government House; Palacio de Tribunales; hot springs at Termas de Reyes.

sans-culottes the French name for the working populace in French towns at the time of the Revolution, generally applied more specifically to the small-time Parisian shopkeepers, craftsmen, wage-earners, and unemployed who were politically active. Their demands for food controls and democratic government made them temporary allies of the Jacobins. [French, = without knee-breeches]

San Sebastian, Basque **Donostia** POP (1991) 170 000, a fortified Basque seaport, fashionable resort, and the capital of Guipúzcoa province, Basque Country, N Spain. It lies on the R Urumea, 469km/291mi N of Madrid. NOTABLE FEATURES Church of St Mary (18c); Mount Urgel Park.

sanserif *noun* (**sans serif**) a style of printing in which the letters have no serifs. [from French *sans*, without + SERIF]

Sanskrit — *noun* a language of ancient India, the religious language of Hinduism since ancient times. — *adj.* relating to or expressed in this language. [from Sanskrit *samskrta*, perfected]
◇ Sanskrit is the name given to the oldest forms of Indo-Aryan. The sacred Hindu tests known as the Vedas were written c.1500–700 BC, and the standardized classical Sanskrit was the language of culture, mathematics, law, and medicine in the Indian subcontinent from c.1000 BC. Sanskrit has influenced the languages of India, Thailand, and Indonesia, and proved to be the key to the reconstruction of Indo-European in the 19c.

Sans Souci a Rococo palace built (1745–7) in Potsdam, Germany, for Frederick II of Prussia. It has been preserved in its original state, and houses several picture galleries.

San Stefano, Treaty of a preliminary treaty (1878) concluding the Russo–Turkish War of 1877–8. Under its terms Russia gained considerable diplomatic advantages and weakened Ottoman power in the Balkans, particularly through the creation of an large Bulgarian state (arguably under Russian influence). Under pressure from Britain and Austro-Hungary the treaty was superseded by a multilateral treaty at the Congress of Berlin (1878), the terms of which were less favourable to Russia, but guaranteed the independence from Turkey of a smaller Bulgaria.

Santa Ana **1** POP (1992) 202 000, the capital of Santa Ana department, El Salvador. It is situated 55km/34mi NW of San Salvador, on the NE slopes of Santa Ana Volcano. Santa Ana is the second-largest city in the country and the business centre of western El Salvador. NOTABLE FEATURES cathedral; Church of El Calvario. **2** a department in El Salvador with the city of Santa Ana as its capital.

Santa Ana POP (1990) 294 000, the capital of Orange County, SW California, USA. It lies on the Santa Ana R and was founded in 1869.

Santa Anna, Antonio López de (1797–1876) Mexican soldier and statesman, born in Jalapa. Following his period as President (1833–6), the Texas revolt (1836) led to his defeat of Texan forces at the Alamo, but also to his being routed at San Jacinto River and imprisoned. As dictator (1839, 1841–5), he returned to power on two occasions (1846, 1853), but was then an exile for many years, until permitted to return to Mexico in 1872.

Santa Barbara POP (1990) 86 000, the resort capital of Santa Barbara County, SW California, USA. It lies on the Santa Barbara Channel of the Pacific Ocean, at the foot of the Santa Ynez Mts, 137km/85mi NW of Los Angeles. It was founded in 1782. NOTABLE FEATURES Santa Barbara Mission (established in 1786), the W headquarters for the Franciscan order; many buildings of Spanish architecture; Vandenburg Air Force Base nearby.

Santa Claus, a jolly old man dressed in red who, in folklore, brings children presents on Christmas Eve or St Nicholas' Day. — Also called *Father Christmas*. [from Dutch dialect *Sante Klaas*, St Nicholas] ◇ Originally, the custom was for a person dressed as a bishop to distribute presents to 'good children' on St Nicholas' feast day (6 Dec). Father Christmas, as he is known today, with a sleigh drawn by reindeer, is a Victorian creation introduced into England about 1840 and much influenced by Charles Dickens's 'Ghosts of Christmas past' in his story *The Christmas Carol* (1843).

Santa Cruz *or* **Santa Cruz de la Sierra** **1** POP (1989e) 529 000, a city in Santa Cruz department, SE Bolivia. It was founded in 1561 by the Spanish and is, today, the second-largest city in the country. It has prospered in recent decades following the discovery of oil and natural gas. NOTABLE FEATURE Plaza 24 de Septiembre, the main square. **2** a department in SE Bolivia with Santa Cruz as its capital.

Santa Cruz POP (1991) 160 000, a province in Patagonia region, S Argentina. AREA 243 943sq km/94 162sq mi. It is the southernmost area of continental Argentina bordered by the Andes and Chile in the W and by the Atlantic Ocean in the E, with the Straits of Magellan to the S. CAPITAL Río Gallegos. NOTABLE FEATURES Cueva de las Manos, caves containing 10 000-year-old paintings of animals and human hands, situated in the N. ECONOMY sheep raising; salt and coal mining; natural gas; oil.

Santa Cruz de Tenerife POP (1991) 189 000, the seaport capital of Santa Cruz de Tenerife province, Canary Is, Spain. It lies on the N coast of Tenerife I.

Santa Fe POP (1990) 117 000, the capital of the state of New Mexico, USA, in Santa Fe County, N central New Mexico. It lies at the foot of the Sangre de Cristo Mts. HISTORY the oldest capital city in the USA, it was founded by the Spanish in 1609; it became the administrative headquarters of a Spanish colonial province and was the centre of Spanish-Native American trade for over 200 years; after Mexico's independence in 1821, Santa Fe became a centre of trade with the USA; it was occupied by US troops during the Mexican War in 1846; following New Mexico's cession to the USA (1848), Santa Fe became capital of the Territory of New Mexico in 1851. NOTABLE FEATURES Palace of the Governors (1610); San Miguel Church (1636); Cathedral of St Francis; Museum of International Folk Art.

Santa Fe **1** POP (1991) 442 000, the river-port capital of Santa Fe province, E central Argentina. It is situated at the mouth of the R Salado and is linked to the R Paraná by a short canal. The city was founded in 1573. Today it is a rail, shipping, commercial, industrial, and agricultural centre. NOTABLE FEATURE Jesuit La Merced Church (1660–1754); Casa de Gobierno; San Francisco Church (1680); Museo Histórico Provincial. **2** a province in E central Argentina with Santa Fe as its capital.

Santa Marta POP (1992e) 287 000, the Caribbean port capital of Magdalena department, N Colombia. The city is a leading seaside resort at the mouth of the R Manzanares. HISTORY the first town founded by the Conquistadores in Colombia in 1525; Simón Bolívar died here in 1830.

Santander POP (1991) 189 000, the capital of Cantabria region and of Santander province, N Spain. A seaport and resort, it lies 393km/244mi N of Madrid. NOTABLE FEATURES Royal Palace; cathedral (13c); Prehistory Museum.

Santarém POP (1981) 102 000, a river-port in Pará state, N Brazil. It is situated at the junction of the Tapajós and Amazon rivers. Santarém was founded in 1661 and is, today, the third-largest town on the Brazilian Amazon.

Santarém, ancient **Scalabis**, or **Praesidium Julium 1** POP (1991) 24 000, the walled capital of Santarém district, central Portugal, 69km/43mi NE of Lisbon. It is the centre for bullfighting in Portugal. NOTABLE FEATURES the Seminario (1676); churches of Santa Clara (13c), Senhor da Graça, and São João de Alporão; Torre das Cabeças. **2** a district in central Portugal with Santarém as its capital.

Santayana, George, originally **Jorge Augustín Nicolás Ruiz de Santayana** (1863–1952) Spanish–US philosopher, poet, and novelist, born in Madrid. He became Professor of Philosophy at Harvard (1907–12), while retaining his Spanish nationality. His writing career began as a poet with *Sonnets and other Verses* (1894), but he later became known as a philosopher and stylist, in such works as *The Life of Reason* (5 vols, 1905–6), *Realms of Being* (4 vols, 1927–40), and his novel *The Last Puritan* (1935). He moved to Europe in 1912, stayed at Oxford during World War I, then settled in Rome.

Santiago *or* **Gran Santiago** *or* **Santiago de Chile** POP (1991e) 5.3m, the capital of Chile, situated in the N central area of the country. It is crossed E–W by the R Mapocho. Santiago is the commercial centre of the republic, serving as the location for over half of Chile's manufacturing industry. HISTORY founded in 1541 by Pedro de Valdivia; became capital in 1818; suffered on several occasions from floods, fires, and earthquakes. NOTABLE FEATURES cathedral; the Avenida O'Higgins (usually called the Alameda) stretches for more than 3km/2mi, lined with ornamental gardens and statues; Santa Lucía Hill, site of Pedro de Valdivia's first fort; Palacio de la Moneda; Parque O'Higgins; Parque Forestal; several museums and churches; the conical hill of San Cristóbal lies to the NE and is ascended by a funicular railway.

Santiago POP (1990) 61 000, the capital of Veraguas province, W central Panama. The town is situated on the Inter-American Highway, in a grain-growing area. It is one of the oldest towns in the country.

Santiago de Compostela, ancient **Campus Stellae**, English **Compostella** POP (1991) 88 000, a city in La Coruña province, Galicia, NW Spain, lying on the R Sar. It was formerly the capital of the Kingdom of Galicia. The shrine of St James made it a world-famous place of pilgrimage during the Middle Ages. The old town is a World Heritage site. NOTABLE FEATURE cathedral (11c–12c).

Santiago de Cuba 1 POP (1989e) 397 000, the seaport capital of Santiago de Cuba province, SE Cuba. It lies on the S coast of the island and is the second-largest city in the country. HISTORY founded in 1514; formerly the capital of the republic; scene of events during the Spanish–American War of 1898, when the town surrendered to US forces; scene of Fidel Castro's 1953 revolution. NOTABLE FEATURES cathedral (1528); Museum of Colonial Art. **2** a province in SE Cuba with Santiago de Cuba as its capital.

Santiago del Estero POP (1991) 202 000, the capital of Santiago del Estero province, N Argentina. It lies on the R Dulce and is the oldest Argentinian town, founded in 1553 by settlers from Peru. Today it is an agricultural, trade, and lumbering centre. NOTABLE FEATURES cathedral; Gothic Church of San Francisco (1590); Wagner Museum.

Santiago (de los Caballeros) 1 POP (1989e) 467 000, a city in central Santiago province, Dominican Republic. It is the second-largest city in the country and the most important trading, distributing, and processing centre in the N. It lies in the fertile Cibao agricultural region. The city was the scene of the decisive battle in the Dominican struggle for independence in 1844. NOTABLE FEATURES cathedral; fort. **2** a province in the Dominican Republic with Santiago as its capital.

Santo Domingo, formerly **Ciudad Trujillo** POP (1990e) 2.2m, the capital of the Dominican Republic. It was founded in 1496 and lies on right bank of the R Ozama in the S part of the country. NOTABLE FEATURES Renaissance cathedral (1514–40); Alcazar Castle (1514).

Santorini, Greek **Santorin**, ancient **Thera** or **Thíra** POP (1982) 2 000, an island in the S Cyclades, lying c.140km/87mi N of Crete. AREA 75sq km/29sq mi. The island rises steeply from the sea to 300m. The last great eruption of its volcano (c.1470 BC), in an explosion four times more powerful than Krakatoa, has been held responsible for the collapse of Minoan civilization although this is not established. The excavated site displays notable wall paintings and three-storeyed houses.

Santorio Santorio see SANCTORIUS.

Santos POP (1991) 429 000, a port in São Paulo state, SE Brazil, situated 63km/39mi SE of São Paulo. It is situated on an island 5km/3mi from the Atlantic coast. Founded in 1534, it is, today, the most important Brazilian port, handling over 40 per cent of all imports and about half of all exports.

São Francisco, River, Portuguese **Rio** a river in E Brazil, 2 900km/1 800mi long. It rises in the Serra de Canastra and flows NE, NW, then SE to enter the Atlantic Ocean at 96km/60mi NE of Aracajú. The river is the main route of access into the interior of E Brazil. Hydroelectricity is generated at several points along its length.

Saône, River, ancient **Arar** a river in E France, length 480km/300mi. Rising in Vosges department, the Saône flows SW, then S to meet the R Rhône at Lyons. It is linked by canal to the Loire, Seine, Marne, Meuse, Mosel, and Rhine.

São Paulo 1 POP (1991) 15.2m, the capital of São Paulo state, SE Brazil. It lies on the R Tietê. The city was founded by Jesuits in 1554 and has developed since the 19c to become the leading commercial and industrial centre in S America. It is the fastest-growing S American city. NOTABLE FEATURES cathedral; Museum of Art; Museum of Brazilian Art; Iparinga Monument; the Anhembi (one of world's largest exhibition halls); Butantan Institute (with snake farm). **2** a state in SE Brazil with São Paulo as its capital.

São Tiago *or* **Santiago** POP (1990) 171 000, the largest island in Cape Verde, in the Sotavento group. AREA 991sq km/382sq mi. It rises to 1 320m at Antonia Peak. CHIEF TOWN Praia (capital of Cape Verde). NOTABLE FEATURES fine beaches at Gamboa, Prainha, and Quebra-Canela; Ribeira Grande, the 15c colonial capital. ECONOMY coffee, sugar, oranges.

São Tomé POP (1984e) 35 000, the seaport capital of the volcanic islands of São Tomé and Príncipe in the Gulf of Guinea. It is situated on Ana de Chaves Bay on the NE coast of São Tomé I.

São Tomé and Príncipe, Portuguese **São Tomé e Príncipe**, official name **Democratic Republic of São Tomé and Príncipe** POP (1992e) 124 000, an equatorial island republic in the Gulf of Guinea, off the coast of W Africa. AREA 963sq km/372sq mi. It comprises São Tomé, Príncipe, and several smaller islands. CAPITAL São Tomé. CHIEF TOWNS Trinidad, São António. TIME ZONE GMT +1. The population includes Mestizo, Angolares, Forros, Serviçaes, Tongas, and Europeans; Roman Catholicism is the main religion. OFFICIAL LANGUAGE Portuguese. CURRENCY the dobra. PHYSICAL DESCRIPTION volcanic islands, heavily forested; São Tomé lies c.440km/275mi off the coast of N Gabon, has an area of 845sq km/326sq mi, and reaches a height of 2 024m; Príncipe, the smaller of the two islands, lies c.200km/125mi off the N coast of Gabon and has similar terrain. CLIMATE tropical; the average annual temperature is 27°C on the coast, 20°C in the mountains; there is a rainy season from Oct to May; the annual average rainfall varies from 500mm to 1 000mm. HISTORY discovered by the Portuguese between 1469 and 1472; became a Portuguese colony in 1522; held by the Dutch (1641–1740), then recovered by Portugal; later a port of call on route to the East Indies; resistance to Portuguese rule led to riots in 1953, and the formation of an overseas liberation movement based in Gabon; gained independence in 1975; a new constitution was introduced in the early 1990s. GOVERNMENT one-party state, with a President and a 55-member National People's Assembly. ECONOMY based on agriculture, employing c.70% of the population; cocoa, copra, palm kernels, coffee; attempts to diversify the economy since 1985 have met with limited success.

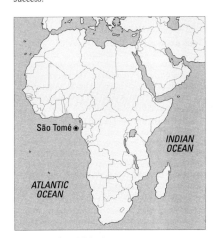

São Tomé and Principe

sap¹ — noun **1** Bot. a liquid containing sugars and other nutrients that circulates within the phloem tissue of plants, and exudes from wounded tissue. **2** vitality. **3** slang a weak or easily fooled person. — verb (**sapped**, **sapping**) **1** to drain sap from. **2** to weaken or exhaust; to drain (eg a person's energy). [from Anglo-Saxon sæp]

sap² — noun a hidden trench by means of which an attack is made on an enemy position. — verb (**sapped**, **sapping**) **1** to attack by means of a sap. **2** to undermine or weaken. [from Italian zappa, spadework]

sapience noun **1** discernment, judgement. **2** often ironic wisdom.

sapient adj. formal, often ironic having or showing good judgement; wise. [from Latin sapere, to be wise]

sapling noun a young tree.

saponification noun Chem. the hydrolysis of an ester by an alkali, resulting in the production of the alcohol from which the ester was derived, together with a salt of the acid. The process is used to convert fats into soap (usually the sodium or potassium salt of stearic or palmitic acid). [from Latin sapo -onis, soap]

Sapper, pseudonym of **Herman Cyril McNeile** (1888–1937) English novelist, born in Bodmin, Cornwall. He trained as a soldier before he achieved fame as the creator of 'Bulldog' Drummond, the aggressively patriotic hero of a series of thrillers written between 1920 and 1937, and including The Final Count (1926).

sapper noun Brit. a soldier, especially a private, in the Royal Engineers.

sapphic adj. **1** literary lesbian. **2** Poetry written in verses of four lines, with a short fourth line. [from Sappho, poetess of ancient Greece, and reputed lesbian]

sapphire noun **1** Geol. any gem variety of the mineral corundum other than ruby, especially the transparent blue variety, although green, yellow, pink, orange, and purple sapphires also occur. It is highly prized as a gemstone, and because of its hardness is also used in record player styluses, etc. **2** the deep blue colour of this stone. [from Greek sappheiros]

Sappho (c.610–c.580 BC) Greek lyric poet, born in Lesbos. A writer of intense love poetry, she went into exile in Sicily, but later returned to Mytilene. Only two of her love odes are extant in full, but many fragments have been found in Egypt.

sappiness noun being full of sap.

Sapporo POP (1991e) 1.7m, the capital of Hokkaido prefecture, W central Hokkaido, Japan. The city was founded in 1871. NOTABLE FEATURE Ainu Museum.

sappy adj. (**sappier**, **sappiest**) **1** said of plants full of sap. **2** full of energy.

saprolite noun Geol. a soft earthy red or brown chemically decomposed rock that is rich in clay. It is formed by chemical weathering of igneous or metamorphic rock (eg as a result of the action of acids in rainwater), especially in humid climates. [from Greek sapros, rotten + lithos, stone]

saprophyte noun Biol. a plant, fungus, or micro-organism that feeds on dead and decaying organic matter. [from Greek sapros, rotten + phyton, plant]

Saqqarah the large necropolis of Memphis in ancient Egypt, where several pharaohs and many noble Egyptians were buried. The most famous surviving monument is the stepped pyramid of Zozer (c.2630 BC). It was designed by Imhotep, and marked a radical advance in pyramid design.

saraband noun **1** a slow formal dance of 17c Spain. **2** a piece of music for, or in the rhythm of, this dance. [from Spanish zarabanda]

Saracen noun **1** a member of a wandering Syrian people of Roman times. **2** a Muslim defending the Holy Land from medieval Christian crusaders. [from Greek Sarakenos]

Saragossa, Spanish **Zaragoza**, ancient **Salduba** POP (1991) 586 000, the capital of Aragón region and of Saragossa province, NE central Spain. Saragossa is an industrial city lying on the R Ebro, 325km/202mi NE of Madrid. It was formerly the residence of the kings of Aragón. During the Peninsular War (1808–9) it was under siege by the French. NOTABLE FEATURES El Pilar and La Seo cathedrals; Exchange (16c); Aljafarería Moorish Palace.

Sarah or **Sarai** **1** a biblical character, wife, and half-sister of Abraham. She accompanied him from Ur to Canaan (Genesis 12–23), and on account of her beauty posed as Abraham's sister

before Pharaoh in Egypt and Abimelech in Gerar, since their desire for her may have endangered her husband's life. Long barren, she eventually gave birth to Isaac as God had promised (Genesis 17.16). **2** a female first name. [from Hebrew, = princess]

Sarah Siddons as the Tragic Muse a painting by Sir Joshua Reynolds (1784, San Marino, California).

Sarajevo POP (1991) 526 000, the capital of Bosnia-Herzegovina republic, lying on the R Miljacka. HISTORY governed by Austria from 1878 to 1918; scene of the assassination of Archduke Francis Ferdinand and his wife (1914), which precipitated World War I; known as a cultural and educational centre; besieged and attacked frequently in the early 1990s in the fighting following the break up of Yugoslavia; a mortar attack on the market in 1994 aroused world opinion and led to a ceasefire.

Saransk POP (1991e) 320 000, the capital of Mordovia, central Russia, lying on the R Insar. The city was founded as a fortress in 1641. NOTABLE FEATURE Church of John the Apostle (1693).

Sarapis see SERAPIS.

Saratoga, Battle of one of the most important engagements of the US War of Independence. Fought (Oct 1777) near modern Schuylerville, New York, the battle saw the defeat of a large British army under John Burgoyne by American continental troops and militia under Horatio Gates. It ended British plans to cut New England off from the rest of the states, and encouraged French intervention on the American side.

Saratov 1 (1991e) 911 000 the river-port capital of Saratov oblast, W central Russia, lying on the R Volga. It was founded in 1590 as a fortress city designed to protect the Volga route from nomad raids. NOTABLE FEATURE Troitskii Cathedral (1689–95). **2** an oblast in W central Russia with the city of Saratov as its capital.

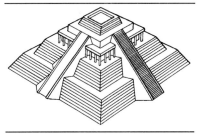

Saqqarah step pyramid

Sarawak POP (1990) 1.7m, a state in E Malaysia, on the NW coast of Borneo. AREA 124 449sq km/48 037sq mi. It is bounded S by Kalimantan (Indonesia), N by the S China Sea, and NE by Brunei and Sabah. PHYSICAL DESCRIPTION consists of a flat, narrow coastal strip, a belt of foothills, and a highly mountainous, forested interior; the highest peak is Mt Murud (2 423m); watered by the R Rajang; there is a national park around Mt Mulu. HISTORY given by the Sultan of Brunei to James Brooke in 1841; ruled by the Brooke family until World War II; became a British protectorate in 1888 and a Crown Colony in 1946. CAPITAL Kuching. ECONOMY oil; rice; sago; rubber; pepper; fishing.

sarcasm noun **1** an ironical expression of scorn or contempt. **2** the use of such remarks. **3** their bitter, contemptuous quality. [from Greek sarkazein, to tear the flesh]

sarcastic adj. **1** containing sarcasm. **2** tending to use sarcasm.

sarcastically adv. in a sarcastic way.

sarcoma *noun* (PL. **sarcomas, sarcomata**) *Medicine* a cancerous tumour developing in connective tissue. [from Greek *sarkoma*, fleshy growth]

sarcophagus *noun* (PL. **sarcophagi, sarcophaguses**) a stone coffin or tomb, especially one decorated with carvings. [from Greek *sarkophagos*, flesh-eating, a supposed quality of the limestone often used]

sardine *noun* a young pilchard, closely related to the herring, and found swimming in shoals, all the members of which are similar in size. It is an important food fish. Sardines for the canning industry are caught mainly off the coasts of France, Portugal, and Spain.
— **like sardines** crowded closely together. [from Greek *sardinos*]

Sardinia, Italian **Sardegna** POP (1991) 1.6m, a region and island of Italy, lying 184km/114mi SW of the promontory of Orbetello, and separated from Corsica by the Strait of Bonifacio. Sardinia is the second-largest island in the Mediterranean Sea. AREA 24 090sq km/ 9 299sq mi; length 272km/169mi; width 144km/89mi. PHYSICAL DESCRIPTION the island is largely hilly, rising to 1 835m in the Monti del Gennargentu; well-wooded in the centre and in the N; the mineral-bearing SW corner is cut off by the fertile alluvial plain of Campidano. HISTORY settled by the Phoenicians; formed part of the Kingdom of Sardinia in the 18c. CAPITAL Cagliari (chief port). CHIEF TOWNS Sassari, Carbonia, Oristano, Iglesias. ECONOMY wine, olives, citrus fruits, vegetables, tobacco, cork, pastoral farming; fishing; sea salt; mining (zinc, lead, manganese, coal); food processing; there are coal and hydroelectric power stations; petrochemicals; tourism.

Sardinia, Kingdom of an Italian kingdom created (1718–20) through the Duchy of Savoy's acquisition of Sardinia, in exchange for Sicily. The kingdom's heart actually remained Savoy and Piedmont, and it is generally called the Kingdom of Sardinia–Piedmont. During the course of the Risorgimento, the kingdom became the main driving force behind unification; Victor Emmanuel II of Sardinia became Italy's first king (1861).

Sardinian — *noun* 1 a native or inhabitant of Sardinia. 2 an Indo-European Romance language spoken by between half and one million people in Sardinia. — *adj.* relating to Sardinia or its people or language.

Sardis the capital of ancient Lydia and the political centre of Asia Minor in the pre-Hellenistic period. It was a flourishing city in Roman imperial times, and contained one of the largest and richest Jewish communities in the Empire.

sardonic *adj.* mocking or scornful. [from Greek *sardonion*, bitter-tasting Mediterranean plant]

sardonyx *noun Geol.* a variety of onyx containing alternating straight parallel bands of white and yellow or orange. [from Greek *sardonyx*]

Sardou, Victorien (1831–1908) French dramatist, born in Paris. His first efforts were failures, but after his marriage he met the actress Virginie Brécourt, for whom he wrote several plays, and his work became widely known in Europe and the USA. His plays include *Les Pattes de mouche* (A Scrap of Paper, 1860), *La Tosca* (1887), and over 60 others.

sargasso *noun* (PL. **sargassos, sargassoes**) a brown ribbon-like seaweed that floats in huge masses. [from Portuguese *sargaço*]

Sargasso Sea a sluggish area of the Atlantic Ocean, between the Azores and the West Indies within the 'Horse Latitudes'. Its location at the centre of clockwise-moving warm surface currents allows great biological activity. There is an abundance of surface gulfweed. The sea is a breeding ground for eels which migrate to Europe.

sarge *noun colloq.* sergeant.

Sargent, John Singer (1856–1925) US painter, born in Florence. Most of his work was done in England, and he became famous as a fashionable portrait painter. He often travelled to the USA, where as well as portraits he worked on decorative paintings for public buildings (eg the *Evolution of Religion* for Boston library).

Sargent, Sir (Harold) Malcolm (Watts) (1895–1967) English conductor, born in Stamford, Lincolnshire. Originally an organist, he first appeared as a conductor when his *Impression on a Windy Day* was performed at a Promenade Concert in 1921. He conducted the Royal Choral Society from 1928, the Liverpool Philharmonic Orchestra (1942–8), and the BBC Symphony Orchestra (1950–7). From 1948 he was in charge of the London Promenade Concerts, and won international popularity for his skill in choral music and sense of occasion.

sari *or* **saree** *noun* (PL. **saris, sarees**) a traditional garment of Hindu women, a single long piece of fabric wound round the body and draped over one shoulder and sometimes the head. [from Hindi *sari*]

Sark, French **Sercq** POP (1991e) 550, the smallest of the four main Channel Is, lying between Guernsey and the Cotentin Peninsula, France. AREA 4sq km/2sq mi. It consists of Great and Little Sark, which are connected by an isthmus. Sark has a separate parliament (the Chief Pleas). The Seigneurie of Sark was established by Elizabeth I; its ruler is known as the Seigneur (if male) or the Dame (if female). No cars are allowed on the island.

sarky *adj.* (**sarkier, sarkiest**) *colloq.* sarcastic.

Sarmatia in Roman times, the area to the N of the Black Sea and the middle and lower Danube, which was occupied by the Sarmatians, a nomadic people closely related to the Scythians. It was never conquered by Rome, but did not escape Roman control altogether: many Sarmatian chieftains were clients of Rome and ruled in her interest.

sarnie *noun slang* a sandwich.

sarong *noun* a Malaysian garment worn by both sexes, a single piece of fabric wrapped around the body to cover it from the waist or chest down. [from Malay *sarung*]

Sarpedon in Greek legend, a son of Zeus, who led the Lycian troops on the Trojan side. He was killed by Patroclus, and carried off by Sleep and Death to Lycia.

sarsaparilla *noun* 1 a tropical American climbing plant with heart-shaped leaves. 2 its dried root, used medicinally. 3 a soft drink flavoured with the root. 4 a liquid medicine prepared from the root. [from Spanish *zarzaparilla*]

Sarto, Andrea del, originally **Andrea d'Agnolo** (1486–1531) Italian painter, born in Florence. He was engaged by the Servites (Servants of the Virgin, an order founded in Florence) to paint a series of frescoes for their Church of the Annunciation (1509–14). Many of his most celebrated pictures are in Florence.

sartorial *adj.* relating to tailoring, or to clothes in general: *sartorial elegance*. [from Latin *sartor*, patcher]

Sartre, Jean-Paul (1905–80) French existentialist philosopher and writer, born in Paris. He taught philosophy at Le Havre, Paris, and Berlin, was imprisoned in Germany (1941), and after his release joined the resistance in Paris. A prominent intellectual, in 1946 (with Simone de Beauvoir) he founded and edited the avant-garde monthly, *Les Temps modernes*. His novels include the trilogy, *Les Chemins de la liberté* (The Roads to Freedom, 1945–9), and (especially after the war) he also wrote many plays, including *Huis clos* (In Camera/No Exit, 1944) and *Le Diable et le bon Dieu* (Lucifer and the Lord, 1951). His philosophy is presented in *L'Etre et le néant* (Being and Nothingness, 1943). In 1964 he published his autobiography *Les Mots* (Words), and was awarded (but declined) the Nobel Prize for Literature.

SAS *abbrev.* Special Air Service.

sash¹ *noun* a broad band of cloth worn round the waist or over one shoulder, originally as part of a uniform. [from Arabic *shash*]

sash² *noun* either of two glazed frames forming a sash window. [from French *châssis*, frame]

sash cord a cord connecting the system of weights and pulleys by which a sash window is opened and held open.

sash window a window consisting of two sashes, one or either of which can slide vertically past the other.

Sask. *abbrev.* Saskatchewan.

Saskatchewan POP (1991) 989 000, a province in W central Canada, bounded S by the USA. AREA 652 380sq km/251 819sq mi. PHYSICAL DESCRIPTION there is a fertile plain occupying two thirds of the province in the S; the N third is in the Canadian Shield; rises to 1 392m in the Cypress Hills in the SW; there are several rivers and many lakes, the largest being L Athabasca in the NW, Reindeer L in the NE, and Wollaston L in the NE. Prince Albert National Park is in the centre of the province. HISTORY first settled by Europeans at the end of the 17c, it became an important fur-trading region; the Hudson's Bay Company land was acquired by Canada in 1870 to become part of Northwest Territories; the Canadian Pacific Railroad arrived in 1882–3, opening the land to agricultural settlement; land disputes between Native Americans and incoming settlers led to the Saskatchewan Rebellion in 1884; it became a province of Canada in 1905. GOVERNMENT governed by a Lieutenant-Governor, an executive Council, and an elected 64-member Legislative Assembly. CAPITAL Regina. CHIEF TOWNS Saskatoon, Moose Jaw, Prince Albert, Yorkton. ECONOMY wheat (about two thirds of Canada's production), barley; cattle, dairy farming; oil, natural gas; potash (largest fields in the world); timber.

Saskatchewan River a river in S Canada, length 1 287km/800mi. It is formed in Saskatchewan by two headstreams which rise in the Rocky Mts of W Alberta. The river flows NE into Manitoba and empties into L Winnipeg. In the days of fur trading it was the main early route to the Western Plains and the mountains.

Saskatoon POP (1991) 186 000, a city in central Saskatchewan, S central Canada, lying on the S Saskatchewan R. First settled in 1882 as a temperance colony, Saskatoon developed in the early 1900s when settlers arrived from the USA. It is the centre of a large grain-growing area. NOTABLE FEATURES the Western Development Museum; Memorial Art Gallery.

sassafras *noun* 1 a N American deciduous tree of the laurel family. 2 its aromatic bark, used as a flavouring and in perfumes and medicine. [from Spanish *sasafrás*]

Sassanids the aggressive Persian dynasty that overthrew the Parthian Empire in AD 224 and became Rome's fiercest challenger in the East. They were driven from Mesopotamia by the Arabs in 636.

Sassari POP (1991e) 120 000, the capital town of Sassari province, Sardinia, Italy. It lies on a limestone plateau in the NW of the island, 176km/109mi NW of Cagliari, and is an agricultural trade centre. NOTABLE FEATURE cathedral (begun in the 12c).

Sassenach — *noun Scot. usually derog.* an English person, a Lowlander. — *adj.* English. [from Gaelic *Sassunach*, from Latin *Saxones*, Saxons]

Sassoon, Siegfried (Lorraine) (1886–1967) English poet and novelist, born in Brenchley, Kent. His experiences in World War I gave him a hatred of war, expressed in *Counterattack* (1918) and *Satirical Poems* (1926). Later collections include *Vigils* (1935) and *Sequences* (1956), and he also wrote a semi-autobiographical trilogy, and three volumes of autobiography which include *The Weald of Youth* (1942).

SAT *abbrev.* **1** in England and Wales, standard assessment task, taken by primary and secondary school pupils at the ages of 7, 11, 14, and 16. The tasks apply to the core and foundation subjects of the national curriculum, which was introduced in 1989. The first tests for seven-year olds were held in 1991, and pilot tests for 14-year olds took place in 1992. In 1993, dissatisfaction with the tests resulted in a boycott of them by many schools. **2** in the USA, Scholastic Aptitude Test, a general examination of verbal and mathematical skills not related to specific course work, taken by high-school pupils wishing to attend university.

Sat *abbrev.* (*also* **Sat.**) Saturday.

sat see SIT.

Satan *noun* **1** in some beliefs, the Devil, the primary evil spirit and the enemy of God. **2** the fallen angel and wicked tempter of Adam and Eve in John Milton's poem *Paradise Lost.* [from Hebrew *satan*, enemy]
◇ Satan is the personification of the evil and negative qualities of humankind: he is tempter, deceiver, liar, the cause of immoral feelings and actions, and has the power of death and destruction over the bodies and souls of human beings. He conventionally resides in the lower atmosphere (in Jewish literature), or hell, a place of fiery torment (in Christianity). The Judaeo-Christian concept is paralleled in Islam (the concepts of *Shaytan* and *Iblic* in the Koran), and in Buddhism (in the form of *Mara*).

satanic *adj.* **1** of or relating to Satan. **2** evil; abominable.

Satanism *noun* the worship of Satan.

Satanist *noun* a person who practices Satanism.

SATB *abbrev.* soprano, alto, tenor, bass (in choral music).

satchel *noun* a small briefcase-like bag for schoolbooks, usually with a shoulder strap. [from Old French *sachel*, little bag]

sate *verb* to satisfy (a desire or appetite) to the full or to excess. [from Anglo-Saxon *sadian*]

satellite *noun* **1** (*in full* **natural satellite**) a celestial body that orbits around a much larger celestial body, eg the Moon (which is a satellite of the Earth, or the Earth (which is a satellite of the Sun). **2** (*in full* **artificial satellite**) a man-made device, especially a spacecraft, that is launched by a rocket into space and placed in orbit around a planet, especially the Earth, used for communication, etc. **3** a nation or state dependent, especially economically or politically, on a larger neighbour. **4** a follower or hanger-on. [from Latin *satelles*, attendant]
◇ All the planets in the solar system except Mercury and Venus appear to have at least one natural satellite, and it is possible that there are some tiny undiscovered satellites around the outer planets. Natural satellites up to a few hundred km across consist mainly of bare rock and are irregular in shape. However, the larger satellites may be cratered (like the Moon), smooth and icy (like Jupiter's Europa), or even have an atmosphere (like Saturn's Titan). The smallest known natural satellite is Deimos (about 12km across), which orbits around Mars, and the largest known is Ganymede (with a diameter of 5 262km), which orbits around Jupiter.

satellite broadcasting *or* **satellite television** *Telecomm.* television transmission using super-high-frequency beam linkage via an artificial satellite.

◇ Such links became possible from 1962 with the launch of Telstar, but direct broadcasting from satellite did not develop until the 1970s when it became possible to relay programmes at sufficient power to serve domestic TV receivers from satellites in fixed geostationary orbit, using small dish antennae of 60mm diameter or less. Commercial direct broadcasting from satellite began in the USA in the 1980s, and in Europe from 1989.

satellite dish *Radio* a dish-shaped aerial for receiving television signals for programmes broadcast via artificial satellite.

satellite town a small town near a larger city, especially one originally developed to prevent the city becoming undesirably large.

sati same as SUTTEE.

satiability *noun* being satiable.

satiable *adj.* capable of being satisfied.

satiate *verb* to satisfy fully or to excess. [from Latin *satiare*, from *satis*, enough]

satiation *noun* satisfaction.

Satie, Erik (Alfred Leslie) (1866–1925) French composer, born in Honfleur. He worked as a café composer and studied under Vincent D'Indy and Albert Roussel. His work, which was in revolt against musical orthodoxy, included the ballet *Parade* (1917), ballads, musical dramas, and whimsical pieces, and had some influence on Claude Debussy, Maurice Ravel, and others.

satiety *noun* the state of being satiated.

satin *noun* silk or rayon closely woven to produce a shiny finish. [from *Zaitun*, Arabic form of the Chinese name of the town where it was originally produced]

satinwood *noun* **1** a shiny light-coloured hardwood used for fine furniture. **2** the E Indian tree that produces it.

satiny *adj.* of or like satin.

satire *noun* **1** a variety of humour aiming at mockery or ridicule, often using sarcasm and irony. **2** any work, eg a play or film, using this kind of humour. [from Latin *satira*, mixture]
◇ In literature and drama, satire has as its motive the exposure and castigation of the follies of the human world and the vices of society. The history of literary satire goes back to the Roman poets Horace and Juvenal, who represent the benign and the bitter aspects respectively. Major satirists in European literature include the dramatist Ben Jonson, Dryden, Pope, Rabelais, Moliere, Volaire, Victor Hugo, Byron, Thackeray, and Flaubert.

satirical *adj.* **1** relating to or of the nature of satire. **2** characterized by satire.

satirist *noun* **1** a writer or performer of satires. **2** a person who frequently uses satire.

satirization *or* **satirisation** *noun* satirizing or being satirized.

satirize *or* **satirise** *verb* to mock or ridicule using satire.

satisfaction *noun* **1** the act of satisfying, or the state or feeling of being satisfied. **2** compensation for mistreatment.

satisfactorily *adv.* in a satisfactory way.

satisfactory *adj.* giving satisfaction; adequate; acceptable.

satisfied *adj.* pleased, contented.

satisfy *verb* (**satisfies**, **satisfied**) **1** to fulfil the needs, desires, or expectations of; to fulfil (eg a desire). **2** to meet the requirements of; to meet (a requirement). **3** to remove the doubts of; to convince. **4** *intrans.* to please; to remove all desire for others: *the taste that satisfies.* **5** to compensate for; to give compensation to. [from Latin *satis*, enough + *facere*, to make]

satisfying *adj.* that satisfies; pleasing.

satrap *noun* a viceroy or governor of a province of the Achaemenid (ancient Persian) Empire. [from Greek *satrapēs*, from Old Persian *khshathrapāvan-*, protector of the kingdom]

satsuma *noun* a thin-skinned seedless type of mandarin orange. [from *Satsuma*, former Japanese province]

Satu Mare 1 POP (1992) 132 000, the capital of the county of Satu Mare, NW Romania. A resort town, it lies on the R Someş near the Hungarian border. **2** a county in NW Romania with Satu Mare as its capital.

saturate *verb* **1** to make soaking wet. **2** to fill or cover with a large amount of something. **3** to add a solid, liquid, or gas to a solution until no more of that substance can be dissolved at a given temperature. **4** to treat an organic chemical compound in such a way that it no longer contains any double or triple bonds. [from Latin *satur*, full]

saturated vapour pressure *Physics* the pressure that is exerted by a vapour which is in equilibrium with the liquid form of the same substance. It is dependent on temperature.

saturation *noun* **1** saturating or being saturated. **2** *Chem.* the point at which a solution contains the maximum possible amount of dissolved solid, liquid, or gas at a given temperature.

saturation point 1 a limit beyond which no more can be added or accepted. **2** *Chem.* same as SATURATION 2.

Saturday *noun* the seventh day of the week. [from Anglo-Saxon *Sæterndæg*, Saturn's day]

Saturday Night and Sunday Morning **1** a novel by Alan Sillitoe (1958). His first, it describes the life of anarchic Nottingham factory-worker Arthur Seaton, who has a zest for life and sexual adventure. **2** a British film based on the novel, directed by Karel Reisz (1960).

Saturn *or* **Saturnus** in Roman mythology, the god of agriculture, identified with the Greek god Cronus. At his annual festival (Saturnalia, 17 Dec) slaves had temporary liberty, and presents were exchanged.

Saturn 1 *Astron.* the sixth planet from the Sun, and the second-largest planet in the solar system. Its orbit lies between those of Jupiter and Uranus, and the planet appears yellowish in colour when viewed through a telescope. **2** (*in full* **Saturn rocket**) any of a group of large US rockets used in the NASA Apollo programme. The Saturn 1B rocket was used to send the first manned Apollo spacecraft into orbit around the Earth, and to launch crews to Skylab. The Saturn V rocket was used to send Apollo spacecraft to the Moon, and to launch Skylab. Saturn rockets were later retired in favour of the space shuttle.
◇ Saturn is about 1 427 km from the Sun, and has a diameter of 120 200km at the equator. It takes 10h 14min to rotate once on its own axis, and 29.5 years to orbit around the Sun. It is best known for its rings. Ring systems have now been discovered around Jupiter, Uranus, and Neptune, but Saturn's rings are by far the brightest. It rotates more rapidly than any other planet except Jupiter, and this has produced a bulge at the equator and flattening at the poles. Saturn's density is only about 13 per cent that of Earth, and it is believed to have a small core composed of rock and iron, surrounded by ice, and covered by liquid hydrogen, ie it does not have a solid surface. Its cloudy atmosphere consists mainly of hydrogen and helium.
The markings on the surface of the planet are swirling clouds of frozen water, methane, ammonia, and other hydrogen compounds. Saturn's ring system is vast, 21 times the diameter of the Earth, but only a few km thick, and consists of countless fragments of rock coated with ice, many of them about 1m across, each individual fragment orbiting around the planet like a tiny moon. When the space probe

Voyager 1 passed by Saturn in Nov 1980, it revealed that there are thousands of closely spaced rings, and not several large rings as was previously thought. The wider gaps between the rings are caused by the gravity of a few tiny satellites pulling the rock particles out of particular orbits. Saturn has 24 satellites, of which Titan, the largest (5 120km in diameter), is the only moon in the solar system with a detectable atmosphere.

saturnalia *noun* **1** (**Saturnalia**) the ancient Roman festival of the god Saturn in mid-December, a time of merry-making and gift-giving. **2** *literary* a scene of rowdy celebration; a wild party.

saturnine *noun literary* **1** grim-faced; unsmiling. **2** melancholy in character. [from the supposed gloomy influence of the planet in astrology]

satyr *noun* **1** a mythological woodland god, part man, part goat, noted for lechery. **2** a lustful man. [from Greek *satyros*]

satyr play *Greek Theatr.* a burlesque performed as comic relief after a series of three classical Greek tragedies. The hero, often Herakles, was presented in a farcical situation, with a chorus of Sileni, or satyrs. The satyr play is characterized by a rapid action, vigorous dancing, and bawdy and outrageous dialogue and gesture.

sauce — *noun* **1** any seasoned liquid that food is cooked or served in or flavoured with after serving. **2** added interest or excitement. **3** *colloq.* impertinence; cheek. — *verb colloq.* to be cheeky to. [from Latin *salsa*, from *sal*, salt]

sauce boat a long shallow jug for serving sauce.

saucepan *noun* a deep cooking pot with a long handle and usually with a lid.

saucer *noun* **1** a small shallow round dish for placing under a tea or coffee cup. **2** something shaped like this. [from Old French *saussiere*]

sauciness *noun* a saucy quality; impertinence.

saucy *adj.* (**saucier**, **sauciest**) *colloq.* **1** impertinent or cheeky; attractively bold or forward. **2** dealing with sex, especially in an amusing way: *saucy postcards*. **3** *said of clothes* smart.

Saudi Arabia, official name **Kingdom of Saudi Arabia**, Arabic **Al-Mamlaka al-Arabiya as-Saudiya** POP (1992e) 15.9m, an Arabic kingdom comprising about four fifths of the Arabian Peninsula, divided into 14 provinces. AREA 2 331 000sq km/899 766sq mi. It is bounded W by the Red Sea, NW by Jordan, N by Iraq, NE by Kuwait, E by the Arabian Gulf, Qatar, and the United Arab Emirates, SE and S by Oman, S and SW by Yemen. CAPITAL Riyadh. CHIEF TOWNS Jeddah, Mecca, Medina, Ta'if, Ad Dammam, Abha. TIME ZONE GMT +3. The population is mainly Arab (90%); Islam is the chief religion. OFFICIAL LANGUAGE Arabic. CURRENCY the riyal. PHYSICAL DESCRIPTION the Red Sea coastal plain is bounded E by mountains; the highlands in the SW include Jebel Abha, Saudi Arabia's highest peak (3 133m); the Arabian Peninsula slopes gently N and E towards the oil-rich Al Hasa plain on the Arabian Gulf; the interior comprises two extensive areas of sand desert, the Nafud in the N and the Great Sandy Desert in the S; the central Najd has some large oases; salt flats are numerous in the E lowlands; a large network of wadis drains NE. CLIMATE hot and dry, with average temperatures varying from 21°C in the N, to 26°C in the S; day temperatures may rise to 50°C in the interior sand deserts; night frosts are common in the N and highlands; the Red Sea coast is hot and humid; average rainfall is low. HISTORY famed as the birthplace of Islam with the holy cities of Mecca, Medina, and Jedda; the modern state was founded by Ibn Saud who, by 1932, united the four tribal provinces of Hejaz in the NW, Asir in the SW, Najd in the centre, and Al Hasa in the E. GOVERNMENT governed as an absolute monarchy based on Islamic law and

Arab Bedouin tradition; a King is both head of state and Prime Minister, assisted by a 26-member Council of Ministers. ECONOMY oil was discovered in the 1930s; now the world's leading oil exporter; reserves account for about a quarter of the world's known supply; rapidly developing construction industry; natural gas; steel; petrochemicals; fertilizers; refined oil products; large areas opened up for cultivation in the 1980s; wheat, dairy produce, dates, grains, livestock; pilgrimage trade.

Saudi Arabia

sauerkraut *noun* shredded cabbage pickled in salt water, a popular German dish. [from German *sauerkraut*, sour cabbage]

Saul a biblical character, the first king to be elected by the Israelites. He conquered the Philistines, Ammonites, and Amalekites, became jealous of his son-in-law David, and quarrelled with the priestly class. Saul fell in battle with the Philistines on Mt Gilboa (1 Samuel 31.5), and was succeeded by David, who had been secretly anointed by Samuel.

Sault Sainte Marie POP (1991) 82 000, a town in S central Ontario, S Canada. It is situated on the N shore of St Mary's R which connects L Huron and L Superior. An international bridge connects Sault Sainte Marie to the town of the same name in Michigan, lying opposite. HISTORY a fort, built on the site in 1751, was taken by the British in 1762; the settlement was destroyed in 1814 by US naval forces; the Soo Canals were built to link L Superior (183m) and L Huron (177m).

sauna *noun* **1** a Finnish-style steam bath, the steam created by pouring water on hot coals. **2** a building or room equipped for this. [from Finnish *sauna*]

saunter — *verb intrans.* (**sauntered, sauntering**) (**saunter along**, **past**, *etc*) to walk at a leisurely pace, often aimlessly; to stroll. — *noun* **1** a lazy walking pace. **2** a leisurely walk; an amble.

saurian *Biol.* — *adj.* of or relating to lizards; lizard-like. — *noun* a lizard. [from Greek *sauros*, lizard]

sausage *noun* **1** a mass of minced and seasoned meat enclosed in a thin tube-shaped casing, usually served hot and whole when small, and cold and in slices when large. **2** any vaguely cylindrical object, especially with rounded ends. — **not a sausage** *colloq.* nothing at all. [from Old French *saussiche*]

sausage meat minced meat of the kind used for making sausages.

sausage roll a small pastry case filled with sausage meat and baked.

Saussure, Ferdinand de (1857–1913) Swiss linguist, born in Geneva, often described as the founder of modern linguistics. He taught historical linguistics at Paris (1881–91), was Professor of Indo-European Linguistics and

Sanskrit (1901–13) and then of General Linguistics at Geneva (1907–13). The work by which he is best known, the *Cours de linguistique générale* (Course in General Linguistics, 1916) was compiled from the lecture notes of his students after his death. His focus on language as an 'underlying system' inspired a great deal of later semiology and structuralism.

sauté — *verb* (**sautés, sautéd** *or* **sautéed, sautéing** *or* **sautéeing**) to fry gently for a short time. — *adj.* fried in this way: *sauté potatoes*. [from French *sauté*, tossed]

Savage, Michael Joseph (1872–1940) New Zealand politician, born in Australia. He went to New Zealand in 1907, became an MP (1919), and Leader of the Labour Party (1933). As Prime Minister (1935–40) of the first Labour government, he presided over a notable set of social reforms.

savage — *adj.* **1** untamed; uncivilized. **2** ferocious: *savage temper*. **3** cruel; barbaric. **4** uncultivated; rugged. — *noun* **1** *old use, now offensive* a member of a primitive people. **2** an uncultured, brutish, or cruel person. — *verb* to attack with ferocity, causing severe injury. [from Old French *sauvage*, wild, from Latin *silvaticus*, of the woods]

savagely *adv.* in a savage way.

savageness *noun* being savage.

savagery *noun* (PL. **savageries**) **1** cruelty or barbarousness; an act of cruelty. **2** the state of being wild or uncivilized.

Savannah POP (1990) 243 000, the seat of Chatham County, E Georgia, USA. It is a major port and tourist centre lying near the mouth of the Savannah R. HISTORY founded in 1733 by James Oglethorpe; held by the British from 1778 until 1782 during the American War of Independence; captured by William Tecumseh Sherman during the Civil War in 1864. NOTABLE FEATURE the city's historic district is designated a National Historic Landmark.

savannah *or* **savanna** dry grassland of the tropics and subtropics, located between areas of tropical rainforest and desert. The length of the arid season prevents widespread tree growth, and the scattered trees which do exist, such as acacia and baobab, are adapted to reduced precipitation levels. Fires, both natural and as a result of human activity, help to promote and maintain grassland.

savant *noun* a male learned person. [from French, from *savoir*, to know]

savante *noun* a female learned person.

save — *verb* **1** to rescue from danger, harm, loss, or failure. **2** (*also* **save something up**) to set it aside for future use. **3** (*also* **save up**) to set money aside for future use. **4** to use economically so as to avoid waste. **5** to cause or allow to escape potential unpleasantness or inconvenience; to spare: *that will save you the trouble of making the trip*. **6** *Sport* to prevent (a ball or shot) from reaching the goal; to prevent (a goal) from being scored. **7** *Relig.* to free from the influence or consequences of sin. **8** *Comput.* to transfer the contents of a computer file from the main memory on to disk or tape for storage, so that data are not lost in the event of an interruption to the power supply. Many word processors save files automatically at regular intervals. — *noun* an act of saving a ball or shot, or preventing a goal. — *prep.* (*also* **save for**) except: *lost all the books save one*. — *conj. old use* (**save that** ...) were it not that: *I would have gone with her, save that she had already left*. [from Latin *salvare*]

Save As You Earn (ABBREV. **SAYE**) in the UK, a savings scheme in which regular monthly payments are made over a five-year period. The sum saved is tax-free, accumulates interest, and is supplemented by a bonus on completion of the five years. The period of saving can be extended to seven years, after which an additional bonus is paid.

saveloy *noun* a spicy smoked pork sausage. [from French *cervelat*]

Savery, Thomas (c.1650–1715) English engineer, born in Shilstone, Devon. He realized that a vacuum could be produced if a steam-filled vessel could be cooled so that the steam condensed, thus allowing the pressure of the atmosphere to act on the piston and do work. This was the first practical steam engine, in use by around 1700.

Save the Children Fund in the UK, the largest international children's charity, founded in 1919 to rescue children from disaster and enforce their rights to longer-term care and education, particularly in developing countries. Its president is the Princess Royal.

Savile, Sir Jimmy (James Wilson Vincent) (1926–) English television and radio personality, born in Leeds. A former miner, he achieved fame as a disc jockey and hosted *Jim'll Fix It* (1975–) on television. He has also worked voluntarily at Leeds Infirmary and uses his celebrity status to raise huge sums of money for deserving causes.

saving — *noun* **1** a thing saved, especially an economy made. **2** (**savings**) money saved up. — *prep. formal* except; save.

saving grace a desirable feature that compensates for undesirable ones.

saviour *noun* **1** a person who saves someone or something from danger or destruction. **2** a person who frees others from sin or evil. **3** (**Saviour**) *Christianity* a name for Christ. [from Middle English *sauveur*]

savoir-faire *noun* **1** expertise. **2** tact. [French, = know what to do]

Savonarola, Girolamo (1452–98) Italian religious and political reformer, born in Ferrara. He became a Dominican in 1474, and as Vicar-General of the Dominicans in Tuscany from 1493, he began to advocate political revolution as a means of restoring religion and morality. When a republic was established in Florence (1494), he fostered a Christian commonwealth with stringent laws to repress vice and frivolity. In 1495 he disregarded a call to Rome to answer a charge of heresy, was excommunicated (1497), and burned in Florence.

savory *noun* (PL. **savories**) any of various aromatic plants of the mint family whose leaves are widely used as a flavouring in cooking. [from Latin *satureia*]

savour — *verb* **1** to taste or smell with relish. **2** to take pleasure in. **3** to flavour or season (food). **4** (**savour of something**) to show signs of it; to smack of it. — *noun* **1** taste or smell as possessed by something. **2** a faint but unmistakable quality. **3** a hint or trace. [from Latin *sapere*, to taste]

savouriness *noun* being savoury.

savoury — *adj.* **1** having a salty or sharp taste or smell; not sweet. **2** pleasant, especially morally pleasing or acceptable: *not a very savoury character.* **3** appetising. — *noun* (PL. **savouries**) a savoury food, especially served as an hors d'oeuvre.

Savoy, House of the rulers (11c–19c) of the duchy of Savoy, a transalpine area in present-day Switzerland and France. Its heyday was from the mid-14c to the mid-15c; thereafter it was hemmed in by French and Spanish monarchies. It suffered from the Italian Wars in the 16c and from conflict with Calvinist Geneva, and fell into decline after the Thirty Years War and the Napoleonic Wars.

savoy *noun* a winter variety of cabbage with wrinkled leaves. [from *Savoie*, the region of France where it was originally grown]

Savoy Operas the operettas by W S Gilbert and Arthur Sullivan, named after the theatre in London where they (from *Iolanthe*, 1882) were performed.

savvy *slang* — *verb trans., intrans.* (**savvies, savvied**) to know or understand. — *noun* **1** common sense; shrewdness. **2** know-how. [from Spanish *saber*, to know]

saw¹ see SEE¹.

saw² — *noun* any of various tools with a toothed metal blade for cutting, hand-operated or power-driven. — *verb* (PAST TENSE **sawed**; PAST PARTICIPLE **sawn**) **1** to cut with, or as if with, a saw. **2** *intrans.* to move to and fro, like a hand-operated saw. [from Anglo-Saxon *sagu*]

Sawchuk, Terry (Terrance Gordon), properly (1929–70) US ice hockey player, born in Winnipeg, Canada. A renowned goalminder, he started his career with the Detroit Red Wings in 1950, and later played for the Boston Bruins, Toronto Maple Leafs, Los Angeles Kings, and New York Rangers. He kept a clean sheet in a record 103 National Hockey League games, and appeared in 971 games (1950–70), a record for a goalminder.

sawdust *noun* dust in the form of tiny fragments of wood, made by sawing.

sawfish *noun* a large ray that has a long snout edged with tooth-like spikes.

sawfly *noun* (PL. **sawflies**) a wasp-like insect which lacks a constricted waist, and uses its large egg-laying tube to deposit eggs deep within plant tissues. The larvae resemble caterpillars, and feed on or bore into plant stems, leaves, or wood.

sawmill *noun* a factory in which timber is cut.

sawn-off shotgun a shotgun with the end of the barrel cut off, making it easier to carry concealed.

Sawyer, Bob a young medical student in Charles Dickens's *The Pickwick Papers.*

Sawyer, Tom See TOM SAWYER, THE ADVENTURES OF.

sawyer *noun* a person who saws timber in a sawmill.

sax *noun colloq.* a saxophone.

Saxe, (Hermann) Maurice, Comte de (Count of), also called **Marshal de Saxe** (1696–1750) French soldier, born in Goslar, the illegitimate son of Augustus II, King of Poland, formerly Elector of Saxony. He served in the French army in the War of the Polish Succession (1733–8), and in the War of the Austrian Succession (1740–8) he invaded Bohemia and took Prague by storm. In 1744 Louis XV appointed him Commander in Flanders, where he won victories at Fontenoy (1745), Raucoux (1746), and Lauffeld (1747), and was promoted to Marshal of France.

Saxe-Coburg-Gotha the name of the British royal family (1901–17). Edward VII inherited it from his father, Prince Albert, the second son of the Duke of Saxe-Coburg-Gotha. The obviously Germanic name was abandoned during World War I to assert the 'Englishness' of the royal family and play down the extent of its German blood.

saxhorn *noun* a musical instrument made of brass tubing, resembling a small tuba, with the mouthpiece set at right angles, and an upright bell. It was patented in the 1840s by the Belgian instrument-maker Adolphe Sax (1814–94), and manufactured in various sizes. Saxhorns are often, and confusingly, known by other names: for example, the alto and tenor saxhorns used in brass bands are known as tenor and baritone horns.

saxifrage *noun* any of a family of rock plants with tufted or mossy leaves and small white, yellow, or red flowers. [from Latin *saxifraga*, rock-breaker]

Saxon — *noun* **1** a member of a Germanic people (see SAXONS). **2** any of various Germanic dialects spoken by them. **3** a native or inhabitant of the region of Saxony in modern Germany. —

adj. relating to the (especially ancient) Saxons. [from Latin *Saxones*, Saxons]

Saxons a Germanic people from the N German plain. With the Angles, they formed the bulk of the invaders who in the two centuries following the Roman withdrawal from Britain (409) conquered and colonized most of what became England. They were especially prominent in Essex, Sussex, and Wessex.

Saxony a German ducal and electoral state. Prominent from the 9c to the 11c, it was reduced by the emperor Frederick I to two small areas on the R Elbe (1180–1422), but dynastic alliances enlarged the Saxon state on the Middle Elbe in the 15c. Frederick the Wise adopted Lutheranism (1524), which established Saxony's Protestant leadership, and it prospered in the 16c. The reign of John George I (1611–56) marked its steady eclipse by Brandenburg, and new duchies (eg Hanover) were formed out of Lower Saxony. Under the Catholic elector Frederick Augustus (reigned 1694–1733), Saxony's prestige improved with the acquisition of the Polish Crown, but King Frederick Augustus I of Saxony allied himself with Napoleon I and lost two fifths of his territory at the Congress of Vienna (1814–15). Saxony was merged in the North German Confederation (1866) and the German Reich (1871).

saxophone *noun* a wind instrument with a long S-shaped metal body. [named after Adolphe Sax (1814–94), Belgian instrument-maker]
◇ It is made of metal, has a wide conical bore with finger keys along its length, and an upturned bell. Though made in a variety of sizes and pitches, the most frequently used are the soprano, alto, tenor, and baritone; these make up the saxophone quartet in larger jazz and dance bands. In orchestras, the instrument is most often used singly.

saxophonist *noun* a person who plays the saxophone.

say — *verb* (PAST TENSE AND PAST PARTICIPLE **said**) **1** to utter or pronounce. **2** to express in words: *say what you mean.* **3** to state as an opinion: *I say we should refuse.* **4** to suppose: *say he doesn't come, what do we do then?* **5** to recite or repeat: *say a blessing.* **6** to judge or decide: *difficult to say which is best.* **7** (**say for** or **against something**) to argue in favour of it or against it: *a lot to be said for it.* **8** to communicate: *she talked for ages but didn't actually say much / what is the poem trying to say?* **9** to indicate: *the clock says 10 o'clock.* **10** to report or claim: *said to be still alive.* **11** *intrans., trans.* to make a statement (about); to tell: *I'd rather not say.* — *noun* **1** a chance to express an opinion: *you've had your say.* **2** the right to an opinion; the power to influence a decision: *have no say in the matter.* — *interj. North Amer., esp. US* an expression of surprise, protest, or sudden joy.

— **it goes without saying** it is obvious.
not to say indeed; even: *expensive, not to say extortionate.*
that is to say in other words.
there's no saying it is impossible to guess or judge.
[from Anglo-Saxon *secgan*]

Sayan Mountains a mountain range mainly in S Siberian Russia, and extending into N Mongolia. The E Sayan Mts stretch 1 090km/677mi SE from the lower R Yenisei, forming the boundary between Russia and Mongolia in the E. Their highest peak is Munku-Sardyk (3 491m). The W Sayan Mts lie entirely within Russia, stretching 640km/398mi NE from the Altay Mts. The Sayan Mts yield gold, coal, graphite, silver, and lead.

SAYE *abbrev.* Save As You Earn.

Sayers, Dorothy L(eigh) (1893–1957) English detective-story writer, born in Oxford. Her novels, beginning with *Clouds of Witness* (1926), relate the adventures of her hero Lord Peter Wimsey in various accurately observed milieux — eg advertising in *Murder Must Advertise* (1933) and bell-ringing in *The Nine Tailors* (1934). She also earned a reputation as a Christian apologist with her religious plays, radio broadcasts, and essays.

saying *noun* **1** a proverb or maxim. **2** an expression.

Say's Law in economics, a principle expounded in 1803 by the French political economist Jean Baptiste Say (1767–1832) that 'supply creates its own demand'. It was effectively countered by J M Keynes in the 1930s.

say-so *noun* **1** the right to make the final decision. **2** an unsupported claim or assertion.

Sb *symbol Chem.* antimony. [from Latin *stibium*]

SBN *abbrev.* Standard Book Number (see ISBN).

SC *or* **S.C.** *abbrev.* South Carolina.

Sc *symbol Chem.* scandium.

scab — *noun* **1** a crust of dried blood formed over a healing wound. **2** a contagious skin disease of sheep. **3** a plant disease caused by a fungus, producing crusty spots. **4** *derog. slang* a worker who defies a union's instruction to strike. — *verb intrans.* (**scabbed, scabbing**) **1** (*also* **scab over**) to become covered by a scab. **2** *slang* to work as a scab. [from Anglo-Saxon *sceabb*]

scabbard *noun* a sheath for a sword or dagger. [from Middle English *scauberc*]

scabbiness *noun* being scabby.

scabby *adj.* (**scabbier, scabbiest**) **1** covered with scabs. **2** *derog. colloq.* contemptible; worthless.

scabies *noun Medicine* a contagious skin disease that causes severe itching of the skin, especially at night, and may lead to secondary bacterial infection. The itching sensation is produced by the secretion of the itch mite (*Sarcoptes scabiei*), which bores under the skin to lay its eggs. [from Latin, from *scabere*, to scratch]

scabious *noun* any of a family of Mediterranean flowering plants with long stalks and dome-shaped flower heads. [from Latin *scabiosa herba*, scabies plant, from its use in curing scabies]

scabrous *adj.* **1** *said of skin, etc* rough and flaky or scaly. **2** bawdy; smutty. [from Latin *scaber*, rough]

Scafell *or* **Scawfell** the highest mountain peak in England, situated in the Lake District, Cumbria, NW England. HEIGHT 977m.

scaffold *noun* **1** a framework of metal poles and planks used as a temporary platform from which building repair or construction is carried out. **2** a makeshift platform from which a person is hanged. **3** any temporary platform. [from Old French *escadafault*]

scaffolding *noun* **1** a building scaffold or arrangement of scaffolds. **2** materials used for building scaffolds.

Scala, La *or* **Teatro alla Scala** a leading international opera house in Milan, Italy, originally opened in 1778.

scalar *Maths.* — *adj.* denoting a quantity that has magnitude but no direction, eg distance, speed, and mass. — *noun* a scalar quantity. See also VECTOR. [from Latin *scala*, ladder]

scald — *verb* **1** to injure with hot liquid or steam. **2** to treat with hot water so as to sterilize. **3** to heat to just short of boiling point. — *noun* an injury caused by scalding. [from Latin *excaldare*, to bathe in warm water]

scale¹ — *noun* **1** a series of markings or divisions at regular known intervals, for use in measuring; a system of such markings or divisions. **2** a measuring instrument with such markings. **3** the relationship between actual size and size as represented on a model or drawing. **4** a complete sequence of notes in music, especially of those

between two octaves. **5** any graded system, eg of employees' salaries. **6** extent or level relative to others: *on a grand scale*. — *verb* **1** to climb. **2** to change the size of (something), making it larger (*scale up*) or smaller (*scale down*) while keeping to the same proportions.
— **to scale** with all sizes and distances in correct proportion to the real thing.
[from Latin *scala*, ladder]

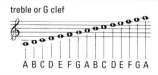

treble or G clef

A B C D E F G A B C D E F G A

musical scale

scale² — *noun* **1** any of the small thin plates that cover the skin of fish and reptiles. **2** a flaky piece of anything, especially skin. **3** tartar on the teeth. **4** a crusty white deposit formed when hard water is heated, eg in kettles. — *verb* **1** to remove the scales from (eg a fish), or scale from (eg a kettle). **2** to remove in thin layers. **3** *intrans.* to come off in thin layers or flakes. [from Old French *escale*, husk]

scale³ *noun* **1** (**scales**) an instrument for weighing. **2** either of the pans of a balance. **3** (**the Scales**) the constellation and sign of the zodiac Libra.
— **tip** *or* **turn the scales 1** to have one's weight measured at a specified amount: *tip the scales at 80kg*. **2** to prompt a firm decision; to be the decisive factor.
[from Norse *skal*, pan of a balance]

scale insect a small bug that feeds on the sap of plants and is wingless, often lacking legs as well, so called because many of the females are covered with a waxy or horny scale. Scale insects often completely cover leaves, stems, and fruits, and they do immense damage to crops.

scalene *adj., said of a triangle* having each side a different length. [from Greek *skalenos*, uneven]

scallawag same as SCALLYWAG.

scallion *noun* any vegetable of the onion family that has a small bulb and long edible leaves, eg the leek and the spring onion. [from Old French *escalogne*]

scallop — *noun* **1** an edible shellfish that has a pair of hinged, fan-shaped shells. **2** one of these shells, especially when served filled with food. **3** any of a series of curves that together form a wavy edge, eg on fabric. — *verb* (**scalloped, scalloping**) **1** to shape (an edge) in scallops. **2** to bake in a scallop shell or small shallow dish. [from Old French *escalope*]

scallywag *or* **scallawag** *noun colloq.* a naughty child; a rascal.

scalp — *noun* **1** the part of the head covered, or usually covered, by hair; the skin at this part. **2** a piece of this skin with its hair, formerly taken from slain enemies as a trophy, especially by some tribes of Native Americans. — *verb* **1** to remove the scalp of. **2** *colloq.* to buy up (eg theatre tickets) for resale at inflated prices. [from Middle English *scalp*]

scalpel *noun* a small surgical knife with a thin blade. [from Latin *scalpellum*, small knife]

scaly *adj.* (**scalier, scaliest**) **1** covered with scales. **2** like scales. **3** peeling off in scales.

scam *noun slang* a trick or swindle.

scamp *noun* a mischievous person, especially a child. [from Old French *escamper*, to decamp]

scamper — *verb intrans.* (**scampered, scampering**) to run quickly taking short steps, especially in play. — *noun* **1** an act of scampering. **2** a scampering movement or pace. [see SCAMP]

scampi *noun* **1** (*pl.*) large prawns. **2** a dish of these, usually deep-fried in breadcrumbs. [from plural of Italian *scampo*, shrimp]

scan — *verb* (**scanned, scanning**) **1** to read through or examine carefully. **2** to look over quickly. **3** *Medicine* to examine (the body, especially an internal part of it) without physical penetration, by any of various techniques, eg by ultrasound or by computerized axial tomography (CAT). **4** *Engineering* to search (an area) by means of radar or by sweeping a beam of light over it. **5** *Comput.* to examine (data) on a magnetic disk. **6** to examine the rhythm of (a piece of poetry). **7** *intrans. said of verse* to conform to a pattern of rhythm. — *noun* **1** an act of scanning. **2** *Medicine* an image obtained by examining the body, especially an internal part of it, using ultrasound, computerized axial tomography, etc. [from Latin *scandere*, to climb]

scandal *noun* **1** widespread public outrage and loss of reputation; an event or fact causing this. **2** any extremely objectionable fact or situation. **3** malicious gossip. [from Greek *skandalon*, stumbling-block]

scandalize *or* **scandalise** *verb* to shock or outrage.

scandalmonger *noun* a person who spreads malicious gossip.

scandalous *adj.* disgraceful; outrageous.

scandalously *adv.* in a scandalous way; to a scandalous extent.

Scandinavia the countries of Norway, Sweden, and Finland. Iceland and Denmark are often considered part of Scandinavia, but are geographically separate.

Scandinavian — *noun* **1** a native or inhabitant of Scandinavia. **2** a group of northern Germanic languages spoken in Scandinavia. They are usually divided into two groups: *Continental*, ie Swedish, Norwegian, and Danish; and *Insular*, ie Icelandic and Faeroese. — *adj.* relating to Scandinavia or its people or languages.

scandium *noun Chem.* (SYMBOL **Sc**, ATOMIC NUMBER **21**) a soft silvery-white metal with a pinkish tinge (a member of the lanthanide series), which has no major uses, although its oxide is used in ceramics and as a catalyst. [from the name *Scandinavia*, where it was discovered]

scanner *noun* a person or device that scans.

scanning electron microscope *Biol.* (ABBREV. **SEM**) an electron microscope that produces a three-dimensional image of an object, allowing the surface structure of a relatively thick specimen, eg a tissue sample, to be examined.

scansion *noun* **1** the act or practice of scanning poetry. **2** a poem's particular pattern of rhythm. [from Latin *scansio*]

scant *adj.* **1** in short supply. **2** meagre; inadequate. [from Norse *skamt*]

scantily *adv.* in a scanty way; hardly, barely.

scantiness *noun* being scant.

scanty *adj.* (**scantier, scantiest**) small in size or amount; barely enough: *scanty clothing* / *scanty meal*.

Scapa Flow an area of open water in the Orkney Is, Scotland, surrounded by the islands of Mainland, Hoy, Flotta, S Ronaldsay, and Burray. It was a British naval base during both World Wars. In 1919 German warships were scuppered there.

Scapegoat, The a painting by William Holman Hunt (1856).

scapegoat *noun* a person made to take the blame or punishment for the mistakes of others. [from ESCAPE + GOAT, from the biblical Jewish practice of symbolically loading the sins of the people on to a goat which was then released into the wilderness]

scapula *noun* (PL. **scapulae, scapulas**) *Medicine* the shoulder-blade. [from Latin *scapula*]

scapular — *adj. Medicine* of the scapula. — *noun* a monk's garment consisting of a broad cloth strip with a hole for the head, hanging loosely over a habit in front and behind.

scar[1] — *noun* **1** a mark left on the skin after a wound has healed. **2** a permanent damaging emotional effect. **3** a blemish. **4** a mark on a plant where a leaf was formerly attached. — *verb trans., intrans.* (**scarred, scarring**) to mark or become marked with a scar. [from Greek *eschara*]

scar[2] *noun* a steep rocky outcrop on the side of a hill or mountain. [from Norse *sker*, low reef]

scarab *noun* **1** any of various dung-beetles, especially the black dung-beetle, regarded as sacred by the ancient Egyptians. **2** an image or carving of the sacred beetle, or a gemstone carved in its shape. [from Latin *scarabaeus*]

scarab

Scarborough POP (1981) 38 000, a coastal resort town in Scarborough district, North Yorkshire, N England. It lies on the North Sea, 25km/16mi N of Bridlington. In the 4c Scarborough was a Roman signal station. It is now England's oldest spa town, sometimes known as 'Queen of the Yorkshire coast'. NOTABLE FEATURES castle (12c); Museum of Regional Archaeology.

scarce — *adj.* **1** not often found; rare. **2** in short supply. — *adv.* scarcely: *could scarce see it through the mist.*
— **make oneself scarce** *colloq.* to leave or stay away.
[from Old French *eschars*]

scarcely *adv.* **1** only just. **2** hardly ever. **3** not really; not at all: *it is scarcely a reason to hit him.*

scarcity *noun* (PL. **scarcities**) a scarce state; a lack.

scare — *verb* **1** *trans., intrans.* to make or become afraid. **2** to startle. **3** (*also* scare someone *or* something away *or* off) to drive them away by frightening them. — *noun* **1** a fright. **2** a sudden and widespread (often unwarranted) feeling of alarm provoked by foreboding news: *a bomb scare.* [from Norse *skirra*, to avoid]

Scarecrow, the one of Dorothy's companions in Frank L Baum's *The Wonderful Wizard of Oz.*

scarecrow *noun* **1** a rough model of a human figure set up in a field, etc to scare birds off crops. **2** *colloq.* a raggedly dressed person. **3** *colloq.* a very thin person.

scaremonger *noun* a person who causes alarm by spreading rumours of (especially imminent) disaster.

scaremongering *noun* causing unnecessary alarm.

scarf[1] *noun* (PL. **scarves, scarfs**) a strip or square of fabric worn around the neck, shoulders, or head for warmth or decoration. [perhaps from Old French *escarpe*, sash or sling]

scarf[2] — *noun* a glued or bolted joint made between two ends, especially of timber, cut so as to overlap and produce a continuous flush surface. — *verb* to join by means of such a joint.

Scarfe, Gerald (1936–) English cartoonist, born in London. His cartoons are based on extreme distortion (eg Mick Jagger's lips are drawn larger than the rest of his face), and have appeared in *Punch* since 1960, *Private Eye* since 1961, and elsewhere, especially the *Sunday Times* since 1967. He also designed the animated sequences for the film *Pink Floyd: The Wall* (1982) and has worked as a theatrical designer.

Scargill, Arthur (1938–) English trade union leader, born in Leeds. Active in the Labour Party and the National Union of Mineworkers, he became President of the NUM in 1982, and a member of the Trades Union Congress General Council. A powerful orator, he is known for his strong defence of British miners through a socialist politics that has often brought his union into conflict with government, particularly during the miners' strike of 1984–5.

scarification *noun* scarifying or being scarified.

scarify *verb* (**scarifies, scarified**) **1** to make scratches or shallow cuts on the surface of. **2** to break up the surface of soil with a tool such as a wire rake, without turning the soil over. **3** to hurt with severe criticism. [from Greek *skariphos*, etching tool]

scarlatina *noun Medicine* scarlet fever. [from Italian *scarlattina*]

Scarlatti, (Pietro) Alessandro (Gaspare) (1660–1725) Italian composer, born in Palermo, Sicily. A leading figure in Italian opera, he was musical director at the court in Naples (1683–1702, 1709–25) and founded the Neapolitan school of opera. He reputedly wrote over 100 operas, of which 40 survive complete (eg *Tigrane*, 1715), 10 masses, c.700 cantatas, and oratorios, motets, and madrigals.

Scarlatti, (Guiseppe) Domenico (1685–1757) Italian composer, the founder of the modern piano technique, born in Naples, the son of Alessandro Scarlatti. From 1711 in Rome he was *maestro di cappella* to the Queen of Poland, for whom he composed several operas, and he also served in Lisbon and Madrid. As choirmaster of St Peter's, Rome (1714–19), he wrote much church music. A skilled harpsichordist, he is noted for his 555 harpsichord concertos.

scarlet *noun* a bright red colour. [from Persian *saqalat*, scarlet cloth]

scarlet fever an infectious disease causing fever, inflammation of the nose, throat, and mouth, and a rash on the body.

scarlet woman *old use or humorous* a sexually promiscuous woman, especially a prostitute.

Scarman, Leslie George Scarman, Baron (1911–) English jurist and law reformer, born in London. He was called to the Bar in 1936. He became a High Court judge in 1961 and was the first Chairman of the Law Commission (1965). He left the Law Commission to go to the Court of Appeal (1973), and then went to the House of Lords as a Lord of Appeal in Ordinary (1977–86). His investigation of the cause of the Brixton and Notting Hills riots (1981) resulted in a much-discussed report. With Lord Devlin, he campaigned for a reassessment of the case of the Guildford Four.

scarp *noun* **1** an escarpment. **2** the inner side of a defensive ditch, nearest to or flush with the wall of a castle, etc. [from Italian *scarpa*]

scarp and dip *Geol.* the two slopes formed by the outcropping of a bed of sedimentary rock. The scarp and dip are usually steep and relatively gentle slopes, respectively.

scarper *verb intrans.* (**scarpered, scarpering**) *colloq.* to run away; to leave quickly and unnoticed. [from Italian *scappare*, to escape]

scarves see SCARF[1].

scary *adj.* (**scarier, scariest**) *colloq.* causing fear or alarm.

scat[1] *verb intrans.* (**scatted, scatting**) *colloq., especially as a command* to go away; to run off. [perhaps from SCATTER]

scat[2] — *noun* jazz singing consisting of improvised sounds, not words. — *verb intrans.* (**scatted, scatting**) to sing jazz in this way. [perhaps imitative]

scathing *adj.* scornfully critical. [from Norse *skathe*, injury]

scathingly *adv.* in a scathing way.

scatological *adj.* **1** relating to or involving scatology. **2** characterized or preoccupied with obscenity.

scatology *noun* **1** preoccupation with the obscene, especially with excrement and related bodily functions. **2** *Medicine* the study of excrement for the purpose of diagnosis. [from Greek *skor*, dung + -LOGY]

scatter — *verb* (**scattered, scattering**) **1** to lay or throw haphazardly. **2** *trans., intrans.* to depart or send off in different directions. — *noun* **1** an act of scattering. **2** a quantity of scattered things. **3** *Statistics* a measure of the extent to which the measurements of two random variables, plotted as paired values on a graph, are grouped close together or scattered apart. It indicates whether the mean value is likely to be representative of all the measurements. [from Middle English *scatter*]

scatterbrain *noun colloq.* a person incapable of organized thought.

scatterbrained *adj.* muddle-headed.

scatter diagram *Maths.* a graph which shows the extent to which two random variables, plotted as paired values, are grouped close together or scattered apart.

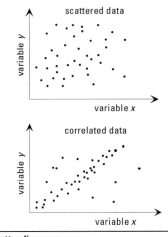

scatter diagrams

scattering *noun* **1** dispersion. **2** something that is scattered. **3** a small amount.

scatty *adj.* (**scattier, scattiest**) *colloq.* **1** mentally disorganized. **2** crazy; daft. [a shortening of SCATTERBRAINED]

scavenge *verb* **1** *intrans.* to search among waste for usable things. **2** *trans. Chem.* to remove impurities from. [from Old French *scawage*, inspection]

scavenger *noun* **1** an animal that feeds on refuse or decaying flesh. **2** a person who searches among rubbish for usable things.

ScD *abbrev. Scientiae Doctor* (Latin), Doctor of Science.

SCE *abbrev.* Scottish Certificate of Education.

scenario *noun* (PL. **scenarios**) **1** a rough written outline of a dramatic work, eg a film; a synopsis. **2** a detailed script. **3** a hypothetical situation or sequence of events. [from Italian *scenario*]

scene *noun* **1** the setting in which a real or imaginary event takes place. **2** a unit of action in a play or film. See also ACT. **3** any of the pieces making up a stage or film set, or the set as a whole. **4** a landscape, situation, etc as seen by someone: *a delightful scene met their eyes.* **5** an embarrassing display of emotion in public: *make a scene.* **6** *colloq.* a state of affairs with regard to a particular activity: *the current music scene.* **7** *colloq.* a liked or preferred area of interest or activity: *not my scene.*
— **behind the scenes 1** out of sight of the audience. **2** unknown to, or out of sight of, the public.
come on the scene to arrive; to become part of the current situation.
set the scene to describe the situation in which an event takes place.
[from Greek *skene*, tent, stage]

scenery *noun* **1** landscape, especially when attractively rural. **2** the items making up a stage or film set.

scenic *adj.* **1** of, being, or including attractive natural landscapes: *a scenic trip.* **2** of or relating to scenery on stage or in film.

scent — *noun* **1** the distinctive smell of a person, animal, or plant. **2** a trail of this left behind: *dogs on the scent.* **3** a series of findings leading to a major discovery: *police on the scent of the drug baron.* **4** perfume. — *verb* **1** to smell; to discover by the sense of smell. **2** to sense; to be aware of by instinct or intuition. **3** to impart a smell, especially a pleasant one. [from Latin *sentire*, to perceive]

sceptic *noun* **1** a person who believes that nothing can be known with absolute certainty. **2** a person who questions widely accepted (especially religious) beliefs. [from Greek *skeptikos*, thoughtful]

sceptical *adj.* doubtful, tending to be incredulous.

scepticism *noun* **1** doubt, or the disposition to doubt. **2** a philosophical tradition that doubts the possibility of human knowledge. **3** agnosticism.
◇ An extreme version, held by the followers of Pyrrho of Elis, maintains that it is never possible to have justified beliefs about anything, including the truth of scepticism itself. Less extreme scepticism is usually directed at particular sources of knowledge, such as perception, memory, or reason.

sceptre *noun* a ceremonial rod carried by a monarch as a symbol of sovereignty. [from Greek *skeptron*, staff]

Sch *abbrev.* schilling.

Schaffhausen, French **Schaffhouse 1** POP (1990) 50 000, an industrial town and the capital of Schaffhausen canton, NE Switzerland. Lying on the R Rhine, 37km/23mi N of Zürich, it is one of the best-preserved of Switzerland's many medieval towns. NOTABLE FEATURES Kastel Munot (1564–85); Minster (1087–1150); falls and rapids on the Rhine are nearby. **2** a canton in NE Switzerland with Schaffhausen as its capital.

Schaudinn, Fritz Richard (1871–1906) German zoologist and microbiologist, born in Röseningken, E Prussia. Director of the Department of Protozoological Research at the Institute for Tropical Diseases in Hamburg, he demonstrated the amoebic nature of tropical dysentery and discovered the spirochaete *Spirochaeta pallida*, now known as *Treponema pallidum*, which causes syphilis (1905).

Schawlow, Arthur Leonard (1921–) US physicist, and co-inventor of the laser, born in Mount Vernon, New York. Professor at Stanford University from 1961, he played a central role in laying down the theoretical framework of the laser and had started to construct one around the time that Theodore Maiman produced the first

working laser at Hughes Research Laboratories in California. He later worked on the development of laser spectroscopy, and shared the 1981 Nobel Prize for Physics with Nicolas Bloembergen and Kai Siegbahn.

schedule — *noun* **1** a list of activities or events planned to take place at specific times. **2** the state of happening on time according to plan: *behind schedule.* **3** any list or inventory. **4** a timetable. **5** a supplement to a document. — *verb* **1** to plan (something) to happen at a specific time. **2** to put on a schedule. [from Latin *schedula*, from *scheda*, strip of papyrus]

Scheele, Carl Wilhelm (1742–86) Swedish chemist, born in Stralsund (now in Germany). He was apprenticed to an apothecary, and later worked at Malmö, Stockholm, Göteborg, Uppsala, and Köping. He recognized that air was a mixture of more than one compound, isolated oxygen, discovered chlorine and molybdenum, and prepared several new acids. In 1775 his experiments on arsenic resulted in the discovery of copper arsenide, a green pigment which became known as 'Scheele's green'.

Schelde *or* **Scheldt, River**, French **Escaut** a river in NW Europe, length 435km/270mi. Rising in Aisne department, Picardy, N France, it flows N and NE through Belgium to Antwerp. The river turns NW and flows to meet the North Sea through two estuaries (East and West Schelde) in the Netherlands. The Schelde is connected by canal to several other N European rivers.

schema *noun* (PL. **schemata**) **1** a diagram or plan. **2** an outline or synopsis. [from Greek *schema*, form]

schematic *adj.* **1** following a particular plan or arrangement. **2** in the form of a diagram or plan.

schematization *or* **schematisation** *noun* schematizing.

schematize *or* **schematise** *verb* to represent by means of a diagram or plan.

scheme — *noun* **1** a plan of action. **2** a system or programme: *a pension scheme.* **3** a careful arrangement of different parts: *a colour scheme.* **4** a secret plan to cause harm or damage. **5** a diagram or table. — *verb intrans.* to plan or act secretly and usually maliciously. [see SCHEMA]

schemer *noun* a person who schemes.

scherzo *noun* (PL. **scherzos**, **scherzi**) a lively piece of music, especially a vigorous or light-hearted movement in a symphony or sonata. [from Italian *scherzo*, joke]

Schiaparelli, Elsa (1890–1973) Italian fashion designer, born in Rome. She lived in the USA, then went to Paris in 1920. She designed and wore a sweater, as a result of which she received orders from a US store, which started her in business in 1929. Her designs were inventive and sensational, and she was noted for her use of colour, including 'shocking pink', and her original use of traditional fabrics.

Schiaparelli, Giovanni Virginio (1835–1910) Italian astronomer, born in Savigliano, Piedmont. Head of the Brera Observatory in Milan, he studied meteors and comets, and detected linear markings on the surface of Mars that he termed *canali* (channels).

Schiller, (Johann Christoph) Friedrich (von) (1759–1805) German dramatist, poet, and historian, born in Marbach, widely regarded as the national dramatist. His first play, *Die Räuber* (The Robbers, 1781), had a revolutionary appeal that made it an instant success. He also wrote the poem *An die Freude* (Ode to Joy, later set to music by Beethoven in his choral symphony), the dramatic trilogy *Wallenstein* (1796–9), the romantic tragedy *Maria Stuart* (1800), and *Wilhelm Tell* (1804).

schilling *noun* the standard unit of currency in Austria, divided into 100 groschen. [from German *schilling*]

Schindler's List a US film (1993) directed by Steven Spielberg. Based on Thomas Keneally's book *Schindler's Ark* (1982, republished as *Schindler's List*, 1994), it is filmed in black and white and shows some of the grim truths of the holocaust. It won seven Oscars, including Best Film and Best Director.

schism *noun* **1** *Relig.* separation from the main group, or into opposing groups. **2** the act of encouraging such separation. **3** a breakaway group formed. [from Greek *schisma*, split]
◇ In the Christian Church, schism is deliberate separation from the main group on matters of Church order and discipline rather than doctrine. Roman Catholic theology has traditionally treated the separation of the Orthodox Church and the Churches of the Reformation as schismatic in the sense that they are no longer in communion with the papacy and are thus outside the true Church. However, this is now more commonly regarded as internal division in the one Church of Christ, rather than a matter of external separation from it.

schismatic *adj.* relating to or involving schism.

schist *noun* *Geol.* any of a group of common coarse-grained metamorphic rocks that characteristically contain broad wavy bands corresponding to zones of minerals, eg mica, hornblende, talc, and graphite, that readily split into layers. [from Greek *schistos*, split]

schistosomiasis *noun* *Medicine* a tropical disease caused by infestation with parasitic flukes belonging to the genus *Schistosoma*. The flukes pass through the blood circulation, and may affect other organs, such as the liver, intestines, and bladder. The disease is transmitted by drinking water contaminated with human sewage. [from Greek *schistos*, split]

schizo *colloq.* — *noun* (PL. **schizos**) a schizophrenic. — *adj.* schizophrenic.

schizoid — *adj.* showing some of the qualities of schizophrenia, eg extreme shyness and indulgence in fantasy, but without definite mental disorder. — *noun* a schizoid person. [from Greek *schizein*, to split + -OID]

schizophrenia *noun* any of various forms of a severe mental disorder characterized by loss of contact with reality, impairment of thought processes, a marked personality change, loss of emotional responsiveness, and social withdrawal. [from Greek *schizein*, to split + *phren*, mind]
◇ Patients with schizophrenia often feel that their thoughts and actions are controlled by external forces, and trivial events and objects take on an inappropriately significant meaning. Some sufferers become totally inactive, while others become violently emotional, or fearful of persecution. The causes of the disorder are not fully understood, but hereditary factors and social stresses are thought to play a major role. Schizophrenia is a form of psychosis, and it is treated with certain drugs, hospitalization in severe cases (until the patient's condition has stabilized), and psychiatric counselling prior to rehabilitation within the community, with the aim of giving the patient social independence.

schizophrenic — *noun* a person suffering from schizophrenia. — *adj.* relating to or suffering from schizophrenia.

Schlegel, August Wilhelm von (1767–1845) German poet and critic, born in Hanover. A leading figure of the Romantic movement, he became Professor of Literature and Fine Art at Jena in 1798 and with his brother Friedrich von Shlegel, founded the literary journal *Das Athenaeum* (1798–1800). He lectured at Berlin (1801–4), and from 1818 until his death was Professor of Literature at Bonn. Although he wrote his own poetry and sonnets (eg *Gedichte*, 1800), he is better known for his translation into German of Shakespeare.

Schleiden, Matthias Jakob (1804–81) German botanist, born in Hamburg, where his father was municipal physician. He abandoned a law career to study science, and later became Professor of Botany at Jena and Dorpat. He explained the role of the cell nucleus in the formation of new cells, and did much to establish the science of plant cytology.

Schleiermacher, Friedrich (Ernst Daniel) (1768–1834) German theologian and philosopher, widely held to be the founder of modern Protestant theology, born in Breslau. A preacher in Berlin (1796), and a professor at Halle (1804–6) and Berlin (from 1810), he was a leader of the movement which led to the union in 1817 of the Lutheran and Reformed Churches in Prussia. His most important work is *Der christliche Glaube* (The Christian Faith, 1821–2).

schlep *or* **schlepp** *slang* — *verb* to carry, pull, or drag with difficulty. — *noun* **1** a clumsy, stupid, or incompetent person. **2** a journey or procedure requiring great effort or involving great difficulty. [from Yiddish *schlep*]

Schlesinger, Arthur M(eier) Jnr (1917–) US historian, born in Columbus, Ohio. He was Professor of History at Harvard (1954–61) and special assistant to President Kennedy (1961–3). His publications include the Pulitzer prizewinners *The Age of Jackson* (1945) and *A Thousand Days: John F Kennedy in the White House* (1965). He then became Professor of Humanities at New York (1966) and President of the American Institute of Arts and Letters (1981).

Schlesinger, John (Richard) (1926–) English actor and film, stage, and opera director, born in London. He directed art documentary films for television, and made his first feature film, *A Kind of Loving*, in 1962, followed by *Billy Liar* (1963). His interpretation of Thomas Hardy's *Far from the Madding Crowd* (1967), *Midnight Cowboy* (1969), which won him an Oscar, and *Sunday, Bloody Sunday* (1971) all showed his versatility. Later productions in the USA include *Marathon Man* (1976), *Honky Tonk Freeway* (1980), *Believers* (1987), and *Pacific Heights* (1990).

Schleswig-Holstein POP (1991e) 2.6m, the northernmost state of Germany. It is bounded N by Denmark and includes the North Frisian Is. AREA 15 721sq km/6 068sq mi. HISTORY it was the focus of a dispute between Denmark and Prussia in the 19c, leading to war (1863) and its annexation by Prussia (1866); in 1920 allied forces held a plebiscite giving the N part of Schleswig to Denmark and the S part, including Holstein, to Germany. CAPITAL Kiel. CHIEF TOWNS Lübeck, Flensburg. ECONOMY shipbuilding; machinery; foodstuffs; electrical engineering; tourism (the coast between Lübeck and Flensburg is Germany's most extensive swimming and sailing resort area).

Schlick, Moritz (1882–1936) German philosopher, one of the leaders of the 'Vienna Circle' of logical positivists, born in Berlin. He taught at Rostock and Kiel, and from 1922 was Professor of Inductive Sciences at Vienna. An early exponent of Einstein's relativity theories, his major works include *Allgemeine Erkenntnislehre* (General Theory of Knowledge, 1918) and *Fragen der Ethik* (Problems of Ethics, 1930). He was murdered on the steps of the university by a deranged student.

Schlieffen, Alfred, Graf von (Count of) (1833–1913) Prussian soldier, born in Berlin. As Chief of General Staff (1891–1905), he devised the Schlieffen Plan (1895), on which German strategy was unsuccessfully based in World War I. He envisaged a German breakthrough in Belgium and the defeat of France within six weeks by a major right-wheel flanking movement through Holland, which would cut off Paris from the sea, meanwhile holding off the Russians with secondary forces.

Schliemann, Heinrich (1822–90) German archaeologist, born in Neubukow. He had a successful business career from which he retired early to realize his ambition of finding the site of the Homeric poems by excavating the tell at Hisarlik in Asia Minor, the traditional site of Troy. From 1871 he discovered nine superimposed city sites, one of which contained a considerable treasure (found 1873) which he (wrongly) identified as Priam's. He also excavated several other Greek sites (eg Mycenae).

schlock *noun* **1** inferior quality; shoddy production. **2** a shoddy or defective article. [from Yiddish *schlock*, from German *Schlag*, a blow]

schmaltz *noun colloq.* excessive sentimentality, especially in music or other art. [from Yiddish *schmaltz*, from German *Schmalz*, cooking fat]

schmaltzy *adj.* (**schmaltzier, schmaltziest**) characterized by schmaltz.

Schmidt, Bernhard Voldemar (1879–1935) Estonian optical instrument-maker, born on the island of Naissaar, near Tallin. Working at the Hamburg Observatory in Bergedorf, he devised a method to overcome aberration of the image formed by spherical mirrors and lenses by the introduction of a correcting plate at the centre of curvature (1932). The Schmidt telescope has been much used in sky surveys, the best-known example being that installed on Mount Palomar.

Schmidt, Helmut (Heinrich Waldemar) (1918–) German politician, born in Hamburg. After service in World War II, he studied at Hamburg, joined the Social Democratic Party in 1946, and became a member of the Bundestag in 1953. He was Minister of Defence (1969–72) and then of Finance (1972–4), when he established a firm basis for Germany's continued economic growth. On succeeding Willy Brandt as Chancellor (1974–82) he described his aim as the 'political unification of Europe in partnership with the United States'.

Schmidt, Maarten (1929–) Dutch-born US astronomer, born in Groningen. He moved to the USA in 1959 to join the staff of the Hale Observatories. He showed that the peculiarities of the spectrum of an astronomical object discovered by Alan Sandage were caused by a massive 'Doppler redshift', which implied that the object is receding from the Earth at nearly 16 per cent of the speed of light; such objects are now known as 'quasars'.

schnapps *noun* in N Europe, any strong dry alcoholic spirit, especially Dutch gin distilled from potatoes. [from German *Schnapps*, dram of liquor]

Schnauzer *noun* a German breed of dog, terrier-like with a thick wiry coat, marked eyebrows, moustache, and beard. The top of the head is flat, and it has short pendulous ears. [from German *Schnauze*, snout]

Schneider Trophy a flying trophy for seaplanes first presented in 1913. After being won outright by Great Britain in 1931 the contest ceased, but the races were revived in the 1980s.

schnitzel *noun* a veal cutlet. [from German *Schnitzel*]

Schoenberg *or* **Schönberg, Arnold (Franz Walter)** (1874–1951) Austro–Hungarian Jewish composer, born in Vienna. Largely self-taught, in his 20s he lived by orchestrating operettas while composing such early works as the string sextet *Verklärte Nacht* (Transfigured Night, 1899). His sought-after personal musical style was emerging in these works, but they were not well received — his *Chamber Symphony* caused a riot at its first performance (1907) as it abandoned the traditional concept of tonality. He became known for his concept of '12-tone' or 'serial' music, used in most of his later works. At the end of World War I he taught in Vienna and Berlin, until exiled by the Nazi government in 1933. He later settled in California, and took US nationality (1941).

scholar *noun* **1** a learned person, especially an academic. **2** a person who studies; a pupil or student. **3** a person receiving a scholarship. [from Latin *scholaris*; see SCHOOL]

scholarly *adj.* **1** showing evidence of extensive study. **2** typical of work produced by scholars: *a book too scholarly to be popular*.

scholarship *noun* **1** a sum of money awarded for the purposes of further study, usually to an outstanding student. **2** the achievements or methods of a scholar.

scholastic *adj.* **1** of or relating to learning; academic; educational. **2** of or relating to scholasticism. [from Greek *scholastikos*]

scholasticism *noun* **1** the system of (especially religious and moral) teaching, based on the writings of the Greek philosopher Aristotle, that dominated W Europe in the Middle Ages. **2** stubborn adherence to traditional teaching methods and values.
◇ The translation of Aristotle's writings into Latin provided medieval scholars and theologians with new material for reflection and criticism. This led to the synthesis of Aristotelian philosophy and Christian theology by, for example, Thomas Aquinas and Duns Scotus.

Schönbrunn Palace a Baroque palace in Vienna, designed (1696–1730) by Fischer von Erlach for Emperor Leopold I, and converted by Nikolaus Pacassi for Maria Theresa's use in the 1740s.

Schöne Müllerin, Die (The Fair Maid of the Mill) a song cycle (1823) comprising 20 settings for male voice and piano composed by Franz Schubert for poems by Wilhelm Müller (1794–1827), telling of a happy love affair with a tragic ending.

school¹ — *noun* **1** a place where a formal general education is received especially as a child or teenager. **2** a place offering formal instruction in a particular subject, often part of a university: *art school*. **3** the body of students and teachers that occupy any such place. **4** the period of the day or year during which such a place is open to students: *stay behind after school*. **5** a group of painters, writers, or other artists sharing the same style or master. **6** any activity or set of surroundings as a provider of experience: *factories are the schools of life*. **7** *colloq.* a group of people meeting regularly for some purpose, eg gambling: *a card school*. — *verb* **1** to educate in a school. **2** to give training of a particular kind to. **3** to discipline. [from Greek *schole*, leisure, lecture-place]

school² — *noun* a group of fish, whales, or other marine animals swimming together. — *verb intrans.* to form, or move about in, a school. [from Dutch *school*]

schoolchild *noun* a child who attends a school.

School for Scandal, The a play by Richard Brinsley Sheridan (1777). It is a comedy which follows the pursuits of the scandal-mongering hypocrite, Joseph, and his good-natured but reckless brother, Charles, until their uncle adopts various disguises to test their characters.

schoolhouse *noun* **1** a building used as a school, especially in a rural area. **2** a house for a teacher within the grounds of a school.

schooling *noun* education or instruction, especially received at school.

school-leaver *noun* a young person recently completing a course of education and no longer attending a school.

schoolmarm *noun colloq.* **1** North Amer., esp. US a schoolmistress. **2** a woman with old-fashioned manners or attitudes, especially regarding sex.

schoolmarmish *adj.* like or typical of a schoolmarm.

schoolmaster *noun* a male schoolteacher or head of a school.

schoolmistress *noun* a female schoolteacher or head of a school.

School of Athens, The a fresco by Raphael (1509–11, Stanza della Segnatura, Vatican). It depicts a gathering of philosophers and mathematicians in ancient Greece, including Plato and Aristotle.

School of Pont-Aven a group of painters who, under the influence of Paul Gauguin, cultivated the style of painting known as Synthetism. The name of the group comes from the town of Pont-Aven in Brittany, where Gauguin lived periodically between 1886 and 1990, and the style was influenced by the simple and spiritual lives of the rural Bretons.

School of the Air in Australia, a two-way radio educational service for children living in isolated areas. It was begun in South Australia in 1951 to supplement correspondence teaching and reduce feelings of isolation.

schoolteacher *noun* a person who teaches in a school.

schooner *noun* 1 a fast sailing-ship with two or more masts. 2 a large sherry glass. 3 *North Amer., esp. US* a large beer glass. [in 18c English *skooner* or *scooner*, possibly from dialect *scoon*, to skim]
◇ The masts are rigged with fore-and-aft sails; on classic two-masted schooners the mainmast is taller than the foremast. The first vessel of the type was launched at Gloucester, Massachusetts, in 1713, and they were chiefly used for coastal trade and fishing in the days of sail.

Schopenhauer, Arthur (1788–1860) German philosopher, born in Danzig. He taught at Berlin (1820), where he combatively held his lectures at the same times as Hegel, whose ideas he rejected, but he failed to attract students. He then lived in retirement as a scholar at Frankfurt am Main. His chief work, *Die Welt als Wille und Vorstellung* (The World as Will and Idea, 1819), emphasizes the central role of human will as the creative, primary factor in understanding. His conception of the will as a blind, irrational force led him to a rejection of Enlightenment doctrines and to pessimism.

schottische *noun* 1 a folk dance, originally from Germany, with short steps and hops, like a slow polka. 2 a piece of music for such a dance. [from German *der schottische Tanz*, the Scottish dance]

Schrödinger, Erwin (1887–1961) Austrian physicist, born in Vienna. He held several professorships in Germany until the rise of the Nazi regime; from 1933 he worked in Oxford, Ganz (Austria), and Dublin. Inspired by the proposal that particles will in some circumstances behave like waves, he introduced his celebrated wave equation which describes the behaviour of such systems. For this fundamental contribution to the theory of quantum mechanics he shared the 1933 Nobel Prize for Physics with Paul Dirac.

Schubert, Franz (Peter) (1797–1828) Austrian composer, born in Vienna. At 11 he became a member of the chapel choir at the imperial court, and with little formal training began to compose. From 1817 he lived precariously as a composer and teacher, until he met the operatic baritone Johann Michael Vogl and founded the successful 'Schubertiads' (private and public accompanied recitals of his songs) that made them both known throughout Vienna. His major works include the 'Trout' piano quintet (1819), his C major symphony (1825), and his B minor symphony (1822), known as the 'Unfinished'; but he is particularly remembered as a great exponent of German songs (lieder) which number c.600, and he wrote much choral and chamber music.

Schumann, Robert (Alexander) (1810–56) German composer, born at Zwickau. He studied law in Leipzig, then turned to piano-playing, but

injured a finger (1832) and gave up performing for writing and composing. Until 1840 almost all his many compositions were for the piano. He then married Clara Wieck (the daughter of his piano teacher Friedrich Wieck), under whose influence he began to write orchestral works, notably his A minor piano concerto (1845) and four symphonies. He also wrote chamber music and a large number of songs (lieder).

Schuschnigg, Kurt von (1897–1977) Austrian politician, born in Riva. He served in World War I, practised law, was elected a Christian Socialist deputy (1927), and became Minister of Justice (1932) and of Education (1933). As Chancellor (1934–8), his attempt to prevent Hitler occupying Austria led to his imprisonment until 1945. He then lived in the USA, where he became Professor of Political Science at St Louis (1948–67).

schwa *noun* 1 the indistinct English vowel sound that occurs in unstressed syllables, as in the first and last syllables of *together* in normal speech, and in other words such as *to* and *the* in rapid speech. 2 the phonetic symbol (ə) used to represent this sound. [from Hebrew *schewa*]

Schwarzenberg, Felix (Ludwig Johann Friedrich) (1800–52) Austrian statesman, born in Krummau. He became Prime Minister during the 1848 Revolution, sought Russian military aid to suppress the Hungarian rebellion (1849), and demonstrated Austrian superiority over Prussia at the Olmütz Convention (1850). He created a centralized, absolutist, imperial state and also temporarily restored Habsburg domination of European affairs.

Schwarzenegger, Arnold (1947–) Austrian-born US film actor, born in Thal, near Graz. A dedicated body-builder, and former Mr Universe, he first appeared in *Hercules Goes Bananas* (1969). Later films include *Conan the Barbarian* (1981), *The Terminator* (1984), *Kindergarten Cop* (1988), *Terminator 2* (1991), and *The Last Action Hero* (1993).

Schwarzkopf, Dame (Olga Maria) Elisabeth (Friederike) (1915–) German soprano, born in Janotschin. She made her début in 1938 in Berlin, and sang in the Vienna State Opera (1944–8) and at Covent Garden (1949–52). She specialized at first in coloratura roles but later appeared as a lyric soprano, especially in recitals of lieder (German songs).

Schwarzschild, Karl (1873–1916) German astronomer, born in Frankfurt, who became director of observatories at Göttingen and Potsdam. While serving on the Russian front during World War I, he wrote important papers on Einstein's general theory of relativity and predicted the existence of 'black holes'.

Schweitzer, Albert (1875–1965) German medical missionary, theologian, musician, and philosopher, born in Kaysersberg. In 1896 he vowed to live for science and art until he was 30, and then devote his life to serving humanity. He became a curate at Strasbourg (1899), taught at the university (1902), and was appointed principal of the theological college (1903). His religious writing includes *Von Reimarus zu Wrede* (The Quest of the Historical Jesus, 1906), and major works on St Paul. Despite his international reputation in music and theology, he turned to studying medicine in 1905, and after qualifying (1913) departed with his wife to set up a hospital to fight leprosy and sleeping sickness in Lambaréné, French Equatorial Africa. He was awarded the Nobel Peace Prize in 1952.

Schwerin POP (1991e) 128 000, the capital of Mecklenburg-Pomerania state, NE Germany. It lies SW of Rostock and is surrounded by 11 lakes. Formerly the capital of Mecklenburg, between 1952 and 1990 it was the capital of Schwerin county in East Germany. NOTABLE FEATURES palace; Gothic cathedral (13c); Art Museum.

Schwyz POP (1990) 41 000, the capital town of Schwyz canton, central Switzerland, situated 35km/22mi E of Lucerne. The town and canton gave their name to the whole country, and the flag of Schwyz (a white cross on a red ground) has become the national flag. The canton of Schwyz formed the Swiss Confederation in 1291 together with the cantons of Uri and Anterwalden. NOTABLE FEATURES Church of St Martin (18c); town hall (1642–3); museum.

sciatic *adj.* 1 relating to the hip or the region round the hip. 2 affected by sciatica. [from Latin *sciaticus*, from Greek *ischion*, hip-joint]

sciatica *noun* intense and intermittent pain in the lower back, buttocks, and backs of the thighs caused by pressure on the sciatic nerve that runs from the pelvis to the thigh.

SCID *abbrev. Medicine* severe combined immunodeficiency.

science *noun* 1 the systematic observation and classification of natural phenomena in order to learn about them and formulate laws which can then be verified by further investigation. 2 the body of knowledge obtained in this way, or any specific subdivison of it, eg astronomy, chemistry, genetics. 3 any area of knowledge obtained using, or arranged according to, formal principles: *political science*. 4 acquired skill or technique, as opposed to natural ability. [from Latin *scientia*, knowledge]

science fiction fiction presenting a view of life in the future, especially incorporating space travel and other technological developments the writer imagines will be current at the future time portrayed.
◇ The first novelist to explore this theme was Jules Verne, with four novels (1863–73) including *Twenty Thousand Leagues under the Sea*. H G Wells brought greater scientific rigour to his five novels at the end of the 19c (eg *The Time Machine*, 1895). Hugo Gernsback's journal *Amazing Stories* (first published 1926) established the popularity of the genre; but major authors such as Ray Bradbury, Arthur C Clarke, and Isaac Asimov did not appear until after World War II. The 'new wave' of science fiction writers includes J G Ballard, Brian Aldiss, and Thomas Disch; and there is a specialist sub-genre of computer science fiction which was pioneered by William Gibson.

Science Museum a museum in S Kensington, London, which houses the most important British collection of scientific, technological, and medical exhibits. The collection was separated from the Victoria and Albert Museum in 1909, and has since expanded.

science park a group of establishments combining scientific research with commerce, often attached to a university.

scientific *adj.* 1 of, relating to, or used in science. 2 displaying the kind of principled approach characteristic of science: *not very scientific but it works*.

scientifically *adv.* in a scientific way; by scientific means.

scientist *noun* a student of or expert in science.

sci-fi *noun colloq.* science fiction.

scilicet *adv. formal, only in writing* namely; that is to say. [from Latin *scire licet*, it is permitted to know]

Scilly, Isles of POP (1987e) 1 900, a group of c.140 islands and islets SW of Land's End, Cornwall, SW England. AREA 16sq km/6sq mi. It is administered by the Duchy of Cornwall and includes the five inhabited islands of St Mary's, St Martin's, Tresco, St Agnes, and Bryher. The coasts are notorious for shipwrecks. CAPITAL Hugh Town on St Mary's I. ECONOMY horticulture, agriculture; tourism. NOTABLE FEATURE Bronze Age settlements.

scimitar *noun* a Middle-Eastern sword with a curved single-edged blade, usually broadening towards the tip. [perhaps from Persian *shimshir*]

scintilla *noun literary* a hint or trace; an iota. [from Latin *scintilla*, spark]

scintillate *verb intrans.* 1 *Physics, said of an atom* to emit a flash of light after having been struck by a photon or a particle of ionizing radiation. **2** to sparkle or send out sparks. **3** to capture attention with one's vitality or wit. [from Latin *scintilla*, spark]

scintillating *adj.* that scintillates.

scintillation *noun* **1** *Physics* the emission of a flash of light by an atom as it returns to its normal energy state after having been raised to a higher energy state by collision with a photon or a particle of ionizing radiation. *Phosphors* produce light in this way. **2** *Astron.* the twinkling of stars due to rapid changes in their brightness caused by variations in the density of the atmosphere through which the light rays pass.

scintillation counter *Physics* a device for detecting very low levels of radiation. It contains a medium, usually a solid or liquid, which scintillates (emits light) when charged particles or radiation fall on it. The scintillation medium is connected to a photomultiplier, which produces detectable pulses of current (corresponding to each scintillation) that are either counted or added together to give a numerical value.

scion *noun* **1** *Bot.* a piece of plant tissue, usually a shoot, that is inserted into a cut in the outer stem of another plant (the *stock*) when making a graft. **2** a descendant or offspring. [from Old French *cion*]

Scipio Africanus Major, Publius Cornelius (236–c.183 BC) Roman general of the Second Punic War. His victory at Ilipa (206 BC) forced the Carthaginians out of Spain, and his defeat of Hannibal at Zama (202 BC) broke the power of Carthage altogether and he was honoured with the title 'Africanus'. He remained in the forefront of affairs until forced into retirement by his political enemies of the 180s BC.

scissors *pl. noun* a one-handed cutting tool with two long blades joined in the middle so as to pivot with cutting edges coming together. [from Latin *cisorium*, cutting tool]

SCLC *abbrev.* Southern Christian Leadership Council.

sclera see SCLEROTIC.

sclerosis *noun* abnormal hardening or thickening of body tissue, organs, or blood vessels. [from Greek *skleros*, hard]

sclerotic — *noun Anat.* in vertebrates, the white fibrous outer layer of the eyeball, which is modified at the front of the eye to form the transparent cornea. — Also called *sclera*. — *adj.* **1** hard, firm. **2** relating to or affected with sclerosis. [from Greek *skleros*, hard]

scoff[1] — *verb intrans.* (often **scoff at someone** or **something**) to express scorn or contempt; to jeer. — *noun* an expression of scorn; a jeer.

scoff[2] — *verb trans., intrans. colloq.* to eat (food) rapidly and greedily. — *noun slang* food. [from Scots *scaff*, food]

scoffing *adj.* scornful.

scold — *verb* to reprimand angrily. — *noun old use* a nagging or quarrelsome person, especially a woman. [from Norse *skald*]

scolding *noun* a bout of fault-finding, a telling-off.

scollop same as SCALLOP.

sconce *noun* a candlestick with a handle, or one fixed by bracket to a wall. [from Latin *absconsa*, dark lantern]

scone *noun* a small round flattish plain cake, usually halved and spread with butter and jam. [from Scot. *scone*]

scoop — *verb* **1** (*also* **scoop something up**) to lift or dig it with a sweeping circular movement. **2** (*also* **scoop something out**) to empty or hollow it with such movements. **3** to do better than (rival newspapers) in being the first to publish a story. — *noun* **1** any of various spoon-like implements for handling or serving food. **2** a hollow shovel-like part of a mechanical digger. **3** a scooping movement. **4** a quantity scooped. **5** a news story printed by one newspaper in advance of all others. [from Old Dutch *schoppe*, shovel]

scoot *verb intrans. colloq.* to go away quickly.

scooter *noun* **1** a child's toy vehicle consisting of a board on a two-wheeled frame with tall handlebars, propelled by pushing against the ground with one foot while standing on the board with the other. **2** (*also* **motor-scooter**) a small-engined motorcycle with a protective front shield curving back at the bottom to form a supporting board for the feet which joins the casing containing the engine at the back of the vehicle.

scope *noun* **1** the size (of a subject or topic). **2** the range of topics dealt with. **3** the limits within which there is the freedom or opportunity to act. **4** range of understanding: *beyond his scope*. [from Greek *skopos*, point watched]

-scope *combining form* forming words denoting an instrument for viewing, examining, or detecting: *telescope*. [from Greek *skopeein*, to view]

-scopic *combining form* forming words: **1** relating to instruments with names ending in *-scope*: *telescopic*. **2** relating to observation or observed size: *microscopic*.

-scopy *combining form* forming words denoting observation or examination, usually with the use of instruments ending in *-scope*: *microscopy*.

scorbutic *adj. Medicine* relating to or suffering from scurvy. [from Latin *scorbuticus*]

scorch — *verb* **1** *trans., intrans.* to burn or be burned slightly on the surface. **2** to dry up or wither. **3** to injure with severe criticism or scorn. — *noun* **1** a scorched area. **2** a mark made by scorching. [from Middle English *skorken*]

scorcher *noun colloq.* an extremely hot day.

scorching *adj.* that scorches; burning.

score — *verb* **1** *trans., intrans.* to achieve (a point, etc) in games. **2** *trans., intrans.* to keep a record of points gained during (a game). **3** to make cuts or scratches in the surface of; to mark (eg a line) by a shallow cut. **4** (*also* **score something out**) to cancel it with a line drawn through it. **5** to be equivalent to (a number of points): *black king scores three*. **6 a** to break down (music) into parts for individual instruments or voices. **b** to adapt (music) for instruments or voices other than those originally intended. **7** to compose music for (a film or play). **8** *intrans.* to achieve a rating; to be judged or regarded: *always score low in written tests / this film scores high for entertainment value*. **9** *intrans. slang* to obtain drugs for illegal use. **10** (**score with someone**) *slang, often offensive* to succeed in having sexual intercourse with them. — *noun* **1** a number of points, etc scored. **2** an act of scoring a point, etc. **3** a scratch or shallow cut, especially made as a mark. **4** a set of twenty: *three score*. **5** (**scores**) very many; lots: *have scores of letters to write*. **6** *colloq.* (**the score**) the current situation; the essential facts: *what's the score?* **7** a written copy of music scored. **8** the music from a film or play. **9** (**the score**) a reason; grounds: *accepted on the score of suitability*. **10** matter; concern; aspect: *no worries on that score*. **11** a grievance or grudge: *settle old scores*. **12** a record of amounts owed. **13** *slang* a successful attempt to obtain drugs for illegal use. **14** *slang, often offensive* an act of sexual intercourse, regarded as a conquest or achievement.
— **over the score** *colloq.* beyond reasonable limits; unfair.

score off someone to humiliate them for personal advantage.
[from Anglo-Saxon *scoru*]

scoreboard *noun* a board on which the score in a game is displayed, altered as the score changes.

scorer *noun* **1** a person who scores a point, etc. **2** a person who keeps a written record of the score during a game.

scorn — *noun* mocking contempt. — *verb* **1** to treat with scorn. **2** to reject with scorn. [from Old French *escarn*, mockery]

scornful *adj.* contemptuous.

scornfully *adv.* in a scornful way.

Scorpio *noun* (PL. **Scorpios**) **1** *Astron.* (also **Scorpius**) the Scorpion, a large bright zodiacal constellation of the S hemisphere. It contains many star clusters that are visible through binoculars, and its brightest star is the supergiant *Antares*. **2** the eighth sign of the zodiac, the Scorpion. **3** a person born under the sign, between 23 Oct and 21 Nov.

scorpion *noun* any of about 650 species of an invertebrate animal belonging to the order Scorpiones, and related to the spider, found in hot regions, especially deserts, worldwide. It has eight legs, powerful pincers resembling the claws of a lobster, and a long thin segmented abdomen or 'tail' that is carried arched over its back, and bears a sharp poisonous sting at the tip. [from Greek *skorpios*]
◇ Scorpions range from 0.5cm to 20cm in length, and they hunt by night, feeding almost exclusively on insects and spiders, and only stinging their prey if it offers resistance. The ferocity of scorpions has been much exaggerated, and in fact they only sting humans if provoked, but the poison of some species can be fatal.

scorpion

Scorsese, Martin (1942–) US film director, born in Queens, New York. As a student at New York University he made a number of short films, then worked towards his first feature, *Who's That Knocking at My Door?* (1969). His work has sought to illuminate masculine aggression and sexual inequality and he has frequently questioned traditional American values. His many successful films include *Alice Doesn't Live Here Anymore* (1974), *Taxi Driver* (1976), *Raging Bull* (1980), *Goodfellas* (1990), *Cape Fear* (1991), and *The Age of Innocence* (1993).

Scot *noun* a native of Scotland. [from Latin *Scottus*]

Scot. *abbrev.* **1** Scotland. **2** Scottish.

Scotch — *adj., said of things, especially products; not now usually said of people* Scottish. — *noun* Scotch whisky. [from SCOTTISH]

scotch — *verb* **1** to ruin or hinder (eg plans). **2** to reveal (especially rumours) to be untrue. — *noun* any of the lines marked on the ground for hopscotch.

Scotch broth a thick soup made with barley and chopped vegetables.

Scotch egg a hard-boiled egg in a sausage-meat case, fried in breadcrumbs.

Scotch mist very fine rain, common in the Scottish Highlands.

Scotch terrier see SCOTTISH TERRIER.

Scotch whisky whisky distilled in Scotland from barley or other grain.

scot-free *adj.* unpunished or unharmed. [from obsolete *scot*, payment, tax]

Scotland POP (1981) 5.1m, the northern constituent part of the United Kingdom, comprising all the mainland N of the border that runs from the Solway Firth to Berwick-upon-Tweed, and the island groups of the Outer and Inner Hebrides, Orkney, and Shetland. It is divided into 12 regions and 53 districts. Scotland is bounded W and N by the Atlantic Ocean, E by the North Sea and S by England. AREA 78 742sq km/30 394sq mi; maximum length 441km/274mi; maximum width 248km/154mi. CAPITAL Edinburgh. CHIEF TOWNS Glasgow, Dundee, Aberdeen. CURRENCY the pound sterling. PHYSICAL DESCRIPTION divided into the Southern Uplands (rising to 843m at Merrick), the Central

Lowlands (the most densely populated area) and the Northern Highlands (divided by the fault line following the Great Glen, and rising to 1 344m at Ben Nevis); there are 787 islands, most of which lie off the heavily-indented W coast and only c.60 exceed 8sq km/3sq mi; there are several wide estuaries on the E coast, primarily the Firths of Forth, Tay, and Moray; the interior has many freshwater lochs, the largest being Loch Lomond (70sq km/27sq mi) and the deepest Loch Morar (310m); the longest river is the R Tay (192km/119mi). HISTORY Roman attempts to limit incursions of N tribes were marked by the building of both the Antonine Wall and Hadrian's Wall; there were the beginnings of unification in the 9c, and wars between England and Scotland during the Middle Ages; Scottish independence was declared by Robert Bruce, and recognized in 1328; the Stuarts succeeded to the throne in the 14c and united the crowns of Scotland and England in 1603; parliaments were united under the Act of Union in 1707; there were unsuccessful Jacobite rebellions in 1715 and 1745; a proposal for devolution failed in a referendum in 1979; Scotland has a separate legal and educational system, and other institutions which are distinct from those of England or Wales; three Scottish banks have the right to issue banknotes. ECONOMY industries are mainly in the Central Belt but heavy industry (such as shipbuilding, steel, vehicles) declined throughout the 1980s, with the closure of many coal pits; whisky; oil services on the E coast; electronics; textiles; agriculture and forestry; fishing and fish farming; tourism.

Scotland Yard, properly **New Scotland Yard** the headquarters of the Metropolitan Police at Westminster in London, although the title is often used to indicate the Criminal Investigation Department (CID). Its name derives from its original site by Great Scotland Yard in Whitehall, London.

Scots — *adj.*, *said especially of law and language* Scottish. — *noun* any of the dialects related to English used in (especially Lowland) Scotland. [from Scots *Scottis*, Scottish]

Scotsman *or* **Scotswoman** *noun* a native of Scotland.

Monarchs of Scotland	
1005–34	Malcolm II
1034–40	Duncan I
1040–57	Macbeth
1057–8	Lulach
1058–93	Malcolm III, 'Canmore'
1093–4	Donald III (Donald Bane)
1094	Duncan II
1094–7	Donald III (Donald Bane)
1097–1107	Edgar
1107–24	Alexander I
1124–53	David I
1153–65	Malcolm IV, 'the Maiden'
1165–1214	William I, 'the Lion'
1214–49	Alexander II
1249–86	Alexander III
1286–90	Margaret ('Maid of Norway')
1290–2	Interregnum
1292–6	John Balliol
1296–1306	Interregnum
1306–29	Robert I, 'the Bruce'
1329–71	David II
1371–90	Robert II
1390–1406	Robert III
1406–37	James I
1437–60	James II
1460–88	James III
1488–1513	James IV
1513–42	James V
1542–67	Mary, Queen of Scots
1567–1625	James VI

Scots pine a coniferous tree of Europe and Asia, the only native British pine.

Scott, Sir George Gilbert (1811–78) English architect, born in Gawcott, Buckinghamshire. He became Professor of Architecture at the Royal Academy in 1868. Influenced by Augustus Pugin, he was the leading practical architect of the British Gothic revival, responsible for the building or restoration of many ecclesiastical and civil buildings, including the Albert Memorial (1862–3), St Pancras Station and Hotel in London (1865), and Glasgow University (1865).

Scott, Paul (Mark) (1920–78) English novelist, born in London. He served with the Indian Army in India and Malaya (1943–6), then worked as a literary agent until 1960. His reputation is based on four novels collectively known as the *Raj Quartet* (1965–75); they are *The Jewel in the Crown* (1965), *The Day of the Scorpion* (1968), *The Towers of Silence* (1971), and *A Division of the Spoils* (1975). They give an exhaustive account of the British withdrawal from India.

Scott, Sir Peter (Markham) (1909–89) British artist, ornithologist, and broadcaster, born in London. An Olympic sportsman (dinghy sailing), he served in the navy in World War II. He began to exhibit his paintings of bird scenes in 1933, and after the war led several ornithological expeditions to Iceland, Australasia, and the Pacific. His writing and television programmes did much to popularize natural history.

Scott, R(obert) F(alcon) (1868–1912) English Antarctic explorer, born near Devonport, Devon. He joined the navy in 1881, and commanded the National Antarctic Expedition (1901–4) which explored the Ross Sea area, and discovered King Edward VII Land. In 1910 he led a second expedition to the South Pole (17 Jan 1912), only to discover that the Norwegian expedition under Roald Amundsen had beaten them by a month. All members of his party died, and their bodies and diaries were found by a search party eight months later. He was posthumously knighted, and the Scott Polar Research Institute at Cambridge was founded in his memory.

Scott, Sir Walter (1771–1832) Scottish novelist and poet, born in Edinburgh. He trained as a lawyer (1792), and began to write ballads in 1796. His first major publication was the popular ballad collection, *The Minstrelsy of the Scottish Border* (3 vols, 1802–3), which was followed by other romances including *Marmion* (1808) and *The Lady of the Lake* (1810). He then turned to writing novels, which fall largely into three groups. His Scottish historical novels include *Waverley* (1814), *Old Mortality* (1816), *Rob Roy* (1818), *The Heart of Midlothian* (1818), and *A Legend of Montrose* (1819). Those which take up themes from the Middle Ages and Reformation times include *Ivanhoe* (1819) and *The Talisman*

Regions of Scotland

Region	Area sq km	sq mi	Population[1]	Admin centre	Former counties	New districts
Borders	4 672	1 803	105 000	Newton St Boswells	Berwick, Peebles, Roxburgh, Selkirk, part of Midlothian	Berwickshire, Ettrick & Lauderdale, Roxburgh, Tweeddale
Central	2 631	1 016	273 000	Stirling	Clackmannan, most of Stirling, parts of Perth and W Lothian	Clackmannan, Falkirk, Stirling
Dumfries & Galloway	6 370	2 459	148 000	Dumfries	Dumfries, Kirkcudbright, Wigtown	Annandale & Eskdale, Nithsdale, Stewartry, Wigtown
Fife	1 307	505	350 000	Glenrothes	Fife	Dunfermline, NE Fife, Kirkcaldy
Grampian	8 704	3 360	522 000	Aberdeen	Aberdeen, Banff, Kincardine, most of Moray	Aberdeen, Banff & Buchan, Gordon, Kincardine & Deeside, Moray
Highland	25 391	9 801	206 000	Inverness	Caithness, Inverness, Nairn, Ross & Cromarty, Sutherland parts of Argyll and Moray	Badenoch & Strathspey, Caithness, Inverness, Lochaber, Nairn, Ross & Cromarty, Sutherland, Skye & Lochalsh
Lothian	1 755	677	751 000	Edinburgh	E Lothian, Midlothian, W Lothian	Edinburgh, E Lothian, Midlothian, W Lothian
Strathclyde	13 537	5 225	2 300 000	Glasgow	Ayr, Bute, Dunbarton, Lanark, Renfrew, most of Argyll, part of Stirling	Argyll & Bute, Bearsden & Milngavie, Clydebank, Clydesdale, Cumnock & Doon Valley, Cunninghame, Cumbernauld & Kilsyth, Dumbarton, E Kilbride, Eastwood, Glasgow, Hamilton, Inverclyde, Kilmarnock & Loudoun, Kyle & Carrick, Monklands, Motherwell, Renfrew, Strathkelvin
Tayside	7 493	2 892	395 000	Dundee	Angus, Kinross, most of Perth	Angus, Dundee, Kinross, Perth
Orkney	976	377	20 000	Kirkwall		
Shetland	1 433	553	23 000	Lerwick		
Western Isles	2 898	1 119	29 000	Stornoway		

[1] 1992 census, provisional figures

(1825), and his remaining books are those from *Woodstock* (1826) until his death. His last years were spent in immense labours for his publishers in an attempt to recover from bankruptcy which followed the collapse of his publishing ventures in 1826.

Scott a male first name, after the surname and originally associated with Scotland.

Scottie see SCOTTISH TERRIER.

Scottish *adj.* of Scotland or its people. [from Anglo-Saxon *Scottisc*]

Scottish Ballet a Scottish dance company, which resulted in 1969 when the Western Theatre Ballet in Bristol (co-founded by Peter Darrell (1929–87) in 1957) divided into two. Most dancers went to Scotland to form the Scottish Theatre Ballet under Darrell, who created new works such as the *Tales of Hoffmann* (1972), and some went to Manchester to form the Northern Ballet.

Scottish Chamber Orchestra an ensemble founded in Edinburgh (1974). Sir Peter Maxwell Davies has been its conductor and composer since 1985, and it tours all over the world.

Scottish Cup, also called the **SFA Cup** a football competition organized by the Scottish Football Association, and held annually in Scotland since 1874.

Scottish National Party (ABBREV. **SNP**) a political party formed in 1928 as the National Party of Scotland, which merged with the Scottish Party in 1934. Its principal policy aim is independence for Scotland from the UK. It first won a seat at a by-election in 1945. Its greatest success was in the 1974 general election, when it took nearly a third of Scottish votes and won 11 seats. Led by Alex Salmond (1955–) since 1990, it won three seats in the 1992 election.

Scottish Office in the UK, the government department, established in 1885, which deals with Scottish affairs. It has five main departments (Agriculture and Fisheries, Environment, Industry, Education, and Home and Health), and is headed by the Secretary of State for Scotland. It is based in Edinburgh.

Scottish Opera a Scottish opera company, co-founded (1962) by Sir Alexander Gibson, its first artistic director, and based since 1975 in the Theatre Royal, Glasgow. Gibson conducted a notable performance of Richard Wagner's *Ring* cycle in 1971.

Scottish terrier, a breed of dog with a long body, short legs, and a short erect tail. It has a long head, with eyebrows, moustache, and beard, short erect ears, and a thick wiry coat, almost reaching the ground. — Also called *Scottie*, *Scotch terrier*.

scoundrel *noun* a person without principles or morals; a rogue or villain.

scour¹ — *verb* **1** to clean by hard rubbing. **2** to flush clean with a jet or current of water. **3** to wash sheep wool in order to remove grease and impurities. — *noun* **1** an act of scouring. **2** (**scours**) diarrhoea in animal livestock. [from Latin *excurare*, to cleanse]

scour² *verb* to make an exhaustive search of (eg an area). [from Norse *skur*, storm, shower]

scourer *noun* **1** a person who scours. **2** a device or container for scouring.

scourge — *noun* **1** a cause of great suffering to many people: *cancer is the scourge of Western society.* **2** a whip used for punishing. — *verb* **1** to cause suffering to; to afflict. **2** to whip. [from Latin *excoriare*, to flay]

Scouse *colloq.* — *noun* **1** the dialect of English spoken in Liverpool. **2** a Scouser. — *adj.* of Liverpool, its people, or their dialect. [a short form of *lobscouse*, a sailor's stew]

Scouser *noun colloq.* a native of Liverpool.

scout — *noun* **1** *Mil.* a person or group sent out to observe the enemy and bring back information. **2** (**talent scout**) a person whose job is to discover and recruit talented people, especially in the fields of sport and entertainment. **3** (*often* **Scout**; *formerly* **Boy Scout**) a member of the Scout Association, a worldwide youth organization promoting outdoor skills and community spirit. **4** *colloq.* a search: *have a scout around for it in my bag.* — *verb intrans.* **1** to act as a scout. **2** (*often* **scout about** *or* **around**) *colloq.* to make a search: *scouting about for new premises.* [from Old French *escouter*]

Scout Association an organization of boys aged between 11 and 16 formed to teach good citizenship and proficiency in outdoor activities, founded (1908) as the Boy Scout movement by Robert Baden-Powell. It now operates in over 100 nations and has over 14 million members, and includes Cub Scouts or Wolf Cubs (aged 8–11), and Venture Scouts (aged 16–29).

Scouter *noun* an adult leader in the Scout Association.

scow *noun* a large flat-bottomed barge for freight. [from Dutch *schouw*]

scowl — *verb intrans.* **1** to wrinkle the brow in displeasure or anger. **2** to look disapprovingly, angrily, or threateningly. — *noun* a scowling expression. [from Middle English *scowl*]

SCR *abbrev.* senior common room.

Scrabble, originally **Criss Cross** *trademark* a board game for 2–4 players first devised in 1931. Each player begins with seven lettered tiles from a pool of 100, and uses them in turn to form possible words, in a crossword pattern. Words are scored from the values assigned to each letter. British national Scrabble championships were inaugurated in 1971, and US tournaments in 1973.

scrabble — *verb intrans.* to scratch, grope, or struggle frantically. — *noun* an act of scrabbling. [from Dutch *schrabben*, to scratch]

scrag — *noun* **1** (*also* **scrag-end**) the thin part of a neck of mutton or veal, providing poor-quality meat. **2** an unhealthily thin person or animal. — *verb* (**scragged, scragging**) *colloq.* **1** to wring the neck of; to throttle. **2** to attack angrily; to beat up. [perhaps from CRAG]

scragginess *noun* being scraggy.

scraggy *adj.* (**scraggier, scraggiest**) unhealthily thin; scrawny.

scram *verb intrans.* (**scrammed, scramming**) *colloq.*, *often as a command* to go away at once. [perhaps from SCRAMBLE]

scramble — *verb* **1** to crawl or climb using hands and feet, especially frantically. **2** *intrans.* to struggle violently against others: *starving people scrambling to grab food.* **3** to cook (eggs) whisked up with milk. **4** to throw together haphazardly; to jumble. **5** to rewrite (a message) in code form, for secret transmission; to transmit (a message) in a distorted form via an electronic scrambler. **6** *intrans.* said *of aircraft or air crew* to take off immediately in response to an emergency. — *noun* **1** an act of scrambling. **2** a violent struggle to beat others in getting something. **3** a walk or half-climb over rough ground. **4** an immediate take-off in an emergency. **5** a cross-country motorcycle race. [perhaps from SCRABBLE]

scrambler *noun Electron.* an electronic device that modifies signals transmitted by radio or telephone so that they can only be made intelligible by means of a special decoding device. Scramblers are used to transmit secret communications, to protect television broadcasting rights, etc.

scrambling circuit a circuit used to protect the security of sound, data, or video signals in communication systems. The original signal is coded by a scrambler before transmission and interpreted by a decoder at the receiver. The

technique prevents unauthorized personnel gaining access to the signals during transmission.

scramjet *noun* a jet engine in which compressed air is drawn into the engine by means of turbo fans and mixed with fuel to improve combustion at a supersonic speed. [from *supersonic combustion ramjet*]

scrap¹ — *noun* **1** a small piece; a fragment. **2** the smallest piece or amount: *not a scrap of advice.* **3** waste material. **4** (**scraps**) leftover pieces of food. — *verb* (**scrapped, scrapping**) to discard as useless or abandon as unworkable. [from Norse *skrap*]

scrap² *colloq.* — *noun* a fight or quarrel. — *verb intrans.* (**scrapped, scrapping**) to fight or quarrel.

scrapbook *noun* a book with blank pages on which newspaper cuttings, etc can be mounted.

scrape — *verb* **1** to push or drag (something, especially a sharp object) along (a hard or rough surface). **2** *intrans.* to move along a surface with a grazing action. **3** (*also* **scrape something off**) to remove it from a surface with such an action. **4** to damage by such contact: *scraped his elbow.* **5** *intrans.* to make savings through hardship: *scrimp and scrape.* **6** *intrans.* to slide the foot backwards when bowing: *bow and scrape.* — *noun* **1** an instance, or the action, of dragging or grazing. **2** a part damaged or cleaned by scraping. **3** *colloq.* a difficult or embarrassing situation; a predicament. **4** *colloq.* a fight or quarrel.
— **scrape through** *or* **by** to manage or succeed (in doing something) narrowly or with difficulty: *just scraped through the interview.*
scrape something together *or* **up** to collect it little by little, usually with difficulty.
[from Anglo-Saxon *scrapian*]

scraper *noun* **1** a person who scrapes. **2** a scraping tool, instrument, or machine.

scraperboard *or* **scratchboard** *noun* a technique used mainly by commercial illustrators for producing sharply defined designs similar in appearance to linocuts. The board is coated with two layers, black over white or vice versa, and the artist scrapes or scratches away the top surface using a set of special blades. See also SGRAFFITO.

scrap heap **1** a place where unwanted objects, eg old furniture, are collected. **2** the state of being discarded or abandoned: *consign the idea to the scrap heap.*

scrapie *noun Agric.* an often fatal disease of sheep, in which there is progressive degeneration of the central nervous system. In one form of the disease there is uncontrollable itching, which the animal attempts to relieve by rubbing itself against trees and other objects, resulting in wool loss. [from Old English *scrapian* or Old Norse *skrapa*]

scrappily *adv.* in a scrappy way.

scrappiness *noun* a scrappy state.

scrappy *adj.* (**scrappier, scrappiest**) not uniform, continuous, or flowing; disjointed; fragmented; bitty.

scratch — *verb* **1** to rub or drag (a sharp or pointed object) across (a surface), causing damage or making marks. **2** to make (eg a mark) by such action. **3** *trans., intrans.* to rub (the skin) lightly with the fingernails, eg to relieve itching. **4** (*usually* **scratch something out** *or* **off**) to cross it out or cancel it. **5** *intrans.* to make a grating noise. **6** *intrans.* to withdraw from a contest. — *noun* **1** a mark made by scratching. **2** an act of scratching. **3** a superficial wound or minor injury. — *adj.* **1** hastily got together; improvised: *a scratch meal.* **2** said *of a competitor* not given a handicap.
— **from scratch** from the beginning; without the benefit of preparation or previous experience.
scratch the surface to deal only superficially with an issue or problem.

up to scratch *colloq.* meeting the required or expected standard.
[from Middle English *scratch*]

scratchily *adv.* in a scratchy way.

scratchiness *noun* being scratchy.

scratch video a video film produced by piecing together images from other films.

scratchy *adj.* (**scratchier, scratchiest**) 1 making the marks or noises of scratching. 2 causing or likely to cause itching.

scrawl — *verb trans., intrans.* to write or draw untidily or hurriedly. — *noun* untidy or illegible handwriting.

scrawly *adj.* (**scrawlier, scrawliest**) *said of writing* careless, untidy.

scrawniness *noun* a scrawny state.

scrawny *adj.* (**scrawnier, scrawniest**) very thin and bony.

Scream, The a painting by Edvard Munch (1893). He later used the same design in a woodcut. The painting was stolen from the National Gallery in Oslo early in 1994, but recovered in May of that year.

scream — *verb* 1 *trans., intrans.* to utter or cry out in a loud high-pitched voice, eg in fear, pain, or anger. 2 *intrans.* to laugh uproariously. 3 *intrans.* (**scream past, through,** *etc*) to go at great speed, especially making a shrill noise: *the train screamed through the tunnel.* 4 (**scream at someone**) *usually said of something unpleasant or unwelcome* to be patently obvious or apparent: *the orange curtains scream at you / his incompetence screamed at them.* — *noun* 1 a loud piercing cry or other sound. 2 *colloq.* an extremely amusing person, thing, or event. [from Anglo-Saxon *scræmen*]

scree *noun Geol.* 1 loose fragments of rock debris that cover a mountain slope, or pile up below bare rock faces or summits. 2 a slope covered with such material. [from Norse *skritha*, landslip]

screech — *noun* a harsh shrill cry, voice, or noise. — *verb* 1 *trans., intrans.* to utter a screech or as a screech. 2 *intrans.* to make a screech: *screeching brakes.* [from Middle English *schrichen*]

screech owl the barn owl, whose call is more of a screech than a hoot.

screechy *adj.* (**screechier, screechiest**) like a screech, shrill and harsh.

screed *noun* a long, often tedious, speech or piece of writing. [from Anglo-Saxon *screade*, shred]

screen — *noun* 1 a movable set of hinged panels, used to partition part of a room off for privacy. 2 a single panel used for protection against strong heat or light. 3 the part of a television set on which the images are formed. 4 a white (usually cloth) surface on to which films or slides are projected. 5 (*often* **the screen**) the medium of cinema or television: *a star of stage and screen.* 6 *Cricket* a sight-screen. 7 a windscreen. — *verb* 1 (*usually* **screen something off**) to separate or partition it with a screen. 2 to show at the cinema or on television. 3 to subject to an examination, eg to test (someone) for reliability or check for the presence of disease. [from Old French *escran*]

screen dump *Comput.* the action of sending the contents of a screen display to a printer or file, eg by pressing a specified function key.

screenplay *noun* the text of a film, comprising dialogue, stage directions, and details for sets.

screen printing *or* **screen process** a printing technique in which ink is forced through a fine silk or nylon mesh, with areas to be left blank blocked chemically.

screen-saver *noun Comput.* a program which temporarily blanks out a screen display, or displays a pre-set pattern, when a computer is switched on but is not in active use.

screen test a filmed audition to test an actor's suitability for a film role.

screen writer a writer of screenplays for film, television, etc.

screw — *noun* 1 a type of nail with a spiral ridge down its shaft and a slot in its head, driven firmly into place using a twisting action with a special tool. 2 any object similar in shape or function. 3 *Snooker, Billiards* a shot in which sidespin or backspin is put on the ball. 4 *slang* a prison officer. 5 *coarse slang* an act of sexual intercourse. 6 *coarse slang* a person judged by sexual prowess or suitability as a sexual partner. 7 *slang* wages. — *verb* 1 to twist (a screw) into place. 2 a (**screw something up** *or* **together**) to attach or assemble it by means of screws. b (**screw up** *or* **together**) to be attached or assembled by means of screws. 3 to push or pull with a twisting action. 4 (**screw something from** *or* **out of someone**) *colloq.* to obtain it by intense persuasion or threats: *tried to screw more money out of them.* 5 *colloq.* to swindle. 6 *Snooker, Billiards* to put sidespin or backspin on (the cue ball). 7 *trans., intrans. coarse slang* to have sexual intercourse with (someone).
— **have one's head screwed on the right way** *colloq.* to be a sensible person.
have a screw loose *colloq.* to be slightly mad or crazy.
put the screws on someone *colloq.* to use pressure on them, especially in the form of threats of violence.
screw someone up *North Amer. slang* to cause them to become extremely anxious, nervous, or psychologically disturbed.
screw something up *slang* to ruin or bungle it.
screw up one's courage to prepare oneself for an ordeal or difficulty.
[from Old French *escroue*]

screwball *noun slang North Amer., esp. US* a crazy person; an eccentric.

screwdriver *noun* a hand-held tool with a metal shaft whose shaped end fits into the slot on a screw's head, turned repeatedly to twist a screw into position.

screwed-up *adj. slang, said of a person* extremely anxious, nervous, or psychologically disturbed.

screw top 1 a round lid that is screwed off and on to open and re-seal a bottle or other container. 2 a container with such a top.

screw-top *adj.* having a screw top.

screwy *adj.* (**screwier, screwiest**) *colloq.* crazy; eccentric.

Scriabin, Aleksandr Nikolayevich (1872–1915) Russian composer and pianist, born in Moscow. He studied at the Moscow Conservatory with Rachmaninov and Nikolai Medtner, and became Professor of the Pianoforte (1898–1904). His compositions, which include a piano concerto, three symphonies, two tone poems, and 10 sonatas, show an increasing reliance on extramusical factors (even coloured light, as in *Prometheus*, 1910), and the influence of religion and occultism.

scribble — *verb* 1 *trans., intrans.* to write quickly or untidily. 2 *intrans.* to draw meaningless lines or shapes absent-mindedly. — *noun* 1 untidy or illegible handwriting. 2 meaningless written lines or shapes. [from Latin *scribere*, to write]

scribbler *noun derog.* a worthless writer.

scribbly *adj.* (**scribblier, scribbliest**) like a scribble; scribbled.

scribe *noun* 1 a person employed to make handwritten copies of documents before printing was invented. 2 a Jewish lawyer or teacher of law in biblical times. 3 a tool with a pointed blade for scoring lines on wood or metal. [from Latin *scriba*, from *scribere*, to write]

Scribner, Charles (1821–71) US publisher, born in New York City. In 1846 he co-founded the New York publishing firm that bears his name. His *Scribner's Monthly* (1870–81) became *Scribner's Magazine* (1887–1939).

scrim *noun* heavy cotton fabric used as lining in upholstery, and in bookbinding.

scrimmage — *noun* a fist-fight or brawl. — *verb intrans.* to take part in a scrimmage. [a variant of SKIRMISH]

scrimp *verb intrans.* to live economically; to be frugal or sparing: *scrimp and save.* [from Scot. *scrimp*]

scrimpy *adj.* (**scrimpier, scrimpiest**) scanty.

scrimshank *verb intrans. colloq.* to evade work or duties.

scrimshanker *noun* a person who evades work or duties, a skiver.

scrip *noun* 1 a scrap of writing paper. 2 *colloq.* a doctor's prescription. 3 *Commerce* a provisional certificate issued before a formal share certificate is drawn up. [a shortened form of PRESCRIPTION and SUBSCRIPTION]

script — *noun* 1 the printed text, or the spoken dialogue, of a play, film, or broadcast. 2 a system of characters used for writing; an alphabet: *Chinese script.* 3 handwriting. 4 an examination candidate's answer paper. — *verb* to write the script of (a play, film, or broadcast). [from Latin *scriptum*, from *scribere*, to write]

scriptural *adj.* relating to or derived from scripture.

scripture *noun* 1 the sacred writings of a religion. 2 (**Scriptures**) the Christian Bible. [from Latin *scriptura*, from *scribere*, to write]

scriptwriter *noun* a person who writes scripts.

scrivener *noun Hist.* a person who drafts, or makes handwritten copies of, legal or other official documents. [related to SCRIBE]

scrofula *noun old use Medicine* former name for tuberculosis of the lymph nodes, especially of the neck. [from Latin *scrofulae*, from *scrofa*, a sow, apparently prone to it]

scrofulous *adj.* affected by scrofula.

scroll — *noun* 1 a roll of paper or parchment written on, now only a ceremonial format, eg for academic degrees. 2 an ancient text in this format: *the Dead Sea Scrolls.* 3 a decorative spiral shape, eg in stonework or handwriting. — *verb trans., intrans.* (*often* **scroll up** *or* **down**) to move the displayed text on a computer screen up or down to bring into view data that cannot all be seen at the same time. [from Middle English *scrowle*]

Scrooge, Ebenezer the miserly, misanthropic moneylender in Charles Dickens's *A Christmas Carol*.

Scrooge *noun* a miserly person.

scrotal *adj.* relating to or in the region of the scrotum.

scrotum *noun* (PL. **scrota, scrotums**) the bag of skin enclosing the testicles in mammals. [from Latin *scrotum*]

scrounge *verb trans., intrans. colloq.* to get (something) by shamelessly asking or begging; to cadge or sponge: *scrounged a fiver off his old granny.* [from dialect *scrunge*, to steal]

scrounger *noun* a person who scrounges.

scrub¹ — *verb* (**scrubbed, scrubbing**) 1 *trans., intrans.* to rub hard, especially with a brush, to remove dirt. 2 to clean by hard rubbing. 3 (*also* **scrub up**) *said of a surgeon, etc* to wash the hands and arms thoroughly before taking part in an operation. 4 *colloq.* to cancel or abandon (eg plans). — *noun* an act of scrubbing. [from Old German *schrubben*]

scrub² *noun* **1** an area of land with a poor soil or low rainfall, covered with vegetation consisting mainly of dwarf or stunted trees and evergreen shrubs. **2** an inferior domestic animal of mixed or unknown parentage. **3** a small or insignificant person. [a variant of SHRUB]

scrubber *noun offensive slang* **1** an unattractive woman. **2** a woman who regularly indulges in casual sex.

scrubby *adj.* (**scrubbier, scrubbiest**) **1** covered with scrub. **2** stunted. **3** insignificant.

scrubland *noun* an area covered with scrub.

scruff¹ *noun* the back of the neck; the nape.

scruff² *noun colloq.* a scruffy person.

scruffily *adv.* in a scruffy way.

scruffiness *noun* a scruffy state.

scruffy *adj.* (**scruffier, scruffiest**) shabbily dressed and untidy-looking.

scrum — *noun* **1** *Rugby* a formation of players from both teams, hunched and with arms and heads tightly interlocked; a re-starting of play in which the ball is thrown into such a formation and struggled for with the feet. **2** *colloq.* a riotous struggle. — *verb intrans.* (**scrummed, scrumming**) (*usually* **scrum down**) to form a scrum. [a shortening of SCRUMMAGE]

scrum half *Rugby* the player from each side who puts the ball into scrums.

scrummage *Rugby* — *noun* a scrum. — *verb intrans.* to form a scrum. [a variant of SCRIMMAGE]

scrummy *adj.* (**scrummier, scrummiest**) *colloq.* scrumptious.

scrumptious *adj. colloq.* **1** delicious. **2** delightful.

scrumpy *noun* (PL. **scrumpies**) strong dry cider with a harsh taste, especially as brewed in SW England. [from dialect *scrump*, withered apples]

scrunch — *verb* **1** *trans., intrans.* to crunch or crumple, or become crunched or crumpled. **2** *intrans.* to make a crunching sound. — *noun* an act, or the sound, of scrunching.

scrunch-dry *verb* to squeeze (hair) into bunches during blow-drying to give it more body.

scruple — *noun* **1** (*usually* **scruples**) a sense of moral responsibility that makes one reluctant or unwilling to do wrong: *has no scruples.* **2** a unit of weight equal to 20 grains. — *verb intrans.* to be hesitant or unwilling because of scruples: *wouldn't scruple to steal if we were starving.* [from Latin *scrupulus*, pebble, anxiety]

scrupulous *adj.* **1** taking great care to do nothing morally wrong. **2** paying careful attention to even the smallest details.

scrupulously *adv.* **1** in a scrupulous way. **2** with great attention to detail.

scrutineer *noun* a person who scrutinises something, especially the collecting and counting of votes.

scrutinize *or* **scrutinise** *verb* to subject to scrutiny; to look at carefully.

scrutiny *noun* (PL. **scrutinies**) **1** a close and thorough examination or inspection. **2** a penetrating or critical look. [from Latin *scrutari*, to search]

scuba *noun* a portable breathing device for underwater divers, consisting of one or two cylinders of compressed air connected to a mouthpiece via a breathing tube. [from *self-contained underwater breathing apparatus*]

Scud *noun* a surface-to-surface missile of a kind made in the former Soviet Union.

scud — *verb intrans.* (**scudded, scudding**) **1** *said especially of clouds* to sweep quickly across

the sky. **2** *Naut.* to sail swiftly under the force of a strong wind. — *noun* cloud, rain, or spray driven by the wind.

Scudamore, Peter (1958–) English National Hunt jockey. He was champion jockey for the first time in 1981–2, and in 1985 rode his first winner for trainer Martin Pipe. He was champion jockey for seven consecutive seasons (1986–93), and broke the season record with 221 wins in 1988–9. In 1993 he retired and turned to training, having ridden a record 1 677 winners.

Scudamour, Sir the grieving knight in Edmund Spenser's *The Faerie Queene*, whose wife Amoret has been snatched from him on their wedding-day by Busirane.

scuff — *verb trans., intrans.* **1** to graze or scrape, or become grazed or scraped, through wear. **2** to drag (the feet) when walking. — *noun* an area worn away by scuffing. [imitative]

scuffle — *noun* a confused fight or struggle. — *verb intrans.* to take part in a scuffle.

scull — *noun* **1** either of a pair of short light oars used by a lone rower. **2** a racing boat propelled by a solitary rower using a pair of such oars. **3** a large single oar at the stern, moved from side to side to propel a boat. — *verb* to propel with a scull or sculls.

sculler *noun* a person who sculls or rows.

scullery *noun* (PL. **sculleries**) a room, attached to the kitchen in a large house, where basic kitchen work, eg washing up and chopping vegetables, is done. [from Old French *escuelerie*]

sculpt *verb* **1** *trans., intrans.* to carve or model (clay, etc). **2** to create (a solid model of something) in clay, etc. **3** to create a solid model of (someone or something) in clay, etc. [from Latin *sculpere*, to carve]

sculptor *noun* a person who practises sculpture.

sculptural *adj.* **1** relating to sculpture. **2** having the qualities of sculpture.

sculpture — *noun* **1** the art of carving or modelling with clay, wood, stone, plaster, etc. **2** a work or works of art produced in this way. — *verb trans., intrans.* to sculpt.

sculptured *adj., said of physical features* fine and regular, like those of figures in classical sculpture.

scum — *noun* **1** dirt or waste matter floating on the surface of a liquid. **2** *colloq., derog.* a contemptible person or people. — *verb* (**scummed, scumming**) to remove the scum from (a liquid). [from Old Dutch *schum*, foam]

scumbag *noun derog. slang* a contemptible person.

scumbling *noun Art* a technique in painting, developed by the Venetian school, in which colour is applied using a dragging, stippling, or dabbing motion to produce a textured effect. In oil painting, a scumble is an opaque layer of paint laid over another opaque layer of a darker colour or tone, so that parts of the lower layer show through. In watercolour, the dabbing motion of the brush has the effect of bringing out the texture of the paper. [perhaps related to SCUM]

scummy *adj.* (**scummier, scummiest**) **1** covered with a layer of scum. **2** *slang* contemptible; despicable.

Scunthorpe POP (1992e) 62 000, a town in Scunthorpe district, Humberside, NE England. It lies 33km/20mi NE of Doncaster.

scupper¹ *verb* (**scuppered, scuppering**) **1** *colloq.* to ruin or put an end to (eg plans). **2** to deliberately sink (a ship).

scupper² *noun Naut.* a hole or pipe in a ship's side through which water is drained off the deck.

scurf *noun* **1** dandruff. **2** any flaking or peeling substance. [from Anglo-Saxon *scurf*]

scurfy *adj.* (**scurfier, scurfiest**) covered or affected with scurf.

scurrility *noun* **1** being scurrilous. **2** a scurrilous comment or remark.

scurrilous *adj.* insulting or abusive, and unjustly damaging to the reputation: *scurrilous remarks.* [from Latin *scurrilis*, from *scurra*, buffoon]

scurry — *verb intrans.* (**scurries, scurried**) (**scurry along, away,** *etc*) to move hurriedly, especially with short quick steps. — *noun* (PL. **scurries**) **1** an act, or the sound, of scurrying. **2** a sudden brief gust or fall, eg of wind or snow; a flurry. [from *hurry-scurry*, a reduplication of HURRY]

scurvy — *noun Medicine* a disease caused by deficiency of vitamin C due to lack of fresh fruit and vegetables in the diet. It is characterized by swollen bleeding gums, subcutaneous bleeding (caused by weakening of the walls of small blood vessels), anaemia, bruising, and pain in the joints. — *adj.* (**scurvier, scurviest**) vile; contemptible. [from Anglo-Saxon *scurf*]

scut *noun* a short tail, especially of a rabbit, hare, or deer. [from Middle English *scut*]

Scutari, Lake, Albanian **Ligen i Shkodrës**, Serbo-Croatian **Skadarsko Jezero**, ancient **Lacus Labeatis** the largest lake in the Balkans, situated in Montenegro and NW Albania. AREA 370sq km/143sq mi. The lake has underwater springs, and the town of Shkodër is on its SW shore.

scutellum *noun Bot.* a structure, supposed to be the cotyledon, by which a grass embryo absorbs the endosperm. [from Latin *scutella*, tray]

scuttle¹ *noun* a container for a small amount of coal, usually kept near a fire. [from Anglo-Saxon *scutel*]

scuttle² — *verb intrans.* to move quickly with short steps; to scurry. — *noun* a scuttling pace or movement. [related to SCUD]

scuttle³ — *verb* **1** to deliberately sink (a ship) by making holes in it. **2** to ruin (eg plans). — *noun* a lidded opening in a ship's side or deck. [from Old French *escoutille*, hatchway]

scuzzy *adj. North Amer. slang* filthy, scummy; sleazy. [perhaps a mixture of SCUM and FUZZY]

Scylla and Charybdis *Greek Mythol.* a sea monster and a whirlpool on each side of the Straits of Messina between Italy and Sicily, so situated that the avoidance of one forced a ship closer to the other.

— **between Scylla and Charybdis** faced with danger on both sides, so that avoidance of one involves exposure to the other.

scythe — *noun* a tool with a handle and a long curved blade, for cutting tall crops or grass by hand with a sweeping action. — *verb* to cut with a scythe. [from Anglo-Saxon *sithe*]

Scythians in Greco-Roman times, a nomadic people of the Russian steppes who migrated to the area N of the Black Sea in the 8c BC. They destroyed the Cimmerians who previously lived there, and established their empire which survived until the 2c AD .

SD *abbrev.* **1** (*also* **S. Dak.**) South Dakota. **2** *Maths.* standard deviation.

SDA *abbrev.* Scottish Development Agency.

SDI *abbrev.* Strategic Defence Initiative.

SDLP *abbrev.* Social and Democratic Labour Party.

SDP *abbrev.* Social Democratic Party.

SE *abbrev.* **1** south-east *or* south-eastern. **2** *Maths.* standard error.

Se *symbol Chem.* selenium.

sea *noun* **1** (*usually* **the sea**) the continuous expanse of salt water that covers about 70 per cent of the Earth's surface, and surrounds the continental land masses. **2** any geographical divi-

sion of this, usually smaller than an ocean, eg the Mediterranean Sea. **3** an area of this with reference to its calmness or turbulence: *choppy seas.* **4** a large inland saltwater lake, eg the Dead Sea. **5** a vast expanse or crowd: *a sea of worshippers.*
— **all at sea** completely disorganized or at a loss.
at sea in a ship on the sea.
go to sea to become a sailor.
put *or* **put out to sea** to start a journey by sea. [from Anglo-Saxon *sæ*]

Largest Seas		
	Area	
Name	sq km	sq mi
Coral Sea	4 791 000	1 849 200
Arabian Sea	3 863 000	1 492 000
Mediterranean Sea	2 510 000	968 900
S China (Nan) Sea	c.2 320 000	895 500
Bering Sea	2 261 100	872 800
Bay of Bengal	2 172 000	839 000
Sea of Okhotsk	1 590 000	614 000
Gulf of Mexico	1 507 600	581 900
Gulf of Guinea	1 533 000	592 000
Barents Sea	1 405 000	542 000
Norwegian Sea	1 383 000	534 000
Gulf of Alaska	1 327 000	512 000
Hudson Bay	c.1 230 250	475 000
Greenland Sea	1 205 000	465 000
Arufura Sea	1 037 000	400 000
Philippine Sea	1 036 000	400 000
Sea of Japan	1 012 900	390 900
E Siberian Sea	901 000	348 000
Kara Sea	883 000	341 000
E China Sea	664 000	256 000
Andaman Sea	564 900	218 000
North Sea	520 000	201 000
Black Sea	507 900	196 000
Red Sea	453 000	175 000
Baltic Sea	414 000	160,000
Arabian Gulf	238 800	92 200
St Lawrence Gulf	238 300	92 000

Oceans are excluded.

sea anchor a device, especially a canvas funnel, dragged by a moving ship to slow it or prevent it drifting off course.

sea anemone any of various solitary marine invertebrates, closely related to corals and found in all the oceans, attached by their bases to submerged weeds and rocks. They are usually brightly coloured, with a cylindrical body and numerous stinging tentacles surrounding the mouth, giving the animal a flower-like appearance.

sea anemone

sea bed the bottom or floor of the sea.
seaboard *noun* a coast.
Seaborg, Glen Theodore (1912–) US atomic scientist, born in Ishpeming, Michigan. Working at the University of California at Los Angeles at Berkeley, he first produced plutonium, and contributed to the development of the atomic bomb. His team later synthesized the transuranic elements of atomic number 95–101, and he shared the 1951 Nobel Prize for Chemistry with Edwin McMillan. From 1961 to 1971 he was Chairman of the US Atomic Energy Commission.
seaborgium *noun Chem.* (SYMBOL **Sg**, ATOMIC NUMBER **106**) an artificially manufactured chemi-

cal element with a half-life of less than a second, discovered in 1974, but not officially named until Mar 1994, after confirmation of its discovery. [named after the US atomic scientist Glen Theodore Seaborg]

sea breeze a breeze blowing inland from the sea.

sea change a complete change or transformation.

sea cow a dugong or manatee.

sea cucumber a typically sausage-shaped soft-bodied marine invertebrate, with a mouth at one end surrounded by up to 30 tentacles. It has a leathery skin containing minute bony structures (ossicles), and is found on or near the sea bed, from shallow water to the deep sea.

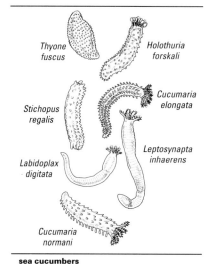

Thyone fuscus
Holothuria forskali
Stichopus regalis
Cucumaria elongata
Labidoplax digitata
Leptosynapta inhaerens
Cucumaria normani

sea cucumbers

sea dog an old or experienced sailor.

sea eagle any of several fish-eating eagles that live near the sea.

seafarer *noun* a person who travels by sea, a sailor.

seafaring *adj.* travelling by or working at sea.

sea-floor spreading *Geol.* the hypothesis that the oceanic crust is expanding outwards (sideways) away from the oceanic ridges at the rate of 1cm to 10cm per year, as a result of the welling up of magma. Together with the theory of continental drift, it has been incorporated into the theory of plate tectonics.

seafood *noun* shellfish and other edible marine fish.

seagoing *adj., said of a ship* designed for sea travel.

Seagull, The a play by Anton Chekhov (1896). A story involving would-be artists, frustrated love, and suicide, the naturalism of its treatment of ordinary people was so revolutionary that the play was a failure until its 1898 Moscow revival.

seagull same as GULL[1].

sea horse any of various small fish found among weeds in warm coastal waters. It is covered with bony plates and swims in an upright position, with its elongated head bent at right angles to its body, so that it resembles a chessboard knight. It feeds on plankton, and anchors itself by curling its long thin tail around seaweed.

sea kale a plant of European coastal waters, with edible spiky green leaves.

seal[1] — *noun* **1** a device, eg a strip of plastic or metal, serving to keep something closed, damage to which is proof of interference. **2** a piece of rubber or other material serving to keep a joint airtight or watertight. **3** a piece of wax or other

material attached to a document and stamped with an official mark to show authenticity. **4** such a mark: *the royal seal.* **5** an engraved metal stamp or ring for making such a mark. **6** an object given, or a gesture made, as a pledge or guarantee. **7** a decorative adhesive label or stamp. — *verb* **1** (*also* **seal something up**) to make it securely closed, airtight, or watertight with a seal. **2** to fix a seal to, or stamp with a seal. **3** to decide or settle: *seal someone's fate / seal a business agreement.* **4** to paint (eg wood) with a substance that protects against damage, eg by weather.
— **seal something off** to isolate an area, preventing entry by unauthorized persons.
set one's seal to something to authorize, approve, or formally endorse it.
[from Latin *sigillum*, from *signum*, mark]

seal[2] — *noun* **1** any of various marine mammals belonging to the family Phocidae which have streamlined bodies which may be smooth-skinned or furry, limbs modified to form webbed flippers, and are found mainly in cool coastal waters, especially near the poles. Most seals live in colonies on the shore during the breeding season. **2** sealskin. — *verb intrans.* to hunt seals. [from Anglo-Saxon *seolh*]
◊ True seals have no external ears, and almost hairless bodies, unlike fur seals and sea lions, which belong to a different family. They are strong swimmers, and while submerged they can close their nostrils to prevent water from entering their lungs. On land, seals move laboriously by dragging themselves on their bellies. The common seal is up to 2m long, and feeds mainly on flatfishes, sand eels, and a variety of crustaceans and molluscs. The pups are born in May and June, and can swim almost immediately. Seals have been widely hunted for their blubber (which forms a thick insulating layer beneath the skin), and for the fur of the pups of some species. The annual seal culls that take place in some parts of the world are the subject of international controversy.

sealant *noun* any material used for sealing, especially one painted on to protect against weathering or wear.

sea legs ability to resist seasickness and walk steadily on the deck of a rolling ship.

sea level the mean level of the surface of the sea between high and low tides; the point from which land height is measured.

sealing-wax *noun* a waxy mixture of shellac and turpentine used for seals on documents.

sea lion any of a number of species of marine mammal with small ears (unlike true seals), long whiskers, paddle-like forelimbs, and large hind flippers, found in coastal waters of the N Pacific, and close to the S American and Australasian coasts. Sea lions feed on fish and squid, and breed in colonies on beaches.

seal of approval *often facetious* official approval.

sealskin *noun* **1** the skin of a furry seal, or an imitation of it. **2** a garment made from this.

Sealyham terrier a breed of dog, developed during the 19c on the Sealyham estate,

sea horse

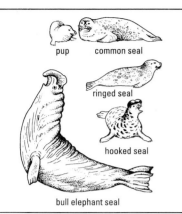

pup   common seal

ringed seal

hooked seal

bull elephant seal

seals

Haverfordwest, Wales. It has a long body with short legs, a short erect tail, a long head with eyebrows, moustache, and beard, short pendulous ears, and a thick wiry coat of pale hair.

seam — *noun* **1** a join between edges, especially one sewn or welded. **2** a layer of coal or ore in the earth. **3** a wrinkle or scar. — *verb* **1** to join edge to edge. **2** to scar or wrinkle. [from Anglo-Saxon *seam*]

seaman *noun* a sailor below the rank of officer.

seamanship *noun* sailing skills, including navigation.

Seamas *or* **Seamus** a male first name. [an Irish Gaelic form of JAMES]

seamer *noun Cricket* a ball delivered by seam bowling, in which the seam of the ball is used by the bowler to make the ball swerve in flight, or first to swerve and then to break in the opposite direction in pitching.

seaminess *noun* being seamy.

seamless *adj.* **1** having no seams; made from a single piece. **2** seeming to be a unified whole; showing no signs of having been pieced together.

seamstress *noun* a woman who sews, especially professionally.

seamy *adj.* (**seamier**, **seamiest**) sordid; disreputable. [from SEAM]

Sean a male first name. [an Irish Gaelic form of JOHN]

séance *or* **seance** *noun* a meeting at which a person attempts to contact the spirits of dead people on behalf of other people present. [from French *séance*, sitting]

sea otter a mammal native to N Pacific coasts, that lives mostly in the water, and has thick insulating fur, small front feet that are not webbed, and a broader body than freshwater otters. It feeds mainly on shellfish.

Sea Peoples seafaring marauders, probably from the Mycenaean world, who destroyed the Hittite empire in Anatolia in c.1200 BC, and penetrated as far south as Egypt before being checked and dispersed. The Achaeans may have been among the invaders.

sea pink same as THRIFT 2.

seaplane *noun* an aeroplane designed to take off from and land on water.

seaport *noun* a coastal town with a port for seagoing ships.

SEAQ *abbrev.* Stock Exchange Automated Quotation.

sear — *verb* **1** to scorch. **2** to wither. — *noun* a mark made by scorching. [from Anglo-Saxon *searian*, to dry up]

search — *verb* **1** *trans., intrans.* to carry out a thorough exploration to try to find something. **2** to check the clothing or body of (a person) for

concealed objects. **3** to examine closely: *search one's conscience.* **4** (*also* **search something out**) to uncover it after a thorough check or exploration. — *noun* an act of searching.

— **in search of something** searching for it.

search me *colloq.* an expression of ignorance about something.
[from Old French *cerchier*, from Latin *circare*, to go around]

Searchers, The a US film directed by John Ford (1956). A Western starring John Wayne, it is a complex tale of revenge and self-discovery which examines the values of the western genre itself.

searching *adj.* that seeks to discover the truth by intensive examination or observation: *a searching inquiry.*

searchlight *noun* **1** a pivoting exterior light with a powerful beam, used to monitor an area in darkness. **2** its beam.

search party a group of people taking part in an organized search for a missing person or thing.

search warrant a document, issued by a justice of the peace, giving a police officer the legal right to search premises.

searing *adj.* burning; intense.

Searle, Ronald (William Fordham) (1920–) English cartoonist, painter, and writer, born in Cambridge. He served in World War II, and the drawings he made during his three years' imprisonment by the Japanese helped to establish his reputation as a artist. After the War he became widely known as the creator of the macabre schoolgirls of 'St Trinians'.

Sears Tower the tallest building in the world, situated in Chicago, Illinois. It was designed by Fazlur Khan, and built in 1970–4 for Sears, Roebuck and Co. It has 110 storeys and reaches a height of 443m.

seascape *noun* a picture of a scene at sea.

Sea Scout a member of a division of the Scout Association that provides training in seamanship.

seashell *noun* the empty shell of an oyster, mussel, or other mollusc.

seashore *noun* the land immediately adjacent to the sea.

seasick *adj.* suffering from seasickness.

seasickness *noun* nausea brought on by the rolling or dipping motion of a ship.

seaside *noun* (*usually* **the seaside**) a coastal area, especially a holiday resort.

season — *noun* **1** any of the four major periods (spring, summer, autumn, and winter), into which the year is divided according to differences in weather patterns and other natural phenomena. **2** a period of the year during which a particular sport is played or some other activity carried out: *fishing season / holiday season.* **3** any period having particular characteristics: *rainy season / our busy season.* **4** a period during which a particular fruit or vegetable is in plentiful supply. — *verb* (**seasoned**, **seasoning**) **1** to flavour (food) by adding salt, pepper, or other herbs and spices. **2** to prepare (eg timber) for use. **3** to make mature or experienced: *seasoned travellers.* **4** to tone down or temper. **5** to add interest or liveliness to.

— **in season 1** *said of food* available, as determined by its growing season. **2** *said of game animals* for which the legal right to hunt exists, according to the time of year. **3** *said of a female animal* ready to mate; on heat.

out of season 1 *said of food* not yet available. **2** *said of game animals* not yet to be hunted. [from Old French *seson*]

seasonable *adj.* **1** *said of weather* appropriate to the season. **2** coming at the right time; opportune.

seasonal *adj.* available, happening, or taking place only at certain times of the year.

seasonal affective disorder *Psychol.* (ABBREV. **SAD**) a recurrent change in mood occurring at a particular time of year, especially a pattern of repeated depression during the winter months, for which treatment with bright lights at either end of the day has been shown to be effective.

seasoned *adj.* **1** flavoured. **2** matured, conditioned.

seasoning *noun* any substance used to season food.

Seasons, The (Die Jahreszeiten) an oratorio (1801) by Joseph Haydn to a libretto by Gottfried van Swieten (1733–1803), based on a poem by the English poet James Thomson (1700–48).

season ticket a ticket giving the right to a specified or unlimited number of visits or journeys during a fixed period.

Seaspeak *noun* the common name for *Essential English for International Maritime Use*, developed in the 1980s to facilitate international communication at sea. It uses a restricted English vocabulary with standardized grammar and fixed syntactic and lexical routines devised to avoid ambiguity and ensure clarity, particularly in radio communication.

Sea Symphony, A the first symphony by Ralph Vaughan Williams (1903–9, revised 1923), for soprano and baritone soloists, chorus, and orchestra, to a text based on poems by Walt Whitman.

seat — *noun* **1** a thing designed for sitting on, eg a chair or bench. **2** the part of it on which one sits. **3** a place for sitting, eg in a cinema or theatre, often reserved; a reservation for such a place. **4** the buttocks. **5** the part of a garment covering the buttocks. **6** the base of an object, or any part on which it rests or fits. **7** a position in Parliament or local government; a position on a committee or other administrative body. **8** an established centre: *seats of learning.* **9** a large country house. — *verb* **1** to assign a seat to, eg at a dinner table. **2** to provide seats for: *the car seats five.* **3** to place in any situation or location. **4** to fit firmly and accurately.

— **be seated** to sit down.

take a *or* **one's seat** to sit down.
[from Norse *sæti*]

seat belt a safety belt that prevents a passenger in a vehicle from being thrown violently forward in the event of a crash.

-seater *combining form* forming words meaning 'having seats for a specified number of people': *a three-seater sofa.*

seating *noun* the number or arrangement of seats, eg in a dining-room.

The Seasons		
N Hemisphere	S Hemisphere	Duration
Spring	Autumn	From vernal/autumnal equinox (c. 21 Mar) to summer/winter solstice (c. 21 Jun)
Summer	Winter	From summer/winter solstice (c. 21 Jun) to autumnal/spring equinox (c. 23 Sept)
Autumn	Spring	From autumnal/spring equinox (c. 23 Sept) to winter/summer solstice (c. 21 Dec)
Winter	Summer	From winter/summer solstice (c. 21 Dec) to vernal/autumnal equinox (c. 21 Mar)

Seattle POP (1990) 2m, the capital of King County, W central Washington, USA. It lies on the E shore of Puget Sound and is the financial, commercial, and cultural centre of the Pacific NW. Founded in 1851, it developed rapidly as a seaport after the 1897 Alaskan gold rush and the opening of the Panama Canal. It is the main port serving Alaska. The economy is dominated by the Boeing aerospace company. There are several scenic and recreational areas nearby. NOTABLE FEATURES Space Needle, a tower 183m high with a revolving restaurant and observation deck; Seattle Art Museum. [named after Chief Seattle of the Duwamish and Suquamish tribes.]

sea urchin the common name for any of 800 species of echinoderm, related to the starfish and brittle stars, but having a spherical or heart-shaped shell formed by fusion of the five arms. The shell is covered by sharp protective spines that may be poisonous, and most species walk on rows of tube feet (similar to those of starfish) that are pushed out through small holes in the shell.

seaward — *adj.* facing or moving toward the sea. — *adv.* (*also* **seawards**) towards the sea.

seaweed *noun* 1 *Bot.* common name for any of a number of large marine algae. 2 such plants collectively.

seaworthiness *noun* a seaworthy state.

seaworthy *adj., said of a ship* fit for a voyage at sea.

sebaceous *adj.* of, like, or secreting sebum. [from Latin *sebaceous*]

sebaceous gland *Anat.* any of the tiny glands, found in the skin of mammals, which open into hair follicles just beneath the skin surface. It secretes *sebum*, an oily substance that protects the skin by preventing evaporative water loss and the entry of bacteria.

Sebastian, St (d.AD 288) Roman martyr, a native of Narbonne. A captain of the Praetorian Guard, he was secretly a Christian, and when his belief was discovered, Diocletian ordered his death by arrows. The archers did not quite kill him and he was nursed back to life, but when he upbraided the tyrant for his cruelty he was beaten to death with rods. His feast day is 20 Jan.

Sebastian 1 the twin brother of Viola in Shakespeare's *Twelfth Night*, who shows no hesitation in marrying Olivia. 2 The wicked and power-hungry brother of Alonso in Shakespeare's *The Tempest* who, along with Antonio, plots Alonso's murder. 3 a male first name. [from Greek *sebastos*, august, venerable]

Sebastiano del Piombo, originally **Sebastiano Luciano** (c.1485–1547) Venetian painter, called *del Piombo* ('of the Seal') from his appointment in 1523 as sealer of briefs to Pope Clement VII. He studied under Giovanni Bellini, and went to Rome (c.1510), where he worked with Michelangelo. His works include the *Raising of Lazarus* (1519, National Gallery, London) and the *Flagellation* (1516–24, St Pietro in Montorio, Rome).

Sebastopol, Russian **Sevastopol** POP (1991e) 367 000, a port in the Crimea, Ukraine. It lies on the SW shore of a peninsula separating the Sea of Azov from the Black Sea. HISTORY founded in 1783; besieged by the British and French for nearly a year in 1854–5 during the Crimean War; taken by the Germans during World War II; the Soviets regained control in 1944. A naval base, Sebastopol is also the centre of a region noted for its health resorts.

Sebha POP (1988e) 122 000, a city in Sebha province, W central Libya. It is built around an oasis.

sebum *noun Zool.* an oily substance, produced by the sebaceous glands, that lubricates the skin and hair. It provides a thin surface film which also protects the skin from excessive dryness by reducing water loss, and has an antibacterial effect. [from Latin *sebum*, grease]

SEC *abbrev.* Securities and Exchange Commission.

Sec. *abbrev.* Secretary.

sec[1] *noun colloq.* a second: *wait a sec.*

sec[2] *adj.* 1 *said of wine* dry. 2 *said of champagne* medium sweet. [from French *sec*, dry]

sec[3] *abbrev.* secant.

sec. *abbrev.* second.

SECAM *abbrev. Séquential Couleur à Mémoire* (French): a coding system for colour television developed in France in the 1960s, and later adopted in the USSR, Eastern Europe, and certain Middle East countries. See also NTSC, PAL.

secant *noun* (ABBREV. **sec**) 1 *Geom.* a straight line that cuts a curve in two or more places. 2 *Maths.* for a given angle in a right-angled triangle, the ratio of the length of the hypotenuse to the length of the side adjacent to the angle under consideration; the reciprocal of the cosine of an angle. [from Latin *secans*, from *secare*, to cut]

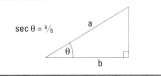

$\sec \theta = {}^a/_b$

secant

secateurs *pl. noun* small sharp shears for pruning bushes. [from French *secateurs*]

secede *verb intrans.* to withdraw formally, eg from a political or religious body or alliance. [from Latin *secedere*, to go apart]

Secession, Right of a US constitutional doctrine that enabled individual states to leave (or secede from) the Federal Union. Espoused by 11 Southern slave-holding states when Abraham Lincoln was elected President (1861), the doctrine hastened the American Civil War, during which it was discredited.

secession *noun* 1 seceding. 2 a group of seceders.

seclude *verb* 1 to keep away from others; to isolate. 2 to keep out of view. [from Latin *secludere*]

secluded *adj.* 1 away from people and noise; private and quiet. 2 hidden from view.

seclusion *noun* the state of being secluded; peacefulness and privacy.

Secombe, Sir Harry (Donald) (1921–) Welsh entertainer, born in Swansea. In 1947 he became a regular on the radio show *Variety Bandbox*, then with Peter Sellers, Spike Milligan, and Michael Bentine he performed in the highly popular *Goon Show* (1951–9). In addition to countless variety shows, he has appeared in *Humpty Dumpty* (1959), *Pickwick* (1963), *The Four Musketeers*, (1967) and *The Plumber's Progress* (1975). Also a popular singer with numerous albums to his credit, his films include *Oliver!* (1968) and *Song of Norway* (1970), and he has written for the magazine *Punch*.

second[1] — *adj.* 1 next after the first, in order of sequence or importance. 2 alternate: *every second week.* 3 additional; supplementary: *have a second go.* 4 subordinate; inferior: *second to none.* 5 so similarly talented as to be worthy of the same name: *a writer described as a second Shakespeare.* 6 *Mus.* indicating an instrument or voice with a subordinate role to, or a slightly lower pitch than, another: *second soprano.* — *noun* 1 a person or thing next in sequence after the first. 2 the second gear in an engine. 3 a second-class honours degree. 4 an assistant to a boxer or duellist. 5 (**seconds**) flawed goods sold at reduced prices.

6 (**seconds**) *colloq.* a second helping of food. 7 (**seconds**) *colloq.* the second course of a meal. 8 a Cub Scout or Brownie Guide next in rank to a sixer. — *verb* 1 to declare formal support for (a proposal, or the person making it). 2 to give support or encouragement of any kind to. 3 to act as second to (a boxer or duellist). — *adv.* in second place: *came second in the race.* [from Latin *secundus*]

second[2] *noun* 1 (ABBREV. **sec, s**) an SI unit of time, equal to $\frac{1}{60}$ of a minute, and defined as the duration of 9 192 631 770 periods of the radiation corresponding to the transition between two hyperfine levels of the ground state of the caesium-133 atom. 2 a unit of angular measurement equal to $\frac{1}{3600}$ of a degree or $\frac{1}{60}$ of a minute. 3 a moment: *wait a second.* [from Latin *secunda minuta*, secondary minute]

second[3] *verb* (with stress on *-cond*) to transfer temporarily to a different post, place, or duty. [from French *en second*, in the second rank]

secondary *adj.* 1 of lesser importance than the principal or primary concern; subordinate. 2 developed from something earlier or original: *a secondary infection.* 3 *said of education* between primary and higher or further; for pupils between ages 11 and 18. See also PRIMARY, TERTIARY. [from Latin *secundarius*]

secondary cell *Physics* an electrolytic cell that must be charged before use by passing an electric current through it, and can then be recharged when necessary.

secondary colour a colour obtained by mixing two primary colours, eg orange.

secondary growth *or* **secondary thickening** *Bot.* 1 the increase in girth of a stem or root that results from the activity of cambium after elongation has ceased. 2 the formation by a cell of a secondary wall.

secondary picketing picketing of firms that have business connections with the employer against whom action is being taken.

secondary sexual characteristics *Zool.* features other than the reproductive organs that distinguish males from females after the onset of puberty, eg beard growth in human males, breast development in human females.

secondary stress *Linguistics* the second-strongest stress in a word, etc. See also PRIMARY STRESS.

second best the next after the best. — **come off second best** *colloq.* to lose.

second-best *adj.* 1 next after the best. 2 somewhat inferior.

second childhood senility; dotage.

second class the class or category below the first in quality or value.

second-class — *adj.* 1 relating to the class below the first. 2 of a poor standard; inferior. 3 not having as many rights or privileges as others: *a second-class citizen.* — *adv.* by second-class mail or transport.

second cousin a child of one's parent's first cousin.

second-degree *adj. Medicine* denoting the second most serious of the three degrees of burning, with blistering but not permanent damage to the skin.

seconder *noun* a person who seconds a proposal or seconds the person making it.

second hand the pointer on a watch or clock that measures the time in seconds.

second-hand — *adj.* 1 previously owned or used by someone else. 2 not directly received or obtained, but coming via an intermediary: *second-hand information.* — *adv.* 1 in a second-hand state: *buy furniture second-hand.* 2 not directly, but from someone else: *heard it second-hand.*

second lieutenant an army or navy officer of the lowest commissioned rank, the rank below lieutenant.

secondly *adv.* in the second place; as a second consideration.

secondment *noun* a temporary transfer to another position.

second nature a habit so firmly fixed as to seem an innate part of a person's nature.

second person see PERSON.

second-rate *adj.* inferior; substandard.

second sight the supposed power to see into the future or to see things happening elsewhere.

second-strike capability *Mil.* in nuclear warfare, the capability of a state to launch a counter-attack following a first strike by an enemy.

second thoughts 1 doubts: *having second thoughts*. 2 a process of reconsidering and reaching a different decision: *on second thoughts*.

second wind 1 the recovery of normal breathing after exertion. 2 a burst of renewed energy or enthusiasm.

secrecy *noun* 1 the state or fact of being secret. 2 the ability or tendency to keep information secret. [from Middle English *secretie*, from *secre*, secret]

secret — *adj.* 1 hidden from or undisclosed to others, or to all but a few. 2 whose activities are unknown to or unobserved by others: *a secret army*. 3 tending to conceal things from others; secretive. — *noun* 1 a piece of information not revealed, or not to be revealed, to others. 2 an unknown or unrevealed method of achievement: *the secret of eternal youth*. 3 a fact or purpose that remains unexplained; a mystery.
— **in secret** secretly; unknown to others. [from Latin *secretus*, set apart]

Secret Agent, The a novel by Joseph Conrad (1907). It is set in a dilapidated shop in Soho, London, and centres on the life of Verloc, a Russian double agent.

secret agent a member of the secret service; a spy.

secretaire *noun* same as ESCRITOIRE. [from French *secretaire*, secretary]

secretarial *adj.* relating to secretaries or their work.

secretariat *noun* 1 the administrative department of any large organization, especially a legislative body. 2 its staff or premises. [from French *secrétariat*]

secretary *noun* (PL. **secretaries**) 1 a person employed to perform administrative or clerical tasks. 2 the member of a club or society responsible for its correspondence and business records. 3 a senior civil servant assisting a government minister or ambassador. [from Latin *secretarius*, person spoken to in confidence]

secretary-bird *noun* a long-legged, long-tailed, snake-eating African bird of prey.

secretary-general *noun* the principal administrative official in a large (especially political) organization.

Secretary of State 1 in the UK, a minister at the head of a major government department. 2 in the US, the head of the department dealing with foreign affairs.

secrete¹ *verb*, *said of a gland or similar organ* to form and release (a substance) for use in the body, or as an excretion. [related to SECRET]

secrete² *verb* to hide away or conceal. [related to SECRET]

Secret Garden, The a children's novel by Frances Hodgson Burnett (1911). It is set in Yorkshire and describes how a spoilt orphan finds happiness after discovering a hidden garden.

secretion *noun* 1 a substance secreted. 2 the process of secreting.

secretive *adj.* inclined not to reveal things to others; fond of secrecy.

secretiveness *noun* being secretive.

Secret Life of Walter Mitty, The a short story by James Thurber (1932). It describes the escapist fantasies of henpecked urban hero, Walter Mitty.

secretly *adv.* 1 in secret. 2 in concealment.

secretory *adj.* that secretes.

secret police a police force operating in secret to stamp out opposition to the government.

secret service a government department responsible for espionage and matters of national security.
◇ Also known as *intelligence service*. In democratic countries, it is usually kept separate from internal security agencies, whereas in such countries as the former USSR, the KGB was responsible both for external espionage and internal counter-intelligence. In the USA, the external espionage is carried out by the CIA with the FBI dealing with internal security: the corresponding agencies in the UK are MI5 and MI6.

secret society an association or group whose activites are kept secret from the world at large and whose members usually take an oath of secrecy.

sect *noun* a religious or other group whose views and practices differ from those of an established body or from those of a body from which it has separated. [from Latin *secta*, a following]
◇ Religious sects are usually distinctive and exclusive, claiming to possess true belief, correct ritual, and warranted standards of conduct. They commonly accept and reject persons on the basis of some test of worthiness, and demand strict conformity and complete personal involvement, often to the point of rejection of all previous attachments.

sectarian — *adj.* 1 of, relating to, or belonging to a sect. 2 having, showing, or caused by hostility towards those outside one's own group or belonging to a particular group: *sectarian violence*. — *noun* a member of a sect, especially a bigoted person.

sectarianism *noun* loyalty or excessive attachment to a particular sect or party.

section — *noun* 1 any of the parts into which a thing is or can be divided, or from which it is constructed. 2 a subdivision of an army platoon. 3 *Geom.* the surface formed when a plane cuts through a solid geometric figure. 4 the act of cutting through a solid figure. 5 a plan or diagram showing a view of an object as if it had been cut through. 6 *Biol.* a thin slice of a specimen of tissue that is prepared for examination under a microscope. 7 *Medicine* in surgery, the act or process of cutting, or the cut or division made. — *verb* (**sectioned**, **sectioning**) *Medicine* to issue an order for the compulsory admission of (a person suffering from mental illness) to a psychiatric hospital under the relevant section of mental health legislation, eg the Mental Health Act in the UK. [from Latin *secare*, to cut]

sectional *adj.* 1 made in sections. 2 relating, or restricted, to a particular group or area.

Section d'Or a group of French painters who were active between 1912, when they held an exhibition in Paris, and 1914. Their style was related to Cubism, and showed a particular interest in a system of proportion.

sector *noun* 1 a part of an area divided up for military purposes. 2 a separate part into which any sphere of activity, eg a nation's economy, can be divided: *the public and private sectors*. 3 a portion of a circle formed by two radii and the part of the circumference lying between them. [from Latin *sector*, cutter]

secular *adj.* 1 not religious or ecclesiastical; civil or lay. 2 relating to this world; not heavenly or spiritual. 3 *said of members of the clergy* not bound by vows to a particular religious order. 4 occurring only once in a lifetime, century, or age. [from Latin *saecularis*, from *saeculum*, generation, century]

secularism *noun* the view that society's values and standards should not be influenced or controlled by religion or the Church.

secularist *noun* a person who favours secularism.

secularize *or* **secularise** *verb* to make secular.

secure — *adj.* 1 free from danger; providing freedom from danger. 2 free from trouble or worry. 3 firmly fixed or attached. 4 not likely to be lost or taken away; assured: *a secure job*. — *verb* 1 to fasten or attach firmly. 2 to get or gain possession of. 3 to make free from danger or risk. 4 to guarantee. [from Latin *securus*, from *se-*, without + *cura*, care]

securely *adv.* in a secure way.

Securities and Exchange Commission (ABBREV. **SEC**) in the USA, a body set up in 1934 during the Great Depression to regulate and control the issue of shares by corporations. It ensures that statements about the stocks being sold are accurate, and generally regulates the way US stock markets operate.

Securities and Investments Board (ABBREV. **SIB**) in the UK, an agency set up in 1985 to regulate the activities of investment business. It has power, under the Financial Services Act (1986), to oversee the activities of various self-regulatory organizations which have been set up to control aspects of the UK's financial markets. These include the Investment Management Regulatory Board (IMRO), dealing with investment managers; the Financial Intermediaries, Managers and Brokers Regulatory Association (FIMBRA), covering independent life assurance and unit trust salesmen and brokers; the Life Assurance and Unit Trust Companies (LAUTRO); and the Securities Association, monitoring some 700 firms, including investment banks, provincial stockbrokers, and securities dealers. The SIB can subpoena documents and witnesses, and initiate prosecutions. It has no powers in relation to takeovers or insider dealing.

security *noun* (PL. **securities**) 1 the state of being secure. 2 freedom from the possibility of future financial difficulty. 3 protection from physical harm, especially assassination. 4 freedom from vulnerability to political or military takeover: *national security*. 5 something given as a guarantee, eg of repayment of a loan. 6 (*usually* **securities**) a certificate stating ownership of stocks or shares; the monetary value represented by such certificates.

security blanket 1 a blanket or other familiar piece of cloth carried around by a toddler for comfort. 2 any familiar object whose presence provides a sense of security or comfort.

security risk a person or activity considered to be a threat to a nation's security, eg because of a likelihood of giving away military secrets.

SED *abbrev.* Scottish Education Department.

Sedan, Battle of the crucial French defeat (1870) of the Franco–Prussian War, which ended the Second Empire in France. Marshal MacMahon's plan to relieve the French Rhine Army, besieged in Metz, was foiled when German forces under Field Marshal Moltke encircled Sedan, causing Napoleon III to surrender the town with 83 000 men, and then advanced on Paris.

sedan *noun* 1 *Hist.* (*also* **sedan chair**) a large enclosed chair which can be lifted and carried on horizontal poles. 2 *North Amer.* a saloon car.

sedate¹ *adj.* 1 calm and dignified in manner. 2 slow and unexciting. [from Latin *sedare*, to still]

sedate² *verb* to make calm by means of a sedative. [from Latin *sedare*, to still]

sedately *adv.* in a sedate way.

sedation *noun Medicine* the act of calming, or state of being calmed, especially by means of sedative drugs.

sedative — *noun Medicine* any agent, especially a drug, that has a calming effect and is used to treat insomnia, pain, delirium, etc. Sedatives have been largely superseded by tranquillizers as a treatment for anxiety and nervous tension. — *adj., said of a drug, etc* having a calming effect.

Seddon, Richard John, known as **King Dick** (1845–1906) New Zealand politician and Prime Minister, born in Eccleston, Lancashire, UK. He settled in New Zealand in 1866, and entered parliament in 1879. As Prime Minister (1893–1906) he led a Liberal Party government remembered for its social legislation (eg the introduction of old-age pensions).

sedentary *adj.* **1** *said of work* involving much sitting. **2** *said of a person* spending much time sitting; taking little exercise. [from Latin *sedere*, to sit]

sedge *noun* any plant resembling a grass or rush and belonging to the family Cyperaceae, especially *Cladium mariscus*, or any of about 200 species of the genus *Carex*. *Cladium mariscus* has saw-edged leaves, and often dominates the vegetation of fens and swamps in warmer regions. *Carex* is found virtually worldwide in poorly drained areas, but is especially common in alpine and marshy subarctic habitats. It produces tufts of grass-like leaves, tiny flowers lacking petals, and oval beaked fruits. Its stems are triangular in cross-section. [from Anglo-Saxon *secg*]

Sedgemoor, Battle of a battle (5 Jul 1685) near Bridgwater, Somerset, which ended the Duke of Monmouth's rebellion against James VII of Scotland and II of England. The rebel army received popular support and outnumbered the royal army by 4 000 to 2 500, but desertions provoked a disastrous night attack. Monmouth was executed, and his supporters suffered under Lord Chief Justice Jeffreys' 'Bloody Assizes'.

Sedgwick, Adam (1785–1873) English geologist, born in Dent, Cumbria. Professor at Cambridge, he studied the geology of Wales and introduced the Cambrian system in 1835. With Roderick Murchison he studied the Lake District, the Alps, and SW England, where they first identified the Devonian system.

sediment *noun* **1** insoluble solid particles that have settled at the bottom of a liquid in which they were previously suspended. **2** *Geol.* solid material such as rock fragments, or plant or animal debris, that has been deposited by the action of gravity, wind, water, or ice, especially such material that has settled at the bottom of a sea, lake, or river. [from Latin *sedimentum*, from *sedere*, to sit]

sedimentary *adj.* **1** relating to or of the nature of sediment. **2** *Geol.* denoting any of a group of rocks, eg clay, limestone, coal, sandstone, that have formed as a result of the accumulation and compaction of layers of sediment, itself consisting of small particles of pre-existing rock that have been transported from their place of origin by water, wind, ice, or gravity.

sedimentation *noun* **1** *Geol.* the process of accumulating or depositing sediment in layers, eg during the formation of sedimentary rock. **2** *Chem.* the settling of solid particles from a suspension, either naturally as a result of gravity, or as a result of centrifugation.

sedition *noun* speech, writing, or action encouraging public disorder, especially rebellion against the government. [from Latin *seditio*, a going apart]

seditious *adj.* **1** relating to or involving sedition. **2** encouraging or taking part in sedition.

Sedley, Amelia one of the two women at the centre of William Makepeace Thackeray's *Vanity Fair*, who marries George Osborne and is forced into a life of poverty. Other family members include her huge brother Joseph, known as 'the Collector of Boggley Wallah', and their parents, Mr and Mrs Sedley.

seduce *verb* **1** to entice into having sexual relations. **2** to tempt, especially into wrongdoing. [from Latin *seducere*, to lead aside]

seduction *noun* seducing or being seduced.

seductive *adj.* **1** sexually very attractive and charming. **2** creating, or designed to create, the mood for sex: *seductive lighting*. **3** tempting; enticing.

seductively *adv.* in a seductive way.

seductiveness *noun* being seductive.

sedulity *noun* being sedulous, diligence.

sedulous *adj. formal* **1** steadily hardworking and conscientious; diligent. **2** painstakingly carried out. [from Latin *sedulus*]

sedum *noun* any of a family of rock plants with fleshy leaves and white, yellow, or pink flowers. [from Latin *sedum*]

see¹ *verb* (PAST TENSE **saw**; PAST PARTICIPLE **seen**) **1** to perceive with the eyes. **2** *intrans.* to have the power of vision. **3** to watch: *see a play*. **4** *trans., intrans.* to understand: *I don't see what you mean.* **5** to be aware of or know, especially by looking: *I see from your letter that you're married.* **6** *trans., intrans.* to find out: *wait and see.* **7** to meet up with; to be in the company of: *not seen her for ages.* **8** to spend time with, especially romantically: *seeing a married woman.* **9** to speak to or consult: *asking to see the manager.* **10** to receive as a visitor: *the manager refused to see me.* **11** to make sure of something: *see that you lock the door.* **12** (**see to something**) attend to it; take care of it: *will you see to it?* **13** to imagine, especially to regard as likely; to picture in the mind: *can't see him agreeing / can still see her as a little girl.* **14** to consider: *see her more as a writer than a politician.* **15** *intrans.* (**see something in someone**) to find an attractive feature in them: *it is hard to know what he sees in her.* **16** to be witness to as a sight or event: *do not wish to see her hurt / now seeing huge increases in unemployment.* **17** to escort: *see you home.* **18** to refer to for information: *see page 5.* **19** *Cards* to match the bet of by staking the same sum: *see you and raise you five.*

— **see about something** to attend to a matter or concern.

see fit to do something to think it appropriate or proper to do it.

see into something to investigate it; to look into it.

see the light 1 to discover religious feelings within oneself. **2** to recognize the merits of, and adopt, some widely held point of view.

see someone off 1 to accompany them to a place of departure. **2** *colloq.* to get rid of them by force.

see someone out 1 to escort them out of a building, etc. **2** to outlive them.

see something out to stay until the end of it.

see over something to inspect it; to look over it.

see things to have hallucinations.

see through something 1 to discern what is implied by an idea or scheme, etc. **2** to recognize an essential truth underlying a lie, trick, etc.

see something through to participate in it to the end.

see you later *colloq.* an expression of temporary farewell.

see² *noun* **1** the post of bishop. **2** the area under the religious authority of a bishop or archbishop. [from Latin *sedes*, seat]

Seebeck, Thomas Johann (1770–1831) Estonian-born German physicist, born in Tallin. He investigated optical polarization in stressed glass (1812), and discovered thermoelectricity (1822), the production of an electric current when

heat is applied to a junction of two metals, now much used in thermocouples for temperature measurement.

seed — *noun* (PL. **seeds**, **seed**) **1** *Bot.* in flowering and cone-bearing plants, the highly resistant structure that develops from the ovule after fertilization, and is capable of developing into a new plant. It contains the developing embryo and a food store, surrounded by a protective coat or *testa*. In flowering plants, but not in cone-bearing plants, the seeds are contained within a fruit which develops from the ovary wall. Seed dispersal by wind, animals, or water enables plants to colonize new areas. **2** a source or origin: *the seeds of the idea*. **3** *literary* offspring; descendants. **4** *literary* semen. **5** *Sport* a seeded player. — *verb* **1** *intrans.* *said of a plant* to produce seeds. **2** to plant (seeds). **3** to remove seeds from (eg a fruit). **4** *Chem.* to use a single crystal to induce the formation of more from a concentrated solution. **5** *Microbiol.* to add bacteria, viruses, etc to (a culture medium). **6** *Sport* to rank (a player in a tournament) according to his or her likelihood of winning; to arrange (a tournament) so that high-ranking players only meet each other in the latter stages of the contest.

— **go to seed 1** (*also* **run to seed**) *Bot.*, *said of a plant* to stop flowering prior to the development of seed. **2** *colloq.* to allow oneself to become unkempt or unhealthy through lack of care. [from Anglo-Saxon *sæd*]

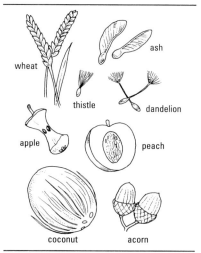

wheat · ash · thistle · dandelion · apple · peach · coconut · acorn

seeds

seedbed *noun* **1** a piece of ground prepared for the planting of seeds. **2** an environment in which something (especially undesirable) develops.

seed drill *Agric.* a farm implement that is used to sow seeds in rows by making a series of furrows, dropping the seeds into them, and covering them with soil.

seeded *adj.* **1** with the seeds removed. **2** bearing or having seeds. **3** sown. **4** *Sport, said of a tournament player* who has been seeded.

seedhead *noun* a compact mass or cluster of seeds on a plant.

seedless *adj.* bearing no or few seeds.

seedling *noun* a young plant grown from seed.

seed-pearl *noun* a tiny pearl.

seed-potato *noun* a potato kept for planting, from which a new potato plant grows.

seedy *adj.* (**seedier**, **seediest**) **1** *said of a fruit, etc* full of seeds. **2** *said of a plant* at the stage of producing seeds. **3** *colloq.* mildly ill. **4** *colloq.* shabby or run-down; dirty or disreputable: *seedy areas of town*.

Seeger, Pete (1919–) US folk singer, songwriter, guitarist, and banjo player, born in New York City. After studying sociology at Harvard, he travelled the USA learning folk songs, then with Woodie Guthrie he organized the Almanac Singers (1940–2), whose repertoire of radical songs marked the start of the 'protest' movement in contemporary folk-music. Later, with the Weavers, he had such folk hits as 'Good-night Irene' and 'On Top of Old Smokey'. Other well-known hits include 'Little Boxes', 'Where Have All the Flowers Gone?', and 'We Shall Overcome', which he adapted from a traditional song. He is an activist on issues of ecology, politics, and individual liberties.

seeing — *noun* the ability to see; the power of vision. — *conj.* (*also* **seeing that**) given (that); since: *seeing you are opposed to the plan, I shall not pursue it.*

seek *verb* (PAST TENSE AND PAST PARTICIPLE **sought**) **1** to look for. **2** to try to get or achieve. **3** to try or endeavour: *seeking to please.* **4** to take oneself off to; to go to get: *seek shelter in a cave.* **5** to ask for: *sought his advice.*
— **seek something** *or* **someone out** to search intensively for and find them. [from Anglo-Saxon *secan*]

seem *verb intrans.* **1** to appear to the eye; to give the impression of (being). **2** to be apparent; to appear to the mind: *there seems to be no good reason for refusing.* **3** to think or believe oneself (to be, do, etc): *I seem to know you from somewhere.* [from Norse *soemr*, fitting]

seeming *adj.* apparent.

seemingly *adv.* apparently.

seemly *adj.* (**seemlier, seemliest**) *old use* fitting; suitable.

seen see SEE[1].

seep *verb intrans.*, *said of a liquid* to escape slowly, through or as if through a narrow opening. [perhaps from Anglo-Saxon *sipian*, to soak]

seepage *noun* **1** seeping. **2** liquid that has seeped.

seer *noun* **1** a person who predicts future events; a clairvoyant. **2** a person of great wisdom and insight; a prophet. [literally 'a person who sees', from SEE[1]]

seersucker *noun* lightweight cotton or linen cloth with a crinkly appearance. [from Persian *shir o shakkar*, milk and sugar]

seesaw — *noun* **1** a plaything consisting of a plank balanced in the middle, allowing people, especially children, seated on its ends to propel each other up and down by pushing off the ground with the feet. **2** an alternate up-and-down or back-and-forth movement. — *verb intrans.* (**seesawed, seesawing**) to move alternately up-and-down or back-and-forth. [a reduplication of SAW[2], from the sawing action]

seethe *verb intrans.* **1** *said of a liquid* to churn and foam because or as if boiling. **2** to be extremely agitated, especially with anger. [from Anglo-Saxon *seothan*]

seething *adj.* **1** that seethes; boiling. **2** furious.

see-through *adj.* said especially of a fabric or clothing, able to be seen through; translucent.

Sefadu POP (1974) 76 000, the capital of Kono district, Eastern province, Sierra Leone. It is situated 113km/70mi NE of Bo.

Seferis, pseudonym of **George Seferiades** (1900–71) Greek poet and diplomat, born in Smyrna. He was appointed as consul in London (1931), and was Greek ambassador to Britain (1957–62). His poetry includes *Logbook* (3 vols, 1940, 1944, 1965) in which he sees himself as a tormented Odysseus longing to return to his native land. He was awarded the Nobel Prize for Literature in 1963.

segment — *noun* (with stress on *seg*-) **1** a part, section, or portion. **2** *Geom.* in a circle or ellipse, the region enclosed by an arc (a segment of the circumference) and its chord (a straight line

drawn from one end of the arc to the other). **3** *Zool.* each of a number of repeating units in the body of certain animals, eg some worms. — *verb* (with stress on *-ment*) to divide into segments. [from Latin *segmentum*, from *secare*, to cut]

segmentation *noun* **1** division into segments, or an instance of this. **2** repeated cell division in a fertilized ovum.

Ségou **1** POP (1987) 89 000, the river-port capital of Ségou region, central Mali. It is situated 200km/124mi NE of Bamako on the R Niger and is the centre of an irrigation scheme based on the R Niger. **2** a region of central Mali with Ségou as its capital.

Segovia, Andrés (1893–1987) Spanish guitarist, born in Linares. Largely self-taught, he gave his first concert in 1909, and quickly gained an international reputation. Influenced by the Spanish nationalist composers, he evolved a revolutionary guitar technique that allowed the performance of a wide range of music, and many modern composers composed works for him.

Segovia the capital of Segovia province, Castilla-León, NW central Spain. It lies 87km/54mi NW of Madrid. NOTABLE FEATURES the Roman aqueduct and old town are a World Heritage site; cathedral (16c); Moorish citadel; El Parral monastery; Churches of St Martin and St Esteban.

Segrè, Emilio (1905–89) US physicist, born in Rome. Dismissed from his post in Palermo under Mussolini's regime (1938), he moved to the USA, where he worked at the University of California at Berkeley and on the atom bomb development project during World War II. In 1937 he discovered the first entirely man-made element, technetium, and he was later involved in the discoveries of astatine and plutonium (1940). In 1955 his research team discovered the anti-proton (the antiparticle of the proton), and for this work he shared the 1959 Nobel Prize for Physics with Owen Chamberlain.

segregate *verb* to separate (a group or groups) from others or from each other. [from Latin *se*-, apart + *grex*, flock]

segregated *adj.* separated out, isolated.

segregation *noun* **1** enforced separation into groups. **2** systematic isolation of one group, especially a racial or ethnic minority, from the rest of society.

segregational *adj.* involving or characterized by segregation.

Séguin, Marc (1786–1875) French mechanical and civil engineer, born in Annonay. His principal achievements were in engineering, notably his association with the development of wire-rope suspension bridges from 1825 onwards, and his invention of the multi-tubular (fire-tube) boiler which he patented in 1827, successfully used in a locomotive in 1829.

Seifert, Jaroslav (1901–86) Czech poet, born in Prague. His major works include *The Carrier Pigeon* (1929), *The Hands of Venus* (1936), and *Put Out The Lights* (1938), and with his post-war volume *A Helmet of Earth* (1945) he was established as the national poet. He refused all compromise after the Communist takeover in 1948. He was awarded the Nobel Prize for Literature in 1984.

seigneur *noun* a feudal lord, especially in France. [from French *seigneur*]

Seikan Tunnel a major rail tunnel (54km/34mi long) beneath the Tsugara Strait, Japan, constructed between 1964 and 1988. It links Tappi Saki, Honshu, with Fukushima, Hokkaido.

Seine, River the third-longest river in France, length 776km/482mi. Rising in the Langres Plateau, NW of Dijon, it flows NW through the Champagne Pouilleuse, W and S across the Brie region, then NW through Paris, where it is an

important feature of the city, to Normandy. It then discharges into the English Channel. There are several canal links to other major rivers.

seine — *noun* a large fishing net kept hanging vertically underwater by means of floats and weights. — *verb trans., intrans.* to catch (fish) with a seine. [from Anglo-Saxon *segne*]

seismic *adj.* **1** of or relating to earthquakes. **2** *colloq.* gigantic: *an increase of seismic proportions.* [from Greek *seismos*, a shaking]

seismograph *noun* an instrument that measures and records the force of earthquakes. [from Greek *seismos*, a shaking + -GRAPH]

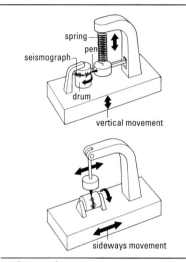

seismograph

seismography *noun* the scientific study of earthquakes.

seismological *adj.* relating to or involving seismology.

seismologist *noun* a scientist skilled in seismology.

seismology *noun* *Geol.* the branch of geology concerned with the scientific study of earthquakes, including their origin and effects, and possible methods by which they may be predicted. [from Greek *seismos*, a shaking + -LOGY]

seize *verb* **1** to take or grab suddenly. **2** to affect suddenly and deeply; to overcome: *seized by panic.* **3** to take by force; to capture. **4** to take legal possession of. **5** (**seize on** *or* **upon something**) to use or exploit it eagerly: *they seized every chance to embarrass us.*
— **seize up** *said of a machine or engine* to become stiff or jammed, eg through overuse or lack of lubrication. [from Old French *saisir*]

seizure *noun* **1** the act of seizing. **2** a sudden attack of an illness, especially producing spasms or loss of movement.

Sejanus, Lucius Aelius (d.31 AD) prefect of the Praetorian Guard (14–31). He effectively assumed control in Rome after the emperor Tiberius's retirement to Capri (26). He systematically eliminated possible successors to Tiberius, such as Agrippina's sons, so that he himself might wield supreme power after Tiberius's death as regent for his young grandson Gemellus. Tiberius became aware of his plans and had him executed.

Sekmet see SAKHMET.

Sekondi-Takoradi POP (1988) 104 000, a major seaport and the capital of Western region, S Ghana. It lies on the Gulf of Guinea, 180km/112mi SW of Accra. HISTORY founded by the Dutch in the 16c; Sekondi expanded after the construction of a railway to Tarkwa from 1898 to

1903, and merged with Takoradi in 1946; formed an important supply base during World War II.

Selangor POP (1990) 2m, a state in W Peninsular Malaysia, on the Strait of Malacca. AREA 7 997sq km/3 087sq mi. HISTORY became a British protectorate in 1874; separated from the federal territory of Wilayah Persekutuan in 1981. CAPITAL Shah Alam. ECONOMY rubber; tin; commerce.

Selby, Prideaux John (1788–1857) English naturalist, born in Alnwick, Northumberland. A Fellow of University College, Oxford, he was appointed high sheriff of Northumberland in 1823. He produced *Illustrations of British Ornithology* (19 vols, 1821–34), the first book of British birds to be shown life-size, and *Illustrations of Ornithology* (1825–43). He also co-founded and edited the *Magazine of Zoology and Botany* (1837).

seldom *adv.* rarely. [from Anglo-Saxon *seldum*]

select — *verb* to choose from among several. — *adj.* **1** picked out in preference to others. **2** to which entrance or membership is restricted; exclusive. [from Latin *seligere*]

select committee *Politics* a committee made up of members of a legislature, whose task is to examine a specific subject, such as education or defence. The two main types are the *ad hoc committee*, which ceases to exist when its prescribed task is completed, and the *permanent* or *standing committee*, which normally lasts for an electoral term and investigates particular policy areas or the actions of government departments.

selection *noun* **1** the act or process of selecting or being selected. **2** a thing or set of things selected. **3** a range from which to choose. **4** natural selection. **5** artificial selection.

selective *adj.* **1** exercising the right to reject some in favour of others. **2** able or tending to select; discriminating. **3** involving only certain people or things; exclusive.

selectivity *noun* the ability to discriminate.

selectness *noun* being select.

selector *noun* a person who selects.

Selene in Greek mythology, the goddess of the Moon, daughter of Hyperion, and sister of Helios and Eos. She was depicted as a charioteer (the head of one of her horses may be seen among the Elgin Marbles). She later became identified with the Greek goddess Artemis.

Selenga, River a river in N central Asia. It is 992km/616mi long. The river rises to the E of Uliastay, in W Mongolia, and flows E. It is joined by the Orhon Gol close to the Russian border and turns W to enter the SE of L Baikal.

selenite *noun Geol.* a variety of gypsum that occurs as clear colourless crystals. [from Greek *selene*, moon]

selenium *noun Chem.* (SYMBOL **Se**, ATOMIC NUMBER **34**) a metalloid element that exists as several different allotropes, one of which conducts electricity in the presence of light, and is used in photoelectric cells, photographic exposure meters, and xerography (photocopying). It is also a semiconductor, used in electronic devices, and an important trace element in plants and animals. [from Greek *selene*, moon]

Seles, Monica (1973–) Yugoslav tennis player, born in Novi Sad, Yugoslavia. She moved to the USA in 1986. She has won the French Open three times (1990–2), the US Open twice (1991–2), and the Australian Open three times (1991–3). In 1992 she was defeated by Steffi Graf in the Wimbledon singles final. During a tournament in Hamburg in Apr 1993, she was injured in a knife attack by a member of the crowd and was unable to take part in any further championships in that year.

Seleucids a Hellenistic Greek dynasty founded by Seleucus I Nicator, the general of Alexander the Great. His successors were all called Seleucus or Antiochus. Initially, the Seleucid empire stretched from Asia Minor to NW India, but its power and extent were reduced after the defeat of Antiochus III by Rome in 188 BC; by 64 BC, all that remained was the Syrian heartland.

Seleucus I Nicator, also called **the Conqueror** (c.358–281 BC) Macedonian general, founder of the Seleucid dynasty. After the death of Alexander the Great (323 BC) he rose from being satrap of Babylonia (321 BC) to being the ruler of an empire (312 BC) which stretched from Asia Minor to India. He assumed the title of king in 305 BC, and founded a new, more central capital at Antioch in N Syria (300 BC). He was killed by Ptolemy Ceraunus, the son of Ptolemy I Soter.

self — *noun* (PL. **selves**) **1** personality, or a particular aspect of it. **2** a person as a whole, a combination of characteristics of appearance and behaviour: *his usual happy self*. **3** personal interest or advantage. — *pron. colloq.* myself, yourself, himself, or herself. [from Anglo-Saxon *seolf*]

self- *combining form* forming words meaning: **1** by or for oneself; in relation to oneself: *self-doubt / self-inflicted*. **2** acting automatically: *self-closing*.

self-abuse *noun* masturbation.

self-addressed *adj.* addressed by the sender for return to him- or herself.

self-appointed *adj.* acting on one's own authority, without being asked or chosen by others.

self-assertion *noun* self-asserting, being self-assertive.

self-assertive *adj.* always ready to make others aware of one's presence or opinions, especially arrogantly or aggressively.

self-assurance *noun* self-confidence.

self-assured *adj.* self-confident.

self-catering *adj., said of accommodation* in which guests or residents have facilities for preparing their own meals.

self-centred *adj.* interested only in oneself and one's own affairs.

self-coloured *adj.* **1** of the same colour all over. **2** in its natural colour; undyed.

self-confessed *adj.* as openly admitted by oneself: *a self-confessed cheat.*

self-confidence *noun* total absence of shyness; confidence in one's own abilities.

self-confident *adj.* confident of one's own powers, sometimes arrogantly so.

self-conscious *adj.* ill at ease in company as a result of feeling oneself to be observed by others.

self-consciousness *noun* being self-conscious.

self-contained *adj.* **1** *said of accommodation* of which no part is shared with others. **2** content to be on one's own; independent. **3** needing nothing added; complete.

self-control *noun* the ability to control one's emotions and impulses.

self-controlled *adj.* characterized by or showing self-control.

self-defence *noun* **1** the act or techniques of defending oneself from physical attack. **2** the act of defending one's own rights or principles.

self-denial *noun* the act or practice of denying one's own needs or wishes.

self-determination *noun* **1** the freedom to make one's own decisions without interference from others. **2** a nation's freedom to govern itself, without outside control.

self-drive *adj., said of a hired vehicle* to be driven by the hirer.

self-effacement *noun* being self-effacing.

self-effacing *adj.* tending to avoid making others aware of one's presence or one's achievements, because of shyness or modesty.

self-employed *adj.* working on one's own behalf and under one's own control, rather than as an employee.

self-esteem *noun* one's opinion, especially good opinion, of oneself; self-respect.

self-evident *adj.* clear enough to need no explanation or proof.

self-explanatory *adj.* easily understood; needing no further explanation.

self-fulfilling *adj., said of a forecast, etc* which, by virtue of its being made, has the effect of bringing about the results it predicts: *a self-fulfilling prophecy.*

self-governing *adj.* controlling itself, not controlled from outside by others.

self-government *noun* being self-governing.

self-harming *noun* the habitual practice of inflicting physical damage on oneself.

self-heal a perennial plant (*Prunella vulgaris*), widespread in Europe, with creeping rooting stems that carpet the ground. Its upright flowering shoots bear oval leaves and terminate in dense heads of violet-blue two-lipped flowers. Its name derives from the fact that it was formerly used as a medicinal herb.

self-help *noun* the practice of solving one's own problems using abilities developed in oneself, rather than relying on assistance from others.

self-importance *noun* being self-important; arrogance.

self-important *adj.* having an exaggerated sense of one's own importance; arrogant; pompous.

self-imposed *adj.* forced on oneself by oneself, not imposed by others.

self-indulgence *noun* being self-indulgent, or an instance of this.

self-indulgent *adj.* giving in, or tending to give in, to one's own wishes or whims.

self-inflicted *adj.* inflicted by oneself on oneself.

selfing *noun Biol.* self-fertilization, self-pollination.

self-interest *noun* one's own personal welfare or advantage.

self-interested *adj.* characterized by self-interest.

selfish *adj.* **1** tending to be concerned only with personal welfare, not the welfare of others. **2** *said of an act* revealing such a tendency.

selfishness *noun* being selfish, or an instance of this.

selfless *adj.* **1** tending to consider the welfare of others before one's own. **2** *said of an act* revealing such a tendency.

selflessness *noun* being selfless, or an instance of this.

self-made *adj.* having acquired wealth or achieved success through one's own efforts, rather than through advantages given by birth.

self-opinionated *adj.* tending to insist that one's own opinions, forcefully stated, are superior to all others.

self-pity *noun* excessive grumbling or moaning about one's own misfortunes.

self-pollination *noun Bot.* in flowering plants, the transfer of pollen from the anther of the stamen to the stigma of the same flower.

self-possessed *adj.* calm and controlled, especially in an emergency.

self-possession *noun* calmness.

self-preservation *noun* the protection of one's own life; the instinct underlying this.

self-raising *adj.*, *said of flour* containing an ingredient to make dough or pastry rise.

self-reliance *noun* reliance on one's own abilities and resources, etc.

self-reliant *adj.* never needing or seeking help from others; independent.

self-respect *noun* respect for oneself and concern for one's dignity and reputation.

self-respecting *adj.* having self-respect.

self-restraint *noun* the act of controlling, or the capacity to control, one's own desires or feelings.

Selfridge, Harry Gordon (1858–1947) US-born British merchant, born in Ripon, Wisconsin. He joined a trading firm in Chicago, and was made a junior partner in 1892. While visiting London in 1906, he bought a site in Oxford Street, where he built the large department store which bears his name (opened 1909).

self-righteous *adj.* having too high an opinion of one's own goodness, and intolerant of other people's faults.

self-righteousness *noun* being self-righteous.

self-sacrifice *noun* the sacrifice of one's own wishes or interests for the sake of other people's.

self-sacrificing *adj.* characterized by self-sacrifice.

selfsame *adj.* very same; identical.

self-satisfaction *noun* self-satisfying, being self-satisfied.

self-satisfied *adj.* feeling or showing complacent or arrogant satisfaction with oneself or one's achievements; smug.

self-sealing *adj.* **1** *said of an envelope* whose flap is coated with an adhesive which sticks without being moistened. **2** *said eg of a tyre* capable of automatically sealing small punctures.

self-seeker *noun* someone who looks mainly to their own interests or advantage.

self-seeking — *adj.* preoccupied with one's own interests and the opportunities for personal advantage. — *noun* behaviour of this kind.

self-service — *noun* a system, especially in catering, in which customers serve themselves and pay at a checkout. — *adj.*, *said of a restaurant, etc* operating such a system.

self-serving *adj.* benefiting or seeking to benefit oneself, often to the disadvantage of others.

self-starter *noun* **1** an electric starting device in a vehicle's engine. **2** *colloq.* a person who requires little supervision in a job, being able to motivate himself or herself and use his or her own initiative.

self-styled *adj.* called or considered so only by oneself: *a self-styled superstar.*

self-sufficiency *noun* being self-sufficient.

self-sufficient *adj.*, *said of a person or thing* able to provide oneself or itself with everything needed to live on or survive.

self-supporting *adj.* **1** earning enough money to meet all one's own expenses. **2** self-sufficient. **3** needing no additional supports or attachments to stay firmly fixed or upright.

self-willed *adj.* strongly or stubbornly determined to do or have what one wants.

Selina a female first name. [of uncertain origin; perhaps from Greek *selene*, moon]

Seljuqs *or* **Seljuks** a family of Turkish mercenary soldiers that rose to conquer much of Asia Minor in the 11c–12c. Converts to the Muslim faith, they became sultans in the area of present-day Syria and E Turkey. Their decline in the 13c

was brought on by Mongol pressure from the east and their defeat at Kösedagh (1243).

Selkirk *or* **Selcraig, Alexander** (1676–1721) Scottish sailor, born in Largo, Fife, whose story suggested that of Daniel Defoe's *Robinson Crusoe*. He joined the South Sea buccaneers, quarrelled with his captain, and at his own request was put ashore on the island of Juan Fernández (1704). He lived there alone until 1709, when he was discovered and brought back to Britain.

sell — *verb* (PAST TENSE AND PAST PARTICIPLE **sold**) **1** to give to someone in exchange for money: *she sold it to her brother / can I sell you a crate of whisky?* **2** to have available for buying. **3** (**sell at** *or* **for something**) to be available for buying at a specified price. **4** *intrans.* to be bought by customers; to be in demand. **5** to cause to be bought; to promote the sale of: *the author's name sells the book.* **6** to persuade (someone) to acquire or agree to something, especially by emphasizing its merits or advantages: *it was difficult to sell them the idea.* **7** (**sell one thing for another**) to lose or betray (eg one's principles) in the process of getting something (especially dishonourable). — *noun* **1** the style of persuasion used in selling: *the hard sell.* **2** *colloq.* a trick or deception. — **sell someone down the river** *colloq.* to betray them. **sell something off** to sell remaining goods quickly and cheaply. **sell out of something** to sell one's entire stock of it. **sell out to someone** to betray one's principles or associates to another party: *he sold out to the opposition.* **sell someone** *or* **something short** *colloq.* to understate their good qualities. **sell up** to sell one's house or business. [from Anglo-Saxon *sellan*, to hand over]

Sellafield, formerly **Windscale** a nuclear power plant in Cumbria, NW England, on the Irish Sea coast, W of Gosforth. It processes and discharges nuclear waste which is divided into the three categories of high, intermediate, and low waste. These categories are treated in different ways: the first is turned from liquid into glass blocks by a process called vitrification and stored on site; the second (solids) is mixed with concrete and stored in stainless steel on site; the third (gloves etc) is compacted and stored underground at a nearby village. In 1993 the government authorized BNFL's introduction of the Thorp nuclear reprocessing plant at Sellafield, despite vigorous opposition from Greenpeace.

sell-by date a date on a manufacturer's or distributor's label indicating when goods, especially foods, are considered no longer fit to be sold.

seller *noun* a person who sells or is selling something.

Sellers, Peter (1925–80) English actor and comedian, born in Southsea. He worked as a stand-up comic and impressionist then entered radio and performed with Spike Milligan, Harry Secombe, and Michael Bentine in the *Goon Show* (1951–9). One of the stalwarts of British film comedy in the 1950s and 1960s, he was acclaimed in *The Ladykillers* (1955) and *I'm Alright Jack*, and established his international reputation with *Lolita* (1962) and *Dr Strangelove* (1963). Perhaps best remembered for playing the incompetent French detective Inspector Clouseau in the *Pink Panther* films (1963–77), he received an Academy Award nomination for *Being There* (1979).

seller's market *Commerce* a situation where demand exceeds supply and sellers may control the price of a commodity, product, etc. The term is frequently applied in the housing market.

Sellotape — *noun* *trademark* a type of transparent adhesive tape, especially for use on paper. — *verb* to stick with Sellotape.

sell-out *noun* an event for which all the tickets have been sold.

sell-through *noun* retail sale, especially of video cassettes.

Selous Game Reserve a game reserve established upon the Rufiji R system, central Tanzania, in 1905. The park, which is still largely unexplored, is noted for the variety of its scenery and wildlife. It is a World Heritage site.

selvage *or* **selvedge** *noun* an edge of a length of fabric woven so as to prevent fraying. [from SELF + EDGE]

selves see SELF.

Selwyn a male first name, after the surname. [of obscure origin; Anglo-Saxon and Norman sources have been suggested]

Selwyn-Lloyd, (John) Selwyn (Brooke) Lloyd, Baron (1904–78) English Conservative politician, born in the Wirral. In 1930 he became a barrister, and practised in Liverpool. He became an MP in 1945 and was appointed Minister of State (1951), Supply (1954–5), and Defence (1955). As Foreign Secretary (1955–60) he defended Anthony Eden's policy on Suez, and as Chancellor of the Exchequer he introduced the 'pay pause' (1960–2). He was then appointed Lord Privy Seal and Leader of the House (1963–4), and Speaker of the House of Commons (1971–6).

Selznick, David O(liver) (1902–65) US film producer, born in Pittsburgh. After working for M-G-M and RKO, he founded his own company in 1937, which at its peak made *Gone with the Wind* (1939). His other works included *Rebecca* (1940), *The Third Man* (1949), and *A Farewell to Arms* (1957).

SEM *abbrev.* *Maths.* standard error of the mean.

semantic *adj.* of or relating to meaning. [from Greek *semantikos*, significant]

semantically *adv.* in a semantic way; in terms of semantics.

semantics *sing. noun* the branch of linguistics that deals with meaning.

semaphore — *noun* **1** a system of signalling in which flags, or simply the arms, are held in positions that represent individual letters and numbers. **2** a signalling device, especially a pole with arms that can be set in different positions. — *verb trans., intrans.* to signal using semaphore or a semaphore. [from Greek *sema*, sign + *-phoros*, bearer]

◇ Semaphore was widely used in visual telegraphy, especially at sea, before the advent of electricity. Old-style railway signals are a simple form of semaphore, with a single arm having two positions to indicate 'stop' and 'go'.

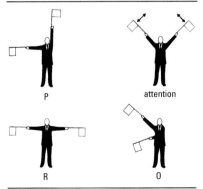

semaphore

Semarang POP (1990e) 1.2m, a fishing port and the capital of Java Tengah province, central Java, Indonesia. It has a large Chinese population. NOTABLE FEATURES Gedung Batu Cave; Mudu War Memorial; Klinteng Sam Poo Kong Temple.

semblance *noun* **1** appearance, especially superficial or deceiving. **2** a hint or trace. [from Old French *sembler*, to seem]

Semele in Greek mythology, the daughter of Cadmus, and mother by Zeus of Dionysus. She asked Zeus to appear in his divine glory before her, and was consumed in fire. Her unborn son (Dionysus) was made immortal.

semen *noun* a thick whitish liquid containing sperm, ejaculated by the penis. See also SEMINAL. [from Latin *semen*, seed]

semester *noun* an academic term lasting half an academic year. [from Latin *semestris*, six-monthly]

semi *noun* (PL. **semis**) *colloq.* a semi-detached house.

semi- *prefix* forming words meaning: **1** half: *semiquaver.* **2** partly: *semiconscious.* **3** occurring twice in the stated period: *semiannual.* [from Latin *semi*, half]

semi-automatic *adj.* **1** partially automatic. **2** *said of a firearm* continuously reloading bullets, but only firing one at a time.

semibreve *noun* the longest musical note in common use, equal to half a breve, two minims, or four crotchets.

semicircle *noun* **1** one half of a circle. **2** an arrangement in this form.

semicircular *adj.* having the form of a semicircle.

semicircular canal *Anat.* in the inner ear of mammals, one of the three fluid-filled semicircular tubes that are involved in the maintenance of balance.

semicolon *noun* a punctuation mark (;) indicating a pause stronger than that marked by a comma and weaker than that marked by a full stop. Its principal use is to separate clauses, as in *We will bring the drink; you can provide the food.*

semiconductor *noun Electron.* a crystalline material that behaves either as an electrical conductor or as an insulator, depending on the temperature and the purity of the material, eg silicon, germanium. Semiconductors are used to make diodes, transistors, photoelectric devices, etc.
◇ The electrical conductivity of a semiconductor can be increased by raising the temperature or by adding small amounts of impurities (*doping*), such as arsenic or boron. Some impurities increase the number of electrons (negative charges) available for carrying current, to give an *n*-type semiconductor. Others reduce the number of electrons, creating 'holes' in the semiconductor that behave like positive charges and also enable a current to flow, giving a *p*-type semiconductor.
A semiconductor diode consists of a single piece of silicon, one half of which is doped as *n*-type and the other half as *p*-type, that allows current to pass through it in one direction only. A transistor consists of three differently doped regions (*p*-*n*-*p* or *n*-*p*-*n*). Semiconductors are used in the form of silicon chips in the integrated circuits of computers, calculators, automatic control systems, etc.

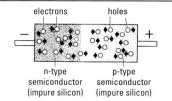

electrons · holes

n-type semiconductor (impure silicon) · p-type semiconductor (impure silicon)

semiconductor diode

semi-detached — *adj.*, *said of a house* forming part of the same building with another house on one side. — *noun* a semi-detached house.

semi-final *noun* in competitions, either of two matches, the winners of which play each other in the final.

semi-finalist *noun* a competitor who qualifies for a semi-final.

seminal *adj.* **1** highly original and at the root of a trend or movement: *seminal writings.* **2** of or relating to seed, semen, or reproduction in general. [from Latin *semen semin*, seed]

seminally *adv.* in a seminal way.

seminar *noun* **1** a small class for the discussion of a particular topic between students and a tutor. **2** any meeting set up for the purpose of discussion. [from Latin *seminarium*, seed-plot]

seminarian *noun* **1** a student in a seminary or in a seminar. **2** a Roman Catholic priest educated in a foreign seminary. **3** a teacher in a seminary.

seminary *noun* (PL. **seminaries**) **1** a college for the training of members of the clergy. **2** *old use* a school, especially for girls. [see SEMINAR]

seminiferous tubule *Anat.* in mammals, any of many long tightly coiled tubules that form the bulk of the testes, and in which the sperm are produced. [from Latin *semen semin-*, seed]

Seminole a Muskogean-speaking Native American group of SE USA, descended from Creeks who settled in Florida in the late 18c. They fought whites encroaching on their territory and eventually surrendered to US troops in the 1820s and 1830s, and moved to reservations in Oklahoma.

semiology *noun* same as SEMIOTICS.

semiotic *adj.* **1** relating to signs and symbols. **2** relating to semiotics. **3** relating to or resembling symptoms of disease.

semiotics *sing. noun* the study of human communication, especially the relationship between words and the objects or concepts they refer to. [from Greek *semeiotikos*, of signs; *semeion*, sign + -LOGY]
◇ Semiotics is a multi-disciplinary area of study which has its roots in the pioneering work on language by the Swiss linguist Ferdinand de Saussure and the US philosopher C S Peirce. It is often divided into three main branches: *syntax*, the study of how linguistic items can be transformed into other linguistic items; *semantics*, the study of meaning and reference; and *pragmatics*, the study of how context affects linguistic interpretation.

Semipalatinsk, formerly **Semipalatka** POP (1991e) 345 000, the river-port capital of Semipalatinsk region, NE Kazakhstan. It is situated on the R Irtysh and was founded as a fortress in 1718.

semi-permeable *adj.* **1** only partly permeable. **2** *Biol.* denoting a membrane through which only certain molecules can pass, eg it may be permeable to water but impermeable to sugars and salts.

semi-precious *adj.*, *said of a gem* considered less valuable than a precious stone.

semi-professional — *adj.* **1** engaging only part-time in a professional activity. **2** *said of an activity* engaged in only as a part-time profession. — *noun* a semi-professional person.

semiquaver *noun* a musical note equal to half a quaver or one-sixteenth of a semibreve.

Semiramis in Greek mythology, a queen of Assyria, who was the wife of Onnes and then Ninus. Later she reigned alone, and founded many cities including Nineveh and Babylon.

semi-skilled *adj.* having or requiring a degree of training less advanced than that needed for specialised work.

Semites a group of peoples found in SW Asia. In antiquity they included the Ammonites, Amorites, Assyrians, Babylonians, Canaanites, and Phoenicians. The most prominent modern Semitic peoples include the Jews and the Arabs.

Semitic — *noun* any of a group of Afro-Asiatic languages that includes Hebrew, Arabic, and Aramaic. — *adj.* **1** relating to or speaking any such language. **2** relating to Semites. **3** relating to the Jews; Jewish.

semitone *noun* half a tone in the musical scale, the interval between adjacent notes on a keyboard instrument.

semi-tropical *adj.* subtropical.

semivowel *noun* **1** a speech sound having the qualities of both a vowel and a consonant, such as the sounds represented by the letters *y* and *w*. **2** a letter representing such a sound.

Semmelweis, Ignaz Philipp (1818–65) Hungarian obstetrician, born in Buda (now Budapest). From 1845 he worked in the first obstetrical clinic of the Vienna general hospital, and introduced antiseptics with positive results, although his ideas met with much opposition. In the later bacteriological age he came to be seen as a pioneer of antiseptic obstetrics.

semolina *noun* hard particles of wheat not ground into flour during milling, used to thicken soups and make puddings. [from Italian *semolino*, diminutive of *semola*, bran]

Semper, Gottfried (1803–79) German architect and theorist, born in Hamburg. He was Professor at the Dresden Academy (1834–49), taught in Zürich (1855–71), and then worked in Vienna. His designs include the Dresden Opera House (1837–41, rebuilt 1878). He also wrote the influential *Der Stil in den technischen und tektonischen Kunsten* (Style in the Technical and Tectonic Arts, 1860–3).

Semtex *noun trademark* a powerful type of plastic explosive.

SEN *abbrev.* State Enrolled Nurse.

Sen. *abbrev.* **1** senate. **2** senator. **3** senior.

Senanayake, Don Stephen (1884–1952) Sri Lankan statesman, born in Colombo. After working on his father's rubber estate, he entered the Legislative Council in 1922, founded the co-operative society movement in 1923, and was elected to the State Council in 1931, where he was Minister of Agriculture for 15 years. Following independence, he became Prime Minister (1947–52), as well as Minister of Defence and External Affairs.

senate *noun* (*often* **Senate**) **1** the chief legislative and administrative body in ancient Rome. **2** a law-making body, especially the upper chamber of the national assembly in the USA, Australia, and other countries. **3** the governing council in some British universities. [from Latin *senatus*, from *senex*, old man]
◇ The Roman Senate was an advisory body, first to the kings, then the consuls, and finally the emperor. Its members were drawn from the patrician class; later in the Republic it was made up of ex-magistrates.
The US Senate is made up of 100 members, presided over by the Vice President. Each state is represented by two senators; two thirds are elected to serve for six years with the remainder chosen every two years. It has the power of 'advice and consent' on presidential treaties and appointments.

senator *noun* (*often* **Senator**) a member of a senate.

senatorial *adj.* **1** relating to or characteristic of a senator. **2** made up of senators.

send *verb* (PAST TENSE AND PAST PARTICIPLE **sent**) **1** to cause or order to go or be conveyed or transmitted. **2** to force or propel: *sent me flying.* **3** to cause to become or pass into a specified state: *sent him into fits of laughter / sent me mad.* **4** to bring about, especially by divine providence: *a plague sent by God.* **5** *old slang use* to put into a state of ecstasy; to thrill.

— **send away for something** to order goods by post.

send someone down 1 *colloq.* to send them to prison. **2** to expel them from university.

send for someone to ask or order them to come; to summon them.

send for something to order it to be brought or delivered.

send something in to offer or submit it by post.

send someone off to dismiss them, especially from the field of play in sport.

send something off to dispatch it, especially by post.

send off for something to order goods by post.

send something on 1 to re-address and re-post a letter, etc; to forward it. **2** to post or send it, so as to arrive in advance of oneself.

send something out 1 to distribute it by post. **2** to dispatch it.

send someone out for something to send them to fetch it.

send someone or **something up** *Brit. colloq.* to ridicule or parody them.

[from Anglo-Saxon *sendan*]

Sendai POP (1991e) 931 000, the capital of Miyagi prefecture, NE Honshu, Japan. It is situated on W Ishinomaki-wan Bay. The town is a base for tours to local hot springs and spas.

sender *noun* **1** a person who sends something, especially by post. **2** a transmitting device.

Sendero Luminoso (Shining Path) a Maoist rural guerrilla movement of uncompromisingly revolutionary character operating in the Peruvian central Andes (and also capable of mounting terrorist actions in cities) in the 1980s and 1990s. In September 1992 its leader Abimael Guzman was captured and sentenced to life imprisonment.

send-off *noun* a display of good wishes from an assembled crowd to a departing person or group.

send-up *noun Brit. colloq.* a parody or satire.

Seneca, Lucius Annaeus, also called **the Younger** (c.5 BC–AD 65) Roman philosopher, statesman, and author, born in Córdoba, Spain, the son of Seneca (the Elder). He was banished to Corsica (41–9) by Claudius and recalled by Agrippina, who entrusted him with the education of her son Nero. Made consul by Nero in 57, his high moral aims gradually incurred the Emperor's displeasure, and he withdrew from public life. Drawn into conspiracy, he was condemned, and committed suicide in Rome. The publication of his *Tenne Tragedies* in 1581 was important in the evolution of Elizabethan drama, which took from them the five-act division.

Seneca an Iroquois-speaking Native American group, who settled in present-day W New York State and E Ohio. A member of the Iroquois League, they expanded through warfare in the 17c, and supported the British during the American Revolution, which led to the destruction of their villages by US troops, and their settlement on reservations in 1797. The present-day population is c.4 600.

Senefelder, Aloys (1771–1834) Bavarian inventor, born in Prague. He became an actor and playwright, and accidentally discovered the technique of lithography by using a grease pencil on limestone (1796). After various trials he opened an establishment of his own in Munich.

Senegal, official name **Republic of Senegal**, French **République du Sénégal** POP (1992e) 7.7m, a country in W Africa, divided into 10 regions. AREA 196 840sq km/75 980sq mi. It is bounded N by Mauritania, E by Mali, S by Guinea and Guinea-Bissau, W by the Atlantic Ocean, and surrounds The Gambia on three sides. CAPITAL Dakar. CHIEF TOWNS Thiès, Kaolack, St Louis, Ziguinchor. TIME ZONE GMT. The population consists mainly of Wolof (36%), Fulani (17.5%), and Serer (16.5%) groups; Islam is the chief religion with most of the remainder of the population following local beliefs. OFFICIAL LANGUAGE French. CURRENCY the franc CFA. PHYSICAL DESCRIPTION the most westerly country in Africa; the coast is characterized by dunes, mangrove forests, and mudbanks; an extensive low-lying basin of savannah and semi-desert vegetation lies to the N; seasonal streams drain to the R Sénégal; the S rises to c.500m. CLIMATE tropical with a rainy season between Jun and Sep; high humidity levels and high night-time temperatures, especially on the coast; rainfall decreases from the S (1 000–1 500mm) to the N (300–350mm); the average annual rainfall at Dakar is 541mm and the average temperature ranges from 22°C to 28°C. HISTORY part of the Mali Empire in the 14c–15c; the French established a fort at Saint-Louis in 1659; incorporated as a territory within French West Africa in 1902; became an autonomous state within the French community in 1958; joined with French Sudan as the independent Federation of Mali in 1959; withdrew in 1960 to become a separate independent republic; joined with The Gambia to form the Confederation of Senegambia in 1982–9. GOVERNMENT governed by a President (elected for a five-year term), Prime Minister, Cabinet, and 120-member National Assembly. ECONOMY mainly agricultural, employing c.75% of the workforce; groundnuts, cotton, sugar, millet, sorghum, manioc, maize, rice, livestock; phosphate, titanium, zirconium, iron ore, gold, oil, natural gas, salt; fishing; timber; agricultural processing; textiles; chemicals; cement; footwear; shipbuilding and repairing; tourism.

Senegal

Sénégal, River a river in W Africa. The upper course above Bafoulabé is known as the R Bafing. Its length including the Bafing is 1 635km/1 016mi and it is navigable as far as Bafing at high water. The river rises in the Fouta Djallon Massif (Guinea), and flows N and NW, forming the N frontier of Senegal with Mauritania. It enters the Atlantic Ocean at St Louis.

Senegambia, Confederation of an association between The Gambia and Senegal, begun in 1982. It was designed to integrate military, economic, communications, and foreign policies, and to establish joint institutions while preserving independence and sovereignty. It proved to be of limited value, and was ended by mutual agreement in 1989.

senescence *noun Biol.* the changes that take place in a living organism during the process of ageing, eg the production of flowers and fruit in plants. Different parts of an organism do not necessarily age at the same rate, eg senescent leaves are shed by deciduous trees in the autumn.

senescent *adj. formal* growing old; ageing. [from Latin *senescere*, to grow old]

seneschal *noun* a steward in charge of the household or estate of a medieval lord or prince. [from Old French, = old servant]

senile *adj.* **1** displaying the feebleness of mind or body brought on by old age. **2** of or caused by old age. [from Latin *senilis*, from *senex*, old]

senile dementia mental deterioration brought on by old age.

senility *noun* **1** old age. **2** mental deterioration in old age.

senior — *adj.* **1** (*often* **senior to someone**) **a** older than someone. **b** higher in rank or authority than someone. **2** of or for schoolchildren over the age of 11. **3** *North Amer.* of final-year college or university students. **4** older than a person of the same name, especially distinguishing parent from child: *James Smith, Senior.* — *noun* **1** a person who is older or of a higher rank. **2** a pupil in a senior school, or in the senior part of a school. **3** *North Amer.* a final-year student. [from Latin *senior*, older]

senior citizen an elderly person, especially one retired.

seniority *noun* **1** the state of being senior. **2** a privileged position earned through long service in a profession or with a company.

senior service (*usually* **the senior service**) the Royal Navy.

Senna, Ayrton (1960–94) Brazilian racing driver, born in Sao Paulo. His first Grand Prix was in Brazil in 1984 with the Toleman team. He was then with Lotus (1985–7), and McLaren (1988–). He was Formula One world champion in 1988, 1990, and 1991, but lost his title to Nigel Mansell in 1992. He was killed when he crashed during the San Marino Grand Prix.

senna *noun* **1** any of a family of tropical trees and shrubs that produce long seed pods. **2** a laxative prepared from the dried pods. [from Arabic *sana*]

Sennacherib (d.681 BC) King of Assyria (704–681 BC), the son of Sargon II and grandfather of Assurbanipal. He is known mainly for his conquest of Babylon (689 BC), and his rebuilding of the city of Nineveh. He figures prominently in the Old Testament, because of his attack on Jerusalem.

Sennett, Mack, originally **Michell Sinott** (1880–1960) US film producer, born in Richmond, Quebec. He worked in the theatre as a comic in burlesque companies, and from 1908 in silent films. He later formed his own company and made hundreds of shorts, establishing a whole generation of players and a tradition of knockabout slapstick under the name of Keystone Komics (1912) and later the Sennett Bathing Beauties (1920). He received a Special Academy Award in 1937.

sensation *noun* **1** awareness of an external or internal stimulus, eg heat, pain, or emotions, as a result of its perception by sensory receptors or sense organs of the nervous system, and subsequent interpretation by the brain. **2** a physical feeling: *a burning sensation in my mouth.* **3** an emotion or general feeling. **4** a sudden widespread feeling of excitement or shock; also, the cause of this. [from Latin *sensatio*, from *sentire*, to feel]

sensational *adj.* **1** causing, or intended to cause, widespread excitement, intense interest, or shock. **2** *colloq.* excellent; marvellous. **3** of the senses.

sensationalism *noun* the practice of, or methods used in, deliberately setting out to cause widespread excitement, intense interest, or shock.

sensationalist *noun* **1** a person who aims to cause a sensation. **2** a person who believes that the senses are the ultimate source of all knowledge.

sensationally *adv.* in a sensational way.

sense — *noun* **1** any of the faculties used by an animal to obtain information about its external or internal environment. The five main senses are

sight, hearing, smell, taste, and touch, and in most vertebrates these stimuli are received and recognized by specialized sense organs that relay sensory information to the brain for interpretation. **2** an awareness or appreciation of, or an ability to make judgements regarding, some specified thing: *sense of direction / bad business sense*. **3** (*often* **senses**) soundness of mind; reasonableness: *lost his senses*. **4** wisdom; practical worth: *no sense in doing it now*. **5** a general feeling, not perceived using any of the five natural powers: *a sense of guilt*. **6** overall meaning: *understood the sense of the passage, if not all the words*. **7** specific meaning. **8** general opinion; consensus: *the sense of the meeting*. — *verb* **1** to detect a stimulus by means of any of the five main senses. **2** to be aware of something by means other than the five main senses: *sensed that someone was following me*. **3** to realize or comprehend.
— **come to one's senses 1** to act sensibly after a period of foolishness. **2** to regain consciousness.
in a sense in one respect; in a way.
make sense 1 to be able to be understood. **2** to be wise or reasonable.
[from Latin *sensus*, from *sentire*, to feel]

Sense and Sensibility a novel by Jane Austen (1811). Her first published novel, it describes the life and loves of the contrasting Dashwood sisters.

sense-datum *noun* (PL. **sense-data**) that which is received immediately through the stimulation of a sense organ, unaffected by inference or other knowledge. It is how a thing appears to be to one person, not how it really is, nor how it appears to someone else. Hallucinations and dreams are therefore included in the definition of sense-data.

senseless *adj.* **1** unconscious. **2** unwise; foolish.

senselessly *adv.* in a senseless way.

senselessness *noun* being senseless.

sense organ *Physiol.* in animals, any organ consisting of specialized receptor cells that are capable of responding to a particular stimulus, eg light, sound, smell. In mammals the main sense organs are the eyes, ears, nose, skin, and taste buds of the tongue.

sensibility *noun* (PL. **sensibilities**) **1** the ability to feel or have sensations. **2** the capacity to be affected emotionally; sensitivity: *sensibility to his grief*. **3** (**sensibilities**) feelings, when easily offended or hurt. [see SENSIBLE]

sensible *adj.* **1** wise; having or showing reasonableness or good judgement. **2** perceptible by the senses. **3** able to feel; sensitive: *sensible to pain*. [from Latin *sensibilis*]

sensibly *adv.* in a sensible way.

sensitive *adj.* **1** responding readily, strongly, or painfully: *sensitive to our feelings*. **2** able to feel or respond. **3** easily upset or offended. **4** about which there is much strong feeling or difference of opinion: *sensitive issues*. **5** *said of documents, etc* not for public discussion or scrutiny, eg because involving matters of national security or embarrassing to the government. **6** *said of scientific instruments* reacting to or recording very small changes. **7** *Photog.* responding to the action of light. **8** *Physics* responding to the action of some force or stimulus: *pressure-sensitive*. [from Latin *sensitivus*, from *sentire*, to feel]

sensitively *adv.* in a sensitive way.

sensitive plant a perennial plant (*Mimosa pudica*), native to S America, a common weed in tropical regions, and often cultivated in cooler climates as a novelty. It has a prickly stem, and leaves divided into narrow leaflets. The leaves close up at night, and this response can also be triggered at greater speed by touching the plant. After a short period the leaflets return to their original position.

sensitivity *noun* **1** a sensitive quality or inclination. **2** being sensitive or reacting to an allergen, drug, or other external stimulus. **3** the readiness and delicacy of an instrument in recording changes.

sensitization *or* **sensitisation** *noun* sensitizing or being sensitized.

sensitize *or* **sensitise** *verb* to make sensitive.

sensor *noun Electr.* any device that detects or measures a change in a physical quantity, eg temperature, light, or sound, usually by converting it into an electrical signal. Examples of sensors include burglar alarms, smoke detectors, microphones, and photocells.

sensory *adj.* of the senses or sensation. [from Latin *sensorium*, brain, seat of the senses]

sensory nerve *Anat.* a nerve that relays nerve impulses from sensory receptor cells and sense organs to the central nervous system (the brain and spinal cord). [from Latin *sensorius*, from Latin *sentire* to feel]

sensual *adj.* **1** of the senses and the body rather than the mind or the spirit. **2** suggesting, enjoying, or providing physical (especially sexual) pleasure. **3** pursuing physical pleasures, especially those derived from sex or food and drink. [from Latin *sensus*, sense]
◆ Often confused with *sensuous*.

sensuality *noun* **1** the quality of being sensual. **2** indulgence in physical pleasures.

sensuous *adj.* **1** appealing to or designed to stimulate the senses aesthetically, with no suggestion of sexual pleasure. **2** pleasing to the senses. **3** very aware of what is perceived by the senses. [from Latin *sensus*, sense]
◆ Often confused with *sensual*.

sensuously *adv.* in a sensuous way.

sensuousness *noun* being sensuous.

sent see SEND.

sentence — *noun* **1** a sequence of words forming a meaningful and more or less complete grammatical structure, usually with a subject and verb and making a statement, asking a question, or making an exclamation. In the Roman and other European alphabets, a written or printed sentence usually begins with a capital letter and ends with a full stop, question mark, or exclamation mark. **2** a punishment determined by a court or judge; its announcement in court. — *verb* **1** to announce the punishment to be given to (someone). **2** to condemn to a punishment: *sentenced him to five years' imprisonment*.
— **pass sentence on someone** to announce the punishment to be given to someone.
[from Latin *sententia*, opinion]

sententious *adj.* **1** tending to lecture others on morals. **2** full of, or fond of using, sayings or proverbs. [from Latin *sententiosus*, full of meaning]

sententiousness *noun* being sententious.

sentience *noun* being sentient.

sentient *adj.* able to feel; capable of sensation: *sentient beings*. [from Latin *sentire*, to feel]

sentiment *noun* **1** an emotion, especially when expressed. **2** emotion or emotional behaviour in general, especially when considered excessive, self-indulgent, or insincere. **3** (*often* **sentiments**) an opinion or view. [from Latin *sentimentum*, from *sentire*, to feel]

sentimental *adj.* **1** easily feeling and expressing tender emotions, especially love, friendship, and pity. **2** provoking or designed to provoke such emotions, especially in large measure and without subtlety. **3** closely associated with, or moved (to tears) by, fond memories of the past: *objects of sentimental value*.

sentimentalism *noun* sentimentality.

sentimentalist *noun* a person who indulges in sentimentalism.

sentimentality *noun* **1** a sentimental quality or inclination. **2** a tendency to indulge in sentiment or to affect fine feelings.

sentimentalize *or* **sentimentalise** *verb* **1** *intrans.* to behave sentimentally. **2** *trans.* to react to emotionally, rather than taking a frank and practical approach.

Sentimental Journey, A, in full **A Sentimental Journey through France and Italy** a novel by Laurence Sterne (1768). His second and last, it is a comic travel book narrated by Parson Yorick.

sentimentally *adv.* in a sentimental way.

sentimental novel a type of fiction, popular in the 18c, concerned with the idea that honourable and moral behaviour (especially of a virtuous heroine) would be justly rewarded. Examples include Samuel Richardson's *Pamela* (1740) and *Clarissa* (1747–8), and Oliver Goldsmith's *The Vicar of Wakefield* (1766).

sentinel *noun* a sentry. [from French *sentinelle*]

sentry *noun* (PL. **sentries**) a soldier or other person on guard to control entry or passage.

sentry-box *noun* a small open-fronted shelter for a sentry.

Seoul *or* **Sŏul** POP (1990) 10.6m, special city and capital of South Korea, in the Han River Valley. HISTORY founded in the 14c; called Hanyang until the 20c; seat of the Yi Dynasty government from 1392 to 1910; badly damaged in the Korean War. NOTABLE FEATURES Kyongbok-kung Palace (14c, rebuilt in 1867), including the National Museum and National Folk Museum; Ch'angdö-kung Palace (1405, rebuilt in 1611); Toksu-kung Palace, including the Museum of Modern Art; Chongmyo (ancestral tablets of the Yi Dynasty); Namdaemun (Great South Gate, reconstructed in 1448); Pagoda Park; Seoul Grand Park; Seoul Land (South Korean version of Disneyland).

Sep *or* **Sep.** *abbrev.* September.

sepal *noun Bot.* in a flower, one of the modified leaves, usually green but sometimes brightly coloured, that together form the *calyx* which surrounds the petals and protects the developing flower bud. [from French *sépale*]

separability *noun* being separable.

separable *adj.* able to be separated. [from Latin *separabilis*]

separate — *verb* (pronounced -rate) **1** to set, take, keep, or force apart (from others or each other). **2** *intrans.* to move apart; to become detached; to cease to be or live together. **3** (*also* **separate up**) to divide or become divided into parts. — *adj.* (pronounced -rət) **1** distinctly different or individual; unrelated: *a separate issue*. **2** physically unattached; isolated. — *noun* (pronounced -rət) (*usually* **separates**) a piece of clothing intended for wear with a variety of others, not forming part of a suit. [from Latin *separare*]

separateness *noun* being separate.

Separate Tables a play by Terence Rattigan (1954), subdivided into two one-act plays: *Table by the Window* and *Table Number Seven*. Set in a hotel dining-room, it examines emotional inadequacies and social isolation in the lives of the guests.

separation *noun* **1** the act of separating or the state or process of being separated. **2** a place or line where there is a division. **3** a gap or interval that separates. **4** an arrangement, approved mutually or by a court, under which a husband and wife live apart while remaining married, usually prior to divorce.

separation of powers a political doctrine which argues that, to avoid tyranny, the three branches of government (legislature, executive, and judiciary) should be separated as far as possible, with their relationships governed by checks and balances. The US Constitution is an example of an attempt at separation of all three powers, while parliamentary systems such as that of the UK do not have complete separation of legislature and executive.

separatism *noun* **1** a tendency to separate or to be separate. **2** support for separation. **3** the practices and principles of separatists.

Séparatisme a French-Canadian independence movement which has played a significant role in Canadian politics since the 1960s. One of the largest groups was the *Rassemblement Démocratique pour l'Indépendence* which was important in the 1966 defeat of Jean Lesage (1912–80), and gained strength after the defeat of the *Parti Québecois* by the Liberals (1985). Initially the federal government responded with such initiatives as the Royal Commission on Bilingualism and Biculturalism. As Liberal Prime Minister (1968–79 and 1980–4), Pierre Trudeau (1919–) reasserted the tradition of tolerant Canadianism for which Sir Wilfrid Laurier (1841–1919) had stood, in the hope that the province might be prevented from becoming racist and introverted.

separatist *noun* a person who encourages, or takes action to achieve, independence from a country or an established institution, eg a Church.

Separatists a Christian group founded (1580) in England by Robert Browne, and exiled to Holland. Critical of the 'impure' national Church, they sought to model theirs on the New Testament concept of the gathered church of Christians, a belief that influenced Congregationalism.

separator *noun* a person, thing, or machine that separates.

sepek takraw a court game popular in SE Asia, played on a badminton court by two teams of three players with a rattan palm ball. The ball is propelled over a central net using any part of the body other than the arms and hands. [from Malay *sepek*, kick + Thai *takraw*, rattan ball]

Sephardim the descendants of the Jews who lived in Spain and Portugal before 1492, when they were expelled for not accepting Christianity and became refugees in N Africa, Turkey, and Italy. Subsequently they migrated to N Europe and the Americas, where during the 16c–17c they kept distinct from other Jews (especially those from central Europe) and became noted for their cultural achievements. They preserved their own rituals, customs, dialect (Ladino), and pronunciation of Hebrew. [Hebrew, = Spaniards]

sepia *noun* **1** a yellowish-brown tint used in photography. **2** a dark reddish-brown colour. **3** a pigment of this colour, obtained from a fluid secreted by the cuttlefish. [from Greek *sepia*, cuttlefish]

sepoy *noun Hist.* an Indian soldier in service with a European (especially British) army. [from Urdu and Persian *sipahi*, horseman]

sepsis (PL. **sepses**) *noun Medicine* the presence of disease-causing micro-organisms, especially viruses or bacteria, and their toxins in the body tissues, which can result in infection, inflammation, and eventual destruction of the affected areas. [from Greek *sepsis*, putrefaction]

Sept *or* **Sept.** *abbrev.* **1** September. **2** Septuagint.

sept *noun* a clan, especially in Ireland. [an alteration of SECT]

septa see SEPTUM.

September *noun* the ninth month of the year. [from Latin *September*, seventh, ie the seventh month in the original Roman calendar]

septennial *adj.* **1** occurring once every seven years. **2** lasting seven years. [from Latin *septem*, seven + *annus*, year]

septet *noun* **1** a group of seven musicians. **2** a piece of music for seven performers. **3** any group or set of seven. [from Latin *septem*, seven]

septic *adj.* **1** *Medicine, said of a wound* contaminated with disease-causing bacteria. **2** putrefying. [from Greek *septikos*; related to SEPSIS]

septicaemia *noun* blood-poisoning. [from Greek *septikos*, putrefied + *haima*, blood]

septic tank a tank, usually underground, in which sewage is broken down by the action of bacteria.

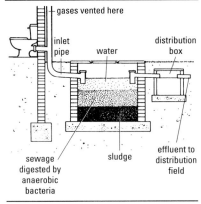

septic tank

septuagenarian — *adj.* between 70 and 79 years old. — *noun* a septuagenarian person. [from Latin *septuaginta*, seventy]

Septuagesima *noun* the third Sunday before Lent, apparently so called by analogy with Quadragesima and Quinquagesima; the 70th day (in fact, the 64th day) before Easter. [from Latin *septuagesimus*, seventieth]

Septuagint a translation into Greek of the Hebrew Bible, named from a legend in the *Letter of Aristeas* (2c BC) which described it as the work of 72 scholars, six from each of the 12 tribes of Israel. Begun c.3c BC, it was for the Greek-speaking Jews in the Diaspora. It has a different order of books from that in the Hebrew canon, and also contains some works not in that canon. When it was adopted by Christians as their preferred version of the Old Testament, it lost favour among the Jews. [from Latin *septuaginta*, 70]

septum *noun* (PL. **septa**) *Anat.* any partition between cavities, eg nostrils, or areas of soft tissue. [from Latin *saeptum*, fence]

septuple — *adj.* being seven times as much or as many; sevenfold. — *verb trans., intrans.* to multiply or increase sevenfold. [from Latin *septuplus*]

septuplet *noun* any of seven children born at the same time to the same mother.

sepulchral *adj.* **1** of a tomb; of burial. **2** suggestive of death or burial; gloomy; funereal.

sepulchre — *noun* a grave or burial vault. — *verb* to bury in a sepulchre; to entomb. [from Latin *sepulcrum*]

sequel *noun* **1** a book, film, or play that continues an earlier story. **2** a result or consequence. [from Latin *sequi*, to follow]

sequence *noun* **1** a series of things following each other in a particular order; the order they follow. **2** a succession of short pieces of action making up a scene in a film. **3** *Maths.* a set of values in which each is a fixed amount greater or smaller than its predecessor, as determined by a given rule. [from Latin *sequi*, to follow]

sequencing *noun* the process of determining the order of amino acids in a protein or of nucleotides in DNA or RNA.

sequential *adj.* **1** following a particular order. **2** consequent; of which each element is a direct consequence of its predecessor.

sequester *verb* (**sequestered, sequestering**) **1** to set apart or isolate. **2** to seclude: *a sequestered garden*. **3** *Legal* to sequestrate. [from Latin *sequester*, depository]

sequestrate *verb Legal* to remove from someone's possession until a dispute or debt has been settled. [from Latin *sequestrare*, from *sequester*, depository]

sequestration *noun* sequestrating or being sequestrated.

sequestrator *noun* a person who sequestrates.

sequin *noun* a tiny round shiny disc of foil or plastic, sewn on a garment for decoration. [from Italian *zecchino*]

sequined *adj.* covered or decorated with sequins.

Sequoia or **Sequoyah**, also called **George Guess** (c.1770–1843) American half-Cherokee scholar, born in Taskigi, North Carolina. He was a major figure behind the decision of the Cherokee to adopt as much as possible of White culture, while retaining their own identity, and personally invented an alphabet for their language. A genus of giant coniferous trees was named after him (*Sequoia*).

Sequoia a national park in E California, USA, established in 1890. It is situated in the Sierra Nevada, E of Fresno. AREA 1 631sq km/630sq mi. The enormous ancient sequoia trees are the park's special feature.

sequoia *noun* either of two types of gigantic Californian coniferous tree, the big tree or giant sequoia, or the redwood. [named after the Cherokee scholar Sequoiah]

seraglio *noun* (PL. **seraglios**) **1** a harem. **2** *Hist.* a Turkish palace, especially that of the sultans at Constantinople. [from Italian *serraglio*, from Persian *saray*, palace]

seraph *noun* (PL. **seraphs, seraphim**) an angel of the highest of the nine celestial orders. [from Hebrew *seraph*]

seraphic *adj.* of or like a seraph.

Serapis or **Sarapis** a compound deity, combining the names and aspects of two Egyptian gods, Osiris and Apis, to which were further added features of major Greek gods, such as Zeus and Dionysus. The god was introduced to Alexandria by Ptolemy I in an attempt to unite Greeks and Egyptians in common worship.

Serbia POP (1991) 9.8m, a constituent republic of Yugoslavia. AREA 88 361sq km/34 107sq mi. It is bounded by Croatia to the NW, Hungary to the N, Romania to the NE, Bulgaria to the E, Macedonia to the S, and Albania and Bosnia-Herzegovina to the W. The provinces of Kosovo and Vojvodina were autonomous until 1990 when the each lost their autonomous status to Serbia. It forms a mountainous area with deep river valleys. HISTORY a former kingdom of the Balkan Peninsula, it was incorporated into Yugoslavia in 1918 and was established as a constituent republic in 1946. Serb minority populations are substantial in Croatia and Bosnia-Herzegovina and civil war between the ethnic groups followed their declarations of independence from Yugoslavia. CAPITAL Belgrade.

Serbo-Croat *noun* a Slavonic language spoken in Serbia, Croatia, etc; the main language of the former Yugoslavia.

SERC *abbrev.* Science and Engineering Research Council.

Serena a female first name. [from Latin *serenus*, serene, calm]

serenade — *noun* **1** a song or tune performed at night under a woman's window by her suitor. **2** any musical piece with a gentle tempo suggestive of romance. **3** a piece of classical music of symphony length but lighter in tone and for a smaller orchestra. — *verb* to entertain (a person) with a serenade. [from Latin *serenus*, bright clear sky]

serendipitous *adj.* discovered by luck or chance.

serendipity *noun* the state of frequently making lucky finds. [from the folk tale 'The Three Princes of *Serendip*' (= Sri Lanka)]

serene *adj.* 1 *said of a person* calm; at peace. 2 *said of a sky* cloudless. 3 (**Serene**) a word incorporated in the titles of members of some European royal families: *Her Serene Highness.* [from Latin *serenus*, clear]

serenely *adv.* with a serene manner.

Serengeti a national park in N Tanzania, established in 1951. AREA 14 763sq km/ 5 698sq mi. It is noted for its wildlife, especially wildebeest, gazelle, zebra, impala, buffalo, topi, eland, kongoni, giraffe, elephant, hyena, and lion. The Serengeti is famous for the mass migratory treks of the grass-eating animals and their predators as they follow the rains to new grazing grounds. It is a World Heritage site.

serenity *noun* a serene quality.

serf *noun* in medieval Europe, a worker of near-slave status, bought and sold with the land on which he or she worked. [from Latin *servus*, slave]

serfdom *noun* the condition of a serf; bondage.

serge *noun* a hard-wearing twilled fabric, especially of wool. [from Old French *serge*]

sergeant *noun* 1 a non-commissioned officer of the rank next above corporal in the armed forces. 2 a police officer of the rank between constable and inspector. [from Old French *sergent*, from Latin *serviens*, servant]

sergeant-at-arms *noun* (also **serjeant-at-arms**) an officer of a court or parliament, responsible for keeping order.

sergeant-major *noun* a non-commissioned officer of the highest rank in the armed forces.

serial — *noun* 1 a story published or broadcast in regular instalments. 2 a periodical. — *adj.* 1 appearing in instalments. 2 forming a series or part of a series.

serialism *noun Mus.* the technique of using a series (or succession) of related notes as the basis for a musical composition. The most common type is 12-note serialism (as first arrived at by Arnold Schoenberg in the 1920s), in which the twelve notes of the chromatic scale are reordered to form one of a possible 479 001 600 different series. Once the series has been established it can be treated in various ways, eg presented vertically as chords or horizontally as melodic lines, played backwards, or turned upside down, etc.

serialization *or* **serialisation** *noun* production in instalments.

serialize *or* **serialise** *verb* to publish or broadcast (a story, etc) in instalments.

serial killer a person committing a succession of murders.

serial number any of a set of consecutive numbers printed on identical products to identify them as a batch.

series *noun* (PL. **series**) 1 a number of similar, related, or identical things arranged or produced one after the other. 2 a television or radio programme in which the same characters appear, or a similar subject is addressed, in regularly broadcast shows. 3 *Maths.* in a sequence of numbers, the sum obtained when each term is added to the previous ones. 4 *Physics* an electric circuit whose components are arranged so that the same current passes through each of them in turn. 5 *Geol.* a group of rocks, fossils, or minerals that can be arranged in a natural sequence on the basis of cer-

tain properties, eg composition. [from Latin *series*, chain, row]

series circuit *Physics* an electric circuit in which the circuit components are connected end to end, so that the same amount of current flows through all the components one after the other.

serif *noun* a short decorative line or stroke on the end of a printed letter, as in E as opposed to the sanserif (= without serifs) E.

serigraph *noun* a print made by silk-screen process. [from Latin *sericum*, silk + Greek *graphe*, writing]

serine *noun Biochem.* an amino acid that is found in proteins. [from Greek *serikos*, silken]

seriocomic *adj.* having both serious and comic elements or qualities.

serious *adj.* 1 solemn; not light-hearted or flippant. 2 dealing with important issues: *a serious newspaper.* 3 severe: *a serious accident.* 4 important; significant: *serious differences of opinion.* 5 earnest; sincere; not joking: *I am serious about doing it.* [from Latin *serius*]

seriously *adv.* in a serious way.

seriousness *noun* being serious.

serjeant see SERGEANT.

sermon *noun* 1 a public speech about morals, religious duties, or some aspect of religious doctrine, especially one forming part of a church service. 2 a lengthy moral or advisory speech. [from Latin *sermo*, discourse]

sermonize *or* **sermonise** *verb intrans.* to moralize.

Sermon on the Mount a collection of Christ's ethical teaching, recorded in Matthew 5–7 as preached on a mountainside early in Christ's ministry, but in Luke 6.17–49 as on a plain or level place. Christ taught the crowd on true adherence to God's law, love of enemies, the Lord's Prayer, material anxieties, and the Golden Rule. Matthew's version includes the Beatitudes.

serology *noun Biol.* the branch of biology that is concerned with the study of blood serum and its constituents, especially antibodies and antigens.

seropositive *adj., said of a person* having blood that is shown by tests to be infected by the specific disease tested for, usually Aids.

serotonin *noun Physiol.* a hormone that is found mainly in the brain, blood platelets, and intestinal tissues, but also occurs in many other body tissues. It acts as a neurotransmitter in the central nervous system, and is also a vasoconstrictor, ie it causes narrowing of blood vessels by stimulating their contraction. [from SERUM + TONIC]

serous *adj.* 1 of or relating to serum. 2 *said of a liquid* resembling serum; watery.

serpent *noun* 1 a snake. 2 a sneaky or malicious person. [from Latin *serpens*, creeping thing]

serpentine — *adj.* 1 snake-like. 2 winding; full of twists and bends. — *noun Geol.* a soft green or white rock-forming mineral derived from magnesium silicates, so called because it is often mottled like a snake's skin. The two main forms are *chrysotile* (the main source of asbestos) and *antigorite*. Serpentine is also used to make ornaments.

SERPS *abbrev.* state earnings-related pension scheme.

serrated *adj.* having notches or teeth like the blade of a saw. [from Latin *serra*, saw]

serration *noun* 1 a saw-edged condition. 2 a sawlike tooth.

serried *adj.* closely packed or grouped together: *soldiers in serried ranks.* [from French *serrer*, to put close together]

serum *noun* (PL. **sera**) (*in full* **blood serum**) the straw-coloured fluid component of blood that remains after removal of the blood cells and clotting factors. It contains specific antibodies, and can therefore be used as a vaccine to confer protection against specific diseases. [from Latin *serum*, whey]

servant *noun* 1 a person employed by another to do household work. 2 a person who acts for the good of others in any capacity: *public servant.*

serve — *verb* 1 to work for the benefit of: *served the community well.* 2 *intrans.* to carry out duties as a member of some body: *serve on a committee.* 3 *intrans.* to act as a member of the armed forces: *served in the marines / served in France.* 4 *trans., intrans.* to give assistance to (customers); to provide to customers. 5 *trans., intrans.* to respond to the needs or demands of (someone): *shoes have served me well / if my memory serves me.* 6 *trans., intrans.* to bring, distribute, or present (food or drink) to (someone). 7 to provide specified facilities to: *trams serving the entire city.* 8 *intrans., trans.* to be of use; to fulfil a need; to suffice: *there's no chair, but this box will serve / it will serve our purpose.* 9 *intrans.* to have a specified effect or result: *his long speech served to delay proceedings.* 10 to undergo as a requirement: *serve an apprenticeship.* 11 *trans., intrans.* to put (the ball) into play in racket sports. 12 to work for as a domestic servant. 13 to deliver or present a legal document: *served him with a writ / served a summons on her.* — *noun Sport* an act of serving.
— **serve someone right** *colloq.* to be the misfortune or punishment that they deserve.
[from Latin *servire*, to serve]

server *noun* 1 a person who serves. 2 *RC Church* a person who assists a priest during mass. 3 a fork, spoon, or other instrument for distributing food.

service — *noun* 1 work performed for or on behalf of others; use or usefulness; a favour, or any act with beneficial results: *do someone a service / your services are no longer required / the car has given me good service / can I be of service?* 2 employment or engagement as a member of an organization working to serve or benefit others in some way; such an organization: *a public service / the civil service.* 3 assistance given to customers. 4 a facility provided: *the bus company runs a great service.* 5 an occasion of worship or other religious ceremony; the words, etc used on such an occasion: *the marriage service.* 6 a complete set of crockery: *a dinner service.* 7 a periodic check of the workings of a vehicle or other machine. 8 an act of putting the ball into play in racket sports; the game in which it is a particular player's turn to do so; the stroke used: *lose one's service / a poor service.* 9 a service charge: *service not included.* 10 (*often* **services**) any of the armed forces. 11 employment as a domestic servant. 12 (*attributive*) for use by domestic servants: *service entrance.* 13 (*attributive*) of the army, navy, or air force. — *verb* 1 to subject to a periodic (especially mechanical) check. 2 *said of a male animal* to mate with (a female).
— **at someone's service** ready to serve or give assistance to someone.
be of service to someone to help them; to be useful to them.
in service 1 in use; operating. 2 working as a domestic servant.
[from Latin *servitium*, from *servire*, to serve]

serviceability *noun* being serviceable.

serviceable *adj.* 1 capable of being used. 2 giving long-term use; durable.

service area a group of establishments near a motorway or major road, providing refuelling, restaurant, and toilet facilities.

service charge a percentage of a restaurant or hotel bill added on to cover (at least nominally) the cost of service.

service flat a rented flat with the cost of certain services, eg domestic cleaning, included in the rent.

service industry an industry whose business is providing services, eg dry-cleaning, rather than manufacturing goods.

serviceman *noun* a male member of any of the armed forces.

service station a petrol station providing additional facilities for motorists, eg car-washing.

servicewoman *noun* a female member of any of the armed forces.

serviette *noun* a table napkin. [from Old French *serviette*]

servile *adj.* 1 slavishly respectful, obedient, or attentive; fawning. 2 of, relating to, or suitable for slaves: *servile tasks*. [from Latin *servilis*]

Servile Wars the collective name for the official attempts to suppress the slave uprisings of the late 2c BC and early 1c BC in Sicily and S Italy. The most serious was the revolt led by Spartacus, in which tens of thousands of slaves were involved. It took the Romans two years to suppress it (73–71 BC).

servility *noun* being servile.

serving *noun* a portion of food served at one time; a helping.

servitude *noun* 1 slavery. 2 dependence: *servitude to drugs*. [from Latin *servitudo*, from *servus*, slave]

servo *or* **servomechanism** *noun* (PL. **servos**) an automatic device used to control machinery. An error in the operation of the machine produces an electrical signal which is amplified and used to power a *servomotor*, which corrects the error until the error signal falls to zero. Servos (servomechanisms) are used in satellite-tracking systems, power-steering systems on some cars, and to control robots and keep ships on course. [from Latin *servus*, servant]

sesame *noun* a SE Asian plant cultivated for its edible seeds, used in cooking and cooking-oil production. [from Greek *sesamon*]

Sesostris a legendary Egyptian king, recorded in the historian Herodotus, who was alleged to have conquered vast areas of Europe, Asia, and N Africa. He was probably a compound of the three Egyptian pharaohs of that time (20c–19c BC) and Rameses II (13c BC).

sessile *adj.* 1 *said of a flower or leaf* attached directly to the plant, rather than by a short stalk. 2 *said of a part of the body* attached directly to the body. 3 *said of an animal* stationary; immobile. [from Latin *sessilis*, low, squat]

session *noun* 1 a meeting of a court, council, or parliament; a period during which such meetings are regularly held. 2 a period of time spent engaged in one particular activity. 3 an academic term or year. — **in session** *said of a committee, etc* conducting or engaged in a meeting. [from Latin *sessio*, a sitting]

sessional *adj.* relating to a session or sessions.

sestet *noun* 1 a poem or verse of six lines. 2 the last six lines of a sonnet. 3 a group of six people or things; a sextet. [from Italian *sestetto*, from Latin *sextus*, sixth]

Set *or* **Seth** in ancient Egyptian religion, a god associated with evil forces and rebellion, depicted with the head of an animal with a long muzzle. He was the brother of Osiris, whom he murdered, and he was himself murdered by Horus, the son of Osiris.

set¹ — *verb* (**setting**; PAST TENSE AND PAST PARTICIPLE **set**) 1 to put into a certain position or condition: *set high up / set free / set fire to*. 2 *trans., intrans.* to make or become solid, rigid, firm, or motionless: *the cement has not set / set someone's jaw*. 3 to fix, establish, or settle: *set a date*. 4 to put into a state of readiness: *set the table*. 5 to adjust (an instrument) to the correct reading: *set a clock*. 6 to adjust (a device) so that its controls are

activated at a fixed time. 7 to fix (a broken bone) in its normal position, for healing. 8 to impose or assign as an exercise or duty: *set a test*. 9 to present or fix as a lead to be followed: *set an example / set the tone*. 10 to place on or against a background, or in surroundings: *diamonds set in a gold bracelet / a poem set to music*. 11 to stir, provoke, or force into activity: *set me thinking / set her to work*. 12 to treat (hair) so as to stay firm in the required style. 13 to place as a value or consideration of worth: *set a high price on honesty / set great store by*. 14 *intrans. said of the sun or moon* to disappear below the horizon. 15 to arrange (type) for printing. 16 *said of a plant* to produce (seed). 17 to decorate: *a bracelet set with diamonds*. — *noun* 1 form; shape: *the set of his jaw*. 2 posture or bearing. 3 the area within which filmed action takes place; the scenery and props used to create a particular location in filming. 4 the process of setting hair; a hairstyle produced by setting: *a shampoo and set*. — *adj.* 1 fixed; allowing no alterations or variations: *a set menu*. 2 never changing: *set in his ways*. 3 predetermined or conventional: *set phrases*. 4 ready, prepared. 5 about to receive or experience; due: *set for a pay rise*. 6 (**set on something**) determined to do it: *dead set on resigning*. 7 assigned; prescribed: *set texts for study*. — **set about someone** to attack them.

set about something to start or begin it: *set about digging the garden*.

set one thing against another 1 to compare or contrast them. 2 to deduct one from the other: *set expenses against tax*.

set one person against another to make them mutually hostile: *set him against his own family*.

set something *or* **someone apart** to reveal them to be different, especially superior.

set something aside 1 to disregard or reject it. 2 to put it away for later use.

set something back 1 to delay or hinder its progress. 2 to cause it to return to an earlier and less advanced stage: *changes that will set the health service back decades*. 3 *slang* to cost: *set me back a fiver*.

set something down 1 to record it in writing. 2 to judge or view: *set the scheme down as a failure*.

set someone down to allow them to leave a vehicle at their destination.

set forth to begin a journey.

set something forth to propose or explain it: *set forth her views*.

set in to become firmly established: *winter has set in*.

set off to start out on a journey.

set someone off to provoke them into action or behaviour of a particular kind: *set them off laughing*.

set something off 1 to cause or start it: *set off a terrible argument*. 2 to detonate an explosive. 3 to show it off to good advantage; to enhance its appearance. 4 to deduct it from another source; to offset it.

set on someone to attack them.

set someone *or* **something on someone** to order them to attack: *set the dogs on him*.

set out to begin a journey.

set something out 1 to present or explain it: *set out her proposals*. 2 to lay it out for display.

set out to do something to resolve or intend to do it: *set out to make me look foolish*.

set to 1 to begin working; to apply oneself to a task. 2 to start fighting or arguing.

set someone up 1 to put them into a position of guaranteed security: *the inheritance has set him up for life*. 2 to improve or restore their health. 3 *slang* to trick them into becoming a target for blame or accusations.

set something up 1 to bring it into being or operation; to establish it. 2 to arrange a meeting. etc. 3 to erect something: *set the tents up over here*. [from Anglo-Saxon *settan*]

set² *noun* 1 a group of related or similar things regarded as a complete unit. 2 *Maths.* a group of objects (known as *elements*) that have at least one characteristic in common, so that it is possible to

decide exactly whether a given element does or does not belong to that group, eg the set of even numbers. 3 a complete collection of pieces needed for a particular activity: *a chess set / a train set*. 4 one of the major divisions of a match in some sports, eg tennis, subdivided into games. 5 a group of people with common characteristics or interests. 6 an instrument for receiving television or radio broadcasts. 7 the songs or tunes performed at a concert. [from Old French *sette*]

◇ In mathematics, a particular set is usually denoted by a capital letter, eg N, and the members of that set are enclosed within curly brackets, eg {2, 4, 6,...}. The symbol ∈ indicates that a specific element is a member of a specific set, eg 2 ∈ N. The symbol ⊂ indicates that one set is a *subset* (is contained within) another, eg if a set S = {2,4} is a subset of a set N of even numbers, then this can be written S ⊂ N. The symbol ∩ indicates the *intersection* of two sets, eg N ∩ P is the set of all elements that are members of both N and P. The *universal set* is the set of all elements, and an empty set has no elements. *Venn diagrams* are often used to represent the relationships between sets.

set³ *or* **sett** *noun* 1 a badger's burrow. 2 a block of stone or wood used in paving. [see SET¹]

set-aside the policy of taking agricultural land out of production, used to reduce surpluses of specific commodities. It has been widely applied in the USA, and farmers in European Community countries are currently being encouraged to withdraw a proportion of their land from cereal production to reduce Community grain surpluses; they are compensated by specific payments or by guaranteed markets for their remaining production.

setback *noun* 1 a check or reversal to progress. 2 a disappointment or misfortune.

Seth, Vikram (1952–) Indian poet, novelist, and travel writer, born in Calcutta and educated at universities in England, the USA, and China. His first poetry collection was *Mappings* (1980). His travel book, *From Heaven Lake: Travels Through Sinkiang and Tibet*, appeared in 1983. His first novel, *The Golden Gate* (1986), written in verse, describes the lives of the contemporary Californian professional classes. His following novel was even more ambitious. At over 1 300 pages, *A Suitable Boy* (1993) is one of the longest single-volume novels in English. Set in immediate post-independence India, it is a love story which encompasses a vast number of characters and attempts a complete portrait of Indian social, political, and cultural life.

Seth 1 a biblical character, the third son of Adam. 2 a male first name. [a Hebrew name, = substitute, compensation]

set piece 1 a carefully prepared performance or sequence of movements. 2 an arrangement of fireworks on a scaffold, etc.

set square a triangular (usually plastic) plate used as an aid to drawing lines and angles.

settee *noun* a sofa. [from SETTLE²]

setter *noun* any of various breeds of dog originally trained to stand rigid to signal that a hunted animal has been scented.

setting *noun* 1 a position in which an instrument's controls are set. 2 a a situation or background within or against which action takes place. b the scenery and props used in filming a scene. 3 (*also* **place setting**) a set of cutlery, crockery, and glassware laid out for use by one diner. 4 a mounting for a jewel.

settle¹ *verb* 1 *trans., intrans.* to make or become firmly, comfortably, or satisfactorily positioned or established. 2 *trans., intrans.* (**settle something** *or* **settle on something**) to come to an agreement about it: *settle an argument / settle on a date*. 3 *intrans.* to come lightly to rest. 4 *trans., intrans.* (*also* **settle down** *or* **settle someone down**) to make or become calm, stable, or disciplined after a period of noisy excitement or upheaval. **5** *trans., intrans.* to establish a permanent home or colony (in). **6** *trans., intrans.* (*also* **settle up**) to pay off or clear (a debt): *I will settle a bill / you settle up with them.* **7** *intrans.* to sink to the bottom of something; to sink lower. **8** to transfer ownership of legally: *settled her estate on her son.* — **settle for something** to accept it as a compromise or in place of something more suitable. [from Anglo-Saxon *setlan*, to place]

settle[2] *noun* a wooden bench with arms and a solid high back, often with a storage chest fitted below the seat. [from Anglo-Saxon *setl*]

Settlement, Act of an important British statute (1701) which determined the succession of the English throne after the death of Queen Anne and her heirs, if any. It excluded the Catholic Stuarts from the succession, which was to pass to the Electress Sophia of Hanover, descendant through the female line of James VI of Scotland and I of England. Future monarchs were to be communicant members of the Church of England, and were not permitted to leave the country without the consent of Parliament.

settlement *noun* **1** the act of settling or the state of being settled. **2** a community or colony of recently settled people. **3** an agreement, especially ending an official dispute. **4** subsidence. **5** an act of legally transferring ownership of property; a document enforcing this.

settler *noun* a person who settles in a country that is being newly populated.

set-to *noun* **1** a fight or argument. **2** a fierce contest.

Setúbal 1 POP (1991) 84 000, an industrial seaport and the capital of Setúbal district, S Portugal. It lies at the mouth of the R Sado, 32km/20mi SE of Lisbon. **2** a district in S Portugal with Setúbal as its capital.

set-up *noun* **1** *colloq.* an arrangement or set of arrangements. **2** *slang* a trick to get a person unjustly blamed or accused.

Seurat, Georges (Pierre) (1859–91) French artist, born in Paris. He set up a studio in Paris, where his works included *Une Baignade, Asnières* (1883–4, Tate, London) and *Sunday Afternoon on the Island of La Grande Jatte* (1884–6, Chicago). His colour theories were influential, and one of his main achievements was the marrying of an Impressionist palette to classical composition (see Divisionism).

Sevastopol, Siege of the main engagement (1854–5) of the Crimean War. Britain, France, and Turkey attacked Russia's main naval base in the Black Sea in order to reduce its alleged threat to the status quo in the Ottoman Empire and the Mediterranean. It took 12 months and many casualties to capture Sevastopol. The Russian surgeon Nikolai Pirogov played a similar role inside the fortifications to that of Florence Nightingale outside.

seven — *noun* **1** the number or figure 7; any symbol for this number. **2** the age of 7. **3** something, eg a garment or a person, whose size is denoted by the number 7. **4** a playing-card with 7 pips. **5** a set of 7 people or things. **6** 7 o'clock. **7** a score of 7 points. — *adj.* **1** 7 in number. **2** aged 7. [from Anglo-Saxon *seofon*]

Seven against Thebes in Greek legend, seven champions who attacked Thebes to deprive Eteocles of his kingship. They were led by his brother Polynices and were defeated by another seven champions at the seven gates of Thebes. Later the sons of the Seven, the Epigoni, led by Adrastus, succeeded in destroying the city.

Seven Days Battles the final conflict (25 Jun–1 Jul 1862) in the Peninsular Campaign during the American Civil War, in which the Union drive to capture Richmond was halted.

sevenfold — *adj.* **1** equal to 7 times as much or as many. **2** divided into, or consisting of, 7 parts. — *adv.* by 7 times as much.

Seven Sacraments, The two series of paintings by Nicolas Poussin (1640s).

Seven Samurai (Shichinin No Samurai) a Japanese film directed by Akira Kurosawa (1954). Set in 16c Japan, it tells of civilized settlers defending their farms from plundering bandits with the help of samurai warriors.

seven seas (*usually* **the seven seas**) the oceans of the world: the Arctic, Southern, N Atlantic, S Atlantic, Indian, N Pacific, and S Pacific Oceans.

Seven Sleepers of Ephesus in medieval legend, seven persecuted Christians who fled into a cave at the time of the emperor Decius (AD 250) They slept for 200 years, emerging in AD 447 at the time of Theodosius II. The story was thought to confirm the resurrection of Christ.

seventeen — *noun* **1** the number or figure 17; any symbol for this number. **2** the age of 17. **3** something, eg a garment or a person, whose size is denoted by the number 17. **4** a set of 17 people or things. — *adj.* **1** 17 in number. **2** aged 17. [from Anglo-Saxon *seofon*, seven + *tien*, ten]

seventeenth *noun, adj.* **1** the position in a series corresponding to 17 in a sequence of numbers. **2** one of 17 equal parts.

seventh *noun, adj.* **1** the position in a series corresponding to 7 in a sequence of numbers. **2** one of 7 equal parts. **3** *Mus.* a tone or semitone less than an octave; a note at that interval from another, or a combination of two tones separated by that interval.

seventh heaven a state of intense happiness or joy.

seventhly *adv.* as seventh in a series.

Seventh Seal, The (Det Sjunde Inseglet) a Swedish film directed by Ingmar Bergman (1957). Depicted through the experiences of a knight (played by Max Von Sydow) who returns from the Crusades, it is an enigmatic allegory about man's relationship with God and Death.

seventies *pl. noun* **1** the period of time between one's seventieth and eightieth birthdays. **2** the range of temperatures between seventy and eighty degrees. **3** the period of time between the seventieth and eightieth years of a century.

seventieth *noun, adj.* **1** the position in a series corresponding to 70 in a sequence of numbers. **2** one of 70 equal parts.

seventy — *noun* (PL. **seventies**) **1** the number or figure 70; any symbol for this number. **2** the age of 70. **3** a set of 70 people or things. — *adj.* **1** 70 in number. **2** aged 70. [from Anglo-Saxon *seofontig*]

Seven Wise Men of Greece seven men famed in antiquity for their wisdom. The lists vary, but Solon of Athens, Thales of Miletus, Bias of Priene, and Pittacus of Mytilene are common to all of them. These and all the others mentioned belonged to the period 620–550 BC.

Seven Wonders of the Ancient World the most renowned man-made structures of the ancient world. They included the Pyramids of Egypt, the Hanging Gardens of Babylon, the Tomb of Mausolus at Halicarnassus, the Temple of Artemis at Ephesus, the Colossus of Rhodes, the Statue of Zeus at Olympia, and the Pharos of Alexandria.

Seven Years War a major European conflict (1756–63) rooted in the rivalry between Austria and Prussia and the imminent colonial struggle between Britain and France in the New World and the Far East. The two opposing power blocs were Austria, France, Russia, Sweden, and Saxony against Prussia, Britain, and Portugal.

sever *verb* (**severed**, **severing**) **1** to cut off physically: *severed limbs.* **2** to break off or end: *severed relations with them.* [from Latin *separare*, to separate]

several — *adj.* **1** more than a few, but not a great number. **2** different and distinct; respective: *went their several ways.* — *pron.* quite a few people or things. [from Old French *several*, separate]

severally *adv. formal* separately or singly: *travelling severally.*

severance *noun* **1** severing or being severed. **2** separation.

severance pay compensation paid by an employer to an employee dismissed through no fault of his or her own.

severe *adj.* **1** extreme and difficult to endure; marked by extreme conditions. **2** very strict towards others. **3** suggesting seriousness and a lack of informality; austere. **4** having serious consequences; grave. **5** rigorous; demanding. [from Latin *severus*]

severe combined immunodeficiency *Medicine* (ABBREV. **SCID**) a severe form of congenital immunological deficiency.

Severed Head, A a novel by Iris Murdoch (1961). It describes the complicated sexual relationships between three women and three men.

severely *adv.* in a severe way; to a severe degree.

severity *noun* being severe; strictness, harshness, gravity.

Severn, River a river in SE Wales and W England, length 354km/220mi. It rises on Plynlimon Fawr, central Wales, and flows NE and E to Shrewsbury, then SE and S through Worcester and Gloucester. It forms a wide estuary into the Bristol Channel. The Severn is navigable to Gloucester and is known for the Severn bore, a tidal wave of c.2m. The 988m-long

---

Seven Wonders of the World

Originally compiled by Antipater of Sidon, a Greek poet, in the 100s BC.

Pyramids of Egypt Oldest and only surviving 'wonder'. Built in the 2000s BC as royal tombs, about 80 are still standing. The largest, the Great Pyramid of Cheops, at el-Gizeh, was 147m (481ft) high.

Hanging Gardens of Babylon Terraced gardens adjoining Nebuchadnezzar's palace said to rise from 23–91m (75–300ft). Supposedly built by the king about 600 BC to please his wife, a princess from the mountains, but they are also associated with the Assyrian Queen Semiramis.

Statue of Zeus at Olympia Carved by Phidias, the 12m (40ft) statue marked the site of the original Olympic Games in the 400s BC. It was constructed of ivory and gold, and showed Zeus (Jupiter) on his throne.

Temple of Artemis (Diana) at Ephesus Constructed of Parian marble and more than 122m (400ft) long with over 100 columns 18m (60ft) high, it was begun about 350 BC and took some 120 years to build. Destroyed by the Goths in AD 262.

Mausoleum at Halicarnassus Erected by Queen Artemisia in memory of her husband King Mausolus of Caria (in Asia Minor), who died 353 BC. It stood 43m (140ft) high. All that remains are a few pieces in the British Museum and the word 'mausoleum' in the English language.

Colossus of Rhodes Gigantic bronze statue of sun-god Helios (or Apollo); stood about 36m (117ft) high, dominating the harbour entrance at Rhodes. The sculptor Chares supposedly laboured for 12 years before he completed it in 280 BC. It was destroyed by an earthquake in 224 BC.

Pharos of Alexandria Marble lighthouse and watchtower built about 270 BC on the island of Pharos in Alexandria's harbour. Possibly standing 122m (400ft) high, it was destroyed by an earthquake in 1375.

Severn Bridge crosses the river between Aust in Somerset and Beachley on the Gwent border.

Severus, Lucius Septimius (c.146–211 AD) Roman emperor (193–211) and founder of the Severan dynasty (193–235), the first Roman emperor to be born in Africa (at Leptis Magna, of Romanized Punic stock). He spent the early years of his reign securing his position against his rivals (eg Pescennius Niger, governor of Syria). Once established, he effected many reforms, and showed a particularly close interest in the army and the law. His final years were spent in Britain, where he tried unsuccessfully to restore order in the N of the province.

Sévigné, Madame de, *née* **Marie de Rabutin-Chantal** (1626–96) French writer, born in Paris. She was a member of French court society, and in 1669 she began a series of letters which lasted over 25 years, recounting the inner history of her time in great detail and in a natural, colloquial style. The letters were published posthumously in 1725.

Seville, Spanish **Sevilla**, ancient **Hispalis** POP (1991) 659 000, the river-port capital of Seville province, Andalusia, S Spain. It lies on the R Guadalquivir, 538km/334mi SW of Madrid. HISTORY Seville was a Moorish cultural centre between the 8c and the 13c; in the 16c it was an important trading port with the Americas; the painters Velázquez and Murillo were born here in 1599 and 1617 respectively. notable features the 15c cathedral (the largest Gothic church in the world, with the tomb of Columbus), the Moorish citadel (Alcazar), and the Archivo de Indias constitute a World Heritage site; Maria Luisa Park; Fine Arts Museum; Pilate's House; Palace of St Telmo; Scipio's Roman settlement of Italica, with a fine amphitheatre, is 7km/4mi NW.

Sèvres porcelain French royal porcelain factory originally in Vincennes, founded c.1745 to produce soft and hard paste luxury porcelain. The early products included many figures in white unglazed 'biscuit' ware, but the factory's speciality became items with exquisitely painted vignettes against richly coloured plain grounds with elaborate gilding.

sew *verb* (PAST PARTICIPLE **sewn**, **sewed**) **1** to stitch, attach, or repair (especially fabric) with thread, by hand with a needle or by machine. **2** to make (garments) by stitching pieces of fabric together. **3** *intrans.* to perform such tasks: *can you sew?*
— **sew something up 1** to mend or join it by sewing. **2** *slang* to arrange or complete it successfully.
[from Anglo-Saxon *siwian*]

sewage *noun* waste matter, especially excrement, carried away in drains. [from SEWER]

sewage farm a place where sewage is treated so as to be usable as manure.

Seward Peninsula a peninsula in Alaska, USA, separating Kotzebue Sound in the N from Norton Sound in the S. It is the westernmost point of the N American continent.

Sewell, Anna (1820–78) English novelist, born in Yarmouth, Norfolk. She was an invalid for most of her life, and is remembered for the children's novel, *Black Beauty* (1877), the story of a horse.

sewer *noun* a large underground pipe or channel for carrying away sewage from drains and water from road surfaces; a main drain. [from Old French *essever*, to drain off]

sewerage *noun* **1** a network of sewers. **2** drainage of sewage and surface water using sewers.

sewing *noun* **1** the act of sewing. **2** something that is being sewn.

sewing-machine *noun* a machine for sewing, especially an electric machine for sewing clothes, etc.

sex — *noun* **1** either of the two classes male and female — into which animals and plants (or certain parts of plants) are divided according to their role in reproduction. **2** membership of one of these classes, or the attributes that determine this. **3** sexual intercourse, often including other love-making activities. — *adj.* **1** of or relating to sexual matters in general: *sex education*. **2** of or based on the fact of being male or female: *sex discrimination*. — *verb* to identify the sex of (an animal). [from Latin *sexus*]

sexagenarian — *adj.*, *said of a person* aged between 60 and 69. — *noun* a person of this age. [from Latin *sexaginta*, sixty]

Sexagesima *noun* the second Sunday before Lent, apparently so called by analogy with Quadragesima and Quinquagesima; the 60th day (in round numbers) before Easter. [from Latin *sexagesimus*, sixtieth]

sex appeal sexual attractiveness.

sex chromosome *Genetics* any chromosome that carries the genes which determine the sex of an organism. In mammals, including humans, females have two identical sex chromosomes, known as X-chromosomes, and males have an X-chromosome together with a smaller chromosome known as a Y-chromosome.

sexed *adj.* having a desire as specified to engage in sexual activity: *highly sexed*.

sexily *adv.* in a sexy way.

sexiness *noun* being sexy.

sexism *noun* contempt shown for a particular sex, usually by men of women, based on prejudice or stereotype.

sexist — *noun* a person whose beliefs and actions are characterized by sexism. — *adj.* relating to or characteristic of sexism.

sexless *adj.* **1** neither male nor female. **2** having no desire to engage in sexual activity. **3** *derog.* sexually unattractive.

sex linkage *Genetics* the tendency for certain inherited characteristics to occur predominantly or exclusively in one of the sexes because the genes for those characteristics are carried on the sex chromosomes (usually the X-chromosome), eg the hereditary disorder haemophilia occurs predominantly in human males.

sexologist *noun* a person who studies human sexual behaviour.

sexology *noun* the study of sexual behaviour, especially in humans.

sexploitation *noun* the commercial exploitation of sex in films and other media.

sext *noun* the fourth of the canonical hours. [from Latin *sexta hora*, the sixth hour]

sextant *noun* an instrument like a small telescope mounted on a graded metal arc, used in navigation and surveying for measuring distance by means of angles. [from Latin *sextans*, sixth, the arc being one sixth of a full circle]

sextet *noun* **1** a group of six singers or musicians, or a piece of music for these. **2** any set of six. [a variant of SESTET]

sex therapy *Medicine* a form of therapy that deals with physical and psychological problems relating to sexual intercourse.

sexton *noun* a person who looks after church property, often also having bell-ringing, grave-digging and other duties. [from SACRISTAN]

sextuple — *noun* a value or quantity six times as much. — *adj.* **1** sixfold. **2** made up of six parts. — *verb trans.*, *intrans.* to multiply or increase sixfold. [from Latin *sextuplus*]

sextuplet *noun* any of six children born at the same time to the same mother.

sexual *adj.* **1** concerned with or suggestive of sex or love-making. **2** relating to sexual repro-duction involving the fusion of two gametes to form a zygote. **3** of, relating to, or according to membership of, the male or female sex.

sexual abuse subjection to sexual activity likely to cause physical or psychological harm.

sexual harassment harassment in the form of unwelcome, often offensive, sexual advances or remarks, usually made by men towards women, especially in the workplace.

sexual intercourse the insertion of a man's penis into a woman's vagina, usually with the release of semen into the vagina.

sexuality *noun* a sexual state or condition.

sexually transmitted disease (ABBREV. **STD**) any disease that is characteristically transmitted by sexual intercourse, formerly known as venereal disease, eg AIDS, gonorrhoea, syphilis.

sexual reproduction a form of reproduction in which new individuals are produced by the fusion of two unlike gametes (specialized reproductive cells). The gametes are typically male (a sperm) and female (an ovum or egg).
◇ During sexual reproduction, two gametes that are haploid (each having a single chromosome set) fuse to form a *zygote* that is diploid (having a double chromosome set). The zygote then divides repeatedly and develops into a new individual. Gametes are formed by a special type of cell division, known as *meiosis*, that not only halves the chromosome number, but also results in rearrangement of the genetic material. The main advantage of sexual reproduction is that it involves the mixing of genetic material from two parent organisms, resulting in offspring that differ genetically both from the parents and from each other. It is this genetic variation that brings new vigour to a species.

sexy *adj.* (**sexier**, **sexiest**) *colloq.* **1** sexually attractive; arousing sexual desire. **2** currently popular or interesting: *sexy products*.

Seychelles, official name **Republic of Seychelles** POP (1992e) 72 000, an island group in the SW Indian Ocean, N of Madagascar, comprising 115 islands. AREA 453sq km/175sq mi (land). The group includes Mahé (AREA 153sq km/59sq mi), Praslin (AREA 38sq km/15sq mi), and La Digue (AREA 10sq km/4sq mi). CAPITAL Victoria (on Mahé). TIME ZONE GMT +4. The population is largely descended from 18c French colonists and their freed African slaves; Roman Catholicism is the chief religion. OFFICIAL LANGUAGES Creole; French and English are spoken. PHYSICAL DESCRIPTION the islands fall into two main groups; the first, a compact group of 41 granitic islands rising steeply from the sea, includes Mahé and its nearest neighbours; these islands are mountainous, rising to 906m on Mahé; the steep forest-clad slopes drop down to

Seychelles

coastal lowlands with a vegetation of grass and dense scrub; the second is a group of low-lying coralline islands and atolls which are situated to the SW. CLIMATE tropical with a rainfall that varies with altitude and is higher on the S sides of the islands; the wettest months are Nov–Mar; the Seychelles are rarely affected by tropical storms. HISTORY visited by Vasco da Gama in 1502; colonized by the French in 1768; captured by Britain in 1794; incorporated as a dependency of Mauritius in 1814; became a separate colony in 1903; became an independent republic within the Commonwealth in 1976; there was a coup in 1977; became a one-party state in 1979; opposition parties were permitted from 1991. GOVERNMENT governed by a President, elected for a five-year term, a Council of Ministers, and a 25-member unicameral National Assembly. ECONOMY fruit; vegetables; livestock; fishing; cinnamon; copra; from the 1970s, tourism expanded to become the most important industry by the 1990s; diversifying small industry; brewing; soap; plastics; furniture; cigarettes; soft drinks; steel fabricated goods.

Seyfert, Carl Keenan (1911–60) US astronomer, born in Cleveland, Ohio. He worked at several US observatories, and became famous for his work on a group of galaxies (named after him), which have very bright bluish star-like nuclei and characteristic spectra, now thought to be the low-luminosity cousins of quasars.

Seyhan, ancient **Sarus** a river in S central Turkey. It is c.64km/40mi SW of Sivas and flows SW past Adana to discharge into the Mediterranean Sea. The river is 560km/348mi long. Cotton and grapes are grown in its valley. A dam on the river at Adana provides flood control, irrigation, municipal water and electricity.

Seymour, Jane (c.1509–37) the third queen-consort of Henry VIII and the sister of Protector Somerset. A lady-in-waiting to Henry's first two wives (Catherine of Aragon and Anne Boleyn), she married him 11 days after Anne's execution. She died soon after the birth of her son, the future Edward VI.

Sezession the name adopted by a number of groups of modern artists in Germany between c.1890 and World War I, who seceded from the orthodox academic bodies to form their own exhibiting societies. The Munich Sezession was founded in 1882, Vienna in 1897, Berlin in 1899. [German, = secession]

SF or **sf** abbrev. science fiction.

sf or **sfz** abbrev. sforzando.

SFA abbrev. Scottish Football Association.

Sfax 1 POP (1989) 222 000, the seaport capital of Sfax governorate, E Tunisia. It lies 240km/150mi SE of Tunis and is the second largest city in the country. HISTORY built on the site of Roman and Phoenician settlements; occupied by the Sicilians in the 12c and the Spaniards in the 16c; also a base for Barbary pirates; the modern city was built after 1895. NOTABLE FEATURES Museum of Folk Arts and Traditions; Archaeological Museum. **2** a governorate in E Tunisia with Sfax as its capital.

Sforza dukes of Milan during the High Renaissance, whose dubious claims to the duchy were typical of Renaissance politics. Francesco (1401–66) became duke after the deaths of the last Visconti duke (1450) whose daughter he had married. Francesco's second son Ludovico (Il Moro 'the Moor', 1451–1508) usurped the dukedom (1481) from his nephew, for whom he was regent (Ludovico's elder brother was murdered in 1476). He was a patron of the arts and made the court of Milan the most splendid in Europe. Louis XII of France claimed the duchy and defeated and imprisoned Ludovico.

sforzando adv., adj. Mus. to be played with sudden emphasis. [from Italian sforzando]

sfumato noun a term used in art history for the smooth imperceptible transitions from one colour to the other achieved by such artists as Leonardo da Vinci and Correggio. This softening of outlines was a technical advance on the harsh and precise method of other quattrocentro (15c) Florentine painters (for example, Botticelli), and helped 16c masters to achieve greater naturalism. [from Italian, from fumo, smoke]

sgraffito or **graffito** noun (PL. **sgraffiti**) a technique in art in which one colour is laid over another and the top layer scratched away to form a design, by revealing the colour beneath. It is used in pottery decoration, and on plasterwork in medieval and Renaissance buildings. [from Italian sgraffito, from Latin ex-, + Greek graphein, to write]

Sgt abbrev. Sergeant.

sh interj. hush; be quiet. [imitative]

Shaba, formerly **Katanga** the southernmost region in Zaire, rich in minerals.

shabbily adv. in a shabby way.

shabbiness noun being shabby.

shabby adj. (**shabbier**, **shabbiest**) **1** said especially of clothes or furnishings old and worn; threadbare; dingy. **2** said of a person wearing such clothes. **3** nasty; mean: shabby conduct. [from Anglo-Saxon sceabb]

Shabuoth or **Shavuoth** or **Shavuot** noun the Jewish 'Feast of Weeks', celebrated seven weeks after the first day of Passover to commemorate the giving of the Law to Moses. [from Hebrew Shabuoth]

shack — noun a roughly built hut. — verb (usually **shack up with someone**) slang to live with them, usually without being married.

shackle — noun **1** either of a pair of metal bands, joined by a chain, locked round a prisoner's wrists or ankles to limit movement. **2** anything that restricts freedom. **3** a U-shaped metal loop closed over by a bolt, used for fastening ropes or chains together. — verb to restrain with, or as if with, shackles. [from Anglo-Saxon sceacul]

Shackleton, Sir Ernest Henry (1874–1922) Irish explorer, born in Kilkee, Co Kildare, Ireland (now Irish Republic). He was a junior officer in Scott's National Antarctic Expedition (1901–3), and reached a point 155.2km/97mi from the South Pole in his own expedition of 1909. In 1915 his ship Endurance was crushed in the ice, and he and five others made a perilous journey of 1 300km/800mi to bring relief to the crew. He died in S Georgia during a fourth Antarctic expedition.

shad noun (PL. **shad**, **shads**) any of a family of edible herring-like fish. [from Anglo-Saxon sceadd]

shade — noun **1** the blocking or partial blocking out of sunlight, or the dimness caused by this. **2** an area from which sunlight has been wholly or partially blocked. **3** such an area represented in a drawing or painting. **4** the state of appearing comparatively unimpressive: lived in the shade of his brother's achievements / her singing puts mine in the shade. **5** any device used as a shield from direct light; a lampshade. **6** a colour, especially one similar to but slightly different from a principal colour. **7** a slight amount; a touch. — verb **1** to block or partially block out sunlight from. **2** to draw or paint so as to give the impression of shade. **3** (usually **shade off** or **away**) to change gradually or unnoticeably. [from Anglo-Saxon sceadu]

shadiness noun being shady.

shading noun the representation of areas of shade, eg by close parallel lines in a drawing.

shadoof or **shaduf** noun an apparatus for lifting water from rivers and watercourses and transferring it to the land or into a trough. It consists of a bucket suspended from a counterpoised pivoted rod, and is chiefly used for irrigation in the flood plain of the Nile. [from Egyptian Arabic shaduf]

shadow — noun **1** a dark shape on a surface, produced when an object stands between the surface and a source of light. **2** an area darkened by the blocking out of light. **3** a slight amount; a hint or trace. **4** a sense of gloom or foreboding: cast a shadow over the proceedings. **5** a greatly weakened or otherwise reduced version: a shadow of her former self. **6** a constant companion. **7** a person following another closely and secretively. — verb **1** to follow closely and secretively. **2** to put into darkness by blocking out light. — adj. denoting a spokesperson or persons with the main opposition political party, who would become minister if the party were elected to power: shadow Foreign Secretary. [from Anglo-Saxon sceadwe, accusative case of sceadu see SHADE]

shadow-box verb intrans. to practise shadow-boxing.

shadow-boxing noun boxing against an imaginary opponent as training.

shadow cabinet Politics a body made up of leading members of an opposition party ready to take office should their party assume power. In the UK, members of the shadow cabinet have 'portfolios' corresponding to the various governmental posts and are their party's official spokespeople on matters relating to that area.

shadow-mask tube a type of cathode-ray tube for colour television, in which electron beams from three separate guns, modulated by the red, green, and blue signals, are deflected by the scanning system through holes on the shadow-mask plate to fall on minute phosphor dots of the appropriate colour making up the screen. The dots glow according to the intensity of the beam reaching them.

shadow puppets puppets which are manipulated to cast a shadow on a screen. There are two major techniques: the two-dimensional figure worked by sticks from below, as in Balinese and Javanese shadow theatre; and puppets worked from behind with sticks at right angles to the screen and the figures pressed close to its surface, as in Chinese and Turkish shadow theatre.

shadowy adj. **1** dark and not clearly visible. **2** darkened by shadows.

Shadwell, Thomas (c.1642–92) English dramatist, born in Brandon, Norfolk. He wrote the successful satirical comedy, The Sullen Lovers (1668), and other 'comedies of manners' (eg Epsom-Wells, 1672) in which he satirized such people as John Dryden, continuing their literary feud. (In turn, Dryden ridiculed Shadwell in MacFlecknoe, 1682). He succeeded Dryden as Poet Laureate in 1689.

shady adj. (**shadier**, **shadiest**) **1** sheltered, or giving shelter, from sunlight. **2** colloq. disreputable; probably dishonest or illegal.

SHAEF abbrev. Supreme Headquarters of the Allied Expeditionary Force.

Shaffer, Peter (Levin) (1926–) English dramatist, born in Liverpool. His plays are variations on the themes of genius and mediocrity, faith and reason, and the nature of God. Among his major ones are The Royal Hunt of the Sun (1964), Equus (1973), Amadeus (1979), and the comedy Lettice and Lovage (1987).

shaft noun **1** the long straight handle of a tool or weapon. **2** any long straight part, eg a revolving rod that transmits motion in vehicle engines. **3** a vertical passageway, especially one through which a lift moves. **4** either of the projecting parts of a cart, etc to which a horse or other animal is fastened. **5** a thing moving or aimed with the directness or violent force of an arrow or missile: shaft of light / shafts of sarcasm. **6** Archit. the long middle part of a column, between the base and the capital. [from Anglo-Saxon sceaft]

Shaftesbury, Anthony Ashley Cooper, 1st Earl of (1621–83) English statesman, born in Wimborne St Giles, Dorset. A member of the Short Parliament (1640) and of the Barebones Parliament (1653), he was made one of Cromwell's Council of State, but from 1655 was in opposition. At the Restoration he was Chancellor of the Exchequer (1661–72), a member of the court cabal (1667), an earl (1672), and Lord Chancellor (1672–3). Dismissed in 1673, he led the opposition to the succession of James, Duke of York (later James II). Charged with treason in 1681, he was acquitted, but fled to Holland in 1682.

Shaftesbury, Anthony Ashley Cooper, 3rd Earl of (1671–1713) English philosopher, born in London, the grandson of the 1st Earl of Shaftesbury. He entered parliament in 1695, but ill health drove him from politics to literature. One of the leading English deists, he is best-known for his essays, collected as *Characteristics of Men, Manners, Opinions, Times* (1711).

Shaftesbury, Anthony Ashley Cooper, 7th Earl of (1801–85) English factory reformer and philanthropist, born in London. He entered parliament in 1826, and as the main spokesman of the factory reform movement he piloted successive Factory Acts (1847, 1859) through parliament, regulated conditions in the coal mines (1842), and provided lodging houses for the poor (1851). A committed Christian, he was also a leader of the evangelical movement within the Church of England.

shaft grave *Archaeol.* a deep burial, especially a group of six tombs behind the Lion's Gate at the W end of the citadel of Mycenae in Greece.
◇ Each tomb was used for between two and five burials of members of a princely or royal family, and contained the first evidence of the flowering of a rich and advanced society on the Greek mainland in the 16c BC. In the rectangular, rock-cut, wooden-roofed chambers were finely crafted gold, silver, and bronze artefacts, including death masks, drinking vessels, weapons, and armour. The first five tombs were excavated in 1876 by Heinrich Schliemann, who believed (erroneously) that he had uncovered the tombs of Agamemnon and his contemporaries.

shag[1] *noun* **1** a ragged mass of hair. **2** a long coarse pile or nap on fabric. **3** tobacco coarsely cut into shreds. [from Anglo-Saxon *sceacga*]

shag[2] *noun* a species of cormorant which has a shaggy tuft on its head. [see SHAG[1]]

shag[3] *coarse slang* — *verb* (**shagged**, **shagging**) **1** to have sexual intercourse with. **2** to tire. — *noun* an act of sexual intercourse.

shagginess *noun* a shaggy state.

shaggy *adj.* (**shaggier, shaggiest**) **1** *said of hair or fur* rough and untidy in appearance. **2** *said of a person or animal* having shaggy hair or fur.

shaggy dog story a rambling story or joke amusing only because of its ridiculous length and pointlessness.

shagreen *noun* **1** coarse grainy leather, especially made from the skin of a horse or donkey. **2** the rough skin of a shark or ray, used as an abrasive. [from Turkish *sagri*, horse's rump]

Shah, Eddy (Selim Jehane) (1944–) English newspaper magnate and novelist, born in Cambridge. He worked in theatre and television before launching the *Sale and Altrincham Messenger* in 1974, and the *Stockport Messenger* in 1977. He came to national attention when he confronted the unions over working practices, and won a protracted strike. In 1986 he launched the *Today* newspaper, and was its Chairman and Chief Executive until 1988. He then launched the *Post*, which folded after a few months. His novels include *Ring of Red Roses* (1991), and *The Lucy Ghosts* (1992).

shah *noun Hist.* a title of the former rulers of Iran. [from Persian *shah*]

Shah Jahan (1592–1666) Mughal Emperor of India (1628–58), born in Lahore (now in Pakistan). His reign saw two wars in the Deccan (1636, 1655), the subjugation of Bijapur and Golconda (1636), and attacks on the Uzbegs and Persians. A ruthless but able ruler, the magnificence of his court was unequalled. He built the Taj Mahal as the tomb of his beloved third wife, Mumtaz Mahal.

shake — *verb* (PAST TENSE **shook**; PAST PARTICIPLE **shaken**) **1** to move with quick, often violent to-and-fro or up-and-down movements. **2** (*also* **shake something up**) to mix it in this way. **3** to wave violently and threateningly. **4** *trans., intrans.* to tremble or cause to tremble, totter, or shiver. **5** to cause intense shock or agitation within: *revelations that shook the nation.* **6** (*also* **shake someone up**) to disturb or upset them greatly. **7** to cause to waver; to weaken: *shook my confidence.* **8** *intrans.* to shake hands. — *noun* **1** an act or the action of shaking. **2** *colloq.* a very short while; a moment. **3** (**the shakes**) *colloq.* a fit of uncontrollable trembling. **4** a milk shake.
— **no great shakes** *colloq.* of no great importance, ability, or worth.
shake a leg *colloq.* to hurry up or get moving.
shake down to go to bed, especially in a makeshift bed.
shake someone down *slang* to extort money from them.
shake something down *slang* to search it thoroughly.
shake hands with someone to greet someone by clasping hands.
shake one's head to move one's head from side to side as a sign of rejection or disagreement.
shake something *or* **someone off 1** to get rid of them; to free oneself from them. **2** to escape from them.
shake someone up *colloq.* to stimulate them into action, from a state of lethargy or apathy.
shake something up *colloq.* to reorganize it thoroughly.
[from Anglo-Saxon *sceacan*]

shakedown *noun colloq.* **1** a makeshift bed, originally made by shaking down straw. **2** an act of extortion. **3** *chiefly North Amer.* a trial run or operation to familiarize personnel with equipment and procedures.

shake-out *noun colloq.* same as SHAKE-UP.

shaker *noun* a container from which something, eg salt, is dispensed by shaking, or in which something, eg a cocktail, is mixed by shaking.

Shakers the popular name for members of the United Society for Believers in Christ's Second Appearing, a millenarian sect founded in England under the leadership of 'Mother' Ann Lee (1736–84), a psychic visionary believed to be the second Incarnation of Christ. Led to America by her in 1774, they became communitarian and pacifist, and their popular name arose from their ecstatic dancing. Their strict celibacy led to their virtual disappearance by the late 20c.

Shakespeare, William (1564–1616) English dramatist and poet, born in Stratford-upon-Avon, Warwickshire. He became an actor in London and when the theatres were closed for the plague (1592–4), he wrote the long poems *Venus and Adonis* and *The Rape of Lucrece.* His sonnets fall into two groups: 1 to 126 are addressed to a fair young man, and 127 to 154 to a 'dark lady' who captivates both the young man and the poet. From 1594 he acted with the Lord Chamberlain's company of players, later 'the King's Men', the company that built the Globe Theatre (1598) and for which he wrote many of his 37 plays. His prolific output brought him success in the fields of comedy, history, and tragedy. Great popular success at the Globe was accompanied by acclaim at court.

Shakespeare a statue of William Shakespeare by Louis François Roubiliac (1758, British Museum).

Shakespearean *or* **Shakespearian** *adj.* relating to or characteristic of the literary works or style of William Shakespeare.

shake-up *noun colloq.* a fundamental change or reorganization.

shakily *adv.* in a shaky way, unsteadily.

shakiness *noun* being shaky.

shako *noun* (PL. **shakos, shakoes**) a tall nearly cylindrical military cap with a plume. [from Hungarian *csákó*]

shaky *adj.* (**shakier, shakiest**) **1** trembling, as with weakness or illness. **2** *colloq.* not solid, sound, or secure.

shale *noun Geol.* a fine-grained black, grey, brown, or red sedimentary rock formed by the compression of clay, silt, or sand under the weight of overlying rocks. Shales are easily split into thin layers. [from Anglo-Saxon *scealu*]

Shalimar Gardens a garden designed by the Mughal emperor Jahangir for his wife, Nur Jahan, in 1616. The garden is laid out on four terraces by Dal Lake, in Kashmir, India.

shall *verb, aux.* expressing: **1** the future tense of other verbs, especially when the subject is *I* or *we*. **2** determination, intention, certainty, and obligation, especially when the subject is *you, he, she, it,* or *they*: *they shall succeed / you shall have what you want / he shall become king / you shall not*

Plays of Shakespeare		
Title	Date	Category
The Two Gentleman of Verona	1590–1	comedy
Henry VI Part One	1592	history
Henry VI Part Two	1592	history
Henry VI Part Three	1592	history
Titus Andronicus	1592	tragedy
Richard III	1592–3	history
The Taming of the Shrew	1593	comedy
The Comedy of Errors	1594	comedy
Love's Labour's Lost	1594–5	comedy
Richard II	1595	history
Romeo and Juliet	1595	tragedy
A Midsummer Night's Dream	1595	comedy
King John	1596	history
The Merchant of Venice	1596–7	comedy
Henry VI Part One	1596–7	history
The Merry Wives of Windsor	1597–8	comedy
Henry IV Part Two	1597–8	history
Much Ado About Nothing	1598	dark comedy
Henry V	1598–9	history
Julius Caesar	1599	Roman
As You Like It	1599–1600	comedy
Hamlet, Prince of Denmark	1600–1	tragedy
Twelfth Night, or What You Will	1601	comedy
Troilus and Cressida	1602	tragedy
Measure for Measure	1603	dark comedy
Othello	1603–4	tragedy
All's Well That Ends Well	1604–5	dark comedy
Timon of Athens	1605	romantic drama
The Tragedy of King Lear	1605–6	tragedy
Macbeth	1606	tragedy
Antony and Cleopatra	1606	tragedy
Pericles	1607	romance
Coriolanus	1608	Roman
The Winter's Tale	1609	romance
Cymbeline	1610	comedy
The Tempest	1611	comedy
Henry VIII	1613	history

kill. **3** a question implying future action, often with the sense of an offer or suggestion, especially when the subject is *I* or *we*: *what shall we do?* / *shall I give you a hand?* [from Anglo-Saxon *sceal*]

shallot *noun* a plant of the onion family, with a smallish oval bulb growing in clusters. [from Old French *eschalote*]

Shallow the fatuous Justice in Shakespeare's *Henry IV Part II* and *The Merry Wives of Windsor*.

shallow — *adj.* **1** having little depth. **2** not profound or sincere; superficial. — *noun* (*often* **shallows**) a shallow place or part, especially in water. [from Middle English *schalowe*]

shalom *noun, interj.* a Jewish greeting or farewell. [from Hebrew *shalom*, peace (be with you)]

Shalott, The Lady of see LADY OF SHALOTT, THE.

shalt the form of the verb **shall** used after *thou*.

shaly *adj.* consisting of or like shale.

sham — *adj.* false; pretended; insincere. — *verb trans., intrans.* (**shammed, shamming**) to pretend or fake. — *noun* **1** anything not genuine. **2** a person who shams; especially an impostor.

shaman *noun* (PL. **shamans**) a priest who uses magic, especially his ability to make his spirit leave his body, to cure illness, commune with gods and spirits, prophesy, influence the weather and food supply, etc. [from Russian *shaman*]

shamanism *noun* a religion, especially of N Asia, dominated by shamans and belief in their powers.

shamanistic *adj.* relating to shamanism.

shamble — *verb intrans.* (**shamble along, past,** *etc*) to walk with slow, awkward, tottering steps. — *noun* such a walk or pace. [from SHAMBLES, suggesting trestle-like legs]

shambles *sing. noun* **1** *colloq.* a confused mess; a state of total disorder. **2** a meat market. **3** a slaughterhouse. **4** a scene of slaughter or carnage. [from Anglo-Saxon *scamel*, stool]

shambling — *noun* awkward or unsteady progress. — *adj.* that shambles; awkward and unsteady.

shambolic *adj. colloq.* totally disorganized; chaotic.

shame — *noun* **1** an embarrassing or degrading sense of guilt, foolishness, or failure as a result of one's own actions or those of another person associated with one. **2** the capacity to feel this. **3** disgrace or loss of reputation; a person or thing bringing this. **4** a regrettable or disappointing event or situation. — *verb* **1** to cause to feel shame. **2** (**shame someone into something**) to provoke them into taking action by inspiring feelings of shame: *shamed him into telling the truth.* **3** to bring disgrace on. — **put someone to shame** to make them seem inadequate by comparison. [from Anglo-Saxon *sceamu*]

shamefaced *adj.* **1** showing shame or embarrassment. **2** modest or bashful. [originally *shamefast*, held by shame]

shamefacedly *adv.* with a shamefaced manner.

shameful *adj.* bringing or deserving shame; disgraceful.

shamefully *adv.* in a shameful way.

shameless *adj.* **1** showing no shame; not capable of feeling shame. **2** done entirely without shame; blatant.

shamelessly *adv.* in a shameless way.

shamelessness *noun* being shameless.

shammy *noun* (PL. **shammies**) *colloq.* a chamois leather.

shampoo — *noun* (PL. **shampoos**) **1** a soapy liquid for washing the hair and scalp. **2** a similar liquid for cleaning carpets or upholstery. **3** a treatment with either liquid. — *verb* (**shampoos, shampooed**) to wash or clean with shampoo. [from Hindi *champo*, squeeze]

shamrock *noun* any of various plants whose green leaves have three rounded leaflets, eg clover, used as the national emblem of Ireland. [from Irish Gaelic *seamrog*]

Shandy, Walter the flamboyant, loquacious father of Tristram in Laurence Sterne's *Tristram Shandy*. Also his genial old soldier brother Toby (Capt Tobias), who is only fleetingly distracted from his overriding interest in war games by the attentions of Widow Wadman.

shandy *noun* (PL. **shandies**) a mixture of beer and lemonade or ginger beer.

Shane a male and more recently a female name. [an anglicization of SEAN]

Shanghai POP (1990) 13.3m, the largest city in China. AREA 5 800sq km/2 239sq mi (municipality). It is a port situated in the E part of the country, on the Yellow Sea, on the Huangpu and Wusong rivers. HISTORY developed in the Yuan period as a cotton centre; trading centre in the 17c–18c; opened to foreign trade in 1842. NOTABLE FEATURES People's Park; People's Square; Jade Buddha Temple (1882), Longhua Temple (c.7c); Industrial Exhibition Hall; Museum of Natural History; Songjiang County Square Pagoda and Dragon Wall (11c); Yu Yuan (Garden of Happiness), built in 1577, the basis for 'willow pattern' chinaware.

shanghai *verb* (**shanghais, shanghaied, shanghaiing**) *colloq.* **1** to kidnap and send to sea as a sailor. **2** to trick into any unpleasant situation. [named after Shanghai in China, from the former use of this method in recruiting sailors for trips to the East]

shank *noun* **1** the lower leg of an animal, especially a horse, between the knee and the foot. **2** a cut of meat from the (especially upper) leg of an animal. **3** a shaft or other long straight part. [from Anglo-Saxon *sceanca*, leg]

Shankar, Ravi (1920–) Indian sitar player, born at Varanasi. He took up a professional career as a player and composer in the 1940s. Through his foreign tours and recordings he has done much to make Indian classical music more widely known.

Shanklin see SANDOWN.

shanks's pony *colloq.* one's own legs as a means of travelling.

Shannon, Claude Elwood (1916–) US applied mathematician and pioneer of communication theory, born in Gaylord, Michigan. After graduating from the Massachusetts Institute of Technology, he worked at the Bell Telephone Laboratories (1941–72). His work helped translate circuit design from an art into a science, and its central tenet — that information can be treated like any other quantity and can be manipulated by a machine — had a profound impact on the development of computing.

Shannon, Gaelic **Rineanna** POP (1991) 8 000, a town in Clare county, Munster, W Irish Republic. It lies W of Limerick, near the R Shannon.

Shannon, River the longest river in the Irish Republic, length c.385km/240mi. It rises in Cavan county, Ulster, and flows SW through L Allen, L Ree, and L Derg to Limerick Bay. It is navigable for most of its length. There is hydroelectric power at Ardnacrusha.

shan't shall not.

shantung *noun* a plain and usually undyed silk fabric with a rugged, slightly coarse finish. [from *Shantung*, province in China where it was originally made]

shanty¹ *noun* (PL. **shanties**) a roughly built hut; a shack. [from Canadian French *chantier*, woodcutter's cabin]

shanty² *noun* (PL. **shanties**) a rhythmical song of a kind formerly sung by sailors working in unison. [from French *chanter*, to sing]

shanty town an area in which poor people live in makeshift or ramshackle housing.

SHAPE *abbrev.* Supreme Headquarters Allied Powers Europe.

shape — *noun* **1** the outline or form of anything. **2** a person's body or figure. **3** form, person, etc: *an assistant in the shape of my brother.* **4** a desired form or (especially physical) condition: *get the contract into shape / keep in shape.* **5** condition generally: *in bad shape.* **6** an unidentifiable figure: *shapes lurking in the dark.* **7** a mould or pattern. **8** a figure, especially geometric. — *verb* **1** to give a particular form to; to fashion. **2** to influence to an important extent: *shaped history.* **3** to devise or develop to suit a particular purpose. — **shape up** *colloq.* **1** to appear to be developing in a particular way: *is shaping up rather well.* **2** to be promising; to progress or develop well. **take shape 1** to take on a definite form. **2** to become recognizable as the desired result of plans or theories. [from Anglo-Saxon *scieppan*]

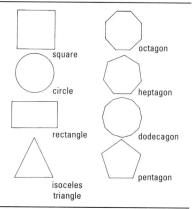

square
octagon
circle
heptagon
rectangle
dodecagon
isoceles triangle
pentagon

shapes

shapeless *adj.* **1** not having a regular describable shape. **2** unattractively shaped.

shapelessness *noun* being shapeless.

shapeliness *noun* being shapely.

shapely *adj., said especially of the human body* well proportioned; attractively shaped.

Shapley, Harlow (1885–1972) US astronomer, born in Nashville, Missouri. Working at Mount Wilson Observatory in California (1914–21), his research indicated that the Sun is near the edge of our stellar system and not at its centre as had been the accepted view. His new model of our galaxy was soon adopted, and he was appointed Director of Harvard College Observatory in 1921.

shard *or* **sherd** *noun* a fragment of something brittle, usually pottery, especially when found on an archaeological site. [from Anglo-Saxon *sceard*]

share¹ — *noun* **1** a portion given to or contributed by each of several people or groups. **2** any of the units into which the total wealth of a business company is divided, ownership of which gives the right to a portion of the company's profits. — *verb* **1** (**share something** or **share in something**) to have joint possession or use of it, or joint responsibility for it, with another or others. **2** (*also* **share something out**) to divide it into portions, distributed to each of several people or groups. [from Anglo-Saxon *scearu*]

share² *noun* a ploughshare. [from Anglo-Saxon *scear*]

shareholder *noun* a person who owns shares in a company.

share-out *noun* a division into shares; a distribution.

shareware *noun Comput.* software readily available for a nominal fee.

Shari'ah the sacred law of Islam, which embraces all aspects of a Muslim's life. The Shari'ah has four sources: the *Koran* (Koran), the *sunna* or 'practice' of the Prophet Mohammed, *'ijma* or consensus of opinion, and *qiyas* or 'reasoning by analogy'.

Sharjah *or* **Shariqah** POP (1985) 269 000, the third largest of the United Arab Emirates, situated NE of Dubai. AREA 2 600sq km/1 004sq mi. CAPITAL Sharjah. ECONOMY offshore oil production began in 1974; natural gas; ship and vehicle repairing; cement; paper bags; steel products; paint.

shark *noun* **1** any of various large fishes belonging to the class Elasmobranchii, found in seas worldwide, but most common in tropical waters. Sharks have a skeleton made of cartilage, a spindle-shaped body, skin covered with tooth-like scales, and a tail fin with a long upper lobe and a shorter lower lobe. **2** *colloq.* a ruthless or dishonest person, especially one who swindles or exploits. [perhaps from German *Schurke*, scoundrel; the second sense may be a different word]
◇ Sharks have been in existence for at least 500m years, and their sharp teeth are in fact modified and enlarged scales. Unlike bony fishes, they lack a swim bladder (which provides buoyancy), so must swim continuously in order to avoid sinking. They range in size from the dogfish, which is about 1.5m long, to the whale shark, which is the largest living fish, up to 15m in length. The whale shark and basking shark feed on plankton, but many species, including the porbeagle and great white shark, which have crescent-shaped mouths on the underside of their snouts, are carnivorous, and hunt their prey by scent. The great white shark has been known to attack humans.

hammerhead shark

Shark Bay a bay in the Indian Ocean off Western Australia. Its main port is Carnarvon, on the Gascoyne River. It is a World Heritage site.

sharkskin *noun* **1** leather made from a shark's skin. **2** smooth rayon fabric with a dull sheen.

Sharon a female first name. [from the biblical place-name]

Sharp, Becky, in full **Rebecca Sharp** one of the two women at the centre of William Makepeace Thackeray's *Vanity Fair*, who marries Rawdon Crawley and leads an increasingly unprincipled and promiscuous life.

Sharp, Cecil (James) (1859–1924) English collector of folk songs and dances, born in London. He practised law in Australia, but then turned to music, worked as an organist, and published several collections of British and US folk material. He returned to England in 1892 and founded the Folk-Dance Society in 1911.

sharp — *adj.* **1** having a thin edge that can cut or a point that can pierce. **2** having a bitter pungent taste. **3** severely felt: *sharp pain.* **4** sudden and acute: *sharp increases / a sharp bend.* **5** quick to perceive, act, or react; keenly intelligent: *sharp-witted.* **6** abrupt or harsh in speech. **7** easily perceived; clear-cut: *in sharp contrast.* **8** sarcastic: *sharp-tongued.* **9** *colloq.* stylish. **10** *Mus.* higher in pitch by a semitone: *C sharp.* **11** *Mus.* out of tune by being slightly too high in pitch. — *noun* **1** *Mus.* a sharp note; a sign indicating this ♯. **2** *colloq.* a practised cheat: *a card sharp.* — *adv.* **1** punctually; on the dot. **2** suddenly: *pulled up sharp.* **3** *Mus.* untunefully high in pitch.
— **look sharp** *colloq.* to hurry up.
[from Anglo-Saxon *scearp*]

sharpen *verb trans., intrans.* (**sharpened, sharpening**) to make or become sharp.

sharpener *noun* a person or tool that sharpens.

sharper *noun colloq.* a practised cheat; a sharp.

Sharpeville a black African township in Transvaal province, NE South Africa, situated S of Johannesburg. It was the scene of the Sharpeville massacre in 1960 and the centre of the Sharpeville Students National Resistance Movement.

Sharpeville massacre an incident on 21 Mar 1960, when police opened fire on a crowd demonstrating against laws restricting non-white movements and requiring non-whites to carry identification cards (the so-called *pass laws*), killing 69 people and wounding 180 others. It led to the banning of both the ANC and the PAC and remains a symbolic day for all black nationalists in South Africa.

sharply *adv.* in a sharp way; harshly.

sharpness *noun* a sharp quality.

sharp practice dishonesty; cheating.

sharpshooter *noun* a good marksman.

sharpshooting *noun* accurate shooting.

Shatt al-Arab a tidal river formed by the union of the Tigris and Euphrates rivers, SE Iraq. It flows 192km/119mi SE through marshland to enter the Arabian Gulf. The river forms part of the Iraq–Iran border in its lower course. It has a wide delta, containing the world's largest date-palm groves and is navigable for ocean-going vessels as far as Basra. An international commission in 1935 gave control to Iraq, but disputes over navigational rights continued, and were one of the issues that led to the outbreak of the Iran–Iraq War in 1980.

shatter *verb* (**shattered, shattering**) **1** *trans., intrans.* to break into tiny pieces, usually suddenly or forcefully. **2** to destroy completely, or cause to break down: *shattered hopes.* **3** to upset greatly. **4** *colloq.* to tire out; to exhaust.

shattered *adj. colloq.* exhausted, extremely upset.

shattering *adj.* that shatters; devastating.

shave — *verb* **1** to cut off (hair) from (the face or other part of the body) with a razor or shaver. **2** *intrans.* to shave one's growth of beard in this way. **3** to remove thin slivers from the surface of (especially wood) with a bladed tool. **4** to graze the surface of, or narrowly miss, in passing. — *noun* **1** an act or the process of shaving one's growth of beard. **2** a narrow miss or escape: *a close shave.* **3** a tool for shaving wood. [from Anglo-Saxon *sceafan*]

shaven *adj.* shaved.

shaver *noun* **1** an electrical device with a moving blade or set of blades for shaving hair. **2** *old colloq.* use a young boy.

shaving *noun* **1** the removal of hair with a razor. **2** a thin sliver, especially of wood, taken off with a sharp tool.

Shaw, Anna Howard (1847–1919) US minister and feminist, born in Newcastle upon Tyne,

UK. Her family migrated to the USA, and after a youth of considerable privation she had a university education, became a Methodist minister, joined in the Women's Christian Temperance Union, and after striking up a friendship with Susan B Anthony became active in the women's suffrage movement. She was President of the National American Women's Suffrage Association (1904–15).

Shaw, Artie, originally **Arthur Arshawsky** (1910–) US bandleader and clarinettist, born in New York City. He tried novel writing and numerous music jobs before he found success as leader of a swing band, notably with 'Begin the Beguine' (1938), 'Star Dust' (1940), and 'Moonglow' (1941), and rivalled Benny Goodman as a clarinet soloist. Notoriously, he married eight times, and his wives included the actresses Lana Turner, Ava Gardner, and Evelyn Keyes. He quit music altogether in 1955.

Shaw, George Bernard (1856–1950) Irish dramatist, essayist, and pamphleteer, born in Dublin. He moved to London in 1876 and in 1882 turned to socialism, joined the committee of the Fabian Society, and began writing critical essays. He wrote over 40 plays: among his early successes were *Arms and the Man* (1894), *Candida* (1897), and *The Devil's Disciple* (1897), followed by *Man and Superman* (1903) and *Major Barbara* (1905). Later plays include *Pygmalion* (1913), an 'anti-romantic' comedy (adapted as a musical play, *My Fair Lady*, in 1956, filmed in 1964), *Heartbreak House* (1919), *Saint Joan* (1923) and *The Apple Cart* (1929). He was also a lifelong advocate and practitioner of vegetarianism. He left money in his will for the devising of a new English alphabet on phonetic principles (which came to be called 'Shavian'). In 1935 he was awarded the Nobel Prize for Literature.

Shaw, (Richard) Norman (1831–1912) English architect, born in Edinburgh. He worked in many styles ranging from Gothic Revival to neo-Baroque, and became a leader of the trend away from Victorian style back to traditional Georgian design. His designs include the Old Swan House, Chelsea, (1876), New Scotland Yard (1888), and the Piccadilly Hotel (1905).

shawl *noun* a large single piece of fabric used as a loose covering for the head or shoulders, or for wrapping a baby in. [from Persian *shal*]

Shawnee an Algonkian-speaking Native American group who originally settled in Ohio, but who were pushed out of the area by the Iroquois. They were defeated in 1794 by US forces at the battle of Fallen Timbers, and were divided up into three sections and settled in Oklahoma. The present-day population is c.2 200.

she *pron.* the female person or animal, or thing thought of as female (eg a ship), named before or understood from the context. [from Anglo-Saxon *seo*]

sheaf — *noun* (PL. **sheaves**) a bundle, especially of reaped corn, tied together. — *verb* (*also* **sheave**) to tie up in a bundle. [from Anglo-Saxon *sceaf*]

shear — *verb* (PAST TENSE **sheared**; PAST PARTICIPLE **shorn**) **1** to clip or cut off with a large pair of clippers. **2** to cut the fleece off (a sheep). **3** (*usually* **be shorn of something**) to be stripped or deprived of it: *was shorn of all authority.* **4** *trans., intrans.* (*also* **shear off**) *said of metal* to twist or break under strain. — *noun* **1** (**shears**) a two-bladed cutting-tool like a large pair of scissors; clippers. **2** a twisting or breaking of metal under strain. [from Anglo-Saxon *sceran*]

shearer *noun* a person who shears sheep.

shearwater *noun* **1** a petrel with a long slender bill, dark plumage on the upper part of the body, and pale plumage beneath. Some species with long wings and tail are found over the open ocean, and fish in flight. Species with shorter wings and tail fish while swimming near coasts. **2** a skimmer.

sheath *noun* **1** a covering for the blade of a sword or knife. **2** a long close-fitting covering. **3** *old use* a condom. **4** a straight tight-fitting dress. [from Anglo-Saxon *sceath*]

sheathe *verb* to put into, or protect or cover with, a sheath.

sheave, and **sheaves**. See SHEAF.

Sheba, Queen of (c.10c BC) a biblical character, mentioned in 1 Kings 10 and 2 Chronicles 9. A monarch from either SW Arabia (modern Yemen) or N Arabia, she journeyed to the splendid court of Solomon in Jerusalem to test his wisdom and exchange gifts.

shebang *noun slang* affair; matter: *the whole shebang*.

shed[1] *noun* a wooden or metal outbuilding of any size, for working in or for storage or shelter. [from SHADE]

shed[2] *verb* (**shedding**; PAST TENSE AND PAST PARTICIPLE **shed**) **1** to release or cause to flow: *shed tears*. **2** to cast off or get rid of: *shed a skin / shed jobs*. **3** to cast: *shed light on*. **4** to allow to flow off: *this fabric sheds water*. [from Anglo-Saxon *sceadan*]

she'd *contr.* **1** she had. **2** she would.

sheen *noun* shine; glossiness; lustre. [from Anglo-Saxon *scene*]

Sheena a female first name. [an anglicization of *Sine*, a Gaelic form of JANE]

sheep *noun* (PL. **sheep**) **1** any of various wild or domesticated species of a herbivorous mammal, belonging to the family Bovidae, and having a stocky body covered with a thick woolly fleece. It is kept as a farm animal worldwide for its meat and wool. **2** a meek person, especially one who follows or obeys unquestioningly. **3** a member of a congregation (thought of as being looked after by the pastor). [from Anglo-Saxon *sceap*]
◇ The sheep was probably first domesticated by humans about 12 000 years ago, and there are now over 400 breeds of the common domestic sheep (*Ovis aries*), which vary greatly in size and shape, and in the colour and texture of the fleece. The Merino sheep provides the best wool. Sheep can be grazed on poor soil, and in medieval England they were a major source of wealth. Today they are reared in very large numbers in Australia, New Zealand, and South Africa.

sheep-dip *noun* an approved chemical used to disinfect sheep in a dipping bath, in order to control parasitic diseases such as sheep scab.

sheepdog *noun* **1** a dog trained to herd sheep. **2** any of various breeds of dog originally trained to herd sheep.

sheepish *adj.* embarrassed because of having done something wrong or foolish.

sheepishly *adv.* in a sheepish way.

sheepishness *noun* being sheepish.

sheepshank *noun* a knot used for shortening a rope.

sheepskin *noun* **1** a sheep's skin with the wool left on it, or a rug or piece of clothing made from it. **2** leather made from sheep's skin.

sheer[1] — *adj.* **1** complete; absolute; nothing but: *sheer madness*. **2** *said of a cliff, etc* vertical or nearly vertical. **3** so fine as to be almost transparent. — *adv.* **1** completely. **2** vertically or nearly vertically: *rock face rising sheer*. [from Middle English *schere*]

sheer[2] *verb intrans.* (**sheer off, away**, *etc*) **1** to change course suddenly; to swerve. **2** to move (away), especially from a person or thing disliked or feared.

Sheerness POP (1981) 11 000, a port and resort town on the I of Sheppey, Kent, SE England.

sheet[1] — *noun* **1** a large broad piece of fabric, especially for covering the mattress of a bed.

2 any large broad piece or expanse. **3** a piece (of paper), especially of a size for writing on. **4** a pamphlet or newspaper. — *verb* **1** to provide or cover with sheets. **2** *intrans. said of rain, ice, etc* to form, or fall in, a sheet-like mass. [from Anglo-Saxon *scete*]

sheet[2] *noun Naut.* a controlling rope attached to the lower corner of a sail. [from Anglo-Saxon *sceata*, corner]

sheet-anchor *noun* **1** an extra anchor for use in an emergency. **2** a person or thing relied on for support, especially in a crisis; a last hope. [originally *shoot-anchor*]

sheeting *noun* fabric used for making sheets.

sheet music music printed on loose sheets of paper.

Sheffield POP (1992e) 531 000, an industrial city and county town in South Yorkshire, N England. It lies on the R Don and is separated from Manchester to the W by the High Peak of Derbyshire. HISTORY Mary Queen of Scots was imprisoned here from 1570 to 1584; the city developed as a cutlery-manufacturing town in the early 18c and as a steel town in the 19c; city status was achieved in 1893; there was major rebuilding after bomb destruction during World War II. NOTABLE FEATURES Cathedral Church of St Peter and St Paul (dating from the 12c); Mappin Art Gallery, Ruskin Gallery; Crucible Theatre; Abbeydale Industrial Hamlet; Cutlers' Hall (1832).

Sheffield plate an imitation silver plate made from copper sheet rolled between films of silver. The technique was discovered (c.1742) by a Sheffield cutler, Thomas Boulsover (1706–88).

Sheherezade *or* **Scheherezade** a symphonic suite by Nicolai Rimsky-Korsakov (Op 35, 1888), based on the Arabian Nights stories.

sheikh *or* **sheik** *noun* **1** the head of an Arab tribe, village or family. **2** a Muslim leader. [from Arabic *shaikh*, old man]

sheikhdom *or* **sheikdom** *noun* the territory of a sheikh.

Sheila a female first name. [an anglicized spelling of Irish Gaelic *Sile*]

sheila *noun colloq. Austral., New Zealand* a woman or girl. [from the name SHEILA]

shekel *noun* **1** the standard unit of currency in Israel, divided into 100 agorot. **2** an ancient Jewish coin and weight. **3** (**shekels**) *slang* money. [from Hebrew *sheqel*]

Shekinah the term for God's special presence with his people, Israel; in rabbinic works, his immanence, often associated with particular locations where he consecrated a place or object, and linked with the motifs of light and glory. Some later Jewish philosophers considered it a created entity distinct from God. [Hebrew, = dwelling, residence]

Shelburne, William Petty Fitzmaurice, 2nd Earl of (1737–1805) British statesman, born in Dublin. After being President of the Board of Trade (1763) and Secretary of State (1766), he became Prime Minister (1782–3) on the death of Rockingham, but resigned when outvoted by the coalition between Charles Fox and James North.

sheldrake *noun* a male shelduck.

shelduck *noun* a large brightly coloured duck of Europe, Africa and Asia. [from dialect *sheld*, pied + DUCK]

shelf *noun* (PL. **shelves**) **1** a (usually narrow) horizontal board for laying things on, fixed to a wall or as part of a cupboard, etc. **2** a sandbank or rocky ledge, especially partially submerged. — **on the shelf 1** *said of a person or thing* no longer used, employed, or active. **2** *said of a person* no longer likely to have the opportunity to marry, especially because of being too old. [from Anglo-Saxon *scylf*]

shelf-life *noun* the length of time that a stored product remains usable.

shell — *noun* **1** *Bot.* the hard protective layer that surrounds the seed, nut, or fruit of some plants. **2** *Zool.* the tough protective structure that covers the body of certain animals, eg molluscs (snails and shellfish), crabs, lobsters, turtles, and tortoises. It is usually made of calcium carbonate, chitin, or a horny or bony material, and is built up in layers from the inside. **3** the protective outer covering of an egg, eg the hard chalky covering of a bird's egg, or the leathery covering of a reptile's egg. **4** the empty covering of a mollusc, found on the seashore. **5** any hard outer case. **6** a round of ammunition for a large-bore gun, eg a mortar; a shotgun cartridge. **7** an empty framework or outer case, the early stage of construction or the undestroyed remains of something, eg a building. **8** *Comput.* a program that acts as a user-friendly interface between an operating system and the user. **9** *Chem.* one of a series of concentric spheres representing the possible orbits of electrons as they revolve around the nucleus of an atom. Depending on its atomic number, an atom may have from one to seven such shells, and only a certain number of electrons can occupy each shell. Electrons in unfilled shells can participate in the formation of chemical bonds. — Also called *orbital*. **10** a person very much weaker than before in body or personality. **11** a narrow light rowing-boat for racing. — *verb* **1** to remove the shell from. **2** to bombard with (eg mortar) shells.
— **come out of one's shell** to become more friendly or sociable.

shell something out *colloq.* to pay it out or spend it.
[from Anglo-Saxon *scell*]

she'll *contr.* she will; she shall.

shellac — *noun* **1** a yellow or orange resin produced by the lac insect and others. **2** a solution of this in alcohol, used as a varnish. — *verb* (**shellacked, shellacking**) to coat with shellac. [from SHELL + LAC]

Shelley, Mary (Wollstonecraft), *née* **Godwin** (1797–1851) English writer, born in London. She eloped with Shelley in 1814, and married him two years later. She wrote several novels, of which *Frankenstein, or the Modern Prometheus* (1818) is the best-known, travel books and journals, and edited Shelley's poems and other works after his death (1823).

Shelley, Percy Bysshe (1792–1822) English Romantic poet, born in Horsham, Sussex. He was expelled from Oxford for his pamphlet, *The Necessity of Atheism* (1811). He married Harriet Westbrook (1811) and settled in Keswick, where he was influenced by William Godwin, and wrote his poem *Queen Mab* (1813). He formed a liaison with Godwin's daughter, Mary, with whom he eloped (1814), accompanied by her half-sister, Jane 'Claire' Clairmont. They travelled on the continent, where he first met Byron at Lake Geneva (1816), and in the same year he married Mary when his first wife drowned herself. From 1818 he lived in Italy, became reacquainted with Byron, and wrote the bulk of his poetry, including 'The Ode to the West Wind' and the verse dramas *Prometheus Unbound* (1818–19) and *Hellas* (1822–4). He was drowned near Leghorn.

Shelley a female first name, after the surname and several place-names.

shellfish *noun* **1** common name for an edible aquatic invertebrate that has a hard shell or exoskeleton, especially a mollusc or crustacean, eg prawn, crab, lobster, shrimp. **2** a collective term for such animals.

shelling *noun* **1** removing the shell or shells. **2** bombarding with ammunition, bombing.

shell-shock *noun* nervous breakdown caused by prolonged exposure to combat conditions.

shell-shocked *adj.* affected with shell-shock.

shell suit a tracksuit of very lightweight multi-coloured fabric, commonly used as everyday casual wear.

Shelter, also called the **National Campaign for Homeless People** in the UK, a charity founded in 1966, funded mainly by voluntary contributions, to provide help for the homeless and to campaign on their behalf.

shelter — *noun* **1** protection against weather or danger. **2** a place or structure giving this. — *verb* (**sheltered**, **sheltering**) **1** to protect from danger or the effects of weather. **2** *intrans.* to take cover.

sheltered *adj.* **1** protected from the effects of weather. **2** kept ignorant of the world's unpleasantnesses: *a sheltered upbringing.*

sheltered housing flats or bungalows specially designed for the elderly or disabled, especially in a safe enclosed complex, with a resident warden.

shelve *verb* **1** to store on a shelf. **2** to fit with shelves. **3** to postpone the use or implementation of; to abandon. **4** to remove from active service. **5** *intrans. said of ground* to slope gently.

shelves see SHELF.

shelving *noun* **1** material for use as shelves. **2** shelves collectively.

Shem a biblical character, Noah's eldest son, the brother of Ham and Japheth. He too escaped the Flood, and lived for 600 years (Genesis 11). His descendants are listed in Genesis 10, where he is depicted as the legendary father of 'Semitic' peoples, meant to include the Hebrews.

Shema an ancient Jewish prayer, traced at least to the 2c BC. Incorporating Deuteronomy 6.4–9, 11.13–21 and Numbers 15.37–41, it begins 'Hear, O Israel: The Lord our God, the Lord is one'. It introduces the Jewish morning and evening prayers, precedes the Amidah and is itself preceded by two benedictions. [Hebrew, = hear]

Shenandoah, River a river in West Virginia and Virginia, USA, length 88km/55mi. It is formed at the junction of the North Fork and South Fork rivers and flows NE to meet the Potomac R near Harper's Ferry. NOTABLE FEATURE Shenandoah National Park.

shenanigans *pl. noun colloq.* **1** boisterous misbehaviour. **2** foolish behaviour; nonsense. **3** underhand dealings; trickery.

Shenyang, formerly **Mukden** POP (1990) 4.8m, the capital of Liaoning province, NE China, and the area's largest industrial city. HISTORY trading centre for nomads in the 11c; became capital of Manchu state in 1625; attacked by the

Japanese in 1931, which led to the establishment of the Japanese puppet state of Manchukuo; occupied by Nationalists in 1945; taken by the communists in 1948; renamed in 1949. NOTABLE FEATURES Imperial Palace (1625–36); Dongling (tomb of Nurhachi, founder of Manchu state); Beiling (tomb of Nurhachi's son and heir, Abukai).

shepherd — *noun* **1** a person who looks after sheep. **2** *literary* a religious minister. — *verb* to guide or herd (a group or crowd). [from Anglo-Saxon *sceaphirde*, sheep herd]

shepherdess *noun old use* a female shepherd.

Shepherd of Hermas a popular 2c Christian work purportedly from Hermas, a Roman slave who was freed and became a merchant. The work is divided into visions, mandates, and similitudes (or parables), and is named 'the Shepherd' after the angel of repentance who appears in one of the visions. Its strong moral earnestness and stress on the need for penitence after baptism appealed to parts of the early Church, but it was excluded from the New Testament canon.

shepherd's pie a baked dish of minced meat with mashed potatoes on the top.

shepherd's purse a small annual weed (*Capsella bursa-pastoris*), found almost everywhere, and having a rosette of oblong lobed leaves and white cross-shaped flowers. The seed capsules are heart-shaped, reminiscent of an old-style peasant's purse.

Shepparton POP (1991) 31 000, a city in Goulburn statistical division, N Victoria, Australia. It is located in the fertile Goulburn Valley. NOTABLE FEATURES Shepparton Arts Centre; International Village, featuring worldwide tourist information.

Sheraton, Thomas (1751–1806) English cabinet maker, born in Stockton-on-Tees, Durham. He settled in London (c.1790), wrote a *Cabinetmaker's Book* (1794), and produced a range of neoclassical designs which had a wide influence on contemporary taste in furniture.

sherbet *noun* **1** a fruit-flavoured powder, or a fizzy drink made from it. **2** a drink of sweetened fruit juices in Middle Eastern countries. [from Turkish and Persian *serbet*]

sherd see SHARD.

Shere Khan the ferocious tiger in Rudyard Kipling's *The Jungle Book*.

Sheridan, Philip H(enry) (1831–88) US soldier, born in Albany, New York. He commanded a Federal cavalry division at the beginning of the Civil War, and took part in many of the campaigns. In 1864 he was given command of the Army of the Shenandoah, when he turned the valley into a barren waste and defeated General Lee. Victory at Five Forks (1865) followed, and Sheridan was active in the final battles which led to Lee's surrender. He succeeded Sherman as general-in-chief (1883) and died having never lost a battle.

Sheridan, Richard Brinsley (Butler) (1751–1816) Anglo-Irish dramatist, born in Dublin. His successful comedy of manners, *The Rivals* (1775), was followed by several other comedies and farces, notably *School for Scandal* (1777). He became manager of Drury Lane Theatre in 1778, and a Whig MP in 1780.

sheriff *noun* **1** the chief police officer in a US county. **2** the chief judge of a sheriff court. **3** the chief representative of the monarch in an English county, whose duties are now mainly ceremonial. [from Anglo-Saxon *scir*, shire + *gerefa*, reeve]

sheriff court a court in a Scottish town or region dealing with civil actions and trying all but the most serious crimes.

Sherman, William Tecumseh (1820–91) US soldier, born in Lancaster, Ohio. He was

appointed general in the Union army during the Civil War, during which his most famous campaign was the capture of Atlanta in 1864, followed by his famous 'March to the Sea', when his 60 000 men destroyed everything in their path. After capturing Savannah, he moved north through the Carolinas, and gained further victories which hastened the Confederate surrender.

Sherpa *noun* a member of an Eastern Tibetan people living high on the south side of the Himalayas. [from Tibetan *shar*, east + *pa*, inhabitant]

Sherrington, Sir Charles Scott (1857–1952) English physiologist, born in London. Professor in London, Liverpool, and Oxford, his research on the nervous system constituted a landmark in modern physiology. He shared the 1932 Nobel Prize for Physiology or Medicine with Lord Adrian.

sherry *noun* (PL. **sherries**) a fortified wine ranging in colour from pale gold to dark brown, strictly speaking one produced in or near the S Spanish town of *Jerez*.

Sherwood Forest an area of heath and woodland, mainly in Nottinghamshire, UK, where medieval kings hunted deer. It is famed for being the home of Robin Hood.

shes *noun* a female person or animal: *a she-wolf.* [from Anglo-Saxon *seo*]

she's *contr.* **1** she is. **2** she has.

She Stoops to Conquer, or The Mistakes of a Night a play by Oliver Goldsmith (1773). It is a comedy criticizing the snobbery of London through characters such as Marlow, who is too bashful to woo anyone but servant girls, and Tony Lumpkin, who mischievously gives him directions to the house of the wealthy Hardcastles instead of to an inn.

Shetland or **The Shetland Islands**, formerly **Zetland** POP (1992e) 23 000, a group of c.100 islands off the coast of NE Scotland, lying 80km/50mi NE of the Orkney Is. AREA 1 433sq km/553sq mi. MAIN ISLANDS Mainland, Unst, Yell, Fetlar, Whalsay. Around 20 of the islands are inhabited. PHYSICAL DESCRIPTION a low-lying group; the highest point is Ronas Hill on N Mainland (450m). CAPITAL Lerwick (on Mainland). HISTORY annexed by Norway in the 9c, then by Scotland in 1472; in Nov 1939 it was the target of the first German air-raid on Britain during World War II; there was a serious oil spillage in 1993 from the grounded tanker, *Braer.* ECONOMY cattle and sheep raising; knitwear; fishing; oil services at Lerwick and Sandwick; oil terminal at Sullom Voe. NOTABLE FEATURES there are several prehistoric remains; Staneydale Temple (on W Mainland), a Neolithic or early Bronze Age hall; Jarlshof (on S Mainland), the remains of three villages occupied from the Bronze to the Viking Age; Mousa Broch (on Mousa, dating from the Iron Age). The small Shetland ponies are well-known for their strength and hardiness.

Shetland pony (PL. **Shetland ponies**) a breed of small sturdy pony with a long thick coat, originally bred in the Shetland Isles.

SHF Radio super high frequency.

Shia or **Shiah** *noun* one of the two main branches of Islam, the branch which regards Mohammed's son-in-law, Ali, as his true successor as leader of Islam. See also SUNNI. [from Arabic *shia*, sect]

◇ After the murder of Ali, his followers continued to support his claim to the Muslim caliphate and became known as *Shi'at* or *Shi'a Ali* ('partisans of Ali') or, more commonly, *Shi'is*, usually anglicized as *Shiites*. Today around 99 per cent of Iranians and 60 per cent of Iraqis are Shiites.

shiatsu or **shiatzu** *noun Medicine* a Japanese massage technique that aims to heal disorders and promote health by the application of pressure, especially with the fingers and palms of the hands, to parts of the body that are distant from

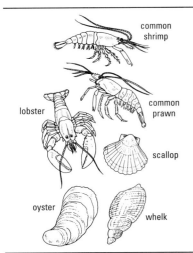

common
shrimp

lobster

common
prawn

scallop

oyster

whelk

shellfish

the affected region. — Also called *acupressure*. [from Japanese, = finger pressure]

shibboleth *noun* **1** a common saying. **2** a slogan, custom, or belief, especially if considered outdated. **3** a use of a word, phrase, or pronunciation that characterizes members of a particular group. [a Hebrew word of uncertain meaning (probably either 'ear of corn', or 'flooded stream'), used in Judges 12.5–6 as an oral test by which Jephthah and his Gileadites detected the enemy Ephraimites, who could not pronounce *sh*]

shield — *noun* **1** a piece of armour carried to block an attack with a weapon. **2** a representation of this, usually a vertical rectangle with a rounded bottom, used as an emblem. **3** a medal or trophy shaped (perhaps only vaguely) like this. **4** a protective plate or screen. **5** a person or thing that protects from danger or harm. — *verb* to protect from danger or harm. [from Anglo-Saxon *sceld*]

shift — *verb* **1** *trans., intrans.* to change the position or direction of; to change position or direction. **2** to transfer, switch, or re-direct: *shift the blame on to someone else.* **3** to change (gear in a vehicle). **4** to remove or dislodge. **5** *intrans. colloq.* to move quickly. — *noun* **1** a change, or change of position. **2** one of a set of consecutive periods into which a 24-hour working day is divided. **3** the group of workers on duty during any one of these periods. **4** a handy method of proceeding or dealing with something; an expedient. **5** a trick or other underhand scheme. — **shift one's ground** to adopt a new opinion, position in an argument, etc. [from Anglo-Saxon *sciftan*, to divide]

shiftily *adv.* in a shifty way.

shiftiness *noun* being shifty.

shiftless *adj.* **1** having no motivation or initiative. **2** inefficient.

shifty *adj.* (**shiftier**, **shiftiest**) *said of a person or behaviour* sly, untrustworthy, or dishonest.

Shihchiachuang see SHIJIAZHUANG.

Shiite — *noun* a Muslim who is an adherent of Shia. — *adj.* of or relating to Shia.

Shijiazhuang *or* **Shihchiachuang** POP (1990) 1.4m, the capital of Hebei province, N China. NOTABLE FEATURES Longcang Temple Stele (Sui dynasty); Zhuanlunzang Pavilion (10c); to the N lies the 6c Buddhist Monastery of Longxing Si, containing a 10c bronze statue of Guanyin, the Goddess of Mercy (22m high, with 42 arms).

Shikoku POP (1990) 4.2m, the smallest of the four main islands of Japan. AREA 18 795sq km/ 7 255sq mi. It lies S of Honshu and E of Kyushu and is bounded in the N by the Seto Naikai Sea, and in the S by the Pacific Ocean. The island is mountainous with a wooded interior, and has a subtropical climate. CHIEF TOWNS Matsuyama, Takamatsu. ECONOMY rice, wheat, tobacco, soya beans; orchards; copper; camphor.

shilling *noun* **1** in the UK before the introduction of decimal currency, a monetary unit and coin worth one twentieth of £1 or 12 old pence (12d). **2** the standard unit of currency in several E African countries. [from Anglo-Saxon *scilling*]

shilly-shally *verb intrans.* (**shilly-shallies**, **shilly-shallied**) to be slow to make up one's mind; to be indecisive. [reduplication of *shall I?*]

Shiloh the site of an ancient city in central Palestine c.14km/9mi north of Bethel. Noted as the central sanctuary of the tribes of Israel during the conquest and settlement of Palestine under the tribal judges, it also sheltered the Ark of the Covenant, but was destroyed c.1050 BC, when the Ark was captured by the Philistines.

Shiloh, Battle of an engagement (6–7 Apr 1862) in the American Civil War in SW Tennessee, in which Union forces under General Grant defeated Confederate forces under Albert Sidney Johnston (1803–62), incurring heavy losses of 13 000 Union and 11 000 Confederate casualties.

Shilton, Peter (1949–) English footballer, born in Leicester. He made his international début for England in 1970 and became a fixture in the England side for the next 18 years. He became the first England goalkeeper to gain 100 caps, and has won all the major honours in the game, including League championship and European Cup medals. In 1989 he won his 109th English cap, surpassing the record previously held by Bobby Moore. He played for Leicester City, Stoke City, and Nottingham Forest, with whom he achieved his greatest successes. After a spell with Southampton he joined Derby County, then became player-manager for Plymouth Argyle in 1992.

shim — *noun* a thin washer, or a metal or plastic strip, used to fill a gap between machine parts, especially gears. — *verb* (**shimmed**, **shimming**) to fill or adjust with a shim.

shimmer — *verb intrans.* (**shimmered**, **shimmering**) to shine quiveringly with reflected light. — *noun* a quivering gleam of reflected light. [from Anglo-Saxon *scimerian*]

shimmery *adj.* that shimmers.

shin — *noun* **1** the bony front part of the leg below the knee. **2** the lower part of a leg of beef. — *verb trans., intrans.* (**shinned**, **shinning**) (*usually* **shin up**) to climb by gripping with the hands and legs. [from Anglo-Saxon *scinu*]

shinbone *noun* the tibia.

shindig *noun colloq.* **1** a lively party or celebration. **2** a noisy disturbance; a commotion. [perhaps from SHINTY]

shine — *verb* (PAST TENSE AND PAST PARTICIPLE **shone**, sense 3 **shined**) **1** *intrans.* to give out or reflect light. **2** to direct the light from: *shone the torch in my face.* **3** to make bright and gleaming by polishing. **4** *intrans.* to command attention or be outstandingly impressive: *she shines at maths.* — *noun* **1** shining quality; brightness; lustre. **2** sunny weather: *rain or shine.* — **take a shine to someone** *colloq.* to like them on first acquaintance. [from Anglo-Saxon *scinan*]

shiner *noun colloq.* a black eye.

shingle[1] *noun Geol.* a mass of small rounded pebbles that have been worn smooth by the action of water, often found in a series of parallel ridges on seashores.

shingle[2] — *noun* **1** a thin rectangular (especially wooden) roof-tile. **2** a woman's short hairstyle, cropped at the back. — *verb* **1** to tile with shingles. **2** to cut in a shingle. [from Latin *scindula*, wooden tile]

shingles *sing. noun Medicine* herpes zoster, a painful viral infection in which acute inflammation of the nerve ganglia produces a series of blisters on one side of the body along the path of the affected nerves, especially in the area of the waist or ribs, but sometimes around the face. It is caused by the same virus that is responsible for chickenpox in children. [from Latin *cingulum*, belt]

shingly *adj.* **1** covered with or consisting of shingle. **2** of the nature of shingle.

Shining Path see SENDERO LUMINOSO.

Shinkansen in Japan, the New Tokaido Line, a standard gauge line from Tokyo to Osaka for high-speed trains (commonly known as 'bullet trains'), completed in 1964. The network is being extended to cover all main Honshu routes. Unlike many of the old lines, it has been commercially successful.

Shinto the indigenous religion of Japan, so named in the 8c to distinguish it from Buddhism, although it subsequently incorporated many Buddhist features. Its derivation from the nature-worship of Japanese folk religions is reflected in ceremonies appealing to the mysterious powers of nature (*kami*) for benevolent treatment and protection. By the 8c divine origins were ascribed to the Emperor and his family, to whom State Shinto had to show loyalty and obedience. In the 19c it was divided into Shrine (*jinga*) Shinto and Sectarian (*kyoho*) Shinto; the former was regarded as a 'state cult' and the latter was officially recognized as a religion but ineligible for state support. State Shinto lost its official status in 1945. [from Japanese *Shinto*, from Chinese *shen*, god + *tao*, way]

Shintoism *noun* the beliefs and practices of Shinto.

Shintoist — *noun* an adherent of Shinto. — *adj.* of or relating to Shinto.

shinty *noun* (PL. **shinties**) **1** a stick-and-ball game played by two teams of 12. **2** the stick or ball used for this game.

◇ The game originated in Ireland more than 1 500 years ago, then was taken to Scotland and is now popular especially in the Scottish Highlands. The playing pitch is up to 155m long and 73m wide with goals, known as *hails*, one at each end. The object is to score goals by using the *caman* (stick) to propel the ball.

Shinwell, Manny (Emmanuel) Shinwell, Baron (1884–1986) English Labour politician, born in London. A 'street-corner' socialist in Glasgow, he became an MP (1922), held junior office in the interwar Labour governments, and in the postwar Labour government was Minister of Fuel and Power, when he nationalized the mines (1946), Secretary of State for War (1947), and Minister of Defence (1950–1). Well known for his party political belligerence, in his later years he mellowed into a backbench 'elder statesman'.

shiny *adj.* (**shinier**, **shiniest**) **1** reflecting light; polished to brightness. **2** *said of part of a piece of clothing* at which the fabric has been badly worn, leaving a glossy surface.

ship — *noun* **1** any large boat intended for sea travel. **2** *colloq.* a spaceship or airship. — *verb* (**shipped**, **shipping**) **1** to send or transport by ship, or any other means. **2** (**ship someone off**) *colloq.* to send them away: *shipped the children off to their grandparents.* **3** *Naut.*, *said of a boat* to have (water, eg waves) coming on board over the side. **4** *Naut.* to bring on board a boat or ship: *ship oars.* — **when one's ship comes in** *or* **comes home** when one becomes rich. [from Anglo-Saxon *scip*]

◇ The first sea-going vessels of which pictorial records survive were Egyptian (from c.1500 BC), ships propelled by oars and a simple square sail. The Greeks, Phoenicians, and Romans made great strides in ship design, but it was not until multi-masted ships, inspired by Chinese junks, were introduced into the West in the 13c that the great age of sail began in Europe. Three-masted ships such as the deep, broad carrack and the Portuguese caravel were common by the 15c; the slimmer, square-sterned galleon appeared in the mid-16c; and the peak of sailing refinement was reached c.1820 with the development in the USA of the clipper ship. Both the clippers and later steel-hulled windjammers were rendered obsolete by steamships, which had developed sufficiently by c.1860 to challenge the sailing ship's supremacy. Despite the development of the diesel engine in 1892, larger passenger ships were powered by steam turbines until the late 1970s. Today only about 3% of the world's ships are powered by steam.

-ship *suffix* forming words denoting: **1** rank, position, or status: *lordship.* **2** a period of office or rule: *during his chairmanship.* **3** a state or condition: *friendship.* **4** a type of skill: *craftsmanship.* **5** a group of individuals: *membership.* [from Anglo-Saxon *-scipe*]

shipboard *adj.* taking place, or situated, on board a ship.

shipmate *noun* a fellow sailor.

shipment *noun* **1** a cargo or consignment (not necessarily one sent by ship). **2** the act or practice of shipping cargo.

Ship of Cheops, an ancient Egyptian funeral ship found dismantled at Giza in 1954 in one of five boat pits around the Pyramid of Cheops (♁–2566 BC) The ship was reconstructed and measures 44m long with a beam of 6m.

shipping *noun* **1** ships as traffic. **2** the commercial transporting of freight, especially by ship.

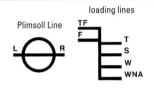

loading lines

Plimsoll Line

LR	Lloyd's Register	
TF	tropical fresh water	
F	fresh water	
T	tropics	
S	summer (equivalent to Plimsoll Line)	
W	winter	
WNA	winter in North Atlantic	

Plimsoll and loading lines used in shipping

shipshape *adj.* in good order; neat and tidy.

Shipton, Eric (Earle) (1907–77) English mountaineer. He spent many years climbing in E and central Africa, and obtained much of his knowledge of the East during his terms as consul-general in Kashgar (1940–2, 1946–8) and Kunming (1949–51). Between 1933 and 1951 he either led or was member of five expeditions to Mt Everest, and helped pave the way for the successful Hunt-Hillary expedition of 1953.

shipwreck — *noun* **1** the accidental sinking or destruction of a ship. **2** the remains of a sunken or destroyed ship. **3** ruin; disaster. — *verb* **1** *trans., intrans.* to be or cause to be the victim of accidental sinking or destruction. **2** to ruin (eg plans).

shipwright *noun* a person who builds or repairs (especially wooden) ships.

shipyard *noun* a place where ships are built and repaired.

Shiraz POP (1986) 848 000, the fifth largest city in Iran and the capital of Shiraz district, Fars province, SW Iran. The city lies 184km/114mi NE of Bushehr, its port on the Arabian Gulf. Shiraz was the capital of Persia between 1750 and 1779. It is noted for its wines, rugs, hand-woven textiles, silverwork, and mosaics.

shire *noun* a county. [from Anglo-Saxon *scir*, authority]

shire horse a large strong horse bred for pulling carts, etc, originally in the Midlands.

Shires *pl. noun* (**the Shires**) the rural areas of England as opposed to the towns, specifically the Midland counties or the fox-hunting counties of Leicestershire and Northamptonshire.

shirk *verb trans., intrans.* to avoid doing (work) or carrying out (a duty). [perhaps from German *Schurke*, scoundrel]

shirker *noun* a person who avoids work or responsibilities.

Shirley a female and formerly also a male first name, after the surname and several place-names.

shirt *noun* a piece of clothing of cotton, silk, etc for the upper body, usually with a collar and buttons down the front, especially worn by men under a jacket.
— **keep one's shirt on** *colloq.* to control one's temper.

put one's shirt on something *colloq.* to bet all one has on it.
[from Anglo-Saxon *scyrte*]

shirt dress *or* **shirtwaister** a woman's dress with a shirt-like bodice.

shirtsleeve *noun* a sleeve of a shirt.
— **in one's shirtsleeves** not wearing a jacket or coat.

shirt-tail *noun* the flap hanging down at the back of a shirt.

shirty *adj.* (**shirtier, shirtiest**) *colloq.* bad-tempered; annoyed.

shish kebab SEE KEBAB.

shit *or* **shite** *coarse slang* — *noun* **1** faeces. **2** an act of defecating. **3** *derog.* rubbish; nonsense. **4** *derog.* a despicable person. — *verb* (**shitting**; PAST TENSE AND PAST PARTICIPLE **shit, shitted**) *intrans.* to defecate. — *interj.* an expression of annoyance or disappointment. [from Anglo-Saxon *scitan*, to defecate]

shitty *adj.* (**shittier, shittiest**) *coarse slang* **1** filthy; soiled with, or as if with, shit. **2** *derog.* mean; despicable.

Shiva one of the three deities of the Hindu triad (*Trimurti*). A complex god of contrasting features (creation and destruction, good and evil, fertility and asceticism), he is also the original Lord of the Dance (*Nataraja*). His symbolic representations include a phallic emblem denoting procreation, and he is often depicted holding weapons and having three eyes.

shiver¹ — *verb intrans.* (**shivered, shivering**) to quiver or tremble, eg with fear, or as a result of involuntary movement of the muscles in response to low temperatures. — *noun* an act of shivering; a shivering movement or sensation.
— **the shivers** *colloq.* a fit of shivering.
[from Middle English *chivere*]

shiver² — *noun* a splinter or other small fragment. — *verb trans., intrans.* (**shivered, shivering**) to shatter. [from Middle English *scifre*]

shivery *adj.* inclined to shiver or to cause shivers.

Shkodër, Italian **Scutari**, ancient **Scodra 1** POP (1989) 80 000, a market town and the capital of Shkodër province, NW Albania. It lies to the SE of L Scutari and was formerly the capital of Albania. **2** a province in NW Albania with Shkodër as its capital.

shoal¹ — *noun* **1** a large number of fish swimming together. **2** a huge crowd; a multitude or swarm. — *verb intrans.* to gather or move in a shoal. [from Anglo-Saxon *scolu*, a troop]

shoal² — *noun* **1** an area of shallow water in a river, lake, or sea where sediment has accumulated, often hazardous to shipping. **2** such an accumulation of sediment. — *verb trans., intrans.* to make or become shallow. [from Anglo-Saxon *sceald*, shallow]

shock¹ — *noun* **1** a strong emotional disturbance, especially a feeling of extreme surprise, outrage, or disgust; also, a cause of this. **2** a convulsion caused by the passage of an electric current through the body. **3** a heavy jarring blow or impact. **4** *Medicine* **a** a state of extreme physical collapse that occurs when the blood pressure within the arteries becomes too low to maintain an adequate blood supply to the tissues, eg as a result of haemorrhage, coronary thrombosis, severe burns, dehydration, major surgery, drug overdose, or a sudden extreme emotional disturbance. The main symptoms of shock are a weak pulse, lowered blood pressure and body temperature, and sweaty pallid skin. **b** *Scot. or dialect* a stroke. — *verb* **1** to cause to feel extreme surprise, outrage, or disgust. **2** to shake or jar suddenly and forcefully. [from French *choc*]

shock² *noun* a bushy mass of hair.

shock³ — *noun* a number of sheaves of corn propped up against each other to dry. — *verb* to

set up to dry in this way. [from Middle English *schokke*]

shock absorber a device, such as a coiled spring, in the suspension system of a vehicle, that damps vibrations caused by the wheels passing over bumps in the road, absorbing the shock waves that would otherwise jar the body of the vehicle, and so ensuring a smoother ride for passengers.

shocking *adj.* **1** extremely surprising, outrageous, or disgusting. **2** *colloq.* very bad.

Shockley, William Bradford (1910–89) US physicist, born in London. Working at the Bell Telephone Laboratories, he developed the point-contact transistor and later the junction transistor; these devices led to the miniaturization of circuits in radio, television, and computer equipment. He shared the 1956 Nobel Prize for Physics with John Bardeen and Walter Brattain, and from 1963 to 1974 was professor at Stanford University.

shock tactics any course of action that seeks to achieve its object by means of suddenness and force.

shock therapy see ELECTRO-CONVULSIVE THERAPY.

shock wave *Physics* an exceptionally intense sound wave, caused by a violent explosion or the movement of an object at a speed greater than that of sound. An explosion will produce a pressure shock wave in the surrounding air. A thunderclap is a shock wave caused by the rapid heating of air by lightning.

shod see SHOE.

shoddily *adv.* in a shoddy way.

shoddiness *noun* being shoddy.

shoddy *adj.* (**shoddier, shoddiest**) **1** of poor quality; carelessly done or made. **2** of the nature of a cheap imitation.

shoe — *noun* **1** either of a pair of shaped outer coverings for the feet, especially made of leather or other stiff material, usually finishing below the ankle. **2** anything like this in shape or function. **3** a horseshoe. — *verb* (**shoeing**; PAST TENSE AND PAST PARTICIPLE **shod**) to fit (usually a horse) with shoes.
— **in someone's shoes** in the same situation as them; in their place.
[from Anglo-Saxon *scoh*]

shoehorn *noun* a curved shaped piece of metal, plastic or (originally) horn, used for gently levering a foot into a shoe.

shoelace *noun* a string or cord for fastening a shoe.

Shoemaker, Willie (William Lee), also called **the Shoe** (1931–) US jockey, born in Fabens, Texas. He has won more races than any other jockey, nearly 9 000 winners between 1949 and his retirement in 1989. In 1953 he rode a world record 485 winners in one season.

shoestring *noun North Amer.* a shoelace.
— **on a shoestring** *colloq.* with or using a very small amount of money.

shoe tree a support put inside a shoe to preserve its shape when not being worn.

shogi *noun* a Japanese form of chess, played on a squared board, each player having 20 pieces. [from Japanese *shogi*]

Shogun a Japanese general, and the head of a system of government which dates from 1192, when a military leader received the title *seii-tai-shogun* ('Barbarian Quelling Generalissimo') from the emperor. Most important were members of the Tokugawa Shogunate (1603–1868), who ruled as military dictators while the emperor remained a powerless figurehead. The shoguns' rule strictly regulated and controlled life down to the smallest detail. The system ended in 1868.

Sholokhov, Mikhail Aleksandrovich (1905–84) Russian novelist, born near

Veshenskaya. He served in the Red Army (1920–2), became a writer, and is best known for his novel tetralogy *And Quiet Flows the Don* (4 vols, 1928–40) and other novels of Cossack life. He was awarded the Nobel Prize for Literature in 1965.

Shona a group of Bantu-speaking agricultural peoples of E Zimbabwe, who include the Manyika, Kalanga, and Haranga. They were a powerful state during the 13c–15c, with their capital at Great Zimbabwe, and they resisted encroachment of white pioneers in the 1890s, but were ruthlessly suppressed. The present-day population is c.5m.

Shona a female first name. [a form of the Scottish Gaelic name *Seonaid*, or a shortening of CATRIONA]

shone see SHINE.

shoo — *interj.* an expression used to chase away a person or animal. — *verb* (**shooed, shooing**) (**shoo someone** *or* **something away** *or* **off**) to chase them away by, or as if by, shouting 'Shoo!'. [imitative]

shook see SHAKE.

shoot — *verb* (PAST TENSE AND PAST PARTICIPLE **shot**) **1** *trans., intrans.* to fire (a gun or other weapon, or bullets, arrows or other missiles). **2** to hit, wound, or kill with a weapon or missile. **3** to direct forcefully and rapidly: *shot questions at them.* **4** *trans., intrans.* to move or cause to move or progress extremely fast: *that last victory shot them to the top of the table.* **5** *trans., intrans.* Sport to strike (the ball, etc) at goal. **6** *trans., intrans.* to film, or take photographs (of). **7** *intrans.* said of pain to dart with a stabbing sensation. **8** *intrans.* said of a plant to produce new growth; (especially of a vegetable) to produce unwanted flowers and seeds. **9** *colloq.* to pass through (a set of traffic lights at red) without stopping. **10** *colloq.* to pass quickly through: *shoot rapids.* **11** *slang* to play a game of (eg pool or golf); to have as a score at golf. **12** *slang* to inject (especially oneself) with (drugs) illegally. — *noun* **1** an act of shooting. **2** a new or young plant growth. **3** an outing to hunt animals with firearms; an area of land within which animals are hunted in this way.

— **shoot someone** *or* **something down 1** to fire guns at an aircraft so as to make it crash. **2** to kill with gunfire. **3** to dismiss mercilessly with criticism or ridicule.

shoot one's mouth off *colloq.* to speak indiscreetly or boastfully.

shoot up to grow or increase extremely quickly. [from Anglo-Saxon *sceotan*]

shooter *noun* **1** a person or thing that shoots. **2** *colloq.* a gun.

shooting brake *old use* an estate car.

shooting star a meteor.

shooting-stick *noun* a sturdy pointed walking-stick whose two-part handle folds out to form a small seat.

shop — *noun* **1** a place where goods (or services) are sold. **2** a place in which (especially manual) work of a particular kind is carried out: *machine shop.* — *verb* (PAST TENSE AND PAST PARTICIPLE **shopped, shopping**) **1** *intrans.* to visit a shop or shops in order to buy goods. **2** *trans. slang* to inform on (someone), eg to the police.

— **all over the shop** *colloq.* scattered everywhere; in numerous places.

shop around 1 to compare the price and quality of goods in various shops before deciding to buy. **2** *colloq.* to explore the full range of options available before committing oneself to any.

shut up shop *colloq.* to stop trading, whether at the end of the working day or permanently.

talk shop *colloq.* to talk about one's work, especially in a tedious way. [from Anglo-Saxon *sceoppa*, treasury]

shop assistant a person serving customers in a shop.

shop floor 1 the part of a factory where the manual work is carried out. **2** the workers in a factory, as opposed to the management.

shopkeeper *noun* a person who owns and manages a shop.

shoplift *verb* to steal goods from shops.

shoplifter *noun* a person who shoplifts.

shoplifting *noun* stealing goods from shops.

shopper *noun* **1** a person who shops. **2** a shopping bag or basket.

shopping *noun* **1** the activity of visiting shops to buy goods. **2** goods bought in shops.

shopping centre 1 an area containing a large number of shops of different kinds. **2** a collection of different shops under one roof, often providing other facilities, eg restaurants and toilets.

shop-soiled *adj.* slightly dirty or spoiled from being used as a display in a shop.

shop steward a worker elected by others to be an official trade union representative in negotiations with the management.

shopwalker *noun* a person who supervises shop assistants in a large department store.

shore¹ *noun* **1** land bordering on the sea or any area of water. **2** (**shores**) *literary* lands; countries: *foreign shores.* [from Middle English *schore*]

shore² — *noun* a prop. — *verb* (*usually* **shore something up**) **1** to support it with props. **2** to give support to it; to sustain or strengthen it. [from Old Dutch *schore*]

shoreline *noun* the line formed where land meets water.

shorn see SHEAR.

Short, Nigel (1965–) English chess player. He became the world's youngest chess grandmaster, and Britain's youngest champion, at the age of 19. In Jan 1993, he defeated Dutchman Jan Timman to become the first British chess world championship challenger for over 100 years. He was defeated in his challenge against world champion Gary Kasparov, which began in Sep 1993 after much controversy surrounding the organization of the event.

short — *adj.* **1** of little physical length; not long. **2** of little height. **3** brief; concise. **4** *said of a temper* easily lost. **5** rudely or angrily abrupt; curt. **6** (**short of** *or* **on something**) lacking in it; not having enough of it; deficient. **7** *said of the memory* tending not to retain things for long. **8** *said of pastry* crisp and crumbling easily. **9** *said of betting odds* providing the winner with only a small profit; near even. **10** *said of a vowel sound* being the briefer of two possible lengths of vowel. **11** *Cricket, said of fielding positions* relatively close to the batsman. — *adv.* **1** abruptly: *stopped short.* **2** (**short of** ...) without going as far as ...; except: *tried every kind of persuasion short of threats.* — *noun* **1** a drink of an alcoholic spirit. **2** a short cinema film shown before the main feature. **3** a short circuit. — *verb trans., intrans.* to short-circuit.

— **be caught** *or* **taken short** *colloq.* to have an urgent need to urinate or defecate.

fall short to be less than a required, expected, or stated amount.

for short as an abbreviated form.

go *or* **run short of something** not to have enough of it.

in short concisely stated.

short and sweet *colloq.* agreeably brief.

short for something an abbreviated form of it. [from Anglo-Saxon *sceort*]

shortage *noun* a lack or deficiency.

shortbread *noun* a rich sweet crumbly biscuit made with flour, butter, and sugar.

shortcake *noun* **1** shortbread. **2** a dessert cake consisting of a biscuit base topped with fruit, served with cream.

short-change *verb* **1** to give (a customer) less than the correct amount of change, whether by accident or intentionally. **2** *colloq.* to treat dishonestly; to cheat.

short circuit a connection across an electric circuit with a very low resistance, usually caused accidentally, eg by an insulation failure. Short circuits can pass a very high current which may damage electrical equipment or be a fire hazard.

short-circuit *verb* to cause a short circuit in (an electrical circuit).

shortcoming *noun* a fault or defect.

short cut 1 a quicker route between two places. **2** a method that saves time or effort.

shorten *verb trans., intrans.* (**shortened, shortening**) to make or become shorter.

shortening *noun* butter, lard or other fat used for making pastry more crumbly.

shortfall *noun* **1** a failure to reach a desired or expected level. **2** the amount or margin by which something is deficient: *a shortfall of £100.*

shorthand — *noun* **1** any of various systems of strokes and dots representing speech sounds and groups of sounds, used as a fast way of recording speech in writing. **2** any method of abbreviated writing. — *adv.* using any such system.

◇ Shorthand was popular in ancient Greece and Rome (a system invented in 63 BC by a Roman freeman, Marcus Tullius Tiro, was used for more than 1 000 years) Several methods were used from the 16c–18c, and the 19c saw the development of systems which are still widely used today, such as those of Isaac Pitman and John Robert Gregg. It has been widely used in commerce and industry, and in the courts of law, for taking records of the proceeding of meetings, and for the dictation of correspondence.

short-handed *adj.* understaffed.

shorthorn *noun* a breed of cattle with short horns.

shortie same as SHORTY.

shortlist — *noun* a selection of the best candidates from the total number submitted or nominated, from which the successful candidate will be chosen. — *verb* to place on a shortlist.

short-lived *adj.* lasting only for a short time.

shortly *adv.* **1** soon. **2** in a curt or abrupt manner.

shortness *noun* **1** being short. **2** deficiency.

shorts *pl. noun* trousers extending from the waist to anywhere between the upper thigh and the knee.

short shrift discourteously brief or disdainful consideration: *their suggestions were given short shrift.*

short-sighted *adj.* **1** *said of a person* affected by myopia, and able to see clearly only those objects that are relatively near. **2** *said of a person, plan etc* lacking foresight; showing a lack of foresight.

short-sightedness *noun* the condition of being short-sighted.

short story a work of prose narrative shorter than a novel (usually of not more than around 10 000 words), often concentrating on a single episode or experience and its effect. The modern short story began in the mid-19c with Edgar Allan Poe, and was confirmed as a major literary genre by Maupassant in France, and Turgenev and Chekhov in Russia. Many important 20c writers have favoured the form for its concentration and atmospheric potential.

Short Take-Off and Landing (ABBREV. **STOL**) a fixed-wing aircraft specially designed for taking off from a short rolling start. These aircraft usually accomplish their function by special aerodynamic devices providing high lift, coupled with an ability to perform well at low forward speeds. During World War II, the best-known of the slow-speed STOL observation aircraft was the Fieseler Fi 156 Storch.

short-tempered *adj.* easily made angry.

short-term *adj.* **1** concerned only with the near future. **2** lasting only a short time.

short wave a radio wave with a wavelength of between 10 and 100 metres.

short-winded *adj.* easily running out of breath.

shorty *noun* (PL. **shorties**) *colloq.* a shorter-than-average person or thing.

Shoshoni a Native American people who once lived in California, Nevada, Utah, and Wyoming. They were semi-nomadic hunter-gatherers; Wind River and N Shoshoni acquired horses and hunted the buffalo on the Plains. The Comanche split from the Wind River group and became feared raiders in the SW. The present-day population is c.9 000, mostly on reservations.

Shostakovich, Dmitri Dimitriyevich (1906–75) Russian composer, born in St Petersburg. He studied at the Conservatory there, and composed his first symphony in 1925. At first his music was highly successful, but his operas and ballets were later criticized by government and press for failing to observe the principles of 'Soviet realism'. Reinstated by his Fifth Symphony (1937), he subsequently composed prolifically in all forms, and wrote 15 symphonies; violin, piano, and cello concertos; chamber music; and choral works. His son Maxim (1938–) is a pianist and conductor.

shot¹ *noun* **1** an act of firing a gun; the sound of a gun being fired. **2** small metal pellets fired in clusters from a shotgun. **3** a person considered in terms of ability to fire a gun accurately: *a good shot.* **4** *Sport* an act of shooting or playing a stroke. **5** a photograph. **6** a single piece of filmed action recorded without a break by one camera. **7** a heavy metal ball thrown as a field event in athletics. **8** *colloq.* an attempt: *have a shot at.* **9** *colloq.* a turn or go: *it's my shot now.* **10** *colloq.* an injection. **11** *colloq. North Amer., esp. US* a drink of alcoholic spirit. **12** *old use* the launch of a spacecraft, especially a rocket: *moon shot.* — **call the shots** *colloq.* to give the orders; to be in charge. **like a shot** extremely quickly; without hesitating. **a shot in the arm** an uplifting or reviving influence; a boost. **a shot in the dark** a wild guess. [from Anglo-Saxon *sceot*]

shot² past tense and past participle of SHOOT. — *adj.* **1** *said of a fabric* woven with different-coloured threads and in such a way that movement produces the effect of changing colours. **2** streaked with a different colour. — **be** *or* **get shot of someone** *or* **something** *colloq.* be rid of them.

shotgun *noun* a gun with a long wide smooth barrel for firing clusters of pellets.

shotgun wedding *or* **shotgun marriage** a marriage into which the couple has been forced, especially because of the woman's pregnancy.

shot put an athletics event in which a heavy metal ball is thrown from the shoulder as far as possible.

shot-putter *noun* an athlete who puts the shot.

should *verb, aux.* expressing: **1** obligation, duty, or recommendation; ought to: *you should brush your teeth regularly.* **2** likelihood or probability: *he should have left by now.* **3** condition: *if I should die before you.* **4** (with first person pronouns) a past tense of *shall* in reported speech: *I told them I should be back soon.* **5** statements in clauses with *that*, fol-

lowing expressions of feeling or mood: *it seems odd that we should both have had the same idea.* **6** (with first person pronouns) doubt or polite indirectness in statements: *I should imagine he's left / I should think I'll get the job.* **7** *literary* purpose: *in order that we should not have to leave.* [from Anglo-Saxon *sceolde*]

shoulder — *noun* **1** the part of the body between the neck and upper arm. **2** the part of a garment covering this. **3** the part of an animal's or bird's body where the foreleg or wing joins the trunk. **4** a cut of meat consisting of the animal's upper foreleg. **5** (**shoulders**) the person as a bearer of burdens; capacity to bear burdens: *a lot of responsibility on his shoulders / have broad shoulders.* **6** any object or part resembling a human shoulder. **7** either edge of a road. — *verb* (**shouldered, shouldering**) **1** to bear (eg a responsibility). **2** to carry on one's shoulders. **3** to thrust with the shoulder. — **straight from the shoulder** *colloq.* frankly and forcefully. **put one's shoulder to the wheel** to get down to some hard work; to begin making a great effort. **rub shoulders with someone** *colloq.* to meet or associate with them. **shoulder arms** to bring one's rifle to a vertical position tight in to the right side with the barrel against the shoulder. **a shoulder to cry on** a person to tell one's troubles to. **shoulder to shoulder** together in friendship or agreement; side by side. [from Anglo-Saxon *sculdor*]

shoulder blade the broad flat triangular bone behind either shoulder; the scapula.

shoulder strap a strap worn over the shoulder to support a garment or bag.

shouldn't *contr.* should not.

shout — *noun* **1** a loud cry or call. **2** *colloq.* a turn to buy a round of drinks. — *verb trans., intrans.* (also **shout out**) to utter (with) a loud cry or call. — **shout someone down** to force them to give up speaking, or make it impossible to hear them, by means of persistent shouting.

shove — *verb* **1** *trans., intrans.* to push or thrust with force. **2** *colloq.* to place or put, especially roughly: *shove it in the bag.* — *noun* a forceful push. — **shove off 1** to start a boat moving by pushing against the shore or jetty. **2** *colloq.* to go away. [from Anglo-Saxon *scufan*]

shovel — *noun* **1** a tool with a deep-sided spade-like blade and a handle, for lifting and carrying loose material. **2** a machine or device with a scooping action. — *verb* (**shovelled, shovelling**) **1** to lift or carry with, or as if with, a shovel. **2** to take crudely, rapidly and in huge quantities: *shovelling food into her mouth.* [from Anglo-Saxon *scofl*, from *scufan*, to shove]

shoveller *noun Zool.* a duck that frequents marshes and muddy shallows, having a long rounded spade-like bill.

show — *verb* (PAST PARTICIPLE **shown, showed**) **1** *trans., intrans.* to make or become visible or noticeable. **2** to present or give to be viewed. **3** to display or exhibit. **4** to prove, indicate, or reveal. **5** to teach by demonstrating: *showed me how to draw.* **6** to lead, guide, or escort: *show you to your room.* **7** to give: *show him some respect.* **8** to represent or manifest: *exam results show a marked improvement.* **9** *intrans. said of a cinema film* to be part of a current programme: *now showing at the local Odeon.* **10** *intrans. slang* to appear or arrive: *what time did he show?* — *noun* **1** an entertainment or spectacle of any kind. **2** an exhibition. **3** a pretence: *a show of friendship between sworn enemies.* **4** a display of true feeling: *no show of emotion.* **5** outward appearance: *all done for show.* **6** *colloq.* proceedings; affair: *who's running the show?* **7** *old colloq. use* effort; attempt: *jolly good show.*

— **have something** *or* **nothing to show** have, or not have, a reward or benefit for one's efforts. **on show** on display; available to be seen. **show off** to display oneself or one's talents precociously, inviting attention or admiration. **show off something** to display it to good effect: *the cream rug shows off the red carpet nicely.* **show something off** to display it proudly, inviting admiration. **show up 1** *colloq.* to arrive; to turn up. **2** to be clearly visible. **show someone up** to embarrass or humiliate them in public. **show something up** to make it seem inadequate or inferior by comparison. [from Anglo-Saxon *sceawian*, to look]

showbiz *noun colloq.* show business.

show business the entertainment industry.

showcase *noun* **1** a glass case for displaying objects, eg in a museum or shop. **2** any setting in which a person or thing is displayed to good advantage.

showdown *noun colloq.* a fight or other contest settling a long-term dispute.

shower — *noun* **1** a sudden but brief fall of rain, snow, or hail. **2** a device producing a stream of water for bathing under, usually while standing. **3** a room or cubicle fitted with such a device or devices. **4** an act of bathing under such a device. **5** a sudden (especially heavy) burst or fall: *a shower of bullets / a shower of abuse.* **6** *colloq.* a bunch of worthless people. — *verb* (**showered, showering**) **1** *trans., intrans.* to cover, bestow, fall, or come abundantly: *showered them with gifts / arrows showering down from the battlements.* **2** *intrans.* to bathe under a shower. **3** *intrans.* to rain in showers. [from Anglo-Saxon *scur*]

showery *adj.* (**showerier, showeriest**) raining in showers.

showiness *noun* being showy.

showing *noun* **1** an act of exhibiting or displaying. **2** a screening of a cinema film. **3** a performance. **4** a display of behaviour as evidence of a fact: *on this showing, he certainly won't get the job.*

showjumper *noun* a horse or rider that takes part in showjumping.

showjumping *noun* a competitive sport in which riders on horseback take turns to jump a variety of obstacles, often against time. ◇ In most competitions, each pair of horse and rider has one attempt at clearing the fences. Those that clear the fences and incur no penalty points are then involved in a 'jump-off' against the clock, where speed as well as accuracy are important. Showjumping is one of the three elements which make up the equestrian competition known as the *three-day-event*.

showman *noun* **1** a person who owns or manages a circus, a stall at a fairground, or other entertainment. **2** a person skilled in displaying things, especially personal abilities, so as to attract maximum attention.

showmanship *noun* skilful display or a talent for it.

shown see SHOW.

show-off *noun colloq.* a person who shows off to attract attention; an exhibitionist.

showpiece *noun* **1** an item in an exhibition. **2** a thing presented as an excellent example of its type, to be copied or admired.

showroom *noun* a room where examples of goods for sale, especially relatively expensive items, are displayed.

showy *adj.* (**showier, showiest**) **1** attractively and impressively bright. **2** ostentatious; gaudy; flashy.

shoyu *noun* a rich Japanese sauce made from soy beans naturally fermented with wheat or barley. [from Japanese]

shrank see SHRINK.

shrapnel *noun* **1** flying fragments of the casing of any exploding shell. **2** an explosive shell, filled with pellets or metal fragments, detonated shortly before impact. [from H *Shrapnel* (1761–1842), British inventor of the pellet-filled shell]

shred — *noun* **1** a thin strip cut or ripped off. **2** the smallest piece or amount: *not a shred of evidence*. — *verb* (**shredded, shredding**) to reduce to shreds by cutting or ripping. [from Anglo-Saxon *screade*]

shredder *noun* a device or machine for shredding documents.

Shreveport POP (1990) 334 000, the seat of Caddo parish, NW Louisiana, USA. It lies on the Red R, 28km/17mi E of the Texan border. Founded in 1837, it developed rapidly after the discovery of oil in 1906; oil and natural gas remain the major industries in Shreveport.

shrew *noun* **1** a small nocturnal mammal, resembling a mouse, found in Europe, Asia, N and S America, and Africa, and having velvety fur, small eyes, and a pointed snout. It is extremely active, and must feed almost continuously on worms, insects, etc, in order to survive. The Etruscan shrew, which weighs only 2g, is the world's smallest mammal. **2** a quarrelsome or scolding woman. [from Anglo-Saxon *screawa*]

shrewd *adj.* having or showing good judgement gained from practical experience.

shrewdly *adv.* in a shrewd way.

shrewdness *noun* being shrewd.

shrewish *adj.* **1** like a shrew. **2** scolding.

Shrewsbury, Anglo-Saxon **Scrobesbyrig** POP (1992e) 93 000, the county town of Shropshire, W central England, situated in Shrewsbury and Atcham district. It lies on the R Severn, 63km/39mi NW of Birmingham. HISTORY the Roman city of Uriconium lies to the E; Shrewsbury was the headquarters of Edward I during the struggle for Wales; the Battle of Shrewsbury was fought here in 1403. NOTABLE FEATURES Church of St Mary; abbey church; Rowley's Mansion (1618); castle (11c). [from Anglo-Saxon *scrobesbyrig*, town in the wood]

shriek — *verb trans., intrans.* to cry out with a piercing scream. — *noun* such a cry.

shrift see SHORT SHRIFT.

shrike *noun* any of various hook-billed songbirds that feed on insects or small birds and animals, some species being noted for impaling their prey on thorns, etc. [from Anglo-Saxon *scric*]

shrill — *adj., said of a sound, voice etc* high-pitched and piercing. — *verb* to utter in such a voice.

shrillness *noun* a shrill quality.

shrimp — *noun* **1** a small edible long-tailed shellfish, smaller than a prawn. **2** *colloq.* a very small slight person. — *verb intrans.* to fish for shrimps.

Shrimp Girl, A a portrait by William Hogarth (c.1759, National Gallery, London).

shrimping *noun slang* the practice of sucking a partner's toes for sexual stimulation.

shrimp plant a bushy perennial plant (*Beloperone guttata*), native to Mexico, and so called because its flower spikes superficially resemble a shrimp. It has arching stems, oval leaves, and white hooded flowers, almost hidden by overlapping pinkish bracts.

shrine *noun* **1** a sacred place of worship. **2** the tomb of a saint or other holy person, or a monument erected near it. **3** any place or thing greatly respected because of its associations. [from Anglo-Saxon *scrin*]

shrink — *verb* (PAST TENSE **shrank**; PAST PARTICIPLE **shrunk**, as adj. **shrunken**) **1** *trans., intrans.* to make or become smaller, especially through exposure to heat, cold or moisture. **2** (**shrink from something**) to move away in horror or disgust. **3** (**shrink from something**) to be reluctant do it. — *noun slang* a psychiatrist. [from Anglo-Saxon *scrincan*]

shrinkage *noun* the act or amount of shrinking.

shrinking violet *colloq.* a shy hesitant person.

shrink-wrap *verb* to wrap in clear plastic film that is then shrunk, eg by heating, so as to fit tightly.

shrivel *verb trans., intrans.* (**shrivelled, shrivelling**) (*also* **shrivel up**) to make or become shrunken and wrinkled, especially through drying out.

Shropshire, sometimes abbreviated **Salop** POP (1992e) 413 000, a county in W central England, divided into six districts. AREA 3 490sq km/1 347sq mi. It is bounded W by Powys and Clwyd in Wales and drained by the R Severn. CHIEF TOWNS Shrewsbury (county town), Telford, Oswestry, Wellington, Ludlow. ECONOMY agriculture (especially dairy farming, cattle, sheep, cereals); engineering. NOTABLE FEATURE Ironbridge Gorge Open-air Museum.

Shropshire Lad, A a collection of poems by A E Housman (1896). They are largely nostalgic in tone, recalling life in a semi-imaginary Shropshire.

shroud — *noun* **1** a cloth in which a dead body is wrapped. **2** anything that obscures, masks or hides: *shrouds of fog*. — *verb* **1** to wrap in a shroud. **2** to obscure, mask, or hide: *proceedings shrouded in secrecy*. [from Anglo-Saxon *scrud*, garment]

Shrove Tuesday the day in the Christian calendar before Ash Wednesday, on which it was customary to confess one's sins; Pancake Day. [from Anglo-Saxon *scrifan*, to confess sins]

shrub *noun Bot.* a woody plant, without a main trunk, which branches into several main stems at or just below ground level. [from Anglo-Saxon *scrybb*, scrub]

shrubbery *noun* (PL. **shrubberies**) a place, especially a part of a garden, where shrubs are grown.

shrubby *adj.* (**shrubbier, shrubbiest**) **1** like or having the character of a shrub. **2** covered with shrubs.

shrug — *verb trans., intrans.* (**shrugged, shrugging**) to raise (the shoulders) briefly as an indication of doubt or indifference. — *noun* an act of shrugging.
— **shrug something off 1** to get rid of it with ease. **2** to dismiss (especially criticism) lightly.

shrunk, shrunken see SHRINK.

shudder — *verb intrans.* (**shuddered, shuddering**) to tremble, especially with fear or disgust. — *noun* **1** such a trembling movement or feeling. **2** a heavy vibration or shaking.
— **shudder to think** to be inwardly embarrassed or appalled when imagining some consequence, etc.

shuffle — *verb* **1** *trans., intrans.* to move (one's feet) with short quick sliding movements; to walk in this way. **2** to rearrange or mix up roughly or carelessly. **3** to jumble up (playing cards) into a random order. — *noun* **1** an act or sound of shuffling. **2** a short quick sliding of the feet in dancing.

shuffleboard *or* **shovelboard** *noun* a popular deck game played aboard ship. A larger version of shove-halfpenny, it is played by pushing wooden discs with long-handled drivers into a scoring area.

shufti *noun colloq.* a look or glance: *have a shufti at this*. [from Arabic *shufti*, literally 'have you seen?']

shun *verb* (**shunned, shunning**) to avoid or keep away from. [from Anglo-Saxon *scunian*]

shunt — *verb* **1** to move (a train or carriage) from one track to another. **2** to move around; to change the place or places of. **3** to transfer (eg a task) on to someone else, as an evasion. — *noun* **1** an act of shunting or being shunted. **2** a conductor diverting part of an electric current. **3** a railway siding. **4** *colloq.* a minor collision between vehicles.

shush — *interj.* be quiet! — *verb* to command to be quiet by, or as if by, saying 'Shush!'. [imitative]

shut — *verb trans., intrans.* (**shutting**; PAST TENSE AND PAST PARTICIPLE **shut**) **1** to place or move so as to close an opening: *shut a door / the door shut*. **2** to close or cause to close over, denying open access to the contents: *shut the cupboard / the book shut*. **3** not to allow access (to): *shut the shop / the office shuts at weekends*. — *adj.* not open; closed.
— **shut down** *or* **shut something down** to stop or cause it to stop working or operating, for a time or permanently.
shut someone *or* **something in** to enclose or confine them.
shut something off to switch it off; to stop the flow of it.
shut someone *or* **something out 1** to prevent them coming into a room, building, etc. **2** to exclude them. **3** to block out (eg light).
shut up *colloq.* to stop speaking.
shut someone up 1 *colloq.* to make them stop speaking. **2** to confine them.
shut something up to close and lock premises, for a time or permanently: *shut up shop*. [from Anglo-Saxon *scyttan*, to bar]

shutdown *noun* **1** a temporary closing of a factory or business. **2** a reduction of power in a nuclear reactor, especially as a safety measure.

Shute, Nevil, originally **Nevil Shute Norway** (1899–1960) English writer, born in Ealing, Middlesex. He became an aeronautical engineer, and began to write novels in 1926. After World War II, he emigrated to Australia, which became the setting for most of his later books, notably *A Town Like Alice* (1949), and *On the Beach* (1957).

shuteye *noun slang* sleep.

shutter — *noun* **1** a movable exterior cover for a window, especially either of a pair of hinged wooden panels. **2** a device in a camera that opens and closes at a variable speed, exposing the film to light. — *verb* (**shuttered, shuttering**) to fit or cover (a window) with a shutter or shutters.
— **put up the shutters** *colloq.* to stop trading, for the day or permanently.

shuttle — *noun* **1** in weaving, the device carrying the horizontal thread (the *weft*) backwards and forwards between the vertical threads (the *warp*). **2** the device carrying the lower thread through the loop formed by the upper in a sewing-machine. **3** an aircraft, train, or bus running a frequent service between two places, usually at a relatively short distance from one another. — *verb trans., intrans.* to move or cause to move or travel back and forth. [from Anglo-Saxon *scytel*, dart]

shuttlecock *noun* a cone of feathers or of feathered plastic, with a rounded cork fixed on its narrow end, hit back and forth in badminton.

Shwe Dagon Pagoda a Buddhist pilgrimage site in Rangoon, Burma (Myanma). It consists of a gold-plated shrine (stupa) 98m high. Tradition holds that the Shwe Dagon houses eight of the Buddha's hairs, and that a pagoda has occupied this site for over 2 000 years.

Shwezigon Pagoda a pagoda erected in the 11c near Pagan, Burma (Myanma) as a reliquary shrine for a tooth and a bone of the Buddha. It is the centre of an annual festival.

shy[1] — *adj.* (**shyer, shyest** *or* **shier, shiest**) **1** *said of a person* embarrassed or unnerved by the company or attention of others. **2** easily scared; timid. **3** (**shy of something**) wary or distrustful of it. **4** *colloq.* short in payment by a specified amount: *10p shy.* — *verb intrans.* (**shies**, **shied**) **1** to jump suddenly aside or back, startled. **2** (*usually* **shy away**) to move away mentally, showing reluctance: *shied away from arguing with them.* — *noun* (PL. **shies**) an act of shying. [from Anglo-Saxon *sceoh*, timid]

shy² — *verb* (**shies**, **shied**) to throw (eg a stone). — *noun* (PL. **shies**) **1** a throw. **2** a fairground stall where balls are thrown to knock over objects, especially coconuts.

Shylock the Jewish money-lender in Shakespeare's *The Merchant of Venice*, who claims his pound of flesh from Antonio.

shyly *adv.* with a shy manner.

shyness *noun* being shy.

shyster *noun slang North Amer., esp. US* an unscrupulous or disreputable person, especially in business. [probably from *Scheuster*, a disreputable 19c US lawyer]

SI *abbrev.* Système International d'Unités. An international system of scientific units in which the fundamental quantities are length, time, mass, electric current, temperature, luminous intensity, and amount of substance, and the corresponding units are the metre, second, kilogram, ampere, kelvin, candela, and mole. [from French *Système International*]

Si *symbol Chem.* silicon.

si same as TI.

sial *noun Geol.* the granite rocks rich in silica and aluminium that form the upper layer of the Earth's crust. It is equivalent to the upper part of the continental crust, above the sima. See also SIMA. [from *silica* and *alumina*]

Sialkot POP (1981) 302 000, a city in Punjab province, E Pakistan, E of the R Chenab. NOTABLE FEATURES ancient fort; mausoleum of the Sikh apostle Nanak.

Siam see THAILAND.

Siamese — *adj.* relating to Siam (now Thailand) in SE Asia, or its people or language. — *noun* **1** a native of Siam. **2** the language of Siam. **3** a Siamese cat.

Siamese cat a fawn-coloured smooth-haired domestic cat with blue eyes and a small head.

Siamese twins 1 twins born with a piece of flesh joining one to the other. **2** any two people always together.

Sian see XI'AN.

Sian a female first name. [a Welsh form of JANE]

Sian Ka'an a reserve covering over 5 000sq km/1 900sq mi in the Yucatán Peninsula, Mexico. In addition to the flora and fauna of the region, the reserve also protects numerous Maya archaeological sites and the way of life of the descendants of the Maya people. It is a World Heritage site.

SIB *abbrev.* Security and Investments Board.

Sibelius, Jean (Julius Christian) (1865–1957) Finnish composer, born in Tavastehus. A passionate nationalist, he abandoned a legal career for music study, and wrote a series of symphonic poems (eg *Swan of Tuonela*) based on episodes in the Finnish epic *Kalevala*. A state grant enabled him to devote himself entirely to composition from 1897, and his seven symphonies (he destroyed the eighth), symphonic poems (notably *Finlandia*, 1899) and violin concerto won him national and international popularity.

Siberia a vast geographical region in Russia, comprising the N third of Asia. AREA c.7 511 000sq km/2 900 000sq mi. It extends from the Ural Mts in the W to the Pacific Ocean in the E, and from the Arctic Ocean in the N to the Kazakhstan Steppes and the Chinese and Mongolian frontiers in the S. The region includes the Arctic islands of Severnaya Zemlya, New Siberian Is, and Wrangel I; Sakhalin and the Kuril Is lie off the Pacific coast. PHYSICAL DESCRIPTION the W Siberian Lowlands stretch over 1 500km/1 000mi from the Ural Mts in the W to the R Yenisei in the E; the Central Siberian Plateau lies between the R Yenisei in the W and the R Lena in the E; the E Siberian Highlands lie to the E; along Siberia's S margins lie the Amur R, the Sayan Mts, and the Altay Mts, rising to 4 506m at Gora Belukha; there are c.155 000 rivers, notably the Ob, Yenisei, and Lena; tundra extends c.320km/200mi inland along the Arctic coast. CLIMATE Siberia has an extreme continental climate; average winter temperatures are generally below –18°C, and January temperatures in the NE average –51°C; summer temperatures are relatively high, with a July average of 15–18°C in the areas which are coldest in winter; precipitation is generally low. CHIEF TOWNS Novosibirsk, Omsk, Krasnoyarsk, Irkutsk, Khabarovsk, Vladivostok (all lie on the Trans-Siberian Railway). HISTORY Russian conquest of Siberia by the Cossacks began in the 16c, and they possessed all of W Siberia by the 17c; the area was soon used as a penal colony and place of exile for political prisoners; fur trade declined in the 18c and mining became the chief economic activity; Russian settlement on a large scale occurred with the construction of the Trans-Siberian Railway (1892–1905); after the 1917 revolution vast areas were occupied by counter-revolutionary armies which were overthrown by Soviet forces in 1922; Siberia underwent dramatic economic development under the five-year plans, relying heavily on forced labour and population resettlement to establish mining, industrial, and agricultural installations. ECONOMY coal; timber; gold; iron; nickel; dairying; cereal; cattle; reindeer; maize; sorghum; soya beans; hydroelectric power.

Siberian Plateau, Central, Russian **Sredne Sibirskoye Ploskogorye** an upland region in E Siberia, Russia, lying between the R Yenisei in the W and the R Lena in the E. Its average height ranges from 300m to 800m.

Siberut an island 140km/87mi off the W coast of Sumatra, Indonesia. AREA 500sq km/193sq mi. It is a nature and 'traditional use' reserve area

protecting the dwarf gibbon, pig-tailed langur, Mentawi leaf monkey, and Mentawi macaque.

sibilance *or* **sibilancy** *noun* hissing.

sibilant — *adj.* of, like, or pronounced with a hissing sound. — *noun* a consonant with such a sound, eg *s* and *z*. [from Latin *sibilare*, to hiss]

Sibley, Antoinette (1939–) English dancer, born in Bromley, Kent. She trained with the Royal Ballet, and appeared as a soloist for the first time in 1956 when, due to the principal dancer's illness, she was given the main role in *Swan Lake* and became famous overnight. Her partnership with Anthony Dowell was one of enchanting compatibility and they were dubbed the 'Golden Pair'. Two of her most celebrated roles were in Frederick Ashton's *The Dream* and Kenneth MacMillan's *Manon*.

sibling *noun* a brother or sister. [from Anglo-Saxon *sibb*, relationship + -LING]

Sibyl *or* **Sibylla** in Greek and Roman antiquity, a name for many prophetesses who uttered predictions, supposedly in a state of ecstasy brought about by divine possession. The most famous was said to live in a cave at Cumae in Campania; there is a scene in Virgil's *Aeneid* in which Aeneas visits her. Sybilline books, or books of prophecies, were deposited at Rome in the age of the kings, and were guarded by two patricians. A collection of such books still existed in the 4c AD. Because of later religious associations, Sibyls featured in Christian art and literature.

Sibylline Books *Roman Hist.* prophetic books offered to Tarquinus Superbus by the Cumaean Sibyl, of which he ultimately bought three for the price he had refused to give for nine, these three being held in the Capitol and referred to by the ancient Roman senate in times of emergency and disaster; also, a later set made after the first collection was destroyed by fire in 83 BC.

sic *adv.* a term used in brackets after a word or phrase in a quotation that appears to be a mistake, to indicate that it is in fact quoted accurately. [from Latin *sic*, thus, so]

Sicilian Vespers the wholesale massacre (1282) of the French in Sicily. The first killings occurred during a riot in a church outside Palermo at vespers (evensong) on Easter Monday in 1282, hence the incident's name. It began the Sicilian revolt against Charles of Anjou, King of Naples-Sicily, and a war that ended in 1302.

Sicily, Italian **Sicilia** POP (1991) 5m, the largest and most populous island in the Mediterranean Sea, separated from the mainland of Italy by the narrow Strait of Messina. Together with some small neighbouring islands, it constitutes an autonomous region of Italy. AREA 25 706sq km/ 9 922sq mi; length 288km/179mi; width 192km/119mi. PHYSICAL DESCRIPTION a mountainous island; the Monti Nebrodi in the N rise to nearly 2 000m; there is a large earthquake zone on the E coast, culminating in Europe's largest active volcano, Mt Etna (3 323m), the island's highest point. CAPITAL Palermo. CHIEF TOWNS Trapani, Messina, Catania. HISTORY settled by the Greeks in the 8c BC, it became a Roman province in the 3c BC; conquered by the Normans in the 11c; the harsh rule of Charles of Anjou led to a Sicilian revolt known as the 'Sicilian Vespers' in 1282; in the 14c Sicily came under Spanish rule through the House of Aragon; the Kingdom of the Two Sicilies was finally formed in 1504, consisting of Sicily and the S part of Italy; Garibaldi's conquest of Sicily in 1860 led to its unification with Italy one year later. ECONOMY the area is under-developed, with considerable poverty; intensive vegetable growing, fruit, wine in the fertile coastal areas (especially around Marsala); arable and pastoral farming in the dry interior; fishing; salt extraction; petrochemicals; food processing; potash; asphalt; marble; tourism.

SI Units

Name of unit	Abbreviation of unit name	Physical quantity	Symbol
metre	m	length	*l*
kilogram	kg	mass	*m*
second	s	time	*t*
ampere	A	electric current	*I*
kelvin	K	thermodynamic temperature	*T*
candela	cd	luminous intensity	*I*
mole	mol	amount of substance	
radian	rad	plane angle	α, β, θ, etc
steradian	sr	solid angle	Ω, ω

sick — *adj.* **1** vomiting; feeling the desire to vomit. **2** ill; unwell. **3** relating to ill health: *sick pay.* **4** extremely annoyed; disgusted. **5** mentally deranged. **6** (**sick of someone** *or* **something**) thoroughly weary or fed up with them. **7** *said of humour* exploiting subjects like death and disease in an unpleasant way. **8** *colloq.* very inadequate in comparison: *makes my effort look a bit sick.* — *noun colloq.* vomit. — *verb trans., intrans. (usually* **sick something up**) to vomit. [from Anglo-Saxon *seoc*]

sick-bay *noun* a room where ill or injured people are treated, eg in a place of work.

sick building syndrome *Medicine* a disorder first diagnosed among office workers in the 1980s, typical symptoms including headache, fatigue, and sore throat. It is thought to be caused by inadequate ventilation or air-conditioning.

sicken *verb* (**sickened, sickening**) **1** to cause to feel like vomiting. **2** to annoy greatly or disgust. **3** *intrans.* (**sicken for something**) to show symptoms of an illness: *sickening for the flu.*

sickening *adj.* that sickens.

sickeningly *adv.* in a sickening way.

Sickert, Walter (Richard) (1860–1942) German-born British artist, born in Munich. After three years on the English stage, he turned to art and worked in Paris with Degas, whose techniques influenced his pictures of music hall interiors and London life. The Camden Town Group (later the London Group) was formed under his leadership (c.1910) and he became a major influence on later English painters. His works include *Ennui* (c.1913, Tate Gallery, London).

sickle *noun* a tool with a short handle and a curved blade for cutting grain crops with a sweeping action. [from Anglo-Saxon *sicol*]

sick-leave *noun* time taken off because of sickness.

sickle-cell anaemia *Medicine* a hereditary blood disorder, common in African peoples, in which the red blood cells contain an abnormal type of haemoglobin. As a result, the cells become sickle-shaped and very fragile, and their rapid removal from the circulation leads to anaemia. The disease confers resistance to certain forms of malaria, but is itself incurable.

sickly — *adj.* (**sicklier, sickliest**) **1** susceptible to illness; often ill. **2** of or suggesting illness. **3** inducing the desire to vomit: *a sickly smell.* **4** unhealthy-looking: *a sickly plant.* **5** weakly and contemptibly sentimental. — *adv.* to an extent that suggests illness: *sickly pale.*

sickness *noun* **1** an illness; ill-health. **2** vomiting. **3** nausea.

sick verse a modern term used to describe a type of poetry (from any period) that is macabre, satirical, or unsettlingly humorous and whose themes are misfortune, death, disease, decay, cruelty, mental illness, etc Many poets have written verse which would qualify for the label 'sick'. Examples include Edgar Allan Poe's 'The Raven' and 'The Sleeper', John Betjeman's 'Death in Leamington'; and Sylvia Plath's 'Surgeon at 2am' and 'In Plaster'.

Siddons, Sarah, *née* **Kemble** (1755–1831) British actress, born in Brecon, Wales, the eldest child of Roger Kemble. A member of her father's theatre company from her earliest childhood, she gained a great reputation in the provinces, played at Drury Lane in 1782, and thereafter became the queen of the stage, unmatched as a tragic actress.

side — *noun* **1** any of the usually flat or flattish surfaces that form the outer extent of something; any of these surfaces other than the top and bottom, or other than the front, back, top, and bottom. **2** an edge or border, or the area adjoining this: *at the side of the road.* **3** either of the parts or areas produced when the whole is divided up the middle: *the right side of your body.* **4** either of the broad surfaces of a flat or flattish object: *two sides of a coin.* **5** any of the lines forming a geometric figure. **6** any of the groups or teams, or opposing positions, in a conflict or competition. **7** an aspect: *saw a different side to him.* **8** the slope of a hill. **9** the part of the body between armpit and hip. **10** a part of an area of land; district: *the north side of the town.* **11** father's or mother's family or ancestors: *related to him on her mother's side.* **12** *Brit. colloq.* television channel: *on the other side.* **13** *slang* a pretentious or superior air: *to put on side.* — *adj.* **1** located at the side: *side entrance.* **2** subsidiary or subordinate: *side road.* — *verb intrans.* (**side with someone**) to adopt their position or point of view; to join forces with them.

— **let the side down** to disappoint one's own group, or frustrate its efforts, by falling below the standards set by its other members.

on *or* **to one side** in or to a position removed from the main concern; aside.

on the side as a secondary job or source of income, often dishonestly or illegally.

on the ... side *colloq.* rather ...; of a ... nature: *found his comments a bit on the offensive side.*

side by side 1 close together. **2** with sides touching.

take sides to support one particular side in a conflict or argument.

[from Anglo-Saxon *side*]

sideboard *noun* **1** a large piece of furniture consisting of shelves or cabinets mounted above drawers or cupboards. **2** a sideburn.

sideburn *noun* the line of short hair growing down in front of each of a man's ears.

sidecar *noun* a small carriage for one or two passengers, fixed to the side of a motorcycle.

side effect an additional unexpected (usually undesirable) effect, especially of a drug.

sidekick *noun colloq.* a close friend, partner, or deputy.

sidelight *noun* **1** a small light fitted on each outside edge of the front and rear of a motor vehicle, used in fading daylight. **2** a light on each side of a moving boat or ship, one red, one green. **3** light coming from the side.

sideline *noun* **1** a line marking either side boundary of a sports pitch. **2** (**sidelines**) the areas just outside these boundaries; the area to which non-participants in any activity are confined. **3** a business, etc carried on in addition to regular work.

sidelong *adj., adv.* from or to one side; not direct or directly: *a sidelong glance.*

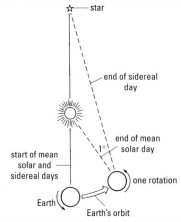

sidereal time

sidereal *adj. formal* of, relating to, or determined by the stars: *sidereal year.* [from Latin *sidus*, star]

siderite *noun Geol.* a brown, grey, greenish, or yellowish mineral form of ferrous carbonate (FeCO$_3$) that occurs in sedimentary deposits, hydrothermal veins (veins formed from magma containing a high proportion of hot water), and some metamorphic rocks. It is an important ore of iron. [from Greek *sideros*, iron]

side-saddle — *noun* a horse's saddle enabling a woman in a skirt to sit with both legs on the same side. — *adv.* sitting in this way.

sideshow *noun* a stall with some form of amusement or game at a fair, beside a circus, etc.

sidespin *noun* a spinning motion imparted to a struck ball that causes it to rotate about its vertical axis while going forward. See also BACKSPIN, TOPSPIN.

side-splitting *adj.* provoking uproarious laughter.

side-step — *verb* to avoid by, or as if by, stepping aside. — *noun* a step taken to one side.

sideswipe *noun* **1** a blow coming from the side, not head-on. **2** a criticism or rebuke made in passing, incidentally to the main discussion.

sidetrack *verb* to divert the attention of away from the matter in hand.

sidewalk *noun North Amer., esp. US* a pavement.

sideways *adv., adj.* **1** from, to, or towards one side. **2** with one side foremost: *slid sideways into the wall.*

side whiskers sideburns.

sidewinder *noun* **1** a snake which moves by pushing its head forward on to the ground, then winding the body forwards and sideways until it lies stretched out to one side; meanwhile the head is moved forward again. By repeating this action, it is able to move rapidly over soft sand. This method is used by several species, especially vipers, but no species uses it all the time. **2** the N American horned rattlesnake, which usually moves by this method.

Sidgwick, Henry (1838–1900) English moral philosopher, born in Skipton, Yorkshire. He lectured at Cambridge and became Professor of Moral Philosophy in 1883. His best-known work, *Methods of Ethics* (1874), is an analytical examination of various theories in moral philosophy, and a sophisticated defence of utilitarianism. He was a founder and the first President of the Society for Psychical Research in 1882.

Sidgwick, Nevil Vincent (1873–1951) English chemist, born in Oxford. Professor at Oxford, he became renowned for his work on molecular structure and his formulation of a theory of valency.

Sidi bel Abbès 1 POP (1987) 153 000, the chief town of Sidi bel Abbès department, N Algeria. It lies 56km/35mi S of Oran. HISTORY originally a walled town, and a military post under French occupation; headquarters of the French Foreign Legion until 1962. **2** a department in N Algeria with Sidi Bel Abbès as its capital.

siding *noun* a short dead-end railway line on to which wagons, etc can be moved temporarily from the main line.

sidle *verb intrans.* to go or move slowly and cautiously or secretively, avoiding notice. [a back-formation from obsolete *sideling*, sideways]

Sidmouth (of Sidmouth), Henry Addington, 1st Viscount (1757–1844) English Tory statesman, born in London. He became an MP in 1783, was Speaker of the House (1789–1801) and when Pitt (the Younger) resigned, was Prime Minister (1801–4) until Pitt resumed his ministry. His administration negotiated the Peace of Amiens (1802), which held for barely a year. He later became Home Secretary under Liverpool (1812–21), but was unpopular for coercive measures such as the Six Acts of 1819.

Sidney, Algernon (1622–83) English Whig politician, born in Penshurst, Kent. He fought for the Parliamentary army in the English Civil War and was wounded at Marston Moor (1644). In 1645 he entered parliament, and served as governor in several cities. An extreme Republican, he resented Cromwell's assumption of power, and retired to Penshurst (1653–9). After the Restoration he lived on the Continent, but in 1677 was pardoned and returned to England. However, in 1683, he was implicated in the Rye House Plot, and beheaded in London.

Sidney, Sir Philip (1554–86) English poet, born in Penshurst, Kent. He travelled in Europe (1572–5), was knighted in 1582, and was appointed governor of Flushing in 1585. He spent the last year of his life in the Netherlands, where he assisted in the struggle against Spain and successfully plotted an attack on the town of Axel, before being fatally wounded at Zutphen. His literary work, which was not published until after his death, includes the unfinished pastoral romance, *Arcadia* (1590), a sonnet cycle, *Astrophel and Stella* (1591), and the *Defence of Poesie* (1595).

Sidney a male and occasionally female first name, after the surname. [perhaps from *Saint-Denis* in France]

Sidon *or* **Saida** POP (1990e) 38 000, a seaport in W Lebanon, on the Mediterranean Sea. It lies 35km/22mi N of Tyre, at the centre of a well-watered coastal plain. The ancient city was founded in the third millennium BC and was once noted for its glass and purple dyes. NOTABLE FEATURES Crusader Castle; ruins of the Phoenician Temple of Echmoun nearby.

SIDS *abbrev.* sudden infant death syndrome.

Sieff (of Brimpton), Israel Moses Sieff, Baron (1889–1972) English commercial executive, born in Manchester. He was a schoolfellow of Simon Marks, who became his brother-in-law, and together they developed Marks and Spencer. He succeeded Lord Marks as Chairman (1964–7). His son Marcus Joseph (1913–) was Chairman of Marks and Spencer (1972–84), President (1984–5), and has been Honorary President since 1985.

siege *noun* 1 an attempt to capture a fort or town by surrounding it with troops and forcing surrender. 2 a police operation using similar tactics, eg to force a criminal out of a building.
— **lay siege to a place** to subject it to a siege. [from Old French *sege*, seat]

Siegfried a music drama by Richard Wagner (1857, first performed 1876), the second part of the three-part cycle *Der Ring des Nibelungen*.

Sielmann, Heinz (1917–) German naturalist and nature film photographer, born in Königsberg. He began to make films in 1938, and won the German Oscar for documentary films three years running (1953–5). He evolved techniques enabling him to film the inside of animal lairs and birds' nests, which revolutionized the study of animal behaviour.

Siemens, (Ernst) Werner von (1816–92) German electrical engineer, brother of William Siemens, born in Lenthe, Hanover. He developed the telegraphic system in Prussia, and in 1847 established Siemens & Halske, which evolved into one of the great electrical engineering firms. He devised numerous electrical instruments, discovered the self-acting dynamo (1867), and determined the electrical resistance of different substances; the SI unit of electrical conductance is named after him.

Siemens, Sir (Charles) William, German (**Karl**) **Wilhelm** (1823–83) German-born British electrical engineer, brother of Werner von Siemens, born in Lenthe, Hanover. As manager in England of the firm of Siemens Brothers, he was actively engaged in the construction of telegraphs, designed a steamship for cable-laying, promoted electric lighting, and patented many inventions. In 1861 he designed a steel furnace which became the most widely used in the world.

siemens *noun* the standard unit of electrical conductance. [named after Werner von Siemens]

Siena POP (1990e) 58 000, the capital of Siena province, Tuscany, central Italy. It lies 70km/44mi S of Florence and is a major tourist city. From this area comes the brown pigment known as sienna. HISTORY founded by the Etruscans; became a rival of Florence in the 12c; centre of the Ghibelline faction; influential centre of medieval art. NOTABLE FEATURES cathedral (13c); 13c Gothic town hall (Palazzo Pubblico) with a notable tower; Palazzo Buonsignori (14c); Church of San Domenico (13c–14c); House of St Catherine of Siena; university (13c). EVENT the Palio, a parade and traditional horse race around the main square.

Sienese School a school of art which flourished in Siena in the 14c and early 15c. Sienese art is more decorative and less dramatic than that of Florence, and has deep roots in the Gothic and Byzantine traditions. Artists included Duccio, Martini, and the Lorenzetti brothers.

Sienkiewicz, Henryk (Adam Alexander Pius) (1846–1916) Polish novelist, born near Luków. He travelled in the USA, and in the 1870s began to write articles, short stories, and novels. His major work was a war trilogy about 17c Poland, beginning with *With Fire and Sword* (1884), but his most widely-known book is the story of Rome under Nero, *Quo Vadis* (1896). He was awarded the Nobel Prize for Literature in 1905.

sienna *noun* 1 a pigment obtained from a type of earth with a high clay and iron content. 2 its colour, browny-yellow in its original state (*raw sienna*), reddish-brown when roasted (*burnt sienna*). [named after Siena in Italy]

sierra *noun* a mountain range in Spanish-speaking countries and the US, especially when jagged. [from Spanish *sierra*, a saw]

Sierra Club a US private, non-profit-making conservation organization. It was founded by the Scottish-born US naturalist and writer, John Muir (1838–1914) in 1892.

Sierra Leone, official name **Republic of Sierra Leone** POP (1992e) 4.4m, a coastal republic in W Africa, divided into four provinces. AREA 72 325sq km/27 917sq mi. It is bounded N by Guinea, SE by Liberia, and S and SW by the Atlantic Ocean. CAPITAL Freetown. CHIEF TOWNS Bo, Sefadu, Makeni, Kenema, Lunsar. TIME ZONE GMT. The population is chiefly African (eg Mende, Temne); local beliefs and Islam are the chief religions. OFFICIAL LANGUAGE English; Krio is also widely spoken. CURRENCY the leone. PHYSICAL DESCRIPTION length, 322km/200mi; width 290km/180mi; a low narrow coastal plain; the W half rises to an average height of 500m in the Loma Mts; the highest point is Loma Mansa (1 948m); the Tingi Mts in the SE rise to 1 853m. CLIMATE equatorial, with a rainy season from May to Oct; the highest rainfall is on the coast; temperatures are uniformly high throughout the year, c.27°C; the average annual rainfall at Freetown is 3 436mm. HISTORY the area was first visited by Portuguese navigators and British slave traders; land was bought from local chiefs by English philanthropists who established settlements for freed slaves in the 1780s; became a British Crown Colony in 1808; the hinterland was declared a British protectorate in 1896; gained independence in 1961; became a republic in 1971; following the adoption of a new constitution in 1991 with provision for multiparty politics, there was a military coup in 1992 resulting in the suspension of political activity and the dissolution of the new constitution. ECONOMY mining is the most important sector of the economy; diamonds represent c.60% of exports; bauxite, gold, titanium, iron ore, columbium, limestone, salt, aluminium, chromite; over 70% of the population is involved in subsistence agriculture, chiefly rice, coffee, cocoa, ginger, palm kernels, cassava,

citrus fruits; food processing; soap; timber; furniture.

Sierra Leone

Sierra Nevada a mountain range in W USA, mainly in E California. It extends NW–SE for 725km/450mi between the Cascade and Coastal ranges. Mt Whitney, at 4 418m, is the highest point in the USA outside Alaska. The Yosemite, Sequoia, and Kings Canyon national parks are located in the Sierra Nevada.

Sierra Nevada a mountain range in Andalusia, S Spain. It rises to 3 481m at Mulhacén, the highest peak in continental Spain.

Sierra Nevada de Mérida a mountain range in W Venezuela. It is a spur of the Andes, with a length of 500km/300mi and width of 50–80km/30–50mi. It rises to 5 007m at Pico Bolívar, the highest peak in Venezuela. The world's highest cable railway runs to Pico Espejo which is 4 765m high.

siesta *noun* a sleep or rest after the midday meal in hot countries. [from Spanish *siesta*]

sieve — *noun* a utensil with a meshed or perforated bottom, used to separate solids from liquids or large particles from smaller ones. — *verb* to strain or separate with a sieve.
— **have a head** *or* **memory like a sieve** to be habitually forgetful.
[from Anglo-Saxon *sife*]

sievert *noun* Physics (ABBREV. **Sv**) the SI unit of radiation dose equivalent, equal to the absorbed dose multiplied by its relative biological effectiveness. It therefore takes account of the fact that different types of radiation cause differing amounts of biological damage, and it is used in radiation safety measurements. [named after the Swedish physicist R M Sievert]

sieve tube *Bot.* in the phloem tissue of a flowering plant, any of the tubular structures, each consisting of a column of long cells joined end to end, through which organic compounds manufactured in the leaves by photosynthesis are transported to the rest of the plant.

Sièyes, Emmanuel Joseph, Comte (Count), also called **Abbé Sièyes** (1748–1836) French cleric and political theorist, born in Fréjus. His pamphlet, *Qu'est-ce que le tiers-état?* (What is the Third Estate?, 1789) stimulated bourgeois awareness and won him great popularity. He became a member of the National Convention, and later served on the Committee of Public Safety (1795) and in the Directory. In 1799, he helped to organize the revolution of 18th Brumaire (in which Napoleon overthrew the Directory), and became a member of the Consulate. He was exiled at the Restoration (1815), but returned after the July Revolution (1830).

sift *verb* 1 to pass through a sieve in order to separate out lumps or larger particles. 2 to separate out by, or as if by, passing through a sieve. **3** to examine closely and discriminatingly. [from Anglo-Saxon *siftan*, from *sife*, sieve]

sigh — *verb* **1** *intrans.* to release a long deep breath, especially indicating sadness, longing, or relief. **2** *intrans.* to make a similar sound, especially suggesting breakdown or failure: *heard the engine sigh.* **3** to express with such a sound. — *noun* an act or the sound of sighing.
— **sigh for someone** or **something** *literary* to regret, grieve over, or yearn for them.
[from Anglo-Saxon *sican*]

sight — *noun* **1** the power of seeing; vision. **2** a thing seen. **3** one's field of vision, or the opportunity to see things that this provides: *catch sight of / within/out of sight.* **4** (*usually* **sights**) a place, building, etc that is particularly interesting to see: *seeing the sights of the town.* **5** a device on a firearm through or along which one looks to take aim. **6** opinion or judgement: *just a failure in his sight.* **7** *colloq.* a person or thing unpleasant to look at: *looked a sight without his teeth in.* — *verb* **1** to get a look at or glimpse of. **2** to adjust the sight of (a firearm). **3** to aim (a firearm) using the sight.
— **at** or **on sight 1** as soon as seen. **2** without previous view or study.
lose sight of something or **someone 1** to no longer be able to see them. **2** to fail to keep them in mind; to no longer be familiar with them.
a sight more *colloq.* a great deal or great many more: *a sight more people than expected.*
a sight for sore eyes a very welcome sight.
set one's sights on something to decide on it as an ambition or aim.
sight unseen without seeing or having seen the thing in question beforehand: *buy a house sight unseen.*
[from Anglo-Saxon *sihth*]

sighted *adj.* having the power of sight; not blind.

sightless *adj.* blind.

sight-read *verb trans., intrans.* to play or sing from music not previously seen.

sight-reading *noun* playing or singing from printed music that one has not seen before.

sight-screen *noun* any of a set of large white movable screens at either end of a cricket ground, providing a background against which the batsman can see the ball clearly.

sightsee *verb intrans.* to go sightseeing.

sightseeing *noun* visiting places of interest.

sightseer *noun* a person who goes sightseeing.

sigillography *noun* the study of seals used on documents, etc as a sign of authenticity. It is particularly useful in historical studies as a means of identifying, dating, and validating documents. [from Latin *sigillum*, diminutive of *signum*, sign + Greek *graphe*, writing]

Sigiriya an ancient city in central Sri Lanka, and the rock which rises 180m above it. The rock is surmounted by a palace built in the 5c by King Kasyapa I. Sigiriya is renowned not only for its ruins, but also for the frescoes adorning the western cliffs of the rock. It is a World Heritage site.

Sigismund I, known as **the Old** (1467–1548) King of Poland (1506–48) and a great patron of the Renaissance. His court was troubled by factions stirred up by his second wife, the daughter of the Duke of Milan, and the Protestant Reformation (from 1518) raised new troubles. In a war with Russia he lost Smolensk (1514), but gained E Prussia (1525) and Moldavia (1531).

Sigismund (**Emperor**) (1368–1437) Holy Roman Emperor (1410–37), the son of Charles IV. He became King of Hungary (1387), German King (1411), and King of Bohemia (1419). In 1396 he was defeated by the Ottoman Turks at Nicopolis, but later conquered Bosnia, Herzegovina, and Serbia. As Emperor, he induced the pope to call the Council of Constance to end the Hussite schism (1414), but

did not provide the 'safe conduct' he had granted John Huss, and permitted him to be burned. This led to the refusal by the Hussites to recognize his succession in Bohemia, and ultimately to the Hussite wars (1420–33).

sign — *noun* **1** a printed mark with a meaning; a symbol: *a multiplication sign.* **2** an indication: *signs of improvement.* **3** a board or panel displaying information for public view. **4** a signal: *gave me the sign to enter by waving his hat.* **5** a sign of the zodiac. — *verb* **1** to write a signature on; to confirm one's assent to with a signature. **2** to write (one's name) as a signature. **3** *trans., intrans.* to employ or become employed with the signing of a contract: *they have signed a new player / he has signed for another team.* **4** *trans., intrans.* to give a signal or indication. **5** *trans., intrans.* to communicate using sign language.
— **sign something away** to give it away or transfer it by signing a legally binding document.
sign in to record one's arrival, eg at work, by writing one's name.
sign someone in to give someone (eg a non-member) official permission to enter a club, etc by signing one's name.
sign off 1 to bring a broadcast to an end. **2** to remove oneself from the register of unemployed people.
sign someone off to dismiss them from employment.
sign on *colloq.* to register oneself as unemployed; to sign one's name as a formal declaration that one is (still) unemployed, as part of a regular report to an unemployment office.
sign someone on to engage them, eg for work.
sign up to engage oneself, eg with an organization (especially the army) or for a task, by signing a contract.
sign someone up to engage them for work by signing a contract.
[from Latin *signum*]

signal — *noun* **1** a message in the form of a gesture, light, sound, etc, conveying information or indicating the time for action. **2** (*often* **signals**) the apparatus used to send such a message, eg coloured lights or movable arms or metal poles on a railway network. **3** an event that marks the moment for action to be taken: *their arrival was a signal for the party to begin.* **4** any set of transmitted electrical impulses received as a sound or image, eg in television, or the message conveyed by them. — *verb* (**signalled**, **signalling**) **1** *trans., intrans.* to transmit (a message) using signals. **2** to indicate: *a fall in interest rates signalled increased trading in sterling.* — *adj.* notable: *a signal triumph.* [from Latin *signum*]

signal-box *noun* the building from which signals on a railway line are controlled.

signalize or **signalise** *verb* to distinguish; to make notable.

signally *adv.* notably.

signalman *noun* a controller of railway signals.

signal-to-noise ratio *Electron.* the ratio of the power of a desired electrical signal to the power of the unwanted background signal or noise. It is usually expressed in decibels.

signatory — *noun* (PL. **signatories**) a person, organization, or state that is a party to a contract, treaty, or other document. — *adj.* being a party to a contract, etc: *signatory nations.*

signature *noun* **1** one's name written by oneself as a formal mark of authorization, acceptance, etc. **2** an indication of key (*key signature*) or time (*time signature*) at the beginning of a line of music. **3** a large sheet of paper with a number of printed pages on it, folded to form a section of a book; a letter or number at the foot of such a sheet, indicating the sequence in which such sheets are to be put together. [from Latin *signare*, to sign]

signature tune a tune used to identify or introduce a particular radio or television programme or performer.

signet *noun* a small seal used for stamping documents, etc. [from Latin *signum*, sign]

signet-ring *noun* a finger ring carrying a signet.

significance *noun* meaning or importance. [see SIGNIFY]

significance test *Maths.* a test which is used to demonstrate the probability that observed patterns cannot be explained by chance.

significant *adj.* **1** important; worth noting. **2** having some meaning; indicating or implying something.

significant figure or **significant digits** *Maths.* the number of digits that contribute to a number and so denote its value to a specified degree of accuracy, eg the value 5 068.35 is accurate to six significant figures. If written as 5 068, it is accurate to four significant figures.

significantly *adv.* in a significant way; to a significant degree.

signify *verb* (**signifies**, **signified**) **1** to be a sign of; to suggest or mean. **2** to denote; to be a symbol of. **3** *intrans.* to be important or significant. [from Latin *signum*, sign + *facere*, to make]

sign language any form of communication using bodily gestures to represent words and ideas, especially a formal system of hand gestures used by deaf people.

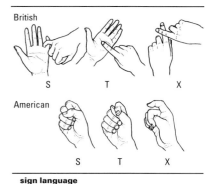

British

American

sign language

sign of the cross a Christian sign made in representation of the cross, by moving the hand from the forehead to the chest and then across to each shoulder, or by making a similar movement in front of oneself.

sign of the zodiac see ZODIAC.

signpost — *noun* a post carrying a sign giving information to motorists or pedestrians. — *verb* to mark (a route) with signposts.

Sigurd in Norse mythology, (eg the *Volsungasaga*), the son of Sigmund the Volsung, who kills Fafnir the dragon and wins Brunhild. He marries Gudrun, having forgotten Brunhild, and is killed by Gudrun's brother Gutthorn. Virtually the same story is told of Siegfried in German legends (eg the *Nibelungenlied*).

Sihanoukville, formerly **Kompong Som**, **Kampong Som**, **Kampong Saom**, **Kompong Saom** a seaport in S Cambodia, on the Gulf of Thailand. The city was completed in 1960 and is the chief deepwater port and commercial centre of Cambodia.

Sikes, Bill a brutal, villainous housebreaker in Charles Dickens's *Oliver Twist.*

Sikh — *noun* a follower of Sikhism. — *adj.* relating to the Sikhs or their beliefs or customs. [from Hindi *Sikh*, disciple]

Sikhism a religion founded by the Guru Nanak (1469–1539) in the Punjab area of N India, which combines elements from Hinduism and Islam. Called a religion of the gurus, through worship, meditation, and service it seeks union with God, the true guru, whose divine word has come to humanity through the 10 historical gurus (Nanak and his nine successors). The line ended in 1708, since when the Sikh community has been called guru. The *Adi Granth*, their sacred scripture, is also called a guru. The Sikh understanding of life is closely related to Punjab identity.

symbol of the Sikh community

Sikh Wars two campaigns (1845–6, 1848–9) between the British and the Sikhs which led to the British conquest and annexation of the Punjab, NW India (Mar 1849).

Sikkim POP (1991) 407 000, a state in NE India, in the E Himalayas. AREA 7 299sq km/2 817sq mi. It is bounded W by Nepal, N by China, and E by China and Bhutan. Sikkim is inhabited mostly by Lepchas, Bhutias, and Nepalis. The state religion is Mahayana Buddhism, but many of the population are Hindu. HISTORY ruled by the Namgyal Dynasty from the 14c until 1975; part of the British Empire from 1866 to 1947; became a protectorate of India in 1950; voted to become a state in 1975. CAPITAL Gangtok. GOVERNMENT governed by a 32-member Assembly. ECONOMY rice, maize, millet, cardamom, soya beans, fruit, tea; cigarettes; copper; zinc; lead; watches; carpets; woodwork; silverwork.

Sikorski, Władysław (Eugeniusz) (1881–1943) Polish soldier and politician, born in Galicia (part of modern Poland). He fought in the Russian-Polish War (1920–1), then became Commander-in-Chief (1921) and Prime Minister (1922–3). After Piłsudski's coup (1926) he retired and wrote military history in Paris. He returned to Poland in 1938, but was refused a command and fled to France to become Commander of the Free Polish forces and (from 1940) premier of the Polish government in exile in London. He was killed in an air crash in Gibraltar.

Sikorsky, Igor (Ivan) (1889–1972) US aeronautical engineer, born in Kiev, Russia. Educated at St Petersburg and Kiev, he built and flew the first four-engined aeroplane (1913), then emigrated to the USA (1919) and founded the Sikorsky Aero Engineering Corporation (1923). He built several flying boats, and in 1939 produced the first successful helicopter.

silage *noun* animal fodder made from forage crops such as grass, maize, kale, etc, which are compressed and then preserved in a succulent condition by controlled fermentation in an airtight tower or *silo*. [from SILO]

Silas 1 in the New Testament, a companion of St Paul. **2** a male first name. [a shortening of the Greek name *Simouanus*, from Latin *silva*, wood]

Silas Marner a novel by George Eliot (1861). It centres around the life of Silas, an outcast linen-weaver who finds happiness when he adopts Eppie, an abandoned child.

Silbury Hill an artificial chalk mound, 40m high, erected in c.2700 BC near Avebury in S England. It is the largest prehistoric barrow in Europe.

Silchester, Latin **Calleva Atrebatum** one of the three main Belgic towns (*oppida*) of pre-Roman Britain, situated SW of Reading. It was also a prosperous place in Roman times until its mysterious abandonment at an unknown date.

silence — *noun* **1** absence of sound or speech, or a period marked by this. **2** failure or unwillingness to disclose information or give away secrets. — *verb* to cause to stop speaking, stop making a

noise, or stop giving away information. — *interj.* be quiet.
— **in silence** without speaking.
[from Latin *silere*, to be quiet]

silencer *noun* a device fitted to a gun barrel or engine exhaust to muffle noise.

silent — *adj.* **1** free from noise. **2** not speaking; not mentioning or divulging something. **3** unspoken but expressed: *silent joy.* **4** not pronounced: *the silent p in pneumonia.* **5** *said of a cinema film* that has no soundtrack. — *noun* a silent film.

silently *adv.* without making any sound; in silence.

silent partner same as SLEEPING PARTNER.

Silenus in Greek mythology, a demigod, who fostered and educated Dionysus, and is represented as a festive old man, usually drunk.

Silesia, Czech **Slezsko**, Polish **Śląsdusk**, German **Schlesien** a region in E central Europe on both banks of the R Oder in SW Poland, N central Czech Republic, and SE Germany. It is bounded to the S by the Sudetes Mts. This largely industrial region includes the coal-mining and metal industries of Katowice and other nearby cities. HISTORY possession of the region was disputed between Austria and Prussia during the 17c–18c; part of Silesia was held by Germany until 1919 when the region was divided into Upper and Lower Silesia; the greater part was granted to Poland in 1945.

silhouette — *noun* **1** a dark shape seen against a light background. **2** an outline drawing of a person, esp a portrait in profile, usually filled in with black. — *verb* to represent, or cause to appear, as a silhouette. [named after E de *Silhouette* (1709–67), French finance minister]

silica *noun Geol.* a hard white or colourless vitreous (glassy) solid that is the commonest constituent of the Earth's crust. — Also called *silicon dioxide*.
◇ Silica occurs in the form of quartz, sand, and flint, and also as silicate compounds in rocks, eg chalcedony. It is used in the manufacture of glass, glazes, and enamels, and silica gel is used as a drying agent. Various forms of silica, eg amethyst, opal, are prized as gemstones.

silica gel *Chem.* a highly absorbent form of silica that is used as a drying and dehumidifying agent, and as a catalyst in many chemical processes.

silicate *noun Chem.* **1** any of a group of chemical compounds containing silicon, oxygen, and one or more metals. Natural silicates are the main components of most rocks and many minerals, eg clay, mica, feldspar, garnet, beryl. **2** any salt of silicic acid.

silicon *noun* (SYMBOL **Si**, ATOMIC NUMBER **14**) a non-metallic element that occurs naturally as silicate minerals in clays and rocks, and as silica (silicon dioxide) in sand and quartz. It is the second most abundant element in the Earth's crust (after oxygen). [from Latin *silex*, flint]
◇ Silicon does not normally conduct electricity, but when minute amounts of certain other elements are added to a pure silicon crystal, it becomes a semiconductor. Silicon is used to make transistors and silicon chips containing microcircuits for computers, calculators, and other electronic equipment. It is also added to alloys to increase their strength and hardness, and is used in photoelectric cells for cameras and exposure meters, and in the manufacture of refractory materials, heat-resistant glass, and ceramics.

silicon carbide *Chem.* (FORMULA **SiC**) a hard iridescent bluish-black crystalline compound, widely used as an abrasive, in cutting, grinding, and polishing instruments, and in light-emitting diodes to produce green or yellow light. – Also called *carborundum*.

silicon chip 1 *Electron.* a very thin piece of silicon or other semiconductor material, only a few

millimetres square, on which all the components of an integrated circuit are arranged. Large numbers of silicon chips are connected together to form the circuits of modern computers. – Also called *chip, microchip.* **2** popular term for an integrated circuit.

silicone *noun Chem.* any of a large group of synthetic polymers consisting of chains of alternating silicon and oxygen atoms, with various organic groups linked to the silicon atoms. Silicone materials usually occur in the form of oily liquids, waxes, plastics, or rubbers, are resistant to heat and water, and do not conduct electricity. They are used in lubricants, electrical insulators, paints, protective coatings, water repellents, and adhesives. Their use in surgical breast implants is the subject of controversy.

Silicon Valley a high technology area of W California, USA, situated in Santa Clara County between Palo Alto and San José. It is a world centre for electronics, computing, and database systems. [named after the non-metallic element, silicon, used in computer micro-chip circuitry]

silicosis *noun* a lung disease caused by prolonged inhaling of dust containing silica.

silk *noun* **1** a fine soft fibre produced by the silkworm. **2** thread or fabric made from such fibres. **3** (*usually* **silks**) a garment made from such fabric. **4** the silk gown worn by a Queen's or King's Counsel; the rank conferred by this.
— **take silk** *said of a barrister* to be appointed a Queen's or King's Counsel.
[from Anglo-Saxon *seolc*, from Latin *sericum*]

silken *adj. literary* **1** made of silk. **2** as soft or smooth as silk.

silkiness *noun* a silky quality.

Silk Road an ancient trade route from E China to central Asia and Europe. HISTORY from the 2c AD, the best-known route ran from Xi'an through the Hexi Corridor to the E Mediterranean coast; during the Sui Dynasty (581–618), a route further N ended at Istanbul. In exchange for silk, China received grapes, cotton, chestnuts, lucerne, and pomegranates. Chinese techniques for silkworm breeding, iron-smelting, paper-making, and irrigation spread W. The route also brought Buddhism to China.

silk-screen see SCREEN PRINTING.

silkworm *noun* the caterpillar of the silk moth, domesticated for centuries in India, China, and Japan to provide silk on a commercial basis. The silkworm is fed on mulberry leaves, and when fully grown it spins a cocoon which may contain up to 900m (over half a mile) of unbroken silk thread.

silky *adj.* (**silkier**, **silkiest**) **1** soft and shiny like silk. **2** *said of a person's manner or voice* suave.

sill *noun* the bottom part of a framework around an opening such as a window or door; also, a ledge of wood, stone, or metal forming this. [from Anglo-Saxon *syll*]

sillabub see SYLLABUB.

sillily *adv.* in a silly way.

silliness *noun* **1** being silly. **2** silly behaviour.

Sillitoe, Alan (1928–) English novelist and short story writer, born in Nottingham. Before serving in the RAF, he worked in a bicycle factory for several years. This produced the subject matter for his first and most popular novel, *Saturday Night and Sunday Morning* (1958). Other works include the short story collection *The Loneliness of the Long Distance Runner* (1959), and the recent novels *Last Loves* (1990) and *Leonard's war: a love story* (1991).

silly — *adj.* (**sillier**, **silliest**) **1** not sensible; foolish; frivolous. **2** dazed; senseless. **3** *Cricket* in a position very near the batsman: *silly mid-on.* **4** senseless: *knocked him silly.* — *noun* (PL. **sillies**) *colloq.* a foolish person. [from Anglo-Saxon *sælig,* happy]

silo *noun* (PL. **silos**) **1** an airtight pit or tall round tower for storing grain or silage. **2** an underground chamber housing a missile ready for firing. [from Spanish *silo*, from Greek *siros*, pit]

silt — *noun* fine sand and mud deposited by flowing water. — *verb trans., intrans.* (usually **silt up**) to become or cause to become blocked by silt. [from Middle English *sylt*]

Silurian *adj. Geol.* denoting the period of geological time between the Ordovician and Devonian periods, lasting from about 440 to 395 million years ago. During this time marine life predominated, and towards the end of the period the first jawed fish and primitive land plants appeared. [from Latin *Silures*, an ancient people of Wales]

silvan same as SYLVAN.

Silvanus *or* **Sylvanus** in Roman religion, the god of uncultivated land, especially woodland, similar to Faunus, the god of animals. He was sometimes identified with the Greek god Pan.

Silver, Long John the scheming, one-legged pirate in Robert Louis Stevenson's *Treasure Island*, who has a parrot called Capt Flint.

silver — *noun* **1** (SYMBOL **Ag**, ATOMIC NUMBER **47**) a soft white lustrous precious metal that is malleable, ductile, and an excellent conductor of heat and electricity. It tarnishes in air, forming a dark deposit of silver sulphide. **2** coins made of this metal. **3** articles made of (or coated with) this metal, especially cutlery and other tableware. **4** a silver medal. — *adj.* **1** of a whitish-grey colour: *silver-haired*. **2** denoting a 25th wedding or other anniversary. — *verb* **1** to apply a thin coating of silver to. **2** to give a whitish metallic sheen to. [from Anglo-Saxon *seolfor*]
◇ Silver occurs naturally as the free metal and in various ores, including argentite (silver sulphide) and horn silver (silver chloride). It is used in jewellery, ornaments, mirrors, coins, electrical contacts, and for electroplating tableware. It is alloyed with mercury to form amalgam for use in dental fillings, and with small amounts of copper to form sterling silver. Silver halides are sensitive to light and are used in photographic emulsions.

silver birch a species of birch tree with silvery-white peeling bark.

silverfish *noun* a small wingless silver-coloured insect common in houses.

Silver Ghost a luxury car introduced by Rolls-Royce in 1906. By 1914 it had earned the reputation of being the 'best car in the world'. Later models, such as the Twenty, Phantom, Silver Dawn, Silver Cloud, Silver Shadow, and Silver Wraith, continued this tradition.

silver lining a positive aspect of an otherwise unpleasant or unfortunate situation.

silver medal a medal of silver awarded especially in sporting competitions, usually to the person in second place.

silver nitrate *Chem.* (FORMULA **AgNO₃**) a colourless crystalline compound, soluble in water and sensitive to light, used in photographic film, silver plating, ink manufacture, mirror silvering, hair dyes, and in the form of a cream or lotion for removing warts and treating skin injuries.

silver plate 1 a thin coating of silver on metal objects, eg cutlery. **2** such objects coated with silver.

silver-plated *adj.* plated with silver.

silver screen (the silver screen) *colloq.* the film industry or films in general.

silverside *noun* a fine cut of beef from just below the rump.

silversmith *noun* a person who makes or repairs articles made of silver.

Silverstone a motor racing circuit near Towcester, Northamptonshire. It was the site of the first world championship Grand Prix in 1950. Since 1987 it has been the home of the British Grand Prix.

silvery *adj.* **1** having the colour or shiny quality of silver. **2** having a pleasantly light ringing sound: *silvery bells*.

Silves POP (1991) 11 000, a town in the Algarve, S Portugal. It lies on the R Arade, 36km/22mi NE of Lagos and was formerly the Moorish capital of the Algarve. NOTABLE FEATURES Moorish Castle; cathedral (13c); Church of the Misericordia.

Silvia the duke of Milan's fair daughter in Shakespeare's *The Two Gentlemen of Verona*, who attracts the attentions of both Valentine and Proteus.

silviculture *noun technical Bot.* the cultivation of forest trees, or the management of woodland to produce timber, etc. [from Latin *silva*, wood + CULTURE]

sima *noun Geol.* the basaltic rocks rich in silica and magnesium that form the lower layer of the Earth's crust. It is equivalent to the oceanic crust and the lower part of the continental crust, beneath the sial. See also SIAL. [from SILICON and MAGNESIUM]

Simbirsk, formerly **Ulyanovsk** (1924–91) **1** POP (1991e) 668 000, the river-port capital of Simbirsk oblast, W central Russia. HISTORY founded as a fortress in 1648; the birthplace of Lenin (1870); renamed after his family name, Ulyanov, in 1924. NOTABLE FEATURE Palace of Books (1847). **2** an oblast in W central Russia with Simbirsk as its capital.

Simenon, Georges (Joseph Christian) (1903–89) Belgian detective-story writer, born in Liège. In Paris he became one of the most prolific authors of his day, and wrote several hundred novels under a variety of pseudonyms. He revolutionized detective fiction with his tough, morbidly psychological Inspector Maigret series, which began in 1933.

Simeon, Tribe of one of the 12 tribes of ancient Israel, descended from Jacob's second son by Leah. Its territory was in the southern extremity of Palestine, south of Judah, into which it seems to have been nearly absorbed.

Simeon Stylites, St (AD 387–459) Syrian ascetic and the earliest Christian 'pillar' saint. He lived nine years without leaving his monastery cell, then became revered as a miracle-worker. Around 420, he established himself on top of a pillar c.20m high in Telanessa, near Antioch, where he spent the rest of his life preaching to crowds. His many imitators were known as *stylites*. His feast day is 5 Jan (W) or 1 Sep (E). [*Stylites* is from Greek, = pillar-dweller]

simian — *noun* a monkey or ape. — *adj.* relating to or resembling monkeys or apes. [from Latin *simia*, ape]

Simien a national park situated in a region of mountains in N Ethiopia. It was established in 1969 to protect threatened native species such as the lion-maned gelada baboon and the Ethiopian ibex. The park is a World Heritage site.

similar *adj.* having a close resemblance to something; of the same kind, but not identical; alike. [from Latin *similis*, like]

similarity *noun* (PL. **similarities**) **1** being similar, likeness. **2** resemblance.

similarly *adv.* in a similar way.

simile *noun* a figure of speech in which a thing is described by being likened to something, usually using *as* or *like*, as in *eyes sparkling like diamonds*, and in set phrases such as *bold as brass*.

similitude *noun formal* similarity; resemblance. [see SIMILAR]

Simla a hill station in Himachal Pradesh state, N India. It stands at an altitude of c.2 200m and is situated NE of Chandigarh, to which it is linked by rail. Simla was established in 1819 as the former summer capital of British India.

simmer — *verb* (**simmered**, **simmering**) **1** *trans., intrans.* to cook or cause to cook gently at just below boiling point. **2** *intrans.* to be near to an outburst of emotion, usually anger. — *noun* a simmering state.
— **simmer down** to calm down after a commotion, especially an angry outburst.
[from Middle English *simperen*]

Simnel, Lambert (c.1475–1535) English pretender, a joiner's son, who in 1487 was set up in Ireland, first as a son of Edward IV, and then as the Duke of Clarence's son, Edward, Earl of Warwick, whom Henry VII had imprisoned in the Tower. Crowned in Dublin as 'Edward VI' (1487), he landed in Lancashire with 2 000 German mercenaries, but was defeated at Stoke, Nottinghamshire. He later made his peace with Henry VII, who employed him as a scullion and falconer.

simnel *noun* a sweet marzipan-covered fruit cake, traditionally baked at Easter or Mid-Lent. [from Latin *simila*, fine flour]

Simon, Claude (Eugene Henri) (1913–) French novelist, born in Tananarive, Madagascar. He joined the Resistance during World War II and later earned a living producing wine at Salses. His novels include *Le Vent* (The Wind, 1957), *L'Herbe* (The Grass, 1958), and *Le Palace* (The Palace, 1962). He was awarded the Nobel Prize for Literature in 1985.

Simon a male first name, an English form of *Simeon*; it is borne by several New Testament characters, including two apostles. [of uncertain origin; perhaps a Hebrew name meaning 'hearing', or a Greek name meaning 'snub-nosed']

Simon (of Stackpole Elidor), John (Allsebrook) Simon, 1st Viscount (1873–1954) English Liberal politician and lawyer, born in Manchester. He entered parliament in 1906, and was Attorney-General (1913–15) and Home Secretary (1915–16), but resigned from the Cabinet because he opposed conscription. Deserting the Liberals to form the Liberal National Party, he supported Ramsay MacDonald's coalition governments and became Foreign Secretary (1931–5), Home Secretary in the Conservative government (1935–7), Chancellor of the Exchequer (1937–40), and Lord Chancellor in Winston Churchill's wartime coalition (1940–5).

simony *noun* the practice of buying or selling a religious post or other privilege. [from *Simon Magus*, biblical sorcerer who offered money for the power to convey the gift of the Holy Spirit]

simper — *verb* (**simpered**, **simpering**) **1** *intrans.* to smile in a foolishly weak manner. **2** to express by or while smiling in this way. — *noun* a simpering smile.

simple *adj.* **1** easy; not difficult. **2** straightforward; not complex or complicated. **3** plain or basic; not elaborate or luxurious. **4** down-to-earth; unpretentious. **5** *often ironic* foolish; gullible; lacking intelligence. **6** plain; mere; not altered or adulterated: *the simple facts*. **7** *Grammar*, *said of a sentence* consisting of only one clause. See also COMPOUND, COMPLEX. [from Latin *simplus*, *simplex*]

simple fracture a fracture of the bone only, with no breaking of the skin.

simple harmonic motion *Physics* (ABBREV. **SHM**) a periodic motion in which the restoring influence acting towards the rest position is proportional to the displacement from rest, as in a pendulum undergoing small swings.

simple interest interest paid only on the basic sum initially borrowed, rather than on an ever-increasing amount which is this basic sum with interest progressively added. See also COMPOUND INTEREST.

simple-minded *adj.* **1** lacking intelligence; foolish. **2** over-simple; unsophisticated.

simple-mindedness *noun* being simple-minded.

simple sentence, a sentence consisting of one clause. See also COMPOUND SENTENCE, COMPLEX SENTENCE.

simpleton *noun* a foolish or unintelligent person.

simplicity *noun* a simple state or quality.

simplification *noun* **1** simplifying or being simplified. **2** something that is simplified.

simplify *verb* (**simplifies**, **simplified**) to make less complicated or easier to understand. [from Latin *simplus, simplex, simple* + *facere*, to make]

simplistic *adj.* unrealistically straightforward or uncomplicated. [see SIMPLE]

simplistically *adv.* in a simplistic way.

Simplon Pass, Italian **Passa del Sempione** a mountain pass through the S Bernese Alps, lying between Brig, Switzerland and Domodossola, Italy. HEIGHT 2 006m. It was built on the orders of Napoleon between 1801 and 1805. The opening of a 20km-long tunnel in 1906 has diminished the importance of the road route.

simply *adv.* **1** in a straightforward, uncomplicated way. **2** just: *simply not true*. **3** absolutely: *simply marvellous*. **4** merely: *simply wanted to help*.

Simpson, Sir James Young (1811–1870) Scottish obstetrician, born in Bathgate. He trained in Edinburgh, where he became Professor of Midwifery in 1840. He introduced chloroform as an anaesthetic, and was the first to use ether as an anaesthetic in labour.

Simpson, O(renthal) J(ames) (1947–) US footballer, born in San Francisco. He joined the Buffalo Bills in 1968, and led the League as top rusher four times (1972–76). He rushed for a record 2 002 yards in 1973, and in 1975 had a then record 25 touchdowns in one season. Occupations since his retirement include actor and sports commentator.

Simpson Desert a desert in SE Northern Territory and SW Queensland, central Australia. AREA c.145 000sq km/56 000sq mi. Scrubland and sand dunes are characteristic of the area.

simulate *verb* **1** to produce a convincing re-creation of (a real-life event or set of conditions).

2 to pretend to have, do, or feel. [from Latin *simulare*]

simulated *adj.* imitation: *simulated leather*.

simulation *noun* simulating; something that is simulated.

simulator *noun* a device that simulates required conditions, eg for training purposes: *flight simulator*.

simulcast *noun* **1** a programme broadcast simultaneously on radio and television. **2** the transmission of a programme in this way. [a shortening of *simultaneous broadcast*]

simultaneous *adj.* happening, or done, at exactly the same time. [from Latin *simul*, at the same time]

simultaneous equations *Maths.* two or more equations whose variables have the same values in both or all the equations.

simultaneously *adv.* at the same time.

sin¹ — *noun* **1** an act that breaks a moral and especially a religious law or teaching. **2** the condition of offending a deity by committing a moral offence. **3** an act that offends common standards of morality or decency; an outrage. **4** *old colloq.* use a great shame. — *verb intrans.* (**sinned**, **sinning**) to commit a sin.
— **live in sin** *colloq.* to live together as husband and wife without being married.
[from Anglo-Saxon *synn*]
◇ What are popularly regarded as 'sins', ie greed, hate, cruelty, lying, and especially sensuality, are regarded as the consequences of the primary sin of turning away from God and his commandments. The distinction between sin and crime is that the former always involves offence against God, whereas the latter is only a violation of civil law. The overall Christian view is that everything that causes human beings to fall short of the glory of God and the demands of love is sin. Muslims view sin under two different headings: a fault or shortcoming that happens inadvertently (*dhanb*), and wilful sin (*ithm*). Even wilful sin may be overcome by repentance and accepting God's forgiveness.

sin² *abbrev.* sine.

Sinai POP (1990e) 229 000, a desert peninsula and governorate in NE Egypt. AREA 60 174sq km/23 227sq mi. It is bounded by Israel and the Gulf of Aqaba in the E, and Egypt and the Gulf of Suez in the W. The N coastal plain rises S to mountains reaching 2 637m at Mt Catherine (Egypt's highest point) and 2 286m at Mt Sinai. Tourist resorts in the S include Sharm el Sheikh, Dahab, Ras Muhammad, and Nuweiba. HISTORY a battlefield since ancient times; taken by Israel in 1967; returned to Egypt following the peace agreement in 1984. CAPITAL El Arish. ECONOMY oil, manganese; some livestock and agriculture in irrigated areas.

Sinai, Mount, also called (in the Hebrew Bible) **Horeb** a mountain of uncertain location, traditionally placed among the granite mountains of the S Sinai peninsula, but sometimes located in Arabia east of the Gulf of Aqabah. God revealed himself to Moses there, and made a covenant with Israel when he gave Moses the Ten Commandments on tablets of stone (Exodus 19–20).

Sinanthropus See PEKING MAN.

Sinatra, Frank (Francis Albert) (1915–) US singer and actor, born in Hoboken, New Jersey, now widely recognized as one of the greatest singers of popular songs. With the Tommy Dorsey orchestra (1940–2) his hit records included 'I'll Never Smile Again' and 'Without a Song', and he starred on radio and in movies (eg *Anchors Aweigh*, 1945). His appeal waned, until his acting role in the film *From Here to Eternity* (1953) won awards and led to several choice film roles. His revival as an actor led to new singing opportunities, and he produced a masterful series of recordings (1956–65), especially the albums *For Swinging Lovers, Come Fly With Me*, and *That's Life*. His highly publicized and controversial personal life includes four marriages (eg to Ava Gardner and Mia Farrow).

since — *conj.* **1** during or throughout the period between now and some earlier stated time. **2** as; because. — *prep.* during or throughout the period between now and some earlier stated time. — *adv.* **1** from that time onwards. **2** ago: *five years since*. [from Middle English *sithens*]

sincere *adj.* genuine; not pretended or affected. [from Latin *sincerus*, clean]

sincerely *adv.* in a sincere way.

sincerity *noun* being sincere.

Sinclair, Sir Clive (Marles) (1940–) English electronics engineer and inventor. He

---

Some Common Similes

as bald as a coot	as happy as a lark *or* a sandboy *or* as Larry	as right as a trivet *or* as rain
as black as ink *or* pitch	as happy as the day is long	as ripe as a cherry
as blind as a bat	as hard as nails	as safe as houses
as blue as the sky	as high as a kite	as sharp as a razor
as bold as brass	as innocent as a lamb	as sick as a dog *or* a parrot
as bright as a button	as keen as mustard	as silent as the grave
as brown as a berry	as large as life	as slippery as an eel
as calm as a millpond	as light as a feather	as sober as a judge
as clean as a whistle	as light as down	as soft as a baby's bottom
as clear as a bell *or* as crystal *or* (*ironically*) as mud	as like as two peas in a pod *or* (*ironically*) chalk and cheese	as sound as a bell
as cold as charity *or* ice	as lively as a cricket	as sound as a roach
as cool as a cucumber	as mad as a hatter *or* a March hare	as steady as a rock
as cross as two sticks	as merry as a grig	as stiff as a poker
as daft as a brush	as near as a touch	as straight as a die
as dead as a dodo *or* a door-nail *or* as mutton	as neat as as ninepence	as strong as a horse
as deaf as a post	as often as not	as stubborn as a mule
as different as chalk and cheese	as old as Adam *or* Methuselah *or* the hills	as sure as a gun *or* as eggs is eggs
as drunk as a lord *or* a piper	as plain as a pikestaff	as thick as a plank
as dry as a bone	as pleased as Punch	as thick (= conspiratorial) as thieves
as dull as ditchwater	as poor as a church mouse	as thick (= stupid) as two short planks
as easy as falling off a log *or* as winking	as proud as a peacock	as thin as a rake
as fair as a rose	as pure as the driven snow	as tough as leather *or* old boots
as fit as a fiddle	as quick as lightning	as ugly as sin
as flat as a pancake	as quiet as a mouse	as warm as toast
as free as a bird	as red as a beetroot	as weak as a kitten
as fresh as a daisy *or* as paint	as regular as clockwork	as wet as a drowned rat
as good as gold	as rich as Croesus	as white as a sheet *or* as snow
as green as grass		as wise as an owl

launched his own electronics research and manufacturing company which developed and successfully marketed a wide range of calculators, miniature television sets, and personal computers. He later manufactured a small three-wheeled 'personal transport' vehicle (the 'C-5'), powered by a washing-machine motor and rechargeable batteries; it was widely rejected as unsafe and impractical. Other designs include an electric bicycle called the Zike (1992).

Sinclair, Upton (Beall) (1878–1968) US novelist, born in Baltimore. He became a journalist, and found success with his novel *The Jungle* (1906), which exposes meat-packing conditions in Chicago. Later novels, including *Metropolis* (1908) and *King Coal* (1917), became increasingly moulded by his socialist beliefs.

Sinclair C-5 a small three-wheeled 'personal transport' vehicle developed by Sir Clive Sinclair.

Sind POP (1985e) 21.7m, a province in SE Pakistan. AREA 140 914sq km/54 393sq mi. It is bounded E and S by India and SW by the Arabian Sea. CAPITAL Karachi. The province has fertile, low-lying, and generally flat land dissected by the R Indus. HISTORY invaded by Alexander the Great in 325 BC; arrival of Islam in the 8c; became part of the Chandragupta Ganges Empire and the Delhi Empire; under British rule in 1843; became an autonomous province in 1937 and a province of Pakistan in 1947. ECONOMY rice, cotton, barley, oilseed; irrigation from the Sukkur Barrage in the N.

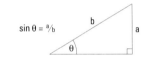

$\sin \theta = {}^{a}/_{b}$

sine

sine *noun Maths.* (ABBREV. **sin**) in trigonometry, a function of an angle in a right-angled triangle, defined as the length of the side opposite the angle divided by the length of the hypotenuse (the longest side). [from Latin *sinus*, curve, bay]

Sinead a female first name. [an Irish Gaelic form of JANET]

sinecure *noun* a paid job involving little or no work. [from Latin *sine*, without + *cura*, care]

sine die indefinitely; with no future time fixed. [Latin, = without a day]

sine qua non an essential condition or requirement. [Latin, = without which not]

sinew *noun* 1 a strong piece of fibrous tissue joining a muscle to a bone; a tendon. 2 (**sinews**) physical strength; muscle. 3 (*often* **sinews**) strength or power of any kind, or a source of this. [from Anglo-Saxon *sinu*]

sine wave *Maths.* a waveform whose shape resembles that obtained by plotting a graph of the size of an angle against the value of its sine. Simple harmonic motion can be represented by a sine wave.

sinewy *adj.* 1 lean and muscular. 2 strong; tough; vigorous.

sinfonietta *noun* 1 an orchestral piece, usually in several movements but shorter and on a smaller scale than a symphony, eg Janáček's *Sinfonietta* (1926). 2 a small symphony or chamber orchestra, such as the London Sinfonietta (founded 1968). [from Italian, a diminutive of *sinfonia*]

sinful *adj.* wicked; involving sin, morally wrong.

sing *verb* (PAST TENSE **sang**; PAST PARTICIPLE **sung**) 1 *trans., intrans.* to speak (words) in a musical, rhythmic fashion, especially to the accompaniment of music. 2 to cause to pass into a particular

state with such sound: *sang him to sleep*. 3 *intrans.* to make a sound like a musical voice; to hum, ring, or whistle: *the kettle singing on the stove* / *bullets singing past his ears*. 4 *intrans.* to suffer a ringing sound: *my ears were singing*. 5 *intrans. slang* to inform or confess.

— **sing out** to shout or call out.

sing someone's praises to praise them enthusiastically.

[from Anglo-Saxon *singan*]

sing. *abbrev.* singular.

Singapore, official name **Republic of Singapore** POP (1992e) 2.8m, a republic at the S tip of the Malay Peninsula, SE Asia. AREA 618sq km/238sq mi. It consists of the island of Singapore and about 50 adjacent islets; the main island is linked to Malaysia by a causeway across the Johore Strait. CAPITAL Singapore. TIME ZONE GMT +8. The population is largely Chinese (77%) but also includes Malay (15%), Indian (7%), and others; the majority are Buddhist or Muslim. OFFICIAL LANGUAGES English, Chinese, Tamil; Malay is the national tongue. CURRENCY the Singapore dollar. PHYSICAL DESCRIPTION the highest point of low-lying Singapore I is at Bukit Timah (177m); the island measures c.42km/26mi by 22km/14mi at its widest; an important deep-water harbour lies to the SE. CLIMATE equatorial, with high humidity, an average annual rainfall of 2 438mm, and a daily temperature range from 21°C to 34°C. HISTORY originally part of the Sumatran Sri Vijaya kingdom; leased by the British East India Company, on the advice of Sir Stamford Raffles, from the Sultan of Johore in 1819; Singapore, Malacca, and Penang were incorporated as the Straits Settlements in 1826; they became a British Crown Colony in 1867; occupied by the Japanese from 1942 until 1945; self-government was established in 1959; part of the Federation of Malaya from 1963 until its establishment as an independent state in 1965. GOVERNMENT a Prime Minister, elected every four years, leads a single-chamber parliament of 81 members, elected for four-year terms. ECONOMY major transshipment centre; oil refining, rubber, food processing, chemicals, electronics, ship repair, financial services, fishing.

PACIFIC OCEAN

Singapore

INDIAN OCEAN

Singapore

Singapore *or* **Singapore City** POP (1992e) 2.8m, the capital of Singapore, on the SE coast of Singapore I. It is one of the world's busiest seaports and the third largest oil refining centre. The city is a thriving commercial centre and a distribution base for many international companies. The first container port in SE Asia opened here in 1972. NOTABLE FEATURES Tiger Balm Gardens; St Andrew's Cathedral; Sultan Mosque; Monkey God Temple, Poh Toh Temple, Siang Lin-Si Temple; House of Jade; National Museum; Botanical Gardens; Raffles Hotel.

singe — *verb trans., intrans.* (**singed**, **singeing**) to burn lightly on the surface; to scorch or become scorched. — *noun* a light surface burn. [from Anglo-Saxon *sengan*]

Singer, Isaac (Bashevis) (1904–91) US Yiddish writer, born in Radzymin, Poland. He emigrated to the USA in 1935, where he became a journalist and US citizen. His books are set among the Jews of Poland, Germany, and America. His novels include *The Family Moskat* (1950) and *The Magician of Lublin* (1960), and his short stories *Gimpel the Fool and Other Stories* (1957). He was awarded the Nobel Prize for Literature in 1978.

singer *noun* 1 a person or bird that sings. 2 a person who sings professionally.

singing *noun* 1 the performing of songs. 2 the sound of singing or a sound like it; ringing.

Singin' in the Rain a US film directed by Stanley Donen (1952). A highly colourful musical starring Gene Kelly, it is the story of the making of a Hollywood film in the 1920s and its actors' off-screen intrigues.

single — *adj.* 1 of which there is only one; solitary. 2 unmarried, especially never having been married. 3 for use by one person only: *a single room*. 4 valid for an outward journey only; not return. 5 (*used for emphasis*) even one: *not a single person*. 6 *said of a flower* having only one set of petals. — *noun* 1 a single room. 2 a ticket for an outward journey only. 3 a record with only one track on each side. 4 a pound coin or note. 5 *Cricket* one run. — *verb* (**single someone** *or* **something out**) to pick them from among others. [from Latin *singuli*, one by one]

single-breasted *adj., said of a coat or jacket* having only one row of buttons and a slight overlap at the front.

single combat fighting between two individuals.

single-figure *adj.* denoting a number from 1 to 9.

single figures the numbers from 1 to 9.

single file a line of people standing or moving one behind the other.

Single Form a sculpture by Dame Barbara Hepworth (1963).

single-handed *adj., adv.* done, etc by oneself, without help from others.

single-handedly *adv.* without any help.

Single Integrated Operational Plan (ABBREV. **SIOP**) the all-embracing military plan for the deployment and use of US nuclear forces. It is subject to continual updating according to policy.

single-lens reflex see CAMERA.

single-minded *adj.* determinedly pursuing a single aim or object.

single-mindedly *adv.* in a single-minded way.

single-mindedness *noun* being single-minded.

single parent a mother or father bringing up a child alone.

singles *noun* a sports match with one player on each side.

singles bar a bar intended as a meeting place for unmarried or unattached people.

singlet *noun* a man's vest or other vest-like garment. [see SINGLE]

singleton *noun* a solitary person or thing, especially the only playing-card of a particular suit in a hand.

singly *adv.* one at a time; individually.

singsong — *noun* an informal bout of singing for pleasure. — *adj., said of a speaking voice, etc* having a fluctuating or monotonous rhythm.

Singspiel *noun* a type of German comic opera with spoken dialogue, popular in the 18c and early 19c. Famous examples include Mozart's *Die Entführung aus dem Serail* (The Abduction from the Seraglio, 1782), and *Die Zauberflöte* (The Magic Flute, 1781). The term was later applied in Germany to musical comedy. [German, = singing play]

singular — *adj.* **1** single; unique. **2** extraordinary; exceptional. **3** strange; odd. **4** *Grammar* denoting or referring to one person, thing, etc as opposed to two or more than one. See also PLURAL. — *noun Grammar* a word or form of a word expressing the idea of one person, thing, etc as opposed to two or more than two. [from Latin *singularis*]

singularity *noun* **1** being singular. **2** peculiarity, individuality.

singularly *adv.* **1** extraordinarily. **2** strangely. **3** singly. **4** very.

Sinhalese — *noun* **1** (PL. **Sinhalese**) a member of a people living in Sri Lanka. **2** the Indo-European language spoken by this people, derived from Sanskrit. — *adj.* relating to this people or their language. [from Sanskrit *Simhala*, Sri Lanka]
◇ The Sinhalese are the largest (74%) ethnic group of Sri Lanka, descended from N Indians who came to the area in the 5c BC. They are predominantly Buddhist, and have an occupational caste system.

Sining see XINING.

sinister *adj.* **1** suggesting or threatening evil or danger. **2** *Heraldry* on the left side of the shield, from the bearer's point of view, not the observer's. See also DEXTER. [from Latin *sinister*, left, thought by the Romans to be the unlucky side]

Sinitic — *adj.* denoting a group of languages belonging to the Sino-Tibetan family, used mainly in China and Taiwan. — *noun* the languages forming this group.

sink — *verb* (PAST TENSE **sank**; PAST PARTICIPLE **sunk**, as adj. **sunken**) **1** *trans.* to fall or cause to fall and usually remain below the surface of water. **2** *intrans.* to collapse downwardly or inwardly; to fall because of a collapsing base or foundation. **3** *intrans.* to produce the sensation of a downward collapse within the body: *my heart sank at the news.* **4** to embed: *sank the pole into the ground.* **5** to pass steadily (and often dangerously) into a worse state. **6** (*also* **sink in**) to penetrate or be absorbed. **7** to invest (money) heavily. **8** *colloq.* to ruin the plans of; to ruin (plans): *we are sunk.* **9** *intrans.* *said of the sun* to disappear slowly below the horizon. **10** *colloq.* to send (a ball) into a pocket in snooker, billiards, etc and into the hole in golf. — *noun* a wall-mounted basin with built-in water supply and drainage.
— **sink in** *colloq.* to be fully understood or realized.
[from Anglo-Saxon *sincan*]

sinker *noun* a weight used to make something, eg a fishing-line, sink.

sink unit a piece of kitchen furniture consisting of a sink and draining-board with cupboards underneath.

sinner *noun* a person who sins or has sinned.

Sinn Féin an Irish political party which developed during the period 1905–8 under Arthur Griffith in support of Irish independence from Britain. By the end of World War I it had become the main Irish nationalist party. It formed a separate assembly from the UK parliament, and succeeded in creating the Irish Free State (1922). Following the Anglo-Irish Treaty (1921), it split to form the two main Irish parties, and in 1970 it split again into official and provisional wings. It has remained active in Northern Ireland, and has close contacts with the Irish Republican Army (IRA). In early 1994 Gerry Adams (leader of Sinn Féin since 1984) responded to an invitation from President Clinton to visit him in the USA. [from Gaelic, = ourselves alone]

Sino- *combining form* forming words meaning 'Chinese': *Sino-Soviet.* [from Greek *Sinai*, Chinese]

Sinologist *noun* an expert in Sinology.

Sinology *noun* the study of China in all its aspects, eg cultural and political.

Sino-Tibetan — *adj.* denoting the family of languages spoken in China, Tibet, and Burma (Myanmar). It consists of some 300 languages, including the eight Chinese (or Sinitic) languages, Tibetan, and Burmese. — *noun* the languages forming this group.

Sintra, formerly **Cintra** POP (1981) 20 000, a small resort town in Lisbon district, central Portugal, lying 12km/7mi N of Estoril. It was formerly the summer residence of the Portuguese royal family. NOTABLE FEATURES National Palace (14c–15c); Moorish Castle, Pena Palace.

sinuosity *or* **sinuousness** *noun* being sinuous.

sinuous *adj.* **1** having many curves or bends; meandering. **2** having a twisting and turning motion. [see SINUS]

sinus *noun Anat.* a cavity or depression filled with air, especially in the bones of the face in mammals, or blood, especially in the brain and certain blood vessels. [from Latin *sinus*, curve]

sinusitis *noun* inflammation of the lining of the sinuses.

Siobhan a female first name. [an Irish Gaelic form of JANE]

Sion, German **Sitten** POP (1990e) 25 000, the capital of Valais canton, SW Switzerland. It lies 80km/50mi S of Bern. The city has been a bishopric since the 6c. It is a market town for wine, fruit, and vegetables from the Rhône valley. NOTABLE FEATURES former cathedral (10c–13c); town hall (17c); Church of Notre-Dame (12c–13c); bishop's fortress (1294).

Sion see ZION.

Sion a male first name. [a Welsh form of JOHN, from Anglo-Norman *jean*]

SIOP *abbrev.* Single Integrated Operational Plan.

Sioux, also called **Dakota** a group of Native American peoples belonging to the Plains people culture. They moved from further north into present-day N and S Dakota, acquired horses, fought wars against other groups, and hunted the buffalo. They were later involved in clashes with advancing white settlers and prospectors, and despite several victories (eg against General Custer at the battle of the Little Bighorn in 1876) they were finally defeated at Wounded Knee (1890). The present-day population is c.48 000, mostly on reservations.

Sioux City POP (1990) 115 000, the seat of Woodbury County, W Iowa, USA, lying at the junction of the Big Sioux and Missouri rivers. It is a shipping and trade centre in an agricultural region.

Sioux Falls POP (1990) 124 000, the seat of Minnehaha County, SE South Dakota, USA, lying on the Big Sioux R. Established in 1857, it became a city in 1883 and is now the largest city in the state and an industrial and commercial centre.

sip — *verb trans., intrans.* (**sipped**, **sipping**) to drink in very small mouthfuls. — *noun* **1** an act of sipping. **2** an amount sipped at one time. [perhaps a variation of SUP]

siphon *or* **syphon** — *noun* **1** an inverted U-tube that can be used to transfer liquid from one container at a higher level into another at a lower level, provided that the tube is filled with liquid initially. Siphons are used to empty inaccessible containers, eg car petrol tanks. **2** a bottle from which a liquid, especially soda water, is forced by pressure of gas. **3** *Zool.* in certain animals, eg bivalve molluscs, an organ resembling a tube

through which water flows in and out. — *verb* (**siphoned**, **siphoning**) (*usually* **siphon something off**) **1** to transfer liquid from one container to another using such a device. **2** to take something slowly and continuously from a store or fund. [from Greek *siphon*, pipe]

sir *noun* **1** (**Sir**) a title used before the Christian name of a knight or baronet. **2** a term of politeness or respect used in addressing a man. [see SIRE]

Siraj ud Daula, originally **Mirza Muhammad** (c.1732–57) ruler of Bengal under the nominal suzerainty of the Mughal Empire. He came into conflict with the British over their fortification of Calcutta, and marched on the city in 1756. The British surrender led to the infamous Black Hole of Calcutta incident, for which he was held responsible. Following the recapture of Calcutta, the British under Clive joined forces with his general Mir Jafar and defeated him at Plassey (1757).

Sir Charles Grandison an epistolary novel by Samuel Richardson (1754). It describes the life of a virtuous gentleman, focusing on the question of divided love.

sire — *noun* **1** the father of a horse or other animal. **2** *old use* a term of respect used in addressing a king. — *verb, said of an animal* to father (young). [from Old French, from Latin *senior*, elder]

Siren in Greek mythology, a creature, half-woman and half-bird, who lured sailors to death by her singing. Odysseus was able to sail past the Sirens' island by stopping the ears of his crew with wax and by having himself bound to the mast. In later legends the Sirens drown themselves after this defeat.

siren *noun* **1** a device that gives out a loud wailing noise, usually as a warning signal. **2** an irresistible woman thought capable of ruining men's lives.

Sirius *Astron.* the Dog Star, the brightest star in the night sky, in the constellation Canis Major. Viewed from N European latitudes, Sirius never rises very high above the southern horizon, usually twinkling violently through the unsteady atmosphere.

sirloin *noun* a fine cut of beef from the upper side of the part of the back just in front of the rump. [from French *surlonge*, from *sur*, above + *longe*, loin]

sirocco *noun* (PL. **siroccos**) a dry hot dust-carrying wind blowing into S Europe from N Africa. [from Italian *sirocco*, from Arabic *sharq*, east wind]

Sirte, Gulf of, Arabic **Khalij Surt** a gulf in the Mediterranean Sea, off the coast of N Libya. It is situated between Misratah in the W and Benghazi in the E. Access to the Gulf waters is an area of dispute between Libya and the USA.

sis *noun colloq.* sister.

sisal *noun* a strong fibre from the leaves of the agave plant of central America, used to make rope. [from *Sisal*, the Mexican port from where it was first exported]

siskin *noun* a yellowish-green Eurasian songbird of the finch family. [from Old Dutch *siseken*]

Sisley, Alfred (1839–99) French Impressionist painter and etcher, who trained under Charles Gleyre (1806–74) in Paris. His work was exhibited in four of the Impressionist exhibitions (1874–86). He painted landscapes almost exclusively, particularly in the valleys of the Seine, Loing, and Thames.

sissy *or* **cissy** *noun* (PL. **sissies**) *derog.* a weak, cowardly person. [see SISTER]

sister — *noun* **1** a female child of the same parents as another. **2** a nun. **3** a senior female nurse, especially one in charge of a ward. **4** a close female associate; a fellow female member of a profession, class or racial group. — *adj.* of the same origin or design: *a sister ship.* [from Anglo-Saxon *sweostor* or Norse *systir*]

sisterhood *noun* **1** the state of being a sister or sisters. **2** a religious community of women; a body of nuns. **3** a group of women with common interests or beliefs.

sister-in-law *noun* (PL. **sisters-in-law**) **1** the sister of one's husband or wife. **2** the wife of one's brother.

sisterliness *noun* being sisterly.

sisterly *adj.*, *said of a woman or her behaviour* like a sister, especially in being kind and affectionate.

Sistine Chapel a chapel in the Vatican, built in 1475–81 for Pope Sixtus IV. It is notable for a series of frescoes executed on its ceiling and altar wall by Michelangelo. It is the scene of papal elections, and is also the home of the Sistine Choir.

Sistine Madonna a painted altarpiece by Raphael (c.1512–13, Dresden Gallery).

Sisyphus in Greek mythology, a Corinthian king who was a famous trickster. In the Underworld he was condemned to roll forever a large stone up a hill, from the summit of which it always rolled down again.

sit *verb* (**sitting**; PAST TENSE AND PAST PARTICIPLE **sat**) **1** *intrans.* to rest the body on the buttocks or hindquarters. **2** *intrans. said of a bird* to perch or lie. **3** *intrans. said of an object* to lie, rest, or hang: *a cup sitting on the shelf / the dress sits nicely around her waist.* **4** *intrans.* to lie unused: *tools sitting in the shed.* **5** *intrans.* to hold a meeting or other session: *court sits tomorrow.* **6** *intrans.* to be a member, taking regular part in meetings: *sit on a committee.* **7** to take (an examination); to be a candidate for (a degree or other award). **8** to conduct to a seat; to assign a seat to: *sat me next to him.* **9** *intrans.* to be or exist in a specified comparison or relation: *his smoking sits awkwardly with his being a doctor.* **10** *intrans.* to serve as an artist's or photographer's model. — **be sitting pretty** *colloq.* to be in a very advantageous position. **sit back 1** to sit comfortably, especially with the back rested. **2** to merely observe, taking no action, especially when action is needed. **sit down** *or* **sit someone down** to adopt or cause them to adopt a sitting position. **sit down under something** to submit meekly to an insult, etc. **sit in on something** to be present at it, especially without taking part. **sit in for someone** to act as a substitute or deputy for them. **sit on someone** *colloq.* to force them to say or do nothing. **sit on something** *colloq.* **1** to delay taking action about a matter in one's care. **2** to keep it secret; to suppress it. **sit something out 1** to stay until the end of it. **2** to take no part in a dance or game. **sit tight 1** to maintain one's position determinedly. **2** to wait patiently. **sit up 1** to bring oneself from a slouching or lying position into an upright sitting position. **2** to remain out of bed longer than usual. **3** to take notice suddenly or show a sudden interest. [from Anglo-Saxon *sittan*]

sitar *noun* a guitar-like instrument of Indian origin, with a long neck, rounded body and two sets of strings. [from Hindi *sitar*]

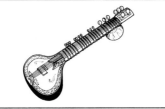
sitar

sitcom *noun colloq.* a situation comedy.

sit-down — *noun colloq.* a short rest in a seated position. — *adj.* **1** *said of a meal* for which the diners are seated. **2** *said of a strike* in which the workers occupy the workplace until an agreement is reached.

site *noun* **1** the place where something was, is, or is to be situated. **2** an area set aside for a specific activity: *camping site.* [from Latin *situs*, position]

Site of Special Scientific Interest see SSSI.

Sithole, Rev Ndabaningi (1920–) Zimbabwean clergyman and politician, born in Nyamandhlovu, Rhodesia. He began as a teacher (1941–53), and after studying in the USA (1955–8) became a Congregationalist minister. A member of the National Democratic Party, he became President of the Zimbabwe African National Union (ZANU) in 1963 and, as an advocate of violent resistance by black African nationalists, joined Robert Mugabe in his struggle against Joshua Nkomo. After a period of detention in the 1960s, he was eclipsed by Mugabe, and later moved into a close political alliance with Bishop Abel Muzorewa.

sit-in *noun* an occupation of a building, etc as a protest.

Sitka a national monument on W Baranof Island, SE Alaska, USA. It was the scene of the last stand of the Tlingit people against the Russians in 1804. The town and naval base of Sitka are nearby.

Sitka spruce *Bot.* a spruce tree (*Picea sitchensis*), with sharp blue-green needles, grown for its timber.

sitter *noun* **1** a person who poses for an artist or photographer. **2** a baby-sitter.

sitting *noun* **1** a period of continuous action: *wrote it at one sitting.* **2** a turn to eat for any of two or more groups too numerous to eat at the same time in the same place. **3** a period of posing for an artist or photographer. **4** a session or meeting of an official body.

Sitting Bull, Sioux name **Tananka Iyotake** (1834–90) warrior chief of the Dakota Sioux, born near Grand River, S Dakota. He was a leader in the Sioux War of 1876–7, after which he escaped to Canada, but surrendered in 1881. After touring as a feature of Buffalo Bill's Wild West Show, he returned to his people, but was killed during the army's suppression of the Ghost Dance messianic religious movement (which predicted the disappearance of all whites and the return of dead Sioux people and buffaloes).

sitting duck *or* **sitting target** a person or thing in a defenceless position, easily attacked, criticized, etc.

sitting-room *noun* a room, especially in a private house, for relaxing in; a living-room.

sitting tenant a tenant occupying a property when it changes ownership.

situate *verb* to put in a certain position or set of circumstances. [from Latin *situare*, to position]

situation *noun* **1** a set of circumstances; a state of affairs. **2** a position or location. **3** a job: *situations vacant.*

situation comedy a comedy in series form in which the same characters are featured in a more or less fixed set of surroundings.

sit-up *noun* a physical exercise in which, from a lying position, the torso is raised up and over the thighs, often with the hands behind the head.

Sitwell, Dame Edith (1887–1964) English poet, born in Scarborough, Yorkshire, the sister of Osbert and Sacheverell Sitwell. She first came to attention as editor of an annual anthology of new poetry, *Wheels* (1916–21), and the first volume of her own experimental poetry, *Façade*

(1923), was (with William Walton's music) given a controversial public reading in London. Other works include *Street Songs* (1942), *The Outcasts* (1962), and her autobiography, *Taken Care Of* (1965).

Sitwell, Sir Osbert (1892–1969) English writer, born in London, the brother of Edith and Sacheverell Sitwell. He served in World War I, began writing poetry, and acquired notoriety with his satirical novel of the Scarborough social scene, *Before the Bombardment* (1927). He is best known for his five-volume autobiographical series, which begins with *Left Hand: Right Hand* (1944).

Sitwell, Sir Sacheverell (1897–1988) English poet and art critic, born in Scarborough, Yorkshire, the brother of Edith and Osbert Sitwell. He served in the British army, travelled in Spain and Italy, and wrote *Southern Baroque Art* (1924) and *German Baroque Art* (1927). His many volumes of poetry cover a period of over 60 years, from *The People's Palace* (1918) to *An Indian Summer* (1982).

six — *noun* **1** the number or figure 6; any symbol for this number. **2** the age of 6. **3** something, eg a garment or a person, whose size is denoted by the number 6. **4** a group of 6 people or things. **5** a playing-card with 6 pips. **6** 6 o'clock. **7** a score of 6 points. **8** *Cricket* a hit scoring 6 runs. **9** a team of (more or less) 6 Cub Scouts or Brownie Guides. — *adj.* **1** 6 in number. **2** aged 6. — **at sixes and sevens** in a state of total disorder or confusion.

knock someone for six *colloq.* **1** to defeat or ruin them completely. **2** to shock or surprise them greatly.

six of one and half a dozen of the other equal; equally acceptable or unacceptable; the same on both sides.
[from Anglo-Saxon *siex*]

Six, Les the French composers Auric, Durey, Honegger, Milhaud, Poulenc, and Tailleferre, who performed together for a few years from 1917.

Six Characters in Search of an Author (Sei personaggi in cerca d'autore) a play by Luigi Pirandello (1921). It is an exploration of the relationship between appearance and reality, actual life and the theatre, through the staging of a play in which characters already dropped by the author appear with the actors.

sixer *noun* the Cub Scout or Brownie Guide leader of a six.

sixfold — *adj.* **1** equal to six times as much or as many. **2** divided into, or consisting of, six parts. — *adv.* by six times as much.

six-pack *noun* a pack containing six items sold as one unit, especially a pack of six cans of beer.

sixpence *noun* a former small British silver coin worth six old pennies (6d), equivalent in value to 2½p.

sixpenny *adj.* worth or costing six old pennies.

sixteen — *noun* **1** the number or figure 16; any symbol for this number. **2** the age of 16. **3** something, eg a garment or a person, whose size is denoted by the number 16. **4** a set of 16 people or things. — *adj.* **1** 16 in number. **2** aged 16. [from Anglo-Saxon *siextene*]

sixteenth *noun, adj.* **1** the position in a series corresponding to 16 in a sequence of numbers. **2** one of 16 equal parts.

sixth *noun, adj.* **1** the position in a series corresponding to 6 in a sequence of numbers. **2** one of six equal parts. **3** *Mus.* an interval of five diatonic degrees; a tone at that interval from another, or a combination of two tones separated by that interval.

sixth form the stage in secondary education in which school subjects are taught to a level that prepares for higher education.

sixth-former *noun* a member of a sixth form.

sixthly *adv.* as sixth in a series.

sixth sense an unexplained power of intuition by which one is aware of things not seen, heard, touched, smelled, or tasted.

sixties *pl. noun* **1** the period of time between one's sixtieth and seventieth birthdays. **2** the range of temperatures between sixty and seventy degrees. **3** the period of time between the sixtieth and seventieth years of a century, especially this period of the 20c.

sixtieth *noun, adj.* **1** the position in a series corresponding to 60 in a sequence of numbers. **2** one of sixty equal parts.

Sixtus IV, originally **Francesco della Rovere** (1414–84) Italian pope, born in Cella Ligura, Genoa. A famous Franciscan preacher, he became a cardinal (1467), and was pope from 1471. His nepotism led to many abuses, and although he fostered learning and built the Sistine Chapel, he lowered the moral authority of the papacy. His alliance with the Venetians in 1482 led to a general Italian war.

sixty — *noun* (PL. **sixties**) **1** the number or figure 60; any symbol for this number. **2** the age of 60. **3** a set of 60 people or things. — *adj.* **1** 60 in number. **2** aged 60. [from Anglo-Saxon *siextig*]

size[1] — *noun* **1** length, breadth, height or volume, or a combination of all or any of these. **2** largeness: *astonished by its size*. **3** any of a range of graded measurements, eg of garments. — *verb* **1** to measure in order to determine size. **2** to sort or arrange according to size. **3** (**size something or someone up**) to judge their nature, quality, or worth. [from Old French *sise*]

size[2] — *noun* a weak kind of glue used to stiffen paper and fabric, and to prepare walls for plastering and wallpapering. — *verb* to treat with size.

sizeable *or* **sizable** *adj.* fairly large.

Sizewell a nuclear power station in Suffolk, England. Its gas-cooled, graphite-moderated reactors came into operation in 1966. It is the site of the first UK pressurized light-water-moderated and -cooled reactor (Sizewell B), due to open in 1994.

sizzle — *verb intrans.* **1** to make a hissing sound when, or as if when, frying in hot fat. **2** *colloq.* to be in a state of intense emotion, especially anger or excitement. — *noun* a sizzling sound. [imitative]

Sjælland a group of islands in Danish territorial waters, lying between Jutland and S Sweden. AREA 7 514sq km/2 900sq mi. It includes Zealand (Sjælland), Møn, Samsø, Amager, and Saltho.

ska *noun* a style of Jamaican popular music, developed in the 1960s, played on trumpet, saxophone, etc, in an unpolished style with loud, blaring rhythms. [perhaps in imitation of the characteristic sound of the music]

Skagerrak an arm of the Atlantic Ocean, which links the North Sea with the Baltic Sea by way of the Kattegat. It is bounded to the N by Norway and to the S by Denmark; length 240km/150mi; width 135km/84mi. The main arm of the Skagerrak is the Oslo Fjord.

Skanda in Hindu mythology, the god of War and the son of Shiva. He was also responsible for the demons who brought disease.

Skanderbeg, originally **George Castriota**, or **Kastrioti** (1405–68) Albanian patriot, of Serb descent. Carried away by Ottoman Turks at the age of seven, he was brought up a Muslim, and became a favourite commander of Sultan Murad II, who gave him his name Skanderbeg, a combination of *Iskander* ('Alexander') and the rank of Bey. In 1443 he changed sides, renounced Islam, drove the Turks from Albania, and for 20 years he maintained Albanian independence. After his death however, opposition to the Turks collapsed.

Skara Brae a Neolithic village of c.3100–2500 BC on the Bay of Skaill, Stromness, Orkney, exposed below sand dunes by storms in 1850. It supported a population of c.30–40, and comprises a tight cluster of nine squarish turf-roofed stone huts with alleys between.

skate[1] — *noun* **1** a boot with a device fitted to the sole for gliding smoothly over surfaces, either a steel blade for use on ice (*ice-skate*) or a set of small wheels for use on wooden and other surfaces (*roller-skate*). **2** the blade of an ice-skate. — *verb intrans.* to move around on skates.
— **get one's skates on** *colloq.* to hurry up.
skate on thin ice to risk danger or harm, especially through lack of care or good judgement.
skate over *or* **round something** to avoid dealing with or considering a difficulty. [from Old French *eschasse*, stilt]

skate[2] *noun* (**skate**, **skates**) a large flat edible fish of the ray family. [from Norse *skata*]

skateboard *noun* a narrow shaped board mounted on sets of small wheels, for riding on in a standing or crouching position.

skater *noun* a person who skates.

skating *noun* moving on skates.

skedaddle *verb intrans. colloq.* to run away quickly.

Skegness POP (1981) 16 000, a resort town in E Lindsey district, Lincolnshire, E central England. It lies on the North Sea coast, 30km/19mi NE of Boston. There is a bird reserve just S of the town.

skein *noun* a loose coil of wool or thread. [from Old French *escaigne*]

skeletal *adj.* **1** like a skeleton. **2** existing in outline only.

skeleton *noun* **1** the framework of bones that supports and often protects the body of an animal, and to which the muscles are usually attached. **2** an initial basic structure or idea upon or around which anything is built. **3** *colloq.* an unhealthily thin person. [from Greek *skeleton soma*, dried body]
◊ Vertebrates (animals with backbones), such as mammals (including humans), birds, and fish, have an internal skeleton or *endoskeleton* made of bone or cartilage. It supports the tissues and organs of the body, and protects soft internal organs such as the lungs. The muscles are attached to the bones of the skeleton by means of tendons, and when they contract they pull against the bones, causing them to move. The point of articulation or contact between two or more bones of the skeleton is known as a joint, different types of joint allowing varying degrees of movement.
Some invertebrates (animals without backbones), such as insects, have an external skeleton or *exoskeleton*, consisting of a rigid covering that is external to the body. In insects and crustaceans it is made of a hard material called *chitin*, and in molluscs, eg snails, it consists of a chalky shell. In certain invertebrates, such as the earthworm, there is a *hydrostatic skeleton*, consisting of a long tube containing fluid under pressure.

Skeleton Coast a national park in NW Namibia, established in 1971. It runs along the Atlantic Ocean coast between Walvis Bay and the Angolan frontier. AREA 16 390sq km/6 326sq mi.

skeleton in the cupboard *or* **skeleton in the closet** a shameful fact concerning oneself or one's family that one tries to keep secret.

skeleton key a key filed in such a way that it can open many different locks.

skeleton staff a set of staff reduced to a bare minimum.

Skelmersdale POP (1981) 43 000, a town in Wigan urban area and W Lancashire district, Lancashire, NW England. It is situated 10km/6mi W of Wigan, and was designated a 'new town' in 1961.

Skelton, John (c.1460–1529) English satirical poet, born in Norfolk. He was court poet to Henry VII, tutor to Prince Henry (VIII), took holy orders in 1498, and became rector of Diss in 1502. He produced some translations and elegies in 1489, but became known for his satirical vernacular poetry, including *Colyn Cloute* (1522).

sketch — *noun* **1** a rough drawing quickly done. **2** a rough plan or outline. **3** any of several short pieces of comedy presented as a programme. — *verb* **1** *trans., intrans.* to do a rough drawing or drawings (of). **2** to give a rough outline of. [from Greek *schedios*, offhand]

sketchily *adv.* in a sketchy way.

sketchiness *noun* being sketchy.

sketchy *adj.* (**sketchier**, **sketchiest**) lacking detail; not complete or substantial.

skew — *adj.* slanted; oblique; askew. — *verb* **1** *trans., intrans.* to slant or cause to slant. **2** to distort. — *noun* a slanting position: *on the skew*. [from Old French *eschuer*]

skewbald — *adj., said of an animal, especially a horse* with patches of white and another colour (other than black). — *noun* a skewbald horse.

skewer — *noun* a long wooden or metal pin pushed through chunks of meat, etc which are to be roasted. — *verb* (**skewered**, **skewering**) to fasten or pierce with, or as if with, a skewer. [from dialect *skiver*]

skewness *noun* *Maths.* a measure of the degree of asymmetry about the central value of a distribution.

skew-whiff *adj., adv. colloq.* lying in a slanted position; awry.

ski — *noun* (PL. **skis**) **1** a long narrow strip of wood, metal or plastic, upturned at the front, for gliding over snow, attached to each of a pair of boots or to a vehicle. **2** (*also* **water-ski**) a similar object worn on each foot for gliding over water. — *verb* (**skis**, **skied** *or* **ski'd**, **skiing**) *intrans.* to move on skis, especially as a sport or leisure activity. [from Norse *skith*, piece of split wood]

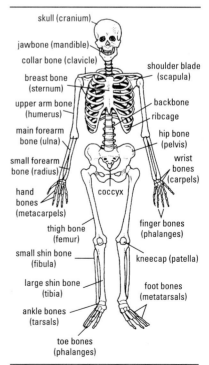

skull (cranium)
jawbone (mandible)
collar bone (clavicle)
breast bone (sternum)
upper arm bone (humerus)
main forearm bone (ulna)
small forearm bone (radius)
hand bones (metacarpels)
thigh bone (femur)
small shin bone (fibula)
large shin bone (tibia)
ankle bones (tarsals)
toe bones (phalanges)

shoulder blade (scapula)
backbone
ribcage
hip bone (pelvis)
wrist bones (carpels)
coccyx
finger bones (phalanges)
kneecap (patella)
foot bones (metatarsals)

human skeleton

Skiathos an island in the N Sporades, Greece, lying in the W Aegean Sea, 4km/2.5mi from the mainland. AREA 48sq km/18sq mi. CHIEF TOWN Skiathos. It is a popular holiday resort.

skid — *verb intrans.* (**skidded, skidding**) **1** *said of a wheel, etc* to slide along without revolving. **2** *said of a vehicle* to slide at an angle, especially out of control. — *noun* an instance of skidding.
— **put the skids under someone** *colloq.* **1** to cause them to hurry. **2** to bring about their downfall.

Skiddaw a mountain in the Lake District of Cumbria, NW England, lying to the E of Bassenthwaite. HEIGHT 928m.

skid pan a special slippery track on which drivers learn to control skidding vehicles.

skid row the poorest or most squalid part of a town.

Skien POP (1991e) 48 000, an ancient town and the river-port capital of Telemark county, SE Norway. It lies on the R Skiensalv.

skier *noun* a person who skis.

skiff *noun* a small light boat. [from French *esquif*]

skiing *noun* the art of propelling oneself along snow while standing on skis, and with the aid of poles.
◇ Skiing is a popular pastime and sport that dates from c.2500 BC. Competitive skiing takes two forms: *Alpine skiing*, which consists of the downhill and slalom (a zig-zag course through markers), both races against the clock; and *Nordic skiing*, which incorporates cross-country skiing, the biathlon, and ski-jumping. Other forms include *ski-flying* (hang-gliding on skis) and *skijoring* (being towed behind a vehicle or horse), as well as several freestyle varieties.

Skikda, formerly **Philippeville 1** POP (1987) 129 000, the chief town of Skikda department, NE Algeria. It is a seaport on the Mediterranean coast, W of 'Annaba. The town was founded by the French in 1838. NOTABLE FEATURE Museum of Punic and Roman Antiquities. **2** a department in NE Algeria.

skilful *adj.* having or showing skill.

skilfully *adv.* in a skilful way.

ski lift a device for carrying skiers to the top of a slope so that they can ski down.

skill *noun* **1** expertness; dexterity. **2** a talent or accomplishment, naturally acquired or developed through training. [from Norse *skil*, distinction]

skilled *adj.* **1** *said of people* possessing skill; trained, experienced. **2** *said of work* requiring skill or showing the use of skill.

skillet *noun* a small long-handled frying-pan or saucepan. [perhaps from Norse *skjola*, bucket]

skim *verb* (**skimmed, skimming**) **1** to remove (floating matter) from the surface of (a liquid). **2** *trans., intrans.* to brush or cause to brush against or glide lightly over (a surface): *skimming stones on the sea / bird's wings skimming (over) the water.* **3** *trans., intrans.* (**skim through something**) to read it superficially. [from Old French *escume*, scum]

skimmed milk *or* **skim milk** milk from which the cream has been removed.

skimmer *noun* a bird that inhabits tropical freshwater and coasts in America, Africa, India, and SE Asia, related to the tern, and having a lower bill longer and narrower than the upper one. It catches fish by flying low with its lower bill cutting the water surface. — Also called *shearwater*.

skimp *verb intrans.* (**skimp on something**) to spend, use, or give too little or only just enough of it. [perhaps from SCANT + SCRIMP]

skimpily *adv.* in a skimpy way.

skimpiness *noun* being skimpy.

skimpy *adj.* (**skimpier, skimpiest**) **1** inadequate; barely enough. **2** *said of clothes* leaving much of the body uncovered.

skin — *noun* **1** the tough flexible waterproof covering of the human or animal body. **2** the outer covering of certain fruits and vegetables. **3** complexion: *greasy skin.* **4** an animal hide, with or without fur or hair attached. **5** a semi-solid coating on the surface of a liquid. **6** a container for liquids made from an animal hide. — *verb* (**skinned, skinning**) **1** to strip the skin from. **2** to injure by scraping the skin from. **3** *slang* to cheat or swindle.
— **by the skin of one's teeth** very narrowly; only just.
get under someone's skin *colloq.* **1** to greatly annoy and upset them. **2** to become their consuming passion.
no skin off one's nose *colloq.* not a cause of even slight concern or nuisance to one.
save one's skin to save oneself from death or other harm.
[from Norse *skinn*]
◇ In humans and animals the skin consists of a thin outer layer (the *epidermis*), which is continually being renewed as dead cells are shed from its surface, and a thicker underlying layer (the *dermis*), which is composed of a network of collagen and elastic fibres containing blood and lymph vessels, sensory nerve endings, hair follicles, sweat and sebaceous glands, and smooth muscle. The skin is an important sense organ, sensitive to touch, pressure, changes in temperature, and painful stimuli. It prevents fluid loss and dehydration, and protects the body from invasion by micro-organisms and parasites. In warm-blooded animals it has an important role in temperature regulation, heat loss being achieved by sweating and by dilation of the skin capillaries. In order to conserve heat, the skin capillaries contract and the hairs on the surface are raised, trapping a layer of warm air next to the skin.

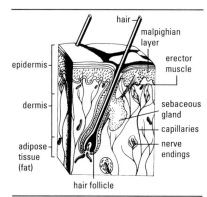

a section through the human skin

skin-deep *adj.* superficial.

skin-diver *noun* a person who practises skin-diving.

skin-diving *noun* underwater swimming with no wet suit and only simple breathing and other equipment.

skin flick *slang* a pornographic film.

skinflint *noun colloq.* a very ungenerous person.

skinful *noun* (PL. **skinfuls**) *slang* a large amount of alcohol, enough to make one thoroughly drunk.

skinhead *noun* a person with closely cropped hair, especially a white youth with tight jeans, heavy boots and anti-establishment attitudes.

skink *noun* a lizard found in tropical and temperate regions worldwide, and usually having a long thin body and short legs (some species are without legs). Its head often bears large flat scales, and it has a broad rounded tongue. Many species burrow, and most feed on invertebrates, although the larger species eat plants. [from Greek *skinkos*]

Skinner, B(urrhus) F(rederic) (1904–90) US psychologist, born in Susquehanna, Pennsylvania. A behaviourist, he taught at Harvard, and invented the 'Skinner box' (a chamber containing mechanisms for an animal to operate and an automatic device for presenting rewards) to advance studies of animal behaviour. His social and political views have reached the public through *Walden Two* (1948) and *Beyond Freedom and Dignity* (1971).

skinny *adj.* (**skinnier, skinniest**) *said of a person* very thin.

skinny-dip *verb intrans. colloq.* to go swimming naked.

skinny-dipping *noun colloq.* naked swimming.

skint *adj. slang* without money; hard up. [from *skinned*]

skin-tight *adj.*, *said of a piece of clothing* very tight-fitting.

skip¹ — *verb* (**skipped, skipping**) **1** *intrans.* to go along with light springing or hopping steps on alternate feet. **2** *intrans.* to make jumps over a skipping-rope. **3** to omit, leave out or pass over. **4** *colloq.* not to attend (eg a class in school). — *noun* a skipping movement.
— **skip it!** *colloq.* forget it; ignore it; it is not important.
[from Middle English *skippen*]

skip² *noun* **1** a large metal container for rubbish from eg building work. **2** a large (especially wicker) chest, eg for storing theatrical costumes. **3** a lift in a coal mine. [a variant of *skep*, beehive]

skipper — *noun* the captain of a ship, aeroplane or team. — *verb* (**skippered, skippering**) to act as skipper of. [from Old Dutch *schipper*, shipper]

skipping-rope *noun* a rope swung backwards and forwards or twirled in a circular motion by the person skipping or by two other people each holding an end, for jumping over as exercise or as a children's game.

skirl — *noun* the high-pitched screaming sound of bagpipes. — *verb intrans.* to make this sound.

skirmish — *noun* **1** a brief battle during a war, especially away from the main fighting. **2** any minor fight or dispute. — *verb intrans.* to engage in a skirmish. [from Old French *escarmouche*]

Skiros POP (1982) 3 000, the largest island in the N Sporades, Greece, in the Aegean Sea. AREA 209sq km/81sq mi; length 36km/22mi; maximum width 14km/9mi. PHYSICAL DESCRIPTION the coast is heavily indented; cultivated land is mainly restricted to the valleys in the N half of the island. ECONOMY handicrafts, particularly hand-weaving and furniture; tourism.

skirt — *noun* **1** a woman's garment that hangs from the waist. **2** the part of a woman's dress from the waist down. **3** any part or attachment resembling a skirt, eg the flap around the base of a hovercraft. **4** a cut of beef from the rear part of the belly; the flank. **5** (*also* **a bit of skirt**) *offensive slang* a woman regarded as an object of sexual desire. — *verb* **1** to border. **2** to pass along or around the edge of. **3** to avoid confronting (eg a problem). [from Norse *skyrta*, shirt]

skit *noun* a short satirical piece of writing or drama.

skittish *adj.* **1** lively and playful. **2** frequently changing mood or opinion; capricious. **3** *said of a horse* easily frightened.

skittle *noun* **1** each of the upright targets used in a game of skittles. **2** (**skittles**) a game in which balls are rolled towards a set of (usually nine or ten) free-standing bottle-shaped wooden or plastic targets, the object being to knock over as many of these as possible.

skive *verb intrans. colloq.* (**skive off**) to evade work or a duty, especially through laziness.

skiver *noun* a person who avoids work.

skivvy *colloq.* — *noun derog.* (PL. **skivvies**) a servant, especially a woman, who does unpleasant household jobs. — *verb intrans.* (**skivvies**, **skivvied**) to work as, or as if, a skivvy.

Skopje *or* **Skoplje**, Turkish **Usküp**, ancient **Scupi** POP (1991) 563 000, the capital of Macedonia. It is an industrial city lying on the R Vardar. HISTORY capital of Serbia in the 14c; largely destroyed by an earthquake in 1963. NOTABLE FEATURES old town and bazaar; Ethnographic Museum; Daut Pasha Hammam, the largest Turkish bath-house in the Balkans (1489); Mustapha Pasha Mosque; Museum of Contemporary Art.

Skorzeny, Otto (1908–75) Austrian soldier, born in Vienna, noted for his commando-style operations in World War II. He joined the Nazi Party (1930), was mobilized into the SS, and fought in France, Serbia, and Russia (1939–43). He freed Mussolini from internment in a mountain hotel on the Gran Sasso Range (1943), abducted Miklós Horthy, the Regent of Hungary (1944), but failed to capture Marshal Tito. During the German counter-offensive in the Ardennes (1944), he carried out widespread sabotage behind Allied lines. He was tried at Nuremberg as a war criminal, but was acquitted (1947).

Skraelings the name given by the Vikings to the native peoples — principally Beothuk and Inuit — they encountered in Greenland and N America. *Skraelingsland* was Labrador. [from Old Norse *skraelinga*, pitiful wretch]

skua *noun* any of various large predatory gull-like birds. [from Norse *skufr*]

skulduggery *noun* unscrupulous or dishonest behaviour; trickery. [from Scots *sculduddery*, unchastity]

skulk *verb intrans.* **1** to sneak off. **2** to hide or lurk, planning mischief. [from Norse *skulk*]

skull *noun* **1** in vertebrates, the hard cartilaginous or bony framework of the head, including the cranium (which encloses the brain), face and jaws. **2** *colloq.* the head or brain. [from Norse]

skull and crossbones a representation of a human skull with two bones arranged in an X underneath, used formerly as a pirate's symbol, now as a symbol of death or danger.

skullcap *noun* a small brimless cap fitting closely on the head.

skunk *noun* **1** any of several small American mammals related to the weasel, and best known for the foul-smelling liquid which it squirts from musk glands at the base of its tail in order to deter predators, and the bold black and white warning coloration of its fur. Skunks feed on insects, mice, frogs, eggs, etc. **2** *derog.* a despised person. [from Algonquian (Native American) language *segonku*]

sky — *noun* (PL. **skies**) **1** the apparent dome of space in which the Sun, Moon and stars can be seen; the heavens. **2** the appearance of this area as a reflection of weather: *dismal skies.* — *verb* (**skies**, **skied**) to mishit (a ball) high into the air.
— **the sky's the limit** there is no upper limit, eg to the amount of money that may be spent.
to the skies in a lavish or extremely enthusiastic manner: *praise him to the skies.*
[from Norse, = cloud]

Skyamsen see THUNDERBIRD.

sky-blue *noun* bright light blue, the colour of a cloudless sky.

sky-diver *noun* a person who practises sky-diving.

sky-diving *noun* free-falling from an aircraft, often involving performing manoeuvres in mid-

air, with a long delay before the parachute is opened.

Skye an island in Highland region, W Scotland, and the second largest island in the Inner Hebrides. AREA 1 665sq km/643sq mi. PHYSICAL DESCRIPTION Skye is separated from the mainland to the E by the Sound of Sleat; the Cuillin Hills lie in the SW, rising to 1 008m in Sgurr Alasdair; in the N are Quiraing (542m) and Storr (721m); the island is much indented by sea-lochs. CHIEF TOWN Portree. ECONOMY crofting, fishing, sheep, cattle, tourism. NOTABLE FEATURES Dunvegan Castle; Kilmuir Croft Museum; Clan Donald Centre at Ardvasar; Dunsgiath Castle; Skye Water Mill and Black House.

Skye terrier a small long-haired terrier originally bred on the island of Skye.

sky-high *adv. adj.*, said especially of prices very high.

skyjack *verb slang* to hijack (an aircraft).

Skylab *noun Astron.* the first US space station, launched from the Kennedy Space Center in May 1973, and manned, over a period of nine months, by three crews of three men each. It contained a workshop for experiments on the medical and biological effects of weightlessness, an observatory with telescopes and a coronograph for monitoring the Sun, and cameras and remote-sensing equipment for obtaining detailed information about the Earth's surface.

skylark — *noun* the common lark, which sings when flying vertically and hovering. — *verb intrans. old use* to lark about.

skylight *noun* a (usually small) window in a roof or ceiling.

skyline *noun* the outline of buildings, hills and trees seen against the sky.

skyscraper *noun* an extremely tall building.
◇ The term was first used at the end of the 19c to describe the multi-storey buildings being constructed in New York and other US cities. Very tall buildings are now a common feature of urban landscapes worldwide, although skyscapers are still particularly associated with the USA, which has some of the most famous (and tallest) examples, including the Empire State Building and Chrysler Building in New York, and the Sears Tower in Chicago.

skyward — *adj.* towards the sky. — *adv.* (*also* **skywards**) towards the sky.

skyway *noun* a route used by aircraft.

slab — *noun* a thick flat rectangular piece, slice or object. — *verb* (**slabbed**, **slabbing**) to pave with concrete slabs.

slack¹ — *adj.* **1** loose; not pulled or stretched tight. **2** not careful or diligent; remiss. **3** not busy. **4** *said of the tide, etc* still; neither ebbing nor flowing. — *noun* **1** a loosely hanging part. **2** a period of little trade or other activity. — *verb* (*often* **slack off**) **1** *intrans.* (*also* **slack off** *or* **up**) to become slower; to slow one's working pace through tiredness or laziness. **2** *trans., intrans.* to make or become looser. **3** *intrans.* to become less busy. **4** *trans., intrans.* to make or become less rigid and more easy or relaxed. [from Anglo-Saxon *slæc*]

slack² *noun* coal dust or tiny fragments of coal. [from Old German *slecke*]

slacken *verb* same as SLACK *VERB*.

slacker *noun* a person who does not work hard enough; a shirker.

slacks *pl. noun old use* a type of loose casual trousers.

slag¹ — *noun* **1** waste material formed on the surface of molten metal ore. **2** waste left over from coal mining. — *verb intrans.* (**slagged**, **slagging**) *said of molten metal ore* to throw up a surface layer of slag. [from Old German *slagge*]

slag² *verb* (**slagged**, **slagging**) *slang* (**slag someone off**) to criticize them harshly or speak disparagingly about them.

slag³ *noun derog. slang* a person, especially a woman, who regularly has casual sex with different people.

slag heap a hill or mound formed from coal-mining waste.

slain see SLAY.

slake *verb* **1** *literary* to satisfy or quench (thirst, desire, or anger). **2** to cause (lime) to crumble by adding water. [from Anglo-Saxon *slacian*]

slaked lime *Chem.* calcium hydroxide prepared by adding water to quicklime (calcium oxide) in a process that evolves much heat, known as slaking.

slalom *noun* a race, on skis or in canoes, in and out of obstacles on a winding course. [from Norwegian *slalom*]

slam¹ — *verb* (**slammed**, **slamming**) **1** *trans., intrans.* to shut loudly and with violence. **2** *trans., intrans.* (*usually* **slam against, into**, *etc*) *colloq.* to make or cause to make loud heavy contact. **3** *slang* to criticize severely. — *noun* the act or sound of slamming.

slam² see GRAND SLAM, LITTLE SLAM.

slammer *noun* (**the slammer**) *slang* prison.

slander — *noun* **1** a false and damaging spoken statement about a person. **2** the making of such statements. — *verb* (**slandered**, **slandering**) to speak about in such a way. See also LIBEL. [from Old French *esclandre*, from Greek *skandalon*, snare, scandal]
◇ In law, although slander usually takes the form of words, it may also be any sound or gesture intended to defame. The term is not recognized in Scots law.

slanderous *adj.* **1** *said of words, reports, etc* characterized by slander. **2** *said of a person* given to the use of slander, using slander.

slang — *noun* words and phrases used only very informally, not usually in writing or polite speech, and often only by members of a particular social group or profession. — *verb* to speak abusively to (someone) using coarse language.

slanging match *colloq.* an angry exchange of abuse.

slangy *adj.* (**slangier, slangiest**) **1** of the nature of slang. **2** using slang.

slant — *verb* **1** *intrans.* to be at an angle, not horizontal or vertical; to slope. **2** to present (information, etc) in a biased way, or for a particular audience or readership. — *noun* a sloping position, surface, or line. — *adj.* sloping; lying at an angle. [from Middle English *slent*]

slanting *adj.* that slants.

slap — *noun* **1** a blow with the palm of the hand or anything flat. **2** the sound made by such a blow, or by the impact of one flat surface with another. — *verb* (**slapped, slapping**) **1** to strike with the open hand or anything flat. **2** to bring or send with a slapping sound: *slapped the newspaper down on the table.* **3** *colloq.* to apply thickly and carelessly: *slapped make-up on her face.* — *adv. colloq.* **1** exactly or precisely: *slap in the middle.* **2** heavily; with a slap: *fell slap on his face.*
— **slap someone down** *colloq.* to reject or contradict them abruptly.
a slap in the face *colloq.* an insult or rebuff.
a slap on the back *colloq.* congratulations.
a slap on the wrist *colloq., often facetious* a mild reprimand.
[from German dialect *slapp*; originally imitative]

slap and tickle *humorous colloq.* kissing and cuddling; sexual activity of any kind.

slap-bang *adv. colloq.* **1** exactly or precisely: *slap-bang in the middle.* **2** directly and with force: *drove slap-bang into the wall.*

slapdash *adj.* careless and hurried.

slap-happy *adj. colloq.* **1** cheerfully carefree or careless. **2** punch-drunk.

slapstick *noun* comedy in which the humour is derived from boisterous antics of all kinds. [from a mechanical sound-effects device, used to punctuate (comic) stage fights with loud reports]

slap-up *adj. colloq., said of a meal* lavish; extravagant.

slash¹ — *verb* **1** *trans., intrans.* to make sweeping cuts or cutting strokes, especially repeatedly. **2** *colloq.* to reduce suddenly and drastically. — *noun* **1** a long (especially deep) cut. **2** a sweeping cutting stroke. **3** (*also* **slash mark**) an oblique line in writing or printing; a solidus.

slash² *coarse slang* — *verb intrans.* to urinate. — *noun* an act of urinating. [perhaps from Scot. dialect, large splash]

slash and burn *Agric.* a system of agriculture, common in tropical regions, in which trees and natural undergrowth are cut down and burned, and crops are then grown on the bare soil for a few years until it loses its fertility. The process is then repeated in a new area.

slat *noun* a thin strip, especially of wood or metal. [from Old French *esclat*]

slate¹ — *noun* **1** *Geol.* a shiny dark grey metamorphic rock, formed by the compression of clays and shales, that is easily split into thin flat layers, and is used for roofing and flooring. **2** a roofing tile made of this. **3** *formerly* a piece of this for writing on. **4** a record of credit given to a customer: *put it on my slate.* **5** a dull grey colour. — *verb* to cover (a roof) with slates.
— **a clean slate** a fresh start, released from all previous obligations, faults, or commitments. [from Old French *esclate*]

slate² *verb colloq.* to criticize extremely harshly. [from Norse *slate*]

slating *adj.* **1** covering with slates. **2** a covering of slates. **3** materials for covering with slates.

slatted *adj.* having or composed of slats.

slattern *noun old use* a woman of dirty or untidy appearance or habits. [from dialect *slatter*, to slop]

slatternliness *noun* being slatternly.

slatternly *adj.* slovenly.

slaughter — *noun* **1** the killing of animals for food. **2** cruel and violent murder. **3** the large-scale indiscriminate killing of people or animals. — *verb* (**slaughtered**, **slaughtering**) **1** to subject to slaughter. **2** *colloq.* to defeat resoundingly; to trounce. [from Norse *slatr*, butchers' meat]

slaughterhouse *noun* a place where animals are killed to be sold for food; an abattoir.

Slav *noun* a member of any of various central and E European peoples speaking Slavonic languages such as Russian, Bulgarian, and Polish. [from Latin *Sclavus*]

slave — *noun* **1** *Hist.* a person owned by and acting as servant to another, with no personal freedom. **2** a person who works extremely hard for another; a drudge. **3** a person submissively devoted to another. **4** (**a slave to something**) a person whose life is dominated by some activity or thing: *a slave to her work.* — *verb intrans.* to work hard and ceaselessly. [from Old French *esclave*, originally 'Slav', the Slavs being much-conquered peoples in the Middle Ages]

slave-driver *noun* **1** *Hist.* a person employed to ensure that slaves work hard. **2** *colloq.* a person who demands very hard work from others.

slaver¹ *noun Hist.* **1** a person engaging in the buying and selling of slaves. **2** a ship for transporting slaves.

slaver² — *noun* spittle running from the mouth. — *verb intrans.* (**slavered**, **slavering**) **1** to let spittle run from the mouth; to dribble. **2** *colloq.* to talk nonsense.

slavery *noun* **1** the state of being a slave. **2** the practice of owning slaves. **3** extremely hard work; toil.
◇ There have been different types and conditions of slavery. At one extreme, slaves might be worked to death, as in the Greek mining camps of the 5c–4c BC. At the other, slaves were used less as chattels and more as servants, working in households, and to an extent even administering them and acting as tutors to young children. Slaves were often captured enemies, or were created as a means of punishment, or through an organized slave trade. It became of significant economic importance with the European conquest of S and Central America and the need to have a labour force to work the new sugar and coffee plantations. Slaves were shipped from Africa in huge numbers (as many as two million between 1680 and 1786 by the British slavers alone). Slavery was outlawed in the British Empire in 1833, but persisted in the S states of the USA until 1865. It is now outlawed in most countries.

Slaves, The two sculptures by Michelangelo (c.1513–15, Louvre, Paris). They were originally intended for the tomb of Pope Julius II.

Slavic *adj.* relating to the Slavs.

Slavic languages *or* **Slavonic languages** the NE branch of the Indo-European languages, often grouped with the Baltic languages. Slavic languages are divided into South Slavic (eg Bulgarian), West Slavic (eg Polish), and East Slavic (eg Russian). The form known as Old Church Slavonic has written records dating from the 9c, and its later form, Church Slavonic, is still used today as the liturgical language of the Eastern Orthodox Church. The most widely spoken Slavic language is Russian with c.150 million speakers; Polish has c.40 million speakers, and Serbo-Croat has c.18 million speakers. The East Slavic languages are written using the Cyrillic alphabet.

slavish *adj.* **1** rigid or unwavering in following rules or instructions. **2** very closely copied or imitated; unoriginal. **3** of or like a slave.

slavishly *adv.* in a slavish way.

Slavonic — *noun* a group of Central and Eastern European languages that includes Russian, Polish, Czech, Slovak, Serb, and Slovenian. — *adj.* of these languages, the peoples speaking them, or their cultures. [see SLAV]

Slawkenbergius the author of a Latin essay on noses in Laurence Sterne's *Tristram Shandy*.

slay *verb* (PAST TENSE **slew**; PAST PARTICIPLE **slain**) *old use, literary* to kill. [from Anglo-Saxon *slean*]

slayer *noun* a person who kills.

sleaziness *or* **sleaze** *noun* a sleazy quality.

sleazy *adj.* (**sleazier**, **sleaziest**) *colloq.* **1** dirty and neglected-looking. **2** cheaply suggestive of sex or crime; disreputable.

sled — *noun* a sledge. — *verb intrans.* (**sledded**, **sledding**) to sledge. [from Old German *sledde*]

sledge — *noun* **1** a vehicle with ski-like runners for travelling over snow, drawn by horses or dogs. **2** a child's toy vehicle of similar design, propelled by the hands or feet; a toboggan. — *verb intrans.* **1** to travel by sledge. **2** to play on a sledge. [from Old Dutch *sleedse*]

sledgehammer *noun* a large heavy hammer swung with both arms. [from Anglo-Saxon *slecg*, from *slean*, to strike]

sleek — *adj.* **1** *said of hair, fur, etc* smooth, soft and glossy. **2** having a well-fed and prosperous appearance. **3** insincerely polite or flattering. — *verb* to smooth (especially hair). [a form of SLICK]

sleep — *noun* **1** in humans and many animals, a readily reversible state of natural unconsciousness during which the body's functional powers are restored, and physical movements are minimal. In most mammals and birds it occurs at regular daily intervals. **2** a period of such rest. **3** *colloq.* mucus that collects in the corners of the eyes during such rest. **4** *poetic* death. — *verb usually intrans.* (PAST TENSE AND PAST PARTICIPLE **slept**) **1** to rest in a state of sleep. **2** to be motionless, inactive or dormant. **3** *trans.* to provide or contain sleeping accommodation for: *the caravan sleeps four.* **4** *colloq.* to be in a dreamy state, not paying attention. **5** *poetic* to be dead.
— **go to sleep 1** to pass into a state of sleep. **2** *colloq., said of a limb* to be temporarily numb through lack of blood circulation.

lose sleep over something *colloq.* to be worried or preoccupied by it.

put someone *or* **something to sleep 1** to anaesthetize them. **2** *euphemistic* to kill an animal painlessly with an injected drug.

sleep around to engage in casual sexual relations.

sleep in 1 to sleep later than usual in the morning. **2** to sleep at one's place of work; to live in.

sleep something off to recover from it by sleeping.

sleep on something to delay taking a decision about it until the following morning.

sleep out 1 to sleep out of doors. **2** to sleep away from one's place of work; to live out.

sleep with someone to have sexual relations with them.
[from Anglo-Saxon *slæp*]

sleeper *noun* **1** a person who sleeps, especially in a specified way: *a light sleeper.* **2** any of the horizontal wooden or concrete beams supporting the rails on a railway track. **3** a railway carriage providing sleeping accommodation for passengers; a train with such carriages. **4** *colloq.* a record, film, book, etc, which suddenly becomes popular after an initial period of uninterest.

sleepily *adv.* in a sleepy way.

sleepiness *noun* being sleepy.

sleeping-bag *noun* a large quilted sack for sleeping in when camping, etc.

Sleeping Beauty, The (Spyashchaya krasavitsa) a ballet by Piotr Ilyich Tchaikovsky (1890), based on Charles Perrault's tale *La belle au bois dormant.*

Sleeping Gypsy a painting by Henri Rousseau (1897, Museum of Modern Art, New York).

sleeping partner a partner who invests money in a business without taking part in its running.

sleeping pill a pill which contains a sedative drug that induces sleep.

sleeping policeman each of a series of low transverse humps built into the surface of a road, intended to slow down motor traffic in residential areas, parks, etc.

sleeping sickness a disease, often fatal, causing violent fever and extreme drowsiness, transmitted by the tsetse fly of Africa.

sleepless *adj.* **1** during which one is or was unable to sleep. **2** unable to sleep.

sleepwalk *verb intrans.* to indulge in sleepwalking; to walk while asleep.

sleepwalker *noun* a person who sleepwalks.

sleepwalking *noun* a condition in which the affected person walks about while asleep, with the eyes either open or closed, but on waking has no memory of the event. In adults it may be a symptom of stress. – Also called *somnambulism.*

sleepy *adj.* (**sleepier**, **sleepiest**) **1** feeling the desire to sleep; drowsy. **2** suggesting sleep or drowsiness: *sleepy music.* **3** characterized by quietness and a lack of activity: *a sleepy village.*

sleepyhead *noun colloq.* **1** a person who often feels sleepy, or who needs a lot of sleep. **2** a person who tends to daydream a lot.

sleet — *noun* rain mixed with snow or hail. — *verb intrans.* to rain simultaneously with snow or hail.

sleety *adj.* (**sleetier, sleetiest**) characterized by sleet, carrying sleet.

sleeve *noun* **1** the part of a garment that covers the arm. **2** any tube-like cover. **3** the cardboard or paper envelope in which a record is stored.
— **up one's sleeve** held secretly in reserve, for possible later use.
[from Anglo-Saxon *slefe*]

sleeveless *adj.* having no sleeves.

sleigh — *noun* a large horse-drawn sledge. — *verb intrans.* to travel by sleigh. [from Dutch *slee*]

sleight of hand skill in moving the hands quickly and deceptively, in the performing of magic tricks. [from Norse *slægth*, cunning]

slender *adj.* **1** attractively slim. **2** narrow; slight: *by a slender margin*. **3** meagre: *slender means*.

slept see SLEEP.

sleuth — *noun* a detective. — *verb intrans.* to work as a detective. [from Norse *sloth*, trail]

slew[1] see SLAY.

slew[2] — *verb trans., intrans.* to twist or cause to twist or swing round, especially suddenly and uncontrollably. — *noun* an instance of slewing.

slewed *adj. slang* extremely drunk.

slice — *noun* **1** a thin broad piece, or a wedge, cut off. **2** *colloq.* a share or portion: *a slice of the business*. **3** a kitchen tool with a broad flat blade for sliding under and lifting solid food. **4** *Sport* a stroke causing a ball to spin sideways and curve away in a particular direction; the spin imparted. — *verb* **1** to cut up into slices. **2** (*also* **slice something off**) to cut it off as or like a slice: *sliced a piece off the end*. **3** *intrans.* to cut deeply and easily; to move easily and forcefully, as if cutting with a knife: *a boat slicing through the water*. **4** to strike (a ball) with a slice. [from Old German *slizan*, to split]

slicer *noun* a person or machine that slices.

slick — *adj.* **1** dishonestly or slyly clever. **2** impressively and only superficially smart or efficient: *slick organization*. **3** smooth and glossy; sleek. — *verb* to smooth (especially hair). — *noun* (*also* **oil slick**) a wide layer of spilled oil floating on the surface of water. [from Anglo-Saxon *slician*, to smooth]

slickenside *noun Geol.* a smooth rock surface that has become polished and striated as a result of grinding or sliding against an adjacent rock mass during slippage along a fault plane. The striations are sometimes mistaken for fossils. [from SLICK]

slicker *noun* **1** a sophisticated city-dweller. **2** a shifty or swindling person.

slide — *verb* (PAST TENSE AND PAST PARTICIPLE **slid**) **1** *trans., intrans.* to move or cause to move or run smoothly along a surface. **2** *trans., intrans.* to move or place softly and unobtrusively: *slid the letter into his pocket*. **3** *intrans.* to lose one's footing; to slip. **4** *intrans.* to pass gradually, especially through neglect or laziness: *slid back into his old habits*. — *noun* **1** an act or instance of sliding. **2** any part that glides smoothly, eg the moving part of a trombone. **3** an apparatus for children to play on, usually with a ladder to climb up and a narrow sloping part to slide down. **4** a small glass plate on which specimens are placed to be viewed through a microscope. **5** a small transparent photograph viewed in magnified size by means of a projector. **6** a large decorative hair-clip.
— **let something slide** to allow a situation to deteriorate.
[from Anglo-Saxon *slidan*]

slide-rule *noun* a hand-held mechanical device, now largely superseded by the pocket calculator, used to perform quick numerical calculations, especially multiplication or division. It consists of a ruler bearing several logarithmic scales that can be moved in relation to each other.

sliding scale a scale, eg of fees charged, that varies according to changes in conditions, eg unforeseen difficulties in performing the service requested.

Sliema POP (1990) 14 000, the largest town in Malta, situated on the N coast of the main island. It is a residential and resort town which lies across Marsamxett Harbour from Valletta.

slight — *adj.* **1** small in extent, significance or seriousness. **2** slender. **3** lacking solidity; flimsy. **4** lacking substance or value: *slight works of literature*. — *verb* to insult by ignoring or dismissing abruptly; to snub.
— **not in the slightest** not at all; not even to the smallest degree.
[from the root seen in Anglo-Saxon *eorthslihtes*, close to the ground]

slightly *adv.* to a small extent, in a small way.

Sligo, Gaelic **Sligeach** POP (1991) 55 000, a county in Connacht province, W Irish Republic, bounded N by the Atlantic Ocean. AREA 1 795sq km/693sq mi. PHYSICAL DESCRIPTION Sligo is watered by the R Moy; the Ox Mts lie to the W. CAPITAL Sligo. ECONOMY cattle, dairy farming, coal. The county is associated with the poet W B Yeats.

Sligo POP (1991) 18 000, the seaport capital of Sligo county, Connacht, W Irish Republic. It lies at the head of Sligo Bay where it meets the R Garrogue. NOTABLE FEATURE megalithic stones at nearby Carrowmore.

slily see SLYLY.

slim — *adj.* (**slimmer, slimmest**) **1** attractively thin; slender. **2** of little thickness or width. **3** not great; slight: *a slim chance*. — *verb intrans.* (**slimmed, slimming**) to make oneself slim, especially by diet and exercise. [from Dutch *slim*, crafty]

slime *noun* **1** any thin unpleasantly slippery or gluey mud-like substance. **2** any mucus-like substance secreted, eg by snails. [from Anglo-Saxon *slim*]

slime mould *Biol.* a small simple organism, resembling a fungus and usually consisting of a naked mass of protoplasm, that lives in damp habitats and feeds on dead or decaying plant material. Slime moulds reproduce by means of spores, and for convenience are usually classified as fungi.

slimily *adv.* in a slimy way.

sliminess *noun* a slimy quality.

slimmer *noun* a person who is trying to lose weight.

slimming *noun* losing weight.

Slim (of Yarralumla and of Bishopston), William (Joseph) Slim, 1st Viscount (1891–1970) English soldier, born in Bristol, Gloucestershire. In World War I he served in Gallipoli and Mesopotamia, and in World War II his greatest achievement was to lead his reorganized forces, the famous 14th 'forgotten' army, to victory over the Japanese in Burma. Appointed field marshal in 1948, he was Chief of the Imperial General Staff (1948–52) and a successful Governor-General of Australia (1953–60).

slimy *adj.* (**slimier, slimiest**) **1** like, covered with or consisting of slime. **2** *colloq.* exaggeratedly and unpleasantly obedient or attentive; obsequious.

sling[1] — *noun* **1** a cloth hoop supporting an injured arm, one end hanging round the neck and the arm passed through the other end. **2** a primitive weapon for launching stones, consisting of a strap or pouch in which the stone is placed and swung round fast. **3** a strap or loop for hoisting, lowering or carrying a weight. — *verb* (PAST TENSE AND PAST PARTICIPLE **slung**) **1** *colloq.* to throw, especially with force; to fling. **2** to hang loosely: *a jacket slung over his shoulder*. **3** to launch from a sling.

— **sling one's hook** *slang* to go away.

sling[2] *noun* a drink of alcoholic spirit (especially gin) and water, sweetened and flavoured.

slingback *noun* a shoe with no cover for the heel, just a strap passing round it to hold the shoe on.

slingshot *noun North Amer., esp. US* a catapult.

slink *verb intrans.* (PAST TENSE AND PAST PARTICIPLE **slunk**) to go or move sneakingly or ashamedly. [from Anglo-Saxon *slincan*]

slinkily *adv.* in a slinky way.

slinkiness *noun* being slinky.

slinky *adj.* (**slinkier, slinkiest**) *colloq.* **1** said of *clothing* attractively close-fitting. **2** slender. **3** said of *a person* walking with slow rolling movements that emphasize the body's curves.

slip[1] — *verb* (**slipped, slipping**) **1** *intrans.* to lose one's footing and slide accidentally. **2** *intrans.* to slide, move, or drop accidentally. **3** to place smoothly, quietly, or secretively: *slipped the envelope into her pocket*. **4** (**slip in, out,** *etc*) to move quietly and unnoticed. **5** *trans., intrans.* to move or cause to move smoothly with a sliding motion. **6** to pull free from smoothly and swiftly; to suddenly escape from: *the dog slipped its lead / the name has slipped my mind*. **7** (*also* **slip up**) to make a slight mistake inadvertently. **8** *colloq.* to give or pass secretly: *slipped him a fiver*. **9** *intrans. colloq.* to lose one's former skill or expertise, or control of a situation. **10** to dislocate (especially a spinal disc). — *noun* **1** an instance of losing one's footing and sliding accidentally. **2** a minor and usually inadvertent mistake: *a slip of the tongue/pen*. **3** a woman's loose undergarment worn under a dress or skirt. **4** a loose covering for a pillow. **5** a slipway. **6** *Cricket* a fielder standing near to and roughly in line with the wicket-keeper on the on side; (*also* **slips**) this fielding position.
— **give someone the slip** *colloq.* to escape from them adroitly.
let something slip 1 to reveal it in speech accidentally. **2** to fail to take advantage of something (eg an opportunity).
[from Old German dialect *slippen*]

slip[2] *noun* **1** a small strip or piece of paper. **2** a small pre-printed form. **3** a mere youngster; an exceptionally slender person: *just a slip of a girl*. [from Middle English *slippe*]

slip[3] *noun* a creamy mixture of clay and water used for decorating and casting pottery. [from Anglo-Saxon *slipa*, paste]

Slipher, Vesto Melvin (1875–1969) US astronomer, born in Mulberry, Indiana. He worked at the Lowell Observatory in Arizona, becoming its director in 1926. He determined the periods of rotation of Uranus, Jupiter, Saturn, Venus and Mars (1912), and discovered the general recession of most galaxies from the Earth, a result which indicated that our universe is expanding.

slip-knot *noun* **1** a knot undone simply by pulling one end of the cord. **2** a knot finishing off a noose, and slipping along the cord to adjust the noose's size.

slip-on *noun* a shoe or other item of clothing that is easily put on, without laces, buttons, or other fastenings.

slipped disc a dislocation of the layer of cartilage between any of the vertebrae, causing painful pressure on a spinal nerve.

slipper *noun* a soft loose laceless indoor shoe.

slippered *adj.* wearing a slipper or slippers.

slipperiness *noun* being slippery.

slippery *adj.* **1** so smooth as to cause slipping. **2** difficult to catch or keep hold of. **3** unpredictable or untrustworthy.

slippy *adj.* (**slippier, slippiest**) *colloq., said of a thing* liable to slip; slippery.

slip road a road for joining or leaving a motorway.

slipshod *adj.* untidy and careless or carelessly done.

slipstream *noun* 1 an area of decreased wind resistance immediately behind a moving vehicle or other object. 2 a stream of air driven back by a moving vehicle, especially an aircraft.

slip-up *noun colloq.* a minor and usually inadvertent mistake.

slipway *noun* a ramp that slopes into water, for launching boats.

slit — *noun* a long narrow cut or opening. — *verb* (**slitted**, **slitting**) 1 to cut a slit in. 2 to cut into strips. [from Middle English *slitten*]

slither — *verb intrans.* (**slithered**, **slithering**) 1 to slide or slip unsteadily while walking, eg on ice. 2 to move slidingly, like a snake. — *noun* a slithering movement. [from Anglo-Saxon *slidrian*]

slithery *adj.* slippery.

sliver — *noun* a long thin piece cut or broken off. — *verb intrans.* (**slivered**, **slivering**) to become broken or cut into slivers. [from Anglo-Saxon *slifan*, to cleave]

slivovitz *noun* a dry colourless plum brandy from E Europe. [from Serbo-Croat *šljivovica*, from *šljiva*, plum]

Sloane, Sir Hans (1660–1753) British physician and naturalist, born in Killyleagh, Co Down, Ireland. He settled in London as a physician, but spent 1685–6 in Jamaica, where he collected a herbarium of 800 species. His museum and library of 50 000 volumes and 3 560 manuscripts formed the nucleus of the British Museum.

slob *colloq.* — *noun* a lazy, untidy or coarse person. — *verb intrans.* (**slobbed**, **slobbing**) (*usually* **slob about** *or* **around**) to move or behave in a lazy, untidy or slovenly way. [from Irish Gaelic *slab*, mud]

slobber — *verb intrans.* (**slobbered**, **slobbering**) 1 to let saliva run from the mouth; to dribble or slaver. 2 (**slobber over something**) *colloq.* to express extreme or excessive enthusiasm or admiration for it. — *noun* dribbled saliva. [from Middle English *slobber*]

slobbish *or* **slobby** *adj.* (**slobbier**, **slobbiest**) like a slob; lazy, untidy.

sloe *noun* the blackthorn fruit or bush. [from Anglo-Saxon *sla*]

sloe gin gin flavoured by having sloes soaked in it.

slog *colloq.* — *verb* (**slogged**, **slogging**) 1 to hit hard and wildly. 2 to labour or toil. — *noun* 1 a hard wild blow or stroke. 2 extremely tiring work.

slogan *noun* a phrase used to identify a group or organization, or to advertise a product. [from Gaelic *sluagh*, army + *gairm*, cry]

sloop *noun* a single-masted sailing boat with fore-and-aft sails. [from Dutch *sloep*]

Slop, Dr the incapable, belligerent doctor in Laurence Sterne's *Tristram Shandy*.

slop — *verb* (**slopped**, **slopping**) (*often* **slop about** *or* **around**) 1 *trans., intrans.* to splash or cause to splash or spill violently. 2 *intrans. colloq.* to move or behave in an untidy or slovenly way. — *noun* 1 spilled liquid. 2 (*often* **slops**) unappetizing watery food. 3 (**slops**) waste food. 4 (**slops**) liquid food fed to pigs. 5 (**slops**) urine and excrement. 6 gushy sentiment. — **slop out** *intrans.* said of *prisoners* to empty slops (sense 5). [from Anglo-Saxon *cusloppe*, cow dung]

Slope, the Rev Obadiah the smarmy chaplain in Anthony Trollope's 'Barsetshire' novels, who figures most prominently in *Barchester Towers*, in which his indiscreet flirtations cause him to be dismissed from his post.

slope — *noun* 1 a position or direction that is neither level nor upright; an upward or downward slant. 2 a slanting surface; an incline; the side of a hill or mountain. 3 a specially prepared track for skiing, on the side of a snow-covered hill or mountain. — *verb intrans.* 1 to rise or fall at an angle. 2 to be slanted or inclined. — **slope off** *colloq.* to leave furtively. [from Anglo-Saxon *aslupan*, to slip away]

Sloper, Catherine the plain heroine of Henry James's *Washington Square*, whose prospective inheritance stands in the way of her happiness.

sloppily *adv.* in a sloppy way.

sloppiness *noun* being sloppy.

sloppy *adj.* (**sloppier**, **sloppiest**) 1 wet or muddy. 2 watery. 3 *said of language, work, etc* inaccurate, careless.

slosh — *verb* 1 *trans., intrans.* (*often* **slosh about** *or* **around**) to splash or cause to splash or spill noisily. 2 *slang* to strike with a heavy blow. — *noun* 1 the sound of splashing or spilling. 2 slush; a watery mess. 3 *slang* a heavy blow. [a form of SLUSH]

sloshed *adj. colloq.* drunk.

slot — *noun* 1 a small narrow rectangular opening into which something is fitted or inserted. 2 a time, place, or position within a schedule, eg of broadcasts or airport take-offs and landings. — *verb* (**slotted**, **slotting**) 1 (*also* **slot something in**) to fit or insert it, or place it in a slot. 2 to make a slot in. [from Old French *esclot*]

sloth *noun* 1 a herbivorous tree-dwelling mammal, belonging to the same order (Edentata) as armadillos and anteaters, and found in tropical forests of America. It has long slender limbs, and is noted for its very slow movements. 2 the desire to avoid all activity or exertion; laziness; indolence. [from Anglo-Saxon *slæwth*, from *slaw*, slow]

◇ Despite the fact that it belongs to the order Edentata (meaning 'without teeth'), the sloth has nine teeth on each side of its mouth. It uses its long curved claws, which resemble hooks, to hang from tree branches, and its hands and feet are covered with a fold of skin that joins the fingers and toes. Each of the body hairs is grooved and often contains algae, giving the animal a greenish appearance which provides very effective camouflage in the forest. Sloths feed on leaves and fruit, and include two-toed and three-toed species.

slothful *adj.* inactive, lazy.

slot machine a machine operated by inserting a coin in a slot, eg a vending machine or fruit machine.

slouch — *verb intrans.* to sit, stand, or walk with a tired or lazy drooping posture. — *noun* 1 such a posture. 2 *colloq.* (**no slouch at something**) a person who is able or competent in some respect: *she's no slouch at dancing.*

Slough POP (1992e) 103 000, an industrial town in Slough district, Berkshire, S England. It lies 30km/19mi W of central London. London Heathrow airport is nearby.

slough¹ *noun* 1 a mud-filled hollow. 2 an area of boggy land; a mire. 3 *literary* a state of deep and gloomy emotion: *in a slough of depression.* [from Anglo-Saxon *sloh*]

slough² — *noun* any part of an animal cast off or moulted, especially a snake's dead skin. — *verb* 1 to shed (eg a dead skin). 2 to cast off or dismiss (eg worries). [from Middle English *sloh*]

Slovakia *or* **Slovak Socialist Republic**, Czech **Slovenská** POP (1992e) 5.3m, a landlocked republic lying in E Europe. It is bounded to the N by Poland, E by the Ukraine, S by Hungary, SW by Austria, and W by the Czech Republic. AREA 49 035sq km/18 927sq mi. CAPITAL Bratislava. CHIEF TOWNS Košice, Banská Bystrica,

Presov. TIME ZONE GMT +1. CURRENCY the Slovak koruna. The population is mainly Slovak (86%) and Hungarian (11%) in origin; Christianity is the chief religion. OFFICIAL LANGUAGE Slovak. PHYSICAL DESCRIPTION the Tatra Mts in the N rise to 2 655m at Gerlachovsky. CLIMATE continental — hot in summer, cold in winter. HISTORY part of Great Moravia in the 9c, it belonged to the Magyar Empire from the 10c; became a province of Czechoslovakia in 1918; became an independent republic in 1993. GOVERNMENT a President is elected for five years by the legislative National Council; the Prime Minister and the Cabinet hold executive power. ECONOMY agriculture, especially cereals, wine, and fruit.

Slovakia

sloven *noun* a slovenly person.

Slovenia, Slovenian **Slovenija** POP (1993e) 2m, a mountainous republic in central Europe, bounded N by Austria, W by Italy, S by Croatia, and E by Hungary. AREA 20 251sq km/7 817sq mi. CAPITAL Ljubljana. CHIEF TOWNS Maribor, Kranj, Celje, Koper. TIME ZONE GMT +1. CURRENCY the tolar. Most of the population is of Slovenian origin: Roman Catholicism is the chief religion. OFFICIAL LANGUAGE Slovene. PHYSICAL DESCRIPTION the land is forested and mountainous, linked to Austria by a number of pass roads; it drops down towards the Adriatic coast; the chief rivers in the republic are the Sava and Drava. HISTORY settled by Slovenians in the 6c, it was later controlled by Slavs and Franks; it was part of the Austro-Hungarian Empire until 1918 when it joined with Croatia, Montenegro, Serbia, and Bosnia Herzegovina to form the Kingdom of Serbs, Croats, and Slovenes; renamed as Yugoslavia in 1929 and became a people's republic in 1946; full independence from Yugoslavia was achieved in 1991. GOVERNMENT the Prime Minister and Cabinet of Ministers hold executive power; legislative power is held by a bicameral National Assembly consisting of a State Chamber and a State Council. ECONOMY maize, wheat, sugar beet, potatoes; livestock; timber; lignite; textiles; vehicles; steel; coal; lead; mercury.

slovenliness *noun* being slovenly.

slovenly — *adj.* careless, untidy or dirty in appearance, habits or methods of working. — *adv.* in a slovenly manner.

slow — *adj.* 1 having little speed or pace; not moving fast or quickly. 2 taking a long time, or longer than usual or expected. 3 *said of a watch or clock* showing a time earlier than the correct time. 4 not quickly or easily learning, understanding or appreciating. 5 progressing at a boringly gentle pace: *a slow film.* 6 not allowing fast progress or movement: *traffic was slow / a golf course with slow greens.* 7 needing much provocation in order to do something: *slow to get angry.* 8 *said of business* slack. 9 *said of photographic film* needing a relatively long exposure time. — *adv.* in a slow manner. — *verb trans., intrans.* (*also* **slow down** *or* **up**) to reduce or cause to reduce speed, pace, or rate of progress. [from Anglo-Saxon *slaw*]

slowcoach *noun colloq.* a person who moves or works at a slow pace.

slowly *adv.* at a slow rate, in a slow way.

slow motion 1 a speed of movement in film or television that is much slower than real-life movement, created by increasing the speed at which the camera records the action. 2 an imitation of this in real-life movement.

slow-motion *adj.* having or using slow motion.

slowness *noun* being slow.

slow neutron *Physics* a neutron with a relatively low energy content, which can be captured by the nucleus of an atom, and is used to initiate various nuclear reactions, especially nuclear fission.

slow-worm *noun* a small legless Eurasian lizard with a snake-like body. [from Anglo-Saxon *slawyrm*; the first part is not related to SLOW but has been assimilated to it]

SLR *abbrev.* single-lens reflex. See CAMERA.

sludge *noun* 1 soft slimy mud. 2 muddy sediment. 3 sewage. 4 half-melted snow; slush. [probably from SLUSH]

sludgy *adj.* (**sludgier, sludgiest**) like or consisting of sludge.

slug¹ *noun* any of various terrestrial molluscs belonging to the same class (Gastropoda) as snails, but having a long fleshy body and little or no shell. Slugs are found in damp habitats worldwide, and many of them are garden pests. ◇ Slugs vary in length from 6 to 200mm, and the mantle (a thick layer of skin) that is present in snails is reduced to a small *saddle* on the back. Slugs are most active at night, or after rain, and most feed near ground level, although some species can climb trees. They are hermaphrodite, and there is usually a two-way exchange of sperm between mating pairs, each member of the pair subsequently laying eggs. Most slugs feed on decaying vegetation, but some eat the leaves or underground parts of growing plants, while others eat only fungi. Shelled slugs, which bear a small ear-shaped shell on the hind end of the body, feed on earthworms and other slugs.

slug² *noun* 1 *colloq.* a bullet. 2 *Printing* a solid line or section of metal type produced by a composing machine.

slug³ *colloq.* — *noun* a heavy blow. — *verb* (**slugged, slugging**) to strike with a heavy blow.

slug⁴ *noun colloq.* a large gulped mouthful of liquid, especially alcohol spirit.

sluggard *noun old use* a lazy, inactive person.

sluggish *adj.* 1 unenergetic; lazy; inactive. 2 less lively, active or responsive than usual: *the engine is a bit sluggish.*

sluice — *noun* 1 a channel or drain for water. 2 (*also* **sluice-gate**) a valve or sliding gate for controlling the flow of water in such a channel. 3 a trough for washing gold or other minerals out of sand, etc. 4 an act of washing down or rinsing. —

Slovenia

verb 1 to drain by means of a sluice. 2 to wash down or rinse by throwing water on. [from Old French *escluse*, from Latin *excludere*, to shut out]

slum — *noun* 1 a run-down, dirty, usually overcrowded house. 2 (*often* **slums**) an area of such housing. — *verb intrans.* (**slummed, slumming**) 1 to visit a socially deprived area, especially out of curiosity or for amusement. 2 to adopt the tastes or behaviour of members of a lower social class, out of pretentiousness.
— **slum it** *colloq., often facetious* to experience circumstances that are less affluent or more squalid than one is used to.

slumber *poetic* — *noun* sleep. — *verb intrans.* (**slumbered, slumbering**) to sleep. [from Middle English *slumeren*]

slumbering *adj.* sleeping.

slumberous *adj.* 1 inviting or causing sleep. 2 sleepy.

slummy *adj.* (**slummier, slummiest**) *colloq.* like a slum; run-down or squalid.

slump — *verb intrans.* 1 to drop or sink suddenly and heavily, eg with tiredness: *slumped into an armchair.* 2 *said of trade, etc* to decline suddenly and sharply. — *noun* a serious and usually long-term decline, eg in a nation's economy.

slung see SLING.

slunk see SLINK.

slur — *verb* (**slurred, slurring**) 1 *trans., intrans.* to pronounce (words) unclearly, eg through drunkenness. 2 to speak or write about very disparagingly. 3 to mention only briefly or deal with only superficially. 4 *Mus.* to sing or play as a flowing sequence without pauses. — *noun* 1 a disparaging remark intended to damage a reputation. 2 a slurred word or slurring way of speaking. 3 *Mus.* a flowing pauseless style of singing or playing.

slurp — *verb* to eat or drink noisily with a sucking action. — *noun* a slurping sound. [from Dutch *slurpen*, to sip audibly]

slurry *noun* (PL. **slurries**) 1 a runny mixture of solid particles and water, especially watery concrete. 2 liquid manure that is either treated to form fertilizer, or stored in a lagoon or tank from which it can be piped on to fields or distributed by tanker.

slush *noun* 1 half-melted snow. 2 any watery half-liquid substance. 3 sickly sentimentality.

slush fund a fund of money used for dishonest purposes, eg bribery, especially by a political party.

slushy *adj.* (**slushier, slushiest**) like or consisting of slush.

slut *noun derog.* 1 a woman who regularly engages in casual sex. 2 a prostitute. 3 an untidy or dirty woman.

sluttish *adj.* characteristic of a slut; dirty and untidy.

Sluys, Battle of a naval battle fought (1340) in the Zwyn estuary in Flanders, the first major English victory in the Hundred Years War. Edward III personally commanded the English fleet, which destroyed or captured all but 24 of the 200 French ships.

Sly, Christopher the coarse, drunken tinker in Shakespeare's *The Taming of the Shrew*, who is made to watch the play after being assured that he is really of noble standing.

sly *adj.* (**slyer, slyest** *or* **slier, sliest**) 1 clever; cunning. 2 secretive; secretively deceitful or dishonest. 3 playfully mischievous: *a sly smile.*
— **on the sly** *colloq.* secretly or furtively. [from Norse *slægr*]

slyly *or* **slily** *adv.* in a sly way.

SM *abbrev.* 1 sado-masochism. 2 sadomasochistic.

Sm *symbol Chem.* samarium.

smack¹ — *verb* 1 *trans.* to slap, especially with the hand. 2 *trans., intrans. colloq.* to hit loudly and heavily: *her head smacked against the wall.* 3 to part (the lips) loudly, with relish or in pleasant anticipation. — *noun* 1 an act, or the sound, of smacking. 2 a loud enthusiastic kiss. — *adv. colloq.* 1 directly and with force: *drove smack into the tree.* 2 precisely: *smack in the middle.* [from Old Dutch *smacken*]

smack² — *verb intrans.* (**smack of something**) 1 to have the flavour of it. 2 to have a suggestion or trace of it. — *noun* 1 taste; distinctive flavour. 2 a hint or trace. [from Anglo-Saxon *smæc*]

smack³ *noun* a small single-masted fishing boat. [from Dutch *smak*]

smack⁴ *noun slang* heroin.

smacker *noun* 1 *colloq.* a loud enthusiastic kiss. 2 *slang* a pound sterling or a dollar.

small — *adj.* 1 little in size or quantity. 2 little in extent, importance or worth; not great. 3 humble; unpretentious. 4 petty: *small-minded.* 5 young: *a small child.* 6 *said of a printed or written letter* lower-case; not capital. 7 humiliated: *feel small.* — *noun* 1 the narrow part, especially of the back. 2 (**smalls**) *colloq.* underclothes. — *adv.* 1 on a small scale. 2 into small pieces. [from Anglo-Saxon *smæl*]

small ads *colloq.* short advertisements in a newspaper, advertising items for sale, etc.

small arms hand-held firearms.

small beer something unimportant.

small change coins of little value.

small fry *colloq.* 1 (*sing., pl.*) a person or thing, or people or things, of little importance or influence. 2 (*pl.*) young children.

smallholder *noun* a person who farms a smallholding.

smallholding *noun* a small area of cultivated land, in the UK under 20 hectares in area, usually devoted to one aspect of farming, eg market gardening or raising goats; also, a general term for a small farm.

small hours (**the small hours**) the hours immediately after midnight.

small-minded *adj.* narrow-minded; pettyminded.

smallness *noun* being small.

smallpox *noun Medicine* a highly contagious viral disease, characterized by fever, vomiting, backache, and a rash that usually leaves permanent pitted scars (pocks) on the skin. Once responsible for millions of deaths, smallpox has been gradually eradicated by immunization programmes.

small print the details of a contract or other undertaking, often printed very small, especially when considered likely to contain unattractive conditions that the writer of the contract does not want to be noticed.

small screen (**the small screen**) television, as opposed to cinema.

small talk polite conversation about trivial matters.

small-time *adj.* operating on a small scale.

smarm — *verb* 1 to smooth or flatten (the hair) with an oily substance. 2 *intrans. colloq.* to be exaggeratedly and insincerely flattering or respectful. — *noun colloq.* exaggerated or insincere flattery.

smarmily *adv.* in a smarmy way.

smarminess *noun* being smarmy.

smarmy *adj.* (**smarmier, smarmiest**) *colloq.* 1 ingratiatingly flattering or respectful. 2 selfconsciously suave or charming.

smart — *adj.* 1 neat and well-dressed. 2 clever; astute; shrewd. 3 expensive and sophisticated: *a*

smart hotel. **4** *said of pain, etc* sharp and stinging. **5** brisk: *at a smart pace.* **6** computer-guided or electronically controlled: *a smart bomb.* **7** *colloq.* impressive; excellent. — *verb intrans.* **1** to feel or be the cause of a sharp stinging pain. **2** to feel or be the cause of acute irritation or distress. **3** *intrans.* to suffer harsh consequences or punishment. — *noun* a sharp stinging pain. — *adv.* in a smart manner.
— **look smart** to hurry up.
[from Anglo-Saxon *smeortan*]

smart alec *or* **smart aleck** *colloq.* a person who thinks himself or herself cleverer than others; a know-all.

smart-alecky *adj.* characteristic of a smart-alec.

smart card a plastic card like a bank card, fitted with a microprocessor (including a memory) instead of a magnetic strip, used in commercial transactions, telecommunications, etc.

smart drug a drug designed to enhance mental powers or perception.

smarten *verb trans., intrans.* (**smartened**, **smartening**) (*also* **smarten up**) to make or become smarter; to brighten up.

smartly *adv.* in a smart way; promptly, quickly.

smartness *noun* being smart.

smash — *verb* **1** *trans., intrans.* to break violently into pieces; to destroy or be destroyed in this way. **2** *trans., intrans.* to strike with violence, often causing damage; to burst with great force: *smashed his fist down on the table / smashed through the door.* **3** *colloq.* to break up or ruin completely: *smash an international drugs ring.* **4** to hit (a ball) with a smash. — *noun* **1** an act, or the sound, of smashing. **2** a powerful overhead stroke in racket sports. **3** *colloq.* a road traffic accident. **4** *colloq.* a smash hit. — *adv.* with a smashing sound. [imitative]

smash-and-grab *adj. colloq., said of a robbery* carried out by smashing a shop window and snatching the items on display.

smashed *adj. colloq.* extremely drunk.

smasher *noun colloq.* a person or thing very much liked or admired.

smash hit *colloq.* an overwhelming success, especially a song, film, play, etc.

smashing *adj. colloq.* excellent; splendid.

smash-up *noun colloq.* a violent road traffic accident.

smattering *noun* **1** a few scraps of knowledge. **2** a small amount scattered around. [from Middle English *smateren*, to rattle]

smear — *verb* **1** to spread (something sticky or oily) thickly over (a surface). **2** *trans., intrans.* to make or become blurred; to smudge. **3** to say or write abusively damaging things about (someone). — *noun* **1** a greasy mark or patch. **2** a damaging criticism or accusation; a slur. **3** an amount of a substance, especially of cervical tissue, placed on a slide for examination under a microscope. **4** *colloq.* a smear test. [from Anglo-Saxon *smeru*, fat, grease]

smear campaign a series of verbal or written attacks intended to defame and discredit an individual, group, or institution.

smear test an examination, under a microscope, of a small amount of tissue from a woman's cervix, to test for the presence of cervical cancer.

smeary *adj.* sticky, greasy; showing smears.

Smeaton, John (1724–92) English civil engineer, born in Austhorpe, near Leeds. He abandoned a law career to work as a scientific instrument-maker, and began to research the mechanics of waterwheels and windmills. He produced the novel design for the third Eddystone lighthouse, and improved the perfor-

mance of the atmospheric steam engine of Thomas Newcomen; he also engineered several important harbours and bridges.

smegma *noun* a thick white secretion produced by the glands of the foreskin of the penis. [from Greek *smegma*, soap]

smell — *noun* **1** the sense by which one becomes aware of the odour of things, located in the nose. **2** the quality perceived by this sense; (an) odour or scent. **3** an unpleasant odour. **4** an act of using this sense: *have a smell of this.* — *verb* (PAST TENSE AND PAST PARTICIPLE **smelled**, **smelt**) **1** to be aware of, or take in, the odour of. **2** (**smell of something**) to give off an odour of it. **3** *intrans.* to give off an unpleasant odour. **4** to be aware of by intuition; to recognize signs or traces of: *I smell a government cover-up.* **5** (**smell of something**) to show signs or traces of it: *an organization smelling of corruption.*
— **smell someone** *or* **something out** to track them down by smell, or as if by smell. [from Middle English *smel*]

smelliness *noun* being smelly.

smelling-salts *pl. noun* crystals of ammonium carbonate, whose strong sharp odour stimulates consciousness after fainting.

smelly *adj.* (**smellier**, **smelliest**) *colloq.* unpleasant-smelling.

smelt¹ *verb* to melt (ore) in order to separate out the metal it contains. [from Old German *smelten*]

smelt² see SMELL.

smelt³ *noun* (PL. **smelts**, **smelt**) any of various small silvery edible fish of the salmon family. [from Anglo-Saxon *smylt*]

smelter *noun* **1** a person whose work is smelting metal. **2** an industrial plant where smelting is done.

Smetana, Bedřich (1824–84) Czech composer, born in Litomyšl. He studied in Prague, and in 1848 opened a music school with the financial support of Franz Liszt. He conducted in Sweden (1856–9), and became conductor of the new National Theatre in Prague (1866), for which his operas were composed. His compositions, intensely national in character, include nine operas, notably *Prodaná nevěsta* (The Bartered Bride, 1866), and many chamber and orchestral works, including the series of symphonic poems *Má Vlast* (My Country, 1874–9).

smidgen *or* **smidgeon** *or* **smidgin** *noun colloq.* a very small amount: *add a smidgen of paprika.* [origin uncertain]

Smike the simple, illegitimate son of Ralph Nickleby in Charles Dickens's *Nicholas Nickleby.*

smile — *verb* **1** *intrans.* to turn up the corners of the mouth, often showing the teeth, usually as an expression of pleasure, favour or amusement. **2** (**smile at someone** *or* **something**) to react to them with such an expression. **3** to show with such an expression: *smiled his agreement.* **4** (**smile on someone** *or* **something**) to show favour towards someone. — *noun* an act or way of smiling. [from Middle English *smilen*]

Smiles, Samuel (1812–1904) Scottish writer and social reformer, born in Haddington, E Lothian. He settled as a surgeon in Leeds, but left medicine for journalism, edited the *Leeds Times* (1838–42), and became involved in railway companies until 1866. His main work was a guide to self-improvement, *Self-Help* (1859), with its short lives of great men and the admonition 'Do thou likewise'. He also wrote many biographical and moral books.

smirch — *verb* **1** to make dirty; to soil or stain. **2** to damage or sully (a reputation, etc); to besmirch. — *noun* **1** a stain. **2** a smear on a reputation. [from Old French *esmorcher*, to hurt]

smirk — *verb intrans.* to smile in a self-satisfied or foolish manner. — *noun* such a smile. [from Anglo-Saxon *smercian*]

smite *verb* (PAST TENSE **smote**; PAST PARTICIPLE **smitten**) *usually literary* **1** to strike or beat with a heavy blow or blows. **2** to kill. **3** to afflict. **4** to cause to fall immediately and overpoweringly in love: *not fail to be smitten by such beauty.* **5** *intrans.* to come suddenly and forcefully: *the king's authority smote down on him.* [from Anglo-Saxon *smitan*, to smear]

Smith, Adam (1723–90) Scottish economist and philosopher, born in Kirkcaldy, Fife. He became Professor of Logic at Glasgow in 1751, and became Professor of Moral Philosophy the following year. In 1776 he moved to London, where he published *An Inquiry into the Nature and Causes of the Wealth of Nations* (1776), the first major work of political economy. This examined in detail the consequences of economic freedom, such as division of labour, the function of markets, and the international implications of a *laissez-faire* economy.

Smith, Bessie (Elizabeth), known as the **Empress of the Blues** (1894–1937) US blues singer, born in Chattanooga, Tennessee. Raised in poverty in the US South, she ran away as a teenager with Ma Rainey's Rabbit Foot Minstrels, a black revue. After working in vaudeville and small theatres, she began recording with great success in 1923, and rose quickly to become an outstanding black artiste with her blues-based repertoire, vivacious stage presence, and magnificent voice.

Smith, Delia (1941–) English cookery writer and broadcaster. She began writing for the *Evening Standard* (1972–85), and published her first cookery book, *How to Cheat at Cooking*, in 1973. Her many television series and subsequent publications have attracted a large popular following, and by the time she presented *Delia Smith's Christmas* (television programme and book, 1990), she had sold five million copies of her cookery books. A more recent bestseller is *Delia Smith's Summer Collection* (1993).

Smith, Dodie, pseudonym **C L Anthony** (1896–1990) British dramatist, novelist, and theatre producer. She started as an actress but turned to writing and produced several plays including *Dear Octopus* (1938). She is best known for her children's book *The Hundred and One Dalmations* (1956).

Smith, Hamilton Othanel (1931–) US molecular biologist, born in New York City. Professor at Johns Hopkins University, he found that bacteria produce restriction enzymes which can split the DNA strand of invading virus particles so that they are inactivated. His work allowed new methods of genetic engineering and DNA structure determination. He shared the 1978 Nobel Prize for Physiology or Medicine with Werner Arber and Daniel Nathans.

Smith, Ian (Douglas) (1919–) Zimbabwean politician, and farmer, born in Selukwe. He fought in World War II, became an MP (1948) and in 1961 a founder of the Rhodesian Front. As Prime Minister of Rhodesia (1964–79), in 1965 he declared UDI (Unilateral Declaration of Independence) without African majority rule, which resulted in the imposition of increasingly severe economic sanctions and an intensive guerrilla war. He negotiated without success with various British governments. Following the Lancaster House Agreement and the setting up of an independent constitution, he was elected MP for the Republican Front. He remained a vigorous opponent of Robert Mugabe.

Smith, John (1580–1631) English adventurer, born in Willoughby, Lincolnshire. He fought in France and Hungary, where he was captured by the Turks and sold as a slave, but he escaped to Russia and joined an expedition to colonize Virginia (1607). Saved from a Native American tribe by the chief's daughter Pocahontas, his experience in dealing with the tribal people led to his being elected president of the colony

(1608–9). He wrote valuable accounts of his travels, and died in London.

Smith, John (1938–94) Scottish Labour politician. Called to the Scottish Bar in 1967, he was made a QC in 1983. He entered the House of Commons in 1970, and served in the administrations of Harold Wilson and James Callaghan, becoming Trade Secretary in 1978. In Opposition, he was Front Bench Spokesman on Trade, Energy, Employment, and Economic Affairs (1987–92). He succeeded Neil Kinnock as Labour Party Leader in 1992.

Smith, Joseph (1805–44) US religious leader, the founder of Mormonism, born in Sharon, Vermont. He was first 'called' as a prophet in 1820, was later told of a hidden gospel written on golden plates in 'reformed Egyptian', and on the night of 22 Sep 1827 the sacred records were apparently delivered into his hands on a hill near Palmyra, New York. The *Book of Mormon* (1830) contains a postulated history of America to the 5c of the Christian era, supposedly written by a prophet named Mormon. Smith was to be the instrument of the Church's re-establishment, and despite ridicule and hostility, the new 'Church of Jesus Christ of Latter-day Saints' (founded 1830) rapidly gained converts. He founded the Nauvoo community, Illinois (1840), where he allegedly practised polygamy ('spiritual wives'). Imprisoned for conspiracy, he was killed by a mob who broke into the jail where he and his brother Hyram were awaiting trial.

Smith, Dame Maggie (Margaret Nathalie) (1934–) English actress, born in Ilford, Essex. She made her stage début with the Oxford University Dramatic Society in a production of *Twelfth Night* (1952) and appeared in New York as one of the *New Faces of '56*. Gaining increasing critical esteem for her performances, she joined the National Theatre to act in *Othello* (1963), *Hay Fever* (1966), and *The Three Sisters* (1970) among others. Her tour de force in film was in *The Prime of Miss Jean Brodie* (1969), which gained her an Academy Award. Later stage work includes *Virginia* (1980) and Peter Shaffer's *Lettice and Lovage* (1987, written as a birthday present to her). Her selection of film roles shows a penchant for eccentric comedy and acid spinsters, and includes award-winning performances in *California Suite* (1978), *A Private Function* (1984, BAFTA Award for Best Actress), *A Room With a View* (1985), and *The Lonely Passion of Judith Hearne* (1987). In 1992 she was the Mother Superior in *Sister Act* and a wizened Wendy in *Hook*, and made a welcome return to the stage as Lady Bracknell in *The Importance of Being Earnest*.

Smith, Stevie, pseudonym of **Florence Margaret Smith** (1902–71) English poet and novelist, born in Hull, Yorkshire. She wrote three novels, (eg *Novel on Yellow Paper*, 1936), but made her reputation principally as a humorous poet on serious themes. Her works of poetry, which are often illustrated by her comic line-drawings, include *A Good Time Was Had By All* (1937), and *Not Waving but Drowning* (1957).

Smith, Tommy (Thomas) (1967–) Scottish jazz musician, composer and bandleader, born in Luton, Bedfordshire, of Scottish parents. Brought up in Edinburgh, as a teenage prodigy he made television and radio performances with internationally known musicians, as well as two records. After studying in the USA, he brought his own quartet Forward Motion to play in Europe, and in 1986 joined vibraphone player Gary Burton's quintet. Thereafter based in Scotland, he plays wind synthesizer as well as saxophone, and leads a variety of groups in jazz and jazz-related settings.

Smith, William (1769–1839) English civil engineer and geologist, born in Churchill, Oxfordshire. Engineer to the Somerset Coal Canal (1794–9), his survey work introduced him to a variety of rock sequences of different ages; he used fossils to identify strata and fix their position in the succession. He settled in London in 1804, and is often regarded as the father of English geology.

smith *noun, combining form* **1** a person who makes articles in (a particular) metal: *silversmith*. **2** a blacksmith. **3** a person who makes skilful use of something: *wordsmith*. [from Anglo-Saxon *smith*]

smithereens *pl. noun colloq.* tiny fragments: *smashed it to smithereens*. [from Irish Gaelic *smidirín*, diminutive of *smiodar*, fragment]

Smithfield an area just outside the walls of the City of London, in former times the scene of tournaments, trials, fairs, and cattle markets. It is noted for its meat market.

Smithsonian Institution a research institution in Washington, DC, USA. It was endowed in 1826 by the English scientist James Smithson (1765–1829), established by an Act of Congress in 1846, and opened in 1855. It administers a number of art, history, and science museums, scientific research centres, and is the parent organization of several autonomous artistic and academic establishments.

smithy *noun* (PL. **smithies**) a blacksmith's workshop.

smitten past participle of SMITE. — *adj.* in love; obsessed.

SMMT *abbrev.* Society of Motor Manufacturers and Traders.

smock *noun* **1** any loose shirt-like garment worn, eg by artists, over other clothes for protection, especially one slipped over the head. **2** a woman's long loose-fitting blouse. **3** *Hist.* a loose-fitting overall of coarse linen worn by farmworkers. [from Anglo-Saxon *smoc*]

smocking *noun* decorative stitching used on gathered or tucked material.

smog *noun* fog mixed with smoke and fumes. [from SMOKE + FOG]

smoggy *adj.* (**smoggier**, **smoggiest**) like or full of smog.

smoke — *noun* **1** a visible cloud given off by a burning substance, and consisting of tiny particles of carbon dispersed in a gas or a mixture of gases, eg air. **2** visible fumes or vapours. **3** *colloq.* the act of or time spent smoking tobacco. **4** *colloq.* a cigarette or cigar. — *verb* **1** *intrans.* to give off smoke or visible fumes or vapours. **2** *trans., intrans.* to inhale and then exhale the smoke from burning tobacco or other substances in a cigarette, cigar, or pipe, especially as a habit. **3** to preserve or flavour food by exposing it to smoke. — **go up in smoke 1** to be completely destroyed by fire. **2** *said of plans, etc* to be ruined completely; to come to nothing. **the smoke** or **big smoke** *colloq.* the nearby big city; a country's capital city. **smoke someone** or **something out 1** to drive an animal into the open by filling its burrow with smoke. **2** to uncover someone or something by persistent searching or investigation. [from Anglo-Saxon *smoca*]

smoked *adj.* **1** cured or treated with smoke. **2** darkened by smoke.

smokeless *adj.* **1** *said of a fuel* giving off little or no smoke when burned, eg coke. **2** *said of an area* **a** in which the use of smoke-producing fuel is prohibited. **b** in which tobacco-smoking is prohibited.

smoker *noun* **1** a person who smokes tobacco products. **2** a railway carriage in which tobacco-smoking is permitted.

smokescreen *noun* **1** a cloud of smoke used to conceal the movements of troops, etc. **2** anything said or done to hide or deceive.

smokestack *noun* **1** a tall industrial chimney. **2** a funnel on a ship or steam train.

smokiness *noun* being smoky.

smoking — *noun* **1** the practice of inhaling the fumes from burning cigarettes or other forms of tobacco. **2** a process used to preserve and improve the flavour of some foods (eg ham, some cheeses), which are exposed to wood smoke (usually from oak or ash) for long periods. — *adj.* in which tobacco-smoking is allowed.
◇ Cigarette smoking is addictive, and is known to be a causative factor in the development of several diseases, including lung cancer, throat cancer, and heart and respiratory disorders. The risk of lung cancer increases with the number of cigarettes smoked per day, and in a number of countries there have been anti-smoking advertising campaigns and a ban on the advertising of tobacco products on television. Cigarette packets and press advertisements also carry government health warnings.

smoky *adj.* (**smokier**, **smokiest**) **1** giving out much or excessive smoke. **2** filled with (especially tobacco) smoke. **3** having a smoked flavour. **4** hazy, especially in colour: *smoky blue*. **5** made dirty by smoke.

Smolensk POP (1991e) 350 000, the river-port capital of Smolensk oblast, W central Russia, lying on the upper R Dnieper. HISTORY in the 9c it was the chief town of the large Slav tribe of Krivichi; part of Russia from 1654; severely damaged during World War II. NOTABLE FEATURE Cathedral of the Assumption (12c).

Smollett, Tobias (George) (1721–71) Scottish novelist, born in Cardross, Dunbartonshire. He settled in London as a surgeon in 1744, turned to writing, and achieved success with his first works, the picaresque novels *The Adventures of Roderick Random* (1748) and *The Adventures of Peregrine Pickle* (1751). He spent several years in journal editing, translating, and writing historical and travel works, and retired to Italy in 1768. His final work was the epistolary novel *Humphry Clinker* (1771).

smolt *noun* a young salmon migrating from fresh water to the sea. [from Scot. *smolt*]

smooch *colloq.* — *verb intrans.* **1** to kiss and cuddle. **2** to dance slowly in an embrace. — *noun* a period of smooching.

smoochy *adj.* (**smoochier**, **smoochiest**) *said of music* sentimental, romantic.

smooth — *adj.* **1** having an even regular surface; not rough, coarse, bumpy or wavy. **2** having few or no lumps; of even texture. **3** free from problems or difficulties: *a smooth journey*. **4** characterized by steady movement and a lack of jolts: *a smooth ferry crossing*. **5** not sharp or bitter: *a smooth sherry*. **6** very elegant or charming, especially self-consciously or insincerely so. — *verb* **1** (*also* **smooth something down** *or* **out**) to make it smooth. **2** (*usually* **smooth over something**) to cause a difficulty, etc to seem less serious or important. **3** to make easier: *smooth the way to promotion*. — *adv.* smoothly: *a smooth-running system*. — *noun* the easy, pleasurable, or trouble-free part or aspect: *take the rough with the smooth*. [from Anglo-Saxon *smoth*]

smoothie *or* **smoothy** *noun* (PL. **smoothies**) *colloq.* a very elegant or charming person, especially one self-consciously or insincerely so.

smoothly *adv.* in a smooth way.

smooth muscle *Anat.* see INVOLUNTARY MUSCLE.

smoothness *noun* being smooth.

smooth snake a harmless European snake having smooth scales and a dark horizontal line on the side of the head. It lives on dry heathland or open woodland, and feeds mainly on lizards.

smooth-talking *or* **smooth-tongued** *adj.* **1** exaggeratedly and insincerely flattering. **2** charmingly persuasive.

smorgasbord *noun* an assortment of hot and cold savoury dishes served as a buffet. [from

Swedish *smörgåsbord*, from *smörgås*, open sandwich + *bord*, table]

smote see SMITE.

smother *verb* (**smothered, smothering**) **1** *trans., intrans.* to kill with or die from lack of air, especially with an obstruction over the mouth and nose; to suffocate. **2** to extinguish (a fire) by cutting off the air supply, eg by throwing a blanket over it. **3** to cover with a thick layer: *bread smothered with jam.* **4** to give an oppressive or stifling amount to: *smothered the children with love.* **5** to suppress or contain (eg laughter). [from Middle English *smorther*, from Anglo-Saxon *smorian*]

smoulder — *verb intrans.* (**smouldered, smouldering**) **1** to burn slowly or without flame. **2** to linger on in a suppressed state: *smouldering anger.* — *noun* a smouldering fire or emotion. [from Middle English *smolder*]

smudge — *noun* **1** a mark or blot spread by rubbing. **2** a faint or blurred shape, eg an object seen from afar. — *verb* **1** to make a smudge on or of. **2** *intrans.* to become a smudge.

smudgy *adj.* (**smudgier, smudgiest**) smudged.

smug *adj.* (**smugger, smuggest**) arrogantly pleased with oneself; self-satisfied. [from German dialect *smuck*, neat]

smuggle *verb* **1** to take (goods) into or out of a country secretly and illegally, eg to avoid paying duty. **2** to bring or take secretly, usually breaking a rule or restriction. [from German dialect *smuggeln*]

smuggler *noun* a person who smuggles.

smuggling *noun* illegal import or export; conveying illegally.

smugly *adv.* in a smug way.

smugness *noun* being smug.

smut — *noun* **1** soot. **2** a speck of dirt or soot. **3** mildly obscene language, pictures or images. **4** any of a group of parasitic fungi, some of which cause a serious disease of cereal crops such as wheat, maize, and oats, characterized by the appearance of masses of black spores, resembling soot, on the leaves and other plant surfaces. **5** the disease caused by such a fungus, which may incur serious economic losses as it affects important cereal crops such as wheat, maize, and oats. — *verb* (**smutted, smutting**) to dirty or affect with smut. [from Middle English *smotten*, to stain]

Smuts, Jan (Christian) (1870–1950) South African general and statesman, born in Malmesbury, Cape Colony. He became a lawyer, fought in the second Boer War (1899–1902), and entered the House of Assembly in 1907. He held several Cabinet posts, led campaigns against the Germans in SW Africa and Tanganyika, was a member of the Imperial War Cabinet in World War I, and succeeded Louis Botha as Prime Minister (1919–24). He was a significant figure at Versailles, and was instrumental in the founding of the League of Nations. As Minister of Justice under Hertzog, his coalition with the Nationalists in 1934 produced the United Party, and he became premier again (1939–48).

smuttiness *noun* being smutty.

smutty *adj.* (**smuttier, smuttiest**) **1** dirtied by smut. **2** mildly obscene.

Smyrna see IZMIR.

Smythe, Pat see KOECHLIN-SMYTHE, PAT.

Sn *symbol Chem.* tin.

snack *noun* a light meal quickly taken, or a bite to eat between meals. [perhaps from Old Dutch *snacken*, to snap]

snack bar a café, kiosk, or counter serving snacks.

snaffle — *noun* a simple bridle-bit for a horse. — *verb* **1** to fit (a horse) with a snaffle. **2** *colloq.* to take sneakily or without permission.

snag — *noun* **1** a problem or drawback. **2** a sharp or jagged edge on which clothes, etc could get caught. **3** a hole or tear in clothes, etc caused by such catching. **4** a part of a tree submerged in water, hazardous to navigation. — *verb* (**snagged, snagging**) to catch or tear on a snag. [from perhaps Norse *snagi*, peg]

snail *noun* any of over 80 000 species of mollusc belonging to the same class (Gastropoda) as slugs, but carrying a coiled or conical shell on its back, into which the whole body can be withdrawn for safety. Snails are found worldwide and include marine, freshwater, and terrestrial species.

— **at a snail's pace** extremely slowly. [from Anglo-Saxon *snæl*]

◇ The snail has a soft body with a muscular foot on which it creeps forward with a gliding movement. The front end of the body merges into the head, which bears one or two pairs of tentacles, a pair of eyes (frequently at the tips of the longer tentacles), and a horny tongue or *radula* bearing rasping teeth. The part of the body that remains within the shell is covered with a layer of thick skin called the *mantle*, and the shell is formed by certain parts of this structure. Land snails tend to flourish on soils rich in calcium, which they need for their shells. Most of them are herbivores, but there are carnivorous species which feed on earthworms.

snake — *noun* **1** any of about 2 300 species of a carnivorous reptile having a long narrow body covered with scaly skin, and belonging to the same order (Squamata) as lizards, but differing from lizards in that it lacks limbs, moveable eyelids, or visible ears. Snakes are found in all parts of the world except the polar regions, New Zealand, Hawaii, and Ireland. **2** any long and flexible or winding thing or shape. **3** *colloq.* (**snake in the grass**) a treacherous person; a friend revealed to be an enemy. — *verb intrans.* to move windingly or follow a winding course. [from Anglo-Saxon *snaca*]

◇ Snakes have a long deeply forked tongue which they use as a sense organ to taste their surroundings and to follow scent trails (they have no sense of hearing). They feed on small mammals, lizards, birds, eggs, insects, and fish, which they swallow whole. When a snake swallows large prey, it can 'unhinge' its jaws, allowing an animal more than twice the diameter of the snake's head to be swallowed. Only about 300 species are venomous, and have poison glands which release venom into hollow or grooved teeth or *fangs*, which they use to inject venom into their prey when they bite. Most snakes travel by side-to-side movements of the body, gliding forwards as their sides press against any small projections in the ground. Some species burrow underground, many live on the ground, and some climb trees or swim in fresh or salt water. Most snakes lay eggs, but a few species give birth to live young.

snakebite *noun* **1** the wound or poisoned condition caused by the bite of a venomous snake. **2** *colloq.* a drink of cider and beer or lager in equal measures.

snake-charmer *noun* a street entertainer who seemingly induces snakes to perform rhythmical movements, especially by playing music.

Snake River a river in NW USA. It is the longest tributary of the Columbia River, with a total length of c.1 600km/1 000mi. Rising in NW Wyoming, it flows through Idaho (via the Snake R Plain) along part of the Oregon–Idaho and Washington–Idaho borders into Washington. It joins the Columbia R near Pasco. Its major tributaries are the Bruneau, Boise, Owyhee, Grande Ronde, Clearwater, and Palouse. Snake R, which is used for irrigation and hydroelectricity, contains several gorges, the largest being Hell's Canyon.

snakes and ladders a game played with counters and dice on a board marked with an ascending path on which ladders allow short cuts

to the goal and snakes force one to go back towards the beginning.

snakily *adv.* in a snaky way, like a snake.

snaky *adj.* (**snakier, snakiest**) **1** like a snake, especially long, thin, and flexible or winding. **2** treacherous or cruelly deceitful.

snap — *verb* (**snapped, snapping**) **1** *trans., intrans.* to break suddenly and cleanly with a sharp cracking noise: *snapped the stick over his knee.* **2** *trans., intrans.* to move quickly and forcefully with a sharp sound: *the lid snapped shut.* **3** *intrans.* (**snap at something**) to make a biting or grasping movement towards it. **4** (**snap at someone**) to speak abruptly with anger or impatience. **5** *colloq.* to take a photograph of, especially spontaneously and with simple equipment. **6** *intrans. colloq.* to lose one's senses or self-control suddenly. — *noun* **1** the act or sound of snapping. **2** *colloq.* a photograph, especially taken spontaneously and with simple equipment. **3** a catch or other fastening that closes with a snapping sound. **4** a crisp biscuit or savoury. **5** (*also* **cold snap**) a sudden brief period of cold weather. **6** a card game in which all the cards played are collected by the first player to shout 'snap' whenever matching cards are laid down by consecutive players. — *interj.* **1** the word shouted in the card game. **2** the word used to highlight any matching pair. — *adj.* taken or made spontaneously, without long consideration: *a snap decision.* — *adv.* with a snapping sound.

— **snap one's fingers 1** to make a short loud snapping sound by flicking one's fingers sharply, usually to attract attention. **2** to show contempt or defiance.

snap out of it *colloq.* to bring oneself out of a state or condition, eg of sulking or depression.

snap something up to acquire or seize it eagerly: *snapped up the opportunity.* [probably from Dutch *snappen*]

snapdragon *noun* an antirrhinum, a garden plant whose flower, when pinched, opens and closes like a mouth.

snapper *noun* a deep-bodied fish that is widespread and locally common in tropical seas, so called because it has long conical front teeth and highly mobile jaws. Some species are a valuable food fish.

snappily *adv.* in a snappy way, curtly.

snappiness *noun* being snappy.

snappy *adj.* (**snappier, snappiest**) **1** irritable; inclined to snap. **2** smart and fashionable: *a snappy dresser.* **3** lively: *at a snappy tempo.*

— **make it snappy**! *colloq.* hurry up!; be quick about it!

snapshot *noun* a photograph, especially taken spontaneously and with simple equipment.

snare — *noun* **1** an animal trap, especially one with a string or wire noose to catch the animal's foot. **2** anything that traps or entangles. **3** the set of wires fitted to a snare drum. — *verb* to trap or entangle in, or as if in, a snare. [from Anglo-Saxon *sneare*]

snare drum a medium-sized drum sitting horizontally, with a set of wires fitted to its underside that rattle sharply when the drum is struck.

snarl¹ — *verb* **1** *intrans. said of an animal* to growl angrily, showing the teeth. **2** *trans., intrans.* to speak or say aggressively in anger or irritation. — *noun* **1** an act of snarling. **2** a snarling sound or facial expression.

snarl² — *noun* **1** a knotted or tangled mass. **2** a confused or congested situation or state. — *verb trans., intrans.* (*also* **snarl up**) to make or become knotted, tangled, confused, or congested. [related to SNARE]

snarl-up *noun colloq.* any muddled or congested situation, especially a traffic jam.

snatch — *verb* **1** to seize or grab suddenly. **2** *intrans.* to make a sudden grabbing movement.

3 to pull suddenly and forcefully: *snatched her hand away*. **4** *colloq.* to take or have as soon as the opportunity arises: *snatch a bite to eat.* — *noun* **1** an act of snatching. **2** a fragment overheard or remembered: *a few snatches of the old song.* **3** a brief period: *snatches of rest between long shifts.* **4** *colloq.* a robbery. [from Middle English *snacchen*]

snazzily *adv.* in a snazzy way.

snazzy *adj.* (**snazzier, snazziest**) *colloq.* fashionably smart or elegant.

SNCF *abbrev.* Société Nationale des Chemins de Fer Français (French) French national railways.

Snead, Sam(uel) Jackson, also called **Slammin' Sam** (1912–) US golfer, born in Hot Springs, Virginia. He turned professional in 1934, and was the winner of a record 84 tournaments on the US Professional Golfers Association (PGA) Tour between 1936 and 1965. He won the British Open in 1946, the US PGA championship in 1942, 1949, and 1951, and the US Masters in 1949, 1952, and 1954.

sneak — *verb* **1** *intrans.* to move or go quietly and avoiding notice. **2** to bring or take secretly, especially breaking a rule or prohibition: *sneaked a girl into his room / sneak a look at the letter.* **3** *intrans. colloq.* to inform about someone. — *noun colloq.* a person who sneaks; a tell-tale. [perhaps from Anglo-Saxon *snican*, to creep]

sneakers *pl. noun esp. North Amer., esp. US* sports shoes; training shoes.

sneakily *adv.* in a sneaky way.

sneaking *adj., said of a feeling, etc* slight but not easy to suppress.

sneak thief a thief who enters premises through unlocked doors or windows, without breaking in.

sneaky *adj.* (**sneakier, sneakiest**) done or operating with secretive unfairness or dishonesty; underhand.

sneer — *verb* **1** *intrans.* to show scorn or contempt, especially by drawing the top lip up at one side. **2** *trans.* to say scornfully or contemptuously. — *noun* an expression of scorn or contempt made with a raised lip, or otherwise.

sneering *adj.* contemptuous, scornful.

sneeze — *verb intrans.* to blow air out through the nose suddenly, violently, and involuntarily, especially because of irritation in the nostrils. — *noun* an act or the sound of sneezing.
— **not to be sneezed at** *colloq.* not to be disregarded or overlooked.
[from Anglo-Saxon *fnesan*]

Snell, Willebrod van Roijen, Latin **Snellius** (1580–1626) Dutch mathematician, born in Leiden. Professor at Leiden, he discovered the law of refraction named after him, which relates the angles of incidence and refraction of a ray of light passing between two media of different refractive index.

Śniardwy the largest lake in Poland. AREA 114sq km/44sq mi; depth 23m. It is situated in Suwałki voivodship, in the NE part of the country.

snick — *noun* **1** a small cut; a nick. **2** *Cricket* a glancing contact with the edge of the bat. — *verb* **1** to make a small cut in. **2** *Cricket* to hit with a snick.

snicker same as SNIGGER.

snide *adj.* expressing criticism or disapproval in an indirect way intended to offend.

sniff — *verb* **1** *intrans.* to draw in air through the nose in short sharp bursts, eg when crying. **2** *trans., intrans.* (**sniff something** or **sniff at something**) to smell it in this way. **3** to inhale the fumes from (a dangerous or addictive substance). — *noun* an act or the sound of sniffing.
— **not to be sniffed at** *colloq.* not to be disregarded or overlooked: *an offer not to be sniffed at.*

sniff someone or **something out** to discover or detect them by, or as if by, the sense of smell. [imitative]

sniffer dog a dog specially trained to seek out or locate illicit or dangerous substances (eg illegal drugs, explosives, etc) by smell.

sniffily *adv.* in a sniffy way.

sniffle — *verb intrans.* to sniff repeatedly, eg because of having a cold. — *noun* **1** an act or the sound of sniffling. **2** (*also* **sniffles**) *colloq.* a slight cold.

sniffy *adj.* (**sniffier, sniffiest**) *colloq.* **1** contemptuous or disdainful. **2** sniffing repeatedly, or feeling that one wants to, because of having a cold.

snifter *noun slang* a drink of alcohol, especially alcoholic spirit; a tipple or dram. [from dialect *snift*, to sniff]

snigger — *verb intrans.* (**sniggered, sniggering**) to laugh quietly in a foolish or mocking way. — *noun* such a laugh. [imitative]

snip — *verb* (**snipped, snipping**) to cut, especially with a single quick action or actions with scissors. — *noun* **1** an act or the action of snipping. **2** a small piece snipped off. **3** a small cut or notch. **4** *colloq.* a bargain. **5** *colloq.* a certainty; a thing easily done. [from Dutch *snippen*]

snipe — *noun* **1** a marshland wading-bird with a long straight bill. **2** a quick verbal attack or criticism. — *verb intrans.* (**snipe at someone**) **1** to shoot at them from a hidden position. **2** to criticize them bad-temperedly. [from Middle English *snipe*]

sniper *noun* a person who shoots from a concealed position.

snippet *noun* a scrap, eg of information. [see SNIP]

snitch *slang* — *noun* **1** the nose. **2** an informer. — *verb* **1** *intrans.* to betray others; to inform. **2** *trans.* to steal; to pilfer.

snitcher *noun slang* an informer.

snivel — *verb intrans.* (**snivelled, snivelling**) **1** to whine or complain tearfully. **2** to have a runny nose. — *noun* an act of snivelling. [from Anglo-Saxon *snofl*, mucus]

SNO *abbrev.* **1** Scottish National Orchestra (now RSNO). **2** Scottish National Opera.

snob *noun* **1** a person who places too high a value on social status, admiring those higher up the social ladder and despising those lower down. **2** a person who judges a thing solely according to the values of those people regarded as socially or intellectually superior: *a wine snob.*

snobbery *noun* **1** snobbishness. **2** snobbish behaviour.

snobbish *adj.* characteristic of a snob.

snobbishness *noun* being snobbish.

snobby *adj.* (**snobbier, snobbiest**) snobbish.

snog *slang* — *verb intrans.* (**snogged, snogging**) to kiss and cuddle. — *noun* a kiss and cuddle.

snood *noun* **1** a pouch of netting or fabric worn by women on the back of the head, to keep hair in a bundle. **2** a hood formed from a piece of woollen material, worn as a fashion garment. [from Anglo-Saxon *snod*]

snook
— **cock a snook at someone** *colloq.* **1** to put the thumb to the nose and wave the fingers at them, as a gesture of contempt or defiance. **2** to express open contempt for them.

snooker — *noun* **1** a game in which long leather-tipped sticks are used to force a white ball to knock coloured balls into holes on the corners and sides of a large cloth-covered table. **2** in this game, a position in which the path between the white ball and the target ball is obstructed by another ball. — *verb* (**snookered, snookering**) **1**

in snooker, to force (an opponent) to attempt to hit an obstructed target ball. **2** *colloq.* to thwart (a person or plan).

snoop — *verb intrans.* to go about inquisitively; to pry. — *noun* **1** an act of snooping. **2** a person who snoops. [from Dutch *snoepen*, to eat or steal]

snooper *noun* a person who snoops.

snootily *adv.* in a snooty way.

snootiness *noun* being snooty.

snooty *adj.* (**snootier, snootiest**) *colloq.* haughty; snobbish.

snooze — *verb intrans.* to sleep lightly; to doze. — *noun* a period of light sleeping, especially when brief; a nap.

snore — *verb intrans.* to breathe heavily and with a snorting sound while sleeping. — *noun* an act or the sound of snoring. [imitative]

snorkel — *noun* **1** a rigid tube through which air from above the surface of water can be drawn into the mouth while one is swimming just below the surface. **2** a set of tubes on a submarine extended above the surface of the sea to take in air and release exhaust gases. — *verb intrans.* (**snorkelled, snorkelling**) to swim with a snorkel. [from German *Schnorchel*]

Snorri Sturluson (1179–1241) Icelandic poet and historian, born in Hvammur. In 1215 he was elected supreme judge of the island, but later incurred the ill-will of King Haakon, who had him murdered. His main works were the *Prose Edda* and the *Heimskringla*, a series of sagas about the Norwegian kings up to 1177.

snort — *verb* **1** *intrans. said especially of animals* to force air violently and noisily out through the nostrils; to make a similar noise while taking air in. **2** *trans., intrans.* to speak or say in this way, especially expressing contempt or anger. **3** *slang* to inhale (a powdered drug, especially cocaine) through the nose. — *noun* **1** an act or the sound of snorting. **2** *colloq.* a small drink of alcoholic spirit. **3** *slang* an amount of a powdered drug inhaled in one breath. [from Middle English *snorten*]

snot *noun colloq.* **1** *coarse slang* mucus of the nose. **2** *derog.* a contemptible person. [from Anglo-Saxon *gesnot*]

snottily *adv. colloq.* in a snotty way.

snottiness *noun colloq.* being snotty.

snotty *adj.* (**snottier, snottiest**) *colloq.* **1** *coarse slang* covered or dripping with nasal mucus: *snotty-nosed kids.* **2** haughty; having or showing contempt. **3** *derog.* contemptible; worthless: *I don't want your snotty advice.*

snout *noun* **1** the projecting nose and mouth parts of certain animals, eg the pig. **2** *colloq.* the human nose. **3** any projecting part. [from Old German *snut*]

Snow, C(harles) P(ercy) Snow, 1st Baron (1905–80) English novelist and physicist, born in Leicester. He was a Fellow (1930–50) of, and a tutor (1935–45) at, Christ's College, Cambridge, and published his first work in 1932. His major works include a cycle of novels which portray English life from 1920 onwards, starting with *Strangers and Brothers* (1940), and including *The Masters* (1951), *The New Men* (1954), and *Corridors of Power* (1964). His controversial *Two Cultures* (Rede lecture, 1959) discussed the dichotomy between science and literature and his belief in closer contact between them.

Snow, John (1813–58) English anaesthetist and epidemiologist, born in York. He practised in London from 1836, and during severe cholera outbreaks traced the cause to contaminated water supplies. Also a pioneer anaesthetist, he did fundamental experimental work on ether and chloroform, and devised apparatus to administer anaesthetics.

snow — *noun* **1** frozen water vapour falling to the ground in soft white flakes, or lying on the ground as a soft white mass. **2** a fall of this: *heavy snows*. **3** *colloq.* flickering white speckles on a television screen caused by interference or a poor signal. **4** *slang* cocaine. — *verb intrans., said of snow* to fall.

— **be snowed under** be overwhelmed with work, etc.

snow someone in *or* **up** to bury or block them with snow.

[from Anglo-Saxon *snaw*]

Snowball an idealistic character, representing Trotsky, who is driven out by Napoleon in George Orwell's *Animal Farm*.

snowball — *noun* a small mass of snow pressed hard together, used by children as a missile. — *verb* **1** *trans., intrans.* to throw snowballs (at). **2** *intrans.* to develop or increase rapidly and uncontrollably.

snowberry *noun* (PL. **snowberries**) *Bot.* **1** a N American shrub (*Symphoricarpos albus*) of the honeysuckle family. **2** a white berry of this shrub.

snow-blind *adj.* affected by snow blindness.

snow blindness severely (but temporarily) impaired eyesight caused by prolonged exposure of the eyes to bright sunlight reflected by snow.

snowboard — *noun* a board resembling a wheel-less skateboard, used on snow. — *verb intrans.* to ski on a snowboard.

snowboarding *noun* the sport of skiing on a snowboard.

snowbound *adj.* shut in or prevented from travelling because of heavy falls of snow.

snow bunting a black-and-white bunting of Arctic regions, a winter visitor in Britain. In summer, it is partly tawny.

snowcap *noun* a cap of snow, as on the polar regions or a mountain-top.

snow-capped *adj., said especially of mountains* with a covering of snow on the top.

Snowdon, Anthony Charles Robert Armstrong-Jones, 1st Earl of (1930–) English photographer and designer, born in London. He was married to Princess Margaret from 1960 to 1978 and was created Earl in 1961. A freelance photojournalist since 1951, he became a *Vogue* photographer in 1954. His portraits of famous people often capture unusual facets of character. He also designed the Aviary of the London Zoo (1965), and has devoted much effort to recording the plight of the handicapped, both in photographic studies and in television documentaries.

Snowdon, Welsh **Yr Wyddfa** a mountain in Gwynedd, the highest point in Wales. It has five peaks and rises to 1 085m; a rack railway runs from Llanberis to the main peak. It is the major feature of Snowdonia National Park.

Snowdonia a national park in Gwynedd, N Wales, established in 1951. It is characterized by rugged mountains and deep valleys. NOTABLE FEATURE Snowdon (the highest peak in England and Wales). AREA 2 140sq km/826sq mi.

snowdrift *noun* a bank of snow blown together by the wind.

snowdrop *noun* a European plant of the daffodil family producing small white drooping flowers in early spring.

snowfall *noun* **1** a fall of snow. **2** an amount of fallen snow.

snowflake *noun* any of the single small feathery clumps of crystals of frozen water vapour that snow is made up of.

snow goose a white Arctic American goose with black-tipped wings.

snow leopard, a large wild cat, now an endangered species, with long soft creamy or pale-grey fur patterned with black rosette spots,

found in the mountains of central Asia. — Also called *ounce*.

snowline *noun* the level or height on a mountain or other upland area above which there is a permanent covering of snow, or where snow accumulates seasonally.

snowman *noun* a crude human figure made of packed snow.

snowmobile *noun* a motorized vehicle, on skis or tracks, for travelling on snow.

snowplough *noun* **1** a large shovel-like device for clearing snow from roads or tracks. **2** a vehicle or train fitted with this.

snowshoe *noun* either of a pair of racket-like frameworks strapped to the feet for walking over deep snow.

Snow White and the Seven Dwarfs a US film directed by Walt Disney (1937). It is an animated fairy tale about a girl taking refuge from her wicked stepmother in the dwarfs' forest home until a Prince Charming ultimately rescues her.

snowy *adj.* (**snowier, snowiest**) **1** abounding or covered with snow. **2** white like snow. **3** pure.

Snowy Mountains Scheme in SE Australia, a construction project carried out 1949–72, first proposed in 1881. The object of the Scheme was to divert the Snowy River inland into the Murrumbidgee River and to build dams and power stations to provide hydroelectricity and irrigation.

snowy owl *Zool.* an owl native to northern regions of the N hemisphere, that inhabits tundra, marshes, and Arctic islands, and is so called because it has mainly white plumage. It hunts during the day and feeds on mammals and birds up to the size of Arctic hares and ducks. It nests on the ground.

SNP *abbrev.* Scottish National Party.

Snr *or* **snr** *abbrev.* senior.

snub — *verb* (**snubbed, snubbing**) to insult by openly ignoring, rejecting, or otherwise showing contempt. — *noun* an act of snubbing. — *adj., said of a nose* short and flat. [from Norse *snubba*, to scold]

snuff[1] — *noun* powdered tobacco for inhaling through the nose. — *verb intrans.* to take snuff. [from Old Dutch *snuffen*, to snuffle]

snuff[2] — *verb* **1** (*also* **snuff something out**) to extinguish a candle. **2** to snip off the burnt part of the wick of (a candle or lamp). **3** (*also* **snuff something out**) to put an end to it: *tried to snuff out all opposition.* — *noun* the burnt part of the wick of a lamp or candle.

— **snuff it** *slang* to die.

[from Middle English *snoffe*]

snuffbox *noun* a small lidded (especially metal) container for snuff.

snuffle — *verb* **1** *intrans.* to breathe, especially breathe in, through a partially blocked nose. **2** *trans., intrans.* to say or speak in a nasal tone. **3** *intrans.* to snivel. — *noun* **1** the sound of breathing through a partially blocked nose. **2** (**the snuffles**) *colloq.* a slight cold. [see SNUFF[1]]

snuff movie *or* **snuff film** *slang* a pornographic film in which the climax is the real-life murder of one of the participants.

snug — *adj.* (**snugger, snuggest**) **1** enjoying or providing warmth, comfort, and shelter; cosy. **2** comfortably close-fitting. — *noun* a small comfortable room or compartment in a pub.

snuggery *noun* (PL. **snuggeries**) *Brit.* a small comfortable room or compartment in a pub.

snuggle *verb intrans.* (*usually* **snuggle down** *or* **in**) to settle oneself into a position of warmth and comfort.

snugly *adv.* in a snug way.

Snyder, Solomon Halbert (1938–) US psychiatrist and pharmacologist, born in Washington. Professor at Johns Hopkins Medical School, he successfully demonstrated the presence of opiate receptors in nervous tissue (1973), opening the way for the study of the body's naturally occurring morphine-like substances, enkephalins and endorphins.

SO *abbrev.* standing order.

so[1] — *adv.* **1** to such an extent: *so expensive that nobody buys it.* **2** to this, that, or the same extent; as: *this one is lovely, but that one is not so nice.* **3** extremely: *she is so talented!* **4** in that state or condition: *promised to be faithful, and has remained so.* **5** also; likewise: *she's my friend and so are you.* **6** used to avoid repeating a previous statement: *you've to take your medicine because I said so.* — *conj.* **1** therefore; thereafter: *he insulted me, so I hit him.* **2** (*also* **so that** ...) in order that: *lend me the book, so that I can read it.* — *adj.* the case; true: *you think I'm mad, but it's not so.* — *interj.* used to express discovery: *so, that's what you've been doing!*

— **and so on** *or* **and so forth** *or* **and so on and so forth** and more of the same; continuing in the same way.

just so neatly, precisely, or perfectly: *with her hair arranged just so.*

... or so approximately: *five or so days ago.*

so as to ... in order to ...; in such a way as to ...

so be it used to express acceptance or defiant resignation.

so much *or* **many 1** such a lot: *so much work to do!* **2** just; mere: *politicians squabbling like so many children.*

so much for ... nothing has come of ...; that has disposed of or ruined: *so much for all our plans!*

so to speak *or* **to say** used as an apology for an unfamiliar or slightly inappropriate expression.

so what? *colloq.* that is of no importance or consequence at all.

[from Anglo-Saxon *swa*]

so[2] same as SOH.

soak — *verb* **1** *trans., intrans.* to stand or leave to stand in a liquid for some time. **2** to make thoroughly wet; to drench. **3** (*also* **soak in** *or* **through**) to penetrate or pass. **4** (*also* **soak something up**) to absorb it. — *noun* **1** an act of soaking. **2** *colloq.* a long period of lying in a bath. **3** *colloq.* a person who habitually drinks a lot of alcohol. [from Anglo-Saxon *socian*]

soaked *adj.* **1** drenched, saturated, steeped. **2** *colloq.* drunk.

soaking *adj.* wet, drenched.

so-and-so *noun colloq.* **1** a person whose name one does not know or cannot remember. **2** used in place of a vulgar word: *you crafty little so-and-so!*

Soane, Sir John (1753–1837) English architect, born in Goring, Oxfordshire. He travelled in Italy (1777–80) and became Professor of Architecture at the Royal Academy (1806). His designs include the Bank of England (1792–1833, now rebuilt) and Dulwich College Art Gallery (1811–14).

soap — *noun* **1** a sodium or potassium salt of a fatty acid (an acid derived from a fat) that is soluble in water and has detergent properties, ie it dissolves grease and acts as a wetting agent. **2** such a substance used as a cleaning agent in the form of a solid block, liquid, or powder. **3** *colloq.* a soap opera. — *verb* to apply soap to.

— **soap someone up** *colloq.* to charm or persuade them with flattery.

[from Anglo-Saxon *sape*]

soapbox *noun* an improvised platform for public speech-making, originally an upturned crate for carrying soap.

soap opera a radio or television series dealing with the daily life and troubles of a regular group of characters, originally applied to those sponsored in the USA by soap manufacturing companies.

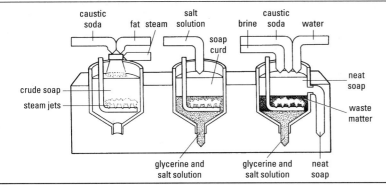

caustic soda — fat steam — salt solution — brine — caustic soda — water

soap curd

neat soap

crude soap

steam jets

waste matter

glycerine and salt solution — glycerine and salt solution — neat soap

soap manufacture

soapstone *noun* a soft (usually grey or brown) variety of the talc mineral, widely used for ornamental carvings.

soapy *adj.* (**soapier**, **soapiest**) **1** like soap. **2** containing soap. **3** smeared with soap. **4** covered with soapsuds.

soar *verb intrans.* **1** to fly high into the air. **2** to glide through the air at a high altitude. **3** to rise sharply to a great height or level: *temperatures soaring*. [from Old French *essorer*, to expose to air by raising up]

sob — *verb* (**sobbed**, **sobbing**) **1** *intrans.* to cry uncontrollably with intermittent gulps for breath. **2** *trans.* to say while crying in this way. — *noun* a gulp for breath between bouts of crying. [imitative]

sober — *adj.* **1** not at all drunk. **2** serious or solemn; not frivolous. **3** suggesting sedateness or seriousness rather than exuberance or frivolity: *sober clothes*. **4** plain; unembellished: *the sober truth*. — *verb trans., intrans.* (**sobered**, **sobering**) (**sober down** *or* **sober someone down**) to become or make someone quieter, less excited, etc. (**sober up** *or* **sober someone up**) to become or make someone free from the effects of alcohol. [from Latin *sobrius*, from *se-*, not + *ebrius*, drunk]

sobering *adj.* provoking serious reflection: *a sobering thought*.

Sobers, Gary, properly **Sir Garfield (St Aubrun)** (1936–) West Indian cricketer, born in Barbados. An all-rounder, he is the only man to score 8 000 Test runs and take 200 wickets. During his career (1953–74) he scored 28 315 runs in first-class cricket (average 54.87) and took 1 043 wickets (average 27.74). He scored 365 not out against Pakistan in 1958, a Test cricket world record until 1994 (broken by Brian Lara). In 1968, playing for Nottinghamshire against Glamorgan, he scored a record 36 runs in one over. He retired in 1974.

sobriety *noun* the state of being sober, especially not drunk. [from Latin *sobrietas*]

sobriquet *or* **soubriquet** *noun literary* a nickname. [from French *sobriquet*]

sob-story *noun colloq.* a story of personal misfortune told in order to gain sympathy.

Soc. *abbrev.* **1** Socialist. **2** Society.

soca *noun* a type of Caribbean calypso incorporating elements of American soul music. [from SOUL + CALYPSO]

so-called *adj.* known or presented as such (with the implication that the term is wrongly or inappropriately used): *a panel of so-called experts*.

soccer *noun* Association Football. [formed from the abbreviation *assoc.* = association]

Sochi POP (1991e) 342 000, a seaport in Krasnodar krai, S Russia. It stretches for over 30km/19mi along the E shore of the Black Sea. Founded as a spa in 1910, Sochi is today an important holiday and health resort. NOTABLE FEATURE fortress ruins (1838).

sociability *or* **sociableness** *noun* being sociable.

sociable *adj.* **1** fond of the company of others; friendly. **2** characterized by friendliness: *a sociable meeting*. [from Latin *sociabilis*; see SOCIAL]

sociably *adv.* in a sociable way.

social — *adj.* **1** of or for people or society as a whole: *social policies*. **2** relating to the organization and behaviour of people in societies or communities: *social studies*. **3** tending or needing to live with others; not solitary: *social creatures*. **4** intended for or promoting friendly gatherings of people: *a social club*. — *noun* **1** a social gathering, especially one organized by a club or other group. **2** (**the social**) *colloq.* social security. [from Latin *socius*, companion]

social action *Politics* action taken by a group or movement to achieve some reform or to promote a particular cause, outside the normal or formal channels of a government or political system, and aimed at gaining support from the wider public. Social action is normally associated with radical politics and with groups such as Greenpeace and animal rights organizations.

social anthropology the study of living societies with a view to establishing, by comparison, the range of variation in social organization, institutions, etc, and the reasons for these differences.

social behaviourism a school of thought in social psychology which holds that all observable social action is in response to the hidden needs, desires, and beliefs of the deeper 'self'. The social construction of an individual's sense of self was given particular prominence through the work of social psychologist George Herbert Mead (1863–1931), who demonstrated that the individual's conception of himself, and how he appears to others, is a product of social interaction.

Social Chapter a section of the Maastricht Treaty comprising seven Articles which set out the social policy of the EC. It concerns such matters as employment policies, living and working conditions, health and safety, equal opportunities for women, and protection for pensioners and the unemployed. Ratification of the treaty by all EC member states would lead to agreement on directives including social security, redundancy, and employment conditions for non-EC workers. The Social Chapter was signed by all EC leaders in Dec 1989, except for John Major who negotiated an opt-out clause, regarding the Social Chapter as a step back to socialist corporatism.

social cleansing the killing or forced removal of those considered socially undesirable from a particular area.

social climber *often derog.* a person who seeks to gain higher social status, often by despicable methods.

social contract an agreement between individuals within a society to work together for the benefit of all, often involving the sacrifice of some personal freedoms.

social democracy a branch of socialism, which emerged in the late 19c after the break-up of the First International (see INTERNATIONAL), and which supports gradual social change through reform within a framework of democratic politics rather than by revolutionary means.

social democrat **1** a supporter of social democracy. **2** a member of a social democratic party.

Social Democratic Party (ABBREV. **SDP**) a UK political party formed in 1981 by a 'gang of four' who broke away from the Labour Party: David Owen, Shirley Williams, Roy Jenkins, and Bill Rogers (1928–). Although it espoused socialist principles, the Party was a moderate centrist one. The SDP formed an electoral pact with the Liberals in 1981, but failed to break the two-party 'mould' of British politics. It merged with the Liberal Party in 1988 to become the Social and Liberal Democratic Party, although a rump, led by David Owen, remained in existence as the SDP until 1990.

social engineering a term used (often critically) to describe the techniques dominant social groups may use to manipulate the subordinate population. It is applied in particular to the policies of government that lack democratic accountability.

socialism a political doctrine or system which aims to create a classless society by removing the nation's wealth (land, industries, transport systems, etc) out of private and into public hands. Socialist ideas appeared in classical times, but was not systemized as a poltical doctrine in Europe until industrialization in the 18c and 10c.

socialist — *noun* a supporter of socialism. — *adj.* relating to or characteristic of socialism.

Socialist Realism in literature and art, the official style of the former Soviet Union and of other socialist states, intended to appeal to the masses by representing ordinary workers in a positive light. The Hungarian critic Georg Lukács was a major proponent, and Russian self-exile Andrei Sinyavsky (1925–) a noted antagonist.

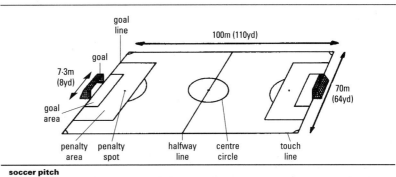

goal line

100m (110yd)

goal

7·3m (8yd)

70m (64yd)

goal area

penalty area — penalty spot — halfway line — centre circle — touch line

soccer pitch

socialite *noun* a person who mixes with people of high social status.

socialization *or* **socialisation** *noun* **1** the act or process of socializing. **2** the process by which infants and young children become aware of society and their relationships with others.

socialize *or* **socialise** *verb* **1** *intrans.* to meet with people on an informal, friendly basis. **2** *intrans.* to circulate among guests at a party; to mingle. **3** to organize into societies or communities.

socially *adv.* in a social way.

social mobility the way individuals or groups move (upwards or downwards) from one status or class position to another within the social hierarchy. Individuals may be upwardly mobile by, for example, education, marriage, or occupation. Entire social groups may also be mobile, by using their resources to enhance their position, eg occupational groups may improve their status by 'professionalizing' their expertise.

social realism *Art* a term current in art criticism since World War II, referring to pictures which treat 'real-life' subjects in a way that challenges the values of 'bourgeois' society. It has been applied to works by members of the US Ashcan School, and in Europe to Italian artist Renato Guttoso (1912–87).

social sciences those subjects that deal with the organization and behaviour of people in societies and communities, including sociology, anthropology, economics, and history.

social scientist an expert in social science.

social security **1** a system by which members of a society pay money into a common fund, from which payments are made to individuals in times of unemployment, illness, and old age. **2** a payment or scheme of payments from such a fund.

social services services provided by local or national government for the general welfare of people in society, eg housing, education, and health.

social work work in any of the services provided by local government for the care of underprivileged people.

social worker an official who carries out social work.

Société Anonyme Inc a gallery of modern art (1920–50) founded by Katherine Dreier, Marcel Duchamp, and Man Ray. The organization promoted contemporary art in the USA through a series of exhibitions and lectures, and introduced the work of artists such as Paul Klee, Joán Miró, and Kurt Schwitters to the country.

society *noun* (PL. **societies**) **1** mankind as a whole, or a part of it such as one nation, considered as a single community. **2** a division of mankind with common characteristics, eg of nationality, race, or religion. **3** an organized group or association. **4** the rich and fashionable section of the upper class: *a society wedding.* **5** *formal* company: *prefers the society of women.* [from Latin *societas*]

Society Islands, French **Archipel de la Société** POP (1988) 163 000, an archipelago of French Polynesia, comprising the Windward Is (including Tahiti) and the Leeward Is. AREA 1 535sq km/592sq mi. PHYSICAL DESCRIPTION there are two clusters of volcanic and coral islands in a 720km/450mi chain stretching NW–SE. CAPITAL Papeete (Tahiti). HISTORY discovered by Capt Cook in 1769; became a French protectorate in 1844 and a French colony in 1897. ECONOMY phosphates; copra; vanilla; mother-of-pearl. [named by Capt Cook after the Royal Society]

Society of Independent Artists a US society formed in New York in 1916 to hold open art exhibitions to which anyone could submit work without having to pass a selection commit-

tee. It was based on the French Salon des Indépendants, and the only work rejected at the first exhibition in 1917 was Marcel Duchamp's exhibit of a urinal, entitled *Fountain*.

socio- *combining form* forming words meaning 'social, of society or sociology': *socioeconomic*.

sociobiology *noun Psychol.* the integrated study of the biological basis of social behaviour, based on the assumption that all behaviour is adaptive.

sociogram *noun* a graphic representation of a network of social relationships.

sociolinguistics *sing. noun* the study of the relationships between language and the society which uses it. The subject is wide-ranging and includes: analysis of varieties used in a community, (including standard and non-standard forms) and the contexts in which they are appropriate; the language of different social class and caste groups; and male and female speech.

sociological *adj.* **1** relating to or involving sociology. **2** dealing or concerned with social questions and problems of human society.

sociologist *noun* an expert in sociology.

sociology *noun* the scientific study of the nature, structure, and workings of human society. [from Latin *socius*, companion + -LOGY]

sociometry *noun* a technique for mapping social networks. The networks are based on respondents ranking those people they find more or less desirable. The technique can be used by psychologists to build up a theory of association between people.

sock[1] *noun* a fabric covering for the foot and ankle, sometimes reaching to the knee, worn inside a shoe or boot.
— **pull one's socks up** *colloq.* to make an effort to do better.
put a sock in it *slang* to become silent; to be quiet.
[from Anglo-Saxon *socc*, light shoe]

sock[2] *slang* — *verb* to hit with a powerful blow. — *noun* a powerful blow.
— **sock it to someone** *slang* to make a powerful impression on them.

socket *noun* **1** a specially-shaped hole or set of holes into which something is fitted: *an electrical socket.* **2** a hollow structure in the body into which another part fits: *a ball-and-socket joint.* [from Old French *soket*]

socle *noun Archit.* a plain projecting block or plinth at the base of a wall, column, or pier. [from French, from Latin *socculus*, diminutive of *soccus*, a shoe]

Socrates (469–399 BC) Greek philosopher, born in Athens, one of the three great figures (with Plato and Aristotle) in ancient philosophy. His technique, the so-called 'Socratic method', was to ask for definitions of such morally significant concepts as piety and justice, and to elicit contradictions from the responses, thus exposing the ignorance of the responder and motivating deeper enquiry into the concepts. He opposed tyranny, and was tried on charges of impiety and corruption of the youth, found guilty, and sentenced to death by drinking hemlock. He wrote nothing himself but his personality and doctrines were immortalized in Plato's dialogues.

Socratic *adj.* relating to the Greek philosopher Socrates, his philosophy, or his method of teaching or inquiry by a series of questions and answers.

sod[1] *noun* **1** a slab of earth with grass growing on it; a turf. **2** *poetic* the ground. [from Old German *sode*]

sod[2] *coarse slang* — *noun* **1** a term of abuse for a person. **2** a person in general: *lucky sod.* — *verb* used as an exclamation of annoyance or contempt: *sod the lot of them.*
— **sod all** *coarse slang* nothing at all.

sod off *coarse slang* go away.
[a shortening of SODOMITE]

soda *noun* **1** a common name given to any of various compounds of sodium in everyday use, eg sodium carbonate (*washing soda*) or sodium bicarbonate (*baking soda*). **2** soda water. **3** *North Amer., esp. US* a fizzy soft drink of any kind. [from Latin *soda*]

soda ash *Chem.* the common name for the commercial grade of anhydrous sodium carbonate (Na_2CO_3), a greyish-white powder that is soluble in water, and used in soaps, detergents, paper and glass manufacture, and petroleum refining.

soda bread bread in which the raising ingredient is baking soda, not yeast.

soda fountain *North Amer., esp. US* a counter in a shop from which fizzy drinks, ice-cream, and snacks are served.

soda lime *Chem.* a solid mixture of sodium or potassium hydroxide and calcium oxide, consisting of greyish-white granules that are used as a drying agent, and to absorb carbon dioxide gas.

soda water water made fizzy by the addition of carbon dioxide, widely used as a mixer with alcoholic spirits.

sodden *adj.* **1** heavy with moisture; thoroughly soaked. **2** made lifeless or sluggish, especially through excessive consumption of alcohol: *drink-sodden brain.*

sodding *adj. coarse slang* a general term of disparagement.

Soddy, Frederick (1877–1965) English chemist, born in Eastbourne. Professor at Glasgow, Aberdeen, and Oxford, he studied radioactivity and verified that radium produces helium when it decays. He discovered isotopes (1913), and also demonstrated that when an atom of a radioactive element emits an alpha particle, it is transformed into an isotope of an element two places down in the periodic table, but when it emits a beta particle it moves one place higher. He was awarded the 1921 Nobel Prize for Chemistry.

Söderblom, Nathan (1866–1931) Swedish theologian, born in Trönö. Ordained in 1893, he became Professor of Theology at Uppsala (1901–14), and primate of the Swedish Lutheran Church. A leader in the ecumenical movement, he strove for peace, and received the Nobel Peace Prize in 1930.

Södertälje, formerly **Tälje** POP (1992e) 82 000, an industrial town in Stockholm county, SE Sweden. A suburb of Stockholm on the Södertälje Canal (1807–19), it developed from a Viking trading station situated between L Mälar and the Baltic Sea.

sodium *noun Chem.* (SYMBOL **Na**, ATOMIC NUMBER **11**) a soft silvery-white metal that occurs mainly as sodium chloride (common salt) in seawater and underground deposits.
◊ Pure sodium is so reactive with air and water that it is normally stored under oil. It is used in alloys, as a reducing agent in chemical reactions, as a coolant in nuclear reactors, and in non-glare lighting, eg in street lamps. Its compounds, especially sodium chloride, sodium hydroxide (caustic soda), and sodium carbonate (soda), are widely used in the chemical industry. Sodium is an essential element of the diet, and plays a central role in maintaining the pH balance of living cells, and in the transmission of nerve impulses. [from SODA]

sodium bicarbonate *Chem.* same as SODIUM HYDROGENCARBONATE.

sodium carbonate *Chem.* (FORMULA Na_2CO_3) a white powder or crystalline solid, that dissolves in water to form an alkaline solution, and readily forms hydrates on exposure to air. It is used as a water softener and food additive, and in glass making, photography, and the manufacture of various sodium compounds. — Also called *washing soda, soda ash.*

sodium chloride *Chem.* (FORMULA **NaCl**) a white crystalline salt, soluble in water, obtained from underground deposits of the mineral halite, and from seawater. It has been used since ancient times for seasoning and preserving food, and is also used as a de-icing and water-softening agent, and in the manufacture of chlorine, sodium hydroxide, hydrochloric acid, and many other chemicals. – Also called *common salt, salt, table salt.*

sodium hydrogencarbonate *Chem.* (FORMULA **NaHCO₃**) a white crystalline or powdery solid, soluble in water, used in antacids to treat indigestion, and in baking powder, powder-based fire extinguishers, carbonated beverages, and ceramics. – Also called *sodium bicarbonate, bicarbonate of soda, baking soda.*

sodium hydroxide *Chem.* (FORMULA **NaOH**) a white crystalline solid that dissolves in water to form a strongly alkaline solution. It absorbs carbon dioxide and water from the air, and is prepared by the electrolysis of brine. Sodium hydroxide is used in the manufacture of soap, detergents, pharmaceuticals, oven cleaners, rayon, and paper, in petroleum refining, and as an intermediate in the manufacture of chemical compounds. It is highly corrosive to living tissue, especially the eyes. – Also called *caustic soda, soda.*

sodium nitrate *Chem.* (FORMULA **NaNO₃**) a toxic colourless crystalline solid with a bitter taste, soluble in water, that decomposes when heated and explodes at high temperatures. It is used in the manufacture of explosives, fireworks, matches, nitrate fertilizers, and glass, and is also used as a food preservative, especially for cured meats.

Sodom and Gomorrah two of five 'cities of the plain' in ancient Palestine, legendary for their sinful (especially sexually perverse) people, perhaps now submerged under the south end of the Dead Sea or located to the south-east of the Dead Sea. Genesis 18–19 tells of how Lot and his family were warned to flee from their home in Sodom just before God destroyed the city.

sodomite *noun* a person who engages in sodomy.

sodomize *or* **sodomise** *verb* to practise sodomy on.

sodomy *noun* **1** a form of intercourse in which the penis is inserted into the anus of a man or woman; buggery. **2** sexual intercourse between a man and an animal. [from *Sodom,* a biblical city renowned for vice]

Sod's law *slang* a facetious maxim stating that if something can go wrong, it will go wrong, or that the most inconvenient thing that could happen is what is most likely to happen.

sofa *noun* an upholstered seat with a back and arms, for two or more people. [from Arabic *suffah*]

sofa bed a piece of furniture designed to be converted from a sofa to a bed and vice versa.

soffit *noun Archit.* a term variously applied to the under surface (or intrados) of an arch; to a ceiling on the underside of a stair; and to the underside of the top of a door or window opening. [from Italian *soffito,* ultimately from Latin *suffigere,* to fasten beneath]

Sofia, Bulgarian **Sofiya**, Latin **Serdica** POP (1991e) 1.2m, the capital of Bulgaria, situated on a plateau in the W. HISTORY a Roman town from the 1c until the 4c; under Byzantine rule from the 6c to the 9c; under Turkish rule from 1382 until 1878; became capital in 1878. NOTABLE FEATURES Mausoleum of Georgi Dimitrov; Alexander Nevsky Memorial Cathedral (1880s); St George Rotunda (4c); Church of St Sofia (6c).

soft — *adj.* **1** easily yielding or changing shape when pressed; pliable. **2** *said of fabric, etc* having a smooth surface producing little or no friction.

3 quiet: *a soft voice.* **4** of little brightness: *soft colours.* **5** kind or sympathetic, especially excessively so. **6** not able to endure rough treatment or hardship. **7** lacking strength of character; easily influenced. **8** weak in the mind; simple: *soft in the head.* **9** weakly sentimental. **10** *said of water* low in or free from mineral salts and so lathering easily. **11** tender; loving: *soft words.* **12** *colloq.* requiring little effort; easy: *a soft job.* **13** *said of drugs* not severely addictive. **14** with moderate rather than hardline or extreme policies: *the soft left.* **15** *said of the consonants c and g* pronounced as in *dance* and *age* respectively. — *adv.* softly: *speaks soft.*

— **soft on someone** *colloq.* **1** lenient towards them. **2** infatuated with them. [from Anglo-Saxon *softe*]

softball *noun* a game similar to baseball, played with a larger, softer ball.
◊ As in baseball, the object is to score runs by completing a circuit of a 18.3m (60ft) diamond-shaped pitch. The principal difference between baseball and softball is in the method of pitching: in softball, it is done underarm.

soft-boiled *adj., said of eggs* boiled for a short while only, leaving the yolk soft.

soft drink a non-alcoholic drink.

soften *verb trans., intrans.* (**softened, softening**) to make or become soft or softer.
— **soften someone up** to prepare them for an unwelcome or difficult request.

softener *noun* a substance added to another to increase its softness, pliability, etc, especially a substance used to soften water.

soft furnishings rugs, curtains, and other articles made of fabric.

soft-hearted *adj.* kind-hearted and generous; compassionate.

soft iron *Chem.* a form of iron that has a low carbon content, and is unable to retain magnetism. It is used to make the cores of electromagnets, motors, generators, and transformers.

soft option the easier or easiest of several alternative courses of action.

soft palate *Anat.* the fleshy muscular back part of the palate.

soft pedal a pedal on a piano pressed to make the sound from the strings less lingering or ringing.

soft-pedal *verb* (**soft-pedalled, soft-pedalling**) *colloq.* to tone down, or avoid emphasizing or mentioning: *the government were soft-pedalling the scheme's disadvantages.*

soft porn *colloq.* pornography in which sexual acts are not shown or described explicitly.

soft sell the use of gentle persuasion as a selling technique, rather than heavy-handed pressure.

soft-soap *verb colloq.* to speak flatteringly to, especially in order to persuade or deceive.

soft-spoken *adj.* having a soft voice, and usually a mild manner.

soft spot a fondness: *have a soft spot for.*

soft touch *slang* a person easily taken advantage of, especially one giving money willingly.

software *noun Comput.* the programs that are used in a computer system (eg operating systems, and applications programs such as word-processing or database programs), and the magnetic disks, tapes, etc, on which they are recorded, as opposed to the computer's electronic, electrical, magnetic, and mechanical components, which form the hardware. See also HARDWARE.

soft water *Chem.* water that naturally contains very low levels of calcium and magnesium salts, or from which these salts have been removed artificially. It lathers easily with soap, and does not cause scaling of kettles, boilers, etc.

softwood *noun* **1** *Bot.* the wood of a coniferous tree, eg pine. The name is misleading, as some softwoods are in fact very hard and durable. **2** *Bot.* any tree which produces such wood. See also HARDWOOD.

softy *or* **softie** *noun* (PL. **softies**) *colloq.* **1** a person easily upset. **2** a weakly sentimental person. **3** a person not able to endure rough treatment or hardship.

SOGAT *abbrev.* Society of Graphical and Allied Trades.

soggily *adv.* in a soggy way.

sogginess *noun* being soggy.

soggy *adj.* (**soggier, soggiest**) **1** thoroughly wet; saturated. **2** *said of ground* waterlogged; boggy. [from dialect *sog, bog*]

Sogne Fjord, Norwegian **Sognefjorden** the largest fjord in Norway, in Sogn og Fjordane county, on the W coast of Norway. An inlet of the Norwegian Sea, it extends E inland for 204km/127mi. Average width 5km/3mi; maximum depth 1 245m.

soh *noun Mus.* in tonic sol-fa, the fifth note of the major scale. [from the first syllable of the word *solve* in a medieval Latin hymn, certain syllables of which were used to name the notes of the scale]

Sŏul see SEOUL.

Soho a district of central London noted for its restaurants, theatres, and nightclubs. The area was once a royal park, and its name derives from an ancient hunting cry.

soil¹ *noun* **1** the mixture of fragmented rock and plant and animal debris that lies on the surface of the Earth, above the bedrock. It contains water and air, as well as living organisms such as bacteria, fungi, and invertebrate animals. **2** *literary* country; land: *on foreign soil.* [from Latin *solum,* ground]

soil² — *verb* **1** to stain or make dirty. **2** to bring discredit on; to sully: *soiled reputation.* — *noun* **1** a stain. **2** dirt. **3** dung; sewage. [from Old French *souil,* wallowing-place]

soil horizon see SOIL PROFILE.

soil profile a vertical section through the soil revealing a series of basic soil levels: the surface layer or topsoil containing humus; the upper subsoil containing little organic matter but rich in soil mineral washed down from the topsoil; the lower subsoil of partially weathered mineral material; and the bedrock from which the upper layers may be derived. Each level may be further classified according to its composition.

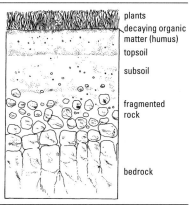

soil profile

soil science the scientific study of soil and its management as a medium for plant growth. It includes the cultivation, drainage, and irrigation of soil, and the control of its nutrient content, acidity, and salinity.

soirée or SOIREE *NOUN* **1** a formal party held in the evening. **2** an evening of entertainment of any kind. [French, = evening]

sojourn *formal — noun* a short stay. — *verb intrans.* to stay for a short while. [from Old French *sojorner*]

Soka Gakkai a new religious movement in Japanese Buddhism that was founded (1937) by Tsunesaburo Makiguchi. Part of the Nichiren Buddhist tradition, its message that Buddhahood is within the grasp of all, that happiness is a key human possibility, that salvation is available through reciting the mantra known as the *daimoku*, and that this age is the age of salvation, made it attractive in postwar Japan, and it grew rapidly in 1945–60 under Josei Toda. Its strong organization is based on 'family units' and the achievement of worldly goals; it also sponsors its own political party. [from Japanese, = value creating society]

Sokodé POP (1987e) 55 000, the chief town of Centrale region, Togo. It is situated 305km/190mi N of Lomé, in the midst of Togo's forest lands. The Fazao-Malfakassa National Park lies to the SW. ECONOMY cotton; groundnuts; livestock.

sol¹ same as SOH.

sol² *noun Chem.* a type of colloid that consists of small solid particles dispersed in a liquid.

sola *noun* an Indian plant, the pith of which was used to make pith helmets. [from Hindi *sola*]

solace — *noun* comfort in time of disappointment or sorrow; also, a source of comfort. — *verb* **1** to provide with such comfort. **2** to bring relief from. [from Latin *solari*, to comfort in distress]

solacement *noun* solace, consolation.

solar *adj.* **1** of or relating to the sun. **2** of, by, or using energy from the sun's rays: *solar-powered*. [from Latin *sol*, sun]

solar battery *Electr.* a battery consisting of a number of solar cells.

solar cell *Electr.* an electric cell that converts solar energy (from sunlight) directly into electricity. Solar cells are an expensive and relatively inefficient source of large-scale power, but are used in pocket calculators, light meters, etc. Arrays of solar cells, known as *solar panels*, are used to power satellites and spacecraft. — Also called *photovoltaic cell*.

solar energy energy that is radiated from the Sun, mainly in the form of heat and light, and only a minute proportion of which falls on the Earth. It is required for photosynthesis, which is essential for the survival of living organisms. ◇ Solar energy is a non-polluting and renewable energy source that can be harnessed directly to provide domestic or industrial heating. Flat or concave solar panels containing pipes through which water is circulated absorb solar energy, and the heated water is then stored in insulated tanks, from which it can be released through a system of radiators when required. Solar energy can also be converted to electric current by photoelectric cells (solar cells), which are used to provide an electricity source for spacecraft, artificial satellites, light meters, pocket calculators, etc.

solar flare *Astron.* a sudden release of energy in the vicinity of an active region on the Sun's surface, generally associated with a sunspot.

solarium *noun* (PL. **solariums, solaria**) **1** a room or establishment equipped with sun-beds. **2** a conservatory or other room designed to allow exposure to sunlight.

solar plexus an area in the abdomen in which there is a concentration of nerves radiating from a central point.

solar system the Sun, and the system of nine major planets (Mercury, Venus, Earth, Mars, Jupiter, Saturn, Uranus, Neptune, and Pluto), together with their natural satellites, and the

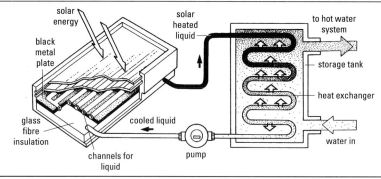
use of solar energy

asteroids (minor planets), comets, and meteors that revolve around it, held in their orbits by the Sun's gravitational pull.
◇ All the orbiting bodies in the solar system move in almost the same plane. The Sun and the planets were formed about 4 600 million years ago, when a dark cloud of gas and dust particles many light years in diameter condensed into a cluster of young stars, one of which was the Sun. The nine major planets developed inside a flat rotating disc of gas and dust that formed around the Sun as it contracted to become a star. Thousands of minor planets or asteroids orbit around the Sun in the wide zone between the orbits of Mars and Jupiter. The comets have long elliptical orbits and pass close to the Sun before swinging back past the outer planets and beyond the solar system. Particles of dust also orbit the Sun in loose clouds and become meteors when they flash down through the Earth's atmosphere.

solar wind *Astron.* a stream of charged particles that flows outward from the Sun in all directions at speeds of over one million kph. It passes the Earth and the other planets as it moves through the solar system.

sold past tense and past participle of SELL.
— **sold on something** *colloq.* convinced or enthusiastic about it.

solder — *noun Engineering* any of several alloys with a low melting point, often containing tin and lead, applied when molten to the joint between two metals to form an airtight seal. — *verb* (**soldered, soldering**) to join two pieces of metal, without melting them, by applying a layer of molten alloy to the joint between them and allowing it to cool and solidify. [from Latin *solidare*, to strengthen]

soldering-iron *noun* a tool with a probe-like part, usually electrically heated, used to melt and apply solder.

soldier — *noun* **1** a member of a fighting force, especially a national army. **2** a member of an

army below officer rank. — *verb intrans.* (**soldiered, soldiering**) to serve as a soldier.
— **soldier on** to continue determinedly in spite of difficulties.
[from Old French *soudier*, from *soude*, pay]

soldierly *adj.* like a soldier.

soldier of fortune a person willing to serve in any army that pays him or her.

sole¹ — *noun* **1** the underside of the foot. **2** the underside of a shoe or boot, especially the part not including the heel. **3** the flattish underside of anything. — *verb* to fit (a shoe or boot) with a sole. [from Latin *solum*, bottom]

sole² *noun* (PL. **sole, soles**) a flatfish found in shallow waters in tropical and temperate regions, with a slender brown body and both eyes on the left side of the head. It is an important food fish, the Dover sole being especially highly prized. [from Latin *solea*]

sole³ *adj.* **1** only. **2** exclusive: *has sole rights to the story*. [from Latin *solus*, alone]

solecism *noun* **1** a mistake in the use of language. **2** an instance of bad or incorrect behaviour. [from Greek *soloikismos*]

solecistic *adj.* of the nature of or involving solecism.

solely *adv.* **1** alone; without others: *solely to blame*. **2** only; excluding all else: *done solely for profit*.

solemn *adj.* **1** done, made, etc in earnest: *a solemn vow*. **2** of a very serious and formal nature; suggesting seriousness: *a solemn occasion / solemn music*. **3** glum or sombre in appearance. [from Latin *sollemnis*, annual, customary, appointed]

solemnity *noun* (PL. **solemnities**) **1** being solemn. **2** a solemn ceremony.

solemnization or **solemnisation** *noun* solemnizing or being solemnized.

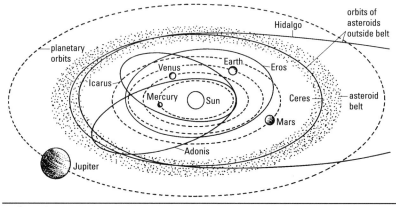
solar system

solemnize *or* **solemnise** *verb* **1** to perform (especially a marriage) with a formal or religious ceremony. **2** to make solemn.

Solemn League and Covenant an alliance (Sep 1643) between the English parliament and the Scottish rebels against Charles I. Parliament promised £30 000 a month to the Scots and the introduction of full Presbyterianism in England; the Scots agreed to provide an army to the hard-pressed Parliamentarians to fight Charles. The pact facilitated the Parliamentary victory in the first of the English Civil Wars, but Presbyterianism was never fully implemented.

solemnly *adv.* in a solemn way.

solenoid *noun* a cylindrical coil of wire that produces a magnetic field when an electric current is passed through it. Solenoids often contain a movable iron or steel core that can be used to operate a switch, relay, circuit breaker, etc. [from Greek *solen*, tube]

Solent, The a channel separating the I of Wight from mainland England. It is a major shipping route from Southampton and is also used for yacht racing.

sol-fa *noun* a system of musical notation in which the notes of a scale are represented by syllables, especially by *doh, re, me, fah, soh, la, ti,* written down or sung. [from *sol* (a form of SOH) + FAH]

Solferino, Battle of an indecisive engagement (20 Jun 1859) between Austrians and invading Franco-Piedmontese forces in Lombardy. Extremely heavy casualties on both sides so revolted Napoleon III that he offered the Austrians an armistice without even consulting his Piedmontese allies.

solicit *verb* (**solicited, soliciting**) **1** *formal* to ask for, or for something from: *solicit aid from other countries / solicited me for advice.* **2** *intrans. said of a prostitute* to approach people with open offers of sex for money. **3** *formal* to require or call for. [from Latin *solicitare*]

solicitation *noun* **1** an act of soliciting, an earnest request. **2** an invitation.

solicitor *noun* a lawyer who prepares legal documents, gives legal advice, and (in the lower courts only) speaks on behalf of clients.

solicitor-advocate *noun Scot. Legal* a solicitor with the right to represent clients in the High Court or Court of Session.

Solicitor-General in the UK, one of the government's law officers, who is a member of the House of Commons and junior to the Attorney-General. The Solicitor-General for Scotland holds a similar position.

solicitous *adj.* **1** (**solicitous about** *or* **for someone** *or* **something**) anxious or concerned about them. **2** (**solicitous to do something**) willing or eager to do it.

solicitously *adv.* in a solicitous way.

solicitude *noun* **1** anxiety or uneasiness of mind. **2** the state of being solicitous.

solid — *adj.* **1** in a form other than a liquid or a gas, and resisting changes in shape. **2** of the same nature or material throughout; pure: *a solid oak table.* **3** firmly constructed or attached; not easily breaking or loosening. **4** difficult to undermine or destroy; sound: *solid support for the scheme.* **5** not hollow. **6** without breaks; continuous: *waited for four solid hours.* **7** competent, rather than outstanding: *a solid piece of work.* — *noun* **1** *Chem.* a state of matter in which the constituent molecules or ions can only vibrate about fixed positions, and are unable to move freely. It has a definite shape, and at a specific temperature (the melting point) becomes a liquid. **2** *Geom.* a three-dimensional geometric figure. **3** (**solids**) non-liquid food. **4** (**solids**) particles of solid matter in a liquid. [from Latin *solidus*]

solid angle *Geom.* a three-dimensional cone-shaped angle representing the region subtended

at a point by a *surface,* as opposed to a line in the case of a two-dimensional (plane) angle. The unit of measurement of solid angles is the steradian.

Solidarity an organization established (Sep 1980) in Poland as the National Committee of Solidarity (*Solidarnos'c'*) to co-ordinate the activities of the emerging independent trade union following protracted industrial unrest, notably in the Lenin shipyard in Gdańsk. Its first president was Lech Wałesa (later to become President of Poland). It organized a number of strikes in early 1981 for improved wages and conditions, and became a force for major political reform. It attempted to seek reconciliation with the Polish government through proposing a council for national consensus, but suffered continuous harassment and was rendered largely ineffective by the declaration of martial law (Dec 1981) and by being made illegal. It remained underground, but came back into the political arena in mid-1988. Following its successes in the 1989 elections, Solidarity entered into a coalition government with the communists, and one of its members (Tadeusz Mazowiecki) eventually became prime minister.

solidarity *noun* mutual support and unity of interests and actions among members of a group.

solidification *noun* solidifying or being solidified.

solidify *verb trans., intrans.* (**solidifies, solidified**) to make or become solid.

solidity *noun* being solid.

solidly *adv.* in a solid way.

solid-state *adj.* **1** *Electron.* denoting an electronic device or component, eg a semiconductor or transistor, that functions by the movement of electrons through solids, and contains no heated filaments or vacuums. **2** *Physics* denoting the branch of physics concerned with the study of matter in the solid state, especially the electrical properties of semiconductors at the atomic level.

solidus *noun* a printed line sloping from right to left, eg separating alternatives, as in *and/or*; a stroke or slash mark. [from Latin *solidus*]

Solihull POP (1981) 95 000, a town in the West Midlands, central England. It forms a suburb of SE Birmingham. NOTABLE FEATURE National Exhibition Centre.

soliloquize *or* **soliloquise** *verb intrans.* to speak a soliloquy.

soliloquy *noun* (PL. **soliloquies**) **1** an act of talking to oneself, especially a speech in a play, etc in which a character reveals thoughts or intentions to the audience by talking aloud. **2** the use of such speeches as a device in drama. [from Latin *solus*, alone + *loqui*, to speak]

◇ The soliloquy was a convention much used by Elizabethan and Jacobean dramatists; there are supreme examples in Shakespeare's *Hamlet, Macbeth,* and *Othello,* and in Christopher Marlowe's *Dr Faustus.* It has been used rarely since more naturalistic forms of drama appeared towards the end of the 19c: isolated exceptions occur, eg in T S Eliot's *Murder in the Cathedral* and Robert Bolt's *A Man for all Seasons.*

Solingen POP (1991e) 163 000, an industrial city in North Rhine-Westphalia state, W central Germany. It lies in the Ruhr Valley, 22km/14mi SE of Düsseldorf. During World War II it was badly bombed.

solipsism *noun Philos.* the theory that one's own self is the only thing whose existence one can be sure of. [from Latin *solus*, alone + *ipse*, self]

solipsist *noun* a believer in solipsism.

solitaire *noun* **1** any of several games for one player only, especially one whose object is to eliminate pegs or marbles from a board and leave only one. **2** a single gem in a setting on its own. **3** *North Amer., esp. US* the card game patience. [from French; related to SOLITARY]

solitariness *noun* a solitary state.

solitary — *adj.* **1** single; lone. **2** preferring to be alone; not social. **3** without companions; lonely. **4** remote; secluded. — *noun* **1** a person who lives alone, especially a hermit. **2** *colloq.* solitary confinement. [from Latin *solitarius*, from *solus*, alone]

solitary confinement imprisonment in a cell by oneself.

solitude *noun* the state of being (especially pleasantly) alone or secluded. [from Latin *solitudo*, from *solus*, alone]

solmization *or* **solmisation** *noun Mus.* in musical reference and training, a system in which syllables are used to designate the notes of the hexachord. The system used in Western music from medieval times is attributed to the French music theorist and teacher Guido d'Arezzo (d.c.1050), who fitted the first syllables of each of the first six lines of a plainsong Latin hymn to the notes of the hexachord to make: *ut* (later changed to *do*), *re, mi, fa, sol,* and *la* (*si* or *ti* was added later). The modern sight-singing and ear-training systems of *tonic sol-fa, solfeggio* (in Italy), and *solfège* (in France) are based on these syllables. [from French *solmisation*, related to the terms SOL[1] + MI]

solo — *noun* (PL. **solos**) a piece of music, or a passage within it, for a single voice or instrument, with or without accompaniment. — *adj.* performed alone, without assistance or accompaniment. — *adv.* alone: *fly solo.* [from Italian *solo*, from Latin *solus*, alone]

soloist *noun* a person who performs a solo or solos.

Solomon (10c BC) **1** a biblical character who was King of Israel, the second son of David and Bathsheba. His splendid reign saw the kingdom expand and the great Temple in Jerusalem erected, but high taxation and alliances with heathen courts bred discontent which led to the disruption of the kingdom under his son Rehoboam (1 Kings 1–14 and 2 Chronicles 1–13). A legendary figure in Judaism, Solomon was credited with extraordinary wisdom, and his name became attached to several biblical and extra-canonical writings. **2** a male first name. [from the Hebrew name *Shlomo*, from *shalom*, peace]

Solomon, John (William) (1931–) British croquet player. He made his international début against New Zealand in 1950 at age 19, and never missed an England Test Match between 1950 and 1973. He won a record 10 Open croquet championships (1953, 1956, 1959, 1961, 1963–8), the men's championship 10 times between 1951 and 1972, the Open doubles championship 10 times (all with Edmond Cotter) between 1954 and 1969, and the mixed doubles title once (with Freda Oddie) in 1954. He was winner of the President's Cup a record nine times.

Solomon Islands POP (1991e) 326 000, an independent country consisting of an archipelago of several hundred islands in the SW Pacific Ocean. The islands stretch c.1 400km/ 870mi between Papua New Guinea in the NW and Vanuatu in the SE. AREA 27 556sq km/ 10 637sq mi. CAPITAL Honiara. CHIEF TOWNS Gizo, Auki, Kirakira. TIME ZONE GMT +11. Most of the population is Melanesian (93%); Protestantism is the chief religion. OFFICIAL LANGUAGE English; pidgin English is also spoken. CURRENCY the Solomon Island dollar. PHYSICAL DESCRIPTION comprises the six main islands of Choiseul, Guadalcanal, Malaita, New Georgia, Makira, and Santa Isabel; the large islands have forested mountain ranges of mainly volcanic origin, deep, narrow valleys, and coastal belts lined with coconut palms; they are ringed by reefs; the highest point is Mt Makarakomburu (2 477m) on Guadalcanal, the largest island. CLIMATE equatorial; the average temperature is 27°C; high humidity; rainfall averages c.3 500mm per year. HISTORY discovered by the Spanish in 1568; the S

Solomon Is were placed under British protection in 1893; the outer islands were added to the protectorate in 1899; the scene of fierce fighting in World War II; gained independence in 1978. GOVERNMENT the British Monarch is represented by a Governor-General; the Prime Minister leads a parliament of 38 members elected for four years. ECONOMY based on agriculture; forestry; livestock; fisheries; taro; rice; bananas; yams; copra; oil palm; fish processing, food processing; crafts.

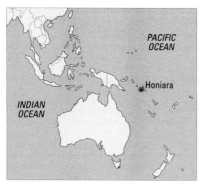

Solomon Islands

Solomon Sea see CORAL SEA.

Solomon's seal a perennial plant (*Polygonatum multiflorum*), native to Europe and Asia, which has arching stems, oval leaves borne in two rows on the stem, and white bell-shaped flowers that hang in clusters beneath the stem.

Solon (7c–6c BC) Athenian statesman. As chief archon, he enacted many economic, constitutional, and legal reforms, and paved the way for the development of democracy in Athens. He abolished enslavement for debt, instituted a new currency, and granted citizenship to foreign craftsmen settling in Athens. Draco's legal code was largely repealed and a more humane one introduced.

Solovetsky Islands an island archipelago in the White Sea, Archangel (Arkhangelsk) oblast, Russia. The three islands form a World Heritage site.

solstice *noun* either of the times when the sun is furthest from the equator: the longest day (*summer solstice*) around Jun 21 in the N hemisphere and the shortest day (*winter solstice*) around Dec 21 in the N hemisphere. [from Latin *solstitium*, the standing still of the sun]

Solti, Sir Georg (1912–) Hungarian-born British conductor, born in Budapest. He appeared as a pianist aged 12, studied with Béla Bartók, Ernst von Dohnányi, and Zoltan Kodály, and assisted Bruno Walter and Arturo Toscanini at the Salzburg Festival (1935–7). World War II forced him to give up his post as conductor of the Budapest Opera, and he worked in Switzerland until 1946, when he became director at the Munich Staatsoper (until 1952) and later at Frankfurt (1952–61) and Covent Garden, London (1961–71). He later conducted the Chicago Symphony Orchestra and the London Philharmonic, and made a pioneering recording of Richard Wagner's *Ring* cycle for the Decca company. He took British nationality in 1972.

solubility *noun* a soluble state.

soluble *adj.* **1** denoting a substance (a *solute*) that is capable of being dissolved in a liquid (a *solvent*). **2** capable of being solved or resolved. [from Latin *solubilis*]

solute *noun Chem.* any substance that is dissolved in a solvent (eg water) to form a solution. [from Latin *solutus*, from *solvere*, to loosen]

solution *noun* **1** the process of finding an answer to a problem or puzzle; also, the answer sought or found. **2** *Chem.* a homogeneous mixture consisting of a solid or gas (the *solute*) and the

liquid (the *solvent*) in which it is completely dissolved. **3** the act of dissolving or the state of being dissolved: *in solution.* **4** *Maths.* in a mathematical equation, the value that one or more of the variables must have for that equation to be valid. [from Latin *solutio*]

solvable *adj.* capable of being solved.

solvation *noun Chem.* the interaction between the ions of a solute and the molecules of a solvent, which enables an ionic solid to dissolve in a solvent to form a solution, or to swell or form a gel in the presence of a solvent. If the solvent is water, the process is referred to as hydration. [from Latin *solvere*, to loosen]

solve *verb* to discover the answer to (a puzzle) or a way out of (a problem). [from Latin *solvere*, to loosen]

solvency *noun* ability to pay all debts.

solvent — *adj.* **1** able to pay all one's debts. **2** in a solution, the liquid in which a solid or gas (the *solute*) is dissolved, eg water and organic chemicals such as ethanol (alcohol), ether, and acetone. — *noun* a solvent substance.

solvent abuse, inhalation of the intoxicating fumes given off by various solvents, eg adhesives, petrol, or fuel gases such as butane in cigarette-lighter refills, in order to induce euphoria. Solvent abuse is an increasingly common practice among children, especially teenagers. It is highly addictive, and damages the brain and lungs, as well as the mucous membranes that line the nasal cavity. — Also called *glue-sniffing.*

Solway Firth an inlet of the Irish Sea which separates Cumbria in England from Dumfries and Galloway in Scotland. It is the estuary of the Esk and Eden rivers, length c.65km/40mi; the width at its mouth is c.40km/25mi. The Solway Firth is noted for its salmon fisheries.

Solzhenitsyn, Aleksandr (Isayevich) (1918–) Russian writer, born in Kislovodsk. He fought in World War II, and was imprisoned in a Russian labour camp (1945–53). His first novel, *One Day in the Life of Ivan Denisovich* (1962), was acclaimed both in the USSR and the West, but his subsequent denunciation of Soviet censorship led to the banning of his later, semi-autobiographical novels, *Cancer Ward* (1968) and *The First Circle* (1968). He was expelled from the Soviet Writers' Union in 1969, and awarded the Nobel Prize for Literature in 1970 (received in 1974). His later books include *The Gulag Archipelago* (3 vols, 1973–6), a factual account of the Stalinist terror, for which he was arrested and exiled (1974). He settled in the USA, and in 1990 his Russian citizenship was restored to him, and the treason charges against him were dropped in 1991.

Som. *abbrev.* Somerset.

Soma in Hindu mythology, an intoxicating, probably hallucinogenic, drink extracted from a plant, drunk by both gods and men. It is personified as a god in the *Rig Veda* texts.

Somali a Cushitic-speaking people of Somalia and parts of Kenya, Ethiopia, and Djibouti. Roughly two thirds of the Somali population is made up by the Samaal (nomadic herders who live inland); the Saab are farmers and traders who live along the coast. They are divided into many traditionally autonomous groups, who have a powerful sense of cultural unity based largely on Islam and the Somali language.

Somalia, official name **Somali Democratic Republic**, Arabic **Jamhuriyadda Dimugradiga Somaliya** POP (1992e) 9.2m, a NE African republic, divided into 16 regions. AREA 686 803sq km/ 265 106sq mi. It is bounded NW by Djibouti, W by Ethiopia, SW by Kenya, E by the Indian Ocean, and N by the Gulf of Aden. CAPITAL Mogadishu. CHIEF TOWNS Hargeisa, Berbera, Kismayu. TIME ZONE GMT +3. Islam is the chief religion. OFFICIAL LANGUAGE Somali, Arabic. CURRENCY the Somali shilling. PHYSICAL DESCRIPTION occupies the E Horn of Africa where a dry

coastal plain broadens to the S and rises inland to a plateau at nearly 1 000m; forested mountains on the Gulf of Aden coast rise to 2 416m at Mt Shimbiris. CLIMATE considerable variation in climate; Berbera on the N coast has an annual average rainfall of 61mm and average maximum daily temperatures of 29–42°C; more rainfall from Apr to Sep on the E coast; Mogadishu has an annual average rainfall of 490mm and average daily maximum temperatures of 28–32°C; serious and persistent threat of drought. HISTORY settled by the Muslims in the 7c; Italian, French, and British interests after the opening of the Suez Canal in 1869; after World War II, Somalia was formed by the amalgamation of Italian and British protectorates; it gained independence in 1960; since the 1960s there has been territorial conflict with Ethiopia (which has a large Somali population); military coup in 1969; a new constitution was adopted in 1979; in the early 1990s there was Civil War and the population faced starvation; the NE region seceded as the Somaliland Republic; UN troops secured routes for relief convoys carrying food aid. GOVERNMENT governed by a President, a Council of Ministers, and a People's Assembly of 171 elected members and six appointed deputies; new constitution in 1991. ECONOMY a largely nomadic people (70%) raising cattle, sheep, goats, camels; cultivation close to rivers; bananas, sugar, spices, cotton, rice, citrus fruits, maize, sorghum, oilseeds, tobacco; textiles; cigarettes; food processing; fishing; some tin, gypsum, uranium, iron ore; difficult communications within the country are being helped by a major road-building programme.

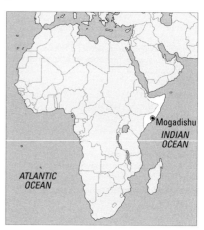

Somalia

somatic *adj. Medicine, Biol.* **1** of the body, rather than the mind. **2** of the body, as opposed to reproduction: *somatic cells.* [from Greek *soma*, body]

somatotrophin *noun Physiol.* growth hormone. [from Greek *soma*, body]

sombre *adj.* **1** sad and serious; grave. **2** dark and gloomy. **3** suggesting seriousness, rather than light-heartedness. [from French *sombre*, perhaps from Latin *sub*, under + *umbra*, shade]

sombrely *adv.* in a sombre way.

sombrero *noun* (PL. **sombreros**) a man's straw or felt hat with a very wide brim, popular in Mexico. [from Spanish *sombrero*, from *sombra*, shade]

some — *adj.* **1** denoting an unknown or unspecified amount or number of. **2** of unknown or unspecified nature or identity: *some problem with the engine.* **3** quite a lot of: *have been waiting for some time.* **4** at least a little: *try to feel some excitement.* **5** a poor example of: *some friend you are!* **6** *colloq.* an excellent or impressive example of: *that was some shot!* — *pron.* **1** certain unspecified things or people: *some say he should resign.* **2** an unspecified amount or number: *give him some, too.* — *adv.* **1** to an unspecified extent: *play some more.* **2** approximately: *some twenty feet deep.* [from Anglo-Saxon *sum*]

-some *suffix* forming words meaning: **1** causing or producing: *troublesome.* **2** inviting: *cuddlesome.* **3** tending to: *quarrelsome.* **4** a group of the specified number of people or things: *a foursome.* [from Anglo-Saxon *-sum*]

somebody *pron.* **1** an unknown or unspecified person; someone. **2** a person of importance: *tried to be somebody.*

someday *adv.* at an unknown or unspecified time in the future.

somehow *adv.* **1** in some way not yet known. **2** for a reason not easy to explain.

Some Like It Hot a US film directed by Billy Wilder (1959). It is a comedy about two men (played by Tony Curtis and Jack Lemmon) who cross-dress to escape gangland conflict and have various encounters while in disguise.

someone *pron.* somebody.

somersault — *noun* a leap or roll in which the whole body turns a complete circle forwards or backwards, leading with the head. — *verb intrans.* to perform such a leap or roll. [from Latin *supra*, over + *saltus*, leap]

Somerset POP (1992e) 473 000, a county in SW England, divided into five districts. AREA 3 451sq km/1 332sq mi. It is bounded N by the Bristol Channel and Avon, E by Wiltshire, S by Dorset, and W by Devon. PHYSICAL DESCRIPTION the uplands in the W include Exmoor and the Brendon and Quantock Hills; the Mendip Hills are in the NE and the Blackdown Hills in the S. CHIEF TOWNS Taunton (county town), Bridg'water, Yeovil. ECONOMY agriculture (especially dairy farming); light engineering; beverages (especially cider); footwear; food processing; tourism. NOTABLE FEATURES Cheddar Gorge; Wookey Hole limestone caves.

Somerset House a building in the Strand, London, designed by Sir William Chambers to house the Royal Academy (now in Burlington House) and government offices, and built (1776–86) on the site of the 16c residence of Protector Somerset (1506–52). It formerly housed the General Register Office of England and Wales, and is now used to accommodate the Inland Revenue and the Courtauld Institute.

Somerset Maugham a portrait painting by Graham Sutherland (1949).

Somers (of Evesham), John Somers, 1st Baron (1651–1716) English Whig statesman, born in Worcester. An MP from 1689, he helped to draft the Declaration of Rights (1689), and after the Revolution of 1688 held several posts under William III, including Lord Chancellor (1697). As William's most trusted minister, he was the object of frequent attacks, which led to his impeachment (and acquittal) in 1701. He was President of the Privy Council under Anne (1708–14).

something — *pron.* **1** a thing not known or not stated: *take something to eat.* **2** an amount or number not known or not stated: *something short of 1 000 people / aged about 40 something.* **3** a person or thing of importance: *make something of oneself / make something out of a casual remark.* **4** a certain truth or value: *there is something in what you say.* **5** *colloq.* an impressive person or thing: *that meal was really something!* — *adv.* to some degree; rather: *the garden looks something like a scrapyard.* — **something of a ...** to some extent: *she's something of a local celebrity.*

sometime *adv.* at an unknown or unspecified time in the future or the past.

sometimes *adv.* occasionally.

somewhat *adv.* rather; a little. — **somewhat of** ... ... to some extent: *has lost somewhat of his strength.*

somewhere *adv.* in or to some place or degree, or at some point, not known or not specified.

Somme, Battle of the a major World War I British offensive (1 Jul–19 Nov 1916) launched by Commander-in-Chief Douglas Haig against German troops in NW France. It developed into the bloodiest battle in world history, with more than one million casualties, and by the time the attack was abandoned, the Allies had advanced only 16km/10mi from previous positions. The battle formed part of the war of attrition on the Western Front.

Somme, River a river in N France, length 245km/152mi. Rising near St Quentin in Aisne department, it flows SW then NW and W to the English Channel near Saint-Valéry-sur-Somme. Canals link the Somme to the waterways of the industrial N. Some of the worst fighting of World War I took place here in 1916.

Sommerfeld, Arnold (1868–1951) German physicist, born in Königsberg (now Kaliningrad, Russia). Professor at Clausthal, Aachen, and Munich, he developed the theory of the gyroscope. He also researched wave spreading in wireless telegraphy, applied quantum theory to multi-electron atoms, and evolved a theory of the behaviour of electrons in metals.

somnambulism *noun formal* sleepwalking. [from Latin *somnus*, sleep + *ambulare*, to walk]

somnambulist *noun* a sleepwalker.

Somnath, Temple of a famous Shiva temple in SW Gujarat, India. Its fabled wealth attracted the attention of Mahmud of Ghazni, who sacked it in 1024 to remove its jewels and (according to tradition) its wonderful gates. The event contributed to a tradition of Muslim intolerance and ferocity among N Indian Hindus.

somnolence *noun* sleepiness, drowsiness.

somnolent *adj. formal* sleepy or drowsy; causing sleepiness or drowsiness. [from Latin *somnus*, sleep]

Somoza (García) Anastasio (1896–1956) Nicaraguan dictator, born in San Marcos, Nicaragua. After being educated in the USA, as chief of the National Guard he established himself in supreme power in the early 1930s, and retained it until assassinated. His sons Luis Somoza Debayle (1923–67) and Anastasio Somoza Debayle (1925–80) continued dynastic control of Nicaragua until the 1979 revolution.

son[1] *noun* **1** a male child. **2** a male person closely associated with, or seen as developing from, a particular activity or set of circumstances: *a son of the Russian revolution.* **3** a familiar and often patronizing term of address used to a boy or man. **4** (**the Son**) *Christianity* Christ considered as the second person of the Trinity. [from Anglo-Saxon *sunu*]

son[2] *noun* a style of Cuban music played with claves, bongo drums, and guitar. [from Spanish *son*, sound]

sonar *noun* a system that is used to determine the location of underwater objects, eg submarines, shipwrecks, shoals of fish, by transmitting ultrasound signals from the bottom of a ship and measuring the time taken for their echoes to return when they strike an obstacle (*active sonar*). *Passive sonar* uses a listening device to locate sources of underwater sounds. [from *sound navigation and ranging*]

sonata *noun* a piece of classical music, in three or more movements, for a solo instrument, especially the piano. [from Italian *sonata*, from *sonare*, to sound]

sonata form the plan or form most often used since c.1750 in the design of the first movement (and occasionally the slow movement and finale) of a sonata or symphony. It is divided into three basic sections: exposition, development, and recapitulation.

sonatina *noun* a short sonata, usually one which is relatively straightforward technically. [from Italian, a diminutive of *sonata*]

Sondheim, Stephen (Joshua) (1930–) US composer and lyricist, born in New York City. He studied lyric-writing with Oscar Hammerstein II and wrote the lyrics for Leonard Bernstein's *West Side Story* (1957). His own highly successful musicals, including *A Funny Thing Happened on the Way to the Forum* (1962), *A Little Night Music* (1972), and *Sweeney Todd* (1979), have contributed to the revival of the musical in the USA.

son et lumière a dramatic night-time outdoor spectacle with lights, music, and narration on a particular theme, often staged at and presenting the history of a famous building. [French, = sound and light]

song *noun* **1** a set of words to be sung, usually with accompanying music. **2** the musical call of certain birds. **3** singing: *poetry and song.* **4** a bargain price: *going for a song.* — **make a song and dance about something** *colloq.* to make an unnecessary fuss about it. [from Anglo-Saxon *sang*]

songbird *noun* any of various kinds of bird with a musical call.

song cycle a set of songs, often to words by a single poet and connected by some common theme or narrative thread: usually intended to be performed complete. Beethoven's *An die ferne Geliebte* ('To the distant Beloved') is one of the earliest examples; later examples include Franz Schubert's *Winterreise* ('Winter Journey'), Gustav Mahler's *Kindertotenlieder* ('Songs on the Death of Children'), and Ralph Vaughan Williams's *On Wenlock Edge*.

Song of Solomon *or* **Song of Songs** a book of the Hebrew Bible and Old Testament, probably a collection of love songs, although sometimes considered a single poem or drama between two lovers, usually dated c.3c BC. It speaks of the ecstatic love between Solomon and his wife.

Song of the Earth, The see LIED VON DER ERDE, DAS.

Songs of Innocence and Experience a collection of poems and etchings by William Blake (*Songs of Innocence*, 1789; *Songs of Experience*, 1794). The first book contains mainly poems on the state of childhood, while the second shows the effects of adult experience on the childlike mind.

songster *noun old use* a talented (especially male) singer.

songstress *noun old use* a talented female singer.

Songs without Words (Lieder ohne Worte) piano pieces collected into eight books of six pieces each, composed by Felix Mendelssohn (1830–45). *Lied ohne Worte* (Song without Words) is both the title of a piece he wrote for cello and piano (Op 109, 1845) and a term invented by him for lyrical songs such as these, which have a distinctive song-like melody.

song thrush a common European thrush, well known for its tuneful call.

sonic *adj.* **1** relating to or using sound or sound waves. **2** travelling at (approximately) the speed of sound. [from Latin *sonus*]

sonic boom a loud boom that is heard when an aircraft flying through the Earth's atmosphere reaches supersonic speed, ie passes through the sound barrier. It is heard at the point where a high-pressure shock wave reaches the Earth's surface. The first aircraft to experience this phenomenon was the Bell XS-1 piloted by Capt Charles (Chuck) Yeager on 14 Oct 1947.

son-in-law *noun* (PL. **sons-in-law**) the husband of one's daughter.

sonnet *noun* a poem with 14 lines of 10 or 11 syllables each and a regular rhyming pattern. [from Italian *sonetto*]

◇ The sonnet was introduced in 13c Italy, and had become a major poetic form across Europe by the 16c. Early examples in English include the cycles *Astrophil and Stella* (1591) by Sir Philip Sydney and *Amoretti* (1595) by Edmund Spenser; Shakespeare's sequence of 154 sonnets was published in 1609. There have been major revivals of the form, especially by the Romantic poets (Keats, Wordsworth, Shelley), and poets of the Victorian period (Elizabeth Barrett Browning, Dante Gabriel Rossetti); and developments of its traditional forms (eg by Gerard Manley Hopkins). The traditional forms are: the Petrarchan, structured as octave and sestet, rhyming *abbabba, cdecde*; the Spenserian, of three quatrains and a couplet, rhyming *abab, bcbc, cdcd, ee*; and the Shakespearian, of three quatrains and a couplet, rhyming *abab, cdcd, efef, gg*.

Sonnets from the Portuguese a sonnet-sequence by Elizabeth Barrett Browning (in *Poems*, 1850). They are love poems written for Robert Browning; 'the Portuguese' was his pet name for her.

sonny *noun* a familiar (often condescending) term of address used to a boy or man.

Son of Man a term found in Jewish and Christian literature, especially in the New Testament Gospels as a self-designation of Jesus. The term's significance is debated: in Aramaic it is an idiomatic reference to 'man' in general, and possibly also a circumlocution for 'I', but in eg Daniel 7.13 it refers to the one who will be exalted at the end of the age and given complete sovereignty.

sonority *or* **sonorousness** *noun* a sonorous quality or character.

sonorous *adj.* **1** sounding impressively loud and deep. **2** giving out a deep clear sound when struck: *a sonorous bell.* **3** *said of language* impressively eloquent. [from Latin *sonare*, to sound]

Sons and Lovers a novel by D H Lawrence (1913). It is set in a mining village in Nottinghamshire and describes the lives of the members of the Morel family.

Sons of Liberty an organization in the American Revolution that provided popular leadership in the resistance movement against Britain. Composed mainly of merchants, lawyers, artisans, and small traders, it operated as an organized inter-colonial group against the Stamp Act in 1765–6, and later helped to set up the First Continental Congress (1774). The term was also used for all Americans involved in the revolutionary movement.

soon *adv.* **1** in a short time from now or from a stated time. **2** quickly; with little delay. **3** willingly: *would sooner pay the fine than go to prison.*
— **as soon as** ... at or not before the moment when: *will pay you as soon as I receive the goods.*
as soon ... as ... used to state that the first alternative is slightly preferable to the second: *would just as soon die as marry him.*
no sooner ... than ... immediately after ... then: *no sooner had I mentioned his name than he appeared.*
no sooner said than done *said of a request, promise, etc* immediately fulfilled.
sooner or later eventually.
[from Anglo-Saxon *sona*]

soot *noun* a black powdery substance produced when coal or wood is burned; smut. [from Anglo-Saxon *sot*]

soothe *verb* **1** to bring relief from (a pain, etc). **2** to comfort or calm (someone). [from Anglo-Saxon *gesothian*, to confirm as true]

soothing *adj.* that soothes.

soothsay *verb intrans.* to foretell or divine.

soothsayer *noun* a person who predicts the future; a seer. [from archaic *sooth*, truth + SAY]

sooty *adj.* (**sootier**, **sootiest**) **1** covered with soot. **2** like or consisting of soot.

sop — *noun* **1** (*often* **sops**) a piece of food, especially bread, dipped in a liquid, eg soup. **2** something given or done as a bribe or in order to pacify someone. — *verb* (**sopped**, **sopping**) (*usually* **sop something up**) to mop or soak it up. [from Anglo-Saxon *sopp*]

Soper, Donald (Oliver) Soper, Baron (1903–) English Methodist minister, born in London. Widely known for his open-air speaking on London's Tower Hill, he was superintendent of the West London Mission (1936–78), and has written many books on Christianity and social questions, and especially on international issues from the pacifist angle.

Sophia (1630–1714) Electress of Hanover, born in The Hague, the youngest daughter of Elizabeth Stuart (the daughter of James I of England) and Frederick Elector Palatine, who was also elected King of Bohemia (1618). In 1658 she married Ernest Augustus, Duke of Brunswick-Lüneburg, who became the first Elector of Hanover. She was the mother of George, Elector of Hanover, who became George I of Britain. Sophia was named in the Act of Settlement (1701) as the Protestant successor to the English Crown after Anne, but died before her.

Sophia a female first name. [from Greek *sophia*, wisdom]

Sophia Alexeyevna (1657–1704) Regent of Russia (1682–9), daughter of Tsar Alexey Mikhailovich and his first wife, Maria Miloslavskaya, born in Moscow. On the death of her brother, Tsar Fyodor Alexeyevich (1682), she opposed the accession of her half-brother, Peter (the future Peter the Great), and used a popular uprising in Moscow to press the candidature of her mentally deficient brother, Ivan. Ivan (V) and Peter were proclaimed joint Tsars, with Sophia as Regent. Supported by leading boyars (aristocrats) she became the *de facto* ruler of Russia, until removed from power in 1689 by a faction of the nobility.

sophism *noun* a convincing but false argument or explanation, especially one intended to deceive. [from Greek *sophisma*, clever device, from *sophia*, wisdom]

sophist *noun* a person who employs sophism.

sophisticate — *verb* to make sophisticated. — *noun* a sophisticated person. [from Latin *sophisticare*, to adulterate]

sophisticated *adj.* **1** having or displaying a broad knowledge and experience of the world, especially of artistic and intellectual things; appealing to or frequented by people with such knowledge and experience. **2** complex and subtle: *sophisticated weaponry / sophisticated arguments.*

sophistication *noun* being sophisticated.

sophistry *noun* (PL. **sophistries**) **1** plausibly deceptive or fallacious reasoning, or an instance of this. **2** the art of reasoning speciously.

Sophists a collection of 5c BC Greek itinerant teachers of rhetoric, statecraft, and philosophy, the most influential of whom was Protagoras of Abdera. They are portrayed in the dialogues of Plato, usually as dialectical opponents of Socrates, more interested in winning arguments than in finding out the truth. Their philosophical doctrines typically included the denial of a real world beyond the world of appearances, scepticism about the gods, and a belief in the perfectibility of humans.

Sophocles (c.496–406 BC) Greek tragic dramatist, born in Colonus Hippius. He wrote 123 plays, of which only seven survive: *Ajax, Electra, Women of Trachis, Philoctetes*, and his three major plays *Oedipus Rex, Oedipus at Colonus*, and *Antigone*. He played an important part in Athenian public life, and assisted Pericles in the war against the Samians (440 BC).

sophomore *noun* North Amer., esp. US a second-year student at a school or university. [from Greek *sophos*, wise + *moros*, foolish]

soporific — *adj.* **1** causing sleep. **2** extremely slow and boring: *a soporific speech.* — *noun* a sleep-inducing drug. [from Latin *sopor*, deep sleep + *facere*, to make]

Sopot, German **Zoppot** POP (1990) 47 000, a resort town in Gdańsk voivodship, N Poland. It is situated 10km/6mi NW of Gdańsk, between wooded slopes and the Bay of Gdańsk. Sopot forms part of the *Tri-City* with Gdańsk and Gdynia. NOTABLE FEATURES hydrotherapy treatment centre; open-air opera; racecourse.

soppily *adv.* in a soppy way.

soppiness *noun* **1** being soppy. **2** soppy behaviour.

sopping *adj., adv.* (*also* **sopping wet**) thoroughly wet; soaking.

soppy *adj.* (**soppier**, **soppiest**) *colloq.* weakly sentimental. [from SOP]

soprano *noun* (PL. **sopranos**) **1** a singing voice of the highest pitch for a woman or a boy; also, a person having this voice. **2** a musical part for such a voice. **3** a musical instrument high or highest in pitch in relation to others in its family. [from Italian *soprano*, from Latin *supra*, above]

Sopwith, Sir Thomas Octave Murdoch (1888–1989) British aircraft designer and sportsman, born in London. He won a prize for the longest flight across the English Channel in 1910, and founded the Sopwith Aviation Company in 1912, building many of the aircraft used in World War I, such as the Sopwith Camel. He later became Chairman and President of the Hawker Siddeley Group.

Sopwith Camel the most successful combat aircraft of World War I, so named because of its hump-backed shape. Its extreme manoeuvrability was the downfall of many inexperienced pilots and caused one Camel pilot to liken it to flying a 'gyroscope with wings'.

sorbet *noun* a dish of sweetened fruit juice, frozen and served as a kind of ice-cream; a water ice. [from French *sorbet*, from Arabic *sharbah*, drink]

sorbitol *noun Chem.* (FORMULA $C_6H_8(OH)_6$) a white crystalline carbohydrate, soluble in water, that is used in cosmetics, toothpastes, resins, and pharmaceuticals, and as a food additive and sweetening agent. It is used by diabetics as a substitute for sugar.

Sorbonne see PARIS, UNIVERSITY OF.

Sorby, Henry Clifton (1826–1908) English geologist and metallurgist, born in Woodbourne, Sheffield. He was the first to study rocks in thin section under the microscope, demonstrating that this could reveal much about their mode of origin, and also adapted the technique for the study of metals by treating polished surfaces with etching materials.

sorcerer *noun* a person who practises sorcery.

sorceress *noun* a woman who practises sorcery.

sorcery *noun* the performing of magic using the power of supernatural forces, especially of black magic using the power of evil spirits. [from Old French *sorcerie*]

sordid *adj.* **1** repulsively filthy; squalid. **2** morally revolting; ignoble. [from Latin *sordidus*, dirty]

sordino *noun* (PL. **sordini**) *Mus.* a mute (or damper) used to soften or deaden the sound of a musical instrument. The indication on musical scores that a part or passage is to be played *con sordino* means 'with the mute'; the term *senza sordino* means 'without the mute'. [from Italian, from Latin *surdus*, deaf, noiseless]

sore — *adj.* **1** painful when touched; tender. **2** *North Amer., esp. US* angry or resentful. — *noun* a diseased spot or area, especially an ulcer or boil. — **stick out like a sore thumb** *colloq.* to be awkwardly obvious or noticeable, especially by being different or out of place. [from Anglo-Saxon *sar*]

sorely *adv.* acutely; very much.

sore point a subject causing much anger or resentment when raised.

sorghum *noun* **1** a cereal of the genus *Sorghum* belonging to the grass family (Gramineae), and having broad leaves and a tall pithy stem bearing dense terminal clusters of small grains. It is resistant to drought, and can be grown in semi-arid tropical regions such as Mexico and the Sudan. The most important species is *S.vulgare* (guinea corn), cultivated as a staple food crop in much of Africa and parts of Asia, and as feedstuff for animal livestock in America and Australia. The juice extracted from the cane of sweet varieties of sorghum is used as a source of molasses. **2** syrup obtained from this plant. [from Italian *sorgo*]

sorority *noun* (PL. **sororities**) a women's club or society, especially any of several such societies in a US university. [from Latin *soror*, sister]

sorrel[1] *noun* any of various sour-tasting herbs of the dock family, used medicinally and in salads. [from Old French *sorele*, from *sur*, sour]

sorrel[2] — *adj.* of a reddish-brown or light chestnut colour. — *noun* a horse of this colour. [from Old French *sorel*]

sorrow — *noun* **1** grief or deep sadness arising from loss or disappointment. **2** a cause of this. — *verb intrans.* to have or express such feelings. [from Anglo-Saxon *sorg*]

sorrowful *adj.* **1** full of sorrow; sad, dejected. **2** causing, showing, or expressing sorrow.

sorrowfully *adv.* in a sorrowful way.

sorry — *adj.* (**sorrier**, **sorriest**) **1** (*often* **sorry for something**) feeling regret or shame about something one has done or for which one is responsible. **2** (**sorry for someone**) feeling pity or sympathy towards them. **3** pitifully bad: *in a sorry state.* **4** contemptibly bad; extremely poor: *a sorry excuse.* — *interj.* **1** used as an apology. **2** *said as a question* asking for something just said to be repeated. [from Anglo-Saxon *sarig*, wounded, influenced in meaning by SORROW]

sort — *noun* **1** a kind, type, or class. **2** *colloq.* a person: *not a bad sort.* — *verb* **1** to arrange into different groups according to type or kind. **2** *colloq.* to put right. **3** *colloq.* to deal with, especially to punish. — **a sort of** ... something like a: *a sort of bottle with a tube attached.* **of a sort** *or* **of sorts** of an inferior or untypical kind: *an author of a sort / a container of sorts.* **out of sorts** *colloq.* **1** slightly unwell. **2** peevish; bad-tempered. **sort of** ... *colloq.* rather ...; ... in a way; ... to a certain extent: *feeling sort of embarrassed.* **sort someone out** *colloq.* to deal with them firmly and decisively. **sort something out 1** to separate it out from a mixed collection into a group or groups according to kind. **2** to put it into order; to arrange it methodically. **3** to resolve the difficulties relating to it; to put it right. [from Latin *sortis*, a lot, from *sortiri*, to draw lots]

sortie — *noun* **1** a sudden attack by besieged troops. **2** an operational flight by a single military aircraft. **3** *colloq.* a short trip to an unpleasant or unfamiliar place. — *verb intrans.* (**sortied**, **sortieing**) to make a sortie. [from French *sortie*, from *sortir*, to go out]

sorus *noun* (PL. **sori**) *Bot.* a cluster of sporangia or soredia. [from Greek *soros*, heap]

SOS *noun* **1** a ship's or aircraft's call for help, consisting of these letters repeated in Morse code. **2** *colloq.* any call for help. [letters chosen for ease of transmission and recognition in Morse code]

Sosigenes (fl. c.40 BC) Alexandrian astronomer and advisor to Julius Caesar in his reform of the calendar. He recommended the introduction of a calendar year of 365.25 days, and inserted an extra 67 days into the year 46 BC to bring the months back into register with the seasons. The Julian calendar was replaced in 1582 by the improved Gregorian system.

so-so *adj., adv. colloq.* neither very good nor very bad; passable; middling.

sostenuto *adv., adj. Mus.* in a steady flowing way, without cutting short any notes. [from Italian *sostenuto*, sustained]

sot *noun old use* a person who is continually drunk. [from Old French *sot*]

Sotheby, John (1740–1807) English auctioneer and antiquarian. He became a director (1780–1800) of the firm founded by his uncle, then known as Leigh and Sotheby, which was transferred to the Strand, London, in 1803.

Sotheby's an art auction firm founded in London by bookseller Samuel Baker in 1744. The firm originally concentrated on auctioning books, manuscripts, and prints until the end of World War I, when paintings and other works of art became its chief sellers. It has been US-owned since 1983.

Sotho-Tswana a group of Sotho-speaking peoples of Botswana, Lesotho, the Transvaal, Orange Free State, and N Cape, distinct from the other main South African group of Bantu-speakers, the Nguni. The main sub-groupings are: the various Tswana groups, traditionally independent chiefdoms; the S Sotho of Lesotho and the Orange Free State, who were united in a single political unit in the early 19c; the Pedi and other N Sotho peoples of the N Transvaal.

sottish *adj.* **1** like a sot. **2** befuddled with drink.

sotto voce 1 in a quiet voice, so as not to be overheard. **2** *Mus.* very softly. [from Italian *sotto voce*, below the voice]

sou *noun* **1** a former French coin of low value. **2** *colloq.* the smallest amount of money: *haven't a sou.* [from French *sou*]

sou' *combining form Naut.* south: *a sou'wester.*

soubrette *noun* a minor female part in a play, especially that of an impudent, flirtatious, or intriguing maid. [from French *soubrette*, from Provençal *soubreto*, coy]

soubriquet see SOBRIQUET.

soufflé *noun* a light sweet or savoury baked dish, a frothy mass of whipped egg-whites with other ingredients mixed in. [from French *soufflé*, from *souffler*, to puff up]

sough — *noun* a sighing sound made by the wind blowing through trees. — *verb intrans.* to make this sound. [from Anglo-Saxon *swogan*, to rustle]

sought past tense and past participle of SEEK.

sought-after *adj.* desired; in demand.

souk *noun* a market-place in Muslim countries. [from Arabic *suq*]

soukous a central African style of dance music, originating in Zaire, combining guitar, drumming, and vocal melodies. [from French *secouer*, to shake]

soul — *noun* **1** the non-physical part of a person, with personality, emotions, and intellect, widely believed to survive in some form after the death of the body. **2** emotional sensitivity; ordinary human feelings of sympathy: *a singer with no soul / cruelty committed by brutes with no soul.* **3** essential nature: *recognize the soul of the political movement.* **4** motivating force; leader: *the soul of the revolution.* **5** (**the soul of** ...) a perfect example of ...; a personification of: *she is the soul of discretion.* **6** *colloq.* a person: *a kind soul.* **7** soul music. — *adj.* relating to Black American culture: *soul food.*

◇ The concept derives from Plato, for whom it was a metaphysical entity, ultimately incorruptible and eternal. In religious thought the soul is widely regarded as a divine or immortal element imprisoned in the human body, which is liberated at death and continues to exist in disembodied form or is reincarnated in a new body.

soul-destroying *adj.* **1** extremely dull, boring, or repetitive. **2** extremely difficult to tolerate or accept emotionally.

soulful *adj.* having or expressing deep feelings, especially of sadness.

soulfully *adv.* in a soulful way.

soulless *adj.* **1** having no emotional sensitivity or ordinary human sympathy. **2** *said of a task, etc* for which no human qualities are required; extremely monotonous or mechanical. **3** *said of a place* bleak; lifeless.

soul mate a person with whom one shares the same feelings, thoughts, and ideas.

soul music a jazzier, more mainstream type of blues music, typically earthy and emotional in tone, usually dealing with love.

soul-searching *noun* critical examination of one's own conscience, motives, actions, etc.

Soult, Nicolas Jean de Dieu (1769–1851) French soldier, born in Saint-Amans-La-Bastide. Created Marshal of France by Napoleon in 1804, he led the French armies in the Peninsular War (1808–14) until he was defeated at Toulouse (1814). He opportunistically turned Royalist after Napoleon's abdication, but joined him in the Hundred Days, and acted as his Chief-of-Staff at Waterloo. Exiled until 1819, he was gradually restored to all his honours, and presided over three ministries of Louis Philippe (1832–4, 1839–40, 1840–7).

Sound, The, Danish **Øresund** a strait between Zealand I, Denmark, and S Sweden. It connects the Kattegat with the Baltic Sea. Its narrowest section is 6km/4mi wide.

sound[1] — *noun* **1** *Physics* periodic vibrations that are propagated through a medium, eg air, as pressure waves, so that the medium is displaced from its equilibrium state. Unlike electromagnetic radiation, such as light, sound cannot travel through a vacuum. **2** the noise that is heard as a result of such periodic vibrations. **3** audible quality: *the guitar has a nice sound.* **4** the mental impression created by something heard: *don't like the sound of that.* **5** aural material, eg spoken commentary and music, accompanying a film or broadcast: *sound editor.* **6** *colloq.* volume or volume control, especially on a television set. **7** (*often* **sounds**) *slang* music, especially pop music: *the sounds of the 60s.* — *verb* **1** *trans., intrans.* to produce or cause to produce a sound. **2** *intrans.* to create an impression in the mind when heard: *sounds like fun.* **3** to pronounce: *does not sound his h's.* **4** to announce or signal with a sound: *sound the alarm.* **5** *Medicine* to examine by tapping or listening. See also SOUND[3] VERB 2. — **sound off** *intrans. colloq.* to state one's opinions forcefully, especially one's complaints angrily. [from Latin *sonus*]

◇ The pitch of a sound depends on its frequency or wavelength, high-pitched sounds having higher frequencies than low-pitched ones. The loudness of a sound depends on the height (known as the *amplitude*) of its waves. Quiet sounds have a small amplitude, and loud sounds have a large amplitude. Sound travels at different speeds in different media, such that the denser the medium, the faster sound travels, eg sound travels faster in water than in air. High-frequency sounds with short wavelengths also travel further before fading. Young people can hear sounds with frequencies between about 20 hertz (cycles per second) and 20 000 hertz, but the range of frequencies that can be heard gets smaller with increasing age. Different animals hear at different frequencies, eg bats can hear up to 120 000 hertz, crickets up to 100 000 hertz, and frogs up to 50 000 hertz.

sound² — *adj.* **1** not damaged or injured; in good condition; healthy. **2** sensible; well-founded; reliable: *sound advice.* **3** acceptable or approved of. **4** *said especially of punishment, etc* severe, hard, thorough: *a sound spanking.* **5** *said of sleep* deep and undisturbed. — *adv.* deeply: *sound asleep.* [from Anglo-Saxon *gesund*]

sound³ — *verb* **1** to measure the depth of (especially the sea). **2** *Medicine* to examine (a hollow organ, etc) with a probe (see also SOUND¹ *verb* 5). — *noun* a probe for examining hollow organs.
— **sound someone out** to try to discover their opinions or intentions.
[from Old French *sonder*]

sound⁴ *noun* a narrow passage of water connecting two seas or separating an island and the mainland; a strait. [from Anglo-Saxon *sund*]

Sound and the Fury, The a novel by William Faulkner (1929). It is a multiple narrative which relates in four different accounts the degeneration of the white Compson family in the Deep South.

sound barrier the resistance an aircraft meets when it reaches speeds close to the speed of sound. At this point the power required to increase speed rises steeply because of the formation of shock waves.

soundbite *noun* a short and succinct statement delivered on television or radio by a public figure, usually in a form inviting quotation.

soundboard *noun Comput.* a printed circuit board added to a computer to provide or enhance sound effects.

sound-box *noun* the hollow body of a violin, guitar, etc.

sound effects artificially produced sounds matching actions in film, broadcasting or theatre.

sounding *noun* **1** the act of measuring depth, especially of the sea. **2** a depth measured. **3** (*often* **soundings**) a sampling of opinions or (eg voting) intentions.

sounding-board *noun* **1** a board over a stage or pulpit directing the speaker's voice towards the audience. **2** a means of testing the acceptability or popularity of ideas or opinions.

soundly *adv.* in a sound way; sensibly, correctly.

Sound of Music, The a US film directed by Robert Wise (1965). Based on the true story of the Von Trapp family's escape to neutral Switzerland in 1938, it is a musical focusing on a carefree young governess (played by Julie Andrews) who gradually falls in love with her widowed employer.

soundtrack *noun* **1** a band of magnetic tape along the edge of a cinematographic film, on which the sound is recorded. **2** a recording of the music from a film or broadcast.

soup *noun* a liquid food made by stewing meat, vegetables, or grains.
— **in the soup** *slang* in trouble or difficulty.

soup something up *colloq.* to make changes to a vehicle or its engine to increase its speed or power.
[from Old French *soupe*]

soupçon *noun literary, facetious* the slightest amount; a hint or dash. [from French *soupçon*, suspicion]

soup kitchen a place where volunteer workers supply free food to people in need.

soupy *adj.* (**soupier**, **soupiest**) having the appearance or consistency of soup.

sour — *adj.* **1** having an acid taste or smell, similar to that of lemon juice or vinegar. **2** rancid or stale because of fermentation: *sour milk.* **3** sullen; miserable: *sour-faced old man.* **4** bad, unsuccessful, or inharmonious: *the marriage turned sour.* — *verb trans., intrans.* to make or become sour, especially bad, unsuccessful, or inharmonious. [from Anglo-Saxon *sur*]

source *noun* **1** the place, thing, person, or circumstance from which anything begins or develops; origin. **2** the point where a river or stream begins. **3** a person, or a book or other document, providing information or evidence. [from Latin *surgere*, to rise]

sour cream cream deliberately made sour by the action of bacteria, for use in savoury dishes.

sour grapes envy and resentment in the form of pretended dislike or disapproval of the thing or person envied.

sourly *adv.* in a sour way, with a sour expression.

sourpuss *noun colloq.* a habitually sullen or miserable person.

Sousa, John Philip (1854–1932) US composer and bandmaster, born in Washington, DC. His early training as a conductor was gained with theatre orchestras, and in 1880 he led the US Marine Band. His own band (formed 1892) won an international reputation, and he became known as the composer of over 100 rousing military marches, 10 comic operas (eg *El Capito*), and as the inventor of the sousaphone (a large brass wind instrument like the tuba).

souse — *verb* **1** to steep or cook in vinegar or white wine. **2** to pickle. **3** to plunge in a liquid. **4** to make thoroughly wet; to drench. — *noun* **1** an act of sousing. **2** the liquid in which food is soused. **3** *North Amer., esp. US* pickle; any pickled food. [from Old German *sulza*]

soused *adj. slang* drunk.

Sousse 1 POP (1989) 101 000, the port capital of Sousse governorate, NE Tunisia. It lies 115km/71mi SE of Tunis. HISTORY founded by the Phoenicians in the 9c BC; destroyed by the Vandals in AD 434. NOTABLE FEATURES Mosque Zakak; the Great Mosque (850); Hanafite Mosque; Ribat Fortress (9c); Sousse Medina, a World Heritage site. **2** a governorate in NE Tunisia with Sousse as its capital.

soutane *noun* the robe or cassock worn by a Roman Catholic priest. [from French *soutane*, from Latin *subtus*, beneath]

South, The a region of the USA covering the SE central states, generally considered to be separated from the North by the Mason–Dixon Line and Ohio R. In its broad usage it includes the states of Virginia, North Carolina, South Carolina, Georgia, Florida, Alabama, Louisiana, Mississippi, Tennessee, Arkansas, and parts of Texas, Oklahoma, Missouri, West Virginia, Kentucky, Maryland, and Delaware. The term is also more narrowly used to refer to those states which formed the Confederacy during the American Civil War (1861–5). A geographically diverse region, it includes mountainous and hilly areas (eg the S Appalachians), areas of coastal plain bordering the Atlantic Ocean and the Gulf of Mexico, and the prairies of Texas.

south — *noun* (*also* **the south** *or* **the South**) the direction to the right of a person facing the rising sun in the N hemisphere; directly opposite north; any part of the earth, a country, a town, etc lying in this direction. — *adv.* towards the south. — *adj.* **1** of, facing, or lying in the south; on the side or in the part nearest the south. **2** *said of the wind* blowing from the south. [from Anglo-Saxon *suth*]

South Africa, official name **Republic of South Africa**, Afrikaans **Republiek van Suid-Afrika** POP (1992e) 39.8m, a republic in the S of the African continent, divided into the four provinces of Cape, Natal, Orange Free State, and Transvaal. AREA 1 233 404sq km/476 094sq mi. It is bounded NW by Namibia, N by Botswana, NE by Zimbabwe, Mozambique, and Swaziland, E and SE by the Indian Ocean, and SW and W by the S Atlantic Ocean; Lesotho is landlocked within its borders. The country includes the independent homelands of Bophuthatswana, Ciskei, Transkei, and Venda, and also the six non-independent national states of Gazankulu,

Lebowa, QwaQwa, KwaZulu, KaNgwane, and KwaNdebele. CAPITAL Pretoria (administrative); Bloemfontein (judicial), Cape Town (legislative); the largest city is Johannesburg. TIME ZONE GMT +2. The population is 70% black African, 18% white, 3% Asian, and 9% coloured; Christian, Hindu, and Muslim beliefs are followed. OFFICIAL LANGUAGES English and Afrikaans; many African languages are also spoken. CURRENCY the rand. PHYSICAL DESCRIPTION occupies the S extremity of the African plateau, fringed by fold mountains and a lowland coastal margin to the W, E, and S; the N interior comprises the Kalahari Basin, scrub grassland, and arid desert, at an altitude 650–1 250m; the peripheral highlands rise to over 1 200m; the Great Escarpment rises E to 3 482m at Thabana Ntlenyana; the Orange R flows W to meet the Atlantic; its chief tributaries are the Vaal and Caledon rivers. CLIMATE subtropical in the E, with lush vegetation; the average monthly rainfall at Durban is 28mm in Jul, 130mm in Mar, the annual average is 1 101mm; dry moistureless climate on the W coast; the annual average rainfall at Cape Town is 510mm, with minimum daily temperatures of 7°C in Jul, to an average maximum of 26°C in Jan–Feb; desert region further N, with an annual average rainfall of less than 30mm. HISTORY originally inhabited by Khoisan tribes; many Bantu tribes arrived from the N after c.1000; the Portuguese reached the Cape of Good Hope in the late 15c; settled by the Dutch in 1652; arrival of the British in 1795; British annexation of the Cape in 1814; Great Trek by the Boers NE across the Orange R to Natal in 1836; the first Boer republic was founded in 1839; Natal was annexed by the British in 1846, but the Boer republics of Transvaal (founded 1852) and Orange Free State (1854) received recognition; discovery of diamonds in 1866 and gold in 1886 led to rivalry between the British and the Boers; South African Wars in 1880–1 and 1899–1902; in 1910 Transvaal, Natal, Orange Free State, and Cape Province were united to form the Union of South Africa, a dominion of the British Empire; it became a sovereign state within the Commonwealth in 1931 and formed an independent republic in 1961; Botswana and Lesotho obtained independence in 1966; Swaziland gained independence in 1968; independence was granted by South Africa to Transkei in 1976, Bophuthatswana in 1977, Venda in 1979, and Ciskei in 1981, but was not recognized internationally; politics were dominated by the treatment of the non-white majority; from 1948, the apartheid policy resulted in the development of separate political institutions for different racial groups; Africans were considered permanent citizens of the 'homelands' to which each tribal group was assigned and were given no representation in the South African Parliament; continuing racial violence and strikes led to the declaration of a state of emergency in 1986; several countries imposed economic and cultural sanctions (especially in the field of sport) in protest at the apartheid system; progressive dismantling of apartheid by the government from 1990; negotiations towards a non-racial democracy were marked by continuing violent clashes; in 1994 free democratic elections resulted in the formation of a multi-racial government, led by the ANC. ECONOMY industrial growth as a result of 19c gold and diamond discoveries — over half of the country's export income is from gold; cheap African labour is used for new products and technologies; grain; wool; sugar; tobacco; cotton; citrus fruit; dairy products; livestock; fishing; motor vehicles; machinery; chemicals; fertilizers; textiles; clothes; metal products; electronics; computers; tourism; uranium; metallic ores; asbestos.

South African Native National Congress see AFRICAN NATIONAL CONGRESS.

South America the fourth-largest of the continents, extending c.7 500km/5 000mi N to S.

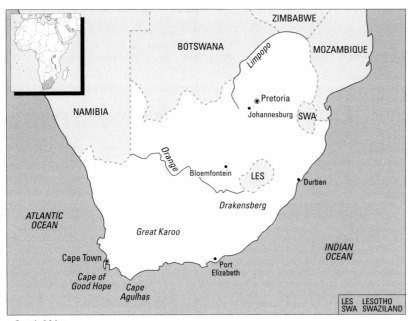

South Africa

AREA c.18m sq km/7m sq mi. It is linked to N America in the NW by the isthmus of Panama. The continent is bounded N by the Caribbean Sea, E by the Atlantic Ocean, and W by the Pacific Ocean. It includes Argentina, Bolivia, Brazil, Chile, Colombia, Ecuador, Guyana, Paraguay, Peru, Surinam, Uruguay, and Venezuela. Outlying islands include the Falkland Is, Galapagos Is, and Tierra del Fuego. PHYSICAL DESCRIPTION the Andes run almost the full W length, rising to 6 969m at Aconcagua; the largest lake is Titicaca; the major river basins are the Orinoco, Paraná, and Amazon (containing the world's largest tropical rainforest). HISTORY there is considerable evidence of early S American Indian kingdoms, notably the Incas, destroyed by Spanish and Portuguese invaders during the 16c; most countries achieved independence following war in the early 19c.

Southampton, Henry Wriothesley, 3rd Earl of (1573–1624) English courtier, born in Cowdray, Sussex. He was known as a patron of poets, notably Shakesepeare, who dedicated to him both *Venus and Adonis* (1593) and *The Rape of Lucrece* (1594). His involvement in the rebellion of the 2nd Earl of Essex (1601) led to his imprisonement, but he was released by James I, and he died in the Netherlands while leading English volunteers against Spain.

Southampton, Latin **Clausentum**, Anglo-Saxon **Hamwih** POP (1992e) 208 000, a major port in Southampton district, Hampshire, S England. It lies on Southampton Water, at the mouth of the R Test and R Itchen. The port, which has four tides daily, handles container traffic and passenger ships. HISTORY a site of both Roman and Saxon settlements; the *Mayflower* set sail to N America from here in 1620; the *Titanic* sailed from here on her disastrous maiden voyage in 1912; Southampton became a city in 1964. NOTABLE FEATURES St Michael's Church (1070); Guildhall (15c); 14c wool house now housing a maritime museum; *Mayflower* Memorial.

South Australia POP (1992e) 1.5m, a state in S Australia. AREA 984 000 sq km/380 000sq mi. It comprises seven statistical divisions. The state is bordered in the S by the Great Australian Bight and the Southern Ocean. PHYSICAL DESCRIPTION consists largely of desert, notably the Great Victoria Desert and Nullarbor Plain; fertile agricultural land in the SE corner of the state is irrigated by the Murray R; the coastline is dissected by the Spencer and St Vincent gulfs; the dry salt

lakes inland include Eyre, Torrens, Gairdner, and Frome; the state rises in the S to the Gawler Ranges N of the Eyre Peninsula, and in the E to the Flinders and Mt Lofty ranges; Mt Woodroffe is the highest point in the state at 1 440m. HISTORY established as a British Crown Colony in 1836; between 1863 and 1901, South Australia included most of Northern Territory; became a state in 1901. CAPITAL Adelaide. CHIEF TOWNS Whyalla, Mount Gambier, Port Pirie, Port Augusta. ECONOMY wheat, barley, fruit; wool; meat; wine; oil refining; natural gas; copper, silver, lead mining; supplies 95% of the world's opals; oranges and other citrus fruit are grown in irrigated orchards along the Murray R and almost half of Australia's wine is produced from the Barossa Valley, N of Adelaide. NOTABLE FEATURES Woomera Prohibited Area (weapons-testing range) extends across the Great Victoria Desert into Western Australia; a 9 600km/6 000mi-long Dingo Fence protects southern grazing sheep from wild dogs.

South Bank Centre a music and arts complex built on the South Bank of the R Thames in London, England. Begun in 1951 for the Festival of Britain, it comprises the Royal Festival Hall, the Queen Elizabeth Hall, the Purcell Room, the Hayward Gallery, the National Film Theatre, and the National Theatre.

South Bend POP (1990) 106 000, the seat of St Joseph County, N Indiana, USA, lying on the St Joseph R. It achieved city status in 1865. NOTABLE FEATURE University of Notre Dame nearby.

southbound *adj.* going or leading towards the south.

South Carolina POP (1990) 3.6m, a state in SE USA, divided into 46 counties. AREA 80 580sq km/ 31 104sq mi. It is known as the 'Palmetto State'. PHYSICAL DESCRIPTION bounded E and SE by the Atlantic Ocean; rivers include the Pee Dee, Edisto, Savannah (which forms most of the Georgia border), Wateree, and Congaree, the latter two joining to form the Santee; the Blue Ridge Mts lie in the extreme NW; the highest point is Mt Sassafras, at 1 085m; there is flat and (in the S) swampy coastland, cut by numerous rivers and creeks to form the famous Sea Islands which attract thousands of tourists; the ground rises inland towards the rolling Piedmont, the agricultural and manufacturing centre; reservoirs in the centre of the state include L Murray, L Marion, and L Moultrie. HISTORY it was settled by the

French at Port Royal in 1562; included in the Carolina grant of 1663, it was returned to the Crown in 1729; after the battle of Guilford Courthouse in 1781 it came under American control; the eighth of the original 13 states to ratify the Constitution in 1788, it was the first state to secede from the Union in 1860; Confederate forces attacked Fort Sumter on 12 Apr 1861, starting the Civil War; slavery was abolished in 1865; South Carolina was readmitted to the Union in 1868. CAPITAL Columbia. CHIEF TOWNS Charleston, Greenville, Spartanburg. ECONOMY textiles and clothing based on the large cotton crop; lumber, chemicals, machinery, foodstuffs; tobacco, soya beans, poultry, cattle, dairy products, peaches, peanuts, sweet potatoes, corn; fishing is a major industry.

South China Sea the west arm of the Pacific Ocean. The boundary to the NW, SW and W is formed by the SE Asian coast; to the N it is bounded by Taiwan, to the E by the Philippines, and to the SE by Borneo. AREA c.2 320 000sq km/ 895 500sq mi. Its maximum depth is 5 490m at the NE basin and its shallowest point is c.60m in the SE. The Gulfs of Tongkin and Kampong are the principal arms of this sea, which is subject to violent typhoons. Numerous island groups are scattered throughout the sea and it is an important fishing region.

Southcott, Joanna (c.1750–1814) English religious fanatic, born in Dorset, who declared herself (c.1792) to be the woman in Revelation 12 who would give birth to the second Prince of Peace. Although she died soon after the date of the supposed birth, she had attracted many followers, whose belief that she would rise again continued until the early 20c.

South Dakota POP (1990) 711 000, a state in N central USA, divided into 66 counties and known as the 'Coyote State'. AREA 199 723sq km/77 093sq mi. PHYSICAL DESCRIPTION the state is crossed by the Missouri R and the Big Sioux R; the Bois de Sioux R and Minnesota R form part of the E border; in the SW corner of the state the Black Hills rise; the highest point is Mt Harney Peak (2 207m); W of the Missouri R is a semi-arid, treeless plain, one third of which is owned by Sioux Native Americans; severe erosion has formed the barren Badlands, where there are many ancient marine and land fossils; rich, fertile plains lie E of the Missouri R. HISTORY it became part of the USA following the Louisiana Purchase in 1803; in 1861 it was included in Dakota Territory; when gold was discovered in the Black Hills in 1874 the population swelled; the territory separated from North Dakota and became the 40th state of the Union in 1889. CAPITAL Pierre. CHIEF TOWNS Sioux Falls, Rapid City, Aberdeen. ECONOMY cattle, wheat, hogs, dairy products, corn, soya beans, oats; meat packing, food processing; the town of Lead in the Black Hills is the nation's leading gold-mining centre; the state is the USA's second-largest gold and beryllium producer. NOTABLE FEATURE Mt Rushmore (in the Black Hills), on which are carved the faces of former US presidents George Washington, Abraham Lincoln, Thomas Jefferson, and Theodore Roosevelt.

South Downs Way a long-distance footpath following the South Downs of East and West Sussex, S England. It stretches 129km/80mi from Eastbourne to Harting.

south-east — *noun* **1** the direction midway between south and east. **2** (**the south-east** or **South-East**) an area lying in this direction. — *adv.* in this direction. — *adj.* of, facing, or lying in the south-east.

South East Asia Treaty Organization (ABBREV. **SEATO**) an organization founded in 1954 to secure SE Asia against communist 'aggression'. The signatories to the treaty were Australia, France, New Zealand, Pakistan, the Philippines, Thailand, UK, and USA. SEATO, whose headquarters were in Bangkok, was phased out in the 1970s.

southeaster *noun* a wind blowing form the south-east.

south-easterly — *adj., adv.* **1** south-east. **2** *said of the wind* blowing from the south-east. — *noun* (PL. **south-easterlies**) a wind blowing from the south-east.

south-eastern *adj.* to the south-east.

Southend, properly **Southend-on-Sea** POP (1992e) 165 000, a resort town co-extensive with Southend-on-Sea district, Essex, SE England. It lies on the estuary of the R Thames, 57km/35mi E of London. NOTABLE FEATURES famous pier (2km/1.2mi long); 12c Prittlewell Priory Museum.

southerly — *adj.* **1** *said of a wind, etc* coming from the south. **2** looking, lying, etc towards the south. — *adv.* to or towards the south. — *noun* (PL. **southerlies**) a southerly wind.

southern *adj.* **1** of or in the south. **2** facing or directed towards the south.

Southern Alps a mountain range in W central South I, New Zealand. It measures c.320km/200mi NE–SW. The range includes New Zealand's highest peaks, Mt Cook, Mt Tasman, and Mt Dampier. There are 19 named peaks exceeding 3 000m. The two mountain passes, the Haast Pass and Arthur's Pass, are the only routes which allow E–W travel. Mountain-climbing and skiing are popular in this area.

Southern Christian Leadership Council (ABBREV. **SCLC**) a US civil rights organization, formed (1957) by Martin Luther King and other ministers to promote racial integration, primarily in the South, through non-violent protest. After his death the organization lost much of its moral authority, though it remained an important platform for later leaders such as Jesse Jackson.

southerner *noun* a person who lives in or comes from the south, especially the southern part of England or of the USA.

southern lights (the southern lights) the aurora australis.

southernmost *adj.* situated furthest south.

Southern Ocean *or* **Antarctic Ocean** the S regions of the Atlantic, Indian, and Pacific Oceans surrounding Antarctica. Its narrowest point is the Drake Passage between S America and the Antarctic Peninsula, measuring 1 110km/690mi.

Southey, Robert (1774–1843) English poet and writer, born in Bristol. He studied law, and settled in Keswick where, with William Wordsworth and Samuel Taylor Coleridge, he became one of the 'Lake Poets'. Originally a radical in politics, in 1809 he began to contribute to the Tory *Quarterly Review*. He was made Poet Laureate in 1813, and his works include the poem 'The Holly Tree', *A Vision of Judgement* (1821), and *Lives* of *Nelson* (1813), *Wesley* (1820), and *Bunyan* (1830).

South Georgia a barren, mountainous, snow-covered island in the S Atlantic Ocean, about 500km/300mi E of the Falkland Is. AREA c.3 750sq km/1 450sq mi; length 160km/100mi. It is a British Dependent Territory administered from the Falkland Is. Research stations are maintained here and on the neighbouring Bird I. Grytviken is the only village. The explorer, Ernest Shackleton, is buried on the island. HISTORY discovered by the London merchant De la Roche in 1675; Captain Cook landed in 1775; British annexation in 1908 and 1917; a sealing and whaling centre until 1965; invaded by Argentina and recaptured by Britain in 1982.

South Glamorgan POP (1992e) 410 000, a county in S Wales, divided into two districts. AREA 416sq km/161sq mi. It is bounded N and W by Mid Glamorgan, E by Gwent, and S by the

Bristol Channel. CAPITAL Cardiff. ECONOMY agriculture (Vale of Glamorgan); steel; plastics; engineering; vehicle components; food processing. NOTABLE FEATURE Welsh Folk Museum at Cardiff.

South Island POP (1991) 882 000, the larger and southernmost of the two main islands of New Zealand. AREA 153 978sq km/59 435sq mi. It is separated from North I by the Cook Strait, and from Stewart I in the S by the Foveaux Strait. PHYSICAL DESCRIPTION fertile plains on the coast give way to mountains; the Southern Alps run through the centre, including Mt Cook at 3 764m, the highest point in New Zealand; to the W is Westland, a narrow forested strip; to the E is Canterbury Plain, the largest area of flat lowland; there are numerous bays and fjords to the SW. CHIEF TOWNS Christchurch, Invercargill, Dunedin, Nelson. ECONOMY tobacco; hops; coal; cement; timber; greenstone; sheep; pottery; fruit; tourism.

South Korea *or* **Korea**, official name **Republic of Korea**, Korean **Tae Han Minguk** POP (1993e) 43.9m, a republic in E Asia occupying the S half of the Korean peninsula. AREA 98 913sq km/38 180sq mi. It consists of nine provinces and four special cities with provincial status (Seoul, Inchon, Taegu, Pusan). It is bordered W by the Yellow Sea, E by the Sea of Japan, S by the Korean Strait, and N by North Korea, from which it is separated by a demilitarized zone. CAPITAL Seoul. TIME ZONE GMT +9. The population is mainly Korean, with a small Chinese minority; the main religions are Confucianism, Shamanism, Christianity, and Buddhism. OFFICIAL LANGUAGE Korean. CURRENCY the won. PHYSICAL DESCRIPTION the Taebaek Sanmaek Range runs N–S along the E coast, reaching heights of over 900m; it descends through a series of ridges to broad, undulating coastal lowlands; c.3 000 islands off the W and S coasts; the largest is Cheju do, on which is situated Korea's highest peak, 1 950m. CLIMATE extreme continental climate, with cold winters and hot summers; typhoons possible in the wettest months (Jun–Sep); average daily temperatures at Seoul are –9–0°C (Jan), 22–31°C (Aug); rainfall minimum 20mm (Feb), maximum 376mm (Jul). HISTORY ruled by the ancient Choson dynasty until the 1c BC; split into three rival kingdoms, united in 668 by the Silla dynasty; succeeded by the Koryo dynasty in 935; Yi dynasty in 1392–1910; independence recognized by China in 1895; annexation by Japan in 1910; in 1945 the country was entered by Russia (from the N) and the USA (from the S) to enforce the Japanese surrender, dividing the country by the 38th parallel of latitude; North Korean forces invaded in 1950; UN forces assisted South Korea in stopping the advance in 1950–3; military coup in 1961; assassination of Park Chung Hee in 1979; summit talks with North Korea in 1990. GOVERNMENT governed by a President, elected indirectly by a 5 000-member Electoral College for a single five-year term; the President leads and appoints a State Council; a 299-member National Assembly is elected for four years. Korea is an official observer at the United Nations, not holding UN membership. ECONOMY light consumer goods, with a shift towards heavy industries; petrochemicals, textiles, electrical machinery, footwear, steel, ships, fish; one of the world's largest deposits of tungsten; only one fifth of Korea is suitable for cultivation; rice, barley, wheat, beans, grain, tobacco; cattle, pigs, poultry, fishing.

South Orkney Islands, Spanish **Orcadas del Sur** a group of islands in the S Atlantic Ocean, NE of the Graham Peninsula. AREA 620sq km/239sq mi. The main islands are Coronation, Signy, Laurie, and Inaccessible. They are barren and uninhabited, apart from when used for scientific research. The islands are claimed by Argentina.

southpaw *colloq.* — *noun* a left-handed person, especially a left-handed boxer (ie one who leads with the right hand). — *adj.* left-handed.

South Pole (the South Pole) the southernmost point of the Earth's axis of rotation, at 90°S, longitude 0°, in central Antarctica.

Southport POP (1981) 91 000, a coastal resort town in Sefton borough, Merseyside, NW England. It lies on the Irish Sea, S of the estuary of the R Ribble, 24km/15mi N of Liverpool. The original 'garden city', Southport is also a notable golfing area (at Birkdale).

South Sandwich Islands a group of small, uninhabited islands in the S Atlantic Ocean, lying c.720km/450mi SE of South Georgia. It is a British Dependent Territory, administered from the Falkland Is. HISTORY discovered by Captain Cook in 1775; annexed by Britain in 1908 and 1917.

South Sea (the South Sea) the southern part of the Pacific Ocean.

South Sea Bubble a financial crisis in Britain (1720) that arose out of speculation mania generated by parliament's approval of the South Sea Company's proposal to take over three fifths of the National Debt. Many investors were ruined in the aftermath, but Robert Walpole's plan for stock transfer retrieved the situation and made his reputation.

South Shetland Islands a group of mountainous islands in the S Atlantic Ocean. The islands lie 880km/550mi SE of Cape Horn. They are used occasionally for scientific bases.

South Shields POP (1981) 87 000, a town in North Tyneside borough, Tyne and Wear, England. It lies opposite North Shields, on the S bank of the R Tyne, 12km/8mi E of Gateshead. South Shields is part of the Tyneside urban area.

southward *or* **southwards** *adv., adj.* towards the south.

Southwark POP (1987e) 217 000, a borough of central Greater London, England. Lying S of the R Thames, it includes the suburbs of Bermondsey, Southwark, and Camberwell. The area was formerly famous for its inns and its Elizabethan theatres (notably the Globe Theatre). NOTABLE FEATURES Southwark Cathedral (13c); Dulwich College (1621); Guy's Hospital (1721); Imperial War Museum.

Southwell, Robert (1561–95) English poet and martyr, born in Horsham, Norfolk. He became a Jesuit and was ordained in 1584. He travelled to England as a missionary in 1586, aiding persecuted Catholics, but was betrayed, tortured, and executed in London. Beatified in 1929, he is known for his devotional lyrics (eg 'The Burning Babe'), and for several prose treatises and epistles.

south-west — *noun* **1** the direction midway between south and west. **2** (**the south-west** *or* **South-West**) an area lying in this direction. — *adv.* in this direction. — *adj.* of, facing, or lying in the south-west.

South West Africa People's Organization (ABBREV. **SWAPO**) the main

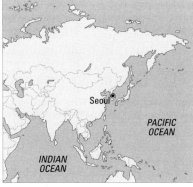

South Korea

nationalist movement for SW Africa (Namibia), founded in 1958 as the Ovambo People's Organization. It organized the guerrilla war against the South African administration of the country. Based initially in Tanzania and then Zambia, the guerrilla movement established bases in Angola in the 1970s and became embroiled in the general conflict involving South Africa, the National Union for the Total Independence of Angola (UNITA), and the MPLA government (Movimento Popular de Libertaçao de Angola) in Luanda with its Cuban and Soviet support. An international agreement was reached in Geneva (1988) which linked Namibia's independence with Cuban withdrawal from Angola and the cessation of South African support for UNITA. The ensuing 1989 election saw SWAPO win over half the votes and a majority of seats and then form the first independent government.

southwester *noun* a wind blowing form the south-west.

south-westerly — *adj., adv.* **1** south-west. **2** *said of the wind* blowing from the south-west. — *noun* (PL. **south-westerlies**) a wind blowing from the south-west.

south-western *adj.* to the south-west.

South Yemen see YEMEN.

South Yorkshire see YORKSHIRE, SOUTH.

souvenir *noun* a thing bought, kept, or given as a reminder of a place, person, or occasion; a memento. [from French *souvenir*]

sou'wester *noun* a seaman's waterproof hat with a large flap-like brim at the back. [a contraction of SOUTHWESTER]

sovereign — *noun* **1** a supreme ruler or head, especially a monarch. **2** a former British gold coin worth £1. — *adj.* **1** having supreme power or authority: *a sovereign ruler.* **2** politically independent: *a sovereign state.* **3** outstanding; unrivalled; utmost: *sovereign intelligence.* [from Old French *sovrain*]

sovereignty *noun* (PL. **sovereignties**) **1** supreme and independent political power or authority. **2** a politically independent state.

soviet — *noun* **1** any of the councils that made up the local and national governments in the former Soviet Union. **2** (**Soviet**) a native or inhabitant of the former Soviet Union. — *adj.* (**Soviet**) of the former Soviet Union. [from Russian *sovet*, council]

Soviet Union, official name **Union of Soviet Socialist Republics** (**USSR**), Russian **Soyuz Sovyetskikh Sotsialisticheskikh Republik** (**Cyrillic alphabet**, **CCCP**) a former federation of 15 Union Republics which, until its dissolution in 1991, jointly formed the world's largest sovereign state. In addition to the Union Republics (Soviet Socialist Republics (SSR)) there were twenty Autonomous Soviet Socialist Republics (ASSR), and several smaller divisions (krays, oblasts, autonomous oblasts, and autonomous okrugs). AREA 22 402 076sq km/8 647 201sq mi. CAPITAL Moscow. PHYSICAL DESCRIPTION the area occupied by the USSR was bordered in the W by Romania, Turkey, Hungary, Czechoslovakia, Poland, Finland, and Norway, and S by Iran, Afghanistan, China, Mongolia, and North Korea; it was divided by the Ural Mts into European and Asian sectors. HISTORY under Empress Catherine the Great, Russia had become a great power, its territory extending into S and E Asia; the 1917 Revolution ended the monarchy, initiating a five year struggle between the Mensheviks and the Bolsheviks; the first Soviet government was headed by Lenin; in the 1920s Stalin began vigorous socialist reforms, including the collectivization of agriculture and rapid industrialization; territories were extended W after World War II, creating a corridor of Communist-dominated countries between the USSR and W Europe; a long period of Cold War between East and West began at this time; the Soviets intervened to sup-

press the 1956 Hungarian uprising and the 1968 Czech programme of liberalization; Afghanistan was invaded between 1979 and 1988; there was a series of disarmament agreements in the 1980s with a new approach to international relations (*glaznost*); constitutional reforms were implemented in 1989; Communist power weakened and local independence movements emerged; Lithuania, Estonia, and Latvia became independent sovereign states in 1991; Georgia also became independent in 1991; Russia, Belorussia, and the Ukraine then formed the Commonwealth of Independent States; they were soon joined by Armenia, Azerbaijan, Moldavia, Kazakhstan, Kirghizia, Tajikistan, Turkmenistan, and Uzbekistan; in Dec 1991 the Soviet Union was formally dissolved.

sow[1] *verb* (pronounced like *so*) (PAST TENSE **sowed**; PAST PARTICIPLE **sown**, **sowed**) **1** to plant (seed); to plant (land) with (crops of a particular kind). **2** to introduce or arouse: *sowed the seeds of doubt in his mind.* [from Anglo-Saxon *sawan*]

sow[2] *noun* (pronounced like *now*) an adult female pig. [from Anglo-Saxon *sugu*]

Soweto POP (1988e) 864 000, a black African township in Transvaal province, NE South Africa. It is linked by rail (5km/3mi) to industrial W Johannesburg. Resistance to the teaching of Afrikaans in schools led to student riots in April 1976, when several hundred people were killed. [derived from the official title, South-West Township]

soya bean *or* **soy bean 1** any of numerous varieties of an annual plant (*Glycine max*) of the pulse family native to SW Asia but widely cultivated for its edible seeds (beans). **2** the edible seed of this plant, which is rich in protein and oil. Soya-bean oil is used as a cooking oil and in the manufacture of margarine, soap, enamels, paints, and varnishes. The residue left after oil extraction is used as a protein concentrate for human diets, and as a feed for animal livestock. Soya beans are also ground into flour, fermented to make soy sauce, and used to make soya milk and bean curd (used as a meat substitute). [from Japanese *shoyu*]

soya bean

Soyinka, Wole, in full **Akinwande Oluwole Soyinka** (1934–) Nigerian writer, born near Abeokuta. He became a play-reader at the Royal Court Theatre, where his first play, *The Invention*, was performed in 1955. He returned to Ibadan in 1959, founded two theatre companies, and built up a new Nigerian drama, written in English but using the words, music, and dance of the traditional festivals. From 1967 to 1969 he was a political prisoner, and was later Professor of Comparative Literature at the Ife University (1976–85), and Professor of Africana Studies and Theatre at Cornell University (1988–92). His writing is concerned with the tension between old and new in modern Africa, and includes his first novel, *The Interpreters* (1964), and the poetic collection *A Shuttle in the Crypt* (1972). He was awarded the Nobel Prize for Literature in 1986.

soy sauce a salty brown sauce made from soya beans, widely used in Eastern (especially

Chinese) cooking. [from Chinese *shi-yu*, salt bean oil]

sozzled *adj. colloq.* drunk.

spa *noun* **1** a mineral water spring. **2** a town where such a spring is or was once located. [from *Spa*, a Belgian town]

Spaak, Paul Henri (1899–1972) Belgian politician, born in Brussels. He was the first socialist Prime Minister (1938–9), Foreign Minister with the government-in-exile during World War II, and in 1946 President of the first General Assembly of the United Nations. After his later periods as premier (1946, 1947–9), he was instrumental in setting up the EEC as Foreign Minister again (1954–7, 1961–8), and also served as Secretary-General of NATO (1957–61).

space — *noun* **1** the three-dimensional medium in which all matter exists. **2** a portion of this; room: *enough space in the garden for a pool.* **3** an interval of distance; a gap. **4** an empty place: *a space at our table.* **5** a period of time: *within the space of ten minutes.* **6** (*also* **outer space**) all those regions of the Universe that lie beyond the Earth's atmosphere: *space technology / intergalactic space.* — *verb* (*usually* **space something out**) to arrange things with intervals, or greater intervals, of distance or time between each.

— **spaced out** *slang* in a dazed or stupefied state from, or as if from, the effects of drugs. [from Latin *spatium*]

space age — *noun* (*usually* **the space age**) the present period in history, in which travel in space has become possible. — *adj.* (**space-age**) **1** technologically very advanced. **2** having a futuristic appearance.

spacecraft *noun* a manned or unmanned vehicle for travel in space or for orbiting the Earth.

Space Invaders *trademark* any of various video games in which players use buttons or levers to fire at invading creatures descending the screen.

Spacelab *noun Astron.* a self-contained research laboratory, developed by the European Space Agency, that is carried in the cargo bay of the NASA space shuttle.

space law a branch of international law which is concerned with rights in air space and outer space. Foreign aircraft have no right to fly over the territory or territorial waters of another state. In practice, states enter into bilateral agreements to permit use of each other's air space. The Outer Space Treaty of 1967 provides that outer space may be used by all states.

spaceman *or* **spacewoman** *noun* a male or female traveller in space.

space platform a space station.

space probe *Astron.* an unmanned spacecraft that is designed to study conditions in space, especially on or around one or more planets or their natural satellites, and to transmit scientific data back to Earth.

space shuttle a reusable crewed US launch vehicle, used to put a payload such as a satellite, space probe, scientific equipment, or the Spacelab module, into space. First launched in 1981, it was developed by NASA to make repeated journeys into space, taking off like a rocket but landing on a runway like an aircraft. In 1986 the second shuttle, *Challenger*, was destroyed together with its crew in an explosion 73 seconds after launching.

space sickness *Astron.* a collection of symptoms, similar to those of travel sickness, experienced by astronauts during their first few days in space, until their bodies have adapted to conditions of weightlessness.

space station a large orbiting spacecraft that is designed to provide accommodation and scientific and technological research facilities in space for crews of astronauts over periods of weeks or months, eg Skylab, Salyut, Mir. Space stations enable detailed astronomical observations to be made, and long-term experiments on the effects of weightlessness to be conducted. All space stations to date have been large Earth-orbiting satellites.

space suit *Astron.* a suit specially designed for use in space travel.

space–time continuum reality regarded as having four dimensions: length, breadth, height, and time.

space walk *Astron.* an excursion by one or more astronauts, wearing pressurized space suits, outside their spacecraft while in space.

spacious *adj.* having ample room or space; extending over a large area.

spaciousness *noun* being spacious.

Spade, Sam the cynical, 'hard-boiled' private detective in Dashiel Hammett's novel *The Maltese Falcon*, and other stories.

spade[1] *noun* **1** a long-handled digging tool with a broad metal blade which is pushed into the ground with the foot. **2** a child's toy version of this, usually of plastic: *bucket and spade.*
— **call a spade a spade** to speak plainly and frankly.
[from Anglo-Saxon *spadu*]

spade[2] *noun* **1** any of the suit of playing-cards that carries an emblem like a black inverted heart. **2** (**spades**) this suit. **3** *offensive slang* a black person. [from Greek *spathe*, broad blade]

spadework *noun* hard or boring preparatory work.

spadix *noun* (PL. **spadices**) *Bot.* a fleshy spike of flowers. [from Greek *spadix -ikos*, a torn-off branch]

spaghetti *noun* pasta in the form of long thin string-like strands. [from Italian *spaghetti*, from *spago*, cord]

Spaghetti Junction *Brit.* a popular name for the complex system of intersecting motorways at Gravelly Hill, Birmingham, with many underpasses and overpasses designed to carry large volumes of traffic from and to the M6, A38, and A5127. Hence, any complex interchange which resembles the intertwined strands of cooked spaghetti.

spaghetti western a western film shot in Europe with an international cast, typically by an Italian director, and typically violent and melodramatic.

Spain, Spanish **España**, official name **Kingdom of Spain**, Spanish **Reino de España**, ancient **Iberia**, Latin **Hispana** POP (1992e) 39.1m, a country in SW Europe, occupying four fifths of the Iberian Peninsula, and including the Canary Is, Balearic Is, and several islands off the coast of N Africa, as well as the Presidios of Ceuta and Melilla in N Morocco. It is divided into 17 regions. AREA 492 431sq km/190 078sq mi (mainland); 504 750sq km/194 834sq mi (total area). Mainland Spain is situated between the Atlantic Ocean and the Mediterranean Sea, bounded in the N by France across the Pyrenees, and in the W by Portugal. CAPITAL Madrid. CHIEF TOWNS Barcelona, Valencia, Seville, Saragossa, Málaga. time zone GMT +1. OFFICIAL LANGUAGE Spanish (Castilian); Catalan, Galician, and Basque are also spoken in certain regions. Roman Catholicism is the chief religion. CURRENCY the peseta. PHYSICAL DESCRIPTION the country consists mainly of a furrowed central plateau (the Meseta, average height 700m) crossed by mountains; the Andalusian or Baetic Mts in the SE rise to 3 478m at Mulhacén; the Pyrenees in the N rise to 3 404m at Pico de Aneto; rivers run E–W, notably the Tagus, Ebro, Guadiana, Miño, Duero, Guadalquivir, Segura, and Júcar. CLIMATE the Meseta has a continental climate, with hot summers, cold winters, and low rainfall; there is high rainfall in the mountains, with deep winter

snow; the S Mediterranean coast has the warmest winter temperatures on the European mainland. HISTORY early inhabitants included Iberians, Celts, Phoenicians, Greeks, and Romans; there was Muslim domination from the 8c; Christian reconquest completed by 1492; Spain became a monarchy following the unification of the Kingdoms of Castile, León, Aragón, and Navarre, largely achieved by 1572; in the 16c the Spanish exploration of the New World led to the growth of the Spanish Empire; there was a period of decline after the Revolt of the Netherlands in 1581; the Spanish Armada was defeated in 1588; the War of the Spanish Succession lasted from 1702 to 1713; Spain was involved in the Peninsular War against Napoleon in 1808–14; war with the USA in 1898 led to the loss of Cuba, Puerto Rico, and the remaining Pacific possessions; dictatorship under Primo de Rivera (1923–30) was followed by exile of the King and establishment of the Second Republic in 1931; military revolt headed by General Franco in 1936 led to Civil War and a Fascist dictatorship; Prince Juan Carlos of Bourbon, nominated to succeed Franco in 1969, acceded to the throne in 1975; a democratic constitution was implemented in 1978; in 1981 an attempted military coup failed; the Basque separatist movement, ETA, has carried out a number of terrorist attacks. GOVERNMENT the country is governed by a bicameral parliament (*Cortes*) comprising a 257-member Congress of Deputies elected for four years and a 208-member Senate; since 1978 there has been a move towards local government autonomy with the creation of 17 self-governing regions; Spain has been a member of the EC since 1986. ECONOMY the traditionally agricultural economy is gradually being supplemented by varied industries; textiles, iron, steel, shipbuilding, electrical appliances, cars, cork, salt, wine, potash, forestry, fishing, tourism; coal, lignite, sulphur, zinc, lead, wolfram, copper.

spake *old use* past tense of SPEAK.

Spallanzani, Lazaro (1729–99) Italian biologist and naturalist, born in Scandiano, Modena. He became a priest, and was also professor at Reggio, Modena, and Pavia. He disproved the theory of spontaneous generation, and in 1780 demonstrated the true nature of digestion, and the functions of spermatozoa and ova. He also successfully artificially inseminated several animals.

Spam *noun trademark* tinned processed meat made mainly from pork. [from *spiced ham*]

span — *noun* **1** the length between the supports of a bridge or arch. **2** a measure of length equal to the distance between the tips of thumb and little finger on an extended hand, conventionally taken as 9in (23cm). **3** (*often in compounds*) length from end to end in distance or time: *the wingspan of an aircraft / the timespan of the war.* — *verb* (**spanned**, **spanning**) to extend across or over. [from Anglo-Saxon *spann*]

Spandex *or* **spandex** *noun trademark* **1** a synthetic elastic fibre made chiefly from polyurethane. **2** a fabric made from this. [an inversion of EXPAND]

spandrel *or* **spandril** *noun* the triangular space between the curve of an arch and the enclosing mouldings, string-course, etc. It also refers, particularly in 20c architecture, to an infill panel below a window.

spangle — *noun* a small piece of glittering material, especially a sequin. — *verb* **1** to decorate (eg a piece of clothing) with spangles. **2** *intrans.* to glitter. [from Anglo-Saxon *spang*, clasp]

Spanglish *noun* a language consisting of a mixture of English and Spanish words and phrases, especially that used in Hispanic communities in the USA.

Spaniard *noun* a native or citizen of Spain. [from Old French *Espaignart*]

spaniel — *noun* any of several breeds of dog with long drooping ears and a silky coat. — *adj.* expressing unwavering devotion or subservience: *his spaniel eyes.* [from Old French *espaigneul*, Spanish dog]

Spanish — *noun* **1** (**the Spanish**) the people of Spain. **2** their language, also spoken in the southern USA and Central and S America. — *adj.* relating to Spain, its people, or their language. [from *Spain* + -ISH]
◇ A Romance language spoken worldwide by c.125–150 million people as a mother-tongue, and by a further 30–130 million people as a second language. Before becoming the standard language of the unified Spanish state in the 13c, Spanish as it is known today was spoken only in the kingdoms of Castile and Aragon in NE Spain. There was a strong Arabic influence resulting from the Moorish occupation from the 8c to the 15c, and the status of Spanish as a world language has largely resulted from Spanish occupation of large parts of Central and S America.

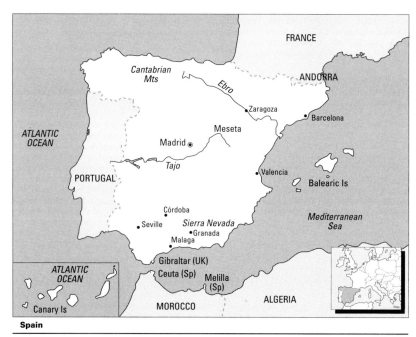

Spain

Spanish–American War a brief conflict (1898) that grew out of US intervention in the Cuban revolution for independence, which resulted in Cuban independence under US suzerainty and the US acquisition of Puerto Rico and the Philippines.

Spanish–American Wars of Independence the wars fought (1810–26) in S America, following Napoleon's invasion of Spain (1808). The semi-independent governments set up (1810) by reformers in the major S American colonies were rejected both by royalists in the colonies and by the Spanish King Ferdinand VII (restored 1813). The ensuing wars were fought in two main theatres: (1) Venezuela, New Granada, and Quito, where Simón Bolívar was the leading patriot general, and (2) Argentina and Chile, from where General José de San Martín mounted an invasion of the Vice-royalty of Peru, still held by Spain (1820–1). The final liberation of Peru was effected in 1824 by Bolívar. The last Spanish garrisons in S America, in Callao (Peru) and on the island of Chiloé (Chile), surrendered to the patriots in 1826.

Spanish Armada a fleet of 130 Spanish ships sent by Philip II of Spain to invade England (1588) and gain control of the English Channel. The invasion was in retaliation for English support of Protestant rebels in the Netherlands, the execution of Mary, Queen of Scots (1587), and raids on Spanish shipping, such as Sir Francis Drake's at Cádiz (1587). The fleet was routed by English attacks off Gravelines (28–29 Jul), and 44 ships were lost in battles and during the flight home around Scotland and Ireland.

Spanish Civil War the conflict (1936–9) between supporters and opponents of the Second Spanish Republic (1931–6). The 'Republicans' included moderates, socialists, communists, and Catalan and Basque regionalists and anarchists. The 'Nationalists' included monarchists, Carlists, conservative Catholics, and fascist Falangists. The armed forces were divided, and both sides attracted foreign assistance: the Republic from the USSR and the International Brigades; the Nationalists from fascist Italy and Nazi Germany. A gradual Nationalist advance led to their victory, achieved under the leadership of General Franco.

Spanish guitar a six-stringed acoustic guitar of the kind normally used for playing classical and folk music.

Spanish Main the mainland area of Spanish S America, known until the 19c for its pirates. It extends from Panama to the Orinoco R estuary in Venezuela.

Spanish Riding School a school of classical horsemanship situated in Vienna, Austria, founded in the late 16c. The school is famous for its white Lipizzaner horses, bred especially for *haute école* ('high school') riding, and originally imported from Spain.

Spanish Succession, War of the a conflict fought (1702–13) ostensibly over the throne of Spain in several theatres (eg the Netherlands, Italy, the Iberian Peninsula) between the Grand Alliance of The Hague (1701: England, the Holy Roman Empire, and the United Provinces of the Netherlands), and France (Louis XIV) and Spain. Hostilities arose after the death without heir of the last Habsburg ruler in Spain, Charles II, who nominated Philip, Duke of Anjou and grandson of Louis XIV, to succeed him, to the disappointment of the other powers. The general European war was concluded by the Peace of Utrecht (1713), which confirmed the Bourbon succession in Spain, and by the Peace of Rastatt (1714).

Spanish Town POP (1991) 92 000, the capital of St Catherine parish, Middlesex county, S Jamaica. It is situated on the R Cobre, 18km/11mi W of Kingston. Spanish Town is the second-largest city in Jamaica, serving a rich agricultural area. It was the capital from 1535 to

1872. NOTABLE FEATURES cathedral (1655); ruins of the King's House (1762); court house (1819); Folk Museum; White Marl Arawak Museum.

Spanish Tragedy, The a play by Thomas Kyd (c.1589). Written in blank verse, it is a tragedy set in Spain about a father planning revenge for his son's murder after failing to win justice legally.

spank — *verb* to smack on the buttocks with the flat of the hand, usually several times as a punishment. — *noun* such a smack. [imitative]

spanker *noun* a fore-and-aft sail on the aftermost mast (mizzenmast) of a sailing ship, used to take advantage of a following wind.
◇ Originally, the spanker was an additional sail hoisted in fair weather in place of the lowest square-rigged sail on the mizzenmast. From about 1840, it became the standard sail taking the place of the square mizzen course.

spanking — *noun* a series of spanks, especially as a punishment. — *adv. colloq.* absolutely; strikingly: *a spanking new watch.* — *adj. colloq.* **1** brisk: *a spanking pace.* **2** impressively fine; striking.

spanner *noun* a tool for turning a nut or bolt, a lever with a shaped end.
— **throw a spanner in the works** to frustrate or upset a plan or system.
[from German, from *spannen*, to stretch]

spar[1] *noun* a strong thick pole of wood or metal, especially one used as a mast or beam on a ship. [from Norse *sperra*]

spar[2] *verb intrans.* (**sparred**, **sparring**) (*often* **spar with someone**) **1** to engage in boxing practice with a partner; to box against an imaginary opponent, for practice. **2** to engage in lively and light-hearted argument. [perhaps from Old French *esparer*, to kick out]

spar[3] *noun, combining form* any of various translucent non-metallic minerals splitting easily into layers: *feldspar / fluorspar.* [from Old German *spar*]

spare — *adj.* **1** held in reserve as a replacement. **2** available for use; unoccupied: *a spare seat next to me.* **3** lean; thin. **4** frugal; scanty. — *verb* **1** to afford to give or give away. **2** to refrain from harming, punishing, killing, or destroying: *spare his life / spare their feelings.* **3** to avoid causing or bringing on: *will spare your blushes.* **4** to avoid incurring: *no expense spared.* — *noun* a duplicate kept in reserve for use as a replacement.
— **go spare** *slang* to become extremely angry or distressed.
to spare left over; surplus to what is required.
[from Anglo-Saxon *sparian*]

spare part a part, for a machine, etc, held in reserve to replace an existing identical part that becomes faulty.

spare ribs ribs of pork with only a small amount of meat on them.

spare tyre **1** an extra tyre carried to replace a punctured tyre. **2** *colloq.* a band of fat just above a person's waist.

sparing *adj.* economical or frugal, often to the point of inadequacy or meanness.

sparingly *adv.* economically, frugally.

Spark, Dame Muriel (**Sarah**) (1918–) Scottish writer, born in Edinburgh. She was editor of *Poetry Review* (1947–9), and has published poetry, short stories, and critical biographies. She is best known for her novels, which include *Memento Mori* (1959), *The Prime of Miss Jean Brodie* (1961, filmed with Maggie Smith in the title role, 1968), *The Driver's Seat* (1970), and *Symposium* (1990). She now lives in Italy.

spark — *noun* **1** a tiny red-hot glowing particle thrown off by burning material, or by the friction between two hard (especially metal or stone) surfaces. **2** an electrical charge flashing across a gap between two conductors. **3** a trace, hint, or glimmer: *not a spark of intelligence.* **4** a lively, witty, or

intelligent person: *a bright spark.* — *verb intrans.* to throw off sparks.
— **spark something off** to stimulate or provoke it, especially as the final cause of several.
[from Anglo-Saxon *spærca*]

spark gap *Engineering* the space between two electrodes across which a high-voltage spark passes.

sparkle — *verb intrans.* **1** to give off sparks. **2** to shine with tiny points of bright light. **3** *said of wine, etc* to give off bubbles of carbon dioxide; to effervesce. **4** to be impressively lively or witty. — *noun* **1** an act of sparkling; sparkling appearance. **2** liveliness; vivacity; wit. [a diminutive of SPARK]

sparkler *noun* **1** a hand-held firework that gives off sparks. **2** *colloq.* a diamond or other impressive jewel.

sparkling *adj.* that sparkles.

spark plug *or* **sparking plug** in a petrol engine, an insulated plug supporting two electrodes between which a high-voltage spark passes, igniting the explosive mixture of fuel and air in the cylinder.

sparring partner **1** a person with whom a boxer practises. **2** a person with whom one enjoys a lively argument.

sparrow *noun* **1** any of various small grey or brown perching birds with a short conical bill adapted for cracking seeds, found in many parts of the world. The continual cheeping and chirruping of house sparrows serves to keep together large flocks, which feed, dust-bathe, and roost together. **2** (**in compounds**) applied to some similar small birds: *hedge sparrow.* [from Anglo-Saxon *spearwa*]

sparrow-hawk *noun* a short-winged bird of prey of the falcon family.

sparse *adj.* thinly scattered or dotted about; scanty. [from Latin *spargere*, to scatter]

sparsely *adv.* in a sparse way.

sparseness *or* **sparsity** *noun* being sparse.

Warrior figure, Sparta

Sparta, Greek **Spartí** POP (1991) 16 000, the capital town of Lakonia department, Peloponnese region, S Greece. Lying on the R Evrotas, 50km/31mi SW of Athens, Sparta was refounded on an ancient site in 1834. HISTORY one of the leading city-states of ancient Greece, with an oligarchic form of government and militaristic outlook that caused idealistic conflict with democratic Athens. Sparta defeated Athens in the Peloponnesian War (431–401 BC), but was unable to sustain an effective leadership of the Greek world, and declined rapidly in the Roman and later periods.

Spartacists, German *Spartakusbund* a left-wing revolutionary faction, led by Rosa

Luxemburg and Karl Liebknecht (1871–1919) in 1917, which advocated ending World War I and worked for a German socialist revolution. Initially part of the Independent SPD (Social Democratic Party of Germany), it formed the core of the German Communist Party (KPD) when the latter was founded in 1919. Luxemburg and Liebknecht were murdered in disturbances during the German revolution in early 1919.

Spartacus (d.71 BC) Thracian-born slave and gladiator at Capua, who led a slave uprising against Rome (73–71 BC). With an army of c.90 000 slaves and dispossessed, he inflicted numerous defeats on the Roman armies sent against him, until he was defeated and killed by Crassus (71 BC). He and his supporters were crucified along the Appian Way.

spartan — *adj.* **1** *said eg of living conditions* austere; frugal; harshly basic. **2** militaristic. — *noun* a spartan person. [from *Sparta*, an ancient Greek city noted for its austerity]

spasm *noun* **1** a sudden uncontrollable jerk caused by a contraction of the muscles. **2** a short period of activity; a spell. **3** a sudden burst of emotion: *spasm of anger*. [from Greek *spasma*, contraction]

spasmodic *adj.* occurring in or consisting of short periods; not constant or regular; intermittent.

spasmodically *adv.* in a spasmodic way.

spastic — *noun* **1** a person suffering from spastic paralysis. **2** *derog. slang* a clumsy or useless person. — *adj.* affected with spastic paralysis. [from Greek *spastikos*; see SPASM]

spastic paralysis permanent uncontrollable jerky muscle movement caused by injury to the muscle-controlling part of the brain.

spat[1] see SPIT[1].

spat[2] *colloq.* — *noun* a trivial or petty fight or quarrel. — *verb intrans.* (**spatted**, **spatting**) to engage in a spat. [probably imitative]

spat[3] *noun* either of a pair of cloth coverings fitting round the ankles and over the tops of the shoes. [an abbreviation of obsolete *spatterdash*, a long gaiter protecting the trousers from mud splashes]

spate *noun* a sudden rush or increased quantity; a burst: *received a spate of complaints*.
— **in spate** *said of a river* fast-flowing due to flooding.

spathe *noun Bot.* a large petal-like bract that surrounds and protects a certain type of flower-head, known as a *spadix* (a large cylindrical fleshy axis), eg in lords-and-ladies. [from Greek *spathe*, a broad blade]

spatial *adj.* of or relating to space. [from Latin *spatium*, space]

spatter — *verb trans., intrans.* (**spattered**, **spattering**) to splash in scattered drops or patches. — *noun* **1** a quantity spattered. **2** the act of spattering.

spatula *noun* a mixing or spreading tool with a broad blunt (often flexible) blade. [from Latin *spatula*, broad blade]

spawn — *noun* the eggs of frogs, fish, and molluscs, laid in water in a soft transparent jelly-like mass. — *verb* **1** *intrans. said of frogs, fish, etc* to lay eggs. **2** *trans.* to give rise to; to lead to: *the film's success spawned several sequels*. [from Old French *espandre*, to shed]

spay *verb* to remove the ovaries from (a female animal). [from Old French *espeier*, to cut with a sword]

SPCK *abbrev.* Society for Promoting Christian Knowledge.

speak *verb* (PAST TENSE **spoke**; PAST PARTICIPLE **spoken**) **1** *trans., intrans.* to utter words; to talk. **2** (*also* **speak to** *or* **with someone**) *said of one person or several* to talk to someone, or to each other:

they haven't spoken for years / may I speak with you for a moment. **3** to make a speech. **4** to communicate, or be able to communicate, in (a particular language): *he speaks French well and German fluently*. **5** *intrans.* (**speak of something**) to make mention of it; to refer to it. **6** *intrans.* to convey meaning: *actions speak louder than words*.
— **be on speaking terms** to be sufficiently friendly or familiar to hold a conversation.
speak for someone to give an opinion on their behalf: *I will be there, but I can't speak for the others*.
speak for itself to have an obvious meaning; to need no further explanation or comment.
speak one's mind to say boldly what one thinks.
speak out *intrans.* **1** to speak openly; to state one's views forcefully. **2** to speak more loudly.
speak up *intrans.* to speak more loudly.
no ... to speak of no ... worth mentioning: *received no education to speak of*.
[from Anglo-Saxon *specan*]

speakeasy *noun* (PL. **speakeasies**) *slang* a bar or other place selling alcohol illicitly during Prohibition.

speaker *noun* **1** a person who speaks, especially one making a formal speech. **2** a loudspeaker. **3** (*also* **Speaker**) the person presiding over debate in a law-making assembly, eg the House of Commons.

speaking clock *Brit.* a telephone service in which the exact time is given by means of a recorded message.

spear — *noun* **1** a weapon consisting of a long pole with a sharp (especially metal) point, for throwing from the shoulder. **2** a spiky plant shoot, eg a blade of grass. — *verb* to pierce with, or as if with, a spear. [from Anglo-Saxon *spere*]

spearhead — *noun* the leading part of an attacking force. — *verb* to lead (a movement, campaign, or attack).

spearmint *noun* **1** a common variety of mint plant, from which a flavouring is made for use in sweets, toothpaste, etc. **2** the flavouring.

spec[1]
— **on spec** *colloq.* as a speculation or gamble, in the hope of success: *wrote to them on spec, asking for a job*.
[a shortening of SPECULATION]

spec[2] *noun colloq.* specification.

special — *adj.* **1** distinct from, especially better than, others of the same kind; exceptional. **2** designed for a particular purpose. **3** not ordinary or common: *special circumstances*. **4** particular; great: *make a special effort*. — *noun* a special thing or person, eg an extra edition of a newspaper or a train running a particular service. [from Latin *specialis*]

Special Air Service (ABBREV. **SAS**) a British army unit specializing in secret and anti-terrorist operations. It was first formed in 1941 as a special commando unit to parachute behind enemy lines, and was revived as a regular unit of the British army in 1952 for special operations. It saw action during the Falklands campaign of 1982. Its motto is 'Who Dares Wins'.

Special Branch a British police department dealing with matters of political security.

special constable a member of a reserve police force, called upon eg in times of national emergency.

special delivery a delivery of post outside normal delivery times.

Special Drawing Rights (ABBREV. **SDRs**) the rights which can be exercised by members of the International Monetary Fund to draw on a pool of mixed currencies (US dollar, British pound, Japanese yen, French franc, German mark) set up by the Fund for use in emergencies. The facility is available to solve temporary balance of payments problems.

special education the education of children with special needs, especially those physically or mentally handicapped.

specialism *noun* **1** a subject of study one specialises in. **2** the act of specialising in some subject.

specialist *noun* **1** a person whose work, interest, or expertise is concentrated on a particular subject. **2** an organism with a narrow range of food and habitat preferences.

speciality *or North Amer.* **specialty** *noun* (PL. **specialities**, **specialties**) **1** a thing specialized in: *seafood is the restaurant's speciality*. **2** a special feature, service, or product.

specialization *or* **specialisation** *noun* specializing.

specialize *or* **specialise** *verb* **1** (*often* **specialize in something**) to devote all one's efforts to, or reserve one's best efforts for, one particular activity, field of study, etc. **2** to adapt to be used for a specific purpose.

specialized *or* **specialised** *adj.* adapted, developed, or modified for a particular purpose.

special licence a licence allowing a marriage to take place at short notice, without the usual legal formalities.

specially *adv.* **1** in a special way. **2** for a special purpose.

Special Operations Executive (ABBREV. **SOE**) an organization set up (Jul 1940) with British War Cabinet approval in response to Winston Churchill's directive to 'set Europe ablaze'; it later also operated in the Far East. It promoted and co-ordinated resistance activity in enemy-occupied territory until the end of World War II.

special school a school designed for the teaching of children with particular needs, especially arising from physical or mental handicaps.

speciation *noun Biol.* the process whereby one or more new species are formed from an existing species, eg as a result of geographical separation of different populations of the parent species.

specie *noun technical* money in coin form, as distinct from notes. [from Latin *in specie*, in kind]

species *noun* (PL. **species**) **1** the fundamental unit in plant and animal classification, consisting of a group of organisms that are able to interbreed among themselves and produce fertile offspring. Related species are grouped into genera, and some species may be divided into subspecies, varieties, breeds, etc. **2** *Chem.* a particular type of atom, molecule, or ion. **3** a kind or type. [from Latin *species*, kind, appearance]

speciesism *noun* the assumption that humans are superior to all other species of animals and are therefore justified in exploiting them for their own use.

specific — *adj.* **1** of a particular nature; precisely identified. **2** precise in meaning; not vague. — *noun* **1** (*usually* **specifics**) a specific detail, eg of a plan or scheme. **2** a drug used to treat a specific disease. [from Latin *species*, kind + *facere*, to make]

specifically *adv.* **1** in a specific way. **2** as a specific instance.

specification *noun* **1** (*often* **specifications**) a detailed description of a thing built or constructed. **2** the nature and quality of the parts that it is made up of: *a car with a hi-tech specification*. **3** the act of specifying.

specific gravity relative density.

specific heat capacity see HEAT CAPACITY.

specify *verb* (**specifies**, **specified**) **1** to refer to or identify precisely. **2** to state as a condition or requirement. [see SPECIFIC]

specimen *noun* **1** a sample or example of something, especially an object studied or put in a collection. **2** a sample of blood, urine, or tissue on which medical tests are carried out. **3** *colloq.* a person of a particular kind: *an ugly specimen*. [from Latin, from *specere*, to see]

specious *adj.* seeming to be good, sound, or just, but really false or flawed: *specious arguments*. [from Latin *species*, appearance]

speciousness *or* **speciosity** *noun* being specious.

speck *noun* a small spot, stain, or particle. [from Anglo-Saxon *specca*]

speckle — *noun* a little spot, especially one of several on a different-coloured background. — *verb* to mark with speckles. [a diminutive of SPECK]

speckled *adj.* covered or marked with specks or speckles.

specs *pl. noun colloq.* spectacles.

spectacle *noun* **1** a thing seen; a sight, especially impressive, wonderful, or ridiculous. **2** a public display or exhibition. **3** (**spectacles**) a pair of lenses held in a frame over the eyes, used to correct faulty eyesight.
— **make a spectacle of oneself** to behave in a way that attracts ridicule or scorn.
[from Latin *spectaculum*, from *specere*, to look at]
◇ Convex lenses help those who are long-sighted; concave lenses those who are short-sighted. Bifocal spectacles have lenses where the upper and lower parts have different curvatures, enabling the wearer to focus on distant and near objects respectively. Spectacles were first developed in the late Middle-Ages, but it was not until the 17c that lenses were accurately ground to specific requirements.

spectacled bear the only bear native to the S hemisphere, found in forests in the W foothills of the Andes. It has a small body with dark fur, and is so called because there are pale rings around its eyes. It builds platforms in trees from broken branches, and feeds mainly on plant material.

spectacular — *adj.* **1** impressively striking to see or watch. **2** remarkable; dramatic. — *noun* a spectacular show or display. [see SPECTACLE]

spectacularly *adv.* in a spectacular way.

spectate *verb intrans.* to be a spectator; to look on.

spectator *noun* a person who watches an event or incident. [from Latin, from *spectare*, to look]

spectral *adj.* relating to or like a spectre.

spectre *noun* **1** a visible ghost; an apparition. **2** a haunting fear; the threat of something unpleasant. [from French *spectre*, from Latin *specere*, to look at]

spectrometer *noun* an instrument for measuring spectra in terms of wavelength and energy.

spectroscope *noun Chem.* an optical instrument that is used to produce a spectrum for a particular chemical compound, which can then be observed and analysed in order to identify the compound, determine its structure, etc.

spectrum *noun* (PL. **spectra**, **spectrums**) **1** *Physics* (*in full* **visible spectrum**) the band of colours (red, orange, yellow, green, blue, indigo, and violet) produced when white light is split into its constituent wavelengths by passing it through a prism. **2** a continuous band or a series of lines representing the wavelengths or frequencies of electromagnetic radiation (eg visible light, X-rays, radio waves) emitted or absorbed by a particular substance. **3** any full range: *the whole spectrum of human emotions*. [from Latin *spectrum*, appearance]

speculate *verb intrans.* **1** (*often* **speculate on** *or* **about something**) to consider the circumstances or possibilities regarding it, usually without any factual basis and without coming to a definite conclusion. **2** to engage in risky financial transactions, usually in the hope of making a quick profit. [from Latin *speculari*, to look out]

speculation *noun* **1** speculating or a result of speculating. **2** a risky investment of money for the sake of large profit.

speculative *adj.* involving speculation.

speculator *noun* a person who speculates, especially financially.

speculum *noun* **1** *Optics* a mirror with a reflective surface, usually of polished metal. **2** *Medicine* an instrument that is used to enlarge the opening of a body cavity so that the interior may be inspected. [from Latin *speculum*, mirror, from *specere*, to look at]

sped see SPEED.

speech *noun* **1** the ability to speak. **2** a way of speaking: *slurred speech*. **3** that which is spoken; spoken language. **4** a talk addressed to other people. [from Anglo-Saxon *spec*]

speechify *verb intrans.* (**speechifies**, **speechified**) *colloq.* to make (especially long and tedious) speeches.

speechless *adj.* temporarily unable to speak, because of surprise, shock, emotion, etc.

speech recognition *Comput.* the understanding of an individual's speech patterns, or of continuous speech, by a computer.

speech therapist a person who provides speech therapy.

speech therapy the treatment of speech and language disorders.

Speed the clownish servant of Valentine in Shakespeare's *The Two Gentlemen of Verona*, who suggests to his master that Silvia is in love with him (Valentine).

speed — *noun* **1** rate of movement or action. **2** quickness; rapidity: *with speed*. **3** a gear setting on a vehicle: *five-speed gearbox*. **4** a photographic film's sensitivity to light. **5** *slang* amphetamines. — *verb intrans.* (PAST TENSE AND PAST PARTICIPLE **sped**) **1** to move quickly. **2** to drive at a speed higher than the legal limit.
— **at speed** quickly.
speed up *or* **speed something up** to increase speed or cause it to increase in speed.
[from Anglo-Saxon *sped*]

speedboat *noun* a motor boat capable of high speeds.

speed bump a low hump across a road intended to slow down traffic.

speedily *adv.* in a speedy way, with haste.

speed limit the maximum speed a vehicle may legally travel at on a given stretch of road.

speedo *noun* (PL. **speedos**) *colloq.* a speedometer.

speed of light *Physics* (SYMBOL *c*) the speed at which electromagnetic waves, including visible light, travel through empty space, ie a vacuum. The speed of light is about 3×10^8 metres per second, the highest speed possible in the universe.

speedometer *noun* an instrument that indicates the speed at which a motor vehicle is travelling. It often incorporates an odometer that displays the total mileage.

speed trap a stretch of road over which police monitor the speed of vehicles, often with electronic equipment.

speedway *noun* **1** racing on lightweight motorcycles round a cinder track. **2** the track used.

speedwell *noun* a plant of the foxglove family, with small blue or pink flowers.

speedy *adj.* (**speedier**, **speediest**) fast; prompt; without delay.

Speenhamland system a local attempt in Britain to improve the operation of the old Poor Laws at a time of crisis. Named from a Berkshire parish, it was introduced in 1795 and comprised scales of relief for labourers which were dependent both on the prevailing price of bread and the size of labourers' families. The principles spread to many southern and eastern parishes in the early 19c, but received criticism from political economists for 'encouraging the poor to breed'.

Speer, Albert (1905–81) German architect and Nazi government official, born in Mannheim. He joined the Nazi Party (1931) and became Hitler's chief architect (1934) and Minister of Armaments (1942). More concerned with technology and administration than ideology, he openly opposed Hitler in the final months of World War II, and was the only Nazi leader at Nuremberg to admit responsibility for the regime's actions. Imprisoned for 20 years in Spandau, Berlin, after his release in 1966 he became a writer.

Speightstown a town on the NW coast of the island of Barbados, N of Bridgetown.

Speke, John Hanning (1827–64) English explorer, born in Bideford, Devon. He served in India, and in 1854 went with Richard Francis Burton to search for the equatorial lakes of Africa. They discovered L Tanganyika (1858), then Speke travelled on alone. He found the lake which he named Victoria and identified as the source of the Nile. His claims to have discovered the source of the Nile were doubted by Burton and others in England, and so he set out on a second expedition (1860–3). On his return, his claims were again challenged, and on the day he was to defend his discovery in public, he accidentally shot and killed himself while hunting near Corsham, Wiltshire.

spelaeology *or* **speleology** *noun* **1** the scientific study of caves. **2** cave-exploring. [from Greek *spelaion*, cave + -LOGY]

spell[1] *verb* (PAST TENSE AND PAST PARTICIPLE **spelt**, **spelled**) **1** *trans., intrans.* to write or name the letters making up (a word or words) in their correct order. **2** to form (a word) when written in sequence: *B, A, D spells 'bad'*. **3** to indicate clearly: *his angry expression spelt trouble*.
— **spell something out 1** to read, write, or speak the letters of (a word) one by one. **2** to explain something clearly and in detail.
[from Old French *espeller*]

spell[2] *noun* **1** a set of words which, especially when spoken, is believed to have magical power. **2** the influence of such power: *cast a spell on someone*. **3** a strong attracting influence; a fascination. [from Anglo-Saxon *spell*, narrative, from *spellian*, to speak or announce]

spell[3] *noun* a period, eg of illness, work, or weather of a particular kind. [from Anglo-Saxon *spelian*, to act for another]

spellbinding *adj.* causing one to be spellbound.

spellbound *adj.* completely charmed or fascinated, as if held by magical power.

spelling *noun* **1** ability to spell. **2** a way a word is spelt.

spelling reform a movement that aims to make English spelling more regular in relation to speech. Many schemes have been suggested, both in Britain and the USA, with the aim of standardizing and simplifying spelling. Examples include: standardizing systems, such as *Regularized English*, which make use of the existing alphabet; augmenting or supplementing systems, such as *i.t.a.*, which add new symbols to the regular alphabet; and, supplanting schemes, such as George Bernard Shaw's *Proposed British Alphabet*, in which an entirely new set of symbols is introduced.

spelt see SPELL[1].

spelunking *noun North Amer.* the sport or activity of exploring caves; potholing. [from Latin *spelunca*, from Greek *spelynx*, a cave]

Spence, Sir Basil (Urwin) (1907–76) Scottish architect, born in Bombay, India. He gradually emerged as the leading postwar British architect, with his fresh approach to new university buildings, the pavilion for the Festival of Britain (1951), and his best-known work, the new Coventry Cathedral (1951), which boldly merged new and traditional structural methods. He was Professor of Architecture at Leeds (1955–6) and at the Royal Academy (1961–8).

Spencer, Herbert (1820–1903) English evolutionary philosopher, born in Derby. He held various jobs (including that of subeditor at *The Economist*, 1848–53) before becoming a full-time writer. A firm (pre-Darwinian) believer in evolution, his main work is the nine-volume *System of Synthetic Philosophy* (1862–93), which brought together biology, psychology, sociology, and ethics. He was a leading advocate of 'Social Darwinism', and coined the phrase 'survival of the fittest'.

Spencer, Sir Stanley (1891–1959) English painter, born in Cookham, Berkshire. He served in World War I and was an official war artist in World War II. He produced many purely realistic landscapes, but his main works are religious and interpret the Bible in terms of everyday life (eg *Resurrection: Port Glasgow*, 1950, Tate, London). His best-known work is his decorative scheme of murals of army life for the Sandham Memorial Chapel, Burghclere (1926–33). Other works include *The Resurrection: Cookham* (1922–7, Tate, London).

Spencer Jones, Sir Harold see JONES, SIR HAROLD SPENCER.

spend *verb* (PAST TENSE AND PAST PARTICIPLE **spent**) **1** *trans., intrans.* to use up or pay out (money). **2** to use or devote (eg time or energy): *needed to spend a few hours on the cleaning.* **3** to use up completely; to exhaust: *their passion was spent.* — **spend a penny** *colloq.* to urinate. [from Latin *expendere*]

Spender, Sir Stephen (Harold) (1909–) English poet and critic, born in London. In the 1930s he became associated with the group of 'modern poets', which also included W H Auden and Louis MacNeice. He was co-editor of *Horizon* (1939–41) and *Encounter* (1953–67), and Professor of English at London (1970–7). His many poetic works include *Poems from Spain* (1939), *Ruins and Visions* (1942), and *The Generous Days* (1971). His *Collected Poems 1930–85* were published in 1985, and the novel *The Temple* in 1988.

spendthrift *noun* a person who spends money freely and carelessly.

Spengler, Oswald (1880–1936) German philosopher of history, born in Blankenburg. He taught mathematics before devoting himself to *Der Untergang des Abendlandes* (The Decline of the West, 2 vols, 1918–22), which argues that all cultures are subject to the same cycle of growth and decay in accordance with predetermined 'historical destiny'. His views were admired by the Nazis.

Spenser, Edmund (c.1552–99) English poet, born in London. He obtained a place in the Earl of Leicester's household, which led to a friendship with Sir Philip Sidney. His first original work was a sequence of pastoral poems, *The Shepheards Calendar* (1579). He became secretary to the Lord Deputy in Ireland (1580), and acquired Kilcolman

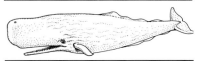

sperm whale

Castle, Co Cork, where he settled in 1586; the castle was burnt by rebels in 1598, but he escaped with his wife to London. The first three books of his major work, *The Faerie Queene*, were published in 1590, and the second three in 1596, but the poem was left unfinished at his death.

spent past tense and past participle of SPEND. — *adj.* used up; exhausted.

sperm *noun* **1** in animals, the small motile male gamete (reproductive cell) that locates, penetrates, and fertilizes the female gamete (the egg or ovum). In mammals it is produced in the testes, and consists of a head containing a nucleus but very little cytoplasm, and a long flagellum or 'tail' that lashes to move the sperm forward. **2** semen, a fluid containing millions of such gametes, together with nutrients, produced in the reproductive organs of male mammals, and introduced into the reproductive tract of the female during copulation. [from Greek *sperma*, seed]

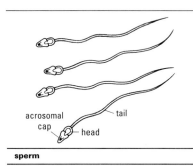

acrosomal cap
tail
head

sperm

spermaceti *noun* a white translucent waxy solid present in the tissue behind the forehead of the sperm whale, and thought to be involved in echo-location. It is used to make candles, soap, cosmetics, and ointments.

spermatogenesis *noun Zool.* the formation of sperm in the testes.

spermatophyte *noun Bot.* any plant belonging to the division Spermatophyta, which includes all seed-bearing plants. [from Greek *sperma -atos*, seed, semen, from *speirein*, to sow]

spermatozoon *noun* (PL. **spermatozoa**) *Biol.* in male animals, a mature sperm cell.

sperm bank a refrigerated store of semen for use in artificial insemination.

spermicide *noun* a substance that kills sperm, used in conjunction with various methods of barrier contraception, eg the condom and the diaphragm.

sperm whale the largest of the toothed whales, with an enormous head (representing a third of the total body length) and a square snout. It is found in all the oceans, and is most common in warm seas. It is now an endangered species, having been widely hunted for spermaceti, found in a large cavity in the head, and for ambergris, produced in the intestines; both substances are used in the cosmetics and perfume industry.

Sperry, Elmer Ambrose (1860–1930) US inventor and electrical engineer, born in Cortland, New York. He invented many new devices, including a new-type dynamo, arc-light, and searchlight, and founded several companies for their manufacture. His chief invention was the gyroscopic compass (1911) and stabilizers for ships and aeroplanes.

Sperry, Roger Wolcott (1913–) US neuroscientist, born in Hartford, Connecticut. He taught at Chicago University, and was later professor at the California Institute of Technology. His early experiments helped to establish the means by which nerve cells are connected in particular ways in the central nervous system.

Later he established that each hemisphere of the brain possesses specific higher functions, the left side controlling verbal activity and processes such as writing and reasoning, the right side being more responsive to music, face, and voice recognition. He shared the 1981 Nobel Prize for Physiology or Medicine with David Hubel and Torsten Wiesel.

spew — *verb trans., intrans.* **1** to vomit. **2** to pour or cause to pour or stream out. — *noun* vomit. [from Anglo-Saxon *spiowan*, to spit]

Spey, River a river in Highland and Grampian regions, NE Scotland, length 171km/106mi. Rising near Corrieyairack Pass, SE of Fort Augustus, it flows NE into Spey Bay, to the E of Lossiemouth. In the lower reaches the Spey is the fastest-flowing river in Britain. It is noted for its salmon fishing.

Speyer Cathedral a Romanesque cathedral founded by Conrad I (c.990–1039) in 1030 at Speyer, SW Germany. The church, which is noted for its royal tombs and crypt, has required reconstruction on several occasions, most recently after World War II. It is a World Heritage site.

SPF *abbrev.* sun protection factor.

sphagnum *noun* (PL. **sphagna**) any moss of the genus *Sphagnum*, the main constituent of peat bogs in temperate regions. It has a spongy structure that retains water, and is used as a packing material, eg for potting plants. [from Greek *sphagnos*]

sphalerite *noun Geol.* a yellowish-brown to brownish-black mineral form of zinc sulphide (ZnS), usually with a resinous lustre, commonly found in coarse or fine granular masses in association with galena. It is the principal ore of zinc, and is also a source of cadmium. — Also called *zinc blende*. [from Greek *sphaleros*, deceptive, from its resemblance to galena]

sphere *noun* **1** a round solid figure with a surface on which all points are an equal distance from the centre; a globe or ball. **2** a field of activity. **3** range or extent: *extend one's sphere of influence.* **4** a class or circle within society: *moves in a different sphere.* [from Greek *sphaira*]

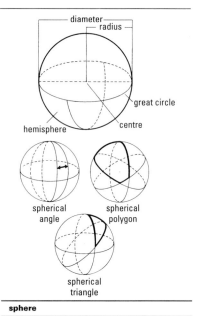

diameter
radius
great circle
centre
hemisphere
spherical angle
spherical polygon
spherical triangle

sphere

spherical *adj.* sphere-shaped.

spheroid *noun* a solid figure that is obtained by rotating an ellipse about its major axis (producing an elongated sphere) or its minor axis (producing a flattened sphere).

sphincter *noun* a ring of muscle that expands and contracts to open and close the entrance to a cavity in the body: *anal sphincter.* [from Greek *sphingein*, to bind tight]

sphinx *noun* **1** (**Sphinx**) *Greek Mythol.* a monster with the head of a woman and the body of a lion, which killed travellers who could not solve the riddles it set. **2** (*also* **Sphinx**) a stone carving or other representation of a sphinx, especially the huge monument near the Egyptian pyramids at Giza. **3** a mysterious or enigmatic person. [from Greek *sphigx*, probably from *sphiggo*, to squeeze]

sphygmomanometer *or* **sphygmometer** *noun Medicine* an instrument for measuring blood pressure in the arteries, consisting of an inflatable cuff for the arm connected to a column of mercury with a graduated scale which indicates blood pressure in millimetres of mercury. [from Greek *sphygmos*, pulse]

spice — *noun* **1** any of numerous strong-smelling vegetable substances used to flavour food, eg pepper, ginger, and nutmeg. **2** such substances collectively. **3** something that adds interest or enjoyment: *variety is the spice of life.* — *verb* **1** to flavour with spice. **2** (*also* **spice something up**) to add interest or enjoyment to it. [from Old French *espice*]

Spice Islands see MOLUCCAS.

spick and span neat, clean, and tidy. [from obsolete *spick and span new*, extension of Middle English *span new*, brand new]

spicy *adj.* (**spicier**, **spiciest**) **1** tasting or smelling of spices; pungent; piquant. **2** *colloq.* dealing with (especially sexual) scandal.

spider *noun* **1** any of at least 32 000 species of invertebrate animal having eight legs and two main body parts, belonging to the order Araneae, and found in virtually all habitats, including Antarctica. **2** a thing resembling this creature, eg a multi-pointed rest used in snooker. [from Anglo-Saxon *spithra*, from *spinnan*, to spin]
◇ All spiders have fangs for seizing their prey, and most have poison glands to subdue insects before they are killed and eaten, but only a few spiders are poisonous to humans, eg the black widow. Most spiders produce silk, which they spin from organs at the end of the abdomen, called *spinnerets.* The silk is used to build webs or traps in which their prey is caught. Almost all spiders lay out a line of silk as they move about, anchoring it at intervals, rather like a mountaineer's safety line. Spiders range in size from species less than 0.5mm in diameter to the giant bird-eating spider of S America, which has a legspan of up to 25cm. Without spiders the Earth would rapidly become overrun with insects.

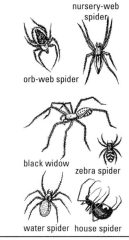

nursery-web spider

orb-web spider

black widow

zebra spider

water spider   house spider

spiders

spider monkey an American tree-dwelling monkey with long thin limbs and a long tail.

spider plant a perennial plant (*Chlorophytum comosum*) that has fleshy roots, long narrow curved leaves, and a branched flower stalk bearing white flowers and tufts of small leaves that root on contact with the soil, and develop into new plants. A variety with cream-striped leaves is widely grown as a house plant.

spidery *adj.* **1** thin and untidy: *spidery handwriting.* **2** full of spiders.

spiel *noun colloq.* **1** a long rambling story, especially given as an excuse: *gave me this whole spiel about missing the train.* **2** plausible talk, especially sales patter. [from German *spiel*, play]

Spielberg, Steven (1947–) US film director and producer, born in Cincinnati. He worked first in television, but achieved a blockbuster success with *Jaws* (1975), and followed this with *Close Encounters of the Third Kind* (1977) and *ET, The Extra-Terrestrial* (1982). Other films include *Raiders of the Lost Ark* (1981), *Poltergeist* (1983), *Indiana Jones and the Temple of Doom* (1984), *Gremlins* (1984), *The Color Purple* (1885), *Who Framed Roger Rabbit?* (1988), and *Jurassic Park* (1993). Despite his commercial success, he failed to win an Oscar until 1994, when he was voted Best Director for *Schindler's List* (1993).

spiffing *adj.* old *colloq.* use excellent; splendid.

spigot *noun* **1** a plug used to stop up the vent hole in a cask. **2** a tap fitted to a cask. [from Provençal *espigot*]

spike[1] — *noun* **1** a thin sharp point. **2** a pointed piece of metal, eg one of several on railings or the soles of running-shoes. **3** (**spikes**) running-shoes with such soles. **4** a large metal nail. — *verb* **1** to strike, pierce, or impale with a pointed object. **2** *colloq.* to make (a drink) stronger by adding alcohol or extra alcohol.
— **spike someone's guns** *colloq.* to spoil their plans.
[from Anglo-Saxon *spicing*]

spike[2] *noun Bot.* a long pointed inflorescence (flower-head) bearing small stalkless flowers along its length, eg plantain, or bearing small secondary spikes or *spikelets* which branch from it, eg grasses and sedges. The youngest flowers are at the tip of the stem and the oldest ones near its base. [from Latin *spica*, ear of corn]

spikelet *noun Bot.* a structure peculiar to the flower heads of grasses, and consisting of one to several reduced flowers enclosed in a series of small bracts. The inflorescence (flower head) of the grass consists of a large number of spikelets arranged in many different ways, according to the species.

spikenard *noun* **1** a sweet-smelling Indian plant with purple flowers. **2** an oil or ointment made from it. [from Latin *spica nardi*]

spikily *adv.* in a spiky way.

spikiness *noun* being spiky.

spiky *adj.* (**spikier**, **spikiest**) **1** having spikes or pointed ends. **2** *colloq.* bad-tempered.

spill[1] — *verb* (PAST TENSE AND PAST PARTICIPLE **spilt**, **spilled**) **1** *trans., intrans.* to run or cause to run or flow out from a container, especially accidentally. **2** *intrans.* to come or go in large crowds, especially quickly: *spectators spilling out of the stadium.* **3** to shed (blood, especially of other people). **4** *colloq.* to throw from a vehicle or saddle. — *noun* **1** an act of spilling. **2** *colloq.* a fall, especially from a vehicle or horse.
— **spill the beans** *colloq.* to reveal confidential information, usually inadvertently.
[from Anglo-Saxon *spillan*]

spill[2] *noun* a thin strip of wood or twisted paper for lighting a fire, candle, etc.

spillage *noun* **1** the act of spilling. **2** an amount spilt.

Spillane, Mickey, properly **Frank Morrison Spillane** (1918–) US popular novelist, born in New York City. He wrote for pulp magazines to pay for his education, and produced his first novel *I, the Jury* in 1947. His novels featuring the private detective Mike Hammer inspired many films and a television series. *Kiss Me Deadly* (1952) is a typical example of his work, in its representation of sadism, sex, and violence.

spilt see SPILL[1].

spin — *verb* (**spinning**; PAST TENSE AND PAST PARTICIPLE **spun**) **1** *trans., intrans.* to rotate or

Spices		
English name	Species	Origin
allspice	*Pimenta officinalis*	America, W Indies
annatto	*Bixa orellana*	S America, W Indies
asafoetida	*Ferula assa-fetida*	W Asia
bay	*Laurus nobilis*	Mediterranean, Asia Minor
caraway	*Carum carvi*	Europe, Asia
cardamom	*Elettaria cardamomum*	SE Asia
cayenne	*Capsicum frutescens*	America, Africa
chilli pepper	*Capsicum annuum*	America
cinnamon	*Cinnamomum zeylanium*	Ceylon
cloves	*Eugenia caryophyllata*	Moluccas
cocoa	*Theobroma cacoa*	S America
coconut	*Cocus nucifera*	Polynesia
coriander	*Coriandrum sativum*	S Europe
cumin	*Cuminum cyminum*	Mediterranean
curry leaf	*Murraya koenigi*	India
fennel	*Foeniculum vulgare*	S Europe
fenugreek	*Trigonella foenum-graecum*	India, S Europe
ginger	*Zingiber officinale*	SE Asia
mace	*Myristica fragrans*	Moluccas
mustard, black	*Brassica niger*	Europe, Africa, Asia, America
mustard, white	*Sinapis alba*	Europe, Asia
nutmeg	*Myristica fragrans*	Moluccas
paprika	*Capsicum annuum*	S America
pepper	*Piper nigrum*	India
sassafras	*Sassafras albidum*	N America
sesame	*Sesamum indicum*	tropics
soya	*Glycine max*	China
tamarind	*Tamarindus indica*	Africa
turmeric	*Curcuma longa*	SE Asia
vanilla	*Vanilla fragrans*	C America

cause to rotate repeatedly, especially quickly. **2** to draw out and twist (fibres, etc) into thread. **3** to construct from thread. **4** to throw or strike (a ball) so that it rotates while moving forward, causing deviation through the air or on impact with the ground or a second ball. **5** *intrans.* to have a revolving sensation that disorientates: *my head was spinning.* **6** to dry in a spin-drier. — *noun* **1** an act of spinning or a spinning motion. **2** rotation in a ball thrown or struck. **3** a nose-first spiral descent in an aircraft, especially uncontrolled. **4** *colloq.* a short trip in a vehicle, for pleasure. — **spin something out 1** to prolong an activity. **2** to cause it to last longer by economical use. **spin a yarn** to tell a story, especially a long improbable one. [from Anglo-Saxon *spinnan*]

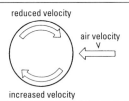

reduced velocity

air velocity

increased velocity

effect of spin on a ball

spina bifida *Medicine* a congenital defect in which one or more vertebrae fail to unite during the development of the embryo, resulting in protrusion of part of the spinal cord through the backbone. It may cause permanent paralysis of the legs, and mental retardation. The condition can now be diagnosed by amniocentesis during pregnancy, so that termination is possible if desired. [from Latin *spina bifida*, split spine]

spinach *noun* **1** a plant of the beet family. **2** its dark green succulent leaves eaten as a vegetable. [from Old French *espinache*, from Arabic *isfanakh*]

spinal *adj.* of or relating to the spine.

spinal column the spine.

spinal cord a cord-like mass of nerve tissue running along the spine and connecting the brain to nerves in all other parts of the body.

spinal nerve *Anat.* in humans, any of 31 pairs of nerves that arise from the spinal cord and extend to all parts of the body, forming many branches as they do so. Each spinal nerve contains a bundle of sensory nerve fibres, which relay information to the brain, and a bundle of motor nerve fibres, which relay information from the brain.

spin bowler *Cricket* a slow bowler who spins the ball sharply with his fingers as he releases it.

spindle *noun* **1** a rod with a notched or tapered end, for twisting the thread in spinning. **2** a pin or axis on which anything turns. **3** *Biol.* in the cytoplasm of a cell, a structure consisting of protein fibres to which chromosomes become attached during cell division. [from Anglo-Saxon *spinel*, from *spinnan*, to spin]

spindly *adj.* (**spindlier, spindliest**) *colloq.* long, thin, and frail-looking.

spin doctor *colloq.* a person, such as a senior public relations advisor to a politician or political party, who is employed to influence public opinion by putting a favourable bias or 'spin' on information when it is presented to the public or to the media. The term originated in the USA in the 1980s.

spin-drier *or* **spin-dryer** *noun* a machine that forces the water out of wet laundry by spinning it at high speed in a revolving drum.

spindrift *noun* spray blown from the crests of waves. [a Scot. variation of obsolete *spoondrift*, from *spoon*, to be blown by the wind + DRIFT]

spin-dry *verb* to partly dry (wet laundry) by using a spin-dryer.

spine *noun* **1** in vertebrates, the flexible bony column consisting of a row of vertebrae connected by cartilage discs. It surrounds and protects the spinal cord, and articulates with the skull, ribs, and pelvic girdle. **2** the narrow middle section of a book's cover, covering the part where the pages are fastened in. **3** in certain plants and animals, eg cacti, hedgehogs, one of many sharply pointed structures that provide protection against predators. **4** *colloq.* courage; strength of character: *he has little spine.* [from Latin *spina*, thorn]

spine-chiller *noun* a frightening story, thought, or happening.

spine-chilling *adj. colloq.* frightening; scary.

spineless *adj.* **1** having no spine; invertebrate. **2** *colloq.* lacking courage or strength of character.

spinet *noun* a musical instrument like a small harpsichord. [from Italian *spinetta*]

spinnaker *noun* a large triangular sail set at the front of a yacht.

spinner *noun* **1** a spin-drier. **2** an angler's lure shaped so as to spin in the water when the line is pulled. **3** *Cricket* a spin bowler, or a ball bowled by one.

spinneret *noun Zool.* in spiders and some insects, a small tubular organ from which silk is produced.

spinney *noun* (PL. **spinneys**) *Bot.* a small wood containing undergrowth, especially one that consists of thorn-bearing trees and shrubs. [from Latin *spinetum*, thorn-hedge]

spinning-jenny *noun* an early type of spinning machine, with several spindles.

spinning-wheel *noun* a machine for spinning thread, consisting of a spindle driven by a hand- or foot-operated wheel.

spin-off *noun* **1** a side-effect or by-product, especially valuable. **2** a thing developed from an earlier product or idea, eg a television series derived from a successful film.

Spinoza, Benedict de, Hebrew **Baruch** (1632–77) Dutch-Jewish philosopher and theologian, born in Amsterdam. His interest in optics, the new astronomy, and Cartesian philosophy made him unpopular, and he was expelled from the Jewish community in 1656. His major works include the *Tractatus Theologico-Politicus* (1670), which despite its anonymity made him famous, and his *Ethica* (published posthumously, 1677). In 1673 he refused the professorship of philosophy at Heidelberg.

spinster *noun* a woman who has never been married, especially when elderly. [from Middle English *spinnestere*, woman who spins thread]

spinsterhood *noun* the status of a spinster.

spiny *adj.* (**spinier, spiniest**) **1** *said of plants or animals* covered with spines. **2** troublesome; difficult to deal with: *a spiny problem.*

Spion Kop, Battle of a battle (1900) in the second Boer War which was part of the British attempt to relieve Ladysmith, a Natal town besieged by the Boers since October 1899. The British attempt to take a nearby hill led eventually to defeat and 1 500 casualties. Together with the reverse at Vaal Krantz in the same week, it continued their succession of defeats suffered during the early months of the war.

spiracle *noun Zool.* in insects, any of various openings (arranged in 10 pairs) along the side of the body that are used for breathing. Each spiracle represents the external opening of a trachea (a flexible air tube that penetrates the body tissues). [from Latin *spiraculum*, from *spirare*, to breath]

spiraea *or* **spirea** *noun* a deciduous shrub of the genus *Spiraea*, native to north temperate regions. It has narrow to broadly oval leaves, and dense clusters of white or pink flowers. It is a popular ornamental plant. [from Greek *speiraia*, privet, from *speira*, coil]

spiral — *noun* **1** the pattern made by a line winding outwards from a central point in near-circles of ever-increasing size. **2** the pattern made by a line winding downwards from a point in near-circles of the same or ever-increasing size, as if round a cylinder or cone. **3** a curve or course following such a pattern. **4** a gradual but continuous rise or fall, eg of prices. — *adj.* of the shape or nature of a spiral. — *verb intrans.* (**spiralled, spiralling**) to follow a spiral course or pattern. [from Greek *speira*, coil]

spirally *adv.* in a spiral way.

spire *noun* a tall thin structure tapering upwards to a point, especially a tower on a church roof. [from Anglo-Saxon *spir*, shoot, sprout]

spirit — *noun* **1** the force within a person that is or provides the will to live: *sad news broke his spirit.* **2** this force as an independent part of a person, widely believed to survive the body after death, and sometimes visible as a ghost. **3** a supernatural being without a body: *evil spirits.* **4** one's thoughts, concerns, etc (as opposed to one's actual presence): *be with you in spirit, though not in person.* **5** (usually **spirits**) emotional state; mood: *in high spirits.* **6** overall atmosphere or feeling generated by several people together: *enter into the spirit of the party / team spirit.* **7** courage; liveliness or vivacity. **8** the underlying essential meaning or intention as distinct from literal interpretation: *in accordance with the spirit, not the letter, of the law.* **9** a distilled alcoholic liquid for drinking, eg whisky, brandy, or gin. **10** *Chem.* a volatile liquid obtained by distillation. — *verb* (**spirited, spiriting**) (*usually* **spirit something** or **someone away** *or* **off**) to carry or convey mysteriously or magically. [from Latin *spiritus*, breath]

spirited *adj.* **1** full of courage or liveliness. **2** (*in compounds*) showing a particular kind of spirit, mood, or attitude: *high-spirited / public-spirited.*

spirit-lamp *noun* a lamp fuelled by methylated or other spirit as opposed to oil.

spirit level a flat-edged bar with a short liquid-filled glass tube set inside it, showing the perfect levelness of a surface on which it is placed when a large bubble in the liquid lies between two markings on the tube.

Spirit of Saint Louis the plane in which Charles A Lindbergh made the first solo non-stop transatlantic flight from New York to Paris on 20 May 1927. It achieved a top speed of 200kph/120mph and took 33.5h to complete the trip.

Spirit of the Age, The a collection of essays by William Hazlitt (1825). They give character sketches and critical overviews of various of his contemporaries (eg Samuel Taylor Coleridge, Sir Walter Scott) from the Romantic and pre-Romantic period.

spiritual — *adj.* **1** of or relating to the spirit or soul, rather than to the body or to physical things. **2** religious: *a spiritual leader.* — *noun* (*also* **Negro spiritual**) a religious song developed from the communal singing traditions of black people in the southern USA. [from Latin *spiritualis*; see SPIRIT]

spiritualism *noun* belief in, or the practice of, communication with the spirits of dead people through a medium, a specially sensitive person. ◇ As an organized religion, spiritualism has been practised mainly in the West, especially in Europe and the USA, from the middle of the 19c. Its adherents believe in God, and believe that they may better understand his laws through communication with the spirits of the dead.

spiritualist *noun* a person who believes in or practises spiritualism.

spirituality *noun* **1** a spiritual state. **2** something that is spiritual.

spiritually *adv.* in a spiritual way.

spirituous *adj.* containing alcohol obtained by distillation.

spirochaete *noun Biol.* any of a group of non-rigid spiral-shaped Gram-negative bacteria, many of which feed on dead organic matter, although some are parasitic and live in the intestines and genital regions of animals, causing various diseases, including syphilis in humans. [from Greek *speira*, a coil + *chaite*, hair, mane]

spirogyra *noun* a filament-like green alga of the genus *Spirogyra*, found in ponds and streams, either floating or fixed to stones. It consists of filaments or chains of cells containing green chloroplasts which form a spiral within each cell. Division of the cells leads to an increase in length of the filament, and broken fragments can form new filaments.

spit[1] — *verb* (**spitting**; PAST TENSE AND PAST PARTICIPLE **spat**) **1** *intrans.* to expel saliva from the mouth, often as a gesture of contempt. **2** (*also* **spit something out**) to force (eg food) out of the mouth. **3** to emit in a short explosive burst: *the frying pan spat hot oil on me.* **4** to speak or utter with hate or violence. **5** *intrans. said of rain* to fall in light intermittent drops. — *noun* **1** saliva spat from the mouth; spittle. **2** (**the spit** *or* **very spit of someone** *or* **something**) *colloq.* an exact likeness of them; a spitting image: *he's the very spit of his father.*
— **spit it out** *colloq.* (*usually as a command*) to speak out what one is hesitating to say. [from Anglo-Saxon *spittan*]

spit[2] *noun* **1** a long thin metal rod on which meat is skewered and held over a fire for roasting. **2** a long narrow strip of land jutting out into the sea. [from Anglo-Saxon *spitu*]

Spitalfields an area in the East End of London, which flourished as a centre of silk-weaving from the late 17c (when Huguenot weavers settled there) until the late 19c. It lies on the site of a 12c spittle-house, or hospital.

spit and polish *colloq.* rigorous attention to cleanliness and tidiness, especially in the armed forces.

spit-and-sawdust *adj.* lacking luxury or refinement, like the sawdust-covered floors of many pubs in former times.

spite — *noun* the desire to hurt or offend; ill-will. — *verb* to annoy or offend intentionally.
— **in spite of someone** *or* **something** regardless of them; in opposition to their efforts. [see DESPITE]

spiteful *adj.* motivated by spite; vengeful, malicious.

spitefully *adv.* in a spiteful way.

spitefulness *noun* **1** being spiteful. **2** a spiteful act or remark.

Spitfire a one-seat fighter aeroplane introduced into the RAF in 1938, which proved to be one of the most influential aeroplanes during World War II. The Spitfire XIV had a top speed of 580kph/440mph and was armed with two 20mm cannons complemented by two 50in machine guns or four 303in machine guns. Some also had the facility to make bomb raids. After an illustrious service it was withdrawn in 1954.

spitfire *noun* a hot-tempered person, especially a woman or girl.

Spitsbergen see SVALBARD.

spitting image *colloq.* an exact likeness; a double.

spittle *noun* saliva, especially when spat from the mouth; spit. [from Anglo-Saxon *spætl*]

spittoon *noun* a container for spitting into, especially a bucket on the floor of a pub in former times.

Spitz, Mark (Andrew) (1950–) US swimmer, born in Modesto, California. He earned worldwide fame at the 1972 Olympics by winning seven gold medals, all in world record time. He also won two golds in the 1968 Games, and set a total of 26 world records between 1967 and 1972. He turned professional in 1972, and later appeared in several films.

spiv *noun colloq.* a man, typically flashily dressed, engaging in small-time trade in illicit or stolen goods.

spivvy *adj.* (**spivvier, spivviest**) characteristic of a spiv.

splash — *verb* **1** *trans., intrans.* to cause large drops of (a liquid or semi-liquid substance) to be thrown about. **2** *intrans. said of such a substance* to fly around or land in large drops. **3** to make wet or dirty with such drops. **4** to print or display boldly: *photograph splashed across the front page.* — *noun* **1** a sound of splashing. **2** an amount splashed. **3** a stain made by splashing. **4** an irregular spot or patch: *splashes of colour.* **5** *colloq.* a small amount of liquid; a dash.
— **make a splash** to attract much attention, especially deliberately.

splash down *said of the crew or crew capsule of a space rocket* to land at sea.

splash out on something *or* **someone** *colloq.* to spend a lot of money on them. [originally *plash*, probably imitative]

splashdown *noun* a landing at sea of the crew or crew capsule of a space rocket.

splat — *noun* the sound made by a soft wet object striking a surface. — *adv.* with this sound: *fell splat on the floor.* [imitative]

splatter — *verb trans., intrans.* (**splattered, splattering**) to splash with or in small scattered drops. — *noun* a splashing sound, especially when repeated or continuous.

splay *verb* to spread (eg the fingers). [related to DISPLAY]

spleen *noun* **1** a small delicate organ, situated on the left side of the abdomen, beside the liver and beneath the diaphragm in man. It produces phagocytes, which remove bacteria and other foreign bodies from the bloodstream, and it destroys red blood cells that are no longer functional. The spleen acts as a reservoir for blood, and if ruptured must be surgically removed. **2** bad temper; spitefulness. [from Greek *splen*]

splendid *adj.* **1** magnificent; impressively grand or sumptuous. **2** very good; excellent. [from Latin *splendidus*, shining, brilliant]

splendidly *adv.* in a splendid way.

splendiferous *adj. colloq.* splendid. [from SPLENDOUR + -*ferous* from other words with this ending (from Latin *ferre*, to carry)]

splendour *noun* the state or quality of being splendid. [from Latin *splendor*]

splenetic *adj.* **1** (*also* **splenic**) relating to the spleen. **2** bad-tempered; spiteful; full of spleen.

splice — *verb* **1** to join (two pieces of rope) by weaving the strands of one into the other. **2** to join (two pieces of film, magnetic tape, etc) end to end with an adhesive. — *noun* a join made in either of these ways.
— **get spliced** *colloq.* to get married. [from Dutch *splissen*]

splint *noun* a piece of wood strapped to a broken limb to fix it in position while the bone heals. [from Old Dutch *splinte*]

splinter — *noun* a small thin sharp piece broken off a hard substance, eg wood or glass. — *verb trans., intrans.* (**splintered, splintering**) to break into splinters. [see SPLINT]

splinter group a small (especially political) group formed by individuals breaking away from a larger one.

Split, Italian **Spalato** POP (1991) 207 000, a seaport and city in W Croatia, situated on the Adriatic coast. NOTABLE FEATURES Roman Emperor Diocletian's Palace (3c AD), a World Heritage site; cathedral.

split — *verb* (**splitting**; PAST TENSE AND PAST PARTICIPLE **split**) **1** *trans., intrans.* to break or cause to break apart or into pieces, especially lengthways. **2** (*also* **split up** *or* **split something up**) to separate or cause it to separate into smaller amounts or groups. **3** (*also* **split up** *or* **split someone up**) to break or cause them to break away from each other or from a group through disagreement. **4** *intrans. slang* to go away or leave. **5** (**split on someone**) *slang* to inform on them. — *noun* **1** a lengthways break or crack. **2** a separation or division through disagreement. **3** a dessert of fruit, especially a banana, sliced open and topped with cream or ice-cream. **4** (**the splits**) an acrobatic leap or drop to the floor with the legs splayed in a straight line, each leg at right angles to the torso.
— **split the difference 1** *said of two people or parties* to compromise by each making an equal concession. **2** to divide a remaining amount equally.
split hairs to make or argue about fine and trivial distinctions.
split one's sides *colloq.* to laugh uncontrollably. [from Dutch *splitten*]

split infinitive an infinitive with an adverb or other word between the particle *to* and the verb, as in *to really believe*.
◆ The split infinitive in English is often regarded as grammatically or stylistically incorrect, but it is historically well attested and is common in current usage.

split-level *adj.* consisting of, or existing on, more than one level.

split pea a dried pea split in half, used in soups and stews.

split personality the displaying of two or more distinct types of behaviour by a single person, a feature of various mental disorders, especially schizophrenia.

split second a fraction of a second.

split-second *adj.* made or occurring in a fraction of a second: *a split-second decision.*

splitting *adj., said of a headache* intense, severe.

splodge — *noun* a large splash, stain, or patch. — *verb* to mark with splodges.

splurge — *noun* a spending spree or extravagance. — *verb intrans.* to spend extravagantly.

splutter — *verb* (**spluttered, spluttering**) **1** *intrans.* to make spitting sounds and throw out drops of liquid, sparks, etc. **2** *trans., intrans.* to speak or say haltingly or incoherently, eg through embarrassment. — *noun* the act or noise of spluttering. [originally SPUTTER, from Dutch *sputteren*, influenced by SPLASH]

Spock, Benjamin McLane (1903–) US paediatrician, born in New Haven, Connecticut. Practising in Manhattan from 1933, he transformed the attitudes of the postwar generation to their babies with his book *The Common Sense Book of Baby and Child Care* (1946), which sold more than 30 million copies. A vocal opponent of the Vietnam War, he helped to form the People's Party, running for the US presidency in 1972 and the vice-presidency in 1976.

Spode, Josiah (1754–1827) English potter, born in Stoke-on-Trent, Staffordshire. In 1770 he founded a firm which manufactured pottery, porcelain, and stoneware. He was made potter to George III in 1806. After merging in 1833 with William Taylor Copeland (1797–1868), the firm also made numerous white imitation marble (*Parian*) figures.

spoil — *verb* (PAST TENSE AND PAST PARTICIPLE **spoilt, spoiled**) **1** to impair, ruin, or make useless or valueless. **2** to make selfish and unable to accept hardship or disappointment by consistently indulging all demands or wishes: *a spoilt child.* **3** *intrans. said of food* to become unfit to eat. — *noun* (**spoils**) **1** possessions taken by force; plunder: *the spoils of war.* **2** any benefits or rewards.
— **be spoiling for something** to seek out a fight or argument eagerly. [from Latin *spolium*, plunder]

spoiler *noun* **1** a flap on an aircraft wing that reduces lift and so assists descent. **2** a fixed horizontal fin on a car that increases its roadholding at high speeds.

Spoils of Poynton, The a novel by Henry James (1897). It is a melancholic love-story turning on the importance to each character of the furnishings of a country manor.

spoilsport *noun colloq.* a person who spoils, or refuses to join in, the fun of others.

Spokane POP (1990) 361 000, the capital of Spokane County, E Washington, USA. It lies on the Spokane R, near the Idaho state border. Founded in 1872, it became a city in 1891. Today, it is the commercial centre for the inland farming, forestry, and mining areas of E Washington (the 'Inland Empire'). NOTABLE FEATURES art centre; museum; Episcopal and Roman Catholic cathedrals.

spoke¹ see SPEAK.

spoke² *noun* any of the radiating rods or bars attaching the rim of a wheel to its centre.
— **put a spoke in someone's wheel** to upset their plans, especially maliciously.
[from Anglo-Saxon *spaca*]

spoken past participle of SPEAK. — *adj.* **1** uttered or expressed in speech. **2** (*in compounds*) speaking in a particular way: *soft-spoken*.
— **be spoken for 1** to be reserved or taken. **2** *said of a person* to be married, engaged, or in a steady relationship.

spokesman *noun* (PL. **spokesmen**) a person appointed to speak on behalf of others or of a government, business, etc.

spokesperson *noun* a spokesman or spokeswoman (without regard to gender).

spokeswoman *noun* (PL. **spokeswomen**) a woman appointed to speak on behalf of others or of a government, business, etc.

Spoleto, Latin **Spoletium** POP (1990e) 61 000, a town in Perugia province, Umbria, central Italy. It is situated 96km/60mi NE of Rome, on a rocky hill overlooking the R Tressino. NOTABLE FEATURES cathedral (11c); San Salvatore Basilica (4c); Roman theatre, amphitheatre, bridge, and triumphal arch.

spoliation *noun* robbing; plundering. [from Latin *spoliare*]

spondaic *adj.* consisting of or written in spondees.

spondee *noun* a foot (= unit of poetical rhythm) consisting of two long syllables. [from Greek *spondeios*]

sponge — *noun* **1** the common name for any of about 3 000 species of an aquatic invertebrate animal belonging to the phylum Porifera. Almost all species are marine, although a few are found in fresh water. Sponges are the most primitive multicellular animals, and consist of a large cluster of cells, resembling a plant, always fixed to a solid object such as a rock. **2** the soft porous skeleton of this animal, from which the jelly-like flesh has been removed by allowing it to dry and then beating the sponge to dislodge the dried debris. It can hold a large amount of water and remains soft when wet, and is widely used in baths. **3** a piece of this material, or a similar absorbent synthetic material, used for cleansing surfaces. **4** a sponge cake or pudding. **5** an act of cleaning with a sponge. **6** *colloq.* a person who is regularly drunk. — *verb* **1** to wash or clean with a sponge and water. **2** (**sponge off** *or* **on someone**) to live by taking advantage of others' generosity. [from Greek *spongia*]
◇ Sponges vary widely in shape, some species being thin and flat, while others are round, vase-shaped, or branched like a twig. All of them have a skeleton made of limestone, silica, or horny fibres. Sponges feed by filtering food particles

from water that is drawn in through small pores scattered over the body surface, and passed out through a large opening at the top of the animal.

sponge bag a small waterproof bag for carrying toiletries in when travelling.

sponge cake *or* **sponge pudding** a very light cake or steamed cake-like pudding.

sponger *noun colloq.* a person who sponges off others.

spongy *adj.* (**spongier**, **spongiest**) soft and springy, and perhaps absorbent, like a sponge.

sponsor — *noun* **1** a person or organization that finances an event or broadcast in return for advertising. **2** a person who promises a sum of money to a participant in a forthcoming fundraising event. **3** a person who offers to be responsible for another, especially a godparent. **4** a person who submits a proposal, eg for new legislation. — *verb* (**sponsored**, **sponsoring**) to act as a sponsor for. [from Latin *spondere*, to promise]

sponsored *adj.* **1** having a sponsor or sponsors. **2** *said of an activity or event* financially supported by sponsors.

sponsorship *noun* sponsoring.

spontaneity *noun* being spontaneous.

spontaneous *adj.* **1** unplanned and voluntary or instinctive, not provoked or invited by others. **2** occurring naturally or by itself, not caused or influenced from outside. **3** *said of a manner or style* natural; not affected or studied. [from Latin *sponte*, of one's own accord]

spontaneous combustion the catching fire of a substance as a result of heat generated within it, not applied from outside.

spontaneous generation *Biol.* the theory, now discredited, that living organisms, eg bacteria, can arise spontaneously from non-living matter.

spoof *colloq.* — *noun* **1** a satirical imitation; a parody. **2** a light-hearted hoax or trick. — *verb* to subject to a spoof. [originally the name of a hoaxing game]

spook *colloq.* — *noun* a ghost. — *verb* to frighten or startle. [from Old German *spok*]

spooky *adj.* (**spookier**, **spookiest**) *colloq.* suggestive of ghosts or the supernatural; eerie.

spool *noun* a small cylinder on which thread, photographic film, tape, etc is wound; a reel. [from Old German *spole*]

spoon — *noun* **1** a kitchen utensil with a handle and a round or oval shallow bowl-like part, for eating, serving, or stirring food. **2** the amount a spoon will hold. — *verb* **1** to lift (food) with a spoon. **2** *intrans. old use* to kiss and cuddle. [from Anglo-Saxon *spon*]

spoonbill *noun* any bird of a family similar to the ibises, with a long flat broad bill that is spoon-shaped at the tip.

Spooner, William Archibald (1844–1930) English Anglican clergyman and educationalist, Dean (1876–89) and Warden (1903–24) of New College, Oxford. As an albino he suffered all his life from weak eyesight but he surmounted his disabilities and earned a reputation for kindness. His nervous tendency to transpose initial letters or half-syllables in speech (metathesis) became known as the spoonerism.

spoonerism *noun* an accidental and often comic slip in speech which reverses the positions of the first sounds of a pair of words, as in *shoving leopard* for *loving shepherd*. [named after Rev. W A Spooner]

spoon-feed *verb* **1** to feed (eg a baby) with a spoon. **2** to supply (someone) with everything needed or required, making any personal effort unnecessary.

spoonful *noun* (PL. **spoonfuls**) the amount a spoon will hold.

spoor *noun* the track or scent left by an animal. [from Dutch *spoor*, track]

sporadic *adj.* occurring from time to time, at irregular intervals; intermittent. [from Greek *sporados*, scattered]

sporadically *adv.* in a sporadic way; from time to time.

sporangium *noun* (PL. **sporangia**) *Bot.* in fungi and some plants, the hollow structure within which the spores are produced. [from Greek *spora*, seed]

spore *noun* an asexual reproductive structure, usually consisting of one cell, from which a new organism or stage in the life cycle develops either immediately or after a resting period, without the need for fusion with another cell. Spores are produced in large numbers by fungi, bacteria, some protozoans, and certain plants, eg ferns, mosses. [from Greek *spora*, seed]

sporophyll *or* **sporophyl** *noun Bot.* in certain plants, a leaf (often highly modified) that bears sporangia. [from Greek *spora*, seed + *phyllon*, leaf]

sporophyte *noun Bot.* in plants whose life cycle shows alternation of generations, a plant of the generation that produces spores and reproduces asexually. [from Greek *spora*, seed]

sporran *noun* a leather pouch worn hanging in front of the kilt in Scottish Highland dress. [from Gaelic *sporan*]

sport — *noun* **1** an activity or competition designed to test physical skills. **2** such activities collectively. **3** the pleasure or amusement gained from such an activity: *hunting for sport*. **4** good-humoured fun: *did it in sport*. **5** *colloq.* a person who cheerfully accepts defeat, inconvenience, or being the butt of jokes: *a good sport*. **6** *literary* a person or thing manipulated or controlled by outside influences; a plaything. **7** *Biol.* an animal or especially a plant that possesses abnormal characteristics as a result of a mutation. — *verb* to wear or display, especially proudly.
— **make sport of someone** *or* **something** *old use* to make fun of them.
[a shortening of DISPORT]

sporting *adj.* **1** of or relating to sport: *sporting achievements*. **2** having or displaying fairness or generosity of character.
— **a sporting chance** a reasonable chance of success.

sportingly *adv.* in a sporting way.

sportive *adj.* playful.

Sports, Book of a statement (1618, reissued 1633) by King James I of England that specified which sports could be legally performed on Sundays after divine services, aiming to resolve quarrels between the gentry and the Puritans.

sports car a small fast car, especially a two-seater, whose body sits close to the ground.

Sports Council in Great Britain, an organization which promotes sport and recreation.

sports jacket a man's jacket for casual wear.

sportsman *or* **sportswoman** *noun* **1** a person who takes part in sport. **2** a person who plays fair and accepts defeat cheerfully.

sportsmanlike *adj.* characteristic of a sportsman, fair, sporting.

sportsmanship *noun* being sportsmanlike.

sportswoman *noun* a woman taking part in sport.

sporty *adj.* (**sportier**, **sportiest**) **1** fond of, and often taking part in, sport. **2** *said of a car* that looks like or handles like a sports car.

spot — *noun* **1** a small mark or stain. **2** a drop of liquid. **3** a small amount, especially of liquid. **4** an eruption on the skin; a pimple. **5** a place. **6** *colloq.* a small amount of work: *did a spot of ironing*. **7** a place or period within a schedule or programme: *a five-minute comedy spot*. **8** *colloq.* a spotlight. — *verb* (**spotted, spotting**) **1** to mark with spots. **2** to see; to catch sight of. **3** to watch for and record the sighting of (eg trains). **4** to search for (new talent). **5** *intrans. said of rain* to fall lightly.

— **in a tight spot** *colloq.* in trouble or difficulty. **knock spots off someone** *or* **something** *colloq.* to be overwhelmingly better than them. **on the spot 1** immediately and often without warning: *motorists caught speeding are fined on the spot.* **2** at the scene of some notable event. **3** in an awkward situation, especially one requiring immediate action or response: *put someone on the spot.*
[from Norse *spotti*, small bit]

spot check an inspection made at random and without warning.

spotless *adj.* absolutely clean; unblemished.

spotlessly *adv.* so as to be spotless.

spotlessness *noun* being spotless.

spotlight — *noun* **1** a concentrated circle of light on a small area, especially of a theatre stage; also, a lamp casting this light. **2** (**the spotlight**) the attention or gaze of others: *put him in the spotlight.* — *verb* (PAST TENSE AND PAST PARTICIPLE **spotlit, spotlighted**) **1** to illuminate with a spotlight. **2** to direct attention to; to highlight.

spot-on *adj. colloq.* **1** exactly right; perfectly accurate. **2** precisely what was required; excellent.

spotted *adj.* **1** having spots, covered with spots. **2** stained, marked.

spotted dick suet pudding containing dried fruit.

spotter *noun* a person who spots (eg trains).

spottiness *noun* being spotty.

spotty *adj.* (**spottier, spottiest**) **1** marked with a pattern of spots. **2** whose skin, especially of the face, has many spots on it.

spouse *noun* a husband or wife. [from Latin *sponsus*, from *spondere*, to promise]

spout — *noun* **1** a projecting tube or lip through which liquid flows or is poured. **2** a jet or stream of liquid, eg from a fountain or the blowhole of a whale. — *verb* **1** to flow or cause to flow out in a jet or stream. **2** *trans., intrans.* to speak or say, especially at length and boringly. — **up the spout** *slang* **1** ruined or damaged beyond repair. **2** pregnant.
[from Middle English *spouten*]

sprain — *verb* to injure (a ligament) by sudden overstretching or tearing. — *noun* such an injury, which causes painful swelling, and may take several months to heal.

sprang see SPRING.

sprat *noun* a small edible fish of the herring family. [from Anglo-Saxon *sprot*]

sprawl — *verb intrans.* **1** to sit, lie, or fall lazily with the arms and legs spread out wide. **2** to spread or extend in an irregular, straggling, untidy way: *sprawling towns.* — *noun* a sprawling position. [from Anglo-Saxon *spreawlian*, to move convulsively]

spray¹ — *noun* **1** a fine mist of small flying drops of liquid. **2** a liquid designed to be applied as a mist: *hairspray.* **3** a device for dispensing a liquid as a mist; an atomiser or aerosol. — *verb* **1** to apply or dispense (a liquid) in spray form. **2** to apply a spray to. **3** to subject to a heavy and widespread stream: *sprayed the car with bullets.* [from Old Dutch *sprayen*]

spray² *noun* a small branch of a tree or plant with leaves and flowers attached, used for decoration. [perhaps from Anglo-Saxon *spræc*, twig]

spray-gun *noun* a container with a trigger-operated aerosol attached, for dispensing liquid, eg paint, in spray form.

spread — *verb* (PAST TENSE AND PAST PARTICIPLE **spread**) **1** *trans., intrans.* to apply, or be capable of being applied, in a smooth coating over a surface. **2** (*also* **spread out** *or* **spread something out**) to extend or cause it to extend or scatter, often more widely or more thinly. **3** (*also* **spread something out**) to open it out or unfold it. **4** *trans., intrans.* to transmit or be transmitted or distributed: *flies spread disease / rumours began to spread.* — *noun* **1** the act or extent of spreading. **2** a food in paste form, for spreading on bread, etc. **3** a pair of facing pages in a newspaper or magazine. **4** *colloq.* a lavish meal. **5** *colloq.* increased fatness around the waist and hips: *middle-aged spread.* [from Anglo-Saxon *sprædan*]

spread-eagled *adj.* with arms and legs stretched wide.

spreadsheet *noun* a computer program that enables numerical data to be entered and displayed in a table of rows and columns. The user can then instruct the program to perform mathematical operations on the data. Spreadsheets are widely used for business and financial planning, bookkeeping, and analysis of experimental data.

spree *noun* a period of extravagance or excess, especially in spending money or drinking alcohol. [perhaps from Scots *spreath*, cattle raid]

sprig *noun* a small shoot or twig: *sprig of heather.*

sprightliness *noun* being sprightly, liveliness.

sprightly *adj.* **1** lively and quick-moving. **2** performed at a brisk pace. [related to SPRITE]

spring — *verb* (PAST TENSE **sprang**; PAST PARTICIPLE **sprung**) **1** *intrans.* to leap with a sudden quick launching action. **2** *intrans.* to move suddenly and swiftly by elastic force. **3** (*also* **spring up**) to appear or come into being suddenly. **4** *intrans.* to develop or originate. **5** (**spring something on someone**) to present or reveal it suddenly and unexpectedly. **6** to fit (eg a mattress) with springs. **7** *slang* to secure the escape of (a prisoner) from jail. — *noun* **1** a metal coil that can be stretched or compressed, and returns to its original shape when released. Springs store energy when distorted, and slowly unwinding springs can be used to release energy at a controlled rate, eg to turn the mechanism of some clocks and watches. Springs are also used to absorb shock waves, eg in the shock absorbers of some motor vehicles. **2** any place where water emerges from underground and flows on to the Earth's surface or into a body of water such as a lake. Springs may be permanent or intermittent, and they often occur at points where the water table reaches the ground surface. Spring water may contain large amounts of dissolved minerals, and is highly valued as drinking water. **3** the season between winter and summer, when most plants begin to grow. **4** a sudden vigorous leap. **5** the ability of a material to return rapidly to its original shape after a distorting force, eg stretching, bending, compression, has been removed: *the mattress has lost its spring.* **6** a lively bouncing or jaunty quality: *a spring in his step.* [from Anglo-Saxon *springan*]

Spring Awakening (Frühlings Erwachen) a play by Frank Wedekind (1891). Judged too shocking to be performed in Britain until 1963, it tells of two 14-year-old lovers whose parents' narrow-minded attitude leads to abortion and death, suggesting the theme of a repressive society that should not ignore signs of puberty in its children.

spring balance a device that measures weight by the downward pull on a large spring to which the weighed object is attached.

springboard *noun* **1** a board that springs up after being jumped on, used by divers and gymnasts as a launching device. **2** anything that serves to get things moving.

springbok *noun* a South African antelope renowned for its high springing leap when running.

spring chicken 1 a very young chicken valued for its tender edible flesh. **2** *colloq.* a young person.

spring-clean *verb trans., intrans.* to carry out spring-cleaning, to clean out thoroughly.

spring cleaning a thorough cleaning of a house, traditionally carried out in spring.

springer *noun* a large spaniel with a domed head.

Springfield POP (1990) 190 000, the capital of the state of Illinois, USA, in Sangamon County, central Illinois. It was settled in 1818 and became a city in 1840. It has become a major commercial centre. The 16th US President, Abraham Lincoln, lived and was buried here.

Springfield POP (1990) 241 000, the seat of Greene County, SW Missouri, USA. Established in 1829, it is now an industrial, trade, and shipping city. It is the tourist centre for the Ozark Mts. NOTABLE FEATURE Museum of the Ozarks.

Springfield POP (1990) 530 000, the seat of Hampden County, SW Massachusetts, USA. It lies on the Connecticut R, 8km/5mi N of the Connecticut border. The game of basketball was devised at Springfield College. NOTABLE FEATURES Springfield Armoury (1794–1968); Basketball Hall of Fame.

springiness *noun* a springy quality.

spring onion an onion picked when young, while just a tiny white bulb with long thin shoots, usually eaten raw in salads.

Springsteen, Bruce (Frederick Joseph) (1949–) US rock singer, guitarist, and songwriter, born in Freehold, New Jersey. From the release of his first album, *Greetings From Asbury Park, NJ* (1973), he was hailed by critics as the new Bob Dylan, but it was not until *Born To Run* (1975) that he met with major commerical success. By the mid-1980s he had become a leading rock star, and had other successful albums including *Born in the USA* (1985).

springtail *noun* a blind primitively wingless insect that is often extremely abundant in soils or leaf litter, and leaps by means of a forked spring organ folded up on the underside of the abdomen.

spring tide a tidal pattern that occurs twice a month, when the difference in level between high and low tides is greatest. It occurs at full and new moon, when the Earth, Moon, and Sun are aligned so that the combined gravitational pull of the Moon and Sun makes high tides higher and low tides lower.

springtime *noun* the season of spring.

springy *adj.* (**springier, springiest**) readily springing back into its original shape when released; elastic; resilient.

sprinkle *verb* **1** to scatter in, or cover with a scattering of, tiny drops or particles. **2** to arrange or distribute in a thin scattering: *houses sprinkled across the valley.* [from Anglo-Saxon *springan*, to spring]

sprinkler *noun* a device that sprinkles, especially one sprinkling water over plants or on a fire to extinguish it.

sprinkling *noun* a small amount thinly scattered.

sprint — *noun* **1** a race at high speed over a short distance. **2** a burst of speed eg at the end of a long race. — *verb trans., intrans.* to run at full speed. [from Norse *sprinta*]

Sprinter in the UK, the generic name for a Class 15X diesel-driven train used since 1986. It is employed on inter-urban and country routes.

sprinter *noun* an athlete who sprints.

sprit *noun* a small diagonal spar used to spread a sail. [from Anglo-Saxon *spreot*, pole]

sprite *noun* **1** *Folklore* a playful fairy; an elf or imp. **2** a number of pixels that can be moved in a group around a screen, eg those representing a figure in a computer game. [from Old French *esprit*, spirit]

spritsail *noun* a sail spread wide by a sprit.

spritzer *noun* a drink of white wine and soda water. [from German *spritzen*, to spray]

sprocket *noun* **1** any of a set of teeth on the rim of a driving wheel, eg fitting into the links of a chain or the holes on a strip of film. **2** a wheel with sprockets.

sprout — *verb* **1** *trans., intrans.* to develop (a new growth, eg of leaves or hair). **2** (*also* **sprout up**) to grow or develop; to spring up. — *noun* **1** a new growth; a shoot or bud. **2** a Brussels sprout. [from Anglo-Saxon *sprutan*]

spruce¹ *noun* **1** an evergreen cone-bearing tree with a thick pyramid-shaped growth of needle-like leaves. **2** the wood of this tree. [from Obsolete *Pruce*, Prussia]

spruce² *adj.* neat and smart, especially in appearance and dress.
— **spruce up** or **spruce someone up** to smarten up or make them smart.
[from smart 16c clothing made of *spruce leather* from *Pruce*, Prussia]

sprung see SPRING.

sprung rhythm *Poetry* a term invented by the poet Gerard Manley Hopkins to describe his own metrical system which related back to techniques used in Old and Middle English alliterative verse. It is close to the rhythm of natural speech, with mixed feet and frequent single stressed syllables. Hopkins' rediscovery, description, and use of sprung rhythm had a major influence on the work of T S Eliot, Dylan Thomas, and other major modern poets.

spry *adj.* (**spryer**, **spryest**) **1** lively; active. **2** light on one's feet; nimble.

spryly *adv.* nimbly.

spryness *noun* being spry.

spud *noun colloq.* a potato. [from Middle English *spudde*, short knife]

spume — *noun* foam or froth. — *verb intrans.* to make spume. [from Latin *spuma*, from *spuere*, to spew]

spumy *adj.* (**spumier**, **spumiest**) foaming.

spun see SPIN.

spunk *noun* **1** *colloq.* courage; mettle. **2** *coarse slang* semen. [from Irish Gaelic *sponc*, tinder]

spunky *adj.* (**spunkier**, **spunkiest**) *colloq.* courageous; spirited.

spur — *noun* **1** a device with a spiky metal wheel, fitted to the heel of a horse-rider's boot, dug into the horse's side to make it go faster. **2** anything that urges or encourages greater effort or progress. **3** a spike or pointed part, eg on a cock's leg. **4** a ridge of high land that projects out into a valley. — *verb* (**spurred**, **spurring**) (*usually* **spur someone on**) to urge them on.
— **on the spur of the moment** suddenly; on an impulse.
[from Anglo-Saxon *spura*]

spurge *noun* any of various plants producing a bitter, often poisonous, milky juice formerly used as a laxative. [from Old French *espurge*, from Latin *expurgare*, to purge]

spurious *adj.* **1** not what it seems or claims to be; false. **2** based on false or mistaken reasoning. [from Latin *spurius*, false]

spurn *verb* to reject (eg a person's love) scornfully. [from Anglo-Saxon *spurnan*]

Spurs, Battle of the a battle (16 Aug 1513) between France and England, who had joined the Holy League of the pope, Spain, and Venice against the French. Henry VIII laid siege to Thérouanne, near St Omer (Pas-de-Calais), and the English managed to beat off the French reliev-

ing force in this battle (so called because of the precipitate French retreat).

spurt — *verb trans., intrans.* to flow out or cause to flow out in a sudden sharp jet. — *noun* **1** a jet of liquid suddenly flowing out. **2** a short spell of intensified activity or increased speed.

Sputnik *noun* the name given to the series of 10 Earth-orbiting artificial satellites launched by the former Soviet Union in 1957 and 1958. Sputnik 1 was the world's first artificial satellite, and Sputnik 2 carried the dog 'Laika', the first terrestrial animal to be transported into space. [named after the first Soviet satellite, literally = 'travelling companion']

sputter same as SPLUTTER. [imitative]

sputum *noun* (PL. **sputa**) saliva mixed with mucus that is coughed up from the bronchial passages. — Also called *phlegm*. [from Latin *sputum*, from *spuere*, to spit]

spy — *noun* (PL. **spies**) **1** a person employed by a government or organization to gather information about political enemies or competitors. **2** a person observing others in secret. — *verb* (**spies**, **spied**) **1** (*also* **spy on someone**) to act as a spy; to keep a secret watch on someone. **2** to catch sight of; to spot.
— **spy someone** or **something out** to discover or uncover them by spying.
[from Old French *espier*]

spyglass *noun* a small telescope.

spyhole *noun* a peephole.

spy ship a ship specially equipped to collect and relay information on the position and movements of enemy ships, submarines, etc. In the past, spy ships were frequently disguised as commercial, especially fishing, vessels; with the development of advanced satellite technology their importance has diminished.

spy story a form of fiction based on the theme of espionage. Important landmarks in the development of the genre were the stories by Willian Le Queux (1864–1927), Erskine Childers' *The Riddle of the Sands* (1903), Joseph Conrad's *The Secret Agent* (1907), and John Buchan's *The Thirty-Nine Steps* (1915). Between the wars Somerset Maugham, Eric Ambler, and Graham Greene presented spies in a realistic and unsensational way; Ian Fleming glamorized the role of spy in his James Bond stories of the 1950s; and in the 1960s there was a return to a more realistic form by writers such as John Le Carré and Len Deighton.

sq. *abbrev.* square.

SQL *abbrev. Comput.* structured query language, a standard programming language used to access information from databases.

squab *noun* **1** a young unfledged bird, especially a pigeon. **2** a short fat person.

squabble — *verb intrans.* to quarrel noisily, especially about something trivial. — *noun* a noisy (especially petty) quarrel.

squabby *adj.* (**squabbier**, **squabbiest**) short and fat; stumpy.

squad *noun* **1** a small group of soldiers, often twelve, drilling or working together. **2** any group of people working together. **3** a set of players from which a sporting team is selected. [from Italian *squadra*, square]

squaddy or **squaddie** *noun* (PL. **squaddies**) *slang* an ordinary soldier; a private.

squadron *noun* **1** a group of between 10 and 18 military aircraft, the principal unit of an air force. **2** a group of warships sent on a particular mission. **3** a division of an armoured regiment of soldiers. [from Italian *squadrone*; related to SQUAD]

squadron leader an air force officer of the rank below wing commander, in charge of a squadron.

squalid *adj.* **1** disgustingly filthy and neglected. **2** morally repulsive; sordid. See also SQUALOR. [from Latin *squalidus*, dirty]

squall — *noun* **1** *Meteorol.* a storm consisting of sudden and short-lived violent gusts of wind. **2** a loud cry; a yell. — *verb* **1** *trans., intrans.* to yell. **2** *said of a wind* to blow in a squall.

squally *adj.* characterized by squalls.

squalor *noun* the state of being squalid. [from Latin *squalor*, roughness]

squander *verb* (**squandered**, **squandering**) to use up wastefully.

square — *noun* **1** a two-dimensional figure with four sides of equal length and four right angles. **2** anything shaped like this. **3** an open space in a town, usually roughly square in shape, and including the surrounding buildings. **4** an L-shaped or T-shaped instrument with which angles can be measured or straight lines drawn. **5** the figure produced when a number is multiplied by itself. **6** *colloq.* a person with traditional or old-fashioned values or tastes. — *adj.* **1** square-shaped. **2** measured in length and breadth; of an area equal to a square whose sides are the stated length: *an area of three square metres / one room is three metres square.* **3** less rounded than normal: *a square jaw.* **4** measuring almost the same in breadth as in length or height: *a squat, square-framed man.* **5** fair; honest: *a square deal.* **6** (**all square**) equal; with each side owing nothing. **7** complete; outright: *a square denial.* **8** *colloq.* having traditional or old-fashioned values or tastes. — *verb* **1** to make square in shape, especially to make right-angled. **2** to multiply (a number) by itself. **3** (*also* **square up** or **square something up**) to pay off or settle a debt. **4** to make the scores in (a match) level. **5** (**square something with someone**) to get their approval or permission for it. **6** (**square with something**) to agree or correspond with it. **7** to mark with a pattern of squares. — *adv.* **1** solidly and directly: *hit me square on the jaw.* **2** fairly; honestly.
— **back to square one** *colloq.* back to the beginning, with no progress made.
square the circle to do the impossible.
square up to something to face up to a task, difficulty, etc and prepare to tackle it.
[from Old French *esquarre*, from Latin *quadra*]

			Square	Cube
Squares and Roots				
No.	Square	Cube	root	root
1	1	1	1.000	1.000
2	4	8	1.414	1.260
3	9	27	1.732	1.442
4	16	64	2.000	1.587
5	25	125	2.236	1.710
6	36	216	2.449	1.817
7	49	343	2.646	1.913
8	64	512	2.828	2.000
9	81	729	3.000	2.080
10	100	1 000	3.162	2.154
11	121	1 331	3.317	2.224
12	144	1 728	3.464	2.289
13	169	2 197	3.606	2.351
14	196	2 744	3.742	2.410
15	225	3 375	3.873	2.466
16	256	4 096	4.000	2.520
17	289	4 913	4.123	2.571
18	324	5 832	4.243	2.621
19	361	6 859	4.359	2.668
20	400	8 000	4.472	2.714
25	625	15 625	5.000	2.924
30	900	27 000	5.477	3.107
40	1 600	64 000	6.325	3.420
50	2 500	125 000	7.071	3.684

square-bashing *noun slang* military drill on a barracks square.

square bracket each of a pair of printed brackets ([ ]), chiefly used to contain special information such as comment by an editor of a text.

square cloth a fabric in which the number of warp and weft threads per centimetre is approximately equal. It is more expensive to make than most fabrics and is mainly used where a woven design has a square repeat sequence.

square dance a folk dance performed by couples in a square formation.

Square Deal the popular name for the domestic policies of US President Roosevelt (especially the enforcement of the Anti-Trust Acts), coined by Roosevelt in 1902.

square leg *Cricket* a fielding position level with the batsman, at some distance from him, and facing his back; also, a fielder in this position.

squarely *adv.* **1** square. **2** at right angles.

square meal a good nourishing meal.

square root *Maths.* a number or quantity that when multiplied by itself gives a particular number, eg the square root of 9 (written as $\sqrt{9}$ or $9^{\frac{1}{2}}$) is 3, because $3 \times 3 = 9$.

squaring the circle *Geom.* an attempt by the ancient Greeks to construct a square of exactly the same area as a circle, using only a ruler and compass. It puzzled mathematicians for centuries, and was proved to be impossible by Ferdinand von Lindemann in 1882.

squash¹ — *verb* **1** to crush or flatten by pressing or squeezing. **2** *intrans.* to force one's body into a confined space. **3** to suppress or put down (eg a rebellion). **4** to force into silence with a cutting reply. — *noun* **1** a concentrated fruit syrup, or a drink made by diluting this. **2** a crushed or crowded state. **3** (*also* **squash rackets**) a game for two players on a walled indoor court, played with rackets and a small hard rubber ball. [from Old French *esquacer*, to crush]

squash² *noun North Amer., esp. US* **1** any marrow-like vegetable of the cucumber family. **2** any of the plants bearing them. [from Narragansett (Native American language) *askutasquash*]

squashy *adj.* (**squashier, squashiest**) *colloq.* soft and easily squashed.

squat — *verb intrans.* (**squatted, squatting**) **1** to take up, or be sitting in, a low position with the knees fully bent and the weight on the soles of the feet. **2** to occupy an empty building without legal right. — *noun* **1** a squatting position. **2** an empty building unlawfully occupied. **3** *colloq.* a squat thrust. — *adj.* short and broad or fat. [from Old French *esquatir*, to crush]

squatter *noun* a person unlawfully occupying an empty building.

squat thrust a fitness exercise in which, from an all-fours position, the feet are made to jump

forwards so that the knees touch the elbows, then back again.

squaw *noun offensive* a Native American woman or wife. [from Massachusett (Native American language) *squa*]

squawk — *noun* **1** a high-pitched croaking cry, like that of a parrot. **2** a loud protest or complaint. — *verb intrans.* **1** to make a high-pitched croaking cry. **2** to complain loudly. [imitative]

squawky *adj.* (**squawkier, squawkiest**) **1** characterized by or like squawks. **2** tending to squawk.

squeak — *noun* **1** a short high-pitched cry or sound, like that of a mouse or a rusty gate. **2** (*also* **narrow squeak**) a narrow escape; a victory or success achieved by the slimmest of margins. — *verb trans., intrans.* to utter a squeak or with a squeak.

— **squeak through something** to succeed in it by a narrow margin. [imitative]

squeakiness *noun* being squeaky.

squeaky *adj.* (**squeakier, squeakiest**) **1** characterized by squeaks. **2** tending to squeak.

squeaky clean *colloq.* **1** spotlessly clean. **2** virtuous, impeccable; above reproach or criticism. [originally used of wet hair, which squeaks when pulled]

squeal — *noun* a long high-pitched cry or yelp, like that of a pig or a child in pain. — *verb* **1** *trans., intrans.* to utter a squeal or with a squeal. **2** *intrans. colloq.* to inform or tell tales. **3** *intrans.* to complain or protest loudly. [imitative]

squealer *noun* **1** a person or thing that squeals. **2** a bird or animal that squeals, especially a piglet. **3** *colloq.* an informer.

squeamish *adj.* **1** slightly nauseous. **2** easily made nauseous. [from Old French *escoymous*]

squeegee *noun* a device with a rubber blade for scraping water off a surface, eg a window. [a fanciful variation of SQUEEZE]

squeegie *noun* someone who washes the windscreens of cars stopped at traffic lights, in the hope of being tipped by drivers. [a variant of SQUEEGEE]

Squeers, Wackford the cruel, one-eyed school proprietor in Charles Dickens's *Nicholas Nickleby*. Other family members include his wife Mrs Squeers and his son Wackford.

squeeze — *verb* **1** to grasp or embrace tightly. **2** to press forcefully, especially from at least two sides. **3** to press or crush so as to extract (eg

juice); to extract (eg toothpaste) by pressing or crushing. **4** *intrans.* to force one's body into or through a confined space. **5** (**squeeze something out of someone**) to obtain it from them by hard persuasion or extortion. — *noun* **1** an act of squeezing. **2** a crowded or crushed state: *it's a bit of a squeeze with four on the sofa.* **3** an amount of fruit juice, etc got by squeezing. **4** a restriction, especially on spending or borrowing money.

— **put the squeeze on someone** *colloq.* to pressurize them into giving something. [from Anglo-Saxon *cwysan*, to press]

squeeze-box *noun colloq.* an accordion or concertina.

squeezer *noun* a person, device, or machine, etc that squeezes (especially fruit).

squelch — *noun* a loud gurgling or sucking sound made by contact with a thick sticky substance, eg wet mud. — *verb intrans.* to make this sound. [imitative]

squelchy *adj.* (**squelchier, squelchiest**) having a squelching feeling.

squib *noun* **1** a small firework that jumps around on the ground before exploding. **2** a satirical criticism or attack; a lampoon. [perhaps imitative]

squid

squid *noun* (PL. **squid, squids**) any of about 350 species of marine mollusc, related to the octopus and cuttlefish, with a torpedo-shaped body supported by an internal horny plate, two well-developed eyes, eight sucker-bearing arms surrounding the mouth, and two longer tentacles. Squid feed on fish, which they seize with their arms and tentacles, and they are capable of changing colour to match their surroundings, and emitting a cloud of dark ink when threatened by predators. Squid is a popular food item in some parts of the world.

squiffy *adj.* (**squiffier, squiffiest**) *colloq.* slightly drunk; tipsy.

squiggle *noun* a wavy scribbled line. [perhaps from SQUIRM and WRIGGLE]

squiggly *adj.* (**squigglier, squiggliest**) characterized by squiggles.

squinch *noun Archit.* a small arch running diagonally across each corner of a square building or room, creating an octagonal base on which a tower or circular dome may be supported.

squint — *noun* **1** the condition of having one or both eyes set slightly off-centre, preventing parallel vision. **2** *colloq.* a quick look; a peep. — *verb intrans.* **1** to be affected by a squint. **2** to look with eyes half-closed; to peer. — *adj.* **1** squinting. **2** *colloq.* not properly straight or centred. [perhaps from Dutch *schuinte*, slant]

Squire, the the courtly son of the Knight in Chaucer's *The Canterbury Tales*, who tells the tale of Cambuscan and his daughter, Canacee.

squire *noun* **1** an owner of a large area of rural land, especially the chief landowner in a district. **2** *colloq.* a term of address used between men. [see ESQUIRE]

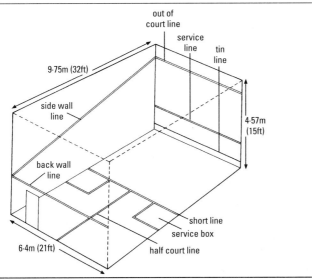

out of court line
service line
tin line
9·75m (32ft)
service box
short line
service box
half court line
side wall line
back wall line
4·57m (15ft)
6·4m (21ft)

squash court

squirm — *verb intrans.* **1** to wriggle. **2** to feel or show embarrassment, shame, or nervousness, often with slight wriggling movements of the body. — *noun* a squirming movement. [perhaps connected with WORM]

squirrel *noun* any of various medium-sized rodents belonging to the family Sciuridae, found almost worldwide, and having a large soft bushy tail and long strong hind legs. Squirrels are noted for grasping their food, mainly seeds and nuts, in their front paws as they feed. [from Greek *skiouros*, from *skia*, shade + *oura*, tail]
◇ The grey squirrel (*Sciurus carolinensis*), a N American species that has become a pest in the UK and other countries, has a grey coat, with light-coloured fringes on the tail. The red squirrel (*Sciurus vulgaris*), which lives mainly in coniferous woodland, where it feeds on cones and shoots, has a rich chestnut coat, and is the only native tree squirrel in Europe. In the UK it has been replaced in most areas by the introduced grey squirrel. *Flying squirrels* glide from tree to tree by extending a furred membrane which stretches between the front and back legs.

squirt — *verb trans., intrans.* to shoot out or cause (a liquid) to shoot out in a narrow jet. — *noun* **1** an act of squirting or an amount of liquid squirted. **2** *colloq.* a small or insignificant person, especially when arrogant. [imitative]

squish — *noun* a gentle splashing or squelching sound. — *verb intrans.* to make, or move with, this sound. [imitative]

Sr¹ *abbrev.* (*used after a name*) Senior: *John Smith, Sr.*

Sr² *symbol Chem.* strontium.

Srebrenica a town in E Bosnia-Herzegovina mainly inhabited by Bosnian Muslims who suffered attack and siege by Bosnian Serbs during the civil war (1992–). A key centre of Muslim resistance, its pre-war population of 10 000 grew to 60 000 due to a huge influx of refugees. One of six 'safe areas' declared by the UN, the enclave was made the centre of a 15sq km demilitarized zone.

Sri-Jayawardenapura the administrative seat of government in Sri Lanka, located in an E suburb of Colombo.

Sri Lanka, formerly **Ceylon**, official name **Democratic Socialist Republic of Sri Lanka** POP (1992e) 17.4m, an island state in the Indian Ocean. A series of coral islands known as Adam's Bridge links Sri Lanka across the Palk Strait with the Indian subcontinent. The country is divided into nine provinces. AREA 65 610sq km/ 25 325sq mi. The island is bounded by the Bay of Bengal in the E and the Gulf of Mannar in the W. CAPITAL Sri-Jayawardenapura, a suburb of, Colombo. CHIEF TOWNS Jaffna, Kandy, Galle. TIME ZONE GMT +5.5. The population consists of Sinhalese (74%), Tamils (18%), and Muslims (7%); Buddhism, Hinduism, Christianity, and Islam are the chief religions. OFFICIAL LANGUAGES Sinhala, English, Tamil. CURRENCY the Sri Lankan rupee. PHYSICAL DESCRIPTION a pear-shaped island, which measures 440km/273mi long and 220km/137mi wide; low-lying areas in the N and S, surrounding the S central uplands; the highest peak is Pidurutalagala at 2 524m; the coastal plain is fringed by sandy beaches and lagoons; the N region is generally arid in the dry season; nearly half the country is tropical monsoon forest or open woodland. CLIMATE high temperatures and humidity in the N plains; the average daily temperatures at Trincomalee are 24–33°C; temperatures in the interior are reduced by altitude; the greatest rainfall is on the SW coast and in the mountains. HISTORY the Sinhalese (from N India) colonized part of the island in the 5c BC; many Tamil invasions from S India; Portuguese conquered coastal areas in the 15c; taken by the Dutch in 1658; British occupation in 1796; became a British colony in 1802; whole island united for the first time in 1815; Tamil

labourers were brought in from S India during colonial rule, to work on coffee and tea plantations; given Dominion status in 1948; became an independent republic in 1972; in the early 1980s Tamil separatists began fighting government forces for control of Tamil majority areas; the fighting remained mainly in the Jaffna Peninsula. GOVERNMENT governed by a President, elected for a six-year term, and a 225-member National State Assembly, which sits for six years; acute political tension exists between the Buddhist Sinhalese majority and the Hindu Tamil minority, who wish to establish an independent state in the N and E. ECONOMY agriculture employs 46% of the labour force; rice, rubber, tea, coconuts, spices, sugar cane; timber; fishing; graphite, coal, precious and semi-precious stones; electricity produced largely by water power; textiles; chemicals; paper; rubber; tobacco; food processing; oil; wood; metal products.

Sri Lanka

Srinagar POP (1991) 586 000, the summer capital of Jammu-Kashmir state, N India. It lies in the Vale of Kashmir, on the R Jhelum. The city was founded in the 6c. NOTABLE FEATURES Buddhist ruins; mosque (1623).

SRN *abbrev.* State Registered Nurse.

SS¹ *abbrev.* **1** Saints. **2** steamship.

SS² *abbrev. Schutzstaffel* ('protective squad') a Nazi organization founded (1925) as Hitler's small personal bodyguard. It was expanded by Heinrich Himmler into an élite, black-uniformed force which within the Third Reich controlled a dominant repressive apparatus, responsible for concentration camps and racial extermination policy. By 1939 it numbered about 250 000 and had its own armed detachments known as the *Waffen* ('armed') SS.

SSP *abbrev.* statutory sick pay.

SSSI *abbrev.* in the UK, Site of Special Scientific Interest, areas designated by the Nature Conservancy Council for the purposes of conservation, including wildlife habitats, interesting geological or physiographical features, and habitats for rare plants and animals. In return for compensation, management agreements may be made between the council and site landowners to protect them. In Northern Ireland, there are 36 equivalent Areas of Special Scientific Interest (ASSI).

St *abbrev.* **1** Saint. **2** Street.

st. *abbrev.* stone (the unit of weight).

stab — *verb* (**stabbed, stabbing**) **1** to wound or pierce with a pointed instrument or weapon. **2** (**stab at something**) to make a quick thrusting movement towards it with something sharp. **3** *intrans.* to produce a sharp piercing sensation: *stabbing pain.* — *noun* **1** an act of stabbing. **2** a stabbing sensation. **3** *colloq.* a try: *have a stab at.*
— **stab someone in the back** to slander or betray them, especially in a cowardly way. [from Middle English *stab*]

stability *noun* the state or quality of being stable. [from Latin *stabilitas*]

stabilization *or* **stabilisation** *noun* stabilizing or being stabilized.

stabilize *or* **stabilise** *verb trans., intrans.* to make or become stable or more stable.

stabilizer *or* **stabiliser** *noun* **1** one or more aerofoils used to give stability to an aircraft. **2** a device used to reduce rolling and pitching of a ship. **3** each of two small wheels fitted to the back wheel of a child's bicycle to give it added stability. **4** any substance that prevents deterioration or breakdown of another substance when added to it. **5** a chemical substance that allows food ingredients that would not otherwise mix well to remain together in a homogeneous state. For example, stabilizers prevent the coagulation of oil droplets in salad cream. **6** *Econ.* any of various factors in a modern economic system which help to keep the economy stable, avoiding the worst effects of trade cycle fluctuations. They mainly relate to fiscal policy, in that tax receipts will change with rises and falls in income; and may also include direct intervention by government, as in a programme of public works.

stable¹ *adj.* **1** firmly balanced or fixed; not likely to wobble or fall. **2** firmly established; not likely to be abolished, overthrown, or destroyed: *a stable government.* **3** regular or constant; not erratic or changing: *the patient's condition is stable.* [from Latin *stabilis*]

stable² *noun* **1** a building in which horses are kept. **2** a place where horses are bred and trained. **3** *colloq.* a number of people or things with a common background or origin, eg a number of athletes trained by the same coach. [from Latin *stabulum*]

staccato *adj., adv.* **1** *Mus.* with notes played as a series of short, abrupt, audibly separate units rather than as a flowing sequence. **2** with, or consisting of, a series of short distinct sounds. [from Italian *staccato*, from *distaccare*, to separate]

stack — *noun* **1** a large neat pile of hay or straw. **2** any large neat pile. **3** (*usually* **a stack of** *or* **stacks of something**) *colloq.* a large amount. **4** a large industrial chimney: *smokestack.* — *verb* **1** to arrange in a stack or stacks. **2** to pre-arrange (playing-cards) in a pack so as to allow cheating. **3** to arrange (circumstances, etc) to favour or disadvantage a particular person. **4** to arrange (aircraft waiting to land) into a queue in which each circles the airport at a different altitude. [from Norse *stakkr*, haystack]

stadium *noun* (PL. **stadiums, stadia**) a large sports arena with spectators' seats on different tiers. [from Greek *stadion*]

Staël, Madame de, pseudonym of **Anne Louise Germaine Necker, Baroness of Staël-Holstein** (1766–1817) French writer, born in Paris, the daughter of the financier Jacques Necker. Both before and after the French Revolution, her Paris *salon* became a centre of political discussion. In 1803 she was forced to leave Paris, and visited Weimar, Berlin, and Vienna. She wrote novels, plays, essays, historical and critical works, and political memoirs, and became known with her *Lettres* (Letters, 1788) on Jean Jacques Rousseau, and achieved European fame with her romantic novel, *Corinne* (1807). Her major work, *De L'Allemagne* (Germany), was published in London in 1813.

staff — *noun* (*usually treated as pl.*) **1** the total number of employees working in an establishment or organization. **2** the employees working for or assisting a manager. **3** *Mil.* the officers assisting a senior commander. **4** (PL. **staffs, staves**) any stick or rod carried in the hand. **5** *Mus.* a set of lines and spaces on which music is written. — *verb* to provide (an establishment) with staff.

staff nurse a qualified nurse next below a sister in rank.

Stafford POP (1981) 62 000, the county town of Staffordshire, central England. Writer Izaak Walton was born here in 1593. NOTABLE FEATURES castle (11c); churches of St Mary and St Chad; William Salt Library (18c); Shire Hall; Borough Hall; Guildhall.

Staffordshire POP (1992e) 1.1m, a county in central England, divided into nine districts and including The Potteries urban area. AREA 2 716sq km/1 048sq mi. Lying in the basin of the R Trent, it is bounded W by Shropshire, NW by Cheshire, E by Derbyshire, SE by Warwickshire, and S by the West Midlands and Hereford and Worcester. CHIEF TOWNS Stafford (county town), Stoke-on-Trent, Newcastle under Lyme, Burton-upon-Trent. ECONOMY agriculture; coal; pottery; brewing. NOTABLE FEATURES Vale of Trent; Cannock Chase.

Staffs. *abbrev.* Staffordshire.

staff sergeant the senior sergeant in an army company.

stag — *noun* **1** an adult male deer, especially a red deer. **2** *slang* a person who buys shares in the hope of selling them immediately for a profit. — *adj.* male; of or for men only. [from Anglo-Saxon *stagga*]

stag beetle a beetle with large antler-like jaw parts.

stag beetle

stage — *noun* **1** a platform on which a performance takes place. **2** any of several distinct and successive periods. **3** a part of a journey or route. **4** (**the stage**) the theatre as a profession or art form. **5** *colloq.* a stagecoach. — *verb* **1** to present as a performance; to present a performance of (a play). **2** to pre-arrange to happen in a particular way. **3** to organize or hold as an event. [from Old French *estage*, storey, tier]

Stagecoach a US film directed by John Ford (1939). One of the first westerns, it is about the hazardous journey of a stagecoach party who are joined by a fugitive from justice called The Ringo Kid (John Wayne).

stagecoach *noun* a large horse-drawn coach formerly carrying passengers and mail on a regular fixed route.

stage directions instructions relating to actors' movements, and often sound and lighting effects, written as part of the script of a play.

stage fright nervousness felt by an actor or other performer or speaker when about to appear in front of an audience, especially for the first time.

stagehand *noun* a person responsible for moving scenery and props in a theatre.

stage-manage *verb* **1** to be the stage manager of (a play). **2** to pre-arrange to happen in a certain way, in order to create a particular effect.

stage manager a person supervising the arrangement of scenery and props for a play.

stage-struck *adj.* having an overwhelming desire to be an actor.

stage whisper **1** an actor's loud whisper intended to be heard by the audience. **2** any loud whisper intended to be heard by people other than the person addressed.

stagflation *noun* inflation in an economy without the expected growth in employment or demand for goods. [from STAGNATION + INFLATION]

stagger — *verb* (**staggered, staggering**) **1** *intrans.* to walk or move unsteadily. **2** to cause extreme shock or surprise to. **3** to arrange so as to take place or begin at different times: *we need to stagger working hours.* — *noun* **1** an act of staggering. **2** (**staggers**) a disease of the brain in horses and cattle, causing staggering. **3** (**the staggers**) giddiness. [from Norse *staka*, to push]

staggering *adj.* that staggers; shockingly surprising.

staginess *noun* being stagy, artificiality.

staging *noun* **1** scaffolding, or the planks used for walking on; any temporary platform. **2** the putting on of a play or other spectacle.

stagnant *adj.* **1** *said of water* not flowing; dirty and foul-smelling because of not flowing. **2** not moving or developing; dull and inactive. [from Latin *stagnum*, pond]

stagnate *verb intrans.* to be or become stagnant.

stagnation *noun* **1** stagnating. **2** being stagnant.

stag party *or* **stag night** a party for men only, especially in honour of a man about to be married.

stagy *adj.* (**stagier, stagiest**) theatrical; artificial or affected.

Stahl, Georg Ernst (1660–1734) German chemist, born in Ansbach. Professor at Halle and personal physician to the King of Prussia, he propounded the idea that although physiological processes could largely be explained in terms of chemistry, each organism was directed by a life force or 'anima'. He is best known for introducing the erroneous 'phlogiston' theory of combustion which prevailed until the end of the 18c.

staid *adj.* serious or sober in character or manner, especially to the point of being dull. [an obsolete past participle of STAY]

stain — *verb* **1** *trans., intrans.* to make or become marked or discoloured, often permanently. **2** to change the colour of (eg wood) by applying a liquid chemical. — *noun* **1** a mark or discoloration. **2** a liquid chemical applied (eg to wood) to bring about a change of colour. **3** a cause of shame or dishonour: *a stain on his reputation.* [from Middle English *steynen*, to paint]

stained glass decorative glass coloured by a chemical process, especially used in church windows.

Staines POP (1981) 53 000, a town in Spelthorne district, Surrey, SE England. Part of the Greater London urban area, it lies at the junction of the R Thames and the R Colne, 27km/17mi W of London.

stainless steel any of a group of iron alloys containing chromium and nickel that are highly resistant to corrosion (rusting) and abrasion, and have a high tensile strength. Stainless steel can be polished to a bright shine, and is used to make cutlery, surgical instruments, ball bearings, turbine blades, exhaust pipes, etc.

stair *noun* **1** any of a set of indoor steps connecting the floors of a building. **2** (*also* **stairs**) a set of these. [from Anglo-Saxon *stæger*]

staircase *or* **stairway** *noun* a set of stairs, often including the stairwell.

stairwell *noun* the vertical shaft containing a staircase.

stake¹ — *noun* **1** a stick or post, usually with one end pointed, knocked into the ground as a support, eg for a young tree or a fence. **2** (**the stake**) *formerly* a post to which a person is tied to be burned alive as a punishment; the punishment. — *verb* to support or fasten to the ground with a stake.

— **stake a claim** to assert or establish a right or ownership.

stake something out 1 to mark the boundary of (a piece of land) with stakes. **2** *colloq.* to place (a person or a building) under surveillance. [from Anglo-Saxon *staca*]

stake² — *noun* **1** a sum of money risked in betting. **2** an interest, especially financial: *have a stake in the project's success.* **3** (**stakes**) a prize, especially in horse-racing. — *verb* **1** to risk as a bet. **2** to give (especially financial) support to.

— **at stake 1** to be won or lost; wagered. **2** at risk; in danger.
[perhaps from Old Dutch *staken*, to place]

stake-out *noun colloq.* surveillance of a person or building.

stalactite *noun* an icicle-like mass of limestone attached to the roof of a cave, etc, formed by the dripping of water containing limestone. [from Greek *stalaktos*, a dripping]

stalagmite *noun* a spiky mass of limestone sticking up from the floor of a cave, etc, formed by the dripping of water from a stalactite. [from Greek *stalagma*, a drop]

stale *adj.* **1** *said of food* not fresh, and therefore dry and unpalatable. **2** *said of air* not fresh; musty. **3** overused and no longer interesting or original. **4** out of condition because of over-training or overstudy. [from Old French *estaler*, to halt]

stalemate *noun* **1** *Chess* a position from which a player cannot move without leaving his or her king in check, resulting in a draw. **2** a position, in any contest or dispute, from which no progress can be made nor winner emerge; a deadlock. [from Middle English *stale*, stalemate + MATE²]

staleness *noun* a stale quality.

Stalin, Joseph, originally **Iosif Vissarionovich Dzhugashvili** (1879–1953) Georgian Marxist revolutionary and later virtual dictator of the USSR (1928–53), born in Gori, Georgia, the son of a cobbler and ex-serf. After joining a Georgian Social Democratic organization (1898), he became active in the revolutionary underground, and was twice exiled to Siberia (1902, 1913). As a leading Bolshevik he played an active role in the October Revolution, and became People's Commissar for Nationalities in the first Soviet government and a member of the Communist Party Politburo. In 1922 he became General Secretary of the Party Central Committee, a post he held until his death, and also occupied other key positions which enabled him to build up enormous personal power in the Party and government apparatus. After Lenin's death (1924) he pursued a policy of building 'socialism in one country', and gradually isolated and disgraced his political rivals, notably Trotsky. In 1928 he launched the campaign for the collectivization of agriculture during which millions of peasants perished, and began the first five-year plan for the forced industrialization of the economy. Between 1934 and 1938 he inaugurated a massive purge of the Party, government, armed forces, and intelligentsia in which millions of so-called 'enemies of the people' were imprisoned, exiled, or shot. In 1938 he signed the Non-Aggression Pact with Hitler which bought the Soviet Union two years' respite from involvement in World War II. After the German invasion (1941), the USSR became a member of the Grand Alliance, and Stalin, as war leader, assumed the title of Generalissimus. He took part in the conferences of Teheran, Yalta, and Potsdam, which resulted in Soviet military and political control over the liberated countries of postwar Eastern and central Europe. From 1945 until his death he resumed his repressive measures at home, and held foreign policies which contributed to the Cold War between the Soviet Union and the West. When he died, his body was displayed in the Lenin Mausoleum, from which it was removed in 1961 and buried near the Kremlin. He was posthumously denounced by Khrushchev at the 20th Party Congress (1956) for crimes against the Party and for building a 'cult of personality'.

Under Mikhail Gorbachev many of Stalin's victims were rehabilitated, and the whole phenomenon of 'Stalinism' officially condemned by the Soviet authorities.

Stalingrad, Battle of a major battle (1942–3) in World War II, fought during the winter in and around Stalingrad (now Volgograd) on the R Volga. Regarded as a major turning-point in the Allied victory over Nazi Germany, the battle was a victory for Soviet forces. The German 6th army surrendered (Feb 1943) after losing 70 000 lives, and yielded 91 000 prisoners-of-war to the Russians.

Stalinism *noun Politics* the rigorous rule of Stalin in the period 1929–53, characterized by socialism, centralization of power, the total subservience of society and culture to political ends, and the suppression of political opponents.

stalk¹ *noun* **1** *Bot.* the main stem of a plant, or the stem that attaches a leaf, flower, or fruit to the plant. **2** any slender connecting part. [from Anglo-Saxon *stalu*]

stalk² *verb* **1** to hunt, follow, or approach stealthily. **2** *intrans.* to walk or stride stiffly or proudly. [from Anglo-Saxon *stealcian*]

stalker *noun* a person who stalks.

stalking-horse *noun* **1** a horse behind which a hunter hides while approaching the hunted animal. **2** a person or thing used to conceal real plans or intentions, especially a planned attack.

stall¹ — *noun* **1** a compartment for housing a single animal in a cowshed, stable, etc. **2** a platform or stand on which goods or services for sale are displayed or advertised. **3** a church seat with arms, especially one in the choir or chancel. **4** (**stalls**) the seats on the ground floor of a theatre or cinema. **5** an act of stalling a vehicle or its engine. — *verb* **1** *trans., intrans. said of a motor vehicle or its engine* to cut out or cause it to cut out unintentionally. **2** to put (an animal) into a stall. [from Anglo-Saxon *stall*]

stall² — *verb* **1** to delay. **2** *intrans.* to do something in order to delay something else; to be evasive. — *noun* an act of stalling; a delaying tactic. [from obsolete *stale*, decoy]

stallion *noun* an uncastrated adult male horse, especially one kept for breeding. [from Old French *estalon*]

stalwart — *adj.* **1** strong and sturdy. **2** unwavering in commitment and support; reliable. — *noun* a stalwart supporter. [from Anglo-Saxon *stælwierthe*, serviceable]

stamen *noun Bot.* in a flowering plant, the male reproductive structure, consisting of a stalk-like *filament* bearing a specialized chamber (the *anther*), within which pollen grains are produced. The number and arrangement of the stamens are often used as an aid to identification of a flower. [from Latin *stamen*, warp thread]

Stamford POP (1990) 203 000, a city in Fairfield County, SW Connecticut, USA. It is situated on Long Island Sound and is a residential suburb for New York City. Stamford was established in 1641 and achieved city status in 1893.

stamina *noun* energy needed to withstand prolonged physical or mental exertion. [an old plural of STAMEN]

stammer — *noun* an inability to utter, without hesitation, certain speech sounds at the beginning of words, resulting in a repetition of the sound; the resulting repetition. — *verb trans., intrans.* (**stammered**, **stammering**) to speak or say with a stammer. [from Anglo-Saxon *stamerian*]

stamp — *verb* **1** *trans., intrans.* to bring (the foot) down with force. **2** *intrans.* to walk with a heavy tread. **3** to imprint or impress (a mark or design); to imprint or impress (something) with a mark or design. **4** to fix or mark deeply: *the number was stamped on his memory.* **5** to prove to be; to

characterize: *his lies stamp him as untrustworthy.* **6** to fix a postage or other stamp on. — *noun* **1** a small piece of gummed paper bearing an official mark and indicating that a tax or fee has been paid, especially a postage stamp. **2** an instrument for stamping a mark or design; the mark or design stamped. **3** a characteristic mark or sign: *the crime bears the stamp of a professional.* **4** an act of stamping the foot.

— **stamp something out 1** to put out a fire by stamping on it. **2** to put an end to an activity or practice, especially an illicit one. [from Anglo-Saxon *stampian*]

Stamp Act a British Act passed (1765) by the administration of George Grenville (1712–70) which levied a direct tax on all papers required in discharging official business in the American colonies. The first direct tax levied without the consent of the colonial assemblies, it caused much discontent in the colonies, and was withdrawn by the Rockingham government (1766).

stamp duty a tax on the drawing up of certain legal documents, eg those transferring ownership of property.

stampede — *noun* **1** a sudden wild rush of animals, especially when alarmed. **2** an excited or hysterical rush by a crowd of people. — *verb intrans.* to rush in a herd or crowd. [from Spanish *estampar*, to stamp]

stamping-ground *noun* a person's usual haunt or place of action. [originally used of wild animals]

stance *noun* **1** position or manner of standing, eg when preparing to play a stroke in sport. **2** point of view. [from Latin *stare*, to stand]

stanch same as STAUNCH².

stanchion *noun* an upright beam or pole serving as a support. [from Old French *estançon*]

stand — *verb* (PAST TENSE AND PAST PARTICIPLE **stood**) **1** (*also* **stand up**) to be in, or move into, an upright position supported by the legs or a base. **2** *trans., intrans.* to place or situate, or be placed or situated. **3** *intrans.* to be a particular height: *the tower stands 300 feet tall.* **4** to tolerate or put up with: *could not stand them / how can you stand it?* **5** *intrans.* to be in a particular state or condition: *I stand corrected / the score stands at 3–1.* **6** *intrans.* to be in a position to do something: *we stand to make a lot of money.* **7** *intrans.* to continue to apply or be valid: *the decision stands.* **8** (**stand for something**) *said of a symbol or device* to represent or signify it. **9** *intrans.* to be a candidate, especially in an election. **10** to withstand or survive: *stood the test.* **11** *colloq.* to buy (something) for (someone): *stood me lunch.* — *noun* **1** a base on which something is supported: *a cake-stand.* **2** a stall displaying or advertising goods or services for sale. **3** a structure with sitting or standing accommodation for spectators. **4** a rack or other device on which coats, hats, umbrellas, etc may be hung. **5** an attitude or course of action resolutely adopted: *take a stand against further building.* **6** an act of resisting attack: *make a stand.* **7** *Cricket* a partnership between batsmen, expressed in terms of the time it lasts or the runs scored.

— **stand by 1** to be in a state of readiness to act. **2** to look on without taking the required or expected action: *stood by and watched them go.*

stand by someone to give them loyalty or support, especially in time of difficulty.

stand down to resign, especially in favour of someone else.

stand for something to tolerate or allow it: *will not stand for it.*

stand in for someone to act as a substitute for them.

stand off to stay some distance away.

stand one's ground to maintain one's position resolutely; to refuse to give in.

stand out to be noticeable or prominent.

stand out for something to persist in demanding or seeking a concession, etc; to hold out.

stand out for *or* **against something** to remain resolutely in favour of or opposed to it.

stand up 1 to assume a standing position; to stand. **2** to prove to be valid on examination: *an argument that will stand up in court.*

stand someone up *colloq.* to fail to keep an appointment with them.

stand up for someone *or* **something** to be outspoken in one's support for or defence of them.

stand up to someone *or* **something** to face or resist someone (eg an opponent); to withstand something (eg hard wear or criticism). [from Anglo-Saxon *standan*]

standard — *noun* **1** an established or accepted model; a thing with which others are compared so as to be measured or judged. **2** a level of excellence, value, or quality. **3** (*often* **standards**) a principle of behaviour or morality adhered to. **4** a flag or other emblem, especially one carried on a pole. **5** an upright pole or support. **6** something, especially a song, that has remained popular over the years. — *adj.* **1** of the normal or accepted kind, without variations or additions. **2** typical; average; unexceptional. **3** accepted as supremely authoritative: *the standard text on the subject.* **4** *said of language* accepted as correct by educated native speakers. [from Old French *estandart*]

standard-bearer *noun* **1** a person carrying a flag. **2** the leader of a movement or cause.

standard deviation *Maths.* (ABBREV. **SD**) a measure of the spread of a sample of numbers about their arithmetic mean, widely used in statistics. It is equal to the square root of the variance (the mean of the squares of the deviations of each number from the mean of the sample).

Standard English the form of English taught in schools, and used, especially in formal situations, by the majority of educated English speakers.

standard error *or* **standard error of the mean** *Maths.* (ABBREV. **SE**, **SEM**) a measure of the extent to which the mean of a sample of a population represents the mean of the population from which the sample is drawn. It is equal to the standard deviation divided by the root of the number of observations, and is widely used in statistics.

Standard Grade in Scotland, a two-year course taken by (usually) secondary school pupils at around the age of 16. It is available on a variety of subjects, and is examined on three separate levels: Credit, General, and Foundation. Pupils usually sit examinations at two of these levels.

standardization *or* **standardisation** *noun* standardizing or being standardized.

standardize *or* **standardise** *verb* to make (all examples of something) uniform in kind, size, shape, etc.

standard lamp a lamp on a pole with a base that sits on the floor.

standard temperature and pressure (ABBREV. **STP**) *Physics* the standard conditions that are used as a basis for experimental measurements and calculations involving quantities that vary with temperature and pressure, by convention a standard temperature of 273.15K (0°C) and a standard pressure of 101 325 pascals (1 atmosphere); formerly known as normal temperature and pressure.

stand-by *noun* **1** a state of readiness to act, eg in an emergency. **2** a person or thing in this role. **3** *said of air travel* a system of allocating spare seats to passengers without a reservation, once the booked seats have been taken.

stand-in *noun* a deputy or substitute.

standing — *noun* **1** position, status, or reputation. **2** duration. — *adj.* **1** done, taken, etc in or from a standing position: *a standing ovation.* **2** permanent; regularly used: *a standing joke.*

standing order 1 an instruction from an account-holder to a bank to make fixed payments from the account to a third party at regular intervals. **2** an order placed with a shopkeeper for a regular supply of something.

standing wave *Physics* a wave that results from interference between waves of the same wavelength travelling in opposite directions, eg on a guitar string, where a wave passes along the string and is reflected back along itself when it reaches the end of the string. — Also called *stationary wave*.

Standish, Myles (c.1584–1656) English colonist, born probably in Ormskirk, Lancashire. After serving in the Netherlands, he sailed with the *Mayflower* in 1620, and became military head of the first American settlement in Plymouth, and treasurer of the colony (1644–9).

stand-off *or* **stand-off half** *noun Rugby* a half-back who stands away from the scrum and acts as a link between the scrum-half and the three-quarters.

stand-offish *adj.* unfriendly or aloof.

standpipe *noun* a vertical pipe leading from a water supply, especially one providing an emergency supply in the street when household water is cut off.

standpoint *noun* a point of view.

St Andrews POP (1981) 11 000, a town in NE Fife district, Fife, E Scotland. It lies on the S side of St Andrews Bay, 17km/11mi SE of Dundee. A popular tourist destination, St Andrews has been associated with golf since the 16c. The St Andrews Royal and Ancient Golf Club (1754) is the ruling authority on the game and the Old Course has hosted the British Open on many occasions. The town's university is the oldest in Scotland, founded in 1412. NOTABLE FEATURES West Port (city gate, dating from 1589); remains of castle (1200) and cathedral (12c–13c); repertory theatre; arts centre.

standstill *noun* a complete stop, with no progress being made at all.

Stanhope, James Stanhope, 1st Earl (1675–1721) British soldier and statesman, born in Paris. He entered parliament as a Whig in 1701, and commanded in Spain during the War of the Spanish Succession (1701–14). He was Secretary of State for Foreign Affairs under George I, and became his Chief Minister in 1717.

Stanislavsky, professional name of **Konstantin Sergeyevitch Alexeyev** (1863–1938) Russian actor, theatre director, and teacher, born in Moscow. He co-founded the Moscow Society of Art and Literature (1888) and in 1898 he helped to found the Moscow Arts Theatre, an influential company. His teaching on acting and his system of actor-training were major contributions to 20c theatre. See also METHOD.

Stanisław II (August) Poniatowski (1732–98) the last King of Poland (1764–95), born in Wołczyn. He travelled to St Petersburg in 1757, and became a favourite of the future empress, Catherine II. Through her influence he was elected king, but was unable to stop the partitions of Poland (1772, 1793) by Russia and Prussia. Despite the rebellion led by Thaddeus Kosciusko, the country was partitioned again in 1795.

stank see STINK.

Stanley, Sir Henry Morton, originally **John Rowlands** (1841–1904) Welsh explorer and journalist, born in Denbigh, Wales. He went as cabin boy to New Orleans in 1859, where he was adopted by a merchant named Stanley. He joined the *New York Herald* in 1867, and as its special correspondent he travelled to Abyssinia and Spain. In 1869 he was told to 'find Livingstone' in Africa. He left Zanzibar for Tanganyika in 1871 and encountered Livingstone in Ujiji. In 1874 Stanley led a second expedition which explored L Tanganyika, and traced the

Congo to the sea. In 1879, on a third expedition, he founded the Congo Free State, and in 1887–9 a further expedition went to the aid of Emin Pasha in the Sudan. He became a British citizen in 1892, and an MP (1895–1900).

Stanley, Wendell Meredith (1904–71) US biochemist, born in Ridgeville, Indiana. He isolated the tobacco mosaic virus (1935) and showed it to contain protein and nucleic acid; he went on to isolate other plant viruses and independently noted that viruses can cause cancer. Professor at the University of California from 1940, he shared the 1946 Nobel Prize for Chemistry with John Northrop and Howard Sumner.

Stanley, Mount a massif in the Ruwenzori Range, on the frontier between Zaire and Uganda. It rises to 5 110m at Margherita Peak, the highest point in Zaire and Uganda.

Stanley a male first name, after the surname and place-name. [from Anglo-Saxon *stan*, stone + *leah*, wood]

Stanley POP (1991) 2 000, the port capital of the Falkland Is, situated on the E coast of East Falkland.

Stanley Cup an end-of-season ice hockey series between the winners of the two conferences in the National Hockey League (NHL) in the USA and Canada. It was first presented in 1893 by Lord Stanley of Preston, then Governor-General of Canada.

Stanleyville see KISANGANI.

Stannaries the former tin-mining districts of Cornwall, UK, lying within the lands of the Duchy of Cornwall. Formerly, the tin miners of the Stannaries held special privileges, including the right to send representatives to the Stannary Parliament and to administer their own courts.

Stant, Charlotte one of the two women at the centre of Henry James's *The Golden Bowl*, who marries Adam Verver.

St Anton am Arlberg a winter sports resort in the Lechtal Alps (Arlberg Massif), Vorarlberg, W Austria.

stanza *noun* a verse in poetry. [from Italian *stanza*]

stapes *noun* (PL. **stapes**) *Anat.* a small stirrup-shaped bone in the middle ear. Together with two other bones, the malleus and incus, it transmits sound waves from the eardrum to the inner ear. [from late Latin *stapes*, stirrup]

staphylococcus *noun Biol.* a spherical Gram-positive bacterium of the genus *Staphylococcus*, that occurs on the skin and mucous membranes of humans and other animals. Some species can cause boils and abscesses, food poisoning, pneumonia, and osteomyelitis (inflammation of the bone marrow). [from Greek *staphyle*, bunch of grapes + *kokkos*, a grain]

staple[1] — *noun* **1** a U-shaped wire fastener for paper, forced through the paper from a special instrument into which it is loaded. **2** a U-shaped metal nail. — *verb* to fasten or attach with a staple or staples. [from Anglo-Saxon *stapol*, post, support]

staple[2] — *adj.* **1** principal; main: *staple foods*. **2** of principal importance as a traded article. — *noun* a staple product or ingredient. [from Old Dutch *stapel*, shop, warehouse]

stapler *noun* an instrument for driving staples through paper.

Staples, The see FARNE ISLANDS.

star — *noun* **1** a celestial body, often visible in the night sky, consisting of a sphere of gaseous material held together entirely by its own gravitational field, and generating heat and light energy by means of nuclear fusion reactions deep within its interior. **2** loosely used to refer to these bodies and the planets, comets, and meteors. **3** a representation of such a body in the form of a fig-

ure with five or more radiating points, often used as a symbol of rank or excellence. **4** (**the stars**) **a** the planets regarded as an influence on people's fortunes. **b** a horoscope. **5** a celebrity, especially from the entertainment world. **6** a principal performer. **7** an asterisk. — *verb* (**starred, starring**) **1** *trans., intrans.* to feature or appear as a principal performer. **2** to decorate with stars. **3** to asterisk. — **see stars** to see spots of light before one's eyes, eg as a result of a heavy blow to the head. [from Anglo-Saxon *steorra*]
◇ Many stars shine for thousands of millions of years before they run out of nuclear fuel. Their heat is generated from deep within, where hydrogen is converted to helium, with the release of large amounts of nuclear energy. Stars are formed by the condensation of a cloud of gas and dust, and they belong to different groups. Some develop into *blue giants* (very hot stars) that explode as *supernovae*, and could become *black holes* or *neutron stars*. Smaller stars at the end of their life expand to form *red giants* (relatively cool stars) and then shrink to form *white dwarfs* (small faint stars). Although stars are moving rapidly through space, they are so distant that the star patterns appear to have remained fixed since the time when they were first recorded.

starboard — *noun* the right side of a ship or aircraft, as viewed when facing forwards. — *adj., adv.* of, on, or towards the right side. [from Anglo-Saxon *steorbord*, steering board]

Starbuck the careful and earnest chief mate on the *Pequod*, in Herman Melville's *Moby Dick*.

starch — *noun* **1** *Biochem.* a carbohydrate that occurs in all green plants, where it serves as an energy store, usually in the form of small white granules in seeds, tubers, etc. **2** a preparation of this substance used to stiffen cloth fabrics and to make paper. Starch extracted from potatoes and cereals is also widely used in the food industry. **3** stiffness of manner; over-formality. — *verb* to stiffen with starch. [from Anglo-Saxon *stercan*, to stiffen]
◇ Starch is a polysaccharide consisting of long often branched chains of glucose molecules. It is a major source of dietary carbohydrate for humans and animals, and during digestion it is broken down by enzymes such as amylase and maltase to form glucose, which can then be used as an energy source. Foods rich in starch include potatoes, cereals, eg maize and rice, and foods made from flour, eg bread and pasta. A solution of iodine turns blue-black in the presence of starch, and this chemical reaction is used as a test for starch and iodine.

Star Chamber, Court of the the royal prerogative court in Britain for hearing subjects' petitions and grievances, increasingly prominent under the Tudors and early Stuarts. Its privy councillors and two chief justices dealt swiftly and efficiently with cases, particularly those involving public order, and it was used against government opponents by Charles I. The Long Parliament abolished it in 1641.

starchily *adv.* in a starchy way.

starchiness *noun* a starchy quality.

starchy *adj.* (**starchier, starchiest**) **1** like or containing starch. **2** stiff in manner; over-formal.

star cluster *Astron.* a group of stars physically associated in space, and held together by mutual gravitational attraction.

star-crossed *adj. literary* ill-fated; doomed.

stardom *noun* the state of being a celebrity.

stardust *noun* an imaginary dust that blinds the eyes to reality and fills them with romantic illusions.

stare — *verb intrans.* to look with a fixed gaze. — *noun* **1** an act of staring. **2** a fixed gaze. — **be staring someone in the face 1** *said of a solution, etc* to be readily apparent, but unnoticed. **2** *said of a misfortune, etc* to be menacingly imminent.

stare someone out or **down** to stare more fixedly at someone staring back, causing them to look away. [from Anglo-Saxon *starian*]

starfish *noun* the popular name for any of about 16 000 species of marine invertebrate animals belonging to the class Asteroidea, and having a number of arms (usually five) radiating outward from a central disc-like body.

◇ Most starfish are yellow, orange, pink, or red in colour, and are found in shallow seas. Like sea urchins and brittlestars, they are *echinoderms*, ie the body of the adult has five-rayed symmetry, is typically covered with rough spiny skin, and contains water-filled tubes, slender branches of which emerge through the body wall as *tube feet*. In starfish the tube feet are arranged in rows along the underside of each arm, and each tube foot ends in a sucker which can grip stones and other surfaces and pull the animal along. The mouth is on the underside of the central disc. Starfish feed mainly on molluscs, worms, crustaceans, and fish, and they can grow new arms to replace any that are lost.

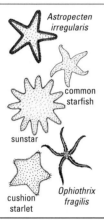

Astropecten irregularis

common starfish

sunstar

cushion starlet

Ophiothrix fragilis

starfish

star fruit the smooth-skinned yellow fruit of a SE Asian tree, the carambola, star-shaped in cross-section.

stargazer *noun colloq.* **1** *facetious* an astronomer or astrologer. **2** a daydreamer.

stargazing *noun* **1** studying the stars. **2** daydreaming.

Stari Most a bridge in Mostar, S Bosnia-Herzegovina, designed by the Turkish architect Hajrudin and built (1566) using mortar made from egg whites and goats' hair. It was destroyed by Serbo-Croat forces in 1993 during their bombardment of the Muslim area of the town.

Stari Ras a former Serbian city located near the present-day town of Novi Pazar in Yugoslavia. It became the first capital of independent Serbia in the 12c, but little now remains of the city apart from the 13c monastery of Sopocani, founded by King Uros I. It is a World Heritage site.

stark — *adj.* **1** severely bare, harsh, or simple. **2** plain; unembellished: *the stark truth.* **3** utter; downright. — *adv.* utterly; completely. [from Anglo-Saxon *stearc*, hard, strong]

starkers *adj. colloq.* stark-naked.

stark-naked *adj.* completely naked. [from Middle English *stert-naked*, from Anglo-Saxon *steort*, tail + *nacod*, naked]

starlet *noun* a young actress, especially in films, regarded as a star of the future.

starlight *noun* the light from the stars.

Starling, Ernest Henry (1866–1927) English physiologist, born in London. Professor at University College London, he discovered (with William Bayliss) the pancreatic secretion *secretin* (1902), and for this and similar chemical messengers they coined the word 'hormone'. His studies of cardiovascular physiology did much to elucidate the physiology of the blood circulation.

starling *noun* a small common songbird with dark glossy speckled feathers and a short tail. [from Anglo-Saxon *stærling*]

starlit *adj.* lit by the stars.

Star of Bethlehem a star mentioned in the New Testament which heralded the birth of Christ and guided magi from the East to the birthplace in Bethlehem (Matthew 2.1–12). Although sometimes considered a comet (Halley's comet c.11 BC), a supernova, or a conjunction of Jupiter and Saturn in the constellation Pisces (c.7 BC), these 'explanations' are inadequate for the sustained presence or movement that is described.

Star of David a six-pointed star, formed by two overlaid equilateral triangles, a very ancient symbol which in the last two centuries has come to symbolize Judaism. It was also adopted by 19c Zionism, appears on Israel's national flag today as a blue design against white, and (in red) signifies the society in Israel that corresponds to the Red Cross.

starry *adj.* (**starrier, starriest**) **1** filled or decorated with stars. **2** shining brightly.

starry-eyed *adj.* **1** naïvely idealistic or optimistic. **2** radiantly happy or affectionate.

Starry Night a painting by Vincent van Gogh (1889, Museum of Modern Art, New York).

Stars and Stripes (**the Stars and Stripes**) the national flag of the USA.

Star-Spangled Banner, The the national anthem of the USA, adopted in 1931. The words were written in 1814 by US lawyer Frances Scott Key (1780–1843), after the British bombardment of Fort McHenry, and put to music by English composer John Stafford Smith (1750–1836).

star-studded *adj. colloq.*, *said of the cast of a film, etc* featuring many well-known performers.

START *abbrev.* Strategic Arms Reduction Talks (or Treaty).

start — *verb* **1** *trans., intrans.* to begin; to bring or come into being. **2** *trans., intrans.* (*also* **start up** or **start something up**) to set or be set in motion, or put or be put into a working state. **3** (*also* **start off** or **out**) to be at first: *started out as an accountant.* **4** (*also* **start off** or **out**) to begin a journey, or an enterprise compared to a journey, eg a career. **5** (*also* **start something up**) to establish it or set it up. **6** (*also* **start something off**) to initiate it or get it going; to cause or set off. **7** *intrans.* to begin a journey: *started for home at midday.* **8** *intrans.* to flinch or shrink back suddenly and sharply, eg in fear or surprise. **9** *intrans. colloq.* to pick a quarrel. **10** to drive (an animal) from a lair or hiding-place. — *noun* **1** the first or early part. **2** a beginning, origin, or cause. **3** the time or place at which something starts. **4** an advantage given or held at the beginning of a race or other contest. **5** a help in or opportunity for beginning, eg in a career. **6** a sudden flinching or shrinking back.

— **for a start** as an initial consideration; in the first place.

start on someone to become suddenly and violently hostile towards them; to turn on them.

to start with 1 in the beginning. **2** in the first place. [from Middle English *sterten*]

starter *noun* **1** a person who gives the signal for a race to begin. **2** any of the competitors, horses, greyhounds, etc assembled for the start of a race. **3** (**starter motor**) an electric motor that is used to start the engine of a motor vehicle. **4** *colloq.* the first course of a meal.

— **for starters** *colloq.* in the first place; for a start.

starting-block *noun Athletics* a device consisting of a shaped block against which an athlete braces the feet at the start of a race, especially a sprint.

startle *verb* **1** to give a sudden fright to. **2** to surprise. [from Anglo-Saxon *steartlian*, to stumble or struggle]

startling *adj.* that startles, surprising.

star turn the principal item or performer in a show.

starvation *noun* a potentially fatal form of malnutrition caused by eating insufficient quantities of food over a long period, or by total lack of food, eg under conditions of famine or extreme poverty.

starve *verb* **1** *trans., intrans.* to suffer or cause to suffer extreme ill-health, or die, through lack of food. **2** *intrans. colloq.* to be very hungry. **3** (**starve something** or **someone of something**) to cause them to suffer a severe lack of it: *starved the project of funds.* **4** (**starve someone into something**) to force them into behaviour of a particular kind by withholding or preventing access to food. [from Anglo-Saxon *steorfan*, to die]

Star Wars a US film directed by George Lucas (1977). It is a science-fiction story of a conflict which pits youthful hero Luke Skywalker (Mark Hamill) and his pilot Han Solo (Harrison Ford) against the evil Darth Vader.

Star Wars *colloq.* the US Strategic Defence Initiative, SDI.

stash *slang* — *verb* to put into a hiding-place. — *noun* a hidden supply or store, or its hiding-place.

Stasi *abbrev.* the former East German secret police, abolished in 1990. [from German, shortened from *Staatssicherheitsdienst*, state security service]

state — *noun* **1** the condition, eg of health, appearance, or emotions, in which a person or thing exists at a particular time. **2** a territory governed by a single political body; a nation. **3** any of a number of locally governed areas making up a nation or federation under the ultimate control of a central government, as in the US. **4** (*often* **State** or **the State**) the political entity of a nation, including the government and all its apparatus, eg the civil service and the armed forces. **5** *colloq.* an emotionally agitated condition. **6** *colloq.* a confused or untidy condition. — *adj.* **1** relating to or controlled or financed by the State, or a federal state. **2** ceremonial: *a state visit by the Queen.* — *verb* **1** to express clearly; to affirm or assert. **2** to specify.

— **lie in state** *said of a dead person* to be ceremonially displayed to the public before burial.

the States the United States of America. [from Latin *status*, from *stare*, to stand]

State Department the oldest and most senior department of the US government, established (Jul 1789) by the fourth Act of Congress. Headed by a Secretary of State, it is responsible to the President for the conduct of foreign affairs.

State Earnings-Related Pension Scheme (ABBREV. **SERPS**) in the UK, the state pension scheme. It was introduced in 1979 and is additional to the basic pension; the amount a pensioner receives is related to how much they earned when they were in employment. Employees can 'contract out' of SERPS if they are in a company pension scheme, or (since 1988) if they start a personal pension scheme.

State Enrolled Nurse, a nurse qualified to perform many nursing tasks. See also STATE REGISTERED NURSE.

stateless *adj.* having no nationality or citizenship.

stateliness *noun* a stately quality.

stately *adj.* (**statelier, stateliest**) noble, dignified and impressive in appearance or manner.

stately home a large grand old private house, usually one open to the public.

statement *noun* **1** a thing stated, especially a formal written or spoken declaration. **2** a record of finances, especially one sent by a bank to an account-holder detailing the holder's transactions within a particular period. **3** the act of stating.

Staten Island POP (1990) 379 000, an island and a borough of New York City, USA, co-extensive with Richmond County. AREA 153sq km/59sq mi. The island is separated from New Jersey by the Kill van Kull and Arthur Kill channels, and from Long Island by the Narrows. It was first settled in 1641. ECONOMY oil refining; shipbuilding; paper; printing.

state of affairs a situation or set of circumstances.

state of emergency the suspension of normal law and order procedures and the introduction of strict control of the population by the military, in order to deal with a crisis, revolution, or other trouble.

state of play the situation at a particular moment.

state of the art the current level of advancement achieved by the most modern, up-to-date technology or thinking in a particular field.

state-of-the-art *adj.* most modern and best.

State Registered Nurse, in England and Wales, a nurse with advanced training, qualified to perform all nursing tasks. See also STATE ENROLLED NURSE, REGISTERED GENERAL NURSE.

stateroom *noun* **1** a large room in a palace, etc used for ceremonial occasions. **2** a large private cabin on a ship.

States General the most important central institution of the Netherlands, which dated from a medieval Burgundian institution and represented the federal union of the provinces of Holland, Zeeland, Gelderland, Utrecht, Friesland, Groningen and Overyssel. Although the body was abolished at the 1795 Revolution, the name was revived in the 1814 constitution.

Stateside *or* **stateside** *colloq.* — *adj.* of or in the USA. — *adv.* to or towards the USA.

statesman *noun* (PL. **statesmen**) an experienced and distinguished politician.

statesmanlike *adj.* **1** diplomatic. **2** suitable for or worthy of a statesman or stateswoman.

statesmanship *noun* the skill of a statesman or stateswoman.

stateswoman *noun* (PL. **stateswomen**) an experienced and distinguished female politician.

static — *adj.* **1** not moving; stationary. **2** fixed; not portable. **3** tending not to move around or change. **4** relating to statics. — *noun* **1** (*in full* **static electricity**) an accumulation of electric charges that remain at rest instead of moving to form a flow of current, eg electricity produced by friction between two materials, such as hair and a plastic comb. **2** a sharp crackling or hissing sound that interferes with radio and television signals, and is caused by static electricity or atmospheric disturbance. [from Greek *statikos*, bringing to a standstill]

statics *sing. noun* the branch of mechanics dealing with the action of forces on objects in equilibrium.

station — *noun* **1** a stopping-place for passenger trains or buses, with facilities for refuelling, ticket-purchasing, etc. **2** a local headquarters or depot, eg of a police force. **3** a building equipped for some particular purpose, eg electricity generation. **4** a radio or television channel, or the buildings from which it is broadcast. **5** a position within a class structure. **6** a post or place of duty. — *verb* (**stationed**, **stationing**) to appoint to a post or place of duty. [from Latin *statio*, from *stare*, to stand]

stationary *adj.* **1** not moving; still. **2** not changing. [related to STATION]

stationary wave *Physics* same as STANDING WAVE.

stationer *noun* a person or shop selling stationery. [from Latin *statio*, shop]

stationery *noun* paper, envelopes, pens, and other writing materials.

stationmaster *noun* the official in charge of a railway station.

Stations of the Cross a form of popular devotion in the Roman Catholic and some Anglican Churches. It consists of meditating on a series of 14 pictures or carvings recalling the Passion of Christ from his condemnation to his burial.

station wagon *North Amer., esp. US* an estate car.

statistical *adj.* relating to or determined by statistics.

statistical linguistics, the study of language using statistical techniques, especially the study of the frequency and distribution of specific letters, words, and forms in texts and spoken language. See also MATHEMATICAL LINGUISTICS.

statistically *adv.* according to statistics.

statistician *noun* a person who collects and analyses statistics.

statistics *noun* **1** (*sing.*) *Maths.* the branch of mathematics concerned with the collation, classification, and interpretation of numerical data, usually by analysing a representative sample of a population (a group of people, objects or items of data). It also includes the analysis of possible relationships (correlations) between different sets of data, and the prediction of events on the basis of probability. **2** (*usually* **statistics**) an item of numerical information collected and presented in an ordered way. [from German *Statistik*, study of political facts and figures, from Latin *status*, state]

statue *noun* a sculpted, moulded, or cast figure, especially of a person or animal, usually life-size or larger, often erected in a public place. [from Latin *statua*]

statuesque *adj.*, *said of a human figure* like a statue, tall and well-proportioned and dignified and imposing in appearance.

statuette *noun* a small statue.

stature *noun* **1** height of body. **2** greatness; eminence. [from Latin *statura*, from *stare*, to stand]

status *noun* **1** rank or position in relation to others, within society, an organization, etc. **2** legal state, eg with regard to adulthood, marriage, or citizenship. **3** importance. [from Latin *status*]

status quo (*usually* **the status quo**) the situation at a given moment, usually before a significant event such as a war. [from Latin, = the state in which]

status symbol a possession or privilege regarded as an indication of a person's high (especially social) status.

statute *noun* **1** a law made by the legislative assembly of a country and recorded in a formal document. **2** a permanent rule drawn up by the leader or leaders of an organization. [from Latin *statutum*, that which is set up]

statute book a formal written record of all the laws passed by a parliament, etc.

statutorily *adv.* according to statute.

statutory *adj.* **1** required or prescribed by law or a rule. **2** usual or regular, as if prescribed by law.

Staudinger, Hermann (1881–1965) German chemist, born in Worms. Educated at Halle, he held several academic posts before becoming

professor at Freiburg (1926–51). He was awarded the 1953 Nobel Prize for Chemistry for his pioneering work on the chemistry of polymers, which contributed to the development of plastics.

Stauffenburg, Claus, Graf von (Count of) (1907–44) German soldier, born in Jettingen. He initially welcomed Hitler's advent to power, but quickly became alienated by Nazi brutality. A colonel on the German general staff in 1944, he placed the bomb at Hitler's feet in an unsuccessful attempt to assassinate him at Rastenburg (20 Jul 1944), and was shot the following day.

staunch[1] *adj.* loyal; trusty; steadfast. [from Old French *estanche*, watertight]

staunch[2] *verb* to stop the flow of (especially blood from a wound). [from Old French *estanchier*]

Staunton, Sir George, alias **George Robertson** the rash lover, and eventual husband, of Effie Deans in Sir Walter Scott's *The Heart of Midlothian*.

Stavanger POP (1992e) 100 000, the seaport capital of Rogaland county, SW Norway. It lies on a S branch of the Bokn Fjord, 304km/189mi SW of Oslo. Founded in the 8c, it is an important North Sea oil centre. NOTABLE FEATURE St Swithin's Cathedral (12c).

stave — *noun* **1** any of the vertical wooden strips joined to form a barrel or tub. **2** any (especially wooden) bar, rod, or shaft, eg a rung on a ladder. **3** *Mus.* same as STAFF *noun* 5. **4** a verse of a poem or song. — *verb* **1** (PAST TENSE AND PAST PARTICIPLE **stove**, **staved**) (*often* **stave something in**) to smash a hole in it. **2** (PAST TENSE AND PAST PARTICIPLE **staved**) (*usually* **stave something off**) to delay the onset of it; to ward it off. [a back-formation from STAVES, plural of STAFF]

staves plural of STAFF, STAVE.

stay[1] — *verb* (PAST TENSE AND PAST PARTICIPLE **stayed**) **1** *intrans.* to remain in the same place or condition, without moving or changing. **2** *intrans.* to reside temporarily, eg as a guest. **3** *intrans.* to remain or linger in order to share or join in something: *will you stay for dinner?* **4** to suspend or postpone (eg legal proceedings). **5** to control or restrain (eg anger). **6** *intrans. Scot.* to reside permanently; to live. — *noun* **1** a period of temporary residence; a visit. **2** a suspension of legal proceedings, or a postponement of a legally enforceable punishment: *grant a stay of execution*.

— stay in to remain indoors, especially not to go out socially.

stay put *colloq.* to remain where one or it is.

stay up to remain out of bed beyond one's usual bedtime.

[from Latin *stare*, to stand]

stay[2] *noun* **1** a prop or support. **2** any of a number of strips of bone or metal sewn into a corset to stiffen it. **3** (**stays**) a corset stiffened in this way. [from Old French *estaye*]

stay[3] *noun* a rope or cable with which a pole, etc is anchored to the ground to keep it upright. [from Anglo-Saxon *stæg*]

stay-at-home *colloq.* — *adj.* tending to prefer the peaceful routine of domestic life to a busy and varied social life. — *noun* a stay-at-home person.

stayer *noun colloq.* a person or animal with great powers of endurance.

staying power stamina; endurance.

STD *abbrev.* **1** sexually transmitted disease. **2** subscriber trunk dialling.

STD code a telephone code for a town or other area, used before a subscriber's individual number when telephoning from outside the area.

stead

— in someone's stead in place of them.

stand someone in good stead to prove useful to them.

[from Anglo-Saxon *stede*, place]

steadfast *adj.* firm; resolute; determinedly unwavering. [from Anglo-Saxon *stede*, place + *fæst*, fixed]

steadfastly *adv.* in a steadfast way.

steadfastness *noun* being steadfast.

Steadicam *noun trademark* a harness device fitted with shock absorbers, on which a film camera is mounted to produce steady shots while the camera operator moves.

steadily *adv.* in a steady way.

steadiness *noun* being steady.

steady — *adj.* (**steadier, steadiest**) **1** firmly fixed or balanced; not tottering or wobbling. **2** regular; constant; unvarying. **3** stable; not easily disrupted or undermined. **4** having a serious or sober character. — *verb trans., intrans.* (**steadies, steadied**) to make or become steady or steadier. — *adv.* in a steady manner. — *interj.* (**steady on!**) an exhortation to be careful or restrained.
— **go steady with someone** *colloq.* to have a steady romantic relationship with them.
[see STEAD]

steady-state theory *Astron.* in cosmology, the generally unaccepted theory that the universe has always existed. In order to account for the observed expansion of the universe, it is postulated that there is continuous spontaneous creation of matter.

steak *noun* **1** fine quality beef for frying or grilling, or a thick slice of this. **2** beef for stewing or braising in chunks. **3** a thick slice of any meat or fish. [from Norse *steik*, roast]

steakhouse *noun* a restaurant specialising in beef steaks.

steal — *verb* (PAST TENSE **stole**; PAST PARTICIPLE **stolen**) **1** *trans., intrans.* to take away (another person's property) without permission or legal right, especially secretly. **2** to obtain by cleverness or trickery: *steal a kiss*. **3** to fraudulently present (another person's work, ideas, etc) as one's own. **4** *intrans.* to go stealthily. — *noun colloq.* **1** a bargain; a thing easily obtained. **2** *North Amer., esp. US* an act of stealing. [from Anglo-Saxon *stelan*]

stealth *noun* **1** softness and quietness of movement, avoiding notice. **2** secretive or deceitful behaviour. [related to STEAL]

stealthily *adv.* in a stealthy way.

stealthy *adj.* (**stealthier, stealthiest**) acting or done with stealth; furtive.

steam — *noun* **1** the gaseous state of water, ie water at a temperature higher than its boiling point. It is colourless, forming a mist of tiny water droplets, and is often used as a source of power or energy, eg in steam engines. **2** *colloq.* power, energy, or speed: *run out of steam*. **3** (*attributive*) powered by steam: *a steam generator*. — *verb* **1** *intrans.* to give off steam. **2** to cook or otherwise treat by exposure to steam. **3** *intrans.* to move under the power of steam. **4** *intrans. colloq.* to go at speed.
— **be steamed up** *colloq.* to be very angry or excited.
let off steam to release anger or energy built up inside one.
steam up *said of a transparent or reflective surface* to make or become clouded by tiny water droplets formed from condensed steam.
under one's own steam by one's own efforts alone.
[from Anglo-Saxon]

steam-boat see STEAMSHIP.

steamer *noun* **1** a ship whose engines are powered by steam. **2** a two-tier pot in which food in the upper tier is cooked by the action of steam from water heated in the lower tier.

steam iron an electric iron in which steam from a built-in water tank is released on to the

laundry through holes in the iron's base, to help smooth out creases.

steamroller — *noun* a large vehicle, originally and still often steam-driven, with wheels consisting of huge solid metal cylinders, driven over newly made roads to flatten the surface. — *verb colloq.* **1** to use overpowering force or persuasion to secure the speedy movement or progress of. **2** to crush (opposition, etc).

steamship *or* **steam-boat** *noun* a boat powered by steam.

steam turbine *Engineering* a balanced wheel, with a large number of blades round its rim, which converts the kinetic energy of moving steam into the mechanical energy of rotation. Steam turbines are often used to drive electricity generators in power stations.

steamy *adj.* (**steamier, steamiest**) **1** full of, or made cloudy by, steam. **2** *colloq.* involving or featuring sexual passion; erotic.

stearic acid *Chem.* a saturated long-chain fatty acid, consisting of a colourless waxy solid that is soluble in alcohol and ether but insoluble in water. It is the commonest fatty acid in animal and vegetable fats and oils, and is used as a lubricant, and in pharmaceutical products, cosmetics, candles, and food packaging. Its sodium and potassium salts are used to make soap. — Also called *octadecanoic acid*. [from Greek *stear steatos*, suet, tallow]

steed *noun literary* a horse thought of as something to ride on. [from Anglo-Saxon *steda*, stallion]

Steel, Sir David (Martin Scott) (1938–   ) Scottish politician, born in Kirkcaldy, Fife. He became a Liberal MP in 1965, sponsored a controversial bill to reform the laws on abortion (1966–7), and was active in the anti-apartheid movement. He became Liberal Chief Whip (1970–5), then succeeded Jeremy Thorpe to become the last Liberal leader (1976–88). In 1981 he led the Party into an Alliance with the Social Democratic Party, and after the 1987 general election he negotiated a merger with the SDP, but declined entering the leadership contest (won by Paddy Ashdown). Since then Steel has been Liberal Democrat MP for Tweeddale, Ettrick, and Lauderdale.

steel — *noun* **1** any of a number of iron alloys containing small amounts of carbon and, in some cases, additional elements, eg chromium, nickel, manganese, silicon, molybdenum. **2** a rough-surfaced rod made of this alloy, on which knives are sharpened by hand. **3** hardness or strength, especially of a person's character. — *verb* (*usually* **steel oneself**) to harden oneself or prepare oneself emotionally, especially for something unpleasant or unwelcome. [from Anglo-Saxon *style*]
◇ *Carbon steels* contain only small amounts of other metals, whereas *alloy steels* contain significant amounts, eg stainless steel contains at least 12% chromium, which renders it highly resistant to corrosion. Steel is made by removing impurities from molten iron or scrap steel and then adding an accurately measured amount of carbon and other elements. It is used to make motor vehicles, ships, bridges, machinery, tools, etc.

steel band a band, of a kind originating in the West Indies, with percussion instruments made from steel petrol drums.

steel blue a deep greyish-blue colour.

Steele, Sir Richard (1672–1729) Irish essayist, dramatist, and politician, born in Dublin. He wrote three successful comedies, and in 1707 became editor of *The London Gazette*. He is best known for the satirical, political, and moral essays which formed much of the content of the periodicals *The Tatler* (1709–11), which he founded, and *The Spectator* (1711–12), which he co-founded with Addison. He was appointed supervisor of Drury Lane Theatre by George I.

steel wool thin strands of steel in a woolly mass, used for polishing and scouring.

steelworks *sing. or pl. noun* a factory where steel is manufactured.

steely *adj.* (**steelier, steeliest**) **1** hard and unyielding: *a steely gaze*. **2** steel-blue.

steep¹ *adj.* **1** rising or sloping sharply. **2** *colloq.*, *said of a price, rate, etc* unreasonably high. [from Anglo-Saxon *steap*]

steep² *verb trans., intrans.* to soak thoroughly in liquid.
— **be steeped in something** to be closely familiar with something (eg a subject of knowledge) or influenced by it.
[from Middle English *stepen*]

steepen *verb trans., intrans.* (**steepened, steepening**) to make or become steep or steeper.

steeple *noun* **1** a tower forming part of a church or temple, especially one with a spire. **2** the spire itself. [from Anglo-Saxon *stepel*]

steeplechase — *noun* **1** a horse race round a course with hurdles, usually in the form of man-made hedges. **2** a track race for humans, with very high hurdles and a water jump. — *verb intrans.* to take part in a steeplechase.

steeplechaser *noun* a horse that runs in a steeplechase.

steeplejack *noun* a person who repairs steeples and tall chimneys.

steeply *adv.* with a steep incline, decline, or slope; abruptly.

steepness *noun* being steep.

steer¹ *verb* **1** *trans., intrans.* to guide or control the direction of (a vehicle or vessel). **2** to guide the course or movements of, eg with tuition, persuasion, or force. **3** to follow (a particular course).
— **steer clear of someone** *or* **something** to avoid them.
[from Anglo-Saxon *styran*]

steer² *noun* a young bull or male ox, especially one castrated and reared for beef. [from Anglo-Saxon *steor*]

steerage *noun* **1** *old use* the cheapest accommodation on board a passenger ship, traditionally near the rudder. **2** the act or practice of steering.

steering committee 1 a committee deciding on the nature and order of topics to be discussed by a parliament, etc. **2** a committee in charge of the overall direction pursued by a business or other organization.

steering-wheel *noun* a wheel turned by hand to control the wheels of a vehicle or the rudder of a vessel.

Stefan, Josef (1835–93) Austrian physicist, born near Klagenfurt. Professor at Vienna and Director of the Institute for Experimental Physics there, he proposed Stefan's law (1879) (or the Stefan–Boltzmann law), that the amount of energy radiated per second from a black body is proportional to the fourth power of its absolute temperature. He used this law to make the first satisfactory estimate of the Sun's surface temperature.

stegosaurus *noun* a herbivorous dinosaur, up to 7.5m in length, that lived during the Jurassic period. It had a small head, a high domed back bearing two rows of large vertical bony plates, and a long tail. [from Greek *stegos*, roof + *saurus*, lizard]

Steichen, Edward (Jean) (1879–1973) US photographer, born in Luxembourg, and taken to the USA as a child. He joined Alfred Stieglitz in setting up the American Photo-Secession Group in 1902, and through their gallery in New York City exercised considerable influence in establishing photography as an acceptable form of modern art. He was Director of Photography at the New York Museum of Modern Art (1945–62).

Stein, Gertrude (1874–1946) US writer, born in Allegheny, Pennsylvania. She settled in Paris, where she was absorbed into the world of experimental art and letters. She was revered as a critic in Paris, and her home became a salon for artists and writers between the two World Wars. Her main works include *Three Lives* (1908), *Tender Buttons* (1914), in which she tried to apply the theories of Cubist art to writing, and her most widely-read book, *The Autobiography of Alice B Toklas* (1933).

Stein, Peter (1937–) German theatre director, born in Berlin. His first production (1967) established him as a leading avant-garde director in Germany. Since 1970 he has been responsible for a remarkable series of collective creations at the Berlin Schaubuhne.

stein *noun* a large metal or earthenware beer mug, often with a hinged lid. [from German *stein*]

Steinbeck, John (Ernst) (1902–68) US novelist, born in Salinas, California. He studied at Stanford, but did not take a degree, and worked as a labourer while writing. He became known with his novel *Tortilla Flat* (1935), which foreshadows his major work *The Grapes of Wrath* (1939), a study of the poor in the face of disaster and threatened disintegration. Other books include *Of Mice and Men* (1937), *East of Eden* (1952), and the humorous *Cannery Row* (1945). He was awarded the Nobel Prize for Literature in 1962.

Steinberger, Jack (1921–) German-born US physicist, born in Bad Kissingen. Professor at Columbia University and a researcher at CERN, the European centre for nuclear research in Geneva, he proved the existence of a fundamental particle known as the 'neutral pion' and showed that there are two distinct types of neutrino. He shared the 1988 Nobel Prize for Physics with Leon Lederman and Melvin Schwartz.

Steiner, George (1929–) British critic and scholar, born in Paris. He taught at Princeton and Cambridge, and became Professor of English and Comparative Literature at the University of Geneva in 1974. His influential books include *The Death of Tragedy* (1960), *Language and Silence* (1967), *After Babel* (1975), and *Antigones* (1984).

Steiner, Rudolf (1861–1925) Austrian social philosopher, the founder of anthroposophy, born at Kraljevec. He studied science and mathematics, edited Goethe's scientific papers, was temporarily influenced by the theosophists, then established his first 'school of spiritual science', or 'Goetheanum', in Dornach, Switzerland (1912). His aim was to integrate the psychological and the practical dimensions of life into an educational, ecological, and therapeutic basis for spiritual and physical development. Many schools and research institutions arose from his ideas, notably the Rudolf Steiner Schools for maladjusted and handicapped children.

Steinway, Heinrich Engelhard, originally **Steinweg** (1797–1871) German-born US piano-maker, born in Wolfshagen. He fought in the Prussian army at the battle of Waterloo, and in 1836 set up a piano factory in Brunswick. In 1850 he transferred the business to New York, where he introduced many innovations into the instrument, such as a cast-iron frame.

stele *or* **stela** *noun* (PL. **stelae**) an ancient stone pillar or upright slab, usually carved or engraved. [from Greek *stele*]

Stella a female first name. [from Latin *stella*, star]

stellar *adj.* of, like, or relating to a star or stars. [from Latin *stella*, star]

stem¹ — *noun* **1** the central part of a plant, growing upward from the root, or the part by which a leaf, flower, or fruit is attached to a

branch. **2** the long thin supporting part of a wine glass. **3** any long slender part. **4** *Linguistics* the usually unchanging base of a word, to which inflectional affixes are added. See also ROOT. — *verb intrans.* (**stemmed**, **stemming**) (**stem from something** *or* **someone**) to originate or derive from them. [from Anglo-Saxon *stemn*]

stem² *verb* (**stemmed**, **stemming**) to stop (the flow of something). [from Norse *stemma*]

stench *noun* a strong and extremely unpleasant smell. [from Anglo-Saxon *stenc*, smell]

stencil — *noun* **1** a drawing or printing plate with parts cut out to form lettering or a design that is copied on to a surface by laying the plate on the surface and inking or painting over the cut out parts. **2** the lettering or design produced in this way. — *verb* (**stencilled**, **stencilling**) to print or produce by means of a stencil. [from Old French *estinceller*, to sparkle]

Stendhal, pseudonym of **Marie Henri Beyle** (1783–1842) French writer, born in Grenoble. He was a soldier under Napoleon, settled in Paris in 1821, and after the 1830 Revolution was appointed consul at Trieste and Civitavecchia. He wrote biographies and critical works on music, art, and literature, but was best known for his novels, notably *Le Rouge et le noir* (The Red and the Black, 1831) and *La Chartreuse de Parme* (The Charterhouse of Parma, 1839).

Sten gun a lightweight portable machine-gun, the standard submachine-gun of the British Army from 1942 onwards. [named after *Shepherd* and *Turpin*, its designers, and *Enfield* as in BREN GUN]

Stenmark, Ingemark (1956–) Swedish skier, born in Tärnaby, 61km/100mi S of the Arctic Circle. He won the slalom and the giant slalom at the 1980 Olympics with an 8cm metal plate in his ankle following an accident the previous year. Between 1974 and 1989 he won a record 86 World Cup races, including a record 13 in the 1979 season. He was overall champion three times (1976–8), won 15 slalom/giant slalom titles, and five world titles. He retired in 1989.

Steno, Nicolaus, also known as **Niels Stensen** (1638–86) Danish physician, naturalist, and theologian who made major advances in anatomy, geology, crystallography, palaeontology, and mineralogy. Personal physician to the Grand Duke of Tuscany and Royal Anatomist at Copenhagen, he became a priest in 1675, and gave up science on being appointed Vicar-Apostolic to N Germany and Scandinavia. He discovered Steno's duct of the parotid gland, a salivery gland in front of the ear, and investigated the function of the ovaries. He also pointed out the true origin of fossil animals (1669), and contended that sedimentary strata were laid down in former seas.

stenographer *noun North Amer., esp. US* a shorthand typist.

stenographic *adj.* relating to or recorded in shorthand.

stenography *noun* the skill or practice of writing in shorthand. [from Greek *stenos*, narrow + *graphein*, to write]

stentorian *adj. literary, said of a voice* loud and strong. [from *Stentor*, a Greek herald in the Trojan War who according to Homer had a voice as loud as 50 men (*Iliad* 5.783–5)]

Step *noun trademark* a method of exercise based on stepping on and off a small platform of adjustable height, usually in time to music.

step — *noun* **1** a single complete action of lifting then placing down the foot in walking or running. **2** the distance covered in the course of such an action. **3** a movement of the foot (usually one of a pattern of movements) in dancing. **4** (*often* **steps**) a single (often outdoor) stair, or any stair-like support used to climb up or down. **5** the sound of a foot being laid on the ground in walk-

ing. **6** a single action or measure taken in proceeding towards an end or goal. **7** a degree or stage in a scale or series. **8** a way of walking; gait. **9** (**steps**) a stepladder. — *verb intrans.* (**stepped**, **stepping**) **1** to move by taking a step or steps, especially slowly, quietly or carefully. **2** (*usually* **step on something**) to lay one's foot on it. **3** (**step into something**) to enter into it or become involved in it, especially easily or casually. **4** to go or come: *step this way*.

— **in step 1** walking or marching in unison, with corresponding feet hitting the ground at the same time. **2** in harmony or unison.
out of step not in step.
step by step gradually.
step down to resign from a position of authority.
step something down to reduce the rate, intensity, etc of it.
step in 1 to take up a position or role as a substitute or replacement. **2** to intervene in an argument.
step on someone *colloq.* to treat them harshly or with contempt.
step on it *colloq.* to hurry up.
step out 1 to walk quickly and confidently with long strides. **2** *colloq.* to go out socially.
step something up to increase the rate, intensity, etc of it.
watch one's step 1 to walk with careful steps, avoiding danger. **2** to proceed with caution, taking care not to anger or offend others.
[from Anglo-Saxon *steppe*]

step- *combining form* indicating a relationship not by blood but through a second or later marriage or partnership. [from Anglo-Saxon *steop*, originally orphan]

stepbrother and **stepsister**. *noun* the son or daughter of a stepfather or stepmother.

stepchild *noun* a stepson or stepdaughter.

stepfather and **stepmother**. *noun* the second or later husband of a mother or wife of a father.

Stephano the drunken butler of Alonso, and companion of Trinculo in Shakespeare's *The Tempest*.

stephanotis *noun* a twining evergreen perennial plant (*Stephanotis floribunda*), native to Madagascar, and having glossy oval leaves and heavily scented white waxy tubular flowers. It is often used in bridal bouquets, and is also a popular house plant. [from Greek *stephanos*, wreath]

Stephen (c.1090–1154) the last Norman King of England (1135–54), son of Stephen, Count of Blois, and Adela, the daughter of William the Conqueror. Although he had sworn to accept Henry I's daughter, Empress Matilda, as Queen, he seized the English Crown and was also recognized as Duke of Normandy on Henry's death (1135). Though captured at the battle of Lincoln (Feb 1141), he was released nine months later after Matilda's supporters had been routed at Winchester. He was unable to defend the Norman Empire mainly because of his other military burdens such as the major offensives of the Scots in the north (David I of Scotland annexed the N English counties by 1141) and the Angevins in the south. By 1144–5 Matilda's husband, Count Geoffrey of Anjou, had conquered Normandy. Stephen was also repeatedly challenged by baronial rebellions, and after 18 years of virtually continuous warfare, he was forced in 1153 to accept Matilda's son, the future Henry II, as his lawful successor.

Stephen I (997–1038) the patron saint and first King of Hungary. He formed a kingdom out of Pannonia and Dacia, organized the Christian Church, and introduced many social and economic reforms. Pope Sylvester II bestowed upon him the title of 'Apostolic King' and, according to tradition, St Stephen's Crown, which is now a Hungarian national treasure. He was canonized in 1083; his feast day is 16 Aug.

Stephen, St (1c AD) a New Testament character, possibly a Hellenist, and the first Christian martyr (Acts 6–7). One of the seven chosen to manage the finances and alms of the early Church, he was charged by the Jewish authorities for speaking against the Temple and the Law, tried by the Sanhedrin, and stoned to death by the crowds in Jerusalem. His feast day is 26 Dec.

Stephen, Sir Leslie (1832–1904) English man of letters, born in London. The father of Vanessa Bell and Virginia Woolf, he was ordained at Cambridge in 1859, but later rejected Christianity and became an agnostic. He settled in London (1864), contributed to many periodicals, and became editor of *The Cornhill Magazine* (1871) and of the first 26 volumes of the new *Dictionary of National Biography* (1885–91). He wrote several literary biographical studies, and a major critical work, *The History of English Thought in the Eighteenth Century* (1876).

Stephen 1 a male first name, borne by the first Christian martyr (Acts 6 and 7). 2 a male first name. [from Greek *stephanos*, crown, wreath]

Stephenson, George (1781–1848) British inventor, born in Wylam, Northumberland. He worked in a colliery, received a basic education at night school, and in 1812 became engine-wright at Killingworth. There he invented the first locomotive (1814). His most famous engine, the 'Rocket', was built in 1829. He subsequently worked as an engineer and consultant for several companies.

Stephenson, Robert (1803–59) British civil engineer, born in Willington Quay in Northumberland. He assisted his father George Stephenson in surveying the Stockton and Darlington Railway, worked as a mining engineer in Colombia, and managed his father's locomotive engine-works at Newcastle. He attained independent fame for many bridge designs including his tubular design for the Britannia bridge over the Menai Straits in Wales (1850), and became an MP in 1847.

Stephenson, Sir William, also called **Intrepid** (1896–1989) Canadian secret intelligence chief, born of Scottish descent in Point Douglas, near Winnipeg. He became involved in British secret intelligence through visits to Germany to buy steel in the early 1930s. His information on Enigma, the German cipher machine, led to MI6's acquisition of a prototype in 1939. In 1940 he was appointed British intelligence chief in N and S America, representing the interests of MI5, MI6, and Special Operations Executive. The novelist Ian Fleming, a member of his wartime staff, is said to have adopted Stephenson as the model for the character 'M' in the James Bond books.

Stephenson's Rocket the train with which George Stephenson won the Liverpool–Manchester railway run in 1829. The *Rocket* reached a speed of 56kph/36mph and confirmed the train as being a viable method of transportation in the growing industrial market.

stepladder *noun* a short ladder with flat steps, not rungs, made free-standing by means of a supporting frame attached by a hinge at the ladder's top.

step-parent *noun* a stepfather or stepmother.

steppe *noun* an extensive dry grassy and usually treeless plain, especially that in SE Europe and Asia extending E from the Ukraine through to the Manchurian plains of China. Large areas of steppe are important for wheat-growing (eg in Ukraine). [from Russian *step*]

Steppenwolf, Der a novel by Herman Hesse (1927). It is a surrealist narrative which presents the reflections of an outsider.

stepping-stone *noun* 1 a large stone in a stream, etc, with a surface above the water level, stepped on to cross the stream. 2 a means of gradual progress.

stepson *or* **stepdaughter** *noun* the son or daughter of a second or later husband or wife, from an earlier marriage or partnership.

-ster *suffix* denoting a person with regard to some characteristic, activity, membership of a group, etc: *youngster / trickster / gangster.*

steradian *noun Geom.* (ABBREV. **sr**) the SI unit of measurement for solid (three-dimensional) angles. It is equal to the solid angle formed at the centre of a sphere when an area on the surface of the sphere equal to the square of the sphere's radius is joined to the centre. [from Greek *stereos*, solid + RADIAN]

stereo — *noun* 1 stereophonic reproduction of sound: *broadcast in stereo*. 2 (PL. **stereos**) a hi-fi system giving a stereophonic reproduction of sound. — *adj.* stereophonic.

stereo- *combining form* forming words meaning 'solid, three-dimensional'. [from Greek *stereos*, solid]

stereochemistry *noun Chem.* the branch of chemistry that is concerned with the study of the three-dimensional arrangement of atoms within molecules, and the way in which such arrangements affect the chemical properties of the molecules. [from Greek *stereos*, solid]

stereophonic *adj. Electron.* denoting the reproduction of sound by means of two or more independent sound channels leading to separate loudspeakers, in order to simulate the depth and physical separation of different sounds that would be experienced at a live performance.

stereophonically *adv.* by means of stereophony.

stereophony *noun Physics* the reproduction of sound by means of two or more independent sound channels leading to separate loudspeakers, in order to simulate the depth and physical separation of different sounds that would be experienced at a live performance. [from Greek *stereos*, solid]

stereoscopic *adj. Optics* denoting an instrument such as a special type of camera or microscope that produces an apparently binocular (three-dimensional) image by presenting a slightly different view of the same object to each eye.

stereoscopically *adv.* by stereoscopic means.

stereoscopic photography *Photog.* the recording and presentation of paired images which give the viewer an impression of solidity and depth. A basic system was developed in 1845 using two cameras 65mm apart (the width between the human eyes), which produced apparently three-dimensional images when viewed in a device that allowed each eye to see only its appropriate right-eye and left-eye record. Twin-lens or stereoscopic cameras produce pairs of colour transparencies which may be mounted, or shown on two projectors each fitted with a polarizing filter orientated at right angles to each other. The viewer wears spectacles with corresponding polarizing filters so that each eye sees only the correct image. Similar principles are applied in cinematography.

stereotype — *noun* 1 an over-generalized idea, impression, or point of view allowing for no individuality or variation. 2 a person or thing conforming to such an idea, etc. 3 a solid metal printing plate cast from a mould taken from a plate on which the text consists of individual letters pieced together. — *verb* to think of or characterize in an over-generalized way.

stereotyped *adj.* 1 *Printing* produced by means of a stereotype. 2 *said of opinions, etc* fixed, unchangeable; conventionalized, conforming to a stock image or cliché.

sterile *adj.* 1 biologically incapable of producing offspring, fruit, or seeds. 2 made free of germs. 3 producing no results; having no new ideas. [from Latin *sterilis*, barren]

sterility *noun* being sterile, inability to reproduce.

sterilization *or* **sterilisation** *noun* 1 the treatment of food, surgical or laboratory equipment, etc, with heat, chemicals or radiation in order to destroy all living micro-organisms. 2 a surgical operation that is performed on a human or animal so that offspring can no longer be produced. It may be achieved by vasectomy in men, cutting and tying of the Fallopian tubes in women, or complete removal of the sex organs in other mammals.

sterilize *or* **sterilise** *verb* to make sterile.

sterling — *noun* British money. — *adj.* 1 of British money. 2 good quality; worthy; reliable. 3 authentic; genuine. 4 *said of silver* of at least 92.5 per cent purity. [from Anglo-Saxon *steorra*, star, from the markings on early Norman pennies]

Stern, Otto (1888–1969) US physicist, born in Sohrau, Germany. Professor at Hamburg and the Carnegie Institute of Technology in Pittsburgh, he carried out his best-known experiment in collaboration with Walther Gerlach (1920–1); this provided fundamental proof of the quantum theory prediction that an atom should possess a magnetic moment which can only be oriented in two fixed directions relative to an external magnetic field. He was awarded the 1943 Nobel Prize for Physics.

stern¹ *adj.* 1 extremely strict; authoritarian. 2 harsh, severe, or rigorous. 3 unpleasantly serious or unfriendly in appearance or nature. [from Anglo-Saxon *styrne*]

stern² *noun* the rear of a ship or boat. [from Norse *stjorn*, steering]

sternal *adj.* relating to or in the region of the sternum.

Sterne, Laurence (1713–68) Irish novelist, born in Clonmel, Co Tipperary. He was ordained in 1738, and appointed to a living in Yorkshire. He is best known for his comic novel, *The Life and Opinions of Tristram Shandy* (1759–67). From 1762 he lived mainly abroad, for health reasons, and published the novel *A Sentimental Journey through France and Italy* in 1768.

sternly *adv.* with a stern manner.

sternness *noun* being stern.

sternum *noun* (PL. **sternums**, **sterna**) the breastbone, the broad vertical bone in the chest to which the ribs and collarbone are attached. [from Greek *sternon*, chest]

steroid *noun* 1 *Biochem.* any of a large group of fat-soluble organic compounds that have a complex molecular structure consisting of four carbon rings, and are widely distributed in living organisms. 2 *Medicine* a drug containing such a compound. 3 an anabolic steroid. [from STEROL + -OID]
◇ Naturally occurring steroids include the sex hormones (eg progesterone, testosterone), the corticosteroid hormones secreted by the adrenal glands, the bile salts, and cholesterol (a major component of cell membranes). Synthetic steroids form the active ingredients of most oral contraceptives, and are also used in the treatment of arthritis and asthma, and as immunosuppressants to prevent the rejection of foreign tissue by the immune system during transplant surgery. Long-term treatment with large doses of steroids can have serious side-effects, including lowered resistance to infection, and loss of calcium from the bones.

sterol *noun Biochem.* any of a group of colourless waxy solid steroid alcohols found in plants, animals, and fungi, eg cholesterol. [a shortening of CHOLESTEROL and similar words]

stertorous *adj. formal, said of breathing* noisy; with a snoring sound. [from Latin *stertere*, to snore]

stet *verb* (**stetted**, **stetting**) *Printing* in proof-reading, an instruction to ignore a correction and let the existing text stand. [from Latin *stet*, let it stand]

stethoscope *noun* an instrument for listening to sounds made inside the body, eg the heartbeat, consisting of a small concave disc, placed on the body, with attached tubes carrying the sound to earpieces. [from Greek *stethos*, chest + *skopeein*, to look at]

stetson *noun* a man's broad-brimmed felt hat with a high crown, concave at the top, worn especially by cowboys. [named after John Stetson (1830–1903), American hat-maker]

stevedore *noun* a person employed to load and unload ships; a docker. [from Spanish *estibador*, packer]

Stevenage POP (1992e) 76 000, a town in Stevenage district, Hertfordshire, SE England, situated 45km/28mi N of London. In 1946 it was the first 'new town'.

Stevens, Wallace (1879–1955) US poet, born in Reading, Pennsylvania. He became a journalist and lawyer, then joined an insurance company in Hartford. *Harmonium*, his first collection of philosophical verse, appeared in 1923. Further works include *The Man with the Blue Guitar* (1937), *Notes Toward a Supreme Fiction* (1942), and *The Auroras of Autumn* (1950). His *Collected Poems* were published in 1954.

Stevenson, Adlai (Ewing) (1900–65) US Democratic politician, born in Los Angeles. He became a lawyer, took part in several European missions for the State Department (1943–5), and became Governor of Illinois (1948). He helped to found the United Nations (1946), stood twice against Eisenhower as presidential candidate (1952, 1956), and was the US delegate to the UN (1961–5).

Stevenson, Ian (1918–) US Professor of Psychiatry, born in Montreal, Canada. He has conducted full-time research in parapsychology at the University of Virginia since 1967. His numerous publications include the series *Cases of the Reincarnation Type*.

Stevenson, Robert Louis (Balfour) (1850–94) Scottish writer, born in Edinburgh. An invalid for much of his childhood, he studied engineering, but then became a lawyer (1875). He travelled extensively in France and wrote travel sketches, essays, and short stories for magazines. The romantic adventure story, *Treasure Island*, brought him fame in 1883, and entered him on a course of romantic fiction which includes *Kidnapped* (1886), *The Strange Case of Dr Jekyll and Mr Hyde* (1886), *The Master of Ballantrae* (1889), and the unfinished *Weir of Hermiston* (1896). He moved to Samoa for the sake of his health in 1889 and died there five years later.

Stevenson screen a shelter for meteorological instruments, particularly thermometers, providing protection from solar radiation. It is a white, wooden box with louvred sides to give ventilation. It was invented by Thomas Stevenson (1818–87), the father of Robert Louis Stevenson.

stew — *verb* **1** to cook (especially meat) by long simmering. **2** to cause (tea) to become bitter and over-strong by letting it brew for too long. **3** *intrans. colloq.* to be in a state of worry or agitation. — *noun* **1** a dish of food, especially meat, cooked by stewing. **2** *colloq.* a state of worry or agitation.
— **stew in one's own juice** *colloq.* to suffer the consequences of one's own (often ill-advised) actions.
[from Old French *estuve*, stove]

steward — *noun* **1** an attendant on a passenger ship or aircraft. **2** a person supervising crowd movements during a sporting event or public march. **3** a person overseeing catering and associated arrangements in a hotel or club. **4** a person employed to manage another person's property and affairs, eg on a country estate. **5** a senior official monitoring the conduct of jockeys during a horse race. — *verb* to serve as a steward of. [from Anglo-Saxon *stigweard*, hall-keeper]

stewardess *noun* a female attendant on a passenger ship or aircraft.

Stewart, Jackie (John Young) (1939–) Scottish motor racing driver, born in Milton, Dunbartonshire. He started in 99 races, and won 27 world championship races between 1965 and 1973, a record until surpassed by Alain Prost in 1987. He was world champion in 1969, 1971, and 1973. He retired at the end of 1973, and took up a career in broadcasting. He also reached Olympic standard in clay pigeon shooting.

Stewart, James (Maitland) (1908–) US film actor, born in Indiana, Pennsylvania. He started in films in 1935, establishing a character of integrity in *You Can't Take It With You* (1938), and *The Philadelphia Story* (1940), for which he won an Oscar. After distinguished service in World War II, he made some westerns (1950–5) and two successes for Alfred Hitchcock, *Rear Window* (1954) and *Vertigo* (1958). His later work included *Fools' Parade* (1971) and *Right of Way* (television, 1983).

Stewart Island POP (1986) 542, an island of New Zealand, to the S of South I, across the Foveaux Strait. AREA 1 735sq km/670sq mi. It is a refuge for animal and bird life. Mt Anglem is the highest point, at a height of 977m. The small settlement of Oban on Halfmoon Bay is the main urban centre on this largely uninhabited island. ECONOMY fishing.

Stewart (of the Glens), James a character in Robert Louis Stevenson's *Catriona*, who is wrongly accused, but eventually acquitted, of the murder of Colin Campbell.

stewed *adj. colloq.* drunk.

Stibitz, George Robert (1904–) US mathematician and computer scientist, born in Dayton, Ohio. Working at Bell Telephone Laboratories, he constructed a binary adder and a 'complex number calculator', the Model I; he later designed program-controlled calculators for the military during World War II, although these were soon superseded by the electronic digital computer.

stick¹ *noun* **1** a twig or thin branch taken from or which has fallen from a tree. **2** any long thin piece of wood shaped for a particular purpose, eg striking the ball in hockey, or playing a percussion instrument. **3** a long thin piece of anything, eg celery. **4** (*usually* **sticks**) a piece of furniture, especially one of few. **5** *colloq.* verbal abuse, criticism, or mockery. **6** (**the sticks**) *colloq.* a rural area when considered remote or unsophisticated. **7** *colloq.* a person: *a funny old stick*.
— **get hold of the wrong end of the stick** to misunderstand a situation, a statement, etc.
[from Anglo-Saxon *sticca*]

stick² *verb* (PAST TENSE AND PAST PARTICIPLE **stuck**) **1** to push or thrust (especially something long and thin or pointed). **2** to fasten by piercing with a pin or other sharp object: *stick it up with drawing-pins*. **3** *trans., intrans.* to fix, or be or stay fixed, with an adhesive. **4** *intrans.* to remain persistently: *an episode that sticks in my mind*. **5** *trans., intrans.* to make or be unable to move; to jam or lock. **6** to confine. **7** (**stick to something**) **a** to remain faithful to something undertaken (eg a promise). **b** not to stray from something (eg a matter under discussion). **8** *intrans. said of criticism, etc* to continue to be considered valid. **9** *colloq.* to place or put: *just stick it on the table*. **10** *colloq.* to bear or tolerate: *could not stick it any longer*.
— **stick around** *colloq.* to remain or linger.
stick at something 1 to continue doggedly with it. **2** to hesitate or refuse to do it for reasons of principle: *will stick at nothing in order to succeed*.
stick by someone to remain loyal or supportive to them.

stick in one's throat *colloq.* to be extremely difficult to say or accept, usually for reasons of principle.
stick out 1 to project or protrude. **2** to be obvious or noticeable; to stand out.
stick something out 1 to cause it to project or protrude. **2** *colloq.* to endure it.
stick out for something to continue to insist on it; to refuse to yield.
stick together to remain loyal and supportive to each other.
stick up *colloq.* to project upwards; to stand up.
stick up for someone to speak or act in their defence.
[from Anglo-Saxon *stician*]

sticker *noun* an adhesive label, especially one displaying a message or advertisement in the window of a shop, a car, etc.

stickiness *noun* a sticky quality.

sticking-plaster *noun* adhesive plaster used to dress wounds.

stick insect a tropical insect with a long twig-like body and legs.

stick-in-the-mud *noun colloq.* a person boringly opposed to anything new or adventurous.

stickleback *noun* a small spiny-backed fish of northern rivers. [from Anglo-Saxon *sticel*, prick + BACK]

stickler *noun* (**a stickler for something**) a person who fastidiously insists on it. [from Anglo-Saxon *stihtan*, to set in order]

sticky *adj.* (**stickier**, **stickiest**) **1** able or likely to stick to other surfaces. **2** *said of the weather* warm and humid; muggy. **3** *colloq., said of a situation, etc* difficult; awkward; unpleasant.
— **a sticky end** *colloq.* an unpleasant end or death.

sticky-fingered *adj. colloq.* prone to pilfering.

sticky tape a strong tape for binding, fastening or joining, with an adhesive substance on one side.

sticky wicket *noun colloq.* a difficult or awkward situation.

Stieglitz, Alfred (1864–1946) US photographer, born in Hoboken, New Jersey. He founded the American Photo-Secession Group with Edward Steichen in 1902. He consistently influenced the development of creative photography as an art form through his magazine *Camera Work* (1903–17) and his gallery of modern art in New York City.

Stiernhielm, Georg (1598–1672) Swedish poet, born in Vika. Ennobled by Gustavus Adolphus (1594–1632), he was the favourite court poet of Queen Christina, and is known as the father of Swedish poetry. Besides much lyric poetry, his works include a didactic allegorical poem, *Hercules* (1647).

stiff — *adj.* **1** not easily bent or folded; rigid. **2** *said of limbs, joints, etc* lacking suppleness; not moving or bending easily. **3** *said of a punishment, etc* harsh; severe. **4** *said of a task, etc* difficult; arduous. **5** *said of a wind* blowing strongly. **6** *said of a manner* not natural and relaxed; over-formal. **7** thick in consistency; viscous. **8** *colloq., said of an alcoholic drink* not diluted or only lightly diluted; strong. — *adv. colloq.* to an extreme degree: *bored me stiff*. — *noun slang* a corpse.
— **have** or **keep a stiff upper lip** to show or maintain self-control and resignation in the face of disappointment or unpleasantness.
[from Anglo-Saxon *stif*]

stiffen *verb trans., intrans.* (**stiffened**, **stiffening**) to make or become stiff or stiffer.

stiffly *adv.* in a stiff way.

stiff-necked *adj.* arrogantly obstinate.

stiffness *noun* a stiff quality.

stiffware *noun* software that is difficult or impossible to modify because of having been customized or having incomplete documentation, etc.

stifle *verb* **1** *intrans.* to experience difficulty in breathing, especially because of heat and lack of air. **2** to kill by stopping the breathing; to smother. **3** to suppress (a feeling or action). [perhaps from Old French *estouffer*, to smother]

stifling *adj.* unpleasantly hot or airless.

stigma *noun* (PL. **stigmas**, sense 4 **stigmata**) **1** shame or social disgrace. **2** a blemish or scar on the skin. **3** *Bot.* in a flower, the sticky surface at the tip of the style that receives pollen. **4** *Zool.* any of a variety of pigmented markings or spots, eg the wingspot of certain butterflies. **5** (**stigmata**) *Christianity* marks resembling the wounds of Christ's crucifixion, said to have appeared on the bodies of certain holy people. [from Greek *stigma*, tattoo-mark, brand]

stigmatization *or* **stigmatisation** *noun* stigmatizing or being stigmatized.

stigmatize *or* **stigmatise** *verb* to describe or regard as shameful.

stilboestrol *or* North Amer. **stilbestrol** *noun* a synthetic oestrogen. [from Greek *stilbein*, to shine]

stile *noun* a step, or set of steps, built into a fence or wall. [from Anglo-Saxon *stigel*]

stiletto *noun* (PL. **stilettos**) **1** (*also* **stiletto heel**) a high thin heel on a woman's shoe. **2** *colloq.* a shoe with such a heel. **3** a dagger with a narrow tapering blade. [from Italian *stiletto*, diminutive of *stilo*, dagger]

still¹ — *adj.* **1** motionless; inactive. **2** quiet and calm; tranquil. **3** *said of a drink* not fizzy. — *adv.* **1** continuing as before, now or at some future time. **2** up to the present time, or the time in question; yet. **3** even then; nevertheless. **4** quietly and without movement: *sit still.* **5** (*with comparatives*) to a greater degree; even: *older still.* — *verb* **1** *trans., intrans.* to make or become still. **2** to calm, appease, or put an end to. — *noun* **1** stillness; tranquillity. **2** a photograph, especially of an actor in or a scene from a cinema film, used for publicity purposes. [from Anglo-Saxon *stille*]

still² *noun* an apparatus in which an alcoholic spirit is distilled. [see DISTIL]

stillborn *adj.* **1** dead when born. **2** *said of a project, etc* doomed from the start.

still life *noun* (PL. **still lifes**) **1** a painting, drawing, or photograph of an object or objects, eg a bowl of fruit, rather than of a living thing. **2** this kind of art or photography.

stillness *noun* being still; a still quality.

still room 1 a room in which distilling is carried out. **2** a housekeeper's pantry in a large house.

stilt *noun* **1** either of a pair of long poles with supports for the feet part way up, on which a person can walk around supported high above the ground. **2** any of a set of props on which a building, jetty, etc is supported above ground or water level. [from Middle English *stilte*]

stilted *adj.*, *said of language* unnatural-sounding, especially over-formal. [see STILT]

Stilton *noun* a strong white English cheese, often with blue veins. [from *Stilton* in Cambridgeshire, S England]

stimulant *noun, adj.* any substance, especially a drug, that produces an increase in the activity of a particular body system or function, eg caffeine, nicotine, amphetamines.

stimulate *verb* **1** to cause physical activity, or increased activity, in (eg an organ of the body). **2** to initiate or get going. **3** to excite or arouse the senses; to animate or invigorate. **4** to create interest and enthusiasm in (someone). [from Latin *stimulare*]

stimulating *adj.* that stimulates; exciting.

stimulation *noun* **1** stimulating. **2** something that stimulates.

stimulus *noun* (PL. **stimuli**) a change in some aspect of the external or internal environment of an organism that causes a response in a cell, tissue, or organ, eg in the nervous system of animals. [from Latin *stimulus*, goad]

sting — *noun* **1** in certain animals and plants, a defensive puncturing organ that can pierce skin and inject poison or venom, eg the spine of a sting-ray, the hairs of a stinging nettle. **2** the injection of poison from an animal or plant. **3** a painful wound resulting from the sting of an animal or plant. **4** any sharp tingling pain. **5** any sharply wounding quality or effect, eg that of a vicious insult. **6** *slang* a trick, swindle, or robbery. — *verb* (PAST TENSE AND PAST PARTICIPLE **stung**) **1** to pierce, poison, or wound with a sting. **2** *intrans.* to produce a sharp tingling pain. **3** (**sting someone into something**) to goad or incite them into action of a particular kind. **4** *slang* to cheat, swindle or rob; to cheat by overcharging. [from Anglo-Saxon *stingan*, to pierce]

stingily *adv.* in a stingy way.

stinginess *noun* being stingy.

stinging *adj.* that stings.

stinging nettle same as NETTLE.

stingray *noun* a ray with a long whip-like tail tipped with spikes capable of inflicting severe wounds.

stingy *adj.* (**stingier**, **stingiest**) ungenerous; mean; miserly. [from *stinge*, a dialect form of STING]

stink — *noun* **1** a strong and very unpleasant smell. **2** *colloq.* an angry complaint or outraged reaction; a fuss: *kick up a stink.* — *verb* (PAST TENSE **stank**, **stunk**; PAST PARTICIPLE **stunk**) **1** *intrans.* to give off a stink. **2** (*usually* **stink something out**) to fill a place with a stink. **3** *intrans. colloq.* to be contemptibly bad or unpleasant. **4** *intrans. colloq.* to be morally disgusting. [from Anglo-Saxon *stincan*, to smell]

stink bomb a small bomb-like container releasing a foul-smelling gas when broken as a practical joke.

stinker *noun colloq.* **1** a very difficult task, question, etc. **2** a dishonest, cheating, or otherwise unpleasant person.

stinkhorn *noun* a fungus (*Phallus impudicus*), found in woodland. When immature it resembles a white egg, which then ruptures to release the fast-growing fruiting body, which consists of a white spongy hollow stem and a swollen conical ridged cap which is covered wtih dark olive-green slime containing the spores. Its pungent nauseating smell attracts insects, which eat the slime and disperse the spores.

dog stinkhorn

stinking — *adj.* **1** that stinks. **2** *colloq.* very unpleasant. — *adv. colloq.* extremely; disgustingly: *stinking rich.*

stint — *verb trans., intrans.* (**stint on something**) to be mean or grudging in the giving or supplying of it. — *noun* an allotted amount of work.

— **without stint** liberally; unreservedly. [from Anglo-Saxon *styntan*, to dull]

stipend *noun* a salary or allowance, especially one paid to a member of the clergy. [from Latin *stipendium*, tax]

stipendiary — *adj.* receiving a stipend. — *noun* (PL. **stipendiaries**) a person receiving a stipend.

stipendiary magistrate *Legal* in England and Wales, a salaried and legally qualified magistrate, found in London and other large towns. Most magistrates are lay people receiving only travelling expenses and a small allowance, and having no formal legal training.

stipple — *verb* **1** to paint or draw in dots or dabs, rather than lines or masses of colour. **2** to give a finish of tiny raised bumps to (wet cement, plaster, etc), creating a grainy effect. — *noun* a pattern produced by stippling. [from Dutch *stippelen*, diminutive of *stippen*, to dot]

stipulate *verb* to state as a necessary condition. [from Latin *stipulari*]

stipulation *noun* **1** stipulating. **2** a contract or a condition of agreement.

stir¹ — *verb* (**stirred**, **stirring**) **1** to mix or agitate (a liquid or semi-liquid substance) by repeated circular strokes with a spoon or other utensil. **2** to arouse the emotions of; to move. **3** *intrans.* to make a slight or single movement. **4** (*also* **stir something up**) to cause or provoke (eg trouble). **5** *intrans.* to get up after sleeping; to become active after resting. **6** *intrans. colloq.* (*also* **stir it**) to make trouble. — *noun* **1** an act of stirring (a liquid, etc). **2** an excited reaction; a commotion: *cause a stir.* [from Anglo-Saxon *styrian*]

stir² *noun slang* prison.

stir-crazy *noun slang North Amer., esp. US* emotionally disturbed as a result of being confined, especially in prison.

stir-fry — *verb* to cook lightly by brisk frying on a high heat with little oil. — *noun* a dish of stir-fried food.

Stirling, James (1926–92) Scottish architect and town planner, born in Glasgow. He worked as an architect in private practice from 1956 until his death. His early designs in Britain include the Engineering Building at Leicester University (1959–63), the History Faculty Building at Cambridge University (1964), and the Florey Building at Queen's College, Oxford (1966). He also worked in Europe, where his designs include the Neue Staatsgalerie in Stuttgart, Germany (1980–4), with its much-imitated twisting curved glass entrance wall, and the Braun industrial complex in Melsungen (1992). His later work in Britain includes the Clore Gallery, an extension built on to the Tate Gallery to house the Turner collection (1987). He also produced a design for the redevelopment of the site at No 1 Poultry in the City of London (awaiting construction), which provoked a long-running controversy between traditionalists and modernists.

Stirling POP (1981) 39 000, the capital of Central Region, central Scotland. It lies on the S bank of the R Forth, 34km/21mi NE of Glasgow. HISTORY Stirling Castle was recaptured from the English by William Wallace in 1297; it was taken by Edward I of England in 1304 and held until 1314 when Bruce won at Bannockburn; the castle later became a favourite royal residence. NOTABLE FEATURES Stirling Castle (12c); the ruins of Cambuskenneth Abbey (1147), scene of Bruce's parliament (1326); Church of the Holy Rude (1414); MacRobert Arts Centre; Smith Art Gallery and Museum; Wallace Monument (1870), 2km/1.3mi NE.

Stirling Range a mountain range in SW Western Australia. It extends 64km/40mi parallel with the SW coast. The range rises to 1 109m at Bluff Knoll.

stirrer *noun colloq.* a person who enjoys stirring up trouble.

stirring *adj.* arousing strong emotions.

stirrup *noun* **1** either of a pair of metal loops hanging on straps from a horse's saddle, serving as the rider's footrests. **2** any strap or loop supporting or passing under a foot. [from Anglo-Saxon *stigrap*, from *stigan*, to mount + *rap*, rope]

stirrup cup an alcoholic drink given to a person, originally a rider, about to leave.

stirrup pump a portable hand-operated pump that draws water from a bucket, etc, used in fighting small fires.

stitch — *noun* **1** a single interlinking loop of thread or yarn in sewing or knitting. **2** a complete movement of the needle or needles creating such a loop. **3** any of various ways in which such loops are interlinked. **4** a single interlinking loop of surgical suture. **5** a sharp ache in the side resulting from physical exertion. **6** *colloq.* the least scrap of clothing: *without a stitch on.* — *verb* (*also* **stitch something up**) to join or close it, or decorate it, with stitches. — **in stitches** *colloq.* helpless with laughter. **stitch someone up** *slang* to trick them, especially to betray or double-cross them. [from Anglo-Saxon *stice*, prick]

stitchwort *noun* *Biol.* a perennial plant, found in woods and hedgerows throughout Europe, that has thin brittle stems, narrow leaves, and small white flowers, so called because it was formerly used to treat a 'stitch' or pains in the side.

stoat *noun* a small flesh-eating mammal, closely related to the weasel, and having a long slender body and reddish-brown fur with white underparts. In northern regions the fur turns white in winter, during which time it is known as ermine and is highly prized by the fur trade. Stoats are found throughout Europe and Asia, and also in N America, where they are known as short-tailed weasels. [from Middle English *stote*]

stock — *noun* **1** (*also* **stocks**) the total amount of goods of a particular kind stored in a shop, warehouse, etc. **2** a supply kept in reserve. **3** equipment or raw material in use: *rolling stock.* **4** liquid in which meat or vegetables have been cooked, used as a base for a soup, sauce, etc. **5** the shaped wooden or plastic part of a rifle or similar gun, held against the firer's shoulder. **6** farm animals; livestock. **7** the money raised by a company through the selling of shares. **8** the total shares issued by a particular company or held by an individual shareholder. **9** a group of shares bought or sold as a unit. **10** ancestry; descent: *of peasant stock.* **11** any of various Mediterranean plants of the wallflower family, cultivated for their bright flowers. **12** (**stocks**) a wooden device into which an offender was formerly fastened to be displayed for public ridicule, held by the head and wrists, or wrists and ankles. **13** reputation; standing. — *adj.* **1** of a standard type, size, etc, constantly in demand and always kept in stock. **2** *said of a phrase, etc* much used, especially so over-used as to be meaningless. — *verb* **1** to keep a stock of (something) for sale. **2** to provide with a supply: *a well-stocked drinks cabinet.* — **in stock** currently held for sale on the premises. **out of stock** not in stock. **stock up on something** to acquire or accumulate a stock of it. **take stock** to make an inventory of all stock held on the premises at a particular time. **take stock of something** to make an overall assessment of something (especially circumstances). [from Anglo-Saxon *stocc*, stick]

stockade — *noun* a fence or enclosure made from tall heavy posts, built for defence. — *verb* to protect or defend with a stockade. [from Spanish *estacada*]

stockbroker *noun* a person who buys and sells stocks and shares for customers in return for a fee.

stockbroking *noun* the buying and selling of stocks and shares for clients.

stock car a car modified for a kind of track racing in which deliberate colliding is allowed.

stock cube a small cube of compressed meat or vegetable extract, added to water to make stock.

stock exchange a market for the trading of stocks and shares by professional dealers on behalf of customers; also a building housing this.

Stock Exchange Automated Quotations (ABBREV. **SEAQ**) in the UK, a system introduced in 1986 in the London Stock Market for trading securities. It is a computerized market-making activity which enables member firms to buy and sell and quote prices for specific securities. The prices are therefore known to all continuously.

Stockhausen, Karlheinz (1928–) German composer, born in Mödrath. He studied under Frank Martin and Olivier Messiaen, joined the *Musique Concrète* group in Paris, and experimented with compositions based on electronic sounds. In Cologne, he helped to found the electronic music studio (1953) and was appointed Professor of Composition at the Hochschule für Musik (1971). He has written orchestral, choral, and instrumental works, including some which combine electronic and normal sonorities, such as *Kontakte* (1960), and parts of a large operatic cycle, *Licht* (Light).

Stockholm POP (1992e) 679 000, the capital of Sweden and the country's largest city. It is situated on a group of islands and on the adjacent mainland where L Mälar joins the Saltsjö, an arm of the Baltic Sea. The seaport, founded in 1255, was an important trading centre of the Hanseatic League; in 1436 it became capital. NOTABLE FEATURES Royal Palace (18c); German Church (17c); National Museum; Drottningholm Palace (royal family residence and a World Heritage site).

stockily *adv.* in a stocky way.

stockiness *noun* being stocky.

stockinet *or* **stockinette** *noun* a stretchy knitted fabric used especially for undergarments. [perhaps a contraction of *stocking-net*]

stocking *noun* **1** either of a pair of close-fitting coverings for women's legs, self-supported or supported by suspenders, made of fine semi-transparent nylon or silk. **2** a sock. [related to STOCK]

stockinged *adj.*, *said of the feet* wearing only socks, stockings, or tights, and not shoes.

stock-in-trade *noun* the basic equipment, techniques, personal qualities, etc needed for a particular trade or activity.

stockist *noun* a person or shop that stocks a particular item.

stockjobber *noun* *Stock Exchange* in the UK until 1986, a middleman buying and selling stocks and shares for stockbrokers.

stock market a stock exchange, or the trading carried on there.
◊ A stock market 'crash' is a situation in which the price of stocks falls dramatically, resulting in many bankruptcies. The most famous case was the Wall Street crash of 1929, and a less dramatic crash occurred in Oct 1987 in most world stock markets.

stockpile — *noun* an accumulated reserve supply. — *verb* to accumulate a (usually large) reserve supply of.

Stockport POP (1992e) 289 000, a town in Stockport borough, Greater Manchester, NW England. It lies 10km/6mi SE of Manchester, at the junction of the R Tame and the R Goyt where they form R Mersey.

stockroom *noun* a storeroom, especially in a shop.

stock-still *adj.*, *adv.* motionless.

stocktaking *noun* **1** the process of making a detailed inventory of all stock held on the premises of a shop, factory, etc at a particular time. **2** the process of making an overall assessment (eg of the present situation).

Stockton POP (1990) 481 000, an inland seaport and city in San Joaquin County, central California, USA. It is on a deep-water channel to the San Joaquin R, c.105km/65mi E of San Francisco. The city was founded in 1847.

Stockton-on-Tees POP (1981) 87 000, a town in Stockton-on-Tees district, Cleveland, NE England, lying on the R Tees Estuary. It developed from the time of the opening of the Stockton–Darlington railway in 1825.

stocky *adj.* (**stockier, stockiest**) *said of a person or animal* broad and strong-looking, especially when not tall.

stockyard *noun* a large yard or enclosure in which cattle are kept temporarily, eg to be sorted for market.

stodge — *noun* food that is heavy, filling, and usually fairly tasteless. — *verb* to stuff with food.

stodginess *noun* a stodgy quality.

stodgy *adj.* (**stodgier, stodgiest**) **1** of the nature of stodge. **2** boringly conventional or serious.

stoic *noun* **1** a stoical person. **2** *Philos.* see STOICS. [from Greek *Stoa Poikile*, Painted Porch, where Zeno taught]

stoical *adj.* **1** accepting suffering or misfortune uncomplainingly. **2** indifferent to both pain and pleasure.

stoically *adv.* in a stoical way, stoical.

stoichiometry *noun* *Chem.* the branch of chemistry that is concerned with the relative proportions in which atoms or molecules react together to form chemical compounds. [from Greek *stoicheion*, element]

stoicism *noun* **1** acceptance of suffering and misfortune. **2** (**Stoicism**) the philosophy of the Stoics.

Stoics philosophers belonging to a school of the Hellenistic-Roman age, founded by Zeno of Citium at the end of the 4c BC, and developed by Chrysippus, Seneca, Epictetus, and Marcus Aurelius. Like the Cynics, their philosophy developed in a period of insecurity in the Hellenistic world with the decline in power of the Greek city-states. Its main emphasis was on the development of self-sufficiency in the individual, whose duty was to conform only to the dictates of natural order to which all people belonged equally.

stoke *verb* (*often* **stoke up**) **1** to put coal or other fuel in (eg the furnace of a boiler). **2** to arouse or intensify (eg passion or enthusiasm). **3** *intrans. colloq.* to fill oneself with food. [from Dutch *stoken*]

stokehold *noun* the boiler room on a steamship.

Stoke-on-Trent POP (1992e) 253 000, an industrial city in Staffordshire, central England. It forms part of the Potteries urban area, lying on the R Trent, 217km/135mi NW of London. It is the largest clayware producer in the world. The potter Josiah Wedgwood and the novelist Arnold Bennett were born here in 1730 and 1867 respectively. NOTABLE FEATURE Wedgwood Museum at Barlaston (7km/4mi S).

Stoker, Bram (Abraham) (1847–1912) Irish writer, born in Dublin. He studied law and science, and partnered Henry Irving in running the Lyceum Theatre from 1878. He wrote several books, of which the best-known is the classic horror tale *Dracula* (1897).

stoker *noun* a person who stokes a furnace, especially on a steamship or steam train.

Stokes, Sir George Gabriel (1819–1903) Irish mathematician and physicist, born in Skreen, Sligo. Professor at Cambridge and Conservative MP for the University, he first used spectroscopy as a means of determining the chemical compositions of the Sun and stars, studied diffraction, identified X-rays as electromagnetic waves produced by sudden obstruction of cathode rays, and formulated 'Stokes' law' expressing the force opposing a small sphere in its passage through a viscous fluid.

Stokowski, Leopold (Antonin Stanislaw Bolesławawicz) (1882–1977) US conductor of Polish origin, born in London. He built up an international reputation as a conductor with the orchestras of Philadelphia (1912–36), New York (1946–50), and Houston (1955–60), and is also known for his music in such films as Walt Disney's *Fantasia* (1940). In 1962 he founded the American Symphony Orchestra in New York City.

STOL *abbrev.* Short Take-Off and Landing.

stole¹ see STEAL.

stole² — *noun* 1 a woman's scarf-like garment, often of fur, worn round the shoulders. 2 a scarf-like garment worn ceremonially by members of the clergy, with ends hanging down in front. [from Greek *stole*]

stolen see STEAL.

stolid *adj.* showing little or no interest or emotion; impassive. [from Latin *stolidus*, dull]

stolidity *or* **stolidness** *noun* being stolid.

stolidly *adv.* in a stolid way.

stolon *noun Bot.* a runner. [from Latin *stolo stolonis*, twig, sucker]

Stolypin, Peter Arkadyevich (1862–1911) Russian statesman, born in Dresden. Following service in the Ministry of the Interior (from 1884) he became Governor of Saratov province (1903–6), where he put down peasant uprisings and helped to suppress the revolutionary upheavals of 1905. As Prime Minister (1906–11), he introduced a series of agrarian reforms, which had only limited success. In 1907 he suspended the Second Duma (national assembly), and arbitrarily limited the franchise.

stoma *noun* (PL. **stomata**) 1 a small opening or pore in the surface of a living organism, eg a mouth-like opening in animals, or one of the tiny pores on the stems and undersurfaces of leaves in plants. 2 *Medicine* the opening that is made in the abdominal wall during a surgical operation such as a colostomy. See also STOMATA.

stomach — *noun* 1 the large sac-like organ situated between the oesophagus and the duodenum, into which food passes after it has been swallowed. It secretes gastric juice containing hydrochloric acid and the enzyme pepsin, which initiates protein digestion. Contractions of the muscular stomach walls reduce the partially digested food to a semiliquid mass. 2 *loosely* the area around the abdomen; the belly. 3 (**the stomach for something**) *colloq.* courage; determination: *do you have the stomach for a fight? / has no stomach for exercise.* — *verb* 1 *colloq.* to bear or put up with: *cannot stomach his arrogance.* 2 to digest (food) easily. [from Greek *stomachos*, from *stoma*, mouth]

stomach-ache *noun* a pain in the abdominal area, especially from indigestion.

stomach pump a device for drawing out stomach contents, usually a syringe with an attached tube passed down the throat.

stomata *pl. noun* 1 see STOMA. 2 *Bot.* the specialized pores present in large numbers on the aerial parts of a plant, particularly on the undersurface of the leaf. They allow the exchange of air and carbon dioxide between the plant and the surrounding atmosphere, and the loss of water vapour from the plant during the process of tran-

spiration. Each pore is surrounded by two *guard cells*, which control the opening and closing of the stomata in response to the general availability of water to the plant.

stomatal *adj.* relating to or in the region of a stoma.

stomp — *verb intrans.* to stamp or tread heavily. — *noun* a kind of lively jazz dancing with stamping movements. [see STAMP]

Stone, Sir (John) Richard (Nicholas) (1913–91) English economist, born in London. He was a government economist during World War II, Director of the Department of Applied Economics (1945–55), and then Professor of Economics (1955–80) at Cambridge. He was awarded the Nobel Prize for Economics in 1984 for his development of the complex models on which worldwide standardized national income reports are based.

stone — *noun* 1 the hard solid material of which rocks are made. 2 a small fragment of rock, eg a pebble. 3 a shaped piece of stone designed for a particular purpose, eg millstone. 4 a gemstone. 5 the hard seed of any of several fruits, eg peach. 6 a hard and often painful mass formed within the gall bladder, kidney, etc, and usually requiring surgical removal. 7 (PL. **stone**) a UK measure of weight equal to 14 pounds or 6.35 kilograms. 8 a dull light grey colour. — *verb* 1 to pelt with stones. 2 to remove the stone from (fruit). — *adv.* (*in compounds*) completely: *stone-deaf / stone-cold.*
— **leave no stone unturned** to try all possibilities or make every possible effort.
a stone's throw *colloq.* a short distance. [from Anglo-Saxon *stan*]

Stone Age *noun* the earliest period in human history, during which primitive tools and weapons were made of stone.

stonechat *noun* a small brownish European bird whose song is like two stones knocking together.

stone circle *Archaeol.* a near-circular or circular ring of prehistoric standing stones (or *henges*) of the late Neolithic and Early Bronze Age found in N Europe (particularly in Britain and Ireland). Their exact function is unkown, although they may have been temples in which celestial events, the passing of the seasons, and the fertility of the land and people could be celebrated.

stonecrop *noun* any of about 300 species of succulents, mostly perennials, of the genus *Sedum*, native to north temperate regions, and having fleshy leaves that may be very narrow or almost circular, and star-like flowers with five

petals, which are usually yellow, but sometimes white or red. Some species are popular ornamentals for rock gardens.

stone curlew a large wading bird like a plover, that nests on stony ground.

stoned *adj. slang* 1 under the influence of drugs. 2 very drunk.

Stonehenge a prehistoric sanctuary near Amesbury, S England, 130km/80mi W of London. It was in use c.3100–1100 BC, and was constructed in three phases: the first (c.2800 BC) consisted of a low bank and ditch of earth c.110m in diameter; the second (c.2100 BC), which no longer exists, consisted of a double ring of 80 pillars of S Wales bluestone; the third (c.2000 BC) is a 30m diameter lintelled circle and inner horseshoe of 80 dressed sarsen (sandstone) blocks, each weighing 20–50 tonnes. Alignment on the midsummer sunrise/midwinter sunset implies prehistoric use for seasonal festivals, but the association with the druids dates only from 1905, and has no historical basis. It is a World Heritage site.

stonemason *noun* a person skilled in shaping stone for building work.

Stone Mountain Memorial a memorial carving on the exposed face of Stonewall Mountain in NW Georgia, USA. The work, which was completed in 1972, depicts Confederate leaders Jefferson Davis, Robert E Lee, and 'Stonewall' Jackson.

stonewall *verb intrans.* to hold up progress intentionally, eg by obstructing discussion or by batting extremely defensively in cricket.

stoneware *noun* hard coarse pottery made of clay with a high silica content or of clay with flint mixed in.

stonewashed *adj., said of a fabric* given a faded appearance through the abrasive action of small pieces of pumice stone.

stonily *adv.* in a stony way.

stony *adj.* (**stonier, stoniest**) 1 covered with stones. 2 having a hard unfriendly or unfeeling appearance or quality: *stony-hearted.* 3 *colloq.* stony-broke.

stony-broke *adj. colloq.* having absolutely no money; penniless.

stood see STAND.

stooge *noun* 1 a performer serving to provide a comedian with opportunities for making jokes, often also the butt of the jokes. 2 an assistant, especially one given unpleasant tasks or otherwise exploited.

stool *noun* 1 a seat without a back. 2 a footstool. 3 a single piece of faeces.
— **fall between two stools** to lose two opportunities by hesitating between them or trying for both.
[from Anglo-Saxon *stol*]

stoolball *noun* an old-fashioned 11-a-side bat-and-ball game resembling cricket and rounders. The batter uses a wooden bat resembling a tennis racket to defend a wicket or stool (a wooden board 1.4m from the ground), which the underarm bowler attempts to hit. Runs are scored in a similar way to cricket.

stool-pigeon *noun* 1 a police informer. 2 a decoy bird, originally a pigeon stuck to a stool, used by a hunter to lure others.

stoop¹ — *verb intrans.* 1 to bend the upper body forward and down. 2 to walk with head and shoulders bent forward. 3 (**stoop to something**) to lower oneself to do it; to deign or condescend to do it. — *noun* a stooped posture. [from Anglo-Saxon *stupian*]

stoop² *noun North Amer., esp. US* an open porch; a veranda. [from Dutch *stoep*]

stoop³ see STOUP.

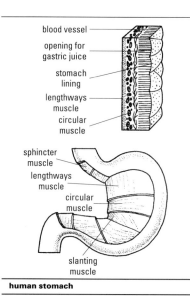

blood vessel
opening for gastric juice
stomach lining
lengthways muscle
circular muscle
sphincter muscle
lengthways muscle
circular muscle
slanting muscle

human stomach

Stonehenge

stop — *verb* (**stopped, stopping**) **1** *trans., intrans.* to bring or come to rest, a standstill or an end; to cease or cause to cease moving, operating, or progressing. **2** to prevent. **3** to withhold or keep back. **4** (*also* **stop something up**) to block, plug, or close it. **5** to deduct (money) from wages. **6** to instruct a bank not to honour (a cheque). **7** *colloq.* to stay or reside temporarily. **8** *Mus.* to adjust the vibrating length of (a string) by pressing down with a finger. **9** *slang* to receive (a blow). — *noun* **1** an act of stopping. **2** a place stopped at, eg on a bus route. **3** the state of being stopped; a standstill. **4** a device that prevents further movement. **5** a full stop. **6** a set of organ pipes of uniform tone; a keyboard knob that brings them all into use at once. **7** (*also* **f-stop**) any of a graded series of sizes that a camera's aperture can be adjusted to. **8** a speech sound made by suddenly releasing a build-up of air behind the lips, teeth, tongue, etc.
— **pull out all the stops** to make one's best effort.
put a stop to something *or* **someone** to cause them to end, especially abruptly.
stop at nothing to be prepared to do anything, no matter how unscrupulous, in order to achieve one's aim.
stop down to reduce the size of the aperture in a camera.
stop off *or* **over** to break one's journey.
[from Anglo-Saxon *stoppian*]

stopcock *noun* a valve controlling the flow of liquid in a pipe, operated by an external lever usually controlled by the level of the liquid in a cistern, etc.

Stopes, Marie Charlotte Carmichael (1880–1958) British pioneer advocate of birth control, suffragette, and palaeontologist, born in Edinburgh. In 1904 she became the first female science lecturer at Manchester. Alarmed at the unscientific way in which men and women embarked upon married life, she wrote a number of books on the subject, including *Married Love* (1918) which covers the subject of birth control. This work caused a storm of controversy. She later founded the first birth control clinic in N London (1921).

stopgap *noun* a temporary substitute.

stop-off *noun* a brief or temporary stop during a longer journey.

stop-over *noun* same as STOP-OFF.

stoppage *noun* **1** an act of stopping or the state of being stopped. **2** an amount deducted from wages. **3** a stopping of work, as in a strike.

Stoppard, Tom, originally **Tom Straussler** (1937–) British dramatist, born in Zlín, Czechoslovakia. His family moved to England in 1946 and he made his name with *Rosencrantz and Guildenstern are Dead* (1967). Other plays include the philosophical satire *Jumpers* (1972), *Travesties* (1974), and the romantic comedy, *The Real Thing* (1982). He has also written a novel, short stories, television plays, and film scripts.

stopper *noun* a cork, plug, or bung.

stop press 1 late news inserted into a newspaper after printing has begun, in a specially reserved space. **2** the space itself.

stopwatch *noun* a watch for accurate recording of elapsed time, used for timing races, etc.

storage *noun* **1** the act of storing or the state of being stored. **2** space used for storing things. **3** the process of storing information in a computer's memory.

storage device *Comput.* any piece of computer equipment, such as a magnetic disk, on which data may be stored.

storage heater an electric heater consisting of a casing enclosing a stack of bricks with a high heat capacity. It accumulates and stores heat, usually overnight during off-peak periods, and then slowly releases it by convection to the surrounding air during the daytime.

store — *noun* **1** a supply kept in reserve. **2** a shop, especially when large and one of a chain. **3** (*also* **stores**) a place where stocks or supplies are kept, eg a warehouse. **4** a computer's memory. — *verb* **1** to put aside for future use. **2** (*also* **store something up**) to build up a reserve supply of it. **3** to put something (eg furniture) into a warehouse for temporary safekeeping. **4** to put into a computer's memory.
— **in store 1** kept in reserve; ready to be supplied. **2** destined to happen; imminent.
set *or* **lay store by something** to value something (especially a quality or attribute) highly.
[from Latin *instaurare*, to provide or restore]

storehouse *noun* a place where things are stored.

Storey, David (Malcolm) (1933–) English novelist and playwright, born in Wakefield, Yorkshire. His plays include *The Contractor* (1969), *The Changing Room* (1972), and *Life Class* (1974), which is set in an art college. His first novel *This Sporting Life* (1960) is set in the world of rugby league. Other novels, including *Saville* (1976, Booker Prize), use autobiographical material from his South Yorkshire mining background, as does the play *In Celebration* (1969). His poems *Storey's Lives* were published in 1992.

storey *noun* (PL. **storeys**) a level, floor, or tier of a building. [from Latin *historia*, picture, story, from the pictures with which medieval windows were decorated]

stork

stork *noun* **1** any of various species of large wading bird, related to the heron, with long legs, a long bill and neck, and usually with loose black and white plumage, mostly found near water in warm regions of the world. In folklore the white stork is associated with childbirth. **2** (**the stork**) this bird as the imaginary bringer of babies. [from Anglo-Saxon *storc*]

storm — *noun* **1** an outbreak of violent weather, with severe winds and heavy falls of rain, hail, or snow, often with thunder and lightning. **2** a violent reaction, outburst or show of feeling. **3** a furious burst, eg of gunfire or applause. — *verb* **1** *intrans.* to go or come loudly and angrily. **2** to say or shout angrily. **3** *Mil.* to make a sudden violent attack on.
— **a storm in a teacup** *colloq.* much fuss about something unimportant.
take someone *or* **something by storm 1** to enthral or captivate them totally and instantly. **2** *Mil.* to capture a place by storming.
[from Anglo-Saxon *storm*]

Stormberg, Battle of one of the battles (1899) in the 'black week' when the British suffered several reverses during the Boer War. They were defeated while attempting to take an important railway junction to the south of the Orange R, one of the keys to Bloemfontein.

storm centre 1 the centre of a storm, where air pressure is lowest. **2** any focus of trouble or controversy.

storm door a second outer door, giving extra protection from bad weather.

Stormont a suburb of E Belfast and site of a castle which housed the seat of government in Northern Ireland (1921–72). The Northern Ireland parliament, created by the Government of Ireland Act 1920, comprised a Senate and a House of Commons, both dominated by Protestants. It had jurisdiction over domestic affairs in the province until suspended by the Northern Ireland (Temporary Provisions) Act, 1972, which established direct rule from Westminster.

storm petrel see PETREL.

stormtrooper *noun* **1** a soldier trained in methods of sudden violent attack. **2** *Hist.* a member of a branch of the Nazi army with a terrorist function.

stormy *adj.* (**stormier, stormiest**) **1** affected by storms or high winds. **2** violent; passionate: *a stormy relationship*.

Stornoway POP (1981) 8 600, the port capital of Western Isles Region, NW Scotland, situated on the E coast of the island of Lewis. NOTABLE FEATURES An Lanntair Art Gallery; Museum Nan Eilean Steornabhagh.

story *noun* (PL. **stories**) **1** a written or spoken description of an event or series of events, real or imaginary. **2** (*also* **short story**) a piece of fiction much shorter than a novel, usually published as one of a collection. **3** the plot of a novel, play, or film. **4** a news article. **5** *colloq.* a lie.
— **the story goes that** ... it is widely said or believed that ...
[from Latin *historia*]

storyline *noun* the plot of a novel, play, or film.

stoup *or* **stoop** *noun* a basin for holy water. [from Norse *staup*]

Stourbridge POP (1981) 56 000, a town in Dudley borough, West Midlands, central England. It lies on the R Stour, 16km/10mi SW of Birmingham.

stout — *adj.* **1** rather fat. **2** hard-wearing; robust. **3** courageous; steadfastly reliable. — *noun* dark beer with a strong malt flavour. [from Dutch *stout*]

stout-hearted *adj.* courageous; steadfastly reliable.

stoutly *adv.* in a stout way.

stoutness *noun* being stout.

stove¹ *noun* **1** a domestic cooker. **2** any cooking or heating apparatus, eg an industrial kiln. [from Anglo-Saxon *stofa*]

stove² see STAVE.

stow *verb* (*often* **stow away**) **1** to pack or store, especially out of sight. **2** *intrans.* to hide on a ship, aircraft, or vehicle in the hope of travelling free. [from Anglo-Saxon *stow*, place]

stowage *noun* **1** a place for stowing things. **2** a charge made for stowing goods.

stowaway — *noun* a person who stows away on a ship, etc. — *adj.* **1** travelling as a stowaway. **2** able to be folded up and carried or stored easily.

Stowe, Harriet (Elizabeth) Beecher (1811–96) US novelist, born in Litchfield, Connecticut. She became a teacher, and in 1836 married a professor of theology and settled in Brunswick, Maine. She became famous through her novel, *Uncle Tom's Cabin* (1852), which immediately focused anti-slavery sentiment in the North. Her other novels include *Dred* (1856) and *The Minister's Wooing* (1859), and she also wrote essays and poems.

STP *abbrev.* standard temperature and pressure.

Strabane, Gaelic **An Srath Ban** POP (1991) 12 000, a market town in Strabane district, Co Tyrone, W Northern Ireland. An Irish border town, it lies where the Mourne and Finn rivers meet to form the R Foyle.

strabismus *noun Medicine* a squint. [from Greek *strabismos*]

Strabo (c.60 BC–after AD 21) Greek geographer and historian, born in Amasia in Pontus, Asia Minor. He visited Greece and Egypt, and seems to have settled in Rome after AD 14. Only a few fragments remain of his 47-volume historical work, but his *Geographica* in 17 books has survived almost complete, and provides extensive observations on the Mediterranean area, as well as copious references to previous writers.

Strachey, (Giles) Lytton (1880–1932) English biographer, born in London. He lived in London, and became a member of the Bloomsbury group of writers and artists. He began his writing career as a critic, but turned to biography and became famous with his *Eminent Victorians* (1918), which radically altered the nature of the genre. Later works include *Queen Victoria* (1921) and *Elizabeth and Essex* (1928).

straddle *verb* **1** to stand or sit with one leg or part on either side of. **2** to part (the legs) widely. **3** *colloq.* to adopt a neutral or non-committal attitude towards. [related to STRIDE]

Stradivari *or* **Stradivarius, Antonio** (c.1644–1737) Italian violin maker, born in Cremona. A pupil of Niccolo Amati, he experimented with the design of string instruments and perfected the Cremona type of violin, assisted by his sons Franceso (1671–1743) and Omobono (1679–1742). It is thought that he made over 1 000 violins, violas, and violoncellos, of which around 650 still exist.

strafe *verb* to attack with heavy machine-gun fire from a low-flying aircraft. [from German *strafen*, to punish]

Strafford, Thomas Wentworth, 1st Earl of (1593–1641) English statesman, born in London. He entered parliament in 1614 and served with the Opposition (1625–8), but after being appointed President of the North (1628), he supported Charles I. As Lord Deputy of Ireland from 1632 he imposed firm rule, and in 1639 he became the King's principal adviser, but after failing to suppress the rebellion in Scotland (Bishop's Wars 1639–40), he was impeached by the Long Parliament. Despite a famous defence at Westminster, he was executed on Tower Hill.

straggle *verb intrans.* **1** to grow or spread untidily. **2** to lag behind or stray from the main group or course.

straggler *noun* a person who trails along behind.

straggly *adj.* (**stragglier, straggliest**) straggling.

straight — *adj.* **1** not curved, bent, curly, or wavy. **2** without deviations or detours; direct. **3** level; not sloping, leaning, or twisted. **4** frank;

open; direct. **5** respectable; not dishonest, disreputable, or criminal. **6** neat; tidy. **7** successive; in a row. **8** *said of a drink, especially alcoholic* undiluted; neat. **9** with all debts and favours paid back. **10** not comic; serious. **11** *colloq.* conventional in tastes and opinions. **12** *slang* heterosexual. — *adv.* **1** in or into a straight line, position, or posture. **2** following an undeviating course; directly. **3** immediately. **4** honestly; frankly. — *noun* **1** a straight line or part, eg of a race track. **2** *slang* a heterosexual person. **3** *Cards* a running sequence of five cards, irrespective of suit.

— **go straight** *colloq.* to renounce criminal activities and live an honest life.

the straight and narrow an honest, respectable, sober way of life.

straight away immediately.

straight up *colloq.* honestly; really.

[from Anglo-Saxon *streht*, from *streccan*, to stretch]

straighten *verb* (**straightened, straightening**) (*often* **straighten out** *or* **up**) **1** *trans., intrans.* to make or become straight. **2** to resolve, disentangle, or put into order.

straight face an unsmiling face hiding a desire to laugh.

straight fight a contest in which there are only two candidates or sides.

straightforward *adj.* **1** without difficulties or complications; simple. **2** honest and frank.

straight man a comedian's stooge.

strain¹ — *verb* **1** to injure or weaken (oneself or a part of one's body) through over-exertion. **2** *intrans.* to make violent efforts. **3** to make extreme use of or demands on. **4** to pass through or pour into a sieve or colander. **5** (**strain something off**) to remove it by the use of a sieve or colander. **6** to stretch or draw tight. **7** (**strain at something**) to tug it forcefully. **8** *intrans.* to feel or show reluctance or disgust; to balk. — *noun* **1** an injury caused by over-exertion, especially a wrenching of the muscles. **2** an extreme or excessive effort made by, or demand made on, the mind or the body. **3** the fatigue resulting from such an effort. **4** an absence of friendliness and openness; tension. **5** *Physics* a measure of the deformation of an object when it is subjected to stress. It is equal to the change in dimension, eg change in length, divided by the original dimension, eg original length. **6** (*also* **strains**) a melody or tune, or a snatch of one. **7** one's tone in speech or writing. [from Old French *estraindre*, from Latin *stringere*, to stretch tight]

strain² *noun* **1** a group of animals (especially farm livestock), or plants (especially crops), that is artificially maintained by inbreeding, etc, in order to retain certain desirable characteristics. **2** a group of bacteria or viruses of the same species that possess a particular characteristic that distinguishes them from other such groups of the same species. **3** an element of a person's character, especially when inherited. [from Anglo-Saxon *streon*, a begetting]

strained *adj.* **1** *said of an action, a person's manner, etc* not natural or easy; forced. **2** *said of an atmosphere* not friendly or relaxed; tense.

strainer *noun* a sieve or colander.

strait — *noun* **1** (*often* **straits**) a narrow strip of water that links two larger areas of ocean or sea. **2** (**straits**) difficulty; hardship: *dire straits.* — *adj. old use* narrow; strict. [from Old French *estreit*, from Latin *stringere*, to draw tight]

straitened *adj.*

— **in straitened circumstances** having very little money or assets.

straitjacket *noun* **1** a jacket used to restrain the arms of a person with violent tendencies, with long sleeves crossed at the chest and tied behind. **2** a thing that prevents freedom of development or expression.

strait-laced *adj.* strictly correct in moral behaviour and attitudes; prudish or puritanical.

Straits Settlements the name given to the former British Crown Colony which consisted of Singapore, Malacca, the Dindings, Penang, and Province Wellesley. All became part of Malaysia in 1963, and Singapore became independent in 1965.

strand¹ — *verb* **1** to run (a ship) aground. **2** to leave in a helpless position, eg without transport. — *noun literary* a shore or beach. [from Anglo-Saxon *strand*, seashore]

strand² *noun* **1** a single thread, fibre, length of hair, etc, whether alone or twisted or plaited with others to form a rope, cord, or braid. **2** a single element or component part.

strange *adj.* **1** not known or experienced before; unfamiliar or alien. **2** not usual, ordinary, or predictable; difficult to explain or understand; odd. **3** vaguely ill or ill at ease. [from Latin *extraneus*, foreign]

strangely *adv.* in a strange way; as a strange circumstance.

strangeness *noun* a strange quality.

stranger *noun* **1** a person whom one does not know. **2** a person from a different place, home town, family, etc. **3** (**a stranger to something**) a person unfamiliar with or inexperienced in something (usually an experience).

Strangers and Brothers an 11-volume novel sequence by C P Snow, which starts with the novel *George Passant* (originally called *Strangers and Brothers*, 1940). The sequence covers more than 30 years in the life of the narrator, barrister Lewis Eliot. Other volumes include *The Masters* (1951), *The Corridors of Power* (1964), and *Last Things* (1970).

Strangford Lough an inlet of the North Channel, E Northern Ireland, separated from the sea to the E by the Ards Peninsula. Its narrow entrance at the S is c.1km/0.8mi wide and 8km/5mi long. The inlet itself is 27km/17mi long and 6km/4mi wide with several islands.

strangle *verb* **1** to kill or attempt to kill by squeezing the throat with the hands, a cord, etc. **2** to hold back or suppress (eg a scream or laughter). **3** to hinder or stop the development or expression of. [from Latin *strangulare*]

stranglehold *noun* **1** a choking hold in wrestling. **2** a position of total control; a severely repressive influence.

strangler *noun* a person who strangles.

strangulate *verb* **1** *Medicine* to press or squeeze so as to stop the flow of blood or air. **2** to strangle. [see STRANGLE]

strangulation *noun* being strangled.

Stranraer POP (1981) 11 000, the port capital of Wigtown district, Dumfries and Galloway, SW Scotland. It lies at the head of Loch Ryan and is an important ferry port for crossings between Scotland and Northern Ireland. NOTABLE FEATURE Wigtown District Museum.

Strap the loyal and generous friend of Roderick in Tobias Smollett's *Roderick Random.*

strap — *noun* **1** a narrow strip of leather or fabric by which a thing is hung, carried, or fastened. **2** (*also* **shoulder strap**) either of a pair of strips of fabric by which a garment hangs from the shoulders. **3** a leather belt used to give a beating as punishment; (**the strap**) such a beating. **4** a hanging loop providing a hand-hold for a standing passenger on a bus or train. — *verb* (**strapped, strapping**) **1** (**strap someone** *or* **something in** *or* **up**) to fasten or bind them with a strap or straps. **2** to beat with a strap. [a dialect form of STROP]

strapped *adj.* (**strapped for something**) *colloq.* short of something (especially cash).

strapping *adj.* tall and strong-looking.

Strasberg, Lee (1901–82) US theatre director, actor, and teacher, born in Budzanow, Austria. He gained a reputation with the Theatre Guild of New York and in 1931 helped to form the Group Theatre, with which he evolved a technique (influenced by Stanislavsky) which became known everywhere as 'the Method'. He exercised great influence as director of the Actors Studio (1949–82), and his pupils included Marlon Brando, Ann Bancroft, and Paul Newman. See also METHOD.

Strasbourg, German **Strassburg**, ancient **Argentoratum** POP (1990) 389 000, the industrial and commercial capital of Alsace region and of Bas-Rhin department, NE France. It lies on the R Ill, W of its junction with the R Rhine. Strasbourg is the sixth-largest city in France and the country's largest river port. HISTORY part of a bishopric since 1003, it became a free imperial city in the 13c; in the 15c printing was developed here by Gutenberg; ceded to France in 1697; taken by Germany in 1871; returned to France in 1918. It is, today, the seat of the Council of Europe, the European Parliament, the European Commission of Human Rights, and the European Science Foundation. Strasbourg is the main tourist centre in Alsace and the venue of numerous conferences. NOTABLE FEATURES Gothic Cathedral of Notre-Dame (begun in 1015–it has a noted 14c astronomical clock); Château des Rohan (1728–42); old town hall; Palais de l'Europe (1972–7); La Petite France (16c quarter of old Strasbourg).

strata see STRATUM.

stratagem *noun* a trick or plan, especially one for deceiving an enemy or gaining an advantage. [from Greek *strategema*, act of generalship]

strategic *adj.* **1** relating to strategy or a strategy. **2** *said of weapons* designed for a direct long-range attack on an enemy's homeland, rather than for close-range battlefield use.

strategically *adv.* in a strategic way.

Strategic Arms Limitation Talks (ABBREV. **SALT**) the name given to two rounds of talks held between the USA and USSR to limit their nuclear weapons arsenals and slow down the arms race. The first began in Helsinki in 1969, and an agreement (SALT I) was reached in 1972, the year SALT II talks began, which reached an agreement in 1979. However the USSR's refusal to allow on-site verification led to a hardening of attitudes in the West, and after the Soviet invasion of Afghanistan, US ratification of SALT II (1979) was doomed. Nevertheless, both countries initially kept to the limitations established; the arms situation was ultimately transformed by the Reagan–Gorbachev arms reduction accord, the revolutions of 1989, and the break-up of the USSR in 1991.

Strategic Arms Reduction Talks (ABBREV. **START**) discussions held between the USA and the USSR, which began in 1982–3 after President Reagan came to power and resumed after Mikhail Gorbachev became General Secretary in 1985. Their aim was to reduce the number of long-range missiles and their nuclear warheads. Agreements were reached on the abolition of intermediate-range nuclear missiles in 1987 (the INF Treaty) and on conventional forces in Europe in 1990 (the CFE Treaty). President Bush agreed the START I Treaty with President Gorbachev in 1991 and the START II Treaty with President Boris Yeltsin in 1993. The two powers agreed to cut their long-range nuclear capability by two thirds within 10 years.

strategic capability *Politics* the capability of states with long-range nuclear missiles and aircraft to make war or carry out reprisals. Various categories include first-strike capability, second-strike capability, and the ability to carry out a pre-emptive strike.

Strategic Defence Initiative (ABBREV. **SDI**) also called **Star Wars** a military pro-gramme introduced in 1983 by US President Ronald Reagan. Its purpose was to provide a defence system (based on satellite, laser, and high-energy particle technology) for the destruction of hostile ballistic missiles when the latter were still in the atmosphere after launch. Research into SDI was carried out in various countries including the UK and the former USSR. The programme was scrapped in 1993 by President Bill Clinton; it had cost in total c.30 billion dollars. A scaled-down version of it was introduced, named the Ballistic Missile Defence Programme.

strategic studies the academic study of the military, political, economic, and technological factors which affect the relations between nations. It reviews the continuous process of military relations between nations in war and peace, and has risen to particular prominence in the age of nuclear weapons (compare MILITARY SCIENCE).

strategist *noun* a person skilled in strategy.

strategy *noun* (PL. **strategies**) **1** the process of, or skill in, planning and conducting a military campaign. **2** a long-term plan for future success or development. [from Greek *strategia*, from *stratos*, army + *agein*, to lead]

Stratford-upon-Avon POP (1981) 22 000, a town in Stratford-upon-Avon district in Warwickshire, central England. It lies on the R Avon, 13km/8mi SW of Warwick. The dramatist and poet William Shakespeare was born here in 1564. NOTABLE FEATURES Royal Shakespeare Theatre (season Apr–Jan); Shakespeare's birthplace; Anne Hathaway's Cottage; Holy Trinity Church (where Shakespeare and his wife are buried).

strath *noun* *Scot.* a broad flat valley. [from Gaelic *srath*]

Strathclyde POP (1992e) 2.3m, a region in W and central Scotland, divided into 19 districts. It is bounded by Highland Region in the N, Central Region in the NE, Lothian and Borders in the E, Dumfries and Galloway in the S, and by the Atlantic Ocean in the W. AREA 13 537sq km/ 5 225sq mi. PHYSICAL DESCRIPTION it encloses the basin of the R Clyde; to the N of the Clyde there are lochs, mountains, and islands (notably Mull, Jura, Islay, and Arran); the lower part of the Clyde comprises Glasgow and Clydeside, the industrial centre of Scotland, containing c.50% of the country's population; part of the Southern Uplands lies to the S of the Clyde. CAPITAL Glasgow. CHIEF TOWNS Paisley, Motherwell, Greenock, Airdrie, Dumbarton, Hamilton, East Kilbride, Coatbridge, Kilmarnock.

strathspey *noun* (PL. **strathspeys**) a Scottish folk dance similar to but slower than the reel, or a piece of music for it. [from *Strathspey* (the valley of the River Spey) in Scotland]

stratification *noun* **1** the formation of strata. **2** a stratified condition.

stratify *verb* (**stratifies, stratified**) **1** *Geol.* to deposit (rock) in layers or strata. **2** to classify or arrange into different grades, levels, or social classes. [from Latin *stratum* (see STRATUM) + *facere*, to make]

stratigraphy *noun* *Geol.* the branch of geology concerned with the origin, composition, and age of rock strata, especially sedimentary rocks, and the sequence in which they have been laid down. It has important applications in prospecting for minerals, especially petroleum, and the interpretation of archaeological excavations.

Strato *or* **Straton of Lampsacus** (d.c.269 BC) Greek philosopher, the third head of the school which Aristotle founded. His writings are lost, but he seems to have worked mainly to revise Aristotle's physical doctrines, denying any role to theological explanations in nature.

stratosphere *noun* *Meteorol.* the layer of the Earth's atmosphere that extends from about 12km to about 50km above the Earth's surface, and contains the ozone layer. It lacks clouds and winds, and its temperature remains relatively constant. [from STRATUM + -*sphere* as in ATMOSPHERE]

stratospheric *adj.* of or in the stratosphere.

Stratton, Charles (Sherwood), also called **Tom Thumb** (1838–83) American midget showman, born in Bridgeport, Connecticut. He stopped growing at six months, and stayed 63cm/25in until his teens, eventually reaching 101cm/40in. He was exhibited in Barnum's American Museum from the age of five, under the name of General Tom Thumb, and became famous throughout the USA and Europe.

stratum *noun* (PL. **strata**) **1** a layer of sedimentary rock. **2** a layer of cells in living tissue. **3** a layer of the atmosphere or the ocean. **4** a level, grade, or social class. [from Latin *stratum*, something spread]

stratus *noun* (PL. **strati**) *Meteorol.* a wide horizontal sheet of low grey layered cloud. [see STRATUM]

Strauss, Johann, known as **the Elder** (1804–49) Austrian violinist, conductor, and composer, born in Vienna. He founded with Josef Lanner the Viennese Waltz tradition, and toured widely in Europe with his own orchestra. He composed several marches, notably the *Radetzky* (1848), and numerous waltzes, but was eclipsed by his son Johann 'the Younger'.

Strauss, Johann, known as **the Younger**, and **Johann Strauss II** (1825–99) Austrian violinist, conductor, and composer, born in Vienna, the son of Johann Strauss 'the Elder'. He studied law, but turned to music and toured with his own orchestra. He wrote over 400 waltzes, notably *The Blue Danube* (1867) and *Tales from the Vienna Woods* (1868), as well as polkas, marches, several operettas, including *Die Fledermaus* (1874), and the concert piece *Perpetuum Mobile*. His brothers Josef (1827–70) and Eduard (1835–1916) were conductors and Josef also composed waltzes.

Strauss, Richard (1864–1949) German composer, born in Munich. He began to compose at the age of six, and his first publications date from 1875. He held many posts as conductor, but is best known for his symphonic poems, such as *Till Eulenspiegels lustige Streiche* (Till Eulenspiegel's Merry Pranks, 1894–5), *Also sprach Zarathustra* (Thus Spoke Zarathustra, 1895–6), and *Ein Heldenleben* (A Hero's Life, 1897–8), and his operas, notably *Der Rosenkavalier* (1911) and *Ariadne auf Naxos* (Ariadne on Naxos, 1912). He also wrote concertos, songs, and several small-scale orchestral works.

Stravinsky, Igor (Fyodorovich) (1882–1971) Russian-born US composer, born in Oranienbaum, near St Petersburg. He studied law, but then turned to musical composition under Rimsky-Korsakov and made his name with his music for the Diaghilev ballets *The Firebird* (1910), *Petrushka* (1911), and *The Rite of Spring* (1913). Essentially an experimenter, he later concentrated on Neoclassicism, as in his ballet *Pulcinella* (1920), based on Pergolesi, the opera-oratorio *Oedipus Rex* (1927), and the choral *Symphony of Psalms* (1930). Other major compositions include the *Symphony in C major* (1940), the opera *The Rake's Progress* (1951), and *Requiem Canticles* (1966), in which he adopted serialism.

straw *noun* **1** the dried cut stems and leaves of cereal crops that remain after removal of the grains by threshing. Straw may be ploughed back into the soil, burned as stubble, or used as litter or feedstuff for animal livestock. It is also used for thatching, and woven into hats, baskets, etc. **2** a single stalk. **3** a thin hollow tube for sucking up a drink. **4** a pale yellow colour.

— **clutch at straws** to resort in desperation to an alternative that is unlikely to succeed.

the last straw the last in a whole series of disagreeable incidents, breaking one's tolerance or resistance.

the short straw the worst of all possible outcomes or options.
[from Anglo-Saxon *streaw*]

strawberry *noun* (PL. **strawberries**) **1** a trailing perennial plant of the genus *Fragaria*, that produces white flowers and propagates by means of runners or stolons. It is widely cultivated in temperate regions for its edible fruit. **2** the juicy red 'fruit' of this plant, which consists of tiny pips or *achenes* (the true fruits) embedded in the surface of a swollen fleshy receptacle. It may be eaten raw, preserved by canning or freezing, or used to make jam. It is also used as a flavouring in confectionery. **3** the flavour or colour of the fruit. [from Anglo-Saxon *streawberige*, perhaps from the straw-like appearance of the plant stem]

strawberry blonde *noun* a woman with reddish-blonde hair.

strawberry mark a reddish birthmark.

straw poll *or* **straw vote** an unofficial vote, especially taken on the spot, to get some idea of general opinion.

stray — *verb intrans.* **1** to wander away from the right path or place, usually unintentionally. **2** to move away unintentionally from the main or current topic in thought, speech, or writing. **3** to depart from an accepted or required pattern of moral behaviour. — *noun* a lost or homeless pet or child. — *adj.* not the result of a regular or intended process; random; casual. [from Old French *estraier*, to wander]

streak — *noun* **1** a long irregular stripe or band. **2** a flash of lightning. **3** an element or characteristic: *a cowardly streak*. **4** a short period; a spell: *a lucky streak*. **5** *colloq.* a naked dash through a public place. — *verb* **1** to mark with a streak or streaks. **2** *intrans.* to move at great speed; to dash. **3** *intrans. colloq.* to make a dash naked through a public place. [from Anglo-Saxon *strica*, stroke]

streaked *adj.* having streaks.

streaker *noun colloq.* a person who makes a naked dash in public (see STREAK *verb* 3).

streakiness *noun* a streaky quality.

streaky *adj.* (**streakier, streakiest**) **1** marked with streaks. **2** *said of bacon* with alternate layers of fat and meat.

stream — *noun* **1** a very narrow river; a brook or rivulet. **2** any constant flow of water or other liquid. **3** a continuously moving line or mass, eg of vehicles. **4** an uninterrupted burst or succession, eg of insults. **5** general direction, trend, or tendency. **6** any of several groups into which school pupils are broadly divided according to ability, subdivided into classes. — *verb* **1** *intrans.* to flow or move continuously and in large quantities or numbers. **2** *intrans.* to float or trail in the wind. **3** to divide (pupils) into streams. [from Anglo-Saxon *stream*]

streamer *noun* **1** a long paper ribbon used to decorate a room. **2** a roll of coloured paper that uncoils when thrown. **3** a long thin flag.

streaming *noun* the placing of children into higher or lower groups or classes according to their general ability. In the UK, it was general practice before the introduction of comprehensive education, and is being reintroduced in some schools, particularly at secondary level.

streamline *verb* to make streamlined.

streamlined *adj.* **1** *said of a vehicle, aircraft, or vessel* shaped so as to move smoothly and efficiently with minimum resistance to air or water. **2** *said of an organization, process, etc* extremely efficient, with little or no waste of resources, excess staff, unnecessary steps, etc.

streamlining *noun* **1** a condition of air or fluid flow such that no turbulence occurs. **2** the design of machinery or apparatus so that its shape creates a minimum of turbulence, either when moving (as in motor cars and aircraft), or when static

(as in fixed structures that stand in a flow of air or water). **3** the refining of any system to optimize efficiency.

stream of consciousness **1** the continuous succession of thoughts and feelings that form an individual's conscious experience. **2** a narrative style which imitates this, as in James Joyce's *Ulysses*.

Streep, Meryl, originally **Mary Louise Streep** (1949–) US actress, born in Baking Ridge, New Jersey. She acted on Broadway before her film début in *Julia* (1977). Since then she has gained Academy Awards for *Kramer Vs Kramer* (1979) and *Sophie's Choice* (1982), and critical acclaim for *The French Lieutenant's Woman* (1981), *Out of Africa* (1985), and *Postcards From The Edge* (1986).

street *noun* **1** a public road, especially one in a town with pavements and buildings at the side or sides. **2** the road and the buildings together. **3** the people in the buildings or on the pavements: *tell the whole street*.

on the street *or* **streets** *colloq.* **1** homeless. **2** practising prostitution, especially soliciting.
streets ahead of someone *or* **something** *colloq.* much more advanced than or superior to them.
up someone's street *colloq.* suited to their tastes or abilities.
walk the streets **1** to walk from street to street. **2** to solicit as a prostitute on the street.
[from Anglo-Saxon *stræt*]

streetcar *noun North Amer., esp. US* a tram.

Streetcar Named Desire, A **1** a play by Tennessee Williams (1947, Pulitzer Prize). Set in a New Orleans slum, it depicts the fiercely antagonistic relationship between the neurotic Southern belle Blanche Du Bois and her surly brother-in-law Stanley Kowalski. **2** a US film directed by Elia Kazan (1951), based on the play, starring Vivien Leigh and Marlon Brando.

street credibility (*also colloq.* **street cred**) popularity with or acceptability from fashionable urban society.

street hockey a form of hockey played on roller skates, first popularized in the USA, and now also played in the UK. It is so called because it was first played by children on street corners, although it is now generally played in enclosed areas, such as playgrounds.

streetwalker *noun colloq.* a prostitute who solicits.

streetwise *adj. colloq.* experienced in, and able to survive, the ruthlessness of urban life.

Streicher, Julius (1885–1946) German journalist and politician, born in Fleinhausen. He was associated with Hitler in the early days of Nazism, and took part in the 1923 putsch. A ruthless persecutor of the Jews, he incited anti-Semitism through the newspaper *Der Stürmer*, which he founded and edited. He was hanged at Nuremberg as a war criminal.

Streisand, Barbra, originally **Barbara Joan Streisand** (1942–) US actress and singer, born in New York City. Starting as a nightclub singer, stage and television appearances brought her the lead in the Broadway show *Funny Girl*, which she repeated in the 1968 film version to win an Oscar. Her film comedies and musicals include *Hello, Dolly!* (1969), *What's Up Doc?* (1972), and *A Star is Born* (1976), for which she won a Best Song Oscar. She directed and acted in *Yentl* (1983) and *Prince of Tides* (1991).

strength *noun* **1** the quality or degree of being physically or mentally strong. **2** the ability to withstand pressure or force. **3** degree or intensity, eg of emotion or light. **4** potency, eg of a drug or alcoholic drink. **5** forcefulness of an argument. **6** a highly valued quality or asset. **7** the number of people, etc needed or normally expected in a group, especially in comparison to those actually present or available: *with the workforce only at half strength*.

— **go from strength to strength** to achieve a series of successes each surpassing the last.
on the strength of something on the basis of it; judging by it.
[from Anglo-Saxon *strengthu*]

strengthen *verb trans., intrans.* (**strengthened, strengthening**) to make or become stronger.

strenuosity *or* **strenuousness** *noun* being strenuous.

strenuous *adj.* requiring, or performed with, great effort or energy. [from Latin *strenuus*]

strenuously *adv.* in a strenuous way.

streptococcus *noun* (PL. **streptococci**) **1** (**Streptococcus**) *Biol.* a genus of non-motile spherical bacteria that occur in pairs or chains. **2** any bacterium of this genus, which includes many harmless species, as well as serious pathogens of humans and animals that cause conditions such as scarlet fever and pneumonia. [from Greek *streptos*, twisted + *kokkos*, berry]

streptomycin *noun* an antibiotic used to treat various bacterial infections. [from Greek *streptos*, twisted + *mykes*, fungus]

Stresemann, Gustav (1878–1929) German politician, born in Berlin. Having entered the Reichstag in 1907 as a National Liberal, he became Leader of the Party, and later founded and led its successor, the German People's Party. He was Chancellor of the new German (Weimar) Republic (1923), then Minister of Foreign Affairs (1923–9). Pursuing a policy of conciliation, he helped to negotiate the Locarno Pact (1925) and secured the entry of Germany into the League of Nations (1926). He shared the 1926 Nobel Peace Prize with Aristide Briand.

stress — *noun* **1** physical or mental overexertion. **2** *Physics* the force exerted per unit area on a body that tends to cause that body to deform. **3** a physical or emotional reaction, or both, to a mentally or emotionally demanding event or situation (eg bereavement or overwork) that has a harmful effect on the general health and functioning of the body. Some physical disorders are worsened, if not caused by, mental stress, eg stomach ulcer, eczema, migraine, certain allergies. **4** importance, emphasis, or weight laid on or attached to something. **5** emphasis on a particular syllable or word. — *verb* **1** to emphasize or attach importance to. **2** to pronounce with emphasis. **3** to subject to mental or physical stress. [a shortening of DISTRESS]

stressful *adj.* affected by or causing stress.

stress-mark *noun* a mark used to indicate stress.

stretch — *verb* **1** *trans., intrans.* to make or become temporarily or permanently longer or wider by pulling or drawing out. **2** *intrans.* to extend in space or time. **3** (*also* **stretch out** *or* **stretch something out**) to straighten and extend the body or part of the body, eg when waking or reaching out. **4** *trans., intrans.* to make or become tight or taut. **5** (*also* **stretch something out**) to lay it out at full length. **6** *intrans.* to be extendable without breaking. **7** *trans., intrans.* to last or cause to last longer through economical use. **8** (*also* **stretch something out**) to prolong it. **9** to make extreme demands on or severely test (eg resources or physical abilities). **10** to exaggerate (the truth). — *noun* **1** an act of stretching, especially (a part of) the body. **2** a period of time; a spell. **3** an expanse, eg of land or water. **4** capacity to extend and expand. **5** a straight part on a race-track or course. **6** *colloq.* a difficult task or test: *will be a bit of a stretch*. **7** *slang* a term of imprisonment.

— **at a stretch** **1** continuously; without interruption. **2** with difficulty.
stretch a point to agree to something not strictly in keeping with the rules; to bend the rules.

stretch one's legs to take a short walk to invigorate oneself after inactivity. [from Anglo-Saxon *streccan*]

stretcher *noun* a length of canvas or other sheeting with poles attached, for carrying a sick or wounded person in a lying position.

stretcher-bearer *noun* a person who carries a stretcher.

stretchiness *noun* a stretchy quality.

stretchy *adj.* (**stretchier, stretchiest**) *said of materials* able or tending to stretch.

Strether, Lambert the conscientious editor sent to Paris to bring home Chad Newsome in Henry James's *The Ambassadors*.

strew *verb* (PAST TENSE **strewed**; PAST PARTICIPLE **strewed, strewn**) 1 to scatter untidily: *papers were strewn across the floor*. 2 to cover with an untidy scattering: *the floor was strewn with papers*. [from Anglo-Saxon *streowian*]

strewth *interj. old colloq. use* an expression of surprise or annoyance. [from *God's truth*]

stria *noun* (PL. **striae**) *Geol., Biol.* any of a series of parallel grooves in rock, or furrows or streaks of colour in plants and animals. [from Latin *stria*, furrow]

striated *adj.* marked with striae, striped.

striated muscle *Anat.* a voluntary muscle.

striation *noun* marking with striae.

stricken *adj.* deeply affected, especially by grief or disease. [an old past participle of STRIKE]

strict *adj.* 1 demanding obedience or close observance of rules; severe. 2 *said of instructions, etc* that must be closely obeyed. 3 observing rules or practices very closely: *strict Catholics*. 4 exact; precise: *the strict sense of the word*. 5 complete: *in the strictest confidence*. [from Latin *stringere*, to tighten]

strictly *adv.* 1 with a strict manner. 2 (*also* **strictly speaking**) as a strict interpretation: *they have, strictly, broken the law*.

strictness *noun* being strict.

stricture *noun* 1 a severe criticism. 2 *Medicine* abnormal narrowing of a passage. [see STRICT]

stride — *noun* 1 a single long step in walking. 2 the length of such a step. 3 a way of walking in long steps. 4 (*usually* **strides**) a measure of progress or development: *make great strides*. 5 a rhythm, eg in working, aimed for or settled into: *put me off my stride*. 6 (**strides**) *slang* trousers. — *verb* (PAST TENSE **strode**; PAST PARTICIPLE **stridden**) 1 *intrans.* to walk with long steps. 2 *intrans.* to take a long step. 3 to step or extend over. — **take something in one's stride** to achieve it or cope with it effortlessly, as if part of a regular routine. [from Anglo-Saxon *stridan*]

stridency *noun* a strident quality.

strident *adj.* 1 *said of a sound, especially a voice* loud and harsh. 2 forcefully assertive; compelling. [from Latin *stridere*, to creak]

stridently *adv.* in a strident way.

strife *noun* 1 bitter conflict or fighting. 2 *colloq.* trouble of any sort; hassle. [from Old French *estrif*]

strigil *noun* 1 in ancient Greece and Rome, a scraper used to clean the skin after bathing. 2 in bees, a mechanism for cleaning the antennae. [from Latin *strigilis*]

strike — *verb* (PAST TENSE AND PAST PARTICIPLE **struck**) 1 to hit; to give a blow to; to come or bring into heavy contact with. 2 to make a particular impression on (someone): *they struck me as a strange couple*. 3 to come into the mind of; to occur to. 4 to cause (a match) to ignite through friction. 5 (*usually* **strike at someone** *or* **something**) to attempt to hit them. 6 *trans., intrans.*

said of a clock to indicate the hours, half-hours, and quarter-hours with chimes. 7 *intrans.* to happen suddenly: *disaster struck*. 8 *intrans.* to make a sudden attack. 9 to afflict suddenly; to cause to become by affliction: *struck dumb*. 10 to introduce or inject suddenly: *the thought struck terror into them*. 11 to arrive at or settle (eg a bargain or a balance). 12 to find a source of (eg oil). 13 (**strike on something**) to come upon or arrive at something (especially an idea) by chance. 14 *intrans.* to stop working as part of a collective protest against an employer. 15 to dismantle (a camp). 16 to make (a coin) by stamping metal. 17 to adopt (a posture or attitude). 18 to lower (a flag). 19 *trans., intrans.* to draw (a line) in order to cross something out. — *noun* 1 an act of hitting or dealing a blow. 2 a usually collective on-going refusal to work, as a protest against an employer. 3 a prolonged refusal to engage in a regular or expected activity, eg eating, as a protest. 4 a military attack, especially by aircraft. 5 a discovery of a mineral source, eg gold. 6 the knocking down of all pins with a single ball in tenpin bowling. 7 *Cricket* the position of being the batsman bowled at: *take strike*. 8 *Baseball* a ball swung at but missed by the batter. — **on strike** taking part in an industrial or other strike.

strike it lucky *or* **rich** to enjoy luck or become rich suddenly and unexpectedly.

strike something *or* **someone off** to remove their name from a professional register, eg of doctors, because of misconduct.

strike out 1 to aim blows wildly. 2 to set out determinedly on a journey or effort. 3 *Baseball* to be dismissed by means of three strikes (see STRIKE *noun* 8).

strike someone out *Baseball* to dismiss a batter by means of three strikes (see STRIKE *noun* 8).

strike something out to cross it out or efface it.

strike up *said of a band, etc* to begin to play.

strike something up to start something (especially a conversation or friendship). [from Anglo-Saxon *strican*]

◇ An official strike is one which has been formally agreed by the members of a trade union, whereas an unofficial strike occurs where action is taken by employees without the formal support of the union. Since the passing of the Trade Union Act (1984), unions in the UK are required to hold a secret ballot of members before strike action is formally declared.

strike-breaker *noun* a person who continues to work while others strike, or who is brought in to do the job of a striking worker.

strike pay an allowance paid by a trade union to a member on strike.

striker *noun* 1 a worker taking part in a strike. 2 *Football* a player with an attacking role.

striking *adj.* 1 impressive or arresting. 2 noticeable; marked. 3 on strike.

Strindberg, (Johan) August (1849–1912) Swedish dramatist and novelist, born in Stockholm. He first achieved fame with the novel *The Red Room* (Röda Rummet, 1879), followed by several plays and collections of short stories. His plays *The Father* (Fadren, 1887) and *Miss Julie* (Fröken Julie, 1888) showed him to be an important exponent of naturalistic drama. Later plays were more symbolic in form and religious in theme.

string — *noun* 1 thin cord, or a piece of this. 2 any of a set of pieces of stretched wire, catgut, or other material vibrated to produce sound in various musical instruments. 3 (**strings**) the orchestral instruments in which sound is produced in this way, usually the violins, violas, cellos, and double basses collectively; also used of the players. 4 a set of things, eg pearls threaded together. 5 a series or succession. 6 (**strings**) undesirable conditions or limitations: *no strings attached*. 7 any cord-like thing, eg a nerve or tendon. — *verb* (PAST TENSE AND PAST PARTICIPLE

strung) 1 to fit or provide with a string or strings. 2 to tie with string. 3 to thread (eg beads) on a string. 4 to remove the stringy parts from (eg a bean pod). 5 (*also* **string out**) to extend in a string.

— **pull strings** *colloq.* to use one's influence, or relationships with influential people, to get something done.

pull the strings *colloq.* to be the ultimate, although not usually apparent, controller of a situation or person.

string someone along to keep them in a state of deception or false hope.

string along with someone to go along with them for company.

string something out to extend or stretch it in a long line.

string someone up *colloq.* to kill them by hanging.

string something up to hang, stretch, or tie it with string, or as if with string. [from Anglo-Saxon *streng*]

stringency *noun* being stringent.

stringent *adj.* 1 *said of rules, terms, etc* severe; rigorous; strictly enforced. 2 marked by a lack of money. [from Latin *stringere*, to draw together]

stringently *adv.* in a stringent way.

stringer *noun* 1 a horizontal beam in a framework. 2 a journalist employed part-time to cover a particular town or area.

stringiness *noun* a stringy quality.

stringy *adj.* (**stringier, stringiest**) 1 like string, especially thin and thread-like. 2 *said of meat or other food* full of chewy fibres.

strip — *noun* 1 a long narrow piece. 2 a lightweight uniform worn by members of a sports team. 3 a striptease performance. — *verb* (**stripped, stripping**) 1 (*also* **strip something off**) to remove it by peeling or pulling off; to remove the surface or contents of something in this way. 2 (**strip someone of something**) to divest or dispossess them of something (eg property or dignity). 3 to remove the clothes of. 4 *intrans.* (*also* **strip off**) to take one's clothes off. 5 (*also* **strip something down**) to take it completely to pieces; to dismantle it. [from Anglo-Saxon *strypan*]

strip cartoon a sequence of drawings, eg in a newspaper, telling a comic or adventure story.

strip club a club in which striptease artistes perform.

stripe — *noun* 1 a band of colour. 2 a chevron or coloured band on a uniform, indicating rank. — *verb* to mark with stripes. [from Old Dutch *stripe*]

striped *adj.* having or marked with stripes.

strip light *or* **strip lighting** a light or lighting using tube-shaped fluorescent lamps.

stripling *noun literary* a boy or youth. [a diminutive of STRIP]

stripper *noun* 1 a striptease artiste. 2 a substance or appliance for removing paint, varnish, etc.

strip search a thorough search of the body of a person who has been made to take off his or her clothes, to check for concealed drugs or smuggled items.

strip-search *verb* to search (a person's naked body).

striptease *noun* an entertainment in which a person undresses to music in a slow and sexually exciting way.

stripy *adj.* (**stripier, stripiest**) marked with stripes; striped.

strive *verb intrans.* (PAST TENSE **strove**; PAST PARTICIPLE **striven**) 1 to try extremely hard; to struggle. 2 to contend; to be in conflict. [from Old French *estriver*]

strobe noun **1** same as STROBE LIGHTING. **2** a stroboscope. [from Greek *strobos*, whirling]

strobe lighting equipment for producing a powerful rapidly flashing light which, directed on a moving body, creates an effect of jerky movement, widely used in discotheques, etc.

strobilus noun *Bot.* a conical reproductive structure composed of spore-bearing leaves, known as *sporophylls*, occurring in cone-bearing plants (eg pine and other conifers) and horsetails. — Also called *cone*. [from Greek *strobile*, a conical plug of lint, *strobilos*, a spinning top, whirl, pine cone]

strobo-flash noun photographic recording of a moving object by a series of brief exposures at regular intervals using sequential electronic flash lighting during the period when the camera shutter is open. In cinematography, strobe-lighting with electronic flash sychronized to the camera frame rate produces sharp images of fast moving subjects.

stroboscope noun an instrument that uses a flashing light (strobe light) to measure or set the speed of rotating shafts, propellers, etc When the speed of the strobe light is equal to that of the rotating object, the latter appears to be stationary. Stroboscopes are used to set the ignition timing of car engines. [from Greek *strobos*, whirling + -SCOPE]

strode see STRIDE.

Stroessner, Alfredo (1912–) Paraguayan dictator, born in Encarnación. He took up a military career, fought in the Chaco War, and became President (1954–89). He was re-elected at regular intervals, but forced to stand down after a coup, when he went into exile in Brazil.

stroke — noun **1** an act of striking; the way a thing is struck, especially the technique used in striking a ball in sport. **2** a single movement with a pen, paintbrush, etc, or the line or daub produced. **3** a single complete movement in a repeated series, as in swimming or rowing. **4** the total linear distance travelled by a piston in the cylinder of an engine. **5** a particular named style of swimming. **6** the striking of a clock, or its sound. **7** a gentle caress or other touching movement. **8** (**stroke of**) an act or occurrence that reveals the presence of something, eg genius or luck. **9** a sloping line used to separate alternatives in writing or print; a solidus. **10** a sudden interruption to the supply of blood to the brain, caused by thrombosis (formation of a blood clot in an artery), embolism (a detached clot circulating in the bloodstream), or haemorrhage (the rupture of a blood vessel in or leading to the brain). It causes a sudden loss of consciousness, often resulting in paralysis of one side of the body, which may be temporary or permanent, and is often accompanied by loss of speech. Stroke is one of the major causes of death worldwide. **11** *colloq.* the least amount of work: *not done a stroke all day.* — verb **1** to caress in kindness or affection, often repeatedly. **2** to strike (a ball) smoothly and with seeming effortlessness. — **at a stroke** with a single action. **on the stroke of** ... precisely at (a particular time). [from Anglo-Saxon *strac*]

stroll — verb *intrans.* to walk in a slow leisurely way. — noun a leisurely walk. [perhaps from German *strolchen*, from *Strolch*, tramp]

Strong, Sir Roy (Colin) (1935–) English art historian and museum director, born in London. He became assistant keeper at the National Portrait Gallery, London, in 1959, and its Director in 1967. He was Director of the Victoria and Albert Museum (1974–87).

strong adj. **1** exerting or capable of great force or power. **2** able to withstand rough treatment; robust. **3** *said of views, etc* firmly held or boldly expressed. **4** *said of taste, light, etc* sharply felt or experienced; intense; powerful. **5** *said of coffee,* alcoholic drink, etc relatively undiluted with water or other liquid; concentrated. **6** *said of an argument* having much force; convincing. **7** (**strong on something**) excelling in it; well-skilled or versed in it. **8** *said of language* bold or straightforward; rude or offensive. **9** *said of prices, values, etc* steady or rising. **10** *said of a syllable* stressed. **11** *said of a group, etc* numbering so many: *a gang fifty strong.*
— **come on strong** *colloq.* to be strongly, often disconcertingly, persuasive or assertive.
going strong *colloq.* flourishing; thriving. [from Anglo-Saxon *strang*]

strongarm — adj. *colloq.* **1** aggressively forceful. **2** making use of physical violence or threats. — verb to compel with aggressive forcefulness or threats of violence.

strongbox noun a safe, or other sturdy lockable box for storing money or valuables.

stronghold noun **1** a fortified place of defence, eg a castle. **2** a place where there is strong support (eg for a political party).

strongly adv. **1** in a strong way. **2** to a strong degree: *strongly flavoured.*

strong point a feature or attribute in which a person excels.

strongroom noun a room in which valuables or prisoners are held for safekeeping, designed to be difficult to penetrate.

strong verb in English, German, etc, an irregular verb with different vowels in different tenses, as *sing, sang, sung* and *write, wrote, written.*

strontium noun *Chem.* (SYMBOL **Sr**, ATOMIC NUMBER **38**) a soft silvery-white highly reactive metal that is a good conductor of electricity. It is used in certain alloys, and as a 'getter' for removing traces of gas from vacuum tubes. Its compounds burn with a bright red flame and are used in flares and fireworks. The radioactive isotope strontium-90 occurs in radioactive fallout, and is a recognized health hazard because it becomes incorporated into bone. [from the name *Strontian* in Scotland, where it was discovered]

strop — noun a strip of coarse leather or other abrasive material on which razors are sharpened. — verb (**stropped, stropping**) to sharpen (a razor) on a strop. [from Latin *struppus*, thong]

stroppy adj. (**stroppier, stroppiest**) *colloq.* quarrelsome, bad-tempered, and awkward to deal with. [probably from OBSTREPEROUS]

Stroud POP (1981) 38 000, a market town in Stroud district, Gloucestershire, SW central England. It lies on the R Frome, 13km/8mi S of Gloucester.

strove see STRIVE.

struck past tense and past participle of STRIKE. — **struck on someone** or **something** *colloq.* infatuated with them; enthusiastic about them.

structural adj. of or relating to structure, or a basic structure or framework.

structural formula *Chem.* a formula that is used to represent the exact arrangement of the atoms within a molecule of a chemical compound, as well as its composition.

structuralism noun an approach to various areas of study, eg literary criticism and linguistics, which seeks to identify underlying patterns or structures, especially as they might reflect patterns of behaviour or thought in society as a whole.

structuralist — noun a person who believes in structuralism. — adj. relating to or characterized by structuralism.

structurally adv. in a structural way; as regards structure.

structure — noun **1** the way in which the parts of a thing are arranged or organized. **2** a thing built or constructed from many smaller parts. — verb to put into an organized form or arrangement. [from Latin *structura*, from *struere*, to build]

strudel noun a baked roll of thin pastry with a filling of fruit, especially apple. [from German *strudel*, whirlpool, from the rolling]

struggle — verb *intrans.* **1** to move the body around violently in an attempt to get free. **2** to strive vigorously or make a strenuous effort under difficult conditions. **3** to make one's way with great difficulty. **4** to fight or contend. — noun **1** an act of struggling. **2** a task requiring strenuous effort. **3** a fight or contest. [from Middle English *strogelen*]

strum — verb *trans., intrans.* (**strummed, strumming**) to play (a stringed musical instrument, or a tune on it) with sweeps of the fingers or thumb rather than with precise plucking. — noun an act or bout of strumming.

strumpet noun *old use* a prostitute, or a woman who engages in casual sex.

strung see STRING.

strut¹ — verb *intrans.* (**strutted, strutting**) to walk in a proud or self-important way. — noun a strutting way of walking. [from Anglo-Saxon *strutian*]

strut² noun a bar or rod used to support weight or take pressure; a prop.

strychnine noun a deadly poison obtained from the seeds of a tropical Indian tree, used medicinally in small quantities as a nerve stimulant. [from Greek *strychnos*, nightshade]

Stuart or **Stewart, House of** a Scottish royal family commencing with Robert I (reigned 1371–90) which succeeded to the English throne in 1603 with the accession of James VI and I, the cousin of Elizabeth I, and the great-grandson of Henry VIII's sister Margaret. The Stuart line ended with the death of Queen Anne (1714), although a pretender laid claim to the throne as late as 1745.

Stuart or **Stewart, Prince Charles Edward (Louis Philip Casimir)**, also called **the Young Pretender**, and **Bonnie Prince Charlie** (1720–88) claimant to the British Crown, born in Rome, the son of James Edward Stuart, and the focus of Jacobite hopes. In 1744 he went to France to head the planned invasion of England, but after the defeat of the French fleet he was unable to leave for over a year. He landed with seven followers at Eriskay in the Hebrides (Jul 1745) and raised his father's standard at Glenfinnan, proclaiming him as James VIII of Scotland and III of England. The clansmen flocked to him, Edinburgh surrendered, and he kept court at Holyrood. Following victory over the government forces at Prestonpans, he invaded England, but turned back at Derby and was routed at Culloden Moor (1746) by the Duke of Cumberland, who ruthlessly suppressed the rising. Charles was hunted for five months before, with the help of Flora Macdonald and disguised as her maid 'Betty Burke', he crossed from Benbecula to Portree. He landed in Brittany, then lived in France and Italy, where (after his father's death in 1766) he assumed the title of Charles III of Great Britain.

Stuart or **Stewart, Prince James (Francis Edward)**, also called **the Old Pretender** (1688–1766) claimant to the British throne, the only son of James II and VII and his second wife Mary of Modena, born in London. As a baby he was taken to St Germain, and proclaimed successor on his father's death (1701). After failing to land in Scotland in 1708, he served with the French in the Low Countries. In 1715 he landed at Peterhead during the Jacobite rising, but left Scotland some weeks later and lived thereafter mainly in Rome.

Stuart see ALICE SPRINGS.

Stuart a male first name, after the surname. [the French form of the name *Stewart*; related to STEWARD]

stub — *noun* **1** a short piece, eg of a cigarette or a pencil, left after the rest has been used up. **2** the part of a cheque or ticket kept by the issuer as a record. — *verb* (**stubbed, stubbing**) **1** to accidentally bump the end of (one's toe) against a hard surface. **2** (*also* **stub something out**) to extinguish a cigarette or cigar by pressing the end against a surface. [from Anglo-Saxon *stubb*]

Stubai Alps, German **Stubaier Alpen** a mountain range of the E Alps in Tirol state, W Austria. The range rises to 3 507m at Zuckerhütl. It has numerous glaciers.

Stubb the easy-going, careless second mate on the *Pequod*, in Herman Melville's *Moby Dick*.

stubbiness *noun* being stubby.

stubble *noun* **1** the mass of short stalks left in the ground after a crop has been harvested. **2** a short early growth of beard. [from Old French *estuble*]

stubbly *adj.* **1** characterized by or having stubble. **2** of the nature of stubble.

stubborn *adj.* **1** resolutely or unreasonably unwilling to change one's plans or opinions; obstinate. **2** determined; unyielding. **3** difficult to treat, remove, or deal with: *stubborn stains*.

stubbornly *adv.* in a stubborn way.

stubbornness *noun* being stubborn.

Stubbs, George (1724–1806) English anatomist, painter, and engraver, born in Liverpool. He specialized in horses, and is best known for his book the *Anatomy of the Horse* (1766), which is illustrated by his own engravings. His paintings include many of horses and sporting life.

stubby *adj.* (**stubbier, stubbiest**) short and broad or thick-set.

STUC *abbrev.* Scottish Trades Union Congress.

stucco — *noun* (PL. **stuccos, stuccoes**) any kind of plaster or cement used for coating, or moulding decorative shapes on to, outside walls. — *verb* (**stuccos** or **stuccoes, stuccoed** or **stucco'd**) to coat with or mould out of stucco. [from Italian *stucco*, from Old German *stucchi*, coating]

stuck past tense and past participle of STICK[2].
— **be stuck for something** *colloq.* to be in need of it or at a loss for it.
be stuck with someone or **something** to be unable to get rid of an unwelcome person or thing.
get stuck in *slang* to set about an activity with energy or aggression.
stuck on someone *colloq.* fond of or infatuated with them.

stuck-up *adj. colloq.* snobbish; conceited.

stud[1] — *noun* **1** a rivet-like metal knob fitted on to a surface, eg of a garment, for decoration. **2** any of several knob-like projections on the sole of a sports boot, giving added grip. **3** a fastener,

House of Stuart	
1371–90	Robert II
1390–1406	Robert III
1406–37	James I
1437–60	James II
1460–88	James III
1488–1513	James IV
1513–42	James V
1542–67	Mary, Queen of Scots
1567–1625	James VI of Scotland
	(as James I of England, 1603–25)
1625–49	Charles I
1649–59	Commonwealth and Protectorate
1660–85	Charles II
1685–8	James VII and II
1689–1702	William III
	(joint ruler, with Mary, 1689–94)
1702–14	Anne

eg fixing a collar to a shirt, consisting of two small discs on either end of a short bar or shank. **4** a press stud. — *verb* (**studded, studding**) **1** to fasten or decorate with a stud or studs. **2** (**be studded with something**) to be covered with a dense scattering of it. [from Anglo-Saxon *studu*, post]

stud[2] *noun* **1** a male animal, especially a horse, kept for breeding. **2** (*also* **stud farm**) a place where animals, especially horses, are bred. **3** a collection of animals kept for breeding. **4** *colloq.* stud poker. **5** *slang* a man who has or claims great sexual energy and prowess.
— **at stud** or **out to stud** kept for breeding purposes.
[from Anglo-Saxon *stod*]

Studenica Monastery a Serbian monastery, founded in 1183 near Usće. The complex includes several churches noted for their medieval frescoes. It is a World Heritage site.

student *noun* **1** a person following a formal course of study, especially in further education. **2** (**a student of something**) a person with an informed interest in a subject. [from Latin *studere*, to be zealous]

Students for a Democratic Society (ABBREV. **SDS**) a radical splinter group of the movement opposed to US involvement in Vietnam, founded at Columbia University, New York City. It advocated social disruption and violence, and spread to over 200 universities, but was subject to factionalism. Two of its members were sentenced in the Chicago Conspiracy Trial of 1969.

studied *adj.*, *said of an attitude, expression, etc* carefully practised and adopted or produced for effect; unspontaneous and affected.

studio *noun* (PL. **studios**) **1** the workroom of an artist or photographer. **2** a room in which music recordings, cinema films, or television or radio programmes are made. **3** (**studios**) the premises of a company making any of these. [from Italian; see STUDY]

studio couch a couch, often backless, that converts into a bed.

studio flat a small flat with one main room acting as living, eating, sleeping, and often cooking area.

studious *adj.* **1** having a serious, hard-working approach to study. **2** painstaking or painstakingly carried out. [see STUDY]

studiously *adv.* in a studious way.

studiousness *noun* being studious.

stud poker a form of poker in which bets are placed on hands in which some of the cards are laid face up.

study — *verb* (**studies, studied**) **1** *trans., intrans.* to devote oneself to the gaining of knowledge of (a subject); to take an educational course in (a subject). **2** to look at or examine closely, or think about carefully. — *noun* (PL. **studies**) **1** the act or process of studying. **2** (**studies**) work done in the process of acquiring knowledge. **3** a careful and detailed examination or consideration: *undertook a careful study of the problem*. **4** a work of art produced for the sake of practice, or in preparation for a more complex or detailed work. **5** a piece of music intended to exercise and develop the player's technique. **6** a private room where quiet work or study is carried out. [from Latin *studere*, to be zealous, from *studium*, zeal]

study skills the ability to study effectively and to use and develop skills, such as effective reading (how to skim, scan, slow down at important stages, make notes, use an index, etc), information gathering and the proper use of library and resource centre facilities, revision techniques, and an understanding of one's own learning strategies.

stuff — *noun* **1** any material or substance. **2** luggage or equipment; belongings. **3** *literary*

matter; essence: *the very stuff of life*. **4** *old use* cloth, especially woollen. — *verb* **1** to fill the hollow or hollowed-out part of (eg a chicken or pepper) with a seasoned mixture of other foods. **2** to fill to capacity or over. **3** to cram or thrust into something. **4** to fill out the disembodied skin of (an animal) to recreate its living shape. **5** to feed (oneself) gluttonously. **6** (*also* **stuff something up**) to block something (eg a hole, or the nose with mucus). **7** *slang* to defeat overwhelmingly. **8** *slang* to dispose of (something angrily rejected) however one wishes: *you can stuff your job!* **9** *offensive slang* to have sexual intercourse with (a woman).
— **do one's stuff** *colloq.* **1** to display one's talent or skill. **2** to perform the task required of one.
get stuffed! *coarse slang* an expression of anger or contemptuous dismissal.
know one's stuff *colloq.* to have a thorough knowledge of the subject with which one is concerned.
[from Old French *estoffe*]

stuffed shirt *derog. colloq.* a conservative or pompous person.

stuffily *adv.* in a stuffy way.

stuffiness *noun* being stuffy.

stuffing *noun* **1** padding used to stuff children's toys, cushions, animal skins, etc. **2** a seasoned mixture of foods with which another item of food is stuffed.
— **knock the stuffing out of someone** *said of an arduous task, etc* to deprive them rapidly of strength or force; to exhaust them.

stuffy *adj.* (**stuffier, stuffiest**) **1** lacking fresh, cool air; badly ventilated. **2** *colloq.* pompous. **3** *colloq.* boringly formal, conventional, or unadventurous; staid.

stultify *verb* (**stultifies, stultified**) **1** to make (eg efforts) appear useless or foolish. **2** to dull the mind of, eg with tedious tasks. [from Latin *stultus*, foolish + *facere*, to make]

stultifying *adj.* that stultifies.

stumble — *verb intrans.* **1** to lose one's balance and pitch forwards after accidentally catching or misplacing one's foot. **2** to walk unsteadily. **3** to speak with frequent hesitations and mistakes. **4** to make a mistake in speech or action. — *noun* an act of stumbling.
— **stumble across** or **on something** to find or encounter it by chance.
[from Middle English *stomble*]

stumbling-block *noun* **1** an obstacle or difficulty. **2** a cause of failure or faltering.

stump — *noun* **1** the part of a felled or fallen tree left in the ground. **2** the short part of anything, eg a limb, left after the larger part has been removed. **3** *Cricket* any of the three thin vertical wooden posts forming the wicket; (**stumps**) the whole wicket, including the bails. — *verb* **1** to baffle or perplex. **2** *intrans.* to walk stiffly and unsteadily, or heavily and noisily. **3** *Cricket* to dismiss (a batsman stepping wholly beyond the crease) by disturbing the wicket with the ball.
— **stump up** *colloq.* to pay up.
[from Middle English *stumpe*]

stumpiness *noun* being stumpy.

stumpy *adj.* (**stumpier, stumpiest**) short and thick.

stun *verb* (**stunned, stunning**) **1** to make unconscious, eg by a blow to the head. **2** to make unable to speak or think clearly, eg through shock. **3** *colloq.* to impress greatly; to astound. [from Old French *estoner*, to astonish]

stung see STING.

stunk see STINK.

stunner *noun colloq.* a person or thing of overwhelming beauty or attractiveness.

stunning *adj. colloq.* **1** outstandingly beautiful. **2** extremely impressive.

stunningly *adv.* in a stunning way.

stunt[1] *verb* to prevent (growth or development) to the full, or prevent the full growth or development of. [from Anglo-Saxon *stunt*, dull, stupid]

stunt[2] *noun* **1** a daring act or spectacular event intended to show off talent or attract publicity. **2** a dangerous or acrobatic feat performed as part of the action of a film or television programme.

stunted *adj.* dwarfed, under-developed.

stuntman *or* **stuntwoman** *noun* a person hired to take the place of an actor when stunts are being filmed.

stupa *noun* an Indian cairn or mound originally constructed over the ashes of an emperor or some other great person, such as the Buddha. Later they were used to house the ashes of Buddhist monks and holy relics. [from Sanskrit *stūpa*]

stupefaction *noun* stupefying or being stupefied.

stupefy *verb* (**stupefies**, **stupefied**) **1** to make senseless, eg with drugs or alcohol. **2** to amaze or astound. **3** to confuse or bewilder. [from Latin *stupere*, to be struck senseless + *facere*, to make]

stupefying *adj.* that stupefies.

stupendous *adj.* **1** astounding. **2** *colloq.* astoundingly huge or excellent. [from Latin *stupere*, to be stunned]

stupendously *adv.* in a stupendous way.

stupid *adj.* **1** having or showing a lack of common sense, or a slowness to understand. **2** made senseless or stupefied, eg with drugs. **3** *colloq.* trivial; unimportant. [from Latin *stupidus*, senseless]

stupidity *noun* a stupid state or condition; extreme foolishness.

stupidly *adv.* in a stupid way.

stupor *noun* a state of near-unconsciousness in which there is little or no response to external stimuli. It is usually caused by drugs, alcohol, etc. [from Latin *stupor*, insensibility]

sturdily *adv.* in a sturdy way.

sturdiness *noun* being sturdy.

sturdy *adj.* (**sturdier**, **sturdiest**) **1** *said of limbs, etc* thick and strong-looking. **2** strongly built; robust. **3** healthy; vigorous; hardy. [from Old French *estourdi*, stunned]

sturgeon *noun* a large long-snouted fish of northern seas, from which caviar is obtained. [from Old French *sturgeon*]

sturgeon

Sturm, Der (The Storm) an art magazine (1910–32) and (Galerie Der Sturm) an art gallery (1912–24) founded in Berlin by Herwarth Walden (1878–1941). They were used to promote avant-garde art in Germany (eg the works of the Blaue Reiter group).

Sturm und Drang a revolutionary literary movement in late-18c Germany, which rejected classical values in favour of subjective feeling and artistic creativity. An important tributary of the Romantic movement, its main proponents were Goethe, Schiller, and Herder. [German, = storm and stress]

Sturtevant, Alfred Henry (1891–1970) US geneticist, born in Jacksonville, Illinois. He produced the first chromosome map of the fruit-fly *Drosophila* in 1911, and did much to establish the basis for the chromosomal theory of heredity. From 1928 he was professor at the California Institute of Technology.

stutter — *noun* **1** an inability to utter, without hesitation, certain speech sounds especially at the beginnings of words, resulting in repetition of the sounds; a stammer. **2** the resulting repetition. — *verb trans., intrans.* (**stuttered, stuttering**) to speak or say with a stutter. [from obsolete *stut*]

Stuttgart POP (1991e) 576 000, the capital of Baden-Württemberg state, Germany. It lies on the R Neckar, 61km/38mi SE of Karlsruhe, and is part of a major fruit and wine area. HISTORY founded in the 10c; former capital of the kingdom of Württemberg and seat of the Reichstag National Assembly; badly bombed during World War II. The philosopher Georg Hegel was born here in 1770. NOTABLE FEATURES castle (originally 13c, much of it is rebuilt); palace (18c); St Leonard's Church (15c); Stiftskirche (12c); Liederhall; mineral springs.

Stuyvesant, Peter (1592–1672) Dutch administrator, born in Scherpenzeel. He joined the Dutch West India Company, was made Governor of Curaçao, and then directed the colony of New Netherland (1647–64). He proved a vigorous but arbitrary ruler, a rigid Sabbatarian (observer of the Sabbath), and an opponent of political and religious freedom, but did much for the commercial prosperity of New Amsterdam (later New York City) until his reluctant surrender to the English (1664).

STV *abbrev.* **1** Scottish Television. **2** single transferable vote (a method of voting for proportional representation).

sty[1] *noun* (PL. **sties**) a pen in which pigs are kept. [from Anglo-Saxon *stig*, pen, hall]

sty[2] *or* **stye** *noun* (PL. **sties, styes**) a tiny swelling on the eyelid, at the base of the lash. [from Anglo-Saxon *stigan*, to rise]

style — *noun* **1** a manner or way of doing something, eg writing, speaking, painting, or designing buildings. **2** a distinctive manner that characterizes a particular author, painter, filmmaker, etc. **3** kind; type; make. **4** a striking quality, often elegance or lavishness, considered desirable or admirable: *she dresses with style*. **5** the state of being fashionable: *gone out of style*. **6** a pointed tool used for engraving. **7** *Bot.* in a flower, the often elongated part of the carpel that connects the stigma to the ovary. — *verb* **1** to design, shape, or groom in a particular way. **2** to name or designate: *a self-styled expert*. [from Latin *stilus*, writing tool, literary style]

stylish *adj.* elegant; fashionable.

stylishly *adv.* in a stylish way.

stylist *noun* **1** a trained hairdresser. **2** a writer, artist, etc who pays a lot of attention to style.

stylistic *adj.* relating to artistic or literary style.

stylistically *adv.* in a stylistic way; as regards style.

stylistics *sing. noun* Linguistics the systematic study of style, ranging from features of language which can be identified with an individual (eg Shakespeare's style, Joyce's style), to those which identify major occupation groups (eg legal style, journalistic style), and those characteristic of speakers and writers in particular situations (eg parliamentary style).

stylize *or* **stylise** *verb* to give a distinctive or elaborate style to, especially creating an impression of unnaturalness.

stylized *or* **stylised** *adj.* conventionalized, not naturalistic.

stylobate *noun Archit.* a continuous platform of masonry supporting a row of columns. Greek Doric columns had no pedestal and were built on a stepped stylobate. [from Greek *stylobates*, from *stylos* a column, + *bates*, from *bainein*, to walk, tread]

stylometry *or* **stylometrics** *sing. noun* a method of studying literary style by means of a statistical analysis of a text. Such studies have an

important function in plotting historical changes in style, and in investigating questions of disputed authorship. [from Greek *stylos*, style + *metron*, a measure]

stylus *noun* (PL. **styluses, styli**) **1** the needle-like part on the end of the arm of a record-player, that picks up the sound from the record's grooves. **2** the cutting tool used to produce the grooves in a record. [related to STYLE]

stymie — *verb* (**stymies, stymied, stymieing** *or* **stymying**) to prevent, thwart, or frustrate. — *noun* (PL. **stymies**) **1** *Golf* a situation in which an opponent's ball blocks the path between one's own ball and the hole, possible before the introduction of markers. **2** any tricky situation.

styptic *Medicine* — *noun* any substance that is used to stop or prevent bleeding, either by causing the blood vessels to contract, or by accelerating the clotting of the blood. It is used to treat minor cuts, as well as bleeding disorders such as haemophilia. — *adj., said of a substance* having an astringent action. [from Greek *styptikos*, contracting]

Styx in Greek mythology, the principal river of the Underworld, which was so terrible that the gods in Homer swore strict oaths by it. The souls of the dead were ferried across it by Charon. It was also the name of a river in Arcadia.

SU *abbrev.* Scripture Union.

suave *adj.* **1** polite and charming, especially insincerely so. **2** *loosely* smart and fashionable. [from Latin *suavis*, sweet]

suavely *adv.* with a suave manner.

suavity *noun* being suave; suave behaviour.

sub *colloq.* — *noun* **1** a submarine. **2** a substitute player. **3** (*also* **subs**) a subscription fee. **4** a small loan or an advance payment of wages, to help one subsist. **5** a subeditor. — *verb* (**subbed, subbing**) **1** *intrans.* to act as a substitute. **2** *trans., intrans.* to subedit or work as a subeditor.

sub- *prefix* forming words meaning: **1** under or below: *submarine*. **2** secondary; lower in rank or importance: *sublieutenant*. **3** imperfectly; less than: *subhuman*. **4** a part or division of: *subcommittee*. [from Latin *sub*, under, near]

subaltern *noun* any army officer below the rank of captain. [from Latin *subalternus*, from *sub*, under + *alter*, another]

subaqua *adj.* of, for, or for use in underwater activities. [from SUB- + Latin *aqua*, water]

subatomic *adj.* **1** smaller than an atom. **2** existing or occurring within an atom.

subatomic particle *Physics* a general term for any particle that is smaller than an atom, eg electron, neutron, proton, neutrino, quark, meson. All subatomic particles are either bosons (force particles) or fermions (matter particles).

subconscious — *noun* **1** the mental processes of which a person is not consciously aware. **2** *Psychol.* in psychoanalysis, the part of the mind that contains all the memories, associations, and feelings that can readily be brought back to conscious awareness after having been repressed. — *adj.* denoting mental processes of which a person is not consciously aware.

subconsciously *adv.* in a subconscious way; in the subconscious.

subcontinent *noun* a large part of a continent that is distinctive in some way, eg by its shape or culture.

subcontract — *noun* a secondary contract, by which the hired person or company hires another to carry out the work. — *verb* to employ (a worker), or pass on (work), under the terms of a subcontract.

subcontractor *noun* a person or company employed under the terms of a subcontract.

subculture *noun* the customs, tastes, and activities of a particular group within society.

subcutaneous *adj. Medicine* under the skin. [from Latin *sub*, under + *cutis*, skin]

subdirectory *noun Comput.* a directory of files that is contained within another, parent directory.

subdivide *verb* to divide (a part) into even smaller parts.

subdivision *noun* **1** a second or further division. **2** a section produced by subdividing.

subdue *verb* to overpower and bring under control; to suppress or conquer (feelings or an enemy). [from Latin *subducere*, to remove]

subdued *adj.* **1** *said of lighting, etc* soft, or made softer; toned down. **2** *said of a person* uncharacteristically quiet or in low spirits.

subedit *verb trans., intrans.* (**subedited, subediting**) to act as a subeditor of (a text, newspaper, etc).

subeditor *noun* **1** a person who selects and prepares material to be printed, eg in a newspaper or magazine, for the ultimate approval of an editor. **2** a person who assists with various editing tasks.

subfusc — *adj.* dusky; sombre. — *noun* dark formal clothes worn at some universities. [from Latin *subfuscus*, dark brown]

subito *adv. Mus.* suddenly, immediately, as in *piano subito*, suddenly soft. [from Italian *subito*]

subject — *noun* (with stress on *sub-*) **1** a matter or topic under discussion or consideration. **2** an area of learning that forms a course of study. **3** a person or thing represented by an artist or writer. **4** a person on whom an experiment or operation is performed. **5** a person under the ultimate rule of a monarch or government; a citizen. **6** *Grammar* a word or phrase referring to the person or thing that performs the action of an active verb or receives the action of a passive verb. *The doctor* is the subject in *the doctor saw us*, and *we* is the subject in *we were seen by the doctor*. — *adj.* (with stress on *sub-*) (*often* **subject to something** *or* **someone**) **1** showing a tendency; prone. **2** exposed; open. **3** governed; dependent. **4** ruled by a monarch or government. — *adv.* (**subject to something**) conditionally upon it: *you may go, subject to your parent's permission.* — *verb* (with stress on *-ject*) (*often* **subject someone to something** *or* **someone**) **1** to cause them to undergo or experience something unwelcome. **2** to make one person subordinate to or under the control of another. [from Latin *subjectus*, thrown under]

subjection *noun* subjecting or being subjected.

subjective *adj.* **1** based on personal thoughts and feelings; not impartial or objective. See also OBJECTIVE. **2** *Grammar* indicating or referring to the subject of a verb; nominative.

subjectively *adv.* in a subjective way.

sub judice under consideration by a court, and therefore not to be publicly discussed or remarked on. [Latin, = under a judge]

subjugate *verb* to bring under one's control; to make obedient or submissive. [from Latin *sub*, under + *jugum*, yoke]

subjugation *noun* subjugating or being subjugated.

subjunctive *Grammar* — *noun* **1** a set of verb forms, or mood, used to express condition, wish or uncertainty, eg 'If I *were* you' and 'I suggest he *leave* now'. **2** a verb form of this kind. — *adj.* in or of the subjunctive. [from Latin *subjungere*, to join to]

sublet *verb* (**subletting**; PAST AND PAST PARTICIPLE **sublet**) to rent out to another person (property one is renting from someone else).

sublimate — *noun Chem.* the solid product formed during the process of sublimation. — *verb* **1** *Chem.* to carry out the process of sublimation. **2** *Psychol.* to channel an undesirable impulse towards the attainment of a more morally or

socially acceptable goal. [from Latin *sublimare*, to elevate or exalt]

sublimation *noun* **1** *Chem.* the conversion of a solid, eg iodine or dry ice (solid carbon dioxide), directly into a gas or vapour without the intermediate formation of a liquid; the reverse process, in which the vapour condenses to form a solid or *sublimate*. **2** *Psychol.* the channelling of an undesirable impulse towards the attainment of a more morally or socially acceptable goal.

sublime — *adj.* **1** of the highest or noblest nature, usually morally or spiritually. **2** overwhelmingly great; supreme. — *verb trans., intrans. Chem.* to change from a solid to a vapour without passing through the liquid state.
— **from the sublime to the ridiculous** passing in consideration from something serious or elevated to something silly or trivial.
[from Latin *sublimis*, in a high position]

sublimely *adv.* to a sublime degree.

subliminal *adj.* existing or occurring below the threshold of ordinary awareness. [from Latin *sub*, under + *limen*, threshold]

subliminal advertising advertising in the form of pictures shown during a film or television programme for a split second only, so that the viewer's subconscious mind registers them without the viewer knowing.

subliminally *adv.* in a subliminal way.

sublimity *noun* **1** being sublime. **2** something that is sublime.

submachine-gun *noun* a lightweight portable machine-gun fired from the shoulder or hip.

submarine — *noun* a vessel, especially military, able to travel beneath the surface of the sea. — *adj.* under the surface of the sea.
◇ Early submarines were strictly speaking 'submersibles'; a World War II U-boat, for example, would typically have spent 85 per cent of its time on the surface, diving only to escape detection or when approaching or attacking enemy shipping. With the installation of nuclear reactors, modern vessels may remain submerged for many weeks or even months, ranging across the oceans and patrolling the high seas undetected.

submariner *noun* a person who goes to sea in a submarine.

submerge *verb* **1** *trans., intrans.* to plunge or sink under the surface of water or other liquid. **2** to overwhelm or inundate, eg with work. [from Latin *sub*, under + *mergere*, to plunge]

submersible — *adj.*, *said of a vessel* able to operate under water. — *noun* a submersible vessel; a submarine.

submersion *noun* submersing or being submersed.

submission *noun* **1** an act of submitting. **2** a thing submitted, eg for consideration or approval. **3** submissiveness.

submissive *adj.* willing or tending to submit; meek; obedient.

submissively *adv.* in a submissive way.

submissiveness *noun* being submissive.

submit *verb* (**submitted, submitting**) **1** *intrans.* (*also* **submit to someone**) to give in, especially to the wishes or control of another person; to stop resisting them. **2** *trans.* to offer (oneself) as a subject of experiment or other treatment. **3** to offer or present (eg a proposal) for formal consideration by others. [from Latin *sub*, beneath + *mittere*, to send]

subnormal *adj.* less than normal, especially with regard to intelligence.

subordinate — *adj.* (pronounced *-nət*) (*often* **subordinate to someone**) lower in rank or importance than them; secondary. — *noun* (pronounced *-nət*) a subordinate person or thing. — *verb* (pronounced *-nate*) (*often* **subordinate one person** *or* **thing to another**) to regard or treat as them as subordinate. [from Latin *sub*, below + *ordo*, rank]

subordinate clause *Grammar* a clause that acts like a noun, adjective, or adverb and is not able to function as an independent sentence, as in 'the book *that you gave me for Christmas* was fascinating'.

subordination *noun* subordinating or being subordinated.

suborn *verb* to persuade (someone) to commit a crime or other wrong, eg with a bribe. [from Latin *sub*, secretly + *ornare*, to equip]

Subotica, Hungarian **Szabadka** POP (1991) 151 000, the largest town in the province of Vojvodina, Yugoslavia. NOTABLE FEATURE Palic health resort nearby.

subplot *noun* a subsidiary plot coinciding with the main action in a play or story.

subpoena — *noun* a written order legally obliging a person to appear in a court of law at a specified time; a summons. — *verb* (**subpoenaed, subpoena'd**) to serve with a subpoena. [from Latin *subpoena*, under penalty]

subroutine *noun Comput.* a self-contained part of a computer program which performs a specific task and which can be called up at any time during the running of the main program.

subscribe *verb* **1** *trans., intrans.* to contribute or undertake to contribute (a sum of money), especially on a regular basis. **2** (*usually* **subscribe to something**) to undertake to receive regular issues of a magazine, etc in return for payment. **3** (**subscribe to something**) to agree with or believe in a theory, idea, etc. **4** to write one's name at the bottom of (a document, picture, etc). [from Latin *sub*, at the bottom + *scribere*, to write]

subscriber *noun* **1** a person who subscribes. **2** the user of a telephone line.

subscriber trunk dialling a telephone system in which customers make long-distance calls direct, without the help of an operator.

subscript *Printing* — *adj.*, *said of a character* set below the level of the line, as the number 2 in

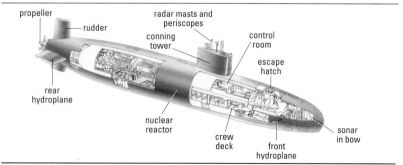

nuclear submarine

H_2O. — *noun* a subscript character. [related to SUBSCRIBE]

subscription *noun* **1** a payment made in subscribing. **2** an advance order, especially of a book before its official publication. **3** the act of subscribing. [related to SUBSCRIBE]

subsequent *adj., adv.* (*also* **subsequent to** **something**) happening after or following it. [from Latin *sub*, after + *sequi*, to follow]

subsequently *adv.* later; thereafter.

subservience *noun* a subservient state.

subservient *adj.* **1** ready or eager to submit to the wishes of others, often excessively so. **2** subordinate. [from Latin *sub*, under + *servire*, to serve]

subset *noun* **1** *Maths.* a set that forms part of a larger set. A set X is said to be a subset of a set Y if all members of set X are included in set Y. **2** *Biol.* a term used in immunology for a functionally or structurally different population of cells within a single cell type.

subside *verb intrans.* **1** *said of land, buildings, etc* to sink to a lower level; to settle. **2** *said of noise, feelings, etc* to become less loud or intense; to die down. [from Latin *sub*, down + *sidere*, to settle]

subsidence *noun* subsiding, settling, sinking.

subsidiarity *noun* the concept of a central governing body permitting its member states, branches, etc to take decisions on issues thought to be best dealt with at a local level.

subsidiary — *adj.* **1** of secondary importance; subordinate. **2** serving as an addition or supplement; auxiliary. — *noun* (PL. **subsidiaries**) **1** a subsidiary person or thing. **2** a company controlled by another, usually larger, company or organization. [related to SUBSIDE]

subsidize *or* **subsidise** *verb* **1** to provide or support with a subsidy. **2** to pay a proportion of the cost of (a thing supplied) in order to reduce the price paid by the customer. **3** *loosely* to pay the expenses of. [related to SUBSIDE]

subsidy *noun* (PL. **subsidies**) **1** a sum of money given, eg by a government to an industry, to help with running costs or to keep product prices low. **2** financial aid of this kind. [related to SUBSIDE]

subsist *verb intrans.* **1** (**subsist on something**) to live or manage to stay alive by means of it. **2** *formal* (**subsist in something**) to be based on it; to consist of it: *the team's success subsists in their fitness.* [from Latin *subsistere*, to stand still or firm]

subsistence *noun* **1** the means of existence; livelihood. **2** (*attributive*) *said of wages, etc* just enough to provide basic necessities.

subsistence farming farming in which almost all the produce is used to feed and support the farmer's family, with no surplus left to sell.

subsoil *noun* *Geol.* the layer of soil that lies beneath the topsoil (the layer that is normally used for cultivation). It contains chemical compounds that have leached from the topsoil, but very little organic matter.

subsonic *adj.* relating to, being, or travelling at speeds below the speed of sound.

subspecies *noun* *Biol.* a taxonomic subdivision of a species, with some morphological differences from the other subspecies and often with a different geographical distribution or ecology.

substance *noun* **1** the matter or material that a thing is made of. **2** a particular kind of matter with a definable quality: *a sticky substance*. **3** the essence or basic meaning of something spoken or written. **4** touchable reality; tangibility: *ghosts have no substance*. **5** solid quality or worth: *food with no substance*. **6** foundation; truth: *no substance in the rumours*. **7** wealth and influence: *woman of substance*. [from Latin *substantia*]

substandard *adj.* inferior; not up to the required or expected standard.

substantial *adj.* **1** considerable in amount, extent or importance. **2** of real value or worth. **3** *said of food* nourishing. **4** solidly built. **5** existing as a touchable thing; material; corporeal. **6** relating to a thing's basic nature or essence; essential. **7** wealthy and influential; well-to-do. [see SUBSTANCE]

substantially *adv.* in a substantial way; to a substantial degree.

substantiate *verb* to prove or support; to confirm the truth or validity of. [see SUBSTANCE]

substantiation *noun* **1** proof, validation. **2** being proved or validated.

substantive — *adj.* **1** of significant importance or value. **2** relating to the essential nature of something. — *noun* *Grammar* a noun. [from Latin *substantivus*]

substantively *adv.* in a substantive way.

substitute — *noun* a person or thing that takes the place of, or is used instead of, another. — *verb* (**substitute something** *or* **substitute one thing for another**) to use or bring into use as a substitute. — *adj.* acting as a substitute. [from Latin *sub*, under + *statuere*, to set]

substitution *noun* **1** the process of substituting or being substituted. **2** something that is substituted.

substrate *noun* **1** *Biol.* the material or medium on which a living organism (eg a plant or bacterium) grows, or to which it is attached. It may provide nutrients (eg agar, used for growing bacterial cultures), or it may merely provide support (eg soil). **2** *Electron.* a piece of ceramic, semiconductor material, plastic, glass, etc, on which an integrated circuit is fabricated, and which provides mechanical support or insulation. **3** *Biochem.* the substance on which an enzyme acts during a biochemical reaction. **4** any surface to which a substance such as a paint, dye, or laminate adheres. [from Latin *substernere substrat-*, to spread beneath]

substratum *noun* (PL. **substrata**) *technical* **1** an underlying layer. **2** a foundation or foundation material.

subsume *verb* **1** to take into, or regard as part of, a larger, more general group or category. **2** *loosely* to take over. [from Latin *sub*, under + *sumere*, to take]

subsumption *noun* subsuming or being subsumed.

subtend *verb, said of a line or a side of a geometric figure* to be opposite to (an arc or an angle). [from Latin *sub*, under + *tendere*, to stretch]

subterfuge *noun* a trick or deception that evades, conceals, or obscures; also, trickery in general: *a clever subterfuge / resorted to subterfuge*. [from Latin *subter-*, secretly + *fugere*, to flee]

subterranean *adj.* existing or operating underground, or in secret. [from Latin *sub*, under + *terra*, earth]

subtext *noun* **1** an unstated message conveyed through the form of a play, film, book, or picture. The subject may be implied by the use of pauses or silence, or by the shape of the plot or the patterns of imagery used. **2** more loosely, anything implied but not stated in ordinary speech or writing, especially in extended conversation.

subtitle *noun* **1** (*usually* **subtitles**) a printed translation of the dialogue of a foreign film, appearing bit by bit at the bottom of the screen. **2** a second title, usually expanding on or explaining the main title.

Subtle the roguish charlatan of the title in Ben Jonson's *The Alchemist*.

subtle *adj.* **1** not straightforwardly or obviously stated or displayed. **2** *said of distinctions, etc* difficult to appreciate or perceive. **3** *said of flavours, etc* extremely faint or delicate. **4** carefully or craftily discreet or indirect. [from Latin *sub*, under + *tela*, web]

subtlety *noun* (PL. **subtleties**) **1** being subtle; subtle behaviour. **2** a subtle point or argument.

subtly *adv.* in a subtle way.

subtract *verb* to take (one number or quantity) from another; to deduct. [from Latin *sub*, away + *trahere*, to draw]

subtraction *noun* the process of subtracting.

subtropical *adj.* relating to or typical of the areas of the world that lie between the tropics and the temperate zone, and that have a near-tropical climate or experience tropical conditions for part of the year.

suburb *noun* (*often* **suburbs**) a district, especially residential, on the edge of a town or city. [from Latin *sub*, near + *urbs*, city]

suburban *adj.* **1** of or in a suburb. **2** narrow in outlook; narrowly genteel or middle-class.

suburbia *noun often derog.* suburbs and their inhabitants and way of life regarded collectively.

subvention *noun* a grant or subsidy. [from Latin *subvenire*, to come to help]

subversion *noun* the act or practice of subverting (usually a government).

subversive — *adj.* likely or tending to subvert or undermine government or authority. — *noun* a subversive person.

subvert *verb* **1** to undermine or overthrow (a government or other legally established body). **2** to corrupt (a person); to undermine (a principle, etc). [from Latin *subvertere*, to overturn]

subway *noun* **1** a passage for pedestrians under a road or railway. **2** an underground passage for pipes and cables. **3** *North Amer., esp. US* an underground railway.

succeed *verb usually intrans.* **1** to achieve an aim or purpose. **2** to develop or turn out as planned. **3** to do well in a particular area or field. **4** *trans.* to come next after; to follow. **5** (*also* **succeed to something**) to take up a position, etc, following on from someone else. [from Latin *succedere*, to go next after]

success *noun* **1** the quality of succeeding or the state of having succeeded; a favourable development or outcome. **2** the attainment of fame, power, or wealth. **3** a person who has attained any such quality, or who is judged favourably by others. **4** a thing that turns out as planned, or that is judged favourably by others.

successful *adj.* **1** resulting in success. **2** achieving the required outcome. **3** prosperous, flourishing.

successfully *adv.* in a successful way; with success.

succession *noun* **1** a series of people or things coming one after the other. **2** the right or order by which one person or thing succeeds another. **3** the sequential development of plant communities on a site, especially a lake in which sitting occurs. — **in succession** one after the other.

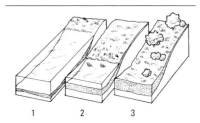

1: open lake fringed by marsh
2: lake begins to silt up and marsh spreads
3: grass and trees grow over filled-in lake

succession

successive *adj.* immediately following another or each other.

successively *adv.* in a successive way; with one following another.

successor *noun* a person who follows another, especially who takes over the job or position of another.

succinct *adj., said of something written or said* brief and precise; concise. [from Latin *succinctus*]

succinctly *adv.* in a succinct way.

succinctness *noun* a succinct quality.

Succoth same as SUKKOTH.

succour *formal* — *noun* help or relief in time of distress or need. — *verb* to give succour to. [from Latin *succurrere*, to run to help]

succubus *noun* (PL. **succubi**) a female evil spirit which is supposed to have sexual intercourse with sleeping men. See also INCUBUS. [from Latin *succuba*, prostitute]

succulence *noun* a succulent quality.

succulent — *noun* a plant which has fleshy stems and leaves adapted for storing water. Succulents are common in arid regions and also in places where water is present but not readily available because the soil contains high levels of salts, eg saltmarshes. Such plants often have thick waxy cuticles, or reduced or inrolled leaves, eg cacti, *Sedum* species (stonecrops). — *adj.* **1** relating to such a plant. **2** *said of food* tender and juicy. [from Latin *sucus*, juice]

succumb *verb intrans.* (**often succumb to someone** *or* **something**) **1** to give in to pressure, temptation, or desire. **2** to die of something (especially a disease). [from Latin *sub*, under + *cumbere*, to lie down]

such — *adj.* **1** of that kind, or the same or a similar kind: *you cannot reason with such a person.* **2** so great: *not such a fool as to believe that.* — *adv.* extremely: *such a lovely present.* — *pron.* a person or thing, or people or things, like that or those just mentioned: *chimps, gorillas, and such.*
— **as such 1** in or by itself alone. **2** as it is described.
such as ... for example ...
[from Anglo-Saxon *swilc*]

such-and-such — *adj.* of a particular but unspecified kind. — *pron.* a person or thing of this kind.

suchlike — *adj.* of the same kind. — *pron.* things of the same kind.

Suchow see SUZHOU.

suck — *verb* **1** *trans., intrans.* (*also* **suck something in** *or* **up**) to draw (liquid) into the mouth. **2** to draw liquid from (eg a juicy fruit) with the mouth. **3** (*also* **suck something in** *or* **up**) to draw it in by suction. **4** to rub (eg one's thumb or a pencil) with the tongue and inside of the mouth, with an action similar to sucking in liquids. **5** to draw the flavour from (eg a sweet) with squeezing and rolling movements inside the mouth. **6** to draw milk from (a breast or udder) with the mouth. **7** *intrans. North Amer. slang* to be contemptible or contemptibly bad. — *noun* an act or bout of sucking.
— **suck up to someone** *colloq.* to flatter them or be obsequious to them, in order to gain favour. [from Anglo-Saxon *sucan*]

sucker *noun* **1** in certain animals, an organ that is adapted to adhere to surfaces by suction, in order to assist feeding, locomotion, etc. **2** a similar man-made device designed to adhere to a surface by creating a vacuum. **3** a shoot arising from an underground stem or root that grows underground and then emerges to form a new plant capable of independent existence. **4** *colloq.* a person easily deceived or taken advantage of. **5** *colloq.* a person who is gullible or vulnerable in some way: *a sucker for lending money.*

suckle *verb* **1** to feed (a baby) with milk from one's breast or udder. **2** *trans., intrans.* to suck milk from (a breast or udder). [related to SUCK]

Suckling, Sir John (1609–42) English poet and dramatist, born in Whitton, Middlesex. He lived at court in London, but involvement in political intrigue led him to flee the country, and he died (it is said by his own hand) in Paris. His plays include *Aglaura* (1637), and his major lyrics are included in *Fragmenta Aurea* (1646).

suckling *noun* a young baby or animal still suckling its mother's breast.

Sucre, Antonio José de (1793–1830) S American soldier-patriot, born in Cumaná, Venezuela. He was Bolívar's lieutenant, defeated the Spaniards at Ayacucho (1824), and became the first President (1826) of Bolivia. He resigned in 1828, took service with Colombia, and won the battle of Tarqui (1829) against Peru, but was assassinated the following year.

Sucre, formerly **Chuquisaca** POP (1989e) 106 000, a city in Oropeza province, S central Bolivia. It stands at an altitude of 2 705m. The city is the official judicial and legal capital of Bolivia and the capital of Chuquisaca region. HISTORY founded in 1538; a revolutionary centre against Spain in the 18c. NOTABLE FEATURES colonial Legislative Palace (where the Declaration of Independence was signed); Santo Domingo (Palace of Justice); 17c cathedral and museum; Churches of San Miguel and San Francisco.

sucrose *noun Chem.* (FORMULA $C_{12}H_{22}O_{11}$) a white soluble crystalline sugar consisting of a molecule of glucose linked to a molecule of fructose. It occurs in most plants, and is extracted from sugar cane and sugar beet for use as a sweetener in food and drinks. — Also called *cane-sugar*. [from French *sucre*, sugar]

suction *noun* **1** the act or power of sucking. **2** a drawing or adhering force created by a difference or reduction in air pressure. [from Latin *sugere*, to suck]

Sudan, official name **Democratic Republic of Sudan**, Arabic **Jamhuryat es-Sudan al-Democratia** POP (1992e) 26.7m, a NE African republic, divided into seven regions. AREA 2 504 530sq km/966 749sq mi. It is bounded N by Egypt, NW by Libya, W by Chad, SW by the Central African Republic, S by Zaire, SE by Uganda and Kenya, E by Ethiopia, and NE by the Red Sea. CAPITAL Khartoum. CHIEF TOWNS Port Sudan, Wad Medani, Khartoum North, Omdurman. TIME ZONE GMT +2. Most of the population are Nilotic, Negro, Nubian, or Arab; Islam (Sunni) and local beliefs are the chief religions. OFFICIAL LANGUAGE Arabic. CURRENCY the Sudanese pound. PHYSICAL DESCRIPTION the largest country on the African continent, astride the middle reaches of the R Nile; the E edge is formed by the Nubian Highlands and an escarpment rising to over 2 000m on the Red Sea; the Imatong Mts in the S rise to 3 187m at Kinyeti, the highest point in Sudan; the Darfur Massif is located in the W; the White Nile flows N to meet the Blue Nile at Khartoum. CLIMATE desert conditions in the N with minimal annual rainfall of 160mm at Port Sudan, increasing S to 1 000mm; in the hottest months (Jul–Aug), the temperature rarely falls below 24°C in the N. HISTORY Christianized in the 6c; Muslim conversion from the 13c; Egyptian control of N Sudan in the early 19c; a religious leader who announced himself the *Mahdi* (the 'expected one') began to unify W and central areas of the country and in 1881 he initiated a revolution which led to the fall of Khartoum in 1885; combined British–Egyptian offensive in 1898, leading to a jointly administered condominium; gained independence in 1956; the constitution was suspended after a military coup in 1989; N–S rivalry has contributed to years of instability, several coups, and severe food shortages. ECONOMY dominated by agriculture, employing over 75% of the people; large-scale irrigation schemes, fed by dams; commercial farming in the N and livestock farming in the S; cotton, sugar, groundnuts, castor seeds, sorghum, wheat; gum arabic (80% of world supply); reserves of copper, lead, iron ore, chromite, manganese, gold, salt; food processing; sugar; textiles; soap; shoes; soft drinks; beer; paper products; cement; development hindered by a poor transport system; the only main paved highway (Khartoum–Port Sudan) was completed in 1980.

Sudan

Sudbury POP (1991) 93 000, a town in E central Ontario, S Canada. HISTORY developed after the arrival of the railway in 1883 and the discovery of copper ore; achieved city status in 1930. The economy of the area relies on mining of various metals and minerals. NOTABLE FEATURE Canada Centennial Numismatic Park.

sudden *adj.* happening quickly or unexpectedly.
— **all of a sudden** suddenly.
[from Old French *soudain*]

sudden death *Sport* a method of deciding a tied contest by declaring the winner to be the player or team that scores first in an extra period.

sudden infant death syndrome (ABBREV. **SIDS**) *Medicine* the sudden unexpected death of an apparently healthy baby, often at night, for which no adequate cause can be found on clinical or post-mortem examination. See also COT DEATH.

suddenly *adv.* unexpectedly and without warning.

suddenness *noun* being sudden.

sucrose

Sudeten *or* **Sudetenland** a mountainous territory on the Polish–Czech border, comprising the Sudetic Mts which rise to 1 603m at Sněžka. During World War II the name also applied to the parts of Bohemia and Moravia occupied by German-speaking people. It was occupied by Germany in 1938 and restored to Czechoslovakia in 1945.

sudorific *Medicine* — *adj., said of a drug* causing sweating. — *noun* a sudorific drug. [from Latin *sudor*, sweat + *facere*, to make]

suds *pl. noun* a mass of bubbles produced on water when soap or other detergent is dissolved. [perhaps from Old Dutch *sudse*, marsh]

sue *verb trans., intrans.* to take legal proceedings against (a person or company). [from Old French *suir*, from Latin *sequi*, to follow]

suede *noun* soft leather given a velvet-like finish. [from French *gants de Suède*, gloves from Sweden]

Suess, Eduard (1831–1914) Austrian geologist, born in London. Professor in Vienna, the greater part of his life was devoted to the study of the evolution of the features of the Earth's surface, particularly the problems of mountain building. His theory that there had once been a great supercontinent made up of the present southern continents was a forerunner of modern theories of continental drift.

suet *noun* hard fat from around the kidneys of sheep or cattle, used to make pastry and puddings. [from Latin *sebum*, fat]

Suetonius, in full **Gaius Suetonius Tranquillus** (AD 75–160) Roman biographer and antiquarian. He became Hadrian's secretary, but lost his post when he was compromised in a court intrigue. He then devoted himself to writing, and his best-known work is *De vita Caesarum* (The Lives of the First Twelve Caesars). His other writings, on major Roman literary figures, survive only in fragments.

Suez, Arabic **El Suweis 1** POP (1990e) 392 000, the seaport capital of Suez governorate, E Egypt. It is situated on the Gulf of Suez at the S end of the Suez Canal, 129km/80mi E of Cairo. **2** a governorate in E Egypt with Suez as its capital.

Suez Canal a canal connecting the Mediterranean and Red seas, in NE Egypt. It passes through L Timsah and the Great and Little Bitter Lakes. Built by Ferdinand de Lesseps from 1859 until 1869, its length is 163km/101mi, including 11km/7mi of approaches to Suez (S end) and Port Said (N end). The minimum width is 60m and the minimum draught is 16m. HISTORY under the 1882 Convention, it is open to vessels of any nation except in wartime; it was controlled by the British from 1882 until 1956; nationalized by Egypt in 1956; blocked by Egypt during war with Israel in 1967; re-opened in 1975. It is a major international waterway and a substantial Egyptian economic asset.

Suez Crisis a political crisis (1956) regarding the Suez Canal. Intensive rearmament by Egypt, the Egyptian nationalization of the Suez Canal, and the establishment of a unified command with Jordan and Syria aimed at surrounding and eliminating Israel, led in October to a pre-emptive strike by Israel in Sinai. Following this attack, the UK and France asked both sides to withdraw from the Canal Zone and agree to temporary occupation. When this was rejected by Egypt, the British and French invaded, but had to withdraw following diplomatic action by the USA and USSR, and Israel was also forced to relinquish the Sinai Peninsula. There have been many allegations of collusion between Israel, France, and the UK.

Suff. *abbrev.* Suffolk.

suffer *verb* (**suffered, suffering**) **1** *trans., intrans.* to undergo or endure (mental or physical pain or other unpleasantness). **2** (**suffer from something**) to be afflicted with an illness.

3 *intrans.* to deteriorate (as a result of something). **4** to tolerate: *not suffer fools gladly.* **5** *old use* to allow: *suffer little children to come unto me.* [from Latin *sub*, under + *ferre*, to bear]

sufferance
— **on sufferance** tolerated, but not welcomed or encouraged.

sufferer *noun* a person who suffers.

suffering *noun* pain or distress.

suffice *verb* **1** *intrans.* to be enough, or be good enough for a particular purpose. **2** *trans.* to satisfy (a person).
— **suffice it to say** ... it is enough to say ... [from Latin *sufficere*]

sufficiency *noun* (PL. **sufficiencies**) a sufficient amount.

sufficient *adj.* enough; adequate. [from Latin *sufficere*, to suffice]

sufficiently *adv.* in a sufficient way; to a sufficient degree.

suffix — *noun* a word element added to the end of a word or word stem to mark a grammatical inflection or form a derivative, eg the *-s* in *monkeys* and the *-tude* in *certitude*. — *verb* to add as a suffix. [from Latin *suffixus*, fixed underneath]

suffocate *verb* **1** *trans., intrans.* to kill with or die from lack of air, eg with an obstruction over the mouth and nose. **2** *intrans.* to experience difficulty in breathing because of heat and lack of air; to stifle. **3** to subject to an oppressive amount of something. [from Latin *suffocare*, from *sub*, under + *fauces*, throat]

suffocating *adj.* that suffocates.

suffocation *noun* suffocating or being suffocated.

Suffolk POP (1992e) 648 000, a county in E England, divided into seven districts. AREA 3 797sq km/1 466sq mi. It is bounded E by the North Sea, N by Norfolk, W by Cambridgeshire, and S by Essex. CHIEF TOWNS Ipswich (county town), Lowestoft, Felixstowe, Bury St Edmunds. ECONOMY engineering; fishing; high technology; agriculture (wheat, barley, sugar beet); food processing; horse breeding. NOTABLE FEATURES Sizewell; Sutton Hoo Ship Burial.

suffragan *noun* **1** a bishop appointed as assistant to another bishop. **2** any bishop considered as an archbishop's subordinate. [from Latin *suffraganeus*, assistant]

suffrage *noun* the right to vote in political elections. [from Latin *suffragium*, a vote]

suffragette *noun* any of a group of women who campaigned strenuously for women's suffrage in Britain in the early 20c.
◇ In England, Emeline Pankhurst (1858–1928) and her daughters were leading figures in the struggle for women's suffrage before World War I. The vote was granted to women over 30 in 1918, and to women over the age of 21 in 1929.

suffuse *verb, said of colour, light, etc* to cover or spread throughout. [from Latin *suffundere*, to pour beneath]

suffusion *noun* suffusing or being suffused.

Sufi *noun* an adherent of Sufism; a Muslim mystic.

Sufism *Relig.* an Islamic mystical movement which represents a move away from the legalistic approach in Islam to a more personal relationship with God, and whose adherents aspire to lose themselves in the ultimate reality of the Divinity by constant repetition of the *dhikr* or 'mentioning of God'. [from Arabic *çūfī*, probably 'man of wool', from *çuf*, wool (as worn by ascetics)]

Sugar, Alan (Michael) (1947–) English entrepreneur, born in London. He founded AMSTRAD (the name is a contraction of Alan M Sugar Trading) in 1968. The company expanded rapidly during the personal-computer boom of

the 1980s, but ran into problems with the slump at the end of that decade. As a result, Sugar bought the company back into his own private ownership. He has been Chairman of Tottenham Hotspur football club since 1991.

sugar — *noun* **1** any of a group of white crystalline carbohydrates that are soluble in water and typically have a sweet taste. Sugars are widely used as sweeteners in confectionery, desserts, soft drinks, etc. **2** common name for sucrose (table sugar), which is obtained from the pith of sugar cane, or from sugar beet. **3** *colloq.* a term of endearment. — *verb* (**sugared, sugaring**) **1** to sweeten with sugar. **2** to sprinkle or coat with sugar.
— **sugar the pill** to make something unpleasant easier to deal with or accept.
[from Arabic *sukkar*]
◇ The two main groups of sugars are the simple sugars or *monosaccharides*, eg glucose, fructose, and galactose, and the *disaccharides*, which consist of two monosaccharides linked together, eg sucrose (consisting of glucose and fructose molecules), and lactose (consisting of glucose and galactose molecules). In the human body, sugars are converted into glucose, which is then broken down to provide energy during respiration. In sugar refining, the sweet juice extracted from crushed sugar cane or sugar beet is boiled until crystals form. Dark brown sticky crystals (muscovado sugar) form first, followed by light brown crystals (demerara sugar), and finally dry white fine-grained crystals (castor sugar).

Sugar Act a British statute (1764) that attempted for the first time to raise colonial revenue without reference to the colonial assemblies, aimed at imposing customs duties and preventing illegal trade. The colonials responded with protest, but not outright resistance, and the Act was sporadically enforced until the complete breakdown of British–American relations.

sugar-beet *noun* a variety of beet (*Beta vulgaris*), widely cultivated in Europe and the USA for its large white conical root, which contains up to 20 per cent sucrose (sugar). It is the most important source of sugar in temperate regions.

sugar cane *noun* a tall tropical grass (*Saccharum officinarum*) that resembles bamboo but has soft jointed stalks up to 6m in height. It is native to Asia, but is cultivated in tropical and subtropical regions worldwide as one of the two main sources of sugar (the other is sugar beet). The stalks are cut once a year, crushed, and soaked in water to extract the juice which contains sugar (sucrose or cane sugar). The sugary solution is then concentrated by evaporation, and sucrose gradually crystallizes out, leaving a residue of molasses. The raw sugar is brown, and can be purified further to give white sugar. Cuba and India are the two largest producers of cane sugar.

sugar daddy *colloq.* an elderly man with a young girlfriend on whom he lavishes money and gifts.

sugared *adj.* **1** sugar-coated, candied. **2** containing sugar.

sugariness *noun* a sugary quality.

sugar-maple *noun* a N American maple tree from whose sap sugar is obtained.

sugar soap a substance for cleaning or stripping paint.

sugary *adj.* **1** like sugar in taste or appearance. **2** containing much or too much sugar. **3** *colloq.* exaggeratedly or insincerely pleasant or affectionate; cloying.

suggest *verb* **1** to put forward as a possibility or recommendation. **2** to make one think of; to create an impression of. **3** to cause one to think or conclude. [from Latin *suggerere*, to put under]

suggestible *adj.* easily influenced by suggestions made by others.

suggestion *noun* **1** a thing suggested; a proposal or recommendation. **2** a hint or trace. **3** the creation of a belief or impulse in the mind of a hypnotised person. **4** the act of suggesting.

suggestive *adj.* **1** (**suggestive of something**) causing one to think of it; creating an impression of it. **2** provoking thoughts or feelings of a sexual nature.

suggestively *adv.* in a suggestive way.

Suicheng see LIUPANSHUI.

suicidal *adj.* **1** involving or indicating suicide. **2** that will result in suicide or ruin. **3** *said of a person* inclined or likely to commit suicide.

suicide *noun* **1** the act, or an instance, of killing oneself deliberately. **2** a person who deliberately kills himself or herself. **3** the bringing about of one's own downfall, often unintentionally: *the minister's speech was political suicide.* [from Latin *sui*, of oneself + *caedere*, to kill]

suit — *noun* **1** a set of clothes, usually a jacket with trousers or a skirt, made from the same material and designed to be worn together. **2** an outfit worn on specific occasions or for a specific activity. **3** any of the four groups into which a pack of playing-cards is divided. **4** a legal action taken against someone; a lawsuit. — *verb* **1** *trans., intrans.* to be acceptable to or what is required by. **2** to be appropriate to, in harmony with, or attractive to.
— **follow suit 1** to play a card of the same suit as the card first played. **2** to do the same as someone else has done.
suit oneself to do what one wants to do, especially without considering others.
[from Old French *sieute*, from *sivre*, to follow]

suitability *noun* being suitable.

suitable *adj.* that suits; appropriate or agreeable.

suitably *adv.* in a suitable way.

suitcase *noun* a portable travelling case for clothes, with flat stiffened sides and a handle.

suite *noun* **1** a set of rooms forming a self-contained unit within a larger building. **2** a matching set of furniture. **3** *Mus.* a set of instrumental movements in related keys. **4** a group of followers or attendants. [from French *suite*]

suitor *noun* **1** *old use* a man courting a woman for love or marriage. **2** a person who sues; a plaintiff. [see SUIT]

Sukarno *or* **Soekarno, Ahmed** (1902–70) Indonesian politician, born in Surabaya, Java. He formed the Indonesia National Party in 1927, was imprisoned by the Dutch in Bandung (1929–31), and lived in exile until 1942, when he was made leader during the Japanese occupation. When Indonesia was granted independence, he became the first President (1945–66). His popularity waned as the country suffered increasing internal chaos and poverty, and his government was accused of corruption. When an abortive communist coup (1965) led to student riots and a takeover by the army, his powers gradually devolved on to General Suharto, and Sukarno finally retired in 1968.

Sukhothai an ancient ruined city in Thailand. It lies 440km/273mi N of Bangkok. The city was founded in the mid-13c when the nation of Thailand came into being. It was the former capital of the Thai-Khmer state and is, today, a historical park.

Sukkoth *or* **Succoth**, a Jewish harvest festival commemorating the period when the Israelites lived in tents in the desert during the Exodus from Egypt. — Also called *Feast of Tabernacles*. [from Hebrew *sukkoth*, huts]

Sukkur *or* **Sakhar** POP (1981) 191 000, a city in Sind province, Pakistan. It lies on the E bank of the R Indus, 360km/224mi NE of Karachi. The Sukkur (Lloyd) Barrage was built between 1928 and 1932 and comprises a dam 58m high, with seven canals irrigating 18m sq km/7m sq mi of land.

Sulaiman *or* **Suleyman I**, known as **the Magnificent** (1494–1566) Ottoman Sultan (1520–66), who conquered Belgrade, Budapest, Rhodes, Tabriz, Baghdad, Aden, and Algiers, and added them to his dominions. His fleets dominated the Mediterranean, although he failed to capture Malta. His system of laws regulating land tenure earned him the name Kanuni ('lawgiver'), and he was a great patron of arts and architecture.

Sulawesi *or* **Celebes** an island in Indonesia, off E Borneo. It is divided into four provinces. These are South Sulawesi (capital Ujung Pandang), Central Sulawesi (capital Palu), South East Sulawesi (capital Kendari), and North Sulawesi (capital Manado). The island is mountainous and forested. The Sangir Is form part of Sulawesi. ECONOMY rice; tuna; maize; kapok; copra; nickel; coal; asphalt; mica; sulphur; salt.

sulk — *verb intrans.* to be silent or unsociable out of petty resentment or bad temper. — *noun* (*also* **the sulks**) a bout of sulking. [perhaps from Anglo-Saxon *aseolcan*, to slack or be slow]

sulkily *adv.* with a sulky manner.

sulkiness *noun* being sulky.

sulky *adj.* (**sulkier, sulkiest**) sulking; inclined to sulk.

Sulla, Lucius Cornelius, also called **Felix** ('**Lucky'**) (138–78 BC) Roman politician and dictator (82–79 BC). His feud with Marius, begun in Africa in 107 BC during the Jugurthine War, twice plunged Rome into civil war in the 80s BC. In 88 BC he chose to lead his army against the state rather than surrender to Marius his command of the war against Mithridates. He defeated Mithridates, and on returning to Rome (83 BC) used his forces to defeat the Marians and secure his own (illegal) position. Appointed 'Dictator' in 82 BC, he set about reforming the state, and enacted a number of measures to boost the authority of the Senate. He retired in 79 BC.

sullen *adj.* **1** silently and stubbornly angry or unsociable. **2** *said of skies, etc* dismal. [from Latin *solus*, alone]

sullenly *adv.* with a sullen manner.

sullenness *noun* being sullen.

Sullivan, Sir Arthur (Seymour) (1842–1900) English composer, born in London. At first an organist in London, his association with the theatre began in 1867, and from 1871 he was known for his collaboration with W S Gilbert in 14 comic operas, including *HMS Pinafore* (1878), *The Pirates of Penzance* (1879), and the *Mikado* (1885). He also composed a grand opera, *Ivanhoe* (1891), cantatas, ballads, a *Te Deum*, and hymn tunes (eg for 'Onward Christian Soldiers').

Sullivan, Jim (James) (1903–77) Welsh rugby player, born in Cardiff. He played rugby union for Cardiff before joining Wigan rugby league club in 1921. He kicked a world record 2 859 goals, including a record 22 in one game (Wigan v Flimby & Fothergill, 1925). He was player-coach of Wigan (1932–46), and later became coach to Rochdale Hornets and St Helens.

Sullivan, Louis (Henry) (1856–1924) US architect, born in Boston. He began to practise in Chicago with his partner, Dankmar Adler (1844–1900), and became known as the 'Father of Modernism'. One of the first to design skyscrapers, his works include the Wainwright Building in St Louis (1890–1) and the Carson, Pirie and Scott Store in Chicago (1899-1904).

Sullom Voe an oil terminal in Shetland, Scotland, linked by pipeline to the Hutton, Ninian, Lyell, Dunlin, Thistle, and Murchison oil fields.

Sully, Maximilien de Béthune, Duc de (Duke of) (1560–1641) French Huguenot soldier, financier, and statesman, born in Rosny. He fought in the later stages of the Wars of Religion (1574–98) and was wounded at Ivry (1590). He was instrumental in arranging the marriage of Henry of Navarre (Henry IV) to Maria de' Medici (1600), and became the King's trusted Chief Minister. His major achievement was the restoration of the economy after the civil wars.

sully *verb* (**sullies, sullied**) **1** to tarnish or mar (a reputation, etc). **2** *literary* to make dirty. [from Anglo-Saxon *sylian*, to defile]

Sully Prudhomme, pseudonym of **René François Armand Prudhomme** (1839–1907) French poet, born in Paris. A leader of the Parnassian movement, his early *Stances et poèmes* (1865) was well-received, and his later works include the didactic poems *La Justice* (Justice, 1878) and *Le Bonheur* (Happiness, 1888). His *Oeuvres* appeared in eight volumes between 1883 and 1908. He was awarded the first Nobel Prize for Literature in 1901.

sulphate *noun* a salt of sulphuric acid.

sulphide *noun* a compound containing sulphur and another element.

sulphonamide *noun* Chem. **1** an amide of a sulphonic acid. **2** *Medicine* any of a group of drugs containing such a compound that prevent the growth of bacteria, formerly widely used to treat bacterial infections in humans, and to prevent infections of wounds and burns during World War II, but now largely superseded by antibiotics such as penicillin.

sulphur *noun* (SYMBOL **S**, ATOMIC NUMBER **16**) a yellow solid non-metallic element that forms several allotropes, including two stable crystalline forms. — Also called *brimstone*.
◊ Sulphur occurs naturally as the free element in the form of powdery masses or thick crystals in volcanic regions, deposits around hot springs, and deep underground deposits. It also occurs in various minerals, and as an impurity in coal and petroleum, and is present in all living organisms, as it is a constituent of the amino acids cysteine and methionine, which are found in most proteins. The main uses of sulphur are in the vulcanization (hardening) of rubber and the manufacture of sulphuric acid, but it is also used in fungicides (eg 'flowers of sulphur'), insecticides, gunpowder, matches, fertilizers, as well as sulphonamide drugs for the treatment of bacterial infections.
[from Latin *sulfur*]

sulphur dioxide *Chem.* (FORMULA SO_2) a colourless gas with a strong pungent odour that is soluble in water and alcohol. It is a reducing agent, and is used as a bleach for paper and straw, and as a food preservative, fumigant, and solvent. It is also used in metal refining, paper pulping, and the manufacture of sulphuric acid. It is produced by the burning of fossil fuels and other sulphur-containing compounds, and is a major cause of acid rain and other forms of atmospheric pollution.

sulphuric acid *Chem.* (FORMULA H_2SO_4) a colourless odourless oily liquid that is highly corrosive, and strongly acidic when diluted with water. It is widely used in the manufacture of organic chemicals, fertilizers, explosives, detergents, paints, and dyes, and as a laboratory reagent. Dilute sulphuric acid is used as an electrolyte in car batteries, and for electroplating.

sulphurous *adj.* of, like, or containing sulphur.

sulphurous acid *Chem.* (FORMULA H_2SO_3) a colourless weakly acidic solution of sulphur dioxide in water, that is a reducing agent and is used as a bleach, antiseptic, and preservative, and in brewing and wine-making, paper and textile manufacture, and the refining of petroleum products.

sultan *noun* the ruler of any of various Muslim countries, especially the former ruler of the Ottoman empire. [from Arabic *sultan*]

sultana *noun* **1** the wife or concubine of a sultan. **2** the mother, sister, or daughter of a sultan. **3** a pale seedless raisin.

sultrily *adv.* in a sultry way.

sultriness *noun* being sultry.

sultry *adj.* (**sultrier, sultriest**) **1** *said of the weather* hot and humid; close. **2** *said of a person* having an appearance or manner suggestive of sexual passion; sensual. [from obsolete *sulter*, to swelter]

sum — *noun* **1** the amount produced when numbers or quantities are added together. **2** an amount of money. **3** an arithmetical calculation, especially of a basic kind. — *verb* (**summed, summing**) (*usually* **sum up** *or* **sum something up**) **1** to summarize. **2** to express or embody the complete character or nature of. **3** to make a quick assessment of. **4** *said of a judge* to review the main points of a case before the jury retires. — **in sum** briefly; to sum up. [from Latin *summa*, top]

sumac *noun Bot.* **1** any tree or shrub of the genus *Rhus*. **2** its dried leaves and shoots, used in dyeing. [from Arabic *summaq*]

Sumatra, Indonesian **Sumatera** POP (1990) 20.5m, an island in W Indonesia, S of the Malay Peninsula. AREA 473 606sq km/182 812sq mi. It is 1 760km/1 094mi long and 400km/250mi wide. Sumatra is the fifth-largest island in the world and includes the Riau archipelago in the E and the the Mentawi Is in the W. HISTORY centre of the Buddhist kingdom of Sri Vijaya in the 7c–13c; discovered by Marco Polo in the 13c; separatist movement followed Indonesian independence in 1949. CHIEF TOWNS Medan, Jambi, Padang, Pekanbaru, Banda Aceh. PHYSICAL DESCRIPTION the Bukit Barisan Range in the W rises to 3 805m at Gunung Kerinci; the Batanghari is the longest river in Sumatra; much of the SE third of the island is swamp and marshland. ECONOMY oil, tin, bauxite, gold, natural gas; rubber; coffee, tea, pepper.

Sumatran rhinoceros a species of rhinoceros found in Asia, and having two horns. It is unusual in that the young are covered with thick brown hair, which is gradually lost as the animal matures.

Sumer the name given to the part of Lower Mesopotamia between Babylon and the Persian Gulf. It is the place where the world's first urban civilization evolved during the 4th millennium BC; among its city-states were Eridu, Ur, and Uruk. Its writing system is the earliest example of cuneiform, and surviving art forms date from c.2500 BC, and include the stone statues of Gudea and many coloured bas-reliefs.

Sumgait POP (1991e) 236 000, a town in Azerbaijan, on the W coast of the Caspian Sea. Lying 45km/28mi NW of Baku, it was developed after 1949 in connection with the republic's chemical and metallurgical industries. ECONOMY ferrous metallurgy (pipe-rolling plant). NOTABLE FEATURE Palace of Culture (1958).

summarily *adv.* in a summary way.

summarize *or* **summarise** *verb* to make or present a summary of.

summary — *noun* (PL. **summaries**) a short account outlining the main points. — *adj.* done or performed quickly and without the usual attention to details or formalities. [from Latin *summarium*]

summary offence *Legal* an offence subject to trial in a magistrates' or (in Scotland) sheriff court (courts of *summary jurisdiction*). Basically, most summary offences are the less serious criminal cases, although the magistrates' and sheriff courts may also try certain indictable offences such as theft.

summation *noun* **1** the process of finding the sum; addition. **2** a summary or summing-up. [from Latin *summare*, to sum up]

summer — *noun* **1** the warmest season of the year, between spring and autumn, extending from about May to Sep in the N hemisphere. **2** *literary* a time of greatest energy, happiness, etc; a heyday. — *adj.* of, occurring in, or for use in the summer. [from Anglo-Saxon *sumer*]

summerhouse *noun* any small building or shelter designed to provide shade in a park or garden.

summer school a course of study held during the summer, eg at a university.

summertime *noun* the season of summer.

summer time time one hour ahead of Greenwich Mean Time, adopted in Britain during the summer months for daylight-saving purposes.

summery *adj.* typical of or suitable for summer.

summing-up *noun* a review of the main points, especially of a legal case by the judge before the jury retires.

summit *noun* **1** the highest point of a mountain or hill. **2** the highest attainable level of achievement or development, eg in a career. **3** (*also* **summit meeting** *or* **conference**) a conference between heads of government or other senior officials. [from Latin *summum*, highest]

summon *verb* (**summoned, summoning**) **1** to order (a person) to come or appear, eg in a court of law. **2** to order or call upon (someone) to do something. **3** (**summon something up**) to gather or muster (eg one's strength or energy). [from Latin *summonere*, to warn secretly]

Summoned by Bells an autobiography in blank verse by Sir John Betjeman (1960). It mainly describes his education at Oxford.

Summoner, the the avaricious, lecherous, and corrupt writ-bearer in Chaucer's *The Canterbury Tales*, who tells a bawdy story about a greedy friar.

summons — *noun* (PL. **summonses**) **1** a written order legally obliging a person to attend a court of law at a specified time. **2** any authoritative order to come or to do something. — *verb* to serve with a summons.

sumo *noun* traditional Japanese wrestling between contestants of great bulk, won by forcing the opponent to the ground or out of the circular unroped ring. [from Japanese *sumo*]

sump *noun* **1** a small tank inside a vehicle engine from which oil is carried around the moving parts. **2** any pit into which liquid drains or is poured. [from Dutch *somp*]

sumptuary *adj.* **1** relating to or regulating expense. **2** controlling extravagance. [from Latin *sumptuarius*, from *sumptus*, cost]

sumptuous *adj.* superbly rich and luxurious. [from Latin *sumptuosus*, from *sumptus*, cost]

sum total the complete or final total.

Sumy POP (1991e) 301 000, a city in NE Ukraine, lying on the R Psel. It was founded in 1652.

Sun *or* **Sun.** *abbrev.* Sunday.

sun — *noun* **1** (*usually* **the Sun**) the central object of the solar system, around which the planets revolve, held in their orbits by its gravitational pull. It is the nearest star to Earth, and its heat and light energy enable living organisms to survive on Earth. **2** the heat and light of this star. **3** any star with a system of planets revolving around it. — *verb* (**sunned, sunning**) to expose (oneself) to the sun's rays. — **under the sun** anywhere; on earth. [from Anglo-Saxon *sunne*]

◇ Compared with other stars the Sun is relatively small and dim, but because it is only 150

million km from Earth, it appears large and bright. It consists of a glowing ball of gas (mainly hydrogen and helium) 1.4 million km in diameter, and over 100 times the diameter of the Earth. It is the source of light and heat for the Earth and other planets, and its surface temperature is about 6 000°C, but the temperature in its central core, which is the site of the nuclear reactions that provide its heat and light energy, is believed to be about 15 million °C. The Sun is about 4 600 million years old, and is about halfway through its expected life cycle.

The shining surface of the Sun is known as the *photosphere*. This is the region where *sunspots* occur, and glowing hydrogen clouds known as *prominences* arise from it. Charged atomic particles, mainly electrons, pour into space from the Sun, causing a phenomenon known as the *solar wind*, and near the Sun's surface they produce its characteristic bright halo or *corona*, which can only be seen when the Sun's brilliant disc is hidden during a total eclipse. The Sun will shine for thousands of millions of years, and eventually it will expand to become a *red giant*, and the Earth's oceans will boil. The Sun will then shrink to form a *white dwarf*.

sunbathe *verb intrans.* to expose one's body to the sun, in order to get a suntan.

sunbathing *noun* exposing oneself to the sun.

sunbeam *noun* a ray of sunlight.

sunbed *noun* a bed-like device with sun-lamps fitted above (and often beneath a transparent screen one lies on), for artificially tanning the whole body.

sunburn *noun* soreness and reddening of the skin caused by over-exposure to the sun.

sundae *noun* a portion of ice-cream topped with fruit, nuts, syrup, etc.

Sunda Islands an island group in Indonesia. It comprises the Greater Sunda Is (consisting of Java, Sumatra, Borneo, and Sulawesi, with their small adjacent islands) and Nusa Tenggara, which were formerly called the Lesser Sunda Is (consisting of Bali, Lombok, Sumba, Sumbawa, Flores, and Timor, with their small islands).

Sundarbans a national park in India and Bangladesh. It was established in 1973 to protect the mangrove habitat of the Ganges Delta and its wildlife, particularly India's largest surviving population of tigers. AREA c.10 000sq km/3 900sq mi. The park is a World Heritage site.

Sunday *noun* **1** the first day of the week and for most Christians the day of worship and rest. **2** *colloq.* a newspaper appearing on this day. — **a month of Sundays** a very long time. [from Anglo-Saxon *sunnan dæg*, day of the sun]

Sunday best one's best clothes, (especially formerly) considered the most suitable for wearing to church.

Sunday school a class for the religious instruction of children, held on Sundays, usually in church buildings.

Sunderland, Robert Spencer, 2nd Earl of (1641–1702) English statesman, born in Paris. He became an influential adviser of, successively, Charles II, James II, and William III. Although he was dismissed as Secretary of State in 1681 for voting to exclude James from the succession, he was reinstated in 1683 and became Chief Minister under James (1685) and a Catholic (1688). On William's accession he fled to Europe, but after renouncing his Catholicism he was allowed to return in 1691, and was Lord Chancellor for a brief period in 1697.

Sunderland, formerly **Wearmouth** POP (1981) 196 000, a port town in Sunderland borough, Tyne and Wear, NE England. It lies at the mouth of the R Wear, 16km/10mi SE of Newcastle upon Tyne, on the site of a monastery (founded in 674). NOTABLE FEATURES museum; art gallery.

sundew *noun Bot.* an insectivorous plant of the genus *Drosera*, found in bogs and on sandy heaths where nitrogen is scarce. The leaves are covered with long sticky hairs that trap insects which are then digested by the plant, providing it with an important source of extra nitrogen.

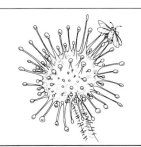

leaf of sundew plant

sundial *noun* an instrument that uses sunlight to tell the time, by the changing position of the shadow that a vertical arm casts on a horizontal plate with graded markings.

sundown *noun* sunset.

sundry — *adj.* various; assorted; miscellaneous. — *noun* (in *pl.* **sundries**) various small unspecified items; oddments. — **all and sundry** everybody. [from Anglo-Saxon *syndrig*]

Sundsvall POP (1992e) 94 000, a seaport and commercial town in SE Västernorrland county, E Sweden, lying on the Gulf of Bothnia. Since the 6c it has been an important trading centre; it received its charter in 1624.

sunfish *noun* a large and distinctive fish that is widespread in open waters of tropical and temperate seas, and has a compressed almost circular body, 1m to 2m in length, a small mouth, and teeth fused into a sharp beak.

sunflower *noun* a tall annual plant (*Helianthus annuus*) that produces large yellow flowerheads up to 30cm in diameter on tall stems up to 3m in height. It is widely cultivated for its seeds, which are rich in edible oil, and as a garden plant. Sunflower-seed oil is used as a cooking oil, and in the manufacture of margarine, soap, paints, and varnishes.

Sunflowers the title of several paintings by Vincent van Gogh. One version (1888) is in the Tate Gallery, London, another in the Van Gogh Museum in Amsterdam, and a third on exhibit in Tokyo.

sung see SING.

sunglasses *pl. noun* glasses with tinted lenses, worn to protect the eyes from sunlight, not to correct eyesight.

sunk see SINK.

sunken past participle of SINK. — *adj.* **1** situated or fitted at a lower level than the surrounding area. **2** *said of the cheeks, etc* made hollow through ill health.

sun-lamp *noun* a lamp emitting light similar in nature to sunlight, used therapeutically and for artificially tanning the skin.

sunlight *noun* light from the sun.

sunlit *adj.* lit by the sun.

sun lounge a room with large windows for letting in maximum sunlight.

Sunni *noun* one of the two main branches of the Islamic religion, regarding the teachings of Mohammed himself as supremely authoritative. See also SHIA. [from Arabic *sunnah*, rule]
◇ Sunnis represent 'orthodoxy' in Islam, and comprise about 80 per cent of all Muslims. They recognize the first four caliphs as following the right course (*rashidun*) and accept the authority of the *Sunna* or *Sunnah* ('path'), traditional Muslim

law based on biographical stories about the Prophet Muhammad and constituting a secondary source of revelation to that which is written down in the Koran.

Sunnite — *noun* an adherent of the Sunni. — *adj.* relating to the Sunni.

sunny *adj.* (**sunnier, sunniest**) **1** filled with sunshine or sunlight. **2** cheerful; good-humoured.

sunrise *noun* the sun's appearance above the horizon in the morning; also, the time of day represented by this.

sunroof *noun* a transparent panel in a car roof, for letting in sunlight, often opening for ventilation.

sunset *noun* the sun's disappearance below the horizon in the evening; also, the time of day represented by this.

sunshade *noun* **1** a sort of umbrella for protecting one from the sun. **2** an awning.

sunshine *noun* **1** fair weather, with the sun shining brightly. **2** the light or heat of the sun. **3** a place where one can be in the light or heat of the sun. **4** an informal term of address, often used in a condescending or scolding tone.

sunspot *noun* **1** *Astron.* a relatively dark patch on the Sun's surface (the photosphere), representing a region that is cooler than the rest of the photosphere, and caused by an intense magnetic field erupting from within the Sun. **2** *colloq.* a holiday resort renowned for sunny weather.

sunstroke *noun* a severe condition of collapse and fever brought on by over-exposure to the sun.

suntan *noun* a browning of the skin through exposure to the sun or a sun-lamp.

sun-tanned *adj.* having a suntan, brown-skinned.

Sun Temple a richly sculptured Hindu temple built in the 13c in Konarak, Orissa, India. The temple itself represents seven horses pulling the chariot of Surya, the Sun-god.

suntrap *noun* a sheltered place which receives a large amount of sunshine.

sun-up *noun* sunrise.

Sun Yixian *or* **Sun Yat-sen** (1866–1925) founder and early leader of China's Nationalist Party, born in Xiangshen, Guangdong province. He was educated in Hawaii and in Hong Kong, where he trained as a doctor. Alarmed by the weakness and decay of China, he founded the Society for the Revival of China. On a visit to London, he was kidnapped by the Chinese legation, and released through the intervention of the Foreign Office. He then helped to organize risings in S China. After the assassination of his follower, Sung Chiao-jen, civil war ensued (1913), and he set up a separate government at Guangzhou (Canton). He died in Beijing (Peking), widely accepted as the true leader of the nation.

Suomenlinna, Fortress of, Swedish **Sveaborg** a fortress (built 1748) on islands off the coast of Helsinki, Finland. It is a World Heritage site.

sup — *verb* (**supped, supping**) **1** to drink in small mouthfuls. **2** *colloq.* to drink (alcohol). — *noun* a small mouthful; a sip. [from Anglo-Saxon *supan*]

super¹ — *adj., interj. colloq.* extremely good; excellent. — *noun* something of superior quality or grade, eg petrol. [from Latin *super*, above]

super² *noun colloq.* **1** a superintendent. **2** a supernumerary, especially a supernumerary actor.

super- *combining form* forming words meaning: **1** great or extreme in size or degree: *supertanker*. **2** above or beyond: *supernatural*. **3** outstanding: *superhero*. [from Latin *super*, above]

superannuated *adj.* **1** made to retire and given a pension; pensioned off. **2** old and no longer fit for use. [from Latin *super*, above + *annus*, year]

superannuation *noun* **1** an amount regularly deducted from wages as a contribution to a company pension. **2** the pension received. **3** retirement.

superb *adj.* **1** *colloq.* outstandingly excellent. **2** magnificent; majestic. [from Latin *superbus*, proud]

superbly *adv.* in a superb way.

Super Bowl in the USA, a professional football game established in 1967. It is the championship match of the National Football League, held annually between the winning teams in the American Football Conference and the National Football Conference.

supercharge *verb* **1** to increase the power and performance of (a vehicle engine). **2** to charge or fill (eg an atmosphere) with an intense amount of an emotion, etc.

supercharger *noun Engineering* a mechanical pump or compressor that is used to increase the amount of air taken into the cylinder of an internal combustion engine, in order to burn the fuel more rapidly and so increase the power output.

supercilious *adj.* **1** self-important. **2** arrogantly disdainful. [from Latin *super*, above + *cilium*, eyelid]

superciliously *adv.* with a supercilious manner.

superciliousness *noun* a supercilious quality.

superconductivity *noun Physics* the complete loss of electrical resistance exhibited by many metals and alloys at temperatures close to absolute zero (−273°C). Various materials, eg certain ceramics, have recently been discovered that show superconductivity at much higher temperatures, close to that of liquid nitrogen. Superconducting coils are used in some large electromagnets and particle accelerators, where they produce very strong magnetic fields.

superconductor *noun Physics* a material which exhibits superconductivity.

supercooling *noun Physics* the cooling of a liquid to a temperature below that considered to be its freezing point.

superego *noun Psychol.* in psychoanalysis, the part of the mind that is concerned with moral conscience or judgement, and so sets standards for the ego, causing it discomfort when it accepts unworthy impulses from the id.

supererogation *noun* the doing of more than is required. [from Latin *super*, above + *erogare*, to pay out]

superficial *adj.* **1** of, on, or near the surface. **2** not thorough or in-depth; cursory. **3** only apparent; not real or genuine. **4** lacking the capacity for sincere emotion or serious thought; shallow. [from Latin *super*, above + *facies*, face]

superficiality *noun* a superficial quality.

superficially *adv.* in a superficial way.

superfluidity *noun Physics* the property of zero resistance to flow (ie zero viscosity) exhibited by liquid helium at temperatures below −271°C. At these temperatures, helium exhibits unusual properties, including the ability to creep out of a container in apparent defiance of gravity.

superfluity *noun* (PL. **superfluities**) **1** being superfluous. **2** a thing that is superfluous. **3** a superabundance.

superfluous *adj.* more than is needed or wanted; surplus. [from Latin *superfluus*, overflowing]

supergiant *noun* a bright star of enormous size and low density, such as Betelgeuse and Antares.

supergrass *noun slang* a police informer whose information has led to large numbers of arrests.

superheterodyne receiver *Radio* a radio receiver in which the frequency of the incoming signal is reduced by mixing it with another signal generated inside the receiver. The resulting intermediate frequency is easier to amplify and manipulate than the initial frequency.

super high frequency *Radio* (ABBREV. **SHF**) a radio frequency in the range 3 000 to 30 000 MHz.

superhuman *adj.* beyond ordinary human ability or knowledge.

superimpose *verb* to lay or set (one thing) on top of another.

superimposition *noun* **1** superimposing or being superimposed. **2** something that is superimposed.

superintend *verb* to supervise. [from Latin *superintendere*]

superintendence *noun* superintending.

superintendent *noun* **1** a police officer above the rank of chief inspector. **2** a person who superintends.

Superior, Lake the largest of the N American Great Lakes, and the largest freshwater lake in the world. AREA 82 103sq km/31 692sq mi; length 563km/350mi; breadth 257km/160mi; maximum depth 405m. The lake, 35% of which lies in Canada, forms part of the US–Canadian boundary. Connected with L Huron in the SE via St Mary's R (the Soo canals), L Superior receives the Nipigon, Kaministikwia, Pigeon, and St Louis rivers. There are several islands, including Isle Royale (a US national park).

superior — *adj.* (*often* **superior to someone** *or* **something**) **1** higher in rank or position. **2** better in a particular way. **3** of high quality. **4** arrogant; self-important. **5** *Printing, said of a character* set above the level of the line; superscript. — *noun* **1** a person of higher rank or position. **2** the head of a religious community. [from Latin *superus*, set above]

superiority *noun* **1** a superior state. **2** preeminence. **3** advantage.

superior planet *Astron.* a planet whose orbit around the Sun lies outside that of the Earth, ie Mars, Jupiter, Saturn, Uranus, Neptune, and Pluto.

superlative — *adj.* **1** superior to all others; supreme. **2** *Grammar, said of an adjective or adverb* expressing the highest degree of a particular quality, eg *nicest, most beautiful.* — *noun Grammar* the superlative form, or an adjective or adverb in this form. [from Latin *superlativus*]

superman *noun* (PL. **supermen**) **1** a man with extraordinary strength or ability. **2** a fictional man with superhuman powers.

supermarket *noun* a large self-service store selling food and other goods.

supernatant *noun Chem.* the clear layer of liquid above a precipitate or a sediment that has settled. [from SUPER- + Latin *natare*, to swim, float]

supernatural — *adj.* of, relating to, or being phenomena that cannot be explained by the laws of nature or physics. — *noun* (**the supernatural**) supernatural phenomena.

supernova *noun* (PL. **supernovae, supernovas**) a star that suddenly becomes millions of times brighter as a result of a catastrophic explosion, so that it may dominate an entire galaxy of stars. A supernova explosion occurs when a massive star has exhausted all the nuclear fuel in its central core, which then collapses. Supernovas occur relatively rarely, and take several weeks or months to fade.

supernumerary — *adj.* additional to the normal or required number; extra. — *noun* (PL.

supernumeraries) **1** a supernumerary person or thing. **2** an actor without a speaking part. [from Latin *super*, above + *numerus*, number]

superoxide *noun Chem.* **1** any of various chemical compounds that are very powerful oxidizing agents and contain the O_2^- ion, which is highly toxic to living tissues. **2** any oxide that reacts with an acid to form hydrogen peroxide and oxygen.

superphosphate *noun Chem.* the most important type of phosphate fertilizer, made by treating calcium phosphate in the form of the mineral apatite, bone ash, or slag with sulphuric acid (which yields a fertilizer containing 16 to 20 per cent phosphorus) or phosphoric acid (which yields a fertilizer containing 45 to 50 per cent phosphorus).

superpower *noun* a nation with outstanding political, economic, or military influence, especially the USA or the former USSR.

superscript *Printing* — *adj., said of a character* set above the level of the line, as the number 2 in 10^2. — *noun* a superscript character. [from Latin *super*, above + *scribere*, to write]

supersede *verb* **1** to take the place of (often something outdated or no longer valid). **2** to set aside in favour of another. [from Latin *supersedere*, to sit above]

supersession *noun* superseding or being superseded.

supersonic *adj.* **1** faster than the speed of sound. **2** *said of aircraft* capable of supersonic speeds. [from Latin *super*, above + *sonus*, sound]

supersonically *adv.* in a supersonic way.

superstar *noun* an internationally famous celebrity, especially from the world of film, popular music, or sport.

superstition *noun* **1** belief in an influence that certain (especially commonplace) objects, actions, or occurrences have on events, people's lives, etc. **2** a particular opinion or practice based on such belief. **3** any widely held but unfounded belief. [from Latin *superstitio*, fear of the supernatural]

superstitious *adj.* **1** relating to or involving superstition. **2** believing, following, or practising superstition.

superstring *noun Physics* a theory that has been proposed to explain the properties of elementary particles and the forces between them, and that takes account of both quantum theory and relativity.

◇ It is suggested that extremely short string-like objects (about 10^{35}m in length) with a very high energy content are the fundamental objects in the Universe, which would have to exist in 10 or 26 dimensions, rather than just the three dimensions of space and the one dimension of time that have been detected to date. No direct experimental evidence has yet been obtained for the existence of superstrings.

superstructure *noun* any part built above another (especially main) part, eg those parts of a ship above the main deck.

supertax *noun colloq.* a surtax.

supertitle same as SURTITLE.

supervene *verb intrans.* to occur as an (especially unexpected) interruption to some process. [from Latin *supervenire*, to come upon]

supervention *noun* supervening.

supervise *verb* to be in overall charge of; to oversee. [from Latin *supervidere*, to see over]

supervision *noun* supervising; inspection; control.

supervisor *noun* a person who supervises.

supervisory *adj.* relating to or involving supervision.

supine *adj.* **1** lying on one's back. **2** passive or lazy. [from Latin *supinus*]

supper *noun* **1** a light evening meal. **2** a late-night snack taken in addition to and later than the main evening meal. [from Old French *soper*]

supplant *verb* to take the place of, often by force or unfair means. [from Latin *supplantare*, to trip up]

supple *adj.* **1** *said of joints, etc* bending easily; flexible. **2** *said of a person* having flexible joints. [from Latin *supplex*, bending the knees]

supplely *or* **supply** *adv.* in a supple way.

supplement — *noun* **1** a thing added to make something complete or to make up a deficiency. **2** an extra section added to a book to give additional information or to correct previous errors. **3** a separate part added to a newspaper or magazine on certain occasions, eg on Sundays. — *verb* to add to, or make up a lack of. [from Latin *supplementum*, a filling up]

supplementary *adj.* additional; added to supply what is needed.

supplementary benefit a former name for INCOME SUPPORT.

supplementation *noun* **1** supplementing. **2** something that is added.

suppleness *noun* a supple quality.

supplicant — *noun* a person who supplicates or entreats. — *adj.* supplicating; entreating.

supplicate *verb trans., intrans.* (**supplicate someone** *or* **to someone**) to make a humble and earnest request or entreaty to them. [from Latin *supplicare*, to beg on one's knees]

supplication *noun* **1** supplicating. **2** an earnest or humble petition. **3** an earnest prayer or entreaty for a special blessing.

supplier *noun* a person or organization that supplies a particular commodity.

supply — *verb* (**supplies, supplied**) **1** (**supply someone with something** *or* **something to someone**) to provide or furnish them with it. **2** to satisfy (eg a need); to make up (a deficiency). — *noun* (PL. **supplies**) **1** an amount supplied, especially regularly. **2** an amount that can be drawn from and used; a stock. **3** (**supplies**) necessary food or equipment gathered or taken on a journey, etc. **4** a source of some public utility, eg water or gas. **5** *Econ.* the total amount of a commodity being produced for sale. **6** degree of availability: *in short supply.* **7** a person, especially a teacher, acting as a temporary substitute. **8** the act of supplying. [from Latin *supplere*, to fill up]

supply-side an economic approach based on the theory that supply creates demand, and proposing that the most effective method of increasing national output and the level of employment is through the removal of tax disincentives. Thus, if personal taxes are reduced, people work harder and there will be a significant rise in output; also, if taxes on profit are reduced it will encourage investment which will again improve output.

support — *verb* **1** to keep upright or in place; to keep from falling; to bear the weight of. **2** to give active approval and encouragement to. **3** to provide with the means necessary for living or existing. **4** to maintain a loyal interest in the fortunes of (a sporting team), especially by regular attendance at matches. **5** to reinforce the disputed accuracy or validity of (eg a theory or claim). **6** to speak in favour of (a proposal, etc). **7** to play a part subordinate to (a leading actor). **8** to perform as an introduction to (the main item in a musical concert, etc). **9** to bear or tolerate. — *noun* **1** the act of supporting or the state of being supported. **2** a person, group, or thing that supports; a supporting act in a concert, etc. [from Latin *supportare*, to hold up]

supporter *noun* a person who supports a cause or proposal, or who supports an institution such as a sports team or political party.

supporting *adj.* giving support.

supportive *adj.* providing support, especially active approval and encouragement.

suppose *verb* 1 to consider likely or probable; to regard as certain or probable. 2 to treat (a possibility) as a fact for the purposes of forming an argument or plan: *let us suppose he does not come.* 3 *said of a theory* to require (a factor or assumption) to be true in order to be itself valid. [from Latin *supponere*, to substitute]

supposed *adj.* generally believed to be so or such (but considered doubtful by the speaker). — **supposed to** ... 1 expected or required to be or do something: *are we supposed to reply?* 2 (*often ironical, as a reproof*) reputed to have or be something: *you are supposed to be an adult.*

supposedly *adv.* as is supposed.

supposition *noun* 1 the act of supposing. 2 that which is supposed; a mere possibility or assumption, not a fact.

suppositional *adj.* hypothetical, conjectural, supposed.

supposititious *adj.* based on supposition; hypothetical.

suppository *noun* (PL. **suppositories**) *Medicine* a soluble container of medicine that is solid at room temperature and can be inserted into the rectum or vagina. [from Latin *suppositorium*, from *supponere*, to place underneath]

suppress *verb* 1 to hold in or restrain (feelings, etc). 2 to put a stop to or crush (eg a rebellion). 3 to prevent from broadcasting or circulating; to prevent from being broadcast, circulated, or otherwise made known. 4 to moderate or eliminate (interference) in an electrical device. [from Latin *supprimere*, to press down]

suppression *noun* 1 suppressing or being suppressed. 2 stopping. 3 concealing.

suppressor *noun* 1 a person who suppresses. 2 a device for suppressing electrical interference.

suppurate *verb intrans.*, *said of a wound, etc* to gather and release pus. [from Latin *suppurare*]

suppuration *noun* 1 the process of suppurating. 2 the formation or secretion of pus. 3 the coming to a head of a boil or similar eruption.

supra *adv.* above; further up the page or earlier in the book. [from Latin *supra*]

supra- *combining form* forming words meaning 'above, beyond': *supranational.* [from Latin *supra*, above]

supranational *adj.* 1 in or belonging to more than one nation. 2 overriding national sovereignty.

supremacy *noun* 1 supreme power or authority. 2 the state of being supreme.

Suprematism a form of modern art based on four simple shapes: rectangle, circle, triangle and cross. The movement was started in Russia (c.1913) by Kasimir Malevich, who painted a square divided diagonally into black and white on a white background. The movement culminated in his *White on White* series (white square on a white background) in 1918–19.

supreme *adj.* 1 of highest rank, power or importance; greatest. 2 most excellent; best. 3 greatest in degree; utmost. [from Latin *supremus*, highest]

Supreme Court in the USA, the highest federal court, created in 1789. Its members (nine since 1869) are appointed by the president with the advice and consent of the Senate. In addition to its jurisdiction relating to appeals, the court also exercises oversight of the Constitution through the power of judicial review of the Acts of state, and federal legislatures, and the executive.

Supreme Headquarters Allied Expeditionary Force (ABBREV. **SHAEF**) a force

formally established (13 Feb 1944) under US General Eisenhower, with British Air Chief Marshal Tedder as Deputy Supreme Commander, to mount the Allied invasion of occupied Europe.

supremely *adv.* to a supreme degree.

supremo *noun* (PL. **supremos**) *colloq.* 1 a supreme head or leader. 2 a boss. [from Spanish; see SUPREME]

sur-¹ *prefix* forming words meaning 'over, above, beyond'. [from French *sur*]

sur-² *prefix* a form of *sub-* used before some words beginning with *r*: *surrogate.*

sura *or* **surah** *noun* a chapter of the Koran. [from Arabic *sura*, step]

Surabaya *or* **Surabaja** POP (1990e) 2.4m, the second-largest city in Indonesia and the industrial seaport capital of Java Timor province, E Java. It lies at the mouth of the R Kali Mas. The city is a naval base, with port facilities located at Tanjung Perak. Surabaya has been an important trading centre since the 14c.

Surat POP (1991) 1.5m, a port in Gujarat state, W India. It is situated on the Gulf of Cambay, 240km/150mi N of Bombay. HISTORY a rich trading centre of the Mughal Empire in the 17c and the 18c; first British trading post in India in 1612; headquarters of the British East India Company until 1687. Surat is noted for its textiles (brocades, silks, etc) and diamond cutting.

surcharge — *noun* 1 an extra charge. 2 an alteration printed on or over something, especially a new valuation on a stamp. 3 an amount over a permitted load. — *verb* 1 to impose a surcharge on. 2 to print a surcharge on or over. 3 to overload.

surd *noun* 1 *Maths.* an irrational number that is a root of a rational number, so can never be determined exactly, eg $\sqrt{3}$. 2 an arithmetic expression involving the sum or difference of such numbers, eg $\sqrt{3} + \sqrt{6}$. [from Latin *surdus*, deaf]

sure — *adj.* 1 confident beyond doubt in one's belief or knowledge; convinced. 2 guaranteed or certain (to happen, etc). 3 (**sure of something**) unquestionably destined for it or assured of it. 4 undoubtedly true or accurate: *a sure sign.* 5 reliably stable or secure. — *adv. colloq.* certainly; of course.
— **be sure to** ... not to fail to do something.
for sure definitely; undoubtedly.
make sure to take the necessary action to remove all doubt or risk; to be certain.
sure enough *colloq.* in fact; as was expected.
to be sure certainly; admittedly.
[from Old French *sur*, from Latin *securus*, with care]

sure-fire *adj. colloq.* sure to succeed; infallible.

sure-footed *adj.* 1 not stumbling or likely to stumble. 2 not making, or not likely to make, mistakes.

surely *adv.* 1 without doubt; certainly. 2 *used in questions and exclamations* it must be that ...; it is hoped or expected that: *surely you are not leaving already!*

sureness *noun* being sure.

surety *noun* (PL. **sureties**) 1 security against loss or damage, or a guarantee that a promise will be fulfilled; also, a thing given as security. 2 a person who agrees to become legally responsible for another person's behaviour. [see SURE]

surf — *noun* the foam produced by breaking waves. — *verb intrans.* to go surfing.

Surface, Charles and **Joseph** the brothers of contrasting character in Richard Brinsley Sheridan's *The School for Scandal.* Charles, an amiable but spendthrift layabout, is in love with Maria while Joseph, a mean hypocrite, spreads vicious rumours about him while himself trying to seduce Lady Teazle. Their rich uncle Sir Oliver

disguises himself as Mr Premium to assess their characters.

surface — *noun* 1 the upper or outer side of anything, often with regard to texture or appearance. 2 the upper level of a body or container of liquid. 3 external appearance, rather than underlying reality. 4 a geometric figure that is flat or two-dimensional, not solid. 5 (*attributive*) **a** at, on, or relating to a surface. **b** superficial: *surface politeness.* — *verb* 1 to give the desired finish or texture to the surface of. 2 *intrans.* to rise to the surface of a liquid. 3 *intrans.* to become apparent; to come to light. 4 *intrans. colloq.* to get out of bed. [from French *surface*]

surface mail mail sent overland or by ship, as opposed to *airmail*.

surface tension *Physics* the force that causes a liquid to behave as if it has an elastic surface skin. It is caused by the attraction between molecules of a liquid at its surface, which causes the liquid to change shape in order to mimimize its surface. For this reason a water drop on a flat surface tends to dome upwards, but if detergent is added to it, reducing surface tension, the water will spread out and wet the surface. Surface tension is responsible for capillary action. See also CAPILLARITY.

surfactant *noun Chem.* 1 any soluble substance that reduces the surface tension of a liquid, or reduces the surface tension between two liquids or between a solid and a liquid. Surfactants are used as detergents, wetting agents, emulsifiers, and foaming agents. 2 *Zool.* a substance secreted by the cells lining the alveoli of the lungs that prevents the walls of the alveoli from sticking together. [a contraction of *surface-active agent*]

surfboard *noun* a long narrow shaped fibreglass board that a surfer stands or lies on.

surfcasting *noun* fishing from the shore by casting into surf.

surfeit — *noun* 1 an excess. 2 the stuffed or sickened feeling resulting from any excess, especially over-eating or over-drinking. — *verb* to feed or otherwise indulge until stuffed or disgusted. [from Old French *surfait*, excess]

surfer *noun* a person who goes surfing.

surfing *noun* the sport of riding a surfboard along on the crests of large breaking waves.

surge — *noun* 1 a sudden powerful mass movement, especially forwards. 2 a sudden sharp increase. 3 a violent rush of emotion. 4 a rising and falling of a large area of sea, without individual waves; a swell. — *verb intrans.* to well up, move, increase, or swell suddenly and with force. [from Latin *surgere*, to rise]

surgeon *noun* 1 a doctor specializing in surgery. 2 a military doctor. [from Old French *surgien*, from Greek *kheirurgia*; see SURGERY]

surgery *noun* (PL. **surgeries**) 1 the treatment of disease or injury by cutting into the patient's body to operate directly on, or remove, the affected part. 2 the place where, or period of the day during which, a community doctor or dentist carries out treatment. 3 a set period during which a local MP or councillor is available to be consulted by the public. [from Greek *kheirurgia*, from *kheir*, hand + *ergon*, work]

surgical *adj.* relating to, for use in, or by means of surgery.

surgically *adv.* by means of surgery.

surgical spirit methylated spirit, with small amounts of castor oil, oil of wintergreen and other substances, used for cleaning wounds and sterilising medical equipment.

Surinam *or* **Suriname**, official name **Republic of Surinam** POP (1992e) 438 000, a republic in NE South America, divided into nine districts. AREA 163 265sq km/63 020sq mi. It is bounded W by Guyana, S by Brazil, E by French

Guiana, and N by the Atlantic Ocean. CAPITAL Paramaribo. CHIEF TOWNS Brokopondo, Nieuw Amsterdam. TIME ZONE GMT –3.5. The population originates from the following groups: E Indian (37%), Creole (31%), and Javanese (15%); several religions are followed. OFFICIAL LANGUAGE Dutch. CURRENCY the Surinam guilder. PHYSICAL DESCRIPTION diverse natural regions, ranging from coastal lowland through savannah to mountainous upland; the coastal strip is mostly covered by swamp; the highland interior in the S is overgrown with dense tropical forest. CLIMATE tropically hot and humid, with two rainy seasons in May–Jul and Nov–Jan; Paramaribo temperatures range from 22–33°C; the average monthly rainfall is 310mm in the N and 67mm in the S. HISTORY sighted by Columbus in 1498; first settled by the British in 1651; taken by the states of Zeeland in 1667; captured by the British in 1799; restored to the Netherlands in 1818; became an independent republic in 1975; c.40% of the population emigrated to the Netherlands following independence; military coups in 1980 and 1990. GOVERNMENT the 1987 constitution provides for a 51-member National Assembly elected for five years, and a President elected by the Assembly. ECONOMY lack of foreign exchange has hindered development of the economy, which is based on mining and agriculture; bauxite mining provides c.80% of export income; sugar cane, rice, citrus fruits, coffee, bananas, oil palms, cacao, fishing; vast timber resources.

Surinam

surliness *noun* being surly.

surly *adj.* (**surlier**, **surliest**) abrupt and impolite in manner or speech. [from obsolete *sirly*, haughty]

surmise — *verb* to conclude from information available; to infer. — *noun* **1** a conclusion drawn from such information. **2** the act of drawing such a conclusion; conjecture. [from Old French *surmettre*, to accuse]

surmount *verb* **1** to overcome (problems, obstacles, etc). **2** to be set on top of; to crown. [from Old French *surmunter*]

surmountable *adj.* capable of being surmounted.

surname *noun* a family name or last name, as opposed to a forename or Christian name. [from French *surnom*]

surpass *verb* **1** to go or be beyond in degree or extent; to exceed. **2** to be better than. [from French *surpasser*]

surpassed *adj.* bettered.

surplice *noun* a loose wide-sleeved white linen garment worn ceremonially over the robe of members of the clergy and choir singers. [from Latin *superpellicium*, overgarment]

surplus — *noun* **1** an amount exceeding the amount required or used. **2** *Commerce* the amount by which income is greater than expenditure. — *adj.* left over after needs have been met; extra. [from French *surplus*]

surprise — *noun* **1** a feeling of mental disorientation caused by an encounter with something sudden or unexpected; also, the thing encountered. **2** the act of catching someone unawares; the state of being caught unawares. — *verb* **1** to cause to experience surprise by presenting with or subjecting to something unexpected. **2** to come upon unexpectedly or catch unawares. **3** to capture or attack with a sudden unexpected manoeuvre. — **take someone by surprise** to surprise them abruptly; to catch them unawares. [from Old French *surprendre*, to take over]

surprised *adj.* **1** taken unawares. **2** shocked, startled, amazed.

Surprise Symphony Haydn's Symphony No.94 in G (1791), named because a loud drumbeat suddenly sounds during the slow movement.

surprising *adj.* causing surprise.

surreal *adj.* dreamlike, in the style of Surrealism.

Surrealism a movement in modern art and literature which flourished between the Wars, mainly in France. The first Surrealist manifesto of André Breton (1924) proposed the subversion of 19c Realism by the three related means of humour, dream, and counter-logic (the absurd). The term is now used to describe the heightened or disordered perception and registration of reality, by whatever means. The basic idea was to free the artist from the demands of logic, and to penetrate beyond everyday consciousness to the 'super-reality' that lies behind. It drew on Sigmund Freud's theory of the subconscious and many pictures by Salvador Dali, René Magritte, and Yves Tanguy seek to recreate the fantasy world of dreams. Other leading Surrealists include Max Ernst, Giorgio de Chirico, and Jean Arp, and its influence is clear in many works by Pablo Picasso and Paul Klee. In literature, the movement is illustrated by the poetry of Louis Aragon and Paul Eluard, the plays of Eugène Ionesco and Samuel Beckett, and the novels of Jean Genet and William S Burroughs.

Surrealist — *noun* an adherent of Surrealism. — *adj.* relating to or characteristic of Surrealism.

surrealistic *adj.* suggestive or characteristic of Surrealism.

surrender — *verb* (**surrendered, surrendering**) **1** *intrans.* to admit defeat by giving oneself up to an enemy; to yield. **2** (**surrender to something**) to allow oneself to be influenced or overcome by a desire or emotion; to give in. **3** to give or hand over, voluntarily or under duress. — *noun* the act of surrendering. [from Old French *surrendre*]

surreptitious *adj.* done secretly or sneakily. [from Latin *sub*, secretly + *rapere*, to snatch]

surreptitiously *adv.* in a surreptitious way.

surreptitiousness *noun* being surreptitious.

Surrey, Henry Howard, Earl of (c.1517–47) English courtier and poet, born in Hunsdon, Hertfordshire. He accompanied Henry VIII to France in 1532, was knighted in 1542, and served in Scotland, France, and Flanders. On his return in 1546, he was found guilty of treason, and beheaded. He is remembered for his love poetry, in which he pioneered the use of blank verse and the Elizabethan sonnet form.

Surrey POP (1992e) 1m, a county in SE England, which is divided into 11 districts. AREA 1 679sq km/648sq mi. It is bounded E by Kent, S by East Sussex and W Sussex, SW by Hampshire, NW by Berkshire, and NE by Greater London. The Thames, Mole, and Wey rivers run through this largely residential county and it is crossed E–W by the North Downs. CHIEF TOWNS Kingston-upon-Thames, Guildford, Reigate, Leatherhead, Staines, Woking. NOTABLE FEATURES Box Hill, Leith Hill, Runnymede; Royal Botanic Gardens (at Kew).

surrogacy *noun* (PL. **surrogacies**) **1** the state of being surrogate or a surrogate. **2** the use of a surrogate, especially a surrogate mother.

surrogate — *adj.* standing in for another. — *noun* a surrogate person or thing. [from Latin *sub*, in the place of + *rogare*, to ask]

surrogate mother a woman who carries and gives birth to a baby on behalf of another couple, especially through artificial insemination with the man's sperm.

surround — *verb* **1** to extend all around; to encircle. **2** to exist as a background situation to; to make up the particular context or environment of. **3** (**surround oneself with people or things**) to maintain around oneself a large following of people or collection of things. — *noun* a border or edge, or an ornamental structure fitted round this. [from Old French *suronder*]

surrounding *adj.* that surrounds; encompassing, neighbouring.

surroundings *pl. noun* environment; the places and things round about.

surtax *noun* an additional tax, especially on incomes above a certain level.

Surtees, John (1934–) English racing driver and motorcyclist, born in Westerham, Kent, the only man to win world titles on two and four wheels. He won the 350cc motor cycling world title in 1958–60, and the 500cc title in 1956, and 1958–60 (all on an MV Augusta). He then turned to car racing, and won the 1964 world title driving a Ferrari. He later became a racing car manufacturer.

Surtees, Robert Smith (1803–64) English sporting writer, born in The Riding, Northumberland. He edited *New Sporting Magazine* (1831–6), and WROTE a series of sporting novels, including *Handley Cross* (1843), which introduces the character of Mr Jorrocks, grocer and sportsman.

surtitle *or* **supertitle** *noun* each of a sequence of captions projected on to a screen visible to the audience above the stage during the performance of a foreign-language opera or play, giving a running translation of the libretto or dialogue as it is performed. The term was first used in Canada in the 1980s; *supertitle* is more common in the USA.

Surtsey Island a volcanic island off the S coast of Iceland. AREA 1.9sq km/0.7sq mi. It was formed in 1963 by volcanic eruption and is now a nature reserve. Surtsey constitutes one of the Icelandic Westman Is.

surveillance *noun* the act of keeping a close watch over a person, eg a suspected criminal. [from French; see SURVEY]

surveillance TV closed circuit television with security applications, such as supervision of customer areas in banks, building societies, supermarkets, and shopping complexes, and the monitoring of unattended locations. Small monochrome cameras sensitive to low light levels are fitted with wide-angled lens to give maximum coverage from a fixed or remotely-controlled viewpoint; pictures may be recorded or viewed from a central location.

survey — *verb* (with stress on -*vey*) (**surveys, surveyed**) **1** to look at or examine at length or in detail, in order to get a general view. **2** to examine (a building) in order to assess its condition or value. **3** to measure land heights and distances in (an area) for the purposes of drawing a detailed map. — *noun* (with stress on *sur-*) (PL. **surveys**) **1** a detailed examination or investigation, eg to find out public opinion or customer preference. **2** an inspection of a building to assess condition or value. **3** a collecting of land measurements for map-making purposes. [from Old French *surveoir*, from Latin *super*, over + *videre*, to see]

surveyor *noun* a person who surveys land or buildings.

survival *noun* **1** surviving, living on. **2** anything that continues to exist after others of its kind have disappeared, or beyond the time to which it naturally belongs.

survive *verb* **1** *trans., intrans.* to remain alive or relatively unharmed in spite of (a dangerous experience); to come through. **2** to live on after the death of. **3** *intrans.* to remain alive or in existence. [from Latin *super*, beyond + *vivere*, to live]

surviving *adj.* that survives, living on.

survivor *noun* a person who survives.

Surya the Sun-god in Hindu mythology, who was the son of Indra, the pre-eminent god of the Rig-Veda.

sus same as SUSS.

Susa, Greek **Shusan** an ancient city of Elam and the capital of the Achaemenid Empire under Darius I and his successors. It is the site of the world's best preserved ziggurat.

Susan a female first name. [from the Hebrew name *Shushannah*, lily]

susceptibility *noun* (PL. **susceptibilities**) **1** the state or degree of being susceptible. **2** (**susceptibilities**) feelings; sensibilities.

susceptible *adj.* **1** (**susceptible to something**) suffering readily from something (eg a disease or something unwelcome); prone to it. **2** in whom strong feelings, especially of love, are easily aroused. **3** (**susceptible to something**) capable of being influenced by something (eg persuasion). **4** (**susceptible of something**) open to it; admitting of it: *a ruling susceptible of several interpretations*. [from Latin *suscipere*, to take up]

sushi *noun* a Japanese dish of small cakes of cold rice topped with raw fish or vegetables. [from Japanese *sushi*]

Suslov, Mikhail Andreyevich (1902–82) Soviet politician, born in Shakhovskoye. He joined the Communist Party in 1921, and was a member of the Central Committee from 1941 until his death. An ideologist of the Stalinist school, he became a ruthless and strongly doctrinaire administrator. Very different from Khrushchev in temperament and political outlook, he opposed Khrushchev's measures to destroy the Stalin 'cult of personality', his economic reforms, and his foreign policy, and was instrumental in unseating him in 1964.

suspect — *verb* (with stress on *-spect*) **1** to consider likely. **2** to think (a person) possibly or probably guilty of a crime or wrongdoing. **3** to doubt the truth or genuineness of. — *noun* (with stress on *sus-*) a person suspected of committing a crime, etc. — *adj.* (with stress on *sus-*) thought to be possibly false, untrue or dangerous; dubious. [from Latin *suspicere*]

suspend *verb* **1** to hang or hang up. **2** to bring a halt to, especially temporarily. **3** to delay or postpone. **4** to remove from a job, a team, etc temporarily, as punishment or during an investigation of a possible misdemeanour. **5** to keep small insoluble solid particles more or less evenly dispersed throughout a fluid (a liquid or a gas). [from Latin *suspendere*]

suspended animation a state in which a body's main functions are temporarily slowed down to an absolute minimum, eg in hibernation.

suspended sentence a sentence of imprisonment not actually served unless the offender commits another crime within a specified period.

suspender-belt *noun* a woman's belt-like undergarment with attached suspenders.

suspenders *pl. noun* **1** elastic straps for holding up women's stockings. **2** elastic straps for holding up men's socks. **3** *North Amer.* braces for trousers.

suspense *noun* a state of nervous or excited uncertainty. [related to SUSPEND]

suspenseful *adj.* full of suspense.

suspension *noun* **1** the act of suspending or the state of being suspended. **2** a system of springs and shock absorbers that connect the axles of a car to the chassis, and absorb some of the unwanted vibrations transmitted from the road surface. **3** a system in which small insoluble solid particles are more or less evenly dispersed throughout a fluid (a liquid or gas).

suspension bridge a bridge in which the road or rail surface hangs on vertical cables themselves attached to thicker cables stretched between towers.

suspicion *noun* **1** the feeling of suspecting. **2** an act of suspecting; a belief or opinion based on intuition or slender evidence. **3** a slight quantity; a trace.
— **above suspicion** too highly respected to be suspected of a crime or wrongdoing.
under suspicion suspected of a crime or wrongdoing.
[related to SUSPECT]

suspicious *adj.* **1** (*often* **suspicious of** *or* **about something**) suspecting or tending to suspect guilt, wrongdoing, or danger. **2** arousing suspicion; dubious.

suspiciously *adv.* in a suspicious way.

suss *or* **sus** *slang* — *verb* (*also* **suss someone** *or* **something out**) **1** to discover them, or to discover their character, especially by intuition. **2** to assess or establish by taking a look. — *noun* **1** a suspect. **2** suspicion, or suspicious behaviour. [a shortening of SUSPECT or SUSPICION]

Sussex a former county of England. It was divided into East Sussex and West Sussex in 1974, West Sussex gaining part of S Surrey.

Sussex, East POP (1992e) 721 000, a county in SE England, divided into seven districts. AREA 1 795sq km/693sq mi. PHYSICAL DESCRIPTION bounded S by the English Channel, N by Kent, and W by West Sussex; drained by the R Ouse; the South Downs run parallel to the coast; part of the Weald lies in the N of the county. CHIEF TOWNS Lewes (county town); Brighton; Eastbourne; Bexhill; Hastings. ECONOMY agriculture, electronics, furniture, service industries; the S coast is an important tourist area. NOTABLE FEATURES Beachy Head; Ashdown Forest; Romney Marsh; castles at Bodiam, Hastings, Lewes, and Pevensey; site of the Battle of Hastings.

Sussex, Kingdom of a kingdom of the Anglo-Saxon heptarchy, situated between Kent and Wessex, and founded probably by c.500 AD. After its reduction to a dependency of Mercia in the late 8c, it never regained the status of a kingdom, and was annexed to Wessex in the 9c.

Sussex, West POP (1992e) 713 000, a county in S England, divided into seven districts. AREA 1 989sq km/768sq mi. PHYSICAL DESCRIPTION bounded S by the English Channel, E by East Sussex, N by Surrey, and W by Hampshire; drained by the Adur and Arun rivers; the South Downs run parallel to the coast. CHIEF TOWNS Chichester (county town), Worthing, Crawley, Horsham. ECONOMY agriculture; horticulture; tourism; electronics; light engineering. NOTABLE FEATURES the Weald; Arundel and Bamber castles; Petworth House; Goodwood.

sustain *verb* **1** to maintain the energy or spirits of; to keep going. **2** to suffer or undergo (eg an injury). **3** to judge (especially a barrister's objection to an opposing barrister's question or comment in court) to be valid. **4** to bear the weight of; to support. **5** to keep in existence, especially over a long period; to maintain. [from Latin *sustinere*]

sustained *adj.* maintained.

sustained-yield cropping *Environ.* the removal of a natural resource, eg trees, fish, at at a rate that does not irreparably deplete or damage the population.

sustenance *noun* that which keeps up energy or spirits, especially food and drink. [related to SUSTAIN]

Sutherland, Graham (Vivian) (1903–80) English artist, born in London. He worked mainly as an etcher until 1930, then made his reputation as a painter of romantic, mainly abstract landscapes. He was an official war artist (1941–5), and later produced several memorable portraits, including *Somerset Maugham* (1949) and the controversial depiction of *Winston Churchill* (1954), which was destroyed on the orders of Lady Churchill. His other works include the *Crucifixion* (1944) in St Matthew's Church, Northampton, and the tapestry *Christ in Glory*, hung in Coventry Cathedral in 1962.

Sutherland, Dame Joan (1926–) Australian operatic soprano, born in Sydney. She made her début in *Dido and Aeneas* (Sydney, 1947), then went to London (1951) and joined the Royal Opera at Covent Garden (1952–88). She gained international fame in 1959 with her roles in Donizetti's *Lucia di Lammermoor* and Handel's *Samson*. She sang regularly all over the world, including a triumphant Australian tour with her own company in 1965, until she retired (1990). In 1954 she married the Australian conductor Richard Bonynge (1930–).

Sutlej, River a river in Asia. At 1 370km/850mi, it is the longest of the five rivers of the Punjab. The river rises in Tibet and flows NW as the Xiangquan He. It enters India, meandering through the Himalayas, and flows SW to its confluence with the R Chenab, E of Alipur in Pakistan. The combined stream flows SW for 81km/50mi to meet the Indus. Its water is used for irrigation and hydroelectric power, particularly at the Bhakara Dam in India.

suttee *noun* **1** a former Hindu custom in which a widow sacrifices herself by being burned alive on her dead husband's funeral fire. **2** a Hindu woman who sacrifices herself in this way. [from Sanskrit *sati*, true wife]

Sutton Coldfield POP (1981) 103 000, a largely residential town in Birmingham borough, West Midlands, central England. It lies 11km/7mi NE of Birmingham. NOTABLE FEATURE Sutton Park.

Sutton Hoo ship burial the grave of an Anglo-Saxon king, probably Raedwald of East Anglia (d.624/5), discovered beneath a barrow on the R Deben near Woodbridge, E England, in 1939. Excavations revealed a 40-oar open rowing boat (4.25m in beam and 27m long) with a wooden burial chamber containing silver plate, gold jewellery, coins, weapons, and domestic equipment (now in the British Museum).

suture — *noun* **1** the thread used in sewing up wounds. **2** a stitch or seam made with such thread. — *verb* to sew up (a wound). [from Latin *sutura*, seam]

Suva POP (1986) 70 000, the capital and chief port of Fiji. It lies on the SE coast of Viti Levu I and is overlooked by Tholoisuva Forest Park.

Suwon *or* **Suweon** POP (1990) 645 000, the industrial capital of Kyonggi province, NW Korea. It lies 48km/30mi S of Seoul. NOTABLE FEATURES reconstructed fortress walls and gates; Korean Folk Village nearby.

suzerain *noun* **1** a nation or state that has control over another. **2** a feudal lord. [from French *suzerain*]

suzerainty *noun* the position or power of a suzerain.

Suzhou or **Suchow**, formerly **Wuhsien** POP (1990) 707 000, a city in Jiangsu province, E China. It lies on the banks of the Grand Canal. HISTORY first settled in c.1000 BC; became capital of the Kingdom of Wu in 518 BC. NOTABLE FEATURES over 150 ornamental gardens, including Canglang (Surging Wave) Pavilion (c.1044), Shizilin (Lion Grove, 1350), and Wangshi Yuan (Garden of the Master of the Nets, 12c); Huqiu (Tiger Hill) is a 2 500-year-old artificial hill (height 36m), built by the King of Wu as a tomb for his father.

Svalbard POP (1991) 3 000, a Norwegian island group in the Arctic Ocean, c.650km/400mi N of the Norwegian mainland. AREA 62 000sq km/ 23 900sq mi. It consists of four large and several smaller islands. CHIEF ISLANDS Spitsbergen, Nordaustlandet, Edgeøya, Barentsøya, Prins Karls Forland. CHIEF TOWN Longyearbyen. HISTORY discovered in 1596; incorporated into Norway in 1925. ECONOMY coal; phosphate; asbestos; iron ore; galena; sphalerite; chalcopyrite; limestone dolerite; anhydrite.

Svedberg, Theodor (1884–1971) Swedish physical chemist, born in Fleräng, near Valbo. Professor at Uppsala, he developed a very high speed centrifuge known as the ultracentrifuge as a means of following optically the sedimentation of particles too small to be seen in the most powerful microscopes of the time, and was awarded the 1926 Nobel Prize for Chemistry.

svelte adj. of attractively slim build. [from French svelte]

Sveshtari tomb a 3c BC tomb, located near the village of Sveshtari in N Bulgaria. The tomb, which was discovered in 1982, is noted for its 10 caryatids and the frieze which decorates the burial chamber. It is a World Heritage site.

SW abbrev. **1** short wave. **2** south-west or south-western.

swab — noun **1** a piece of cotton wool or gauze used to clean wounds, apply antiseptics, etc. **2** a sample of some bodily fluid taken for examination. **3** a mop used for cleaning floors, ships' decks, etc. **4** slang a worthless person. — verb (**swabbed, swabbing**) to clean or clean out with, or as if with, a swab. [from Old Dutch swabbe]

Swabia a medieval German duchy, extending from the R Rhine in the W to the Alps in the S, Bavaria in the E, and Franconia in the N, containing the cities of Strasbourg, Constance, and Augsburg. The Peasants War of 1524–5 began here, because of disputes between landlords and peasants, the increase of imperial authority, and the spread of Lutheran doctrines.

Swabian League an alliance formed (1488) by 22 Imperial German towns, the Imperial Knights' League of St George, and ecclesiastical princes (eg Mainz, Bavaria, Baden) to support the Holy Roman Empire. Its army was involved in suppressing the Peasants War (1524–5), but the League was disbanded (1534) because of religious divisions caused by the Reformation.

swaddle verb **1** to bandage. **2** to wrap (a baby) in swaddling-clothes. [from Anglo-Saxon swæthel, bandage]

swaddling-clothes pl. noun strips of cloth formerly wrapped round a newborn baby to restrict movement.

swag — noun **1** slang stolen goods. **2** Austral. a traveller's pack or rolled bundle of possessions. **3** a garland hung between two points, or a carved representation of one. — verb intrans. (**swagged, swagging**) to sway or sag. [from Norse sveggja, to cause to sway]

swagger — verb intrans. (**swaggered, swaggering**) **1** to walk with an air of self-importance. **2** to behave arrogantly. — noun **1** a swaggering way of walking or behaving. **2** colloq. the quality of being showily fashionable or smart. — adj. colloq. showily fashionable or smart. [see SWAG]

swagger-stick noun a short cane carried by a military officer.

swagman noun Austral. a traveller on foot, especially an itinerant workman, who carries a swag.

Swahili **1** a group of Bantu-speaking peoples of the coast and islands of E Africa, ethnically and culturally an amalgam of African groups and Arab immigrants entering the area continually since ancient times. **2** the language spoken by those people, which probably replaced Arabic from about the 13c, and is today spoken as a lingua franca throughout E Africa.

swain noun old use, poetic **1** a country youth. **2** a young male lover or suitor. [from Anglo-Saxon swan]

swallow¹ — verb **1** to transfer (food or drink) from the mouth to the oesophagus (gullet) by a muscular movement of the tongue. **2** intrans. to move the muscles of the throat as if performing such an action; to gulp. **3** (also **swallow something up**) to make it an indistinguishable and inseparable part of a larger mass; to engulf or absorb it. **4** to stifle or repress (one's pride, tears, etc). **5** to accept (an insult, etc) meekly and without retaliation. **6** colloq. to believe unquestioningly. — noun **1** an act of swallowing. **2** an amount swallowed at one time. [from Anglo-Saxon swelgan]

swallow² noun a small fast-flying insect-eating bird with long pointed wings and a long forked tail. [from Anglo-Saxon swalwe]

swallow dive a dive during which the arms are held out at chest level until just before the entry into water.

swallowtail butterfly a large colourful butterfly with hindwings extended into slender tails. The adults and larvae are usually distasteful to predators.

swam see SWIM.

swami noun a Hindu religious teacher. [from Hindi svami, lord, master]

swamp — noun an area of land that is permanently waterlogged but has a dense covering of vegetation, especially trees and shrubs, eg mangroves in certain tropical regions, reeds or willows in some temperate regions. — verb **1** to overwhelm or inundate. **2** to cause (a boat) to fill with water. **3** to flood. [from Old Dutch somp]

swampy adj. (**swampier, swampiest**) having many swamps; of the nature of or like a swamp.

Swan, Sir Joseph Wilson (1828–1914) British chemist, inventor, and industrialist, born near Sunderland. He became a manufacturing chemist, patented the carbon process for photographic printing in 1864, and invented the dry plate and bromide paper. He also invented electric lamps which anticipated and later improved Thomas Edison's model, and was the first to produce practicable artificial silk.

swan — noun any of six species of a large graceful aquatic bird with a long slender neck, powerful wings, and webbed feet, belonging to the same family (Anatidae) as ducks and geese. — verb intrans. (**swanned, swanning**) colloq. (**swan off, around**, etc) to spend time or wander irresponsibly or idly. [from Anglo-Saxon] ◇ The mute swan (Cygnus olor), which despite its name has a variety of calls, and hisses violently if disturbed, is native to Europe and Asia, but has been introduced to many other parts of the world. It is about 1.5m long, weighs about 16kg, and has pure white plumage and an orange bill with a prominent black knob at its base. Swans are strong fliers, and they feed mainly on plants. They graze grass on land, and they feed in water by lowering their long necks below the water surface. Mute swans pair for life.

Swan Hill POP (1986) 9 000, a town in Northern Mallee statistical division, N Victoria, Australia. It lies on the Murray R. NOTABLE FEATURES Pioneer Settlement (open-air museum); Clockworld, a collection of over 500 clocks and watches from the past 300 years.

swank colloq. — verb intrans. to boast or show off. — noun boastfulness.

swanky adj. (**swankier, swankiest**) colloq. **1** boastful. **2** showily smart or fashionable.

Swan Lake (Lebedinoye ozero) a ballet by Piotr Ilyich Tchaikovsky (1877). It tells of a prince's fight for the love of the Swan Queen.

Swan River a major watercourse of SW Western Australia. It rises as the Avon R in the hills near Corrigin, flows past Perth, and enters the Indian Ocean at Fremantle. It also receives the Helena and Canning rivers. Its total length, including the Avon R, is 386km/241mi. Established in 1829, the Swan River Settlement was the first colonial settlement in Western Australia. Swanland is a fertile region producing wheat, fruit, wine, wool, and timber.

Swanscombe skull the partial female skull of an archaic form of Homo sapiens found at Swanscombe near London in 1935–6. Its possible age is 250 000 years.

Swansea, Welsh **Abertawe** POP (1992e) 190 000, a port city and county town in Swansea district, West Glamorgan, S Wales. It lies on the Bristol Channel at the mouth of the R Neath where it enters Swansea Bay. The city was chartered in 1158–84. NOTABLE FEATURES Norman Castle; Royal Institution of South Wales (1835); Guildhall; Industrial and Maritime Museum; marina.

swan song the last performance or piece of work by a musician, artist, etc before death or retirement.

swap or **swop** — verb trans., intrans. (**swapped, swapping**) (**swap things** or **one thing for another**) to exchange them. — noun **1** an exchange. **2** a thing exchanged or offered in exchange. [from Middle English swappen]

SWAPO abbrev. South-West Africa People's Organization.

swarm¹ — noun **1** a large group of bees flying off in search of a new home. **2** any large group of insects or other small creatures on the move. **3** a crowd of people on the move. — verb intrans. **1** to gather, move, or go in a swarm. **2** (**be swarming with people or things**) said of a place to be crowded or overrun with them. [from Anglo-Saxon swearm]

swarm² verb trans., intrans. (often **swarm up**) to climb (especially a rope or tree) by clasping with the hands and knees or feet.

swarthiness noun having a dark complexion.

swarthy adj. (**swarthier, swarthiest**) of dark complexion. [from Anglo-Saxon sweart]

swashbuckling adj., said of a story, film, etc full of adventure and excitement. [from obsolete swash, to make noisy violent movements + BUCKLER]

swastika noun a plain cross with the ends bent at right angles, usually clockwise, an ancient religious symbol and the adopted badge of the Nazi party. [from Sanskrit svastika, from svasti, well-being]

swat — verb (**swatted, swatting**) to crush (especially a fly) with a heavy slapping blow. — noun such a blow. [from Old French esquatir, to crush]

swatch noun **1** a sample, especially of fabric. **2** a collection of fabric samples.

swath or **swathe** noun **1** a strip of grass or corn, etc cut by a scythe, mower, or harvester; also, the width of this. **2** a broad strip, especially of land. [from Anglo-Saxon swæth, track]

swathe¹ — verb to wrap or bind in fabric, eg clothes or bandages. — noun a bandage; a wrapping, especially of cloth. [from Anglo-Saxon *swathian*]

swathe² see SWATH.

sway — *verb* **1** *trans., intrans.* to swing or cause to swing from side to side, especially slowly and smoothly. **2** *intrans.* to waver between two opinions or decisions. **3** to persuade to take a particular view or decision. — *noun* **1** a swaying motion. **2** control or influence.
— **hold sway** to have authority or influence. [perhaps from Norse *sveigja*, to bend]

Swazi a Bantu-speaking agricultural and pastoral people living in Swaziland and adjoining parts of southern Africa. They are one of the Nguni peoples, and were formed into a kingdom in the early 19c. Swaziland gained its independence since 1968, and is governed by traditional Swazi institutions with the king as head of state.

Swaziland, official name **Kingdom of Swaziland** POP (1992e) 792 000, a monarchy in SE Africa, divided into four administrative districts. AREA 17 363sq km/6 702sq mi. It is bounded N, W, S, and SE by South Africa, and NE by Mozambique. CAPITAL Mbabane. TIME ZONE GMT +2. Most of the population is of Swazi origin; Christianity and local beliefs are the chief religions. OFFICIAL LANGUAGES English (government, business) and Siswati. CURRENCY the lilangeni (plural, emalangeni). PHYSICAL DESCRIPTION a small country, 192km/119mi N–S and 144km/89mi E–W; mountainous Highveld in the W; the highest point in Swaziland is Emblembe at 1 862m; the more populated Middleveld in the centre descends to 600–700m; the rolling, bush-covered Lowveld in the E is irrigated by river systems. CLIMATE humid, near temperate climate in the W, with an average annual rainfall of 1 000–2 280mm; subtropical and drier in the centre; tropical in the E, with relatively little rain (500–890mm, susceptible to drought); the average annual temperature is 16°C in the W, and 22°C in the E. HISTORY arrival of Swazi in the area, in the early 19c; boundaries with the Transvaal were decided, and independence was guaranteed in 1881 and again in 1884; the British agreed to Transvaal administration of Swaziland in 1894 but, after the South African War, Swaziland became a British High Commission territory in 1903; gained independence in 1968. GOVERNMENT the monarch, who holds executive, legislative, and judicial power, chooses a Cabinet and a Prime Minister; governed by a bicameral parliament consisting of a 50-member National Assembly and a 20-member Senate;. ECONOMY agriculture employs 70% of the population; maize, groundnuts, beans, sorghum, sweet potatoes, cotton, tobacco, pineapples, rice, sugar cane, citrus; several hydroelectric schemes; asbestos; iron ore; coal; wood products; sugar refining; canning; food and drink processing; textiles; cement; paper; chemicals; televisions.

Swaziland

swear *verb* (PAST TENSE **swore**; PAST PARTICIPLE **sworn**) **1** *intrans.* to use indecent or blasphemous language. **2** to promise or assert solemnly or earnestly, as if by taking an oath. **3** (**swear to something**) to solemnly state it to be unquestionably true. **4** (**swear someone to something**) to bind them to a solemn promise: *I swore him to secrecy.*
— **swear by someone** *or* **something 1** to appeal to a deity as a witness of one's solemn promise or statement. **2** *colloq.* to put complete trust in something (eg a certain product or remedy).
swear someone in to introduce them formally into a post, or into the witness box, by requesting them to take an oath.
swear off something *colloq.* to promise to renounce it or give it up. [from Anglo-Saxon *swerian*]

swear-word *noun* a word regarded as obscene or blasphemous.

sweat — *noun* **1** the salty moisture that the body gives off through the skin's pores during physical exertion, exposure to heat, nervousness or fear. **2** the state, or a fit, of giving off such moisture. **3** *colloq.* any activity that causes the body to give off such moisture. — *verb* (PAST TENSE AND PAST PARTICIPLE **sweated**, **sweat**) **1** *intrans.* to give off sweat through one's pores. **2** *intrans.* to release a sweat-like moisture, as cheese does when warm. **3** *intrans. colloq.* to be nervous, anxious or afraid. **4** to exercise (eg a racehorse) strenuously, to the point of producing sweat. **5** to cook (eg onions) slowly so as to release and retain the juices.
— **in a sweat** *colloq.* in a worried or anxious state.
no sweat! *slang* **1** that presents no problems. **2** okay!
sweat blood *colloq.* **1** to work extremely hard. **2** to be in a state of extreme anxiety.
sweat it out *colloq.* to endure a difficult or unpleasant situation to the end, especially to wait at length in nervous anticipation. [from Anglo-Saxon *swætan*]

sweatband *noun* a strip of elasticated fabric worn around the wrist or head to absorb sweat when playing sports.

sweated labour hard work for long hours with poor pay and conditions; also, people carrying out this work.

sweater *noun* a knitted jersey or pullover, of a kind worn before and after hard exercise.

sweatshirt *noun* a long-sleeved jersey of a thick soft cotton fabric with a fleecy lining, originally worn for sports.

sweatshop *noun* a workshop or factory in which sweated labour is demanded.

sweatsuit *noun* a loose-fitting suit of sweatshirt and trousers, usually tight-fitting at the wrists and ankles, worn especially by athletes.

sweaty *adj.* (**sweatier**, **sweatiest**) **1** causing sweat. **2** covered with sweat, wet or stained with sweat. **3** smelling of sweat.

Swede *noun* a native or citizen of Sweden.

swede *noun* a large turnip with yellow flesh, originally introduced from Sweden.

Sweden, Swedish **Sverige**, official name **Kingdom of Sweden**, Swedish **Konungariket Sverige** POP (1993e) 8.7m, a kingdom in N Europe, occupying the E side of the Scandinavian Peninsula, divided into 24 countries (*Län*). AREA 411 479sq km/158 830sq mi. It is bounded E by Finland, the Gulf of Bothnia, and the Baltic Sea, SW by the Skagerrak and Kattegat, and W and NW by Norway. CAPITAL Stockholm. CHIEF TOWNS Gothenburg, Malmö, Uppsala, Norrköping, Västerås, Örebro, Linkoping. TIME ZONE GMT +1. The population is mainly of Teutonic descent; the chief religion is Lutheran Protestantism. OFFICIAL LANGUAGE Swedish. CURRENCY the Swedish krona. PHYSICAL DESCRIPTION there is a large

amount of inland water (9%), the chief lakes being Vänern, Vättern, and Mälar; there are many coastal islands, notably Gotland and Öland; c.57% of the country is forested; the Kjölen Mts in the W form much of the boundary with Norway; the highest peak is Kebnekaise (2 111m); several rivers flow SE towards the Gulf of Bothnia; there are many waterfalls. CLIMATE typically continental, with a considerable range of temperature between summer and winter, except in the SW, where winters are warmer; enclosed parts of the Baltic Sea often freeze in winter; the average number of days with a mean temperature below freezing increases from 71 in Malmö to 184 at Haparanda near the Arctic Circle. HISTORY formed from the union of the kingdoms of the Goths and Svears in the 7c; the Danes continued to rule in the extreme S (Skåne) until 1658; Sweden was united with Denmark and Norway under Danish leadership in 1389; this union ended in 1527, following a revolt led by Gustavus Vasa, founder of modern Sweden; Norway was acquired from Denmark in 1814; the union with Norway was dissolved in 1905; Sweden has been a neutral country since 1814. GOVERNMENT a representative and parliamentary democracy, with a monarch as head of state; governed by a Prime Minister and a single-chamber parliament (*Riksdag*) of 349 elected members. ECONOMY a gradual shift from the traditional emphasis on raw materials (timber and iron ore) to advanced technology; transportation equipment; electronics; electrical equipment; chemicals; engineering; steelmaking; non-ferrous metals; hydroelectricity provides 70% of the country's power; c.57% of Sweden is forested; wheat, barley, oats; hay; sugar beet, peas, grain; cattle; fishing; tourism.

Sweden

Swedenborg, Emmanuel, originally **Swedberg** (1688–1772) Swedish mystic and scientist, born in Stockholm. As assessor in the college of mines (1716–47), he wrote books on algebra, navigation, astronomy, and chemistry, and in 1734 he published *Opera Philosophica et Mineralia* (Philosophical and Logical Works), a mixture of metallurgy and metaphysical speculation on the creation of the world. Curious dreams convinced him that he had direct access to the spiritual world. He communicated his spiritual explorations in *Arcana Coelestia* (Heavenly Arcana, 8 vols, 1749–56), and spent the rest of his life expounding his doctrines in such works as *The New Jerusalem* (1758). In 1787 his followers (known as Swedenborgians) in London formed the Church of the New Jerusalem.

Swedish — *noun* **1** the language of Sweden. **2** (**the Swedish**) the people of Sweden; Swedes. — *adj.* relating to Sweden or its people or language.
◇ Swedish is a Germanic language belonging to the continental Scandinavian group. It is spoken by c.8 million people in Sweden, Finland, and parts of the USA.

sweep — *verb* (PAST TENSE AND PAST PARTICIPLE **swept**) **1** (*also* **sweep up** *or* **sweep something up**) to clean (a room, a floor, etc), or remove (dirt,

dust, etc), with a brush or broom. **2** to take, carry, or push suddenly and with irresistible force. **3** to force or inspire into taking an unwanted or unintended direction or course of action. **4** to lift, gather, or clear with a forceful scooping or brushing movement. **5** *intrans.* to move, pass, or spread smoothly and swiftly, or uncontrollably. **6** *intrans.* to walk (especially with garments flowing) impressively or arrogantly. **7** to pass quickly over, making light contact. **8** *intrans.* to extend curvingly and impressively into the distance. **9** *said of emotions, etc* to affect suddenly and overpoweringly. **10** to cast or direct (eg one's gaze) with a scanning movement. — *noun* **1** an act of sweeping. **2** a sweeping movement. **3** a sweeping line, eg of a road or landscape. **4** *colloq.* a sweepstake. **5** *colloq.* a chimney-sweep.
— **sweep something under the carpet** to hide or ignore something (especially unwelcome facts, difficulties, etc).
[from Anglo-Saxon *swapan*, to sweep]

sweeper *noun* **1** a person who sweeps. **2** a device or machine used for sweeping. **3** *Sport* a player covering the whole area behind a line of defenders.

sweeping — *adj.* **1** *said of a search, change, etc* wide-ranging and thorough. **2** *said of a statement* too generalized; indiscriminate. **3** *said of a victory, etc* impressive; decisive. — *noun* (*usually* **sweepings**) a thing swept up.

sweepingly *adv.* **1** with a sweeping gesture or movement. **2** indiscriminately, comprehensively.

sweepstake *noun* **1** a system of gambling in which the prize money is the sum of the stakes of all those betting. **2** a horse race in which the winning owner receives sums of money put up by all the other owners.

Sweet, Henry (1845–1912) English philologist, born in London. He became Reader in Phonetics at Oxford, where he pioneered Anglo-Saxon studies. His works include Old and Middle English texts, primers, and dictionaries, and a historical English grammar. He was the probable source for Professor Higgins in George Bernard Shaw's *Pygmalion*.

sweet — *adj.* **1** tasting like sugar; not sour, salty or bitter. **2** pleasing to any of the senses, especially smell and hearing. **3** *said of air or water* fresh and untainted. **4** *said of wine* having some taste of sugar or fruit; not dry. **5** likeable; charming. **6** *colloq.* (**sweet on someone**) fond of them; infatuated with them. — *noun* **1** any small sugar-based confection for sucking or chewing. **2** a dessert. **3** a person one loves or is fond of. [from Anglo-Saxon *swete*]

sweet-and-sour — *adj.* cooked in a sauce that combines sugar with vinegar or fruit juice. — *noun* a sweet-and-sour dish.

sweetbread *noun* the pancreas of a young animal, especially a calf, used as food.

sweetcorn *noun* kernels of a variety of maize, eaten young while still sweet.

sweeten *verb* (**sweetened, sweetening**) **1** to make (food) sweet or sweeter. **2** (*also* **sweeten someone up**) *colloq.* to make them more agreeable or amenable, eg by flattery. **3** *colloq.* to make (eg an offer) more acceptable or inviting, by making changes or additions.

sweetener *noun* **1** an agent for sweetening food, especially one other than sugar (see also ARTIFICIAL SWEETENER). **2** *colloq.* an additional and usually illicit inducement made to an offer to make it more attractive, especially a bribe.

sweetheart *noun* **1** a term of endearment. **2** *old use* a lover.

sweetie *noun colloq.* **1** a sweet confection for sucking or chewing. **2** a term of endearment. **3** a lovable person.

sweetly *adv.* in a sweet way.

sweetmeat *noun* any small sugar-based confection or cake.

sweetness *noun* a sweet quality.

sweet nothings the endearments that lovers say to each other.

sweet pea a European climbing plant with delicate fragrant brightly-coloured flowers.

sweet pepper 1 a fruit native to the New World, consisting of a hollow fleshy pod, usually red, green, or yellow in colour. **2** the plant which produces such fruit.

sweet potato the potato-like root of a tropical American climbing plant, with pinkish violet or grey skin and yellow or pink, slightly sweet flesh.

sweet talk *colloq.* flattery intended to persuade.

sweet-talk *verb colloq.* to persuade with flattery.

sweet tooth a fondness for sweet foods.

sweet-toothed *adj.* fond of sweet things.

sweet william a perennial plant (*Dianthus barbatus*), native to S Europe, having elliptical leaves sheathing its stem, and dense compact heads of dark red or pink flowers; garden varieties also include white and spotted forms.

swell — *verb* (PAST TENSE **swelled**; PAST PARTICIPLE **swollen, swelled**) **1** (*also* **swell up** *or* **out**, *or* **swell something up** *or* **out**) to become or make it bigger or fatter through injury or infection, or by filling with liquid or air. **2** *trans., intrans.* to increase or cause to increase in number, size, or intensity. **3** *intrans.* to become visibly filled with emotion, especially pride. **4** *intrans. said of the sea* to rise and fall in smooth masses, without forming individual waves. **5** *intrans. said of a sound* to become louder, then die away. — *noun* **1** a heaving of the sea without waves. **2** an increase in number, size or intensity. **3** an increase in volume of sound or music, followed by a dying away. **4** *old colloq. use* a person who dresses smartly and fashionably. **5** *old colloq. use* a prominent member of society. — *adj. chiefly North Amer. colloq.* excellent. [from Anglo-Saxon *swellan*]

swelling *noun* an area on the body swollen through injury or infection.

swelter — *verb intrans.* (**sweltered, sweltering**) to sweat heavily or feel oppressively hot. — *noun* a sweltering feeling or state. [from Anglo-Saxon *sweltan*, to die]

sweltering *adj.*, *said of the weather* oppressively hot.

swept see SWEEP.

swerve — *verb intrans.* **1** to turn or move aside suddenly and sharply, eg to avoid a collision. **2** to deviate from a course of action. — *noun* an act of swerving; a swerving movement. [from Middle English *swerve*]

Sweyn *or* **Swegn**, also called **Forkbeard** (d.1014) King of Denmark (987–1014) and England (1013–14), the son of Harold Blue-tooth, and the father of Canute. He first attacked England in 994, and during his final campaign in 1013, conquered the whole country and was recognized as King, while Ethelred the Unready withdrew to exile in Normandy.

Swift, Jonathan (1667–1745) Anglo-Irish clergyman and satirist, born in Dublin of English parents. He moved to England where he became secretary to the diplomat, Sir William Temple. During a visit to Ireland, he was ordained in the Anglican Church (1695), and he later became Dean of St Patrick's in Dublin (1714). He wrote several poems then turned to prose satire, attacked religious dissension in *A Tale of a Tub* (1704), and produced a wide range of political and religious essays and pamphlets. His best-known works include the satire *Gulliver's Travels*

(1726), *Moll Flanders* (1722), and *A Journal of the Plague Year* (1722).

swift — *adj.* **1** fast-moving; able to move fast. **2** done, given, etc quickly or promptly. — *noun* a small fast-flying insect-eating bird similar to the swallow but with longer wings and a shorter tail. [from Anglo-Saxon *swift*]

swiftly *adv.* quickly.

swiftness *noun* being swift.

swig *colloq.* — *verb trans., intrans.* (**swigged, swigging**) to drink in gulps, especially from a bottle. — *noun* a large draught, or gulp.

swill — *verb* **1** to rinse by splashing water round or over. **2** *colloq.* to drink (especially alcohol) greedily. — *noun* **1** any mushy mixture of scraps fed to pigs. **2** disgusting food or drink. **3** *colloq.* a gulp of beer or other alcohol. [from Anglo-Saxon *swilian*, to wash]

swim — *verb* (**swimming**; PAST TENSE **swam**; PAST PARTICIPLE **swum**) *usually intrans.* **1** to propel oneself through water by moving the arms and legs or (in fish) the tail and fins. **2** *trans.* to cover (a distance) or cross (a stretch of water) in this way. **3** to float. **4** (**be swimming in** *or* **with something**) to be flooded or awash with it. **5** to be affected by dizziness. **6** to move or appear to move about in waves or whirls. — *noun* **1** a spell of swimming. **2** the general flow of events.
— **in the swim** *colloq.* up to date with, and often involved in, what is going on around one. [from Anglo-Saxon *swimman*]

swim bladder *Zool.* in bony fishes, an internal structure that can be filled with air and so used to control buoyancy of the fish in the water.

swimmer *noun* a person who swims.

swimming the act of propelling oneself through water without any mechanical aids. The earliest reference to it as a sport is in Japan in 36 BC. There are four competition strokes: the *breast stroke* (developed in the 16c); the *front crawl* (or *freestyle*); *backstroke*; and *butterfly* (developed in the 20c). In competitions there are also relays, involving four swimmers, and medley races, which are a combination of all four strokes. In major events the pool is normally 50m long and divided into eight lanes. Race lengths range from 50m to 1 500m.

swimming-bath *noun* (*also* **swimming-baths**) a swimming-pool, usually indoors.

swimming-costume *noun* a swimsuit.

swimmingly *adj. colloq.* smoothly and successfully.

swimming-pool *noun* an artificial pool for swimming in.

swimsuit *noun* a garment worn for swimming.

Swinburne, Algernon Charles (1837–1909) English poet and critic, born in London. He travelled in Europe, and became associated with the Pre-Raphaelite Brotherhood. He made his name with his play *Atalanta in Calydon* (1865), a drama in Greek form, and the first of his series of *Poems and Ballads* (1866). Other works include *Songs before Sunrise* (1871), the Arthurian romance *Tristram of Lyonesse* (1882), and several critical studies.

swindle — *verb* to cheat or trick; to obtain by cheating or trickery. — *noun* **1** an act of swindling. **2** anything that is not what it is presented as being. [from German *schwindeln*, to be giddy]

swindler *noun* a person who swindles.

Swindon, Major the conscientious British officer in George Bernard Shaw's *The Devil's Disciple*, who serves as the butt of General Burgoyne's sarcasm during the trial of Richard Dudgeon.

Swindon POP (1981) 129 000, an old market town in Thamesdown district, Wiltshire, S England. Situated 113km/70mi W of London, it developed into an industrial town with the arrival of the Great Western Railway in the 19c. NOTABLE FEATURES Great Western Railway Museum (1962); the White Horse of Uffington is 9km/5mi E.

swine *noun* (PL. **swine**, in sense 2 **swines**) **1** a pig. **2** a despicable person. [from Anglo-Saxon *swin*, pig]

swing — *verb* (PAST TENSE AND PAST PARTICIPLE **swung**) **1** *trans., intrans.* to open, close, or move to and fro in a curving motion, pivoting from a fixed point. **2** *trans., intrans.* to move or cause to move or turn with a sweeping or swaying movement or movements. **3** *intrans.* to undergo a sudden sharp change or changes, eg of opinion, mood or direction. **4** *colloq.* to arrange or fix; to achieve the successful outcome of. **5** *colloq.* to determine or settle the outcome of (eg an election in which voters were initially undecided). **6** *intrans. colloq.* to throw a punch at someone. **7** *intrans. colloq., said of a social function* to be lively and exciting. **8** *intrans. colloq.* to enjoy oneself with vigour and enthusiasm. **9** *intrans. colloq.* to be promiscuous. **10** *intrans.* to be hanged. **11** *Mus.* to perform as swing. — *noun* **1** an act, manner, or spell of swinging. **2** a swinging movement. **3** a seat suspended from a frame or branch, for a child to swing on. **4** a sudden sharp change, eg in mood or pattern of voting. **5** a swinging stroke with a golf club, cricket bat, etc; the technique of a golfer. **6** *Mus.* jazz or jazz-like dance music with a simple regular rhythm, popularized by bands in the 1930s. **7** usual routine or pace: *get back into the swing of things*.
— **in full swing** at the height of liveliness.

swing the lead *slang* to make up excuses to avoid work.

swings and roundabouts *colloq.* a situation in which advantages and disadvantages are equal. [from Anglo-Saxon *swingan*]

swingboat *noun* a fairground ride in the form of a boat-shaped swinging carriage.

swing bridge a bridge that swings open to let boats through.

swing door a door hinged so as to open in both directions.

swingeing *adj.* hard to bear; severe. [from Anglo-Saxon *swengan*, to shake]

swinger *noun old slang use* **1** a person who has a very active social life, especially with much dancing and drinking. **2** a promiscuous person.

swinging *adj.* **1** moving or turning with a swing. **2** *colloq.* lively and exciting.

swinish *adj.* **1** like a swine. **2** filthy. **3** voracious.

swipe — *verb* **1** to hit with a heavy sweeping blow. **2** (**swipe at someone** *or* **something**) to try to hit them. **3** *colloq.* to steal. — *noun* a heavy sweeping blow. [from Anglo-Saxon *swipian*, to beat]

swirl — *verb trans., intrans.* to flow or cause to flow or move with a whirling or circling motion. — *noun* such a motion.

swish[1] — *verb trans., intrans.* to move or cause to move with a brushing or rustling sound. — *noun* a brushing or rustling sound or movement. [imitative]

swish[2] *adj. colloq.* smart and stylish.

Swiss — *adj.* of or relating to Switzerland, its people, or the dialects of German and French spoken by them. — *noun* (PL. **Swiss**) **1** a native or citizen of Switzerland. **2** either of the dialects of German and French spoken in Switzerland.

Swiss cheese plant monstera.

Swiss Family Robinson, The (Der schweizerische Robinson) a novel by Johann David Wyss (4 vols, 1812–27). It is a didactic adventure tale about a family shipwrecked on a desert island.

Swiss Guards the papal police corps, originally instituted by Pope Julius II (reigned 1503–13) and recruited from the mercenaries of the cantons of the Swiss confederacy, whose reputation as infantrymen was established after their victories over the Burgundian cavalry in 1476. Their dark blue, yellow, and red uniforms were designed by Michelangelo.

Swiss lake dwellings prehistoric settlements around the Swiss lakes, first identified in 1854 at Obermeilen, L Constance, by Swiss archaeologist Ferdinand Keller (1800–81), when abnormally low water revealed extensive timber piling. Over 200 comparable Neolithic sites preserved by waterlogging were subsequently revealed (1860–75).

Swiss roll a cylindrical cake made by rolling up a thin slab of sponge spread with jam or cream.

Switch *noun trademark* a method of paying for goods in the UK, using a plastic card which automatically debits the relevant amount from the user's bank account.

switch — *noun* **1** a manually operated or automatic device that is used to open or close an electric circuit, eg a lever or button that makes or breaks a pair of contacts, or a solid-state switch with no moving parts, eg a transistor. **2** a change; an exchange or change-over. **3** a long flexible twig or cane. **4** *North Amer., esp. US* a set of railway points. — *verb* **1** (**switch something on** *or* **off**) to turn an appliance on or off by means of a switch. **2** *trans., intrans.* to exchange (one thing or person for another), especially quickly and without notice. **3** *trans., intrans.* to transfer or change over (eg to a different system). **4** to beat with a switch.
— **switch off** *colloq.* to stop paying attention. (**switch someone on**) *colloq.* to make them aware of something.

switch something on *colloq.* to bring on eg charm or tears at will, to create the required effect.

switchback *noun* **1** a road with many twists and turns and upward and downward slopes. **2** a roller-coaster.

switchboard *noun* **1** a board on which incoming telephone calls are connected manually or electronically. **2** a board from which various pieces of electrical equipment are controlled.

switched-on *adj. colloq.* **1** well informed or aware. **2** under the influence of drugs.

Swithin *or* **Swithun, St** (d.862) English saint and divine, adviser to Egbert, and Bishop of Winchester from 852. On 15 Jul 971 his body was to have been exhumed by monks and buried in the rebuilt Winchester cathedral, but the task was delayed by heavy rains. There is now a belief that if it rains on St Swithin's Day (15 Jul), it will rain for 40 days more.

Switzerland, French **La Suisse**, German **Schweiz**, Italian **Svizzera**, ancient **Helvetia**, official name **Swiss Confederation**, French **Confédération Suisse**, German **Schweizerische Eidgenosseschaft**, Italian **Confederazione Svizzera** POP (1992e) 6.9m, a landlocked European republic, divided into 23 cantons (these include six demicantons). AREA 41 228sq km/ 15 914sq mi. It is bounded E by Liechtenstein and Austria, S by Italy, W by France, and N by Germany. CAPITAL Bern. CHIEF TOWNS Zurich (largest city), Lucerne, St Gallen, Lausanne, Basle, Geneva. TIME ZONE GMT +1. The Swiss are predominantly of Alpine descent, with a strong Nordic element; chief religions are Roman Catholicism and Protestantism. LANGUAGES German (65%), French (18%), Italian (12%), and Romansch (1%); many of the Swiss speak more than one of these. CURRENCY the Swiss franc. PHYSICAL DESCRIPTION the Alps run roughly E–W in the S; the highest peak is Dufourspitze (4 634m); the average height of the Pre-Alps in the NW is 2 000m; the Jura Mts run SW–NW; the central plateau is, at an average altitude of 580m, is fringed by large lakes; chief rivers are the Rhine, Rhône, Adige, Inn, and the tributaries of the Po; there are c.3 000sq km/1 160sq mi of glaciers, notably the Aletsch; major lakes include Constance, Zurich, Lucerne, Neuchâtel, and Geneva, and the N of L Maggiore. CLIMATE a temperate climate, varying greatly with relief and altitude; there are warm summers, with considerable rainfall; winter temperatures average 0°C; average annual rainfall in the central plateau is c.1 000mm; average annual temperature is 7–9°C; the Föhn, a warm wind, is noticeable in the Alps during late winter and spring. HISTORY part of the Holy Roman Empire in the 10c; the Swiss Confederation was created in 1291, when the cantons of Uri, Schwyz, and Unterwalden formed a defensive league; the Confederation expanded during the 14c and was the centre of the Reformation in the 16c; Swiss independence and neutrality was recognized under the Treaty of Westphalia in 1648; the country was conquered by Napoleon, who in 1798 instituted the Helvetian Republic; in 1815 it was organized as a confederation of 22 cantons; a federal constitution was adopted in 1848; Switzerland was neutral in both World Wars. GOVERNMENT governed by a parliament comprising a 46-member Council of States (*Ständerat*) and a 200-member National Council (*Nationalrat*); elected for four years; a president is elected yearly. ECONOMY increased specialization and development in high-technology products; machinery; precision instruments; watches; drugs; chemicals; textiles; dairy farming; wheat, potatoes, sugar beet, grapes, apples; an all-year tourist area; a major financial centre with the headquarters of many international organizations.

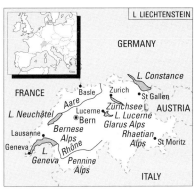

Switzerland

swivel — *noun* a joint between two parts enabling one part to turn or pivot independently of the other. — *verb trans., intrans.* (**swivelled, swivelling**) to turn or pivot on a swivel, or as if on a swivel. [from Anglo-Saxon *swifan*, to turn round]

swivel chair a chair in which the seat pivots on the base, and can be spun right round.

swizz *noun colloq.* a thing that, in reality, is disappointingly inferior to what was cheatingly promised.

swizzle — *noun* **1** a frothy cocktail with a rum or gin base. **2** *colloq.* a swizz. — *verb colloq.* to cheat with a swizz.

swizzle-stick *noun* a thin stick used to stir cocktails and other drinks.

swollen see SWELL.

swoon — *verb intrans.* **1** to faint. **2** (**swoon over someone** *or* **something**) to go into raptures or fits of adoration for them. — *noun* an act of swooning. [from Middle English *iswowen*]

swoop — *verb intrans.* **1** to fly down with a fast sweeping movement. **2** to make a sudden forceful attack; to descend or pounce. — *noun* **1** an act of swooping. **2** a swooping movement. [from Anglo-Saxon *swapan*, to sweep]

swop see SWAP.

sword *noun* **1** a weapon like a large heavy knife, with a long blade sharpened on one or both edges. **2** (**the sword**) violence or destruction, especially in war.
— **cross swords with someone** to encounter them as an opponent.
[from Anglo-Saxon *sweord*]

1: 16c two-handed sword 3: 15c cut and thrust
2: 17c rapier 4: 19c sword

swords

sword dance **1** in Scotland, a dance, often by a solo dancer, with steps over an arrangement of swords laid on the ground. **2** in northern England, a dance for a group of dancers carrying long flexible swords with which they perform a number of movements and create various patterns.

swordfish *noun* a large sea-fish with a very long and pointed upper jaw used as a weapon.

Sword in the Stone, The a children's novel by T H White (1937). It is the first part of his Arthurian sequence, *The Once and Future King* (1958).

sword of Damocles *literary* any imminent danger or disaster.

swordplay *noun* **1** the activity or art of fencing. **2** lively argument.

swordsman *noun* a man skilled in fighting with a sword.

swordsmanship *noun* skill in using a sword.

swordstick *noun* a hollow walking-stick containing a short sword or dagger.

swordtail *noun* a small colourful freshwater fish native to streams and swamps of Central America, up to 12cm in length, and green in colour with an orange side stripe. In the male the lower edge of the tail is prolonged to form the 'sword'. It is a popular aquarium fish, with many varieties produced by selective breeding.

swore see SWEAR.

sworn past participle of SWEAR. — *adj.* bound or confirmed by, or as if by, having taken an oath: *sworn enemies*.

swot *colloq.* — *verb trans., intrans.* (**swotted**, **swotting**) **1** to study hard and seriously. **2** (*also* **swot something up**) to study it intensively, especially at the last minute. — *noun* a person who studies hard, especially single-mindedly or in order to impress a teacher. [a variant of SWEAT]

swum see SWIM.

swung see SWING.

Sybaris an ancient Greek city in S Italy founded in c.720 BC. Its citizens were notorious for their wealth and luxurious lifestyle — whence the term 'sybarite'. It was obliterated in 510 BC by the neighbouring town of Croton, and never refounded.

sybarite *noun* a person devoted to a life of luxury and pleasure. [originally an inhabitant of *Sybaris*, an ancient Greek city in S Italy, noted for its luxury]

sybaritic *adj.* luxurious.

Sybil a female first name. [from the Greek name *Sybilla* or *Sibylla*]

sycamore *noun* **1** a deciduous tree of Europe and Asia, with large five-pointed leaves and seedcases that spin when they fall. **2** *North Amer.* any American plane tree. **3** the wood of any of these trees. [from Greek *sykomoros*, from *sykon*, fig]

sycophancy *noun* the behaviour of a sycophant, flattery.

sycophant *noun* a person who flatters in a servile way; a crawler. [from Greek *sykophantes*, informer, swindler]

sycophantic *adj.* characteristic of a sycophant or sycophancy.

Sycorax the witch, and mother of Caliban, mentioned but never seen in Shakespeare's *The Tempest*.

Sydenham, Thomas (1624–89) English physician, born in Wynford Eagle, Dorset. From 1655 he practised in London, and stressed the importance of observation rather than theory in clinical medicine. Among a wide variety of important contributions to medicine, he wrote *Observationes Medicae* (1667) and a treatise on gout (1683), distinguished the symptoms of venereal disease (1675), and recognized hysteria as a distinct disorder. He gave his name to the mild convulsions of children, 'Sydenham's chorea' (St Vitus's dance), and to the medicinal use of liquid opium, 'Sydenham's laudanum'.

Sydney POP (1990e) 3.7m, the state capital and a port of New South Wales, Australia, situated on the shore of Port Jackson. Sydney statistical division comprises 44 municipalities and shires. It was founded as the first British settlement in 1788 and is now the largest city in Australia and a major centre of commerce, culture, and finance. NOTABLE FEATURES two cathedrals; two major harbours (Sydney, Port Botany); Sydney Harbour Bridge (1932); Sydney Opera House on Bennelong Point Peninsula; State Parliament House; National Art Gallery (1871); The Rocks (heritage area); Darling Harbour; Chinatown; National Maritime Museum. Sydney Cup Week (horse racing) takes place in April.

Sydney Harbour Bridge an arch bridge in Sydney, Australia, the widest and heaviest arch bridge in the world, built 1923–32. The length of the main arch is 503m, and the highest point is 134m above sea level. The bridge provides a rail and road link across the harbour.

Sydney Opera House an opera house in Sydney, Australia. It was designed in 1956 by Danish architect Joern Utzon (1918–) for an international competition. He resigned in 1966 in the political controversy over the escalating costs of the project. It was completed in 1973, having cost over $100 million to build.

SYHA *abbrev.* Scottish Youth Hostels Association.

Sykes–Picot Agreement a secret agreement (9 May 1916) negotiated by Sir Mark Sykes (for Britain) and Georges Picot (for France) to partition the Ottoman Turkish Empire after World War I. France was to be the dominant power in Syria and Lebanon, and Britain in Transjordan, Iraq, and N Palestine; the rest of Palestine was to be under international control, and an Arab state was to be established.

syllabary *noun* a writing system in which the basic units, or *graphemes*, correspond to spoken syllables. Examples of syllabic writing systems include the ancient Cypriot syllabary of the 6c–3c BC; and present-day Amharic, Cherokee, and Japanese *kana*.

syllabi see SYLLABUS.

syllabic *adj.* relating to syllables, or the division of words into syllables.

syllabification *noun* division into syllables.

syllabify *verb* (**syllabifies**, **syllabified**) to divide (a word) into syllables.

syllable *noun* **1** each of the distinct parts that a spoken word can be divided into. Each part consists of one or more sounds and usually includes a vowel. The word *telephone* has three syllables, *tiger* has two, and *book, dance,* and *shape* have one each. **2** the slightest sound: *they hardly uttered a syllable all evening.*
— **in words of one syllable** in simple language; frankly.
[from Greek *syllabe*]

syllabub *or* **sillabub** *noun* a frothy dessert made by whipping a sweetened mixture of cream or milk and wine.

syllabus *noun* (PL. **syllabuses**, **syllabi**) a series of topics prescribed for a course of study; also, a booklet or sheet listing these. [from a misreading of Latin *sittybas*, from Greek *sittyba*, book-label]

syllogism *noun* an argument in which a conclusion, valid or invalid, is drawn from two independent statements using logic, as in *All dogs are animals, foxhounds are dogs, therefore foxhounds are animals.* [from Greek *syllogismos*, a reasoning together]

syllogistic *adj.* relating to or involving syllogism.

sylph *noun* **1** in folklore, a spirit of the air. **2** a slender, graceful woman or girl. [word created by Paracelsus, a medieval alchemist]

Sylphides, Les (The Sylphs), originally entitled *Chopiniana* a one-act ballet by Frédéric Chopin (1907). Anna Pavlova danced in the first performance, which was choreographed by Michel Fokine.

sylph-like *adj.* like a sylph, slim.

Sylt the largest of the German North Frisian Is, lying off the Schleswig-Holstein coast. AREA 99sq km/38sq mi; length 37km/23mi. It is a popular summer resort.

sylvan *adj. literary* of woods or woodland; wooded. [from Latin *silva*, a wood]

Sylvanus see SILVANUS.

Sylvester II, originally **Gerbert of Aurillac** (c.940–1003) French pope, born in Aurillac. His erudition in chemistry, mathematics, and philosophy led people to suspect him of being in league with the devil. Said to have introduced Arabic numerals and to have invented clocks, he became Abbot of Bobbio (982) and Archbishop of Ravenna (988), and as pope (from 999) he upheld the primacy of Rome against the separatist tendencies of the French Church.

Sylvester, James Joseph (1814–97) English mathematician, born in London.

Sydney Opera House

Professor at University College London, the University of Virginia, Woolwich, Johns Hopkins University, and Oxford, he was one of the founders of the algebraic theory of invariants which became a powerful tool in resolving physical problems.

symbiosis *noun* (PL. **symbioses**) **1** a close association between two organisms of different species, usually to the benefit of both partners. In many cases such a relationship is essential for mutual survival, eg a lichen represents a symbiotic relationship between a fungus and an alga. **2** *Psychol.* a mutually beneficial relationship between two people who are dependent on each other. [from Greek *syn*, together + *bios*, livelihood]

symbiotic *adj.* relating to or involving symbiosis.

symbol *noun* **1** a thing that represents or stands for another, usually something concrete or material representing an idea or emotion, eg the colour red representing danger. **2** a letter or sign used to represent a quantity, idea, object, operation, etc, such as the × used in mathematics to represent the multiplication process or £ used for pound sterling. [from Greek *symbolon*, token]

Symbols in General Use

&,	ampersand (*and*)
&c.	et cetera
@	at; per (in costs)
×	by (measuring dimensions, eg 3 × 4)
£	pound
$	dollar (also peso, escudo, etc in certain countries)
¢	cent (also centavo, etc in certain countries)
©	copyright
®	registered
¶	new paragraph
§	new section
"	ditto
*	born (in genealogy)
†	died
*	hypothetical or unacceptable form (in linguistics)
☠	poison; danger
♂, □	male
♀, ○	female
⊞	bishop's name follows
☏	telephone number follows
☞	this way
✂ ✄⋯	cut here

In astronomy

●	new moon
☽	moon, first quarter
○	full moon
☾	moon, last quarter

In meteorology

▲▲▲	cold front
●●●	warm front
▲▼▲▼	stationary front
▲▲●●	occluded front

In cards

♥	hearts
♦	diamonds
♠	spades
♣	clubs

symbolic *adj.* **1** (*often* **symbolic of something**) being a symbol of it; standing for it. **2** relating to symbols or their use.

symbolically *adv.* in a symbolic way.

symbolic interactionism a sociological theory, developed by the Chicago school of sociologists in the 1930s, which attempts to explain patterns of behaviour in terms of the meanings and symbols that people share in everyday interaction, and which emphasizes that mutual understanding depends on people continually monitoring, checking, and negotiating the meaning of what they say and how they behave.

symbolism *noun* **1** the use of symbols, especially to express ideas or emotions in literature, cinema, etc. **2** (*often* **Symbolism**) a 19c movement in art and literature making extensive use of symbols.
◇ A Symbolist Manifesto was published in 1886 by Jean Moréas (1856–1910). Though principally a literary movement espoused by the French poets Charles Pierre Baudelaire, Stéphane Mallarmé, Paul Verlaine, and Arthur Rimbaud, it had a profound effect on music (eg Claude Debussy), drama (eg Maurice Maeterlinck and Paul Claudel), and on painting (eg Pierre Cécile Puvis de Chavannes, Odilon Redon, and Gustave Moreau). The combination in unexpected ways of natural objects and symbols in Symbolist art ultimately contributed to the development of Surrealism. Paul Gauguin was influenced by Symbolist ideas, as were certain members of the Nabis, in their attempts to challenge the principles of naturalism and express inner ideas and inspiration.

symbolist *noun* an artist or writer who uses symbolism (see also SYMBOLISM).

symbolize *or* **symbolise** *verb* to be a symbol of; to stand for.

symmetrical *adj.* having symmetry.

symmetrically *adv.* in a symmetric way.

symmetry *noun* (PL. **symmetries**) **1** exact similarity between two parts or halves, as if one were a mirror image of the other. **2** the arrangement of parts in pleasing proportion to each other; also, the aesthetic satisfaction derived from this. [from Greek *syn*, together + *metron*, measure]

sympathetic *adj.* **1** (*also* **sympathetic to someone** *or* **something**) feeling or expressing sympathy for them. **2** amiable, especially because of being kind-hearted. **3** acting or done out of sympathy. **4** in keeping with one's mood or feelings; agreeable. **5** *Biol.* or or relating to the sympathetic nervous system.

sympathetically *adv.* in a sympathetic way.

sympathetic nervous system *Zool.* in vertebrates, a subdivision of the autonomic nervous system. The activity of the sympathetic nervous system tends to increase the heart rate, constrict blood vessels, and generally prepare the body for action. It has the opposite effects to the parasympathetic nervous system.

sympathize *or* **sympathise** *verb intrans.* (**sympathize with someone**) to feel or express sympathy for them.

sympathizer *or* **sympathiser** *noun* a person who sympathizes.

sympathy *noun* (PL. **sympathies**) **1** a deep and genuine understanding of the sadness or suffering of others, often shown in expressions of sorrow or pity. **2** (*often* **sympathy for** *or* **with someone**) loyal or approving support for them or agreement with them. **3** affection between people resulting from their understanding of each other's personalities. [from Greek *syn*, with + *pathos*, suffering]

symphonic *adj.*, *said of music* suitable for performance by a symphony orchestra.

Symphonie Fantastique, in full *Symphonie fantastique, épisode de la vie d'un artiste (Fantastic Symphony: Episode in the Life of an Artist)* a symphony by Hector Berlioz (Op 14, 1830), an example of programme music, written for the Irish actress Harriet Smithson (1800–54), whom he later married.

symphony *noun* (PL. **symphonies**) **1** a long musical work in several parts, or movements, played by a full orchestra. **2** an instrumental passage in a musical work which consists mostly of singing. **3** *literary* a pleasing combination of parts, eg shapes or colours. [from Greek *syn*, together + *phone*, sound]
◇ From c.1765, the classical form of the symphony (as exemplified in works by Joseph Haydn, Mozart, Beethoven, and Franz Schubert) was usually in four movements: a fast movement, a slow movement, a minuet or scherzo, and a finale. In the 19c, the structure was varied a great deal, sometimes by expansion or contraction, or with the introduction of voices.

symphony orchestra a large orchestra capable of playing large-scale orchestral music.

Symplegades in Greek mythology, the Clashing Rocks, situated at the entrance to the Black Sea, through which the *Argo* had to pass.

Symposium, The a dialogue by Plato (c.384 BC). It describes a drinking party in which Socrates and others converse about love.

symposium *noun* (PL. **symposia**, **symposiums**) **1** a conference held to discuss a particular (especially academic) subject. **2** a collection of essays by different writers on a single topic. [from Greek *symposion*, a drinking-party with intellectual discussion]

symptom *noun* **1** *Medicine* an indication of the presence of a disease or disorder, especially something perceived by the patient and not outwardly visible, eg pain, nausea, dizziness. **2** an indication of the existence of a (usually unwelcome) state or condition: *increasing crime as a symptom of moral decline*. [from Greek *symptoma*, happening, attribute]

symptomatic *adj.* serving as a symptom.

synagogue *noun* **1** a Jewish place of worship and religious instruction. **2** a Jewish religious assembly or congregation. [from Greek *synagoge*, assembly]

synapse *noun Anat.* in the nervous system, a region where one neurone (nerve cell) communicates with the next. There is a minute gap between the two cells, across which nerve impulses are transmitted by means of a chemical substance known as a *neurotransmitter*. [from Greek *synapsis*, contact, junction]

synapsis *noun* **1** *Biol.* the pairing of chromosomes of paternal and maternal origin during meiosis. **2** *Medicine* a synapse. [from Greek *synapsis*, contact, junction]

synch *or* **sync** *colloq.* — *noun* synchronization, especially of sound and picture in film and television. — *verb* to synchronize.

synchromesh *noun* a gear system which matches the speeds of the gear wheels before they are engaged, avoiding shock and noise in gear-changing. [a shortening of *synchronized mesh*]

synchronic *or* **synchronical** *adj.* *Linguistics* concerned with the study of a language as it exists at a particular point in time, without reference to its past history or development: the opposite of *diachronic*.

Synchronism a US movement in abstract art (c.1913–18). It is often considered as an American version of Orphism: its principal exponents, Stanton MacDonald-Wright (1890–1973) and Morgan Russell (1886–1953), were influenced by Robert Delaunay and František Kupka in Paris. As in Orphism, faceted Cubist-inspired shapes combined with rich colours were characteristic of the style.

synchronization *or* **synchronisation** *noun* the process of synchronizing or being synchronized.

synchronize *or* **synchronise** *verb* **1** *trans.*, *intrans.* to happen or cause to happen, move, or operate in exact time with (something else or each other). **2** to project (a film) or broadcast (a television programme) so that the action, actors' lip movements, etc precisely match the sounds or words heard. [from Greek *syn*, together + *chronos*, time]

synchronized swimming a sport in which a swimmer or group of swimmers performs a sequence of gymnastic and balletic movements in time to music. Individual and group competitions have recently become official events in the Olympic Games.

synchronous *adj.* in time with something; synchronized.

synchrotron *noun Physics* a particle accelerator that is used to accelerate electrons and protons which travel around a hollow ring at increasing speed. Synchrotrons are an important experimental tool in particle physics. [from Greek *syn*, together + *chronos*, time + ELECTRON]

syncline *noun Geol.* a large generally U-shaped fold in the stratified rocks of the Earth's crust. [from Greek *syn*, together + *klinein*, to cause to lean]

syncopate *verb* to alter (the rhythm of music) by putting the stress on beats not usually stressed. [see SYNCOPE]

syncopation *noun* 1 syncopating. 2 the beat or rhythm produced by syncopating.

syncope *noun* 1 *Medicine* a fit of fainting. 2 the dropping of a letter or syllable in the middle of a word, eg in *o'er*, the poetic version of *over*. [from Greek *synkope*, a cutting short]

sync pulse 1 *Broadcasting* in a television signal, a pulse transmitted at the beginning of each line and field to ensure correct scanning rate on reception. 2 *Cinema* in motion pictures, a series of signals linked to the camera frame rate recorded on the separate sound magnetic tape for subsequent matching to the picture (see also SYN-CHRONIZATION).

syndic *noun* the person representing a university, company, or other body in business or legal matters. [from Greek *syndikos*, advocate, representative]

syndicalism *noun* a form of trade-unionism favouring the transfer of the ownership of factories, etc to the workers themselves. [from French *syndicalisme*, from Greek *syndikos*, representative]

syndicate — *noun* (pronounced *-kət*) 1 any association of people or groups working together on a single project. 2 a group of business organizations jointly managing or financing a single venture. 3 an association of criminals organizing widespread illegal activities. 4 an association of journalists selling material to a variety of newspapers. — *verb* (pronounced *-kate*) 1 to form into a syndicate. 2 to organize or sell by means of a syndicate. [from Old French *syndicat*, from Greek *syndikos*, representative]

syndication *noun* syndicating or being syndicated.

Syndics of the Drapers Guild, The a group portrait by Rembrandt (1662, Rijksmuseum, Amsterdam).

syndrome *noun* 1 a set of symptoms that represent a specific (physical or mental) illness. 2 a pattern or series of events, observed qualities, etc characteristic of a particular problem or condition. [from Greek *syndrome*, a running together]

synecdoche *noun* a figure of speech in which a part of something is used to refer to or denote the whole thing, or the whole to refer to or denote a part, as *wiser heads* meaning *wiser people*. [from Greek *synekdoche*, a receiving together]

synergy *or* **synergism** *noun Biol.* the phenomenon in which the combined action of two or more compounds, especially drugs or hormones, is greater than the sum of the individual effects of each compound. [from Greek *synergia*, co-operation]

Synge, J(ohn) M(illington) (1871–1909) Irish dramatist, born near Dublin. He studied

music in Europe, then turned to writing. On the advice of W B Yeats, he settled among the people of the Aran Islands (1899–1902), an experience which provided the material for his plays, the best-known of which is *The Playboy of the Western World* (1907). He had a profound influence on the next generation of Irish playwrights, and was a director of the Abbey Theatre, Dublin, from 1904.

synod *noun* a local or national council of members of the clergy; also, a meeting of this. [from Greek *synodos*, meeting]

synonym *noun* a word having the same, or very nearly the same, meaning as another. [from Greek *syn*, with + *onoma*, name]

synonymous *adj.* (*often* **synonymous with something**) 1 having the same meaning. 2 very closely associated in the mind: *for many, football is synonymous with hooliganism.*

synopsis *noun* (PL. **synopses**) *noun* a brief outline, eg of the plot of a book; a summary. [from Greek *syn*, together + *opsis*, view]

synoptic *adj.* of the nature of a synopsis; giving or taking an overall view.

Synoptic Gospels the Gospels of Matthew, Mark, and Luke, which describe the events of Christ's life from a similar point of view.

synovia *noun* an oily liquid produced by the body to lubricate the joints. [a term invented by Paracelsus]

synovial *adj.* relating to or in the region of the synovia.

syntactic *or* **syntactical** *adj.* relating or belonging to syntax.

syntax *noun* the positioning of words in a sentence and their relationship to each other; also, the grammatical rules governing this. [from Greek *syn*, together + *tassein*, to put in order]

synthesis *noun* (PL. **syntheses**) 1 the process of putting together separate parts to form a complex whole. 2 the result of such a process. 3 *Chem.* any process whereby a complex chemical compound is formed from simpler compounds or elements, especially via a series of chemical reactions. [from Greek *syn*, together + *thesis*, a placing]

synthesiser *or* **synthesizer** *noun* a musical instrument, especially a keyboard, that produces sound electronically, especially one also reproducing the sounds of other instruments.

synthesize *or* **synthesise** *verb* 1 to combine (simple parts) to form (a complex whole). 2 to create by chemical synthesis.

synthesizer *or* **synthesiser** *noun* an integrated set of electronic devices for generating and modifying musical sounds. It usually includes one or more keyboards, loudspeakers, oscillators, filters, and devices for frequency and amplitude modulation. One of the earliest and best known was developed by Robert A Moog (1934–). Before c.1975, synthesizers could produce only one note at a time, but more recently polyphonic types have been developed, including digital systems based on microprocessors. There are a wide variety of types and sizes used in the production of both live and pre-recorded music.

synthetic *adj.* 1 created artificially by combining chemical substances; not natural; man-made. 2 not sincere; sham. [from Greek *synthetikos*, skilled at putting together]

synthetically *adv.* in a synthetic way.

Synthetism a term sometimes used by art critics to refer to the Symbolist artists, to distinguish them from the Symbolist poets. It is also sometimes applied to the group known as the Nabis.

syphilis *noun Medicine* a sexually transmitted disease caused by infection with the bacterium *Treponema pallidum*, characterized by painless

ulcers which appear on the genitals, and heal spontaneously after several weeks, to be followed by fever, headache, fatigue, and a faint red rash. If untreated with antibiotics, the disease may over a period of years result in heart damage, blindness, paralysis, and death. [from *Syphilus*, the infected hero of a 16c Latin poem]

syphilitic *adj.* relating to or affected with syphilis.

syphon see SIPHON.

Syracuse, Italian **Siracusa** POP (1990e) 125 000, the seaport capital of Syracuse province, Sicily, Italy, situated 53km/33mi SE of Catania. HISTORY founded by Greek settlers in 734 BC; a leading cultural centre in the 5c BC; taken by the Romans in 212 BC. The mathematician Archimedes and the poet Theocritus were born here. NOTABLE FEATURES cathedral (640); Greek theatre (5c BC); Roman amphitheatre, temples, and aqueducts.

Syracuse POP (1990) 660 000, the seat of Onondaga County, central New York, USA. It lies 19km/12mi S of the W end of L Oneida. Syracuse developed in association with salt works during the 1780s and later at the junction of the Erie and Oswego canals. It became a city in 1847.

Syr Darya, ancient **Jaxartes** a river predominantly in Kazakhstan, formed by the junction of the Naryn and Kara Darya rivers, in the W section of the Tien Shan Mts, Uzbekistan. It discharges into the Aral Sea. In total the river is 2 212km/1 375mi long and the area of its drainage basin is 219 000sq km/84 600sq mi. The cotton-growing areas along the river's course are irrigated by its waters and it is also the source for hydroelectric power at the Chardara and Toktogul stations.

Syria, Arabic **Suriya**, official name **Syrian Arab Republic**, Arabic **Al-Jumhuriyah al-Arabiyah as-Suriyah** POP (1992e) 13m, a republic in the Middle East, divided into 14 governorates (*mohofazats*). AREA 185 180sq km/ 71 479sq mi. It is bounded W by the Mediterranean Sea and Lebanon, SW by Israel and Jordan, E by Iraq, and N by Turkey. CAPITAL Damascus. CHIEF TOWNS Aleppo, Homs, Hama, Latakia. TIME ZONE GMT +2. The population is mainly Arab (90%); Islam (74% Sunni Muslim, 16% Alawite Druze and other sects) and Christianity (10%) are the chief religions. OFFI-CIAL LANGUAGE Arabic. CURRENCY the Syrian pound. PHYSICAL DESCRIPTION behind a narrow Mediterranean coastal plain, the Jabal al Nusayriyah mountain range rises to c.1 500m; steep drop in the E to the Orontes R valley; the Anti-Lebanon range in the SW rises to 2 814m at Mt Hermon; open steppe and desert to the E. CLI-MATE coastal Mediterranean climate, with hot, dry summers and mild, wet winters; desert or semi-desert climate in 60% of country, with an annual rainfall below 200mm; the *khamsin* wind causes temperatures to rise to 43–49°C; in Damascus the average annual rainfall is 225mm, and average temperatures range from 7°C in Jan, to 27°C in Jul. HISTORY part of the Phoenician Empire and the Persian Empire; conquered by Alexander I; part of the Roman and Byzantine empires; conquered by Muslim Arabs in the 7c; conquered by Turks in the 11c; the scene of many Crusader battles in the Middle Ages; part of the Ottoman Empire in 1517; brief period of independence in 1920, then made a French mandate; gained independence in 1946; merged with Egypt and Yemen to form the United Arab Republic in 1958; re-established itself as an independent state under its present name in 1961; the Golan Heights region was seized by Israel in 1967; after the outbreak of civil war in Lebanon in 1975, Syrian troops were sent to restore order; Syrian soldiers were part of the international coalition force which opposed Iraq in the Gulf War; took part in the Middle East peace talks in 1992 which gave rise to hopes of agreement being reached with Israel. GOVERNMENT governed by a President, elected for a seven-year term; a 250-member People's Council is elected for a four-year term. ECONOMY since 1974, oil has been the most important source of export revenue; cotton; phosphate; textiles; beverages; tobacco; cement; oil refining; food processing; tourism; cotton, wheat, barley, rice, olives, millet, sugar-beet, fruit; cattle breeding, poultry; the Euphrates Dam Project, begun in 1978, supplies 97% of domestic electricity demand, and is intended to increase the area of arable land by 6 400sq km/2 500sq mi.

Syria

Syriac — *noun* **1** the ancient Aramaic dialect of Syria. **2** a modern form of this dialect, spoken by c.1m people in the Middle East and the USA. — *adj.* relating to or spoken or written in either of these dialects.

syringa *noun* **1** the mock orange shrub. **2** the lilac shrub. [see SYRINGE]

syringe — *noun* **1** a medical instrument for injecting or drawing off liquid, consisting of a hollow cylinder with a plunger inside and a thin hollow needle attached. **2** a similar device used in gardening, cooking, etc. — *verb* to clean, spray or inject using a syringe. [from Greek *syrinx*, tube]

Syrinx in Greek mythology, a nymph pursued by Pan. She called on the Earth to help, and so sank down into it and became a reed-bed. Pan cut some of the reeds, and made his panpipes from them.

syrinx *noun* (PL. **syringes**, **syrinxes**) **1** a pan-pipe or set of panpipes. **2** *Zool.* the sound-producing organ of a bird, consisting of several vibrating membranes. [from Greek *syrinx*, a reed, panpipes; see SYRINX]

syrup *noun* **1** a sweet sticky almost saturated solution of sugar in water, obtained from various plants, eg sugar-cane, maple, corn, or manufactured commercially, eg golden syrup. It is widely used in cooking, baking, etc. **2** a solution of sugar in water used to preserve canned fruit. **3** any sugar-flavoured liquid medicine. **4** *colloq.* exaggerated sentimentality or pleasantness of manner. [from Arabic *sharab*]

syrupy *adj.* of the consistency of or like syrup.

system *noun* **1** a set of interconnected or inter-related parts forming a complex whole: *the trans-*

port system / the human digestive system. **2** an arrangement of mechanical, electrical or electronic parts functioning as a unit. **3** a way of working; a method. **4** efficiency of organization; methodicalness. **5** one's mind or body regarded as a set of interconnected parts: *get the illness out of your system.* **6** (**the system**) society, or the network of institutions that control it, usually regarded as an oppressive force. [from Greek *systema*]

systematic *adj.* **1** making use of, or carried out according to, a clearly worked-out plan or method. **2** methodical.

systematically *adv.* in a systematic way.

systematics *Biol.* the scientific study of the classification of living organisms into a hierarchical series of groups which emphasizes their natural interrelationships. The main categories of modern classifications are (in order of increasing generality) species, genus, family, order, class, phylum (in animals) or division (in plants), and kingdom.

systematization *or* **systematisation** *noun* systematizing or being systematized.

systematize *or* **systematise** *verb* to organize or arrange in a methodical way.

system building *Archit.* methods designed to increase the speed of construction by manufacturing component parts of a building ready for later assembly on site. Many modern buildings are constructed from prefabricated components, such as steel and timber frames, preformed roofing and exterior wall cladding, and windows.

system date *Comput.* the current date as specified by an operating system, used to record a user's operations or to begin pre-set programs, etc.

systemic *adj. Medicine, Biol.* relating to or affecting the whole body or the whole plant.

systemically *adv.* in a systemic way.

systems analysis **1** the detailed analysis of all phases of activity of a commercial, industrial, or scientific organization, usually with a computer, in order to plan more efficient methods and better use of resources, or to determine whether computerization of certain processes would be appropriate. **2** *Comput.* the detailed investigation and analysis of some human task, usually in business, commerce, management, industry, or scientific research, in order to determine whether and how it can be computerized, followed in appropriate cases by the design, implementation, and evaluation of a computer system that can perform the task.

systems analyst a person who carries out systems analysis.

systole *noun Medicine* contraction of the heart muscle, during which blood is pumped from the ventricle into the arteries. Together with *diastole* (relaxation of the muscle) it represents a single heartbeat. [from Greek *systole*]

systolic *adj. Medicine* relating to systole, when the heart pumps out blood.

Szczecin, German **Stettin** POP (1992e) 414 000, the industrial river-port capital of Szczecin voivodship, NW Poland. It lies on R Oder, 60km/37mi from the Baltic Sea and includes the area of Mie(du)dzyodrze, with 5km/3mi of docks, canals, and transshipment facilities. HISTORY achieved urban status in 1243; became a member of the Hanseatic League in 1360; under Prussian rule from 1720 to 1945; badly damaged in World War II; ceded to Poland in 1945. NOTABLE FEATURES St James's Cathedral; castle (16c); city walls (13c–14c).

Szeged POP (1991e) 176 000, the river-port capital of Csongrád county, S Hungary, lying on the R Tisza. It is the cultural centre of the S Alföld. NOTABLE FEATURES medicinal baths; castle (1242); Votive Church.

Székesfehérvár, German **Stuhlweissenburg**, ancient **Alba Regia** POP (1991e) 109 000, the capital of Fejér county, W central Hungary. It is the ancient capital of the Hungarian kingdom. The city, which was badly damaged during World War II, serves as a market centre. NOTABLE FEATURES cathedral; Episcopal Palace; Garden of Ruins with remains of an 11c royal cathedral.

Szent-Györgyi, Albert von Nagyrapolt (1893–1986) Hungarian-born US biochemist, born in Budapest. He lectured at Groningen and Cambridge, became professor at Szeged and Budapest, and later became director of research institutes in Massachusetts. He discovered the protein actin, isolated vitamin C, and made important studies of biological combustion, muscle contraction, and cellular oxidation. He was awarded the 1937 Nobel Prize for Physiology or Medicine.

Szewinska, Irena, *née* Kirszenstein (1946–) Polish athlete, born in Leningrad (now St Petersburg), Russia. She established herself at the 1964 Olympics with a silver medal in the long jump, and a gold in Poland's relay squad. She set world records at 100m and 200m in 1965, won three gold medals at the European championships in 1966, and took the Olympic 200m title in 1968 in world record time. In 1976 she won the Olympic 400m title in a world record time of 49.28sec. She appeared in her fifth Olympics at Moscow in 1980.

Szilard, Leo (1898–1964) Hungarian-born US physicist, born in Budapest. In 1933 he fled from Nazi Germany to England, and in 1938 emigrated to the USA, where he began work on nuclear physics at Columbia University. In 1934 he had taken out a patent on nuclear fission as an energy source, and with Enrico Fermi, he developed the first fission reactor (1942); he also contributed to the development of the atomic bomb.

Szombathely, German **Steinamanger**, ancient **Sabaria** POP (1990e) 86 000, the capital of Vas county, W Hungary, lying on R Gyöngyös. NOTABLE FEATURES cathedral; Franciscan church (14c); 17c Dominican Church; Garden of Ruins with excavations of a 4c imperial palace.

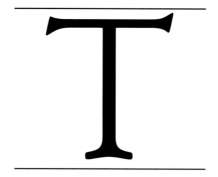

T¹ *or* **t** *noun* (PL. **Ts, T's, t's**) **1** the twentieth letter of the English alphabet. **2** something shaped like a T, eg a pipe which is used to join three separate pipes together.
— **to a T** exactly; perfectly well.

T² *abbrev. Mus.* tenor.

T³ *symbol Chem.* tritium.

t *or* **t.** *abbrev.* **1** ton. **2** tonne. **3** troy (weight).

TA *abbrev.* Territorial Army.

Ta *symbol Chem.* tantalum.

ta *interj. Brit. colloq.* thank you. [imitative of a young child's pronunciation]

tab¹ — *noun* **1** a small flap, tag, strip of material, etc attached to an article, for hanging it up, opening it, holding it, etc for identification. **2** a small strip of material attached to a garment for hanging it up. **3** *North Amer.* a bill, eg in a restaurant.
— *verb* (**tabbed, tabbing**) to fix a tab to.
— **keep tabs on someone** *or* **something** *colloq.* to keep a close watch or check on them.
pick up the tab *North Amer.* to pay the bill.
[probably originally a dialect word]

tab² *noun* a key on a typewriter or word processor which sets and then automatically finds the position of the margins and columns needed to arrange information in a table. [an abbreviation of TABULATOR]

tabard *noun* a short, loose, sleeveless jacket or tunic, worn especially by a knight over his armour, or, with the arms of the king or queen on the front, by a herald. [from Old French *tabart*]

Tabari, Abu Jafar Mohammed Ben Jarir al- (839–923) Arab historian, born in Amol, Persia. He travelled throughout the Middle East collecting scholarly material, and wrote a major commentary on the Koran and a history of the world from creation until the early 10c, which provided a basis for later historical and religious studies.

Tabasco *noun* trademark a hot sauce made from a pungent type of red pepper. [named after *Tabasco* in Mexico]

tabbouleh *noun* a Mediterranean salad made with cracked wheat which has been soaked especially in lemon juice and mixed with chopped vegetables, especially tomatoes, cucumber, and garlic. [from Arabic *tabbula*]

tabby — *noun* (PL. **tabbies**) **1** (*also* **tabby cat**) **a** a usually grey or brown cat with darker stripes. **b** any female domestic cat. **2** a kind of silk with irregular wavy shiny markings. — *adj.* having darker stripes or wavy markings. [from *Al-Attabiyah* in Baghdad where the silk was first made]

tabernacle *noun* **1** (*also* **Tabernacle**) *Hist.* the tent carried by the Israelites across the desert during the Exodus, used as a sanctuary for the Ark of the Covenant. **2** *RC Church* a receptacle in which the consecrated bread and wine are kept. **3** a place of worship of certain nonconformist Christian denominations.
— **Feast of Tabernacles** see SUKKOTH.
[from Latin *tabernaculum*, tent]

Tabitha 1 in the New Testament, a Christian woman of Joppa, restored to life by Peter (Acts 9.36–41). **2** a female first name. [of Aramaic origin, = gazelle]

tabla *noun* a pair of small drums played with the hands in Indian music. [from Hindi, from Arabic]

tablature *noun* an old system of musical notation (chiefly of the 16c and 17c), tailored to a particular instrument or group of instruments, and indicating the keys, frets, etc, to be used rather than the pitch to be sounded. Examples include lute tablature which used letters and numerals on lines representing the strings of the instrument, and German organ tablature, which used letters in conjunction with rhythmic signs. Nowadays tablature is used only for the guitar and ukulele. [from French, from medieval Latin *tabulatura*, from Latin *tabula*, a board]

table — *noun* **1** a piece of furniture consisting of a flat horizontal surface supported by a leg or legs. **2** the people sitting at a table. **3** the food served at a particular table or in a particular house: *keeps a good table.* **4** a group of words, figures, etc arranged systematically in columns and rows. **5** a multiplication table. **6** any flat level surface. **7** *Hist.* a slab of stone or wood inscribed with laws. **8** a tableland. **9** a broad flat surface cut on a gem. — *verb* **1** *Brit.* to put forward for discussion. **2** *North Amer.* to postpone discussion of a bill, etc indefinitely. **3** to make or enter into a table; to tabulate.
— **at table** having a meal.
on the table under discussion.
turn the tables on someone to reverse a situation, so that they are at a disadvantage where previously they had an advantage.
[from Latin *tabula*, board, tablet]

tableau *noun* (PL. **tableaux**) **1** a picture or pictorial representation of a group or scene. **2** (*also* **tableau vivant**) a group of people on stage forming a silent motionless scene from history, literature, etc. [from French]

tablecloth *noun* an often decorative cloth for covering a table, especially during meals.

table d'hôte (PL. **tables d'hôte**) a meal with a set number of choices and a set number of courses offered for a fixed price, especially to residents in a hotel. [from French *table d'hôte*, host's table]

tableland *noun Geol.* a broad high plain or a plateau, usually with steep sides and rising sharply from the surrounding lowland.

table licence a licence to sell and serve alcohol only with meals.

table linen tablecloths and napkins.

table mat a mat for protecting the top of a table from the heat of dishes from the oven and warmed plates.

Table Mountain a mountain in SW Cape province, South Africa. HEIGHT 1 086m. It is a flat-topped central massif flanked on either side by the Lion's Head and Devil's Peak. The mountain is often shrouded in cloud, known as the 'Tablecloth'. Kirstenbosch National Botanical Gardens are situated on the E slopes and Cape Town lies at the foot.

tablespoon *noun* **1** a spoon which is larger than a dessert spoon and is used for serving food. **2** the amount a tablespoon will hold.

tablespoonful *noun* (PL. **tablespoonfuls**) the amount a tablespoon will hold.

tablet *noun* **1** a small, solid, measured amount of a medicine or drug; a pill. **2** a solid flat piece of something, eg soap. **3** a slab of stone or wood on which inscriptions may be carved. [from Old French *tablete*, from Latin *tabula*, board]

table tennis a game based on tennis which is played indoors on a table with small bats and a light hollow ball.
◇ The centre of the table has a net 15.25cm (6in) high stretched across it. The ball is hit over the net and into the opposing half of the table. The object is to force one's opponent to make an error and not return the ball successfully. The winner is the first to reach 21 points with at least a two-point lead. Known as *ping-pong* in the early part of the 20c, it is particularly popular in China and Korea.

tableware *noun* dishes, plates, cutlery, etc for use at table.

tabloid *noun* a newspaper with relatively small pages (approximately 12×16in, 30×40cm), especially one written in an informal and often sensationalist style and with many photographs. See also BROADSHEET. [from TABLET]

taboo *or* **tabu** — *noun* **1** anything which is forbidden for religious reasons or by social custom. **2** any system which forbids certain actions as being unclean or holy. — *adj.* forbidden or prohibited as being a taboo. — *verb* to forbid (a custom, the use of a word, etc) as a taboo. [from Tongan (the language of Tonga) *tabu*, unclean, holy]

tabor *noun* a small, single-headed drum played with one hand while the same player plays a pipe or fife with the other. [from Old French *tabour*]

Tabriz, ancient **Tauris** POP (1986) 972 000, the capital of Tabriz district, NW Iran. It is the fourth-largest city in the country and an industrial and commercial centre. The city is vulnerable to earthquakes. NOTABLE FEATURES ruined 15c Blue Mosque and citadel.

tabular *adj.* arranged in systematic columns; in the form of or according to a table. [from Latin *tabularis*, from *tabula*, board]

tabulate *verb* to arrange (information) in tabular form. [from Latin *tabulare*, from *tabula*, board]

tabulation *noun* tabulating.

tabulator *noun* **1** see TAB². **2** a machine which reads data from a computer storage device, especially punched cards, and prints it out on continuous sheets of paper.

Tachism *or* **Tachisme** *noun Art* a term used, especially in France, to describe a movement in mid-20c abstract painting which coincided with the development of action painting in the US. Paint was laid on in thick patches intended to be interesting in themselves, irrespective of whether a motif was represented. Its exponents included Jean Dubuffet (1901–85), Jean Bazaine (1904–75), and Nicholas de Staâl (1914–55). [from French *tache*, blob (of paint)]

tachograph *noun* a device which records the speed a vehicle travels at and the distance travelled in a particular period of time, used especially in lorries and coaches. [from Greek *tachos*, speed]

tachometer *noun* a device which measures the speed of a machine or vehicle.

tachycardia *noun Medicine* abnormally rapid beating of the heart. [from Greek *tachys*, swift + *kardia*, heart]

tacit *adj.* understood but not actually stated; implied; inferred. [from Latin *tacitus*, silent]

tacitly *adv.* without speaking, silently.

tacitness *noun* silence.

taciturn *adj.* saying little; quiet and uncommunicative. [from Latin *taciturnus*, from *tacere*, to be silent]

taciturnity *noun* a taciturn or uncommunicative quality.

taciturnly *adv.* in a taciturn way.

Tacitus, in full **Publius** or **Gaius Cornelius Tacitus** (c.55–120 AD) Roman historian. He became a praetor, established a great reputation as an orator, and became consul in 97. His major works are two historical studies, the 12-volume *Historiae* (Histories), of which only the first four books survive whole, and the *Annales* (Annals), of which only eight out of possibly 18 books have been completely preserved.

tack — *noun* **1** a short nail with a sharp point and a broad flat head. **2** a long loose temporary stitch used especially to hold material together while it is being sewn properly. **3** the direction of a sailing ship which is sailing into the wind at an angle, stated in terms of the side of the sail that the wind is blowing against: *on the starboard tack*. **4** a sailing ship's zigzag course formed by sailing with first one side of the sail to the wind and then the other. **5** a direction, course of action, or policy. **6** riding harness, saddle, and bridle, etc for a horse. **7** stickiness. — *verb* **1** (*also* **tack something down**) to fasten or attach it with tacks. **2** to sew with long loose temporary stitches. **3** (*also* **tack something on**) to attach or add it as a supplement. **4** *intrans. said of a sailing ship or its crew* to sail into the wind at an angle with first one side of the sail to the wind and then the other so as to sail in a zigzag course and be able to progress forwards. **5** to change the tack of (a ship) to the opposite one. **6** *intrans.* to change one's direction, course of action, or policy abruptly. [from Middle English *tak*]

tackily *adv.* in a tacky way.

tackiness¹ *noun* **1** a tacky quality. **2** stickiness. **3** vulgarity.

tackle — *noun* **1** *Sport* an act of trying to get the ball away from a player on the opposing team. **2** the equipment needed for a particular sport or occupation. **3** a system of ropes and pul-

leys for lifting heavy objects. **4** the ropes and rigging on a ship. — *verb* **1** to grasp or seize and struggle with, especially to try and restrain. **2** to try to **deal** with or solve (a problem). **3** *trans., intrans. Sport* to try to get the ball from (a player on the opposing team). [from Middle English *takel*, gear]

tacky¹ *adj.* (**tackier, tackiest**) slightly sticky.

tacky² *adj.* (**tackier, tackiest**) *colloq.* shabby; vulgar.

taco *noun* (PL. **tacos**) in Mexican cooking, a thin flat corn disc (tortilla), fried and filled with meat. [from Mexican Spanish]

Tacoma POP (1990) 586 000, the port capital of Pierce County, W central Washington, USA. It is 40km/25mi S of Seattle, lying on Commencement Bay, an inlet of Puget Sound. Tacoma is a major NW Pacific container port and a tourist centre. HISTORY settled in 1868; developed as the terminus of the North Pacific Railroad; became a city in 1875. NOTABLE FEATURES Chinese museums; Fort Nisqually.

tact *noun* **1** an awareness of the best or most considerate way to deal with others so as to avoid offence, upset, antagonism, or resentment. **2** skill or judgement in handling difficult situations; diplomacy. [from Latin *tactus*, touch]

tactful *adj.* having or showing tact.

tactfully *adv.* with tact.

tactfulness *noun* a tactful quality.

tactic *noun* a tactical manoeuvre. [from Greek *taktikos*, fit for arranging]

tactical *adj.* **1** relating to or forming tactics. **2** skilful; well-executed and well-planned. **3** *said of a bomb, missile, etc* used to support other military operations.

tactically *adv.* in a tactical way; as regards tactics.

tactical voting the practice of voting for a candidate one does not support but who is the most likely to defeat another candidate that one supports even less.

tactician *noun* a person who is good at tactics or successful planning.

tactics *noun* **1** (*sing.*) the art or science of employing and manoeuvring troops to win or gain an advantage over the enemy. **2** (*sing.*) skill in or the art of using whatever means are available to achieve an end or aim. **3** (*pl.*) the plans, procedure, means, etc followed.

tactile *adj.* **1** of or having a sense of touch. **2** perceptible to the sense of touch. [from Latin *tactilis*, from *tangere*, to touch]

tactless *adj.* lacking tact.

tactlessly *adv.* without tact.

tactlessness *noun* lack of tact.

Tadmur *or* **Tadmor**, Greek **Palmyra** POP (1987e) 22 000, an ancient city in Hims governorate, central Syria. It lies 208km/129mi NE of Damascus. HISTORY financial capital of the E world in the 1c–2c and many of its fine examples of Hellenistic art and architecture date from this period; on the ancient caravan route from the Arabian Gulf to the Mediterranean Sea. NOTABLE FEATURES many examples of Hellenistic art and architecture; numerous temples, including the Temple of Bâl; Monumental Arch; various tombs on the slopes of the hills to the E. The city is a World Heritage site.

tadpole *noun* the larval stage of many frogs and toads, resembling a fish, which lives in water and initially has a round or oval body, a characteristic fin-covered tail, and gills. [from Middle English *taddepol*, from *tadde*, toad + *pol*, head]

Taegu POP (1990) 2.2m, a special city in SE South Korea, the largest inland city after Seoul. It is a market centre situated in the heart of the country's apple growing area. NOTABLE FEATURES Haeinsa Temple (802) with the Tripitaka

Koreana, a set of 80 000 wooden printing blocks engraved with Buddhist scripture (13c); Tonghwasa Temple nearby (17c).

Taejon POP (1990) 1.1m, the capital of Ch'ungch'ongnam province, central South Korea. It was badly damaged in the Korean War. The Yusong Hot Springs and the Kyeryongsan National Park lie to the W of the city.

taekwondo *noun* a Korean martial art and combat sport similar to karate. [from Korean *tae*, kick + *kwon*, fist + *do*, method]

taffeta *noun* a stiff shiny cloth woven from silk or some silk-like material, eg rayon. [from Persian *taftan*, to twist]

taffrail *noun* a rail round a ship's stern. [from Dutch *tafereel*, panel]

Taffy *noun* (PL. **Taffies**) *slang, often offensive* a Welshman. [from Welsh *Dafydd*, David]

Taft, William Howard (1857–1930) US statesman, the 27th President, born in Cincinnati, Ohio. He became a lawyer, Solicitor-General (1890), the first civil governor of the Philippine Is (1901), Secretary of War (1904–8), and President (1909–13). From 1913 he was Professor of Law at Yale, and from 1921 Chief Justice. His son Robert Alphonso (1889–1953) became a US Senator (1938) and Republican leader (1939–53), but was defeated as presidential candidate on four occasions.

Taft–Hartley Act, offical name the **National Management Relations Act** the US labour legislation (1947) that outlawed 'unfair' labour practices (eg the closed shop) and demanded that unions supply financial reports and curtail their political activities. It also gave the US government the power to postpone major strikes endangering national health or safety for a cooling-off period of 80 days.

tag¹ — *noun* **1** a piece of material, paper, leather, etc that carries information (eg washing instructions or the price) about the object to which it is attached. **2** an electronic device such as a bracelet or anklet which transmits radio signals and is used to supervise the movements of a prisoner or offender outside of prison. **3** a metal or plastic point on the end of a shoelace or cord. **4** a loose hanging flap or piece of loose hanging cloth. **5** a trite or common quotation used especially for effect. **6** the final speech in a play, or refrain in a song, added to make the moral or point clear. — *verb* (**tagged, tagging**) **1** to put a tag or tags on. **2** to attach or fasten (something). **3** (**tag along, on**, *etc*) to follow or accompany, especially when uninvited. [from Middle English *tagge*]

tag² — *noun* a children's game in which one child chases the others and tries to catch or touch one of them, who then becomes the chaser. — *verb* (**tagged, tagging**) to catch or touch in or as if in the game of tag.

Tagalog — *noun* an Austronesian language spoken as a first language by c.12 million people on the island of Luzon in the Philippines. A standardized version of the language, known as Pilipino, is taught along with English in schools. — *adj.* relating to or spoken or written in Tagalog.

Taganrog POP (1991e) 294 000, a seaport in Rostov oblast, S Russia. It lies on the NE shore of the Gulf of Taganrog in the Sea of Azov. In 1698 it was founded by Peter I as a fortress and naval base. The dramatist Anton Chekhov was born here in 1860.

tagliatelle *noun* pasta made in the form of long narrow ribbons. [from Italian *tagliatelle*]

Tagore, Rabindranath (1861–1941) Indian poet and philosopher, born in Calcutta. In 1901 he founded the Santiniketan near Bolpur, a communal school to blend Eastern and Western philosophical and educational systems. He is best known for his poems (eg *Gitanjali*, Song Offering, 1912), and short stories (eg *Galpaguccha*, A Bunch of Stories, 1912), and he also wrote several plays and novels. He was awarded the Nobel Prize for Literature in 1913 and was knighted in 1915 — an honour which he resigned in 1919 as a protest against British policy in the Punjab.

Tagus, River, Spanish **Río Tajo**, Portuguese **Tejo** a river in Spain and Portugal, length 1 007km/626mi. Rising in the Sierra de Albarracin, E Spain, it flows 785km/488mi SW to the Portuguese border, which it follows for 44km/27mi. South of Vila Franca de Xira, it opens out into an estuary at Lisbon Bay. In 1976, 229sq km/88sq mi of the estuary were given reserve status. The river is navigable for 212km/132mi to Abrantes.

tahini *noun* a thick paste made from ground sesame seeds. [from Arabic *tahine*, from *tahan*, to grind]

Tahiti, French **Archipel de Tahiti** POP (1988) 116 000, the largest island of French Polynesia, S Pacific Ocean, belonging to the Windward group of the Society Is. AREA 1 042sq km/402sq mi. It became a French colony in 1880 and was the home of Paul Gauguin from 1891 to 1893 and from 1895 to 1901. CAPITAL Papeete. PHYSICAL DESCRIPTION the island is 48km/30mi long and rises to 2 237m at the volcanic peak of Mt Orohena. ECONOMY vanilla, coconuts, copra, sugar cane; tourism.

Tahoua POP (1988) 52 000, the capital of Tahoua department, SW central Niger, 360km/224mi NE of Niamey.

Tai a national park in Guiglo and Sassandra departments, SW Ivory Coast. It was established in 1972 and is a World Heritage site. AREA 3 300sq km/1 300sq mi.

Tai, Mount, Chinese **Taishan** the most revered of China's five sacred mountains, and a key geological, religious, and cultural site in Shandong province. Evidence of settlement dates back 400 000 years, and the area is rich in fossils, medicinal plants, ancient ruins, and temples. It is a World Heritage site.

Tai — *adj.* denoting a family of c. 40 languages used in SE Asia, principally in Thailand, Laos, Vietnam, and parts of China. It is usually divided into three groups, south-western, central, and northern, and includes Thai, Lao (or Laotian), Shan, and Yuan. — *noun* the languages forming this family.

t'ai chi *or* **t'ai chi ch'uan** a Chinese system of exercise and self-defence in which good balance and co-ordination mean that minimum effort is used, developed especially by doing extremely slow and controlled exercises. [from Chinese, = great art of boxing]

Taichung *or* **Taizhong** POP (1992e) 777 000, an independent municipality and the third-largest city in Taiwan. It is the economic, cultural, and commercial centre of the central part of the country.

Taif, At POP (1980e) 300 000, a summer resort town in Mecca province, W central Saudi Arabia. It lies 64km/40mi SE of Mecca, on a high plateau, at an altitude of 1 158m. It is the unofficial seat of government during the summer. The town is situated at the centre of a fruit-growing district and is noted for its wine.

taiga *noun* Geog. in northern parts of the N hemisphere, the large area of predominantly coniferous forest located S of the arctic and sub-arctic tundra regions. [from Russian *taiga*]

tail¹ — *noun* **1** the often quite long and relatively thin part of an animal's body that projects from the lower or rear end of the back; the feathers that project from the rear of a bird's body; the end part of a snake's body. **2** anything which has a similar form, function, or position as a creature's tail: *the tail of a shirt/kite*. **3** a lower, last, or rear part: *the tail of the storm*. **4** the rear part of an aircraft including the rudder and tailplane. **5** the trail of luminous particles following a comet.

6 (**tails**) the reverse side of a coin, that side which does not bear a portrait or head. **7** (**tails**) a tailcoat. **8** (**tails**) evening dress for men, usually including a tailcoat and white bow tie. **9** *colloq.* a person who follows and keeps a constant watch on someone else. **10** *offensive slang* women thought of as sexual objects. — *verb* **1** to remove the stalks (from fruit or vegetables). **2** (**tail someone** *or* **tail after someone**) to follow them closely.

— **tail away** *or* **off** to become gradually less, smaller, or weaker.

turn tail to turn round and run away.

with one's tail between one's legs completely defeated or humiliated.
[from Anglo-Saxon *tægel*]

tail² *noun* Legal a limiting of who may inherit property to one person and that person's heirs, or to some other particular class of heirs. [from Old French *taillier*, to cut]

tailback *noun* a long queue of traffic stretching back from an accident, roadworks, etc blocking the road.

tailboard *noun* a hinged or removable flap at the rear of a lorry, cart, or wagon.

tailcoat *noun* a man's formal black jacket which is cut away below the waist in the front and has a long divided, tapering tail which is slit to the waist.

tailed *adj.* **1** having a tail. **2** with the tail removed.

tail end the very end or last part.

tailgate *noun* **1** the rear door which opens upwards on a hatchback vehicle. **2** the lower gate of a canal lock. **3** *North Amer.* a tailboard.

Tailleferre, Germaine (1892–1983) French pianist and composer, born in Park-St-Maur. One of the group of young French composers known as 'Les Six', she wrote chamber music, a ballet (*Le Marchand d'oiseaux*), a piano concerto, and songs.

tailless *adj.* lacking a tail.

tail-light *noun* North Amer. the usually red light on the back of a car, train, bicycle, etc.

Tailor, The a painting by Giovanni Battista Moroni (16c, National Gallery, London).

tailor — *noun* a person who makes suits, jackets, trousers, overcoats, etc to measure, especially for men. — *verb* (**tailored**, **tailoring**) **1** *trans., intrans.* to make and style (garments) so that they fit well. **2** to make suitable for particular or special circumstances. [from Old French *taillour*]

tailor-bird *noun* a small Asian bird that sews leaves together to make a nest.

tailored *adj.* **1** tailor-made. **2** *said of a person* dressed in clothes which fit well.

tailoress *noun* rare a female tailor.

tailor-made — *adj.* **1** *said of clothes* made by a tailor to fit a particular person well. **2** well suited or adapted for a particular purpose. — *noun* a tailor-made piece of clothing.

tailpiece *noun* **1** a piece at the end or tail. **2** a design or engraving at the end of a chapter. **3** a strip of wood at the bottom of some stringed instruments (eg a violin) from which the strings are stretched across the bridge to the pegs.

tailplane *noun* a small horizontal wing at the rear of an aircraft.

tailspin *noun* an aircraft's spiral dive with the nose facing down.

tail wind a wind blowing in the same direction as that in which a ship, aircraft, etc is travelling.

Taimyr, Lake see TAYMYR, LAKE.

Tainan *or* **T'ai-nan** POP (1992e) 690 000, an independent municipality and the oldest city in Taiwan. It lies on the SW coast of Taiwan I. Tainan was the capital from 1684 to 1687. NOTABLE FEATURES oldest Confucian temple in Taiwan (1665); Yi T'sai Castle (1874).

taint — *verb* **1** *trans., intrans.* to affect or be affected by pollution, putrefaction, or contamination. **2** to contaminate morally; to infect with evil. **3** to affect slightly with something bad. — *noun* **1** a spot, mark, or trace of decay, contamination, infection, or something bad or evil. **2** a corrupt or decayed condition. [from Middle English *taynt*, struck + Old French *teint*, from Latin *tingere*, to dye]

tainted *adj.* contaminated, polluted.

taipan *noun* a venomous snake native to NE Australia and New Guinea, one of the world's most deadly snakes, and the largest Australian snake. It is brown with a paler head, and feeds mainly on small mammals. [an Aboriginal name]

Taipei *or* **Taibei**, also **T'ai-pei** POP (1992e) 2.7m, the capital of Taiwan. It lies at the NW end of the island and is one of the fastest-growing cities in Asia. HISTORY occupied by the Japanese from 1895 until 1945; became the seat of the Nationalist Government in 1949. NOTABLE FEATURES National Palace Museum; Chung Cheng Memorial Hall; Lung Shan (Dragon Mountain) Temple (1740, rebuilt several times).

Tairov, Aleksandr Yakovlevich, originally **Kornblit** (1885–1950) Russian theatre director and actor, born in Rovno. He acted in Kiev, Petersburg, Rīga, and Simbirsk (1905–13), then directed at the Free Theatre in Moscow, before founding the Moscow Chamber Theatre with his wife in 1914. As director he pioneered a 'synthetic theatre' of abstract balletic movement.

Taiwan, formerly **Formosa**, official name **Republic of China** POP (1992e) 20.6m, an island republic consisting of Taiwan I and several smaller islands, divided into 16 counties (*hsien*). AREA 36 000sq km/13 896sq mi. It lies c.130km/80mi off the SE coast of China from which it is separated to the W by the Taiwan Strait; it is bounded S by the S China Sea, N by the E China Sea, and E by the Pacific Ocean. CAPITAL Taipei. CHIEF TOWNS Kaohsiung, Taichung, Keelung. TIME ZONE GMT +8. The population is mainly Han Chinese (98%); several religions are practised. OFFICIAL LANGUAGE Mandarin Chinese. CURRENCY the new Taiwan dollar. PHYSICAL DESCRIPTION the island is c.395km/245mi long, 100–145km/60–90mi wide; a mountain range runs N–S, covering two thirds of the island; the highest peak is Yu Shan (3 997m); the low-lying land is mainly on the W; crossed by the Tropic of Cancer. CLIMATE tropical monsoon-type climate; annual rainfall is generally over 2 000mm; the wettest period is in summer (May–Sep), when it is also hot and humid; typhoons bring heavy rains between Jul and Sep; mild and short winters; the average daily temperature at Taipei is 12–19°C in Jan, and 24–33°C in Jul–Aug; the monthly rainfall is 71mm in Dec and 290mm in Jun. HISTORY discovered by the Portuguese in 1590; conquered by Manchus in the 17c; ceded to Japan in 1895; returned to China in 1945; the Nationalist government was moved here in 1949; in 1991 Taiwan officially recognized the People's

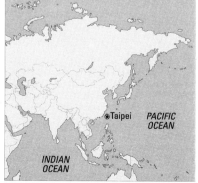

Taiwan

Republic of China for the first time in over 40 years. GOVERNMENT governed by a President, who appoints a Premier; the National Assembly has 920 members; Parliament (*Yuan*) has 313 members. ECONOMY changed from agriculture to industry since the 1950s; high technology; textiles; footwear; electronics; plastics; cement; furniture; consumer goods; iron and steel; petrochemicals; machinery; plywood; canned food; small deposits of coal, natural gas, limestone, marble, asbestos; fish; sugar, bananas, pineapples, citrus fruits, vegetables, tea.

Taiyuan *or* **Yangku** POP (1990) 2.2m, the capital of Shanxi province, E central China. HISTORY founded during the W Zhou Dynasty; development was promoted by Western powers in the late 19c. NOTABLE FEATURES Shanxi Museum; Jinci temples from the N Wei Dynasty are located c.25km/15mi SE.

Tajikistan *or* **Tadzhikistan**, Tajik **Respublika i Tojikiston**, Russian **Tadzhikskaya** POP (1991e) 5.5m, an republic in SE Middle Asia. AREA 143 100sq km/55 200sq mi. It is bounded W and N by Uzbekistan, N by Kirghizia, E by China, and S by Afghanistan. CAPITAL Dushanbe. CHIEF TOWNS Khudzand, Kulyab, Kurgan-Tyube. Islam is the main religion. OFFICIAL LANGUAGE Tajik. CURRENCY the rouble. PHYSICAL DESCRIPTION the Tien Shan, Gissar-Alai, and Pamir ranges cover over 90% of the area; Communism Peak reaches 7 495m; the R Amudarya flows E–W along the S border; the largest lake is L Kara-Kul. HISTORY became a Soviet Socialist Republic in 1929; achieved full independence in 1991; Civil War began in 1992. ECONOMY oil, natural gas, coal; lead, zinc; machinery, metalworking; chemicals; food processing; cotton; wheat, maize, vegetables, fruit; hot mineral springs and health resorts.

Tajikistan

Taj Mahal a mausoleum constructed (1639–48) at Agra in Uttar Pradesh, India, for Mumtaz Mahal, the favourite wife of the Mughal emperor, Shah Jahan. It is built of white marble and inlaid with semi-precious stones and mosaic work. It is a World Heritage site.

Takamine, Jokichi (1834–1922) Japanese-born US chemist, born in Takaoka. In 1887 he opened a factory in Japan to make superphosphate fertilizer; he later moved to the USA and set up an industrial biochemical laboratory there. In 1891 he isolated adrenaline in crystalline form from the adrenal glands. This was the first time that a hormone was isolated in pure form from a natural source.

take — *verb* (PAST TENSE **took**; PAST PARTICIPLE **taken**) **1** (*often* **take something down, off, out**, *etc*) to reach out for and grasp, lift, pull, *etc* (something chosen or known); to grasp, enter, *etc* for use: *take a book from the shelf / take my car if you like.* **2** to carry, conduct, or lead to another place: *take him some grapes / talents which will take her far.* **3** to do or perform: *take a walk / take one's revenge.* **4** to get, receive, occupy, obtain, rent, or buy: *take a holiday / take two eggs.* **5** to agree to have or

accept: *take advice / take office / will you take a cheque?* **6** to accept as true or valid: *take her word for it.* **7** to adopt or commit oneself to: *take a decision / take her side in the argument.* **8** to endure or put up with: *cannot take his arrogance.* **9** to need or require: *it will take all day to finish / a verb which takes a direct object.* **10** to use as a means of transport: *take the bus.* **11** to make (a written note of something): *take the minutes of the meeting / take notes.* **12** to make (a photographic record); to make a photographic record of (someone or something): *decided to take a few colour slides / shall I take you by the bridge?* **13** to study or teach: *take French at night school.* **14** to remove, use, or borrow without permission: *took her coat by mistake.* **15** to proceed to occupy: *take a seat.* **16** to come or derive from: *a quotation taken from Proust.* **17** to have room or strength to support: *the shelf won't take any more books.* **18** to consider as an example. **19** to consider or think of in a particular way; to mistakenly consider (someone) to be someone or something: *took her to be a teacher / do you take me for a fool?* **20** to capture or win. **21** (**take someone** *or* **be taken with someone**) to be charmed and delighted by them. **22** to eat or drink: *take medicine / take sugar in coffee.* **23** to conduct or lead: *this road will take you the station.* **24** to be in charge or control of; to run: *take the meeting.* **25** to react to or receive in a specified way: *take the news well.* **26** to feel: *take pride in one's work.* **27** to turn to for help, refuge, etc. **28** (*also* **take something away** *or* **off**) to subtract it. **29** to go down or into: *took the first road on the left.* **30** to deal with or consider: *take the first two questions together.* **31** *intrans.* to have or produce the expected or desired effect: *the vaccination didn't take.* **32** *intrans. said of seeds, etc* to begin to send out roots and grow. **33** to measure: *take a temperature.* **34** (**be taken ill**, *etc*) to become suddenly ill, etc. **35** to understand. **36** to have sexual intercourse with. — *noun* **1** a scene filmed or piece of music recorded during an uninterrupted period of filming or recording. **2** the amount or number taken (eg of fish caught) at one time. **3** the amount of money taken in a shop, business, etc over a particular period of time: *the day's take.*

— **take after someone** to be like a parent or relation in appearance or character.

take against someone to dislike them immediately.

take someone apart to criticize or defeat them severely.

take something apart to separate it into pieces or components.

take someone back 1 to make them remember the past. **2** to receive back a former partner, lover, etc, after an estrangement.

take something back 1 to withdraw or retract a statement or promise. **2** to regain possession of something. **3** to return something to an original or former position. **4** to return something bought from a shop for an exchange or refund.

take a degree to study for and obtain a university or college degree.

take something down 1 to make a written note or record of it. **2** to demolish or dismantle it. **3** to lower it.

take someone down 1 to escort them to dinner. **2** to make less powerful or self-important; to humble: *take him down a peg or two.*

take someone in 1 to include them. **2** to give them accommodation or shelter. **3** to deceive or cheat them.

take something in 1 to include it. **2** to understand and remember it. **3** to make a piece of clothing smaller. **4** to do paid work in one's home: *take in washing.* **5** to include a visit to it: *we can take in a restaurant on the way home.*

take it 1 to be able to bear suffering, trouble, difficulty, etc: *tell me the worst, I can take it.* **2** to assume: *I take it that you'll be able to come.*

take it from me you can believe me.

take it out of someone *colloq.* to exhaust their strength or energy.

take it out on someone *colloq.* to vent one's anger or frustration on an innocent person.

take it upon oneself to take responsibility.

take off 1 *said of an aircraft or its passengers* to leave the ground. **2** to depart or set out, especially by aeroplane: *took off for Madrid.* **3** *colloq., said of a scheme, product, etc* to become popular and successful and expand quickly.

take someone off to imitate or mimic them.

take something off 1 to remove something, especially clothing. **2** to deduct something. **3** to spend a period of time away from work on holiday, resting, etc.

take on *colloq.* to be greatly upset or distraught.

take someone on 1 to give them employment. **2** to challenge or compete with them: *decided to take them on at snooker.*

take something on 1 to agree to do it; to undertake it. **2** to acquire a new meaning, quality, appearance, etc. **3** *said of an aircraft, ship, etc* to admit new passengers, fuel, cargo, etc on board.

take something out 1 to remove or extract it. **2** to obtain on application: *take out insurance / take out a warrant.*

take someone out 1 to go out with them or escort them in public. **2** *slang* to kill, defeat, or destroy them.

take over *or* **take something over** to assume control, management, or ownership of it.

take to someone *or* **something 1** to develop a liking for them. **2** to begin to do something regularly. **3** to turn to something as a remedy or for refuge.

take someone up 1 to become their patron or supporter. **2** *said of an activity, interest, etc* to absorb them.

take something up 1 to lift or raise it. **2** to use or occupy space or time. **3** to become interested in it and begin to do it: *take up the violin.* **4** to shorten a piece of clothing. **5** to resume a story, account, etc after a pause. **6** to assume or adopt: *take up residence in July.* **7** to accept an offer.

take someone up on something 1 to accept their offer, proposal, challenge, etc. **2** to discuss a point or issue first raised by them.

take something up with someone to discuss a matter with them: *take it up with your MP.*

take up with someone to become friendly with them; to begin to associate with them. [from Anglo-Saxon *tacan*]

takeaway — *noun* **1** a cooked meal prepared and bought in a restaurant but taken away and eaten somewhere else, eg at home. **2** a restaurant which provides such meals. — *adj.* **1** *said of cooked food* prepared in a shop or restaurant for the customer to take away. **2** *said of a shop or restaurant* providing such meals.

take-home pay the salary that one actually receives after tax, national insurance, and pension contributions have been deducted.

take-off *noun* **1** an instance of an aircraft leaving the ground. **2** an act of imitating or mimicking. **3** a place from which one takes off, jumps, etc; a starting-point. See also TAKE OFF.

takeover *noun* the act of taking control of something, especially a company by buying the majority of its shares.

taker *noun* a person who takes or accepts something, especially a bet.

take-up *noun* the act or extent of claiming or accepting something, eg state benefit.

take-up rate the number of people who claim a benefit to which they are entitled or who accept an offer.

taking — *adj.* attractive; charming. — *noun* (**takings**) the amount of money taken at a concert, in a shop, etc; receipts.

Talamanca Range–La Amistad Reserve a reserve on the Costa Rica–Panama border. It stretches from the Pacific Ocean to the Atlantic Ocean, encompassing a wide range of ecosystems, and providing a unique habitat for many species. AREA 50 000sq km/19 000sq mi. The reserve is a World Heritage site.

Talbot, William Henry Fox (1800–77) English pioneer of photography, born in Melbury Abbas, Dorset. He became an MP in 1833. In 1838 he succeeded in making photographic prints on silver chloride paper, which he termed 'photogenic drawing', and later developed and patented the Calotype process.

talc or **talcum** noun **1** Geol. a soft greasy white, green, or grey mineral form of magnesium silicate, which when purified consists of a white powder. It is used in talcum powder and other cosmetics, French chalk, lubricants, and paper coatings, and as a filler in paints, plastics, and rubber. **2** talcum powder. [from Persian talk]

Talca POP (1991e) 183 000, the capital of Maulé region and of Talca province, central Chile. HISTORY founded in 1692; destroyed by earthquakes in 1742 and 1928, then completely rebuilt; Chilean independence was declared here in 1818. The province is noted as the greatest wine-producing area in Chile. NOTABLE FEATURE O'Higgins Museum.

Talcahuano POP (1991e) 251 000, a port in Concepción province, central Chile. It lies on a peninsula 12km/7mi N of Concepción and is the site of Chile's main naval base and dry docks.

talcum powder a fine, often perfumed, powder made from purified talc, used on the body.

tale noun **1** a story or narrative. **2** a false or malicious story or piece of gossip; a lie.
— **tell tales** to disclose secret or private information, especially about another person's wrongdoing to someone in authority. [from Anglo-Saxon talu]

tale-bearer noun a person who repeats malicious or false gossip.

talent noun **1** a special or innate skill, aptitude, or ability, especially for art, music, etc. **2** high general or mental ability. **3** a person or people with such skill or ability. **4** colloq. attractive members of the opposite sex as a group. **5** Hist. a measure of weight and unit of currency used eg by the ancient Greeks and Romans. [from Anglo-Saxon talente, from Latin talentum]

talented adj. having talent or aptitude.

talent scout or **talent spotter** a person whose job is to find and recruit talented amateurs, especially singers and dancers, for professional engagements.

Tale of a Tub, A a prose satire by Jonathan Swift (1704). It is primarily a religious satire which centres on the actions of three brothers when they are each left a coat by their father.

Tale of Two Cities, A a novel by Charles Dickens (1859). It is set in London and Paris at the time of the French Revolution.

Tales from the Vienna Woods (Geschichten aus dem Wienerwald) a waltz by Johann Strauss, the Younger (Op 325, 1868).

Tales of Hoffmann, The (Les Contes d'Hoffmann) an opera by Jacques Offenbach (produced posthumously, 1881), based on tales by E T A Hoffmann. The story is set in a beer cellar where Hoffmann is drinking with his 'muse' Nicklausse and is visited by Lindorf, his rival for the affections of the opera-singer Stella. Each of the three acts tells of one of his disastrous love affairs, involving a doll, a singer, and a courtesan, and in each his enemy is played by Lindorf, who finally wins Stella.

Taliesin (6c) Welsh bard, possibly mythical, known only from a collection of poems in The Book of Taliesin (late 13c). His name is given in the Saxon Genealogies added to the 9c Historia Britonum of Nennius.

Talisman, The a novel by Sir Walter Scott (1825). The second of the Tales of the Crusaders, it

describes the adventures in the Holy Land of the Scottish knight Sir Kenneth.

talisman noun (PL. **talismans**) a small object such as a stone which is supposed to have magic powers to protect its owner from evil, bring good luck, or work magic; a charm or amulet. [from Greek telesma, rite, consecrated object]

talismanic adj. of the nature of a talisman.

talk — verb **1** intrans. (often **talk to** or **with someone**) to express one's ideas, feelings, and thoughts by means of spoken words; to have a conversation or discussion. **2** to discuss: talk business. **3** intrans. to use or be able to use speech: is the baby beginning to talk yet? **4** to express in speech; to utter: talk nonsense. **5** intrans. to gossip. **6** intrans. to give away secret information. **7** to use (a language) or speak in it: talk Dutch. **8** to get (oneself) into a certain state by talking: talked themselves hoarse. **9** (**talk someone into** or **out of something**) to persuade them by talking to do or not to do something: tried to talk him out of jumping. **10** intrans. to have influence: money talks. **11** intrans. to give a talk or lecture: our guest speaker will talk on potholing. — noun **1** a conversation or discussion. **2** (often **talks**) a formal discussion or series of negotiations. **3** an informal lecture. **4** gossip or rumour, or the subject of it: the talk of the town. **5** fruitless or impractical discussion or boasting: his ideas are just talk. **6** a particular way of speaking or communicating: baby talk.
— **now you're talking** colloq. now you are saying something welcome.

talk back to answer rudely, impudently, or boldly.

talk big colloq. to talk boastfully.

talk someone down 1 to silence them by speaking more loudly or aggressively. **2** to help a pilot or aircraft to land by sending instructions over the radio.

talk down to someone to talk patronizingly or condescendingly to them.

talk something out 1 to resolve a problem or difference of opinion by discussion. **2** Brit. to defeat a bill or motion in parliament by prolonging discussion of it until there is not enough time left to vote on it.

talk something over to discuss it thoroughly.

talk round something to discuss all aspects of a subject, problem, etc without reaching a decision or coming to a conclusion.

talk someone round to bring them to one's own way of thinking by talking persuasively.

you can't talk colloq. you are in no position to criticize or disagree.
[from Middle English talken]

talkative adj. talking a lot.

talker noun a person who talks, especially at length or in some specified way.

talkie noun colloq. a cinema film with sound, especially one of the first such films.

talking-point noun a subject for discussion.

talking-shop noun a place for discussion and argument and not action.

talking-to noun colloq. a ticking-off; a scolding or reproof.

tall adj. **1** of above average height. **2** having a stated height: six feet tall. **3** difficult to believe; extravagant: a tall story. **4** difficult or demanding: a tall order. [from Middle English tal, from Anglo-Saxon getæl, swift, ready]

Tallahassee POP (1990) 234 000, the capital of the state of Florida, USA, situated in Leon County, NW Florida. HISTORY originally a settlement of the Apalachee Native Americans; it became state capital in 1824; the ordinance of secession from the Union was adopted here in 1861.

tallboy noun a tall chest of drawers, sometimes on short legs and with an upper and slightly smaller section standing on a lower larger one.

Talleyrand-Périgord, Charles Maurice de, Prince of Benevento (1754–1838)

French statesman, born in Paris. Educated for the Church, he was ordained (1779), appointed Bishop of Autun (1788), elected to the Estates General, and made President of the Assembly (1790). He lived in exile in England and the USA until after the fall of Robespierre. As Foreign Minister under the Directory (1797–1807), he helped to consolidate Napoleon's position as Consul (1802) and Emperor (1804). Alarmed by Napoleon's ambitions however, he resigned in 1807 and became leader of the anti-Napoleonic faction. He became Foreign Minister under Louis XVIII and represented France with great skill at the Congress of Vienna (1814–15). He then lived mainly in retirement, but was Louis Philippe's chief adviser at the July Revolution, and was appointed French Ambassador to England (1830–4).

Tallien, Jean Lambert (1767–1820) French revolutionary politician, born in Paris. As President of the Convention (1794), he was denounced by Robespierre, but conspired with Comte de Barras and Joseph Fouché to bring about Robespierre's downfall. He became a member of the Council of Five Hundred under the Directory (1795–9), and accompanied Napoleon to Egypt (1798).

Tallinn, formerly German **Revel Reval** (to 1917) POP (1990e) 484 000, the seaport capital of Estonia, lying on the S coast of the Gulf of Finland. It has extensive military and naval installations. HISTORY a member of the Hanseatic League; taken by Russia in 1710; capital of independent Estonia between 1918 and 1940; occupied by Germany during World War II. NOTABLE FEATURES citadel (13c); former Governor's Palace (1767–73); Toomkirik (cathedral, 13c–15c).

Tallis, Thomas (c.1505–1585) English musician, 'the father of English cathedral music', born in London. In 1575 Elizabeth I granted him, with William Byrd, a monopoly for printing music and music paper in England. One of the greatest contrapuntists of the English School, an adaptation of his plainsong responses, and his setting of the Canticles in D Minor, are still in use. He wrote much church music, including a motet in 40 parts, Spem in alium.

tallness noun being tall.

tallow noun hard fat from sheep and cattle melted down and used to make candles, soap, etc. [from Middle English talg]

tally — noun (PL. **tallies**) **1** an account or reckoning, eg of work done, debts, or the score in a game. **2** Hist. a stick which could have notches cut in it to show debts and accounts, and which could then be split in half lengthways so that each party could have a record of the deal. **3** a distinguishing or identifying mark or label. **4** a counterpart; a corresponding part. — verb (**tallies**, **tallied**) **1** intrans. to agree, correspond, or match. **2** to record or mark (a number, score, etc) on, or as if on, a tally. [from Latin talea, stick]

tally clerk a person who checks a ship's cargo against an official list.

tally-ho interj. a cry to the hounds at a hunt when a fox has been sighted.

tallyman noun **1** a person who keeps a tally. **2** a person who sells goods on credit, especially from door to door.

Talmud noun the body of Jewish civil and canon law. [Hebrew, = instruction]

Talmudic adj. relating to or contained in the Talmud.

Talmudist noun a scholar of the Talmud.

talon noun a hooked claw, especially of a bird of prey. [from Latin talus, heel]

talus noun (PL. **tali**) Anat. the ankle bone. [from Latin talus, ankle]

tamable or **tameable** adj. capable of being tamed.

Tamale POP (1988e) 151 000, the capital of Northern region, Ghana. The city is situated 430km/267mi N of Accra and is an educational and commercial centre.

Tamara a female first name. [a Caucasian name, possibly from Hebrew *tamar*, date-palm]

tamari *noun* a concentrated sauce made of soya beans and salt, used especially in Japanese cookery. [from Japanese]

tamarind *noun* **1** a tropical evergreen tree which bears yellow flowers and brown seed-pods. **2** the pod of this tree, filled with a reddish-black slightly acid pulp used as food and to make cooling drinks. [from Arabic *tamr-hindi*, Indian date]

tamarisk *noun* a tropical or Mediterranean shrub or tree with slender branches and small pink or white flowers, usually found on seashores. [from Latin *tamarix*]

Tambo, Oliver (1917–93) South African politician, born in Bizana, Transkei. He joined the African National Congress Youth League in 1944, and rose to be a member of the ANC executive (1949), Secretary-General (1955), and Deputy President (1958–67). He then went into exile and was President of ANC in exile from 1977. He returned to South Africa in 1990 as titular Leader of the Party, but gave up this position in 1991 through ill health.

tambour *noun* **1** a drum. **2** a frame for embroidery consisting of two hoops which hold the fabric taut while stitches are sewn. **3** an embroidery done on such a frame. [from Old French]

tambourine *noun* a small round drum with skin stretched tight on one side only, with small discs of metal in the rim that jingle when the drum is struck with the hand. [from Old Dutch *tamborijn*, small drum]

Tambov 1 POP (1991e) 334 000, the capital of Tambov oblast, S central Russia, lying on a tributary of the R Oka. It was founded in 1636 as a fortress to defend Moscow. **2** an oblast in S central Russia with Tambov as its capital.

Tamburlaine the Great a play in two parts by Christopher Marlowe (c.1587). Written in blank verse, it tells the story of the rise of Tamburlaine (Timur) from shepherd to ferocious ruler. His ruthlessness leads to the deaths of the Turkish emperor and his Queen in a cage and is curbed only by his love for Zenocrate.

tame — *adj.* **1** *said of animals* used to living or working with people; not wild or dangerous. **2** *said of land, etc* changed by people from a natural wild state; cultivated. **3** docile, meek, and submissive. **4** dull and unexciting; insipid: *a tame ending to an otherwise exciting story.* — *verb* **1** to make (an animal) used to living or working with people. **2** to make meek and humble; to deprive the spirit of; to subdue. [from Anglo-Saxon *tam*]

tamely *adv.* in a tame way.

tameness *noun* a tame quality.

tamer *noun* a person who tames animals.

Tamerlaine see TIMUR.

Tamil — *noun* **1** a member of a people living in S India and Sri Lanka. **2** the language spoken by this people. — *adj.* of or relating to this people or their language.

Tamil Nadu, formerly **Madras** POP (1991) 55.9m, a state in S India. AREA 130 069sq km/50 207sq mi. It is bounded E and S by the Bay of Bengal and is separated from Sri Lanka by the Palk Strait and the Gulf of Mannar. The population is mainly Hindu. PHYSICAL DESCRIPTION Cape Comorin forms the most southerly point; there are several hill ranges and rivers. HISTORY part of the Chola Empire in the 10c–13c; the first British trading settlement was established in 1611; largely under British control by 1801; the boundaries of Mysore state altered

in 1956 and 1960; renamed Tamil Nadu in 1968. CAPITAL Madras. GOVERNMENT governed by a 63-member Legislative Council and a 234-member Legislative Assembly. ECONOMY rice, maize, pulses, millets, sugar cane, cotton, oilseed, tobacco, coffee, tea, rubber, pepper; coal, chromite, bauxite, limestone, manganese; textiles; tanning; machinery; tyres; forestry.

Taming of the Shrew, The a play by William Shakespeare (1592). It is apparently a comedy about love and marriage, but the story of the strong-minded Katherina's enforced subservience to Petruchio (a task originally undertaken so that his friend can court her younger sister) provides serious comment on the role of women in society.

Tammany Hall a US political machine of the Democratic party in New York City and State. It was originally a club (the Society of Tammany) founded in 1789, notorious in the late 19c and early 20c for its political corruption. Its power declined in the 1932 election, and although revived for a short time, it no longer exists as a power in New York politics.

Tammerfors see TAMPERE.

Tammuz or **Thammuz**, earlier form **Dumuzi** a Babylonian god of fertility and agriculture who was beloved by Ishtar (in Syria by Astarte). Each year he returned from the underworld then died again, his death mourned by funeral chants, a ritual which symbolized the agricultural cycle.

Tam O'Shanter a narrative poem by Robert Burns (1791). It describes Tam's drunken witness of a witches' gathering with the Devil in Alloway Kirk and his desperate ride to evade capture.

tam-o'-shanter *noun* a Scottish flat round cloth or woollen cap which fits tightly round the brows and has a full crown, often with a bobble in the middle. [after the hero of Robert Burns's poem]

tamoxifen *noun Medicine* a drug that inhibits the effects of oestrogens, and is used in the treatment of advanced breast cancer. It has been suggested that it may have useful preventive effects in certain women at relatively high risk of developing breast cancer. It is also used to stimulate ovulation in the treatment of infertility.

tamp *verb* **1** to fill up (a hole containing explosive) with earth, cement, etc before setting off the explosion. **2** to drive or force down (eg ballast on a railway) by repeated blows.

Tampa POP (1990) 280 000, the seat of Hillsborough County, W Florida, USA, lying on the NE coast of Tampa Bay. Today Tampa is a port and resort town; it developed from 1824 around a military base and was later a cigar-making centre. NOTABLE FEATURES David Falk and Tampa theatres; Museum of Science and Industry; Tampa Museum; Busch Gardens.

tamper *verb intrans.* (**tampered, tampering**) **1** to interfere or meddle, especially in a harmful way. **2** to attempt to corrupt or influence, especially by bribery. [a form of TEMPER]

Tampere, Swedish **Tammerfors** POP (1992e) 174 000, the second-largest city in Finland, situated in Häme province, SW Finland. It lies on the Tammerkoski Rapids by L Näsijärvi, c.160km/100mi NW of Helsinki. Established in 1779, it developed as an industrial centre in the 19c. NOTABLE FEATURES cathedral (20c); open-air theatre.

tamper-evident *adj., said of packaging* designed in such a way that it is obvious when it has been tampered with.

Tampico POP (1990) 272 000, a seaport in Tamaulipas state, NE Mexico, situated on the Gulf of Mexico.

tampion or **tompion** a plug, especially a protective plug placed in the muzzle of a gun

when not in use. [from French *tampon*, from *tapon*, a plug of cloth]

tampon — *noun* a plug of cottonwool or other soft absorbent material inserted into a cavity or wound to absorb blood and other secretions, especially one for use in the vagina during menstruation. — *verb* (**tamponed, tamponing**) to insert a tampon in. [from Old French, from *tape*, plug]

Tamsin a female first name. [of Cornish origin, originally a contracted form of *Thomasina*]

tam-tam *noun* a percussion instrument similar to a gong, but made of thinner metal and having no central boss. While a gong produces a definite pitch, the tam-tam's sound is made up of a dissonant mixture of frequencies varying with the size of the instrument. [from Hindi]

Tamworth POP (1992e) 71 000, a town linked with Fazeley in Tamworth district, Staffordshire, central England. It lies on the R Tame, 21km/13mi NE of Birmingham. In the 8c King Offa maintained a royal palace and mint here. NOTABLE FEATURES Church of St Editha (14c); Castle Museum.

tan¹ — *noun* **1** the brown colour of the skin after exposure to the sun's ultraviolet rays. **2** a tawny brown colour. **3** oak bark or other material, used especially for tanning hides. — *adj.* tawny brown in colour. — *verb* (**tanned, tanning**) **1** *trans., intrans.* to make or become brown in the sun. **2** to convert (hide) into leather by soaking it in a solution containing tannin, mineral salts, or manmade chemicals. **3** *colloq.* to beat. [from Latin *tannum*, oak bark]

tan² *abbrev. Maths.* tangent (see TANGENT 2).

Tana, Lake, Amharic **Tana Hāyk** a lake in W central Ethiopia. AREA 3 600sq km/1 400sq mi. It lies at an altitude of 1 829m and is the source of the Blue Nile. The lake is noted for the 40 monasteries which are located on islands.

Tanagra figurines a type of small terracotta statuette from Tanagra in Greece. Most examples date from the 3c BC, and represent draped female figures.

Tananarive see ANTANANARIVO.

Tancred (c.1076–1112) Norman crusader, grandson of Robert Guiscard. He went on the First Crusade, distinguished himself in the sieges of Nicaea, Tarsus, Antioch, Jerusalem, and Ascalon, and was given the principality of Tiberias (1099). He also ruled at Edessa and Antioch, where he died.

tandem — *noun* **1** a type of long three-wheeled bicycle for two people, with two seats and two sets of pedals placed one behind the other. **2** a team of two horses harnessed one behind the other, or a carriage drawn by it. **3** any two people or things which follow one behind the other. — *adv.* one behind the other, especially on a bicycle, or with two horses harnessed one behind the other: *ride tandem / drive tandem.*
— **in tandem 1** with one behind the other. **2** together or in partnership.
[a pun on Latin *tandem*, at length, at last]

tandoori *noun* food cooked on a spit over charcoal in a clay oven. [from Hindi *tandoor*, clay oven]

Tane in Maori mythology, the god of forests, and the son of Rangi (Heaven) and of Papa (Earth). He separated Rangi and Papa, thus permitting the world to exist.

tang *noun* **1** a strong or sharp taste, flavour or smell. **2** a trace or hint. **3** the pointed end of a knife, sword, chisel, etc that fits into and is held firmly by the handle. [from Norse *tange*, point]

Tanga 1 POP (1988) 188 000, the seaport capital of Tanga region, NE Tanzania. It lies on the Indian Ocean, opposite Pemba I, and is the country's second-largest port, situated at the centre of an agricultural area. **2** a region in NE Tanzania with Tanga as its capital.

Tanganyika, Lake a freshwater lake in E central Africa. It is situated mostly along the Tanzania–Zaire frontier. Small areas fall within the Zambian (S) and Burundian (NW) frontiers. With a length of 645km/401mi from NW to SE and an area of 32 900sq km/12 700sq mi, it is the longest and second-largest lake (after L Victoria) in Africa. At a depth of 1 400m, it is the deepest lake in Africa and the second-deepest in the world (after L Baikal in Russia). The lake is 25–80km/15–50mi wide. Main ports are at Kigoma (Tanzania), Kalémié (Zaire), and Bujumbura (Burundi). Small-scale naval warfare took place on the lake between British and German forces in 1915–16.

tangent — *noun* **1** *Geom.* a straight line that touches a curve at one point, and has the same gradient (slope) as the curve at the point of contact. At a maximum or minimum, the tangent to a curve has a gradient of zero. **2** (ABBREV. **tan**) *Maths.* in trigonometry, a function of an angle in a right-angled triangle, defined as the length of the side opposite the angle divided by the length of the side adjacent to it. — *adj.* being or forming a tangent.
— **at a tangent** in a completely different direction or course.
[from Latin *tangere*, to touch]

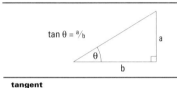
$$\tan \theta = {}^a\!/_b$$

tangent

tangential *adj.* **1** of or along a tangent. **2** not of central importance to; incidental; peripheral.

tangentially *adv.* in the direction of a tangent; at a tangent.

tangerine — *noun* **1** a tree producing a variety of mandarin orange with a loose reddish-orange skin and flesh. **2** an orange produced by this tree. **3** the reddish-orange colour of this fruit. — *adj.* reddish-orange. [named after *Tangier*, a port on the Moroccan coast]

tangibility *noun* the quality of being tangible.

tangible *adj.* **1** able to be felt by touch. **2** real or definite; material: *tangible evidence*. [from Latin *tangibilis*]

tangibly *adv.* in a tangible way.

Tangier *or* **Tangiers**, French **Tanger**, ancient **Tingis** POP (1992e) 566 000, a seaport in Nord-Ouest province, N Morocco. It is situated at the W end of the Strait of Gibraltar and occupies an important strategic position at the entrance to the Mediterranean Sea. HISTORY held in past centuries by the Vandals, Byzantines, and Arabs; occupied by the Portuguese in 1471, and later by the Spanish, English, and then the Moors; established in 1923 as an international zone, governed by Britain, France, Spain, and Italy; Spanish occupation in World War II; international administration removed in 1956; became a part of Morocco in 1959; free port status was restored in 1962. NOTABLE FEATURES royal summer residence; kasbah fortress; Dar Shorfa Palace; Caves of Hercules on the coast to the W.

tangle — *noun* **1** an untidy and confused or knotted state or mass, eg of hair or fibres. **2** a confused or complicated state or situation. — *verb* **1** *trans., intrans.* said especially of hair, fibres, etc to become or make them untidy, knotted, and confused. **2** (**tangle with someone**) *colloq.* to become involved with them, especially in conflict, a struggle, or an argument. **3** *colloq.* to trap or hamper the movement of. [from Middle English *tangilen*]

tangled *adj.* full of tangles.

tango — *noun* (PL. **tangos**) a dance of Argentinian origin with dramatic stylized body positions and long pauses, or a piece of music for this. — *verb intrans.* (**tangoes**, **tangoed**) to perform this dance. [from American Spanish *tango*]

Tangshan *or* **T'angshan** POP (1990) 1m, a city in E Hebei province, N China, situated SE of Beijing.

tangy *adj.* (**tangier**, **tangiest**) having a fresh sharp smell or flavour.

Tanizaki, Junichiro (1886–1965) Japanese novelist, born in Tokyo. He became known in the West only after the translation in 1957 of his long novel *The Makioka Sisters* (1943–8), a notable example of descriptive realism. His later novels include *The Key* (1960) and *Diary of a Mad Old Man* (1962).

tank — *noun* **1** a large container for holding, storing, or transporting liquids or gas. **2** the amount a tank will hold. **3** a heavy steel-covered vehicle armed with guns and moving on Caterpillar® tracks. — *verb* (*often* **tank up** *or* **tank something up**) **1** to fill the tank of (a vehicle) with fuel. **2** *trans., intrans. slang* to drink or cause to drink heavily and become very drunk. **3** to store in a tank. **4** *intrans.* to move like a tank, especially quickly and heavily. [from Gujurati (Indian language) *tankh*, reservoir, and Portuguese *tanque*, pond]
◇ The first practical tanks were devised and used in action by the British in 1916. While there was limited development between the World Wars, by 1939 the Germans had fast-moving, hard-hitting machines, which were central to the *Blitzkrieg* attacks on Poland, France, and Russia. During World War II, the USSR produced the powerful T-34, the first mass-produced tank, and the main Allied tank after 1942 was the US M4 Sherman. Huge armoured battles were fought on the E and W fronts, and the tank emerged as the most important land weapon, both in World War II and in later conflicts, such as the Gulf War. Modern vehicles are equipped with advanced night vision devices, laser range-finders, and fire-control computers.

tankard *noun* a large silver, pewter, or pottery drinking-mug, often with a hinged lid, used especially for drinking beer. [from Middle English]

tanker *noun* **1** a ship or large lorry which transports liquid in bulk. **2** an aircraft which transports fuel and is usually able to refuel other aircraft in flight.

tankful *noun* (PL. **tankfuls**) the amount a tank will hold.

tanned *adj.* **1** having a suntan. **2** *said of hide* cured, treated.

Tannenberg, Battle of a World War I battle (26–30 Aug 1914) between Russian and German forces. The Russian army under General A V Samsonov was completely routed, 100 000 prisoners-of-war were taken, and Samsonov committed suicide. German nationalists claimed the victory as revenge for the defeat of the Teutonic Knights by Russian, Polish, and Lithuanian forces at the first battle of Tannenberg (Grunwald) in 1410.

tanner[1] *noun* a person who tans leather, especially as a profession.

tanner[2] *noun Brit. old colloq. use* a sixpence.

tannery *noun* (PL. **tanneries**) a place where hides are tanned.

Tannhäuser the name of both a legendary German knight and a 13c minstrel, combined in a popular 16c ballad. It tells of a man who seeks forgiveness for a life of pleasure but, being refused absolution by the pope, returns to his former ways.

Tannhäuser, in full ***Tannhäuser und der Sängerkrieg auf dem Wartburg (Tannhäuser***

and the Singing Contest on the Wartburg) an opera by Richard Wagner (1845), based on the medieval legend about Venus (goddess of love) presiding over a debauched court (the Venusberg). After a year at the Venusberg, Tannhäuser prays to the Virgin Mary to reappear in the real world. His return and reunion with Elisabeth lead to a singing contest for her hand in marriage, but his songs of erotic passion shock and he is sent to seek absolution from the pope, only to return apparently unredeemed.

tannic acid *or* **tannin** any of several substances obtained from certain tree barks and other plants, used in tanning leather, dyeing, ink-making, and in medicine, also occurring in, and giving a distinctive flavour to, red wine and tea.

tanning *noun* **1** browning of the skin due to exposure to ultraviolet light. **2** converting hides into leather.

Tannoy *noun trademark* a communication system with loudspeakers, used for making announcements in public buildings, eg railway stations.

Tansley, Sir Arthur George (1871–1955) English botanist, born in London. He lectured at University College London and at Cambridge before becoming professor of botany at Oxford in 1927. He founded the precursor of the Ecological Society, published *Practical Plant Ecology* (1923) and *The British Isles and their Vegetation* (1939), and contributed to anatomical and morphological botany as well as physiology.

tansy *noun* (PL. **tansies**) a wild plant with small heads of yellow flowers and pungent leaves used in cooking and formerly in medicine. [from Greek *athanasia*, immortality]

tantalization *or* **tantalisation** *noun* the process of tantalizing or being tantalized.

tantalize *or* **tantalise** *verb* to tease or torment (someone) by keeping something wanted just out of reach. [named after *Tantalus*, in Greek mythology]

tantalizing *or* **tantalising** *adj.* teasing; tormenting.

tantalizingly *or* **tantalisingly** *adv.* in a tantalizing way.

tantalum *noun Chem.* (SYMBOL **Ta**, ATOMIC NUMBER 73) a hard bluish-grey metal that is resistant to corrosion and has a high melting point. It is used to make certain alloys, especially for nuclear reactors, as well as electronic components, chemical equipment, and dental and surgical instruments. [named after Tantalus because of certain supposedly tantalizing characteristics of its chemistry]

Tantalus in Greek mythology, a king of Phrygia in Lydia, who committed various crimes. For these he was punished in the Underworld by being made to stand in a pool which receded when he bent to drink, and by being unable to reach the fruits which hung over his head.

tantalus *noun* a case in which decanters holding whisky, sherry, etc are visible but locked up.

tantamount *adj.*
— **tantamount to something** having the same effect or result as something; as good as it; equivalent to it.
[from Old French *tant amunter* or Italian *tanto montare*, to amount to as much]

Tantra *or* **tantra** *noun* any of a number of Hindu or Buddhist texts giving religious teaching and ritual instructions which may include descriptions of spells, magical formulas, mantras, meditative practices, and rituals to be performed. The practice of Tantra requires instruction by a guru. [from Sanskrit *tantra*, thread, fundamental doctrine]

tantrum *noun* a fit of childish or petulant bad temper.

Tanzania, official name **United Republic of Tanzania** POP (1992e) 27.8m, an E African repub-

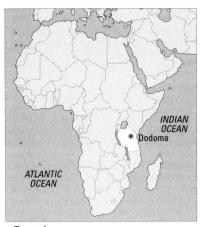

Tanzania

lic, divided into 22 regions. AREA 939 652sq km/362 706sq mi. It is bounded S by Mozambique and Malawi, SW by Zambia, W by Zaire, NW by Burundi, Rwanda, and Uganda, N by Kenya, and E by the Indian Ocean. It includes the islands of Zanzibar, Pemba, and Mafia. CAPITAL Dodoma. CHIEF TOWNS Dar es Salaam, Zanzibar, Mwanza, Tanga, Arusha. TIME ZONE GMT +3. The population is mainly of Bantu origin; on the mainland, Christianity is the chief religion and on Zanzibar it is almost entirely Islam. OFFICIAL LANGUAGES English, Swahili. CURRENCY the Tanzanian shilling. PHYSICAL DESCRIPTION the largest E African country, just S of the Equator; the coast is fringed by long sandy beaches protected by coral reefs; the coastal plain rises towards a central plateau with an average elevation of 1 000m; high grasslands and mountain ranges lie to the centre and S; the Rift Valley branches around L Victoria in the N, where there are several high volcanic peaks, notably Mt Kilimanjaro (5 895m); the extensive Serengeti plain lies to the W; the E branch of the Rift Valley runs through central Tanzania from NE of L Victoria, containing several lakes; the W branch runs S down the W side of L Victoria, and includes L Tanganyika and L Rukwa. CLIMATE hot, humid, and tropical on the coast and offshore islands; the average temperatures are c.23°C during Jun–Sept and 27°C during Dec–Mar; average annual rainfall is over 1 100mm; hot and dry on the central plateau, with an average annual rainfall of 250mm; semitemperate at altitudes above 1 500m; permanent snow on high peaks. HISTORY early links with Arab, Indian, and Persian traders; the Swahili culture developed between the 10c–15c; Zanzibar was the capital of the Omani empire in the 1840s; exploration of the interior by German missionaries and British explorers in the mid-19c; Zanzibar became a British protectorate in 1890; German East Africa was established in 1891; British mandate to administer Tanganyika in 1919; became the first E African country to gain independence and become a member of the Commonwealth in 1961; became a republic in 1962; Zanzibar given independence as a constitutional monarchy with the Sultan as head of state; the Sultan was overthrown in 1964, and an Act of Union between Zanzibar and Tanganyika led to the United Republic of Tanzania; a multiparty system was approved in 1992; drought in several areas in 1992. GOVERNMENT governed by a President, elected for a five-year term, a Cabinet, and a National Assembly of 243 members serving a five-year term; agreement in 1993 to a separate government for Tanganyika (mainland Tanzania). ECONOMY largely based on agriculture: rice, sorghum, coffee, sugar, cloves (most of the world's market), coconuts, tobacco, cotton; reserves of iron, coal, tin, gypsum, salt, phosphate, gold, diamonds, oil; food processing; cement; cigarettes; tourism centres on Mt

Kilimanjaro, beaches and reefs, national parks, and the five game reserves.

Taoism   **1** a Chinese philosophical system based on the teachings of Lao-tzu (c.6c BC) and others, advocating a life of simplicity and non-interference with the natural course of events. **2** a religion supposedly based on this system of philosophy, but also including magic, alchemy, and the worship of many gods. [from Chinese *tao*, way]

Taoist — *noun* a follower of Taoism. — *adj.* characteristic of or relating to Taoism.

Taos, Pueblo de a pueblo settlement in the town of Taos, New Mexico, USA. It consists of two large communal dwellings, four and five storeys high, built in c.1100 and still inhabited. It is a World Heritage site.

tap[1] — *noun* **1** a quick or light touch, knock, or blow, or the sound made by this. **2** tap-dancing. **3** a piece of metal attached to the sole and heel of a shoe for tap-dancing. — *verb* (**tapped**, **tapping**) **1** to strike or knock lightly. **2** to strike or knock lightly with (something). **3** (*also* **tap something out**) to produce it by tapping: *tap out a message.* **4** (**tap at** *or* **on something**) to strike it with a light but audible blow. [from Middle English *tappen*]

tap[2] — *noun* **1** a device consisting of a valve, with a handle for opening and shutting it, attached to a pipe for controlling the flow of liquid or gas. **2** a peg or stopper, especially in a barrel. **3** a receiver for listening to and recording private conversations, attached secretly to a telephone wire. **4** an act of attaching such a receiver to a telephone wire. **5** the withdrawal of fluid from a place, especially *Medicine* from a cavity in the body. **6** a screw for cutting an internal thread. — *verb* (**tapped**, **tapping**) **1** to get liquid from (a barrel, cavity in the body, etc) by piercing it or opening it with, or as if with, a tap. **2** to let out (liquid) from a vessel by opening, or as if by opening, a tap. **3** to get sap from (a tree) by cutting into it. **4** to attach a receiver secretly to (a telephone wire) so as to be able to hear private conversations. **5** to start using (a source, supply, etc). **6** *colloq.* (**tap someone for something**) to obtain money from them. — **on tap 1** *said of beer* stored in casks from which it is served. **2** ready and available for immediate use. [from Anglo-Saxon *tæppa*]

tapas *pl. noun* light savoury snacks or appetizers, especially those based on Spanish foods and cooking techniques, and served with drinks. [from Spanish *tapas*]

tap-dance — *noun* a dance performed wearing shoes with metal on the soles and toes so that the dancer's rhythmical steps can be heard clearly. — *verb intrans.* to perform a tap-dance.

tap-dancer *noun* a person who tap-dances.

tap-dancing *noun* dancing wearing shoes fitted with taps.

tape — *noun* **1** a narrow strip of woven cloth used for tying, fastening, etc. **2** (*in full* **magnetic tape**) a strip of thin plastic or metal wound on spools, used for recording sounds or images. **3** anything which has been recorded on magnetic tape; a tape- or video-recording. **4** (*in full* **adhesive tape**) a strip of thin paper or plastic with a sticky surface, used for fastening, sticking, etc. **5** a string or paper ribbon stretched above the finishing line on a race track. **6** a tape-measure. — *verb* **1** to fasten, tie, or seal with tape. **2** *trans., intrans.* to record (sounds or images) on magnetic tape. — **have something** *or* **someone taped** *colloq.* to understand them or be able to deal with them. [from Anglo-Saxon *tæppe*]

tape deck a tape recorder and player used to record sound or video signals on to magnetic tape, or to play back such a recording. It usually

forms part of an integrated sound system that may also include a compact-disc player, record turntable, radio tuner, etc.

tape-measure *noun* a length of plastic, cloth, or thin flexible metal tape, marked with inches, feet, and yards or centimetres and metres for measuring.

taper — *noun* **1** a long thin candle. **2** a long waxed wick or spill for lighting candles or fires. **3** a gradual lessening of diameter or width towards one end. — *verb trans., intrans.* (**tapered**, **tapering**) (*also* **taper off**) **1** to make or become gradually narrower towards one end. **2** to make or become gradually less. [from Anglo-Saxon *tapor*]

tape-record *verb* to record (sounds) on magnetic tape.

tape recorder a machine that is used to record sound or video signals on magnetic tape, and play them back.
◇ During audio recording, sound signals are first converted into electric current by means of a microphone. As the tape travels past an electromagnetic recording head, the electrical signals are stored on tape as a magnetic pattern. The tape is then rewound to enable the user to listen to the recording. During replay, as it passes the head again, the magnetic pattern on the tape is converted into electrical signals which are then amplified into the original sound. Some tape recorders are small enough to be carried in a pocket, the sound being played back through headphones instead of loudspeakers.

tape-recording *noun* **1** recording sound on tape. **2** a sound recording made on tape.

tapered *or* **tapering** *adj.* having a taper.

tapestried *adj.* covered or decorated with tapestry.

tapestry *noun* (PL. **tapestries**) **1** a thick woven textile with an ornamental design (often a picture) on it, used for curtains, wall-hangings, chair coverings, etc. **2** embroidery or an embroidery usually done with wool on canvas, which imitates the designs and pictures and the heavy texture of tapestry. [from Old French *tapisserie*, carpeting]

tapeworm *noun Zool.* any of a group of segmented flatworms that live as parasites in the intestines of humans and other vertebrates.

tapioca *noun* hard white grains of starch from the cassava plant, often made into a pudding

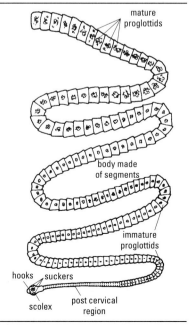

tapeworm

with sugar and milk. [from Tupí (S American Indian language) *tipioca*, juice squeezed out]

Tapiola in the Finnish poem *Kalevala*, the forest, the land of Tapio, the god of hunting. It was used as a motif by Sibelius.

tapir *noun* (PL. **tapir**, **tapirs**) any of three species of brown or black-and-white nocturnal mammal, related to the horse and rhinoceros, and similar in size to a donkey, but with shorter legs and a long flexible snout. Tapirs are found near water in tropical forests of Central and S America and SE Asia, where they browse on water plants and low-growing vegetation on land. [from Tupí (S American Indian language) *tapira*]

tappet *noun* a lever or projection that transmits motion from one part of a machine to another, especially in an internal-combustion engine from the camshaft to the valves. [from TAP[1]]

taproom *noun* a bar serving alcoholic drinks, especially beer direct from casks.

taproot *noun Bot.* a long straight main root of a plant, from which smaller lateral roots develop. In certain plants, eg carrot, it functions as a food store.

taps *pl. noun* **1** a bugle call for lights out, also used at military funerals. **2** in the Guide movement, a song sung at the end of a meeting or round a campfire in the evening.

tar[1] — *noun* **1** a dark sticky pungent liquid obtained by distillation of coal or wood, or by petroleum refining. It consists of a mixture of hydrocarbons, phenols, and free carbon, and is used in road construction, and as a wood preservative and antiseptic. **2** a similar substance, especially the residue formed from smoke from burning tobacco. — *verb* (**tarred**, **tarring**) to cover with tar.
— **tar and feather someone** to cover them with tar and then feathers as a punishment.
tarred with the same brush having the same faults.
[from Anglo-Saxon *teoru*]

tar[2] *noun old colloq. use* a sailor. [perhaps an abbreviation of TARPAULIN]

Tara a prehistoric hillfort, 40km/23mi NW of Dublin, the traditional seat of the kings of Ireland from pre-Christian times to the death of Maél Sechnaill II of Meath in 1022. Its earthworks include the Mound of the Hostages, a megalithic passage grave dating from the early third millennium BC.

Tara a female first name, after the place-name.

taramasalata *noun* a creamy pink paste made from the smoked roe of fish, especially cod, and olive oil and garlic. [from modern Greek, from *taramus*, preserved roe, and *salata*, salad]

tarantella *noun* a lively country dance from S Italy, or a piece of music for it. [named after *Taranto* in S Italy]

tarantula *noun* **1** a European wolf spider, named after the town of Taranto in Italy, where according to legend its bite was fatal unless the bitten person danced until exhausted. **2** any of a family of large tropical spiders with a fist-sized body and long hairy legs, which live in short burrows in the ground, and run down their prey instead of trapping it in webs. They hunt nocturnally, and although capable of catching small birds, they feed mainly on small insects which they kill instantly by injecting a poison. [from Italian *tarantola*]

tarantula

Tar Baby, the a character in Joel Chandler Harris's *Uncle Remus*.

Tarbes the capital of Hautes-Pyrénées department, Midi-Pyrénées region, S France. It lies on the left bank of the R Adour, 37km/23mi SE of Pau. Originally a Roman settlement and then the ancient capital of the province of Bigorre, it is now an industrial and commercial city. NOTABLE FEATURES cathedral (12c–14c); National Stud Farm (Les Haras, founded in 1806); Jardin Mussey.

tarboosh *noun* a hat like a fez, sometimes worn with a turban. [from Arabic *tarbush*]

— tarboosh

tarboosh

tardily *adv.* slowly, late.

tardiness *noun* being late or delayed.

tardy *adj.* (**tardier**, **tardiest**) **1** slow to move, progress, or grow; sluggish. **2** slower to arrive or happen than expected; late. [from Latin *tardus*, slow]

tare[1] *noun* **1** any of several vetches, especially those grown for food or fodder. **2** (*usually* **tares**) *Biblical* a weed which grows in cornfields. [from Middle English]

tare[2] *noun* **1** the weight of the wrapping paper or container in which goods are packed. **2** an allowance made for this. **3** the weight of a vehicle without its fuel, cargo, or passengers. [from Arabic *tarhah*, that which is thrown away]

target — *noun* **1** an object aimed at in shooting practice or competitions, especially a flat round board marked with concentric circles and with a bull's-eye in the centre. **2** any object or area fired or aimed at. **3** a person or thing which is the focus of ridicule or criticism. **4** a result aimed at; a goal. **5** *old use* a small buckler or round shield. — *verb* (**targeted**, **targeting**) **1** to direct or aim (something). **2** to make (a person, place, or thing) a target or the object of an attack. [from Old French *targe*, shield]

Targets a series of paintings by Jasper Johns (from c.1954).

Targum *or* **targum** *noun Relig.* an Aramaic version or paraphrase of the Hebrew Scriptures, probably originally composed orally (c.1c BC) when the Torah was read aloud in the synagogues, since most Jews of the time understood Aramaic rather than Hebrew, and later written in the rabbinic period. [from Chaldaean *targūm*, interpretation]

tariff *noun* **1** a list of prices or charges: *a hotel tariff*. **2** the tax or duty to be paid on a particular class of goods imported or exported. **3** a list of such taxes and duties. [from Arabic *tarif*, explanation]

Tarim Basin the largest inland basin in China. AREA 530 000sq km/205 000sq mi. It is bounded by the Kunlun and Altun Shan ranges in the S and the Tien Shan Range in the N. The land becomes dry towards the centre with salt lakes and desert, including the Taklimakan Shamo, the largest desert in China (AREA 327 000sq km/126 000sq mi). The area is rich in salt and non-ferrous metals. Nuclear testing takes place in the region.

Tarim He a river in NW China, in the N Tarim Basin. Its length is 2 179km/1 354mi. It is the largest inland river in China, fed by glaciers and melting snow from the Tien Shan Mts in the N. The river course changes constantly as a result of seepage and evaporation along its middle and lower course.

Tarkenton, Fran(cis) (1940–) US footballer, born in Richmond, Virginia. He played for the Minnesota Vikings and New York Giants (1961–78), and gained 47 003 yards by passing, a National Football League record. He later became a sports commentator and management consultant.

tarlatan *noun* an open, transparent muslin, used for stiffening garments. [from French *tarlatane*]

Tarlton *or* **Tarleton, Richard** (d.1588) English clown who first performed with Leicester's Men, but joined Queen Elizabeth's Men on the formation of that company in 1583. He became a famous and skilful entertainer, specializing in the dramatic jigs which were a popular feature in the playhouses.

tarmac *noun* **1** tarmacadam. **2** a surface covered with tarmac, especially an airport runway.

tarmacadam *noun* a mixture of small stones bound together with tar, used to make road surfaces, etc.

tarn *noun Geol.* a small, often circular, mountain lake, especially one formed in a cirque. [from Norse *tjörn*]

tarnish — *verb* **1** to make (metal) dull and discoloured, especially through the action of air or dirt. **2** *intrans. said of metal* to become dull and discoloured. **3** to spoil or damage (eg someone's reputation). — *noun* **1** a loss of shine or lustre. **2** a discoloured or dull film on the surface of metal. [from Old French *ternir*, to make dull]

tarnishable *adj.* capable of tarnishing.

taro *noun Bot.* a plant of the genus *Colocasia* of the arum family, widely cultivated in the Pacific islands for its edible rootstock. [from Polynesian]

tarot *noun* **1** a pack of 78 playing cards consisting of four suits of 14 cards and a fifth suit of 22 trump cards. It is used for playing several different games or in fortune-telling. **2** any of the 22 trump cards in this pack, which are decorated with allegorical pictures. [from Italian *tarocchi*]
◇ The 78-card pack first appeared in Italy in the 14c. The modern pack generally contains 54 cards: 32 suit cards, 21 trumps (or tarots), and 1 joker.

tarot cards

tarpaulin *noun* heavy canvas which has been made waterproof, especially with tar; also, a sheet of this. [from TAR[1] + PALL[1]]

Tarpeia in Roman legend, a Roman woman who betrayed the Capitol to the Sabines, in return for 'what they wore on their left arms' (meaning gold rings). Instead, they kept their side of the bargain by throwing their shields on her and crushing her to death.

Tarquin the name of two kings of Rome of the 6c BC, Tarquinius Priscus and Tarquinius Superbus. Tarquinius Priscus is traditionally believed to have been the fifth king of Rome and Tarquinius Superbus the seventh, and final, king before the formation of the Republic.

Tarquinius or **Tarquin Sextus** the son of the king of Rome in Shakespeare's *The Rape of Lucrece*, who is banished after raping Lucretia.

Tarquinius Superbus, also called **the Proud** (6c BC) the last king of Rome, possibly of Etruscan extraction, whose overthrow (510 BC) marked the end of monarchy in Rome, and the beginning of the Republic.

tarragon *noun* a European herb with narrow, pungent leaves used in cooking, eg for flavouring vinegar. [from Greek *drakon*, dragon]

Tarragona, Latin **Tarraco** POP (1991) 110 000, the port capital of Tarragona province, Catalonia, NE Spain. It is situated 534km/332mi NE of Madrid. NOTABLE FEATURES Roman aqueduct and amphitheatre, Cyclopean walls; cathedral (12c–13c); Archaeological Museum.

tarriness *noun* a tarry quality.

tarry[1] *verb intrans.* (**tarries, tarried**) **1** to linger or stay in a place. **2** to be slow or late in coming, doing something, etc. [from Middle English *taryen*, to delay]

tarry[2] *adj.* (**tarrier, tarriest**) like tar or covered with tar.

tarsal *adj. Anat.* relating to the bones of the tarsus (the foot and ankle). — *noun* in terrestrial vertebrates, any of the bones that form the tarsus. [from Greek *tarsos*, the flat of the foot]

Tarsus POP (1990) 188 000, a town in Iáel province, S Turkey, lying on the W bank of the R Pamuk. Ancient Tarsus was one of the most important cities in Asia Minor. The town was the birthplace of St Paul.

tarsus *noun* **1** *Anat.* the bones forming the upper part of the foot and ankle. **2** *Biol.* the extremity of a limb in insects, usually a five-jointed foot. **3** *Anat.* the firm connective tissue that supports and stiffens the eyelid. [from Greek *tarsos*, the flat of the foot]

tart[1] *adj.* **1** sharp or sour in taste. **2** *said of a remark, etc* brief and sarcastic; cutting. [from Anglo-Saxon *teart*, rough]

tart[2] — *noun* **1** a pastry case, especially one without a top, with a sweet filling such as fruit or jam. **2** *derog. slang* a female prostitute or promiscuous woman. — *verb* (*usually* **tart someone** or **something up**) *slang* to decorate or embellish them, especially in a showy or tasteless way. [from Old French *tarte*]

tartan *noun* **1** a distinctive checked pattern which can be produced with checks of different widths and different colours, especially one of the very many designs which are each associated with a different Scottish clan. **2** a woollen cloth or garment woven with such a design. [from Old French *tiretaine*]

Tartar — *noun* **1** (*also* **Tatar**) a member of a group of peoples, including Mongols and Turks, which overran Asia and parts of Europe in the Middle Ages. **2** (*also* **Tatar**) a member of a people related to the Turks living especially in Soviet central Asia. **3** (*also* **Tatar**) the language spoken by this people. **4** (**tartar**) a violent or fierce person. — *adj.* relating to the Tartars or their language. [from Latin *Tartarus*, from Persian *Tatar*, perhaps influenced by Greek *Tartaros*, hell]

tartar *noun* **1** a hard deposit, consisting mostly of calcium salts, that forms on the teeth. **2** a deposit that forms a hard brownish-red crust on the insides of wine casks during fermentation. [from Greek *tartaron*]

tartaric acid an organic acid consisting of a white or colourless crystalline solid, that occurs naturally in grapes and other fruit, and can also be manufactured synthetically. It is used in baking powder, food additives, dyeing, tanning, textile processing, printing, mirror silvering, photographic chemicals, and ceramics.

tartar sauce or **tartare sauce** mayonnaise flavoured with chopped pickles, capers, olives, and parsley, often served as a dressing for fish. [from French *sauce tartare*]

Tartarus in Greek mythology, the name of the part of the Underworld where those who offended the gods were punished. The Titans were thrust down there after their rebellion, and infamous criminals were tortured.

tartly *adv.* with a tart manner.

tartness *noun* being tart, sharpness.

tartrazine *noun Food Science* a yellow powder, soluble in water, that is used as an artificial colouring in foods, drugs, and cosmetics. It can produce allergic reactions in some people, and has been associated with hyperactivity in children. [from TARTAR]

Tartuffe, ou L'Imposteur a play by Molière (1664). An attack on religious hypocrisy, it is the story of how Tartuffe deceives Orgon with an effective show of piety, which is successful until he tries to seduce Orgon's wife.

tarty *adj.* (**tartier, tartiest**) *derog. slang* **1** *said of a woman or women's clothing* blatantly sexual or promiscuous. **2** cheap, showy, and vulgar.

Tarutao a marine national park in Thailand. It comprises a group of 51 islands 30km/19mi off the W coast, near the Thailand–Malaysia frontier, N of the Langkawi Is. AREA 1 400sq km/540sq mi.

Tarzan see TARZAN OF THE APES.

Tarzan of the Apes a novel by Edgar Rice Burroughs (1914). It is the first of his many stories featuring the aristocratic British boy who is brought up by apes in the jungle.

Tashkent POP (1990e) 2.1m, the capital of Uzbekistan. It is situated in the foothills of the Tien Shan Mts. HISTORY the oldest city in central Asia, known in the 1c BC; taken by Russia in 1865; virtually rebuilt after earthquake damage in 1966. NOTABLE FEATURES Islamic centres of Kukeldash (c.17c) and Barakkhana (c.15c–16c).

Tashtego the bold Native American harpooner on the *Pequod* in Herman Melville's *Moby Dick*.

task *noun* a piece of work to be done or required, especially one which is unpleasant or difficult; a chore.
— **take someone to task** to scold or criticize them.
[from Old French *tasque*]

task-force *noun* **1** *Mil.* a temporary grouping of different units, eg land, sea, and air forces, under a single commander to undertake a specific mission. **2** any similar grouping of individuals for a specific purpose.

taskmaster or **taskmistress** *noun* a man or woman who sets and supervises the work of others, especially strictly or severely.

Tasman, Abel Janszoon (1603–c.1659) Dutch navigator, born in Groningen. He was sent in quest of the 'Great South Land' by Antony Van Diemen (1593–1645), Governor-General of Batavia, and in 1642 discovered the area he named Van Diemen's Land (now Tasmania) and New Zealand, followed by Tonga and Fiji (1643). He made a second voyage (1644) to the Gulf of Carpentaria and the NW coast of Australia.

Tasmania, formerly **Van Diemen's Land** (to 1856) POP (1992e) 470 000, an island state of Australia, separated from the mainland by the Bass Strait. AREA 67 800sq km/26 200sq mi (main island). It is divided into four statistical divisions and is the smallest Australian state. The state includes the main island of Tasmania, and several smaller islands, notably King I (1 099sq km/424sq mi), Flinders I (1 374sq km/530sq mi), and Bruny I (362sq km/140sq mi). PHYSICAL DESCRIPTION the Central Plateau of the main island's mountainous interior rises to 1 617m at Mt Ossa; the most fertile regions lie along the NW and E coasts and along the river valleys of the midlands and SE plateau. CLIMATE temperate and maritime; influenced by the westerly 'Roaring Forties' winds. HISTORY the first Aborigines to settle here 25 000 years ago crossed the land bridge now formed by the Bass Strait; European discovery by Abel Tasman in 1642; the first European settlement was established in 1803 when Tasmania became a British dependency of New South Wales; Port Arthur on the E coast became the largest penal colony in Australia (1803–25); Tasmania became a separate colony in 1825; a Legislative Council was established in 1851; in 1901 Tasmania joined the Commonwealth of Australia. CAPITAL Hobart. CHIEF TOWNS Devonport, Launceston, Burnie-Somerset, Queenstown, New Norfolk. ECONOMY sheep, cattle, pigs, cereals, apples, hogs; wood, paper, chemicals, machinery, textiles; mining of tin, copper, zinc, lead, silver, gold, coal; abundant hydroelectric power; tourism. NOTABLE FEATURES Western Tasmania Wilderness National Parks; numerous unique plants and animals, notably the Tasmanian Devil, a carnivorous marsupial.

Tasmanian devil a small ferocious bear-like marsupial now found only in Tasmania.

Tasmanian devil

Tasmanian Wilderness the uninhabited and partly unexplored part of SW Tasmania, including the South West National Park. It is a World Heritage site.

Tasman Sea a part of the Pacific Ocean separating E Australia and Tasmania from New Zealand. The sea is linked to the Indian Ocean by the Bass Strait. It sinks to depths of 4 570m in the Tasman Abyssal Plain. [named after the Dutch explorer Abel Tasman]

Tass the official news agency of the former Soviet Union. [an acronym of Russian *Telegrafnoe Agentsvo Sovietskovo Soyuza*, Telegraph Agency of the Soviet Union]

tassel — *noun* **1** a decoration (eg on a curtain, cushion, or lampshade) consisting of a hanging bunch of threads tied firmly at one end and loose at the other. **2** a tassel-like flower-head on some plants, especially maize. — *verb* (**tasselled, tasselling**) **1** to adorn with tassels. **2** *intrans. said of* maize to grow tassels. [from Old French *tassel*]

Tassili N'Ajjer a national park in E Algeria, established in 1972. It lies at the NE of the Hoggar Mts. Many prehistoric cave paintings of animals and people can be found on a sandstone plateau within the park. AREA c.1 000sq km/390sq mi.

Tasso, Torquato (1544–95) Italian poet, born in Sorrento. His first work was the romantic poem, *Rinaldo* (1562). After joining the court of the Duke of Ferrara, he wrote his epic on the capture of Jerusalem during the first crusade, *Gerusalemme Liberata* (Jerusalem Liberated, 1581). He later rewrote this work, in response to criticisms, as *Gerusalemme Conquistata* (1593).

tastable *adj.* capable of being tasted.

taste — *verb* **1** *trans., intrans.* to perceive the flavour of (food, drink, or some other substance) by means of the sensation produced on the surface of the tongue. **2** to try or test a food or drink

by eating or drinking a small amount of it. **3** *trans., intrans.* to be aware of or recognize the flavour of: *I can taste nutmeg in this cake.* **4** (**taste of something**) to have a particular flavour. **5** to eat or drink, especially in small quantities or with enjoyment: *had not tasted food for days.* **6** to experience: *taste defeat.* — *noun* **1** the particular sensation produced when food, drink, or other substances are placed on the tongue. **2** the quality or flavour of a food, drink, or other substance that is perceived by this sense: *dislike the taste of onions.* **3** an act of tasting or a small quantity of food or drink tasted. **4** a first, usually brief experience of something. **5** a liking or preference: *a taste for exotic holidays / the film was not to her taste.* **6** the ability to judge, and appreciate, what is suitable as well as being fine, elegant, or beautiful: *show good taste in clothes / a joke in poor taste.*
— **to taste** as needed to give a pleasing flavour: *add water to taste.*
[from Old French *taster*]
◇ The sensation of taste is produced by stimulation of the taste buds (specialized sensory receptors) when food is moistened by the saliva (dry food cannot be tasted). Nerve impulses are relayed via the glossopharyngeal and lingual nerves to the brain, where they are interpreted as taste, which is often classified as sweet, sour, bitter, or salty, but is usually some combination of these.

taste bud any of the cells on the surface of the tongue which are sensitive to flavour.

tasteful *adj.* showing good judgement or taste.

tastefully *adv.* in a tasteful way.

tastefulness *noun* a tasteful quality.

tasteless *adj.* **1** lacking flavour. **2** showing a lack of good taste or judgement.

tastelessly *adv.* in a tasteless way.

tastelessness *noun* being tasteless.

taster *noun* a person whose job is to taste and judge the quality of food or drink.

tastily *adv.* in a tasty way.

tastiness *noun* a tasty quality.

tasting *noun* a social event at which wine or some other food or drink is sampled.

tasty *adj.* (**tastier, tastiest**) **1** having a good, especially savoury, flavour. **2** *colloq.* interesting or attractive.

tat¹ *noun Brit. colloq.* rubbish or junk. [a shortening of TATTY]

tat² *verb trans., intrans.* (**tatted, tatting**) to make (lace for trimming) by hand with a small shuttle from sewing-thread.

ta-ta *interj. Brit. colloq.* good-bye.

Tatar see TARTAR.

Tate, Sir Henry (1819–99) English sugar magnate, art patron, and philanthropist, born in Chorley, Lancashire. He patented a method for cutting sugar cubes in 1872 and attained great wealth as a Liverpool sugar refiner. The Tate Gallery, to which he donated his private art collection, is named after him.

Tate Gallery a gallery in London housing the chief collection of British art and modern foreign art. It was opened in 1897 as a branch of the National Gallery, but became administratively autonomous in 1915, and fully independent in 1955. The Clore Gallery, which houses the Turner Collection, was opened in 1987. The Tate Gallery, Liverpool, opened in 1988 and the Tate Gallery, St Ives, in 1993.

Tati, Jacques, originally **Jacques Tatischeff** (1908–82) French actor and film producer, born in Pecq. He began in music-hall, and directed his first film in 1931. After *Jour de Fête* (The Big Day, 1947), directed and written by himself, he made his reputation as the greatest film comedian of the postwar period, notably in *Les Vacances de Monsieur Hulot* (Mr Hulot's Holiday, 1953) and

Mon Oncle (My Uncle, 1958), which won several awards.

Tatra Mountains, Czech **Tatry** the highest mountain group in the Carpathians and in the Czech Republic and Slovakia. Situated in the central Carpathian Mts, it comprises the High Tatra (*Vysoké Tatry*) and the Low Tatra (*Nízké Tatry*). Gerlachovsky at 2 655m is the highest point. The High Tatra National Park was established in 1948.

tatter *noun* (*usually* **tatters**) a torn ragged shred of cloth, especially of clothing.
— **in tatters 1** *said of clothes* in a torn and ragged condition. **2** *said of an argument, theory, etc* completely destroyed.
[from Middle English, from Norse *torturr*, rag]

tattered *adj.* ragged or torn.

tattily *adv.* in a tatty way.

tattiness *noun* being tatty.

tatting *noun* **1** delicate knotted lace trimming made by hand with a small shuttle from sewing-thread. **2** the process of making such lace.

tattle — *noun* idle chatter or gossip. — *verb* **1** *intrans.* to chat or gossip idly. **2** *trans.* to give away (secrets) by chatting idly or gossiping. [from Old Dutch *tatelen*]

tattler *noun* a chatterer, a gossip.

tattoo¹ — *verb* (**tattoos, tattooed**) to mark (coloured designs or pictures) on (a person or part of the body) by pricking the skin and putting in indelible dyes. — *noun* (PL. **tattoos**) a design tattooed on the skin. [from Tahitian *tatau*]

tattoo² *noun* (PL. **tattoos**) **1** a signal by drum or bugle calling soldiers to quarters, especially in the evening. **2** an outdoor military entertainment with marching troops, military bands, etc, usually given in the evening. **3** a rhythmic beating, tapping, or drumming. [from earlier *taptoo*, from Dutch *taptoe*, the tap of a barrel (is to be) shut]

tattooer or **tattooist** *noun* a person who tattoos skin.

tatty *adj.* (**tattier, tattiest**) *colloq.* shabby and untidy. [from TATTER]

Tatum, Art (Arthur) (1910–56) US jazz pianist, born in Toledo, Ohio. Although near-blind from birth, he was a professional musician from his teens, and became the first supreme jazz keyboard virtuoso and a very influential swing-style pianist, most effective as a soloist or leading a piano-bass-guitar trio. His technical skills astounded other musicians, for he embellished the melodies of popular songs in ways that seemed to press the limits of dexterity, and which extended the harmonic bounds of jazz.

Ta-t'ung see DATONG.

Taufa'ahau, also called **King George Tupou I' of Tonga** (1797–1893) a chief of the district of Ha'apai and an able and ambitious leader. By 1852 he had made himself king over the various chieftainships in Tonga, and had unified the group under his control. The royal dynasty he established continues to rule Tonga.

taught see TEACH.

Taung skull the million-year-old partial skull and brain cast of a young *Australopithecus africanus*, found in Taung, South Africa, in 1924. This was the first discovery of a creature seemingly intermediate between ape and man ('the missing link').

taunt — *verb* to tease, say unpleasant things to, or jeer at in a cruel and hurtful way. — *noun* a cruel, unpleasant, and often hurtful or provoking remark.

taunting — *noun* teasing, goading. — *adj.* that taunts.

tauntingly *adv.* with taunts.

Taunton POP (1981) 49 000, the county town of Somerset, SW England, situated in Taunton

Deane district. It lies on the R Tone, in the Vale of Taunton Deane. HISTORY founded in 705; the rebellion of Perkin Warbeck ended here in 1497; in 1685 the Duke of Monmouth was crowned king here. The town is famous for its cider. NOTABLE FEATURES 12c castle hall, where the Bloody Assizes were held in 1685; Somerset County Museum.

taupe — *noun* a brownish-grey colour. — *adj.* of this colour. [from French *taupe*, mole]

Taupo, Lake a lake in central North I, New Zealand. AREA 606sq km/234sq mi. It fills an old volcanic crater. Measuring 40km/25mi long and 27km/17mi wide, it is the largest lake in New Zealand. The town of Taupo is situated at the NE side of the lake. A geothermal power scheme is based in this area. There are thermal pools at Tokaanu. The lake is used as a reservoir and is also popular for fishing and watersports.

Taurean — *noun* a person born under the sign Taurus. — *adj.* relating to this sign.

Taurus *noun* **1** *Astron.* the Bull, a conspicuous northern constellation of the zodiac, which includes the Crab Nebula, and the Pleiades (Seven Sisters) and Hyades star clusters. Its brightest star is the red giant Aldebaran. **2** the second sign of the zodiac, the Bull. **3** a person born between 21 Apr and 20 May, under this sign. [from Latin *taurus*, bull]

Taurus Mountains, Turkish **Toros Dağlari** a mountain chain in S Turkey, extending in a curve from L Eğridir, roughly parallel to the Mediterranean coast as far as the R Seyhan. It forms the S border of the Anatolian Plateau. Its highest peak is Ala Dağlari (3 910m) and its NW extension across the R Seyhan is called the *Anti-Taurus*. The Cilician Gates are situated in the SE; they constituted an important pass in ancient times. Mineral deposits include chromium, copper, silver, zinc, iron, and arsenic.

taut *adj.* **1** pulled or stretched tight. **2** showing nervous strain or anxiety. **3** *said of a ship* in good condition. [from Middle English *toht*, tight]

tauten *verb trans., intrans.* (**tautened, tautening**) to make or become taut.

tautological or **tautologous** *adj.* relating to or involving tautology.

tautology *noun* (PL. **tautologies**) **1** the use of words which repeat the meaning found in other words already used, as in *I myself personally.* **2** *Logic* a statement which is necessarily always true. [from Greek *tautologos*, from *tauto*, same + *legein*, to say]

Tavener, John (Kenneth) (1944–) English composer, born in London. He was a pupil of Lennox Berkeley, and was first recognized as a composer with the cantata *The Whale* (1966). His music is predominantly choral and religious (he was converted to the Russian Orthodox faith in 1974), and includes *Ultimos ritos* (Last Rites, 1972) for soloists, chorus, and orchestra, and a sacred opera *Therese* (1979). His more recent works include *The Protecting Veil* (1987) for cello and strings, and *The Repentant Thief* (1990) for clarinet, percussion, and strings.

tavern *noun* an inn or public house. [from Latin *taberna*, shed]

taverna *noun* in Greece, a type of guesthouse with a bar, popular as holiday accommodation; also, a Greek restaurant. [from modern Greek, from Latin *taberna*, shed]

tawdrily *adv.* in a tawdry way.

tawdriness *noun* being tawdry.

tawdry *adj.* (**tawdrier, tawdriest**) cheap and showy and of poor quality. [from *St Audrey lace*, lace sold at fairs held on the feast day of St Audrey, 17 Oct]

Tawney, R(ichard) H(enry) (1880–1962) British economic historian, born in Calcutta, India. He became active in the Workers'

Educational Association at Rochdale, Lancashire, and was its President from 1928 to 1944. He was Professor of Economic History at London (1931–49). He wrote a number of studies in English economic history, particularly of the Tudor and Stuart periods.

tawny — *noun* a yellowish-brown colour. — *adj.* (**tawnier, tawniest**) of this colour. [from Old French *taune*]

tawny owl a tawny-coloured European owl.

taws *or* **tawse** *noun Scot.* a leather strap divided into strips at one end, formerly used for corporal punishment in schools. [pl. of obsolete *taw*, whip]

tax — *noun* **1** a contribution towards a country's expenses raised by the government from people's salaries, property, and from the sale of goods and services. **2** a strain, burden, or heavy demand. — *verb* **1** to impose a tax on (a person, goods, etc) or take tax from (a salary). **2** to put a strain on or make a heavy demand on. **3** (**tax someone with something**) to accuse them of it. **4** *Legal* to assess (costs). [from Latin *taxare*, to appraise]

taxable *adj.* capable of being taxed.

taxation *noun* the act or system of imposing taxes.
◇ Taxation is the means by which governments raise money to finance their activities. Taxation may be direct, eg taxes paid by individuals on their income, or indirect, eg taxes levied on goods for sale.

tax-deductible *adj.*, *said of expenses, etc* eligible for deduction from taxable income.

Tax-Exempt Special Savings Account (ABBREV. **TESSA**) in the UK, a savings scheme introduced in 1991 in which payments (regular or irregular, up to an overall maximum of £9 000) are made over a five-year period. The sum accumulated gathers interest and is tax-free; if any withdrawals are made before the end of the five years, the interest becomes taxable.

tax-free *adj.*, *adv.* without payment of tax.

tax haven a country or state with a low rate of taxation compared to one's own.

taxi — *noun* (PL. **taxis**) a car which may be hired together with its driver to carry passengers on usually short journeys, and which is usually fitted with a taximeter for calculating the fare. — *verb* (**taxis, taxied, taxiing** *or* **taxying**) **1** *intrans. said of an aircraft or its pilot* to move along the ground slowly before or after take-off or landing under its own power. **2** to cause (an aircraft) to move in this way. **3** *intrans., trans.* to travel or cause to be conveyed in a taxi. [a shortening of *taximeter cab*]

taxicab *noun* same as TAXI *noun*.

taxidermist *noun* a person who practises taxidermy.

taxidermy *noun* the art of preparing, stuffing, and mounting animal skins and birds so that they present a lifelike appearance. [from Greek *taxis*, arrangement + *derma*, skin]

Taxi Driver a US film directed by Martin Scorsese (1976). It depicts the horrors of contemporary urban life through the feelings of disgust, religious anxiety, sexual inadequacy, and violence of one man (played by Robert De Niro).

Taxila the chief city of the Achaemenid satrapy of Gandhara, now a major archaeological site covering 65sq km/25sq mi in Punjab, Pakistan. Excavations have revealed three distinct cities: the earliest dates from c.400 BC; the second was occupied successively by Bactrian Greeks, Scythians, Parthians, and Kushans; the third was founded in c.130 AD and flourished for over five centuries. It is a World Heritage site.

taximeter *noun* a meter fitted to a taxi which monitors the time taken and the distance travelled, and displays the fare due. [from French *taximètre*, from *taxe*, tax + *mètre*, meter]

taxing *adj.* requiring a lot of mental or physical effort; demanding.

taxi rank a place where taxis stand until hired.

taxis *noun Biol.* the movement of a single cell (eg a gamete, bacterium, or protozoan) in response to an external stimulus from a specific direction (eg light). Such behaviour is only shown by cells that have some means of locomotion. [from Greek *taxis*, from *tassein* to arrange]

taxonomic *adj.* relating to or involving classification.

taxonomist *noun* a scientist who classifies plants and animals.

taxonomy *noun Biol.* the theory and techniques of describing, naming, and classifying living and extinct organisms on the basis of their anatomical and morphological features (*classical taxonomy*), similarities in the structure of their proteins and nucleic acids (*biochemical taxonomy*), the number, size, and shape of their chromosomes (*cytotaxonomy*), or quantitative assessments of their similarities and differences (*numerical taxonomy*). [from Greek *taxis*, arrangement + *nomos*, law]

taxpayer *noun* a person who pays or is liable for tax or taxes.

Taylor, Elizabeth (Rosemond) (1932–) US film actress, born in London, England. A film star since her childhood in the USA, she was first seen as an adult in *The Father of the Bride* (1950). Her later films include *Cat on a Hot Tin Roof* (1958) and *Butterfield 8* (1960, Academy Award). In *Cleopatra* (1962) she co-starred with Richard Burton (later one of her eight husbands), with whom she also made *Who's Afraid of Virginia Woolf?* (1966, Academy Award). Her television films include *Between Friends* (1983) and *Sweet Bird of Youth* (1986).

Taylor, Frederick W(inslow) (1856–1915) US engineer, born in Philadelphia. He developed the concept of rational principles underlying engineering and engineering management. He discovered the process of heat treatment of high-speed steel (1898), but is better known for the development of time-and-motion study, which he established as an important management tool.

Taylor, Sir Geoffrey Ingram (1886–1975) English physicist and applied mathematician, born in London. Professor at Cambridge, his many original investigations on the mechanics of fluids and solids were applied to meteorology, oceanography, and aircraft, and Jupiter's Great Red Spot. He proposed in 1934 the idea of dislocation in crystals, a form of atomic misarrangement which enables the crystal to deform at a stress less than that of a perfect crystal.

Taymyr *or* **Taimyr, Lake** a lake in N Siberia, Russia, lying on the N Taymyr Peninsula. AREA 4 560sq km/1 760sq mi; length 250km/155mi; maximum depth 26m. It is frozen over from Sep to Jun.

Tay, River the longest river in Scotland, length 192km/119mi. Rising on Ben Lui in the Grampians, it flows NE, E, then SE to enter the Firth of Tay, extending 40km/25mi NE to the North Sea at Buddon Ness. Its tributaries include the Tummel, Isla, and Earn. The Tay is noted for salmon fishing; it is crossed at Dundee by the two Tay Bridges (rail and road).

Tayside POP (1981) 395 000, a Region in E Scotland, divided into three districts. AREA 7 493sq km/2 892sq mi. It is bounded N by Grampian and Highland Regions, NW by Strathclyde, W and S by Central Region, SE by Fife, and E by the Firth of Tay and the North Sea. PHYSICAL DESCRIPTION the Grampian Mts lie in the NW; the 'Highland line', which separates the Highlands from the Lowlands, runs NE through the region; the Sidlaw Hills lie to the N of the Firth of Tay and the Ochil Hills to the S; drained by the Tay, Isla, Ericht, Earn, and South Esk rivers; the largest lochs are Rannoch, Tummel,

and Tay. CAPITAL Dundee. CHIEF TOWNS Forfar, Arbroath, Montrose, Perth. ECONOMY farming; tourism.

TB *abbrev.* tuberculosis.

Tb *symbol Chem.* terbium.

Tbilisi, formerly **Tiflis** (to 1936) POP (1991e) 1.3m, the capital of Georgia, lying on the R Kura, between the Greater and Lesser Caucasus Mts. HISTORY founded in the 5c; since ancient times it has been a trading point between Europe and India; anti-Russian demonstrations in 1981; over 100 people were killed during four months of fighting when opposition forces tried to overthrow President Gamsakhurdia in 1991. NOTABLE FEATURES Citadel of Narikala ruins (4c–17c); Anchiskhati Church (6c); Sioni Cathedral (6c–7c).

tbsp *abbrev.* tablespoon or tablespoonful.

Tc *symbol Chem.* technetium.

t-cell *noun* a kind of lymphocyte involved in cellular immunity that matures in the thymus gland in mammals. [from the initial letter of THYMUS + CELL]

Tchad see CHAD.

Tchaikovsky, Piotr Ilyich (1840–93) Russian composer, born in Kamsko-Votkinsk. He began as a civil servant, joined the St Petersburg Conservatory in 1862, and moved to Moscow (1865), where he became known for his operas, second symphony, and first piano concerto. Unsuited to marriage, he left his bride after a month (1877) and retired to the country to devote himself to composition. Among his greatest works are the ballets *Swan Lake* (1876–7), *The Sleeping Beauty* (1890), and *The Nutcracker* (1892), the last three of his six symphonies, two piano concertos, and several tone poems, notably *Romeo and Juliet* and *Italian Capriccio*.

Tchogha Zanbil the site in SW Iran of a religious centre built in the 13c BC by King Untash Napirisha. The city comprises three palaces, five underground tombs, 10 temples, and a ziggurat. It is a World Heritage site.

TCM *abbrev.* traditional Chinese medicine.

TCP *abbrev. trademark* an antiseptic and disinfectant. [from the full name *trichlorophenylmethyliodasalicyl*]

Te *symbol Chem.* tellurium.

te see TI.

tea *noun* **1** a small evergreen tree or shrub, especially *Camellia sinensis* (of the camellia family), which has pointed leathery leaves and white fragrant flowers, and grows to a height of about 4m in the wild, although in cultivation it is pruned to the height of a small shrub to encourage the production of new shoots. Tea is native to Burma and Assam, but is now cultivated in China, Japan, India, Sri Lanka, and elsewhere for its leaves. The shoot tips with the first two leaves are picked, allowed to wither, and then rolled, fermented, and dried. When infused with boiling water they make a popular beverage. **2** the dried leaves of this plant prepared for sale. **3** a beverage prepared by infusing the dried leaves of this plant with boiling water. It contains tannins, which give the drink its characteristic flavour, and caffeine, which is a stimulant, and it may be served either hot or iced. **4** a similar drink made from the leaves or flowers of other plants: *peppermint tea*. **5** a light afternoon meal at which tea, sandwiches, and cakes are served. **6** *Brit.* a light cooked meal, usually less substantial than the midday meal, served early in the evening. [from S Chinese *te*]

tea bag a small bag or sachet of thin paper containing tea, infused in boiling water in a pot or cup.

tea break a pause for tea or other refreshments in working hours.

tea caddy a small container for tea leaves.

teacake *noun* a glazed currant bun, usually eaten toasted.

teach *verb* (PAST TENSE AND PAST PARTICIPLE **taught**) **1** to give knowledge to; to instruct in a skill or help to learn. **2** to give lessons in (a subject). **3** *intrans.* to give lessons in a subject, especially professionally. **4** *said of circumstances, experience, etc* to cause to learn or understand, especially by example, experience, or punishment: *experience had taught her to be cautious.* **5** to encourage (someone) to do what is required or acceptable (often with irony, as in the first example): *I'll teach you to be so rude / that'll teach you to be more polite.*
— **teach school** *North Amer.* to be a teacher in a school.
[from Anglo-Saxon *tæcan*]

teachable *adj.* **1** able, willing, or quick to learn. **2** capable of being taught.

teacher *noun* a person who teaches, especially professionally in a school.

tea chest a tall light wooden box in which tea is packed for export, or for storing things in.

teach-in *noun* an informal lecture, demonstration and discussion, or a series of these given one after the other and usually on the same day, by experts in a particular subject.

teaching *noun* **1** the work or profession of a teacher. **2** that which is taught, especially guidance or doctrine.

teaching hospital a large hospital where medical students are taught.

tea cloth 1 a small cloth for decorating and protecting the surface of a table or trolley. **2** a tea towel.

tea-cosy *noun* a cover to keep a teapot warm.

teacup *noun* **1** a medium-sized cup used especially for drinking tea. **2** the amount a teacup will hold.

teacupful *noun* (PL. **teacupfuls**) the amount a teacup will hold.

teahouse *noun* a restaurant in China or Japan where tea and light refreshments are served.

teak *noun* **1** a large tree which grows in India, Malaysia, etc. **2** its hard yellowish-brown wood used for making furniture. [from Malayalam (S Indian language) *tekka*]

teal *noun* any of several kinds of small freshwater duck of Europe and America. [from Middle English *tele*]

tea leaf 1 a leaf of the tea plant, or a part of the leaf. **2** (**tea leaves**) the leaves remaining in the pot or cup after the tea made from them has been drunk. **3** *slang* a thief.

team — *noun* **1** a group of people forming one side in a game. **2** a group of people working together. **3** two or more animals working together, especially in harness together. — *verb* **1** *intrans., trans.* (**team up with someone**) to form a team for some common action. **2** to harness (horses, oxen, etc) together. **3** to match (clothes). [from Anglo-Saxon *team*, child-bearing, offspring]

team spirit willingness to work together as part of a team and suppress individual needs and desires.

teamster *noun* **1** a driver of a team of animals. **2** *North Amer., esp. US* a lorry-driver.

Teamsters' Union in the USA, the International Brotherhood of Teamsters, Chauffeurs, Warehousemen, and Helpers of America, the largest US labour union, with over 1.5m members. It was founded in 1903, expelled from the AFL/CIO in 1957 for corruption, and re-affiliated in 1987.

team-work *noun* co-operation between those who are working together on a task.

Te Anau, Lake a lake in SW South I, New Zealand. AREA 344sq km/133sq mi. It is situated on the E edge of Fiordland National Park. Measuring 61km/38mi long and 10km/6mi wide, it is the second-largest lake in New Zealand, and the largest on South I. There are glow-worm caves on its W side. The lake is used for water sports.

teapot *noun* a pot with a spout and handle used for making and pouring tea.

Teapot Dome Scandal a US government scandal (1923) during the Harding administration. It involved the lease of naval oil reserves at Teapot Dome (Wyoming) and Elk Hills (California) by the Secretary of the Interior Albert B Fall, who allowed no competition to the bids of two men from oil companies from whom he had previously received large loans of money. Fall was eventually fined and imprisoned for one year.

tear[1] *noun* **1** a drop of clear saline liquid, secreted by the lachrymal gland, that moistens and cleans the front of the eyeball, or overflows from it in response to irritation of the eye, or as a result of emotion, especially sorrow. **2** any pear- or tear-shaped drop or blob.
— **in tears** crying; weeping.
[from Anglo-Saxon *tear*]

tear[2] — *verb* (PAST TENSE **tore**; PAST PARTICIPLE **torn**) **1** to pull or rip apart by force. **2** (**tear at something**) to pull it violently or with tearing movements. **3** to make (a hole, etc) by, or as if by, tearing or ripping. **4** *intrans.* to come apart; to be pulled or ripped apart: *material that tears easily.* **5** (*also* **tear someone away**) to remove or take them by force; to force or persuade them to leave. **6** *intrans.* (**tear along, away, off,** *etc*) to rush; to move with speed or violence. — *noun* **1** a hole or other damage caused by tearing. **2** an act of tearing. **3** damage: *wear and tear.*
— **be torn** to be unable to decide between two or more options.
tear a strip off someone *colloq.* to rebuke or reprimand them severely.
tear someone apart to cause them severe suffering or distress.
tear something down to pull it down or demolish it using force.
tear one's hair out to be in despair with impatience and frustration.
tear into someone to attack them physically or verbally.
tear something up 1 to tear it into pieces, especially to destroy it. **2** to remove from a fixed position by violence: *the wind tore up several trees.*
[from Anglo-Saxon *teran*]

tearaway *noun Brit. colloq.* an undisciplined and reckless young person.

teardrop *noun* a single tear.

tear duct a short tube opening in the inner corner of the eye, for carrying tears to the eye or draining them into the nose.

tearful *adj.* **1** inclined to cry or weep. **2** with much crying or weeping; covered with tears. **3** causing tears to be shed; sad.

tearfully *adv.* in a tearful way.

tearfulness *noun* being tearful.

tear gas a gas which causes stinging, blinding tears, and temporary loss of sight, used eg to control riots.

tearing *adj.* furious; overwhelming: *a tearing hurry.*

tear-jerker *noun colloq.* a sentimental play, film, book, etc intended to make people feel sad and cry.

tear-jerking *adj.* sentimental.

tearless *adj.* without tears or sorrow.

tearoom *noun* a restaurant where tea, coffee, cakes, etc are served.

tea rose a hybrid rose which is supposed to smell of tea.

tear-stained *adj., said of the face or cheeks* marked with the traces of tears.

tease — *verb* **1** *trans., intrans.* to annoy or irritate deliberately or unkindly. **2** *trans., intrans.* to laugh at or make fun of playfully or annoyingly. **3** to persuade (someone) to agree to something, especially by continual coaxing. **4** *trans., intrans.* to arouse (someone) sexually without satisfying that desire. **5** to comb wool, flax, hair, etc to remove tangles and open out the fibres. **6** to raise a nap on (cloth) by scratching or brushing, especially with teasels. **7** to backcomb (the hair). — *noun* **1** a person or thing that teases. **2** an act of teasing.
— **tease something out 1** to separate it from something in which it is entangled. **2** to clarify an obscure point by discussion, etc.
[from Anglo-Saxon *tæsan*, to card]

teasel *or* **teazel** *or* **teazle** *noun* **1** a plant whose prickly flower heads were formerly used to raise a nap on woollen or woven cloth. **2** an artificial substitute for the teasel. [from Anglo-Saxon *tæsel*]

teasel

teaser *noun* **1** a puzzle or tricky problem. **2** a person who enjoys teasing others.

teashop *noun* a (usually small) restaurant where tea and light refreshments are served; also, a shop where tea is sold.

teasing — *noun* the act or practice of teasing. — *adj.* that teases; taunting, tantalizing.

teasingly *adv.* in a teasing way.

teaspoon *noun* **1** a small spoon for use with a teacup. **2** the amount a teaspoon will hold.

teaspoonful *noun* (PL. **teaspoonfuls**) the amount a teaspoon will hold.

teat *noun* **1** the nipple of a breast or udder. **2** a piece of shaped rubber attached to a bottle through which a baby can suck milk. [from Old French *tete*]

tea towel a cloth for drying dishes after they have been washed.

tea tray a tray on which tea, usually with sandwiches and cakes, is served.

tea trolley a small trolley from which tea, sandwiches, and cakes are served.

Teazle, Sir Peter the elderly husband of the frivolous Lady Teazle in Richard Brinsley Sheridan's *The School for Scandal*, who is also the guardian of Maria.

Tebbit, Norman (Beresford) Tebbit, Baron (1931–) English Conservative politician, born in Enfield, Greater London. He entered parliament in 1970 and served in Margaret Thatcher's governments as Employment Secretary (1981–3), and Secretary for Trade and Industry (1983–5). His career was interrupted in 1984 when both he and his wife were badly hurt after the IRA bombing of the Grand Hotel in Brighton. In 1985 he became Chancellor of the Duchy of Lancaster and Chairman of the Party, but following the successful 1987 election campaign, relations with Mrs Thatcher cooled and he returned to the backbenches, until his retirement from parliament in 1992.

tec *noun colloq.* a detective.

tech *noun colloq.* a technical college.

tech. *abbrev.* **1** technical. **2** technology.

technetium *noun Chem.* (SYMBOL **Tc**, ATOMIC NUMBER **43**) a radioactive metallic element that is produced artificially by bombarding molybdenum with neutrons. It has 16 radioactive isotopes, and there are no known natural sources of the element. [from Greek *technetos*, artificial]

technical *adj.* **1** having knowledge of, specializing in, or relating to a practical skill or applied science, especially those sciences which are useful to industry. **2** *said especially of language* relating to a particular subject or requiring knowledge of a particular subject to be understood. **3** according to a strict interpretation of the law or rules. **4** of or showing a quality of technique: *playing of technical brilliance*. [from Greek *technikos*, from *techne*, art]

technical college a college of further education that teaches practical skills and applied sciences necessary to industry and business.

technical drawing 1 the drawing of plans, machinery, electrical circuits, etc with compasses, rulers, etc for business and industry. **2** a drawing done for business or industry.

technical hitch a mechanical fault.

technicality *noun* (PL. **technicalities**) **1** a technical detail or term. **2** a usually trivial or petty detail caused by a strict interpretation of the law or rules. **3** the state of being technical.

technical knockout a decision by a referee that a boxer has been defeated even though he or she has not been knocked out.

technically *adv.* in a technical way; strictly speaking: *technically, they are criminals*.

technician *noun* **1** a person specialized or skilled in a practical art or science: *a dental technician*. **2** a person employed to do practical work in a laboratory. [from Greek *techne*, art]

Technicolor *trademark* a process of producing colour cinema film by placing several copies of a scene, each one produced using different colour filters, on top of each other.

technique *noun* **1** proficiency or skill in the practical or formal aspects of an art, especially painting, music, sport, etc: *a singer with a beautiful voice but poor technique*. **2** mechanical or practical skill or method: *study the techniques of film-making*. **3** a way of achieving one's purpose skilfully; a knack. [from French, from Greek *technikos*, from *techne*, art]

techno *noun* a style of pop music that makes uses of electronic effects, especially to produce unmelodic sounds. [from TECHNOLOGY]

technobabble *noun colloq.* language that overuses technical jargon, eg specialized words, acronyms, and abbreviations used in computing, etc.

technocracy *noun* (PL. **technocracies**) the government of a country or management of an industry by technical experts. [from Greek *techne*, art + -CRACY]

technocrat *noun* a member of or believer in technocracy.

technocratic *adj.* relating to or typical of technocracy.

technological *adj.* relating to or involving technology.

technologist *noun* a person skilled in technology and its applications.

technology *noun* (PL. **technologies**) **1** the practical use of scientific knowledge in industry and everyday life. **2** practical sciences as a group. **3** the technical skills and achievements of a particular time in history, civilization, or group of people. [from Greek *technologia*, systematic treatment]

◊ Technology was transformed during the Industrial Revolution by the development of the steam engine, which was subsequently replaced by internal combustion engines (petrol engines,

diesel engines, and eventually gas turbines) that provided a reliable source of power for manufacturing, transport, and agriculture. The development of electronics in the 20c revolutionized communications and led to the development of computers. Important milestones in technology include the development of the printing press, microscope, telescope, electric battery, camera, refrigerator, telephone, light bulb, motor car, radio, tape recorder, aeroplane, television, jet engine, radar, optical fibre, video recorder, artificial satellite, laser, and microcomputer.

tectonics *sing. noun* **1** *Geol.* the study of structures which form the earth's crust and the forces which change it. See also PLATE TECTONICS. **2** the art or science of building and construction. [from Greek *tekton*, builder]

Tecumseh (c.1768–1813) Shawnee tribal chief. He joined his brother 'The Prophet' in a rising against the whites, but it was suppressed at Tippecanoe (1811). He passed into English service, commanded the Indian allies in the War of 1812, and died fighting in Canada.

Ted *noun Brit. colloq.* a Teddy boy.

Tedder (of Glenguin), Arthur William Tedder, 1st Baron (1890–1967) Scottish airman, born in Glenguin, Stirlingshire. During World War II he directed research and development at the Air Ministry, served as Commander-in-Chief (RAF) in the Middle East Air Force, moved on to the Mediterranean theatre (1943), and became Deputy Supreme Commander of the Allied Expeditionary Force under Eisenhower (1943–5), after which he was appointed Marshal of the RAF (1945).

teddy[1] *noun* (PL. **teddies**) (*also* **teddy bear**) a child's stuffed toy bear. [named after 'Teddy', the pet-name of Theodore Roosevelt, who was well known as a bear hunter]

teddy[2] *noun* (PL. **teddies**) a woman's one-piece undergarment consisting of a chemise and panties.

Teddy boy *Brit. colloq.* an unruly or rowdy adolescent, especially one in the 1950s who dressed in Edwardian-style clothes. [from *Teddy*, a familiar form of *Edward*]

Te Deum (PL. **Te Deums**) a Latin hymn of praise and thanksgiving, or a musical setting of it. [from its first words *Te Deum laudamus*, You God we praise]

tedious *adj.* tiresomely long-winded or dull; monotonous. [from Latin *taedere*, to weary]

tediously *adv.* in a tedious way.

tediousness *noun* being tedious.

tedium *noun* tediousness; boredom. [from Latin *taedere*, to weary]

tee[1] *noun* a phonetic spelling for the letter *T*. See also T[1].

tee[2] *noun* **1** *Golf* **a** a small peg with a concave top, or a small pile of sand, used to support a ball when the first shot is taken at the beginning of a hole. **b** the small area of level ground where the first shot is taken at the beginning of a hole. **2** a mark aimed at in quoits or curling.
— **tee off** to play one's first ball at the beginning of a golf hole.
tee up to place a golf ball on a tee ready for a stroke.

teem[1] *verb intrans.* **1** (**teem with people or things**) to be full of them or abound in them: *a resort teeming with tourists*. **2** to be present in large numbers; to be plentiful: *fish teem in this river*. [from Anglo-Saxon *teman*, to give birth]

teem[2] *verb intrans.* (*usually* **teem down**) *said of water, especially rain* to pour in torrents. [from Norse *toema*, to empty]

teen *noun* **1** (**teens**) the years of a person's life between the ages of 13 and 19. **2** (**teens**) the numbers from 13 to 19. **3** *colloq.* (*usually* **teens**) a teenager. [from Anglo-Saxon *tien*, 10]

teenage *adj.* **1** (*also* **teenaged**) in one's teens. **2** relating to or suitable for people in their teens.

teenager *noun* a person aged between 13 and 19.

teeny *or* **teensy** *adj.* (**teenier**, **teeniest**) *colloq.* tiny. [from TINY + WEE[1]]

teenybopper *noun colloq.* a young teenager, usually a girl, who enthusiastically follows the latest trends in clothes and pop music.

teeny-weeny *or* **teensy-weensy** *adj. colloq.* very tiny.

teepee see TEPEE.

Tees, River a river in NE England, length 127km/79mi. Rising on Cross Fell in the Pennines, Cumbria, the R Tees flows SE through Durham county, along the North Yorkshire border, and into Cleveland. Here it passes through Teesside and develops into a broad estuary that meets the North Sea below Middlesbrough. It is linked to the R Tyne as part of the UK's first regional water grid system, supplying water to the industrial NE. The upper river valley is known as Teesdale.

tee shirt see T-SHIRT.

Teesside POP (1981) 383 000, a heavily industrialized urban area surrounding the estuary of the R Tees in Cleveland, NE England. It includes Stockton-on-Tees, Redcar, Thornaby, and Middlesbrough.

teeter *verb intrans.* (**teetered**, **teetering**) **1** (**teeter about**, **along**, *etc*) to stand or move unsteadily; to wobble. **2** to hesitate or waver. [from Middle English *titeren*]

teeth see TOOTH.

teethe *verb intrans.* (**teethed**, **teething**) *said of a baby* to develop or cut milk teeth. [from Middle English *tethen*]

teething *noun* cutting teeth.

teething ring a small hard ring for a baby to chew while teething.

teething troubles problems or difficulties at the beginning of a project, or with a new piece of machinery, etc.

teetotal *adj.* never taking alcoholic drink. [probably connected with 'total abstinence (from alcohol)'; used by a campaigner for total abstinence in a speech in 1833]

teetotaller *noun* a person who abstains from alcoholic drink.

tefillen *or* **tephillin** *pl. noun Judaism* phylacteries consisting of two black leather cubes with leather straps, bound over the head and arm, and worn during Jewish morning prayers, except on sabbaths and festivals. Also, the scriptural texts contained in the cubes. [from Hebrew *tephillāh*, prayer]

TEFL *abbrev.* teaching English as a foreign language.

Teflon *noun trademark* PTFE (polytetrafluoroethene), a polymer with a high melting point, which is resistant to chemical attack. It is widely used to coat the inside of cooking pans to give them a non-stick surface.

Tegucigalpa POP (1989) 608 000, the capital of Honduras. It comprises two distinct towns, the almost flat Comayagüela and the hilly Tegucigalpa, separated by the R Choluteca. HISTORY founded as a mining camp in 1524; became the capital in 1880. NOTABLE FEATURES cathedral (18c); Church of Virgen de los Dolores (18c).

Teheran *or* **Tehran 1** POP (1990e) 6.8m, the capital of Iran and of Tehran province, situated in the N of the country. It stands at an altitude of 1 200–1 700m. HISTORY superseded Isfahan as the capital of Persia in 1788; extensively modernized after 1925. NOTABLE FEATURES Niavaran, Golestan, Marmar, Saadabad, and Baharstan palaces; Shahyad Tower, symbol of modern Iran. **2** a province in N Iran with Tehran as its capital.

Teheran Conference the first inter-Allied conference (28 Nov–1 Dec 1943) of World War II, attended by Stalin, Franklin D Roosevelt, and Winston Churchill. The subjects discussed were the co-ordination of Allied landings in France with the Soviet offensive against Germany, Russian entry in the war against Japan, and the establishment of a postwar international organization. Failure to agree on the future government of Poland foreshadowed the start of the Cold War.

Tehran see TEHERAN.

Teide, Pico de the highest peak in Spain, situated in the Teide National Park on the island of Tenerife, Canary Is. HEIGHT 3 718m.

Teifi a river in Dyfed, W Wales, length 80km/50mi. It rises in the Cambrian Mts of central Wales and flows SW and W to meet Cardigan Bay at Cardigan.

Teilhard de Chardin, Pierre (1881–1955) French geologist, palaeontologist, Jesuit priest, and philosopher, born in Sarcenat. Ordained in 1911, he became Professor of Geology at the Institut Catholique in Paris (1918) and went on palaeontological expeditions in China and central Asia. His unorthodox ideas led to a ban on his teaching and publishing but he was nevertheless awarded academic distinctions for his work in Cenozoic geology and palaeontology. His major work, *Le Phénomène humain* (The Phenomenon of Man), is based on his scientific thinking and argues that humanity is in a continuous process of evolution towards a perfect spiritual state.

Teisserenc de Bort, Leon Philippe (1855–1913) French physicist and meteorologist, born in Paris. Chief of the Central Meteorological Bureau in Paris, he used kites and hydrogen-filled balloons carrying instruments for measuring pressure, temperature, and humidity. He discovered and named the stratosphere (as distinct from the troposphere) in the upper atmosphere.

Te Kanawa, Dame Kiri (Janette) (1944–) New Zealand operatic soprano, born in Gisborne, Auckland. After winning many awards in New Zealand and Australia she went to London, where she made her début with the Royal Opera Company (1970). She has since taken a wide range of leading roles, and in 1981 sang at the wedding of the Prince and Princess of Wales.

tel. *abbrev.* telephone.

Tel Aviv-Jaffa POP (1990e) 322 000, the largest conurbation in Israel, comprising the twin cities in the W of Tel Aviv and Jaffa in Tel Aviv district. It is a commercial port on the Mediterranean Sea. HISTORY Tel Aviv was founded in 1909 as a suburb of Jaffa, the most ancient port in Israel; it was the transitional seat of government in 1948–9 before Jerusalem became the capital of Israel; Tel Aviv and Jaffa officially joined as one municipality in 1949. NOTABLE FEATURES Franciscan Monastery of St Peter (1654).

tele- *combining form* forming words meaning: **1** at, over, or to a distance: *telegram*. **2** television: *teletext*. **3** telephone: *telesales*. [from Greek *tele*, far]

tele-ad *noun* an advertisement placed in a newspaper by telephone.

telebanking *noun* a system which enables banking transactions to be carried out by means of a telecommunications network. This is most commonly achieved through a view data system or an interactive computer link, or sometimes over an interactive cable television network, with provision for the user to send signals to the bank.

telecast — *verb* (PAST TENSE AND PAST PARTICIPLE **telecast, telecasted**) to broadcast by television. — *noun* a television broadcast.

telecaster *noun* a television broadcaster.

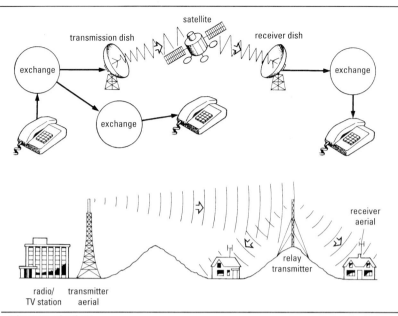

telecommunications

telecommunication *or* **telecommunications** *noun* any process or group of processes that allows the transmission of audible or visible information, or data, over long distances by means of electrical or electronic signals, eg telephone, radio, television, telegraph, fax, radar, data transmission.
◇ Information such as speech, computer data, radio signals, television programmes, etc, is usually transmitted in the form of *digital signals*, consisting of a series of electrical pulses that contain a coded version of all the original information. The signal is used to modulate a high-frequency carrier wave, which is subsequently picked up by a receiver and demodulated (separated from the signal). Large numbers of transmitters and receivers are linked together to form telecommunications networks.

telecommuter *noun* a person working at home and communicating with an office by telephone, computer link, etc.

telecommuting *noun* same as TELEWORKING.

teleconferencing the facility for conducting conferences or meetings between people in two or more remote locations by video, audio, and/or computer links which allow communication in real time between the participants.

telecottage *noun* a building situated in a rural area and equipped with computers and electronic communication links, used by a number of people for teleworking.

telegram *noun* a message sent by telegraph and delivered in printed form, now used (in the UK) only for messages sent abroad and replaced by *Telemessage* for inland messages.

telegraph — *noun* a system of or instrument for sending messages or information to a distance, especially by sending electrical impulses along a wire. — *verb* **1** *trans., intrans.* to send (a message) to (someone) by telegraph. **2** to give a warning of (something which is to happen) without being aware of doing so. **3** *intrans.* to signal. [from French *télégraphe*]

telegrapher *or* **telegraphist** *noun* a person who operates a telegraph.

telegraphese *noun* the jargon or abbreviated language used for telegrams.

telegraphic *adj.* **1** of or by telegraph or telegram. **2** concisely worded.

telegraphically *adv.* by means of the telegraph.

telegraphy *noun* the science or practice of sending messages by telegraph.

telekinesis *noun* the moving of objects at a distance without using physical force, eg by willpower. [from TELE- + Greek *kinesis*, movement]

telekinetic *adj.* relating to or involving telekinesis.

Tel el Amarna a short-lived Egyptian city on the E bank of the R Nile, c.250km/150mi S of Cairo. It was founded (c.1350 BC) by the heretic pharoah Akhenaton as both a royal residence and administrative capital, was abandoned on his death, and subsequently demolished. Notable finds include the painted bust of Akhenaton's queen, Nefertiti, found in 1911–12 and now in Berlin, Germany.

Tel-El-Kebir, Battle of an engagement (1882) between British and Egyptian forces which resulted in the British becoming the effective rulers of Egypt. It followed a period of increasing Egyptian ambition to extend her power, which had led to a financial crisis. In 1881 an army faction under Col 'Urabi Pasha (c.1840–1911) forced the Egyptian Khedive Ismail to appoint a new ministry with 'Urabi as Minister for War. Regarding this as a dangerous destabilization of the country, the British bombarded Alexandria using naval force and landed an army led by Sir Garnet Wolseley, who defeated 'Urabi at Tel-el-Kebir.

Telemachus in Greek legend, the son of Odysseus and Penelope. He set out to find his father, and visited Nestor and Menelaus. Later he helped Odysseus fight Penelope's suitors.

Telemann, Georg Philipp (1681–1767) German composer, born in Magdeburg. He taught himself music by learning to play a wide range of instruments and studying the scores of the masters. He held several posts as kapellmeister, notably at Frankfurt (1712–21), and was musical director of the Johanneum at Hamburg from 1721. Ranked in his lifetime above his friend J S Bach, and admired by George Frideric Handel, his popularity waned from his death until the 1930s. A prolific composer, his works include church music, 46 passions, over 40 operas, oratorios, many songs, and much instrumental music.

telemarketing a marketing system that uses the telephone to recruit and provide a service for prospective clients.

Telemessage *noun Brit. trademark* a message sent by telex or telephone and delivered in printed form, replacing the telegram within the UK.

telemeter *noun Engineering* an instrument that is used to take measurements and send the readings obtained, usually by means of electrical or radio signals, to a location remote from the site of measurement. Telemeters are used to relay information from spacecraft, to transmit meteorological data, and to determine the conditions inside nuclear reactors.

telemetric *adj.* involving or by means of a telemeter.

telemetry *noun* scientific measurement of distances.

teleological *adj.* relating to or involving teleology.

teleologist *noun* a believer in or supporter of teleology.

teleology *noun* the doctrine that the universe, all phenomena, and natural processes are directed towards a goal or are designed according to some purpose. [from Greek *telos*, end + -LOGY]

telepathic *adj.* relating to or involving telepathy.

telepathically *adv.* in a telepathic way; by means of telepathy.

telepathist *noun* a person who studies or practises telepathy.

telepathy *noun* the communication of thoughts directly from one person's mind to another's without using any of the five known senses. [from TELE- + Greek *pathos*, feeling]

telephone — *noun* **1** an instrument with a mouthpiece and an earpiece mounted on a handset, for transmitting human speech in the form of electrical signals or radio waves, enabling people to communicate with each other over a distance. Most modern telephones have a push-button dialling mechanism. **2** the system of communication that uses such an instrument. — *verb* **1** to seek or establish contact and speak to (someone) by telephone. **2** to send (a message, etc) by telephone. **3** *intrans.* to make a telephone call. — **on the telephone 1** connected to the telephone system. **2** talking to someone by means of the telephone.
◇ The earpiece (receiver) of a telephone contains a small loudspeaker, and the mouthpiece (transmitter) contains a small carbon microphone. Sound waves produced by the caller's voice vibrate a metal diaphragm in the microphone that compresses carbon granules and alters their electrical resistance. These changes cause variations in an electric current which travels along the telephone line. At the recipient's earpiece, the varying current causes an electromagnet to vibrate another diaphragm, which produces sound waves that reproduce the caller's voice. International telephone systems use cables (which are increasingly made of optical fibres instead of metal), and communications satellite links.

telephone box *or* **telephone booth** a small enclosed or partly-enclosed compartment containing a telephone for public use.

telephone directory *or* **telephone book** a book listing the names, addresses, and telephone numbers of telephone subscribers in a particular area.

telephone exchange see EXCHANGE.

telephonic *adj.* relating to or involving the telephone.

telephonist *noun* a telephone switchboard operator.

telephony *noun* the use or system of communication by means of the telephone.

telephoto *adj.* relating to telephotography.

telephotographic *adj.* relating to or involving telephotography.

telephotography *noun* the photographing of distant objects with lenses which produce large images.

telephoto lens a camera lens which produces large images of distant or small objects.

teleprinter *noun* an apparatus with a keyboard which types messages as they are received by telegraph and transmits them as they are typed.

Teleprompter *noun trademark* a device placed next to a television or film camera and out of sight of the audience, which displays the script to the speaker.

telesales *pl. noun* (*also* **teleselling**) the selling of goods or services by telephone.

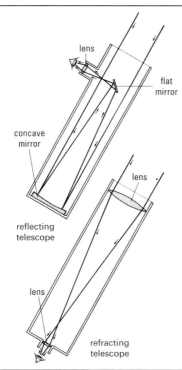

reflecting and refracting telescopes

telescope — *noun* **1** an optical instrument containing a powerful magnifying lens or mirror that makes distant objects appear larger. **2** a radio telescope. — *verb* **1** *intrans.* to be in the form of several cylinders which slide into each other for opening and closing, like the sections of a folding telescope. **2** to collapse part within part like a folding telescope. **3** *trans., intrans.* to crush or compress, or become crushed or compressed, under impact. [from TELE- + Greek *skopeein*, to see]
◇ There are two main types of astronomical telescope. A *refracting telescope* uses lenses to form a magnified inverted (upside-down) image, whereas a *reflecting telescope* has a large curved mirror for gathering light, which is reflected off a second mirror into the eyepiece. Large astronomical telescopes always use mirrors, because they are easier to manufacture and mount than lenses. Binoculars consist of two telescopes side by side.

telescopic *adj.* **1** of or like a telescope; performed with a telescope. **2** able to be seen only through a telescope. **3** *said of a lens* able to discern and magnify distant objects. **4** made in sections which slide into each other.

telescopically *adv.* in a telescopic way.

telescopic sight a small telescope used as a sight on a rifle.

teleshopping *noun* the purchase or ordering of goods from home, using an electronic communications network. A list of food and goods available to the shopper are displayed on a television screen, and these can be ordered directly over the communications link.

teletext *noun* a news and information service that is produced and regularly updated by a television company, eg Ceefax, operated by the BBC. It is transmitted using the spare lines in the video signal, and can be viewed on television sets fitted with a suitable receiver and decoder.

telethon *noun* a usually day-long television programme broadcast to raise money for charity. [from TELEVISION + MARATHON]

Teletype *noun trademark* a type of teleprinter.

televangelist *noun North Amer., esp. US* an evangelical preacher who preaches and conducts religious services regularly on television. [from TELEVISION + EVANGELIST]

televise *verb* to broadcast by television.

television *noun* **1** an electronic system that is used to convert moving images and sound into electrical signals, which are then transmitted by radio waves or by cable to a distant receiver that converts the signals back to images and sound. It is widely used for entertainment and educational purposes. **2** (*also* **television set**) a device with a picture tube and loudspeakers that is used to receive picture and sound signals transmitted in this way. **3** television broadcasting in general. See also COLOUR TELEVISION.
◇ Modern television systems use electronic scanning to analyse and reconstruct the images that are to be broadcast. A television camera lens focuses an image of the scene to be filmed on to a photoelectric screen within the camera. A beam of electrons rapidly scans this image, line by line, and produces an electric current that varies in magnitude according to the brightness of the part of the image that is being scanned. The varying electrical signal produced is known as the *picture signal*.
Sound signals from microphones and the picture signal from the camera are made to modulate VHF or UHF carrier waves that are broadcast from the transmitter mast, picked up by the receiver's television aerial, and demodulated within the receiver (television set). A beam of electrons scans the screen of the picture tube, tracing out a series of lines across it so rapidly that the viewer has the illusion of seeing a complete picture. The picture signal is used to control the brightness of the lines and so reconstruct the original scene, and the sound signal is fed to the loudspeaker. The broadcast pictures are shown in such rapid succession (25 pictures per second in Europe) that they give the impression of smooth movement.
Closed-circuit television (CCTV) conveys pictures from a camera directly to the screen of a cathode-ray tube by cable. It is used for educational purposes, and for security surveillance of banks, shops, etc.

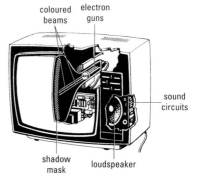

television set

televisual *adj.* of or suitable for being broadcast by television.

televisually *adv.* in a televisual way; by means of television.

teleworking *noun* working from home by means of an electronic communication link with an office.

telex (*also* **Telex**) — *noun* **1** *Telecomm.* an international telecommunications network that uses teleprinters (devices that transmit and receive telegraph messages in the form of coded electrical signals) and radio and satellite links to enable subscribers to the network to send and receive messages to each other. Unlike fax, telex can transmit one message to several receivers simultaneously. **2** a teleprinter used in such a network. **3** a message received or sent by such a network. — *verb trans., intrans.* to send a message to someone via such a network. [from TELEPRINTER + EXCHANGE]

Telford, Thomas (1757–1834) British engineer, born in Westerkirk, Dumfries. He began as a stonemason, taught himself architecture, and in 1787 became surveyor of public works for Shropshire. He planned the Ellesmere (1793–1805) and Caledonian (1803–23) canals as well as the road from London to Holyhead with the Menai Suspension Bridge (1825), and built in all over 1 600km/1 000mi of road, 1 200 bridges, as well as harbours, docks, and other buildings.

Telford's bridge and castle, Conway

Telford a town in Shropshire, W central England, designated a 'new town' in 1963. It comprises three previous urban areas and is situated on the R Severn, 55km/34mi NW of Birmingham.

Tell, William (15c) legendary Swiss patriot of Bürglen in Uri, whose name first occurs in a chronicle of 1470. A famous crossbow marksman, he reputedly saved his native district from Austrian oppression. According to tradition, he was compelled by the tyrannical Austrian governor to shoot an apple off his own son's head from a distance of 80 paces. Later, Tell slew the tyrant, and so initiated the movement which secured the independence of Switzerland. Similar tales are found in the folklore of many countries.

tell¹ *verb* (PAST TENSE AND PAST PARTICIPLE **told**) **1** (**tell someone something** *or* **tell something to someone**) to inform or give information to someone in speech or writing. **2** *trans., intrans.* (**tell of something** *or* **tell someone of something**) to relate or give an account of something. **3** to command or instruct. **4** to express in words: *tell lies.* **5** to discover or distinguish: *you can tell it by its smell / it is sometimes difficult to tell Brie from Camembert.* **6** (**tell on someone**) to give away secrets about them. **7** to make known or give away. **8** (**tell on someone**) *said of an ordeal, etc* to have a noticeable effect on them. **9** *intrans., trans.* to know or recognize (something) definitely: *can never tell when he's lying.* **10** to assure. **11** (**tell**

against someone) *said of evidence, circumstances, etc* to be unfavourable to their case, cause, etc.
— **all told** in all; with all taken into account: *there were thirty all told.*
take a telling to do as one is told without having to be asked again.
tell people *or* **things apart** to distinguish between them.
tell someone off 1 to scold or reprimand them. **2** to count them off and detach them on some special duty.
you're telling me! *colloq.* an exclamation of agreement.
[from Anglo-Saxon *tellan*]

tell² *or* **tel** *noun Archaeol.* especially in the Middle East, an artificial mound or hill formed from the accumulated remains of former settlements. [from Arabic *tall*, hill]

Teller, Edward (1908–) Hungarian–US physicist, born in Budapest. He left Germany in 1933, lectured in London and Washington (1935), and contributed profoundly to the modern explanation of solar energy, anticipating the theory behind thermonuclear explosions. Later he collaborated in the construction of the first nuclear fission pile in Chicago, and the development of fission and hydrogen bombs. In 1963 he became professor at California University.

teller *noun* **1** a person who tells especially stories. **2** a bank employee who receives money from and pays it out to members of the public. **3** a person who counts votes.

telling *adj.* having a great or marked effect.

tellingly *adv.* in a telling way.

telling-off *noun* a mild scolding.

telltale — *noun* **1** a person who spreads gossip and rumours, especially about another person's private affairs or misdeeds. **2** any of various devices for recording or monitoring a process, machine, etc. — *adj.* revealing or indicating something secret or hidden.

tellurian — *adj.* of or living on the earth. — *noun* an inhabitant of the earth, especially in science fiction. [from Latin *tellus*, earth]

tellurium *noun Chem.* (SYMBOL **Te**, ATOMIC NUMBER 52) a brittle silvery-white metalloid element obtained from gold, silver, and copper ores. It is added to alloys of lead or steel to increase their hardness, and is also used in semiconductors, glass, and ceramics, and as a catalyst. [from Latin *tellus*, earth]

Tellus see GAEA.

telly *noun* (PL. **tellies**) *colloq.* television; a television set.

telophase *noun Biol.* the final stage of cell division, that occurs once in mitosis and twice in meiosis. The two sets of chromosomes aggregate at opposite poles of the spindle, and a nuclear membrane forms around each set, resulting in the production of two daughter nuclei. [from Greek *telos*, end, purpose]

Tel Quel a French journal of cultural criticism (1960–82), founded by writer Philippe Soller. It provided a platform for many radical interventions in the overlapping fields of art, literature, philosophy, politics, semiotics, and psychoanalysis by such writers as Barthes, Derrida, Foucault, Kristeva, and Todorov. A Symbolist manifesto by Jean Moréas (1886) set out their ideas, which were expounded by Arthur Symons in *The Symbolist Movement in Literature* (1899).

Telstar *noun* any of a series of communications satellites, industrially funded but launched by NASA. *Telstar 1* was the first satellite to relay live television pictures across the Atlantic Ocean, in Jul 1962.

Telugu — *noun* a Dravidian language of SE India and parts of Malaysia with c.35–55 million speakers. — *adj.* relating to or spoken or written in Telugu.

Tema POP (1988e) 110 000, a seaport in Greater Accra region, S Ghana. It lies E of Accra and has the largest artificial harbour in Africa, opened in 1962.

temerity *noun* rashness or boldness; an unreasonable lack of fear. [from Latin *temeritas*]

temp — *noun* an employee, especially a secretary, typist, or other office worker, employed on a temporary basis. — *verb intrans.* to work as a temp.

temp. *abbrev.* **1** temperature. **2** temporary.

Tempe POP (1990) 142 000, a health resort in Maricopa County, S central Arizona, USA, situated 15km/9mi E of Phoenix. It was settled in 1872.

temper — *noun* **1** a characteristic state of mind; mood or humour: *have an even temper.* **2** a state of calm; composure; self-control: *lose one's temper.* **3** a state of uncontrolled anger: *in a temper.* **4** a tendency to have fits of uncontrolled anger. **5** the degree of hardness and toughness of metal or glass. — *verb* (**tempered**, **tempering**) **1** to soften or make less severe: *temper firmness with understanding.* **2** *Engineering* to heat a metal, hardened alloy (eg steel), or glass to a certain temperature and then allow it to cool slowly, in order to toughen it by reducing its hardness and making it less brittle. **3** to bring clay, plaster, or mortar to the desired consistency by moistening it with water and kneading it. **4** to tune (the notes on a keyboard instrument) so that the intervals between them are correct.
— **out of temper** irritable; peevish; fractious. [from Latin *temperare*, to mix in due proportion]

tempera *noun* **1** a method of painting in which powdered pigment is mixed with an emulsion made usually of egg yolks and water. **2** an emulsion, especially one made with egg yolks and water, into which powdered pigments are mixed to produce paint. **3** a painting produced using tempera. [from Italian *temperare*, to mix in due proportion]

temperament *noun* **1** a person's natural character or disposition which governs the way he or she behaves and thinks. **2** a sensitive, creative, and excitable or emotional personality. **3** an adjustment made to the intervals between notes on an instrument's keyboard to allow the instrument to play in any key. [from Latin *temperamentum*, a mixing in due proportion, in this case for the four humours believed in the Middle Ages to govern one's physical and mental characteristics]

temperamental *adj.* **1** given to extreme changes of mood; quick to show emotion, anger, irritability, etc. **2** *said of a machine, etc* not working reliably or consistently. **3** of or caused by temperament.

temperamentally *adv.* in a temperamental way.

temperance *noun* **1** moderation, self-restraint, especially in controlling one's appetite or desires. **2** moderation or complete abstinence from alcoholic drink. [from Latin *temperantia*, moderation, sobriety]

temperate *adj.* **1** moderate and self-restrained, especially in appetite, consumption of alcoholic drink, and behaviour. **2** not excessive; moderate. **3** *said of a climate or region* having temperatures which are mild, and neither tropical nor polar. [from Latin *temperatus*]

temperately *adv.* in a temperate way.

temperateness *noun* a temperate quality.

temperate zones those parts of the earth having moderate temperatures, lying between the tropic of Cancer and the Arctic Circle, and the tropic of Capricorn and the Antarctic Circle.

temperature *noun* **1** the degree of hotness or coldness of an object or medium (eg air or water), as measured by a thermometer. Heat always flows from a region of higher temperature to one of lower temperature. **2** a body temperature above normal (37°C or 98.6°F), regarded as an indicator of ill health if it is significantly higher than normal. — Also called *fever*. [from Latin *temperatura*, proportion]

◇ Temperature is a measure of the average kinetic (vibrational) energy of the constituent atoms or molecules of an object or medium. At the lowest possible temperature, known as *absolute zero*, the atoms or molecules have lost all their kinetic energy. The SI unit of temperature, measured from absolute zero, is the kelvin, but temperature is also expressed in degrees Celsius and Fahrenheit.

Tempest, The a play by William Shakespeare (c.1611). It is a romantic comedy, with deeper undertones, revolving around the magical powers of Prospero, who enforces the assistance of various spirits (including Ariel and the monster Caliban) in his interference in the lives of the shipwrecked humans on the island and in his supervision of Miranda's meetings with Ferdinand.

tempest *noun* **1** a violent storm with very strong winds. **2** a violent uproar. [from Latin *tempestas*, season, storm]

tempestuous *adj.* **1** of or like a tempest; very stormy. **2** *said of a person, behaviour, etc* violently emotional; passionate.

tempestuously *adv.* in a tempestuous way.

tempestuousness *noun* a tempestuous quality.

tempi see TEMPO.

Templars the Poor Knights of Christ and of the Temple of Solomon; an international religious–military order, whose members were subject to monastic vows. Named from the location of its headquarters (near the site of the Jewish Temple in Jerusalem), the order was founded (c.1120) chiefly to protect pilgrims to the Holy Land. It developed into a great army and acquired wealth and property, but was suppressed by Pope Clement V in 1312.

template *or* **templet** *noun* **1** a piece of metal, plastic, or wood cut in a particular shape and used as a pattern when cutting out material, drawing, etc. **2** a small wooden beam or block placed in a wall to help spread and support the weight or load. **3** the coded instructions carried by a molecule for the formation of a new molecule of the same type. [from Latin *templum*, small piece of timber]

Temple, Shirley (1928–) US child film actress, born in Santa Monica, California. During 1934–8 she appeared in more than 20 feature films, such as *Stand Up and Cheer* (1934) and *Bright Eyes* (1934). She appeared as a teenager in a few films without great success, but in her married status as Mrs S T Black she entered politics, and was US Ambassador to Ghana (1974–6).

Temple, Sir William (1628–99) English diplomat and essayist, born in London. A diplomat from 1655, he became Ambassador at The Hague and negotiated the Triple Alliance (1668) against France. In 1677 he helped arrange the marriage of the Prince of Orange to the Princess Mary, daughter of James, Duke of York (later James II). After the revolution he declined a political post in order to devote himself to literature. His essay style was a major influence on 18c writers, including Jonathan Swift, who was his secretary.

Temple, William (1881–1944) English Anglican prelate and Archbishop of Canterbury, born in Exeter. Ordained in 1908, he was Bishop of Manchester (1921–9), Archbishop of York (1929–42), and of Canterbury (1942–4). An outspoken advocate of social reform, he crusaded against usury, slums, and dishonesty, and in favour of the reform of Church structures and the ecumenical movement.

Temple a group of buildings, including the 12c Temple Church, in Fleet St, London. They were established on land once owned by the Knights Templar (a medieval religious order), and have housed the law offices of the Inner and Middle Temples for centuries.

temple¹ *noun* **1** a building in which people worship, especially in ancient and non-Christian religions, and in particular Christian sects such as the Mormons. **2** *Hist.* either of the two successive religious buildings built by the Jews in Jerusalem, one before and one after the exile in Babylon. **3** a place devoted to a particular purpose: *a temple to literature.* **4** *North Amer., esp. US* a synagogue, especially in Reform or Conservative Judaism. [from Latin *templum*]

temple² *noun* either of the flat parts of the head at the side of the forehead in front of the ear. [from Latin *tempus*]

temple³ *noun* a device in a loom which keeps the cloth stretched. [from Latin *templum*, small piece of timber]

Temple Bar a site at the junction of the Strand and Fleet St, London, where from 1301 a gateway marked the boundary of the Cities of London and Westminster. The original gateway was replaced in 1672 by one designed by Christopher Wren; in 1878 this was in turn replaced by a statue of a griffin.

Temple, Jerusalem the central shrine of Jewish worship and its priesthood, established under Solomon. The Babylonian king Nebuchadnezzar destroyed it in c.587/6 BC, but rebuilt it (as the Second Temple) after the return from exile (515 BC). Extended by Herod the Great (beginning c.20 BC), it was barely finished before Titus destroyed it during the Jewish revolt of AD 70. Still unrestored today, its site is now partly occupied by the late 7c Muslim mosque, the Dome of the Rock.

Temple of Heaven a group of buildings in Beijing (Peking), in which the Emperors formerly conducted their devotions. The complex was laid out in 1406–20.

Temple of the Tooth the Dalada Maligawa, a Buddhist pilgrimage site in Kandy, Sri Lanka. The shrine was built to house one of the Buddha's teeth, which is believed to have been conveyed to Sri Lanka in 1590.

templet see TEMPLATE.

tempo *noun* (PL. **tempos, tempi**) **1** the speed at which a piece of music should be or is played. **2** rate or speed. [from Italian *tempo*]

temporal¹ *adj.* **1** of or relating to time, often in being relatively short. **2** of worldly or secular life as opposed to religious or spiritual life. **3** *Grammar* relating to tense or the expression of time. [from Latin *temporalis*, from *tempus*, time]

temporal² *adj.* of or close to the temples on either side of the head. [from Latin *tempus*, temple]

temporally *adv.* in a temporal way.

temporarily *adv.* in a temporary way; not permanently.

temporariness *noun* being temporary.

temporary — *adj.* lasting, acting, used, etc for a limited period of time only. — *noun* (PL. **temporaries**) a worker employed temporarily; a temp. [from Latin *temporarius*, from *tempus*, time]

temporization *or* **temporisation** *noun* avoidance of a decision or commitment.

temporize *or* **temporise** *verb intrans.* **1** to avoid taking a decision or committing oneself to some course of action, to gain time and perhaps win a compromise. **2** to adapt oneself to circumstances or what the occasion requires. [from Latin *tempus*, time]

temporizer *or* **temporiser** *noun* a person who temporizes.

tempt *verb* **1** to seek to attract and persuade (someone) to do something, especially something wrong or foolish. **2** to attract or allure. **3** to be strongly inclined to do something. **4** to risk provoking, especially by doing something foolhardy: *tempt fate.* [from Latin *temptare*, to probe, test]

temptation *noun* **1** an act of tempting or the state of being tempted. **2** something that tempts.

Temptation of St Anthony a painting by Hieronymous Bosch (Lisbon).

tempter *noun* **1** a person who tempts. **2** (**the Tempter**) *Relig.* the Devil.

tempting *adj.* attractive; inviting; enticing.

temptingly *adv.* in a tempting way.

temptress *noun* a female tempter.

tempura *noun* a Japanese dish of seafood or vegetables deep-fried in batter. [from Japanese]

Ten. *abbrev.* Tennessee.

Ten, The a group of US Expressionist artists founded in 1935. Members included Mark Rothko and Adolph Gottlieb, and they held exhibitions until 1940.

ten — *noun* **1** the number or figure 10; any symbol for this number. **2** the age of 10. **3** something, especially a garment or a person, whose size is denoted by 10. **4** a playing-card with 10 pips. **5** a set of 10 things, people, etc. **6** 10 o'clock. **7** a score of 10 points. — *adj.* **1** 10 in number. **2** aged 10. [from Anglo-Saxon *ten*]

tenability *noun* being tenable.

tenable *adj.* **1** able to be believed, upheld, or maintained. **2** *said of a post or office* to be held or occupied for a specified period only or by a specified person. [from Latin *tenere*, to hold]

tenacious *adj.* **1** holding or sticking firmly. **2** determined; persistent; obstinate. **3** *said of memory* retaining information extremely well; retentive. [from Latin *tenere*, to hold]

Temple of the Tooth

tenaciously *adv.* in a tenacious way.

tenaciousness *or* **tenacity** *noun* being tenacious.

tenancy *noun* (PL. **tenancies**) **1** the temporary renting of property or land by a tenant. **2** the period during which property or land is so rented.

tenant — *noun* **1** a person who pays rent to another for the use of property or land. **2** an occupant. — *verb* to occupy as a tenant. [from Latin *tenere*, to hold]

tenanted *adj.* occupied by a tenant.

tenant farmer a farmer who farms land rented from another person, especially on an estate.

tenantry *noun* all of the tenants, usually of an estate or a landlord.

tench *noun* (PL. **tench**) a European freshwater fish with a dark green or brownish body, related to the carp. [from Old French *tenche*]

Ten Commandments *or* **Decalogue** the fundamental laws of the Jews, which, according to the Bible, were given by God to Moses on Mt Sinai and set the terms of God's covenant with the Jewish people. Slightly variant forms of the 'ethical' decalogue are found in Exodus 20 and Deuteronomy 5, but a 'cultic' variant (covering major Jewish feasts and offerings) appears in Exodus 34.14–26. Deuteronomy 9 tells how God inscribed them on two tablets of stone which were then deposited in the Ark of the Covenant. The 'ethical' decalogue contains the commands: (1) that the God of Israel shall be acknowledged as one and unique, (2) worship of images is prohibited, (3) misuse of the Lord's name is prohibited, (4) the Sabbath must be observed, (5) one's parents must be honoured, (6–10) murder, adultery, theft, false testimony, and coveting one's neighbours goods are prohibited.

tend[1] *verb* **1** to take care of; to look after; to wait on. **2** (**tend to something**) to attend to it: *tended to all his needs.* [from ATTEND]

tend[2] *verb intrans.* **1** (**tend to** *or* **towards something**) to be likely or inclined to it. **2** to move slightly, lean, or slope in a specified direction. [from Latin *tendere*, to stretch]

tendency *noun* (PL. **tendencies**) **1** a likelihood of acting or thinking, or an inclination to act or think, in a particular way. **2** a general course, trend, or drift. **3** a faction or group within a political party or movement.

tendentious *adj.* having a particular bias, tendency, or underlying purpose.

tendentiously *adv.* in a tendentious way.

tendentiousness *noun* being tendentious.

tender[1] *adj.* **1** soft and delicate; fragile. **2** *said of meat* easily chewed or cut. **3** easily damaged or grieved; sensitive: *a tender heart.* **4** easily hurt when touched, especially because of having been hurt before: *her arm is still bruised and tender.* **5** loving and gentle: *tender words.* **6** easily moved to love, pity, guilt, etc: *a tender conscience.* **7** youthful and vulnerable: *of tender years.* **8** requiring gentle or careful handling. [from Old French *tendre*, from Latin *tener*]

tender[2] — *verb* **1** to offer or present (an apology, resignation, etc). **2** (**tender for something**) to make a formal offer to do work or supply goods for a stated amount of money and within a stated period of time. — *noun* a formal offer, usually in writing, to do work or supply goods for a stated amount of money and within a stated period of time.
— **put something out to tender** to invite tenders for a job or undertaking.
[from Old French *tendere*, to stretch]

tender[3] *noun* **1** (*often in compounds*) a person who looks after something or someone: *bartender.* **2** a small boat which carries stores or passengers to and from a larger boat. **3** a railway wagon attached to a steam-engine to carry fuel and water.

tender[4] see TEND[1].

tenderfoot *noun* (PL. **tenderfeet**, **tenderfoots**) an inexperienced newcomer or beginner.

tender-hearted *adj.* kind and sympathetic; easily made to feel love or pity.

tender-heartedly *adv.* in a tender-hearted way.

tender-heartedness *noun* being tender-hearted.

Tender is the Night a novel by F Scott Fitzgerald (1934). It centres on the disintegrating life of US psychiatrist Dick Diver.

tenderize *or* **tenderise** *verb* to make (meat) tender by pounding it or by adding an acidic substance.

tenderizer *or* **tenderiser** *noun* a pounding instrument or a substance that tenderizes meat.

tenderloin *noun* a cut from the tenderest part of the loin of pork, beef, etc.

tenderly *adv.* in a tender way.

tenderness *noun* being tender.

tendinitis *or* **tendonitis** *noun* inflammation of a tendon.

tendon *noun* a cord of strong, fibrous tissue that joins a muscle to a bone or some other structure. [from Latin *tendo*]

tendril *noun Bot.* a long, often spirally twisted, thread-like extension of a stem, leaf, or petiole, by means of which many climbing plants attach themselves to solid objects for support. [from Old French *tendron*, shoot]

tendrilled *adj.* having a tendril or tendrils.

tenement *noun* **1** *North Amer., Scot.* a large building divided into several self-contained flats or apartments. **2** a self-contained flat or room within such a building. [from Latin *tenementum*, from *tenere*, to hold]

Tenerife see CANARY ISLANDS.

tenet *noun* a belief, opinion, or doctrine. [from Latin *tenet*, he, she, or it holds]

tenfold — *adj.* **1** 10 times as much or as many. **2** divided into, or consisting of, 10 parts. — *adv.* by 10 times as much.

ten-gallon hat *North Amer., esp. US* a hat worn by cowboys, with a broad brim and high crown.

Teng Hsiao-p'ing see DENG XIAOPING.

Tengri the Mongol god of heaven, the organizer and ruler of the world. He was believed to be great and merciful, and to show his anger by sending thunderstorms.

Tenkodogo the chief town in E central Burkina. It is located 137km/85mi from Ouagadougou on the route to Lomé (Ghana).

Ten Lost Tribes of Israel the 10 tribes of Israel taken captive by Assyria in 721 BC and merged (hence 'lost') with the Assyrians. British Israelites claim them to be the ancestors of the British and American peoples, but this theory is largely discredited.

Tenn. *abbrev.* Tennessee.

Tennant Creek POP (1991) 4 000, a town in Northern Territory, Australia, between Darwin and Alice Springs. It has been an important gold and, since the 1950s, copper mining centre. The Devil's Marbles, an outcrop of weathered round granite boulders, are in a scenic reserve 113km/70mi to the S.

tenner *noun colloq.* a £10 note.

Tennessee POP (1990) 5m, a state in SE central USA, divided into 95 counties. AREA 109 149sq km/42 132sq mi. It is known as the 'Volunteer State'. CAPITAL Nashville. CHIEF TOWNS Memphis, Knoxville, Chattanooga. PHYSICAL DESCRIPTION the Mississippi R follows the W border; the Holston and French Broad Rivers form the Tennessee R; the highest point is Clingmans Dome (2 025m); in the E lie the Great Smoky Mts, Cumberland Plateau, narrow river valleys, and heavily forested foothills, which severely restrict farming; the fertile 'bluegrass' country in the centre is ideal for livestock and dairy farming; in the W is a rich floodplain where most of the state's cotton is grown; many lakes were created by the Tennessee Valley Authority's damming of the Tennessee and Cumberland rivers. HISTORY visited by Hernando de Soto in 1540 and claimed for France, but ceded in 1763; explored by Daniel Boone in 1769; the temporary state of Franklin was formed in 1784, after the War of Independence; the Federal government created the Territory of the United States South of the Ohio (Southwest Territory) in 1790; admitted to the Union in 1796 as the 16th state; seceded in 1861; the scene of many battles during the Civil War, including Shiloh, Chattanooga, and Stone River; slavery was abolished in 1865; re-admitted to the Union in 1866; the Ku Klux Klan was founded at Pulaski in 1866. ECONOMY tobacco; soya beans; hay; cotton; cattle and dairy products; chemicals; processed foods; textiles; electrical equipment; coal; cement; the nation's largest producer of zinc and pyrites; several popular tourist areas.

Tennessee River a river in SE USA. It is formed near Knoxville, Tennessee, by the confluence of the French Broad and Holston rivers. Flowing for a total of 1 398km/869mi (including the French Broad), the river forms part of the Alabama–Mississippi border and enters into Kentucky to join the Ohio R at Paducah. The major tributaries are the Little Tennessee, Clinch, Hiwasee, Elk, and Duck. It is used for irrigation, flood-control, and hydroelectric power.

Tennessee Valley Authority (ABBREV. **TVA**) an independent US government agency created by Act of Congress in 1933. It is responsible for development in the Tennessee R basin and has provided hydroelectric power cheaply, changing the basis of the state economy from agriculture to industry.

Tenniel, Sir John (1820–1914) English artist, born in London. He became known as a *Punch* cartoonist (from 1851) and book illustrator, notably in his work for *Alice's Adventures in Wonderland* (1865) and *Through the Looking-glass* (1872).

tennis *noun* **1** (*in full* **lawn tennis**) a game in which two players or two pairs of players use rackets to hit a light ball across a net on a grass-covered or hard rectangular court. **2** real tennis. [from Old French *tenetz*, hold!, take!]

Tennis Court Oath an oath taken (1789) on a tennis court at Versailles, France, by representatives of the Third Estate locked out of their assembly place. Declaring themselves to be the National Assembly, the deputies swore never to separate until a constitution was established for France.

tennis elbow painful inflammation of the elbow caused by over-exercise (typically by playing tennis) or over-work.

Tennyson, Alfred, 1st Baron, also called **Alfred, Lord Tennyson** (1809–92) English poet, born in Somersby, Lincolnshire. His first collections, *Poems Chiefly Lyrical* (1830) and *Poems* (1833), were not well received, but his reputation was established by a revised volume in 1842. His major works include the elegy *In Memoriam* (1850), *Maud: a Monodrama* (1855), and a series of poems on the Arthurian theme, *Idylls of the King* (1859–85). He also wrote several plays, and was made Poet Laureate in 1850.

Tenochtitlan the island capital of L Texcoco, now beneath Mexico City, from which the Aztecs dominated Mexico from c.1344–5 to the Spanish Conquest in 1519.

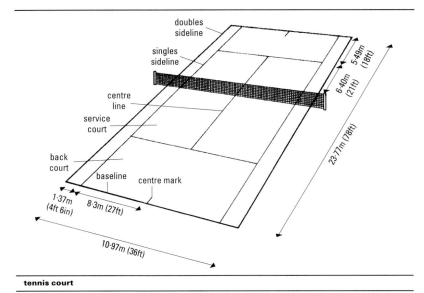

tennis court

tenon — *noun* a projection at the end of a piece of wood, etc, formed to fit into a socket or mortise in another piece. — *verb* **1** to fix with a tenon. **2** to cut a tenon in. [from Latin *tenere*, to hold]

tenor *noun* **1** a singing voice of the highest normal range for an adult man; also, a singer having this voice. **2** an instrument, eg a viola, recorder, or saxophone, with a similar range. **3** music written for a voice or instrument with such a range. **4** the general course or meaning of something written or spoken. **5** a settled or general course or direction, eg of a person's life. [from Latin *tenor*, from *tenere*, to hold]

tenpin bowling a game in which 10 skittles are set up at the end of an alley and a ball is rolled at them with the aim of knocking as many down as possible.

Tenrikyo a Japanese faith-healing missionary sect, founded by a female shaman Nakayama Miki (1798–1887). Its chief religious centre is her birthplace, Tenri, near the ancient capital of Nara. [Japanese, = teaching of heavenly truth]

tense¹ *noun Grammar* a form of verb that shows the time of its action in relation to the time of speaking and whether that action is completed or not. [from Latin *tempus*, time]

tense² — *adj.* **1** feeling, showing, or marked by emotional, nervous, or mental strain. **2** tightly stretched; taut. — *verb trans., intrans.* to make or become tense. [from Latin *tendere*, to stretch]

tensely *adv.* in a tense way.

tenseness *noun* being tense.

tensile *adj.* **1** able to be stretched. **2** relating to or involving stretching or tension. [from Latin *tensilis*, from *tendere*, to stretch]

tensile strength *Physics* a measure of the ability of a material to resist tension, equal to the minimum stress (force per unit cross-sectional area) required to break it. The tensile strength of a material is influenced by the way in which it is manufactured, and by processes such as tempering.

tensility *noun* a tensile quality or condition.

tension — *noun* **1** an act of stretching, the state of being stretched, or the degree to which something is stretched. **2** mental or emotional strain, excitement, or anxiety, usually accompanied by physical symptoms. **3** strained relations or underlying hostility between people, countries, etc. **4** *Physics* a force which causes a body to be stretched or elongated. **5** electromotive force. **6** *Knitting* the tightness or looseness of wool as

one knits, measured as the number of stitches to the inch. — *verb* to give the required tightness or tension to. [from Latin *tensio*, from *tendere*, to stretch]

tent — *noun* **1** a shelter made of canvas or other material supported by poles or a frame and fastened to the ground with ropes and pegs, that can be taken down and carried from place to place. **2** anything like a tent in form or function, especially a clear plastic device placed over the head and shoulders to control the oxygen supply to a sick person. — *verb* **1** *intrans.* to camp in a tent. **2** to cover or shelter with a tent. [from Old French *tente*, from Latin *tendere*, to stretch]

tentacle *noun* **1** any of the long thin flexible appendages growing on the head or near the mouth of many invertebrate animals (eg sea anemone, octopus) used as sense organs, or for defence, grasping prey, or attachment to surfaces. **2** in certain insectivorous plants (eg sundew) any of the sticky hairs on the leaves that serve to trap insects. [from Latin *tentare*, to feel]

tentacled *adj.* having tentacles.

tentacular *adj.* belonging to or like a tentacle.

tentative *adj.* **1** not finalised or completed; provisional. **2** uncertain; hesitant; cautious. [from Latin *tentare*, to try]

tentatively *adv.* in a tentative way.

tentativeness *noun* being tentative.

tenter *noun* a frame on which cloth is stretched, especially so that it dries in without losing its shape.

tenterhook *noun* a sharp hooked nail used for fastening cloth to a tenter.
— **on tenterhooks** in a state of impatient suspense or anxiety.

tenth — *noun* **1** one of 10 equal parts. **2** the last of 10; the next after the ninth. **3** *Mus.* an interval of an octave plus a third. **4** *Mus.* a note which is an octave plus a third above or below another. — *adj.* being the last of 10 or in an equivalent position. — *adv.* **1** in tenth position. **2** as the tenth point, etc.

tenthly *adv.* as the tenth point, etc.

tenuous *adj.* **1** slight; with little strength or substance. **2** thin; slim. [from Latin *tenuis*, thin]

tenuously *adv.* in a tenuous way.

tenuousness *noun* being tenuous.

tenure *noun* **1** the holding of an office, position, or property. **2** the length of time an office, position, or property is held. **3** the holding of a position, especially a university teaching job, for a

guaranteed length of time or permanently. **4** the conditions by which an office, position, or property is held. [from Latin *tenere*, to hold]

tenured *adj.* having tenure of office or property.

Ten Years War a nationalist Cuban uprising (1868–78) against Spanish colonial rule. The rebels accepted their defeat in the Pact of Zanjón (Feb 1878) which promised reform and representation, but the only positive outcome of the conflict was the abolition of slavery.

Tenzing Norgay, also called **Sherpa Tenzing** (1914–86) Nepalese mountaineer, born in Tsa-chu near Makalu. He made his first climb as a porter with a British Everest expedition in 1935, and later climbed many of the Himalayan peaks. In 1953 he succeeded in reaching the Everest summit with Edmund Hillary, for which he was awarded the George Medal. He later became head of the Institute of Mountaineering at Darjeeling.

Teotihuacán an Aztec city, 30km/20mi NE of Mexico City, which flourished c.450–650 and was destroyed and burnt c.700. Its remains include the 70m high Pyramid of the Sun, the Pyramid of the Moon, and the *Ciudadela* or royal palace, with its Temple of Quetzalcoatl. It is a World Heritage site.

tepee *or* **teepee** *noun* a Native American tent formed of skins stretched over a conical frame of poles. [from Dakota (Native American language) *tipî*]

tepid *adj.* **1** slightly or only just warm; lukewarm. **2** not enthusiastic. [from Latin *tepidus*]

tepidity *noun* a tepid quality.

tepidly *adv.* in a tepid way; to a tepid degree.

tequila *noun* a Mexican spirit used as the basis for many alcoholic drinks. [named after *Tequila*, a district in Mexico]

ter- *prefix* forming words meaning 'three, threefold, thrice'. [from Latin *ter*, thrice]

terabyte *noun Comput.* a unit of storage capacity equal to 2^{40} or 1 099 511 627 776 bytes. [from Greek *teras*, monster, + BYTE]

teratogen *noun Medicine* an agent or procedure that interferes with the normal development of the fetus, and leads to the development of physical abnormalities. [from Greek *teras*, *-atos*, monster]

terbium *noun Chem.* (SYMBOL **Tb**, ATOMIC NUMBER 65) a silvery metal that is a member of the lanthanide series, and is used in semiconductor devices and phosphors. [from *Ytterby* in Sweden, where it was discovered]

terce *noun* the third of the canonical hours, originally said at the third hour (ie 9 am). See also COMPLINE, LAUDS, MATINS, NONE², SEXT, VESPERS. [from Latin *tertia pars*, third part]

tercel *or* **tiercel** *noun* a male hawk. [from Old French *tercel*]

tercentenary *or* **tercentennial** — *noun* (PL. **tercentenaries**) a three-hundredth anniversary. — *adj.* of three hundred years. [from Latin *ter*, thrice + CENTENARY]

tercet *noun* a set of three lines in a poem which rhyme or which are connected by rhyme to a preceding or following group of three lines. [from Italian *terzetto*, from *terzo*, third]

teredo *noun* (PL. **teredos**) any of several molluscs which bore into wooden ships. [from Greek *teredon*, boring worm]

Terence (Publius Terentius Afer) (c.190–159 BC) Roman comic poet, born in Carthage, N Africa. After being freed from slavery, he was introduced to Roman society with the success of his first play, *Andria* (The Andrian Girl, 166 BC). His six surviving comedies are Greek in origin and scene, and four of them are directly based on Menander. Many of his conventions were later used by European dramatists.

Terence a male first name. [from the Roman family name *Terentius*]

Terengganu POP (1990) 752 000, a state in NE Peninsular Malaysia. AREA 12 928sq km/ 4 990sq mi. HISTORY formerly a fief of Malacca and then of Johor, before coming under the rule of Thailand; ceded to Britain in 1909. CAPITAL Kuala Terengganu. ECONOMY fishing; offshore oil.

Teresa of Avila, St (1515–82) Spanish saint and mystic, born in Avila. She entered a Carmelite there in 1533, and was noted for her asceticism and sanctity. To re-establish the ancient Carmelite rule, in 1562 she founded the first of her 16 religious houses, and in 1568 she helped St John of the Cross found the first community of reformed Carmelite friars. Among her writings are her autobiography *The Way of Perfection*, and the mystical work *The Interior Castle*. Canonized in 1622, she was the first woman to be given the title of Doctor of the Church (1970). Her feast day is 15 Oct.

Tereshkova, Valentina (1937–) Soviet cosmonaut and the first woman to fly in space, born in Maslennikovo. She worked in a textile factory, qualified as a sports parachutist, and entered training as a cosmonaut in 1962, becoming a solo crew member of the three-day *Vostok 6* flight launched on 16 Jun 1963. She was made a hero of the Soviet Union, and became a member of the Central Committee of the Soviet Communist Party in 1971.

tergiversate *verb intrans. formal* **1** to turn one's back. **2** to change sides. **3** to speak or act evasively. [from Latin *tergum*, back + *versare*, to turn]

tergiversation *noun formal* **1** turning one's back. **2** evasion.

term — *noun* **1** a word or expression, especially one used with a precise meaning in a specialized field: *a scientific term*. **2** (**terms**) language used; a particular way of speaking: *criticized him in no uncertain terms*. **3** a limited or clearly defined period of time. **4** the end of a particular time, especially the end of pregnancy when the baby is about to be born. **5** (**terms**) a relationship between people or countries: *be on good terms*. **6** (**terms**) the rules or conditions of an agreement: *terms of sale*. **7** (**terms**) fixed charges for work or a service. **8** one of the usually three divisions into which the academic and school year is divided. **9** the time during which a court is in session. **10** *Maths.* a quantity which is joined to another by either addition or subtraction. **11** *Maths.* one quantity in a series or sequence. **12** *Logic* a word or expression which may be a subject or a predicate of a proposition. — *verb* to name or call.
— **come to terms** to give way or submit; to yield.
come to terms with someone *or* **something 1** to come to an agreement or understanding with someone. **2** to find a way of living with or tolerating some personal trouble or difficulty.
in terms of ... in relation to ...; using the language and value of ... as a basis.
[from Latin *terminus*, boundary]

termagant *noun* a scolding, brawling, and overbearing woman. [from Old French *Tervagan*, a mythical deity believed in the Middle Ages to be worshipped by Muslims and introduced into morality plays as a scolding, overbearing character]

Terman, Lewis Madison (1877–1956) US psychologist, born in Johnson County, Indiana. At Stanford University he developed an English version of the Binet-Simon intelligence test and introduced Terman Group Intelligence Tests into the US army in 1920. He initiated the use of the term IQ (Intelligence Quotient) in his *The Measurement of Intelligence* (1916).

Terme the national museum of Rome, which contains an important collection of Greek and Roman art. It is housed in the ancient Diocletian Baths.

terminability *noun* being terminable.

terminable *adj.* able to come or be brought to an end. [from Latin *terminus*, boundary]

terminal — *adj.* **1** *said of an illness* causing death; fatal. **2** *said of a patient* having an illness which will cause death. **3** *colloq.* extreme; acute: *terminal laziness*. **4** forming or occurring at an end, boundary, or terminus. **5** of a term or occurring every term. — *noun* **1** an arrival and departure building at an airport. **2** a large station at the end of a railway line or for long-distance buses and coaches. **3** a point in an electric circuit or electrical device at which the current leaves or enters it, or by which it may be connected to another device. **4** a device consisting usually of a keyboard and visual display unit, which allows a user to communicate with and use a distant computer. **5** an installation at the end of a pipeline or at a port where oil is stored and from where it is distributed. [from Latin *terminalis*, from *terminus*, boundary]

terminally *adv.* **1** in a terminal way. **2** fatally.

terminal velocity the constant velocity reached by an object falling through a fluid (a gas or liquid) under the influence of gravity, with no net force acting on it.

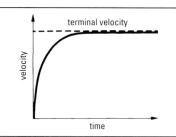
terminal velocity

terminate *verb* **1** *trans., intrans.* to bring or come to an end. **2** *intrans. formal* to end or conclude in a specified way or at a specified time: *the conference terminated in/with a panel discussion*. **3** to end (a pregnancy) artificially before its term. **4** to form a boundary or limit to. **5** *intrans. formal* to stop; to go no further: *the train terminates at Vienna*. [from Latin *terminare*, to set a limit to]

terminate-and-stay-resident program *Comput.* (ABBREV. **TSR**) a program which remains in memory once activated, even while it is not running, and which can be reactivated quickly using a pre-set key, etc.

termination *noun* **1** an act of ending or the state of being brought to an end. **2** an artificially induced miscarriage or abortion. **3** a final result.

terminological *adj.* relating to or involving terminology.

terminologically *adv.* as regards terminology.

terminologist *noun* an expert in terminology.

terminology *noun* (PL. **terminologies**) the words and phrases used in a particular subject or field. [from Latin *terminus*, term]

Terminus in Roman mythology, the god of boundary marks, where his statue or bust was sometimes placed. His stone on the Capitol was within the temple of Jupiter Optimus Maximus, but was not allowed to be covered.

terminus *noun* (PL. **termini**, **terminuses**) **1** the end of a railway line or bus route, usually with a station. **2** an extreme or final point. **3** a stone marking a boundary. [from Latin *terminus*, boundary, limit]

termite *noun* any of about 200 species of social insect that live in highly organized colonies of up

to a million insects, found mainly in the tropics, although a few species occur in the USA. Many termites feed on living plants and are regarded as pests, while wood-boring species cause damage to trees, structural timber of buildings, etc. [from Latin *termes*, white ant]

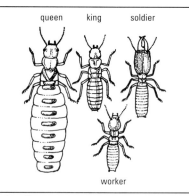

queen   king   soldier

worker

termites

terms of reference a description or definition of the basis and scope of an undertaking, inquiry, etc.

tern *noun* any of several sea-birds which are smaller than gulls and have long wings and a long forked tail. [from Scandinavian]

ternary *adj.* **1** having three parts. **2** *Maths.* using three as a base. [from Latin *ternarius*]

terpene *noun Chem.* any of a group of unsaturated hydrocarbons that are present in plant resins and also form the main constituents of essential oils such as rose and jasmine oil. They are used in the manufacture of camphor and menthol. [from *terpentin*, an old form of TURPENTINE]

Terpsichore in Greek mythology, one of the Muses, usually associated with dancing or lyric poetry.

terpsichorean *adj.* of or relating to dancing.

terrace — *noun* **1** each one of a series of raised level banks of earth, like large steps on the side of a hill, used for cultivation. **2** a row of identical and connected houses, properly one overlooking a slope, or the street on to which they face. **3** a raised, level, paved area by the side of a house. **4** (*usually* **terraces**) open areas rising in tiers round a sports ground, where spectators stand. — *verb* to form into a terrace or terraces. [from Latin *terracea*]

terrace house *or* **terraced house** *Brit.* a house which is part of a terrace.

terracotta — *noun* **1** an unglazed brownish-orange earthenware made from a mixture of sand and clay and used for pottery, statuettes, and building. **2** its brownish-orange colour. — *adj.* made of, or the colour of, terracotta. [from Italian *terracotta*, baked earth]

terra firma dry land as opposed to water or air; solid ground. [from Latin *terra firma*, firm land]

terrain *noun* a stretch of land, especially with regard to its physical features or as a battle area. [from Latin *terrenus*, from *terra*, earth]

terrapin *noun* **1** in the UK, any small freshwater turtle. **2** in the USA, an edible turtle. [from a Native American language]

terrapin

terrarium *noun* (PL. **terraria, terrariums**) **1** an enclosed area or container in which small land animals are kept. **2** a large globe-shaped sealed glass jar in which plants are grown. [from Latin *terra*, earth]

terrestrial — *adj.* **1** relating to dry land or to the Earth. **2** denoting animals or plants that are found on dry land, rather than in aquatic environments or in the air. **3** of this world; worldly; mundane. **4** *said of broadcast signals* sent by a land transmitter and not by satellite. — *noun* an inhabitant of the earth. [from Latin *terrestris*, from *terra*, earth]

terrible *adj.* **1** *colloq.* very bad: *a terrible singer.* **2** *colloq.* very great; extreme: *a terrible gossip.* **3** causing great fear or terror. **4** causing suffering or hardship and requiring great strength or fortitude. [from Latin *terribilis*, from *terrere*, to frighten]

terribly *adv.* **1** *colloq.* very: *terribly happy.* **2** in a terrible way; to a great degree: *hurts terribly.*

terrier *noun* any of several breeds of small dog bred originally to hunt animals in burrows. [from Old French *chien terrier*, dog of the earth]

terrific *adj.* **1** *colloq.* marvellous; excellent. **2** *colloq.* very great or powerful: *a terrific storm.* **3** very frightening; terrifying. [from Latin *terrificus*, frightful]

terrifically *adv.* **1** in a terrific way. **2** *colloq.* extremely.

terrified *adj.* extremely frightened.

terrify *verb* to make very frightened; to fill with terror. [from Latin *terrificare*]

terrifying *adj.* causing extreme fright.

terrine *noun* **1** an oval or round earthenware dish in which food may be cooked and served. **2** food cooked or served in such a dish, especially pâté. [from Old French *terrin*, earthen]

territorial — *adj.* **1** of or relating to a territory. **2** limited or restricted to a particular area or district. **3** *said especially of birds and animals* likely to establish its own territory and defend it from others of the same species. — *noun* (**Territorial**) *Brit.* a member of the Territorial Army.

Territorial Army (ABBREV. **TA**) also called **the Terriers**, formerly **the Territorial Force** a British reserve military force, first formed in 1908. Its volunteers receive continuous training on a part-time basis, and are intended to provide direct reinforcement to the British Army of the Rhine, or to act in home defence.

territorial waters the sea surrounding a state which is considered to belong to it.

territory *noun* (PL. **territories**) **1** a stretch of land; a region. **2** the land under the control of a ruler, government, or state. **3** an area of knowledge, interest, or activity. **4** an area or district for which a travelling salesman or distributor is responsible. **5** an area which a bird or animal treats as its own and defends against others of the same species. **6** (*often* **Territory**) part of a country (usually a federal state such as the USA) with an organized government but without the full rights of a state. [from Latin *territorium*, the land round a town]

Terror, Reign of the extreme phase (1793–4) of the French Revolution, characterized by the systematic execution of c.40 000 political opponents of the Jacobins and supposed sympathizers of the Counter-Revolution, who were brought before the Revolutionary Tribunal and guillotined.

terror *noun* **1** very great fear or dread. **2** something or someone which causes such fear. **3** *colloq.* a troublesome or mischievous person, especially a child. **4** a time of, or government by, terror. [from Latin *terror*]

terrorism *noun* the systematic and organized use of violence and intimidation to force a government, community, etc to act in a certain way or accept certain demands.

◊ It may be 'official', as under Stalin, or 'unofficial', as employed by various opposition and underground movements. Terrorism may be confined to a specific territory or may have an international dimension, manifest in hijackings and hostage-taking.

terrorist — *noun* a person who practises terrorism. — *adj.* relating to or involving terrorism.

terrorize *or* **terrorise** *verb* **1** to frighten greatly. **2** to control or coerce (someone) by threatening violence.

terror-stricken *adj.* feeling very great uncontrollable fear.

Terry, Dame (Alice) Ellen (1848–1928) English actress, born in Coventry, West Midlands. Born into an acting family, she appeared on stage at the age of eight, played in Bristol from 1862, and established herself as the leading Shakespearean actress in London, dominating the English and US theatre (1878–1902) in partnership with Henry Irving. In 1903 she entered theatre management, and toured and lectured widely.

terry — *noun* an absorbent fabric with uncut loops on one side used especially for towels. — *adj.* made of this fabric.

terse *adj.* **1** *said of language* brief and concise; succinct. **2** abrupt and rude; curt. [from Latin *tersus*, rubbed clean]

tersely *adv.* in a terse way.

terseness *noun* a terse quality.

tertiary — *adj.* **1** third in order, degree, importance, etc. **2** *said of education* coming after secondary, eg university or college. See also PRIMARY, SECONDARY. **3** *Geol.* (**Tertiary**) relating to the first period of the Cenozoic era, lasting from about 65 million to 2 million years ago, and subdivided into the Palaeocene, Eocene, Oligocene, Miocene, and Pliocene epochs. During this period mammals evolved rapidly, although many large mammals died out at the end of the period when the climate became colder, and flowering plants became widespread. Mountain ranges such as the Alps, Himalayas, Andes, and Rockies were formed towards the beginning of the period. **4** relating to rocks formed during this period. — *noun* (PL. **tertiaries**) **1** (**Tertiary**) the first geological period of the Cenozoic era. **2** a lay person who is affiliated to a monastic order and who follows a slightly modified form of that order's rule. [from Latin *tertius*, third]

Tertullian, in full **Quintus Septimus Florens Tertullianus** (c.160–220AD) Christian theologian, born in Carthage. Following his conversion in c.196, his opposition to worldliness in the Church culminated in his becoming a leader of the Montanist sect (c.207). The first to produce major Christian works in Latin, he had a profound influence on the development of ecclesiastical language, and also wrote against heathens, Jews, and heretics.

Teruel, ancient **Turba** POP (1987e) 28 000, the capital of Teruel province, Aragón, E central Spain. It lies on the R Turia, 302km/188mi from Madrid. NOTABLE FEATURES cathedral (16c); Los Arcos Aqueduct; Church of St Peter; the town's Mudéjar architecture, a mixture of Christian and Islamic influences, constitutes a World Heritage site.

Terylene *noun trademark* a light tough synthetic fabric of polyester fibres.

terza rima *Prosody* an Italian verse-form in triplets, rhyming *aba bcb cdc*. [Italian, = third rhyme]

Teshub in Hurrian mythology, the god of the thunderstorm, and the son of Kumarbi. He dethroned Kumarbi and became the supreme god, and later successfully defended himself against an attack from the giant Ullikummi.

TESL *abbrev.* teaching English as a second language.

Tesla, Nikola (1856–1943) Yugoslav-born US physicist and electrical engineer, born in Smiljan, Croatia. In 1884 he emigrated to the USA, where he became a prolific and highly innovative inventor. His inventions included improved dynamos, transformers, electric bulbs, and the high-frequency coil which now bears his name; he also did much to promote the use of alternating current electricity supply.

tesla *noun Physics* (ABBREV. **T**) the SI unit of magnetic flux density, defined as a magnetic flux of one weber per square metre. [named after the US physicist Nikola Tesla]

TESSA *abbrev.* Tax-Exempt Special Savings Account.

tessellate *verb* to form into or mark like a mosaic, especially with tesserae or checks. [from Latin *tessella*, small square piece of stone]

tessellated *adj.* chequered.

tessellation *noun* a regular pattern of small squares, such as that found on mosaic tiles. [from Latin *tessellare*]

tessera *noun* (PL. **tesserae**) a square piece of stone, glass, etc used in mosaics. [from Latin *tessera*]

tessitura *noun* the natural range of the pitch or compass of a particular voice or of a vocal or instrumental part in a particular piece. A particular singer or vocal part may be said to have or require a high or low tessitura. [from Italian *tessitura*, texture]

Tess of the D'Urbervilles, in full ***Tess of the D'Urbervilles, A Pure Woman*** a novel by Thomas Hardy (1891). It describes the tragic fate of Tess Durbeyfield, a poor villager's daughter.

test¹ — *noun* **1** a critical examination or trial of a person's or thing's qualities, abilities, etc. **2** anything used as the basis of such an examination or trial, eg a set of questions or exercises: *long-distance running is a test of endurance.* **3** a short, minor, usually written examination: *a spelling test.* **4** a test match. **5** *Chem.* anything used to distinguish, detect, or identify a substance; a reagent. — *verb* **1** to examine (someone or something, abilities, qualities, etc), especially by trial. **2** *trans., intrans.* to examine (a substance) to discover whether another substance is present or not: *test the water for microbes.* **3** *intrans.* to achieve a stated result in a test: *test positive for the virus.* [from Old French, from Latin *testa* or *testum*, earthenware pot]

test² *noun Biol.* a hard outer covering or shell of certain invertebrates. [from Latin *testa*, tile]

testa *noun Biol.* the hard outer covering of a seed.

testable *adj.* capable of being tested.

testaceous *adj.* **1** *Biol.* covered by a protective shell-like material, or consisting of such a material. **2** of a reddish-brown colour.

Test Act a British Act passed (1673) to curb Catholic influence at the court of Charles II. Every office holder had to take Oaths of Supremacy and Allegiance, take communion according to the rites of the Church of England, and make a declaration against transubstantiation. The Act necessitated the resignation of the King's brother James, Duke of York, as Lord High Admiral, and remained in force until 1828.

testament *noun* **1 a** a written statement of one's wishes, especially of what one wants to be done with one's property after death. **b** a will: *last will and testament.* **2** proof, evidence, or tribute. **3** a covenant between God and Man. **4** (**Testament**) **a** either of the two main divisions of the Bible, the *Old Testament* and the *New Testament.* **b** a copy of the New Testament. [from Latin *testamentum*, from *testis*, witness]

testamentary *adj.* **1** relating to a test or will. **2** bequeathed or done by will.

testate *adj. Legal* having made and left a valid will. [from Latin *testari*, to make a will]

testator *noun Legal* a person who leaves a will at death.

testatrix *noun Legal* a female testator.

test case *Legal* a case whose outcome will serve as a precedent for all similar cases in the future.

test drive a trial drive of a car by a prospective owner to test its performance.

test-drive *verb* to test (a car) by taking a trial drive.

tester *noun* **1** a person who tests. **2** a thing used for testing.

testes see TESTIS.

testicle *noun* a testis. [from Latin *testis*, witness (of male virility)]

testicular *adj.* relating to or affecting the testicles.

testify *verb* (**testifies, testified**) **1** *intrans.* to give evidence in court. **2** (**testify to something**) to serve as evidence or proof of it. **3** *intrans.* to make a solemn declaration (eg of one's faith). **4** to declare solemnly: *testify one's sorrow.* [from Latin *testificari*, from *testis*, witness]

testily *adv.* in a testy way.

testimonial *noun* **1** a letter or certificate giving details of one's character, conduct, and qualifications. **2** a gift presented (often in public) as a sign of respect or as a tribute to personal qualities or services.

testimony *noun* (PL. **testimonies**) **1** a statement made under oath, especially in a law court. **2** evidence: *a testimony to her intelligence.* **3** a declaration of truth or fact. [from Latin *testimonium*, from *testis*, witness]

testiness *noun* being testy.

testing *noun* the assessment of an individual pupil's level of knowledge, skill, etc by a variety of methods. In schools, it may be a formal examination based on course work, or continuous assessment over a term or a year, or a combination of the two.

testis *noun* (PL. **testes**) *Anat.* in male animals, either of the two reproductive glands that produce sperm and, in vertebrates, also secrete male sex hormones, eg testosterone. During development the testes of mammals usually descend from the body cavity into the scrotum, so that the sperm are stored at slightly below body temperature. [from Latin *testis*]

test match in various sports, especially cricket, a match forming one of a series played by the same two international teams.
◇ Test matches are played regularly between the major cricketing nations: England, Australia, New Zealand, West Indies, India, and Pakistan.

testosterone *noun Physiol.* the main male sex hormone, a steroid that is secreted primarily by the testes. It controls the growth and funtioning of the male sex organs, and the appearance of male secondary sexual characteristics such as beard growth and deepening of the voice. [from Latin *testis*, testicle]

test paper **1** a list of questions forming a short, minor examination. **2** paper which has been soaked in some substance so that it changes colour when it comes into contact with certain chemicals.

test pilot a pilot who tests new aircraft by flying them.

test tube a thin glass tube closed at one end, used in chemical tests or experiments.

test-tube baby **1** *Medicine* a baby born as a result of fertilization (under laboratory conditions) of one of the mother's ova by male sperm, followed by implantation of the fertilized ovum in the mother's uterus (womb). **2** formerly, a child born as a result of artificial insemination.

testy *adj.* (**testier, testiest**) irritable; bad-tempered; touchy. [from Old French *testif*, headstrong]

tetanus *noun* **1** *Medicine* an infectious and potentially fatal disease caused by the bacterium *Clostridium tetani*, which usually enters the body through a wound and releases a toxin that affects the nervous system. The main symptoms are fever and painful muscle spasms that result in rigidity, especially of the mouth and facial muscles, and may lead to convulsions and inability to breathe. — Also called *lockjaw*. **2** the state of prolonged contraction of a muscle caused by rapidly repeated stimuli. [from Greek *tetanos*, from *teinein*, to stretch]

tetchily *adv.* in a tetchy way.

tetchiness *noun* being tetchy.

tetchy *adj.* (**tetchier, tetchiest**) irritable; peevish.

tête-à-tête — *noun* (PL. **tête-à-têtes**) a private conversation or meeting between two people. — *adj., adv.* in private; intimate, intimately. [from French *tête-à-tête*, head to head]

tether — *noun* a rope or chain for tying an animal to a post or confining it to a particular spot. — *verb* (**tethered, tethering**) to tie or restrain with a tether.
— **at the end of one's tether** having reached the limit of one's patience, strength, resources, etc.
[from Norse *tjothr*]

Tet Offensive a campaign (Jan–Feb 1968) in the Vietnam War. On 30 Jan 1968, the Buddhist 'Tet' holiday, the Viet Cong launched an attack against US bases and more than 100 S Vietnamese towns, including the US Embassy in Saigon and the city of Hue. US public opinion was shocked by the scale of death and destruction, and support for the war declined rapidly. The offensive proved to be a turning-point in the war: on 31 Mar 1968, President Lyndon B Johnson announced an end to escalation and a new readiness to negotiate.

Tétouan *or* **Tetuán** POP (1992e) 864 000, a city in Tétouan prefecture, Nord-Ouest province, NE Morocco. It lies 60km/37mi SE of Tangier. HISTORY settled by Moorish exiles from Spain in the 15c; captured by the Spanish in 1860.

tetra *noun* any of many small colourful freshwater fish from S and Central America, about 3cm to 10cm in length. It is a popular aquarium fish. [a shortening of the former genus name *Tetragonopterus*]

tetra- *combining form* forming words meaning 'four'. [from Greek *tetra-*, from *tettares*, four]

tetrachloromethane *noun Chem.* (FORMULA CCl_4) a toxic colourless strong-smelling liquid, insoluble in water, formerly used as a solvent for fats, waxes, laquers, and rubber, as a dry-cleaning reagent, and in certain types of fire-extinguisher. It is now known to be carcinogenic, and has been largely replaced by safer chemicals. — Also called *carbon tetrachloride*.

tetracycline *noun Medicine* any of a group of antibiotics obtained from *Streptomyces* bacteria and used to treat a wide range of bacterial infections, eg acne, respiratory infections, syphilis.

tetrad *noun* a group of four. [from Greek *tetras*]

tetragon *noun* a plane figure with four angles and four sides. [from Greek *tetragonon*]

Tetragrammaton *noun* the Hebrew name of God written using four letters, in the English alphabet given as either YHWH (Yahweh) or JHVH (Jehovah). [from Greek, from *tetra-*, four + *gramma*, letter]

tetrahedron *noun* a solid figure having four plane faces with three angles each; a three-sided pyramid. [from Greek *tetraedron*]

tetrameter *noun* a line of verse with four measures. [from Greek *tetrametros*, from *tetra-*, four + *metron*, measure]

tetrapod *noun Zool.* an animal with four limbs, adapted for living on land. Tetrapods include amphibians, reptiles, birds, and mammals. [from Greek *tetrapous*, four-footed]

Tetzel, Johann (c.1465–1519) German monk, born in Pirna, Saxony. He became a Dominican in 1489, and was appointed in 1516 to sell indulgences to raise money for the building of St Peter's in Rome. This he did with great ostentation, which provoked Martin Luther's 95 Wittenberg theses, and his own reply.

Teuton *noun* **1** any speaker of a Germanic language. **2** *Hist.* a member of an ancient Germanic tribe from N Europe. [from Latin *Teutoni* or *Teutones*, the Teutons]

Teutonic — *adj.* **1** relating to the Germanic languages or peoples speaking these languages. **2** German. — *noun* Germanic.

Teutonic Knights members of the Order of St Mary of the Germans, a religious-military order founded c.1190 and inspired by crusading ideals. By the 14c they controlled the E Baltic lands of the Livonian Knights, Prussia, and E Pomerania. The Order was dissolved in Germany in 1809, but re-established in Austria in 1834.

Te Wahipounamu a national park in South Island, New Zealand. It incorporates the former national parks of Westland, Mount Cook, and Fiordland. It is a World Heritage site.

Tex. *abbrev.* Texas.

Texas POP (1990) 17.7m, a state in SW USA, which is divided into 254 counties. AREA 691 003sq km/266 807sq mi. It is known as the 'Lone Star State' and is the second-largest state in the USA. CAPITAL Austin. CHIEF TOWNS Houston, Dallas, San Antonio, El Paso, Fort Worth. PHYSICAL DESCRIPTION bounded SE by the Gulf of Mexico and SW by Mexico; rivers include the Red, Sabine, Trinity, Brazos, and Colorado; the Rio Grande forms the state's entire international border with Mexico; the Davis and Guadalupe Mts lie in the extreme W; the highest point is Guadalupe Peak (2 667m); much of the E is hilly, forested country with cypress swamps and cotton and rice cultivation; extensive oil fields underlie the land here; the Gulf coastal plains around Houston are heavily industrialized; heavy industry in the drier S coastal region; intensive agriculture in the irrigated lower Rio Grande Valley, producing citrus fruits and winter vegetables; the richest agricultural land is in the centre and N (the Blackland prairies); the S central plains and Edwards Plateau have vast wheat and cotton farms and cattle ranches; the far N is dry, barren, and mountainous. HISTORY first settled by the Spanish in the late 1600s; first American settlement in 1821; American rebellion after a request for separate statehood was turned down by Mexico in 1835; Texas declared independence, but defeated by Mexican General Santa Anna at

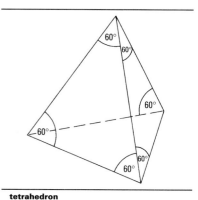

tetrahedron

the Alamo in 1836; Mexican army then defeated by Sam Houston at San Jacinto in 1836; independence of Texas was recognized; an independent republic for 10 years; admitted to the Union as the 28th state in 1845; US–Mexican War, with Mexican defeats at Palo Alto and Resaca de la Palma; joined the Confederate states in the Civil War (the only state not to be overrun by Union troops); re-admitted to the Union in 1870; the economy was transformed in 1901 by the discovery of extensive oil deposits. ECONOMY the nation's leading producer of oil and natural gas; chemicals; processed foods; machinery; fabricated metals; major producer of cattle, sheep, and cotton; wheat, sorghum, rice, vegetables; dairy produce; fishing; tourism.

Tex-Mex *adj., said of food, music, etc* typically Mexican but with elements either taken from, or adapted through contact with, American culture.

text *noun* **1** the main body of printed words in a book as opposed to the notes, illustrations, etc. **2** the actual words of an author or piece of written work as opposed to commentary on them. **3** a short passage from the Bible taken as the starting-point for a sermon or quoted in authority. **4** a theme or subject. **5** a book, novel, play, etc forming part of a course of study. **6** the words written or displayed on a visual display unit. [from Latin *texere*, to weave]

textbook *noun* **1** a book containing the standard principles and information of a subject. **2** (*attributive*) conforming to or as if conforming to the guidance of a textbook; exemplary.

textile — *noun* **1** any cloth or fabric made by weaving or knitting. **2** fibre, yarn, etc suitable for weaving into cloth. — *adj.* of, relating to, manufacturing, or suitable for being woven into, such cloth. [from Latin *textilis*, from *texere*, to weave]

text linguistics the study of the structure of all forms of linguistic text which have a communicative function, eg essays, notices, road signs, scripts, poems, and conversations. This includes analysis of the ways in which elements of the text cohere in a sequence, and of the ways in which the content is structured from the point of view of grammar, vocabulary, pronunciation, and graphic layout.

textual *adj.* relating to, found in, or based on a text or texts.

textually *adv.* **1** in or as regards the text. **2** in the words of the text.

textural *adj.* relating to texture.

texture — *noun* **1** the way the surface of a material or substance feels when touched. **2** the way that a piece of cloth looks or feels, caused by the way in which it is woven. **3** the structure of a substance as formed by the size and arrangement of the smaller particles which form it, especially as seen, touched, or tasted: *cheese with a crumbly texture.* **4** the structure of a piece of music, writing, work of art, etc as formed by the individual parts which form it. — *verb* to give a particular texture to (eg food or fabric). [from Latin *texere*, to weave]

textured *adj.* having a texture.

texturize *or* **texturise** *verb* to give a particular texture to (eg food or fabric).

Tezcatlipoca in Aztec mythology, 'the smoking mirror', a malevolent sorcerer who introduced the custom of human sacrifice to Mexico. He was the enemy and opposite of Quetzalcoatl, and had the animal form of a jaguar.

TGV *abbrev. train à grande vitesse* (French), a high-speed rail service which began in 1981 on the Paris–Lyon line. A second service was launched in 1990 running between Paris, Le Mans, and Tours. In the same year, a TGV train broke the world speed record. In May 1993, the first section of the proposed high-speed rail link between London and Paris was opened, between Paris and Lille. TGV trains carry passengers at a maximum

cruising speed of 300kph/186mph. [French, = high-speed train]

TGWU *abbrev.* Transport and General Workers' Union.

Th *symbol Chem.* thorium.

Th. *abbrev.* Thursday.

-th¹ *or* **-eth** *suffix* forming ordinal numbers and fractions from cardinal numbers: *fourth / one fiftieth.* [from Anglo-Saxon *-tha, -the*]

-th² *suffix* forming nouns denoting an action or process, or a state or condition: *death / filth / width.* [from Anglo-Saxon *-thu, -tho, -th*]

Thabana-Ntlenyana, Mount *or* **Mount Thadentsonyane** a mountain in E Lesotho, in the Drakensberg Mts. HEIGHT 3 482m. It is the highest peak in Lesotho and the highest peak in Africa S of Mt Kilimanjaro.

Thackeray,   William   Makepeace (1811–63) English novelist, born in Calcutta, India. He became a journalist, and first attracted attention with his work in *Punch* (1842), in which he exploited the theme of English snobbery and the view of society as seen by the butler ('Jeames's Diary'). His major novels, which were all published as monthly serials, include *Vanity Fair* (1847–8), *Pendennis* (1848), *Henry Esmond* (1852), and *The Newcomes* (1853–5). In 1860 he became the first editor of *The Cornhill Magazine*, where much of his later work appeared.

Thai — *noun* the official language of Thailand, the largest of the Tai language family of SE Asia. It is spoken by c.30 million people and has a wide range of dialects. — *adj.* relating to or spoken or written in Thai.

Thailand, Thai **Muang Thai**, formerly **Siam**, official name **Kingdom of Thailand** POP (1992e) 57.8m, a kingdom in SE Asia, which is divided into 72 provinces (*changwats*). AREA 513 115sq km/198 062sq mi. It is situated N and W of the Gulf of Thailand and bounded W by the Andaman Sea, W and NW by Burma (Myanma), NE and E by Laos, E by Cambodia, and S by Malaysia. CAPITAL Bangkok. CHIEF TOWNS Chiang Mai, Nakhon Ratchasima. TIME ZONE GMT +7. Ethnic groups include Thai (75%) and Chinese (14%); Buddhism is the chief religion. OFFICIAL LANGUAGE Thai. CURRENCY the baht. PHYSICAL DESCRIPTION the central agricultural region is dominated by the floodplain of the Chao Praya R; a NE plateau rises above 300m and covers one third of the country; mountainous N region rising to 2 595m at Doi Inthanon; a narrow, low-lying S region separates the Andaman Sea from the Gulf of Thailand and is covered in tropical rainforest; mangrove-forested islands off the coast. CLIMATE equatorial climate in the S; tropical monsoon climate in the N and centre. HISTORY evidence of Bronze Age communities in 4 000 BC; the Thai nation was founded in the 13c; it is the only country in S and SE Asia to have escaped colonization by a European power; occupied by the Japanese during World War II; military-controlled government for most of the time after 1945; mass demonstrations in 1992 resulted in the fall of the military-controlled government and led to a reduction in the power of the military. GOVERNMENT the King is head of state, advised by a 12-member Privy Council; governed by a Prime Minister, a Cabinet, and a bicameral National Assembly consisting of a 347-member House of Representatives and a 264-member Senate. ECONOMY agriculture is the most important economic activity; rice, manioc, maize, bananas, pineapple, sugar cane; rubber, teak; textiles; electronics; cement; chemicals; food processing; tourism; tin (world's third-largest supplier), tungsten (world's second-largest supplier), manganese, antimony, lead, zinc, copper, natural gas.

thalamus *noun* (PL. **thalami**) *Anat.* in the forebrain of vertebrates, either of two egg-shaped masses of grey matter that lie within the cerebral

hemispheres. The thalamus relays sensory nerve impulses to the cerebral cortex. [from Greek *thalamos*, inner room, bedroom]

thalassaemia   or   thalassemia   *noun* *Medicine* a hereditary disorder, most common in the Mediterranean region, characterized by the presence of an abnormal form of haemoglobin in the red blood cells. The main symptom is anaemia, which may be severe if the disorder is inherited from both parents. [from Greek *thalassa*, sea + *haima*, blood]

thalassotherapy *noun* a form of treatment to detoxify and relax the body, involving the application of mud and seaweed compresses, seawater baths, and massage. [from Greek *thalassa*, sea]

Thaleia see THALIA.

Thales (c.620–c.555 BC) Greek natural philosopher, traditionally regarded as the first philosopher, born in Miletus. His mercantile journeys took him to Egypt and Babylon, where he acquired land-surveying and astronomical techniques, and is said to have predicted the solar eclipse in 585 BC. None of his writings survive, but Aristotle attributes to him the doctrine that water is the original substance from which all things are derived.

Thalia *or* **Thaleia** in Greek mythology, the Muse of comedy and idyllic poetry.

thalidomide *noun* a drug formerly used as a sedative but withdrawn in 1961 because it was found to cause malformation of the fetus if taken by the mother in early pregnancy.

thallium *noun Chem.* (SYMBOL **Tl**, ATOMIC NUMBER **81**) a soft bluish-white metal that is used in electronic equipment, experimental alloys, and optical glass. Its compounds, which are highly poisonous, are used as pesticides. [from Greek *thallos*, a green shoot, so called because of the bright green line in its spectrum]

thalloid *adj. Bot.* relating to a thallus.

thallus *noun* (PL. **thalluses**, **thalli**) *Biol.* in fungi, lichens, seaweeds, etc, a flattened and sometimes branched structure that is not differentiated into stems, leaves, and roots. [from Greek *thallos*, young shoot]

Thames, River, Latin **Tamesis** a river in S England, length 352km/219mi. It rises in the Cotswold Hills, SE Gloucestershire; flows E and SE through Oxfordshire, Berkshire, Surrey, and Greater London; approaches the North Sea in a long, wide estuary between Essex and the N coast of Kent; navigable as far as London by large ships. Chief tributaries include the Cherwell, Thame, Lea, Colne, Roding, Kennet, Mole, Wey, and Medway rivers; the upper part beyond Oxford is often called the Isis; it is joined by the Grand Union Canal near Brentford. The river is known as the *Pool* at London Bridge. Two embankments were built at London, from Blackfriars Bridge to Westminster (1864), and from Westminster Bridge to Vauxhall (1866). A tidal barrier was constructed across the approach to London in 1983 to reduce the risk of floods. The Thames Conservancy Board was established

Thailand

in 1857; administration of the river below Teddington was given to the Port of London Authority in 1908. [from Latin *tamesis*, dark river]

Thames Barrier in the UK, a movable tidal barrier built (1983) across the R Thames at Woolwich, near London, to reduce the risk of floods to the city. Spanning 520m, it consists of curved gates which can be rotated into position, and is the largest tidal barrier in the world.

than — *conj.* **1** used to introduce the second part of a comparison, or that part which is taken as the basis of a comparison: *she is older than he is.* **2** used to introduce the second, and usually less desirable or rejected, option in a statement of alternatives: *would rather go swimming than play football.* **3** except; other than: *be left with no alternative than to resign.* — *prep.* in comparison with: *someone older than him.* [from Anglo-Saxon *thonne*]

thanatology *noun Medicine* the medical and legal study of death, its causes and phenomena. [from Greek *thanatos*, death + -LOGY]

thane *noun Hist.* **1** in Anglo-Saxon England, a person holding land from the king or some other superior in exchange for military service. **2** a person holding land from a Scottish king, (but not in return for military service); a Scottish feudal lord. [from Anglo-Saxon *thegn*]

Thanet, Isle of POP (1987e) 127 000, an urban area in E Kent, SE England, in which the towns of Margate, Broadstairs, and Ramsgate are situated. It was originally an island.

thank — *verb* **1** to express gratitude to: *thanked him for his help.* **2** to hold responsible for: *have only yourself to thank for your failure.* — *noun* (*usually* **thanks**) **1** gratitude or an expression of gratitude. **2** thank you: *thanks for the present.*
— **no thanks to someone** *or* **something** in spite of them; no gratitude being due to them.
thank God *or* **goodness** *or* **heavens** an expression of relief.
thanks to ... as a result of ...; because of ...
thank you a polite expression acknowledging a gift, help, or offer.
[from Anglo-Saxon *thancian*]

thankful *adj.* grateful; relieved and happy.

thankfully *adv.* **1** in a thankful manner. **2** in a way that invites one's thanks: *thankfully, it didn't rain.*

thankfulness *noun* being thankful.

thankless *adj.* bringing no thanks, pleasure, or profit.

thanklessly *adv.* in a thankless way.

thanklessness *noun* being thankless.

thanksgiving *noun* **1** a formal act of giving thanks, especially to God. **2** (**Thanksgiving** *or* **Thanksgiving Day**) *North Amer.* a public holiday for giving thanks, occurring on the fourth Thursday in November in the USA and the second Monday in October in Canada.

Thant, U (1909–74) Burmese diplomat, born in Pantanaw. He was a teacher who took up government work when Burma became independent (1948), and became the country's United Nations representative (1957). His period as Secretary-General of the UN (1962–71) was marked by his major diplomatic role during the Cuban crisis, the formulation of a plan to end the Congolese Civil War (1962), and the mobilization of a UN peace-keeping force in Cyprus (1964).

Thapsus, Battle of a battle (46 BC) in N Africa in which the forces of Julius Caesar won a decisive victory over those of Pompey. It paved the way for Caesar's dictatorship.

Thar Desert *or* **(Great) Indian Desert** an arid region in NW India and E Pakistan, S Asia. AREA c.320 000sq km/124 000sq mi; 800km/500mi long and 400km/250mi wide. It lies between the Aravalli Range in the E and the Indus and Sutlej rivers to the W. The desert is bounded S by the Rann of Kutch and crossed by irrigation canals in

the N and W, the largest of which is the Rajasthan Canal.

Tharp, Twyla (1941–) US dancer, choreographer, and director, born in Portland, Indiana. She studied with Martha Graham and Merce Cunningham, and danced with Paul Taylor's company (1963–5). Then she formed her own group, and made new work for other ballet and modern dance companies, eg the American Theatre Ballet. Flippant, throwaway movement and humour in her works disguises meticulous structure and comment on social issues, as in *Push Comes to Shove* (1976). Her work also includes the dance in the films *Hair* (1979) and *White Nights* (1985).

that — *adj.* (PL. **those**) **1** indicating the thing, person, or idea already mentioned, specified, or understood. **2** indicating someone or something that is farther away or is in contrast: *not this book, but that one.* — *pron.* (PL. **those**) **1** the person, thing, or idea just mentioned, already spoken of, or understood. **2** a relatively distant or more distant person, thing, or idea. — *rel. pron.* used instead of *which, who,* or *whom,* to introduce a relative clause which defines, distinguishes, or restricts the person or thing mentioned in the preceding clause: *all the children that were late.* — *conj.* used to introduce a noun clause, or a clause showing reason, purpose, consequence, a result, or expressing a wish or desire: *spoke so quickly that no one could understand / oh, that the holiday would never end!* — *adv.* **1** to the degree or extent shown or understood: *won't reach that far.* **2** *colloq., dialect* to such a degree that; so: *they are that unsociable they never leave the house.*
— **all that** *colloq.* very: *not all that good.*
that's that that is the end of the matter.
[from Anglo-Saxon *thæt*]

thatch — *noun* **1** a roof covering of straw, reeds, etc. **2** anything resembling such a roof, especially thick hair on the head. — *verb trans., intrans.* to cover (a roof or building) with thatch. [from Anglo-Saxon *theccan*]

Thatcher, Margaret (Hilda) Thatcher, Baroness, *née* **Roberts** (1925–) English Conservative politician and Prime Minister (1979–90), born in Grantham, Lincolnshire. She worked as a research chemist, was called to the Bar (1954), entered parliament (1959), and was Minister of Education (1970–4). In 1975 she replaced Edward Heath to become the first woman party leader in British politics. Under her leadership, the Conservative Party moved towards a more right-wing position. Her 11-year government instituted the privatization of nationalized industries and national utilities, tried to institute a market in state-provided health care and education, and reduced the role of local government as a provider of services. Elected for a third term of office in 1987, by 1988 she had become the longest-serving premier of the 20c. She resigned (Nov 1990) following a challenge to her leadership as a result of the controversy which followed her opposition to full monetary and economic union with Europe, and she did not stand for parliament in the 1992 election.

thatcher *noun* a person who thatches.

Thatta monuments a group of monuments in Thatta, the former capital of Sind in present-day Pakistan. The monuments include the 17c Great Mosque built by Shah Jahan, and graves in the 'City of Mausoleums', a necropolis covering 15sq km/6sq mi. It is a World Heritage site.

thaw — *verb* **1** *trans., intrans. said of snow or ice* to melt or cause it to melt. **2** *trans., intrans.* (*also* **thaw out** *or* **thaw something out**) *said of anything frozen, eg food* to become or cause it to become unfrozen; to defrost. **3** *intrans.* to become warm enough to begin to melt snow and ice: *it is beginning to thaw.* **4** *trans., intrans.* (*also* **thaw out** *or* **thaw something out**) to make or become less stiff and numb with cold. **5** *trans.,*

intrans. (*also* **thaw out** *or* **thaw something out**) to make or become more friendly or relaxed. — *noun* **1** an act or process of thawing. **2** a period of weather warm enough to begin to thaw ice and snow. [from Anglo-Saxon *thawian*]

the — *definite article* **1** used to refer to a particular person or thing, or group of people or things, already mentioned, implied, or known. **2** used to refer to a unique person or thing: *the Pope.* **3** used before a singular noun to refer to all the members of that group or class: *a history of the novel.* **4** used before certain titles and proper names. **5** used before an adjective or noun describing an identified person: *William the Conqueror.* **6** used after a preposition to refer to a unit of quantity, time, etc: *a car which does forty miles to the gallon / paid by the hour.* — *adv.* **1** used before comparative adjectives or adverbs to indicate (by) so much or (by) how much: *the sooner the better.* **2** used before superlative adjectives and adverbs to indicate an amount beyond all others: *like this book the best.* [from Anglo-Saxon *the,* who, which, that, replacing *se,* that]

Thea a female first name. [from the Greek word meaning 'goddess']

theatre *noun* **1** a building or area outside specially designed for the performance of plays, operas, etc. **2** a large room with seats rising in tiers, eg for lectures. **3** (*also* **the theatre**) the writing and production of plays in general. **4** *Brit.* a specially equipped room in a hospital where surgery is performed. **5** a scene of action or place where events take place: *theatre of war.* **6** (**the theatre**) the world and profession of actors and theatre companies. **7** *North Amer.* a cinema. [from Greek *theatron,* from *theaesthai,* to see]
◇ In Renaissance Italy, plays were produced indoors for the first time, and from the 16c new theatres were built all over Europe. With the development of the proscenium arch, scenic illusion played a dominant role in Western theatre, although this pictorial tradition has been appropriated to a large extent by film and television in the 20c. This has led to a rediscovery in modern western theatre of the effectiveness of open stages, emblematic staging, and the direct presentational styles of such popular forms as the *commedia dell'arte* and the mumming play. The influence of ancient and high-developed theatrical traditions, such as those found in Chinese, Indian, and Japanese theatre, is also strongly evident in much more modern theatre.

theatre-in-the-round *noun Theatr.* a style of staging plays in a theatre with a central stage surrounded on all sides by the audience. Modern theatre-in-the-round developed in the 1930s, particularly for avant-garde productions in Russia, England, and the USA.

Theatre of the Absurd, a term for certain plays of the 1950s, in which the absurdity of man's condition was mirrored in a dramatic form of unreal situations without traditional narrative continuity or meaningful and coherent dialogue. The term is applied to works by Samuel Beckett (notably *Waiting for Godot,* 1953), Eugène Ionesco, Jean Genet, Arthur Adamov, and Harold Pinter. See also ABSURDISM.

Theatre Workshop an English theatre company founded (1945) by Joan Littlewood in Manchester. Based in London at the Theatre Royal, Stratford East, from 1953, it is best remembered for such shows as *The Hostage* and *Oh, What a Lovely War.* The company finally dispersed in 1973.

theatrical — *adj.* **1** of theatres or acting. **2** *said of behaviour, a gesture, etc* done only for effect; artificial and exaggerated. — *noun* (**theatricals**) dramatic performances.

theatricality *noun* a theatrical quality.

theatrically *adv.* in a theatrical way.

Thebes 1 the ancient capital of Upper Egypt, which was situated on the R Nile, where the town of Luxor now stands. It is the location of many pharaonic temples and tombs, including Tutankhamen's. It is a World Heritage site. **2** in ancient Greece, one of the most powerful city-states in Boeotia. It is prominent in Greek legend (the Oedipus cycle is based there), and though in historical times it was rarely able to rival Athens and Sparta, under Epaminondas in the 370s BC it succeeded briefly in being the leading power in Greece. It is now the capital town of Boeotia department, SE Greece, 52km/32mi NW of Athens.

thee *pron. old use, dialect* the objective form of *thou*. [from Anglo-Saxon]

theft *noun* **1** stealing; an act of stealing. **2** something stolen. [from Anglo-Saxon *thiefth*]
◇ In law, theft is the dishonest taking of property belonging to another person, with the intention of permanently depriving that person of the property.

their *adj.* **1** of or belonging to them. **2** his or her: *has everyone got their books with them?* [from Norse *thierra*]

theirs *pron.* a person or thing that belongs to them.
— **of theirs** belonging to them.

theism *noun* the belief in the existence of God or a god, especially one revealed supernaturally to man. See also DEISM. [from Greek *theos*, god]
◇ Theism is a feature of Jewish, Islamic, and Christian faith, and is contrasted with both *deism* and *pantheism*. All adhere to the belief in a single divine being, transcendent and personal, who created the world, and who, although involved with it and related to the creation, is distinct from it. This creator is intelligent, powerful, and moral, and can act through his creation for the good of mankind; as a personal being he can also reveal himself to humans.

theist *noun* a person who believes in theism.

theistic *adj.* relating to or involving theism.

Thelma a female first name, popularized by the 19c novelist Marie Corelli. [perhaps from Greek *thelems*, will]

them — *pron.* **1** people or things already mentioned or spoken about, or understood or implied. **2** *colloq., dialect* those. **3** *old use* themselves. — *adj. colloq., dialect* those. [from Norse *thiem*]

theme *noun* **1** the subject of a discussion, speech, or piece of writing. **2** *Mus.* a short melody which forms the basis of a piece of music and which is developed and repeated with variations. **3** a repeated or recurring image or idea in literature or art. **4** a brief essay or written exercise. [from Greek *thema*]

theme park a large amusement park in which all of the rides and attractions are based on a particular theme, such as outer space.
◇ The first theme park was Disneyland, at Anaheim, California, opened in 1955 and based on Walt Disney's cartoon characters.

theme song *or* **theme tune** a song or melody that is associated with, and usually played at the beginning and end of, a film, television, or radio programme, or which is associated with a particular character.

Themis in Greek mythology, the goddess of established law and justice, often depicted carrying a pair of scales. She was the second consort of Zeus, and the mother of the Horae and the Moerae.

Themistocles (c.523–c.458 BC) Athenian politician and naval strategist. He persuaded the Athenians to develop Piraeus as a port (493 BC) and use their rich silver deposits to expand their fleet (483 BC). The fleet won a naval victory over the Persians at Salamis (480 BC), and laid the foundations of the Athenian maritime empire. The pro-Spartan faction in Athens plotted his downfall after he had persuaded the city to raise

the height of its walls (c.470 BC) and he was ostracized and fled to Asia.

themselves *pron.* **1** the reflexive form of *they* and *them*: *they helped themselves.* **2** used for emphasis: *they did it themselves.* **3** their normal selves: *they aren't feeling themselves today.* **4** *colloq.* himself or herself: *nobody needs to blame themselves.*

then — *adv.* **1** at that time. **2** soon or immediately after that: *looked at him, then turned away.* **3** in that case; that being so; as a necessary consequence: *what would we do then?* / *if you're tired, then you should rest.* **4** also; in addition. **5** used to continue a narrative after a break or digression: *by the time she got to the top, then, it had started to snow.* **6** used especially at the end of questions which ask for an explanation, opinion, etc, or which ask for or assume agreement: *your mind is made up, then?* / *that was a bit of a shock, then, wasn't it?* — *noun* that time: *until then.* — *adj.* being or acting at that time: *the then Prime Minister.*
— **then and there** at that very time and on that very spot.
[from Anglo-Saxon *thonne*]

thence *adv. old use, formal* **1** from that place or time. **2** from that cause; therefore. [from Middle English *thennes*]

thenceforth *or* **thenceforward** *adv. old use, formal* from that time or place forwards.

theo- *combining form* forming words meaning 'of God or a god'. [from Greek *theos*, god]

theocracy *noun* (PL. **theocracies**) government by a deity or by priests representing a deity; also, a state ruled in this way. [from Greek *theos*, god + *kratos*, power]

theocrat *noun* a divine or deified ruler.

theocratic *adj.* relating to or involving theocracy.

theocratically *adv.* in a theocratic way.

Theocritus (c.310–250 BC) Greek pastoral poet, born (probably) in Syracuse. He lived in Cos, and at the court of Ptolemy II Philadelphus in Alexandria. About 30 of his poems survive, though the authenticity of some have been disputed. His short pastoral poems, representing a single scene, came to be called 'idylls' (*eidullia*), and influenced Tennyson and the pastoral poets of the Renaissance.

theodolite *noun* an instrument for measuring horizontal and vertical angles when surveying land. [from Latin *theodolitus*]

Theodora (c.500–47) Byzantine empress (527–47), a former actress and the mistress then wife of Justinian. She had considerable influence in political affairs, and intervened on behalf of Justinian during the Nika riots (532). She also introduced legislation promoting the rights of women.

Theodorakis, Mikis (1925–) Greek composer, born in Khios. His first ballet *Antigone* was produced in 1959 at Covent Garden, London. On his return to Greece (1961), he became intensely critical of the Greek musical and artistic establishment. When the right-wing government took power in 1967, he was imprisoned and his music banned, but after worldwide appeals he was released (1970). Often inspired by the history, traditions, and folk tunes of Greece, his prolific musical output includes oratorios, ballets, song cycles, and music for film scores such as *Zorba the Greek* (1965).

Theodore a female first name. [from Greek *Theodoros*, from *theos*, god + *doron*, gift]

Theodoric *or* **Theoderic**, known as **the Great** (AD 455–526) King of the Ostrogoths (471–526), who invaded Italy in 489 and defeated the barbarian ruler, Odoacer. His long reign secured tranquillity and prosperity for Italy, where the Goths and the Romans continued as distinct nations, each with its own tribunals and laws. He established his capital at Ravenna.

Theodoric a male first name. [of Germanic origin, = people-rule]

Theodosian Code a codification of the law promulgated throughout the Roman Empire in AD 438 by the emperor Theodosius II. Its 16 books summarized all the laws that had been enacted since the beginning of the reign of Constantine the Great (AD 312).

Theodosius I, also called **the Great** (c.346–95 AD) Roman emperor of the East (379–94) and sole emperor (394–5). He campaigned against the Goths but allowed them to settle south of the Danube as allies of Rome (382). He championed orthodox Christianity and in 391 ordered the closing of all pagan temples and banned all pagan cults. After the murder of Western emperor Valentinian II (392), Theodosius marched against and defeated the puppet emperor Eugenius (394), and ruled as sole Roman emperor until his death.

Theodosius II (401–50 AD) Eastern Roman emperor (408–50), the grandson of Theodosius I and, like him, a champion of orthodox Christianity. He is chiefly remembered for his codification of the Roman law (the Theodosian Code, 438).

theolinguistics *sing. noun* the study of language used in the theory and practice of religious belief, eg by theologians, biblical scholars, ministers and preachers, etc.

theologian *noun* a person who studies, or is an expert in, theology.

theological *adj.* relating to or involving theology.

theologically *adv.* in a theological way; as regards theology.

theology *noun* (PL. **theologies**) **1** the study of God, religion, religious belief, and revelation. **2** a particular system of theology and religion: *Catholic theology.* [from Greek *theos*, god + *logos*, word, reason]
◇ In Christianity, it is understood as the systematic clarification of the historical beliefs of the Church. It has been divided into natural theology, ie that which can be known about God from nature or by reason alone, and revealed theology, ie that which can only be known through the self-disclosure or revelation of God.

Theophrastus (c.372–286 BC) Greek philosopher, born in Eresus, Lesbos. He studied under Plato in Athens, and became the close friend of Aristotle, and head of the Peripatetic school after Aristotle's death. He was responsible for preserving many of Aristotle's works, along with many fragments of the works of the Presocratics.

theorbo *noun* a type of large lute with six strings above a fretted fingerboard, and seven or eight additional unstopped bass strings with a separate pegbox. It was widely used in the 17c as a continuo instrument. [from Italian *teorba*, variant of *tuorba*, travelling bag]

theorem *noun Maths.* a scientific or mathematical statement which makes certain assumptions in order to explain observed phenomena, and which has been proved to be correct. [from Greek *theorema*, subject for contemplation]

theoretical *or* **theoretic** *adj.* **1** concerned with or based on theory rather than practical knowledge or experience. **2** existing in theory only; hypothetical. **3** dealing with theory only; speculative.

theoretically *adv.* in a theoretical way; in terms of theory rather than practice.

theoretician *noun* someone who specializes in or is concerned with the theoretical aspects of a subject rather than its practical use.

theorist *noun* **1** a person who speculates or invents theories. **2** a theoretician.

theorize *or* **theorise** *verb intrans.* to devise theories; to speculate.

theory *noun* (PL. **theories**) **1** a series of ideas and general principles which seek to explain some aspect of the world: *theory of relativity*. **2** an idea or explanation which has not yet been proved; a conjecture. **3** the general and usually abstract principles or ideas of a subject: *music theory*. **4 a** ideal, hypothetical, or abstract situation. **b** ideal, hypothetical, or abstract reasoning: *a good idea in theory*. [from Greek *theoria*, from *theoreein*, to view]

theosophic *or* **theosophical** *adj.* relating to or involving theosophy.

theosophically *adv.* in a theosophical way.

theosophist *noun* a person who believes in theosophy.

theosophy *noun* (PL. **theosophies**) a religious philosophy which is based on the belief that a knowledge of God can be achieved through intuition, mysticism, and divine inspiration, especially a modern movement which combines this with elements from Hinduism and Buddhism, such as a belief in reincarnation. [from Greek *theos*, god + *sophia*, wisdom]

Thera see SANTORINI.

therapeutic *adj.* **1** of, concerning, or contributing to the healing and curing of disease. **2** bringing a feeling of general well-being. [from Greek *therapeuein*, to take care of, to heal]

therapeutically *adv.* in a therapeutic way.

therapeutics *sing. noun Medicine* the branch of medicine concerned with the treatment and cure of diseases.

therapist *noun Medicine* a person who treats physical or mental diseases and disorders of a particular kind by means other than surgery or drugs, eg speech therapist, physiotherapist.

therapy *noun* (PL. **therapies**) the treatment of physical or mental diseases and disorders by means other than surgery or drugs. [from Greek *therapeuein*, to take care of, to heal]

Theravada the form of Buddhism commonly found in S Asia (Sri Lanka, Burma, Thailand, Cambodia, and Laos). Its doctrines remain essentially as they were in the 3c BC, and it is generally distinguished from the later Mahayana Buddhism in its rejection of the theory of Bodhisattvas.

there — *adv.* **1** at, in, or to a place or position. **2** at that point in speech, a piece of writing, performance, etc: *don't stop there*. **3** in that respect: *I agree with him there*. **4** used to begin a sentence when the subject of the verb follows the verb instead of coming before it: *there are no mistakes in this*. **5** used at the beginning of a sentence to emphasise or call attention to that sentence: *there goes the last bus*. **6** used after a noun for emphasis: *that book there is the one you need*. **7** *colloq., dialect* used between a noun and *this* or *that*, etc for emphasis: *that there tractor*. — *noun* that place or point. — *interj.* used to express sympathy, satisfaction, approval, encouragement, etc or to comfort.

— **have been there before** *slang* to have been in the same, especially unpleasant, situation before.

there and then at that very time and on that very spot.

there you are 1 *said when giving something to someone* this is what you need or want. **2** expressing satisfaction or triumph.
[from Anglo-Saxon *thær*]

thereabouts *or* **thereabout** *adv.* near that place, number, amount, degree, or time.

thereafter *adv. formal* from that time on.

thereby *adv. formal* **1** by that means. **2** in consequence.

therefore *adv.* for that reason; as a consequence.

therein *adv. formal* in or into that or it.

thereof *adv. formal* of or from that or it.

thereon *adv. formal* on or onto that or it.

Theresa *or* **Teresa** a female first name. [possibly of Greek origin, connected with the island of *Therasia*; the spelling *Teresa* is influenced by the Italian and Spanish forms, and in particular by the name of St Teresa of Avila]

Theresa (of Calcutta), Mother, originally **Agnes Gonxha Bojaxhiu** (1910–) Roman Catholic nun and missionary in India, born in Yugoslavia. She went to India in 1928, taught at a convent school in Calcutta, and took her final vows in 1937. She became principal of the school, but left in 1948 to work alone in the slums. After medical training in Paris, she opened her first school for destitute children in Calcutta, started the Missionaries of Charity sisterhood (1950), opened her House for the Dying (1952), and in 1957 began work with lepers and in many disaster areas of the world. She was awarded the Pope John XXIII Peace Prize in 1971, and the Nobel Peace Prize in 1979.

Theresa of Lisieux, originally (**Marie Françoise**) **Thérèse Martin**, also called **the Little Flower**, and **St Theresa of the Child Jesus** (1873–97) French saint, born in Alençon. A religious child, she entered the Carmelite convent of Lisieux in Normandy at the age of 15, and remained there until her death from tuberculosis nine years later. She wrote an account of her life (*Histoire d'une me*, Story of a Soul, 1898) which shows how the most ordinary person can attain sainthood by following her 'little way' of simple, childlike Christianity. Canonized in 1925, in 1947 she was associated with Joan of Arc as patron saint of France; her feast day is 1 Oct.

thereto *adv. formal* to that or it; in addition.

thereunder *adv. formal* under that or it.

thereupon *adv. formal* **1** on that matter or point. **2** immediately after it or that.

therm *noun* a unit of heat equal to 100 000 British thermal units, used to measure gas used or sold. [from Greek *therme*, heat]

thermal — *adj.* **1** of, caused by, or producing heat. **2** *said of clothing* designed to prevent the loss of heat from the body. — *noun* a rising current of warm air, used by birds, gliders, and hang-gliders to move upwards. [from Greek *therme*, heat]

Thermalite *noun trademark* a manufactured material used to make building-blocks, light and effective as insulation.

thermally *adv.* in a thermal way; by means of heat.

thermal printer *Comput.* a printer which uses heat-sensitive paper, producing visible characters by the action of heated wires.

thermic lance a torch-like cutting device for resistant steel and alloys which depends on the fact that iron will burn in oxygen. It consists of a main nozzle (for a stream of oxygen) with a subsidiary nozzle for acetylene which preheats the metal to the temperature at which it will begin to burn in the stream of oxygen.

Thermidor the *coup d'état* of 16–27 Jul 1794 or 8–9 Thermidor Year II, when Robespierre and his Jacobin supporters were overthrown, ending the most radical phase of the French Revolution. The instigators of Thermidor included the former Jacobins Joseph Fouché and Paul Barras who, with members of the National Convention, set about dismantling the machinery of the Reign of Terror.

thermion *noun* an electrically charged particle emitted by an extremely hot or incandescent substance. [from Greek *therme*, heat]

thermionic *adj.* relating to thermions.

thermionic emission *Physics* the emission of electrons from a heated material, usually a metal surface.

thermionics *pl. noun Physics* the branch of electronics concerned with the study of the processes involved in thermionic emission. It is mainly concerned with the design of thermionic valves and electron guns, which draw away electrons emitted from a heated metal surface, so producing a beam of electrons that can be used for a range of different purposes.

thermionic valve *Electron.* an electron tube (vacuum tube) that emits electrons from an electrically heated cathode into a vacuum. Formerly widely used in amplifiers, switches, and other electrical devices, thermionic valves have now largely been superseded by transistors.

thermistor *noun Physics* a device in which the electrical resistance decreases rapidly as its temperature rises. Thermistors are used in electronic circuits for measuring or controlling temperature, eg electronic switches and thermometers. [a contraction of *thermal resistor*]

thermo- *combining form* forming words denoting heat. [from Greek *therme*, heat]

thermocouple *noun* a device for measuring temperature, consisting of two different metallic conductors welded together at their ends to form a loop. When the two junctions are kept at different temperatures, a voltage is generated between them, the size of which can be measured and is directly related to the temperature difference between the two junctions.

thermodynamic *adj.* relating to or involving thermodynamics.

thermodynamically *adv.* in a thermodynamic way; in terms of thermodynamics.

thermodynamics *sing. noun Physics* the branch of physics concerned with the study of the relationship between heat and other forms of energy, especially mechanical energy, and the behaviour of physical systems in which temperature is an important factor.

thermoelectric *adj.* relating to or involving thermoelectricity.

thermoelectricity *noun Electr.* an electric current generated by a difference in temperature in an electric circuit, especially between a pair of junctions where two different metals are in contact, eg a thermocouple. Thermoelectric devices incorporating a radioactive heat source are used to power heart pacemakers.

thermography *noun* **1** a technique for the conversion of invisible heat energy into a visible picture, used for military purposes, and for nocturnal studies of wildlife. **2** *Medicine* the analysis of heat emitted from the skin of a patient's body as infrared radiation, which is converted to a visible image representing warmer and cooler regions of the skin, and is used in the diagnosis of certain medical disorders, eg underlying tumours. It is widely used in mammography to detect breast cancer.

thermoluminescence dating *Archaeol.* a method of dating ancient pottery, burnt flint, calcite, and sediments by measuring the energy accumulated in the crystal lattice of its inclusions of quartz, through the breakdown over time of naturally occurring uranium.

thermometer *noun* an instrument for measuring temperature, often consisting of a narrow calibrated sealed glass tube filled with a liquid whose properties vary with temperature, eg mercury, which expands (rises) as the temperature increases, and contracts (falls) as it decreases.

thermonuclear *adj.* **1** using or showing nuclear reactions which can only be produced at extremely high temperatures. **2** relating to or involving thermonuclear weapons.

thermopile *noun Physics* a device consisting of several thermocouples connected together, that is used to detect and measure the intensity of thermal radiation.

thermoplastic — *noun Chem.* a polymer that can be repeatedly softened and hardened, without any appreciable change in its properties, by heating and cooling it. — *adj.* denoting such a material.

Thermopylae a pass between mountains and sea in central Greece. The Greeks under Leonidas held the pass for three days in the battle of Thermopylae in 480 BC before being defeated by the Persians, who went on to invade Attica, capture Athens, and sack the Acropolis.

Thermos *noun trademark* (also **Thermos flask**) a kind of vacuum flask. [from Greek *thermos*, hot]

thermosetting *adj.*, *said of plastics* becoming permanently hard after a single melting and moulding.

thermosphere *noun* the layer of the Earth's atmosphere that is situated above the mesosphere, and in which the temperature rises steadily with increasing height, although the actual heat content is very low because the air is so thin. The thermosphere includes the ionosphere.

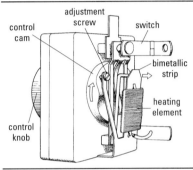

thermostat

thermostat *noun* a device that is used to maintain the temperature of a system at a constant preset level. [from THERMO- + Greek *-states*, causing to stand]

◇ A thermostat consists of a temperature sensor (usually a bimetallic strip) connected to a switching device in an electric circuit that controls the supply of electricity or fuel. If the temperature falls below the preset level, then the circuit is completed, switching the system on. When the temperature rises above the desired level, the circuit is broken, switching the system off. Thermostats are used to regulate the temperature of central heating systems in rooms and buildings, and in water heaters, ovens, refrigerators, washing machines, irons, car engines, machinery, etc.

thermostatic *adj.* relating to or operated by a thermostat.

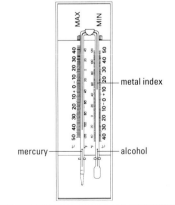

maximum and minimum thermometer

thermostatically *adv.* by means of a thermostat.

thesaurus *noun* (PL. **thesauruses, thesauri**) 1 a book which lists words and their synonyms according to sense. 2 any book, eg a dictionary or encyclopedia, which gives information about a particular field, quotations, etc. [from Greek *thesauros*, treasury]

these see THIS.

Theseus in Greek legend, a king and national hero of Athens, who features in the story of Oedipus, Procrustes, the Argonauts, and others. With Ariadne's help he killed the Minotaur; he conquered the Amazons, and married their queen, Hippolyta; later, he married Phaedra.

thesis *noun* (PL. **theses**) 1 a long written essay or report, especially one based on original research and presented for an advanced university degree such as the MSc, MLitt, or PhD. 2 an idea or proposition to be supported or upheld in argument. 3 an unproved statement put forward as a basis for argument or discussion. [from Greek *thesis*, a setting down]

Thespian — *adj.* of or relating to tragedy, or to drama and the theatre in general. — *noun facetious* an actor or actress. [from Greek *Thespis* (lived c.534 BC), Greek poet and reputed founder of Greek tragedy]

Thessalonians, Letters of Paul to the two New Testament writings of Paul to the church he founded in the capital of the Roman province of Macedonia. In the first letter (perhaps c.50 AD), he defends his earlier ministry in Thessalonica against Jewish propaganda, appears gratified at their perseverance despite persecution, and instructs them about ethical matters and Christ's second coming. The second letter (his authorship of which is disputed) is similar, but emphasizes the persecution of the community, and counters the belief that the Day of the Lord had already arrived.

Thessaloníki see SALONICA.

Thessaly, Greek **Thessalía** POP (1991) 731 000, a fertile agricultural region in E Greece, bounded W by the Pindus Mts, and E by the Aegean Sea. AREA 14 037sq km/5 418sq mi. CAPITAL Larisa. HISTORY an independent state in ancient Greece; became part of the Roman province of Macedonia; under Turkish control in the 14c; the region was annexed by Greece in 1881. In ancient times, the horses of Thessaly were renowned.

Thetford POP (1981) 20 000, a town in Breckland district, Norfolk, E England. It lies at the junction of the Thet and Ouse rivers, 20km/12mi N of Bury St Edmunds. Thetford was the 11c residence of the kings of East Anglia. NOTABLE FEATURE Ancient House Museum (15c).

Thetis in Greek mythology, a nereid loved by Zeus and Poseidon, destined to bear a son greater than his father. Because of this, she was forced to marry a mortal (Peleus), and she became the mother of Achilles.

they *pron.* 1 the people, animals, or things already spoken about or being indicated. 2 people in general. 3 people in authority. 4 *colloq.* he or she: *anyone can help if they want.* [from Norse *their*]

they'd *contr.* 1 they had. 2 they would.

they'll *contr.* 1 they will. 2 they shall.

they're *contr.* they are.

they've *contr.* they have.

thiamine *Biochem.* a member of the vitamin B complex that is found in yeast, wheatgerm, peas, beans, and green vegetables. It is required for the metabolism of carbohydrates, and deficiency of the vitamin causes the disorder beriberi. — Also called *vitamin B$_1$*. [from Greek *theion*, sulphur + AMINE]

thick — *adj.* 1 having a relatively large distance between opposite sides. 2 having a specified distance between opposite sides: *one inch thick.* 3 having a large diameter: *a thick rope.* 4 *said of a line, handwriting, etc* broad. 5 *said of liquids* containing a lot of solid matter; viscous: *thick soup.* 6 having many single units placed very close together; dense: *thick hair.* 7 difficult to see through: *thick fog.* 8 (**thick with something**) covered with or full of it: *a room thick with smoke.* 9 great in number: *insults were flying thick and fast.* 10 *said of speech* not clear. 11 *said of an accent* marked; pronounced. 12 *colloq.*, *said of a person* stupid; dull. 13 *colloq.* (**thick with someone**) friendly or intimate: *is very thick with the new manager.* 14 *colloq.* unfair: *that's a bit thick!* — *adv.* thickly. — *noun* (**the thick**) 1 the busiest, most active, or most intense part: *in the thick of the fighting.* 2 the thickest part of anything.
— **as thick as thieves** very friendly.
through thick and thin whatever happens; in spite of any difficulties.
[from Anglo-Saxon *thicce*]

thicken *verb* (**thickened, thickening**) 1 *trans.*, *intrans.* to make or become thick or thicker. 2 *intrans.* to become more complicated: *the plot thickens.*

thickening *noun* 1 something used to thicken liquid. 2 the process of making or becoming thicker. 3 a thickened part.

thicket *noun* a dense mass of bushes and trees. [from THICK]

thickhead *noun colloq.* a stupid person.

thick-headed *adj. colloq.* 1 stupid. 2 unable to think clearly because of a cold, too much alcohol, etc.

thickly *adv.* in a thick way; so as to be thick.

thickness *noun* 1 the state, quality, or degree of being thick. 2 a layer. 3 the thick part of something.

thickset *adj.* 1 heavily built; having a thick, short body. 2 growing or planted close together.

thick-skinned *adj.* not easily hurt by criticism or insults; insensitive.

thief *noun* (PL. **thieves**) a person who steals, especially secretly and often without violence. [from Anglo-Saxon *theof*]

Thiers, (Louis) Adolphe (1797–1877) French statesman and historian, born in Marseilles. He became a lawyer and journalist, then held several posts in the government of Louis Philippe, and was twice Prime Minister (1836, 1839). He supported Napoleon in 1848, but was banished in the *coup d'état* of 1851. He re-entered the Chamber in 1863 as a critic of Napoleon's policies, and after the collapse of the Second Empire became chief of the executive power in the provisional government, suppressed the Paris Commune, and was elected first President of the Third Republic (1871–3). Defeated by a coalition of monarchists, he resigned in 1873. His most ambitious literary work was the 20-volume *L'histoire du consulat et de l'empire* (History of the Consulate and the Empire, 1845–62).

Thiès 1 POP (1992e) 201 000, the capital of Thiès region, W Senegal. It lies 55km/34mi E of Dakar. The city is an African cultural and craft centre, noted for its tapestries. 2 a region in W Senegal with Thiès as its capital.

thieve *verb trans.*, *intrans.* to steal.

thieving — *noun* stealing. — *adj.* that thieves.

thievish *adj.* given to stealing.

thievishly *adv.* in a thievish way.

thievishness *noun* being thievish.

thigh *noun* the fleshy part of the leg between the knee and hip in humans, or the corresponding part in animals. [from Anglo-Saxon *theoh*]

thigh bone the bone of the leg between the hip-joint and the knee.

thimble *noun* **1** a small metal, ceramic, or plastic cap worn on the finger to protect it and push the needle when sewing. **2** a metal ring with a concave groove on the outside, fitted into a loop formed by splicing a rope in order to prevent chafing. [from Anglo-Saxon *thymel*]

thimbleful *noun* (PL. **thimblefuls**) the amount a thimble will hold, especially used for a very small quantity of liquid.

Thimphu *or* **Thimbu** *or* **Tashi Chho Dzong** POP (1980e) 9 301, the official capital of Bhutan, central Asia. It lies on the R Raidak. HISTORY founded in 1581, this fortified town was a major monastery; capital since 1962. NOTABLE FEATURE Tashi Chho Dzong Castle.

thin — *adj.* (**thinner, thinnest**) **1** having a relatively short distance between opposite sides. **2** having a relatively small diameter: *thin string*. **3** *said of a line, handwriting, etc* narrow or fine. **4** *said of people or animals* not fat; lean (often too lean). **5** *said of liquids* containing very little solid matter. **6** set far apart; not dense or crowded: *thin hair*. **7** rarefied: *thin air*. **8** few in number: *good books are thin on the ground*. **9** weak; lacking in body: *thin blood*. **10** not convincing or believable: *a thin disguise*. **11** *colloq.* difficult; uncomfortable; unpleasant: *have a thin time of it*. — *adv.* thinly. — *verb trans., intrans.* (**thinned, thinning**) (*usually* **thin out** *or* **thin something out**) to make or become thin, thinner, sparser, or less dense. [from Anglo-Saxon *thynne*]

thin air nowhere: *disappear into thin air*.

thine *old use, dialect* — *pron.* something which belongs to thee. — *adj.* (used before a vowel instead of *thy*) of or belonging to thee. — **of thine** of or belonging to thee. [from Anglo-Saxon *thin*]

thing *noun* **1** any object, especially one that is inanimate. **2** any object that cannot, need not, or should not be named. **3** any fact, quality, idea, etc that can be thought about or referred to. **4** an event, affair, or circumstance: *things are getting out of hand*. **5** a quality: *generosity is a great thing*. **6** *colloq.* a person or animal, especially when thought of as an object of pity: *poor thing!* **7** a preoccupation, obsession, or interest: *have a thing about horses*. **8** what is needed or required: *it's just the thing*. **9** an aim: *the thing is to do better next time*. **10** (**things**) personal belongings, especially clothes. — **do one's own thing** *colloq.* to do what one likes doing best, or what it is natural for one to do. **make a thing of something** to make a fuss about it or exaggerate its importance. **one of those things** something that must be accepted or cannot be avoided. [from Anglo-Saxon *thing*]

thingummy *or* **thingamy** *or* **thingummyjig** *or* **thingummybob** *noun* (PL. **thingummies**) *colloq.* someone or something whose name is unknown, forgotten, or deliberately not used.

think — *verb* (PAST TENSE AND PAST PARTICIPLE **thought**) (*often* **think something** *or* **think about** *or* **of something**) **1** *intrans., trans.* **a** to have or form ideas in the mind. **b** to have as a thought in one's mind. **2** *trans., intrans.* to consider, judge, or believe: *thought the world was flat / think of oneself as a great singer*. **3** *trans., intrans.* to intend or plan; to form an idea of: *think about going to London / couldn't think of being so unkind / think no harm*. **4** *trans., intrans.* to imagine, expect, or suspect: *did not think there would be any trouble*. **5** (**think of someone** *or* **something**) to keep them in one's mind; to consider them: *think of the children first*. **6** *trans., intrans.* (**think of something** *or* **to do something**) to remember it: *did not think to tell her / couldn't think of his name*. **7** (**think of something**) to form or have an idea about it: *think of a plan*. **8** to have one's mind full of. **9** to bring into a specified condition by thinking. — *noun colloq.* an act of thinking.

— **think better of something** *or* **someone 1** to change one's mind about something on further thought. **2** to think that someone would not be so bad as to do something wrong: *I thought better of him than that*.

think highly *or* **well** *or* **badly**, *etc* **of someone** to have a high, good, bad, etc opinion of them.

think little of something *or* **not think much of something** to have a very low opinion of it.

think something out 1 to consider or plan it carefully. **2** to solve a problem by thinking about all the aspects of it.

think something over to consider all the advantages and disadvantages of an action, decision, etc; to reflect on it.

think something through to think carefully about all the possible consequences of a plan, idea, etc, especially so as to reach a conclusion as to its wisdom or value.

think twice about something to hesitate before doing something; to decide in the end not to do it.

think something up to invent or devise it. [from Anglo-Saxon *thencan*]

Thinker, The a sculpture in bronze by Auguste Rodin (1904).

thinker *noun* a person who thinks, especially deeply and constructively or in a specified way: *an original thinker / a shallow thinker*.

thinking — *noun* **1** the act of using one's mind to produce thoughts. **2** opinion or judgement: *what is your thinking on this?* — *adj., said of people* using the mind intelligently and constructively. — **put on one's thinking-cap** *colloq.* to think carefully or reflect, especially to try to solve a problem or come up with an idea.

think tank *colloq.* a group of experts who research into an area to find solutions to problems and think up new ideas.

thinly *adv.* in a thin way; so as to be thin.

thinner *noun* a liquid such as turpentine that is added to paint or varnish to dilute it.

thinness *noun* being thin.

thin-skinned *adj.* sensitive; easily hurt or upset.

thio- *combining form Chem.* forming words denoting the presence of sulphur in a compound. [from Greek *theion*, sulphur]

thiosulphate *noun Chem.* an ester or salt of thiosulphuric acid (an unstable acid that readily decomposes to form sulphur and sulphurous acid), containing the $S_2O_3^{2-}$ ion. Thiosulphates are used in photography as fixing agents.

Thíra see SANTORINI.

third — *adj.* **1** coming next after second in time, place, order, or rank; last of three. **2** being one of three equal parts. **3** being the forward gear which is one faster than second in a gearbox, eg in a motor vehicle. — *noun* **1** one of three equal parts. **2** (*also* **third gear**) the gear which is one faster than second in a gearbox, eg in a motor vehicle. **3** the third position in time, place, order, or rank; also, the person or thing occupying that position. **4** *Mus.* an interval of three notes (counting inclusively) along the diatonic scale. **5** *Mus.* a note which is separated by such an interval from another. **6** *Brit.* (*also* **third class**) an honours degree of the third, and usually lowest, class. — *adv.* in the third position: *come third in the race*. [from Anglo-Saxon *thridda*]

third class the class or rank next (especially in quality) after second.

third-class *adj., adv.* of or in the position, class, or rank next after or below the second.

third degree prolonged and intensive interrogation, usually involving physical and mental intimidation.

third-degree *adj. Medicine* denoting the most serious of the three degrees of burning, with damage to the lower layers of skin tissue.

third dimension the depth or thickness of an object which distinguishes a solid object from a flat one.

thirdly *adv.* in the third place; as the third reason, etc.

Third Man, The 1 a novel by Graham Greene. **2** a British film directed by Carol Reed (1949), with screenplay by Graham Greene. It is a thriller set in Vienna, starring Joseph Cotten and Orson Welles.

third party a person who is indirectly involved, or involved by chance, in a legal action, contract, etc between usually two principals.

third-party *adj., said of insurance* covering damage done by or injury done to a person other than the insured.

third person see PERSON.

third-rate *adj.* of very bad or inferior quality.

Third Reich see REICH.

Third World (**the Third World**) the developing or underdeveloped countries in Africa, Asia, and Latin America.
◇ Third World nations, whether poor or one of the oil-rich countries, tend to adopt a position of neutrality in their relations with the major political power blocs, and thereby constitute a third force or influence in world politics.

thirst — *noun* **1** the need to drink, or the feeling of dryness in the mouth that this causes. **2** a strong and eager desire or longing. — *verb intrans.* **1** to have a great desire or long for something. **2** *old use* to be thirsty. [from Anglo-Saxon *thyrstan*]

thirstily *adv.* with a thirsty manner.

thirstiness *noun* being thirsty.

thirsty *adj.* (**thirstier, thirstiest**) **1** needing or wanting to drink. **2** eager or longing. **3** causing thirst.

thirteen — *noun* **1** the number or figure 13; any symbol for this number. **2** the age of 13. **3** something, especially a garment or a person, whose size is denoted by the number 13. **4** a set of 13 people or things. — *adj.* **1** 13 in number. **2** aged 13. [from Anglo-Saxon *threotine*]

Thirteen Colonies the American provinces that revolted against British rule and declared independence in 1776. From N–S they were New Hampshire, Massachusetts, Rhode Island, Connecticut, New York, New Jersey, Pennsylvania, Delaware, Maryland, Virginia, North Carolina, South Carolina, and Georgia. There was actually a fourteenth, as Vermont separated from New York.

thirteenth *noun, adj.* **1** the position in a series corresponding to 13 in a sequence of numbers. **2** one of 13 equal parts.

thirties *pl. noun* **1** the period of time between one's thirtieth and fortieth birthdays. **2** the range of temperatures between thirty and forty degrees. **3** the period of time between the thirtieth and fortieth years of a century.

thirtieth *noun, adj.* **1** the position in a series corresponding to 30 in a sequence of numbers. **2** one of 30 equal parts.

thirty — *noun* (PL. **thirties**) **1** the number or figure 30; any symbol for this number. **2** the age of 30. **3** a set of 30 people or things. — *adj.* **1** 30 in number. **2** aged 30. [from Anglo-Saxon *thritig*]

thirty-eighth parallel the boundary line proposed for the partition of Korea at the Potsdam Conference (1945), after the defeat of Japan (which had annexed Korea in 1910). In 1948 the Democratic People's Republic of Korea was proclaimed, but not recognized by the Western powers. Since the Korean War, the 38th parallel again forms the line of division between North and South Korea.

Thirty-Nine Articles a set of doctrinal formulations for the Church of England, issued (after several earlier efforts) under Elizabeth I in 1563. Finally adopted as a whole by the Convocation of 1571, they do not comprise a creed, but rather a general Anglican view on a series of contentious matters (eg the presence of Christ in the Eucharist, the authority of Scriptures and the Councils, and the doctrine of predestination) in order to maintain the unity of the Anglican churches and Anglican Communion. Church of England clergy have been required since 1865 to affirm these principles in general terms.

Thirty-Nine Steps, The a novel by John Buchan (1915). The first and best-known of his Richard Hannay thrillers, it has been filmed several times.

36 Views of Mount Fuji a series of landscape prints by Hokusai (c.1826–33).

Thirty Tyrants the Spartan-backed clique which seized power in Athens towards the end of the Peloponnesian War (404 BC), overthrew the democracy, and instituted a reign of terror. They were overthrown in 403 BC and the democracy restored.

Thirty Years War a complex phase (1618–48), specifically German in origin, of an intermittent power struggle between the kings of France and the Habsburg rulers of the Holy Roman Empire and Spain (1491–1715). Meanwhile there was developing confrontation between militant Calvinism and re-invigorated, post-Tridentine Catholicism, and an underlying constitutional conflict between the Holy Roman Emperor and the German princes (as in the Bohemian Revolt, 1618). With the defeat (1620) of Elector Frederick V and intervention by other powers (eg Sweden, Transylvania, Denmark, France), the conflict intensified and spread. As Spain collapsed, the Emperor became isolated and opened negotiations (1643–8) which ended the German war, at the Peace of Westphalia.

this — *pron.* (PL. **these**) **1** a person, animal, thing, or idea already mentioned, about to be mentioned, indicated, or otherwise understood from the context. **2** a person, animal, thing, or idea which is nearby, especially which is closer to the speaker than something else. **3** the present time or place. **4** an action, event, circumstance: *what do you think of this?* — *adj.* **1** being the person, animal, thing, or idea which is nearby, especially closer than something else: *this book or that one.* **2** being the person, animal, thing, or idea just mentioned, about to be mentioned, indicated, or otherwise understood. **3** relating to today, or time in the recent past ending today: *this morning / have been working on it these last few days.* **4** *colloq.* (used instead of *a* or *the* for emphasis) being a person, animal, thing, or idea not yet mentioned: *then I had this bright idea.* — *adv.* to this (extreme) degree or extent: *I didn't think it would be this easy.* — **this and that** *colloq.* various minor unspecified actions, objects, etc. [from Anglo-Saxon *thes*]

Thistle, The Most Ancient and Most Noble Order of the a Scottish order of knighthood, probably instituted by James III of Scotland. Under the sovereign there are 16 members (Knights of the Thistle), who rank just below the Knights of the Garter (the most prestigious in the UK). Their Latin motto is *Nemo me impune lacessit* ('No-one provokes me with impunity'; Scots 'Wha daur meddle wi me?'), and the ribbon is green.

thistle *noun* any of several plants with prickly purple flowers, the national emblem of Scotland. [from Anglo-Saxon *thistel*]

thistledown *noun* the fluffy hairs attached to thistle seeds.

thither *adv.* old use, literary, formal to or towards that place. [from Anglo-Saxon *thider*]

thixotropy *noun Physics* the property of certain fluids, especially gels, which show a decrease in viscosity when stirred or shaken, eg 'jelly' paints. [from Greek *thixis*, action of touching, + *tropos*, turn]

tho' *poetic* same as THOUGH.

thole[1] *or* **tholepin** *noun* either one of a pair of pins in the side of a boat to keep an oar in place. See also ROWLOCK. [from Anglo-Saxon *thol*]

thole[2] *verb Scot. old use* to endure or tolerate. [from Anglo-Saxon *tholian*, to suffer]

tholos *or* **tholus** *noun* (PL. **tholoi, tholi**) a term loosely applied to any round building. More specifically, a dome-shaped or 'beehive' tomb common in the Mycenaean period, and the name by which the classical Greek tomb at Epidaurus (c.350 BC) is known.

Thomas, St (1c AD) one of the 12 Apostles of Jesus Christ. John's Gospel calls him Didymus ('the twin'), and relates how he doubted the Resurrection until he touched the wounds of the risen Christ (John 20). Early church traditions describe him subsequently as a missionary to the Parthians or a martyr in India. Many later apocryphal works bear his name, such as the Gospel, Acts, and Apocalypse of Thomas. The patron saint of Portugal, his feast day is 21 Dec.

Thomas, Dylan (Marlais) (1914–53) Welsh poet, born in Swansea. He worked as a journalist, and established himself as a poet in 1934 with the publication of *18 Poems*. Other poetic works include *Deaths and Entrances* (1946), and his *Collected Poems 1934–52* (1952). His best-known work is the radio 'play for voices', *Under Milk Wood* (1954). His prose output includes the unfinished novel, *Adventures in the Skin Trade* (1955).

Thomas, Sir George (Alan) (1881–1972) British badminton player, born in Istanbul, Turkey. He was the winner of a record 21 All-England titles between 1903 and 1928, including the singles title four times (1920–3). In 1934 he was elected President of the International Badminton Federation, a post he held for 21 years, and in 1939 presented a Cup (the 'Thomas Cup') to be contested by national teams. He represented England for 27 years at badminton, was also an international at lawn tennis and chess, and was twice British chess champion.

Thomas, R(onald) S(tuart) (1913–) Welsh poet, born in Cardiff. He was ordained in 1936 and became a rector in the Church of Wales (1942–78). His collections include *Song at the Year's Turning* (1955), *The Bread of Truth* (1963), *Laboratories of the Spirit* (1975), and *Counterpoint* (1990).

Thomas 1 in the New Testament, the name of one of the twelve Apostles. **2** a male first name. [from Greek *Didymos*, twin]

Thomas Aquinas, St see AQUINAS, ST THOMAS.

Thomas Becket, St see BECKET, ST THOMAS (A).

Thomism in Christian philosophical theology, the name given to the doctrines of Thomas Aquinas, and to later schools claiming descent from him.

Thompson, Benjamin see RUMFORD, BENJAMIN THOMPSON, COUNT.

Thompson, Daley (Francis Morgan) (1958–) British decathlete, born in London, the son of a Nigerian father and a Scottish mother. His first major honour was the 1978 Commonwealth Games, which he retained in 1982 and 1986. He was world champion (1983), European champion (1982, 1986), and Olympic champion (1980, 1984). In 1988 he was affected by injury and finished fourth. He broke the world record four times between 1980 and 1984. He retired in 1992.

Thompson, Emma (1959–) English actress, born in London. A graduate of Newnham

College, Cambridge, she began performing as a member of the Cambridge Footlights and worked as a comedienne and in the long-running West End musical *Me and My Girl* (1985–6) before her award-winning roles in John Byrne's television series *Tutti Frutti* (1987), and in *Fortunes of War* (1988) as the witty, vulnerable Olivia Manning. Married to Kenneth Branagh since 1989, she has appeared opposite him on stage in *Look Back in Anger* (1989) and in such films as *Henry V* (1989), *Dead Again* (1991), *Peter's Friends* (1992), and *Much Ado About Nothing* (1993). Her other films include *Howard's End* (1992), for which she received the Academy Award for Best Actress, and *The Remains of the Day* (1993) for which she received another Oscar nomination.

Thomsen, Christian see THREE-AGE SYSTEM.

Thomson, Elihu (1853–1937) English-born US inventor, born in Manchester. One of the pioneers of the electrical manufacturing industry in the USA, he co-operated in 700 patented electrical inventions, which included the three-phase alternating-current generator and arc lighting. With Edwin James Houston, he founded the Thomson–Houston Electric Company (1883), which merged with Thomas Edison's firm in 1892 to form the General Electric Company.

Thomson, Sir George Paget (1892–1975) English physicist, born in Cambridge, son of J J Thomson. Professor at Aberdeen and Imperial College, London, he became Master of Corpus Christi College at Cambridge in 1952. He shared the 1937 Nobel Prize for Physics with Clinton Davisson for the discovery, separately and by different methods, of electron diffraction by crystals.

Thomson, James (1700–48) Scottish poet, born in Ednam, Roxburgh. He is best known for his four-part work, *The Seasons* (1730), the first major nature poem in English. Other works include the ode 'Rule, Britannia', from *Alfred, a Masque* (1740), and the Spenserian allegory, *The Castle of Indolence* (1748).

Thomson, Sir J(oseph) J(ohn) (1856–1940) English physicist, born near Manchester, the discoverer of the electron. Professor at Cambridge, he showed in 1897 that cathode rays are rapidly moving particles, and by measuring their speed and specific charge deduced that these 'corpuscles' (electrons) must be nearly 2 000 times smaller in mass than the lightest known atomic particle, the hydrogen ion. He was awarded the 1906 Nobel Prize for Physics.

Thomson, Sir (Charles) Wyville (1830–82) Scottish marine biologist and oceanographer, born in Bonsyde, Linlithgow. Professor at Cork, Belfast, and Edinburgh, he was famous for his deep-sea researches, and in 1872 was appointed scientific head of the *Challenger* round-the-world expedition.

Thomson Kelvin, William see KELVIN, WILLIAM THOMSON, 1ST BARON OF LARGS.

Thomson (of Fleet), Roy (Herbert) Thomson, 1st Baron (1894–1976) British newspaper and television magnate, born in Toronto, Canada. He set up his own radio transmitter in North Bay (1931), founding what later became the NBC network, and starting other radio stations. After buying many Canadian and US newspapers, he settled in Edinburgh on acquiring his first British paper, *The Scotsman* (1952), bought the Kemsley newspapers in 1959 (including the *Sunday Times*, to which he added the first colour supplement in 1962), and in 1966 took over *The Times*.

Thonburi a suburb of Bangkok, Thailand. It lies on the W bank of the Chao Phraya R. Thonburi was the capital of Thailand from 1767 to 1782. NOTABLE FEATURES temples, including the Wat Arun ('Temple of the Dawn').

thong *noun* a narrow strip of leather used eg to fasten something, or as the lash of a whip. [from Anglo-Saxon *thwang*]

Thor, also called **the Hurler** in Norse mythology, the god of Thunder, son of Odin and Frigga. He was armed with a magic hammer (called Miolnir) and belt, and was the strongest of the gods. At Ragnarok (the last battle) he was destined to fight with the Midgard-Serpent, kill it, and then die.

thoracic *adj.* relating to or in the region of the thorax.

thorax *noun* (PL. **thoraxes**, **thoraces**) the part of the body between the head and abdomen, in humans the chest, and in insects the middle section that bears the wings and legs. [from Greek *thorax*, breastplate]

Thoreau, Henry David (1817–62) US essayist and poet, born in Concord, Massachusetts. Around 1839 he began his walks and studies of nature which became his major occupation. In 1845 he built himself a shanty in the woods by Walden Pond, near Concord, where his writings included *Walden, or Life in the Woods* (1854). After his death, several books were published, based on his daily journal (from 1835) of his walks and observations, including *Summer* (1884) and *Winter* (1887).

thorium *noun Chem.* (SYMBOL **Th**, ATOMIC NUMBER **90**) a silvery-grey radioactive metal used in X-ray tubes, photoelectric cells, and sunlamps. The isotope thorium-232 is used as a nuclear fuel in breeder reactors, as it decays to form uranium-233 when bombarded with neutrons. [from *Thor*, the Scandinavian god of thunder]

thorn *noun* **1** a hard, sharp point sticking out from the stem or branch of certain plants. **2** a shrub bearing thorns, especially a hawthorn. **3** a constant irritation or annoyance: *a thorn in one's side*. [from Anglo-Saxon]

Thorndike, Edward Lee (1874–1949) US psychologist, born in Williamsburg, Massachusetts. As professor at Teachers College, Columbia (1904–40), he formulated important theories of educational psychology and of the psychology of animal learning. He devised intelligence tests and stressed the effect of chance associations in educational processes.

Thorndike, Dame (Agnes) Sybil (1882–1976) English actress, born in Gainsborough, Lincolnshire. Though trained as a pianist, she entered the theatre in 1904, eventually playing a great variety of male and female roles, including in 1924 the title role in the first English performance of George Bernard Shaw's *Saint Joan*. She was a notable member of the Old Vic Company during World War II.

thorny *adj.* (**thornier**, **thorniest**) **1** full of or covered with thorns. **2** difficult; causing trouble or problems.

thorough *adj.* **1** *said of a person* extremely careful and attending to every detail. **2** *said of a task, etc* carried out with great care and great attention to detail. **3** complete; absolute: *a thorough waste of time*. [from Anglo-Saxon *thurh*]

thoroughbred — *noun* **1** an animal, especially a horse, bred from the best specimens carefully developed by selective breeding over many years. **2** (**Thoroughbred**) a breed of racehorse descended from English mares and Arab stallions of the early 18c. **3** a racehorse belonging to this breed. — *adj.* **1** *said of an animal, especially a horse* bred from the best specimens; pure-bred. **2** (**Thoroughbred**) of or being a Thoroughbred.

thoroughfare *noun* **1** a public road or street. **2 a** a road or path that is open at both ends. **b** the right of passage through this.

thoroughgoing *adj.* **1** extremely thorough. **2** utter; out-and-out: *a thoroughgoing villain*.

thoroughly *adv.* in a thorough way; to a thorough degree.

thoroughness *noun* being thorough.

Thorpe, (John) Jeremy (1929–) English Liberal politician. He became a barrister in 1954, and entered parliament in 1959. Leader of the Liberal Party from 1967, he resigned in 1976 following a series of allegations concerning a previous homosexual relationship with a Mr Norman Scott. In 1979, shortly after losing his seat in the general election, he was acquitted of charges of conspiracy and incitement to murder Mr Scott.

those see THAT.

Thoth in Egyptian religion, originally a Moon-god, later the god of words, magic, and scribes. He was sometimes depicted with the head of an ibis, sometimes as a baboon. In the Underworld he recorded the souls of the dead. He was usually identified with the Greek god Hermes Trismegistos.

Thoth

thou¹ *pron. old use, dialect* you (singular). [from Anglo-Saxon *thu*]

thou² *noun* (PL. **thou**, **thous**) **1** *colloq.* a thousand. **2** a unit of length equal to one thousandth of an inch.

though — *conj.* **1** despite the fact that. **2** if or even if: *I wouldn't marry him though he was the richest man in the world*. **3** and yet; but: *we like the new car, though not as much as the old one*. — *adv.* however; nevertheless.
— **as though** ... as if ...
[from Norse *tho*]

thought past tense and past participle of THINK. — *noun* **1** an idea, concept, or opinion. **2** the act of thinking. **3** serious and careful consideration: *give some thought to the problem*. **4** the faculty or power of reasoning. **5** the intellectual ideas which are typical of a particular place, time, group, etc: *recent scientific thought*. **6** intention, expectation, or hope. [from Anglo-Saxon *thoht*]

thoughtful *adj.* **1** thinking deeply, or appearing to think deeply; reflective. **2** showing careful or serious thought: *a thoughtful reply*. **3** thinking of other people; considerate.

thoughtfully *adv.* in a thoughtful way.

thoughtfulness *noun* being thoughtful.

thoughtless *adj.* **1** not thinking about other people; inconsiderate. **2** showing a lack of careful or serious thought; rash.

thoughtlessly *adv.* in a thoughtless way.

thoughtlessness *noun* being thoughtless.

Thousand, Expedition of the in Italian history, the expedition of 1 146 volunteer Red Shirts led by Garibaldi to assist Sicilian rebels against Bourbon rule.

thousand — *noun* (PL. **thousands**, **thousand**) **1** the number or figure 1 000; any symbol for this number, eg M. **2** anything having 1 000 parts, etc. **3** (*usually* **thousands**) *colloq.* a large unspecified number or amount. — *adj.* numbering 1 000.
— **one in a thousand** an extremely rare or special person or thing.
[from Anglo-Saxon *thusend*]

Thousand and One Nights, The see ARABIAN NIGHTS.

thousandth *noun*, *adj.* **1** the position in a series corresponding to 1 000 in a sequence of numbers. **2** one of 1 000 equal parts.

Thrace, Greek **Thráki** a NE region of Greece, bounded N by Bulgaria, E by Turkey, and S by the Aegean Sea. It is divided between Turkey, Greece, and Bulgaria. In ancient times, it was inhabited by the Greeks from the 8c BC. Its power passed to Persia (6c–5c BC), Macedonia (4c–2c BC), and Rome (2c BC; it became a Roman province in AD 46). It was under Turkish rule from the 15c until the late 19c. In classical times, it formed part of an area associated with the worship of Dionysus.

thrall *noun* **1** a person who is in the power of another person or thing; a slave. **2** (*also* **thraldom**) the state of being in the power of another person or thing; slavery: *be held in thrall by her beauty*. [from Anglo-Saxon *thræl*]

thrash — *verb* **1** to beat soundly, especially with blows or a whip. **2** to defeat thoroughly or decisively. **3** (*usually* **thrash about**, **around**, *etc*) to move around violently or wildly. **4** *trans., intrans.* to thresh (corn, etc). — *noun* **1** an act of thrashing. **2** *colloq.* a party. **3** *colloq.* thrash metal music.
— **thrash something out** to discuss a problem, etc thoroughly to try to solve it.
[from Anglo-Saxon *therscan*]

thrashing *noun* **1** a beating. **2** threshing.

thrash metal a style of music combining heavy metal and punk rock rhythms, often with violent lyrics or subject matter.

thread — *noun* **1** a very thin strand of glass, silk, cotton, or wool, especially when several such strands are twisted together for sewing. **2** any naturally formed very thin strand of fibre, such as that forming a spider's web. **3** anything like a thread in length and narrowness. **4** the projecting spiral ridge round a screw, bolt, or in a nut. **5** a continuous connecting element or theme in a story, argument, etc: *lost the thread of what he was saying*. **6** a thin seam or vein of ore or coal. — *verb* **1** to pass a thread through (eg the eye of a needle). **2** to pass (tape, film, etc) into or through something to put it into its correct position. **3** to string (beads) on a thread or length of string. **4** *trans., intrans.* to make (one's) way carefully (through eg narrow streets or crowded areas). **5** to streak (hair, the sky, etc) with narrow patches of a different colour. **6** to provide (eg a bolt) with a screw thread.
— **hang by a thread** to be in a very precarious or dangerous state or position.
[from Anglo-Saxon *thræd*]

threadbare *adj.* **1** *said of material or clothes* worn thin; shabby. **2** *said of a person* wearing such clothes. **3** *said of a word, excuse, etc* commonly used and meaningless; hackneyed; feeble.

threadworm *noun Zool.* a nematode worm of the genus *Enterobius*, which resembles a small piece of thread and lives as a parasite in the large intestine of humans, mainly affecting children. It rarely causes any symptoms apart from itching around the anus.

threat *noun* **1** a warning that one is going to or might hurt or punish (someone). **2** a sign that something dangerous or unpleasant is or may be about to happen. **3** a source of danger. [from Anglo-Saxon *threat*, affliction]

threaten *verb* (**threatened**, **threatening**) **1** to make or be a threat to. **2** to give warning that (something unpleasant or dangerous is or may be about to happen). **3** *intrans. said of something unpleasant or dangerous* to seem likely to happen: *a storm was threatening*.

threatening *adj.* **1** making threats. **2** imminent.

threateningly *adv.* in a threatening way.

three — *noun* **1** the number or figure 3; any symbol for this number, eg III. **2** the age of 3.

3 something, especially a garment or a person, whose size is denoted by the number 3. **4** a playing-card with 3 pips. **5** a set of 3 things or people. **6** 3 o'clock. **7** a score of 3. — *adj.* **1** 3 in number. **2** aged 3. — *pron.* 3 things or people. [from Anglo-Saxon *thrie*]

Three-Age System the chronological division of Old World prehistory into three successive ages of Stone, Bronze, and Iron. The scheme was devised (1819) by Christian Jürgensen Thomsen (1788–1865), who used it to classify the collections of the new National Museum in Copenhagen. The subdivision of the Stone Age into Palaeolithic (Old Stone Age) and Neolithic (New Stone Age) originated in the English archaeologist Sir John Lubbock's *Prehistoric Times* (1865). The term Mesolithic (Middle Stone Age), was also coined in the 1860s.

three-dimensional *adj.* **1** having or appearing to have three dimensions, ie height, width, and depth. **2** *said especially of fictional characters* developed or described in detail and therefore lifelike.

Three Emperors' League, German *Dreikaiserbund* an entente (1873, renewed 1881 and 1884) between emperors William I of Germany, Francis Joseph of Austria-Hungary, and Alexander II of Russia. Designed by Bismarck to protect Germany by isolating France and stabilizing SE Europe, it was largely superseded by the Dual Alliance (1879) of Germany and Austria-Hungary, and lapsed in 1887.

threefold — *adj.* **1** three times as much or as great. **2** divided into, or consisting of, three parts. — *adv.* by three times as much.

Three Graces, The a neoclassical sculpture by Antonio Canova, commissioned by the 6th Duke of Bedford in 1814.

three-legged race a race run between pairs of runners who have their adjacent legs tied together.

three-line whip a written notice to politicians belonging to a particular party that they must attend a vote in parliament and vote in the way in which they are instructed.

Three Musketeers, The (Les Trois Mousquetaires) a novel by Alexandre Dumas (1844). It is set mainly in Paris at the time of Louis XIII and describes the adventurous life of D'Artagnan when he joins forces with the three Musketeers, Athos, Porthos, and Aramis.

threepence *noun Brit. Hist.* in the UK before the introduction of decimal currency, the sum of three pence (3d).

threepenny *adj. Brit. Hist.* **1** worth or costing threepence. **2** of little worth or value.

threepenny bit *or* **threepenny piece** *Brit. Hist.* a coin worth threepence.

three-ply — *noun* anything which has three layers or strands bound together, especially wood or wool. — *adj.* having three layers or strands.

three-point turn a reversing of the direction of a motor vehicle by moving forward, then backward, then forward again while turning round.

three-quarter — *adj.* being three-quarters of the full amount or length. — *noun Rugby* any of the four players positioned between the full back and the scrum half and stand-off half.

three Rs see R¹.

Three Sisters, The (Tri sestry) a play by Anton Chekhov (1901). It is a realistic and gentle account of three Moscow women living in the country whose various dreams are recognized but never realized.

threesome *noun* a group of three.

Three Worlds theory the theory that sees the world as three main blocs of countries, defined by their economic status: the developed capitalist economies (the First World), the developed communist countries (the Second World), and underdeveloped countries (the Third World), which covers most of Latin America and recently independent African and Asian states. The Third World, which resists definition by its diversity and includes the oil-rich countries alongside the poorest countries, tends to adopt a position of neutrality, thereby dividing the world politically in three. Some (including the United Nations) recognize a 'Fourth World' of the 25 poorest nations.

threnodial *or* **threnodic** *adj.* relating to or of the nature of a threnody.

threnodist *noun* a person who composes or performs a threnody.

threnody *noun* (PL. **threnodies**) a song or ode of lamentation, especially for a person's death. [from Greek *threnos*, lament + *oide*, song]

threonine *noun Biochem.* an amino acid that is found in certain proteins. [a rearrangement of Greek *erythro-*, red]

thresh *verb trans., intrans.* **1** to separate the grain or seeds from the stalks of cereal plants by beating, a procedure that is now often performed by a combine harvester at the time of cutting. **2** to beat or strike. **3** (**thresh about** *or* **around**) to move violently or wildly. [from Anglo-Saxon *therscan*]

thresher *noun* **1** a machine or person that threshes corn, etc. **2** a large shark with a long whip-like tail.

threshold *noun* **1** a piece of wood or stone forming the bottom of a doorway. **2** any doorway or entrance. **3** a starting-point: *on the threshold of a new career.* **4** *Biol.* the minimum intensity of a stimulus, eg pain, that is required to produce a response in a cell or organism, and below which there is no response. **5** *Biol.* the membrane potential that must be reached before an impulse is initiated in a nerve cell. **6** *Physics* the minimum value of a quantity or variable that must be reached before it has a specified effect. [from Anglo-Saxon *therscold*]

threw see THROW.

thrice *adv. old use, literary* three times; three times as much. [from Anglo-Saxon *thriwa*]

thrift *noun* **1** careful spending, use, or management of resources, especially money. **2** a wild plant with narrow bluish-green leaves and dense round heads of pink flowers, usually found near the coast. [from Norse, = prosperity]

thriftily *adv.* in a thrifty way.

thriftiness *noun* being thrifty.

thriftless *adj.* not thrifty; extravagant.

thrifty *adj.* (**thriftier, thriftiest**) showing thrift; economical; frugal.

thrill — *verb* **1** *trans., intrans.* to feel or cause to feel a sudden strong glowing, tingling, or throbbing sensation, especially of excitement, emotion, or pleasure. **2** *trans., intrans.* to vibrate or quiver. **3** *intrans. said of a feeling* to pass quickly with a glowing or tingling sensation: *excitement thrilled through her.* — *noun* **1** a sudden tingling feeling of excitement, happiness, or pleasure. **2** something, eg an event, which causes such a feeling. **3** a shivering or trembling feeling caused especially by fear, terror, or distress. [from Anglo-Saxon *thyrlian*, to pierce]

thriller *noun* an exciting novel, play, or film, usually involving crime, espionage, or adventure.

thrilling *adj.* that thrills, exciting.

thrillingly *adv.* in a thrilling way.

thrip *noun* (PL. **thrips, thripses**) a minute slender black insect which lives on flowers. [from Greek *thrips*, woodworm]

thrive *verb* (PAST TENSE **throve, thrived**; PAST PARTICIPLE **thriven, thrived**) *intrans.* **1** to grow strong and healthy. **2** to prosper or be successful, especially financially. [from Norse *thrifa*, to grasp]

thriving *adj.* that thrives; prosperous.

thro' *or* **thro.** through.

throat *noun* **1** the top part of the passage which leads from the mouth and nose to the stomach. **2** the front part of the neck. **3** something resembling a throat in form or function, especially a narrow passageway or opening.
— **cut one's own throat** to cause one's own ruin or downfall.
cut someone's throat to kill or injure someone by slitting open their throat.
stick in one's throat *said of an unwelcome or unpalatable thought* to be impossible to say, believe, or accept.
[from Anglo-Saxon *throte*]

throatily *adv.* in a throaty way.

throatiness *noun* being throaty.

throaty *adj.* (**throatier, throatiest**) *said of a voice* deep and hoarse.

throb — *verb intrans.* (**throbbed, throbbing**) **1** to beat, especially with unusual force in response to excitement, emotion, exercise, or pain. **2** to beat or vibrate with a strong, regular rhythm. — *noun* a regular beat; pulse. [from Middle English *throbben*]

Throckmorton, Sir Nicholas (1515–71) English diplomat, who fought at Pinkie (1547) and became Ambassador to France and Scotland. In 1569 he was imprisoned for promoting the scheme to marry Mary, Queen of Scots, to the Duke of Norfolk, but was soon released. His daughter Elizabeth married Sir Walter Raleigh. His nephew Francis was executed (1584) for planning a conspiracy to overthrow Elizabeth I.

throe *noun* (usually **throes**) a violent pang or spasm, especially during childbirth or before death.
— **in the throes of something** involved in a difficult or painful struggle with it; suffering under it: *in the throes of a severe storm.*
[from Middle English *throwe*]

thrombin *noun Biochem.* an enzyme that causes the blood to clot by converting the soluble protein fibrinogen into the insoluble protein fibrin, which then forms a network of fibres.

thrombosis *noun* (PL. **thromboses**) *Pathol.* the formation of a thrombus (blood clot) in a blood vessel, obstructing the flow of blood to the tissue supplied by the vessel. Formation of a thrombus in an artery to the heart (coronary thrombosis) causes heart attack, and the formation of a blood clot in an artery to the brain is one cause of stroke. [from Greek *thrombosis*, curdling]

thrombotic *adj.* relating to or caused by thrombosis.

thrombus *noun Pathol.* a blood clot in a blood vessel. [from Greek *thrombus*, clot]

throne — *noun* **1** the ceremonial chair of a monarch or bishop, used on official occasions. **2** the office or power of the sovereign: *come to the throne.* — *verb* to place on a throne. [from Greek *thronos*, seat]

throng *noun* a crowd of people or things, especially in a small space; a multitude. **1** to crowd or fill: *people thronging the streets.* **2** *intrans.* to move in a crowd; to come together in great numbers: *an audience thronging into a theatre.* [from Anglo-Saxon *gethrang*]

throstle *noun old use, poetic* a song thrush. [from Anglo-Saxon *throstle*]

throttle — *noun* **1** a valve which regulates the amount of fuel, steam, etc supplied to an engine; also, the pedal or lever that controls this. **2** the throat or windpipe. — *verb* **1** to injure or kill by choking or strangling. **1** to prevent from being said, expressed, etc; to suppress. **2** to control the flow of (fuel, steam, etc to an engine) using a valve.

— **throttle back** or **down** to reduce the speed of an engine by closing the throttle to reduce the amount of fuel, steam, etc supplied to it. [from Middle English *throtelen*, to strangle]

through — *prep.* 1 going from one side or end of to the other: *a road through the village.* 2 from place to place within; everywhere within: *searched through the house.* 3 from the beginning to the end of: *read through the magazine.* 4 *North Amer.* up to and including: *Tuesday through Thursday.* 5 because of: *lost his job through stupidity.* 6 by way of, means of, or agency of; by: *related through marriage.* — *adv.* 1 into and out of; from one side or end to the other. 2 from the beginning to the end. 3 into a position of having completed, especially successfully: *sat the exam again and got through.* 4 to the core; completely: *soaked through.* 5 *Brit.* in or into communication by telephone: *put the caller through.* — *adj.* 1 *said of a journey, route, train, ticket, etc* going all the way to one's destination without requiring a change of line, train, etc or a new ticket. 2 *said of traffic* passing straight through an area, town, etc without stopping. 3 going from one surface, side or end to another: *a through road.*
— **be through** to have no further prospects or intentions in some regard: *is through as a businessman.*
be through with someone to have no more to do with them.
be through with something to have finished or completed it.
through and through completely. [from Anglo-Saxon *thurh*]

throughout — *prep.* 1 in all parts of. 2 during the whole of. — *adv.* 1 in every part; everywhere: *a house with carpets throughout.* 2 during the whole time: *remain friends throughout.*

throughput *noun* the amount of material put through a process, especially a computer or manufacturing process.

Through The Lens (ABBREV. **TTL**) it refers to an exposure meter or automatic control system activated by light passing through the camera lens itself, rather than by a separate external photocell.

Through the Looking-Glass, in full *Through the Looking Glass and What Alice Found There* a children's novel by Lewis Carroll (1871, dated 1872). It is a sequel to *Alice's Adventures in Wonderland*, describing the fantastic characters Alice meets when she walks through a mirror.

throw — *verb* (PAST TENSE **threw**; PAST PARTICIPLE **thrown**) 1 *trans.*, *intrans.* to propel or hurl through the air with force, especially with a rapid forward movement of the hand and arm. 2 to move or hurl into a specified position, especially suddenly or violently. 3 to put into a specified condition, especially suddenly: *threw them into confusion.* 4 to direct, cast, or emit: *a candle throwing shadows on the wall / throw a glance.* 5 *colloq.* to puzzle or confuse. 6 *said of a horse* to make (its rider) fall off. 7 *Wrestling, Judo* to bring (one's opponent) to the ground. 8 to move (a switch or lever) so as to operate a mechanism. 9 to make (pottery) on a potter's wheel. 10 *colloq.* to lose (a contest) deliberately, especially in return for a bribe. 11 *trans.*, *intrans.* to roll (dice) on to a flat surface. 12 to obtain (a specified number) by throwing dice. 13 to have or suffer: *throw a tantrum.* 14 to give (a party). 15 to deal (a punch). 16 to cause (one's voice) to appear to come from elsewhere. — *noun* 1 an act of throwing or instance of being thrown. 2 the distance something is thrown. 3 *colloq.* an article, item, turn, etc: *sell them at £2 a throw.* 4 *Geol.* the amount by which a fault in a stratum is displaced vertically.
— **throw something about** or **around** to throw it in various directions; to scatter it.
throw something away 1 to discard it or get rid of it. 2 to fail to take advantage of it; to waste or lose it through lack of care.

throw something back to delay or hinder its progress to a specified extent: *the problem threw us back six months.*
throw someone back on something to force them to rely on it.
throw back to something to revert to some earlier, ancestral character or type.
throw something in 1 to include or add it as a gift or as part of a bargain at no extra cost. 2 to contribute a remark to a discussion, especially casually.
throw in one's hand *colloq.* to give up or abandon what one is doing.
throw in the towel or **sponge** *colloq.* to give up or abandon a struggle.
throw oneself into something to begin doing it with great energy or enthusiasm.
throw something off 1 to get rid of it: *throw off a cold.* 2 to write or say it in an offhand or careless way. 3 to remove clothing hurriedly.
throw something on to put on clothing hurriedly.
throw oneself on something to rely or depend on someone's goodwill, sympathies, mercy, etc.
throw something open 1 to open it suddenly and widely. 2 to allow anyone to enter or take part in it.
throw something out 1 to get rid of it; to reject or dismiss it. 2 to say it in a casual or offhand manner. 3 to cause it to extend or project, especially from a main body: *throw out a new wing.*
throw someone out 1 to expel them. 2 to confuse or disconcert them.
throw someone over to leave or abandon someone, especially a lover.
throw people together *said of circumstances, etc* to bring them into contact by chance.
throw something together to construct it hurriedly or temporarily.
throw up *colloq.* to vomit.
throw something up 1 to give it up or abandon it. 2 to build or erect it hurriedly.
throw up one's hands to raise them in the air quickly, usually as a sign of despair, horror, etc. [from Anglo-Saxon *thrawan*, to twist]

throwaway *adj.* 1 meant to be thrown away after use. 2 said or done casually or carelessly.

throwback *noun* reversion to earlier or ancestral characteristics, or an instance of this.

throw-in *noun Football, Basketball* an act of throwing the ball back into play from a sideline.

thru *North Amer., esp. US* same as THROUGH.

thrum[1] — *verb* (**thrummed**, **thrumming**) 1 *trans.*, *intrans.* to strum idly (on a stringed instrument). 2 *intrans.* to drum or tap with the fingers. 3 *intrans.* to hum monotonously. — *noun* repetitive strumming, or the sound of this. [imitative]

thrum[2] *noun* 1 an unwoven end of thread remaining on a loom when the woven fabric has been cut away, or a group of such threads. 2 any loose thread or fringe. [from Anglo-Saxon *thrum*]

thrush[1] *noun* any of several common small or medium-sized songbirds with brown feathers and a spotted chest. [from Anglo-Saxon *thrysce*]

thrush[2] *noun* 1 a fungal infection, especially of children, which causes white blisters in the mouth, throat, and lips. 2 a similar infection in the vagina. 3 an inflammation affecting the sole of a horse's hoof.

thrust — *verb* (PAST TENSE AND PAST PARTICIPLE **thrust**) 1 to push suddenly and violently. 2 (**thrust something on** or **upon someone**) to force them to accept it; to impose it on them. 3 (**thrust through something**) to pierce or stab it. 4 (**thrust at something**) to make a lunge at it. 5 (**thrust into, through, etc**) to force one's way. — *noun* 1 a sudden or violent movement forward, a push or lunge. 2 *Aeron.* the force produced by a jet or rocket engine that propels an aircraft or rocket forward. The magnitude of thrust depends on the mass and velocity of the gases expelled from the rear of the vehicle. 3 an

attack or lunge with a pointed weapon; a stab. 4 an attack, especially by a military force on the enemy's territory, or a verbal attack on them. 5 the strong continuous pressure that one part of an object exerts against another. 6 the main theme, message or gist, eg of an argument. 7 determination; drive. [from Norse *thrysta*]

thrust stage *Theatr.* a stage that extends beyond the proscenium arch into the auditorium.

Thucydides (c.460–c.400 BC) Athenian historian. He fought in the Peloponnesian War but was forced into exile after losing the colony of Amphipolis to the Spartans (424 BC). He lived in exile for 20 years, during which time he wrote his eight-volume *History of the Peloponnesian War*.

thud — *noun* a dull sound like that of something heavy falling to the ground. — *verb intrans.* (**thudded**, **thudding**) to move or fall with a thud. [from Anglo-Saxon *thyddan*, to strike]

thug *noun* 1 a violent or brutal man or criminal. 2 (**Thug**) *Hist.* a member of a religious organization of robbers and murderers in India. [from Hindi *thag*, thief, cheat]

thuggery *noun* violent behaviour.

thuggish *adj.* characteristic of a thug; violent, brutal.

Thule an Inuit settlement in NW Greenland, lying on the coast of Hayes Halvø Peninsula. It was founded as a Danish trading post in 1910. There are scientific installations and a Danish–US airforce base nearby. Thule is also the name given by the ancients to the most northerly land of Europe, an island described in c.310 BC by the Greek navigator Pytheas.

thulium *noun Chem.* (SYMBOL **Tm**, ATOMIC NUMBER **69**) a soft silvery-white metal that is a member of the lanthanide series and is used as a source of X-rays and gamma rays. The dust of this metal is a fire hazard. [from Latin *Thule*]

thumb — *noun* 1 in humans, the two-boned digit on the inner side of the hand, set lower than and at a different angle to the other four digits. 2 the part of a glove or mitten covering this finger. 3 in other animals, the digit corresponding to the human thumb. — *verb* 1 *trans.*, *intrans.* (**thumb through something**) to turn over the pages of a book, magazine, etc to glance at the contents. 2 to smudge or wear with the thumb. 3 to ask for or obtain (a lift) in a motor vehicle by signalling to passing drivers with the thumb. 4 *intrans.* to travel by thumbing lifts; to hitchhike.
— **all thumbs** awkward and clumsy.
thumbs down a sign indicating failure, rejection, or disapproval.
thumbs up a sign indicating success, best wishes for success, satisfaction, or approval.
under someone's thumb completely controlled or dominated by someone. [from Anglo-Saxon *thuma*]

thumb index a series of notches, each with a letter or word in them, cut into the outer edges of pages of a book for quick reference.

thumb-nail — *noun* the nail on the thumb. — *adj.* brief and concise.

thumbscrew *noun Hist.* an instrument of torture which crushes the thumbs.

thumbtack *noun North Amer.* a drawing-pin.

thump — *noun* a heavy blow, or the dull sound of a blow. — *verb* 1 to beat or strike with dull-sounding heavy blows. 2 *intrans.* to throb or beat violently. 3 (*also* **thump something out**) to play (a tune), especially on a piano, by pounding heavily on the keys. 4 (**thump along, around,** *etc*) to move with heavy pounding steps. [imitative]

thumping *colloq.* — *adj.* very big: *a thumping lie.* — *adv.* very: *a pair of thumping great boots.*

Thun, French **Thoune** POP (1990) 83 000, a town in Bern canton, W central Switzerland, lying on the R Aare near L Thun. Its old town is on a long, narrow island in the middle of the river, which is connected to the modern town by numerous bridges. It is a gateway to the Bernese Alps. NOTABLE FEATURE castle (1191).

thunder — *noun* **1** a deep rumbling or loud cracking sound heard after a flash of lightning, caused by the lightning causing gases in the atmosphere to expand suddenly. **2** a loud deep rumbling noise. — *verb* (**thundered, thundering**) **1** *intrans.* said of thunder to sound or rumble. **2** *intrans.* to make a noise like thunder while moving: *tanks thundering over a bridge.* **3** to say or utter in a loud, often aggressive, voice. [from Anglo-Saxon *thunor*]

Thunder Bay POP (1991) 114 000, a port and resort in S Ontario, S Canada, lying on the NW shore of L Superior. It was created in 1970 by the union of Fort William and Port Arthur. NOTABLE FEATURE Centennial Park.

Thunderbird, also called **Skyamsen** in NW Native American religion, a totem figure in the form of a bird. Lightning flashed from its eye and it fed on killer whales. The chief of the Thunderbirds was Golden Eagle (Keneun).

Thunderbird

thunderbolt *noun* **1** a flash of lightning immediately followed by thunder. **2** a sudden and unexpected event. **3** a supposed destructive stone, missile, etc falling to earth in a flash of lightning.

thunderclap *noun* a crash of thunder, something startling or unexpected.

thundercloud *noun* a large cloud charged with electricity which produces thunder and lightning.

thundering *colloq.* — *adj.* very great: *a thundering idiot.* — *adv.* very: *a thundering great error.*

thunderous *adj.* like thunder, especially in being very loud, threatening, or violent.

thunderously *adv.* with a thunderous noise.

thunderstorm *noun* a storm with thunder and lightning and usually heavy rain.

thunderstruck *adj.* overcome by surprise; astonished.

thundery *adj.* warning of, or likely to have or bring, thunder.

Thur *or* **Thur.** *abbrev.* Thursday.

Thurber, James (Grover) (1894–1961) US writer and cartoonist, born in Columbus, Ohio. He became a journalist and made his reputation on the staff of *The New Yorker* from 1927. His drawings first appeared in his book *Is Sex Necessary?* (1929), and there are several anthologies of his work, which often combine humorous essays with characteristic doodles. His works include the short story *The Secret Life of Walter Mitty* (1932), *Thurber's Dogs* (1955) and the posthumous *Vintage Thurber* (1963).

thurible *noun* a censer. [from Latin *thus*, incense]

Thuringia a historic area of Germany, a frontier region against the Slavs that included the Harz Mts and Thuringian Forest. Controlled by various dynasties, from the 10c Dukes of Saxony to the House of Wettin (1265), it was divided between Saxony, Hesse-Kassel, and others from 1485 to 1920, and was subsequently a part of East Germany.

Thuringian Forest, German **Thüringer Wald** a region of forest land in Thuringia state, S Germany. It is a popular tourist region with a winter sports resort at Oberhof.

Thurs *or* **Thurs.** *abbrev.* Thursday.

Thursday *noun* the fifth day of the week. [from Anglo-Saxon *thunresdæg*, the day of Thunor, the god of thunder]

Thurso POP (1981) 8 900, a port town in Caithness district, Highland region, N Scotland. It lies on the N coast, at the head of the R Thurso, 30km/19mi NW of Wick. NOTABLE FEATURES St Peter's Church (17c), Thurso Folk Museum.

thus *adv.* **1** in the way or manner shown or mentioned; in this manner. **2** to this degree, amount, or distance: *thus far.* **3** therefore; accordingly. [from Anglo-Saxon *thus*]

Thutmose I (2nd millenium BC) King of Egypt (c.1526–1508 BC), who is believed to have come to the throne through marriage to Amhose, the sister of King Amenhotpe I. He waged war in Nubia and in Syria, where he campaigned as far as the Euphrates. He constructed the fourth and fifth pylons (monumental gateways) at the Temple of Amun in Karnak, and erected a pair of granite obelisks, one of which still stands. His burial in the Valley of the Kings established a pattern for royal internments which was followed for the next 400 years.

Thutmose III *or* **Thothmes** *or* **Tuthmosis** (d.1450 BC) King of Egypt (c.1504–1450 BC), of the 18th dynasty. He re-established Egyptian control over Syria and Nubia, and extended his territories to Carchemish on the Euphrates. He built a festival hall and the seventh pylon at Karnak, and erected many obelisks, including one at Heliopolis (now in London, 'Cleopatra's Needle'). In the early years of his reign, he ruled jointly with Hatshepsut, his aunt/stepmother.

thwack — *noun* a blow with something flat, such as a bat, or the noise made by it. — *verb* to strike (something) with such a noise. [imitative]

thwart — *verb* to prevent or hinder (a person, plans, etc). — *noun* a seat for a rower lying across a boat. [from Norse *thvert*, across]

thy *adj.* old use, dialect of or belonging to thee. [from Middle English, from THINE]

Thyestes in Greek mythology, a son of Pelops, who inherited the curse upon that house. His children were killed and their flesh set before him in a dish by his brother Atreus. Later, he became the father of Aegisthus.

thyme *noun* any of several herbs and shrubs, especially those with sweet-smelling leaves which are used to season food. [from Greek *thymon*]

thymine *noun* Biochem. one of the bases, derived from pyrimidine, that is found in the nucleic acid DNA. [from Greek *thymos*, thymus gland]

thymus *noun* (PL. **thymi**) (*in full* **thymus gland**) Anat. in vertebrates, a gland just above the heart, which in the newborn plays an important role in the development of the immune response to invasion of the body by pathogens or other foreign particles. It enlarges between birth and puberty, and gradually shrinks during adulthood. [from Greek *thymos*]

thyroid — *noun Physiol.* (*in full* **thyroid gland**) in vertebrates, a shield-shaped gland situated in the neck, in front of the trachea. It secretes several hormones, including thyroxine, which controls growth, development, and metabolic rate. Deficiency of iodine in the diet can lead to enlargement of the thyroid, forming a goitre. — *adj.* **1** relating to the thyroid gland or thyroid cartilage. **2** shield-shaped. [from Greek *thyreoeides*, shield-shaped]

thyroid cartilage the principle cartilage in the larynx which projects in men to form the Adam's apple.

thyroid hormone *Physiol.* any of various hormones, especially thyroxine and triiodothyronine, that are secreted by the thyroid gland and are required for normal mental and physical development, and for the growth and functioning of the body tissues.

thyroxine *or* **thyroxin** *noun* **1** *Physiol.* an iodine-containing compound that is the principal hormone secreted by the thyroid gland. **2** a synthetic form of this compound, administered in order to treat underactivity of the thyroid gland.

thyself *pron.* old use, dialect Relig. **1** the reflexive form of *thou* and *thee.* **2** used for emphasis.

Ti *symbol Chem.* titanium.

ti *or* **te** *noun Mus.* in tonic sol-fa, the seventh note of the major scale. [earlier *si*, from the initial sounds of *Sancte Iohannes* in a medieval Latin hymn, certain syllables and sounds of which were used in naming the notes of the scale]

Tiahuanaco an ancient urban and ceremonial settlement near the S end of L Titicaca, Bolivia. It was occupied c.1500 BC–AD 1200, and flourished particularly c.500–1000 AD with a population of c.30 000. The ceremonial core is notable for the Akapana, a stone platform-mound 200m square and 15m high.

Tiananmen Square the largest public square in the world, covering 40ha and lying before the gate to the Imperial Palace ('Gate of Heavenly Peace') in central Beijing (Peking). The People's Republic was proclaimed here in Sep 1949. In Jun 1989, it was the scene of mass protests against the Chinese government by students and others, who were crushed by troops of the Chinese Army with an undisclosed number of dead.

Tianjin *or* **Tientsin** *or* **T'ien-ching** POP (1990) 9.4m, a major port city in E China, 50km/31mi W of Bo Hai Gulf, on the Hai He R. China's largest artificial harbour was built here during the Japanese occupation (1937–45) and was designated in 1952. The city is designated as a special economic zone. HISTORY founded in the Warring States period (403–221 BC); developed in the Middle Ages as a grain port; attacked by the British and the French in 1860; badly damaged by an earthquake in 1976; reconstruction was completed in 1982. NOTABLE FEATURES Tianjin Art Museum; Industrial Exhibition Hall; many European-style buildings and Victorian mansions.

tiara *noun* **1** a women's jewelled ornament for the head, similar to a crown. **2** the pope's three-tiered crown. [from Greek]

Tiber, River, Italian **Tevere**, ancient **Tiberis** the second-longest river in Italy, length 405km/252mi. Rising in the Etruscan Apennines on Monte Fumaiolo, it flows S and SW through Rome and discharges into the Tyrrhenian Sea.

Tiberias, Hebrew **Tevarya** POP (1988e) 31 000, a holiday resort town in Northern district, NE Israel. It lies on the W shore of L Tiberias and was named after the Roman emperor, Tiberius. Its medicinal hot springs have been known since ancient times. Tiberias is one of the four holy cities of the Jews. NOTABLE FEATURE Monastery of St Peter.

Tiberias, Lake *or* **Sea of Galilee**, Hebrew **Yam Kinneret**, ancient **Sea of Chinnereth** a lake in Northern district, NE Israel. AREA 166sq km/64sq mi; length 23km;

width 12km; maximum depth 46m. It lies in the Jordan Valley, 210m below sea level. The lake is fed and drained by the R Jordan and serves as Israel's largest reservoir, with water piped as far as the Negev. Around the lake, there are many centres of historic and scriptural interest, especially connected with the life of Jesus. The first kibbutz was founded just S of the lake in 1909.

Tiberius, originally **Tiberius Julius Caesar Augustus** (42 BC–AD 37) Roman emperor (14–37), the son of Livia, and stepson and successor of the emperor Augustus. He was conservative by nature and sought to continue Augustus's policies and consolidate his achievements. His reign was marred by treason trials and executions, and in 26 he left Rome to live on the island of Capri, leaving the praetorian prefect Sejanus in control of Rome. He had Sejanus executed (31) following a plot against him, and entered on a reign of terror which made him loathed in Rome.

Tibesti Mountains a mountain range in N central Africa, the highest in the Sahara. It is largely situated in NW Chad and partly in Libya and Sudan. AREA 100 000sq km/38 600sq mi; length 480km/300mi. Emi Koussi is the highest peak at 3 415m. The range is volcanic in origin and is extremely rugged with spectacular rock formations created by wind erosion.

Tibet or **Xizang** POP (1990) 2.2m, an autonomous region in SW China. AREA 1 221 600sq km/471 538sq mi. Burma (Myanma) lies on its SE border, Bhutan and Nepal on its S border, and India on its S and W borders. PHYSICAL DESCRIPTION situated on the Tibet Plateau, the highest in the world, at an average altitude of 4 000m; the Himalayas lie to the S, on the border with India, Nepal, and Bhutan, where the mountains rise to 8 848m at Mt Everest; in the N lies the Kunlun Shan Range; the major farming area is situated in the S valleys; there are several rivers and lakes in the region — the largest salt-water lake is Nam Co, NW of Lhasa. HISTORY dominated by Buddhist lamas from the 7c until the departure of the Dalai Lama into exile in 1959; ruled by the Mongols from 1279 until 1368; controlled by the Manchus in the 18c; Chinese rule was restored in 1951, and full control was asserted after a revolt in 1959. Most monasteries and temples are now closed or officially declared historical monuments, but many people still worship daily. There are thought to be fewer than 1 000 lamas in Tibet, compared to almost 110 000 monks in 2 500 monasteries prior to 1959. CAPITAL Lhasa. ECONOMY wheat, peas, rapeseed; sheep, yak, and goat raising; forestry; medicinal musk; caterpillar fungus; textiles; mining of chromium, iron, copper, lead, zinc, borax, salt, mica, gypsum.

Tibetan — noun **1** a native or citizen of Tibet (the Tibet Autonomous Region of China). **2** the main language of Tibet. — adj. relating to Tibet or its people or language, etc.

Tibetan Buddhism see LAMAISM.

Tibet Plateau or **Qinghai-Tibet Plateau**, Chinese **Xizang Gaoyuan** a plateau in W and SW China. It includes Tibet, Qinghai, W Sichuan province, and SW Gansu province. At an average altitude of 4 000m, it is the highest plateau in the world, known as 'the roof of the world'. AREA 2.3m sq km/0.9m sq mi. It is bounded S by the Himalayas, N by Kunlun Shan and Qilian Shan ranges, W by the Karakoram Range, and E by the Hengduan Shan Range. PHYSICAL DESCRIPTION several internal ranges separate the basins, valleys, and lakes; it is the source of many rivers of E, SE, and S Asia, including the Yangtze, Yellow, Mekong, Salween, Indus, Brahmaputra, and Tarim; major farming region in the S; uplift continues at over 10mm per year. CLIMATE the S is warm and humid; the centre and N are cold and dry, with ice and snow for six months each year.

tibia noun (PL. **tibias, tibiae**) **1** the inner and usually larger of the two bones between the knee and ankle in man, or the bone corresponding to this in other animals; the shinbone. **2** the fourth joint of an insect's leg. [from Latin tibia, shinbone]

Tibullus (c.54–19 BC) Roman elegiac poet, born (probably) in Gabii. He fought in Aquitania, but withdrew from military life and became a member of a literary circle in Rome. Two books of elegies, written largely on the theme of love, were published in his lifetime and the other works under his name are almost certainly by other authors.

tic noun **1** an habitual nervous, involuntary movement or twitch of a muscle, especially of the face. **2** an habitual and usually involuntary response or behaviour. [from French tic]

tick¹ — noun **1** a usually soft regular tapping or clicking sound, such as that made by a watch or clock. **2** Brit. colloq. a moment. **3** a small mark, usually a line with an acute angle at the bottom, used to show that something is correct, to mark off items on a list which have been dealt with, etc. — verb **1** intrans. said eg of a clock, to make a sound like a tick. **2** (usually **tick away**) said of time to pass steadily. **3** to mark with a written tick. **4** (also **tick something off**) to count something (eg an item on a list) by marking a tick beside it. — **tick someone off** colloq. to scold them mildly. **tick over 1** to function or work quietly and smoothly at a relatively gentle or moderate rate. **2** said of an engine to idle. **what makes someone tick** colloq. their underlying character and motivation. [from Middle English tek, little touch]

tick² noun **1** any of several bloodsucking, spider-like insects living on the skin of some animals, eg dogs and cattle. **2** any of several bloodsucking flies living on the skins of eg sheep and birds. [from Anglo-Saxon ticia]

tick³ noun **1** the strong cover of a mattress, pillow, or bolster. **2** (also **ticking**) the strong, coarse, usually striped, cotton fabric from which such covers are made. [from Greek theke, case]

tick⁴ noun Brit. colloq. credit: buy it on tick. [a shortening of TICKET]

ticker noun **1** anything that ticks, eg a watch. **2** colloq. the heart.

ticker-tape noun formerly continuous paper tape with messages, especially up-to-date share prices, printed by a telegraph instrument.

ticket — noun **1** a printed piece of paper or card which shows that the holder has paid a fare (eg for travel on a bus or train) or for admission (eg to a theatre or cinema), or has the right to use certain services (eg a library). **2** an official notice issued to someone who has committed a motor offence, such as speeding or parking illegally. **3** a tag or label, especially one showing the price, size, etc of the item to which it is attached. **4** North Amer. a list of candidates put up for election by a particular political party. **5** the principles of a particular political party. **6** slang a certificate discharging a soldier from the army. **7** slang a licence or permit, especially one allowing the holder to work as a ship's master or pilot. **8** colloq. exactly what is required, proper, or best: just the ticket. — verb (**ticketed, ticketing**) to give or attach a ticket or label to. [from Old French estiquier, to attach, stick]

ticket of leave a pass issued to convicts in Australia as a reward for good behaviour; it was a form of parole which could be issued for four, six, or eight years, depending on whether the sentence was for seven years, fourteen years, or life. About 30 per cent of convicts received tickets of leave by 1840.

ticking-off noun colloq. a mild scolding.

tickle — verb **1** to touch (a person or part of the body) lightly and so as to provoke a tingling or light prickling sensation or laughter. **2** intrans. said of a part of the body to feel a tingling or light prickling sensation. **3** colloq. to amuse or entertain. **4** to catch (a fish, especially a trout) by rub-

bing it gently underneath so that it moves backwards into one's hands allowing one to put one's fingers into its gills. — noun **1** an act of tickling. **2** a tingling or light prickling sensation. — **tickled pink** or **to death** colloq. very pleased or amused. [from Middle English tikelen]

ticklish adj. **1** sensitive to tickling. **2** said of a problem, etc difficult to manage or deal with; needing careful handling.

ticklishness noun being ticklish.

tick-tack noun a system of communication based on hand signals, used eg by bookmakers at a racecourse to exchange information about the odds they are offering.

tidal adj. relating to or affected by tides.

tidally adv. **1** in a tidal way. **2** by the tide or tides.

tidal wave 1 a popular (but unscientific) name for a tsunami. **2** a loose term for an unusually large ocean wave.

tidbit noun North Amer. a titbit.

tiddler noun Brit. colloq. **1** a small fish, especially a stickleback or a minnow. **2** a small person or thing.

tiddly¹ adj. (**tiddlier, tiddliest**) Brit. colloq. slightly drunk.

tiddly² noun Brit. colloq. little.

tiddlywinks sing. noun a game in which players try to flick small flat plastic discs into a cup using larger discs.

tide noun **1** the twice daily rise and fall of the water level in the oceans and seas that is caused by the gravitational pull of the Sun and especially the Moon. Two fixed 'bulges' of water are pulled out on either side of the Earth, which moves through them as it rotates, giving high tides and low tides. Spring tides occur at full and new moon, while neap tides occur at quarter moon. **2** the level of the water, especially the sea, as affected by this: high tide. **3** a sudden or marked trend: the tide of public opinion. **4** (in compounds) a time or season, especially of some festival: Whitsuntide. — verb **1** intrans. to drift with or be carried on the tide. **2** (**tide someone over**) to help them deal with a problem, difficult situation, etc for a time. [from Anglo-Saxon tid]

tidemark noun **1** a mark showing the highest level that the tide has reached or usually reaches. **2** Brit. colloq. a mark left on a bath which shows how high it was filled. **3** Brit. colloq. a dirty mark on the skin which shows the limit of washing.

tideway noun a channel in which a tide runs, especially that part of a river which has a tide.

tidily adv. in a tidy way; so as to be tidy.

tidiness noun being tidy; a tidy state.

tidings pl. noun news. [from Anglo-Saxon tidung]

tidy — adj. (**tidier, tidiest**) **1** neat and in good order. **2** methodical. **3** colloq. large; considerable. — verb (**tidies, tidied**) (also **tidy something away** or **up**) to make it neat; to put things away or arrange them neatly. [from Middle English, seasonable]

tie — verb (**tying**) **1** to fasten with a string, ribbon, rope, etc. **2** to make (string, ribbon, etc) into a bow or knot, or to make a bow or knot in. **3** intrans. to be fastened with a knot, string, ribbon, etc: a dress that ties at the back. **4** intrans. to have the same score or final position as another competitor or entrant (in a game, contest, etc). **5** (also **tie someone down**) to limit or restrict the way they lead their life: be tied down by family responsibilities. **6** Mus. **a** to mark (notes of the same pitch) with a curved line showing that they are to be played as a continuous sound rather than individually. **b** Mus. to play (notes of the same pitch) in this way. — noun **1** a narrow strip of material worn, especially by men, round the

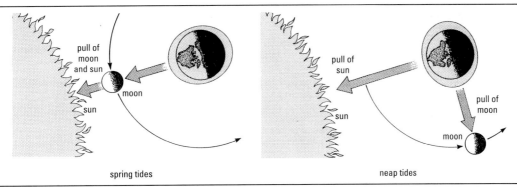

spring and neap tides

neck under a shirt collar and tied in a knot or bow at the front. **2** a strip of ribbon, rope, cord, chain, etc for binding and fastening. **3** something that limits or restricts one's freedom. **4** a link or bond: *ties of friendship*. **5** a match, competition, etc in which the result is an equal score for both sides; also, the score or result achieved. **6** *Brit.* a game or match to be played, especially in a knockout competition. **7** a rod or beam holding parts of a structure together. **8** *Mus.* a curved line above two or more notes of the same pitch showing that they are to be played as a continuous sound rather than individually. **9** *North Amer.* a sleeper.
— **tie someone down** to bind them to a decision or commitment.
tie in with something to be in or be brought into connection; to correspond or be made to correspond.
tie up to moor or dock.
tie someone up 1 to bind them securely. **2** to keep them busy. **3** to block or restrict their progress, movement, or operation.
tie something up 1 to attach and fasten it securely with string, especially to make into a parcel with string. **2** to invest money, funds, etc so that it cannot be used for other purposes.
tie up with something to be in or be brought into connection; to correspond or be made to correspond.
[from Anglo-Saxon *tiegan*]

tie beam a horizontal beam connecting the lower ends of rafters so that they do not move apart.

tie-break *or* **tie-breaker** *noun* an extra game, series of games, or question that decides which of the competitors or teams is to win a match which has ended in a draw.

tied cottage *Brit.* a cottage on an employer's land which is rented out to employees.

tied house *Brit.* a public house which may only sell the beer of a particular brewery.

tie-dyed *adj.* treated with tie-dyeing.

tie-dyeing *noun* a technique of dyeing fabrics to produce patterns, in which parts of the fabric are tied tightly to stop them absorbing the dye.

tie-in *noun* **1** a connection or link. **2** something which is presented at the same time as something else, especially a book which is published to coincide with a film or television programme.

T'ien-ching see TIANJIN.

Tien Shan *or* **Tyan Shan** a mountain range in central Asia, on the border of Kirghizia and China. It separates the Tarim Basin in the N from the Dzungarian Basin in the S and has glaciers up to 70km/40mi long. The range stretches for 2 500km/1 500mi, with passes at Shengli Daban and Qijiaojing. It is higher in the W than in the E, rising to 7 439m at Peak Pobedy. There are rich deposits of coal, rock salt, and metals. Dense forests cover the N slopes and the S slopes are mainly grassland.

Tientsin see TIANJIN.

tie-pin *or* **tie-clip** *noun* an ornamental clasp fixed to a tie to hold it in place.

Tiepolo, Giovanni Battista (1696–1770) Italian artist, born in Venice. He became renowned as a decorator of buildings throughout Europe. Examples of his work can be found in the ceiling paintings of the Würzburg and Madrid palaces, where his imaginary skies are filled with floating, gesticulating Baroque figures. His son Giandomenico Tiepolo (1727–1804) is known for his engravings and etchings, especially the series on the *Flight into Egypt*.

tier — *noun* any series of levels placed one above the other, eg of seats in a theatre. — *verb* to place in tiers. [from Old French *tire*, sequence]

tiercel see TERCEL.

Tiergarten a park covering 255ha in Berlin, Germany. It was originally a royal hunting ground which was landscaped and opened to the public in the 18c. The park was re-established, after being severely damaged during World War II.

Tierra del Fuego POP (1991) 70 000, an island group at the extreme S of South America. AREA 73 746sq km/28 467sq mi. The E side (about one third) belongs to Argentina (National Territory), and the remainder belongs to Chile. It is bounded by the Magellan Strait to the N, Atlantic Ocean to the E, the Pacific Ocean to the W, and the Beagle Channel to the S. Monte Darwin at 2 438m is the highest point. The southernmost point is at Cape Horn. CAPITAL (Argentina) Ushuaia, the southernmost town in the world. CAPITAL (Chile) Punta Arenas. ECONOMY sheep; timber; fishing; oil; natural gas. A dispute over the islands at the E end of Beagle Channel was resolved in 1985 in favour of Chile.

tiff — *noun* a slight, petty quarrel. — *verb intrans.* to have a tiff; to squabble.

Tiffany, Charles Lewis (1812–1902) US goldsmith and jeweller, born in Killingly, Connecticut, founder of Tiffany & Co. He began dealing in fancy goods in New York in 1837, and by 1883 had become one of the largest manufacturers of silverware in the USA. He held official appointments to 23 royal patrons, including the Tsar of Russia and Queen Victoria.

Tiffany a female first name. [from Greek *theophania*, revelation of God]

tiffin *noun old use* a light meal taken in the middle of the morning, especially by members of the British raj in India. [from obsolete *tiff*, to sip]

tig same as TAG[2].

tiger *noun* **1** a carnivorous cat (*Panthera tigris*), and the largest member of the cat family (Felidae), native to Asia, and having a fawn or reddish coat with black or brownish-black transverse stripes, and white underparts. **2** the male of this species. **3** a fierce, cruel person. TIGRESS [from Greek *tigris*]
◇ Tigers are found mainly in forests and tall grassland of S and E Asia, but have also adapted

to life in rocky mountainous regions. A large male may be up to 2.7m in length (including the tail), and females are slightly smaller. The striped coat provides excellent camouflage when the animal is hunting in forests during the day. In India there have been rare cases of white tigers. Tigers are excellent swimmers but, unlike most cats, poor climbers. They depend mainly on their keen hearing when stalking their prey, which includes deer, antelope, wild pigs, smaller mammals such as porcupines and monkeys, and sometimes fish and turtles. Old or injured tigers seek easy prey, occasionally including humans. The numbers of tigers in the wild have been greatly reduced by hunting and deforestation.

tigerish *adj.* like a tiger, especially fiery-tempered.

tiger lily a tall lily with black- or purple-spotted orange or yellow flowers.

tiger moth any of several moths with long striped and spotted wings.

Tigger the tiger in A A Milne's *The House at Pooh Corner*.

tight — *adj.* **1** fitting very or too closely. **2** stretched so as not to be loose; tense; taut. **3** fixed or held firmly in place: *a tight knot*. **4** (*usually in compounds*) made so as to not let air, water, etc pass in or out: *watertight*. **5** difficult or posing problems: *in a tight spot*. **6** strictly and carefully controlled: *keep a tight rein on one's emotions*. **7** *said of a contest or match* closely or evenly fought. **8** *said of a schedule, timetable, etc* not allowing much time. **9** *colloq.* mean; miserly. **10** *colloq.* drunk. **11** *said of money or some commodity* in short supply; difficult to obtain. — *adv.* tightly; soundly; completely. [from Norse *thettr*]

tighten *verb trans., intrans.* (**tightened, tightening**) to make or become tight or tighter.

tight-fisted *adj.* mean and ungenerous with money.

tight-knit *adj.* closely organized or united.

tight-lipped *adj.* with the lips firmly closed in determination to say or reveal nothing.

tightly *adv.* in a tight way; so as to be tight.

tightness *noun* being tight.

tightrope *noun* **1** a tightly-stretched rope or wire on which acrobats balance. **2** a difficult situation which requires careful, fair handling if a potential disaster is to be avoided.

tights *pl. noun* a close-fitting usually nylon or woollen garment covering the feet, legs and body to the waist, worn by women, dancers, acrobats, etc.

Tigray *or* **Tigre** POP (1992e) 2.9m, a region in NE Ethiopia. AREA 65 900sq km/25 437sq mi. PHYSICAL DESCRIPTION the W half is mountainous, with peaks including Mokada (2 295m); the low-lying E half has a large section below sea level at the centre of the Danakil Depression. CAPITAL Mekele. Tigray was one of the areas most severely affected by the drought in the 1980s, and was a centre of resistance to the government. The people are mostly nomadic herders in the N and agriculturalists in the S.

tigress noun **1** a female tiger. **2** a fierce or passionate woman.

Tigris, River, Arabic **Shatt Dijla**, Turkish **Dicle** a river in SE Turkey and Iraq, length 1 850km/1 150mi. It rises in E central Turkey and flows generally SE through Iraq. It joins the Euphrates 64km/40mi NW of Basra to form the Shatt al-Arab. The Tigris is navigable to Baghd(a bar)d for shallow-draft vessels. Several dams are used for flood control and irrigation. In ancient times the Tigris served as an important transportation route and along its banks are the ruins or sites of ancient Mesopotamian cities such as Nineveh, Seleucia, Ashur, and Calah.

Tijuana POP (1990) 743 000, a border town in NW Baja California Norte, NW Mexico. It lies on the Pacific Ocean at the frontier with California, USA. Tijuana is a resort town with casinos and nightclubs.

Tikal National Park an ancient Maya city in the Petén rainforest of N Guatemala, settled by 250 BC, at its peak in the 7c–8c AD, and abruptly abandoned in c.900. Monuments include palaces, plazas, 10 reservoirs, and six temple pyramids. It is a World Heritage site.

tike same as TYKE.

tikka noun in Indian cookery, meat that is marinated in yoghurt and spices and cooked in a clay oven. [from Hindi]

Tilak, Bal Gangadhar (1856–1920) Indian nationalist, scholar, and philosopher, born in Ratnagiri. After teaching mathematics, he was owner and editor of two weekly newspapers. A militant member of the 'extremist' wing within the Indian National Congress, he was twice imprisoned by the British for his nationalist activities. He helped to found the Home Rule League in 1914.

Tilburg POP (1992e) 161 000, an industrial city in North Brabant province, S Netherlands. It lies on the Wilhelmina Canal, 54km/34mi SE of Rotterdam. Tilburg is the largest commercial and cultural city in the S of the Netherlands and a centre of Catholicism.

Tilbury POP (1981) 12 000, a port town in Thurrock district, Essex, SE England. It lies on the R Thames Estuary, E of London, and is part of the Grays-Tilbury urban area. It provides docks for London and the SE.

tilde noun a mark ~ placed over a noun in Spanish to show that it is pronounced *ny* and over *a* and *o* in Portuguese to show they are nasalized. [from Spanish]

tile — noun **1** a flat, thin slab of fired clay, or a similar one of cork or linoleum, used to cover roofs, floors, walls, etc. **2** a tube-shaped piece of clay used for building drains. **3** a small, flat, rectangular piece used in some games. — verb to cover with tiles.
— **on the tiles** having a wild time socially, usually including a lot of drinking and dancing. [from Anglo-Saxon *tigele*, from Latin *tegula*]

tiler noun a maker or setter of tiles.

tiling noun **1** tiles as a group. **2** a tiled area. **3** the act of covering a surface with tiles.

till¹ — prep. up to the time of: *wait till tomorrow.* — conj. up to the time when: *go on till you reach the station.* See also UNTIL. [from Anglo-Saxon *til*]

till² noun a container or drawer in which money taken from customers is put, now usually part of a cash register. [from Middle English *tylle*, to draw]

till³ verb to prepare and cultivate (land) for growing of crops. [from Anglo-Saxon *tilian*, to aim at]

tillable adj., said of land capable of being tilled; arable.

tillage noun **1** the preparing and cultivating of land for crops. **2** land which has been tilled.

tiller¹ noun the lever used to turn the rudder of a boat. [from Old French *telier*, weaver's beam]

tiller² noun **1** a sapling. **2** a shoot growing from the bottom of the original stalk. **3** a sucker. [from Anglo-Saxon *telgor*, twig]

tiller³ noun a person who tills the land.

Tilley, Vesta, professional name of **Lady de Frece**, *née* **Matilda Alice Powles** (1864–1952) English music hall entertainer, born in Worcester. She first appeared as 'The Great Little Tilley', aged four, in Nottingham, and later became a celebrated male impersonator. Her many popular songs included 'Burlington Bertie' and 'Following in Father's Footsteps'.

Tilsit, Treaties of agreements (1807) made by France with Russia and Prussia. After spectacular victories at Jena and Auerstät, and the battle of Friedland, Napoleon I imposed a blockade on continental trade with Britain, and established the Grand Duchy of Warsaw and the Kingdom of Westphalia. Prussia was much reduced and subordinated to France.

tilt — verb **1** trans., intrans. to slope or cause to slope; to be or put in a slanting position. **2** intrans. (**tilt at someone or something**) to charge at or attack them. **3** intrans. to fight on horseback with a lance; to joust. **4** to point (a lance) or attack with (a lance) as if in a joust. **5** to forge (steel, etc) using a tilt-hammer. — noun **1** a slant; a sloping position or angle. **2** an act of tilting. **3** a joust. **4** a thrust, charge, or attack with a lance during a joust. **5** an attack, disagreement, or contest.
— **at full tilt** at full speed or with full force. [from Anglo-Saxon *tealt*, tottering]

tilth noun Agric. the physical condition of the soil surface after cultivation, eg after ploughing. It may be fine or coarse, depending on the size of the clods of soil. [from Anglo-Saxon]

tilt-hammer noun a heavy pivoted hammer lifted by a cam, used in forging.

timber — noun **1** wood, especially prepared for building or carpentry. **2** trees suitable for this; forest or woodland. **3** a wooden beam in the framework of especially a ship or house. — interj. used to warn that a tree has been cut and is going to fall. — verb (**timbered, timbering**) **1** to provide timber or beams for. **2** to cover in timber. [from Anglo-Saxon]

timbered adj. **1** built completely or partly of wood. **2** said of land covered with trees; wooded.

timber line the line or level of high ground above which trees do not grow.

timbre noun the distinctive quality of the tone produced by a musical instrument or voice, as opposed to pitch and loudness. [from Old French, = bell]

timbrel noun a small tambourine. [from Old French *timbre*, bell]

Timbuktu, French **Tombouctou** POP (1976) 20 000, a town in Gao region, N Mali. It lies 690km/429mi NE of Bamako. The adjoining town of Kabara serves as a port on the R Niger. HISTORY settled in the 11c; became a chief centre of Muslim learning; declined after a conquest by Morocco in the 16c; taken by the French in 1893. NOTABLE FEATURES Djinguereber Mosque (13c), Sankore Mosque (14c), Sidi Yahya Mosque (15c).

time — noun **1** the continuous passing and succession of minutes, days, years, etc. **2** a particular point in time expressed in hours and minutes, or days, months and years, and as can be read from a clock or watch or told by a calendar. **3** any system for reckoning or expressing time: *East European Time.* **4** (*also* **times**) a point or period which is marked by some event or some particular characteristic: *at the time of her marriage / Edwardian times.* **5** the period required or available for, suitable for or spent doing some particular activity. **6** an unspecified interval or period: *stayed there for a time.* **7** one of a number or series of occasions or repeated actions: *been to Spain three times.* **8** (**times**) expressing multiplication: *three times two is six.* **9** a period or occasion, especially a personal one, characterized by some quality or experience: *a good time / hard times.* **10** a particular period being considered, especially the present. **11** colloq. a prison sentence: *do time.* **12** an apprenticeship. **13** the point at which something ends, eg a section of a game. **14** Brit. the time when a public house must close. **15** the moment at which childbirth or death is expected. **16** the hours and days that one spends at work. **17** a rate of pay for work: *double time.* **18** Mus. any of several different rhythms and speeds: *waltz time.* **19** Mus. the speed at which a piece of music is to be played. — adj. that can be set to function at a particular moment or during a particular period: *a time switch on a heating system.* — verb **1** to measure the time taken by (an event, journey, etc). **2** to arrange, set, or choose the time for. **3** trans., intrans. to keep or beat, or cause to keep or beat, time (with).
— **against time** with as much speed as possible because of the need or wish to finish by a certain time.
ahead of time earlier than expected or necessary.
all in good time in due course; soon enough.
all the time continually.
at times occasionally; sometimes.
behind time late.
behind the times out-of-date; old-fashioned.
for the time being meanwhile; for the moment.
from time to time occasionally; sometimes.
have no time for someone or something to have no interest in or patience with them; to despise them.
have the time of one's life to enjoy oneself very much.
in good time early.
in no time very quickly.
in one's own time 1 in one's spare time when not at work. **2** at the speed one prefers.
in time early enough.
in time with someone or something at the same speed or rhythm as them.
kill time to pass time aimlessly while waiting on events.
make good time to travel as quickly as, or more quickly than, one had expected or hoped.
no time at all colloq. a very short time.
on time at the right time; not late.
pass the time of day to exchange greetings and have a brief, casual conversation.
take one's time not to hurry; to work as slowly as one wishes.
time and time again again and again; repeatedly.
time out of mind for longer than anyone can remember.
[from Anglo-Saxon *tima*]

time-and-motion study a study of the way work is done in a factory, company, etc with a view to increasing efficiency.

time bomb a bomb that has been set to explode at a particular time.

time capsule a box containing objects chosen as typical of the current age, buried or otherwise preserved for discovery in the future.

time clock an apparatus with a clock which stamps on cards the time of arrival and departure of eg factory workers.

time code a series of digitally coded signals appearing sequentially (as hours, minutes, and seconds) on a magnetic tape of a video or audio recording, and sometimes on film, to provide specific identification and location of each frame, etc, in editing and post-production.

time exposure a photograph taken by exposing the film to the light for a relatively long period of time, usually a few seconds.

time-honoured *adj.* respected and upheld because of being a custom or tradition.

timekeeper *noun* **1** a person who records the time, eg that worked by employees or taken by a competitor in a game. **2** a clock or watch, especially thought of in terms of its accuracy: *a good timekeeper*. **3** an employee thought of in terms of punctuality.

timekeeping *noun* **1** beating, marking, or observing time. **2** punctuality.

time lag the interval or delay between connected events or phenomena.

time-lapse photography a series of photographs taken of a subject at regular intervals and from the same viewpoint, to record some process or development, such as plant growth, cloud formation, metallic corrosion, or traffic flow. When filmed as successive single frames, subsequent projection at normal speed provides a rapid presentation of changes which are slow or gradual in real time.

timeless *adj.* **1** not belonging to or typical of any particular time or date. **2** unaffected by time; ageless; eternal.

timelessly *adv.* **1** in a timeless way. **2** with no reference to time.

timelessness *noun* being timeless.

time limit a fixed length of time during which something must be done and finished.

timeliness *noun* being timely; punctual, opportune.

timely *adj.* coming at the right or a suitable moment.

Time Machine, The a novel by H G Wells (1895). It is an allegory set in the year 802701 describing the divided two-tier society of the Eloi and the Morlocks.

Time of Troubles a period (1598–1613) of intense social and political turmoil in Russia that involved successive crises, civil war, famines, Cossack and peasant revolts, foreign invasions, and widespread material destruction. It ended with a national uprising against the invading Poles, and the election of the first Romanov tsar, Mikhail.

time out *North Amer.* a brief pause or period of rest, especially in a game.
— **take time out from something** to take a break from some activity, eg work.

timepiece *noun* an instrument for keeping time, especially one which is larger than a watch but which does not chime.

timer *noun* **1** a device like a clock which switches an appliance on or off at pre-set times. **2** a person or instrument that records the time taken by someone or something.

Times, The British daily newspaper, founded in 1785 as the *Daily Universal Register*. Renamed *The Times* in 1788, it gradually gained a reputation for accurate reportage and independent editorial comment, and became Britain's most influential newspaper, a symbol of the British Establishment. Alfred Harmsworth was one of the owners of *The Times* (1908–22). In 1981 it was purchased by Rupert Murdoch.

Times Square a public square in Manhattan, New York City, situated at the junction of Broadway, 42nd Street, and 7th Avenue, and at the centre of the city's theatre district. It takes its name from the Times Tower, built in 1904 to house the offices of the *New York Times*.

time-served *adj.* having completed an apprenticeship; fully trained.

timeserver *noun* a person who changes his or her behaviour or opinions to fit those held by people in general or by someone in authority.

time-sharing *noun* **1** a scheme whereby a person buys the right to use a holiday home for the same specified period within the year for an agreed number of years. **2** a system which allows many users with individual terminals to use a single computer at the same time.

time sheet a record of the time worked by a person on a daily, weekly, or monthly basis, and often used as a basis for calculating pay.

time signal a signal, especially broadcast on the radio, which gives the exact time.

time signature *Mus.* a sign consisting of two numbers one above the other (the lower one indicating the value of the note used as the basic beat and the upper one the number of these to the bar), placed after the key signature at the beginning of a piece of music to show the rhythm it is to be played in, or in the middle of a piece where the rhythm changes.

timetable — *noun* **1** a list of the depature and arrival times of trains, coaches, buses, etc. **2** a plan showing the order of events, especially of classes in a school. — *verb* to arrange or include in a timetable; to schedule or plan.

time warp in science fiction, etc, a hypothetical distortion in the time continuum, allowing one to pass from the present to the past or the future, or to stand still in the present.

timeworn *adj.* worn through long use; old.

time zone any one of the 24 more or less parallel sections into which the world is divided longitudinally, all places within a given zone generally being at the same standard time.

Timgad the former Roman city of Thaugadi in NE Algeria. It was founded by the emperor Trajan in AD 100, and abandoned after the 5c. It is a World Heritage site.

timid *adj.* easily frightened or alarmed; nervous; shy. [from Latin *timidus*]

timidity *noun* a timid state; nervousness, shyness.

timidly *adv.* in a timid way.

timing *noun* the regulating and co-ordinating of actions and events to achieve the best possible effect, especially the regulating of the speed of dialogue, action, and interaction between characters in a play, film, etc.

Timişoara, Magyar **Temesvár** POP (1992) 334 000, the capital of Timiş county, W Romania, lying on the Bega Canal. HISTORY ceded to Romania in 1919; in 1989 many civilians were killed in the violent suppression of demonstrations against the treatment of Hungarian minorities; this sparked a more general uprising against the Ceauşescu regime. NOTABLE FEATURES two cathedrals; Hunyadi Castle (15c).

Timor POP (1992) 791 000, a mountainous island in SE Asia, in the Sunda group, NW of Australia. AREA 33 912sq km/13 090sq mi. It was divided between Portugal and Holland in 1859. West Timor (former Dutch Timor) was included in Indonesia at independence, and is administered as part of the province of Nusa Tenggara Timur. CAPITAL Kupang. ECONOMY coffee, coconuts. The former Portuguese territory of East Timor declared itself independent as the Democratic Republic of East Timor in 1975. It was invaded by Indonesian forces and annexed, but the claim was not recognized by the United Nations. It is now administered by Indonesia as the province of Timor Timur. An independence movement is active. CAPITAL Dili. ECONOMY maize, coffee.

timorous *adj.* very timid; frightened. [from Latin *timere*, to fear]

timorously *adv.* timidly.

timorousness *noun* a timid quality or state.

Timor Sea a section of the Pacific Ocean, SE of the Indonesian island of Timor, and NW of Northern Territory, Australia. It lies over a wide continental shelf, with depths of 110m, but it deepens off Timor I.

Timoshenko, Semyon Konstantinovich (1895–1970) Soviet soldier, born in Furmanka, the Ukraine. He joined the Tsarist army (1915), and took part in the defence of Tsaritsyn in the Revolution (1917). During World War II he broke Finnish resistance during the Russo-Finnish War (1940), then commanded in the Ukraine, but failed to stop the German advance (1942). He also served as People's Commissar of Defence and improved the system of army training.

Timothy 1 in the New Testament, a companion of St Paul. **2** a male first name. [from Greek *Timotheus*, from *time*, honour + *theos*, god]

Timothy, Letters of Paul to two New Testament writings or Pastoral Letters, attributed (arguably) to Paul. Both are addressed to Paul's close companion Timothy (Acts 16.1; Thessalonians 3.2), but mostly concern questions of Church order and discipline, and problems with false teachers who were spreading gnostic and Jewish speculations; the second however does refer to Paul's personal experiences and circumstances.

timothy grass *Bot.* a perennial grass (*Phleum pratense*) used for fodder and pasture. [named after Timothy Hanson, who promoted its cultivation in America in the early 18c]

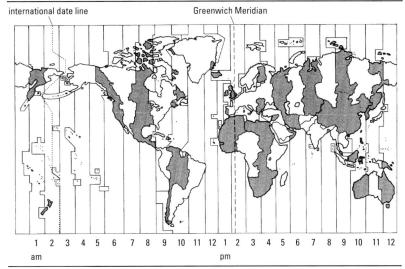

international date line   Greenwich Meridian

1 2 3 4 5 6 7 8 9 10 11 12 1 2 3 4 5 6 7 8 9 10 11 12
   am   pm

international time zone

timpani or **tympani** pl. noun a set of two or three kettledrums. [from Italian]

timpanist or **tympanist** noun a person who plays the timpani.

Timur, also called **Timur Lenk**, Turkish for **Timur the Lame**, English **Tamerlane**, or **Tamburlaine** (1336–1405) Tatar conqueror, born near Samarkand. After he ascended the throne of Samarkand (1369), he subdued nearly all Persia, Georgia, and the Tatar Empire, and conquered all the states between the Indus and the lower Ganges (1398). He won Damascus and Syria from the Mameluke sovereigns of Egypt, then defeated the Turks at Angora (1402), when he took Sultan Bajazet prisoner. He planned to conquer China, but died on the way.

tin — noun **1** Chem. (SYMBOL **Sn**, ATOMIC NUMBER **50**) a soft silvery-white metal that exists as three different allotropes, and is obtained from ores such as cassiterite (tinstone). It is used as a thin protective coating for steel, eg in 'tin' cans, and as a component of various alloys, eg bronze, pewter, solder. Tin compounds are used in dyeing, and as fungicides and catalysts. **2** an airtight metal container, often composed of steel coated with a thin layer of tin, used for storing food. **3** any of several containers of different shapes and sizes made usually of tin or aluminium and in which food is cooked. **4** the amount a tin will hold. **5** a strip of tin along the bottom of the front wall of a squash court. **6** Brit. slang money. — adj. made of tin. — verb (**tinned**, **tinning**) **1** to pack (food) in tins; to can. **2** to cover or coat with tin. [from Anglo-Saxon]

Tinbergen, Jan (1903–) Dutch economist, born in The Hague. His major contribution was the econometric modelling of cyclical movements in socio-economic growth. He was Director of the Central Planning Bureau in the Netherlands (1945–55), and also worked with developing countries. He was jointly awarded the first Nobel Prize for Economics in 1969.

Tinbergen, Nikolaas (1907–88) Dutch ethologist, born in The Hague. He taught at Leiden and later at Oxford, and is considered to be one of the founders of ethology, the study of animal behaviour in relation to the environment to which it is adapted. His research centred round the patterns of animal behaviour in nature, showing that many are stereotyped. He shared the 1973 Nobel Prize for Physiology or Medicine with Konrad Lorenz and Karl von Frisch.

tincture — noun **1** a slight flavour, trace, or addition. **2** a slight trace of colour; hue; tinge. **3** a solution of a drug in alcohol for medicinal use. — verb to give a trace of a colour, flavour, etc to. [from Latin tinctura, dyeing]

tinder noun dry material, especially wood, which is easily set alight and can be used as kindling. [from Anglo-Saxon tynder]

tinder-box noun **1** Hist. a box containing tinder, a flint and steel for striking a spark to light a fire. **2** a volatile and potentially dangerous situation.

Tin Drum, The (Die Blechtrommel) **1** a novel by Günter Grass (1959). His first, it is set against a backdrop of Nazism. It is the autobiography of Oskar Matzerah, who is detained in a mental hospital for a murder he did not commit. **2** a French–German film directed by Volker Schlöndorff (1979). Based on part of Grass's novel, it is an allusive account of wartime Poland, focusing on three-year-old Oskar (played by David Bennent) who resolves to stop growing.

tine noun a slender prong or tooth, eg of a comb, fork, or antler. [from Anglo-Saxon tind]

tinea noun Medicine any of a group of common fungal infections of the skin, and sometimes the nails, eg athlete's foot, which affects the skin between the toes. [from Latin tinea, moth, bookworm, etc]

tinfoil noun tin, aluminium or other metal in the form of very thin, paper-like sheets, used especially for wrapping food.

tinful noun (PL. **tinfuls**) the amount a tin will hold.

Ting, Samuel Chao Chung (1936–) US physicist, born in Ann Arbor, Michigan. He worked at the European nuclear research centre (CERN) in Geneva, Columbia University, in Hamburg and at the Massachusetts Institute of Technology. In 1974 his research team discovered an elementary particle known as the 'J/ψ particle'; for this work he shared the 1976 Nobel Prize for Physics with Burton Richter.

ting noun a high, metallic tinkling sound such as that made by a small bell. [imitative]

ting-a-ling noun a ringing or tinkling.

tinge — noun **1** a trace or slight amount of colour. **2** a trace or hint of (eg a quality or feeling). — verb **1** to give a slight colour to. **2** to give a trace or hint of a feeling, quality, etc to. [from Latin tingere]

tingle — verb trans., intrans. to feel or cause to feel a prickling or slightly stinging sensation, as with cold or embarrassment. — noun a prickling or slightly stinging sensation. [from Middle English tinglen, a variant of tinklen, to tinkle]

tingling or **tingly** adj. that tingles.

tin god **1** a self-important pompous person. **2** a person or thing held in excessively or unjustifiably high esteem.

tin hat slang a military steel helmet.

Tinian POP (1980) 899, an island of the N Mariana Is, W Pacific Ocean. AREA 101sq km/39sq mi. It lies 5km/3mi SW of Saipan and is 18km/11mi long. The island has four long runways which were built by the USA during World War II. A plaque commemorates the launching of the Hiroshima bombing mission in 1945. NOTABLE FEATURE site of ancient stone columns.

tininess noun a tiny size.

tinker — noun **1** a travelling mender of pots, pans, and other household utensils. **2** Scot., Irish a Gypsy. **3** colloq. a mischievous or impish person, especially a child. — verb intrans. (**tinkered**, **tinkering**) **1** (often **tinker about** or **around**) to work in an unskilled way, meddle or fiddle with machinery, etc, especially to try to improve it. **2** to work as a tinker. [from Middle English tinkere, worker in tin]

Tinkerbell the fairy in J M Barrie's Peter Pan.

tinkle — verb **1** trans., intrans. to make or cause to make a sound of or like the ringing or jingling of small bells. **2** intrans. colloq. to urinate. — noun **1** a ringing or jingling sound. **2** colloq. a telephone call. **3** colloq. an act of urinating. [from Middle English tinken, to click or tink]

tinkly adj. (**tinklier**, **tinkliest**) tinkling.

tinned adj. **1** coated or plated with tin. **2** preserved in tins, canned.

tinnily adv. with a tinny sound.

tinniness noun a tinny quality.

tinnitus noun Medicine any noise (ringing, buzzing, whistling, etc) in the ears that is not caused by external sounds. It is frequently associated with deafness due to ageing or continuous exposure to loud noise, but may also be caused by ear infections or disease, high blood pressure, or drugs such as aspirin or quinine. [from Latin tinnire to ring]

tinny adj. (**tinnier**, **tinniest**) **1** of or like tin, especially in appearance or taste. **2** not solid and durable; flimsy; shoddy. **3** said of sound thin and high-pitched.

tin-opener noun any of several tools for opening tins of food.

Tin Pan Alley a nickname coined c.1900 for the popular music-publishing centre of New York City situated on 28th Street and 6th Avenue, and later near 49th Street.

tin plate thin sheet iron or steel coated with tin.

tinpot adj. Brit. colloq. cheap; of poor quality.

tinsel — noun **1** a long strip of glittering coloured metal or plastic threads used as a decoration especially at Christmas. **2** anything which is cheap and showy. — adj. of or like tinsel, especially in being cheap and showy. [from Old French estincele, spark]

tinselly adj. **1** like or full of tinsel. **2** gaudy.

tinsmith noun a worker in tin and tin plate.

tint — noun **1** a variety or (usually slightly) different shade of a colour. **2** a variety of a colour, especially one made softer by adding white. **3** a pale or faint colour used as a background for printing. **4** shading produced by engraving parallel lines close together. **5** a hair dye. — verb to give a tint to; to colour slightly. [from Latin tingere, to colour]

Tintern Abbey a poem by William Wordsworth (in Lyrical Ballads, 1798). It is primarily a reflection on the formative power of nature on humankind.

tintinnabulation noun a ringing of bells. [from Latin tintinnabulum, bell]

Tintoretto, pseudonym of **Jacopo Robusti** (1518–94) Venetian painter, born (probably) in Venice. His major works include two paintings of the Last Supper (1547 and c.1592–4, Venice), The Last Judgement (c.1560, Venice) and the Paradiso, famous for its great size (1588, Venice). From 1564 he was employed in decorating the Albergo, and the Halls of the Scuola di San Rocco and its church, which contains an iconographical scheme from the Old and New Testaments, including the Crucifixion (1565) and Annunciation (1583–7).

Tin Woodman, the one of Dorothy's companions in Frank L Baum's The Wonderful Wizard of Oz.

tiny adj. (**tinier**, **tiniest**) very small. [from Middle English tine]

Tiny Tim the crippled youngest son of Bob Cratchit, and a paragon of goodness, in Charles Dickens's A Christmas Carol.

tip¹ — noun **1** the usually small pointed end of something. **2** a small piece forming an end or point: a rubber tip on a walking-stick. **3** a tea leafbud. — verb (**tipped**, **tipping**) **1** to put or form a tip on. **2** (**tip in**) to attach (a loose sheet) into a book. **3** to remove a tip from.
— **on the tip of one's tongue** about to be or almost said, but not able to be because not quite remembered.
[from Middle English]

tip² — verb (**tipped**, **tipping**) **1** trans., intrans. (also **tip up** or **tip something up**) to lean or cause to lean or slant. **2** (also **tip something out**) to remove or empty (something) from its container, surface, etc by overturning or upsetting that container or causing that surface to slant. **3** Brit. to dump (rubbish). — noun **1** a place for tipping rubbish, coal, etc. **2** colloq. a very untidy place.
— **tip over** trans., intrans. to knock or fall over; to overturn.
[from Middle English typen, to overturn]

tip³ — noun **1** a gift of money given to a servant, waiter, taxi driver, etc in return for service done well. **2** a piece of useful information; a helpful hint or warning. **3** a piece of inside information which may lead to financial gain, such as the name of a horse likely to win a race, or a company whose shares are likely to become more valuable. — verb (**tipped**, **tipping**) to give a tip to.
— **tip someone off** to give them a piece of useful or secret information.

[perhaps from TIP⁴]

tip⁴ — *noun* a light blow or tap. — *verb* (**tipped**, **tipping**) to hit or strike lightly. [from Middle English]

Tipasa a village on the N coast of Algeria. It stands on the ruins of the ancient city of Tipasa. HISTORY the original settlement was founded in the 5c BC and passed through many hands, from Phoenician to Roman, before it was abandoned in the 5c. It is a World Heritage site.

tip-off *noun* a piece of useful or secret information, or the disclosing of this.

tipped *adj.* having a tip.

Tipperary, Gaelic **Thiobrad Árann** POP (1991) 133 000, a county in Munster province, S central Irish Republic. PHYSICAL DESCRIPTION the Silvermine Mts lie to the N, the Galty Mts to the S, and the Slieve Ardagh Hills to the W; the R Suir runs through the county. CAPITAL Clonmel. It is a rich dairy-farming area and a centre for horse and greyhound breeding.

tippet *noun* 1 a shoulder-cape of fur or cloth. 2 a long band of cloth or fur worn as part of some official costumes, eg by the clergy over the surplice during morning and evening prayers. [from TIP¹]

Tippett, Sir Michael (Kemp) (1905–) English composer, born in London. He was director of music at Morley College (1940–51) and first attracted attention with his chamber music and Concerto for Double String Orchestra (1939), then his oratorio *A Child of our Time* (1941), reflecting the problems of the 1930s and 1940s, won him wide recognition. A convinced pacifist, he was imprisoned as a conscientious objector during World War II. His operas include *The Midsummer Marriage* (1952), *King Priam* (1962), and *The Knot Garden* (1970), and among his other works are four symphonies, a piano concerto, and string quartets.

Tipp-Ex *or* **Tippex** *noun trademark* a correction fluid, usually opaque white, for covering over mistakes in typing or writing.

tipple *colloq.* — *verb trans., intrans.* to drink alcohol regularly in relatively small amounts. — *noun* a person's favourite alcoholic drink.

tippler *noun* a habitual drinker of alcohol.

tipsily *adv.* in a tipsy way.

tipsiness *noun* being tipsy.

tipstaff *noun* (PL. **tipstaffs**, **tipstaves**) 1 a metal-tipped staff which is a symbol of office. 2 a sheriff's officer. [from TIP¹ + STAFF]

tipster *noun* a person who gives tips, especially as to which horses to bet on.

tipsy *adj.* (**tipsier**, **tipsiest**) *colloq.* slightly drunk. [from TIP²]

tiptoe — *verb intrans.* to walk quietly or stealthily on the tips of the toes. — *noun* the tips of the toes. — *adv.* on the tips of the toes.

tiptop *colloq.* — *adj., adv.* excellent; first-class. — *noun* the very best; the height of excellence.

TIR *abbrev. Transports Internationaux Routiers* (French), International Road Transport, a continental haulage organization.

tirade *noun* a long angry speech, harangue, or denunciation. [from French]

Tirana *or* **Tiranë** POP (1989) 239 000, the capital of Albania and of Tirana district. It lies in a valley in the foothills of the Kruja-Dajti Mts, 40km/25mi from the Adriatic Sea. Tirana is the country's main political, economic, and cultural centre. HISTORY founded by the Turks in the early 17c; became the capital of Albania in 1920; occupied by Italian and German troops during World War II. The residential area of the town was built by the Italians between 1939 and 1943.

tire¹ *verb* 1 *trans., intrans.* to make or become physically or mentally weary and in need of rest.

2 (**tire of something**) to lose patience with it; to have had enough of it; to become bored with it. [from Anglo-Saxon *teorian*]

tire² *North Amer.* same as TYRE.

tired *adj.* 1 wearied; exhausted. 2 (**tired of something** *or* **someone**) no longer interested in them; bored with them. 3 lacking freshness and showing the effects of time and wear, especially in being limp and grubby or hackneyed.

tiredly *adv.* in a tired way.

tiredness *noun* being tired, weariness.

tireless *adj.* never becoming weary or exhausted.

tirelessly *adv.* in a tireless way.

tirelessness *noun* being tireless.

Tiresias in Greek mythology, a blind Theban prophet, who takes a prominent part in Sophocles' plays about Oedipus and Antigone. Later legends account for his wisdom by saying that he had experienced the life of both sexes.

tiresome *adj.* troublesome and irritating; annoying; tedious.

tiresomely *adv.* in a tiresome way.

tiresomeness *noun* being tiresome.

tiring *adj.* that tires.

tiro *or* **tyro** *noun* (PL. **tiros**, **tyros**) a beginner or novice. [from Latin, = recruit]

Tirol *or* **Tyrol** POP (1991e) 630 000, a state in W Austria, bounded N by Germany and S by Italy. AREA 12 647sq km/4 882sq mi. PHYSICAL DESCRIPTION drained by the R Inn; lakes include the Achensee, Walchsee, Tristacher See, and Schwarzsee. CAPITAL Innsbruck. HISTORY the S Tirol was ceded to Italy in 1919. ECONOMY hydroelectric power; agriculture, forestry, powder metallurgy, diesel engines, vehicles, optical instruments; it is a leading state for tourism, especially winter sports (eg at Kitzbühel).

Tirol Alps *or* **Bavarian Alps**, German **Bayerische Alpen** a mountain range extending E and W from L Constance to Salzburg. Its highest peak is the Zugspitze (2 962m). The Allgäu Alps form the W section of the range.

Tirpitz, Alfred (Friedrich) von (1849–1930) German admiral, born in Küstrin. He joined the Prussian navy in 1865 and rose to be Lord High Admiral (1911). As Secretary of State for the imperial navy (1897–1916), he raised and commanded a fleet to challenge British supremacy of the seas (1914–16). He advocated unrestricted submarine warfare, and resigned when this policy was opposed.

Tiruchchirappalli *or* **Trichinopoly** POP (1991) 387 000, a city in Tamil Nadu, S India. It lies on the Kaveri R. The city is an educational, religious, and commercial centre, noted for its gold, silver, and brass working. NOTABLE FEATURES fort; Shrine of Sringam; Monument to Shiva.

Tiryns an ancient Greek town in the Argolid near Mycenae, famous for the remains of its fortified Bronze Age palace. Large parts of its Cyclopean walls still stand.

'tis *contr.* old use or poetic it is.

Tiselius, Arne Wilhelm Kaurin (1902–71) Swedish chemist, born in Stockholm. Professor at the University of Uppsala, he investigated serum proteins by electrophoretic analysis, and in chromatography evolved new methods for the analysis of colourless substances. He was awarded the 1948 Nobel Prize for Chemistry, and was President of the Nobel Foundation (1960–4).

Tissot, James Joseph Jacques (1836–1902) French painter, born in Nantes. He was influenced by Degas in Paris, then in the 1870s he settled in London, painting scenes of Victorian life. As a result of a visit to Palestine in 1886, he produced a series of watercolours of the life of Christ.

tissue *noun* 1 a group of cells with a similar structure and particular function in an animal or plant: *muscle tissue*. 2 a piece of thin soft disposable paper used as a handkerchief or as toilet paper. 3 (*in full* **tissue paper**) fine thin soft paper, used eg for protecting fragile objects. 4 fine thin delicate woven fabric. 5 an interwoven mass or collection: *a tissue of lies*. [from Old French *tissu*, woven cloth]

tissue culture *Biol.* the growth of isolated plant or animal cells, tissues, or organs under controlled conditions in a sterile growth medium. Important applications include the large-scale propagation of plants, development of disease-free plants, and the production of drugs from plant tissues. Tissue culture is also used for medical research on the behaviour of cancer cells, and the growth of human skin cultures to provide tissue grafts for patients with burns.

Tisza, River, Czech **Tisa**, Russian **Tissa** the longest tributary of the R Danube in E Europe. It is 962km/598mi long and is navigable for 780km/485mi. Rising in the W Ukrainian Carpathian Mts, it flows S into the Great Plain of Hungary, where it is used for irrigation and hydroelectricity. It enters the Danube SW of Belgrade. There are major land reclamation schemes along its course.

tit¹ *noun* any of several small agile songbirds. [from Middle English *tite*]

tit²
— **tit for tat** blow for blow; repayment of injury with injury.

tit³ *noun* 1 *slang* a teat. 2 *coarse slang* a woman's breast. [from Anglo-Saxon *titt*]

Titan 1 in Greek mythology, any of the 12 children of Uranus and Gaea, members of the older generation of gods. After Zeus and the Olympians took power, the Titans made war on them but were defeated and imprisoned in Tartarus (see also OLYMPIAN). 2 *Astron.* Saturn's largest natural satellite, 5 120km in diameter, the second-largest moon in the solar system, the only one with a detectable atmosphere.

titan *noun* a person or thing of very great strength, size, intellect, or importance.

Titaness in Greek mythology, a female Titan.

Titania 1 in Greek mythology, a female Titan identified with the Moon. 2 In Shakespeare's *A Midsummer Night's Dream*, she is the queen of the fairies and consort of Oberon, and is tricked into falling in love with Bottom, the Weaver.

Titanic a 46 329 gross tons British luxury passenger liner owned by White Star Line, which collided with an iceberg in the N Atlantic Ocean on her maiden voyage from Southampton to New York in Apr 1912. Lifeboat capacity was inadequate, and only about 700 lives were saved out of a total of over 2 000. The wreck of the vessel (broken into two pieces) was discovered in 1985, explored, and photographed on the sea bed.

titanic *adj.* having great strength or size; colossal; gigantic.

titanium *noun Chem.* (SYMBOL **Ti**, ATOMIC NUMBER 22) a silvery-white metal that is used to make strong light corrosion-resistant alloys for components of aircraft, missiles, etc. Its oxide is used as a dielectric in capacitors, and as a white pigment (titanium white). [from TITAN]

titbit *noun* a choice or small tasty morsel eg of food or gossip. [from TIDE 4 + BIT¹]

titfer *noun slang* a hat. [shortened from rhyming slang *tit for tat* (see TIT²)]

tithable *adj.* subject to the payment of tithes.

tithe — *noun* 1 (*often* **tithes**) *Hist.* a tenth part of a person's annual income or produce, paid as a tax to support the church or clergy in a parish. 2 a tenth part. — *verb* 1 to demand a tithe or tithes from. 2 *intrans.* to pay a tithe or tithes. [from Anglo-Saxon *teotha*, tithe, tenth]

Titian, in full **Tiziano Vecellio** (c.1490–1576) Venetian painter, born in Pieve di Cadore. He assisted Giorgione with the paintings on the Fondaco dei Tedeschi (1508), and his early paintings display Giorgione's influence (eg *Sacred and Profane Love*, c.1515). His own revolutionary style becomes apparent after c.1516 (eg in the *Assumption of the Virgin*, 1516–18, Venice). He painted three mythological subjects for the Duke of Ferrara, *Feast of Venus* (c.1515–18), *Bacchanal* (c.1518, both Prado, Madrid), and the richly-coloured *Bacchus and Ariadne* (c.1523, National Gallery, London). Also belonging to this period is the portrait *Man with a Glove* (c.1520, Louvre, Paris). From 1530, he also painted many pictures for Emperor Charles V, and this period also includes his *Venus of Urbino* (c.1538, Florence) and *Ecce Homo* (1543, Vienna). He later executed a series of works on mythological scenes for Philip of Spain, and in his last years painted several religious and mythological subjects, including the *Rape of Europa* (c.1560), *The Fall of Man* (c.1570, Madrid), *Christ Crowned with Thorns* (c.1570, Munich), and the unfinished *Pietà* (1573–6).

Titian — *noun* a bright reddish-gold colour. — *adj.* of this colour. [named after the painter TITIAN]

Titicaca, Lake the largest lake in S America and the highest large lake in the world (3 812m). AREA 8 289sq km/3 200sq mi; length 177km/110mi; width 56km/35mi; maximum depth 475m. It is situated in SE Peru and W Bolivia and forms a major transportation artery between the two countries. The lake divides into two parts, L Chucuito and L Uinamarca, connected by the Strait of Tiquina. The mining centre, Matilde, lies on the NE shore. The lake is a hunting, fishing, and sailing resort. It contains 36 islands, including Titicaca and Coati with archaeological remains. Copacabana, on the SW shore, served as a place of recreation for the Royal Inca family. NOTABLE FEATURES sanctuary and 17c temple (a Franciscan monastery) with a statue of the Virgin de Copacabana (1576), a place of pilgrimage; ruins of the ancient centre of the Tiahuanaco Empire are located nearby.

titillate *verb* 1 to excite gently, especially in a sexual way. 2 to tickle. [from Latin *titillare*]

titillating *adj.* that titillates.

titillation *noun* 1 titillating or being titillated. 2 something that titillates.

titivate *verb trans., intrans. colloq.* to smarten up or put the finishing touches (to). [earlier *tidivate*, from TIDY + -*vate* from words such as *elevate* and *cultivate*]

titivation *noun* titivating.

title — *noun* 1 the distinguishing name of a book, play, work of art, piece of music, etc. 2 an often descriptive heading, eg of a chapter in a book or a legal document. 3 a word of address used before a person's name to show acquired or inherited rank, an honour, occupation, or attainment. 4 a title page. 5 (*often* **titles**) written material on film giving credits, dialogue, etc. 6 *Legal* a right to the possession or ownership of property. 7 *Sport* a championship. 8 a book or publication. 9 a book or publication as distinct from a copy and as listed in a catalogue. — *verb* to give a title to. [from Latin *titulus*]

titled *adj.* having a title, especially one that shows noble rank.

title deed a document proving legal ownership.

title page the page at the beginning of a book which gives the name and address of the publisher, the title, author, and cataloguing information, etc.

title role the role of the character in a play or film from which that play or film takes its name, eg *King Lear*.

titmouse *noun* (PL. **titmice**) same as TIT[1]. [from Middle English *titemose*]

Tito, also called **Marshal Tito**, originally **Josip Broz** (1892–1980) Yugoslav statesman, born near Klanjec. He served with the Austro-Hungarian army in World War I, was taken prisoner by the Russians, and became a communist. He was imprisoned for conspiring against the regime in Yugoslavia (1928–9), and became Secretary of the Communist Party (1937). In World War II he organized partisan forces against the Axis conquerors (1941), and afterwards became the country's first communist Prime Minister (1945) and President (1953–80). He broke with Stalin and the Cominform (Communist Information Bureau) in 1948 to develop Yugoslavia's independent style of communism (or 'Titoism'), and played a leading role in the association of non-aligned countries.

Titograd, formerly **Podgorica** (to 1948) POP (1991) 118 000, the capital of Montenegro, Yugoslavia, lying on the R Morava, N of L Scutari. The Roman Emperor Diocletian was born here in AD 245. [named after Marshal Tito, the former President of Yugoslavia]

titrate *verb Chem.* to determine the concentration of a chemical substance in a solution by the process of titration. [from French *titre*, title, qualification]

titration *noun Chem.* a method of *volumetric analysis* (a form of chemical analysis) in which the concentration of a particular solution is determined by adding measured amounts of another solution of known concentration until the endpoint is reached, as indicated by a colour change or precipitation.

titre *noun* 1 *Chem.* the concentration of a solution as determined by titration with a standard solution of known concentration. 2 *Biol.* the concentration of a particular virus present in a suspension. 3 the concentration of an antibody present in a sample of serum.

titter *colloq.* — *verb intrans.* (**tittered, tittering**) to giggle or snigger. — *noun* a giggle or snigger.

tittle *noun* 1 a small written or printed sign, mark or dot. 2 a very small particle. [from Latin *titulus*, title]

tittle-tattle — *noun* idle or petty gossip or chatter. — *verb intrans.* to gossip or chatter idly.

titty *noun* (PL. **titties**) a child's word for TIT[3].

titular *adj.* 1 having the title of an office or position but none of the authority or duties. 2 being or having a title. [from Latin *titulus*, title]

titularly *adv.* 1 in respect of name, style, or title. 2 in name only.

Titus, originally **Titus Flavius Vespasianus** (AD 39–81) Roman emperor (79–81), the elder son and successor of Vespasian. He was a popular ruler, but is execrated in Jewish tradition for his destruction of Jerusalem (70) and suppression of the Jewish Revolt. His brief reign was marred by many natural calamities, notably the eruption of Vesuvius (79). He was called 'the darling of the human race' by Suetonius.

Titus 1 in the New Testament, a companion of St Paul. 2 a male first name. [from the Roman first name *Titus*]

Titus, Letter of Paul to a New Testament writing or Pastoral Letter, attributed to Paul. The letter addresses problems of Church order and false (possibly gnostic) teachers, with specific instructions about the importance of sound doctrine, the selection of elders and bishops, family and social relationships, and submission to rulers and authorities.

Tizard, Sir Henry Thomas (1885–1959) English chemist and administrator, born in Gillingham, Kent. In 1918–19 he was Assistant Controller of Experiments and Research for the RAF, and he later served as Secretary of the Department of Scientific and Industrial Research, Rector of Imperial College and President of Magdalen College, Oxford. He then became

Chairman of the Defence Policy Research Committee and of the Advisory Council on Scientific Policy until his retirement in 1952.

tizzy *or* **tizz** *noun* (PL. **tizzies**) *colloq.* a nervous, highly excited or confused state.

T-junction *noun* a junction at which one road meets another at a right angle but does not cross it.

Tl *symbol Chem.* thallium.

Tlaloc in Aztec religion, the god of rain, to whom children were sacrificed in time of drought. The features of his face were formed of serpents, representing lightning.

TLC *abbrev. facetious* tender loving care.

Tlemcen, ancient **Pomaria** 1 POP (1987) 127 000, the chief town of Tlemcen department, NW Algeria. It lies 113km/70mi SW of Oran and was the capital of major Moroccan dynasties from the 12c to the 16c. Despite French occupation from 1842, the town has a well-preserved Muslim culture. NOTABLE FEATURES Almovarid Great Mosque (1135), Grand Mosque; Museum of Bel Hassane. 2 a department in NW Algeria with the town of Tlemcen as its capital.

Tlingit a Native American group of the Pacific NW coast (from Prince William Sound to S Alaska), who lived mainly by fishing and hunting. They are famed for their art, which includes woven blankets and wooden sculptures.

Tm *symbol Chem.* thulium.

TN *abbrev.* Tennessee.

TNT *abbrev.* trinitrotoluene.

to — *prep.* 1 towards; in the direction of; with the destination of. 2 used to express as a resulting condition, aim, or purpose: *turn to stone / boil the fruit to a pulp / made to order / to my surprise.* 3 as far as; until: *a lie from beginning to end / five miles from the house to the station / bear the scars of the attack to this day.* 4 used to introduce the indirect object of a verb: *he sent it to us.* 5 used to express addition: *add one to ten.* 6 used to express attachment, connection, contact, or possession: *put his ear to the door / the key to the lock.* 7 before the hour of: *ten minutes to three.* 8 used to express response or reaction to a situation, event, etc: *rise to the occasion / dance to the music.* 9 used to express comparison or proportion: *win by two goals to one / second to none.* 10 used before an infinitive or instead of a complete infinitive: *he asked her to stay but she didn't want to.* — *adv.* 1 in or into a nearly closed position: *pulled the window to.* 2 back into consciousness: *he came to a few minutes later.* 3 near at hand. 4 in the direction required.

— **to and fro** backwards and forwards.

toing and froing movement backwards and forwards in an agitated way.

[from Anglo-Saxon]

Toad the car-driving, temperamental master of Toad Hall in Kenneth Grahame's *The Wind in the Willows*.

toad *noun* 1 a tailless amphibian belonging to the family Bufonidae of the order Anura (which also includes frogs), and having a short squat head and body, and dry skin covered with warts that contain poison glands which help to deter predators. 2 an obnoxious or repellent person. [from Anglo-Saxon *tade*]

◊ The hind legs of toads are shorter than those of frogs, and this restricts them to hopping or walking, rather than leaping. The common toad (*Bufo bufo*), native to Europe and Asia, is usually brown, but its skin may range from brick-red to grey or green in colour, and tends to match the colour of the ground on which the animal lives. Toads hibernate in winter, and in spring they migrate to their breeding grounds, often covering large distances, usually at night, to return to favoured ponds where large numbers of toads congregate.

toadflax *noun* a plant with flax-like leaves and yellow flowers.

toad-in-the-hole *noun Brit.* sausages cooked in Yorkshire pudding batter.

toadstool *noun* any of various fungi, most of which are poisonous or inedible, that produce a fruiting body consisting of an umbrella-shaped cap, on the underside of which are numerous spore-bearing gills, supported by a stem. See also MUSHROOM.

toady — *noun* (PL. **toadies**) a person who flatters someone else, does everything he or she wants and hangs on his or her every word; a sycophant. — *verb trans., intrans.* (**toady to someone**) to flatter them and behave obsequiously towards them.

toadyish *adj.* characteristic of a toady.

toadyism *noun* the activities and behaviour of a toady.

Toamasina *or* **Tamatave** POP (1990e) 145 000, a port on the E coast of Madagascar, on the Indian Ocean. Lying 367km/228mi NE of Antananarivo, it is the main port of Madagascar and a popular tourist resort. The town is surrounded by sugar-cane plantations. NOTABLE FEATURE Ivoloina Gardens nearby.

toast — *verb* **1** to make (especially bread) brown by exposing it to direct heat, eg under a grill. **2** *intrans. said especially of bread* to become brown in this way. **3** *trans., intrans.* to make or become warm by being exposed to heat, eg a fire. **4** to drink ceremonially in honour of or to the health or future success of. — *noun* **1** bread which has been browned by being exposed to direct heat, eg under a grill. **2** an act of drinking to a person's honour, health, or future success. **3** a person whose honour, health, or future success is drunk to. **4** a very admired person or thing: *her singing is the toast of the festival.* **5** the wish conveyed when drinking to someone's honour, etc. [from Latin *tostus*, roasted; sense 4 of the verb and senses 2, 3, 4, and 5 of the noun reflect the idea that a woman's name (ie as the person whose health is being drunk to) would flavour the wine like spiced toast]

toasted *adj.* cooked or heated by toasting.

toaster *noun* an electric machine for toasting bread.

toasting-fork *noun* a fork with a long handle, used to toast bread in front of a fire.

toastmaster *or* **toastmistress** *noun* a man or woman who announces the toasts to be drunk at a ceremonial dinner.

toast rack a small rack for holding slices of toast.

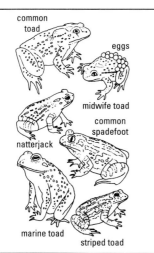

common toad
eggs
midwife toad
common spadefoot
natterjack
marine toad
striped toad

types of toad

tobacco *noun* (PL. **tobaccos, tobaccoes**) **1** a fast-growing annual or shrubby perennial plant of the genus *Nicotiana*, belonging to the same family (Solanaceae) as the potato. It is thought to be native to tropical America, and has large leaves and tubular greenish, yellow, pink, or red flowers. The leaves of certain species, especially *N. tabacum*, contain nicotine, a poisonous alkaloid compound that is an addictive stimulant. The plant requires a warm humid climate and a fertile well-drained soil. Much of the tobacco that is used in cigars is grown in the Caribbean. **2** the dried leaves of this plant, which are used to make cigarettes, cigars, pipe tobacco, and snuff. [from Spanish *tabaco*]

tobacco plant

tobacconist *noun* a person or shop that sells tobacco, cigarettes, cigars, pipes, etc.

Tobago POP (1990) 50 000, an island in the West Indies. AREA 300sq km/116sq mi. It forms part of the Republic of Trinidad and Tobago. CHIEF TOWN Scarborough. The island was united with Trinidad in 1889. NOTABLE FEATURES luxury hotel-conference centre at Rocky Point; tourist complex at Minster Point.

-to-be *combining form* forming words meaning 'of the future, soon to become': *mother-to-be.*

Tobias a male first name. [of Hebrew origin, = the Lord is good]

toboggan — *noun* a long, light sledge which curves up at the front, used for riding over snow and ice. — *verb intrans.* to ride on a toboggan. [from Native American *topagan*]

tobogganing *noun* the activity or sport of riding on a toboggan.

tobogganist *or* **tobogganer** *noun* a person who rides on a toboggan.

Tobruk *or* **Tubruq** POP (1979) 34 000, a seaport in Darnah province, N Libya. It lies on the Mediterranean coastline. HISTORY occupied by the Italians in 1911; important battle site in World War II: taken by the Australians in Jan 1941, then changed hands several times until finally taken by the British in late 1942.

Toby jug a pottery jug in the form of a seated figure, usually a stout man smoking a pipe and wearing a tricorn hat which forms the pouring lip. The jugs seem to have been introduced by Ralph Wood (1715–72) and his son in Burslem, Staffordshire, in the second half of the 18c.

toccata *noun* a piece of music for a keyboard instrument intended to show off the performer's skill and touch in a series of runs and chords before breaking into a fugue. [from Italian, from *toccare*, to touch]

Toc H a Christian fellowship founded (1915) as a club for British soldiers serving in Belgium. The club is non-sectarian, and now engages in a wide range of social work in the English-speaking world. [from *Toc* (telegrapher's code for *T*) + *H*, from *Talbot House* in Belgium where it held its first meetings]

tocopherol *noun* vitamin E. [from Greek *tokos*, offspring + *pherein*, to bear; so called from its apparent necessity for reproduction]

Tocqueville, Alexis (Charles Henri Maurice Clérel) de (1805–59) French historian and political scientist, born in Verneuil. He became a lawyer (1825), and in 1831 went to the USA to report on the prison system. On his return, he published *De la Démocratie en Amerique* (Democracy in America, 1835), a penetrating political study that made his name in Europe. He became a member of the Chamber of Deputies (1839), and in 1849 was Vice-President of the Assembly and briefly Minister of Foreign Affairs. After Louis Napoleon's coup, he retired to his estate and wrote one volume of *L'Ancien Régime et la Révolution* (The Old Regime and the Revolution, 1856), but he died before completing another volume.

tocsin *noun* an alarm bell or warning signal. [from French]

tod
— **on one's tod** *Brit. colloq.* alone.
[rhyming slang *on one's Tod Sloan*, on one's own]

today — *noun* **1** this day. **2** the present time. — *adv.* **1** on or during this day. **2** nowadays; at the present time. [from Anglo-Saxon *to dæg*]

Todd, Mike, originally **Avrom Hirsch Goldbogen** (1909–58) US showman, born in Minneapolis. In 1927 he went to Hollywood as a soundproofing expert, staged a real 'Flame Dance' spectacle at the Chicago World Fair (1933), and produced plays, musical comedies, and films, including a jazz version of Gilbert and Sullivan, *The Hot Mikado* (1939). He sponsored the 'TODD-AO' wide-screen process, used for his greatest film, *Around the World in Eighty Days* (1956, Academy Award).

Todd (of Trumpington), Alexander Robertus Todd, Baron (1907–) Scottish chemist, born in Glasgow. Professor at Manchester and Cambridge, he made important studies of the chemistry of natural products, including vitamins B_1, E, and B_{12}. He was awarded the 1957 Nobel Prize for Chemistry for research which established the manner in which sugar molecules and phosphate groups are attached to the four chemical DNA bases to form nucleotides, the building blocks of DNA.

toddle — *verb intrans.* **1** to walk with unsteady steps, as or like a young child. **2** *colloq.* to take a casual walk; to stroll or saunter. **3** (**toddle off**) *colloq.* to leave; to depart. — *noun* **1** a toddling walk. **2** *colloq.* a casual walk or stroll. [originally a dialect form; origin unkown]

toddler *noun* a very young child who is just beginning or has just learnt to walk.

toddy *noun* (PL. **toddies**) a drink made of spirits, sugar, hot water, lemon juice and sometimes spices. [from Hindi *tari*, from *tar*, palm]

Todi, Jacopone da (c.1230–1306) Italian religious poet, born in Todi, in Spoleto. He became a Franciscan in 1278, and was imprisoned (1298–1303) for satirizing Pope Boniface VIII. He is credited with the authorship of the *Stabat Mater* and other Latin hymns, and he also wrote *laudi spirituali* ('spiritual praises'), which were important in the development of Italian drama.

to-do *noun* (PL. **to-dos**) *colloq.* a fuss, commotion, or bustle.

toe — *noun* **1** in humans, any of the five digits at the end of each foot, whose main function is to assist balance and walking. **2** the front part of a shoe, sock etc covering the toes. **3** in other animals, the digit corresponding to the human toe. **4** the lower, often projecting end of eg a tool or area of land. — *verb* **1** to kick, strike, or touch with the toes. **2** to provide (eg a stocking, sock or shoe) with a toe.

— **on one's toes** alert and ready for action.

toe the line *colloq.* to act according to the rules.

tread on someone's toes to offend or upset them.

turn up one's toes *colloq.* to die. [from Anglo-Saxon *ta*]

toe-cap *noun* a piece of metal or leather covering the toe of a boot or shoe.

toe-hold *noun* **1** a place to anchor one's toes, eg when climbing. **2** a small initial or beginning position.

toenail *noun* a nail covering a toe.

toerag *noun slang* a despicable or contemptible person.

toff *noun Brit. slang* an upper-class and usually smartly dressed person. [from *tuft*, a titled undergraduate]

toffee *noun* a sticky sweet which is usually either chewy or hard, made from boiling sugar and butter, and sometimes nuts, etc.

toffee-apple *noun* an apple covered with a thin layer of toffee on a stick.

toffee-nosed *adj. Brit. colloq.* conceited; stuck-up.

tofu *noun* a curd made from soya beans, with a creamy colour and bland flavour, used especially in Japanese cooking. [from Japanese, from Chinese *dou fu*, rotten beans]

tog¹ — *noun* (**togs**) clothes. — *verb trans., intrans.* (**togged**, **togging**) (**tog up** *or* **tog oneself up**) to dress in one's best or warmest clothes. [from Middle English, from Latin *toga*, toga]

tog² *noun* a unit for measuring the warmth of fabrics and clothes. [perhaps from TOG¹]

toga *noun Hist.* a loose outer garment worn draped round the body by a citizen of ancient Rome. [from Latin]

togaed *adj.* wearing a toga.

together — *adv.* **1** with someone or something else; in company: *travel together.* **2** at the same time: *all arrived together.* **3** so as to be in contact, joined or united. **4** by action with one or more other people: *managed to persuade him together.* **5** in or into one place: *gather together.* **6** continuously: *chatting on the phone for hours together.* **7** *colloq.* into a proper or suitable order or state of being organized: *get things together.* — *adj. colloq.* well organized; competent.
— **together with** ... in company with ...; in addition to ...
[from Anglo-Saxon *to gæthere*]

togetherness *noun* a feeling of closeness, mutual sympathy and understanding, and of belonging together.

toggle — *noun* **1** a fastening, eg for garments, consisting of a small bar of wood, plastic, etc which will pass one way only through a loop of material, rope, etc. **2** a pin, bar or crosspiece placed through a link in a chain, loop in a rope, etc to prevent the chain, rope, etc from slipping. **3** *Comput.* a keyboard command which turns a particular feature (eg bold type or read-only mode) alternately on or off. — *verb* **1** to provide or fasten with a toggle. **2** *Comput.* **a** (**toggle something on** *or* **off**) to turn a particular feature, eg bold type or read-only mode alternately on and off using the same keyboard command. **b** *intrans.* to move between different features, modes, files, etc using a keyboard command. [originally a nautical term; origin unknown]

toggle switch 1 *Electr.* a switch consisting of a projecting spring-loaded lever that can be moved to either of two positions, as a result of which an electric circuit is either opened or closed. **2** *Comput.* a key on a computer keyboard that operates in a similar manner, and is used to turn a particular feature, such as bold type, on or off.

Togliatti see TOLYATTI.

Togo, official name **Republic of Togo**, French **République Togolaise** POP (1992e) 3.8m, a

republic in W Africa, divided into five regions. AREA 56 600sq km/21 848sq mi. It is bounded W by Ghana, N by Burkina, and E by Benin; its S coastline lies on the Bight of Benin. CAPITAL Lomé. CHIEF TOWNS Sokodé, Kpalimé, Atakpamé. TIME ZONE GMT. The chief ethnic groups are Hamitic in the N and Ewe in the S; local beliefs and Christianity are the chief religions. OFFICIAL LANGUAGE French; many local languages are also spoken. CURRENCY the franc CFA. PHYSICAL DESCRIPTION Togo rises from the lagoon coast of the Gulf of Guinea, past low-lying plains to the Atakora Mts, which run NE–SW across the N of the country; the highest peak is Pic Baumann (986m); flat plains lie to the NW. CLIMATE tropical; rain throughout the year in the S; one rainy season in the N between Jul and Sep; the average annual rainfall at Lomé on the coast is 875mm. HISTORY formerly part of the Kingdom of Togoland; German protectorate from 1884 to 1914; mandate of the League of Nations in 1922, divided between France (French Togo) and Britain (part of British Gold Coast); trusteeships of the United Nations in 1946; French Togo became an autonomous republic within the French Union in 1956; British Togoland voted to join the Gold Coast (Ghana) in 1957; French Togo gained independence in 1960; military coups in 1963 and 1967; return to civilian rule in 1980; an unstable period in the early 1990s as the country began to move towards democracy. GOVERNMENT governed by a President, a Cabinet, and a 77-member National Assembly, elected for five years. ECONOMY largely agricultural: coffee, cocoa, cotton, cassava, maize, rice, timber; phosphates; bauxite; limestone; iron ore; marble; cement; steel; oil refining; food processing; crafts; textiles; beverages.

Togo

To His Coy Mistress a love poem by the 17c poet Andrew Marvell.

toil¹ — *verb intrans.* **1** to work long and hard; to labour. **2** to make progress or move forwards with great difficulty or effort. — *noun* long, hard work. [from Old French *toiler*, to contend]

toil² *noun* (*usually* **toils**) a trap or snare. [from French *toile*, cloth, from Latin *tela*, web]

toilet *noun* **1** a bowl-like receptacle for the body's waste matter, with a water supply for washing this into a drain. **2** a room containing such a receptacle. **3** (*also* **toilette**) the act of washing, dressing, and arranging one's hair. [from French *toilette*, cloth]

toilet paper *or* **toilet tissue** thin absorbent paper used for cleaning the body after urination and defecation.

toilet roll a roll of toilet paper.

toiletry *noun* (PL. **toiletries**) an article or cosmetic used when washing, arranging the hair, and making up.

toilet water a light perfume containing a lot of alcohol.

toilsome *adj.* involving long, hard work.

toilworn *adj.* wearied by hard work.

Tojo, Hideki (1885–1948) Japanese soldier and politician, born in Tokyo. He became military attaché in Germany (1919), served in Manchuria as Chief-of-Staff (1937–40), and during World War II was Minister of War (1940–1) and Prime Minister (1941–4). Arrested in 1945, he attempted to commit suicide, but was hanged as a war criminal.

Tokay *noun* a sweet, heavy, aromatic wine made at *Tokay* in Hungary.

Tokelau, formerly **Union Islands** POP (1986e) 2 000, a non-Self Governing island Territory under New Zealand administration. AREA 10.1sq km/3.9sq mi. It consists of three small atolls (Atafu, Nukunonu, Fakaofo) in the S Pacific Ocean, c.3 500km/2 200mi NE of New Zealand. The inhabitants are citizens of New Zealand. The chief settlement is Nukunonu. TIME ZONE GMT –11. Most of the population are Polynesian. OFFICIAL LANGUAGES Tokelauan, English. CURRENCIES the dollar (New Zealand); the tala (Western Samoa). PHYSICAL DESCRIPTION each atoll consists of low-lying, scrub-covered, reef-bound islets encircling a lagoon. CLIMATE hot and humid, tempered by trade winds. HISTORY became a British protectorate in 1877; annexed in 1916, and included with the Gilbert and Ellice Islands Colony; returned to separate status in 1925, under the administrative control of New Zealand, but substantially self-governing at local level. ECONOMY copra, coconuts, breadfruit, pawpaw, bananas; pigs, fowl; the principal revenue earners are copra, stamps, souvenir coins, and handicrafts.

token — *noun* **1** a mark, sign, or distinctive feature. **2** anything serving as a reminder or souvenir; a keepsake. **3** a voucher worth a stated amount of money which can be exchanged for goods of the same value. **4** a small coin-like piece of metal or plastic which is used instead of money, eg in slot machines. — *adj.* done or given as a token and therefore of no real value.
— **by the same token** also; in addition; for the same reason.
[from Anglo-Saxon *tacen*]

tokenism *noun* the principle or practice of doing very little of something in pretence that one is committed to it, eg of employing one black person to avoid charges of racism.

Tok Pisin an English-based Melanesian pidgin spoken by about 1 million people in Papua New Guinea. Strongly influenced by native languages, it is now spoken by some as a mother tongue, and has thus become a creole.

Tokugawa, Ieyasu (1542–1616) Japanese soldier, who became the third of the three great historical unifiers of Japan (after Nobunaga and Hideyoshi), born in E Japan. He took power after the battle of Sekigahara (1600), and founded the Tokugawa shogunate (1603–1868). He completed Edo Castle (now Tokyo Imperial Palace) as his headquarters, and instituted an all-pervading centralized control of Japanese life, the effects of which are still felt.

Tokyo POP (1991e) 8.2m, the seaport capital of Japan, in Kanto region, E Honshu. It lies on the N shore of Tokyo-wan bay, on the R Sumida. HISTORY founded as the village of Edo in the 12c; became the headquarters of the Tokugawa shogunate in 1603; became the imperial capital in 1868; severe earthquake damage in 1923; heavily bombed in World War II. There are major problems of atmospheric pollution and traffic congestion. NOTABLE FEATURES over 100 universities; Tokyo Tower (1958), the tallest metal tower in the world; Ginza shopping district; Idemitsu Art Gallery; Imperial Palace (17c); Meiji Shrine; Asakusa Kannon Temple (645); Disneyland (1983), 10km/6mi to the SE.

tolbooth or **tollbooth** noun **1** an office where tolls are or were collected. **2** old use Scot. a town hall. **3** Scot. a prison.

told see TELL.

Toledo, Latin **Toletum** POP (1987e) 58 000, the capital of Castilla-La Mancha region and of Toledo province, Spain. It lies on the R Tagus, 71km/44mi SW of Madrid. Toledo was formerly the capital of the Visigothic kingdom of Castile and of Spain. NOTABLE FEATURES Moorish citadel; cathedral (13c–17c); El Greco's House; Churches of St Thomas and St Romanus; Santa Cruz Museum (containing paintings by El Greco); the old city is a World Heritage site.

Toledo POP (1990) 614 000, the seat of Lucas County, NW Ohio, USA. It is a port situated at the mouth of the Maumee R, at the W end of L Erie and is one of the country's largest rail centres. Toledo was formed by the union of two settlements in 1833. It was involved in the 'Toledo War' (1835–6), a boundary dispute between Ohio and Michigan. NOTABLE FEATURES Museum of Art; Zoological Gardens; Crosby Gardens; Fort Meigs State Memorial; Bluebird Passenger Train.

tolerability noun being tolerable.

tolerable adj. **1** able to be borne or endured. **2** fairly good.

tolerably adv. in a tolerable way; to a tolerable degree.

tolerance noun **1** the ability to be fair towards and accepting of other people's religious, political, etc beliefs or opinions. **2** the ability to resist or endure pain or hardship. **3** Medicine the ability of a person to adapt to the effects of a drug, so that increased doses are required to produce the same effect. **4** Biol. lack of reactivity to a particular antigen that would normally cause an immune response. **5** Biol. the ability of a plant or animal to survive extreme environmental conditions, eg drought, low temperature.

tolerant adj. **1** tolerating the beliefs and opinions of others. **2** capable of enduring unfavourable conditions, etc. **3** indulgent, permissive. **4** able to take drugs without showing serious side effects.

tolerantly adv. in a tolerant way.

tolerate verb **1** to bear or endure (pain or hardship); to put up with. **2** to be able to resist the effects of (a drug). **3** to treat fairly and accept (a person with different religious, political, etc beliefs or opinions). **4** to allow to be done or exist. [from Latin tolerare]

toleration noun **1** the act of tolerating. **2** the practice of allowing people to practise religions which are different to the established religion of the country.

Tolkien, J(ohn) R(onald) R(euel) (1892–1973) British philologist and writer, born in Bloemfontein, South Africa. He was Professor of Anglo-Saxon (1925–45) and of English Language and Literature (1945–59) at Oxford. His interest in language and saga are at the root of his well-known fantasy novels, which include The Hobbit (1937), The Lord of the Rings (3 vols, 1954–5), and The Silmarillion (1977).

toll¹ — verb **1** trans., intrans. to ring (a bell) with slow, measured strokes. **2** said of a bell to announce, signal, or summon by ringing with slow measured strokes. — noun the act or sound of tolling. [from Middle English tollen, to entice, lure]

toll² noun **1** a fee or tax paid for the use of some bridges and roads. **2** the cost in damage, injury, or lives of some disaster. [from Anglo-Saxon toll]

tollgate noun a gate or barrier across a road or bridge which is not lifted until travellers have paid the toll.

Tolpuddle martyrs agricultural labourers in Tolpuddle, Dorset, who in 1833 were organized into a trade union by a Methodist preacher,

George Loveless (1796–1874), convicted of taking illegal oaths, and transported. The action provoked substantial protests, and the labourers were eventually pardoned.

Tolstoy, Leo Nikolayevich, Count (1828–1910) Russian writer, moralist, and mystic, born in Yasnaya Polyana, Tula province. He joined the army in 1851, became known for his short stories, and fought in the Crimean War (1854–5). He then travelled abroad, married in 1862, and settled on his Volga estate, where he wrote his epic story of Russia during the Napoleonic Wars, War and Peace (1865–9), followed by Anna Karenina (1875–7). His subsequent spiritual crisis culminated in such works as A Confession (1879–82) and What I Believe (1883), and he made over his fortune to his wife and lived poorly as a peasant under her roof. His doctrines founded a sect, and Yasnaya Polyana became a place of pilgrimage.

Toltecs a people (or peoples) dominant in most of central Mexico between c.900 and 1150, the last such culture prior to the Aztecs. Their capital was at Tula, 80km/50mi north of Mexico City, but the most impressive Toltec ruins are at Chichen Itzá in the Yucatn, where a branch of the culture survived beyond the fall of its central Mexican hegemony.

Toluca or **Toluca de Lerdo** POP (1990) 488 000, the capital of México state, central Mexico. At an altitude of 2 675m, it is situated 66km/41mi W of Mexico City and was founded in 1535. NOTABLE FEATURES Churches of Tercer Orden and Vera Cruz, Convent of Carmen; Museo de Bellas Artes, Museo del Arte Popular; Palacio de Gobierno.

toluene noun Chem. (FORMULA $C_6H_5CH_3$) a toxic organic compound, consisting of a colourless flammable liquid, derived from benzene and insoluble in water, used as an industrial solvent and as an intermediate in the manufacture of the explosive trinitrotoluene (TNT), high-octane petrol, and various other organic chemicals.

Tolyatti or **Togliatti**, formerly **Stavropol** (to 1964) POP (1991e) 655 000, a town in Samara oblast, Russia, lying on a reservoir of the R Volga. HISTORY founded in 1738; the town was relocated in the mid-1950s when it was flooded by the reservoir of the nearby hydroelectric power plant.

Tom, Uncle the noble, Christian black slave in Harriet Beecher Stowe's Uncle Tom's Cabin, who is murdered on the instructions of his master, Simon Legree.

tom noun a male of various animals, especially a male cat. [an abbreviation of the name Thomas]

tomahawk noun a small axe used as a weapon by Native Americans. [from Algonkian (Native American language group) tamahaac]

Tomar POP (1991) 14 000, a town in Santarém district, central Portugal, lying on the R Nabão. NOTABLE FEATURES Convent of Christ, a World Heritage site; Church of São João Baptista.

tomato noun (PL. **tomatoes**) **1** a round or oval fleshy, juicy fruit, usually red or yellow in colour, eaten as a vegetable eg in salads. **2** the plant bearing this fruit. [from Aztec tomatl]

tomb noun **1** a chamber or vault for a dead body, either below or above ground, and often serving as a monument; a grave. **2** a hole cut in the earth or rock for a dead body. **3** (**the tomb**) poetic death. [from Greek tymbos]

Tombaugh, Clyde William (1906–) US astronomer, born in Streator, Illinois. Working at Lowell Observatory, he discovered Pluto in 1930. He later became professor at the University of New Mexico.

tombola noun a lottery in which winning tickets are drawn from a revolving drum. [from Italian tombolare, to tumble]

tomboy noun a girl who likes rough and adventurous games and activities.

Tom Brown's Schooldays a novel by Thomas Hughes (1857). It describes the experiences of a young boy at a public school.

tombstone noun an ornamental stone placed over a grave, on which the dead person's name, etc is engraved.

tomcat noun a male cat.

Tom, Dick, and Harry anybody at all; people in general.

tome noun a large, heavy and usually learned book. [from Greek tomos, slice]

tomfool — noun an absolute fool. — adj. absolutely foolish. [from Middle English Thome fole, Tom the fool]

tomfoolery noun (PL. **tomfooleries**) stupid or foolish behaviour, or an instance of it; nonsense.

Tom Jones, The History of a novel by Henry Fielding (1749). It describes the wandering life of Tom, who is abandoned as a baby.

Tommy noun (PL. **Tommies**) colloq. a private in the British army. [from Tommy Atkins, the name used on specimens of official forms]

tommygun noun a type of submachine gun. [named after J T Thompson (1860–1940), its American inventor]

tommy-rot noun colloq. absolute nonsense.

tomography noun Medicine a diagnostic scanning technique, especially one involving the use of X-rays or ultrasound, in which a clear image of internal structures in a single plane of a body tissue at a specified depth and angle is obtained. [from Greek tomos, cut + -GRAPHY]

Tomonaga, Sin-Itiro (1906–79) Japanese physicist, born in Kyoto. Professor at Tokyo University, he developed a relativistic quantum description of the interaction between a photon and an electron. For the resulting theory of 'quantum electrodynamics' he shared the 1965 Nobel Prize for Physics with Richard Feynman and Julian Schwinger.

tomorrow — noun **1** the day after today. **2** the future. — adv. **1** on the day after today. **2** in the future. [from Anglo-Saxon tomorgen]

Tom Sawyer, The Adventures of a novel by Mark Twain (1876). It describes the adventures of mischievous young Tom in the Missouri town of St Petersburg.

Tomsk 1 POP (1991e) 507 000, the river-port capital of Tomsk oblast, W central Siberia, Russia. It lies on the R Tom, 60km/37mi from its confluence with the R Ob. Founded in 1604, it was a major Siberian trade centre before the Trans-Siberian railway bypassed the town in the 1890s. **2** an oblast in W central Siberia, Russia, with Tomsk as its capital.

Tom Thumb, in full **Tom Thumb, a Tragedy** a burlesque drama by Henry Fielding (1730). It is a satire on the conventions of heroic drama.

tomtit noun a tit, especially a bluetit.

tom-tom noun a usually small-headed drum beaten with the hands. [from Hindi tam-tam, imitative]

-tomy combining form (PL. **-tomies**) Medicine forming words denoting removal by surgery: episiotomy. [from Greek tome, from temnein, to cut]

ton noun **1** Brit. (in full **long ton**) a unit of weight equal to 2 240 lb (approximately 1 016.05kg). **2** North Amer. (in full **short ton**) a unit of weight equal to 2 000 lb (approximately 907.2kg). **3** (in full **metric ton**; also **tonne**) a unit of weight equal to 1 000kg (approximately 2 204.6 lb). **4** (in full **displacement ton**) a unit used to measure the amount of water a ship displaces, equal to 2 240 lb or 35 cubic feet of seawater. **5** (in full **register ton**) a unit (originally a tun of wine) used to measure a ship's internal capacity, equal to 100 cubic feet. **6** (*in full* **freight ton**) a unit for measuring the space taken up by cargo, equal to 40 cubic feet. **7** (*usually* **tons**) *colloq.* a lot. **8** *colloq.* a speed, score, sum, etc of 100. See also TONNAGE. [a variant of TUN]

tonal *adj.* of or relating to tone or tonality.

tonality *noun* (PL. **tonalities**) **1** *Mus.* the organization of all of the notes and chords of a piece of music in relation to a single tonic. **2** the colour scheme and tones used in a painting.

Tone, (Theobald) Wolfe (1763–98) Irish nationalist, born in Dublin. He was called to the Bar in 1789, acted as secretary of the Catholic Committee, helped to organize the United Irishmen, but had to flee to the USA and to France (1795). He induced France to invade Ireland on two occasions, and was captured during the second expedition. He was condemned to be hanged, but committed suicide in Dublin.

tone — *noun* **1** a musical or vocal sound with reference to its quality and pitch. **2** *Mus.* a sound having a definite pitch. **3** a quality or character of the voice expressing a particular feeling, mood, etc. **4** the general character or style of spoken or written expression. **5** *Mus.* the interval between, or equivalent to that between, the first two notes of the major scale. **6** high quality, style, or character: *his coarse jokes lowered the tone of the meeting.* **7** the quality, tint, or shade of a colour. **8** the harmony or general effect of colours. **9** firmness of the body, a bodily organ or muscle. — *verb* **1** *intrans.* (**tone in**) to fit in well; to harmonize. **2** to give tone or the correct tone (to). **3** *intrans.* to take on a tone or quality.

— **tone down** *or* **tone something down** to become or make it softer or less harsh in tone, colour, force, etc.

tone up *or* **tone something up** to become or make it stronger, healthier, more forceful, etc. [from Greek *tonos*, tension]

tone-deaf *adj.* unable to distinguish accurately between notes of different pitch.

tone-deafness *noun* being tone-deaf.

tone language a language in which differing pitch levels, or tones, are used to alter the meaning of a word, or to signal a grammatical feature such as a change of tense. In Mandarin Chinese, for example, the word *ma* can mean 'mother', 'horse', 'hemp', or 'scold', depending on the tone used.

toneless *adj.* without variation in sound, pitch, expression, etc.

tonelessly *adv.* in a toneless manner.

tone pad *Comput.* an electronic device similar to a remote control for a television, etc, which allows data to be input into a central computer from a distance, usually via a telephone link.

tone poem a piece of music not divided into movements and which is based on a story or literary or descriptive theme.

tong *noun* a Chinese guild or secret society, especially one responsible for organized crime and gang warfare. [from S Chinese dialect *tong*, meeting hall]

Tonga, formerly **Friendly Islands** POP (1991e) 103 000, an independent island group in the SW Pacific Ocean, 2 250km/1 400mi NE of New Zealand. AREA 646sq km/249sq mi. CAPITAL Nuku'alofa. TIME ZONE GMT +13. Most of the population are of Tongan origin (98%); Protestantism is the chief religion. OFFICIAL LANGUAGE English. CURRENCY the pa'anga. PHYSICAL DESCRIPTION consists of 169 islands, 36 of which are inhabited, divided into three main groups (coral formations of Ha'apai and Tongatapu-Eua, mountainous Vava'u); the largest island is Tongatapu, with two thirds of the population and an area of 260sq km/100sq mi; the W islands are mainly volcanic and some are still active; they rise to a height of 500–1 000m; the highest point is the extinct volcano of Kao (1 014m). CLIMATE

semi-tropical; the average annual temperature at Tongatapu is 23°C and the average annual rainfall is 1 750mm; there are occasional hurricanes in the summer months. HISTORY became a British protectorate in 1899, under its own monarchy; gained independence in 1970. GOVERNMENT governed by a Sovereign, Privy Council, and a unicameral Legislative Assembly of Cabinet Members, nobles, and elected people's representatives. ECONOMY largely based on agriculture; copra, coconuts, bananas, watermelons, yams, taro, cassava, groundnuts, rice, maize, tobacco, sugar cane; tourism and cottage handicrafts are small but growing industries.

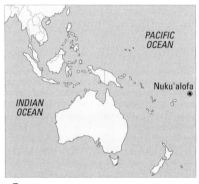

Tonga

Tongariro an active volcano rising to 1 968m in Tongariro National Park in central SW North I, New Zealand. AREA 765sq km/295sq mi. Other active volcanoes, Ruapehu and Ngauruhoe, are also located within the park's boundaries. The park was established in 1894. There are many historical Maori sites in the area.

Tongeren, French **Tongres** POP (1991e) 30 000, a rural market town in S Limburg province, Belgium, lying on the R Jeker. Founded in the 1c, it is the oldest town in Belgium. NOTABLE FEATURE Basilica of Our Lady.

Tongking *or* **Tongkin, Gulf of** a gulf in Indo-China, situated E of Vietnam and W of Hainan I, China. It is an inlet of the South China Sea.

tongs *pl. noun* a tool consisting of two arms joined by a hinge or pivot, for holding and lifting objects. [from Anglo-Saxon *tang*]

tongue — *noun* **1** in certain animals, the fleshy muscular organ attached to the floor of the mouth, covered with a mucous membrane, and bearing groups of taste buds on its upper surface. Its functions include tasting, licking, and manipulating food in preparation for chewing and swallowing. In human beings it is the main organ of speech. **2** the tongue of some animals, eg the ox and sheep, used as food. **3** the ability to speak. **4** a particular language. **5** a particular manner of speaking: *a sharp tongue.* **6** anything like a tongue in shape. **7** a narrow strip of land that reaches out into water. **8** the clapper in a bell. **9** a flap in the opening of a shoe or boot. **10** a projecting strip along the side of a board that fits into a groove in another. — *verb* **1** to touch or lick with the tongue. **2** *intrans. Mus.* to play a wind instrument by tonguing. **3** *Mus.* to produce (notes) by tonguing.

— **find one's tongue** to be able to speak again after a shock which has left one speechless.

hold one's tongue to say nothing; to keep quiet.

lose one's tongue to be left speechless with shock, horror, etc.

speak in tongues *Biblical* to speak in wholly or partly unknown languages.

with one's tongue in one's cheek, *or* **tongue in cheek** with ironic, insincere, or humorous intention.

[from Anglo-Saxon *tunge*]

tongue-tie *noun* a speech impediment which is caused by an abnormally small fold of skin under the tongue not allowing full movement of the tongue.

tongue-tied *adj.* **1** speechless, especially because of shyness or embarrassment. **2** suffering from tongue-tie.

tongue-twister *noun* a phrase or sentence that is difficult to say quickly, usually because it contains a series of similar consonant sounds, eg *She sells sea shells by the sea shore.*

tonguing *noun Mus.* a way of playing a wind instrument which allows individual notes to be articulated separately by the tongue opening and blocking the passage of air.

tonic — *noun* **1** a medicine that increases strength, energy, and the general wellbeing of the body. **2** anything that is refreshing or invigorating. **3** same as TONIC WATER. **4** *Mus.* the first note of a scale, the note on which a key is based. — *adj.* **1** increasing strength, energy, and wellbeing. **2** invigorating. **3** *Mus.* of or being the tonic. **4** producing (especially muscular) tension. [from Greek *tonikos*]

tonic sol-fa a way of teaching music which represents notes by syllables, with *doh* as the keynote for major keys and *lah* that for minor keys.

tonic water a fizzy soft drink flavoured with quinine.

tonight — *noun* the night of this present day. — *adv.* on or during the night of the present day. [from Anglo-Saxon *to niht*]

Tonlé Sap, English **Great Lake** a freshwater lake situated in W central Cambodia. AREA 2 850sq km/1 100sq mi (during the dry season). It lies in a depression on the Cambodian Plain, where it acts as a natural flood reservoir. The lake is linked to the Mekong R by the Tonlé Sap R; the confluence of the two rivers is at Phnom Penh. During the wet season, the height is raised by c.9m and the area is almost tripled. The lake and river are an important communications route.

tonnage *noun* **1** the space available in a ship for carrying cargo, measured in tons. **2** the total carrying capacity of a country's merchant shipping, measured in tons. **3** a duty or tax on ships based on their cargo-carrying capacity. **4** a duty on cargo by the ton. [originally a tax or duty levied on each *tun* of wine carried by a ship.] See also TON.

tonne *noun* a unit of weight equal to 1 000kg (2 204.6 lb) (see also TON 3). [from French]

tonner *noun* (*in compounds with a numeral*) a ship, lorry, etc that can carry the specified number of tons: *a 10-tonner.*

tonsil *noun* either of two almond-shaped lumps of tissue at the back of the mouth. They produce lymphocytes (white blood cells associated with antibody formation) and have an important role in preventing infection. During childhood they often become swollen, resulting in tonsillitis. [from Latin *tonsillae*, pl.]

tonsillectomy *noun* (PL. **tonsillectomies**) a surgical operation to remove the tonsils.

tonsillitis *noun* inflammation of the tonsils.

tonsorial *adj. often facetious* relating to barbers or hairdressing. [from Latin *tondere*, to clip or shave]

tonsure — *noun* **1** a shaved patch on the crown of a monk's or priest's head. **2** the act of shaving the crown of a monk's or priest's head as part of the rite of entering a monastic order or the priesthood. — *verb* to shave the head of, especially as a tonsure. [from Latin *tonsura*, from *tondere*, to clip or shave]

tonsured *adj.* wearing a tonsure.

tontine *noun* an annuity scheme in which several subscribers share a common fund, with their individual benefits increasing as members die until only one member is left alive and receives everything or until a specified date at which the proceeds will be shared amongst the survivors. [named after Lorenzo *Tonti* (c. 1653), the Italian-born Parisian banker who invented it]

ton-up *adj. old slang use, usually said of a motorcyclist* travelling or having travelled at more than 100mph, especially often and recklessly.

too *adv.* **1** to a greater extent or more than is required, desirable, or suitable: *too many things to do.* **2** in addition; as well; also: *enjoy swimming and like cycling too.* **3** what is more; indeed: *they need a good holiday, and they'll get one, too!* [a stressed form of TO]

took see TAKE.

Tooke, John Horne, originally **John Horne** (1736–1812) English radical politician, born in London. He became a lawyer, and in 1760 a vicar. In 1771, in support of the self-government for the American colonists and parliamentary reform, he formed the Constitutional Society. His spirited opposition to an enclosure bill drew the attention of a Mr Tooke of Purley in Surrey (later his friend and benefactor); this led to his new surname and *The Diversions of Purley* (1786), written while in prison for supporting the American cause. Tried for high treason in 1794, he was acquitted, and became an MP in 1801.

tool — *noun* **1** an implement, especially one used by hand, for cutting, digging, etc, such as a spade, hammer, etc. **2** the cutting part of a machine tool. **3** a thing used in or necessary to a particular trade or profession: *books are the tools of a librarian's job.* **4** a person who is used or manipulated by another, especially for selfish or dishonest reasons. **5** *coarse slang* a penis. — *verb* **1** to work or engrave (eg stone or leather) with tools. **2** (*also* **tool up** *or* **tool something up**) to equip a factory, etc or become equipped with the tools needed for production. **3** (**tool along**, **around**, *etc*) *colloq.* to drive or ride casually. [from Anglo-Saxon *tol*]

toolbag *noun* a bag for carrying and storing tools.

toolbox *noun* a box for carrying and storing tools.

toolkit *noun* a set of tools, especially those required for a particular trade or purpose.

toolmaker *noun* a person who makes or repairs machine tools.

toolmaking *noun* **1** producing tools. **2** the production or repair of machine tools.

toot — *noun* a quick, sharp blast of a trumpet, whistle, horn, etc. — *verb trans., intrans.* to sound or cause (a trumpet, horn, etc) to sound with a quick, sharp blast. [imitative]

tooth — *noun* (PL. **teeth**) **1** in vertebrates, any of the hard structures, usually embedded in the upper and lower jaw bones, that are used for biting and chewing food. **2** in invertebrates, any similar structure that is used for rasping or grinding food, or that resembles a vertebrate tooth. **3** one of many equally spaced projections around the edge of a gear wheel. **4** anything like a tooth in shape, arrangement or function, such as one of a series of cogs on a wheel or points on a comb. **5** an appetite or liking, especially for sweet foods: *a sweet tooth.* **6** (**teeth**) enough power or force to be effective. — *verb* **1** to provide with teeth. **2** *intrans. said of cogs* to interlock.
— **in the teeth of something** against it; in opposition to it.
long in the tooth *colloq.* old.
set one's teeth on edge to cause a sharp pain in the teeth such as that caused by eating something very cold; to cause to wince; to irritate severely.
take the teeth out of something to make it harmless.
tooth and nail fiercely and with all one's strength.

[from Anglo-Saxon *toth*]
◇ Teeth are used mainly for tearing, cutting, and grinding food to prepare it for swallowing and digestion, but in many animals they are also used to seize and kill prey, or for grooming. The number, arrangement, and type of teeth vary between different animals, depending on their diet. In mammals, each tooth consists of a central core of soft tissue (the *pulp*), which is richly supplied with nerves and blood vessels. The pulp is surrounded by a layer of *dentine* (a bony substance), and the part of the tooth that projects above the gum (the *crown*) is covered with a layer of enamel, the hardest material in the body, which is highly resistant to wear. The crown of the tooth may bear one or more projections called *cusps*, and the lower part of the tooth (the *root*) is embedded in a socket in the jaw bone, and is covered with cement instead of enamel.
In humans, the first set of teeth, consisting of 20 *deciduous* or *milk* teeth, is gradually replaced from about six years of age by 32 *permanent* teeth. These consist of chisel-shaped *incisors* for cutting, situated at the front of each jaw, and behind them the pointed *canine* teeth, for tearing food. Behind the canines are the *molars* and *premolars*, which have uneven surfaces for grinding and chewing food.

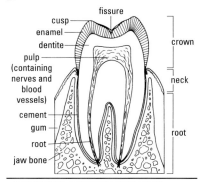

longitudinal section of a molar tooth

toothache *noun* an ache or pain in a tooth, usually as a result of dental caries (tooth decay). It also occurs during teething.

toothbrush *noun* a brush for cleaning the teeth.

toothily *adv.* in a toothy manner.

toothless *adj.* **1** without teeth. **2** powerless or ineffective.

toothpaste *noun* a paste used to clean the teeth.

toothpick *noun* a small sharp piece of wood, plastic, etc for picking out food from between the teeth.

toothpowder *noun* a powder used to clean the teeth.

toothsome *adj.* appetising; delicious; attractive.

toothy *adj.* (**toothier**, **toothiest**) showing or having a lot of especially large, prominent teeth.

tootle — *verb intrans.* **1** to toot gently or continuously. **2** (**tootle about**, **round**, *etc*) *colloq.* to go about casually, especially by car. — *noun* **1** a tootling sound. **2** *colloq.* a trip or drive. [from TOOT]

tootsie *or* **tootsy** *noun* (PL. **tootsies**) *colloq.* **1** a foot. **2** a toe.

Toowoomba POP (1991) 76 000, a city in Darling Downs statistical division, Queensland, Australia. It lies 130km/80mi W of Brisbane and serves as a commercial centre for the rich agricultural Darling Downs area. NOTABLE FEATURES Early Settlers Museum; St Matthew's Church (1859).

top[1] — *noun* **1** the highest part, point, or level of anything. **2** the highest or most important rank or position, or the person holding this: *top of the class.* **3** the upper edge or surface of something: *the table-top.* **4** a lid or piece for covering the top of something. **5** a garment for covering the upper half of especially a woman's body. **6** the highest or loudest degree or pitch: *the top of one's voice.* **7** (**the tops**) *colloq.* the very best person or thing. **8** (*usually* **tops**) the part of a root vegetable that is above the ground. **9** *Brit.* top gear. — *adj.* at or being the highest or most important. — *verb* (**topped**, **topping**) **1** to cover or form the top of, especially as a finishing or decorative touch: *top a cake with cream.* **2** to remove the top of. **3** to rise above or be better than; to surpass. **4** to reach the top of. **5** *slang* to kill. **6** *Golf* to hit the upper half of (the ball).
— **from top to toe** completely; from head to foot.
on top of something 1 in control of it. **2** in addition to it. **3** very close to it.
on top of the world in the very best of spirits.
top something off to put a finishing or decorative touch to it.
top something out to put the highest stone on a building.
top something up 1 to refill (a glass, container, etc) that has been partly emptied. **2** to provide money to bring (a grant, wage, money supply, etc) to the required or desirable total.
top someone up to refill their partly emptied glass, container, etc: *let me top you up with more coffee.*
[from Anglo-Saxon]

top[2] *noun* a wooden or metal toy which spins on a pointed base.
— **sleep like a top** to sleep very soundly.
[from Anglo-Saxon]

topaz *noun* an aluminium silicate mineral, found in gneisses and granites, that sometimes occurs in the form of enormous hard crystals, the pale yellow variety being most highly prized as a semi-precious gemstone. [from Greek *topazos*]

top boot a high boot with a band of different coloured leather round the top.

top brass *colloq.* the highest-ranking (especially military) officers or personnel.

topcoat *noun* an overcoat.

top coat a final coat of paint.

top dog *colloq.* the most important or powerful person in a group.

top drawer the highest level, especially of society.

top-dress *verb* to apply a top-dressing to.

top-dressing *noun Agric.* **1** manure or fertilizer applied to a growing crop. **2** the application of manure or fertilizer to a growing crop.

tope[1] *verb intrans.* to drink alcohol to excess. [a variant of obsolete *top*, to drink]

tope[2] *noun* a small shark found in European waters. [from a Norfolk dialect word]

Topeka POP (1990) 161 000, the capital of the state of Kansas, USA, in Shawnee County, E Kansas. It lies on the Kansas R, 88km/55mi W of Kansas City. Settled by anti-slavery colonists in 1854, it became capital in 1861. Topeka is a marketing and processing centre for agricultural products, particularly cattle and wheat, and is noted for its psychiatric research.

toper *noun* a drunkard.

top-flight *adj.* of the best or highest quality.

topgallant *noun* the mast or sail above the topmast and topsail.

top gear *Brit.* the combination of gearwheels which allows a vehicle to travel at its fastest speeds.

Top Hat a US film directed by Mark Sandrich (1935). It is a dance musical created for starring partnership Fred Astaire and Ginger Rogers.

top hat a man's tall, cylindrical hat, often made of silk, worn as part of formal dress.

top-heavy *adj.* **1** having the upper part too heavy for, or disproportionately large in comparison with, the lower. **2** *said of a company, administration, etc* having too many senior staff in proportion to junior staff.

topi *or* **topee** *noun* (PL. **topis, topees**) a helmet-like lightweight hat worn in hot countries as protection against the sun. [from Hindi, = hat]

topiary — *noun* (PL. **topiaries**) **1** the art of cutting trees, bushes and hedges into ornamental shapes. **2** an example of this. — *adj.* of or relating to topiary work. [from Latin *topia*, landscape gardening]

topic *noun* a subject or theme. [from Greek *topos*, place]

topical *adj.* **1** relating to matters of interest at the present time; dealing with current affairs. **2** relating to a particular place; local. **3** of a topic or topics.

topicality *noun* being topical.

topically *adv.* in a topical way; so as to be topical.

topknot *noun* a crest, tuft of hair, piece of added hair, or a knot of ribbons, etc, on the top of the head.

topless *adj.* **1** having no top. **2** *said of a woman's clothing* leaving the breasts exposed. **3** *said of a woman* with her breasts exposed. **4** *said of a place* where women go topless: *topless beaches.*

topmast *noun* the second mast, usually directly above the lower mast.

topmost *adj.* being the very highest of all.

top-notch *adj. colloq.* of the very best quality; superb.

topographical *adj.* relating to or involving topography.

topographically *adv.* in a topographical way; in terms of topography.

topography *noun* (PL. **topographies**) **1** the natural and man-made features on the surface of land, such as rivers, mountains, valleys, bridges and railway lines; also, a description or map of these. **2** the describing or mapping of such features. **3** the mapping or describing of the surface of any object or body. [from Greek *topos*, place + *graphein*, to describe]

topological *adj.* relating to or involving topology.

topologically *adv.* in a topological way; in terms of topology.

topology *noun Geom.* the branch of geometry concerned with those properties of a geometrical figure that remain unchanged even when the figure is deformed by bending, stretching, twisting, etc. For example, a ring shape (torus) painted on a rubber sheet can be distorted by stretching, but will always have a hole at its centre. The standard map of the London Underground system is a topological diagram, because it shows the lines joining the various stations, but is not to scale, ie the distances are distorted. [from Greek *topos*, place + -LOGY]

two topologically equivalent figures

Topolski, Feliks (1907–89) Polish-born British painter, draughtsman, and illustrator. He went to England in 1935, and worked as an official war artist (1940–5). His publications include *Topolski's Chronicle* (1953–79 and 1982–9), a draughtsman's record of contemporary life in various countries. His large paintings include the mural *The Coronation of Elizabeth II*, which is housed in Buckingham Palace.

topper *noun colloq.* a top hat.

topping — *noun* something that forms a covering or garnish for food. — *adj. Brit. old colloq.* use excellent.

topple *verb trans., intrans.* **1** (*also* **topple over**) to cause to fall, fall, or make as if to fall as if top-heavy. **2** to overthrow or be overthrown. [from TOP[1]]

topsail *noun* a square sail set across the topmast.

top-secret *adj.* very secret, especially officially classified so.

topside — *noun* **1** a lean cut of beef from the rump. **2** the side of a ship above the waterline. — *adj., adv.* on deck.

topsoil *noun* the uppermost layer of soil, rich in organic matter, that is disturbed during cultivation, eg ploughing. Most plant roots develop in this layer.

topspin *noun* a spin given to a ball by hitting it sharply on the upper half with a forward and upward stroke to make it travel higher, further, or more quickly.

Topsy the mischievous black child in Harriet Beecher Stowe's *Uncle Tom's Cabin*, who is the playmate of Little Eva.

topsy-turvily *adv.* in a topsy-turvy way.

topsy-turviness *noun* being topsy-turvy.

topsy-turvy *adj., adv.* **1** upside down. **2** in confusion. [from TOP[1] + obsolete *terve*, to turn over]

toque *noun* a woman's small, close-fitting, brimless or nearly brimless hat. [French]

tor *noun* a high rock or a pile of rocks or boulders found on the summit of a hill in an area of hard bedrock, eg on Dartmoor in the UK. [from Anglo-Saxon *torr*]

Torah *noun Judaism* **1** the Pentateuch. **2** the scroll on which this is written, used in a synagogue. **3** the whole body of Jewish literature and law, both written and oral, and including the Old Testament and Talmud. [from Hebrew, instruction]

Torbay POP (1987e) 118 000, an urban area in Devon, SW England. It was formed in 1968 and includes the resort towns of Torquay, Paignton, and Brixham.

torc see TORQUE.

torch *noun* **1** *Brit.* a small portable light powered by electric batteries. **2** a piece of wood or bundle of cloth, etc used to give light. **3** any source of heat, light, illumination, enlightenment, etc.
— **carry a torch for someone** to feel (especially unrequited) love for them.
[from Old French *torche*, from Latin *torquere*, to twist]

torchlight *noun* the light of a torch or torches.

tore see TEAR[2].

toreador *noun* a bullfighter, especially one on horseback. [from Spanish]

torero *noun* (PL. **toreros**) a bullfighter on foot. [from Spanish]

torii *noun* a Japanese Shinto temple gateway, generally orange-red in colour, but sometimes unpainted, giving the name of the deity. At shrines of the harvest god, or the fox deity (Inari), those wanting good fortune may donate torii with their names. [from Japanese]

torment — *noun* (with stress on *tor-*) **1** very great pain, suffering or anxiety. **2** something that causes this. — *verb* (with stress on *-ment*) **1** to cause great pain, suffering, or anxiety to. **2** to pester or harass (eg a child or animal). [from Latin *tormentum*]

tormentil *noun* a perennial plant (*Potentilla erecta*) with leaves composed of three (sometimes more) leaflets, silvery below, with margins toothed towards the tip. It bears clusters of bright yellow flowers, and is widely distributed on cultivated land, heaths, and garden lawns. [from Old French *tormentille*, from Latin *tormentum*, torment, because it was used to numb pain]

tormentor *noun* a person who torments.

torn see TEAR[2].

Tornado a multi-role combat aircraft produced by Panavia Aircraft, it had its first flight on 27 Oct 1979. It was used in the airforces of Britain, Germany, and Italy.

tornado *noun* (PL. **tornadoes**) *Meteorol.* a violently destructive storm consisting of a funnel-shaped rotating column of air which can be seen extending downward from thunder clouds to the ground surface, tracing a narrow path across the land. Tornadoes can reach speeds of over 350kph, and cause considerable destruction in the Gulf states and central and S plains of the USA, and Australia. [from Spanish *tronada*, thunderstorm]

the scroll of the Torah in its case

Torness a nuclear power station near Dunbar, East Lothian, Scotland. It came into operation, using gas-cooled reactors, in 1987.

Tornio, River, Swedish **Torne älv** a river in N and NE Sweden, length 566km/352mi. It issues from L Torneträsk in NW Sweden and flows SE and S, forming part of the Swedish–Finnish border in its lower course. At Tornio on the border with Finland, it enters the Gulf of Bothnia.

Toronto POP (1991e) 3.9m, the capital of Ontario province, SE Canada, and the country's second largest city. It lies on the N shore of L Ontario, at the mouth of the R Don and is a leading commercial and cultural centre. HISTORY the French built a fort here in 1749; the site was occupied by the British in 1759; United Empire Loyalists settled in 1793, naming the settlement York; it became capital of Upper Canada in 1796; during the War of 1812 it was twice captured by the Americans; in 1834 it became a city and was named Toronto; in 1837 it was the centre of a separatist rebellion; since 1867 it has been Ontario's capital. NOTABLE FEATURES Art Gallery of Ontario; Sigmund Samuel Canadiana Gallery; Osgoode Hall (1828); old City Hall (1891–9) with a 91m-high clock tower; Fort York (1793, restored in 1934); Ontario Centennial Centre of Science and Technology; O'Keefe Centre (home of the Canadian Opera Company); several theatres; a ballet; Toronto Symphony Orchestra.

torpedo — *noun* (PL. **torpedos, torpedoes**) **1** a long, self-propelling, underwater missile which explodes on impact with its target (usually a ship) and can be fired from submarines, ships, and aircraft. **2** any of several rays found in warm seas with organs on the head which can give an electric shock. **3** *North Amer.* a small container holding an explosive charge, used in warfare as eg a firework or fog-signal. — *verb* (**torpedoes, torpedoed**) **1** to attack with torpedoes. **2** to wreck or destroy (eg a plan). [from Latin *torpedo*, numbness, electric ray, from *torpere*, to be numb] ◇ The first practical torpedo dates from the middle of the 19c. In modern warfare, guided torpedoes are a key anti-submarine weapon, equipped with sonar-seeking heads which identify and track underwater sounds and computerized systems to guide them towards the source of the noise.

torpedo boat a small fast warship armed with torpedos.

torpedo ray see ELECTRIC RAY.

torpid *adj.* **1** sluggish and dull; lacking in energy. **2** unable to move or feel; numb. **3** *said of a hibernating animal* dormant. [from Latin *torpidus*, from *torpere*, to be numb]

torpidity *noun* a torpid state; numbness.

torpidly *adv.* with a torpid manner.

torpor *noun* **1** drowsiness, sluggishness, apathy. **2** numbness. [from Latin, from *torpere*, to be numb]

Torquay POP (1981) 58 000, a resort town in Torbay, Devon, SW England. It lies 30km/19mi S of Exeter and is a centre for recreational sailing. NOTABLE FEATURES Torr Abbey (12c); Kent's Cavern.

torque *noun* **1** (*also* **torc**) *Hist.* a necklace made of metal twisted into a band, worn by the ancient Britons and Gauls. **2** *Physics* a measure of the tendency of a force to cause an object to rotate about an axis. It is defined as the magnitude of the force multiplied by the distance between the force and the point about which it causes rotation. [from Latin *torquere*, to twist]

Torquemada, Tomás de (1420–98) Spanish Dominican monk, born in Valladolid. A Dominican prior in Segovia (1452–74), he persuaded Ferdinand and Isabella to ask the pope to sanction the institution of the 'Holy Office' of the Inquisition. As first Inquisitor-General of Spain from 1483, he displayed pitiless cruelty, and was responsible for the expulsion of the Jews from Spain (1492) and c.2 000 burnings.

Torquil a male first name. [of Norse origin, associated with the name of the god *Thor*]

torr *noun Physics* a unit of pressure equal to 133.3 pascals, that will support a column of mercury 1mm high. It is used to measure very low pressures, eg in high-vacuum technology. [named after the Italian mathematician Evangelista Torricelli]

Torrens, Lake a salt lake in S central South Australia, W of the Flinders Ranges. AREA 5 775sq km/2 229sq mi; 240km/150mi long and 65km/40mi wide.

torrent *noun* **1** a great rushing stream or downpour of water, lava, etc. **2** a violent or strong flow, eg of questions, abuse, etc. [from Latin *torrens*, boiling]

torrential *adj., said of rain, etc* falling in torrents; extremely heavy.

Torres Strait a channel between the Coral Sea in the E and the Arafura Sea in the W, to the N of Cape York, Queensland, Australia. The strait, which is 130km/80mi wide, was discovered in 1606. The Torres Strait Is, which may be the remains of a land bridge linking Asia and Australia, were annexed by Queensland in the 19c. They are inhabited by Polynesians, Melanesians, and Aborigines.

Torrey, John (1796–1873) US botanist, born in New York City. Professor at West Point, the US Military Academy, and at Cornell, he later became Chief Assayer at the US Assay Office in New York (1854). He founded the New York Lyceum of Natural History and prepared several floras for N America. His collection of over 50 000 plant species formed the basis for the herbarium of the New York Botanical Gardens.

Torricelli, Evangelista (1608–47) Italian physicist and mathematician, probably born in Faenza. The successor of Galileo as professor to the Florentine Academy, he discovered that it is because of atmospheric pressure that water will not rise above 33 feet in a suction pump, and gave the first description of a mercury barometer or 'torricellian tube' (1644).

torrid *adj.* **1** *said of the weather* so hot and dry as to scorch the land. **2** *said of land* scorched and parched by extremely hot, dry weather. **3** passionate; intensely emotional. [from Latin *torridus*, from *torrere*, to parch]

Tórshavn *or* **Thorshavn** POP (1992e) 16 000, the seaport capital of the Faroe Is, lying on the SE coast of Strømø I.

torsion *noun* **1** the act or process of twisting something by applying force to one end while the other is held firm or twisted in the opposite direction. **2** the state of being twisted in this way. [from Latin *torsio*, from *torquere*, to twist]

torsional *adj.* relating to or involving torsion.

torso *noun* (PL. **torsos**) **1** the main part of the human body, without the limbs and head. **2** a nude statue of this. [from Italian, from Latin *thyrsos*, stalk]

tort *noun Legal* any wrongful act other than breach of contract for which an action for damages or compensation may be brought. [from Latin *tortum*, wrong] ◇ A tort is actionable in the civil courts and the usual remedies are damages and/or an injunction. Examples include negligence, trespass, nuisance, and defamation.

Tortelier, Paul (1914–90) French cellist, conductor, and composer, born in Paris, where he made his début in 1931. His solo career began with the Concertgebouw, Amsterdam (1946), and with Beecham in London (1947); he subsequently toured worldwide. A leading soloist, he was also a distinguished teacher (his masterclasses were televised), and a composer of cello music and of the international anthem *The Great Flag* for the United Nations Organization. His son Yan Pascal (1947–) is a conductor and violinist.

tortilla *noun* a Mexican thin round maize cake cooked on a griddle and usually eaten hot with a filling or topping of meat or cheese. [from Spanish *torta*, cake]

tortoise *noun* any of various slow-moving toothless reptiles having a high domed shell into which the head, short scaly legs, and tail can be withdrawn for safety. Tortoises are found in warm regions, and live on land, unlike turtles, which are aquatic. [from Latin *tortuca*] ◇ Tortoises first appeared on Earth about 200 million years ago, and have changed very little since then. Most tortoises live in tropical and subtropical regions (except Australasia), and each day they bask in the Sun's heat, in order to warm their bodies, and then search for food, mainly leaves, flowers, and fruit. Tortoises living in temperate regions hibernate in winter, burying themselves in soft earth or dead leaves. The Galapagos giant tortoise, whose shell may be up to 1.5m long, has been known to live for up to 177 years.

tortoise

tortoiseshell — *noun* **1** the brown and yellow mottled shell of a sea turtle, used in making combs, jewellery, and decorative inlay in furniture. **2** a butterfly with mottled orange or red and brown or black wings. **3** a domestic cat with a mottled orange and brown coat. — *adj.* made of or mottled like tortoiseshell.

tortuous *adj.* **1** full of twists and turns. **2** not straightforward, especially in being devious or involved. [from Latin *tortuosus*, from *torquere*, to twist]

tortuously *adv.* in a tortuous way.

tortuousness *noun* being tortuous.

torture — *noun* **1** the infliction of severe pain or mental suffering, especially as a punishment or as a means of persuading someone to give information. **2** great physical or mental suffering, or a cause of this. — *verb* **1** to subject to torture. **2** to cause to experience great physical or mental suffering. **3** to force out of a natural state or position; to distort. [from Latin *tortura*, torment]

torturous *adj.* **1** causing torture. **2** causing distortion.

torturously *adv.* in a torturous way.

Toruń, German **Thorn** POP (1992e) 202 000, an industrial river port and the capital of Toruń voivodship, N central Poland. It lies on the R Vistula and was the birthplace of Copernicus. NOTABLE FEATURES Church of St John (13c); Palace of the Bishops of Kuyawy (1693); castle (13c); Ethnographical Museum; Burghers' Manor (15c).

torus *noun* **1** *Anat.* a rounded swelling or projection on a body part. **2** *Bot.* the receptacle of a flower, ie the tip of the flower stalk, on which the sepals, petals, stamens, and carpels are borne. **3** *Geom.* a curved surface with a hole in it, resembling a doughnut, obtained by rotating a circle about an axis lying in the same plane as the circle. [from Latin *torus*, bulge, swelling]

Torvill, Jayne (1957–) British figure skater, born in Nottingham, the partner of Christoper Dean (1958–). They were world ice-dance champions (1981–4), and Olympic and European champions in 1984. Their highly acclaimed performances included an interpretation of music from Ravel's *Bolero*, and the musical, *Barnum*. They retired from competitive skating in 1984, and turned professional. They competed again in the 1994 Winter Olympics, winning bronze medals.

Tory — *noun* (PL. **Tories**) **1** a member or supporter of the British Conservative Party. **2** *Hist.* a member or supporter of a major English political party from the 17c to mid-19c which favoured royal authority over that of Parliament, supported the established Church and was against political and social reform, superseded by the Conservative Party. See also WHIG. **3** *North Amer. Hist.* a supporter of the British Crown during the American Revolution. — *adj.* **1** relating to or supporting the Tories. **2** Conservative. [from Irish Gaelic *tóraí*, bandit, outlaw]

Toryism *noun* the principles of the Tories; Conservatism.

Tosca an opera by Giacomo Puccini (1900). Set in Rome in the year 1800, the story tells how Tosca, who is the painter Cavaradossi's lover, unwittingly leads the sadistic chief of police Scarpia to his villa, where a political fugitive is hiding. Scarpia tortures Cavaradossi, and offers to arrange a mock execution in exchange for sexual favours from Tosca. She agrees, but stabs Scarpia. He had lied about the mock execution and Cavaradossi is shot, after which Tosca jumps from the castle battlements.

Toscanini, Arturo (1867–1957) Italian conductor, born in Parma. In 1886 while playing the cello in Rio de Janeiro, he was suddenly called upon to replace the conductor, and presented a triumphant performance of *Aida*. He later conducted at La Scala, Milan (1898–1908), the Metropolitan Opera House, New York

(1908–15), the New York Philharmonic (1926–36), the Bayreuth (1930–1) and Salzburg (1934–7) festivals, and founded the National Broadcasting Orchestra of America (1937–53).

toss — *verb* **1** to throw up into the air. **2** (*usually* **toss something away**, **aside**, **out**, *etc*) to throw it away or discard it casually or carelessly. **3** (*also* **toss about**, **around**, *etc*) to move restlessly or from side to side repeatedly: *toss sleeplessly all night.* **4** (*also* **toss about** *or* **toss something about**) to be thrown or throw it from side to side repeatedly and violently: *a ship tossed by the storm.* **5** to jerk (the head), especially as a sign of impatience or anger. **6** *trans., intrans.* to throw (a spinning coin) into the air and guess which side will land facing up, as a way of making a decision or settling a dispute. **7** to settle a dispute with (someone) by tossing a coin: *toss him for the last cake.* **8** to coat (food, especially salad) by gently mixing it in a dressing. **9** *said of a horse, etc* to throw (its rider). **10** *said of an animal* to throw (a person) into the air with its horns. **11** to discuss or consider in, or as if in, light-hearted or casual debate: *toss various ideas back and forth in one's head.* — *noun* **1** an act or an instance of tossing. **2** a fall from a horse. **3** *coarse slang* the slightest amount: *not give a toss.*
— **argue the toss** to dispute a decision.
toss off *Brit. coarse slang* to masturbate.
toss something off 1 to drink it quickly, especially in a single swallow. **2** to produce it quickly and easily.
toss up to throw a spinning coin into the air and guess which side will land facing upwards, as a way of making a decision or settling a dispute.

toss-up *noun* **1** *colloq.* an even chance or risk. **2** an act of tossing a coin.

tot[1] **1** a small child; a toddler. **2** a small amount of spirits: *a tot of whisky.*

tot[2] *verb* (**totted**, **totting**) **1** (*also* **tot something up**) to add it together. **2** (*also* **tot up**) *said of money, etc* to increase. [an abbreviation of TOTAL]

total — *adj.* whole; complete. — *noun* the whole or complete amount, eg of various things added together. — *verb* (**totalled**, **totalling**) **1** *trans., intrans.* to amount to a specified sum. **2** (*also* **total something up**) to add it up to produce a total. **3** *North Amer. slang* to wreck or destroy (especially a vehicle) completely. [from Latin *totalis*, from *totus*, all]

total internal reflection *Optics* the complete reflection of a ray of light at the boundary of one medium with another, eg glass and air. It forms the basis for the reflection of light inside optical fibres, so that all of the light is reflected back into the fibre and 'trapped'.

totalitarian — *adj.* of or relating to a system of government by a single party which allows no opposition and which demands complete obedience to the State. — *noun* a person in favour of such a system.

totalitarianism *noun* totalitarian practices and systems.

totality *noun* **1** completeness. **2** a complete number or amount.

Totalizator, also called the **the Tote** a method of placing bets at horse race or greyhound meetings, first tried at Newmarket and Carlisle on 2 Jul 1928. All money invested is returned to winning punters, less expenses and taxes.

totalizer *noun* **totaliser** same as TOTALIZATOR.

totally *adv.* **1** completely. **2** absolutely.

total recall *Psychol.* the power of remembering accurately in full detail.

Tote see TOTALIZATOR.

tote *verb* (**tote something about** *or* **around**) *colloq.* to carry, drag, or wear it.

tote bag a large bag for carrying shopping.

totem *noun* **1** a natural object, especially an animal, used as the badge or sign of a tribe or an individual person among North American Indians. **2** an image or representation of this. [from Ojibwa (N American Indian language) *nintotem*, my totem, from *ote-*, to live in a village]

totemic *adj.* **1** relating to a totem or totems. **2** having or characterized by totems.

totemism *noun* the rituals, customs, and taboos associated with the use of totems as the foundation of a social system of obligation and restriction.

totem pole 1 a large wooden pole on which totems are carved and painted. **2** an order of rank; a hierarchy.

totem poles

To the Lighthouse a novel by Virginia Woolf (1927). It is a stream-of-consciousness narrative focusing on the impressions of the Ramsay family and their guests while they are holidaying on the west coast of Scotland.

totter — *verb intrans.* (**tottered**, **tottering**) **1** to move unsteadily or weakly. **2** to sway or tremble as if about to fall. **3** *said of a system of government, etc* to be on the verge of collapse. — *noun* a weak and unsteady movement or gait. [from Middle English *toteron*]

tottery *adj.* shaky.

totting-up *noun* **1** adding-up. **2** *Brit.* accumulation of penalties for motoring offences, eventually resulting in disqualification.

toucan *noun* a tropical American fruit-eating bird with a huge beak and brightly coloured feathers. [from Tupí (S American Indian language) *tucana*, imitative of its cry]

toucan

touch — *verb* **1** to bring something (eg one's hand) into contact, especially lightly, with (something), especially so as to feel: *he touched her cheek gently.* **2** *said of an object* to come into contact with (something else): *the branch touched the window.* **3** *intrans.* to feel, push, or strike something lightly, especially with the hand or foot. **4** *intrans.* to be in contact with something else without overlapping. **5** to make (someone) feel pity, sympathy, quiet pleasure, etc: *was touched by his sad story.* **6** to have an effect on. **7** to be of concern to: *a matter which doesn't touch you.* **8** to have dealings with: *wouldn't touch a job like that.* **9** to use, especially to eat or drink: *I never touch chocolate.* **10** to reach: *the temperature touched 100°.* **11** to be as good as; to equal or rival: *no one can touch her at chess.* **12** to mark slightly or delicately; to make a usually slight, sometimes harmful, impression on: *a sky touched with pink.* **13** to draw or paint with light strokes. **14** (**touch on** *or* **upon something**) to speak of or discuss briefly or in passing. **15** to disturb by handling, meddling, etc: *someone's touched my papers.* **16** (**touch someone for something**) *slang* to ask for and receive money as a loan or gift from them: *tried to touch him for £50.* — *noun* **1** an act of touching or the sensation of being touched. **2** the sense by which the existence, nature, texture and quality of objects can be perceived through physical contact with the hands, feet, skin, lips, etc. **3** the particular texture and qualities of an object as perceived through contact with the hands, etc: *the silky touch of the fabric against her skin.* **4** a small amount or quantity; a trace or hint. **5** a slight attack (eg of an illness). **6** a slight stroke or mark. **7** a detail which adds to or complements the general pleasing effect or appearance: *put the finishing touches to the portrait / a few vases of flowers are an elegant touch.* **8** a distinctive or characteristic style or manner: *a woman's touch.* **9** a musician's individual manner or technique of touching or striking the keys of a keyboard instrument or strings of a string instrument to produce a good tone. **10** an artist's or writer's individual style or manner of working. **11** the ability to respond or behave with sensitivity and sympathy: *have a wonderful touch with animals.* **12** contact; communication: *out of touch with recent developments / in touch with old school friends.* **13** (**a touch ...**) *colloq.* a bit ...; rather: *a touch too much make-up.* **14** *Rugby etc* the ground outside the touchlines. **15** *slang* an act of asking for and receiving money from someone as a gift or loan. **16** *slang* a person who can be persuaded to give or lend money: *a soft touch.* **17** a test with, or as if with, a touchstone.
— **touch and go** of a very uncertain outcome.
touch down *said of an aircraft or spacecraft* to land.
touch something down *Rugby* to put the ball on the ground behind the goal-line, either behind one's own as a defensive move or behind the opponent's when scoring a try.
touch something off 1 to cause it to explode, eg by touching it with a flame. **2** to cause it to begin; to trigger it.
touch someone up *slang* to touch or fondle them so as to excite sexually; to molest them sexually.
touch something up to improve it by adding small details to or correcting or hiding the minor faults of.
[from Old French *tuchier*]

touchdown 1 the point of contact of an aircraft with the ground on landing. **2** *Rugby* the action of touching the ball down to score.

touché *interj.* an expression used to acknowledge: **1** a hit in fencing. **2** a point scored in an argument or made in retaliation. [French, = touched]

touched *adj.* **1** feeling pity, sympathy, quiet pleasure, etc. **2** *colloq.* slightly mad.

touchily *adv.* in a touchy manner.

touchiness *noun* being touchy.

touching — *adj.* causing one to feel pity or sympathy; moving. — *prep.* concerning.

touchingly *adv.* in a touching way.

touch judge *Rugby* a linesman.

touchline *noun* *Football, Rugby* either of the two lines marking the side boundaries of the pitch.

touchpaper *noun* paper steeped in saltpetre for firing gunpowder.

touch screen *Comput.* a visual display unit screen that doubles as an input device, and is operated by being touched.

Touchstone the Fool at Duke Frederick's court and the companion in exile of Rosalind and Celia in Shakespeare's *As You Like It*, whose ascerbic wit and word-spinning win him the heart of Audrey.

touchstone *noun* **1** a test or standard of judging the quality of something. **2** a hard black flint-like stone used for testing the purity and quality of gold and silver alloys which, when rubbed on this stone, leave a coloured mark which indicates the amount of alloy.

touch-type *verb intrans.* to type without looking at the typewriter keyboard.

touch-typing *noun* the act or skill of typing without watching the keyboard.

touch-typist *noun* a person who is skilled in touch-typing.

touchwood *noun* wood which can be used as tinder, especially because it is dry or decayed.

touchy *adj.* (**touchier, touchiest**) *colloq.* **1** easily annoyed or offended. **2** needing to be handled or dealt with with care and tact.

tough — *adj.* **1** strong and durable; not easily cut, broken, torn, or worn out. **2** *said of food* difficult to chew. **3** *said of people and animals* strong and fit and able to endure hardship. **4** difficult to deal with or overcome; testing. **5** severe and determined; unyielding; resolute. **6** rough and violent; criminal. **7** *colloq.* unlucky; unjust; unpleasant: *tough luck.* — *noun* a rough, violent person, especially a bully or criminal.
— **get tough with someone** *colloq.* to begin to deal with them more strictly or severely. [from Anglo-Saxon *toh*]

toughen *verb* (**toughened, toughening**) (*also* **toughen up** *or* **toughen someone up**) to become or make them tough or tougher.

toughly *adv.* in a tough way.

toughness *noun* a tough quality.

Toulon, Latin **Tilio Martius** POP (1990) 438 000, a fortified naval port and the capital of Var department, Provence-Alpes-Côte d'Azur region, SE France. It lies on the Mediterranean Sea, 70km/43mi SE of Marseilles and is the most important naval port in France. HISTORY renowned in Roman times for a purple dye obtained from a shellfish; a major naval station in World War I; in 1942 the French fleet was scuttled here in order to prevent capture by Germany. NOTABLE FEATURES Gothic Cathedral of Sainte-Marie-Majeure (11c–12c); Naval Museum; opera house; zoo.

Toulouse, ancient **Tolosa** POP (1990) 608 000, the capital of Midi-Pyrénées region and of Haute Garonne department, S France. It lies on the R Garonne and the Canal du Midi, 213km/132mi SE of Bordeaux and is the fourth largest city in the country. The city, which was capital of the former province of Languedoc, is the cultural and economic centre of S France with important electronics and aircraft industries. It is known as the 'red city' because of its numerous brick buildings. NOTABLE FEATURES Catholic Institute of Toulouse (1877); Church of St-Sernin (11c–12c); Gothic Church of the Jacobins (1216); Cathedral of St-Etienne (11c–17c); observatory; botanical gardens; university (1229).

Toulouse-Lautrec (-Monfa), Henri (Marie Raymonde) de (1864–1901) French painter and lithographer, born in Albi. At the age of 14 he broke both his legs, which then ceased to grow. He settled in Montmartre in 1884, where he painted and drew the cabaret stars, prostitutes, barmaids, clowns, and actors of that society, as in *The Bar* (1898, Zürich) and *At the Moulin Rouge* (1892, Chicago). He also depicted fashionable society (eg *At the Races*, 1899) and produced several portraits. Over 600 of his works are in the Musée Lautrec in Albi.

toupee *noun* a small wig or hair-piece worn usually by men to cover a bald patch. [from French *toupet*, tuft of hair]

tour — *noun* **1** an extended journey round a place stopping at various places along the route and usually returning to one's starting-point at the end: *a coach tour of Italy.* **2** a visit round a particular place: *a tour of the cathedral.* **3** a journey round a place with frequent stops for business or professional engagements along the route, eg by a theatre company or a sports team visiting from abroad. **4** an official period of duty or military service, especially abroad. — *verb* **1** *trans., intrans.* to make a tour of (a place). **2** *said of a theatre company* to travel from place to place giving performances of (a play). [from Old French, from Greek *tornos*, tool for making circles]

Touraine a former province of central France, now occupying the department of Indre-et-Loire and part of Vienne. It became part of France in 1641 and was known for its Huguenot silk-weaving trade. The chief town in Touraine was Tours.

tour de force (PL. **tours de force**) a feat of strength or skill; an outstanding performance or effort. [French, = turning movement]

Tour de France a bicycle race, generally considered to be the world's most gruelling, first held in France in 1903. Riders have to cover approximately 4 800km/3 000mi of (usually) French countryside during a three-week period each July. The race is divided into c.21 daily stages, each of which is timed, and the winner is the cyclist who has the lowest aggregate time.

Tourette's syndrome *Medicine* a disorder that usually starts in childhood, and is characterized by severe and multiple nervous tics, and coprolalia (involuntary obscene speech). Its cause is unknown. [named after the French physician Gilles de la Tourette]

tourism *noun* **1** the practice of travelling to and visiting places for pleasure and relaxation. **2** the industry providing services, eg accommodation and catering, for tourists.

tourist — *noun* **1** a person who travels for pleasure and relaxation. **2** a member of a sports team visiting from abroad. — *adj.* of or suitable for tourists, often in being cheap or reasonably priced.

tourist class the cheapest class of passenger accommodation on a ship or in an aircraft.

touristy *adj. derog.* designed for or full of tourists.

tourmaline *noun Geol.* any of a group of aluminium silicate minerals containing boron, and found in many igneous and metamorphic rocks. Tourmaline crystals, which may be transparent or coloured, are used as semi-precious gem-stones, especially the pink, blue, and green varieties. [from Sinhalese *tormalliya*, cornelian]

Tournai, Flemish **Doornik**, ancient **Tornacum** POP (1992e) 78 000, an administrative and cultural town in W Hainaut province, Belgium. It lies on the R Scheldt near the Belgian–French border, 22km/14mi E of Lille, France. Founded in AD 275, it is the second oldest town in Belgium. NOTABLE FEATURE cathedral (11c–12c, restored in the 19c).

tournament *noun* **1** a competition, eg in tennis or chess, between many players for a championship, usually played in heats. **2** *Hist.* in the Middle Ages, a competition in which knights on horseback fought with usually blunted lances and swords. [from Old French *torneiement*]

tournedos *noun* (PL. **tournedos**) a small round thick fillet of beef. [from French]

Tourneur, Cyril (c.1575–1626) English dramatist. He published several poems, but is known for his two plays, *The Revenger's Tragedy* (1607, sometimes assigned to John Webster or Thomas Middleton), and *The Atheist's Tragedy* (1611).

tourney — *noun* (PL. **tourneys**) a medieval tournament. — *verb intrans.* (**tourneys, tour-**

neyed) to take part in a medieval tournament. [from Old French *torneie*]

Tournier, Paul (1898–1986) Swiss physician and writer, born in Geneva. A general practitioner in private practice in Geneva, he discovered religious faith through contact with the Oxford Group in 1932, and thereafter emphasized the need to treat his patients as whole humans. His books, many best-sellers, included *A Doctor's Casebook in the Light of the Bible* (1954) and *Learning to Grow Old* (1972).

tourniquet *noun* a bandage or other device for tying very tightly round an arm or leg to stop the flow of blood through an artery. [from French, from *tourner*, to turn]

Tours, ancient **Caesarodunum**, or **Turoni** POP (1990) 272 000, the capital of Indre-et-Loire department, Centre region, W central France. An industrial and commercial city, it lies between the Loire and Cher rivers, 206km/128mi SW of Paris. HISTORY an episcopal see in the 3c; grew up around the tomb of St Martin (who died in 397), becoming a place of pilgrimage and centre of healing; the Huguenot silk industry developed here in the 15c–16c. The writer Honoré de Balzac was born here in 1799. NOTABLE FEATURES Cathedral of St-Gatien (12c–16c); several silk museums; Museum of Touraine Wines; Art Museum.

Tours of Dr Syntax, The a series of books commenting on the social scene illustrated by Thomas Rowlandson and published by Rudolph Ackermann (1812–21).

tousle — *verb* to make (especially hair) untidy; to tangle or dishevel. — *noun* a tousled mass. [from Middle English *touselen*]

Toussaint L'Ouverture, originally **François Dominique Toussaint** (1746–1803) Haitian revolutionary leader, born a slave in Saint Domingue (called Haiti since 1804). Freed in 1777, in 1791 he joined the insurgents, and by 1797 was effective ruler of the former colony. He drove out British and Spanish expeditions, restored order, and aimed at independence, but Napoleon sent a new expedition to Saint Domingue and proclaimed the re-establishment of slavery. Toussaint was arrested and died in a French prison. His surname ('the opening') comes from his bravery in once making a breach in enemy ranks.

tout — *verb* **1** *intrans.* to try persistently to persuade people to buy something, give support, etc: *tout for trade.* **2** to try persistently to persuade (someone) to buy (something). **3** to advertise or praise strongly or aggressively. **4** *intrans.* to spy on racehorses in training to gain information about their condition and likely future performance. — *noun* **1** a person who buys up large numbers of tickets for a popular sporting event, concert, etc and sells them at inflated prices to members of the public. **2** a person who spies on racehorses in training and passes information about their condition, etc to people wishing to bet on them. **3** a person who touts for trade, especially persistently or aggressively. [from Middle English *tuten*, to peep out]

tow[1] *verb* **1** to pull (a ship, barge, car, trailer, etc) by rope, chain or cable behind the vehicle one is driving. **2** *said of a vehicle* to pull (a ship, barge, car, etc) along by rope, chain or cable. **3** an act of towing or the state of being towed. **4** something towed, eg a car.
— **in tow 1** (*also* **on** *or* **under tow**) *said of a vehicle* being towed. **2** *said of a person* following or accompanying as a companion or escort: *she arrived late with several men in tow.* **3** *said of a person* under one's protection, guidance, or control. [from Anglo-Saxon *togian*]

tow[2] *noun* coarse, short, or broken fibres of flax or hemp prepared for spinning into rope. [from Anglo-Saxon *tow-*]

towards *or* **toward** *prep.* **1** in the direction of: *travel towards Boston / turn towards him.* **2** in relation or regard to: *a strange attitude towards the new manager.* **3** as a contribution to: *donate £1 000 towards the cost of a new hospital.* **4** near; just before: *towards midnight.* [from Anglo-Saxon *toweard*, future]

towbar *noun* a short rigid bar at the back of a car for towing a caravan or trailer.

tow-coloured *adj.*, *said of hair* very fair.

towel — *noun* **1** a piece of absorbent cloth or paper for drying oneself, washed dishes, etc. **2** a sanitary towel. — *verb* (**towelled**, **towelling**) **1** to rub, wipe, or dry with a towel. **2** *slang* to thrash. [from Old French *toaille*]

towelling *noun* **1** an absorbent cotton cloth for making towels. **2** *slang* a thrashing.

tower — *noun* **1** a tall, narrow, usually circular or square structure forming part of a larger, lower building such as a church or castle or standing alone, built for defence, as a lookout, for machinery, etc. **2** a fortress, especially one with one or more towers: *the Tower of London.* — *verb intrans.* (**towered**, **towering**) (*often* **tower above something** *or* **someone**) to reach a great height or rise high above them.
— **a tower of strength** someone who is a great help or support.

tower over someone to be considerably taller than or superior to them.
[from Anglo-Saxon *torr*]

tower block a very tall residential or office building.

Tower Bridge the easternmost bridge on the R Thames, London, designed by Sir Horace Jones (1819–87) and Sir John Wolfe Barry (1836–1918), and opened in 1894. It can open to allow large ships in and out of the Pool of London.

towering *adj.* **1** reaching a great height; very tall or elevated. **2** *said of rage, fury, etc* intense; violent.

Tower of London a palace-fortress started by the Normans in the 11c. From the 15c to the 18c the Tower was notorious as a state prison and the scene of many executions, including that of Ann Boleyn. It is now the depository of the royal coronation regalia.

tow-head *noun* a person with very fair or tousled hair.

tow-headed *adj.* **1** fair-haired. **2** having tousled hair.

towline *or* **towrope** *noun* a rope, chain, or cable used for towing.

town *noun* **1** an urban area with relatively defined boundaries and a name, smaller than a city but larger than a village. **2** the central shopping or business area in a neighbourhood. **3** the principal town in an area, or the capital city of a country, regarded as a destination: *went into town on Thursday.* **4** the people living in a town. **5** city or urban life in general as opposed to the countryside and rural life. **6** the permanent residents of a town as opposed to *gown*, the members of its university.
— **go out on the town** *colloq.* to enjoy the entertainments offered by a town, especially its restaurants and bars.

go to town *colloq.* to do something very thoroughly or with great enthusiasm or expense.
[from Anglo-Saxon *tun*, enclosure, manor]

town clerk *Brit. Hist.* (until 1974) a secretary and legal advisor to a town council.

town council an elected governing body of a town.

town councillor a member of a town council.

town crier *Hist.* a person whose job is to make public announcements in the streets of a town.

townee *or* **townie** *noun colloq.*, *often derog.* a person living in a town, especially as opposed to a person living in the countryside or a member of a town's university.

Townes, Charles Hard (1915–) US physicist, born in Greenville, South Carolina. Working at Columbia University, he produced the first operational maser (Microwave Amplification by Stimulated Emission of Radiation), the forerunner of the laser. He later held professorships at the Massachusetts Institute of Technology and the University of California, and shared the 1964 Nobel Prize for Physics with Nikolai Basov and Alexander Prokhorov.

town gas a flammable gas, obtained from coal and consisting of a mixture of methane, hydrogen, and carbon, formerly used as an industrial and domestic fuel, and now largely superseded by natural gas.

town hall the building where the official business of a town is carried out.

town house 1 a terraced house, especially a fashionable one, and often with the living room on an upper floor. **2** a person's house in town as opposed to his or her house in the country.

Town Like Alice, A a novel by Nevil Shute (1949). It is set during World War II and describes the capture by the Japanese, and the later romantic reunion, of Jean Paget and Joe Harman. Its various settings include the bleakly-portrayed town of Alice Springs, Australia.

town planning the planning and designing of the future development of a town.

townscape *noun* the general appearance of or visual impression created by a town.

townsfolk *pl. noun* the people living in a town or city.

Townshend (of Rainham), Charles Townshend, 2nd Viscount (1674–1738) English Whig statesman, born in Raynham, Norfolk. He became Secretary of State under George I (1714–16, 1721–30) and was a leading figure in the Whig ministry with his brother-in-law Robert Walpole. He became known as 'turnip Townshend' for his interest in agricultural improvement, and for his proposal to use turnips in crop rotation.

Townshend Acts the taxes imposed (1767) by the British parliament on five categories of goods imported into the American colonies, after successful colonial resistance to the Stamp Act (1765). Resistance to them led to the repeal of four categories (1770), but the tax on tea remained in effect until the Boston Tea Party. The Acts are named after the British Chancellor of the Exchequer Charles Townshend (1725–67), who sponsored them.

township *noun* **1** *South Afr.* an urban area where black and coloured citizens live. **2** *Brit. Hist.* a division of a large parish. **3** *North Amer.* a subdivision of a county with some degree of local government. **4** *North Amer.* an area of land or district 36 miles square. **5** *Austral.* a small town or settlement.

townsman *or* **townswoman**. *noun* a man or woman living in a town or city.

townspeople *pl. noun* the people living in a town or city.

Townsville POP (1990) 116 000, an industrial port and resort in Northern statistical division, Queensland, NE Australia, situated on Cleveland Bay. The city was founded in 1864 and is the largest in tropical Australia. NOTABLE FEATURES the Great Barrier Reef Marine Park Authority Headquarters; Australian Institute of Marine Science; Magnetic I is a tourist centre.

towpath *noun* a path beside a canal or river formerly used by horses towing barges.

Towy, Welsh **Tywi** a river in Dyfed, SW Wales, length 108km/67mi. It rises in the Cambrian Mts of central Wales and flows SW to meet Carmarthen Bay.

toxaemia *noun* **1** *Medicine* blood poisoning caused by the presence of a bacterial toxin in the bloodstream, released from a local site of bacterial infection such as an abscess. It may also occur as a result of kidney failure. **2** a serious complication that sometimes occurs in late pregnancy, characterized by a sudden increase in blood pressure, oedema (abnormal retention of fluid in the body tissues), and the excretion of protein in the urine. [from Greek *toxikon*, poison for the tips of arrows + *haima*, blood]

toxaemic *adj.* relating to or affected with toxaemia.

toxic *adj.* **1** poisonous. **2** of or caused by a poison or toxin. [from Greek *toxikon pharmakon*, poison for the tips of arrows, from *toxon*, bow]

toxicity *noun* (PL. **toxicities**) **1** the degree to which a substance is poisonous. **2** the state of being poisonous.

toxicologist *noun* an expert in toxicology.

toxicology *noun* the scientific study of poisons.

toxic shock syndrome a potentially fatal condition in women, marked by flu-like symptoms and a drop in blood pressure, caused by blood-poisoning which is itself caused by a toxin developing in a high-absorbency tampon which is kept too long in the body during menstruation.

toxin *noun* any poison produced naturally by plants, animals, bacteria, etc, especially in a body.

toxocara *noun Zool.* any of various roundworms, especially *Toxocara canis* and *T.cati*, which live as parasites in the intestines of dogs and cats, respectively. When transmitted to humans they cause the disease toxocariasis, which often results in damage to the retina of the eye. [from Greek *toxikon*, poison for the tips of arrows + *kara*, head]

toxoid *noun Biol.* a toxin that has been treated so as to remove its toxic properties without destroying its ability to stimulate the production of antibodies, eg chemically treated preparations of diphtheria and tetanus toxins are used as vaccines.

toy — *noun* **1** an object made, especially for a child, to play with. **2** *often derog.* anything, especially a gadget, intended to be or thought of as being for amusement or pleasure rather than practical use. **3** something which is very small, especially a dwarf breed of dog. — *adj.* **1** made to be played with, especially in imitation of something real: *a toy oven.* **2** being a dwarf breed. — *verb intrans.*
— **toy with someone** to flirt or amuse oneself amorously with them. (**toy with something**) to play with it in an idle way and without much interest: *toy with one's food.*
[from Middle English *toye*, dalliance]

toy boy *colloq.* a usually young man who is the lover of a woman much older than himself.

Toynbee, Arnold (Joseph) (1889–1975) English historian, born in London. He served in the Foreign Office in both World Wars, and attended the Paris peace conferences (1919 and 1946). He was Professor of Modern Greek and Byzantine History at London (1919–24) and director of the Royal Institute of International Affairs, London (1925–55). The *History of the World* (10 vols, 1934–54) was his major work.

Toynbee Hall the first university settlement (institutions through which universities provide support to deprived inner city communities), founded in E London in 1885. It was named after Arnold Toynbee, who dedicated himself to improving the quality of life of the urban poor.

Toyota Motor Corporation the parent company of the Japanese Toyota group, and the largest automobile manufacturer in Japan. It was founded in 1933, and expanded rapidly during the 1960s and 1970s. It exports its vehicles and automotive parts and products to many overseas countries.

trabeated construction *Archit.* a method of building in which vertical load-bearing posts are used to support horizontal beams, without the use of arches and vaults. Classical Greek architects used this method, especially for large public buildings, with columns supporting the structure externally and internally. [from Latin *trabs*, beam]

trace[1] — *noun* **1** a mark or sign that some person, animal, or thing has been in that place. **2** a track or footprint. **3** a very small amount that can only just be detected. **4** a tracing. **5** a line marked by the moving pen of a recording instrument. **6** a visible line on a cathode ray tube showing the path of a moving spot. **7** a supposed physical change in the brain or cells of the nervous system caused by learning. — *verb* **1** to track and discover by or as if by following clues, a trail, etc. **2** to follow step by step: *trace the development of medicine.* **3** to make a copy of (a drawing, design, etc) by covering it with a sheet of semi-transparent paper and drawing over the visible lines. **4** to outline or sketch (an idea, plan, etc). **5** (*also* **trace back** *or* **trace something back**) to date or be dated back to a specified time: *can trace the name back to the sixteenth century.* [from Old French, from Latin *trahere*, to draw]

trace[2] *noun* either of two ropes, chains, or straps attached to an animal's collar, etc for pulling a carriage, cart, etc.
— **kick over the traces** to become independent or rebellious.
[from Old French *trais*, from Latin *trahere*, to pull]

trace element a chemical element that is required in very small quantities for the growth, development, and general health of a living organism, eg zinc, copper, molybdenum. Trace elements are usually toxic if absorbed in large quantities.

tracer *noun* **1** a person or device that traces. **2** a bullet, etc which leaves a smoke-trail behind it by which its flight path can be seen. **3** a substance, especially a radioactive element, whose course through the body, or effect on it, can be observed.

tracer bullet *or* **tracer shell** a bullet or shell containing a charge of chemical compound (such as phosphorus) which glows brightly as it travels through the air, indicating in darkness or the fog of war the path of the bullet or shell and its efficacy in reaching its target.

tracery *noun* (PL. **traceries**) **1** ornamental open stonework used to form a decorative pattern, especially in the top part of a Gothic window. **2** a finely patterned decoration or design.

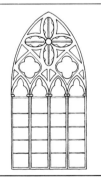

tracery

trachea *noun* (PL. **tracheae**) the passage which carries air into and out of the lungs from the larynx; the windpipe. [from Greek *tracheia arteria*, rough artery]

tracheotomy *or* **tracheostomy** *noun* (PL. **tracheotomies, tracheostomies**) *Medicine* a surgical operation in which an incision is made through the front of the neck into the trachea

(windpipe), usually to provide an alternative airway when breathing is obstructed, eg during diphtheria, or when the larynx is blocked by a tumour. [from TRACHEA + Greek *tome*, a cutting]

trachoma *noun* *Medicine* a contagious eye disease, common in the Third World, caused by the bacterium *Chlamydia trachomatis*, which is transmitted by flies. The main symptoms are inflammation and scarring of the conjunctiva, redness, and pain. If untreated it may spread to the cornea, causing blindness. [from Greek *trachoma*, roughness]

tracing *noun* **1** a copy of a drawing made on semi-transparent paper. **2** an act of tracing.

tracing-paper *noun* thin, semi-transparent paper used for tracing drawings.

track — *noun* **1** a mark or trail left by the passing of a person, animal, or thing, especially a footprint. **2** a rough path, especially one beaten by feet. **3** a specially prepared course, especially for racing. **4** a railway line, ie the parallel rails, the space in between, and the sleepers and stones below. **5** a length of railing along which something, eg a curtain, moves. **6** the groove cut in a record by the recording instrument. **7** one of several items, eg a song or movement of a symphony, recorded on a disc or tape. **8** one of several paths on magnetic recording tape that receives information from a single input channel. **9** one of a series of parallel paths on magnetic recording tape that contains a single sequence of signals. **10** *Comput.* an area that is created on the surface of a magnetic disc during the process of formatting, and within which data can be stored. **11** the line or course of travel or movement. **12** the line or course of thought, reasoning, etc. **13** the predetermined line of travel of an aircraft. **14** the continuous band of metal plates used instead of wheels on heavy vehicles designed to travel over rough surfaces, eg a tank. **15** the distance between a pair of wheels as measured between those parts of the wheels which actually touch the ground. — *verb* **1** to follow the marks, footprints, etc left by (a person or animal). **2** to follow and usually plot the course of (a spacecraft, satellite, etc) by radar. **3** *intrans.* to move a television or film camera in towards, parallel to or away from the object being filmed. **4** *said of stylus or laser beam* to extract information from (a recording medium, eg a vinyl record or a compact disc). **5** *intrans.* *said of a vehicle's rear wheels* to run exactly in the course of the front wheels.
— **across the tracks** *colloq.* a socially disadvantaged area of town.
in one's tracks exactly where one is standing.
keep *or* **lose track of something** to keep or fail to keep oneself informed about its progress or whereabouts.
make tracks *colloq.* to leave; to set out.
on the track of someone *or* **something** following, pursuing, or looking for them.
track someone *or* **something down** to search for and find them after a thorough search or by following a track.
the wrong side of the tracks a poor or disadvantaged urban area.
[from Old French *trac*]

trackball *or* **trackerball** *noun* *Comput.* a ball mounted in a small box linked to a computer terminal, rotated with the palm to move a cursor correspondingly on a screen.

tracker dog a dog specially trained to search for people, especially criminals.

track event *Athletics* a race. See also FIELD EVENT.

tracking *noun* **1** the balance of the arm on a gramophone so that the needle remains correctly positioned in the groove. **2** *Electr.* a leakage of current between two insulated points caused by moisture, dirt, etc.

tracking station a station equipped with radar to follow and plot the courses of spacecraft, satellites, etc.

track record a record of past performance.

track shoe a shoe with a spiked sole worn by a runner.

tracksuit *noun* a warm suit worn by athletes, etc when exercising, or to keep the body warm before and after performing.

tract *noun* **1** an area of land, usually of indefinite extent. **2** a system in the body with a particular function formed by a series of connected organs and glands: *the digestive tract.* **3** a short essay or book, especially on a religious subject. [from Latin *trahere*, to draw]

tractability *noun* being tractable.

tractable *adj.* easily managed, controlled, or used; pliant; docile. [from Latin *tractabilis*]

tractably *adv.* in a tractable way.

Tractarianism *noun* *Relig.* the system of religious opinion which sought the revival of high doctrine and ceremonial in the Church of England, promulgated in the *Tracts for the Times* (1833–41) by Keble, Newman, Pusey, Hurrell, Fronde, and others; also known as the Oxford Movement. It led to Anglo-Catholicism and ritualism, and has remained influential in certain quarters of Anglicanism.

traction *noun* **1** the action of pulling, state of being pulled or the force used in pulling. **2** *Medicine* a steady pulling on a muscle or limb using a series of pulleys and weights, to correct some condition or problem. **3** the grip of a wheel, tyre, etc on the surface on which it moves. [from Latin *tractio*, from *trahere*, to pull]

tractional *or* **tractive** *adj.* relating to or involving traction.

traction engine a heavy steam-powered road vehicle formerly used for pulling heavy loads, eg farm machinery, and as a mobile power source.

tractor *noun* **1** a slow-moving motor vehicle with two large rear wheels for pulling especially farm machinery, heavy loads, etc. **2** a traction engine. [from Latin, from *trahere*, to pull]

Tracy, Spencer (Bonadventure) (1900–67) US film actor, born in Milwaukee, Wisconsin. He played on Broadway before his feature-film début in *Up the River* (1930). He won Academy Awards for *Captains Courageous* (1937) and *Boys' Town* (1938), and often played opposite Katharine Hepburn, such as in the comedies *Woman of the Year* (1942) and *Pat and Mike* (1952), and in *Bad Day at Black Rock* (1955) and *Judgement at Nuremberg* (1961). His last film was *Guess Who's Coming to Dinner* (1967).

Tracy *or* **Tracey** a female first name. [originally a contraction of THERESA]

trad — *noun* *Brit. colloq.* traditional jazz, the style of jazz music first played in the 1920s and 1930s and which originated in New Orleans. — *adj.* traditional.

trade — *noun* **1** the buying and selling of goods or services. **2** business and commerce, especially as opposed to a profession or landed property; also, the people involved in this. **3** a personal occupation or job, especially one requiring skill; a craft: *a carpenter by trade.* **4** the people and companies engaged in a particular business or occupation: *the building trade.* **5** customers: *the lunchtime trade.* **6** business at a particular time or for a particular market: *the tourist trade / a seasonal trade in woolly hats.* **7** (**trades**) the trade winds. — *verb* **1** (**trade in something**) to buy and sell a particular type of goods. **2** *intrans.* to engage in trade (with a person or country). **3** to exchange (one commodity) for another.
— **trade something in** to give it as part payment for something else.
trade something off to give it in exchange for something else, usually as a compromise.
trade on something to take unfair advantage of a factor, especially a person's generosity, etc. [from Middle English, = course, path]

Trade and Industry, Department of
(ABBREV. **DTI**) (in the UK) the government department that is responsible for the country's policies on industry and commerce, including international trade, competition policy and consumer protection, energy development, science and technological research, and company legislation.

trade cycle the pattern of changing levels of activity in an economy over a period of time. High points of activity are *booms*, and low points are *recessions* or *slumps*. Economists have identified that a typical trade cycle lasts seven or eight years, though much longer trends have also been identified.

trade gap the amount by which a country's imports are greater than its exports.

trade-in a commodity that is traded in exchange for another, especially a used vehicle.

trademark *noun* **1** a name, word, or symbol, especially (*in full* **registered trademark**) one that is officially registered and protected by law, used to represent a company or individual and shown on all of the goods made or sold by that company or individual. **2** a distinguishing characteristic or feature.
◇ In the USA, trademarks often include the symbol ®, signifying that the mark has been registered.

tradename *noun* **1** a name given to an article or product, or group of these, by the trade which produces them. **2** a name under which a company or individual does business. **3** a name serving as a trademark.

trade-off an exchange, especially a compromise.

trader *noun* **1** a person who trades, often one who owns or runs a shop, or who trades in a particular group of goods. **2** a ship used for trade.

tradescantia *noun* any of several widely cultivated plants with attractive, often variegated, leaves. [named after John Tradescant (c.1567–1637), English gardener, naturalist, and traveller]

tradesman *or* **tradeswoman** *noun* (PL. **tradesmen**) **1** a person engaged in trade, especially a shopkeeper. **2** a skilled worker.

tradespeople *pl. noun* people engaged in trade.

Trades Union Congress a national organization formed from representatives of the individual trade unions, which meets annually to discuss working conditions and the economy in the country at large.

tradeswoman *noun* (PL. **tradeswomen**) a woman engaged in trade, especially a shopkeeper.

trade union *or* **trades union** an organization of workers or employees formed to protect their interests and to improve working conditions.
◇ The trade union movement developed in the early years of the 19c, growing rapidly after the repeal of the Combination Laws in 1824–5. In 1834, six Dorset labourers were sentenced to transportation for attempting to press for higher wages, becoming famous as the 'Tolpuddle Martyrs'. Since then trade unions have played an important role in industrial relations, and have developed in all Western nations over the last 150 years. The Conservative governments in the UK (from 1979) brought forward legislation which is aimed at curbing the power of the trade unions.

trade unionism the principles and practices of trade unions.

trade unionist a member of a trade union.

trade wind a wind that blows continually towards the equator and is deflected westward by the eastward rotation of the earth.

trading estate *Brit.* an area in a town which is developed for industry and business.

trading post a store in a remote or sparsely populated region.

trading stamp a stamp given to a customer in return for a certain amount of money spent on goods in a store, and which may be collected and exchanged for an item supplied by the company issuing the trading stamp.

tradition *noun* **1** the handing down of doctrines, beliefs, customs, etc from generation to generation. **2** a doctrine, belief, custom, story, etc that is passed on. **3** a particular body of doctrines, beliefs, customs, etc belonging to a particular group of people, religion, country, family, etc. **4** the continuous development of a body of artistic, literary, or musical principles or conventions. [from Latin *traditio*, from *tradere*, to give up]

traditional *adj.* **1** belonging to or derived from tradition. **2** of the nature of or being a tradition.

traditionalism *noun* belief in the importance of, respect for and often excessive following of tradition.

traditionalist — *noun* a person who favours tradition. — *adj.* relating to or involving tradition.

traditional jazz see TRAD.

traditionally *adv.* in a traditional way; in terms of tradition.

traduce *verb* to say or write unpleasant things about; to malign. [from Latin *traducere*, to lead across]

traducement *noun* traducing, slander.

traducer *noun* a person who traduces, a slanderer.

Trafalgar, Battle of the most famous naval engagement (21 Oct 1805) of the Napoleonic Wars. Fought off Cape Trafalgar, Spain, between the British and Franco-Spanish fleets, the British triumph was marred by the death of Nelson at the moment of victory, but it destroyed Napoleon I's hopes of invading England and established British naval supremacy for a century.

Trafalgar, Cape, Latin **Promontorium Lunosis**, Arabic **Tarif-al-ghar** a cape on the Atlantic coast of Cádiz province, SW Spain. It is the scene of Nelson's defeat of the French and Spanish fleet in 1805. [from Arabic *tarif-al-ghar*, cape of the cave]

traffic — *noun* **1** the vehicles, ships, aircraft, etc moving along a route. **2** the movement of vehicles along a route. **3** illegal or dishonest trade. **4** trade; commerce. **5** the transporting of goods or people on a railway, air or sea route, etc. **6** the goods or people transported along a route. **7** dealings or communication between groups or individuals. — *verb* (**trafficked**, **trafficking**) **1** (**traffic in something**) to deal or trade in it, especially illegally or dishonestly. **2** to deal in (a particular type of goods). [from Old French *trafique*]

traffic island see ISLAND.

trafficker *noun* a dealer or trader, usually in illegal goods.

traffic lights a system of red, amber, and green lights which controls traffic at road junctions, pedestrian crossings, etc.

traffic warden *Brit.* a person whose job is to control the parking of vehicles in towns and report parking offences.

tragedian *noun* **1** an actor who specialises in tragic roles. **2** a person who writes tragedies.

tragedienne *noun* an actress who specialises in tragic roles.

tragedy *noun* (PL. **tragedies**) **1** a serious drama, film, opera, etc in which the main character or characters are eventually destroyed through a combination of events, circumstances and per-

sonality problems. **2** such plays as a group or genre. **3** any sad play, film, book, etc, especially one ending with an unnecessary or untimely death. **4** a serious disaster. **5** any sad event. [from Greek *tragoidia*, from *tragos*, goat + *oide*, song]

tragic *adj.* **1** sad, especially because of death or destruction; intensely distressing. **2** relating to or in the style of tragedy. [from Greek *tragikos*]

tragically *adv.* in a tragic way; so as to be tragic.

tragicomedy *noun* (PL. **tragicomedies**) a play or event which includes a mixture of both tragedy and comedy. [from Latin *tragicomoedia*]

tragicomic *adj.* having the nature of a tragicomedy, combining comedy and tragedy.

tragicomically *adv.* in a tragicomic way.

Traherne, Thomas (c.1636–74) English mystical writer, born in Hereford. He became rector of Credenhill (1657), and later moved to London where he was appointed chaplain to the lord keeper of the great seal. The unpublished manuscripts of his *Poetical Works* (1903) and *Centuries of Meditations* (1908) were discovered by chance on a London street bookstall in 1896.

trail — *verb* **1** *trans., intrans.* to drag or be dragged loosely along the ground or other surface, especially behind one. **2** (*usually* **trail along**, **behind**, *etc*) to walk or move along slowly and wearily. **3** to drag (a limb, etc) especially slowly and wearily: *a bird trailing a broken wing.* **4** *trans., intrans.* to fall or lag behind (eg a competitor) in eg a race or contest, often by a stated number of points. **5** to follow the track or footsteps of. **6** *trans., intrans.* to grow or encourage (a plant) to grow so long that it droops over or along a surface towards the ground. — *noun* **1** a track, series of marks, footprints, etc left by a passing person, animal or thing, especially one followed in hunting. **2** a rough path or track through a wild or mountainous area. **3** anything which drags or is drawn behind. **4** the part of a gun carriage that rests on the ground when the limber is detached.
— **trail away** *or* **off** *said especially of a sound* to become fainter.
[from Middle English *trailen*]

trailblazer *noun* a person who blazes a trail (see BLAZE[2]); a pioneer.

trailblazing — *noun* breaking new ground, pioneering. — *adj.* pioneering.

trailer *noun* **1** a usually two-wheeled cart for towing behind a car, used eg for transporting small boats. **2** the rear section of an articulated lorry, as opposed to the cab. **3** *North Amer.* a caravan. **4** a series of brief extracts from a film or programme prepared as an advertisement for it.

train — *noun* **1 a** a string of railway carriages or wagons with a locomotive. **b** *loosely* a locomotive. **2** a back part of a long dress or robe that trails behind the wearer. **3** the attendants following or accompanying an important person. **4** a connected series of events, actions, ideas, or thoughts. **5** a number of things in a string or connected line, eg a line of animals or vehicles carrying baggage. **6** a line of gunpowder, etc laid to fire a charge. **7** a set of connected wheels which act on each other to transmit motion. — *verb* **1** to teach or prepare (a person or animal) for something through instruction, practice, or exercises. **2** *intrans.* to be taught, or prepare oneself to be taught, through instruction, practice, or exercises: *trained as a nurse.* **3** (**train for something** *or* **train someone for something**) to prepare oneself or prepare them for performance (eg in a sport) by instruction, practice, exercise, diet, etc: *training for the marathon.* **4** to point or aim (eg a gun) at or focus (eg a telescope) on a particular object or in a particular direction: *the guns were all trained on the front gates.* **5** to make (a plant, tree, etc) grow in a particular direction: *train the ivy* *along the wall.* **6** *intrans.* to travel by train. [from Old French *trahiner*, to drag]

train-bearer *noun* a person who carries the train of a person's dress or robe.

trained *adj.* having received training; prepared, tamed.

trainee *noun* a person who is being trained for a job.

trainer *noun* **1** a person who trains racehorses, athletes, sportsmen and -women, etc. **2** *Brit.* a soft running shoe with a thick sole. **3** a machine or device used in training, eg an aircraft with two sets of controls for training pilots.

training *noun* **1** the act or process of being prepared for something, of being taught or learning a particular skill and practising it until the required standard is reached: *go into training for the marathon.* **2** the state of being physically fit: *out of training.*

train-spotter *noun* a person who notes the numbers of railway locomotives or rolling stock as a hobby.

train-spotting *noun* the activity of a train-spotter.

traipse *or* **trapes** — *verb intrans.* to walk or trudge along idly or wearily. — *noun* a long, tiring walk.

trait *noun* a distinguishing feature or quality, especially of a person's character. [from French, from Latin *trahere*, to draw]

traitor *noun* **1** a person who commits treason and betrays his or her country to the enemy. **2** a person who betrays a friend's trust. [from Latin *tradere*, to give up]

traitorous *adj.* like a traitor; treacherous.

traitorously *adv.* in a traitorous way.

traitress *noun old use* a female traitor.

Trajan, originally **Marcus Ulpius Trajanus** (c.53–117 AD) Roman emperor (98–117), selected as successor by Nerva for his military skills. He was the first emperor after Augustus to expand the Roman Empire significantly. He defeated Dacia in 106, and the wealth from its gold mines enabled him to launch an ambitious building programme, especially in Rome, where his constructions included a new forum.

trajectory *noun* (PL. **trajectories**) *Physics* the curved path followed by an object that has been projected into the air (a *projectile*), eg a rocket, guided missile, or bullet. [from Latin *trajectorius*, casting over]

Tralee, Gaelic **Tráighlí** POP (1991) 18 000, the capital of Kerry county, Munster province, SW Irish Republic. It lies NE of the Slieve Mish Mts.

tram *noun* **1** an electrically-powered passenger vehicle which runs on rails laid in the streets. **2** a truck or wagon running on rails in a mine.

tramcar *noun* same as TRAM 1.

tramline *noun* **1** (often **tramlines**) either of a pair of rails forming the track on which trams run. **2** (**tramlines**) *colloq.* the lines marking the sides of a tennis or badminton court and the lines parallel to them inside the court.

trammel — *noun* **1** a dragnet for fishing in which a fine inner mesh is carried by fish through the coarse outer mesh, thus trapping the fish in a pocket. **2** (*usually* **trammels**) anything which hinders or prevents free action or movement. — *verb* (**trammelled**, **trammelling**) **1** to catch or entangle, especially in a trammel. **2** to hinder or prevent the free movement of. [from Old French *tramail*, net]

tramp — *verb* **1** (*usually* **tramp about, up,** *etc*) to walk with firm, heavy footsteps. **2** *intrans.* to make a journey on foot, especially heavily or wearily: *tramp over the hills.* **3** to walk heavily and wearily on or through: *tramp the streets.* **4** to walk (a specified distance) heavily and wearily: *tramp*

six miles across the open moor. **5** *intrans.* to live as a tramp. **6** to tread or trample. — *noun* **1** a person with no fixed home or job, who travels from place to place on foot and who lives by begging and doing odd jobs. **2** a long and often tiring walk especially in the country. **3** the sound of heavy, rhythmic footsteps. **4** (*in full* **tramp steamer**) a cargo boat with no fixed or regular route. **5** *slang* a promiscuous or immoral woman. **6** an iron plate on the sole of a shoe to protect it, eg when digging. [from Middle English *trampen*]

trample — *verb trans.,* *intrans.* **1** (**trample something** *or* **on something**) to tread on it heavily or roughly: *trampled on the flower-bed.* **2** to press or be pressed down by treading or being trodden on: *cigarette ash trampled into the carpet.* **3** to treat someone dismissively or with contempt: *trampled all over them / trampled over their feelings.* — *noun* an act of trampling or the sound made by trampling. [from Middle English *tramplen*, to stamp]

trampoline — *noun* a piece of tough canvas attached to a framework by cords or rope and stretched tight, for acrobats, gymnasts, children, etc to jump on. — *verb intrans.* to jump, turn somersaults, etc on a trampoline. [from Italian *trampolino*, springboard]

tramway *noun* **1** a system of tracks for trams. **2** a tram system.

trance *noun* **1** a sleep-like or half-conscious state in which one loses the ability to react to stimuli such as pain. **2** a dazed or absorbed state. **3** a usually self-induced state in which one may experience religious or mystical ecstasy. [from Latin *transire*, to go across]

trannie *or* **tranny** *noun* (PL. **trannies**) *Brit. colloq.* a transistor radio.

tranquil *adj.* quiet; peaceful; undisturbed. [from Latin *tranquillus*]

tranquillity *noun* a tranquil state or quality; calmness.

tranquillize *or* **tranquillise** *verb trans.,* *intrans.* to make or become calm, peaceful, or less tense or restore or be restored to such a state, especially through drugs.

tranquillizer *or* **tranquilliser** *noun* a drug that acts on the central nervous system and has a calming and relaxing effect. Major tranquillizers, eg chlorpromazine, are used to treat severe mental disorders such as schizophrenia. Minor tranquillizers, eg diazepam, are used to relieve anxiety and tension, but may become addictive if taken for prolonged periods.

tranquilly *adv.* in a tranquil way.

trans *abbrev.* **1** transitive. **2** translation; translated.

trans- *prefix* forming words meaning: **1** across; beyond; on the other side of: *transatlantic.* **2** through. **3** into another state or place: *transform.* [from Latin *trans*, across]

transact *verb* to conduct or carry out (business). [from Latin *transigere*, to force through]

transaction *noun* **1** something transacted, especially a business deal. **2** (**transactions**) the published reports of papers read, discussions, decisions taken, etc at a meeting of a learned society. **3** an act of transacting.

transactor *noun formal* a person who transacts, a negotiator.

transalpine *adj.* situated or happening beyond the Alps (originally as viewed from Rome). [from Latin *transalpinus*]

transatlantic *adj.* **1** crossing the Atlantic. **2** situated on the other side of the Atlantic. **3** relating to or originating from the other side of the Atlantic.

Transcaucasia a geographical region in both Europe and Asia, extending S from the Greater Caucasus to the Turkish and Iranian frontiers,

between the Black Sea in the W and the Caspian Sea in the E. It comprises the republics of Georgia, Azerbaijan, and Armenia, which from 1922 to 1936 formed the Transcaucasian SFSR (one of the consituent republics of the former USSR). Its chief towns include Kutaisi, Batumi, Tbilisi, Kirovabad, and Baku.

transceiver *noun* a piece of radio equipment which both receives and transmits signals.

transcend *verb* **1** to be beyond the limits or range of: *transcend the bounds of human experience.* **2** to be better or greater than; to surpass or excel. **3** to overcome or surmount: *transcend all difficulties.* [from Latin *transcendere*, to climb over]

transcendence *or* **transcendency** *noun* transcending.

transcendent *adj.* **1** going beyond in excellence; surpassing or excelling. **2** beyond usual human knowledge or experience. **3** *said especially of a deity* existing outside the material or created world and independent of it.

transcendental *adj.* **1** going beyond usual human knowledge or experience. **2** going beyond in excellence; surpassing or excelling. **3** supernatural or mystical. **4** vague, abstract, or abstruse.

transcendentalism *noun* any philosophical system concerned with what is constant, innate and a priori, independent of and a necessary prerequisite to experience.

transcendentally *adv.* in a transcendental way.

transcendental meditation a system of meditation for relieving anxiety, promoting spiritual wellbeing, and achieving physical and mental relaxation through the (usually silent) repetition of a mantra.

transcendental number *Maths.* an irrational number (a number that cannot be expressed as a ratio of two integers) that is not algebraic, eg π.

transcontinental — *adj., said especially of a railway* crossing a continent. — *noun* something that crosses a continent, eg a railway.

transcribe *verb* **1** to write out (a text) in full, eg from notes: *take shorthand notes to be transcribed later.* **2** to copy (a text) from one place to another: *transcribed the poem into her album.* **3** to write out (a spoken text). **4** *Mus.* to arrange (a piece of music) for an instrument or voice that it was not originally composed for. **5** to record any form of information on a suitable storage medium. **6** *Comput.* to transfer data from one computer storage device to another, eg from tape to disk, or from the main memory of a computer to a storage device, or from a storage device to the main memory. [from Latin *transcribere*]

transcript *noun* a written or printed copy, especially a legal or official copy of court proceedings. [from Latin *transcriptum*]

transcription *noun* **1** the act of transcribing. **2** something transcribed; a transcript. [from Latin *transcriptio*]

Transdanubia, Hungarian **Dunántúl** a geographical region in Hungary, lying W of the R Danube and extending to the Hungarian Alps and S to the R Drava. A hilly and fertile region, noted for livestock and wine production, it occupies one third of Hungary.

transducer *noun* **1** *Electr.* a device that converts energy from one form to another, eg a loudspeaker, which converts electrical energy into sound waves. **2** *Electr.* a device that converts a physical quantity, such as sound, light, or temperature, into an electrical signal, eg a microphone or photoelectric cell. Because electrical signals can be measured, transducers are used in many types of sensor. [from Latin *transducere*, to lead across]

transept *noun* each of the two arms forming the part of a cross-shaped church that is at right angles to the nave; also, the area formed by these two arms. [from Latin *transeptum*, from *trans*, across + *saeptum*, enclosure]

transfer — *verb* (**transferred, transferring**) **1** *trans., intrans.* to move from one place, person, or group to another. **2** *intrans.* to change from one vehicle, line, or passenger system to another. **3** *Legal* to give the right to or ownership of (property) to someone. **4** to move (a design) from one surface to another. — *noun* **1** an act of transferring or the state of being transferred. **2** a design or picture that can be transferred from one surface to another. **3** any person or thing that is transferred. **4** *Legal* the changing of the right to property from one person to another; conveyance. **5** *Legal* any document which records such a change in the right to property. **6** *North Amer.* a ticket allowing a passenger to continue a journey on another route. [from Latin *transferre*, to carry across]

transferable *adj.* capable of being transferred.

transference *noun* **1** the act of transferring from one person, place, or group to another. **2** *Psychol.* an unconscious transferring of one's emotions, fears, anxieties, etc to another person or thing, especially to a psychoanalyst during therapy.

transfer orbit *Astron.* the flight path taken by a spacecraft as it moves from one orbit to another.

transfer pricing *Commerce* the price charged when an article is passed from one part or department of a company to another. When such a transfer is across national boundaries, as with multinational companies, the company may avoid taxes in one country by artificially fixing the price.

transfer RNA *Genetics* (ABBREV. **tRNA**) a small molecule of RNA (ribonucleic acid) whose function is to carry specific amino acids from the cytoplasm to the specialized structures known as ribosomes that are the site of protein manufacture in living cells.

Transfiguration, The a painting of the Transfiguration of Christ by Raphael (unfinished, c.1517–20, Vatican).

transfiguration *noun* **1** a change in appearance, especially to something more beautiful, glorious, or exalted. **2** (**Transfiguration**) **a** *Christianity* the radiant change in Christ's appearance described in Matthew 17.1–2. **b** a Church festival held on 6 Aug to commemorate this.

transfigure *verb* to change the appearance of, especially so as to make more beautiful, glorious or exalted. [from Latin *transfigurare*]

transfix *verb* **1** to cause (someone) to be unable to move through surprise, fear, horror, etc. **2** to pierce through with, or as if with, a pointed weapon. [from Latin *transfigere*, to pierce through]

transfixion *noun* transfixing or being transfixed.

transform *verb* **1** to change the appearance, nature, or function of completely and often dramatically. **2** *intrans.* to undergo a complete and often dramatic change of appearance, function, or nature. **3** *Maths.* to change the form but not the value of (an equation or algebraic expression). **4** to change the voltage or type of (a current), eg from alternating to direct. [from Latin *transformare*]

transformation *noun* **1** transforming or being transformed. **2** a change of form, constitution, or substance.

transformational grammar *Linguistics* a system of generative grammar in which elements or structures can be derived from others or related to others by using a set of rules to convert the basic structure of a sentence into the forms in which they will occur in the language.

transformer *noun Electr.* an electromagnetic device, usually consisting of two coils of wire (the input or *primary* and the output or *secondary*) wound on the same iron core, and used to transfer electrical energy from one alternating current circuit to another, with an increase or decrease in voltage. Transformers are used to provide a low-voltage domestic supply from high-voltage mains electricity, and to provide even lower voltages for the operation of electrical appliances, eg television sets.

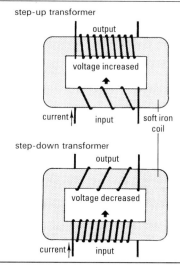

transformer

transfuse *verb* **1** to transfer (blood or plasma from one person) into the blood vessels of another. **2** to cause to pass, enter, or diffuse through. **3** to cause (fluid) to pass from one vessel to another. [from Latin *transfundere*, to pour out]

transfusion *noun* **1** (*in full* **blood transfusion**) the introduction of whole blood directly into a person's bloodstream by allowing it to drip under gravity through a needle inserted in a vein. **2** the introduction of a component of whole blood (eg plasma) or saline solution into a person's bloodstream in a similar manner, eg to treat shock.
◇ Blood transfusion is usually performed to replace blood that has been lost as a result of injury, severe burns, surgery, etc, or that is of defective quality as a result of disease. Donated blood that is to be used for transfusion is carefully tested and then stored in a blood bank until required. The blood group of the donor must be compatible with that of the recipient.

transgenic *adj. Genetics* containing genetic material introduced, usually in the form of DNA, from another species.

transgress *verb* **1** *trans., intrans.* to go beyond the limits set by, break, or violate (divine law, a rule, etc). **2** to overstep (a limit or boundary). [from Latin *transgredi*, to step across]

transgression *noun* **1** the act of breaking rules, divine law, etc. **2** a fault, crime, or sin.

transgressor *noun* a person who transgresses, a sinner.

tranship same as TRANSSHIP.

transhumance *noun* the transfer of livestock, most often cattle or sheep, between summer and winter pastures. It is characteristic of many mountainous regions, where entire families may move with their flocks to high altitude pastures, and, in Arctic regions where livestock are moved to more northerly pastures in summer. [from Spanish *trashumar*, from Latin *trans*, across beyond + *humus* ground]

transience *or* **transiency** *noun* a transient quality.

transient — *adj.* lasting, staying, or visiting for a short time only; passing quickly. — *noun* **1** a temporary resident or worker. **2** a short, sudden surge of voltage or current. [from Latin *transire*, to cross over]

transiently *adv.* in a transient way.

transistor *noun* **1** *Electron.* a semiconductor device with three electrodes, used as a switch or to amplify (strengthen) electric current in electronic circuits. Transistors have superseded valves because they are smaller, more efficient, and cheaper to produce. They are used to amplify signals in radio receivers, television sets, etc, and complex circuits containing thousands of transistors can be constructed on silicon chips. **2** (*in full* **transistor radio**) a small portable radio using transistors. [from TRANSFER + RESISTOR]

transistorize *or* **transistorise** *verb* to fit with a transistor or transistors.

transistorized *or* **transistorised** *adj.* equipped or powered with transistors.

transit — *noun* **1** the carrying or movement of goods or passengers from place to place or across or through a place. **2** a route or passage: *transit by sea.* **3** *North Amer., esp. US* the transport of passengers or goods on public, usually local, routes. **4** the passage of a heavenly body across a meridian. — *verb* (**transited, transiting**) to pass across or through.
— **in transit** *said of goods or passengers* in the process of being taken from or travelling from one place to another.
[from Latin *transitus*, from *transire*, to cross over]

transit camp a camp for the temporary accommodation of soldiers, refugees, etc on the way to their permanent destination.

transit instrument an astronomical instrument for observing the passage of a heavenly body across the meridian; generally a telescope mounted on a fixed horizontal axis so as to sweep the meridian in a vertical plane. It may be used for correcting clocks, and as a means of determining longitude.

transition *noun* **1** a change or passage from one place, state, subject, etc to another. **2** *Mus.* a change from one key to another. **3** *Archit.* the gradual change from one style to another, especially from Norman to Early English. [from Latin *transitio*, from *transire*, to cross over]

transitional *or* **transitionary** *adj.* involving transition; temporary.

transitionally *adv.* in a transitional period, during a transition.

transition element *Chem.* in the periodic table, any of a group of metallic elements that have only partially filled inner electron shells, eg copper, cobalt, iron. As a result, they tend to show variable valency and form highly coloured compounds. Many of them are used as catalysts. — Also called *transition metal.*

transitive *adj.* Grammar, *said of a verb* having a direct object, such as the verb *hit* in the phrase *hit the ball.* [from Latin *transitivus*]

transitively *adv.* in a transitive way.

transit lounge an airport lounge for passengers waiting for a connecting flight.

transitorily *adv.* briefly, for a short time.

transitoriness *noun* being transitory.

transitory *adj.* lasting only for a short time; transient. [from Latin *transitorius*, from *transire*, to cross over]

transit visa a visa which allows a person to pass through a country but not to stop in it.

Transkei POP (1991e) 3.5m, an independent black homeland in SE South Africa. AREA 42 200sq km/16 300sq mi. It lies between the Kei and Mtamvuna rivers on the Indian Ocean and is the traditional territory of the Xhosa people. Around 15% of the population are commuters or migrant workers in South Africa. CAPITAL Umtata. HISTORY achieved self-government status in 1963; granted independence by South Africa (not recognized internationally) in 1976. ECONOMY forestry; livestock; maize, sorghum, coffee, tea, sugar cane.

translate *verb* **1** to express (a word, speech, written text, etc) in another language, with the same meaning. **2** *intrans.* to do this, especially as a profession. **3** *intrans. said of a written text, etc* to be able to be expressed in another language: *poetry does not always translate well.* **4** to put or express (eg an idea) in plainer or simpler terms. **5** to interpret the significance or meaning of (an action, behaviour, etc). **6** *trans., intrans.* to change or be changed into or show or be shown as: *need to translate their ideas into reality.* **7** to change or move from one state, condition, person, place, etc to another. **8** *Ecclesiastical* to transfer (a bishop) from one see to another. **9** to move (the relics of a saint) from one place to another. **10** *Relig.* to remove to heaven, especially without death. [from Latin *translatum*, from *transferre*, to carry across]

translation *noun* **1** a word, speech, written text, etc that has been put into one language from another. **2** the act of translating. **3** *Genetics* in a living cell, the process by which the coded genetic information within messenger RNA molecules is used to specify the order in which individual amino acids are added to a growing chain of protein that is being manufactured within the cell. Translation takes place on specialized structures called *ribosomes.*

translational *adj.* relating to or involving translation.

translator *noun* a person who translates, especially as a profession.

transliterate *verb* to write (a word, name, text, etc) in the letters of another alphabet. [from TRANS- + Latin *litera*, letter]

transliteration *noun* **1** the process of transliterating. **2** a letter or word that is transliterated.

translocation *noun Bot.* in higher plants, the transport of soluble organic compounds (manufactured in the leaves by photosynthesis) to the rest of the plant via the specialized conducting tissue known as phloem.

translucence *or* **translucency** *noun* a translucent quality.

translucent *adj.* **1** allowing light to pass and be diffused through; semi-transparent. **2** clear. [from Latin *translucere*, to shine through]

translucently *adv.* in a translucent way.

transmigrate *verb intrans.* **1** *said of a soul in some beliefs* to pass into another body at death. **2** to move from one home or abode to another; to migrate. [from Latin *transmigrare*]

transmigration *noun* the act or process of transmigrating.

transmissible *adj.* capable of being transmitted.

transmission *noun* **1** an act of transmitting or the state of being transmitted. **2** something transmitted, especially a radio or television broadcast. **3** the system of parts in a motor vehicle which transfers power from the engine to the wheels. [from Latin *transmissio*]

transmit *verb* (**transmitted, transmitting**) **1** to pass or hand on (especially a message or infection). **2** *trans., intrans.* to send out (signals) by radio waves. **3** *trans., intrans.* to broadcast (a radio or television programme). **4** to allow the passage of (eg light or sound); to act as a medium for. [from Latin *transmittere*]

transmitter *noun* **1** a person or thing that transmits. **2** *Radio* the equipment that converts electrical signals into modulated radio waves for broadcasting. **3** *Telecomm.* the part of a telephone mouthpiece that converts sound waves into electrical signals. **4** *Physiol.* a neurotransmitter.

transmogrification *noun* a strange transformation.

transmogrify *verb* (**transmogrifies, transmogrified**) *facetious* to transform, especially in shape or appearance and often in a surprising or bizarre way.

transmutable *adj.* capable of being changed into something else.

transmutation *noun* the process of transmuting; change of form.

transmute *verb* **1** to change the form, substance, or nature of. **2** to change (one chemical element) into another. **3** *Alchemy* to change (base metal) into gold or silver. [from Latin *transmutare*]

transom *noun* **1** a horizontal bar of wood or stone dividing a window, or placed across the top of a door separating it from a window or fanlight above. **2** a lintel. **3** (*in full* **transom window**) a small window over the lintel of a door or larger window. **4** any of several crossbeams in the stern of a boat. [from Old French *traversin*]

transparency *noun* (PL. **transparencies**) **1** the state of being transparent. **2** a small photograph on glass or rigid plastic mounted in a frame and viewed by being placed in a projector or other device which shines light behind it.

transparent *adj.* **1** able to be seen through; clear. **2** easily seen through, understood, or recognized; obvious; evident. **3** frank and open; candid. [from Latin *transparere*, to shine through]

transparently *adv.* in a transparent way; openly, visibly.

transpiration *noun* **1** transpiring. **2** exhalation through the skin. **3** emission of water vapour in plants.

transpire *verb* **1** *intrans. said especially of something secret* to become known; to come to light: *it later transpired that he had been in Paris.* **2** *intrans. loosely* to happen: *what transpired next?* **3** *trans., intrans. Bot., said of a plant* to lose water vapour into the atmosphere by evaporation, especially through the stomata on the lower surfaces of leaves. **4** to give off in the form of vapour. [from Latin *transpirare*, to breathe through]

transplant — *verb* **1** to transfer (an organ, skin, etc) from one person or part of the body to another. **2** to move (especially a growing plant) from one place to another. — *noun* **1** an operation in which an organ, skin, etc is transferred from one person or part of the body to another. **2** anything which has been transplanted, especially an organ, skin, or plant. [from Latin *transplantare*]

transplantation *noun* the transfer of an organ or tissue from one person (the donor), who may be alive or recently dead, to another (the recipient), or from one part of the body to another. ◇ The most successful transplants to date have been achieved with the kidney, and in cases of severe kidney failure a transplant is the only alternative to regular use of a dialysis machine, but its availability as a treatment is limited by the number of suitable donors. Other organs and tissues that have been transplanted are the heart, lungs, liver, bone marrow (for treatment of leukaemia), and cornea of the eye. Skin and bone grafting involve transplantation within the same person.

With the exception of the cornea, transplanted organs from another person are normally treated as foreign material by the body's immune system, and are therefore rejected and destroyed. During transplant surgery the likelihood of rejection can be greatly reduced by careful matching of donor and recipient, and by the use of immunosuppressive drugs. In bone-marrow transplant operations, the patient's immune system can be rendered inactive by radiation treatment.

transport — *verb* **1** to carry (goods, passengers, etc) from one place to another. **2** *Hist.* to

send to a penal colony overseas. **3** (*usually* **be transported**) to be affected with strong feelings: *was transported with grief.* — *noun* **1** the transporting of people, goods, etc from place to place; also, a system or business for this. **2** a means of getting or being transported from place to place: *I have no transport at the moment.* **3** (*often* **transports**) strong emotion, especially of pleasure or delight; ecstasy. **4** a ship, aircraft, lorry, etc used to carry soldiers or military equipment and stores. **5** *Hist.* a criminal or convict who has been sentenced to transportation. [from Latin *transportare*]

transportable *adj.* capable of being transported.

transportation *noun* **1** the act or transporting or process of being transported. **2** a means of being transported; transport. **3** *Hist.* the punishment of prisoners by sending them to a penal colony overseas.

transport café *Brit.* an inexpensive restaurant on or near a main road, used especially by lorry drivers.

transporter *noun* someone or something that transports, especially a heavy vehicle for carrying large goods.

transposable *adj.* capable of being transposed.

transpose *verb* **1** to cause (two or more things, letters, words, etc) to change places. **2** to change the position of (a thing) in a sequence or series. **3** *Mus.* to perform or rewrite in a different key. **4** *Maths.* to move (a term) to the other side of an equation and reverse the sign accompanying it. [from Middle English *transposen*, to transmute]

transposition *noun* **1** transposing or being transposed. **2** something transposed.

transputer *noun Comput.* a chip capable of all the functions of a microprocessor, including memory, and able to process in parallel rather than sequentially. [from TRANSISTOR + COMPUTER]

transsexual *noun* **1** a person belonging anatomically to one sex who adopts the physical characteristics or social behaviour, etc of the opposite sex. **2** a person who has had medical or surgical treatment to alter the external sexual features to resemble those of the opposite sex.

transship *verb trans., intrans.* (**transshipped, transshipping**) to transfer from one ship or form of transport to another.

transshipment *noun* the process of transshipping; changing from one conveyance to another.

Trans-Siberian Railway a rail route extending across Siberia in Russia, originally between terminals at Chelyabinsk in the Urals (now extended to Moscow) and Vladivostok on the Pacific. It was constructed 1891–1905, with an extension around L Baykal completed in 1917. The line, which has played a major role in the development of Siberia, is now largely electrified.

transubstantiate *verb* to change into another substance. [from Latin *transubstantiare*]

transubstantiation *noun Christianity* the doctrine, especially in the Roman Catholic and Eastern Orthodox churches, that the bread and wine become the actual body and blood of Christ when consecrated during the Eucharist, but with their appearance remaining unchanged.

transuranic *adj. Chem.* having an atomic number greater than that of uranium.

transuranic element *Chem.* any chemical element with an atomic number greater than 92 (the atomic number of uranium). Such elements are artificially manufactured and radioactive, most of them having short half-lives.

Transvaal POP (1985) 8.6m, a province in South Africa. AREA 262 499sq km/101 325sq mi. It is bounded N by the Limpopo R following the frontiers with Botswana and Zimbabwe. The Transvaal Drakensberg Mts lie to the SE. CAPITAL

Pretoria. CHIEF TOWNS Johannesburg, Krugersdorp, Vereeniging. HISTORY settled by the Boers after the Great Trek of 1831; gained independence in 1852, recognized by Britain; known as the South African Republic; annexed by Britain in 1877; the Boer rebellion in 1880–1 led to restoration of the republic; annexed as a British colony in 1900; granted self-government in 1906; joined the Union of South Africa in 1910. ECONOMY the most prosperous province in the country; gold; diamonds; iron; oil; engineering; hydroelectricity; cereals; tobacco; clothing; forestry.

transverse *adj.* placed, lying, built, etc crosswise or at right angles. [from Latin *transvertere*, to turn across]

transversely *adv.* in a transverse direction or position.

transverse stage *Theatr.* an open stage positioned in the middle of an auditorium and stretching from wall to wall, dividing the audience into two groups facing each other across the acting area.

transverse wave *Physics* a wave motion in which the disturbance of the medium occurs at right angles to the direction of propagation of the wave, eg ripples on water.

transvestism *noun* the practices of transvestites.

transvestite *noun* a person, especially a man, who derives sexual pleasure from wearing the clothes of the opposite sex. [from Latin *trans*, across + *vestire*, to dress]

Transylvania, Magyar **Erdély**, German **Siebenbürgen** a geographical region and former province of N and central Romania, separated from Wallachia and Moldavia by the Carpathian Mts. It was formerly a principality that became part of the Austro-Hungarian Empire, and was then incorporated into Romania in 1918. Part of the region was ceded to Hungary by Hitler in World War II. CHIEF TOWNS Cluj-Napoca, Braşov.

Transylvanian Alps *or* **Southern Carpathian Mountains**, Romanian **Carpaţii Meridionali** the S branch of the E European Carpathian Mts, situated in central Romania. The highest peak in the range is Negoiul (2 548m); it is also the highest point in Romania. The range includes the National Park of Retezat.

trap — *noun* **1** a device or hole, usually with bait attached, for catching animals. **2** a plan or trick for surprising a person into speech or action, or catching someone unawares: *a speed trap.* **3** a trapdoor. **4** a bend in a pipe, especially a drainpipe, which fills with liquid to stop foul gases passing up the pipe. **5** a light, two-wheeled carriage pulled by a single horse. **6** a device for throwing a ball or clay pigeon into the air. **7** a box-like compartment from which a greyhound is released at the beginning of a race. **8** a bunker or other hazard on a golf course. **9** *slang* the mouth. **10** (**traps**) *Jazz* drums or other percussion instruments. — *verb* (**trapped**, **trapping**) **1** to catch (an animal) in a trap. **2** to catch (a person) out or unawares, especially with a trick. **3** to set traps in (a place). **4** to stop and hold in or as if in a trap. **5** *intrans.* to act as a trapper. [from Anglo-Saxon *treppe*]

trapdoor *noun* a small door or opening in a floor or ceiling.

trapes see TRAIPSE.

trapeze *noun* a swing-like apparatus consisting of a short horizontal bar hung on two ropes, on which gymnasts or acrobats perform tricks. [from French *trapèze*, trapezium]

trapezium *noun* (PL. **trapeziums**, **trapezia**) **1** *Brit.* a quadrilateral with one pair of opposite sides parallel. **2** *North Amer., esp. US* a quadrilateral with no sides parallel (see also TRAPEZOID 1). **3** any quadrilateral that is not a parallelogram. [from Greek *trapezion*, from *trapeza*, table]

trapezoid *noun* **1** *Brit.* a quadrilateral with no sides parallel. **2** *North Amer., esp. US* a quadrilateral with one pair of opposite sides parallel (see also TRAPEZIUM 1). [from Greek *trapeza*, table]

trapper *noun* a person who traps animals and sells their fur.

trappings *pl. noun* clothes or ornaments suitable for a particular occasion, ceremony, office, or person. [from Old French *drap*, cloth]

Trappist — *noun* a member of a branch of the Cistercian order of monks with a severe rule which includes a vow of silence. — *adj.* relating to the Trappists. [from *La Trappe*, in France, where the order was founded]

Trappists the popular name of the Cistercians of the More Strict Observance, centred on the monastery of La Trappe, France, until 1892. The Order continues throughout the world, devoted to divine office, and noted for its austerity (eg perpetual silence, and abstention from meat, fish, and eggs).

traps *pl. noun* personal luggage. [from Old French *drap*, cloth]

trash *noun* **1** *North Amer., esp. US* rubbish; waste material or objects. **2** nonsense. **3** a worthless person or worthless people. **4** a worthless object or worthless objects. [from Middle English *trasches*]

trashcan *noun North Amer., esp. US* a dustbin.

trashily *adv.* in a trashy way.

trashiness *noun* a trashy quality.

trashy *adj.* (**trashier, trashiest**) worthless.

Trás-os-Montes a former region of NE Portugal, bounded N and E by Spain. The population of this mountain area is concentrated in the fertile valleys, where grapes and fruit are grown. Sheep and goats graze on the bare upland plateaux. [from Portuguese *trás-os-montes*, beyond the mountains]

trattoria *noun* (PL. **trattorias**, **trattorie**) an Italian restaurant. [from Italian *trattoria*]

trauma *noun* (PL. **traumas**, **traumata**) **1** a physical injury or wound. **2** a state of shock caused by a physical wound or injury. **3** an emotional shock which may have long-term effects on behaviour or character. [from Greek *trauma*, wound]

traumatic *adj.* **1** relating to, resulting from, or causing physical wounds. **2** of or causing an emotional shock with long-term effects. **3** *colloq.* distressing; frightening; unpleasant.

traumatically *adv.* in a traumatic way.

traumatize *or* **traumatise** *verb* to cause physical or emotional trauma to.

Traun, Lake, German **Traunsee**, or **Gmundner See** a lake in Reutte district, Tirol state, central Austria. AREA 25sq km/15sq mi; length 12km/7mi; width 3km/2mi; maximum depth 191m. Summer resorts in the area include Gmunden, Traunkirchen, Ebensee, and Rindbach. Water sports are popular.

travail — *noun* **1** painful or extremely hard work or labour. **2** the pain of childbirth; labour. — *verb intrans.* to work hard or with pain, especially in childbirth. [from Old French]

travel — *verb usually intrans.* (**travelled**, **travelling**) **1** to go from place to place; to journey, especially abroad or far from home. **2** *trans.* to journey through, across, or over (a region, country, etc). **3** *trans.* to journey across (a stated distance). **4** to be capable of withstanding a usually long journey: *her children don't travel well.* **5** to journey from place to place as a sales representative. **6** to move: *light travels in a straight line.* **7** to move or pass deliberately and steadily from one point to another: *her eyes travelled over the horizon.* **8** *said especially of machinery* to move along a fixed course. **9** *colloq.* to move quickly. — *noun* **1** an act of travelling. **2** (*usually* **travels**) a journey or tour,

especially abroad: *get back from one's travels.* **3** the distance or speed travelled by machinery. [from Middle English]

travel agency an office dealing in airline, coach, ship, and train tickets, hotel accommodation, etc for journeys and holidays.

travel agent a person who runs a travel agency.

travelled *adj., combining form* **1** having travelled especially abroad a lot. **2** travelled along; frequented: *a well-travelled road.*

traveller *noun* **1** a person who travels. **2** *old use* a travelling sales representative. **3** *Brit. colloq.* a gypsy.

traveller's cheque a cheque issued by a bank, which can be exchanged for the currency of another country when in that country.

travelogue *noun* a film, article, talk, etc about travel, especially an individual's trip to a particular place or region.

travel sickness nausea and vomiting experienced as a result of motion during travel by car, boat, aircraft, etc.

Traven, B, pseudonym of **Benick Traven Torsvan** (1890–1969) US writer, thought to have been born in Chicago of Swedish (or German) parents. Little is known about his background, although he is thought to have lived in Mexico from the 1930s. He is best known as the author of *The Treasure of the Sierra Madre* (1935), on which the celebrated film by John Huston is based. Other novels include *The Death Ship* (1926) and *The Rebellion of the Hanged* (1936).

traversal *adj.* the action of traversing or crossing.

traverse — *verb* **1** to go across or through. **2** to lie or reach across: *a bridge traversing a deep gorge.* **3** *trans., intrans.* to climb, walk, or ski at an angle across (a slope) rather than straight up or down. **4** *intrans.* to move sideways or to one side. **5** to examine or consider (a subject, problem, etc) carefully and thoroughly. **6** to move (especially the barrel of a large gun) to one side while keeping it horizontal. **7** to oppose or thwart. **8** to survey by traverse. — *noun* **1** an act of crossing or traversing. **2** a path or passage across eg a rock face or slope. **3** something that lies across. **4** a sideways movement. **5** the movement of the barrel of a large gun to one side while being kept horizontal. **6** a survey by measuring straight lines from point to point and the angles between. **7** an obstruction. — *adj.* being or lying across; oblique. [from Latin *traversare*]

travesty — *noun* (PL. **travesties**) a ridiculous or crude distortion: *a travesty of justice.* — *verb* (**travesties**, **travestied**) to make a travesty of. [from French *travestir*, to disguise]

Traviata, La an opera by Giuseppe Verdi (1853). The story focuses on the consumptive courtesan Violetta, with whom the shy and sensitive Alfredo falls in love. However, his father wishes to protect the family's reputation and secretly asks Violetta to deny his son, which leads to much misunderstanding and heartache until someone enlightens Alfredo. [Italian, = the fallen woman]

travolator *or* **travelator** *noun* a moving ramp which transports people or goods horizontally, or at a slight incline (see also ESCALATOR).

trawl — *noun* **1** (*in full* **trawl-net**) a large bag-shaped net with a wide mouth, used to catch fish at sea. **2** a wide-ranging or extensive search. — *verb trans., intrans.* **1** to search (the sea, an area of sea, etc) for (fish) with a trawl. **2** to search through (a large number of things, people, etc) thoroughly, especially before finding the one required: *had to trawl through hundreds of applications.* [from Old Dutch *tragel*]

trawler *noun* **1** a fishing-boat used in trawling. **2** a person who trawls.

tray *noun* **1** a flat piece of wood, metal, plastic, etc usually with a low edge, for carrying dishes, crockery, etc. **2** a very shallow lidless box forming a drawer in eg a wardrobe or trunk, or used for displaying articles in a cabinet. [from Anglo-Saxon *trig*]

treacherous *adj.* **1** not able to be trusted; ready or likely to betray. **2** having hidden hazards and dangers. [from Old French *trechier*, to cheat]

treacherously *adv.* in a treacherous way.

treacherousness *noun* **1** being treacherous. **2** treachery.

treachery *noun* (PL. **treacheries**) betraying someone or their trust, disloyalty; also, an act of betrayal or disloyalty.

treacle *noun* **1** (*also* **black treacle**) the thick dark sticky liquid that remains after the crystallization and removal of sugar from extracts of sugar-cane or sugar-beet. **2** molasses. [from Greek *theriake*, an antidote to the bites of wild beasts, from *therion*, wild beast. The word gradually came to be applied to the sugary substance in which the antidote was taken rather than to the antidote itself]

tread — *verb* (PAST TENSE **trod**; PAST PARTICIPLE **trodden**, **trod**) **1** (**tread on something**) to put a foot or feet on it; to walk or step on it. **2** to step or walk on, over, or along. **3** to crush or press (eg into the ground) with a foot or feet; to trample: *tread grapes / was treading ash into the carpet.* **4** to wear or form (a path, hole, etc) by walking. **5** to perform by walking. **6** (**tread on someone**) to suppress them; to treat them cruelly. **7** *said of a male bird* to copulate with (a female bird). — *noun* **1** a manner, style, or sound of walking: *a heavy tread.* **2** an act of treading. **3** a mark made by treading; a footprint or track. **4** the thick, grooved, and patterned surface of a tyre that grips the road. **5** that part of a wheel that touches the rail. **6** that part of a rail that the wheels touch. **7** that part of the sole of a shoe that touches the ground. **8** the horizontal part of a step or stair on which the foot is placed.
— **tread water** to keep oneself afloat and upright in water by making a treading movement with the legs and a circular movement with the hands and arms.
[from Anglo-Saxon *tredan*]

treadle — *noun* a pedal for one or both feet that drives a machine, eg a sewing-machine or loom. — *verb intrans.* to work a treadle. [from Anglo-Saxon *tredel*, step]

treadmill *noun* **1** an apparatus for producing motion consisting of a large wheel turned by people (especially formerly prisoners) or animals treading on steps inside or around it. **2** a monotonous and dreary routine. **3** an exercise machine consisting of a continuous moving belt whose speed can be regulated to make the user walk, jog, or run.

treason *noun* **1** (*also* **high treason**) disloyalty to or betrayal of one's country, sovereign, or government. **2** any betrayal of trust or act of disloyalty. [from Old French *traison*]
◇ In the UK, the law on treason includes the unlawful acts of conspiring or inciting to kill the monarch, and insurrection. The person who commits an act of treason must owe allegiance to the Crown, either because he or she is a British subject, or if not a British subject, because he or she has accepted the protection of the Crown. In the USA, treason is defined in Article III, section 3, of the Constitution.

treasonable *adj.* of, being or involving treason.

treasonably *adv.* in a treasonable way.

treasure — *noun* **1** wealth and riches, especially in the form of gold, silver, precious stones and jewels, etc which have been accumulated over a period of time and which can be hoarded. **2** any thing of great value. **3** *colloq.* a much loved and valued helper, friend, etc. — *verb* **1** to value greatly or think of as very precious. **2** (*usually* **treasure something up**) to preserve it or collect it for future use or as something of value: *treasured up all his old school photographs.* [from Old French *tresor*]

treasure hunt **1** a hunt for treasure. **2** a game in which players try to be the first to find a hidden prize by solving a series of clues whose answers lead to its location.

Treasure Island a novel by Robert Louis Stevenson (1883). It describes the adventures of young Jim Hawkins in his hunt for buried treasure.

treasurer *noun* **1** the person in a club, society, etc who is in charge of the money and accounts. **2** an official responsible for public money, eg in a local council.

treasure-trove *noun Legal* treasure or money that is found hidden usually in the earth and whose owner is unknown, deemed to be the property of the Crown. [from Old French *trover*, to find]

treasury *noun* (PL. **treasuries**) **1** a place where treasure is stored. **2** (**Treasury**) the government department in charge of a country's finances, especially the collection and distribution of income from tax, etc; also, the building which houses this. **3** the income or funds of a state, government, organization, or society. **4** a store of valued items, eg a book containing popular poems, stories, or quotations.

Treasury bench the front bench in the House of Commons where the Prime Minister, Chancellor of the Exchequer, and other senior members of the Government sit.

treat — *verb* **1** to deal with or behave towards (a person or thing) in a certain manner: *treated him badly / treat it as a joke.* **2** to care for or deal with (a person, illness, injury, etc) medically. **3** to put through a process or apply something to: *treat the wood with creosote.* **4** (**treat someone to something**) to provide them with food, drink, entertainment, or a gift at one's own expense: *she treated herself to a new dress.* **5** to speak or write about; to discuss. **6** (**treat of something**) to deal with or discuss a subject, especially in writing. **7** (**treat with someone**) to negotiate with another nation, person, etc to settle a dispute, end a war, etc. — *noun* **1** an outing, meal, present, etc given as a gift by one person to another. **2** any source of pleasure or enjoyment, especially when unexpected.
— **a treat** *colloq.* very good or well: *they looked a treat.*
[from Old French *traitier*]

treatise *noun* a formal piece of writing with deals with a subject in depth. [from Old French *tretis*, from *traitier*, to treat]

treatment *noun* **1** the medical or surgical care given to a patient, or to cure an illness. **2** an act or the manner of dealing with someone or something, often in a literary, musical, or artistic treatment: *rough treatment / the painter's characteristic treatment of light and shadow.*
— **the full treatment** *colloq.* the appropriate or usual treatment, especially when lavish or generous.

treaty *noun* (PL. **treaties**) **1** a formal agreement between states or governments. **2** an agreement between two parties or individuals, especially for the purchase of property. [from Old French *trete*]

Trebizond, Turkish **Trabzon** a city on the Black Sea coast of present-day Turkey, former capital of the Christian empire (1204–1461), founded by Alexius Comnenus. It was the outpost of Greek culture in Asia Minor until the Greek defeat by the Turks in 1922.

treble — *noun* **1** anything which is three times as much or as many. **2** *Mus.* a soprano; a person, especially a boy, having a soprano singing voice; a part written for this voice. **3** *Mus.* an instrument with a similar range; in a family of instruments, the member with the highest range. **4** a high-pitched voice or sound. **5** the higher part of the audio frequency range of a radio, record, etc. **6** a cumulative bet on three races in which the original money bet plus winnings on the first race is (if successful) bet on the second, and then the total bet on the third. **7** the narrow inner ring of a dartboard, which scores three times the stated score; also, a hit on this. — *adj.* **1** three times as much or as many; threefold; triple. **2** for, being, or having a treble voice. **3** *said of a voice* high-pitched. — *adv.* with a treble voice: *sing treble.* — *verb trans., intrans.* to make or become three times as much a person, especially a boy, having a soprano singing voice; a part written for this voice. [from Latin *triplus*, triple]

treble chance a way of betting with football pools in which the chance of winning depends on the number of draws and home and away wins forecast by the competitor.

treble clef a sign at the beginning of a piece of written music which places the note G (a fifth above middle C) on the second line of the staff.

trebly *adv.* three times as much; to a threefold degree.

trecento *noun* the 14c, usually with reference to Italian art. [Italian, = three hundred (shortened from *mille trecento*, thirteen hundred)]

treddle same as TREADLE.

Tree, Sir (Herbert Draper) Beerbohm (1853–1917) English actor-manager, born in London. He had a commercial education in Germany but became an actor, took over the Haymarket theatre (1887), and built His Majesty's theatre (1897), where he rivalled Henry Irving's productions at the Lyceum. He founded the Royal Academy of Dramatic Art in 1904, where the first production of George Bernard Shaw's *Pygmalion* (1914) was a great sucess.

tree — *noun* **1** *Bot.* a tall woody perennial plant which typically has one main stem or trunk, and usually only bears branches on its upper part, so giving rise to a distinct crown of foliage. Apart from the loss of leaves in deciduous species, the aerial parts do not die back at the end of each growing season. **2** anything like a tree, especially in having branches leading from a main trunk, eg a diagram with a branched structure: *a family tree.* **3** (*also in compounds*) a wooden frame or support for holding things: *shoe tree.* **4** *old use* a cross for crucifixion. **5** *old use* a gallows or gibbet. — *verb* to drive or chase up a tree.
— **at the top of the tree** at the top of one's profession.
up a tree *North Amer. colloq.* in difficulties.
[from Anglo-Saxon *treow*]

tree creeper a small bird that runs up tree trunks in search of insects on which to feed.

tree fern a fern with a thick woody stem covered in dead leaf bases and bearing a crown of leaves at its apex, found mainly in tropical regions, and so called because it resembles a tree in size and shape.

tree frog a frog adapted to live in trees, that has sucker-like discs on its fingers and toes to facilitate climbing.

treeless *adj.* having no trees.

tree line same as TIMBER LINE.

Trees an early series of abstract paintings by Piet Mondrian.

tree shrew a small SE Asian mammal with a long tail (which may be bushy or have a tufted tip) and a long thin shrew-like muzzle. It lives in trees and on the ground, feeds on insects and fruit, and resembles ancestral mammals of 220 million years ago.

tree snake any snake which spends much of its life in trees. The term is applied to many unrelated species.

tree surgeon a person who is skilled in tree surgery.

tree surgery *Bot.* the treatment of diseased or damaged trees, especially by cutting off dead branches, filling cavities, and providing supports.

treetop *noun* the top of a tree.

trefoil *noun* **1** a leaf which is divided into three sections. **2** any plant having such leaves, eg clover. **3** anything with three lobes or sections. **4** a carved ornament or decoration with three lobes or sections. [from Latin *trifolium*, from *tres*, three + *folium*, leaf]

trefoil arch *Archit.* an arch constructed in a trefoil shape with two rounded arches on either side of and below a third arch whose central point is drawn from the cusp formed by the arcs of the two lower arches.

trek — *verb intrans.* (**trekked**, **trekking**) **1** to make a long, hard journey. **2** *South Afr.* to make a journey by ox-wagon. — *noun* **1** a long, hard journey. **2** *South Afr.* a journey by ox-wagon. [from Dutch *trekken*, to draw (a vehicle or load)]

trellis — *noun* a frame or network of narrow wooden strips used to support climbing plants. — *verb* (**trellised**, **trellising**) to provide or support with a trellis. [from Old French *trelis*]

trellised *adj.* **1** having or formed like a trellis. **2** trained on a trellis.

tremble — *verb intrans.* **1** to shake, eg with cold, fear, weakness, etc. **2** to quiver or vibrate. **3** to feel fear or anxiety. — *noun* **1** a trembling movement; a shudder or tremor. **2** (**trembles**) a disease of livestock, especially cattle, causing muscular weakness, shaking, and constipation.

— **go in fear and trembling of someone** or **something** *often facetious* to be extremely afraid of them.

[from Latin *tremere*, to shake]

trembling *adj.* **1** that trembles. **2** afraid.

tremblingly *adv.* with trembling.

trembling poplar the aspen.

trembly *adj.* (**tremblier**, **trembliest**) trembling or likely to tremble.

tremendous *adj.* **1** enormous; huge. **2** *colloq.* very good or remarkable. [from Latin *tremendus*, to be trembled at]

tremendously *adv.* in a tremendous way; to a tremendous degree.

Tremiti Islands a rocky limestone archipelago in Puglia region, S Italy, in the Adriatic Sea. AREA 3sq km/1sq mi. The main islands are San Domino, San Nicola, Caprara. It is a popular area for scuba diving.

tremolo *noun* (PL. **tremolos**) *Mus.* **1** a trembling effect produced by rapidly repeating a note or notes, produced especially by a stringed or keyboard instrument. **2** a similar effect produced in singing by fluctuating the pitch of the note sung. **3** a device in an organ for producing a trembling effect. [from Italian]

tremor *noun* **1** a shaking or quivering. **2** a slight vibration or trembling movement, especially a slight earthquake. **3** a thrill. [from Latin *tremor*]

tremulous *adj.* **1** trembling, especially with fear, worry, nervousness, or excitement. **2** *said of a line drawn, words written, etc* written by a shaky hesitant hand and so weak and wavering. [from Latin *tremulus*, from *tremere*, to shake]

tremulously *adv.* in a tremulous way.

tremulousness *noun* a tremulous quality.

trench — *noun* **1** a long narrow ditch dug in the ground, especially one used to protect soldiers from enemy gunfire. **2** a long narrow deep depression in the sea floor, usually having steep sides. **3** a long narrow depression in the Earth's surface, produced by erosion or by movements of the Earth's crust. — *verb* **1** to dig a trench or trenches (in). **2** to provide (a place) with a trench as fortification. [from Old French *trenche*, cut]

trenchancy *noun* a trenchant quality.

trenchant *adj.* **1** cutting; keen. **2** incisive; penetrating. **3** forthright; vigorous. [from Old French *trenchant*, cutting]

trenchantly *adv.* in a trenchant way.

Trenchard (of Wolfeton), Hugh Montague, 1st Viscount (1873–1956) English airman, born in Taunton, Somerset. He joined the army in 1893, served in India, South Africa, and W Africa, and developed an interest in aviation. He commanded the Royal Flying Corps in World War I, helped to establish the RAF (1918), was the first Chief of Air Staff (1918–29), and was appointed Marshal of the RAF (1927). As Commissioner of the London Metropolitan Police (1931–5), he founded the police college at Hendon.

trench coat a waterproof coat with a belt and epaulettes, based on the style of a military raincoat.

trencher *noun* **1** *Hist.* a wooden plate or board for serving food. **2** (*in full* **trencher-cap**) a square flat hat worn by academics; a mortarboard. [from Old French *trenchour*, from *trenchier*, to cut]

trencherman *noun* a person who eats well or heartily.

trench warfare warfare in which each side uses trenches from which to attack the enemy.

trend — *noun* **1** a general direction or tendency. **2** the current general movement in fashion, style, or taste. — *verb intrans.* to turn or have a tendency to turn in a specified direction: *trend north / trend towards socialism*. [from Anglo-Saxon *trendan*]

trendily *adv.* in a trendy way.

trendsetter *noun* a person who sets a fashion.

trendsetting *noun* creating a new fashion.

trendy — *adj. Brit. colloq.* (**trendier**, **trendiest**) following the latest fashions, often without thinking or using one's own discrimination or taste. — *noun* (PL. **trendies**) a trendy person.

Trent, Little Nell the child companion and support of her ageing grandfather in Charles Dickens's *The Old Curiosity Shop*. Her dissolute brother is Frederick Trent.

Trent, Council of a Council of the Roman Catholic Church, held (1545–63) in Trento, Italy. Called to combat Protestantism and to reform the discipline of the Church, it spearheaded the Counter-Reformation by clarifying many points of doctrine and practice.

Trent, River a river in N Staffordshire, central England, length 275km/171mi. Rising S of Biddulph, it flows SE, then E and NE through Derbyshire, Nottinghamshire, and Humberside to meet the estuary of the R Humber near Whitton. It is linked by canal to many industrial towns in the Midlands.

Trent Affair an incident (1861) between the USA and Britain during the American Civil War, in which the USS *San Jacinto* removed two officials of the Confederate States from the British ship *Trent* while in international waters. There was considerable British anger until the Confederate officials were released by the American Secretary of State.

Trento, Latin **Tridentum**, German **Trient**, English **Trent** POP (1991e) 102 000, the capital of Trentino-Alto Adige region and of Trento province, N Italy. It is situated on the left bank of the R Adige. NOTABLE FEATURES cathedral (11c–12c); Castello del Buon Consiglio (13c, enlarged in the 16c); Church of Santa Maria Maggiore (16c), where the Council of Trent met between 1545 and 1563.

Trenton POP (1990) 326 000, the capital of the state of New Jersey, USA. It is situated in Mercer County, W New Jersey, USA, on the E bank of the R Delaware, 45km/30mi E of Philadelphia. HISTORY settled by English Quakers in the 1670s;

scene of a British defeat by George Washington in 1776 (marked by a 47m-high monument); became state capital in 1790; achieved city status in 1792. NOTABLE FEATURES State House complex; William Trent House.

trepan — *noun* a small cylindrical saw formerly used for removing part of a bone, especially the skull, during surgery. — *verb* (**trepanned**, **trepanning**) to remove (a piece of bone) with a trephine. [from Greek *trypaein*, to bore]

trephine — *noun* a surgical instrument used for removing circular sections of bone, especially from the skull, during surgery, now used instead of the trepan. — *verb* to remove (a piece of bone) with a trephine. [from Latin *tres fines*, three ends]

trepidation *noun* fear or nervousness. [from Latin *trepidare*, to hurry with alarm]

Trésaguet, Pierre Marie Jerome (1716–96) French civil engineer, born in Nevers. He made his career in the Corps des Ponts et Chaussées, becoming inspector-general of the Corps in 1775. He is best known for the improved method of road construction he introduced, involving the use of a base layer of stones with progressively smaller sizes towards the surface. He also emphasized the importance of good drainage and regular maintenance.

trespass — *verb intrans.* (*often* **trespass on** *or* **upon someone** *or* **something**) **1** to enter someone else's property without the right or permission to do so. **2** to intrude into a person's time, privacy, rights, etc. **3** *old use* to sin. — *noun* **1** the act of entering someone else's property without the right or permission to do so. **2** an intrusion into someone's time, privacy, etc. **3** *old use* a sin. [from Latin *transpassare*, to step across]

◇ In England and Wales, trespass is usually a civil offence, although in certain circumstances, such as trespass by squatting, it may be a criminal offence. The term is not used in Scots law.

trespasser *noun* **1** a person who trespasses. **2** *old use* a sinner.

tress *noun* **1** a long lock or plait of hair. **2** (**tresses**) a woman's or girl's long hair. [from Old French *tresse*]

trestle *noun* a support, eg for a table, consisting of a horizontal beam resting at each end on a pair of legs sloping outwards. [from Old French *trestel*, from Latin *transtrum*, transom]

trestle table a table consisting of a board or boards supported by trestles.

Trethowan, Sir (James) Ian (Raley) (1922–90) English journalist and broadcaster, born in High Wycombe. From the *Yorkshire Post*, he moved to ITN as a television newscaster in 1956. With the BBC from 1961, he was political commentator and then managing director of radio (when the Home, Light, and Third programmes became Radio 1, 2, 3, and 4), before returning to television and becoming director general (1977–82).

Tretyakov Gallery an art gallery in Moscow, of which the museum building was designed by Viktor M Vasnetsov (1848–1926) and erected in 1901–2. The gallery passed into state ownership in 1918. It houses exhibits of Russian painting and sculpture from the 11c to the present. A new gallery is presently under construction.

Trevelyan, G(eorge) M(acaulay) (1876–1962) English historian, born in Welcombe, Warwickshire. After serving in World War I, he became Professor of Modern History at Cambridge (1927–40). Best known as a pioneer social historian, his *English Social History* (1944) is a companion volume to his *History of England* (1926).

Treves, French **Trèves**, German **Trier**, ancient **Augusta Treverorum** POP (1991e) 98 000, a river port in Rhineland-Palatinate state, W central

Germany. It lies on the R Mosel, near the Luxembourg border. One of Germany's oldest towns, it has been a bishopric since the 4c. It is a considerable centre of wine production and the wine trade. Karl Marx was born here in 1818. NOTABLE FEATURES Roman Catholic Theological College; Porta Nigra (2c), basilica (4c), cathedral (11c–12c), all World Heritage sites.

Trevithick, Richard (1771–1833) British engineer and inventor, born in Illogan, Cornwall. He became a mining engineer at Penzance, and over 1796–1801 invented a steam carriage, which ran between Camborne and Tuckingmill, and which in 1803 was run from Leather Lane to Paddington via Oxford Street. He later went to Peru and Costa Rica (1816–27), where his engines were introduced into the silver mines.

Trevor a male first name, after the surname and several Welsh place-names.

trews *pl. noun* trousers, especially of tartan cloth. [from Irish amd Scots Gaelic *triubhas*]

tri- *combining form* forming words meaning 'three, three times, threefold'. [from Latin *tres* and Greek *treis*, three]

triad *noun* **1** any group of three people or things. **2** a chord consisting of three notes, usually a base note and those notes a third and a fifth above it. **3** any of several Chinese secret societies, especially one involved in organized crime or drug trafficking. **4** in Welsh literature, a group of three sayings, stories, etc about related subjects. [from Greek *treis*, three]

triadic *adj.* relating to or consisting of triads.

Trial, The (Der Prozess) a novel by Franz Kafka (1925). It presents the sinister scenario of a man being arrested, tried, and put to death for no apparent reason.

trial *noun* **1** a legal process by which a person accused of a crime or misdemeanour is judged in a court of law. **2** an act of trying or testing; a test. **3** trouble, worry, or vexation, or a cause of this: *her son is a great trial to her.* **4** *Sport* a preliminary test of a player's or athlete's skill and fitness, especially before choosing which players or athletes to include in a team. **5** a test of a vehicle's performance held especially over rough ground or a demanding course. **6** a competition, usually over rough ground, to test skills in handling high-performance cars or motorcycles. **7** any competition testing the skills of animals: *sheepdog trials.* **8** an attempt.
— **on trial 1** the subject of a legal action in court. **2** undergoing tests or examination before being permanently accepted or approved.
trial and error the trying of various methods, alternatives, etc until the correct or suitable one is found.
[from Old French, from *trier*, to try]

trial run a test of a vehicle, piece of machinery, etc or rehearsal of a play, to assess effectiveness.

Triamond the Knight of Friendship in Spenser's *The Faerie Queene*, who marries Canacee, the sister of his friend Cambell.

triangle *noun* **1** a plane (two-dimensional) figure with three sides and three angles, whose sum is always 180°; a three-sided polygon. **2** anything with a similar shape. **3** a musical percussion instrument consisting of a metal bar shaped into a triangle with one corner left open that is struck with a small hammer. **4** an emotional relationship or love affair involving three people. [from Latin *triangulum*]

triangular *adj.* **1** in the shape of a triangle. **2** involving three people or parties.

triangularity *noun* a triangular form.

triangularly *adv.* in a triangular way.

triangulate *verb* to survey (an area) by dividing it up into a series of triangles, eg when map-making.

triangulation *noun* the process or result of triangulating.

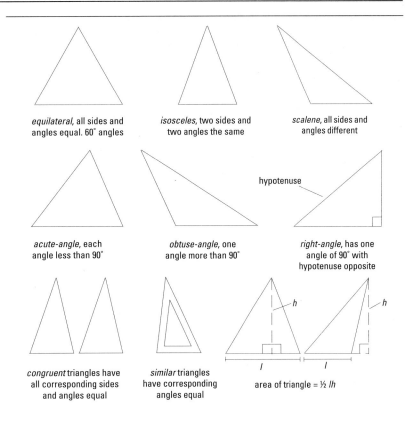

equilateral, all sides and angles equal. 60° angles

isosceles, two sides and two angles the same

scalene, all sides and angles different

hypotenuse

acute-angle, each angle less than 90°

obtuse-angle, one angle more than 90°

right-angle, has one angle of 90° with hypotenuse opposite

congruent triangles have all corresponding sides and angles equal

similar triangles have corresponding angles equal

area of triangle = ½ *lh*

triangles

Triassic *adj. Geol.* relating to the earliest period of the Mesozoic era, lasting from about 250 million to 210 million years ago. During this time the first dinosaurs and large sea reptiles appeared, and ammonites were common. The first small mammals also appeared, and conifers became widespread, forming luxuriant forests. [from Latin *trias*, triad]

triathlete *noun* an athlete who competes in the triathlon.

triathlon *noun* an athletic contest consisting of three events, usually swimming, running, and cycling. [from TRI- + DECATHLON]

tribal *adj.* of a tribe or tribes.

tribalism *noun* **1** the system of tribes as a way of organizing society. **2** the feeling of belonging to a tribe.

tribally *adv.* in a tribal way; in terms of tribes.

tribe *noun* **1** a group of families, clans, or communities who are linked by social, economic, and political ties, who often have a common ancestor and usually have a common culture, dialect, and leader. **2** a group of people with a common interest, profession, etc. **3** *Hist.* any of the three divisions of the ancient Romans, the Latins, Etruscans, and Sabines. **4** *Hist.* any of the twelve divisions of the Israelites, each of which was believed to be descended from one of the twelve patriarchs. **5** *Biol.* in plant and animal classification, a subdivision of a family, consisting of several similar or closely related genera. [from Latin *tribus*, one of the divisions of the ancient Roman people]

tribesman *or* **tribeswoman** *noun* (PL. **tribesmen**) a man, or woman, who belongs to a tribe.

tribulation *noun* great sorrow or trouble, or a cause of this. [from Latin *tribulatio*, from *tribulare*, to afflict]

tribunal *noun* **1** a court of justice. **2** a group of people appointed to inquire into some matter or

dispute and to adjudicate or give judgement. **3** a seat or bench in a court for a judge or judges. [from Latin *tribunus*]

tribune[1] *noun* **1** *Hist.* a high official elected by the ordinary people of ancient Rome to defend their rights and interests. **2** a champion or defender of the rights of the common people. [from Latin *tribunus*]

tribune[2] *noun* **1** a raised area, dais, or stand. **2** a bishop's throne. [from Latin *tribuna*]

tributary — *noun* (PL. **tributaries**) **1** a stream or river flowing into a larger river or lake. **2** a person or nation paying tribute to another. — *adj.* **1** *said of a stream or river* flowing into a larger river or lake. **2** paid or owed as tribute. **3** paying tribute. [from Latin *tributarius*]

tribute *noun* **1** something given or said as an expression of praise, thanks, admiration, or affection. **2** a sign or evidence of (something valuable, effective, worthy of praise, etc): *her success was a tribute to all her hard work.* **3** *Hist.* a sum of money paid regularly by one nation or ruler to another in return for protection or as an acknowledgement of submission. [from Latin *tributum*]

tricarboxylic acid cycle *Biochem.* Kreb's cycle.

trice
— **in a trice** in a very short time; almost immediately.
[from Middle Dutch *trisen*, to pull or haul]

triceps *noun* any muscle attached to a bone or bones in three places, especially the large muscle at the back of the arm which straightens the elbow. [from Latin *triceps*, three-headed]

triceratops *noun* a four-legged herbivorous dinosaur, with a bony frill round its neck, one horn over each eye and one on its nose. [from Greek *trikeratos*, three-horned + *ops*, face]

Trichinopoly see TIRUCHCHIRAPPALLI.

trichinosis *noun Medicine* a disorder caused by infestation with a parasitic nematode worm

(*Trichinella spiralis*), usually as a result of eating raw or partially cooked pork containing the worm's larvae, The main symptoms are nausea, diarrhoea, fever, and pain and stiffness in the muscles. [from Greek *trichinos*, of hair + -OSIS]

trichloromethane *noun* *Chem.* same as CHLOROFORM.

trichology *noun* the scientific study of the hair and its diseases. [from Greek *trix*, hair + -LOGY]

trick — *noun* **1** something which is done or said to cheat, deceive, fool, or humiliate someone. **2** a deceptive appearance, especially one caused by the light; an illusion. **3** a mischievous act or plan; a prank or joke. **4** a clever or skilful act or feat which astonishes, puzzles, or amuses. **5** a habit or mannerism: *he has a trick of scratching his nose when he's angry.* **6** a special technique or knack: *a trick of the trade.* **7** a feat of skill which can be learned. **8** the cards played in one round of a card game and which are won by one of the players. **9** *slang* a prostitute's client. **10** *Naut.* a period of duty at the helm. — *adj.* **1** intended to deceive or give a certain illusion: *trick photography.* **2** able to or designed for the performing of tricks. — *verb* **1** to cheat, deceive, or defraud. **2** (**trick someone into** *or* **out of something**) to make them do as one wants, or to gain something from them, by cheating or deception: *tricked him into donating his life savings.* — **do the trick** *colloq.* to do or be what is necessary to achieve something.

trick or treat *chiefly North Amer.* the children's practice of dressing up on Hallowe'en to call at people's houses for small gifts, threatening to play a trick if they are not given one.

trick someone *or* **something out** *or* **up** to dress or decorate them fancily.

up to one's tricks *colloq.* behaving in one's usual deceitful or tiresome way.

[from Old French *trique*]

trickery *noun* (PL. **trickeries**) an act or the practice of deceiving or cheating.

trickily *adv.* in a tricky way.

trickiness *noun* being tricky.

trickle — *verb* **1** *trans., intrans.* to flow or cause to flow in a thin slow stream or drops. **2** *intrans.* to move, come, or go slowly and gradually. — *noun* a thin slow stream, flow, or movement. [from Middle English *triklen*]

trickster *noun* a person who deceives or cheats, or plays tricks.

tricky *adj.* (**trickier**, **trickiest**) **1** difficult to handle or do; needing skill and care. **2** inclined to trickery; sly; deceitful. **3** clever in tricks; resourceful; adroit.

tricolour *noun* a three-coloured flag, especially one with three equal stripes of different colours, such as the French and Irish flags. [from Latin *tricolor*]

tricoloured *adj.* three-coloured.

tricot *noun* **1** a hand-knitted woollen fabric. **2** a soft, slightly ribbed cloth for women's garments. [from French *tricot*, knitting]

tricycle — *noun* **1** a vehicle with three wheels, two at the back and one at the front, driven by pedals. **2** a light, three-wheeled car for the use of a disabled person. — *verb intrans.* to ride a tricycle.

tricyclist *noun* a person who rides a tricycle.

trident *noun* **1** *Hist.* a spear with three prongs, especially as carried by a sea-god, such as Neptune or Britannia, or a Roman gladiator. **2** (**Trident**) a ballistic missile with several warheads which can each be programmed to attack a different target, fired from a submarine. [from Latin *tridens*, having three teeth]

Tridentine — *adj.* relating to the Council of Trent (1545–63) or the traditional Catholic beliefs and doctrines reaffirmed there as a reaction to Protestantism and the Reformation. —

noun a member of the Roman Catholic Church who follows the traditional doctrine affirmed at the Council of Trent. [from Latin *Tridentum*, Trent]

Trident missile the US Navy's third-generation submarine-launched ballistic missile system, following on from the earlier Polaris and Poseidon missiles. The first version, Trident C-4, became operational in the USA in 1980, followed at the end of the the the decade by the larger Trident D-5. The British Royal Navy began to replace its Polaris submarine fleet with Trident submarines at the beginning of the 1990s. The missile has a range of 11 000km/6 835mi, carries up to 14 individually targetable re-entry vehicles (MIRVS), and has a navigation system giving it accuracy equivalent to its land-based counterparts, although it is launched from a moving platform.

tried *adj.* **1** tested and proved to be good, efficient, etc. **2** (*in phrases and compounds*) having had one's patience put to strain: *sorely tried.*

triennial *adj.* **1** happening once every three years. **2** lasting three years. [from Latin *triennis*]

triennially *adv.* every three years.

Trier see TREVES.

trier *noun* a person who tries hard.

Trieste POP (1991e) 231 000, the capital of Trieste province, Friuli-Venezia Giulia region, NE Italy. It is the largest port on the Adriatic coast. It is also capital of the Free Territory of Trieste, an area established by the UN in 1947 and divided in 1954 into Italian and Yugoslav zones (the latter is less populous with its headquarters at Capodistria). NOTABLE FEATURES town hall (1874); Cathedral of San Giusto (14c); Church of Sant'Antonio (1849); castle (15c–18c).

trifle — *noun* **1** anything of very little value. **2** a very small amount. **3** a dessert made typically of sponge-cake soaked in sherry and spread with jam or jelly and fruit and topped with custard and whipped cream. — *verb* **1** (**trifle with someone** *or* **something**) to treat a person or a person's feelings frivolously and insensitively. **2** *intrans.* to act, behave, or talk idly. **3** (**trifle something away**) to spend or pass time idly; to waste an opportunity, etc. [from Old French *trufe*, mockery, deceit]

trifling *adj.* **1** unimportant; trivial. **2** frivolous.

trig *noun colloq.* trigonometry.

trigger — *noun* **1** a small lever which releases a catch or spring to set a mechanism going, especially one which is squeezed to fire a gun. **2** anything which starts a train of actions or reactions. — *verb* (**triggered**, **triggering**) (*also* **trigger something off**) to start a train of actions, reactions, events, etc. [from Dutch *trekken*, to pull]

trigger-happy *adj. colloq.* likely to shoot or react violently without thinking or with very little provocation.

Triglav the highest peak in Slovenia, situated in the Julian Alps in the NW of the country. HEIGHT 2 863m.

triglyceride *noun Biochem.* any of a large number of chemical compounds, consisting of a glycerol molecule combined with three fatty acids, that are present in most fats.

triglyph *noun Archit.* a tablet with three parallel grooves, forming part of a Doric frieze. [from Greek *triglyphos*, from *glyphein*, to carve]

trigonometrical *or* **trigonometric** *adj.* relating to or involving trigonometry.

trigonometrical point a fixed point, often a point on a hilltop, whose position as the vertex of a triangle is calculated astronomically and which is used as an aid to map-making.

trigonometric function *or* **trigonometric ratio** *Maths.* any function of an angle that is defined by the relationship between the angles and sides in a right-angled triangle, eg sine, cosine, tangent, secant, cosecant, cotangent.

trigonometry *noun Maths.* the branch of mathematics that is concerned with the relationships between the sides and angles of triangles, especially by use of the trigonometric functions (sine, cosine, and tangent). It is an important mathematical tool, and also has practical applications in navigation and surveying. [from Greek *trigonon*, triangle + *metron*, measure]

trig point *noun colloq.* same as TRIGONOMETRICAL POINT.

trike *noun colloq.* a tricycle.

Trikhonís, Lake the largest lake in Greece, situated in W central Greece, 16km/10mi NE of Missolonghi. AREA 96 513sq km/37 254sq mi; length 19km/12mi; width 4.8km/3mi.

trilateral *adj.* having three sides. [from Latin *tri-*, three + *latus*, side]

trilaterally *adv.* **1** on three sides. **2** concerning three countries or parties.

Trilby a novel by George du Maurier (1894). It describes how a young female singer (Trilby) falls under the controlling influence of another musician (Svengali).

trilby *noun* (PL. **trilbies**) *Brit.* a soft felt hat with an indented crown and narrow brim. [named after *Trilby*, the heroine of the novel of the same name by George du Maurier, in the stage version of which such a hat was worn]

trilingual *adj.* **1** able to speak three languages fluently, as or like a native speaker. **2** written or spoken in three languages. [from TRI- + Latin *lingua*, tongue]

trill — *noun* **1** *Mus.* a sound produced by playing or singing a note and a note higher than it repeatedly and in rapid succession. **2** a shrill warbling sound made by a songbird. **3** a consonant sound, especially an 'r' sound, produced by rapidly vibrating the tongue. — *verb trans., intrans.* to play, sing, or pronounce (something) with a trill. [from Italian *trillo*]

trillion *noun* **1** in North America, and increasingly in the UK, a million millions (10^{12}). **2** formerly in Britain, a million million millions (10^{18}). **3** (*also* **trillions**) *colloq.* an enormous number or amount. [from TRI- + MILLION]

trillionth *noun, adj.* a million millionth.

trilobite *noun* **1** *Zool.* an extinct marine arthropod having a flat oval body divided lengthwise into three lobes. Trilobites were abundant from the Cambrian to the Permian periods. **2** the fossilized remains of this animal. [from Greek *trilobos*, three-lobed]

trilogy *noun* (PL. **trilogies**) a group of three plays, novels, poems, operas, etc which are related, often by theme. [from Greek *trilogia*]

Trim, Corporal the faithful garrulous servant of Toby in Laurence Sterne's *Tristram Shandy*.

trim — *verb* (**trimmed**, **trimming**) **1** to make neat and tidy, especially by clipping. **2** (*also* **trim something away** *or* **off**) to remove it by, or as if by, cutting: *trim hundreds of pounds off the cost.* **3** to make less by, or as if by, cutting: *trim costs.* **4** to decorate with ribbons, lace, ornaments, etc. **5** to adjust the balance of (a ship, submarine, or aircraft) by moving its cargo, ballast, etc. **6** to arrange (a ship's sails) to suit the weather conditions. **7** *intrans.* to hold a neutral or middle course between two opposing individuals or groups. **8** *intrans.* to adjust one's behaviour to suit current trends or opinions, especially for self-advancement. — *noun* **1** a haircut which neatens but does not change a person's hairstyle. **2** proper order or condition: *in good trim.* **3** material, ornaments, etc used as decoration. **4** the decorative additions to a car, including the upholstery, internal and external colour scheme, and chrome and leather accessories. **5** the set or balance of a ship on the water. **6** *said of a ship* the state of being ready, especially with the sails in proper order, for sailing. **7** the inclination of an aircraft in flight, especially with reference to the horizon. **8** parts removed by trimming. — *adj.* (**trimmer, trimmest**) **1** in good order; neat and tidy. **2** clean-cut; slim. [from Anglo-Saxon *trymian,* to strengthen]

trimaran *noun* a boat with three hulls placed side by side. [from TRI- + CATAMARAN]

trimester *noun* a period of three months, especially in the US one forming an academic term. [from Latin *trimestris,* of three months]

trimly *adv.* in a trim way.

trimmer *noun* **1** a person or thing that trims. **2** a person who adjusts his or her behaviour to suit current trends and opinions, especially for self-advancement. **3** a short horizontal beam on a floor into which the ends of joists are fitted.

trimming *noun* **1** ribbon, lace, or other decoration added to clothing, etc. **2** (**trimmings**) the traditional or usual sauce, garnish, accompanying vegetables, etc served with a particular dish. **3** (**trimmings**) parts cut or trimmed off.

trimness *noun* being trim.

Trimurti the Hindu triad, which manifests the cosmic functions of the Supreme Being, as represented by the gods Brahma, Vishnu, and Shiva. Brahma is the balance between the opposing principles of preservation and destruction, symbolized by Vishnu and Shiva respectively. [Sanskrit, = having three forms]

Trincomalee *or* **Trinkomali** POP (1981) 44 000, the seaport capital of Trincomalee district, Eastern province, Sri Lanka. It lies 257km/160mi NE of Colombo on Koddiyar Bay, at the mouth of the R Mahaweli. HISTORY one of the earliest Tamil settlements; taken by the British in 1795; principal British naval base during World War II after the fall of Singapore. NOTABLE FEATURES deep-water harbour praised by Lord Nelson in 1770 as the finest harbour in the world; ruins of the Temple of a Thousand Columns (3c BC); Hindu temple; Fort Fredrick at the foot of the Swami Rock.

Trinculo the bullying jester of Alonso, and companion to Stephano, in Shakespeare's *The Tempest.*

Trinidad and the Valley de Los Ingenios a town in Sancti Spíritus province, central Cuba. It is a World Heritage site.

Trinidad and Tobago, official name **Republic of Trinidad and Tobago** POP (1992e) 1.3m, a republic comprising the southernmost islands of the Lesser Antilles chain, SE Caribbean Sea, just off the S American mainland. AREA 5 128sq km/1 979sq mi. CAPITAL Port of Spain. CHIEF TOWNS San Fernando, Arima, Scarborough. TIME ZONE GMT –4. The population is mainly of East Indian or African descent; Roman Catholicism and Hinduism are the chief religions. OFFICIAL LANGUAGE English. CURRENCY the Trinidad and Tobago dollar. PHYSICAL DESCRIPTION the island of Trinidad is roughly rectangular in shape; separated from Venezuela in the S by the 11km/7mi-wide Gulf of Paria; crossed by three mountain ranges; the N range includes El Cerro del Aripo (940m); the remainder of the land is low-lying, with large areas of mangrove swamps along the coasts; Pitch Lake in the SW is the world's largest reservoir of natural asphalt; Tobago lies 30km/19mi NE; the Main Ridge extends along most of the island, rising to 576m. CLIMATE tropical, with an annual average temperature of 29°C; the average rainfall is 1 270mm in the W, 3 048mm in the NE. HISTORY visited by Columbus in 1498; Trinidad was settled by Spain in the 16c; ceded to Britain in 1802; Tobago became a British colony in 1814; became a joint British Crown Colony in 1899; independent member of the Commonwealth in 1962; republic in 1976. GOVERNMENT governed by a President elected for a five-year term and bicameral parliament, comprising a 31-member Senate and a 36-member House of Representatives. ECONOMY

based on the oil and gas industry; an industrial complex on the W coast of Trinidad includes a steel mill, ammonia plants, and facilities for producing methanol and urea; cement; oil refining; petrochemicals; asphalt; processing of sugar; cocoa; coffee; fruit; the main tourist centre is on Tobago.

Trinidad and Tobago

Trinitarian — *noun* a person who believes in the doctrine of the Trinity. — *adj.* relating to or believing in the doctrine of the Trinity. See also UNITARIAN.

Trinitarianism *noun* the beliefs of the Trinitarians.

trinitrotoluene *noun Chem.* a highly explosive yellow crystalline solid that is used as an explosive, and in certain photographic chemicals and dyes. [from TRI- + NITRO- + *toluene,* a liquid organic chemical]

trinity *noun* (PL. **trinities**) **1** the state of being or a group of three. **2** (**Trinity**) in Christian theology, the unity of three persons, the Father, Son, and Holy Spirit, in a single Godhead. **3** (**Trinity** *or* **Trinity Sunday**) the Sunday after Whit Sunday, kept as a festival in honour of the Trinity. **4** (**Trinity** *or* **Trinity term**) the university or law term beginning after Easter. [from Latin *trinitas*]

Trinity College of Music a conservatory founded (1872) in London specifically to teach church music. Since 1876 however, the curriculum has included music of all kinds for performers and teachers. The college is recognized as a teaching school of London University.

Trinity House the lighthouse authority for England and Wales, the Channel Islands, and Gibraltar. It is one of the principal pilotage authorities, and also supervises the maintenance of navigation marks carried out by local harbour authorities. Its pilotage role is undergoing a fundamental change, with control being gradually devolved to local port management.

trinket *noun* a small, worthless article, especially a cheap ornament or piece of jewellery.

trinketry *noun* a collection of such articles.

trio *noun* (PL. **trios**) **1** a group of three. **2** *Mus.* a group of three instruments, players, or singers, or a piece of music composed for it. **3** *Mus.* a contrastive central section of a minuet, scherzo, or march. [from Italian]

trip — *verb* (**tripped, tripping**) **1** *trans., intrans.* (*also* **trip over** *or* **up**) to stumble or cause to stumble. **2** *trans., intrans.* (*also* **trip up**) to make or cause to make a mistake. **3** to catch (someone) in a fault or mistake. **4** *intrans.* (*usually* **trip along**) to walk, skip, or dance with short light steps. **5** *intrans.* to move or flow smoothly and easily: *words tripping off the tongue.* **6** *intrans.* to take a trip or excursion. **7** *intrans. slang* to experience the hallucinatory effects of a drug, especially LSD. **8** *trans., intrans.* to activate or cause (a device or mechanism) to be activated, especially suddenly. **9** to perform (a dance) with quick, light, agile steps. — *noun* **1** a short journey or excursion, usually to a place and back again. **2** a catching of the foot; a stumble. **3** a short light step or skip. **4** a striking part or catch which activates a mechanism. **5** an error or blunder. **6** *slang* a hallucinatory experience caused by taking a drug, espe-

cially LSD. **7** *slang* an intensely emotional experience. [from Old French *triper*]

tripartite *adj.* **1** divided into three parts. **2** involving or concerning three parts, groups, people, etc. [from Latin *tripartitus*]

tripe *noun* **1** parts of the stomach of a cow or sheep, used as food. **2** *colloq.* nonsense; rubbish. [from Old French]

triple — *adj.* **1** three times as great, as much, or as many. **2** made up of three parts or things. **3** *Mus.* having three beats to the bar. — *verb trans., intrans.* to make or become three times as great, much, or many. — *noun* **1** three times the (usual) amount. **2** a group or series of three. [from Latin *triplus*]

Triple Alliance, War of the, also called **Paraguayan War** a devastating war fought (1864–70) by Paraguay against the combined forces of Brazil, Argentina, and Uruguay (the Triple Alliance). Provoked by the ambitions of the Paraguayan dictator Francisco Solano López (1826–70), his eventual defeat by the Allies (mostly Brazilian troops) reduced Paraguay's male population by nine-tenths.

triple bond *Chem.* a covalent bond formed between two atoms that share three pairs of electrons between them.

Triple Crown a term used in many sports to describe the winning of three major events. In British horse racing it is the Derby, 2 000 Guineas, and St Leger; in US racing, the Preakness Stakes, Kentucky Derby, and Belmont Stakes. In British Rugby Union it is the beating of the other three Home countries in the international championship.

Triple Entente a series of agreements between Britain and France (1904) and Britain and Russia (1907) initially to resolve outstanding colonial differences. It aligned Britain to France and Russia (who had concluded a military alliance in 1893–4) and in 1914 became a military alliance.

triple glazing three layers of glass separated by air spaces to give improved thermal and acoustic insulation. It provides insulation significantly greater than that from double glazing.

triple jump an athletic event in which competitors try to cover the greatest distance with a type of jump consisting of a hop, skip, and a jump.

triple point *Chem.* the temperature and pressure at which the solid, liquid, and gaseous phases of a particular substance are in equilibrium.

triplet *noun* **1** one of three children or animals born to the same mother at the same time. **2** a group or set of three. **3** *Mus.* a group of three notes played in the time usually given to two. **4** a group of three rhyming verses in a poem. [from TRIPLE]

triple time musical time with three beats to the bar. Simple triple time has beats divisible by two, as in 3:2, 3:4, 3:8. Compound triple time has beats divisible by three, as in 9:4, 9:8, 9:16.

triplicate — *adj.* **1** having three parts which are exactly alike. **2** being one of three identical copies. **3** tripled. — *noun* any of three identical copies or three parts which are exactly alike. — *verb* to make three copies of.
— **in triplicate** three times; on three separate copies of the same document. [from Latin *triplicatus*]

triplication *noun* the process of triplicating.

triply *adv.* three times as much.

tripod *noun* **1** a stand with three legs for supporting a camera. **2** a stool or table with three legs or feet. [from Latin *tripous*]

Tripoli, Arabic **Tarabulus,** or **Tarabulus al-Gharb,** ancient **Oea** POP (1990e) 1.5m, the seaport capital of Libya. It is situated on the

Mediterranean coast, 345km/214mi SW of Malta. HISTORY founded by the Phoenicians, and later developed by the Romans; important Axis base in World War II; bombed in 1941–2 and occupied by the British in 1943; bombed by the US Air Force in response to alleged terrorist activities in 1986. NOTABLE FEATURE arch of Marcus Aurelius (1c BC); the old city partly surrounded by Byzantine and mediaeval walls.

Tripoli, Arabic **Trâblous**, Greek **Tripolis**, ancient **Oea** POP (1990e) 160 000, the seaport capital of Tripoli division, Ash Shamaïl region, NW Lebanon. It is the second largest city in the country and the trade centre for N Lebanon and NW Syria. There are two Palestinian refugee camps located nearby. NOTABLE FEATURES Tower of the Lion; Crusader Castle of St Gilles (12c); Mamelukes' Grand Mosque (13c).

Tripolitania a former province of W Libya, lying between Tunis and Cyrenaica. HISTORY under Turkish control from the 16c until 1911; under Italian control until 1943; under British control until 1952.

tripos noun an honours examination for the BA degree at Cambridge University. [from Latin *tripus*, tripod]

tripper noun 1 *Brit. often derog.* a person who goes on a journey for pleasure; a tourist. 2 *slang* a person who takes a drug, especially LSD, and experiences its hallucinatory effects.

triptych noun a picture or carving on three panels which are joined together by hinges to form a single work of art, often used as an altarpiece. See also DIPTYCH. [from Greek *triptychos*, threefold]

Tripura POP (1991) 2.8m, a state in E India. AREA 10 477sq km/4 044sq mi. It is bounded N, W, and S by Bangladesh. The terrain is mostly hilly and forested. HISTORY became a state of India in 1949; its status changed to union territory in 1956; reverted to a state in 1972. CAPITAL Agartala. GOVERNMENT governed by a 60-member Legislative Assembly. ECONOMY rice, wheat, tea, cotton, jute, oilseed, sugar cane; food processing; steel; handicrafts.

trip-wire noun a hidden wire which sets off a mechanism of some kind, such as an alarm or bomb, when someone trips over it.

trireme noun an ancient Greek warship with three banks of rowers on each side. [from Latin *triremis*]
◇ Triremes were used by the Greeks, Phoenicians, and Romans. Speeds of up to 9 knots are claimed for short distances. A typical Roman example of the 1c BC was crewed by c.140 rowers and armed with a ram, a drawbridge for boarding enemy galleys, and a catapult.

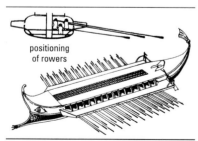

positioning of rowers

trireme

trisect verb to divide into three usually equal parts. [from TRI- + Latin *secare*, to cut]

trisection noun trisecting, dividing into three equal parts.

Tristan and Isolde (Tristan und Isolde) an opera by Richard Wagner (1865). The tale begins with Tristan bringing Isolde from Brittany to marry his uncle, King Mark, in Cornwall. It is revealed that Isolde had once cured Tristan (although he had just killed her fiancé) and now loves him. They drink a death potion together, which is actually an aphrodisiac, and they continue as lovers in King Mark's castle, with tragic results (see TRISTRAM).

Tristan da Cunha POP (1988) 297, a small volcanic island in the S Atlantic Ocean, about midway between southern Africa and South America. AREA 98sq km/38sq mi. Its volcanic cone rises to 2 060m. The inhabitants are the descendants of a British garrison, established in 1816 during Napoleon's exile in St Helena. In 1922 the island became a dependency of St Helena. The population is centred on the settlement of Edinburgh. In 1961 the islanders were evacuated after a volcanic eruption, but returned in 1963. There are three uninhabited islands nearby. ECONOMY fishing (crayfish); crafts; postage stamps.

Tristram or **Tristan** 1 in Arthurian legend, a knight who was sent to woo Iseult (Isolde) on behalf of his uncle, King Mark of Cornwall. He fell in love with her himself, after they had mistakenly drunk the same love-potion. He then fled to Brittany, where he married Iseult of the White Hands. Later, when he was dying from a wound, he sent for Iseult to heal him; she arrived too late because of his wife's deceit, and died at his side. 2 a male first name. [from the Celtic name *Drystan*, tumult]

Tristram Shandy, The Life and Opinions of a novel by Laurence Sterne (1759–67). It is an innovative, digressive narrative following the fortunes of the narrator, Tristram, and his family. It is often regarded as the prototype of the 20c 'stream-of-consciousness' novel.

trite adj., *said of a remark, phrase, etc* having no meaning or effectiveness because repeated or used so often; hackneyed. [from Latin *tritus*, rubbed]

tritely adv. in a trite way.

triteness noun a trite quality.

tritium noun *Chem.* (SYMBOL ^{3}H, T) a radioactive isotope of hydrogen that contains two neutrons and one proton in its nucleus. It undergoes radioactive decay to form beta particles, and is used in scientific research to label compounds with radioactivity so that they can be traced by the radiation they emit. It is also used in hydrogen bombs and luminous paints. [from Greek *tritos*, third]

Triton 1 in Greek mythology, the son of Poseidon and Amphitrite. He is depicted in art as a fish from the waist down, and blows a conchshell to command the waves. The beings of similar form (mermen) who serve Poseidon are often referred to as Tritons. 2 *Astron.* the largest natural satellite of Neptune, 2 700km in diameter. It orbits the planet in the opposite direction to the other moons.

triumph — noun 1 a great or notable victory, success, or achievement. 2 the great joy or feeling of elation felt on winning a great victory, etc. 3 *Hist.* the procession accompanying the entry into ancient Rome of a general who had won a great victory over a foreign enemy. — verb intrans. 1 to win a victory or be successful. 2 to celebrate a victory or success. 3 to enjoy a feeling of triumph over someone. [from Latin *triumphus*]

triumphal adj. of or celebrating a triumph.

triumphal arch *Archit.* a free-standing gateway of purely aesthetic or symbolic function, usually monumental in proportion and built of stone. Triumphal arches were first built in Rome in the 2c BC, usually to celebrate a military victory. The most famous example today is the Arc de Triomphe d'Etoile in Paris, built in 1806–35.

triumphant adj. 1 having won a victory or achieved success. 2 feeling or showing great joy or elation at, or celebrating, a victory or success.

triumphantly adv. in a triumphant way.

Triumph of Caesar a series of nine tempera paintings by Andrea Mantegna (begun c.1486, Hampton Court).

Triumph of the Will (Triumph Des Willens) a German film directed by Leni Riefenstahl (1934). It is a technically innovative and accomplished record of the 1934 Nazi Party rally at Nuremberg, condemned by many as a propagandist glorification of the Nazi ethic.

Triumph of Venice, The a ceiling painting by Paolo Veronese (c.1535, Ducal Palace, Venice).

triumvir noun (PL. **triumviri**, **triumvirs**) any one of a group of three people sharing office or supreme power. [from Latin, from *trium virorum*, of three men]

triumviral adj. relating to or designating a triumvir.

triumvirate noun a group of three people sharing office or supreme power.
◇ In ancient Rome, the name given commonly to the unofficial coalition between Caesar, Pompey, and Crassus in 60 BC; also, the name given to the joint rule from 43 BC of Antony, Octavian, and Lepidus.

trivalence or **trivalency** noun being trivalent.

trivalent adj. *Chem.* having a valency of three. [from TRI- + Latin *valere*, to be strong]

Trivandrum or **Trivandram** POP (1991) 524 000, the capital of Kerala state, SW India. It lies 1 255km/780mi SE of Bombay, on the Malabar coast. The city is a commercial and cultural centre, known for its wood and ivory carving. NOTABLE FEATURE early 18c temple to Vishnu.

trivet noun 1 a three-legged stand or bracket which hooks on to a grate for holding cooking vessels over a fire. 2 a stand for a hot dish, pot, teapot, etc at table. [from Anglo-Saxon *trefet*]

trivia pl. noun unimportant or petty matters or details. [from Latin *trivium*, place where three ways meet]

trivial adj. 1 of very little importance. 2 *said of a person* only interested in unimportant things; frivolous. 3 commonplace; ordinary.

triviality noun (PL. **trivialities**) 1 being trivial. 2 something that is trivial.

trivialization or **trivialisation** noun trivializing or being trivialized.

trivialize or **trivialise** verb to make or treat as if trivial or unimportant.

trivially adv. in a trivial way; to a trivial extent.

Trivial Pursuit *trademark* a board quiz game developed in Canada in 1979. Players advance by answering questions correctly on a variety of subjects and move coloured discs round a circular board, filling in segments of the disc as they progress. When a player's disc has been filled, the player may advance to the centre of the board. The first player to answer a question correctly (the subject area having been selected by the other players) after reaching the central area is declared the winner.

trochee noun *Prosody* a foot consisting of one long syllable followed by one short one. [from Greek *trochaios pous*, running foot]

trod, trodden see TREAD.

troglodyte noun a person who lives in a cave. [from Greek *troglodytes*, one who creeps into holes]

troika noun 1 a Russian vehicle drawn by three horses abreast. 2 a team of three horses harnessed abreast. 3 any group of three people working as a team, especially sharing power. [from Russian]

Troilus in Greek legend, a prince of Troy, the son of Priam and Hecuba, who was killed by Achilles. In medieval stories, he is the lover of Cressida (eg in Chaucer's *Troilus and Criseyde*).

Troilus and Cressida a play by William Shakespeare (1609). It is set during the Trojan war and depicts the ill-fated love-affair of Troilus and Cressida.

Troilus and Criseyde a poem by Geoffrey Chaucer (c.1385–90). It draws on Boccaccio's *Il Filostrato*.

Trojan — *noun* **1** *Hist.* a citizen or inhabitant of ancient Troy in Asia Minor. **2** a person who works, fights, etc extremely hard or courageously. — *adj.* relating to ancient Troy or its inhabitants or citizens. [from Latin *Trojanus*, from *Troja*, Troy]

Trojan Horse 1 in Greek legend, a huge wooden horse built by the Greeks during the Trojan War and left behind on the beach, on the pretence of having abandoned the siege of Troy. The Trojans were told that it was an offering to Athena, and broke down their city wall to bring it inside. At night, Greek warriors emerged and opened the gates to allow the capture of the city. **2** *Comput.* a disruptive part of a program which lies dormant until activated by certain circumstances, causing damage to data but unable either to replicate itself or to attach itself to other programs.

Trojan War in Greek legend, the 10-year conflict between the Greeks and Trojans, which began when Paris carried off Helen, the wife of Menelaus, and ended in the sacking of Troy. The story was the subject of Homer's *Iliad*, and is dated to the 12c or 13c BC.

Trojan Women a play by Euripides (c.415 BC). An anti-war statement, it is a tragedy about the aftermath of the fall of Troy and its effects on both armies.

troll[1] *noun Scandinavian Mythol.* an imaginary, ugly, evil-tempered, human-like creature, usually a dwarf or a giant. [from Norse]

troll[2] — *verb* **1** *trans., intrans.* to fish by trailing bait on a line through water. **2** *intrans. old use, facetious* to stroll or saunter. — *noun* the bait used in trolling, or a line holding this. [from Middle English *trollen*, to roll or stroll]

trolley *noun* (PL. **trolleys**) **1** *Brit.* a small cart or basket on wheels used for conveying luggage, shopping, etc. **2** *Brit.* a small table, usually with a shelf underneath, mounted on castors or wheels, used for conveying food, crockery, etc in the home or a restaurant. **3** a bed on wheels for transporting patients in hospital. **4** *Brit.* a small wagon or truck running on rails. **5** a trolley wheel. **6** *Brit.* a trolley bus. **7** *North Amer.* a trolley car.
— **off one's trolley** *colloq.* daft; crazy.
[probably from TROLL[2]]

trolley bus a vehicle providing public transport which receives power from a trolley wheel and overhead electric wires.

trolley car *North Amer.* a vehicle providing public transport which runs on rails like a tram and receives power from a trolley wheel and overhead electric wires.

trolley wheel a small grooved wheel which collects current from an overhead electric wire and transmits it down a pole to power the vehicle underneath.

trollop *noun* a promiscuous or disreputable woman. [perhaps from TROLL[2]]

Trollope, Anthony (1815–82) English novelist, born in London. He joined the Post Office in 1834, and in 1841 became postal surveyor in Ireland, where he began to write. His first novel in the Barsetshire series, *The Warden*, appeared in 1855, and was followed by such successful books as *Barchester Towers* (1857), *Framley Parsonage* (1861), and *The Last Chronicle of Barset* (1867). A political series of novels followed, known as the Palliser novels, including *Phineas Finn* (1869) and *The Eustace Diamonds* (1873). Among his later novels were *The Way We Live Now* (1875) and *Mr Scarborough's Family* (1883).

trombone *noun* a brass musical wind instrument, on which the pitch of notes is altered by sliding a tube in and out. [from Italian, from *tromba*, trumpet]

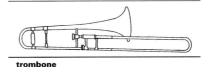

trombone

trombonist *noun* a person who plays the trombone.

Tromp, Maarten (Harpertszoon) (1598–1653) Dutch admiral, born in Briel. He is known for his defeat of a superior Spanish fleet off Gravelines and won the battle of the Downs, both in 1639. Knighted by Louis XIII of France (1640) and by Charles I of England (1642), he then fought the French pirates based on Dunkirk, and his encounter with Blake in 1652 started the Anglo-Dutch Wars. Victorious off Dover, he was defeated by a superior English fleet off Portland, and finally off Terhejide, near Schevingen. His son Cornelis was also a naval commander, who shared the glory of Ruyter's Four Days' battle during the second Anglo-Dutch wars (1666).

trompe l'oeil (PL. **trompe l'oeils**) a painting or decoration which gives a convincing illusion of reality. [French, = deceives the eye]
◊ The success of a *trompe l'oeil* depends not on its aesthetic value, which is often minimal, but on its ability to so deceive the eye that the spectator is convinced of the material reality of the objects represented. For example, according to Pliny, the ancient Greek painter Zeuxis painted grapes so realistic that birds tried to peck them. The device is also used in interior decoration to create a three-dimensional illusion on flat surfaces.

Tromsø POP (1991e) 51 000, the seaport capital of Troms county, N Norway. It lies on a small island between South Kvaløy and the mainland. The largest town in N Norway, it was founded in the 13c and received its municipal charter in 1794. It is used as a base for expeditions to the Arctic. NOTABLE FEATURES observatory for the study of the aurora borealis; Tromsdalen Church (1975); Tromsø Museum.

Trondheim, formerly **Nidaros**, later German **Trondhjem**, or **Drontheim** POP (1992e) 140 000, the seaport capital of Sør-Trøndelag county, central Norway, lying at the mouth of R Nidelv, on the S shore of Trondheim Fjord. Trondheim is a former capital of Norway, first becoming capital during the Viking period. It was occupied by the Germans between 1940 and 1945. NOTABLE FEATURES cathedral (1066–93); Royal Palace (18c); Church of Our Lady (13c).

Troödos Mountains a mountain range in central Cyprus. It rises to 1 951m at Mt Olympus, the highest peak on the island.

Troon POP (1981) 14 000, a town and golf resort in Kyle and Carrick district, Strathclyde, W Scotland. It lies at the N end of Ayr Bay, 9km/6mi N of Ayr.

troop — *noun* **1** (*usually* **troops**) armed forces; soldiers. **2** a group or collection, especially of people or animals. **3** a division of a cavalry or armoured squadron. **4** a large group of Scouts, divided into patrols. — *verb intrans.* (**troop along, off**, *etc*) to move as a group.
— **troop the colour** to parade the regiment's flag ceremonially.
[from Old French *trope*]

trooper *noun* **1** a private soldier, especially one in a cavalry or armoured unit. **2** a cavalry soldier's horse. **3** *North Amer., esp. US* a policeman mounted on a horse or motorcycle. **4** *Brit.* a troop-ship.

Trooping the Colour in the UK, a military ceremony that takes place annually in June to mark Elizabeth II's official birthday. It originated as the display of the regimental standard to the troops, but now consists of a ceremony on Horse Guards Parade, London, when the Queen reviews one of the seven regiments of her personal guard, and its flag, or 'colour', is paraded before her.

troop-ship *noun* a ship for transporting soldiers.

trope *noun* a word or expression used figuratively. [from Greek *tropos*, turn]

trophy *noun* (PL. **trophies**) **1** a cup, medal, plate, etc awarded as a prize for victory or success in some contest, especially in sport. **2** something which is kept in memory of a victory or success, eg in hunting. **3** a memorial of victory, especially in ancient Greece or Rome, originally captured weapons, armour, and other spoils, set up on or near the field of victory. **4** a representation of such a memorial, eg on a medal or monument. [from Greek *tropaion*]

tropic — *noun* **1** either of two imaginary circles running round the earth at 23° 27″ north (the *Tropic of Cancer*) or 23° 27″ south (the *Tropic of Capricorn*) of the equator. **2** (**tropics**) the part of the earth lying between these two circles, noted for its hot dry weather. — *adj.* same as TROPICAL. [from Greek *tropikos*]

tropical *adj.* **1** relating to, found in, or originating from the tropics. **2** very hot; passionate. **3** luxuriant.

tropically *adv.* in a tropical way or situation.

tropical medicine *Medicine* the branch of medicine that specializes in diseases that are prevalent in tropical regions. The most important tropical diseases worldwide are malaria, schistosomiasis, leprosy, and river blindness, all of which are potentially curable, although the facilities for their treatment are often inadequate in the countries where they occur.

Tropic of Capricorn see TROPIC.

tropism *noun Biol.* the growth movement of a plant in response to an external stimulus such as gravity or light, usually by curving towards or away from the source. For example, plant roots grow vertically downward in response to gravity (positive geotropism). [from Greek *tropos*, turning]

troposphere *noun Meteorol.* the lowest layer of the Earth's atmosphere, extending from the Earth's surface to a height of about 8km over the Poles, and about 17km over the Equator. Weather conditions, in the form of clouds, convection currents, etc, occur within the troposphere, and the temperature steadily decreases with increasing height. [from Greek *tropos*, turn + SPHERE]

Trot *noun derog. colloq.* **1** a Trotskyist. **2** any supporter of the extreme left.

trot — *verb* (**trotted, trotting**) **1** *intrans. said of a horse* to move at a steady, fairly fast pace, moving each diagonal pair of legs together to give a bouncy gait. **2** to cause (a horse) to move in this way. **3** *intrans.* to move or proceed at a steady, fairly brisk pace. — *noun* **1** the pace at which a horse, rider, etc moves when trotting. **2** an act of trotting. **3** (**the trots**) *slang* diarrhoea.
— **on the trot** *colloq.* **1** one after the other. **2** continually moving about; busy.
trot something out *colloq.* to produce a story, excuse, etc habitually and unthinkingly.
[from Old French *troter*]

troth *noun old use* faith or fidelity.
— **plight one's troth** to promise to be faithful and true in marriage.
[from Anglo-Saxon *treowth*, truth]

Trotsky, Leon, also called **Lev Davidovich Bronstein** (1879–1940) Russian Jewish revolutionary, born in Yanovka, Ukraine. In 1898 he was arrested as a Marxist and exiled to Siberia, but he escaped (1902), joined Lenin in London, and in the abortive 1905 Revolution was President of the St Petersburg Soviet. He then worked as a revolutionary journalist in the West, and returned to Russia in 1917, when he joined the Bolsheviks and played a major role in the October Revolution. In the Civil War he was Commissar for War, and created the Red Army. After Lenin's death (1924) his influence began to decline. Stalin, who opposed his theory of 'permanent revolution', ousted him from the Party, and he was exiled to central Asia (1927) and expelled from the Soviet Union (1929). He continued to agitate as an exile, and was sentenced to death in his absence by a Soviet court (1937). He finally found asylum in Mexico, but was assassinated there by one of Stalin's agents.

Trotskyism a development of Marxist thought by Leon Trotsky. Essentially a theory of permanent revolution, Trotskyism stressed the internationalism of socialism and encouraged revolutionary movements abroad, which conflicted with Stalin's 'socialism in one country'. Trotskyism has since inspired other extreme left-wing revolutionary movements but they are factionally divided, and have little support ouside some Western capitalist states.

Trotskyist or **Trotskyite** — noun a supporter of Trotskyism. — adj. relating to or involving Trotskyism.

trotter noun 1 a horse trained to trot in harness. 2 (usually **trotters**) a pig's foot used as food.

Trotwood, Betsey the eccentric and reclusive great-aunt of David in Charles Dickens's *David Copperfield*.

troubadour noun Hist. any of a number of lyric poets in S France and N Italy in the 11c to 13c who wrote, usually in Provençal, about a highly idealized form of love. [from Provençal *trobar*, to find]

trouble — noun 1 distress, worry, or concern, or a cause of this. 2 bother or effort, or a cause of this: *go to a lot of trouble / the dog was no trouble*. 3 a problem or difficulty: *your trouble is that you're too generous*. 4 (often **troubles**) public disturbances and unrest. 5 illness or weakness: *heart trouble*. 6 malfunction; failure: *engine trouble*. 7 the state of expecting a child when not married: *get into trouble*. — verb 1 trans., intrans. to feel or cause to feel distress, worry, concern, anger, or sadness to. 2 to cause physical distress or discomfort to. 3 used in polite requests to put to inconvenience: *might I trouble you to open the window a little?* 4 intrans. to make any effort or take pains: *he didn't even trouble to tell me what had happened*. 5 to disturb or agitate (eg the surface of water).
— **be asking for trouble** colloq. to behave in a way likely to bring problems or difficulties on oneself.
in trouble in difficulties, especially because of doing something wrong or illegal.
take trouble over with something to perform or treat it carefully and assiduously.
[from Old French *trubler*, from Latin *turbare*, to disturb]

troubled adj. agitated, disturbed.

troublemaker noun a person who continually and usually deliberately causes trouble, worry, problems, etc to others.

troubleshooter noun 1 a person who is employed to find and solve problems, eg with machinery or in a company. 2 a person employed to mediate in disputes.

troubleshooting noun the solving of problems.

troublesome adj. causing worry or difficulty.

troublesomely adv. in a troublesome way.

troublous adj. old use, literary full of troubles; disturbed.

trough noun 1 a long narrow open container used for feeding animal livestock. 2 a channel, drain, or gutter. 3 a long narrow hollow between two waves. 4 *Meteorol.* a long narrow area of low atmospheric pressure; the opposite of a ridge. 5 a low point. [from Anglo-Saxon *trog*]

trounce verb to beat or defeat completely.

trouncing noun a beating.

troupe noun a group or company of performers. [from French, from Latin *troppus*, troop]

trouper noun 1 a member of a troupe. 2 an experienced, hard-working, and loyal colleague.

trouser- combining form of trousers: *trouser-buttons*.

trousers pl. noun an outer garment for the lower part of the body, reaching from the waist and covering each leg separately down to the ankle.
— **wear the trousers** colloq. to be the member of a household who makes the decisions.
[from Irish and Scots Gaelic *triubhas*, trews]

trousseau noun (PL. **trousseaux, trousseaus**) a bride's set of new clothes and linen, traditionally bought for her wedding and for married life. [from French, from *trousse*, bundle]

trout noun (PL. **trout, trouts**) 1 any of several usually freshwater fish of the salmon family. 2 derog. slang an unpleasant, interfering old person, usually a woman. [from Anglo-Saxon *truht*]

Trout Quintet Franz Schubert's Piano Quintet in A (D667, 1819), named after the variations on his song 'Die Forelle' (c.1817) which appear in the fourth movement.

Trovatore, Il (The Troubadour) an opera by Giuseppe Verdi (1853). Set in 15c Spain, the story arises from the burning of a gypsy by the Di Luna family for 'bewitching' one of the old Count's sons; in anger her daughter Azucena threw the baby concerned on the pyre (but it was actually her own son). Years later, her supposed son Manrico 'the Troubadour' and the young Count di Luna fight a duel over Leonore. Thinking Manrico dead, Leonore plans to enter a convent; he prevents her but is imprisoned and executed by the Count (actually his brother) — thus the old gypsy's death is avenged.

trove see TREASURE-TROVE.

Trowbridge POP (1981) 28 000, the county town of Wiltshire, S England, situated in West Wiltshire district. It lies 12km/7mi SE of Bath.

trowel noun 1 a small, hand-held tool with a flat blade, used for applying and spreading mortar, plaster, etc. 2 a similar tool with a slightly curved blade, used for potting plants, etc. [from Latin *trulla*, scoop]

Troy, Sergeant Francis the dazzling, unprincipled Sergeant who betrays Fanny Robin and marries Bathsheba Everdene in Thomas Hardy's *Far from the Madding Crowd*.

Troy, Turkish **Truva,** ancient **Troy,** or **Ilium** an ancient ruined city in Çanakkale province, W Turkey. The archaeological site lies S of the Dardanelles near Hisarlik. At a time now identified with the Mycenaean period, it was attacked and besieged by a Greek army for 10 years (the Trojan War), according to the *Iliad*. From the Stone Age to Roman times, over a period of 4 000 years, the city was rebuilt on the same site nine times. It was originally excavated by Heinrich Schliemann in the 1870s, and the occupation level known as Troy VIIa is thought to be the city of the Greek legend.

troy noun (in full **troy weight**) a system of weights used for precious metals and gemstones, with 12 ounces or 5 760 grains to the pound. [from *Troyes* in France]

Troyes, ancient **Augustobona Tricassium** POP (1990) 123 000, the capital of Aube department, Champagne-Ardenne region, NE central France. It is on the braided channel of the R Seine, 150km/93mi SE of Paris. A bishopric since the 4c, it was capital of the old province of Champagne. It is a traditional centre of the hosiery trade. NOTABLE FEATURES Cathedral of St Peter and St Paul (13c–16c); Church of St Urbain (13c); Church of Ste Madeleine (16c); former Abbey of St Loup, with a famous library; Museum of Fine Arts; Hosiery Museum.

truancy noun playing truant.

truant — noun someone who stays away from school or work without good reason or without permission. — verb intrans. to be a truant.
— **play truant** to stay away from school without good reason and without permission.
[from Old French]

truce noun 1 an agreement to stop fighting, usually temporarily. 2 a temporary break in fighting, hostilities, feuding, etc. [from Middle English *trewes*, from Anglo-Saxon *treow*, truth]

Trucial States the former name of the United Arab Emirates of Abu Dhabi, Ajman, Dubai, Fujairah, Ras al Khaimah, Sharja, and Umm al Qaiwain on the Persian Gulf and Gulf of Oman. The name derives from a truce signed between the ruling sheiks and Great Britain in 1820. In 1892 they accepted British protection.

truck¹ — noun 1 Brit. an open railway wagon for carrying goods. 2 North Amer. a heavy motor vehicle for transporting goods; a lorry. 3 a frame with four or more wheels supporting a railway carriage. 4 any wheeled vehicle, trolley, or cart for moving heavy goods. — verb 1 to put on or transport by truck. 2 intrans. chiefly North Amer. to work as a truck driver.

truck² — noun 1 exchange of goods; commercial dealings. 2 payment of wages in goods rather than money. 3 colloq. small goods or wares. 4 colloq. odds and ends; rubbish. 5 North Amer., esp. US market-garden produce, such as vegetables and fruit. — verb trans., intrans. to give (goods) in exchange; to barter.
— **have no truck with someone** or **something** have no part in or dealings with them. [from Old French *troquer*, to exchange]

trucker noun North Amer. a person who drives a lorry, especially over long distances.

trucking noun transporting by trucks.

truckle — noun (in full **truckle-bed**) a low bed that may be wheeled under a larger bed for storage. — verb intrans. to submit or give in passively or weakly. [from Latin *trochlea*, pulley]

truculence or **truculency** noun 1 being truculent. 2 truculent behaviour.

truculent adj. aggressively defiant, quarrelsome, or discourteous. [from Latin *trux*, wild, fierce]

truculently adv. with a truculent manner.

trudge — verb 1 intrans. (usually **trudge along, over,** etc) to walk with slow and weary steps. 2 to cover (a stated distance, ground, etc) slowly and wearily. — noun a long and tiring walk.

true — adj. 1 agreeing with fact or reality; not false or wrong: *a true story*. 2 real; genuine; properly so called: *the spider is not a true insect*. 3 accurate or exact: *a photograph doesn't give a true idea of the size of the building*. 4 faithful; loyal: *be true to one's word*. 5 conforming to a standard, pattern, type, or expectation: *behave true to form*. 6 in the correct position; well-fitting; accurately adjusted. 7 said of a compass bearing measured according to the earth's axis and not magnetic north. 8 honest; sincere: *twelve good men and true*. — adv. 1 certainly: *true, she isn't very happy here*. 2 truthfully. 3 faithfully. 4 honestly. 5 accurately or precisely. 6 accurately in tune: *sing true*. 7 conforming to ancestral type: *breed true*. — verb to bring or restore (eg machinery) into an accurate or required position.
— **come true** said of a dream, hope, etc to happen in reality.
out of true not in the correct position; not straight or properly balanced. [from Anglo-Saxon *treow*]

true airspeed *Aeron.* (ABBREV. **TAS**) the actual speed of an aircraft as it moves through the air, calculated by correcting the value obtained from an airspeed indicator (the *indicated airspeed*) for altitude, temperature, density, and pressure.

true-blue — *adj.* **1** extremely loyal. **2** *Brit.* being an extremely orthodox supporter of the Conservative party. — *noun* a true-blue person.

true-love *noun* a beloved person; a sweetheart.

trueness *noun* being true.

true north the direction of the north pole (rather than the direction of magnetic north).

Truffaut, François (1932–84) French film critic and director, born in Paris. His career as a critic from 1953 led to his 'auteur' concept of film-making. In 1959 he made his first feature film as director/actor/co-scriptwriter, *Les Quatre Cents Coups* (The 400 Blows), effectively launching the French *Nouvelle Vague* movement. Other films include *Tirez sur le Pianiste* (Shoot the Pianist, 1960), *Jules et Jim* (1962), *Fahrenheit 451* (1966), and *La Nuit américaine* (Day for Night, 1972), for which he received an Oscar.

truffle *noun* **1** any of several dark round fungi which grow underground and are considered a delicacy. **2** a usually round sweet made typically with cream, butter, chocolate, and rum, and coated in cocoa. [from Latin *tuber*, lump, swelling]

trug *noun Brit.* a shallow rectangular basket used for carrying garden tools, plants, etc. [perhaps a variant of TROUGH]

truism *noun* a statement which is obviously true; a commonplace.

Trujillo POP (1990e) 532 000, the capital of La Libertad department, NW Peru. The city was founded by Pizarro in 1536. NOTABLE FEATURES cathedral, several convents, monasteries, and colonial churches.

Truk POP (1990) 54 000, a member of the Federated States of Micronesia, W Pacific Ocean. AREA 127sq km/49sq mi. It comprises the 11 high volcanic islands in the Truk lagoon and numerous outlying atolls. CAPITAL Moen. More than 60 ships of the Japanese wartime fleet lie sunk at various depths in the lagoon, one of the largest in the world.

truly *adv.* **1** really: *truly believe it to be for the best.* **2** genuinely; honestly. **3** faithfully. **4** accurately; exactly. **5** properly; rightly.

Truman, Harry S (1884–1972) US Democratic statesman, the 33rd President, born in Lamar, Missouri. Elected to the Senate in 1934, he was chairman of a special committee investigating defence, Vice-President (1944), and President (1945–53) on the death of Franklin D Roosevelt. His decisions included the dropping of the first atom bomb on Japan, the postwar loan to Britain, the establishment of NATO (1949), and the sending of US troops to withstand the communist invasion of South Korea (1950). He promoted the policy (the Truman Doctrine) of giving military and economic aid to countries threatened by communist interference, and in the USA itself he introduced a liberal programme or 'Fair Deal' of economic reform.

trump[1] — *noun* **1** (**trumps**) the suit of cards which has been declared to have a higher value than any other suit. **2** (*also* **trump card**) **a** a card of this suit, which has a higher value than a card of the other suits. **b** a secret advantage. **3** *colloq.* a helpful, reliable, or fine person. — *verb* **1** *trans.*, *intrans.* to defeat (an ordinary card or a trick with no trumps) by playing a trump. **2** to win a surprising victory or advantage over (a person, plan, idea, etc).
— **come up** *or* **turn up trumps** *said of a person* to be unexpectedly useful or helpful in difficult circumstances.
trump something up to invent or make up false evidence, accusations, etc.

[a variant of TRIUMPH]

trump[2] *noun old use, poetic* a trumpet.
— **the last trump** *Relig.* the trumpet call to wake the dead on the Day of Judgement.
[from Old French *trompe*]

trumped-up *adj.*, *said of evidence, accusations, etc* invented or made up; false.

trumpery — *noun* (PL. **trumperies**) **1** showy but worthless articles. **2** rubbish. — *adj.* showy but worthless. [from Old French *tromper*, to deceive]

trumpet — *noun* **1** a brass musical instrument with a narrow tube and flared bell and a powerful, high, clear tone. **2** anything like this in shape, such as the corona of a daffodil or a horn, or sound. **3** the loud cry of an elephant. — *verb* (**trumpeted**, **trumpeting**) **1** *intrans. said of an elephant* to make a loud cry. **2** *intrans.* to blow a trumpet. **3** to make known or proclaim loudly. [from Old French *trompette*]
◇ The trumpet has been used as a solo and orchestral instrument since the 17c. In earlier orchestral instruments, the fundamental pitch could only be altered by fitting pieces of tubing of various lengths, known as 'crooks'; from c.1830 valves performed the same function more easily.

trumpet

trumpeter *noun* a person who plays the trumpet.

trumpeter swan a black-billed American swan, the largest of the world's swans.

Trumpler, Robert Julius (1886–1956) Swiss-born US astronomer, born in Zürich. After moving to the USA he joined the staff of the Allegheny and Lick observatories, and became professor at the University of California. His discovery that starlight can be absorbed by interstellar material (1930) led to an important reassessment of the distance scale of our galaxy.

truncate — *verb* to cut so as to shorten. — *adj.*, *said eg of a leaf* having the base or tip cut square. [from Latin *truncare*]

truncation *noun* the process of truncating or being truncated.

truncheon *noun* **1** a short, thick heavy stick, carried by police officers. See also BATON. **2** a staff of authority or office. [from Old French *tronchon*, stump]

trundle *verb trans.*, *intrans.* (*usually* **trundle along**, **through**, *etc*) to move or roll heavily and clumsily. [from Anglo-Saxon *trendel*]

trunk *noun* **1** the main stem of a tree without the branches and roots. **2** a person's or animal's body without the head and limbs. **3** the main part of anything. **4** a large rigid box or chest for storing or transporting clothes and personal items. **5** *North Amer.* the boot of a car. **6** the long, muscular nose of an elephant. **7** (**trunks**) men's close-fitting shorts or pants worn especially for swimming. [from Latin *truncus*]

trunk call *Brit.* a long-distance telephone call.

trunk line 1 a main telephone line between large towns or cities. **2** a main railway line.

trunk road a main road between large towns.

Truro POP (1981) 19 000, the county town of Cornwall, SW England, situated in Carrick district. It lies on the R Truro, 20km/12mi SW of St Austell. NOTABLE FEATURES cathedral (1880–1910); Pendennis Castle (1543).

truss — *noun* **1** a framework, eg of wooden or metal beams, supporting a roof, bridge, etc. **2** a belt, bandage, or other device worn to support a hernia. **3** a bundle of hay or straw. **4** a cluster of flowers or fruit at the top of a main stalk or stem. **5** *Archit.* a corbel. — *verb* (*often* **truss something** *or* **someone up**) **1** to tie up or bind (someone) tightly. **2** to tie up the wings and legs of (a fowl) before cooking. **3** to support (a roof, bridge, etc) with a truss. [from Old French *trousse*]

trust — *noun* **1** belief or confidence in, or reliance on, the truth, goodness, character, power, ability, etc of someone or something. **2** charge or care: *the child was placed in my trust.* **3** the state of being responsible for the conscientious performance of some task: *be in a position of trust.* **4** a task assigned to someone in the belief that they will perform it well and conscientiously. **5** credit: *put it on trust.* **6** an arrangement by which money or property is managed by one person for the benefit of someone else. **7** an amount of money or property managed by one person for the benefit of another. **8** a group of business firms working together to control the market in a particular commodity, beat down competition, and maximise profits. — *adj.* held in trust. — *verb* **1** (**trust someone** *or* **trust in someone**) to have confidence or faith in them; to depend or rely on them: *we must trust her to cope.* **2** to allow (someone) to use or do something in the belief that they will behave responsibly, honestly, etc: *I wouldn't trust him with your new car.* **3** (**trust something** *or* **someone to someone**) to give them into the care of that person: *trusted the children to their grandfather.* **4** *trans.*, *intrans.* to be confident; to hope or suppose: *I trust you had a good journey.* **5** to give credit to.
— **take something** *or* **someone on trust** to accept or believe them without verification. [from Norse *traust*]

trustee *noun* **1** a person who manages money or property for someone else. **2** a member of a group of people managing the affairs and business of a company or institution.

trusteeship *noun* the status or position of a trustee.

trustful *or* **trusting** *adj.* willing to have confidence or trust in others; confiding.

trustfully *or* **trustingly** *adv.* in a trustful or trusting way.

trustfulness *noun* being trustful.

trust fund money or property held in trust, eg until the owner comes of age.

trustily *adv.* faithfully, honestly.

trustiness *noun* being trusty.

Trust Territory a non-self-governing area, the administration of which was supervised by the United Nations under Article 75. Trust territories were former mandated territories of the League of Nations and former possessions of the Axis powers. The Trusteeship Agreements with the UN asked the administering country to prepare the people for independence and encourage the development of human rights. All territories had obtained self-governing status by 1986.

trustworthily *adv.* in a trustworthy way.

trustworthiness *noun* being trustworthy.

trustworthy *adj.* able to be trusted or depended on.

trusty — *adj.* (**trustier**, **trustiest**) able to be trusted or depended on. — *noun* (PL. **trusties**) a trusted person, especially a convict given special privileges for good behaviour.

truth *noun* **1** the state of being true, genuine, or factual. **2** the state of being truthful; sincerity; honesty. **3** that which is true. **4** that which is established or generally accepted as true: *scientific truths.* **5** strict adherence to an original or standard.
— **to tell the truth** *or* **truth to tell** really; actually.
[from Anglo-Saxon *treowth*]

truthful *adj.* **1** *said of a person* telling the truth. **2** true; realistic.

truthfully *adv.* in a truthful way.

truthfulness *noun* being truthful.

Truth or Consequences *or* **Truth or C**, formerly **Hot Springs** (to 1950) POP (1980) 5 000, a town in Sierra County, SW New Mexico, USA, lying on the R Grande. The new name was adopted by the citizens of the town following a vote to accept an offer made by the presenter of a famous radio programme: if the town adopted the name of his show, he would hold a yearly fiesta with the programme presented from there.

try — *verb* (**tries, tried**) **1** *trans., intrans.* to attempt or make an effort (at); to seek to attain or achieve. **2** (*also* **try something out**) to test it or experiment with it in order to assess its usefulness, value, quality, etc. **3** to judge or conduct the legal trial of (someone). **4** to examine all the evidence in (a case) in a law court. **5** to exert strain or stress on: *try the limits of his patience.* — *noun* (PL. **tries**) **1** an attempt or effort. **2** *Rugby* the score of three points (in Rugby League) or five points (in Rugby Union) gained by a player who succeeds in placing the ball over the opponent's goal line with his or her hand.

— **try one's hand at something** to see if one can do it, especially at a first attempt.

try something on to put on (clothes, shoes, etc) to check the fit and appearance.

try it on *Brit. colloq.* to attempt to deceive someone, or to test their patience or tolerance.

try something *or* **someone out** to test their qualities or capabilities.
[from Old French *trier*, to sift]

trying *adj.* causing strain or anxiety; stretching one's patience to the limit.

try-on *noun Brit. colloq.* an attempt to deceive, or to test a person's patience.

try-out *colloq.* a test or trial.

trypsin *noun Biochem.* a digestive enzyme secreted by the pancreas that catalyses the partial breakdown of protein. [from Greek *tripsis*, rubbing, because it was first obtained by rubbing down the pancreas with glycerine]

tryptophan *or* **tryptophane** *noun Biochem.* an essential amino acid that is found in proteins.

trysail *noun* a small strong fore-and-aft sail used in a storm.

tryst *old use Scot. literary* — *noun* **1** an arrangement to meet someone, especially a lover. **2** the meeting place. **3** (*also* **trysting-place**) the place where such a meeting takes place. — *verb intrans.* to make a tryst. [from Old French *triste*, a hunter's station]

tuatara

Tsaochuang see ZAOCHUANG.

tsar *or* **czar** *or* **tzar** *noun* **1** *Hist.* the title given to the former emperor of Russia. **2** a despot or tyrant. [from Latin *Caesar*, family name of the earliest Roman emperors]

Tsaratanana, Massif du a mountain range in N Madagascar which rises to 2 876m at Maromokotra. The Ambre Mountain Nature Reserve lies to the N.

tsarevitch *or* **czarevitch** *or* **tzarevitch** *noun Hist.* the title given to the eldest son of a tsar or tsarina.

tsarina *or* **czarina** *or* **tzarina** *noun Hist.* **1** the title given to a woman who rules Russia as empress. **2** the title given to the wife or widow of a tsar.

Tsavo a national park in SE Kenya, established in 1948. It is the home of many African herd animals, as well as of the lion, hippopotamus, and rhinoceros. AREA 20 800sq km/8 000sq mi.

TSB *abbrev.* Trustee Savings Bank.

Tselinograd, formerly **Akmolinsk** (to 1961) POP (1991e) 286 000, a city in NE Kazakhstan, lying on the R Ishim. The city was founded as a fortress in 1830.

tsetse *noun* (*in full* **tsetse-fly**) an African fly which feeds on human and animal blood and transmits several dangerous diseases including sleeping sickness. [from Tswana (a southern African language) *tsetse*]

T-shirt *or* **tee shirt** *noun* a light casual shirt, often made of stretchy material, with no collar and usually short sleeves.

Tsinan see JINAN.

Tsingtao see QINGDAO.

Tsiolkovsky, Konstantin Eduardovich (1857–1935) Russian astrophysicist and rocket pioneer, born in Izheskaye in the Spassk district. Self-educated, he independently developed the kinetic theory of gases, and published his visionary ideas on the use of rockets for space exploration in 1903. From 1911 he developed the basic theory of rocketry, and also multi-stage rocket technology (1929); towards the end of his life his work began to be recognized.

T-square *noun* a T-shaped ruler for drawing right angles.

TSR *abbrev. Comput.* terminate-and-stay-resident.

tsunami *noun* (PL. **tsunamis**) a fast-moving highly destructive wave that steadily increases in height as it approaches the shore, associated with movement of the Earth's surface under the sea, such as a volcanic eruption or a landslide. It is sometimes loosely referred to as a tidal wave, but is not associated with the tides. Tsunamis can cause severe structural damage and loss of life. [from Japanese *tsu*, harbour + *nami*, wave]

Tswana see SOTHO-TSWANA.

Tswett *or* **Tsvett, Mikhail Semenovich** (1872–1919) Russian organic chemist, born in Asti, Italy. Brought up in Switzerland, he studied at Kazan University, then taught in Warsaw and Tarto. He devised a percolation method of separating plant pigments in 1906, thus making the first chromatographic analysis.

TT *abbrev.* **1** teetotal. **2** Tourist Trophy.

TTL *abbrev.* Through The Lens.

Tuamotu Archipelago POP (1988) 12 000, an island group of French Polynesia, E of the Society Is. AREA 826sq km/319sq mi. It consists of two parallel ranges of 78 atolls, the largest group of coral atolls in the world. MAIN ISLANDS Rangiroa, Hao, Fakarava. The area has been used for nuclear testing by the French since 1962.

Tuareg a Berber-speaking pastoral people of the central Sahara and the N Sahel zone of W Africa. A traditionally highly stratified feudal society, in the past they were caravan traders and feared raiders. Many died during the severe drought of the short 1970s. The present-day population is c.900 000.

tuatara *noun* a rare lizard-like reptile, native to islands off the coast of New Zealand, green or orange-brown in colour, and up to 650mm in length. In the male there is a crest of tooth-like spines along the back. It is nocturnal, and feeds on invertebrates, small vertebrates, and birds' eggs. [from Maori, = spine on the back]

Tuatha de Danann, Old Irish **the people of the goddess Danu** in Old Irish mythology, a race of wise beings who came to Ireland c.1500 BC, and became the ancient gods of the Irish. They were conquered by the Milesians,

and retreated into tumuli (ancient burial mounds) near the R Boyne.

tub *noun* **1** any of various large, low, round wooden, metal, or plastic containers, usually for holding water. **2** a small, round plastic or cardboard container for holding cream, ice-cream, yoghurt, etc. **3** a bath. **4** the amount a tub will hold. **5** *colloq.* a slow and often clumsy boat. [from Middle English *tubbe*]

tuba *noun* a musical instrument made from brass tubing curved elliptically, with three to five valves, a mouthpiece set at right angles, and a wide upturned bell. It is the largest and lowest in pitch of the brass instruments and was included as an orchestral instrument from the mid-19c. It is made in various sizes, some of which are known by other names. [from Latin and Italian *tuba*]

tuba

tubbiness *noun* being tubby.

tubby *adj.* (**tubbier, tubbiest**) *colloq.* plump; podgy. [from TUB]

tube *noun* **1** a long hollow cylinder used for conveying liquids or as a container. **2** a similar long hollow structure in an animal or plant body: *bronchial tubes.* **3** a cylindrical container made from soft metal or plastic with a cap at one end, used for holding paste which is got out by squeezing. **4** *Brit.* an underground railway, especially in London; also a train running on this. **5** a cathode ray tube. **6** *North Amer.* a thermionic valve. **7** *slang* a television set.

— **go down the tubes** *slang* to fail dismally; to be ruined.
[from Latin *tubus*, pipe]

tubeless *adj.*, *said of a tyre* having no inner tube.

tuber *noun* **1** *Bot.* in certain plants, a swollen underground root (eg dahlia tuber) or stem (eg potato tuber) which functions as a food storage organ, enabling the plant to survive between one growing season and the next. It also allows the propagation of new plants from buds on the surface of stem tubers. **2** *Anat.* a thickened region or swelling. [from Latin *tuber*, swelling]

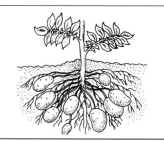

potato tuber

tubercle *noun* **1** a small round swelling or lump, eg on a bone. **2** a small round swelling in an organ, especially one caused by a bacillus and characteristic of tuberculosis. [from Latin *tuberculum*, small swelling]

tubercular *or* **tuberculous** *adj.* **1** affected by or suffering from tuberculosis. **2** of or having tubercles.

tuberculin *noun* a preparation in the form of a sterile liquid prepared from a culture of the bacillus which causes tuberculosis, used to test for and treat the disease.

tuberculin-tested *adj., said of milk* from cows that have been tested for and certified free from tuberculosis.

tuberculosis *noun* (ABBREV. **TB**) any of various infectious diseases of humans and animals, caused by the bacterium *Mycobacterium tuberculosis*. [from Latin *tuberculum*, small swelling]
◇ The commonest form of TB is *pulmonary tuberculosis* (formerly known as consumption), which affects the lungs and associated lymph nodes, and is still a major cause of death in some parts of the world. The disease is characterized by the formation of *tubercles* (lesions resembling nodules) in the affected tissues. These often heal spontaneously, but in some cases they spread rapidly through the lungs, or the bacteria spread via the bloodstream to other sites in the body, eg bones. The main symptoms are fever, weight loss, and the spitting of blood, although it is common for infection to occur without symptoms. Tuberculosis can be cured by treatment with various antibiotics, especially streptomycin.

tuberculous *see* TUBERCULAR.

tuberous *adj.* **1** having tubers. **2** of the nature of or like a tuber.

tubful *noun* (PL. **tubfuls**) the amount a tub will hold.

tubing *noun* a length of tube or system of tubes, or material for this.

Tübingen POP (1991e) 80 000, a town in Baden-Württemberg state, SW Germany. It lies on the R Neckar, 27km/17mi S of Stuttgart.

Tubman, Harriet (c.1820–1913) US abolitionist and rescuer of slaves, born in Dorchester Co, Maryland. She escaped from slavery in Maryland (1849), and from then until the Civil War she was active on the dangerous slave escape route (the 'Underground Railroad') into the South. Famous among abolitionists, she counselled John Brown before his attempt to launch the Harper's Ferry slave insurrection (1859). During the Civil War (1861–5) she was a Northern spy and scout, but she was denied a federal pension until 1897.

Tubruq *see* TOBRUK.

tub-thumper *noun* a passionate or ranting public speaker or preacher.

tub-thumping *noun* declamatory or rousing public speaking.

Tubuai Islands *or* **Austral Islands**, French **Iles Tubuai** POP (1988) 7 000, a volcanic island group of French Polynesia. AREA 137sq km/53sq mi. It lies 528km/328mi S of the Society Is and comprises a 1 300km/800mi chain of volcanic islands and reefs. MAIN ISLANDS Rimatara, Rurutu, Tubuai, Raivaevae, Rapa. The chief settlement is Mataura (Tubuai). ECONOMY coffee; copra.

tubular *adj.* **1** made or consisting of tubes or tube-shaped pieces. **2** shaped like a tube.

tubular bells a set of brass tubes tuned to different pitches, suspended in a large frame in the same arrangement as a keyboard, and struck with a short mallet to simulate the sounds of bells. They are used in orchestral and operatic music, and are also known as *chimes*.

tubule *noun* a small tube in an animal or plant body.

TUC *abbrev.* Trades Union Congress.

tuck — *verb* **1** (**tuck something in, up,** *etc*) to push or fold the outer edges of something together or into a specified position, especially to make it secure or tidy. **2** (*usually* **tuck something up**) to draw or put it into a folded position: *tucked her legs up*. **3** (**tuck someone in** *or* **up**) to fold the edges of the bedclothes tightly round

them. **4** to put in a confined or hidden place: *tuck it away out of sight.* **5** to make a tuck or tucks in (a piece of clothing, etc). — *noun* **1** a flat pleat or fold sewn in a garment or piece of material. **2** *Brit. colloq.* food, especially sweets, cakes, and pastries eaten by school children.
— **tuck something away** *colloq.* to eat large quantities of food heartily.
tuck in *or* **tuck into something** *colloq.* to eat heartily or greedily.
[from Anglo-Saxon *tucian*, to disturb]

tucker *noun Hist.* a piece of material, lace, etc drawn over the bodice of a low-cut dress.
— **best bib and tucker** *colloq.* best clothes.
[from TUCK]

tuck shop *Brit.* a small shop selling sweets, cakes, pastries, etc in or near a school.

Tucson POP (1990) 667 000, the seat of Pima County, SE Arizona, USA. It lies on the Santa Cruz R, 172km/107mi SE of Phoenix. Tucson is an industrial centre and a major tourist and health resort. HISTORY the Spanish founded the Presidio of San Augustín de Tuguison in 1776; ceded to the USA in 1853, it was state capital from 1867 until 1877 and became a city in 1883. NOTABLE FEATURES Davis-Monthan Air Force Base nearby.

Tucumán *see* SAN MIGUEL DE TUCUMAN.

Tudor — *adj.* **1** relating to the royal family which ruled England from 1485 to 1603 or this period in English history. **2** in or of the style of architecture characteristic of this period, which involved using a lot of wood both internally and externally. — *noun* a member of the House of Tudor.

House of Tudor	
1485–1509	Henry VII
1509–47	Henry VIII
1547–53	Edward VI
1553–8	Mary I
1558–1603	Elizabeth I

Tudor, House of a N Wales family of landed gentry, one of whose descendants married a Plantagenet in the early 15c. Elevated to the peerage in the mid-15c, it became a ruling dynasty in England in 1485, when Henry (later Henry VII), 2nd Earl of Richmond and son of Margaret Beaufort (a Lancastrian claimant to the Crown), overthrew Richard III. It ended with the death of Elizabeth I in 1603.

Tue *or* **Tue.** *abbrev.* Tuesday.

Tues *or* **Tues.** *abbrev.* Tuesday.

Tuesday *noun* the third day of the week. [from Anglo-Saxon *Tiwesdaeg*, Tiw's day (Tiw being the Anglo-Saxon god of war)]

tufa *noun Geol.* a deposit of calcium carbonate, usually consisting of white spongy porous masses in the form of an incrustation around a spring or along a stream, especially in an area of limestone rock. [from Italian, from Latin *tofus*, soft stone]

tufaceous *adj.* **1** consisting of tufa. **2** of the nature or texture of tufa.

tuff *noun* a rock composed of fine volcanic fragments and dust. [from French *tuf*, from Latin *tofus*, soft stone]

tuffaceous *adj.* **1** consisting of volcanic tuff. **2** having the properties of tuff.

tuffet *noun* **1** a low seat. **2** a small mound. [a variant of TUFT]

tuft *noun* a small bunch or clump of grass, hair, feathers, wool, etc attached to or growing together at the base. [from Middle English]

tufted *adj.* **1** having or forming a tuft or tufts. **2** growing in tufts.

tufty *adj.* (**tuftier, tuftiest**) **1** covered with or full of tufts. **2** forming a tuft or tufts; consisting of or growing in tufts.

tug — *verb trans., intrans.* (**tugged, tugging**) **1** (**tug at**) to pull sharply and strongly. **2** to tow (a ship) with a tugboat. — *noun* **1** a strong sharp pull. **2** a hard struggle. **3** a small boat with a very powerful engine, for towing larger ships and barges. [from Middle English *toggen*, from Anglo-Saxon *teon*]

tugboat *noun* same as TUG *NOUN* 3.

tug-of-love *noun* a dispute over the guardianship of a child, eg between divorced parents.

tug-of-war *noun* **1** a contest in which two people or teams pull at opposite ends of a rope, trying to pull their opponents over a centre line. **2** any hard struggle between two opposing sides.

Tuileries the name given to formal gardens laid out in the 17c by Le Nôtre in Paris. They are all that remain of the former Tuileries Palace built for Catherine Medici in the 16c, and destroyed by fire in 1871.

tuition *noun* **1** teaching or instruction, especially when paid for, or in a college or university. **2** the fee paid for teaching or instruction. [from Latin *tuitio*, protection]

Tula [1] POP (1991e) 544 000, the industrial capital of Tula oblast, W Russia. It lies on the R Upa, 193km/120mi S of Moscow. The Imperial Small Arms Factory was founded here by Peter the Great in 1712. NOTABLE FEATURE Uspenskii Cathedral (1762–4). **2** an oblast in W Russia with the city of Tula as its capital.

Tula an ancient Mesoamerican city, c.65km/ 40mi NW of Mexico City, from which the Toltecs dominated central Mexico. It developed from c.750, and was destroyed in c.1168.

tulip *noun* **1** any spring-flowering perennial plant of the genus *Tulipa*, which has an underground bulb and produces a single cup-shaped flower in a variety of bright colours on a long leafy stem. Tulips are native to the Mediterranean region, but several thousand ornamental garden varieties are cultivated on a commercial scale in the Netherlands for export. **2** the flower of this plant. [from Turkish *tulbend*, turban]

tulip tree a tall N American tree of the magnolia family, with tulip-like flowers.

tulip tree

Tull, Jethro (1674–1740) English agriculturist, born in Basildon, Berkshire. Educated at Oxford, he became a lawyer, but turned to farming. He introduced several new farming methods, including the invention of a seed drill which planted seeds in rows (1701).

Tullamore, Gaelic **Tulach Mhór** POP (1991) 9 000, the capital of Offaly county, Leinster province, central Irish Republic. NOTABLE FEATURE the nearby abbey at Durrow was founded by St Columba.

tulle *noun* a delicate thin netted cloth made of silk or rayon. [from *Tulle* in France, where it was first made]

Tulliver, Maggie the dark-haired, spirited heroine of George Eliot's *The Mill on the Floss*. The novel also features her mother and father, Mr and Mrs Tulliver, and her unimaginative brother Tom.

Tulsa POP (1990) 709 000, the seat of Tulsa County, NE Oklahoma, USA. It is a port on the Arkansas R. Settled as a Creek Native American village in the 1830s, the modern city developed in the 1880s with the coming of the railway. It is a major national centre of the petroleum industry. NOTABLE FEATURE Gilcrease Institute of Art.

tum *noun* a child's word for 'stomach'.

tumble — *verb* **1** *trans., intrans.* (usually **tumble down, over**, *etc*) to fall or cause to fall headlong, especially suddenly or clumsily. **2** *intrans.* to fall or collapse suddenly, especially in value or amount. **3** (**tumble about, around**, *etc*) to roll over and over or toss around helplessly. **4** *intrans.* to perform as an acrobat, especially turning somersaults. **5** *intrans.* to move or rush in a confused, hasty way: *tumble out of the car*. **6** to rumple or disorder: *tumble the bedclothes*. **7** (**tumble to something**) *colloq.* to understand, realize, or become aware of it suddenly: *tumbled to their intentions*. **8** to dry (wet clothes or washing) in a tumble-drier. — *noun* **1** an act of tumbling. **2** a fall. **3** a somersault. **4** a confused or untidy state or heap. [from Anglo-Saxon *tumbian*]

tumbledown *adj.*, said of a building falling to pieces; ramshackle.

tumble-drier *or* **tumble-dryer** *noun* a machine for drying wet clothes and washing by tumbling them in a current of warm air.

tumble-dry *verb trans., intrans.* (**tumble-dries, tumble-dried**) to dry (laundry) in a tumble-drier.

tumbler *noun* **1** a large drinking glass without a stem or handle. **2** the amount a tumbler will hold. **3** an acrobat, especially one who performs somersaults. **4** a tumble-drier. **5** the part of a lock which holds the bolt in place until it is moved by a key. **6** the part of a firearm which is released by the trigger and forces the hammer forward. **7** (*also* **tumbler-box**) a machine with a revolving drum in which gemstones are polished.

tumblerful *noun* (PL. **tumblerfuls**) the amount a tumbler will hold.

tumbleweed *noun* a plant that snaps off above the root, curls into a ball and rolls around in the wind.

tumbling-barrel *noun* same as TUMBLER 7.

tumbrel *or* **tumbril** *noun* **1** a two-wheeled cart which tips over backwards to empty its load, used eg on farms. **2** *Hist.* a similar cart used to take those sentenced to death to the guillotine during the French Revolution. [from Old French *tomberel*, from *tomber*, to fall]

tumescence *noun* **1** becoming tumid. **2** a swelling.

tumescent *adj.* swollen or becoming swollen, especially with blood as a response to sexual stimulation. [from Latin *tumescere*, to swell up]

tumid *adj.* **1** swollen or enlarged. **2** *said of writing, speech, etc* bombastic; inflated. [from Latin *tumidus*, from *tumere*, to swell]

tumidity *noun* being tumid.

tumidly *adv.* in a tumid manner.

tummy *noun* (PL. **tummies**) a child's word for 'stomach'. [a childish pronunciation of STOMACH]

tummy-button *noun colloq.* the navel.

tumorous *adj.* relating to or of the nature of a tumour.

tumour *noun* **1** *Pathol.* an abnormal growth of tissue that may be malignant (cancerous) or benign, and develops within or on the surface of normal body tissue. **2** any swelling that is not caused by inflammation. [from Latin *tumor*, from *tumere*, to swell]

tumular *or* **tumuli** see TUMULUS.

tumult *noun* **1** a great or confused noise, especially made by a crowd; an uproar. **2** a violent or angry commotion or disturbance. **3** the state of feeling confused and usually violent emotions: *a mind in tumult*. [from Latin *tumultus*, from *tumere*, to swell]

tumultuous *adj.* **1** with great noise or confusion: *a tumultuous welcome*. **2** disorderly; unruly. **3** agitated.

tumultuously *adv.* in a tumultuous way, uproariously.

tumulus *noun* (PL. **tumuli**) *Archaeol.* an ancient burial mound or barrow. [from Latin, from *tumere*, to swell]

tun *noun* **1** a large cask, especially for ale or wine. **2** *Hist.* the amount such a cask holds, being 252 gallons of wine or 216 gallons of ale, used as a unit of measure for liquids. [from Middle English *tunne*]

tuna *noun* (PL. **tuna, tunas**) **1** any of several large marine fish with a streamlined body, pointed head, and coarse oily flesh, related to the mackerel, and found in warm temperate and tropical seas, eg bluefin tuna, yellowfin tuna, albacore (an important food fish). Tuna are the only fish that have a body temperature higher than that of the surrounding water. **2** the flesh of this fish used as food. [from Greek *thynnos*]

tunable *or* **tuneable** *adj.* capable of being tuned.

Tunbridge Wells *or* **Royal Tunbridge Wells** POP (1992e) 102 000, a spa town in Tunbridge Wells district, Kent, SE England. It is situated 50km/31mi SE of London. Iron-rich springs were discovered here in 1606 and the town became a fashionable health resort in the 17c–18c. The 'Royal' affixed to its name in 1909 is a legacy of the visits made by Queen Victoria.

tundra *noun Geog.* the vast relatively flat treeless zone, with permanently frozen subsoil, found mainly in the arctic regions of Alaska, N Canada, and Siberia. Its vegetation consists of dwarf trees and shrubs, grasses, sedges, mosses, and lichens. [from Lappish]

tune — *noun* **1** a pleasing succession of musical notes; a melody. **2** the correct, or a standard, musical pitch. **3** harmony; agreement: *in tune with current fashions*. — *verb* **1** *trans., intrans.* (*also* **tune up**) to adjust (a musical instrument or instruments, their keys or strings, etc) to the correct or a standard pitch. **2** *trans., intrans.* (*also* **tune in**) to adjust (a radio receiver) to pick up signals from a required frequency or station, or for a particular programme: *tune in to the local radio station.* **3** to adjust (an engine, machine, etc) so that it runs properly and efficiently.

— **call the tune** *colloq.* to be in charge.

change one's tune to change one's attitude, opinions, approach or way of talking.

in tune 1 *said of a voice or musical instrument* having or producing the correct or a required pitch: *sing in tune.* **2** having the same pitch as other instruments or voices: *the two guitars are not in tune.*

out of tune not in tune.

to the tune of ... *colloq.* amounting to the sum or total of ...

[a Middle English variant of TONE]

tuneful *adj.* **1** having a good, clear, pleasant, etc tune; melodious. **2** full of music.

tunefully *adv.* in a tuneful way.

tunefulness *noun* being tuneful.

tuneless *adj.* without a good, pleasant, etc tune; not melodious.

tunelessly *adv.* in a tuneless way.

tunelessness *noun* being tuneless.

tuner *noun* **1** a person whose profession is tuning instruments, especially pianos. **2** *Electron.* an electronic circuit that acts as a filter for radio or television broadcast signals, by selecting one

specific frequency, eg the channel selector on a television set. **3** a knob, dial, etc, that is used to adjust a radio to different wavelengths corresponding to different stations. **4** a radio that is part of a stereo sound system.

tungsten *noun Chem.* (SYMBOL **W**, ATOMIC NUMBER **74**) a very hard silvery-white metal that is resistant to corrosion and has the highest melting point of any metal. It is used in steel alloys for turbine blades and cutting tools, and in filaments for electric light bulbs, X-ray tubes and television sets. Tungsten carbides are used as abrasives. — Also called *wolfram*. [from Swedish, = heavy stone]

Tungurahua an Andean volcano in central Ecuador. HEIGHT 5 016m. It is situated 30km/19mi SE of Ambato. The spa town of Baños lies at its N foot. The volcano is dormant, although it emits vapours from time to time. It erupted in 1886, devastating Baños.

Tunguska, River a river in N Russia, length 3 200km/2 000mi. It comprises three tributaries of the R Yenisei, known as the Lower, Stony, and Upper Tunguska.

tunic *noun* **1** a loose, sleeveless garment reaching usually to the hip or knee and usually with a belted or gathered waist, as worn in ancient Greece and Rome, or as a type of simple modern dress. **2** a close-fitting usually belted jacket with a high collar worn as part of a soldier's or policeman's uniform. **3** *Biol.* a covering membrane or layer. [from Latin *tunica*]

tuning-fork *noun* a two-pronged metal instrument invented in 1711 by the English trumpeter John Shore (c.1662–1752). When the tuning fork is struck and made to vibrate, it produces a single note virtually free from overtones, to which voices and instruments can adjust their pitch.

Tunis POP (1990e) 1.6m, the seaport capital of Tunisia. It lies 240km/150mi from Sicily, in a strategic position on the Mediterranean Sea. HISTORY Phoenician origin, later dominated by Carthage; achieved capital status in 1236; captured by the Turks in 1533 and gained notoriety as a pirate base; occupied by the French from 1881 until 1956. NOTABLE FEATURES Great Mosque of Zitouna (9c); Dar Ben Abdullah (19c house); Palace of Dar Hussein; Museum of Islamic Art, Dar Beb Abdallah Museum, Dar Lasram Museum, Bardo National Museum. The Medina of Tunis is a World Heritage site.

Tunisia, official name **Republic of Tunisia**, Arabic **Al Djoumhouria Attunusia** POP (1992e) 8.4m, a N African republic, divided into 18 governorates (*gouvernorats*). AREA 164 150sq km/63 362sq mi. It is bounded W by Algeria, SE by Libya, and NE and N by the Mediterranean Sea. CAPITAL Tunis. CHIEF TOWNS Bizerta, Sousse, Sfax, Gabes. TIME ZONE GMT +1. The population is mainly Arabic (98%); Islam is the chief religion. OFFICIAL LANGUAGE Arabic; French is also spoken. CURRENCY the dinar. PHYSICAL DESCRIPTION the Atlas Mts in the NW rise to 1 544m at Chambi; the central depression runs W–E, containing several salty lakes; dry, sandy upland lies to the S. CLIMATE Mediterranean climate on the coast, with hot, dry summers and wet winters; the daily maximum temperature is 14–33°C; the average annual rainfall is 420mm at Tunis and over twice this level in the Atlas Mts; further S, rainfall decreases and temperatures can be extreme. HISTORY variously ruled by Phoenicians, Carthaginians, Romans, Byzantines, Arabs, Spanish, and Turks; became a French protectorate in 1883; gained independence in 1956; the monarchy was abolished and a republic was declared in 1957. GOVERNMENT a 141-member National Assembly, elected every five years; a President, also elected for five years, appoints a Prime Minister and Cabinet. ECONOMY agriculture employs 50% of the population, but is of declining importance; the world's fourth-largest producer of olive oil; olives, wheat, barley, henna, almonds, cork, citrus fruits, dates, grapes, vegetables; livestock; fishing; sugar refining; oil refining; cement; tyres; textiles; carpets; food processing; paper; tourism; the world's fifth largest producer of phosphates; oil, iron ore, lead, zinc; reserves of gold, barite, fluorspar.

Tunisia

Tunja POP (1992e) 112 000, the capital of Boyacá department, E central Colombia. It is situated in an arid, mountainous area, at an altitude of 2 819m. HISTORY one of the oldest cities in Colombia and the seat of the Zipa (one of the two Chibcha kings); refounded as a Spanish city in 1539; the decisive Battle of Boyacá was fought 16km/10mi to the S in 1818. notable features Church of Santo Domingo (begun in 1594); Santa Clara Chapel (1580); Parque Bosque de la Republica; Casa del Fundador Suárez Rendón (1540–3, now a museum).

tunnel — *noun* **1** a man-made underground passage for pedestrians, vehicles, trains, etc through or under some obstruction such as a hill or river. **2** an underground passage dug by an animal such as a mole. **3** a period of difficulty, problems, stress or exceptionally hard work: *light at the end of the tunnel.* — *verb* (**tunnelled, tunnelling**) **1** (**tunnel through, under,** *etc*) to make a tunnel through, under, etc. **2** *intrans.* to pass through, or as if through, a tunnel. **3** (**tunnel one's way**) to make one's way by digging a tunnel. [from Old French *tonel*, cask]

tunnel vision 1 a medical condition in which one is unable to see objects other than those straight ahead. **2** the inability or unwillingness to consider other viewpoints on or the wider implications of a situation.

tunny *noun* (PL. **tunnies**) (*also* **tunny-fish**) tuna. [from Greek *thynnos*]

tup *Brit.* — *noun* a ram. — *verb* (**tupped, tupping**) *said of a ram* to copulate with (a ewe). [from Middle English *tupe*]

Tupolev, Andrei Nikolaevich (1888– 1972) Soviet aircraft designer, born in Pustomezovo. From 1922 he headed the design office of the central aerohydrodynamics institute in Moscow, producing over 100 types of aircraft, and in 1955 he built the first Soviet civil jet, the Tu–104. In 1968 he completed the first test flight of a supersonic passenger aircraft, the Tu–144.

tuppence, tuppenny see TWOPENCE, TWOPENNY.

Tupungato, Cerro a mountain on the border between Argentina and Chile. HEIGHT 6 800m. It lies c.80km/50mi SE of Cerro Aconcagua.

Turandot an opera by Giacomo Puccini (1924–6). Completed after Puccini's death (1924) by Franco Alfano (1876–1954), it is a story set in Peking, focusing on the cruel and bewitching emperor's daughter Turandot, who presides over the execution of any suitor who fails to answer

three riddles. The unknown prince Calaf succeeds in the test, but offers to die anyway if Turandot can discover his name; this she attempts to do by torturing his friend Liù, who refuses to tell and kills herself. At last Turandot understands the nature of true love and her icy exterior melts.

Turangalîla-Symphonie a symphony in 10 movements for a large orchestra by Olivier Messiaen (1948). [from Sanskrit *Turangalîla,* play about the passage of time, movement, and rhythm]

turban *noun* **1** a man's headdress consisting of a long cloth sash wound round the head or a cap, worn especially by Muslims and Sikhs. **2** a woman's headdress or hat similar to this. [from Persian *dulband*]

turbaned *adj.* wearing a turban.

turbid *adj.* **1** *said of liquid, etc* cloudy; not clear. **2** thick or dense. **3** confused; disordered. [from Latin *turbidus,* from *turba,* disturbance]

turbidity *noun* a turbid quality.

turbidly *adv.* in a turbid way.

turbine *noun* a balanced wheel, with a large number of blades around its rim, that converts the kinetic energy of a moving fluid (such as water, steam, or gas) that passes over the blades into the mechanical energy of rotation. Steam turbines and water turbines are used to drive electricity generators in power stations, and gas turbines are used to power jet-propelled aircraft. [from Latin *turbo,* whirlwind]

turbo- *combining form* forming words meaning 'having or driven by a turbine'. [from Latin *turbo,* whirlwind]

turbocharger *noun* a supercharger operated by the exhaust gases of an engine, thereby boosting its power.

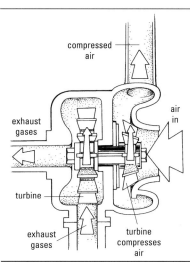

compressed air

air in

exhaust gases

turbine

exhaust gases

turbine compresses air

turbocharger

turbofan *noun* a jet engine driven by a gas turbine in which part of the power developed is used to drive a fan which blows air out of the exhaust and so increases thrust.

turbojet *noun* a jet engine consisting of a compressor and a turbine in which the gas energy produced is directed through a nozzle to produce thrust; also, an aircraft powered by this.

turboprop *noun* a jet engine in which the turbine drives a propeller; also, an aircraft powered by this.

turbot *noun* (PL. **turbot, turbots**) a large flatfish highly valued as food. [from Old French]

turbulence *noun* **1** a disturbed, wild, or unruly state. **2** *Meteorol.* the irregular movement of the atmosphere, causing gusts of wind. **3** *Physics* the movement of particles of a fluid (a liquid or a gas) in an irregular manner so that there are continual

changes in the magnitude and direction of motion, eg during the flow of air across an aircraft wing, or the movement of a liquid through a pipe. [from Latin *turbulentia,* from *turba,* turmoil]

turbulent *adj.* **1** violently disturbed; wild; unruly. **2** *Meteorol.* in a state of turbulence; stormy. **3** causing disturbance or unrest.

turbulently *adv.* in a turbulent way.

turd *noun* **1** *coarse slang* a lump of excrement. **2** *coarse slang* a worthless or despicable person. [from Anglo-Saxon *tord*]

tureen *noun* a large deep dish with a cover from which food, especially soup, is served at table. [from Old French *terrin,* earthen]

Turenne, Henri de la Tour d'Auvergne, Vicomte de (Viscount of) (1611–75) French soldier, born in Sedan, son of the Protestant Duc de Bouillon, and grandson of William the Silent. His uncles, the Princes of Orange, taught him good soldiering, and in the Thirty Years War (1618–48) he fought with distinction for the armies of the Protestant alliance. He captured Breisach (1638) and Turin (1640), and for gaining Roussillon from the Spaniards (1642) was made Marshal of France (1643). In the civil wars of the Frondes, he joined the *frondeurs* at first, but then switched sides — his campaigning (1652–3) saved the young King Louis XIV and Mazarin's government. In the Franco–Spanish war he conquered much of the Spanish Netherlands after defeating Condé at the battle of the Dunes (1658), and he won lasting fame for his campaigns in the United Provinces during the Dutch War (1672–5).

turf — *noun* (PL. **turfs, turves**) **1** the surface of the soil consisting of grass and matted roots. **2** a square piece cut from this. **3** a slab of peat. **4** (**the turf**) horse-racing, the race-course or the racing world. **5** *slang* area of operation or influence; territory. — *verb* to cover with turf.
— **turf something** *or* **someone over, out,** *etc Brit. colloq.* to throw or expel them: *turfed him out of the house / turf the book over here.* [from Anglo-Saxon]

turf accountant *Brit.* a bookmaker.

turfy *adj.* (**turfier, turfiest**) **1** covered with or consisting of turf. **2** like turf. **3** associated with turf.

Turgenev, Ivan (Sergeyevich) (1818–83) Russian novelist, born in Orel province. He joined the Russian civil service in 1841, but left in 1843 to take up literature. His first studies of peasant life, *A Sportsman's Sketches* (1852), made his reputation, but were perceived by the government as an attack on serfdom. His praise of Gogol resulted in banishment to his country estates. After that he spent much time in Europe, writing nostalgically about Russia. His major novel, *Fathers and Sons* (1862), was poorly received in Russia, but successful in England. He also wrote poetry, plays, short stories, and tales of the supernatural.

turgescence *noun* **1** swelling up. **2** swollenness.

turgescent *adj.* swelling; growing big. [from Latin *turgere,* to swell]

turgid *adj.* **1** swollen; inflated or distended. **2** *said of language* sounding important but meaning very little; pompous. [from Latin *turgere,* to swell]

turgidity *noun* a turgid quality.

turgidly *adv.* in a turgid way.

Turin, Italian **Torino**, ancient **Augusta Taurinorum** POP (1990e) 1m, the capital of Piedmont region, NW Italy and of Turin province. It lies on the left bank of the R Po. HISTORY founded by the Taurini; a Roman colony under Augustus; capital of the Kingdom of Sardinia in 1720; centre of the 19c Risorgimento; first capital of the Kingdom of Italy until 1865.

NOTABLE FEATURES Porta Palatina (Roman city gate); cathedral (15c); Palazzo Reale (1646–58); Palazzo Carignano (1680); Palazzo Madama (1718–20).

Turin, Shroud of, also called **Holy Shroud** a relic, alleged to be the burial-sheet of Jesus Christ, known since the 14c, and preserved in a cathedral in Turin since 1578. On it there is an image (clearer when viewed on a photographic negative) of a man's body, with markings that seem to correspond to the stigmata of Jesus. Controversy over its authenticity resulted in the use of three independent radiocarbon-dating tests in 1988, which dated the shroud to between 1260 and 1390.

Turing, Alan Mathison (1912–54) English mathematician and computer pioneer, born in London. He joined the National Physical Laboratory in 1945, and later worked at Manchester University. He made important contributions to the design and programming of early computers, and introduced the notion of an idealized computer (the 'Turing machine'). He committed suicide at Wilmslow, Cheshire.

Turk — noun **1** a person from the modern state of Turkey or the former Ottoman Empire. **2** any speaker of a Turkic language. **3** derog. a wild or unmanageable person. — adj. Turkish. [from Persian and Arabic]

Turkana, Lake, formerly **Lake Rudolf** (to 1979) a lake in NW Kenya and Ethiopia. AREA 6 405sq km/2 472sq mi; length 290km/180mi; width 56km/35mi; depth c.70m. It lies 400km/250mi N of Nairobi in Kenya and the N extremity extends into Ethiopia. The area of the lake is important for fossil hominid finds. High evaporation is causing the lake to shrink and so become increasingly salty.

Turkey, Turkish **Türkiye**, official name **Republic of Turkey**, Turkish **Türkiye Cumhuriyeti** POP (1992e) 58.8m, a republic lying partly in Europe and partly in Asia, divided into 67 provinces. AREA 779 452sq km/300 868sq mi. The W area (Thrace) is bounded by the Aegean Sea and Greece, and N by Bulgaria and the Black Sea; the E area (Anatolia) is bounded by Georgia, Armenia, Azerbaijan, and Iran, and S by Iraq, Syria, and the Mediterranean Sea. CAPITAL Ankara. CHIEF TOWNS Istanbul, Izmir, Adana, Bursa, Gaziantep. TIME ZONE GMT +3. The population consists largely of Turks (85%) and Kurds (12%); Islam is the chief religion. OFFICIAL LANGUAGE Turkish. CURRENCY the Turkish lira. PHYSICAL DESCRIPTION the Turkish Straits (the Dardanelles, Sea of Marmara, and Bosporus) connect the Black Sea in the NE and the Mediterranean Sea in the SW; it is a mountainous country at an average height of 1 100m; ranges extend W–E along the N and S coasts of Anatolia; average altitude of the high central plateau is 1 000–2 000m; the Taurus Mts cover the entire S part of Anatolia; E Anatolia is the highest region, and the highest peak is Mt Ararat (5 165m); the alluvial coastal plains are 20–30km/12–19mi wide; chief rivers include the Kizil Irmak, Sakarya, and Seyhan; the R Tigris and the R Euphrates have their origins in Turkey. CLIMATE a typically Mediterranean climate on the Aegean and Mediterranean coasts, with hot, dry summers and warm, wet winters; further E along the Black Sea coast, rainfall becomes heavy in summer and autumn; rainfall is low on the interior plateau, with cold winters and warm or hot summers and occasional thunderstorms. HISTORY modern Turkey includes the area known as Asia Minor, and many Greek colonies (now major archaeological sites) were established; part of the empire of Alexander I, and of the Byzantine Empire; in the 13c, the Seljuk Sultanate was replaced by the Ottoman Sultanate in NW Asia Minor; the Turkish invasion of Europe began with the Balkans in 1375; in 1453 Constantinople fell to the Turks; the empire was at its peak in the 16c under Sulaiman the Magnificent, but in the

17c the Turks were pressed back by Russian and Austrian armies; in the 19c Turkey was regarded by Britain as a bulwark against Russian expansion but, following alleged Armenian massacres, Britain abandoned its support of Turkey; the Young Turks seized power in 1908 and became embroiled in the Balkan War (1912–13); Turkey allied with Germany during World War I; the Republic of Turkey was founded in 1923 following the Young Turk Revolution, led by Kemal Atatürk; he introduced a policy of westernization and economic development; Turkey was neutral throughout most of World War II, before siding with the Allies; there were military coups in 1960 and 1980; relations with Greece were strained, leading to an invasion of Cyprus in 1974; the SE of Turkey has been under martial law since the mid-1980s as a result of fierce fighting between Kurds in the area and government force; earthquake in 1992. GOVERNMENT the constitution provides for a single-chamber, 450-member National Assembly; a President appointed by the Assembly holds office for seven years, appointing a Prime Minister and a Council of Ministers. ECONOMY agriculture employs over 60% of the workforce, the principal products being cotton, tobacco, cereals, figs, silk, olive oil, dried fruits, nuts, mohair, wool, and hides; there is a wide range of important mineral resources, including chrome, coal, lignite, copper concentrate, and sulphur; there is oil in E Turkey; manufacturing industries include food processing, textiles, iron and steel, cement, leather goods, glass, and ceramics; tourism is increasing; many Turks find work in Europe, especially Germany.

turkey noun (PL. **turkeys**) **1** a large gamebird related to the grouse and pheasant, indigenous to woodland in N and Central America; domesticated varieties are now intensively farmed in most parts of the world. It has dark plumage with a green sheen, and a bare blue or red head with red wattles (loose flaps of skin). The male has a fanlike tail and a large protuberance on its neck. **2** the flesh of this bird used as food, eaten particularly at Christmas and (in the USA) at Thanksgiving. **3** North Amer. slang a stupid or inept person. **4** North Amer. slang a play, film, etc that is a complete failure.

— **talk turkey** North Amer. slang to talk bluntly or frankly; to talk business.

[originally used of a guinea fowl imported from Turkey, and later wrongly applied to the American bird]

Turkic — noun the family of Asian languages to which Turkish, Tatar, Uzbek, etc belong. — adj. of this family of languages or the people who speak them.

Turkish — adj. of Turkey, its people, language, etc. — noun the official language of Turkey.
◇ Turkish belongs to the Altaic family of languages, and is spoken by c.27–45m people in Turkey, Bulgaria, and some surrounding areas.

Turkish Bath, The a painting by Jean Auguste Dominique Ingres (1859–62, Louvre, Paris).

Turkish bath a bath in which the bather first sweats in a hot room filled with steam, is then washed and massaged, and finally takes a cold shower.

Turkish coffee strong, usually very sweet black coffee.

Turkish delight a sticky, jelly-like sweet usually flavoured with rose water or lemon and dusted with icing sugar.

Turkmenistan, Turkmenian **Turkmenostan Respublikasy**, Russian **Turkmenskaya** POP (1991e) 3.7m, a republic in SW Middle Asia. AREA 488 100sq km/188 400sq mi. It is bounded N by Kazakhstan and Uzbekistan, S by Iran and Afghanistan, and W by the Caspian Sea; c.80% of the country is occupied by the Kara Kum desert; the people live mainly around oases. CAPITAL Ashkhabad. CHIEF TOWNS Chardzhou, Mary, Krasnovodsk, Nebit-Dag. TIME ZONE GMT +3. Most of the population are Turkomans (72%), Russians (10%), and Uzbeks (9%); Islam (Sunni) is the chief religion. OFFICIAL LANGUAGE Turkmenian. CURRENCY the manat. PHYSICAL DESCRIPTION low-lying with hills in the S; mainly desert; the chief river is the Amudarya. CLIMATE continental, hot and arid in the large desert areas. HISTORY proclaimed a Soviet Socialist Republic in 1924; gained independence in 1991. ECONOMY oil refining; chemicals; food processing; rugs; machinery; cotton; silk; Turkmenistan is noted for Turkoman horses and Karakul sheep.

Turks and Caicos Islands POP (1990) 12 000, a British Colony comprising a pair of island groups which form the SE archipelago of the Bahamas chain. AREA 500sq km/200sq mi. They lie 920km/570mi SE of Miami. CAPITAL Cockburn Town (Grand Turk). TIME ZONE GMT –5. The population is mainly of African

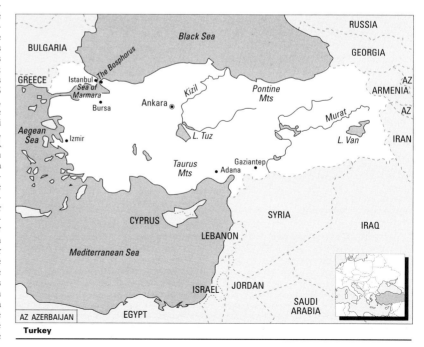

Turkey

descent; Christianity is the chief religion. OFFICIAL LANGUAGE English. CURRENCY the US dollar. PHYSICAL DESCRIPTION the Turks Is and Caicos Is are separated by 35km/22mi; there are c.30 islands and cays, only six of which are inhabited. CLIMATE subtropical; the average annual rainfall on Grand Turk is 525mm, but it tends to be higher on the Caicos Is; temperatures are 24–27°C in winter and 29–32°C in summer; occasional hurricanes. HISTORY discovered by the Spanish in 1512; linked formally to the Bahamas in 1765; transferred to Jamaica in 1848; became a British Crown Colony in 1972; achieved internal self-government in 1976. GOVERNMENT the British Sovereign is represented by a Governor, who presides over an eight-member Council. ECONOMY corn, beans; fishing, fish-processing; tourism is a rapidly expanding industry.

Turku, Swedish **Åbo** POP (1992e) 160 000, the seaport capital of Turku-Pori province, SW Finland. It lies on R Aurajoki near the river's mouth on the Gulf of Bothnia. It is Finland's third largest city. HISTORY established in the 11c, it was capital of Finland until 1812; a peace between Sweden and Russia was signed here in 1743. NOTABLE FEATURE Rantasipi Congress Centre.

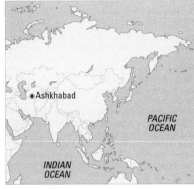

Turkmenistan

turmeric noun **1** an E Indian plant of the ginger family. **2** the dried powdered underground stem of this plant, used as a spice (eg in curry powder) and as a yellow dye. [from Latin *terra merita*, merited earth]

turmoil noun wild confusion, agitation or disorder; upheaval: *a mind in turmoil.*

turn — verb **1** trans., intrans. to move or go round in a circle or with a circular movement. **2** trans., intrans. to change or cause to change position so that a different side or part comes to the top or front: *turn the pages slowly / turn to face the sun / turn it inside out.* **3** intrans. to change direction or take a new direction: *turn left at the corner.* **4** trans., intrans. to direct, aim or point or be directed, aimed or pointed: *turn one's thoughts to supper.* **5** to go round: *turn the corner.* **6** trans., intrans. to become or cause to become or change to something specified: *turn the book into a film / love which turned to hate / turn nasty.* **7** trans., intrans. to change or cause to change colour: *the shock turned his hair white / the leaves begin to turn in September.* **8** trans., intrans. said of milk to make or become sour. **9** to make into a circular or rounded shape, especially on a lathe or potter's wheel. **10** to perform with a rotating movement: *turn somersaults.* **11** intrans. to move or swing around a point or pivot: *a gate turning on its hinge / turn on one's heels.* **12** to pass the age or time of: *turn forty.* **13** (**turn to someone** or **something**) to appeal to or have recourse to them for help or support. **14** (**turn to something**) to come to consider or pay attention to it: *the conversation turned to discussing holiday plans.* **15** (also **turn something out**) to put it into a specified position by, or as if by, inverting it; to tip it out: *turned the dough out on to the table.* **16** trans., intrans. said of the stomach to feel or cause it to feel nausea or queasi-

ness. **17** trans., intrans. said of the head to become or cause it to become giddy. **18** to translate. **19** (**turn against someone** or **turn one person against another**) to become or make them hostile or unfriendly. **20** to remake (part of a piece of clothing, sheet, etc) by putting the worn outer part on the inside: *turn a collar.* **21** to give an elegant form to. **22** intrans. said of the tide to begin to flow in the opposite direction. **23** to make (a profit, etc). — noun **1** an act of turning; a complete or partial rotation: *a turn of the wheel.* **2** a change of direction, course, or position: *a turn to the right.* **3** a point or place where a change of direction occurs. **4** a direction, tendency, or trend: *the twists and turns of the saga.* **5** a change in nature, character, condition, course, etc: *a turn for the worse / an unfortunate turn of events.* **6** an opportunity or duty that comes to each of several people in rotation or succession: *her turn to bat.* **7** inclination or tendency: *be of a pessimistic turn of mind.* **8** a distinctive style or manner: *a blunt turn of phrase.* **9** an act of a stated kind, usually good or malicious. **10** colloq. a sudden feeling of illness, nervousness, shock, faintness, etc: *gave her quite a turn.* **11** a short walk or ride. **12** each of a series of short acts or performances, eg in a circus or variety theatre; also, each performer. **13** a single coil or twist of eg rope or wire. **14** (**the turn of the month**, **year**, **century**, **etc**) the end of one month, year, century, etc and the beginning of the next. **15** Mus. an ornament in which the principal note is preceded by that next above it and followed by that next below it.

— **at every turn** everywhere, at every stage; continually.

by turns one after another in order; in succession.

in turn one after another in order; in succession.

on the turn 1 said of the tide starting to change direction. **2** said of milk on the point of going sour.

out of turn 1 out of the correct order. **2** at a moment that is inappropriate or discourteous: *he apologized for speaking out of turn.*

serve a turn to be enough or adequate for present purposes or needs.

take turns or **take it in turn** said of two or more people to share a task by acting or working one after the other in rotation.

to a turn cooked to exactly the right degree.

turn and turn about one after the other; each taking a turn.

turn aside or **turn something aside** to look away, or turn (one's eyes, gaze, face, concentration, etc) to another direction.

turn away to move or turn to face the opposite direction.

turn someone away to send them away or reject them; to refuse them admittance.

turn back or **turn someone back** to return or cause them to return in the opposite direction.

turn one's back on someone or **something** to leave them for good; to have no more to do with them.

turn something down to reduce the level of light, noise, etc produced by something by, or as if by, turning a control.

turn someone or **something down** to refuse or reject them.

turn one's hand to something to undertake a task, etc, or have the ability for it.

turn in 1 to bend inwards. **2** colloq. to go to bed.

turn someone or **something in** to hand them over to someone in authority.

turn something in to give, achieve, or register a good performance, score, etc.

turn someone or **something loose** to set a person or animal free.

turn off 1 to leave a straight course or a main road: *followed the car until it turned off down a side street.* **2** said of a road to lead from a main road.

turn someone off colloq. to cause them to feel dislike or disgust, or to lose (especially sexual) interest.

turn something off 1 to cause water, electricity, etc, or a machine to stop flowing or operating

by, or as if by, turning a knob or pushing a button or switch. **2** to operate a knob, button, tap, switch, etc so that something stops.

turn on or **upon someone** to attack them physically or verbally, usually suddenly or violently.

turn someone on colloq. **1** to cause them to feel excitement, pleasure, or (especially sexual) interest. **2** to cause them to feel a heightened sense of awareness, especially with hallucinogenic drugs.

turn on or **upon something** to depend on it: *the whole argument turns on a single point.*

turn something on 1 to cause electricity, etc, or a machine to flow or operate by or as if by turning a knob. **2** to operate a knob, button, tap, switch, etc so that something begins to work.

turn out 1 to bend outwards. **2** to happen or prove to be: *she turned out to be right.* **3** to leave home for a public meeting or event: *hundreds of people turned out to vote.* **4** colloq. to get out of bed.

turn someone out 1 to send them away; to make them leave; to expel them. **2** to call soldiers, a guard, etc for duty.

turn something out 1 to put a light, etc out or off by or as if by turning a knob. **2** to make or produce something. **3** to empty or clear a room, etc, especially for cleaning or to check the contents.

turn someone or **something out** to dress, equip, or groom them: *was well turned out.*

turn over 1 to roll oneself over when in a lying position. **2** said of an engine to start and run at low speed.

turn over something to handle or do business to the amount specified: *turned over five million in the first year.*

turn something over 1 to turn it so that the hidden or reverse side becomes visible or faces upwards. **2** to roll it over. **3** to start an engine so that it runs at low speed. **4** to consider it carefully.

turn someone or **something over 1** to surrender them to an authority. **2** slang to rob them.

turn round 1 to turn to face in the opposite direction. **2** said of a loaded vehicle to arrive, be unloaded, and depart again.

turn something round to receive and deal with a matter, the arrival of loaded vehicles, etc in the appropriate manner: *able to turn an order round in an hour.*

turn to something to begin a task, undertaking, etc.

turn up 1 to appear or arrive. **2** to be found, especially by accident or unexpectedly.

turn something up 1 to increase the flow, intensity, or strength of sound, light, etc produced by a machine by, or as if by, turning a knob. **2** to discover facts, evidence, etc. **3** to shorten a piece of clothing or its hem by folding part up and stitching it in place. **4** to turn it so as to make the hidden or reverse side visible. [from Anglo-Saxon *turnain* and Old French *torner*]

turnabout or **turnaround** noun **1** an act of turning to face the opposite way. **2** a complete change or reversal of direction or opinion.

Turnberry a championship golf course in Ayrshire, Scotland, reconstructed after World War II, when it was used as an airstrip.

turncoat noun a person who turns against or leaves his or her party, principles, etc and joins the opposing side.

Turner, J(oseph) M(allord) W(illiam) (1775–1851) English landscape artist and watercolourist, born in London. He spent three years in collaboration with Thomas Girtin producing topographical watercolours. He then took to oils and his early works include *Shipwreck* (1805), *Frosty Morning* (1813), and *Crossing the Brook* (1815). He visited Italy, and his second visit (1829) marks the beginning of his last major artistic period, which includes *The Fighting Téméraire* (1839) and *Rain, Steam and Speed* (1844), both in the National Gallery, London.

Turner, Nat (1800–31) US slave insurrectionary, born in Southampton Co, Virginia. He learned to read, and in 1831 made plans for a slave uprising. Leading a force of eight, he succeeded in killing 51 whites, but the revolt quickly collapsed, and after six weeks in hiding he was captured and hanged.

Turner, Tina, originally **Anna Mae Bullock** (1938–) US singer and film actress, born in Brownsville, Tennessee. In 1956 she joined Ike Turner's band the Kings of Rhythm, and later she became his wife (1958–78). Together with some successful recordings (eg 'River Deep Mountain High', 1966), Tina's sexually provocative stage image attracted attention, as did their 1969 tour with the Rolling Stones. Her comeback solo career has resulted in such successes as the song 'What's Love Got to Do with It?' (1984), the album *Private Dancer* (1984), and film roles in eg *Tommy* (1975) and *Mad Max beyond Thunderdome* (1985), and she also appeared at the end of the film about her life: *What's Love Got to Do with It* (1993).

turner *noun* a person or thing that turns, especially a person who works with a lathe.

turning *noun* **1** a place where one road branches off from another. **2** a road which branches off from another. **3** the art of using a lathe to form curves in wood, metal, etc. **4** (**turnings**) the shavings from an object turned on a lathe.

turning-circle *noun* the smallest possible circle in which a vehicle can turn round.

turning-point *noun* a time or place at which a turn or significant change is made.

turnip *noun* **1** a plant of the cabbage family with a large round white or yellowish root. **2** the root of this vegetable used as food or animal fodder. [from TURN, with reference to its rounded shape + Latin *napus*, turnip]

turnkey *noun* (PL. **turnkeys**) *Hist.* a person who keeps the keys in a prison; a gaoler.

turnoff *noun* **1** a road which branches off from a main road. **2** *colloq.* a person or thing that causes dislike or disgust.

turn of phrase one's way of expressing oneself, especially if distinctive; an instance of this: *has an amusing turn of phrase.*

Turn of the Screw, The a story by Henry James (1898). It is a ghostly tale of ambiguous apparitions narrated by an obsessive governess.

turn-on *noun slang* a person or thing that causes especially sexual excitement.

turn-out *noun* **1** the number of people attending a meeting, celebration, event, etc. **2** an outfit or set of clothes or equipment. **3** the quantity of goods produced or on display.

turnover *noun* **1** the total value of sales in a business during a certain time. **2** the rate at which stock is sold and replenished. **3** the rate at which money or workers pass through a business. **4** *Biol.* within a living organism, eg in bone tissue, the rate at which molecules that are undergoing breakdown are being replaced by new molecules. **5** *Biol.* in an ecosystem, the rate at which members of a population of plants or animals that are lost as a result of death or emigration are being replaced by reproduction or by the immigration of new members. **6** a small pastry with a fruit or jam filling.

turnpike *noun* **1** *Hist.* a gate or barrier across a road or bridge which is not lifted until travellers have paid the toll. **2** *North Amer., esp. US* a motorway on which a toll is paid.

turnstile *noun* a revolving gate with metal arms which allows only one person to pass through at a time, usually after payment of a fee.

turntable *noun* **1** the revolving platform on which a record turns on a record-player. **2** a revolving platform for turning railway engines and other vehicles.

turn-up *noun* **1** *Brit.* a piece of material folded up at the bottom of a trouser-leg. **2** (**a turn-up for the book**) an unexpected and usually pleasant surprise; a surprising piece of good luck.

turpentine *noun* **1** a thick oily resin obtained from certain trees, eg pines. **2** (*in full* **oil of turpentine**) a clear essential oil distilled from this resin used in many commercial products, especially solvent and paint thinners. [from Greek *terebinthos*, a tree yielding turpentine]

Turpin, Dick (Richard) (1705–39) English robber, born in Hempstead, Essex. He was, successively or simultaneously, butcher's apprentice, cattle- and horse-thief, smuggler, housebreaker, and highwayman. He worked in partnership with another highwayman, Tom King, whom he shot dead by accident. The legend surrounding Turpin also tells of his ride to York on a mare called Black Bess, recounted in Harrison Ainsworth's *Rookwood* (1824). Eventually Turpin was arrested and hanged in York.

turpitude *noun* baseness; vileness; depravity. [from Latin *turpitudo*]

turquoise *noun* **1** *Geol.* a hard opaque mineral, light blue or green in colour, consisting of copper aluminium phosphate, and formed by the alteration of aluminium-rich rock by surface waters. It is a valuable gemstone and ornamental material. **2** the colour of this stone. [from Old French *turkeis*, Turkish, as first brought from Persia through Turkey or Turkestan]

turret *noun* **1** a small tower on a castle or other building. **2** (*in full* **gun-turret**) a small revolving tower-like structure on warships, tanks, etc on which guns are mounted. **3** that part of a lathe which holds the cutting tool. [from Latin *turris*, tower]

turreted *adj.* **1** having turrets. **2** formed like a tower or a long spiral.

turtle *noun* **1** any of several large marine reptiles of the order Chelonia, with a short broad body protected by a bony shell which tends to be flatter than that of its land-dwelling relatives (the tortoises), and limbs that have evolved as flippers. All turtles return to land to lay their eggs, and several species have become endangered as a result of their exploitation for food (including their eggs) and tortoiseshell. **2** *North Amer.* a tortoise or terrapin.
— **turn turtle** *said of a boat, etc* to turn upside down; to capsize. [from Latin *tortuca*]

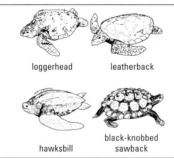

loggerhead   leatherback

hawksbill   black-knobbed sawback

turtles

turtledove *noun* any of several wild doves noted for their soft cooing and apparent affection for mates and young. [from Latin *turtur*]

turtle-neck *noun* a high round close-fitting neck; also, a piece of clothing having this, especially a jersey.

turtle soup soup made from the flesh and fat of a female turtle.

turves see TURF.

Tuscan — *adj.* **1** denoting an order of classical architecture, introduced by the Romans. It is a simplified version of Doric with an unfluted shaft on the column and minimal decoration on capital and entablature. **2** relating to Tuscany in Italy. — *noun* a native of Tuscany.

Tuscany, Italian **Toscana** POP (1991) 3.6m, a mountainous region in W central Italy, with fertile valleys and a marshy coastal plain. AREA 22 989sq km/8 874sq mi. CAPITAL Florence. CHIEF TOWNS Pisa, Siena, Lucca, Leghorn. ECONOMY industry is mainly in the valley of the Arno, including iron and lignite mines and marble quarries; the valley is an important agricultural area and is the home of Chianti wine; tourism is focused on traditional centres of art, notably Florence, Siena, and Pisa.

Tusculum an ancient town in the mountains SE of Rome, near modern Frascati. It was originally an independent Latin town during the first millennium BC, but by the late Republic it had become a fashionable country retreat for wealthy Romans.

tusk *noun* one of a pair of long, curved, pointed teeth which project from the mouth of certain animals including the elephant, walrus and wild boar. [from Anglo-Saxon *tusc*]

tusked *adj.* having tusks.

tusker *noun* an elephant, walrus, wild boar, etc with well-developed tusks.

Tussaud, Marie, *née* **Grosholtz**, known as **Madame Tussaud** (1761–1850) Swiss modeller in wax, born in Strasbourg. She was apprenticed in Paris to her uncle, Dr Curtius, whose wax museums she inherited (1794). After the Revolution, she attended the guillotine to take masks from the severed heads, and later toured Britain with her life-size portrait waxworks. In 1835 she set up a permanent exhibition in Baker St, London, which was burnt down in 1925 and re-opened in Marylebone Rd (1928). Her work remaining there includes Marie Antoinette, Napoleon, and Burke and Hare in the Chamber of Horrors.

tussle — *noun* a sharp or vigorous struggle or fight. — *verb intrans.* to struggle or fight vigorously. [from Middle English *tusen*]

tussock *noun* a clump of grass or other vegetation.

tussocky *adj.* **1** full of tussocks. **2** forming tussocks.

tut or **tut-tut** — *interj.* an expression of mild disapproval, annoyance or rebuke. — *verb intrans.* (**tutted, tutting**) to express mild disapproval, annoyance or rebuke by saying 'tut' or 'tut-tut'. — *noun* an act of saying 'tut' or 'tut-tut'. [originally a conventional spelling representation of the sound, also represented by *tch* or *tsk*, made with the tongue against the inner gums to express mild disapproval, etc]

Tutankhamen (14c BC) King of Egypt (1361–1352 BC) of the 18th dynasty, the son-in-law of the pharaoh, Akhenaton. He came to the throne at the age of 12 and died aged about 18. He is remembered chiefly for his tomb at Thebes, which was discovered intact in 1922 by Lord Carnarvon and Howard Carter.

tutelage *noun* **1** the state or office of being a guardian. **2** the state of being under the care of a guardian. **3** tuition or instruction. [from Latin *tutela*, guard]

tutelary *adj.* **1** having the power or role of a guardian over someone. **2** of a guardian. **3** giving protection. [from Latin *tutelaris*, from *tutela*, guardian]

tutor — *noun* **1** a university or college teacher who teaches students individually or in small groups, or who is responsible for the general welfare and progress of a certain number of students. **2** a private teacher. **3** *Brit.* an instruction book. — *verb trans., intrans.* (**tutored, tutoring**) to act as a tutor to (a pupil). [from Latin *tutor*, guardian]

tutorial — *noun* a lesson given by a university or college tutor to an individual student or small group of students. — *adj.* of a tutor or tuition by a tutor.

tutorially *adv.* **1** in a tutorial way. **2** by a tutor, in a tutorial.

tutorship *noun* the office or position of tutor.

Tutsi, also called **Batusi**, **Tussi**, **Watusi** an ethnic group whose members live in Burundi and Rwanda. They moved into the area in the 14c–15c, and have formed the traditional aristocracy in both countries. Since the 1960s there has been a struggle for power with the members of the Hutu tribe who form the majority of the population.

tutti *Mus.* — *adv.* with all the instruments and singers together. — *noun* a piece of music to be played or sung by all the instruments and singers together. [from Italian]

tutti-frutti *noun* an ice cream or other sweet containing or flavoured with mixed fruits. [from Italian, = all fruits]

tut-tut see TUT.

tutu *noun* a female ballet dancer's very short, stiff, spreading skirt. [from French]

Tuvalu, formerly **Ellice Islands** (to 1976) POP (1992e) 12 000, an independent island group in the SW Pacific, 1 050km/650mi N of Fiji. AREA 26sq km/10sq mi. CAPITAL Fongafale on Funafuti atoll. TIME ZONE GMT +12. The majority of the population are Polynesian; Protestantism is the chief religion. CHIEF LANGUAGES Tuvaluan, English. CURRENCY the Australian dollar. PHYSICAL DESCRIPTION comprises nine low-lying coral atolls, running NW–SE in a chain 580km/360mi long. CLIMATE hot and humid; the average annual temperature is 30°C and the average annual rainfall is 3 535mm. HISTORY invaded by Samoans in the 16c; became a British protectorate as the Ellice Is in 1892; administered as a colony jointly with the Gilbert Is (now Kiribati) from 1915; separate constitution, following the 1974 referendum; gained independence in 1978. GOVERNMENT the British monarch is represented by a Governor-General; governed by a Prime Minister, Cabinet, and a unicameral 12-member parliament. ECONOMY copra, tropical fruit; fishing; crafts; postage stamps.

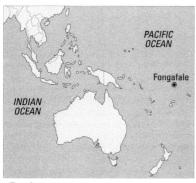

Tuvalu

tu-whit tu-whoo a conventional spelling representation of an owl's hoot.

tux *noun North Amer. colloq.* a tuxedo.

tuxedo *noun* (PL. **tuxedos**) a dinner-jacket, or an evening suit which includes such a jacket. [named after a fashionable club at *Tuxedo* Park, New York]

Tuzla a town in NE Bosnia-Herzegovina, one of six 'safe areas' declared by the UN during the civil war (1992–). Its airport was closed to humanitarian flights during the struggle between Muslim and Bosnian Serb forces, causing discussions in NATO over whether to use air strikes to attempt to force its re-opening.

TV *abbrev.* television.

TVEI *abbrev.* Technical and Vocational Education Initiative, a scheme intended to give school students more job-oriented and technological courses.

TVP *abbrev.* textured vegetable protein, a form of protein from vegetable sources which has a meat-like texture, used in food as a substitute for meat.

TWA *abbrev.* Trans-World Airlines.

twaddle — *noun colloq.* nonsense; senseless or silly writing or talk. — *verb intrans.* to speak or write nonsense.

Twain, Mark, pseudonym of **Samuel Langhorne Clemens** (1835–1910) US writer, born in Florida, Missouri. He adopted his pen name from a well-known call of the man sounding the river in shallow places ('mark twain' meaning 'by the mark two fathoms'). In 1867 he wrote *Innocents Abroad* (1869), which established his reputation as a humorist. His two best-known works are the novels *Tom Sawyer* (1876) and *Huckleberry Finn* (1884), which are drawn from his own boyhood experiences. Other works include *A Tramp Abroad* (1880) and *A Connecticut Yankee in King Arthur's Court* (1889).

twain *noun* old use two: *in twain*. [from Anglo-Saxon *twegen*]

twang — *noun* **1** a sharp ringing sound like that produced by plucking a tightly-stretched string. **2** a nasal quality or tone of voice. **3** *colloq.* a local or regional intonation. — *verb trans., intrans.* to make or cause to make a twang. [imitative]

twangy *adj.* (**twangier, twangiest**) making a twanging sound.

twat *noun coarse slang* **1** a worthless, unpleasant or despicable person. **2** the female genitals.

tweak — *verb* to pull or twist with a sudden jerk. — *noun* a sudden sharp pull or twist. [related to TWITCH]

twee *adj. Brit. colloq.* too pretty, sweet, quaint or sentimental. [from *tweet*, a childish pronunciation of SWEET]

Tweed, River a river in SE Scotland and NE England, length 155km/96mi. Rising in SW Borders region at Tweed's Well, NW of Moffat, it flows generally E and forms part of the border between Scotland and England before entering the North Sea at Berwick-upon-Tweed.

tweed *noun* **1** a thick, rough woollen cloth usually with coloured flecks in it, made originally in Scotland and used for suits, jackets, etc. **2** (**tweeds**) clothes, especially a suit, made of this material. [from Scots *tweedling*, twilling or *tweeled*, twilled]

Tweedledum and Tweedledee the fat, contrary twins encountered by Alice in Lewis Carroll's *Through the Looking-Glass*.

tweedy *adj.* (**tweedier, tweediest**) **1** of or like tweed. **2** typical of people who enjoy a hearty, outdoors life and pastimes such as fishing and shooting, for which it is traditional to wear tweed clothing.

tweely *adv.* in a twee way.

'tween *contr.* old use between.

tweeness *noun* a twee quality.

tweet — *noun* a melodious chirping sound made by a small bird. — *verb intrans.* to chirp melodiously. [imitative]

tweeter *noun* a loudspeaker used to reproduce high-frequency sounds. See also WOOFER.

tweezers *pl. noun* a small pair of pincers for pulling out individual hairs, holding small objects, etc. [from obsolete *tweeze*, a surgeon's case of instruments]

twelfth — *noun* **1** one of 12 equal parts. **2** the last of 12; the next after the eleventh. — *adj.*

coming after the eleventh. — *adv.* **1** in twelfth position. **2** as the twelfth point, etc. [from Anglo-Saxon *twelfta*]

Twelfth Day the twelfth day after Christmas, 6 Jan.

twelfthly *adv.* as the twelfth point, etc.

twelfth man *Cricket* a reserve member of a team.

Twelfth Night the evening before the twelfth day after Christmas (5 Jan) or the evening of the day itself (6 Jan).

Twelfth Night, or What You Will a play by William Shakespeare (1600–2). It is a comedy revolving around the near-identical twins, Sebastian and Viola, who are separated on being shipwrecked. Viola's disguise as a man leads to much confusion and intrigue among the society in which she finds employment, particularly when her brother turns up in the same town.

twelve — *noun* **1** the number or figure 12; any symbol for this number. **2** the age of 12 years. **3** something, especially a garment or a person, whose size is denoted by 12. **4** a set of 12 things, people, etc. **5** a score of 12 points. **6** 12 o'clock. **7** *Brit.* a film classified as being suitable for people of twelve years and over. — *adj.* **1** 12 in number. **2** aged 12. [from Anglo-Saxon *twelf*]

twelvefold — *adj.* **1** 12 times as much or as many. **2** divided into or consisting of 12 parts. — *adv.* by 12 times as much.

twelvemonth *noun old use* a year.

Twelve Tables the first codification of Roman law, drawn up by a commission of 10 men in 451–450 BC. Their publication (on 12 tablets) was produced under pressure from the plebeians, and was intended to curb the power of the patricians. Although the original tablets themselves do not survive, quotations from them in ancient authors give indications of the wide areas of law with which they dealt.

twelve-tone *adj. Mus.* of or relating to music based on a pattern formed from the 12 notes of the chromatic scale.

twenties *pl. noun* **1** the period of time between one's 20th and 30th birthdays. **2** the range of temperatures between 20 and 30 degrees. **3** the period of time between the 20th and 30th years of a century.

twentieth *noun, adj.* **1** the position in a series corresponding to 20 in a sequence of numbers. **2** one of 20 equal parts.

twenty — *noun* (PL. **twenties**) **1** the number or figure 20; any symbol for this number. **2** the age of 20. **3** a set of 20 people, things, etc. **4** a bank note worth 20 pounds. **5** a score of 20 points. — *adj.* **1** 20 in number. **2** aged 20. [from Anglo-Saxon *twentig*]

twerp or **twirp** *noun colloq.* a silly or contemptible person.

twice *adv.* **1** two times; on two occasions. **2** double in amount: *twice as much*. [from Middle English *twiges*, from Anglo-Saxon *twige*]

twiddle — *verb* **1** to twist (something) round and round: *twiddle the knob on the radio*. **2** (**twiddle with something**) to play with it or twist it round and round idly. — *noun* **1** an act of twiddling. **2** a curly mark or ornament. — **twiddle one's thumbs 1** to move one's thumbs in a circular movement round and round each other, usually as a sign of boredom. **2** to have nothing to do. [perhaps from TWIRL, TWIST, TWITCH, FIDDLE]

twiddler *noun* a person who twiddles.

twiddly *adj.* (**twiddlier, twiddliest**) full of twiddles, ornamented.

twig[1] *noun* a small shoot branch of a tree, bush, etc. [from Anglo-Saxon]

twig[2] *verb trans., intrans.* (**twigged, twigging**) *colloq.* to understand (a joke, situation, etc) especially suddenly. [from Irish Gaelic *tuigim*, I understand]

twiggy *adj.* **1** like a twig. **2** full of twigs.

twilight — *noun* **1** the faint light in the sky when the sun is just below the horizon immediately before sunrise or especially immediately after sunset. **2** the time of day when this occurs. **3** dim light or partial darkness. **4** a period of decline in strength, health or importance, especially after a period of vigorous activity: *the twilight of his life.* — *adj.* of or at to twilight; shadowy; dim. [from Anglo-Saxon *twi*, two + LIGHT]

twilight zone 1 a decaying area of a city or town situated typically between the main business and commercial area and the suburbs. **2** any indefinite or intermediate state or position.

twilit *adj.* lit by or as if by twilight.

twill — *noun* a strong woven cloth worked to give an appearance of parallel diagonal lines. — *verb* to weave (fabric) with a twill. [from Anglo-Saxon *twilic*, woven of double thread]

twilled *adj.* woven with a twill.

twilling *noun* weaving cloth with a twill.

twin — *noun* **1** either of two people or animals born of the same mother at the same time. **2** either of two people or things that are very like or closely associated with each other. **3** (**the Twins**) Gemini. **4** (*also* **twin crystal**) a compound crystal consisting of two crystals or parts of crystals which have grown together so that each one or part is a mirror image of the other. — *adj.* **1** being one of or consisting of a pair born of the same mother at the same time. **2** being one of or consisting of very similar or closely connected parts. — *verb* (**twinned**, **twinning**) **1** *trans., intrans.* to bring or come together closely or intimately. **2** to link (a town) with a counterpart in another country to encourage cultural, social, and economic exchanges and co-operation. **3** *intrans.* to give birth to twins. **4** *trans., intrans.* to form into or grow as a twin crystal. [from Anglo-Saxon *twinn*]

twin bed a single bed which is one of a matching pair.

twine — *noun* **1** strong string or cord made of twisting two or more threads of cotton, hemp, etc together. **2** a coil or twist. **3** an act of twisting or clasping. — *verb* **1** to twist together; to interweave. **2** to form by twisting or interweaving. **3** *trans., intrans.* to twist or coil round: *ivy twining round the old tree trunk.* [from Anglo-Saxon *twin*, double or twisted thread]

twin-engined *adj.* having a pair of engines.

twinge — *noun* **1** a sudden sharp stabbing or shooting pain. **2** a sudden sharp pang of emotional pain, bad conscience, etc. — *verb trans., intrans.* to feel or cause to feel a sharp pain or pang. [from Anglo-Saxon *twengan*, to pinch]

twinkle — *verb* **1** *intrans. said of a star, etc* to shine with a bright, flickering light. **2** *intrans. said of the eyes* to shine or sparkle with amusement or mischief. **3** to give off (light) with a flicker. — *noun* **1** a gleam or sparkle in the eyes. **2** a flicker or glimmer of light. **3** an act of twinkling. — **in a twinkle** *or* **in the twinkle of an eye** in a moment or very short time. [from Anglo-Saxon *twinclian*]

twinkling — *adj.* shining brightly; scintillating. — *noun* **1** the time occupied by a wink; an instant. **2** scintillation of the stars. — **in a twinkling** *or* **in the twinkling of an eye** in a moment or very short time.

twinkly *adj.* (**twinklier**, **twinkliest**) twinkling.

twinset *noun Brit.* a matching sweater and cardigan.

twin town a town which has been linked to a town abroad to encourage cultural, social and economic exchanges and co-operation.

twirl — *verb trans., intrans.* to turn, spin, or twist round. — *noun* **1** an act of twirling. **2** a curly

mark or ornament, especially one made with a pen. [from TWIST + WHIRL]

twirly *adj.* full of twirls, twirling.

twirp see TWERP.

twist — *verb* **1** *trans., intrans.* to wind or turn round, especially by moving only a single part, or different parts in opposite directions: *twist the knob / he twisted round in his seat.* **2** *intrans.* to follow a winding course: *a road twisting through the mountains.* **3** *trans., intrans.* to wind around or together: *twist the pieces of string together / a piece of wire was twisted round his leg.* **4** to force or wrench out of the correct shape or position with a sharp turning movement: *twist an ankle.* **5** to distort the form, meaning, implication or balance of: *twisted his face into an ugly sneer / twist her words / a twisted mind.* **6** to remove or break off with a sharp turning movement: *twist the button off.* **7** to form by winding or weaving. **8** *intrans.* to dance the twist. **9** *trans., intrans.* to take or give a spiral or coiled form (to). — *noun* **1** the act of twisting. **2** something formed by twisting or being twisted. **3** a turn or coil; a bend. **4** a sharp turning movement which pulls something out of shape; a wrench. **5** an unexpected event, development or change, eg of direction. **6** a distortion of form, nature or meaning. **7** an eccentricity or perversion. **8** a length of thread, cord, silk, etc formed by twisting two or more strands together. **9** a twisted roll of bread or tobacco. **10** a curl of citrus peel used to flavour a drink. **11** a screw of paper, especially one containing a collection of small items such as sweets. **12** (*usually* **the twist**) a dance, popular in the 1960s, involving twisting movements of the legs and hips. — **round the twist** *colloq.* mad; crazy.

twist someone's arm *colloq.* to apply especially moral pressure to someone to make them act in the way one wants. [from Middle English *twisten*, to divide]

twisted *adj.* **1** full of twists, coiled, distorted. **2** *colloq.* mentally sick or perverted.

twister *noun* **1** *Brit. colloq.* a dishonest or deceiving person; a swindler. **2** *North Amer.* a tornado.

twisty *adj.* (**twistier**, **twistiest**) **1** full of twists or turns. **2** dishonest.

twit[1] *noun colloq.* a fool or idiot. [perhaps from TWIT[2]]

twit[2] *verb* (**twitted**, **twitting**) to tease or criticize, usually pleasantly or affectionately. [from Anglo-Saxon *ætwitan*, to reproach]

twitch — *verb* **1** *intrans.* to move jerkily. **2** (**twitch something** *or* **twitch at something**) to pull or pluck it sharply or jerkily. — *noun* **1** a sudden sharp pull or jerking movement. **2** a sudden spasm of a muscle, especially one caused by nervousness; a tic. [related to Anglo-Saxon *twiccian*, to pluck]

Twitcher, Jemmy one of Capt MacHeath's band of unashamed thieves in John Gay's *The Beggar's Opera.*

twitcher *noun* **1** a person or thing that twitches. **2** *colloq.* a bird-watcher whose main interest is to spot as many rare birds as possible.

twitchily *adv.* in a twitchy way.

twitchy *adj.* (**twitchier**, **twitchiest**) *colloq.* nervous.

twitter — *noun* **1** a light, repeated chirping sound made by especially small birds. **2** *colloq.* a nervous or excited state: *be all of a twitter.* — *verb* (**twittered**, **twittering**) **1** *intrans. said especially of a bird* to make a light, repeated chirping sound or similar high-pitched trembling sounds. **2** to say or utter with such a chirping sound. **3** *intrans.* to make small nervous or excited movements. [imitative]

twittery *adj.* habitually twittering.

two — *noun* **1** the number or figure 2; any symbol for this number. **2** the age of 2. **3** something,

especially a garment or a person, whose size is denoted by the number 2. **4** something with 2 parts or members. **5** a playing-card with 2 pips. See also DEUCE[1]. **6** 2 o'clock. **7** a score of 2. — *adj.* **1** 2 in number. **2** aged 2. — *pron.* two people or things.

— **in two** in or into two pieces.

put two and two together to come to a usually obvious conclusion from the available evidence.

that makes two of us *colloq.* the same is true of me too.

[from Anglo-Saxon *twa*]

two-bit *adj. North Amer. colloq.* cheap; petty; small-time.

two-edged *adj.* double-edged.

two-faced *adj.* deceitful; hypocritical; insincere.

twofold — *adj.* **1** twice as much or as many. **2** divided into or consisting of two parts. — *adv.* by twice as much.

Two Gentlemen of Verona, The a play by William Shakespeare (1592–3). It is a comedy about the gentlemen friends Valentine and Proteus, and the demands that their conflicting love interests make on their friendship.

two-handed *adj.* **1** having, needing or for two hands or people. **2** able to use both hands equally well.

twopence *or* **tuppence** *noun Brit.* **1** the sum of two pence, especially before the introduction of decimal coinage. **2** a coin of the value of two pence in decimal coinage.

— **not care twopence** *colloq.* to not care at all.

twopenny *or* **tuppenny** *adj. Brit.* **1** worth or costing twopence. **2** *colloq.* cheap; worthless.

two-piece — *adj., said of a suit, etc* having two matching or complementary pieces or parts. — *noun* a two-piece suit, etc.

two-ply — *adj.* having two strands or layers. — *noun* (PL. **two-plies**) knitting wool or yarn made of two strands of wool twisted together.

Twort, Frederick William (1877–1950) English bacteriologist, born in Camberley, Surrey. Professor in London from 1919, he studied Jöhne's disease (a chronic intestinal disorder in cattle, sheep, and goats) and methods of culturing organisms, and discovered 'bacteriophages', the viruses which attack certain bacteria.

two-seater *noun* a vehicle, aircraft or seat for two people.

two-sided *adj.* **1** having two sides which are different. **2** having two aspects; controversial.

twosome *noun* **1** a game, dance, etc for two people. **2** a pair of people; a couple.

two-step *noun* a ballroom dance in duple time, or a piece of music for it.

two-stroke *adj., said of an internal combustion engine* having a cycle consisting of one up and one down stroke of a piston.

2001: A Space Odyssey a British film directed by Stanley Kubrick (1968). It is the the story of a journey through space by two astronauts (played by Keir Dullea and Gary Lockwood) that explores the development of humankind.

Two Thousand Guineas see CLASSICS.

two-time *verb trans., intrans. colloq.* to deceive or be unfaithful to (a husband, wife, lover, etc).

two-timer *noun colloq.* a person who two-times another.

two-tone *adj.* having or made up of two colours or two shades of the same colour, or two sounds.

two-way *adj.* **1** able to move, moving or allowing movement in two opposite directions: *a two-way street.* **2** *said of a radio, telephone, etc* able to both send and receive messages. **3** *said of communication between two people or groups* in which both participate equally and responsibility and gains are shared. **4** able to be used in two ways.

TX *abbrev.* Texas.

Tyan Shan see TIEN SHAN.

Tybalt the violent nephew of Lady Capulet in Shakespeare's *Romeo and Juliet*, who kills Mercutio and is himself killed by Romeo.

Tyche in Greek mythology, the goddess of chance or luck, prominent in the Hellenistic period. She was identified with the Roman goddess Fortuna.

tycoon *noun* a rich and powerful businessman or businesswoman. [from Japanese *taikun*, great prince]

Tyger, The a poem by William Blake (in *Songs of Innocence and of Experience*, 1794). One of his best-known poems, it addresses a tiger which symbolises strength and terror of God's creation (as opposed to the gentle innocence of a lamb).

tying see TIE.

tyke *noun* **1** a dog, especially a mongrel. **2** *Brit. originally dialect* a rough or coarse man. **3** *colloq.* a small, often cheeky child. [from Norse *tik*, bitch]

Tyler, Wat (Walter) (d.1381) English leader of the Peasants' Revolt (1381). He was chosen as leader by the rebels of Kent, after they had taken Rochester Castle. At the Smithfield conference with Richard II in London, where they demanded an end to serfdom and more freedom of labour, blows were exchanged, and Tyler was wounded by the Mayor of London, William Walworth. He was taken to St Bartholomew's Hospital, where Walworth had him dragged out and beheaded.

Tylor, Sir Edward Burnett (1832–1917) English anthropologist, born in London. He travelled with US ethnologist John Christy (1810–65) to Mexico, where they studied Toltec remains. He then devoted himself to anthropology, became Keeper of the University Museum at Oxford (1883), and the first Professor of Anthropology (1895–1909). A leading Darwinian anthropologist, he synthesized theories concerning the 'evolution' of technology and of religious ideas.

tympanic *adj.* **1** relating to or in the region of the eardrum. **2** relating to or representing a drum.

tympanic membrane same as TYMPANUM 1.

tympani, tympanist see TIMPANI.

tympanum *noun* (PL. **tympana**, **tympanums**) **1** *Anat.* the eardrum. **2** *Archit.* the recessed usually triangular face of a pediment. **3** *Archit.* a space between a lintel and an arch over it. **4** a drum or drumhead. [from Greek *tympanon*, kettledrum]

Tynan, Kenneth (1927–80) English theatre critic, born in Birmingham. As a drama critic, notably for the *Observer* (1954–63), he was one of the first to champion John Osborne and the other new playwrights of the time. He became literary manager of the National Theatre (1963–9), an editor in films and television, and achieved further fame with his controversial revue *Oh, Calcutta!* (1969).

Tyndale *or* **Tindale** *or* **Hutchins, William** (d.1536) English translator of the Bible, born (probably) in Slymbridge, Gloucestershire. He became a chaplain and tutor to a family, and was sympathetic to humanist learning. In 1524 he went to Hamburg, visited Martin Luther in Wittenberg, then began printing his translation of the English New Testament in Cologne (1525). Later he began work on an Old Testament translation in Antwerp (1531), but before it was finished he was accused of heresy, imprisoned, and put to death in Vilvorde, Belgium.

Tyndall, John (1820–93) Irish physicist, born in Leighlin-Bridge, County Carlow. Professor at the Royal Institution, he discovered in 1869 the

'Tyndall effect', the scattering of light by colloidal particles in solution, thus making a light beam visible when viewed from the side. He also correctly explained the blue colour of the sky.

Tyne, River a river in NE England, length 48km/30mi. It is formed by the confluence of the North Tyne and the South Tyne, NW of Hexham, Northumberland. The South Tyne rises on Cross Fell, E Cumbria; the North Tyne rises in the Cheviot Hills, and is dammed to form Kielder Water Reservoir. The Tyne flows E across Kielder Moor and through Tyne and Wear to meet the North Sea between Tynemouth and South Shields. The river serves the industrial towns of Newcastle, Jarrow, Gateshead, Wallsend, and South Shields, and is linked to the R Tees as part of the UK's first regional water grid system. It is navigable for 13km/8mi above Newcastle.

Tyne and Wear POP (1992e) 1.1m, a metropolitan county area in NE England, divided into five districts. Controlled by a metropolitan county council until 1986, the area is now administered by metropolitan district councils. AREA 540sq km/208sq mi. PHYSICAL DESCRIPTION it is bounded E by the North Sea, N and W by Northumberland, and S by Durham; drained by the Tyne and Wear rivers. The area has been highly industrialized since the Industrial Revolution. It suffered a serious decline following the Great Depression, notably in shipbuilding. Tyne and Wear is now designated as a special development area, with considerable diversification of industry. CHIEF TOWNS Newcastle upon Tyne (administrative centre), Gateshead, Jarrow, Wallsend, Sunderland.

Tyneside POP (1981) 782 000, an urban area in Tyne and Wear, NE England. It includes Newcastle upon Tyne, Gateshead, Jarrow, Felling, Hebburn, Newburn, Longbenton-Killingworth, Wallsend, and North and South Shields.

Tynwald *noun* the parliament of the Isle of Man. [from Norse *thing*, assembly + *völlr*, field]

type — *noun* **1** a class or group of people, animals or things which share similar characteristics; a kind or variety. **2** the general character, nature or form of a particular class or group. **3** *colloq.* a person, especially of a specified kind: *a quiet type of person.* **4** a person, animal or thing that is a characteristic example of its group or class. **5** a small metal block with a raised letter or character on one surface, used for printing. **6** a set of such blocks. **7** a set of such blocks of a particular kind: *italic type.* **8** printed letters, characters, words, etc. **9** *Biol.* the actual specimen on which the description of a new species or genus is based. — *verb* **1** *trans., intrans.* to write (words, text, etc) using a typewriter or word processor. **2** to be a characteristic example or type of; to typify. **3** *Medicine, Biol.* to decide the type of (eg a blood sample); to classify. [from Greek *typos*, blow, mark]

typecast — *verb* (PAST TENSE AND PAST PARTICIPLE **typecast**) to cast (an actor or actress) regularly in the same kind of part. — *adj., said of an actor or actress* regularly cast in the same kind of part.

typeface *noun* a set of letters, characters, etc of a particular design or style.

typescript *noun* any typewritten document, manuscript or copy.

typeset *verb* (**typesetting**; PAST TENSE AND PAST PARTICIPLE **typeset**) *Printing* to arrange (type) or set (a page, etc) in type ready for printing.

typesetter *noun* a person or machine that sets type ready for printing.

typewrite *verb trans., intrans.* (PAST TENSE **typewrote**; PAST PARTICIPLE **typewritten**) to produce (text) with a typewriter.

typewriter *noun* a machine with a keyboard for writing in characters resembling print.

◇ In older manual machines, a sytem of levers connects each key to the appropriate type bar (which bears both upper- and lower-case letters); the type bars are arranged in a semicircle so that each strikes the centre of the machine, with the paper and inked ribbon moving on after each strike. The first practical typewriter was invented in the USA in 1867 by Christopher Scholes. The older mechanical machines have largely been replaced by electric or electronic typewriters, and by word processors.

typewriting *noun* **1** the act of process of using a typewriter. **2** text produced by a typewriter.

typhoid — *noun* (also **typhoid fever**) *Medicine* a serious and sometimes fatal infection of the digestive system caused by the bacterium *Salmonella typhi*, transmitted by contaminated food and drinking water, and characterized by fever, a rash of red spots on the front of the body, abdominal pain, and sometimes delirium. — *adj.* relating to or resembling typhus. [from Greek *typhos*, fever + *eidos*, likeness]

typhoon *noun Geol.* a tropical storm, characterized by revolving winds, that occurs over the NW Pacific Ocean and the South China Sea. [from Chinese *da feng*, great wind + Greek *typhon*, whirlwind]

typhus *noun Medicine* any of a group of infectious diseases caused by rickettsiae (small spherical or rodlike parasitic micro-organisms) and transmitted to humans by lice, fleas, ticks, or mites carried by rodents. The main symptoms are fever, severe headache, a red skin rash, and delirium. [from Greek *typhos*, fever]

typical *adj.* (often **typical of someone** *or* **something**) **1** having or showing the usual characteristics; being a characteristic or representative example. **2** showing the usual, expected, undesirable characteristics of behaviour, attitude, etc: *a hostile reaction is typical of him.* **3** of, relating to or being a representative or characteristic specimen or type. **4** foreshadowing; symbolic. [from Latin *typicalis*, from Greek *typos*, blow, mark]

typically *adv.* in a typical way; as is typical.

typify *verb* (**typifies**, **typified**) **1** to be an excellent or characteristic example of. **2** to represent by a type or symbol; to symbolize. [from Greek *typos*, blow, mark + Latin *facere*, to make]

typing *noun* typewriting.

typist *noun* a person who types, especially as an occupation.

typo *noun* (PL. **typos**) an error made in the typesetting of a text, such as the use of one letter in mistake for another. [an abbreviation of *typographical error*]

typographer *noun* a person skilled in typography.

typographic *or* **typographical** *adj.* **1** relating to or involving printing or typography. **2** printed.

typographically *adv.* in a typographic way; in terms of typography.

typography *noun* **1** the art or occupation of composing type and arranging texts for printing. **2** the style and general appearance of printed matter which has been typeset. [from Latin *typographia*]

Tyr in Norse mythology, the god of battle, who guards the other gods. He lost one hand in the mouth of the Fenris wolf.

tyrannical *or* **tyrannous** *adj.* of or like a tyrant; oppressive; despotic.

tyrannically *or* **tyrannously** *adv.* in a tyrannical way.

tyrannize *or* **tyrannise** *verb trans., intrans.* to rule or treat (a person or people) in a cruel, unjust and oppressive way.

tyrannosaur *or* **tyrannosaurus** *noun* the largest flesh-eating dinosaur, which lived during the Cretaceous period, and grew to a height of 6m, walking on its hind legs, the front legs being much reduced. It is thought to have used the powerful claws on its hind legs to kill its prey, which consisted mainly of herbivorous dinosaurs. [from Greek *tyrannos*, tyrant, after DINOSAUR]

tyranny *noun* (PL. **tyrannies**) **1** cruel, unjust, and oppressive use of authority or power. **2** absolute, cruel and oppressive government by a single tyrant or group of tyrannical people. **3** a state under such government. **4** a cruel, unjust or oppressive act. [from Latin *tyrannia*, from Greek *tyrannos*, tyrant]

tyrant *noun* **1** a cruel, unjust, and oppressive ruler with absolute power. **2** a person who uses authority or power cruelly and unjustly. [from Greek *tyrannos*]
◇ In Greek city states of the 7c and 6c BC, the term was constitutional and also largely non-judgemental, referring to an absolute ruler who had seized power illegally. It was not until the 5c BC that it acquired the meaning 'cruel and oppressive ruler'.

Tyre, Arabic **Sour** POP (1990e) 14 000, a Mediterranean fishing port in SW Lebanon. The ancient city was the most important commercial centre in the E Mediterranean, noted for silk, glass, and Tyrean purple dye. Excavations since 1947 have uncovered remains of Crusader, Arab, Byzantine, and Graeco-Roman cities. There are several Roman remains, including one of the largest hippodromes of the Roman period. It is a World Heritage site.

tyre *noun* a thick rubber and usually air-filled or hollow ring placed over a wheel, and forming the contact with the ground. Tyres usually no longer have inner tubes, and grip is improved by a carefully designed tread and a system of grooves and

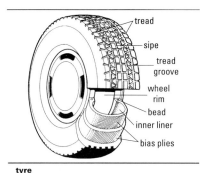

tyre

slits (sipes) which aid in water dispersal. [a variant of *tire*, headdress]

tyro see TIRO.

Tyrol see TIROL.

Tyrone, James the aging one-time screen-star driven to drink in Eugene O'Neill's *Long Day's Journey into Night*. The play also features his morphine-addicted wife Mary and their two sons, the cynical and hard-drinking Jamie, and the consumptive and depressive Edmund.

Tyrone, Gaelic **Tir Eoghain** POP (1981) 143 000, a county in W Northern Ireland. AREA 3 136sq km/1 210sq mi. It is bounded N by Co Londonderry, E by Lough Neagh, SE by Co Armagh, SW by Co Fermanagh, and S by the Republic of Ireland. PHYSICAL DESCRIPTION a hilly county, with the Sperrin Mts rising in the N to 683m at Mt Sawel; drained by the Blackwater, Foyle, and Strule rivers. CHIEF TOWNS Omagh (county town), Dungannon, Cookstown, Strabane. ECONOMY oats, potatoes, turnips; flax; sheep; cattle.

tyrosine *noun Biochem.* an amino acid that is found in proteins. [from Greek *tyros*, cheese]

Tyrrhenian Sea an arm of the Mediterranean Sea, bounded by the Italian Peninsula, Sicily, Sardinia, and Corsica. Major ports are Naples and Palermo.

Tyson, Mike (**Michael Gerald**) (1966–) US boxer, born in New York City. He turned professional in 1985, and 15 of his first 25 opponents were knocked out in the first round. He beat Trevor Berbick (1952–) for the World Boxing Council version of the world heavyweight title in 1986, to become the youngest heavyweight champion (20 yr 145 days), and added the World Boxing Association title in 1987, when he beat James Smith (1954–). In Aug 1987, he beat Tony Tucker (1958–) to become undisputed world champion, a title he held until Feb 1990, when he was defeated by James 'Buster' Douglas. In 1992 he was sentenced to six years in jail for charges including rape.

Tyumen **1** POP (1991e) 494 000, the capital of Tyumen oblast, SW Siberia, Russia, lying on the R Nitsa. HISTORY founded in 1585 on the site of a Tatar settlement; the first settled Russian town E of the Ural Mts; formerly an important centre of trade with China. **2** an oblast in SW Siberia, Russia, with Tyumen as its capital.

tzar, tzarevitch, tzarina see TSAR.

tzatziki *noun* a Greek dish made of yoghurt and finely chopped cucumber, flavoured with mint and garlic, and eaten as a dip. [from modern Greek]

tzigane *noun* a Hungarian gypsy. [from Hungarian *cigány*, gypsy]

Tz'u Hsi see CI XI.

Tzu-po see ZIBO.

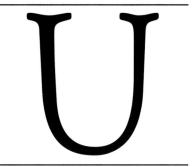

U

U¹ *or* **u** *noun* (PL. **Us**, **U's**, **u's**) **1** the twenty-first letter of the English alphabet. **2** anything shaped like the letter.

U² *adj. Brit. colloq., said especially of language* typical of or acceptable to the upper classes (see NON-U).

U³ *abbrev.* **1** unionist. **2** united. **3** *Brit.* universal, denoting a film designated as suitable for people of all ages.

U⁴ *symbol Chem.* uranium.

U-2 Incident on 1 May 1960 a US U-2 spy plane was brought down over Sverdlovsk in the USSR (now Yekaterinburg, Russia). After US denials, Premier Nikita Khrushchev produced the pilot and some photographs of military installations, and so President Eisenhower claimed the flights were essential for US national security. At the Paris Summit Meeting a few days later, Khrushchev withdrew Eisenhower's invitation to visit the USSR, and demanded that he condemn the flights, but the President refused, and Khrushchev walked out of the summit, blaming the USA for its failure.

UB40 *noun* in the UK, a registration card issued by the Department of Employment to an unemployed person.

Ubangi, River, French **Oubangui** a major tributary of the R Zaire, in N and W central Africa. It is 1 060km/660mi long; including the longest headstream (the R Uele), it measures 2 250km/1 400mi. The river follows the frontier between the Central African Republic and Zaire to join the R Zaire 97km/60mi SW of Mbandaka.

ubiquitous *adj.* found or seeming to be found everywhere; ever-present. [from Latin *ubique*, everywhere]

ubiquity *noun* existence everywhere.

U-boat *noun* a German submarine (especially of World Wars I and II). [from German *Unterseeboot*, undersea-boat]

Ucayali, River a river in E Peru. It is one of the Amazon's main headstreams, formed by the union of the Apurímac and Urubamba rivers. The Ucayali flows c.1 600km/1 000mi N, joining the R Marañón to form the Amazon 88km/55mi SW of Iquitos. It is navigable for its entire length by small craft.

UCCA *abbrev.* Universities Central Council on Admissions.

Uccello, Paolo, originally **Paolo di Dono** (1397–1475) Florentine painter, born in Pratovecchio. He trained under Lorenzo Ghiberti, worked in Venice as a mosaicist (1425–31), then settled in Florence, where he applied the principles of perspective to his paintings. His works include *The Flood* (1447–8, Florence), in which his use of perspective and foreshortening gives a starkly realistic effect, and *St George and the Dragon* (c.1460, National Gallery, London).

Udall, Nicholas (1504–56) English dramatist, born in Southampton. He was headmaster of Eton (c.1534–41) and made many classical translations, but is chiefly remembered as the author of the first major comedy in English, *Ralph Roister Doister* (c.1553, published 1567).

udder *noun* in certain mammals, such as cows and goats, the bag-like structure which hangs beneath the body and contains the mammary glands that secrete milk. Each gland has its own teat or nipple from which the milk is sucked. [from Anglo-Saxon *uder*]

UDI *abbrev.* Unilateral Declaration of Independence.

Udine POP (1990e) 98 000, the industrial capital of Udine province, Friuli-Venezia Giulia region, NE Italy, situated 61km/38mi NW of Trieste. It suffered severe bombing in World War II. NOTABLE FEATURES castle (16c); cathedral; town hall (15c).

UEFA *abbrev.* Union of European Football Associations.

Ufa POP (1990e) 1.1m, the industrial capital of Bashkortostan, S central Russia. It lies in the Ural Mts, on the R Ufa, at its confluence with the Dema and Zilim rivers. It was founded as a fortress in 1586.

UFC *abbrev.* Universities Funding Council.

Uffizi a museum and art gallery in Florence, Italy, which houses one of the world's greatest collections of works by Italian masters. The Renaissance palace was designed by Giorgio Vasari in 1560, and opened to the public by the Medici family in the 17c. In May 1993, the west wing of the gallery was seriously damaged in a bomb blast, and several works of art were damaged, with three of them being completely destroyed.

UFO *noun* (PL. **UFOs**, **UFO's**) *colloq.* an unidentified flying object, any unrecognizable flying vehicle presumed to be from another planet or outer space.

ufology *noun* the study of unidentified flying objects.

Uganda, official name **Republic of Uganda** POP (1992e) 18.7m, an E African republic, divided into 10 provinces. AREA 238 461sq km/92 029sq mi. It is bounded S by Rwanda, Tanzania and L Victoria, E by Kenya, N by Sudan, and W by Zaire. CAPITAL Kampala. CHIEF TOWNS Jinja, Mbale, Tororo, Soroti, Entebbe. TIME ZONE GMT +3. The chief ethnic group is Ganda; Christianity (66%) is the chief religion. OFFICIAL LANGUAGE English; Luganda and Swahili are also spoken. CURRENCY the New Uganda shilling. PHYSICAL DESCRIPTION landlocked country, mainly on a plateau with an elevation of between 900m and 1 000m; dry savannah or semi-desert N of L Kyoga; the population is concentrated in the fertile L Victoria basin; the W Rift Valley runs along Uganda's frontier with Zaire; straddling the frontier is the Mt Stanley massif, including Margherita Peak (5 110m), the highest point in Uganda and Zaire; main lakes include Victoria (SE), George (SW), Edward (SW), Albert (W), Kwania (central), Kyoga (central), and Bisina (formerly L Salisbury, in the E); the two main rivers are the upper reaches of the R Nile: the Victoria Nile and the Albert Nile. CLIMATE the highest rainfall is in the mountains to the W and SW and along the shores of L Victoria, exceeding 1 500mm per year; daily temperatures at Entebbe on the N shore of the lake are 24–28°C; central and NE areas receive less than 1 000mm of rain annually. HISTORY Bantu-speaking peoples migrated into SW Uganda c.500 BC; organized into several kingdoms by the 14c AD; discovered by Arab traders in the 1830s; explored by John Hanning Speke in the 1860s; granted to the British East Africa Company in 1888; the Kingdom of Buganda became a British protectorate in 1893; other territory was included by 1903; gained independence in 1962; Dr Milton Obote assumed all powers in 1966; a coup was led by General Idi Amin Dada in 1971; he expelled all Asian residents who were not Ugandan citizens; reacting to Amin's repressive regime, Tanzanian troops and Ugandan exiles marched on Kampala, overthrowing the government in 1979; a further coup took place in 1985; in 1993 the government instituted a policy of returning property to Asians who had been expelled by Amin. GOVERNMENT Parliament normally consists of 126 members; governed by a National Resistance Council which is part-elected and part-appointed by the President; a Cabinet appointed by the Council is led by a Prime Minister. ECONOMY agriculture is the main economic activity; coffee, cotton, tea, tobacco, sugar, maize, millet, yams, sorghum, groundnuts; livestock; fishing; textiles; fertilizers; food processing; plywood; brewing; tungsten; copper, tin, beryl, phosphate, limestone.

Uganda

Ugarit an ancient Canaanite city on the coast of N Syria opposite Cyprus. It was at its height in the late Bronze Age (c.1450–1200 BC) and enjoyed wide contacts with the Egyptians, the Hittites, and the Mycenaeans. It was destroyed by the Sea peoples in c.1200 BC. Excavations have uncovered ancient religious texts written in cuneiform script (eg the *Ras Shamra* texts).

UGC *abbrev.* University Grants Committee (replaced, 1979, by UFC).

ugh *interj.* an exclamation of dislike or disgust, also used to represent a cough or grunt.

ugli *noun* (PL. **uglis, uglies**) a fruit that is a cross between a grapefruit, a tangerine, and a seville orange, with wrinkly green and yellow skin. [from UGLY, from its appearance]

ugly *adj.* (**uglier, ugliest**) **1** unpleasant to look at. **2** morally repulsive or offensive. **3** threatening or involving danger or violence. **4** bad-tempered.

ugly duckling a person or thing initially thought ugly or worthless but growing to be outstandingly beautiful or highly valued.

UHF *abbrev.* ultra-high frequency.

Uhlenbeck, George Eugene (1900–88) Dutch–US physicist, born in Batavia (now Jakarta), Indonesia. Professor at the University of Michigan, he first proposed that electrons in atoms can have intrinsic 'spin' angular momentum as well as orbital angular momentum to explain experimental results; this was later confirmed by quantum theory.

UHT *abbrev.* **1** ultra-heat-treated. **2** ultra-high-temperature.
◇ UHT milk is sterilized by raising its temperature to 132–150°C for one or two seconds. Such treatment gives it a shelf-life of several months, and minimizes loss of nutrients, but alters the flavour.

Ujung Pandang, formerly **Makassar** *or* **Macassar** (to 1973) POP (1980) 709 000, the seaport capital of Sulawesi Selatan province, Indonesia. It lies in the SW corner of Sulawesi I and is an important trade centre of E Indonesia. The city was established by the Dutch in 1607 and became a free port in 1848.

UK *abbrev.* United Kingdom.

UKAEA *abbrev.* United Kingdom Atomic Energy Authority.

ukase *noun* a command issued by a supreme ruler, especially the Tsar in Imperial Russia. [from Russian *ukaz*]

Ukraine, Ukrainian **Ukrainia**, Russian **Ukrainskaya** *or* **Ukraina** POP (1992e) 52.2m, a republic in E Europe, divided into 25 oblasts. AREA 603 700sq km/233 028sq mi. It is bounded SW by Moldavia and Romania, W by Hungary, Slovakia, and Poland, N by Belorussia, E by Russia, and S by the Black Sea. CAPITAL Kiev. CHIEF TOWNS Kharkov, Donetsk, Odessa, Dnepropetrovsk, Lvov, Zaporozhye, Krivoy Rog. The population is mainly Ukrainian and Russian. TIME ZONE GMT +2. LANGUAGES Ukrainian, Russian. CURRENCY the karbovanet. PHYSICAL DESCRIPTION generally a plain with high elevations in the W, S, and SE; the Ukrainian Carpathian Mts in the W rise to 2 061m at Mt Goveria; the Crimean Peninsula separates the Black Sea from the Sea of Azov; the Crimean Mts lie along the S coast of the peninsula; chief rivers are the Dnieper, Dniester, Severskiy Donets, and Prut; there are many reservoirs and lakes. HISTORY inhabited by Scythians in ancient times, then invaded by Goths, Huns, and Khazars; centre of power in Kiev overrun by the Golden Horde in the 14c; ruled by Lithuania in the 14c–15c, and under Polish rule in the 16c; many fled Polish rule and formed resistance (Cossacks); gradually became part of Russia in the 17c–18c; declared independence in 1918 but Kiev occupied by Soviet troops; became a Soviet Socialist Republic in 1922; Chernobyl nuclear disaster in 1986; declaration of independence in 1991; dispute with Russia about control of the Black Sea fleet and the status of the Crimean peninsula; economic deterioration in the 1990s with high inflation. ECONOMY coal (from the large Donets coalfield), iron ore; manufacturing industries include metallurgy, machinery, fertilizers, fibres, synthetic resins, plastics, dyes, rubber products, and food processing; natural gas, oil refining; a major grain-exporting republic; other agricultural products are wheat, sugar beet, sunflower, cotton, flax, tobacco, soya, hops, fruit, and vegetables; tourism on the Crimean coast.

Ukraine

ukulele *or* **ukelele** *noun* a small guitar, usually with four strings. [from Hawaiian *ukulele*, jumping flea]

Ulan Bator *or* **Ulaanbaatar**, formerly **Urga** (to 1924) POP (1991e) 575 000, the capital of Mongolia and of Selenge county in the centre of the country. It is surrounded by the Khenti Mts. HISTORY founded as Urga in 1639, centre of Lamaistic religion in Mongolia; served as a trading centre on caravan routes between Russia and China in the 18c; became capital in 1921.

Ulanova, Galina (Sergeyevna) (1910–) Russian ballerina, born in St Petersburg. After making her début at the Kirov Theatre in 1928, she rose to become its leading ballerina, and queen of the Bolshoi Ballet. She won the Stalin prize four times and the Lenin prize once (1957), and has appeared in several films made by the Moscow State Ballet Company. Around 1962 she retired from the stage but continued to teach at the Bolshoi.

Ulan-Ude, formerly **Verkhneudinsk** (to 1934) POP (1991e) 362 000, the industrial capital of Buryatia, SE Siberia, Russia. It lies on the R Selenga, 75km/47mi E of L Baikal, and was founded in 1666 as a Cossack winter encampment. NOTABLE FEATURE Odigitrievskii Cathedral (1741–85).

Ulbricht, Walter (1893–1973) East German Communist politician, born in Leipzig. A cabinetmaker by trade, he entered politics in 1912, and in 1928 became Communist deputy for Potsdam. He left Germany on Hitler's rise (1933) and spent most of his exile in the USSR, until he returned in 1945 as head of the German Communist Party, and became deputy premier of the German Democratic Republic and General Secretary of the Party (1950). He was largely responsible for the 'sovietization' of East Germany, and built the Berlin Wall in 1961.

ulcer *noun* **1** *Pathol.* an open sore, often accompanied by inflammation, on the surface of the skin or of a mucous membrane lining a body cavity, eg peptic ulcer. Ulcers may be caused by a wide range of diseases (especially sexually transmitted diseases) and disorders, injury, restricted blood circulation, stress, etc. **2** a continuing source of harm or evil. [from Latin *ulceris*]

ulcerate *verb trans., intrans.* to form an ulcer on or in a part of the body.

ulceration *noun* the process or result of ulcerating.

ulcerous *adj.* **1** like an ulcer. **2** affected with ulcers.

Uleaborg see OULU.

Ulfilas *or* **Wulfila** (c.311–83AD) Cappadocian prelate and translator of the Bible, born among the Goths north of the Danube. Consecrated a missionary bishop to the Visigoths by Eusebius of Nicomedia in 341, after seven years' labour he was forced to migrate with his converts across the Danube. He devised the Gothic alphabet, and carried out the first translation of the Bible into a Germanic language.

Ullapool POP (1981) 1 200, a port town and tourist resort in Ross and Cromarty district, Highland region, NW Scotland, situated on the E shore of Loch Broom. NOTABLE FEATURE Ullapool Museum.

Ullswater the second-largest lake in England, situated in the Lake District, Cumbria. It lies SW of Penrith. The lake measures 12km/7mi long and 1km/0.6mi wide, with a depth of 64m.

Ulm POP (1991e) 109 000, an industrial and commercial city in Baden-Württemberg state, Germany. It lies on the R Danube, 72km/45mi SE of Stuttgart. In 1805 Napoleon defeated Austria nearby. The physicist Albert Einstein was born here in 1879. NOTABLE FEATURE Gothic Minster (1377–1529), with the world's highest spire (161m).

ulna *noun* (PL. **ulnae, ulnas**) *Anat.* the inner and longer of the two bones of the human forearm, or the corresponding bone in the forelimb or wing of other vertebrates. [from Latin *ulna*, elbow, arm]

ulnar *adj.* of or in the region of the ulna.

Ulric a male first name. [from Anglo-Saxon, from *wulf*, wolf + *ric*, power]

Ulster 1 a name commonly used to refer to Northern Ireland. **2** POP (1991) 232 000, a province in the Irish Republic, comprising the counties of Cavan, Donegal, and Monaghan. AREA 8 012sq km/3 093sq mi. Donegal is separated by part of Connacht, lying W of Northern Ireland; Cavan and Monaghan lie to the S of Northern Ireland. CHIEF TOWNS Donegal, Letterkenny, Cavan, Monaghan. HISTORY a former kingdom, and one of the four traditional provinces of Ireland; divided into 9 counties in the 16c; the land was confiscated by the English Crown, and distributed to Protestant English and Scots settlers in the 17c; following refusal by the Protestant counties of Ulster to accept the new Irish Free State, the province was divided in 1921 between Northern Ireland and the Irish Republic.

ulster *noun* a man's loose heavy double-breasted overcoat. [from Ulster in Northern Ireland, where it was first made]

ult. *abbrev.* **1** ultimate or ultimately. **2** ultimo.

ulterior *adj., said of motives, etc* other than what is apparent or admitted. [from Latin, from *uls*, beyond]

ultimate — *adj.* **1** last or final. **2** most important; greatest possible. **3** fundamental; basic. **4** *colloq.* best; most advanced. — *noun* (**the ultimate**) *colloq.* the best or most advanced one of its kind. [from Latin *ultimus*, last]

ultimately *adv.* in the end; finally.

ultimatum *noun* (PL. **ultimatums, ultimata**) a final statement declaring an intention to take hostile action unless a specified condition is fulfilled. [see ULTIMATE]

ultimo *adj., in business letters* of last month: *your letter of the tenth ultimo.* [from Latin *ultimus*, last]

Ultra a British security classification (the very highest) given during World War II to intelligence gathered from the breaking of the key German military codes used with their 'Enigma' encryption device. 'Ultra' intelligence was available to the British high command from the outset of the war, and was of crucial importance during the Battle of Britain and the Battle of the Atlantic.

ultra- *combining form* forming words meaning: **1** beyond in place, range, or limit: *ultra-microscopic*. **2** extreme or extremely: *ultra-Conservative*. [from Latin *ultra*, beyond]

ultra-high frequency (ABBREV. **UHF**) a radio frequency between 300 and 3000MHz.

ultramarine *noun* a deep blue pigment used in paints, originally made by grinding lapis lazuli, a blue stone from Asia. [from Latin *ultra marinus*, overseas, from where the stone was imported]

ultramontane — *adj.* **1** beyond the mountains, especially the Alps. **2** *RC Church* denoting a faction in favour of supreme papal authority on doctrinal matters. — *noun* **1** a person living on the other side of the Alps. **2** *RC Church* a member of the ultramontane faction. [from Latin *ultra*, beyond + *mons*, mountain]

Ultramontanism a movement in Roman Catholicism that advocated papal authority and the centralization of the Church. It originated in N Europe (eg France) from where its adherents looked southwards beyond the Alps to receive guidance from the pope and the Roman Catholic Church in Rome. It gained impetus after the French Revolution (1789), and reached its high point with the First Vatican Council (1870) when papal infallibility was declared. [from medieval Latin *ultramontanus*, beyond the mountains]

ultrasonic *adj.* relating to or producing ultrasound.

ultrasonically *adv.* in an ultrasonic way; by ultrasonic means.

ultrasonics *sing. noun* the study of ultrasound, a branch of physics.

ultrasound *noun* sound consisting of waves with frequencies higher than 20 000 Hz, and which are therefore above the upper limit of normal human hearing. It is widely used in medical diagnosis (especially during pregnancy when X-rays would be damaging), sonar systems, and for cleaning and degreasing industrial tools, and detecting flaws and impurities in metals.

ultrasound scan a medical examination of an internal part, especially a fetus, by directing ultrasound waves through it to produce an image on a screen.

ultraviolet (ABBREV. **UV**) *adj.* denoting electromagnetic radiation with wavelengths in the range 4 to 400nm, ie in the region between violet light and X-rays. Ultraviolet radiation emitted by the Sun can cause burning of human skin, even though most of the radiation is absorbed by the ozone layer before it reaches the Earth. [from ULTRA- + VIOLET, because it is beyond the violet end of the visible spectrum]

ululate *verb intrans.* to howl, wail, or screech. [from Latin *ululare*]

ululation *noun* a howling or wailing.

Uluru a national park in Northern Territory, central Australia. AREA c.1 300sq km/500sq mi. It is an area of continuing cultural and religious significance to the Aboriginal people, and is a World Heritage site. NOTABLE FEATURES the Olgas, a series of steep-sided rock domes; Ayers Rock.

Ulysses see ODYSSEUS.

Ulysses a novel by James Joyce (1922). It is set in Dublin and is loosely based on the events of Homer's *Odyssey*, describing one day in the lives of Leopold Bloom, his wife Molly, and Stephen Dedalus.

U-matic *trademark* the first helical-scan videotape cassette recorder introduced by Sony (1970), initially for the professional non-broadcast market, widely used for all forms of industrial video production.

umbel *noun Bot.* an inflorescence (flower-head) in which a cluster of flowers with stalks of equal length arise from the same point on the main stem. This umbrella-shaped arrangement is found in plants belonging to the family Umbelliferae, eg cow parsley, hogweed. [from Latin *umbella*, sunshade]

umbellate *adj.* **1** constituting an umbel. **2** having an umbel or umbels.

umbelliferous *adj. Bot.* denoting a plant with flowers growing in umbels.

umber *noun* a dark yellowish-brown mineral in soil, used as a pigment in paints. [from Italian *terra di umbra*, shadow earth or Umbrian earth]

Umberto I (1844–1900) King of Italy (1878–1900), born in Turin. He fought in a war against Austria (1866), and as King brought Italy into the Triple Alliance with Germany and Austria (1882). He supported Italian colonialism in Africa, but his popularity declined after Italy's defeat by the Ethiopians at Adowa (1896), and he was assassinated in Monza.

Umberto II (1904–83) the last King of Italy (1946), born in Racconigi. He succeeded to the throne on the abdication of his father, Victor Emmanuel III, but he too abdicated a month later, after a national referendum had declared for a republic.

umbilical *adj.* relating to the umbilicus or the umbilical cord.

umbilical cord a long flexible tube-like organ by which a fetus is attached to the placenta, and through which it receives nourishment.

umbilicus *noun Medicine* the navel. [from Latin *umbilicus*]

umbra *noun* (PL. **umbrae**, **umbras**) **1** the darkest part of a shadow, at the centre. **2** any shadow, especially that cast by the moon on the earth during an eclipse of the sun. [from Latin *umbra*, shade, shadow]

umbrage *noun* offence, especially in the phrases *give umbrage / take umbrage*. [from Old French *ombrage*, from Latin *umbra*, shadow]

umbrella *noun* **1** a device carried to give shelter against rain, etc, consisting of a rounded fabric canopy on a lightweight folding framework fitted around a central handle. **2** a thing, eg an organization, providing protection or overall cover for a number of others. [from Italian *ombrella*, from *ombra*, shade]

umbrella bird any of three species of bird with black plumage, native to tropical forests of S America. It has a crest of raised feathers on the crown of its head which, when opened during courtship, resembles an umbrella.

umbrella bird

Umbrellas, The a painting by Pierre Auguste Renoir (c.1881–4, National Gallery, London).

Umbria POP (1991) 823 000, a region in central Italy. AREA 8 456sq km/3 264sq mi. PHYSICAL DESCRIPTION watered chiefly by the streams of the upper Tiber basin; L Trasimeno, W of Perugia, is the largest lake on the Italian Peninsula; the Appenines rise in the E of the region. During the Renaissance, the region was the home of the Umbrian school of painting; painters included Raphael and Perugino. CAPITAL Perugia. CHIEF TOWNS Foligno, Terni. ECONOMY a prosperous farming region; corn, olives, wine, sugar beet, tobacco; market gardening; sheep farming; industry around Terni, Narni, and Foligno (chemicals, metalworking); textiles and crafts in Perugia and Spoleto.

Umeå POP (1992e) 93 000, the seaport capital of Västerbotten county, N Sweden. It lies on the Gulf of Bothnia at the mouth of the R Ume. HISTORY developed with the rise of the woodworking industry in the late 19c.

UMIST *abbrev.* University of Manchester Institute of Science and Technology.

umlaut *noun* in Germanic languages: **1** a change in the pronunciation of a vowel under the influence of a front vowel in a following syllable (especially in a suffix). **2** a mark consisting of two dots placed above a vowel that undergoes or has undergone this change. [from German *um*, around + *Laut*, sound]

Umm al Qaiwain POP (1985) 29 000, a member state of the United Arab Emirates. AREA 750sq km/290sq mi. It lies between Sharjah and Ras al Khaimah. CAPITAL Umm al Qaiwain. ECONOMY fishing; light industry; agriculture is concentrated in the fertile enclave of Falaj al Mualla.

Ummayyad Mosque the mosque at Damascus in Syria built (705–15) on the site of a Christian church to John the Baptist, and believed to incorporate the reliquary shrine of the saint's head.

umpire — *noun* a person supervising play in various sports, eg cricket and tennis, enforcing the rules and deciding disputes. — *verb trans., intrans.* to act as umpire in a match. [from Old French *nomper*, not a peer or equal]

umpteen *adj. colloq.* very many; innumerable. [from obsolete *umpty*, a great deal + -*teen*, from *thirteen*, etc]

umpteenth *noun, adj.* the latest or last of very many.

UN *abbrev.* United Nations.

un- *prefix* forming words denoting the opposite or reversal of the root word: *unacceptable / unplug / unperson*. [from Anglo-Saxon *un*]

'un *contr. colloq.* one: *that's a nice 'un*.

Una 1 the beautiful virgin eventually betrothed to the Redcrosse Knight in Book I of Edmund Spenser's *The Faerie Queene*, who represents truth in its purest and most virtuous form. **2** a female first name. [from Irish Gaelic, from Latin *unus*, one]

unable *adj.* not having sufficient strength, skill, or authority; not able to do something.

unaccountable *adj.* **1** impossible to explain. **2** not answerable or accountable.

unaccountably *adv.* in an unaccountable way; so as to be unaccountable.

unaccustomed *adj.* **1** (**unaccustomed to something**) not used to or accustomed to it. **2** not usual or customary.

unadopted *adj., said of a road* for which the local authority has no responsibility regarding maintenance, etc.

unadulterated *adj.* **1** pure or neat; not mixed with anything else. **2** sheer; absolute.

unadvised *adj.* **1** not advised; without advice. **2** unwise; ill-advised.

unadvisedly *adv.* in an unadvised way; against advice.

unaffected *adj.* **1** sincere or genuine, not pretended or affected; free from pretentiousness. **2** not affected.

unalienable same as INALIENABLE.

unalloyed *adj., said of joy, pleasure, etc* pure; sheer; not mixed with feelings of sadness or anxiety.

Un-American Activities Committee in the USA, a committee of the House of Representatives, established (1938) to consider the loyalty of federal government employees. Although supposed to identify communists, it was notorious for harassing individuals whose political opinions offended committee members. Later called the International Security Committee, it was abolished in 1975.

unanimity *noun* unanimous agreement.

unanimous *adj.* **1** all in complete agreement. **2** *said of an opinion, decision, etc* shared or arrived at by all, with none disagreeing. [from Latin *unus*, one + *animus*, mind]

unanswerable *adj.* that can not be denied or disproved.

unapproachable *adj.* whose manner discourages informality; unfriendly; stand-offish.

unarmed *adj.* without weapons.

unasked *adj.* **1** not asked. **2** not asked for; uninvited.

unassailable *adj.* not able to be challenged or destroyed.

unassuming *adj.* modest or unpretentious.

unattached *adj.* **1** not in a steady romantic or sexual relationship with another person. **2** not attached, associated, or connected.

unattended *adj.* **1** not accompanied or watched over. **2** not listened to or paid attention.

unavailing *adj., said of efforts, etc* futile; of no avail.

unaware *adj.* having no knowledge of something; not aware.

unawares *adv.* **1** unexpectedly; by surprise. **2** without knowing or realizing.

unbalanced *adj.* **1** not in a state of physical balance. **2** lacking mental balance; deranged. **3** lacking impartiality; biased.

unbearable *adj.* too unpleasant to bear; intolerable.

unbearably *adv.* in an unbearable way; to an unbearable degree.

unbecoming *adj.* **1** not suited to the wearer. **2** not proper or fitting.

unbeknown *or* **unbeknownst** *adv.* (**unbeknown to someone**) *colloq.* unknown to them; without their knowledge.

unbelief *noun* lack of (especially religious) belief.

unbelievable *adj.* **1** too unusual or unexpected to be believed. **2** *colloq.* remarkable; astonishing.

unbelievably *adv.* in an unbelievable way; so as to be unbelievable.

unbeliever *noun* a person who does not believe (especially in a particular religion).

unbelieving *adj.* not believing, without belief.

unbend *verb* (PAST TENSE AND PAST PARTICIPLE **unbent**) **1** *intrans.* to become less formal in manner or behaviour. **2** *trans.* to straighten or release from a bent position.

unbending *adj.* strict or severe; inflexible.

unbidden *adj., adv. literary* not requested, solicited, or summoned up; spontaneous or spontaneously.

unblushing *adj.* shameless; brazen.

unborn *adj.* **1** *said of a baby* not yet born. **2** of or in the future.

unbosom *verb* (**unbosomed, unbosoming**) (*often* **unbosom oneself**) to speak openly about what is on one's mind; to free oneself of worries or troubles by talking about them.

unbounded *adj.* limitless; infinite.

unbowed *adj.* **1** not bowed or bent. **2** not conquered or forced to yield.

unbridled *adj.* fully and freely felt or expressed; unrestrained.

unburden *verb* (**unburdened, unburdening**) **1** to remove a load or burden from. **2** (*often* **unburden oneself**) to relieve oneself of troubles or worries by confessing them to another person.

uncalled-for *adj., said of a remark, etc* not warranted or deserved, especially unjustifiably rude or aggressive.

uncannily *adv.* in an uncanny way.

uncanniness *noun* being uncanny.

uncanny *adj.* **1** strange or mysterious. **2** beyond ordinary human ability.

uncared-for *adj.* not well looked-after; neglected.

unceremonious *adj.* **1** without ceremony; informal. **2** with no regard for politeness or dignity; direct and abrupt.

unceremoniously *adv.* in an unceremonious way.

uncertain *adj.* **1** not sure, certain or confident. **2** not definitely known or decided. **3** not to be depended upon. **4** likely to change. **5** lacking confidence; hesitant.

uncertainty *noun* (PL. **uncertainties**) **1** an uncertain state. **2** something that is uncertain.

uncertainty principle *Physics* the notion that it is impossible to determine the exact position and momentum of a moving particle simultaneously. — Also called *Heisenberg uncertainty principle.*

uncharted *adj.* **1** *said of territory, etc* which has never been fully explored or mapped in detail. **2** not yet examined or investigated.

unchristian *adj.* against the principles or spirit of Christianity; uncharitable.

uncial — *adj., said of a form of writing* in large rounded letters with flowing strokes, of a kind used in ancient manuscripts. — *noun* **1** an uncial letter or form of writing. **2** a manuscript written in uncials. [from Latin *uncia*, inch]

uncircumcised *adj.* **1** not circumcised. **2** not Jewish; gentile.

uncivil *adj.* lacking courtesy; rude.

uncivilly *adv.* in an uncivil way.

unclasp *verb* **1** to unfasten the clasp on. **2** to relax one's clasp on. **3** to cause (one's hand) to relax and open up.

uncle *noun* **1** the brother or brother-in-law of a father or mother; the husband of an aunt. **2** *colloq.* a form of address used by a child to a male friend of his or her parents. **3** *slang* a pawnbroker. [from Latin *avunculus*]

unclean *adj.* **1** morally or spiritually impure. **2** *said of an animal* regarded for religious reasons as unfit to be used as food.

unclear *adj.* not clear; uncertain; vague.

Uncle Remus, in full **Uncle Remus, His Songs and His Sayings** The first of several volumes of verse and tales by Joel Chandler Harris (1881). They are based on black folklore and feature animals endowed with human characteristics (eg Brer Rabbit, Brer Fox).

Uncle Sam a nickname for the US government, or a personification of the USA. [supposedly from the initials 'US' stamped on boxes of meat supplied to the government in the War of 1812 by Samuel Wilson (1766–1854) of Troy, New York, who was known locally as Uncle Sam]

Uncle Tom *noun offensive* a black person who behaves subserviently to whites.

Uncle Tom's Cabin, in full **Uncle Tom's Cabin, or, Life among the Lowly** a novel by Harriet Beecher Stowe (1852). It tells how the loyal slave, Uncle Tom, is savagely murdered by his brutal master, Simon Legree.

Uncle Vanya (Dyadya Vanya) a play by Anton Chekhov (1900). A revised version of his play *The Wood Demon*, it is set in a country house and examines the futility of the lives of such inhabitants as Uncle Vanya and his niece Sonya.

unclothe *verb* **1** to take the clothes off. **2** to uncover or reveal.

uncomfortable *adj.* **1** not comfortable. **2** feeling, involving, or causing discomfort or unease.

uncomfortably *adv.* in an uncomfortable way; so as to be uncomfortable.

uncommon *adj.* **1** rare or unusual. **2** remarkably great; extreme.

uncommonly *adv.* in an uncommon way; to an uncommon degree.

uncompromising *adj.* **1** refusing to compromise or submit. **2** sheer; out-and-out.

uncompromisingly *adv.* in an uncompromising way.

unconcern *noun* lack of interest or concern; indifference.

unconcerned *adj.* **1** indifferent. **2** not anxious.

unconcernedly *adv.* with an unconcerned manner.

unconditional *adj.* straightforward, with no conditions imposed; absolute.

unconditionally *adv.* in an unconditional way; without conditions.

unconscionable *adj.* **1** without conscience or scruples. **2** outrageous; unthinkable; unreasonable; excessive.

unconscious — *adj.* **1** *said of a person or animal* in a state of insensibility, characterized by loss of awareness of the external environment, and inability to respond to sensory stimuli. **2** denoting any mental activity of which a person is unaware: *unconscious actions.* **3** (**unconscious of something**) not actively thinking about it. — *noun Psychol.* (**the unconscious**) in psychoanalysis, the part of the mind that contains memories, thoughts, and feelings of which one is not consciously aware, but which may be manifested as dreams, psychosomatic symptoms, or certain patterns of behaviour.

unconsciously *adv.* not consciously, unintentionally.

unconstitutional *adj.* not allowed by or consistent with a nation's constitution.

unconstitutionally *adv.* in an unconstitutional way.

uncork *verb* **1** to remove the cork from (a bottle). **2** *colloq.* to release (eg emotion) from a pent-up state.

uncouple *verb* to undo the coupling of or between; to disconnect.

uncouth *adj.* coarse in behaviour, manners or language. [from Anglo-Saxon *uncuth*, unfamiliar (ie with social graces)]

uncover *verb* (**uncovered, uncovering**) **1** to remove the cover from. **2** to reveal or expose. **3** *intrans.* to take off one's hat as a mark of respect.

uncrowned *adj.* **1** *said of a monarch* not yet crowned. **2** having the status but not a formal title; denoting an acknowledged master of expert in something: *the uncrowned king of swindlers.*

UNCTAD *abbrev.* United Nations Conference on Trade and Development.

unction *noun* **1** *Christianity* the act of ceremonially anointing a person with oil. **2** the oil used. **3** ointment of any kind. **4** soothing words or thoughts. **5** the kind of sincerity in language or tone of voice that provokes, or is the result of, deep emotion. **6** affected charm, sincerity, or religious feeling. [from Latin *ungere*, to anoint]

unctuous *adj.* **1** insincerely and excessively charming. **2** oily; greasy. [from Latin *unctuosus*]

uncured *adj., said of food, especially meat and fish* not dried, salted, or smoked.

uncut *adj.* **1** not cut. **2** *said of a book* whose pages have not been cut open. **3** *said of a book, film, etc* with no parts cut out. **4** *said of a gemstone* not cut into a regular shape.

undated *adj.* not dated; lacking a date.

undeceive *verb* to free from a mistaken belief; to reveal the truth to.

undecided *adj.* **1** not having decided; not able to decide. **2** about which no decision has been made.

undeniable *adj.* **1** not able to be denied; obviously true. **2** clearly and indisputably excellent.

undeniably *adv.* so as to be undeniable.

under — *prep.* **1** below or beneath; on the downward-facing surface of. **2** at the foot of. **3** less than; short of. **4** lower in rank than. **5** during the reign or administration of. **6** subjected to, receiving, or sustaining: *under consideration / under pressure.* **7** in the category or classification of. **8** according to: *under the terms of the agreement.* **9** in view of; because of: *under the circumstances.* **10** propelled by: *under sail.* **11** *said of a field* planted with (a particular crop). — *adv.* **1** in or to a lower place, position, or rank. **2** into a state of unconsciousness. — *adj.* **1** lower. **2** subordinate. — **under way** in motion; in progress. [from Anglo-Saxon *under*]

under- *combining form* forming words meaning: **1** beneath or below: *underfoot.* **2** too little in quantity or degree; insufficient or insufficiently: *underexpose / underpay.* **3** lower in rank or importance: *under-secretary.* **4** less than: *underbid.* **5** less or lower than expectations or potential: *underdeveloped.*

underachieve *verb intrans.* to be less successful than expected, especially academically; to fail to fulfil one's potential.

underachiever *noun* a person who is less successful than expected.

under-age *adj.* **1** *said of a person* below an age required by law. **2** *said of an activity, etc* carried on by an under-age person.

underarm *adj. adv., said of a style of bowling in sports* with the arm kept below the level of the shoulder.

underbelly *noun* (PL. **underbellies**) **1** the part of an animal's belly facing the ground. **2** any underside that resembles a belly. **3** (*also* **soft underbelly**) any unprotected part vulnerable to attack.

undercarriage *noun* **1** the landing-gear of an aircraft, including wheels, shock absorbers, etc. **2** the chassis of a road vehicle.

undercharge *verb* **1** to charge (a person) too little money. **2** to put an insufficient charge in (eg an electrical circuit or explosive device).

underclothes *pl. noun or* **underclothing**. *noun* underwear.

undercoat — *noun* **1** a layer of paint applied as preparation for the top or finishing coat. **2** the kind of paint used. **3** a layer of fur or hair beneath the top layer. — *verb* to apply an undercoat to.

undercover *adj.* working, or carried out, in secret.

undercurrent *noun* **1** an unseen current under the (often still) surface of a body of water. **2** an underlying trend or body of opinion, especially different from the one perceived.

undercut — *verb* (**undercutting**; PAST TENSE AND PAST PARTICIPLE **undercut**) **1** to offer goods or services at a lower price than (a competitor). **2** to cut away the underside of. **3** to apply backspin to (a ball). — *noun* the underside of a sirloin, ie the fillet.

underdog *noun* **1** the less highly regarded competitor, not expected to win. **2** the losing competitor. **3** a person dominated by another.

underdone *adj.* not cooked to the proper or required degree.

underemployed *adj.* **1** given less work than could realistically be done. **2** given work that fails to make good use of the skills possessed.

underemployment *noun* **1** insufficient use of something. **2** a state of having too large a part of a labour force unemployed.

underestimate — *verb* to make too low an estimate of the value, capacity, or extent of. — *noun* too low an estimate.

underfelt *noun* an old type of underlay, made of felt.

underfoot *adv.* under the feet of a walking or running person or people.

undergarment *noun* an item of underwear.

undergo *verb* (**undergoes**; PAST TENSE **underwent**; PAST PARTICIPLE **undergone**) to endure, experience, or be subjected to. [from Anglo-Saxon *undergan*]

undergraduate *noun* a person studying for a first degree in a higher education establishment.

underground — *noun* (*usually* **the underground**) **1** a place or area below ground level. **2** a system of electric trains running in tunnels below ground. **3** a secret paramilitary organization fighting a government or occupying force. **4** any artistic movement seeking to challenge or overturn established (usually social as well as artistic) views and practices. — *adj.* **1** existing or operating below the surface of the ground. **2** of or belonging to any political or artistic underground. — *adv.* **1** to a position below ground level. **2** into hiding.

Underground Railroad in US history, a network of safe houses, hiding places, and routes to aid escaped American slaves to reach freedom in the North or Canada. Never formally organized, it was active as early as 1786, but was most widespread from 1830 to 1860. Estimates suggest that it may have assisted some 50 000 runaways.

undergrowth *noun* a thick growth of shrubs and bushes among trees.

underhand *or* **underhanded** — *adj.* **1** secretively deceitful or dishonest; sly. **2** underarm. — *adv.* in an underhand way.

underlay — *verb* (PAST TENSE AND PAST PARTICIPLE **underlaid**) to lay underneath, or support or provide with something laid underneath. — *noun* a thing laid underneath another, especially felt or rubber matting laid under a carpet for protection.

underlie *verb* (**underlying**; PAST TENSE **underlay**; PAST PARTICIPLE **underlain**) **1** to lie underneath. **2** to be the hidden cause or meaning of (an attitude, event, etc), beneath what is apparent, visible, or superficial.

underline *verb* **1** to draw a line under (eg a word or piece of text). **2** to emphasize.

underling *noun derog.* a subordinate.

underlying *adj.* **1** lying under or beneath. **2** fundamental, basic: *the underlying causes.*

undermentioned *adj.* mentioned or named below or later in the text.

Under Milk Wood a radio drama by Dylan Thomas (broadcast, 1954). It describes a day in the lives of various characters in the small Welsh town of 'Llareggub'.

undermine *verb* **1** to dig or wear away the base or foundation of. **2** to weaken or destroy, especially gradually and imperceptibly.

underneath — *prep., adv.* beneath or below; under. — *noun* a lower or downward-facing part or surface. [from Anglo-Saxon *underneothan*]

underpants *pl. noun* a man's undergarment covering the body from the waist or hips to (especially the tops of) the thighs.

underpass *noun* **1** a tunnel for pedestrians under a road or railway; a subway. **2** a road or railway passing under another.

underpin *verb* (**underpinned, underpinning**) **1** to support from beneath, usually temporarily, with brickwork or a prop. **2** *fig.* to give strength or support to.

underplay *verb* to understate or reduce the emphasis on.

underprivileged *adj.* deprived of the basic living standards and rights enjoyed by most people in society.

underproduce *verb trans., intrans.* to produce less than the required or potential amount of something.

underproduction *noun* producing less than expected or possible.

underrate *verb* to underestimate.

underrated *adj.* **1** underestimated. **2** rated at less than real worth.

underseal — *noun* an anti-rusting substance painted on to the underside of a motor vehicle. — *verb* to apply such a substance to.

under-secretary *noun* (PL. **under-secretaries**) a subordinate to a secretary of state, especially a junior minister or senior civil servant.

undersell *verb* (PAST TENSE AND PAST PARTICIPLE **undersold**) to sell goods or services at a lower price than (a competitor).

undersexed *adj.* experiencing sexual desire less frequently or less intensely than the average person.

undershoot *verb* (PAST TENSE AND PAST PARTICIPLE **undershot**) **1** *said of an aircraft* to land short of (a runway). **2** to fall short of (a target, etc).

underside *noun* the downward-facing side or surface.

undersigned *adj.* whose names are signed below: *we, the undersigned, ...*

undersized *adj.* of less than the usual size.

underskirt *noun* a thin skirt-like undergarment worn under a dress or skirt.

understaffed *adj.* having insufficient staff.

understand *verb* (PAST TENSE AND PAST PARTICIPLE **understood**) **1** to grasp with the mind the meaning, nature, explanation, or implication of. **2** to know, believe, or infer, from information received. **3** to have a sympathetic awareness of the character or nature of. **4** *intrans.* to grasp what is said. **5** *intrans.* to be sympathetic. [from Anglo-Saxon *understandan*]

understandable *adj.* capable of being understood; reasonable.

understandably *adv.* **1** in an understandable way. **2** so as to be understood.

understanding — *noun* **1** the act of understanding, or the ability to understand. **2** a person's perception or interpretation of information received. **3** an informal agreement. **4** a sympathetic harmony of viewpoints. **5** a condition agreed upon: *on the understanding that you stay for six months.* — *adj.* sympathetic to, or keenly aware of, the feelings and opinions of others.

understate *verb* to describe as being less or more moderate than is really the case, or to express in very restrained or moderate terms, often for ironic or dramatic effect.

understatement *noun* something that is understated.

understood past tense and past participle of UNDERSTAND. — *adj.* **1** implied but not expressed or stated. **2** realized without being, or needing to be, openly stated.

understudy — *verb trans., intrans.* (**understudies, understudied**) to study (a role), or study the role of (an actor), so as to be able to take over if the need arises. — *noun* (PL. **understudies**) a person who understudies.

undertake *verb* (PAST TENSE **undertook**; PAST PARTICIPLE **undertaken**) **1** to accept (a duty, responsibility, or task). **2** to promise or agree. [from Middle English *undertaken*, to entrap]

undertaker *noun* a person whose job is organizing funerals and preparing dead bodies for burial or cremation.

undertaking *noun* **1** a duty, responsibility, or task undertaken. **2** a promise or guarantee. **3** the work of an undertaker.

Under the Volcano a novel by Malcolm Lowry (1947). It describes the last day in the life of Geoffrey Firmin, the alcoholic, ex-British Consul in Cuernavaca, Mexico.

undertone *noun* **1** a quiet tone of voice. **2** an underlying quality, emotion, or atmosphere. **3** a subdued sound or shade of a colour.

undertook see UNDERTAKE.

undertow *noun* **1** the strong current that flows away from the shore underneath a breaking wave. **2** any undercurrent that flows in the opposite direction to the surface current.

undervalue *verb* to place too low a value on.

underwater *adj., adv.* below the surface of water.

underwear *noun* clothes worn under shirts, trousers, dresses, and skirts.

underwent see UNDERGO.

underworld *noun* **1** the world of organized crime. **2** *Mythol.* a world beneath the earth's surface, the home of the souls of the dead.

underwrite *verb* (PAST TENSE **underwrote**; PAST PARTICIPLE **underwritten**) **1** to agree to finance (a commercial venture), and accept the loss in the event of failure. **2** to agree to buy, or find a buyer for, leftover shares from (a sale of shares to the public). **3** to issue (an insurance policy), accepting the risk involved.

underwriter *noun* a person who underwrites insurance.

undesirable — *adj.* unpleasant or objectionable in some way. — *noun* a person or thing considered undesirable.

undesirably *adv.* in an undesirable way; to an undesirable extent.

undid see UNDO.

undies *pl. noun colloq.* items of (especially women's) underwear.

undo *verb* (**undoes**; PAST TENSE **undid**; PAST PARTICIPLE **undone**) **1** *trans., intrans.* to open, unfasten, or untie. **2** to cancel or reverse the effect or result of. **3** *facetious, literary* to bring about the downfall of: *I am undone!*

undoing *noun* downfall or ruin, or the cause of it.

undone *adj.* **1** unfinished. **2** unfastened. **3** ruined.

undoubted *adj.* beyond doubt or question; clear; evident.

undoubtedly *adv.* without doubt, certainly.

undreamed-of *or* **undreamt-of** *adj.* not imagined, especially thought never to be likely or possible.

undress — *verb* **1** to take the clothes off. **2** *intrans.* to take one's clothes off. — *noun* **1** nakedness, or near-nakedness. **2** casual or informal dress. **3** ordinary uniform as opposed to full military dress.

Undset, Sigrid (1882–1949) Norwegian novelist, born in Kalundborg, Denmark. Her major novels are *Kristin Lavransdatter* (1920–2), a 14c trilogy, and the series *Olav Audunssön* (4 vols, 1925–7). She became a Catholic in 1924 which influenced her later work, most of which had contemporary settings. She was awarded the Nobel Prize for Literature in 1928.

undue *adj.* inappropriately or unjustifiably great; excessive.

undue influence a strong influence over another person, considered to have prevented that person from exercising free will.

undulant fever a remittent fever with swelling of the joints and enlarged spleen; it is caused by the bacterium which produces brucellosis in animals and is transmitted to man by goat's or cow's milk.

undulate *verb intrans.* **1** to move in or like waves. **2** to be wavy. [from Latin *unda*, wave]

undulation *noun* **1** undulating. **2** a wave-like motion or form. **3** waviness. **4** a wave.

unduly *adv.* excessively; unreasonably.

undying *adj.* everlasting; eternal.

unearned *adj.* **1** *said of income* gained through investments, interest on savings, etc, rather than as wages or fees. **2** not deserved.

unearned income income, such as dividends and interest earned on savings, that is not remuneration for work done.

unearth *verb* **1** to dig up out of the ground. **2** to discover by searching or rummaging.

unearthliness *noun* an unearthly state or quality.

unearthly *adj.* **1** weird; ghostly. **2** *colloq.* outrageous, especially outrageously early: *at this unearthly hour.* **3** not of this earth; heavenly or hellish.

unease *or* **uneasiness** *noun* an uneasy state or quality.

uneasily *adv.* in an uneasy way.

uneasy *adj.* (**uneasier, uneasiest**) **1** nervous, anxious, or unsettled; ill at ease. **2** unlikely to prove lasting; unstable. **3** causing anxiety; unsettling.

uneaten *adj.* not eaten.

uneconomic *adj.* not conforming to the principles of sound economics, especially unprofitable.

uneconomical *adj.* not economical; wasteful.

UN Economic and Social Council the 54-member body elected by the UN General Assembly. It supervises the work of various committees, commissions, and expert bodies in the economic and social area, and co-ordinates the work of UN specialized agencies.

unemployed — *adj.* **1** not having a paid job. **2** not in use. — *noun* (**the unemployed**) unemployed people.

unemployment *noun* **1** the state of being unemployed. **2** the number of unemployed people.
◇ Unemployment in Britain has peaked at three million or more in two periods in the 20c, the first in the Great Depression of the 1930s and the second in the early 1980s. The methods used to calculate the total number of unemployed people have varied over the years and it is therefore difficult to make accurate comparisons between the official statistics and 'real' levels of unemployment.

unemployment benefit a regular payment made to an unemployed worker through the national insurance scheme.

unequal *adj.* **1** not equal in quantity, value, or rank. **2** not evenly matched or balanced. **3** (**unequal to something**) unable to carry it out, deal with it, etc. **4** not uniform; varying.

unequalled *adj.* not matched by any other; without equal; supreme.

unequivocal *adj.* clearly stated or expressed; unambiguous.

unequivocally *adv.* in an unequivocal way.

unerring *adj.* consistently true or accurate; never making an error or missing the mark.

UNESCO *abbrev.* United Nations Educational, Scientific, and Cultural Organization.

uneven *adj.* **1** not smooth or flat; bumpy. **2** *said of a contest* with sides poorly matched; unequal. **3** not uniform or consistent; varying.

uneventful *adj.* during which nothing interesting or out of the ordinary happens; uninteresting, routine.

uneventfully *adv.* routinely; without much happening.

unexampled *adj.* **1** unprecedented. **2** unequalled.

unexceptionable *adj.* so inoffensive, excellent, or suitable as to make criticism or objection impossible.

unexceptional *adj.* ordinary; run-of-the-mill.

unfailing *adj.* remaining constant; never weakening or failing.

unfailingly *adv.* without fail.

unfair *adj.* **1** not fair or just. **2** involving deceit or dishonesty.

unfairly *adv.* in an unfair way.

unfairness *noun* being unfair; an instance of this.

unfaithful *adj.* **1** breaking faith with a sexual partner by having a sexual relationship with someone else. **2** not loyal. **3** not true to a promise. **4** not accurate as a copy or reproduction.

unfathomable *adj.* **1** that cannot be understood or fathomed. **2** too deep to measure or fathom.

unfavourable *adj.* **1** not encouraging or helping; adverse. **2** not liking, agreeing, or approving.

unfavourably *adv.* in an unfavourable way; so as to be unfavourable.

unfeeling *adj.* unsympathetic; hard-hearted.

unfettered *adj.* not controlled or restrained.

Unfinished Symphony Franz Schubert's Symphony No.8 in B minor (D759, 1822). Only the first two movements were completed.

unfit *adj.* **1** not meeting required standards; not good enough. **2** not fit, especially physically.

unfitted *adj.* **1** not provided with fittings. **2** not adapted or suited.

unflappability *noun* being unflappable.

unflappable *adj. colloq.* never becoming agitated or alarmed; always remaining calm.

unflappably *adv.* in an unflappable way.

unfledged *adj.* **1** *said of a bird* not yet having developed adult flight feathers. **2** young and inexperienced.

unflinching *adj.* showing a fearless determination in the face of danger or difficulty.

unfold *verb* **1** to open out the folds of; to spread out. **2** *intrans.* to be opened out or spread out. **3** *intrans.* to develop, or be revealed, gradually.

Unforgiven a US film directed by Clint Eastwood (1992). It is a sombre revival of the Western, set in a town where the sherriff (played by Gene Hackman) has outlawed firearms. Eastwood stars as an ageing killer hired by the women in a brothel to avenge the slashing of one prostitute's face.

unforgiven *adj.* not forgiven.

unforgiving *adj.* not ready or disposed to forgive; intolerant.

unfortunate — *adj.* **1** having bad luck. **2** resulting from or constituting bad luck: *an* *unfortunate injury.* **3** regrettable. — *noun* an unfortunate person.

unfortunately *adv.* as is unfortunate; regrettably.

unfounded *adj.* not based on fact; without foundation; groundless.

unfreeze *verb* (PAST TENSE **unfroze**; PAST PARTICIPLE **unfrozen**) **1** *trans., intrans.* to thaw or cause to thaw. **2** to free (eg prices or funds) from a restriction or control imposed, eg by a government.

unfrock same as DEFROCK.

unfunny *adj.* not funny; not amusing.

unfurl *verb trans., intrans.* to open out from a rolled-up or tied-up state.

ungainliness *noun* an ungainly manner.

ungainly *adj.* (**ungainlier, ungainliest**) awkward and ungraceful in movement. [from obsolete *gainly*, graceful]

Ungaretti, Giuseppe (1888–1970) Italian poet, born in Alexandria, Egypt. He fought in the Italian army in World War I, and was Professor of Italian Literature at São Paulo, Brazil (1936–42), and at Rome (1942–58). His collection, *Il porto sepolto* (The Buried Port, 1916), which is characterized by symbolism, compressed imagery, and modern verse structure, lies at the foundation of the hermetic movement. Later works include *Il dolore* (Sorrow, 1947), and *Vito d'un uomo* (Life of a Man, 1969).

Ungaro, Emanuel (Maffeolti) (1933–) French fashion designer, born in Aix-en-Provence of Italian parents. He trained to join the family tailoring business, but went instead to Paris in 1955, where he worked for a small tailoring firm, and later joined Cristóbal Balenciaga. In 1965 he opened his own house, with Sonia Knapp designing his fabrics. Initially featuring rigid lines, his styles later softened. In 1968 he produced his first ready-to-wear lines.

Ungava-Quebec Crater see CHUBB CRATER.

UN General Assembly the plenary body which controls much of the UN's work, supervises the subsidiary organs, sets priorities, and debates major issues of international affairs.

ungodliness *noun* being ungodly.

ungodly *adj.* **1** wicked or sinful. **2** *colloq.* outrageous, especially outrageously early.

ungovernable *adj., said of a temper, etc* uncontrollable.

unguarded *adj.* **1** without guard; unprotected. **2** showing a lack of caution or alertness.

unguardedly *adv.* in an unguarded way.

unguent *noun* ointment. [from Latin *unguere*, to anoint]

ungulate *Biol.* — *adj.* hoofed. — *noun* a hoofed mammal. [from Latin *ungula*, hoof, claw]

unhand *verb old use, literary* to let go of; to take one's hands off.

unhappily *adv.* in an unhappy way, sadly.

unhappiness *noun* being unhappy, sadness.

unhappy *adj.* (**unhappier, unhappiest**) **1** sad; in low spirits. **2** being the result of, or bringing, misfortune; unfortunate.

unhealthily *adv.* in an unhealthy way.

unhealthiness *noun* an unhealthy state.

unhealthy *adj.* (**unhealthier, unhealthiest**) **1** suffering from, or showing evidence of, ill health. **2** damaging to health. **3** causing or likely to cause anxiety or worry; psychologically damaging. **4** flouting or corrupting moral standards.

unheard *adj.* **1** not heard. **2** not heeded; ignored.

unheard-of *adj.* **1** not known to have ever happened or been done before; unprecedented. **2** not at all famous; unknown.

unhinge *verb* to cause (a person, or a person's mind) to become unbalanced.

unhinged *adj.* **1** *said of a door, etc* off the hinges. **2** *said of a person* deranged, crazy.

unholy *adj.* (**unholier, unholiest**) **1** wicked; sinful; irreligious. **2** *colloq.* outrageous; frightful.

unholy alliance an alliance that seems unnatural, especially because it is between adversaries, often formed for malicious purposes against a third party.

unhorse *verb* to throw or force (a rider) off a horse.

uni *noun colloq.* a university.

uni- *combining form* forming words meaning 'one, a single': *unidirectional*. [from Latin *unus*, one]

unicameral *adj.* having only one law-making body or chamber.

UNICEF *abbrev.* United Nations Children's Fund.

unicellular *adj.* denoting an organism or structure that consists of a single cell, eg bacteria, protozoa, and many spores.

unicorn *noun* a mythical animal in the form of a (usually white) horse with a long straight horn on its forehead. [from Latin *cornu*, horn]
◇ In medieval legend it could be captured only by a virgin putting its head in her lap. It seems likely that the unicorn was based on stories of the rhinoceros.

unicycle *noun* an acrobat's cycle consisting of a single wheel with a seat and pedals attached.

unicyclist *noun* a person who rides a unicycle.

Unidad Popular a coalition of six left-wing political parties in Chile (Communists, Socialists, Radicals, and three minor groups) formed to support the presidential candidacy and government (1970–3) of Salvador Allende. [from Spanish *unidad popular*, popular unity]

unidentified *adj.* **1** not identified. **2** too strange to identify.

unidentified flying object see UFO.

unification *noun* the act of unifying, or the state of being unified. [from UNI- + Latin *facere*, to make]

Unification Church, also called **the Moonies** a religious movement founded (1954) in Korea by the Rev Sun Myung Moon. Its teachings, based on Moon's book *Divine Principle*, which includes a special interpretation of the Bible and revelations allegedly from God, posit that the purpose of creation was to establish a perfect family, but the Fall frustrated its realization until its fulfilment in Moon and his wife. Its rituals include mass weddings conducted by Moon, and it insists that 'unification' requires unreserved commitment from its adherents. It has extensive commercial interests, and some of its activities have generated public hostility, bringing accusations of brainwashing.

uniform — *noun* a distinctive set of clothing worn by members of a particular organization or profession. — *adj.* not changing or varying in form or nature. [from UNI- + Latin *forma*, form]

uniformed *adj.* wearing a uniform.

uniformitarianism *noun Geol.* the principle which states that the results of past geological events resemble the results of geological processes and phenomena occurring in the present, and can be used to explain them.

uniformity *noun* a uniform state or quality.

Uniformity, Acts of a series of Acts passed (1549, 1552, 1559, 1662) by English parliaments aimed at imposing religious uniformity by requiring the use of the Church of England liturgy as contained in the Book of Common Prayer (various editions, 1549–1662). The Act of

1552 penalized Catholic recusants, and that of 1662 excluded dissenting Protestant clergy.

uniformly *adv.* in a uniform way.

unify *verb* (**unifies, unified**) to bring together to form a single unit or whole. [from UNI- + Latin *facere*, to make]

unilateral *adj.* affecting, involving, or done by only one person or group among several. [from UNI- + Latin *latus*, side]

unilateralism *noun* a policy or practice of unilateral action, especially unilateral nuclear disarmament.

unilateralist — *noun* a person who supports unilateralism. — *adj.* relating to or involving unilateralism.

unilaterally *adv.* in a unilateral way; by or on one side alone.

unimpeachable *adj.* indisputably reliable or honest.

uninspired *adj., said of a performance, etc* lacking feeling or imagination; dull.

uninspiring *adj.* that fails to inspire interest, enthusiasm, or emotion.

uninterested *adj.* not taking an interest; not interested. See also DISINTERESTED.

UN International Court of Justice the body of 15 judges appointed by the UN Security Council and the General Assembly. As only states can bring issues before it, its jurisdiction depends on the consent of the states who are a party to a dispute. It also offers advisory opinions to various organs of the UN.

union *noun* **1** the act of uniting or the state of being united. **2** an association of people or groups united in a common (especially political) purpose. **3** a trade union. **4** an organization concerned with the welfare of the students in a college, university, etc; also, the building housing this, often also the site of canteen and recreational facilities. **5** agreement or harmony. **6** *formal* marriage; wedlock. **7** *Maths.* a set comprising the members of two smaller sets. **8** *formal* sexual intercourse. [from Latin *unio*, from *unus*, one]

Union, Acts of the Acts which joined England in legislative union with Scotland (1707) and Ireland (1800). The 1707 Act enabled 45 Scottish MPs to join the new House of Commons of Great Britain, and 16 peers to join the House of Lords; the Scottish legal system, however, remained separate. The 1800 Act created the United Kingdom of Great Britain and Ireland (in effect 1801–1922). Union was brought about after the collapse of the Irish rebellion (1798) in order to increase British security in the French wars. The Irish parliament was abolished; 100 Irish MPs were added to the UK House of Commons, and 32 peers to the Lords. The Churches of England and Ireland were united.

union flag the Union Jack.

unionism *noun* **1** the principle or policy of combining. **2** the principles and practices of trade unions.

unionist *noun* **1** a person supporting or believing in trade unions. **2** a person in favour of creating or maintaining a political union between states or countries, especially (**Unionist**) between Northern Ireland and Britain.

unionization *or* **unionisation** *noun* the process or policy of unionizing.

unionize *or* **unionise** *verb* **1** to recruit into a trade union. **2** to organize (a workforce), or the workforce of (a company), into a trade union.

Union Jack the national flag of the United Kingdom, combining the crosses of St George, St Andrew, and St Patrick.

Union Movement a party formed (1948) by Sir Oswald Mosley to succeed his New Party (1931) and the British Union of Fascists (1932). It put up candidates in 1959–66, but failed to secure many votes. Its main platform was opposition to immigration, but it also aimed to unite Europe into a vast market to buy from and sell to Africa. Mosley gave up the leadership in 1966, and the movement soon died out.

Union of European Football Associations (ABBREV. **UEFA**) a football organization founded in 1954 by the representatives of the association football governing bodies of 30 European nations, and now consisting of 34 members. UEFA is responsible for organizing the three major European club tournaments: the Champions' Cup, the Cup Winners' Cup, and the UEFA Cup. It also runs its own European championship, a World Cup style of competition for national teams.

unique *adj.* **1** being the only one of its kind; having no equal. **2** (**unique to something** *or* **someone**) belonging solely to *or* associated solely with them. **3** *colloq.* extremely unusual or excellent. [from Latin *unicus*, from *unus*, one]

uniquely *adv.* in a unique way; to a unique degree.

uniqueness *noun* being unique.

unisex *adj.* suited to, for use by, or wearable by, both men and women.

unison *noun* **1** *Mus.* sameness of pitch in voices or instruments; the state of singing or playing all in the same pitch. **2** the state of acting all in the same way at the same time. **3** complete agreement. [from UNI- + Latin *sonus*, sound]

unit — *noun* **1** a single item or element regarded as the smallest subdivision of a whole; a single person or thing. **2** a set of mechanical or electrical parts, or a group of workers, performing a specific function within a larger construction or organization. **3** a standard measure of a physical quantity, such as time or distance, specified multiples of which are used to express its size, eg SI units. **4** *Physics* a kilowatt-hour. **5** an item of furniture combining with others to form a set; a set of such items. **6** any whole number less than 10. **7** any subdivision of a military force. — *adj.* relating to the quantity of one, eg unit mass. [see UNITY]

Unitarian — *noun* a member of a religious group originally comprising Christians who believed God to be a single entity rather than a Trinity of Father, Son, and Holy Spirit, now including members holding a broad spectrum of beliefs. — *adj.* relating to this group.
◇ As an organized group, the Unitarians date back to the Anabaptists at the time of the Reformation. John Biddle (1615–62) is regarded as their founder in England. Modern Unitariansism is based on reason and conscience, rather than scriptural authority, and has no formal doctrine or creed.

Unitarianism *noun* the beliefs of Unitarians.

unitary *adj.* **1** of a unit or units. **2** characterized by unity or uniformity.

unite *verb* **1** *trans., intrans.* to make or become a single unit or whole. **2** *trans., intrans.* to bring or come together in a common purpose or belief. **3** to have (eg features or characteristics) in combination. [from Latin *unire*]

united *adj.* **1** joined together, combined. **2** in combination, resulting from union.

United Arab Emirates, Arabic **Ittihad al-Imarat al-Arabiyah**, formerly **Trucial States** POP (1992e) 1.6m, a federation comprising seven internally self-governing emirates, in the E central Arabian Peninsula. AREA 83 600sq km/32 300sq mi. It is bounded N by the Arabian Gulf, E by Oman, and S and W by Saudi Arabia. CAPITAL Abu Dhabi. CHIEF TOWNS Dubai, Sharjah, Ras al Khaimah. TIME ZONE GMT +4. The population is 19% Emirian, 23% other Arabs, and 50% S Asian; Islam is the chief religion. OFFICIAL LANGUAGE Arabic. CURRENCY the dirham. PHYSICAL DESCRIPTION located along the S shore (Trucial Coast) of the Arabian Gulf; Al

United Arab Emirates

Fujairah has a coastline along the Gulf of Oman; salt marshes predominate on the coast; barren desert and gravel plain inland; the Hajar Mts in Al Fujairah rise to over 1 000m. CLIMATE hot with limited rainfall; winter temperatures average 21°C, with high humidity (70%+); less humid in summer, with maximum temperatures rising to 45°C; sandstorms are common; the average annual rainfall in Abu Dhabi is 32mm. HISTORY a peace treaty with Britain was signed by rulers of the Trucial States in 1820; the new state formed by six emirates was established in 1971; Ras al Khaimah joined in 1972. GOVERNMENT governed by a Supreme Council comprising the hereditary rulers of the seven emirates. ECONOMY an important commercial and trading centre; the economy is based on oil and gas with Abu Dhabi the major producer, followed by Dubai; iron and steel; petrochemicals; construction; ship repairing; fishing; light industry; tourism; saline water supplies have restricted agriculture to the oases and the irrigated valleys of the Hajar Mts: vegetables, fruits, dates, dairy farming.

United Gold Coast Convention (ABBREV. **UGCC**) a political party (founded 1947), led originally by Dr J B Danquah (1895–1965), the first organization to seek self-government within a short timeframe. For a while its General Secretary was Kwame Nkrumah, but he broke away to form the more radical Convention People's Party (CPP) and defeated the UGCC in the 1951 elections, after which the latter was dissolved.

United Irishmen, Society of a society formed (1791) in Belfast by Protestant lawyer Wolfe Tone, which supported the French Revolution and espoused both religious equality and parliamentary reform, with support at first primarily located in Ulster. United Irishmen became increasingly associated with support for Catholicism, and the Society was instrumental in organizing French support for the unsuccessful Irish rebellion of 1798, after which it declined.

United Kingdom (ABBREV. **UK**) in full **United Kingdom of Great Britain and Northern Ireland** POP (1989e) 57.2m, a kingdom in W Europe, comprising England, Scotland, Wales, and Northern Ireland. AREA 244 755sq km/94 475sq mi. CAPITAL London. CHIEF TOWNS Belfast, Birmingham, Bradford, Cardiff, Edinburgh, Glasgow, Leeds, Liverpool, Manchester, Newcastle upon Tyne, Sheffield. The population is 81.5% English, 9.6% Scottish, 2.4% Irish, 1.9% Welsh, and 2% West Indian, Asian, and African; Christianity is the chief religion. OFFICIAL LANGUAGE English; Welsh and Gaelic are spoken by minorities. CURRENCY the pound sterling. HISTORY Wales was effectively joined to England in 1301, then Scotland was joined under one crown in 1603 (and by legislative union in 1707), and Ireland in 1801 (the United Kingdom of Great Britain and Ireland); the present name dates from 1922, following the establishment of the Irish Free State. GOVERNMENT a kingdom with a monarch as head of state; governed by a bicameral Parliament comprising an elected 650-member House of Commons, and a House of Lords with hereditary peers, life peers, Anglican bishops, and law lords; a Cabinet is appointed by the Prime Minister.

United Kingdom Atomic Energy Authority (ABBREV. **UKAEA**) an authority set up by the Atomic Energy Authority Act in 1954, which has prime responsibility for research and the development of nuclear power in the UK on behalf of the government.

United Nations (ABBREV. **UN**) an organization formed to maintain world peace and foster international co-operation, formally established on 24 Oct 1945 with 51 founder countries (178 members in 1992). The UN Charter, which was drafted during World War II by the USA, UK, and USSR, remains virtually unaltered despite the growth in membership and activities. There are

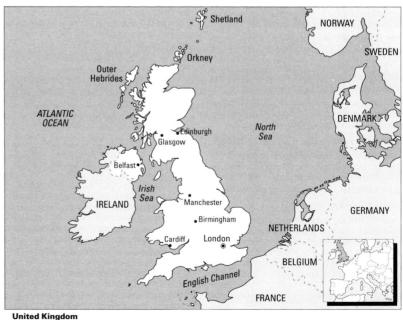

United Kingdom

six 'principal organs': the General Assembly; the Security Council; the Secretariat; the International Court of Justice; the Economic and Social Council; and the Trusteeship Council. In addition to the organs established under the Charter, there is a range of subsidiary agencies, many with their own constitutions and membership, and some pre-dating the UN. The main agencies are the Food and Agriculture Organization, the Intergovernmental Maritime Consultative Organization, the International Atomic Energy Authority, the International Bank for Reconstruction and Development ('World Bank'), the International Civil Aviation Organization, the International Development Association, the International Finance Corporation, the International Fund for Agricultural Development, the International Labour Organization, the International Monetary Fund, the United Nations Educational, Scientific, and Cultural Organization, the Universal Postal Union, the International Telecommunication Union, the World Meterological Organization, and the World Health Organization. It is generally seen as a forum where states pursue their national interest, rather than as an institution of world government, but it has considerable impact. See panel p. 1330.

United Nations Conference on Trade and Development (ABBREV. **UNCTAD**) an organ of the UN, established by the 1964 General Assembly to consider how to increase international trade and promote economic development. It meets irregularly, though its executive board meets annually, and provides the main forum through which underdeveloped countries can liaise with the major economic powers.

United Nations Educational, Scientific, and Cultural Organization (ABBREV. **UNESCO**) an organization founded (1946) to promote collaboration among nations through education, science, and culture. In the 1980s, concern among the non-communist industrialized countries over the organization's administrative inefficiency and its allegedly inappropriate political aims led to the departure of the USA (1985), which had a major impact financially, and also of the UK (1985) and Singapore. UNESCO's headquarters are in Paris, and in 1992 there were 166 member states.

United Provinces of the Netherlands the seven sovereign states of the Dutch Republic (Holland, Zeeland, Gelderland, Utrecht, Friesland, Groningen, and Overijssel), roughly comprising the present kingdom of the Netherlands, but originally part of the Burgundian lands until they achieved independence from the Spanish Crown in the Eighty Years War (1568–1648). Also known as the Dutch Republic, it declined in the 18c and collapsed during the Revolutionary Wars (1795).

United Service Organizations (ABBREV. **USO**) in the USA, an association of agencies, founded in 1941. It includes the YMCA, YWCA, and the Salvation Army, and aims to provide for the social and recreational needs of the US armed forces.

United States military academies in the USA, federal training institutions for people who want to become officers in the US armed forces. The United States Air Force (USAF) Academy was formed by Act of Congress in 1948, and is located near Colorado Springs, USA. The United States Military Academy was founded in 1802, and is now in West Point on the Hudson River, New York State. The United States Naval Academy was founded in 1845, and is in Annapolis, Maryland. Women have been admitted to these institutions since 1976. The United States Coast Guard (USCG) Academy was founded in 1876, and has been located at New London, Connecticut, since 1936.

United Nations Membership	
1945	Argentina, Australia, Belgium, Belorussian SSR, Bolivia, Brazil, Canada, Chile, China (Taiwan) (to 1971), Colombia, Costa Rica, Cuba, Czechoslovakia, Denmark, Dominican Republic, Ecuador, Egypt, El Salvador, Ethiopia, France, Greece, Guatemala, Haiti, Honduras, India, Iran, Iraq, Lebanon, Liberia, Luxembourg, Mexico, Netherlands, New Zealand, Nicaragua, Norway, Panama, Paraguay, Peru, Philippines, Poland, Saudi Arabia, South Africa, Syria, Turkey, Ukrainian SSR, USSR, UK, USA, Uruguay, Venezuela, Yugoslavia
1946	Afghanistan, Iceland, Sweden, Thailand
1947	Pakistan, Yemen
1948	Burma
1949	Israel
1950	Indonesia
1955	Albania, Austria, Bulgaria, Kampuchea (formerly Cambodia), Sri Lanka (formerly Ceylon), Finland, Hungar, Ireland, Italy, Jordan, Laos, Libya, Nepal, Portugal, Romania, Spain
1956	Japan, Morocco, Sudan, Tunisia
1957	Ghana, Malaya (Malasia, 1963)
1958	Guinea
1960	Benin (formerly Dahomey), Burkina Faso (formerly Upper Volta), Cameroon, Central African Republic, Chad, Congo, Ivory Coast (Côte d'Ivoire), Cyprus, Gabon, Madagascar, Mali, Niger, Nigeria, Senegal, Somalia, Togo, Zaire
1961	Mauritania, Mongolia, Sierra Leone, Tanganyika (within Tanzania, 1964)
1962	Algeria, Burundi, Jamaica, Rwanda, Trinidad and Togabo, Uganda
1963	Kenya, Kuwait, Zanzibar (within Tanzania, 1964)
1964	Malawi, Malta, Zambia, Tanzania
1965	Gambia, Maldives, Singapore
1966	Barbados, Botswana, Guyana, Lesotho
1968	Equatorial Guinea, Mauritius, Swaziland
1970	Fiji
1971	Bahrain, Bhutan, China (People's Republic of), Oman, Qatar, United Arab Emirates
1973	Bahamas, German Democratic Republic, German Federal Republic
1974	Bangladesh, Grenada, Guinea-Bissau
1975	Cape Verde, Comoros, Mozambique, Papua New Guinea, São Tomé and Principe, Surinam
1976	Angola, Seychelles, Western Samoa
1977	Djibouti, Vietnam
1978	Dominica, Solomon Islands
1979	St Lucia
1980	St Vincent and the Grenadines, Zimbabwe
1981	Antigua and Barbuda, Belize, Vanuatu
1983	St Christopher and Nevis
1984	Brunei
1990	Namibia, Yemen (formerly North Yemen and South Yemen) (Germany replaced GDR and GFR)
1991	Estonia, Latvia, Lithuania, Marshall Islands, Micronesia, North Korea, Russia, South Korea
1992	Armenia, Azerbaijan, Kazakhstan, Kirgizia, Moldavia, San Marino, Tadzhikistan, Turkmenistan, Uzbekistan

Prime Ministers of the United Kingdom			
1721–42	Robert Walpole	1855–8	Viscount Palmerston (Henry John Temple)
1742–3	Earl of Wilmington (Spencer Compton)	1858–9	Earl of Derby (Edward George Stanley)
1743–54	Henry Pelham	1859–65	Viscount Palmerston (Henry John Temple)
1754–6	Duke of Newcastle (Thomas Pelham-Holles)	1865–6	Lord John Russell
1756–7	Duke of Devonshire (William Cavendish)	1866–8	Earl of Derby (Edward George Stanley)
1757–62	Duke of Newcastle (Thomas Pelham-Holles)	1868	Benjamin Disraeli
1762–3	Earl of Bute (John Stuart)	1868–74	William Ewart Gladstone
1763–5	George Grenville	1874–80	Benjamin Disraeli
1765–6	Marquess of Rockingham (Charles Watson Wentworth)	1880–5	William Ewart Gladstone
1766–70	Duke of Grafton (Augustus Henry Fitzroy)	1885–6	Marquess of Salisbury (Robert Gascoyne-Cecil)
1770–82	Lord North (Frederick North)	1886	William Ewart Gladstone
1782	Marquess of Rockingham	1886–92	Marquess of Salisbury (Robert Gascoyne-Cecil)
1782–3	Earl of Shelburne (William Petty-Fitzmaurice)	1892–4	William Ewart Gladstone
1783	Duke of Portland (William Henry Cavendish)	1894–5	Earl of Rosebery (Archibald Philip Primrose)
1783–1801	William Pitt the Younger	1895–1902	Marques of Salisbury (Robert Gascoyne-Cecil)
1801–4	Henry Addington	1902–5	Arthur James Balfour
1804–6	William Pitt the Younger	1905–8	Henry Campbell-Bannerman
1806–7	Lord Grenville (William Wyndham)	1908–16	Herbert Henry Asquith
1807–9	Duke of Portland	1916–22	David Lloyd George
1809–12	Spencer Perceval	1922–3	Andrew Bonar Law
1812–27	Earl of Liverpool (Robert Banks Jenkinson)	1923–4	Stanley Baldwin
1827	George Canning	1924	James Ramsay MacDonald
1827–8	Viscount Goderich (Frederick John Robinson)	1924–9	Stanley Baldwin
1828–30	Duke of Wellington (Arthur Wellesley)	1929–35	James Ramsay MacDonald
1830–4	Earl Grey (Charles Grey)	1935–7	Stanley Baldwin
1834	Viscount Melbourne (William Lamb)	1937–40	Arthur Neville Chamberlain
1834–5	Robert Peel	1940–5	Sir Winston Churchill
1835–41	Viscount Melbourne (William Lamb)	1945–51	Clement Attlee
1841–6	Robert Peel	1951–5	Sir Winston Churchill
1846–52	Lord John Russell	1955–7	Anthony Eden
1852	Earl of Derby (Edward George Stanley)	1957–63	Harold Macmillan
1852–5	Lord Aberdeen (George Hamilton-Gordon)	1963–4	Alex Douglas-Home
		1964–70	Harold Wilson
		1970–4	Edward Heath
		1974–6	Harold Wilson
		1976–9	James Callaghan
		1979–90	Margaret Thatcher
		1990–	John Major

United Nations Agencies

Abbreviated form	Full title	Area of concern
ILO	International Labour Organization	Social justice
FAO	Food and Agriculture Organization	Improvement of the production and distribution of agricultural products
UNESCO	United Nations Educational, Scientific and Cultural Organization	Stimulation of popular education and the spread of culture
ICAO	International Civil Aviation Organization	Encouragement of safety measures in international flight
IBRD	International Bank for Reconstruction and Development	Aid of development through investment
IMF	International Monetary Fund	Promotion of international monetary co-operation
UPU	Universal Postal Union	Uniting members within a single postal territory
WHO	World Health Organization	Promotion of the highest standards of health for all people
ITU	International Telecommunication Union	Allocation of frequencies and regulation of procedures
WMO	World Meteorological Organization	Standardization and utilization of meteorological observations
IFC	International Finance Corporation	Promotion of the international flow of private capital
IMCO	Inter-governmental Maritime Consultative Organization	The co-ordination of safety at sea
IDA	International Development Association	Credit on special terms to provide assistance for less developed countries
WIPO	World Intellectual Property Organization	Protection of copyright, designs, inventions etc
IFAD	International Fund for Agriculture Development	Increase of food production in developing countries by the generation of grants or loans

United States of America (ABBREV. **USA**) also called **United States**, and often **America** POP (1992e) 225m, a federal republic in N America and the fourth-largest country in the world. AREA 9 160 454sq km/3 535 935sq mi. It includes the detached states of Alaska and Hawaii. The mainland is bounded N by Canada, E by the Atlantic Ocean, S by the Gulf of Mexico, and W by the Pacific Ocean. Several other islands are formally associated with the USA; these are Puerto Rico, American Samoa, Guam, Virgin Is (of the USA), Northern Marianas, and Palau. TIME ZONES GMT –5 (E coast) to –8 (Pacific Coast), Alaska GMT –9, Hawaii GMT –10.CAPITAL Washington DC. CHIEF TOWNS New York, Chicago, Los Angeles, Philadelphia, Detroit, Houston. In the 19c, millions of immigrants arrived from Europe

and the Far East, many of them refugees, leading to the description of the USA as the 'melting pot' of nations; more recently, large numbers of Spanish-speaking people have arrived, mainly from Mexico and the West Indies; of the many ethnic groups, most are of European origin (including 6.2% Hispanic), and 11% African-American, 1.6% Asian and Pacific, and 0.7% Native American, Inuit, and Aleut. Christianity is the chief religion. OFFICIAL LANGUAGE English; there is a sizeable Spanish-speaking minority. CURRENCY the US dollar. PHYSICAL DESCRIPTION the E Atlantic coastal plain is backed by the Appalachian Mts from the Great Lakes in the N to Alabama in the S; this series of parallel ranges includes the Allegheny, Blue Ridge, and Catskill mountains; to the S the plain broadens out

towards the Gulf of Mexico and into the Florida Peninsula; to the W, the Gulf Plains stretch N to meet the higher Great Plains from which they are separated by the Ozark Mts; further W, the Rocky Mts rise to over 4 500m; the highest point is Mt McKinley, Alaska, at 6 194m; the lowest point is in Death Valley (–86m); drainage in the N is into the St Lawrence R or the Great Lakes; in the E, the Hudson, Delaware, Potomac, and other rivers flow E into the Atlantic Ocean; the central plains of the United States are drained by the great Red River–Missouri–Mississippi River System and by other rivers flowing into the Gulf of Mexico; in the W the main rivers are the Columbia and Colorado. CLIMATE varies from conditions in hot tropical deserts (in the SW) to those typical of Arctic continental regions; most regions are affected by westerly depressions that can bring changeable weather; rainfall is heaviest in the Pacific NW, lightest in the SW; in the Great Plains, wide temperature variation is the result of cold air from the Arctic as well as warm tropical air from the Gulf of Mexico; on the W coast the influence of the Pacific Ocean results in a smaller range of temperatures between summer and winter; on the E coast there is a gradual increase in winter temperatures southwards; the states bordering the Gulf of Mexico are subject to hurricanes and tornadoes moving NE from the Caribbean Sea. HISTORY first settled by migrant groups from Asia over 25 000 years ago; these Native Americans remained undisturbed until the region was explored by the Norse (9c) and the Spanish (16c), who settled in Florida and Mexico; in the 17c, there were settlements by the British, French, Dutch,Germans, and Swedish; many black Africans were introduced as slaves to work on the plantations; in the following century, British control grew; a revolt of the English-speaking colonies in the War of Independence (1775–83) led to the creation of the United States of America, which then lay between the Great Lakes, the Mississippi, and Florida; the Declaration of Independence was made on 4 Jul 1776; Louisiana was sold to the USA by France in 1803 (the Louisiana Purchase) and the westward movement of settlers began; Florida was ceded by Spain in 1819, and further Spanish states joined the Union between 1821 and 1853; in

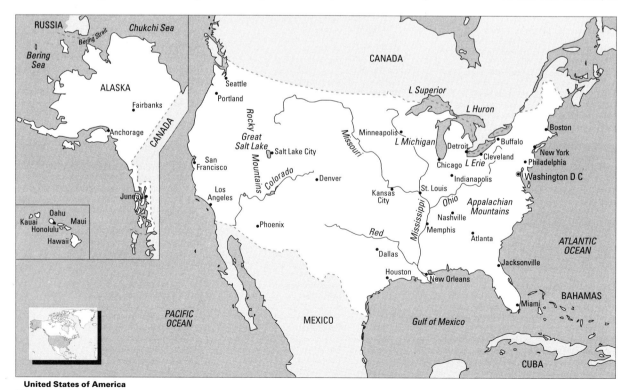

Presidents of the USA

Vice-Presidents in parentheses

1789–97	George Washington (1st) (John Adams)
1797–1801	John Adams (2nd) (Thomas Jefferson)
1801–9	Thomas Jefferson (3rd) (Aaron Burr, 1801–5) (George Clinton, 1805–9)
1809–17	James Madison (4th) (George Clinton, 1809–12) no Vice-President 1812–13 (Elbridge Gerry, 1813–14) no Vice-President 1814–17
1817–25	James Monroe (5th) (Daniel D Tompkins)
1825–9	John Quincy Adams (6th) (John C Calhoun)
1829–37	Andrew Jackson (7th) (John C Calhoun, 1829–32) no Vice-President 1832–3 (Martin Van Buren, 1833–7)
1837–41	Martin Van Buren (8th) (Richard M Johnson)
1841	William Henry Harrison (9th) (John Tyler)
1841–5	John Tyler (10th) no Vice-President
1845–9	James K Polk (11th) (George M Dallas)
1849–50	Zachary Taylor (12th) (Millard Fillmore)
1850–3	Millard Fillmore (13th) no Vice-President
1853–7	Franklin Pierce (14th) (William R King, 1853) no Vice-President 1853–7
1857–61	James Buchanan (15th) (John C Breckinridge)
1861–5	Abraham Lincoln (16th) (Hannibal Hamlin, 1861–5) (Andrew Johnson, 1865)
1865–9	Andrew Johnson (17th) no Vice-President
1869–77	Ulysses S Grant (18th) (Schuyler Colfax, 1869–73) (Henry Wilson, 1873–5) no Vice-President 1875–7
1877–81	Rutherford B Hayes (19th) (William A Wheeler)
1881	James A Garfield (20th) (Chester A Arthur)
1881–5	Chester A Arthur (21st) no Vice-President
1885–9	Grover Cleveland (22nd) (Thomas A Hendricks, 1885) no Vice-President 1885–9
1889–93	Benjamin Harrison (23rd) (Levi P Morton)
1893–7	Grover Cleveland (24th) (Adlai E Stevenson)
1897–1901	William McKinley (25th) (Garret A Hobart, 1897–9) no Vice-President 1899–1901 (Theodore Roosevelt, 1901)
1901–9	Theodore Roosevelt (26th) no Vice-President 1901–5 (Charles W Fairbanks, 1905–9)
1909–13	William Howard Taft (27th) (James S Sherman, 1909–12) no Vice-President 1912–13
1913–21	Woodrow Wilson (28th) (Thomas R Marshall)
1921–3	Warren G Harding (29th) (Calvin Coolidge)
1923–9	Calvin Coolidge (30th) no Vice-President 1923–5 (Charles G Dawes, 1925–9)
1929–33	Herbert Hoover (31st) (Charles Curtis)
1933–45	Franklin D Roosevelt (32nd) (John Nance Garner, 1933–41) (Henry A Wallace, 1941–5) (Harry S Truman, 1945)
1945–53	Harry S Truman (33rd) no Vice-President 1945–9 (Alben W Barkley, 1949–53)
1953–61	Dwight D Eisenhower (34th) (Richard M Nixon)
1961–3	John F Kennedy (35th) (Lyndon B Johnson)
1963–9	Lyndon B Johnson (36th) no Vice-President 1963–5 (Hubert H Humphrey, 1965–9)
1969–74	Richard M Nixon (37th) (Spiro T Agnew, 1969–73) no Vice-President Oct–Dec 1973 (Gerald Ford, 1973–4)
1974–7	Gerald Ford (38th) no Vice-President Aug–Dec 1974 (Nelson A Rockefeller 1974–7)
1977–81	Jimmy Carter (39th) (Walter F Mondale)
1981–9	Ronald Reagan (40th) (George Bush)
1989–93	George Bush (41st) (J Danforth Quayle)
1993–	Bill Clinton (42nd) (Al Gore)

1860–1, 11 Southern states left the Union over the slavery issue, and formed the Confederacy; the Civil War (1861–5) ended in victory for the North, and the Southern states later rejoined the Union; as a result of the North's victory, slavery was abolished in 1865; in 1867 Alaska was purchased from Russia, and the Hawaiian Is were annexed in 1898 (both admitted as states in 1959); entered World War I on the side of the Allies in 1917; Native Americans were given the right to become US citizens in 1924; in 1929 the stockmarket on Wall Street crashed, resulting in the great economic depression; after the Japanese attack on Pearl Harbor in 1941 the USA entered World War II; assassination of President J F Kennedy in 1963; the campaign for black civil rights developed in the 1960s, accompanied by much civil disturbance; from 1964 to 1975 the USA intervened in the Vietnamese Civil War, supporting non-Communist South Vietnam; led the space exploration programme of the 1960s and 1970s (in 1969 US astronaut Neil Armstrong was the first person on the Moon); the Watergate scandal (1972–4) forced President Richard Nixon to resign; in 1986 further scandal over arms sales to Iran to fund Contra rebels in Nicaragua; Wall Street crashed again in 1987; Cold War between the USA and the USSR came to an end in 1989; in the 1991 Gulf War US troops led the assault against Saddam Hussein following Iraq's invasion of Kuwait; in 1992 there was rioting in Los Angeles and other cities over racial issues; the worst storms to hit the USA in the 20c resulted in deaths in 17 states in 1993. GOVERNMENT the Congress consists of two bodies: a 435-member House of Representatives elected for two-year terms, and a 100-member Senate elected for six-year terms; a President, who is elected every four years by a College of State Representatives, appoints an Executive Cabinet responsible to Congress; the USA is divided into 50 federal states and the District of Columbia, each state having its own two-body legislature and Governor. ECONOMY in the 20c the USA has become the chief industrial nation in the world, with vast mineral and agricultural resources, a highly diversified economy, and an advanced system of communications and transportation; increases in consumption in the 1980s led to an unfavourable balance of trade, and the need to reduce public spending. See panels, pp. 1332–33.

United States Open a golf tournament, the second-oldest of golf's four major tournaments, first held in Newport, Rhode Island on 4 Oct 1895. It is now played over 72 holes at a different course each year. See also US OPEN.

United States Trust Territory of the Pacific Islands a territory situated in the W Pacific Ocean, N of Papua New Guinea. It formerly comprised the Commonwealth of the N Mariana Is, the Federated States of Micronesia, the Republic of Palau, and the Marshall Is. The population was mostly Micronesian, with some Polynesian. OFFICIAL LANGUAGE English. HISTORY administered by Japan in the inter-war years; placed under UN trusteeship in 1947; the Northern Mariana Is became a self-governing commonwealth of the USA in 1978 and the Federated States of Micronesia and the Marshall Is each achieved independence in 1991; Palau is the last remaining component. ECONOMY based on agriculture; fisheries; tourism; coconuts, sugar cane, cassava, yams, copra; fish processing.

Unit One a group of avant-garde British artists formed in 1933. Leading members included the sculptors Henry Moore and Barbara Hepworth, and the painter Paul Nash.

unit price the price per item of goods supplied.

unit trust 1 an investment scheme in which clients' money is invested in various companies, with the combined shares purchased divided into units which are allocated in multiples to each client according to the individual amount invested. **2** a financial organization operating such a scheme.

Unity a female first name, after the concept of *unity*.

unity *noun* (PL. **unities**) **1** the state of being a single unified whole; oneness. **2** a single unified whole. **3** agreement or harmony between different members or elements. **4** *Maths.* the number 1. [from Latin *unitas*, from *unus*, one]

Univ. *abbrev.* University.

univalency *noun Chem.* a univalent state.

univalent *adj. Chem.* monovalent, ie describing an atom of an element that has a valency of one.

universal *adj.* **1** of the universe. **2** of, relating to, or affecting the whole world or all people. **3** of, relating to, or affecting all the people or things in a particular group. **4** *colloq.* widespread; general; all-round.

universal indicator *Chem.* a mixture of several chemical indicators, used to measure the pH (relative acidity or alkalinity) of a solution, that shows a whole range of different colours corresponding to different pH values.

universality *noun* being universal.

universal joint *or* **universal coupling** a joint allowing movement in all directions.

universally *adv.* in a universal way; everywhere.

universe *noun* **1** the cosmos, ie the whole of space and all the galaxies, stars, planets, moons, asteroids, and other bodies contained within it. **2** the world; all people. [from Latin *universus*, whole]
◇ It is thought that the universe was formed after the Big Bang, which probably took place 13 to 20 billion years ago. It has been expanding ever since, and contains millions of galaxies, collected into clusters and superclusters, rather than being scattered evenly throughout space.

university *noun* (PL. **universities**) **1** a higher education institution with the authority to award degrees, traditionally in non-vocational subjects. **2** its buildings, staff, or students. [from Latin *universitas*, group of scholars]
◇ Universities usually provide courses leading to

US States

Population: figures to the nearest 100 000 from the 1990 population census. Abbreviations are given after each state name: the first is the common abbreviation, the second the ZIP (postal) code.

Alabama (Ala; AL)
Entry to Union 1819 (22nd)
Pop 4.1m
Nickname Camellia State, Heart of Dixie
Inhabitant Alabamian
Area 133 911 sq km/51 705 sq mi
Capital Montgomery
Bird Yellowhammer *Fish* Tarpon
Flower Camellia *Tree* Southern Pine

Alaska (Alaska; AK)
Entry to Union 1959 (49th)
Pop 587 000
Nickname Mainland State, The Last Frontier
Inhabitant Alaskan
Area 1 518 748 sq km/586 412 sq mi
Capital Juneau
Bird Willow Ptarmigan *Fish* King Salmon
Flower Forget-me-not
Gemstone Jade *Tree* Sitka Spruce

Arizona (Ariz; AZ)
Entry to Union 1912 (48th)
Pop 3.8m
Nickname Apache State, Grand Canyon State
Inhabitant Arizonan
Area 295 249 sq km/113 966 sq mi
Capital Phoenix
Bird Cactus Wren *Flower* Giant Cactus
Gemstone Turquoise *Tree* Paloverde

Arkansas (Ark; AR)
Entry to Union 1836 (25th)
Pop 2.4m
Nickname Bear State, Land of Opportunity
Inhabitant Arkansan
Area 137 749 sq km/53 171 sq mi
Capital Little Rock
Bird Mockingbird *Flower* Apple Blossom
Gemstone Diamond *Tree* Pine

California (Calif; CA)
Entry to Union 1850 (31st)
Pop 30.9m
Nickname Golden State
Inhabitant Californian
Area 411 033 sq km/158 706 sq mi
Capital Sacramento
Animal California Grizzly Bear
Bird California Valley Quail
Fish South Fork Golden Trout
Flower Golden Poppy
Tree California Redwood

Colorado (Colo; CO)
Entry to Union 1876 (38th)
Pop 3.5m
Nickname Centennial State
Inhabitant Coloradan
Area 269 585 sq km/104 061 sq mi
Capital Denver
Animal Rocky Mountain Bighorn Sheep
Bird Lark Bunting *Flower* Columbine
Gemstone Aquamarine *Tree* Blue Spruce

Connecticut (Conn; CT)
Entry to Union 1788 (5th)
Pop 3.3m
Nickname Nutmeg State, Constitution State
Inhabitant Nutmegger
Area 12 996 sq km/5 017 sq mi
Capital Hartford
Bird American Robin *Flower* Mountain Laurel
Gemstone Garnet *Tree* White Oak

Delaware (Del; DE)
Entry to Union 1787 (1st)
Pop 689 000
Nickname Diamond State, First State
Inhabitant Delawarean
Area 5 296 sq km/2 045 sq mi
Capital Dover
Bird Blue Hen Chicken *Flower* Peach Blossom
Tree American Holly

District of Columbia (DC; DC)
Pop 589 000
Inhabitant Washingtonian
Area 174 sq km/67 sq mi
Capital Washington
Bird Woodthrush *Flower* American Beauty Rose
Tree Scarlet Oak

Florida (Fla; FL)
Entry to Union 1845 (27th)
Pop 13.5m
Nickname Everglade State, Sunshine State
Inhabitant Floridian
Area 151 934 sq km/58 647 sq mi
Capital Tallahassee
Bird Mockingbird *Flower* Orange Blossom
Gemstone Agatized Coral *Tree* Sabal Palm

Georgia (Ga; GA)
Entry to Union 1788 (4th)
Pop 6.8m
Nickname Empire State of the South, Peach State
Inhabitant Georgian
Area 152 571 sq km/58 892 sq mi
Capital Atlanta
Bird Brown Thrasher *Flower* Cherokee Rose
Tree Live Oak

Hawaii (Hawaii; HI)
Entry to Union 1959 (50th)
Pop 1.2m
Nickname Aloha State
Inhabitant Hawaiian
Area 16 759 sq km/6 469 sq mi
Capital Honolulu
Bird Nene *Flower* Hibiscus *Tree* Kukui

Idaho (Idaho; ID)
Entry to Union 1890 (43rd)
Pop 1.1m
Nickname Gem State
Inhabitant Idahoan
Area 216 422 sq km/83 564 sq mi
Capital Boise
Bird Mountain Bluebird *Flower* Syringa
Gemstone Idaho Star Garnet
Tree Western White Pine

Illinois (Ill; IL)
Entry to Union 1818 (21st)
Pop 11.6m
Nickname Prairie State, Land of Lincoln
Inhabitant Illinoisan
Area 145 928 sq km/56 328 sq mi
Capital Springfield
Bird Cardinal *Flower* Butterfly Violet
Tree White Oak

Indiana (Ind; IN)
Entry to Union 1816 (19th)
Pop 5.7m
Nickname Hoosier State
Inhabitant Hoosier
Area 93 716 sq km/36 185 sq mi
Capital Indianapolis
Bird Cardinal *Flower* Peony
Tree Tulip Tree

Iowa (Iowa; IA)
Entry to Union 1846 (29th)
Pop 2.8m
Nickname Hawkeye State, Corn State
Inhabitant Iowan
Area 145 747 sq km/56 275 sq mi
Capital Des Moines
Bird Eastern Goldfinch *Flower* Wild Rose
Tree Oak

Kansas (Kans; KS)
Entry to Union 1861 (34th)
Pop 2.5m
Nickname Sunflower State, Jayhawker State
Inhabitant Kansan
Area 213 089 sq km/82 252 sq mi
Capital Topeka
Animal Bison *Bird* Western Meadowlark
Flower Native Sunflower *Tree* Cottonwood

Kentucky (KY; KY)
Entry to Union 1792 (15th)
Pop 3.8m
Nickname Bluegrass State
Inhabitant Kentuckian
Area 104 658 sq km/40 410 sq mi
Capital Frankfort
Bird Cardinal *Flower* Goldenrod
Tree Kentucky Coffee Tree

Louisiana (La; LA)
Entry to Union 1812 (18th)
Pop 4.3m
Nickname Pelican State, Sugar State, Creole State
Inhabitant Louisianian
Area 123 673 sq km/47 738 sq mi
Capital Baton Rouge
Bird Eastern Brown Pelican *Flower* Magnolia
Tree Bald Cypress

Maine (Maine; ME)
Entry to Union 1820 (23rd)
Pop 1.2m
Nickname Pine Tree State
Inhabitant Downeaster
Area 86 153 sq km/33 255 sq mi
Capital Augusta
Bird Chickadee *Flower* White Pine Cone and Tassel
Gemstone Tourmaline
Tree Eastern White Pine

Maryland (Md; MD)
Entry to Union 1788 (7th)
Pop 4.9m
Nickname Old Line State, Free State
Inhabitant Marylander
Area 27 090 sq km/10 460 sq mi
Capital Annapolis
Bird Baltimore Oriole *Fish* Striped Bass
Flower Black-eyed Susan *Tree* White Oak

Massachusetts (Mass; MA)
Entry to Union 1788 (6th)
Pop 6m
Nickname Bay State, Old Colony
Inhabitant Bay Stater
Area 21 455 sq km/8 284 sq mi
Capital Boston
Bird Chickadee *Flower* Mayflower
Tree American Elm

Michigan (Mich; MI)
Entry to Union 1837 (26th)
Pop 9.4m
Nickname Wolverine State, Great Lake State
Inhabitant Michigander
Area 151 579 sq km/58 527 sq mi
Capital Lansing
Bird Robin *Fish* Trout
Flower Apple Blossom *Gemstone* Chlorastrolik
Tree White Pine

Minnesota (Minn; MN)
Entry to Union 1858 (32nd)
Pop 4.5m
Nickname Gopher State, North Star State
Inhabitant Minnesotan
Area 218 593 sq km/84 377 sq mi
Capital St Paul
Bird Loon *Fish* Walleye
Flower Moccasin Flower
Gemstone Lake Superior Agate
Tree Red Pine

Mississippi (Miss; MS)
Entry to Union 1817 (20th)
Pop 2.6m
Nickname Magnolia State
Inhabitant Mississippian
Area 123 510 sq km/47 689 sq mi
Capital Jackson
Bird Mockingbird *Flower* Magnolia
Tree Magnolia

US States contd.

Missouri (Mo; MO)
Entry to Union 1821 (24th)
Pop 5.2m
Nickname Bullion State, Show Me State
Inhabitant Missourian
Area 180 508 sq km/69 697 sq mi
Capital Jefferson City
Bird Bluebird *Flower* Hawthorn
Tree Dogwood

Montana (Mont; MT)
Entry to Union 1889 (41st)
Pop 824 000
Nickname Treasure State, Big Sky Country
Inhabitant Montanan
Area 380 834 sq km/147 046 sq mi
Capital Helena
Bird Western Meadowlark *Flower* Bitterroot
Gemstone Sapphire, Agate
Tree Ponderosa Pine

Nebraska (Nebr; NE)
Entry to Union 1867 (37th)
Pop 1.6m
Nickname Cornhusker State, Beef State
Inhabitant Nebraskan
Area 200 342 sq km/77 355 sq mi
Capital Lincoln
Bird Western Meadowlark *Flower* Goldenrod
Gemstone Blue Agate *Tree* Cottonwood

Nevada (Nev; NV)
Entry to Union 1864 (36th)
Pop 1.3m
Nickname Silver State, Sagebrush State
Inhabitant Nevadan
Area 286 341 sq km/110 528 sq mi
Capital Carson City
Bird Mountain Bluebird *Flower* Sagebrush
Tree Single-leaf Piñon

New Hampshire (NH; NH)
Entry to Union 1788 (9th)
Pop 1.1m
Nickname Granite State
Inhabitant New Hampshirite
Area 24 032 sq km/9 279 sq mi
Capital Concord
Bird Purple Finch *Flower* Purple Lilac
Tree White Birch

New Jersey (NJ; NJ)
Entry to Union 1787 (3rd)
Pop 7.8m
Nickname Garden State
Inhabitant New Jerseyite
Area 20 168 sq km/7 787 sq mi
Capital Trenton
Bird Eastern Goldfinch *Flower* Purple Violet
Tree Red Oak

New Mexico (N Mex; NM)
Entry to Union 1912 (47th)
Pop 1.6m
Nickname Sunshine State, Land of Enchantment
Inhabitant New Mexican
Area 314 914 sq km/121 593 sq mi
Capital Santa Fe
Animal Black Bear *Bird* Roadrunner
Fish Cutthroat Trout *Flower* Yucca
Gemstone Turquoise *Tree* Piñon

New York (NY; NY)
Entry to Union 1788 (11th)
Pop 18.1m
Nickname Empire State
Inhabitant New Yorker
Area 127 185 sq km/49 108 sq mi
Capital Albany
Bird Bluebird *Flower* Rose
Gemstone Garnet *Tree* Sugar Maple

North Carolina (NC; NC)
Entry to Union 1789 (12th)
Pop 6.8m
Nickname Old North State, Tar Heel State
Inhabitant North Carolinian
Area 136 407 sq km/52 669 sq mi
Capital Raleigh
Animal Grey Squirrel *Bird* Cardinal

Fish Channel Bass *Flower* Dogwood
Gemstone Emerald *Tree* Longleaf Pine

North Dakota (N Dak; ND)
Entry to Union 1889 (39th)
Pop 638 000
Nickname Flickertail State, Sioux State
Inhabitant North Dakotan
Area 183 111 sq km/70 702 sq mi
Capital Bismarck
Bird Western Meadowlark *Fish* Northern Pike
Flower Wild Prairie Rose
Gemstone Teredo petrified wood
Tree American Elm

Ohio (Ohio; OH)
Entry to Union 1803 (17th)
Pop 11m
Nickname Buckeye State
Inhabitant Ohioan
Area 107 041 sq km/41 330 sq mi
Capital Columbus
Bird Cardinal *Flower* Scarlet Carnation
Tree Buckeye

Oklahoma (Okla; OK)
Entry to Union 1907 (46th)
Pop 3.2m
Nickname Sooner State
Inhabitant Oklahoman
Area 181 083 sq km/69 919 sq mi
Capital Oklahoma City
Bird Scissor-tailed Flycatcher
Flower Mistletoe *Tree* Redbud

Oregon (Oreg; OR)
Entry to Union 1859 (33rd)
Pop 3m
Nickname Sunset State, Beaver State
Inhabitant Oregonian
Area 251 409 sq km/97 044 sq mi
Capital Salem
Animal Beaver *Bird* Western Meadowlark
Fish Chinook Salmon *Flower* Oregon Grape
Gemstone Thunder Egg *Tree* Douglas Fir

Pennsylvania (Pa; PA)
Entry to Union 1787 (2nd)
Pop 12m
Nickname Keystone State
Inhabitant Pennsylvanian
Area 117 343 sq km/45 308 sq mi
Capital Harrisburg
Animal Whitetail Deer *Bird* Ruffed Grouse
Flower Mountain Laurel *Tree* Hemlock

Rhode Island (RI; RI)
Entry to Union 1790 (13th)
Pop 1m
Nickname Little Rhody, Plantation State
Inhabitant Rhode Islander
Area 3 139 sq km/1 212 sq mi
Capital Providence
Bird Rhode Island Red *Flower* Violet
Tree Red Maple

South Carolina (SC; SC)
Entry to Union 1788 (8th)
Pop 3.6m
Nickname Palmetto State
Inhabitant South Carolinian
Area 80 580 sq km/31 104 sq mi
Capital Columbia
Animal Whitetail Deer *Bird* Carolina Wren
Fish Striped Bass *Flower* Yellow Jessamine
Tree Cabbage Palmetto

South Dakota (S Dak; SD)
Entry to Union 1889 (40th)
Pop 711 000
Nickname Sunshine State, Coyote State
Inhabitant South Dakotan
Area 199 723 sq km/77 116 sq mi
Capital Pierre
Animal Coyote *Bird* Ring-necked Pheasant
Flower Pasque *Gemstone* Fairburn Agate
Tree Black Hills Spruce

Tennessee (Tenn; TN)
Entry to Union 1796 (16th)
Pop 5m

Nickname Volunteer State
Inhabitant Tennessean
Area 109 149 sq km/42 132 sq mi
Capital Nashville
Animal Raccoon *Bird* Mockingbird
Flower Iris *Gemstone* Pearl *Tree* Tulip Poplar

Texas (Tex; TX)
Entry to Union 1845 (28th)
Pop 17.7 m
Nickname Lone Star State
Inhabitant Texan
Area 691 003 sq km/266 807 sq mi
Capital Austin
Bird Mockingbird *Flower* Bluebonnet
Gemstone Topaz *Tree* Pecan

Utah (Utah; UT)
Entry to Union 1896 (45th)
Pop 1.8m
Nickname Mormon State, Beehive State
Inhabitant Utahn
Area 219 880 sq km/84 874 sq mi
Capital Salt Lake City
Bird Sea Gull *Flower* Sego Lily
Gemstone Topaz *Tree* Blue Spruce

Vermont (Vt; VT)
Entry to Union 1791 (14th)
Pop 570 000
Nickname Green Mountain State
Inhabitant Vermonter
Area 24 899 sq km/9 611 sq mi
Capital Montpelier
Animal Morgan Horse *Bird* Hermit Thrush
Flower Red Clover *Tree* Sugar Maple

Virginia (Va; VA)
Entry to Union 1788 (10th)
Pop 6.4m
Nickname Old Dominion State, Mother of
Presidents
Inhabitant Virginian
Area 105 582 sq km/40 755 sq mi
Capital Richmond
Bird Cardinal *Flower* Dogwood
Tree Flowering Dogwood

Washington (Wash; WA)
Entry to Union 1889 (42nd)
Pop 5.1m
Nickname Evergreen State, Chinook State
Inhabitant Washingtonian
Area 176 473 sq km/68 119 sq mi
Capital Olympia
Bird Willow Goldfinch *Fish* Steelhead Trout
Flower Western Rhododendron
Gemstone Petrified Wood
Tree Western Hemlock

West Virginia (W Va; WV)
Entry to Union 1863 (35th)
Pop 1.8m
Nickname Panhandle State, Mountain State
Inhabitant West Virginian
Area 62 758 sq km/24 224 sq mi
Capital Charleston
Animal Black Bear *Bird* Cardinal
Flower Big Rhododendron *Tree* Sugar Maple

Wisconsin (Wis; WI)
Entry to Union 1848 (30th)
Pop 5m
Nickname Badger State, America's Dairyland
Inhabitant Wisconsinite
Area 145 431 sq km/56 136 sq mi
Capital Madison
Animal Badger, Whitetail Deer *Bird* Robin
Fish Muskellunge *Flower* Wood Violet
Tree Sugar Maple

Wyoming (Wyo; WY)
Entry to Union 1890 (44th)
Pop 466 000
Nickname Equality State
Inhabitant Wyomingite
Area 253 315 sq km/97 780 sq mi
Capital Cheyenne
Bird Meadowlark *Flower* Indian Paintbrush
Gemstone Jade *Tree* Cottonwood

bachelor, master, and doctoral level, and a high priority is given to research. Vocational courses may also be offered, leading to qualifications in such professions as medicine, engineering, and the law. In the UK, many former polytechnics have recently been upgraded to universities offering degree courses, principally in technical and vocational areas.

University of California in the USA, a university with nine campuses, originally founded in 1853 as the College of California in Oakland. It became the University of California in 1868, and moved to its main campus in Berkeley in 1873. Its other campuses include Davis, Irvine, Los Angeles, San Diego, Riverside, San Francisco, Santa Cruz, and Santa Barbara.

univocalic — *adj.* using only one vowel. — *noun* writing, especially verse, that uses only one vowel throughout, as in *no fool so gross to bolt Scotch collops hot*, from a poem by C C Bombaugh written in 1890.

UNIX or Unix *noun trademark Comput.* a type of operating system designed to handle large file transfers and allow multi-user access of data. [from UNI-, influenced by *Multics*, an operating system developed in the 1960s]

unkempt *adj.*, *said of hair* uncombed. *said of general appearance* untidy; dishevelled. [from Anglo-Saxon *uncembed*, uncombed]

unkind *adj.* unsympathetic, cruel, or harsh.

unknown — *adj.* **1** not known; unfamiliar. **2** not at all famous. — *adv.* (**unknown to someone**) without their knowledge. — *noun* an unknown person or thing.

Unknown Political Prisoner, The a sculpture by Barbara Hepworth (1953).

unknown quantity a person or thing whose precise identity, nature, or influence is not known or cannot be predicted.

Unknown Soldier, also called **the Warrior** an unnamed soldier, who is taken to represent all those who died in World War I, and whose grave commemorates all war dead. The countries which have such a memorial include France (beneath the Arc de Triomphe); the UK (in Westminster Abbey); and the USA (in Arlington National Cemetery).

unladen *adj.* not carrying a load.

unleaded *adj.*, *said of petrol* not containing lead additives, eg antiknocking agents. In the UK it is cheaper than leaded petrol, and most new cars are designed to use it, in an attempt to reduce environmental pollution from exhaust fumes.

unlearn *verb* (PAST TENSE AND PAST PARTICIPLE **unlearnt, unlearned**) **1** to try actively to forget; to rid one's memory of. **2** to free oneself from (eg an acquired habit).

unlearned[1] *adj.* having no learning; uneducated.

unlearned[2] or unlearnt *adj.* **1** *said of a lesson, etc* not learnt. **2** *said of a skill, etc* not acquired by learning; instinctive; innate.

unleash *verb* **1** to release (eg a dog) from a leash. **2** to release or give free expression to (eg anger).

unleavened *adj.*, *said of bread* made without yeast, and therefore rather flat and hard.

unless *conj.* if not; except if. [from Middle English *unlesse*]

unlettered *adj.* **1** uneducated. **2** illiterate.

unlike — *prep.* **1** different from. **2** not typical or characteristic of. — *adj.* different; dissimilar.

unlikelihood or unlikeliness *noun* an unlikely state.

unlikely *adj.* **1** probably untrue. **2** not expected or likely. **3** not obviously suitable; improbable.

unlimited *adj.* **1** not limited or restricted. **2** *loosely* very great or numerous.

unlined *adj.* **1** not having a lining: *an unlined jacket.* **2** free from lines: *she had a youthful unlined face.*

unlisted *adj.* not entered on a list, especially on a list of telephone numbers or companies quoted on the Stock Exchange.

unlit *adj.* not having lights or lighting.

unload *verb* **1** *trans.*, *intrans.* to remove (cargo) from (a vehicle). **2** *trans.*, *intrans.* to remove the ammunition from (a gun). **3** to dispose of. **4** to relieve (oneself or one's mind) of troubles or anxieties by telling them to another; to get rid of (troubles) in this way.

unlock *verb* **1** to undo the lock of. **2** to free from being locked up. **3** to release or let loose.

unlooked-for *adj.* **1** unexpected. **2** not deliberately encouraged or invited.

unloose or unloosen *verb* (**unloosened**, **unloosening**) **1** to make less tight; to loosen. **2** to set free.

unloved *adj.* not loved.

unluckily *adv.* **1** in an unlucky way; as a result of bad luck. **2** I am sorry to say; unfortunately.

unlucky *adj.* (**unluckier**, **unluckiest**) **1** bringing, resulting from, or constituting bad luck. **2** having, or tending to have, bad luck.

unmade *adj.* **1** not yet made. **2** *said of a bed* with bedclothes not rearranged neatly after being slept in. **3** *said of a road* with no proper surface (eg of tarmac).

unmake *verb* to cancel or destroy the (especially beneficial) effect of.

unman *verb* (**unmanned, unmanning**) *old use, literary* to cause to lose self-control, especially to overcome with emotion.

unmanned *adj.* **1** *said especially of a vehicle or spacecraft* not manned, especially controlled remotely or automatically. **2** *old use, literary* deprived of self-control.

unmannerliness *noun* being unmannerly.

unmannerly *adj.* bad-mannered; impolite.

unmarried *adj.* not married, usually when never having been married.

unmask *verb* **1** to remove a mask or disguise from. **2** to reveal the true identity or nature of.

unmentionable — *adj.* not fit to be mentioned or talked about, especially because considered indecent. — *noun* (**unmentionables**) *humorous* underwear.

unmerciful *adj.* **1** merciless. **2** unpleasantly great or extreme.

unmistakable or unmistakeable *adj.* too easily recognizable to be mistaken for anything or anyone else.

unmistakably or unmistakeably *adv.* in an unmistakable way; as is unmistakable.

unmitigated *adj.* **1** not lessened or made less severe. **2** unqualified; absolute; out-and-out: *an unmitigated rogue.*

unmoved *adj.* **1** still in the same place. **2** not persuaded. **3** not affected by emotion.

unnamed *adj.* **1** not named or specified; anonymous. **2** not baptized.

unnatural *adj.* **1** contrary to the way things usually happen in nature. **2** contrary to ordinary human nature, especially intensely evil, cruel, or disgusting. **3** insincere; affected.

unnaturally *adv.* in an unnatural way; to an unnatural degree.

unnerve *verb* **1** to weaken the courage or confidence of. **2** to cause to feel ill at ease.

unnerving *adj.* that unnerves, unsettling.

unnilpentium *noun Chem.* (SYMBOL **Unp**, ATOMIC NUMBER 105) an artificially manufactured metallic element that has six isotopes, all with half-lives of a fraction of a second; sometimes referred to as nielsbohrium.

unnilquadium *noun Chem.* (SYMBOL **Unq**, ATOMIC NUMBER 104) a radioactive metallic element, formed by bombarding californium with

carbon nuclei, that has 10 isotopes with half-lives of up to 70 seconds.

unnilseptium *noun Chem.* (SYMBOL **Uns**, ATOMIC NUMBER 107) an artificially manufactured radioactive chemical element.

unnumbered *adj.* **1** not given a number. **2** too numerous to be counted; innumerable.

UNO *abbrev.* United Nations Organization.

unobtrusive *adj.* not noticeable or prominent.

unobtrusively *adv.* in an unobtrusive way.

unpack *verb* **1** to take out of a packed state. **2** to empty (eg a suitcase) of packed contents.

unpaid *adj.* not paid: *unpaid bills / an unpaid job.*

unparalleled *adj.* so remarkable as to have no equal or parallel.

unparliamentary *adj.* contrary to the established procedures by which, or to the spirit in which, a parliament is conducted.

unperson *noun* a person whose existence is officially denied or ignored, often by removing his or her name from official records.

unpick *verb* to undo (stitches); to take (a sewn article) to pieces by undoing the stitching.

unpleasant *adj.* not pleasant; disagreeable.

unpleasantly *adv.* in an unpleasant way; to an unpleasant extent.

unpleasantness *noun* **1** the quality of being unpleasant. **2** *euphemistic* an unpleasant incident, especially a disagreement involving open hostility.

unplug *verb* to remove the plug from.

unpopular *adj.* generally disliked.

unpopularity *noun* an unpopular state or quality.

unpractical *adj.* having no practical skills; not good at practical tasks. See also IMPRACTICAL.

unpractised *adj.* **1** having had little or no practice or experience. **2** not or not yet put into practice.

unprecedented *adj.* not known to have ever happened before; without precedent.

unprepossessing *adj.* **1** unappealing; unattractive. **2** not creating or likely to create a good impression.

unprincipled *adj.* having or showing a lack of moral principles.

unprintable *adj.* not fit to be printed, especially because of being obscene or libellous.

unprofessional *adj.* violating the rules governing, or the standards of conduct expected of, members of a particular profession.

unputdownable *adj. colloq.*, *said of a book* so absorbing as to compel one to read to the end without a break.

unqualified *adj.* **1** not having any formal qualifications; lacking the formal qualifications required for a particular job, etc. **2** not limited or moderated in any way. **3** absolute; out-and-out: *an unqualified success.* **4** not competent.

unquestionable *adj.* beyond doubt or question.

unquestionably *adv.* as cannot be questioned; undoubtedly.

unquestioning *adj.* not arguing or protesting; done, etc without argument or protest.

unquestioningly *adv.* without questioning or protesting.

unquiet *literary* — *adj.* anxious; ill at ease; restless. — *noun* disquiet.

unquote *interj.* used in speech to indicate the end of a quotation. See also QUOTE.

unravel *verb trans.*, *intrans.* (**unravelled, unravelling**) **1** to take or come out of a knitted or woven state back into a strand or strands. **2** to take or come out of a tangled state. **3** to make or become clear after being confusing or obscure.

unread *adj.* **1** *said of a book, etc* that has not been read. **2** *said of a person* having read few books.

unreadable *adj.* **1** illegible. **2** too difficult to read. **3** not worth reading.

unready *adj.* **1** not ready. **2** not acting quickly; hesitant.

unreal *adj.* **1** not real; illusory or imaginary. **2** *colloq.* exceptionally strange, ridiculous, or excellent.

unreality *noun* lack of reality.

unrelenting *adj.* **1** refusing to change viewpoint or chosen course of action. **2** not softened by feelings of mercy or pity. **3** constant; relentless; never stopping.

unremitting *adj.* not easing off or abating; constant; never stopping.

unrequited *adj., said of love* not felt in return by the loved person.

unreserved *adj.* **1** not booked or reserved. **2** open and sociable in manner; showing no shyness or reserve. **3** not moderated or limited; unqualified.

unreservedly *adv.* without reservation.

unrest *noun* **1** a state of (especially public) discontent bordering on riotousness. **2** anxiety; unease.

unrivalled *adj.* far better than any other; unequalled.

unroll *verb trans., intrans.* **1** to open out from a rolled state. **2** *intrans.* to become unrolled.

unruffled *adj.* **1** *said of a surface* smooth. **2** *said of a person* not agitated or flustered.

unruliness *noun* **1** being unruly. **2** unruly behaviour.

unruly *adj.* (**unrulier**, **unruliest**) noisily disobedient or disorderly, especially habitually.

unsaddle *verb* **1** to take the saddle off (a horse). **2** to throw (a rider) from a horse; to unhorse.

unsafe *adj.* **1** not safe or secure; dangerous. **2** *said of a conclusion or decision* based on insufficient or suspect evidence.

unsaid *adj.* not said, especially when it might have been or should have been said. See also UNSAY.

unsaturated *adj. Chem.* **1** *said of an organic chemical compound* containing at least one double or triple bond between its carbon atoms, eg unsaturated fats. **2** *said of a solution* not containing the maximum amount of a solid or gas (*solute*) that can be dissolved in it.

unsavoury *adj.* unpleasant or distasteful.

unsay *verb* (PAST TENSE AND PAST PARTICIPLE **unsaid**) to take back or withdraw (something said). See also UNSAID.

unscathed *adj.* not harmed or injured.

unscramble *verb* **1** to interpret (a coded or scrambled message). **2** to take out of a jumbled state and put in order.

unscrew *verb* **1** to remove or loosen by taking out screws, or with a twisting or screwing action. **2** to loosen (a screw).

unscrupulous *adj.* without scruples or moral principles.

unseasonable *adj.* **1** not appropriate to the time of year. **2** coming at a bad time; inopportune.

unseat *verb* **1** to remove from an official post or position, especially a parliamentary seat. **2** to throw or knock off a seat, or off a horse.

UN Secretariat a body of the UN, under the Secretary-General. It employs c.16 000 at the

UN's headquarters in New York City and 50 000 worldwide. The staff are answerable only to the UN, not national governments, and are engaged in considerable diplomatic work. The Secretary-General is often a significant person in international diplomacy and is able to take independent initiatives.

UN Security Council the 15-member UN body which has its primary role the maintainance of international peace and security; its decisions, unlike those of the General Assembly, are binding on all other members. It is dominated by the five permanent members (China, France, UK, Russia, and USA) who each have the power of veto over any resolutions; the remaining 10 are elected for two-year periods. It is empowered to order mandatory sanctions, call for cease-fires, and establish peacekeeping forces (these forces were awarded the Nobel Peace Prize in 1988). The use of the veto has prevented it from intervening in a number of disputes, such as Vietnam.

unseemliness *noun* being unseemly.

unseemly *adj.* not fitting, especially because of being indecent.

unseen *adj.* **1** not seen or noticed. **2** *of a text for translation* not seen in advance by the examinee.

unselfish *adj.* having or showing concern for others; generous-spirited.

unselfishly *adv.* in an unselfish way.

unselfishness *noun* being unselfish.

unsettle *verb* **1** to disturb from a fixed or stable position or state. **2** to cause to become ill at ease.

unsettled *adj.* **1** lacking stability; changing or likely to change. **2** not relaxed or at ease. **3** *said of a debt* unpaid.

unshakable *or* **unshakeable** *adj., said of beliefs, or the person holding them* firm; steadfast.

unsightliness *noun* being unsightly.

unsightly *adj.* (**unsightlier**, **unsightliest**) not pleasant to look at; ugly.

unskilled *adj.* not having or requiring any special skill or training.

unsociable *adj.* disliking or avoiding the company of other people.

unsocial *adj.* **1** annoying, or likely to annoy, other people; antisocial. **2** *said of working hours* falling outside the normal working day.

unsold *adj.* not sold.

unsophisticated *adj.* **1** not sophisticated. **2** free from insincerity or artificiality.

unsound *adj.* **1** not reliable; not based on sound reasoning. **2** not firm or solid.
— **of unsound mind** *Legal* mentally ill; insane.

unsparing *adj.* **1** giving generously or liberally. **2** showing no mercy.

unspeakable *adj.* **1** not able to be expressed in words. **2** too bad, wicked, or obscene to be spoken about.

unspeakably *adv.* in an unspeakable way.

unspent *adj.* not spent.

unstinting *adj.* giving (eg praise) generously or liberally.

unstop *verb* **1** to free from being stopped or blocked. **2** to draw out the stop or stopper from.

unstoppable *adj. colloq.* whose progress can not be stopped.

unstrung *adj.* **1** with strings removed. **2** unnerved.

unstuck *adj.* loosened or released from a stuck state.
— **come unstuck** *said of a plan, etc* to go wrong.

unstudied *adj.* not affected; natural and spontaneous.

unsung *adj., said of people or their achievements* not praised or recognized.

unsure *adj.* **1** uncertain, doubtful: *he was unsure if the painting was genuine.* **2** precarious: *an unsure foothold.* **3** insecure; not assured: *he was unsure of himself in large gatherings of people.* **4** untrustworthy: *an unsure character.*

unswerving *adj.* not deviating from a belief or aim; steadfast.

untamed *adj.* not tame; wild.

untangle *verb* to disentangle.

untaxed *adj.* **1** not taxed. **2** not charged with any fault.

Unter den Linden a boulevard running between Mark-Engels Platz and the Brandenburg Gate, in Berlin, Germany. It was formerly a stately avenue lined with linden (lime) trees and historic buildings, many of which were destroyed during World War II.

Untersee see ZELLER SEE.

unthinkable *adj.* **1** too unusual to be likely; inconceivable. **2** too unpleasant to think about.

unthinking *adj.* **1** inconsiderate. **2** careless.

unthrone *verb* to dethrone.

untidily *adv.* in an untidy or disorderly way.

untidy — *adj.* (**unidier**, **untidiest**) not tidy; messy, disordered. — *verb* (**untidies**, **untidied**) to make untidy (something that was previously tidy).

untie *verb* **1** to undo from a tied state. **2** to remove the constraints on; to set free.

until — *prep.* **1** up to the time of. **2** up to the time of reaching (a place); as far as: *slept until Paris.* **3** (*with a negative*) before: *not until Wednesday.* — *conj.* **1** up to the time that. **2** (*with a negative*) before: *not until I say so.* [see TILL¹]

untimeliness *noun* being untimely.

untimely *adj.* **1** happening before the proper or expected time. **2** coming at an inappropriate or inconvenient time.

unto *prep. old use* to.

untold *adj.* **1** not told. **2** too severe to be described. **3** too many to be counted.

untouchable — *adj.* **1** not to be touched or handled. **2** discouraging physical contact. **3** above the law. — *noun* **1** an untouchable person or thing. **2** *formerly* in India, a member of the lowest social class, or caste, whose touch was regarded by members of higher castes as a contamination.

untoward *adj.* **1** inconvenient; unfortunate. **2** adverse; unfavourable.

untried *adj.* **1** not attempted or tested. **2** not yet submitted to a legal trial.

untrue *adj.* **1** not true. **2** not accurate. **3** unfaithful.

UN Trusteeship Council a body of the UN that oversees the transition of UN Trust territories to self-government. Its members are China, France, Russia, the UK, and the USA.

untruth *noun* **1** the fact of being untrue. **2** a lie.

untruthful *adj.* not truthful; lying.

unused *adj.* **1** brand new; never used. **2** (**unused to something**) not used or accustomed to it.

unusual *adj.* not usual; uncommon; rare.

unusually *adv.* in an unusual way; to an unusual degree.

unutterable *adj.* so extreme or intense as to be impossible to express in words.

unvarnished *adj., said of an account or report* not exaggerated or embellished.

unveil *verb* **1** to remove a veil from (a person's face). **2** *intrans.* to remove one's veil. **3** to remove a curtain or other covering from (a plaque, etc) as part of a formal opening ceremony. **4** to reveal or make known for the first time.

unveiling *noun* **1** removal of a veil. **2** the ceremony of opening or presenting something new.

unvoiced *adj.* **1** unspoken. **2** *Phonetics* pronounced without vibrating the vocal cords; voiceless.

unwaged *adj.* not in paid employment.

unwell *adj.* ill.

unwieldiness *noun* being unwieldy.

unwieldy *adj.* large and awkward to carry or manage; cumbersome. [from WIELD]

unwilling *adj.* having or showing a lack of willingness; reluctant.

unwillingly *adv.* in an unwilling way.

unwillingness *noun* being unwilling.

unwind *verb* (PAST TENSE AND PAST PARTICIPLE **unwound**) **1** *trans., intrans.* to take or come out of a coiled or wound position. **2** *intrans. colloq.* to relax.

unwise *adj.* not prudent; ill-advised; foolish.

unwisely *adv.* in an unwise way.

unwitting *adj.* **1** not realizing or being aware. **2** done without being realized or intended. [from WIT]

unwittingly *adv.* without knowing.

unwonted *adj.* not usual or habitual. [from WONT]

unwound see UNWIND.

unwritten *adj.* **1** not recorded in writing or print. **2** *said of a rule or law* not formally enforceable, but traditionally accepted and followed.

unzip *verb* (**unzipped**, **unzipping**) to unfasten or open by undoing a zip.

up — *prep.* at or to a higher position on, or a position further along: *climbed up the stairs / walking up the road.* — *adv.* **1** at or to a higher position or level: *lift it up / turn up the volume / prices went up.* **2** at or to a place higher up, or a more northerly place. **3** in or to a more erect position: *stood up.* **4** fully or completely: *use up / eat up.* **5** into the state of being gathered together: *saved up for it / parcel up the presents.* **6** in or to a place of storage or lodging: *put them up for the night.* **7** out of bed: *got up.* **8** to or towards: *went up to the town / travelling up to London / walked up to him.* — *adj.* **1** placed in, or moving or directed to, a higher position. **2** out of bed: *he's not up yet.* **3** having an advantage; ahead: *two goals up / £5 up after the first bet.* **4** *said of a road* under repair. **5** appearing in court: *up before the judge.* **6** *said of the sun* above the horizon. **7** relating to or providing (especially rail) transport to, rather than away from, a major place: *the up train.* — *verb* (**upped**, **upping**) **1** to raise or increase. **2** *intrans. colloq.* to proceed boldly or unexpectedly to act or speak; to get up (and do something): *he upped and left her.* — *noun* **1** a success or advantage. **2** a spell of good luck or prosperity.

— **be well up on** or **in something** to have a thorough knowledge of it.

it's all up with someone *colloq.* there is no hope for them.

not up to much *colloq.* not good at all; no good.

on the up-and-up *colloq.* **1** steadily becoming more successful. **2** honest; on the level.

something is up something is wrong or amiss.

up against someone or **something 1** situated or pressed close against them. **2** faced with difficulties, etc.

up and about or **up and doing** out of bed and active.

up for something 1 presented or offered for (eg discussion or sale). **2** under consideration for a job or post.

up front *colloq.* **1** openly or candidly. **2** *said of money paid* in advance.

up to ... **1** immersed or embedded as far as ... **2** dependent on: *it's up to you.* **3** capable of ...; equal to: *are you up to meeting them?* **4** thinking about doing or engaged in doing: *was up to his usual tricks.* **5** as good as: *not up to his standard.*

up to the minute completely up to date.

up with ... **1** abreast of ... **2** even with ... **3** an expression of enthusiastic approval or support: *up with Christmas!*

what's up? what's the matter? what's wrong? [from Anglo-Saxon *up* or *upp*]

up-and-coming *adj.* beginning to become successful or well known.

Upanishads the last section of the Hindu scriptures (the Veda), composed in Sanskrit between 800 and 400 BC. The name, meaning 'to sit near', refers to the secret transmission of these teachings by gurus.

upbeat — *adj. colloq.* cheerful; optimistic. — *noun Mus.* the unstressed beat, at which a conductor raises the baton.

upbraid *verb* to scold or reproach. [from Anglo-Saxon *upbregdan*]

upbringing *noun* the all-round instruction and education of a child, intended to form his or her character and values.

up-country — *adj., adv.* to or in the regions away from the coast; inland. — *noun* the inland regions.

update — *verb* (with stress on *-date*) to make or bring up to date. — *noun* (with stress on *up-*) an act of updating.

Updike, John (Hoyer) (1932–) US writer, born in Shillington, Pennsylvania. He wrote poetry, stories, and criticism for the *New Yorker* magazine from 1955. His novels, which explore human relationships in contemporary US society, include *Rabbit, Run* (1960), *Couples* (1968), *Rabbit is Rich* (1981, Pulitzer Prize), *The Witches of Eastwick* (1984), and *Rabbit at Rest* (1990, Pulitzer Prize). He has also published several collections of short stories, selected in *Forty Stories* (1987).

up-end *verb* **1** to turn upside down. **2** to put into disorder or disarray.

upfront *adj. colloq.* **1** candid; open. **2** *said of money* paid in advance.

upgrade *verb* **1** to promote (a person). **2** to increase the grade or status of (a job or post). **3** to improve the quality of.

upheaval *noun* a change or disturbance that greatly disrupts.

upheld see UPHOLD.

Up-Helly-Aa *noun* a midwinter festival, derived from an older Celtic fire festival, held on the last Tuesday of January in Lerwick, Shetland. It now includes guisers and the ceremonial burning of a replica Viking long boat. [from *up*, at an end, finished + Scots *haliday*, holiday; ie the end of the Yule holiday]

uphill — *adj.* **1** sloping upwards; ascending. **2** *said of a task, etc* requiring great effort; arduous. — *adv.* up a slope.

uphold *verb* (PAST TENSE AND PAST PARTICIPLE **upheld**) **1** to support (an action), defend (a right) or maintain (the law). **2** to declare (eg a court judgement) to be correct or just; to confirm.

upholster *verb* (**upholstered**, **upholstering**) to fit with upholstery. [from UPHOLD, in the obsolete meaning 'to keep in good condition']

upholstered *adj.* fitted with upholstery.

upholsterer *noun* a person who upholsters furniture.

upholstery *noun* **1** the springs, stuffing, and covers of a chair or sofa. **2** the work of an upholsterer.

UPI *abbrev.* United Press International.

upkeep *noun* the task of keeping something in good order or condition, or the cost of this.

upland *noun* (*often* **uplands**) a high or hilly region.

uplift — *verb* (with stress on *-lift*) **1** to fill with an invigorating happiness, optimism, or awareness of the spiritual nature of things. **2** *formal* to lift up; to collect. — *noun* (with stress on *up-*) an uplifting influence or effect.

uplifting *adj.* cheering, inspiring with hope.

upload *verb intrans., trans. Comput.* to send (data) from one computer to another, eg by means of a telephone line and modem.

up-market *adj.* high in price, quality, or prestige.

upmost *adj., adv.* uppermost.

upon *prep.* on or on to.

— **upon my word!** *old use* an exclamation of surprise.

upper — *adj.* **1** higher; situated above. **2** high or higher in rank or status. — *noun* **1** the part of a shoe above the sole. **2** *slang* a drug that induces euphoria.

— **on one's uppers** *colloq.* extremely short of money; destitute.

upper-case *adj.* consisting of capital letters.

upper class the highest social class; the aristocracy.

upper-class *adj.* belonging or relating to the upper class.

upper crust *adj. colloq.* the upper class.

upper-crust *adj. colloq.* same as UPPER-CLASS.

uppercut *noun* a forceful upward blow with the fist, usually under the chin.

upper hand (**the upper hand**) a position of advantage or dominance.

upper house or **upper chamber** the second and normally smaller part of a two-chamber (bicameral) parliament, such as the House of Lords in the UK.

uppermost *adj., adv.* at, in or into the highest or most prominent position.

uppish or **uppity** *adj. colloq.* arrogant or snobbish. [from UP]

Uppsala 1 POP (1992e) 171 000, the capital of Uppsala county, E Sweden, situated 64km/40mi NW of Stockholm. It is an educational centre, with a university (1477) and many other academic institutions. NOTABLE FEATURES cathedral (13c–15c), with the tombs of Gustavus Vasa and other kings; castle (16c). **2** a county in E Sweden with Uppsala as its capital.

upright — *adj.* **1** standing straight up; erect or vertical. **2** having integrity or moral correctness. — *adv.* into an upright position. — *noun* **1** a vertical (usually supporting) post or pole. **2** an upright piano.

upright piano a piano with strings arranged vertically in a case above the keyboard.

uprising *noun* a rebellion or revolt.

uproar *noun* an outbreak of noisy and boisterous behaviour, especially angry protest. [from Dutch *oproer*, from *oproeren*, to stir up]

uproarious *adj.* **1** *said of laughter* loud and unrestrained. **2** provoking such laughter.

uproariously *adv.* in an uproarious way, with uproar.

uproot *verb* **1** to pull (a plant) out of the ground completely, with the root attached. **2** to take completely away from surroundings settled into.

ups-a-daisy or **upsy-daisy** *interj.* an expression of encouragement to a child one is lifting up, or helping up from a fall.

ups and downs spells of success and failure; changes of fortune.

upscale *adj. colloq.* of or designed to appeal to the wealthier in society; up-market.

upset — *verb* (with stress on *-set*) (**upsetting**; PAST TENSE AND PAST PARTICIPLE **upset**) **1** to cause to be emotionally distressed. **2** to ruin or spoil (eg plans). **3** to disturb the proper balance or function of (a person's stomach). **4** to knock over. —

noun (with stress on *up-*) **1** a disturbance, eg of plans or digestion. **2** an unexpected result or outcome. — *adj.* emotionally distressed.

upset price the lowest price a seller will accept, and the price at which bidding starts at an auction.

upsetting *adj.* causing upset.

upshot *noun* (**the upshot**) the final outcome or ultimate effect.

upside *noun* **1** the upper part or side of anything. **2** *colloq.* a positive or favourable aspect.

upside down *adj., adv.* (*also, as adj.,* **upside-down**) **1** with the top part at the bottom; upturned or inverted. **2** in or into complete confusion or disorder.

upsides *adj.* (**upsides with someone**) *Brit. colloq.* even with them, especially through revenge or retaliation.

upstage — *adj., adv.* **1** at or towards the back of a theatre stage. **2** *slang* arrogant or arrogantly. — *verb* **1** to move upstage and force (an actor) to turn his or her back to the audience when speaking to one. **2** to direct attention away from (a person) on to oneself.

upstairs — *adj., adv.* **1** on or to an upper floor. **2** *colloq.* in or to a senior or more senior position. — *noun* an upper floor, especially the part of a house above the ground floor.

upstanding *adj.* **1** honest; respectable; trustworthy. **2** having a healthily erect posture. — **be upstanding** *formal* to stand up.

upstart *noun derog.* an arrogant young person with rapidly acquired power or wealth.

upstream *adv.* towards the source of a river or stream and against the current.

upsurge *noun* a sudden sharp rise or increase; a surging up.

upsy-daisy see UPS-A-DAISY.

uptake
— **quick** *or* **slow on the uptake** *colloq.* quick or slow to understand or realize.

upthrust *noun Physics* the upward force that tends to make an object immersed in a liquid float.

uptight *adj. colloq.* **1** nervous; anxious; tense. **2** angry; irritated. **3** *North Amer., esp. US* strait-laced; conventional.

up to date *or* **up-to-date 1** containing all the latest facts or information. **2** knowing or reflecting the latest trends.

upturn — *noun* an increase in (especially economic) activity; an upward trend. — *verb* to turn over, up, or upside-down.

upward — *adv.* (**upwards**) to or towards a higher place, a more important or senior position, or an earlier era. — *adj.* moving or directed upwards.
— **upwardly mobile** *colloq.* moving, or in a position to move, into a higher social class or income bracket.

upwards of ... more than: *upwards of a thousand people.*

upwardly *adv.* in an upward direction.

upwind — *adv.* **1** against the direction of the wind; into the wind. **2** in front in terms of wind direction; with the wind carrying one's scent towards (eg an animal one is stalking). — *adj.* going against or exposed to the wind.

Ur an ancient city-state of Sumer, lying to the SE of Babylon, the early home of the Jewish patriarch Abraham. It was at its height in the third millennium BC, when it twice became the capital of Sumer. It was destroyed by Elam in c.2000 BC, and though it recovered it never attained its former greatness. It was finally abandoned in the 4c BC.

uracil *noun Biochem.* one of the bases, derived from pyrimidine, that is present in the nucleic acid RNA. [from UREA + ACETIC]

uraemia *or* **uremia** *noun Medicine* the presence of excessive amounts of urea and other nitrogenous waste products in the blood, one of the first symptoms of kidney failure. [from Greek *ouron*, urine + *haima*, blood]

Uralic — *adj.* denoting a family of languages descended from an ancestor spoken in the N Ural Mountains over 7 000 years ago. The major languages include Finnish, Estonian, and Lapp, with an isolated member, Magyar, spoken in Hungary. Uralic languages have a written history dating from the 13c. — *noun* the languages forming this family.

Ural Mountains *or* **The Urals**, Russian **Uralskiy Khrebet** a mountain range in Russia and Kazakhstan, forming the traditional boundary between Europe and Asia, and separating the E European Plain in the W from the W Siberian Lowlands in the E. The range extends 1 750km/1 087mi S from Novaya Zemlya in the Arctic Ocean to the N Kazakhstan border. The relief consists of low, parallel N–S ridges, generally 200–1 000m high; the N Urals contain the highest peak, Mt Narodnaya (1 894m); a plateau forms the central Urals, crossed by several transport routes including the Trans-Siberian Railway; the S Urals consist of several parallel ranges, reaching a maximum width of 150–200km/ 100–125mi; the area is heavily forested and there are rich mineral deposits including oil, iron ore, coal, copper, manganese, gold, aluminium, potash, bauxite, asbestos, zinc, lead, silver, nickel, and gemstones. Cities in the region include Magnitogorsk and Yekaterinburg; the central and S parts of the region are heavily industrialized.

Urania in Greek mythology, the Muse of astronomy, usually depicted with a globe and compass.

uraninite *noun Geol.* a hard slightly greasy black, brown, grey, or greenish mineral form of uranium oxide that is often associated with thorium, lead, radium, or the rare earth elements, and is highly radioactive. It is the principal ore of uranium.

uranium *noun Chem.* (SYMBOL **U**, ATOMIC NUMBER **92**) a dense silvery-white radioactive metal, originally discovered in pitchblende in 1789, but now mainly obtained from the ore uraninite. [after the planet *Uranus*, discovered shortly before the metal]
◇ Uranium has three natural isotopes. Uranium-234 is used in nuclear research. Uranium-238 represents about 99% of naturally occurring uranium, and is non-fissionable, but can be converted to fissionable plutonium-239 in a breeder reactor. It can also be used to date geological samples because of its long half-life (4.5 billion years). Uranium-235 (0.7% of natural uranium) does undergo nuclear fission to release large amounts of energy, and is used as fuel for nuclear reactors and nuclear weapons. The mining and extraction of uranium, and its use as a nuclear fuel, generate large amounts of radioactive waste that is difficult to dispose of safely without causing long-term environmental pollution.

Uranus 1 (*also* **Ouranus**) in Greek mythology, the earliest sky-god, the personification of Heaven. His children by Gaea (Earth) included the Titans and the Cyclops. He was displaced by Cronus, who castrated him and as a result separated Heaven and Earth. **2** *Astron.* the seventh planet from the Sun. Its orbit lies between those of Saturn and Neptune.
◇ Uranus is about 2 872 million km from the Sun, and has a diameter of 52 000km at the equator. It takes 17 hours 24 minutes to rotate once on its own axis, and 84 years to orbit around the Sun. It rotates on its axis in the opposite direction to all the other planets except Venus (and possibly Pluto). Uranus has a faint ring system composed of 11 rings, and 15 natural satellites, the largest being Titania (1 600km across) and the

smallest Miranda (480km across). All the satellites have icy surfaces covered with craters, and one of them, Ariel, has immense valleys.
Little was known about Uranus until the space probe *Voyager 2* sent back information in 1986. The planet has a rocky core covered with ice, and a thick atmosphere consisting mainly of hydrogen and helium, together with methane and ammonia, but unlike the other outer planets it has virtually no cloud markings. The axis of rotation of Uranus is tilted at an angle of 98°, so during its orbit around the Sun its poles lie almost in the plane of its orbit, and parts of the planet's surface are in continuous day, and then continuous night, for almost 40 Earth years.

Urartu an ancient state which flourished from the 9c BC to the 7c BC in the mountains of E Turkey around L Van. Urartu was often engaged in hostilities with neighbouring Assyria.

Urban VIII (1568–1644) Italian pope, born in Florence. He was papal legate in France (1601), became a cardinal (1606), and as pope (1623–44) supported Cardinal Richelieu's policy against the Habsburgs in the Thirty Years War, and carried out much ecclesiatical reform. A great scholar and supporter of the arts, he issued several condemnations of heresy, which included the writings of Galileo Galilei and Cornelius Otto Jansen.

urban *adj.* of, relating to, or situated in a town or city; not rural. [from Latin *urbs*, city]

urbane *adj.* **1** having refined manners; courteous. **2** sophisticated; civilized; elegant. [from Latin *urbanus*, of the town]

urban guerrilla a person carrying out terrorist activities in urban areas.

urbanity *noun* an urbane quality.

urbanization *or* **urbanisation** *noun* the process of urbanizing.

urbanize *or* **urbanise** *verb* to make (a district) less rural and more town-like.

urban renewal the clearing and redevelopment of slums, etc, in large cities and towns.

urban renewal project the demolition of old or run-down areas in a city to allow construction of new buildings, or the installation of modern amenities and the repair of structurally sound buildings in such areas.

urchin *noun* **1** a mischievous child. **2** a dirty, raggedly dressed child. **3** a sea-urchin. [from Old French *heriçon*, from Latin *ericus*, hedgehog]

Urdu — *noun* the official literary language of Pakistan, related to Hindi but with many words from Arabic and Persian. — *adj.* in or relating to Urdu.
◇ Urdu is an Indo-Aryan language of the Indo-European family. It has c.25–40m speakers in Pakistan and Bangladesh, and is also spoken among Muslims in India. The language is written in Arabic script.

urea *noun Biochem.* a compound, white and crystalline when purified, formed during amino acid breakdown in the liver of mammals, and excreted in the urine. It is also manufactured synthetically for use as a component of plastics, pharmaceuticals, fertilizers, and animal-feed additives. [from Greek *ouron*, urine]

ureter *noun Anat.* one of the two tubes through which urine is carried from the kidneys to the bladder. [from Greek *oureter*, from *ouron*, urine]

urethra *noun* (PL. **urethras**, **urethrae**) the tube through which urine passes from the bladder out of the body. [from Greek *ourethra*, from *ouron*, urine]

urethritis *noun* inflammation of the urethra.

Urey, Harold Clayton (1893–1981) US chemist, born in Walkerton, Indiana. He taught at Johns Hopkins University, Columbia University, and Chicago, and played a major role in the development of the atomic bomb. In 1932 he discovered deuterium, or 'heavy hydrogen', and for this work he was awarded the 1934 Nobel Prize for Chemistry.

urge — *verb* **1** to persuade forcefully or incite. **2** to beg or entreat. **3** to advise or recommend earnestly. **4** (*also* **urge someone** *or* **something on**) to drive (eg horses) onwards. — *noun* a strong impulse, desire, or motivation. [from Latin *urgere*]

urgency *noun* an urgent state or condition.

urgent *adj.* **1** needing immediate attention or action. **2** *said of a request, etc* forcefully and earnestly made. [from Latin *urgere*, to urge]

urgently *adv.* with urgency.

uric *adj.* relating to or present in urine.

uric acid *Biochem.* an organic acid that is the main form in which nitrogenous waste products are excreted by birds and reptiles. In humans, the deposition of uric acid crystals in the joints is the main cause of gout.

Urim and Thummim objects of uncertain description, kept in the breastplate and vestments of the Israelite high priest. They were apparently used to discern God's answer to 'yes'-or-'no' questions put to him, and served either as gemstones catching the light (if Hebrew *urim* means 'lights') or as flat markers used in casting lots (if *urim* means 'curse' and *thummim* means 'perfect').

urinal *noun* **1** any receptacle designed for men to urinate into. **2** a room containing such receptacles. [from Old French, from Latin *urinalis*, of urine]

urinary *adj.* of or relating to urine or the passing of urine.

urinate *verb intrans.* to discharge urine.

urination *noun* the act of urinating.

urine *noun Zool.* a liquid, consisting mainly of water containing urea, uric acid, and other nitrogenous waste products, that is produced by the kidneys and stored in the bladder. It is passed to the outside of the body via the urethra in most mammals, and via the cloaca in most non-mammalian vertebrates. [from Latin *urina*, from Greek *ouron*]

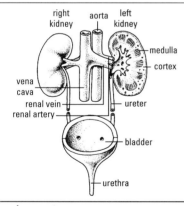

urinary system

urn *noun* **1** a vase with a rounded body, a small narrow neck, and a (usually square) base. **2** such a vase used to contain a dead person's ashes. **3** a large metal cylinder with a tap and an internal element for heating water or making large quantities of tea or coffee. [from Latin *urna*]

Urnes Stave Church a 12c church constructed of wooden staves in Urnes, Sogn og Fjordane county, Norway. It is a World Heritage site.

urology *noun Medicine* the branch of medicine concerned with the treatment of diseases and disorders of the male and female urinary tracts, and the male genital tract. [from Greek *ouron*, urine + -LOGY]

ursine *adj.* **1** of or relating to bears. **2** bear-like. [from Latin *ursus*, bear]

Ursula, St (4c AD) a legendary saint and martyr, who is especially honoured in Cologne, Germany, where she is said to have been slain with 11 000 virgins by a horde of Huns while returning home from a pilgrimage to Rome. She is the patron saint of many educational institutes, particularly the teaching order of the Ursulines, and her feast day is 21 Oct.

Ursula a female first name. [from the Latin name *Ursula*, a diminutive of *ursa*, little she-bear]

Ursulines the members of the Order of St Ursula, which was founded (1535) in Brescia, Italy, by St Angela Merici, named after the 4c legendary saint and martyr. Now spread worldwide, the congregations of sisters engage mainly in the education of girls.

Uruguay

Uruguay, official name **Oriental Republic of Uruguay**, Spanish **República Oriental del Uruguay** POP (1992e) 3.1m, a republic in E South America, divided into 19 departments. AREA 176 215sq km/68 018sq mi. It is bounded E by the Atlantic Ocean, N by Brazil, and W by the R Uruguay and Argentina. CAPITAL Montevideo. CHIEF TOWNS Salto, Paysandú, Mercedes, Las Piedras. TIME ZONE GMT –3. The population is mainly of European origin; Roman Catholicism is the chief religion. OFFICIAL LANGUAGE Spanish. CURRENCY the nuevo peso. PHYSICAL DESCRIPTION grass-covered plains of the S rise N to a high sandy plateau; the R Negro flows SW to meet the R Uruguay on the Argentine frontier. CLIMATE temperate with warm summers and mild winters; the average annual rainfall at Montevideo is 978mm with an average temperature of 16°C. HISTORY originally occupied by the Charrúas people; discovered by the Spanish in 1515; became part of the Spanish Vice-royalty of Río de la Plata in 1726; province of Brazil between 1814 and 1825; gained independence in 1828; unrest caused by Tupamaro guerrillas in the late 1960s and early 1970s; military rule until 1985. GOVERNMENT a President is advised by a Council of Ministers, and a bicameral legislature consists of a 30-member Senate and a 99-member Chamber of Deputies, both elected for five years. ECONOMY traditionally based on livestock and agriculture; meat, wool, hides, maize, wheat, sorghum, rice, citrus fruit, potatoes, vegetable oils; fishing; food processing and packing; cement; chemicals; textiles; leather; steel; light engineering.

Uruguay, River, Portuguese **Rio Uruguai** a river in S America. It is c.1 600km/1 000mi long, but is navigable only in its lower course. The river rises in S Brazil and flows W, SW, and S along the Brazil–Argentina and Uruguay–

Argentina borders, joining the R Paraná above Buenos Aires to form the R Plate. Concepción del Uruguay in Argentina, and Paysandu in Uruguay are the main ports.

Uruk an ancient city-state of Sumer, lying to the NW of Ur. It is the site of the earliest writing ever found, and the home of the legendary Mesopotamian hero, Gilgamesh. Although it came under the domination of Ur in c.2100 BC, it outlasted its powerful neighbour, and survived well into the Parthian period (3c AD).

Urumqi *or* **Urumchi** *or* **Wu-lu-k'o-mu-shi** POP (1990) 1.4m, the capital of Xinjiang autonomous region, NW China. It served as the Communist headquarters in the 1930s and 1940s.

US *abbrev.* United States (of America).

us *pron.* **1** the speaker or writer together with another person or other people; the object form of *we*. **2** all or any people; one. **3** *colloq.* me: *give us a hand.* — **be us** *colloq.* to be suited to us: *breakdancing is just not us.* [from Anglo-Saxon *us*]

USA *abbrev.* United States of America.

USA a trilogy of novels by John Dos Passos (1938). It includes *The 42nd Parallel* (1930), *1919* (1932), and *The Big Money* (1936), and offers a wide picture of American life in the early 20c.

usable *adj.* capable of being used.

USAF *abbrev.* United States Air Force.

usage *noun* **1** the act or way of using. **2** custom or practice. **3** the way language is used in practice; a word or expression commonly used. [from Old French *usage*]

Usborne, Mount a mountain on the island of East Falkland. HEIGHT 705m. It is situated c.65km/40mi W of Stanley and is the highest point in the Falkland Is.

use¹ — *verb* **1** to put to a particular purpose. **2** to consume; to take as a fuel. **3** to treat (a person) as a means to benefit oneself; to exploit. **4** *slang* to take (especially drugs or alcohol) habitually. **5** *old use* to behave (well or badly) towards. — **used to something** *or* **someone** accustomed to them: *she's not used to exercising / they're not used to us yet.* — *verb aux.* was or were formerly: *they used to be friends / she didn't use to be/used not to be so grumpy.* **be used up** *colloq.* be tired or exhausted. **use something up 1** to exhaust supplies, etc. **2** to finish off an amount left over. [from Latin *uti*, to use]

use² *noun* **1** the act of using. **2** the state of being (able to be) used: *go out of use / not in use.* **3** a practical purpose a thing can be put to. **4** the quality of serving a practical purpose: *it's no use complaining. Is this spanner any use?* **5** the ability or power to use (eg a limb). **6** the length of time for which a thing is, will be, or has remained serviceable: *should give you plenty of use.* **7** the habit of using; custom. — **have no use for something** *or* **someone 1** to have no need of them. **2** *colloq.* to dislike or despise them. **make use of someone** to exploit a person. **make use of something** to put it to a practical purpose. [from Latin *usus*, from *uti*, to use]

used *adj.* not new; second-hand.

useful *adj.* **1** serving a helpful purpose, or various purposes. **2** (**useful at something**) *colloq.* skilled or proficient in it. — **come in useful** to prove to be useful.

usefully *adv.* in a useful way.

usefulness *noun* being useful.

useless *adj.* **1** serving no practical purpose. **2** (**useless at something**) *colloq.* not at all proficient at it.

uselessly *adv.* in a useless way; so as to be useless.

uselessness *noun* being useless.

user *noun* a person who uses something.

user-friendly *adj.* designed to be easy or pleasant to use, or easy to follow or understand.

usher — *noun* **1** a person who shows people to their seats, eg in a church or theatre. **2** a court official who guards the door and maintains order. **3** an official who escorts, or introduces people to, dignitaries on ceremonial occasions. — *verb* **1** (**usher someone in** *or* **out**) to conduct or escort them into or out of a building, room, etc. **2** (**usher something in**) *literary* to be a portent of it; to herald it. [from Old French *ussier*, from Latin *ostiarius*, doorkeeper]

usherette *noun* a woman who shows people to their seats in a theatre or cinema.

USM *abbrev.* Unlisted Securities Market.

US Marines *or* **US Marine Corps** a world-famous fighting force, created by Congress in 1798, which served with distinction in the Pacific in World War II and during the Korean and Vietnam Wars. Marines are traditionally known as 'leathernecks', from the leather collars on the early uniforms.

USN *abbrev.* United States Navy.

US Open an international lawn tennis championship now held annually at Flushing Meadow, near New York. It was first held in 1881 as the US championships, and was renamed the US Open in 1968.

Uspallata a pass in the Andes between Mendoza in Argentina and Santiago in Chile. It lies at the foot of Aconcagua and rises to 3 900m. The statue of Christ of the Andes was erected in 1904 to commemorate peaceful boundary settlements.

USS *abbrev.* United States Ship or Steamer.

USSR *abbrev.* Union of Soviet Socialist Republics (see SOVIET UNION).

Ustinov, Sir Peter (Alexander) (1921–) British actor and playwright, born in London, the son of white Russian parents. He first appeared on the stage in 1938, and he later worked in films as an actor (eg *Spartacus*, 1960; *Death on the Nile*, 1978), writer, and producer, and in broadcasting as a satirical comedian. A prolific playwright, his works include *The Love of Four Colonels* (1951), *Romanoff and Juliet* (1956), *Overheard* (1981), and the novel *The Old Man and Mr Smith* (1990).

Ust-Kamenogorsk POP (1991e) 333 000, a city in NE Kazakhstan. It is situated on the R Irtysh and was founded in 1720 as a fortress.

usual — *adj.* done, happening, etc most often; customary. — *noun* (**the usual**) *colloq.* the thing regularly requested, done, etc.
— **as usual** as regularly happens.
[from Latin *usualis*]

usually *adv.* ordinarily, normally.

Usumacinta, River a river in Guatemala and Mexico. It is formed by the meeting of the Pasión and Chixoy rivers on the border and follows a winding course NW to enter the Gulf of Mexico at Frontera. Its length (with the Chixoy, which rises in Guatemala) is c.965km/600mi, but it is only navigable for 480km/300mi.

usurer *noun* a moneylender.

usurious *adj.* **1** relating to or involving usury. **2** *said of interest* excessive.

usurp *verb* to take (eg power) or assume (eg authority) by force, without right, or unjustly. [from Latin *usurpare*, to take possession of by use]

usurpation *noun* the act of usurping.

usurper *noun* a person who usurps.

usury *noun* **1** the practice of lending money at an unfairly or illegally high rate of interest. **2** such a rate of interest. [from Latin *usura*, from *uti*, to use]

US War of Independence see AMERICAN REVOLUTION.

UT *or* **Ut.** *abbrev.* Utah.

Utah POP (1990) 1.8m, a state in W USA, divided into 29 counties. AREA 219 880sq km/ 84 874sq mi. It is known as the 'Beehive State'. PHYSICAL DESCRIPTION rivers include the Colorado and Green; contains the Great Salt Lake in the NW, the largest saltwater lake in the country (2 590sq km/1 000sq mi); L Utah is a freshwater lake S of Great Salt Lake; the Wasatch Range, part of the Rocky Mts, runs N–S through the state; the Uinta Mts lie to the NE; Kings Peak (4 123m) is the highest point; deep canyons dissect the mountainous and sparsely inhabited E region; major cities (containing four fifths of the population) lie along the W foothills of the Wasatch Range; the Great Basin is further W and the arid Great Salt Lake Desert is in the NW. HISTORY the first white exploration was made by the Spanish in 1540; discovery of the Great Salt Lake in 1824; arrival of the Mormons in 1847; acquired by the USA through the Treaty of Guadalupe Hidalgo in 1848; Utah Territory, a large area including the present state, was organized in 1850; several petitions for statehood were denied because of the Mormons' practice of polygamy; antagonism between the Mormon Church and Federal law over this issue led to the 'Utah War' in 1857–8; joined the Union as the 45th state in 1896. CAPITAL Salt Lake City. CHIEF TOWNS Provo, Ogden. ECONOMY cattle, sheep, poultry, hay, wheat, barley, sugar-beet; copper; petroleum; coal; aerospace research; machinery, transportation equipment, electronic components, fabricated metals; food processing; tourism is important (Arches, Bryce Canyon, Glen Canyon National Recreation Area, Zion National Park).

utensil *noun* an implement or container, especially for everyday use. [from Latin *utensilis*, fit for use]

uterine *adj.* **1** relating to or in the region of the uterus. **2** *said of siblings* having the same mother but different fathers.

uterus *noun* (PL. **uteri**) *Anat.* in the lower abdomen of female mammals, the pear-shaped hollow muscular organ (extending upward from the vagina, and linked to the oviducts or Fallopian tubes) in which the embryo or fetus develops and is nourished until birth. At the time of birth, the embryo is expelled from the body as a result of strong muscular contractions of the uterus. — Also called *womb*. [from Latin *uterus*]

Uther Pendragon in Arthurian legend, a king of Britain, who was the father of King Arthur by Ygerna, the wife of Duke Gorlois of Cornwall.

Utica POP (1990) 69 000, the seat of Oneida County, central New York state, USA. It lies on the Mohawk R, 75km/47mi E of Syracuse. NOTABLE FEATURE Munson–Williams–Proctor Institute (art).

utilitarian — *adj.* **1** intended to be useful rather than beautiful. **2** caring (too much) about usefulness and not (enough) about beauty. **3** of or relating to utilitarianism. — *noun* a supporter of utilitarianism. [see UTILITY]

utilitarianism *noun* a set of values based on the belief that an action is morally right if it benefits the majority of people.

utility — *noun* (PL. **utilities**) **1** usefulness. **2** a useful thing. See also PUBLIC UTILITY. — *adj.* designed for usefulness, rather than beauty. [from Latin *utilis*, useful, from *uti*, to use]

utilization *or* **utilisation** *noun* utilizing or being utilized.

utilize *or* **utilise** *verb* to make practical use of; to use. [see UTILITY]

utmost — *adj.* **1** greatest possible. **2** furthest; outermost. — *noun* the greatest possible degree or extent: *tried his utmost to win.* [from Anglo-Saxon *utemest*]

Utopia a political essay by Sir Thomas More on the theme of perfect government. It is written in Latin, and uses the device of an ideal republic named *Utopia.* [from Greek *ou topos*, no place]

utopia *noun* any imaginary place or situation of ideal perfection.

utopian *adj.* unrealistically ideal.

Utrecht, Latin **Trajectum ad Rhenum 1** POP (1990e) 1m, the capital of Utrecht province, W Netherlands. It lies on the R Kromme Rijn and the Amsterdam–Rhine Canal, 32km/20mi SE of Amsterdam, forming the NE end of the Randstad conurbation. It is an important political and cultural city, and a centre for trade fairs. HISTORY centre of the Utrecht school of painters (17c); scene of the Union of Utrecht (1579) and the Treaties of Utrecht (1713–14). NOTABLE FEATURES Cathedral of St Michael (1254); Maliebaan (1636); Paushuize (1523, Pope's House); several museums and old churches. **2** a province in W Netherlands with Utrecht as its capital.

Utrecht, Peace of the treaty (1713) which ended the War of the Spanish Succession, signed by England, the Dutch Republic, Spain, and France, with the other powers agreeing later. By its terms Philip of Anjou became King Philip V of Spain, but the S Netherlands went to the Austrian Habsburgs, along with Spanish parts of Italy. England obtained Gibraltar (from Spain) and parts of Canada (from France). The Dutch stopped French encroachments and obtained some possessions in Gelderland.

Utrecht School a group of Dutch painters who went to Rome early in the 17c and were influenced by Caravaggio. They included Dirck van Baburen (c.1595–1624), Gerard van Honthorst (1590–1656), and Hendrik Terbrugghen (1588–1629).

utricle *noun* **1** *Medicine* the larger of the cavities of the inner ear. **2** *Biol.* any pouch-like part in plants and animals. [from Latin *utriculus*, small bag]

Utrillo, Maurice (1883–1955) French painter, born in Paris. Despite acute alcoholism he was a prolific artist, and produced picture-postcard views of the streets of Paris, particularly old Montmartre.

Uttar Pradesh POP (1991) 139.1m, a state in N central India. AREA 294 413sq km/113 643sq mi. It is bounded to the N by Nepal and China and is crossed by several rivers and canals. HISTORY known as the Bengal Presidency until 1833, then divided into the provinces of Agra and Oudh; in 1857 the Indian Mutiny began at Meerut; came under one administration in 1877; called United Provinces of Agra and Oudh in 1902; renamed United Provinces in 1935; adopted present name in 1950. CAPITAL Lucknow. GOVERNMENT governed by a 108-member Legislative Council and a 426-member Legislative Assembly. OFFICIAL LANGUAGE Hindi. The state is the largest producer of food-grains in India.

utter[1] *verb* (**uttered, uttering**) **1** to express or give out as speech or a sound; to speak. **2** *Legal* to put (counterfeit money) into circulation. [from Middle English *uttren*, from Anglo-Saxon *ut*, out]

utter[2] *adj.* complete; total; absolute. [from Anglo-Saxon *utor*, outer]

utterance *noun* **1** the act of uttering; the ability to utter. **2** a thing uttered.

utterly *adv.* completely, absolutely.

uttermost *adj.* utmost.

Uttley, Alison (1884–1976) English writer of children's stories, born in Derbyshire. She was widowed in 1930, and turned to writing to support herself and her young son. *The Country Child*

(1931) was followed by a series of books, mainly for children, which revealed her knowledge of the countryside. Many are in the Beatrix Potter tradition, featuring popular characters such as Little Grey Rabbit and Sam Pig.

U-turn *noun* **1** a manoeuvre in which a vehicle is turned to face the other way in a single continuous movement. **2** a complete reversal of direction, eg of government policy.

UV *or* **uv** *abbrev.* ultraviolet.

UVF *abbrev.* Ulster Volunteer Force.

uvula *noun* (PL. **uvulas**, **uvulae**) the fleshy part of the soft palate that hangs over the back of the tongue at the entrance to the throat. [from Latin *uvula*, small grape]

uvular *adj.* relating to or produced by the uvula.

Uxmal an ancient Maya city, 80km/50mi S of Merida in the Yucatan Peninsula, Mexico. It covered 60ha, flourished c.600–1000, and was finally abandoned in c.1450. Its ceremonial buildings include the Temple of the Magician on its huge pyramid, and the so-called Governor's Palace, erected on a triple terrace.

uxorious *adj.* greatly or submissively fond of one's wife. [from Latin *uxor*, wife]

Uzbekistan, Uzbek **Ozbekiston Respublikasy**, Russian **Uzbekskaya** POP (1991e) 20.7m, a republic in central and N Middle Asia. AREA 447 400sq km/172 696sq mi. It is bounded to the S by Afghanistan, SW by Turkmenistan, W and NE by Kazakhstan, NW by the Aral Sea, and E by Kirghizia and Tajikistan. CAPITAL Tashkent. CHIEF TOWNS Samarkand, Andizhan, Namangan. TIME ZONE GMT +5. The population is mainly Uzbek (71%) with Russian (8%), Tajik (5%), and Kazakh minorities; the chief religion is Islam. OFFICIAL LANGUAGE Uzbek. CURRENCY the rouble. PHYSICAL DESCRIPTION large area occupied by the Kyzyl-Kum desert; the chief rivers are the Amudarya, Syr-Darya, and Chirchik. HISTORY proclaimed a Soviet Socialist Republic in 1924; declaration of independence in 1991; strong Uzbek nationalism resulted in vio-

Uzbekistan

lent confrontation with Tajiks in the early 1990s. ECONOMY coal, oil, oil refining; metallurgy; fertilizers; machinery; cotton, silk; food processing; intensive cultivation with the aid of irrigation.

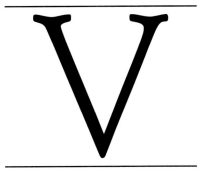

V

V¹ *or* **v** *noun* (PL. **Vs, V's, v's**) **1** the twenty-second letter of the English alphabet. **2** a thing shaped like the letter V.

V² *abbrev.* volt.

V³ *symbol* **1** *Chem.* vanadium. **2** the Roman numeral for 5.

v *or* **v.** *abbrev.* **1** verb. **2** versus. **3** very. **4** *vide* (Latin): see, refer to.

V-1 *abbrev.* Vergeltungswaffe-1.

V-2 *abbrev.* Vergeltungswaffe-2.

VA *or* **Va.** *abbrev.* Virginia.

Vaal River a river in South Africa. Its length is 1 200km/750mi. It rises in SE Transvaal, close to the Swaziland frontier, and flows W, then SW along the border between Transvaal and Orange Free State. It is dammed at Bloemhof. The Vaal is a major tributary of the Orange R, which it joins SW of Kimberley.

Vaasa, Swedish **Vasa,** formerly **Nikolainkaupunki 1** POP (1991e) 36 000, the seaport capital of Vaasa province, SW Finland. It lies on the Gulf of Bothnia, 352km/219mi NW of Helsinki. HISTORY established in 1606; destroyed by fire in 1852; rebuilt on the present site in c.1860; briefly capital in 1917. **2** a province in SW Finland with the town of Vaasa as its capital.

Vac POP (1990) 34 000, a river port and summer resort in Pest county, N central Hungary. It lies on the R Danube, 32km/20mi N of Budapest. NOTABLE FEATURES Baroque triumphal arch; cathedral.

vac *noun colloq.* a vacation, especially between terms at a university or college.

vacancy *noun* (PL. **vacancies**) **1** the state of being vacant. **2** an unoccupied job or post. **3** an unoccupied room in a hotel or guesthouse.

vacant *adj.* **1** empty or unoccupied. **2** having, showing, or suggesting an absence of thought, concentration, or intelligence. [from Latin *vacare,* to be empty]

vacantly *adv.* absently, without concentration: *stared vacantly into the distance.*

vacate *verb* to leave or cease to occupy (a house or an official position). [from Latin *vacare,* to be empty]

vacation — *noun* **1** *North Amer., esp. US* a holiday. **2** a holiday between terms at a university, college, or court of law. — *verb intrans. North Amer., esp. US* to take a holiday. [from Latin *vacatio,* freedom, exemption]

vaccinate *verb* to administer a vaccine to, giving immunity from a disease.

vaccination *noun* the act or process of inoculating with a vaccine.

vaccine *noun Medicine* a liquid preparation containing dead or weakened micro-organisms (such as bacteria or viruses), or products derived from

them, which have lost their virulence but still behave as antigens. Vaccines are used in vaccination to confer temporary or permanent immunity to a bacterial or viral disease by stimulating the body to produce antibodies to a specific bacterium or virus. They are usually either injected into the bloodstream or given by mouth. [from Latin *vaccinus,* from *vacca,* cow]

vacillate *verb intrans.* to change opinions or decisions frequently; to waver. [from Latin *vacillare*]

vacillation *noun* constant wavering or hesitation; indecision.

vacuity *noun* (PL. **vacuities**) **1** the state or quality of being vacuous. **2** a foolish thought or idea. **3** *formal* an empty space.

vacuole *noun Biol.* a space within the cytoplasm of a living cell that is filled with air or liquid (eg water or cell sap), and is surrounded by a membrane known as a *tonoplast* that controls the movement of substances in to and out of the vacuole. Plant cells characteristically have one large vacuole, and animal cells usually have a number of small ones. [from French *vacuole,* little vacuum]

vacuous *adj.* **1** unintelligent; stupid; inane. **2** *said of a look or expression* blank; conveying no feeling or meaning. **3** empty. **4** having no meaning or purpose. [from Latin *vacuus,* empty]

vacuously *adv., said of an expression* without feeling or meaning; blankly: *then he stared vacuously back at me.*

vacuum — *noun* (PL. **vacuums,** or in technical use **vacua**) **1** a space from which all matter has been removed. **2** a space from which all or almost all air or other gas has been removed. **3** a feeling or state of emptiness. **4** a condition of isolation from outside influences. **5** *colloq.* a vacuum cleaner. — *verb trans., intrans.* (**vacuumed, vacuuming**) *colloq.* to clean with a vacuum cleaner. [from Latin *vacuus,* empty]

vacuum cleaner an electrically powered cleaning device that lifts dust and dirt by suction.

vacuum flask a container for preserving the temperature of liquids, especially drinks. It consists of a double-skinned glass bottle with a vacuum sealed between the layers, fitted inside a protective metal or plastic container.

vacuum-packed *adj.* sealed in a container from which most of the air has been removed.

vacuum tube 1 *Electr.* an electron tube containing an electrically heated electrode (the cathode) that emits electrons which flow through a vacuum to a second electrode (the anode). — Also called *valve.* **2** a thermionic valve.

vade-mecum *noun* a handbook of practical information carried for frequent reference. [from Latin *vade mecum,* literally 'go with me']

Vadim, Roger, originally **Roger Vadim Plemiannikov** (1928–) French film director,

born in Paris. The success of *Et Dieu Créa la Femme* (And God Created Woman, 1956), starring his wife Brigitte Bardot (as a 'sex-kitten'), paved the way for further sex-symbol presentations of his later wives: Annette Stroyberg in *Les Liaisons Dangereuses* (Dangerous Liaisons, 1959), Jane Fonda in *Barbarella* (1968), and his mistress, Catherine Deneuve, in *La Vice et La Vertue* (Vice and Virtue, 1962).

Vaduz POP (1991e) 5 000, the capital of Liechtenstein and of Oberland district, lying in the Rhine Valley. NOTABLE FEATURES 12c castle (rebuilt in the 20c); Red House; Prince's Picture Gallery; State Art Collection; Postal Museum.

vagabond — *noun* a person who lives an unsettled wandering life, especially one regarded as lazy or worthless. — *adj.* wandering; roving. [from Latin *vagari,* to wander]

vagary *noun* (PL. **vagaries**) an unpredictable and erratic act or turn of events. [from Latin *vagari,* to wander]

vagina *noun* in the reproductive system of most female mammals, the muscular canal that leads from the cervix of the uterus to the exterior. It receives the penis during sexual intercourse, and is the passage down which the fetus passes at the time of birth. [from Latin *vagina,* sheath]

vaginal *adj.* relating to or associated with the vagina.

vaginismus *noun Medicine* spasmodic contraction of the muscles surrounding the vagina, which may be associated with fear of or aversion to sexual intercourse, or have physical causes.

vagrancy *noun* the unsettled state of a vagrant.

vagrant — *noun* a person who has no permanent home or place of work. — *adj.* **1** wandering; roving. **2** uncertain; unsettled. [from Old French *wakerant,* roaming]

vague *adj.* **1** of an indistinct or imprecise nature. **2** thinking, expressing, or remembering without clarity or precision. [from Latin *vagus,* wandering]

vaguely *adv.* in a vague or uncertain manner; roughly or imprecisely: *was vaguely thinking of going out.*

vagueness *noun* a vague state; unclear or indistinct thought.

vagus *Anat.* in vertebrates, the tenth cranial nerve, branches of which carry motor nerve fibres to many internal organs, such as the heart, lungs, stomach, kidneys, and liver. [from Latin *vagus,* wandering]

Váh, River a river in the Slovak Republic, length 392km/244mi. Rising on the slopes of the Low Tatra as two headstreams, it flows S to meet the R Danube at Komárno.

vain *adj.* **1** having too much pride in one's appearance, achievements, or possessions; conceited. **2** having no useful effect or result; futile.

— **in vain** without success; fruitlessly.
take someone's name in vain to refer to them in a disrespectful way, especially in anger or surprise.
[from Latin *vanus*, empty]

vainglorious *adj. literary* boasting; extremely proud.

vainglory *noun literary* extreme boastfulness; excessive pride in oneself. [from Old French *vaine gloire*]

vainly *adv.* **1** in a vain manner. **2** unsuccessfully.

Vakhtangov, Evgeny Bagrationovich (1883–1923) Russian theatre director, actor, and teacher, born in Vladikavkaz, Armenia. He became an actor with the Moscow Arts Theatre in 1911, and from 1920 was head of the Third Studio, which after 1926 became the Vakhtangov Theatre. In all aspects of his work he combined Stanislavsky's and Meyerhold's methods, stressing the expressiveness of the actor, with his concept of 'fantastic realism' informing his most influential productions.

valance *noun* a decorative strip of fabric hung over a curtain rail or round the frame of a bed. [possibly from Old French *valer*, to descend]

Valcamonica a site in Lombardy, N Italy, where 130 000 rock engravings dating from the 7c BC to the 1c AD have been excavated. The carvings have proved to be an important record for reconstructing the economic and cultural life of the period. It is a World Heritage site.

Valdivia, Pedro de (c.1510–1559) Spanish soldier, born near La Serena, Estremadura. He went to Venezuela and then to Peru, where he became lieutenant to Francisco Pizarro. On the expedition to Chile he founded Santiago (1541), Concepción (1550), and Valdivia (1552). He was killed by Araucanians while attempting to relieve the siege at Tucapel.

vale *noun literary* a valley. [from Latin *vallis*]

valediction *noun* a farewell. [from Latin *vale*, farewell + *dicere*, to say]

valedictory *adj.* signifying or accompanying a farewell: *gave a valedictory wave*.

valence *noun Chem.* same as VALENCY.

valence electron *Chem.* an electron in one of the outer shells of an atom that participates in the formation of chemical bonds with other atoms, resulting in the production of molecules.

Valencia POP (1989e) 2.1m, an autonomous region in E Spain, occupying a narrow coastal area from the Ebro delta to the R Segura. AREA 23 260sq km/8 978sq mi. PHYSICAL DESCRIPTION the central plateau is cut by several rivers which water some of Spain's most fertile land; there is intensive irrigation. HISTORY a former Moorish kingdom; captured by El Cid in 1094; under Spanish rule from 1238. CAPITAL Valencia. The region includes the popular tourist resorts of the Costa Blanca and Costa del Azahar. ECONOMY main agricultural crops are maize, wheat, lucerne, vegetables, and fruit; car plant at Almusafes.

Valencia POP (1991) 753 000, the industrial capital of Valencia autonomous region and of Valencia province, E Spain. It lies on the R Turia. NOTABLE FEATURES Serranos Military Towers (14c); cathedral (13c–15c); Silk Exchange; Ceramics Museum; Fine Arts Museum.

Valencia POP (1990e) 1.3m, the capital of Carabobo state, N Venezuela, and the third largest city in the country. It lies on the R Cabriales, 5km/3mi from L Valencia. The city is famous for its oranges. NOTABLE FEATURE cathedral (18c).

valency *or* **valence** *noun* (PL. **valencies**, **valences**) *Chem.* a positive number that denotes the combining power of an atom of a particular element. It is equal to the number of hydrogen

atoms or their equivalent with which it could combine to form a compound, eg in water (H_2O), hydrogen has a valency of one and oxygen has a valency of two. [from Latin *valentia*, strength, capacity]

Valentine 1 a male and occasionally female first name. **2** one of the two idealistic 'gentlemen' in Shakespeare's *The Two Gentlemen of Verona*, who falls in love with Silvia. [from the Latin name *Valentinus*, from *Valens*, healthy]

valentine *noun* **1** a card or other message given, often anonymously, as a token of love or affection on St Valentine's Day (14 Feb). **2** the person it is given to.
◊ The custom of choosing a valentine, though nominally associated with the saint's day, is probably derived from the ancient Roman festival of Lupercalia, or from association with the season when birds choose their mates.

Valentino, originally **Valentino Garavani** (1933–) Italian fashion designer, born in Rome. He studied fashion in Milan and Paris, then worked for Jean Dessès and Guy Laroche in Paris. He opened his own house in Rome in 1959, and achieved worldwide recognition with his 1962 show in Florence. He has opened numerous ready-to-wear shops throughout Europe, the USA, and Japan.

Valentino, Rudolph (1895–1926) US film actor, born in Castellaneta, Italy. He emigrated to the USA in 1913, and first appeared on stage as a dancer. In 1919 he made his screen début in *The Four Horsemen of the Apocalypse*, and his performances in *The Sheikh* (1921), *Blood and Sand* (1922), and other silent film dramas made him the leading 'screen lover' of the 1920s.

Valera, Eamon de (1882–1975) Irish politician, Prime Minister, and President, born in New York City. Active in various Republican movements, he was a commandant in the 1916 rising, and was arrested and narrowly escaped the firing squad. He became an MP in 1917, leader of Sinn Féin (1917–26), President of Dáil Eireann, and in 1926 became leader of Fianna Fáil, his newly-formed Republican opposition party, which won the 1932 elections. In spite of his colourful early career, his leadership as Prime Minister (1932–48, 1951–4, 1957–9), and President (1959–73), was moderate, and he opposed extremism and religious intolerance.

valerian *noun* **1** any of a family of small flowering plants of Europe and Asia. Its roots have medicinal properties. **2** a sedative drug prepared from its root. [from medieval Latin *valeriana herba*, from the name *Valerius*]

Valerie a female first name. [from the Roman family name *Valeria*, from *valere*, to be healthy]

Valéry, (Ambroise) Paul (Toussaint Jules) (1871–1945) French poet and critic, born in Sète. His poetic works, showing the influence of the Symbolists, include *La Jeune Parque* (The Young Fate, 1917) and *Charmes* (1922). He also wrote several philosophical and literary prose works, and his notebooks appeared posthumously as *Cahiers* (29 vols, 1957–60).

valet — *noun* a man's personal servant. — *verb* (**valeted**, **valeting**) **1** *intrans.* to work as a valet. **2** to clean out (a car) as a service. [from French *valet*, related to VARLET]

valeta see VELETA.

Valetta see VALLETTA.

valetudinarian *formal* — *adj.* **1** relating to or suffering from a long-term or chronic illness. **2** anxious about one's health; hypochondriac. — *noun* a valetudinarian person. [from Latin *valetudo*, state of health]

Valhalla in Norse mythology, a great hall built by Odin to house warriors who die bravely in battle. [from Norse *Valhöll*, from *valr*, the slain + *höll*, hall]

valiant *adj.* outstandingly brave and heroic. [from Latin *valere*, to be strong]

valiantly *adv.* bravely; heroically: *the doctors worked valiantly to save many lives*.

valid *adj.* **1** based on truth or sound reasoning. **2** *said of a ticket or official document* legally acceptable for use. **3** *said of a contract* drawn up according to proper legal procedure. [from Latin *validus*, strong]

validate *verb* to make valid; to confirm the validity of.

validation *noun* making valid; validating.

validity *noun* **1** the state of being valid or acceptable for use. **2** soundness of an argument or proposition.

valine *noun Biochem.* an essential amino acid that is found in proteins. [from *valeric acid*]

valise *noun North Amer.*, esp. *US* a small overnight case or bag. [from French *valise*, suitcase]

Valium *noun trademark* a type of tranquillizing drug.

Valkyrie *Scandinavian Mythol.* a handmaiden of Odin, one of twelve who accompanied the souls of slain heroes to Valhalla. See also WALKÜRE. [from Norse *Valkyrja*, from *valr*, the slain + *kjosa*, to choose]

Valladolid POP (1991) 328 000, the industrial capital of Castilla-Léon region and of Valladolid province, W central Spain. It lies on the R Pisuerga, 193km/120mi NE of Madrid. HISTORY seat of the Castilian and then the Spanish court in the Middle Ages; Ferdinand and Isabella of Castile were married here in 1469; the explorer Christopher Columbus died in Valladolid. NOTABLE FEATURES cathedral (16c); Cervantes Museum; Santa Cruz College; university (1346).

Valle d'Aosta, French **Val d'Aoste** POP (1991) 117 000, an autonomous region in NW Italy, bounded W by France and N by Switzerland. Its population is mostly French-speaking. AREA 3 263sq km/1 260sq mi. PHYSICAL DESCRIPTION contains the valleys of the Dora and the Baltea, and the Valle d'Aosta itself, running SE from Mont Blanc. It has been an important valley since ancient times, being the access route to the Great and Little St Bernard Passes through the Alps. CAPITAL Aosta. ECONOMY wine-growing; livestock; tourism.

Vallée de Mai a nature reserve on Praslin I in the Seychelles. It is noted as the unique habitat of the coco-de-mer palm. Around 4 000 trees, many of them over 800 years old, grow in the reserve, which is a World Heritage site.

Valletta *or* **Valetta** POP (1990) 9 000, the port capital of Malta, lying on a peninsula between the Grand Harbour and the Marsamxett Harbour. It was founded by the Knights of St John in 1566. NOTABLE FEATURES Palace of the Grand Masters; St John's Co-Cathedral (16c); National Museum of Fine Arts. Valletta is a World Heritage site.

valley *noun* (PL. **valleys**) **1** a long flat area of land, usually containing a river or stream, flanked on both sides by higher land, eg hills or mountains. Valleys are most commonly formed by the action of rivers, but may also occur as a result of movements of the Earth's crust (eg faulting), the action of glaciers, or wind erosion. **2** any trough or hollow between ridges, eg on an M-shaped roof. [from Latin *vallis*]

Valley Forge a state park in Chester County, Pennsylvania, USA. It is situated 7km/4mi SE of Phoenixville, on the R Schuylkill. HISTORY the winter headquarters of George Washington in 1777–8.

Valley of the Kings a remote limestone wadi (river valley) on the W bank of the R Nile at Luxor, 650km/400mi S of Cairo. The tombs of the Egyptian kings of the New Kingdom

(XVIII–XX Dynasties, 1550–1070 BC) and their families are cut into its walls.

Valois, Ninette de see DE VALOIS, NINETTE.

Valois Dynasty a ruling dynasty of France from the accession of Philip VI, Count of Valois (1328) to the death of Henry III (1589). The succession was maintained in the direct male line from the 14c until Louis XII of the Orléans branch assumed the Crown (1498). The last three Valois kings (Francis II, Charles IX, and Henry III) were all childless.

valorous *adj. literary* showing valour; courageous.

valour *noun North Amer.* **valor** courage or bravery, especially in battle. [from Latin *valere*, to be strong]

Valparaíso 1 POP (1991e) 296 000, a port and the capital of Valparaíso region, central Chile, situated in Valparaíso province. It is the main port in the country and a major commercial centre. The city was founded in 1536, but most of the old buildings have been destroyed by earthquakes. The lower and upper areas are connected by winding roads and funicular railways. A lift runs from the Plaza Aduana to the Paseo Veintiuno de Mayo terrace on Cerro Artillería, giving a panoramic view. NOTABLE FEATURES cathedral; Naval Academy. **2** a region in central Chile with the city of Valparaíso as its capital.

valuable — *adj.* of considerable value or usefulness. — *noun* (*usually* **valuables**) personal possessions of high financial or other value.

valuably *adv.* to a valuable degree or extent.

valuation *noun* **1** an assessment of the monetary value of something, especially from an expert or authority. **2** the value arrived at.

value — *noun* **1** worth in monetary terms. **2** the quality of being useful or desirable; the degree of usefulness or desirability. **3** the quality of being a fair exchange: *value for money*. **4** (**values**) moral principles or standards. **5** *Maths.* a quantity represented by a symbol or set of symbols. **6** *Mus.* the duration of a note or rest. — *verb* **1** to consider to be of a certain value, especially a high value; to esteem. **2** to assess the value of. [from Latin *valere*]

value-added tax a tax on goods and services sold. It is calculated on the difference between the cost of raw materials and production, and the market value of the final product.
◊ In the UK, the tax is administered and collected by HM Customs and Excise. Certain goods and services are not subject to the tax; these include food, children's clothes, and books, newspapers, and magazines. The standard rate of 17½ per cent is applied to most other goods and services. Businesses with the appropriate registration may offset or reclaim the VAT which they pay on their inputs against any tax charged on their outputs or sales.

valued *adj.* considered valuable or precious; highly prized: *a valued friend.*

value judgement an assessment of worth or merit based on personal opinion rather than objective fact.

valueless *adj.* having little or no value.

valuer *noun* a person who makes a valuation, especially professionally.

valve *noun* **1** any device that regulates the flow of a fluid (a liquid or gas) through a pipe by opening or closing an aperture, or that allows flow in one direction only. **2** *Anat.* in certain tubular organs, a flap of membranous tissue that allows flow of a body fluid, such as blood, in one direction only, eg the valves in the heart and veins. **3** *Electron.* a thermionic valve. **4** any of a set of finger-operated devices that control the flow of air through some brass musical instruments, producing different notes. **5** *Bot.* any of the sections that are formed when a capsule or other dry fruit

opens to shed its seeds at dehiscence. **6** *Zool.* either half of the hinged shell of a bivalve mollusc such as a cockle or clam. [from Latin *valva*, folding door]

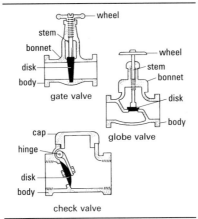

three types of valve

valvular *adj.* **1** having valves. **2** functioning as a valve.

vamoose *verb intrans. North Amer., esp. US slang* (usually as a command) to depart hurriedly; to clear off. [from Spanish *vamos*, let us go]

vamp¹ *colloq.* — *noun* a woman who flaunts her sexual charm, especially in order to exploit men. — *verb* **1** to seduce (a man) with intent to exploit. **2** *intrans.* to behave like a vamp. [a shortening of VAMPIRE]

vamp² — *noun* the part of a shoe or boot that covers the toes. — *verb* **1** (**vamp something up**) **a** to refurbish it or do it up; to prepare something old or out of date for re-use by making alterations. **b** to make up from bits and pieces. **2** to improvise (a simple musical accompaniment). [from Old French *avanpié*, forefoot]

vampire *noun* **1** a dead person who supposedly rises from the grave at night to suck the blood of the living. **2** a person who ruthlessly exploits others. [from German *Vampir*]
◊ According to Slavic folklore, the bite of a vampire turns the victim also into a vampire. They may be repelled by crucifixes, garlic, and daylight, and can be destroyed by being beheaded or pierced through the heart with a wooden stake. Bram Stoker's *Dracula* (1897) popularized the myth.

vampire bat a bat of Central and S America that pierces the skin of animals and humans and sucks their blood.

vampire bat

van¹ *noun* **1** a commercial road vehicle with storage space at the rear, lighter than a lorry or truck. **2** *Brit.* a railway carriage in which luggage and parcels are carried, often also where the guard travels. [a shortening of CARAVAN]

van² *noun* **1** a vanguard. **2** the forefront: *in the van of progress.* [a shortening of VANGUARD]

vanadium *noun Chem.* (SYMBOL **V**, ATOMIC NUMBER **23**) a soft silvery-grey metal that is used to increase the toughness and shock resistance of

steel alloys, eg for components of cars. Its compounds are used in ceramics and glass, and as industrial catalysts. [after *Vanadis*, a name of the Norse goddess Freyja]

Van Allen, James Alfred (1914–) US physicist, born in Mount Pleasant, Iowa. During World War II he developed the radio proximity fuse, a device fitted to explosive projectiles that made use of radio waves to detect the proximity of targets. He was also involved in the launching of the USA's first satellite, Explorer I (1958), and identified from satellite observations the Van Allen belts, two doughnut-shaped zones in which the Earth's magnetic field traps Earth-bound high-speed charged particles.

Van Allen belt *Astron.* either of two rings of intense radiation that encircle the Earth at distances of about 1 000km to 5 000km and 15 000km to 25 000km. They consist of electrically charged particles trapped by the Earth's magnetic field, the outer zone consisting mostly of electrons, and the inner one of protons. [named after James Van Allen]

Vanbrugh, Sir John (1664–1726) English playwright and Baroque architect, born in London. He scored a success with his comedies *The Relapse* (1696) and *The Provok'd Wife* (1697), and became a theatre manager with Congreve. As architect, he designed Castle Howard, Yorkshire (1702) and Blenheim Palace, Oxfordshire (1705–20).

Van Buren, Martin (1782–1862) US Democratic statesman, the eighth President, born in Kinderhook, New York. He became a lawyer, state Attorney-General (1816), Senator (1821), a founder-member of the Democratic Party (1824), Governor of New York (1828), Secretary of State (1829), and Vice-President (1832). During his presidency (1837–41) the financial panic of 1837 meant that his plan for a treasury independent of private banks created opposition, and he was overwhelmingly defeated by the Whigs in 1840. He was unsuccessful in 1848 as the Free Soil presidential candidate, promoting the antislavery cause.

Vance, Cyrus R(oberts) (1917–) US lawyer and politician, born in Clarksburg, West Virginia. He served in the navy before practising law, then held a number of government posts, and served as Secretary of State under President Carter. He resigned in 1980 over the handling of the crisis when US diplomats were being held hostage in Iran. In 1991 he was appointed UN special envoy in Yugoslavia, and the following year became Co-Chairman with Lord Owen of the Yugoslavia Peace Conference (1992–3).

Vancouver, George (c.1758–98) English navigator and explorer, born in King's Lynn, Norfolk. He sailed with James Cook on his second and third voyages and, promoted captain (1794), did survey work in Australia, New Zealand, and the west coast of N America, sailing round the island later named after him (1795).

Vancouver POP (1991e) 1.6m, an industrial seaport in SW British Columbia, SW Canada. It lies opposite Vancouver I, between Burrard Inlet in the N and Fraser R in the S. It is the third largest city in Canada. HISTORY settled in c.1875, named Granville; reached by railway in 1886; in the same year it became a city and received its current name. NOTABLE FEATURES Lipsett Indian Museum in Hastings Park; Stanley Park, with zoo, aquarium, and totem poles; art gallery; Lions Gate Bridge (longest bridge in the Commonwealth); Chinatown, the second largest Chinese community in N America. [named after Capt George Vancouver]

Vandal — *noun* a member of a Germanic people (see VANDALS). — *adj.* relating to the Vandals.

vandal *noun* a person who wantonly damages or destroys works of art or other property.

vandalism *noun* wanton damage to works of art or other property.

vandalize *or* **vandalise** *verb* to inflict wilful and senseless damage on (property).

Vandals a Germanic people, originally perhaps from the Baltic area, who settled in the Danube valley in the 4c AD. Pushed west by the Huns, they invaded Gaul (406), crossed into Spain, conquered Roman Africa (429–39), and sacked Rome (455). The Byzantine general Belisarius reconquered N Africa in 533–4.

Van de Graaff, Robert Jemison

(1901–67) US physicist, born in Tuscaloosa, Alabama. At Princeton in 1929 he constructed the first working model of his 'van de Graaff generator', in which electric charge could be built up on a hollow metal sphere, achieving potentials of over a million volts. Working at the Massachusetts Institute of Technology, he adapted it for use as a particle accelerator and for the production of high-energy X-rays.

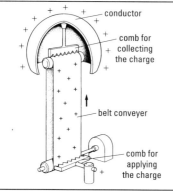

conductor
comb for collecting the charge
belt conveyer
comb for applying the charge

Van de Graaff generator

Vanderbilt, Cornelius (1794–1877) US financier, born in Staten Island, New York. He became the owner of a fleet of passenger and cargo steamships running to Boston and up the Hudson. In 1849, during the gold rush, he established a route to California, and during the Crimean War, a line of steamships to Le Havre. He sold his ships in 1862, and became a railroad financier. He endowed Vanderbilt University in Nashville, Tennessee.

Vanderbilt, Harold S(tirling) (1884–1970) US industrialist, born in Oakdale, New York. He developed the current scoring system for contract bridge while playing aboard the SS Finland on a journey from Los Angeles to Havannah in 1925.

Van der Post, Sir Laurens (Jan) (1906–) South African writer, born in Philippolis. He served with the commandos during World War II, and on his return to South Africa made several voyages of exploration to the interior. He has written novels, but is best known for his books in the mixed genres of travel, anthropology, and metaphysical speculation. These include *Venture to the Interior* (1952) and *The Lost World of the Kalahari* (1958). The influence of Jung is pervasive in his work.

van der Waals, Johannes Diderik (1837–1923) Dutch physicist, born in Leiden. In 1873 he discovered the equation named after him, defining the physical state of a gas or liquid. He became professor at the University of Amsterdam, and was awarded the 1910 Nobel Prize for Physics.

van der Waals' force *Physics* any of the weak attractive forces that exist between atoms or molecules. [named after the Johannes Diderik van der Waals]

van de Velde, Henri see VELDE, HENRI VAN DE.

Van Diemen's Land see TASMANIA.

Vane, Sir Henry (1613–62) English statesman, born in Hadlow, Kent. He travelled in Europe, became a Puritan, and sailed for New England (1635), where he was Governor of Massachusetts. After losing popularity for advocating religious toleration, he returned (1637), entered parliament, and became joint Treasurer of the Navy. He helped to impeach Strafford, promoted the Solemn League and Covenant, and supported the Parliamentary cause in the Civil War. During the Commonwealth he was appointed one of the Council of State (1649–53), but he opposed Cromwell's becoming Lord Protector in 1653, and retired from politics. On Cromwell's death he returned to public life (1659), opposed the Restoration, and was imprisoned and executed.

vane *noun* **1** a weathervane. **2** each of the blades of a windmill, propeller, or revolving fan. [from obsolete *fane*, flag, weathercock]

Vänern, Lake the largest lake in Sweden, situated in the SW of the country. AREA 5 585sq km/2 156sq mi; length 146km/91mi; maximum depth 98m. The chief towns on its banks are Karlstad, Vänersborg, Lidköping, and Mariestad.

Vanessa a female first name, devised by Jonathan Swift from the name of Esther Vanhomrigh.

Van Eyck, Jan (c.1389–1441) Flemish painter, born (possibly) in Maaseik or Maastricht. He worked for John of Bavaria at The Hague (1422–4), and from 1425 for Philip Duke of Burgundy, mainly in Bruges. A major exponent of the new realistic approach to painting in the 15c Netherlands, his works include *Man in a Red Turban* (1433) and *Arnolfini and his Wife* (1434), both in the National Gallery, London.

Van Gogh, Vincent (Willem) (1853–90) Dutch Post-Impressionist painter, born in Groot-Zundert. He worked in an art dealer's and was an evangelist preacher in Le Borinage (1878–80). He painted the first of his major works, *The Potato Eaters* (1885, Amsterdam) in Nuenen. He then studied in Paris (1886–8), where he developed his individual style: one of the pioneers of Expressionism, he used colour primarily for its emotional appeal. In 1888 he settled in Arles, where his art was transformed by the light and colour, and his paintings inspired by the Provençal landscape include *Sunflowers* (several versions, one bought by a Japanese businessman in 1987 for £24 750 000). Other works from this period include *Night Café* (1888). He showed increasing signs of mental disturbance (after a quarrel with Paul Gauguin, he cut off part of his own ear), and was placed in an asylum in St Rémy (1889–90). His paintings from that time include *Starry Night* (Museum of Modern Art, New York) and many sketches and paintings of cypress trees. He then stayed in Auvers-sur-Oise, where at the scene of his last painting, *Cornfields with Flight of Birds* (Amsterdam), he shot himself, and died two days later.

vanguard *noun* **1** the part of a military force that advances first. **2 a** a person or group that leads the way, especially by setting standards or forming opinion. **b** a leading position: *in the vanguard of discovery*. [from French *avant-garde*, advance guard]

vanilla *noun* **1 a** a Mexican climbing orchid. **b** its pod. **2** a flavouring substance obtained from the pod, used in ice cream, chocolate, and other foods. [from Spanish *vainilla*, small pod]

vanish *verb intrans.* **1** to disappear suddenly. **2** to cease to exist; to die out. [from Latin *evanescere*, from *vanus*, empty]

vanishing cream moisturizing cream that leaves no trace on the skin.

vanishing point 1 the point at which parallel lines extending into the distance appear to meet. **2** the point at which something disappears completely.

vanitas *noun Art* a type of still-life picture, produced mainly by 17c Dutch artists such as Bailly (1584–1657), in which symbolic motifs such as skulls, hourglasses, and old books feature as reminders of the vanity of earthly pleasures and the transience of human life and aspirations. [from a phrase in the Vulgate (Eccles. 1.2): *vanitas vanitatum, omnia vanitas*, vanity of vanities, all is vanity]

vanity *noun* (PL. **vanities**) **1** the quality of being vain or conceited. **2** a thing one is conceited about. **3** futility or worthlessness. [from Latin *vanitas*]

vanity bag *or* **vanity case** a woman's small case for cosmetics and make-up.

Vanity Fair a novel by William Makepeace Thackeray (1847–8). It is set during the Napoleonic Wars and follows the interlinked fortunes of the two very different heroines, Amelia Sedley and Becky Sharp.

vanity unit a piece of furniture combining a dressing-table and washbasin.

Van, Lake, Turkish **Van Gölü** the largest lake in Turkey, situated in mountainous E Anatolia. AREA 3 173sq km/1 225sq mi; length 120km/75mi; width 80km/50mi. The ancient Armenian civilization grew up around its shores. ECONOMY fishing; salt extraction.

Vannes, ancient **Dariorigum** POP (1990) 49 000, the port capital of Morbihan department, Brittany, NW France. It lies on the Gulf of Morbihan, 107km/66mi NW of Nantes. NOTABLE FEATURES picturesque Old Town; Château Gaillard (Brittany's first parliament building); Cathedral of St-Pierre (13c–19c); 14–17c fortifications with 14c Constable's Tower.

vanquish *verb literary* to defeat or overcome. [from Latin *vincere*]

vantage *noun* an advantage, especially in tennis. [from Old French *avantage*, related to ADVANTAGE]

vantage point a position affording a clear overall view or prospect.

Vanua Levu a mountainous, volcanic island in the SW Pacific Ocean. AREA 5 556sq km/2 145sq mi; length 176km/109mi. It is the second largest of the Fiji Is, situated 32km/20mi NE of Viti Levu. The Great Sea Reef is the third longest barrier reef in the world. CHIEF TOWN Labasa. ECONOMY coconut plantations, sugar, copra; gold; tourism.

Vanuatu, formerly **New Hebrides**, official name **Republic of Vanuatu** POP (1992e) 154 000, an independent republic comprising an irregular Y-shaped island chain in the SW Pacific Ocean. AREA 14 763sq km/5 698sq mi. It lies 400km/250mi NE of New Caledonia. Vanuatu comprises 12 islands and 60 islets, the largest being Espiritu Santo, Malakula, and Éfaté. CAPITAL Port-Vila (on Éfaté). TIME ZONE GMT +11. The population is mainly Melanesian (95%); Roman Catholicism is the chief religion. OFFICIAL LANGUAGES English, French; Bislama is the national language. CURRENCY the vatu. PHYSICAL DESCRIPTION mainly volcanic and rugged, with raised coral beaches fringed by reefs; the highest peak (on Espiritu Santo) rises to 1 888m; there are several active volcanoes; densely forested, with

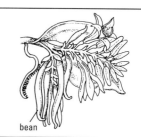

bean

vanilla plant

narrow strips of cultivated land on the coast. CLIMATE tropical, with a hot and rainy season in Nov–Apr when cyclones may occur; annual temperatures at Port-Vila are 16–33°C, and the average annual rainfall is 2 310mm. HISTORY visited by the Portuguese in 1606; under Anglo-French administration as the condominium of the New Hebrides in 1906; gained independence as the Republic of Vanuatu in 1980. GOVERNMENT governed by a President, Prime Minister, and Cabinet, and a representative 46-member Assembly. ECONOMY agriculture includes yams, breadfruit, taro, manioc, bananas, copra, cocoa, coffee; cattle, pigs; manganese; fish processing, foodstuffs; crafts; tourism is rapidly increasing, especially from cruise ships.

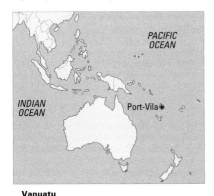

Vanuatu

van Vleck, John Hasbrouck (1899–1980) US physicist, born in Middletown, Connecticut. He was educated at Harvard, where he returned to teach in 1934. He founded the modern theory of magnetism based on quantum theory, and also devised theories of magnetic behaviour in crystals. For this work he shared the 1977 Nobel Prize for Physics with Philip Anderson and Nevill Mott.

Van Winkle, Rip see RIP VAN WINKLE.

vapid adj. **1** dull; uninteresting. **2** having little taste, colour, or smell. [from Latin vapidus, flat-tasting]

vapidity noun a vapid state or condition.

vaporization or **vaporisation** noun the act or process of vaporizing.

vaporize or **vaporise** verb **1** to convert into vapour. **2** intrans. to become vapour; to evaporate. **3** to destroy by reducing to vapour.

vapour noun **1** a gas that can be condensed to a liquid by pressure alone, without being cooled. It consists of atoms or molecules, dispersed in the air, that have evaporated from the surface of a substance that normally exists in the form of a liquid or solid: water vapour. **2** (**the vapours**) old use a feeling of depression, or of faintness, formerly thought to be caused by gases in the stomach. [from Latin vapor]

vapour pressure Chem. the pressure exerted by the atoms or molecules of a vapour. If the vapour is in equilibrium with the liquid with which it is in contact, the pressure is referred to as the saturated vapour pressure.

vapour trail a white trail of condensed water vapour from the engine exhausts of a high-flying aircraft.

Varanasi see BENARES.

Vardon, Harry (1870–1937) British golfer, born in Grouville, Jersey. He won the British Open a record six times (1896, 1898–9, 1903, 1911, 1914), and the US Open in 1900, the first overseas winner. He tied for second place in the 1920 United States Open at the age of 50. He is remembered for his overlapping grip which is still known as the 'Vardon grip'.

Varèse, Edgard (1885–1965) US composer, born of Italo-French parentage in Paris, where his

teachers included D'Indy and Busoni. Until World War I he was active in movements to bring music to the French people, then he settled in the USA (1915), founded the New Symphony Orchestra (1919), and organized the International Composers' Guild (1921). Almost entirely orchestral, his work often uses unconventional percussion instruments, and its abstract nature is reflected in such titles as Hyperprism (1923) and Ionisation (1931).

Vargas, Getúlio (Dornelles) (1883–1954) Brazilian politician, born in São Borja. Elected a Federal deputy in 1923, in 1930 he seized power by revolution and became President of Brazil (1930–45, 1950–4). His government did much to unify Brazil, but from 1937, when he dissolved Congress and suppressed all political parties and trade unions, he governed as a mild dictator. In 1945 he was ousted by popular demand for a democratic constitution, but under this was elected back to office (1950). Four years later, in the face of mounting opposition, he committed suicide.

Vargas Llosa, Mario (1936–) Peruvian novelist, born in Arequipa. He was educated at military school in Lima, and lived in Paris, London, and Barcelona before returning to Peru in 1974. His novels include La ciudad y los perros (The Time of the Hero, 1962), Pantaleon y las visitidores (Captain Pantoja and the Special Service, 1973), and La tia Julia y el escribidor (Aunt Julia and the Scriptwriter, 1978), an inventive comedy which was made into a television series in Colombia. He stood as a candidate for the Peruvian presidency in 1990.

variability noun the state or condition of being variable.

variable — adj. **1** varying or tending to vary; not steady or regular; changeable. **2** that can be varied or altered. — noun **1** a thing that can vary unpredictably in nature or degree. **2** a factor which may change or be changed by another. **3** Maths. in an algebraic expression or equation, a symbol, usually a letter, for which one or more quantities or values may be substituted, eg in the expression $3x$, x is a variable. **4** Astron. denoting a star whose brightness changes over a period of time.

variably adv. in a way that varies or is changeable.

variance noun **1** the state of being different or inconsistent: there was some variance between them. **2** Statistics a quantity equal to the square of the standard deviation.

— **at variance** in disagreement or conflict. [from Latin varientia difference, related to VARY]

variant — noun **1** a form of a thing that varies from another form, eg the ending of a story, or one of several permissible spellings of a word. **2** an example that differs from a standard. — adj. **1** different. **2** differing from a standard.

variation noun **1** the act or process of varying or changing. **2** a thing that varies from a standard. **3** the extent to which a thing varies from a standard. **4** a passage of music in which the main melody is repeated with some (slight) changes. **5** Biol. differences in characteristics, eg size, colouring, between individual members of the same plant or animal species, due to environmental differences, differences in genetic make-up, or (more often) both. **6** differences in characteristics between parents and their offspring, due to mutations, or (more often) to the rearrangement of genetic material that occurs during sexual reproduction.

varicoloured adj. having parts in different colours. [from Latin varius, various + **colour**]

varicose adj. **1** Medicine denoting a superficial vein that is abnormally swollen and twisted, so that it produces a raised and often painful knot on the skin surface, usually of the legs. Varicose veins may be inherited or caused by poor circula-

tion. **2** denoting an ulcer that forms as a result of the development of such a vein. [from Latin varix, varicose vein]

varied adj. having variety; diverse.

variegated adj. Bot. denoting leaves or flowers with patches of two or more colours. [from Latin variegatus, from varius, changing]

variegation noun Bot. in certain plants, the occurrence of patches of two or more colours on the leaves or flowers. Variegation may be an inherited characteristic, as in certain species of ivy, or it may be caused by a viral infection.

variety noun (PL. **varieties**) **1** any of various types of the same thing; a kind or sort. **2** the quality of departing from a fixed pattern or routine; diversity. **3** a plant or animal differing from another in certain characteristics, but not enough to be classed as a separate species; a race, breed, or strain. **4** a form of theatrical entertainment consisting of a succession of acts of different kinds. [from Latin varietas]
◇ Variety was a term coined in the 1880s to describe the newly-built theatres which replaced the old music-halls attached to public houses. However, variety continues to be synonymous with music-hall in the UK, applied both to the shows and to the individual acts performing in them: the equivalent term in the USA is vaudeville.

various adj. **1** several different: worked for various companies. **2** different; disparate; diverse: their interests are many and various. [from Latin varius, changing]

variously adv. in different ways or at different times.

varlet noun old use **1** a menial servant. **2** a rascal or rogue. [from Old French vaslet]

varmint noun North Amer., esp. US slang a troublesome animal or person. [a variant form of VERMIN]

Varna, formerly **Stalin** (1949–56), Latin **Odessus 1** POP (1991e) 321 000, the resort capital of Varna province, E Bulgaria. It lies in a bay of the Black Sea, 469km/291mi E of Sofia. It is the third largest town in Bulgaria, with the country's largest harbour. HISTORY site of Hungarian defeat by the Turks (1444). NOTABLE FEATURES Roman thermae and baths; gold hoard from 3500–3000 BC discovered in the Varna Necropolis (1972); museums, theatre; art gallery; opera house. **2** a province in E Bulgaria with the town of Varna as its capital.

Varna, Battle of a three-month siege and battle (1828) between Russian and Turkish troops during the Russo-Turkish war, which took place at the fortress of Varna on Bulgaria's Black Sea coast. The Turkish garrison fell in October 1828, and was occupied by Russian forces.

varnish — noun **1** an oil-based liquid containing resin, painted on a surface such as wood to give a hard transparent and often glossy finish. **2** any liquid providing a similar finish, eg on fingernails. **3** a superficial attractiveness or impressiveness, especially masking underlying shoddiness or inadequacy; a gloss. — verb **1** to apply varnish to. **2** to make superficially appealing or impressive. [from French vernis]

Varro, Marcus Terentius (116–27 BC) Roman scholar and author, born in Reate. He was politically opposed to Caesar and fought under Pompey in the Civil War and was legate in Spain. Pardoned by Caesar, he was appointed public librarian (47 BC), but under the second triumvirate, Antony placed his name on the list of the proscribed. He wrote over 600 books, covering a wide range of subject matter, but only his work on agriculture (De re rustica) and part of his book on Latin survive.

varsity noun colloq. (PL. **varsities**) **1** Brit. a university, especially with reference to sport.

2 *North Amer.* the principal team representing a college in a sport.

Varuna in Hindu mythology, the god of world order. He reigned in association with Mitra, and was a personification of the essential natural forces of the world.

vary *verb* (**varies, varied**) **1** *intrans.* to change, or be of different kinds, especially according to different circumstances. **2** *trans., intrans.* to make or become less regular or uniform and more diverse. [from Latin *variare*, from *varius*, various]

varying *adj.* changing, especially according to circumstances.

varyingly *adv.* in a changing way; with change.

vas *noun* (PL. **vasa**) *Biol.* a vessel, tube, or duct carrying liquid. [from Latin *vas*, vessel]

Vasa see VAASA.

Vasa Dynasty a royal dynasty which provided Sweden's monarchs, with two exceptions, from 1523 to 1818. Originally a minor noble family, it gained the throne for the first time in the person of Gustav I Vasa, who finally broke the Danish-dominated Kalmar Union and carried through the Reformation. He was succeeded by three of his sons: Erik XIV, John III and (after the deposition of John's son, Sigismund) Charles IX. The latter's son, Gustav II Adolf, was a great statesman and soldier, whose daughter, Christina, abdicated in 1654 in favour of her cousin, Charles X. His son, Charles XI, introduced absolute monarchy, but this was again abolished after the death of his childless son, Charles XII. The abdication of the latter's sister, Ulrika Eleonora, in 1720 brought a breach in the line with the accession of her husband, Frederick I. His successor, Adolf Frederick, was descended from Charles IX's sister, and his son, Gustav III, had even less of the blood in his veins. The line ended with his brother, Charles XIII, who died without heirs.

Vasarely, Victor (1908–) Hungarian-born French painter, born in Pecs. He moved to Paris in 1930, and became one of the leading exponents of Op Art. From c.1947 he painted abstract pictures using repeated geometrical shapes, arranged in such a way as to create an impression of movement. He has also experimented with Kinetic Art. He has had two museums in Provence dedicated to him, and also one in Pecs, Hungary.

vascular *adj. Biol.* relating to the blood vessels of animals or the sap-conducting tissues (*xylem* and *phloem*) of plants. [from Latin *vasculum*, from *vas*, vessel]

vascular bundle *Bot.* in higher plants (eg flowering plants, conifers, ferns), any of numerous thin strands of vascular tissue (conducting tissue), running upwards through the roots and stem and extending into the leaves, composed of xylem (which transports water and mineral salts absorbed by the roots) and phloem (which conducts sugars manufactured during photosynthesis in the leaves).

vascular tissue *Biol.* describing tissue within which water, nutrients, and other materials are transported from one part of a living organism to another, ie the blood vessels of animals, and the xylem and phloem of plants.

vas deferens (PL. **vasa deferentia**) *Biol.* the duct from each testicle that carries sperm to the penis. [from Latin *deferre*, to carry away]

vase *noun* an ornamental glass or pottery container, especially one for holding cut flowers. [from Latin *vas*, vessel]

vasectomy *noun* (PL. **vasectomies**) *Medicine* a surgical operation involving the tying and cutting of the vas deferens in order to produce male sterility without loss of sexual desire or potency. It is an increasingly popular method of contraception. [from Latin *vas*, vessel + -ECTOMY]

Vaseline *noun trademark* an ointment consisting mainly of petroleum jelly.

vasoconstrictor *noun Physiol.* any agent (eg a hormone, drug, or nerve) that stimulates blood vessels to contract, so that they become narrower. [from Latin *vas*, vessel]

vasodilator *noun Physiol.* any agent (eg a hormone, drug, or nerve) that stimulates blood vessels to dilate, so that they become wider. [from Latin *vas*, vessel]

vasopressin *noun Physiol.* a hormone, released by the pituitary gland, that increases blood pressure and the absorption of water by the kidneys, so that less water is excreted from the body. [from Latin *vas*, vessel]

vassal *noun* **1** *Hist.* a person acting as a servant to, and fighting on behalf of, a medieval lord in return for land or protection. **2** a person or nation dependent on or subservient to another. [from Latin *vassus*, servant]

vassalage *noun Hist.* the condition of vassals; a system of using vassals.

Vassar College in the USA, a college in Poughkeepsie, New York, founded by US merchant Matthew Vassar (1792–1868), and opened in 1865. It was initially for women only, but became co-educational in 1968.

vast *adj.* extremely great in size, extent, or amount. [from Latin *vastus*, desolate, huge]

vastly *adv.* to a considerable extent: *was vastly different.*

vastness *noun* a vast state or space; immensity.

VAT *abbrev.* value-added tax.

vat *noun* a large barrel or tank for storing or holding liquids, especially alcoholic drinks. [Anglo-Saxon *fæt*]

Vatican *noun* (*usually* **the Vatican**) **1** the palace and official residence of the pope in Rome. **2** the authority of the pope. [from Latin *Mons Vaticanus*, Vatican Hill]

Vatican City *or* **Vatican**, Italian **Stato della Città del Vaticano** POP (1992e) c.1 000, an independent papal sovereign state, on the W bank of the R Tiber, and the smallest state in the world. AREA 0.4sq km/0.2sq mi. The state is surrounded on all sides by Rome, Italy. It includes St Peter's, the Vatican Palace and Museum, several buildings in Rome, and the pope's summer villa at Castel Gandolfo. There are three entrances to the City (in the care of the Pontifical Swiss

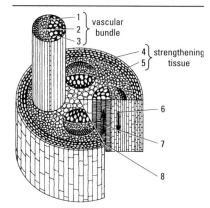

1: vessels and tracheids (xylem)
2: cambium
3: sieve tubes (phloem)
4: sclerenchyma fibres
5: collenchyma cells
6: water and mineral salts in xylem elements
7: organic food materials in phloem elements
8: parenchyma cells (packing tissue)

vascular bundle

Guard): 'The Bronze Doors' at the end of the right-hand colonnade, the Arch of Charlemagne or 'Arch of the Bells', and the Via di Porta Angelica. TIME ZONE GMT +1. OFFICIAL LANGUAGE Latin; Italian is widely spoken. HISTORY created in 1929 by the Lateran Treaty between the pope and Mussolini's government; this treaty ended the dispute arising from Italian occupation of the Papal States and the seizure of Rome in 1870; the state is protected by the 1954 La Haye Convention. GOVERNMENT the Supreme Pontiff of the Roman Catholic Church, the Pope, is Head of State, elected for life by the Sacred College of Cardinals and has full legislative, judicial, and executive powers. NOTABLE FEATURES the City, designated a World Heritage site, contains several great museums and works of art; it issues its own stamps and coinage.

Vatican Councils two councils of the Roman Catholic Church. The First (1869–70) was called by Pope Pius IX to deal with doctrine, discipline and canon law, foreign missions, and the relationship between Church and State. Its decree on papal infallibility resulted in the Ultramontanists' triumph. The Second (1962–5) was called by Pope John XXIII, to attempt to renew religious life and update the belief, structure, and discipline of the Church (*aggiornamento*). Its reforms in liturgy and its ecumenical outlook have had far-reaching effects throughout the Christian world.

Vatican Library one of the world's major libraries, situated in Vatican City. It was formally established by Pope Nicholas V (1397–1455) and enriched by subsequent popes. The present building was built for Sixtus V (1585–90) by the architect Fontana. It has holdings of over 65 000 manuscripts, 7 000 incunabula, and 1 000 000 other volumes.

Vatican Museums a series of art museums occupying part of the papal palaces in Vatican City. They include the Pio-Clementino Museum founded by Clement XIV (1769–74), the Pinacoteca founded by Pius VI (1755–99), the Chiaramonti Sculpture Museum founded by Pius VII (1800–23), and the Gregorian Etruscan Museum and the Egyptian Museum founded by Gregory XVI (1831–46).

vatman *noun* (PL. **vatmen**) *Brit.* a customs and excise officer responsible for collecting VAT.

Vättern, Lake *or* **Vetter** *or* **Wetter** the second largest lake in Sweden, lying E of L Vänern, in the S of the country. AREA 1 912sq km/738sq mi. It extends 130km/81mi from Askersund in the N to Jönköping in the S; its maximum width is 30km/19mi. The Göta Canal connects Lake Vättern with the Baltic Sea.

Vauban, Sebastien le Prestre de (1633–1707) French soldier and military engineer, born in Saint Léger. He served in the Frondes (1651) and joined the government forces (1653). By 1658 he was chief engineer under Turenne and served with him at the siege of Lille (1667). He brought about a revolution in siege warfare and fortification by directing siege operations throughout Louis XIV's campaigns and surrounding the kingdom with a cordon of fortresses (1667–88). He was created Marshal of France in 1703.

vaudeville *noun North Amer., esp. US* variety entertainment; music hall. [from French *vaudeville*, originally of 15c songs composed in *Vau de Vire* in Normandy]
◇ As with the English music-halls, new variety theatres replaced the old beer-halls in the USA in the 1880s. The removal of variety acts to these new custom-built theatres led to the development of vaudeville as one of the most popular and respectable forms of family entertainment, especially in the period from the 1890s to 1925. In France, the term was originally used for dumb shows with songs performed at the Paris fairs, and later for the light satirical songs popular in the 18c theatres.

Vaughan, Henry (1622–95) Welsh religious poet, born in Newton-by-Usk, Breconshire. A doctor by profession, his best-known works are the meditations, *Silex Scintillans* (1650) and the prose devotions *The Mount of Olives* (1652). His other writings include elegies and translations.

Vaughan a male first name. [from the Welsh name *Vychan*, small one]

Vaughan Williams, Ralph (1872–1958) English composer, born in Down Ampney, Gloucestershire. He studied under Sir Charles Stanford, Max Bruch, and Maurice Ravel, and developed a national style of music which derived from English choral tradition, especially of the Tudor period, and folksong. His early successes include the choral *Sea Symphony* (1910), set to words by Walt Whitman, and the orchestral *Fantasia on a Theme by Thomas Tallis* (1910) for strings. He composed nine symphonies, the ballet *Job* (1930), the opera *The Pilgrim's Progress* (1948–9) and numerous choral works. He also wrote for the stage, as in his music for *The Wasps* (1909), and for films, such as *Scott of the Antarctic* (1948), and composed many songs and hymns.

vault[1] — *noun* **1** an arched roof or ceiling, especially in a church. **2** an underground chamber used for storage, or as a burial tomb. **3** a wine cellar. **4** a fortified room for storing valuables, eg in a bank. **5** *poetic* the sky or heaven. — *verb* **1** to build in the shape of an arch. **2** to provide with an arched roof or ceiling. [from Old French *voute*, from Latin *volvere*, to roll]

vault[2] — *verb trans., intrans.* to spring or leap over, especially assisted by the hands or a pole. — *noun* an act of vaulting. [from Latin *volvere*, to roll]

vaulting *adj.* excessive or immoderate, especially of ambition or pride.

vaulting-horse *noun* a padded wooden block on legs, vaulted over by gymnasts.

vaunt — *verb trans., intrans.* to boast or behave boastfully about. — *noun* a boast. [from Latin *vanitare*, from *vanus*, vain]

vauntingly *adv.* in a boastful manner.

Vauquelin, Nicolas-Louis (1763–1829) French chemist, born in Saint-André-d'Hébertot. He began his career as an assistant to pharmacists, and later became professor in Paris. In 1798 he discovered chromium and some of its compounds; he later investigated the compounds of beryllium.

Vavilov, Nikolai Ivanovich (1887–1943) Russian plant geneticist, born in Moscow. He assembled the world's largest collection of seeds, and established a network of 115 experimental stations across the USSR. He formulated the principle of diversity which postulates that, geographically, the centre of greatest diversity represents the origin of a cultivated plant. His international reputation was challenged by Trofim Denisovich Lysenko, who denounced him at a genetics conference; arrested in 1940, he died of starvation in a Siberian labour camp.

VC *abbrev.* **1** Vice Chancellor. **2** Victoria Cross.

VCR *abbrev.* video cassette recorder.

VD *abbrev.* venereal disease.

VDQS *abbrev. vins délimités de qualité supérieure* (French) wines of superior quality from approved vineyards.

VDU *abbrev.* visual display unit.

've *contr.* (usually after pronouns) have: *we've / they've.*

veal *noun* the flesh of a calf, used as food. [from Old French *veel*, from Latin *vitulus*, calf]

vector *noun* **1** *Maths.* a quantity which has both magnitude and direction, eg force, velocity, acceleration. It is often represented by an arrow pointing in an appropriate direction, whose length is proportional to its magnitude. Two vec-

tors can be added graphically by constructing a *parallelogram of vectors* in which they form adjacent sides. See also SCALAR. **2** *Aeron.* the course of an aircraft or missile. **3** *Medicine* any agent, such as an insect, that is capable of transferring a pathogen (a disease-causing micro-organism) from one organism to another, eg from an animal to man, usually without itself contracting the disease, eg the vector of the malaria parasite is the *Anopheles* mosquito. **4** *Biol.* in genetic engineering, a vehicle used to transfer DNA from one organism to another to make *recombinant DNA* (DNA containing sequences from different sources). [from Latin *vector*, carrier]

Veda the 'sacred knowledge' of the Hindus (c.1500 BC), contained in the four collections: the *Vedas*, the *Brahmanas* appended to them, and the *Aranyakas* and *Upanishads*, which serve as an epilogue or conclusion. Originally the Veda consisted of the Rig-veda (sacred songs or hymns of praise), Sama-veda (melodies and chants used by priests during sacrifices), and Yajur-veda (sacrificial formulae); the Athara-veda (spells, charms, and exorcistic chants) were added later. The Aranyakas and Upanishads deny that ritual sacrifice is the only means to liberation, and introduce monistic doctrine. Eventually understood as the fulfilment of Vedic aspirations, they are called the *Vedanta* ('the end of the Veda'). [from Sanskrit *veda*, knowledge]

Vedanta a system of medieval Indian thought expressed in commentaries on the *Brahma Sutras*, which in turn were inspired by the *Upanishads*. Shankara (788–820) founded Advaita Vedanta, whose most distinctive doctrines are that *Brahman* (Holy Power) and *atman* (self) are identical, and that the world of separate selves is an illusion.

Vedic — *adj.* relating to the Hindu Vedas. — *noun* the old Sanskrit language of the Vedas.

Vedic Age a period (1500–600 BC) in the history of India which began with the migration of Indo-European tribes (Indo-Aryans) to N India. It was a time of transition from nomadic pastoralism to settled village communities, when cattle represented the main form of wealth and there was religious worship of personified forces of nature and abstract divinities, centred on a ritual of sacrifice.

veduta *noun* (PL. **vedute**) *Art* a painting depicting a panoramic view of a place, usually a city, in a topographically accurate and decorative manner. Canaletto produced many such views of Venice, which were especially popular with 18c English gentlemen on the Grand Tour, who collected picturesque records of places they visited. [from Italian *veduta*, view]

veer — *verb intrans.* **1** to move abruptly in a different direction. **2** *said of the wind* to change direction clockwise. — *noun* a change of direction. [from French *virer*]

veg *colloq.* — *noun* a vegetable or vegetables. — *verb intrans.* (**veg out**) *colloq.* to be inactive or engage in mindless activity, especially after a period of over-exertion.

Vega (Carpio), Lope (Félix) de (1562–1635) Spanish dramatist and poet, born in Madrid. He served in the Armada and first made

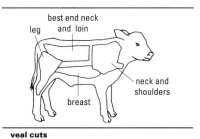

best end neck
leg   and loin
neck and shoulders
breast

veal cuts

his mark as a ballad writer; after 1588 he produced a wide range of historical and contemporary dramas including about 2 000 plays and dramatic pieces, of which over 400 have survived.

vegan — *noun* a person who does not eat meat, dairy products, or any foods containing animal fats or extracts, often also avoiding wool, leather, and other animal-based substances. — *adj.* **1** of or for vegans. **2** *said of a meal or diet* excluding such foods. [a contraction of VEGETARIAN]

veganism *noun* the principles and practices adopted by vegans.

vegeburger *noun* a flat cake resembling and served like a hamburger, made with vegetables, soy beans, etc instead of meat. [from VEGETARIAN + HAMBURGER]

vegetable — *noun* **1** a plant or any of its parts, other than fruits and seeds, that is used for food, eg roots, tubers, stems, or leaves. **2** loosely used to refer to some fruits that are used for food, eg tomato, marrow. **3** the edible part of such a plant. **4** *offensive colloq.* a person almost totally incapable of any physical or mental activity because of severe brain damage. — *adj.* relating to plants. [from Latin *vegetabilis*, from *vegetus*, lively]

vegetable marrow a marrow.

vegetable oil any of various oils obtained from plants, used especially in cooking and cosmetics.

vegetal *adj.* consisting of or relating to vegetables or to plant life in general. [from Latin *vegetalis*]

vegetarian — *noun* a person who does not eat meat or fish. — *adj.* **1** of or for vegetarians. **2** denoting food or a diet that contains no meat or fish. [from VEGETABLE + suffix *-arian*]

vegetarianism *noun* the principles and practices adopted by vegetarians.

vegetate *verb intrans.* **1** to live a dull inactive life. **2** to live or grow as a vegetable. [from Latin *vegetare*, to animate]

vegetation *noun* **1** *Bot.* a collective term for plants. **2** *Bot.* the plants of a particular area, which may be very diverse or belong to just one or a few species, depending on climatic conditions, the nature of the soil, and human activity.

vegetative *adj.* **1** of plants or vegetation. **2** *Biol.* denoting asexual reproduction in plants or animals, as in bulbs, corms, yeasts, etc. **3** *Bot.* denoting a phase of plant growth as opposed to reproduction.

vegetative propagation *Bot.* any form of asexual reproduction in plants (ie reproduction without the formation of seeds), which gives rise to new plants known as clones which are genetically identical to the parent plant. Natural methods of vegetative propagation include the production of bulbs, tubers, corms, rhizomes, stolons, etc, and artificial methods include grafting and the taking of cuttings. Vegetative propagation is widely used in horticulture as it allows the mass production of plants with desirable traits that might be lost in breeding.

veggie *noun colloq.* **1** a vegetarian. **2** a vegetable.

vehemence *noun* strong and forceful feeling.

vehement *adj.* expressed with strong feeling or firm conviction; forceful; emphatic. [from Latin *vehemens*, eager]

vehemently *adv.* with strong feeling; forcefully.

vehicle *noun* **1** a conveyance for transporting people or things, especially a self-powered one. **2** a person or thing used as a means of communicating ideas or opinions: *newspapers as vehicles for political propaganda.* **3** a neutral substance in which a drug is mixed in order to be administered, eg a syrup. **4** a substance in which a pigment is transferred to a surface as paint, eg oil or water. [from Latin *vehere*, to carry]

vehicular *adj.* relating to or for the use of vehicles: *no vehicular access*.

veil — *noun* **1** a fabric covering for a woman's head or face, forming part of traditional dress in some societies. **2** a covering of fine netting for a woman's head, which may be attached to a hat or headdress, worn for decoration or ceremonially, eg by a bride. **3** the hoodlike part of a nun's habit. **4** (**the veil**) *literary* the vocation of a nun. **5** anything that covers or obscures: *a veil of secrecy*. — *verb* **1** to cover, or cover the face of, with a veil. **2** to conceal or partly conceal; to disguise or obscure: *veiled threats*.

— **draw a veil over something** to conceal it discreetly; to avoid mentioning it.

take the veil to become a nun.

[from Latin *velum*, curtain]

vein *noun* **1** any blood vessel, apart from the pulmonary vein, that carries deoxygenated blood back towards the heart. Veins have thin walls, and contain valves which ensure that blood can only flow in one direction. **2** *loosely* any blood vessel. **3** a thin sheetlike deposit of one or more minerals, eg quartz, deposited in a fracture or joint in the surrounding rock. **4** a streak of different colour, eg in cheese. **5** in a leaf, any of a large number of thin branching tubes containing the vascular (conducting) tissues, ie the xylem and phloem. **6** in an insect, any of the tubes of chitin that stiffen and support the membranous structure of the wings. **7** a mood or tone: *written in a sarcastic vein*. **8** a distinct characteristic present throughout; a streak. [from Latin *vena*]

veined *adj.* having veins or different-coloured streaks.

veiny *adj.* streaked with veins; having prominent veins.

Vejle **1** POP (1990e) 46 000, the seaport capital of Vejle county, E Jutland, Denmark. It is a manufacturing town, lying at the head of Vejle Fjord. NOTABLE FEATURES St Nicholas's Church (13c); 28km/17mi W is Billund, with Legoland, a miniature town built of Lego plastic bricks. **2** a county in E Jutland, Denmark, with the town of Vejle as its capital.

Velázquez, Diego (Rodríguez de Silva) (1599–1660) Spanish painter, born in Seville. His early works include religious scenes eg *The Adoration of the Magi* (1619, Prado, Madrid) and domestic genre pieces eg *The Old Woman Cooking Eggs* (1618, Edinburgh). Sometimes, as in *Christ in the House of Martha* (National Gallery, London), these two themes are combined. In 1623 he moved to Madrid and became a court painter. He visited Italy (1629–31), which transformed his sombre, naturalistic style into a more colourful approach, influenced by Titian. He is best known for his three late works, *Las Meninas* (1655, Maids of Honour) and *Las Hilanderas* (c.1657, The Tapestry Weavers) in the Prado, Madrid, and *Venus and Cupid*, known as the *Rokeby Venus* (c.1651) in the National Gallery, London. Other works include *The Crucifixion* (Prado, Madrid).

Velcro *noun trademark* a fastening material consisting of two nylon surfaces, one of tiny hooks, the other of thin fibres, which bond tightly when pressed together but are easily pulled apart.

veld *or* **veldt** *noun* a wide grassy plane with few or no trees, especially in southern Africa. [from Dutch *veld*, field]

Velde, Henri van de (1863–1957) Belgian architect, born in Antwerp. He began as a painter and became one of the originators of the Art Nouveau style of architecture. With his pupil Gropius, he founded the Deutscher Werkbund (a movement for improving manufacturing design) in Germany. He also established the Weimar School of Arts and Crafts (1906) from which developed the Bauhaus school. His designs include the Werkbund Theatre in Cologne (1914).

veleta *or* **valeta** *noun* a ballroom dance or dance tune with a fast waltz-like rhythm. [from Spanish *veleta*, weathercock]

Veliko Tŭrnovo **1** POP (1991e) 74 000, the capital of Veliko Tŭrnovo province, E central Bulgaria. It lies on the R Yantra, 241km/150mi NE of Sofia. HISTORY capital of the second Bulgarian Kingdom (1187–1393). NOTABLE FEATURES Tsarevets Hill with its fortress walls; Patriarch's Palace; Royal Palace and defensive tower; Forty Martyrs Church (1230); Renaissance Museum. **2** a province in E central Bulgaria with the town of Veliko Tŭrnovo as its capital.

Velingrad POP (1991) 26 000, a spa town in Pazardzhik province, S Bulgaria, situated in the Rhodope Mts. It is a well-known therapeutic centre, with 70 thermal springs.

vellum *noun* **1** a fine kind of parchment, originally made from calfskin. **2** a manuscript written on such parchment. **3** thick cream-coloured writing-paper. [from Old French *velin*, from *veel*, calf]

velocity *noun* (PL. **velocities**) **1** *technical* rate of motion in a particular direction. **2** *loosely* speed. [from Latin *velox*, swift]

velour *or* **velours** *noun* any fabric with a velvet-like pile, used especially for upholstery. [from French *velours*, related to VELVET]

velvet — *noun* **1** a fabric, usually nylon or silk, with a very short soft closely woven pile on one side. **2** the soft skin that covers the growing antlers of deer, and is rubbed off as they mature. — *adj.* **1** made of velvet. **2** soft or smooth like velvet.

— **on velvet** *colloq.* in a comfortable position of safety or wealth.

[from late Latin *velvettum*, from Latin *villus*, tuft]

velveteen *noun* cotton fabric with a velvet-like pile.

velvet glove apparent gentleness or lenience concealing strength or firmness, especially with allusion to the phrase *an iron hand in a velvet glove*.

velvet revolution the peaceful transition from communism to democracy in Czechoslovakia in 1989.

velvety *adj.* having the quality of velvet; smooth.

Ven. *abbrev.* Venerable.

vena cava (PL. **venae cavae**) *Anat.* either of the two large veins (the superior vena cava and the inferior vena cava) that carry deoxygenated blood to the right atrium (auricle) of the heart. [from Latin *vena cava*, hollow vein]

venal *adj.* **1** willing to be persuaded by corrupt means, especially bribery. **2** *said of behaviour* dishonest; corrupt. [from Latin *venum*, goods for sale]

venality *noun* a venal state or conduct; susceptibility to corruption.

venally *adv.* dishonestly; corruptly.

venation *noun Biol.* **1** the arrangement of veins in the wing of an insect. **2** the arrangement of veins in the leaf of a plant. [from Latin *vena*, vein]

vend *verb* to sell or offer for sale (especially small wares). [from Latin *vendere*, to sell]

vendee *noun Legal* a buyer, especially of property.

Vendée, Wars of the French counter-revolutionary insurrections in the western provinces against the central government in Paris. The brutal rising in La Vendée (1793), when priests and nobles encouraged the conservative peasantry to rebel against the Convention's conscription and anticlerical policies, was a precedent for other provincial revolts in 1795, 1799, 1815, and 1832.

vender *noun formal* a seller of goods, especially at a market: *fruit-vender*.

vendetta *noun* **1** a bitter feud in which the family of a murdered person takes revenge by

killing the murderer or a relative. **2** any long-standing bitter feud or quarrel. [from Italian, from Latin *vindicta*, revenge]

vending machine a coin-operated machine dispensing small wares such as sweets, drinks, and cigarettes.

Vendôme, Louis Joseph, Duc de (Duke of) (1654–1712) French soldier, born in Paris, the great-grandson of Henry IV. He fought in the Dutch campaign of 1672, and in the War of the Grand Alliance (1689–97). He commanded in Italy and Flanders during the War of the Spanish Succession (1701–14), during which he was victorious at Cassano (1705) and Calcinato (1706), defeated at Oudenarde by Marlborough, and recalled after the loss of Lille (1708). Sent to Spain in 1710 to aid Philip V, he recaptured Madrid, and defeated the English at Brihuega and the Austrians at Villaviciosa.

vendor *noun Legal* a seller, especially of property.

veneer — *noun* **1** a thin layer of a fine material (especially wood) fixed to the surface of an inferior material to give an attractive finish. **2** a false or misleading external appearance, especially of a favourable quality: *a veneer of respectability*. — *verb* to put a veneer on. [from Old French *fornir*, to furnish]

venerable *adj.* **1** deserving to be greatly respected or revered, especially on account of age or religious association. **2** (**Venerable**) **a** *Church of E.* a title given to an archdeacon. **b** *RC Church* a title given to a person due to be declared a saint. [from Latin *venerabilis*]

venerate *verb* to regard with deep respect or awe; to revere. [from Latin *venerari*]

veneration *noun* the paying of deep respect; devotion.

venereal *adj.* **1** *said of a disease or infection* transmitted by sexual intercourse. **2** relating to, resulting from, or for the treatment of such diseases. [from Latin *venereus*, from *Venus*, Roman goddess of love]

venereal disease *Medicine* former name for a sexually transmitted disease.

Venetia a female first name. [origin uncertain; perhaps related to a Celtic word meaning 'blessed']

Venetian — *adj.* relating to Venice in NE Italy. — *noun* a native or citizen of Venice. [from Latin *Venetia*, Venice]

Venetian blind a window blind consisting of horizontal slats strung together, one beneath the other, and tilted to let in or shut out light.

Venetian School the art associated with Venice, beginning with the building of the Basilica of St Mark in the 11c. Painting developed from the 14c onwards and became one of the great traditions in Renaissance Europe. Leading masters included Bellini, Giorgione, Titian, Veronese, and Tintoretto. The Baroque period saw the building of magnificent churches, and the 18c saw a final flowering in painting, with G B Tiepolo, Canaletto and Guardi.

Venezuela, official name **Republic of Venezuela**, Spanish **República de Venezuela** POP (1992e) 20.3m, the most northerly country in S America, divided into 20 states, two territories, and one federal district. AREA 912 050sq km/ 352 051sq mi. It is bounded N by the Caribbean Sea, E by Guyana, S by Brazil, and SW and W by Colombia. CAPITAL Caracas. CHIEF TOWNS Maracaibo, Ciudad Guayana, Valencia, Barquisimeto. TIME ZONE GMT –4. Most of the population is mestizo (67%) or of European origin (21%); Roman Catholicism is the chief religion. OFFICIAL LANGUAGE Spanish. CURRENCY the bolívar. physical description the Guiana Highlands in the SE cover over half the country; the Venezuelan Highlands lie in the W and along the coast, reaching heights of over 5 000m; there

Venezuela

are lowlands around L Maracaibo and in the valley of the Orinoco R, which crosses the country S–NE. CLIMATE generally hot and humid; one rainy season from Apr to Oct; annual temperatures at Caracas are 13–27°C, monthly rainfall between 10mm and 109mm; annual rainfall on the coast increases from very low amounts around L Maracaibo to 1 000mm in the E; in the Guiana Highlands to the SE, annual rainfall is c.1 500mm. HISTORY originally inhabited by Caribs and Arawaks; seen by Columbus in 1498; Spanish settlers in 1520; frequent revolts against Spanish colonial rule; independence movement under Bolívar, leading to the establishment of the State of Gran Colombia (Colombia, Ecuador, Venezuela) in 1821; became an independent republic in 1830; there were two unsuccessful attempted coups in 1992. GOVERNMENT governed by an elected two-chamber National Congress, comprising a Senate and a 196-member Chamber of Deputies; a President is advised by a Council of Ministers. ECONOMY largely an agricultural country until the 1920s, when the development of oil from Maracaibo transformed the economy: over 90% of export revenue is now derived from oil; iron ore, natural gas, aluminium, gold, nickel, iron, copper, manganese; cement; steel; chemical; food; shipbuilding; vehicles; 20% of the land is under cultivation: coffee, cocoa, maize, tobacco, sugar; dairy and beef cattle.

Venezuelan Boundary Dispute a dispute between Britain and Venezuela over the boundary of British Guiana (now Guyana). In 1895 this provoked a brief but acute crisis in Anglo-American relations that involved the USA forcing Britain to accept arbitration. The issue was settled in 1899.

vengeance *noun* punishment inflicted as a revenge; retribution.
— **with a vengeance 1** forcefully or violently. **2** to a great degree: *foolishness with a vengeance.*
[from Old French, from Latin *vindicare*, to avenge]

vengeful *adj.* **1** eager for revenge. **2** carried out in revenge. [from obsolete *venge*, to avenge]

venial *adj.*, *said of a sin or weakness* forgivable; excusable. [from Latin *venia*, pardon]

veniality *noun* a venial state, with reference to sin or weakness.

venial sin *RC Church* a minor sin, not involving loss of divine grace. See also MORTAL SIN.

Venice, Italian **Venezia**, Latin **Venetia** POP (1991e) 318 000, the seaport capital of Veneto region and of Venice province, NE Italy. It lies on the Gulf of Venice, at the head of the Adriatic Sea. Situated 4km/3mi from the Italian mainland in a salt-water lagoon, it is separated from the

Adriatic Sea by narrow spits of land. The city is built on 118 small islands, and crossed by numerous canals, notably the Grand Canal, the main traffic artery. Connection with the mainland is by a causeway for road and rail traffic and by ferries; gondolas and water buses (*vaporettos*) are the main form of city transport. The houses and palaces are built on piles. HISTORY an influential and independent trading republic from the 10c; played an important role during the Italian Renaissance (the Venetian School of painting, the operas of Monteverdi); ruled by a Doge until the late 18c; joined Italy in 1866; developed as a major tourist centre in the 19c–20c; there has been fresh anxiety since the 1980s over the risk to the city from flooding and pollution. NOTABLE FEATURES Venice and the lagoon are World Heritage sites; St Mark's Cathedral (11c) and Campanile (99m-high bell-tower, rebuilt from 1905 until 1912); Old Mint; Doge's Palace (14c–15c); Bridge of Sighs (c.1595); Church of Santi Giovanni e Paolo (14c); Accademia di Belle Arti.

Venice Preserv'd, or a Plot Discovered a play by Thomas Otway (1682). A tragedy written in blank verse, it stems from the secret marriage of Belvidera, a Senator's daughter, and Jaffeir, who joins a plot against the Venetian state. His betrayal of the conspirators results in his own tragic downfall.

Vening Meinesz, Felix Andries (1887–1966) Dutch geophysicist, born in The Hague. Professor at Utrecht and Delft, he used a submarine to make the first marine gravity determinations in the Pacific in 1923. His later voyages led him to deduce the presence of 'subduction zones', where down-buckling of oceanic crust occurs.

venison *noun* the flesh of a deer, used as food. [from Old French, from Latin *venari*, to hunt]

Venn, John (1834–1923) English logician, born in Drypool, Hull. A Fellow of Caius College, Cambridge, he is best known for his use of 'Venn diagrams', pictorially representing the relations between sets.

Venn diagram *Maths.* a diagram that is used to illustrate the relationships between mathematical sets, consisting of a rectangle that represents the universal set, within which individual sets are denoted by circles. Intersecting sets are indicated by two or more overlapping circles, and a subset is shown as a smaller circular area within a circle. [named after John Venn]

venom *noun* **1** a poisonous liquid that some creatures, including scorpions and certain snakes, inject in a bite or sting. **2** spitefulness, especially in language or tone of voice. [Latin *venenum*, poison]

venomous *adj.* **1** inflicting venom; poisonous. **2** spiteful.

venous *adj.* relating to or contained in veins. [from Latin *vena*, vein]

vent[1] *noun* a slit in a garment, especially upwards from the hem at the back of a jacket or coat, for style or ease of movement. [from French *fente*, slit]

vent[2] — *noun* **1** an opening allowing air, gas, or liquid into or out of a confined space. **2** the passage inside a volcano, through which lava and gases escape. **3** *Biol.* the anus of a bird or other small animal. — *verb* **1** to make a vent in. **2** to let in or out through a vent. **3** to release (especially emotion) freely.
— **give vent to something** to express one's feelings or emotions openly.
[from French *éventer*, to expose to air]

ventilate *verb* **1** to allow fresh air to circulate throughout. **2** to cause (blood) to take up oxygen. **3** to supply air to (the lungs). **4** to expose to public examination or discussion. [from Latin *ventilare*, from *ventus*, wind]

ventilation *noun* the act or process of ventilating; circulation of fresh air.

ventilator *noun* **1** a device that circulates or draws in fresh air. **2** a machine that ventilates the lungs of a person whose respiratory system is damaged.

Ventnor POP (1981) 7 000, a health resort in South Wight district, Isle of Wight, S England. It lies on the SE coast of the island, on cliff-side terraces. The poet Algernon Charles Swinburne is buried in the churchyard at Bonchurch nearby.

ventral *adj.* **1** *Anat.* denoting the lower surface of an animal that walks on four legs, of any invertebrate, or of a structure such as a leaf or wing. **2** denoting the front surface of the body of an animal that walks upright, eg a human being. **3** denoting a structure that is situated on or just beneath such a surface. [from Latin *venter*, abdomen]

ventrally *adv.* in relation to the abdomen or belly.

ventricle *noun* **1** *Anat.* in mammals, either of the two lower chambers of the heart, which have thick muscular walls. Contraction of the right ventricle pumps deoxygenated blood to the lungs, whereas contraction of the left ventricle pumps oxygenated blood to the rest of the body via the aorta. **2** *Anat.* in vertebrates, any of several fluid-filled cavities within the brain. [from Latin *ventriculus*]

ventricular *adj.* relating to or situated in a ventricle.

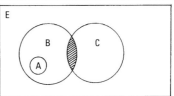

A is a subset of B, B and C are intersecting sets, and E is the universal set

Venn diagram

ventriloquism *noun* the art of speaking in a way that makes the sound appear to come from elsewhere, especially a dummy's mouth; throwing the voice. [from Latin *venter*, belly + *loqui*, to speak]

ventriloquist *noun* a person who performs ventriloquism, especially as entertainment.

ventriloquize or **ventriloquise** *verb intrans.* to perform ventriloquism.

Ventris, Michael (George Francis) (1922–1956) English linguist, born in Wheathampstead, Hertfordshire. As a teenager he heard Arthur Evans lecture on the undeciphered Minoan scripts found on tablets excavated at palace sites in Crete (Linear B), and determined to decipher them. Although an architect by training, after World War II he devoted much

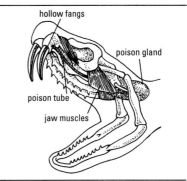

hollow fangs

poison gland

poison tube

jaw muscles

venom-injecting devices

of his time to analysis of the texts, and in 1952 announced that the language of Linear B was early Greek, a conclusion later confirmed by other scholars.

venture — *noun* **1** an exercise or operation involving danger or uncertainty. **2** a business project, especially one involving risk or speculation. **3** an enterprise attempted. — *verb* **1** *trans., intrans.* **a** to be so bold as to; to dare: *ventured to criticize the chairman.* **b** (**venture out** or **forth**) to dare to go out, especially outdoors: *reluctant to venture out in bad weather.* **2** to put forward or present in the face of possible opposition: *ventured a different opinion.* **3** to expose to danger or chance; to risk.
— **venture on something** to attempt something dangerous.
[shortening of ADVENTURE]

venture capital money supplied by individual investors or business organizations for a new, especially speculative, business enterprise.

venturer *noun* **1** a person who takes part in a venture or enterprise. **2** *Hist.* a participant in a trading scheme.

Venture Scout a member of the senior branch of the Scout movement.

venturesome *adj.* **1** prepared to take risks; enterprising. **2** involving danger; risky.

venue *noun* **1** the chosen location for a sports event or entertainment. **2** *Legal* the place where a court case is to be tried, or the district from which the jurors are chosen. **3** a meeting-place. [from Latin *venire*, to come]

venule *noun Biol.* **1** a branch of a vein in an insect's wing. **2** any of the small-calibre blood vessels into which the capillaries empty, and which join up to form veins. [from Latin *venula*, diminutive of *vena*, vein]

Venus in Roman mythology, originally a goddess of the vegetable garden who became identified with Aphrodite, the Greek goddess of love.

Venus *Astron.* the second planet from the Sun. Its orbit lies between those of Mercury and Earth, and it is clearly visible from the Earth. It resembles a bright star, and can be seen some time before and after the true stars become visible. For this reason it is sometimes called the 'evening star' or 'morning star'.
◇ Venus is about 109 million km from the Sun, and has a diameter of 12 104km at the equator. It takes 243 days to rotate once on its own axis, and 224.7 days to orbit around the Sun, ie its 'day' is longer than its 'year'. Venus rotates on its axis in the opposite direction to all the other planets except Uranus (and possibly Pluto). It is almost exactly the same size as the Earth, but its surface reaches a maximum temperature of 480°C, hotter than that of any other planet.
Venus has a thick atmosphere almost entirely composed of carbon dioxide, and sulphuric acid droplets form dense clouds. Sunlight passes through the atmosphere and falls on the rocky surface of the planet, which warms up and reflects heat back into the atmosphere, where it is trapped by the insulating layer of carbon dioxide. The trapped heat releases more carbon dioxide from the rocks, so that the insulating layer becomes even more efficient. This escalating greenhouse effect is responsible for the very high surface temperatures of the planet. In 1992 the space probe *Magellan* was used to map 95% of the surface of Venus, which is obscured by clouds. Mountain peaks up to 12km high and various features resembling volcanoes were charted.

Venus de Milo a statue in marble of a seminude Aphrodite (c.150 BC, Louvre, Paris). It was found in Melos in 1820.

Venus flytrap an insectivorous plant (*Dionaea muscipula*), native to the bogs of North and South Carolina, with leaves consisting of two parts hinged together. When an insect touches the

inner surface of the leaf, it is trapped as the two halves snap shut. The plant then secretes digestive enzymes that enable it to absorb nitrogen and other nutrients from the dead insect.

Venus flytrap

Vera a female first name. [from a Russian name meaning 'faith'; associated with Latin *verus*, true]

veracious *adj. formal* truthful. [from Latin *verus*, true]

veracity *noun formal* truthfulness.

Veracruz 1 POP (1990) 328 000, a seaport in Veracruz state, E Mexico. It lies on the Gulf of Mexico and is the principal port of entry for the country. The city was the site of the Cortés landing in 1519. NOTABLE FEATURES Palacio Municipal (17c); Castle of San Juan de Ulúa (1565); Baluarte de Santiago Fort; City Museum. **2** a state in E Mexico with Jalapa Enríquez as its capital.

veranda or **verandah** *noun* a sheltered terrace attached to a house or other building. [from Portuguese *varanda*, balcony]

verb *noun* a word that belongs to a grammatical class denoting an action, experience, occurrence, or state, eg *do, feel, happen, remain.* [from Latin *verbum*, word]

verbal *adj.* **1** relating to or consisting of words: *verbal abuse.* **2** spoken, not written: *verbal communication.* **3** *Grammar* relating to verbs.

verbalism *noun* excessive attention paid to words used, rather than to ideas expressed, especially in literary criticism.

verbalize or **verbalise** *verb* **1** to express in words. **2** *intrans.* to use too many words; to be verbose.

verbally *adv.* in speech, not in writing: *communicated with them verbally.*

verbal noun a form of a verb that functions as a noun, eg 'to err is human' and 'swimming keeps you fit'.

verbatim *adj., adv.* using exactly the same words; word-for-word. [from Latin *verbatim*]

verbena *noun* any of a group of plants of mild and tropical climates, with clusters of fragrant flowers, used in herbal medicine and cosmetics. [from Latin *verbena*, sacred bough]

verbiage *noun* **1** the use of language that is wordy or needlessly complicated, and often meaningless. **2** such language. [from Old French *verbeier*, to chatter]

verbose *adj.* using or containing too many words; boringly or irritatingly long-winded. [from Latin *verbosus*]

verbosity *noun* using or containing too many words; long-windedness.

verdancy *noun* a lush quality; freshness.

verdant *adj.* **1** covered with lush green grass or vegetation. **2** of a rich green colour. **3** naïve or unsophisticated; green. [from Old French *verdeant* from Latin *viridis* green]

Verdi, Giuseppe (Fortunino Francesco) (1813–1901) Italian composer, born in Le Roncole, Parma. After studying in Milan, he began to write operas, and achieved his first major success with *Nabucco* (1842). *Rigoletto* (1851), *Il Trovatore* (1853), and *La Traviata* (1853) established him as the leading Italian operatic

composer of the day. His spectacular *Aida* was commissioned for the new opera house in Cairo, built in celebration of the Suez Canal (1871). Apart from the *Requiem* (1874), there was then a lull in output until, in his old age, he produced *Otello* (1887) and *Falstaff* (1893).

verdict *noun* **1** a decision arrived at by a jury in a court of law. **2** any decision, opinion, or judgement. [from Latin *veredictum*, truly said]

verdigris *noun Chem.* a bluish-green coating of basic copper salts, especially copper carbonate, that forms as a result of corrosion when copper, brass, or bronze surfaces are exposed to air and moisture for long periods. [from Old French *verd de Grèce*, green of Greece]

verdure *noun literary* lush green vegetation, or its rich colour. [from Latin *viridis*, green]

Vereeniging, Peace of the treaty (1902) which ended the Boer War, signed in Pretoria. The Boers won three important concessions: amnesty for those who had risen in revolt within the Cape Colony; a promise that the British would deny the franchise to Africans until after the Boer republics were returned to representative government; and additional financial support for reconstruction. It also guaranteed that the political relationship of whites and blacks in South Africa would not undergo significant change.

verge¹ — *noun* **1** a limit, boundary, or border. **2** a strip of grass bordering a road. **3** a point or stage immediately beyond or after which something exists or occurs: *on the verge of tears.* — *verb* **1** to serve as the border or boundary of. **2** (**verge on something**) to be close to being or becoming something specified: *enthusiasm verging on obsession.* [from Latin *virga*, rod]

verge² *verb intrans.* **1** to slope or incline in a specified direction. **2** (**verge to** or **towards something**) to move or tend to or towards it. [from Latin *vergere*, to bend]

Vergeltungswaffe-1 (ABBREV. **V-1**) also called **buzz-bomb** a small winged and pilotless aircraft powered by a pulse jet motor, developed by the German Luftwaffe. It carried a tonne of high explosive several hundred miles at a speed of c.800kph/500mph, slow enough for some to be intercepted by gunfire and high speed aircraft. Between 1944 and 1945, 5 823 were launched against Britain. [German, = revenge weapon]

Vergeltungswaffe-2 (ABBREV. **V-2**) a guided ballistic missile developed by the German army, which began rocket experiments under the direction of Wernher von Braun in 1937. Because of its very high speed, it could not be intercepted by gun or aircraft. It was unstoppable, but wildly inaccurate. Between Sep 1944 and Mar 1945, 1 054 fell on Britain.

verger *noun* **1** a church official who assists the minister and acts as caretaker. **2** an official who carries the ceremonial staff of a bishop or other dignitary. [from Latin *virga*, rod]

Verges the peevish constable and associate of Dogberry in Shakespeare's *Much Ado About Nothing.*

Vergina the ancient capital of Macedonia. It is notable archaeologically for the excavation in 1977 of the reputed grave of Philip of Macedon, the father of Alexander the Great. The tomb included a gold casket holding cremated bones and a gold wreath of acorns and oak leaves.

verifiable *adj.* capable of being verified or established as true.

verification *noun* establishing as true or valid; verifying.

verify *verb* (**verifies, verified**) to check or confirm the truth or accuracy of. [from Latin *verus*, true + *facere*, to make]

verily *adv. old use* truly; really. [related to VERY]

verisimilitude *noun formal* **1** the quality of appearing to be real or true. **2** a statement or proposition that sounds true but may not be. [from Latin *verus*, true + *similis*, like]

veritable *adj. formal* accurately described as such; real: *a veritable genius!* [from Latin *verus*, true]

veritably *adv. formal* truly, really.

Verity a female first name. [from Latin *veritas* truth]

verity *noun* (PL. **verities**) **1** a true statement, especially one of fundamental wisdom or importance; a maxim. **2** truthfulness. [from Latin *verus*, true]

Verklärte Nacht (Transfigured Night) a string sextet by Arnold Schoenberg (Op 4, 1899), which he arranged for orchestra in 1917.

Verlaine, Paul (Marie) (1844–96) French poet, born in Metz. He joined the civil service, mixed with the leading Parnassian writers, and achieved success with his second book of poetry, *Fêtes galantes* (Feasts of Elegance, 1869). In 1872 he began to travel with the poet Rimbaud, but their association ended in Brussels (1873) when Verlaine was imprisoned for shooting him. While in prison for two years, he wrote *Romances sans paroles* (Songs Without Words, 1874). He became a Catholic, then taught French in England, where he wrote *Sagesse* (Wisdom, 1881). In 1877 he returned to France, where he wrote critical studies, notably *Les Poètes maudits* (Cursed Poets, 1884), short stories, and sacred and profane verse.

Vermeer, Jan (1632–75) Dutch painter, born in Delft. He gained some recognition in his lifetime in Holland, but he made little effort to sell and as a result, his art was forgotten until 19c researchers re-established his reputation. He painted small, detailed domestic interiors, notable for their use of perspective and treatment of the various tones of daylight. Fewer than forty of his paintings are known, including the *Allegory of Painting* (c.1665, Vienna), *Woman reading a Letter* (c.1662, Amsterdam), *Girl with a Pearl Earring* (The Hague), *Woman with a Water Jug* (c.1658–60, New York), and *View of Delft* (c.1660, The Hague).

vermicelli *noun* **1** pasta in very thin strands, thinner than spaghetti. **2** tiny splinters of chocolate used for desserts and cake decoration. [from Italian *vermicelli*, little worms]

vermiform *adj.* like a worm; worm-shaped. [from Latin *vermis*, worm]

vermiform appendix *Medicine* the appendix.

vermilion *noun* **1** a bright scarlet colour. **2** a pigment of this colour, consisting of sulphide of mercury. [from Latin *vermiculus*]

vermin *noun* (*usually as pl.*) **1** a collective name for wild animals that spread disease or generally cause a nuisance, especially rats and other rodents. **2** detestable people. [from Latin *vermis*, worm]

verminous *adj.* like vermin; parasitic; vile.

Vermont POP (1990) 570 000, a New England state in NE USA, divided into 14 counties. AREA 24 899sq km/9 611sq mi. PHYSICAL DESCRIPTION the Green Mts run N–S through the centre; rivers drain W from the mountains into L Champlain which forms much of the W border, and E into the Connecticut R which forms much of the E border; the highest point is Mt Mansfield (1 339m); Vermont is known as 'the Green Mountain State'. HISTORY explored by Champlain in 1609; first permanent settlement established by the English at Fort Dummer in 1724; New York and New Hampshire both laid claim to the area, but the independent state of Vermont was proclaimed in 1777; the 14th state to be admitted to the Union, in 1791. CAPITAL Montpelier. CHIEF TOWN Burlington. ECONOMY forestry and timber products; arable farming, grazing, dairy products; maple syrup; marble, granite; tourism.

vermouth *noun* an alcoholic drink consisting of wine flavoured with aromatic herbs, originally wormwood. [from German *Wermut*, wormwood]

vernacular — *noun* (*usually* **the vernacular**) **1** the native language of a country or people, as opposed to a foreign language that is also in use. **2** the form of a language as commonly spoken, as opposed to the formal or literary language. **3** the language or jargon of a particular group. **4** *humorous* slang or indecent language. — *adj.* **1** of or in the vernacular. **2** local; native. [from Latin *vernaculus*, native]

vernal *adj.* relating or appropriate to spring. [from Latin *ver*, spring]

vernal equinox *Astron.* the equinox that occurs annually around 21 Mar, when the Sun's path crosses the celestial equator S–N, so that day and night are of equal length.

vernalization *or* **vernalisation** *noun Bot.* the process whereby germinating seeds or seedlings are exposed to low temperatures in order to ensure that they flower subsequently.

vernally *adv.* as regards spring; in spring.

Verne, Jules (1828–1905) French novelist, born in Nantes. From 1848 he wrote opera libretti, and in 1863 developed a new vein in fiction, merging scientific exploration with exotic adventure. His best-known books are *Voyage au centre de la terre* (Journey to the Centre of the Earth, 1864), *Vingt mille lieues sous les mers* (Twenty Thousand Leagues under the Sea, 1870), and *Le Tour du monde en quatre-vingts jours* (Around the World in Eighty Days, 1873). Several successful films have been made from his novels.

Vernier, Pierre (1584–1638) French scientific instrument-maker, born in Ornans. He spent most of his life serving the King of Spain in the Low Countries, and in 1631 invented the famous auxiliary scale named after him to facilitate an accurate reading of a subdivision of an ordinary scale.

vernier *noun* a small sliding device on some measuring instruments, eg barometers and theodolites, used to measure fractions of units. [named after Pierre Vernier]

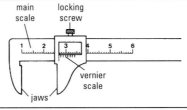

vernier callipers

Vernon, Diana the vivacious niece of Sir Hildebrand, who eventually marries Francis Osbaldistone, in Sir Walter Scott's *Rob Roy*.

Vernon, Edward (1684–1757) British admiral. He joined the navy in 1700, and was also an MP (1727–41). In 1739, during the War of Jenkins' Ear, his capture of Portobello from the Spanish made him a national hero. During the Jacobite rebellion of 1745 his position in the Channel successfully kept the standby Gallic reinforcements in their ports. His coat, made of a cloth known as grogram, earned him the nickname 'Old Grog', and when he ordered the navy rum ration to be mixed with water, it was given the name 'grog'.

Vernon a male first name, after the surname.

Verona POP (1991e) 259 000, the capital of Verona province, Veneto region, N Italy, lying on the R Adige. It is a market centre for agricultural produce. NOTABLE FEATURES many Roman and medieval remains, notably a large amphitheatre; cathedral (12c); Church of San Giorgio in Braida

(16c); Castel Vecchio (1354–5); Church of San Zeno Maggiore (11c–12c).

Veronese, Paolo, pseudonym of **Paolo Caliari** (c.1528–88) Venetian decorative painter, born in Verona. He worked in Verona and Mantua, then settled in Venice (1555), where he came to rank with Titian and Tintoretto. The Church of San Sebastiano in Venice contains many pictures of the period before his visit to Rome (1560). His major paintings include *The Marriage Feast at Cana* (1562–3, Louvre, Paris), *The Adoration of the Magi* (1573, National Gallery, London), and a 'Last Supper', the *Feast in the House of Levi* (1573, Venice), which brought him before the Inquisition for trivializing religious subjects. Other works include *The Triumph of Venice* on the ceiling of the Ducal Palace in Venice (c.1535).

Veronica a female first name. [a Latin form of Greek *Berenice*; associated with Latin *vera icon*, true image]

veronica *noun* a plant of the foxglove family, of mild and cold climates, with small blue, pink, or white flowers.

Verrazano-Narrows Bridge a major steel suspension bridge across the entrance to New York Harbour, from Brooklyn to Staten I, constructed in 1959–64. It is named after the Italian explorer Giovanni da Verrazano (1485–1528) and has a main span of 1 298m.

Verrocchio, Andrea del, properly **Andrea del Cione** (c.1435–88) Florentine sculptor, painter, and goldsmith, born in Florence. Of the paintings ascribed to him, only the 'Baptism' in the Uffizi is certain, and this was completed by Leonardo da Vinci, whom he taught. He is best known for his equestrian statue of Colleoni at Venice, and for his bronze *David* (c.1476) in the Bargello, Florence.

verruca *noun* (PL. **verrucas**, **verrucae**) *Medicine* a wart, especially one on the sole of the foot. [from Latin *verruca*, wart]

Versailles a chateau built (17c) for Louis XIII at the village of Versailles, near Paris, and transformed under Louis XIV into a palace. Later extensions were the Grand Trianon and the Petit Trianon. Ransacked during the French Revolution, it was restored to its original state and has been the scene of the signing of several peace treaties, including that at the end of World War I (1919). It is a World Heritage site.

Versailles, Treaty of a peace treaty drawn up (1919) near Paris between Germany and the Allied powers. Of the 434 Articles, the most controversial was Article 231, which assigned responsibility to Germany and her allies for causing World War I, and established liability for reparation payments. Germany lost all overseas colonies, and much territory to Poland in the east. The Rhineland was demilitarized and to be occupied by Allied troops for up to 15 years, and German armed forces were strictly limited.

versatile *adj.* **1** adapting easily to different tasks. **2** having numerous uses or abilities. [from Latin *versatilis*, from *vertere*, to turn]

versatility *noun* the ability to be adaptable.

verse *noun* **1** a division of a poem; a stanza. **2** poetry, as opposed to prose. **3** a poem. **4** a division of a song. **5** any of the numbered subdivisions of the chapters of the Bible. [from Latin *versus*, line, row]

versed *adj.* (**versed in something**) familiar with it or skilled in it.

versification *noun* composing verses or turning into verses.

versifier *noun* a person who writes verses.

versify *verb* (**versifies**, **versified**) **1** *intrans.* to write poetry. **2** to express as, or turn into, a poem. [from Latin *versificare*, to put into verse]

version *noun* any of several types or forms in which a thing exists or is available, eg a particular edition or translation of a book, or one person's account of an incident. [from Latin *versio*, from *vertere*, to turn]

verso *noun* (PL. **versos**) **1** the back of a loose sheet of printed paper. **2** the left-hand page of two open pages. See also RECTO. [Latin *verso folio*, turned leaf]

versus *prep.* **1** (in a contest or lawsuit) against. **2** *colloq.* in comparison to. [from Latin *versus*]

Vert, Cap see CAPE VERDE.

vertebra *noun* (PL. **vertebrae**) *Anat.* in vertebrates, any of the small bones or cartilaginous segments that form the backbone. Each vertebra contains a central canal through which the spinal cord passes. [from Latin *vertebra*, from *vertere*, to turn]

vertebral *adj.* relating to the vertebra.

vertebrate — *noun Zool.* any animal that has a backbone consisting of bony or cartilaginous vertebrae enclosing a spinal cord. Vertebrates include fish, amphibians, reptiles, birds, and mammals. — *adj.* relating to an animal that has a backbone.

vertex *noun* (PL. **vertexes, vertices**) **1** the highest point; the peak or summit. **2** *Maths.* the point opposite the base of a geometric figure, eg the pointed tip of a cone. **3** *Maths.* the point where the two sides of an angle meet in a polygon, or where three or more surfaces meet in a polyhedron. [from Latin *vertex*, summit, whirlpool]

vertical — *adj.* **1** perpendicular to the horizon; upright. **2** running from top to bottom, not side to side. **3** of or at a vertex. **4** relating to, involving, or running through all levels within a hierarchy, all stages of a process, etc, rather than just one. — *noun* a vertical line or direction.

vertical integration *Commerce* a business situation in which a company expands by buying up its suppliers and/or its customers, thus controlling all the processes of production, from raw materials through to sale of the final product. An example is the oil industry, where all stages can be owned, from oil wells, through tankers and refineries, to petrol stations.

vertically *adv.* in a vertical or upright position.

vertical take-off a take-off by an aircraft directly upwards from a stationary position.

Vertical Take-Off and Landing (ABBREV. **VTOL**) a fixed-wing aircraft specially designed for taking off directly upwards from a stationary position (eg from the deck of a ship). The most successful aircraft of this type is the Harrier Jump Jet fighter-bomber, originally designed (in the UK) by British Aerospace and (in the US) by McDonnell Douglas. It had its first flight in 1966 and entered RAF service in 1969.

vertiginous *adj.* **1** so high or whirling as to bring on vertigo; dizzying. **2** relating to vertigo.

vertigo *noun* a whirling sensation felt when the sense of balance is disturbed; dizziness; giddiness. [from Latin *vertigo*, from *vertere*, to turn]

Verulamium a Belgic town in Roman Britain which stood on the site of present-day St Albans. It was completely destroyed in the Revolt of Boadicea in AD 60, but was later rebuilt and became a focal point for the Romanization of the province.

vervain *noun* a wild verbena. [from Old French *vervaine*]

verve *noun* great liveliness or enthusiasm. [from French *verve*]

Verver, Maggie one of the two women at the centre of Henry James's *The Golden Bowl*, who marries Prince Amerigo. Her wealthy father, Adam, marries Charlotte Stant.

Verwoerd, Hendrik (Freusch) (1901–66) South African politician, born in Amsterdam, the Netherlands. He was educated at Stellenbosch, where he became Professor of Applied Psychology (1927) and Sociology (1933), and edited the nationalist *Die Transvaler* (1938–48). Elected Senator in 1948, he became Minister of Native Affairs (1950) and Prime Minister (1958–66). His administration was marked by the highly controversial policy of apartheid, an attempt on his life (1960), the establishment of South Africa as a republic (1962), and his assassination in Cape Town.

very — *adv.* **1** to a high degree or great extent: *very kind.* **2** (used with *own, same,* and with superlative adjectives) absolutely; truly: *the very same day / my very best effort.* — *adj.* **1** absolute: *the very top.* **2** precise; actual: *this very minute.* **3** mere: *shocked by the very thought.*
— **not very** not at all; the opposite of.
very good *or* **very well** expressions of consent and approval.
[from Old French *verai*, from Latin *verus*, true]

very high frequency (ABBREV. **VHF**) a band of radio frequencies between 30 and 300 MHz.

Very light a coloured flare fired from a pistol, as a signal or to iluminate an area. [invented by E W Very (1852–1910), US naval ordnance officer]

very low frequency (ABBREV. **VLF**) *Radio* a radio frequency in the range 3 to 30kHz.

Vesak *or* **Wesak** *noun* the most widely celebrated of Buddhist festivals, held in May to commemorate the birth, enlightenment, and death of Buddha.

Vesalius, Andreas (1514–64) Belgian anatomist, born in Brussels, one of the first dissectors of human cadavers. He was appointed professor at Padua University, and was Court Physician to the emperor Charles V and his son Philip II of Spain. His greatest work was the *De Humani Corporis Fabrica* (On the Structure of the Human Body, 1543), which set a completely new level of clarity and accuracy in anatomy.

vesicle *noun* **1** *Biol.* any small sac or cavity, especially one filled with fluid, within the cytoplasm of a living cell. **2** *Medicine* a small blister in the skin, containing serum (a clear fluid), usually associated with herpes, eczema, or other skin disorders. **3** *Geol.* a cavity formed by trapped gas bubbles during the solidification of molten lava. [from Latin *vesica*, bladder]

Vespasian, originally **Titus Flavius Vespasianus** (AD 9–79) Roman emperor (69–79), and founder of the Flavian dynasty (69–96). He was declared emperor by the troops in the East, where he was engaged in putting down the Jewish Revolt. He ended the civil wars that had been raging since Nero's overthrow, stabilized the economy, and restored discipline to the army. His many building projects included the Colosseum.

vespers *sing. noun* an evening service in some Christian churches; evensong. [from Latin *vesper*, evening]

Vespucci, Amerigo (1454–1512) Italian explorer, born in Florence. He promoted a voyage to the New World in the track of Columbus, sailed with its commander (1499), and explored the coast of Venezuela. In 1505 he was naturalized in Spain, and from 1508 was pilot-major of the kingdom. His name was given to America through an inaccurate account of his travels published in Lorraine (1507), in which he is represented as having discovered and reached the mainland in 1497.

vessel *noun* **1** a container, especially for liquid. **2** a ship or large boat. **3** a tube or duct carrying liquid, eg blood or sap, in animals and plants. [from Latin *vasis*]

vest — *noun* **1** an undergarment for the top half of the body. **2** *North Amer., esp. US* a waistcoat. — *verb* **1** (**vest something in someone** *or* **someone with something**) to give or bestow legally or officially: *by the power vested in me / the chairman is vested with absolute authority.* **2** *intrans.*

to put on ecclesiastical robes. [from Latin *vestis*, clothing]

Vesta in Roman mythology, the goddess of the hearth. Her sacred fire, and a shrine containing sacred objects, were kept in a round building, and tended by the Vestal Virgins. She was identified with the Greek goddess Hestia.

vestal — *adj.* virginal; chaste. — *noun* **1** a chaste woman, especially a nun. **2** a vestal virgin. [from Latin *vestalis*, of Vesta, the Roman goddess of the hearth and home]

Vestal Virgins in ancient Rome, the aristocratic virgin priestesses of Vesta, the goddess of the hearth. They each served for 30 years, tending the sacred flame which burned perpetually in the Temple of Vesta near the forum.

vested interest **1** an interest a person has in the fortunes of a particular system or institution because that person is directly affected or closely associated. **2** a person or company with such an interest.

Vesterålen *or* **Vesteraalen** an island group in the Norwegian Sea, lying off the NW coast of Norway, just N of the Lofoten group. MAIN ISLANDS Hinnøy, Langøya, Andøa, Hadseløy. ECONOMY fishing, fish processing.

vestibule *noun* an entrance hall. [from Latin *vestibulum*]

vestige *noun* **1** a slight amount; a hint or shred. **2** a surviving trace of what has almost disappeared. **3** *Biol.* a small, fairly functionless part in an animal or plant, once a fully developed organ in ancestors. [from Latin *vestigium*, footprint]

vestigial *adj. Biol.*, *said of an organ* having no function: *a vestigial wing.*

vestment *noun* **1** any of various garments worn ceremonially by members of the clergy and church choir. **2** any ceremonial robe. [from Latin *vestis*, clothing]

papal vestments

chimere

rochet

cassock

vestry *noun* (PL. **vestries**) a room in a church where the vestments are kept, often also used for meetings, Sunday school classes, etc. [from Latin *vestis*, clothing]

Vesuvius, Italian **Vesuvio** an active volcano in Campania region, S Italy, situated 15km/9mi SE of Naples. HEIGHT 1 277m. Its crater circumference is 1 400m with a depth of 216m. HISTORY first recorded eruption was in AD79, overwhelming Pompeii, Herculaneum, and Stabiae; eruptions occurred at long intervals until 1631, and there has been more regular activity since; the last eruption was in 1944. Fruit and vines grow on the lower slopes.

vet¹ — *noun* a veterinary surgeon. — *verb* (**vetted, vetting**) to examine or investigate (especially a person) thoroughly, to check for suitability or reliability.

vet² *noun colloq. North Amer., esp. US* a veteran.

Vetch, Fleda the young heroine who is disappointed in love in Henry James's *The Spoils of Poynton*.

vetch *noun* any of various climbing plants of the pea family with blue or purple flowers, and pods used as fodder. [from Latin *vicia*]

veteran *noun* **1** a person with many years of experience in a particular activity. **2** an old and experienced member of the armed forces. **3** *North Amer., esp. US* an ex-serviceman or -woman. [from Latin *veteranus*, old]

veteran car a very old motor car, specifically one made before 1905.

Veterans' Day 11 Nov, a public holiday in the USA, in honour of veterans of all wars. It was originally instituted as *Armistice Day* after World War I, and was known by that name until 1954.

veterinary — *adj.* concerned with diseases of animals. — *noun* (PL. **veterinaries**) *colloq.* a veterinary surgeon. [from Latin *veterinae*, cattle]

veterinary surgeon *or* **veterinarian** a person qualified to treat diseases of animals.

veto — *noun* (PL. **vetoes**) **1** the right to formally reject a proposal or forbid an action, eg in a lawmaking assembly; the act of using such a right. **2** *colloq.* any prohibition or refusal of permission. — *verb* (**vetoes**, **vetoed**) **1** to formally and authoritatively reject or forbid. **2** *loosely* to forbid. [from Latin *veto*, I forbid]

vex *verb* **1** to annoy or irritate. **2** to worry. [from Latin *vexare*, to shake, to annoy]

vexation *noun* **1** the state or feeling of being vexed. **2** a thing that vexes.

vexatious *adj.* vexing; annoying.

vexed *adj.*, *said of an issue, etc* much discussed or debated.

vexing *adj.* irritating; annoying.

Vézelay church the 12c abbey church of St Madeleine in Vézelay, E France. It is noted both as a major work of Romanesque architecture and as the start of one of the main pilgrimage routes to Santiago de Compostela in Spain. It is a World Heritage site.

Vézère Valley a stretch of the Vézère R valley in S France. Its yield of flint tools and fossilized remains has been formative in the modern understanding of the Old Stone Age. The grottoes, which are noted for their wall paintings and engravings, are a World Heritage site.

VGA *abbrev. Comput.* video graphics array, a computer monitor screen display system able to display several colours at a resolution of 640 x 480 pixels.

VHF *abbrev. Radio* very high frequency.

VHS *abbrev.* Video Home Service.

via *prep.* by way of or by means of; through. [from Latin *via*, way]

viability *noun* feasibility; capable of being maintained.

viable *adj.* **1** *said of a plan, etc* having a chance of success; feasible; practicable. **2** *said of a plant, etc* able to exist or grow in particular conditions. **3** *said of a foetus or baby* able to survive independently outside the womb. [from French *viable*, from Latin *vita* life]

viaduct *noun* a bridge-like structure of stone arches supporting a road or railway across a valley, etc. [from Latin *via*, way + *ducere*, to lead]

vial *noun* a small medicine bottle. [related to PHIAL]

viands *pl. noun formal* items of food; provisions. [from Old French *viande*, food, from Latin *vivenda*]

viaticum *noun* (PL. **viaticums**, **viatica**) **1** the Eucharist given to a dying person. **2** *formal* provisions for a journey. [from Latin *viaticum*, from *via*, way]

vibes *pl. noun colloq.* feelings, sensations, or an atmosphere experienced or communicated. [shortening of *vibration*]

Viborg 1 POP (1990e) 30 000, an ancient city and the industrial capital of Viborg county, N central Jutland, Denmark. NOTABLE FEATURE 12c Gothic cathedral (restored in 1864–76). **2** a county in N central Jutland, Denmark, with the town of Viborg as its capital.

vibrancy *noun* **1** vibrating; quivering. **2** excitement.

vibrant *adj.* **1** extremely lively or exciting; made strikingly animated or energetic. **2** *said of a colour* strong and bright. **3** vibrating. [from Latin *vibrare*, related to VIBRATE]

vibrantly *adv.* in a vibrant or exciting way.

vibraphone *noun* a musical instrument in which horizontal metal bars of different lengths are made to resound electrically when struck with hammers. [from VIBRATE + -PHONE]

vibraphonist *noun* a person who plays the vibraphone.

vibrate *verb* **1** *trans., intrans.* to move a short distance back and forth very rapidly. **2** *intrans.* to ring or resound when struck. **3** *intrans.* to shake or tremble. **4** *intrans.* to swing back and forth; to oscillate. [from Latin *vibrare*, to tremble]

vibration *noun* **1** a vibrating motion. **2** a single movement back and forth in vibrating. **3** (**vibrations**) *colloq.* feelings, sensations, or an atmosphere experienced or communicated.

vibrato *noun* (PL. **vibratos**) a faint trembling effect in singing or the playing of string and wind instruments, achieved by vibrating the throat muscles or the fingers. [from Italian *vibrato*]

vibrator *noun* **1** any device that produces a vibrating motion, eg for massage. **2** a battery-powered vibrating dildo.

vibratory *adj.* causing vibration.

vicar *noun* **1** *Church of E.* the minister of a parish. **2** *RC Church* a bishop's deputy. [from Latin *vicarius*, deputy, substitute]

vicarage *noun* a vicar's residence or benefice.

vicar-apostolic *noun RC Church* a member of the clergy appointed, with the rank of bishop, to a country with no established church structure.

vicar-general *noun RC Church* an official assisting a bishop in administrative matters.

vicarial *adj.* of or serving as a vicar.

vicarious *adj.* **1** experienced not directly but through witnessing the experience of another person: *vicarious pleasure in seeing his children learn.* **2** undergone on behalf of someone else. **3** standing in for another. **4** *said of authority, etc* delegated to someone else. [from Latin *vicarius*, substituted]

Vicar of Christ the pope, regarded as representative of Christ on earth.

Vicar of Wakefield a novel by Oliver Goldsmith (1766). It has a rural setting and follows the changing fortunes of the vicar, Dr Primrose, and his family.

vice[1] *noun* a tool with heavy movable metal jaws, usually fixed to a bench, for gripping an object being worked on. [from French *vis*, screw]

vice[2] *noun* **1** a habit or activity considered immoral, evil, or depraved, especially involving prostitution or drugs. **2** such activities collectively. **3** a bad habit; a fault in one's character. [from Latin *vitium*, blemish]

vice[3] *prep.* **1** in place of. **2** following on from or succeeding. [from the Latin root *vic-*, turn, alteration]

vice- *combining form* forming words meaning 'next in rank to, and acting as deputy for': *vice-admiral / vice-president.* [related to VICE[3]]

vice-chancellor *noun* the deputy chancellor of a university, responsible for most administrative duties.

vicegerency *noun* the office of vicegerent.

vicegerent *noun* a person appointed to act in place of a superior. — *adj.* acting in this capacity. [from VICE[3] + Latin *gerere*, to manage]

Vicente, Gil (c.1470–c.1537) Portuguese dramatist and poet. He accompanied the court and wrote many plays and entertainments in both Spanish and Portuguese. His work, characterized by its lyricism and predominantly comic spirit, includes plays on religious, national, and social themes, as well as farces, and pastoral and romantic plays.

Vicenza, ancient **Vicetia** POP (1991e) 109 000, the capital of Vicenza province, Veneto region, NE Italy. Situated 35km/22mi NW of Padua, on the edge of the Po Plain, it was home to the 16c architect Palladio. NOTABLE FEATURES Basilica Palladiana (1549–1614); Teatro Olimpico; Rotonda; cathedral (15c).

viceregal *adj.* relating to a viceroy.

viceroy *noun* a governor of a province or colony ruling in the name of, and with the authority of, a monarch or national government. [from French *viceroy*]

viceroyalty *or* **viceroyship** *noun* the office or position of viceroy.

vice squad a branch of the police force investigating crimes relating to vice, especially prostitution.

vice versa *adj.* with the order or correspondence reversed; the other way round: *from me to you and vice versa.* [from Latin *vice versa*, the position being reversed, related to VICE[3]]

Vichy, official name **Etat français** (**the French State**) the French political regime in 1940–5, which was established at the spa town of Vichy following Germany's defeat of France (1940). Its head of state was Marshal Philippe Pétain; its other dominant political figure was Pierre Laval, Prime Minister from 1942. Although a client state of Germany, Vichy at first maintained a degree of autonomy.

vicinity *noun* (PL. **vicinities**) **1** a neighbourhood. **2** the area immediately surrounding. **3** the condition of being close; nearness. [from Latin *vicinus*, neighbour]

vicious *adj.* **1** violent or ferocious. **2** spiteful or malicious. **3** extremely severe or harsh. **4** *said of reasoning, etc* incorrect or faulty; unsound. [from Latin *vitiosus*, faulty]

Vicious Circle see HUIS CLOS.

vicious circle 1 a situation in which any attempt to resolve a problem creates others which in turn recreate the first one. **2** an incorrect form of reasoning in which one proposition is supposedly proved on the basis of another which itself depends for its proof on the truth of the first.

viciously *adv.* in a vicious or spiteful way.

viciousness *noun* a vicious or spiteful state or manner.

vicissitude *noun* an unpredictable change of fortune or circumstance. [from Latin *vicissim* by turns]

Vickers–Vimy Biplane the plane used by John Alcock and Arthur Brown in their successful attempt to be the first to fly the Atlantic Ocean. They managed it on 4 Jun 1919 in 16h and 12min, and won £10 000 from the *Daily Mail* for their accomplishment.

Vicksburg POP (1990) 21 000, the seat of Warren County, W Mississippi, USA. It is a port on the Mississippi R, 64km/40mi W of Jackson. The US Mississippi River Commission has its headquarters here and the town is an important processing and shipping centre for a cotton, timber, and livestock area. HISTORY settled in 1791; captured by Union forces during the Civil War (1863) after a long siege the 'Vicksburg

Campaign' gave control of the Mississippi to the North, splitting the Confederacy on a N–S axis. NOTABLE FEATURE National Cemetery nearby, where c.13 000 unknown Union troops are buried, brought from all over the South.

Vicksburg, Battle of a major success (1863) for Union forces during the American Civil War, in which General Ulysses S Grant captured Vicksburg and thus the Mississippi R, splitting the Confederate forces in two. The victory proved Grant's abilities as a general and Lincoln placed him in command of all the Union's western forces. The cause of emancipation was also helped by the use of black units in the campaign.

Vico, Giambattista (1668–1744) Italian historical philosopher, born in Naples. Devoted to literature, history, and philosophy, in 1699 he became Professor of Rhetoric at Naples. In his *Scienza Nuova* (New Science, 1725), now recognized as a landmark in European intellectual history, he attempted to systematize the humanities into a single human science, expounding a theory of the cyclical growth and decline of societies. His theories influenced later scholars such as Goethe and Marx.

victim *noun* 1 a person or animal subjected to death, suffering, ill-treatment, or trickery. 2 a person or animal killed in a sacrifice or ritual. [from Latin *victima*, beast for sacrifice]

victimization *or* **victimisation** *noun* unfair or vindictive treatment.

victimize *or* **victimise** *verb* 1 to single out for hostile or unfair treatment. 2 to cause to be a victim.

Victor a male first name. [from Latin *victor*, conqueror]

victor *noun* the winner or winning side in a war or contest. [from Latin *victor*, from *vincere*, to conquer]

Victor Emmanuel II (1820–78) the first King of Italy (1861–78), born in Turin. As King of Sardinia from 1849, he appointed Conte Camillo Cavour as his Chief Minister (1852). He fought against Austria (1859), winning victories at Montebello, Magenta, and Solferino, and gaining Lombardy. In 1860 Modena, Parma, the Romagna, and Tuscany were peacefully annexed, Sicily and Naples were added by Giuseppe Garibaldi, and Savoy and Nice were ceded to France. Proclaimed king at Turin, he supported Prussia in the Austro-Prussian War (1866), and after the fall of the French Empire (1870) he entered and annexed Rome.

Victor Emmanuel III (1869–1947) King of Italy (1900–46), born in Naples. Initially a constitutional monarch, he defied parliamentary majorities by bringing Italy into World War I on the side of the Allies in 1915, and by offering Mussolini the premiership (1922). Reduced to a figurehead by the Fascist government, he played an important part in effecting Mussolini's fall (1943), but his association with fascism had tainted him forever and he abdicated in 1946, leaving his son as lieutenant-governor.

Victoria, in full **Alexandrina Victoria** (1819–1901) Queen of Great Britain (1837–1901) and (from 1876) Empress of India, born in London, the only child of George III's fourth son, Edward, and Victoria Maria Louisa of Saxe-Coburg, sister of Leopold, King of the Belgians. She clearly understood constitutional principles and the scope of her own prerogative, which she first exercised in 1839 on the fall of Viscount Melbourne's government, when she ignored the precedent which decreed the dismissal of the current ladies of the bedchamber (who had Whig sympathies), resulting in the Bedchamber Crisis. This caused Sir Robert Peel to resign, and the ministry of Melbourne, whom she preferred, was prolonged until 1841. In 1840 she married Prince

Albert of Saxe-Coburg and Gotha, and had four sons and five daughters. Strongly influenced by her husband, with whom she worked in closest harmony, after his death (1861) she went into lengthy seclusion and neglected many duties, which decreased her popularity and motivated a republican movement. But with her recognition as Empress of India, and the celebratory golden (1887) and diamond (1897) jubilees, she rose high in her subjects' favour, and increased the prestige of the monarchy. She had strong preferences for certain (more conservative) Prime Ministers (in particular Melbourne and Benjamin Disraeli) over others (notably Peel and Gladstone), but on Albert's advice did not press these beyond the bounds of constitutional propriety. At various points in her long reign she exercised some influence over foreign affairs, and the marriages of her children had important diplomatic, as well as dynastic, implications in Europe. She was succeeded by her son, Edward VII.

Victoria POP (1991) 71 000, the capital of British Columbia province, W Canada. It lies at the SE end of Vancouver I, on the Juan de Fuca Strait. HISTORY founded as a fur-trading post in 1843; became provincial capital in 1866. NOTABLE FEATURES Parliament Buildings (1893–7); Empress Hotel (1906–8); Thunderbird Park (unique collection of totem poles); Butchart Gardens.

Victoria POP (1992e) 4.5m, the second-smallest state in Australia, situated in the SE of the country. AREA 227 600sq km/87 900sq mi. It comprises 12 statistical divisions and is bordered in the S and E by the Bass Strait and Tasman Sea. PHYSICAL DESCRIPTION to the E is the Great Dividing Range, known in this region as the Australian Alps, with its highest point, Mt Bogong (1 986m); about 36% of the land is occupied by forest; there are several inland lakes which are mostly very salty; irrigation storages include L Eildon on the Goulburn R and L Hume on the Murray R. The SW region is known as Gippsland. One quarter of the Australian population is concentrated into 3% of the state's land. CAPITAL Melbourne. CHIEF TOWNS Geelong, Ballarat. HISTORY visited by Captain Cook in 1770; Melbourne was settled in 1835; separated from New South Wales in 1851; gold was discovered at Ballarat in 1851. ECONOMY produces about one fifth of Australia's agricultural output of wheat, oats, barley, maize, tobacco, hops, fodder crops, citrus fruits, grapes, apples, vegetables, wool, hides, mutton, lamb, dairy products; timber; coal mining (Latrobe Valley is one of the world's largest deposits of brown coal); motor parts; oil and natural gas fields in the Gippsland Basin and Bass Strait.

Victoria POP (1987) 24 000, the seaport capital of the Seychelles. It is situated on the NE coast of Mahé I.

Victoria a female first name; it was little known in Britain before the accession of Queen Victoria, who was named after her German mother. [from Latin *victoria*, victory]

victoria *noun* a large red sweet variety of plum, named after Queen Victoria.

Victoria and Albert Museum a museum of fine and applied arts, opened in London in 1852 as the Museum of Manufactures, and later renamed the Museum of Ornamental Art. The core of the original display was formed from articles bought from the Great Exhibition (1851). It was renamed the Victoria and Albert in 1899, when Queen Victoria laid the foundation stone of the present building.

Victoria Cross (ABBREV. **VC**) in the UK, the highest military decoration, instituted by Queen Victoria in 1886 and awarded 'for conspicuous bravery in the face of the enemy'. It can be conferred posthumously (since 1902), and women are eligible to receive it (since 1920), though none

has. The medal's inscription is 'For valour', and the ribbon is crimson.

Victoria Desert see GREAT VICTORIA DESERT.

Victoria Falls, indigenous name **Mosi oa Tunya** (**'the smoke that thunders'**) the waterfalls on the Zambezi R which lie on the Zambia–Zimbabwe frontier. The falls, which are a major tourist attraction, are 61–108m high and 1 688m wide. They comprise five main falls: Eastern Cataract, Rainbow Falls, Devil's Cataract, Horseshoe Falls, and Main Falls. The towns of Livingstone and Victoria Falls are situated on the Zambia and Zimbabwe sides of the falls respectively. [named in 1855 after Queen Victoria by David Livingstone, the first European to discover the falls]

Victoria Island a sparsely populated island in Northwest Territories, Canada, situated in the Arctic Ocean. It is separated from the Canadian mainland by the Dolphin and Union Strait, Coronation Gulf, Dease Strait, and Queen Maud Gulf. AREA 217 290sq km/83 874sq mi; 515km/320mi long; 274–595km/170–370mi wide. Its coast is deeply indented, with Prince Albert Sound in the SW and Hadley Bay in the N.

Victoria, Lake the largest lake on the African continent, situated in the E. AREA 69 500sq km/26 827sq mi; 400km/250mi long; 240km/150mi wide. Lying at an altitude of 1 300m, it is bounded S by Tanzania, NW by Uganda, and NE by Kenya. It contains several islands, notably the Sese archipelago. The water level was raised by the Owen Falls Dam in 1954. Main lakeside ports are Kisumu in Kenya, and Mwanza in Tanzania. The first European to discover the lake was John Speke in 1858 and it was extensively explored by Sir Henry Stanley in 1875. [originally called Ukewere, it was renamed in honour of Queen Victoria]

Victorian — *adj.* 1 relating to or characteristic of Queen Victoria or the period of her reign (1837–1901). 2 *said of attitudes or values* typical of the strictness or conventionality of this period. — *noun* a person who lived during this period.

Victoriana *pl. noun* objects from, or in a style typical of, the Victorian period in Britain.

Victoria Nile the upper reach of the River Nile, in NW Uganda. It is 420km/260mi long. The river flows generally NW from the N end of L Victoria to enter L Kyoga, then in a NW arc into the Kabalega National Park, passing the Kabalega (Murchison) Falls. It ends in a swampy delta at the NE end of L Albert.

Victoria Peak the principal peak on Hong Kong I. HEIGHT 554m. A peak tramway, opened in 1888, leads to the summit for spectacular views of the city and harbour. [named after Queen Victoria]

victorious *adj.* 1 winning a war or contest. 2 marking or representing a victory.

Victory the name of Admiral Lord Horatio Nelson's flagship at the battle of Trafalgar (1805). It was the seventh vessel in the Royal Navy to bear the name. It is now in permanent dry dock in Portsmouth.

victory *noun* (PL. **victories**) 1 success against an opponent in a war or contest. 2 an occurrence of this. [from Latin *victoria*]

Victory of Samothrace, also called **Nike of Samothrace** an ancient statue of Nike, the goddess of victory, found on the Greek island of Samothrace in 1863, now in the Louvre, Paris.

victual — *noun* (*usually* **victuals**) food; provisions. — *verb* (**victualled**, **victualling**) 1 to supply with victuals. 2 *intrans.* to obtain supplies. [from Latin *victualis*, relating to living]

victualler *noun formal* 1 a shopkeeper selling food and drink. 2 (*in full* **licensed victualler**) *Brit.*

a publican licensed to sell food and alcoholic liquor for consumption on the premises.

vicuña *noun* **1** a S American mammal related to the llama. **2** a cloth or yarn made from its wool. [from Spanish *vicuña*]

Vidal, Gore (1925–) US writer, born in West Point, New York. He served in the army, an experience he draws on in his first novel, *Williwaw* (1946). Other novels include the satirical comedies *Myra Breckinridge* (1968) and *Duluth* (1983), the historical trilogy *Burr* (1974), *1876* (1976), and *Lincoln* (1984) and, more recently, *Empire* (1987), and *Hollywood* (1990). He has also written short stories, plays (eg *Visit to a Small Planet*, 1956), film scripts, and essays.

vide *verb* (as an instruction in a text) refer to; see. [Latin]

videlicet *adv. formal* (especially in writing) namely; that is. [Latin *videre licet* it is allowed to see]

video — *noun* (PL. **videos**) **1** the recording, reproducing, or broadcasting of visual (especially televised) images on magnetic tape. **2** a videocassette or videocassette recorder. **3** a film or programme pre-recorded on videocassette: *now available as a video.* — *adj.* relating to the process of or equipment for recording by video. — *verb* (**videos**, **videoed**) to make a videocassette recording of. [Latin *videre*, to see]

video camera *Photog.* a portable camera that records moving visual images directly on to videotape, which can then be played back on a videocassette recorder and viewed on the screen of a television receiver.

videocassette *noun* a cassette containing videotape, for use in a videocassette recorder.

videocassette recorder (ABBREV. **VCR**) a machine for recording on magnetic tape the sound and video signals of a television broadcast, so that they can be played back on a standard television receiver at a later date. It is also used to play back pre-recorded tapes of motion pictures.

video disc *Telecomm.* a rotating flat circular plate for the reproduction of pre-recorded video programmes on a television receiver. Both picture and sound are recorded as an extremely fine spiral track and the series of pits in the reflective surface of the disc are optically scanned by a laser with the reflected beam read by a photo-diode to produce the signal.

video game an electronically operated game involving the manipulation of images produced by a computer program on a visual display unit. ◇ The first video game appeared in the USA in the 1970s. Many games have war or combat themes or are simulated versions of sports, such as football and golf, or board games. Since the 1980s there has been a rapid expansion in the market in western countries, facilitated by developments in computer technology and the promotional efforts of the major Japanese companies which dominate the field.

Video Home Service (ABBREV. **VHS**) *trademark* a videotape cassette recorder introduced by JVC/Matsushita (1976) for the domestic market, and widely adopted by other manufacturers. It has a playing time of up to eight hours, and is the most internationally popular home VTR (videotape recorder) system.

video nasty *colloq.* an explicitly shocking violent or pornographic film available as a videocassette.

video RAM or VRAM *Comput.* video random access memory, a part of a computer's memory in which data controlling the visual display is stored, sometimes physically separate from the main memory.

video recorder a videocassette recorder.

videotape *noun* magnetic tape on which visual images and sound can be recorded.

videotext *noun* any system in which computerized information is displayed on a television screen, eg teletext.

vie *verb intrans.* (**vying**) (**vie with someone for something**) to compete or struggle with them for some gain or advantage. [from Old French *envier*, to challenge or invite]

Vienna, German **Wien 1** POP (1991) 1.5m, the capital of Austria, at the foot of the Wienerwald on the R Danube, near the borders with Hungary, the Czech Republic, and Slovakia. Its central area is surrounded by the monumental buildings and gardens of the Ringstrasse, developed between 1859 and 1888. The city had associations with many composers during the 18–19c; in World War II it was badly damaged and in subsequent years (1945–55) it was under Allied occupation. NOTABLE FEATURES St Stephen's Cathedral; St Peter's Church; Schottenkirche (12c, rebuilt 1638–48); former Bohemian Court Chancery; Church of Maria am Gestade; Spanish Riding School; Ruprechtskirche (12–13c); Franciscan Church (1603–11); Maria Theresa Monument (1887); Palais Trautson; town hall (1872–83); Baroque Palace of Schönbrunn; Opera House; Burgtheater; Uno-City (1979) is a conference and office complex housing the offices of the United Nations agencies in Vienna. **2** a state in NE Austria, with Vienna as its capital.

Vienna, Congress of a European assembly convened (1814–15) at the instigation of the four victorious powers (Austria, Britain, Prussia, and Russia) to redefine the territorial map of Europe after the defeat of Napoleon I.

Vienna, University of a university founded in Vienna in 1365. It came under state control in 1557, and during the mid-19c reforms were instituted by Maria Theresa, making its medical school the most up-to-date in Europe.

Vienna Boys' Choir an Austrian choir school, founded in 1498 when it was associated with the chapel of the imperial court. There are four choirs, which perform a secular repertoire worldwide, often with the Vienna State Opera.

Vienna Circle a philosophical discussion group founded in Vienna in the early 1920s by Moritz Schlick and invigorated in the late 1920s by Rudolf Carnap. It became an international focus for Logical Positivism, before disintegrating in the 1930s with the rise of Naziism.

Vienna State Opera, German *Staatsoper* an Austrian opera company and its theatre, originally built in 1869 and known as the Vienna Court Opera (*Hofoper*), noted for its performances of Wagner, Mozart, and Strauss. Destroyed in World War II, it reopened in 1955; Herbert von Karajan was among its post-war directors.

Vientiane, Lao **Viangchan** POP (1985) 178 000, the capital of Laos, SE Asia. It is a port on the R Mekong, in the W of the country, close to the Thailand frontier. NOTABLE FEATURES National Museum; National Library; Nam Ngum Dam to the N; That Luang Temple (16c).

Vieta, Franciscus, French **François Viète** (1540–1603) French mathematician, born in Fontenay-le-Comte. He became a privy councillor to Henri IV of France, wrote one of the earliest works on symbolic algebra, and devised methods for solving algebraic equations up to the fourth degree. He also wrote on trigonometry and geometry, and obtained the value of p as an infinite product.

Viet Cong or Vietcong the name given by the Saigon government in 1959 to all the guerrilla forces that fought the South Vietnamese government during the Vietnam War. In 1960 they formed the National Liberation Front, whose demands included the withdrawal of all foreign troops and the overthrow of the government in South Vietnam.

Viet Minh or Vietminh *abbrev.* the Vietnam Doc Lap Dong Minh ('League for the Independence of Vietnam'), an organization formed by Ho Chi Minh in 1941. It included nationalists and communists, and aimed to liberate Vietnam from the Japanese and gain independence from France. In 1945 it formed a government in Hanoi, and its army defeated the French at Dien Bien Phu in 1954.

Vietnam, official name **Socialist Republic of Vietnam**, Vietnamese **Cong Hoa Xa Hoi Chu Nghia Viet Nam** POP (1992e) 69.3m, an independent socialist state in Indo-China, divided into three autonomous cities and 36 provinces. AREA 329 566sq km/127 213sq mi. It is bounded E by the S China Sea (including the Gulf of Tongking in the N), W by Laos and Cambodia, and N by China. CAPITAL Hanoi. CHIEF CITIES Ho Chi Minh (formerly Saigon), Haiphong, Da Nang, Nha Trang. TIME ZONE GMT +7. Most of the population is of Vietnamese origin; Buddhism, Roman Catholicism, Confucianism, and Taoism are the chief religions. OFFICIAL LANGUAGE Vietnamese. CURRENCY the dông. PHYSICAL DESCRIPTION occupies a narrow strip along the coast of the Gulf of Tongking and the South China Sea; broader at the Mekong R Delta, in the S, and along the Red R Valley to the N; the highest peak is Fan si Pan at 3 143m; a limestone plateau in the S stretches W into Cambodia. CLIMATE tropical monsoon-type, dominated by S–SE winds during May–Sep and N–NE winds during Oct–Apr; the average annual rainfall is 1 000mm in the lowlands, 2 500mm in the uplands; high humidity in the rainy season; temperatures are high in the S, cooler in the N during Oct–Apr. HISTORY under the influence of China for many centuries; visited by the Portuguese in 1535; Dutch, French, and English traders arrived in the 17c, with missionaries; the regions of Tongking in the N, Annam in the centre, and Cochin-China in the S united as the Vietnamese Empire in 1802; French conquest in the 19c; French protectorates were established in Cochin-China in 1867, and in Annam and Tongking in 1884; formed the French Indo-Chinese Union with Cambodia and Laos in 1887; occupied by the Japanese in World War II; the communist Viet-Minh League under Ho Chi Minh was formed after the World War II, but not recognized by France; Indo-Chinese War, resulting in French withdrawal in 1946–54; in 1954 an armistice divided the country between the communist 'Democratic Republic' in the N and the 'State' of Vietnam in the S; civil war led to US intervention on the side of South Vietnam in 1965; US withdrawal in 1973; fall of Saigon in 1975; with the defeat of South Vietnam nearly 200 000 Vietnamese fled the country; reunification as the Socialist Republic of Vietnam in 1976; large numbers of refugees tried to find homes in the W in the late 1970s; the Chinese invasion of Vietnam in 1979 greatly increased the number attempting to leave the country by sea; these 'Boat People' have presented non-communist countries with a continuing problem; market reforms are being implemented under Communist Party rule. GOVERNMENT governed by a Prime Minister and a two-chamber legislature, comprising a 496-member National Assembly, elected every five years, and a 15-member Council of State, appointed by the Assembly. ECONOMY over 70% of the workforce is employed in agriculture: rice, maize, sorghum, beans, sugar, sweet potatoes, tea, coffee, rubber, tobacco, groundnuts; fishing; forestry; wood and rubber products; textiles; paper; fertilizers; glass; cement; food processing; light engineering; coal, tin; zinc; offshore oil; the Vietnam War brought depopulation of the countryside, and considerable destruction of forest and farmland; towns overcrowded with refugees have since contributed to the economic problems, as have natural disasters caused by typhoons and flooding.

Vietnam

Vietnamese — *noun* **1** (PL. **Vietnamese**) a native or citizen of Vietnam. **2** an Austro-Asiatic language spoken by c.50 million people in Vietnam, Laos, and Cambodia. There is little known about the early development of the language, largely because of the political and linguistic dominance of China until the 10c. A romanized alphabet known as *Quoc-ngu* ('national language') was introduced in the 17c. — *adj.* relating to Vietnam or its people or language.

Vietnam War, also called the **First and Second Indo-Chinese Wars** a war between communist North Vietnam and non-communist South Vietnam. The first began in 1946 after the breakdown of negotiations between France and the Viet Minh under Ho Chi Minh, and ended with the defeat of the French at Dien Bien Phu in 1954. The subsequent Geneva settlement left North Vietnam under communist rule, and the South ruled first by the emperor Bas Dai (until 1955) and then by Ngo Dinh Diem's dictatorial regime. US aid to the South increased considerably from 1961, and in 1964, following a North Vietnamese attack on US ships, their aircraft had begun bombing the North; by 1968 over 500 000 US troops were involved. These troops were withdrawn in 1973 following opposition to the war in the USA, and hostilities ceased in 1975, when the North's victory was completed with the capture of Saigon (renamed Ho Chi Minh).

view — *noun* **1** an act or opportunity of seeing without obstruction: *a good view of the stage.* **2** something, especially a landscape, seen from a particular point: *a magnificent view from the summit.* **3** range or field of vision: *out of view.* **4** a scene recorded in photograph or picture form. **5** a description or impression: *the book gives a view of life in Roman times.* **6** an opinion; a point of view: *can we have your view on unemployment?* **7** a way of considering or understanding something: *a short-term view of the situation.* — *verb* **1** to see or look at. **2** to inspect or examine. **3** to consider or regard. **4** *trans., intrans.* to watch (a programme) on television; to watch television.
— **have something in view** to have it as a plan or aim.
in view of something taking account of it; because of it.
on view displayed for all to see or inspect.
with a view to something with the hope or intention of achieving it: *bought the house with a view to retiring there.*
[from French *vue*]

viewdata *noun* a system by which computerized information can be displayed on a television screen by means of a telephone link with a computer source.

viewer *noun* **1** any device used for viewing something, especially a photographic slide. **2** a person watching television.

viewfinder *noun* a device on a camera showing the field of vision covered by the lens.

View from the Bridge, A a play by Arthur Miller (1955, Pulitzer Prize). It tells of a hard-working longshoreman who develops a desire for his wife's niece. Following his betrayal of two Italian immigrants illegally working in the community, one of whom has gained the niece's love, he is killed.

viewing *noun* an act or opportunity of seeing or inspecting something, eg an exhibition or a house for sale.

View of Delft a painting by Jan Vermeer (c.1660, The Hague).

View on the Stour a landscape painting by John Constable (1819).

viewpoint *noun* an interpretation of facts received; an opinion or point of view.

vigil *noun* **1** a period of staying awake, usually to guard or watch over a person or thing. **2** the day before a major religious festival, traditionally spent in prayer. **3** a night-time religious service or session of prayer. [from Latin *vigil*, awake, watchful]

vigilance *noun* the state of being watchful or observant. [from Latin *vigilare*, to keep awake]

vigilant *adj.* ready for possible trouble or danger; alert; watchful.

vigilante *noun* a self-appointed enforcer of law and order.

Vigneaud, Vincent du (1901–78) US biochemist, born in Chicago. Professor at Cornell from 1938, he synthesized penicillin and oxytocin (a pituitary hormone), discovered the structure of biotin (one of the group of B vitamins), and was awarded the 1955 Nobel Prize for Chemistry for his work on hormone synthesis.

vignette *noun* **1** a decorative design on a book's title page, traditionally of vine leaves. **2** a photographic portrait with the background deliberately faded. **3** a short literary essay, especially describing a person's character. [from French *vignette*, little vine]

Vignola, Giacomo (Barozzi) da (1507–73) Italian architect, born in Vignola. He became architect to Pope Julius III in Rome, and designed for him the Villa di Papa Giulio (1550–5). The most influential of his many church designs was the church of Il Gesú in Rome (1568–73).

Vigo POP (1991) 275 000, a naval and commercial port in Pontevedra province, Galicia region, NW Spain. It is Spain's chief port for transatlantic traffic. NOTABLE FEATURES Castle of St Sebastian; Castro Castle.

vigorous *adj.* **1** strong and active. **2** forceful; energetic: *had a vigorous approach to life.*

vigorously *adv.* forcefully; energetically.

vigour *noun* **1** great strength and energy of body or mind. **2** liveliness or forcefulness of action. **3** healthy growth (in plants, etc). [from Latin *vigor*]

viking *noun* (often **Viking**) any of the Scandinavian seafaring peoples who raided and settled in much of NW Europe between the 8c and 11c. [perhaps from Anglo-Saxon *wicing*, pirate]

Viking project *Astron.* either of two NASA space probes, *Viking 1* and *Viking 2*, that made the first successful landings on Mars. *Viking 1* landed on Mars in Jul 1976 and continued to send back information to Earth until 1982. *Viking 2* landed in Sep 1976, and although no evidence of life was found on the planet, photographs taken by the probes showed a stony dusty reddish-brown landscape, covered with craters, volcanoes, and gorges, and data sent back to Earth has provided the basis for continuing research on the history and climate of Mars.

Vikings raiders, traders, and settlers from Norway, Sweden, and Denmark, who from the late 8c to the mid-11c conquered and colonized large parts of Britain, Normandy, and Russia; attacked Spain, Morocco, and Italy; traded with Byzantium, Persia, and India; discovered and occupied Iceland and Greenland; and reached the coast of N America. Though brutal and destructive as raiders, as traders they were instrumental in the development of medieval Europe. Their earliest overseas settlements were in the Orkney and Shetland Is, which remained united to the Norwegian Crown until 1472.

Viking house (a reconstruction)

Vila Real 1 POP (1991) 16 000, the capital of Vila Real district, N Portugal. It lies on the R Corgo, 116km/72mi NE of Oporto. The famous Mateus Rosé wine is produced nearby. NOTABLE FEATURES cathedral; Church of São Pedro (16c); Mateus House; Roman Sanctuary of Panoias 7km/4mi SE. **2** a district in N Portugal with the city of Vila Real as its capital.

vile *adj.* **1** evil or wicked. **2** physically repulsive; disgusting. **3** *colloq.* extremely bad or unpleasant. [from Latin *vilis*, worthless, base]

vilification *noun* speaking evil; defamation.

vilify *verb* (**vilifies, vilified**) to say insulting or abusive things about; to malign or defame. [from Latin *vilificare*, to make worthless or base]

Villa, Francisco, also called **Pancho**, originally **Doroteo Arangol** (1877–1923) Mexican revolutionary, born near San Juan del Río, Durango. He had various modest occupations before the Mexican Revolution made him famous as a military commander. In a fierce struggle for control of the Revolution, he was defeated by Venustiano Carranza and withdrew to his strongholds in N Mexico. He eventually made peace with the government (1920) but was murdered in Parral.

villa *noun* **1** a large country house or mansion. **2** a good-sized (especially detached) suburban house. **3** a seaside house let to holidaymakers. [from Latin *villa*, country house]

village *noun* **1** a group of houses, shops, and other buildings smaller than a town and larger than a hamlet, especially in or near the countryside. **2** the people living in it, regarded as a community: *the village has started to gossip.* **3** a residential complex for participants in a major (usually international) sporting event. [from Old French *village*, from Latin *villaticus*]

Village, The a poem by George Crabbe (1783). It offers a harsh, realistic presentation of rural life in opposition to the idyllic depiction favoured by pastoral poets.

villager *noun* an inhabitant of a village.

Villahermosa POP (1990) 390 000, the river-port capital of Tabasco state, SE Mexico. It lies on the R Grijalva. NOTABLE FEATURES Centro de Investigaciones de las Culturas Olmecas; Mayan brick-built ruins of Comalcalco to the NW.

villain *noun* **1** the principal wicked character in a story. **2** any violent, wicked, or unscrupulous person. **3** *colloq.* a criminal. [originally 'a rustic', from Old French *vilein*, serf, from Latin *villanus*, worker on a country estate]

villain of the piece 1 the villain in a story. **2** the person responsible for some trouble or mischief.

villainous *adj.* **1** like or worthy of a villain. **2** *colloq.* extremely bad: *a villainous storm.*

villainy *noun* (PL. **villainies**) wicked or vile behaviour, or an act of this kind.

Villa-Lobos, Heitor (1887–1959) Brazilian composer and conductor, born in Rio de Janeiro. His first published composition was *Salon Waltz* (1908), and a set of *Country Songs* (1910) show his interest in Brazilian folk music and folklore. His many compositions include 12 symphonies, 16 string quartets, five operas, large-scale symphonic poems, and ballets. He is also known for the nine suites *Bachianas Brasileiras* (1930–45), in which he treats Brazilian-style melodies in the manner of Bach. In 1932 he became director of musical education for Brazil, and in 1945 he founded the Brazilian Academy of Music.

villein *noun Hist.* a feudal peasant worker owing allegiance directly to a lord. [a Middle English variant of VILLAIN]

villeinage *noun Hist.* the position or status of villeins.

Villeneuve, Pierre (Charles Jean Baptiste Sylvestre) de (1763–1806) French admiral, born in Valensoles. He commanded the rear division of the French navy in the battle of the Nile, and in 1805 was in charge of the French fleet at Trafalgar, where he was taken prisoner. Released in 1806, he committed suicide on his return journey to Paris to face Napoleon.

Villon, François, pseudonym of **François de Montcorbier** (1431–?) French poet, born in Paris. He served several jail sentences for violent crime, and in 1463 received a death sentence, which was commuted to banishment. The best-known of his surviving work includes *Le Lais* (The Legacy, also known as *Le Petit Testament*), and *Le Grand Testament* (1461).

villus *noun* (PL. **villi**) *Anat.* any of many tiny fingerlike projections that line the inside of the small intestine. The villi absorb the products of digestion, and their presence greatly increases the surface area over which absorption can take place. [from Latin *villus*, wool]

Vilnius, formerly **Wilno** (1920–39) POP (1990e) 593 000, the industrial capital of Lithuania. It is situated on the R Vilnia, near the Belorussian border, in SE Lithuania. HISTORY became capital of Lithuania in 1323; belonged to Poland before becoming part of Russia in 1795; occupied by Germany in World War II; became capital of the newly independent Lithuania in 1991. NOTABLE FEATURES cathedral (1777–1801); Gediminas Castle.

vim *noun colloq.* energy; liveliness. [from Latin *vis*, force]

Vimy Ridge an escarpment 8km/5mi NE of Arras (Pas-de-Calais), a strongly held part of the German defence line on the Western Front in World War I. It was successfully stormed during the Battle of Arras by the Canadian Corps of the British 1st Army (1917), a feat that had much symbolic significance in establishing Canada's identity as an independent nation.

Viña del Mar POP (1991e) 312 000, a seaside town in Valparaíso province, Valparaíso region, central Chile. It lies 9km/6mi from the city of Valparaíso. The town is a residential suburb and a popular S American resort. NOTABLE FEATURES Sporting Club, with racecourse and playing fields; Granadilla Golf Club; casino; sports stadium; Tranque Sausalito (artificial lake); Salinas Golf Course; Cerro Castillo (presidential summer palace); Quinta Vergara (gallery); Teatro Municipal.

vinaigrette *noun* a salad dressing made by mixing oil, vinegar, and seasonings, especially mustard. [from French, from *vinaigre*, vinegar]

Vincent a male first name. [from Latin *vincere*, to conquer]

Vincent de Beauvais, Latin **Vincentius Bellovacensis** (c.1190–c.1264) French Dominican and encyclopedist. Under the patronage of Louis IX, he gathered together the entire knowledge of the Middle Ages in his *Speculum Majus* (Great Mirror). Its three parts, on natural, doc-

trinal, and historical subjects were supplemented by a section on morals in the 14c, by an unknown author.

Vincent de Paul, St (c.1581–1660) French priest and philanthropist, born in Pouy. Ordained in 1600, he was captured by corsairs in 1605, and sold into slavery in Tunis. Once he had persuaded his master to return to the Christian faith, he escaped to France (1607) and formed associations for helping the sick, became almoner-general of the galleys (1619), and in 1625 founded the Congregation of Priests of the Missions (or 'Lazarists', from their priory of St Lazare), and the Sisterhood of Charity (1634). He was canonized in 1737 and his feast day is 27 Sep.

Vincentio, Duke 1 the temperate, wise Governor of Vienna in Shakespeare's *Measure for Measure*, who disguises himself as a friar after abdicating his responsibilities, and orchestrates the happy ending in the play. **2** the father of Lucentio in Shakespeare's *The Taming of the Shrew*.

Vinci, Leonardo da see LEONARDO DA VINCI.

vindicate *verb* **1** to prove to be blameless or beyond criticism. **2** to show to have been worthwhile or justified: *the year's results vindicated their cautious planning*. [Latin *vindicare*, to lay claim to, to avenge]

vindication *noun* proof of blamelessness or worth: *this was a vindication of all they had done*.

vindicatory *adj.* serving to vindicate or prove worthwhile.

vindictive *adj.* **1** feeling or showing spite or hatred. **2** seeking revenge. **3** serving as revenge or retribution. [from Latin *vindicta* vengeance, related to VINDICATE]

vindictively *adv.* spitefully; with malicious revenge.

vindictiveness *noun* a maliciously spiteful state or character.

Vine, Frederick John (1939–88) English geophysicist, educated at St John's College, Cambridge. Professor at the University of East Anglia, he undertook important work which helped to confirm Harry Hess's 'sea-floor spreading' hypothesis, giving further support to the theory of continental drift.

vine *noun* **1** any of various climbing plants that produce grapes. **2** any climbing or trailing plant, including ivy. [from Latin *vinum*, wine]

vinegar *noun* **1** a sour liquid consisting of a dilute solution of acetic acid, produced by the bacterial fermentation of alcoholic beverages such as cider or wine. It is used as a food flavouring, and as a preservative for pickles. **2** the quality of being bad-tempered or peevish. [from French *vinaigre*, from *vin*, wine + *aigre*, sour]

vinegary *adj.* sour like vinegar.

vineyard *noun* a plantation of grape-bearing vines, especially for wine-making.

Vingt, Les a group of 20 modern painters, including Ensor, founded in Brussels in 1884. For ten years they held exhibitions where pictures by leading Post-Impressionists such as Georges Seurat, Paul Gauguin, Paul Cézanne, and Vincent van Gogh were shown.

vingt-et-un *noun* the card game pontoon. [from French *vingt-et-un*, twenty-one]

viniculture *noun* the cultivation of grapes for making wine. [from Latin *vinum*, wine + CULTURE]

viniculturist *noun* a cultivator of grapes for making wine.

Vínland a generalized Norse name meaning 'Berry' or 'Vine Land', applied to the E coast of N America from the time of its first sighting by the Viking Leif Eriksson in c.985. Though the 'Vinland Map', purportedly of the 1440s, is a 20c forgery, accounts of the Norse discovery of

America in Icelandic sagas are confirmed by archaeological evidence.

vino *noun slang* wine, especially of poor quality. [from Spanish and Italian *vino*]

vinous *adj.* **1** of or like wine. **2** resulting from excess of wine: *a vinous complexion*. [from Latin *vinum*, wine]

Vinson Massif the highest range in Antarctica, rising to 5 140m in the Ellsworth Mts.

vintage — *noun* **1** the grape-harvest of a particular year. **2** the wine produced from a year's harvest. **3** the time of year when grapes are harvested. **4** a particular period, especially when regarded as productive: *literature of a postwar vintage*. — *adj.* **1** *said of wine* of good quality and from a specified year. **2** typical of someone's best work or most characteristic behaviour: *the remark was vintage Churchill*. [from Old French *vintage*, from Latin *vinum*, wine]

vintage car *Brit.* an old motor car, specifically one built between 1919 and 1930.

vintner *noun formal* a wine-merchant. [from Old French *vinetier*, from Latin *vinum* wine]

vinyl *noun* **1** any of a group of tough plastics manufactured in various forms, eg paint additives and carpet fibres. **2** *colloq.* plastic long-playing records regarded collectively, as distinct from cassettes and compact discs.

viol *noun* any of a family of Renaissance stringed musical instruments played with a bow. [from Old Provençal *viola*]

Viola the twin sister of Sebastian in Shakespeare's *Twelfth Night* who, disguised as Cesario, becomes page to Orsino, with whom she falls in love.

viola¹ *noun* a musical instrument of the violin family, larger than the violin and lower in pitch. [Italian]
◇ Its pitch is a fifth lower than the violin, and an octave above the cello. It has been used as an orchestral instrument since the 17c, and in chamber music since the 18c. It was formerly known (in English) as the *alto violin* or *tenor violin*.

viola

viola² *noun* any of a group of flowering plants including the violet and pansy. [from Latin *viola*]

violate *verb* **1** to disregard or break (a law or agreement, or an oath). **2** to treat (something sacred or private) with disrespect; to profane. **3** to disturb or disrupt (eg a person's peace or privacy). **4** to rape or sexually abuse. [from Latin *violare*, to treat violently]

violation *noun* an act or the process of violating.

violator *noun* a person who violates an agreement or oath.

violence *noun* **1** the state or quality of being violent. **2** violent behaviour.
— **do violence to someone or something 1** to harm them physically. **2** to spoil or ruin them. **3** to distort their meaning or significance. [from Latin *violentus*, from *vis*, force]

violent *adj.* **1** marked by or using extreme physical force. **2** using, or involving the use of, such force to cause physical harm. **3** impulsively aggressive and unrestrained in nature or behaviour. **4** intense, extreme, vehement: *they took a violent dislike to me*.

violently *adv.* **1** in a violent or aggressive way. **2** extremely; severely; ardently: *she was violently opposed to our involvement.*

violet *noun* **1** any of a group of flowering plants of mild climates with large purple or blue petals; or of various similar but unrelated plants, eg the African violet. **2** a bluish-purple colour. [from Latin *viola*]

violin *noun* **1** a musical instrument with a shaped body and a neck along which four strings are stretched. It is held with one end under the chin and played with a bow. **2** any of the violinists in an orchestra or group: *was first violin.* [from Italian *violino*, little viola]
◇ The four-string violin was developed in the 16c from earlier three-string instruments. Its form has hardly changed since it reached its highest point of perfection between 1650 and 1730, with the result that instruments made in that period, especially by Antonio Stradivari and the Amati and Guarneri families, are still the most sought after and highly valued. Other members of the violin family are the viola, cello, and double bass.

violin

violinist *noun* a violin-player.

violist *noun* a viola- or viol-player.

Viollet-Le-Duc, Eugène (Emmanuel) (1814–79) French architect and archaeologist, born in Paris. He studied in France and Italy, and in 1840 directed the restoration of Sainte Chapelle, Paris. His other restorations included the cathedrals of Notre Dame (begun 1845), Amiens, and Laon, and the Château de Pierrefonds.

violoncellist *noun formal* a cellist.

violoncello *noun* (PL. **violoncellos**) *formal* a cello. [from Italian *violoncello*, a diminutive form]

VIP *abbrev.* very important person.

viper *noun* **1** any of a large family of poisonous snakes found in Europe, Asia, and Africa, characterized by long tubular fangs through which venom is injected into the prey. When the jaws are closed the fangs are folded back against the roof of the mouth. **2** the common European viper, which is the only poisonous snake in the UK. — Also called *adder*. **3** a treacherous or spiteful person. [from Latin *vipera*]

virago *noun* (PL. **viragoes, viragos**) *literary* a loudly fierce or overbearing woman. [from Latin *virago*, manlike woman]

viral *adj.* relating to or caused by a virus.

Virchow, Rudolf (1821–1902) German pathologist and politician, born in Schivelbein, Pomerania. Professor at Würzburg and Berlin, he recognized leukaemia (1845), and studied animal parasites, inflammation, thrombosis and embolism. His *Cellularpathologie* (Cellular Pathology, 1858) established that tumours and all other morbid structures contained cells derived from previous cells. He was a liberal member of the Reichstag (1880–93), forcefully opposing Bismarck.

Virgil or Vergil, in full **Publius Vergilius Maro** (70–19 BC) Roman poet, born in Andes, near Mantua. He studied rhetoric and philosophy in Rome, and later became one of the court poets to Maecenas. His *Eclogues* (37 BC) were received with great enthusiasm. He moved to the country (near Nola) and wrote the *Georgics* (36–29 BC). His epic work, the *Aeneid*, which was incomplete at his death, was written at the request of the emperor Augustus, who wanted a work to celebrate the founder of the Roman nation. His tomb was for many hundreds of years worshipped as a sacred place and his works (in Latin) became the textbooks of W Europe from the Middle Ages to the 20c.

virgin — *noun* **1** a person, especially a woman, who has never had sexual intercourse. **2** a member of a religious order of women sworn to chastity. **3** (**the Virgin**) *RC Church* a name for Mary, the mother of Jesus Christ. **4** (**Virgin**) a portrait or statue of Mary. **5** (**the Virgin**) the sign or constellation Virgo. — *adj.* **1** never having had sexual intercourse; chaste. **2** in its original state; never having been used. [from Latin *virgo*]

virginal¹ *adj.* **1** of or appropriate to a virgin. **2** in a state of virginity.

virginal² *noun* a 16c–17c keyboard instrument like a small harpsichord but with strings set at right angles to the keys (as in the clavichord). [perhaps so called because it was mostly played by young women]

Virgin and Child with St Anne a cartoon (c.1499, National Gallery, London) and painting (c.1501–12, Louvre, Paris) by Leonardo da Vinci.

Virgin Birth *Relig.* the birth of Christ of the Virgin Mary, regarded as an act of God.

Virginia POP (1990) 6.4m, a state in E USA, divided into 95 counties and 41 independent cities. It is known as 'Old Dominion'. AREA 105 582sq km/40 755sq mi. PHYSICAL DESCRIPTION Chesapeake Bay and the Atlantic Ocean lie to the E; the Potomac R follows the Maryland state border; the Rappahannock, York, and James rivers cross the state to Chesapeake Bay; the Blue Ridge Mts lie in the W; Mt Rogers (1 743m) is the highest point; the coastal area in E Virginia is flat and swampy (known as the Tidewater Region); to the W, land rises into the rolling, fertile Piedmont, interrupted further W by the Blue Ridge Mts; W of these lies the Valley of Virginia, a series of beautiful valleys, notably the Shenandoah. HISTORY first permanent British settlement in America made at Jamestown in 1607; one of the first colonies to move for independence; scene of the British surrender at Yorktown in 1781; 10th of the original 13 states to ratify the Constitution in 1788; at the beginning of the Civil War the W counties, loyal to the Union, split from the rest of Virginia, becoming the US state of West Virginia in 1863; scene of several major battles in the Civil War (Richmond was the Confederacy capital); readmitted to the Union in 1870. CAPITAL Richmond. CHIEF TOWNS Norfolk, Virginia Beach, Newport News. ECONOMY tobacco (chief agricultural crop); dairy produce; cattle; hay, corn, peanuts, sweet potatoes, apples; coastal fisheries (especially shellfish); manufactures include chemicals, tobacco products, electrical equipment, and ships; coal mining; scenic mountains, valleys, and shores, as well as the area's history, make tourism a major state industry. [named after Elizabeth I, the 'Virgin Queen']

Virginia a female first name. [from the Roman family name *Virginius*]

Virginia Beach POP (1990) 393 000, an independent city in SE Virginia, USA. It lies on the Atlantic Ocean, 29km/18mi E of Norfolk, and is a major summer resort. NOTABLE FEATURES Cape Henry Memorial (site of the English landing in 1607); Marine Science Museum.

Virginia Company a joint stock company established (1606) to promote English settlement in N America. It founded Virginia (1607) and governed it until 1624, when the company was dissolved, for despite high investments it never returned a profit.

Virginians, The a novel by William Makepeace Thackeray (1857–9). It describes the fortunes of twin brothers in America and England up to the time of the American War of Independence.

Virgin Islands, British POP (1991) 17 000, a British Crown Colony comprising an island group at the NW end of the Lesser Antilles chain in the E Caribbean Sea. AREA 153sq km/59sq mi. It lies c.80km/50mi E of Puerto Rico. CAPITAL Road Town (on Tortola I). TIME ZONE GMT –4. The population is mainly of African or mixed descent; Protestantism is the chief religion. OFFICIAL LANGUAGE English. CURRENCY the US dollar. PHYSICAL DESCRIPTION comprises four large islands (Tortola, Virgin Gorda, Anegada, Jost Van Dyke) and over 30 islets and cays; only 16 islands are inhabited; the highest point is Sage Mt (540m) on Tortola I. CLIMATE sub-tropical; temperatures range from 17°C to 28°C in winter, and 26°C to 31°C in summer; the average annual rainfall is 1 270mm. HISTORY Tortola was colonized by British planters in 1666; a constitutional government was granted in 1774; became part of the Leeward Is in 1872; became a separate Crown Colony in 1956. GOVERNMENT a governor represents the British Sovereign; there is a six-member Executive Council and a Legislative Council of 11 members. ECONOMY over 50% of national income is from tourism; construction; rum; paint; gravel and stone extraction; livestock; coconuts; sugar cane; fruit and vegetables; fish.

Virgin Islands, United States, official name **Virgin Islands of the United States**, formerly **Danish West Indies** (to 1917) POP (1992e) 107 000, an Unincorporated Territory of the USA comprising a group of more than 50 islands in the S and W of the Virgin Is group, Lesser Antilles, Caribbean Sea. AREA 342sq km/132sq mi. It lies 64km/40mi E of Puerto Rico. CAPITAL Charlotte Amalie. TIME ZONE GMT –4. OFFICIAL LANGUAGE English. The chief religion is Protestantism. CURRENCY the US dollar. PHYSICAL DESCRIPTION three main inhabited islands, St Croix, St Thomas, St John; the islands are of volcanic origin; the highest peak is Crown Mt (474m) on St Thomas. CLIMATE the average temperature is 21–29°C in Dec–Mar, and 24–31°C in Jun–Sep; low humidity. HISTORY Denmark colonized St Thomas and St John in 1671, and bought St Croix from France in 1733; purchased by the USA in 1917. GOVERNMENT a governor serves a four-year term, with an elected 15-member unicameral legislature. ECONOMY the chief industry is tourism; St Croix industries include oil and alumina refining, clocks and watches, textiles, rum, fragrances, pharmaceuticals, vegetables, fruit, sorghum.

virginity *noun* the state of being a virgin.

Virgo *noun* (PL. **Virgos**) **1** *Astron.* the Maiden, a large northern constellation of the zodiac, lying between Leo and Libra. It is the second-largest constellation in the sky, and its brightest star is Spica. **2** the sixth sign of the zodiac, the Virgin. **3** a person born under this sign, between 23 Aug and 22 Sep. [from Latin *virgo*, virgin]

virile *adj.* **1** *said of a man* having a high level of sexual desire. **2** displaying or requiring qualities regarded as typically masculine, especially physical strength. **3** *said of a man* able to produce children. **4** relating to or possessing the features of a mature adult male. [from Latin *virilis*, manly]

virility *noun* the state of being virile; showing masculine physical strength.

virological *adj.* relating to the study of viruses.

virology *noun Medicine* the branch of microbiology concerned with the study of viruses and viral diseases.

virtual *adj.* **1** being so in effect or in practice, but not in name: *a virtual state of war.* **2** nearly so: *the virtual collapse of the steel industry.* [from Latin *virtualis*, related to VIRTUE]

virtually *adv.* **1** in practice, though not strictly speaking: *was virtually in charge of us.* **2** almost; nearly: *the war is virtually over.*

virtual reality a computer simulation of a real or artificial environment that gives the user the impression of actually being within the environment and interacting with it. A special visor is worn, containing two tiny television screens (one for each eye), and the user may wear special gloves fitted with sensors.
◇ Virtual reality systems could have important applications in the training of surgeons, aircraft pilots, astronauts, and military personnel, and would enable architects to 'walk' through the interior of proposed building designs. They could also be used in interactive learning programmes, video games, etc.

virtue *noun* **1** a quality regarded as morally good: *he has many virtues, including honesty.* **2** moral goodness; righteousness. **3** an admirable quality or desirable feature: *the virtue of this one is its long life.* **4** virginity, especially in women.
— **by** *or* **in virtue of something** because of it; on account of it.
[from Latin *virtus*, moral excellence, bravery]

virtuosity *noun* brilliance of technique.

virtuoso *noun* (PL. **virtuosos**) **1** a person with remarkable artistic skill, especially a brilliant musical performer. **2** (*attributive*) highly skilful; brilliant: *a virtuoso performance.* [from Italian *virtuoso*, learned, skilful]

virtuous *adj.* possessing or showing virtue; morally sound.

virtuously *adv.* in a virtuous way; with moral rightness.

virulence *noun* **1** causing extreme harm; poisonousness. **2** bitter hostility.

virulent *adj.* **1** *said of a disease* having a rapidly harmful effect. **2** *said of a disease or the organism causing it* extremely infectious. **3** *said of a substance* highly poisonous. **4** bitterly hostile; acrimonious. [from Latin *virulentus*, venomous]

Virunga a national park in the Kivu region of NW Zaire. AREA 120sq km/46sq mi. It includes marshy deltas, savannah, volcanic landscapes, and snow-covered mountains. The park is noted for its wild mammals, particularly its gorilla colonies. It is a World Heritage site.

virus *noun* **1** a non-cellular micro-organism, only visible under an electron microscope, that infects the cells of animals, plants, and bacteria, and can only survive and reproduce within such cells. **2** the organism that causes and transmits an infectious disease. **3** *loosely* a disease caused by such an organism. **4** anything that damages or corrupts. **5** (*in full* **computer virus**) a computer program, written anonymously, that can make copies of itself and spread from one computer to another within a network. Many viruses instruct a computer to change or delete data (eg by erasing hard disks), and they can be spread via floppy disks. Various anti-virus programs have been designed to detect and destroy some of the better known viruses. [from Latin *virus*, venom]
◇ Viruses cause many plant and animal diseases, and human viral diseases include the common cold, influenza, herpes, hepatitis, chickenpox, mumps, measles, smallpox, polio, rabies, and AIDS (which is caused by infection with the human immunodeficiency virus, HIV). Antibiotics have no effect on such diseases, but the vaccines that are available for many of them are very effective.
A mature virus, known as a *virion*, consists of a core of nucleic acid (either DNA or RNA) surrounded by a coat of protein. Such a virus is completely inert while it is outside the cell of another organism, but once it has penetrated the cell wall, it injects a strand of DNA or RNA, which makes copies of itself, and damages or destroys the genetic material of the host cell. The virus then directs the cell to manufacture more identical viruses, and the cell wall eventually ruptures, releasing the newly formed viruses. Oncogenes, which play a role in the development of some forms of cancer, are genes carried by certain

viruses, and they induce normal cells to divide in an uncontrolled manner, forming a tumour.

visa *noun* a permit stamped into a passport to allow the holder to enter or leave the country issuing it. [from Latin *visa*, from *videre*, to see]

visage *noun literary* **1** the face. **2** the usual expression of a face; a countenance. [from French *visage*, face]

vis-à-vis — *prep.* in relation to; with regard to. — *adv.* face-to-face. — *noun* (PL. **vis-à-vis**) a counterpart or opposite number. [from French *vis-à-vis*, face to face]

Visayan Islands an island group in the central Philippines. AREA 61 991sq km/23 929sq mi. It lies N of Mindanao I, S of Luzon I and is bounded by the Sulu Sea in the W and the Philippine Sea in the E. MAIN ISLANDS Cebu, Bohol, Panay, Leyte, Samar, Negros, Masbate. ECONOMY sugar, coconuts.

viscacha *noun* a cavy-like rodent, native to S America, that resembles a large chinchilla, and lives among rocks or in burrows. [from Spanish, from Quechua *huiscacha*]

viscera — *pl. noun Anat.* the internal organs of the body, especially those found in the abdominal cavity. — *adj.* relating to these organs. [from Latin *viscera*, plural of *viscus*; see VISCUS]

visceral *adj.* **1** relating to the viscera. **2** relating to the feelings, especially the basic human instincts as distinct from the intellect.

viscid *adj.* glutinous; viscous. [from Latin *viscum*, bird-lime]

Visconti, Luchino, real name **Count Don Luchino Visconti Di Morone** (1906–76) Italian stage and film director, born in Milan. After working in stage design and opera and ballet production, he was assistant to Jean Renoir. His first film, *Ossessione* (Obsession, 1942), had a strictly realist style and was concerned with social problems. Others included *La Terra Trema* (The Earth Trembles, 1947), *Il Gattopardo* (The Leopard, 1963), and *Morte a Venezia* (Death in Venice, 1971).

viscose *noun* **1** cellulose in a viscous state, able to be made into thread. **2** rayon, a fabric made from such thread.

viscosity *noun* (SYMBOL η) a measure of the resistance of a fluid (a liquid or gas) to flow, caused by internal friction which results in different rates of flow in different parts of the liquid, eg treacle has a higher viscosity than water. The viscosity of liquids decreases with increasing temperature, while that of gases increases.

viscount *noun* a member of the British nobility below an earl and above a baron in rank. [from Old French *visconte*]

viscountcy *or* **viscountship** *noun* the rank of viscount.

viscountess *noun* **1** the wife or widow of a viscount. **2** a woman of the rank of viscount in her own right.

viscous *adj.* **1** of a thick semi-liquid consistency, not flowing easily. **2** *said of liquid* sticky. [from Latin *viscosus*, sticky, from *viscum*, bird-lime]

viscus *noun Medicine* any of the body's large internal organs. See also VISCERA. [from Latin *viscera*]

Vishnu the second Hindu deity in the Hindu triad (*Trimurti*). The preserver of the universe and the embodiment of goodness and mercy, he is believed to have assumed visible form in nine descents (*avataras*): three in non-human form, one in hybrid form, and five in human form, of which his appearances as Rama and Krishna are the most important.

visibility *noun* **1** the state or fact of being visible. **2** the range in which one can see clearly in given conditions of light and weather: *poor visibility / visibility down to 50 yards.*

visible *adj.* **1** able to be seen. **2** able to be realised or perceived; apparent. [from Latin *visibilis*, from *videre*, to see]

visible spectrum *Physics* the range of wavelengths of electromagnetic radiation that can be seen by the human eye, ie visible light, ranging from about 390nm to 780nm. The visible spectrum can be produced by dispersing white light through a prism.

visibly *adv.* so as to be visible or discernible: *they were visibly annoyed.*

Visigoths a Germanic people who fled from the Huns in AD 376 into the Roman Empire and founded several Visigothic kingdoms, which by the 6c extended through Portugal, most of Spain, and S Gaul. They absorbed elements of Roman culture and, despite their official Arian Christianity, allowed Catholic Christianity to coexist. Visigothic civilization decayed after the Arab conquests that began in 711.

vision *noun* **1** the ability to see objects outside the body. Nerve impulses from specialized receptor cells (rods and cones) in the retina are relayed via the optic nerve to the brain, where they are interpreted as a three-dimensional image of the object being viewed. Common defects of vision, including myopia (short-sightedness), hypermetropia (long-sightedness), and astigmatism, can be corrected by wearing spectacles or contact lenses. **2** an image conjured up vividly in the imagination. **3** the ability to perceive what is likely, and plan wisely for it; foresight. **4** an image communicated supernaturally, especially by God. **5** the picture on a television screen, or its quality. **6** a person or thing of overwhelming beauty. [from Latin *visio*, sight]

visionary — *adj.* **1** showing or marked by great foresight or imagination. **2** possible only in the imagination; impracticable; fanciful. **3** capable of seeing supernatural images; seeing such images often. — *noun* (PL. **visionaries**) **1** a person of great foresight. **2** *Relig.* a person to whom supernatural visions are attributed. **3** a person who dreams up idealistic schemes.

vision mixer *Telecomm.* **1** equipment used in video and film production for the combination of visual material from several sources (eg multiple cameras, videotape, etc), and with facilities for transition effects between scenes and image combination at the time of shooting, to create the visual effects required by the director. **2** the operator of this equipment.

visit — *verb* (**visited**, **visiting**) **1** *trans., intrans.* to go or come to see (a person or place) socially or professionally. **2** *trans., intrans.* to go or come to stay (with) temporarily. **3** (**visit something on someone**) to inflict harm or punishment on them. **4** to enter the mind of temporarily. **5** (**visit**

Vishnu

someone with something) *old use* to afflict or trouble them: *were visited with dire consequences.* — *noun* **1** an act of visiting; a social or professional call. **2** a temporary stay. **3** a sightseeing excursion. [from Latin *visitare*, from *visere*, to go to see]

visitant *noun* **1** *Relig.* a person appearing in a supernatural vision; an apparition. **2** a migratory bird, staying temporarily.

visitation *noun* **1** an official visit or inspection. **2** an event regarded as a divine punishment or reward. **3** an instance of seeing a supernatural vision. **4** (**the Visitation**) the visit made by the Virgin Mary to her cousin Elizabeth (Luke 1.39–56); the Christian festival commemorating this, held on 2 Jul.

visiting-card *noun* a card with one's name and address printed on it, left instead of a formal visit.

visitor *noun* **1** someone who visits a person or place. **2** a migratory bird present in a place for a time: *winter visitors.*

visor *noun* **1** the movable part of a helmet, covering the face. **2** (*in full* **sun visor**) a translucent device shaped like the peak of a cap, worn to shade the eyes. **3** a small movable panel above the windscreen on the inside of a motor vehicle, folded down to shade the eyes from sunlight. [from Old French *viser*, from *vis*, face]

vista *noun* **1** a view into the distance, especially when bounded narrowly on both sides, eg by rows of trees. **2** a mental vision extending far into the future or past. [from Italian *vista*, view]

Vistula, River, Polish **Wisła** the longest river in Poland, length 1 047km/651mi. Rising in the Carpathians in SW Poland, it flows NE, N, and NW to meet the Baltic Sea at Gdańsk. It is linked by canal to E and W Europe, and is dammed at Goczałkowice. The river is navigable for 941km/585mi.

visual *adj.* **1** relating to or received through sight or vision: *a visual image.* **2** creating vivid mental images: *visual poetry.* **3** creating a strong impression through what is seen, rather than what is said or heard: *a very visual play.* [from Latin *visus*, sight]

visual aid a picture, film, or other visual material used as an aid to teaching or presenting information.

visual arts (*usually* **the visual arts**) art-forms involving appreciation with the eyes, eg painting, sculpture, film, etc, as distinct from literature, music, etc.

visual display unit (ABBREV. **VDU**) a screen on which information from a computer is displayed.

visualization *or* **visualisation** *noun* **1** the act or process of visualizing. **2** *Psychol.* a technique for improving performance, in which a person learns to create a mental picture of the successful performance of the tasks that are to be achieved. Visualization is also used to increase self-confidence, relieve stress, etc.

visualize *or* **visualise** *verb* to form a clear mental image of.

visually *adv.* as regards sight or vision: *the performance is visually stunning.*

visual purple. See RHODOPSIN.

vital — *adj.* **1** relating to or essential for life: *the vital organs.* **2** determining life or death, or success or failure: *a vital error.* **3** essential; of the greatest importance. **4** full of life; energetic. — *noun* (**vitals**) the vital organs, including the brain, heart, and lungs. [from Latin *vita*, life]

vitality *noun* **1** liveliness and energy. **2** the state of being alive; the ability to stay alive.

vitalization *or* **vitalisation** *noun* the act or process of vitalizing.

vitalize *or* **vitalise** *verb* to fill with life or energy.

vitally *adv.* essentially, urgently: *it is vitally important to go.*

vital statistics **1** statistics concerning births, marriages, deaths and other matters relating to population. **2** *colloq.* a woman's bust, waist, and hip measurements.

vitamin *noun Biochem.* any of various organic compounds that occur in small amounts in many foods, and are also manufactured synthetically. Trace amounts of vitamins are essential for the normal growth and functioning of the body. [from Latin *vita*, life + AMINE]
◇ Vitamin deficiency, eg in areas where famine and malnutrition are common, can cause serious medical disorders known as *deficiency diseases.* Vitamin supplements are not regarded as necessary if a person eats a balanced diet including milk and other dairy products, bread, meat and fish or pulses, and fresh fruit and vegetables.

vitamin A a fat-soluble organic compound found in liver, fish oils, dairy products, and egg yolk. It is required for normal growth and especially the functioning of the light-sensitive rods and cones of the retina of the eye. Deficiency causes night blindness and retarded growth. — Also called *retinol.*

vitamin B₁ thiamine.

vitamin B₂ riboflavin.

vitamin B₆ any of three interconvertible organic compounds found in milk, eggs, liver, cereal grains, yeast, and fresh vegetables. Vitamin B₆ is required for the metabolism of amino acids, and deficiency of the vitamin can cause dermatitis and nervous disorders. — Also called *pyridoxine.*

vitamin B₇ nicotinic acid.

vitamin B₁₂ a member of the vitamin B complex that is found in raw liver, and is required for the oxidation (breakdown) of fatty acids, the manufacture of DNA, and the formation of red blood cells. Deficiency of the vitamin causes pernicious anaemia. — Also called *cyanocobalamin.*

vitamin B complex any of a group of water-soluble vitamins found in yeast, liver, and wheat germ, and referred to either by individual B numbers, eg vitamin B₁, vitamin B₂, or by specific names, eg thiamine, riboflavin.

vitamin C a water-soluble crystalline organic compound found in fresh fruits, especially citrus fruits and blackcurrants, and green vegetables. It is required for the maintenance of healthy bones, cartilage, and teeth, and deficiency of the vitamin causes scurvy. — Also called *ascorbic acid.*

vitamin D either of two fat-soluble steroid compounds, vitamin D₂ (calciferol) and vitamin D₃ (cholecalciferol), found in fish liver oils, egg yolk, and milk, and also formed from cholesterol derivatives in the skin on exposure to sunlight. Vitamin D is required for the deposition of adequate amounts of calcium and phosphates in the bones and teeth, and deficiency in children causes rickets.

vitamin E any of various closely related fat-soluble organic compounds found in wholemeal flour, wheat-germ, and green vegetables. Vitamin E has strong antioxidant properties and may be required for maintenance of the structure of cell membranes. Deficiency causes infertility in some animals, and has been associated with muscular dystrophy in humans. – Also called *tocopherol.*

vitamin K any of various closely related fat-soluble organic compounds found in green leafy vegetables, and also manufactured by bacteria in the intestines, as a result of which deficiency is rare. It is required for the production of several proteins involved in blood clotting.

Vitebsk 1 POP (1991e) 362 000, the industrial river-port capital of Vitebsk region, NE Belorussia. It lies on the R Dvina. **2** a region in NE Belorussia with Vitebsk as its capital.

Vitez a town in central Bosnia-Herzegovina. It became a Croat enclave which was almost surrounded by Muslim-led Bosnian government forces during the civil war (1992–).

vitiate *verb* **1** to impair the quality or effectiveness of (eg an argument); to make faulty or defective. **2** to make (eg a legal contract) ineffectual or invalid. [from Latin *vitiare*, from *vitium*, blemish]

vitiation *noun* the act or process of vitiating.

viticulture *noun* the cultivation of grapes for making wine; viniculture. [from Latin *vitis*, vine + CULTURE]

Viti Levu the largest and most important island of Fiji, in the SW Pacific Ocean. AREA 10 429sq km/4 026sq mi. It is separated from Vanua Levu, 32km/20mi NE, by the Koro Sea. PHYSICAL DESCRIPTION measures 144km/89mi long and 104km/65mi wide; it has a mountainous interior, rising to 1 324m at Tomanivi (Mt Victoria); the lower reaches of the main rivers provide fertile alluvial flats. CAPITAL Suva. ECONOMY gold mining; sugar milling; tourism; experimental irrigated rice projects near Suva. NOTABLE FEATURE Tholoisuva Forest Park.

Vitosha *or* **Vitosa** a winter resort in central W Bulgaria, situated 20km/12mi E of Sofia, at an altitude of 1 810m. It is W Bulgaria's largest ski resort.

vitreous *adj.* **1** relating to or consisting of glass. **2** like glass in hardness, sheen, or transparency: *vitreous china.* [from Latin *vitrum*, glass]

vitreous humour a jelly-like substance inside the eye, between the lens and the retina.

vitrification *noun Engineering, Geol.* the formation of glass or a glassy material under conditions of intense heat.

vitrified *adj.* made into glass or something like glass.

vitrify *verb trans., intrans.* (**vitrifies, vitrified**) to make into or become glass or something like glass, especially by heating. [from Latin *vitrum*, glass + *facere*, to make]

vitriol *noun* **1** concentrated sulphuric acid. **2** a sulphate of a metal, originally one of a glassy appearance. **3** extremely bitter or hateful speech or criticism. [from Latin *vitreus*, of glass]

vitriolic *adj.* extremely bitter or hateful, especially with reference to speech or criticism.

Vitruvius, in full **Marcus Vitruvius Pollio** (1c BC) Roman architect and military engineer. He was in the service of Augustus, and wrote the 10-volume *De Architectura* (On Architecture), the only Roman treatise on architecture still extant.

Vittoria, Spanish **Vitoria** POP (1991) 205 000, the capital of Alava province, Basque Country, N Spain. It is situated 351km/218mi N of Madrid. It was the scene of the French defeat in the Peninsular War (1813). NOTABLE FEATURES Church of St Peter; old and new cathedrals.

vituperate *verb* **1** to attack with abusive criticism or disapproval. **2** *intrans.* to use abusive language. [from Latin *vituperare*, to blame]

vituperation *noun* abusive criticism or language.

vituperative *adj.* abusive.

viva¹ *interj.* long live (someone or something named). [from Spanish and Italian *viva*]

viva² — *noun* (*in full* **viva voce**) (PL. **vivas, viva voces**) an oral examination, usually for an academic qualification. — *verb* (**vivas, vivaed**) to examine orally. [from Latin *viva voce*, by the living voice]

vivace *adj., adv. Mus.* in a lively manner. [from Italian]

vivacious *adj.* attractively lively and animated, especially with reference to a person. [from Latin *vivax*, lively]

vivaciously *adv.* in an attractive lively way.

vivacity *noun* liveliness, animation, especially with reference to a person.

Vivaldi, Antonio (Lucio) (1678–1741) Venetian violinist and composer, born in Venice, known as the 'Red Priest' because of his red hair. He was ordained in 1703, but gave up officiating, and was attached to the Conservatory of the Ospedale della Pietà at Venice (1703–40). The 12 concertos of *L'Estro Armonico* (1712) gave him a European reputation; *The Four Seasons* (1725), an early example of programme music, proved highly popular; and he wrote many operas, sacred music, and over 450 concertos.

vivarium *noun* (PL. **vivariums, vivaria**) any place or enclosure in which live animals are kept, especially in conditions resembling their natural habitat. [from Latin *vivarium*, from *vivere*, to live]

viva voce in speech; orally.

Vivekananda, also called **Narendranath Datta** (1862–1902) Hindu philosopher, born in Calcutta. He first joined the Brahmo Samaj movement, attracted by its policy of social reform. After meeting Ramakrishna, he became his leading disciple and established the headquarters of the Ramakrishna Order at Belur Math on the Ganges, near Calcutta. He attempted to combine Indian spirituality with Western materialism, and was the main force behind the Vedanta movement in the West.

Vivès, Juan Luis, also called **Ludovicus Vives** (1492–1540) Spanish philosopher and humanist, born in Valencia. He became Professor of Humanities at Louvain in 1519. He dedicated his edition of St Augustine's *Civitas Dei* to Henry VIII, who summoned him to England in 1523 as tutor to Princess Mary. His writings include *Adversus Pseudodialecticos* (1570, Against the Pseudo-Dialecticians), and several other works on educational theory and practice. He was imprisoned in 1527 for opposing Henry's divorce, and then lived mostly in Bruges.

Vivian a male and female first name. [from Latin *vivus*, lively]

vivid *adj.* 1 *said of a colour* strong and bright. 2 creating or providing a clear and immediate mental picture: *gave a vivid account of the incident / has a vivid imagination.* 3 full of life; vivacious. [from Latin *vividus*, lively]

vividly *adv.* brightly, clearly, intensely.

vividness *noun* brightness, clarity, intensity.

viviparity *noun* the condition of giving birth to a live offspring.

viviparous *adj.* 1 *Zool.*, *said of an animal* giving birth to live young that have developed within the mother's body, as in humans and most other mammals, instead of laying eggs that develop outside the body. See also OVIPAROUS. 2 *Bot.* denoting a form of asexual reproduction in which new young plants start to develop on the parent plant while still attached to it, as in the spider plant and certain grasses. [from Latin *vivus*, alive + *parere*, to produce]

vivisect *verb* to perform vivisection on.

vivisection *noun* 1 strictly, the practice of dissecting living animals for experimental purposes. 2 loosely used to refer to any form of animal experimentation. [from Latin *vivus*, living + *secare*, to cut] see also ANIMAL EXPERIMENTATION.

vivisectionist *noun* a person who practises or advocates vivisection.

vixen *noun* 1 a female fox. 2 a fierce or spiteful woman. [from Anglo-Saxon *fyxen*]

viz or **viz.** *adv.* namely; that is. [an abbreviation of Latin *videlicet*, from *videre*, to see + *licet*, it is allowed]

vizier *noun* a high-ranking government official in certain Muslim countries. [from Arabic *wazir*, porter, bearer of a burden]

Vlaanderen see FLANDERS.

Vladimir one of the two argumentative tramps in Samuel Beckett's *Waiting for Godot*.

Vladimir (Svyatoslavich) I, known as **the Great** (c.956–1015) Grand Prince of Kiev (c.978–1015). One of ancient Russia's most illustrious rulers, he consolidated the state and led victorious campaigns against the Viatichi, Lithuanians, and Bulgars. Under his rule the economy and culture of Kievan Russia flourished. In 988 he was converted to Christianity, and adopted the Greek Orthodox rite from Byzantium as the official religion of Russia. After his death, Kievan Russia was torn apart by dynastic rivalries among his 12 sons. He was later canonized (feast day 15 Jul).

Vladivostok POP (1991e) 648 000, the seaport capital of Primorskiy krai, Russia, situated on the Sea of Japan. It is the chief Russian port on the Pacific Ocean (kept open during winter by icebreakers) and a base for fishing fleets. The seaport was founded in 1860. Vladivostok is the terminus of the Trans-Siberian Railway.

Vleck, John Hasbrouck van see VAN VLECK, JOHN HASBROUCK.

VLF *abbrev. Radio* very low frequency.

Vlissingen see FLUSHING.

Vlorë or **Vlora**, Italian **Valona**, ancient **Aulon** 1 POP (1989) 72 000, the seaport capital of Vlorë district, SW Albania. It lies on the Bay of Vlorë, 112km/70mi SW of Tiranë. HISTORY a bishopric in the 5c; independence was proclaimed here in 1912. 2 a district in SW Albania with Vlorë as its capital.

Vltava, River, German **Moldau** a river in W Czech Republic, length 427km/265mi. Formed in the Bohemian Forest by the junction of two headstreams, it flows SE and N to meet the R Elbe near Melnik. It is a major source of hydroelectricity, and is navigable for c.80km/50mi.

VMH *abbrev.* Victoria Medal of Honour.

V-neck *noun* 1 the open neck of a garment cut or formed to a point at the front. 2 a garment, especially a pullover, with such a neck.

V-necked *adj.*, *said of clothing* having a V-neck.

VOA *abbrev.* Voice of America.

voc. *abbrev.* vocative.

vocable *noun Linguistics* 1 a spoken word or single sound in a word. 2 a spoken or written word regarded as a series of sounds or letters, rather than as a unit of meaning. [from Latin *vocabulum*, from *vox*, voice]

vocabulary *noun* (PL. **vocabularies**) 1 the words used in speaking or writing a particular language. 2 the words, or range of words, known to or used by a particular person or group. 3 a list of words with translations in another language alongside. 4 a range of artistic or stylistic forms and techniques.

vocal — *adj.* 1 relating to or produced by the voice. 2 expressing opinions or criticism freely and forcefully. — *noun* (**vocals**) the parts of a musical composition that are sung, as distinct from the instrumental accompaniment. [from Latin *vocalis*, from *vox*, voice]

vocal cords *Anat.* in mammals, the two folds of tissue within the larynx that vibrate and produce sound when air is expelled from the lungs. Changes in the tension of the vocal cords, and in the speed of the air flow over them, affect the pitch and volume of the sound produced.

vocalist *noun* a singer, especially in a pop group.

vocalization or **vocalisation** *noun* the act or process of forming sounds.

vocalize or **vocalise** *verb* 1 to utter or produce with the voice. 2 to express in words; to articulate.

vocally *adv.* with the voice; loudly.

vocation *noun* 1 a particular occupation or profession, especially regarded as needing dedication and skill. 2 a feeling of being especially suited for a particular type of work. 3 *Relig.* a divine calling to adopt a religious life or perform good works. [from Latin *vocare*, to call]

vocational *adj.* concerned with, or in preparation for, a particular trade or profession: *vocational training*.

vocational education education aimed at preparing students for their present or future employment. It may take place in colleges of further education, universities, or in the workplace itself. It is also increasingly being offered to secondary school pupils in a wide variety of subjects, and in the form of work experience. Some vocational qualifications are awarded by chartered institutions, others by professional organizations, and others by colleges of further education in conjunction with professional organizations.

vocationally *adv.* as regards vocation or profession.

vocative *Grammar* — *noun* 1 in some languages, the particular form of a word used when a person or thing is addressed directly. 2 a word in this form. — *adj.* in the vocative. [from Latin *vocare*, to call]

vociferate *verb trans.*, *intrans. formal* 1 to exclaim loudly and forcefully. 2 to shout or cry in a loud voice; to bawl. [from Latin *vox*, voice + *ferre*, to carry]

vociferous *adj.* 1 loud and forceful, especially in expressing opinions. 2 expressed loudly and forcefully.

vociferously *adv.* loudly and forcefully.

vociferousness *noun* loudness, forcefulness.

Vodafone *noun trademark* 1 a UK cellular phone system. 2 a cellular phone.

vodka *noun* a clear alcoholic spirit of Russian origin, traditionally made from rye, sometimes from potatoes. [from Russian *vodka*, from *voda*, water]

Vogel, Hans-Jochen (1926–) German politician, born in Göttingen. He was a Minister of Housing and Town Planning (1972–4) and Minister of Justice (1974–81) and also served briefly as governing Mayor of West Berlin (1981) before he succeeded Helmut Schmidt as Leader of the Social Democratic Party (SPD) in 1982 and was the Party's unsuccessful candidate for the chancellorship of West Germany (1983). He succeeded Willy Brandt as Chairman of the SPD (1987–90).

Vogel, Hermann Carl (1841–1907) German astronomer, born in Leipzig. Director of Potsdam Observatory, he introduced photographic methods into stellar spectroscopy, and was the first to measure radial velocities of stars from their spectra. In 1889 he discovered the binary nature of Algol, the first double star to be discovered by analyzing its spectrum.

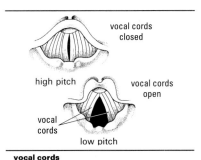

vocal cords

vogue *noun* **1** (*usually* **the vogue**) the current fashion or trend in any sphere. **2** a period of being fashionable or popular: *enjoyed a long vogue.* — **in vogue** in fashion. [French *vogue*]

vogue word a word that is currently fashionable.

voice — *noun* **1** the ability to speak; the power of speech: *lost his voice.* **2** a way of speaking or singing peculiar to each individual: *couldn't recognize the voice.* **3** a tone of speech reflecting a particular emotion: *in a nervous voice.* **4** the sound of a person speaking: *heard a voice.* **5** the ability to sing, especially to sing well: *has no voice / has a lovely voice.* **6** expression in the form of spoken words: *gave voice to their feelings.* **7** a means or medium of expression or communication: *newspapers as the voice of the people.* **8** *Grammar* the status or function of a verb in being either active or passive. — *verb* **1** to express in speech. **2** *Phonetics* to pronounce with a vibration of the vocal cords. — **in good voice** singing well. **with one voice** unanimously. [from Latin *vox*]

voice-box *noun colloq.* the larynx.

voiced *adj.* **1** expressed in speech. **2** *Phonetics* pronounced with a vibration of the vocal cords, as is *z*, but not *s*.

voiceless *adj. Phonetics* not voiced.

Voice of America (ABBREV. **VOA**) in the USA the external broadcasting service of the US Information Agency, founded in 1942.

voice-over *noun* the voice of an unseen narrator in a film or television advertisement or programme.

void — *adj.* **1** not valid or legally binding: *declared the contract null and void.* **2** containing nothing; empty or unoccupied. **3** (**void of something**) free from it. — *noun* **1** an empty space. **2** a space left blank or unfilled. **3** a feeling of absence or emptiness strongly felt. — *verb* **1** to make empty or clear. **2** to invalidate or nullify. **3** to empty (the bladder or bowels). [from Old French *voide*, empty]

voile *noun* any very thin semi-transparent fabric. [from French *voile*, veil]

voivodship any of the 49 provinces of Poland.

Vojvodina POP (1991) 2.1m, a province in N Serbia, Yugoslavia. AREA 21 506sq km/ 8 301sq mi. CAPITAL Novi Sad. The population is mainly Serb (c.50%) with Hungarians, Croats, and Slovaks. The province effectively lost its autonomous status to Serbia in 1990. ECONOMY agriculture; livestock; petroleum; natural gas.

vol *or* **vol.** *abbrev.* volume.

volatile *adj.* **1** changing quickly from a solid or liquid into a vapour. **2** explosive. **3** easily becoming angry or violent. **4** *said of a situation, etc* liable to change quickly, especially verging on violence. [from Latin *volare*, to fly]

volatility *noun* a volatile state.

volatilization *or* **volatilisation** *noun* the process of evaporating or causing to evaporate.

volatilize *or* **volatilise** *verb trans., intrans.* to change, or cause to change, from a solid or liquid into a vapour.

vol-au-vent *noun* a small round puff-pastry case with a savoury filling. [from French *vol-au-vent*, literally 'flight in the wind']

volcanic *adj.* **1** relating to or produced by a volcano or volcanoes. **2** easily erupting into anger or violence: *a volcanic temper.*

volcano *noun* (PL. **volcanoes**) **1** any of various cracks or vents in the Earth's crust through which lava (molten rock), gas, steam, ash, or solid rock material may be forced out on to the Earth's surface, often forming a more or less conical hill or

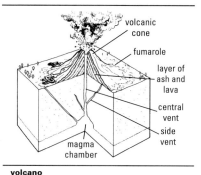

volcano labels: volcanic cone; fumarole; layer of ash and lava; central vent; side vent; magma chamber

volcano

mountain with a central crater. **2** a situation, or a person, likely to erupt into anger or violence. [from Latin *Vulcanus*, Roman god of fire]
◇ Most volcanoes are found along or close to the edges of the plates that form the Earth's crust. Movement of the plates causes the flow of molten rock material, on which the plates are floating, to the surface, leading to volcanic eruptions. There are about 850 active volcanoes in the world, 75 per cent of which are located around the edge of the Pacific plate, often referred to as the 'Ring of Fire'. An erupting volcano can produce thousands of tonnes of lava, which when red-hot can have a temperature of over 1 000°C.

Volcano Islands, Japanese **Kazan Retto** a group of Japanese islands in the W Pacific Ocean.

They include Iwo Jima, Kita Iwo, and Minami Iwo. The islands were administered by the USA from 1945 until 1968, when they were returned to Japan. ECONOMY sulphur; sugar.

Volcanus see VULCAN.

vole *noun* a small rodent related to the lemming, with a smaller tail, blunter snout, and smaller eyes and ears than a mouse, found in Europe, Asia, N Africa, and N America. Voles feed on grasses, seeds, and insects, and can cause serious damage to crops, grassland pastures, and forest plantations. [originally *vole-mouse*, from Norwegian *voll*, field + *mus*, mouse]

Volga, River, ancient **Rha** the longest river in Europe, length 3 531km/2 194mi. Rising in the Valdai Hills, W Russia, it flows generally SE to enter the Caspian Sea, forming a broad delta below Astrakhan. The principal navigable waterway in Russia, it is linked by canal to the Baltic Sea, White Sea, Sea of Azov, and Black Sea. It has many reservoirs on its course and is an important source of hydroelectric power and irrigation (notably for the dry steppe areas to the E).

Volgograd, formerly **Tsaritsyn** (to 1925), **Stalingrad** (1925–61) **1** POP (1990e) 1m, the capital of Volgograd oblast, SW Russia, lying on the R Volga. HISTORY founded in the 16c to protect the Volga trade route; largely destroyed in World War II. **2** an oblast in SW Russia with Volgograd as its capital.

volition *noun* the act of willing or choosing; the exercising of one's will: *did it of her own volition.* [from Latin *velle*, to will]

Major Volcanoes			
Name	Height m	Major eruptions (years)	Last eruption (year)
Aconcagua (Argentina)	6 960	extinct	
Ararat (Turkey)	5 165	extinct	Holocene
Awu (Sangihe Is)	1 327	1711, 1856, 1892	1968
Bezymianny (Russia)	2 800	1955–6	1984
Coseguina (Nicaragua)	847	1835	1835
El Chichón (Mexico)	1 349	1982	1982
Erebus (Antarctica)	4 023	1947, 1972	1986
Etna (Italy)	3 323	122, 1169, 1329, 1536; 1669, 1928, 1964, 1971	1986
Fuji (Japan)	3 776	1707	1707
Galunggung (Java)	2 180	1822, 1918	1982
Hekla (Iceland)	1 491	1693, 1845, 1947–8, 1970	1981
Helgafell (Iceland)	215	1973	1973
Hudson (Chile)	1 740	1971, 1973	1991
Jurullo (Mexico)	1 330	1759–74	1774
Katmai (Alaska)	2 298	1912, 1920, 1921	1931
Kilauea (Hawaii)	1 247	1823–1924, 1952, 1955, 1960, 1967–8, 1968–74, 1983–7	1991
Kilimanjaro (Tanzania)	5 895	extinct	Pleistocene
Klyuchevskoy (Russia)	4 850	1700–1966, 1984	1985
Krakatoa (Sumatra)	818	1680, 1883, 1927, 1952–3, 1969	1980
La Soufrière (St Vincent)	1 234	1718, 1812, 1902, 1971–2	1979
Laki (Iceland)	500	1783	1784
Lamington (Papua New Guinea)	1 780	1951	1956
Lassen Peak (USA)	3 186	1914–5	1921
Mauna Loa (Hawaii)	4 169	1859, 1880, 1887, 1919, 1950	1984
Mayon (Philippines)	2 462	1616, 1766, 1814, 1897, 1968, 1993	1993
Nyamuragira (Zaire)	3 056	1921–38, 1971, 1980	1984
Paricutin (Mexico)	2 774	1943–52	1952
Pelée, Mont (Martinique)	1 397	1902, 1929–32	1932
Pinatubo, Mt (Philippines)	1 462	1391, 1991	1991
Popocatepetl (Mexico)	5 452	1802	1920
Rainier, Mt (USA)	4 395	1st-c BC, 1820	1882
Ruapehu (New Zealand)	2 797	1945, 1953, 1969, 1975	1986
St Helens, Mt (USA)	2 549	1800, 1831, 1835, 1842–3, 1857, 1980–	1987
Santorini/Thira	1 315?	1470 BC, 197 BC, AD 46, 1570–3, 1707–11, 1866–70	1950
Stromboli (Italy)	931	1768, 1882, 1889, 1907, 1930, 1936, 1941, 1950, 1952	1986
Surtsey (Iceland)	174	1963–7	1967
Taal (Philippines)	1 448	1911, 1965, 1969	1977
Tambora (Sumbawa)	2 868	1815	1880
Tarawera (New Zealand)	1 149	1886	1973
Unzen (Japan)	1 360	1360, 1791	1991
Vesuvius (Italy)	1 277	79, 472, 1036, 1631, 1779, 1906	1944
Vulcano (Italy)	502	antiquity, 1444, 1730–40, 1786, 1873, 1888–90	1890

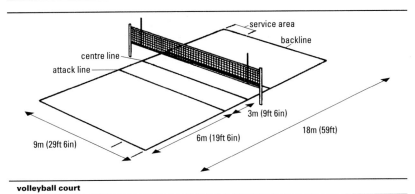

volleyball court

volitional *adj.* relating to volition or the exercise of will.

Volkswagen Beetle the 'people's' car was designed by Ferdinand Porsche in 1938 and approved by Adolf Hitler. It was orignally named the KDF Wagen (*Kraft durch Freude*, or 'Strength through Joy') from the slogan of the National Socialist (ie Nazi) Labour Front. Their philosophy was to create new employment opportunities for the German people and produce a car that any employed person could afford to purchase and run. Sales were initially slow because of World War II but post-war sales exceeded 20 million, making it the most popular car in automobile history.

volley — *noun* (PL. **volleys**) **1** a firing of several guns or other weapons simultaneously. **2** an aggressive outburst, especially of criticism or insults. **3** *Sport* a striking of the ball before it bounces. — *verb* (**volleys, volleyed**) **1** to fire (weapons) in a volley. **2** *Sport* to strike (a ball) before it bounces. [from French *volée*, flight]

volleyball *noun* a game for two teams of six players each, in which a large ball is volleyed back and forth over a high net with the hands. ◇ Originally known as *mintonette*, it was invented by William G Morgan in 1895, at the Holyoke YMCA, Massachusetts. It became an Olympic sport in 1964.

Volpone, or The Fox a play by Ben Jonson (1606). A satiric comedy on senile sensuality and greedy legacy hunters, it focuses on the rich, childless Venetian Volpone who, with the help of the parasitic Mosca, feigns a fatal illness to test the apparent generosity of those who want his inheritance.

Volsungasaga a German prose epic (13c) deriving in part from the Norse *Edda*. It tells the story of the dynasty of the Volsungs, which is linked to that of the Nibelungs.

volt *noun* (SYMBOL **V**) the SI unit of voltage, potential difference, or electromotive force. It is equal to the potential difference between two points if one joule of energy is required to move one coulomb of electric charge from one point to the other. One volt will send a current of one ampere across a resistance of one ohm. [named after the Italian physicist Alessandro Volta]

Volta, Alessandro Giuseppe Anastasio, Count (1745–1827) Italian physicist, born in Como. Professor of Physics at Como and Pavia, he devised many electrical inventions, but is best known for the electrochemical battery, or 'voltaic pile' (1800), which was the first source of continuous or current electricity. His name is given to the SI unit of electrical potential difference, the volt.

Volta, River a river in Ghana. It is formed by the meeting of the Black Volta and White Volta rivers as they enter L Volta, which has been created by the damming of the river to the S at Akosombo. It flows S from the dam to enter the Bight of Benin at Ada. The Volta River Scheme

was designed to supply power, improve irrigation, and help develop bauxite deposits.

voltage *noun Electr.* potential difference expressed as a number of volts.

Voltaire, pseudonym of **François Marie Arouet** (1694–1778) French writer, born in Paris. The major figure of the Enlightenment, he was imprisoned in the Bastille (1717–18) for his writings, and later forced to go into exile in England (1726–9). Back in France, he wrote plays, poetry, historical and scientific treatises, and his *Lettres Philosophiques* (1734). He became royal historiographer, moved to Berlin at the invitation of Frederick the Great (1750–3), and settled near Geneva in 1755, where he wrote the satirical tale, *Candide* (1759). From 1762 he produced a range of anti-religious writings and the *Dictionnaire philosophique* (1764).

volte-face *noun* a sudden and complete reversal, of opinion or policy. [from French *volte-face*, literally 'turning face']

voltmeter *noun Electr.* an instrument that measures voltage.

volubility *noun* the act or process of speaking insistently or volubly.

voluble *adj.* **1** speaking or spoken insistently, uninterruptedly, or with ease. **2** tending to talk at great length. [from Latin *volubilis*, from *volvere*, to roll]

volubly *adv.*, *said of talking* at great length; fluently.

volume *noun* **1** the amount of three-dimensional space occupied by an object, gas, or liquid. **2** loudness of sound; the control that adjusts it on a radio, hi-fi system, etc. **3** a book, whether complete in itself or one of several forming a larger work. **4** an amount or quantity, especially when large: *the volume of traffic*.
— **speak volumes** to be very significant; to say a lot: *their refusal to answer spoke volumes*.
[from Latin *volumen*, roll, scroll]

Volume

Metric units

cubic millimetre (cu mm)
1 000 cu mm = 1 cubic centimetre (cu cm)
1 000 cu cm = 1 cubic decimetre (cu dm) = 1 litre
1 000 cu dm = 1 cubic metre (cu m)
1 000 000 000 cu m = 1 cubic kilometre (cu km)

Imperial units

cubic inch (cu in)
1 728 cu in = 1 cubic foot (cu ft)
27 cu ft = 1 cubic yard (cu yd)
5 451 776 000 cu yd = 1 cubic mile (cu mile)

volumetric analysis *Chem.* a method of chemical analysis in which the unknown concentration of a solution of known volume is determined by adding known volumes of standard solutions of known concentration until the

chemical reaction between the reagents is complete.

voluminous *adj.* **1** *said of clothing* flowing or billowing out; ample. **2** *said of a writer* producing great quantities of writing. **3** *said of writing* enough to fill many volumes.

voluntarily *adv.* willingly; of one's free will.

voluntary — *adj.* **1** done or acting by free choice, not by compulsion. **2** working with no expectation of being paid or otherwise rewarded. **3** *said of work* unpaid. **4** *said of an organization* staffed by unpaid workers; supported by donations of money freely given. **5** *said of a movement, muscle, or limb* produced or controlled by the will.
— *noun* (PL. **voluntaries**) a piece of music, usually for organ, played before, during, or after a church service. [from Latin *voluntarius*, from *velle*, to will]

voluntary muscle *Anat.* muscle that is under conscious control, and produces voluntary movements by pulling against the bones of the skeleton, to which it is attached by means of tendons.
— Also called *striated muscle*.

Voluntary Service Overseas (ABBREV. **VSO**) in the UK, a charity founded in 1958 to send skilled volunteers to work for two-year periods in developing countries. The host government provides a living allowance and accommodation; VSO provides the briefing, airfare, and a grant.

volunteer — *verb* **1** *trans.*, *intrans.* (**volunteer for something**) to offer one's help or services freely, without being persuaded or forced. **2** *intrans.* to go into military service by choice, without being conscripted. **3** to give (information, etc) unasked. **4** *colloq.* to constrain (someone) to perform a task or give help: *I'm volunteering you for playground duty*. — *noun* **1** a person who volunteers. **2** a person carrying out voluntary work. **3** a member of a non-professional army of voluntary soldiers set up during wartime.

voluptuary — *noun* (PL. **voluptuaries**) a person addicted to luxury and sensual pleasures. — *adj.* promoting or characterized by luxury and sensual pleasures. [from Latin *voluptas*, pleasure]

voluptuous *adj.* **1** relating to or suggestive of sensual pleasure. **2** *said of a woman* strikingly attractive sexually. [from Latin *voluptas*, pleasure]

voluptuously *adv.* in a voluptuous way; sensually.

voluptuousness *noun* sensuousness; strong sensual gratification.

volute *noun* **1** a spiral. **2** a scroll carved in stone, especially at the top of a column. **3** one single twist in a spiral shell. [from Latin *volvere*, to roll]

vomit — *verb* (**vomited, vomiting**) **1** *trans.*, *intrans.* to eject the contents of the stomach forcefully through the mouth as a reflex action; to be sick. **2** to emit or throw out with force or violence. — *noun* the contents of the stomach ejected during this process. [from Latin *vomere*]

von Braun, Wernher (1912–77) German-born US rocket pioneer, born in Wirsitz. He founded in 1930 a society for research into space travel and later, with Hitler's backing, perfected the V-2 rockets launched against Britain in 1944. After World War II he was chiefly responsible for the launching of the first US satellite (1958) and, as Director of the Marshal Space Flight Center, he developed the Saturn rocket for the Apollo 8 Moon landing (1969).

von Klitzing, Klaus (1943–) German physicist, born in Schroda. Professor at Munich and later Director of the Max Planck Institute in Stuttgart, he published a paper which illustrated the 'quantum Hall effect' which occurs in semiconductor devices at low temperatures (1977). This caused a major revision of the theory of electric conduction in strong magnetic fields. He was awarded the 1985 Nobel Prize for Physics.

von Laue, Max Theodor Felix (1879–1960) German physicist, born near Koblenz. Professor in Zürich, Frankfurt, and Berlin, he researched optics and relativity theory. In 1912 he discovered that X-rays are diffracted by the three-dimensional array of atoms in crystals; for this work he was awarded the 1914 Nobel Prize for Physics.

Vonnegut, Kurt, Jr (1922–) US novelist, born in Indianapolis. He served with the US Air Force in World War II, and has worked as a reporter, freelance writer, and lecturer. His novels are satirical fantasies, often cast in the form of science fiction, as in *Player Piano* (1952) and *Cat's Cradle* (1963). He is best known for the novel *Slaughterhouse-Five* (1969).

Von Sternberg, Josef, originally **Jonas Sternberg** (1894–1969) Austrian film director, born in Vienna. He worked in silent films in Hollywood in the 1920s as scriptwriter, cameraman, and director, but went to Germany to make his most famous film *Der blaue Engel* (The Blue Angel, 1910) with Marlene Dietrich. This was followed by six more Hollywood features in which she starred, the last being *The Devil is a Woman* (1935).

voodoo — noun **1** witchcraft of a type originally practised by the Black peoples of the West Indies and southern US. **2** the beliefs and practices of the religious cult that developed it, including serpent-worship and human sacrifice. — verb to bewitch using, or as if using, voodoo methods. [from *vodu*, (in various W African languages) spirit, demon]
◇ A blending of Roman Catholicism and W African religion, its followers attend both the church and the voodoo temple, where a priest or priestess leads a ritual invoking the spirits of the voodoo world through magical diagrams, chants, and prayer. Spirits possess the members in trance. It is particularly associated with Haiti.

Voortrekker noun one of the Afrikaner (Boer) farmers from Cape Colony who took part in the Great Trek into the Transvaal in 1836 and following years. They established independent republics in the interior (the Orange Free State and the South African Republic).

voracious adj. **1** eating or craving food in large quantities. **2** extremely eager in some respect: *a voracious reader*. [from Latin *vorare*, to devour]

voraciously adv. in a voracious or eager way; greedily.

voracity noun extreme greed or eagerness.

Voronezh 1 POP (1991e) 900 000, the industrial river-port capital of Voronezh oblast, W Russia. It lies on the R Voronezh and was founded as a fortress in 1586. **2** an oblast in W Russia with Voronezh as its capital.

Voroshilov, Kliment Yefremovich (1881–1969) Soviet soldier and politician, born near Dniepropetrovsk. He joined the Russian Social Democratic Labour Party in 1903, but political agitation soon brought about his exile to Siberia, where he remained until 1914. His role was military rather than political in the 1917 Revolution, and as Commissar for Defence (1925–40) he was responsible for the modernization of the Red Army. Though removed from office after the failure to prevent the German siege of Leningrad, he stayed active in the Communist Party, and became President (1953–60) after Stalin's death.

Vorster, John, originally **Balthazar Johannes Vorster** (1915–83) South African politician, born in Jamestown. He became a lawyer and joined an extreme Afrikaner movement. In 1953 he became a Nationalist MP, and he was Minister of Justice under Verwoerd (1961), whom he succeeded as Prime Minister (1966–78), maintaining the policy of apartheid

and using state power to protect white interests. In 1978, after a scandal over the misappropriation of government funds, he resigned for health reasons, and was elected President, but stood down from this position nine months later when an investigating commission found him jointly responsible.

vortex noun (PL. **vortexes**, **vortices**) **1** a whirlpool or whirlwind; any whirling mass or motion. **2** a situation or activity into which all surrounding people or things are helplessly and dangerously drawn. [from Latin *vortex*, from *vortere*, to turn]

vortical adj. resembling or characteristic of a vortex.

Vorticism a modern art movement started in England in 1913, partly inspired by the Futurists. Leading members included Wyndham Lewis (1884–1957), C R W Nevinson (1889–1946), and Henri Gaudier-Brzeska (1891–1915). Two issues were published of a journal, *Blast* (1914), and an exhibition was held (1915), after which the movement petered out.

Vortigern (5c) semi-legendary British king who, according to Bede, recruited Germanic mercenaries led by Hengist and Horsa to help fight off the Picts after the final withdrawal of the Roman administration from Britain (409). Tradition has it that when these troops revolted, they started the Germanic conquests and settlements in England.

Vosges Mountains, ancient **Vosegus** a range of hills in NE France, near the frontier with Germany. AREA 7 425sq km/2 866sq mi. It extends for 250km/155mi and is separated from the Jura to the S by the Belfort Gap. Ballon de Guebwiller (1 423m) is the highest point. The range forms a classical rift valley landscape; from thickly-wooded hills, rivers descend to the Rhine and the Central Plateau. Skiing and rock climbing are popular.

Voss a novel by Patrick White (1957). It is set in 1845 and describes an ill-fated attempt by explorer Johann Voss to lead a party across Australia.

Vostok a Russian scientific station in Antarctica. The lowest temperature ever recorded on Earth, –88°C, was measured at this site. The South Geomagnetic Pole (1985) is nearby.

votary noun (PL. **votaries**) **1** a person bound by solemn vows to a religious life. **2** a person dedicated to a particular cause or activity. [from Latin *vovere*, to vow]

vote — noun **1** a formal indication of choice or opinion, eg in an election or debate. **2** the right to express a choice or opinion, especially in a national election. **3** a choice or opinion expressed in this way: *a vote in favour of the motion*. **4** the support given by a certain sector of the population, or to a particular candidate or group, in this way: *will attract the middle-class vote*. — verb **1** intrans. to cast a vote (for or against). **2** to decide, state, grant, or bring about by casting votes. **3** to declare support for by casting a vote. **4** colloq. to declare or pronounce by general consent: *the show was voted a success*. **5** colloq. to propose or suggest. — **vote someone** or **something down** to reject or defeat them by voting.
vote someone in to appoint them by voting; to elect them.
[from Latin *votum*, wish]

vote of confidence or **vote of no confidence** a vote taken to show whether the majority support or disapprove of a person or group in authority or leadership.

voter noun a person who votes, or is eligible to vote, in an election.

votive adj. Relig. done or given in thanks to a deity, or to fulfil a vow or promise. [from Latin *vovere*, to vow]

vouch verb intrans. (**vouch for someone or something**) to give a firm assurance or guarantee of their authenticity, trustworthiness, etc. [from Old French *voucher*, to call upon to defend]

voucher noun **1** a ticket or paper serving as proof, eg of the purchase or receipt of goods. **2** a ticket exchangeable for goods or services of a specified value; a token: *gift voucher*.

voucher scheme Education a scheme giving parents a voucher equivalent in value to the average cost of a child's education, which they are then entitled to spend at the school of their choice. The system has been tried on an experimental basis in the USA, and is favoured by some politicians in the UK.

vouchsafe verb trans., intrans. literary to agree or condescend (to do, give, grant, or allow): *vouchsafed me no reply / did not vouchsafe to reply*. [from VOUCH in the sense 'voucher' + SAFE]

voussoir — noun Archit. one of the wedge-shaped stones that form part of the centre line of an arch. Also known as an *arch stone*. — verb to form (an arch) with voussoirs. [from French, from Latin *vol/u bar)tus*, from *volvere*, to roll]

vow — noun a solemn and binding promise, especially one made to or in the name of a deity. — verb to promise or declare solemnly, or threaten emphatically; to swear. [from Latin *vovere*]

vowel noun **1** any speech-sound made with an open mouth and no contact between mouth, lips, teeth, or tongue. **2** a letter, used alone or in combination, representing such a sound — in English the letters *a e i o u* and in some words *y*. [from Latin *vocalis*, from *vox*, voice]

vox pop Broadcasting popular opinion derived from comments given informally by members of the public.

vox populi public opinion; popular belief. [from Latin *vox populi*, voice of the people]

voyage — noun a long journey to a distant place, especially by air or sea or in space. — verb intrans. to go on a voyage; to travel. [from Old French *voiage*, from Latin *viaticum*]

Voyage of the Argo, The, also called **The Argonautica** an epic poem by Apollonius Rhodius (c.3c BC). It describes the voyage to Argo by Jason and the Argonauts in search of the Golden Fleece.

Voyager an aircraft which in 1986 became the first to complete a non-stop flight around the world. The plane, piloted by Dick Ruton and Jeanna Yeager, left Edwards Air Force 100km/60mi NE of Los Angeles on 14 Dec and returned nine days later, travelling 40 251km/25 012mi at an average speed of 186kph/116mph.

voyager noun a person who goes on a voyage.

Voyager project Astron. a multiple space mission undertaken by NASA to make the first detailed exploration beyond Mars, and designed to take advantage of a rare alignment of Jupiter, Saturn, Uranus, and Neptune.
◇ Two US space probes, *Voyager 1* and *Voyager 2*, were launched in 1977. *Voyager 1* flew past Jupiter in 1979, and with a boost from Jupiter's gravity it flew on to Saturn, which it passed in 1980. *Voyager 2* followed the same path as *Voyager 1*, and then used Saturn's gravity to fly on to Uranus, which it passed in 1986, and Neptune, which it passed in 1989.

voyeur noun **1** a person who derives gratification from furtively watching the sexual attributes or activity of others. **2** a person who observes, especially with fascination or intrusively, the feelings of others. [from French *voyeur*, one who sees]

voyeurism noun the practice of spying on others as a means of sexual gratification.

voyeuristic adj. characteristic of a voyeur; spying intrusively.

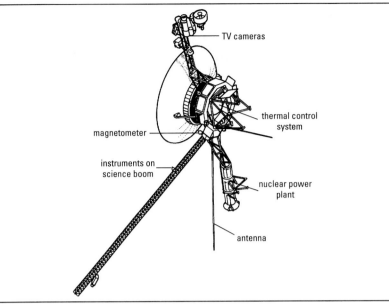

TV cameras

thermal control
system

magnetometer

instruments on
science boom

nuclear power
plant

antenna

Voyager spacecraft

VR *abbrev.* virtual reality.

VRAM same as VIDEO RAM.

Vries, Hugo Marie de see DE VRIES, HUGO MARIE.

vs *or* **vs.** *abbrev.* versus.

VS-300 *abbrev.* the first practical single-rotor helicopter designed in 1939 by Igor Sikorsky. It was based on earlier designs by the Spaniard Juan de la Cierva who first flew the autogiro in 1923. After the basic principles of helicopter flight were established, rapid technical progression occurred on both sides of the Atlantic.

V-sign *noun Brit.* a sign made by raising the first two fingers, an expression of victory with the palm turned outwards or an offensive gesture of contempt with the palm inwards.

VSO *abbrev.* Voluntary Service Overseas.

VSOP *abbrev.* very special old pale: a port, sherry, or brandy between 20 and 25 years old.

VT *or* **Vt.** *abbrev.* Vermont.

VTOL *abbrev.* vertical take-off and landing.

VTR *abbrev.* videotape recorder.

Vulcan *or* **Vulcanus** *or* **Volcanus** in Roman mythology, the god of fire, especially destructive fire and volcanic activity, sometimes called Mulciber. He was identified with the

Greek god Hephaestus, and later given his attributes, such as metal-working.

vulcanite *noun* hard black vulcanized rubber.

vulcanization *or* **vulcanisation** *noun Chem.* the process whereby natural or artificial rubber is hardened and its elasticity increased by treating it with sulphur or sulphur compounds at high temperatures.

vulcanize *or* **vulcanise** *verb* to subject natural or artificial rubber to the process of vulcanization. [see VOLCANO]

vulg. *abbrev.* vulgar.

vulgar *adj.* **1** marked by a lack of politeness or social or cultural refinement; coarse. **2** of or relating to the form of a language commonly spoken, rather than to formal or literary language; vernacular.

vulgar fraction a fraction expressed as one number above another, rather than in decimal form.

vulgarism *noun* **1** a vulgar expression in speech. **2** an example of vulgar behaviour.

vulgarity *noun* (PL. **vulgarities**) coarseness in speech or behaviour, or an instance of it.

vulgarization *or* **vulgarisation** *noun* the act or an instance of vulgarizing.

vulgarize *or* **vulgarise** *verb* **1** to make vulgar. **2** to make, or spoil by making, common or popular.

vulgarly *adv.* **1** in a vulgar or coarse way. **2** *old use* among people generally.

Vulgate a Latin translation of the Christian Bible from Hebrew by Jerome (c.405 AD) to end the confusion caused by the many Old Latin versions. From about the 7c, it emerged in Western Christianity as the preferred Latin version, but was itself revised and corrupted through the centuries. In 1546 it was recognized by the Council of Trent as the official Latin text of the Roman Catholic Church. [from Latin *vulgata editio*, popular edition]

vulnerability *noun* a state of being vulnerable or easily harmed.

vulnerable *adj.* **1** easily hurt or harmed physically or emotionally. **2** easily tempted or persuaded. **3** (**vulnerable to something or someone**) unprotected against physical or verbal attack from them. [from Latin *vulnerare*, to wound]

vulpine *adj.* **1** relating to or resembling a fox or foxes. **2** *formal* cunning like a fox. [from Latin *vulpes*, fox]

vulture *noun* **1** any of various large birds of prey with brown or black plumage, long broad wings, a bare head, and a strongly curved beak, found in both temperate and tropical regions. They feed on carrion and, unlike other birds of prey, they rarely hunt live food. Their beaks are not strong enough to pierce skin, so they wait until carrion has started to decompose, or has been torn open by another scavenger, before they descend in flocks to feed on it. **2** an American vulture or condor, sometimes referred to as a buzzard. **3** a person who exploits, or prepares to exploit, the downfall or death of another. [from Latin *vultur*]

vulva *noun Medicine* the parts surrounding the opening to the vagina; the female genitals. [from Latin *vulva*, wrapping, womb]

vv *or* **vv.** *abbrev.* **1** versus. **2** vice versa.

VW *abbrev.* Volkswagen.

vying present participle of VIE.

Vyshinsky, Andrei Yanuaryevich (1883–1954) Russian jurist and politician, born in Odessa. He joined the Communist Party in 1920, and became Professor of Criminal Law and Attorney-General (1923–5). He was the public prosecutor at the state trials (1936–8) which removed Stalin's rivals, and later became the Soviet delegate to the United Nations (1945–9, 1953–4), and Foreign Minister (1949–53).

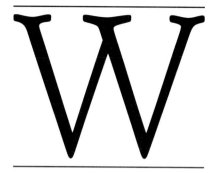

W¹ *or* **w** *noun* (PL. **Ws**, **W's**, **w's**) the twenty-third letter of the English alphabet.

W² *symbol Chem.* tungsten. [from German *Wolfram*]

W³ *abbrev.* **1** watt. **2** West. **3** *Physics* work.

w *abbrev.* **1** *Cricket* wicket. **2** wide. **3** wife. **4** with.

WA *abbrev.* Washington.

WAAC *abbrev.* Women's Army Auxiliary Corps (now WRAC).

WAAF *abbrev.* Women's Auxiliary Air Force (later WRAF).

Waals, Johannes Diderik van der see VAN DER WAALS, JOHANNES DIDERIK.

Wabash River a river in Ohio, Indiana, and Illinois, USA. It rises in W Ohio and flows 764km/475mi across Indiana to meet the Ohio R SW of Evansville.

Wace, Robert (12c) Anglo-Norman poet, born in Jersey. A canon of Bayeux (1160–70), his main work is the *Roman de Brut* (1155), a Norman-French version of Geoffrey of Monmouth's *Historia Regum Britanniae*. He also wrote several verse lives of the saints, and the *Roman de Rou* (1160–74), an epic of the exploits of the Dukes of Normandy.

wacky *adj.* (**wackier**, **wackiest**) *colloq. orig. North Amer., esp. US* eccentric; crazy. [perhaps from WHACK]

Waco POP (1990) 189 000, the seat of McLennan County, central Texas, USA, on the Brazos R. Waco was founded in 1849 and is a trading, shipping, and industrial centre in the heart of the Blacklands. NOTABLE FEATURE Texas Ranger Hall of Fame. [named after a Native American tribe]

wad *noun* **1** a compressed mass of soft material used for packing, padding, stuffing, etc. **2** a thick sheaf or bundle of banknotes, etc. [from Latin *wadda*, from Arabic]

wadding *noun* material used as padding or stuffing.

waddle *verb intrans., said of a duck, or derog. of a person* to sway from side to side in walking. [perhaps related to WADE]

wade *verb trans., intrans.* to walk through deep water; to cross (a river, etc) by wading.
— **wade in** to involve oneself unhesitatingly and enthusiastically in a task, etc.
wade into someone to attack or criticize them fiercely.
wade through something to make one's way laboriously through it: *wading through legal documents*.
[from Anglo-Saxon *wadan*, to go]

wader *noun* **1** a general term for any long-legged bird that wades in marshes, or along the shores of rivers, lakes, or seas, eg curlew, plover, heron, stork, sandpiper, flamingo. Their beaks

are usually specially adapted for extracting food from water, sand, or mud. **2** (**waders**) thigh-high waterproof boots used by anglers, etc.

wadi *noun* a rocky river bed in N Africa and Arabia, dry except during the rains. [from Arabic *wadi*]

Wadi Medani POP (1983) 141 000, the chief city of Central region, E Sudan. It is situated 180km/112mi SE of Khartoum, on the Blue Nile, and is the centre of a cotton-growing area.

Wadman, Widow *or* **Mrs** a neighbour of the Shandy family who is set on marrying Toby in Laurence Sterne's *Tristram Shandy*.

Wafd Party the name of the Egyptian nationalist party responsible for gaining independence from Britain (partial 1922, complete 1936) after a delegation under the nationalist leader Sa'd Zaghlul (c.1857–1927) went to the British High Commissioner (1919). The 'New Wafd' became Egypt's official Opposition Party in 1984, but was replaced as such in 1987 by an alliance headed by the Muslim Brotherhood. [from Arabic, = delegation]

wafer *noun* **1** a thin, light, finely layered kind of biscuit, served eg with ice cream. **2** a thin disc of unleavened bread or rice paper served to communicants at Holy Communion. **3** *Hist.* a thin disc of sticky paste or other adhesive material for sealing letters. **4** *Hist.* a small flat edible capsule of medicine. [from Middle English *wafre*, from Old Dutch *wafer*, variant of *wafel*, waffle]

waffle¹ *noun* a light-textured cake made of batter, with a distinctive grid-like surface pattern. [from Old Dutch *wafel*]

waffle² — *verb intrans.* to talk or write at length but to little purpose. — *noun* talk or writing of this kind.

waffle iron a flat double-sided hinged mould for cooking waffles.

waffler *noun* a person who waffles.

waft — *verb trans., intrans.* to float or cause to float or drift gently, especially through the air. — *noun* a whiff, eg of perfume. [from Middle English *waughter* or *wafter*, escort vessel]

wag — *verb* (**wagged**, **wagging**) **1** *trans., intrans.* to wave to and fro vigorously. *said of a dog or its tail* to wave (its tail) as a sign of pleasure. **2** to shake (one's finger) up and down at someone, while giving advice, a warning, or rebuke. **3** *intrans. said of the tongue, chin, or beard* to move busily in chatter. — *noun* **1** a wagging movement. **2** a habitual joker; someone with a roguish sense of humour; a wit. [from Anglo-Saxon *wagian*]

wage — *verb* to fight (a war or battle). — *noun* **1** (*sing., pl.*) a regular, especially daily or weekly rather than monthly, payment from an employer to an especially unskilled or semi-skilled employee. See also SALARY. **2** (**wages**) *literary*

reward, recompense, or repayment: *the wages of sin is death.* [from Old French *wagier*, to pledge]

wager *old use* — *noun* a bet on the outcome or result of something. — *verb* (**wagered**, **wagering**) to bet; to stake in a bet. [from Old French *wagier*, to pledge]

Wagga Wagga POP (1991) 41 000, a town in Murrumbidgee statistical division, New South Wales, Australia. It lies at the centre of a rich agricultural area to the W of Canberra.

waggish *adj.* **1** amusing. **2** mischievous.

waggle *verb trans., intrans.* to move or cause to move to and fro. [from WAG]

Wagner, (Wilhelm) Richard (1813–83) German composer, born in Leipzig. His early efforts at composition were unsuccessful, and in Paris (1839–42) he made a living by journalism and hack operatic arrangements. His *Rienzi* (1842) was a great success at Dresden, and he was appointed kapellmeister, but his next operas, including *Tannhäuser* (1845), were failures. The poem of the *Ring* cycle was finished in 1852, and in 1853 he began to write *Das Rheingold* (The Rhinegold, performed 1869), followed by *Die Walküre* (The Valkyrie, 1856, performed 1870) and Part I of *Siegfried* (1857, performed 1876). In 1864 he was saved from ruin by the eccentric young King of Bavaria, Ludwig II, who became a fanatical admirer of his work, and offered him every facility at Munich. Since his first wife Minna had died in 1866, Wagner then married Franz Liszt's daughter Cosima, after her divorce from his musical director Hans von Bülow. To fulfil his ambition to give a complete performance of the *Ring* (*Walküre*, *Siegfried*, *Götterdämmerung*, with *Rheingold* as introduction), he established the now famous theatre at Bayreuth, which opened in 1876. *Parsifal*, his last opera, was staged in 1882, a year before his sudden fatal heart attack.

Wagner-Jauregg *or* **Wagner von Jauregg, Julius** (1857–1940) Austrian neurologist and psychiatrist, born in Wels. Professor at Graz and Vienna, he was awarded the 1927 Nobel Prize for Physiology or Medicine for his discovery of a treatment for general paralysis (a late stage of syphilis) by infection with malaria (1917). This 'fever therapy' was abandoned when antibiotics and other better treatments became available.

wagon *or* **waggon** *noun* **1** a four-wheeled vehicle for carrying loads, especially horse-drawn; a cart. **2** an open truck or closed van for carrying railway freight. **3** a tea trolley.
— **on the wagon** *colloq.* temporarily abstaining from alcohol.
off the wagon *colloq.* no longer abstaining from alcohol.
[from Dutch *wagen*]

wagoner *or* **waggoner** *noun* the driver of a wagon.

Wagram, Battle of a victory achieved (1809) by Napoleon I over the Austrians under Archduke Charles (1771–1847), fought northeast of Vienna, notable for the unparalleled concentration of artillery fire. Napoleon forced Austria to seek an armistice and negotiate the Treaty of Vienna (1809).

Wahhabis an Islamic movement which derives from the religious reformer Muhammad ibn Abd al-Wahhab and Muhammad ibn Saud, the ancestor of the present rulers of Saudi Arabia. In the 18c the alliance enabled most of the peninsula to be united under the Saudi banner. In the 20c it was reunified (1902–32) by King Abd al-Aziz, otherwise known as 'Ibn Saud'. Arabs call the followers of Abd al-Wahhab *muwahhidun* or 'unitarians'; *Wahhabis* is an anglicism. They maintain that legal decisions must be based exclusively on the Koran and the *Sunna*. The original Wahhabis banned such things as music, poetry, silk, and jewellery, and in the 20c the *ikhwan* ('brotherhood') have criticized the telephone, radio, and television as innovations not sanctioned by God.

waif *noun* **1** an orphaned, abandoned, or homeless child. **2** any pathetically undernourished-looking child. **3** something unclaimed and apparently ownerless. [from Old French *waif, guaif,* stray beast]

waif-like *adj.* like a waif; thin and underfed.

waifs and strays **1** homeless people, especially children. **2** unclaimed articles; odds and ends.

Waikato, River the longest river in New Zealand, situated on North I. It rises in L Taupo and flows 425km/264mi from the Upper Waikato NW to enter the Tasman Sea, S of Manukau Harbour. The river is a source of hydroelectric power.

Waikiki Beach a resort beach in SE Honolulu, on the Pacific island of Oahu, Hawaii state, USA.

wail — *noun* a long-drawn-out mournful or complaining cry. — *verb intrans., trans.* to make, or utter with, such a cry. *said eg of a siren* to make a similar noise. [perhaps related to Norse *wæla,* to wail]

Wain, John (Barrington) (1925–) English novelist and critic, born in Stoke-on-Trent, Staffordshire. He lectured in English at Reading University (1947–55), became a freelance writer, and was later Professor of Poetry at Oxford (1973–8). His novels include *Hurry on Down* (1953), *The Contenders* (1958), and *Young Shoulders* (1982). Other works include poetry, associated with the Movement, (eg *Weep Before God,* 1961), and several works of criticism.

wainscot *noun Hist.* wooden panelling or boarding covering the lower part of the walls of a room. [perhaps from Dutch *wagen-schot,* wagon partition]

wainscoting *or* **wainscotting** *noun* a wainscot, or material for this.

waist *noun* **1** the narrow part of the human body between the ribs and hips. **2** the part of a garment covering this. **3** a narrow middle part of something such as a violin or a wasp. **4** the middle part of a ship. [from Anglo-Saxon *wæstm,* form, figure]

waistband *noun* the reinforced strip of cloth on a skirt, trousers, etc, that goes round the waist.

waistcoat *noun* a close-fitting, sleeveless, usually waist-length garment worn especially by men under a jacket.

wait *verb* **1** (**wait for something**) to delay action, or remain in a certain place, in expectation of, or readiness for, something: *wait for the bus / wait till you're older.* **2** *intrans. said of a task, etc* to remain temporarily undealt with: *that can wait.* **3** to postpone action for (a period of time). **4** to await (one's turn, etc). **5** *colloq.* to delay eating (a

meal) till someone arrives: *won't wait dinner.* **6** *intrans.* to park one's vehicle briefly at the kerb, etc: *no waiting.* **7** *intrans.* to serve as a waiter or waitress.

— **wait on someone 1** to serve them with food as a waiter or waitress. **2** to act as a servant or attendant to someone. **3** *dialect* to wait for someone. **4** *old use* to pay a respectful visit to someone.

wait up for someone to delay going to bed at night waiting for someone's arrival or return, or some other event.

you wait! an expression used to warn or threaten.

[from Old French *waitier, guaitier,* from Old German *wahten,* to watch]

Waitangi Day 6 Feb, the national day of New Zealand, commemorating the Treaty of Waitangi made between Britain and the Maori chiefs in 1840.

Waite, Terry (Terence Hardy) (1939–) English religious adviser, born in Cheshire. In 1980 he was appointed adviser on Anglican Communion affairs to Robert Runcie, who was then Archbishop of Canterbury. He undertook many overseas assignments and on 20 Jan 1987, while making inquiries in Beirut about European hostages, was kidnapped. Following worldwide efforts to secure his release and that of his fellow hostages, 1 763 days later he was freed.

waiter *or* **waitress** *noun* a man, or woman, who serves people with food at a restaurant, etc.

Waiting For Godot (En Attendant Godot) a play by Samuel Beckett (1956). A highly influential play, it depicts two tramps, Vladimir and Estragon, awaiting the arrival of a being called Godot. Their time is filled with meaningless word-play and other strange events, suggesting the ignorance and paralysis of the human condition.

waiting-list *noun* a list of people waiting for something currently unavailable.

waiting-room *noun* a room for people to wait in, eg at a railway station, doctor's surgery, etc.

Waitz, Grete, *née* **Andersen** (1953–) Norwegian athlete, born in Oslo. Formerly a track champion in the 3 000m, at which she set world records in 1975 and 1976, she has since developed into the world's leading female road athlete. The world marathon champion in 1983, and the Olympic silver medallist in 1984, she has four times set world best times for the marathon. She won the London Marathon in 1983 and 1986, and the New York marathon a record nine times between 1978 and 1988. She has also been the women's cross-country champion five times (1978–81, 1983).

waive *verb* **1** to refrain from insisting upon; to give up (a claim, right, etc). **2** to refrain from enforcing (a rule, penalty, etc). [from Old French *weyver, guaiver,* to abandon]

waiver *noun* the relinquishment of a right, etc, or a written statement confirming this.

Wajda, Andrzej (1926–) Polish film director, born in Suwalki. His first feature film was *Pokolenie* (A Generation, 1954) and he is best known outside Poland for *Czlowiek z marmaru* (Man of Marble, 1977), about the Stalinist era. His varied films include literary adaptations (eg *Crime and Punishment,* 1984), and he has also worked in television and the theatre.

wake[1] — *verb* (PAST TENSE **woke**; PAST PARTICIPLE **woken**) **1** *trans., intrans.* (*also* **wake up** *or* **wake someone up**) to rouse or be roused from sleep. **2** *trans., intrans.* (*also* **wake up** *or* **wake someone up**) to stir or be stirred out of a state of inactivity, lethargy, etc. **3** (**wake up** *or* **wake someone up to something**) to become or make them aware of a fact, circumstance, situation, etc. — *noun* **1** a watch or vigil kept beside a corpse. **2** *dialect* an annual holiday. [from Middle English *waken,*

from Anglo-Saxon *wacan,* to become awake, and *wacian,* to stay awake]

wake[2] *noun* a trail of disturbed water left by a ship, or of disturbed air left by an aircraft.

— **in one's wake** wherever one has been.

in the wake of someone *or* **something** coming after them; resulting from them.

[from Norse *vök,* hole or channel in the ice]

Wakefield POP (1981) 76 000, the administrative centre of West Yorkshire, N England. It is an industrial city situated on the R Calder, 13km/8mi S of Leeds. HISTORY a woollen centre since the 16c; site of the battle of Wakefield (1460) during the Wars of the Roses. NOTABLE FEATURE cathedral.

wakeful *adj.* **1** not asleep; unable to sleep. **2** *said of a night* sleepless. **3** vigilant; alert; watchful.

wakefully *adv.* in a wakeful way.

Wake Island POP (1980) 302, a horseshoe-shaped coral atoll enclosing three islands in the central Pacific Ocean. AREA 10sq km/4sq mi. It is situated 1 200km/750mi N of Kwajalein, Marshall Is. HISTORY annexed by the USA in 1898; a seaplane base opened in 1935; important for trans-Pacific air flights; under the control of the US Air Force since 1972.

Wakem, Philip the sensitive hunchback who is in love with Maggie in George Eliot's *The Mill on the Floss.*

waken *verb* (**wakened, wakening**) **1** *trans., intrans.* to rouse or be roused from sleep, or from inactivity or lethargy. **2** *intrans.* (**waken to something**) to become aware of a fact, situation, etc. [from Anglo-Saxon *wæcnan*]

waking hours the part of the day that one spends awake.

Waksman, Selman Abraham (1888–1973) US biochemist, born in Priluka, in the Ukraine. He moved to the USA in 1910 and eventually became professor at Rutgers University. From 1939 he searched for antibiotics of medical importance, and discovered the first anti-tuberculosis drug streptomycin (1944), as well as several other anti-bacterial agents. He was awarded the 1952 Nobel Prize for Physiology or Medicine.

Walachia see MOLDAVIA AND WALLACHIA.

Walcott, Derek (1930–) West Indian poet and dramatist, born in St Lucia. He founded the Trinidad Theatre Workshop in 1959, has lectured at various US universities, and is visiting Professor of English at Boston University. His early volumes of poetry include *In A Green Night* (1962), *Castaway* (1965), and *The Gulf* (1969). His *Collected Poems* was published in 1986, and he was awarded the Nobel Prize for Literature in 1992.

Walden, in full *Walden, or Life in the Woods* an autobiographical work by Henry David Thoreau (1854). It describes a two-year period in his life when he lived a secluded, self-sufficient life at Walden Pond, near Concord, Massachusetts, USA.

Waldenses *or* **Waldensians** a small Christian community that began as a reform movement initiated in the 12c by Peter Waldo in Lyons, France. Because they rejected the authority of the pope, prayers for the dead, and veneration of the saints, they were excommunicated and persecuted. However they survived, and after the Reformation they continued (as Protestants) mainly in N Italy, with missions in S America.

Waldeyer-Hartz, Wilhelm (1839–1921) German histologist and anatomist, born in Hehlen. Professor at several universities, including Breslau, Strassburg, and Berlin, he established his reputation with his histological studies of cancers, which he classified according to their embryological cells of origin. He also coined the words 'neurone' and 'chromosome'.

Waldheim, Kurt (1918–) Austrian politician, born near Vienna. He served on the Russian front, but was wounded and discharged (1942), then studied at Vienna, and entered the Austrian foreign service (1945). He was appointed Ambassador to Canada (1955–60), Director of Political Affairs at the Ministry (1960–4), Austrian representative at the United Nations (1964–8, 1970–1), Foreign Minister (1968–70), and UN Secretary-General (1972–81). His presidential candidature was controversial because of claims that he had lied about his wartime activities and been involved in anti-Jewish atrocities, but he denied the allegations, and despite international pressure to stop his campaign, he became President (1986–).

Waldsterben *noun Environ.* the dying back of first the shoots and then the larger branches of trees, especially pine trees, as a result of air pollution, first observed in the late 1970s in the Black Forest, Germany, and now occurring in many other countries, including the UK. [German, = forest death]

wale *noun* 1 a raised mark on the skin; a weal. 2 a ridge on cloth, eg the rib on corduroy. 3 *Naut.* a course of planking running along the top edge of a ship's side. [from Anglo-Saxon *walu*, ridge]

Wales, Welsh **Cymru** POP (1987e) 2.8m, a principality and western constituent part of the United Kingdom, divided into eight counties. AREA 20 761sq km/8 014sq mi. It is bounded E by England, W by St George's Channel, N by the Irish Sea, and S by the Bristol Channel, and includes the island of Anglesey off the NW coast. CAPITAL Cardiff. CHIEF TOWNS Swansea, Newport, Merthyr Tydfil, Bangor, Wrexham. The chief religion is Protestantism, with a Roman Catholic minority. OFFICIAL LANGUAGE English; nearly 20% of the population speak Welsh, mainly in the N. PHYSICAL DESCRIPTION rises in the NW to 1 085m at Snowdon in the Snowdonia range; the Cambrian Mts rise in the centre, and the Brecon Beacons in the S; drained by the Severn, Clwyd, Conwy, Dee, Dovey, Taff, Tawe, Teifi, Towy, Usk, and Wye rivers. HISTORY Anglo-Saxon invaders of Britain drove the Brythonic Celts into Wales, calling them *Waelisc*, 'foreign'; in the 8c Welsh territory was lost to Offa, King of Mercia, who built a frontier dyke from the Dee to the Wye; Rhodri Mawr united Wales against the Saxons, Norse, and Danes in the 9c; Edward I of England established authority over Wales, building several castles in the 12c–13c; Edward I's son was created the first Prince of Wales (1301); 14c revolt under Owen Glendower; politically united with England at the Act of Union in 1535; centre of Nonconformist religion since 18c; the political nationalist movement (Plaid Cymru) returned its first MP in 1966; 1979 referendum opposed devolution. ECONOMY industrialized S valleys and the coastal plain are based on local coal; tourism in N

and NW, with seaside resorts and mountains; important source of water for England; slate, lead, steel, engineering, oil refining; fishing, forestry, sheep, dairy products; much light industry in recent decades, following the Great Depression and reduction in coal and steel industries; Royal Mint at Llantrisant.

Wałesa, Lech (1943–) Polish trade unionist, politician, and President, born in Popowo. A former Gdansk shipyard worker, he became leader of the independent trade union, *Solidarity*, which openly challenged the Polish government's economic and social policies. He held negotiations with the leading figures in the Church and State, but was detained by the authorities when martial law was declared in 1981. Released in 1982, he was awarded the Nobel Peace Prize in 1983. His political influence continued and Solidarity effectively formed the first Polish non-Communist government (Sep 1989), a contributory factor in the E European revolution of 1989–90. In 1990 he was elected President in the country's first free elections for 45 years.

walk — *verb* 1 *intrans.* to go in some direction on foot, moving one's feet alternately and always having one or other foot on the ground. 2 *intrans.* to go or travel on foot; to do this for exercise. 3 to travel (a distance) by walking: *walked three miles.* 4 to go about (the streets, countryside, etc) on foot. 5 to accompany, support, or propel (someone who is on foot). 6 to take (a dog) out for exercise. 7 *intrans.* old use to live one's life or behave in a certain manner: *walk in fear / walk tall.* 8 *intrans. facetious* to disappear; to be stolen: *my pen has walked.* — *noun* 1 the motion, or pace, of walking: *she slowed to a walk.* 2 an outing or journey on foot, especially for exercise. 3 a distance walked or for walking: *a three-minute walk.* 4 one's distinctive manner of walking: *they recognized your walk.* 5 a path, especially a broad formal one. 6 a route for walking: *some nice walks in these parts.*
— **walk all over someone** *colloq.* to treat them inconsiderately or arrogantly.
walk away from someone *colloq.* to outdistance them.
walk away from something 1 to ignore or abandon a commitment, responsibility, etc. 2 to escape unhurt from an accident, etc.
walk away with something to win a prize or reward effortlessly.
walk into something to involve oneself in trouble or difficulty through one's own unwariness.
walk off to depart.
walk off with something 1 to win a prize or reward effortlessly. 2 *colloq.* to steal it.
walk out 1 *said of factory workers, etc* to leave the workplace in a body, in declaration of a strike. 2 to depart abruptly from a meeting, etc in protest.
walk out on someone to abandon or desert them.

walk out with someone *old use* to court someone of the opposite sex.
[from Anglo-Saxon *wealcan*]

walkabout *noun* 1 a casual stroll through a crowd of ordinary people by a celebrity, especially a member of the royal family. 2 *Austral.* usually in **go walkabout** a walk alone in the bush by an Australian Aboriginal.

walker *noun* a person who walks, especially for pleasure.

walkie-talkie *noun colloq.* a portable two-way radio carried by police, etc.

walking *adj.* 1 in human form: *a walking encyclopedia.* 2 for the use of walkers: *walking shoes.*

walking frame a metal frame used by an infirm person to provide support while walking.

walking-stick *noun* a stick used for support or balance in walking.

Walkman *noun trademark* a small portable audio cassette recorder, or radio, with headphones.

walk of life one's occupation or profession.

walk-on *adj., said of a part in a play, opera, etc* not involving any speaking or singing.

walkout *noun* a sudden departure, especially of a workforce in declaration of a strike.

walkover *noun colloq.* an easy victory.

Walküre, Die (The Valkyrie) a music drama by Richard Wagner (1856, first performed 1870), the first part of the three-part cycle *Der Ring des Nibelungen*, dealing with the disobedience and punishment of the Valkyrie Brünnhilde.

walkway *noun* a paved path or passage for pedestrians.

wall — *noun* 1 a solid vertical brick or stone construction of narrow width, substantial length, and variable height, serving eg as a barrier, territorial division, or protection. 2 the side of a building or room. 3 anything in some way suggestive of a wall: *a wall of fire / a wall of secrecy.* 4 *Biol.* an outer covering, eg of a cell; the side of a hollow organ or cavity. 5 a sheer rock face. — *verb* 1 to surround with a wall: *a walled garden.* 2 (*usually* **wall something off** *or* **in**) to separate or enclose it with a wall. 3 (**wall something** *or* **someone up**) to block an opening with, or seal something behind, brickwork, etc; to imprison someone in this way.
— **go to the wall** *said of a business* to fail.
have one's back to the wall to be making one's last desperate stand.
up the wall *colloq.* crazy.
walls have ears an exhortation to speak discreetly.
[from Anglo-Saxon *weall*, from Latin *vallum*, rampart]

Counties of Wales

County	Area sq km	sq mi	Population[1]	Admin centre	Former counties	New districts
Clwyd	2 426	936	415 000	Mold	Flint, most of Denbigh	Alyn & Deeside, Colwyn, Delyn, Glyndwr, Rhuddlan, Wrexham, Maelor
Dyfed	5 768	2 226	351 000	Carmarthen	Camarthen, Cardigan, Pembroke	Camarthen, Ceredigion, Dinefwr, Llanelli, Preseli, South Pembrokeshire
Gwent	1 376	531	449 000	Cwmbrăn	Most of Monmouth, part of Brecon	Blaenau Gwent, Islwyn, Monmouth, Newport, Torfaen
Gwynedd	3 869	1 493	240 000	Caernarvon	Anglesey, Caernarvon, Merioneth, part of Denbigh	Abercronwy, Arfon, Dwyfor, Meirionydd, Anglesey (Ynys Môn)
Powys	5 077	1 960	119 000	Llandrindod Wells	Montgomery, Radnor, most of Brecon	Brecknock, Montgomery, Radnor
Mid Glamorgan	1 018	393	543 000	Cardiff	Parts of Glamorgan, Brecon, and Monmouth	Cynon Valley, Merthyr Tydfil, Ogwen, Rhondda, Rhymney Valley, Taff-Ely
South Glamorgan	416	161	410 000	Cardiff	Parts of Glamorgan and Monmouth	Cardiff, Vale of Glamorgan
West Glamorgan	817	315	371 000	Swansea	Part of Glamorgan	Afan, Lliw Valley, Neath, Swansea

[1] 1992 census, provisional figures

wallaby *noun* (PL. **wallabies**) any of more than 20 species of a plant-eating marsupial, belonging to the same family (Macropodidae) as, but smaller than, the kangaroo, and native to Australia and Tasmania. Some wallabies are no larger than rabbits, and several species are endangered. [from Aboriginal *walaba*]

Wallace, Alfred Russel (1823–1913) Welsh naturalist, born near Usk, Gwent. He travelled and collected specimens in the Amazon basin and the Malay Archipelago, and his *Geographical Distribution of Animals* (1876) became the founding text of zoogeography. He conceived the idea of the 'survival of the fittest' as the key to evolution independently of Charles Darwin and around the same time.

Wallace, Lewis, also called **Lew** (1827–1905) US writer and soldier, born in Brookville, Indiana. He served in the Mexican War and the Civil War, became a lawyer, and was Governor of New Mexico (1878–81) and Minister to Turkey (1881–5). He is best known as the author of the successful religious novel *Ben Hur* (1880, filmed 1927 and 1959).

Wallace, William (c.1274–1305) Scottish knight and champion of the independence of Scotland, born probably in Elderslie, near Paisley. He routed the English army at Stirling (1297), and took control of the government of Scotland as 'Guardian', but was defeated by Edward I at Falkirk (1298). He was eventually captured near Glasgow (1305), and was hanged, drawn, and quartered in London. He has entered legend as a hero due to his popular appeal as a national figure resisting foreign oppression.

Wallace Collection a museum of paintings, furnishings, and other objets d'art at Hertford House, London. The collection was created by successive Marquesses of Hertford, especially the fourth, who left it to his son Sir Richard Wallace. It was bequeathed to the nation in 1897.

Wallachia see MOLDAVIA AND WALLACHIA.

wallah *noun* Anglo-Indian (in compounds) a person performing a specified task: *the tea wallah*. [from Hindi *-wala*]

Wallasey POP (1981) 63 000, a town in Wirral borough, Merseyside, NW England, situated on the Wirral Peninsula, N of Birkenhead. It is a dormitory town for Liverpool.

wallbars *pl. noun* a series of horizontal wooden bars supported by uprights lining the walls of a gymnasium, for climbing, hanging from, etc.

Wallenstein *or* **Waldstein, Albrecht (Wenzel Eusebius), Herzog von (Duke of)** (1583–1634) Bohemian soldier, born in Hermanice. During the Thirty Years War (1618–48) he became Commander of the Imperial armies, won a series of victories (1625–9), and gained the titles of the Duke of Mecklenburg and 'General of the Baltic and Oceanic Seas'. His ambition led to his dismissal in 1630, but he was reinstated to defend the empire against Swedish attack. He recovered Bohemia, but was defeated by Gustavus Adolphus at Lützen (1632), and was again dismissed. His intrigues led to an Imperial proclamation of treason, which resulted in his assassination.

Waller, Edmund (1606–87) English poet and politician, born in Coleshill, Buckinghamshire. He became an MP in 1621, and was a member of the Long Parliament in 1640. In 1643 he led a conspiracy ('Waller's plot') against parliament, was arrested, and banished. He is notable for his use of the heroic couplet, and his works include *Poems* (1645).

Waller, Fats (Thomas Wright) (1904–43) US jazz pianist, organist, singer, and songwriter, born in New York City. A professional musician from his teens, he became a brilliant piano player in the stride tradition (a rhythmic style of piano-playing derived from ragtime), and a great, nat-

ural songwriter, eg of such jazz standards as 'Honeysuckle Rose' (c.1928), 'Ain't Misbehavin' (1929), and 'Keepin' Out of Mischief Now' (1932).

wallet *noun* **1** a flat folding case made eg of leather, for holding banknotes, etc, carried in the pocket or handbag. **2** any of various kinds of especially plastic folders or envelopes for holding papers, etc. [from Middle English *wallet*]

walleye *noun* **1** an eye in which the iris has a chalky appearance. **2** an eye that squints away from the nose, so that an abnormal amount of the white shows. [from Norse *wagleygr*]

walleyed *adj.* having a walleye.

wallflower *noun* **1** a sweet-smelling plant with yellow, orange or red flowers. **2** *colloq.* a person who sits all evening at the edge of the dance floor, waiting in vain to be asked to dance.

Wallis, Sir Barnes Neville (1887–1979) English aeronautical engineer and inventor, born in Derbyshire. He joined the Vickers Company in 1911, and designed their airship R100 which successfully crossed the Atlantic. He also designed the Wellesley and Wellington bombers, and the 'bouncing bombs' used during World War II. From 1945 to 1971 he was chief of aeronautical research and development for the British Aircraft Corporation in Weybridge. In the early 1950s he was responsible for the design of the first variable-geometry (swing-wing) aircraft.

Wallis, John (1616–1703) English mathematician, born in Ashford, Kent. He graduated from Cambridge, and took holy orders, but in 1649 became professor at Oxford. His *Arithmetica Infinitorum* (The Arithmetic of Infinitesimals, 1656) anticipated calculus and the binomial theorem. One of the founders of the Royal Society, he also wrote on proportion, mechanics, grammar, logic, and the teaching of the deaf and dumb.

Wallis and Futuna Islands, official name **Territory of the Wallis and Futuna Islands** POP (1992e) 14 000, a French Overseas Territory consisting of an island group in the S central Pacific Ocean, lying NE of Fiji. AREA 274sq km/106sq mi. It comprises the Wallis Is and the Hooru Is, 230km/140mi apart. CAPITAL Matu-Utu (on Uvéa). Most of the population are Polynesian; Roman Catholicism is the chief religion. CURRENCY the franc. PHYSICAL DESCRIPTION the Wallis Is include Uvéa, rising to 145m at Mt Lulu, ringed by low-lying coral reefs; the Hooru Is include Futuna and Alofi, which are mountainous and volcanic; Futuna rises to 765m at Mt Puke; Alofi is uninhabited. CLIMATE warm and damp, with a cyclone season between Oct and Mar. HISTORY became a French protectorate in 1842; changed status to Overseas Territory of France in 1961. GOVERNMENT governed by an administrator, assisted by an elected 20-member Territorial Assembly. ECONOMY subsistence farming; fishing; copra; yams; taro roots; bananas; timber.

Wallonia a French-speaking region in S Belgium. There are c.3.5m Walloons (36% of the Belgian population). The dividing line with Flanders (to the N) consists of a belt of industry from Liège to Tournai. Many Walloon towns are renowned for their art treasures. ECONOMY steel; engineering.

Walloon — *noun* **1** a member of the French-speaking population of S Belgium. **2** their language, a dialect of French. — *adj.* relating to, or belonging to, the Walloons. [from French *Wallon*, from Germanic; literally foreigner]

wallop *colloq.* — *verb* (**walloped, walloping**) to hit or spank vigorously. — *noun* a hit or a thrashing. [from Old French *waloper, galoper*, to gallop]

walloping — *noun* a thrashing. — *adj.* great; whopping: *a walloping great hole*.

wallow *verb intrans.* (often **wallow in something**) **1** to lie or roll about in water, mud, etc.

2 to revel or luxuriate in admiration, etc. **3** to indulge excessively in self-pity, etc. **4** *said of a ship* to roll from side to side making poor headway. **5** *said of an enterprise, project, etc* to fail to progress with speed and efficiency. [from Anglo-Saxon *wealwian*]

wallpaper — *noun* paper used to decorate the interior walls and ceilings of houses, etc. — *verb* to cover (walls) or the walls of (a room) with wallpaper.

Wallsend POP (1981) 45 000, a town in North Tyneside borough, Tyne and Wear, NE England. It is situated on the R Tyne, 6km/4mi E of Newcastle upon Tyne, at the E end of Hadrian's Wall.

Wall Street a street in Manhattan, New York City, where the New York Stock Exchange and other major financial institutions are located. The road follows what was once the walled N boundary of the original Dutch colony.

wall-to-wall *adj.* **1** *said of carpeting* covering the entire floor of a room. **2** *facetious* ever-present; inescapable: *wall-to-wall Muzak*.

wally *noun* (PL. **wallies**) *colloq.* an ineffectual or foolish person. [from the name *Walter*]

walnut *noun* **1** any of various deciduous trees of the genus *Juglans*, found in N temperate regions, with large compound leaves, cultivated for its timber and for its edible nut, which is rich in protein and fat. **2** the round nut produced by this tree, consisting of a wrinkled two-lobed seed surrounded by a hard shell. **3** the hard durable dark-brown or black wood of this tree, which has an attractive grain and is highly prized for furniture-making, cabinetwork, and panelling. [from Anglo-Saxon *wealhhnutu*, foreign nut]

Walpole, Sir Hugh (Seymour) (1884–1941) English novelist, born in Auckland, New Zealand. His many novels, which were popular during his lifetime, include *The Secret City* (1919), *The Cathedral* (1922), and the four-volume family saga, *The Herries Chronicle* (1930–3).

Walpole, Sir Robert, Earl of Orford (1676–1745) English statesman, born in Houghton, Norfolk, whose period in office is widely held to have increased the influence of the House of Commons in the Constitution. He became a Whig MP in 1701, and was made Secretary for War (1708) and Treasurer of the Navy (1710). Sent to the Tower for alleged corruption during the Tory government (1712), he was recalled by George I, and made a Privy Councillor and Chancellor of the Exchequer (1715). Later a leading minister (1721–42) under George I and George II, he was regarded by them as indispensable; one of his rewards was No.10 Downing Street. After the collapse of the South Sea Scheme, he again became Chancellor (1721) and established his supremacy by chairing a small group of ministers (the forerunner of the Cabinet). He became recognized as 'prime minister', a title before then unknown to the Constitution. A shrewd manipulator of men, he took trouble to consult backbench MPs, and followed policies of low taxation designed to win their favour. His popularity decreased in the 1730s over both the Excise Scheme and his determination to avoid foreign wars, and he resigned in 1742.

Walpurga *or* **Walburga, Walpurgis, St** (c.710–c.777) English abbess and missionary, born in Wessex. A Benedictine nun in Wimbourne monastery, Dorset, she travelled with her brother Willibald to Germany, and became Abbess of Heidenheim. Walpurgis Night (30 Apr) is so called from a confusion of the day when her relics were moved to Eichstätt (1 May) and the popular superstitions regarding the flight of witches on that night.

Walpurgis Night the eve of 1 May, when according to German popular superstition witches rode on broomsticks and he-goats to revel with the Devil on high places.

walrus *noun* (PL. **walruses**, **walrus**) a large marine mammal (*Odobenus rosmarus*) belonging to the family Odobenidae, related to the seal, and found in the northern waters of the Atlantic and Pacific oceans. Walruses are usually over 3m in length, and have grey, wrinkled, almost hairless skin, flippers, a broad bristly snout, and two long tusks. [from Dutch *walrus*, literally whale-horse] ◇ Walruses collect in large herds in shallow coastal waters within the Arctic Circle, and they lie on beaches and ice floes, diving to depths of up to 100m to dig mussels and clams from the sea bed with their long tusks. The tusks are also used as defence, and as grapnels to help the animal haul its bulky body out of the water on to the ice. Walruses are normally timid, but will fight to protect their young. Strict conservation measures have saved the Pacific walrus from extinction, but the Atlantic species is still endangered after years of overhunting.

walrus

Walrus and the Carpenter, the two oyster-eating characters whose story is told in the poem of the same name in Lewis Carroll's *Through the Looking-Glass.*

walrus moustache a thick drooping moustache.

Walsall POP (1992e) 263 000, a town in Walsall borough, West Midlands, central England. It is situated 13km/8mi NW of Birmingham. HISTORY centre of the lock and key industry in the 17c. NOTABLE FEATURES England's only lock museum; museum and art gallery.

Walsingham, Sir Francis (c.1530–1590) English statesman, born in Chislehurst, Kent. He became a diplomat, and was made Secretary of State to Elizabeth I (1573–90) and a Privy Councillor. A Puritan sympathizer, and a strong opponent of the Catholics, he developed a complex system of espionage at home and abroad, which enabled him to reveal the plots of Francis Throckmorton and Antony Babington against the Queen. He was one of the commissioners who tried Mary, Queen of Scots at Fotheringay.

Walter, Bruno, originally **Bruno Walter Schlesinger** (1876–1962) German-born US conductor, born in Berlin. He conducted at Cologne while still in his teens, then worked with Mahler in Hamburg and Vienna, directed the Munich Opera (1913–22), and became chief conductor of the Berlin Philharmonic in 1919. On fleeing from the Nazis in 1933 he settled in the USA, where he became chief conductor of the New York Philharmonic (1951). A great exponent of the German romantic tradition, he was noted particularly for his performances of Joseph Haydn, Mozart, and Gustav Mahler.

Walter, Hubert (c.1140–1205) English churchman and statesman. He became Bishop of Salisbury (1189) and accompanied Richard I on the Third Crusade (1190–3). Appointed Archbishop of Canterbury in 1193, he helped to raise the ransom to secure Richard's release from captivity, and to contain the rebellion of the King's brother, John. He was justiciar of England (1193–8), and was responsible for all the business of government. On John's accession (1199) he became Chancellor.

Walter, John (1739–1812) English printer and newspaper publisher, born in London. In 1784 he acquired a printing office in Blackfriars, London,

nucleus of the later Printing House Square buildings, and in 1785 founded *The Daily Universal Register* newspaper, which was renamed *The Times* in 1788 and was later managed by his son and grandson.

Walter a male first name. [of Germanic origin, from *wald*, rule + *hari*, people, army]

Walton, Ernest Thomas Sinton (1903–) Irish physicist, born in Dungarvan, Waterford. With John Cockcroft, he produced the first artificial disintegration of a nucleus by bombarding a lithium nucleus with protons in the first successful use of a particle accelerator (1932); they shared the 1951 Nobel Prize for Physics. He became professor at Trinity College, Dublin, in 1947.

Walton, Izaak (1593–1683) English writer, born in Stafford. In 1621 he settled in London as an ironmonger, but left the city for Staffordshire during the Civil War, and after the Restoration lived in Winchester. He is best known for his treatise on fishing and country life, *The Compleat Angler* (1653), and he also wrote several biographies.

Walton, Sir William (Turner) (1902–83) English composer, born in Oldham, Lancashire. He wrote his first compositions while at Oxford, and became known through his instrumental setting of poems by Edith Sitwell, *Façade* (1921). His works include two symphonies, concertos for violin, viola, and cello, the biblical cantata *Belshazzar's Feast* (1931), and the opera *Troilus and Cressida* (1954). He is also known for his film music, notably Laurence Olivier's *Henry V*, *Hamlet*, and *Richard III*.

waltz — *noun* **1** a slow or fast ballroom dance in triple time. **2** a piece of music for this dance. — *verb intrans.* **1** to dance a waltz. **2** *colloq.* to go or move with easy confidence. [from German *Walzer*, from *walzen*, to roll, dance]

Walvis Bay, Afrikaans **Walvisbaai** POP (1980e) 25 000, a seaport in W central Namibia. It is situated on the Atlantic Ocean coast, 275km/171mi SW of Windhoek. The Walvis Bay enclave (AREA 1 128sq km/435sq mi) is administered by South Africa as part of Cape Province. HISTORY annexed by the Dutch in 1792; taken by Britain in 1878; incorporated into Cape Colony in 1884; remaining a South African enclave after Namibian independence. Walvis Bay handles most of Namibia's trade.

wampum *noun Hist.* shells strung together for use as money among the Native Americans. [from Algonkin (Native American language group) *wampumpeag*, white string of beads]

WAN *abbrev. Comput.* wide area network, a network of computers spread over a wide area, linked by means of telephone lines, etc.

wan *adj.* (**wanner**, **wannest**) pale and pinched-looking from illness, exhaustion, or grief. [from Anglo-Saxon *wann*, dusky, lurid]

wand *noun* **1** a slender rod used eg by magicians or fairies for performing magic. **2** a conductor's baton. **3** a rod carried as a symbol of authority. **4** a slender young shoot; a flexible cane or switch. [from Norse *vöndr*, shoot]

wander — *verb* (**wandered**, **wandering**) **1** to walk or travel about, with no particular destination; to ramble. **2** *said of a stream, etc* to follow a meandering course. **3** to stray, eg from the right path, or from the point of an argument, etc. **4** *said of people, their wits, etc* to become confused, incoherent, or irrational, eg in delirium or advanced age. **5** *said of one's thoughts, etc* to flit randomly. — *noun* a ramble or stroll. [from Anglo-Saxon *wandrian*]

wanderer *noun* a person or animal that wanders.

Wandering Jew in Christian legend, a character who taunted Christ as he carried his cross, and was condemned to wander the Earth until

the end of the world or until Christ's second coming. Various Jews, notably Ahasuerus of Hamburg in 1602, have been identified with the character.

wanderlust *noun* an urge to rove; a liking for keeping on the move. [from German *Wanderlust*, from *wandern*, to travel + *Lust*, desire]

wane — *verb intrans.* **1** *said of the moon* to grow narrower as the sun illuminates less of its surface. **2** to decline in glory or influence. — *noun* the process of waning or declining. — **on the wane** decreasing or declining. [from Anglo-Saxon *wanian*, to lessen]

Wang, An (1920–90) Chinese-born US physicist and computer company executive, born in Shanghai. He emigrated to the USA in 1945, and studied applied physics at Harvard. He played a major role in inventing magnetic core memories for computers, and in 1951 founded Wang Laboratories in Boston. He also invented the electronic calculator, and became a leading manufacturer of minicomputers and word-processing software. He left the company in 1983.

Wanganui, River a river in W North I, New Zealand. It rises NW of L Taupo, then flows S to enter the Tasman Sea 195km/121mi N of Wellington. At 290km/180mi in length, it is the longest navigable river in New Zealand. The town of Wanganui, situated near the mouth of the river, is an outdoor resort area and agricultural centre.

wangle — *verb* to contrive or obtain by persuasion or subtle manipulation. — *noun* an act of wangling.

wank *verb intrans. coarse slang* to masturbate.

Wankel, Felix (1902–88) German mechanical engineer, born in Luhran. He was employed in various engineering works before opening his own research establishment in 1930. In 1956 he produced an alternative internal combustion engine.

wanker *noun coarse slang* **1** a person who masturbates. **2** used as a general term of abuse.

wanly *adv.* with a pale or weak appearance.

wannabe *noun* someone who aspires, usually ineffectually, to a particular lifestyle or image. [representing a colloquial pronunciation of *want to be*]

wanness *noun* being wan; pallor.

want — *verb* **1** to feel a need or desire for. **2** (**want to do something** *or* **want someone to do something**) to wish or require that they do it: *do you want to say something? / she doesn't want you to leave.* **3** (**want in**, **out**, *etc*) *colloq.* to desire to get in, out, etc. **4** *colloq.* ought; need: *you want to take more care / we want to turn left at the school.* **5** *colloq.* to need (a certain treatment, etc): *he wants his head examined.* **6** (**want something** *or* **want for something**) to feel the lack of it: *want for nothing.* **7** to require the presence of: *you are wanted next door.* **8** to desire (someone) sexually. **9** *old use* to fall short by a certain amount: *it wants two minutes to midnight.* — *noun* **1** a need or requirement. **2** *old use* lack: *a want of discretion.* **3** a state of need; destitution: *those in want.* — **for want of something** in the absence of it: *for want of a better word.* **in want of something** needing it. [from Norse *vanta*, to be lacking]

wanted *adj.* being sought by the police on suspicion of having committed a crime, etc.

wanting *adj.* **1** missing; lacking. **2** (**wanting in something**) not having enough of it: *wanting in tact.* **3** not up to requirements: *has been found wanting.*

wanton — *adj.* **1** motivelessly cruel. **2** motiveless: *wanton destruction.* **3** *old use, said of a woman* sexually immoral. **4** *old use* playfully fanciful; whimsical. — *noun old use* a wanton woman. — *verb intrans.* (**wantoned**, **wantoning**) *old use* to play about, flirt, or trifle wantonly. [from Middle English *wantowen*, from Anglo-Saxon *wan-*, not + *togen*, disciplined]

wantonly *adv.* in a wanton manner.

wantonness *noun* being wanton.

wapiti *noun* a large deer of N America. [from Algonkian *wapiti* (Native American language group)]

war — *noun* **1** an openly acknowledged state of armed conflict, especially between nations: *declared war on the French.* **2** a particular armed struggle: *the Iran–Iraq war.* **3** fighting as a science: *the arts of war.* **4** open hostility between people. **5** any long-continued struggle or campaign: *the war against drug-dealing.* **6** fierce rivalry or competition in business: *a trade war.* — *verb intrans.* (**warred, warring**) **1** to fight wars. **2** to conflict one with another: *warring emotions.*
— **go to war** to begin an armed conflict.
have been in the wars *colloq.* to have, or show signs of having, sustained injuries.
[from Old French *werre*]

War and Peace a novel by Leo Tolstoy (1863–9). It is a Russian epic chronicling the lives of three noble families at the time of the war with Napoleon.

war baby a baby born during a war, especially a serviceman's illegitimate child.

Warbeck, Perkin (c.1474–1499) Flemish impostor, pretender to the English throne, born in Tournai, Flanders. In 1492 he appeared at the court of the Duchess of Burgundy, sister of Edward IV of England, and professed to be Richard, Duke of York, the younger of Edward's two sons who had been murdered in the Tower. He made an ineffectual landing in Kent (1495), then landed in Cornwall (1497), but was captured at Beaulieu, Hampshire.

warble[1] *verb intrans., trans.* **1** *said of a bird* to sing melodiously. **2** *said of a person* to sing in a high, tremulous voice; to trill. [from Old French *werbler*]

warble[2] *noun* a swelling under the hide of horses or cattle, especially one containing a maggot.

warbler *noun* any of several small songbirds.

Warburg, Otto Heinrich (1883–1970) German biochemist, born in Freiburg, Baden. He worked at the Kaiser Wilhelm (later Max Planck) Institute in Berlin from 1913, becoming director there in 1953, and made important discoveries concerning cellular respiration, and the activity of cancerous cells. He was awarded the 1931 Nobel Prize for Physiology or Medicine, but as a Jew was prevented from accepting it by Hitler.

war crime a crime, eg ill-treatment of prisoners, massacre of civilians or racial minorities, etc, committed during, and in connection with, a war.

war criminal a person who commits a war crime.

war cry 1 a cry used to rally or hearten troops, or as a signal for charging. **2** a slogan or watchword.

Ward, Dame Barbara (Mary) see JACKSON (OF LODSWORTH), BARONESS.

ward — *noun* **1** any of the rooms in a hospital with beds for patients. **2** any of the areas into which a town, etc is divided for administration or elections. **3** *Legal* a person, especially a minor, under the protection of a guardian or court. **4** a projection inside a lock that fits into a notch in its key, ensuring that the lock cannot be turned by the wrong key. **5** *old use* a watch or guard kept over something. — *verb* (*usually* **ward something off**) **1** to fend off, turn aside, or parry a blow. **2** to keep trouble, hunger, disease, etc away. [from Anglo-Saxon *weard*, protector]

-ward see -WARDS.

war dance a dance performed by primitive tribes before going into battle, or after victory.

warden *noun* **1** a person in charge of a hostel, student residence, old people's home, etc. **2** (*in compounds*) a public official responsible in any of various ways for maintaining order: *traffic warden / game warden.* **3** *North Amer.* the officer in charge of a prison. [from Old French *wardein*]

Warden, The a novel by Anthony Trollope (1855). The first of the 'Barsetshire' novels, it describes how a hospital warden, the Reverend Septimus Harding, is forced to resign in the face of public pressure.

warder *noun* a prison officer. [from Middle English *wardere*, from Old French *warder*, *garder*, to guard]

wardress *noun* a female warder.

Wardrobe a major financial office of 13c–14c English government, which was relied upon particularly by Edward I (reigned 1272–1307) during his extensive military campaigns. Though later superseded by the Chamber and Exchequer systems, the Wardrobe office and its Privy Seal remained important for household administration under the early Stuarts.

wardrobe *noun* **1** a cupboard in which to hang clothes. **2** a personal stock of garments. **3** the stock of costumes belonging to a theatrical company. [from Old French *garderobe*]

wardrobe mistress *or* **wardrobe master** the woman or man in charge of a theatrical company's costumes.

wardroom *noun* the officers' quarters on board a warship.

-wards *or* **-ward** *combining form* forming words denoting direction: *westwards / backwards / homeward.* [from Anglo-Saxon *-weardes*, genitive of *-weard*, towards]

ware *noun* **1** (*in compounds*) manufactured goods of a specified material or for a specified range of use: *glassware / kitchenware.* **2** (*often in compounds*) a particular type of pottery: *Delftware.* **3** (**wares**) goods that one has for sale. [from Anglo-Saxon *waru*]

warehouse *noun* **1** a building in which goods are stored. **2** a large, especially wholesale, shop.

warfare *noun* **1** the activity of waging war. **2** violent conflict.

warfarin *noun Medicine* a crystalline substance that is used as an anticoagulant to prevent the clotting of blood, or to break up existing clots in blood vessels, eg in coronary thrombosis. It is also used as a rat poison. [from *Wisconsin Alumni Research Foundation* (the patent owners)]

war game 1 a mock battle or military exercise providing training in tactics, etc. **2** an elaborate game in which players use model soldiers, knights, etc to enact imaginary battles, etc.

warhead *noun* the front part of a missile, etc containing the explosives.

Warhol, Andy, originally **Andrew Warhola** (c.1926–87) US artist and film-maker, born in Pittsburgh, Pennsylvania. He worked as a commercial designer before becoming a pioneer in 1961 of Pop Art. He used the silk-screen technique to produce brightly-coloured exact reproductions of familiar everyday objects (eg *100 Soup Cans* and *Green Coca-Cola Bottles*, both 1962) and of famous people (eg *Marilyn Monroe*). His films include *Sleep* (1963), a three-hour silent observation of a sleeping man, and *Chelsea Girls* (1967).

warhorse *noun* **1** *Hist.* a powerful horse on which a knight rode into battle. **2** an old soldier or politician still full of fight. **3** a standard, reliable, frequently used, over-familiar musical composition, etc.

warily *adv.* cautiously, watchfully.

wariness *noun* being wary.

warlike *adj.* **1** fond of fighting; aggressive; belligerent. **2** relating to war; military.

warlock *noun* a wizard, male magician, or sorcerer. [from Anglo-Saxon *warloga*]

warlord *noun* a powerful military leader.

warm — *adj.* **1** moderately, comfortably, or pleasantly hot. **2** *said of clothes* providing and preserving heat. **3** *said of work* making one hot. **4** kind-hearted and affectionate. **5** *said of an environment, etc* welcoming and congenial. **6** enthusiastic; whole-hearted: *warm support.* **7** *old use* vehement; indignant: *was warm in her denial of the charge.* **8** *said of colours* suggestive of comfortable heat, typically deep and containing red or yellow. **9** *said of a trail or scent* still fresh enough to follow. **10** *in a children's game, etc* close to guessing correctly or finding the thing sought. **11** *old use, said of one's situation* awkward or dangerous. — *verb* **1** *trans., intrans.* to make or become warm or warmer. **2** (*usually* **warm to something**) to gain in enthusiasm for a task as one performs it. **3** (**warm to someone**) to gain in affection or approval for them.
— **warm up** *or* **warm something up 1** to become or make it warm or warmer. **2** to re-heat food. **3** *said of a party, etc* to become or make it livelier. **4** *said of an engine* to reach, or bring it up to, an efficient working temperature. **5** to exercise the body gently in preparation for a strenuous work-out, race, athletic contest, etc. [from Anglo-Saxon *wearm*]

warm-blooded *adj.* **1** *said of an animal* maintaining its internal body temperature at a relatively constant level, usually above that of the surrounding environment, eg mammals, birds. — Also called *homoiothermic.* **2** *said of a person* passionate, impulsive, or ardent.

warm boot *Comput.* a reboot activated by pressing a computer's reset key or a combination of keys, rather than by switching off and on again at the power source.

war memorial a monument commemorating members of the armed forces who died in war.

warm front *Meteorol.* the edge of a mass of warm air pushing against a mass of cold air.

warm-hearted *adj.* kind, affectionate, and generous.

warming-pan *noun Hist.* a long-handled copper or brass lidded container for hot coals, slid into a bed to warm it up.

warmly *adv.* **1** so as to be warm. **2** enthusiastically; affectionately.

warmonger *noun* a person who tries to precipitate war, or whips up enthusiasm for it.

warmth *noun* **1** the condition of being warm; moderate, pleasant, or comfortable heat. **2** affection or kind-heartedness. **3** passion; vehemence: *the warmth of her denial.* **4** strength or intensity: *the warmth of her love for him.*

warm-up *noun* the act of exercising the body in preparation for an athletic contest, etc.

warn *verb* **1** (*usually* **warn someone of** *or* **about something**) to make aware of possible or approaching danger or difficulty. **2** to advise strongly: *warned them to book early.* **3** to rebuke or admonish, with the threat of punishment for a repetition of the offence; to caution. **4** to inform in advance: *warned him she might be late.* **5** (**warn someone off**) to order them to go away. [from Anglo-Saxon *wearnian*]

Warner, Jack (1892–1978) US film producer, born in London, Ontario. With his three older brothers he worked in film exhibition and distribution, moving into production and setting up studios in 1923. Warners were the first to introduce sound, and the success of *The Jazz Singer* (1927) led to expansion in both cinema ownership and studio resources. Jack supervised the major productions such as *My Fair Lady* (1964) and *Camelot* (1967), but eventually sold his interest and the name to the Canadian company Seven Arts.

warning — *noun* something that happens, or is said or done, that serves to warn. — *adj.* intended, or serving, to warn.

warning coloration *Zool.* brightly coloured patterns occurring on some animals, especially poisonous, unpalatable, or stinging insects. These deter potential predators which learn to associate the coloration with unpalatable prey and avoid it, eg the black-and-yellow stripes on the abdomen of the wasp.

warningly *adv.* so as to warn.

warnography *noun* the presentation of images of war for pleasure. [from WAR + PORNOGRAPHY]

War of 1812 1 the name given to the hostilities (1812–14) between the UK and the USA, caused by some unfulfilled provisions of the Peace of 1783 (which secured American independence) and provoked by Britain's refusal to recognize American neutral and maritime rights, and the failure of both President Thomas Jefferson's embargo policy and the subsequent Non-Intercourse Act to alter British policies. The British, with Native American allies, were victorious against US attempts to gain Canadian land and in burning down the Capitol and the White House in Washington. The peace treaty allowed a mutually beneficial commercial relationship to develop, and marked the achievement of substantive, as well as formal, independence for the USA.

War of the Pacific a war fought (1879–83) by Chile against Peru and Bolivia (in alliance since 1873) which arose out of Chilean grievances in the Bolivian-held Atacama desert. Chile won command of the sea early on, and sent large expeditions to Peru to occupy the capital, Lima (Jan 1881). Peace treaties with Peru (1883) and Bolivia (1904) gave Chile large territorial gains.

War of the Worlds, The a science-fiction novel by H G Wells (1898). It describes the invasion and destruction of England by Martians. A radio adaptation of the novel by Orson Welles (1938) caused panic among many US listeners who believed it to be an actual news report of the invasion of New Jersey.

warp — *verb trans., intrans.* 1 *said of wood and other hard materials* to become or cause to become twisted out of shape through the shrinking and expanding effects of damp and heat. 2 to become or cause to become distorted, corrupted, or perverted. 3 *Naut., said of a vessel* to move it, or be manoeuvred, by hauling on a rope fixed to a position on a wharf. — *noun* 1 an unevenness or twist in wood, etc. 2 a distortion or abnormal twist in personality, etc. 3 a shift or displacement in a continuous dimension, especially time: *caught in a time warp.* 4 *Naut.* a rope used for warping a vessel. 5 *Weaving* the set of threads stretched lengthways in a loom, under and over which the widthways set of threads (the *weft* or *woof*) are passed. [from Anglo-Saxon *weorpan*, to throw]

warpaint *noun* paint put on the face by primitive peoples when going to war.

warpath *noun* the march to war, especially *Hist.* among Native Americans.
— **on the warpath** 1 setting off to fight. 2 *colloq.* in a fighting mood; in angry pursuit.

warrant — *noun* 1 a written legal authorization for doing something, eg arresting someone, or searching property. 2 a certificate such as a licence, voucher, or receipt, that authorizes, guarantees, or confirms something. 3 a justification: *has no warrant for making such an accusation.* 4 a certificate appointing a warrant officer in the armed services. — *verb* 1 to justify: *the circumstances are suspicious enough to warrant a full investigation.* 2 *old use* to assert with confidence; to be willing to bet: *I'll warrant he knows nothing of this.* 3

to guarantee (goods, etc) as being of the specified quality or quantity; to confirm as genuine, worthy, etc. [from Old French *warant, guarant*]

warrantable *adj.* 1 that may be permitted. 2 justifiable.

warrant officer in the armed services, an officer intermediate between a commissioned and non-commissioned officer.

warrantor *noun* a person who gives a warrant or warranty.

warranty *noun* (PL. **warranties**) 1 an assurance of the quality of goods being sold, usually with an acceptance of responsibility for repairs during an initial period of use; a guarantee. 2 an undertaking or assurance expressed or implied in certain contracts.

Warren, Earl (1891–1974) US politician and jurist, born in Los Angeles. An active Republican, he rose through minor state offices to be Governor of California (1943–53). During his time as Chief Justice (1953–69), the US Supreme Court adopted a strongly liberal policy, particularly concerning civil rights. He was responsible in *Brown v. Board of Education of Topeka, Kansas* (1954) for the epochal decision that outlawed school segregation, and was chairman of the federal commission that investigated the assassination of President Kennedy.

Warren, Robert Penn (1905–89) US writer, born in Guthrie, Kentucky. He became Professor of English at Louisiana, Minnesota, and Yale, and established an international reputation with his novel, *All the King's Men* (1943, filmed 1949). He also wrote several other novels, short stories, and volumes of poetry.

Warren a male first name, after the surname. [of Norman origin]

warren *noun* 1 an underground labyrinth of interconnecting tunnels linking numerous rabbit burrows. 2 an overcrowded dwelling or district. 3 any maze of passages. [from Old French *warenne*]

War Requiem a choral work by Benjamin Britten (Op 66, 1962). It comprises settings of nine of Wilfred Owen's poems interpolated into Britten's version of the Requiem Mass.

Warrington POP (1981) 83 000, an industrial town in Warrington district, Cheshire, NW central England. It lies on the R Mersey, 25km/16mi SW of Manchester, and was designated a 'new town' in 1968.

warrior *noun* 1 a skilled fighting man, especially of earlier times. 2 any distinguished soldier. 3 a person notable for stoutness of spirit or indomitability. [from Old French *werreieor*]

Warrior, HMS the name of Britain's first iron armoured warship, commissioned in 1861. Screw-propelled, steam-powered, and ship-rigged, it marked a turning point in warship evolution. In 1929, however, it was relegated to becoming a fuelling pontoon in Milford Haven. It was restored by the Maritime Trust, and is now on permanent display in Portsmouth.

Warsaw, Polish **Warszawa**, German **Warschau**, Russian **Varshava** POP (1991e) 1.7m, the river-port capital of Poland and of Greater Poland voivodship. It is situated on the R Vistula, on the Mazovian Plain. HISTORY established in the 13c; became capital of the Duchy of Mazovia in 1413, and the capital of Poland in 1596; occupied by Germany in both World Wars; Jewish ghetto established in 1940, with the uprising and death of most residents in 1943; largely destroyed in World War II; post-war reconstruction of the medieval old town followed the pre-war street pattern. The physicist and chemist Marie Curie was born here in 1867. NOTABLE FEATURES restored 14c Cathedral of St John; Royal Castle; Adam Mickiewicz Museum of Literature; Łazienkowski Palace; the city centre is a World Heritage site.

Warsaw Pact the name for the East European Mutual Assistance Treaty, signed (1955) in Warsaw by Albania, Bulgaria, Czechoslovakia, E Germany, Hungary, Poland, Romania, and the USSR. Albania withdrew in 1968. The pact established a unified military command for the armed forces of all the signatories, who were committed to giving immediate assistance to one another in the event of an attack in Europe. In part a Soviet bloc response to the formation of NATO by the West, its political purpose was demonstrated when it was used in Czechoslovakia to restore communism, allegedly endangered by the Prague Spring of Alexander Dubček. In the wake of the E European revolution in the winter of 1989–90, the pact effectively disintegrated before it was officially terminated (1991).

warship *noun* a ship equipped with guns, etc for naval battles.

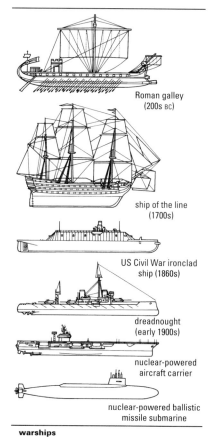

Roman galley
(200s BC)

ship of the line
(1700s)

US Civil War ironclad
ship (1860s)

dreadnought
(early 1900s)

nuclear-powered
aircraft carrier

nuclear-powered ballistic
missile submarine

warships

wart *noun* 1 a small and usually hard benign growth with a horny surface, found on the skin, especially of the fingers, hands, and face, and transmitted by a virus. 2 a small protuberance on a plant surface or the skin of an animal.
— **warts and all** *colloq.* with any blemishes or defects remaining.
[from Anglo-Saxon *wearte*]

warthog *noun* a hairy wild pig of Africa, which has wart-like lumps on its face, and two tusks.

warthog

wartime *noun* a period during which a war is going on.

Warton, Joseph (1722–1800) English literary critic, born in Dunsfold, Surrey. He was headmaster of Winchester College (1766–93), and wrote various poetic works including *Odes* (1746). He is best known for his Classical translations and critical works, which gained him a high reputation.

Warwick, Richard Neville, Earl of, also called **the Kingmaker** (1428–71) English soldier and politician. A Yorkist supporter during the first phase of the Wars of the Roses, he defeated and captured Henry VI at Northampton (1460), had his cousin, Edward of York, proclaimed king as Edward IV (1461), and then destroyed the Lancastrian army at Towton. When Edward tried to assert his independence, Warwick joined the Lancastrians, forced the King to flee to Holland, and restored Henry VI to the throne (1470). He was defeated and killed by Edward IV at the battle of Barnet.

Warwick POP (1981) 22 000, the county town of Warwickshire, central England, situated in Warwick district. It lies on the N bank of the R Avon, 15km/9mi SW of Coventry. HISTORY founded in 914; partly destroyed by fire in 1694. NOTABLE FEATURES Warwick Castle (14c); Lord Leycester Hospital (1383).

Warwicks. *abbrev.* Warwickshire.

Warwickshire POP (1992e) 497 000, a county in central England, divided into five districts. AREA 1 981sq km/765sq mi. It is bounded W by Hereford and Worcester, NW by the West Midlands, N by Staffordshire and Derbyshire, NE by Leicestershire, E by Northamptonshire, and S by Oxfordshire and Gloucestershire. It is drained by the R Avon. CHIEF TOWNS Warwick (county town), Nuneaton, Royal Leamington Spa, Rugby, Stratford-upon-Avon. ECONOMY agriculture; engineering; textiles; tourism. NOTABLE FEATURES castles at Kenilworth and Warwick.

wary *adj.* (**warier, wariest**) **1** alert; vigilant; cautious; on one's guard. **2** distrustful or apprehensive. **3** (*often* **wary of something** *or* **someone**) cautious; suspicious: *should be wary of such invitations.* [from Anglo-Saxon *wær*, to beware]

was see BE.

Wasa a four-masted Swedish warship of 1628 which foundered on her maiden voyage due to poor stability, with a loss of 50 personnel. It was salvaged in 1961 and is preserved in dry dock in Stockholm.

Wash, The a shallow inlet of the North Sea on the E coast of England. It lies between Norfolk and Lincolnshire, and is bounded by a low marshy coast. It receives the Welland, Witham, Nene, and Ouse rivers.

Wash. *abbrev.* Washington.

wash — *verb* **1** to cleanse with water and usually soap or detergent. **2** *intrans.* to cleanse oneself, or one's hands and face, with water, etc. **3** *intrans.* said of a fabric or dye to withstand washing without change or damage. **4** *trans., intrans.* (*usually* **wash** *or* **wash something off, out**, *etc*) *said of dirt or a stain* to be removed, or remove it, through washing. **5** *said of an animal* to lick itself, its young, etc clean. **6** to moisten or flush (eg an injured part) with liquid. **7** (*usually* **wash against** *or* **over something**) *said of a river, the sea, waves, etc* to flow against or over a place, land-feature, etc. **8 a** (*usually* **wash something down** *or* **away**) *said of flowing water* to sweep objects along with it. **b** (*usually* **wash down** *or* **away**) *said of substances, etc* to be swept along by water. **9** *said of flowing water* to gouge out (a channel, etc) in the landscape. **10** to apply watercolour thinly to (a surface, eg a wall). **11** *intrans. colloq.* to stand the test; to bear investigation: *that excuse won't wash.* **12** *Mining* to separate (ore) from earth with a flow of water. **13** *literary* to spread over: *washed with the pale light of morning.* — *noun* **1** the process

of washing or being washed. **2** this process undertaken by a laundry. **3** a quantity of clothes, etc for washing, or just washed. **4** the breaking of waves against something; the sound of this. **5** the rough water or disturbed air left by a ship or aircraft. **6** a lotion or other preparation for cleansing or washing. **7** kitchen slops or brewery waste, etc for giving to pigs; pigswill. **8** a thin application of water colour.
— **be washed out 1** *colloq., said of a person* to be worn out and faded-looking. **2** *said of fabric* to be faded through washing. **3** *said of an outdoor occasion, eg a sports match* to be cancelled because of rain or other bad weather.
be washed up *colloq.* **1** *said of a person* to be exhausted and incapable of further productivity. **2** *said of plans, etc* to have come to nothing.
come out in the wash to turn out satisfactorily in the end.
wash something down 1 to wash walls, etc from top to bottom. **2** to ease a pill down one's throat, or accompany food, with a drink.
wash one's hands of something *or* **someone** to abandon responsibility for them.
wash up *or* **wash something up** to wash dishes.
[from Anglo-Saxon *wæscan*]

washable *adj.* able to be washed without damage.

washbasin *or* **washhand basin** *noun* a shallow sink in which to wash one's face and hands.

washcloth *noun North Amer.* a facecloth or flannel.

washed-out *adj.* **1** *colloq., said of a person* worn out and faded-looking. **2** *said of fabric* faded through washing.

washed-up *adj. colloq., said of a person* exhausted and incapable of further productivity.

washer *noun* **1** *combining form* a machine for washing: *a dishwasher.* **2** a flat ring of rubber or metal for keeping a joint tight, or one of linen for reinforcing the punched holes in ring-binder paper.

washerwoman *noun Hist.* a woman paid to wash clothes.

washhouse *noun Hist.* **1** an outhouse or basement room for washing clothes. **2** a public building for washing clothes in.

washing *noun* clothes to be, or which have just been washed.

washing-machine *noun* a machine for washing clothes.

washing-powder *noun* powdered detergent for washing clothes.

washing soda sodium carbonate crystals, used for washing and cleaning.

Washington, Booker T(aliaferro) (1856–1915) US black leader and educationalist, born a slave in Franklin Co, Virginia. After emancipation (1865), he became a teacher, writer, and speaker on black problems. In 1881 he was appointed principal of the newly-opened Tuskegee Institute, Alabama, and built it up into a major centre of black education. He won white support by his acceptance of the separation of blacks and whites and encouraged blacks to focus on economic rather than social or political equality. His policies were repudiated by the 20c civil rights movement.

Washington, Denzel (1954–) US film actor, born in Mount Vernon, New York. After some television work he made his feature film début in *Carbon Copy* (1981). His role as Steve Biko in *Cry Freedom* (1987) was acclaimed and he won a Best Supporting Oscar for his role in *Glory* (1989). Later appearances include *Malcolm X* (1992) and *Philadelphia* (1993).

Washington, George (1732–99) US soldier and statesman, the first President of the USA, born in Bridges Creek, Virginia. After an informal education, he worked as a surveyor, and first fought in the campaigns of the French and Indian War (1754–63). He then managed the family estate at Mount Vernon, Virginia, became active in politics, and represented Virginia in both the first (1744) and second (1775) Continental Congresses. As commander of American forces he displayed great powers as a strategist and leader of men. Following reverses in the New York area, he retreated through New Jersey and inflicted notable defeats on the enemy at Trenton and Princeton (1777). He suffered defeats at Brandywine and Germantown, but held his army together through the winter of 1777–8 at Valley Forge. After the alliance with France (1778), he forced the surrender of Lord Cornwallis at Yorktown (1781). He then retired to Mount Vernon, and sought to secure a strong government by constitutional means. In 1787 he presided over the Constitutional Convention and became President. Having remained neutral while political parties were formed, he eventually joined the Federalist Party, and retired in 1797.

Washington POP (1990) 5.1m, a state in NW USA, divided into 39 counties. AREA 176 473sq km/68 119sq mi. It is bounded to the N by Canada (British Columbia), NW by the Strait of Juan de Fuca, and W by the Pacific Ocean. Washington is known as the 'Evergreen State'. PHYSICAL DESCRIPTION rivers include the Columbia, Snake, Okanogan, Sanpoil, and

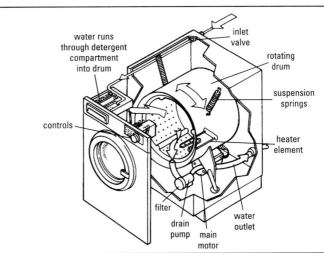

water runs through detergent compartment into drum — inlet valve — rotating drum — suspension springs — heater element — controls — filter — drain pump — main motor — water outlet

washing-machine

Yakima; Olympic Peninsula with the Olympic Mts in the NW (Mt Olympus 2 428m); the highest point is Mt Rainier (4 395m); Mt Saint Helens Volcano (2 549m) in the Cascade Range lies to the SW (erupted in 1980), and North Cascades National Park is in the N. There is a substantial Native American population and there are several reservations in the state. HISTORY Spanish and British explorers visited the coast in the 18c; first settled by Europeans in the late 18c as part of Oregon Territory, a prosperous fur-trading area; Britain and the USA quarrelled over the region until the international boundary was fixed by treaty in 1846 to lie along the 49th parallel; it became a territory in 1853 and joined the Union in 1889, as the 42nd state; after the arrival of the railway in 1887, the state developed through lumbering and fishing; Seattle was an important supply point during the Alaskan gold rush of 1897–9. CAPITAL Olympia. CHIEF TOWNS Seattle, Tacoma, Edmonds, Bellingham. ECONOMY apples (the nation's largest crop); wheat; livestock; dairy produce; aircraft, aerospace; oil refining; food processing; mining (wide range of minerals); a major tourist area.

Washington, DC POP (1990) 3.9m, the capital of the USA, co-extensive with the District of Columbia. It is situated between Maryland and Virginia, on the E bank of the Potomac R, at its junction with the Anacostia R. The city is the US legislative, administrative, and judicial centre. The Federal Government provides most of the city's employment. HISTORY the site was chosen in 1790 by George Washington and planned by Pierre L'Enfant; occupied by the Federal Government in 1800; sacked and burned by the British in 1814.

Washington Monument a marble column in honour of George Washington, designed by Robert Mills (1781–1855) and erected (1848–84) in Washington, DC. The tower, which is 169m high, incorporates many blocks of stone bearing inscriptions from the states, foreign governments, or organizations who donated them.

Washington Square a novel by Henry James (1881). It is set in New York and describes the unhappy life of Catherine Sloper, a plain heiress.

washing-up noun 1 washing dishes after a meal, etc. 2 dishes for washing.

wash leather a chamois leather.

washout noun 1 colloq. a failure or flop. 2 a rained-off event, eg a match.

washroom noun North Amer. a lavatory.

washstand noun Hist. a small table in a bedroom for holding a jug and basin for washing oneself.

washy adj. (**washier, washiest**) colloq. 1 said of a drink watery; weak. 2 feeble; lacking liveliness or vigour. 3 said of colours faded-looking or pallid.

wasn't contr. was not.

WASP abbrev. North Amer. often derog. White Anglo-Saxon Protestant.

wasp noun any of numerous stinging insects having slender bodies and narrow waists, belonging to the same order (Hymenoptera) as bees and ants, and found worldwide. They include both social and solitary species. [from Anglo-Saxon wæsp]
◇ Social wasps usually bear black-and-yellow stripes, and the females inflict painful stings. They include the hornet and the well-known common wasp that appears in late summer. Such wasps use wood fibres and saliva to build intricate nests of wood pulp, which are sometimes found in hollow trees or hanging freely from branches, but are most commonly built below ground or under the roofs of buildings. The social organization of wasps is very similar to that of bees, the nest being dominated by a fertile egg-laying queen, while many workers maintain the nest and feed the young larvae. Males and new queens appear

in late summer, and all the workers die in the autumn, only the newly-mated queens surviving to the following year. The adult common wasp feeds on nectar and ripe fruit, but the developing larvae are fed on other insects and spiders.

waspish adj. sharp-tongued; caustic.

Wasps, The 1 a play by Aristophanes (422 BC). It is a satire on the Athenians' supposed passion for litigation, told through the story of one dog prosecuting another for stealing a piece of cheese. 2 an orchestral suite with an overture (1912), arranged from incidental music for the play (1909) by Ralph Vaughan Williams.

wasp waist a slender waist.

wasp-waisted adj. having a slender waist.

wassail noun old use 1 a festive bout of drinking. 2 a toast made at such an occasion. [from Norse ves heill, be in good health]

wast a form of the past tense of the verb be used with the pronoun thou.

wastage noun 1 the process of wasting; loss through wasting. 2 the amount so lost. 3 loss or reduction through use, natural decay, etc. 4 (also **natural wastage**) reduction of staff through retirement or resignation, as distinct from dismissal or redundancy.

waste — verb 1 to use or spend purposelessly, extravagantly, or to too little useful effect; to squander. 2 to fail to use or make the best of (an opportunity, etc). 3 to throw away unused. 4 to offer (advice, sympathy, etc) where it is unheeded or unappreciated: shall not waste any more sympathy on them. 5 trans., intrans. (also **waste away**) to lose or cause to lose flesh or strength. 6 old use to devastate (territory); to lay waste. — adj. 1 rejected as useless or excess to requirements. 2 said of ground lying unused, uninhabited, or uncultivated. 3 Physiol. denoting material excreted from the body in the urine or faeces. — noun 1 the act, or an instance, of wasting; the condition of being wasted. 2 failure to take advantage of something: a waste of talent. 3 material that is no longer needed and must be disposed of, eg household waste, nuclear waste. 4 refuse; rubbish. 5 Physiol. matter excreted from the body. 6 a devastated or barren region: reduced to a muddy waste. 7 (often **wastes**) a vast tract of uncultivated land, expanse of ocean, etc: the Arctic wastes.
— **go** or **run to waste** to be wasted.
lay something waste to devastate an area, etc. [from Old French wast, guast]

waste disposal the depositing of waste from domestic, industrial, or agricultural sources, the environmental consequences of which are a source of major concern.
◇ The most commonly used methods of waste disposal are burial in landfill sites (consisting of a natural hollow or pit excavated for the purpose), dumping at sea, incineration (burning), and the production of fuel pellets, derived from refuse, which can be used as an energy source. In some heavily urbanized regions there is now a serious shortage of landfill sites, and waste must be transported long distances. Many precautions must be taken during the disposal of toxic and hazardous substances, eg radioactive waste, in order to avoid pollution of water, air, or soil. Recycling is an alternative to the disposal of some waste products, eg paper, glass, scrap metal, and certain plastics.

wasteful adj. causing waste; extravagant.

Waste Land, The a poem by T S Eliot (1922). It offers a symbolic picture of the chaos and disillusion in Europe after World War I.

wasteland noun a desolate and barren region.

waste paper paper discarded as rubbish.

waste-paper basket or **waste-paper bin** a basket or other container for waste paper and other office or household waste.

waste pipe a pipe carrying waste material or waste water from a sink, etc.

waste product 1 a useless by-product of a manufacturing process, etc. 2 a substance excreted from the body during the metabolic and physiological processes.

waster noun an idler, good-for-nothing, or wastrel.

wastrel noun an idle spendthrift; a good-for-nothing.

Watauga Association an agreement (1772) among settlers of present-day NE Tennessee, USA, to establish civil government in the absence of regular institutions, and to obtain land directly from the Native Americans rather than from the British Crown.

watch — verb 1 trans., intrans. to look at or focus one's attention on (someone or something moving, doing something, etc). 2 trans., intrans. to pass time looking at (television, a programme, entertainment, sports event, etc). 3 to guard, look after, or keep an eye on. 4 to keep track of, follow, or monitor: watch developments in the Middle East. 5 to keep (eg a building or person) under observation or surveillance. 6 (**watch something** or **watch for something**) to await one's chance, opportunity, etc. 7 to keep checking on, in case controlling measures or adjustments are necessary. 8 (**watch oneself**) colloq. to take care in one's behaviour or actions. 9 to pay proper attention to: watch where you're going! 10 to take care: watch you don't slip. — noun 1 a small instrument for telling the time, usually worn strapped to the wrist or in the waistcoat pocket. 2 the activity or duty of watching or guarding: keep watch / stayed on watch. 3 Naut. any of the four-hour shifts during which particular crew members are on duty; those on duty in any shift. 4 old use a body of sentries on look-out duty; a watchman or body of watchmen.
— **keep a watch on something** or **someone** to keep them under observation.
on the watch for something seeking or looking out for it.
watch it! be careful!
watch out to be careful.
watch out for something or **someone** to be on one's guard against them; to look out for them.
watch over someone or **something** to guard, look after, or tend to them.
[from Anglo-Saxon wæccan or wacian, to watch]

watchdog noun 1 a dog kept to guard premises, etc. 2 a person or group of people guarding against unacceptable standards, behaviour, etc.

watchful adj. alert, vigilant, and wary.

watchfully adv. in a watchful way.

watchfulness noun being watchful.

watching brief an instruction to a barrister to follow a case on behalf of a client not directly involved.

watchmaker noun a person who makes and repairs watches and clocks.

watchman noun a man employed to guard premises at night.

watchnight service a church service lasting through midnight on Christmas Eve or New Year's Eve.

watchtower noun a tower from which a sentry keeps watch.

watchword noun 1 a catchphrase encapsulating the principles, or used to inspire the members, of a party, group, profession, etc. 2 old use a password.

water — noun 1 (FORMULA. H_2O) a colourless odourless tasteless liquid that freezes to form ice at 0°C and boils to form steam at 100°C, at normal atmospheric pressure. 2 (also **waters**) an expanse of this; a sea, lake, river, etc. 3 (**waters**) the sea round a country's coasts, considered part of its territory. 4 the level or state of the tide: at high/low water. 5 a solution of a substance in

water: *rose water.* **6** (**waters**) water at a spa, etc, containing minerals and formerly considered good for one's health. **7** *Physiol.* any of several fluids secreted by the body, especially urine. **8** (**waters**) the amniotic fluid surrounding the fetus in the womb. **9** the degree of brilliance and transparency of a diamond. — *verb* **1** to wet, soak, or sprinkle with water. **2** to irrigate (land). **3** to dilute (wine, etc). **4** *intrans. said of the mouth* to produce saliva in response to a stimulus activated by the expectation of food. **5** *intrans. said of the eyes* to fill with tears in response to irritation. **6** *trans., intrans.* to let (animals) drink, or (of animals) to drink: *fed and watered.* **7** to give a wavy appearance to the surface of, by wetting and pressing: *watered silk.*
— **by water** by ship.
hold water to prove sound; to be valid.
in deep water in trouble, danger, or difficulty.
like water *colloq.* in large quantities; freely; lavishly: *spending money like water.*
make one's mouth water to make one's saliva flow; to stimulate one's appetite for something.
of the first water of the highest class; first-class; prize.
pass water to urinate.
test the water *or* **waters** to test for a response to an intended course of action.
throw cold water on something *colloq.* to be discouraging or unenthusiastic about an idea, etc.
tread water to keep oneself afloat and upright in deep water, gently moving one's legs and arms to maintain the position.
under water under the surface of the water.
water something down 1 to dilute or thin it with water. **2** to reduce the impact of something; to make it less controversial or offensive.
water under the bridge experiences that are past and done with.
[from Anglo-Saxon *wæter*]
◇ Water is the most abundant liquid on Earth, covering about 70 per cent of the Earth's surface (in liquid or solid form). It is a good solvent for many substances, especially ionic compounds, eg salts, and it has a high heat capacity. Whereas most liquids freeze to form a denser solid, water is most dense at 4°C, when it is still liquid, and then expands as it freezes, as a result of which ice floats. Water occurs in the tissues of all living organisms, and is the main component of body fluids such as blood and lymph. It represents about 66 per cent of human body weight, and humans can only survive without water for a few days. Water is formed by burning hydrocarbon fuels or hydrogen in air, or by allowing an acid to react with a base or an alcohol. It can be broken down into hydrogen and oxygen by electrolysis.

Water-Babies, The, in full *The Water-Babies, A Fairy Tale for a Land-Baby* a children's story by Charles Kingsley (1862–3). It describes the fantastic underwater adventures of a young chimney-sweep.

water bed a waterproof mattress filled with water, or a bed equipped with this.

water biscuit a plain crisp biscuit made from water and flour, eaten with cheese, etc.

water boatman a predatory aquatic bug, distributed worldwide, that swims upside-down in water, using its paddle-like hindlegs. Its forelegs are used to grasp prey.

waterborne *adj.* carried by water.

water boatman

water buffalo an important domestic animal belonging to the cattle family, native to India, Sri Lanka, and SE Asia. It may be black, grey, pink, or white in colour, and has huge ridged horns that curve outwards and upwards. It is noted for its docility, and it provides meat and milk, the skin being used for leather. Wild water buffalo have black coats, are much more aggressive, and live in small herds in swampy areas or by rivers.

water bus a passenger boat sailing regularly across a lake, along a river, etc.

water cannon a device that sends out a powerful jet of water, used for dispersing crowds.

Water-carrier *noun* (**the Water-carrier**) the constellation and sign of the zodiac Aquarius.

water chestnut 1 an aquatic annual plant (*Trapa natans*), native to Asia, Africa, and warm parts of Europe. It produces white flowers and triangular woody fruits, which are rich in starch and fat, and are an important food source in many parts of Asia. **2** a sedge (*Eleocharis tuberosa*), grown in China, that produces edible tubers. **3** the tuber of this plant, eaten as a vegetable, especially in Chinese and Japanese cuisine.

water closet *formal, technical* a lavatory whose pan is mechanically flushed with water.
◇ The first widely used flushing lavatory system was developed by Alexander Cummings in the 1770s. David Bostel developed the more efficient ballcock valve system in 1889, and it is this system which is found in most modern lavatories.

watercolour *noun* **1** a paint thinned with water, not oil. **2** a painting done in such paint.

water-colourist *noun* an artist who works in water colours.

water-cooled *adj., said of an engine, etc* cooled by circulating water.

watercourse *noun* the bed or channel of a stream, river, or canal.

watercress *noun* a cress that grows in water, whose sharp-tasting leaves are used in salads, etc.

water cycle *Chem.* the continuous movement of water between the oceans, the atmosphere, and the land, mainly involving such processes as evaporation and precipitation (eg in the form of rain or snow), and also including interactions with living organisms.

water-diviner *noun* a person who detects underground sources of water, usually with a divining-rod; a dowser.

waterfall *noun* a sudden interruption in the course of a river or stream where water falls more or less vertically for a considerable distance, eg over the edge of a plateau, or where overhanging softer rock has been eroded away.

Waterford POP (1991) 42 000, the capital of Waterford county, Munster province, S Irish Republic. It is a seaport lying at the mouth of the R Suir. NOTABLE FEATURES remains of city walls; cathedral (1793); Blackfriars Priory (1226).

Waterford, Gaelic **Phort Láirge** POP (1991) 51 000, a county in Munster province, S Irish Republic. AREA 1 839sq km/710sq mi. It is bounded S by the Atlantic Ocean. PHYSICAL DESCRIPTION coastal inlets at Youghal, Dungarvan, Tramore, and Waterford (capital); watered by the Suir and Barrow rivers; the Knockmealdown Mts lie in the W. ECONOMY apple growing; cattle; glass making (Waterford crystal); tourism, with popular resorts such as Tramore on the S coast.

waterfowl *noun* **1** a bird living on or near water, especially a swimming bird such as a duck. **2** (*pl.*) swimming game birds in general.

waterfront *noun* the buildings or part of a town along the edge of a river, lake, or the sea.

Watergate a US political scandal (1972–4) that led to the first resignation of a president in US history (Richard Nixon, in office 1968–74). It was named from the hotel and office complex in Washington, DC, the home of the Democratic Party headquarters, where, during the 1972 presidential campaign, burglars were caught whose connections were traced to the White House and to the Committee to Re-elect the President. Investigations by the *Washington Post*, a grand jury, and two special prosecutors revealed the possible involvement of some high officials, and that Nixon himself was aware of illegal measures to cover up this implication.

waterglass *noun* a solution of potassium or sodium silicate in water, used as protective coating, an adhesive, and, especially formerly, for preserving eggs.

waterhole *noun* a pool or spring in a desert area, where animals can drink.

water ice sweetened fruit purée frozen and served as a dessert; a sorbet.

watering-can *noun* a water-container with a handle and spout, for watering plants.

watering-hole *noun* **1** a waterhole. **2** *facetious* a public house.

Watering Place, The a painting by Thomas Gainsborough (1777, Tate, London).

watering-place *noun* Hist. a spa or other place where people go to drink mineral water or bathe.

water jump in a steeplechase, etc, a jump over a water-filled ditch.

water level 1 the height reached by the surface of a body of water. **2** the level below which the ground is waterlogged; a water table. **3** a waterline.

Water Lilies a series of paintings by Claude Monet (1899–1926). Some examples are in the Musée d'Orsay, Paris.

water lily any of various aquatic perennial plants of the genera *Nymphaea* or *Nuphar*, found in both tropical and temperate regions, with large flat circular leaves and conspicuous white, pink, red, or yellow bowl-shaped flowers that float on the surface of still or very slow-moving water.

Highest Waterfalls		
Name	Height	m
Angel (upper fall), Venezuela		979
Itatinga, Brazil		628
Cuquenan, Guyana–Venezuela		610
Ormeli, Norway		563
Tysse, Norway		533
Pilao, Brazil		524
Ribbon, USA		491
Vestre Mardola, Norway		468
Roraima, Guyana		457?
Cleve-Garth, New Zealand		450?

waterline *noun* the level reached by the water on the hull of a floating vessel.

waterlogged *adj.* **1** saturated with water. **2** *said of a boat* so filled or saturated with water as to be unmanageable.

Waterloo, Battle of the final defeat (18 Jun 1815) of Napoleon I, which marked the Emperor's last bid for power in the Hundred Days and ended the Napoleonic Wars. It was a hard-fought battle in which Field Marshal Blücher's Prussian force arrived at the climax to support the Duke of Wellington's mixed Allied force.

Waterloo *noun* the challenge that finally defeats one: *meet one's Waterloo*. [after the battle of Waterloo]

water main a large underground pipe carrying a public water supply.

watermark — *noun* **1** the limit reached by the sea at high or low tide. **2** a manufacturer's distinctive mark in paper, visible when the paper is held up to the light. — *verb* to impress (paper) with a watermark.

water meadow a meadow kept fertile by periodic flooding from a stream.

water melon a melon native to Africa, with dark green coarse skin and red flesh.

watermill *noun* a mill whose machinery is driven by a water wheel.

Water Music a collection of music by George Frideric Handel (1715 or 1717), said to have been written either as a 'peace offering' for George I (elector of the Hanoverian court) because Handel had taken frequent leave to visit London, or for a royal party held on the R Thames. The first group of pieces is in F major and features horn music; the second, in D major, uses trumpets; and the third, in G major and minor, chamber music.

water of crystallization *Chem.* water that is chemically incorporated in definite proportions in crystalline compounds, and can be removed by heating. Such compounds are called *hydrates*. For example, copper(II) sulphate, $CuSO_4.5H_2O$, has five molecules of water of crystallization associated with each molecule of copper(II) sulphate.

water pistol a toy pistol that fires squirts of water.

water pollution *Environ.* the contamination of seas, lakes, rivers, and other bodies of water with artificial fertilizers, pesticides, sewage, industrial waste, and other materials that are considered to be detrimental to living organisms.

water polo a seven-a-side ball game for swimmers; a similar game for canoeists.
◇ When played in a swimming pool, the object is to score goals by propelling the ball into the opposing team's goal at the end of the pool. It was originally known as 'football in water'.

water power the power generated by moving water (including tides and waves) that is used to drive machinery, eg turbines for generating hydroelectricity.

waterproof — *adj.* impenetrable by water; treated or coated so as to resist water. — *verb* to treat so as to make waterproof. — *noun* a raincoat.

water rat *or* **water vole** a swimming rodent inhabiting stream banks.

water rate a charge made for the use of the public water supply.

watershed *noun* 1 the high land separating two river basins. 2 a crucial point after which events take a different turn.

waterside *noun* the edge of a river, lake, or sea.

water ski a ski on which to glide over water, towed by a powered boat.

water-ski *verb intrans.* (**water-skis**, **water-skied** *or* **water-ski'd**) to travel on water skis.

water-skiing *noun* the sport or activity of travelling on water skis.

water-softener *noun* a substance or device used in water to remove minerals, especially calcium, that cause hardness and prevent lathering.

waterspout *noun* *Meteorol.* a tornado that occurs over open water, mainly in the tropics, and consists of a rotating column of water and spray. Waterspouts are potentially hazardous to shipping.

water table *Geol.* the level below which porous rocks are saturated with groundwater.

watertight *adj.* 1 so well sealed as to be impenetrable by water. 2 *said of an argument, etc* without any apparent flaw or weakness; completely sound.

water tower a tower supporting an elevated water tank, from which water can be distributed at uniform pressure.

water vapour water in the form of droplets suspended in the atmosphere, especially where

evaporation has occurred at a temperature below boiling point.

water vole see WATER RAT.

waterway *noun* a channel, eg a canal or river, used by ships or smaller boats.

waterwheel *noun* a wheel that is turned by the force of flowing or falling water on blades or buckets around its rim, formerly used as a source of energy to drive machinery, etc, but now largely superseded by the turbine.

water wings an inflatable device that supports the chest and terminates in wing-like projections, used by children learning to swim.

waterworks *noun* 1 (*sing., pl.*) an installation where water is purified and stored for distribution to an area. 2 (*pl.*) *euphemistic* one's bladder and urinary system. 3 (*pl.*) *facetious* tears; weeping.

watery *adj.* 1 of, or consisting of, water: *the watery depths*. 2 containing too much water; overdiluted; weak or thin: *watery tea*. 3 *said of the sun or sunlight* weak and pale, as when alternating with showers. 4 *said of eyes* inclined to water. 5 *said of a smile, etc* half-hearted; feeble.

Watford POP (1992e) 76 000, a residential and industrial town in Watford district, Hertfordshire, SE England. It lies 26km/16mi NW of London and forms part of the Greater London urban area.

Watson, James Dewey (1928–) US biologist, born in Chicago. Working in Cambridge in 1951, he deduced with Francis Crick and Maurice Wilkins the two-stranded helical structure of DNA, the molecule that carries genetic information in living cells; for this work they shared the 1962 Nobel Prize for Physiology or Medicine. He later became professor at Harvard and Director of the Cold Spring Harbor Laboratory in New York.

Watson, Dr John the impassive, good-hearted sidekick to Sherlock Holmes in Arthur Conan Doyle's *A Study in Scarlet* and other stories.

Watson, Tom (Thomas Sturges) (1949–) US golfer, born in Kansas City, Missouri. He turned professional in 1971 and has won the British Open five times (1975, 1977, 1980, 1982–3), the US Open (1982), and the Masters (1977, 1981).

Watson-Watt, Sir Robert Alexander (1892–1973) Scottish physicist, born in Brechin. By 1935 he had perfected his invention of 'RAdio Detection And Ranging', abbreviated to 'radar', allowing aircraft to be located through the reflection of radio waves. He became scientific adviser to the air ministry in 1940.

Watt, James (1736–1819) Scottish engineer and inventor, born in Greenock. Employed as a mathematical instrument-maker, on surveys for canals and various civil engineering projects, he had begun to investigate steam engines by 1759. His improved model of Thomas Newcomen's engine, incorporating a separate condenser, soon superseded Newcomen's machine as a pumping engine, and many more related inventions followed, including the design of a steam locomotive. The SI unit of power is named after him.

watt *noun* (SYMBOL **W**) *Physics* the SI unit of power, defined as the power that gives rise to the production of energy at the rate of one joule per second. Electrical power is equal to the current (in amperes) multiplied by the voltage (in volts). [named after the UK engineer James Watt]

wattage *noun* electrical power expressed in watts.

Watteau, (Jean) Antoine (1684–1721) French Rococo painter, born in Valenciennes. He worked as a scene painter and a copyist in Paris. His early canvases were mostly military scenes, but he made his reputation with the mytho-

logical *L'Embarquement pour l'Île de Cythère* (Embarkation for the island of Cythera, 1717). He is also known for his *Fêtes galantes* (scenes of gallantry), quasi-pastoral idylls in court dress which became fashionable in high society.

watt hour a unit of electrical energy, the amount of work done by one watt in one hour.

wattle *noun* 1 rods, branches, etc forming a framework for a wall, especially when interwoven. 2 a loose fold of skin hanging from the throat of certain birds, fish, and lizards. 3 any of various Australian acacia trees.

wattle

wattle and daub wattle plastered with mud, as a building material.

wattmeter *noun* *Physics* an instrument for measuring the power consumption (usually in watt-hours or units) in an electric circuit. [named after James Watt]

Waugh, Auberon (Alexander) (1939–) English journalist and novelist, the eldest son of Evelyn Waugh, born in Pixton Park, Dulverton, Somerset. He joined the *Daily Telegraph* in 1960, the same year he published his first novel, *The Foxglove Saga*. He has contributed to most national papers (eg the *New Statesman* and the *Spectator*) as well as *Private Eye* (1970–86), and since 1986 has been editor of the *Literary Review*. His autobiography, *Will This Do?*, appeared in 1991.

Waugh, Evelyn (Arthur St John) (1903–66) English writer, born in London, the father of Auberon Waugh. He quickly established a reputation with such social satirical novels as *Decline and Fall* (1928), *Vile Bodies* (1930), and *Scoop* (1938). He became a Roman Catholic in 1930, and his later books display a more serious attitude, as seen in the religious theme of *Brideshead Revisited* (1945), and his war trilogy, beginning with *Men at Arms* (1952).

wave — *verb* 1 *intrans., trans.* to move (one's hand) to and fro in greeting, farewell, or as a signal; to hold up and move (some other object) in this way for this purpose: *waved her hand to her father / waved their handkerchiefs*. 2 to say (especially goodbye) in this way: *waved them farewell*. 3 (**wave someone off**) to see them off on a journey. 4 *trans., intrans.* to move or cause to move or sway to and fro. 5 to direct with a gesture of the hand: *waved the waiter away*. 6 to put a gentle curl into (hair) by artificial means. — *noun* 1 any of a series of moving ridges on the surface of the sea or some other body of water; such a ridge as it arches and breaks on the shore, etc. 2 *Physics* a regularly repeated disturbance or displacement in a medium (eg water or air). Both electromagnetic radiation (eg light and radio waves) and sound travel as waves. 3 any of the circles of disturbance moving outwards from the site of a shock such as an earthquake. 4 a loose soft curl, or series of such curls, in the hair. 5 a surge or sudden feeling: *a wave of nausea*. 6 a sudden increase in something: *a wave of car thefts / a heat wave*. 7 an advancing body of people: *waves of invaders*. 8 any of a series of curves in an upward-and-

downward-curving line or outline. **9** an act of waving the hand, etc.
— **wave someone** *or* **something aside** to dismiss them as unimportant or intrusive.
[from Anglo-Saxon *wafian*, to wave]
◇ The three main properties of a wave are its *amplitude*, its *wavelength*, and its *frequency*. The amplitude is the maximum displacement of the wave, ie the height measured from the crest of a wave to a trough. The wavelength is the distance between two consecutive waves, and the frequency is the number of peaks or troughs of the wave that pass a particular point over a period of one second.

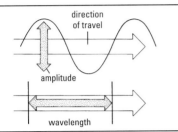

properties of a wave

waveband *noun Radio* a range of frequencies in the electromagnetic spectrum occupied by radio or television broadcasting transmission of a particular type. Broadcasting systems that require a large waveband, eg FM radio, use higher frequencies, which have a larger frequency range.

wavelength *noun Physics* **1** the distance between two successive peaks or two successive troughs of a wave. It is equal to the velocity of the wave divided by its frequency, ie for waves of a given velocity, the higher the frequency the shorter the wavelength. The wavelengths of electromagnetic waves range from several kilometres for some radio waves to less than 10^{-10}m for gamma radiation. Visible light has wavelengths in the range 7×10^7m (for red light) to 4×10^{-7}m (for violet light). **2** the length of the radio wave used by a particular broadcasting station.
— **on the same wavelength** *said of two or more people* speaking or thinking in a way that is mutually compatible.

Wavell (of Eritrea and of Winchester), Archibald Percival Wavell, 1st Earl (1883–1950) English soldier, born in Winchester, Hampshire. He served in South Africa and India, became Lord Allenby's Chief-of-Staff in Palestine, and in 1939 was given the Middle East Command. He defeated the Italians in N Africa, but failed against General Rommel, and in 1941 was transferred to India, where he became Viceroy (1943). He was made field marshal (1943), earl (1947), Constable of the Tower (1948), and Lord-Lieutenant of London (1949).

wave power *or* **wave energy** energy or power derived from the movement of the ocean waves, especially when used for the generation of electricity.

waver *verb intrans.* (**wavered, wavering**) **1** to falter, lessen, weaken, etc. **2** to hesitate through indecision. **3** *said of the voice* to become unsteady through emotion, etc. **4** to shimmer or flicker. **5** to vary or fluctuate between extremes: *wavering between elation and despair.* [from Norse *vafra*, to flicker]

Waverley a novel by Sir Walter Scott (1814). His first, it describes the adventures of young English officer Edward Waverley in the Scottish Highlands during the Jacobite Rebellion.

Wave Rock a unique rock formation in S central Western Australia, near the town of Hyden. It is a wave-shaped granite formation eroded by water and wind, and is estimated to be 2 700m years old.

wavy *adj.* (**wavier, waviest**) **1** *said of hair* falling in waves. **2** *said of a line or outline* curving alternately upward and downward.

wax¹ — *noun* **1** *Chem.* any of a wide variety of solid or semi-solid organic compounds that are typically shiny, easily moulded when warm, and insoluble in water. Mineral waxes, eg paraffin wax, consist of mixtures of hydrocarbons, and are used in candles, polishes, and protective coatings. Natural waxes produced by plants or animals, eg beeswax, and the waxy coatings of certain leaves and fruits, are esters of fatty acids. **2** beeswax. **3** sealing-wax. **4** the sticky, yellowish matter that forms in the ears. — *verb* to use or apply a natural or mineral wax, eg prior to polishing. [from Anglo-Saxon *weax*]

wax² *verb intrans.* **1** *said of the moon* to appear larger as more of its surface is illuminated by the sun. **2** to increase in size, strength, or power. **3** *facetious* to become (eg eloquent, lyrical) in one's description of something. [from Anglo-Saxon *weaxan*, to grow]

waxen *adj.* made of, or similar to, wax.

waxwing *noun Zool.* a songbird of the N hemisphere, which has greyish-brown plumage with a black tail, and a crest on the head. In some individuals there are red wax-like tips to some of the wing feathers. It inhabits woodland and gardens, and feeds on berries and insects.

waxwork *noun* **1** a lifelike model, especially of someone celebrated, made of wax. **2** (**waxworks**) an exhibition of these.

waxy *adj.* (**waxier, waxiest**) like wax in appearance or feel.

way — *noun* **1** a route, entrance, exit, etc providing passage or access somewhere; also, the passage or access provided: *the way into the house / is this the way?* **2** the route, road, or direction taken for a particular journey: *on the way to school / are you going my way?* **3** (*often in compounds*) a track or road: *motorway / London Way.* **4** a direction: *a one-way street / a two-way radio.* **5** position: *the wrong way up.* **6** a distance in space or time: *a little way ahead / Christmas is a long way off.* **7** one's district: *if you're round our way.* **8** the route or path ahead; room to move or progress: *block someone's way / moved out of the way / clear the way for reform.* **9** a means. **10** a distinctive manner or style: *a funny way of walking.* **11** a method: *an easy way to cook fish / do it your own way.* **12** (**ways**) customs: *their ways are not ours.* **13** a characteristic piece of behaviour: *can't stand the way he ignores women.* **14** a habit or routine: *get into the way of taking regular exercise.* **15** a typical pattern or course: *it's always the way.* **16** (**his**, **her**, *etc*, **way** *or* **own way**) what one wants oneself, as opposed to what others want: *always wanting their own way.* **17** a mental approach: *different ways of looking at it.* **18** a respect: *correct in some ways.* **19** an alternative course, possibility, choice, etc: *can't have it both ways / that way we'll save money.* **20** a state or condition: *is in a bad way.* **21** scale: *is in business in a big way.* **22** (**the**, **this**, *or* **that way**) the manner or tendency of a person's feelings, wishes, etc: *if that's the way you want it / I didn't know you felt that way.* **23** used with many verbs to indicate progress: *ate their way through the food.* **24** *Naut.* headway: *made little way that day.* **25** used in indicating the number of portions something is divided into: *divided it three ways.* — *adv. colloq.* far; a long way: *way back in the 60s.*
— **be on** *or* **get on one's way** to make a start on a journey.
by the way incidentally; let me mention while I remember.
by way of ... as a form or means of ...: *he grinned by way of apology.*
by way of a place by the route that passes through it: *went by way of Lincoln.*
come someone's way *said of an opportunity, etc* to become available to them, especially unexpectedly.

give way 1 to collapse or subside. **2** to fail or break down under pressure, etc. **3** to yield to persuasion or pressure.
go out of one's way to make special efforts.
have a way with someone to be good at dealing with them: *has a way with customers.*
have a way with one *colloq.* to have an attractive manner.
have something one's own way to get what one wants with something.
in its, *etc* **own way** as far as it, etc goes; within limits: *is all right in its way.*
in no way not at all.
in the way of ... in the nature of ...: *haven't got much in the way of cash.*
lead *or* **show the way** to act as a guide or inspiration to others.
learn one's way around to accustom oneself to one's new environment, duties, etc.
look the other way to pretend not to notice something.
lose one's way to leave one's intended route by mistake.
make one's way 1 to go purposefully. **2** to progress or prosper: *making her way in life.*
make way for someone *or* **something 1** to stand aside, or make room, for them. **2** to be replaced by them.
no two ways about it that's certain; no doubt about it.
no way *slang* absolutely no possibility.
on the way out becoming unfashionable.
on the way to ... progressing towards ...: *well on the way to becoming a millionaire.*
pay one's way to pay one's own debts and living expenses.
put someone out of the way *euphemistic colloq.* to kill.
see one's way to *or* **clear to doing something** to be agreeable to it.
that's the way! a formula of encouragement or approval.
under way in motion; progressing.
[from Anglo-Saxon *weg*]

waybill *noun* a list giving details of goods and passengers being carried. [from WAY]

wayfarer *noun old use* a traveller, especially on foot. [from WAY + FARE]

wayfaring *noun, adj.* travelling, journeying by road.

Wayland in Norse, German, and Old English legends, a clever inventor, known as Wayland the Smith. He was captured by the Swedish king Nidud, lamed, and forced to work in his smithy. In English tradition, 'Wayland's Smithy' is identified with an ancient site on the Berkshire Downs.

waylay *verb* (PAST TENSE AND PAST PARTICIPLE **waylaid**) **1** to lie in wait for and ambush. **2** to wait for and delay with conversation. [from WAY + LAY²]

wayleave *noun* permission given to pass over another's ground, usually on payment of a fee. [from WAY + LEAVE²]

Wayne, John, originally **Marion Michael Morrison** (1907–79) US film actor, born in Winterset, Iowa. His first success was in *Stagecoach* (1939) and he made over 80 films, typically starring in westerns as a tough but warm-hearted gunfighter or lawman or the equivalent in war films. He won an Oscar for his role in *True Grit* (1969).

Wayne a male first name, after the surname. [from Anglo-Saxon *waegen*, cart]

Way of All Flesh, The a novel by Samuel Butler (1903). It focuses on the life of Edward Pontifex as he struggles to free himself from the religious constraints of his family.

way of life a style of living; the living of one's life according to certain principles.

Way of the World, The a play by William Congreve (1700). It is a Restoration comedy revolving around Mirabell and Millament's courtship and their attempts to gain the approval of Lady Wishfort. It explores the themes of wealth and constancy.

way-out adj. slang excitingly unusual, exotic, or new.

-ways combining form forming words denoting direction or manner: lengthways / edgeways. [from WAY¹]

ways and means methods, especially of obtaining funds; resources.

wayside — noun the edge of a road, or the area to the side of it. — adj. growing or lying near the edge of roads.

— **fall by the wayside** to fail or give up in one's attempt to do something; to drop out.

wayward adj. undisciplined, self-willed, headstrong, wilful, or rebellious. [from AWAY + -WARD]

wazir noun a vizier, a high-ranking official in Muslim countries. [from Arabic wazir]

WBA abbrev. World Boxing Association.

WBC abbrev. World Boxing Council.

WC abbrev. (PL. **WCs**, **WC's**) water closet.

W/Cdr abbrev. Wing Commander.

we pron. used as the subject of a verb: **1** to refer to oneself in company with another or others. **2** to refer to people in general: the times we live in. **3** by a royal person and by writers and editors in formal use, to refer to themselves or the authority they represent. **4** affected to mean 'you': how are we feeling today? [from Anglo-Saxon we]

WEA abbrev. Workers' Educational Association.

weak adj. **1** lacking physical strength. **2** not functioning effectively: a weak heart. **3** liable to give way: a weak link. **4** lacking power: militarily weak. **5** Commerce dropping in value: a weak dollar. **6** too easily influenced by others. **7** yielding too easily to temptation. **8** lacking full flavour: weak tea. **9** said of an argument unsound or unconvincing. **10** faint: a weak signal. **11** half-hearted: a weak smile. **12** (**weak on** or **in something**) defective in some respect; having insufficient of something. [from Norse veikr]

weaken verb (**weakened**, **weakening**) **1** trans., intrans. to make or become weaker. **2** intrans. to yield to pressure or persuasion.

weak-kneed adj. cowardly; feeble.

weakling noun **1** a physically weak person or animal. **2** someone weak in a certain respect: a moral weakling.

weak-minded adj. **1** of feeble intelligence. **2** lacking will or determination.

weak moment a lapse of self-discipline.

weakness noun **1** the condition of being weak. **2** a fault or failing. **3** (**a weakness for something**) a liking for it.

weak verb Grammar a verb inflected by the addition of a regular suffix, eg walked, and not by a change of the main vowel, as with sang and sung.

weal¹ noun a long, raised, reddened mark on the skin caused eg by a slash with a whip or sword. [a variant of WALE]

weal² noun old use welfare: the common weal. [from Anglo-Saxon wela]

Weald, The an area in Kent, Surrey, and Sussex, SE England, situated between the North and South Downs. A fertile agricultural area, it was formerly noted for its extensive woodlands which provided charcoal for the iron industry during the Middle Ages. The term often refers strictly to the area in Kent SW of the greensand ridge from Hythe through Ashford to Westerham. [from Anglo-Saxon weald, wood]

wealth noun **1** riches and property, or the possession of them. **2** abundance of resources: the country's mineral wealth. **3** a large quantity: a wealth of examples. [from Middle English welthe, from Anglo-Saxon wela WEAL²]

wealthy adj. (**wealthier**, **wealthiest**) **1** possessing riches and property; rich. **2** (**wealthy in something**) well supplied with it; rich in it: wealthy in timber.

wean¹ verb **1** to accustom (a baby) to taking food other than its mother's milk: weaned on to solid foods. **2** to break (someone) gradually of a bad habit, etc: how to wean him from drugs. [from Anglo-Saxon wenian, to accustom]

wean² noun Scot. a child. [from WEE + ane, one]

weapon noun **1** an instrument or device used to kill or injure people in a war or fight. **2** something one can use to get the better of others: patience is our best weapon. [from Anglo-Saxon wæpen]

weaponry noun weapons, armament.

wear — verb (PAST TENSE **wore**; PAST PARTICIPLE **worn**) **1** to be dressed in, or have on one's body. **2** to have (one's hair, beard, etc) cut a certain length or in a certain style. **3** to have (a certain expression). **4** intrans. said of a carpet or garment to become thin or threadbare through use. **5** to make (a hole, bare patch, etc) in something through heavy use. **6** intrans. to bear intensive use; to last in use: doesn't wear well. **7** colloq. to accept (an excuse, story, etc) or tolerate (a situation, etc). **8** to tire: worn to a frazzle. **9** (**wear on someone**) to irritate them: all that noise is very wearing on us. — noun **1** (often in compounds) clothes suitable for a certain purpose, person, occasion, etc: menswear. **2** the amount or type of use that eg clothing, carpeting, etc gets: subjected to heavy wear. **3** damage caused through use: machinery showing signs of wear.

— **wear away** or **wear something away** to become or make it thin or disappear completely through rubbing, weathering, etc.

wear down or **wear something down** to become or make it shallower or shorter through rubbing, friction, etc.

wear someone down to tire them, especially with persistent objections or demands.

wearing thin said of an excuse, etc becoming unconvincing or ineffective through over-use.

wear off said of a feeling, pain, etc to become less intense; to disappear gradually.

wear on said of time to pass: as the year wore on.

wear out or **wear something out** to become or make it unusable through use.

wear someone out to tire them utterly; to exhaust them.

wear through said of clothing, etc to develop a hole through heavy wear. [from Anglo-Saxon werian]

wearable adj. capable of being worn.

wear and tear damage sustained in the course of continual or normal use.

wearer noun a person who is wearing something.

wearily adv. with a weary manner.

weariness noun being weary.

wearing adj. exhausting.

wearisome adj. tiring, tedious, or frustrating.

weary — adj. (**wearier**, **weariest**) **1** tired out; exhausted. **2** (**weary of something**) tired by it; fed up with it. **3** tiring, dreary, or irksome. — verb **1** trans., intrans. to make or become weary. **2** intrans. (**weary of something**) to get tired of it. [from Anglo-Saxon werig]

weasel noun a small nocturnal carnivorous mammal, closely related to the stoat and found in most N temperate regions, with a slender body, short legs, and reddish-brown fur with white underparts. It feeds on rodents and small birds, and will sometimes kill animals several times its own size, eg rabbits. [from Anglo-Saxon wesle]

weather — noun the atmospheric conditions in any area at any time, with regard to sun, cloud, temperature, wind, rain, etc. — adj. Naut. on the side exposed to the wind. — verb (**weathered**,

weathering) **1** trans., intrans. to expose or be exposed to the effects of wind, sun, rain, etc; to alter or be altered in colour, texture, shape, etc through such exposure. **2** to come safely through (a storm or stormy situation). **3** Naut. to get to the windward side of (a headland, etc).

— **keep a weather eye open** to keep alert for developments.

make heavy weather of something to make unnecessarily slow and difficult progress with a task.

under the weather colloq. not in good health. [from Anglo-Saxon weder]

weatherbeaten adj. **1** said of the skin or face tanned or lined by exposure to sun and wind. **2** worn or damaged by exposure to the weather.

weatherboard noun **1** a sloping board fitted to the bottom of a door, to exclude rain. **2** any of a series of overlapping horizontal boards covering an exterior wall.

weathercock noun **1** a weathervane in the form of a farmyard cock. **2** derog. a fickle, unreliable person who frequently changes loyalties.

weathering noun Geol. the physical disintegration and chemical decomposition of rocks on or just beneath the Earth's surface, involving little or no transport of the altered rock material, which occurs as a result of exposure to wind, rain, humidity, extremes of temperature (eg frost), atmospheric oxygen, etc.

weatherman noun colloq. a person who presents the weather forecast on radio or television.

Weathermen a radical US splinter group of Students for a Democratic Society, which organized extensive bombing campaigns in 1969–70, claiming that out of the chaos a new brotherhood of man would emerge.

weatherproof adj. designed or treated so as to keep out wind and rain.

weathervane noun a revolving arrow that turns to point in the direction of the wind, having a fixed base with arms for each of the four compass points, mounted eg on a church spire.

weave¹ — verb (PAST TENSE **wove**; PAST PARTICIPLE **woven**) **1** trans., intrans. to make (cloth or tapestry) in a loom, passing threads under and over the threads of a fixed warp; to interlace (threads) in this way. **2** to construct anything (eg a basket, fence, etc) by passing flexible strips in and out between fixed canes, etc; to make by interlacing or intertwining. **3** to devise (a story, plot, etc); to work (details, facts, etc) into a story, etc. — noun the pattern or compactness of the weaving in a fabric: an open weave.

weave² verb intrans. (PAST TENSE AND PAST PARTICIPLE **weaved**) to move to and fro or wind in and out.

— **get weaving** colloq. to get busy; to hurry. [from Middle English weve]

weaver noun a person who weaves. [from Anglo-Saxon wefian]

weaverbird noun Zool. a small sparrow-like bird with a conical bill, found in Africa and Asia, that has bright plumage during the breeding season. The male builds an elaborate flask-shaped nest from strands of grass or palm fronds.

web noun **1** a network of slender threads constructed by a spider to trap insects. **2** old use a piece of weaving or tapestry on a loom. **3** a membrane connecting the toes of a swimming bird or animal. **4** Printing a continuous roll of paper fed through rollers in an offset lithographic printing process. **5** any intricate network: a web of lies, intrigue, etc. [from Anglo-Saxon webb]

Webb, James E(dwin) (1906–) US official and administrator of NASA, born in Tally Ho, North Carolina. He became head of the Bureau of the Budget under President Truman (1946–9), and later his Under-Secretary of State (1949–52). He was chosen by President Kennedy in 1961 to create in NASA an agency capable of successfully undertaking the Apollo Project, and retired from NASA in 1968, a year before the Apollo 11 landing.

Webb, Sidney (James) (1859–1947) English social reformer, historian, and economist, born in London. He became a lawyer, and joined the Fabian Society, where he wrote many powerful tracts, then in 1892 married Beatrice Potter (1858–1943), who was involved with the social problems of the time. Together they led a life of service to socialism and trade unionism, and wrote such works as their classic *History of Trade Unionism* (1894) and *English Local Government* (1906–29, 9 vols). They also started the *New Statesman* (1913). He became an MP (1922), President of the Board of Trade (1924), Dominions and Colonial Secretary (1929–30), and Colonial Secretary (1930–1).

webbed *adj.* **1** having a web. **2** *said of fingers or toes* partially joined together by a membrane of skin.

webbing *noun* strong jute or nylon fabric woven into strips for use as belts, straps, and supporting bands in upholstery.

Weber, Carl Maria (Friedrich) von (1786–1826) German composer and pianist, born near Lübeck. Encouraged by his family, he began to compose (eg *Das Waldmädchen* (1800), later remodelled as *Silvana*) and became conductor of the opera at Breslau (1804). In 1813 he settled in Prague as opera kapellmeister, and was invited by the King of Saxony to direct the German opera at Dresden (c.1816). As founder of German romantic opera, notably *Der Freischütz* (The Freeshooter, 1821), *Euryanthe* (1823), and *Oberon* (1826), he was the forerunner of Richard Wagner. He also wrote several orchestral works, piano, chamber, and church music, and many songs.

Weber, Max (1864–1920) German sociologist, born in Erfuer. His best-known work is *Die protestantische Ethik und der Geist des Kapitalismus* (The Protestant Ethic and the Spirit of Capitalism, 1904), which was a major influence on sociological theory. He also helped to draft the constitution for the Weimar Republic (1919).

Weber, Wilhelm Eduard (1804–91) German scientist, born in Wittenburg. Professor at Göttingen and Leipzig, he developed an electrodynamometer for the absolute measurement of an electric current (1845) and the mirror galvanometer (1849). His most important contribution was to determine the ratio between static and dynamic units of charge, of great importance to later theories of electromagnetism. His name is given to the SI unit of magnetic flux.

weber *noun Physics* (SYMBOL **Wb**) the SI unit of magnetic flux (the total size of a magnetic field). [named after Wilhelm Weber]

Webern, Anton (Friedrich Wilhelm) von (1883–1945) Austrian composer, born in Vienna. He was one of Arnold Schoenberg's first musical disciples and made wide use of 12-tone techniques, which led to several hostile demonstrations when his works were first performed. They include a symphony, cantatas, several short orchestral pieces, chamber music, a concerto for nine instruments, and songs, and have profoundly influenced many later composers. The Nazis banned his music, and he worked as a proof-reader during World War II, then was accidentally shot dead by a US soldier near Salzburg.

web-footed *or* **web-toed** *adj.* having webbed feet.

Webster, John (c.1580–c.1625) English dramatist, who collaborated with other Elizabethan writers, especially Thomas Dekker, but is best known for his two tragedies, *The White Devil* (1612) and *The Duchess of Malfi* (1623).

Webster, Noah (1758–1843) US lexicographer, born in Hartford, Connecticut. He became a lawyer, but returned to teaching, and achieved fame with the first part (later known as

'Webster's Spelling Book') of *A Grammatical Institute of the English Language* (1783). Political articles and pamphlets, lecturing, and journalism occupied him until 1798, when he retired to a life of literary labour in New Haven, Connecticut. He is best known for his *American Dictionary of the English Language* (1828).

Webster–Ashburton Treaty an agreement (1842) between Britain and the USA that established the boundary between NE USA and Canada, negotitated by US Secretary of State Daniel Webster and Alexander Baring, Baron Ashburton. Among specific issues were the disputed territory between Maine and New Brunswick and at the N end of Lake Champlain, the navigation rights on the St John's River, and control of the Mesabi iron deposits.

Wed *or* **Wed.** *abbrev.* Wednesday.

wed *verb* (**wedding**; PAST TENSE AND PAST PARTICIPLE **wedded, wed**) **1** *trans., intrans. old use* to marry. **2** *old use* to join in marriage. **3** (**wed one thing to** *or* **with another**) to unite or combine: *wed firmness with compassion.* [from Anglo-Saxon *weddian*, to promise, marry]

we'd *contr.* we would; we should.

wedded *adj.* **1** (**wedded to something**) devoted or committed to a principle, activity, etc. **2** married; in marriage: *wedded bliss.*

Weddell Sea an arm of the Atlantic Ocean, SE of Argentina. It is bounded by the Antarctic Peninsula in the W, Coats Land in the E, and the S Orkney and Sandwich Is in the N. Ice shelves cover the S extent. [named after James Weddell (1787–1834), who claimed to have discovered the sea in 1823.]

wedding *noun* **1** a marriage ceremony, or the ceremony together with the associated celebrations. **2** any of the notable anniversaries of a marriage, especially the *silver wedding* (25 years), *ruby wedding* (40 years), *golden wedding* (50 years), or *diamond wedding* (60 years). [see WED]

wedding breakfast the celebratory meal served after a wedding ceremony.

wedding cake a rich iced fruit cake usually in several tiers, served to wedding guests.

wedding ring a ring, especially in the form of a plain gold band, given by a bridegroom to his bride, or by a bride and bridegroom to each other, for wearing as an indication of married status.

Wedekind, Frank (1864–1918) German dramatist, born in Hanover. He worked in business and journalism before becoming a cabaret performer, playwright, and producer. He is best known for his unconventional tragedies, in which he anticipated the Theatre of the Absurd: *Spring Awakening* (Frühlings Erwachen, 1891), *Earth Spirit* (Erdgeist, 1895), and *Pandora's Box* (Die Büchse der Pandora, 1903).

wedge — *noun* **1** a piece of solid wood, metal, or other material, tapering to a thin edge, driven into eg wood to split it, or pushed into a narrow gap between moving parts to immobilize them. **2** a wedge-shaped section usually cut from something circular. **3** a shoe heel in the form of a wedge, tapering towards the sole. **4** *Golf* a club with a steeply angled wedge-shaped head for lofting. — *verb* **1** to fix or immobilize in position with, or as if with, a wedge. **2** to thrust or insert: *wedged herself into the corner.*
— **drive a wedge between people** to cause ill-feeling or division between people formerly friendly or united.
the thin end of the wedge something that looks like the small beginning of a significant, usually unwanted, development. [from Anglo-Saxon *wecg*]

Wedgwood, Dame Cicely (Veronica) (1910–) English historian, born in Stocksfield, Northumberland. She became a specialist in 17c history, and wrote such biographies as *Oliver*

Cromwell (1939) and *William the Silent* (1944), and other works including *The Thirty Years' War* (1938).

Wedgwood, Josiah (1730–95) English potter, born in Burslem, Staffordshire. He worked in the family pottery business, became a partner in a Staffordshire firm (1754), and began to devise his own ware. He emulated antique models, producing an unglazed blue jasper ware, with raised designs in white, and a black basalt ware (Wedgwood ware). In 1759 he opened a factory at Burslem, and a decade later opened another near Hanley, which he called 'Etruria', where his concern over social welfare led him to build a village for his workmen. From c.1768–80 he was in partnership with Thomas Bentley (1730–80).

Wedgwood *noun trademark* a type of pottery decorated with white classical figures applied over a distinctive blue background. [named after Josiah Wedgwood]

wedlock *noun old use* the condition of being married.
— **born out of wedlock** born to parents not married to each other; illegitimate. [from Anglo-Saxon *wedlac*]

Wednesday *noun* the fourth day of the week. [from Anglo-Saxon *Wodnes dæg*, the day of Woden (the chief god of the Germanic peoples)]

Weds *or* **Weds.** *abbrev.* Wednesday.

wee[1] *adj.* (**weer, weest**) *colloq. esp. Scot.* small; tiny. [from Middle English *we*, bit, from Anglo-Saxon *wæg*, weight]

wee[2] *or* **wee-wee** *colloq.* — *verb intrans.* (**wees, weed**) to urinate. — *noun* **1** an act of urinating. **2** urine.

weed — *noun* **1** any plant that grows wild and has no specific use or aesthetic value. **2** any plant growing where it is not wanted, especially one that is thought to hinder the growth of cultivated plants such as crops or garden plants. **3** a plant growing in fresh or salt water, eg pondweed, seaweed. *colloq.* marijuana. **4** (**the weed**) *old colloq. use* tobacco. **5** *derog.* an unmanly man, especially of gangling build. — *verb* **1** *trans., intrans.* to uproot weeds from (a garden, flowerbed, etc). **2** (*also* **weed out**) to identify and eliminate eg those who are unwanted or ineffective from an organization or other group. [from Anglo-Saxon *weod*]

weedkiller *noun* a substance used to kill unwanted plants.

weeds *pl. noun old use* the black mourning clothes worn by a widow. [from Anglo-Saxon *wæd*, garment]

weedy *adj.* (**weedier, weediest**) **1** overrun with weeds. **2** *said of a plant* straggly in growth. **3** *derog., said of a person* of gangling or otherwise weak build. **4** feeble; ineffectual.

week — *noun* **1** a sequence of seven consecutive days, usually beginning on Sunday. **2** any period of seven consecutive days. **3** the working days of the week, as distinct from the weekend. **4** the period worked per week: *works a 45-hour week.* — *adv.* by a period of seven days before or after a specified day: *Friday week* (= the Friday after the next one) / *a week last Friday* (= the Friday before the last one) / *a week on Friday/next Friday* (= the Friday after the next one).
— **week in, week out** endlessly; relentlessly. [from Anglo-Saxon *wice*]

weekday *noun* any day except Sunday, or except Saturday and Sunday.

weekend *noun* the period from Friday evening to Sunday night.

weekly — *adj.* occurring, produced, or issued every week, or once a week. — *adv.* every week, or once a week. — *noun* (PL. **weeklies**) a magazine or newspaper published once a week.

weeny *adj.* (**weenier, weeniest**) *colloq.* tiny. [from WEE + TINY or TEENY]

weep — verb (PAST TENSE AND PAST PARTICIPLE **wept**) **1** intrans. to shed tears as an expression of grief or other emotion. **2** (**weep for something** or poetic **weep something**) to lament or bewail it: wept for her lost youth / no poet wept his passing. **3** intrans., trans. said of a wound, seal, etc to exude matter; to ooze. — noun a bout of weeping. [from Anglo-Saxon wepan]

weeping adj., said of a tree variety having low-drooping branches.

weepy — adj. (**weepier, weepiest**) **1** tearful. **2** said of a story, etc making one weep; poignant; sentimental. — noun (PL. **weepies**) colloq. a film, novel, etc of this kind.

weevil noun any of several beetles with an elongated proboscis, that as both adults and larvae can damage fruit, grain, nuts, and trees; any insect that damages stored grain. [from Anglo-Saxon wifel]

wee-wee see WEE[2].

weft noun Weaving the threads that are passed over and under the fixed threads of the warp in a loom. [from Anglo-Saxon weft]

Wegener, Alfred Lothar (1880–1930) German meteorologist and geophysicist, born in Berlin. He is famous for his theory of continental drift, published in 1915, which proposed that there may once have been one supercontinent ('Pangaea') on Earth, which later broke up, the fragments drifting apart to form the continents as they are today. After World War I he joined the German Marine Observatory in Hamburg and became professor at Graz, Austria.

Weierstrass, Karl Theodor Wilhelm (1815–97) German mathematician, born in Ostenfelde. Professor at Berlin, he published relatively little but became famous for his lectures, in which he gave a systematic account of analysis with previously unknown rigour. He made important advances in the theory of elliptic functions, constructed the first accepted example of a continuous function which cannot be differentiated at any point, and showed that every continuous function could be uniformly approximated by polynomials.

Weigel, Helene (1900–71) German actress-manager, born in Austria. She married Bertolt Brecht (1929), and became a leading exponent of his work, particularly in The Mother (Die Mutter, 1932) and Mother Courage and her Children (Mutter Courage und ihre Kinder, 1949). She took control of the Berliner Ensemble after Brecht's death in 1956, and was instrumental in furthering his influence internationally.

weigh verb **1** to measure the weight of. **2** trans., intrans. to have (a certain weight): weighs 8kg / books weigh heavy. **3** (also **weigh something out**) to measure out a specific weight of it: weighed out a pound of flour. **4** (also **weigh something up**) to consider or assess (facts, possibilities, etc). **5** to balance (something) in one's hand so as to feel its weight. **6** (**weigh on** or **upon someone**) to oppress them: her worries weighed heavily on her. **7** (**weigh with someone**) to impress them favourably: your previous experience should weigh with the appointments board. **8** to raise (the anchor) of a ship before sailing: weighed anchor at dawn. — **weigh someone down** to burden, overload, or oppress them. **weigh in** said of a wrestler or boxer before a fight, or of a jockey after a race to be weighed officially. **weigh in with something** colloq. to contribute a comment, etc to a discussion. [from Anglo-Saxon wegan]

weighbridge noun an apparatus for weighing vehicles with their loads, consisting of a metal plate set into a road surface and connected to a weighing device.

weigh-in noun the official weighing in of a wrestler, boxer, or jockey.

weight — noun **1** the heaviness of something; the amount anything weighs. **2** Physics (SYMBOL **W**) the gravitational force acting on a body at the surface of the Earth or another planet, star, or moon. Units of measurement are the newton, dyne, or pound-force. Weight = mass × acceleration due to gravity; therefore an object of constant mass weighs more on the Earth than on the Moon. **3** any system of units for measuring and expressing weight: imperial weight / troy weight. **4** a piece of metal of a standard weight, against which to measure the weight of other objects. **5** (often in compounds) a heavy object used to compress, hold down, or counterbalance: paperweight / counterweight. **6** a heavy load. **7** Athletics a heavy object for lifting, throwing, or tossing. **8** a mental burden: took a weight off my mind. **9** strength or significance in terms of amount: the weight of the evidence. **10** the main thrust or force: the weight of the argument. **11** influence, authority, or credibility: opinions that carry little weight. **12** Statistics a number denoting the frequency of some element within a frequency distribution. — verb **1** to add weight to, eg to restrict movement. **2** to burden or oppress. **3** to arrange so as to have an unevenness or bias: a tax system weighted in favour of the wealthy.

— **pull one's weight** to do one's full share of work, etc.

throw one's weight about colloq. to behave domineeringly.

throw one's weight behind something to give one's full support to it.

worth one's weight in gold exceptionally useful or helpful.

[from Anglo-Saxon wiht]

Weight		

Metric units
milligram (mg)
1 000 mg = 1 gram (g)
1 000 g = 1 kilogram (kg)
100 kg = 1 quintal (q)
1 000 kg = 1 metric ton, or tonne (t)

Imperial units (Avoirdupois)
grain (gr); dram (dr)
7 000 gr = 1 pound (lb)
16 dr = 1 ounce (oz)
16 oz = 1 lb
14 lb = 1 stone
28 lb = 1 quarter
112 lb = 1 hundredweight (cwt)
20 cwt = 1 ton = 2240 lb

Troy weight
24 gr = 1 pennyweight (dwt)
20 dwt = 1 (Troy) ounce = 480 gr

Apothecaries' weight
20 gr = 1 scruple
3 scruples = 1 drachm
8 drachms = 1 (apoth) ounce = 480 gr

weighted mean Maths. see MEAN[3] 2b.

weighting noun a supplement to a salary, usually to compensate for high living costs: London weighting.

weightless adj. **1** weighing nothing or almost nothing. **2** said of an astronaut in space not subject to earth's gravity, so able to float free.

weightlessness noun being weightless.

weightlifter noun a person who specializes in weightlifting.

weightlifting noun the sport or exercise of lifting barbells.

weight-training noun muscle-strengthening exercises performed with the aid of weights and pulleys.

weighty (**weightier, weightiest**) adj. **1** heavy. **2** important, significant, or grave.

Weil, Simone (1909–43) French philosophical writer and mystic, born in Paris. She taught philosophy in several schools, interspersing this with periods of manual labour to experience the working-class life. In 1936 she served in the Republican forces in the Spanish Civil War. In 1941 she settled in Marseilles, where she developed a mystical feeling for the Catholic faith but also a reluctance to join an organized religion. She went to the USA in 1942 and worked for the Free French in London, starving herself to death in Ashford, Kent, in sympathy with the victims of war. Her posthumously published works include La Pesanteur et la Grâce (Gravity and Grace, 1946) and Attente de Dieu (Waiting for God, 1950).

Weill, Kurt (1900–50) German composer, born in Dessau. He studied under Engelbert Humperdinck and Ferrucio Busoni, became a composer of instrumental works, then collaborated with Bertolt Brecht and achieved fame with Die Dreigroschenoper (The Threepenny Opera, 1928). A refugee from the Nazis, he settled in the USA in 1934, and was influenced by the idioms of jazz. His later songs, operas, and musical comedies all contain an element of social criticism, and include Lady in the Dark (1940) and Street Scene (1946).

Weimar POP (1991e) 60 000, a city in Thüringia state, SE Germany, lying on the R Ilm. HISTORY an intellectual centre in the 18c–19c, Weimar has associations with Schiller, Goethe, and Liszt; the constitution of the new Weimar Republic was drawn up here in 1919. NOTABLE FEATURES former concentration camp of Buchenwald nearby; Goethe National Museum; Liszt Museum; observatory; Weimar Castle; Belvedere Castle (18c).

Weimar Republic the name for the German Federal Republic of 1918–33. In 1919 a National Constituent Assembly met at Weimar, and drew up a constitution for the new republic. The government moved from Weimar to Berlin in 1920, but in 1933, two months after becoming Chancellor, Hitler passed an Enabling Act to suspend the Weimar constitution.

Weinberg, Steven (1933–) US physicist, born in New York City. He worked at Columbia University, the University of California, the Massachusetts Institute of Technology, and Harvard, before becoming professor at the University of Texas in 1986. In 1967 he produced the 'electroweak' theory to describe the electromagnetic and weak forces simultaneously. He shared the 1979 Nobel Prize for Physics with Abdus Salam and Sheldon Glashow.

Weinberger, Caspar (Willard) (1917–) US politician. A former lawyer, he was state finance director of California when Ronald Reagan was Governor (1968–9), served in the administrations of Presidents Nixon and Ford, then became Secretary of Defense under President Reagan (1981–87).

weir noun **1** a shallow dam constructed across a river to control its flow. **2** a fish-trap built across a river in the form of a fence. [from Anglo-Saxon wer, enclosure]

weird adj. **1** eerie; uncanny; supernatural. **2** queer; strange; bizarre. [from Anglo-Saxon wyrd, fate]

weirdly adv. in a weird way.

weirdness noun being weird.

weirdo noun (PL. **weirdos**) colloq. someone who behaves or dresses bizarrely.

Weismann, August Friedrich Leopold (1834–1914) German biologist, born in Frankfurt. Professor at Freiburg, he wrote on the development of the Diptera (the order of two-winged insects or flies) and on evolution; his theory of germ-plasm ('Weismannism', a form of neo-Darwinism) raised opposition in Britain.

Weissmuller, Johnny (Peter John), originally **Jonas** (1903–84) US swimmer, born in Freidorf, Romania. In 1922 he made history by becoming the first person to swim 100m in under one minute. He won a total of five Olympic gold medals, including the 100m freestyle at the 1924 and 1928 Olympics. After turning professional in 1932, he became a swimsuit model for a clothing firm, and starred in 12 Tarzan films between 1932 and 1948.

Weizmann, Chaim (Azriel) (1874–1952) Jewish politician, born near Pinsk, Russia. He lectured on chemistry at Geneva and Manchester, then helped to secure the Balfour Declaration of 1917, and became President of the Zionist Organization (1920–30, 1935–46), and of the Jewish Agency (from 1929). He played a major role in the establishment of the state of Israel (1948), and was its first President (1949–52).

Weizsäcker, Carl Friedrich, Baron von (1912–) German physicist, born in Kiel. Professor of Philosophy at Hamburg, he proposed that the source of energy in stars is chain nuclear fusion reactions (1938), and described the 'carbon cycle' sequence of reactions involved. He also suggested a possible mechanism for the formation of the planets.

welch same as WELSH.

welcome — *verb* **1** to receive (a guest, visitor, etc) with a warm greeting or kindly hospitality. **2** to encourage visits from: *the museum welcomes children.* **3** to invite (suggestions, contributions, etc). **4** to approve of (an action, etc): *welcomed her intervention.* **5** to respond with pleasure to: *welcomed the long summer evenings.* — *interj.* an expression of pleasure on receiving someone: *welcome home!* — *noun* the act of welcoming; a reception. — *adj.* **1** warmly received: *was made welcome.* **2** gladly permitted or encouraged (to do or keep something): *you're welcome to borrow it / she's welcome to my old bicycle.* **3** much appreciated: *a welcome cup of tea.*

— **welcome with open arms** to receive warmly, gladly, gratefully, or thankfully.

you're welcome! *used in response to thanks* not at all; it's a pleasure.

[from Anglo-Saxon *wilcuma*, a welcome guest]

weld — *verb* **1** *Engineering* to join two pieces of metal by heating them to melting point and fusing them together, or by applying pressure alone. Welding produces a stronger joint than soldering. **2** to unite or blend together. — *noun* a joint between two metals formed by welding. [a past participle of obsolete *well*, to melt, weld]

welder *noun* a person who welds.

Welensky, Sir Roy (1907–91) Rhodesian politician, born in Salisbury, Southern Rhodesia. A railway worker and trade unionist, he was elected to the Legislative Council of Northern Rhodesia in 1938, and from 1956 to its break-up in 1963 was Prime Minister of the Federation of Rhodesia and Nyasaland.

welfare *noun* **1** the health, comfort, happiness, and general wellbeing of a person, group, etc. **2** social work concerned with helping those in need. **3** financial support given to those in need. [from WELL[1] + FARE]

welfare economics *Econ.* an economic theory devoted to studying how best to distribute the gross national product and a nation's wealth among competing claimants, and the extent to which government interferes with market forces.

welfare state a system in which the government uses tax revenue to look after citizens' welfare, with the provision of free health care, old-age pensions, and financial support for the disabled or unemployed.

◇ The development of modern welfare states was significantly influenced by the Beveridge Report of 1944, and a comprehensive system was established in the UK after World War II, funded out of national insurance contributions and taxation. In recent years, those on the political right have claimed that welfare provision decreases self-reliance and freedom of choice, and government has undertaken major reviews of individual benefits as the cost of provision has increased.

well[1] (**better, best**) — *adv.* **1** competently; skilfully. **2** satisfactorily: *all went well.* **3** kindly: *was well treated.* **4** thoroughly; properly; carefully; fully: *wash it well / wasn't attending very well.* **5** intimately: *don't know her well.* **6** successfully; prosperously: *do well / live well.* **7** approvingly: *thinks well of you.* **8** by a long way: *well past midnight / well ahead.* **9** justifiably: *can't very well ignore him.* **10** conceivably; quite possibly: *may well be right.* **11** understandably: *if she objects, as well she may.* **12** very much: *well worth doing.* **13** used in combination for emphasis: *I'm jolly well going to.* — *adj.* **1** healthy. **2** in a satisfactory state. **3** sensible; advisable: *would be well to check.* — *interj.* **1** used enquiringly in expectation of a response, explanation, etc. **2** used variously in conversation, eg to resume a narrative, preface a reply, express surprise, indignation, doubt, etc.

— **all very well** *colloq., said in response to a consoling remark* satisfactory or acceptable only up to a point.

as well 1 too; in addition. **2** (*also* **just as well**) for all the difference it makes: *I may as well tell you.* **3** (*also* **just as well**) advisable; sensible: *would be as well to buy it now.* **4** (*also* **just as well**) a good thing; lucky: *it was just as well you came when you did.*

as well as ... in addition to ...

do well out of something to profit from it.

leave *or* **let well alone** not to interfere in things that are satisfactory as they are.

mean well to have helpful or kindly intentions.

very well an expression of acceptance in complying with an order, accepting a point, etc.

well and good used to show acceptance of facts or a situation.

well and truly thoroughly; completely.

well away 1 making rapid progress; having got into one's stride. **2** *colloq.* drunk, asleep, etc.

well done! an expression used to congratulate someone on an achievement, etc.

well enough satisfactory within limits.

well off 1 wealthy; financially comfortable. **2** fortunate; successful.

well out of something fortunate to be free of it.

well up in something having a thorough knowledge of it.

[from Anglo-Saxon *wel*]

well[2] — *noun* **1** a lined shaft that is sunk from ground level to a considerable depth below ground in order to obtain a supply of water, oil, gas, etc. **2** a natural spring of water, or a pool fed by it. **3** a shaft, or shaft-shaped cavity, eg that made through the floors of a building to take the staircase: *stairwell.* **4** *Naut.* an enclosure in a ship's hold round the pumps. **5** (*in compounds*) a reservoir or receptacle: *inkwell.* **6** *Legal* the open space in the centre of a law court. **7** a plentiful source of something: *she's a well of information.* — *verb intrans.* (**well up**) *said of a liquid* to spring, flow, or flood to the surface. [from Anglo-Saxon *wella*]

we'll *contr.* we will; we shall.

well-advised *adj.* sensible: *you'd be well-advised to comply.*

Welland Ship Canal a canal in Ontario, E Canada, length 61km/38mi. Generally considered to be part of the St Lawrence Seaway, it links L Erie and L Ontario, bypassing the Niagara Falls. The first canal was opened in 1829, and the modern canal in 1932. It can be used by vessels up to 223m in length.

well-appointed *adj., said of a house, etc* well furnished or equipped.

well-balanced *adj.* **1** satisfactorily proportioned. **2** sane, sensible, and stable.

well-behaved *adj.* behaving with good manners or due propriety.

wellbeing *noun* welfare.

well-born *adj.* descended from an aristocratic family.

well-bred *adj.* having good manners; showing good breeding.

well-built *adj.* **1** strongly built. **2** of muscular or well-proportioned bodily build.

well-connected *adj.* having influential or aristocratic friends and relations.

well-disposed *adj.* inclined to be friendly.

well-earned *adj.* thoroughly deserved.

Weller, Samuel the resourceful valet and faithful companion to Pickwick in Charles Dickens's *The Pickwick Papers*. Other members of his family include his second wife, Mrs Weller, and his father Tony.

Welles, (George) Orson (1915–85) US film director and actor, born in Kenosha, Wisconsin. A radio producer in the USA from 1937, his production of H G Wells's *War of the Worlds* in 1938 was so realistic that it caused panic. He wrote, produced, directed, and acted in the films *Citizen Kane* (1941) and *The Magnificent Ambersons* (1942), and he played Harry Lime in *The Third Man* (1949).

Wellesley (of Norragh), Richard (Colley) Wellesley, 1st Marquis (1760–1842) British administrator, brother of the 1st Duke of Wellington, born in Dangan, Co Meath, Ireland. He became an MP (1784), a Lord of the Treasury (1786), a marquis (1799), and Governor-General of India (1797–1805). Under his administration British rule in India became supreme — the influence of France was extinguished, and the power of the princes reduced by the crushing of Tippoo Sahib, the Sultan of Mysore (1799), and the Marathas (1803). He then returned to England and became Ambassador to Madrid (1805), Foreign Minister (1809), and Lord-Lieutenant of Ireland (1821, 1833).

well-founded *adj., said of suspicions, etc* justified; based on good grounds.

well-groomed *adj., said of a person* of smart, neat appearance.

well-grounded *adj.* **1** *said of an argument, etc* soundly based. **2** having had a good basic training.

Wellhausen, Julius (1844–1918) German biblical scholar and Arabist, born in Hameln. He became professor at Greifswald (1872), Halle (1882), Marburg (1885), and Göttingen (1892), and was best known for his investigations into Old Testament history and source criticism of the Pentateuch. His works include the influential *Prolegomena zur Geschichte Israels* (1883, translated as *History of Israel*, 1885).

wellhead *noun* **1** the source of a stream; a spring. **2** an origin or source. **3** the rim or structure round the top of a well.

well-heeled *adj. colloq.* prosperous; wealthy.

well-informed *adj.* **1** having sound, reliable information on something particular. **2** full of varied knowledge.

Wellington, Arthur Wellesley, 1st Duke of (1769–1852) British soldier and statesman, born in Dublin, Ireland. He joined the army in 1787, defeated Tippoo Sahib, the Sultan of Mysore, in India (1799), became Governor of Mysore, and broke the power of the Marathas. An MP from 1806, he was appointed Irish Secretary in 1807, the year he defeated the Danes during the Copenhagen expedition. In the Peninsular War he drove the French out of Portugal and Spain, and was victorious at Talavera (1809), Salamanca (1812), and Toulouse (1814), for which he was created Duke of Wellington. After Napoleon's escape from Elba, he routed the French at Waterloo (1815). He supported Liverpool's government, and joined it as Master-General of the Ordnance (1818). He also became Constable of the Tower (1826) and army Commander-in-Chief (1827). His period as Prime Minister (1828–30) saw the Tory Party weaken, for it split over the question of Catholic emancipation and disagreed over trade and reform. Wellington's opposition to parliamentary reform brought down his government, which was succeeded by the Whigs. He was Foreign Secretary under Robert Peel (1834–5) and retired from public life in 1846.

Wellington POP (1991) 326 000, the capital city and seat of government of New Zealand, on the S coast of North I. The city was founded in 1840 and became capital in 1865. NOTABLE FEATURES Government Building; Parliament Buildings (1922, 1980); General Assembly Library (1897); War Memorial Museum; St Paul's Cathedral (1866); Michael Fowler Centre; National Art Gallery; National Museum.

wellington *noun* a waterproof rubber or plastic boot loosely covering the foot and calf. [named after the first Duke of Wellington]

well-intentioned *adj.* having good intentions, if an unfortunate effect.

well-judged *adj.* neatly calculated; judicious.

well-knit *adj.* **1** *said of a person* sturdily and compactly built. **2** compactly or soundly constructed.

well-known *adj.* familiar or famous.

well-mannered *adj.* polite.

well-meaning *adj.* well-intentioned.

well-meant *adj.* intended well.

well-nigh *adv.* almost; nearly.

well-oiled *adj.* **1** *colloq.* drunk. **2** *fig.* smoothly operating from thorough practice.

well-preserved *adj.* **1** in good condition; not decayed. **2** youthful in appearance; showing few signs of age.

well-read *adj.* having read and learnt much.

well-rounded *adj.* **1** pleasantly plump. **2** having had a broadly based, balanced upbringing and education. **3** well constructed and complete.

Wells, H(erbert) G(eorge) (1866–1946) English writer, born in Bromley, Kent. He worked as an apprentice draper and teacher before he achieved fame as a novelist with scientific fantasies including *The Time Machine* (1895) and *War of the Worlds* (1898). He also wrote a range of comic social novels which proved highly popular, notably *Kipps* (1905) and *The History of Mr Polly* (1910). A member of the Fabian Society, he was often engaged in public controversy, and wrote several socio-political works dealing with the role of science and the need for world peace (eg *The Outline of History*, 1920, and *The Work, Wealth and Happiness of Mankind*, 1932).

Wells POP (1981) 9 560, a market town in Mendip district, Somerset, SW England. It lies S of the Mendip Hills, 24km/15mi S of Bristol. NOTABLE FEATURES renowned cathedral (12c); 13c Bishop's Palace (13c); Church of St Cuthbert (15c).

well-spoken *adj.* having a courteous, fluent, and usually refined way of speaking.

wellspring *noun* **1** a spring or fountain. **2** a rich or bountiful source.

Well-Tempered Clavier, The (Das Wohltemperirte Klavier) J S Bach's collection of 48 Preludes and Fugues for keyboard. Written in two halves (1722 and 1748) and published in 1800–1, it is sometimes referred to as 'the 48'. The composer named the collection from a term denoting a keyboard tuning suitable for all 24 keys.

well-thought-of *adj.* approved of; respected.

well-timed *adj.* timely; opportune.

well-to-do *adj.* wealthy; financially comfortable.

well-tried *adj.* found reliable from frequent testing.

well-turned *adj.* **1** *old use* attractively formed: *a well-turned ankle*. **2** neatly expressed: *a well-turned phrase*.

well-versed *adj.* thoroughly trained.

well-wisher *noun* someone concerned for one's welfare.

well-woman clinic *Medicine* a clinic that specializes in the diagnosis and treatment of minor gynaecological and sexual disorders, and also offers advice on related health matters.

well-worn *adj.* **1** much worn or used; showing signs of wear. **2** *said of an expression, etc* overfamiliar from frequent use; trite.

welly *noun* (PL. **wellies**) *colloq.* a wellington.

Welsh — *noun* **1** the Celtic language of Wales. **2** (**the Welsh**) the people of Wales. — *adj.* **1** of or belonging to Wales. **2** of or in the language of Wales. [from Anglo-Saxon *welisc*, from *wealh*, Briton, foreigner]
◇ Welsh has a rich literary history dating to the 6c epic poem *Taliesin*, and the prose tales of the *Mabinogion*, preserved in medieval manuscripts which record an oral tradition many centuries older.
Although the numbers of Welsh speakers have declined steadily since 1900, it has equal status with English in Wales, in legal and administrative affairs. Welsh has a literary tradition dating from the 6c, with an oral tradition many centuries older. Welsh language and culture are maintained in a national TV channel and by events such as the National Eisteddfod.

welsh *or* **welch** *verb intrans.* **1** (**welsh on something**) to fail to pay one's debts or fulfil one's obligations. **2** (**welsh on someone**) to fail to keep one's promise to them.

Welshman *or* **Welshwoman** *noun* a person from Wales.

Welsh Office in the UK, the government department established in 1964 which deals with Welsh affairs. Its areas of responsibility include health, social services, agriculture, education, and the arts. It also oversees economic matters and regional planning in Wales. It is headed by the Secretary of State for Wales.

Welsh rabbit *or* **Welsh rarebit** a dish of melted cheese served on toast.

welt — *noun* **1** a reinforcing band or border, eg the ribbing at the waist of a knitted garment. **2** *Shoemaking* a strip of leather fitted round the upper, as a means of attaching it to the sole. **3** a weal raised by a lash or blow. — *verb* **1** to fit a welt. **2** to beat or thrash.

welter — *noun* a confused mass. — *verb intrans.* (**weltered, weltering**) (**welter in something**) to lie, roll, or wallow in it. [from Old Dutch *welteren*]

welterweight *noun* **1** a class for boxers and wrestlers of not more than a specified weight (66.7kg in professional boxing, similar but different weights in amateur boxing and wrestling). **2** a boxer or wrestler of this weight.

welwitschia *noun* a peculiar gymnosperm (cone-bearing plant), *Welwitschia mirabilis*, found only in the deserts of SW Africa, where it obtains moisture from sea fogs. It usually lasts for over a century and has a turnip-like stem which produces two strap-shaped leaves several metres long, which grow throughout the life of the plant. [named after an Austrian traveller F Welwitsch]

Welwyn Garden City POP (1981) 41 000, a town in Hatfield district, Hertfordshire, SE England, situated 10km/6mi NE of St Albans. It was founded in 1919 by Ebenezer Howard and designated a 'new town' in 1948.

Wembley Stadium a football stadium built at Wembley in NE London in 1923. It has a capacity of 78 000, and was the site of the 1948 Olympic Games.

wen *noun* a cyst on the skin, usually the scalp. [from Anglo-Saxon *wenn*]

Wenceslaus *or* **Wenceslas, St**, also called **Good King Wenceslas** (c.907–929) prince-duke of Bohemia, born in Stochov. He was raised as a Christian by his grandmother, and when he came of age (c.924) he was free of his pagan mother's protectorate and could encourage German missionaries to come to Bohemia. He put his duchy under the protection of Henry the Fowler of Germany, and was murdered by his pagan brother Boleslaw. The patron saint of Bohemia, he was regarded as a symbol of Czech nationalism, and his feast day is 28 Sep.

wench — *noun old colloq. use* **1** a girl; a woman. **2** a servant girl. **3** a prostitute. — *verb intrans.* **1** to associate with prostitutes. **2** to go courting girls. [from Anglo-Saxon *wencel*, a child]

wend *verb*
— **wend one's way** to go steadily and purposefully on a route or journey.
[from Anglo-Saxon *wendan*, to go]

Wendy a female first name, devised by J M Barrie in *Peter Pan* (1904).

Wendy house a small playhouse for children constructed of wood or cloth.

went see GO.

Wenzel, Hanni (1956–) Liechtenstein alpine skier, born in Staubirnen, Germany. At the 1980 Olympics she won the gold medal in the slalom and giant slalom, and the silver in the downhill. Her total of four Olympic gold medals is a record for any skier. She was combined world champion and overall World Cup winner in 1980.

wept see WEEP.

were see BE.

we're *contr.* we are.

weren't *contr.* were not.

werewolf *noun* (PL. **werewolves**) *Folklore* a person who changes periodically into a wolf. [from Anglo-Saxon *werwulf*, man-wolf]
◇ Stories of men who were turned, or who at will could turn themselves, into wolves, appear in Ovid and Pliny. In ancient folklore, the transformation usually took place at the full moon, and the werewolf roamed about at night eating infants and sometimes exhuming corpses. It could only be destroyed by a weapon blessed in a chapel dedicated to St Hubert, or in later versions, by a silver bullet.

Wergeland, Hendrik Arnold (1808–45) Norwegian poet, dramatist, and patriot, born in Kristiansand. He is best known for his poetry, notably his *Creation, humanity, and desire* (1830), and the narrative poem *The English pilot* (1844). A leader of the cause of Norwegian nationalism, he became Norway's national poet.

Werner, Abraham Gottlob (1749–1817) German geologist, born in Wehrau, Silesia (now in Poland). A teacher at Freiburg in Saxony from 1775, he was one of the first to frame a classification of rocks, and gave his name to the later discredited Wernerian (or 'Neptunian') theory of deposition, suggesting that crystalline igneous rocks were formed by direct precipitation from sea-water.

Wernicke, Carl (1848–1905) German neurologist and psychiatrist, born in Tarnowitz, Upper Silesia (now in Poland). Professor at Breslau (1885–1904), he studied brain damage leading to aphasia (the loss of certain kinds of language ability). 'Wernicke's area' in the brain is named after him.

wert *old use* a form of the past tense of the verb *be* used with the pronoun *thou*.

Weser, River, ancient **Visurgis** a major river in Germany, length 440km/273mi. Formed by the confluence of the Werra and Fulda rivers at Münden in Lower Saxony, it flows generally N to the North Sea forming an estuary at Bremerhaven. The river is navigable for the length of its course and is connected to the Rhine and Elbe by the Mittelland Canal.

Wesker, Arnold (1932–) English dramatist, born in London. His Jewish background, socialism, and his varied attempts at earning a living (having left school at 14) are important ingredients of his plays, such as in the Kahn family trilogy: *Chicken Soup with Barley*, *Roots*, and *I'm Talking about Jerusalem* (1959–60). Later plays include *The Kitchen* (1959), *Chips with Everything* (1962), *The Friends* (1970), and *Caritas* (1981).

Wesley, John (1703–91) English evangelist and founder of Methodism, born in Epworth, Lincolnshire. Ordained deacon (1725) and priest (1728), he was influenced by the spiritual writings of William Law (1686–1761), and became leader of a small group (the 'Methodists') that had gathered round his brother Charles (1707–88), and which was to grow into a great evangelical movement. Following a failed mission with Charles in Georgia (1735–8), at a meeting in London (1738) he experienced such assurance of salvation during the reading of Martin Luther's preface to the Epistle to the Romans that he was convinced he must bring the same assurance to others. His zeal so alarmed most of the parish clergy that their pulpits were closed to him, and he was driven to preach in the open air in Bristol, where he founded the first Methodist chapel (1739). He then preached in and bought the Foundry at Moorfields, London, which became the headquarters of Methodism. He survived much persecution, and the itineraries of his old age were triumphal processions throughout the country. A prolific writer, he produced grammars, histories, biographies, collections of hymns, his own sermons and journals, and a magazine.

Wesleyan — *adj.* relating to John Wesley, or to Methodism, the Protestant movement founded by him. — *noun* a follower of Wesley or Methodism.

Wessex a kingdom of the Anglo-Saxon heptarchy, with its main centres at Winchester and Hamwic (Southampton). Under Alfred, Wessex (by then incorporating Kent and Sussex) was the only English kingdom to withstand the Vikings. Alfred's successors reconquered the Danelaw, and by 954 had united all England under a single monarchy.

West, Mae (1892–1980) US actress, born in New York City. She performed as a child and spent some years in vaudeville and on Broadway before her first film, *Night After Night* (1932). The series of racy comedies that followed, (eg *I'm No Angel*, 1933) exploited her voluptuousness and often used her own dialogue-script, to the dismay of 1930s censors. Later films included *Myra Breckinridge* (1970).

West, Dame Rebecca, pseudonym of **Cicily Isabel Andrews**, née **Fairfield** (1892–1983) English novelist and critic, born in London. She became a journalist, and is best known for her studies arising out of the Nuremberg war trials, including *The Meaning of Treason* (1947) and *A Train of Powder* (1955). Her novels include *The Judge* (1922), *The Thinking Reed* (1936), and *The Birds Fall Down* (1966).

west — *noun* **1** (*also* **the west** *or* **the West**) the direction in which the sun sets, or any part of the earth, a country, town, etc lying in that direction. **2** (**the West**) **a** the countries of Europe and N America, in contrast to those of Asia; also formerly, the non-communist bloc as distinct from the communist or former communist countries of the East. **b** *Hist.* the part of the US to the west of the Mississippi. — *adj.* **1** in the west; on the side that is on or nearer the west. **2** *said of a wind* blowing from the west. — *adv.* toward the west. — **go west** *colloq.* to be lost or destroyed. [from Anglo-Saxon *west*]

West Bank a region in the Middle East, W of the R Jordan and the Dead Sea. HISTORY part of

the former mandate of Palestine, it was administered by Jordan from 1949 to 1967; seized by Israel in the 1967 War, and remains under Israeli occupation, administered as the district of Judea-Samaria. The area includes Old (East) Jerusalem, as well as Bethlehem, Jericho, Hebron, and Nablus. It has been a focus of territorial aspirations by the Palestine Liberation Organization and was the scene of an uprising (*intifada*) against the Israelis between 1988 and 1993, during which time schools and many shops were closed. Palestinian sources claimed that Israeli troops had killed many Palestinians in their attempts to control the uprising. In 1993, Israel reached agreement with the Palestine Liberation Organization on the implementation of limited Palestinian self-rule, but in 1994 talks faltered following attacks on a mosque in Hebron, and a reprisal attack by Hamas in Afula in N Israel.

West Bengal POP (1991) 68.1m, a state in NE India. AREA 87 853sq km/33 911sq mi. It is bounded NW by Nepal, E by Bangladesh, S by the Bay of Bengal and is crossed by many rivers. The state was created in 1947, when the former province of Bengal was divided between the new state of West Bengal and the Muslim majority districts of East Bengal (now Bangladesh). CAPITAL Calcutta. GOVERNMENT governed by a 295-member Legislative Assembly. ECONOMY rice; foodgrains; oilseed; jute; coal; aluminium, steel; fertilizer; extensive rail network.

westbound *adj.* going or leading towards the west.

West Bromwich POP (1981) 155 000, an industrial town in Sandwell borough, West Midlands, central England. It lies 8km/5mi NW of Birmingham. NOTABLE FEATURE half-timbered Oak House (16c–17c).

West Country the SW counties of England — Somerset, Devon, and Cornwall.

West End a fashionable shopping and theatre area in west central London. It contains over 25 theatres, including the Aldwych, Covent Garden, Drury Lane, and London Palladium.

westering *adj.*, *said of the sun* sinking towards the west.

westerlies *or* **Westerlies** *Meteorol.* winds that blow W–E, most often over the middle latitudes of both hemispheres. In the N hemisphere the westerlies blow from the SW, and in the S hemisphere they blow from the NW.

westerly — *adj.* **1** *said of a wind* coming from the west. **2** looking, lying, etc towards the west. — *adv.* to or towards the west. — *noun* (PL. **westerlies**) a westerly wind. See also WESTERLIES.

Western, Sophia the beautiful, sweet-natured heroine of Henry Fielding's *The History of Tom Jones*, who loves and is loved by Tom. Her roistering father is called Squire Western.

western — *adj.* **1** of or in the west. **2** facing or directed towards the west. — *noun* (**Western**) a film or story about 19c cowboys in the west of the USA.
◇ James Fenimore Cooper established a model for the western story in *The Pioneers* (1823), basing his hero Leatherstocking on Daniel Boone. Davy Crockett and Kit Carson were similarly fictionalized, and journalist E Z C Judson promoted Buffalo Bill Cody to legendary status in dime novels (from 1860), for which Prentiss Ingraham (1843–1904) later wrote over 200 Buffalo Bill stories. The railroad robbery by Butch Cassidy and his Wild Bunch in 1900 occasioned Edwin S Porter's film *The Great Train Robbery* (1903), beginning the tradition of Western films, including *Stagecoach* (1939), *High Noon* (1952), *Shane* (1953), and *Butch Cassidy and the Sundance Kid* (1969).

Western Australia POP (1992e) 1.7m, a state in W Australia, comprising nine statistical divisions. AREA 2 525 500sq km/975 000sq mi. The state is bounded in the S by the Great Australian

Bight, in the W by the Indian Ocean, and in the N by the Timor Sea. One third of the total area of Australia is covered by this state. PHYSICAL DESCRIPTION over 90% of the state is occupied by the Great Plateau at an average altitude of 600m above sea level, and a highest point of 1 245m at Mt Meharry; in the E are the Great Sandy Desert, Gibson Desert, Great Victoria Desert, and the Nullarbor Plain; near the border with Northern Territory is Wolf Crater, the world's second-largest meteorite crater; there are many dry salt lakes in the interior, including L Lefroy and L McLeod; several archipelagoes lie off the coast; principal rivers are the Swan, Avon, Blackwood, Gascoyne, Drysdale, Murchison, Ashburton, and Fitzroy. HISTORY Dutchman Dirk Hartog landed here in 1616, and Englishman William Dampier in 1688; Britain's first non-convict settlement was established on the Swan R in 1829; governed at first by New South Wales; became a separate colony in 1890. CAPITAL Perth. CHIEF TOWNS Port Hedland, Busselton, Albany, Kalgoorlie, Carnarvon. ECONOMY fishing; forestry; wheat; sheep; wine; agricultural machinery; gold, iron ore, nickel, uranium, bauxite, mineral sands, superphosphates, oil and natural gas.

Western Dvina, Russian **Zapadnaya Dvina** a river in NW Russia, Belorussia, and Latvia, length 1 013km/630mi. It discharges into the Gulf of Riga, an inlet of the Baltic Sea. It is frozen over from Dec to Apr.

westerner *noun* a person who lives in or comes from the west, especially the western part of the USA.

Western European Union (ABBREV. **WEU**) an organization of W European nations, founded (1955) to co-ordinate defence and other policies, a replacement for the defunct European Defence Community. Its members are Belgium, France, Germany, Italy, Luxembourg, the Netherlands, Portugal, Spain, and the UK. It contains a Council of Ministers, a representative assembly in the Consultative Assembly of the Council of Europe, and a Standing Armaments Committee which works in co-operation with NATO. In the 1990s it developed as the defence arm of the European Union, bringing together the European members of NATO.

Western Isles POP (1992e) 29 000, an administrative Region in Scotland, consisting of a group of islands off the W coast (the Outer Hebrides). AREA 2 898sq km/1 119sq mi. The group is separated from the mainland by the Minch and Little Minch, and is bounded W by the Atlantic Ocean. Lewis, Harris, North Uist, Benbecula, South Uist, and Barra are the main islands. The name Western Isles is often used to refer to both the Inner and the Outer Hebrides. CAPITAL Stornoway (on Lewis). ECONOMY fishing, cattle, sheep; Harris tweed.

westernmost *adj.* situated furthest west.

Western Reserve the territory in NW Ohio that was successfully claimed (1786) by the state of Connecticut during the final settlement of interstate boundary disputes that dated from the colonial era.

Western Sahara POP (1992e) 250 000, a disputed NW African territory administered by Morocco. AREA 252 126sq km/97 321sq mi. It is bounded by Morocco in the N, Algeria in the NE, Mauritania in the E and S, and the Atlantic Ocean in the W. CAPITAL Laâyoune. CHIEF TOWNS Ad Dakhla, Es Semara. The chief religion is Sunni Muslim. OFFICIAL LANGUAGE Arabic. CURRENCY the Moroccan dirham. PHYSICAL DESCRIPTION a desert area, rich in phosphates. HISTORY visited by Portuguese navigators in 1434; protectorate first claimed by Spain in 1884; partitioned by Morocco and Mauritania after its Spanish status ended in 1975; withdrawal of Mauritania in 1979; the independence movement, *Frente Polisario*, has named it the Saharan Arab Democratic Republic and has set up a 'government in exile'. Saharan guerrillas operate from within Algeria.

Western Sahara

Western Samoa, official name **The Independent State of Western Samoa** POP (1992e) 158 000, an island nation in the SW Pacific Ocean, 2 600km/1 600mi NE of Auckland, New Zealand. AREA 2 842sq km/1 097sq mi. It is divided into 24 districts and comprises two large and seven smaller islands, four of which are inhabited (Upolu, Savai'i, Apolima, Manono). CAPITAL Apia. TIME ZONE GMT –11. The population is mostly of Polynesian origin; Protestantism is the chief religion. OFFICIAL LANGUAGES Samoan, English. CURRENCY the Western Samoan dollar (tala). PHYSICAL DESCRIPTION formed from ranges of extinct volcanoes, rising to 1 829m on Savai'i; many dormant volcanoes (last activity was between 1905 and 1911); thick tropical vegetation; several coral reefs along the coast. CLIMATE tropical; the rainy season is Dec–Apr; average annual temperatures are 22–30°C; average annual rainfall is 2 775mm; hurricanes occur. HISTORY visited by the Dutch in 1772; the 1889 commission divided Samoa between Germany (which acquired Western Samoa) and the USA (which acquired Tutuila and adjacent small islands, now known as American Samoa); New Zealand was granted a League of Nations mandate for Samoa in 1919; UN Trust Territory under New Zealand in 1946; gained independence in 1962. GOVERNMENT governed by a monarch as head of state, a Prime Minister, and a 47-member Legislative Assembly elected for three years. ECONOMY largely agricultural subsistence economy; taro; yams, breadfruit, pawpaws, coconuts, cocoa, bananas; tourism increasing; the internal transportation system depends largely on roads and ferries.

Western Wall, also called the **Wailing Wall** the only surviving part of the Second Temple of Jerusalem and, as such, the most sacred of Jewish sites. It was traditionally a place of prayer and lamentation during the dispersion of the Jews. It is a World Heritage site.

West Germany, German **Bundesrepublik Deutschland** see GERMANY.

West Glamorgan POP (1992e) 371 000, a county in S Wales divided into four districts. AREA 817sq km/315sq mi. It is bounded S by the Bristol Channel, E by Mid Glamorgan, NE by Powys, and W by Dyfed. The Gower Peninsula lies nearby. CAPITAL Swansea. CHIEF TOWNS Neath, Port Talbot. ECONOMY steel, coal, tinplate, aluminium; chemicals; tourism.

West Highland Way a long-distance footpath in Scotland, length 158km/98mi. It stretches from Milngavie near Glasgow to Fort William, and was opened in 1980.

West Highland white terrier a small muscular terrier developed in Scotland, which has a thick coat of white straight hair, a rounded head, and short pointed erect ears.

West Indian — *noun* a native or inhabitant of the West Indies. — *adj.* relating to the West Indies.

West Indies a large archipelago separating the Gulf of Mexico and the Caribbean Sea from the Atlantic Ocean. It stretches between the coasts of Florida and Venezuela and comprises about 1 200 islands, divided into three main groups: the Bahamas, the Greater Antilles, and the Lesser Antilles. The islands are largely autonomous dependencies, Crown Colonies, or independent republics. MAIN ISLANDS Cuba, Hispaniola, Jamaica, Puerto Rico, Trinidad and Tobago, the Windward Is, and the Leeward Is.

West Indies, Federation of the an unsuccessful attempt (1958–62) to establish a single government for the English-speaking West Indies, after the failure of which the countries concerned slowly gained their independence.

Westinghouse, George (1846–1914) US engineer, born in Central Bridge, New York. He patented a railway steam locomotive and many other devices connected with railways, notably the 'Westinghouse air brake' (1869), and founded the Westinghouse Air Brake Company to manufacture this and other appliances. Also a pioneer in the use of alternating current for distributing electric power, he founded the Westinghouse Electrical Company in 1886.

West Irian see IRIAN JAYA.

Westman Islands, Icelandic **Vestmannaeyjar** POP (1991e) 5 000, a group of 15 islands and 30 reefs lying off the S coast of Iceland. The volcanic island of Heimaey erupted in 1973. The island of Surtsey was formed during submarine eruptions between 1963 and 1966. ECONOMY fishing, fish processing.

Westmeath, Gaelic **na h-Iarmhidhe** POP (1991) 62 000, a county in Leinster province, central Irish Republic. AREA 1 764sq km/681sq mi. PHYSICAL DESCRIPTION bounded on the SW by the R Shannon; crossed by the Royal Canal. CAPITAL Mullingar. ECONOMY cattle, agriculture.

West Midlands POP (1987e) 2.6m, a metropolitan county area in central England, divided into seven districts. Controlled by a metropolitan county council until 1986, the area is now administered by metropolitan district councils. AREA 899sq km/559sq mi. CHIEF TOWNS Birmingham (administrative centre), Wolverhampton, West Bromwich, Coventry, Walsall. ECONOMY vehicles; aircraft; engineering.

Westminster, City of a borough of central Greater London, England, N of the R Thames. It includes Hyde Park, St James's Park, Green Park and the suburbs of Paddington, Westminster, and Marylebone. The administrative centre of the UK, it also includes the major tourist area from Westminster Bridge through Trafalgar Square to the West End.

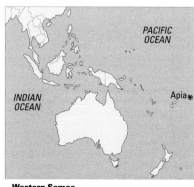

Western Samoa

Westminster, City of POP (1987e) 173 000, a borough in central Greater London, England, lying N of the R Thames. It is the administrative centre of the UK. The borough includes Hyde Park, St James's Park, Green Park, and the suburbs of Paddington, Westminster, and Marylebone. Westminster also comprises the major tourist area from Westminster Bridge through Trafalgar Square to the West End. HISTORY 13c Statutes of Westminster laid the foundations of the development of English law; the Westminster Confession of Faith, produced between 1643 and 1649, is a statement of Presbyterian theology. NOTABLE FEATURES Downing Street; Whitehall; Houses of Parliament; Westminster Hall; Westminster Abbey; Big Ben; Buckingham Palace; St James's Palace; Royal Albert Hall; Tate Gallery; National Gallery; National Portrait Gallery; the Cenotaph, Nelson's Column; Royal Academy.

Westminster, Statutes of part of a comprehensive legislative programme undertaken by Edward I to reform English law and administration. The first Statute (1275) was concerned mainly with criminal matters, notably compulsory trial by jury; the second (1285) covered many fields of law, and facilitated the creation of entailed estates; the third (1290) protected lords' feudal incidents.

Westminster, Treaty of an Anglo-Dutch agreement (1674) that recognized English control of New York. Originally founded as the New Netherlands, the province was conquered by the English in 1664 and again (after a brief period of Dutch control) 10 years later.

Westminster Abbey the collegiate church of St Peter in Westminster, London. It is probable that there was a monastic settlement on this site from the 8c. The first recorded abbey church, consecrated in 1065, was replaced from 1245 by the present building in early English Gothic style; the monastery was dissolved in 1540. The crowning of British sovereigns takes place in the Abbey, and it is the burial place of many monarchs. It is a World Heritage site.

Westminster Assembly a body of 120 clerics and 30 laymen convened (1643) by the English Long Parliament to arrange a religious settlement to replace the Church of England. Dominated by Presbyterians, it produced a directory of public worship to replace the Prayer Book, and the Westminster Confession of Faith. Its influence declined after 1648 when the army, which favoured toleration, increased in power.

Westminster Confession of Faith the main Presbyterian Confession of Faith, adopted (1643) by the Westminster Assembly, England. It delineated the main doctrines of the Christian faith from a Calvinistic perspective, and became the major confessional influence among Reformed Churches of the English-speaking world.

Westmorland a former county of NW England. It has been part of Cumbria since 1974.

Weston-super-Mare POP (1981) 62 000, a resort town in Woodspring district, Avon, SW England. It is situated 28km/17mi SW of Bristol on the Bristol Channel.

Westphalia a NW German principality, first settled by Saxons c.700. It was given to the Archbishop of Cologne (1180) and later became part of the Lower Rhine–Westphalian Circle of the Holy Roman Empire (1512). In 1803–6 it was divided between Brandenburg-Prussia and neighbouring states, and although the name was coined for Napoleon's satellite kingdom (1807), the princes regained possession (1814–15).

Westphalia, Peace of a series of treaties (1648) that ended the Thirty Years War between France and the Holy Roman Empire, and the Eighty Years War between Spain and the Dutch, negotiated in the Westphalian towns of Münster and Osnabrück. It marked the triumph of the

Houses of Parliament, Westminster

French Bourbons over the Habsburgs, and enshrined the concept of *raison d'état* (the primacy of the interests of the sovereign state over other considerations, eg dynastic or religious factors).

West Point a US military academy founded by an Act of Congress in 1802 at the West Point military station on the Hudson River, New York.

West Side Story a musical by Leonard Bernstein to a libretto by Stephen Sondheim on a text by Arthur Laurents (1957). With much dancing and echoes of *Romeo and Juliet* in the plot, it tells of gang warfare and romance in the slums of Manhattan.

West Sussex see SUSSEX, WEST.

West Virginia POP (1990) 1.8m, a state in E USA, divided into 55 counties. AREA 62 758sq km/24 224sq mi. CAPITAL Charleston. CHIEF TOWNS Huntington, Wheeling, Parkersburg, Morgantown. PHYSICAL DESCRIPTION the Ohio R follows the Ohio state border, with several tributaries; the Potomac R forms part of the N border; the Allegheny Mts dominate the E; Mt Spruce Knob (1 481m) is the highest point; rugged, forested, and hilly, most of the state lies in the Allegheny Plateau; known as the 'Mountain State'. HISTORY part of Virginia until the Civil War, when the area remained loyal to the Union; split from Confederate East Virginia in 1861; the 35th state admitted to the Union, as West Virginia in 1863. ECONOMY cattle; dairy products; apples; corn; tobacco; the nation's leading producer of bituminous coal; major producer of natural gas; stone; cement; salt; oil; glass; chemicals; metals; machinery; tourism.

westward *or* **westwards** *adv., adj.* towards the west.

Westward Ho! a novel by Charles Kingsley (1855). It is an adventure novel glorifying English supremacy in the war with the Spanish Armada.

Westwood, Vivienne (1941–) English fashion designer, born in London. Initially a primary-school teacher, she turned her attention to clothes design on meeting Malcolm McLaren. They established a shop in London and became known as the leading creators of punk clothing. Their designs, which used rubber, leather, and bondage gear, were influenced by the paraphernalia of pornography. She split from McLaren in 1983, and became accepted by the mainstream. She was Designer of the Year in 1990 and 1991.

Wet, Christian (Rudolf) de (1854–1922) Afrikaner soldier and statesman, born in Smithfield district, Orange Free State. He distinguished himself in the Transvaal War (1880–1), and was a commander in the second Boer War (1899–1902). In 1907 he became Minister of Agriculture of the Orange River Colony, and in 1914 joined the South African insurrection, but

was captured. Sentenced to six years' imprisonment, he was released in 1915.

wet — *adj.* (**wetter, wettest**) **1** covered or soaked in water, rain, perspiration, or other liquid. **2** *said of the weather* rainy. **3** *said of paint, cement, etc* not yet dried. **4** covered with tears: *wet cheeks.* **5** *said of a baby* having a urine-soaked nappy. **6** *derog. colloq., said of a person* feeble; ineffectual. **7** *North Amer. Hist.* allowing the sale of alcoholic drink. **8** *Chem., said of processes, etc* using liquid. — *noun* **1** moisture. **2** rainy weather; rain. **3** *derog.* a feeble, ineffectual person. **4** *colloq.* a moderate Conservative. — *verb* (**wetting**; PAST TENSE AND PAST PARTICIPLE **wet, wetted**) **1** to make wet; to splash or soak. **2** to urinate involuntarily on: *wet the bed.*
— **wet behind the ears** *colloq.* immature or inexperienced.
wet through completely wet.
[from Anglo-Saxon *wæt*]

wet blanket a dreary, pessimistic person who dampens the enthusiasm and enjoyment of others; a killjoy.

wet dream an erotic dream that causes emission of semen.

wether *noun* a castrated ram. [from Anglo-Saxon *wether*]

wet nurse *Hist.* a woman employed to breastfeed another's baby.

wet suit a tight-fitting rubber suit permeable by water, but conserving body heat, worn by divers, canoeists, yachtsmen, etc.

we've *contr.* we have.

Wexford, Gaelic **Loch Garman** POP (1991) 102 000, a county in Leinster province, SE Irish Republic. AREA 2 352sq km/908sq mi. It is bounded by St George's Channel and the Atlantic Ocean. PHYSICAL DESCRIPTION the coastline is indented with bays and inlets; the Wicklow Mts lie in the N, and the Blackstairs Mts in the W; watered by the Barrow and Slaney rivers. CAPITAL Wexford. CHIEF TOWNS Bannow, Rosslare. ECONOMY agriculture; tourism.

Wexford POP (1991) 15 000, the capital of Wexford county, Leinster province, Irish Republic. It lies at the mouth of the R Slaney where it meets Wexford harbour.

Weyl, Hermann (1885–1955) German mathematician, born in Elmshorn. Professor at Zürich and Göttingen, he moved to Princeton in 1933, and made many important contributions to mathematical theory. Inspired by a brief period with Einstein in Zürich, he also wrote on the mathematical foundations of relativity and quantum mechanics.

Weymouth POP (1992e) 62 000, a port and resort town in Weymouth and Portland district,

Dorset, S England. It is situated 42km/26mi W of Bournemouth.

WFTU *abbrev.* World Federation of Trade Unions.

whack *colloq.* — *verb* to hit sharply and resoundingly. — *noun* **1** a sharp, resounding blow, or the sound of this. **2** one's share of the profits, work, etc.
— **have a whack at something** to try it. [imitative]

whacked *adj.* exhausted.

whacking — *noun* a beating. — *adj. colloq.* enormous; huge.

whale — *noun* any of various large marine mammals belonging to the order Cetacea, distributed worldwide, and having a torpedo-shaped body, two flippers, flat horizontal tail blades, and a blow-hole on the top of the head for breathing. — *verb intrans.* to hunt whales.
— **a whale of a** ... *colloq.* a hugely enjoyable (time, evening, etc).
[from Anglo-Saxon *hwæl*]
◇ Whales evolved over 100 million years ago from four-legged land mammals. Instead of hair they have a thick layer of oily blubber beneath their skin, which provides insulation. They breathe by means of lungs, the front limbs are modified to form flippers, and the nostrils are situated at the top of the head, where they form a blow-hole. After a dive, a whale rises to the surface and 'spouts' to expel used air from its lungs. It then breathes in more air before submerging again. There are two main groups. The *baleen whales* (eg rorquals and blue whales) feed on plankton which they sieve through a row of plates of whalebone or baleen, formed from modified hair, inside the mouth. The *toothed whales* (eg killer and sperm whales, dolphins, and porpoises) are smaller, have teeth, and feed mainly on fish and squid, although the killer whale preys on seals, penguins, and other whales. Most whales swim together in herds known as *schools*, and the blue whale, which can grow to a length of 34m, is the largest animal on earth.

whalebone *noun* the light flexible horny substance of which the plankton-filtering plates in the mouths of toothless whales are composed, used especially formerly for stiffening corsets, etc.

whale oil oil obtained from whale blubber.

whaler *noun* a person or ship engaged in whaling.

whale shark the largest of all fishes, widely distributed in surface waters of tropical seas, up to 18m in length, and weighing up to 20 tonnes. It feeds mainly on small planktonic organisms.

whaling *noun* the activity of hunting and killing whales.

wharf *noun* (PL. **wharfs, wharves**) a landing-stage built along a waterfront for loading and unloading vessels. [from Anglo-Saxon *hwearf*]

wharfage *noun* **1** dues paid for the use of a wharf. **2** accommodation for vessels at a wharf.

wharfinger *noun* the owner or supervisor of a wharf.

Wharton, Edith (Newbold), *née* **Jones** (c.1861–1937) US novelist, born in New York City. She published her first stories, *The Greater Inclination*, in 1899. She wrote mainly about upper-class New York society, and is best known for her novels, *The House of Mirth* (1905), *Ethan Frome* (1911), and *The Age of Innocence* (1920, Pulitzer Prize).

what — *adj., pron.* **1** used in seeking to identify or classify a thing or person: *what street are we in?* / *what woman do you mean?* / *tell me what flowers these are* / *what is that bird?* **2** used in exclamations: *what lies they tell!* / *what a fool!* / *what awful* *clothes! / what she puts up with!* **3** used as a relative, meaning 'the, all, or any (things or people) that': *it is just what I thought / what you need is a holiday / they gave what money they could / what little they have is used sparingly.* — *adv.* to what extent: *what does that matter?*

— **give someone what for** *colloq.* to scold or punish them.

know what's what *colloq.* to know what really goes on, counts, etc; to know the truth of the matter.

so what? *or* **what of it?** *colloq.* why is that important?

what ... for? what is the reason ...?: *what did you do that for?*

what have you *colloq.* other such things.

what's more ... and, more importantly: *they came, and what's more, they stayed all evening.*

what with ... because of ...; taking account of: *we were exhausted, what with all the delays.* [from Anglo-Saxon *hwæt*]

what-d'you-call-it *noun colloq.* a thing whose name one can't remember.

whatever — *adj., pron.* **1** used as an emphatic form of *what*: *whatever shall I do? / take whatever you want / take whatever money you need.* **2** no matter what: *I must finish, whatever happens.* **3** ... at all: *has nothing whatever to do with you.* **4** *colloq.* some or other: *has disappeared, for whatever reason.* **5** used to express uncertainty: *a didgeridoo, whatever that is.*

— ... **or whatever** *colloq.* ... or some such thing.

What Maisie Knew a novel by Henry James (1897). It is set mainly in England and describes the fate of the child Maisie when her parents divorce.

whatnot *noun* **1** a stand with shelves for ornaments, etc. **2** *colloq.* a whatsit. **3** *colloq.* and other similar things: *grammar and whatnot.*

what's-his-name *or* **what's-her-name**, *etc colloq.* a substitute for an unknown or forgotten name.

whatsit *noun colloq.* some unspecified thing, or one whose name one can't remember. [from *what is it?*]

whatsoever *pron., adj.* **1** *poetic* whatever: *whatsoever things are lovely.* **2** used after noun or pronoun in negative sentences: at all: *had no encouragement whatsoever / none whatsoever.*

wheat *noun* a cereal of the genus *Triticum*, belonging to the grass family (Gramineae), and the most important cereal crop in terms of harvested area, native to the Middle East but now cultivated in temperate regions worldwide. It bears a dense cylindrical head of flowers and is the only cereal suitable for making bread, because it contains the elastic protein gluten. There are numerous species and cultivars with different growth properties and yielding different qualities of flour, such as bread wheat (*Triticum aestivum*), and durum wheat (*Triticum durum*), which is used to make pasta. Wheat is also used in breakfast cereals, and soft wheat flour is used in cakes, biscuits, and pastry. [from Anglo-Saxon *hwæte*]

wheatear *noun* a migratory songbird with a white belly and rump. [probably changed from *white arse*]

wheaten *adj.* **1** made of wheat flour or grain. **2** wholemeal.

wheat germ the vitamin-rich embryo of wheat, present in the grain.

wheatmeal *noun* brown flour containing more than 85 per cent of the powdered whole grain (bran and germ), but not as much as wholemeal flour. Its nutritional value is almost as high as that of wholemeal flour, and it is more digestible and yields a more attractive loaf.

wheatsheaf *noun* a sheaf of wheat.

Wheatstone, Sir Charles (1802–75) English physicist, born in Gloucester. He

invented the concertina (1829), and became professor at King's College, London in 1834. In 1837, with William Cooke, he took out a patent for an electric telegraph; he also explained the principle of the 'stereoscope', and invented a sound magnifier for which he introduced the term 'microphone'. Wheatstone's bridge was brought to notice (though not invented) by him.

Wheatstone's *or* **Wheatstone bridge** *Physics* an electric circuit, consisting of four resistors connected in a loop, for measuring the resistance of one resistor of unknown value by comparing it with three other resistors of known values. [named after Sir Charles Wheatstone]

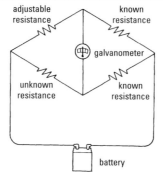

Wheatstone's bridge

wheedle *verb intrans., trans.* to coax or cajole.

wheedler *noun* a person who wheedles.

wheel — *noun* **1** a circular object of varying design rotating on an axle, on which a vehicle moves along the ground. **2** such an object serving as part of a machine or mechanism. **3** a steering-wheel, spinning-wheel, or water wheel. **4** (**wheels**) *chiefly North Amer. colloq.* a motor vehicle for personal use. **5** (**wheels**) the workings of an organization, etc: *the wheels of justice.* **6** *Hist.* a circular instrument of torture on which the victim was stretched. **7** *Betting* a disc or drum on the results of whose random spin bets are made: *a roulette wheel.* **8** a circling or pivoting movement, eg of troops. **9** any progression that appears to go round in a circle: *the wheel of fortune.* — *verb* **1** to fit with wheels: *wheeled vehicles.* **2** to push (a wheeled vehicle or conveyance) or (someone or something) in or on it. **3** *intrans. said of troops, birds, etc* to sweep round in a curve. **4** (*also* **wheel round**) to turn round suddenly; to pivot on one's heel.

— **at** *or* **behind the wheel 1** in the driver's seat. **2** in charge.

wheel and deal to engage in tough business dealing or bargaining.

wheel something out to suggest ideas, etc that have often been connsidered before. [from Anglo-Saxon *hweol*]

wheelbarrow *noun* a hand-pushed cart with a wheel in front and two legs at the rear.

wheelbase *noun* the distance between the front and rear axles of a vehicle.

wheelchair *noun* a chair with wheels in which invalids can be conveyed or convey themselves.

wheel clamp a locking device fitted to a wheel of an illegally parked vehicle in order to immobilize it.

Wheeler, Sir (Robert Eric) Mortimer (1890–1976) English archaeologist, born in Glasgow, Scotland. He was Keeper of the London Museum (1926–44), and carried out notable excavations in Britain at Verulamium (St Albans) and Maiden Castle. Other posts include Director-General of Archaeology in India (1944–7) and Professor at the Institute of Archaeology in London (1948–55). He was well known for his popular accounts of his subject, in books and on television.

wheeler-dealer *noun* a person who uses wheeler-dealing to achieve success.

wheeler-dealing *or* **wheeling and dealing** tough dealing and bargaining in pursuit of one's political or business interests.

wheelhouse *noun* the shelter on a ship's bridge in which the steering-gear is housed.

wheelie bin *Brit. colloq.* a large dustbin in a wheeled frame.

wheel window same as ROSE WINDOW.

wheelwright *noun* a craftsman who makes and repairs wheels and wheeled carriages.

wheeze — *verb intrans.* to breathe in a laboured way with a gasping or rasping noise, when suffering from a lung infection, etc. — *noun* **1** a wheezing breath or sound. **2** *colloq.* a bright idea; a clever scheme. [from Norse *hvæza*]

wheezily *adv.* with wheezing.

wheezy *adj.* (**wheezier**, **wheeziest**) wheezing.

whelk *noun* an edible shellfish with a thick spiral shell. [from Anglo-Saxon *weoloc*]

whelp — *noun* **1** the young of a dog or wolf; a puppy. **2** *old use* an impudent boy or youth. — *verb intrans.* to give birth to puppies or cubs. [from Anglo-Saxon *hwelp*]

when — *adv.* at what time?; during what period?; how soon?: *when does the plane arrive? / I cannot remember when I last saw them.* — *conj.* **1** at the time, or during the period, that: *locks the door when she goes to bed / it happened when I was abroad.* **2** as soon as: *I'll come when I've finished.* **3** at any time; whenever: *come when you can.* **4** but just then: *was about to leave when the telephone rang.* **5** at which time; for at that time: *ring tomorrow, when I'll have more information.* **6** in spite of the fact that; considering that: *why stand when you can sit?* — *pron.* what or which time: *they stayed talking, until when I can't say / since when she hasn't spoken to me / an era when life was harder.* [from Anglo-Saxon *hwænne*]

whence *or* **from whence** — *adv.* **1** from what place?: *enquired whence they had come.* **2** from what cause or circumstance?: *can't explain whence the mistake arose.* — *conj.* **1** to the place from which; from where: *returned to the village / whence they had come.* **2** from which cause or circumstance: *has red hair, whence his nickname 'Ginger'.* [from Middle English *hwannes*]

whenever — *conj.* **1** at any or every time that: *gets furious whenever he fails to get his way.* **2** if ever; no matter when: *I'll be here whenever you need me.* — *adv.* **1** an emphatic form of *when*: *whenever could I have said that?* **2** used to indicate that one does not know when: *at Pentecost, whenever that is.* — ... **or whenever** *colloq.* ... or some such time.

whensoever *adv.* if ever; no matter when.

where — *adv.* **1** in, at, or to which place?; in what direction?: *where is she going? / I don't know where this road takes us.* **2** in what respect?: *showed me where I'd gone wrong.* — *pron.* what place?: *where have you come from?* — *conj., pron.* **1** in, at, or to the, or any, place that; in, at, or to which: *went where he pleased / the village where I was born.* **2** in any case in which: *keep families together where possible.* **3** the aspect or respect in which: *that's where you are wrong.* **4** and there: *stopped at Bradford, where we picked up Jane.* [from Anglo-Saxon *hwær*]

whereabouts — *adv.* (with stress on *-bouts*) where or roughly where? — *sing. or pl. noun* (with stress on *where-*) the position or rough position of a person or thing.

whereas *conj.* **1** when in fact: *she thought she'd failed, whereas she'd done well.* **2** but, by contrast: *I'm a pessimist, whereas my husband is an optimist.*

whereby *rel. pron.* by means of which.

wherefore — *conj., adv. old use Legal* for what reason? — *noun* a reason, as in *the whys and wherefores.*

wherein *old use Legal* — *adv., conj.* in what place⸮; in what respect⸮: *wherein is the justification⸮* — *rel. pron.* in which place or thing.

whereof *rel. pron. old use* of which: *the circumstances whereof I told you.*

whereon *rel. pron. old use* on which.

wheresoever *adv. old use* no matter where.

whereupon *conj.* at which point.

wherever — *rel. pron.* in, at, or to any or every place that: *takes it wherever she goes.* — *conj.* in, at, or to whatever place: *they were welcomed wherever they went.* — *adv.* **1** no matter where: *I won't lose touch, wherever I go.* **2** an emphatic form of where: *wherever can they be⸮* **3** used to indicate that one does not know where: *the Round House, wherever that is.*
— *... or wherever colloq.* ... or some such place.

wherewithal — *rel. pron. old use* with which. — *noun* (**the wherewithal**) the means or necessary resources, especially money.

wherry *noun* (PL. **wherries**) **1** a long light rowing-boat, especially for transporting passengers. **2** a light barge.

whet *verb* (**whetted, whetting**) **1** to sharpen (a bladed tool) by rubbing it against stone, etc. **2** to intensify (someone's appetite or desire). [from Anglo-Saxon *hwettan*]

whether *conj.* **1** used to introduce an indirect question: *asked whether it was raining.* **2** used to introduce an indirect question involving alternative possibilities: *was uncertain whether or not he liked her.* **3** used to state the certainty of something, whichever of two circumstances applies: *promised to marry her, whether or not his parents agreed / the rules, whether fair or unfair, are not our concern.* [from Anglo-Saxon *hwæther*]

whetstone *noun* a stone for sharpening bladed tools.

whew *interj. colloq.* an expression of relief or amazement.

whey *noun* the watery content of milk, separated from the curd in making cheese, junket, etc. [from Anglo-Saxon *hwæg*]

which *adj., pron.* **1** used like *what* in seeking to identify or specify a thing or person, usually from a known set or group: *which twin did you mean⸮ / can't decide which book is better / which did you choose⸮* **2** used like *that* to introduce a defining or identifying clause: *animals which hibernate / the evidence on which it is based / look for the house which lies back from the road.* **3** used to introduce a commenting clause: in this use *that* is not available: *the house, which lies back from the road, is painted red.* **4** used as a relative, meaning 'any that': *take which books you want / tell me which you fancy.* [Anglo-Saxon *hwilc*]

whichever *rel. pron., rel. adj.* **1** the one or ones that; any that: *take whichever are suitable / take whichever coat fits better.* **2** according to which: *at 10.00 or 10.30, whichever is more convenient.* — *adj., pron.* no matter which: *we'll be late, whichever way we go / I'll be satisfied, whichever you choose.*

Whicker, Alan (Donald) (1925–) English broadcaster and journalist, born in Cairo. After World War II he was a war correspondent, reporting on the Inchon landings in Korea before joining the BBC (1957–68), where he worked on the 'Tonight' (1957–65) programme and began his *Whicker's World* documentary series (1958). Thereafter he specialized in travel programmes, including *Whicker Down Under* (1961), *Whicker Within a Woman's World* (1972), *Whicker's World Aboard the Orient Express* (1982), and *Living With Waltzing Matilda* (1987–8.)

whiff *noun* **1** a slight smell. **2** a puff or slight rush: *a whiff of smoke.* **3** a hint: *at the first whiff of scandal.* [imitative]

Whig *Brit. Hist.* — *noun* a member of the Whigs. See also TORY. — *adj.* relating to the Whigs.

[probably from *whiggamore*, a 17c Scottish Presbyterian rebel]

Whiggery *noun* Whig principles.

Whiggish *adj.* relating to or resembling Whigs.

Whig Party in the USA, one of two major US political parties prior to the American Civil War. The Whigs, in opposition to President Andrew Jackson and the Democratic Party from 1834, stood for greater governmental intervention in the economy than their opponents did, but both parties agreed on keeping the slavery issue out of politics. However, when this could no longer be contained the Party collapsed (1854). Henry Clay and Daniel Webster (1782–1852) were prominent Whigs.

Whigs in the UK, a British political party that emerged in 1679–80 as a group agitating for the exclusion of James, Duke of York (later James VII and II) on the grounds of his Catholicism. Probably named from a contraction of 'Whiggamores' (militant Scottish Presbyterians), the Party benefited from the political changes of the Glorious Revolution of 1688 and was dominant in British politics after 1714, when it defended the 'principles of 1688' (eg limited monarchy and the importance of parliament). Most Whig leaders were great landowners who used political patronage to create family-based groupings in parliament. Whig supporters included many from the moneyed and commercial classes, and Nonconformists who (usually mistakenly) looked to the Whigs to provide religious toleration. Whig fortunes waned in the late 18c, and Whigs became leading members of the new Liberal Party from the mid-19c.

while — *conj.* **1** at the same time as. **2** for as long as; for the whole time that: *guards us while we sleep.* **3** during the time that: *happened while we were abroad.* **4** whereas: *he likes camping, while she prefers sailing.* **5** although: *while I see your point, I still cannot agree.* — *adv.* at or during which: *all the months while I was ill.* — *noun* a space or lapse of time: *after a while.* — *verb* (usually **while away** *time, etc*) to pass time in a leisurely or undemanding way.
— **in between whiles** during the intervals.
make it worth someone's while *colloq.* to reward them well for their trouble.
worth one's while worth one's time and trouble.
[from Anglo-Saxon *hwil*]

whilst *conj.* while.

whim *noun* a sudden fanciful idea; a caprice.

whimper — *verb* (**whimpered, whimpering**) **1** *intrans.* to cry feebly or plaintively. **2** *trans.* to say plaintively. — *noun* a feebly plaintive cry. [imitative]

whimsical *adj.* **1** delicately fanciful or playful. **2** odd, weird, or fantastic. **3** given to having whims.

whimsicality *noun* a whimsical quality.

whimsically *adv.* in a whimsical way.

whimsy *noun* (PL. **whimsies**) **1** quaint, fanciful humour. **2** a whim. [see WHIM]

whin *noun* gorse. [probably from Norse *whin*]

whine — *verb usually intrans.* **1** to whimper. **2** to cry fretfully. **3** to complain peevishly. **4** to speak in a thin, ingratiating, or servile voice. **5** *trans.* to say peevishly. — *noun* **1** a whimper. **2** a continuous high-pitched noise. **3** a thin, ingratiating nasal tone of voice. [from Anglo-Saxon *hwinan*]

whinge — *verb intrans. colloq.* to complain irritably. — *noun* a peevish complaint. [from Anglo-Saxon *hwinsian*, to whine]

whinny — *verb intrans.* (**whinnies, whinnied**) *said of a horse* to neigh softly. — *noun* (PL. **whinnies**) a gentle neigh. [imitative]

whip — *noun* **1** a lash with a handle, for driving animals or thrashing people. **2** a member of a parliamentary party responsible for members' discipline, and for their attendance to vote on important issues. **3** a notice sent to members by a party whip requiring their attendance for a vote, urgency being indicated by the number of underlinings: *a three-line whip.* **4** a dessert of any of various flavours made with beaten egg-whites or cream. **5** a whipper-in. — *verb* (**whipped, whipping**) **1** to strike or thrash with a whip. **2** to lash with the action or force of a whip: *a sharp wind whipped their faces.* **3** *trans., intrans.* to move or cause to move with a whip-like motion: *the branch whipped back.* **4** (usually **whip something off, out,** *etc*) to take or snatch it: *whipped out a revolver.* **5** *intrans., trans.* to move smartly: *whipped out of sight.* **6** to rouse, goad, drive, or force into a certain state: *whipped the crowd into a fury.* **7** *colloq.* to steal. **8** to beat (egg-whites, cream, etc) until stiff. **9** to wind cord round (a rope, etc) to prevent fraying. **10** to oversew. **11** *colloq.* to outdo, outwit, or defeat.
— **have the whip hand over someone** *colloq.* to have an advantage over them.
whip something up 1 to arouse support, enthusiasm, or other feelings. **2** to prepare a meal, etc at short notice.
[from Middle English *whippe*]

whipcord *noun* **1** strong, fine, tightly twisted cord. **2** cotton or worsted cloth with a diagonal rib.

whiplash *noun* **1** the lash of a whip, or the motion it represents. **2** (*also* **whiplash injury**) a popular term for a neck injury caused by the sudden jerking back of the head and neck, especially as a result of a motor-vehicle collision.

whipper-in *noun* an assistant to a huntsman, who controls the hounds.

whipper-snapper *noun old colloq. use* a cheeky young lad; any lowly person who behaves impudently.

whippet *noun* a slender dog like a small greyhound, used for racing.

whipping-boy *noun* **1** *Hist.* a boy who is educated with a prince and given whatever beatings the prince has deserved. **2** anyone on whom the blame for others' faults falls.

whipping cream cream that will thicken when whipped.

whipping-top *noun* a top kept spinning by the lash of a whip.

Whipple, Fred Lawrence (1906–) US astronomer, born in Red Oak, Iowa. Professor at Harvard from 1945, he is known especially for his work on comets. In 1950 he put forward the 'dirty snowball' model of the cometary nucleus made of ice and dust, a few kilometres across; this was later confirmed through observations of Halley's comet.

Whipple, George Hoyt (1878–1976) US pathologist, born in Ashland, New Hampshire. Director of a research centre at the University of California, and later professor at University of Rochester in New York, his research led others to a successful liver treatment of anaemia, until then a fatal disease. He shared the 1934 Nobel Prize for Physiology or Medicine with George Minot and William Murphy.

whippoorwill *noun* a species of nightjar native to N America. [imitative of call]

whippy *adj.* (**whippier, whippiest**) *said of a stick or cane* springy; flexible.

whip-round *noun* a collection of money hastily made among a group of people.

whipstock *noun* the handle of a whip.

whirl — *verb* **1** *intrans.* to spin or revolve rapidly. **2** *trans., intrans.* to move with a rapid circling or spiralling motion. **3** *intrans. said of the head* to feel dizzy from excitement, etc. — *noun* **1** a circling or spiralling movement or pattern: *a whirl of smoke / whirls of colour.* **2** a round of intense activity: *a whirl of parties*. **3** a dizzy state. [from Norse *hvirfla*, to turn]

whirligig *noun* **1** a spinning toy, especially a top. **2** a merry-go-round. **3** a dizzying round of activity, progression of events, etc. [from Middle English *whirligigge*, spinning toy]

whirlpool *noun* a violent almost circular eddy of water that occurs in rivers or seas at a point where several strong currents of water travelling in different directions converge, eg at the foot of a a waterfall. Floating objects may be drawn into a depression at the whirlpool's centre.

whirlwind — *noun* a violently spiralling column of air. — *adj.* rapid: *a whirlwind courtship*.

whirlybird *noun colloq.* a helicopter.

whirr *or* **whir** — *verb intrans.* (**whirred**, **whirring**) to turn or spin with a humming noise. — *noun* a whirring sound. [probably from Scandinavian *whirr*]

whisk — *verb* **1** (**whisk something off** *or* **away**) to brush or sweep it lightly: *whisked the crumbs off the table*. **2** to transport rapidly: *was whisked into hospital*. **3** to move with a brisk waving motion: *whisked its tail from side to side*. **4** to beat (egg-whites, cream, etc) till stiff. — *noun* **1** a whisking movement or action. **2** a hand-held implement for whisking egg-whites, etc. **3** a flexible implement for swatting flies. [related to Norse *visk*, wisp]

whisker *noun* **1** any of the long coarse hairs growing round the mouth of a cat, mouse, etc. **2** (**whiskers**) a man's beard, especially the parts growing on his cheeks. **3** the tiniest possible margin; a hair's breadth: *within a whisker of death / escaped by a whisker*. [related to Norse *visk*, wisp]

whiskery *adj.* having whiskers.

whiskey *noun* (PL. **whiskeys**) *Irish, North Amer., esp. US* whisky.

Whiskey Rebellion an insurrection (1794) of farmers in W Pennsylvania and Virginia, USA, against the excise tax imposed by the federal government on the whiskey they made from their grain. The rebellion was suppressed by government forces led by Henry Lee (1756–1818) and Alexander Hamilton.

whisky *noun* (PL. **whiskies**) an alcoholic spirit distilled from a fermented mash of cereal grains, eg barley, wheat, or rye. [from Gaelic *uisge beatha*, literally 'water of life']

whisper — *verb* (**whispered**, **whispering**) **1** *intrans., trans.* to speak or say quietly, breathing rather than voicing the words. **2** *intrans., trans.* to speak or say in secrecy or confidence. **3** *intrans., trans.* to spread a rumour; to rumour: *it's whispered that she's leaving him*. **4** *intrans.* said of a breeze, etc to make a rustling sound in leaves, etc. — *noun* **1** a whispered level of speech: *spoke in a whisper*. **2** (*often* **whispers**) a rumour or hint; whispered gossip: *have been whispers about their divorce*. **3** a soft rustling sound: *the whisper of the breeze*. [from Anglo-Saxon *hwisprian*]

whist *noun* a card game for usually two pairs of players, in which the object is to take a majority of 13 tricks, each trick over six scoring one point. [originally *whisk*]

◊ A trick is won by the highest card played of the suit led, or by the highest trump if any are played. A game is won by the first side to reach five points, and a rubber by the first side to win two games. Whist derives from the 16c game *trump* (or *ruff and honours*), and was regarded as the premier card game from the 18c until the appearance of bridge at the end of the 19c.

whist drive a gathering for whist-playing, with a change of partner after every four games.

whistle — *noun* **1** a shrill sound produced through pursed lips or through the teeth, used to signal, to express surprise, etc. **2** any of several similar sounds, eg the call of a bird, or the shrill sigh of the wind. **3** any of many devices produc-

ing a similar sound, etc, eg one operated by steam on a railway locomotive or kettle, or one blown by a referee to regulate play on the pitch. **4** a simple wind instrument consisting of a wooden or metal pipe with finger holes. — *verb* **1** *intrans., trans.* to produce a whistle through pursed lips or teeth; to perform (a tune), signal, communicate, or summon with this sound. **2** *intrans., trans.* to blow a whistle, or play on a whistle. **3** *intrans. said of a kettle or locomotive* to emit a whistling sound. **4** *intrans. said of the wind* to make a shrill sound. **5** *intrans., trans. said of a bird* to sing. **6** *intrans. said of a bullet, etc* to whizz through the air.

— **blow the whistle on someone** *or* **something** *colloq.* **1** to expose illegal or dishonest practices to the authorities. **2** to declare something to be illegal.

wet one's whistle *colloq.* to have a drink; to quench one's thirst.

whistle for something *colloq.* to expect it in vain.

[from Anglo-Saxon *hwistlian*, to whistle]

Whistler, James (Abbott) McNeill (1834–1903) US artist, born in Lowell, Massachusetts. He left the USA to take up art in Paris, and later in London, where his work was controversially received. He is best known for his evening scenes ('nocturnes'), including *Old Battersea Bridge* (c.1872–5, Tate, London), and for the portrait of his mother (*The Artist's Mother*, 1871–2, Louvre, Paris). He also became known for his etchings and lithographs, especially those dealing with the London riverside.

whistle-stop *adj.* **1** *said of a politician's tour* with a number of short stops, originally at railway stations, for delivering electioneering addresses to local communities. **2** *said of any tour* very rapid, with a number of brief stops.

Whit — *noun* Whitsuntide. — *adj.* of or belonging to Whitsuntide.

whit *noun* (*with a negative*) the least bit: *not a whit worse*. [variant of *wight*, creature]

Whitbread Prize in the UK and Ireland, a literary prize founded in 1971 by Whitbread brewers. It is awarded annually for five categories of literature.

Whitby POP (1981) 13 000, a port and resort town in Scarborough district, North Yorkshire, N England. It lies on the North Sea coast, 27km/17mi NW of Scarborough. HISTORY site of a monastery founded in 657 by St Hilda; the Synod of Whitby met here in 663; Captain Cook sailed from Whitby in 1768. NOTABLE FEATURES abbey (13c); St Mary's Church (12c).

Whitby, Synod of a meeting (663) in Britain where the differences in organization between Roman and Celtic Christianity were debated before Oswiu, King of Northumbria. Roman concepts of Church order prevailed, which resulted in the two Christian traditions in Britain eventually uniting in their acceptance of the authority and practices of Rome.

White, Gilbert (1720–93) English naturalist and clergyman, born in Selbourne, Hampshire. He was curate of Selbourne and Faringdon. His fame is based upon his *Natural History and Antiquities of Selborne* (1789), which gives acute observations on the habits and lives of a wide range of birds, mammals, and insects.

White, Patrick (Victor Martindale) (1912–90) Australian writer, born in London, England. His first novel, *Happy Valley*, appeared in 1939, and after service in World War II, he returned to Australia. He wrote several novels, short stories, and plays, and achieved international success with *The Tree of Man* (1955), and *Voss* (1957). His 'self-portrait' *Flaws in the Glass* was published in 1981. He was awarded the Nobel Prize for Literature in 1973.

White, T(erence) H(anbury) (1906–64) English novelist, born in Bombay, India. He is

best known as the author of the sequence of novels about King Arthur, *The Once and Future King* (1958), which begins with the children's classic *The Sword in the Stone* (1937). Other works include the autobiographical novel, *The Goshawk* (1951).

white — *adj.* **1** of the colour of snow, the colour that reflects all light. **2** (*often* **White**) *said of people* belonging to one of the pale-skinned races; relating to such people. **3** abnormally pale, from shock or illness. **4** *said eg of a rabbit or mouse* albino. **5** *said of hair* lacking pigment, as in old age. **6** *said of a variety of anything* pale-coloured, as distinct from darker types: *white grapes*. **7** *said of wine* made from white grapes or from skinned black grapes. **8 a** *said of flour* having had the bran and wheat germ removed. **b** *said of bread* made with white flour. **9** *said of coffee or tea* with milk or cream added. **10** *poetic, said of the soul, etc* pure; innocent. — *noun* **1** white colour or colouring matter, eg paint; white clothes: *dressed all in white*. **2** (*often* **White**) a white person. **3** (*also* **egg-white**) the clear fluid surrounding the yolk of an egg; albumen. **4** the white part of the eyeball, surrounding the iris. **5** *Games* something white, eg a playing-piece in chess or draughts, a ball in snooker, or ring on an archery target; the player of the white pieces in a board game. **6** (**whites**) household linen, or white clothes, worn eg for cricket or tennis.

— **bleed someone white** to drain or deprive them gradually of resources, wealth, etc.

[from Anglo-Saxon *hwit*]

white ant a termite.

White Australia Policy the unofficial national policy of Australia from 1901 to the late 1960s, designed to exclude non-European migrants. The trade union movement supported the policy on the grounds that it excluded workers who might undermine union wage rates. In the 1950s and 1960s, the Colombo Plan (1950) brought Asian students to Australia, and their presence helped to reduce racial prejudice in the major urban areas. In the late 1960s, the policy was progressively dismantled, and race was replaced as a basis for admission by other criteria such as educational and technical qualifications.

whitebait *noun* the young of various fish, eg herrings, fried and eaten whole.

white blood cell *or* **white corpuscle**, a colourless blood cell, containing a nucleus, whose main functions are to engulf invading micro-organisms and foreign particles, to produce antibodies, or to remove cell debris from sites of injury and infection. There are three main types (monocytes, granulocytes, and lymphocytes), all of which are formed in the bone marrow. — Also called *leucocyte*.

White Canon another name for PREMON-STRATENSIAN.

white-collar *adj.* denoting non-manual workers, in clerical or other professions. See also BLUE-COLLAR.

White Devil, The a play by John Webster (1612). Written in blank verse, it is a tragedy of love, ghosts, and bloodshed, depicting the trial of the treacherous but courageous Vittoria and the revenge plot instigated by the ghost of her lover's wife.

white dwarf a small faint hot star that has reached the last stage of its life, having exhausted the nuclear fuel in its central core and started to collapse under its own gravity. The mass of a white dwarf is similar to that of the Sun, but its diameter is about the same as that of the Earth.

white elephant a possession or piece of property that is useless or unwanted, especially if inconvenient or expensive to keep.

White Ensign see ENSIGN.

white feather a symbol of cowardice.
— **show the white feather** to behave in a cowardly fashion.

Whitefield, George (1714–70) English Methodist evangelist, born in Gloucester. His association with Charles and John Wesley at Oxford made him become an enthusiastic evangelist. Many of his adherents followed the Countess of Huntingdon in Wales, and formed the Calvinistic Methodists, so she appointed him her chaplain, and built and endowed many chapels for him. He also played an important role in the Great Awakening in America.

white fish a general name for white-fleshed sea fish, including whiting, cod, sole, haddock, and halibut.

white flag the signal used for offering surrender or requesting a truce.

whitefly *noun* a small sap-sucking bug, whose body and wings are covered with a white waxy powder. The immature stages are immobile, and are typically found on the underside of leaves. It commonly produces honeydew, and is attended by ants.

white gold a pale lustrous alloy of gold, containing eg platinum or palladium.

white goods large, traditionally white, kitchen appliances such as washing machines, dishwashers, and cookers.

Whitehall a wide thoroughfare lying between Parliament and Trafalgar Squares in London, and by association the offices of central government which line it. All that remains of the Palace of Whitehall, from which the street takes its name, is the 17c banqueting house designed by Inigo Jones.

Whitehead, A(lfred) N(orth) (1861–1947) English mathematician and idealist philosopher, born in Ramsgate. He was Senior Lecturer in Mathematics at Cambridge until 1910. He then taught at London (1910–14), was Professor of Applied Mathematics at Imperial College (1914–24), and was then Professor of Philosophy at Harvard (1924–37). He collaborated with his former pupil, Bertrand Russell, in writing the *Principia Mathematica* (1910–13). Other more popular works include *Adventures of Ideas* (1933) and *Modes of Thought* (1938).

white-headed boy *ironic* a favourite or protégé.

white heat 1 a temperature of metals, etc greater than red heat, at which white light is emitted. 2 *colloq.* the intensest possible keenness, activity, or excitement: *the white heat of technology.*

white hope someone of whom great achievements are expected.

Whitehorse POP (1991) 22 000, the capital of Yukon Territory, NW Canada. It lies on the R Lewes, 145km/90mi E of the Alaskan border. It was founded in 1900 during the Klondike gold rush.

White Horse, Vale of the a valley in Oxfordshire, England, whose name derives from a stylized representation of a horse carved on the chalk hillside, probably during the Iron Age. It was perhaps originally a cult object for the local Celtic tribe, the Belgae.

white horse a white wave crest on a choppy sea.

white-hot *adj.* 1 so hot that white light is given off. 2 intense; passionate.

White House the official residence of the US President, situated on Pennsylvania Avenue in Washington, DC. The 132-room neoclassical mansion was built (1793–1801) from the designs of James Hoban (1762–1831), who also supervised its reconstruction (1814–29) after it was burnt down by the British in 1814. Major restoration work was carried out between 1948 and 1952.

white knight a person who rescues a company financially, especially from an unwanted takeover bid.

white-knuckle *adj. colloq.* causing extreme anxiety, alarm, or terror: *a white-knuckle ride.*

Whitelaw, Willie (William Stephen Ian) Whitelaw, 1st Viscount (1918–) Scottish Conservative politician, born in Nairn. He became an MP in 1955, and after several years as Chief Whip (1964–70), he became Leader of the House of Commons (1970–2), Secretary of State for Northern Ireland (1972–3) and for Employment (1973–4), and Home Secretary (1979–83). Made a viscount in 1983, he was Leader of the House of Lords until 1988.

white lead a mixture of lead carbonate and lead hydroxide in the form of a white powder, used as colouring matter, etc.

white lie a forgivable lie, especially one told to avoid hurting someone's feelings.

white light light, such as that of the sun, containing all the wavelengths in the visible range of the spectrum.

white magic magic used for beneficial purposes, eg to oppose evil, cure disease, etc.

white matter pale fibrous nerve tissue in the brain and spinal cord.

white meat a pale-coloured meat, eg veal, chicken, and turkey. **b** in poultry, the paler meat of the breast as opposed to the darker meat of the leg, etc.

whiten *verb trans., intrans.* (**whitened, whitening**) to make or become white or whiter; to bleach.

whitener *noun* 1 a person or thing that whitens. 2 an artificial substitute for milk in coffee, etc.

whiteness *noun* a white state or quality.

White Nile *or* **Bahr El Ablad** the upper reach of the R Nile in S and E Sudan. The river is 1 900km/1 180mi long and is a continuation of the Albert Nile, which crosses into SE Sudan from NE Uganda at Nimule. It flows generally N to Khartoum, where it is joined from the E by the Blue Nile, forming the R Nile.

white noise noise in which there are a large number of frequencies of roughly equal intensity.

white-out *noun* 1 conditions of poor visibility in snowy weather, when the overcast sky blends imperceptibly with the white landscape. 2 a dense blizzard.

white paper (*also* **White Paper**) a government policy statement printed on white paper, issued for the information of parliament.

white pepper light-coloured pepper made from peppercorns from which the dark outer husk has been removed.

White Plains POP (1990) 49 000, the seat of Westchester County, SE New York State, USA. HISTORY Provincial Congress ratified the Declaration of Independence here (1776); scene of the Battle of White Plains (1776). NOTABLE FEATURE Miller Hill Restoration (Washington's headquarters).

white pudding a spicy sausage made from minced pork, oatmeal, and suet.

White Russia see BELORUSSIA.

White Russians the name collectively given to counter-revolutionary forces led by ex-tsarist officers, who fought unsuccessfully against the Bolshevik Red Army during the Russian Civil War (1918–20). Supported by the military intervention of British, American, French, and Japanese troops, white resistance to the Red Army collapsed when these withdrew.

White Sands an area of white gypsum sand dunes in S New Mexico, USA, designated a national monument in 1933. The first nuclear explosion took place on the surrounding missile testing range in 1945.

white sauce thick sauce made from flour, fat, and milk.

White Sea, Russian **Beloye More** an arm of the Arctic Ocean and an inlet of the Barents Sea, NW Russia. AREA c.95 000sq km/36 700sq mi. The port of Belmorsk is connected to St Petersburg on the Baltic Sea by a 225km-/140mi-long canal system, completed in 1933. Ice-breakers keep some sea channels open in winter. Herring and cod fishing are important.

white slave a girl or woman held against her will, and forced into prostitution.

white spirit a colourless liquid distilled from petroleum and containing a mixture of hydrocarbons, used as a solvent and thinner for paints and varnishes.

white sugar refined sugar.

white tie 1 a white bow tie, part of men's formal evening dress. 2 *as an instruction on an invitation* formal evening dress for men.

whitewash — *noun* 1 a mixture of lime and water, for giving a white coating to especially outside walls. 2 measures taken to cover up eg a disreputable affair, clear a stained reputation, etc. — *verb* to coat, clean up, or conceal with whitewash.

white whale a white toothed whale of arctic waters, related to the dolphin.

whitewood *noun* 1 the light-coloured timber of any of various trees. 2 unstained wood; wood prepared for staining.

Whitgift, John (c.1530–1604) English prelate and Archbishop of Canterbury, born in Grimsby, Lincolnshire. Ordained in 1560, he became Dean of Lincoln (1571), Bishop of Worcester (1577), Archbishop (1583), and Privy Councillor (1586). He attended Elizabeth I at her death-bed, and crowned James VI and I. He vindicated the Anglican position against the Puritans and enforced a policy of uniformity in the Church of England.

whither *old use* — *adv.* 1 to what place: *whither did they go?* 2 in what direction? towards what state: *whither education?* — *conj., rel. pron.* 1 to the, or any, place that; towards which: *went*

White House

whither he was instructed / the mountain pass whither they were headed. **2** towards which place: *some miles away lay London, whither they turned their steps next day.* [from Anglo-Saxon *hwider*]

whiting[1] *noun* a small edible fish related to the cod. [from Middle English *hwitling* or Old Dutch *witinc*]

whiting[2] *noun* ground and washed white chalk, used in putty, whitewash, and silver-cleaner. [see WHITE]

whitish *adj.* somewhat white; nearly white.

whitlow *noun* an inflammation of the finger or toe, especially near the nail. [from Middle English *whitflawe*, white flaw]

Whitman, Walt (1819–91) US poet, born in Long Island, New York. He worked in offices and as a teacher, before turning to journalism. His major poetic work is *Leaves of Grass* (1855), which grew in size with each of the eight succeeding editions. During the Civil War he became a volunteer nurse in the hospitals of the Northern army — an experience which forms much of the subject matter of his later prose works, notably *Democratic Vistas* (1871) and *Specimen Days & Collect* (1882–3). He suffered a stroke in 1873, and left Washington for Camden, New Jersey.

Whitsun *or* **Whitsuntide** *noun* the week beginning with Whit Sunday.

Whit Sunday *or* **Whitsunday** in the Christian Church, the seventh Sunday after Easter, commemorating the day of Pentecost, on which by tradition those newly baptized wore white robes. [from Anglo-Saxon *hwita sunnandæg*, white Sunday]

Whittier, John Greenleaf (1807–92) US Quaker poet and abolitionist, born near Haverhill, Massachusetts. He embarked on a career as a writer and journalist, and his first publication was a collection of poems and stories, *Legends of New England* (1831). In 1840 he settled at Amesbury, where he devoted himself to the cause of emancipation. His later poetic works include *In War Time* (1864), *Snowbound* (1866), and *At Sundown* (1890).

Whittington, Dick (Richard) (c.1358–1423) English merchant, supposed to have been the youngest son of Sir William Whittington of Pauntley in Gloucestershire, on whose death he set out (aged 13) for London, where he found work as an apprentice. He became an alderman and sheriff, Lord Mayor of London (1397), and was a generous benefactor. The legend of his cat is an accepted part of English folklore.

Whittle, Sir Frank (1907–) English aeronautical engineer and inventor, born in Coventry. He joined the RAF as an apprentice (1923), and studied at the RAF College, Cranwell, and at Cambridge University. He invented the jet engine, first flown successfully in a Gloster aircraft in May 1941, and has since acted as consultant and technical adviser to a number of British firms.

whittle *verb* **1** to cut, carve, or pare (a stick, piece of wood, etc). **2** to shape or fashion by this means. **3** (**whittle something away**) to consume it bit by bit; to eat away at it or erode it. **4** (**whittle something down**) to reduce it gradually or persistently: *whittled down the guest list from 200 to 150.* [from Anglo-Saxon *thwitan*, to cut]

Whitworth, Sir Joseph (1803–87) English engineer and inventor, born in Stockport. At the Great Exhibition of 1851 he exhibited many tools and machines. In 1859 he invented a gun of compressed steel, with spiral polygonal bore. He also founded Whitworth scholarships to encourage engineering.

Whitworth, Kathy (Kathrynne Ann) (1939–) US golfer, born in Monahans, Texas. She has won 88 tournaments on the US Women's circuit, including all the women's 'Majors' except the US Open. She turned professional in 1958, and won the US Ladies Professional Golf Association championship four times (1967, 1971, 1975, 1982). She was the leading money-winner in women's golf eight times between 1965 and 1973.

whizz *or* **whiz** *colloq.* — *verb intrans.* (**whizzed**, **whizzing**) **1** to fly through the air, especially with a whistling noise. **2** to move fast. — *noun* an expert.

whizz kid *colloq.* someone who achieves success early, through ability, inventiveness, dynamism, or ambition.

WHO *abbrev.* World Health Organization.

who *pron.* **1** used in seeking to identify a person or people, as the subject of a verb and also commonly as the object of a verb or preposition in place of the more formal *whom*: *who is at the door? / who did you give it to? / asked who else he had seen.* **2** used like *that* to introduce a defining clause: *the boy who was on the train / anyone who wants this can have it.* **3** used to add a commenting clause; in this use, *that* is not available: *Julius Caesar, who was murdered in 44 BC.* — **know who's who** know the important people and what they do. [from Anglo-Saxon *hwa*]

whoa *interj.* a command to stop, especially to a horse.

who'd *contr.* **1** who would. **2** who had.

whodunit *or* **whodunnit** *noun colloq.* a detective novel, play, etc; a mystery. [from *who done it?*, facetiously illiterate for *who did it?*]

whoever *pron.* **1** used as an emphatic form of *who* or *whom*: *whoever is that at the door? / ask whoever you like.* **2** no matter who: *I don't know them, whoever they are / whoever is appointed faces a huge task.* **3** used to indicate that one does not know who: *St Fiacre, whoever he was.* — **... or whoever** *colloq.* ... or some other such person or people.

whole — *noun* **1** all of; not less than. **2** something complete in itself, especially if consisting of integrated parts: *elements that together form a whole.* — *adj.* **1** all of; no less than. **2** in one piece: *swallowed it whole.* **3** unbroken: *only two cups left whole.* **4** *said of food* processed as little as possible. **5** *old use* healthy; well: *the miracle that made him whole.* **6** *colloq.* huge; vast: *a whole pile of work to do.* — *adv. colloq.* completely; altogether; wholly: *a whole new approach.* — **a whole lot** *colloq.* a great deal. **as a whole** in general; taken as a complete group, etc rather than as individuals. **on the whole** considering everything. [from Anglo-Saxon *hal*, healthy]

wholehearted *adj.* sincere and enthusiastic.

wholeheartedly *adv.* in a wholehearted way.

wholemeal *adj.* **1** *said of flour* made from the entire wheat grain. **2** *said of bread* made from wholemeal flour.

wholeness *noun* a whole or complete state.

wholesale — *noun* the sale of goods in large quantities to a retailer. — *adj., adv.* **1** of, or by, this type of sale. **2** on a huge scale and without discrimination: *wholesale destruction.* See also RETAIL.

wholesaler *noun* a wholesale supplier.

wholesome *adj.* **1** attractively healthy: *a wholesome appearance.* **2** promoting health. **3** *old use* morally beneficial. **4** sensible; prudent: *a wholesome respect for mountains.*

wholesomely *adv.* in a wholesome way.

wholesomeness *noun* being wholesome.

whole-tone scale *Mus.* either of two scales produced by beginning on one of any two notes a chromatic semitone apart and ascending or descending in whole tones for an octave. There may be no tonic (or other) relationship between the individual notes in the series. Claude Debussy and others made extensive use of the whole-tone scale in their music.

wholly *adv.* completely; altogether.

whom *pron.* used as the object of a verb or preposition, as the objective case of *who*; it is now often replaced by *who*, especially in less formal usage: **1** in seeking to identify a person: *whom do you want? / to whom are you referring?* **2** used like *that* as a relative in a defining clause: *I am looking for the woman whom I met at the reception.* **3** used to introduce a commenting clause: in this use *that* is not available: *the woman, whom I met at the reception, has disappeared.* [from Anglo-Saxon *hwam*]

whomever *pron. formal* used as the object of a verb or preposition to mean 'any person or people that': *I will write to whomever they appoint.*

whomsoever *pron.* whomever.

whoop — *noun* **1** a loud cry of delight, triumph, etc. **2** a noisy indrawn breath typical in whooping cough. — *verb intrans., trans.* to utter, or say with, a whoop. — **whoop it up** *colloq.* to celebrate noisily.

whoopee *interj.* expressing exuberant delight. — **make whoopee** to celebrate exuberantly.

whooper swan a swan that is easily distinguished by its straight neck and yellow-and-black bill, so called because it makes loud whooping calls when in flight. It breeds in Iceland, N Europe, and Asia, and migrates S in winter.

whooping cough *Medicine* pertussis, a highly contagious disease mainly affecting children, caused by infection of the respiratory tract with the bacterium *Bordetella pertussis*. It is characterized by bouts of violent coughing followed by a sharp drawing in of the breath which produces a characteristic 'whooping' sound.

whoops *interj.* an exclamation of surprise or concern made when one has a slight accident, makes an error, etc or sees someone else do so.

whop *verb* (**whopped**, **whopping**) *colloq.* **1** to hit; to thrash. **2** to defeat soundly.

whopper *old colloq. use noun* **1** anything very large: *a whopper of a fish.* **2** a lie.

whopping *adj. colloq.* huge; enormous.

whore — *noun old offensive use* **1** a prostitute. **2** a sexually immoral or promiscuous woman. — *verb intrans.* **1** *said of a man* to have sexual relations with prostitutes. **2** *said of a woman* to be a prostitute. [from Anglo-Saxon *hore*]

who're *contr.* who are.

whorehouse *noun old colloq. use* a brothel.

whorl *noun* **1** *Bot.* a circular arrangement of several petals, leaves, or other identical structures around the same point on a plant. **2** *Zool.* one of the coils in the spiral shell of a mollusc. **3** a type of fingerprint in which there is a spiral arrangement of the ridges on the skin. [from Anglo-Saxon *hwyrfel*]

who's *contr.* **1** who is. **2** who has.

whose *pron., adj.* **1** belonging to which person or people: *whose is this jacket? / we do not know whose these are.* **2** used to introduce a defining clause: of whom or which: *children whose parents are divorced / buildings whose foundations are sinking.* **3** used to add a commenting clause: *my parents, without whose help I could not have succeeded.* **4** whoever's or whichever's: *take whose advice you will.*

whosoever *pron.* whoever.

why — *adv.* for what reason: *why do you ask? / did not say why she was leaving.* — *rel. pron.* for, or because of, which: *no reason why I should get involved.* — *interj.* **1** expressing surprise, indignation, impatience, recognition, etc: *why, you little monster!* **2** used to challenge an implied criticism:

why, have you any objection? — *noun* a reason: *the whys and wherefores.*

— **why not** used to make or agree to a suggestion: *why don't you ask her?* / *'Like a drink?' 'Why not.'.*
[from Anglo-Saxon *hwi*]

Whymper, Edward (1840–1911) English wood-engraver and mountaineer, born in London. He was trained as an artist on wood, but became better known for his mountaineering than for his book illustrations. During 1860–9 he conquered several hitherto unscaled peaks of the Alps, including the Matterhorn (1865). He later travelled in Greenland, the Andes, and Canada.

WI *abbrev.* **1** West Indies. **2** Wisconsin. **3** in the UK, Women's Institute.

Wichita POP (1990) 485 000, the seat of Sedgwick County, S Kansas, USA, lying on the Arkansas R. It is the largest city in Kansas and the chief commercial and industrial centre in the S of the state. HISTORY settled in 1864; achieved city status in 1871. NOTABLE FEATURE Cow Town (a replica of early Wichita). [named after a Native American tribe]

Wick POP (1981) 7 900, the capital of Caithness district, Highland Region, NE Scotland. It is a fishing port on the NE coast, at the mouth of the R Wick. NOTABLE FEATURES Wick Heritage Centre; Castle Girnigoe (15c) and Castle Sinclair (1606–7) lie to the N.

wick *noun* the string running up through a candle and projecting at the top, that burns when lit and draws up the wax into the flame.
— **get on someone's wick** *slang* to be a source of irritation to them.
[from Anglo-Saxon *weoce*]

wicked *adj.* **1** evil; sinful; immoral. **2** mischievous; playful; roguish. **3** *colloq.* bad: *wicked weather.* [from Anglo-Saxon *wicca*, wizard]

wickedly *adv.* in a wicked way.

wickedness *noun* a wicked state; wicked activity or behaviour.

wicker *adj., said of a fence, basket, etc* made of interwoven twigs, canes, rushes, etc. [from Scandinavian *wicker*]

wickerwork *noun* articles made of such material.

wicket *noun* **1** *Cricket* a row of three small wooden posts stuck upright in the ground behind either crease; the playing area between these; a batsman's stand at the wicket, or his or her dismissal by the bowler: *45 runs for two wickets.* **2** a small door or gate, especially one that can open separately within a large door or gate. [from Old French *wiket*]

wicket-keeper *noun* *Cricket* the fielder who stands immediately behind the wicket.

Wickham, George an unprincipled character who elopes with Lydia in Jane Austen's *Pride and Prejudice.*

Wicklow, Gaelic **Cill Mhantáin**, also called **The Garden of Ireland** POP (1991) 97 000, a county in Leinster province, E Irish Republic. AREA 2 025sq km/782sq mi. It is bounded E by the Irish Sea. PHYSICAL DESCRIPTION watered by the Slaney, Liffey, and Avoca rivers; the Wicklow Mts lie in the W. CAPITAL Wicklow. ECONOMY agriculture; tourism (resorts include Bray).

wide — *adj.* **1** large in extent from side to side. **2** measuring a certain amount from side to side. **3** *said of the eyes* open to the fullest extent. **4** *said of a range, selection, etc* covering a great variety. **5** extensive; widespread: *wide support.* **6** *said of a gap* large: *a wide difference.* **7** general, as opposed to particular: *consider the wider implications.* **8** (**wide of something**) off the mark: *his aim was wide of the target.* — *adv.* **1** over an extensive area: *travelling far and wide.* **2** to the fullest extent: *with legs wide apart.* **3** (**wide of something**) off the mark: *shot wide of the target.* — *noun Cricket* a ball bowled out of the batsman's reach.

— **wide awake** fully awake or alert.

wide open 1 open to the fullest extent. **2** *colloq.* vulnerable; exposed to attack.
[from Anglo-Saxon *wid*]

-wide *combining form* forming words meaning 'throughout the extent of': *nationwide.*

wide-angle lens a camera lens with an extra-wide range of view.

wide boy *colloq.* a shrewd but dishonest operator in business undertakings.

widely *adv.* **1** over a wide area or range. **2** to a great extent.

widen *verb trans., intrans.* (**widened, widening**) to make, or become, wide or wider.

wideness *noun* a wide state or quality.

wide-ranging *adj., said of interests, discussions, etc* covering a large variety of subjects or topics.

widespread *adj.* **1** extending over a wide area. **2** affecting or involving large numbers of people: *widespread agreement.*

widgeon see WIGEON.

widget *noun* a gadget; any small manufactured item or component. [perhaps an alteration of GADGET]

Widnes POP (1981) 56 000, a town in Halton district, Cheshire, NW central England. It is situated 20km/12mi E of Liverpool, on the N bank of the R Mersey.

widow — *noun* **1** a woman whose husband is dead and who has not remarried. **2** *colloq.* a woman whose husband spends much time away from her on some especially sporting pursuit: *golf widows.* — *verb* to leave (someone) a widow or widower. [from Anglo-Saxon *widewe*]

widower *noun* a man whose wife is dead, and who has not remarried.

width *noun* **1** extent from side to side. **2** wideness. **3** the distance from side to side across a swimming-pool. [see WIDE]

widthways *adv., adj.* across the width: *folded widthways.*

Wieland, Christoph Martin (1733–1813) German poet and writer, born near Biberach. He made the first German translation of Shakespeare (1762–6) and wrote a number of popular romances, notably *Agathon* (1766–7). His best-known work is the heroic poem *Oberon* (1780).

Wieland, Heinrich Otto (1877–1957) German chemist, born in Pforzheim. He taught at Munich and in Freiburg before returning to Munich as professor in 1925. He is most famous for his studies of the bile acids (substances stored in the gall bladder which aid the digestion of lipids); for this work he received the 1927 Nobel Prize for Chemistry.

wield *verb* **1** to brandish or use (a tool, weapon, etc). **2** to have or exert (power, authority, influence, etc). [from Anglo-Saxon *wieldan*, to control]

Wieliczka salt mine a salt mine in S Poland which has been worked for over 500 years, and which is still in operation. The mine is noted for its museum of salt mining techniques and equipment, and for its subterranean architecture and sculptures. It is a World Heritage site.

Wien, Wilhelm Carl Werner Otto Fritz Franz (1864–1928) German physicist, born in Gaffken, E Prussia. Professor at Aachen, Giessen, Würzburg, and finally Munich, his chief contribution was on black-body radiation. He showed that the wavelength at which maximum energy is radiated is inversely proportional to the absolute temperature of the body (1893), and formulated an expression for the distribution of energy in a radiation spectrum as a function of wavelength and temperature (for short wavelengths). He was awarded the 1911 Nobel Prize for Physics.

Wien see VIENNA.

Wiener, Norbert (1894–1964) US mathematician, born in Columbia, Missouri. During World War II he studied mathematical communication theory applied to predictors and guided missiles. Professor at the Massachusetts Institute of Technology, his study of the significance of feedback in the handling of information by electronic devices led him to compare this with analogous mental processes in animals; he is now regarded as the founder of 'cybernetics'.

Wiesbaden POP (1991e) 257 000, the capital of Hessen state, Germany. It lies on the R Rhine, 32km/20mi W of Frankfurt am Main. The city is a popular health resort, and also a traditional wine centre; most of the large German Sekt (sparkling wine) cellars are in the area.

Wies Pilgrimage Church an 18c church in Wies, S Germany, which was founded in 1330 to house a miraculously weeping statue of Christ and became the centre of a religious cult. The present building was designed by Dominikus Zimmermann (1685–1766). It is a World Heritage site.

wife *noun* (PL. **wives**) **1** the woman to whom a man is married; a married woman. **2** *old use, dialect (often in compounds)* a woman: *housewife / fishwife.* [from Anglo-Saxon *wif*]

wifely *adj.* of, or considered suitable to, a wife.

Wife of Bath, the the five-times-married, lascivious, cheerful woman in Chaucer's *The Canterbury Tales*, whose tale underlines the value of 'sovereignty' to women.

wig *noun* an artificial covering of hair for the head. [see PERIWIG]

Wigan POP (1981) 89 000, an industrial town in Wigan borough, Greater Manchester, NW England. It lies 27km/17mi NE of Liverpool, on the R Douglas and the Leeds–Liverpool Canal. It has been a borough since 1246. NOTABLE FEATURE Wigan Pier, now a museum, was made famous by George Orwell in *The Road to Wigan Pier* (1932).

wigeon *or* **widgeon** *noun* a wild duck of marshy regions.

wigged *adj.* wearing a wig.

wigging *noun colloq.* a scolding. [see WIG[1]]

wiggle *verb trans., intrans. colloq.* to move, especially jerkily, from side to side or up and down. [related to Anglo-Saxon *wegan*, to move, and Dutch *wiggelen*, to totter]

Wigglesworth, Sir Vincent Brian (1899–) English biologist, born in Kirkham, Lancashire. Professor at Cambridge and director of an insect research centre, he demonstrated the production and secretory cell sources of hormones which selectively activate different genetic components of insects during various stages of their life cycles. This work on insect metamorphosis led to a much greater understanding of their physiology and interactions with the environment.

wiggly *adj.* (**wigglier, wiggliest**) wriggly, wavy.

Wight, Isle of, Latin **Vectis** POP (1987e) 127 000, an island county off the S coast of England, divided into two districts. AREA 381sq km/147sq mi. It lies in the mouth of Southampton Water, separated from Hampshire by the Solent and Spithead. PHYSICAL DESCRIPTION an irregular range of chalk hills running E–W ends at the imposing cliffs of the vertical sandstone Needles near Alum Bay; drained by the R Medina. HISTORY invaded by the Romans in AD 43; during the Civil Wars, Charles I was imprisoned in Carisbrooke Castle. CHIEF TOWNS Newport (county town), Cowes, Ryde, Sandown, Shanklin, Ventnor. ECONOMY agriculture; hovercraft and boat building; electronics; yachting (especially Cowes Regatta Week); tourism. NOTABLE FEATURE Osborne House.

wight *noun old use* a human creature. [from Anglo-Saxon *wiht*]

Wightman Cup an annual lawn tennis competition involving professional women's teams from the USA and UK. It was first held in 1923, and named after the former US player Hazel Wightman (*née* Hotchkiss) (1886–1974). It was discontinued in 1989.

Wigman, Mary, originally **Marie Wiegmann** (1886–1973) German dancer, choreographer, and teacher, born in Hanover. Her career as the most famous German modern dancer of her era began after World War I, when she toured extensively and opened a school in Dresden (1920). She created numerous solo and group dances which typified German Expressionist dancing. Her schools, teaching, and highly dramatic performances provided the focus for the development of a performance form of European modern dance.

Wigmore Hall a concert hall in London, England, where many début performances are made. It opened as the Bechstein Hall in 1901 and was renamed in 1917.

Wigner, Eugene Paul (1902–) Hungarian-born US theoretical physicist, born in Budapest. Professor at Princeton University, he is especially known for his theories of nuclear reactions and the conservation of the angular momentum of electron spin. His calculations were used for the first nuclear reactor in Chicago. He was awarded the 1963 Nobel Prize for Physics.

wigwam *noun* **1** a domed tent-like Native American dwelling made of arched poles covered with skins, bark, or mats. **2** often applied to the cone-shaped dwelling more correctly known as a tepee. [from Abenaki (Native American language) *wikewam*, house]

Wilberforce, William (1759–1833) English politician, evangelist, and philanthropist, born in Hull, Yorkshire. He became an MP (1780), and in 1788 began the movement that resulted in the abolition of the slave trade in the British West Indies (1807). He sought to secure the abolition of all slaves, but had to retire from parliament due to declining health in 1825, and he died one month before the Slavery Abolition Act was passed. His evangelical Christian faith led him to urge the aristocracy to practise 'real Christianity', and to give a moral lead to the poor.

Wilbye, John (1574–1638) English madrigal composer, born in Diss, Norfolk. He was a farmer, who became a household musician at Hengrave Hall (1593–1628), then at Colchester, Essex. He is known for only 66 madrigals, which are renowned for his careful setting of literary texts, and for some translations of Italian poems.

wild — *adj.* **1** *said of animals* untamed; undomesticated; not dependent on man. **2** *said of plants* growing in a natural, uncultivated state. **3** *said of country* desolate, rugged, inhospitable, or uninhabitable. **4** *said of peoples* savage; uncivilized. **5** unrestrained; uncontrolled: *wild fury.* **6** frantically excited: *the spectators went wild.* **7** distraught: *wild with grief.* **8** dishevelled; disordered: *wild attire.* **9** *said of the eyes* staring; scared-looking. **10** *said of weather* stormy: *a wild night.* **11** *said of plans, hopes, etc* crazy; impracticable; unrealistic: *succeeded beyond their wildest dreams.* **12** *said of a guess* very approximate, or quite random. **13** (**wild about someone** *or* **something**) intensely fond of them or keen on them. **14** *colloq.* furious. **15** *slang* enjoyable; terrific. — *noun* **1** (**the wild**) a wild animal's or plant's natural environment or life in it: *returned the cub to the wild.* **2** (**the wild**) lonely, sparsely inhabited regions away from the city.
— **run wild 1** *said of a garden or plants* to revert to a wild, overgrown, uncultivated state. **2** *said eg of children* to live a life of freedom, with little discipline or control.
[from Anglo-Saxon *wilde*]

wild boar a wild ancestor of the domestic pig, native to Europe, NW Africa, and S Asia, and having thick dark hair. The male has tusks.

wild card 1 a competitor lacking the usual or statutory qualifications. **2** *Comput.* a symbol, eg an asterisk, that can be used to represent any character or set of characters in a certain position, in order to identify text strings with variable contents. For example, the specification 'c∗.doc' can be used to denote all file-names that start with 'c' and end with '.doc'.

wildcat — *noun* **1** (*often* **wild cat**) an undomesticated cat of Europe and Asia, which has a longer stouter body and longer legs than those of a domestic cat, and a thick bushy tail which is shorter and ringed, with a black tip. It feeds mainly on hares, grouse, rabbits, and small rodents, but will also attack poultry and lambs. **2** (*often* **wild cat**) any of several small or medium-sized cats, eg lynx, ocelot, as opposed to the lion, tiger, leopard, cheetah, and other large cats. — *adj.* **1** *said of an industrial strike* not called or approved by a trade union. **2** *said of a business scheme* financially unsound or risky; speculative. **3** *said of an oil well* exploratory; experimental.

Wild Duck, The (Vildanden) a play by Henrik Ibsen (1884). It is a tragic story of a photographer, Hjalmar Ekdal, whose daughter kills herself on overhearing that he is perhaps not her father. The mysterious duck kept in the attic symbolizes the various delusions under which the family live.

Wilde, Oscar (Fingal O'Flahertie Wills) (1854–1900) Irish writer, born in Dublin. Renowned for his wit and flamboyant manner among the social and literary circles in London, he became a leading member of the 'art for art's sake' movement. His early work included the novel *The Picture of Dorian Gray* (1891), and the comic plays *Lady Windermere's Fan* (1892) and *The Importance of Being Earnest* (1895). *The Ballad of Reading Gaol* (1898) reveals the effect on him of his prison sentence of two years' hard labour, which was imposed for the then illegal homosexual practices that were exposed during his libel action against the Marquis of Queensberry.

wildebeest *noun* (PL. **wildebeest, wildebeests**) either of two species of large antelope that live in herds on the grasslands of Africa, and resemble cattle in appearance, having a large head, a short thick neck, tufts of hair growing from the throat, and an upright mane. Both sexes have large curved horns. Wildebeest is the main prey of the lion. — Also called *gnu.* [from Afrikaans, from Dutch *wilde*, wild + *beest*, ox]

Wilder, Thornton (Niven) (1897–1976) US writer, born in Madison, Wisconsin. His first novel, *The Cabala* (1926), was followed by the very successful *The Bridge of San Luis Rey* (1927), and the plays *Our Town* (1938) and *The Skin of Our Teeth* (1942), all Pulitzer Prize-winners. His later plays included *The Matchmaker* (1954), the basis of the musical *Hello Dolly* (1964).

Wilderness, Battle of the 1 a conflict (1755) in W Pennsylvania, in which Native Americans and French troops decimated a larger British army under General Edward Braddock, and from which George Washington, who commanded the American auxiliaries, emerged with a considerable military reputation. **2** an indecisive conflict (1864) in the American Civil War between the Union army under General Grant and the Confederate army under General Lee.

wilderness *noun* **1** an uncultivated or uninhabited region. **2** a desolate, pathless area. **3** an overgrown tangle of weeds, etc. **4** *Hist.* a part of a garden or estate deliberately left wild for romantic effect. **5** any daunting maze. **6** *Politics* the state of being without office or influence after playing a leading role.
— **a voice crying in the wilderness** someone with an important message or warning who goes unheeded (in allusion to Matthew 3.3).
[from Anglo-Saxon *wilddeor*, wild beast]

Wilderness Road the early route across the S Appalachian Mts, from the Holston River through Cumberland Gap to Boonesborough on the Kentucky River. It was constructed in 1775 by a party led by Daniel Boone under the sponsorship of Richard Henderson, founder of the Transylvania Company.

Wildfire, Madge see MURDOCKSON, MEG.

wildfire *noun Hist.* a highly flammable liquid used in warfare.
— **spread like wildfire** *said eg of disease, rumour, etc* to spread rapidly and extensively.

wildfowl *sing. or pl. noun* a game bird or game birds, especially waterfowl.

wildfowler *noun* a person who hunts and kills wildfowl.

wildfowling *noun* the activity or sport of hunting and killing wildfowl.

wild-goose chase a search that is bound to be unsuccessful.

wildlife *noun* wild animals, birds, and plants in general.

wildly *adv.* in a wild way; to a wild extent.

wildness *noun* a wild state or quality.

wild pansy see HEARTSEASE.

Wild Strawberries (Smultronstället) a Swedish film directed by Ingmar Bergman (1957). It is a sombre but affirmative depiction of the life of a professor (played by Victor Sjöström) told through his reminiscences and dreams during a car journey.

wild type the form of a species typically occurring under natural breeding conditions, as distinct from mutant types.

Wild West (the Wild West) *Hist.* the part of the US west of the Mississippi, settled during the 19c and legendary for the adventures of its cattlemen and the struggle to gain territory from the Native American population.

wile — *noun* **1** (**wiles**) charming personal ways. **2** a piece of cunning; a ruse, trick, manoeuvre, or stratagem. — *verb* **1** *old use* (**wile someone away**) to lure or entice them. **2** (**wile away time**) to pass time pleasantly; to while away time. [from Anglo-Saxon *wil*; related to GUILE]

Wilfred a male first name. [from Anglo-Saxon, from *wil*, will + *frid*, peace]

Wilfrid *or* **Wilfrith, St** (634–709) English prelate, born in Northumbria. He trained at Lindisfarne, and upheld the replacement of Celtic by Roman religious practices at the Synod of Whitby (664). As Bishop of York (c.665), he was involved in controversy over the organization of the Church in Britain, and was the first churchman to appeal to Rome to settle the issue. His feast day is 12 Oct.

wilful *adj.* **1** deliberate; intentional. **2** headstrong, obstinate, or self-willed. [see WILL²]

wilfully *adv.* in a wilful way.

wilfulness *noun* being wilful.

Wilhelmina (Helena Pauline Maria) (1880–1962) Queen of the Netherlands (1890–1948), born in The Hague. She succeeded her father William III at the age of 10, and her mother acted as regent until 1898. An upholder of constitutional monarchy, she won the admiration of her people, particularly during World War II, when she steadfastly encouraged Dutch resistance to the German occupation, though she herself had to seek refuge in Britain. In 1948, she abdicated in favour of her daughter Juliana, and assumed the title of Princess of the Netherlands.

wili (PL. **wilis**) in Slavic folklore, the spirit of a betrothed maiden who has died before her wedding-day. They haunt highways at night, compelling any passing youth to dance with them until he drops dead. The legend was recorded by

Heinrich Heine and used in the ballet *Giselle* by Théophile Gautier.

wiliness *noun* being wily.

Wilkes, Ashley the aristocratic object of Scarlett O'Hara's infatuation in Margaret Mitchell's *Gone with the Wind*.

Wilkes, John (1727–97) English politician and journalist, born in London. He became an MP (1757), and attacked the ministry (especially the Chief Minister Lord Bute) in his weekly journal, the *North Briton* (1762–3). He was imprisoned, released, then expelled from the House for libel. Re-elected on several occasions, and repeatedly expelled, he came to be seen as a champion of liberty and an upholder of press freedom. In 1774 he became Lord Mayor of London, and was finally readmitted to parliament until his retirement (1790).

Wilkes, Maurice Vincent (1913–) English computer scientist, born in Dudley. He directed the Mathematical (later Computer) Laboratory at Cambridge (1946–80), where he was best known for his pioneering work with EDSAC (Electronic Delay Storage Automatic Calculator), around which he built the world's first computing service.

Wilkes Land the area of Antarctica between Queen Mary Land to the W and Terre Adélie. It lies mostly between 105°E and 135°E. The territory includes the Australian scientific station at Casey which was established in 1961.

Wilkie, Sir David (1785–1841) Scottish painter, born in Cults, Fife. He settled in London following the success of his *Pitlessie Fair* (1804) and *The Village Politicians* (1806). His fame rests mainly on his genre painting in the Dutch style (eg *The Village Festival*). He also painted portraits, and in 1830 was made Painter-in-Ordinary to George IV.

will[1] *verb aux.* used: **1** especially in the second and third persons, to form a future tense. **2** in the first person, to express intention or determination: *we will not give in.* **3** to make requests: *please will you shut the door!* **4** to express commands: *you will apologize to your mother immediately!* **5** to indicate ability: *the table will seat ten.* **6** to indicate readiness or willingness: *any of our branches will exchange the goods / the car simply will not start.* **7** to make an invitation: *will you have a coffee?* **8** to indicate what is bound to be the case: *accidents will happen / the experienced teacher will know when a child is unhappy.* **9** to state what applies in certain circumstances: *an unemployed young person living at home will not receive housing benefit.* **10** to express an assumption or probability: *that will be Ted at the door.* **11** to suggest obstinate resistance to advice: *she will leave her clothes on the floor.* **12** to mean 'will be so good' or 'wish': *consider, if you will..make what you will of that.* See also SHALL, WON'T. [from Anglo-Saxon *wyllan*]

will[2] — *noun* **1** the power of conscious decision and deliberate choice of action: *free will / exercise one's will.* **2** one's own preferences, or one's determination in effecting them: *a clash of wills / I did it against my will.* **3** desire or determination: *the will to live.* **4** a wish or desire: *what is your will?* **5** instructions for the disposal of a person's property, etc after death, or the document containing these. **6** one's feeling towards someone else: *felt no ill-will towards her.* — *verb* **1** to try to compel by, or as if by, exerting one's will: *willed herself to keep going.* **2** *formal* to desire or require that something be done, etc: *Her Majesty wills it.* **3** to bequeath in one's will.

— **at will** as and when one wishes.

with a will eagerly; enthusiastically.

with the best will in the world (*with a negative*) no matter how willing one is or how hard one tries.

[from Anglo-Saxon *willa*]

Willandra Lakes an area in the Murray R Basin, New South Wales, Australia. AREA 6 000sq km/2 300sq mi. It is a World Heritage

area with an extensive system of Pleistocene freshwater lake sites, and it provides a remarkable 'fossil landscape', generally unmodified since the end of the Pleistocene ice age. Certain archaeological discoveries made here have been dated at 30000–40000 BC.

Willemstad POP (1981) 50 000, the capital of the Netherlands Antilles. It is a free port on the SW coast of Curaçao I. The town was established by the Dutch as a trading centre in the mid-17c.

Willendorf a prehistoric site near Krems, lower Austria, with Gravettian occupation dated c.32000–28000 BC. It is celebrated for the 'Willendorf Venus', a large-bellied, heavy-breasted limestone statuette, 11cm high.

William I (Emperor), German **Wilhelm** (1797–1888) King of Prussia (1861–88) and first German Emperor (1871–88), born in Berlin, the second son of Frederick William III. His use of force during the 1848 revolution made him unpopular, and he had to leave Prussia temporarily for London. As King, he consolidated the throne and strengthened the army; Bismarck was placed at the head of the ministry, with Albert von Roon, who devised the new army system, as War Minister. He was victorious against Denmark (1864), Austria (1866), and France in 1871, when he was proclaimed Emperor of Germany. The rapid rise of socialism in Germany led him to take severely repressive measures. He survived several socialist attempts at assassination.

William I (of England), also called **the Conqueror** (c.1028–87) Duke of Normandy (1035–87) and the first Norman King of England (1066–87), the illegitimate son of Duke Robert of Normandy. Edward the Confessor is thought to have nominated him as future King of England in 1051, and so when Harold Godwin took the throne as Harold II, William invaded, defeated and killed Harold at the battle of Hastings, and was crowned king on Christmas Day 1066. This military conquest was enforced by aristocratic colonization — by the time of the Domesday Book (1086), the leaders of Anglo-Saxon society south of the Tees had been almost entirely replaced by a new ruling class of Normans, Bretons, and Flemings, who were tied to William by feudal bonds.

William I (of Scotland), also called **the Lion** (c.1142–1214) King of Scots (1165–1214), the brother and successor of Malcolm IV. In 1173–4 he invaded Northumberland during the rebellion against Henry II, but was captured at Alnwick, and by the Treaty of Falaise (1174) recognized Henry as the feudal superior of Scotland. He nevertheless strengthened Scotland's kingdom, and in 1192 Celestine III declared the Scottish Church free of all external authority save the pope's.

William I (of the Netherlands), Prince of Orange, known as **William the Silent** (1533–84) the first of the hereditary stadholders of the United Provinces of the Netherlands (1572–84), born in Dillenburg, Nassau. He joined the aristocrats who were protesting against the oppressive policies of Philip II of Spain, and in 1568 took up arms against the Spanish Crown. After initial reverses, he recovered the coastal towns, and became stadholder of the Northern provinces, which were united in the Union of Utrecht (1579). He was assassinated at Delft by a Spanish agent, and succeeded by his son, Maurice of Nassau. His nickname comes from his ability to keep secret Henry II's scheme to massacre all the Protestants of France and the Netherlands, confided to him when he was a French hostage in 1559.

William II (Emperor), German **Wilhelm** (1859–1941) German Emperor and King of Prussia (1888–1918), born in Potsdam, the eldest son of Frederick (II) and Victoria (the daughter of Britain's Queen Victoria), and grandson of William I. He dismissed Bismarck (1890), and

began a long period of personal rule. Belligerent in international affairs, he pledged full support to Austria-Hungary after the assassination of the Archduke Francis Ferdinand in Sarajevo (1914), but then had to make strenuous efforts to prevent an international crisis. During World War I he became a mere figurehead, and when the German armies collapsed, and US President Wilson refused to negotiate while he remained in power, he abdicated, fled the country, and settled in the Netherlands.

William II (of England), also called **Rufus** (c.1056–1100) King of England (1087–1100), the second surviving son of William the Conqueror. He fought to recover Normandy from his elder brother Robert Curthose, and from 1096, when Robert departed on the First Crusade, William ruled the duchy. He also led expeditions to Wales (1095, 1097); conquered Carlisle and the surrounding district (1092); and after the death of Malcolm Canmore, exercised some control in Scottish affairs. Criticized as an arbitrary and ruthless ruler, he exploited his rights over the Church and the nobility, quarrelled with Anselm, Archbishop of Canterbury, and caused outrage with his supposed homosexuality. His death by an arrow while hunting was supposed by some to have been a murder ordered by his younger brother, who succeeded him as Henry I.

William III (of Great Britain), also called **William of Orange** (1650–1702) Stadholder of the United Provinces (1672–1702) and King of Great Britain (1689–1702), born in The Hague, the son of William II of Orange and Mary, the eldest daughter of Charles I of England. In 1677 he married his cousin Mary (1662–94), the daughter of James II and Anne Hyde. Invited by seven British notables (the Immortal Seven) to redress the grievances of the country (eg protect the Protestant religion), he landed at Torbay in 1688 with an English and Dutch army, and forced James II to flee. William and Mary were proclaimed joint rulers early the following year. He defeated James's supporters at Killiecrankie (1689) and at the Boyne (1690), then concentrated on the War of the Grand Alliance against France (1689–97), in which he was eventually successful. After withstanding much parliamentary opposition to his proposals, and several assassination plots, he died childless, and the Crown passed to Mary's sister Anne.

William IV (of Great Britain), known as **the Sailor King** (1765–1837) King of Great Britain and Ireland, and King of Hanover (1830–7), born in London, the third son of George III. He entered the navy in 1779, saw service in the USA and the West Indies, became Admiral in 1811, and Lord High Admiral in 1827–8. Since his elder brother had died, he succeeded his eldest brother George IV in 1830. Believed to have been a Whig until his accession, he developed Tory sympathies and did much to obstruct the passing of the first Reform Act (1832). He was the last monarch to use prerogative powers to dismiss a ministry with a parliamentary majority when he sacked the Whig Melbourne (1834) and invited the Tories to form a government. His niece succeeded him as Queen Victoria.

William, in full **William Brown** the mischievous, scheming schoolboy hero of Richmal Crompton's *Just William* and other books.

William a male first name. [of Germanic origin, from *wil*, will + *helm*, helmet]

William of Malmesbury (c.1090–c.1143) English chronicler and Benedictine monk, the librarian of Malmesbury Abbey, Wiltshire. He emphasized the importance of documentary material and non-written sources (eg architectural evidence). His main works are *Gesta Regum Anglorum*, a general history of England from the coming of the Anglo-Saxons; *Gesta Pontificum Anglorum*, an ecclesiastical history of England from the Conversion; and *Historia Novella*, a contemporary narrative of English affairs from c.1125 to 1142.

William of Tyre (c.1130–1185) Chronicler and churchman, born in Palestine of French parents. He entered the service of the Kings of Jerusalem, and was appointed Archbishop of Tyre in 1175. His main work, *Historia rerum in partibus transmarinis gestarum* (History of Deeds in Foreign Parts), deals with the history of Palestine from 614 to 1184, including the 12c Crusades.

William of Wykeham *or* **Wickham** (1324–1404) English churchman and statesman, born in Wickham, Hampshire. Perhaps the son of a serf, he rose in the service of Edward III to become Keeper of the Privy Seal (1363), Bishop of Winchester (1367), and twice Chancellor of England (1367–71, 1389–91). He founded New College, Oxford, and Winchester College.

Williams, (George) Emlyn (1905–87) Welsh playwright and actor, born in Mostyn, Clwyd. His successes as a dramatist began with *A Murder has been Arranged* (1930) and included the psychological thriller, *Night Must Fall* (1935). He appeared in productions of many of his own plays, featured in several films, and gave acclaimed readings from the works of Charles Dickens.

Williams, John (Christopher) (1942–) Australian classical and jazz guitarist, born in Melbourne, Victoria. He studied with Andres Segovia, moved to England (1952), made his professional début in 1958, and taught in London and Manchester. Several classical composers have written works for him, and he has founded various ensembles, including the rock group Sky (1979–84).

Williams, John(ny) (1932–) US composer of film music, born in Long Island, New York. He began as a jazz pianist, then turned to composing for television in the late 1950s. His work includes the Oscar-winning orchestrations of *Fiddler on the Roof* (1971), *Jaws* (1975), *Star Wars* (1977), and *E.T* (1982).

Williams, J(ohn) P(eter) R(hys) (1949–) Welsh rugby player (retired), born in Bridgend, Mid Glamorgan, Wales. He won the Wimbledon junior tennis championship in 1966. He trained in medicine, and played rugby for the London Welsh, Bridgend, Wales, and the British Lions. He made a record 55 appearances for Wales between 1969 and 1981.

Williams, Robin (1952–) US film actor, born in Chicago, Illinois. Following starring roles in such television series as *Happy Days* and *Mork and Mindy* (1978–81), his comic versatility was captured in feature films including *The World According to Garp* (1982) and *Good Morning Vietnam* (1987). Later appearances include *Dead Poets Society* (1989), *Awakenings* (1990), *The Fisher King* (1991), and *Hook* (1991).

Williams, Roger (c.1604–1683) English colonist who founded Rhode Island, born in London. He took Anglican orders, became an extreme Puritan, and emigrated to New England (1630). Refusing to join the congregation in Boston, he moved to Salem, where he was persecuted and banished. He then purchased lands from the Native Americans and founded the city of Providence (1636), where he allowed full religious toleration. In 1643 and 1651 he came to England to procure a charter for his colony, and became its President (1654–8).

Williams, Shirley (Vivien Teresa Brittain) Williams, Baroness (1930–) English politician, daughter of Vera Brittain. A former journalist, she became a Labour MP in 1964, and was Secretary of State for Prices and Consumer Protection (1974–6), and for Education and Science (1976–9). She lost her seat in 1979, became a co-founder of the Social Democratic Party in 1981, and the Party's first elected MP later that year. She lost her seat in the 1983 general election, but remained as the SDP's President (1982–8), and supported the merger between the SDP and the Liberal Party in 1988. That year she became Professor of Elective Politics at Harvard University, but she remains active in British politics.

Williams, Tennessee, pseudonym of **Thomas Lanier Williams** (1911–83) American dramatist, born in Columbus, Mississippi. He achieved success with *The Glass Menagerie* (1944) and his later plays, almost all set in the Deep South against a background of decadence and degradation, include *A Streetcar Named Desire* (1947, Pulitzer Prize), *Cat on a Hot Tin Roof* (1955, Pulitzer Prize), *Suddenly Last Summer* (1958), and *Night of the Iguana* (1961).

Williamsburg POP (1980) 10 000, the seat of James City County, SE Virginia, USA. It is administratively independent of the county, and lies between the York and James rivers, SE of Richmond. HISTORY settled in 1633 (as Middle Plantation, renamed in 1699); served as state capital from 1699 until 1780. NOTABLE FEATURES Colonial Williamsburg is a major building restoration scheme; College of William and Mary (1693).

Williamson, Henry (1895–1977) English writer, born in Bedfordshire. He served in World War I, became a journalist, then turned to farming in Norfolk. He wrote several semi-autobiographical novels, including his long series *A Chronicle of Ancient Sunlight* (1951–69), but is best known for his classic nature stories, including *Tarka the Otter* (1927).

Williamson, Malcolm (Benjamin Graham Christopher) (1931–) Australian-born British composer, born in Sydney. He studied under Sir Eugene Goossens and Elizabeth Lutyens and moved to England in 1953 to begin his career as a solo pianist and organist. His compositions include the operas *Our Man in Havana* (1963) and *The Red Sea* (1972), several works for television and films, ballets, orchestral, vocal, choral, and piano music, and 'cassations', which often involve the audience. He became Master of the Queen's Music in 1975.

William Tell (Guillaume Tell) an opera by Gioacchino Rossini (1829), based on Friedrich von Schiller's version of the legend. Set in early 14c Switzerland against the background of the Swiss rising against the Austrian Habsburg ruler Gessler, it focuses on William Tell, the leader of the rising, and Arnold, one supporter's son, who unfortunately is in love with Gessler's daughter Mathilde. The famous apple-shooting episode was to punish Tell for refusing to bow to Gessler's hat on a pole.

willies *pl. noun* (**the willies**) *colloq.* a feeling of anxiety or unease.

willing *adj.* **1** ready, glad, or not disinclined (to do something). **2** eager and co-operative. **3** voluntarily given. [see WILL²]

willingly *adv.* with a willing manner, readily.

willingness *noun* being willing.

Willis, Thomas (1621–73) English physician, born in Great Bedwin, one of the founders of the Royal Society. He was professor at Oxford, but became famous as a physician in Westminster. His main work was on the anatomy of the brain and on diseases of the nervous system. His *Cerebri anatome* (Anatomy of the Brain, 1664) was the principal study of brain anatomy of its time. In this he described cerebral circulation, discovering the ring of blood vessels now called the 'circle of Willis'.

will-o'-the-wisp *noun* **1** a light sometimes seen over marshes, caused by the combustion of marsh gas (methane). – Also called *ignis fatuus*. **2** something elusive, such as an unattainable goal. [literally 'Will of the torch']

willow *noun* **1** a deciduous tree or shrub of the genus *Salix* found mainly in the N hemisphere, generally growing near water, and having slender flexible branches, narrow leaves, and spikes or catkins of male and female flowers. It is widely cultivated as an ornamental plant, eg weeping willow. **2** the durable yellowish-brown wood of this tree, which is used to make cricket bats, wicker baskets, high-quality drawing charcoal, and furniture. [from Anglo-Saxon *welig*]

willow herb a plant with willow-like leaves and purple flowers.

willow pattern a design used on pottery, usually in blue on a white background, showing a Chinese landscape with a willow tree, bridge, and figures.

willowy *adj.*, *said of a person, especially a woman* slender and graceful.

willpower *noun* the determination, persistence, and self-discipline needed to accomplish something.

Wills, Helen (Newington), married names **Moody, Roark** (1905–) US lawn tennis player, born in Berkeley, California. A renowned baseline player, she won the Wimbledon singles title eight times in nine attempts (1927–30, 1932–3, 1935, 1938). Between 1927 and 1932 she won all the major singles championships (except the Australian) without losing a set. In all, she won 31 Grand Slam events, including seven US singles titles. She also won gold medals in the women's singles and doubles at the 1924 Olympics.

Willstätter, Richard (1872–1942) German chemist, born in Karlsruhe. Professor in Zürich, Berlin, and Munich, he researched the structure and synthesis of natural products, and is especially known for his discoveries concerning the alkaloids and chlorophylls. He was awarded the 1915 Nobel Prize for Chemistry.

willy *or* **willie** *noun* (PL. **willies**) *colloq. especially childish* a penis.

willy-nilly *adv.* whether one wishes or not; regardless. [originally *will I, nill I* (or *will ye, he*, etc), will I, will I not]

Wilmington POP (1990) 579 000, the seat of New Castle County, N Delaware, USA, and the largest city in the state. It is an industrial port at the confluence of Brandywine Creek, the Christina R, and the Delaware R. The city is home to several large corporations and is known as 'the chemical capital of the world'. HISTORY founded by the Swedes as Fort Christina in 1638; taken by the British and renamed Willington in 1731; renamed Wilmington in 1739; achieved city status in 1832. NOTABLE FEATURES State House complex; Winterthur Museum; Hagley Museum.

Wilmington POP (1990) 120 000, the seat of New Hanover County, SE North Carolina, USA. It is the state's largest port, lying close to the Atlantic Ocean, on the Cape Fear R. HISTORY gave the first armed resistance to the Stamp Act in 1765; headquarters of the British troops under Cornwallis in 1781; the last Confederate port to close in the Civil War.

Wilmot Proviso a motion introduced (1846) in US Congress by David Wilmot (Democrat, Pennsylvania) to forbid the expansion of slavery into territory acquired during the Mexican War. It passed the House of Representatives but not the Senate, where the South and the North had equal strength, and was a major step towards the politicization of the slavery issue.

Wilson, Sir Angus (Frank Johnstone) (1913–91) English writer, born in Bexhill, E Sussex. He worked in the British Museum Reading Room (1949–55), and was Professor of English literature at the University of East Anglia (1966–78). He began to write in 1946 and established a reputation with his short stories, *The Wrong Set* (1949). Other works include the novels *Hemlock and After* (1952), *Anglo-Saxon Attitudes* (1956), and *The Old Men at the Zoo* (1961), the play *The Mulberry Bush* (1955), and two volumes of short stories. His *Collected Stories* were published in 1987.

Wilson, Charles Thomson Rees
(1869–1959) Scottish pioneer of atomic and nuclear physics, born in Glencorse, near Edinburgh. Professor at Cambridge, he developed the cloud chamber method of marking the tracks of charged particles, allowing the interactions of atomic particles to be followed. He shared the 1927 Nobel Prize for Physics with Arthur Compton.

Wilson, Edward Osborne (1929–) US biologist, born in Birmingham, Alabama. Professor at Harvard, he has investigated the biological basis of social behaviour, helping to found the subject of sociobiology. His book, *The Insect Societies* (1971), outlined his belief that the same evolutionary forces have shaped the behaviours of insects and other animals including humans.

Wilson, Kenneth Geddes (1936–) US theoretical physicist, born in Waltham, Massachusetts. Professor at Cornell University and Columbus, Ohio, he applied ingenious mathematical methods to the understanding of the magnetic properties of atoms, and later used similar methods in the study of phase changes between liquids and gases, and in alloys. For this work he was awarded the 1982 Nobel Prize for Physics.

Wilson, Robert Woodrow (1936–) US physicist, born in Houston, Texas. He joined Bell Laboratories in New Jersey, becoming head of its radiophysics research department in 1976. There he detected with Arno Penzias background radio waves coming from all directions (1964), now thought to be residual radiation from the 'Big Bang' at the universe's creation. They shared the 1978 Nobel Prize for Physics with Peter Kapitza.

Wilson, (John) Tuzo (1908–93) Canadian geophysicist, born in Ottawa. Professor at the University of Toronto, he identified a new type of movement of tectonic plates, introducing the idea of 'transform faults' (1965); this was an important contribution to theories of continental drift.

Wilson, (Thomas) Woodrow (1856–1924) US statesman, the 28th President, born in Staunton, Virginia. He became a lawyer and university professor, President of Princeton, and Governor of New Jersey (1911). Elected Democratic President in 1912 and 1916, his administration (1913–21) saw the amendments to the constitution of prohibition and women's suffrage, America's participation in World War I, his peace plan proposals (the 'Fourteen Points'), his championship of the League of Nations, and the Senate's rejection of the Treaty of Versailles. He was awarded the Nobel Peace Prize in 1919.

Wilson (of Libya and of Stowlangtoft), Henry Maitland Wilson, 1st Baron
(1881–1964) English soldier, born in London. He fought in South Africa and in World War I, and at the outbreak of World War II was appointed Commander of British troops in Egypt. He led the initial British advance in Libya (1940–1) and the unsuccessful Greek campaign (1941), and became Commander-in-Chief Middle East (1943), field marshal (1944), and Supreme Allied Commander in the Mediterranean theatre (1944). He also headed the British Joint Staff Mission in Washington (1945–7).

Wilson (of Rievaulx), (James) Harold Wilson, Baron (1916–) English Labour politician and Prime Minister, born in Huddersfield. He became an MP in 1945, and was President of the Board of Trade (1947–51) and Opposition spokesman on economic affairs. An able and hard-hitting debater, in 1963 he succeeded Hugh Gaitskell as Leader of the Labour Party, and became Prime Minister (1964–70, 1974–6). His economic plans were badly affected by a balance of payments crisis, which led to very restrictive measures. He was also faced with the problem of

Rhodesian independence, opposition to Britain's proposed entry into the Common Market, and increasing conflict within the Labour Party. Following his third general election victory, he suddenly resigned the Party leadership in 1976.

wilt — *verb intrans.* **1** *Bot.*, *said of a plant organ or tissue* to droop or become limp because there is insufficient water to maintain the individual cells in a turgid state. **2** to droop from fatigue or heat. **3** to lose courage or confidence. — *noun Bot.* one of a number of plant diseases, often caused by fungal infection, in which wilting is the main symptom. [a variant of *wilk*, to wither]

Wilts. *abbrev.* Wiltshire.

Wiltshire POP (1992e) 579 000, a county in S England, divided into five districts. AREA 3 481sq km/1 344sq mi. It is bounded N by Gloucestershire, NE by Oxfordshire, E by Berkshire, SE by Hampshire, S by Dorset, and W by Somerset and Avon. PHYSICAL DESCRIPTION drained by the Avon and Kennet rivers; the chalk downland of Salisbury Plain lies at the centre of the county. CHIEF TOWNS Trowbridge (county town), Salisbury, Swindon, Chippenham. ECONOMY agriculture; engineering; clothing; brewing. NOTABLE FEATURES many ancient prehistoric remains, such as Stonehenge, Avebury, and Silbury Hill; Marlborough Downs; Savernake Forest; Longleat House; Wilton House.

wily *adj.* (**wilier, wiliest**) cunning. [from WILE]

Wimbledon a residential district in Merton borough, S Greater London, England. NOTABLE FEATURES Wimbledon Common; headquarters of the All England Tennis Club. EVENT annual lawn tennis championships (Jun–Jul).

Wimbledon the popular name for the lawn-tennis centre, home of the All England Lawn Tennis and Croquet Club in Wimbledon, S London. It is used each year for the premier international championship tournament. The centre was originally at Worple Road, home of the All England Croquet Club. Tennis was first played there in 1875, and the first championship held in 1877. The club moved to its present site in Church Road in 1922.

wimp[1] *colloq.* — *noun* a feeble person. — *verb intrans.* (**wimp out**) to back out of doing something through feebleness.

wimp[2] *noun Comput.* a user interface incorporating windows, icons, pull-down menus, and a pointing device such as a mouse or trackball.

Wimsey, Lord Peter the aristocratic amateur detective in the crime novels of Dorothy L Sayers, which include *Whose Body?*, *Strong Poison*, and *Gaudy Night*.

win — *verb* (**winning**; PAST TENSE AND PAST PARTICIPLE **won**) **1** *trans.*, *intrans.* to be victorious, come first, or beat one's opponent or rivals in (a contest, race, conflict, war, bet, election, etc). **2** to compete or fight for, and obtain (a victory, prize, etc). **3** to obtain by struggle or effort: *win someone's heart / win a contract.* **4** to earn and get: *win respect.* **5** *old use* to gain the hand of in marriage: *wooed and won her.* **6** to secure for: *her dazzling smile won her the part.* **7** (*also* **win through** *or* **out**) to be successful, or succeed in getting somewhere, after a struggle. — *noun* a victory or success.

— **win someone over** *or* **round** to persuade them to come over to one's side or opinion.

you can't win there's no way to succeed, please someone, etc.

[from Anglo-Saxon *winnan*]

wince — *verb intrans.* to shrink back, start, or grimace, eg in pain or anticipation of it; to flinch. — *noun* a start or grimace in reaction to pain, etc. [from Old French *wencier*, *guenchier*]

winceyette *noun* a soft cotton cloth with a raised brushed surface on both sides. [from Scot. *wincey*, linen or cotton cloth with a mixture of wool]

winch — *noun* **1** a drum-shaped roller round which a rope or chain is wound for hoisting or

hauling heavy loads; a windlass. **2** a crank or handle for setting a wheel, axle, or machinery in motion. — *verb* (*usually* **winch something up** *or* **in**) to hoist or haul it with a winch. [from Anglo-Saxon *wince*]

Winchester, Latin **Venta Belgarum**, Anglo-Saxon **Wintanceaster** POP (1992e) 100 000, the county town of Hampshire, S England, situated in Winchester district. It lies on the R Itchen, 105km/65mi SW of London. HISTORY its Roman settlement was the fifth largest in Britain; became capital of Wessex in 519, and capital of England in 827; William the Conqueror was crowned here as well as in London; the *Domesday Book* was compiled here; from the 14c the city declined into a small provincial town; St Swithin is buried here. NOTABLE FEATURES Gothic cathedral (1079–93), the longest in the world; Winchester College (1382), the oldest public school in England; 12c St Cross Hospital; 13c castle hall, containing a medieval 'replica' of Arthur's Round Table.

wind[1] — *noun* **1** the movement of air, especially horizontally, across the Earth's surface as a result of differences in atmospheric pressure between one location and another. **2** a current of air produced artificially, by a fan, etc. **3** an influence that seems to pervade events: *a wind of change.* **4** one's breath or breath supply: *short of wind.* **5** the scent of game, or, for animals, the scent of a hunter or predator, carried by the wind. **6** gas built up in the intestines; flatulence. **7** empty, pompous, or trivial talk. **8** the wind instruments of an orchestra; their players. — *verb* to deprive of breath temporarily: *was winded by her fall.*

— **before the wind** *said of a ship* sailing with the wind coming from behind it.

break wind to discharge intestinal gas through the anus.

down wind from something receiving, or liable to receive, air laden with the smell, pollutants, etc, from it.

get wind of something to have one's suspicions aroused or hear a rumour, especially of something unfavourable or unwelcome.

get the wind up *colloq.* to become anxious or alarmed.

get one's second wind to recover breath after initial exertion sufficiently to carry on with ease.

in the wind about to happen.

like the wind swiftly.

put the wind up someone *colloq.* to make them anxious or alarmed.

sail close to the wind to be in danger of going beyond an approved limit.

see which way the wind blows to assess current opinions, likely developments, etc.

take the wind out of someone's sails to thwart someone's confident progress; to deflate or humble someone.

[from Anglo-Saxon]

◇ Global wind patterns are largely dependent on the amount of radiation that reaches the Earth's surface, but winds are also influenced by the Earth's rotation, the relative distribution of land and sea, the presence of mountain ranges and other landforms, ocean currents, and local heating and cooling.

wind[2] *verb* (PAST TENSE AND PAST PARTICIPLE **wound**) **1** (*often* **wind** *or* **wind something round** *or* **up**) to wrap or coil, or be wrapped or coiled. **2** *intrans.*, *trans.* to progress on a path with many twists and turns: *winding lanes / the procession wound its way through the streets.* **3** (*also* **wind something up**) to tighten the spring of a clock, watch, or other clockwork device by turning a knob or key.

— **wind down 1** *said of a clock or clockwork device* to slow down and stop working. **2** *said of a person* to begin to relax, especially after a spell of tension or stress.

wind something down 1 to lower it by turning a handle. **2** to reduce the resources and activities of a business or enterprise.

wind up *colloq.* to end up: *wind up in jail.*

wind someone up 1 to make them tense, nervous, or excited. **2** *colloq.* to taunt or tease them.

wind something up 1 to raise it by turning a handle. **2** to tighten the spring of a clock or clockwork device. **3** to conclude or close down a business or enterprise.
[from Anglo-Saxon *windan*]

Windaus, Adolf (1876–1959) German chemist, born in Berlin. Professor at Freiburg, Innsbruck, and Göttingen, his most important research was on the structure of cholesterol and vitamin D; for this work he was awarded the 1928 Nobel Prize for Chemistry.

windbag *noun colloq.* a person full of pompous, tedious, or trivial talk.

wind band a musical ensemble made up of wind instruments.

windbreak *noun* a barrier, eg in the form of a fence or line of trees, giving protection from the wind.

windcheater *noun* a windproof jacket usually of close-woven fabric.

windchill *noun* the extra chill given to air temperature by the wind.

wind cone a windsock.

winder *noun* a person or thing that winds.

Windermere POP (1981) 8 000, a lakeside resort town in South Lakeland district, Cumbria, NW England. It lies on L Windermere, 11km/7mi NW of Kendal, and is a major tourist centre. NOTABLE FEATURES Church of St Martin (15c); Rydal Mount (10km/6mi NW), Wordsworth's home from 1813 to 1850; Brantwood, home of John Ruskin.

Windermere, Lake the largest lake in England, in the Lake District of Cumbria, NW England. It extends 18km/11mi S from Ambleside, with a width of 1.6km/1mi, and is linked to Morecambe Bay by the R Leven. The largest island in the lake is Belle Isle. NOTABLE FEATURE remains of 13c chapel on Ladyholme.

windfall *noun* **1** a fruit, especially an apple, blown down from its tree. **2** an unexpected financial gain, or other piece of good fortune.

wind farm a place where electricity is generated by wind power.

Windhoek POP (1991) 159 000, the capital of Namibia. It lies 1 450km/900mi N of Cape Town, South Africa, at an altitude of 1 650m. HISTORY occupied by South African forces in 1915; capital of German South-West Africa in 1922. NOTABLE FEATURE cathedral.

Windhover, The a poem by Gerard Manley Hopkins, in which he experimented with 'sprung rhythm'.

winding-sheet *noun* a sheet for wrapping a corpse in; a shroud.

wind instrument a musical instrument such as a clarinet, flute, or trumpet, played by blowing air through it.

Wind in the Willows, The a children's novel by Kenneth Grahame (1908). It gives an anthropomorphic description of the riverside lives of several creatures.

windjammer *noun Hist.* a large fast merchant sailing-ship.

windlass *noun* a drum-shaped axle round which a rope or chain is wound for hauling or hoisting weights. [from Norse *windass*, from *vinda*, to wind + *ass*, beam]

windmill *noun* **1** a mechanical device operated by wind-driven sails or vanes that revolve about a fixed shaft, formerly used in W Europe to mill flour. Lightweight metal windmills are used in many developing countries to pump water (eg for land drainage) and to generate electricity. **2** a toy with a set of plastic or paper sails mounted on a stick, that revolve in the wind.

— **tilt at windmills** to attack imaginary opponents (with reference to Cervantes' hero *Don Quixote*, who in a crazed state gave battle to windmills, thinking them to be knights).

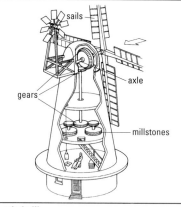

windmill

Windmill at Wijk, The a painting by Jacob van Ruisdael (c.1665, Rijksmuseum, Amsterdam).

window *noun* **1** an opening in a wall to look through, or let in light and air; a wooden or metal frame fitted with panes of glass for placing in such an opening; a pane. **2** the area behind a shop's window, in which to display goods on sale: *the skirt in the window.* **3** a glass-covered opening eg at a railway, theatre, etc, at which to purchase one's ticket. **4** a gap in a schedule, etc available for some purpose. **5** *Comput.* an enclosed rectangular area on the visual display unit of a computer, which can be used as an independent screen. Many operating systems allow several windows to be displayed simultaneously, so that a different file can be worked on or a different program run in each window. [from Norse *windauga*, literally 'wind eye']

window box a box fitted along an exterior window ledge, for growing plants.

window-dressing *noun* **1** the art of arranging goods in a shop window. **2** the art or practice of giving something superficial appeal by skilful presentation.

window-shopping *noun* the activity of eyeing goods in shop windows as the next-best thing to buying them.

windowsill *or* **window ledge** *noun* the interior or exterior ledge running along the bottom of a window.

windpipe *noun* the passage running from the back of the throat to the lungs, through which air is drawn into, and expelled from, the body; the trachea.

wind power a renewable energy source generated from winds in the Earth's atmosphere, used to drive machinery, generate electricity, etc.

Windscale see SELLAFIELD.

windscreen *noun* the front window of a motor vehicle.

windscreen-wiper *noun* a device fitted to the windscreen of a motor vehicle, consisting of a rubber blade on an arm moving in an arc, to keep the windscreen clear of rain.

windshield *noun North Amer.* a windscreen.

windsock *noun* an open-ended cone of fabric flying from a mast, eg at an airport, showing the direction and speed of the wind.

Windsor *or* **New Windsor** POP (1981) 32 000, a town linked with Eton in Windsor and Maidenhead district, Berkshire, S England. It lies W of London, on the R Thames. NOTABLE FEATURES Windsor Castle; Eton College (1540).

EVENTS Royal Windsor Horse Show (May); horse-racing at Royal Ascot (Jun).

Windsor POP (1991) 191 000, an industrial town in S Ontario, SE Canada, lying on the Detroit R, opposite Detroit. HISTORY founded as a Hudson's Bay Company post in 1835; underwent rapid industrial growth in the 19c; during Prohibition in the 1920s, Windsor was the major route for rum-running into the USA. NOTABLE FEATURES Hiram Walker Historical Museum; Point Pelee National Park to the S, notable for birds and butterflies.

Windsor, Bessie Wallis Warfield, Duchess of (1896–1986) wife of Edward VIII, born in Blue Ridge Summit, Pennsylvania. She married (1916–27) Lt E W Spencer of the US Navy, then (1927–36) Ernest Simpson, a US-born Englishman. Well known in London society, she met Edward the Prince of Wales at a country house party in 1931. Following her divorce and his abdication in 1936, they were married in France in 1937. After his death she lived in seclusion in Paris.

Windsor, House of the name of the British royal family since 1917. Unequivocally English, the name resulted from a declaration by George V (a member of the House of Saxe-Coburg-Gotha) because the British monarchy's Germanic surname was felt to be inappropriate, especially during a war against Germany (see FAMILY TREE).

Windsor Castle the largest of England's castles, situated on the R Thames in Windsor, Berkshire. It was founded by William I and first used as a royal residence by Henry I. The process of converting Windsor from a fortress into a palace began in the 16c. In Nov 1992, the interior of the Castle was seriously damaged by fire.

windsurfing *noun* the sport of riding the waves on a sailboard; sailboarding.

windswept *adj.* **1** exposed to strong winds. **2** dishevelled from, or otherwise showing the effects of, exposure to the wind.

wind tunnel *Aeron.* an experimental chamber in which fans blow a controlled stream of air past stationary models of aircraft, cars, trains, etc (or their components), in order to test their aerodynamic properties by simulating the effects of movement through air.

windward — *noun* the side of a boat, etc facing the wind. — *adj.* on this side.

Windward Islands an island group of the Lesser Antilles, in the Caribbean Sea. It lies S of the Leeward Is, from Martinique in the N to Grenada in the S, excluding Trinidad and Tobago. The group is so called because of its exposure to the prevailing NE trade winds. It was formerly the name of a British colony comprising Dominica, St Lucia, St Vincent, and Grenada.

Windward Islands, French **Iles du Vent** POP (1988) 140 000, an island group of the Society Is, French Polynesia. It comprises Tahiti, Moorea, and the smaller Mehetia, Tetiaroa, and Tubuai Manu Is. CAPITAL Papeete. ECONOMY coconuts; tourism.

windy *adj.* (**windier**, **windiest**) **1** exposed to, or characterized by, strong wind: *a windy place / a windy day.* **2** *colloq.*, *said of speech or writing* long-winded or pompous. **3** *colloq.* nervous; uneasy.

wine *noun* **1** an alcoholic drink made from the fermented juice of grapes, or one made from other fruits, plants, etc. **2** the dark red colour of red wine. [from Anglo-Saxon *win*, from Latin *vinum*]

winebibber *noun old use* someone who drinks wine to excess.

wine cellar 1 a cellar in which to store wines. **2** the stock of wine stored there.

wine glass a drinking-glass typically consisting of a bowl on a stem, with a wide base flaring out from the stem.

winery *noun* (PL. **wineries**) a place where wine is prepared and stored.

wineskin *Hist.* the skin of a goat or sheep sewn up and used for holding wine.

wing — *noun* **1** one of the two modified forelimbs of a bird or bat that are adapted for flight. **2** one of two or more membranous outgrowths that project from either side of the body of an

Wine Regions

Australia
Barossa Valley (S Australia)
Coonawarra (S Australia)
Geelong (Victoria)
Glenrowan (Victoria)
Great Western (Victoria)
Hunter Valley (NSW)
McLaren Vale (S Australia)
Riverland (S Australia)
Swan Valley (W Australia)

Eastern Europe
Bulgaria
CIS States
Czech State
Hungary
Romania
Slovakia

France
Alsace
Bordeaux
Burgundy
Beaujolais
Champagne
Loire
Rhône
SE France

Germany
Ahr
Baden
Franken
Mosel-Saar-Ruhr
Rheingau
Rheinhessen (incl. Liebfraumilch)
Rheinpfalz
Saale-Unstrut

Italy
Latium (incl. Frascati)
Lombardy
Tuscany (incl. Chianti)
Piedmont
Veneto (incl. Soave and Valpolicella)
Umbria (incl. Orvieto)

New Zealand
Gisborne
Hawke's Bay
Marlborough

Portugal
Alantejo
Bairrada
Dao
Douro
Oeste
Ribatejo
Setubal

Spain
La Mancha
Penedes
Rias Baixas
Rioja
Rueda

USA
California (incl. Livermore Valley, Napa County, Sonoma County)
New York State

insect and enable it to fly. **3** one of the flattened structures that project from either side of an aircraft body. **4** any of the corner sections of a vehicle body, forming covers for the wheels. **5** a part of a building projecting from the central or main section. **6** the left or right flank of an army or fleet in battle formation. **7** *Football* either edge of the pitch, or the player at either extreme of the forward line. **8** (**wings**) the area at each side of a stage, where performers wait to enter, out of sight of the audience. **9** a group with its own distinct views and character, within a political party or other body. **10** in the Royal Air Force, a unit consisting of several squadrons. **11** (**wings**) *literary* a miraculous surge of speed: *fear lent him wings.* — *verb* **1** to wound in the wing, arm, or shoulder; to wound superficially. **2** (**wing one's way**) to make one's way by flying, or with speed. **3** *poetic* to fly over, or skim lightly. **4** to send (eg an arrow) swiftly on its way.
— **in the wings** waiting for one's turn to perform.
on the wing flying; in flight.
spread one's wings 1 to use one's potential fully. **2** to escape from a confining environment in order to do this.
take wing to fly off.
under someone's wing under their protection or guidance.
[from Norse *vængre*]

Wingate, Orde (Charles) (1903–44) British soldier, born in Naini Tal, India. He was commissioned in 1922, and served in the Sudan (1928–33) and Palestine (1936–9), where he helped create a Jewish defence force. In the Burma theatre (1942) he organized the Chindits — specially trained jungle-fighters who were supplied by air and placed far behind the enemy lines. He was killed in a plane crash in Burma (Myanma).

wing chair an armchair that has a high back with forward-projecting lugs.

wing commander in the Royal Air Force, an officer of the rank below group captain.

winger *noun Football* a player in wing position.

wingless *adj.* not having wings.

wing nut a metal nut with flattened projections for easy turning on a bolt with the finger and thumb.

wingspan *noun* the distance from tip to tip of the wings of an aircraft, or a bird's wings when outstretched.

Winifred a female first name. [from the Welsh personal name *Gwenfrewi*]

wink — *verb intrans., trans.* **1** to shut an eye briefly as a form of informal communication with someone, especially as a conspiratorial signal. **2** (**wink at something**) to ignore an offence or improper procedure deliberately; to pretend

not to notice it. **3** *said of lights, stars, etc* to flicker or twinkle. — *noun* an act of winking.
— **tip someone the wink** *colloq.* to give them a useful hint, valuable information, etc, especially in confidence.
[from Anglo-Saxon *wincian*]

winker *noun old colloq. use* a flashing direction-indicator on a motor vehicle.

winkle — *noun* a small edible snail-shaped shellfish; a periwinkle. — *verb* (**winkle something out**) to force or prise it out. [see PERIWINKLE²]

winkle-picker *noun colloq.* a shoe with a long narrow pointed toe.

Winkler, Hans-Günther (1926–) German show jumper, born in Wuppertal-Barmen, Westphalia. He is the only man to have won five Olympic gold medals at show jumping (the team golds in 1956, 1960, 1964, and 1972, and the individual title on *Halla* in 1956). He won the individual world title on the same horse in 1954 and 1955. He made his German international début in Spain in 1952, and later became team captain.

winner *noun* a person, animal, or vehicle, etc that wins a contest, etc.

Winnie-the-Pooh a collection of children's stories by A A Milne (1926). They describe the antics of the greedy bear Pooh and his friends.

winning — *adj.* **1** attractive or charming: *a winning smile.* **2** securing victory: *the winning shot.* — *noun* (**winnings**) money won, especially in gambling.

winningly *adv.* in a winning way; attractively, persuasively.

winning-post *noun Racing* the post marking the point where a race finishes.

Winnipeg POP (1991e) 652 000, the industrial capital of Manitoba province, central Canada, lying on the Red R where it meets the Assiniboine R. HISTORY established in 1738 as Fort Rouge; became a fur-trading post in 1806; received its current name in 1873; expanded after the arrival of the railway in 1881; severely damaged by flood in 1950. NOTABLE FEATURES railway memorial; Centennial Arts Centre (concert hall, planetarium, museum); Civic Auditorium (home of Winnipeg Symphony Orchestra); Royal Winnipeg Ballet; art gallery.

Winnipeg, Lake a lake in S central Manitoba province, S Canada, located 64km/40mi NE of Winnipeg. It is a remnant of the glacial L Agassiz. AREA 24 390sq km/9 415sq mi; length 386km/240mi; width 88km/55mi. It is drained N into Hudson Bay by the Nelson R.

Winnipesaukee, Lake the largest lake in New Hampshire, NE USA. AREA 184sq km/71sq mi. It is a popular resort area, situated to the N of Concord.

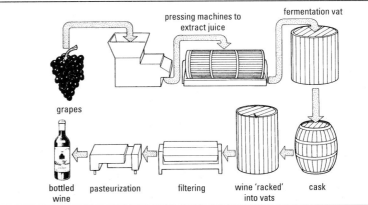

wine production

winnow *verb* **1** to separate chaff from (grain) by blowing a current of air through it or fanning it. **2** (**winnow something out**) to blow (chaff) from grain, to identify and reject what is unwanted from a group or mass. **3** to sift (evidence, etc). [from Anglo-Saxon *windwian*, from *wind*, wind]

wino *noun* (PL. **winos**) *slang* someone, especially a down-and-out, addicted to cheap wine.

Winslow Boy, The a play by Terence Rattigan (1946). It is a psychological study based on the Archer–Shee case, in which a young naval cadet was tried for theft. It focuses on the father's attempts to clear his son's reputation.

winsome *adj. old use* charming; captivating. [from Anglo-Saxon *wynsum*, joyous]

winsomely *adv.* in a winsome way.

winsomeness *noun* a winsome state or quality.

Winston a male first name, after the surname, in turn after the place-name in Gloucestershire; it has been used in the Churchill family since the 17c.

Winston Churchill a portrait painting by Graham Sutherland (1954). It was later destroyed on the instruction of Lady Churchill.

Winston-Salem POP (1990) 144 000, the seat of Forsyth County, N central North Carolina, USA, situated 40km/25mi W of Greensboro. It is the nation's chief tobacco manufacturer. HISTORY Winston was founded in 1849, and Salem in 1766; the towns were united in 1913. NOTABLE FEATURE Old Salem.

winter — *noun* the coldest season of the year, coming between autumn and spring. — *adj.* of or belonging to winter. — *verb intrans.* (**wintered**, **wintering**) to spend the winter in a specified place, usually other than one's normal home. [from Anglo-Saxon *winter*]

wintergreen *noun* **1** an evergreen plant from which an aromatic oil, used medicinally and as a flavouring, is obtained. **2** this oil.

winter sports sports held on snow or ice, eg skiing and tobogganing.

Winter's Tale, The a play by William Shakespeare (1611). It is a romantic comedy depicting King Leontes's unforgiving reaction to his conviction that his virtuous wife Hermione is having an affair with his old friend Polixenes. Later, Perdita, the daughter born in prison, falls in love with the son of Polixenes, eventually bringing about reconciliation.

Winterthur POP (1990) 125 000, a town in Zürich canton, Switzerland. It lies near the R Töss in the Pre-Alpine region, NE of Zürich. NOTABLE FEATURE town hall (18c–19c).

wintertime *noun* the season of winter.

Winthrop, Dolly a kind and caring character in George Eliot's *Silas Marner*.

Winthrop, John (1588–1649) English colonist, born in Groton, Suffolk. He became a lawyer, and in 1629 was appointed Governor of Massachusetts colony, to which post he was re-elected, with brief intervals, throughout his life. He probably had more influence than anyone else in forming the political institutions of the N states of America.

wintriness *noun* a wintry condition.

wintry *adj.* (**wintrier**, **wintriest**) **1** *said of weather, etc* like or characteristic of winter. **2** unfriendly, cold, or hostile: *a wintry expression*.

winy *adj.* (**winier**, **winiest**) having a wine-like flavour.

wipe *verb* **1** to clean or dry with a cloth, on a mat, etc. **2** to dry (dishes). **3** (**wipe something away** *or* **off**) to remove it by wiping. **4** *Comput.* to erase material from a tape or disk. **5** to remove or get rid of: *wiped the incident from his memory.*

6 to pass (a cloth, etc) over, or rub (a liquid, etc) on to, a surface.
— **wipe something out 1** to clean out the inside of it. **2** to remove or get rid of it: *wipe out the memory*. **3** to destroy or obliterate it. [from Anglo-Saxon *wipian*]

wiper *noun* same as WINDSCREEN-WIPER.

wire — *noun* **1** metal drawn out into a narrow flexible strand. **2** a length of this, usually wrapped in insulating material, used for carrying an electric current. **3** a cable connecting point with point in a telecommunications system. **4** a telegram or telegraph. **5** a fence, barrier, etc made of wire; wire netting. — *verb* **1** to send a telegram to; to send (a message) by telegram. **2** (*also* **wire something up**) to fit up or connect up an electrical apparatus, system, etc with wires. **3** (*also* **wire something up**) to fasten or secure it with wire.
— **get one's wires crossed** to misunderstand or be confused about something. [from Anglo-Saxon *wir*]

wire-haired *adj., said of a dog breed* having a coarse, usually wavy coat.

wireless *noun old use* **1** a radio. **2** wireless telegraphy.

wireless telegraphy the transmission of signals by means of electromagnetic waves.

wire netting wires twisted into network for use as fencing, etc.

wiretap *verb* (**wiretapped**, **wiretapping**) to tap (a telephone) or the telephone of (someone).

wire wool a mass of fine wire used for scouring.

wireworm *noun* the hard-bodied worm-like larva of certain beetles, destructive to plant roots.

wiring *noun* **1** the arrangement of wires that connects the individual components of electric circuits into an operating system, eg the mains wiring of a house. **2** the act of securing with, connecting with, or communicating by wire.

wiry *adj.* (**wirier**, **wiriest**) **1** of slight build, but strong and agile. **2** resembling wire. **3** *said of hair* coarse and wavy.

Wis. *abbrev.* Wisconsin.

Wisconsin POP (1990) 5m, a state in N USA, divided into 72 counties, and bounded N by L Superior and N and E by L Michigan. AREA 145 431sq km/56 136sq mi. It is known as the 'Badger State'. PHYSICAL DESCRIPTION rivers include the Mississippi (part of the W border), Menominee (part of the E border), and Wisconsin; L Winnebago lies to the E; part of L Michigan lies within the state boundary; there are over 8 500 lakes; the highest point is Timms Hill (595m); the glaciated terrain in the N and W is largely forested. HISTORY explored by the French, and first settled by French traders in 1670; surrendered to the British in 1763 at the end of the French and Indian wars; ceded to the USA in 1783; contained successively in the Territories of Indiana, Illinois, and Michigan before the Territory of Wisconsin was formed in 1836; became the 30th state to join the Union, in 1848. CAPITAL Madison. CHIEF TOWNS Milwaukee, Green Bay, Racine. ECONOMY dairy products (the nation's largest producer of milk, butter, and cheese); grain, vegetables; brewing; heavy industry in the Milwaukee area; manufactures include timber products, paper, metal products, machinery, electrical equipment, and transport equipment; food processing; winter sports.

wisdom *noun* **1** the ability to make sensible judgements and decisions, especially on the basis of one's knowledge and experience; prudence and common sense. **2** learning; knowledge. **3** the weight of informed opinion: *the current wisdom on whether or not to smack children*. **4** *old use* wise sayings. [from Anglo-Saxon *wisdom*]

wisdom literature in the Hebrew Bible, a group of writings, usually including Proverbs,

Ecclesiastes, the Song of Songs, and Job. The literature is usually traced to a special class of sages in Israel who sought to draw lessons for life from general human experience rather than from revealed religious truths. The influence of wisdom may also be found in other Biblical stories (eg Esther) and in some of the Psalms; in the Apocrypha it also includes Ecclesiasticus and the Wisdom of Solomon.

wisdom tooth any of the last four molar teeth to come through, at the back of each side of the upper and lower jaw.

wise[1] *adj.* **1** having or showing wisdom; prudent; sensible. **2** learned. **3** astute; shrewd; sagacious. **4** (*in compounds*) knowing the ways of: *streetwise / worldly-wise*.
— **be wise to something** *colloq.* to be aware of or informed about it.
none the wiser knowing no more than before.
put someone wise *colloq.* to give them necessary information.
wise up to find out the facts about something. [from Anglo-Saxon *wis*]

wise[2] *noun old use* way: *in no wise to blame.* [from Anglo-Saxon *wise*, manner]

-wise *combining form* forming words denoting: **1** direction or manner: *lengthwise / clockwise / likewise / otherwise*. **2** respect or relevance: *moneywise / business-wise*. [from WISE[2]]

wiseacre *noun derog.* someone who assumes an air of superior wisdom. [from Old Dutch *wijseggher*, soothsayer]

wisecrack *noun* a smart, clever, knowing remark.

wise guy *colloq.* someone full of smart comments; a know-all.

wisely *adv.* in a wise way; with wisdom.

Wiseman, Nicholas (Patrick Stephen) (1802–65) British Roman Catholic churchman, born of an Irish family in Seville, Spain. Raised in Waterford and Ushaw, he entered the English College in Rome, was ordained in 1825, and became Rector of the College (1828–40). His appointment as the first Archbishop of Westminster and a cardinal (1850) led to much religious indignation, which resulted in the Ecclesiastical Titles Assumption Act. His works include the historical novel *Fabiola* (1854).

wise man *old use* **1** a wizard. **2** one of the Magi.

wish — *verb* **1** to want; used especially in expressing one's desire. **2** to desire, especially vainly or helplessly (that something were the case): *I wish you'd sit still. I wish I'd known*. **3** (**wish for something**) **a** to long, especially vainly, for it: *often wished for a quieter life*. **b** to make a wish for it: *wished for a new bicycle*. **4** to express a desire for (luck, success, happiness, etc) to come to someone: *wish you all the best*. **5** to say (good afternoon, etc) to: *wished them good day*. **6** (**wish something on someone**) (*with a negative*) to desire it to be inflicted on them: *wouldn't wish it on my worst enemy*. **7** *colloq.* to impose or inflict: *expect she'll wish herself on us for Christmas*. — *noun* **1** a desire. **2** (*usually* **wishes**) what one wants to be done, etc: *we want to respect your wishes*. **3** (**wishes**) a hope expressed for someone's welfare: *best wishes to your parents*. **4** in fairy tales, traditional ritual, etc, the stating of a desire in expectation or hope of its being magically fulfilled: *make a wish*.
— **wish someone joy of something** *ironic* to wish them well of some liability, commitment, etc that one is glad to be rid of. [from Anglo-Saxon *wyscan*]

Wishart, George (c.1513–46) Scottish reformer and martyr, born in Pitarrow, Kincardineshire. As a schoolmaster in Montrose he incurred a charge of heresy for teaching the Greek New Testament (1538). After travelling on the Continent, he returned to Scotland (1543) and preached the Lutheran doctrine in several towns, but was arrested and burned at St Andrews. One of his converts was John Knox.

wishbone *noun* a V-shaped bone in the breast of poultry.

wishful thinking an over-optimistic expectation that something will happen, arising from one's desire that it should.

wishy-washy *adj.* **1** *said eg of colours* pale and insipid. **2** lacking character; insipid. **3** watery; weak.

wisp *noun* **1** a strand; a thin fine tuft or shred. **2** something slight or insubstantial: *a wisp of a child.*

wispy *adj.* (**wispier, wispiest**) wisp-like; light and fine in texture, flimsy, insubstantial.

wisteria *or* **wistaria** *noun* a deciduous climbing shrub of the genus *Wisteria*, native to E Asia and N America, and having leaves divided into leaflets, and lilac, violet, or white flowers borne in long pendulous clusters. It is often grown for ornament, and can reach a considerable age, developing thick gnarled stems. [named after the American anatomist C Wistar (or Wister)]

wistful *adj.* sadly or vainly yearning. [from old word *wist*, intent]

wistfully *adv.* in a wistful way.

wistfulness *noun* a wistful quality.

wit[1] *noun* **1** humour; the ability to express oneself amusingly. **2** a person with this ability. **3** humorous speech or writing. **4** (*also* **wits**) common sense; intelligence; resourcefulness.
— **at one's wits' end** *colloq.* reduced to despair; utterly at a loss.
have *or* **keep one's wits about one** to be, or stay, alert.
live by one's wits to live by cunning.
scared, *etc* **out of one's wits** extremely scared, etc.
[from Anglo-Saxon *wit*, mind, thought]

wit[2]
— **to wit** *old use Legal* that is to say; namely. [from Anglo-Saxon *witan*, to know]

witch *noun* **1** a person, especially a woman, supposed to have magical powers used usually, but not always, malevolently. **2** a frighteningly ugly or wicked old woman. **3** a dangerously or irresistibly fascinating woman. [from Anglo-Saxon *wicca*]

witchcraft *noun* magic or sorcery of the kind practised by witches.
◇ Witchcraft especially involves the manipulation of natural objects or events; often called *black magic* if harmful to people, *white magic* if beneficial. In Africa, the power of witches is said to be innate, and individuals may not be aware that they are witches. The Christian Church in Europe systematically persecuted witches from the 14c and by the end of the 17c c.200 000 people, mainly women, had been executed. Contemporary witchcraft in the West generally sees itself as an alternative religion, and exercises its magical powers in beneficial ways.

witch doctor a member of a tribal society who is believed to have magic powers, and to be able to cure or harm people by means of them.

witchery *noun* **1** the activities of witches. **2** a bewitching or spellbinding influence; fascination.

Witches, The Three, also called the **Weird Sisters** the mysterious heath-dwellers in Shakespeare's *Macbeth*, who visit their ambiguous prophecies on Macbeth and Banquo.

witch hazel **1** a N American shrub with narrow-petalled yellow flowers, from whose bark an astringent lotion is produced, used to treat bruises, etc. **2** another name for wych-elm. [from Anglo-Saxon *wice*]

witch hunt the hunting down and persecution of an individual or number of individuals, for

alleged political or other types of heresy, behaviour considered dangerous to society, etc.

with *prep.* **1** in the company of: *went with her.* **2** used after verbs of partnering, co-operating, associating, etc: *danced with him / plays with Arsenal.* **3** used after verbs of mixing: *mingled with the crowd.* **4** by means of; using: *raised it with a crowbar.* **5** used after verbs of covering, filling, etc: *plastered with mud / filled with rubbish.* **6** used after verbs of providing: *equipped with firearms.* **7** as a result of: *shaking with fear.* **8** bearing; announcing: *rang with bad news.* **9** in the same direction as: *drift with the current.* **10** at the same time or rate as: *discretion comes with age.* **11** used after verbs of conflict: *quarrelled with her brother / clashes with the curtains.* **12** used after verbs of agreeing, disagreeing, and comparing: *compared with last year / agrees/disagrees with the evidence.* **13** used in describing: *a man with a limp.* **14** used in stating manner: *won with ease / answered with a nod.* **15** because of having: *with your talents, you'll surely get the job.* **16** in spite of having: *with all his money he's still unhappy.* **17** in (the specified circumstances): *I can't go abroad with my mother so ill.* **18** featuring; starring: *'Treasure Island' with Robert Newton.* **19** in the care of: *left it with the porter.* **20** used after verbs of parting: *parted with her sadly / dispensed with his crutches.* **21** regarding: *what shall we do with this? / can't do a thing with my hair / what's wrong with you?* **22** used after adverbs and adverbial phrases in exclamations expressing a wish or order: *down with tyranny! / into bed with you!* **23** *colloq.* understanding: *are you with me?* **24** loyal to; supporting: *we're with you all the way.*
— **with it** *colloq.* fashionable; trendy.
with that ... at that point ...; thereupon ...
[from Anglo-Saxon *with*]

withal *old use* — *adv.* **1** as well; into the bargain. **2** for all that; nevertheless. — *prep.* with: *flesh to bait fish withal.* [from WITH + ALL]

withdraw *verb* (PAST TENSE **withdrew**; PAST PARTICIPLE **withdrawn**) **1** *intrans.* to move somewhere else, especially more private: *withdrew into her bedroom.* **2** *trans., intrans. said of troops* to move back; to retreat or order to retreat. **3** to pull in or back: *withdrew his head into the carriage / withdrew her hand from his.* **4** to take (money) from a bank account for use. **5** *intrans., trans.* to back out or pull out of an activity: *withdrew from the contest.* **6** to take back, or say that one doesn't mean (what one has said): *I withdraw that remark.* **7** *intrans.* (**withdraw from something**) to stop oneself taking a drug to which one is addicted. **8** *intrans.* to become uncommunicative or unresponsive. **9** to discontinue or cancel: *withdraw a service / withdraw an offer.* [from WITH (= away from) + DRAW]

withdrawal *noun* **1** the act or process of withdrawing. **2** a removal of funds from a bank account. **3** *Medicine* the breaking of a drug addiction, with associated physical and psychological symptoms (known as *withdrawal symptoms*), eg trembling, sweating, vomiting, and depression. **4** a retreat into silence and self-absorption. **5** (*also* **withdrawal method**) an unreliable method of contraception in which the penis is removed from the vagina before ejaculation has occurred.

withdrawal symptom any of a number of symptoms such as pain, nausea, or sweating, experienced by someone who is deprived of a drug to which they have become addicted.

withdrawn *adj.* unresponsive, shy, or reserved.

withe *noun* a pliable branch or twig, especially from the willow tree. [from Anglo-Saxon *withthe*]

wither *verb intrans., trans.* (**withered, withering**) **1** *said of plants* to fade or cause to fade, dry up, and die. **2** to fade or cause to fade and disappear: *love that never withers.* **3** to shrivel or cause to shrivel and decay: *withered old bodies.* [possibly a variant of WEATHER]

withered *adj., said of a limb* thin and stunted, from illness, etc.

Withering, William (1741–99) English physician, born in Wellington in Shropshire. He practised medicine in Stafford and Birmingham, and wrote *An Account of the Foxglove* (1785), introducing digitalis, extracted from that plant, as a drug for cardiac disease. He was the first to see the connection between dropsy and heart disease.

withering *adj., said of a glance, remark, etc* such as makes one shrivel up; bitterly contemptuous.

withers *pl. noun* the ridge between the shoulder blades of a horse. [from older *wither*, against]

withhold *verb* (PAST TENSE AND PAST PARTICIPLE **withheld**) to refuse to give or grant; to hold back: *withhold evidence / withhold payment.* [from WITH (=away from) + HOLD]

within — *prep.* **1** inside; enclosed by: *within these four walls / circles within circles.* **2** not outside the limits of; not beyond: *live within one's means / within sight.* **3** in less than (a certain time or distance): *finished within a week / within a hair's breadth of death.* — *adv. old use* inside: *apply within / a voice from within.* [from Anglo-Saxon *withinnan*]

without — *prep.* **1** not having the company of: *went home without him.* **2** deprived of: *can't live without her.* **3** not having: *a blue sky without a cloud.* **4** lacking: *books without covers.* **5** not (behaving as expected or in a particular way): *answered without smiling / did it without being told.* **6** not giving, showing, etc: *complied without a murmur.* **7** not encountering (some expected circumstance): *managed without difficulty / completed the rescue without anyone getting hurt.* **8** not having (something required); in neglect of (a usual procedure): *entered without permission / imprisoned without trial.* **9** not using; not having the help of: *opened it without a key.* **10** if it had not been for: *would have died without their help.* **11** *old use* outside: *without the walls.* — *adv. old use* outside. [from Anglo-Saxon *withutan*]

withstand *verb* to resist or brave: *withstand storms / withstand insults.* [from Anglo-Saxon *withstandan*]

withy *noun* (PL. **withies**) a withe.

witless *adj.* **1** stupid; brainless. **2** crazy. [see WIT[1]]

witness — *noun* **1** someone who sees, and can therefore give a direct account of, an event, occurrence, etc. **2** a person who gives evidence in a court of law. **3** a person who adds his or her own signature to confirm the genuineness of a signature just put on a document, etc. **4** proof or evidence of anything. — *verb* **1** to be present as an observer at (an event, etc). **2** to add one's own signature to confirm the genuineness of (a signature on a document, etc). **3** *said of a period or place, or of a person* to be the setting for, or to live through certain events: *a century that witnessed great medical advances.* **4** *trans., intrans.* (**witness something** *or* **witness to something**) to confirm it: *I can witness to his generosity.* — *prep.* as shown by: *politicians do not get everything right, witness the poll tax.*
— **bear witness to something** to be evidence of it; to give confirmation of it: *a chaotic mess that bore witness to the struggle / was at home all evening, as my husband will bear witness.*
be witness to something to be in a position to observe it: *have never before been witness to such cruelty.*
[from Anglo-Saxon *witnes*, from *witan*, to know]

witness-box *or* **witness-stand** *noun* the enclosed stand from which a witness gives evidence in a court of law.

Witt, Jan de (1625–72) Dutch statesman, the Grand Pensionary (chief minister) of the United Provinces of the Netherlands (1653–72), born in Dort. As leader of the Republican Party, he sought to abolish the office of Stadholder, and to limit the power of the House of Orange. However, when France invaded the Netherlands in 1672, William of Orange was made Stadholder and Commander of the Dutch forces. De Witt's brother, Cornelius, was accused of conspiracy and imprisoned, and when De Witt went to see him in prison at The Hague, they were killed by an infuriated mob.

Witt, Katerina (1965–) German figure skater, born in Karl-Marx-Stadt. The East German champion in 1982, she won the first of six successive European titles in 1983, was world champion in 1984–5 and 1987–8, and Olympic champion in 1984 and 1988.

Wittenberg POP (1990e) 50 000, a town in Saxony-Anhalt state, E central Germany. It lies on the R Elbe, SW of Berlin. HISTORY associated with the beginning of the Reformation in 1517; became part of Prussia in 1814. NOTABLE FEATURES 16c Augustinian monastery where Luther lived; Schlosskirche, on the doors of which Luther nailed his 95 theses; Stadtkirche.

Wittgenstein, Ludwig (Josef Johann) (1889–1951) Austrian-born British philosopher, born in Vienna. He studied mathematical logic at Cambridge under Bertrand Russell (1912–13). While serving in the Austrian army in World War I, he wrote the *Tractatus Logico-philosophicus* (1921), in which he argued that an adequate account of language must recognize that any sentence is a picture of the fact it represents, and that any thought is a sentence. In 1929 he began lecturing at Cambridge, submitting the *Tractatus* as his doctoral dissertation. He was appointed Professor of Mental Philosophy and Logic at Cambridge in 1939, worked at a hospital in London during World War II, and finally resigned his chair in 1947. Between 1936 and 1949 he worked on the *Philosophische Untersuchungen* (Philosophical Investigations, 1953), in which he rejected the doctrines of the *Tractatus*, claiming that linguistic meaning is a function of the *use* to which expressions are put, or the 'language games' in which they play a role.

witticism *noun* a witty remark.

wittily *adv.* in a witty way.

wittiness *noun* a witty quality.

wittingly *adv.* knowingly; consciously. [from Anglo-Saxon *witan*, to know]

witty *adj.* (**wittier**, **wittiest**) able to express oneself cleverly and amusingly. [see WIT¹]

Witwatersrand *or* **The Rand** a region centred on a ridge of gold-bearing rock in S Transvaal province, South Africa. It is 100km/60mi long and 40km/25mi wide. Johannesburg is located near its centre. It is the power house of the South African economy. Gold was discovered here in 1886 and the region produces over half the world's supply. [from Afrikaans *Witwatersrand*, white water's reef]

wives see WIFE.

Wives and Daughters an unfinished novel by Mrs Gaskell (1864–6). Her last, it describes the lives of two families in early 19c England.

wizard — *noun* **1** a man supposed to have magic powers; a magician or sorcerer. **2** *colloq.* (**wizard at** *or* **with something**) a person extraordinarily skilled in some way. — *adj. old colloq. use* marvellous. [from Middle English *wisard*, from *wis*, wise]

Wizard of Oz, The a US film directed by Victor Fleming (1939), based on L Frank Baum's *The Wonderful Wizard of Oz* (1900). It is a magical musical fantasy focusing on Dorothy (Judy Garland) who befriends a scarecrow, a tin man, and a lion in Munchkin Land.

wizened *adj.* shrivelled or wrinkled, especially with age. [from Anglo-Saxon *wisnian*, to dry up]

WNO *abbrev.* Welsh National Opera.

WNP *abbrev.* Welsh National Party.

WO *abbrev.* Warrant Officer.

woad *noun* **1** a plant from whose leaves a blue dye is obtained. **2** this dye used by ancient Britons to paint their bodies. [from Anglo-Saxon *wad*]

wobble — *verb* **1** *intrans., trans.* to rock or cause to rock, sway, or shake unsteadily. **2** *intrans. said of the voice* to be unsteady. **3** *intrans.* to be undecided; to waver. — *noun* a wobbling, rocking, or swaying motion. [from German *wabbeln*]

wobbliness *noun* being wobbly.

wobbly *adj.* (**wobblier**, **wobbliest**) unsteady; shaky.

Wodehouse, Sir P(elham) G(renville) (1881–1975) English novelist, born in Guildford, Surrey. He wrote for various magazines including *Punch*, and was interned in Germany during World War II, after which he settled in the USA. He made his name with *Piccadilly Jim* (1918), but is best known as the creator of Bertie Wooster and his 'gentleman's gentleman' Jeeves, who appear in many volumes of his stories, including *My Man Jeeves* (1919). Other works include a succession of novels, short stories, sketches, and librettos.

Woden see ODIN.

wodge *noun colloq.* a lump, wad, or chunk. [a variant of WEDGE]

woe — *noun* **1** grief; misery. **2** affliction; calamity. — *interj. old use* an exclamation of grief. — **woe betide** ... *old use, facetious* may evil befall, or evil will befall whoever offends in some specified way.

woe is me *old use* alas!
[from Anglo-Saxon *wa*]

woebegone *adj.* dismally sorrowful. [from *begone*, surrounded]

woeful *adj.* **1** mournful; sorrowful. **2** causing woe. **3** disgraceful; pitiful.

woefully *adv.* **1** sorrowfully. **2** disgracefully.

woefulness *noun* a woeful quality.

wog *noun Brit. offensive slang* any non-white person. [perhaps from GOLLIWOG]

Wöhler, Friedrich (1800–82) German chemist, born in Eschersheim. Professor at Göttingen from 1836, he attempted to prepare ammonium cyanate from silver cyanate and ammonium chloride, but instead obtained urea (1827). This was the first demonstration of the production of a natural product from non-organic materials, and revolutionized organic chemistry. He also prepared pure aluminium and beryllium.

wok *noun* an almost hemispherical pan used in Chinese cookery. [from S Chinese *wok*]

woke, woken see WAKE.

Woking POP (1992e) 88 000, a town linked with Byfleet in Woking district, Surrey, SE England. It lies on the R Wey, 40km/25mi SW of London, and forms part of the Greater London urban area.

wold *noun* a tract of open rolling upland. [from Anglo-Saxon *wald*, *weald*, forest]

Wolds Way a long-distance footpath, stretching 115km/71mi from Hull to Filey, N England. It links with the Cleveland Way.

wolf — *noun* (PL. **wolves**) **1** either of two species of carnivorous mammal belonging to the dog family (Canidae), and having erect ears, a long muzzle, and a long bushy tail. **2** *colloq.* a man with an insatiable appetite for sexual conquests. — *verb* (*usually* **wolf something down**) *colloq.* to gobble it greedily.

— **cry wolf** to give a false alarm.

keep the wolf from the door to ward off hunger.

wolf in sheep's clothing a dangerous or powerful person who appears to be harmless. [from Anglo-Saxon]

◇ The grey wolf (*Canis lupus*) was formerly widespread in Europe, Asia, and N America, but is now mainly restricted to the more northerly

and uninhabited areas. It is larger than the red wolf (*Canis rufus*), which is very rare, and confined to a small area of the southern USA. The grey wolf, which has been hunted almost to extinction in the USA, is about 1.5m in length, and usually has a grey coat sprinkled with black, and yellowish-white underparts and legs. Wolves live in open country and forests, hunting by day, and hiding by night under fallen trees, among rocks, or in underground holes. They usually hunt in family groups or in packs of 20 to 40 animals, and can generally outrun their prey, which includes mammals such as deer. Wolves only kill livestock when food is scarce.

grey wolf

wolfcub *noun* **1** a young wolf. **2** (**Wolfcub**) formerly, a Cub Scout.

Wolfe, Thomas (Clayton) (1900–38) US novelist, born in Asheville, North Carolina. He wrote several plays, but is best known for his autobiographical novels, notably *Look Homeward, Angel* (1929) and *Of Time and the River* (1935).

Wolfenden, John Frederick Wolfenden, Baron (1906–85) English educationalist, born in Halifax, Yorkshire. He was headmaster at Uppingham (1934–44) and Shrewsbury (1944–50), and Vice-Chancellor of Reading University from 1950. He was best known for his government investigation of homosexuality and prostitution (the Wolfenden Report, 1957), which called for the legalization of private homosexual acts between consenting adults aged 21 and over. This recommendation became law under the Sexual Offences Act of 1967.

wolfish *adj.* **1** like a wolf. **2** rapacious. **3** ravenous.

wolfishly *adv.* in a wolfish way.

Wolfit, Sir Donald (1902–68) English actor-manager, born in Newark, Nottinghamshire. He began his stage career in 1920, formed his own company in 1937, and became known for his Shakespeare performances. During the Battle of Britain (1940) he instituted the first London season of 'Lunchtime Shakespeare'.

wolfram *Chem. noun* the old name for tungsten. [from German]

Wolfram von Eschenbach (c.1170–c.1220) German poet, born near Anspach, Bavaria. He was a Bavarian knight who is best known for his epic *Parzival* (c.1200–10), from which Richard Wagner derived the libretto of his *Parsifal*. His other works include *Willehalm*, seven *Love Songs*, and two fragments of *Titurel*.

wolfsbane *noun* a poisonous yellow-flowered plant; the aconite.

Wolfsburg POP (1991e) 127 000, a city in Lower Saxony state, N Germany. It is situated 24km/15mi NE of Brunswick, on the Mittelland and Elbe branch canals. Founded in 1938, it is known as the 'Volkswagen town' (site of the car factory).

Wolfson, Sir Isaac (1897–91) Scottish businessman, born in Glasgow. He became Managing Director of Great Universal Stores in 1934, and later Honorary Life President. In 1955 he set up the Wolfson Foundation for the advancement of health, education, and youth activities in the UK and the Commonwealth.

wolf whistle a whistle usually directed at a woman by a man, as a coarse expression of admiration for her appearance.

Wollaston, William Hyde (1766–1828) English chemist, born in East Dereham, Norfolk. He practised as a physician in London until 1800, and by 1805 he had evolved a successful technique of producing platinum in malleable form and built up a lucrative business. Among many diverse achievements, he made improvements to the goniometer, an instrument for measuring the angles between crystal faces, and wrote extensively on atomic theory, realizing that the arrangement of atoms in a molecule must be three-dimensional.

Wollongong POP (1991) 236 000, an urban centre in Illawarra statistical division, SE New South Wales, Australia. It extends 48km/30mi along the coast and includes the towns of Wollongong, Bulli, and Port Kembla.

Wollstonecraft, Mary, later **Mary Godwin** (1759–97) Anglo-Irish feminist, born in London. After working as a teacher and governess, she became a translator and literary adviser. In 1792 she wrote *Vindication of the Rights of Woman* to argue for the equality of the sexes. She was in Paris during the French Revolution, and died in London soon after giving birth to Mary (later, Mary Shelley), her daughter by her second husband William Godwin.

Wolseley (of Wolseley), Garnet Joseph Wolseley, 1st Viscount (1833–1913) British soldier, born in Golden Bridge, Co Dublin, Ireland. He joined the army in 1852, and served in the Burmese War (1852–3), the Crimea (where he lost an eye), the Indian Mutiny (1857), and the Chinese War (1860). He put down the Red River rebellion (1870) in Canada, and commanded in the Ashanti War (1873). Following other posts in India, Cyprus, South Africa, and Egypt, he led the attempted rescue of General Gordon at Khartoum. After the Sudan campaign (1884–5) he was made a viscount and field marshal (1894), and as army Commander-in-Chief (1895–1901) he effected several reforms and mobilized forces for the Boer War (1899–1902). He also wrote military works.

Wolsey, Thomas (c.1475–1530) English cardinal and statesman, born in Ipswich, Suffolk. Ordained in 1498, he was appointed chaplain to Henry VII in 1507, and became Dean of Lincoln. Under Henry VIII, he became Bishop of Lincoln, Archbishop of York (1514), and cardinal (1515). As Lord Chancellor (1515–29), he pursued legal and administrative reforms and was Henry VIII's leading adviser, in charge of the day-to-day running of government. He aimed to make England a major power in Europe, and also had ambitions to become pope, but his policy of supporting first Emperor Charles V (1523) then Francis I of France (1528) in the Habsburg–Valois conflict was unsuccessful, and high taxation caused much resentment. When he acted evasively concerning Henry's divorce from Catherine of Aragon, the King's anger led to his impeachment and the forfeiture of his property. Arrested on a charge of high treason, he died while travelling to London.

Wolverhampton POP (1992e) 248 000, a town in the West Midlands, central England. It is situated 20km/12mi NW of Birmingham, in the industrial 'Black Country'. It was named after Wulfruna (sister of Edgar II) who endowed the first collegiate church here in 994. NOTABLE FEATURE Church of St Peter (15c).

wolverine *noun* a large carnivorous animal of the weasel family, found in the forests of N America, Europe, and Asia. [related to WOLF]

woman — *noun* (PL. **women**) **1** an adult human female. **2** women generally. **3** one's wife or girlfriend. **4** *old use, affected* a female servant or domestic daily help. **5** feminine instincts: *the woman in her longed for a child.* — *adj.* female: *a woman doctor.* [from Anglo-Saxon *wifman*, from *wif*, wife + *man*, man, human]

-woman *combining form* forming words denoting: **1** a woman associated with a specified activity: *policewoman.* **2** a woman who is a native of a specified country or place: *Irishwoman.*

womanhood *noun* **1** the state of being a woman; female adulthood. **2** womankind.

womanish *adj. derog.* **1** associated with women. **2** *said of a man, or his behaviour or appearance* effeminate; unmanly.

womanize or **womanise** *verb intrans. derog. colloq., said of a man* to frequent the company of, or have casual affairs with, women.

womanizer *noun* a person who womanizes.

womankind *noun* women generally.

womanliness *noun* a womanly quality.

womanly *adj.* **1** feminine. **2** considered natural or suitable to a woman.

woman of the world a woman who is mature and widely experienced.

Woman with a Water Jug a painting by Jan Vermeer (c.1658–60, New York City).

womb *noun* **1** the uterus, the organ in female mammals in which the young develop till birth. **2** a place of origin: *the womb of civilization.* **3** *literary* a deep dark centre: *in the womb of the earth.* [from Anglo-Saxon *wamb*]

wombat *noun* a nocturnal marsupial of Australia and Tasmania, well adapted for burrowing, with a compact body, short legs, a large flat head, and no tail. It is the only marsupial with continuously growing incisor teeth. It feeds on grasses, tree roots, and the bark of shrubs. [from Aboriginal *wambat*]

women see WOMAN.

womenfolk *pl. noun* **1** women generally. **2** the female members of a family or society. **3** a man's female relations.

Women in Love a novel by D H Lawrence (1921). It continues the story of the Brangwen sisters, Ursula and Gudrun, who first appeared in *The Rainbow.*

Women in the Garden a painting by Claude Monet (1866–7, Louvre, Paris).

Women's Institutes, National Federation of (ABBREV. **WI**) a voluntary organization for women, founded in Canada in 1897 by Adelaide Hoodles to provide classes in domestic science and home-making. The WI spread to Britain in 1915, and to other Commonwealth countries. There are now some 9 200 institutes in England and Wales, but none in Scotland, which has its own Scottish Women's Rural Institutes (1917). Their activities now include organizing campaigns in response to member's concerns, raising awareness of social issues (eg the effect of rail privatization on rural areas), the publication of books for and by their members, and they run Denman College, a short-stay adult education college in Oxfordshire.

women's liberation a movement, started by women, aimed at freeing them from the disadvantages they suffer in a male-dominated society.

Women's Royal Voluntary Service (ABBREV. **WRVS**) in the UK, an organization formed in 1938 (designated Royal in 1966), which consists of unpaid helpers who do community work. Active in World War II, they pioneered the first home help scheme (1944), and run the meals on wheels service for the housebound elderly, as well as providing voluntary workers for day centres, hospitals, playgroups, prison visiting, and rural transport.

women's studies the study of the history, literature, and contemporary role of women. It is more widely available in further and higher education than in schools, and highlights women's experiences and feminist issues.

won see WIN.

wonder — *noun* **1** the state of mind produced by something extraordinary, new, or unexpected; amazement; awe. **2** something that is a cause of awe, amazement or bafflement; a marvel. — *adj.* notable for accomplishing marvels: *a wonder drug.* — *verb* (**wondered, wondering**) **1** *trans., intrans.* to be curious: *often wondered about her background.* **2** (*also* **wonder at something**) to be surprised by it: *shouldn't wonder if she won / hardly to be wondered at.* **3** to be uncertain or undecided: *I wonder whether to go.* **4** used politely to introduce requests: *I wonder if you could help me?* — **do** or **work wonders** to achieve marvellous results.

no little or **small wonder** it is hardly surprising. [from Anglo-Saxon *wundor*]

wonderful *adj.* **1** arousing wonder; extraordinary. **2** excellent; splendid.

wonderfully *adv.* in a wonderful way; to a wonderful extent.

Wonderful Wizard of Oz, The a children's fantasy by L Frank Baum (1900). The first of a series, it describes the adventures of Kansas girl Dorothy in the magical land of Oz. See also WIZARD OF OZ.

wonderland *noun* **1** an imaginary place full of marvels. **2** a scene of strange unearthly beauty.

wonderment *noun* **1** surprise. **2** curiosity. **3** something that stimulates wonder.

wondrous *adj.* wonderful, strange, or awesome.

wondrously *adv.* in a wondrous way; to a wondrous extent.

wonky *adj.* (**wonkier, wonkiest**) *colloq.* unsound, unsteady, wobbly, crooked or ill-made.

wont *old use* — *adj.* habitually inclined, or accustomed. — *noun* a habit that one has: *it was her wont to rise early.* [from Anglo-Saxon *gewunod,* accustomed]

won't *contr.* will not.

wonted *adj.* customary: *with none of his wonted cheerfulness.*

woo *verb* (**woos, wooed**) **1** *old use, said of a man* to try to win the love of (a woman) especially in the hope of marrying her. **2** to try to win the support of: *woo the voters.* **3** to pursue or seek (fame, success, fortune, etc). [from Anglo-Saxon *wogian*]

Wood, Sir Henry (Joseph) (1869–1944) English conductor, born in London. With Robert Newman he founded (1895) the Promenade Concerts which he conducted annually until his death. He composed operettas and an oratorio *Saint Dorothea* (1889), but his international reputation was gained as a conductor of the Queen's Hall symphony and promenade concerts.

Wood, Mrs Henry, *née* **Ellen Price** (1814–87) English novelist, born in Worcester. She wrote a series of melodramatic novels, of which *East Lynne* (1861) was a longstanding success. From 1867 she owned and edited the monthly magazine *Argosy*, in which many of her novels appeared.

wood — *noun* **1** *Bot.* the hard tissue (secondary xylem) that forms the bulk of woody trees and shrubs. The central *heartwood* provides structural support, enabling many trees to grow to a great height, and is surrounded by the *sapwood*, which is involved in the transport of water from the roots to all other parts of the plant. **2** this material obtained from trees and used as building timber, firewood, and fencing, and for furniture-making, etc. **3** (*also* **woods**) an expanse of growing trees. **4** *Golf* a club with a head made of wood. **5** *Bowls* a bowl. **6** casks or barrels made of wood, for wine or beer: *matured in wood.* — *adj.* made of, or using, wood.

— **not see the wood for the trees** to fail to grasp the broad issue because of over-attention to details.

out of the woods free at last of trouble or danger.

touch wood (*usually as an exclamation*) to touch something wooden as a superstitious guard against bad luck: *no problems so far, touch wood!* [from Anglo-Saxon *wudu*]

wood alcohol methanol.

woodbine *noun* honeysuckle. [from Anglo-Saxon *wudubinde*]

Wood Buffalo a national park in N Alberta and S Northwest Territories, central Canada, established in 1922. AREA 44 807sq km/ 17 296sq mi. PHYSICAL DESCRIPTION Wood Buffalo includes part of Buffalo L and L Claire and part of the Caribou and Birch Mts; the Great Canadian Oil Sands lie to the S; crossed by the Birch, Peace, Buffalo, and Little Buffalo rivers. It is noted for its herds of bison and has been designated a World Heritage site.

woodchuck *noun* a N American marmot. [from Cree (N American Indian language) *otchek*, marten]

woodcock *noun* a long-billed game bird related to the snipe, but with a bulkier body and shorter, stronger legs.

woodcut *noun* a design cut into a wooden block, or a print taken from it.

woodcutter *noun* a person who fells trees and chops wood.

wooded *adj.*, *said of land* covered with trees.

wooden *adj.* **1** made of wood. **2** *said of an actor, performance, etc* stiff, unnatural, and inhibited; lacking expression and liveliness.

wooden-headed *adj.* dull-witted; unintelligent.

woodenly *adv.* in a wooden manner.

woodenness *noun* being wooden.

wooden spoon a booby prize.

Woodhouse, Mr the amiable but hypochondriac father of Emma in Jane Austen's *Emma*.

woodland *noun* (*also* **woodlands**) an area of land planted with relatively short trees that are more widely spaced than those in a forest.

Woodland culture a generic term for the Native American culture of the E USA as far W as the Great Plains (c.700 BC– AD 1500). It is characterized archaeologically by burial mounds, cord-impressed pottery, and tobacco smoking, and its main traditions are *Adena-Hopewell* (c.700 BC– AD 400), centred on S Ohio, and *Mississippian* (c.700–1500 AD).

woodlouse *noun* (PL. **woodlice**) an insect-like creature with a grey, oval, plated body, found in damp places, under stones, bark, etc.

woodpecker *noun* any of about 200 species of tree-dwelling bird found in woodland throughout the world except for Australasia and Madagascar. They are usually brightly patterned with black, white, green, or red, and have a straight pointed chisel-like bill that is used to bore into tree bark in search of insects, and to drill nesting holes.

woodpecker

wood pigeon a common pigeon of the woods, with a white marking round its neck; the ring dove.

wood pulp crushed wood fibres used in paper-making.

woodruff *noun* a white-flowered, sweet-smelling plant. [from Anglo-Saxon *wuduroffe*]

Woodstock Festival a rock festival held over three days at the Woodstock Music and Art Fair near Bethel, New York, and attended by c.450 000 people (Aug 1969). A peaceful gathering, it marked the pinnacle of the flower-power period, and was the subject of a successful film.

Woodward, Robert Burns (1917–79) US chemist, born in Boston. Professor at Harvard and Director of the Woodward Research Institute at Basle, he executed the syntheses of a wide range of biochemical compounds, including strychnine, cholesterol, and chlorophyll, and was awarded the 1965 Nobel Prize for Chemistry. Following his work on the synthesis of vitamin B_{12}, he made important contributions to the theory of chemical reactions.

woodwind *noun* orchestral wind instruments made, or formerly made, of wood, including the flute, oboe, clarinet, and bassoon; the section of the orchestra composed of these.

woodwork *noun* **1** the art of making things out of wood; carpentry. **2** the wooden parts of any structure.

woodworm *noun* (PL. **woodworm**, **woodworms**) the larva of any of several beetles, that bores into wood.

woody *adj.* (**woodier**, **woodiest**) **1** *said of countryside* wooded. **2** resembling, developing into, or composed of wood: *plants with woody stems*.

woody nightshade a purple-flowered climbing plant with poisonous red berries.

wooer *noun* a person who woos.

woof[1] — *noun* the sound of a dog's bark. — *verb intrans.* to give a bark. [imitative]

woof[2] *noun Weaving* the weft. [from Middle English *oof*, with *w* added by association with WEFT and WARP]

woofer *noun Electron.* a large loudspeaker for reproducing low-frequency sounds. See also TWEETER.

Wookey Hole a group of limestone caves near the village of Wookey in Sedgemoor district, Somerset, England, in the Mendip Hills near the R Axe. Prehistoric tools have been found in the caves.

wool — *noun* **1** the soft wavy hair of sheep and certain other animals. **2** this spun into yarn for knitting or weaving. **3** fluffy, curly, or tangled material resembling this: *steel wool.* — *adj.* made of wool; relating to wool or its production.

— **pull the wool over someone's eyes** *colloq.* to deceive them.

[from Anglo-Saxon *wull*]

Woolf, (Adeline) Virginia (1882–1941) English novelist, born in London. In 1912 she married Leonard (Sidney) Woolf (1880–1969), with whom she set up the Hogarth Press (1917). A leading member of the Bloomsbury Group, she wrote biographies and critical essays, and made a major contribution to the development of the novel in such works as *Mrs Dalloway* (1925), *To the Lighthouse* (1927), and *The Waves* (1931), which are noted for their impressionistic, stream-of-consciousness style. Following a history of mental illness, she committed suicide. Her *Diary* (5 vols, 1977–84) and *Letters* (6 vols, 1975–80) were published posthumously.

wool-gathering *noun* absent-mindedness; day-dreaming.

woollen — *adj.* **1** made of wool. **2** producing, or dealing in, goods made of wool: *woollen manufacturers.* — *noun* **1** (*often* **woollens**) a woollen, especially knitted, garment. **2** a woollen fabric.

Woolley, Sir (Charles) Leonard (1880–1960) English archaeologist, born in London. He carried out excavations at Carchemish, Al'Ubaid, and Tell el-Amarna. He subsequently directed the important excavations (1922–34) at Ur in Mesopotamia, which in 1926 uncovered gold and lapis lazuli in the royal tombs. He wrote several popular accounts of his work, notably *Digging up the Past* (1930).

woolliness *noun* a woolly quality.

woolly — *adj.* (**woollier**, **woolliest**) **1** made of wool, like wool, or covered with wool or wool-like fibres, etc; fluffy and soft. **2** vague and muddled: *woolly thinking / woolly-minded.* — *noun colloq.* a woollen, usually knitted garment.

woolly monkey a New World monkey with a large round head, a long grasping tail, and a short dense dark woolly coat. It feeds on fruit and some insects, and if food is plentiful will eat until its abdomen is markedly swollen.

woolly rhinoceros an extinct rhinoceros, once native to Europe and N Asia, about 3.5m in length, and having a thick coat of long hair, and a snout with two horns. It was hunted by humans in Europe 30 000 years ago.

woolsack *noun* the seat of the Lord Chancellor in the House of Lords, a large square wool-stuffed sack.

Woolworth, F(rank) W(infield) (1852–1919) US merchant, born in Rodman, New York. He became a shop assistant in 1873, and in 1879 opened a store in Utica, New York. He then built a chain of stores selling ten-cent goods, and set up the F W Woolworth Company in 1905. At the time of his death the company controlled over 1000 stores from their headquarters in the Woolworth building, New York City. Woolworth stores first opened in Britain in 1910.

Woosnam, Ian (Harold) (1958–) Welsh golfer, born in St Martins, Shropshire. He turned professional in 1976, and made his reputation in 1987 when he won five tournaments, and led Wales to the World Cup. He has been a regular member of Europe's Ryder Cup team since 1983. In 1991, he was the winner of the US Masters.

Wooster, Bertie the rich, good-natured but brainless young man-about-town who is frequently rescued by his butler, Jeeves, in the novels and stories of P G Wodehouse, which include *My Man Jeeves, Carry On, Jeeves,* and *Thank You, Jeeves.*

Wootton (of Abinger), Barbara Frances Wootton, Baroness (1897–1988) English social scientist, born in Cambridge. She became a lecturer in economics at Cambridge, and was director of studies (1927–44) and Professor in Social Studies (1948–52) at London. She was a frequent royal commissioner and London magistrate, best known for her work, *Testament for Social Science* (1950), an attempt to assimilate the social to the natural sciences.

woozily *adv.* in a woozy manner.

woozy *adj.* (**woozier**, **wooziest**) *colloq.* feeling dazed, dizzy, or confused, with senses blurred and hazy.

wop *noun offensive slang* a member of a Latin or Mediterranean race, eg an Italian, especially as an immigrant or visitor. [perhaps from Italian dialect *guappo*, swaggerer]

Worcester, Anglo-Saxon **Wigorna Ceaster** POP (1992e) 86 000, the county town of Hereford and Worcester, W central England. It lies on the R Severn, 38km/24mi SW of Birmingham. HISTORY founded in c.680; site of a Cromwell victory in the Civil War; the Royal Worcester Porcelain Co was established here in 1862. The composer Edward Elgar was born nearby in 1857. NOTABLE FEATURES cathedral (14c); Commandery (11c), founded by St Wulfstan; Guildhall (18c); Dyson Perins Museum.

Worcester porcelain porcelain made at a factory in Worcester, England, founded in 1751 by John Wall (1708–76). The factory is noted for its enamelled and gilded pieces of the late 18c, and its Regency porcelain painted with flowers and figure subjects.

Worcester sauce a strong-tasting sauce used as a seasoning, made with soy sauce, vinegar, and spices. [from *Worcester*, in England, where it was originally made]

word — *noun* **1** the smallest unit of spoken or written language that can be used independently, usually separated off by spaces in writing and printing. **2** a brief conversation on a particular matter: *I'd like a word with you.* **3** any brief statement, message, or communication: *a word of caution / a word to all pet-owners.* **4** news or notice: *any word of Kate? / sent word she'd arrive tomorrow.* **5** a rumour: *the word is they are bankrupt.* **6** one's solemn promise: *give one's word / word of honour.* **7** an order: *expects her word to be obeyed / just say the word.* **8** a word given as a signal for action: *wait till I give the word.* **9** what someone says: *remembered her mother's words.* **10** (**words**) language as a means of communication: *impossible to convey in words.* **11** (**words**) discussion in contrast to action. **12** (**words**) the lyrics of a song, etc; the speeches an actor must learn for a particular part. **13** (**the Word**) *Relig.* the teachings contained in the Bible. **14** a watchword: *mum's the word.* **15** *Comput.* **a** a group of bits or bytes that can be processed as a single unit by a computer. The size of a word varies according to the size of the computer. **b** in word processing, any group of characters separated from other such groups by spaces or punctuation, whether or not it is a real word. — *verb* to express in carefully chosen words: *worded her refusal tactfully.*
— **as good as one's word** careful to keep one's promise.
have words with someone *colloq.* to quarrel with them.
in a word briefly.
in other words saying the same thing in a different way.
in so many words explicitly; bluntly.
my word *or* **upon my word** an exclamation of surprise.
of many *or* **few words** inclined to be talkative (or reserved).
say the word to give one's consent or approval for some action to proceed.
take someone at his *or* **her word** to take an offer, undertaking, etc literally.
take someone's word for it to accept what someone says as true, without verification.
word for word repeated in exactly the same words, or translated into exactly corresponding words.
[from Anglo-Saxon]

word-blindness *noun* dyslexia.

wordclass a set of words that share the same grammatical properties, such as inflectional forms or position in a sentence structure: otherwise known as *part of speech*. The grouping of words into classes was first carried out by the Greeks, and there are eight classes recognized in most grammars: noun, verb, adjective, adverb, pronoun, preposition, conjunction, and interjection.

Worde, Wynkyn de (d.c.1535) London printer, born in Holland or in Alsace. He was a pupil of William Caxton, and in 1491 succeeded to his stock-in-trade. He made great improvements in printing and typecutting, and was the first in England to use italic type.

word game any game or puzzle in which words are constructed, deciphered, etc.

wordily *adv.* in a wordy manner.

wordiness *noun* being wordy.

wording *noun* one's choice and arrangement of words in expressing something.

word of honour one's solemn promise.

word of mouth spoken, in contrast to written, communication.

word-perfect *adj.* able to repeat something accurately from memory.

word-processing *noun* the production of text using a word-processor.

word processor *Comput.* a computer system or program that allows the input, processing, storage, and retrieval of text, and so can perform electronically the tasks of typing and editing letters, documents, and books.
◇ A word processor enables the user to enter text via a keyboard attached to the computer, and to view it on the screen of a visual-display unit (VDU). Text can be manipulated in many different ways, eg to correct errors, to make additions to or delete selected parts of existing text, to copy text from one file to another, or to change the format by moving text around on the screen. The edited document can then be printed out on paper (known as *hard copy*), or stored on a hard or floppy disk. Word processors and microcomputers with word-processing programs, are now very widely used and are rapidly replacing typewriters for many applications.

Wordsworth, Dorothy (1771–1855) the sister and lifetime companion of William Wordsworth, born in Cockermouth, Cumberland. Her *Journals* show a keen sensibility and acute observation of nature, and were a source of poetic imagery to both William Wordsworth and Samuel Taylor Coleridge. In 1829 she suffered a breakdown from which she never fully recovered.

Wordsworth, William (1770–1850) English poet, born in Cockermouth, Cumberland. After a walking tour through France and Switzerland (1790), he developed pro-revolutionary sentiments, and had an affair with a French woman, Annette Vallon, who bore him a daughter. He returned to England (1793), eventually setting up house in Dorset with his sister, Dorothy, where he pursued his vocation as a nature poet. After moving to Alfoxden, Somerset (1797), he wrote with Samuel Taylor Coleridge the *Lyrical Ballads* (1798), the first manifesto of the new Romantic poetry. He spent some time in Germany, then moved to Grasmere (1799) and married Mary Hutchinson (1802). His works include his poetic autobiography, *The Prelude* (1805, published posthumously in 1850), and *Poems in Two Volumes* (1807), which includes the poem 'Intimations of Immortality'. He was made Poet Laureate in 1843.

wordy *adj.* (**wordier**, **wordiest**) using too many words to say something; long-winded, especially pompously so.

wore see WEAR.

work — *noun* **1** physical or mental effort made in order to achieve or make something; labour, study, research, etc. **2** employment: *out of work.* **3** one's place of employment: *leaves work at 4.30.* **4** tasks to be done: *often brings work home with her / housework.* **5** the product of mental or physical labour: *his work has improved / a splendid piece of work.* **6** a literary, artistic, musical, or dramatic composition or creation: *the complete works of Milton.* **7** anything done, managed, made, achieved, etc; activity for some purpose: *good work! / works of charity.* **8** (*in compounds*) things made in the material or with the tools specified; the production of such things: *basketwork / needlework.* **9** (*in compounds*) the parts of a building, etc using a specified material: *stonework / paintwork.* **10** (**works**) building or repair operations: *roadworks / the clerk of works.* **11** (**works**) (*often in compounds*) a rampart or defence: *earthworks.* **12** (**works**) *colloq.* the operating parts of eg a watch or machine; the mechanism. **13** (**works**) (*often in compounds*) the place of manufacture of a specified product: *gasworks.* **14** *colloq.* (**the work**) everything possible, available, or going; the lot: *has a headache, fever, cold – the works!* **15** *Physics* the transfer of energy that occurs when force is exerted on a body to move it. — *adj.* relating to,

suitable for, etc, work: *work clothes.* — *verb* **1** *intrans.* to do work; to exert oneself mentally or physically; to toil, labour, or study. **2** *intrans., trans.* to be employed; to have a job; to perform the tasks and duties involved in a job; to do this for (so many hours a day, etc): *stop working at 65 / works a nine-hour day.* **3** *trans.* to impose tasks on; to cause to labour: *works her staff hard.* **4** *trans., intrans.* to operate, especially satisfactorily: *learn to work a drill / does this radio work?* **5** *intrans.* said of a plan, idea, etc to be successful or effective. **6** *intrans.* to function in a particular way: *most relationships don't work like that.* **7** *intrans.* said of a craftsman to specialize in the use of a specified material: *works in brass.* **8** to shape or fashion (metals or other materials); to make by doing this: *earrings worked in silver.* **9** to cultivate (land). **10** to extract materials from (a mine). **11** to knead (eg dough). **12** to cover (an area) as a salesman, etc. **13** *old use* to sew, embroider, etc (eg a handkerchief). **14** to achieve (miracles, wonders, etc). **15** *colloq.* to manipulate (a system, rules, etc) to one's advantage. **16** (*also* **work someone up**) to rouse or stir up: *work oneself into a rage / too worked-up to think.* **17** *trans., intrans.* to make (one's way), or shift or cause to shift gradually: *work one's way forward / worked the nail out of his sole.* **18** *intrans. said eg of a screw* to become gradually (loose, free, etc). **19** *intrans. said of the face or features* to move uncontrollably with emotion; to contort. **20** to exercise (a part of the body). **21** to earn (one's sea passage) by unpaid work on board.
— **give someone the works** *colloq.* to use every measure available in dealing with someone, by way of eg punishment, coercion, or welcome.
have one's work cut out *colloq.* to be faced with a challenging task.
make short work of something *or* **someone** to deal with them rapidly and effectively.
a ... piece *or* **bit of work** *colloq.* a person, especially with regard to an unfavourable aspect of character or disposition: *a nasty piece of work.*
work in *said of workers protesting against closure, redundancy, etc* to occupy work premises and take over the running of the business.
work something in 1 to add and mix an ingredient into a mixture. **2** to find a place for something; to fit it in.
work something off to get rid of energy or the effects of a heavy meal by energetic activity.
work on something 1 to try to perfect or improve it. **2** to use it as a basis for one's decisions and actions: *working on that assumption.*
work on someone *colloq.* to use one's powers of persuasion on them.
work out 1 to be successfully achieved: *if things work out.* **2** to perform a set of energetic physical exercises.
work something out to solve it; to sort or reason it out.
work someone over *slang* to beat them up.
work to rule to reduce efficiency by working strictly to official working rules, especially as a form of industrial action.
work someone up to excite or agitate them.
work something up to summon up an appetite, enthusiasm, energy, etc.
work up to something to approach a difficult task or objective by gradual stages.
[from Anglo-Saxon *weorc*]

workability *noun* being workable.

workable *adj.* **1** *said of a scheme, etc* able to be carried out; practicable. **2** *said eg of a material, mineral source, etc* able to be worked.

workaday *adj.* **1** ordinary; commonplace. **2** suitable for a work day; practical or everyday; not fine.

workaholic *noun colloq.* a person addicted to work. [formed after ALCOHOLIC]

workbasket *or* **workbox** *noun* a basket or box for holding sewing materials and implements.

workbench *noun* a usually purpose-built table for a mechanic or craftsman.

workday *noun North Amer.* a working day.

worker *noun* **1** a person who works. **2** a person employed in manual work. **3** an employee as opposed to an employer. **4** a male social insect, eg honeybee, ant, that is sterile and whose sole function is to maintain the colony and forage for food. See also DRONE.

workforce *noun* the number of workers engaged in a particular industry, factory, etc; the total number of workers potentially available.

workhouse *noun Hist.* an institution where the poor can be housed and given work to do.

work-in *noun* the occupation of work premises by employees, especially in protest at closure.

working — *noun* **1** (*also* **workings**) the operation or mode of operation of something. **2** the steps, usually noted down, by which the answer to a mathematical problem is reached. **3** (**workings**) excavations at a mine or quarry. — *adj.* **1** *said of a period of time* devoted to work, or denoting that part that is devoted to work. **2** adequate for one's purposes: *a working knowledge of French.*
— **in working order** functioning properly.

working capital money used to keep a business, etc going.

working class the wage-earning section of the population, employed especially in manual labour.

working-class *adj.* relating to the working class.

working day 1 a day on which people go to work as usual. **2** the part of the day during which work is done: *an eight-hour working day.*

working majority *Politics* a majority sufficient to enable a party in office to carry through its legislative programme without the risk of parliamentary defeat.

Working Men's Clubs and Institutes Union in the UK, clubs that provide education and recreation for working men. Originally founded as an alternative to the public house, the Union was created in 1862 by the Rev Henry Solly; initially the clubs did not serve alcohol, but now they provide it at a lower price than in public houses.

working-party *noun* a group of people appointed to investigate and report on something.

Workington POP (1981) 26 000, a port town in Allerdale district, Cumbria, NW England. It lies 48km/30mi SW of Carlisle, at the mouth of the R Derwent. NOTABLE FEATURES remains of the Roman fort of Gabrosentium; Workington Hall (1379).

workload *noun* the amount of work expected of a person or machine.

workman *noun* **1** a man employed to do manual work. **2** anyone performing a craft.

workmanlike *adj.* suitable to, or characteristic of, a good workman.

workmanship *noun* the skill of a craftsman, especially where evident in the appearance of a finished product.

workmate *noun colloq.* someone who works alongside one in one's place of work; a fellow-worker or colleague.

work of art 1 a painting or sculpture of high quality. **2** anything constructed or composed with obvious skill.

workout *noun* a session of physical exercise or training.

workpiece *noun* an object that is being worked on with a machine or tool.

workplace *noun* an office, factory, or other premises where a person is employed.

works council *or* **works committee** a body on which representatives of both employer and employee meet to deal with labour relations within a business.

workshop *noun* **1** a room or building where construction and repairs are carried out. **2** a course of study or work, especially of an experimental kind, for a group of people on a particular project.

workshy *adj. colloq.* lazy; inclined to avoid work.

Works Projects Administration (ABBREV. **WPA**) a US federal agency established (1935–43) under President Roosevelt to combat unemployment during the Great Depression. Originally called the Works Progress Administration, it built transportation facilities, parks, and buildings, and employed some 8 500 000 people, including artists and writers as well as manual workers.

work station a person's seat at a computer terminal.

work study an investigation of the most efficient way of doing a job, especially with regard to time and effort.

work surface *or* **worktop** a flat surface constructed along the top of kitchen installations such as fridge and cupboards, on which to prepare food, etc.

work-to-rule *noun* a period of working to rule by employees.

world — *noun* **1** the earth; the planet we inhabit. **2** any other planet or potentially habitable heavenly body. **3** the people inhabiting the earth; mankind: *tell the world.* **4** human affairs: *the present state of the world.* **5** (*also* **World**) a group of countries characterized in a certain way: *the Third World / the New World.* **6** (*also* **World**) the people of a particular period, and their culture: *the Ancient World.* **7** a state of existence: *in this world or the next.* **8** (**the world**) human existence, especially regarded as oppressive and materialistic, or as distinct from spiritual or intellectual life: *escape from the world.* **9** one's individual way of life or range of experience: *one's own narrow world.* **10** an atmosphere or environment: *enter a world of make-believe.* **11** a particular area of activity: *the world of politics.* **12** a class of living things: *the insect world.* **13** *colloq.* a great deal; a lot: *did her a world of good / are worlds apart.* — *adj.* relating to, affecting, or important throughout, the whole world: *world championships / a world power.*
— **be** *or* **mean all the world to someone** to be important or precious to them.
the best of both worlds the benefits of both alternatives with the drawbacks of neither.
bring someone into the world to give birth to or deliver a baby.
come into the world to be born.
come *or* **go up** *or* **down in the world** to rise (or fall) in social status.
for all the world as if ... exactly as if ...
in the world used for emphasis: *how in the world...? / without a care in the world.*
not for the world not for anything: *wouldn't hurt her for the world.*
on top of the world *colloq.* supremely happy.
out of this world *colloq.* extraordinarily fine; marvellous.
think the world of someone to love or admire them immensely.
[from Anglo-Saxon *weorold*]

World Bank see INTERNATIONAL BANK FOR RECONSTRUCTION AND DEVELOPMENT.

world-beater *noun* a person, product, etc that is supreme in its class.

World Boxing Association (ABBREV. **WBA**) in boxing, a governing body originally founded in the USA in 1920 as the National Boxing Association. It changed to its present name in the early 1960s.

World Boxing Council (ABBREV. **WBC**) in boxing, a governing body founded in 1963.

world-class *adj. Sport* of the highest standard in the world.

World Council of Churches an inter-denominational Council of Churches, formed (1948) in Amsterdam. It originated in the early-20c ecumenical movement, and has the unity of the Church as its main aim. It comprises most of the main-line Christian denominations with the exception of the Roman Catholic Church, with which it retains close contact. Based in Geneva, it has a ruling body or representative Assembly which meets every six or seven years.

World Cup a term used to describe an international sporting competition. The soccer World Cup is the best known, and was first contested in Uruguay in 1930 for the Jules Rimet Trophy. In recent years other sports such as skiing, athletics, rugby league, rugby union, and cricket have inaugurated World Cup competitions.

world-famous *adj.* well known throughout the world.

World Federation of Trade Unions (ABBREV. **WFTU**) an association of world trade union federations, set up in 1945, with its headquarters in Prague. The democratic unions of W Europe and N America broke away in 1949, after a squabble with communist members. It now contains some 92 affiliated national trade union federations, mainly from E Europe.

World Health Organization (ABBREV. **WHO**) a United Nations specialized agency, which was formed in 1948 to advance international co-operation for the improvement in health of peoples in all countries. Primarily concerned with the control of epidemic diseases, vaccination and other programmes, worldwide sanitation, and water supplies, it also acts as a clearing house for information on such topics as drugs, nuclear hazards, and cancer research.

worldliness *noun* a worldly quality.

worldly *adj.* (**worldlier, worldliest**) **1** relating to this world; material, not spiritual or eternal: *worldly possessions.* **2** over-concerned with possessions, money, luxuries, etc; materialistic. **3** shrewd about the ways of the world; knowing and sophisticated in one's outlook.

worldly-wise *adj.* knowledgeable about life; not easily impressed.

Worldly Wiseman, Mr a character in John Bunyan's *The Pilgrim's Progress*, who tries to discourage Christian from embarking on his journey.

world music popular folk music originating in non-western, especially African, cultures.

World Series in baseball, the end-of-season meeting between the winners of the two major Baseball leagues in the USA, the National League (NL) and American League (AL). It was first held in 1903, and is now a best-of-seven series held each October.

world-shaking *adj. colloq.* important; significant; momentous.

World Snooker Championships in snooker, a professional championship first held in 1927 and now held every April at the Crucible, Sheffield, England. It is conducted as a knock-out tournament in which the world's top-ranked 16 players are seeded.

World Trade Center a complex of buildings occupying 6.5ha in Manhattan, New York City. Its two 110-storey skyscrapers were the world's tallest buildings from their completion in 1973, until exceeded by the Sears Tower a year later. It was damaged in a bomb blast in Feb 1993.

world war a war in which most of the major world powers take part, especially those of 1914–18 (*World War I*) and 1939–45 (*World War II*).

World War I a war whose origins lay in the increasingly aggressive foreign policies pursued by Austria-Hungary, Russia and, most significantly, Germany. The assassination of the heir to the Habsburg throne, Francis Ferdinand, at Sarajevo in Bosnia (28 June 1914), triggered the war which soon involved most European states following Austria's declaration of war on Serbia (28 Jul). Russia mobilized in support of Serbia (29–30 Jul); and Germany declared war on Russia (1 Aug), and on France (3 Aug). The German invasion of neutral Belgium (4 Aug) brought the British into the war on the French side. Japan joined Britain, France, and Russia under the terms of an agreement with Britain (1902, 1911), and Italy joined the Allies in May 1915. Turkey allied with Germany (Nov 1914), and they were joined by Bulgaria (Oct 1915). Military campaigning in W Europe centred on France, Belgium, and (later) Italy, and in E Europe on Poland, W Russia, and the Balkans. By the end of 1914, a static defence line had been established from the Belgian coast to Switzerland. The Allies attempted to break the stalemate by the Gallipoli Campaign aimed at re-supplying Russia and knocking out Turkey (Apr 1915–Jan 1916), but failed. On the E and SE fronts, the Central Powers occupied Russian Poland and most of Lithuania, and Serbia was invaded. After staunch resistance, Serbia, Albania and, latterly, Romania were overrun. Naval competition had played a crucial role in heightening tension before 1914, but the only significant naval encounter (Jutland, 1916) proved indecisive. The Allies organized a large offensive for the W Front in 1916, but were forestalled by the Germans, who attacked France at Verdun (Feb–Jul). To relieve the situation, the battle of the Somme was launched, but proved indecisive. The Germans then unleashed unrestricted submarine warfare (Jan 1917) and British food stocks fell perilously low, but the USA declared war on Germany (2 Apr 1917) and the German submarine menace was finally overcome by the use of convoys. By 1917, the Russian armies were broken and revolution broke out in St Petersburg and Moscow after which Lenin's Bolshevik government sued for peace. In March 1918 Germany and her allies imposed the punitive peace of Brest–Litovsk on the USSR (annulled after Germany's defeat). The Germans launched a major attack in the W, but were driven back, with the help of troops from the USA. By September the German Army was in full retreat, and signified its intention to sue for peace on the basis of President Wilson's Fourteen Points. By November, when the armistice was signed, the Allies had recaptured W Belgium and nearly all French territory. Military victories in Palestine and Mesopotamia resulted in a Turkish armistice (31 Oct 1918); Italian victories and a northward advance by Franco-British forces finished Austria-Hungary (and Bulgaria). Estimated combatant war losses were: British Empire, just under 1 million; France, nearly 1.4 million; Italy, nearly half a million; Russia, 1.7 million; USA, 115 000; Germany 1.8 million; Austria-Hungary 1.2 million, and Turkey 325 000. About double these numbers were wounded.

World War II a war (1939–45) whose origins lay in three different conflicts which merged after 1941: Hitler's desire for European expansion and perhaps even world domination; Japan's struggle against China; and a resulting conflict between Japanese ambitions and US interests in the Pacific. The origins of the war in Europe lay in German unwillingness to accept the frontiers laid down in 1919 by the Treaty of Versailles and the National Socialists' expansionist foreign policy. After the German invasion of rump Bohemia-Moravia (Mar 1939), Britain and France pledged support to Poland. Germany concluded an alliance with the USSR (Aug 1939), and then invaded Poland (1 Sep). Britain and France declared war on Germany (3 Sep), but could not prevent Poland from being overrun in four weeks. For six months there was a period of 'phoney war', when little fighting took place, but the Germans then occupied Norway and Denmark (Apr 1940), and Belgium and Holland

were invaded (10 May), followed immediately by the invasion of France. A combination of German tank warfare and air power brought about the surrender of Holland in four days, Belgium in three weeks, and France in seven weeks. Italy declared war on France and Britain in the final stages of this campaign. There followed the Battle of Britain (1940), in which Germany's attempt to win air supremacy over Britain failed. Germany launched submarine (U-boat) attacks against British supply routes, but then moved E and invaded Greece and Yugoslavia (Apr 1941) and, following an Italian military fiasco there, Greece. British military efforts were concentrated against Italy in the Mediterranean and N Africa. After early reverses for Italy, Rommel was sent to N Africa with the German Afrika Corps to reinforce Italian military strength; fiercely contested campaigning continued here for three years until Allied troops finally ejected German and Italian forces in mid-1943, invaded Sicily and then Italy itself, and forced Italy to make a separate peace (3 Sep 1943). In Jun 1941, in line with Hitler's longheld hostility to the USSR, and in his quest for *Lebensraum*, Germany invaded its ally Russia along a 3220km/2 000mi front, and German armies advanced in three formations: to the outskirts of Leningrad in the N, towards Moscow in the centre, and to the Volga River in the S. After spectacular early successes, the Germans were held up by bitter Soviet resistance, and by heavy winter snows and Arctic temperatures, for which they were completely unprepared. From Nov 1942 they were gradually driven back, suffering decisive reverses at Stalingrad (winter 1942–3) and Kursk (May 1943). Leningrad was under siege for nearly 2.5 years (until Jan 1944), and about a third of its population died from starvation and disease. The Germans were finally driven out of the USSR (Aug 1944). A second front was launched against Germany by the Allies (Jun 1944), through the invasion of Normandy, and Paris was liberated (25 Aug). Despite German use of flying bombs and rockets against Allied bases, the Allies advanced into Germany (Feb 1945) and linked with the Russians on the R Elbe (28 Apr). The Germans surrendered unconditionally at Rheims (7 May 1945). In the Far East, Japan's desire for expansion, combined with a US threat of economic sanctions, led to the Japanese attack on Pearl Harbor and other British and US bases (7 Dec 1941), and the USA declared war against Japan the next day. In reply Japan's allies, Germany and Italy, declared war on the USA (11 Dec). Within four months, Japan controlled SE Asia and Burma. Not until Jun 1942 did naval victories in the Pacific stem the advance, and Japanese troops defended their positions grimly. Bitter fighting continued until 1945, when, with Japan on the retreat, the USA dropped two atomic bombs on Hiroshima and Nagasaki (6 and 9 Aug). Japan then surrendered (14 Aug). Casualty figures are not easy to obtain accurately, but approximately 3 million Russians were killed in action, 3 million died as prisoners of war, 8 million people died in occupied Russia, and about 3 million in unoccupied Russia. Germany suffered 3.25 million military casualties, around 6 million total casualties, and lost 1 million prisoners of war. Japan suffered just over 2 million military casualties and just over a quarter of a million civilian deaths. France lost a total of half a million dead, and Britain and the Commonwealth just over 600 000. The USA suffered just over 300 000 casualties. It is also estimated that in the course of the German occupation of a large part of Europe, about 6 million Jews were murdered in extermination and labour camps, along with one million or more other victims.

worldweary *adj.* tired of the world; bored of life.

worldwide *adj.*, *adv.* extending or known throughout the world.

World Wide Fund for Nature (ABBREV. **WWF**) an international voluntary organization, founded in 1961 as the World Wildlife Fund, with its headquarters in Switzerland. Its International President is the Duke of Edinburgh. It aims to create awareness of the need for conservation of endangered wild animals, plants, and places. It adopted its present name in 1988.

worm — *noun* **1** *Zool.* any member of several unrelated groups of small soft-bodied limbless invertebrates (animals with no backbone) that are characteristically long, slender, and cylindrical in shape, eg annelids (segmented worms such as the earthworm) and flatworms (such as tapeworms). **2** any superficially similar but unrelated animal, eg the larva of certain insects. **3** a mean, contemptible, weak, or worthless person. **4** *Mech.* the spiral thread of a screw. **5** (**worms**) any disease characterized by the presence of parasitic worms in the intestines of humans or animals. **6** *Comput.* an unauthorized computer program designed to sabotage a computer system, especially by reproducing itself throughout a computer network. A worm differs from a virus in that it is an independent program rather than a piece of coding. — *verb* **1** (**worm one's way**) to wriggle or manoeuvre oneself gradually: *wormed their way to the front.* **2** (**worm one's way into something**) to insinuate oneself into someone's favour, affections, etc. **3** (*also* **worm something out**) to extract information, etc little by little: *wormed the secret out of them.* **4** to treat an animal that has worms, especially to rid it of these. [from Anglo-Saxon *wyrm*]

wormcast *noun* a coiled heap of sand or earth excreted by a burrowing worm.

worm-eaten *adj.*, *said eg of furniture* riddled with wormholes.

worm gear **1** a gear consisting of a shaft with a spiral thread that engages with and drives a toothed wheel. **2** (*also* **worm wheel**) the toothed wheel driven in this way.

wormhole *noun* a hole left by a burrowing grub, in eg furniture, books, or fruit.

Worms, ancient **Borbetomagus** POP (1991e) 77 000, a river port in Rhineland-Palatinate state, SW Germany. It lies on the R Rhine, 16km/10mi NW of Mannheim; a centre of the wine trade (notably for Liebfraumilch). HISTORY one of the oldest towns in Germany, it was capital of the kingdom of Burgundy in the 5c; scene of many Imperial Diets, notably the Diet of Worms (1521); badly bombed in World War II. NOTABLE FEATURE cathedral (11c–12c).

Worms, Diet of the meetings (1521, 1545) of the estates of the German Empire which decided the fate of religion in 16c Germany. At the first, following papal declarations of heresy and excommunication (1520, 1521), Luther was condemned; at the second, an attempt to heal the religious divisions between Catholics and Lutherans failed amidst suspicion of papal intentions.

wormwood *noun* **1** a bitter-tasting herb from which the flavouring for absinthe is obtained. **2** *old use* acute bitterness or chagrin, or a cause of this. [from Anglo-Saxon *wermod*]

wormy *adj.* (**wormier, wormiest**) like or full of worms.

worn past participle of WEAR. — *adj.* **1** haggard with weariness. **2** showing signs of deterioration through long use or wear.
— **worn out 1** exhausted. **2** too badly worn to be any further use; threadbare.

worried *adj.* anxious, concerned, fretting.

worrier *noun* a person who worries, especially habitually.

worrisome *adj. old use* causing worry; perturbing; vexing.

worry — *verb* (**worries, worried**) **1** *intrans.* to be anxious. **2** to cause anxiety to. **3** to bother or harass. **4** *said of a dog* to tear and pull about with the teeth; to chase and bite (sheep, etc). **5** (**worry at something**) to try to solve a problem, etc. — *noun* (PL. **worries**) **1** a state of anxiety. **2** a cause of anxiety.

— **not to worry** *colloq.* an expression of reassurance.

[from Anglo-Saxon *wyrgan*, to strangle]

worry beads a string of beads for fiddling with, to calm the nerves.

worse — *adj.* comparative of BAD. **1** more bad: *to be blind or deaf – which is worse?* **2** more ill. **3** more grave, serious, or acute. **4** inferior in standard. — *noun* something worse: *worse was to follow.* — *adv.* less well; more badly.

— **go from bad to worse** to get worse; to deteriorate.

might do worse than ... should consider (doing something).

none the worse for ... unharmed by (an accident, bad experience, etc).

the worse for something showing the bad effects of it.

the worse for wear 1 worn or shabby from use. **2** in poor condition.

worse off in a worse situation, especially financially.

[from Anglo-Saxon *wyrsa*]

worsen *verb intrans., intrans.* (**worsened, worsening**) to make or become worse.

worship — *verb* (**worshipped, worshipping**) **1** *trans., intrans.* to honour (God or a god) with praise, prayer, hymns, etc. **2** to love or admire, especially blindly; to idolise. **3** to glorify or exalt (material things, eg money). — *noun* **1** the activity of worshipping. **2** (**His** *or* **Your Worship**) the title used to address or refer to a mayor or magistrate. [from Anglo-Saxon *weorthscipe*, 'worthship']

worshipful *adj.* **1** full of reverence or adoration. **2** (*usually* **Worshipful**) used as a term of respect in the titles of certain dignitaries. **3** worshipping; adoring.

worshipper *noun* a person who worships.

worst — *adj.* **1** most bad, awful, unpleasant, etc. **2** most grave, severe, acute, or dire. **3** most inferior; lowest in standard. — *noun* the worst thing, part, or possibility: *hope the worst is over.* — *adv.* most severely; most badly: *the worst I've ever played.* — *verb* to defeat; to get the better of.

— **at its**, *etc* **worst** in the worst state or severest degree.

at the worst taking the most unfavourable or pessimistic view.

do your worst a formula rejecting or defying a threat, etc.

get the worst of something to lose a fight, argument, etc.

if the worst comes to the worst if the worst happens.

[from Anglo-Saxon *wyrst*]

worsted *noun* **1** a fine strong woollen yarn. **2** fabric woven from this. [from *Worstead*, in Norfolk]

wort *noun* **1** *combining form* a plant: *liverwort.* **2** *Brewing* a dilute solution or infusion of malt, fermented to make beer and whisky. [from Anglo-Saxon *wyrt*, plant, root]

worth — *noun* **1** value; importance; usefulness. **2** financial value. **3** the quantity of anything that can be bought for a certain sum, accomplished in a certain time, etc: *lost a thousand pounds' worth of equipment / three days' worth of work.* — *adj.* **1** having a value of: *a stamp worth £15.* **2** *colloq.* having money and property to the value of: *she's worth two million.* **3** justifying, deserving, meriting, repaying, or warranting: *worth consideration.*

— **for all one is worth** with all one's might.

for all it's *etc* **worth** to the utmost.

for what it's *etc* **worth** worthless though it, etc may be.

worth it worthwhile.

[from Anglo-Saxon *weorth*]

Wörther See a lake in SE Austria, situated in Kärnten state, W of Klagenfurt. AREA 19sq km/7sq mi; length 4km/2.5mi; width 2km/1mi; maximum depth 86m. Veldon, on the lakeside, is the chief town and most fashionable resort in Kärnten. The lake is popular for water sports.

worthily *adv.* in a worthy way; so as to be worthy.

worthiness *noun* a worthy quality.

Worthing POP (1992e) 98 000, a resort town co-extensive with Worthing district, West Sussex, S England. It lies 17km/11mi W of Brighton. HISTORY once a fishing village, it developed into a fashionable coastal resort after its discovery by Princess Amelia, daughter of George III. NOTABLE FEATURES Cissbury Ring (2km/1mi N), a 3c fort and Neolithic flint mines.

worthless *adj.* of no value or merit.

worthlessly *adv.* in a worthless way.

worthlessness *noun* being worthless.

worthwhile *adj.* worth the time, money, or energy expended; useful, beneficial, or rewarding.

worthy — *adj.* (**worthier, worthiest**) **1** *often condescending* admirable; excellent; deserving: *support worthy causes.* **2** (**worthy of something**) deserving it. **3** (**worthy of someone**) suitable to them. — *noun often condescending* an esteemed person; a dignitary: *the village worthies.*

Wotan see ODIN.

would *verb aux.* past tense of WILL used:. **1** in reported speech: *said she would leave at 10.* **2** to indicate willingness, readiness, or ability: *was asked to help, but would not / the radio would not work.* **3** in expressing probability: *they would surely have heard.* **4** in indicating habitual action: *would always telephone at six.* **5** in implying that some happening is predictable or unsurprising: *'She refused.' 'She would.'.* **6** to suggest obstinate resistance to advice: *he would have his own way.* **7** in expressing frustration at some happening: *it would rain, just as we're setting out.* **8** in expressing condition: *in your place, I would have told her.* **9** in making polite invitations, offers, or requests: *would you like to go? / would you rather have a red one? / would you ring her back?* **10** in formulating a desire: *wish she would stop talking.* **11** in politely expressing and seeking opinions: *I would suggest / would you not agree?*

— **would that** ... *old use* if only: *would that I were twenty again.*

[from Anglo-Saxon *wolde*, past tense of *wyllan*]

Would-be, Sir Politic and **Lady** the gullible traveller and his muddle-headed wife in Ben Jonson's *Volpone.*

would-be *adj.* hoping or aspiring to be: *a would-be actor.*

wouldn't *contr.* would not.

wound¹ see WIND².

wound² — *noun* **1** any external injury to living tissue of a human, animal, or plant, caused by physical means such as cutting, piercing, crushing, or tearing. Wounds include bruises, grazes, cuts, and burns. **2** an incision made by a surgeon. **3** an injury caused to pride, feelings, reputation, etc. — *verb trans., intrans.* **1** to inflict a wound on (a person, creature, limb, etc). **2** to injure (feelings, etc). [from Anglo-Saxon *wund*]

Wounded Knee the site in South Dakota of the final defeat (29 Dec 1890) of the Sioux tribe. The 'battle' was in fact a massacre of men, women, and children by US troops, which finally suppressed the Ghost Dance cult inspired by the Paiute Indian religious leader Wovoka.

wove, woven see WEAVE.

wow¹ *colloq.* — *interj.* an exclamation of astonishment or admiration. — *noun* a huge success.

— *verb* to impress hugely. [perhaps originally Scot.]

wow² *noun Electron.* a repeated waver in the pitch of reproduced sound, usually caused by an irregularity in the operating speed of the recording or reproducing apparatus. [imitative]

Wozzeck an opera by Alban Berg, based on Buchner's drama *Woyzeck* (1879). Each scene is based on a musical form (eg suite, rhapsody etc) and there is much use of *sprechgesang* (spoken dialogue), which was invented by Berg's teacher Schoenberg. The story focuses on the soldier Wozzeck, his declining relationship with his unfaithful mistress Marie, and on his own increasing instability.

WPC *abbrev.* woman police constable.

wpm *abbrev.* words per minute..

WRAC *abbrev.* Women's Royal Army Corps.

wrack *noun* **1** seaweed, especially one of the large brown varieties, floating, cast-up, or growing on the beach. **2** destruction. **3** a wreck or wreckage. [from Old Dutch or Old German *wrak*, related to Anglo-Saxon *wræc*, misery, and *wrecan*, to wreak; in sense 2, a variant of RACK²]

WRAF *abbrev.* Women's Royal Air Force.

wraith *noun* **1** a ghost; a spectre. **2** a person of spectral thinness and pallor. [originally Scot.]

Wrangel, Pyotr Nikolayevich, Baron (1878–1928) Russian soldier, born in Aleksandrovsk, Lithuania. He entered military service in 1904 and commanded a cavalry corps during World War I. During the Civil War, he commanded cavalry divisions and the Volunteer Army in the Ukraine, and in 1920 became Commander-in-Chief of the White Russian forces in the south. After the Red Army victory, he fled to Turkey with the remnants of his troops.

Wrangel Island, Russian **Ostrov Vrangelya** a tundra-covered island in the W Chukchi Sea, near the NE extremity of Asia. AREA 5 180sq km/1 999sq mi. It is 120km/75mi long, 72km/45mi wide and rises to 1 097m. The island was named after F P Wrangel (Vrangel), a 19c Russian navigator. It was ceded to Russia in 1924. There is a government Arctic station and trading post on the NE shore. Small settlements of Chukchi and Inuit inhabit the island.

wrangle — *verb intrans.* to quarrel or argue noisily or bitterly. — *noun* a bitter dispute. [from German *wrangeln*, related to WRING]

wrap — *verb* (**wrapped, wrapping**) **1** to fold or wind round something. **2** (*also* **wrap something up**) to cover or enfold it. — *noun* **1** a shawl or stole for the shoulders. **2** a protective covering.

— **keep something under wraps** *colloq.* to keep it secret.

take the wraps off something *colloq.* to reveal it to the public for the first time.

wrapped up in something absorbed in it; engrossed by it.

wrap round 1 *said eg of a piece of clothing* to pass right round with an overlap. **2** *Comput., said of text on a screen* to start a new line automatically as soon as the last character space on the previous line is filled.

wrap up 1 to dress warmly. **2** *slang* to be quiet.

wrap something up *colloq.* to finish it off or settle it finally.

wraparound *or* **wrapround** *adj., said especially of clothing* designed to wrap round.

wrapper *noun* **1** a paper or cellophane cover round a packet, sweet, etc. **2** the dust jacket of a book.

wrapping *noun* (*usually* **wrappings**) any of various types of cover, wrapper, or packing material.

wrasse *noun* a brightly coloured bony sea fish. [from Cornish *wrach*]

wrath *noun literary* anger; fury. [from Anglo-Saxon *wræththo*]

wrathful *adj. literary* angry.

wrathfully *adv. literary* angrily.

wreak *verb* **1** to cause (havoc, damage, etc) on a disastrous scale. **2** to take (vengeance or revenge) ruthlessly on someone. **3** to give unrestrained expression to (one's anger or hatred). [from Anglo-Saxon *wrecan*]

wreath *noun* **1** a ring-shaped garland of flowers and foliage placed on a grave as a tribute, or hung up as a decoration. **2** a victor's crown of especially laurel leaves. **3** (*usually* **wreaths**) a ring, curl, or spiral of smoke, mist, etc. [from Anglo-Saxon *writha*, something coiled, related to WRITHE]

wreathe *verb* **1** to coil, twine, or intertwine. **2** to hang or encircle with flowers, etc. **3** to cover or surround in (smoke, mist, etc). **4** *intrans. said of smoke, etc* to curl, coil, or spiral.

— **wreathed in smiles** smiling broadly or joyously.

wreck — *noun* **1** the destruction, especially accidental, of a ship at sea. **2** a hopelessly damaged sunken or grounded ship. **3** a crashed aircraft; a ruined vehicle. **4** *colloq.* someone in a pitiful state of fitness or mental health. **5** something in so advanced a state of deterioration that it cannot be salvaged. **6** *colloq.* a mess or shambles. **7** the remains of something destroyed: *a wreck of his former self.* — *verb* **1** to break; to destroy. **2** to spoil (eg plans, hopes, a holiday, relationship, etc). **3** to cause the wreck of (a ship, etc). [from Middle English *wrec*, from ODan *wræce*]

wreckage *noun* the remains of things that have been wrecked.

wrecker *noun* **1** someone who criminally ruins anything. **2** *Hist.* someone who deliberately causes a wreck in order to plunder the wreckage. **3** *North Amer.* a person whose job is to demolish buildings, vehicles, etc. **4** *North Amer.* a breakdown vehicle.

Wreck of the Deutschland, The a poem by Gerard Manley Hopkins (1918). It is based on the sinking of the *Deutschland* in the Thames in 1875, in which five Franciscan nuns were among the passengers drowned.

Wren, Sir Christopher (1632–1723) English architect, born in East Knoyle, Wiltshire. He became Professor of Astronomy at Gresham College, London, in 1657, and Professor of Astronomy at Oxford in 1661. After the Great Fire of London (1666), he drew designs for rebuilding the whole city, but his scheme was never implemented. He designed the new St Paul's (1669–1711), and many other churches and public buildings in London, including the Royal Exchange and Greenwich Observatory.

Wren, P(ercival) C(hristopher) (1885–1941) English popular novelist, born in Devon. He had an adventurous early life and joined the French Foreign Legion, an experience which provided him with the background for several novels of adventure, notably *Beau Geste* (1924) and *Beau Sabreur* (1928).

Wren *noun* a member of the Women's Royal Naval Service. [from the initials WRNS]

wren *noun* a very small songbird with short wings and an erect tail. [from Anglo-Saxon *wrenna*]

wrench — *verb* **1** (*often* **wrench something off** *or* **out**) to pull or twist it violently. **2** (**wrench someone away**) to force them to leave. **3** to sprain (an ankle, etc). — *noun* **1** a violent pull or twist. **2** a spanner-like tool for gripping and turning nuts and bolts, etc. **3** a painful parting or separation: *leaving home was always a wrench.* [from Anglo-Saxon *wrencan*]

wrest *verb* **1** to pull or wrench away, especially from someone else's grasp or possession. **2** to

extract with force or difficulty: *wrested an admission from her.* **3** to grab (victory) from the expected victor. **4** to distort or twist (words) from their true meaning. [from Anglo-Saxon *wræstan*]

wrestle — *verb* **1** *trans., intrans.* to fight by trying to grip, throw, and pinion one's opponent; to do this as a sport; to force to some position in this way: *wrestled him to the floor.* **2** *intrans.* to struggle intensely. — *noun* **1** a spell of wrestling. **2** a struggle. [from Anglo-Saxon *wrestlian*]

wrestler *noun* a person who wrestles.

wrestling *noun* the activity or sport of wrestlers.

◇ In most cases the object is to bring the opponent to the ground, although many variations exist. The most popular amateur forms, which are also included in the Olympic Games, are freestyle and Graeco-Roman. There are also many national and regional styles throughout the world including: *sambo*, originating in Russia; *sumo*, the national sport of Japan; and in Britain, *Cumberland and Westmoreland* and *Devon and Cornwall*.

wretch *noun* **1** a miserable, unfortunate, pitiful creature. **2** *humorous* a shamelessly wicked person. [from Anglo-Saxon *wrecca*]

wretched *adj.* **1** pitiable. **2** miserable; unhappy; distressed; distraught. **3** inferior; poor; lowly: *a wretched hovel.* **4** infuriating: *a wretched bore.*

wretchedly *adv.* in a wretched condition or way.

wretchedness *noun* a wretched state or quality.

Wrexham POP (1981) 41 000, a market centre in Wrexham Maelor district, Clwyd, NE Wales. It lies 20km/12mi SW of Chester. NOTABLE FEATURES cathedral; Church of St Giles (15c).

wrick same as RICK[2].

wriggle — *verb* **1** *intrans., trans.* to twist to and fro. **2** *intrans., trans.* to make (one's way) by this means. **3** *intrans.* (**wriggle out of something**) to manage cleverly to evade an awkward situation, disagreeable obligation, etc. — *noun* a wriggling action. [from Old German *wriggeln*]

wriggly *adj.* (**wrigglier, wriggliest**) inclined to wriggle.

Wright, Frank Lloyd (1867–1959) US architect, born in Richland Center, Wisconsin. He became known for his low-built, prairie-style residences, but soon launched out into more controversial designs, and was regarded as the leading designer of modern private dwellings. Among his larger works are the Larkin Building in Buffalo, the Imperial Hotel in Tokyo and the Guggenheim Museum of Art in New York City.

Wright, Joseph, also called **Wright of Derby** (1734–97) English genre and portrait painter, born in Derby. He spent most of his life in Derby, and became well-known for his fireside portrait groups which often show unusual light effects. His industrial works include the depiction of experiments made by candlelight (eg *Experiment with the Air Pump*, 1768, London).

Wright, Orville (1871–1948) US pioneer of aviation, born in Dayton, Ohio. With his brother Wilbur he founded in 1892 the Wright Cycle Company, and they later became the first to fly heavier-than-air powered aircraft (1903) at Kitty Hawk, North Carolina. They formed an aircraft production company (1909), but in 1915 he sold his interests in the business in order to devote himself to aeronautical research.

Wright, Richard (1908–60) US novelist, born in Natchez, Mississippi. He lived in Chicago (1928–45), and became a member of the Communist Party (1932–44). His disenchantment with this experience is the subject of *The God That Failed* (1950). He is most widely known

for *Native Son* (1940), the first substantial novel of US black revolt, and for his autobiography *Black Boy* (1945). After World War II he moved to Paris, and his novels of that period include *The Outsider* (1953).

Wright, Wilbur (1867–1912) US pioneer of aviation, born near Millville, Indiana. With his brother Orville, he was first to fly in a heavier-than-air powered aircraft (1903) and founded an aircraft production company. He died of typhoid.

wright *noun* (*usually in compounds*) a maker or repairer: *playwright / shipwright.* [from Anglo-Saxon *wryhta*]

wring *verb* (PAST TENSE AND PAST PARTICIPLE **wrung**) **1** (*also* **wring something out**) to force liquid from it by twisting or squeezing. **2** to force (information, a consent, etc) from someone. **3** to break (the neck) of a bird, etc by twisting. **4** to keep clasping and twisting (one's hands) in distress. **5** to crush (someone's hand) in one's own, by way of greeting. **6** to tear at (the heart as the supposed seat of the emotions).

— **wringing wet** soaking wet; saturated. [from Anglo-Saxon *wringan*]

wringer *noun Hist.* a machine with two rollers for squeezing water out of wet clothes.

wrinkle[1] — *noun* **1** a crease or line in the skin, especially of the face, appearing with advancing age. **2** a slight crease or ridge in any surface. — *verb trans., intrans.* to develop or cause to develop wrinkles. [from Anglo-Saxon *wrinclian*, to wind round]

wrinkle[2] *noun colloq.* a useful tip; a handy hint. [perhaps from Anglo-Saxon *wrenc*, trick]

wrinkly *adj.* (**wrinklier, wrinkliest**) having wrinkles.

wrist *noun* **1** the joint between the hand and the forearm. **2** the region surrounding the wrist joint. **3** the part of a sleeve covering this. [from Anglo-Saxon]

wristlet *noun* a decorative or supporting band for the wrist.

wristwatch *noun* a watch worn strapped to the wrist.

writ *noun* a legal document by which one is summoned, or required to do or refrain from doing something. [from Anglo-Saxon *writ*]

write *verb* (PAST TENSE **wrote**; PAST PARTICIPLE **written**) **1** *trans., intrans.* to produce (letters, symbols, numbers, words, sentences, etc) on a surface, especially paper, usually using a pen or pencil. **2** to compose or create (a book, music, etc) in manuscript, typescript, on computer, etc; to be the author or composer of. **3** *intrans.* to compose novels, contribute articles to newspapers, etc, especially as a living. **4** to put down; to inscribe. **5** to make or fill in (a document, form, etc): *write a prescription.* **6** *trans., intrans.* to compose (a letter, etc). **7** to say in a letter, article, book, etc. **8** to put up-to-date information in (one's diary, etc). **9** to include (a condition, etc) in a contract, etc: *wrote a new stipulation into his will.* **10** to fill (pages, sheets, etc) with writing. **11** to display all too clearly: *guilt written all over his face.* **12** *Comput.* to transfer (data) to a memory or storage device.

— **write something down 1** to put it down or record it in writing. **2** to reduce its accounting value.

write down to someone to write in a simplified style for their benefit.

write in to write a letter formally to an organization, television programme, etc.

write off to write and send a letter of request.

write something off 1 to damage a vehicle beyond repair. **2** to cancel a debt. **3** to discontinue a project, etc because it is likely to fail. **4** to dismiss something as being of no importance.

write something out 1 to write it in full; to copy or transcribe it. **2** to remove a character or scene from a film, serial, etc.

write something up 1 to write or rewrite it in a final form. **2** to bring a diary, accounts, etc up to date. **3** to write about it or review it, especially approvingly. [from Anglo-Saxon *writan*]

write-off *noun* something that is written off, especially a motor vehicle involved in an accident.

writer *noun* **1** a person who writes, especially as a living; an author. **2** someone who has written a particular thing.

writer's cramp painful cramp of the hand brought on by intensive writing.

write-up *noun* an written or published account, especially a review.

writhe *verb intrans.* **1** to twist violently to and fro, especially in pain or discomfort; to squirm. **2** *colloq.* to feel painfully embarrassed or humiliated. [from Anglo-Saxon *writhan*, to twist]

writing *noun* **1** written or printed words. **2** handwriting. **3** a literary composition, or the art or activity of literary composition. **4** (*usually* **writings**) a literary work: *Bacon's writings.* **5** a form of script: *Chinese writing.*
— **in writing** *said of a promise or other commitment* in written form, especially as being firm proof of intention, etc.
◇ The earliest known writing was developed in Sumeria c.4 000 BC and was pictographic (ie had a character for each item being named), as were many other ancient writing systems. The Greeks developed a phonetic alphabet c.800 BC, and most modern alphabets are phonemic (with some important exceptions, eg the Chinese writing system, which has thousands of characters).

writing-paper *noun* paper for writing letters on.

written past participle of WRITE. — *adj.* expressed in writing, and so undeniable: *a written undertaking.*

written word (the written word) written language, as distinct from spoken language.

WRNS *abbrev.* Women's Royal Naval Service.

Wrocław, German **Breslau 1** POP (1992e) 643 000, the industrial river-port capital of Wrocław voivodship, W Poland, on the R Oder. It is also the historic capital of Lower Silesia. HISTORY founded in the 10c; annexed by Prussia in 1741; the first Polish publications were printed here in 1745; badly damaged in World War II. NOTABLE FEATURES cathedral (13c); Church of St Mary Magdalene (13c–14c); National Museum; world-famous pantomime theatre established by Henryk Tomaszewski. **2** a voivodship in W Poland with the town of Wrocław as its capital.

wrong — *adj.* **1** not correct. **2** mistaken: *quite wrong about her motives.* **3** not appropriate or suitable: *always saying the wrong thing / wrong way up.* **4** not good; not sensible; unjustifiable: *wrong to waste the good weather.* **5** morally bad: *wrong to tell lies.* **6** defective or faulty: *something wrong with the radio.* **7** amiss; causing trouble, pain, etc: *wouldn't cry unless something was wrong with her.* **8** *said of one side of a fabric, garment, etc* intended as the inner, unseen, side. **9** not socially acceptable: *get in with the wrong class of people.* — *adv.* **1** incorrectly: *spelt wrong.* **2** improperly; badly: *timed it wrong.* — *noun* **1** whatever is not right or just: *know right from wrong / do wrong.* **2** any injury done to someone else: *did her wrong.* — *verb* **1** to treat unjustly. **2** to judge unfairly.
— **get on the wrong side of someone** *colloq.* to antagonize them.
get something wrong 1 to give the incorrect answer to it, or do it incorrectly. **2** to misunderstand it.
go wrong 1 *said of plans, etc* to fail to go as intended. **2** to make an error. **3** to stray morally; to fall into bad ways. **4** *said of a mechanical device* to stop functioning properly.
in the wrong guilty of an error or injustice. [from Anglo-Saxon *wrang*]

wrongdoer *noun* a person guilty of an immoral or illegal act.

wrongdoing *noun* evil or wicked action or behaviour.

wrongfoot *verb* **1** *Tennis, etc* to catch (one's opponent) off balance by making an unpredictable shot, etc to a point away from the direction in which they are moving or preparing to move. **2** to contrive to place (an opponent in a dispute, etc) at a tactical or moral disadvantage; to disconcert.

wrongful *adj.* unlawful; unjust.

wrongfully *adv.* wrongly, unjustly, unlawfully.

wrongly *adv.* in the wrong direction or way.

wrote see WRITE.

wroth *adj. old use* angry; full of wrath. [from Anglo-Saxon *wrath*]

wrought *adj.* **1** *old use* made, formed, shaped, or fashioned. **2** *old use* decorated or ornamented. **3** *said of metal* beaten into shape as distinct from being cast. [an old past participle of WORK]

wrought iron a malleable form of iron with a very low carbon content, but containing small amounts of slag as evenly distributed threads or fibres that render it tough and ductile. It is resistant to corrosion, easily welded, and used to make ornamental ironwork, chains, bolts, pipes, rivets, anchors, etc.

wrought-iron *adj.* made of wrought iron.

wrought-up *adj.* over-excited; agitated.

wrung see WRING.

WRVS *abbrev.* Women's Royal Voluntary Service.

wry *adj.* **1** slightly mocking or bitter; ironic. **2** *said of a facial expression* with the features twisted into a grimace, in reaction to a bitter taste, etc. **3** twisted to one side; awry. [from Anglo-Saxon *wrigian*, to turn, twist]

wryneck *noun* a small bird related to the woodpecker, that twists its head to look backwards over its shoulder.

WS *abbrev.* Writer to the Signet.

wt *abbrev.* weight.

Wu, Chien-Shiung (1912–) Chinese-born US physicist, born in Shanghai. Professor at Columbia University, she showed in 1956 that a quantum property known as 'parity' is not conserved in the so-called 'weak interactions' between particles.

Wuhan *or* **Han-kow** *or* **Han-kou** POP (1990) 3.9m, an inland port and the capital of Hubei province, E central China. It lies at the confluence of the Han Shui and Yangtze rivers. The city is a union of the three municipalities of Wuchang, Hankou, and Hanyang. It is the commercial centre of central China. NOTABLE FEATURES Guiyuan Buddhist Temple (c.1600), now a museum; Changjiang Bridge (first modern bridge to cross the Yangtze R, completed in 1957); Red Hill Park in Wuchang, with Yuan Dynasty Pagoda (1307–15).

Wuhsien see SUZHOU.

Wu-lu-k'o-mu-shi see URUMQI.

Wuppertal POP (1991e) 378 000, an industrial city in North Rhine-Westphalia state, W central Germany. It lies on the R Wupper in the Ruhr Valley, 26km/16mi NE of Düsseldorf, and includes the former towns of Barmen, Elberfeld, and Vohwinkel.

wurst *noun* any of various types of large German sausage. [from German literally 'something rolled', related to Latin *vertere*, to turn]

Wurtz, Charles Adolph (1817–84) French Chemist, born in Strasbourg. Professor at the Ecole de Médecine and the Sorbonne in Paris, he carried out important work on phosphorous

acids, and is best known for his pathway for synthesizing the larger alkanes and for the discovery of glycol (an intermediate between alcohol and glycerine) in 1856.

Würzburg POP (1991e) 126 000, an industrial city in Bavaria, S central Germany. It lies on the R Main, 96km/60mi SE of Frankfurt am Main, and is the centre of wine production and trade in Franconia. NOTABLE FEATURES cathedral (11c–13c); St Mary's Chapel (1377–1479); Old Main Bridge (1473–1543); Marienberg (fortress, 13c); Würzburg Residence, an episcopal palace built by Balthasar Neumann in 1719–44, is a World Heritage site.

wuther *verb intrans.* (**wuthered, wuthering**) *dialect, said of the wind* to roar or bluster. [related to Norse *hvitha*, squall]

Wuthering Heights a novel by Emily Brontë (1847). It is a tale of violent passion set on the Yorkshire moors in the contrasting homes of Wuthering Heights and the Grange.

Wu Yue see FIVE HOLY MOUNTAINS.

WV *or* **W. Va.** *abbrev.* West Virginia.

WVS *abbrev.* Women's Voluntary Service (now WRVS).

WWF *abbrev.* World Wide Fund for Nature (earlier World Wildlife Fund).

WY *or* **Wy.** *abbrev.* Wyoming.

Wyatt, Sir Thomas (1503–42) English courtier and poet, born in Allington, Kent. He was knighted (1536), made High Sheriff of Kent (1537), and went on several diplomatic missions. In 1557 his poems, published in *Tottel's Miscellany*, helped to introduce the Italian sonnet and other forms into English literature.

wych-elm *noun* a tree of the elm family native to N Europe and Asia, with drooping branches and smooth bark. [from Anglo-Saxon *wice*]

Wycherley, William (c.1640–1716) English dramatist, born in Clive, Shropshire. He wrote several satirical comedies, notably *The Country Wife* (1675) and *The Plain Dealer* (1677), both based on plays by Molière.

wych hazel same as WITCH HAZEL.

Wycliffe *or* **Wicliffe, John** (c.1330–1384) English religious reformer, born near Richmond, Yorkshire. He taught philosophy at Oxford, then entered the Church, and became rector of Lutterworth, Leicestershire (1374). He was sent to Bruges to discuss ecclesiastical abuses with ambassadors from the pope, but was prosecuted for his unacceptable views. He wrote many popular tracts in English (as opposed to Latin), attacking the Church hierarchy, priestly powers, and the doctrine of transubstantiation, and he issued the first English translation of the Bible. His opinions were condemned; the characteristic of his widely influential teaching, which in many respects anticipated the Reformation, was its insistence on inward religion instead of the formalism of the time. His followers were derisively known as 'Lollards'.

Wye, River 1 a river in central Wales, length 208km/129mi. Rising on Plynlimon, it flows SE and E through Powys, Hereford, and along the Gwent–Gloucestershire border to meet the estuary of the R Severn, S of Chepstow. It is notable for its valley scenery. **2** a river in Buckinghamshire, S central England, length 15km/9mi. It flows SE to meet the R Thames at Bourne End. **3** a river in Derbyshire, central England, length 32km/20mi. Rising near Buxton, it flows SE to join the R Derwent at Rowsley.

Wyler, William (1902–81) US film director, born at Mulhouse, Alsace (then in Germany). He emigrated to the USA in 1922, where he worked in film-making before becoming a director, mainly of westerns. In 1935 his association with Sam Goldwyn resulted in several successes, including the Oscar-winning *Mrs Miniver* (1942) and *The Best Years of Our Lives* (1946). His later films included *Friendly Persuasion* (1956), *Ben Hur* (1959), for which he won another Oscar, and *Funny Girl* (1968).

Wyndham, John, pseudonym of **John Wyndham Parkes Lucas Beynon Harris** (1903–69) English science-fiction writer, born in Knowle, Warwickshire. He began to write science-fiction tales for popular magazines in the late 1920s and achieved fame with his first novel, *The Day of the Triffids* (1951). Other works include the novels *The Kraken Wakes* (1953), *The Chrysalids* (1955), and *The Midwich Cuckoos* (1957), and collections of short stories, including *The Seeds of Time* (1969).

Wynne-Edwards, Vero Copner (1906–) English zoologist, born in Leeds. He taught at Bristol and at McGill University, Montreal, and later became professor at Aberdeen. He introduced the idea of 'group selection' to explain the altruistic behaviour of certain animals; although most of his examples of this have subsequently been explained on the basis of selection acting at the level of the individual, this was an important contribution to evolutionary debate.

Wyo. *abbrev.* Wyoming.

Wyoming POP (1990) 466 000, a sparsely populated state in western USA, divided into 23 counties. AREA 253 315sq km/97 780sq mi. Wyoming is known as the 'Equality State'. PHYSICAL DESCRIPTION rivers include the Snake, Yellowstone, Green, and N Platte; the Wind River Range lies in the W, and the Absaroka Range, Teton Mts, and Bighorn Mts in the N; all form part of the Rocky Mts (largely forested); the highest point is Gannett Peak (4 201m); the eroded 'badlands' are in the extreme NE, with higher tablelands in the SE; in the SW, the South Pass is the natural gateway through the Rocky Mts; the fertile Great Plains area in the E is ranching and farming country; Yellowstone and Grand Teton national parks and the Wind River Native American reservation lie within the state. HISTORY most of the region was acquired by the USA from France in the 1803 Louisiana Purchase; Spain, Britain, and the Republic of Texas all laid claims to other parts; came under total American jurisdiction in 1848; Wyoming Territory was established in 1868; major growth after the arrival of the railway in 1868; the first territory or state to adopt women's suffrage in 1869 and the first to elect a woman governor (in 1924); admitted to the Union as the 44th state in 1890; conflicts between cattle and sheep ranchers in the 1890s; coal, gas, and oil products contributed to an economic boom in the 1970s and 1980s, but lack of diversity has led to economic difficulties, and the mining has caused some severe pollution. CAPITAL Cheyenne. CHIEF TOWNS Casper, Laramie. ECONOMY agricultural products include cattle, sheep, sugar-beets, dairy produce, wool, hay, and barley; an important mining state; oil, natural gas, sodium salts, uranium, coal, gold, silver, iron, and copper; very little manufacturing (petroleum products, timber, and food processing); a major tourist area (with hunting, fishing, and rodeos).

WYSIWYG — *abbrev. Comput.* what you see is what you get, ie the type and characters appearing on screen are as they will appear on the printout. — *noun* a word-processing facility giving text on screen that closely approximates to printed text, with italic and bold type, etc as required.

Wyss, Johann Rudolf (1781–1830) Swiss writer, born in Berne. He collected Swiss tales and folklore, and was Professor of Philosophy at Berne from 1806. He is best known for his completion and editing of *Der Schweizerische Robinson* (The Swiss Family Robinson, 1812–13), written by his father, Johann David Wyss.

Wyszynski, Stepan (1901–81) Polish cardinal, born in Zuzela. Ordained in 1924, he became Bishop of Lublin (1946), Archbishop of Warsaw and Gniezno (1948), and a cardinal (1952). His indictment of the communist campaign against the Church led to his imprisonment (1953), but on his release (1956) he agreed to a reconciliation between Church and State under the Gomulka regime, though relations remained uneasy.

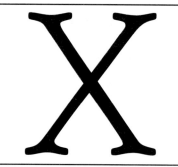

X¹ *or* **x** *noun* (PL. **Xs, X's, x's**) **1** the twenty-fourth letter of the English alphabet. **2** anything in the shape of an X. **3** an unknown or unnamed person.

X² *symbol* **1** *Maths.* (**x**) an unknown quantity. **2** the Roman numeral for 10. **3** a film classified as suitable for people over the age of 17 (in the USA) or 18 (in the UK; now replaced by '18'). **4** a mark used to symbolize a kiss, to indicate an error, the signature of an illiterate person, etc.

x *Maths.* see X².

xanthoma *noun* (PL. **xanthomata**) *Medicine* a small yellowish lump or swelling in the skin, often on the eyelid. It is formed by deposits of fat, and is usually a symptom of high blood cholesterol levels. [from Greek *xanthos*, yellow]

Xanthos-Letoon a Lycian and Roman archaeological site in SW Turkey. Xanthos was first excavated in 1842, and most of the archaeological treasures removed to the British Museum. It is a World Heritage site.

X-chromosome *noun Biol.* the sex chromosome that when present as one half of an identical pair determines the female sex in most animals, including humans. There is only one X-chromosome present in the male sex in most animals. See also Y-CHROMOSOME.

Xe *symbol Chem.* xenon.

Xenakis, Iannis (1922–) Greek composer, born in Braila, Romania. He studied engineering in Athens and worked as an architect for Le Corbusier in Paris, then turned to musical composition (1954) with *Metastasis* for orchestra. He developed a highly complex style which incorporated mathematical concepts of chance and probability (so-called *stochastic music*), as well as electronic techniques, in mainly instrumental and orchestral works.

Xenocrates (c.395–314 BC) Greek philosopher and scientist, born in Chalcedon on the Bosphorus. A pupil of Plato and later head of his Academy, he is thought to have travelled with Aristotle and taken part in foreign diplomatic missions. He wrote prolifically on natural science, astronomy, and philosophy, but only fragments of this output survive.

xenoglossia *noun* the spontaneous use of a language which the speaker has never heard or learned. The power of xenoglossia was ascribed to the Apostles in the early days of Christianity; however, no scientifically attested case of xenoglossia has come to light, though it continues to interest psychical researchers. See also GLOSSOLALIA. [from Greek *xenos*, strange, foreign + *glossa*, tongue]

xenolith *noun Geol.* a piece of foreign material that occurs within a body of igneous rock. [from Greek *xenos*, stranger + *lithos*, stone]

xenon *noun Chem.* (SYMBOL **Xe**, ATOMIC NUMBER **54**) a colourless odourless inert gas (one of the rare or noble gases) that is present in minute traces in the atmosphere. It is used in fluorescent lamps, photographic flash tubes, and lasers. [from Greek *xenos*, stranger]

Xenophanes (c.570–c.480 BC) Greek philosopher, born in Colophon, Ionia. He travelled extensively, and probably lived in Sicily and S Italy. He attacked traditional Greek conceptions of the gods, arguing against anthropomorphism and polytheism.

xenophobe *noun* a person who practises xenophobia.

xenophobia *noun* intense fear or dislike of foreigners or strangers. [from Greek *xenos*, stranger + PHOBIA]

xenophobic *adj.* relating to or practising xenophobia.

Xenophon (c.435–354 BC) Greek historian, essayist, and soldier, born in Attica. A friend and pupil of Socrates, in 401 he served with 10 000 Greek mercenaries under the Persian Prince Cyrus, who was fighting against his brother, Artaxerxes II, the King of Persia. After Cyrus was killed, the Greeks were isolated over 1500km/900mi away from home, but once Xenophon was elected leader, the group successfully fought their way back to the Black Sea. This heroic feat formed the basis of his major work, *Anabasis Kyrou* (The Expedition of Cyrus).

xerographic *adj.* relating to or involving xerography.

xerography *noun* an electrostatic printing process used to make photocopies of printed documents or illustrations. An image of the object to be copied is transferred to a charged drum, and the charge is erased by light reflecting off the white areas of the article. Resinous ink powder (*toner*) adheres to the areas of the drum that remain charged, and is then transferred to paper and fixed to it by heat. [from Greek *xeros*, dry + -GRAPHY]

xerophyte *noun Bot.* a plant that is adapted to grow under conditions where water is very scarce, such as the desert cactus, and showing any of a number of structural modifications, eg swollen stems that serve as a water store, specialized leaves that may be covered in hairs or reduced to spines in order to minimize water loss. [from Greek *xeros*, dry + *phyton*, plant]

Xerox — *noun trademark* **1** a type of photographic process used for copying documents. **2** a copying-machine using this process. **3** a photocopy made by such a process. — *verb* (**xerox**) to photocopy (something) using this process. [see XEROGRAPHY]

Xerxes (c.519–465 BC) Achaemenid king of Persia (485–465 BC), the son of Darius I. He is remembered in the West mainly for the failure of his forces against the Greeks at Salamis (480 BC), Plataea (479 BC), and Mycale.

Xhosa a group of Bantu-speaking peoples of the Transkei and Ciskei, South Africa, including the Ngqika, Gcaleka, and others who fled from Zulu armies in the early 1800s. They are mainly farmers, although many are settled permanently in urban centres. Xhosa is the most widely spoken African language in South Africa. The present-day population is c.5.5m.

Xiamen *or* **Hsia-men** *or* **Amoy** POP (1990) 369 000, a subtropical port city in Fujian province, SE China. It is situated on an island in the Taiwan Strait at the mouth of the Jiulong R and is connected to the mainland by a 5km-/3mi-long causeway, built in 1949. The city lies at the centre of the growing unofficial trade between China and Taiwan. HISTORY first settled during the S Song Dynasty from 1127 until 1279; made an open port in 1842; designated a special economic zone in 1981. NOTABLE FEATURES 10c Nanputo Temple located 5km/3mi to the E; Overseas Chinese Museum.

Xi'an *or* **Sian**, formerly **Changan**, *or* **Siking** POP (1990) 2.9m, the capital of Shaanxi province, central China. It was the first capital of feudal China. NOTABLE FEATURES many pagodas from the Tang Dynasty; Ming Dynasty Drum Tower; 14c Bell Tower; Banpo Neolithic Village (10km/6mi E); Tumulus of Emperor Qin Shihuangdi (30km/18mi E); terracotta warriors of the Emperor Qin, discovered in 1974; Big Wild Goose Pagoda (652); Great Mosque (742); Hua Qing Hot Springs, scene of the Xi'an incident (1936); Zhaoling Tomb of Tang Emperor, Tia Zong.

Xi'an incident the Chinese leader Chiang Kai-shek was held hostage in Xi'an by one of his own commanders, Zhang Xueliang, who demanded an anti-Japanese united front from the nationalist and communist forces. Chou En-Lai had to intervene to secure his release. The united front was achieved.

Xingu a national park in NE Mato Grosso state, W central Brazil. It is crossed by branches of the Xingu R, a S tributary of the Amazon. It was created in 1961 by the Vilas Boas brothers to protect the indigenous tribes. In recent years it has suffered from property developers and new roads now threaten the continued existence of the tribes living there.

Xinhua the national news agency of the People's Republic of China, established as the communist Red China News Agency in 1929 and sometimes known as the New China News Agency.

Xining *or* **Hsining** *or* **Sining** POP (1990) 552 000, the capital of Qinghai province, W central China. It lies NW of Lanzhou.

Xinjiang *or* **Sinkiang** POP (1990) 15.2m, an autonomous region in NW China. AREA 1 646 800sq km/635 665sq mi. CAPITAL Urumqi. ECONOMY wheat; cotton; maize; rice; silkworm cocoons; melons; grapes; sheep and horse raising; forestry; oil; coal; chemicals; textiles.

Xipe Totec in Aztec mythology, 'the flayed lord', a god of springtime renewal. Ceremonies in his honour demanded human sacrifices.

Xiuhtecuhtli in Aztec mythology, the god of fire, sun, and volcanoes. He is sometimes depicted as an old man who carries a burning brazier on his head.

Xizang see TIBET.

Xmas *noun colloq.* Christmas. [formed by substituting *X* for Christ, this being identical to Greek chi = ch]

Xochimilco a suburb of Mexico City, c.25km/15mi from the centre, on Lake Xochimilco. It is noted for its *chinampas* ('floating gardens'), islands in the lake which have formed from rafts made of mud and reeds, and anchored to the lake bed by plant roots. Canals are used for transportation. It is a World Heritage site.

X-ray — *noun* **1** an electromagnetic ray which can pass through many substances that light cannot pass through, producing on photographic film an image of the object passed through. **2** a photograph taken using X-rays. **3** a medical examination using X-rays. — *verb* to take a photograph of (something) using X-rays. [called X because at the time of discovery in 1895, the nature of the rays was unknown]

X-ray astronomy *Astron.* the study of X-ray emissions from celestial objects, using instruments on rockets or satellites (because X-rays from space cannot penetrate the Earth's atmosphere).

X-ray crystallography *Chem.* the study of the arrangement of atoms within a crystal by

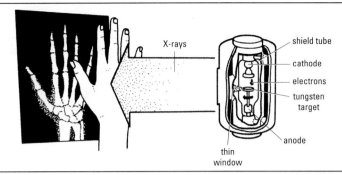

X-rays
shield tube
cathode
electrons
tungsten target
anode
thin window

X-ray

analysis of the diffraction pattern obtained when a beam of X-rays is passed through the crystal. A pattern of spots, corresponding to the arrangement of atoms, is produced on a photographic plate.

X-ray diffraction *Chem.* the characteristic interference pattern produced when X-rays are passed through a crystal, due to the fact that the wavelengths of X-rays are of a similar size to the distance between atoms in crystals. X-ray diffraction forms the basis of X-ray crystallography, which is used to determine the arrangement of atoms within a crystal.

xylem *noun Bot.* the plant tissue that transports water and mineral nutrients from the roots to all other parts of the plant. It consists of vertical chains of two types of conducting cell (vessels and tracheids), and woody fibres. The latter also provide structural support as the 'wood' in the stems of woody plants. See also PHLOEM. [from Greek *xylon*, wood]

xylene *or* **xylol** *noun* a hydrocarbon existing in three isomeric forms, a colourless liquid obtained from coal tar, etc and used eg as a solvent and in the preparation of specimens for microscopy. [from Greek *xylon*, wood]

xylophone *noun* a musical instrument consisting of a series of wooden, or sometimes metal, bars of different lengths, played by being struck by wooden hammers. [from Greek *xylon*, wood + *phone*, sound]

xylophonist *noun* a person who plays the xylophone.

XYZ Affair a diplomatic incident (1797) between the USA and France. It arose when French agents, identified as 'X', 'Y', and 'Z', solicited a bribe from US agents sent to negotiate an end to maritime hostilities.

Y

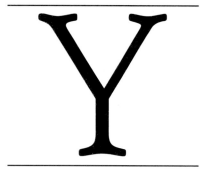

Y¹ *or* **y** *noun* (PL. **Ys**, **Y's**, **y's**) **1** the twenty-fifth letter of the English alphabet. **2** a thing shaped like the letter Y.

Y² *abbrev.* yen.

Y³ *symbol* **1** *Chem.* yttrium. **2** *Maths.* (**y**) the second of two unknown quantities. See also X, Z.

y *symbol Maths.* see Y³.

-y¹ *suffix* forming adjectives with the sense of 'full of', 'characterized by', 'having the quality of', 'keen on', etc: *spotty / icy / shiny / horsey.* [from Anglo-Saxon *-ig*]

-y² an element forming words that are. **1** diminutives or nouns used as terms of affection: *doggy / daddy.* **2** nouns denoting people or things with a particular characteristic: *fatty.* [originally Scots, used in names]

-y³ an element forming nouns denoting. **1** a quality or state: *jealousy / modesty.* **2** an action: *entreaty / expiry.* [from Old French *-ie*]

yacht *noun* a boat or small ship, usually with sails and often with an engine, built for racing or cruising.

yacht club a club for yacht-owners.

yachting *noun* sailing in yachts, especially as a sport.

yachtsman *or* **yachtswoman** *noun* a person who sails a yacht.

yack *derog. slang* — *verb* (**yacked**, **yacking**) *intrans.* to talk at length and often foolishly or annoyingly. — *noun* persistent foolish or annoying chatter. [imitative]

yah *interj.* **1** an exclamation of scorn or contempt. **2** *colloq.* yes.

yahoo *noun* a lout or ruffian. [named after the characters in Swift's *Gulliver's Travels*]

Yahoos a race of dirty, drunken beasts in Jonathan Swift's *Gulliver's Travels*, who are shaped as humans and exist in opposition to the Houyhnhnms, being corrupt, violent, and greedy.

Yahweh *or* **YHWH** the name of the God of Israel. The unvocalized YHWH (known as the Tetragrammaton) is considered by Jews too sacred to pronounce aloud, except by the high priest in the Holy of Holies on the Day of Atonement, and is usually replaced orally by Adonai ('Lord') when read from the Bible. It was vocalized erroneously by Christians as 'Jehovah'. [Hebrew, = (usually) He is/will be, He comes to be/creates, or He causes to fall]

yak¹ *noun* (PL. **yaks**, **yak**) a type of long-haired ox found in Tibet. [from Tibetan *gyag*]

yak² see YACK.

yakitori *noun* a Japanese dish of boneless pieces of chicken grilled on skewers and basted with a thick sweet sauce of sake, mirin, and soy sauce. [from Japanese, from *yaki*, grill + *tori*, bird]

Yale lock *trademark* a type of lock operated by a flat key with a notched upper edge. [from Linus Yale (1821–68), US locksmith]

Yale University in the USA, a university in New Haven, Connecticut, founded in 1701 as the Collegiate School in Clinton, Connecticut. It moved to Old Saybrook, then to New Haven (1716) where it was renamed Yale College after a benefactor, Elihu Yale (1649–1721). It was given its current name in 1886.

Yalow, Rosalyn, née **Rosalyn Sussman** (1921–) US biophysicist, born in New York City. She joined the Bronx Veterans Administration Hospital in 1947, and during the 1950s developed the technique of radio immunoassay, an ultrasensitive method of measuring concentrations of substances in the body such as hormones and enzymes in the blood. She shared the 1977 Nobel Prize for Physiology or Medicine with Roger Guillemin and Andrew Schally.

Yalta Conference a meeting (4–11 Feb 1945) during World War II in Yalta in the Crimea between Churchill, Stalin, and Roosevelt. Among matters agreed were the disarmament and partition of Germany, the Russo–Polish frontier, the establishment of the United Nations, and the composition of the Polish government. In a secret protocol it was also agreed that Russia would declare war on Japan after the war with Germany ended.

Yalu, River a river forming most of the N border between North Korea and NE China. The river rises in the Changbai Shan Range and flows S, W, then SW to flow into Korea Bay.

yam *noun* **1** any of various perennial climbing plants of the genus *Dioscorea*, cultivated in tropical and subtropical regions for its thick edible tuber. Some wild species are a source of a chemi-

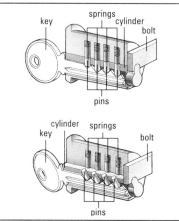

Yale lock

cal compound used in the contraceptive pill. **2** the thick starchy tuber of this plant, which is a major food crop in SE Asia, W Africa, and Central and S America. **3** *North Amer.* a sweet potato. [from Portuguese *inhame*]

Yamagata, Prince Aritomo (1838–1900) Japanese soldier and statesman, born in Hagi. He was adviser to the Emperor, War Minister (1873), Chief-of-Staff (1878), and Prime Minister (1889–91, 1898–1900). His modernization of the military system led to the defeat of China (1894–5) and Russia (1904–5), and the emergence of Japan as a significant force in world politics.

Yamamoto, Yohji (1943–) Japanese fashion designer, born in Tokyo. He started his own company in 1972 and produced his first collection in Tokyo in 1976. After some time in Paris he opened a new headquarters in London in 1987. He designs loose, functional clothes for men and women, featuring a great deal of black, which conceal rather than emphasize the body.

Yamashita, Yashiro (1957–) Japanese judo fighter, born in Kyushu. He won nine consecutive Japanese titles (1977–85), the Olympic open class gold medal (1984), and four world titles (1979, 1981, 1983 at over 95kg, and 1981, open class). He retired in 1985 after 203 consecutive bouts without defeat from 1977.

yammer — *verb* (**yammered**, **yammering**) **1** *intrans.* to complain whiningly; to grumble. **2** *intrans.* to talk loudly and at length. **3** *trans.* to say, especially to make (a complaint), loudly and longly. — *noun* the act or sound of yammering. [from Anglo-Saxon *geomrian*]

Yamoussoukro POP (1984e) 120 000, the capital of the Ivory Coast, in Bouaké department. It is a resort town lying NW of Abidjan. NOTABLE FEATURE presidential residence.

Yamuna *or* **Jumna, River** a river in NW India, 1 370km/850mi long. It rises in the Himalayas of N Uttar Pradesh and flows SW to Delhi, then generally SE to join the R Ganges. Its confluence with the Ganges is one of the most sacred Hindu places. The Taj Mahal at Agra lies on its banks.

Yang, Chen Ning (1922–) Chinese-born US physicist, born in Hofei. Professor at the Institute for Advanced Studies, Princeton, and later Director of the Institute for Theoretical Physics at New York State University, he predicted that the quantum property known as parity was unlikely to be conserved in the so-called weak interactions between particles (1956); this was confirmed experimentally in the same year. He shared the 1957 Nobel Prize for Physics with Tsung-Dao Lee.

yang see YIN.

Yangchow see YANGZHOU.

Yangku see TAIYUAN.

Yangtze River or **Yangtse-kiang** or **Chang Jiang** the longest river in China and third-longest in the world. It is c.6 300km/ 3 900mi long. Rising in the Tanggula Shan Range, it flows E as the Tongtian He, then S as the Jinsha Jiang, becoming the Yangtze after the town of Yibin in S Sichuan. It flows NE through the Sichuan Basin, then through a series of gorges, and across the Hubei Plain to enter the East China Sea at Shanghai. Its drainage area measures over 1 800 000sq km/694 800sq mi. Approximately one quarter of China's cultivated land lies in the densely populated river basin, where the soil is fertile and there are numerous mineral deposits. Around 40% of China's electricity is provided by the river. The Gezhouba Dam near Yichang is one of the largest in the world. The river is navigable for over 940km/ 580mi and is a major transportation artery between E and W China. Bridges at Chongqing, Wuhan, and Nanjing facilitate N–S communication.

Yangzhou or **Yangchow** POP (1990) 313 000, a city in Jiangsu province, E China. It lies on the Yangtze and Hua rivers. The city is an artistic centre for crafts, lacquerware screens, jade carving, and printing. HISTORY first settled during the Spring and Autumn Period (770–476 BC); became a major communications centre after the building of the Grand Canal in the 6c. NOTABLE FEATURES Fajing Si (Tang Dynasty Temple); museum; largest multiple-purpose water control project in China (constructed 1961–1975).

Yank *noun colloq.* a person from the United States. [a shortening of YANKEE]

yank *colloq.* — *noun* a sudden sharp pull. — *verb trans., intrans.* to pull suddenly and sharply.

Yankee *noun* 1 *Brit. colloq.* a person from the United States. 2 *North Amer., esp. US* a person from New England or from any of the northern states of America. [perhaps from Dutch *Jan Kees*, John Cheese, the nickname given by the New York Dutch to the British settlers in Connecticut]

Yanofsky, Charles (1925–) US geneticist, born in New York City. Professor at Stanford, his work on gene mutations has shown that the sequence of bases in the genetic material DNA acts by determining the order of the amino acids which make up proteins, including the enzymes which control biochemical processes.

Yaoundé or **Yaundé** POP (1988e) 776 000, the capital of Cameroon. It lies 210km/130mi E of Douala. HISTORY established as military post by Germans in 1899; occupied by Belgian colonial troops in 1915; became capital of French Cameroon in 1921.

Yap POP (1990) 14 000, one of the Federated States of Micronesia. AREA 119sq km/46sq mi. It comprises the four large islands of Yap, Gagil-Tomil, Map, and Rumung, with some 130 outer islands. CAPITAL Colonia. ECONOMY copra; tropical fruit.

yap — *verb intrans.* (**yapped, yapping**) 1 *said of a puppy or small dog* to give a high-pitched bark. 2 *derog. colloq., said of a person* to talk continually in a shrill voice, often about trivial matters. — *noun* a short high-pitched bark. [imitative]

yappy *adj.* (**yappier, yappiest**) *said of a dog* inclined to yap or bark.

Yard *noun* (**the Yard**) *colloq.* New Scotland Yard, the headquarters of the London Metropolitan Police.

yard[1] *noun* 1 a unit of length equal to 3 feet (0·9144 m). 2 *Naut.* a long beam hung on a mast, from which to hang a sail. [from Anglo-Saxon *gierd*, rod]

yard[2] *noun* 1 (*often in compounds*) an area of (enclosed) ground near a building. 2 (*often in compounds*) an area of enclosed ground used for a special (business) purpose: *a shipyard.* 3 *North Amer.* a

garden. [from Anglo-Saxon *geard*, fence, enclosure]

yardage *noun* the length (or, rarely, the area or volume) of something, measured in yards.

yard-arm *noun Naut.* either of the tapering end-sections of a yard.

Yardie *noun* a member of a criminal organization, originally from and based in Kingston, Jamaica, involved in drug-dealing and related crime. [from Jamaican English *yard*, home, dwelling, or (by Jamaicans abroad) Jamaica]

yardstick *noun* 1 a standard for comparison. 2 a stick exactly one yard long, used for measuring.

yarmulka or **yarmulke** *noun* a skullcap worn by Jewish men. [from Yiddish]

yarn *noun* 1 thread spun from wool, cotton, etc. 2 a story or tale, often lengthy and incredible. 3 *colloq.* a lie.
— **spin a yarn** *colloq.* to tell a long or untruthful story.
[from Anglo-Saxon *gearn*]

Yaroslavl 1 POP (1991e) 638 000, the river-port capital of Yaroslavl oblast, NW Russia. It is the oldest town on the R Volga, founded in c.1024. NOTABLE FEATURE Spaso-Preobrazhenski Monastery (12c). 2 an oblast in NW Russia with Yaroslavl as its capital.

yarrow *noun* a strong-scented composite plant with heads of small white flowers. [from Anglo-Saxon *gearwe*]

yashmak *noun* a veil worn by Muslim women, covering the face below the eyes. [from Arabic *yashmaq*]

Yates, Dornford, pseudonym of **Cecil William Mercer** (1885–1960) English novelist, born in London. He achieved great popularity with an entertaining series of fanciful escapist adventure fiction, including *Berry and Co* (1921).

yaw — *verb intrans.* 1 *said of a ship* to move temporarily from, or fail to keep to, the direct line of its course. 2 *said of an aircraft* to deviate horizontally from the direct line of its course. 3 to move unsteadily; to zigzag. — *noun* an act of yawing.

yawl *noun* 1 a type of small fishing- or sailing-boat, especially one with two masts. 2 a ship's small boat, usually with four or six oars. [from Dutch *jol*]

yawn — *verb intrans.* 1 to open the mouth wide and take a deep involuntary breath when tired or bored. 2 *said of a hole, gap, etc* to be or become wide open. — *noun* 1 an act of yawning. 2 *colloq.* a boring or tiresome event, person, etc. [from Anglo-Saxon *ganian*, to yawn, and *geonian*, to gape widely]

yawning *adj., said of a hole, etc* wide; large.

yaws *sing. noun* an infectious skin disease of tropical countries, causing red swellings.

Yayoi in Japanese archaeology, the period (c.300 BC– AD 300) that follows J(o bar)mon and precedes Kofun. Notable features are rice cultivation, irrigation, and the increasing use of bronze for weapons and tools.

Yb *symbol Chem.* ytterbium.

Y-chromosome *noun Biol.* the smaller of the two sex chromosomes, whose presence determines the male sex in most animals. In male humans there is one Y-chromosome and one X-chromosome. There is no Y-chromosome in human females. See also X-CHROMOSOME.

yd *abbrev.* yard.

ye[1] *pron. old use, dialect* you (plural). [from Anglo-Saxon *ge*]

ye[2] *definite article old or affected use* the: *Ye Olde Englishe Tea Shoppe.* [from the use of *y* by medieval printers as a substitute for the old letter þ representing the *th* -sound]

yea *interj. old use* yes. [from Anglo-Saxon *gea*]

Yeager, Charles Elwood, also called **Chuck** (1923–) US test pilot, born in Myra, West Virginia, the first man to break the sound barrier. He graduated as a fighter pilot in the US Air Force in 1943, and during combat missions he gained 12 victories. On 14 Oct 1947 he flew the Bell X-1 rocket research aircraft to a level speed of more than 670mph, thus 'breaking the sound barrier'; in the Bell X-1A he flew at more than 2.5 times the speed of sound (1953).

yeah *interj. colloq.* yes.

year *noun* 1 the period of time the earth takes to go once round the sun, about 365¼ days; the equivalent time for any other planet. 2 (*also* **calendar year**) the period from 1 Jan to 31 Dec, being 365 days, except in a leap year, when it is 366 days. 3 any period of twelve months. 4 a period of less than 12 months during which some activity is carried on: *At this college, the academic year runs from September to June.* 5 a period of study at school, college, etc over an academic year: *she's in third year now.* 6 students at a particular stage in their studies, considered as a group: *had a meeting with the third year this morning.* See also YEARS.
— **year in, year out** happening, done, etc every year, with tedious regularity.
[from Anglo-Saxon *gear*]

Year Equivalents

Jewish[1] **(AM)**

5752	(9 Sep	1991–27 Sep	1992)
5753	(28 Sep	1992–15 Sep	1993)
5754	(16 Sep	1993–5 Sep	1994)
5755	(6 Sep	1994–24 Sep	1995)
5756	(25 Sep	1995–13 Sep	1996)
5757	(14 Sep	1996–1 Oct	1997)
5758	(2 Oct	1997–20 Sep	1998)
5759	(21 Sep	1998–10 Sep	1999)
5760	(11 Sep	1999–29 Sep	2000)

Islamic[2] **(H)**

1412	(13 Jul	1991–1 Jul	1992)
1413	(2 Jul	1992–20 Jun	1993)
1414	(21 Jun	1993–9 Jun	1994)
1415	(10 Jun	1994–30 May	1995)
1416	(31 May	1995–18 May	1996)
1417	(19 May	1996–8 May	1997)
1418	(9 May	1997–27 Apr	1998)
1419	(28 Apr	1998–16 Apr	1999)
1420	(17 Apr	1999–5 Apr	2000)

Hindu[3] **(SE)**

1913	(22 Mar	1991–20 Mar	1992)
1914	(21 Mar	1992–21 Mar	1993)
1915	(22 Mar	1993–21 Mar	1994)
1916	(22 Mar	1994–21 Mar	1995)
1917	(22 Mar	1995–20 Mar	1996)
1918	(21 Mar	1996–21 Mar	1997)
1919	(22 Mar	1997–21 Mar	1998)
1920	(22 Mar	1998–21 Mar	1999)
1921	(22 Mar	1999–21 Mar	2000)

Gregorian equivalents are given in parentheses and are AD (= Anno Domini).
[1] Calculated from 3761 BC, said to be the year of the creation of the world. AM = Anno Mundi.
[2] Calculated from AD 622, the year in which the Prophet went from Mecca to Medina. H = Hegira.
[3] Calculated from AD 78, the beginning of the Saka era (SE), used alongside Gregorian dates in Government of India publications since 22 Mar 1957. Other important Hindu eras include: Vikrama era (58 BC), Kalacuri era (AD 248), Gupta era (AD 320), and Harsa era (AD 606).

year-book *noun* a book of information updated and published every year, especially one recording the events, etc of the previous year.

yearling — *noun* an animal which is a year old. — *adj., said of an animal* one year old.

yearly — *adj.* 1 happening, etc every year. 2 valid for one year. — *adv.* every year.

yearn *verb intrans.* **1** (**yearn for** *or* **after something** *or* **to do something**) to feel a great desire for it; to long for it. **2** (**yearn to** *or* **towards someone**) to feel compassion for them. [from Anglo-Saxon *giernan*, to desire]

yearning *noun* a strong desire or longing.

years *pl. noun* **1** age: *he is wise for his years.* **2** *colloq.* a very long time. **3** some period of time in the past or future: *in years gone by.*

yeast *noun* any of various single-celled fungi belonging to the genus *Saccharomyces* of the subdivision Ascomycetes, which are round or oval in shape. They reproduce asexually, mainly by budding, in which small outgrowths produced from the body of the parent become detached and eventually develop into new individuals.
◇ Some yeasts normally inhabit certain parts of the body, eg the digestive tract and vagina, but may under certain conditions cause infections such as thrush. Yeasts are capable of fermenting carbohydrates, eg sugars, to produce alcohol and carbon dioxide. *Saccharomyces cerevisiae* is used to bring about fermentation in the baking and brewing industries. In bread-making, carbon dioxide bubbles produced during the fermentation process cause the dough to rise, and in the production of wine and beer, the sugar from fruit, hops, or barley is fermented to alcohol. Yeast is a valuable source of some vitamins of the B group, and yeast extracts are used as savoury spreads for sandwiches, etc.
[from Anglo-Saxon *gist*]

yeasty *adj.* **1** (tasting or smelling) of yeast. **2** frothy. **3** trivial.

Yeats, W(illiam) B(utler) (1865–1939) Irish poet and dramatist, born near Dublin. Initially an art student, in 1889 he published *The Wanderings of Oisin*, a long narrative poem that established his reputation. *The Celtic Twilight*, a book of Irish legends, appeared in 1893. His plays include *The Countess Cathleen* (1892), *The Land of Heart's Desire* (1894), and *Cathleen ni Houlihan* (1903), and he wrote several others for the Abbey Theatre, which he helped to found in 1904. Many of his best-known poems appeared in *The Tower* (1928), *The Winding Stair* (1929), and *A Full Moon in March* (1935). He was a senator of the Irish Free State (1922–8), and was awarded the Nobel Prize for Literature in 1923. His *Collected Poems* were published in 1950.

Yekaterinburg *or* **Ekaterinburg**, formerly **Sverdlovsk** (to 1991) POP (1987e) 84 000, the industrial capital city of Sverdlovsk oblast, E Russia. It lies in the E foothills of the Ural Mts, on the R Iset, and was founded as a military stronghold and trading centre in 1821. Nicholas II was shot with his family at Yekaterinburg.

yell — *noun* a loud shout or cry. — *verb intrans., trans.* to shout or cry out. [from Anglo-Saxon *gellan*]

yellow — *adj.* **1** of the colour of gold, butter, egg-yolk, a lemon, etc. **2** *derog. colloq.* cowardly: *a yellow streak.* (= a tendency to cowardice). **3** *often offensive* (when used as a term of racial description) having a yellow or yellowish skin. **4** (any shade of) the colour of gold, butter, egg-yolk, etc. **5** something (eg material or paint) yellow in colour. — *verb trans., intrans.* to make or become yellow. [from Anglo-Saxon *geolu*]

yellow-bellied *adj. slang* cowardly.

yellow card *noun Football* a yellow-coloured card shown by the referee as a warning to a player being cautioned for a serious violation of the rules. See also RED CARD.

yellow fever *noun* an acute viral disease of tropical America and West Africa transmitted by the bite of a mosquito, causing high fever, jaundice and haemorrhaging.

yellowhammer *noun* a small brownish bunting, the male of which has a yellow head, neck, and breast.

yellowish *adj.* somewhat yellow; close to yellow.

Yellowknife POP (1991) 12 000, the capital of Northwest Territories, N Canada. It is situated on the NW shore of the Great Slave Lake at the mouth of Yellowknife R. HISTORY founded in 1935; capital since 1967.

yellowness *noun* a yellow state or quality.

Yellow Pages *trademark* a telephone directory, or a section of one, printed on yellow paper, in which entries are classified and arranged together according to the nature of the trade or profession of the individuals or companies listed and the services they offer.

Yellow River *or* **Huang Ho** *or* **Huang He** the second-longest river in China. It is 5 464km/3 395mi long. The river rises in Bayan Har Shan Range, W central China and flows NW through Inner Mongolia, then generally E or NE across the country to enter the Bo Hai Gulf. A series of gorges in its upper reaches is used for hydroelectricity. Flooding, formerly a major problem, is now increasingly controlled by dykes. There are several conservancy projects on the upper and middle reaches.

Yellow Sea, Chinese **Hwang Hai** an inlet of the Pacific Ocean. It is bounded by China in the N and W and by North Korea and South Korea in the E. The sea has a maximum width of c.650km/400mi and a maximum depth of c.150m. It was named for its colour, caused by the silt brought down by its rivers.

yellow spot see FOVEA.

Yellowstone the largest US national park, mainly in NW Wyoming, and the first national park in the world. Established in 1872, it has over 3 000 hot springs and geysers, including Old Faithful, a geyser that spurts water at regular intervals; Yellowstone and Jackson lakes also form part of the park. The highest point is at Electric Peak (3 350m). AREA 8 992sq km/ 3 472sq mi.

yelp *verb intrans. noun, said of a dog, etc* (to give) a sharp, sudden cry. [from Anglo-Saxon *gielpan*, to boast]

Yemen, official name **Republic of Yemen** POP (1993e) 13m, a republic in the S of the Arabian Peninsula. AREA 531 570sq km/205 186sq mi. It is bounded N by Saudi Arabia, W by the Red Sea, S by the Gulf of Aden, and E by Oman. CAPITAL San'a (political), Aden (commercial). CHIEF TOWN Ta'iz. TIME ZONE GMT +3. Islam is the chief religion. OFFICIAL LANGUAGE Arabic. CURRENCY the rial and the dinar. PHYSICAL DESCRIPTION a narrow desert plain bordering the Red Sea rises abruptly to mountains at 3 000–3 700m; a flat, narrow coastal plain in the S is backed by mountains rising to almost 2 500m; to the N, a plateau merges with the gravel plains and sand wastes of the Rub al Khali Basin. CLIMATE hot and humid on the coastal strip in the W, with an annual temperature of 29°C; milder in the highlands and winters can be cold; annual rainfall is higher in the N and W than in the E and S; hot all year round in the S, with maximum temperatures over 40°C in Jul and Aug; very high humidity in this area; average temperatures at Aden are 24°C in Jan, 32°C in Jul. HISTORY advanced civilizations developed in S Arabia from c.750 BC; controlled by Muslim caliphate 7c AD; ruled by Egyptian caliphs from c.1000; part of the Ottoman Empire from 16c until 1918; this was followed by the rule of the Hamid al-Din Dynasty until the revolution in 1962; fighting between royalists and republicans continued until 1967, when the republican regime was recognized; border clashes with South Yemen in the 1970s; in South Yemen, the fishing port of Aden was occupied by Britain in 1839; formed part of the Federation of South Arabia in 1963; overrun by the National Liberation Front, British troops withdrew, and a republic was proclaimed in 1967; border disputes with Oman and North Yemen in the 1970s; the

Yemen Arabic Republic (North Yemen) and The People's Democratic Republic of Yemen (South Yemen) formally united in 1990 as the Republic of Yemen. GOVERNMENT governed by a President, a 308-member House of Representatives, a Presidential Council and a Council of Ministers. ECONOMY based on agriculture: livestock, millet, sorghum, vegetables, wheat, barley, fruit, cotton, coffee; irrigation schemes are likely to increase the area under cultivation; Qat, a narcotic leaf, is a major export; textiles; cement; aluminium products; fishing; oil refining.

Yemen

yen[1] *colloq.* — *noun* a desire. — *verb* (**yenned**, **yenning**) (**yen for something**) to feel a longing for it. [from South Chinese dialect *yeen*]

yen[2] *noun* (PL. **yen**) the standard unit of Japanese currency. [from Japanese]

Yenisei *or* **Yenisey, River** a river in central Siberia, Russia, length 3 487km/2167mi. It rises in the E Sayanskiy Khrebet, and flows generally N to enter the Kara Sea via a long estuary. It forms the W boundary of the central Siberian Plateau. The river is navigable for five months on the upper river course, and for three months on the lower course. There are coal reserves in the upper valley and non-ferrous metal deposits near the mouth of the river; the Yenisei also generates hydroelectric power.

yeoman *noun* (PL. **yeomen**) **1** *Hist.* a farmer who owns and works his own land, often serving as a foot-soldier when required. **2** *Mil.* a member of the yeomanry (sense 2). [from Middle English *yoman*; perhaps from earlier *yongman*, young man]

yeomanry *noun* (PL. **yeomanries**) **1** *Hist.* the class of land-owning farmers. **2** a volunteer cavalry force formed in the 18c, now mechanized and forming part of the Territorial Army.

Yeomen of the Guard, also known as **Beefeaters** the oldest of the four corps of the sovereign's personal bodyguard. They wear Tudor-style uniforms and are summoned for special duties only. The Yeomen Warders of the Tower of London wear the same uniforms; their original duty was to guard the Tower, but now they attend the gates and act as guides to the tourists.

Yeovil POP (1981) 37 000, a market town in Yeovil district, Somerset, SW England, situated 34km/21mi E of Taunton. NOTABLE FEATURES Church of St John the Baptist (14c); Cadbury Castle (10km/6mi NE); Montacute House (5km/3mi W).

yep *interj. colloq.* yes.

Yerevan *or* **Erivan** POP (1990e) 1.2m, the industrial capital of Armenia, lying on the R Razdan, 15km/9mi E of the Turkish frontier. HISTORY one of the world's most ancient cities, it was founded in the 7c; ceded to Russia in 1828; badly damaged by earthquake in 1988. NOTABLE FEATURE ruins of a 16c Turkish fortress.

yin-yang symbol

Yerma a play by Federico García Lorca (1934). The second of a trilogy of folk tragedies (including *Blood Wedding*, 1933, and *The House of Bernarda Alba*, 1936), it focuses on a barren woman whose misery and frustration lead her to murder her sterile husband.

yes — *interj.* used to express agreement or consent. — *noun* (PL. **yesses**) an expression of agreement or consent.

yes-man *noun derog.* a person who always agrees with the opinions and follows the suggestions of a superior, employer, etc, especially to curry favour with them.

yesterday — *noun* **1** the day before today. **2** the recent past. — *adv.* **1** on the day before today. **2** in the recent past. [from Anglo-Saxon *giestran dæg*]

yesteryear *noun literary* **1** the past in general. **2** last year.

yet — *adv.* **1** (*also* **as yet**) up till now or then; by now or by that time: *he had not yet arrived.* **2** at this time; now: *you can't leave yet.* **3** at some time in the future; before the matter is finished; still: *she may yet make a success of it.* **4** (*used for emphasis with another, more, or a comparative*) even; still: *yet bigger problems / yet another mistake.* — *conj.* but; however; nevertheless.
— **nor yet** ... and not ... either.
yet again once more.
[from Anglo-Saxon *giet*]

yeti *noun* the abominable snowman, an ape-like creature supposed to live in the Himalayas. [from Tibetan]

Yevtushenko, Yevegeny (Aleksandrovich) (1933–) Russian poet, born in Zima in Siberia. He moved to Moscow in 1944 and his early poetry includes *The Third Snow* (1955). His long narrative poem *Zima Junction* (1956) prompted criticism, as did his *Babi Yar* (1962), which attacked anti-Semitism. His *Collected Poems 1952–90* were published in 1990, and *Stalin's Funeral* in 1991. Other works include several prose works and the play *Under the Skin of the Statue of Liberty* (1972). He has also engaged in acting and photography.

yew *noun* **1** (*also* **yew tree**) a type of evergreen tree with dark needle-like leaves and red berries. **2** its wood. [from Anglo-Saxon *iw*]

Y-fronts *pl. noun* men's or boys' underpants with a Y-shaped front seam.

Yggdrasil in Norse mythology, a giant ash, the World-Tree, which supports the sky, holds the different realms of gods and men in its branches, and has its roots in the Underworld.

YHA *abbrev.* Youth Hostels Association.

Yid *noun offensive* a Jew. [from YIDDISH]

Yiddish *noun, adj.* (of or in) a language spoken by many Jews, based on medieval German, with elements from Hebrew and several other, especially Slavic, languages. [from German *jüdisch*, Jewish]
◇ Yiddish is a Germanic language of the Indo-European family. Originally, it was the language of E European Jews, especially in Poland and Russia, and was a development (in the 9c) of Rhineland German. It spread, with emigration, to the USA, Israel, and elsewhere in Europe, and has had a significant impact on American English. A flourishing literature in the 19c and early 20c has not been significantly added to since the establishment of Hebrew as the official language of Israel (and Judaism). There are approximately 500 000 speakers of Yiddish worldwide.

yield — *verb* **1** to produce an animal product such as meat or milk, or a crop. **2** to give or produce: *shares yield dividends.* **3** *trans., intrans.* to give up or give in; to surrender. **4** *intrans.* to break or give way under force or pressure. — *noun* **1** the amount produced. **2** the total amount of a product produced by an animal or plant, or harvested from a certain area of cultivated land. [from Anglo-Saxon *gieldan*, to pay]

yielding *adj.* **1** submissive. **2** flexible. **3** able to or tending to give way.

yin *noun Chinese Philos.* one of the two opposing and complementary principles of traditional Chinese philosophy, religion, medicine, etc, being the negative, feminine, dark, cold, passive element or force as opposed to the positive, masculine, light, warm, active **yang**. [from Chinese *yin*, dark, *yang*, bright]

Yinchuan *or* **Yinch'uan** POP (1990) 357 000, the capital of Ningxia autonomous region, N China. Situated NE of Lanzhou, the city is a commercial and agricultural centre.

Yin-hsien see NINGBO.

yippee *interj. colloq.* used to show excitement, delight, etc.

ylang-ylang an evergreen tree (*Cananga odorata*) that grows to a height of 25m, native to Malaysia and the Philippines, and cultivated elsewhere. It has large elliptical leaves, and dull yellow fragrant flowers. Ylang-ylang or macassar oil from the flowers is used in perfumes and aromatherapy. [from Tagalog]

YMCA *abbrev.* in the UK, the Young Men's Christian Association, a charity founded in London in 1844 to promote the spiritual, social, and physical welfare of boys and young men. It developed rapidly, particularly in the USA, and is now active in over 90 countries. Its many services include physical education, counselling, and formal education, and it runs residences, cafeterias, and (in the USA) further education institutions and adult night schools.

YMHA *abbrev.* Young Men's Hebrew Association.

yob *noun slang* a bad-mannered, aggressive young person (usually male); a lout or hooligan. [a slang reversed form of *boy*]

yobbo *noun* (PL. **yobbos**) *slang* same as YOB.

yodel — *verb trans., intrans.* (**yodelled**, **yodelling**) to sing (a melody, etc), changing frequently from a normal to a falsetto voice and back again. — *noun* an act of yodelling. [from German dialect *jodeln*]

yodeller *noun* a person who yodels or is yodelling.

yoga *noun* **1** a system of Hindu philosophy showing how to free the soul from reincarnation and reunite it with God. **2** any of several systems of physical and mental discipline based on this, especially (in western countries) a particular system of physical exercises. [from Sanskrit, = union]

yoghurt *or* **yogurt** *or* **yoghourt** *noun* a type of semi-liquid food made from fermented milk, often flavoured with fruit. [from Turkish *yoghurt*]

yogi *noun* a person who practises the yoga philosophy and the physical and mental disciplines associated with it.

Yogyakarta *or* **Yogya** POP (1980) 399 000, the capital of Yogyakarta special territory, S central Java, Indonesia. It is the cultural centre of Java. NOTABLE FEATURES Sultan's Palace (18c); Soino Budoyo Museum; ancient temples of Borobudur and Prambanan.

yoke — *noun* **1** a wooden frame placed over the necks of oxen to hold them together when they are pulling a plough, cart, etc. **2** a frame placed across a person's shoulders, for carrying buckets. **3** something oppressive; a great burden: *the yoke of slavery.* **4** *technical* the part of a garment that fits over the shoulders and round the neck. — *verb trans.* (**yoke one thing to another** *or* **two things together**) **1** to join them under or with a yoke (sense 1). **2** to join or unite them. [from Anglo-Saxon *geoc*]

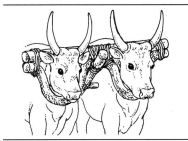

yoke

yokel *noun derog.* an unsophisticated (usually male) person from the country.

Yokohama POP (1991e) 3.2m, the port capital of Kanagawa prefecture, central Honshu, Japan. It is situated on the W shore of Tokyo-wan Bay, to the SW of Tokyo. The city is the fourth largest in Japan, handling 30% of the country's foreign trade. HISTORY the first port to be opened to foreign trade, in 1858; linked to Tokyo by the first Japanese railway in 1872; largely destroyed by an earthquake in 1923, and by bombing in 1945. NOTABLE FEATURES Sankei en Park (19c); silk museum.

yolk *noun* the yellow part of a bird's or reptile's egg. [from Anglo-Saxon *geolca*, from *geolu*, yellow]

Yomeimon Gate, also called **Higurashimon** (**Twilight Gate**) a gateway built in the 17c at the entrance to the inner courtyard of the Toshogu shrine in Nikko, Japan. It is covered with carving, lacquerwork, and gilding.

Yom Kippur the Day of Atonement, an annual Jewish religious festival devoted to repentance for past sins and celebrated with fasting and prayer. [from Hebrew]

Yom Kippur War hostilities (1973) that broke out towards the end of Golda Meir's last term as Israeli premier, when an attack on the State of Israel by Egypt and Syria coincided with Yom Kippur, the holiest day in the Jewish calendar. A cease-fire was reached after three weeks of fighting in which there were heavy losses on both sides.

yon *adj. literary, dialect* that or those. [from Anglo-Saxon *geon*]

yonder *adj., adv.* (situated) in or at that place over there. [from Middle English]

Yonge, Charlotte M(ary) (1823–1901) English novelist, born in Otterbourne, Hampshire. She achieved a great popular success with her *Heir of Redclyffe* (1853), and in all she published some 120 volumes of fiction, High Church in tone, which helped to spread the Oxford Movement. She also published children's books, historical works, and edited a magazine for girls, *The Monthly Packet*.

Yonkers POP (1990) 188 000, a town in Westchester County, SE New York State, USA. It is a residential suburb on the Hudson R, at the N edge of Greater New York, c.24km/15mi N of the city centre. NOTABLE FEATURES St Andrews Golf Course (first course in the USA); Hudson R Museum; Sherwood House. [named after the courtesy title ('Jonkheer') given to the early Dutch settler Adriaen van der Donck]

yonks *noun colloq.* a long time.

yoo-hoo *interj. colloq.* used to attract someone's attention.

yore
— **days of yore** *literary* times past or long ago. [from Anglo-Saxon *geara*, formerly]

Yorick 1 the dead jester in Shakespeare's *Hamlet* whose skull is brought to the surface when Ophelia's grave is being dug. **2** the impetuous parson in Laurence Sterne's *Tristram Shandy*.

York, ancient **Eboracum** POP (1992e) 104 000, a city in North Yorkshire, N England. HISTORY a Roman settlement, founded in AD 71 as capital of the Roman province of Britannia; thereafter a royal and religious centre, and capital of Anglo-Saxon Northumbria; captured by the Danes in 867 and known as Jorvik; expanded rapidly in the 19c as a railway centre. NOTABLE FEATURES 14c city walls; medieval streets eg the Shambles; 12c–15c York Minster (its south transept was badly damaged by fire in 1984, now restored); National Railway Museum; Castle Museum; Jorvik Viking Centre (1984); Theatre Royal.

York, House of a branch of the Plantagenet Dynasty, founded by Edmund of Langley, the fourth son of Edward III and first Duke of York (1385–1402). From this branch came three kings of England: Edward IV, who usurped the throne from the Lancastrian Henry VI; Edward V; and Richard III, who was killed at Bosworth Field and succeeded by Henry VII, first of the Tudors.

yorker *noun Cricket* a ball pitched to a point directly under the bat. [probably from the name *Yorkshire*]

Yorkist *Hist.* — *noun* a supporter of the House of York in the Wars of the Roses. See also LANCASTRIAN. — *adj.* relating to the House of York.

Yorks. *abbrev.* Yorkshire.

Yorkshire, North POP (1992e) 723 000, a county in N England, consisting of six districts. It is the largest county in England, extending from Lancashire in the W to the North Sea in the E; Cumbria, Durham, and Cleveland form its N boundary and West Yorkshire, South Yorkshire, and Humberside form its S boundary. AREA 8 309sq km/3 207sq mi. PHYSICAL DESCRIPTION the Pennines rise in the W; in the E are the Vale of York, North Yorkshire Moors, and Cleveland Hills; drained by the Ouse and Derwent rivers. CHIEF TOWNS Northallerton (county town), Harrogate, Scarborough, Whitby, York. ECONOMY agriculture (cereals, dairy farming, sheep); electrical and mechanical equipment; footwear; clothing; vehicles; plastics; foodstuffs; tourism. NOTABLE FEATURES Fylingdales Radar Station; Rievaulx Abbey; Castle Howard; Fountains Abbey; Yorkshire Dales National Park.

Yorkshire, South POP (1992e) 1.3m, a metropolitan county area in N central England, divided into four districts. Controlled by a metropolitan county council until 1986, the area is now administered by metropolitan district councils. AREA 1 560sq km/602sq mi. It is bounded NW by West Yorkshire, N by North Yorkshire, NE by Humberside, SE by Nottinghamshire and SW by Derbyshire. CHIEF TOWNS Sheffield, Rotherham, Doncaster, Barnsley. ECONOMY agriculture (sheep, arable, dairy farming); coal, steel; engineering.

Yorkshire, West POP (1992e) 2.1m, an industrial metropolitan county area in N England, divided into five districts. Controlled by a metropolitan county council until 1986, the area is now administered by metropolitan district councils. AREA 2 039sq km/787sq mi. It is bounded N and E by North Yorkshire, W by Lancashire, SW by Greater Manchester, and S by Derbyshire and South Yorkshire. PHYSICAL DESCRIPTION drained by the Aire and Calder rivers; Ilkley Moor lies in the NW. CHIEF TOWNS Wakefield (administrative centre), Leeds, Bradford, Huddersfield, Halifax.

ECONOMY wool textiles; coal; engineering, machinery, machine tools. NOTABLE FEATURES Haworth Parsonage (home of the Brontes); Peak District National Park.

Yorkshire Dales a national park in North Yorkshire and Cumbria, England, established in 1954. It is characterized by limestone scenery (eg Kilnsey Crag, Gordale Crag, Malham Cove) and is popular with potholers and fell walkers. The three main peaks are Ingleborough, Whernside, and Pen-y-Ghent. NOTABLE FEATURES Bolton Abbey (Wharfedale); Roman fort at Bainbridge. AREA 1 761sq km/680sq mi.

Yorkshire fog *Bot.* a grass (*Holcus lanatus*) with greyish-green leaves covered with soft hair, which has long white, green, pink, or purple spikelets borne in dense hairy flower-heads.

Yorkshire pudding a baked cake-like pudding of unsweetened batter, served especially with roast beef. [from the name *Yorkshire* in England]

Yorkshire terrier a small long-haired breed of dog.

Yorktown the seat of York County, SE Virginia, USA. It is situated at the mouth of the York R. HISTORY settled in 1631; now in the Colonial National Historical Park; Revolutionary troops under Washington and Rochambeau besieged British forces under Cornwallis here in 1781; also besieged during the Civil War by Union forces under McClellan in 1862.

Yorktown Campaign the final campaign (30 Aug–19 Oct 1781) of the US War of Independence, in which the British army under General Cornwallis was trapped at Yorktown, Virginia, by troops under George Washington and a French fleet under Admiral de Grasse (1722–88). The defeat destroyed the political will on the English side to continue the war, brought about the fall of Lord North, Prime Minister since 1770, and opened the way for peace negotiations.

Yoruba a group of Kwa-speaking peoples of SW Nigeria and Benin, mostly organized in culturally similar but politically autonomous kingdoms, each ruled by a king who is both political and religious head. Their dominant state in the 17c–18c was the kingdom of Oyo, which broke up in the early 19c. Traditional religion still flourishes, although many are Muslims and Christians. The present-day population is 16.5m.

Yoshkar Ola *or* **Ioshkar Ola** POP (1991e) 275 000, the capital of Mari-El republic, central W Russia, lying on the R Kokshaga. The city was founded in 1578.

you *pron.* **1** the person or persons, etc spoken or written to. **2** any or every person: *you don't often see that nowadays*.
— **something is you** *or* **really you**, etc *colloq.* it suits you: *that hat is just you*. [from Anglo-Saxon *eow*, originally accusative and dative of *ge*, ye]

you'd *contr.* **1** you would. **2** you had.

you'll *contr.* **1** you will. **2** you shall.

Young, Arthur (1741–1820) English agricultural and travel writer, born in London. He spent most of his life on a small rented farm in Bradfield, Suffolk, where he carried out agricultural experiments. In 1793 he became secretary to the Board of Agriculture. His writings helped to elevate agriculture to a science, and he was founder-editor of the monthly *Annals of Agriculture* (1784).

Young, Brigham (1801–77) US Mormon leader, born in Whitingham, Vermont. Converted in 1832, he became one of the 12 apostles of the Mormon Church in 1835, and succeeded Joseph Smith as President (1844). After the Mormons were driven from Nauvoo, he led them to Utah (1847), where they founded Salt Lake City. He was appointed Governor of Utah

in 1850, but was replaced in 1857 when an army was sent to establish federal law and suppress polygamy in the territory. He died leaving about $2 500 000 to 17 wives and 56 children.

Young, Cy, properly **Denton True Young** (1867–1955) US baseball player, born in Gilmore, Ohio. He made his senior début in 1890 and played until 1911. During his career he played 906 games, pitched in 706 complete games, and won 511 games, all records.

Young, Thomas (1773–1829) English physicist, physician, and Egyptologist, born in Milverton, Somerset. He became a physician in London in 1800, but devoted himself to scientific research and was briefly professor at the Royal Institution. He became best known in the 19c for his wave theory of light, explaining various interference phenomena; he also contributed to the deciphering of the inscriptions on the Rosetta Stone.

young — *adj.* **1** in the first part of life, growth, development, etc; not old. **2** in the early stages: *The evening is still young.* — *pl. noun* **1** young animals or birds: *Some birds feed their young on insects.* **2** (**the young**) young people in general. [from Anglo-Saxon *geong*]

Younghusband, Sir Francis (Edward) (1863–1942) British explorer, born in Murree, India. He joined the army in 1882, explored Manchuria (1886), and discovered the route from Kashgar into India via the Mustagh Pass. In 1902 he went on the expedition which opened up Tibet to the western world. He wrote much on India and central Asia, and founded the World Congress of Faiths in 1936.

Young Men/Women's Hebrew Association (ABBREV. **YMHA/YWHA**) in the USA, an organization to promote health, social activities, and Jewish culture. The first YMHA was founded in 1854, and the first independent YWHA in 1902.

Young Person's Guide to the Orchestra an orchestral work with a narrator by Benjamin Britten (Op 34, 1946). Originally written for the documentary *The Instruments of the Orchestra*, it consists of variations and fugue on a theme from Purcell's incidental music for the play *Abdelazer* (1695).

youngster *noun colloq.* a young person.

Young Turks the modernizing and westernizing reformers in the early 20c Ottoman Empire. With the support of disaffected army elements under Enver Pasha, they rebelled against Sultan Abd-ul-Hamid II in 1908, and deposed him (1909). The Young Turk revolution helped precipitate Austria-Hungary's occupation of Bosnia-Herzegovina (1908), the similar Greek officers' revolt of 1909, the Italian attack on Libya (1911), and the Balkan Wars (1912–13).

your *adj.* belonging to you. [from Anglo-Saxon *eower*, genitive of *ge*, ye]

Yourcenar, Marguerite, pseudonym of **Marguerite de Crayencour** (1903–87) French novelist, born in Brussels. The daughter of a member of the French aristocracy, she spent her childhood travelling in Europe. In 1937 she left France for the USA, where she took dual US-French nationality. She is best known for her historical novel *Mémoires d'Hadrien* (1951), and for being the first woman to be elected to the Académie Française.

you're *contr.* you are.

yours *pron.* **1** something belonging to you. **2** (**yours faithfully** *or* **sincerely** *or* **truly**) expressions written before a signature at the end of a letter (see FAITHFULLY, SINCERELY, TRULY).
— **... of yours** ... of or belonging to you: *a book of yours*.

yourself *pron.* (PL. **yourselves**) **1** the reflexive form of **you**. **2** used for emphasis. **3** your normal self: *don't seem yourself this morning.* **4** (**by yourself**) alone; without help.

yours truly *colloq.* used to refer to oneself, especially with irony or affected condescension: *then yours truly had to go and fetch it.*

youth *noun* **1** (the state of being in) the early part of life, between childhood and adulthood. **2** the enthusiasm, rashness, etc associated with people in this period of life. **3** a boy or young man. **4** (*pl.*) young people in general.

youth club a place or organization providing leisure activities for young people.

youth custody centre a place where young offenders between the ages of 15 and 21 are detained and given education and training.

youthful *adj.* **1** young, especially in manner or appearance. **2** *said of someone who is not young* young-looking, or having the energy, enthusiasm, etc of a young person. **3** of or associated with youth: *youthful pleasures.*

youthfully *adv.* with a youthful manner.

youthfulness *noun* being youthful; a youthful quality.

youth hostel a hostel providing simple overnight accommodation, especially one that belongs to the Youth Hostels Association.

Youth Hostel Federation, International an organization founded (1932) to co-ordinate the various national youth hostel associations, now found in 58 countries. It includes the Youth Hostels Association (YHA), a British charity founded in 1930 to promote knowledge and care of the countryside by providing simple, low-cost accommodation, mainly for young people on active holidays.

youth hosteller a person who stays at youth hostels, especially regularly.

Youth Hostels Association (ABBREV. **YHA**) see YOUTH HOSTEL FEDERATION, INTERNATIONAL.

Youth Training Scheme see YTS.

you've *contr.* you have.

yowl *verb intrans. noun, said especially of an animal* (to make) a sad cry or howl. [from Middle English *youlen*]

yo-yo — *noun* (PL. **yo-yos**) **1** a toy consisting of a pair of wooden, metal, or plastic discs joined at their centre with a deep groove between them, and with a piece of string attached to and wound round the joining axis within the groove, the toy being repeatedly made to unwind from the string by the force of its weight and rewind by its momentum. **2** anything which resembles such an object in upward and downward movement or variation. — *verb intrans.* (**yo-yoes, yo-yoed**) to rise and fall repeatedly; to fluctuate repeatedly in any way. [originally a trademark]

Ypres, Flemish **Ieper** POP (1991) 35 000, a town in West Flanders province, W Belgium. It lies on the canalized R Ypres, close to the French border. HISTORY long associated with the cloth trade; devastated in World War I (the Battles of Ypres). NOTABLE FEATURES Menin Gate (Menenpoort) Memorial, its graveyards, and the Garden of Peace provide a place of pilgrimage; Cloth Hall (13c); St Martin's Cathedral.

Ypres, Battle of 1 (Oct–Nov 1914) in World War I, the halting of a German offensive to outflank the British Expeditionary Force. It left Ypres (Belgium) and its salient dominated on three sides by German-occupied heights. **2** (Apr–May 1915) a series of German attacks in which poison gas (chlorine) was used for the first time in warfare. It forced the British to shorten their defence line in the Ypres salient. **3** (Jul–Nov 1917). See PASSCHENDAELE, BATTLE OF.

yr *abbrev.* **1** year. **2** your.

YTS *abbrev.* Youth Training Scheme, a British government-sponsored scheme to give training and work-experience to unemployed school-leavers.

ytterbium *noun Chem.* (SYMBOL **Yb**, ATOMIC NUMBER **70**) a silvery-white metallic element. [from the name *Ytterby*, a quarry in Sweden]

yttrium *noun Chem.* (SYMBOL **Y**, ATOMIC NUMBER **39**) a silvery-grey metal that is used in alloys to make superconductors and strong permanent magnets. Its compounds are used in lasers, microwave filters, and red phosphors for colour television sets. [see YTTERBIUM]

Yuan drama music theatre written and produced in China during the Yuan dynasty (1280–1369). Some 150 texts survive.

Yucatán POP (1990) 1.4m, a state in SE Mexico, situated on the N Yucatán Peninsula. AREA 38 402sq km/14 823sq mi. It is bounded N by the Gulf of Mexico. A third of the state is covered by forests and savannah vegetation is common in the drier NW. Yucatán is a name also often given to the whole peninsula, including the states of Quintana Roo and Campeche. CAPITAL Mérida. ECONOMY grain, tropical fruit, sisal, tobacco; timber; sea salt; fishing; textiles; brewing; tourism. NOTABLE FEATURES numerous Mayan ruins, including Chichén Itzá and Uxmal.

yucca *noun* any of a number of household and garden plants, originally from southern USA and Central America, grown for their attractive sword-like leaves and clusters of white flowers.

yucky *adj.* (**yuckier, yuckiest**) *colloq.* disgusting; unpleasant; messy. [from *Yuck* or *yuk*, an expression of disgust]

Yugoslavia or **Jugoslavia**, official name **Federal Republic of Yugoslavia**, Serbo-Croatian **Federativna Republika Jugoslavija** POP (1992e) 10.5m, a federal republic in the Balkan peninsula of SE Europe, consisting of the republics of Serbia and Montenegro. AREA 256 409sq km/98 974sq mi. It is bounded W by Bosnia-Herzegovina and Croatia, N by Hungary, NE by Romania, E by Bulgaria, and S by Macedonia and Albania. CAPITAL Belgrade. CHIEF TOWNS Priština, Subotica. TIME ZONE GMT +2. The population consists largely of Serbs, Montenegrins, Albanians, and Muslims; chief religions are Serbian Orthodox, Roman Catholicism, and Islam. OFFICIAL LANGUAGE Serbo-Croat. CURRENCY the dinar. PHYSICAL DESCRIPTION dominated in the N by the Danube, Tisza, and Sava rivers, with fertile plains in the NE; drained in the centre by the R Morava; ranges in the S are cut by deep river valleys; there are several great lakes in the S; highest point is Durmitor (2522m) in the SW. CLIMATE a Mediterranean climate on the Adriatic coast; a continental climate in the N and NE; rain falls throughout the year; there is a colder upland climate, with winter snow. HISTORY Serbs, Croats, and Slovenes united under one monarch in 1918; renamed Yugoslavia in 1929; civil war between Serbian royalists (Chetniks), Croatian nationalists, and Communists; occupied by Germany during World War II; Federal People's Republic established in 1945; following a break with the Soviet Union in 1948, the country followed an independent form of communism and a general policy of nonalignment; at the end of the 1980s political disagreement between the federal republics increased; in 1989 Slovenia declared its sovereignty and its strong opposition to the Communist Party; in an attempt to preserve Yugoslavian unity the Government announced plans to allow a multiparty system with direct elections, but ethnic unrest in Serbia and Croatia placed further strains on the federal system; Croatia and Slovenia ceded from Yugoslavia in 1991, and Bosnia-Herzegovina in 1992; Macedonia declared its independence in 1992; since 1991 there has been prolonged civil war and atrocities between ethnic factions in Bosnia-Herzegovina, forcing economic sanctions by the UN; a new Federal Republic of Yugoslavia consisting of Serbia and Montenegro was declared in Apr 1992 but is unrecognized by the United

Nations; in 1992 rigorous sanctions were imposed upon Yugoslavia, regarded as a supply route and ally for the Serbian forces in Bosnia-Herzegovina. GOVERNMENT governed by a bicameral Federal Assembly, comprising a 138-member Chamber of Citizens (108 Serb, 30 Montenegrin) and a 40-member Chamber of Republics. ECONOMY the industrial base extended following World War II; machine tools; chemicals; textiles; food processing; wood and metal products; oil refining; increased agricultural output, especially wheat, maize, sugar beet, livestock; wine; forestry; fishing; civil war has severely affected the economic situation in Yugoslavia.

Yugoslavia

Yukawa, originally **Ogawi Hideki** (1907–81) Japanese physicist, born in Tokyo. Professor in Kyoto, he proposed a theory of nuclear forces, suggesting a strong short-range attractive interaction between nucleons (neutrons and protons) through the exchange of massive particles. The existence of the intermediate particles he described (known as 'pions') was later confirmed experimentally, and he was awarded the 1949 Nobel Prize for Physics.

Yukon POP (1991) 28 000, a territory in NW Canada. AREA 483 450sq km/186 600sq mi. It is bounded W by Alaska and N by Mackenzie Bay and the Beaufort Sea. PHYSICAL DESCRIPTION area of plateaux and mountain ranges, rising to 5 950m at Mt Logan; Selwyn Mts in the E; tundra in the N; drained by the Yukon R and tributaries in the S, and the Peel and Porcupine rivers in the N; several lakes. CAPITAL Whitehorse. CHIEF TOWNS Watson Lake, Dawson City, Mayo. ECONOMY minerals; hydroelectric power. HISTORY Hudson's Bay Company fur-trading post was set up in 1842; gold prospectors arrived in 1873; became a district of Northwest Territories in 1895; made a separate territory when the Klondike gold rush was at its height in 1898. GOVERNMENT governed by a five-member Executive Council appointed from a 16-member elected Legislative Assembly.

Yukon River a major river in N America, in Yukon Territory, Canada, and Alaska, USA. Its length to the head of the longest headstream (the Nisutlin) is 3 185km/1 979mi. It rises in the Rocky Mts, near the border with British Columbia, and flows generally NW then W and SW through central Alaska. It then veers NW to enter the Bering Sea in a wide delta near Alakanuk. In NE Alaska it widens into the Yukon Flats for c.320km/200mi of its length the river is 15–30km/9–19mi wide. It is navigable to Dawson for large vessels, and as far as Whitehorse for smaller vessels, but is ice-bound for most of the year (Oct–Jun). The river was a major transportation route to the Dawson gold-mining area during the Klondike gold rush (1897–8).

Yule *noun old use, literary, dialect* **1** Christmas. **2** (**Yuletide**) the Christmas period. [from Anglo-Saxon *geol*]

yummy *adj.* (**yummier, yummiest**) *colloq.* delicious. [from YUM-YUM]

yum-yum *interj.* an expression of delight at or appreciative anticipation of something, especially delicious food. [imitative]

Yunnan see KUNMING.

yuppie *or* **yuppy** *noun* (PL. **yuppies**) *derog. colloq.* an ambitious young professional person working in a city job. [from *y*oung *u*rban *p*rofessional, or *y*oung *u*pwardly-mobile *p*rofessional]

yuppie flu *colloq. Medicine* myalgic encephalomyelitis.

Yu Shan see MORRISON, MOUNT.

Yves a male first name. [a French name, based on a Germanic element meaning 'yew']

YWCA *abbrev.* (in the UK) the Young Women's Christian Association, a charity formed in London in 1877 by the joining of a prayer union and a home for nurses travelling to and from the Crimean War (both established 1855). The movement spread to the USA in 1866, and a world organization was set up in 1892; it is now active in over 80 countries.

YWHA *abbrev.* Young Women's Hebrew Association.

Z¹ or z *noun* (PL. **Zs, Z's, z's**) **1** the last letter of the English alphabet. **2** anything in the shape of this letter.

Z² *symbol Maths.* (**z**) a third unknown quantity.

Z a French–Algerian film directed by Constantin Costa-Gavras (1968). It is a political thriller set in a Mediterranean country, starring Yves Montand as a politician whose 'accidental' death is the centre of controversy.

zabaglione *noun* a dessert made from egg-yolks, sugar, and wine whipped together. [from Italian *zabaglione*]

Zabrze POP (1992e) 206 000, a mining and industrial city in Katowice voivodship, S Poland. It lies W of Katowice and is the second largest city in the upper Silesian industrial region. From 1915 to 1945 it was named Hindenburg after Field Marshal Paul von Hindenburg.

Zacynthus, Greek **Zákinthos**, ancient **Zante** POP (1991) 33 000, the third largest of the Ionian Is, W Greece, situated in the Ionian Sea. AREA 406sq km/157sq mi; length 40km/25mi. CAPITAL Zacynthus. PHYSICAL DESCRIPTION deep and rugged W coast, and a hilly E coast, with a fertile central plain. The island was devastated by earthquakes in 1953. ECONOMY currants; tourism.

Zadar, Italian **Zara** POP (1991) 76 000, a seaport resort in Croatia, lying on the Adriatic Sea. HISTORY conquered by Venice in 1000; passed to Austria in 1797; an enclave of Italy from 1920 to 1947; part of Yugoslavia until Croatia's independence in 1991; experienced severe shelling in the Yugoslav civil war. NOTABLE FEATURES many Venetian buildings; Franciscan friary; cathedral; Roman remains at nearby Nin.

Zadokites the descendants of Zadok, a priest apparently of Aaronic lineage and of the family of Eleazar, who opposed the conspiracy of Abiathar against Solomon, was appointed high priest, and served in Solomon's temple. His family continued to hold this office both until Jerusalem fell (587/6 BC), and in the Second Temple period until the office became a political appointment of the occupying power under Antiochus IV (c.171 BC). The Qumran community continued to look for a renewal of the Zadokite priesthood, and described its own priestly members in these terms. Some derive 'Sadducees' from Zadokites.

Zagreb, German **Agram**, Hungarian **Zágrb**, ancient **Andautonia** POP (1991e) 704 000, the capital of Croatia, lying on the R Sava. It is the chief Croat cultural centre but suffered damage in the fighting following the declaration of independence from Yugoslavia.

Zagros Mountains a major mountain range in W Iran, extending c.1 770km/1 100mi from the Turkish–Armenian border SE along the Arabian Gulf. Mt Sabalan is the highest point at 4 811m. Large basins, one of which holds the shallow but navigable L Urmia, lie to the NW, the most populated area. There is a series of parallel ridges separated by deep valleys in the centre. The country's main oilfields lie along the W foothills of this part of the range. Bare rock and sand dunes are typical of the desolate extreme SE.

Zaharoff, Sir Basil, originally **Basileios Zacharias** (1850–1936) Turkish-born armaments magnate and financier, born in Mugla. He entered the munitions industry and became an influential figure in international politics and finance, amassing a huge fortune in arms deals, oil, shipping, and banking. During World War I he was an Allied agent. He donated large sums of money to public institutions.

Zaire *or* **Zaïre**, official name **Republic of Zaire**, French **République de Zaïre**, formerly **Congo Free State** (1885–1908), **Belgian Congo** (1908–60), **Democratic Republic of the Congo** (1960–71) POP (1992e) 39.9m, a central African republic, divided into nine regions. AREA 2 343 950sq km/904 765sq mi. It is bounded W by the Congo and the Atlantic Ocean, SW by Angola, SE by Zambia, E by Tanzania, Burundi, Rwanda, and Uganda, NE by Sudan, and N and NW by the Central African Republic. CAPITAL Kinshasa. CHIEF TOWNS Lubumbashi, Kisangani, Mbuji-Mayi, Kananga. TIME ZONE GMT +1 (W), +2 (E). There are over 200 ethnic groups, mainly of Bantu origin; Christianity is the chief religion. OFFICIAL LANGUAGE French. CURRENCY the new zaïre. PHYSICAL DESCRIPTION the land rises E from a low-lying basin to a densely-forested plateau, which is bounded E by volcanic mountains marking the western edge of the Great Rift Valley; the Ruwenzori Mts in the NE, on the Ugandan frontier rise to 5 110m in the Mt Stanley Massif; the Mitumbar Mts lie further S; in the Rift Valley the chain of lakes includes Albert, Edward, Kivu, and Tanganyika; a narrow strip of land follows the R Zaire to the Atlantic Ocean and a short 43km/27mi coastline. CLIMATE the country is crossed by the Equator and has a hot and humid climate; the average annual rainfall at Kisangani is 1 700mm; the average maximum daily temperatures range between 28°C and 31°C. HISTORY the Bantu had settled most of Zaire by 1000 AD; the Portuguese were the first Europeans to visit, in 1482; expeditions by Henry Stanley in 1874–7; claimed by King Leopold II of Belgium and recognized in 1895 at the Berlin Conference; the Congo Free State became a Belgian colony in 1908 and was renamed the Belgian Congo; gained independence in 1960; mineral-rich Katanga (later, Shaba) province claimed independence, leading to civil war; UN peace-keeping force present until 1964; renamed Zaire in 1971; further conflict in 1977–8; power struggles in the early 1990s; ethnic unrest in Shaba, Kivu, and Kasai provinces in 1993, resulting in many deaths; GOVERNMENT a one-party state, governed by a President, elected for seven years, a 27-member National Executive Council, and a National Legislative Council of 210 members, elected every five years; ultimate power lies with the Popular Movement of the Revolution, whose higher policy-making body is an 80-member Central Committee. ECONOMY nearly 80% of the population are involved in subsistence farming; livestock, maize, yams, cassava, rice, beans, fruit; cash crops include cotton, sugar, oil palm products, quinquina, coffee, tea, cocoa; extensive mineral reserves; world's biggest producer of cobalt, industrial diamonds, copper; other reserves include tin, manganese, zinc, columbium, tantalum, gold, silver, iron ore, rare-earth metals, offshore oil; cement; textiles; cotton; wood products; tobacco processing; vegetable oil; chemicals; major source of hydroelectricity.

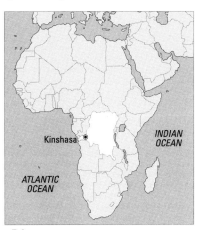

Zaire

Zaire, River, formerly **Congo** a river in central and W Africa. At c.4 670km/2 900mi, it is the second longest river in Africa. It rises as the R Lualaba, which drains L Deleommune in S Zaire, and flows N, crossing the Equator SE of Kisangani, where it becomes known as the R Zaire. It flows NW in an arc across central Africa, then SW, with the Congolese and Zairian capitals of Brazzaville and Kinshasa on opposite banks. The river makes a narrow trench in the Crystal Mts into the extreme W of Zaire, then enters the Atlantic Ocean SE of Pointe-Noire. It is affected by the ocean tide for 100km/60mi upstream. Hydroelectricity is produced from several dams. The first European discovery of the river mouth was by the Portuguese explorer Diogo Cão in 1482, but its extent was appreciated only in the 19c, with explorations by Stanley, Livingstone, and others.

zakat *noun* the obligatory alms tax of 2½ per cent payable by all Muslims as an annual levy on income and capital. It is the third of the five 'pillars' of Islam. [from Persian, from Arabic *zakāh*]

Zakopane POP (1990e) 29 000, the chief town in the High Tatra Mts, S Poland. It lies S of Kraków and is a winter sports and health resort which expanded after the arrival of the railway in 1899.

Zama, Battle of a battle (202 BC) in which the Romans under Scipio Africanus defeated the Carthaginians under Hannibal. It was the culminating battle of the Second Punic War.

Zambezi or **Zambesi, River**, Portuguese **Zambeze** a river in SE Africa. It flows through Angola, Zimbabwe, Zambia, Namibia, and Mozambique. It is one of Africa's major rivers, with a length of c.2 700km/1 700mi. The river rises in NW Zambia, and flows in a large 'S' shape generally SE. It forms the Zambia–Namibia border (the Caprivi Strip). The Victoria Falls, L Kariba, and the Kariba Dam lie on the Zimbabwe–Zambia border. It enters the Mozambique Channel as a marshy delta 210km/130mi NE of Beira. David Livingstone explored its middle course in the early 1850s.

Zambezi Expedition an official British expedition (1858–64), led by David Livingstone, to investigate the potentiality of the R Zambezi for steamship communication with the interior of Africa, aimed also at promoting the destruction of the slave trade. The expedition was a failure: the Zambezi was found to be non-navigable, Livingstone's difficult relations with his associates helped to thwart the scientific objectives, and the missionary endeavours met with disaster.

Zambia, official name **Republic of Zambia**, formerly **Northern Rhodesia** (to 1964) POP (1992e) 8.6m, a republic in southern Africa, which is divided into eight provinces. AREA 752 613sq km/290 509sq mi. It is bounded W by Angola, S by Namibia, SE by Zimbabwe and Mozambique, E by Malawi, NE by Tanzania, and NW by Zaire. CAPITAL Lusaka. CHIEF TOWNS Ndola, Kitwe, Kabwe, Livingstone. TIME ZONE GMT +2. Most of the population is Bantu (99%); Christianity and local beliefs are the chief religions. OFFICIAL LANGUAGE English; local languages are also spoken. CURRENCY the kwacha. PHYSICAL DESCRIPTION occupies a high plateau at an altitude of 1 000–1 400m; the highest point is 2 067m, SE of Mbala; the Zambezi R rises in the N extremity of North-West province. CLIMATE warm-temperate climate on upland plateau; rainy season is Oct–Mar; at Lusaka the average rainfall is 840mm and the maximum average daily temperatures range between 23°C and 35°C; tropical climate in the lower river valleys. HISTORY most ethnic groups at present in Zambia arrived there between 16c and 18c; European influence followed David Livingstone's discovery of the Victoria Falls in 1855; administered by the British South Africa Company under Rhodes; Northern

and Southern Rhodesia were declared a British sphere of influence in 1888; became Northern Rhodesia in 1911; became a British protectorate in 1924; massive copper deposits discovered in late 1920s; joined with Southern Rhodesia and Nyasaland as the Federation of Rhodesia and Nyasaland in 1953; the Federation dissolved in 1963; gained independence in 1964; first multi-party elections since independence held in 1991; an unsuccessful coup attempt was made in 1993. GOVERNMENT governed by a 150-member National Assembly serving five-year terms, a President, Chairman of Cabinet, and Council of Ministers; a multiparty system was introduced in 1991. ECONOMY based on copper and cobalt, which provide over half the national income; gold, lead, silver, zinc; maize, sugar, cassava, millet, sorghum, pulses, groundnuts, cotton, tobacco; cattle; manufacturing industries include copper wire, cement, fertilizer, explosives, vehicle assembly, sugar refining, food processing, textiles, glassware, tyres, bricks, brewing, and oil refining.

Zamboanga or **Zamboanga City** POP (1990) 444 000, a seaport in Zamboanga Del Sur province, W Mindanao, Philippines. It was founded in 1635. NOTABLE FEATURE Fort Pilar (17c).

Zamenhof, L(azarus) L(udwig) (1859–1917) Polish physician and oculist, the inventor of Esperanto, born in Białystok. His aims were to promote international tolerance and world peace, which he hoped to achieve through the use of an artificial language. His textbook, *Lingvo Internacia* was published in 1887 under the pseudonym of 'Doktoro Esperanto'. He withdrew as leader of the Esperanto movement in 1912.

Zamość a city in Zamość province, E Poland, built 1580–1600. Notable features include the 16c–17c houses surrounding the Market Square, the 16c–17c collegiate church, the 16c palace of Chancellor Jan Zamoyski, and the 17c former Zamoyski Academy. It is a World Heritage site.

Zante see ZACYNTHUS.

ZANU *abbrev.* Zimbabwe African National Union.

Zanuck, Darryl F(rancis) (1902–79) US film producer, born in Wahoo, Nebraska. He became a scriptwriter for Warner Brothers in 1924, and was co-founder of Twentieth Century Pictures (later Twentieth Century-Fox) in 1933. Among his many successful films are *The Jazz Singer* (1927), *The Grapes of Wrath* (1940), *The Longest Day* (1962), and *The Sound of Music* (1965).

zany *adj.* (**zanier, zaniest**) amusingly crazy. [from *Zanni*, a N Italian dialect form of *Gianni* or *Giovanni*, John, name of a character in medieval comedies]

Zanzibar POP (1990e) 663 000, an island region of Tanzania. AREA 1 660sq km/641sq mi. It includes several offshore islands, such as Tumbatu in the NW and Kwale in the SW. Zanzibar is separated from the mainland by the 40km-/25mi-wide Zanzibar Channel. The island is 85km/53mi long, 39km/24mi wide, and its highest point is 118m. CAPITAL Zanzibar. HISTORY populated by Bantu peoples (from the mainland), Shiraz Persians, and Arabs; largely Islamic since the 10c; developed under Omani Arab rule into the commercial centre of the W Indian Ocean in the 17c; annexed by Germany in 1885; exchanged for Heligoland in 1890, with Britain establishing a protectorate; gained independence in 1963; the ruling Sultanate was overthrown in 1964 and the People's Republic of Zanzibar was created; joined with Tanganyika and Pemba to form the United Republic of Tanganyika and Zanzibar, later the United Republic of Tanzania.

Zanzibar POP (1988) 158 000, the capital of Zanzibar I, Tanzania. It is situated on the W coast of the island. NOTABLE FEATURE Beit El Ajaib Palace (1833), Dr Livingstone's residence.

Zaozhuang or **Tsaochuang** POP (1990) 381 000, a city in Shandong province, E China. It is situated S of Jinan, in a major coal-mining area.

zap *verb* (**zapped, zapping**) *colloq.* **1** to hit, destroy, shoot, etc, especially suddenly. **2** *Comput.* to delete all the data in (a file) or from (the main memory of a computer). **3** *intrans.* to change television channels frequently using a remote-control device. **4** *trans., intrans.* to move quickly or suddenly. [imitative]

Zapata, Emiliano (1879–1919) Mexican revolutionary, born in Anencuilio, Morelos. He became a sharecropper and local leader, and after the onset of the Mexican Revolution, mounted a land distribution programme in areas under his control. Along with Pancho Villa, he fought the Carranza government, and was eventually lured to his death in the Chinameca hacienda.

Zaporozhye, formerly **Aleksandrovsk** POP (1991e) 897 000, the river-port capital of Zaporozhye region, Ukraine. It is a major industrial and energy-producing centre, founded as a fortress in 1770.

Zapotecs a Precolumbian Middle American Indian civilization of S Mexico (300 BC–AD 300) influenced by Olmec culture. It was centred on Monte Alban, a ceremonial site located on an artificially-levelled hilltop 400m above the Valley of Oaxaca.

zapper *noun colloq.* a remote-control device for a television or video recorder.

ZAPU *abbrev.* Zimbabwe African People's Union.

Zara a female first name. [perhaps of Arabic or Hebrew origin]

Zaria POP (1992e) 345 000, a town in Kaduna state, SW Nigeria. It was founded in the 16c and is situated 145km/90mi SW of Kano.

Zarqa POP (1990e) 515 000, an industrial town in Amman governorate, East Bank, N Jordan. It is the site of much of Jordan's industrialization programme. Large phosphate reserves are located nearby.

zarzuela *noun* a type of popular Spanish opera with spoken dialogue. The Teatro de la zarzuela, opened in Madrid in 1856, was specially built for performances. The modern form of zarzuela may be serious or comic in character. [probably from *La Zarzuela*, a royal palace near Madrid, where productions were first staged in the 17c]

Zatopek, Emil (1922–) Czech track athlete, born in Kopřivnice. After many successes in Czech track events, he won the 10 000m title at the 1948 Olympics. In the succeeding four years he broke 13 world records and won the 5 000m, 10 000m, and the Marathon at the 1952 Olympics. He was also European champion in the 5 000m in 1950, and in the 10 000m in 1950 and 1954. His wife Dana (née Dana Ingrova) won the Olympic javelin title in 1952.

zeal *noun* great, and sometimes excessive, enthusiasm or keenness. [from Greek *zelos*]

Zealand, Danish **Sjælland**, German **Seeland** POP (1976e) 1 987 549, the main island of the Sjælland group, Denmark. AREA 7 016sq km/ 2 708sq mi; length 128km/80mi. The island is bounded by the Kattegat in the N and NW, and the Great Belt in the W; The Sound separates Zealand from Sweden. The island is low-lying, rising to 126m. CHIEF TOWNS Copenhagen, Roskilde, Helsingør. ECONOMY a major agricultural area.

zealot *noun* **1** (**Zealot**) *Hist.* a member of the Zealots. **2** *often derog.* a single-minded and determined supporter of a political cause, religion, etc.

Zealots a militant Jewish sect which came into prominence in Palestine in the 1c AD . Its members were violently opposed to Roman rule in Palestine, and they took part in the revolt against Rome in AD 66 when they seized the fortress of Masada. It was disapproved of by the more traditional Pharisees and Sadducees.

zealous *adj.* enthusiastic; keen.

Zambia

zealously *adv.* enthusiastically.

zebra *noun* (PL. **zebras**, **zebra**) any of three species of a stocky black-and-white striped mammal with a stubby mane, belonging to the same family (Equidae) as the horse and ass, and found in Africa, south of the Sahara. Like horses, zebras are grazing animals and can run very fast. Their main predator is the lion. [from an African language]

zebra crossing *Brit.* a pedestrian crossing marked by black and white stripes.

zebu *noun* a domesticated ox found in parts of Africa and Asia. [from French *zébu*]

Zebulun one of the 12 tribes of ancient Israel, descended from the sixth son of Jacob by Leah. Its territory was in N Israel, a fertile part between the sea of Galilee and the Mediterranean coast, but buffered on each side by other tribes (eg the tribes of Issachar and Manasseh to the S).

Zechariah *or* **Zacharias, Book of** one of 12 so-called 'minor' prophetic writings of the Hebrew Bible and Old Testament, attributed to Zechariah, written (c.520–518 BC) after he returned to Jerusalem from exile. It contains visions of the building of Jerusalem's Temple and of a new messianic age.

zed *Brit.* noun the name of the letter Z. [from French *zède*, from Greek *zeta*]

zee *North Amer.* noun the name of the letter Z.

Zeebrugge a Belgian ferry port, the scene of a major shipping disaster in 1987 in which 193 lives were lost. The main car deck doors of the Townsend Thoresen ferry, *Herald of Free Enterprise*, were left open to the sea, causing it to founder just outside the harbour.

Zeeland POP (1990e) 356 000, a province in W Netherlands, bounded on the S by Belgium and on the W by the North Sea. It lies in the estuary area of the Rhine, Maas, and Schelde rivers. AREA 1 786sq km/689sq mi (land). The entire area has been reclaimed from the sea by artificial dykes, and is mostly below sea level. The 'Delta Plan' is intended to prevent a recurrence of the disastrous flooding of 1953, with sea and river dykes being strengthened and raised. CAPITAL Middelburg. CHIEF TOWNS Flushing, Breskens, Terneuzen. ECONOMY arable farming; fishing.

Zeeman, Sir (Erik) Christopher (1923–) British mathematician. Professor at Warwick University (1964–88) and Principal of Oxford's Hertford College since 1988, his early work developing topology and catastrophe theory was widely applied in physics, social sciences, and economics.

Zeeman, Pieter (1865–1943) Dutch physicist, born in Zonnemaire, Zeeland. Professor at Amsterdam University, he studied the effects of a magnetic field on sodium and lithium light sources, and observed that some lines in the spectrum were split into two or three components; this phenomenon became known as the Zeeman effect. He shared the 1902 Nobel Prize for Physics with Hendrik Lorentz.

Zeffirelli, Franco (1923–) Italian stage, opera, and film director, born in Florence. He began as an actor and designer, and during the 1950s produced many operas. His stage productions include *Romeo and Juliet* at the Old Vic (1960) and *Who's Afraid of Virginia Woolf* in Paris (1964). He also filmed *The Taming of the Shrew* (1966), *Romeo and Juliet* (1968) and *Hamlet* (1990), and the television film *Jesus of Nazareth* (1977). He also produced film versions of the operas *La Traviata* (1983) and *Otello* (1986).

Zeiss, Carl (1816–1888) German optician, born in Weimar. In 1846 he established a factory at Jena which became noted for the production of lenses, microscopes, and other optical instruments.

Zeller See *or* **Untersee** a lake in N Austria, lying N of the Grossglockner. It is an arm of L Constance, to which it is connected by the R Rhine. AREA 4.3sq km/1.7sq mi; length 4km/2.5mi; width 1.5km/0.9mi; maximum depth 68m. The resorts of Zell am See, Saalbach, and Kaprun have combined to form the 'Europa Sport Region'.

Zen *or* **Zen Buddhism** a meditation school of Buddhism. It originated in India and spread to China, where it incorporated elements of Taoism, then was taken by monks returning to Japan in the 12c. Zen stresses the personal experience of enlightenment based on a simple life lived close to nature, and upon methods of meditation which avoid complicated rituals and abstruse thought. In Japan, there are two main Zen bodies: Rinzai, introduced by Eisai (1141–1214), and Soto, introduced by Dogen (1200–53). The former seeks spontaneous enlightenment, while the latter regards it as a more gradual process.

Zend-Avesta *noun* the Zoroastrian sacred writings, comprising the scriptures (the *Avesta*) and a commentary on them (the *Zend*). [from Old Persian *zand*, commentary, *avastak*, text]

zenith *noun* **1** *Astron.* the point on the celestial sphere that is directly above the observer. It is diametrically opposite the nadir. See also NADIR. **2** the highest point. [from Arabic *samt-ar-ras*, direction of the head]

Zenocrate the captive, then wife, of Tamburlaine in Christopher Marlowe's *Tamburlaine the Great*.

Zeno of Citium (c.336–c.265 BC) Greek philosopher, the founder of the Stoic school, born in Citium, Cyprus. He went to Athens in c.315 BC, where he attended Plato's Academy and other philosophical schools, then opened his own school at the *Stoa poikile* ('painted porch'), from which the name of his philosophy derives.

Zeno of Elea (c.490–c.420 BC) Greek philosopher, a native of Elea, Italy. A disciple of Parmenides, he became known for a series of paradoxes, many of which denied the possibility of spatial division or motion. The best-known is 'Achilles and the Tortoise', whose conclusion is that no matter how fast Achilles runs, he cannot overtake a tortoise, if the tortoise has a head start, because the tortoise moves on while Achilles catches up. His arguments influenced Socrates' philosophical technique.

zeolite *noun* *Geol.* any of a group of hydrated aluminosilicate minerals, usually containing sodium, potassium, or calcium. Both natural and synthetic zeolites have an open three-dimensional internal structure, with a net negative charge, into which water molecules and positively charged ions can diffuse. They are widely used as 'molecular sieves' for separating substances, and as water softeners, eg Permutit (which contains sodium ions which are exchanged with the calcium ions in hard water). [from Greek *zeein* to boil (in allusion to the fact that many swell up when heated with a blowpipe) + *lithos*, stone]

Zephaniah, Book of one of 12 so-called 'minor' prophetic writings of the Hebrew Bible and Old Testament, attributed to Zephaniah, son of Cushi and descendant of Hezekiah, active in Josiah's reign (7c BC). It strongly denounces influences from heathen cults on Jewish religion (presumably preparing for Josiah's reforms), proclaims God's judgement on Israel's enemies, and consoles the remnant in Jerusalem who loyally await the 'Day of the Lord'.

zephyr *noun literary* a light, gentle breeze. [from Greek *Zephyros*, the west wind]

Zeppelin, Ferdinand (Adolf August Heinrich) Graf von, Count of (1838–1917) German army officer, born in Constance. He served in the Franco-Prussian War, and in 1897–1900 constructed his first airship, setting up a factory for their construction at Friedrichshafen.

Zeppelin a type of cigar-shped hydrogen-filled airship designed by Ferdinand von Zeppelin. The first was built in 1900 and over 100 were used during World War I. Rapid technological progress in other forms of transport, together with a series of fatal disasters, caused the Zeppelin to become rapidly defunct.

Zermatt POP (1990) 4 000, a fashionable skiing resort in the Pennine Alps, Valais canton, S Switzerland. It is also a popular mountaineering centre. The Matterhorn rises to the SW.

zero — *noun* (PL. **zeros**) **1** the number or figure 0. **2** the point on a scale (eg on a thermometer) which is taken as the base from which measurements may be made: *5 degrees below zero*. **3** zero hour. See also ABSOLUTE ZERO. — *adj.* **1** of no measurable size. **2** *colloq.* not any; no. — *verb* (**zeroes**, **zeroed**) to set to zero on a scale. — **zero in on something 1** to aim for it; to move towards it. **2** to focus one's attention on it. **3** to aim a weapon at it. [from French *zéro*, from Arabic *sifr*]

zero grazing a feeding system, often used on intensively stocked farms, where freshly cut grass is fed to livestock which are confined in a building, yard, or paddock. It makes use of grass from, eg, outlying or unfenced pastures, and reduces wastage from the fouling and selective grazing that often occurs when animals are allowed to graze freely.

zero hour 1 the exact time fixed for something to happen. **2** the time at which a military operation, etc is fixed to begin.

zero-rated *adj.*, *said of goods* on which the buyer pays no VAT, and on which the seller can claim back any VAT he or she has paid.

zest *noun* **1** keen enjoyment; enthusiasm. **2** something that adds to one's enjoyment of something. **3** *Cookery* the peel of an orange or lemon, used for flavouring.

zestful *adj.* keen; full of enjoyment.

zestfully *adv.* with zest.

zeugma *noun* a figure of speech in which an adjective or verb is applied to two nouns although strictly it is appropriate to only one of them, as in *weeping eyes and hearts*. [from Greek *zeugma*, yoking together]

Zeus in Greek mythology, the supreme god, the son of Cronus and Rhea. He defeated Cronus and the Titans, which brought the Olympian gods to supremacy. He had many wives and affairs with mortal women to whom he appeared in various guises. He was usually depicted with thunderbolts and an eagle, and was identified with the Roman god Jupiter.

Zeus, Statue of a colossal statue designed by the Greek sculptor Phidias in c.430 BC, located in the Temple of Zeus at Olympia. It was almost 12m high and wrought in ivory and gold over a core of wood. It was one of the Seven Wonders of the Ancient World.

Zhengzhou *or* **Chengchow** *or* **Chenghsien** POP (1990) 1.8m, the capital of Henan province, N central China. The city is a major market and transportation centre. First settled before 1 000 BC, the modern city stems from the construction of the railway in 1898. NOTABLE FEATURE Henan Provincial Museum.

Zhenjiang *or* **Chinkiang** POP (1990) 368 000, a river port in Jiangsu province, E China. Founded in 545 BC, it lies at the confluence of the Yangtze R and Grand Canal. NOTABLE FEATURE scenic areas known as the 'Three Hills of the Capital Gateway'; the Fahaizdong (Monk Cave) and the Bailongdong (White Dragon Cave); Jinshan Temple (4c); monastery; numerous temples; pavilions; inscribed stone tablets; the Dujinglou (Pavilion for Choosing Prospective Sons-in-Law); the Shijianshi (Testing Swords Stone).

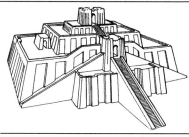

ziggurat

Zhitomir *or* **Jitomir** POP (1991e) 298 000, a city in W central Ukraine. It lies on the R Teterev, 165km/103mi W of Kiev, and was founded in the 9c.

Zhou Enlai *or* **Chou En-Lai** (1898–1975) one of the leaders of the Communist Party of China, and Prime Minister of the Chinese People's Republic from its creation in 1949 until his death. In 1927 he became a member of the Politburo of the Communist Party of China, and served Mao Zedong faithfully, becoming the Party's chief negotiator and diplomat. As Minister of Foreign Affairs (and Prime Minister) he vastly increased China's international influence. During the Cultural Revolution in China (1966–76), he worked to preserve national unity and the survival of government against the forces of anarchy.

Zhoukoudian a village 55km/34mi SW of Beijing (Peking), where fossil remains (Peking man) of the species *Homo erectus* were discovered during the 1920s. A wealth of other items have also been unearthed, and are displayed in an archaeological complex. It is a World Heritage site.

Zhu De *or* **Chu Teh** (1886–1976) one of the founders of the Chinese Red Army, born in Sichuan province. He was closely associated throughout his later career with Mao Zedong (Mao Tse-tung). He took part in the Nanchang Mutiny (1927), his defeated troops joining with those of Mao to form the Jiangxi Soviet. There, he and Mao evolved the idea of 'people's war', beating off attacks by vastly superior Nationalist forces until finally driven out in 1934. The Red Army then undertook the Long March, in which Zhu De was the leading commander.

Zhu Jiang see PEARL RIVER.

Zhukov, Giorgiy Konstantinovich (1896–1974) Soviet soldier, born in Strelkovka. He joined the Red Army in 1918, commanded Soviet tanks in Outer Mongolia (1939), and became army Chief-of-Staff (1941). He lifted the siege of Moscow, and in 1943 his counter-offensive was successful at Stalingrad. In 1944–5 he captured Warsaw, conquered Berlin, and accepted the German surrender. Later Commander of the Russian zone of Germany, he became Minister of Defence (1955), but was dismissed by Khrushchev in 1957.

Zia Ul-Haq, Muhammad (1924–88) Pakistani soldier and politician, born near Jullundhur, Punjab. He served in Burma, Malaya, and Indonesia in World War II, and in the wars with India (1965, 1971), and rose to become general and army Chief-of-Staff (1976). He led a bloodless coup in 1977, and as President (1978–88) he imposed martial law, banned political activity, and introduced an Islamic code of law. Despite international protest, he sanctioned the hanging of former President Bhutto in 1979.

Ziaur Rahman (1935–81) Bangladeshi soldier and politician, who played an important part in the emergence of the state of Bangladesh. Appointed army Chief-of-Staff after the assassination of Mujibur Rahman (1975), he became the dominant figure within the military. When he was President (1977–81), his government was of

a military character, even after the presidential election of 1978 which confirmed his position. He survived many attempted coups, but was finally assassinated in Dhaka.

Zibo *or* **Tzu-po** POP (1990) 2.4m, a city in Shandong province, E China, situated E of Jinan.

Ziegfeld, Florenz (1869–1932) US theatre manager, born in Chicago. He devised the American revue spectacle, based on the *Folies Bergère*. His *Follies of 1907* was the first of an annual series that continued until 1931 and made his name synonymous with extravagent theatrical production. His wide range of other musical productions include *Show Boat* (1927) and *Bitter Sweet* (1929).

ziggurat *noun* a pyramid-like temple in ancient Mesopotamia. [from Assyrian *ziqquratu*, mountain-top]
◇ The ziggurats of ancient Babylonia, Sumer, and Elam were high, regular, pyramidal mounds surmounted by a shrine; access to the shrine was by a series of external stairways and ramps. It is thought that they were built to such great heights in order to form a bridge between man and the gods. Famous examples include the ziggurat of the moon god at Ur and the largest, at Dur-Untash near Susa, which measures 100sq m.

zigzag — *noun* **1** (*usually* **zigzags**) one of two or more sharp bends to right and left in a path, etc. **2** a path, road, etc with a number of such bends. — *adj.*, *said of a path, road, etc* having sharp bends to right and left. — *verb* (**zigzagged**, **zigzagging**) to move in a zigzag path or manner. [from French *zigzag*, from German *Zickzack*]

zilch *noun slang* nothing.

Zillertal Alps, German **Zillertaler Alpen**, Italian **Alpi Aurine** a mountain range in the E Alps of N Italy and the S Tirol of Austria. It extends from the Birnlücke in the E to the Brenner in the W. The highest peak is Hochfeiler (3 510m).

zillion *noun colloq.* a very large but unspecified number. [by analogy with *million*, *billion*, etc]

Zimbabwe, official name **Republic of Zimbabwe**, formerly **Southern Rhodesia** (to 1979) POP (1992) 10.4m, a landlocked republic in southern Africa, divided into eight provinces. AREA 391 090sq km/150 961sq mi. It is bounded S by South Africa, SW by Botswana, NW by Zambia, and NE, E, and SE by Mozambique. CAPITAL Harare. CHIEF TOWNS Bulawayo, Gweru, Mutare. TIME ZONE GMT +2. The majority of the population is Bantu (97%), mainly Shona and Ndebele; Christianity and local beliefs are the chief religions. OFFICIAL LANGUAGE English. CURRENCY the Zimbabwe dollar. PHYSICAL DESCRIPTION high plateau country with the 'Middleveld' ranging in altitude from 900m to 1 200m and the 'Highveld' running SW–NE, with an altitude of 1 200–1 500m; the relief dips towards the Zambezi R in the N and the Limpopo R in the S; the mountains on E frontier rise to 2 592m at Mt Inyangani. CLIMATE generally subtropical, strongly influenced by altitude; warm and dry in the lowlands, with an annual rainfall of between 400mm and 600mm; the mountains in the E receive 1 500–2 000mm of rain annually; the average maximum daily temperatures at Harare, in the Highveld, range between 21°C and 29°C. HISTORY a medieval Bantu kingdom from the 12c–16c, with the capital at Great Zimbabwe; visited by David Livingstone in the 1850s; Southern Rhodesia came under British influence in the 1880s as the British South Africa Company under Cecil Rhodes began its exploitation of the rich mineral resources of the area; divided into Northern and Southern Rhodesia in 1911; Southern Rhodesia became a self-governing British colony in 1923; Northern and Southern Rhodesia and Nyasaland formed a multi-racial federation in 1953; independence of Nyasaland and Northern Rhodesia in 1963; opposition to

the independence of Southern Rhodesia under African rule resulted in a Unilateral Declaration of Independence (UDI) by the White-dominated government in 1965; economic sanctions and internal guerrilla activity forced the government to negotiate with the main African groups; power eventually transferred to the African majority; gained independence as Zimbabwe in 1980; government plans for land distribution announced in 1992 caused unrest among white farmers. GOVERNMENT a bicameral legislature was replaced in 1990 by a new single-chamber parliament, the House of Assembly, with 150 members (120 elected); an executive President combines the posts of head of state and head of government. ECONOMY agriculture involves 70% of the population: maize, sorghum, millet, rice, cassava, vegetables, tobacco, coffee, cotton, tea, groundnuts, wheat, sugar cane; cattle, pigs, poultry, forestry; rich mineral resources include gold, asbestos, nickel, coal, copper, chrome ore, iron ore, tin, silver, cobalt; iron; steel; foodstuffs; drink; tobacco; clothing; footwear; wood; furniture; paper; tourism to the national parks.

Zimbabwe

Zimbabwe, Great an area of stone ruins covering 25ha in SE Zimbabwe. The site was probably occupied from the 4c, and the ruins themselves, which consist of a hilltop stronghold with dwellings below, date from the 8c. It is a World Heritage site.

Zimmer *noun trademark* a three-sided tubular metal frame, used as a support for walking by the disabled or infirm. [the name of the original manufacturer]

zinc *noun Chem.* (SYMBOL **Zn**, ATOMIC NUMBER **30**) a brittle bluish-white metal that occurs in the ores zinc blende (sphalerite) and smithsonite. It is used in dry batteries, various alloys, eg brass and bronze, and as a corrosion-resistant coating to galvanize steel. Its compounds are used in medicines and pigments, and it is an important trace element in plants and animals. [from German *Zink*]

zincite *noun Geol.* a yellow, orange, or dark red mineral form of zinc oxide, often also containing small amounts of manganese, that is an important ore of zinc.

zinc ointment a soothing antiseptic ointment containing zinc oxide.

Zinder, Norton David (1928–   ) US geneticist, born in New York City. His studies using mutants of the bacterium *Salmonella* led him to describe the process of 'bacterial transduction', whereby a gene from one bacterium is moved to another by means of a viral phage particle. This has explained the spread of drug resistance in bacteria, and offered a mechanism of inserting specific genes into a host cell bacterium. He became professor at Rockefeller University in 1964.

Zinder POP (1988) 121 000, the capital of Zinder department, E central Niger. It lies 725km/450mi E of Niamey, on an important trade route to Kano in Nigeria. HISTORY occupied by the French in 1899; colonial capital until the 1920s. NOTABLE FEATURE Sultan's Palace (1860).

zine *noun slang* a magazine, especially one aimed at a special-interest group. [a shortening of MAGAZINE]

zing — *noun* **1** a short high-pitched humming sound, as made by a bullet or vibrating string. **2** *colloq.* zest or vitality. — *verb intrans.* to move very quickly, especially making a high-pitched hum. [imitative]

Zinjanthropus see *Australopithecus*, the former name of *Australopithecus boisei*.

zinnia *noun* an originally tropical American plant cultivated for its showy flowers. [named after J G *Zinn* (1727–59), German botanist]

Zinoviev, Grigoriy Yevseyevich, originally **G Ye Radomyslskiy** (1883–1936) Russian Jewish revolutionary and politician, born in Kherson province, Ukraine. In 1924 he became a member of the ruling Politburo, but because of opposition to Stalin's policies was expelled from the Party (1926). Reinstated in 1928, he was again expelled (1932), and in 1935 was arrested, charged with conspiring in the assassination of Sergei Kirov and for organizing other terrorist activities. He was executed following the first of Stalin's Great Purge trials in Moscow. The so-called Zinoviev letter urging British communists to incite revolution in Britain contributed to the downfall of Ramsay MacDonald's Labour government in the 1924 general elections.

Zinzendorf, Nicolaus Ludwig, Graf von (Count of) (1700–60) German religious leader, who refounded the Moravian Brethren, born in Dresden, where he held a government post. He invited the persecuted Hussite refugees from Moravia to his Lusatin estates in Saxony, where he founded for them the colony of *Herrnhut* ('the Lord's keeping'). His zeal led to conflict with the government and exile from Saxony (1736–48), during which time he was ordained and became Bishop of the Moravian Brethren. He was the author of over 100 books.

Zion *or* **Sion** a term used in the Old Testament and Jewish literature in various ways: for one of the hills in Jerusalem; for the mount on which the Temple was built; for the Temple itself; and symbolically for Jerusalem or even Israel as a whole. Today *Mount Zion* usually denotes the south-west hill in Jerusalem just south of the city wall. [Hebrew, (probably) = fortress or rock]

Zionism *noun* the movement which worked for the establishment of a national homeland in Palestine for Jews and now supports the state of Israel.

Zionist *noun* a supporter of Zionism. — *adj.* characteristic of or supporting Zionism.

zip — *noun* **1** (*also* **zip fastener**) a device for fastening clothes, bags, etc, in which two rows of metal or nylon teeth are made to fit into each other when a sliding tab is pulled along them. **2** a whizzing sound. **3** *colloq.* energy; vitality. — *verb* (**zipped**, **zipping**) **1** *trans., intrans.* (*also* **zip up**) to fasten, or be fastened, with a zip fastener. **2** *intrans.* to make, or move with, a whizzing sound. [imitative]

zip code in the US, a postal code, having the form of a five-figure number. [from zone improvement plan]

zipper *North Amer.* a zip fastener.

zippy *adj.* (**zippier, zippiest**) *colloq.* lively; quick.

zircon *noun Geol.* a hard mineral form of zirconium silicate, which is the main ore of zirconium, and an important source of hafnium and thorium. It occurs in various coloured forms, and

colourless varieties are used as semi-precious gemstones. [from German *Zirkon*; originally from Persian *zargun*, golden]

zirconium *noun Chem.* (SYMBOL **Zr**, ATOMIC NUMBER **40**) a silvery-grey metal that is resistant to corrosion and absorbs neutrons, used in certain alloys, and as a coating for fuel rods in nuclear reactors. Its oxide is used as an electrolyte in fuel cells. [from ZIRCON]

Ziska *or* **Žižka, John** (c.1370–1424) Bohemian Hussite leader, born in Trocznov. He fought against the Poles, Turks, and French, and soon after the murder of John Huss, became Chamberlain to King Wenceslas. During the civil war he was chosen to be leader of the popular party, captured Prague (1421), and erected the fortress of Tabor, from which his party, the Taborites, took its name. Having lost both his eyes in battles, he continued to lead his troops in a series of victories, and compelled Emperor Sigismund to offer the Hussites religious liberty.

zither *noun* a musical instrument consisting of a flat wooden sound-box, one section of which has frets on it, over which strings (usually metal) are stretched, the instrument being played resting on a table or on the player's knees. [from German *Zither*]

Zlatni Pyasǎci, English **Golden Sands** a beach resort in Varna province, E Bulgaria. It lies on the Black Sea, 17km/11mi NE of Varna. It is a centre for international conferences and hydrotherapy treatment.

Zn *symbol Chem.* zinc.

zodiac *noun* **1** (**the zodiac**) *Astron.* the band of sky that extends 8° on either side of the Sun's ecliptic (apparent path). It is divided into 12 equal parts, each containing one of the zodiacal constellations, ie Aries, Taurus, Gemini, Cancer, Leo, Virgo, Libra, Scorpius, Sagittarius, Capricornus, Aquarius, and Pisces. **2** *Astrol.* a chart or diagram, usually circular, representing this belt. [from Old French *zodiaque*, from Greek *zoidiakos*, from *zoidion*, a figure of a small animal]

Zoe a female first name. [from Greek *zoe*, life]

Zog I (1895–1961) Albanian politician and king, born in Burgajet. He became leader of the nationalist party, and as Prime Minister (1922–4) formed a republican government. Forced into exile in 1924, he returned with the assistance of Yugoslavia, became President (1925–8) and proclaimed himself king (1928–39). After Albania was overrun by the Italians (1939), he fled to Britain, formally abdicated (1946), and later lived in Egypt and France.

Zohar the main text of the Jewish Kabbalah. Discovered in Spain in the late 13c, it was said to be the mystical teachings of Rabbi Simeon bar Yochai and his followers, who lived in Palestine in the 2c–3c AD.

Zola, Emile (1840–1902) French novelist, born in Paris. He was a clerk and journalist, then began to write short stories (eg *Contes à Ninon*, 1864). After his first major novel, *Thérèse Raquin* (1867), he began the long series called *Les Rougon-Macquart*, a sequence of 20 books described in the subtitle as 'the natural and social history of a family under the Second Empire'. The series contains such acclaimed studies as *Nana* (1880), *Germinal* (1885), *La Terre* (Earth, 1887), and *La Bête humaine* (The Beast in Man, 1890). In 1898 he espoused the cause of Alfred Dreyfus in his open letter *J'accuse* and was sentenced to imprisonment, but escaped to England, and was given a great welcome on his return after Dreyfus had been cleared.

Zola a female first name. [perhaps a variant of ZOE]

Zollverein a German customs union, officially constituted in 1834, based on the enlarged Prussia of 1814. It comprised all of Germany save the Austrian Empire, Hanover, Brunswick, Oldenburg, and three northern maritime states — a total of 17 states embracing 26 million people — and was an important stage in the German unification process.

Spring Signs
Aries, the Ram 21 Mar-19 Apr
Gemini, the Twins 21 May-21 Jun
Taurus, the Bull 20 Apr-20 May

Summer Signs
Cancer, the Crab 22 Jun-22 July
Leo, the Lion 23 July-22 Aug
Virgo, the Virgin 23 Aug-22 Sep

Autumn Signs
Libra, the Balance 23 Sep-23 Oct
Scorpio, the Scorpion 24 Oct-21 Nov
Sagittarius, the Archer 22 Nov-21 Dec

Winter Signs
Capricorn, the Goat 22 Dec-19 Jan
Aquarius, the Water Bearer 20 Jan-18 Feb
Pisces, the Fishes 19 Feb-20 Mar

signs of the zodiac

zombie or **zombi** *noun* **1** a corpse brought to life again by magic. **2** *derog. colloq.* a slow-moving, stupid, unresponsive, or apathetic person. [from Kongo (W African language) *zumbi*, fetish]

zonal *adj.* **1** relating to a zone or zones. **2** arranged in zones.

zone — *noun* **1** an area or region of a country, town, etc, especially one marked out for a special purpose or by a particular feature. **2** any of the five horizontal bands into which the Earth's surface is divided by the Arctic Circle, the Tropic of Cancer, the Tropic of Capricorn and the Antarctic Circle. — *verb* **1** (**zone something off**) to divide it into zones; to mark it as a zone. **2** to assign to a particular zone. [from Latin *zona*, girdle]

zonked *adj.* **1** *colloq.* exhausted. **2** *slang* under the influence of drugs or alcohol. [imitative]

zoo *noun* a place where wild animals are kept for the public to see, and for study, breeding, etc. [a shortening of ZOOLOGICAL GARDEN]

zoological *adj.* relating to or involving zoology.

zoological garden *formal* a zoo.

zoologically *adv.* in a zoological way; in terms of zoology.

zoologist *noun* a person who studies zoology.

zoology *noun* the scientific study of animals, including their structure, function, behaviour, ecology, evolution, and classification. [from Greek *zoion*, animal + -LOGY]

zoom — *verb* **1** *intrans., trans.* (often **zoom over**, **past**, *etc*) to move or cause to move very quickly, making a loud, low-pitched, buzzing noise. **2** (**zoom away**, **off**, *etc*) to move very quickly. **3** *intrans.* to increase quickly: *prices have zoomed in the past year.* — *noun* the act or sound of zooming.

— **zoom in on someone** or **something** to direct a camera towards them, using a zoom lens to make them appear closer. [imitative]

zoom lens a type of camera lens which can be used to make a distant object appear gradually closer or further away without the camera being moved and without loss of focus.

◇ These lenses are standard for all video cameras, and are widely used in cinematography. They are sometimes fitted to portable projectors to give variable magnification for different screen sizes and distances.

zoophyte *noun Biol.* any of various invertebrate animals which resemble plants, such as sponges, corals and sea anemones. [from Greek *zoion*, animal + *phyton*, plant]

zooplankton *noun Zool.* the part of the plankton that is composed of passively drifting or floating microscopic animals.

Zoroaster, Greek form of **Zarathushtra**, modern form **Zaradusht** (c.630–c.553 BC) Iranian religious leader and prophet, the founder or reformer of the ancient Parsee religion as Zoroastrianism. He appears as a historical person only in the earliest part of the *Avesta*. He apparently had visions of Ahura Mazda, which led him to preach against polytheism. As the centre of a group of chieftains, he carried on a struggle for the establishment of a holy agricultural state against Turanian and Vedic aggressors.

Zoroastrian — *noun* a follower of Zoroastrianism. — *adj.* relating to or characteristic of Zoroastrianism.

Zoroastrianism *noun* an ancient religion of Persian origin founded or reformed by Zoroaster, which teaches the existence of two continuously opposed divine beings, one good and the other evil.

◇ Zoroastrians believed that the spirit of evil, Ahriman, would finally be overcome by Ahura Mazda ('Wise Lord') or God, who would then become fully omnipotent. Their body of scripture was known as the *Avesta*, and rites of worship were performed by priests, or Magi. Zoroastrianism was forced out of Persia by the expansion of Islam.

Zörs a winter sports resort in the Lechtal Alps, Vorarlberg state, W Austria. It lies at an altitude of 1 720m.

zoster *noun* **1** an ancient Greek waist-belt for men. **2** *Medicine* herpes zoster or shingles. [from Greek *zoster*, girdle]

Zouaves a body of troops in the French army, first raised from Algerian tribes in 1830, who dressed in flamboyant Moorish costume. During the American Civil War, several 'Zouave' style volunteer regiments were raised on the US side.

zouk *noun* a style of dance music originating in the French Antilles combining Latin American, African, and Western disco rhythms. [from French]

Zr *symbol Chem.* zirconium.

Zrenjanin, formerly **Veliki Beckerek**, or **Petrovgrad** POP (1991) 81 000, a river-port city in Vojvodina province, N Serbia, Yugoslavia. It lies on the R Begej.

zucchini *noun* (PL. **zucchini**, **zucchinis**) *North Amer., Austral.* a courgette. [from Italian *zucchini*]

Zug 1 POP (1990) 22 000, the capital of Zug canton, central Switzerland. It lies at the NE end of Zuger Zee, 24km/15mi S of Zurich. The town is noted for its kirsch. NOTABLE FEATURE Gothic church (15c–16c). **2** a canton in central Switzerland with the town of Zug as its capital.

Zugspitze the highest peak in Germany, in the Wettersteingebirge of the Bavarian Alps, near the border with Austria. HEIGHT 2 962m. The hotel near the summit is one of Europe's highest atmospheric sampling stations.

Zuider Zee a former shallow inlet of the North Sea in W Netherlands. Since the 1920s it has been divided into the outer Waddenzee (Wadden Sea) and the inner Ijsselmeer, which has been partially reclaimed as polder land.

Zuleika Dobson a novel by Max Beerbohm (1911). It is set in Oxford and tells ironically of the extreme reaction of the male undergraduates to the beautiful heroine Zuleika.

Zulu — *noun* **1** a member of a Bantu people of S Africa. **2** the language of this people. — *adj.* of or pertaining to the Zulus, their language, etc.

Zuni a Native American Pueblo people of the American SW, living in New Mexico and Arizona, similar to the Hopi. A peaceful agricultural people, they were defeated by the Spanish in the 17c. Many are assimilated into US culture, although certain traditions are still intact. The present-day population is c.7 300.

Zurich 1 POP (1991e) 841 000, the largest city in Switzerland and the capital of Zurich canton in the N of the country. A major financial centre, it lies on the R Limmat, at the NW end of L Zurich, 96km/60mi NE of Bern. HISTORY joined the Swiss Confederation in 1351; an important centre during the Reformation and Counter-Reformation. NOTABLE FEATURES Grossmünster (11c–14c); Fraumünster (13c, now restored); town hall (17c); St Peter's Church (13c). **2** a canton in N Switzerland with the city of Zurich as its capital.

Zwickau POP (1991e) 119 000, a mining and industrial city in Saxony state, E central Germany. It lies on the R Mulde, SW of Karl Marx Stadt. HISTORY a free imperial city (1290–1323); the composer Robert Schumann was born here in 1810.

Zwingli, Huldreich or **Ulrich**, Latin **Ulricus Zuinglius** (1484–1531) Swiss Protestant reformer, born in Wildhaus. Ordained in 1506, he became a chaplain to the Swiss mercenaries, and was elected preacher in the Zürich minster (1518). He opposed the selling of indulgences, espoused the Reformed doctrines, and obtained the support of the civil authorities, but in 1524 he disagreed with Martin Luther over the question of the Eucharist, for he rejected the idea of any kind of real presence. War between the cantons followed, and he was killed in an attack on Zurich.

Zwolle POP (1992e) 97 000, the capital of Overijssel province, E Netherlands. It lies on the Zwarte Water, which opens into the Ijsselmeer c.20km/12mi NW of the city. A major cattle market takes place here. Zwolle is associated with Thomas à Kempis, who spent most of his life nearby. NOTABLE FEATURE St Michaelskerk (15c).

Zworykin, Vladimir Kosma (1889–1982) US physicist, born in Mourom, Russia. He worked for the Radio Corporation of America from 1929, and is chiefly remembered for applying the cathode-ray tube to television, a development which he patented in 1928. By 1938 he had developed the first practical television camera which he called the 'iconoscope', and he later contributed to the development of the electron microscope and other electronic devices.

zygote *noun Biol.* the cell that is formed as a result of the fertilization of a female gamete (ovum or egg cell) by a male gamete (sperm or pollen grain). [from Greek *zygon*, yoke]

zymase *noun* any enzyme that catalyses the fermentation of carbohydrates to ethanol (ethyl alcohol). [from Greek *zyme*, leaven]

zymotic *adj.* **1** relating to or causing fermentation. **2** relating to, causing, or like an infectious disease. [from Greek *zymosis*, fermentation]

Key to Maps

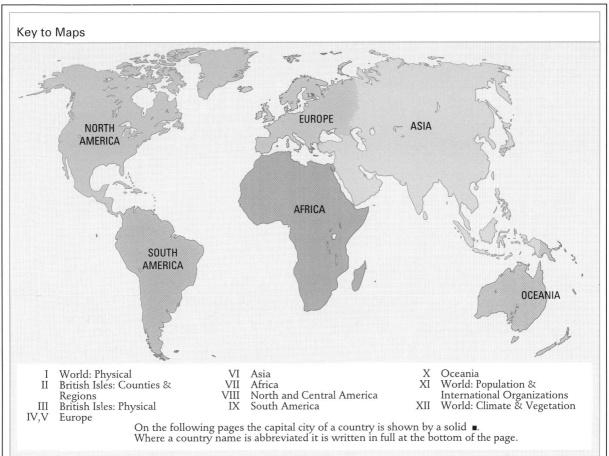

I	World: Physical	VI	Asia	X	Oceania
II	British Isles: Counties & Regions	VII	Africa	XI	World: Population & International Organizations
III	British Isles: Physical	VIII	North and Central America	XII	World: Climate & Vegetation
IV,V	Europe	IX	South America		

On the following pages the capital city of a country is shown by a solid ■.
Where a country name is abbreviated it is written in full at the bottom of the page.

Physical

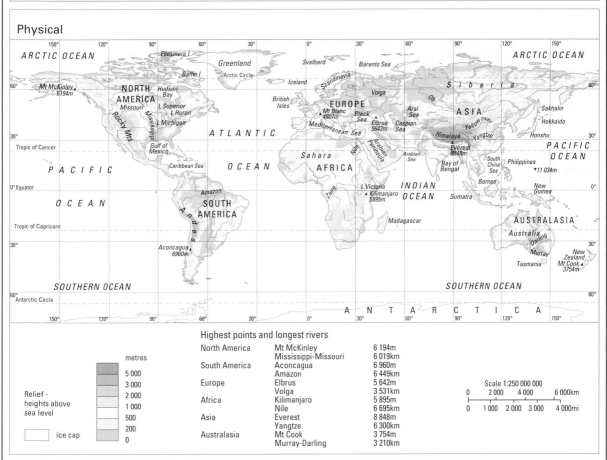

Highest points and longest rivers

North America	Mt McKinley	6 194m
	Mississippi-Missouri	6 019km
South America	Aconcagua	6 960m
	Amazon	6 449km
Europe	Elbrus	5 642m
	Volga	3 531km
Africa	Kilimanjaro	5 895m
	Nile	6 695km
Asia	Everest	8 848m
	Yangtze	6 300km
Australasia	Mt Cook	3 754m
	Murray-Darling	3 210km

Relief - heights above sea level

metres
5 000
3 000
2 000
1 000
500
200
0

ice cap

Scale 1:250 000 000

0   2 000   4 000   6 000km
0   1 000   2 000   3 000   4 000mi

BEDS : BEDFORDSHIRE
BERKS : BERKSHIRE
BUCKS : BUCKINGHAMSHIRE
GM : GREATER MANCHESTER
HERTS : HERTFORDSHIRE
LEICS : LEICESTERSHIRE
LONG : LONGFORD
MG : MID GLAMORGAN
NOTTS : NOTTINGHAMSHIRE
SG : SOUTH GLAMORGAN
SOUTH YORKS : SOUTH YORKSHIRE
STAFFS : STAFFORDSHIRE
WEST YORKS : WEST YORKSHIRE
WG : WEST GLAMORGAN
WM : WEST MIDLANDS

Boundaries liable to change due to review
1994-5. Correct as of April 1994.

• denotes county town/region capital

© Bartholomew 1994

British Isles, Physical

Height above
sea level (metres)

1 000
500
200
100
0

SHETLAND IS
Herma Ness
Yell
Unst
Mainland
Fetlar
Whalsey
Foula
Bresay
Sumburgh
Head

Fair Isle

Westray
Sanday
Stronsay
ORKNEY IS
Mainland
Hoy
South Ronaldsay
Cape Wrath
Pentland Firth
Duncansby Head
Butt of
Lewis
Thurso
The Minch
Lewis
Clisham
▲799
Loch
Shin
Dornoch Firth
St Kilda
Loch
Broom
Harris
Ben Wyvis
▲1045
Moray Firth
Kinnairds
Head
North West Highlands
North
Uist
Skye
Beauly
Spey
Deveron
Don
South
Uist
Little Minch
Cuillin
Hills ▲1009
Loch
Ness
Cairngorms
Ben Macdui
▲1311
Dee
Barra
Rhum
Ben Nevis
▲1344
Grampian Mountains
Outer Hebrides
Coll
Ben Lawers ▲
Ben More
▲966
1214
Tay
Sidlaw Hills
Firth of Tay
Inner Hebrides
Tiree
Mull
Loch
Tay
Firth of Lorn
Loch
Lomond
Loch
Ochil Hills
Jura
Loch
Fyne
Forth
Firth of Forth

ATLANTIC

North
Sea

OCEAN

Islay
Goat Fell
874▲
Arran
Firth of Clyde
Ayr
Clyde
Tweed
Holy I
Malin Head
Rathlin I
Mull of
Kintyre
Merrick
843▲
Southern Uplands
The Cheviot Hills
Errigal Mtn
▲752
Lough
Foyle
Bann
Mts of Antrim
Nith
Annan
Tyne
Lough
Foyle
Mourne
Lough
Neagh
North Channel
Luce
Bay
Solway Firth
Cross Fell
893▲
The Pennines
Tees
Erris
Head
Donegal
Bay
Lower
Lough
Erne
Strangford
Lough
Mull of
Galloway
Lake
District
Scafell Pike
977▲
Cumbrian Mts
North York
Moors
Derwent
Lough
Conn
Upper
Lough
Erne
Mourne
Mts
852
Slieve
Donard
Isle of Man
Morecambe Bay
Wolds
Flamborough Head
Achill I
Moy
Erne
Ribble
Ouse
Wharfe
Yorkshire Wolds
Clew
Bay
Lough
Mask
Lough
Corrib
Suck
Boyne
Irish Sea
Anglesey
Liverpool
Bay
Aire
Don
Spurn Head
Croagh Patrick
765
Mersey
High Peak
636▲
Humber
Lincolnshire
Wolds
Slyne
Head
Lough
Ree
Snowdon
▲1085
Cheshire
Plain
Witham
Galway Bay
Shannon
Dee
Trent
The
Wash
Aran Is
Lough
Derg
Lugnaquillia
Mtn 926 ▲
Wicklow Mts
Cardigan
Bay
Cambrian Mountains
Severn
Welland
The Fens
Norfolk
Broads
Shannon
Suir
Nore
Barrow
Slaney
Avon
Great Ouse
Waveney
Dingle
Bay
Blackwater
Teifi
Wye
Carrantouohill
▲1041
Lee
Carnsore
Point
St David's
Head
St Brides Bay
886▲
Brecon
Beacons
Severn
Cotswold Hills
Chiltern Hills
Chelmer
Dursey
Head
Cape Clear
St Govan's Head
Carmarthen Bay
Avon
Thames
Malborough
Downs
Thames
Isle of
Sheppey
St George's Channel
Lundy
Hartland Pt
Bristol Channel
Exmoor
Forest
Mendip
Hills
Salisbury
Plain
Test
North Downs
South Downs
The Weald
Strait of
Dover
Dungeness
Beachy Head
Exe
N Dorset
Downs
Avon
New
Forest
Solent
Bodmin
Moor
Dartmoor
Tamar
Lyme Bay
Bill of
Portland
Isle of Wight
English Channel
Isles of Scilly
Land's End
Lizard Pt
Start Pt

Scale 1 : 5 000 000
0   50   100   150km
0   25   50   75mi

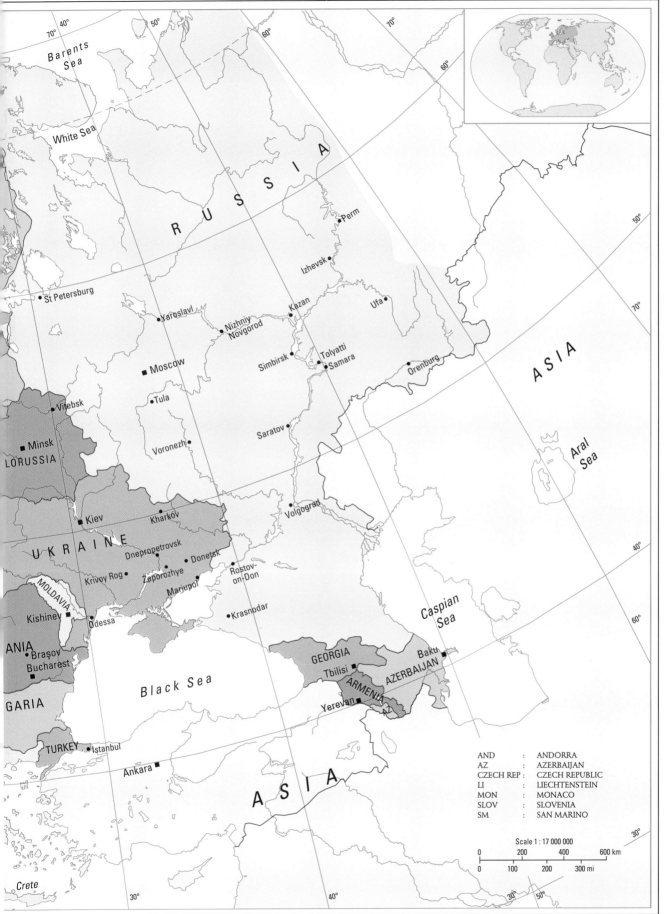

Barents Sea

White Sea

R U S S I A

• Perm

• Izhevsk

• St Petersburg

• Yaroslavl

• Nizhniy Novgorod

• Kazan

• Ufa

• Moscow

• Simbirsk

• Tolyatti
• Samara

• Orenburg

ASIA

• Tula

• Vitebsk

• Saratov

Aral Sea

• Minsk

LORUSSIA

• Voronezh

• Volgograd

U K R A I N E

• Kiev

• Kharkov

• Dnepropetrovsk

• Donetsk

MOLDAVIA

• Krivoy Rog

• Zaporozhye

• Rostov-on-Don

• Mariupol

Caspian Sea

• Kishinev

• Odessa

• Krasnodar

ANIA

• Braşov

• Bucharest

GEORGIA

Baku

GARIA

Tbilisi

AZERBAIJAN

ARMENIA

Black Sea

Yerevan

AZ

TURKEY

• Istanbul

• Ankara

A S I A

Crete

AND	:	ANDORRA
AZ	:	AZERBAIJAN
CZECH REP	:	CZECH REPUBLIC
LI	:	LIECHTENSTEIN
MON	:	MONACO
SLOV	:	SLOVENIA
SM	:	SAN MARINO

Scale 1 : 17 000 000

| 0 | 200 | 400 | 600 km |
| 0 | 100 | 200 | 300 mi |

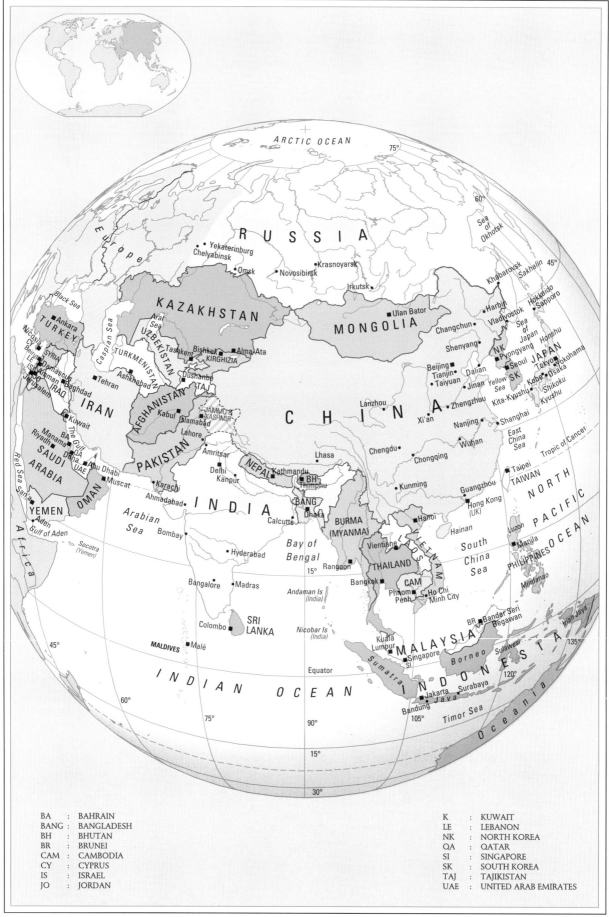

BA	:	BAHRAIN	
BANG	:	BANGLADESH	
BH	:	BHUTAN	
BR	:	BRUNEI	
CAM	:	CAMBODIA	
CY	:	CYPRUS	
IS	:	ISRAEL	
JO	:	JORDAN	

K	:	KUWAIT
LE	:	LEBANON
NK	:	NORTH KOREA
QA	:	QATAR
SI	:	SINGAPORE
SK	:	SOUTH KOREA
TAJ	:	TAJIKISTAN
UAE	:	UNITED ARAB EMIRATES

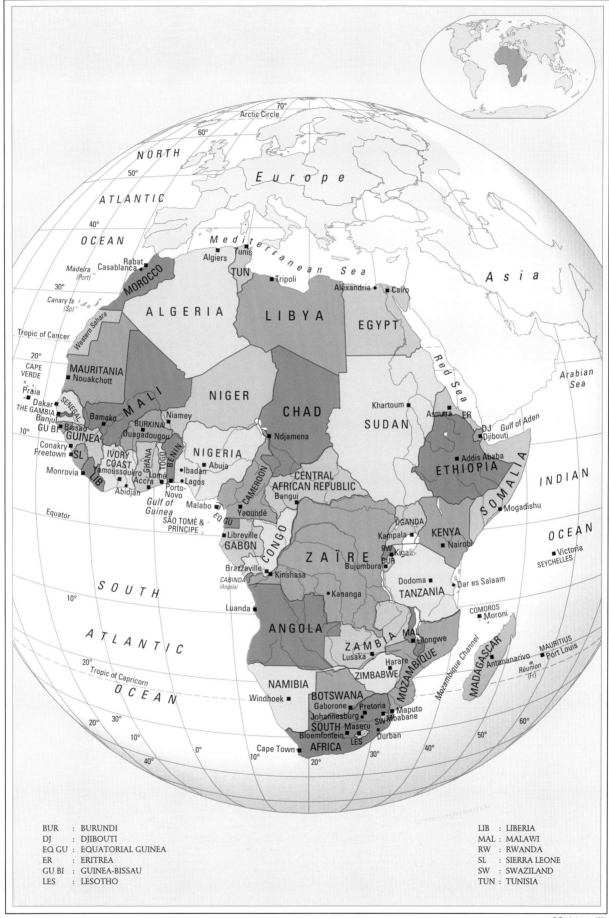

BUR : BURUNDI
DJ : DJIBOUTI
EQ GU : EQUATORIAL GUINEA
ER : ERITREA
GU BI : GUINEA-BISSAU
LES : LESOTHO

LIB : LIBERIA
MAL : MALAWI
RW : RWANDA
SL : SIERRA LEONE
SW : SWAZILAND
TUN : TUNISIA

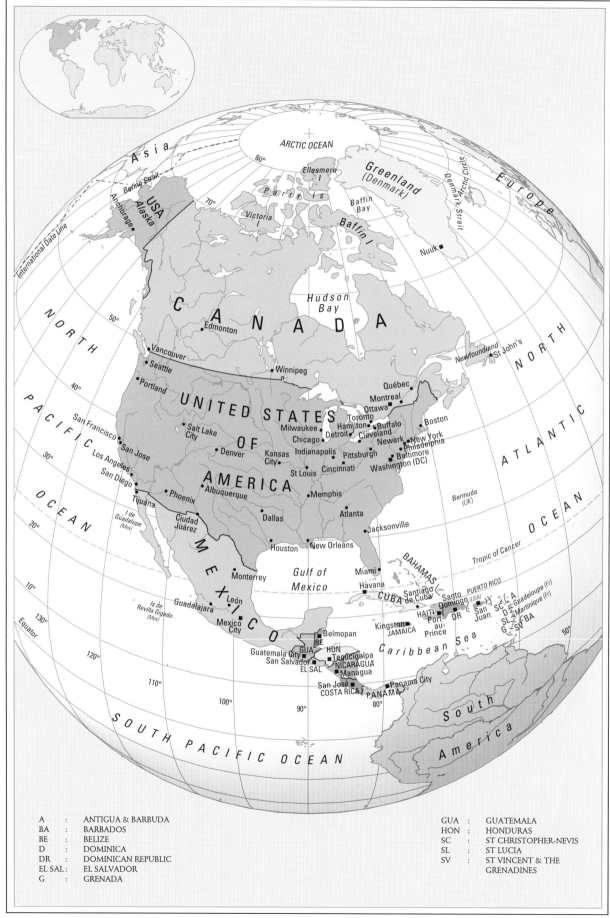

A	:	ANTIGUA & BARBUDA	
BA	:	BARBADOS	
BE	:	BELIZE	
D	:	DOMINICA	
DR	:	DOMINICAN REPUBLIC	
EL SAL	:	EL SALVADOR	
G	:	GRENADA	

GUA	:	GUATEMALA
HON	:	HONDURAS
SC	:	ST CHRISTOPHER-NEVIS
SL	:	ST LUCIA
SV	:	ST VINCENT & THE GRENADINES

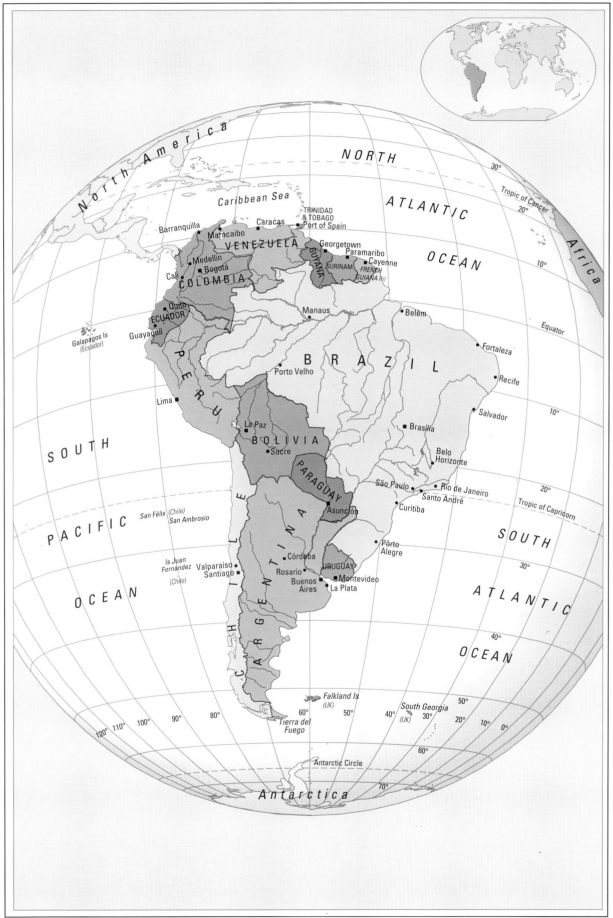

North America

Caribbean Sea

NORTH

ATLANTIC

OCEAN

Africa

30°

Tropic of Cancer

20°

10°

Barranquilla

Maracaibo

Caracas

TRINIDAD & TOBAGO
Port of Spain

Georgetown
Paramaribo
Cayenne

VENEZUELA

GUYANA

SURINAM

FRENCH GUIANA (Fr.)

Medellin

Bogotá

Cali

COLOMBIA

Quito

ECUADOR

Guayaquil

Galapagos Is
(Ecuador)

Manaus

Belém

Equator

P E R U

B R A Z I L

Fortaleza

Recife

Porto Velho

Lima

Salvador

10°

La Paz

B O L I V I A

Sucre

Brasília

Belo Horizonte

SOUTH

PARAGUAY

São Paulo

Rio de Janeiro

Santo André

20°

Tropic of Capricorn

Asunción

Curitiba

PACIFIC

San Félix (Chile)
San Ambrosio

A R G E N T I N A

SOUTH

Pôrto Alegre

ATLANTIC

Is Juan Fernandez
(Chile)

Valparaíso

Santiago

Córdoba

Rosario

URUGUAY

Montevideo

30°

C H I L E

Buenos Aires

La Plata

OCEAN

OCEAN

40°

OCEAN

Falkland Is
(UK)

South Georgia
(UK)

50°

50°

60°

40°

30°

20°

10°

0°

120° 110° 100° 90° 80°

Tierra del Fuego

60°

Antarctic Circle

70°

Antarctica

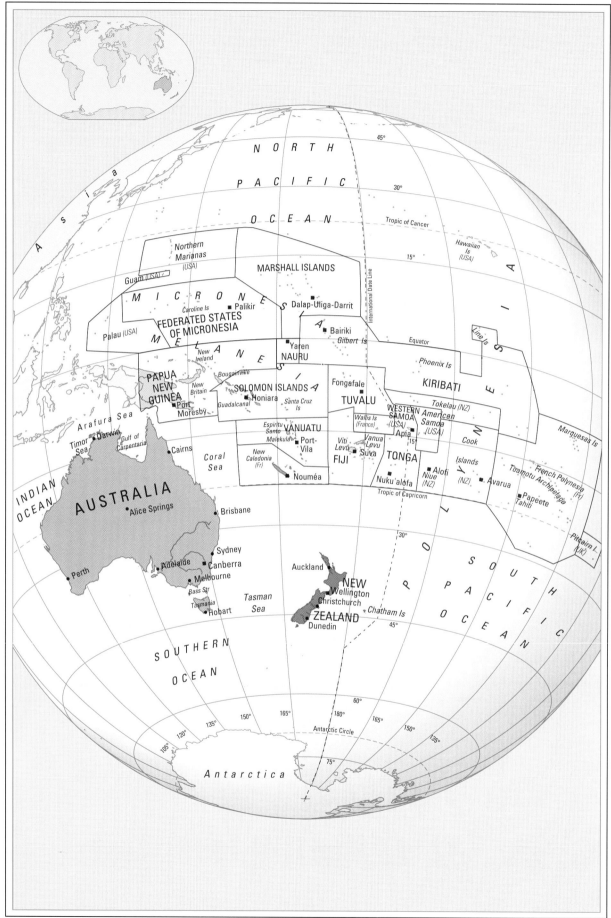

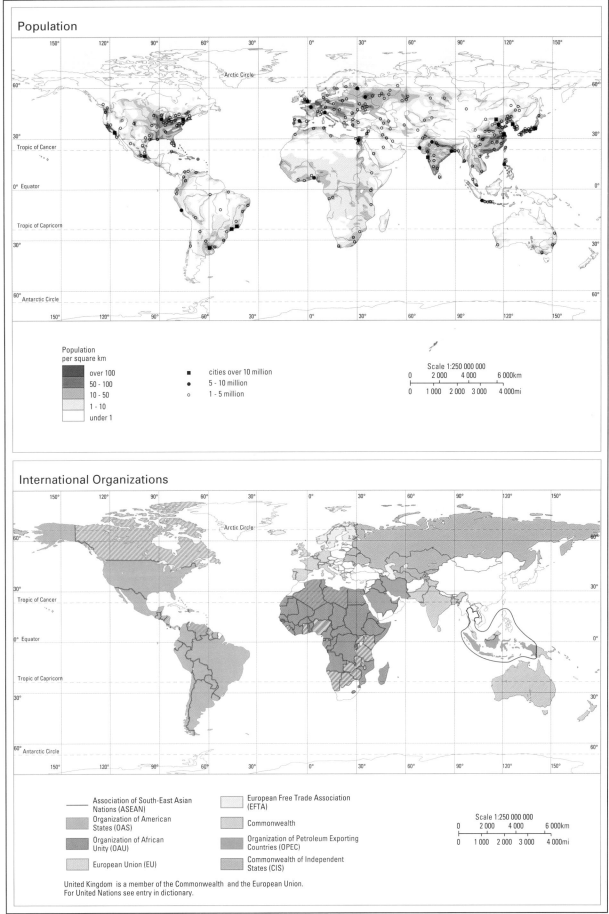

Population

Population
per square km

	over 100
	50 - 100
	10 - 50
	1 - 10
	under 1

■ cities over 10 million
● 5 - 10 million
○ 1 - 5 million

Scale 1:250 000 000

0   2 000   4 000   6 000km

0   1 000 2 000 3 000 4 000mi

International Organizations

— Association of South-East Asian Nations (ASEAN)

Organization of American States (OAS)

Organization of African Unity (OAU)

European Union (EU)

European Free Trade Association (EFTA)

Commonwealth

Organization of Petroleum Exporting Countries (OPEC)

Commonwealth of Independent States (CIS)

Scale 1:250 000 000

0   2 000   4 000   6 000km

0   1 000 2 000 3 000 4 000mi

United Kingdom is a member of the Commonwealth and the European Union.
For United Nations see entry in dictionary.

© Bartholomew 1994

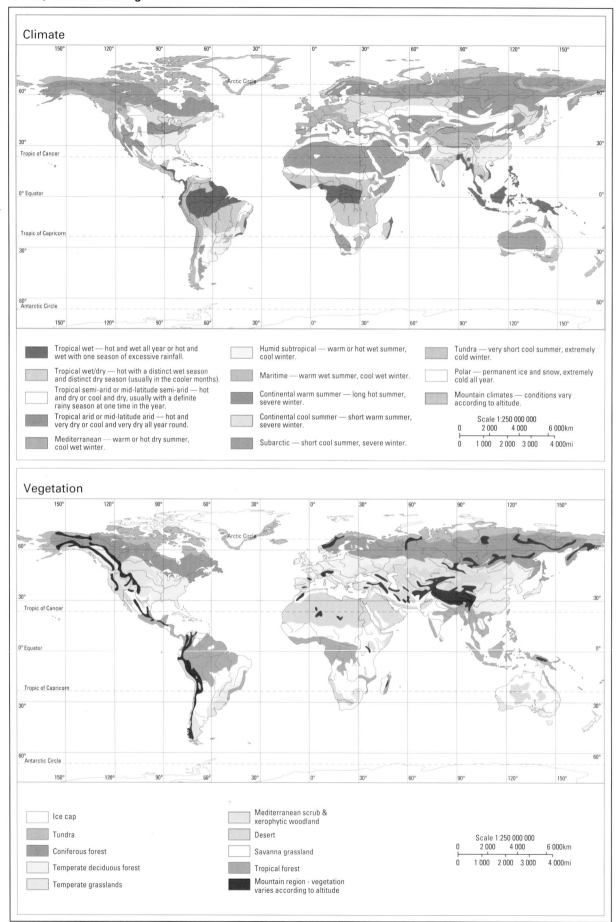

Climate

- Tropical wet — hot and wet all year or hot and wet with one season of excessive rainfall.
- Tropical wet/dry — hot with a distinct wet season and distinct dry season (usually in the cooler months).
- Tropical semi-arid or mid-latitude semi-arid — hot and dry or cool and dry, usually with a definite rainy season at one time in the year.
- Tropical arid or mid-latitude arid — hot and very dry or cool and very dry all year round.
- Mediterranean — warm or hot dry summer, cool wet winter.
- Humid subtropical — warm or hot wet summer, cool winter.
- Maritime — warm wet summer, cool wet winter.
- Continental warm summer — long hot summer, severe winter.
- Continental cool summer — short warm summer, severe winter.
- Subarctic — short cool summer, severe winter.
- Tundra — very short cool summer, extremely cold winter.
- Polar — permanent ice and snow, extremely cold all year.
- Mountain climates — conditions vary according to altitude.

Scale 1:250 000 000
0   2 000   4 000   6 000km
0   1 000   2 000   3 000   4 000mi

Vegetation

- Ice cap
- Tundra
- Coniferous forest
- Temperate deciduous forest
- Temperate grasslands
- Mediterranean scrub & xerophytic woodland
- Desert
- Savanna grassland
- Tropical forest
- Mountain region - vegetation varies according to altitude

Scale 1:250 000 000
0   2 000   4 000   6 000km
0   1 000   2 000   3 000   4 000mi